CONGRESSIONAL QUARTERLY

Almanac

98th CONGRESS
2nd SESSION 1984

VOLUME XL

Congressional Quarterly Inc.

Washington, D.C.

CQ 1984 Almanac

Editor and President
Eugene Patterson

Publisher
Wayne P. Kelley

Deputy Publisher and Executive Editor
Peter A. Harkness

General Manager
Robert C. Hur

Director, Research and Development
Robert E. Cuthriell

EDITORIAL DEPARTMENT

Managing Editor: Kathryn Waters Gest

Assistant Managing Editors: Peg O'Hara, Andy Plattner

Political Editor: Alan Ehrenhalt

News Editors: Martha Angle, Marsha Canfield, John R. Cranford, Michael Glennon, Robin D. Meszoly

Assistant Political Editor: Harrison Donnelly

Reporters: Steve Blakely, Jacqueline Calmes, Nadine Cohodas, Rhodes Cook, Joseph A. Davis, Phil Duncan, John Felton, Pamela Fessler, Stephen Gettinger, Nancy Green, Diane Granat, Rob Gurwitt, Janet Hook, Steven Pressman, Robert Rothman, Dale Tate, Pat Towell, Tom Watson, Elizabeth Wehr, Elder Witt

Production Editor: William L. Bonn

Editorial Coordinator: Colleen McGuiness

Proofreaders: Eugene J. Gabler, Dave Kaplan

Editorial Assistants: Peter Bragdon, Joe Leverone, Rowena Olegario

RESEARCH DEPARTMENT: Michael L. Koempel (Director), Wayne Walker (Assistant Director), Martha Bomgardner (Library Director), Diane Huffman (Indexer), Andre D. Adams, Donald F. Baldini, Charles S. Clark, Bena A. Fein, Thomas E. J. Hazard, Walter Alex Hill, Genevieve Kelley, Nancy Kervin, Barbara L. Miracle, Neal Santelmann, Pamela Walker, Lenore Webb

ART DEPARTMENT: Richard A. Pottern (Director), Robert Redding (Assistant Director), Kathleen A. Ossenfort

PRODUCTION: I. D. Fuller (Manager), Maceo Mayo (Assistant Manager)

COMPUTER SERVICES: Sydney E. Garriss (Manager)

BUSINESS MANAGER: Jonathan C. Angier

MARKETING: Richard A. Shontz (Director), Sandra Stencel (Research Director)

BOOK DEPARTMENT: David R. Tarr (Director), John L. Moore (Assistant Director), Joanne D. Daniels (Director, CQ Press), Kathryn Suarez (Marketing Manager)

NEWSLETTERS: Donald Smith (Editor)

CONGRESSIONAL MONITOR: Michaela Buhler (Editor), Robert Healy (Managing Editor)

EDITORIAL RESEARCH REPORTS: Hoyt Gimlin (Editor), Martha V. Gottron, Richard L. Worsnop (Associate Editors)

WASHINGTON ALERT SERVICE: Ross Evans (Manager), Steve Newman (Editor), Wayne S. Muhlstein (Marketing Manager)

Chairman of the Board: Nelson Poynter (1903-1978)

Library of Congress No. 47-41081
International Standard Book No. 0-87187-346-X

Copyright 1985 by Congressional Quarterly Inc.
1414 22nd Street, N.W., Washington, D.C. 20037

Congressional Quarterly Inc.

Congressional Quarterly Inc. is an editorial research service and publishing company serving clients in the fields of news, education, business and government. Congressional Quarterly, in its basic publication, the CQ Weekly Report, covers Congress, government and politics. Congressional Quarterly also publishes hardbound reference books and paperback books on public affairs. The service was founded in 1945 by Henrietta and Nelson Poynter.

An affiliated service, Editorial Research Reports, publishes reports each week on a wide range of subjects. Editorial Research Reports also publishes hardbound and paperback books.

Almanac Editor: Mary Cohn

Editorial Coordinator: Colleen McGuiness

Assistant Editors: Martha Angle, Marsha Canfield, John R. Cranford, Harrison Donnelly, Michael Glennon, Robin D. Meszoly, Peg O'Hara, Andy Plattner, Elder Witt

Other Contributors: Andre D. Adams, Renee Amrine, Jacqueline Calmes, Nadine Cohodas, Barbara Coleman, Rhodes Cook, Joseph A. Davis, Leslie Ann De Long, Phil Duncan, John Felton, Pamela Fessler, Stephen Gettinger, Diane Granat, Nancy Green, Rob Gurwitt, Janet Hook, Julia McCue, Brian Nutting, Patricia Ann O'Connor, Robert Rothman, Dale Tate, Pat Towell, Tom Watson, Lenore Webb, Elizabeth Wehr

Roll-Call Charts: Bena A. Fein; **Vote Studies:** Wayne Walker

Editorial Assistants: William L. Bonn, Eugene J. Gabler, Dave Kaplan

Indexers: Carolyn McGovern, Jodean Marks, Jenny Adams

Production: I. D. Fuller (manager), Maceo Mayo (assistant manager)

CQ

SUMMARY TABLE OF CONTENTS

TABLE OF CONTENTS

Chapter 1 — 98th Congress, Second Session

Chapter 2 — Defense

Chapter 3 — Foreign Policy

Chapter 4 — Economic Policy

Chapter 5 — Congress and Government

Chapter 6 — Law Enforcement/Judiciary

Chapter 7 — Transportation/Commerce/Consumers

Chapter 8 — Environment/Energy

Chapter 9 — Agriculture

Chapter 10 — Appropriations

Chapter 11 — Health/Education/Welfare

APPENDIXES

Special Reports

Political Report

Voting Studies

Lobby Registrations

Presidential Messages

Public Laws

Roll-Call Charts

Index

Errata

1980 Almanac, p. 3-B, col. 1, paragraph 2: Ronald Reagan's re-election victory was 9.7 (not 7) percentage points.

1982 Almanac, p. 205, box: HR 6685 was a $5.4 billion (not $4.5 billion) bill.

1983 Almanac, p. 4, col. 1, paragraph 2, first sentence should read: There were no changes in chairmen of Senate standing committees. **P. 345**, col. 1, fifth paragraph: HR 1062 was a public bill. **P. 450**, col. 2, ninth paragraph should read: Democrats called the Reagan initiative a good starting point. House Majority Leader Jim Wright, D-Texas, said the president "has come a long way toward" the Democratic position on jobs. **P. 507**, col. 2, first paragraph: Date was Sept. 22 (not 23).

Glossary of Congressional Terms

Act—The term for legislation once it has passed both houses of Congress and has been signed by the president or passed over his veto, thus becoming law. *(See below.)* Also used in parliamentary terminology for a bill that has been passed by one house and engrossed. *(See Engrossed Bill.)*

Adjournment Sine Die—Adjournment without definitely fixing a day for reconvening; literally "adjournment without a day." Usually used to connote the final adjournment of a session of Congress. A session can continue until noon, Jan. 3, of the following year, when, under the 20th Amendment to the Constitution, it automatically terminates. Both houses must agree to a concurrent resolution for either house to adjourn for more than three days.

Adjournment to a Day Certain—Adjournment under a motion or resolution that fixes the next time of meeting. Under the Constitution, neither house can adjourn for more than three days without the concurrence of the other. A session of Congress is not ended by adjournment to a day certain.

Amendment—A proposal of a member of Congress to alter the language, provisions or stipulations in a bill or in another amendment. An amendment usually is printed, debated and voted upon in the same manner as a bill.

Amendment in the Nature of a Substitute—Usually an amendment that seeks to replace the entire text of a bill. Passage of this type of amendment strikes out everything after the enacting clause and inserts a new version of the bill. An amendment in the nature of a substitute also can refer to an amendment that replaces a large portion of the text of a bill.

Appeal—A member's challenge of a ruling or decision made by the presiding officer of the chamber. In the Senate, the senator appeals to members of the chamber to override the decision. If carried by a majority vote, the appeal nullifies the chair's ruling. In the House, the decision of the Speaker traditionally has been final; seldom are there appeals to the members to reverse the Speaker's stand. To appeal a ruling is considered an attack on the Speaker.

Appropriations Bill—A bill that gives legal authority to spend or obligate money from the Treasury. The Constitution disallows money to be drawn from the Treasury "but in Consequence of Appropriations made by Law."

It usually is the case that an appropriations bill provides the actual monies approved by authorization bills, but not necessarily the full amount permissible under the authorization measures. By congressional custom, an appropriations bill originates in the House, and it is not supposed to be considered by the full House or Senate until the related authorization measure is enacted. Under the 1974 Congressional Budget and Impoundment Control Act,

general appropriations bills are supposed to be enacted by the seventh day after Labor Day before the start of the fiscal year to which they apply, but in recent years this deadline rarely has been met.

In addition to general appropriations bills, there are two specialized types. *(See Continuing Resolution, Supplemental Appropriations Bill.)*

Authorization—Basic, substantive legislation that establishes or continues the legal operation of a federal program or agency, either indefinitely or for a specific period of time, or which sanctions a particular type of obligation or expenditure. An authorization normally is a prerequisite for an appropriation or other kind of budget authority. Under the rules of both houses, the appropriation for a program or agency may not be considered until its authorization has been considered. An authorization also may limit the amount of budget authority to be provided or may authorize the appropriation of "such sums as may be necessary." *(See also Backdoor Spending.)*

Backdoor Spending—Budget authority provided in legislation outside the normal appropriations process. The most common forms of backdoor spending are borrowing authority, contract authority and entitlements. *(See below.)* In some cases, such as interest on the public debt, a permanent appropriation is provided that becomes available without further action by Congress. The 1974 budget act places limits on the use of backdoor spending.

Bills—Most legislative proposals before Congress are in the form of bills and are designated by HR in the House of Representatives or S in the Senate, according to the house in which they originate, and by a number assigned in the order in which they are introduced during the two-year period of a congressional term. "Public bills" deal with general questions and become public laws if approved by Congress and signed by the president. "Private bills" deal with individual matters such as claims against the government, immigration and naturalization cases, land titles, etc., and become private laws if approved and signed. *(See also Concurrent Resolution, Joint Resolution, Resolution.)*

Bills Introduced—In both the House and Senate, any number of members may join in introducing a single bill or resolution. The first member listed is the sponsor of the bill, and all members' names following his are the bill's cosponsors.

Many bills are committee bills and are introduced under the name of the chairman of the committee or subcommittee. All appropriations bills fall into this category. A committee frequently holds hearings on a number of related bills and may agree to one of them or to an entirely new bill. *(See also Report, Clean Bill, By Request.)*

Bills Referred— When introduced, a bill is referred to the committee or committees that have jurisdiction over the subject with which the bill is concerned. Under the standing rules of the House and Senate, bills are referred by the Speaker in the House and by the presiding officer in the Senate. In practice, the House and Senate parliamentarians act for these officials and refer the vast majority of bills.

Borrowing Authority—Statutory authority that permits a federal agency to incur obligations and make payments for specified purposes with borrowed money. The 1974 budget act sets limits on new borrowing authority, except in certain instances, to the extent or amount provided in appropriations acts.

Budget—The document sent to Congress by the president early each year estimating government revenue and expenditures for the ensuing fiscal year.

Budget Authority—Authority to enter into obligations that will result in immediate or future outlays involving federal funds. The basic forms of budget authority are appropriations, contract authority and borrowing authority. Budget authority may be classified by (1) the period of availability (one-year, multiple-year or without a time limitation), (2) the timing of congressional action (current or permanent), or (3) the manner of determining the amount available (definite or indefinite).

Budget Process—The congressional budget process is organized around two concurrent resolutions. The deadline for approval of the first resolution is May 15. The resolution must be passed before the House and Senate consider appropriations, revenue and entitlement legislation. The deadline for the second budget resolution is Sept. 15, two weeks before the Oct. 1 start of the next fiscal year. (Congress has failed to meet these deadlines in recent years.) The purpose of the two budget resolutions is to guide and restrain Congress in its actions on appropriations spending and revenue bills. A concurrent resolution does not have the force of law. Consequently, Congress cannot appropriate money, impose taxes or directly limit federal expenditures by means of a budget resolution. Unless it otherwise stipulates, Congress is not bound by the targets in the first budget resolution when it acts on appropriations and tax legislation. The second resolution sets a ceiling on new budget authority and outlays and a floor on revenues for the coming year. After its adoption a point of order can be raised against any legislation that would cause expenditures to exceed or revenues to drop below budgeted amounts. Congress can revise its budget decisions at any time during the fiscal year by adopting supplementary budget resolutions.

Budget Reconciliation—The 1974 budget act provides for a "reconciliation" procedure for bringing existing tax and spending laws into conformity with the congressional budget resolutions. Under the procedure, Congress instructs designated legislative committees to approve measures adjusting revenues and expenditures by a certain amount. The committees have a deadline by which they must report the legislation, but they have the discretion of deciding what changes are to be made. The recommendations of the various committees are consolidated without change by the Budget committees into an omnibus reconciliation bill, which then must be considered and approved by both houses of Congress.

By Request—A phrase used when a senator or representative introduces a bill at the request of an executive agency or private organization but does not necessarily endorse the legislation.

Calendar—An agenda or list of business awaiting possible action by each chamber. The House uses five legislative calendars. *(See Consent, Discharge, House, Private and Union Calendar.)*

In the Senate, all legislative matters reported from committee go on one calendar. They are listed there in the order in which committees report them or the Senate places them on the calendar, but may be called up out of order by the majority leader, either by obtaining unanimous consent of the Senate or by a motion to call up a bill. The Senate also uses one non-legislative calendar; this is used for treaties and nominations. *(See Executive Calendar.)*

Calendar Wednesday—In the House, committees, on Wednesdays, may be called in the order in which they appear in Rule X of the House, for the purpose of bringing up any of their bills from either the House or the Union Calendar, except bills that are privileged. General debate is limited to two hours. Bills called up from the Union Calendar are considered in Committee of the Whole. Calendar Wednesday is not observed during the last two weeks of a session and may be dispensed with at other times by a two-thirds vote. This procedure is rarely used and routinely is dispensed with by unanimous consent.

Call of the Calendar—Senate bills that are not brought up for debate by a motion, unanimous consent or a unanimous consent agreement are brought before the Senate for action when the calendar listing them is "called." Bills must be called in the order listed. Measures considered by this method usually are non-controversial, and debate is limited to a total of five minutes for each senator on the bill and any amendments proposed to it.

Chamber—The meeting place for the membership of either the House or the Senate; also the membership of the House or Senate meeting as such.

Clean Bill—Frequently after a committee has finished a major revision of a bill, one of the committee members, usually the chairman, will assemble the changes and what is left of the original bill into a new measure and introduce it as a "clean bill." The revised measure, which is given a new number, then is referred back to the committee, which reports it to the floor for consideration. This often is a timesaver, as committee-recommended changes in a clean bill do not have to be considered and voted on by the chamber. Reporting a clean bill also protects committee amendments that might be subject to points of order concerning germaneness.

Clerk of the House—Chief administrative officer of the House of Representatives, with duties corresponding to those of the secretary of the Senate. *(See also Secretary of the Senate.)*

Cloture—The process by which a filibuster can be ended in the Senate other than by unanimous consent. A motion for cloture can apply to any measure before the Senate, including a proposal to change the chamber's rules.

A cloture motion requires the signatures of 16 senators to be introduced, and the cloture motion must obtain the votes of three-fifths of the entire Senate membership (60 if there are no vacancies) to end a filibuster, except that in order to end a filibuster against a proposal to amend the standing rules of the Senate, a two-thirds vote of senators present and voting is required. The cloture request is put to a roll-call vote one hour after the Senate meets on the second day following introduction of the motion. If approved, cloture limits each senator to one hour of debate. The bill or amendment in question comes to a final vote after 100 hours of consideration (including debate time and the time it takes to conduct roll calls, quorum calls and other procedural motions). *(See Filibuster.)*

Committee—A division of the House or Senate that prepares legislation for action by the parent chamber or makes investigations as directed by the parent chamber. There are several types of committees. *(See Standing and Select or Special Committees.)* Most standing committees are divided into subcommittees, which study legislation, hold hearings and report bills, with or without amendments, to the full committee. Only the full committee can report legislation for action by the House or Senate.

Committee of the Whole—The working title of what is formally "The Committee of the Whole House (of Representatives) on the State of the Union." The membership is comprised of all House members sitting as a committee. Any 100 members who are present on the floor of the chamber to consider legislation comprise a quorum of the committee. Any legislation, however, must first have passed through the regular legislative or Appropriations committee and have been placed on the calendar.

Technically, the Committee of the Whole considers only bills directly or indirectly appropriating money, authorizing appropriations or involving taxes or charges on the public. Because the Committee of the Whole need number only 100 representatives, a quorum is more readily attained, and legislative business is expedited. Before 1971, members' positions were not individually recorded on votes taken in Committee of the Whole. *(See Teller Vote.)*

When the full House resolves itself into the Committee of the Whole, it supplants the Speaker with a "chairman." A measure is debated and amendments may be proposed, with votes on amendments as needed. *(See Five-Minute Rule.)* When the committee completes its work on the measure, it dissolves itself by "rising." The Speaker returns, and the chairman of the Committee of the Whole reports to the House that the committee's work has been completed. At this time members may demand a roll-call vote on any amendment *adopted* in the Committee of the Whole. The final vote is on passage of the legislation.

Committee Veto—A requirement added to a few statutes directing that certain policy directives by an executive department or agency be reviewed by certain congressional committees before they are implemented. Under common practice, the government department or agency and the committees involved are expected to reach a consensus before the directives are carried out. *(See also Legislative.)*

Concurrent Resolution—A concurrent resolution, designated H Con Res or S Con Res, must be adopted by both houses, but it is not sent to the president for his signature and therefore does not have the force of law. A concurrent resolution, for example, is used to fix the time for adjournment of a Congress. It also is used as the vehicle for expressing the sense of Congress on various foreign policy and domestic issues, and it serves as the vehicle for coordinated decisions on the federal budget under the 1974 Congressional Budget and Impoundment Control Act. *(See also Bills, Joint Resolution, Resolution.)*

Conference—A meeting between the representatives of the House and the Senate to reconcile differences between the two houses on provisions of a bill passed by both chambers. Members of the conference committee are appointed by the Speaker and the presiding officer of the Senate and are called "managers" for their respective chambers. A majority of the managers for each house must reach agreement on the provisions of the bill (often a compromise between the versions of the two chambers) before it can be considered by either chamber in the form of a "conference report." When the conference report goes to the floor, it cannot be amended, and, if it is not approved by both chambers, the bill may go back to conference under certain situations, or a new conference must be convened. Many rules and informal practices govern the conduct of conference committees.

Bills that are passed by both houses with only minor differences need not be sent to conference. Either chamber may "concur" in the other's amendments, completing action on the legislation. Sometimes leaders of the committees of jurisdiction work out an informal compromise instead of having a formal conference. *(See Custody of the Papers.)*

Confirmations—*(See Nominations.)*

Congressional Record—The daily, printed account of proceedings in both the House and Senate chambers, showing substantially verbatim debate, statements and a record of floor action. Highlights of legislative and committee action are embodied in a Daily Digest section of the Record, and members are entitled to have their extraneous remarks printed in an appendix known as "Extension of Remarks." Members may edit and revise remarks made on the floor during debate, and quotations from debate reported by the press are not always found in the Record.

Beginning on March 1, 1978, the Record incorporated a procedure to distinguish remarks spoken on the floor of the House and Senate from undelivered speeches. Congress directed that all speeches, articles and other matter that members inserted in the Record without actually reading them on the floor were to be set off by large black dots, or bullets. However, a loophole allows a member to avoid the bulleting if he delivers any portion of the speech in person.

Congressional Terms of Office—Terms normally begin on Jan. 3 of the year following a general election and are two years for representatives and six years for senators. Representatives elected in special elections are sworn in for the remainder of a term. A person may be appointed to fill a Senate vacancy and serves until a successor is elected; the successor serves until the end of the term applying to the vacant seat.

Consent Calendar—Members of the House may place on this calendar most bills on the Union or House Calendar that are considered to be non-controversial. Bills on the Consent Calendar normally are called on the first and third Mondays of each month. On the first occasion that a bill is called in this manner, consideration may be blocked by the objection of any member. The second time, if there are three objections, the bill is stricken from the Consent Calendar. If less than three members object, the bill is given immediate consideration.

A bill on the Consent Calendar may be postponed in another way. A member may ask that the measure be passed over "without prejudice." In that case, no objection is recorded against the bill, and its status on the Consent Calendar remains unchanged. A bill stricken from the Consent Calendar remains on the Union or House Calendar.

Cosponsor—*(See Bills Introduced.)*

Continuing Resolution—A joint resolution drafted by Congress "continuing appropriations" for specific ongoing activities of a government department or departments when a fiscal year begins and Congress has not yet enacted all of the regular appropriations bills for that year. The continuing resolution usually specifies a maximum rate at which the agency may incur obligations. This usually is based on the rate for the previous year, the president's budget request or an appropriation bill for that year passed by either or both houses of Congress, but not cleared.

Contract Authority—Budget authority contained in an authorization bill that permits the federal government to enter into contracts or other obligations for future payments from funds not yet appropriated by Congress. The assumption is that funds will be available for payment in a subsequent appropriation act.

Controllable Budget Items—In federal budgeting this refers to programs, for which the budget authority or outlays during a fiscal year can be controlled without changing existing, substantive law. The concept "relatively uncontrollable under current law" includes outlays for open-ended programs and fixed costs such as interest on the public debt, Social Security benefits, veterans' benefits and outlays to liquidate prior-year obligations.

Correcting Recorded Votes—Rules prohibit members from changing their votes after the result has been announced. But, occasionally, hours, days or months after a vote has been taken, a member may announce that he was "incorrectly recorded." In the Senate, a request to change one's vote almost always receives unanimous consent. In the House, members are prohibited from changing their votes if tallied by the electronic voting system installed in 1973. If taken by roll call, it is permissible if consent is granted.

Current Services Estimates—Estimated budget authority and outlays for federal programs and operations for the forthcoming fiscal year based on continuation of existing levels of service without policy changes. These estimates of budget authority and outlays, accompanied by the underlying economic and policy assumptions upon which they are based, are transmitted by the president to Congress when the budget is submitted.

Custody of the Papers—To reconcile differences between the House and Senate versions of a bill, a conference may be arranged. The chamber with "custody of the papers" — the engrossed bill, engrossed amendments, messages of transmittal — is the only body empowered to request the conference. By custom, the chamber that asks for a conference is the last to act on the conference report once agreement has been reached on the bill by the conferees. Custody of the papers sometimes is manipulated to ensure that a particular chamber acts either first or last on the conference report.

Deferrals of Budget Authority—Any action taken by U.S. government officials that withholds, delays or precludes the obligation or expenditure of budget authority. The 1974 budget act requires a special message from the president to Congress reporting a proposed deferral. Deferrals may not extend beyond the end of the fiscal year in which the message reporting the deferral is transmitted. *(See also Rescission Bill.)*

Dilatory Motion—A motion made for the purpose of killing time and preventing action on a bill or amendment. House rules outlaw dilatory motions, but enforcement is largely within the discretion of the Speaker or chairman of the Committee of the Whole. The Senate does not have a rule banning dilatory motions, except under cloture.

Discharge a Committee—Occasionally, attempts are made to relieve a committee from jurisdiction over a measure before it. This is attempted more often in the House than in the Senate, and the procedure rarely is successful.

In the House, if a committee does not report a bill within 30 days after the measure is referred to it, any member may file a discharge motion. Once offered, the motion is treated as a petition needing the signatures of 218 members (a majority of the House). After the required signatures have been obtained, there is a delay of seven days. Thereafter, on the second and fourth Mondays of each month, except during the last six days of a session, any member who has signed the petition must be recognized, if he so desires, to move that the committee be discharged. Debate on the motion to discharge is limited to 20 minutes, and, if the motion is carried, consideration of the bill becomes a matter of high privilege.

If a resolution to consider a bill is held up in the Rules Committee for more than seven legislative days, any member may enter a motion to discharge the committee. The motion is handled like any other discharge petition in the House.

Occasionally, to expedite non-controversial legislative business, a committee is discharged by unanimous consent of the House, and a petition is not required. *(Senate procedure, see Discharge Resolution.)*

Discharge Calendar—The House calendar to which motions to discharge committees are referred when they have the required number of signatures (218) and are awaiting floor action.

Discharge Petition—*(See Discharge a Committee.)*

Discharge Resolution—In the Senate, a special motion that any senator may introduce to relieve a committee from consideration of a bill before it. The resolution can be called up for Senate approval or disapproval in the same manner as any other Senate business. *(House procedure, see Discharge a Committee.)*

Division of a Question for Voting—A practice that is more common in the Senate, but also is used in the House, whereby a member may demand a division of an amendment or a motion for purposes of voting. Where an amendment or motion can be divided, the individual parts are voted on separately when a member demands a division. This procedure occurs most often during the consideration of conference reports.

Division Vote—*(See Standing Vote.)*

Enacting Clause—Key phrase in bills beginning, "Be it enacted by the Senate and House of Representatives...." A successful motion to strike it from legislation kills the measure.

Engrossed Bill—The final copy of a bill as passed by one chamber, with the text as amended by floor action and certified by the clerk of the House or the secretary of the Senate.

Enrolled Bill—The final copy of a bill that has been passed in identical form by both chambers. It is certified by an officer of the house of origin (clerk of the House or secretary of the Senate) and then sent on for the signatures of the House Speaker, the Senate president pro tempore and the president of the United States. An enrolled bill is printed on parchment.

Entitlement Program—A federal program such as Social Security or unemployment compensation that guarantees a certain level of benefits to persons or other entities who meet the requirements set by law. It thus leaves no discretion with Congress on how much money to appropriate.

Executive Calendar—This is a non-legislative calendar in the Senate on which presidential documents such as treaties and nominations are listed.

Executive Document—A document, usually a treaty, sent to the Senate by the president for consideration or approval. Executive documents are identified for each session of Congress as Executive A, 97th Congress, 1st Session; Executive B, etc. They are referred to committee in the same manner as other measures. Unlike legislative documents, however, treaties do not die at the end of a Congress but remain "live" proposals until acted on by the Senate or withdrawn by the president.

Executive Session—A meeting of a Senate or House committee (or occasionally of either chamber) that only its members may attend. Witnesses regularly appear at committee meetings in executive session — for example, Defense Department officials during presentations of classified defense information. Other members of Congress may be invited, but the public and press are not allowed to attend.

Expenditures—The actual spending of money as distinguished from the appropriation of funds. Expenditures are made by the disbursing officers of the administration; appropriations are made only by Congress. The two are rarely identical in any fiscal year. In addition to some current budget authority, expenditures may represent budget authority made available one, two or more years earlier.

Filibuster—A time-delaying tactic associated with the Senate and used by a minority in an effort to prevent a vote on a bill or amendment that probably would pass if voted upon directly. The most common method is to take advantage of the Senate's rules permitting unlimited debate, but other forms of parliamentary maneuvering may be used. The stricter rules used by the House make filibusters more difficult, but delaying tactics are employed occasionally through various procedural devices allowed by House rules. *(Senate filibusters, see Cloture.)*

Fiscal Year—Financial operations of the government are carried out in a 12-month fiscal year, beginning on Oct. 1 and ending on Sept. 30. The fiscal year carries the date of the calendar year in which it ends. (From fiscal year 1844 to fiscal year 1976, the fiscal year began July 1 and ended the following June 30.)

Five-Minute Rule—A debate-limiting rule of the House that is invoked when the House sits as the Committee of the Whole. Under the rule, a member offering an amendment is allowed to speak five minutes in its favor, and an opponent of the amendment is allowed to speak five minutes in opposition. Debate is then closed. In practice, amendments regularly are debated more than 10 minutes, with members gaining the floor by offering pro forma amendments or obtaining unanimous consent to speak longer than five minutes. *(See Strike Out the Last Word.)*

Floor Manager—A member who has the task of steering legislation through floor debate and the amendment process to a final vote in the House or the Senate. Floor managers are usually chairmen or ranking members of the committee that reported the bill. Managers are responsible for apportioning the debate time granted supporters of the bill. The ranking minority member of the committee normally apportions time for the minority party's participation in the debate.

Frank—A member's facsimile signature, which is used on envelopes in lieu of stamps, for the member's official outgoing mail. The "franking privilege" is the right to send mail postage-free.

Germane—Pertaining to the subject matter of the measure at hand. All House amendments must be germane to the bill being considered. The Senate requires that amendments be germane when they are proposed to general appropriations bills, bills being considered once cloture has been adopted, or, frequently, when proceeding under a unanimous consent agreement placing a time limit on consideration of a bill. The 1974 budget act also requires that amendments to concurrent budget resolutions be germane. In the House, floor debate must be germane, and the first three hours of debate each day in the Senate must be germane to the pending business.

Grandfather Clause—A provision exempting persons or other entities already engaged in an activity from rules or legislation affecting that activity. Grandfather clauses sometimes are added to legislation in order to avoid antagonizing groups with established interests in the activities affected.

Grants-in-Aid—Payments by the federal government to states, local governments or individuals in support of specified programs, services or activities.

Guaranteed Loans—Loans to third parties for which the federal government in the event of default guarantees, in whole or in part, the repayment of principal or interest to a lender or holder of a security.

Hearings—Committee sessions for taking testimony from witnesses. At hearings on legislation, witnesses usually include specialists, government officials and spokesmen for persons or entities affected by the bill or bills under study. Hearings related to special investigations bring forth a variety of witnesses. Committees sometimes use their subpoena power to summon reluctant witnesses. The public and press may attend open hearings, but are barred from closed, or "executive," hearings. The vast majority of hearings are open to the public. *(See Executive Session.)*

Hold-Harmless Clause—A provision added to legislation to ensure that recipients of federal funds do not receive less in a future year than they did in the current year, if a new formula for allocating funds authorized in the legislation would result in a reduction to the recipients. This clause has been used most frequently to soften the impact of sudden reductions in federal grants.

Hopper—Box on House clerk's desk where members deposit bills and resolutions to introduce them. *(See also Bills Introduced.)*

Hour Rule—A provision in the rules of the House that permits one hour of debate time for each member on amendments debated in the House of Representatives sitting as the House. Therefore, the House normally amends bills while sitting as the Committee of the Whole, where the five-minute rule on amendments operates. *(See Committee of the Whole, Five-Minute Rule.)*

House—The House of Representatives, as distinct from the Senate, although each body is a "house" of Congress.

House as in Committee of the Whole—A procedure that can be used to expedite the consideration of certain measures such as continuing resolutions and, when there is debate, private bills. The procedure, which can be invoked only with the unanimous consent of the House or a rule from the Rules Committee, has procedural elements of both the House sitting as the House of Representatives, such as the Speaker presiding and the previous question motion being in order, and the House sitting as the Committee of the Whole, such as the five-minute rule pertaining.

House Calendar—A listing for action by the House of public bills that do not directly or indirectly appropriate money or raise revenue.

Immunity—The constitutional privilege of members of Congress to make verbal statements on the floor and in committee for which they cannot be sued or arrested for slander or libel. Also, freedom from arrest while traveling to or from sessions of Congress or on official business. Members in this status may be arrested only for treason, felonies or a breach of the peace, as defined by congressional manuals.

Impoundments—Any action taken by the executive branch that delays or precludes the obligation or expenditure of budget authority previously approved by Congress. *(See also Deferrals of Budget Authority, Rescission Bill.)*

Joint Committee—A committee composed of a specified number of members of both the House and Senate. A joint committee may be investigative or research-oriented, an example of the latter being the Joint Economic Committee. Others have housekeeping duties such as the joint committees on Printing and on the Library of Congress.

Joint Resolution—A joint resolution, designated H J Res or S J Res, requires the approval of both houses and the signature of the president, just as a bill does, and has the force of law if approved. There is no practical difference between a bill and a joint resolution. A joint resolution generally is used to deal with a limited matter such as a single appropriation.

Joint resolutions also are used to propose amendments to the Constitution in Congress. They do not require a presidential signature, but become a part of the Constitution when three-fourths of the states have ratified them.

Journal—The official record of the proceedings of the House and Senate. The *Journal* records the actions taken in each chamber, but, unlike the *Congressional Record*, it does not include the substantially verbatim report of speeches, debates, etc.

Law—An act of Congress that has been signed by the president or passed over his veto by Congress. Public bills, when signed, become public laws, and are cited by the letters PL and a hyphenated number. The two digits before the number correspond to the Congress, and the one or more digits after the hyphen refer to the numerical sequence in which the bills were signed by the president during that Congress. Private bills, when signed, become private laws. *(See also Slip Laws, Statutes at Large, U.S. Code.)*

Legislative Day—The "day" extending from the time either house meets after an adjournment until the time it next adjourns. Because the House normally adjourns from day to day, legislative days and calendar days usually coincide. But in the Senate, a legislative day may, and frequently does, extend over several calendar days. *(See Recess.)*

Legislative Veto—A procedure permitting either the House or Senate, or both chambers, to review proposed executive branch regulations or actions and to block or modify those with which they disagree. The specifics of the procedure may vary, but Congress generally provides for a legislative veto by including in a bill a provision that administrative rules or action taken to implement the law are to go into effect at the end of a designated period of time unless blocked by either or both houses of Congress. Another version of the veto provides for congressional reconsideration and rejection of regulations already in effect.

The Supreme Court ruling of June 23, 1983, restricted greatly the form and use of the legislative veto as an unconstitutional violation of the lawmaking procedure provided in the Constitution.

Lobby—A group seeking to influence the passage or defeat of legislation. Originally the term referred to persons frequenting the lobbies or corridors of legislative chambers in order to speak to lawmakers.

The definition of a lobby and the activity of lobbying is a matter of differing interpretation. By some definitions, lobbying is limited to direct attempts to influence lawmakers through personal interviews and persuasion. Under other definitions, lobbying includes attempts at indirect, or "grass-roots," influence, such as persuading members of a group to write or visit their district's representative and state's senators or attempting to create a climate of opinion favorable to a desired legislative goal.

The right to attempt to influence legislation is based on the First Amendment to the Constitution, which says Congress shall make no law abridging the right of the people "to petition the government for a redress of grievances."

Majority Leader—The majority leader is elected by his party colleagues. In the Senate, in consultation with the minority leader and his colleagues, the majority leader directs the legislative schedule for the chamber. He also is his party's spokesman and chief strategist. In the House, the majority leader is second to the Speaker in the majority party's leadership and serves as his party's legislative strategist.

Majority Whip—In effect, the assistant majority leader, in either the House or Senate. His job is to help marshal majority forces in support of party strategy and legislation.

Manual—The official handbook in each house prescribing in detail its organization, procedures and operations.

Marking Up a Bill—Going through the contents of a piece of legislation in committee or subcommittee, considering its provisions in large and small portions, acting on amendments to provisions and proposed revisions to the language, inserting new sections and phraseology, etc. If the bill is extensively amended, the committee's version may be introduced as a separate bill, with a new number, before being considered by the full House or Senate. *(See Clean Bill.)*

Minority Leader—Floor leader for the minority party in each chamber. *(See also Majority Leader.)*

Minority Whip—Performs duties of whip for the minority party. *(See also Majority Whip.)*

Morning Hour—The time set aside at the beginning of each legislative day for the consideration of regular, routine business. The "hour" is of indefinite duration in the House, where it is rarely used.

In the Senate it is the first two hours of a session following an adjournment, as distinguished from a recess. The morning hour can be terminated earlier if the morning business has been completed. Business includes such matters as messages from the president, communications from the heads of departments, messages from the House, the presentation of petitions, reports of standing and select committees and the introduction of bills and resolutions. During the first hour of the morning hour in the Senate, no motion to proceed to the consideration of any bill on the calendar is in order except by unanimous consent. During the second hour, motions can be made but must be decided without debate. Senate committees may meet while the Senate conducts morning hour.

Motion—In the House or Senate chamber, a request by a member to institute any one of a wide array of parliamentary actions. He "moves" for a certain procedure, the consideration of a measure, etc. The precedence of motions, and whether they are debatable, is set forth in the House and Senate manuals. *(See some specific motions above and below.)*

Nominations—Presidential appointments to office subject to Senate confirmation. Although most nominations win quick Senate approval, some are controversial and become the topic of hearings and debate. Sometimes senators object to appointees for patronage reasons — for example, when a nomination to a local federal job is made without consulting the senators of the state concerned. In some situations a senator may object that the nominee is "personally obnoxious" to him. Usually other senators join in blocking such appointments out of courtesy to their colleagues. *(See Senatorial Courtesy.)*

One-Minute Speeches—Addresses by House members at the beginning of a legislative day. The speeches may cover any subject, but are limited to one minute's duration.

Override a Veto—If the president disapproves a bill and sends it back to Congress with his objections, Congress may try to override his veto and enact the bill into law. Neither house is required to attempt to override a veto. The override of a veto requires a recorded vote with a two-thirds majority in each chamber. The question put to each house is: "Shall the bill pass, the objections of the president to the contrary notwithstanding?" *(See also Pocket Veto, Veto.)*

Oversight Committee—A congressional committee, or designated subcommittee of a committee, which is charged with general oversight of one or more federal agencies' programs and activities. Usually, the oversight panel for a particular agency also is the authorizing committee for that agency's programs and operations.

Pair—A voluntary arrangement between two lawmakers, usually on opposite sides of an issue. If passage of the measure requires a two-thirds majority vote, a pair would require two members favoring the action to one opposed to it. Pairs can take one of three forms — specific, general and live. The names of lawmakers pairing on a given vote and their stands, if known, are printed in the *Congressional Record.*

The specific pair applies to one or more votes on the same subject. On special pairs, lawmakers usually specify how they would have voted.

A general pair in the Senate, now rarely used, applies to all votes on which the members pairing are on opposite sides. It usually does not specify the positions of the senators pairing. In a general pair in the House, no agreement is involved. A representative expecting to be absent may notify the House clerk he wishes to make a "general" pair. His name then is paired arbitrarily with that of another member desiring a pair, and the list is printed in the *Congressional Record*. He may or may not be paired with a member taking the opposite position. General pairs in the House give no indication of how a member would have voted.

A live pair involves two members, one present for the vote, the other absent. The member present casts his vote and then withdraws it and votes "present." He then announces that he has a live pair with a colleague, identifying how each would have voted on the question. A live pair subtracts the vote of the member in attendance from the final vote tabulation.

Petition—A request or plea sent to one or both chambers from an organization or private citizens' group asking support of particular legislation or favorable consideration of a matter not yet receiving congressional attention. Petitions are referred to appropriate committees.

Pocket Veto—The act of the president in withholding his approval of a bill after Congress has adjourned. When Congress is in session, a bill becomes law without the president's signature if he does not act upon it within 10 days, excluding Sundays, from the time he gets it. But if Congress adjourns sine die within that 10-day period, the bill will die even if the president does not formally veto it. *(See also Veto.)*

Point of Order—An objection raised by a member that the chamber is departing from rules governing its conduct of business. The objector cites the rule violated, the chair sustaining his objection if correctly made. Order is restored by the chair's suspending proceedings of the chamber until it conforms to the prescribed "order of business."

President of the Senate—Under the Constitution, the vice president of the United States presides over the Senate. In his absence, the president pro tempore, or a senator designated by the president pro tempore, presides over the chamber.

President Pro Tempore—The chief officer of the Senate in the absence of the vice president; literally, but loosely, the president for a time. The president pro tempore is elected by his fellow senators, and the recent practice has been to elect to the office the senator of the majority party with the longest period of continuous service.

Previous Question—A motion for the previous question, when carried, has the effect of cutting off all debate, preventing the offering of further amendments, and forcing a vote on the pending matter. In the House, the previous question is not permitted in the Committee of the Whole. The motion for the previous question is a debate-limiting device and is not in order in the Senate.

Printed Amendment—A House rule guarantees five minutes of floor debate in support and five minutes in opposition, and no other debate time, on amendments printed in the *Congressional Record* at least one day prior to the amendment's consideration in the Committee of the Whole.

In the Senate, while amendments may be submitted for printing, they have no parliamentary standing or status. An amendment submitted for printing in the Senate, however, may be called up by any senator.

Private Calendar—In the House, private bills dealing with individual matters such as claims against the government, immigration, land titles, etc., are put on this calendar. The private calendar must be called on the first Tuesday of each month, and the Speaker may call it on the third Tuesday of each month as well.

When a private bill is before the chamber, two members may block its consideration, which recommits the bill to committee. Backers of a recommitted private bill have recourse. The measure can be put into an "omnibus claims bill" — several private bills rolled into one. As with any bill, no part of an omnibus claims bill may be deleted without a vote. When the private bill goes back to the House floor in this form, it can be deleted from the omnibus bill only by majority vote.

Privilege—Privilege relates to the rights of members of Congress and to the relative priority of the motions and actions they may make in their respective chambers. The two are distinct. "Privileged questions" deal with legislative business. "Questions of privilege" concern legislators themselves.

Privileged Questions—The order in which bills, motions and other legislative measures are considered by Congress is governed by strict priorities. A motion to table, for instance, is more privileged than a motion to recommit. Thus, a motion to recommit can be superseded by a motion to table, and a vote would be forced on the latter motion only. A motion to adjourn, however, takes precedence over a tabling motion and thus is considered of the "highest privilege." *(See also Questions of Privilege.)*

Pro Forma Amendment—*(See Strike Out the Last Word.)*

Public Laws—*(See Law.)*

Questions of Privilege—These are matters affecting members of Congress individually or collectively. Matters affecting the rights, safety, dignity and integrity of proceedings of the House or Senate as a whole are questions of privilege in both chambers.

Questions involving individual members are called questions of "personal privilege." A member rising to ask a question of personal privilege is given precedence over almost all other proceedings. An annotation in the House rules points out that the privilege rests primarily on the Constitution, which gives him a conditional immunity from arrest and an unconditional freedom to speak in the House. *(See also Privileged Questions.)*

Quorum—The number of members whose presence is necessary for the transaction of business. In the Senate and House, it is a majority of the membership. A quorum is 100 in the Committee of the Whole House. If a point of order is made that a quorum is not present, the only business that is in order is either a motion to adjourn or a motion to direct the sergeant-at-arms to request the attendance of absentees.

Readings of Bills—Traditional parliamentary procedure required bills to be read three times before they were passed. This custom is of little modern significance. Normally a bill is considered to have its first reading when it is introduced and printed, by title, in the *Congressional Record*. In the House, its second reading comes when floor consideration begins. (This is the most likely point at which there is an actual reading of the bill, if there is any.) The second reading in the Senate is supposed to occur on the legislative day after the measure is introduced, but before it is referred to committee. The third reading (again, usually by title) takes place when floor action has been completed on amendments.

Recess—Distinguished from adjournment *(see above)* in that a recess does not end a legislative day and therefore does not interrupt unfinished business. The rules in each house set forth certain matters to be taken up and disposed of at the beginning of each legislative day. The House usually adjourns from day to day. The Senate often recesses, thus meeting on the same legislative day for several calendar days or even weeks at a time.

Recognition—The power of recognition of a member is lodged in the Speaker of the House and the presiding officer of the Senate. The presiding officer names the member who will speak first when two or more members simultaneously request recognition.

Recommit to Committee—A motion, made on the floor after a bill has been debated, to return it to the committee that reported it. If approved, recommittal usually is considered a death blow to the bill. In the House, a motion to recommit can be made only by a member opposed to the bill, and, in recognizing a member to make the motion, the Speaker gives preference to members of the minority party over majority party members.

A motion to recommit may include instructions to the committee to report the bill again with specific amendments or by a certain date. Or, the instructions may direct that a particular study be made, with no definite deadline for further action. If the recommittal motion includes instructions to "report the bill back forthwith" and the motion is adopted, floor action on the bill continues; the committee does not actually reconsider the legislation.

Reconciliation—*(See Budget Reconciliation.)*

Reconsider a Vote—A motion to reconsider the vote by which an action was taken has, until it is disposed of, the effect of putting the action in abeyance. In the Senate, the motion can be made only by a member who voted on the prevailing side of the original question or by a member who did not vote at all. In the House, it can be made only by a member on the prevailing side.

A common practice in the Senate after close votes on an issue is a motion to reconsider, followed by a motion to table the motion to reconsider. On this motion to table, senators vote as they voted on the original question, which allows the motion to table to prevail, assuming there are no switches. The matter then is finally closed and further motions to reconsider are not entertained. In the House, as a routine precaution, a motion to reconsider usually is made every time a measure is passed. Such a motion almost always is tabled immediately, thus shutting off the possibility of future reconsideration, except by unanimous consent.

Motions to reconsider must be entered in the Senate within the next two days of actual session after the original vote has been taken. In the House they must be entered either on the same day or on the next day the House is in session.

Recorded Vote—A vote upon which each member's stand is individually made known. In the Senate, this is accomplished through a roll call of the entire membership, to which each senator on the floor must answer "yea," "nay" or, if he does not wish to vote, "present." Since January 1973, the House has used an electronic voting system for recorded votes, including yea-and-nay votes formerly taken by roll calls.

When not required by the Constitution, a recorded vote can be obtained on questions in the House on the demand of one-fifth (44 members) of a quorum or one-fourth (25) of a quorum in the Committee of the Whole. *(See Yeas and Nays.)*

Report—Both a verb and a noun as a congressional term. A committee that has been examining a bill referred to it by the parent chamber "reports" its findings and recommendations to the chamber when it completes consideration and returns the measure. The process is called "reporting" a bill.

A "report" is the document setting forth the committee's explanation of its action. Senate and House reports are numbered separately and are designated S Rept or H Rept. When a committee report is not unanimous, the dissenting committee members may file a statement of their views, called minority views and referred to as a minority report. Members in disagreement with some provisions of a bill may file additional or supplementary views. Sometimes a bill is reported without a committee recommendation.

Adverse reports occasionally are submitted by legislative committees. However, when a committee is opposed to a bill, it usually fails to report the bill at all. Some laws require that committee reports — favorable or adverse — be made.

Rescission Bill—A bill rescinding or canceling budget authority previously made available by Congress. The president may request a rescission to reduce spending or because the budget authority no longer is needed. Under the 1974 budget act, however, unless Congress approves a rescission bill within 45 days of continuous session after receipt of the proposal, the funds must be made available for obligation. *(See also Deferrals of Budget Authority.)*

Resolution—A "simple" resolution, designated H Res or S Res, deals with matters entirely within the prerogatives of one house or the other. It requires neither passage by the other chamber nor approval by the president, and it does not have the force of law. Most resolutions deal with the rules or procedures of one house. They also are used to express the sentiments of a single house such as condolences to the family of a deceased member or to comment on foreign policy or executive business. A simple resolution is the vehicle for a "rule" from the House Rules Committee. *(See also Concurrent and Joint Resolutions, Rules.)*

Rider—An amendment, usually not germane, which

its sponsor hopes to get through more easily by including it in other legislation. Riders become law if the bills embodying them are enacted. Amendments providing legislative directives in appropriations bills are outstanding examples of riders, though technically, legislation is banned from appropriations bills. The House, unlike the Senate, has a strict germaneness rule; thus, riders usually are Senate devices to get legislation enacted quickly or to bypass lengthy House consideration and, possibly, opposition.

Rules—The term has two specific congressional meanings. A rule may be a standing order governing the conduct of House or Senate business and listed among the permanent rules of either chamber. The rules deal with duties of officers, the order of business, admission to the floor, parliamentary procedures on handling amendments and voting, jurisdictions of committees, etc.

In the House, a rule also may be a resolution reported by its Rules Committee to govern the handling of a particular bill on the floor. The committee may report a "rule," also called a "special order," in the form of a simple resolution. If the resolution is adopted by the House, the temporary rule becomes as valid as any standing rule and lapses only after action has been completed on the measure to which it pertains. A rule sets the time limit on general debate. It also may waive points of order against provisions of the bill in question such as non-germane language or against certain amendments intended to be proposed to the bill from the floor. It may even forbid all amendments or all amendments except those proposed by the legislative committee that handled the bill. In this instance, it is known as a "closed" or "gag" rule as opposed to an "open" rule, which puts no limitation on floor amendments, thus leaving the bill completely open to alteration by the adoption of germane amendments.

Secretary of the Senate—Chief administrative officer of the Senate, responsible for overseeing the duties of Senate employees, educating Senate pages, administering oaths, handling the registration of lobbyists, and handling other tasks necessary for the continuing operation of the Senate. *(See also Clerk of the House.)*

Select or Special Committee—A committee set up for a special purpose and, usually, for a limited time by resolution of either the House or Senate. Most special committees are investigative and lack legislative authority — legislation is not referred to them and they cannot report bills to their parent chamber. *(See also Standing Committees.)*

Senatorial Courtesy—Sometimes referred to as "the courtesy of the Senate," it is a general practice — with no written rule — applied to consideration of executive nominations. Generally, it means that nominations from a state are not to be confirmed unless they have been approved by the senators of the president's party of that state, with other senators following their colleagues' lead in the attitude they take toward consideration of such nominations. *(See Nominations.)*

Sine Die—*(See Adjournment Sine Die.)*

Slip Laws—The first official publication of a bill that has been enacted and signed into law. Each is published separately in unbound single-sheet or pamphlet form. *(See also Law, Statutes at Large, U.S. Code.)*

Speaker—The presiding officer of the House of Representatives, selected by the caucus of the party to which he belongs and formally elected by the whole House.

Special Session—A session held after Congress has adjourned sine die. Special sessions are convened by the president.

Spending Authority—The 1974 budget act defines spending authority as borrowing authority, contract authority and entitlement authority *(see above)*, for which budget authority is not provided in advance by appropriation acts.

Sponsor—*(See Bills Introduced.)*

Standing Committees—Committees permanently established by House and Senate rules. The standing committees of the House were last reorganized by the committee reorganization act of 1974. The last major realignment of Senate committees was in the committee system reorganization of 1977. The standing committees are legislative committees — legislation may be referred to them and they may report bills and resolutions to their parent chambers. *(See also Select or Special Committees.)*

Standing Vote—A non-recorded vote used in both the House and Senate. (A standing vote also is called a division vote.) Members in favor of a proposal stand and are counted by the presiding officer. Then members opposed stand and are counted. There is no record of how individual members voted.

Statutes at Large—A chronological arrangement of the laws enacted in each session of Congress. Though indexed, the laws are not arranged by subject matter, and there is not an indication of how they have altered previously enacted laws. *(See also Law, Slip Laws, U.S. Code.)*

Strike from the Record—Remarks made on the House floor may offend some member, who moves that the offending words be "taken down" for the Speaker's cognizance, and then expunged from the debate as published in the *Congressional Record.*

Strike Out the Last Word—A motion whereby a House member is entitled to speak for five minutes on an amendment then being debated by the chamber. A member gains recognition from the chair by moving to "strike out the last word" of the amendment or section of the bill under consideration. The motion is pro forma, requires no vote and does not change the amendment being debated.

Substitute—A motion, amendment or entire bill introduced in place of the pending legislative business. Passage of a substitute measure kills the original measure by supplanting it. The substitute also may be amended. *(See also Amendment in the Nature of a Substitute.)*

Supplemental Appropriation Bill—Legislation appropriating funds after the regular annual appropriation bill *(see above)* for a federal department or agency has been enacted. A supplemental appropriation provides additional budget authority beyond original estimates for programs or activities, including new programs authorized after the enactment of the regular appropriation act, for which the need for funds is too urgent to be postponed until enactment of the next year's regular appropriation bill.

Suspend the Rules—Often a time-saving procedure for passing bills in the House. The wording of the motion, which may be made by any member recognized by the Speaker, is: "I move to suspend the rules and pass the bill. . . ." A favorable vote by two-thirds of those present is required for passage. Debate is limited to 40 minutes and no amendments from the floor are permitted. If a two-thirds favorable vote is not attained, the bill may be considered later under regular procedures. The suspension procedure is in order every Monday and Tuesday and is intended to be reserved for non-controversial bills.

Table a Bill—A motion to "lay on the table" is not debatable in either house, and usually it is a method of making a final, adverse disposition of a matter. In the Senate, however, different language sometimes is used. The motion may be worded to let a bill "lie on the table," perhaps for subsequent "picking up." This motion is more flexible, keeping the bill pending for later action, if desired. Tabling motions on amendments are effective debate-ending devices in the Senate.

Teller Vote—This is a largely moribund House procedure in the Committee of the Whole. Members file past tellers and are counted as for, or against, a measure, but they are not recorded individually. In the House, tellers are ordered upon demand of one-fifth of a quorum. This is 44 in the House, 20 in the Committee of the Whole.

The House also has a recorded teller vote, now largely supplanted by the electronic voting procedure, under which the votes of each member are made public just as they would be on a recorded vote. *(See above.)*

Treaties—Executive proposals — in the form of resolutions of ratification — which must be submitted to the Senate for approval by two-thirds of the senators present. Treaties today are normally sent to the Foreign Relations Committee for scrutiny before the Senate takes action. Foreign Relations has jurisdiction over all treaties, regardless of the subject matter. Treaties are read three times and debated on the floor in much the same manner as legislative proposals. After approval by the Senate, treaties are formally ratified by the president.

Trust Funds—Funds collected and used by the federal government for carrying out specific purposes and programs according to terms of a trust agreement or statute such as the Social Security and unemployment compensation trust funds. Such funds are administered by the government in a fiduciary capacity and are not available for the general purposes of the government.

Unanimous Consent—Proceedings of the House or Senate and action on legislation often take place upon the unanimous consent of the chamber, whether or not a rule of the chamber is being violated. Unanimous consent is used to expedite floor action and frequently is used in a routine fashion such as when a senator requests the unanimous consent of the Senate to have specified members of his staff present on the floor during debate on a specific amendment.

Unanimous Consent Agreement—A device used in the Senate to expedite legislation. Much of the Senate's legislative business, dealing with both minor and controversial issues, is conducted through unanimous consent or unanimous consent agreements. On major legislation, such agreements usually are printed and transmitted to all senators in advance of floor debate. Once agreed to, they are binding on all members unless the Senate, by unanimous consent, agrees to modify them. An agreement may list the order in which various bills are to be considered, specify the length of time bills and contested amendments are to be debated and when they are to be voted upon and, frequently, require that all amendments introduced be germane to the bill under consideration. In this regard, unanimous consent agreements are similar to the "rules" issued by the House Rules Committee for bills pending in the House. *(See above.)*

Union Calendar—Bills that directly or indirectly appropriate money or raise revenue are placed on this House calendar according to the date they are reported from committee.

U.S. Code—A consolidation and codification of the general and permanent laws of the United States arranged by subject under 50 titles, the first six dealing with general or political subjects, and the other 44 alphabetically arranged from agriculture to war. The code is revised every six years, and a supplement is published after each session of Congress. *(See also Law, Slip Laws, Statutes at Large.)*

Veto—Disapproval by the president of a bill or joint resolution (other than one proposing an amendment to the Constitution). When Congress is in session, the president must veto a bill within 10 days, excluding Sundays, after he has received it; otherwise, it becomes law without his signature. When the president vetoes a bill, he returns it to the house of origin along with a message stating his objections. *(See also Pocket Veto, Override a Veto.)*

Voice Vote—In either the House or Senate, members answer "aye" or "no" in chorus, and the presiding officer decides the result. The term also is used loosely to indicate action by unanimous consent or without objection.

Whip—*(See Majority and Minority Whip.)*

Without Objection—Used in lieu of a vote on non-controversial motions, amendments or bills that may be passed in either the House or Senate if no member voices an objection.

Yeas and Nays—The Constitution requires that yea-and-nay votes be taken and recorded when requested by one-fifth of the members present. In the House, the Speaker determines whether one-fifth of the members present requested a vote. In the Senate, practice requires only 11 members. The Constitution requires the yeas and nays on a veto override attempt. *(See Recorded Vote.)*

Yielding—When a member has been recognized to speak, no other member may speak unless he obtains permission from the member recognized. This permission is called yielding and usually is requested in the form, "Will the gentleman yield to me?" While this activity occasionally is seen in the Senate, the Senate has no rule or practice to parcel out time.

How a Bill Becomes Law

This graphic shows the most typical way in which proposed legislation is enacted into law. There are more complicated, as well as simpler, routes, and most bills never become law. The process is illustrated with two hypothetical bills, House bill No. 1 (HR 1) and Senate bill No. 2 (S 2). Bills must be passed by both houses in identical form before they can be sent to the president. The path of HR 1 is traced by a solid line, that of S 2 by a broken line. In practice most bills begin as similar proposals in both houses.

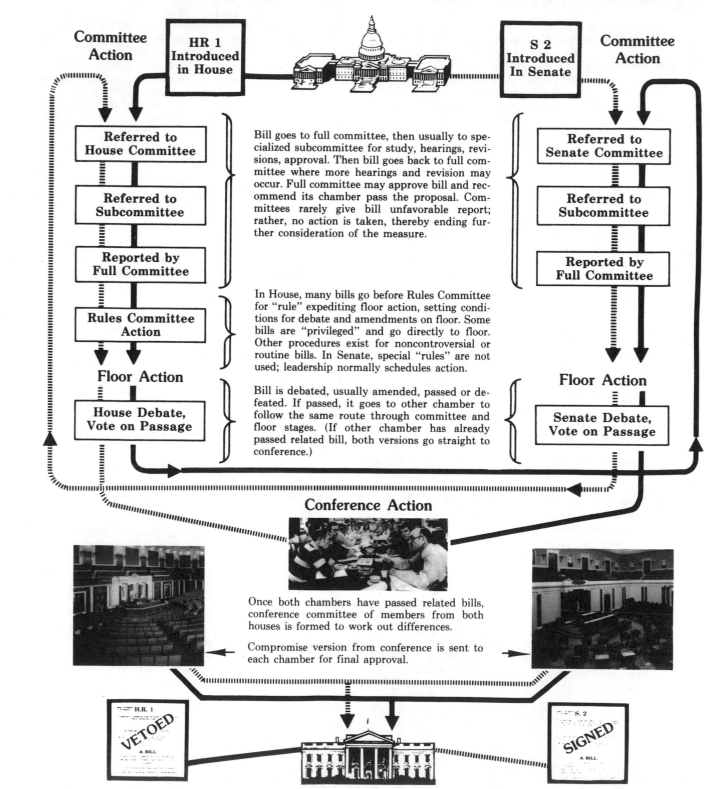

Committee Action

HR 1 Introduced in House

S 2 Introduced In Senate

Committee Action

Referred to House Committee

Referred to Subcommittee

Reported by Full Committee

Bill goes to full committee, then usually to specialized subcommittee for study, hearings, revisions, approval. Then bill goes back to full committee where more hearings and revision may occur. Full committee may approve bill and recommend its chamber pass the proposal. Committees rarely give bill unfavorable report; rather, no action is taken, thereby ending further consideration of the measure.

Referred to Senate Committee

Referred to Subcommittee

Reported by Full Committee

Rules Committee Action

In House, many bills go before Rules Committee for "rule" expediting floor action, setting conditions for debate and amendments on floor. Some bills are "privileged" and go directly to floor. Other procedures exist for noncontroversial or routine bills. In Senate, special "rules" are not used; leadership normally schedules action.

Floor Action

House Debate, Vote on Passage

Bill is debated, usually amended, passed or defeated. If passed, it goes to other chamber to follow the same route through committee and floor stages. (If other chamber has already passed related bill, both versions go straight to conference.)

Floor Action

Senate Debate, Vote on Passage

Conference Action

Once both chambers have passed related bills, conference committee of members from both houses is formed to work out differences.

Compromise version from conference is sent to each chamber for final approval.

H.R. 1 VETOED — A BILL

S. 2 SIGNED — A BILL

Compromise bill approved by both houses is sent to the president, who can sign it into law or veto it and return it to Congress. Congress may override veto by a two-thirds majority vote in both houses; bill then becomes law without president's signature.

The Legislative Process in Brief

Note: Parliamentary terms used below are defined in the Glossary.

Introduction of Bills

A House member (including the resident commissioner of Puerto Rico and non-voting delegates of the District of Columbia, Guam, the Virgin Islands, and American Samoa) may introduce any one of several types of bills and resolutions by handing it to the clerk of the House or placing it in a box called the hopper. A senator first gains recognition of the presiding officer to announce the introduction of a bill. If objection is offered by any senator the introduction of the bill is postponed until the following day.

As the next step in either the House or Senate, the bill is numbered, referred to the appropriate committee, labeled with the sponsor's name, and sent to the Government Printing Office so that copies can be made for subsequent study and action. Senate bills may be jointly sponsored and carry several senators' names. Until 1978, the House limited the number of members who could co-sponsor any one bill; the ceiling was eliminated at the beginning of the 96th Congress. A bill written in the Executive Branch and proposed as an administration measure usually is introduced by the chairman of the congressional committee which has jurisdiction.

Bills—Prefixed with "HR" in the House, "S" in the Senate, followed by a number. Used as the form for most legislation, whether general or special, public or private.

Joint Resolutions—Designated H J Res or S J Res. Subject to the same procedure as bills, with the exception of a joint resolution proposing an amendment to the Constitution. The latter must be approved by two-thirds of both houses and is thereupon sent directly to the administrator of general services for submission to the states for ratification rather than being presented to the president for his approval.

Concurrent Resolutions—Designated H Con Res or S Con Res. Used for matters affecting the operations of both houses. These resolutions do not become law.

Resolutions—Designated H Res or S Res. Used for a matter concerning the operation of either house alone and adopted only by the chamber in which it originates.

Committee Action

A bill is referred to the appropriate committee by a House parliamentarian n the Speaker's order, or by the Senate president. Sponsors may indicate their preferences for referral, although custom and chamber rule generally govern. An exception is the referral of private bills, which a.e sent to whatever group is designated by their sponsors. Bills are technically considered "read for the first time" when referred to House committees.

When a bill reaches a committee it is placed upon the group's calendar. At that time it comes under the sharpest congressional focus. Its chances for passage are quickly determined — and the great majority of bills fall by the legislative roadside. Failure of a committee to act on a bill is equivalent to killing it; the measure can be withdrawn from the group's purview only by a discharge petition signed by a majority of the House membership on House

bills, or by adoption of a special resolution in the Senate. Discharge attempts rarely succeed.

The first committee action taken on a bill usually is a request for comment on it by interested agencies of the government. The committee chairman may assign the bill to a subcommittee for study and hearings, or it may be considered by the full committee. Hearings may be public, closed (executive session), or both. A subcommittee, after considering a bill, reports to the full committee its recommendations for action and any proposed amendments.

The full committee then votes on its recommendation to the House or Senate. This procedure is called "ordering a bill reported." Occasionally a committee may order a bill reported unfavorably; most of the time a report, submitted by the chairman of the committee to the House or Senate, calls for favorable action on the measure since the committee can effectively "kill" a bill by simply failing to take any action.

When a committee sends a bill to the chamber floor, it explains its reasons in a written statement, called a report, which accompanies the bill. Often committee members opposing a measure issue dissenting minority statements which are included in the report.

Usually, the committee "marks up" or proposes amendments to the bill. If they are substantial and the measure is complicated, the committee may order a "clean bill" introduced, which will embody the proposed amendments. The original bill then is put aside and the "clean bill," with a new number, is reported to the floor.

The chamber must approve, alter, or reject the committee amendments before the bill itself can be put to a vote.

Floor Action

After a bill is reported back to the house where it originated, it is placed on the calendar.

There are five legislative calendars in the House, issued in one cumulative calendar titled *Calendars of the United States House of Representatives and History of Legislation.* The House calendars are:

The Union Calendar to which are referred bills raising revenues, general appropriation bills and any measures directly or indirectly appropriating money or property. It is the Calendar of the Committee of the Whole House on the State of the Union.

The House Calendar to which are referred bills of a public character not raising revenue or appropriating money or property.

The Consent Calendar to which are referred bills of a non-controversial nature that are passed without debate when the Consent Calendar is called on the first and third Mondays of each month.

The Private Calendar to which are referred bills for relief in the nature of claims against the United States or private immigration bills that are passed without debate when the Private Calendar is called the first and third Tuesdays of each month.

The Discharge Calendar to which are referred motions to discharge committees when the necessary signatures are signed to a discharge petition.

There is only one legislative calendar in the Senate and one "executive calendar" for treaties and nominations

Progress of Legislation

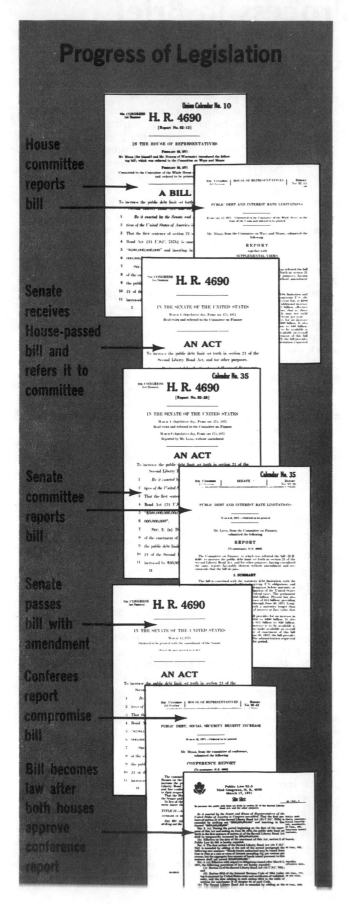

House committee reports bill

Senate receives House-passed bill and refers it to committee

Senate committee reports bill

Senate passes bill with amendment

Conferees report compromise bill

Bill becomes law after both houses approve conference report

submitted to the Senate. When the Senate Calendar is called, each senator is limited to five minutes' debate on each bill.

DEBATE. A bill is brought to debate by varying procedures. If a routine measure, it may await the call of the calendar. If it is urgent or important, it can be taken up in the Senate either by unanimous consent or by a majority vote. The policy committee of the majority party in the Senate schedules the bills that it wants taken up for debate.

In the House, precedence is granted if a special rule is obtained from the Rules Committee. A request for a special rule is usually made by the chairman of the committee that favorably reported the bill, supported by the bill's sponsor and other committee members. The request, considered by the Rules Committee in the same fashion that other committees consider legislative measures, is in the form of a resolution providing for immediate consideration of the bill. The Rules Committee reports the resolution to the House where it is debated and voted upon in the same fashion as regular bills. If the Rules Committee should fail to report a rule requested by a committee, there are several ways to bring the bill to the House floor — under suspension of the rules, on Calendar Wednesday or by a discharge motion.

The resolutions providing special rules are important because they specify how long the bill may be debated and whether it may be amended from the floor. If floor amendments are banned, the bill is considered under a "closed rule," which permits only members of the committee that first reported the measure to the House to alter its language, subject to chamber acceptance.

When a bill is debated under an "open rule," amendments may be offered from the floor. Committee amendments are always taken up first, but may be changed, as may all amendments up to the second degree, i.e., an amendment to an amendment to an amendment is not in order.

Duration of debate in the House depends on whether the bill is under discussion by the House proper or before the House when it is sitting as the Committee of the Whole House on the State of the Union. In the former, the amount of time for debate is determined either by special rule or is allocated with an hour for each member if the measure is under consideration without a rule. In the Committee of the Whole the amount of time agreed on for general debate is equally divided between proponents and opponents. At the end of general discussion, the bill is read section by section for amendment. Debate on an amendment is limited to five minutes for each side.

Senate debate is usually unlimited. It can be halted only by unanimous consent by "cloture," which requires a three-fifths majority of the entire Senate except for proposed changes in the Senate rules. The latter requires a two-thirds vote.

The House sits as the Committee of the Whole when it considers any tax measure or bill dealing with public appropriations. It can also resolve itself into the Committee of the Whole if a member moves to do so and the motion is carried. The Speaker appoints a member to serve as the chairman. The rules of the House permit the Committee of the Whole to meet with any 100 members on the floor, and to amend and act on bills with a quorum of the 100, within the time limitations mentioned previously. When the Committee of the Whole has acted, it "rises," the Speaker returns as the presiding officer of the House and the member appointed chairman of the Committee of the Whole reports the action of the committee and its recommendations (amendments adopted).

VOTES. Voting on bills may occur repeatedly before they are finally approved or rejected. The House votes on the rule for the bill and on various amendments to the bill. Voting on amendments often is a more illuminating test of a bill's support than is the final tally. Sometimes members approve final passage of bills after vigorously supporting amendments which, if adopted, would have scuttled the legislation.

The Senate has three different methods of voting: an untabulated voice vote, a standing vote (called a division) and a recorded roll call to which members answer "yea" or "nay" when their names are called. The House also employs voice and standing votes, but since January 1973 yeas and nays have been recorded by an electronic voting device, eliminating the need for time-consuming roll calls.

Another method of voting, used in the House only, is the teller vote. Traditionally, members filed up the center aisle past counters; only vote totals were announced. Since 1971, one-fifth of a quorum can demand that the votes of individual members be recorded, thereby forcing them to take a public position on amendments to key bills. Electronic voting now is commonly used for this purpose.

After amendments to a bill have been voted upon, a vote may be taken on a motion to recommit the bill to committee. If carried, this vote removes the bill from the chamber's calendar. If the motion is unsuccessful, the bill then is "read for the third time." An actual reading usually is dispensed with. Until 1965, an opponent of a bill could delay this move by objecting and asking for a full reading of an engrossed (certified in final form) copy of the bill. After the "third reading," the vote on final passage is taken.

The final vote may be followed by a motion to reconsider, and this motion itself may be followed by a move to lay the motion on the table. Usually, those voting for the bill's passage vote for the tabling motion, thus safeguarding the final passage action. With that, the bill has been formally passed by the chamber. While a motion to reconsider a Senate vote is pending on a bill, the measure cannot be sent to the House.

Action in Second House

After a bill is passed it is sent to the other chamber. This body may then take one of several steps. It may pass the bill as is — accepting the other chamber's language. It may send the bill to committee for scrutiny or alteration, or reject the entire bill, advising the other house of its actions. Or it may simply ignore the bill submitted while it continues work on its own version of the proposed legislation. Frequently, one chamber may approve a version of a bill that is greatly at variance with the version already passed by the other house, and then substitute its amendments for the language of the other, retaining only the latter's bill designation.

A provision of the Legislative Reorganization Act of 1970 permits a separate House vote on any non-germane amendment added by the Senate to a House-passed bill and requires a majority vote to retain the amendment. Previously the House was forced to act on the bill as a whole; the only way to defeat the non-germane amendment was to reject the entire bill.

Often the second chamber makes only minor changes.

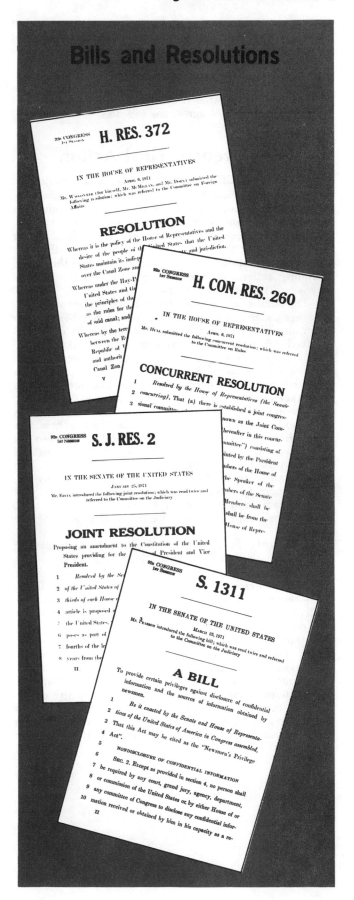

Bills and Resolutions

If these are readily agreed to by the other house, the bill then is routed to the White House for signing. However, if the opposite chamber basically alters the bill submitted to it, the measure usually is "sent to conference." The chamber that has possession of the "papers" (engrossed bill, engrossed amendments, messages of transmittal) requests a conference and the other chamber must agree to it. If the second house does not agree, the bill dies.

Conference, Final Action

CONFERENCE. A conference undertakes to harmonize conflicting House and Senate versions of a legislative bill. The conference is usually staffed by senior members (conferees), appointed by the presiding officers of the two houses, from the committees that managed the bills. Under this arrangement the conferees of one house have the duty of trying to maintain their chamber's position in the face of amending actions by the conferees (also referred to as "managers") of the other house.

The number of conferees from each chamber may vary, the range usually being from three to nine members in each group, depending upon the length or complexity of the bill involved. There may be five representatives and three senators on the conference committee, or the reverse. But a majority vote controls the action of each group so that a larger representation does not give one chamber a voting advantage over the other chamber's conferees.

Theoretically, conferees are not allowed to write new legislation in reconciling the two versions before them, but this curb sometimes is bypassed. Many bills have been put into acceptable compromise form only after new language was provided by the conferees. The 1970 Reorganization Act attempted to tighten restrictions on conferees by forbidding them to introduce any language on a topic that neither chamber sent to conference or to modify any topic beyond the scope of the different House and Senate versions.

Frequently the ironing out of difficulties takes days or even weeks. Conferences on involved appropriation bills sometimes are particularly drawn out.

As a conference proceeds, conferees reconcile differences between the versions, but generally they grant concessions only insofar as they remain sure that the chamber they represent will accept the compromises. Occasionally, uncertainty over how either house will react, or the positive refusal of a chamber to back down on a disputed amendment, results in an impasse, and the bills die in conference even though each was approved by its sponsoring chamber.

Conferees sometimes go back to their respective chambers for further instructions, when they report certain portions in disagreement. Then the chamber concerned can either "recede and concur" in the amendment of the other house, or "insist on its amendment."

When the conferees have reached agreement, they prepare a conference report embodying their recommendations (compromises). The reports, in document form, must be submitted to each house.

The conference report must be approved by each house. Consequently, approval of the report is approval of the compromise bill. In the order of voting on conference reports, the chamber which asked for a conference yields to the other chamber the opportunity to vote first.

FINAL STEPS. After a bill has been passed by both the House and Senate in identical form, all of the original papers are sent to the enrolling clerk of the chamber in which the bill originated. He then prepares an enrolled bill which is printed on parchment paper. When this bill has been certified as correct by the secretary of the Senate or the clerk of the House, depending on which chamber originated the bill, it is signed first (no matter whether it originated in the Senate or House) by the Speaker of the House and then by the president of the Senate. It is next sent to the White House to await action.

If the president approves the bill he signs it, dates it and usually writes the word "approved" on the document. If he does not sign it within 10 days (Sundays excepted) and Congress is in session, the bill becomes law without his signature.

However, should Congress adjourn before the 10 days expire, and the president has failed to sign the measure, it does not become law. This procedure is called the pocket veto.

A president vetoes a bill by refusing to sign it and before the 10-day period expires, returning it to Congress with a message stating his reasons. The message is sent to the chamber which originated the bill. If no action is taken there on the message, the bill dies. Congress, however, can attempt to override the president's veto and enact the bill, "the objections of the president to the contrary notwithstanding." Overriding of a veto requires a two-thirds vote of those present, who must number a quorum and vote by roll call.

Debate can precede this vote, with motions permitted to lay the message on the table, postpone action on it, or refer it to committee. If the president's veto is overridden by a two-thirds vote in both houses, the bill becomes law. Otherwise it is dead.

When bills are passed finally and signed, or passed over a veto, they are given law numbers in numerical order as they become law. There are two series of numbers, one for public and one for private laws, starting at the number "1" for each two-year term of Congress. They are then identified by law number and by Congress — i.e., Private Law 21, 97th Congress; Public Law 250, 97th Congress (or PL 97-250).

98TH CONGRESS, SECOND SESSION

CQ

Organization of Congress

'84 Pressures Shape '85 Leadership Decisions

The 98th Congress adjourned *sine die* Oct. 12, ending a session marred by election-year acrimony and repeated legislative stalemate. For the first time since 1978, lawmakers did not return to Washington for a post-election session. *(Lame-duck sessions, 1982 Almanac p. 6)*

In the Senate, filibuster threats and drawn-out negotiations slowed work on almost every major piece of legislation considered during 1984. Impending retirement limited the influence of Majority Leader Howard H. Baker Jr., R-Tenn., a leader known for his accommodative style, and White House intransigence hindered Republican solidarity on some major issues. In the House, the Democratic leadership faced challenges from junior members of its own party, as well as strident attacks from conservative Republicans.

The frustrations of the 1984 session colored organizational meetings held late in the year for the 99th Congress that was to begin Jan. 3, 1985.

Senate Republicans selected a forceful new majority leader who was expected to discipline Senate operations and stand up to the White House on divisive issues. While Senate Democrats re-elected their top leader, the fact that there was a contest at all reflected the degree of discontent within the party.

Despite considerable ferment for change, Democrats in the House left their leadership and rules essentially intact as they organized for the new Congress. House Republicans likewise made no leadership changes.

Senate

Robert Dole, R-Kan., was elected Senate majority leader in a tight five-way race Nov. 28. In a closed-door caucus of the 53 Republicans who were to serve in the 99th Congress, Dole prevailed over four other contenders, finally defeating Alaskan Ted Stevens on a 28-25 vote in the last round.

The caucus also elected five other new members to the Republican leadership team. The second-ranking leadership slot went to Alan K. Simpson, Wyo., who replaced Stevens as majority whip. Other new GOP leaders were John H. Chafee, R.I., chairman of the Republican Conference; Thad Cochran, Miss., conference secretary; William L. Armstrong, Colo., Policy Committee chairman; and John Heinz, Pa., chairman of the Republican Senate campaign committee.

Republican senators hailed the new leadership as geographically and ideologically balanced. But philosophically, the group seemed tilted toward the party's moderate wing, with several of the Senate's more conservative Republicans losing their bids for leadership slots.

A senator since 1969 and House member for eight years before that, Dole, 61, was the Republican vice presidential nominee in 1976. He also was considered a probable candidate for the presidency in 1988. Dole was viewed as a tough-minded leader, whose strong personality and skills as a negotiator would be useful in pushing legislation through an often unruly Senate.

"If we really want the discipline, I'm willing to provide

it, maybe if we don't even want it all the time," Dole said after his election.

Dole's elevation to majority leader required him to yield his chairmanship of the tax-writing Senate Finance Committee to moderate Bob Packwood, R-Ore. Packwood was replaced in the Commerce Committee chair by John C. Danforth, R-Mo. Another result of the Nov. 28 race was that Richard G. Lugar, R-Ind., who lost his attempt to become leader, took over the Foreign Relations Committee, while Jesse Helms, R-N.C., remained head of the Agriculture Committee.

A Rare Vote

The election Nov. 28 was the first time since 1937 that the selection of a Senate majority leader came down to a vote. There was a contest in 1977 between Democrats Robert C. Byrd, W.Va., and Hubert H. Humphrey, Minn., for the majority leader's job, but Humphrey withdrew from the race on the morning of the Democratic Conference vote. *(1977 Almanac p. 3)*

The 1984 race started soon after Baker announced in January 1983 that he would leave the Senate at the end of the 98th Congress. By fall, there were five entries in the field: Dole, Stevens, Lugar, Pete V. Domenici, N.M., and James A. McClure, Idaho.

98th Congress Leadership

SENATE

President Pro Tempore — Strom Thurmond, R-S.C.
Majority Leader — Howard H. Baker Jr., R-Tenn.
Majority Whip — Ted Stevens, R-Alaska
Republican Conference Chairman — James A. McClure, R-Idaho
Republican Conference Secretary — Jake Garn, R-Utah

Minority Leader — Robert C. Byrd, D-W.Va.
Minority Whip — Alan Cranston, D-Calif.
Democratic Conference Secretary — Daniel K. Inouye, D-Hawaii

HOUSE

Speaker — Thomas P. O'Neill Jr., D-Mass.
Majority Leader — Jim Wright, D-Texas
Majority Whip — Thomas S. Foley, D-Wash.
Caucus Chairman — Gillis W. Long, D-La.

Minority Leader — Robert H. Michel, R-Ill.
Minority Whip — Trent Lott, R-Miss.
Chairman of the Conference — Jack F. Kemp, R-N.Y.
Policy Committee Chairman — Dick Cheney, R-Wyo.

To win, a senator needed the votes of a majority of his Republican colleagues, or 27 votes. The basic rule was that if no senator won a clear majority on the first ballot, the bottom man dropped out. That low-man-out procedure continued until Dole won a majority on the fourth ballot.

On the first ballot, McClure fell out of the race. Domenici was the next to go. On the third ballot, Lugar received 13 votes, leaving the race to Stevens and Dole, with 20 votes each. In the last round, Dole defeated Stevens by a three-vote margin.

With Dole's selection as majority leader, Senate Republicans effectively declared their independence from the White House. Of the five men who sought the job, Dole was the least likely to toe the White House line on legislation. He had disagreed with President Reagan on issues as diverse as taxes, civil rights and food stamps.

Republican Contrasts

The new leadership lineup was a contrast to the picture of the Republican Party that emerged from its 1984 presidential nominating convention in Dallas. There, the party's right wing dominated the drafting of the Republican platform, and pragmatists like Dole were shunted aside. At the convention's end, though, Dole told a reporter, "We're going back to the real world now — it's called Washington."

While Senate Republicans turned to practical leaders like Dole and Simpson, House Republicans increasingly had come under the influence of a group of young conservatives, such as Newt Gingrich, Ga., who preferred confrontation over compromise.

Dole said, however, that because Senate Republicans were in the majority, they had a responsibility to pass the president's program, a burden House Republicans did not bear because they were in the minority.

Senate Democrats

Senate Democrats, although feeling the same pressures for change as the rest of the party, chose to stick with their current leaders for another two years. But they vowed to become more assertive in their role as minority party in 1985.

On Dec. 10, the Democrats voted 32-10 to keep Byrd as minority leader, turning aside a last-minute challenge by Lawton Chiles, Fla. Proxies, counted after the vote was announced, made the tally 36-11.

Alan Cranston, Calif., was unchallenged in his bid to retain the party's No. 2 spot, minority whip. And Daniel K. Inouye, Hawaii, remained as the secretary of the Democratic Conference. All three men had held their posts since 1977.

As he had promised to do if re-elected, Byrd named George J. Mitchell, Maine, to be chairman of the Democratic Senatorial Campaign Committee. Mitchell replaced Lloyd Bentsen, Texas, who did not want to continue in the job.

Byrd, 67, could take only modest comfort from his victory. The fact that Chiles, a cautious, moderate-to-conservative politician, chose to run against him in 1984 signaled the depth of Democratic discontent. Never before had anyone challenged an incumbent Democratic leader in the Senate.

House

As the closed-door caucus of House Democrats opened Dec. 3, an internal challenge to Speaker Thomas P. O'Neill Jr. evaporated and the Massachusetts Democrat was renominated to his fifth and final term as Speaker — a choice ratified by the full House a month later.

While Democrats fought over changes in the budget

Membership Changes, 98th Congress

Senate

Party	Member	Died	Resigned	Successor	Party	Appointed	Sworn In
D	Henry M. Jackson, Wash.	9/1/83		Daniel J. Evans	R	9/8/83*	9/12/83

House

Party	Member	Died	Resigned	Successor	Party	Elected	Sworn In
R	Jack Swigert	12/27/82		Daniel L. Schaefer	R	3/29/83	4/7/83
D	Benjamin S. Rosenthal	1/4/83		Gary L. Ackerman	D	3/1/83	3/2/83
D	Phil Gramm		1/5/83	Phil Gramm	R	2/12/83	2/22/83
D	Phillip Burton	4/10/83		Sala Burton	D	6/21/83	6/28/83
D	Harold Washington		4/30/83	Charles A. Hayes	D	8/23/83	9/12/83
D	Larry P. McDonald	9/1/83		George W. "Buddy" Darden	D	11/8/83	11/10/83
D	Clement J. Zablocki	12/3/83		Gerald D. Kleczka	D	4/3/84	4/10/84
R	Edwin B. Forsythe	3/29/84		H. James Saxton	R	11/6/84	
D	Andy Ireland		Ireland switched to the Republican Party on July 5, 1984.				
D	Carl D. Perkins	8/3/84		Carl C. "Chris" Perkins	D	11/6/84	

* Evans subsequently was elected to fill the remaining five years of the term, expiring Jan. 3, 1989.

process, rules governing the chairmanship of the Budget Committee and limits on House television broadcasts, they could not reach agreement on these issues and stuck with the status quo.

But there was a sense of transition in the caucus. Looking to the 99th Congress and O'Neill's planned retirement at its conclusion, Democratic leaders agreed to open up decision making to a wider variety of Democrats.

There also was a reflective mood in the wake of the Nov. 6 elections, when the Democrats lost 49 states in the presidential race and at least 14 seats in the House. One seat in Indiana remained undecided.

"There was a sense of relief that we were elected and the country didn't turn that many House members out of office," said Jim Moody, D-Wis. "But Democrats are clearly on the defensive in the country and there was apprehension about what's to come."

Although nearly two dozen House rules changes were on the Democratic Caucus agenda, only a handful of minor revisions emerged from the three-day meeting.

Controversial proposals that were rejected or set aside included:

● A rules change to waive a three-term limit to allow Budget Committee Chairman James R. Jones, D-Okla., and senior Budget member Leon E. Panetta, D-Calif., to remain on the committee and compete for the chairmanship in the 99th Congress.

● A plan by David R. Obey, D-Wis., to overhaul the budget process by merging, into one massive bill, a spending blueprint, all appropriations and tax bills, and authorization measures needed to implement the spending plan. It was rejected, 53-176.

● A proposal to limit the time reserved for televised "special order" speeches at the end of each day. After protests from Republicans who called this a "gag rule" and liberal Democrats concerned about restraints on free speech, the plan was dropped.

● A proposal by Thomas J. Downey, D-N.Y., to create a Select Committee on Arms Control. Defeated 103-112, this proposal would have consolidated jurisdiction over arms control that was currently shared by the Foreign Affairs and Armed Services committees.

Democratic Leaders

O'Neill was nominated for Speaker by acclamation Dec. 3, after Texan Charles W. Stenholm abandoned his challenge to O'Neill. Stenholm, the leader of the 33-member Conservative Democratic Forum, had talked about running against O'Neill to demonstrate "Boll Weevil" discontent within the party.

But after a Nov. 30 meeting with O'Neill, Stenholm said it would have been "destructive" for him to run because O'Neill had agreed to concessions that would give conservatives "a voice at the table" when party strategy was discussed.

In his acceptance speech to the caucus, O'Neill, who turned 72 Dec. 9, said he would retire after the 99th Congress. He first announced his retirement plans to reporters in March.

Alluding to Stenholm's complaints, O'Neill said, "Our party is a party of many philosophies. Our diversity is our greatest strength, but it is also the source of great tensions.... We need to listen to all our Democratic colleagues."

After renominating O'Neill for Speaker, the Democrats re-elected Jim Wright, Texas, as majority leader.

Senate Cloture Votes

Following is list of all cloture votes taken by the Senate during 1984. Cloture motions required a three-fifths majority of the total Senate (60 members) for adoption, under a rule adopted in 1975. Previously cloture could be invoked by a two-thirds majority vote of those senators present and voting, except between 1949 and 1959, when the rule required a two-thirds majority of the entire Senate.

Since 1979, Senate rules had required, after no more than 100 hours of post-cloture debate, a final vote on a measure on which cloture had been invoked.

The 12 cloture votes in 1984 brought to 206 the total number of cloture votes taken since the adoption of Rule 22 first allowed them in 1917. *(Previous votes, 1983 Almanac p. 7; 1982 Almanac p. 5; 1981 Almanac p. 10; 1977 Almanac p. 813)*

Issue	Date	Vote
Capital Punishment	Feb. 9, 1984	65-26
Hydroelectric Power Plants	July 30, 1984	60-28
Wilkinson Nomination	July 31, 1984	57-39
Agriculture Appropriations, Fiscal 1985	Aug. 6, 1984	54-31
Agriculture Appropriations, Fiscal 1985	Aug. 8, 1984	68-30
Wilkinson Nomination	Aug. 9, 1984	65-32
Financial Services Competitive Equity Act	Sept. 10, 1984	89-3
Financial Services Competitive Equity Act	Sept. 13, 1984	92-6
Broadcasting of Senate Procedures	Sept. 18, 1984	73-26
Broadcasting of Senate Procedures	Sept. 21, 1984	37-44
Surface Transportation and Uniform Relocation Assistance Act	Sept. 24, 1984	70-12
Continuing Appropriations	Sept. 29, 1984	92-4

O'Neill and Wright reappointed Thomas S. Foley, Wash., as majority whip and Bill Alexander, Ark., as chief deputy whip. The caucus elected Richard A. Gephart, Mo., as its new chairman. He replaced Gillis W. Long, La., who, under caucus rules, had to retire after four years as chairman. Although Gephardt was unopposed, the secret ballot for the chairmanship was 208-5.

Elected by voice vote was Mary Rose Oakar, Ohio, as caucus secretary. She succeeded Geraldine A. Ferraro, N.Y., who gave up her House seat to run for vice president.

Divisive Issues

Special Orders. One of the most volatile issues in the Democratic Caucus was the plan to curb the time devoted to special-order speeches.

The caucus committee on organization, study and review Nov. 19 recommended that special orders at the end of the day should be limited to one hour for Democrats and one hour for Republicans, to be controlled by leaders of each party.

Under existing procedures, an unlimited amount of time could be spent on these speeches by members of either party. Junior House Republicans, led by Gingrich, used the

Vetoes Cast by President Reagan

President Reagan vetoed 17 bills in his fourth year in office, bringing his total vetoes to 39.

Congress overrode one veto in 1984, the only one on which an override attempt was made. That bill was S 684, which authorized $36 million annually for water resources research institutes at land grant colleges in 50 states and some U.S. territories.

Reagan had one veto overridden in 1983 and two in 1982 — for a total of four during his first term.

When Congress is in session, a bill becomes law without the president's signature if he does not act upon it within 10 days, excluding Sundays, from the time he receives it. But if Congress adjourns within that 10-day period, the bill is killed, or pocket-vetoed, without the president's signature. Fourteen of the 17 vetoes in 1984 were pocket vetoes.

1981

1. H J Res 357 (Continuing Appropriations)
   Vetoed: Nov. 23, 1981
   No override attempt
2. HR 4353 (Bankruptcy Fees on Lifetime Communities Inc.)
   Pocket-vetoed: Dec. 29, 1981†

1982

3. S 1503 (Standby Petroleum Allocation)
   Vetoed: March 20, 1982
   Senate sustained March 24: 58-36 *
4. HR 5118 (Southern Arizona Water Rights Settlement Act)
   Vetoed: June 1, 1982
   No override attempt
5. HR 5922 (Urgent Supplemental Appropriations, Fiscal 1982)
   Vetoed: June 24, 1982
   House sustained June 24: 253-151 *
6. HR 6682 (Urgent Supplemental Appropriations, Fiscal 1982)
   Vetoed: June 25, 1982
   House sustained July 13: 242-169 *
7. HR 6198 (Manufacturers Copyright Bill)
   Vetoed: July 8, 1982
   Veto overridden July 13 *
   House: 324-86, July 13
   Senate: 84-9, July 13
8. HR 6863 (Supplemental Appropriations, Fiscal 1982)
   Vetoed: Aug. 28, 1982
   Veto overridden Sept. 10 *
   House: 301-117, Sept. 9
   Senate: 60-30, Sept. 10
9. HR 1371 (Contract Disputes)
   Vetoed: Oct. 15, 1982
   No override attempt
10. S 2577 (Environmental Research and Development)
    Vetoed: Oct. 22, 1982
    No override attempt
11. S 2623 (Indian Controlled Community Colleges)
    Pocket-vetoed: Jan. 3, 1983†
12. HR 5858 (Private Bill for Relief of Certain Silver Dealers)
    Pocket-vetoed: Jan. 4, 1983†
13. HR 7336 (Education Consolidation and Improvement Act Amendments)
    Pocket-vetoed: Jan. 12, 1983†
14. HR 9 (Florida Wilderness Act)
    Pocket-vetoed: Jan. 14, 1983†
15. HR 3963 (Anti-Crime Bill)
    Pocket-vetoed: Jan. 14, 1983†

1983

16. S 366 (Indian Claims Bill)
    Vetoed: April 5, 1983
    No override attempt
17. S 973 (Tax Leasing Plan)
    Vetoed: June 17, 1983
    No override attempt

18. HR 3564 (Feed Grains Bill)
    Vetoed: Aug. 12, 1983
    No override attempt
19. H J Res 338 (Chicago School Desegregation)
    Vetoed: Aug. 13, 1983
    No override attempt
20. S J Res 149 (Dairy Assessment Delay Bill)
    Vetoed: Aug. 23, 1983
    No override attempt
21. HR 1062 (Oregon Land Transfer Bill)
    Vetoed: Oct. 19, 1983
    Veto overridden Oct. 25 *
    Senate: 95-0, Oct. 25
    House: 297-125, Oct. 25
22. HR 4042 (El Salvador Certification)
    Pocket-vetoed: Nov. 30, 1983

1984

23. S 684 (Water Resources Research)
    Vetoed: Feb. 21, 1984
    Veto overridden March 22 *
    Senate: 86-12, March 21
    House: 309-81, March 22
24. S 2436 (Corporation for Public Broadcasting)
    Vetoed: Aug. 29, 1984
25. HR 1362 (Private Bill)
    Vetoed: Oct. 8, 1984
26. S 1967 (Indian Affairs)
    Pocket-vetoed: Oct. 17, 1984†
27. HR 2859 (Private Bill)
    Pocket-vetoed: Oct. 17, 1984
28. S 1097 (NOAA Research and Services Act)
    Pocket-vetoed: Oct. 19, 1984†
29. S 607 (Corporation for Public Broadcasting)
    Pocket-vetoed: Oct. 19, 1984†
30. S 2166 (Indian Health Care Improvement Act)
    Pocket-vetoed: Oct. 19, 1984†
31. HR 6248 (Armed Career Criminal Act of 1984)
    Pocket-vetoed: Oct. 19, 1984†
32. HR 5172 (National Bureau of Standards Authorizations)
    Pocket-vetoed: Oct. 30, 1984†
33. S 540 (Health Research Extension Act of 1984)
    Pocket-vetoed: Oct. 30, 1984†
34. S 2574 (Public Health Service Act Amendments of 1984)
    Pocket-vetoed: Oct. 30, 1984†
35. HR 999 (American Conservation Corps Act of 1984)
    Pocket-vetoed: Oct. 30, 1984†
36. HR 5760 (Indian Affairs)
    Pocket-vetoed: Oct. 30, 1984†
37. HR 723 (Private Bill)
    Pocket-vetoed: Oct. 31, 1984
38. HR 452 (Private Bill)
    Pocket-vetoed: Oct. 31, 1984
39. HR 5479 (Civil Actions and Procedures)
    Pocket-vetoed: Nov. 8, 1984†

* Veto overrides require a two-thirds majority vote of both houses.
† President's memorandum of disapproval issued on this date.

special orders extensively in 1984 to criticize Democrats. As part of House proceedings, their speeches were broadcast live to millions of cable television watchers.

O'Neill partially retaliated in May when he ordered that the television cameras pan the chamber during special orders to show viewers that the chamber was virtually empty. *(Story, p. 206)*

But, still angry about the after-hours attacks, many Democrats called for restrictions on the speeches or a policy change so they would not be broadcast. In addition, some complained that it was expensive for the House to continue in session long after regular legislative business was completed. One estimate set the cost of the speeches at $10,000 an hour, to cover employee salaries, utilities and other expenses.

Despite this grumbling, there was heavy opposition to the proposed restrictions when the caucus considered them Dec. 4. After two days of negotiations between Democrats and Republicans and among the Democrats themselves, the proposal was shelved.

House Republicans, who were adamantly opposed to the new restrictions, were relieved that the Democrats could not reach an agreement.

Obey Budget Plan. Another divisive issue in the Democratic Caucus was Obey's budget proposal. He had been touting it for the past six years, but it was too much for House Democrats to swallow.

Under the Obey plan, the House would vote on one, omnibus budget bill that contained a spending and tax blueprint and all the appropriations and authorization legislation required to carry out the budget.

But the plan did not have the support of the House leadership. And it was strenuously opposed by almost every authorizing committee chairman, many of whom believed that their power would be severely diminished under the Obey budgeting scheme. John D. Dingell, D-Mich., chairman of the Energy and Commerce Committee, led a lobbying effort against the proposal.

After the 53-176 drubbing, Obey said the overriding reason for the defeat was "doubt that the House could ever pass the bill."

Obey's rationale for lumping all fiscal decisions into one bill was to force members to make not only abstract decisions about deficit cutting, but to vote for the cuts as well. Under the existing system, Obey charged, "the only way we can put a budget together is to design one that doesn't reflect what's done."

Public Laws

A total of 408 bills cleared by Congress in 1984 became public laws. Following is a list of the number of public laws enacted since 1967:

Year	Public Laws	Year	Public Laws
1984	408	1975	205
1983	215	1974	404
1982	328	1973	247
1981	145	1972	383
1980	426	1971	224
1979	187	1970	505
1978	410	1969	190
1977	223	1968	391
1976	383	1967	249

The Democratic Caucus did approve a "sense of the caucus" resolution urging that the current budget process be expedited.

House Republicans

House Republicans also caucused during the week of Dec. 3. In a pro forma gesture, they named Minority Leader Robert H. Michel, Ill., as their candidate for Speaker and approved a package of proposed rules changes for the House to consider when it convened Jan. 3, 1985.

Republicans retained their leadership team of Michel as minority leader; Trent Lott, Miss., as whip; and Jack F. Kemp, N.Y., as conference chairman. To replace retiring member Jack Edwards, Ala., as conference vice chairman, the House Republicans chose Lynn Martin, Ill.

Michel in his acceptance speech appeared to endorse the confrontational strategy favored by the group of junior Republicans led by Gingrich.

"The most important thing we have done is rid ourselves of that subservient, timid mentality of the permanent minority," Michel said. "The Republican Party in the House is no longer content to go along. We want to go for broke."

But he added that there was room for both compromise and confrontation. ∎

Members of the 98th Congress, Second Session . . .

As of Oct. 12, 1984
Representatives
D 266; R 167
2 Vacancies*

A

Ackerman, Gary L., D-N.Y. (7)
Addabbo, Joseph P., D-N.Y. (6)
Akaka, Daniel K., D-Hawaii (2)
Albosta, Donald J., D-Mich. (10)
Alexander, Bill, D-Ark. (1)
Anderson, Glenn M., D-Calif. (32)
Andrews, Ike, D-N.C. (4)
Andrews, Michael A., D-Texas (25)
Annunzio, Frank, D-Ill. (11)
Anthony, Beryl Jr., D-Ark. (4)
Applegate, Douglas, D-Ohio (18)
Archer, Bill, R-Texas (7)
Aspin, Les, D-Wis. (1)
AuCoin, Les, D-Ore. (1)

B

Badham, Robert E., R-Calif. (40)
Barnard, Doug Jr., D-Ga. (10)
Barnes, Michael D., D-Md. (8)
Bartlett, Steve, R-Texas (3)
Bateman, Herbert H., R-Va. (1)
Bates, Jim, D-Calif. (44)
Bedell, Berkley, D-Iowa (6)
Beilenson, Anthony C., D-Calif. (23)
Bennett, Charles E., D-Fla. (3)
Bereuter, Douglas K., R-Neb. (1)
Berman, Howard L., D-Calif. (26)
Bethune, Ed, R-Ark. (2)
Bevill, Tom, D-Ala. (4)
Biaggi, Mario, D-N.Y. (19)
Bilirakis, Michael, R-Fla. (9)
Bliley, Thomas J. Jr., R-Va. (3)
Boehlert, Sherwood, R-N.Y. (25)
Boggs, Lindy (Mrs. Hale), D-La. (2)
Boland, Edward P., D-Mass. (2)
Boner, Bill, D-Tenn. (5)
Bonior, David E., D-Mich. (12)
Bonker, Don, D-Wash. (3)
Borski, Robert A., D-Pa. (3)
Bosco, Douglas H., D-Calif. (1)
Boucher, Frederick C., D-Va. (9)
Boxer, Barbara, D-Calif. (6)
Breaux, John B., D-La. (7)
Britt, Robin, D-N.C. (6)
Brooks, Jack, D-Texas (9)
Broomfield, William S., R-Mich. (18)
Brown, George E. Jr., D-Calif. (36)
Brown, Hank, R-Colo. (4)
Broyhill, James T., R-N.C. (10)
Bryant, John, D-Texas (5)
Burton, Dan L., R-Ind. (6)
Burton, Sala, D-Calif. (5)
Byron, Beverly B., D-Md. (6)

C

Campbell, Carroll A. Jr., R-S.C. (4)
Carney, William, R-N.Y. (1)
Carper, Thomas R., D-Del. (AL)
Carr, Bob, D-Mich. (6)
Chandler, Rod, R-Wash. (8)
Chappell, Bill Jr., D-Fla. (4)
Chappie, Gene, R-Calif. (2)
Cheney, Dick, R-Wyo. (AL)
Clarke, James McClure, D-N.C. (11)
Clay, William, D-Mo. (1)
Clinger, William F. Jr., R-Pa. (23)
Coats, Dan, R-Ind. (4)
Coelho, Tony, D-Calif. (15)
Coleman, E. Thomas, R-Mo. (6)
Coleman, Ron, D-Texas (16)
Collins, Cardiss, D-Ill. (7)
Conable, Barber B. Jr., R-N.Y. (30)
Conte, Silvio O., R-Mass. (1)
Conyers, John Jr., D-Mich. (1)
Cooper, Jim, D-Tenn. (4)
Corcoran, Tom, R-Ill. (14)
Coughlin, Lawrence, R-Pa. (13)

Courter, Jim, R-N.J. (12)
Coyne, William J., D-Pa. (14)
Craig, Larry E., R-Idaho (1)
Crane, Daniel B., R-Ill. (19)
Crane, Philip M., R-Ill. (12)
Crockett, George W. Jr., D-Mich. (13)

D

D'Amours, Norman E., D-N.H. (1)
Daniel, Dan, D-Va. (5)
Dannemeyer, William E., R-Calif. (39)
Darden, George W. "Buddy", D-Ga.
Daschle, Thomas A., D-S.D. (AL)
Daub, Hal, R-Neb. (2)
Davis, Robert W., R-Mich. (11)
de la Garza, E. "Kika", D-Texas (15)
Dellums, Ronald V., D-Calif. (8)
Derrick, Butler, D-S.C. (3)
DeWine, Michael, R-Ohio (7)
Dickinson, William L., R-Ala. (2)
Dicks, Norman D., D-Wash. (6)
Dingell, John D., D-Mich. (16)
Dixon, Julian C., D-Calif. (28)
Donnelly, Brian J., D-Mass. (11)
Dorgan, Byron L., D-N.D. (AL)
Dowdy, Wayne, D-Miss. (4)
Downey, Thomas J., D-N.Y. (2)
Dreier, David, R-Calif. (33)
Duncan, John J., R-Tenn. (2)
Durbin, Dick, D-Ill. (20)
Dwyer, Bernard J., D-N.J. (6)
Dymally, Mervyn M., D-Calif. (31)
Dyson, Roy, D-Md. (1)

E

Early, Joseph D., D-Mass. (3)
Eckart, Dennis E., D-Ohio (11)
Edgar, Bob, D-Pa. (7)
Edwards, Don, D-Calif. (10)
Edwards, Jack, R-Ala. (1)
Edwards, Mickey, R-Okla. (5)
Emerson, Bill, R-Mo. (8)
English, Glenn, D-Okla. (6)
Erdreich, Ben, D-Ala. (6)
Erlenborn, John N., R-Ill. (13)
Evans, Cooper, R-Iowa (3)
Evans, Lane, D-Ill. (17)

F

Fascell, Dante B., D-Fla. (19)
Fazio, Vic, D-Calif. (4)
Feighan, Edward F., D-Ohio (19)
Ferraro, Geraldine A., D-N.Y. (9)
Fiedler, Bobbi, R-Calif. (21)
Fields, Jack, R-Texas (8)
Fish, Hamilton Jr., R-N.Y. (21)
Flippo, Ronnie G., D-Ala. (5)
Florio, James J., D-N.J. (1)
Foglietta, Thomas M., D-Pa. (1)
Foley, Thomas S., D-Wash. (5)
Ford, Harold E., D-Tenn. (9)
Ford, William D., D-Mich. (15)
Fowler, Wyche Jr., D-Ga. (5)
Frank, Barney, D-Mass. (4)
Franklin, Webb, R-Miss. (2)
Frenzel, Bill, R-Minn. (3)
Frost, Martin, D-Texas (24)
Fuqua, Don, D-Fla. (2)

G

Garcia, Robert, D-N.Y. (18)
Gaydos, Joseph M., D-Pa. (20)
Gejdenson, Sam, D-Conn. (2)
Gekas, George W., R-Pa. (17)
Gephardt, Richard A., D-Mo. (3)
Gibbons, Sam, D-Fla. (7)
Gilman, Benjamin A., R-N.Y. (22)
Gingrich, Newt, R-Ga. (6)
Glickman, Dan, D-Kan. (4)
Gonzalez, Henry B., D-Texas (20)
Goodling, Bill, R-Pa. (19)
Gore, Albert Jr., D-Tenn. (6)
Gradison, Bill, R-Ohio (2)
Gramm, Phil, R-Texas (6)
Gray, William H. III, D-Pa. (2)
Green, Bill, R-N.Y. (15)

Gregg, Judd, R-N.H. (2)
Guarini, Frank J., D-N.J. (14)
Gunderson, Steve, R-Wis. (3)

H

Hall, Katie, D-Ind. (1)
Hall, Ralph M., D-Texas (4)
Hall, Sam B. Jr., D-Texas (1)
Hall, Tony P., D-Ohio (3)
Hamilton, Lee H., D-Ind. (9)
Hammerschmidt, John Paul, R-Ark. (3)
Hance, Kent, D-Texas (19)
Hansen, George, R-Idaho (2)
Hansen, James V., R-Utah (1)
Harkin, Tom, D-Iowa (5)
Harrison, Frank, D-Pa. (11)
Hartnett, Thomas F., R-S.C. (1)
Hatcher, Charles, D-Ga. (2)
Hawkins, Augustus F., D-Calif. (29)
Hayes, Charles A., D-Ill. (1)
Hefner, W. G. "Bill", D-N.C. (8)
Heftel, Cecil, D-Hawaii (1)
Hertel, Dennis M., D-Mich. (14)
Hightower, Jack, D-Texas (13)
Hiler, John, R-Ind. (3)
Hillis, Elwood, R-Ind. (5)
Holt, Marjorie S., R-Md. (4)
Hopkins, Larry J., R-Ky. (6)
Horton, Frank, R-N.Y. (29)
Howard, James J., D-N.J. (3)
Hoyer, Steny H., D-Md. (5)
Hubbard, Carroll Jr., D-Ky. (1)
Huckaby, Jerry, D-La. (5)
Hughes, William J., D-N.J. (2)
Hunter, Duncan L., R-Calif. (45)
Hutto, Earl, D-Fla. (1)
Hyde, Henry J., R-Ill. (6)

I, J

Ireland, Andy, R-Fla. (10)
Jacobs, Andrew Jr., D-Ind. (10)
Jeffords, James M., R-Vt. (AL)
Jenkins, Ed, D-Ga. (9)
Johnson, Nancy L., R-Conn. (6)
Jones, Ed, D-Tenn. (8)
Jones, James R., D-Okla. (1)
Jones, Walter B., D-N.C. (1)

K

Kaptur, Marcy, D-Ohio (9)
Kasich, John R., R-Ohio (12)
Kastenmeier, Robert W., D-Wis. (2)
Kazen, Abraham Jr., D-Texas (23)
Kennelly, Barbara B., D-Conn. (1)
Kemp, Jack F., R-N.Y. (31)
Kildee, Dale E., D-Mich. (7)
Kindness, Thomas N., R-Ohio (8)
Kleczka, Gerald D., D-Wis. (4)
Kogovsek, Ray, D-Colo. (3)
Kolter, Joe, D-Pa. (4)
Kostmayer, Peter H., D-Pa. (8)
Kramer, Ken, R-Colo. (5)

L

LaFalce, John J., D-N.Y. (32)
Lagomarsino, Robert J., R-Calif. (19)
Lantos, Tom, D-Calif. (11)
Latta, Delbert L., R-Ohio (5)
Leach, Jim, R-Iowa (1)
Leath, Marvin, D-Texas (11)
Lehman, Richard H., D-Calif. (18)
Lehman, William, D-Fla. (17)
Leland, Mickey, D-Texas (18)
Lent, Norman F., R-N.Y. (4)
Levin, Sander M., D-Mich. (17)
Levine, Mel, D-Calif. (27)
Levitas, Elliott H., D-Ga. (4)
Lewis, Jerry, R-Calif. (35)
Lewis, Tom, R-Fla. (12)
Lipinski, William O., D-Ill. (5)
Livingston, Bob, R-La. (1)
Lloyd, Marilyn, D-Tenn. (3)
Loeffler, Tom, R-Texas (21)
Long, Clarence D., D-Md. (2)
Long, Gillis W., D-La. (8)
Lott, Trent, R-Miss. (5)
Pepper, Claude, D-Fla. (18)
Petri, Thomas E., R-Wis. (6)

Lowery, Bill, R-Calif. (41)
Lowry, Mike, D-Wash. (7)
Lujan, Manuel Jr., R-N.M. (1)
Luken, Thomas A., D-Ohio (1)
Lundine, Stan, D-N.Y. (34)
Lungren, Dan, R-Calif. (42)

M

Mack, Connie, R-Fla. (13)
MacKay, Buddy, D-Fla. (6)
Madigan, Edward R., R-Ill. (15)
Markey, Edward J., D-Mass. (7)
Marlenee, Ron, R-Mont. (2)
Marriott, Dan, R-Utah (2)
Martin, David O'B., R-N.Y. (26)
Martin, James G., R-N.C. (9)
Martin, Lynn, R-Ill. (16)
Martinez, Matthew G., D-Calif. (30)
Matsui, Robert T., D-Calif. (3)
Mavroules, Nicholas, D-Mass. (6)
Mazzoli, Romano L., D-Ky. (3)
McCain, John, R-Ariz. (1)
McCandless, Al, R-Calif. (37)
McCloskey, Frank, D-Ind. (8)
McCollum, Bill, R-Fla. (5)
McCurdy, Dave, D-Okla. (4)
McDade, Joseph M., R-Pa. (10)
McEwen, Bob, R-Ohio (6)
McGrath, Raymond J., R-N.Y. (5)
McHugh, Matthew F., D-N.Y. (28)
McKernan, John R. Jr., R-Maine (1)
McKinney, Stewart B., R-Conn. (4)
McNulty, James F. Jr., D-Ariz. (5)
Mica, Daniel A., D-Fla. (14)
Michel, Robert H., R-Ill. (18)
Mikulski, Barbara A., D-Md. (3)
Miller, Clarence E., R-Ohio (10)
Miller, George, D-Calif. (7)
Mineta, Norman Y., D-Calif. (13)
Minish, Joseph G., D-N.J. (11)
Mitchell, Parren J., D-Md. (7)
Moakley, Joe, D-Mass. (9)
Molinari, Guy V., R-N.Y. (14)
Mollohan, Alan B., D-W.Va. (1)
Montgomery, G. V. "Sonny", D-Miss. (3)
Moody, Jim, D-Wis. (5)
Moore, Henson, R-La. (6)
Moorhead, Carlos J., R-Calif. (22)
Morrison, Bruce A., D-Conn. (3)
Morrison, Sid, R-Wash. (4)
Mrazek, Robert J., D-N.Y. (3)
Murphy, Austin J., D-Pa. (22)
Murtha, John P., D-Pa. (12)
Myers, John T., R-Ind. (7)

N

Natcher, William H., D-Ky. (2)
Neal, Stephen L., D-N.C. (5)
Nelson, Bill, D-Fla. (11)
Nichols, Bill, D-Ala. (3)
Nielson, Howard C., R-Utah (3)
Nowak, Henry J., D-N.Y. (33)

O

Oakar, Mary Rose, D-Ohio (20)
Oberstar, James L., D-Minn. (8)
Obey, David R., D-Wis. (7)
O'Brien, George M., R-Ill. (4)
Olin, James R., D-Va. (6)
O'Neill, Thomas P. Jr., D-Mass. (8)
Ortiz, Solomon P., D-Texas (27)
Ottinger, Richard L., D-N.Y. (20)
Owens, Major R., D-N.Y. (12)
Oxley, Mike, R-Ohio (4)

P

Packard, Ron, R-Calif. (43)
Panetta, Leon E., D-Calif. (16)
Parris, Stan, R-Va. (8)
Pashayan, Charles Jr., R-Calif. (17)
Patman, Bill, D-Texas (14)
Patterson, Jerry M., D-Calif. (38)
Paul, Ron, R-Texas (22)
Pease, Don J., D-Ohio (13)
Penny, Timothy J., D-Minn. (1)

. . . Governors, Supreme Court, Cabinet-rank Officers

Pickle, J. J., D-Texas (10)
Porter, John Edward, R-Ill. (10)
Price, Melvin, D-Ill. (21)
Pritchard, Joel, R-Wash. (1)
Pursell, Carl D., R-Mich. (2)

Q, R

Quillen, James H., R-Tenn. (1)
Rahall, Nick J. II, D-W.Va. (4)
Rangel, Charles B., D-N.Y. (16)
Ratchford, William R., D-Conn. (5)
Ray, Richard, D-Ga. (3)
Regula, Ralph, R-Ohio (16)
Reid, Harry, D-Nev. (1)
Richardson, Bill, D-N.M. (3)
Ridge, Tom, R-Pa. (21)
Rinaldo, Matthew J., R-N.J. (7)
Ritter, Don, R-Pa. (15)
Roberts, Pat, R-Kan. (1)
Robinson, J. Kenneth, R-Va. (7)
Rodino, Peter W. Jr., D-N.J. (10)
Roe, Robert A., D-N.J. (8)
Roemer, Buddy, D-La. (4)
Rogers, Harold, R-Ky. (5)
Rose, Charlie, D-N.C. (7)
Rostenkowski, Dan, D-Ill. (8)
Roth, Toby, R-Wis. (8)
Roukema, Marge, R-N.J. (5)
Rowland, J. Roy, D-Ga. (8)
Roybal, Edward R., D-Calif. (25)
Rudd, Eldon, R-Ariz. (4)
Russo, Marty, D-Ill. (3)

S

Sabo, Martin Olav, D-Minn. (5)
St Germain, Fernand J., D-R.I. (1)
Savage, Gus, D-Ill. (2)
Sawyer, Harold S., R-Mich. (5)
Schaefer, Daniel L., R-Colo. (6)
Scheuer, James H., D-N.Y. (8)
Schneider, Claudine, R-R.I. (2)
Schroeder, Patricia, D-Colo. (1)
Schulze, Richard T., R-Pa. (5)
Schumer, Charles E., D-N.Y. (10)
Seiberling, John F., D-Ohio (14)
Sensenbrenner, F. James Jr., R-Wis. (9)
Shannon, James M., D-Mass. (5)
Sharp, Philip R., D-Ind. (2)
Shaw, E. Clay Jr., R-Fla. (15)
Shelby, Richard C., D-Ala. (7)
Shumway, Norman D., R-Calif. (14)
Shuster, Bud, R-Pa. (9)
Sikorski, Gerry, D-Minn. (6)
Siljander, Mark D., R-Mich. (4)
Simon, Paul, D-Ill. (22)
Sisisky, Norman, D-Va. (4)
Skeen, Joe, R-N.M. (2)
Skelton, Ike, D-Mo. (4)
Slattery, Jim, D-Kan. (2)
Smith, Christopher H., R-N.J. (4)
Smith, Denny, R-Ore. (5)
Smith, Larry, D-Fla. (16)
Smith, Neal, D-Iowa (4)
Smith, Robert F., R-Ore. (2)
Smith, Virginia, R-Neb. (3)
Snowe, Olympia J., R-Maine (2)
Snyder, Gene, R-Ky. (4)
Solarz, Stephen J., D-N.Y. (13)
Solomon, Gerald B. H., R-N.Y. (24)
Spence, Floyd, R-S.C. (2)
Spratt, John M. Jr., D-S.C. (5)
Staggers, Harley O. Jr., D-W.Va. (2)
Stangeland, Arlan, R-Minn. (7)
Stark, Fortney H. "Pete", D-Calif. (9)
Stenholm, Charles W., D-Texas (17)
Stokes, Louis, D-Ohio (21)
Stratton, Samuel S., D-N.Y. (23)
Studds, Gerry E., D-Mass. (10)
Stump, Bob, R-Ariz. (3)
Sundquist, Don, R-Tenn. (7)
Swift, Al, D-Wash. (2)
Synar, Mike, D-Okla. (2)

T

Tallon, Robin, D-S.C. (6)
Tauke, Tom, R-Iowa (2)
Tauzin, W. J. "Billy", D-La. (3)
Taylor, Gene, R-Mo. (7)

Thomas, Lindsay, D-Ga. (1)
Thomas, William M., R-Calif. (20)
Torres, Esteban Edward, D-Calif. (34)
Torricelli, Robert G., D-N.J. (9)
Towns, Edolphus, D-N.Y. (11)
Traxler, Bob, D-Mich. (8)

U, V

Udall, Morris K., D-Ariz. (2)
Valentine, Tim, D-N.C. (2)
Vandergriff, Tom, D-Texas (26)
Vander Jagt, Guy, R-Mich. (9)
Vento, Bruce F., D-Minn. (4)
Volkmer, Harold L., D-Mo. (9)
Vucanovich, Barbara F., R-Nev. (2)

W

Walgren, Doug, D-Pa. (18)
Walker, Robert S., R-Pa. (16)
Watkins, Wes, D-Okla. (3)
Waxman, Henry A., D-Calif. (24)
Weaver, James, D-Ore. (4)
Weber, Vin, R-Minn. (2)
Weiss, Ted, D-N.Y. (17)
Wheat, Alan, D-Mo. (5)
Whitehurst, G. William, R-Va. (2)
Whitley, Charles, D-N.C. (3)
Whittaker, Bob, R-Kan. (5)
Whitten, Jamie L., D-Miss. (1)
Williams, Lyle, R-Ohio (17)
Williams, Pat, D-Mont. (1)
Wilson, Charles, D-Texas (2)
Winn, Larry Jr., R-Kan. (3)
Wirth, Timothy E., D-Colo. (2)
Wise, Bob, D-W.Va. (3)
Wolf, Frank R., R-Va. (10)
Wolpe, Howard, D-Mich. (3)
Wortley, George C., R-N.Y. (27)
Wright, Jim, D-Texas (12)
Wyden, Ron, D-Ore. (3)
Wylie, Chalmers P., R-Ohio (15)

X, Y, Z

Yates, Sidney R., D-Ill. (9)
Yatron, Gus, D-Pa. (6)
Young, C. W. Bill, R-Fla. (8)
Young, Don, R-Alaska (AL)
Young, Robert A., D-Mo. (2)
Zschau, Ed, R-Calif. (12)

Delegates

de Lugo, Ron, D-Virgin Islands
Fauntroy, Walter E., D-D.C.
Sunia, Fofo I. F., D-American Samoa
Won Pat, Antonio Borja, D-Guam

Resident Commissioner

Corrada, Baltasar, New Prog.-Puerto Rico

Senators
R 55; D 45

Abdnor, James, R-S.D.
Andrews, Mark, R-N.D.
Armstrong, William L., R-Colo.
Baker, Howard H. Jr., R-Tenn.
Baucus, Max, D-Mont.
Bentsen, Lloyd, D-Texas
Biden, Joseph R. Jr., D-Del.
Bingaman, Jeff, D-N.M.
Boren, David L., D-Okla.
Boschwitz, Rudy, R-Minn.
Bradley, Bill, D-N.J.
Bumpers, Dale, D-Ark.
Burdick, Quentin N., D-N.D.
Byrd, Robert C., D-W.Va.
Chafee, John H., R-R.I.
Chiles, Lawton, D-Fla.
Cochran, Thad, R-Miss.
Cohen, William S., R-Maine
Cranston, Alan, D-Calif.
D'Amato, Alfonse M., R-N.Y.
Danforth, John C., R-Mo.

DeConcini, Dennis, D-Ariz.
Denton, Jeremiah, R-Ala.
Dixon, Alan J., D-Ill.
Dodd, Christopher J., D-Conn.
Dole, Robert, R-Kan.
Domenici, Pete V., R-N.M.
Durenberger, Dave, R-Minn.
Eagleton, Thomas F., D-Mo.
East, John P., R-N.C.
Evans, Daniel J., R-Wash.
Exon, J. James, D-Neb.
Ford, Wendell H., D-Ky.
Garn, Jake, R-Utah
Glenn, John, D-Ohio
Goldwater, Barry, R-Ariz.
Gorton, Slade, R-Wash.
Grassley, Charles E., R-Iowa
Hart, Gary, D-Colo.
Hatch, Orrin G., R-Utah
Hatfield, Mark O., R-Ore.
Hawkins, Paula, R-Fla.
Hecht, Chic, R-Nev.
Heflin, Howell, D-Ala.
Heinz, John, R-Pa.
Helms, Jesse, R-N.C.
Hollings, Ernest F., D-S.C.
Huddleston, Walter D., D-Ky.
Humphrey, Gordon J., R-N.H.
Inouye, Daniel K., D-Hawaii
Jepsen, Roger W., R-Iowa
Johnston, J. Bennett, D-La.
Kassebaum, Nancy Landon, R-Kan.
Kasten, Bob, R-Wis.
Kennedy, Edward M., D-Mass.
Lautenberg, Frank R., D-N.J.
Laxalt, Paul, R-Nev.
Leahy, Patrick J., D-Vt.
Levin, Carl, D-Mich.
Long, Russell B., D-La.
Lugar, Richard G., R-Ind.
Mathias, Charles McC. Jr., R-Md.
Matsunaga, Spark M., D-Hawaii
Mattingly, Mack, R-Ga.
McClure, James A., R-Idaho
Melcher, John, D-Mont.
Metzenbaum, Howard M., D-Ohio
Mitchell, George J., D-Maine
Moynihan, Daniel Patrick, D-N.Y.
Murkowski, Frank H., R-Alaska
Nickles, Don, R-Okla.
Nunn, Sam, D-Ga.
Packwood, Bob, R-Ore.
Pell, Claiborne, D-R.I.
Percy, Charles H., R-Ill.
Pressler, Larry, R-S.D.
Proxmire, William, D-Wis.
Pryor, David, D-Ark.
Quayle, Dan, R-Ind.
Randolph, Jennings, D-W.Va.
Riegle, Donald W. Jr., D-Mich.
Roth, William V. Jr., R-Del.
Rudman, Warren B., R-N.H.
Sarbanes, Paul S., D-Md.
Sasser, Jim, D-Tenn.
Simpson, Alan K., R-Wyo.
Specter, Arlen, R-Pa.
Stafford, Robert T., R-Vt.
Stennis, John C., D-Miss.
Stevens, Ted, R-Alaska
Symms, Steven D., R-Idaho
Thurmond, Strom, R-S.C.
Tower, John, R-Texas
Trible, Paul S. Jr., R-Va.
Tsongas, Paul E., D-Mass.
Wallop, Malcolm, R-Wyo.
Warner, John W., R-Va.
Weicker, Lowell P. Jr., R-Conn.
Wilson, Pete, R-Calif.
Zorinsky, Edward, D-Neb.

Governors
D 35; R 15

Ala.—George C. Wallace, D
Alaska—Bill Sheffield, D
Ariz.—Bruce Babbitt, D
Ark.—Bill Clinton, D
Calif.—George Deukmejian, R
Colo.—Richard D. Lamm, D
Conn.—William A. O'Neill, D

Del.—Pierre S. "Pete" du Pont IV, R
Fla.—Robert Graham, D
Ga.—Joe Frank Harris, D
Hawaii—George Ariyoshi, D
Idaho—John V. Evans, D
Ill.—James R. Thompson, R
Ind.—Robert D. Orr, R
Iowa—Terry Branstad, R
Kan.—John Carlin, D
Ky.—Martha L. Collins, D
La.—Edwin W. Edwards, D
Maine—Joseph E. Brennan, D
Md.—Harry R. Hughes, D
Mass.—Michael S. Dukakis, D
Mich.—James J. Blanchard, D
Minn.—Rudy Perpich, D
Miss.—Bill Allain, D
Mo.—Christopher S. "Kit" Bond, R
Mont.—Ted Schwinden, D
Neb.—Bob Kerrey, D
Nev.—Richard H. Bryan, D
N.H.—John H. Sununu, R
N.J.—Thomas H. Kean, R
N.M.—Toney Anaya, D
N.Y.—Mario M. Cuomo, D
N.C.—James B. Hunt Jr., D
N.D.—Allen I. Olson, R
Ohio—Richard F. Celeste, D
Okla.—George Nigh, D
Ore.—Victor G. Atiyeh, R
Pa.—Richard L. Thornburgh, R
R.I.—J. Joseph Garrahy, D
S.C.—Richard Riley, D
S.D.—William J. Janklow, R
Tenn.—Lamar Alexander, R
Texas—Mark White, D
Utah—Scott M. Matheson, D
Vt.—Richard A. Snelling, R
Va.—Charles S. Robb, D
Wash.—John Spellman, R
W.Va.—John D. "Jay" Rockefeller IV, D
Wis.—Anthony S. Earl, D
Wyo.—Ed Herschler, D

Supreme Court

Burger, Warren E.—Minn., Chief Justice
Blackmun, Harry A.—Minn.
Brennan, William J. Jr.—N.J.
Marshall, Thurgood—N.Y.
O'Connor, Sandra Day—Ariz.
Powell, Lewis F. Jr.—Va.
Rehnquist, William H.—Ariz.
Stevens, John Paul—Ill.
White, Byron R.—Colo.

Cabinet

Baldrige, Malcolm—Commerce
Bell, T. H.—Education
Block, John R.—Agriculture
Clark, William P.—Interior
Dole, Elizabeth Hanford—Transportation
Donovan, Raymond J.—Labor
Heckler, Margaret M.—HHS
Hodel, Donald P.—Energy
Pierce, Samuel R. Jr.—HUD
Regan, Donald T.—Treasury
Shultz, George P.—State
Smith, William French—Attorney General
Weinberger, Caspar W.—Defense

Other Officers With Cabinet Rank

Brock, William E. III—U.S. Trade Representative
Bush, George—Vice President
Casey, William J.—CIA Director
Kirkpatrick, Jeane J.—U.N. Representative
Meese, Edwin III—Counselor to the President
Stockman, David A.—OMB Director

Kentucky 7th District, New Jersey 13th District.

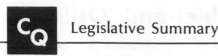

98th Congress Leaves Thorny Legacy for 99th

A year of politics and procrastination on Capitol Hill left many members of the 98th Congress disappointed with their track record and a long list of unsolved problems for the new Congress to address.

Nearly two years after opening on a harmonious note with the passage of a Social Security rescue plan, the 98th Congress ended in partisan discord Oct. 12. The only way lawmakers could wind up their business was to bump the most controversial issues onto the 1985 calendar.

Left for members of the 99th Congress to decide were such questions as whether to continue MX missile production, test anti-satellite weapons and provide aid to Nicaraguan rebels. By deferring these matters until 1985, members avoided votes that could have damaged their re-election chances. And each party hoped to return with an election mandate that would allow it to work its will in 1985.

One of the biggest problems shoved onto 1985's agenda was the massive federal deficit. Although Congress took actions designed to reduce the deficit by $149 billion over three years, the tax increases and spending cuts were viewed as a mere "down payment" on a larger remedy.

Several other contentious issues were almost resolved in 1984, but compromises fell apart in the final days of the session.

These failed efforts included legislation to overhaul the nation's immigration laws, a bill releasing Interstate highway funds to the states and a renewal of the Export Administration Act, which controlled U.S. shipments abroad to protect national security. Also lost in the rush to adjourn was a civil rights measure overturning the Supreme Court's *Grove City* decision, which narrowed the reach of major anti-discrimination laws.

Other measures were abandoned even earlier. The Senate passed banking deregulation legislation, but the House did not. The House passed a renewal of the "superfund" program to clean up toxic wastes, but the Senate did not. Neither house passed bills to decontrol natural gas prices or to extend the Clean Air Act.

Notable Achievements

There were, however, several notable achievements in 1984. Congress sent President Reagan legislation revamping the nation's bankruptcy courts, a bill pressuring states to raise their minimum drinking age to 21, a bill creating a national policy for cable television franchising and bills creating more wilderness areas than Congress had approved in 20 years.

Worried about the influence of the gender gap on the elections, Congress also approved bills of special interest to women, including one expanding pension coverage for women and one enforcing child-support payments.

There also was substantial progress in health legislation. Congress cleared a bill to place stronger health warnings on cigarette packages. It also cleared a measure making low-cost generic drugs more widely available to consumers and an organ transplant bill to create a national computer network to match patients who need transplants with donors of organs.

Second Session Summary

The second session of the 98th Congress ended Oct. 12 when the Senate adjourned *sine die* at 3:17 p.m. The House had adjourned at 3:05 p.m.

Convened at noon on Jan. 23, the session lasted 264 days. Although it was the shortest election-year session since the second session of the 94th Congress in 1976, it ranked as the 43rd longest in history. The third session of the 76th Congress, from Jan. 3, 1940, to Jan. 3, 1941, was the longest on record. *(CQ Guide to Congress 3rd Edition, p. 410)*

The Senate met for 131 days in 1984, the House for 120 days. There were 3,764 bills and resolutions introduced during the session, compared with 8,434 in 1983 and 4,520 in 1982, the second session of the 97th Congress.

President Reagan signed into law 408 public bills cleared by Congress, 193 more than in 1983 and 80 more than in 1982. Reagan vetoed 17 bills in 1984; one veto was overridden and enacted into law without his signature.

During 1984, the House took 408 recorded votes, 90 fewer than in 1983. The Senate took 275 recorded votes, 96 fewer than in 1983.

Following are the recorded congressional vote totals between 1972 and 1984:

Year	House	Senate	Total
1984	408	275	683
1983	498	371	869
1982	459	465	924
1981	353	483	836
1980	604	531	1,135
1979	672	497	1,169
1978	834	516	1,350
1977	706	635	1,341
1976	661	688	1,349
1975	612	602	1,214
1974	537	544	1,081
1973	541	594	1,135
1972	329	532	861

Playing With Dollars

One of the biggest frustrations for members of the 98th Congress was their absorption with budget issues throughout the year.

"All we do is play the money game," griped Sen. Dave Durenberger, R-Minn. "We're not dealing with peace to the world, with feeding the hungry. We just sit around and play with numbers."

Despite its preoccupation with money, Congress was able to clear only five of the 13 regular appropriations bills for fiscal 1985. The major roadblock was a standoff between Reagan and House Democrats over the military budget.

"For five months we were tied up because the damn administration wanted a 13 percent increase on defense and the House wanted 3 percent," Durenberger said. In the end, the administration relented, settling for a 5 percent inflation-adjusted increase over current spending, a compromise between the House level of 3.5 percent and the Senate-passed 7.8 percent increase.

But the lengthy standoff created a legislative backlog as Congress tried to adjourn in early October. Members fought to attach their favorite bills to the last two "must-pass" items — the 1985 continuing spending resolution and a measure to increase the debt limit — and their battles stalled the passage of both urgent measures.

The late approval of the continuing resolution led to a half-day shutdown of federal government offices. And the delays in increasing the debt limit would cost the government $400 million in higher interest costs, according to the Treasury Department.

While legislators spent much of 1984 talking about the evils of the swelling federal deficit, they only took a first step toward a cure. Instead, many members figured they would deal with the problem in 1985 — after the November elections.

Reagan's Record

Unlike his first two years in office, Reagan did not seek sweeping changes in economic policy during the 98th Congress. And he often was forced to adjust his goals in the face of congressional opposition.

On domestic issues, Reagan met many disappointments on Capitol Hill in 1984. The president could not get Congress to approve his social agenda, which featured constitutional amendments to ban abortion and allow school prayer. Nor did Congress adopt his tuition tax credit plan to help parents who sent their children to private schools, or his enterprise zone system, to provide tax relief to businesses that create jobs in depressed areas.

Congress also did not consider Reagan's proposal to lower the minimum wage for teenagers. And it did not act on his call for constitutional amendments requiring a balanced budget and giving the president a veto over items in appropriations bills.

Members also reversed some earlier Reagan policies, restoring budget cuts in social-welfare programs, such as college student aid and maternal and child health programs.

Reagan did, however, win approval of his anti-crime package that included new sentencing procedures and insanity plea restrictions. And while Congress rejected his school prayer amendment, it did agree to an "equal access" proposal, allowing student religious groups to meet in school facilities on the same terms as other extracurricular clubs.

Most of the squabbling between Congress and the president concerned national security issues.

The year started on a dissonant note when members challenged Reagan's actions in Lebanon. By the time Reagan pulled troops out of Beirut in February, he and Congress were arguing about who was to blame for the policy failures in the Middle East.

On Central America, Reagan's policies had mixed success on Capitol Hill. Successful presidential elections in El Salvador quieted congressional debate about that country, enabling Reagan to win approval for most of the military aid he sought for fiscal years 1984 and 1985. But Congress barred the president from providing further aid to anti-government rebels in Nicaragua through Feb. 28, 1985, and said that Reagan must bring a new request to Congress in March if he wanted to continue direct U.S. involvement in the war to oust the leftist government in Nicaragua.

Congress also deferred decisions on two major military matters. Although about $2.5 billion was appropriated to build another 21 MX missiles (in addition to 21 funded in fiscal 1984), the new money could not be spent unless Congress passed two separate resolutions in March 1985 approving more MX production. Congress also imposed a moratorium until March on tests of the anti-satellite missile.

Internal Politics

Partisan warfare was not limited in 1984 to battles between the White House and Congress. Much of the political strife took place within the confines of the Capitol building.

Pre-election partisanship was heightened in the House by the aggressive floor tactics of junior Republicans who were angry that the Democratic leadership would not bring up their conservative agenda.

Almost daily, these Republicans attacked the Democrats in speeches aimed largely at the growing cable television audience watching live broadcasts of House sessions. In May, the simmering dispute erupted into a shouting match between Speaker Thomas P. O'Neill Jr., D-Mass., and Newt Gingrich, R-Ga., one of the leaders of the Republican barrage.

The partisan fighting eventually quieted down, but some Democrats predicted it would recur in 1985.

Both chambers also were handicapped in 1984 by lame-duck leaders. The impending retirement of Senate Majority Leader Howard H. Baker Jr., R-Tenn., put him in a less persuasive position with his rambunctious colleagues. And the announcement by House Speaker Thomas P. O'Neill Jr., D-Mass., that he would retire by the end of 1986 opened the door for more rebellions against his leadership.

The following summarizes the status of major legislation in 1984:

Agriculture

Farm Credit. Bills (HR 1190, S 24) that would have eased repayment terms for federal loans to financially troubled farmers died upon adjournment Oct. 12. But, after opposing the bills for several years, the Reagan administration Sept. 18 reversed course and, using administrative authority, launched a billion-dollar package of farm debt forgiveness and loan guarantees.

The House had passed broader credit plans in 1982 and again in 1983, but the Senate version, approved in 1983 by the Agriculture Committee, did not come to the floor for a vote. A loan deferral amendment passed in 1982 as part of the fiscal 1983 appropriations bill, but failed in conference.

Price Supports. Congress agreed in April to cancel scheduled 1984 and 1985 increases in a major type of price support — known as target prices — for wheat, feed grains, cotton and rice. The support program made cash payments to farmers when market prices for their crops dropped below "target" prices set by law.

The Reagan administration, which sought unsuccessfully in 1981 to end the program, had been working since early 1983 for a freeze. To achieve it, however, administration officials agreed to include in the measure (HR 4072 — PL 98-258) other concessions to farmers, including cash payments for not growing crops in 1985, that appeared to offset savings from the freeze.

Rural Electric. Popular legislation (S 1300, HR 3050) that would have shored up the federal fund that lends money to rural electric and telephone systems failed to clear Congress.

Last-minute attempts to win a Senate vote failed Oct. 10 when Howard M. Metzenbaum, D-Ohio, and Alan K. Simpson, R-Wyo., objected to Senate debate on the bill, which would have revised loan repayment terms both for utilities borrowing from the Rural Electrification Administration (REA) and for REA's substantial debts to the U.S. Treasury.

The bill passed the House March 1 in slightly different form, but ran into trouble in May when Simpson disclosed his objections to its cost, to sales of REA-subsidized power to wealthy corporations, and to REA involvement in the financially troubled nuclear power industry. The Reagan administration also had opposed the bill.

'Sodbuster.' Despite strong bipartisan support, Congress failed to complete landmark legislation (S 663, HR 3457) that would have barred federal price supports and other farm program benefits to farmers who plowed up fragile, easily erodible land.

The Senate approved the so-called "sodbuster" plan in 1982 and again in 1983; the House in May passed a broader soil conservation bill, combining sodbuster language with payments to farmers who instituted long-term conservation practices on fragile crop land. Conferees resolved their differences on the sodbuster language, but when Senate conferees suggested dropping the long-term conservation program, House conferees refused and the conference remained stalemated.

Meanwhile, the Senate Aug. 9 added sodbuster language to the fiscal 1985 agriculture appropriations bill. But conferees on that measure later dropped it, in part, they said, because of objections from House advocates of the long-term conservation program. The sodbuster language had drawn strong support in the farm community. The Reagan administration also backed the sodbuster proposal, but objected strongly to the long-term conservation plan.

Appropriations

Spending Bills. By Oct. 1, the start of fiscal 1985, Congress had cleared only four of its 13 regular appropriations bills: Commerce, State, Justice, Judiciary (HR 5712 — PL 98-411); Energy and Water Development (HR 5653 — PL 98-360); Housing and Urban Development (HR 5713 — PL 98-371); and Legislative Branch (HR 5753 — PL 98-367).

The House passed 10 of its regular appropriations measures; the Senate, eight.

Delayed by disagreement over defense spending and two summer recesses for the political conventions, the most contentious spending measures were put off until the last weeks of the session. Then, Congress was forced to approve four short-term continuing appropriations resolutions — an unprecedented number — before it finally managed, on Oct. 11, to clear a massive $470 billion continuing resolution (H J Res 648 — PL 98-473) to run until the end of fiscal 1985.

Bills covered by the stopgap money bill were: Agriculture, Defense, District of Columbia, Foreign Aid, Interior, Labor, Health and Human Services and Education, Military Construction, Transportation, and Treasury-Postal Service. The bill also contained a major overhaul of the federal criminal code.

Three supplemental spending bills for fiscal 1984 also were enacted. On March 27, Congress cleared a $290 million supplemental measure (H J Res 493 — PL 98-248) earmarking money for food aid to Africa and low-income energy assistance.

H J Res 492 (PL 98-332), including money for African food aid and summer youth employment, cleared June 26 after the deletion of provisions adding money for rebels fighting the Nicaraguan government.

And on Aug. 10 Congress cleared a $6.2 billion measure (HR 6040 — PL 98-396) providing funding for an assortment of government programs. The bill set aside $70 million in military aid to the U.S.-backed government in El Salvador and $700 million for the food stamp program.

Banking/Commerce

Banking Deregulation. A House-Senate standoff over banking reforms blocked enactment of a major deregulation bill that the Reagan administration had favored.

Instead, in a joint statement Oct. 4, the rival chairmen of the House and Senate Banking committees said that "legislation addressing the competitive and regulatory framework of the financial system will be the first priority" of their panels in 1985.

For two years, Senate Banking Chairman Jake Garn, R-Utah, had labored for an administration-backed bill (S 2181) to close legal loopholes and to free banks to engage in securities, real estate and insurance. The Senate overwhelmingly approved a pared-down version (S 2851) Sept. 13.

But Garn's House counterpart, Fernand J. St Germain, D-R.I., steadfastly opposed bank deregulation and pushed his own bill (HR 5916) to close loopholes only. On Sept. 21 he abruptly dropped the fight without taking his bill to the House floor, saying it was pointless to proceed given the differences with the Senate.

Inaction left open the so-called "non-bank bank loophole" through which limited-purpose banks avoided a federal ban on interstate banking. But Garn and St Germain agreed that any future bill would outlaw non-bank banks formed after July 1, 1983.

Telephone Charges. Under pressure from Congress, the Federal Communications Commission (FCC) postponed until June 1985 an order that residential phone customers pay an extra $1 monthly charge.

In 1982, the FCC proposed that local phone companies levy an "access charge" on residences and businesses to offset any loss of long-distance profits after Jan. 1, 1984, when their court-ordered break from parent company American Telephone & Telegraph Co. took effect. The charges were to start in 1984 at $2 monthly for residential lines, and $6 monthly for business lines, rising to more than $10 a month by 1990. Business customers with more than one line began paying the charges May 25, 1984.

But in January, to satisfy congressional critics, the FCC delayed the charges for residents and for small businesses with one line. The Senate then voted not to take up a bill (S 1660) that would have imposed a delay through 1985.

Also, there was no action on a House-passed bill (HR 4102) to ban the charges.

In December, with congressional opposition notably absent, the FCC approved a compromise proposal calling for a $1 a month access charge beginning in June 1985, rising to $2 a month in 1986.

Broadcast Deregulation. Broadcasters lost their fight for freedom from federal regulation of licenses and programming. In both chambers, majorities still supported the 1934 Communications Act's premise that the airwaves — unlike the print press — should be regulated as a scarce public resource.

The industry's campaign was two-pronged. One bill (S 1917) would have repealed several provisions of the 1934 law, including the so-called Fairness Doctrine that required stations to air all sides of public issues. Sponsored by Bob Packwood, R-Ore., the bill was rejected by his Senate Commerce Committee June 13.

Other legislation (S 55, HR 2382) would have given radio and TV station owners more certainty of license renewals and repealed some administrative requirements. The Senate passed S 55 in 1983, but the House bill never got out of the Energy and Commerce Subcommittee on Telecommunications because members demanded public-interest guidelines for programming that the industry would not accept.

Nevertheless, many of the industry-sought changes took effect in September as a result of a rule approved by the pro-deregulation Federal Communications Commission (FCC). The FCC also was studying whether it had authority to repeal the Fairness Doctrine.

Cable Television. After repeated setbacks, a bill (S 66 — PL 98-549) defining national policy for the cable television industry was passed just before adjournment Oct. 12.

For more than two years, cable firms and the cities that granted franchises had fought bitterly over the bill. In 1983, the Senate-passed version was abandoned in the House because some cities complained its terms were too favorable to the industry.

In Congress' final week, the industry and cities agreed to a compromise — their third in two years — and the House approved it Oct. 1. But conservative Senate Republicans opposed an equal-employment provision, and most parties considered the bill dead.

A compromise provision was agreed to Oct. 11, and, within hours, both houses approved the bill. It clarified cities' rights to grant franchises for local cable operators, while limiting city authority over rates and programs. It outlined national procedures for franchise renewals, replacing a confusing hodgepodge of local processes.

Public Broadcasting. President Reagan vetoed two bills that would have restored administration budget cuts for public broadcasting by authorizing three times his funding request.

He said the increases could not be justified in light of the need to lower the budget deficit.

The vetoed bills were:

● S 2436, which authorized $761 million for fiscal 1987-89 for the Corporation for Public Broadcasting (CPB) and $159 million for fiscal 1985-87 to build broadcasting facilities. It was vetoed Aug. 29.

● S 607, which authorized $675 million over three years for CPB and $100 million over three years for the facilities program. Reagan pocket-vetoed the measure Oct. 19.

The administration had proposed a total of $255 million for CPB and sought no funds for the facilities program.

The second veto came in spite of efforts by Sen. Barry Goldwater, R-Ariz., to reach a compromise with the administration. But the president said the proposed funding level in S 607 was still too high.

Failure to enact the reauthorization did not immediately affect funding. Congress had included $200 million for fiscal 1987 for CPB in the Labor, Health and Human Services, Education appropriations bill (HR 6028 — PL 98-619), and $24 million for the facilities in the Commerce, Justice, State and the Judiciary appropriations bill (HR 5712 — PL 98-411).

Television Rerun Rights. Hollywood won its battle with the television networks over the $800 million-a-year market in reruns of television shows.

The Federal Communications Commission (FCC) sparked a storm when it proposed to repeal rules prohibiting ABC, NBC and CBS from having a financial share in shows they aired. Independent producers of those programs, who depended on syndication rights for their profits, asked Congress to stop the agency.

The House passed a bill (HR 2250) to delay the FCC rule's effect until mid-1984 to give Congress time to act. Then, in March 1984, the FCC agreed to a two-year moratorium at the request of President Reagan and a group of senators.

Oil Company Mergers. One of the noisier debates of 1984 — over legislation to curb multibillion-dollar oil company mergers — ended quietly and without action.

Spurred by three record-setting deals, including Standard Oil of California's $13.2 billion acquisition of Gulf Corp., members in both chambers introduced anti-merger bills.

The Senate twice voted against a moratorium on big mergers, and instead, on March 28, called for a study of the issue. But even that proposal, an amendment to a supplemental appropriations bill (H J Res 492), was dropped in a conference committee with the House.

Corporate Takeover Reforms. Facing opposition from the Reagan administration and the Securities and Exchange Commission (SEC), House sponsors dropped a bill to restrain controversial business tactics that were increasingly common in corporate takeover fights.

Among other things, the bill (HR 5693) would have prohibited "greenmail" — the premium price a company paid to get its stock back from a raider — unless other stockholders approved the tactic or were offered the same price for their stock. The bill also would have limited "golden parachutes" — bonus severance packages arranged for executives whose jobs might be lost in a takeover.

The administration said HR 5693 infringed on states' rights to set corporate law. The SEC, which proposed the legislation initially, opposed the bill in the amended form approved by the House Energy and Commerce

Final Days Create Legislative Supermarket . . .

The waning hours of the 98th Congress produced a flurry of attempts to bring home the legislative bacon through special-interest amendments.

As is normally the case, senior members on key committees seemed to fare the best. When the dust settled, they could claim credit for items ranging from money for health research to guarantees that the government would continue to buy local coal.

In some instances, however, the maneuvering doomed otherwise healthy bills.

Much of the pork-barrelling took place on the massive continuing appropriations resolution to fund government agencies (H J Res 648 — PL 98-473). Each year this resolution is among the last pieces of legislation that must be signed, and lawmakers love to add pet projects to it.

But projects also were added to bills ranging from a library aid reauthorization to the remains of a boat safety measure.

Following is a sampling of special-interest provisions that members fought over in the confusion of the last several days of the session:

Defense

Within the massive $274 billion defense appropriations bill contained within the continuing resolution, there was room for a home-state project or two. They included:

● Four new Blackhawk troop helicopters worth about $6 million each for the Alaska National Guard. Sen. Ted Stevens, R-Alaska, facing re-election in November, was chairman of the Appropriations Subcommittee on Defense.

● $6 million to pay for removing asbestos from an Anchorage, Alaska, high school located on Fort Richardson.

● $1.7 million to improve the Devil's Lake, N.D., Municipal Airport runway to accommodate National Guard transport planes. Sen. Mark Andrews, R-N.D., was a member of Stevens' subcommittee.

● A provision continuing the congressional insistence that U.S. bases in Europe run their power plants on coal mined in the United States. For years, the Pennsylvania delegation had prevented bases in Europe from burning coal or oil they could purchase locally.

● Continuing to bar the Army from buying engines for the M-1 tank from anyone other than the Avco Corp., which made them in Connecticut. The Army wanted to have a second contractor also building its tank engines.

● $10 million to start work on a $300 million Army ammunition plant at Joliet, Ill. The money was sought — and heralded — by Sen. Charles H. Percy, R-Ill., who was facing a tough re-election battle.

Congress changed its mind about a pork-barrel maneuver it had made two years earlier when it insisted that the Air Force buy three Boeing 747s. That had been viewed as a sop to Sen. Henry M. Jackson, D-Wash., when the Air Force chose to buy more C-5 transports instead of 747s. Jackson died in 1983. In 1984, the Air Force, which never wanted the 747s, proposed instead to buy three C-5s, all destined for stationing in New York, represented

on Senate Appropriations by Republican Alfonse M. D'Amato. Congress went along.

Education

Helping home-state universities also seemed to be in favor in 1984. In the last-minute rush to reauthorize the politically popular Head Start program, a number of amendments were added. Examples included:

● $6 million for a Center for Excellence in Education at Indiana University. Dan Quayle, R-Ind., was a member of the Senate Labor and Human Resources Committee, which reported the bill (S 2565 — PL 98-558).

● $4 million for a research center to examine the health effects of new energy technologies at the University of Utah. The Labor Committee's chairman was Orrin G. Hatch, a Utah Republican.

● $6 million for cancer screening and research in St. George, Utah, a town that was in the fallout path of early nuclear weapons tests.

Taking no chances, Hatch also had added similar Utah amendments to a reauthorization bill (S 540) for the National Institutes of Health, which also was cleared but was vetoed by President Reagan.

On a more obscure bill that Congress cleared to reauthorize federal aid to libraries (HR 2878 — PL 98-480), four special grants were authorized for universities. Money ($22 million) for all four was later provided in the fiscal 1985 appropriations bill (HR 6028 — PL 98-619) for the Departments of Labor, Health and Human Services (HHS) and Education. The grants were:

● $6.5 million for construction of a library addition at the University of Hartford, an amount sought by Sen. Lowell P. Weicker Jr., R-Conn., a member of the Senate Labor and Human Resources Committee and, more importantly, chairman of the Appropriations subcommittee that provides funding for such projects.

● $9 million to build a handicapped research and training center at the University of Kansas, money sought by the chairman of the Senate Finance Committee, Robert Dole, R-Kan.

● $3.5 million for a facility to house the Carl Vinson Institute of Government at the University of Georgia, a project backed by Sen. Mack Mattingly, R-Ga., and named after a former longtime chairman of the House Armed Services Committee. Vinson, who died in 1981, retired in 1965 after 51 years in the House.

● $3 million for a John W. McCormack Institute of Public Affairs at the University of Massachusetts in Boston. McCormack, who died in 1980, was Speaker of the House from 1962 to 1971. Rep. Joe Moakley, D-Mass., a member of the Rules Committee and the occupant of McCormack's old seat, helped secure the money.

Taxes

The night before the Oct. 12 adjournment, trying to avoid amendments on a debt ceiling increase (H J Res 654 — PL 98-475), the Senate added tax amendments to a minor House-passed revenue measure (HR 2163) and sent the measure back to the House. The process allowed senators to offer the amendments even though it was

. . . Members Arrange to Bring Back the Bacon

clear the House would not consider them at that late date. The House indeed adjourned without considering HR 2163 again.

Among the amendments adopted by the Senate were:

● One by Robert C. Byrd, D-W.Va., to extend an energy tax credit for a West Virginia company making chlor-alkali electrolytic cells, essentially a high-powered battery.

● One by Strom Thurmond, R-S.C., to extend the deadline for a South Carolina firm to sell partnership interests to tax-exempt investors.

● One by William L. Armstrong, R-Colo., expressing the sense of the Senate that the Internal Revenue Service should not prevent military personnel from taking an interest deduction for home mortgage payments they make with their tax-free housing allowances.

Other amendments were withdrawn after their sponsors got Dole to promise to hold hearings in 1985. They included one by Daniel Patrick Moynihan, D-N.Y., to allow employees of Pan American World Services to avoid paying income taxes on free airline tickets given them as a fringe benefit.

Environment

In a couple of cases, special-interest amendments were at least partially responsible for killing bills that might otherwise have been enacted. For example:

● A wetlands protection bill (HR 3082) was passed by the House but eventually died in the Senate, where senators were unhappy over a provision to build a jetty at Oregon Inlet, N.C. That had been added by Rep. Walter B. Jones, D-N.C., chairman of the Merchant Marine and Fisheries Committee, and only survived by nine votes in the House.

● A reauthorization (HR 3282) of the Clean Water Act was passed by the House but died without Senate consideration. At least part of the bill's demise was due to extended squabbling over provisions added by the House to end New York City's dumping of raw sewage into the Hudson River. Some of the sewage wound up on New Jersey beaches, and the provision was backed by Reps. James J. Howard, D-N.J., chairman of the Public Works and Transportation Committee, and Robert A. Roe, D-N.J., chairman of the panel's Water Resources Subcommittee. Another parochial squabble on the bill erupted over an exemption sought for two pulp mills in Alaska by Stevens and Sen. Frank H. Murkowski, R-Alaska.

Members in both chambers loaded the continuing appropriations resolution down with a batch of long-sought water projects. To the dismay of many senior members, these projects all were stripped out of the bill to satisfy White House objections. The projects included:

● The Bonneville Lock and Dam in Oregon and Washington, sought by Mark O. Hatfield, R-Ore., chairman of the Senate Appropriations Committee. Hatfield, who was up for re-election, was upset when House conferees on the continuing resolution agreed to give up on the water projects. The Bonneville project to expand the existing lock was expected to cost $177 million.

● A flood control project along Sowashee Creek in Me-

ridian, Miss., that had been added on the Senate floor for Sen. John C. Stennis, Miss., the senior Democrat on Appropriations. The amendment added $10.9 million.

● Another flood control project in Mississippi along the Pearl River basin, also added as a floor amendment for Stennis and his Republican Mississippi colleague, Thad Cochran. The amendment added $96 million.

But Hatfield and others were not without victories. For example, Congress cleared a bill (HR 2838 — PL 98-478) Hatfield sought to allow logging companies to get out of contracts to buy timber from the federal government at prices higher than they were any longer willing to pay.

Miscellany

Members also won congressional approval of a host of other legislative "cats and dogs" in the final days, most of them in the continuing resolution. Those included:

● An amendment by Sen. Bill Bradley, D-N.J., to add $400,000 to fund a commission to study a 1932-33 famine in the Ukraine.

● An amendment by Sen. Edward M. Kennedy, D-Mass., to add $2 million for a lighthouse at Nantucket, Mass.

● A provision to allow the Small Business Administration (SBA) to provide federal disaster loans to the fishing industry hurt by weather problems related to El Niño, the name given to an unusual change in ocean currents that affected the world's weather. This provision, sought by the California delegation, had dragged a reauthorization (S 1323) of the SBA to its death because of administration opposition to the provision.

● $4 million to establish a U.S. Institute of Peace that had long been sought by Hatfield and retiring Sen. Jennings Randolph, D-W.Va.

● $500,000 in a matching grant for the College of the Virgin Islands, secured by Sen. J. Bennett Johnston, D-La., who was the ranking member of the Energy and Natural Resources Committee, which had jurisdiction over U.S. territories.

● Exemptions to federal noise regulations for foreign flights into airports at Miami and Bangor, Maine. The exemptions were sought by Sens. Lawton Chiles, D-Fla., Paula Hawkins, R-Fla., and William S. Cohen, R-Maine, who argued that they would save American jobs.

● $1 million a year for five years for a new international health program at Johns Hopkins University in Baltimore. The designation of the funds was secured by Rep. Clarence D. Long, D-Md., chairman of the Appropriations Subcommittee on Foreign Operations, who was in a tough re-election fight.

● Blocking the Transportation Department from eliminating the Transportation Systems Center, a research facility in Cambridge, Mass., in the district of House Speaker Thomas P. O'Neill Jr., D-Mass.

● A bill (HR 89 — PL 98-563) to allow foreign-flag cruise ships to carry passengers between Puerto Rico and the U.S. mainland. The measure was sought by Puerto Rico's non-voting member of Congress, Baltasar Corrada, who was leaving the House to run for mayor of San Juan.

Committee Aug. 2.

The SEC objected to a provision doubling from 20 days to 40 days the amount of time that a tender offer — a public invitation to buy stockholders' shares — must be open for stockholders to consider. The SEC argued that 20 days was enough time; the bill's sponsor, Timothy E. Wirth, D-Colo., said stockholders often felt stampeded into selling shares to raiders in a hostile takeover.

Insider Trading. Penalties for using confidential information to profit in the stock market were increased by a bill (HR 559 — PL 98-376) signed into law on Aug. 10.

The House passed the bill in 1983. On June 29, the Senate approved its version (S 910), and House members accepted the minor changes.

The law, sought by the Securities and Exchange Commission, required a person convicted of insider trading to forfeit any gains made (or losses avoided), and to pay civil fines of up to three times the amount of profit. Previously, the penalty was limited to forfeiture of gains. The new law also raised the criminal penalty for defrauding the market from $10,000 to $100,000.

Unisex Insurance. The insurance industry triumphed over women's groups when Congress failed to enact a bill that would have mandated equal insurance benefits and rates for men and women.

No action was taken on the legislation (HR 100, S 372) after March 28, when the House Energy and Commerce Committee approved amendments pushed by the insurance lobby. Supporters in women's and civil rights groups said the changes gutted their bill, and vowed to try again in 1985.

The legislation, part of an anti-discrimination package known as the Economic Equity Act, would have barred insurers from considering gender in computing insurance premiums and benefits.

Product Liability. For the second consecutive Congress, a formidable business alliance got no further than a Senate committee in its push for a law limiting manufacturers' liability for unsafe products.

The Senate Commerce Committee on March 27 approved S 44, a product liability bill sponsored by Bob Kasten, R-Wis., and supported by the Reagan administration. Numerous

business groups had made the bill a top priority, but associations for consumers, plaintiffs' lawyers and women worked for its defeat. Faced with filibuster threats from Ernest F. Hollings, D-S.C., and others, the bill was never brought to the floor.

In 1984, chances for passage were hurt by news reports about thousands of lawsuits filed against the A. H. Robins Co. by women who suffered debilitating infections after using its Dalkon Shield contraceptive device. A provision of S 44, added by Sen. Paul S. Trible Jr., R-Va., at Robins' request, would have allowed only one plaintiff to win compensation from a firm for punitive damages.

Auto Theft Safeguards. To deter car thieves, Congress passed a bill (HR 6257 — PL 98-547) requiring manufacturers to put identification numbers on major parts of automobiles with high theft rates.

Supporters said car theft had grown to a $5 billion-a-year problem, due to organized crime's operation of "chop shops" that dismantled stolen cars and resold the more valuable parts.

Under the measure, car makers would mark 14 parts, to be chosen by the secretary of transportation, on auto lines with above-average theft rates. For example, Ford's Escort subcompacts probably would not be marked, but its Thunderbirds would.

The auto industry balked initially at the cost of marking parts, but the bill had a cap of $15 a car. A provision added at the behest of General Motors Corp. allowed a company to win exemptions from the marking requirement if it sold federally approved anti-theft devices on its car lines as standard equipment.

Credit Card Surcharge. Due to an impasse in the Senate, Congress did not renew a ban on credit card surcharges that expired Feb. 27.

The bill (HR 5026) would have extended until May 31, 1985, a decade-old prohibition against merchants adding fees to cover costs of processing credit card transactions. It was a compromise between the Senate, which voted Feb. 28 to allow surcharges, and the House, where Frank Annunzio, D-Ill., chairman of the Banking Subcommittee on Consumer Affairs, opposed the fees.

The House approved HR 5026 April 3, but the Senate took no action because of threats of amendments

both from senators backing the fees and from those opposed to them.

Retailers had been free since February to impose surcharges. Business lobbyists said few had done so because of legal arguments that the fees would violate federal truth-in-lending laws and state usury statutes.

Congress

Senate TV. Senate Majority Leader Howard H. Baker Jr., R-Tenn., was vanquished in his last drive to bring television cameras and radio microphones into the Senate chamber.

Sporadically during the week of Sept. 17, the Senate debated a resolution (S Res 66) that would have allowed gavel-to-gavel television and radio coverage of its proceedings. But after losing a cloture vote to cut off debate, Baker pulled the measure from the floor Sept. 21, handing a victory to camera-shy senators who claimed that broadcasts would disrupt the Senate's business.

It was Baker's last push for Senate TV because he retired from the Senate at the end of 1984. But William L. Armstrong, R-Colo., pledged to revive the issue in 1985.

Ethics. Questions about the ethical practices of several members of Congress were raised during 1984.

On July 31, the House reprimanded Rep. George Hansen, R-Idaho, following his federal court conviction on charges of filing false financial statements in violation of the 1978 Ethics in Government Act.

In September, the House Committee on Standards of Official Conduct decided to conduct a formal inquiry into allegations that Rep. Geraldine A. Ferraro, D-N.Y., had violated the ethics act by failing to disclose adequately her family's financial holdings. On Dec. 3 the panel decided — reportedly by a vote of 8-2 — that she had technically violated the law about 10 times. However, no action was taken against Ferraro, since she gave up her House seat to run for vice president.

The Senate Ethics Committee Sept. 25 voted to end its staff review of the relationship between Sen. Mark O. Hatfield, R-Ore., and Greek businessman Basil A. Tsakos. The panel concluded there was insufficient evidence that Hatfield improperly helped

Tsakos promote a trans-African pipeline at the same time that the senator's wife was receiving $55,000 from Tsakos. Hatfield said his wife earned the money for real estate work she did for Tsakos.

Senate Committees. A special ad hoc committee to examine the Senate's committee structure recommended changes Nov. 29 designed to make the panels function more efficiently and effectively. The recommendations were submitted to the Rules and Administration Committee for action by the 99th Congress.

The 12-member Temporary Select Committee to Study the Senate Committee System, created June 6 and chaired by Dan Quayle, R-Ind., recommended strictly limiting the number of committee assignments each senator may hold and examining a two-year budget process, among other things.

The panel also went beyond its strict mandate and proposed some alterations in Senate procedures to reduce the parliamentary snarls that increasingly engulfed the Senate. But it stopped short of endorsing a proposal to increase the votes needed to invoke cloture.

Pay for Members. The Senate voted in January to rescind a 3.5 percent raise that members of Congress automatically received Jan. 1, 1984. But the measure (S 2211) was buried in the House Post Office and Civil Service Committee, leaving the raise in effect.

In April, under a budget reconciliation measure, the 3.5 percent salary hike was increased by another half percentage point, for a total 1984 pay raise of 4 percent, bringing lawmakers' annual salaries to $72,600.

On Jan. 1, 1985, members received another 3.5 percent raise, identical to the one recommended for white-collar federal workers, boosting members' salaries to $75,100.

Defense

Defense Budget. After a deadlock that lasted three months, Congress approved a fiscal 1985 defense budget totaling $292.9 billion. That marked a "real" increase of 5 percent above the fiscal 1984 defense appropriation, after the cost of inflation.

Reagan's January budget request of $313 billion for defense would have amounted to a real increase of 13 percent. Under intense congressional pressure to reduce the deficit, Reagan trimmed his request to $299 billion in early May.

Ultimate agreement on a 5 percent growth rate was widely anticipated from the outset of the annual defense budget minuet, but not until the end of the session did protagonists agree on the expected rate, largely because some Republican senators feared that House Democrats would hold out for even deeper cuts.

The Republicans stalled action on the budget resolution and the defense authorization bill (HR 5167 — PL 98-525) until they and House Democrats were ready to cut a single, once-and-for-all deal covering all three pieces of legislation.

Agreed to on Sept. 20, after more than a week of negotiations between House Speaker Thomas P. O'Neill Jr., D-Mass., and Senate Majority Leader Howard H. Baker Jr., R-Tenn., the package set the defense appropriations total (and the defense ceiling in the budget resolution) at $292.9 billion. A $297 billion authorization was agreed to, but that measure only set a ceiling on programs; the appropriations provisions of the continuing resolution (PL 98-473) set the amount actually spent.

MX Missile. The Baker-O'Neill summit also settled the immediate future of the MX missile — by deferring a decision until the spring of 1985.

Congress had agreed in 1983 to build the first 21 production-line missiles. But because of well-organized opposition by liberal arms control activists, this came only after a series of increasingly narrow votes in the Democratic-controlled House.

In 1984, Reagan requested an additional 40 missiles. On May 16, the House narrowly rejected a move to deny the production funds outright. But two weeks later, on May 31, it voted to bar production of additional missiles unless Congress passed a resolution in 1985 approving production.

The Senate approved production of 21 MXs.

Under the Baker-O'Neill agreement, embodied in both the defense authorization and appropriations bills, $2.5 billion for production of up to 21 additional MXs was authorized and appropriated. But none of the money could be spent for the new missiles unless Congress in March 1985 passed two resolutions approving production.

Anti-Satellite Weapon. In the compromise version of the defense appropriations bill, Congress blocked any tests of the anti-satellite (ASAT) missile against a target in space until March 1, 1985. It also prohibited more than three such tests in the remainder of fiscal 1985.

By a hefty margin, the House added to the defense authorization bill (HR 5167) a provision banning any ASAT target tests so long as Moscow continued the moratorium on tests of its own more primitive ASAT, which had been in service for more than a decade. The Senate bill allowed ASAT tests after the president reported to Congress on their rationale and their potential impact on efforts to negotiate ASAT arms control limitations with the Soviet Union.

Conferees provided that no more than two "successful" ASAT target tests would be allowed.

Arms control advocates, who saw ASAT as the opening wedge of a Reagan move to militarize outer space, then turned to the defense appropriations bill to impose further limits on the program. The House version of that measure contained the same conditional test ban as the authorization bill. One of the most contentious defense matters before the conference on the omnibus continuing resolution (H J Res 648 — PL 98-473), the issue was settled with the five-month moratorium on target tests and a three-test limit.

Space Missile Defense. Congress pared more than 20 percent from the first installment of Reagan's "strategic defense initiative" to develop space-based defenses against nuclear missiles. The $1.78 billion budget request was trimmed to $1.4 billion in the defense authorization bill (HR 5167 — PL 98-525).

Arms control advocates had ridiculed the program as "Star Wars." They argued that the program would never work but nevertheless would spur Soviet efforts to match it, opening outer space to the arms race.

Opponents of the strategic defense initiative concentrated on limiting the program's funding in House Appropriations Committee action on the defense appropriations bill. The House approved $1.09 billion and the Senate $1.63 billion; conferees on the continuing resolution (PL 98-473) reached a compromise of $1.4 billion.

Spare Parts Purchasing.
Widely reported instances of exorbitant charges to the Pentagon for spare parts prompted Congress to weigh a raft of legislation designed to forestall abuses.

Several such provisions were incorporated into the defense authorization bill (HR 5167 — PL 98-525), many of them intended to make it easier for the Pentagon to buy parts from their original manufacturer instead of purchasing them through the prime contractor who assembled the parts into a tank, plane or ship.

One provision required prime contractors to identify the subcontractor making each part. Another required Pentagon purchasing officers to check the government's supply inventory before ordering a part, to see whether it was already available.

The bill also required a picture and description of each part to be available at some point in the parts-ordering process so that ordering officials could have some idea of the reasonableness of a quoted price.

Rejected was a House-passed provision to put a seven-year limit on the right of a contractor to withhold technical data on its products from potential competitors.

Economic Affairs

Budget Resolution. On Oct. 1 Congress finally cleared its internal spending and revenue blueprint, the fiscal 1985 budget resolution (H Con Res 280).

Adoption of the conference report on the budget resolution capped a months-long struggle over how to reduce the size of federal deficits, projected to be in the $200 billion range through fiscal 1989.

By assuming tax increases, spending cuts and savings from lower interest rates, the $1.021 trillion fiscal 1985 budget plan showed deficit reductions totaling $149 billion through fiscal 1987.

The budget, which set total 1985 outlays at $932 billion and revenues at $750.9 billion, showed a deficit of $181.1 billion. And despite the deficit reductions, the deficit was projected to continue to increase, to $207.6 billion in fiscal 1987.

Deficit Reduction Package.
During consideration of the fiscal 1985 budget, the House approved a $182 billion deficit reduction plan; the Senate, a $140 billion package.

Both proposals contained a mix of tax increases, entitlement benefit reductions, cuts in discretionary spending, limits on defense spending and savings from lower interest payments on the national debt.

The compromise finally agreed upon by budget conferees envisioned $149.2 billion in deficit cuts through fiscal 1987.

The deficit reduction package was made up of: $50.8 billion in increased revenues; $58.3 billion from smaller increases in the defense budget; $12.2 billion in savings from entitlement and other mandatory benefit programs; $3.9 billion from reductions in non-defense discretionary programs; $18.3 billion from net interest savings; $5.7 billion from offsetting receipts.

The tax component of the deficit reduction plan (HR 4170 — PL 98-369), cleared June 27, centered largely on closing loopholes and other efforts to beef up taxpayer compliance. The bill also extended telephone excise taxes and called for a cutback in real estate depreciation.

The cuts in entitlement spending included a physician fee freeze for Medicare reimbursements and an increase in out-of-pocket health care costs for the elderly.

Despite earlier claims he would not sign a tax increase package until he was assured that an equivalent amount of spending cuts would be made, President Reagan sent a letter to members shortly before the politically difficult vote on HR 4170 to pledge his support.

Debt Limit. As a fitting end to an often tumultuous 98th Congress, the Senate Oct. 12 cleared a necessary extension of the public debt limit (H J Res 654 — PL 98-475) by the skin of its teeth.

It voted 37-30 to raise the limit from $1.573 trillion to $1.824 trillion, which was expected to allow sufficient borrowing authority for the government through fiscal year 1985.

The approval took some prodding, however, by the Senate leadership. Shortly after midnight the same day, members voted 14-46 to defeat the politically unpopular housekeeping measure, which had become symbolic of high government spending. Some senators, who had left town thinking adjournment was at hand, had to be flown back on special Air Force planes for the final vote.

The House automatically approved the extension the week before as part of its adoption of a fiscal 1985 budget resolution, under a 1979 procedure that allowed the House to avoid a direct vote on the debt hike.

The increase was the third for the year. Congress raised the limit $30 billion, from $1.49 trillion to $1.52 trillion, on May 24 (HR 5692 — PL 98-302). It agreed to another increase, to $1.573 trillion, on June 29 (HR 5953 — PL 98-342).

The Senate passed both of the earlier measures by voice vote. But it took two tries in the House to pass the first bill and four tries to pass the second.

Balanced Budget. The Senate Judiciary Committee approved a proposed constitutional amendment Sept. 13 to require a balanced federal budget, but the proposal (S J Res 5) died without full Senate action. It was the second consecutive Congress in which the Republican-controlled Senate, at President Reagan's bidding, sought to push the amendment. In the 97th Congress, the Senate passed a balanced budget amendment, but a companion proposal was rejected by the House.

In the 98th Congress, the House did not consider a balanced budget constitutional amendment. There was an effort to dislodge a proposal from the House Judiciary Committee, but sponsors of that discharge petition failed to get the required 218 signatures.

Fiscal austerity and election-year politics meanwhile helped propel through the House a bill that would have required the president to submit a balanced budget.

On Oct. 2, the House voted 411-11 for the bill (HR 6300) introduced by House Budget Committee Chairman James R. Jones, D-Okla. Despite the fact that GOP members labeled it a political "gimmick," 155 Republicans supported the measure. The bill was not considered by the Senate.

The measure would have required the president to submit a balanced budget, starting with the fiscal 1986 budget, although he would also have been allowed to propose a budget that did not balance. The House and Senate Budget committees would likewise have been required to report balanced budgets.

Budget Reform. After more than two years of study, the House

Rules Committee June 27 approved a bill (HR 5247) to revise — but not overhaul — the congressional budget process.

The main feature of the bill was a compressed timetable for drafting and acting on the budget. The president would have had to submit his budget earlier — by the first Monday after Jan. 3. Deadlines for action on the congressional budget would have been pushed forward. And, under the bill, Congress would not have been allowed to leave for its July 4th recess until work on all 13 regular appropriations bills was completed.

Education

Bilingual Education. A major overhaul of federal aid to bilingual education was approved by Congress as part of an omnibus bill (S 2496 — PL 98-511) to extend 10 expiring programs, including aid for the education of adults, Indians, women and immigrants.

The bill, which was cleared Oct. 4, also extended a part of the impact aid program for school districts that educated the children of federal employees, which had been scheduled to die at the end of fiscal 1984.

The measure cleared after House conferees, faced with the threat of a Senate filibuster, agreed to drop a controversial amendment that would have required public schools to allow moments of silent prayer.

Math and Science Education, School Access. Congress July 25 cleared a measure (HR 1310 — PL 98-377) authorizing $1 billion over two years to improve mathematics and science education, a politically popular measure that had become a lightning rod for controversial amendments. Before the bill was enacted, the new education program was overshadowed by debate over religion in public schools.

Added to the math-science bill was a much-disputed proposal requiring schools to allow voluntary student religious groups to meet in school facilities on the same terms as other extracurricular groups before and after class hours.

The final bill also included a rider to aid magnet schools in communities undergoing desegregation — a compromise drafted by proponents and opponents of reviving a desegregation aid program that had been abolished in 1981.

School Improvement. After more than a year of highly publicized pronouncements about the need to bolster the quality of U.S. schools, legislation responding to those concerns met a mixed record of success.

A bill (HR 5609) that would have set up a broad new program of school-improvement aid, heavily lobbied by the National Education Association, died on the House floor Sept. 13 without having been brought to a vote. Republican plans to introduce amendments on school prayer and other controversial social issues spoiled Democrats' appetite for further action on the measure, which was not brought back to the floor after general debate was completed Sept. 13.

Scholarships to attract bright students into teaching and to keep good teachers in the profession were authorized as part of an omnibus social services bill (S 2565 — PL 98-558) that cleared Congress Oct. 9. A similar scholarship plan had been approved by the House Aug. 8 as a free-standing bill (HR 4477).

Legislation (HR 2708) to improve foreign language instruction was passed Feb. 23 by the House but died in the Senate.

Student Aid. The administration for the second year in a row proposed revamping college student aid to put increased emphasis on student "self help" in paying tuition bills. Congress again turned a cold shoulder to the administration's ideas.

Lawmakers also shunned a proposal (HR 5240) to significantly expand student aid that had been advanced by the chairman of the House Education and Labor Subcommittee on Postsecondary Education, Paul Simon, D-Ill. Simon shelved the plan when his colleagues insisted that the plan was premature and too costly.

In the meantime, Congress voted to maintain existing eligibility standards for Pell grants for needy college students through academic year 1986-87, under an amendment to an omnibus education bill (S 2496 — PL 98-511) that cleared Oct. 4.

Vocational Education. Congress Oct. 4 approved a five-year extension of federal aid to vocational education that put more emphasis on improving and modernizing vocational training.

The measure (HR 4164 — PL 98-524) did not go as far as some members would have liked in giving states the flexibility to use federal money to meet local needs.

It required states to earmark a larger portion of their federal grants for improving access to training for the disadvantaged, handicapped and other groups that traditionally had been poorly served.

The bill authorized $500,000 for a national summit meeting on school improvement. The House had voted in October 1983, in a separate measure (HR 3245), to authorize the summit.

Peace Institute. After years of effort by Sen. Jennings Randolph, D-W.Va., and other members to set up a federal institution dedicated to the study of peace and conflict resolution, Congress in 1984 authorized the establishment of a U.S. Institute for Peace.

Some $6 million in fiscal 1985 and $10 million in 1986 was authorized to establish the institute for peace studies and international affairs, as part of the fiscal 1985 defense authorization bill (HR 5167 — PL 98-525) that cleared Congress Sept. 27.

The peace institute provisions of HR 5167 were similar to a bill (S 564) to establish a U.S. Academy of Peace that was reported in September 1983 by the Senate Labor and Human Resources Committee.

Energy

Natural Gas. Neither chamber brought the volatile issue of natural gas pricing to the floor in 1984.

The Senate deadlocked in November 1983 on proposals for both decontrol and re-control of gas prices, and made no further attempts to deal with the politically treacherous subject.

The House backed away from consideration of a complex measure (HR 4277) reported by the Energy and Commerce Committee May 31 that might have cushioned the effect of the scheduled Jan. 1, 1985, decontrol of approximately half of all U.S. natural gas supplies. The bill was slated for action in September, but it disappeared from the Rules Committee agenda at the last minute after Democratic members complained that the issue could divide the party and hurt the presidential ticket in the Southwest.

The House bill was a shaky compromise that would have allowed changes in the contracts that govern most sales of natural gas. It was vigorously opposed by representatives from Southwestern states.

Synfuels. The embattled U.S. Synthetic Fuels Corporation (SFC) emerged alive from the 98th Congress, but only after Congress amputated more than $7 billion of the $20 billion the corporation began with in 1980.

The SFC was buffeted by accusations that it was mismanaged and a bad economic idea. In April, it lost a quorum on its board and the administration refused to name new directors until the program was slashed.

In July, SFC lost $2 billion as part of the deficit reduction package (PL 98-369). In October, it lost another $5.375 billion as part of the continuing resolution (H J Res 648 — PL 98-473) that gave the government funding for another year.

The administration had asked in the spring that $9 billion be taken away from the SFC. But in September it agreed to the compromise reflected in the continuing resolution and promised to fill five vacancies on the board.

Coastal Zone Management. Legislation to give states greater control over offshore oil and gas leasing through the Coastal Zone Management (CZM) program sank in the 98th Congress.

The Supreme Court Jan. 11 ruled that provisions of the Coastal Zone Management Act of 1972 requiring federal activities "directly affecting" offshore areas to be consistent with approved state CZM plans applied only to actual drilling and production, not to the offering of leases.

The Senate Commerce, Science and Transportation Committee reported a bill (S 2324) June 13 to extend coverage to leasing activities. But it was strongly opposed by some senior senators and never made it to the floor.

The House Merchant Marine and Fisheries Committee had the issue on its agenda for markup in early September, but the committee meeting had to be cut off when Republican members raised procedural obstacles.

The administration strongly opposed the legislation, saying it would give states a veto over offshore leasing and would set back the effort to foster energy independence.

Offshore Revenue Sharing. In the waning days of the session, the Senate shelved legislation (S 2463) to give states a share of money raised from federal offshore oil and gas drilling leases.

House-Senate conferees had agreed on a plan to give states approximately 4 percent of federal revenues from leases off the Outer Continental Shelf. The House approved the conference report Sept. 13, 312-94. But when the measure came up in the Senate in early October, it was blocked by senators who supported the administration's claim that the program would increase the deficit and send money to states that did not participate in offshore drilling.

States had long sought a share of federal revenues from leases off their shores. They received half of the revenues from federal leases on land within their boundaries. S 2463 would have set up a fund, beginning at $300 million in fiscal 1985, for distribution to coastal states according to a formula. Supporters said the plan would compensate states for burdens imposed by offshore development and entice them to permit more offshore exploration for oil and gas.

Energy Emergency Preparedness. Legislation to strengthen the nation's capacity to deal with an interruption in oil supplies foundered.

In the Senate, Energy and Natural Resources Committee Chairman James A. McClure, R-Idaho, pressed the administration to soften its free-market stance and support several standby programs to deal with an energy crisis.

But McClure lost enthusiasm for his bill (S 1678) after Bill Bradley, D-N.J., succeeded in adding an amendment that would have set up a financial assistance program for the needy in the event of high oil prices.

The House Sept. 18 passed a vestigial emergency preparedness bill (HR 3880) that would have required the Energy Department to conduct a test sale of oil from the Strategic Petroleum Reserve. But the Senate failed to act on the measure.

The one related measure that did become law was a bill (HR 4194 — PL 98-239) to extend until June 30, 1985, an antitrust exemption for major U.S. oil companies that participated in the emergency planning activities of the International Energy Agency. That exemption had expired at the end of 1983.

Hoover Dam. Congress stuck to its policy of pricing electric power at what it cost to produce it, rather than what it was worth on the open market, when it gave customers of the Hoover Dam another 30 years of bargain rates.

Contracts governing the sale of power from the dam, located on the Colorado River at the Arizona-Nevada border, had been scheduled to expire in 1987. Legislation (S 268 — PL 98-381) cleared July 31 extended those arrangements until 2017.

Opponents claimed the extension was a giveaway that discouraged conservation and froze out areas in the West that were not already getting power from the dam.

Environment

Hazardous-Waste Control. Congress Oct. 5 cleared a bill (HR 2867 — PL 98-616) to strengthen and extend for four years the nation's main law regulating the handling of hazardous wastes.

The bill banned for the first time the disposal on land of all liquid and some solid hazardous wastes. It also set up the first federal program regulating underground tanks that stored gasoline and other hazardous liquids. In addition, the bill extended controls to generators of small quantities (220 to 2,200 pounds per month) of hazardous waste. This affected tens of thousands of dry cleaners, gas stations and other small businesses.

The bill also closed numerous loopholes in the 1976 Resource Conservation and Recovery Act.

Superfund. The Democratic-controlled House passed a bill (HR 5640) in August to renew and expand the 1980 "superfund" for the cleanup of hazardous-waste dumps, but the bill died in the Republican-controlled Senate. Reagan administration officials had urged Congress to wait until 1985, when the superfund tax on chemical and oil companies expired, to reauthorize the program.

The House Aug. 10 passed its $10.2 billion, five-year renewal of the superfund by a 323-33 vote, and the Senate Environment and Public Works Committee Sept. 13 approved its version by a 17-1 vote. The bill bogged down in the Senate Finance Committee, however, where Chairman Robert Dole, R-Kan., declined to schedule a markup despite pleas from some members.

The Senate delivered a coup de grâce to superfund's chances for renewal in 1984 when it defeated, 38-59, an Oct. 2 effort to add a version of the bill to the fiscal 1985 continuing appropriations resolution (H J Res 648).

Wilderness. Congress cleared more wilderness bills in 1984 than at any time since the 1964 Wilderness Act set up a system for preserving pristine federal lands from drilling, logging, road building and other development. Twenty separate bills for specific states went to President Reagan.

The legislation protected a total of 8.3 million acres in the following states: Arizona, Arkansas, California, Florida, Georgia, Mississippi, Missouri, New Hampshire, New Mexico, North Carolina, Oregon, Pennsylvania, Tennessee, Texas, Utah, Vermont, Virginia, Washington, Wisconsin and Wyoming.

Water Pollution. Bills to reauthorize the nation's main water pollution control law died when Congress adjourned without resolving deep House-Senate differences.

The House passed its Clean Water Act reauthorization (HR 3282) June 26 by a 405-11 vote, after making numerous concessions to environmentalists, industry and other interest groups. The measure authorized more than $24 billion in new spending, mostly for sewage plant construction.

The Senate never took up a bill (S 431) that the Environment and Public Works Committee approved June 28, 1983. That bill reflected the belief of Chairman Robert T. Stafford, R-Vt., that the law was basically sound and should be renewed without major tampering.

Water Projects. Congress failed to authorize or fund new Corps of Engineers' water projects, despite hopes that the 1984 election year would finally end an eight-year construction drought and policy impasse.

Dying as the session ended were two omnibus authorization bills — an $18 billion measure (HR 3678) passed by the House June 29, and a more modest $11 billion measure (S 1739) reported Nov. 17, 1983, by the Senate Environment Committee.

Also doomed was a supplemental appropriation to fund new construction starts. In 1983, the House passed HR 3958, providing $119 million for

43 new projects, and the Senate Appropriations Committee approved a $78 million version for 27 projects.

Efforts to attach both the omnibus authorization and the new starts supplemental to the fiscal 1985 continuing resolution (H J Res 648) during the final days of the session failed in the face of veto threats.

Safe Drinking Water. A compromise rewrite (HR 5959, S 2649) of the safe drinking water law was derailed in last-minute disputes over regulatory language and legal appeals. The bill, intended to end delays in setting national purity standards for drinking water, was forged in lengthy negotiations between environmental and water industry representatives. It won House approval Sept. 18 and, in a somewhat different form, Senate Environment Committee endorsement the following week.

In partial response to Reagan administration objections, sponsors agreed to drop a House-passed groundwater protection plan and make certain other revisions. But they failed to settle differences on wording of the basic health standards, and on a Senate amendment permitting legal appeals around the country.

Clean Air/Acid Rain. For the fourth year in a row, Congress failed to act on a reauthorization of the Clean Air Act. The law's funding authorization expired in 1981, although its regulations remained on the books and Congress had continued to appropriate funds for its enforcement.

Acid rain was the issue that confounded both House and Senate efforts to reauthorize the air pollution control law. The issue split the Northeast, the victim of acid rain, from the Appalachian states and the Midwest, which produced and burned much of the high-sulfur coal thought to cause acid rain. Westerners, largely upwind of the problem, did not want to pay to solve it.

Henry A. Waxman, D-Calif., chairman of the House Energy Sub he sought in fiscal years 1984 and 1985. José Napoleón Duarte, of the center-left Christian Democratic Party, was elected president in May.

The Senate Environment and Public Works Committee reported a clean air bill (S 768) in May. But the measure's acid rain controls were opposed by the Reagan administration, and the bill faced filibuster threats from several senators, including Mi-

nority Leader Robert C. Byrd, D-W.Va. It was never brought to the floor.

Foreign Policy

Foreign Aid. For the third year in a row, Congress failed to enact regular authorizations and appropriations bills for foreign aid programs. Instead, $18 billion worth of foreign aid spending for fiscal 1985 was included in the omnibus continuing resolution (H J Res 648 — PL 98-473) cleared on Oct. 11.

The House passed an aid authorizations bill (HR 5119) May 10, but the Senate never took up its companion measure (S 2582) because of disputes over aid to Central America and because neither the Reagan administration nor the Foreign Relations Committee was able to drum up enough support for the bill.

A last-minute attempt to attach a full authorizations bill to the continuing resolution failed when several Senate Democrats complained that the move was being made behind their backs. Several provisions of the House-passed bill, however, were included in the resolution.

Among major issues handled in the continuing resolution were: approval of $700 million in military aid for Turkey, a cut of $55 million from Reagan's request and $15 million from the 1984 level, signifying congressional unhappiness with Turkey's continued occupation of the northern third of Cyprus; approval of $290 million in aid for population programs, and a ban on the use of U.S. aid for "involuntary" abortions overseas; and a shift of $45 million in aid to the Philippines from military aid to economic aid, as a signal of unhappiness with the dictatorial regime of President Ferdinand E. Marcos.

Nicaragua. President Reagan would be forced to return to Congress in March 1985 if he wanted to continue direct U.S. involvement in the three-year-old war to oust the leftist government of Nicaragua.

Congress Oct. 10-11 approved a compromise that barred the president from providing further aid to anti-government rebels in Nicaragua until after Feb. 28, 1985 — and then only if both chambers of Congress agreed. The compromise was hammered out by House Democrats, who wanted to ban all aid to the guerrillas, and Senate Republicans, who supported the administration's aid to them. It was included in the fiscal 1985 omnibus continuing appropriations resolution (H J Res 648 — PL 98-473).

The compromise also was included in a bill (HR 5399 — PL 98-618) making fiscal 1985 authorizations for the CIA and other intelligence agencies. Congress cleared that measure on Oct. 11.

The administration inflicted much of the political damage on itself, with a decision early in the year to mine several harbors in Nicaragua without telling the Senate Intelligence Committee beforehand. When the mines went off, committee Chairman Barry Goldwater, R-Ariz., exploded in anger at the CIA for sidestepping his panel. Both chambers adopted nonbinding resolutions (HR 2163, H Con Res 290) condemning the mining.

El Salvador. Successful presidential elections in El Salvador quieted congressional debate about that country, enabling Reagan to win approval for most of the military aid he sought in fiscal years 1984 and 1985. José Napoleón Duarte, of the center-left Christian Democratic Party, was elected president in May.

Congress approved two aid supplementals for El Salvador in fiscal 1984: $61.75 million in an "urgent" supplemental (PL 98-332) and $70 million in the year's final supplemental (PL 98-396). That put the year's total at $196.55 million — more than twice the level for fiscal 1983. Reagan had requested $243.5 million.

In the continuing appropriations resolution (H J Res 648 — PL 98-473) for fiscal 1985, Congress appropriated $123.5 million of Reagan's $132.5 million request.

Kissinger Commission Aid. Congress in 1984 enacted only pieces of a sweeping $8.8 billion, six-year program of aid for Central America, recommended in January by a presidential commission headed by former Secretary of State Henry A. Kissinger. Congress approved most of the $1 billion-plus in economic and development aid that the commission recommended for fiscal 1985 — but it rejected a plan to authorize follow-up aid for fiscal years 1986-89.

The Kissinger commission recommendations suffered their biggest setback in the Republican-controlled Senate, where liberal Democrats and Jesse Helms, R-N.C., joined in an unusual coalition to help block the 1985 foreign aid authorizations bill (HR 2582).

Jerusalem Embassy. Two House Foreign Affairs subcommittees on Oct. 2 approved H Con Res 352, calling on the president to move the U.S. Embassy in Israel to Jerusalem, from Tel Aviv. But the measure, which for months had been the subject of intense negotiations between its sponsors and the administration, died at that point because Congress ran out of time to consider it.

The resolution was a watered-down version of a bill (HR 4877, S 2031) that would have required the president to move the embassy to Jerusalem, which Israel claimed as its capital. The administration adamantly opposed any congressional action on the issue because the status of Jerusalem was a sensitive issue in any negotiations between Israel and its Arab neighbors.

Genocide Treaty. A handful of Senate conservatives on Oct. 10 blocked approval of a treaty designed to outlaw genocide. Instead, the Senate on Oct. 11 passed a resolution (S Res 478) expressing approval for the principles stated in the treaty and pledging quick action on it in the 99th Congress.

Formally named the Convention on the Prevention and Punishment of Genocide, the treaty called on signatory nations to take specific steps to prevent acts of genocide and to punish those responsible. But Jesse Helms, R-N.C., and several other conservatives argued that the treaty might undermine U.S. sovereignty. When they threatened to throw up procedural barriers to the treaty's approval, Senate leaders withdrew it. The treaty had been before the Senate since 1949.

Afghanistan. Nearly three years after Sen. Paul E. Tsongas, D-Mass., publicly raised the issue, Congress on Oct. 3-4 completed action on an amended resolution (S Con Res 74) calling on the administration "to effectively support" anti-Soviet rebels in Afghanistan. The administration had opposed the original version of the resolution on the grounds that it might focus attention on Pakistan, through which most supplies for the rebels flowed.

Congress also appropriated $50 million for aid to the rebels in a supplemental spending bill (PL 98-396) for fiscal 1984.

Lebanon and Terror. Terrorist bombings caused turmoil throughout the year for U.S. policy in the Middle East, particularly in Lebanon.

At the beginning of the year, the United States was still reeling from the October 1983 bombing that killed more than 240 U.S. military personnel stationed at the Beirut airport as part of a multinational peacekeeping force. Some 1,600 Marines were hunkered down in bunkers at the airport, and President Reagan was refusing mounting calls in Congress to bring them home. But on Feb. 7, after radical Moslem armies stormed through West Beirut, Reagan suddenly announced he was "redeploying" the Marines to ships offshore. With that, House Democrats dropped plans for action on a resolution (H Con Res 248) that called on Reagan to begin the "prompt and orderly withdrawal" of the Marines.

Reagan subsequently ordered the total withdrawal of Marines from the waters off Lebanon, and the issue died down, except for bursts of recrimination between Reagan and congressional Democrats.

But the Sept. 20 terrorist bombing of a U.S. Embassy annex near Beirut, killing two Americans and a dozen others, reopened the issue. Congress Oct. 5 cleared a bill (HR 6311 — PL 98-533) authorizing $355.3 million to bolster security at U.S. embassies overseas. Of that amount, $110.2 million was appropriated in the fiscal 1985 continuing resolution (H J Res 648 — PL 98-473). HR 6311 also established a new program of rewards for persons providing conclusive information about terrorist acts committed in the United States or directed against U.S. property.

General Government

Freedom of Information. Although the Senate passed the first major overhaul of the Freedom of Information Act (FOIA) in 10 years, the legislation (S 774) remained stalled in a House subcommittee.

The bill would have closed off more information from public view, particularly law enforcement information and data submitted by businesses. It would also have provided incentives for speedy responses to

FOIA requests.

But after numerous hearings, the House Government Operations Subcommittee on Government Information failed to produce a bill that was sufficiently non-controversial to pass in the waning days of the session. Chairman Glenn English, D-Okla., introduced a bill (HR 6414) on Oct. 5 that he said could be used as a starting point in the 99th Congress.

Congress did clear a separate measure (HR 5164 — PL 98-477), which allowed the director of the CIA to close off certain operational files from review provisions of FOIA.

Polygraph Limitation. Legislation to curb the federal government's use of lie detector tests (polygraphs) failed to pass, but the Reagan administration voluntarily pulled back a proposed directive to step up their use.

The directive would have also required about 120,000 federal employees to agree to submit their writings for pre-publication review.

Rep. Jack Brooks, D-Texas, sponsored a bill (HR 4681) that would have banned pre-publication review and limited the use of polygraphs, but the bill never reached the floor because of differences over which agencies should be included in the ban. The Post Office and Civil Service Committee reported a bill exempting the CIA and the National Security Agency, but the Armed Services Committee voted partial exemptions from the polygraph ban for the Defense Department. Other agencies, such as the FBI, wanted exemptions as well.

Handicapped Voting Access. Congress Sept. 12 cleared legislation (HR 1250 — PL 98-435) requiring, as of 1986, that polling places used in national elections be accessible to the elderly and handicapped.

The bill, approved by voice vote in both chambers, also required states without mail or door-to-door registration to provide a reasonable number of accessible registration sites.

The bill also required states to report every even-numbered year to the Federal Election Commission, which would report to Congress, on the number of inaccessible polling places. This provision was to expire after 10 years.

Election Projections. Congress adopted a non-binding resolution (H Con Res 321) urging the media not to predict election results until all polls closed. The House passed the measure June 26, the Senate Sept. 21.

The resolution was a result of members' lingering anger over TV networks' 1980 election coverage, in which Ronald Reagan was called the winner soon after polls closed in the East. Members complained that the early projections discouraged voting in Western states, where polls remained open for several hours.

Pay Equity. The House voted overwhelmingly to require a study of the federal work force to determine if wage differences arose because of sex discrimination, but the Senate killed a similar plan, with a pledge to take up the issue in 1985.

The House bill (HR 5680) was attached to a Senate-passed measure (S 958) making changes in the merit pay system for managers in civil service grades 13-15 and in the Senior Executive Service (SES). That bill never went to conference.

Sen. Alan Cranston, D-Calif., proposed an amendment to the continuing resolution (H J Res 648), requiring a pay equity study, but the Senate voted 41-57 that the amendment was non-germane.

The Senate added the merit pay/SES provisions of S 958 to another House bill (HR 2300 — PL 98-615), cleared Oct. 10, and Cranston secured a promise from Ted Stevens, R-Alaska, chairman of the Governmental Affairs Civil Service Subcommittee, to hold hearings on pay equity in 1985.

Small Business. Congress cleared a measure (HR 4209 — PL 98-577) aimed at increasing the participation of small businesses in the federal procurement process and promoting competition in that process.

But an authorization (S 1323) for Small Business Administration (SBA) programs stalled in conference because the Reagan administration opposed a House-passed provision permitting SBA disaster loans for businesses harmed by the weather pattern known as El Niño. That provision later was added to the continuing resolution (H J Res 648 — PL 98-473), however.

Space Station. A $150 million down payment on a permanent manned space station became law July 16 as part of the fiscal 1985 appropriations bill for the National Aeronautics and Space Administration (HR 5154 — PL 98-361).

Although some scientists questioned the need for embarking on a manned program, funding for research into the station, expected to cost $8 billion by the time it was launched in 1992, passed without opposition. HR 5154 also required NASA to begin planning for an unmanned station.

Congress also cleared other measures (HR 5155 — PL 98-365, HR 3942 — PL 98-575) paving the way for commercial use of Landsat satellites that take pictures of the Earth, and expendable launch vehicles.

Health

Cigarette Labels, Taxes, Safety. Congress approved four sharp new health warnings for cigarette packages and advertisements, specifically identifying such smoking-related risks as cancer and harm to unborn children. Final action came Sept. 26 when the Senate cleared the measure (HR 3979 — PL 98-474).

In a major deficit reduction bill (HR 4170 — PL 98-369), Congress decided to let the existing 16-cents-per-pack federal tax on cigarettes drop to 8 cents on Oct. 1, 1985.

And Congress cleared a bill (HR 1880 — PL 98-567) mandating a study on the feasibility of developing "fire-safe" cigarettes, to minimize risks of cigarette-caused fires.

Generic Drugs. Congress Sept. 12 completed action on landmark legislation (S 1538 — PL 98-417) intended to make many more inexpensive "generic" versions of brand-name drugs available to consumers. The bill also authorized longer patent protection for new brand-name drugs.

Weeks after the bill passed, however, lobbyists for the generic-pharmaceuticals industry objected vehemently to another unrelated patent measure (HR 6286 — PL 98-622) they charged would effectively block the new supply of generic drugs. By the time that measure was cleared by the Senate Oct. 11, it had been shorn of the provisions that disturbed the generic-drug officials, but the issue was expected to resurface in 1985.

Drug Exports. A proposal (S 2878) to repeal a federal ban on the export of American-made drugs that did not meet U.S. health and safety standards was the subject of hearings but died without further action. The administration backed the repeal, but consumer groups and their congressional allies objected.

Heroin. The House Sept. 19, by a vote of 55-355, rejected a bill (HR 5290) to legalize the use of heroin for terminally ill patients with intractable pain. Families of such patients had long sought enactment of the bill, but the American Medical Association and the Reagan administration lobbied strongly against it, arguing that it set a bad precedent and that supplies of the drug might be diverted to illegal use.

Biomedical Research, Health Professions. President Reagan Oct. 30 vetoed two major health bills — one to create an arthritis research institute and reauthorize selected medical research programs (S 540), and one to continue community health programs and subsidies for training health professionals (S 2574).

Reagan said that "adequate authority" to continue the vetoed health programs was provided by the continuing appropriations resolution (H J Res 648 — PL 98-473).

He called the proposed arthritis institute and a second new federal research institute on nursing authorized by S 540 "unnecessary" and "premature." He noted a study of the organizational structure of the entire National Institutes of Health (NIH) was to be released soon.

S 540 also reauthorized funding for the National Cancer Institute and the National Institute of Heart, Lung and Blood Disease.

In vetoing the health professions bill, Reagan noted it authorized 41 percent more in spending than he had requested and continued "obsolete federal subsidies to health professions students" at a time of anticipated surpluses of doctors and nurses.

Medicare/Medicaid. Having imposed new out-of-pocket costs on Medicare beneficiaries and clamped new spending controls on hospitals in previous years, Congress in 1984 ordered a temporary halt to increases in Medicare payments to physicians for patient services.

The doctors' fee freeze, with new restraints to keep doctors from passing on higher charges to Medicare patients, was included in a multi-part deficit reduction package (HR 4170 —

PL 98-369) that cleared in June. The freeze, which extended to October 1985, was challenged in court by the American Medical Association.

Also included in the deficit reduction bill was a new child health assurance plan (CHAP), requiring states to broaden their Medicaid coverage to include more low-income women during pregnancy, and more young children.

Organ Transplant System. Congress completed action Oct. 4 on a bill (S 2048 — PL 98-507) meant to ease logistical problems associated with organ transplant surgery.

The measure provided for a national computerized network to match transplant patients with donated organs, and authorized funds to upgrade and coordinate local and regional organ procurement agencies.

The bill also created a commission to study ethical, legal and other issues raised by the surgery, and outlawed the buying and selling of human organs. The final version omitted a controversial House-passed provision that would have funded, for low-income transplant patients, an expensive new drug used after the surgery.

Housing/Development

Enterprise Zones. President Reagan's proposal to provide tax breaks for businesses that located in designated "enterprise zones" in inner cities and rural areas failed to become law for the third year in a row.

The Senate included the enterprise zone plan in its version of the 1984 deficit reduction act (HR 4170), but it was dropped in conference with the House. Sen. Robert Dole, R-Kan., reintroduced the proposal as a separate bill (S 2914), but it never reached the floor.

Reagan, charging that House Democrats refused to consider the plan, wrote to House Minority Whip Trent Lott, R-Miss., in September, asking the House to consider the plan, but Lott was unable to bring it to the House floor.

Secondary Mortgage Market. A bill to encourage private firms to buy mortgages and sell securities backed by them was signed into law Oct. 3 (S 2040 — PL 98-440).

The bill removed some regulatory

hurdles firms had encountered in entering the secondary mortgage market, and maintained some protections for investors. It also expanded the authority of two federally backed mortgage corporations, allowing them to purchase loans on mobile homes and second mortgages.

Some members of the banking industry wanted to include a provision allowing banks to underwrite mortgage-backed securities. That provision was part of a Senate-passed banking bill (S 2851) that was not considered by the House. A separate proposal allowing issuers of mortgage-backed securities to form new entities called trusts for investment in mortgages (TIMs) to manage mortgage pools was shelved because of disagreement over whether to include the federally chartered mortgage corporations in the plan.

Labor

Conservation Jobs. Congress cleared legislation (HR 999) authorizing $225 million over three years for a program, reminiscent of the Depression-era Civilian Conservation Corps, to put unemployed youths to work on public and Indian lands. But President Reagan, a longtime foe of job-creation programs, vetoed the bill Oct. 30.

A similar measure to establish an American Conservation Corps died in the 97th Congress.

In an effort to overcome administration objections to the bill as passed by the House in March 1983, the Senate substantially cut back the funding before passing its version Oct. 3. The House then overwhelmingly approved the Senate-amended version Oct. 9.

Subminimum Wage. The administration's proposal to lower the minimum wage for teenagers died without being brought to a vote in either the House or the Senate.

The youth subminimum wage, which would apply only in the summer months, was the cornerstone of the administration's policies for combating youth unemployment.

Plans to bring the proposal to the Senate floor as an amendment to other legislation were scuttled by the threat of a filibuster.

Pension 'Equity.' With legislators eager to demonstrate their commitment to women in an election year, Congress cleared a bill (HR 4280 — PL 98-397) designed to make it easier for women to earn retirement benefits under private pension plans.

The measure was cleared Aug. 9 after committee staff members ironed out relatively minor differences between the pension "equity" bills approved in November 1983 by the Senate and on May 22 by the House.

The law expanded pension coverage for workers who left and later went back to a job, and strengthened the pension rights of homemakers whose working spouses died before retirement age. The changes were a key element of a legislative package intended to eliminate economic bias against women.

Pension Insurance. Congress failed to finish work on legislation to shore up the Pension Benefit Guaranty Corporation (PBGC), the federal agency that guaranteed eligible workers would receive retirement income if their pension plans were shut down.

With the PBGC facing a deficit of more than $500 million, legislation (S 1227, HR 3930) was approved by the Senate Labor Committee June 13 and by a House Education and Labor subcommittee in November 1983 to crack down on abuses of the agency's insurance program and increase the premium employers paid into the insurance fund.

But both bills died without seeing further action. Another House bill (HR 5143) would have increased the PBGC premium without overhauling the insurance program. That measure, whose principal purpose was to provide new pension protections for public-sector workers, was reported by the Education and Labor Committee Oct. 4 but went no further.

Disability Benefits. With elections just over the horizon, Congress ended more than two years of legislative bickering and agreed to overhaul a controversial Social Security disability review program.

The bill (HR 3755 — PL 98-460) was designed to make it more difficult for the administration to remove individuals from the disability rolls. The administration's review of disability recipients began in 1981 in response to a congressional mandate to cut down on waste, but after the program was established, members of Congress were besieged with complaints that thousands of eligible individuals were

being dropped from the rolls.

The administration, promising to address complaints administratively, opposed legislation setting a new review standard. Its allies in the Senate blocked legislative action, citing fears that the rolls would again become bloated with ineligible recipients.

But the program's troubles grew. By early 1984, more than half the states had stopped administering the reviews, and courts were routinely overturning the administration on appeals. After a 410-1 House vote for HR 3755 in March, the administration did an about-face and agreed to work with Congress on passing a bill. The final version cleared Sept. 19.

Social Security Cost-of-Living. Plagued by Democratic charges that he would cut Social Security benefits if re-elected, President Reagan took the offensive and proposed July 24 that the elderly receive a cost-of-living allowance (COLA) in January 1985, even if inflation were too low to trigger one. Under existing law, no COLA was allowed if inflation for the previous year was below 3 percent, as it then was expected to be.

The Senate responded quickly and two days later approved a one-year waiver of the trigger. The Democratic-controlled House moved more slowly. Denying Reagan a chance to take full credit for the COLA increase at the Republican convention in August, the House passed its version of the COLA bill (HR 6299) Oct. 2. By then, it was apparent that the year's cost of living would be above 3 percent, and Democrats blasted the president for "needless meddling" with the program. The Senate cleared the bill Oct. 11 (PL 98-604).

Law/Judiciary

Immigration. For the third year in a row, a sweeping immigration reform bill failed to make it through Congress, even though slightly different versions of the measure were passed by both chambers. House-Senate conferees could not agree on a final version of the bill (S 529), which fell victim to heavy lobbying by competing interest groups and the election-year qualms of members.

Conferees, who met 10 times, had ironed out their differences on all but one of the major elements in the bill. The measure would have penalized

employers who knowingly hired illegal aliens, while authorizing the legalization of aliens who came to the United States illegally prior to Jan. 1, 1981.

A conference deadlock over a funding issue doomed the bill. The dispute was over the amount states should get from the federal government to defray social service costs anticipated from the legalization program. The Reagan administration insisted on a $1 billion annual cap for four years, but conferees from states with large illegal alien populations contended this amount would be insufficient.

Crime. Congress cleared major anti-crime legislation Oct. 11 as part of the fiscal 1985 continuing appropriations resolution (H J Res 648 — PL 98-473). The measure was the most wide-ranging crime bill since the 1968 Omnibus Crime Control and Safe Streets Act.

Among the major elements of the crime package were provisions that required federal judges to follow new sentencing guidelines, permitted pretrial detention of dangerous defendants, restricted use of the insanity defense, increased penalties for drug trafficking, created an interagency council to combat drug trafficking and re-established anti-crime grants for states.

President Reagan repeatedly lambasted the House for sitting on a Senate-passed crime package (S 1762), even though the House was working its way through much of the package via individual bills.

Republican House members managed to attach provisions of the Senate bill to H J Res 648. The Senate left the crime package in that measure but made some modifications that subsequently were agreed to by the conference committee.

Bankruptcy. Congress June 29 cleared legislation designed to put the nation's bankruptcy courts on sound legal footing. President Reagan signed it July 10 (HR 5174 — PL 98-353).

In addition to restructuring the courts, the legislation made a number of substantive changes in bankruptcy law. One of the most controversial barred companies filing for bankruptcy from unilaterally abrogating their labor contracts. This provision, the result of relentless lobbying by organized labor, overturned a Feb. 22 Supreme Court decision.

The new law gave overall authority for bankruptcy matters to federal district courts and made bankruptcy judges adjuncts of those courts. It also gave bankruptcy judges authority to deny bankruptcy protection to an individual debtor upon determining that it would be a "substantial abuse" of bankruptcy law to allow a particular consumer to declare bankruptcy and cancel his debts.

Another provision provided expedited procedures for handling bankruptcy cases involving grain elevators and fish-processing plants. That was intended to provide quick relief to farmers and fishermen who sold their goods to storage operations that subsequently went bankrupt.

Civil Rights. The House passed but the Senate refused to act on legislation (HR 5490) to overturn a Feb. 28 Supreme Court decision restricting enforcement of Title IX of the 1972 Education Amendments. That law barred discrimination based on sex in any education "program or activity" receiving federal aid. The court held that the ban did not apply to all activities of a recipient institution, but only to the particular program or activity receiving federal funds.

Three other laws barred discrimination based on race, age or handicap in any "program or activity" receiving federal funds, and civil rights lawyers warned that the ruling in *Grove City College v. Bell* could restrict enforcement of those statutes as well.

HR 5490 would have amended all four laws to make clear that any "recipient" of aid, not simply any "program or activity," would be required to conform to anti-bias laws.

The House passed the bill June 26 by 375-32. The measure was held at the Senate desk, where Majority Leader Howard H. Baker Jr., R-Tenn., could have called it up for consideration at any time. A Senate companion bill (S 2568) stalled in the Labor and Human Resources Committee, where Chairman Orrin G. Hatch, R-Utah, led the opposition.

Hatch and Reagan administration officials contended that the bill would do more than simply restore the law to its pre-*Grove City* state. They said the measure would expand federal civil rights enforcement power.

In mid-September, Baker made clear that he would not bring the House bill to the floor. Senate supporters then sought to attach the measure to the continuing resolution (H J Res 648), a move that touched off a

four-day parliamentary gridlock. On Oct. 2, with no agreement in sight, the Senate finally voted 53-45 to table (kill) the amendment.

School Prayer. Despite pressure from President Reagan and conservative religious groups, Congress refused to approve a constitutional amendment allowing either silent prayer or organized, recited prayer in public schools.

On March 15, the Senate voted 81-15 to table (kill) a proposal that would have allowed silent prayer or meditation in public schools. The proposal was offered as an alternative to a constitutional amendment (S J Res 73) backed by Reagan allowing recited school prayer.

The proposed vocal-prayer amendment fell March 20. Although it received a 56-44 majority, this was 11 votes short of the required two-thirds majority.

The House did not consider a constitutional amendment on prayer. It did, however, attach to a school aid bill (S 2496) language to bar schools from denying individuals the opportunity to engage in moments of silent prayer. The provision was dropped in a conference on the bill, which subsequently was cleared for Reagan's signature.

Trade

Omnibus Trade Bill. Congress Oct. 9 cleared omnibus trade legislation (HR 3398 — PL 98-573) that contained provisions ranging from preferential treatment for exports from developing nations to import relief for the domestic steel industry.

Among other things, the bill:

● Extended for 8½ years the generalized system of preferences (GSP), which lifted duties on some imports from some developing countries.

The bill linked benefits, for the first time, to recipients' steps to open markets to U.S. trade, honor copyrights and other intellectual property and respect worker rights. It also cut benefits for countries with an annual per capita gross national product of more than $8,500.

● Approved duties to offset "upstream subsidies" — government aid such as financing which unfairly lowered the export price of foreign goods.

This provision originally was part of a trade remedies bill (HR 4784)

passed by the House July 26. Other remedies in that bill were dropped.

● Gave the president authority to enforce voluntary restraints on steel imports, which President Reagan had recommended Sept. 18. The authority was linked to steelmakers' steps to modernize equipment and retrain workers. The bill also asked the president to reduce steel imports to between 17 percent and 20.2 percent of the domestic market, and instructed the administration to negotiate voluntary copper import reductions with major foreign copper producers.

● Granted the president authority to negotiate to lower or eliminate barriers on most trade between Israel and the United States, and extended the president's powers to negotiate free-trade agreements with other countries, subject to congressional review.

● Asked, but did not require, the president to negotiate reduced barriers to U.S. wine trade. The provision was a watered-down version of so-called wine "equity" legislation meant to prevent U.S. wine makers from being shut out of European markets by high tariffs or substantially losing domestic sales to foreign imports.

The bill also allowed grape growers to bring unfair-trade complaints to the International Trade Commission.

● Extended to service industries many of the same remedies for unfair foreign trade practices that already applied to goods. The bill authorized the president to negotiate lowered barriers to trade in high-technology items, U.S. investment abroad and services such as banking.

Export Administration. After six months of House-Senate conferences and countless hours of behind-the-scenes negotiations, efforts to renew the Export Administration Act failed. The legislation would have authorized the president to restrict U.S. shipments abroad to protect national security, promote foreign policy and prevent shortages of important commodities.

The House passed a bill (HR 3231) in October 1983; the Senate approved its version March 1. Conferees finally deadlocked after resolving nearly all major differences. In a last-ditch effort, Sen. Jake Garn, R-Utah, Oct. 10 offered a compromise bill (HR 4230) that would have dropped two of the most controversial outstanding issues: a Senate plan to grant the Defense Department more power to review licenses for high-technology exports and a House-backed proposal to cut new commercial bank loans to the government of South Africa.

But the House Oct. 11 reinstated the prohibition on bank loans, which effectively killed the bill's Senate chances.

Trade Adjustment Assistance. Congress failed to renew the trade adjustment assistance program, which aided workers who had lost their jobs because of increased imports. The House requested a two-year extension in the omnibus trade bill (HR 3398), but Senate conferees Oct. 9 rejected the plan. The program, which was to expire Sept. 30, 1985, had been criticized for failing to retrain workers adequately or help them find new jobs.

International Banks. After a struggle that threatened to scuttle some funds earmarked for the international development banks that lend to developing nations, Congress Oct. 11 approved $1.3 billion for the banks as part of the fiscal 1985 continuing resolution (H J Res 648 — PL 98-473).

Also authorized was funding for the International Development Agency (IDA) for the next three years; $750 million was appropriated for the first year of that commitment. Congress also restored $150 million for the remainder of the United States' 1981-84 commitment to IDA's international lending pool. The funds had been cut Aug. 10 from a fiscal 1984 supplemental appropriations bill.

IDA, which made no-interest loans to the world's poorest countries, had drawn fire for its cost, priorities and effectiveness as an instrument of foreign policy. The U.S. pledge of $2.25 billion for the next three years trimmed the previous U.S commitment by 31 percent.

Domestic Content. Domestic content legislation, a priority of labor groups, was rejected for the second year in a row as too strongly protectionist.

A bill (HR 1234) that would require foreign automakers to use a fixed proportion of U.S. parts and labor in cars sold in the United States passed the House in November 1983. But the bill remained bottled up in the Senate Commerce Committee because its chairman, Bob Packwood, R-Ore., was opposed to it.

Although it failed to make much headway, domestic content legislation

remained symbolically important. Many House members backed the bill to signal the Japanese to cut back on exports. Labor groups also used the vote as a test of loyalty.

Foreign Sales Corporations. As part of its June budget deficit down payment plan (HR 4170 — PL 98-369), Congress replaced a major export subsidy that had been criticized as a violation of international trade rules with a less generous but still lucrative tax break. With the switch from Domestic International Sales Corporations (DISCs) to Foreign Sales Corporations (FSCs), Congress wrote off approximately $13.6 billion in deferred taxes for U.S. exporters accumulated since DISCs began in 1971.

DISCs and FSCs were both meant to increase exports by saving companies taxes on foreign sales. However, DISCs existed only on paper and so rarely would actually close down, allowing taxes on their operations to be deferred indefinitely.

The new FSC rules responded to foreign criticisms by requiring beneficiaries to set up an actual business operation abroad. In most cases the FSC tax break would be slightly lower than the DISC deferral.

Industrial Policy. Industrial policy, which at times in 1983 looked as if it might become a rallying cry for Democrats, instead remained largely a collection of ideas looking for supporters. Nevertheless, the concept, which would enlarge the government's role in promoting particular industries, influenced several trade bills, including a steel plan passed Oct. 9 as part of the omnibus trade bill (HR 3398 — PL 98-573).

That plan linked the president's authority to enforce voluntary restraints on steel imports with steel makers' efforts to modernize and retrain workers.

The original industrial policy legislation left many Democrats wary of advancing central planning. In particular, Democrats split in their support for a Bank for Industrial Competitiveness, which would have lent money and promoted stock purchases to finance industrial modernization.

The major industrial policy bill (HR 4360), which contained plans for the bank, was reported by the House Banking Committee in April and by the Energy and Commerce Committee in June, but went no further during the remainder of the session.

Transportation

CAB Sunset. The Civil Aeronautics Board (CAB) went out of business as scheduled Jan. 1, 1985, but its consumer protection powers were given to the Department of Transportation (DOT) under legislation cleared by Congress Sept. 20 and signed into law Oct. 4 (HR 5297 — PL 98-443).

House and Senate versions of the legislation agreed on the major provision of the bill: transferring to DOT the authority to continue consumer-protection rules such as those regulating smoking on flights, baggage damage and bumping of passengers to other flights. But they differed on whether the power to approve airline mergers and to grant antitrust exemptions should go to the Justice Department, as the Senate and the administration wanted, or to DOT, as the House preferred. The final bill accepted the House approach.

Drunken Driving. Despite initial misgivings, President Reagan lobbied for and signed into law a bill to pressure states to raise their minimum drinking age to 21 (HR 4616 — PL 98-363).

The measure, designed to combat drunken driving by young people, whipped through the House and Senate during the week before the July 4 recess, with the House clearing it June 28. The Senate had attached the drunken-driving provisions to HR 4616, a House-passed bill to establish a child safety restraint program.

The law would withhold from states a portion of federal highway funds if they had a minimum drinking age below 21. Reagan at first opposed that approach as an infringement on states' rights, but later he embraced it as a way to reduce the problem of youths driving across state lines to drink in a state with a low drinking age.

The legislation also offered incentives for states to take other steps to combat drunken driving.

Air Bags. Legislation to require automakers to put air bags in new cars lost its impetus soon after July 11, when the Department of Transportation (DOT) issued a regulation supporting mandatory crash protection. The new rule allowed auto manufacturers to choose between air bags, automatically closing seat belts or "crashproof" interiors, but required them to phase in some type of crash protection between 1986 and 1989.

The rule would not apply if states representing two-thirds of the U.S. population passed mandatory seat-belt-use laws by April 1, 1989.

The regulation represented a reversal of course for the Reagan administration, which had opposed government interference in auto manufacturing. In 1981 DOT rescinded a Carter administration rule that would have required passive restraints in cars, but the Supreme Court overturned that action in 1983 and sent the matter back to DOT for reconsideration.

Shipping Act. After years of frustration, the ocean-liner industry persuaded Congress to expand its antitrust immunity for setting prices and dividing routes. The Shipping Act of 1984 (S 47 — PL 98-237), which updated federal regulation of the maritime industry, passed both houses in 1983 but differences were not resolved by conferees until 1984. The Senate adopted the conference report Feb. 23, the House March 6.

The legislation marked the first major change in shipping regulation in more than 20 years. Previous attempts to expand antitrust immunity, which shippers said was necessary to enable them to compete in the international marketplace, had been blocked by consumer groups and members opposed to antitrust immunity.

Highway Construction. For the second consecutive year, Congress failed to pass comprehensive legislation to release to the states money for Interstate highway construction.

Conferees broke up without agreeing on legislation to release more than $7 billion for fiscal 1984 and 1985 from the Highway Trust Fund. The lack of action could cause delays in the completion of the Interstate Highway System, which had been targeted for 1990. A majority of states were virtually out of cash for Interstate construction.

In 1983 Congress deadlocked on bills to release the money, which was raised from gasoline and diesel fuel taxes and other road-related fees. Funds for the first half of fiscal 1984 were approved in March, but legislation to cover the remaining 18 months ran aground.

The House passed its version of the measure (HR 5504) June 7, but

two Senate bills (S 2527, S 3024) were delayed by controversies. S 3024 passed the Senate Oct. 4, but the House's insistence that the bill cover mass transit as well as highways delayed a conference until one day before adjournment. The conference broke up when House members refused to accept a Senate proposal that would have limited funding for special highway and bridge projects.

Veterans

Agent Orange. Congress Oct. 4 cleared a bill (HR 1961 — PL 98-542) requiring the Veterans Administration to set up guidelines for compensating Vietnam veterans suffering from diseases believed to be caused by the herbicide Agent Orange.

The bill also provided temporary disability payments for veterans suffering from two specific diseases. The House version of the bill would have compensated victims of three diseases; the Senate version left to the VA the decision about which diseases to presume were caused by exposure to the herbicide.

G.I. Bill. Congress established a large-scale program of college-level education benefits as part of the defense authorization bill (HR 5167 — PL 98-525). The last such program lapsed in 1976.

The armed services had succeeded well in recruiting in recent years, but Pentagon officials acknowledged that a civilian job shortage was at least partly responsible. Proponents of the existing all-volunteer U.S. military had argued for years that a program of educational benefits would be needed to entice academically talented teenagers into the services once the economy began providing more civilian job opportunities.

The Reagan administration seemed to support the G.I. Bill approach when it took office, but quickly dropped the idea as being too costly.

HR 5167 established a three-year, voluntary test program which, unlike earlier G.I. Bill programs, would require contributions by participants. Any recruit entering military service between June 1985 and July 1988 could join the program for $100 a month for the first year of service. Those in service for three years would then be eligible to receive $300 for each of 36 months in school. The sec-

retary of defense could increase benefit levels for recruits in selected job specialties, to encourage enlistment and re-enlistment.

Welfare

Child Support. A key element of a legislative package designed to remedy economic discrimination against women was enacted Aug. 16, when President Reagan signed a bill (HR 4325 — PL 98-378) to strengthen the collection of delinquent child-support payments.

The measure required states to set up procedures for withholding past-due, court-ordered support payments from wages. It also provided for the withholding of both federal and state income-tax refunds owed to parents who have reneged on their support obligations.

The measure was an important piece of the Economic Equity Act, a package of proposals aimed at improving the treatment of women in such areas as tax law, insurance and pensions.

Child Abuse/Baby Doe. Legislation (HR 1904 — PL 98-457) designed to ensure that severely handicapped infants were not denied the medical treatment they needed to live cleared Congress Sept. 28, after months of negotiations over the emotional issue.

The so-called "Baby Doe" provisions were included in a bill that reauthorized at significantly higher spending levels federal programs to prevent and treat child abuse.

The bill required states, in order to receive federal child protection aid, to have procedures for responding to reports of medical neglect of handicapped infants. But it made clear that doctors would not have to take heroic steps to save the life of an infant if treatment would be futile.

The bill also authorized a new program to help states provide shelter for battered wives and other victims of domestic violence.

Social Services. The politically divisive formula for allocating energy aid for the poor was modified, under an omnibus social services bill (S 2565 — PL 98-558) that cleared Congress Oct. 9.

The change was a compromise designed to respond to complaints of members from warm-weather regions that their constituents were being shortchanged, while protecting cold-weather states from drastic and sudden losses of energy aid. The revised formula was included in a two-year reauthorization bill that included the energy aid, Community Services Block Grants and the Head Start program for disadvantaged preschool children.

The bill was cleared after being adorned with several unrelated amendments to establish new education programs, such as scholarships for teachers and training centers for school administrators.

ACTION. Congress rebuffed the administration's efforts to dismantle Volunteers in Service to America (VISTA), a well-known remnant of the War on Poverty.

Congress May 8 cleared legislation (S 1129 — PL 98-288) that extended VISTA for three years, along with other federally sponsored volunteer programs run by ACTION. The bill authorized $158.4 million in fiscal 1984, rising to $175.2 million in 1986. It included provisions designed to ensure that a minimum number of VISTA volunteers be hired before other programs were financed.

Food Programs. Congress did not complete action on legislation partially restoring some Reagan-era cuts in food stamps and other federal food aid programs. The bills were drafted in response to reports over several years that noticeable numbers of low-income Americans needed more food assistance.

The House in May approved a $9 billion four-year reauthorization (HR 7) of child nutrition programs, which liberalized benefits and eligibility for school meal programs and nearly doubled funding levels for a nutritional program (WIC) for pregnant low-income women and young children.

The House passed a second food-aid bill in August — a billion-dollar food stamp measure (HR 5151) making some relatively modest changes in methods for calculating benefit levels and eligibility. The measure also strengthened the penalties for state program errors.

The Senate Agriculture Committee in May agreed upon a shorter, no-growth WIC reauthorization (S 2722). That bill stalled over disagreements about using it to expand programs.

Congress adjourned without further action on the food aid bills, and expiring child nutrition programs were extended by the continuing resolution (H J Res 648 — PL 98-473), which also made one change in food stamps. That change restored food stamp benefit levels to 100 percent, from 99 percent, of the thrifty food plan, which the government used to measure an inexpensive diet.   ∎

MAJOR CONGRESSIONAL ACTION

CQ

Defense

For the third consecutive year, an intense congressional debate over President Reagan's defense policy focused on two general themes: the pace of Reagan's planned military buildup and the administration's approach to arms control, particularly relating to nuclear weapons.

The upshot of both battles in 1984 was similar to the outcomes in 1982 and 1983. Once again, although Reagan suffered some substantial defeats, the fundamental shape of his Pentagon program survived.

On the arms control front, Congress approved a large number of measures designed to nudge the Reagan team toward new initiatives. Most of these moves had only marginal immediate impact, but two hit uncomfortably close to home for Reagan:

● Congress deferred until early 1985 a decision on whether or not to continue production of the MX intercontinental missile, though it seemed unwilling to kill the project outright.

● And for the first time, Congress blocked — though only for several months — imminent tests of a weapon in hopes that negotiations would bar all such arms. At stake was the anti-satellite missile, or ASAT.

As in earlier years, Reagan's initial budget request went far beyond most assessments of what Congress would seriously consider.

Reagan called for a fiscal 1985 defense budget that was 13.3 percent higher than the fiscal 1984 appropriation, in addition to the cost of inflation. The conventional wisdom was that Congress would approve a "real" post-inflation defense increase on the order of 5 percent.

And 5 percent it was, in the end, but only after a prolonged legislative impasse that stalled the annual defense funding legislation for months. When it came to allocating the reductions of some $20 billion in Reagan's initial request, Congress made its trims in the usual places: corners were cut, production schedules slowed down, lower priority items were shelved.

Proportionally, most of the reduction came in the request for military hardware. But it required neither the cancellation of a single, major program, nor any substantial revision of U.S. military strategy.

The most noticeable change from the 1983 congressional defense debate was a heightened partisanship that, presumably, reflected the fact that 1984 was an election year.

For the first half of the year — until former Vice President Walter F. Mondale had assured his grip on the Democratic presidential nomination — Mondale and his fellow hopefuls jockeyed for the support of Democratic Party activists who had a dovish stance on defense.

Over the same period, the House Democratic leadership took an increasing role in the decade-long battle over the MX, the centerpiece of Reagan's nuclear weapons program.

In large part, that reflected their judgment that the controversial missile symbolized the facets of Reagan's defense posture that Democrats hoped to run against: ballooning budgets, an overreliance on weapons rather than diplomacy as instruments of U.S. global policy, and an emphasis on building up the U.S. nuclear arsenal rather than seeking an immediate freeze on U.S. and Soviet nuclear weapons buildups.

Although the Democrats' combativeness heated up the congressional debate over defense, it seemed to have little effect on the November election. Both major presidential candidates pitched their rhetoric on defense issues toward the political center. Mondale soft-pedaled his emphasis on the nuclear weapons freeze while Reagan stressed his desire to resume arms control talks the Russians had broken off late in 1983.

How Much Is Enough?

In his defense budget request for fiscal 1985, Reagan continued the emphases of his previous three budgets:

● Modernization of all three parts of the so-called nuclear triad — the fleets of land-based missiles, submarine-launched missiles and bombers. The budget would continue production of the MX missile, the Trident submarine missile and the B-1 bomber while allocating billions to the development of wholly new weapons in each of the three classes.

Though the Pentagon's nuclear arsenal continued to absorb only about 15 percent of the annual defense budget, it was consuming a much larger share of the weapons procurement budget than had been the case throughout the 1970s.

● Expansion of the fleet to reach the "600-ship Navy" touted by Reagan during his 1980 presidential campaign. The slogan was shorthand for a fleet built around 15 big aircraft carriers and their escorts. The last of the new carriers had been funded in fiscal 1983, but expensive new escort ships would be budgeted for years to come.

In part, this was because the large number of escort ships built in the late 1950s were wearing out. But the expansion was also aimed at building new ships to carry the Aegis anti-aircraft system, designed to fend off the swarms of anti-ship cruise missiles in the Soviet armory.

● Modernization of the Army's front-line units. Because the day-to-day cost of fighting the Vietnam War and the low defense budgets of the immediate, post-Vietnam period, the Army had gone nearly a decade without introducing major new weapons designed to deal with Soviet forces in Europe.

Accordingly, it was buying concurrently M-1 tanks, Apache missile-armed, anti-tank helicopters, Bradley new armored troop carriers, and a host of less dramatic items.

● Expansion of the fleet of ships and planes designed to

haul U.S. forces overseas for combat. One goal was a surge in construction of amphibious landing ships designed to let Marine Corps units fight their way ashore.

The newer ships would replace ships built in the late 1950s and boost the number of Marines that could be landed at once. Also funded was a hefty increase in the fleet of cargo ships and intercontinental transport planes.

The Road to 5 Percent

Reagan's request for a 13 percent "real" increase was politically dead before it hit the congressional doorstep in early February.

There was virtual unanimity among participants in and observers of the congressional budget process that nothing even close to that rapid an increase would be approved for the Pentagon, given the size of the projected deficit and the stringent budget limits being imposed on politically attractive domestic service programs.

By early May, Reagan had negotiated an overall budget compromise with Senate Republicans — the so-called "Rose Garden agreement" — that included a real defense increase of 7 percent. This would have brought the Pentagon budget for fiscal 1985 down to $299 billion, from the request of $313 billion.

The Democratic-controlled House had settled early on for a 3 percent real defense increase. This was the growth rate that all members of NATO agreed to seek under strong pressure from President Carter's administration.

So on its face, the battle was over where the budget eventually would fall within a range of about 3 percent on either side of $292 billion, the midpoint between the Senate and House figures. That midpoint was equivalent to a real growth of 5 percent. The stage seemed set for a repeat of the previous two years' compromise on 5 percent real growth.

But both the political symbolism of the issue and its recent congressional history worked against an early resolution of the budget question.

As a political symbol, the annual real increase in the Pentagon's budget dated back to the tenure of James Schlesinger as defense secretary to Presidents Nixon and Ford (1973-75). Ever since, a politician's stance on how fast the budget should grow had symbolized:

● Where the official ranked defense within the hierarchy of competing national budget priorities.

● How heavily he would rely on military force as an instrument of U.S. policy abroad.

A decade after the U.S. military involvement in Southeast Asia came to an end, those issues remained crucial for congressional Democrats whose political apprenticeship was spent opposing the Vietnam War policies of Presidents Johnson and Nixon.

For many of these members, the "lessons of Vietnam" translated into a reluctance to use military force as an instrument of global policy and a profound suspicion of the Pentagon's basic competence.

That point of view, however, went into political eclipse toward the end of President Carter's term. Growing Soviet intransigence and a series of international embarrassments — most dramatically, the Iranian seizure of the U.S. Embassy staff in Tehran — left the public evidently more inclined toward the more muscular national posture promised in 1980 by Ronald Reagan and the Republican Party.

The Pentagon's liberal critics lay low in the first years of Reagan's tenure. But they began to reassert their position as the budget crunch following the 1981 tax cut won

them allies. The size of the defense budget, rather than what was in it, was the common ground on which liberals could gain moderate and conservative support for attacks on the Reagan military buildup.

Why So Long?

By June 1984, conference committees working on final versions of the defense authorization bill and the first congressional budget resolution had come to a halt over the issue of real defense growth. And because of the delay in the defense authorization bill, the timetable for producing the companion defense appropriations bill was slipping in each house.

The House conferees on the budget resolution then offered to compromise on a 5 percent growth rate ($292 billion) but that was turned down by Senate Budget Committee Chairman Pete V. Domenici, R-N.M. Ostensibly, Domenici did not want to tie the hands of Senate conferees on the defense authorization bill.

But the previous year's defense budget debate held the key to why Domenici turned down agreement at the very level generally expected to be the final outcome of all the political maneuvering. Domenici and the Senate GOP leadership feared that in future bargaining over appropriations, House Democrats would knock the defense number down further.

Such had been the case in 1983. Then, budget resolution conferees agreed to a post-inflation defense increase of 5 percent for fiscal 1984. But actual appropriations for the fiscal year provided a real increase of only 3.7 percent.

Senate Armed Services Committee Chairman John Tower, R-Texas, the Pentagon's most vigorous Senate champion, blamed the Senate Appropriations Subcommittee on Defense for the shortfall.

In Tower's view, subcommittee Chairman Ted Stevens, R-Alaska, simply had been outbargained in the appropriations conference by his opposite number, House subcommittee Chairman Joseph P. Addabbo, D-N.Y.

Stevens, on the other hand, insisted that his hand had been forced by the budget resolution. The appropriations bill did fall short of the resolution's allowance for new budget authority, he conceded. But the resolution also set a cap on defense outlays — the amount of money actually spent in the fiscal year.

(A sizable fraction of the budget authority appropriated for major weapons is not actually spent that same year. This is because contractors are paid in installments over the several years it takes to build a warship or a fleet of planes.)

The outlay cap and the inevitable give and take of conference negotiations with Addabbo accounted for the lower appropriation in the defense bill, Stevens insisted.

Whatever the reason for the 1983 outcome, GOP senators were determined it would not be repeated in 1984.

They had resolved to cut a deal on defense spending with the Democratic House only once — and to make it stick.

As a result, negotiations dragged on until after Labor Day. On Sept. 20, House Speaker Thomas P. O'Neill Jr., D-Mass., and Senate Majority Leader Howard H. Baker Jr., R-Tenn., with the concurrence of the White House, negotiated a defense agreement that covered the budget resolution, the defense authorization bill and the defense appropriations bill.

To the surprise of few, the figure agreed on was $293 billion — a real increase of about 5 percent.

Again, Arms Control

President Reagan came into the year barely a jump ahead of his political critics on the issues of arms control and nuclear weaponry.

In the course of 1983, the administration had dramatically moderated its confrontational tone toward Moscow, an attitude that had fueled widespread political opposition toward Reagan's nuclear arms program in 1981 and 1982.

The administration also altered its negotiating position in two ongoing arms reduction negotiations with the Soviet Union, in response to critics' charges that the initial Reagan offers were too hard on Moscow to promise agreements. These were the Strategic Arms Reduction Talks (START) dealing with long-range, intercontinental weapons, and the negotiations on intermediate-range nuclear forces (INF) — missiles based in Europe and the Soviet Union.

In return for Reagan's shift of negotiating positions, a small but influential group of House and Senate moderates supported initial production of the controversial MX missile in 1983.

But the narrowing margins by which the House voted for the missile during that year portended rough sledding for the program — and, more generally, for Reagan's nuclear arms posture, in 1984.

As in 1983, the 1984 struggle over fundamental nuclear arms policy crystallized around Reagan's request to continue production of the MX.

Driving the battle were two fundamental issues of nuclear arms policy on which the liberal arms control establishment was at loggerheads with the Reagan administration.

One of the basic issues was whether land-based ballistic missiles were uniquely potent — if only in symbolic terms — among the types of weapons in the nuclear arsenal.

The administration argued that they were, and that Soviet advantages in the number and destructive power of intercontinental missiles (ICBMs) and European-based weapons such as the Soviet SS-20 were unacceptable.

The administration argued that such weapons' speed and accuracy would make it theoretically possible for Moscow to destroy a large slice of the U.S. nuclear force in a surprise attack.

The danger was not so much that this scenario would be played out, the administration emphasized, but that if such an attack were technically possible, the Soviets would be emboldened to take greater risks in challenging U.S. interests than Washington would be willing to take in defending them.

The arms controllers dismissed these "war-fighting" scenarios as implausible, and argued that nuclear war would not remain the relatively limited and orderly minuet that administration strategists were assuming.

The arms control activists contended that nuclear weapons would be so destructive that the two superpowers would "use" them only passively, as threats to deter any use of nuclear weapons by a rival.

For that role, the arms controllers maintained, Soviet advantages in the number and power of ICBMs were offset by U.S. advantages in bombers and missile-launching submarines.

The arms controllers' other fundamental clash with the administration came over "bargaining chips." Would new, more powerful U.S. nuclear weapons encourage Moscow to agree to an acceptable arms control treaty? Or would the Russians start work on new weapons of their own to match the U.S. move?

The administration viewed MX partly as a lever that would induce the Russians to move away from the large, multi-warhead ICBMs that made up the bulk of their nuclear arsenal. If it became clear that the Soviet missiles would be vulnerable to the new U.S. weapon, the reasoning went, Moscow would see its ICBM fleet as a "wasting asset," to be replaced.

On the other hand, the administration's liberal critics described the history of bargaining chips as a sequence of new weapons that never got bargained away, but instead accelerated the arms race.

Battling the MX

In 1984, arms controllers continued the effort, begun in 1983, to whip House Democrats into line on the proposition that MX was a vote of confidence in Reagan's nuclear arms policy.

Well-organized pressure by members and by a coalition of grass-roots lobbies brought the foes of MX to within a hairsbreadth of victory in the year's first MX vote on May 16. Thereupon, a new element appeared in the political equation of the MX battle: Speaker O'Neill and the House Democratic leadership threw their organizational resources into the fray and eked out the last few votes needed to win a symbolic victory over Reagan in a series of MX votes on May 31.

The result of the House voting was that a decision on MX production in fiscal 1985 would be deferred until early 1985 when Congress would have the last word.

In the Senate, too, there was a change in the political dynamic of the MX fight during 1984.

Opposition to MX on traditional arms control grounds remained at about the same level as in 1983: just over 40 senators.

But during the Senate debate on the defense authorization bill in mid-June, a new faction suddenly surfaced. Lawton Chiles, Fla., senior Democrat on the Budget Committee, had recruited several conservative Democrats who approached MX largely as a budgetary issue.

Alliance with these conservatives discomfited some arms controllers, since Chiles expressly endorsed the importance of having some kind of new ICBM in the works as a bargaining chip with the Russians. He refused to vote for canceling MX outright, saying it should be held ready for production in case efforts to develop a new, small ICBM fell through.

But expediency prevailed and the alliance of arms control backers and Chiles' budgeteers came within a vote of blocking MX production in the Senate. Vice President George Bush had to break a tie on the issue.

Space Weapons Fights

As Reagan and the arms controllers squared off over the "old" arms race issue of nuclear missiles, they also sparred through the first round of a battle over space weaponry likely to displace MX as the arms control issue of the rest of the century.

At stake was Reagan's call early in 1983 for a major effort to develop an anti-missile defense, which could involve exotic, new weapons such as lasers based on space satellites.

The Pentagon already had under way extensive research on various elements of the proposed system. But in corralling them all into his so-called strategic defense initiative (SDI), Reagan gave them a bureaucratic focus, more money and the political clout that accrues to programs that hold special interest for the president.

Reagan and a handful of his closest political subordinates insisted that new technologies could make a country-wide defense feasible. This would render nuclear missiles "impotent and obsolete," in Reagan's words.

Most defense scientists ruled out any such revolutionary development, but many argued that SDI might yield a more modest development.

It might not provide a defense sufficiently airtight to protect U.S. cities from a Soviet barrage, but it might provide one good enough to disrupt the careful timing that would have to go into an attack on armored U.S. military targets, including U.S. missiles and command posts.

Traditional arms control backers, who ridiculed Reagan's plan as "star wars," saw it as one more futile effort to beat Moscow in an arms race. Moreover, if the plan went very far, it would have to brush aside the 1972 U.S.-Soviet treaty severely limiting the scope of anti-missile activity in each country.

For fiscal 1985, Congress trimmed Reagan's $1.8 billion SDI request to $1.4 billion, but the significance of that cut for future battles over the new policy was unclear. The reduction of just over 20 percent was within the normal range of arbitrary reductions Congress made for purely budgetary reasons in dozens of military research programs, particularly those like SDI that were years from any practical result.

In addition, the arms control advocates decided early in the year that they would concentrate not on SDI — the real target — but on a surrogate: the anti-satellite missile, or ASAT. Strictly speaking, ASAT was not part of the "star wars" program, but it was to use some of the same technology. Any negotiated ban on "star wars" would severely hamper development of an ASAT.

Moreover, the ASAT fight had an urgency about it that the battle over the fundamental SDI policy lacked. Reagan critics warned that once the missile had been tested against a target satellite, verification of a ban on its deployment would be impossible, because of the ASAT's small size.

So the arms controllers chose as the first test of political strength on the whole panoply of space weapons issues an effort to ban tests of the ASAT against a target in space.

The coalition of arms control lobbyists that had refined its skills on MX, won the ASAT fight in the House by a very large margin in mid-May.

In its final form, the fiscal 1985 defense authorization bill imposed a moratorium on ASAT target tests until March 1, 1985, after which no more than two successful tests could be flown in the rest of fiscal 1985. The companion appropriation bill provided that there could be no more than three ASAT tests in the whole year, successful or not.

—*By Pat Towell*

Congress Authorizes $219 Billion for Defense

Congress approved a $219 billion defense authorization bill (HR 5167 — PL 98-525) for fiscal 1985, reflecting the approach it had taken to President Reagan's defense buildup almost from the outset: agreeing to go along with the plan's fundamental shape, but insisting on lower costs.

The resulting bill, which was passed by the House on Sept. 26 and the Senate on Sept. 27, was typical. Proportionately modest reductions were made in hundreds of programs, but very few of the cuts posed substantial challenges to defense policy. *(Final provisions, p. 53; box, p. 40)*

The issue of the MX intercontinental missile, centerpiece of Reagan's strategic program, stalled the bill for weeks. Disputes over MX and the dollar amount for defense were resolved only by intervention of congressional leaders and the White House. Essentially, Congress decided not to decide on the controversial missile until after the November elections. The program's fate was to be decided by two congressional votes in the spring of 1985. *(Story, p. 59)*

For programs normally in the annual defense bill, the conference report authorized $211.7 billion in fiscal 1985 appropriations. Also included was the authorization for nuclear weapons programs conducted for the Pentagon by the Energy Department. Normally covered by a separate bill, this authorization for $7.4 billion was folded into HR 5167 (H Rept 98-1080).

The annual authorization bill did not directly cover military personnel costs, which were included in the defense appropriations bill. *(Defense appropriations, p. 399)*

However, the authorization measure set military manpower ceilings and other personnel policies with indirect effect on annual personnel costs.

When combined with defense programs not covered by the authorization bill, HR 5167 was to produce a total defense authorization for fiscal 1985 of $297 billion, the amount agreed to by congressional leaders and the administration on Sept. 20.

The leaders also had agreed that actual defense appropriations — included in an omnibus continuing resolution — would be $4.1 billion below the authorization level. *(Continuing resolution, p. 444)*

Deficit Reduction Package

Reagan's original budget had requested $313 billion for defense. But on May 3, under intense pressure from members of Congress to trim the budget deficit, the administration proposed a $13.9 billion reduction in its defense program for fiscal 1985, bringing the request to $299 billion. *(Deficit reduction, p. 143)*

The defense cutback was part of a deficit reduction package negotiated between the White House and Senate Republican leaders in early March. In the usual fashion of the congressional defense funding committees, the Pentagon whittled away at dozens of programs rather than drastically reshaping its original request.

Many of the specific recommendations mirrored changes proposed by the House Armed Services Committee in its version of HR 5167. None of the major strategic weapons programs — the MX and Trident II missiles, the B-1 bomber and the "strategic defense initiative" to develop space-based anti-missile weapons — was to be cut.

About two-thirds of the cuts ($8.5 billion) came from the $107.6 billion earmarked for weapons purchases. About $2.5 billion of the reduction would have no real impact on the Pentagon's program; these cuts reflected fuel price declines and other shifts in the cost of doing business.

House Committee Report

As reported by the House committee on April 19 (H Rept 98-691), HR 5167 authorized $208.1 billion for programs covering roughly 70 percent of the annual defense budget, a cut of $16.4 billion from the president's Feb. 1 request.

The committee bill's personnel provisions would have trimmed $2.2 billion from the administration's personnel budget. Of that reduction, nearly $400 million reflected the committee's approval of a 3.5 percent pay hike for uniformed personnel except recruits, who would receive no pay raise. The administration had requested a 5.5 percent military pay hike.

House Armed Services followed its usual procedures, trimming programs instead of killing major ones. The panel also sought to revive a peacetime G.I. Bill. *(Box, p. 56)*

Nuclear Warfare

MX Missile

In its report on HR 5167, the House committee cut Reagan's $2.9 billion MX production request by $450 million — a reduction from 40 missiles to 30. But the anti-MX campaign hoped to stop all MX production on the House floor.

In November 1983, critics had come within nine votes of blocking procurement of the first 21 production-line versions of the MX missile. Reagan won the day largely by dint of intense lobbying. The large, accurate MX was to offset some 600 similar Soviet missiles already deployed, the administration argued, therefore this would give the Soviets an incentive to agree to deep, mutual reductions in the superpower missile arsenals. *(1983 Almanac p. 195)*

Opponents, led by liberal arms control groups, warned that the new missile would accelerate the nuclear arms race. They hoped that the formidable grass-roots lobby they had organized in 1983 would help kill the missile in 1984.

Midgetman

The committee approved $405.2 million to develop a small, single-warhead ICBM informally dubbed Midgetman, to supplement the multiple-warhead MX. The panel dropped from the request $60 million associated with a controversial plan to equip the missile with maneuverable warheads (called MARV).

According to the Air Force, a warhead that could home in on its target could be needed to make the small missile as accurate as MX, if the MX guidance system could not be repackaged to fit into the much smaller weapon. But the committee warned that such pinpoint accuracy might negate the small missile's alleged advantages from the standpoint of arms control.

The panel endorsed the administration's position that Moscow was responsible for the breakdown in late 1983 of

U.S.-Soviet negotiations to limit long-range and medium-range nuclear weapons. *(1983 Almanac p. 206)*

However, the panel cautioned the administration not to presume that the public would give it a free hand in strategic arms policy just because of Soviet intransigence.

Also approved was a $180.1 million request to develop super-hard missile silos in an attempt to obviate the need for expensive, mobile launchers for the small missile. However, the panel denied $39.6 million sought for testing the feasibility of basing ICBMs deep underground.

Anti-Missile Defense

The panel endorsed the general thrust of Reagan's call for research into the feasibility of developing large-scale, anti-missile defenses. The administration called the controversial program the strategic defense initiative; critics ridiculed it as "Star Wars."

The panel complained, however, that the administration's projected five-year $24 billion research program was ill-defined. Armed Services cut $407 million — about 23 percent — from the president's fiscal 1985 request for $1.78 billion, charging that amount was too high, given budgetary constraints, and that there was too much overlap among different projects under the strategic defense umbrella.

Three-quarters of the cut ($317 million) was imposed on the $721 million requested for development of surveillance equipment to locate and track attacking missiles while space-based lasers or other weapons draw a bead on them.

The $489 million sought to develop lasers and other "directed-energy" weapons was cut by $30 million. The budget to develop interceptor missiles and more conventional anti-missile weapons was trimmed by $60 million, to $296 million.

The panel ordered the secretary of defense to submit a detailed report on plans for the strategic defense program within 90 days of the bill's enactment. It also recommended establishment of a technical advisory board for the project and a liaison committee to explain the program to U.S. allies.

The committee also strongly endorsed the administration's request to begin production of the so-called anti-satellite (or ASAT) guided missile. ASAT was intended to be launched from an F-15 fighter to destroy an orbiting space satellite. The $84.5 million requested to begin ASAT production was approved, as was $120 million of the $143 million sought for development of the weapon. *(Story, p. 62)*

As with several other controversial weapons, the panel emphasized the arms control rationale for ASAT. It cited arguments, made during the Carter administration, that since the Soviet Union had its own ASAT, a U.S. counterpart "may encourage good faith ASAT negotiations."

Strategic Bombers

The $7.1 billion request to buy 34 B-1 bombers (plus components for additional B-1s to be included in the next year's budget) was approved without change. Moreover, the committee warned that any reduction in the fiscal 1985 B-1 budget would be wiped out by increased future costs.

So far, the panel argued, the Pentagon and its contractors were adhering to a commitment to deliver a fleet of 100 bombers for a total cost of $20.5 billion in fiscal 1981 dollars. However, that limitation depended on congressional support for the previously negotiated B-1 production schedule. Any tampering with the plan, the report warned,

would remove the strong incentive to avoid costly frills.

The request for a "stealth" bomber, designed to avoid enemy radars, was secret. The House panel trimmed about $350 million from the request, which was estimated at $1 billion.

Two bomber-related projects were among the several "new starts" which the committee slowed, or deferred, to meet the budget ceiling:

● Development of advanced air-to-surface missiles, or AASM — an acronym Pentagon wordsmiths pronounced "awesome" — was cut from $54.4 million to $20 million.

● Development of a rotary launcher that could be inserted in the bomb bays of B-1s, existing B-52s or "stealth" bombers was stopped, yielding a cut of $79.8 million in procurement funds and $77.3 million in research money. The launcher was designed to carry any combination of conventional bombs, nuclear bombs, cruise missiles or short-range nuclear missiles and to allow the bomber crew to drop them in any sequence.

The committee approved only $10 million of $299.1 million requested for three programs intended to modernize radar jammers and other electronics on existing B-52 and FB-111 bombers.

On the other hand, the committee quadrupled (to $86.6 million) the budget to develop radars and other equipment with which B-52s and other heavy bombers could fire conventionally armed missiles at ground targets, such as Soviet tank columns, from a range of a hundred miles or more. It ordered the Pentagon to plan to begin fielding this so-called "conventional standoff capability" by fiscal 1988.

Submarine Missiles

Of the $1.49 billion requested for the 12th Trident missile-firing submarine, the committee approved $1.15 billion in new funds. It made up the difference with $340 million appropriated in fiscal 1984 to build an escort frigate. The committee killed the frigate, which the administration had not requested in the first place.

Approved without change was the $265.5 million request for components of two more Trident subs budgeted for full funding in future years.

The committee made only minor reductions in the budget for the Trident II missile, which, unlike the Trident I, would be accurate enough to destroy an armored Soviet missile silo with each of its several warheads. To continue development of the new missile, $2.05 billion of the $2.09 billion request was approved.

To finish building the production line for the Trident II and for components to be used in the first batch of missiles, the panel approved $152.4 million of the $162.9 million request.

The panel cut $77 million from the budget in order to end development of the E-6 radio plane. The Boeing 707 jetliner would unfurl a radio antenna several miles long to relay messages to submerged missile subs. The projected $2 billion E-6 fleet would be too expensive, the committee said. It added to the budget $15 million to begin improving the radios aboard the fleet of C-130 cargo planes that currently carried out the radio missions. The C-130s were called TACAMOs — an acronym commonly said to stand for "Take Charge and Move Out."

Missiles in Europe

Under pressure from the budget ceiling, the panel reduced the request for 93 Pershing II missiles and their spare parts ($472.2 million) by 23 missiles to $368.2 million.

Approved without change was $580.1 million for 120 ground-launched cruise missiles (GLCMs) and associated launchers and parts.

Despite strong domestic opposition in several NATO countries, the alliance accepted U.S. deployment of the first of the planned 108 Pershing IIs and the planned 464 GLCMs. The missiles, capable of striking Soviet territory with nuclear warheads from launchers in Western Europe, were intended to offset Soviet deployment of SS-20 missiles able to strike any point on the continent.

U.S.-Soviet talks aimed at limiting such intermediate-range nuclear forces (INF) collapsed in late 1983, when the U.S. missiles were deployed on a NATO timetable agreed to in 1979.

Ground Combat

The only major weapon for which the panel ordered a production increase was the M-1 tank. Because of budgetary limits, the administration had requested only 720 M-1s in fiscal 1985. But the panel insisted on buying 840 in fiscal 1985 and succeeding years. That was the number purchased in fiscal 1984.

According to the committee, the fiscal 1985 cost of continuing to build 840 tanks annually would be $6.1 million less in new budget authority than the $1.76 billion requested for going to a rate of 720 tanks. This assumed that $173.8 million available from earlier budgets would be added to the fiscal 1985 request.

The committee also reiterated its insistence that gas turbine engines for the M-1 be bought only from Avco Corp., which currently supplied the engines. Early in the M-1 production run, Avco had serious cost, schedule and performance difficulties producing the power plants.

In 1984, the House panel and members from areas with Avco plants, arguing that the firm had ironed out the kinks, blocked a Pentagon effort to award future tank engine contracts on a competitive basis.

Tank Hunters

In another exception to its rule of restraining production increases to meet the budget ceiling, the committee approved without change the $1.199 billion requested for 144 Apache missile-armed anti-tank helicopters. In fiscal 1984, 112 of the planes were funded for $1.13 billion.

As in the case of the B-1 bomber, the committee argued that the Pentagon and the Apache's contractors had kept the cost of the helicopter under control, partly because Congress had approved the production schedule. Holding the plane's production rate to 112 in fiscal 1985 would increase the cost per copy some 12 percent ($900,000), the panel warned, and would open the door to further price hikes.

The panel increased the authorization for Copperhead laser-guided anti-tank artillery shells by $44.8 million, to $147.6 million, to reduce the unit cost of the shells and encourage selection of a second contractor to compete for future Copperhead contracts.

Striking Deep

The committee sharply attacked the Air Force for resisting cooperation with the Army to develop so-called "strike deep" technologies. Such radars and missiles were designed to aim non-nuclear warheads at tank columns and other targets up to a few hundred miles behind an enemy's

front lines. The approach had won enthusiastic backing on grounds it could remove the military argument for politically controversial, short-range nuclear weapons in Europe.

The congressional defense panels had urged the Army and Air Force to develop a common radar (called Joint STARS) to locate enemy tanks and a missile (called JTACMS) to attack such targets from ground or airborne launchers.

According to the House committee, the Air Force was insisting on radars that would be different from the Army's and a missile that would take longer to field than the modified versions of existing missiles that the Army was testing. The panel approved the Army requests for Joint STARS ($108.2 million) and JTACMS ($78.98 million) but denied the Air Force requests ($94.97 million and $35.5 million, respectively).

Anti-Aircraft Weapons

Two of the committee's goals were beefing up the anti-aircraft defense of U.S. installations in Europe and encouraging U.S. allies to chip in more toward the cost of alliance defense. To remedy what it saw as Pentagon foot-dragging on both counts, the panel added $350 million to the bill. This was to be used to buy anti-aircraft missiles to be manned by European allies to defend U.S. air bases and missile sites on their territory. The House panel had been a leading proponent of such arrangements for four years.

Largely to meet budgetary limits, the committee trimmed several Army anti-aircraft programs, particularly those for which the projected fiscal 1985 production rate was substantially higher than the fiscal 1984 rate:

● It held the production of Patriot long-range missiles to 440, the number bought in 1984, instead of the 585 requested, for a total savings of $141 million.

● It approved 117 Sergeant York anti-aircraft tanks (also called DIVAD), instead of the 132 requested, and it ordered the Pentagon to reduce Sergeant York purchases from 130 to 117 in fiscal 1984. With various bookkeeping adjustments, including the transfer to fiscal 1985 accounts of the money saved with the smaller fiscal 1984 buy, the net result was a fiscal 1985 authorization of $438.5 million in new budget authority, $77.3 million less than the budget request.

The committee warmly endorsed the DIVAD on its merits, implicitly rejecting critics' allegations that it had failed various performance tests.

Chemical Weapons

An arms control strategy figured prominently in the committee's support for preparing to produce a new family of lethal nerve gas weapons — but without actually manufacturing any of them, the panel emphasized.

At issue were so-called binary munitions. In 1982 and 1983, Congress had refused administration efforts to start building these air bombs and artillery shells, at the insistence of the House. *(1982 Almanac p. 83; 1983 Almanac p. 178)*

During 1984, administration witnesses emphasized, and the House committee underscored, that the $95 million binary weapons procurement request would buy equipment that would be used in weapons assembly lines and components for the weapons. It would not result in a finished product.

The bill sought to require the president to assemble a bipartisan Chemical Warfare Review Commission to recommend whether binary weapons should be made. Chemi-

Defense Authorizations for Fiscal 1985

	Administration Request	House-Passed	Senate-Passed	Final Authorization
		(in billions of dollars)		
Procurement	$107.6	$ 96.6	$100.7	$ 99.5
Research and Development	34.0	30.3	32.6	32.1
Operations and Maintenance	82.7	80.0	80.1	79.9
Military Personnel [1]	70.5	68.3	68.9	68.8
Civil Defense	.3	.2	.2	.2
Subtotal [2]	**$295.1**	**$275.5**	**$282.6**	**$280.5**
Military Construction	10.5	9.2	9.3	9.1
Military Nuclear Programs in Energy Department	7.8	7.4	7.3	7.4
Defense Total	**$313.4**	**$292.1**	**$299.2**	**$297.0**

[1] *Personnel funds were not included in the annual defense authorization bill. These were the amounts that would have to be appropriated to fund the manpower levels and other personnel policies set by the authorization bill.*

[2] *The first five funding categories were traditionally covered, directly or indirectly, by the annual defense authorization bill. Numbers may not add up precisely because of rounding.*

cal weapons production could be resumed — for the first time since 1969 — only after the president reviewed the commission's findings, if he then certified that binary production was dictated by national security requirements and if Congress formally approved the move.

The panel endorsed the administration's contention that Moscow would agree to ban chemical weapons only to head off U.S. replacement of its current stockpile, which the Pentagon and the committee deemed largely obsolete and unusable.

Tactical Air Combat

The Air Force's $5.6 billion request for 198 of its front-line fighter planes — 48 F-15s and 150 F-16s — was cut about 20 percent ($1.1 billion). However, the only change in the number of planes was a reduction to 40 of the more expensive F-15s.

The F-15 cutback accounted for about a quarter of the reduction ($264 million). It reflected the committee's view that the Air Force should abandon plans to increase the F-15 production rate to 96 planes a year. This was part of the service's plan to expand from 36 fighter wings to 40 within five years. The committee deemed such expansion unrealistic in light of budget constraints, and directed the Air Force to plan on 38 fighter wings with an annual F-15 production rate of 42 planes.

The panel approved a separate force of F-15s equipped with electronic gear designed to let the planes attack ground targets at night and in bad weather. But it warned the service that these so-called F-15Es would do little good in wartime if they were destroyed at U.S. air bases that were naked to aerial attack. The committee's approval of the F-15E plan was contingent on:

● Pentagon submission of a master plan for building air defenses around U.S. air bases in Europe.

● A fiscal 1986 budget request that sought at least as much money for air base defense as for F-15Es.

In a slap at a highly popular idea, the committee recommended that the Air Force buy the fiscal 1985 batch of twin-engined F-15s without the warranty offered by the Pratt & Whitney division of United Technologies, maker of the planes' engines. The warranty was one aspect of Pratt & Whitney's hard-fought competition with General Electric for the engine contract.

Sen. Mark Andrews, R-N.D., and other members had cited the Air Force's earlier satisfaction with the warranty in their campaign for legislation to require a general warranty on major weapons.

But according to the Armed Services Committee, Pratt & Whitney wanted $53 million for the F-15 engine warranty, about one-third the cost of the engines themselves, compared with the usual warranty cost of about 5 percent of the cost of the item.

The panel dropped the $53 million and added to the bill a provision waiving the existing law requiring a warranty on the engines.

Though the committee did not reduce the budgeted number of F-16s, it cut some $486 million that, it said, was rendered unnecessary by the completion of the engine competition.

Navy Planes

Requests for all of the Navy's carrier-based combat planes were approved without substantial change:

● $786.9 million for 24 F-14 fighters;

● $2.3 billion for 84 F-18 combination fighters and light bombers;

● $199.5 million for six A-6E medium bombers (a $15.1 million reduction, made up for by unspent funds from earlier years); and

● $742.1 million for 32 AV-8B vertical takeoff light bombers for the Marine Corps.

However, the committee told the Navy to drop plans for large boosts in F-18 and AV-8B production next year and cut $70.4 million budgeted for components that would be used in future years' production runs.

The panel blocked development of an improved version of the A-6E, with new electronics and engines. It argued that an F-14 equipped with the electronics of the F-15E would be a better bomber for the 1990s than a re-worked A-6E, which was based on a 1960s-vintage design.

It dropped $19.6 million earmarked for the A-6E project and added $15 million to study the F-14 plan, but said the Navy could use the funds for the A-6E, after it studied the alternative and after giving the committee prior notification.

Naval Forces

The $13.1 billion shipbuilding request was cut by $1.25 billion without canceling a single major combat ship requested by the administration. For the most part, the trims were achieved by paying for ships with funds appropriated in earlier years, but not spent.

The planned modernization of the carrier *Independence* was approved without change ($583.2 million). The modernization of the battleship *Missouri* to carry long-range cruise missiles also was approved but without providing any of the requested $422.6 million in new budget authority. Unspent funds from earlier appropriations would be enough to cover the cost.

Approved without change was the $532 million request for 180 Tomahawk cruise missiles — similar to the Air Force ground-launched cruise missiles. The Tomahawks would let the renovated battleships and most other large warships strike at ships and land targets hundreds of miles distant.

The panel approved four ships intended to protect U.S. fleets against Soviet cruise missile attack with the Aegis anti-aircraft system: the 14th, 15th and 16th Aegis cruisers ($3.1 billion), and the $1.2 billion DDG-51, the *Arleigh Burke* — first of a new class of destroyers intended to replace some 30 ships due for retirement around 1990.

In approving the cruisers and the *Burke*, the committee implicitly rejected some critics' allegations that Aegis had fared poorly in tests against very low-flying missiles. On May 2, the Navy announced an Aegis cruiser had successfully destroyed several such "sea-skimmer" targets.

Sub Hunting

Four *Los Angeles*-class nuclear submarines, designed chiefly to hunt Soviet subs, were approved as requested ($2.3 billion), as were components for four more of the ships in each of the next two years ($617.8 million).

The panel also approved the $174 million request to begin developing a new submarine, but on condition that the Navy certify that the new vessel could defeat projected Soviet subs. This requirement reflected the committee's unhappiness that new Soviet submarines were faster and could dive deeper than U.S. subs.

To meet the congressional budget ceiling, two other sub hunting programs were scaled back:

● Five P-3C land-based patrol planes (based on the vintage Electra airliner of the 1950s) were approved for fiscal 1985 and future years, instead of the nine requested — a reduction of $188.4 million.

● Three T-AGOS ships, designed to detect submarines hundreds of miles away with huge underwater microphones, were approved (one less than had been requested) — a $63 million cut.

On the other hand, the committee recommended

boosting from 18 to 24 the production rate of LAMPS III anti-submarine helicopters, carried by most surface warships. This required a $72.9 million addition to the bill.

Airlift and Sealift

The two largest air transport programs also came under the budget scalpel:

● Eight KC-10 midair refueling tankers (versions of the DC-10 jetliner) were approved as requested for fiscal 1985, but the panel recommended buying eight rather than 12 more in fiscal 1986, for a reduction of $81 million.

● Eight C-5 cargo planes were approved rather than 10, making a $308.7 million reduction.

Both planes were being purchased under multi-year contracts that permitted minor adjustments in the number of planes bought in any one year so long as the total number purchased in the life of the contract was unchanged.

Marine Landing Forces

The committee approved without major change the requests associated with modernizing the Navy's amphibious landing fleet, designed to let Marine Corps units fight their way ashore against opposition. The largest single item was $406 million for two so-called LSDs, designed to carry combat vehicles and the barges to haul them ashore.

Also approved were:

● $230 million for a dozen air-cushion landing barges (called LCACs) designed to haul tanks ashore at up to 50 mph.

● $213.3 million for 10 CH-53E cargo helicopters, able to haul 16 tons of troops or cargo from ship to shore. This was $10 million less than requested.

● $178.5 million to develop a hybrid airplane/helicopter called JVX intended to fly at twice the speed of a helicopter and replace the Marines' older helicopters. This was $20 million below the request.

The panel also added to the bill $20 million to begin buying for the Army the Arapaho helicopter system: A prefabricated set of helicopter hangars, repair shops and flight decks that could be installed on any commercial container ship. Originally designed to carry Navy anti-submarine helicopters in merchant convoys, Arapaho also could be used to carry Army attack helicopters or transport helicopter units.

Operating Costs

The committee's $78.3 billion recommendation for funds covering routine operating costs (operations and maintenance and various revolving funds) was $2.7 billion less than the budget request.

Typically with these accounts, the lion's share of the reduction reflected marginal "bookkeeping-type" changes rather than any challenge to administration policies.

Just over $1 billion of the cut would have no impact at all on Pentagon operations, according to the committee, since it reflected various fact-of-life changes in projected operating costs. These included a $302.9 million reduction in estimated fuel costs, a $282.6 million decrease in overseas operating costs due to the dollar's increased strength against foreign currencies, and a $280 million re-estimate in the cost of certain supplies.

Nearly $1 billion more was cut by arbitrarily trimming several programs that were budgeted for much more rapid increases than the defense budget as a whole was expected to have.

Almost $500 million came from various cuts intended to underscore the committee's desire that certain wasteful practices exposed by Pentagon auditors be stopped. These included cuts of:

- $125 million to discourage the expensive practice of leasing computers rather than buying them;
- $60 million to cut down on the use of outside consultants, a perennial target of congressional budgeteers;
- $26 million to encourage tighter oversight of the use of telephones for personal calls. The committee seemed particularly incensed at one audit that found the Pentagon billed for $300,000 worth of long-distance calls to a "dial-a-porn" service.

House Floor Action

The House took up HR 5167 on May 15 and passed its $207 billion bill shortly after midnight of the session that began May 31. The vote was 298-98. *(Vote 184, p. 58-H)*

Floor action on the bill was marked by cliffhanger votes on the MX missile, resulting in new controls on the weapon that represented a dramatic setback for Reagan. The House also made clear its suspicion that the administration was not trying hard enough to reach arms control agreements with the Soviet Union. Members adopted, over strong White House opposition, amendments:

- Deleting funds aimed at resuming production of chemical weapons.
- Barring realistic tests of an ASAT unless the Soviet Union tests its own version first.

MX Missile

The House, in the first of two series of votes on the MX missile, on May 16 gave the go-ahead to production of 15 more missiles, subject to conditions. In the second series of votes, in the May 31 session, members tightened those conditions. *(Details, p. 59)*

May 16 Votes. By a vote of 212-218, after intensive lobbying and sophisticated parliamentary maneuvering, the House rejected an amendment offered by Nicholas Mavroules, D-Mass., that would have blocked production of any MXs in fiscal 1985. *(Vote 133, p. 44-H)*

The razor-thin vote marked the fourth time in a year that centrists in the House had saved the controversial missile from its liberal critics. *(Background, 1983 Almanac p. 195)*

The position backed by the House in the seven-hour-long May 16 debate had been hammered out by the centrist group, led by Les Aspin, D-Wis. Under the plan, the 15 missiles could be bought, at a total cost of $1.8 billion, under these conditions: No money would be spent until April 1, 1985, and then only if, in the president's judgment, the Soviets were not indicating a willingness to bargain in good faith for limits on ICBMs such as MX. If they were willing to bargain, the ban would continue.

The Aspin plan was nailed down with a 229-199 vote in favor of an amendment offered by William L. Dickinson, Ala., the senior Armed Services Committee Republican. *(Vote 134, p. 44-H)*

May 31 Votes. After a concerted drive by its Democratic leadership, the House voted to tighten further congressional controls on the 15 MX missiles.

On each of three MX votes in the May 31 session, the House affirmed, by margins of no more than three votes, an amendment offered by Charles E. Bennett, D-Fla. His amendment stated that Congress, not the president, would have the last say on whether to proceed with 15 missiles after April 1, 1985. The decision was to be made by joint resolution. The May 31 votes, all on the same amendment, were not to affect the 21 MXs Congress approved in 1983 in the budget for fiscal 1984. *(Votes 178, 179, 183, p. 58-H)*

Anti-Satellite Missile

On May 23, the House voted to continue for a year a moratorium on realistic tests of an anti-satellite (ASAT) missile, so long as the Soviet Union did likewise. The amendment, authored by George E. Brown Jr., D-Calif., was adopted 238-181. *(Vote 152, p. 50-H)*

As a matter of political strategy, the administration's arms control critics had chosen the ASAT ban as their test run on this bill against Reagan's far-reaching plans to develop weapons for use in outer space. In part, this was because the House Armed Services Committee's $407 million reduction in Reagan's $1.8 billion request to develop a space-based anti-missile system was far larger than the arms controllers had anticipated.

The arms control argument for banning a U.S. test of ASAT against a target in space was that it would be the last clear chance to head off the deployment of weapons with which the United States and the Soviet Union could threaten each other's satellites.

The administration argued that Moscow would agree to abandon its existing ASAT only if confronted by a successfully tested U.S. counterpart. The administration also insisted it saw no way to verify a useful ASAT limitation agreement and that it wanted the U.S. ASAT to be able to destroy Soviet reconnaissance satellites. *(Story, p. 62)*

ASAT backers rallied behind a counter-amendment by Beverly B. Byron, D-Md., that would have allowed the United States as many ASAT tests as the Soviets had. The Soviet system had 20 tests since June 1968, nine successful. The most recent Soviet test — a failure — was in June 1982.

But backers of Brown's amendment worried most about a "middle ground" staked out by Dave McCurdy, D-Okla. McCurdy's amendment would have barred an ASAT target test until March 31, 1985, but then would have allowed testing if the president submitted to Congress a plan for seeking a U.S.-Soviet ASAT ban and certified that he had invited Moscow to resume ASAT negotiations.

At Aspin's urging, the Brown amendment was re-offered by Gore in a slightly different form so that it would receive the first vote; it prevailed 238-181. The House then rejected the Byron amendment twice (once, as re-offered by Samuel S. Stratton, D-N.Y.) on votes of 178-236 and 181-229. The McCurdy amendment then was turned down 186-228. *(Votes 152-155, pp. 50-H, 52-H)*

Nerve Gas Curb

In a replay of action taken by the House in 1982 and 1983, members rejected production funds for binary chemical munitions.

The administration's contention, fervently backed by the House Armed Services Committee, was that U.S. production of the new lethal, nerve gas weapons was needed to prod Moscow to agree to a Reagan-proposed total ban on chemical weapons.

Opponents contended that existing U.S. nerve gas stockpiles were adequate to bring the Soviets to the bargaining table and that a resumption of chemical weapons production after a 15-year hiatus would surrender an important U.S. propaganda advantage.

In 1984, the panel argued that funds in the fiscal 1985 bill would not provide for final assembly of any of the new weapons. This money would only move one step closer to the new weapons, the committee argued, but none would be built until Congress had another vote on whether or not to proceed.

The argument seemed to have no impact and, on an amendment offered May 17 by Ed Bethune, R-Ark., the House deleted the $95 million requested for binary munitions procurement. The vote on the Bethune amendment was 247-179. *(Vote 135, p. 46-H)*

Trident II

On May 17, the House brushed aside, 93-319, an amendment by Ted Weiss, D-N.Y., that would have denied $152 million to begin setting up the production line for the Trident II (or D-5) submarine-launched missile. Weiss' argument embodied the fundamental tenet of liberal arms control orthodoxy: That extremely accurate ballistic missiles, which could threaten a surprise attack on Soviet missile launchers, should be avoided. *(Vote 136, p. 46-H)*

Pershing II

On May 23, the House rejected, 122-294, an amendment by Mike Lowry, D-Wash., that would have blocked temporarily procurement of the authorized 70 Pershing II missiles. The president would have to certify after April 1, 1985, that the Russians were not trying to negotiate in good faith limitations on such weapons. The missiles then could be bought if Congress approved production by a joint resolution. *(Vote 147, p. 50-H)*

The issue resurfaced on May 31, when Ronald V. Dellums, D-Calif., offered an amendment that would have halted the further deployment of Pershing II and cruise missiles until the end of fiscal 1985. The amendment was rejected, 104-291. *(Vote 182, p. 58-H)*

Sea-Launched Cruise Missiles

The House approved an amendment that appeared to block deployment, scheduled to begin in June, of nuclear armed cruise missiles, or SLCMS, aboard warships. The amendment, by Armed Services Committee member Stratton, barred deployment of the missiles unless the president submitted a report on how they could be distinguished from non-nuclear cruise missiles or the Soviet Union deployed its own nuclear SLCMs.

The political significance of the House action was unclear, since Stratton insisted that Soviet missiles already deployed would make deployment of the U.S. SLCM possible under his amendment. The nuclear SLCM opponents, led by Aspin, denied that existing Soviet missiles would have that effect.

Spare Parts

By a vote of 324-75, the House adopted an amendment by Berkley Bedell, D-Iowa, to open up competition for contracts by barring the Pentagon from limiting competition to firms on a list of "qualified bidders."

Bedell's amendment consisted of portions of HR 2133, which had been reported by the Small Business Committee. It was offered as an amendment to an amendment offered by Bill Nichols, D-Ala. The Nichols amendment had been reported as HR 5064 by the Armed Services

Committee. The panel opposed Bedell's move. *(Related story, p. 197)*

Nichols' amendment, like Bedell's, emphasized greater reliance on competitive purchases to prevent excessive price tags for spare parts.

After adopting Bedell's amendment to Nichols' measure, the House adopted the modified Nichols amendment 396-0. *(Vote 170, p. 56-H)*

Central America

On May 23, the House passed an amendment barring introduction of U.S. combat troops into El Salvador and Nicaragua except in case of congressional approval or clear threat of attack on the United States, U.S. personnel or a U.S. embassy.

The amendment, offered by Majority Whip Thomas S. Foley, D-Wash., won the approval of the hawkish Armed Services Committee and was adopted 341-64 after only a few minutes of perfunctory debate. But, as the House settled down after the roll-call vote on the Foley amendment, GOP conservatives mounted a belated attack. *(Vote 156, p. 52-H)*

Henry J. Hyde, R-Ill., blistered his colleagues for a "cowardly" amendment.

To dramatize conservative GOP unhappiness, Thomas F. Hartnett, R-S.C., introduced an amendment that would apply the Foley prohibition to countries in Western Europe, South Korea and the Middle East.

That was rejected 27-379. *(Vote 157, p. 52-H)*

Carroll A. Campbell Jr., R-S.C., then offered an amendment extending the Foley provisions to all of Central America and stipulating the amendment did not limit the president's constitutional power as commander in chief of U.S. armed forces.

When debate resumed the next day, May 24, Foley readily accepted Campbell's amendment and it was agreed to by voice vote.

The conservatives tried one last shot: an amendment by Duncan L. Hunter, R-Calif., waiving the Foley limitation if the president determined "there exists a Soviet, Soviet-bloc, Cuban or other communist threat to the region." That was rejected 99-288. *(Vote 163, p. 54-H)*

Budget Cut Rejected

An amendment by Patricia Schroeder, D-Colo., that would have required the Pentagon to cut about $4.5 billion from the bill's authorization for weapons procurement, was rejected on May 23 by a vote of 173-250. *(Vote 149, p. 50-H)*

Schroeder's amendment would have held appropriations for procurement in fiscal 1985 to 106.5 percent of the amount appropriated in fiscal 1984. Stratton ridiculed it as a move to let members "vote for massive reductions in that terrible old defense budget without actually having to vote to cut a single solitary program."

Senate Committee Action

S 2723 was reported by the Armed Services Committee on May 31 (S Rept 98-500).

For programs traditionally covered by the annual defense authorization bill, the committee recommended $213.5 billion, about $6 billion more than was authorized by the corresponding House bill.

Armed Services also included in S 2723 authorizations totaling $16.6 billion for two programs the House covered in separate legislation: the construction of military facilities and programs conducted on the Pentagon's behalf by the Energy Department.

In addition to the $12.6 billion the bill cut from Reagan's February budget request, the bill included changes in personnel policy that trimmed an additional $1.8 billion from the defense appropriations bill. The annual authorization bill was not to directly authorize personnel costs.

As reported by the Armed Services Committee, the bill authorized real growth of 6.9 percent, the rate agreed to by Reagan and the Senate Republican leadership in their deficit reduction package. As a result of that so-called Rose Garden agreement, the Pentagon trimmed $14.4 billion from its February budget request in May.

However, the administration's revised budget plan had some narrow shaves in the Senate in early May.

A deficit package hammered out by Senate Democrats, which included a real defense growth in fiscal 1985 of only 4 percent, was rejected on a 49-49 tie vote. Another budget plan sponsored by moderate Republicans — also allowing a real defense increase of 4 percent — was turned down 48-46. *(Votes 88, 93, p. 18-S)*

Strategic Weaponry

The committee just about halved the number of MX missiles to be purchased, authorizing 21 for $2.4 billion, the number funded in fiscal 1984. Reagan had requested 40 missiles.

The committee rejected an effort to bar any MX procurement by a 7-11 vote. Gordon J. Humphrey, R-N.H., voted for the ban along with all the Democrats except Sam Nunn, Ga., and John C. Stennis, Miss.

Accurate Warheads. In its May budget revision, the administration had trimmed from two research programs a total of $60 million that had been earmarked to develop a maneuvering re-entry vehicle (or MARV) for ICBMs. Of that reduction, $47.3 million came from the program to develop the small, single-warhead missile dubbed Midgetman; the remaining $12.7 million came from a $108.3 million catchall program to improve missile accuracy.

Earlier MARV development had concentrated on so-called "evader" warheads that would fly pre-programmed maneuvers to outwit Soviet anti-ballistic missile (ABM) systems.

Arms control advocates long had feared that MARVs would be designed not just to evade enemy defenses but to home in on their targets with great accuracy. This would make the prospect of a successful first strike seem more likely than already was the case, they argued, thus destabilizing the U.S.-Soviet nuclear balance.

However, the committee argued that MARVs would be needed to ensure that U.S. missiles could penetrate Soviet defenses, if Moscow decided to throw off the restraints of the 1972 treaty limiting ABMs. The proposed $60 million reduction would delay MARV deployment from 1995 until 1998, according to the panel.

The committee accepted the cut in Midgetman-related MARV work, recommending $358.3 million for the small missile. But it rejected the proposed MARV reduction in the missile accuracy program. Moreover, it increased the accuracy program by $10 million (to a total of $118.3 million), with the added funds to be used for "additional penetration-related research, including consideration of an evader MARV."

Bombers. Authorized without change was the $7.7 billion requested for 34 additional B-1 bombers and related equipment, as was the secret amount requested to develop a so-called "stealth" bomber, designed to avoid enemy detection.

However the bill required the secretary of defense to notify the two Armed Services committees before spending any funds covered by the bill for "any activity having as its objective research, design, demonstration, development or procurement" of more than 100 B-1s.

Nunn and other Democrats feared that the Pentagon might have been contemplating the purchase of more than the announced 100 B-1s, at the expense of delaying production of the "stealth" bomber.

The committee approved $597.8 million of the $626.8 million requested for modifications of the existing fleet of B-52 bombers and $77.3 million to develop a missile launcher that would fit into the bomb bays of B-52s, B-1s or stealth bombers. The launcher would let the planes carry a more varied array of nuclear weapons, including long-range cruise missiles.

Sub-Launched Missiles. The request for a 12th Trident missile-launching submarine was approved without change ($1.5 billion) as was the $265.5 million request for components to be used in future missile subs.

Also approved was all but $5 million of the $2.1 billion requested to continue development of the so-called D-5 or Trident II missile, and $163 million to begin purchasing components for use in Trident II production.

In February, the Pentagon had requested $77.1 million to develop a replacement for its current fleet of TACAMO planes, Hercules transports equipped with five-mile-long antennas to send radio messages to submerged missile subs. The new planes would be modified Boeing 707 jetliners, designated E-6s.

The project was dropped by the administration in the May budget reduction, but was resuscitated almost immediately by the Pentagon.

The Senate committee, a strong supporter of the E-6 program, approved the $77.1 million request, but barred use of the money until the secretary of defense certified a five-year commitment to funding the program.

Strategic Defense. The committee trimmed $150 million from the president's $1.8 billion request to begin developing an anti-ballistic missile defense, including such weapons as laser-armed space satellites. The panel rejected a motion to reduce the program by an additional $200 million by a 7-11 vote, with Jeff Bingaman, D-N.M., joining all 10 Republicans to vote "nay."

Meeting head-on one prominent objection to the project, the committee insisted repeatedly that all research planned for the next few years would be consistent with the 1972 ABM treaty. The panel also echoed the administration's complaint that Soviet ABM efforts might violate the treaty, and ordered an administration report next February on Soviet compliance with the pact.

Missiles in Europe. Like the House, the Senate panel trimmed the authorization for Pershing II missiles from 93 requested ($472 million) to 70 missiles ($399 million), the number actually purchased in fiscal 1984.

Approved without change was the $607 million requested for 120 ground-launched cruise missiles (GLCMs). Under terms of a 1979 NATO agreement, 108 Pershing IIs and 464 GLCMs were being deployed in response to Soviet deployments of more than 350 triple-warhead SS-20 missiles.

Ground Combat

The Democrats' emphasis on conventional force improvements was evident in their losing effort to fund 840 M-1 tanks instead of 720. The committee backed the lower number (costing $1.3 billion) by a 10-7 vote that followed party lines (with Democratic presidential hopeful Gary Hart, Colo., absent).

In May, the administration had trimmed its tank request from 720 M-1s to 600.

Setting the stage for a battle with the House, the committee proposed repealing a ban against finding a second source for the M-1's gas turbine engine.

The Pentagon had favored such "dual-sourcing" to put competitive pressure on the original engine supplier, the Avco Corp., which had technical and schedule problems earlier.

However, the House, in the fiscal 1984 defense authorization bill, banned the second source for the tank engine. That action came at the insistence of members whose districts were home to some of Avco's far-flung employees. They argued that the firm's earlier problems had been corrected and that starting up a second production line would be too expensive.

Helicopters. The committee also turned down the administration's May proposal to cut back production of the Apache, a missile-armed, anti-tank helicopter. The February request for 144 planes ($1.2 billion) had been trimmed to 112 Apaches in fiscal 1985, with a planned annual production rate of 96 planes in each of the following three years.

Skyrocketing price estimates had led the Senate panel to threaten cancellation of the Apache in 1982. But close Pentagon oversight — and a more rapid production rate than originally had been planned — had held the price per plane down to about $14 million since then.

The administration's May plan to cut back on the production rate would boost that price by $1.2 million per copy, the committee warned.

The panel also said that "the slightest cost growth" over the next two years would doom the Army's hopes of buying more than the currently planned 515 Apaches.

An equally stern position was taken toward development of a new helicopter (called LHX). Beginning in the mid-1990s, this small helicopter would replace about 7,000 light helicopters of Vietnam War vintage currently in use for various missions. Since it is the only sizable helicopter production contract in prospect for the 1990s, LHX has elicited keen interest from the helicopter industry.

But the committee, recalling large cost overruns in each of the Army's major helicopter programs for the last decade, warned that similar problems would not be tolerated.

Anti-tank Missiles. The Army's stockpile of one-man anti-tank missiles was becoming obsolete as the Soviets were adopting new kinds of armor protection for the front of their tanks. The committee conceded that armor technology perhaps had outstripped the one-man tank-buster, but it added to the bill two small amounts to keep some options open:

- $9.8 million to develop a more powerful warhead for the current Dragon guided missile.
- $7.8 million to increase the number of Swedish-built AT-4 rocket-launchers purchased. In Army tests, the AT-4 had emerged as the most effective of several small rocket-launchers that could serve as last-ditch anti-tank weapons for infantrymen.

Earlier, the service had canceled the Viper anti-tank rocket at the insistence of the Senate Appropriations Subcommittee on Defense, largely because the rocket could not meet its original goal of dealing with Soviet tanks head-on. But the Armed Services panel said that the AT-4 would be useful, even though it, too, could not penetrate the front of new Russian tanks.

'Deep Strike' Weapons. On the broader issue of how to deal with a massive Soviet ground invasion of Western Europe, the committee seemed headed for a clash with the Army. At stake was a proposed missile, called JTACMS, intended to disrupt an attack by smashing targets up to 200 miles behind an enemy's front lines. It would be guided by an airborne radar called J-STARS.

The basic idea had been widely heralded for several years as a way for NATO to offset the numerical advantages in Central Europe of the Soviet-led Warsaw Pact forces.

In 1983, both Armed Services committees raked the Army and Air Force for their failure to coordinate development of the missile and the radar. In November 1984, the two services announced a common position on both projects, as part of a "treaty" between the two services on the coordination of certain projects.

The Senate committee added to the bill a requirement that the JTACMS be able to throw a 1,000-pound warhead some 120 miles. But under the new Army-Air Force plan, the Army's version of the JTACMS missile was expected to be an artillery rocket (called MLRS) which carried one-third of the payload about one-sixth of the distance specified by the Senate panel.

The committee also questioned whether cruise missiles, favored by the Air Force for its version of JTACMS, could reach their targets in time to be effective. The Army preferred ballistic missiles for its JTACMS.

Like the House, the Senate committee approved the $79 million requested for development of the Army JTACMS but denied the $35.5 million requested for the Air Force version.

Anti-Aircraft Defenses. The committee agreed with the Pentagon's decision in May to fund 117 Sergeant York (or DIVAD) anti-aircraft tanks, rather than the 132 requested in February. Including various funding adjustments, this amounted to a reduction of $90 million in DIVAD production funds (to $438.5 million).

But the panel also barred use of any of the fiscal 1985 DIVAD funds until the initial production-line versions of the weapon had been tested. The committee, professing continued support for DIVAD, dismissed earlier failures of the weapon as routine "growing pains." However, it said it wanted proof that there were not technical flaws in the design.

The committee also approved 440 Patriot long-range anti-aircraft missiles. This is the number approved by the House and essentially the number to which the administration's initial request for 585 missiles had been reduced in May. Compared to the February request, the savings were $141 million.

Anti-Missile Missile. Like the House, the Senate panel sharply reduced the funds requested for the "anti-tactical missile" (ATM) program, to modify the Patriot to intercept short-range Soviet ballistic missiles. Pentagon officials had warned that a non-nuclear Soviet attack in Europe might begin with chemical warheads from such missiles immobilizing NATO air bases.

The committee approved $32.3 million of the $92.3

million request, compared with $15 million approved by the House. The panel cautioned the Army not to expand the program to one that might threaten long-range missiles in contravention of the 1972 ABM treaty.

Tactical Air Combat

The Air Force had requested a total of $6.4 billion for procurement and $472 million for research related to its current and planned fleet of jet fighters.

The committee cut a total of some $790 million from that overall request, but the bulk of the reduction was a byproduct of the Pentagon's selection of a new jet engine for its F-16 fighters, after a fierce competition.

The panel recommended all 150 F-16s requested and 42 of the more sophisticated F-15s. The administration had trimmed its F-15 request from 48 planes to 42 in May.

The committee approved the $98.3 million requested to continue the Air Force's long and troubled effort to develop a radar and infrared television system (called LANTIRN) designed to let pilots attack ground targets at night from low altitudes. But it approved only $118.3 million of the $198.3 million requested to begin LANTIRN production, citing continued testing problems with one part of the device.

Carrier-Based Planes. The Navy's request for fighters and bombers was approved with only minor funding adjustments: 24 F-14 fighters ($783 million), 84 F-18s for use as fighters or small bombers ($2.3 billion), and 32 AV-8B Harriers (a vertical-takeoff small bomber used by the Marines).

In 1982 and 1983, Senate Armed Services recommended ending production of A-6E medium bombers, partly because of the great expense of building planes at the rate of one every two months. Instead, the panel suggested transferring to the Navy the Marine Corps' fleet of some 50 A-6Es.

In 1984, it approved the Navy's request for an additional six A-6Es. But it added to the budget $15 million to develop a version of the F-18 that would carry some of the electronic gear that let the larger A-6E attack ground targets at night.

The panel also added $50 million to the Navy's $19.6 million request to begin developing an improved version of the A-6E. But it told the service to concentrate initially on improving the plane's mechanical reliability and to plan on modifying existing planes rather than building new ones.

Airborne Missiles. The request for 1,000 of the 10-mile-range Sidewinder missiles, to be fired by fighters at other planes, was approved. But the panel authorized $58.6 million in new budget authority instead of the $68.6 million requested because the Navy had found $10 million in unanticipated savings in earlier budgets.

Development glitches were expected to delay by six months production of a new, medium-range (40 miles or so) air-to-air missile (called AMRAAM). Accordingly, the administration had decided in May to trim its request for AMRAAM procurement funds from $413 million to $108 million and to increase the number of existing Sparrow medium-range missiles bought from 1,250 to 1,850 ($388 million). The panel concurred.

Because of testing problems with a new version of the 100-mile-range Phoenix missile, carried only by the Navy's F-14 fighter, the committee trimmed the number of missiles from 400 to 340 ($357 million).

Naval Warfare

Administration plans were approved for the two largest warships involved in this year's budget: a stem-to-stern renovation of the 25-year-old carrier *Independence* ($583 million) and modernization of the World War II battleship *Missouri* to carry cruise missiles.

By using unspent funds from prior budgets, as the administration had proposed in May, the $422.6 million battleship renovation was authorized without requiring any new budget authority in fiscal 1985.

Anti-Missile Defenses. Four ships that would carry the Aegis anti-aircraft system designed to protect U.S. fleets against cruise missile attack were approved as requested: three *Ticonderoga*-class cruisers ($3.1 billion) and the first of a new class of destroyers ($1.2 billion). The Navy said it would need more than 30 of the new destroyers to replace a group of anti-aircraft escort ships that were built around 1960 and would be due for retirement around 1990.

In a new round of a long-running tussle, the committee told the Navy to begin developing an improved version of the Mark 92 anti-aircraft radar used on the more than 50 *Perry*-class missile frigates built or authorized since 1976. The panel added $20 million to the bill for this project and told the Navy to start spending money appropriated for the purpose in prior budgets.

The Navy had objected that the proposed improvement would be too expensive, and would be superfluous since it planned to use these ships to escort convoys far beyond the reach of heavy air raids and heavy jamming.

For development of long-range, portable, land-based radars that could supplement the air defense radars of a U.S. fleet, the committee approved $39 million. In its May budget revision, the administration had recommended a deeper cut (to $32 million) in its original request for $64 million.

Submarines. The committee dismissed the administration's May proposal to drop one of the four *Los Angeles*-class submarines requested in February ($2.3 billion). The subs were designed to attack other submarines.

A construction rate of four ships a year would be needed to achieve the Navy's goal of 100 attack submarines and to maintain it through the 1990s, the committee said. In that decade, subs that were built at the rate of five or more per year in the 1960s would be ready for retirement after 30 years of use.

The committee also approved $162 million of the $174 million requested for a cluster of research programs related to development of a new attack submarine class to succeed the *Los Angeles*-type, of which more than 40 had been built or authorized in the last decade.

Sub Hunters. The committee added six LAMPS III helicopters to the 18 requested, for a total authorization of $400.6 million. These were anti-submarine copters carried by most of the Navy's newer surface warships. The conference report on the fiscal 1984 defense authorization bill had instructed the Pentagon to plan on a steady production rate of 24 LAMPS IIIs per year.

The panel also approved as requested six of the smaller LAMPS Is ($65.9 million), used on some older ships. The committee ordered these helicopters to be assigned to the Naval Reserve and told the Navy to consider continuing the program so that reserve-manned LAMPS Is could reinforce active ships as well as equip reserve-manned ships.

It added to the bill $17 million to test the installation of a more powerful engine in the LAMPS I.

Getting Over There

The committee continued the traditional strong congressional support for beefing up the amphibious fleet designed for Marine Corps landings. Major amphibious-assault items in this bill included two so-called "landing ship docks" or LSDs ($406 million), designed to carry landing barges that would be used to haul tanks and other heavy equipment ashore.

The panel approved the $37.6 million request to convert a large container ship to carry the portable maintenance facilities a Marine landing force would use to set up an airstrip on its beachhead.

Also approved as requested were:

● $39.2 million for components to be used in a $1 billion helicopter carrier due to be included in the fiscal 1986 budget.

● $15 million for components to be used to begin rebuilding seven "landing platform docks" (LPDs) — big amphibious ships similar to LSDs, but carrying more helicopters. These massive overhauls were designed to add 15 years to the ships' usual 30-year life.

For nine air-cushion landing craft, designed to haul tanks ashore from amphibious ships at up to 50 mph, the $199 million request was approved. The panel also approved the $198 million requested to develop the hybrid airplane/helicopter called JVX, to replace the Marines' troop-carrying helicopters in the 1990s.

Cargo Ships. The panel approved $31 million to buy commercial cargo ships to be added to the so-called "ready reserve force," a fleet of mothballed vessels held ready for rapid mobilization to transport U.S. combat forces, at an annual cost of about $500,000 per ship. The number of ships to be bought in fiscal 1985 depended on market forces, but the same amount in the fiscal 1984 budget bought 19 ships.

Pentagon planners long had worried about the availability of U.S.-controlled cargo ships that could be pressed into service to haul military cargoes in case of a war. Not only was the U.S. merchant fleet shrinking, but, unlike its Soviet counterpart, it was made up increasingly of container ships that required elaborate shore facilities. To unload such ships off a landing beach or in a harbor without a container port, the committee approved $44 million to put huge cargo cranes on two commercial container ships now in the reserve fleet.

The committee added to the bill $7.7 million to cut down the time it would take to bring into full service a fleet of four large and very fast container ships currently kept on a standby status.

Air Transport. Four major cargo plane programs were approved without change:

● $1.5 billion for eight huge C-5s, an administration-backed reduction of two planes from the initial budget request.

● $622 million for eight KC-10 midair refueling tankers and related parts and equipment.

● $128.9 million to modify four commercial Boeing 747 jetliners so they could be quickly converted to haul military cargo in case of war, as part of the "civil reserve air fleet."

● $129.3 million to continue development of the C-17 long-range cargo plane, designed to haul tanks and other heavy equipment into primitive airstrips.

For spare parts for Air Force cargo planes alone, the committee approved the revised request for $494.5 million. A portion of this was to replenish spare parts inventories that routinely were "used up" during peacetime operations.

The rest was to build up parts stockpiles that would used to keep the transports flying at a much accelerated pace in wartime.

The service hoped to reach its goal for wartime stocks by fiscal 1988.

Personnel

The committee approved an active-duty manpower level of 2,155,540, nearly 20,000 more men than the level approved in fiscal 1984.

The administration initially had recommended authorization of 2,165,800 active-duty personnel but had trimmed that to 2,158,800 in May.

Instead of the requested 5.5 percent, across-the-board pay raise effective Jan. 1, 1985, the committee approved a 4 percent raise for all personnel except new recruits, the same raise Congress had approved for fiscal 1984.

The administration's proposal for a 5.5 percent pay raise was turned down by a vote of 5-13, with Republican William S. Cohen, Maine, joining Democrats Hart, Bingaman, Carl Levin, Mich., and Edward M. Kennedy, Mass., to vote "aye."

Recruiting. For the Army and Navy, the Pentagon budgeted a total of $304.2 million for recruiting and advertising in fiscal 1985, slightly less than the amount appropriated in fiscal 1984 when allowance was made for the cost of inflation.

The committee pointed out that the Army already had reported a slowdown in inquiries by potential enlistees, and added $14 million to the recruiting and advertising budgets of the two services.

The committee ordered the services to project in detail the number of recruits and their "quality" — measured by aptitude tests or other indicators — that would be needed over five years. This was intended to establish bench marks against which the committee could look for recruiting shortfalls.

G.I. Bill. The committee added to the bill a provision lifting the deadline of Dec. 31, 1989, for the use of education benefits earned by military personnel under the so-called "Vietnam-era G.I. Bill."

This would have given eligible beneficiaries 10 years after they left military service in which to use their benefits. Without this change, the committee warned, up to 400,000 service personnel would have faced the alternatives of leaving the service to go to school or giving up their G.I. Bill benefits.

Since this change would expressly alter the G.I. Bill program for the purposes of military personnel management, the committee provision would have required the Pentagon, rather than the Veterans Administration, to pay for any educational benefits used after Dec. 31, 1989.

The House bill had repealed the limiting date, too, but had gone much further. It incorporated provisions that amounted to a peacetime G.I. Bill, which never were debated on the House floor.

Substantially similar to HR 1400, reported from the House Veterans' Affairs Committee in 1983, the House provision would establish for military personnel a basic monthly educational stipend of $300 for up to 36 months, to be paid for through the budget of the Veterans Administration. *(1983 Almanac p. 418; related story, p. 502)*

Central America, Military Construction

The Senate committee proposed a $1.2 billion cut in the Pentagon's fiscal 1985 budget for building of military facilities. This was a little less than the amount by which the administration trimmed its construction budget request in May.

The panel sought to bring the construction budget down to $9.3 billion — about the same size as was recommended by the House Armed Services Committee in its markup of a separate bill (HR 5604). *(Military construction provisions, p. 64)*

On the controversial issue of Central America, the Senate panel approved by the narrowest possible margin $4.4 million for two facilities that would be used to store U.S. military equipment and ammunition in Honduras. *(Related story, p. 84)*

A motion by Bingaman to delete these funds failed on a 9-9 tie vote. Republican Cohen joined the eight committee Democrats in support of the Bingaman motion.

Warranties, Spare Parts

One provision of S 2723 sought to give the Pentagon more discretion in carrying out a 1983 law requiring manufacturers' warranties on all weapons. *(1983 Almanac p. 494)*

The modifications were hammered out in negotiations between Sen. Mark Andrews, R-N.D., the father of the warranties requirement, and a committee task force on procurement practices headed by Sens. Dan Quayle, R-Ind., and Levin.

The Defense Department and major defense contractors had vigorously opposed the Andrews law, which was incorporated into the fiscal 1984 defense appropriations bill. But the measure appeared to enjoy broad support because of widely publicized instances of expensive weapons that fell short of their performance specifications.

Warranty Revisions. Among the changes in the warranty requirement to which Andrews and the committee agreed was a provision exempting from the requirement the first 10 percent of a weapon's planned production run, or all the weapons contracted for in the first year of full-scale production, whichever number was smaller.

The new requirements also would give the secretary of defense discretion in assessing the penalty against a contractor in case a piece of equipment failed to meet the warrantied standards.

The revision also would stipulate that the Pentagon was free to distinguish between performance specifications — such as speed, range and length of time between major parts failures — that were requirements and other specifications that were goals. Required performance levels would be covered by warranty; goals would not.

Spare Parts Purchasing. The committee also incorporated into the bill its recommendations for preventing extremely high prices for spare parts:

● A requirement that contracts specified in great detail the government's right to the use of manufacturing data associated with the item being purchased.

● A procedure to be established for adjudicating government challenges to contractors' claims that certain data was proprietary.

● The Pentagon inquire of suppliers whether some quantity of items other than the number originally requested would give the government a price break.

● Performance evaluations of Pentagon officials take account of their efforts to increase competition and achieve cost savings in contracting. *(Related story, p. 97)*

Minutiae

● Section 151 of the Senate bill ensured that the deputy secretary of defense, the two under secretaries and the five members of the Joint Chiefs of Staff could continue to be chauffeured to and from work.

Such service, called "domicile-to-duty," was restricted by law to the president, the "heads of executive departments" and senior diplomatic officials. The Pentagon interpreted the law to allow rides for the eight officials covered by section 151. But the General Accounting Office decided that only the secretaries of defense, the Army, the Navy and the Air Force qualified as "heads of executive departments." The Senate committee said that extending the perk to the other eight was "an appropriate and wise use of funds . . . because of the critical and time-sensitive nature of their duties."

● To protect the Marine Corps against exploitation of its insignia, the committee added a provision designating the seal, emblem and initials of the Marine Corps as official "insignia of the United States" and barring their use for any commercial purpose that tended to suggest Pentagon approval.

Senate Floor Action

The Senate took up its version of the defense authorization bill (S 2723) on June 7 and passed it 82-6 at about 4 a.m. June 21 after a marathon session. It authorized some $213.5 billion for weapons procurement, military research and operations. This was about $6 billion more than the House had authorized in the version it passed in the wee hours of June 1. *(Vote 151, p. 27-S)*

As in the House debate, the MX missile proved to be the most hard-fought issue. Ultimately, the Senate authorized 21 of the 40 missiles the president had requested for fiscal 1985, but only on the strength of Vice President George Bush's tie-breaking vote.

MX Missile

Bush's tie-breaking vote came on June 14, on a motion to table, and thus kill, an amendment by Lawton Chiles, D-Fla. Chiles' proposal would have barred funding of additional MX production in 1985. *(Vote 132, p. 24-S)*

The close call for Chiles' MX amendment, in the face of strong White House opposition, reflected several factors in addition to general sensitivity over nuclear arms programs. Fundamentally, it arose out of the fact that support for MX had been tepid, even among its Senate supporters, since the administration abandoned the search for a basing method that would protect the big missile against Soviet attack.

However, this did not translate into Senate willingness to kill the program outright. An amendment to that end by Democrats Patrick J. Leahy, Vt.; Dale Bumpers, Ark., and Levin was rejected June 14 by a 55-41 vote, shortly before the vote on Chiles. This was only slightly narrower than the margin by which the Senate had killed a "no-MX" amendment in 1983. *(Vote 131, p. 24-S; 1983 Almanac p. 186)*

Because Chiles and his cosponsors enjoyed a reputation for moderation and being "strong" on defense, their sponsorship of a relatively complicated amendment seemed to have been taken by some members as a safe way to register unhappiness with MX.

The Senate Armed Services Committee had trimmed the number of missiles authorized from 40 to 21.

Chiles proposed barring production of any MX missiles beyond the 21 authorized in fiscal 1984. But his amendment earmarked $596 million to maintain a "hot" production line — ready to crank out missiles on short notice.

The amendment also earmarked:

• $200 million so the 21 missiles from fiscal 1984 could be used for flight tests.

• $200 million for equipment that would be needed if Congress subsequently decided to deploy MXs in fiscal 1985.

In all, the amendment would have trimmed $1.9 billion from the committee recommendation for ICBM-related programs.

Debate. During the debate on June 14, Chiles insisted that this arrangement would provide the bargaining leverage on Moscow to negotiate an arms control agreement, which had been one part of Scowcroft's rationale for MX production.

Chiles also argued that cessation of MX production would improve the prospects that the Pentagon could speed up development of a much smaller, single-warhead missile dubbed "Midgetman."

Technically, Chiles' amendment was voted on as a part of an amendment offered by Daniel Patrick Moynihan, D-N.Y. Chiles' language accounted for the bulk of the amendment, which also included a Moynihan provision that barred the use of any funds in the bill to deploy any MXs in existing missile silos.

Vote. The vote on the amendment came on a motion to table (and thus kill) it, by Senate Armed Services Committee Chairman John Tower, R-Texas.

As the clerk began to call the roll, Bush took the chair, ready to cast his vote as presiding officer of the Senate, in case of a tie.

With senators scattered around the Capitol when the vote came at nearly 10 p.m., the count took far longer than the regulation 15 minutes.

While the last few were awaited, Moynihan stood in front of Bush, pointing at him with a mischievous grin and saying something. The only words audible from the press gallery were "nerve gas," a reference to the only other times Bush had broken a Senate tie: the two occasions in 1983 when he voted in favor of beginning production of a new kind of lethal chemical weapons. *(1983 Almanac p. 186)*

Nearly nine minutes late, the vote was closed and the clerk announced a 48-48 tie.

"The Senate being equally divided," Bush intoned, "the vice president votes 'aye,' and the motion to table is agreed to."

Strategic Defense Initiative

An effort by Charles H. Percy, R-Ill., and others to trim $100 million from the so-called "strategic defense initiative" (SDI) to develop space-based anti-missile defenses was tabled on June 13 by a 47-45 vote. *(Vote 127, p. 24-S)*

The Armed Services Committee previously had trimmed $150 million from Reagan's $1.77 billion SDI request.

Initially, Percy planned to offer an amendment that would bring the Senate authorization for SDI down to the House-passed figure of $1.33 billion — $257 million less than the Armed Services panel had proposed.

William Proxmire, D-Wis., and Charles McC. Mathias Jr., R-Md., had drafted a more far-reaching amendment

that would have cut $510 million from the panel's figure, bringing the total authorization down to $1.11 billion. That would have been an increase, after inflation, of 7.5 percent in funding for those programs compared with the fiscal 1984 appropriation. On June 11, Proxmire and Mathias cast their lot with Percy's more modest reduction.

But at the very last minute, Percy decided to trim back his amendment further. In order to win the support of Armed Services members Cohen and Nunn, Percy decided to aim at only $100 million in addition to the $150 million cut by the panel.

This would have brought the authorization for the SDI programs down to the level projected by the Pentagon prior to Reagan's speech in March 1983, which proposed the program.

Percy changed the amendment so late that his floor speech on its behalf was typed including the figures for the larger reduction. Those numbers were crossed out and the lower numbers written in with a pen.

Percy's effort was hurt by the absence of three of his Democratic allies — Paul E. Tsongas, Mass.; Edward M. Kennedy, Mass.; and Bumpers. All were in Massachusetts attending a "Salute to Tsongas." Tsongas had announced his retiring from the Senate for health reasons at the end of 1984.

ASAT Compromise

Facing a close Senate vote on the issue of anti-satellite (ASAT) missiles, the administration elected instead to seek compromise in a series of votes June 12. *(Story, p. 62)*

The compromise, reached while the Senate held a 2 1/2-hour-long secret debate, barred ASAT target tests until 30 days after the president had certified to Congress that: "The United States is endeavoring to negotiate in good faith the strictest possible [ASAT] limitations . . . consistent with the national security interests."

The presidential certification, parts of which could be secret, was to describe the proposed limitations the president was prepared to negotiate. It also was to include detailed recommendations to decrease the vulnerability of U.S. satellites to Soviet ASATs.

The deal, offered by John Warner, R-Va., came under harsh attack from conservatives led by Malcolm Wallop, R-Wyo., skeptical of arms control talks. Wallop proposed amending the compromise to say that nothing in the provision would prevent the president from acting "in the national security interest," but that was rejected 45-48. For the most part, the split was along ideological lines, with conservatives backing and liberals opposing Wallop. *(Vote 119, p. 23-S)*

The Senate then rejected a motion to table the Warner amendment, 29-65, and adopted the amendment by a vote of 61-28. *(Votes 120, 121, p. 23-S)*

Military Pay Raises

By a vote of 49-45 on June 14, the Senate tabled, and thus killed, an amendment by Cohen that would have provided a 5.5 percent military pay raise to all ranks, effective Jan. 1, 1985. The Armed Services Committee recommended a 4 percent raise for all ranks but recruits, who were to receive no raise. *(Vote 133, p. 25-S)*

Alliance Burden-Sharing

Widespread unhappiness with U.S. allies was underscored on June 7 by a 91-3 vote approving an amendment by Proxmire dealing with the touchy subject of "burden-sharing" among the United States, its North Atlantic Treaty Organization allies and Japan. *(Vote 114, p. 22-S)*

The non-binding amendment expressed the sense of Congress that the president should "insist" that:

● Major NATO members meet their earlier pledges to increase defense spending by at least 3 percent above the cost of inflation in 1984 and 1985.

● Japan "further increase its defense spending." Because of domestic anti-militarist political pressures since World War II, the Japanese government had held its defense budget to less than 1 percent of the gross national product (GNP). The U.S. defense budget absorbed nearly 7 percent of its GNP.

But by a vote of 76-16, the Senate rejected an amendment by Larry Pressler, R-S.D., that was intended to limit the rate of increased spending for U.S. forces in Europe to the rate at which NATO countries increased their defense budgets. *(Vote 115, p. 22-S)*

Nunn Amendment. On June 20, the issue was more strongly underscored as Nunn proposed an amendment that could have removed up to 90,000 of the 326,000 U.S. troops from Europe, if other NATO members did not carry out defense improvements.

The Nunn amendment was tabled (or killed) 55-41, after six hours of often spirited debate. But the vote seemed to obscure a solidifying agreement that the allies were systematically shirking and that something had to be done. *(Vote 149, p. 27-S)*

The amendment would have frozen the number of U.S. personnel in Europe at 326,000, the number requested for fiscal 1985. The allies could prevent reductions in that level, beginning in 1987, by meeting a 1978 alliancewide pledge to boost defense spending annually in addition to the cost of inflation. Or, the allies could avoid troop withdrawals if they began in 1986 firm five-year programs to meet NATO goals involving ammunition stockpiles and maintenance facilities.

In each of the three years starting in 1987, the United States would lower its European troop ceiling by 30,000 unless either the 3 percent budget increase or the ammunition and facilities buildup had begun.

In the end, the administration carried the day because of tight party discipline and the concern of some senators that the timing was wrong for a hard-nosed approach to the allies.

After killing the Nunn amendment, the Senate voted 94-3 for an amendment offered by Cohen that amounted to Nunn's amendment minus the threatened troop cuts. *(Vote 150, p. 27-S)*

G.I. Bill

In intense procedural wrangling, the Senate June 13 indicated its support for a broad revival of the G.I. Bill, then reversed itself and approved a less sweeping measure to offer educational aid to certain recruits once they completed their military service.

On a 72-20 vote, the Senate passed an amendment introduced by Sen. John Glenn, D-Ohio, which would establish a four-year test program offering $500 a month for three years in educational benefits as a recruiting incentive. *(Vote 126, p. 24-S)*

During 10 hours of debate on June 11 and 13, however, the Senate at first defeated 46-51 a bid to kill a more comprehensive amendment to provide what its sponsors described as a true G.I. Bill. *(Vote 123, p. 23-S)*

That proposal was offered by Sens. William L. Arm-

strong, R-Colo.; Cohen; Spark M. Matsunaga, D-Hawaii; Alan Cranston, D-Calif.; and Ernest F. Hollings, D-S.C. Their amendment would have created a program fully funded by the government to apply to everyone completing three years of active military duty regardless of education or job.

In contrast, Glenn's plan sought to open benefits only to high school graduates recruited for certain job specialties, to be designated by the secretary of defense, for which personnel was in short supply. To qualify, one would have to serve two years of active duty with $250 a month less in pay.

The Senate became entangled in a procedural snarl after Armstrong's amendment survived a tabling attempt. Majority Leader Howard H. Baker Jr., R-Tenn., raised a point of order, objecting that Armstrong's amendment violated congressional budget procedures. This precipitated parliamentary maneuvers and a close vote over whether the budget act should be waived, for which Vice President Bush appeared in the chamber to be on hand in case of a tie. *(Votes 123, 124, p. 23-S)*

But in the end, as some senators switched and others did not vote, Armstrong's amendment was killed on a second tabling amendment, by a vote of 47-45. *(Vote 125, p. 24-S)*

Under the Glenn plan, as revised by a perfecting amendment offered by Tower and approved on a 96-1 vote, benefits for college or post-secondary vocational education would be available for up to 12,500 persons entering military service between Sept. 30, 1984, and Sept. 30, 1988. *(Vote 122, p. 23-S)*

'Stealthy' Attack?

Continuing a battle that dated from 1981, Minority Leader Robert C. Byrd, D-W.Va., offered an amendment to bar the administration from diverting to any other program the secret amount authorized in the bill for the so-called "stealth" bomber, being designed to evade detection by enemy radars.

The fiscal 1985 stealth amendment also was to cover the secret amount authorized for a so-called "advanced cruise missile." That weapon was designed to be launched from bombers and reportedly incorporated stealth design features.

The amendment was agreed to on June 7, 90-0. *(Vote 116, p. 22-S)*

The Senate Armed Services Committee had approved without change the secret amounts requested for these two programs. However, the House bill incorporated hefty reductions in each — possibly trimming as much as $350 million from a stealth bomber request of around $1 billion.

Byrd, Nunn and others warned repeatedly that some Pentagon officials could have been hoping to prolong production of the B-1 bomber by delaying development of the stealth plane, due to replace the B-1.

Central America

The Senate, rejecting a proposal to end U.S. support for anti-government guerrillas in Nicaragua, on June 18 handed Reagan a nominal victory in his Central America policy. But the vote of 58-38 disguised a sharp drop in support among key Democrats at a time when the administration was waging an uphill battle to continue subsidizing civil war in Nicaragua.

Four Democratic members of the Intelligence Committee, who earlier had backed Reagan's policy of arming the

Nicaraguan "contras," bolted on that vote, depriving the administration of strong bipartisan support. The four were Daniel K. Inouye, Hawaii; Lloyd Bentsen, Texas; Moynihan; and Walter D. Huddleston, Ky. Republican panel member Cohen of Maine also bolted.

The administration had counted on Democratic support in the GOP-controlled Senate to counter opposition to its Nicaragua policy in the Democratic-run House.

The Senate's action came on an amendment sponsored by Kennedy. By 58-38, the Senate killed the amendment, which would have prohibited U.S. assistance to the contras in fiscal 1985. *(Vote 141, p. 26-S)*

Earlier June 18, the Senate rejected another Kennedy amendment that sought to prohibit the introduction of U.S. combat troops into Central America, except under several narrow conditions. That amendment was tabled, 63-31. *(Vote 140, p. 25-S)*

Under the troops amendment, the president would not have been allowed to send U.S. soldiers to either El Salvador or Nicaragua unless Congress had declared war or otherwise authorized the deployment. The president also could send troops to those countries if necessary to meet a "clear and present danger of hostile attack" upon the United States, its embassy or its citizens and employees.

Ten days earlier, the administration averted what could have become a contentious debate over its Central America policy by agreeing to drop from the bill $4.4 million to build in Honduras two storage sites for ammunition and equipment intended for use by U.S. forces. *(Story, p. 84)*

Bingaman, whose effort to delete the funds had failed in committee, promised to renew his effort on the Senate floor, but Tower pre-empted that June 8 by offering his own amendment to drop the funds, which was agreed to by voice vote. According to Tower, the administration wanted to "consult on the need for the facilities in the overall context of our foreign policy for the region."

Nuclear Test Bans

A non-binding amendment calling on the president to seek ratification of two nuclear test ban treaties and to resume negotiations of a comprehensive treaty banning all nuclear tests was approved 77-22 on June 20. The measure was offered by Kennedy and Mathias. *(Vote 148, p. 26-S)*

At issue was a treaty signed in 1974 banning underground nuclear weapons tests with a power of more than 150 kilotons — the so-called "threshold test ban treaty" — and one signed in 1976 setting a similar ceiling on the size of underground peaceful nuclear explosions. The Ford and Carter administrations, husbanding their political capital to fight on other issues, had left the two treaties on the shelf.

President Carter began negotiations with the Russians for a comprehensive test ban treaty. But those talks were suspended, along with all other U.S.-Soviet arms control efforts, in early 1980 after the Soviet invasion of Afghanistan.

In 1983, the Reagan administration announced it would not seek ratification of the threshold and peaceful explosions treaties, unless procedures for verifying compliance with the limits were renegotiated. The Russians rejected several requests to reopen those issues, maintaining they would be willing to talk about verification methods after the treaties were ratified.

Senate Foreign Relations Committee Chairman Percy tried to get administration support for approving the treaties since Reagan took office. In 1983, he threatened to sit on the nomination of Reagan's new arms control chief, Kenneth L. Adelman, unless the administration explained its position on the pacts. *(1983 Almanac p. 213)*

In spring of 1984, the test ban lobby groups, Kennedy and Mathias began a concerted push to raise the issue.

According to one lobbyist, Nunn, the Armed Services Committee's influential senior Democrat, was the key to wrapping up a majority of Senate support. Nunn insisted that the original resolution be modified to stipulate that, when the president asked for ratification of the two existing treaties, he could append any "understandings" or "reservations" he thought should be formally attached to the treaty in order to deal with verification problems.

Most test ban supporters rejected the administration's contention that there would be difficulties in verification. Accordingly, they resisted the specific reference to "reservations" for fear it would give color of legitimacy to the administration's position. But in the end, they accepted most of Nunn's demands. After Kennedy and Mathias introduced their original amendment June 20, they accepted Nunn's modification.

GOP conservatives, led by James A. McClure and Steven D. Symms of Idaho, vigorously opposed this amendment, saying U.S. arms control initiatives lulled the public into a false sense of security about the Soviet Union while Moscow continued its arms buildup, to the extent of violating ratified treaties.

After a motion to kill the Kennedy amendment by tabling it was rejected 34-65, the Senate agreed 99-0 to a Symms amendment to the Kennedy amendment. It declared that "in accordance with international law," the United States would not be bound by any treaty the Soviet Union was violating. *(Votes 146, 147, p. 26-S)*

Even after his amendment was agreed to, Symms — and most of the conservatives — voted against the modified Kennedy amendment.

SALT II Limits

The test ban battle followed essentially the same pattern as a fight June 19 on U.S. policy toward certain weapons limits contained in the unratified strategic arms limitation treaty (SALT II).

An amendment by Bumpers called on the president to continue the current policy, which was "not to undercut" the treaty. Bumpers accepted a Nunn amendment stipulating that the policy be continued through Dec. 31, 1985, which was the expiration date of SALT II.

Since the effort to ratify SALT II was shelved after the invasion of Afghanistan, the Carter and Reagan administrations each endorsed the "not undercut" policy, although as a 1980 presidential candidate Reagan had condemned the treaty as slanted toward Soviet interests.

Reagan officials insisted on the circumlocution "not undercut," rather than "observe" or "abide by." They meant it as a signal that they reject the treaty's fairness, while conceding that the United States could benefit by observing it informally.

The basis for that pragmatic judgment was that Soviet nuclear missiles and submarines currently in production could be used to expand the Russian arsenal rapidly, if Moscow did not simultaneously dismantle older weapons to stay within the SALT II limits.

No U.S. production lines threatened the SALT II limits. But that was expected to change late in 1985 when the *Alaska*, seventh of the huge Trident missile-firing submarines, was scheduled to begin sea trials.

Bumpers and Leahy pressed ahead with their amendment, maintaining that they wanted to assemble a broad, bipartisan coalition behind the amendment, rather than simply criticize the administration. Accordingly, they accepted the "not undercut" language and reluctantly agreed to Nunn's insistence that the amendment incorporate the treaty's expiration date.

To accommodate conservatives, Nunn and Percy offered a modification that required a presidential report by Sept. 15, 1984, on Soviet compliance with the "not undercut" policy. Accepted by Bumpers and Leahy, the new language also told the president to "carefully consider" the implications of any change in the U.S. approach to the SALT limits and to consult with Congress before making any changes.

The modified amendment was agreed to 82-17. McClure supported it, but most of the other conservatives voted "nay." *(Vote 144, p. 26-S)*

Sea-Launched Cruise Missiles

Arms control advocates backed down from one showdown with the administration, over sea-launched cruise missiles (SLCMs) armed with nuclear warheads.

Because the new SLCMs were so small — the size of a regular torpedo — and because there was no external difference between nuclear and non-nuclear versions, arms controllers warned for years that limitations on the nuclear version would become impossible once it was deployed.

Mathias and Dave Durenberger, R-Minn., had worked since early May on a non-binding amendment that would have urged a mutual U.S.-Soviet moratorium on nuclear SLCM deployment pending negotiation of a ban on such weapons.

But Navy Secretary John F. Lehman Jr. mounted a vigorous lobbying campaign against the amendment, and SLCM supporters were confident they could beat Mathias when the defense bill went to the Senate floor.

After introducing their amendment on June 19, Mathias and Durenberger accepted a substitute amendment by Cohen. It asked the president to discuss with Moscow, in the appropriate arms control forum, means by which nuclear SLCM limitations could be verified.

The Cohen amendment also told the president to inform the Russians that the United States remained willing to accept "those intrusive, on-site inspection procedures" needed to verify such limits, and that the Soviet Union should accept them, also.

The modified amendment was agreed to by voice vote.

Tension Reduction

The Senate also agreed to two other amendments that signified members' desire to make some effort at reducing risks in the nuclear age. Agreed to by voice vote were amendments:

● By Arlen Specter, R-Pa., urging the president to meet the president of the Soviet Union "at the earliest practical time following thorough preparation" to seek arms reductions.

As adopted, the amendment hewed to the administration line on the need for preparation before a summit. Specter's original language called for a summit meeting "as soon as possible," but that ran into a buzzsaw of opposition.

● By Mark O. Hatfield, R-Ore., Matsunaga, and Jennings Randolph, D-W.Va., to establish a national peace academy, with initial funding of $23.5 million for two years. The idea, which had been before Congress for decades, picked up support in 1984 as a gesture to Randolph, one of its most fervent backers. He was retiring at the end of the session.

Divorced Spouses Rights

By a voice vote, the Senate agreed June 19 to an amendment by Paul S. Trible Jr., R-Va., that would make the divorced but not remarried spouses of military personnel eligible for health care services, commissary privileges and post exchange privileges. Recipients would have to meet the following conditions: that the marriage to the military member lasted for at least 20 years, that the military member served for at least 20 years on active duty, and that the marriage and the term of military service overlapped for at least 15 years.

Under legislation adopted in 1982, such benefits were available only to former spouses who were married to a service member during at least 20 years of the member's active duty service. *(1982 Almanac p. 100)*

Before agreeing to the Trible amendment, the Senate tabled (and thus killed) by a vote of 70-29 an amendment by Roger W. Jepsen, R-Iowa, that would have retained the requirement that the marriage have encompassed 20 years of the military member's active service. *(Vote 145, p. 26-S)*

Other Amendments

By a vote of 80-4 on June 8, the Senate approved a proposal by Byrd providing that the Competition Advocate General, which the bill would establish for each of the armed services, be a general or admiral appointed to the position for a two-year term. *(Vote 117, p. 23-S)*

Other amendments agreed to by voice vote were:

● By McClure, requiring the president to send Congress a report on Soviet compliance with arms control agreements that was prepared in 1983 by the administration's general advisory committee on arms control. Reportedly, the secret document accused Moscow of several arms control violations.

● By McClure, authorizing the use of 10 million ounces of silver from the national defense stockpile to mint coins for sale.

● By Hollings, expressing the sense of Congress opposing extension beyond fiscal 1985 of the current law which limited cost-of-living increases for federal pensions to persons under 62 years of age to one-half the increase granted pensioners 62 and older. *(1982 Almanac p. 514)*

Senate Passage

The bill debated by the Senate for two weeks, S 2723, included authorizations for military construction projects and for defense-related nuclear programs of the Energy Department as well as the weapons, research and operations funds ususally covered by the defense authorization bill.

Before the Senate took its final action on the measure June 21, however, it broke the legislation into separate bills covering weapons and operations, construction and the Energy Department.

It then substituted its version of the weapons and operations bill for provisions of the corresponding House-passed bill and passed the bill as HR 5167.

By voice vote, the Senate then passed as S 2459 the Energy Department section of S 2723.

Hill-White House Negotiations

On June 22, the day after the Senate finished its work on the defense authorization bill, House-Senate conferees met to begin an arduous effort to hammer out a compromise. The two chambers were not very far apart on authorizations for specific programs. But obstacles were posed by both houses' differences over MX and Central America issues.

And an even greater hurdle proved to be the simple question of the total dollar level for the authorization. The Senate-passed figure was part of the overall defense-budget total agreed to by Reagan and Senate Republican leaders in May. In return for trimming some $14 billion from Reagan's earlier defense budget request, Reagan reportedly secured from Senate GOP leaders vows that they would stand by the new total — $299 billion overall for the Defense Department.

That commitment made GOP Senate conferees particularly resistant to House demands for a lower authorization.

After weeks of stalemate, the issue was finally resolved Sept. 20 in a carefully crafted bargain between House Speaker Thomas P. O'Neill Jr., D-Mass., and Senate Majority Leader Baker over the defense number and the future of MX.

The compromise, coming as members of Congress struggled to meet a scheduled Oct. 4 adjournment date, unblocked the way for Congress to act on the budget resolution and the defense appropriations measure, as well as the authorization bill.

The Sept. 20 agreement set fiscal 1985 defense appropriations at $292.9 billion, roughly 5 percent more than the fiscal 1984 appropriation in addition to the cost of inflation.

Of that amount, $2.5 billion was earmarked for buying MX missiles, but with a very large string attached. Only $1 billion could be spent before April 1, 1985; none of it could be used to complete MXs in addition to the 21 funded in fiscal 1984.

The remaining $1.5 billion could be used to complete another 21 new missiles — but only if both houses of Congress voted twice in spring 1985 to approve that course.

Compared with his original fiscal 1985 budget request — $313 billion, including $3.2 billion for 40 MXs — Reagan settled for substantially less on both counts. However, his initial request — which would have amounted to a 13 percent after-inflation increase in defense appropriations — was widely regarded on Capitol Hill as politically unrealistic.

Conference Report

Barely had the Baker-O'Neill agreement been announced than the Senate-House conferees on the defense authorization bill resumed their deliberations. Staff members of the Senate and House Armed Services committees began thrashing out details on Sept. 22. And in a bargaining session that ran into the wee hours of Sept. 25, conferees agreed on a fiscal 1985 defense authorization bill that would allow an overall defense budget of $297 billion.

This was $16 billion less than Reagan had initially requested, but only $2 billion less than the revised budget negotiated between Reagan and Senate Republican leaders in May.

The House passed the conference version of the bill (HR 5167 — H Rept 98-1080) by voice vote Sept. 26. The Senate followed suit Sept. 27.

Because some parts of the defense budget were not covered by the annual authorization bill, the amount actually authorized by the conference report was $219.7 billion.

Under the Baker-O'Neill agreement, Congress would authorize a total of $297 billion for defense and appropriate a total of $292.9 billion for fiscal 1985.

A $292.9 billion appropriation would provide a real increase in defense spending, above the cost of inflation, of 5 percent.

Baker and O'Neill had stepped in to break the authorization conferees' deadlock over the defense budget level and over the immediate future of the MX missiles.

The authorization conference came out much closer to the Senate-passed bill (which would fit into a $299 billion defense budget) than to the House version (which contemplated a $292 billion budget).

Compared with the original budget request, nearly two-thirds of the reduction came from the amounts requested for hardware. The procurement account was cut by 7.5 percent and the research and development account by 5.6 percent. By contrast, 3.4 percent was trimmed from the operations and maintenance request and 2.4 percent from the request for military personnel costs.

Few dramatic differences over major weapons programs confronted the conferees, and some of them were resolved in favor of the higher funding level. For instance, the conferees consented to buy 840 M-1 tanks ($1.8 billion) as agreed to by the House, instead of the 720 requested by Reagan and approved by the Senate.

Of the $1.8 billion requested to develop a space-based anti-missile defense system, the conferees approved $1.6 billion, the amount agreed to by the Senate. The House had trimmed the program, which Reagan critics called "Star Wars," to $1.4 billion.

On the other hand, though the conferees authorized $503 million for 117 DIVAD anti-aircraft tanks, they barred production of the trouble-prone weapons until Congress received reports of successful operational tests.

Nuclear Warfare

The MX Deal. Never at issue in the conference was the $1.7 billion each house had approved as requested to continue MX development. Most leaders of the anti-MX coalition wanted to kill the program outright. However, the MX foes had for the most part taken the more moderate public stance of opposing production of the missile while supporting its development as a bargaining chip for arms control negotiations with Moscow.

The battle focused on procurement funds, of which the administration requested nearly $3.2 billion:

● $1.15 billion for equipment needed to deploy the 21 MXs that were funded in the fiscal 1984 budget.

● $1.79 billion to buy 40 additional missiles.

● $233 million to buy spare parts.

As had been agreed to by the White House and Capitol Hill leaders, the authorization conferees approved a total of $2.5 billion for MX procurement, $148 million of which was earmarked for spares. The remaining $2.352 billion could be used for deployment of the fiscal 1984 missiles and production of up to 21 of the 40 new missiles Reagan had requested.

However, only $1 billion of the $2.5 billion total could be spent before spring of 1985, and not for new missiles. The conferees estimated that deployment of MXs already funded would take up most of that $1 billion. The $1 billion also could be used for spare parts or to ensure that no contracts for MX components were canceled.

The remaining $1.5 billion was to be spent to build the new missiles only if Congress enacted two separate resolutions in March endorsing production. Technically, the point of requiring two resolutions was that one would "release" the authorization of the new missiles and the other would "release" the appropriation.

The practical point of the two-vote requirement agreed to by Baker and O'Neill was to give MX foes two chances to kill the program in the spring. That supposed advantage was lessened, however, by agreement that votes on the two resolutions occur very close together — thus making it difficult for the anti-MX lobby to regroup for the second vote in case they lost the first.

Midgetman. The two houses had made similar, small trims in the $724.5 million request to develop future ICBMs that would be less vulnerable to attack than the MX. The conferees agreed on a total of $701.8 million to develop a small single-warhead missile (nicknamed "Midgetman") and to test new basing methods, including the launchers more heavily armored than the current type.

Because of budgetary limits, the authorization for Pershing II ballistic missiles had been trimmed by both houses from 93 missiles ($456 million) to 70, for which the conferees authorized $375 million.

Anti-Missile Defense. For research on Reagan's proposal to develop a space-based defense against nuclear missiles, the conferees agreed to the Senate-passed figure of $1.63 billion (of $1.78 billion requested). The House had trimmed the authorization to $1.37 billion.

The conferees authorized $32 million (of $93 million requested) to modify the Patriot anti-aircraft missile so it could intercept short-range Soviet missiles in Europe.

Submarine Missiles. Conferees trimmed $16 million from the $2.1 billion requested to develop a new Trident II submarine-launched missile, intended — like MX and Midgetman — to be accurate enough to destroy armored Soviet missile launchers.

For the 12th huge submarine designed to launch Trident missiles, the conference authorized $1.7 billion, all but $47 million of the request. The House had trimmed that amount by $340 million, ordering the Navy to make up the difference with funds authorized in fiscal 1984 for an anti-submarine frigate. The conference action left the frigate authorized.

The House had denied a $77 million request to develop a version of the Boeing 707 airliner into an airborne radio station to communicate with submerged missile subs — a mission called TACAMO (Take Charge And Move Out). According to the Navy, the current fleet of C-130 TACAMO planes was wearing out. The Senate approved the request, but House Armed Services complained that the new program would be too expensive. The conferees allowed $60 million for the Navy to develop either the 707 or an improved C-130 for this mission, with the money embargoed until the Pentagon justified its decision to the two Armed Services panels.

Bombers, Cruise Missiles. Both houses had agreed to the $7.1 billion procurement request for B-1 bombers. But the House had allowed none of the $228 million requested to modernize existing B-52 bombers and only $10 million of the $161 million requested to update FB-111 bombers.

The conferees approved $149 million for B-52 modifi-

cations and the entire $161 million for the FB-111s.

Most of the House cuts in programs to develop "stealthy" weapons that could evade enemy detection evidently were restored by the conferees. The House had trimmed $350 million from the secret request — estimated at $1 billion — to develop the "stealth" bomber and $108 million from the secret amount sought for a new, bomber-launched cruise missile.

All but $100 million was restored to the bomber program and all but $30 million was added back to the cruise missile project.

Arms Control Policies

The conferees agreed to a raft of provisions added in each house that were intended to promote various arms control notions, but which imposed only modest limitations on ongoing weapons programs.

The most concrete arms control provision limited tests of the anti-satellite (or ASAT) missile during fiscal 1985 to two "successful" tests against target satellites. The conferees defined a successful test as one in which both the missile engine and its guidance mechanism worked properly and the missile intercepted the target satellite. But they warned the Pentagon against trying to circumvent the two-test limit by aiming the ASAT to miss the target narrowly.

Target tests could not begin until 15 days after the president notified Congress: that he was endeavoring to negotiate "the strictest possible" ASAT limitation agreement with Moscow, that the test was required for national security reasons and would not gravely impair prospects for such negotiations, and that the test would be consistent with the 1972 treaty limiting anti-ballistic missile systems.

The House bill barred ASAT target tests so long as the Soviets continued their current moratorium on such tests. The Senate bill barred ASAT target tests until 30 days after the president certified he was trying to negotiate "the strictest possible conditions . . . consistent with national security."

The conferees agreed to the $144 million requested for ASAT development. The $84.5 million sought for ASAT procurement had been approved by both houses.

The conferees' other arms control provisions included expressions of the "sense of Congress" that:

● The United States should continue the current policy of "not undercutting" existing arms control accords, so long as Moscow did likewise.

● The president should seek Senate consent to ratification of two treaties limiting underground nuclear explosions that were signed in the mid-1970s but never ratified. The president's request should include whatever reservations or understandings he thought should be attached to the treaties to help make verification of Soviet compliance more reliable.

● The president should try to negotiate with the Russians establishment of jointly staffed "nuclear risk reduction centers" to help the two superpowers deal with nuclear threats by minor powers or terrorists.

The conference report also required the president to report to Congress on several related issues:

● The impact of Reagan's anti-missile defense plan on the 1972 anti-ballistic missile treaty.

● The feasibility of reducing NATO's reliance on short-range nuclear weapons, such as artillery shells.

● The implications for U.S. nuclear strategy of the proposed procurement of extremely accurate nuclear missiles, including the MX, Midgetman and Trident II missiles.

• The theory that a nuclear war would create a "nuclear winter" because of the soot and debris blown into the atmosphere.

• A method for distinguishing nuclear-armed sea-launched cruise missiles (SLCMs) aboard warships from conventionally armed ones. Conferees dropped a House provision that would have barred deployment of the nuclear-armed U.S. Tomahawk missile unless the Soviets deployed a similar one. Arms control advocates warned that problems in telling nuclear from conventional cruise missiles could hinder future agreements to limit nuclear SLCMs.

A Senate-passed provision establishing a "United States Peace Institute," to foster research on non-violent resolution of conflicts, was pared back. The proposed academy was transformed into a research institute that would neither acquire property nor operate as a school. An institute grants program was to be named after retiring Sen. Randolph, a proponent of the academy.

Ground Combat

By tapping $216 million authorized but not spent in fiscal 1984, the conferees approved purchase of 840 M-1 tanks for $1.7 billion. This was $57 million less than the Army had requested to buy only 720 tanks.

Both houses had approved the January request for 144 Apache anti-tank helicopters ($1.3 billion), thus dismissing the administration's May proposal to save $176 million by buying only 112 helicopters.

One major Army program that was pared back, evidently for budgetary reasons, was the Bradley fighting vehicle, an armored troop carrier equipped with anti-tank missiles. The conference approved 680 Bradleys ($992 million) of the 710 requested in January ($1.1 billion). In May, the administration had reduced its Bradley request to 655 vehicles.

Anti-Tank Weapons. Both houses had added $45 million to the $103 million request to buy Copperhead, laser-guided artillery shells, designed to kill tanks. But because of cost and technical problems with the Aquila — a tiny, remote control airplane equipped with a laser to guide Copperheads to their targets — the conferees approved only $44 million of the $100 million requested to buy the planes.

Also approved was $10 million of the $13.8 million requested to develop a mortar shell that could home in on tanks.

In May, the administration proposed to save $120 million by cutting more than half the January request for nearly 22,000 TOW guided missiles, the staple of anti-tank defense for Army and Marine Corps units. Both houses rejected so deep a cut and the conferees authorized $310 million for nearly 19,000 TOWs.

Also agreed to was a Senate provision adding $9.8 million to give the smaller Dragon anti-tank missile a more powerful warhead. And the conferees increased to $42 million the administration's $34 million request for a smaller, one-man anti-tank rocket.

'Deep Strike' Weapons. The conferees agreed to some Pentagon changes in a high-technology scheme for attacking enemy tank columns far behind Soviet lines. However, they insisted on certain characteristics for the new equipment. The new equipment included a 200-mile-range missile (called JTACMS) and two devices to find targets for it: an airborne radar (called JSTARS) and a so-

called "fusion center" to consolidate information from various sources on the whereabouts of potential targets.

Both houses had approved only the $79 million requested for Army development of the missile, rejecting the $36 million requested for the Air Force share of what Congress had insisted be a joint project. The two Armed Services panels complained that the Air Force was ignoring their strong suggestion that the new missile be derived from an existing rocket.

The conferees endorsed a recent Pentagon decision to put the radar on only one plane — a converted jetliner that would orbit far behind NATO lines — instead of developing separate Army and Air Force radar planes. Accordingly, the conferees reduced to $155 million the earlier $203 million JSTARS request.

The secret amount requested for the fusion center was trimmed by $23 million, half the amount the House had wanted to cut. The conferees backed the demand of the House that the center be made more lightweight and easily transportable — and cheaper.

Anti-Aircraft Weapons. The authorization conference was completed five days too early to capitalize on Defense Secretary Caspar W. Weinberger's decision to forgo production of the DIVAD anti-aircraft gun in fiscal 1985.

On Sept. 29, Weinberger trimmed the $516 million requested for 132 DIVADs to $100 million, earmarked for components that would be used to build more guns in fiscal 1986, if the weapon passed some operational tests it had hitherto failed.

In the conference completed early Sept. 25, the authorization conferees had approved $461 million for 117 DIVADs, but barred use of the money until tests had been completed and reported to Congress.

Both houses had earlier agreed to add $32 million to the budget to buy Chaparral short-range anti-aircraft missiles. But because of test delays, they also had agreed to trim from $33 million to $3 million the budget for modernizing the existing Vulcan short-range anti-aircraft gun, which DIVAD was designed to supplant.

Both houses had slowed down production of the Patriot long-range anti-aircraft missile, which earlier had cost and production problems. Of the 550 missiles requested in January ($1.1 billion), 440 were authorized ($976 million).

The conferees agreed to two House additions to beef up anti-aircraft defenses for U.S. forces in Europe: $250 million for the U.S. share of a multi-country anti-aircraft defense for U.S. air bases and missile sites; $25 million to beef up anti-aircraft protection for U.S. Army installations.

Naval Warfare

Nearly $1 billion was cut from the $13 billion request for Navy ships, but without dropping a single major warship from the budget. More than three-quarters of the reduction came from what were essentially bookkeeping adjustments both houses already had made to the bill:

• $598 million — including all $423 million requested to refurbish the mothballed battleship *Missouri* — was available from shipbuilding funds appropriated in earlier years but not needed because of lower-than-predicted contractor bids.

• In light of the continuing pattern of low bidding by Navy contractors, the two houses also dropped $187 million included in the budget to cover anticipated price increases.

The two versions of the bill had approved with no substantial disagreement the budget request for three

Congress Revives Large-Scale G.I. Bill . . .

In the defense authorization bill (PL 98-525), Congress voted to authorize a three-year test program that would revive large-scale educational benefits to any military recruit. But members attached the condition that applicants help pay for the program in monthly contributions.

The first such program, enacted during World War II as part of a "G.I. Bill of Rights," was intended to help people who had served in the military at very low pay re-enter civilian life. It was reinstated during the Korean and Vietnam wars.

The program was repealed in 1976, because men no longer were being drafted and because military pay had gone up substantially. Economic recession helped propel many job seekers into the military, easing serious recruitment problems.

Subsequently, a shrinking pool of potential recruits and an improving economy led to predictions on Capitol Hill that there would be future manpower shortages in the all-volunteer armed forces.

In addition, military personnel who qualified for benefits under the Vietnam-era program faced a Dec. 31, 1989, deadline for using those benefits, a deadline that offered an incentive for servicemen to leave.

House Proposals

In an effort to ease the recruiting crunch, members tried to revive a wide-scale G.I. Bill in 1983. A bill, HR 1400, was reported from the House Veterans' Affairs Committee that would have established a package of education benefits. But it was never brought to the floor. Nor was there any Senate action on the proposal. *(1983 Almanac p. 418)*

In 1984, the House Armed Services Committee incorporated a proposal similar to HR 1400 into the defense authorization bill (HR 5167 — H Rept 98-691), reported April 19. The provision amounted to a peacetime G.I. Bill, establishing for military personnel a basic monthly educational stipend of $300 for up to 36 months, to be paid for through the budget of the Veterans Administration.

The House bill would have repealed the limiting date for the Vietnam-era G.I. Bill benefits.

The proposal for a peacetime G.I. Bill was not debated on the floor, when the House considered HR 5167 in May 1984. But the issue was the focus of intense procedural wrangling in the Senate in June.

Senate Proposals

In its companion bill (S 2723 — S Rept 98-500), the Senate Armed Services Committee also added a provision lifting the Dec. 31, 1989, deadline for the use of education benefits earned by military personnel under the Vietnam G.I. Bill.

The Senate provision would have given eligible beneficiaries 10 years after they leave military service in which to use their benefits. Without this change, the committee warned, up to 400,000 service personnel would have faced the alternatives of leaving the service to go to school or giving up their G.I. Bill benefits.

Since this change sought to alter the G.I. Bill program for the purposes of military personnel management, the committee provision required the Pentagon, rather than the Veterans Administration, to pay for any educational benefits used after Dec. 31, 1989.

During 10 hours of debate on the floor on June 11 and 13, senators indicated support of a broad revival of the G.I. bill, similar to that in the House legislation. But the Senate subsequently reversed itself and approved a less sweeping package.

An amendment was offered that would have created a program fully funded by the government to apply to everyone completing three years of active military duty, regardless of education or job. Similar to the House plan, it was sponsored by Sens. William L. Armstrong, R-Colo.; William S. Cohen, R-Maine; Spark M. Matsunaga, D-Hawaii; Alan Cranston, D-Calif.; and Ernest F.

---

cruisers (a total of $3.1 billion) and the first of a new class of smaller destroyers, carrying a version of the cruisers' Aegis anti-missile defense system. As the first of its kind, the small destroyer carried a $1.5 billion price tag.

In a move that drew objections from arms control activists, the conferees approved $10 million of the $40 million requested to develop a nuclear warhead for the Navy's Standard anti-aircraft missile.

Sub Hunting. The two bills had approved the $2.7 billion requested for four nuclear-powered sub-hunting submarines.

The two Armed Services panels had differed over how best to shift to production of a new version of the Navy's Mark 48 anti-submarine torpedo — the so-called ADCAP (for advanced capability). The ADCAP is designed to cope with the higher speed, deeper diving ability and stronger hulls of new Soviet subs.

The conferees agreed on the Senate committee's plan, authorizing $213 million (of $237 million requested) for Mark 48 production. Of that amount, $89 million was earmarked to continue producing the current Mark 48 while $124 million was to start ADCAP production.

Both versions of the bill had increased by $73 million (to $458 million) the budget for LAMPS III anti-submarine helicopters, carried by most modern classes of cruisers, destroyers and frigates. This would allow a production rate of 24 per year.

The House had proposed to trim from nine planes to five the budget for P-3C long-range, land-based sub-hunters, a version of the 1950s-vintage Electra turboprop airliner. But the conferees authorized nine planes, approving $406 million of the $465 million P-3C request.

Bucking the strong political pressure in favor of competition for weapons contracts, the conferees agreed to order the Navy to replace aging anti-sub helicopters aboard aircraft carriers with a version of the LAMPS III, rather than open the contract to competition. This would save time and money, they insisted.

Landing Troops. For development of the JVX — a hybrid airplane-helicopter, designed to carry a Marine platoon ashore at 300 mph and land without a runway — the conferees approved $188 million of the $198 million re-

...But as a 3-Year Test, With Conditions

Hollings, D-S.C.

The less comprehensive amendment was offered by John Glenn, D-Ohio. It would have established a four-year test program offering $500 a month for three years in educational benefits as a recruiting incentive.

Glenn's plan opened benefits only to high school graduates recruited for certain job specialties, to be designated by the secretary of defense, for which personnel was in short supply. To qualify, a "citizen-soldier," as Glenn dubbed those he hoped to attract, would have to serve two years of active duty and contribute $250 a month.

The Senate became entangled in a procedural snarl after Armstrong's amendment survived a tabling attempt, 46-51. Majority Leader Howard H. Baker Jr., R-Tenn., raised a point of order, objecting that Armstrong's amendment violated congressional budget procedures. This precipitated parliamentary maneuvers and a close vote over whether the budget act should be waived, for which Vice President Bush appeared in the chamber to be on hand in case of a tie. *(Votes 123, 124, p. 23-S)*

But in the end, as some senators switched and others did not vote, Armstrong's amendment was killed on a second tabling amendment, by a vote of 47 to 45. *(Vote 125, p. 24-S)*

Sens. Robert Dole, R-Kan., Jesse Helms, R-N.C., J. Bennett Johnston, D-La., and Edward Zorinsky, D-Neb., voted with Armstrong on the tabling motion and against him when Armstrong moved to waive the budget act. In a second vote to kill Armstrong's amendment, all except for Johnston sided with Armstrong again. But two others, Sens. Slade Gorton, R-Wash., and Nancy Landon Kassebaum, R-Kan., switched to oppose him. Then the Senate swiftly voted for Glenn's measure, 72-20. *(Vote 126, p. 24-S)*.

Backers of the two rival Senate amendments traded sharp charges. While Armstrong defended his plan as cost-effective and as a boon for educational opportunity, critics portrayed it as a costly entitlement program that would lock the government into paying large educational benefits to veterans indefinitely.

Glenn said his GI Bill would cost at most $160 million per year compared to the annual $775 million he said the Armstrong plan would demand within 10 years.

Under the Glenn plan, as revised 96-1 by a perfecting amendment offered by Sen. John Tower, R-Texas, benefits for college or post-secondary vocational education were to be available for up to 12,500 persons entering military service betweeen Sept. 30, 1984, and Sept. 30, 1988. *(Vote 122, p. 23-S)*

Alan K. Simpson, R-Wyo., chairman of the Veterans' Affairs Committee, opposed both amendments. He said they would deter re-enlistments because people will leave "to take advantage" of the educational benefits.

Conference

The conferees agreed to a three-year test program that was to be voluntary. Their report (H Rept 98-1080), cleared by Congress Sept. 27, incorporated the Glenn proposal for contributions, although not in the amount of $250 a month.

Under the conferees' agreement, any recruit entering the service between June 1985 and July 1988 could contribute $100 per month for the first 12 months of service.

That would guarantee payment by the Defense Department of at least $300 per month toward tuition and expenses for 36 months, for a total of $10,800.

The secretary of defense was to have discretion to increase benefit levels for recruits in selected job specialties, to encourage enlistments or re-enlistments.

A separate program would pay $140 per month for educational expenses for 36 months to enlistees in the National Guard or reserve forces who meet certain criteria and enlist for six years.

---

quest.

They also approved a House initiative to add $20 million for the Army to buy Arapaho kits, modular helicopter bases that could be installed on cargo ships for use during an amphibious landing.

Tactical Air Combat

The Armed Services committees differed over Air Force plans for a rapid fighter-plane buildup. The Senate endorsed a rapid increase in the production rate of both F-15s and the less expensive and less capable F-16s. The House committee, citing long-term budget constraints, had called for lower production rates, with more emphasis on the cheaper planes.

The conferees approved 42 F-15s ($2.1 billion) as proposed by the Senate. Both houses had authorized the 150 F-16s requested, but had trimmed the amount from $4.1 billion to $3.4 billion, mostly to reflect the results of a competition to produce the fighter's jet engine.

The production rate issue was reflected in the compromise amounts for so-called long-lead-time components, parts that would be used in planes to be included in the following budget. For each type, the conferees agreed on compromise amounts, about midway between the House-passed amounts and the higher amounts included in the budget and agreed to by the Senate.

For Navy combat planes, the two bills had substantially agreed with the budget request for 24 F-14 fighters ($783 million), 84 smaller F-18 fighters ($2.3 billion) and six A-6E bombers ($200 million).

The conferees sliced $292 million from the $413 million requested for AMRAAM air-to-air missiles. The Air Force deemed this a critical program because AMRAAM would be the first long-range missile that could be carried by the F-16 fighter. But the program had had technical problems.

The HARM missile, designed to be fired from planes to home in on enemy anti-aircraft radars, fared better at the conferees' hands. The House panel had complained about the missile's $385,000 price tag, and trimmed the authorization from 1,674 missiles ($636 million) to 1,349 missiles ($536 million). The conferees' compromise was shaded toward the Senate view: 1,571 missiles for $596 million.

The House provision ordering the Navy to develop a cheaper version of HARM's radar-seeking guidance system was retained in modified form.

Operations and Maintenance

In contrast to the conferees' 8 percent cut in the January request for procurement, they trimmed the $80.9 billion request for operations and maintenance by only $2.6 billion — a reduction of 3 percent.

At that, about 60 percent of the net reduction in the operations and maintenance account came from a handful of reductions the conferees agreed would have no impact on Pentagon activity, since they merely reflected economic changes in the year since the fiscal 1985 budget request was taking final shape. These included reductions of:

● $794 million to reflect lower-than-budgeted fuel prices.

● $480 million to reflect the rise of the dollar against foreign currencies, in countries where U.S. forces were stationed and bought services and supplies from the local economy.

● $270 million for re-estimates in the "prices" that Pentagon supply accounts would "charge" the services for various parts and supplies.

● $93 million to compel the Air Force to squeeze the same amount of overtime from its civilian employees as the other services.

According to Nunn, these savings allowed the conferees to plow back some $470 million into various accounts related to "combat-readiness" that had been reduced in one version of the bill, including equipment overhauls, property maintenance and supply services.

For instance, the conferees added to the budget funds to overhaul three ships, wiping out the Navy's backlog of ships overdue for maintenance.

Personnel Issues

The Senate position on the annual military pay hike prevailed: a 4 percent raise, effective Jan. 1, 1985, for all uniformed personnel except recruits in service less than four months. This was similar to the raise agreed to by the Senate. The House bill authorized a 3.5 percent pay hike, excluding all recruits.

The conferees also agreed to a routine extension through the end of fiscal 1987 of the Pentagon's authority to award cash bonuses for enlistment or re-enlistment in critical job specialties. They raised the ceiling on re-enlistment bonuses from $20,000 to $30,000 but with the proviso that no more than 10 percent of all bonuses paid could exceed $20,000.

Also approved was an increase in the bonus paid to senior enlisted personnel stationed on ships. The conferees commented that this increase should make sea duty more attractive, thus allowing the Navy to keep active-duty personnel at sea longer while relying more on reservists for assignments ashore. The Navy's historic argument for making less use of reservists than the other services is that it needs to reserve most of its shore billets for active-duty sailors who would leave the service if forced to spend too much time at sea.

The conferees retained a House provision establishing a minimum for the proportion of new Air Force recruits who are women. They slightly eased the original House-passed standards, setting the floor at 22 percent of Air Force recruits in fiscal 1988. The House Armed Services Committee had complained that the Air Force had reduced its goal for recruiting women in the early 1980s, even though the national policy against assigning women to combat jobs ruled out proportionally fewer jobs in the Air Force than in any other service.

Reserves. The conferees retained in amended form several House provisions designed to beef up the combat-readiness of reserve forces. Among these were requirements for:

● At least one major reserve mobilization exercise annually.

● A test of the benefits of longer training periods for certain reserve units.

G.I. Bill. For the first time since 1976, a large-scale program of educational benefits would become available to any military recruit under the conference report. *(Story, p. 56)*

The first such program, enacted during World War II as part of a "G.I. Bill of Rights," was intended to help people who had served in the military at very low pay re-enter civilian life. That program was repealed in 1976, because men no longer were being drafted and because military pay had gone up substantially.

The three-year test program agreed to by the conferees was to be voluntary. Any recruit entering the service between June 1985 and July 1988 could contribute $100 per month for the first 12 months of service. That would guarantee payment by the Defense Department of at least $300 per month toward tuition and expenses for 36 months, for a total of $10,800.

The secretary of defense was to have discretion to increase benefit levels for recruits in selected job specialties, to encourage enlistments or re-enlistments.

A separate program would pay $140 per month for educational expenses for 36 months to enlistees in the National Guard or reserve forces who met certain criteria and enlisted for six years.

Divorced Spouses' Rights. Another hotly contested issue involved the rights of military members' former spouses to military fringe benefits — especially medical care coverage.

Under a law passed in 1982, military spouses divorced after the law was enacted were eligible for military medical benefits and access to military commissaries and post exchanges, provided the marriage had lasted for 20 years, the military member had been on active duty for 20 years, and the marriage and the military service had overlapped for 20 years. This was referred to as the "20-20-20" provision.

Organizations of divorced military spouses objected that the 1982 law unfairly excluded spouses who had been divorced before that date. They also argued that the 20-20-20 provision was unrealistic: Many people joined the service in their late teens and retired in their late 30s, after 20 years of service, but did not marry until their early 20s, thus making it unlikely that the marriage and the term of active service would overlap for 20 years.

The conferees made the 20-20-20 provision retroactive. They also made divorced spouses eligible for military medical care if the marriage and the spouse's term of active service overlapped for 15 years. They also ordered the Pentagon to develop by 1986 a program allowing divorced spouses to join a private medical insurance program.

Management Reforms

Spare Parts. Both versions of the authorization bill had included a raft of provisions designed in response to widely reported instances of exorbitant charges to the Pentagon for spare parts.

The conferees agreed to a House-passed requirement that prime contractors identify the subcontractor producing each part so the Pentagon would have the option of buying directly from the producer and cutting out the middleman.

Other House provisions agreed to require that:

● An agency ordering a part check the government's supply system first to see if the part was available.

● A picture and description of each part be available at some point in the parts-ordering process. The intent was to help ordering officials know, for example, that a KX-81726GP was a crescent wrench, and judge whether the seller's price was reasonable.

The conferees rejected a House provision that would have placed an absolute limit of seven years on the period during which a contractor could withhold technical data on its products from potential competitors. *(Related story, p. 197)*

Among the related Senate provisions agreed to by the conferees was one requiring that officers who served as managers of weapons programs did so for a term of four years, to provide continuity in dealing with contractors.

Warranties. Senate-passed amendments to the 1983 law requiring warranties on all major weapons were largely agreed to with some apparently minor changes.

The conferees complained that the Pentagon was not using its authority under existing law to tailor each warranty to the product. For instance, conferees said, a contractor's liability for weapon performance should depend in part on the degree to which the manufacturer enjoyed a free hand — and thus bore full responsibility — for the item's design.

They also charged the Pentagon with ignoring the law's requirement that it seek a congressional waiver of the warranty requirement, in cases for which a warranty would cost more than it was worth.

Joint Chiefs of Staff. The House bill included several provisions intended to increase the authority of the chairman of the Joint Chiefs of Staff. The House Armed Services Committee had complained that the current Joint Chiefs arrangement gave the separate military services too much power to promote their parochial interests. The conferees agreed to let the Joint Chiefs chairman select the officers — the technical advisers — who would serve on the Joint Staff and to force the sometimes balky Joint Chiefs to reach conclusions on controversial issues.

However, the Senate conferees refused to accept other House provisions that would have made the chairman a member of the National Security Council and would have authorized him to give the president military advice in his own right, not merely as spokesman for the Joint Chiefs.

Central America

A provision that the House adopted overwhelmingly in May, barring the introduction of combat troops into El Salvador or Nicaragua without prior congressional approval, was turned into a non-binding expression of the "sense of Congress."

The conferees also asked the secretary of defense to consider regulations that would bar the participation by members of the National Guard or reserve forces as private parties in foreign wars. This was brought on by the death in Nicaragua Sept. 1 of two U.S. reservists who were participating in a guerrilla attack on a Nicaraguan installation.

"Free-lance" military activity risked depriving a reservist's unit of the training he had been given, the conferees argued. Moreover, it might lead to misinterpretation of official U.S. policy toward the particular conflict: "The fact that members were acting as private citizens could be overshadowed by the implication that their membership in the U.S. reserve connotes U.S. government complicity," according to the conferees.

Other Provisions

The conferees retained with minor changes a Senate provision that put a ceiling of 326,414 on the number of U.S. military personnel stationed in Europe. The provision also called on the president to seek commitments from other NATO members to improve the alliance's ability to defend against a Soviet attack without resort to nuclear weapons, through boosting their ammunition stockpiles and building bombproof shelters for fighter planes.

According to the conference report, House conferees feared that the provision could erode alliance cohesion. They promised hearings on the provision's impact in 1985.

Religious Observance. The conference report established a Pentagon advisory committee to investigate possible conflicts between military discipline and the religious practices of military members. The panel was to report to the secretary of defense who would, in turn, report to the Armed Services committees by Feb. 1, 1985.

While drawing the group's charter in broad terms, the conferees insisted that it not lose sight of the issue that gave rise to the provision: whether Jews could wear skullcaps (or yarmulkes) while in uniform.

Getting Respect. The conferees retained a Senate provision barring the unauthorized use of the Marine Corps' emblems on commercial products. Another Senate provision, also agreed to, authorized the Pentagon to provide transportation between home and work for the deputy secretary and the two under secretaries of defense and for the five members of the Joint Chiefs of Staff. ∎

Congress Approves MX, With Tough Conditions

The MX intercontinental missile, the centerpiece of President Reagan's strategic defense program, survived a third year of crucial tests in Congress. In the end, Congress approved 21 of the controversial missiles for fiscal 1985, the same number as it approved in fiscal 1984. *(1983 Almanac p. 195; 1982 Almanac p. 120)*

But there was a major difference: Congress put new strings on the program. Congress agreed that $2.5 billion for 21 MXs would be authorized and appropriated in fiscal 1985. None of that money, however, could be used to build new missiles — in addition to the 21 funded in fiscal 1984 — until after two sets of congressional votes in March 1985 to proceed with the additional production. One set of votes would amount to an endorsement of the authorization of the MX, the other an endorsement of the appropriation.

In 1984, the fight over MX was the symbolic vote of confidence in Reagan's nuclear arms policy. It produced cliff-hanger voting on the floor of each chamber of Congress and contributed to a stalemate in the ensuing House-Senate conference on the defense authorization bill (HR 5167 — PL 98-525) that was only broken after talks between Capitol Hill leaders and the administration. *(Story, p. 37)*

Proponents and opponents of the MX disagreed over two broad issues: the missile's effectiveness as a weapon and its role in arms control efforts.

The administration contended that land-based ballistic missiles like the MX were needed to offset unacceptable advantages the Soviet Union had in such weapons. Liberal arms controllers argued that ICBMs only work in limited-war scenarios and that other kinds of nuclear weapons, such as submarine missiles and bombers, would counter the Soviet threat more effectively.

On the arms control front, the administration made the case that the MX was at least in part a bargaining chip. Opponents of the missile said bargaining chips did not work and the MX was a new step in the arms race.

In 1984, liberal advocates of arms control continued their effort, begun in 1983, to convince House Democrats that a vote for MX represented a vote of confidence in the president's nuclear arms policy — and that vote should be no. Well-organized lobbying by members and at the grassroots level brought the arms control coalition to within a hairsbreadth of victory in the House in mid-May. Then Speaker Thomas P. O'Neill Jr., D-Mass., and the House Democratic leadership threw their organizational resources into the fray and eked out the few votes needed to win a symbolic victory on May 31.

In the Senate, too, there was a change in the political dynamic of the MX fight. Members who opposed the missile gained some support from more conservative Democrats, led by Lawton Chiles, Fla., who saw MX largely as a budget issue. Together, those two goups produced a tie that the administration won by Vice President George Bush's vote.

May 16: First House Test

In his budget request, Reagan had asked for $2.9 billion to produce 40 new missiles in fiscal 1985. The House Armed Services committee cut the request by $450 million — a reduction to 30 missiles.

But MX foes in the House, led by Charles E. Bennett, D-Fla., and Nicholas Mavroules, D-Mass., pushed an amendment that would deny all MX production funds. They would not touch the $1.7 billion authorized to continue development of the missile.

Centrist members of the House, led by Les Aspin, D-Wis., saved the day for the MX program on May 16, hammering out a compromise that would allow 15 missiles to be bought, at a total cost of $1.8 billion under these conditions:

● No money would be spent until April 1, 1985.

● It would only be spent if, in the president's judgment, the Soviets were not indicating a willingness to bargain in good faith for limits on ICBMs. If they were willing to bargain, the ban would continue.

In the May 16 voting, the centrists' legislative craftsmanship and strong White House lobbying prevailed over the anti-MX lobby, which had honed its skills in two years of legislative battles against the MX and for a nuclear freeze resolution. In November 1983, they came within nine votes of killing funding for MX. *(1983 Almanac p. 203)*

While rallying "swing" members looking for a middle-position, Aspin's proposal won the support of members who backed the full Reagan request, but knew it had no chance of passage. Aspin and Joel Pritchard, R-Wash., credited Minority Leader Robert Michel, R-Ill., and other GOP leaders for bringing along conservative Republicans.

The showdown between the MX opponents and the Aspin team took place in a dramatic, seven-hour-long debate May 16, in which rhetorical eloquence took a back seat to parliamentary maneuvering. After the jockeying was over, the Bennett-Mavroules team got a roll-call vote on their "no-MX" amendment. When the seesaw vote was over, the MX opponents had lost, 212-218. The Aspin position was then approved on a 229-199 vote. *(Votes 133, 134, p. 44-H)*

The Switchers

In the welter of lobbying by both sides, 11 members who had supported MX in November 1983 changed their minds and voted on May 16 for no new missiles. Ten who had voted against MX also switched, approving the missile, with the Aspin conditions.

The MX opponents' most prominent trophy was Majority Whip Thomas S. Foley, D-Wash., with whom they completed a sweep of the top House Democratic leadership. Foley had been a charter member of Aspin's group of bipartisan centrists, who had tried since early 1983 to find a political strategy linking support of MX to steps that would promote U.S.-Soviet arms control negotiations.

Others who switched to oppose MX were seven Democrats: James R. Jones, Okla.; Joseph M. Gaydos, Pa.; Walter B. Jones, N.C.; Stephen L. Neal, N.C.; Lindy (Mrs. Hale) Boggs, La.; Robert Garcia, N.Y.; and Ed Jenkins, Ga. Three Republicans switched to oppose MX: Lawrence Coughlin, Pa.; Ed Zschau, Calif.; and F. James Sensenbrenner Jr., Wis.

The 10 who switched from opposing MX to backing the Aspin amendment were Jerry Patterson, D-Calif.; Robin Tallon, D-S.C.; Ike Andrews, D-N.C.; Tim Valentine, D-N.C.; Charlie Rose, D-N.C.; Claude Pepper, D-Fla.; William J. Hughes, D-N.J.; Ron Coleman, D-Texas; Christopher H. Smith, R-N.J.; and Bill Goodling, R-Pa.

May 31: Second House Test

Before the dust had settled on Aspin's May 16 victory, the Democratic leadership began girding for a rematch. On May 20, Common Cause volunteers were rounding up pledges from 500 people to call members who had abandoned their previous opposition to MX in the May 16 voting.

But what really changed the political equation was O'Neill's commitment of skilled Democratic tacticians to the fight against the MX. This task force was led by Richard A. Gephardt, Mo., and Democratic Congressional Campaign Committee Chairman Tony Coelho, Calif. Others in the group were Marty Russo, Ill.; Mavroules; Les AuCoin, Ore.; Thomas J. Downey, N.Y.; Mike Synar, Okla.; Mike Lowry, Wash.; and Peter H. Kostmayer, Pa.

The Gephardt group accepted the basic premise of Aspin's amendment — that 15 new missiles would be authorized in 1985, but that production would not begin before April 1985 and would not begin at all if the Soviets resumed arms talks.

The Gephardt group added the wrinkle that it would be up to Congress, not the president, to decide whether or not to release production funds.

Rounding Up the Votes

With MX backers confining their tactical planning to procedural moves, rather than political persuasion, the MX opponents won out in a series of tight votes on May 31. The MX backers decided to force the issue by offering an amendment that restated the position that the House had adopted on May 16. It was agreed to 203-182. *(Vote 177, p. 56-H)*

Bennett then offered his amendment, requiring a congressional vote after April 1, 1985, before the 15 MXs could be produced. This time the seesaw vote ended in the MX foes' favor, 199-197. *(Vote 178, p. 58-H)*

Jim Courter, R-N.J., demanded a roll-call vote on the amendment to which Bennett's language had just been added, in effect, another vote on the same issue. The Democrats had scattered and the leadership held the vote open for nearly two minutes beyond the allotted 15 before Dante B. Fascell, D-Fla., trotted down the aisle to break a tie, giving the MX foes a 198-197 victory. With rumors rampant that the GOP leadership was trying to round up absent members, the anti-MX forces held their troops in line for a third vote on the issue, 199-196. White House ally Guy Vander Jagt, R-Mich., was retrieved by Air Force jet in time for the third vote, but he was offset by the return of MX foe Gary L. Ackerman, D-N.Y. *(Votes 179, 183, p. 58-H)*

June 14: Close Call in Senate

Two weeks later, on June 14, the GOP-controlled Senate gave the administration a scare on the MX: a tie-vote on an amendment to bar funding of more missiles in 1985 that was broken in the administration's favor by Vice President Bush.

The close call on the no-MX amendment, offered by Chiles, reflected several factors in addition to general sensitivity over nuclear arms programs. Support for MX had been tepid, even among Senate supporters, since the administration abandoned the search for a basing method that would protect the big missile against Soviet attack.

However, this did not mean the Senate was willing to kill the missile. An amendment to that end by Democrats Patrick J. Leahy, Vt., Dale Bumpers, Ark., and Carl Levin, Mich., was rejected June 14 by a 55-41 vote. This was only slightly narrower than the margin by which the Senate had killed a no-MX amendment in 1983. *(Vote 131, p. 24-S; 1983 Almanac p. 186)*

Chiles' reputation for moderation and being "strong" on defense meant his sponsorship of a relatively complicated amendment offered some senators a way to register unhappiness with MX. Chiles had stepped up his involvement in the MX issue after the House imposed its controls on May 31.

The Senate Armed Services Committee had trimmed the number of missiles for fiscal 1985 from 40 to 21. The Senate committee had rejected conditions on the program, dismissing them as providing "the Soviets with veto power over such an important U.S. program."

Chiles, in looking for an MX position different from the one taken by that panel, came up with an alternative that he said would give the United States the bargaining chip of MX without paying full price for it.

The 'Hot' Production Line

Under the Chiles amendment, no new missiles would be built in fiscal 1985, but the production line for the missile would be kept "hot" — ready to start cranking out missiles on short notice. The amendment also earmarked:

● $596 million to maintain the "hot" production line. Chiles argued that for much of the fiscal year, the facilities and employees would be busy catching up on delays in production of the 21 missiles authorized in fiscal 1984.

● $200 million so the 21 missiles from fiscal 1984 could be used for flight tests.

● $200 million for equipment that would be needed if Congress subsequently decided to deploy MXs in fiscal 1985.

In all, the amendment would have trimmed $1.9 billion from the committee recommendation for ICBM-related programs, a point Chiles and cosponsor J. Bennett Johnston, D-La., made in floor debate.

Opponents of the Chiles amendment complained about the mechanics of a "hot" production line that was not producing anything and warned that stopping MX production would reward Soviet intransigence on arms control.

Technically, Chiles' amendment was voted on as a part of an amendment offered by Daniel Patrick Moynihan, D-N.Y. The vote on it came on a motion to table (and thus kill) it, by Senate Armed Services Committee Chairman John Tower, R-Texas.

Four senators who would not vote to kill MX but supported Chiles were known before the vote: Johnston, Lloyd Bentsen, D-Texas, and Charles E. Grassley, R-Iowa, cosponsors of the amendment, and Charles McC. Mathias Jr., R-Md., who had supported the Leahy amendment after having opposed a similar amendment in 1983.

Chiles' other converts included Larry Pressler, R-S.D., Arlen Specter, R-Pa., Russell B. Long, D-La., and Jennings Randolph, D-W.Va.

Bush's vote broke a 48-48 tie. *(Vote 132, p. 24-S)*

Conference and Compromise

House-Senate conferees on the defense bill began meeting June 22, but disputes over the MX and the overall budget number produced a stalemate that continued until Sept. 20.

The two chambers were apart on the number of MXs to be produced in fiscal 1985: 15 voted by the House and 21 by the Senate. But the real sticking point was the House's stipulation that the money could not be spent until April 1 — and then only if Congress approved by concurrent resolution.

As conferees chewed over the MX issue throughout the summer, it became apparent that members would have to delay expenditure of the procurement money. But disputes remained on what role Congress would have in releasing the money when the delay expired. If a production go-ahead depended on an affirmative vote of both houses, as in the House bill, one chamber could block the missile. If Congress only had the right to stop a presidential decision to build the MXs, both houses would have to vote accordingly.

The Final Formula

With the defense authorizations, appropriations and the budget resolution as the major legislation standing between Congress and an October adjournment target, O'Neill and Senate Majority Leader Howard H. Baker Jr., R-Tenn., held two weeks of talks to work out a compromise. The outcome, announced Sept. 20, gave Reagan $2.5

billion for MX procurement, $148 million of which was earmarked for spares. The remaining $2.352 billion could be used for deployment of fiscal 1984 missiles and production of up to 21 new missiles.

However, only $1 billion of the $2.5 billion total could be spent before the spring of 1985, and not for new missiles. Deployment of MXs already funded would take up most of that $1 billion. The $1 billion also could be used for spare parts or to ensure that no contracts for MX components were canceled. The remaining $1.5 billion could be spent to build the new missiles only if Congress enacted two separate resolutions in March 1985, endorsing production.

Technically, the point of requiring two resolutions was that one would "release" the authorization of the new missiles and the other would "release" the appropriation. The practical point of the two-vote requirement was to give MX foes two chances to kill the program. That supposed advantage was lessened, however, by agreement that the votes would occur close together.

The Sept. 20 agreement freed up the authorization bill to clear Congress on Sept. 27. The compromise language also was folded into the defense appropriations portion of an omnibus continuing resolution (H J Res 658 — PL 98-473), which cleared Congress on Oct. 11. ∎

Anti-Satellite Missile Gets New Restrictions

Congress set new restrictions on testing of the anti-satellite missile (ASAT) in fiscal 1985, delaying a test against a target in space until March 1, 1985, limiting the number of tests, and imposing other conditions.

The battle over the ASAT issue represented a test of support for the "new" arena of President Reagan's defense strategy: space weaponry. In much the same way, the fight over the MX missile posed a vote of confidence in the "old" arms race issue of nuclear missiles. *(MX story, p. 59)*

To some degree, conservatives saw in space weaponry a way to break out of the Earth-based nuclear stalemate by rendering the Soviet Union's missiles obsolete. But liberal arms controllers argued that such technology, which they ridiculed as "star wars," was just another attempt to surpass the Soviets, rather than negotiate with them.

The ASAT, a 19-foot-long missile to be fired from an F-15 fighter plane, was designed to destroy Soviet space satellites by homing in on their heat and ramming them. Technically, the ASAT was not part of the president's "strategic defense initiative," a program to develop laser-type weapons that could be aimed from space to destroy earth-launched missiles.

But as the first widely publicized U.S. weapon in years designed for use in outer space, it became a test case on the whole panoply of space weaponry in 1984.

An effort by liberal arms controllers to block it in 1983, with very little advance spadework, had shown surprising strength. The arms control lobby, having honed its skills in the MX battle, went to work on ASAT in 1984 and won a major victory in the House. That set the stage for compromises in the Senate and by House-Senate conferees that put conditions on target testing of the weapon.

A leading ASAT opponent, Charles Montfort of the Union of Concerned Scientists, claimed that in 1984 Congress had set a precedent: imposing a test moratorium on a new weapon.

Background

Many ASAT critics argued that it was critical to block testing of the U.S. version of the weapon against a target in space. Once realistic testing of the weapon was begun, they insisted, the United States and the Soviet Union would be unable to achieve a mutual ban on the weapon.

This was because the U.S. version was so small, in contrast to the huge, ICBM-launched Soviet ASAT, that Moscow could not be sure the U.S. weapon had not been secretly produced.

Administration officials vehemently disagreed, maintaining that any effort to deploy the ASAT covertly would be quickly exposed.

1983 Battles

In the spring of 1983, a group of House members led by Joe Moakley, D-Mass., George E. Brown Jr., D-Calif., and John F. Seiberling, D-Ohio, joined forces with the Federation of American Scientists (FAS) and the Union of Concerned Scientists (UCS), two liberal groups that emphasized a technical approach to arms control issues.

Staffers for those two organizations, the three members and a few other parties began meeting weekly in Moakley's office. Out of these sessions came the first congressional vote on space weapons issues: Brown's amendment to the fiscal 1984 defense authorization bill (PL 98-94) deleting the $19.4 million requested to begin ASAT production. Though the amendment was rejected 177-243, it drew more support than liberal arms control moves usually did. *(1983 Almanac p. 179)*

In the Senate, Armed Services Committee leaders and proponents of a moratorium on space weapons tests negotiated a compromise that was agreed to, 91-0. The amendment, offered by Paul E. Tsongas, D-Mass., barred ASAT tests against targets in space unless the president certified that he was trying to negotiate a ban with the Soviet Union on such weapons. Conferees accepted the amendment. *(1983 Almanac p. 188)*

When the focus of action shifted to the defense appropriations bill, FAS and UCS lobbyists found allies on the House Appropriations Committee in Matthew F. McHugh, D-N.Y., Lawrence Coughlin, R-Pa., and Norman D. Dicks, D-Wash. Their amendment, accepted with modification by the committee, dropped the $19.4 million in ASAT production money and required a report on administration plans to seek arms control agreements dealing with ASAT weapons.

The money was restored in the House-Senate conference on the bill, but the requirement for the report was retained. *(1983 Almanac pp. 480, 494)*

Gearing Up for a New Round

Preparing for the 1984 space weapons policy battles, the FAS and UCS brought several of the arms control and other liberal lobby groups into the coalition against ASAT.

Meanwhile, Brown, Moakley and Seiberling and their allies announced on March 28 that they would seek arms control measures including a mutual ASAT moratorium.

Administration Report

On March 31, the administration submitted, as required under the fiscal 1984 appropriations bill, its report to Congress on an ASAT ban. The administration, while not ruling out curbs on certain types of ASAT activity, concluded that a total ban:

● Could not be verified, even if existing Soviet ASAT weapons were destroyed. In part, the administration argued, this was because the Soviets could use other weapons and space vehicles as substitute ASATs.

● Would prevent production of the U.S. ASAT. To deter Soviet attacks on U.S. satellites, the administration argued, it would be necessary to threaten retaliation against Soviet satellites.

● Would make outer space a sanctuary from which Soviet reconnaissance satellites could guide Soviet attacks on U.S. and allied military targets. *(Text, p. 20-E)*

House Action

In its report on the fiscal 1985 defense authorization bill on April 19 (HR 5167 — H Rept 98-691), the House Armed Services Committee strongly endorsed the administration's request to begin production of the ASAT guided missile. The $84.5 million Reagan had sought to begin ASAT production was approved, as was $120 million of the $143 million he had asked for development of the weapon. The panel emphasized its arms control rationale for ASAT. It cited arguments, made during the Carter administration, that since the Soviet Union had its own ASAT, a U.S. counterpart might "encourage good faith ASAT negotiations." *(Story, p. 37)*

When members debated the issue on the House floor on May 23, ASAT opponents had lined up enough votes in support of a moratorium on realistic tests of the ASAT weapon, so long as the Soviet Union did likewise.

The ASAT amendment, offered by Brown, was needed to head off an ASAT race between the two superpowers, Moakley and other members argued.

ASAT backers rallied behind a counter-amendment by Beverly B. Byron, D-Md., that would have allowed the United States as many ASAT tests as the Soviets had had. (The Soviets then had had 20 tests — nine successful.)

But backers of Brown's amendment worried most about a "middle-ground" staked out by Dave McCurdy, D-Okla. His amendment would have barred an ASAT target test until March 31, 1985, but then would have allowed testing if the president submitted to Congress a plan for seeking a U.S.-Soviet ban and certified that he had invited Moscow to resume ASAT negotiations.

The Brown forces had Albert Gore Jr., D-Tenn., reoffer their amendment in a slightly different form so that it would receive the first vote; it prevailed 238-181. The House then rejected the Byron amendment twice (once, as reoffered by Samuel S. Stratton, D-N.Y.) on votes of 178-236 and 181-229. The McCurdy amendment then was turned down, 186-228. *(Votes 152-155, pp. 50-H, 52-H)*

Senate Action

In its defense bill (S 2723 — S Rept 98-500), reported May 31, the Senate Armed Services Committee set the stage for a potential floor fight by gutting the Tsongas amendment to the 1984 defense bill, which had barred ASAT flight testing pending presidential certification to Congress of willingness to negotiate with the Soviets.

Ultimately, a floor fight was averted after the administration elected to seek a compromise in a series of votes June 12.

Under the Senate panel's version of the defense bill, an ASAT target test would have been banned unless the president certified that continued testing was essential to gaining an ASAT arms control agreement. This provision was tailored to the administration's insistence that:

● A total ban on ASATs, as called for by the Tsongas amendment, could not be verified.

● Development of a U.S. counterpart was necessary to induce Moscow to abandon ASAT.

Pressler Proposal

Meanwhile, Senate ASAT opponents had lowered their sights, figuring that the administration could stave off a flat ban on testing. By mid-May, they had revised an ASAT arms control resolution (S J Res 129), sponsored by Larry Pressler, R-S.D. The new version dropped the call for a test moratorium and exhorted the president to resume talks for "a ban or strict limitations" on ASAT testing and to seek a mutual ban on all space weapons.

Drafters intended the latter provision to amount to a Senate vote of no confidence in Reagan's plan for a space-based anti-missile defense. Accordingly, the administration opposed the resolution strongly, despite its non-binding character.

Though Tsongas was a cosponsor of the Pressler amendment, he also wanted to salvage as much as possible of his original amendment. Tsongas, too, abandoned the goal of a total ASAT ban, seeking instead to bar an ASAT target test only until the president certified a willingness to negotiate with the Russians "the strictest possible limitations" on ASATs.

On the assumption that both the Pressler and Tsongas language would be offered as amendments to the defense authorization bill, the Pressler measure also posed a tactical problem for Tsongas and his supporters.

They regarded theirs as the more serious limitation on the administration — it legally required some administration action before target tests could be carried out. They feared that if Pressler's non-binding amendment were voted on first, it might pass, co-opting their efforts.

Dickering and Compromise

John W. Warner, R-Va., became the interlocutor between the administration and the Tsongas group. Sam Nunn, D-Ga., was part Tsongas ally and part independent player in the bargaining with the administration. Nunn wanted to allow target testing so long as it was linked to serious efforts to limit future ASAT weapons.

When the Senate took up the ASAT issue June 12, Pressler beat Tsongas to the punch and offered the revised S J Res 129 as an amendment.

But before the debate got going in earnest, the Senate went into a two-and-a-half-hour-long secret session, at Warner's insistence, to receive a briefing on Soviet anti-satellite capabilities. When the Senate reopened its doors at about 4:30 p.m., both sides began a vigorous debate. But that was no more than the background to the negotiations among White House officials, Warner, Nunn and Tsongas.

Pressler then withdrew his amendment. Warner offered in its place a compromise, barring ASAT target tests until 30 days after the president had certified to Congress that he was trying to negotiate strict limitations on the weapon.

The presidential certification, parts of which could be secret, would have to describe the proposed limitations the president was prepared to negotiate. It also would have to include detailed recommendations to decrease the vulnerability of U.S. satellites to Soviet ASATs, something on which Nunn had been insistent.

But the deal came under harsh attack from conservatives led by Malcolm Wallop, R-Wyo., who denounced it as one more effort to "make people feel comfortable in this country" by holding out the hope of arms control agreements while forcing the administration to give ground toward Soviet negotiating positions.

Wallop proposed amending the compromise to say that nothing in the provision would prevent the president from acting "in the national security interest," but that was rejected 45-48. For the most part, the split was along ideological lines, with conservatives backing and liberals opposing Wallop. *(Vote 119, p. 23-S)*

Warner was one exception to the pattern, warning that Wallop's amendment would gut his compromise. Also, two liberal Democrats, both up for re-election in fairly conservative states, voted for Wallop: Max Baucus, Mont., and David Pryor, Ark.

The Senate then rejected a motion to table the Warner amendment, 29-65, and adopted the amendment by a vote of 61-28. *(Votes 120, 121, p. 23-S)*

Authorization Conference

Conferees on the defense bill, in their most concrete arms control provision, limited tests of the ASAT missile during fiscal 1985 to two "successful" tests against target satellites. The conferees defined a successful test as one in which both the missile engine and its guidance mechanism worked properly and the missile intercepted the target satellite. But they warned the Pentagon against trying to circumvent the two-test limit by aiming the ASAT to miss the target narrowly.

Target tests were not to begin until 15 days after the president notified Congress: that he was endeavoring to negotiate "the strictest possible" ASAT limitation agreement with Moscow, that the test was required for national security and would not gravely impair prospects for such negotiations, and that the test would be consistent with the 1972 treaty limiting anti-ballistic missile systems. *(1972 Almanac p. 589)*

The conferees agreed to the $144 million requested for ASAT development. The $84.5 million sought for ASAT procurement had been approved by both houses.

Appropriations Legislation

The authorization bill cleared Congress on Sept. 27. But the dickering over ASAT was far from over.

In late September and early October, Congress was wrestling with the massive continuing appropriations resolution (H J Res 648 — PL 98-473). Several anti-ASAT lobbyists credited Joseph P. Addabbo, D-N.Y., chairman of the House Appropriations Subcommittee on Defense, with extracting in the appropriations conference additional White House concessions beyond those in the authorization bill. *(Continuing appropriations, p. 444)*

Addabbo demanded a test moratorium on ASAT. However, one lobbyist said, the House aim was to limit the Pentagon to two tests, regardless of whether they succeeded.

The ASAT issue was one of the most contentious defense matters before the conference on the continuing resolution. When the wrangling was over, the ASAT opponents had won further concessions: tests of the weapon would be delayed until March 1, 1985, at the earliest, and no more than three target tests would be allowed during fiscal 1985.

As a practical matter, it was unclear whether the moratorium until March 1, 1985, would actually delay the ASAT test schedule, which was secret. ∎

$9.1 Billion Authorized for Military Construction

With a warning to NATO allies that they should pay more toward keeping U.S. troops in Europe, Congress voted to authorize $9.13 billion for military construction authorizations in fiscal 1985.

The warning was contained in the conference report on the military construction authorization bill (HR 5604 — PL 98-407), cleared by Congress Aug. 9.

The final version of the bill authorized $104 million less than had been approved by the House and $166 million less than the Senate had voted in their respective versions of the bill.

The House agreed to the conference report by voice vote on Aug. 8; the Senate followed suit the next day.

The $9.13 billion compared to the $7.35 billion authorized in fiscal 1984 (PL 98-115). *(1983 Almanac p. 193)*

President Reagan's original budget request for fiscal 1985 military construction in February was $10.5 billion, roughly $1.36 billion higher than the amount finally authorized. However, the construction request was trimmed to $8.5 billion in early May, when Reagan cut $13.9 billion from his defense budget as part of a deficit-reduction package.

In an omnibus continuing resolution (PL 98-473), Con-

gress appropriated $8.4 billion for military construction projects in fiscal 1985. *(Story, p. 444)*

House Action

Trying not to greatly constrain actual construction work, the House Armed Services Committee cut $1.2 billion from the Pentagon's $10.5 billion authorization request for military construction in fiscal 1985.

The panel approved its bill, HR 5604, May 8, and reported it (H Rept 98-765), on May 15. The bulk of the reductions, adding up to roughly $1 billion, came from what were essentially bookkeeping adjustments. "Free" budget cuts included:

● Across-the-board trims in the construction request for each service, totaling $387.3 million. According to the committee, the job-hungry construction industry provided a "favorable bidding climate," in which the Pentagon could anticipate lower-than-budgeted costs for many projects.

● Provision of only the first year's worth of funding for two new military hospitals. Technically, the panel recommended authorizing $338 million of the $353 million requested for a new hospital at Fort Lewis, Wash., and the entire $201.2 million requested for a hospital at Travis Air Force Base in California. But only a fraction of those totals was approved for appropriation in fiscal 1985: $11.2 million for Fort Lewis and $30 million for Travis.

● Approval of $250 million instead of the $296.7 million requested for the annual U.S. contribution to the North Atlantic Treaty Organization's common fund for building facilities. The committee said its authorization still would meet the U.S. obligation to the fund because of the dollar's strength against Western European currencies.

● Denial of $46 million for facilities on Johnston Island in the South Pacific that had been sought to "detoxify" obsolete chemical weapons stored there. Though funds would have to be appropriated for the project in 1984, the committee said, no new authorization was needed since the funds had been authorized in earlier years.

Those four items accounted for nearly two-thirds of $1.5 billion trimmed by the panel from the administration's military construction request. Additions totaling $253 million brought the net total amount authorized by HR 5604 to $9.3 billion.

The cutbacks were more than half again the $738 million by which the committee had planned to trim the construction request in the course of reducing Reagan's overall defense request by some $19.7 billion.

Facilities in Honduras

The House committee denied an administration request for $8.7 million to construct military facilities in Honduras. The panel complained that the administration had not yet supplied Congress with a comprehensive report on planned U.S. military construction in Central America, as was mandated by last year's defense construction appropriations act (PL 98-116). *(1983 Almanac p. 193)*

Military construction in Honduras, a neighbor country to strife-torn El Salvador and Nicaragua, came under close congressional scrutiny after an unprecedented number of U.S. servicemen participated in joint military exercises there. Critics charged that the administration was trying to circumvent Congress and establish a permanent presence in Honduras at a time when that country was seeking to build a democracy.

The House panel's action deleted $1.5 million the administration had requested for a forward munitions storage area at Palmerola, $4.3 million for a maintenance hangar and barracks there, and $2.9 million for a warehouse, ammunition storage area and fuel storage tank at San Lorenzo.

In all, the committee cut $1.23 billion from President Reagan's $10.5 billion construction request, exceeding its self-imposed goal of trimming $800 million from the combined requests for military construction and civil defense. The civil defense request, which was included in the main defense authorization bill (HR 5167) reported April 19, previously had been trimmed by $62.5 million to $190 million.

Cruise Missiles and NATO

The committee recommended ending the two-year delay in authorizing construction of facilities for U.S. dependents at bases in Europe for ground-launched cruise missiles (GLCMs).

At the same time, it recommended a $96.2 million reduction in Reagan's request for the GLCM facilities. In December 1983, NATO began deploying 464 of these small, drone jet planes and 108 Pershing II ballistic mis-

siles, both of which could strike Soviet territory from the launchers in Western Europe. The deployments aroused ferocious domestic opposition in several of the European countries that had agreed to accept the U.S. missiles.

Since U.S.-Soviet negotiations to ban these and other intermediate-range nuclear force (INF) missiles had begun in late 1981, Congress had insisted that construction at the cruise bases in Europe be held down, to minimize the loss in case the deployment was stopped at the bargaining table. Congress had denied any funds for family housing, schools or other dependents' facilities, telling the Air Force to assign personnel to short-term duty, without families, pending clarification of how permanent the bases would be.

The INF talks broke off in late 1983, when the Soviets walked out to protest the imminent deployment of the cruise and Pershing II missiles. In light of the stalled negotiations, the committee approved $94.8 million requested for dependent-related facilities at Greenham Common in the United Kingdom and Cosimo in Sicily.

In all, the panel approved $159 million of the $254 million requested for cruise facilities. They deferred for one year $52.2 million requested for dependents' facilities at the base under construction in Florennes, Belgium. They also approved only $35 million of the $79 million requested for cruise missile installations at Woensdrecht, the Netherlands, and provided that none of the funds could be spent until the Dutch Parliament ratified the deployment decision. The Dutch government announced June 1 that it would accept cruise missiles but not until 1988, two years later than the date set by NATO.

The panel denied $8.3 million requested for the Navy's air base at Sigonella, Sicily, insisting that NATO should pay for such facilities.

It approved $9.7 million for Army housing and recreational facilities in Greece. But, citing the Greeks' intention eventually to close U.S. bases in that country, the panel told the Navy to make do with existing communications facilities and denied $3.95 million requested to replace them.

Other Facilities

The committee also made the following reductions in the administration's military construction request:

● A $77 million reduction in the request for facilities in a secret location that would be used by the so-called Rapid Deployment Force, or Central Command. This was the umbrella-organization that would command U.S. forces sent to the Middle East or Indian Ocean regions. Of the reduction, $62 million was to await the unnamed country's formal agreement to the U.S. construction plan. The remaining $15.1 million was to build bomb-proof airplane hangars, which the committee opposed.

● A $142 million reduction for the Marine Corps' share of a two-dam water project at the huge Camp Pendleton training center. The committee wanted to await the House Interior Committee's approval of legislation regarding the $263 million water project.

The panel approved $26.9 million for Air Force projects in Oman, at the mouth of the Persian Gulf, but denied $15.1 million requested to build bombproof airplane shelters in that country.

Approved were facilities associated with several strategic weapons:

● $232 million for various projects at the Atlantic coast base for Trident missile submarines in Kings Bay, Ga.

● $96 million to "bed down" the first B-1 squadrons in

South Dakota and Texas.

● $44 million for construction at the prospective MX missile base near Cheyenne, Wyo.

● $16.5 million for facilities at Langley Air Force Base, Va., to handle the anti-satellite missile. *(ASAT story, p. 62)*

Floor Action

On June 22, the House passed the fiscal 1985 military construction bill, authorizing $9.2 billion for military construction projects in fiscal 1985. That was $1.2 billion less than the administration's request.

The bill was passed 312-49 after several amendments were adopted by voice vote. *(Vote 235, p. 74-H)*

The most noteworthy amendment dropped from the bill was $35 million earmarked for ground-launched cruise missile (GLCM) facilities in the Netherlands. Although deployment of the missiles had been controversial, the amendment was not. Supporters and opponents of GLCM deployment agreed that the cut simply reflected the Dutch government's deferral until late 1985 of a final decision on whether to let the missiles be fielded.

Senate Action

The Senate's military construction authorizations package was incorporated into that chamber's omnibus defense bill. The Senate Armed Services Committee reported its bill (S 2723) on May 31 (S Rept 98-500). This measure also included authorizations for weapons procurement, military research, operations and maintenance and the nuclear weapons programs conducted on behalf of the Pentagon by the Energy Department. *(Authorization bill, p. 48)*

Senate Armed Services approved $9.3 billion, for military construction projects. This was a little less than the amount by which the administration trimmed its construction budget request in May, as part of President Reagan's deal with Senate Republicans to lower the projected deficit.

Cuts Without Lost Construction

Compared with its House counterpart, the Senate panel made substantially larger cuts, which, according to the panel, merely reflected economic facts of life and would not affect planned construction. These included:

● $420 million that would not be needed since the committee expected contractors to submit lower-than-anticipated bids.

● $100.6 million to be replaced by funds "left over" from the fiscal 1984 construction appropriation because of low bids.

● $165 million (of the $296.7 million requested) for the U.S. contribution to NATO's Infrastructure fund, a kitty for building facilities of common benefit. The committee agreed with the administration's decision in May that this reduction could be made without effectively cutting the annual U.S. contribution because of the growing strength of the dollar against European currencies.

On the other hand, the Senate committee approved the entire amounts requested for two new military hospitals at Fort Lewis, Wash. ($353 million), and at Travis Air Force Base, 50 miles northeast of San Francisco ($201 million). Technically, the House panel also had authorized the two projects, but it had limited fiscal 1985 appropriations to only those amounts scheduled to be spent in that

year. This trimmed more than $500 million from the House committee's bill.

Honduras Military Facilities

The Senate committee approved by the narrowest possible margin $4.4 million for two facilities that would be used to store U.S. military equipment and ammunition in Honduras.

During the committee markup of S 2723, a motion by Jeff Bingaman, D-N.M., to delete these funds failed on a 9-9 tie vote. William S. Cohen, R-Maine, joined the eight committee Democrats in support of the Bingaman motion.

"These represent the first step toward committing American forces to combat in Central America," Bingaman warned in a statement appended to the committee report. "We may be sliding toward a commitment of U.S. ground forces in Honduras in the absence of adequate public debate." *(Honduras bases, p. 84)*

Floor Action

The Senate began debating its defense bill June 7 and approved it June 21. The administration averted a floor fight over the military bases in Honduras, by agreeing on June 8 to drop the $4.4 million it had requested for equipment and ammunition storage facilities there.

Bingaman had promised to renew his attempt to block the funds on the Senate floor, but Armed Services Committee Chairman John Tower, R-Texas, pre-empted that June 8 by offering his own amendment to drop the funds. The Tower amendment was agreed to by voice vote. According to Tower, the administration wanted to "consult on the need for the facilities in the overall context of our foreign policy for the region."

Alliance Burden-Sharing

The issue of allies' burden-sharing did play a part in the Senate debate, however. Widespread unhappiness with the allies was underscored on June 7 by a 91-3 vote approving an amendment by William Proxmire, D-Wis., dealing with the issue. *(Vote 114, p. 22-S)*

The non-binding amendment expressed the sense of Congress that the president should "insist" that:

● Major NATO members meet their earlier pledges to increase defense spending by at least 3 percent above the cost of inflation in 1984 and 1985.

● Japan "further increase its defense spending." Because of domestic anti-militarist political pressures since World War II, the Japanese government had held its defense budget to less than 1 percent of the gross national product (GNP). The U.S. defense budget absorbed nearly 7 percent of its GNP.

But by a vote of 76-16, the Senate rejected an amendment by Larry Pressler, R-S.D., that was intended to limit the rate of increased spending for U.S. forces in Europe to the rate at which NATO countries increased their defense budgets. *(Vote 115, p. 22-S)*

Nunn Amendment

On June 20, Sam Nunn, D-Ga., proposed an amendment that could have removed up to 90,000 of the 326,000 U.S. troops from Europe, if other NATO members did not carry out defense improvements.

The Nunn amendment was tabled (or killed) 55-41, after six hours of often spirited debate. But the vote seemed to obscure a solidifying agreement that the allies were systematically shirking and that something had to be done. *(Vote 149, p. 27-S)*

The amendment would have frozen the number of U.S. personnel in Europe at 326,000, the number requested for fiscal 1985. The allies could prevent reductions in that level, beginning in 1987, by meeting a 1978 alliance-wide pledge to boost defense spending annually in addition to the cost of inflation. Or, the allies could avoid troop withdrawals if they began in 1986 firm five-year programs to meet NATO goals involving ammunition stockpiles and maintenance facilities.

In each of the three years starting in 1987, the United States would lower its European troop ceiling by 30,000 unless either the 3 percent budget increase or the ammunition and facilities buildup had begun.

Nunn insisted that it was the broader question of military effectiveness — not mere equity — that drove him to offer the amendment.

Without the improvements, Nunn warned, NATO could not offer a serious non-nuclear defense against a Soviet conventional invasion. In that case, he reasoned, the alliance's conventional forces on the continent amounted to no more than a "tripwire," whose destruction would trigger nuclear retaliation against the Soviet Union.

As a practical matter, he told the Senate, the alliance would be capable of little else, without beefed-up ammunition stocks. Though the precise figures were secret, the United States had more than the 30 days' worth of ammunition agreed on as the alliance goal. The other six NATO countries with troops in central Europe averaged less than half the U.S. endurance level.

Tower led the charge against Nunn's amendment, arguing that U.S. deployments to NATO were simply good military sense: "We are not there just to defend the blue-eyed Europeans. It is axiomatic that, when confronted by a very, very powerful adversary . . . , you establish your defense perimeter as close to his shores as possible."

The administration carried the day because of tight party discipline and the concern of some senators that the timing was wrong for a hard-nosed approach to the allies.

Other than William V. Roth Jr., D-Del., who was Nunn's cosponsor, only three Republicans voted with Nunn on the amendment: Pressler; Charles E. Grassley, Iowa; and Gordon J. Humphrey, N.H.

Democrats voted with Nunn except for conservative Howell Heflin, Ala., and five liberals: Christopher J. Dodd, Conn.; Gary Hart, Colo.; George J. Mitchell, Maine; Daniel Patrick Moynihan, N.Y.; and Paul E. Tsongas, Mass. The liberals apparently agreed with Tower that the amendment would be counterproductive.

After killing the Nunn amendment, the Senate voted 94-3 for an amendment offered by William S. Cohen, R-Maine, that amounted to Nunn's amendment minus the threatened troop cuts. *(Vote 150, p. 27-S)*

Passage

The Senate passed S 2723, containing all defense-related authorizations, on June 21. The House passed its separate military construction bill, HR 5604, on June 22. Immediately upon passage of the House bill, the Senate was deemed to have passed its own version of HR 5604 "automatically."

Conference

The conference report on the bill (H Rept 98-962) was filed Aug. 7.

In the report, conferees warned that the refusal of European allies to pay a greater share of the cost of keeping U.S. forces in Europe was "becoming a major issue with the American people. Unless the allies are more forthcoming in their support for U.S. forces, there will be ever increasing pressure to bring U.S. forces home."

Burden-Sharing Complaints

The conferees singled out West Germany for special criticism. In the 1970s, the Bonn government had paid for several construction projects to support U.S. units. But now, the conferees complained, West Germany was refusing to pay for the so-called "master re-stationing plan." Under that plan, three battalions would be moved from their current billets to new facilities a hundred miles closer to the defensive positions along the East German border that U.S. forces would be expected to hold in case of war.

Congress had insisted for years that West Germany pay for the move. Not only would that country be better protected by the repositioned U.S. troops, the reasoning went, but it would profit from the commercial use of the valuable, urban property that the U.S. units currently occupied.

The repositioning plan was on the shelf because of the funding deadlock. Meanwhile, the conferees accused West Germany of similarly tight-fisted behavior on the issue of buying a former rug factory to be used as a headquarters for wartime U.S. supply operations in Europe. They "reluctantly" approved the $13.1 million the Army requested to buy the building. "If the project is turned down, U.S. forces will suffer," they explained.

Like the Senate, the conferees approved $131.7 million for the annual U.S. contribution to NATO's so-called Infrastructure fund, the alliance's kitty for jointly funded construction projects. The House had approved $250 million of the $296.7 million request. But the conferees agreed that the lower amount would meet the U.S. obligation because of the dollar's strength against European currencies.

Central America Facilities

The administration had abandoned its $4.4 million request for two facilities in Honduras to store gear and ammunition that could be used by U.S. troops. However, an added $4.3 million for Honduran facilities for a U.S. Army air reconnaissance unit, which the administration still wanted, had been authorized only by the Senate.

The conferees approved the $4.3 million without comment.

Budget Games

The conferees said they were "displeased" that the Strategic Air Command (SAC) was circumventing the normal budget process, and they told the secretary of the Air Force to put a stop to it.

According to the conferees, SAC, the part of the Air Force operating intercontinental-range nuclear bombers and missiles, was "the only major command of any of the services that, as a matter or routine, seeks to have projects added at the congressional level," that is, by direct appeals to members of Congress.

This undermined the way the Air Force set priorities among construction projects, the conferees said.

Museum Funds

Citing the budgetary restraints on the Pentagon, the Senate had turned down a request for $5.4 million, to be matched with private contributions, for expanding the Air Force museum in Dayton, Ohio. The House strongly supported the request.

The conferees authorized the funds with the proviso that each of the armed services could request federal funds for only one museum of the dozens on various bases around the country.

Shuffling Paper Shufflers

The conferees approved $16 million of the $19.76 million requested to renovate for Navy office use a building in the Washington, D.C., Navy Yard. But they said this did not imply approval of the Navy's long-simmering plan to move into the Navy Yard some 18,000 people in offices scattered around Washington, the vast bulk of them in nearby Virginia suburbs.

The proposal to concentrate Navy administrative offices in the yard had faced adamant opposition from members of the Virginia congressional delegation, including Senate Armed Services Committee member John W. Warner, R-Va. The conference report noted that the 900 people who would be accommodated by the Navy Yard project authorized in this bill currently worked in Washington, D.C., and one of its Maryland suburbs.

Located on the Anacostia River, a mile or so from its junction with the Potomac and only a mile southeast of the Capitol, the Navy Yard once built the Navy's cannons. However, many of the facility's huge industrial buildings long had been idle. ∎

Foreign Policy

President Reagan and his administration continued to use retreat as a strategy in dealing with Congress on foreign policy in 1984.

On matters ranging from the Middle East to Central America, the president backed down and claimed victories when faced with overwhelming opposition in Congress to his most controversial policies. A year of battling with Congress gained Reagan little; on only one issue, aid to El Salvador, did he end the year in measurably better political shape than at the beginning. But by sidestepping confrontations on Lebanon, Middle East arms sales and other issues, Reagan avoided outright defeats and gave himself running room for the future.

Reagan's record in dealing with the world at large was similar. Faced with election year pressures, he concentrated on the symbols of the presidency — a much-televised trip to China in April, a pre-election meeting with Soviet Foreign Minister Andrei A. Gromyko in September. And he tried to avoid hard choices on nuclear arms control, the Arab-Israeli dispute and other pressing matters.

The U.S. experience in Lebanon was perhaps the best example of Reagan's ability to escape lasting political damage from a foreign policy disaster. At the beginning of the year, Marines were hunkered down at the Beirut airport, Congress was demanding their withdrawal and Reagan was refusing to budge because of "vital" U.S. interests in Lebanon. But when the political pressure mounted to the point that Congress seemed likely to force his hand, the president moved swiftly in February to move the Marines out of Lebanon. He won praise for accepting reality; few blamed him for putting the Marines in an exposed position in the first place.

Reagan also maneuvered skillfully between various domestic factions that attempted to influence U.S. foreign policy. On the right, Jesse Helms, R-N.C., and other hardline conservatives continued to complain that Reagan was abandoning his principles by tilting toward China and away from Taiwan, by failing to press hard enough against leftists in Central America and by making election-year overtures to the Soviet Union. At the same time, many liberals in Congress charged that Reagan was forsaking U.S. leadership on human rights, was stalling on arms control negotiations and was relying too heavily on military might to resolve problems that were essentially diplomatic in nature.

These and other divisions were apparent within, as well as outside, the administration. Secretary of State George P. Shultz and Defense Secretary Caspar W. Weinberger at times seemed to be speaking for different administrations: Shultz advocating an activist approach to Third World conflicts and Weinberger counseling caution on the use of troops overseas.

As was the case in Lebanon, Congress stepped into the breach when it appeared that Reagan could not or would not resolve the conflicts within his own administration. By reducing military aid, Congress also set the tone for U.S. policy toward the Philippines, in a year when growing anti-government sentiment there posed a potential threat to important U.S. security interests.

In such cases, however, Reagan responded quickly and with mastery of public debate. Although he adopted positions he previously had opposed, he was widely perceived as leading, rather than following.

Central America

For the third year in a row, Central America was the focal point of foreign policy dissension between Reagan and Congress. But for the first time in that troubled relationship, Reagan and his congressional critics each scored political victories that reduced the need for compromise.

Successful presidential elections in El Salvador guaranteed, at least for the time being, that Congress would readily accept Reagan's requests for military and economic aid to that government, which was fighting leftist guerrillas. And Democrats in Congress prevailed decisively over the president on the issue of aiding anti-government rebels in Nicaragua.

As in previous years, there was a considerable amount of confusion about the short-range tactics and long-range goals of administration policy in Central America.

From Reagan on down, administration officials professed to be pursuing peaceful solutions to the region's problems, particularly the civil wars in El Salvador and Nicaragua. But by supporting guerrillas battling the leftist Nicaraguan regime and by conducting unprecedented military exercises in the region, the United States appeared to be relying more on armed force than on diplomacy and persuasion.

The Reagan administration claimed to be an active supporter of the so-called "Contadora process," in which Colombia, Mexico, Panama and Venezuela were attempting to draft treaties ending Central America's wars. But when the Contadora countries — so named after a Panamanian island where their leaders first met — produced a draft treaty in October, the United States rejected it as too favorable to Nicaragua.

To a certain extent, confusion served the administration's purposes as far as Nicaragua was concerned. The supposedly "covert" aid for the anti-government guerrillas, called "contras," put enormous pressure on Nicaragua's Sandinista regime at little diplomatic and financial cost to the United States. Meantime, offers of negotiation were intended to undercut criticism that Washington was determined to drive the Sandinista leaders from Managua.

Although it may have been successful in frightening and bewildering the Nicaraguans, the ambiguity in administration policy created severe political problems on Capitol Hill. Democrats in both chambers declared that Reagan was conducting an undeclared, illegal war against a sitting government with which the United States had diplomatic relations. And even some Republicans said that aiding the contras was strengthening, rather than weakening, the Sandinistas by raising the spectre of "Yankee imperialism."

Reagan made two attempts to get Congress to appropriate additional funds for the contras, once the $24 million that had been voted in November 1983 ran out. House Democrats, by refusing to compromise on the issue, blocked both moves, giving Reagan the most serious foreign policy defeat he suffered on Capitol Hill during his first term.

The president tried first to win approval for an extra $21 million for the contras in fiscal 1984. But that failed when House Democrats held firm and the Senate, to free up unrelated funds for summer youth job programs, dumped the contra money from a supplemental spending bill.

Reagan sought another $28 million for the contras in his regular fiscal 1985 budget. Again, the House refused to budge, and the result was a one-sided compromise under which Congress approved $14 million under such stringent conditions that the money was likely never to be spent.

Even as dissension increased over the issue of Nicaragua, the long and contentious debate over U.S. involvement in El Salvador came to a close in 1984 because of the presidential election in that troubled country.

Throughout three years of political battles with Congress, Reagan and most of his aides had insisted that the U.S. goal in El Salvador was to provide a "shield" against the leftist insurgency there so that moderate leaders could build a democratic government. If the guerrillas could be held off long enough, according to this theory, government could consolidate its power and demonstrate to the people that democracy promised a better future than leftist revolution.

Critics, citing the rhetoric of some officials such as Fred C. Ikle, the under secretary of defense for policy, said the administration's real goal was the outright defeat of the Salvadoran guerrillas. The proper goal of the United States, the critics said, should be to encourage the Salvadoran government and the guerrillas to negotiate a settlement that would end the war and reduce the influence of the country's military and far right.

Reagan's policy gained a major success in May, when El Salvador's longtime centrist leader José Napoleón Duarte was elected president over rightist Roberto d'Aubuisson. In two trips to Capitol Hill shortly after his May 6 election, Duarte was treated like a conquering hero. He won praise, and congressional commitments for support of his government, with his promises to end human rights abuses, control the military and investigate right-wing death squads.

In the weeks and months after Duarte's election, Congress approved nearly all of Reagan's requests for military and economic aid to El Salvador — without the tough human rights conditions attached to aid in 1981 to 1983.

El Salvador's cause in Congress also was enhanced by the conviction, in May, of five former Salvadoran national guardsmen on charges of murdering four U.S. churchwomen in December 1980. The murder, and the Salvadoran government's subsequent attempt to cover up military involvement in it, had been a major cause of concern in the United States about human rights abuses in El Salvador. Congress had made the case a key test of U.S. policy by

withholding nearly $20 million in military aid to the government until a verdict was reached.

Along with aid to the Nicaraguan rebels and to the Salvadoran government, the third leg of Reagan's policy in Central America was massive build-up of U.S. military involvement, particularly in Honduras.

Beginning in 1983, the United States conducted a series of land and naval exercises that clearly were intended to intimidate Nicaragua and to demonstrate the U.S. commitment to El Salvador and Honduras. One offshoot of the exercises was the construction or expansion of more than a dozen military facilities in Honduras, including several that allegedly were used as bases for the Nicaraguan guerrillas and others that were used for U.S. intelligence-gathering missions. Throughout 1984, the United States had at least 1,000 military personnel in Honduras, a country that was at peace and faced no serious internal insurgency.

Kissinger Commission

In a gamble to quash the debate over Central America, Reagan created a bipartisan presidential commission in 1983 to recommend solutions. But Congress never approved enough of the panel's recommendations to give Reagan the broad political endorsement he sought for his policies.

Headed by former Secretary of State Henry A. Kissinger, the commission concluded in January 1984 that there was a crisis in Central America and that the United States had to "act to meet it, and act boldly."

The panel's prescriptions roughly conformed to those Reagan had been urging on Congress: substantial military support for El Salvador and hefty doses of long-term development and economic aid for all countries in the region. The commission also gave an indirect endorsement to Reagan's supposedly "covert" aid to anti-government guerrillas in Nicaragua.

But the commission's report failed to produce the consensus that Reagan sought for his policies. In large part that was because the commission reflected many of the uncertainties and disagreements about Central America that were running deep in Congress and the American public.

In footnoted dissents that garnered as much attention as the basic text of the report, two commission Democrats objected to aiding the Nicaraguan guerrillas and Kissinger dissented against the commission's recommendations for stiff human rights conditions on aid to El Salvador.

The administration also diluted the impact of the commission's report in February when it proposed legislation to implement nearly all the recommendations — with human rights conditions on El Salvador and the establishment of a new regional aid agency being the major exceptions. That led two key Democratic commissioners, AFL-CIO President Lane Kirkland and former Democratic National Committee Chairman Robert Strauss, to play down their support for the commission recommendations. In turn, Democrats in Congress viewed the commission report, and the implementing legislation, as cosmetics for the Reagan policies they opposed.

Nevertheless, the House adopted the bulk of the commission proposals on May 10, when it passed a foreign aid authorizations bill for fiscal 1985. Although a major victory for Reagan, that action resulted more from optimism generated by Duarte's election as president of El Salvador than from the White House lobbying campaign.

The Kissinger legislation received less charitable treatment in the Republican-controlled Senate. The Foreign Relations Committee deadlocked on Central American issues because one Republican, Helms, refused to endorse commission recommendations, on land reform and other issues, that he viewed as "socialistic."

In its continuing appropriations resolution for fiscal 1985, Congress ultimately adopted only a skeleton of the Kissinger commission recommendations for increased aid to Central America.

Middle East

For all practical purposes, the United States in 1984 withdrew temporarily as a major actor on the Middle East stage. First, by pulling U.S. Marines from their "peacekeeping" duties in Lebanon, and then by reneging on proposed arms sales to Jordan and Saudi Arabia, Reagan reduced the active U.S. presence that had been an important feature of Middle East politics for a dozen years. Without U.S. involvement, whatever slim chance there had been for peace negotiations disappeared.

The retreat from Lebanon was one of the worst foreign policy defeats the United States had suffered in the post World War II era. It diminished immeasurably U.S. prestige in the Middle East, guaranteed that ethnic and religious factions would continue to brutalize Lebanon, and enabled Syria to boast that it had prevailed over the United States.

But by February 1984, Reagan had no alternative, politically, but to withdraw the Marines. More than 260 U.S. military and diplomatic personnel had been killed in terrorist attacks since 1983, and some 1,200 Marines were holed up in bunkers at the Beirut airport, their mission of keeping the peace and bolstering the government of Amin Gemayel an obvious failure. At home, the House was readying to pass a resolution calling for the "prompt and orderly withdrawal" of the Marines, and Reagan was by no means certain that he could head off a similar resolution in the Senate.

On Feb. 7, after Moslem militiamen stormed West Beirut, Reagan announced that the Marines would be "redeployed" to offshore ships. Within a few months, all but a handful of the Marines had vanished and Beirut was once again in the hands of competing paramilitary groups and the Lebanese government was under the effective control of Syria.

Reagan's withdrawal of the proposed arms sales to Jordan and Saudi Arabia was a much less spectacular reversal of policy. But it demonstrated that the president was willing to subordinate his overall goals to the political needs of the moment.

The administration had planned to sell both Jordan and Saudi Arabia a portable anti-aircraft missile called the Stinger. But Israel and its allies in Congress opposed the sales, arguing that the hand-held weapons could fall into the hands of terrorists, thus jeopardizing all air traffic in the Middle East if not the entire world.

After exerting little effort to overcome the opposition, Reagan in March withdrew the sale offer. It was the first time in the 16-year history of direct congressional involvement in arms sales that a president had withdrawn an arms sales proposal without stating that he would resubmit it to Congress at a future date.

An aggravating factor in Reagan's decision was a bitter attack on the United States made by King Hussein of Jordan in an interview with *The New York Times*. The United States could no longer serve as mediator between Israel and its Arab neighbors, Hussein said, because "you obviously have made your choice, and your choice is Israel. Therefore, there is no hope of achieving anything."

Reagan in May sold Saudi Arabia 400 Stinger missiles, using his emergency power to avoid a review by Congress. He said the Saudis needed the missiles to defend their oilfields against attacks by Iran, which was angered by Saudi support for Iraq in the bloody Iran-Iraq war that had been raging since 1980.

The Saudi sale was only the second time, since arms sales laws were enacted in 1968, that a president had used his emergency power to bypass Congress on a major sale. President Carter first used that power in 1979.

At the end of 1984, the administration was weighing another aspect of its choice of Israel as main ally in the Middle East. Suffering its worst economic crisis in history, Israel turned to the United States for massive infusions of emergency aid. Reagan agreed to a substantial boost in military aid, but on the advice of Shultz postponed a decision on increased economic aid until Israel's fragile coalition government agreed on, and began to implement, austerity measures to ease inflation and reduce government spending.

A Breakdown in Congress

The Reagan administration continued to take advantage of Congress' chronic inability to handle its foreign policy oversight chores through established procedures. The administration got much of the foreign aid it wanted, and headed off several moves to torpedo key policies, because Congress could not resolve its internal squabbles.

For the third consecutive year, Congress failed to pass regular bills authorizing and appropriating foreign aid funds. Instead, foreign aid was tucked into a continuing appropriations resolution along with several other government programs — thus reducing the visibility of the always-controversial aid issues and undercutting administration critics on several foreign policy committees.

The most important breakdown in the congressional procedure was the Senate's failure to take up the annual bill to authorize foreign aid programs. The authorizations bill was an important piece of legislation each year because Congress used it to put its imprint on foreign policy. In 1981, for example, Congress used a foreign aid authorizations bill (PL 97-113) to impose human rights conditions on aid to El Salvador.

The House passed its version of the authorizations bill (HR 5119) in May after the administration won a bruising fight over aid to El Salvador. But in the Senate, the badly divided Foreign Relations Committee deadlocked over Central America aid issues and was forced to report a bill without any provisions on aid to that region. The committee's truncated bill included another provision restricting military aid to Turkey that was strongly opposed by the administration. After several months of indecision, Senate leaders decided in August to kill the bill by not allowing it to reach the floor.

The House and Senate Appropriations committees made no serious effort to get floor action on separate foreign aid spending bills. From the beginning of the year, leaders of those committees assumed that the foreign aid bills they produced would be included in an omnibus continuing resolution.

Three of the four foreign policy committees underwent leadership changes during the year.

In January, Rep. Dante B. Fascell, D-Fla., was elected

to chair the House Foreign Affairs Committee, succeeding Clement J. Zablocki, D-Wis. (1949-1983), who died in December 1983. One of the most skillful legislators in the House, Fascell gave the committee new energy and was largely responsible for the House passage of the foreign aid authorizations bill.

The November elections opened up the chairmanships of two other committees. The defeat of Sen. Charles H. Percy, R-Ill., left open the chair of the Foreign Relations Committee, which was taken by Richard G. Lugar, R-Ind. And the defeat of Rep. Clarence D. Long, D-Md., opened the chairmanship of the House Appropriations Subcommittee on Foreign Operations. David R. Obey, D-Wis., took over that panel.

The House and Senate Intelligence committees also underwent major changes at the end of the year because both chambers enforced previously ignored rules that limited the number of years members could serve. Because of expired terms and retirements, the Senate committee lost nine of its 15 members, including Chairman Barry Goldwater, R-Ariz., and Vice Chairman Daniel Patrick Moynihan, D-N.Y., and the House committee lost seven of its 15 members, including Chairman Edward P. Boland, D-Mass., and ranking Republican J. Kenneth Robinson, R-Va.

New leaders of the Senate committee were Chairman Dave Durenberger, R-Minn., and Vice Chairman Patrick J. Leahy, D-Vt. The House committee was taken over by Chairman Lee H. Hamilton, D-Ind., and Bob Stump, R-Ariz.

The Intelligence committees, which had labored in relative obscurity during most of the years after their founding in the mid-1970s, were thrust into the limelight in 1983 and 1984 during the debates on the CIA's aid to Nicaraguan contras.

The Democratic-controlled House committee took the lead in opposing aid to the rebels, while the Republican-controlled Senate panel was a major source of congressional support for the administration position.

The Nicaraguan controversy demonstrated to the two committees that the CIA had shirked its legal responsibility to keep them "fully and currently informed" about covert operations. The most graphic example was the agency's failure to tell the Senate committee in advance about U.S. involvement in the mining of three Nicaraguan harbors. When several foreign ships were damaged by the mines, and word leaked out in April that the CIA was responsible, Goldwater exploded in anger and sent agency director William J. Casey a pithy letter saying "this is no way to run a railroad."

After months of negotiations, Casey and Senate committee leaders on June 6, 1984, signed an agreement governing how the CIA would report in the future on covert operations. The text of the agreement was not made public, but the committee later described its general thrust.

The heart of the agreement, according to the committee, was that the CIA would inform the committee about all activities "planned to be undertaken as part of ongoing covert action programs." Previously, the agency had interpreted a 1980 reporting law as requiring it to notify the committee only of overall covert operations, such as aiding the contras, and not of specific activities within those operations, such as helping the contras to mine harbors.

The House committee sent Casey a letter listing the kinds of activities, such as the mining, about which it wanted advance notice. Casey responded that he preferred the procedure outlined in his agreement with the Senate committee, an aide said.

Foreign Aid

Congress and the Reagan administration in 1984 completed a four-year-long expansion of foreign aid spending that resulted in a substantially increased U.S. commitment to friendly countries around the world.

In 1981, the last fiscal year over which President Carter had primary control, the United States spent $9.4 billion on foreign economic, military and development aid. By 1985, Reagan's fourth budget year, the total had risen by 79 percent to $16.7 billion.

The bulk of the increased spending was for military aid and for assistance geared to bolstering the economies of countries with close political ties to the United States. There were smaller increases in programs designed to advance development and combat poverty in the Third World — but much of those increases were tied more to political than humanitarian purposes.

The biggest increases in foreign aid went to friendly countries in Central America (especially El Salvador) and the Middle East (especially Israel). But pro-U.S. countries throughout the world benefited from the loosening of foreign aid purse strings.

There were several reasons for Congress' newfound willingness to appropriate huge sums for foreign aid:

● The fact that Reagan requested the increases made it easier for conservatives, many of whom previously had opposed foreign aid, to go along.

● Reagan successfully emphasized the "national security" aspects of foreign aid, noting that much of the money went to countries facing real or potential threats from the Soviet Union and its allies.

● Ironically, the collapse of the regular foreign aid authorizations and appropriations processes meant that foreign aid was hidden in omnibus spending bills and thus was given some protection against attacks on the House and Senate floors. For example, governmentwide appropriations bills were used in 1981 and 1984 to disguise new longterm, multibillion-dollar commitments to the International Development Association, the controversial arm of the World Bank that made loans to the world's poorest countries.

—By John Felton

Congress Gives Reagan Aid for El Salvador

After three years of bitter debate between Congress and President Reagan over U.S. policy toward El Salvador, the Central American country faded as a major political issue in 1984. Congress gave the president almost all the additional military aid he requested for fiscal 1984 to help the Salvadoran government battle leftist guerrillas and continued the aid into fiscal 1985.

The changed attitude in Congress resulted largely from the election in May of a moderate, José Napoleón Duarte, as president of El Salvador in a U.S.-backed election that was boycotted by leftist politicians and their guerrilla allies. Duarte was viewed as a centrist figure who would try to negotiate with the guerrillas for an end to the four-year-old civil war and would try to move the country toward greater democratization and respect for human rights.

Within weeks of his election, Duarte visited Capitol Hill and made more progress in winning congressional support for increased aid for his country than the Reagan administration had been able to accomplish in more than three years. His direct, low-key appeal for aid in May and July meetings with congressional leaders helped ensure the passage of $132 million in additional military aid for fiscal 1984 over the $64.8 million approved by Congress in November 1983. By the end of the year, Congress had given El Salvador for fiscal 1984 more than twice the military aid approved for fiscal 1983. Congress also gave the president most of the military aid he requested for El Salvador in fiscal 1985. *(1983 Almanac p. 154)*

The favorable response in Congress to Duarte's election broke a political stalemate which had developed between Congress and the Reagan administration over El Salvador.

Critics of administration policy, mostly House Democrats, had argued that increased military aid merely bolstered Salvadoran right-wing extremists in the military and security police; such extremists have been suspected in the deaths of thousands of civilians and in other human rights abuses. Over Reagan administration objections, Congress since 1981 had treated human rights as a priority issue for Central America.

Congress used its control over the foreign aid budget to impose conditions on the distribution of aid, particularly to El Salvador. The conditions were intended to force progress by the Salvadoran government to end human rights abuses. The president requested increased military aid with no conditions attached.

At the beginning of the year, it appeared as if the political debate over El Salvador was going to continue as Reagan sought increased fiscal 1984 military aid for the Central American country, in "urgent" supplemental appropriations legislation and as part of an $8 billion, five-year program of aid for Central America. Reagan requested an additional $188.7 million for fiscal 1984 and $132.5 million for fiscal 1985.

The Republican-dominated Senate approved an additional $61.75 million on April 5, as part of a $1.15 billion supplemental appropriation (H J Res 492). *(Supplemental bill, p. 429)*

But House members on both the Foreign Affairs and Appropriations committees tried to resist further aid in fiscal 1984 until the presidential election was held in El Salvador. After the election runoff on May 6, the House acted favorably on the extra $61.75 million for fiscal 1984. By fall, an additional $70 million for fiscal 1984 also had been approved by Congress. *(Story, p. 439)*

Although Congress was unable to pass a foreign aid authorization bill for the third year in a row, both houses incorporated most of the funds Reagan requested for El Salvador for fiscal 1985 in a continuing appropriations resolution (PL 98-473) which cleared just before the adjournment of the 98th Congress in October. *(Story, p. 444)*

The funds were granted because El Salvador's new president, Duarte, promised members of Congress that he would respect human rights, control the military and carry out other changes demanded by Congress since 1981. Some Democrats, led by House Majority Leader Jim Wright, D-Texas, said Congress should support Duarte by giving him all the aid he said he needed. Withholding aid, they said, would weaken Duarte's bargaining power with the military, long the dominant force in El Salvador.

Rep. Michael D. Barnes, D-Md., chairman of the House Foreign Affairs Subcommittee on Western Hemisphere Affairs and a long-time critic of administration policies in El Salvador, said of Duarte's election, "We'll be a lot more receptive to requests from Napoleón Duarte than from a military dictatorship."

Conditions

Congress continued to insist, however, that the distribution of authorized military aid be conditioned on progress in El Salvador on human rights issues and land reform. One of the most controversial issues between the administration and its Democratic congressional critics had been a certification process that had governed El Salvador's aid in 1982 and 1983. The certification law (PL 97-113) banned military aid to El Salvador unless the president certified every 180 days that the Salvadoran government was trying to end human rights abuses and moving ahead on land reform and free elections. *(1981 Almanac p. 182)*

PL 97-113 expired on Sept. 30, 1983, and Reagan later vetoed a bill (HR 4042) that would have reinstated it for fiscal 1984. But in an effort to win further military aid for fiscal 1984, Reagan moved to meet liberals part way by offering to impose human rights conditions on the military aid, as long as there was no threat of a cutoff of aid.

Congress attached a new certification requirement, however, to the "urgent" supplemental appropriation bill, which included a portion of the increased military aid the president sought for fiscal 1984. Complying with that law, the State Department issued a report on July 12. For the first time in two years, the Reagan administration and its most persistent critics agreed that the government of El Salvador had made significant progress in curtailing killings of civilians by so-called "death squads."

Aid Highlights

In February 1983, Reagan requested $86.3 million in military aid for El Salvador in fiscal 1984. A supplemental request for $178.7 million in military aid was submitted in February 1984 as part of a broader Central American aid package, bringing the military aid request for fiscal 1984 to $265 million.

Congress approved a total of $196.5 million for fiscal 1984 in three steps: $64.8 million in a continuing appropriations resolution (PL 98-151) cleared in November 1983; $61.75 million in an urgent supplemental bill (PL 98-332), cleared on June 26; and $70 million in the final supplemental (PL 98-396), cleared on Aug. 10. *(Box, p. 76)*

Of the $61.75 million in the urgent supplemental, $32 million was used to pay back the Pentagon for equipment and supplies that Reagan had shipped to El Salvador on an emergency basis in April. Reagan had used a special authority allowing him to waive for up to 120 days a requirement that foreign countries pay cash for military supplies from the United States.

The total of $196.5 million in military aid included $18.5 million in Foreign Military Sales (FMS) loan guarantees; $176.5 million in Military Assistance Program (MAP) grants and $1.5 million in International Military Education and Training (IMET) aid.

For fiscal 1984 economic aid, Congress approved $120 million in PL 98-151 and $90 million in PL 98-396, matching Reagan's full request. Congress also approved $71.3 million in development aid, of which $30 million was in the supplemental. *(Previous aid, 1983 Almanac p. 124)*

For fiscal 1985, Reagan requested $132.5 million in military aid. Congress provided $128.25 million in the continuing appropriations resolution (PL 98-473) which cleared Congress on Oct. 11. Of the total, $111.75 million was in MAP grants, $15 million was in FMS low-interest loans, and $1.5 million was for military training. The continuing resolution also included $195 million in Economic Support Fund aid, a slight cut from the Reagan request of $210 million.

1984 Requests

Neither house in the first session of the 98th Congress acted on a regular foreign aid appropriations bill for fiscal 1984. Foreign aid recommendations by the House and Senate Appropriations committees were incorporated in the fiscal 1984 omnibus continuing appropriations resolution covering departments and agencies whose regular funding bills never cleared Congress. The bill included $64.8 million in military aid for El Salvador.

PL 98-151 gave the administration the discretion to determine how much would be in grants and how much would be in the form of loans.

Of the total amount approved by Congress, 30 percent was withheld until Salvadoran authorities substantially concluded their investigation into the cases of five former national guardsmen accused of murdering four U.S. churchwomen in December 1980, brought the accused to trial and obtained a verdict. *(Box, p. 80)*

The continuing resolution also withheld 10 percent of the total amount until the president certified to Congress that the Salvadoran regime had not taken any actions that would "modify, alter, suspend or terminate" the two major portions of the land reform program in a manner that would be detrimental to the rights of those who intended to benefit from the program. The president also was required to certify that the Salvadoran government "continues to make documented progress" in the land reform program.

However, the two withholdings combined were not to exceed 30 percent of the aid.

The continuing resolution allowed the administration to provide economic aid for El Salvador at the requested levels: $120 million in economic aid and $38 million in development assistance.

The bill earmarked $3 million of the economic aid for helping the Salvadoran government improve its judicial system.

State Department Report

The Reagan administration began its efforts in 1984 for increased military aid for El Salvador by launching a vigorous campaign to convince Congress that it was serious about forcing the Salvadoran government to end human rights abuses. The first step was a report issued by the State Department on Jan. 16 acknowledging that "continued abuse of human rights remains a central problem" in El Salvador, particularly a resurgence in killings in 1983 by "death squads." But the report said specific measures had been taken under U.S. pressure "to control the death squads and to exert stricter discipline over members of the armed forces."

The State Department's findings also covered a broader range of political and security issues than did the four reports issued in 1982 and 1983. A senior State Department official said that the United States and El Salvador had reached a "tacit understanding" that involved the crackdown by the Salvadoran government and "our taking a second look at the levels of assistance" the government needed to fight leftist guerrillas. The official said the report was part of an effort "to demonstrate conclusively that it was the administration, not simply Congress, that had an interest in human rights in El Salvador."

The report also said that extra money was needed for training and for weapons in 1984 for an expanded and improved Salvadoran army. Plans called for adding about 6,500 men to the 26,000-man army. To get the extra money, officials said, Reagan was willing to accept limited conditions requiring El Salvador to improve its human rights record — as long as the conditions did not threaten an eventual cutoff of aid.

Kissinger Commission Findings

The report had followed by a few days the release of the findings of the National Bipartisan Commission on Central America, chaired by former Secretary of State Henry A. Kissinger. In a Jan. 11 report to the president, the commission recommended that the United States give El Salvador "significantly increased levels of military aid as quickly as possible." *(Kissinger commission, p. 93)*

Embracing most of the commission's recommendations, the president on Feb. 3 unveiled his $8 billion, five-year aid package for Central America. The proposal included the following amounts for El Salvador for 1984: military, $178.7 million; economic, $90 million, and development, $44 million. For fiscal 1985, the requests were: military, $132.5 million; economic, $210 million and development, $131.1 million.

Reagan also accepted the commission recommendation that military assistance to El Salvador be linked to improvements in human rights conditions. However, Reagan rejected conditions that would give Congress a role in deciding whether El Salvador merited the aid. "We believe the administration is in the best position to control the spigot," a senior administration official told reporters. Reagan's proposal required that he report to Congress twice each year on the human rights situation in El Salvador.

Administration Arguments

Secretary of State George P. Shultz told the Senate Foreign Relations Committee on Feb. 23 that the Salvadoran government had been taking steps, such as cracking down on right-wing "death squads" in response to U.S. administration pressure, not because of any threat that the aid would be stopped. But administration officials made little headway in persuading some committee members that El Salvador's government and military would not continue to resist fundamental changes and would respond only when faced with a cutoff of aid.

The administration also had trouble convincing many members that El Salvador needed nearly a fivefold increase in military aid for fiscal 1984 and 1985. Shultz and Defense Secretary Caspar W. Weinberger said the aid was needed to break the stalemate in the war between the Salvadoran government and the leftist guerrillas.

They also blamed Congress for failing in the past to approve enough military aid for El Salvador. Because of the "stop-and-start" pattern of congressional funding, Weinberger told the House Foreign Affairs panel Feb. 9, the Salvadoran army "cannot plan effectively, must hoard scarce ammunition and is forced to engage in selected operations as ways of conserving limited and uncertain supplies."

During February there were reports that Reagan planned to use emergency powers to provide some of the aid he was seeking for El Salvador without approval of Congress. Members were outraged, but Shultz told the House Appropriations Foreign Operations Subcommittee on March 6: "One way or another, we're going to provide the resources that are needed."

The State Department decided not to use emergency powers and instead, to seek the money from the Senate Appropriations Committee, which had approved all of Reagan's previous requests for aid.

'URGENT' SUPPLEMENTAL APPROPRIATIONS

The administration said it needed more money for El Salvador because Congress had cut Reagan's request for fiscal 1984 and blocked the expenditure of some money that it did approve. Of Reagan's original $86.3 million request, Congress had approved $64.8 million and also banned the administration from spending 30 percent of the approved amount — $19.4 million — until the Salvadoran government obtained a verdict in the case of the former national guardsmen accused of murdering four U.S. churchwomen in 1980.

Administration officials contended that Congress intended the $64.8 million to cover only part of fiscal 1984, in the expectation that Reagan would ask for more. But Clarence D. Long, D-Md., who as chairman of the House Appropriations Subcommittee on Foreign Operations helped set the $64.8 million figure, said that the amount "was supposed to last the whole year."

Although the president sought $178.7 million in extra military aid funds for fiscal 1984, he said El Salvador urgently needed at least $92.75 million just to keep its army going at existing levels of operation for the coming months. However, Defense Department documents provided to the Senate Armed Services Committee by the Pentagon indicated that little more than half the amount — about $50 million — was needed for ammunition, weapons and other supplies to sustain the Salvadoran army through fiscal 1984.

The president also said that El Salvador needed emergency military supplies to thwart guerrilla attacks on the March 25 presidential election. Congressional critics noted that none of the supplies covered by this additional aid were likely to reach El Salvador before the election.

Administration Strategy

The administration plan was to get the Senate Appropriations Committee to add the $92.7 million for El Salvador to a House-passed supplemental appropriations bill (H J Res 492) that would provide $150 million in emergency food aid to Africa. The move was coupled with an attempt to add $21 million for the rebels ("contras") fighting the leftist Nicaraguan government to a bill (H J Res 493) providing $200 million for low-income energy assistance in the United States. *(Nicaragua aid, p. 86)*

The administration reasoned that both H J Res 492 and H J Res 493 were "must" legislation which the House could not afford to risk in a confrontation with the administration. But the ploy failed when the amendment to add the Nicaraguan aid to H J Res 493 failed by a one-vote margin. Stunned by the defeat, administration backers withheld action on the request for El Salvador until administration officials could bring more pressure to bear on the committee.

Senate Committee Action

On March 14, the committee approved the funds for El Salvador by a voice vote after rejecting, 13-16, an effort to delay action. The committee also included a requirement that the aid be contingent on reports from the president that human rights concerns were being met.

Bob Kasten, R-Wis., offered the amendment containing the administration request, saying it was necessary to ensure that the March 25 election in El Salvador proceeded peacefully. "Without the funds," Kasten said, "the armed forces will collapse."

But Daniel K. Inouye, D-Hawaii, said the administration failed to provide documents justifying the urgency of the aid and offered a motion to defer action until the administration proved it was crucial.

Inouye argued that Congress should wait to see who won the Salvadoran election. One presidential candidate, Roberto d'Aubuisson, had been linked to the right-wing "death squads," which had been accused of killing thousands of civilians. "We have no knowledge about who will use the funds," Inouye said. "It is of some consequence."

He offered an amendment to defer action on the money for El Salvador. Although three Republicans — Appropriations Committee Chairman Mark O. Hatfield, R-Ore., Mark Andrews, R-N.D., and Lowell P. Weicker Jr., R-Conn. — voted in favor of the amendment with most of the committee Democrats, the Inouye amendment failed 13-16.

Kasten's proposal to add the $92.7 million for El Salvador to H J Res 492 also included a requirement that the administration certify to Congress that El Salvador had made progress toward free elections, freedom of association, the establishment of a rule of law and an effective judicial system, termination of killings by death squads and prosecution of those guilty of crimes.

At the suggestion of Dennis DeConcini, D-Ariz., Kasten modified his proposal to require a certification every 60 days, instead of requiring only one certification.

Arlen Specter, R-Pa., called for a stiffer plan requiring El Salvador to establish a special investigative prosecuting unit to expedite bringing alleged death squad members to justice. Fifty percent of the aid would be withheld until the Reagan administration certified, 60 days after the establishment of the prosecuting unit, that the unit was working.

But that might violate the Salvadoran constitution,

El Salvador Aid: A Record of Approval . . .

Aid to El Salvador was one of the most controversial issues on Capitol Hill since President Reagan took office in 1981. Following is a summary of congressional action on Salvadoran assistance.

Fiscal 1981

Congress approved $5.5 million in military aid in fiscal 1981, and Presidents Carter and Reagan used their emergency powers to provide another $30 million, for a total of $35.5 million.

The $5.5 million formally approved by Congress was included in a continuing resolution (PL 96-536) for 1981, cleared in December 1980.

Of the $30 million in aid provided under emergency powers, Carter gave $5 million on Jan. 17, 1981, three days before leaving office; he used his authority to "draw down" Defense Department money to send foreign military aid without congressional approval. Reagan provided $20 million on March 2, 1981, using the drawdown authority. Reagan sent another $5 million later in March with the approval of the House and Senate Appropriations committees.

Congress also approved $44.9 million in economic aid, and $91.1 million in development, food, housing and other aid. *(1981 Almanac p. 184)*

Fiscal 1982

Congress approved $27 million in military aid, and Reagan provided another $55 million under his Defense drawdown authority, for a total of $82 million.

The $27 million was included in a foreign aid appropriations bill (PL 97-121), cleared in December 1981. Congress had not passed a regular aid spending bill since then, in large part because of disputes about aid to El Salvador.

Reagan sent the $55 million in January 1982 in response to a guerrilla attack on a military airport outside San Salvador.

Reagan subsequently asked for another $35 million, but Congress refused. It was the only outright rejection on Capitol Hill of any Reagan request for aid to El Salvador.

Congress approved $115 million in economic aid and $77.5 million in development, food and other aid. *(1981 Almanac p. 339; 1982 Almanac p. 219)*

Fiscal 1983

Congress approved $81.3 million in military aid, 60 percent of Reagan's request. The aid included: $26.3 million in loans and grants under a continuing resolution (PL 97-377); $30 million in loans that were "reprogrammed," or transferred, from other countries in April 1983 with the approval of the House and Senate Appropriations committees and the Senate Foreign Relations Committee; and $25 million in grants approved in an omnibus supplemental appropriations bill (PL 98-63).

Reagan's original military aid request, submitted in February 1982, was for $61.3 million. But in March 1983, after Congress had approved only $26.3 million, Reagan

submitted a supplemental request for $110 million, putting the total amount he had sought at $136.3 million.

Congress approved Reagan's full requests of $140 million in economic aid and $87.1 million in development and food aid programs. *(1983 Almanac p. 154; 1982 Almanac p. 242)*

Fiscal 1984

Congress approved a total of $196.55 million in military aid in three steps: $64.8 million in a continuing appropriations resolution (PL 98-151) cleared in November 1983; $61.75 million in an "urgent" supplemental spending bill (PL 98-332) cleared on June 26; and $70 million in the final supplemental (PL 98-396), cleared on Aug. 10.

Of the $61.75 million in the urgent supplemental, $32 million was used to pay back the Pentagon for equipment and supplies that Reagan had shipped to El Salvador on an emergency basis in April. Reagan had used a special authority allowing him to waive for up to 120 days a requirement that foreign countries pay cash for military supplies from the United States.

Reagan's original request for the year, submitted in February 1983, was for $86.3 million. But the president's supplemental request, submitted in February 1984 as part of a broader Central American aid package, was for $178.7 million on top of the $64.8 million that Congress already had approved. So, for comparison purposes, Congress gave Reagan $196.55 million of the $243.5 million he ultimately requested — or 81 percent.

For economic aid, Congress approved $120 million in the continuing resolution and $90 million in the supplemental, matching Reagan's full request. El Salvador also received $64.8 million in development aid and $54.3 million in food aid.

Fiscal 1985

Congress approved $128.25 million of the $132.5 million that Reagan requested for military aid. The approved amount included $111.75 million in grants, $15 million in loans and $1.5 million for military training. The money was included in the fiscal 1985 continuing appropriations resolution (PL 98-473).

Two conditions were placed on the military grants: only half of the money could be spent before March 1, 1985, unless the president got approval from the two Appropriations committees to spend at a faster rate; and $5 million was held in escrow until the Salvadoran government conducted a trial and obtained a verdict in the case of two U.S. land reform advisers killed in January 1981.

Congress also approved $195 million of Reagan's $210 million request for economic aid. Based on overall amounts in the continuing resolution, the administration allocated another $80 million in development aid and $51.1 million in food aid for El Salvador.

All aid to El Salvador was to be suspended if the elected president was deposed by military coup or decree.

... On One of Most Controversial Issues

This chart shows U.S. aid to El Salvador for each fiscal year since 1981. President Reagan took office in January 1981.

(in millions of dollars)

Program Request	1981	1982	1983	1984	1985
Foreign Military Sales loans	$ 10.0	$ 16.5	$ 46.5	$ 18.5	$ 15.0
Military Assistance Program grants	0	8.5	33.5	176.5	111.75
Defense Department drawdown	25.0[1]	55.0[1]	0	(32.0)[2]	0
International Military Education and Training	.5	2.0	1.3	1.5	1.5
Total, Military Aid	**$35.5**	**$ 82.0**	**$ 81.3**	**$196.5**	**$128.25**
Economic Support Fund	44.9	115.0	140.0	210.2	195.0
Development Aid	32.8	36.2	58.8	64.8	80.0
Food for Peace	26.3	34.4	46.7	54.3	51.1
Disaster Aid	2.6	6.9	0	0	0
Total, Non-Military Aid	**$106.6**	**$192.5**	**$245.5**	**$329.3**	**$326.1**

[1] *Presidents Carter and Reagan in 1981 and 1982 used section 506 (a) of the Foreign Assistance Act of 1961 to send military aid to El Salvador without congressional approval.*

[2] *President Reagan in April 1984 used section 21 (D) of the Arms Export Control Act to send military aid to El Salvador in advance of appropriations; the $32 million was included in the Military Assistance Program grant total for fiscal 1984.*

CIA Role in Salvador Election

Charges that the Central Intelligence Agency subsidized the U.S.-favored candidate in the May 6 presidential runoff in El Salvador cast doubt on the validity of that election. Despite the reports, however, Congress gave President Reagan the military and economic aid he sought to help the newly-elected president, José Napoleón Duarte, battle leftist guerrillas and promote democracy within his country.

Sen. Jesse Helms, R-N.C., charged on May 8 that the CIA and the State Department "rigged" the election in favor of Duarte, who was the candidate of the Christian Democratic Party.

The White House denied taking sides in the election, although the CIA admitted to the two congressional Intelligence committees that it supplied aid to Duarte but not to his opponent.

The runoff election pitted Duarte against Roberto d'Aubuisson of the Republican National Alliance Party.

On May 9, before the Salvadoran Central Election Council finished counting the ballots, d'Aubuisson withdrew his party's involvement from the count, claiming that the election was fraudulent because of active U.S. support for Duarte. D'Aubuisson said that if illegal ballots were thrown out, he would be the winner.

The charges by Helms and d'Aubuisson forced into the open a long-simmering dispute in Congress about the propriety of U.S. support for selected candidates in the election. There had been no question that the administration favored Duarte, because of the candidates considered to have a chance of winning, he was widely perceived as the most moderate.

The administration feared that if d'Aubuisson won, Congress would suspend all military aid to El Salvador.

Helms charged that the United States provided Duarte "comprehensive across-the-board services," including money for precinct organizers, radio and television advertisements and computer voter registration.

Others on Capitol Hill said the CIA had given more than $360,000 to Duarte's party and more than $100,000 to the conservative National Conciliation Party, which also opposed d'Aubuisson. Its candidate, Francisco José Guerrero, ran third in the first round of voting March 25.

Helms' charges paralleled claims by d'Aubuisson's supporters that the U.S. Embassy had backed the Duarte campaign by funding grass-roots organizing by the Salvadoran Communal Union, the country's largest labor group, and by paying for political advice through the Venezuelan Institute for Popular Education, a consulting agency. The administration confirmed that U.S. aid was given to pro-Duarte labor unions.

Nevertheless, members of Congress who went to El Salvador as official observers maintained that the election had been conducted honestly. "I can say to you without any doubt that it was a free and open election," said Rep. J. J. Pickle, D-Texas, on May 10.

Kasten suggested.

Kasten also said Specter's amendment would negate the committee's intent to provide $93 million in assistance, and he proposed an alternative that would not have withheld funds.

Pete V. Domenici, R-N.M., arguing against both plans, said, "We should not be writing foreign policy in this committee." His motion to table (kill) Specter's amendment carried, 21-3.

Senate leaders late March 22 announced an agreement with the Reagan administration to cut the $92.7 million by one-third. Under the terms of the agreement, Inouye was to offer an amendment to cut the Salvadoran aid from $92.7 million to $61.7 million.

Inouye originally had intended to offer an amendment to cut the figure to $49.2 million, the amount the Pentagon has indicated was necessary to carry on existing activities through the end of fiscal 1984. Inouye agreed to add $12.5 million more to provide necessary medical supplies and training.

Senate Floor Action

Action by the Senate on H J Res 492 was postponed until after the March 25 Salvadoran election when Edward M. Kennedy, D-Mass., warned that he would object to any attempt to bring the bill up any sooner. Kennedy and others left often the possibility of cutting funds below the $61.7 million, particularly if d'Aubuisson won the election.

A clear-cut winner did not emerge from the March 25 election, which meant a runoff election had to be held May 6 between Duarte and d'Aubuisson. During floor debate March 29 on the Salvadoran aid portion of H J Res 492, Kennedy argued against appropriating any new military assistance to El Salvador until it was clear who would be in charge of the government. Instead of the $61.7 million, Kennedy proposed $21 million to last through the runoff election.

Senators who observed the March 25 election spoke emotionally of their experience, arguing that the nation was moving toward democracy and deserved aid.

After nine days of debate, the Senate passed H J Res 492 on April 5, containing the $61.7 million for El Salvador. Although H J Res 492 had contained only the $150 million African food aid when it had passed the House, as approved by the Senate it became a $1.15 billion "urgent" supplemental appropriation for fiscal 1984.

H J Res 492 passed by a vote of 76-19. On passage, 53 Republicans voted with 23 Democrats to support the package, while Weicker was the only Republican voting against it. *(Vote 56, p. 12-S)*

Partial Victories for Democrats

Democratic critics got the full-scale debate they sought on Reagan's policies but won only partial victories. They succeeded with an amendment requiring funds to El Salvador to be cut off if there were a military coup there, and they secured a pledge from the Intelligence Committee to probe possible Central Intelligence Agency involvement in Salvadoran death squad activity.

Kennedy April 2 offered his promised amendment to cut Salvadoran funding from $61.75 million to $21 million. Inouye said he was sympathetic to Kennedy's aims, but he said he wanted a compromise that would pass. Another proposal April 2 by John Melcher, D-Mont., would have cut funding to $35.4 million, but it would have sliced more deeply into military aid than Kennedy's. Melcher included

$7.9 million in military aid while all of the $21 million in Kennedy's plan was military aid. Melcher also proposed $13.5 million in medical aid and $14 million in food aid.

Kennedy's amendment failed by a 25-63 vote, and Melcher's, 24-63. *(Votes 46, 47, p. 11-S)*

On April 4, the Senate adopted by voice vote an amendment, opposed by the Reagan administration, to cut off funds to El Salvador in the event of a military coup against the newly elected government.

Kennedy April 3 proposed withholding 15 percent of the funds, or $9.26 million, until the Salvadoran government obtained a verdict in the 1981 murders of two U.S. labor advisers in that country.

Opponents argued that since the case was far from resolution, the amendment amounted to a 15 percent cut. Inouye noted that in the United States in 1982, out of 100 arrests for murder, 32 of those arrested were not prosecuted. "How can we hold El Salvador to a higher standard?" he asked.

Kennedy, his voice rising, shot back, "We are not talking about unsolved murders. We are talking about organized assassination squads."

The Senate tabled Kennedy's amendment, 69-24. *(Vote 48, p. 11-S)*

Republican Specter then proposed withholding 30 percent of the money, or $18.5 million, until the 1980 deaths of four U.S. churchwomen were solved.

A similar Specter amendment had been added to the fiscal 1984 foreign aid appropriation, and as a result, $19 million in military aid to El Salvador had not been spent. *(1983 Almanac p. 164)*

Specter argued that the Salvadoran government should be pressured to bring the case to trial. But Patrick J. Leahy, D-Vt., said that Specter's 1983 amendment should preclude any new Salvadoran aid at all. He proposed, as a substitute, that no more money be sent until the murders were resolved.

Specter, arguing that a total ban went too far, said, "It is unwise to tie the hands of the administration totally."

Kasten's motion to table his amendment carried, 54-39, which also had the effect of killing Leahy's substitute. *(Vote 49, p. 11-S)*

The Senate later adopted, by voice vote, an amendment by Daniel Patrick Moynihan, D-N.Y., adding $500,000 to protect jurors and witnesses in the trial of the alleged killers of the churchwomen.

Kennedy proposed a further restriction, to prohibit military aid after May 31, 1984, unless the administration certified by June 30, 1984, that the Salvadoran government had agreed to participate in unconditional negotiations with all parties in the conflict in that country, including the leftist guerrillas. The amendment was tabled, 63-26. *(Vote 50, p. 11-S)*

Provisions in Senate Bill

As passed by the Senate, H J Res 492 appropriated $61.75 million for El Salvador, including $49.25 million in military aid and $12.5 million in medical aid. Funds were to be cut off in the event of a military coup in that country.

The president was to certify to Congress within 60 days after enactment, and every 60 days thereafter, that the government of El Salvador had demonstrated progress toward free elections, freedom of association, establishment of an effective judicial system, land reform and the termination of activities of death squads.

H J Res 492 also included:

● $7 million for refugee assistance to El Salvador.
● $500,000 for witness and juror protection in the case of the four murdered U.S. churchwomen.

House-Senate Differences

Although the Senate action was encouraging for the administration, it was not at all clear in early April that the $61.75 million in H J Res 492 would survive when the bill had to be reconciled with the original House version.

Administration officials continued to insist that additional aid was needed urgently. House Democrats and members of the Senate Appropriations Subcommittee on Foreign Operations offered opposing views on how to provide additional money without congressional appropriation. The Democrats wanted Reagan to use a process called "reprogramming," which involved transferring aid money from one country to another. Either the Senate or the House Foreign Operations Subcommittee could veto such a fund transfer.

Long, chairman of the House Appropriations Foreign Operations Subcommittee, agreed to a $32.5 million reprogramming — if Reagan would make new demands for reforms by the Salvadoran government on human rights and other issues.

But the Senate Appropriations Foreign Operations Subcommittee, headed by Kasten, refused to go along, saying that Long was attempting to impose his own conditions on El Salvador and was unilaterally cutting aid to $32.5 million. Kasten wanted Reagan to use emergency powers to provide the aid.

On April 13, the White House announced Reagan's decision to invoke Section 21D of the Arms Export Control Act (PL 90-629), which allowed foreign countries in an emergency to have up to 120 days to pay for U.S. arms shipments.

White House spokesman Larry Speakes said El Salvador needed ammunition, weapons, helicopters and other items "to prevent unnecessary loss of life and to assure security" for its presidential election runoff May 6.

Other administration officials said Reagan would not exceed the $32.5 million that House leaders had agreed to support during negotiations on April 12-13.

Administration officials justified Reagan's action during appearances April 26 before the House Appropriations Subcommittee on Foreign Operations. William Schneider Jr., under secretary of state for security assistance, said Reagan used his emergency power "reluctantly" and "only after exhaustive consultations failed to find a compromise that was acceptable to a majority of both houses of Congress and the administration."

Although only $32 million was sent, Schneider said the administration was insistent that Congress approve the $61.75 million, part of which would be used to pay for the $32 million in emergency aid.

Conference Report Adopted

Democrats delayed further action on H J Res 492 until after the May 6 election runoff in El Salvador. On May 24, the House agreed by a vote of 267-154 to the $61.75 million the Senate had added to H J Res 492. Seventy-five Southern and 40 Northern Democrats joined 152 Republicans in supporting the aid while 136 Northern and 13 Southern Democrats and only five Republicans opposed it. *(Vote 161, p. 52-H)*

Several Democratic critics of the administration's Central American policy, including Long, backed the aid to

U.S. Churchwomen: Human Rights Symbol

For four years, Congress battled the Reagan administration over conditioning military aid to El Salvador on that country's progress toward ending abuses in human rights.

One focus of that struggle was the killing of four U.S. churchwomen in 1980 and the delays in finding and then prosecuting five Salvadoran former national guardsmen accused of the crime.

The oft-delayed trial of the five men became a symbol of the Salvadoran government's resistance to prosecuting those responsible for human rights violations. Congress froze $19.44 million of $64.8 million in military aid to El Salvador pending a verdict in the case. The money was part of the fiscal 1984 continuing appropriations resolution (PL 98-151) enacted in November 1983.

On the evening of Dec. 2, 1980, Maryknoll nuns Ita Ford and Maura Clark, returning to El Salvador from their order's annual conference in Managua, were met at the San Salvador airport by Sister Dorothy Kazel, an Ursuline nun, and Jean Donovan, a lay social worker.

The four left the airport in a white Toyota van, but were stopped by national guardsmen at a nearby checkpoint. The guardsmen abducted the churchwomen, drove them some 15 miles to a deserted rural area, raped them, and shot them, leaving their bodies by the roadside. Later that evening, the guardsmen set the women's van afire. Local villagers discovered the bodies the next day.

The former national guardsmen were convicted of the crime on May 24, 1984.

Within hours of the verdict, at a tiny courtroom in Zacatecoluca, some members of Congress made speeches and issued statements taking credit for the verdict. Oth-

ers, particularly the harshest critics of U.S. policy in El Salvador, cited the alleged role of that country's guard officials in covering up the case.

A retired U.S. judge, Harold R. Tyler Jr., who investigated the case for the State Department, said pressures from Congress and restrictions on military aid were contributing — but not decisive — factors in the convictions.

Tyler gave most credit for the verdict to U.S. Embassy employees who cracked an early cover-up by the Salvadoran national guard and to several officials in that country.

Perhaps the most provocative aspect of Tyler's report was the flat assertion that the high officials of the Salvadoran national guard covered up the guard's involvement in the murders.

Tyler's report said "it is quite possible" that Carlos Eugenio Vides Casanova, then head of the guard and Salvadoran defense minister at the time of the report, "was aware of, and for a time acquiesced in, the cover-up."

While the report offered no direct proof for the allegation against Vides Casanova, it speculated, for example, that he was informed of the cover-up efforts of Major Lizandro Aepeda Velasco, who headed the guard's own secret investigation of the murders.

"It seems unlikely that a mid-level officer like Zepeda would have undertaken the obstructive actions he did without approval or encouragement from somewhere higher," the report said.

In spite of those findings, Tyler credited Vides Casanova for pursuing the case once the U.S. Embassy developed evidence proving that the five guardsmen committed the murders.

El Salvador, apparently swayed by Salvadoran President-elect Duarte, who visited Capitol Hill during the week.

The House voted 376-36 for the conference report (H Rept 98-792). *(Vote 160, p. 52-H)*

The Senate on June 25 adopted the conference report on the H J Res 492 and the House cleared the $1.1 billion fiscal 1984 urgent supplemental for the president on June 26 (PL 98-332).

The monthlong delay between House passage on May 24 and Senate approval on June 26 resulted from a deadlock that had developed over the level of covert aid for the Nicaraguan "contras" that House and Senate leaders and the administration could accept.

In addition to the $61.75 million, PL 98-332 also:

● Required the president to report every 60 days, during the remainder of fiscal 1984, on the following issues in El Salvador: elections, the administration of justice, freedom of association, government actions to curtail death squads, the development of a medical evacuation and training system, the training of the armed forces, the status of ammunition and supplies for the military, and land reform.

● Required the president to submit a report to Congress on the whereabouts of military equipment sent since 1980 to El Salvador, and the location of military personnel trained with U.S. funds.

● Required the immediate cutoff of military aid in the event of a military coup in El Salvador.

● Stated the sense of the Senate that the U.S. should provide military equipment to El Salvador to suppress guerrilla terrorism.

'REGULAR' SUPPLEMENTAL APPROPRIATIONS

After H J Res 492 cleared Congress, work began on a "regular" supplemental appropriation for fiscal 1984 (HR 6040). The House Appropriations Committee originally had intended to begin work on the bill in mid-June. But it postponed action at that time because the bill had become loaded down by special interest items, with members ready to offer some 25 amendments adding at least $1 billion to its cost.

House Committee Action

As approved by the committee, the bill had $131 million for Central America, of which $25 million was for economic aid for El Salvador. The president had requested $117 million in additional military aid to add to the $64.8 million approved in November 1983 and the $61.75 million cleared on June 26.

But after little debate, the Appropriations panel on a 13-21 vote refused to add some $359 million in Central

American aid to the bill. Only two Democrats, Charles Wilson and Jack Hightower, both of Texas, voted for the added Central American aid.

Two days before the committee action, Reagan said, on a nationally televised news conference, that the Democrats' "niggardly treatment" of El Salvador was "comparable to letting El Salvador slowly bleed to death."

House Floor Action

When the House voted on the $5.5 billion supplemental appropriations bill on Aug. 1, an effort by Jack F. Kemp, R-N.Y., to add an additional $359 million for military and economic assistance for Central America was ruled out of order.

Kemp argued that the United States needed to strengthen its support of the Duarte government. "I think each and every one of us wants to do something to help implement the democratic reforms that not only are coming, but must continue to come in El Salvador."

But Long said more U.S. money would go to Central America in fiscal 1985, obviating the need for additional funds in the last two months of the current fiscal year. Long raised a point of order against the Kemp amendment on the grounds that it would have provided funds not authorized by legislation. Jack Brooks, D-Texas, who was presiding over the House during the debate, wasted no time in sustaining Long's objection.

Senate Action

On Aug. 2, one day after the House had approved HR 6040, the Senate Appropriations Committee reported its version of HR 6040, which was $1.4 billion larger than the House-passed bill and which included $565 million in economic and military assistance to Central American countries compared with the $131 million in the House bill. The total included the $117 million in military aid requested by the president for El Salvador in fiscal 1984.

The Senate passed its version of the supplemental bill shortly after midnight on Aug. 9, some 10 hours after the chamber had begun debating the measure. The vote on final passage was 62-32. *(Vote 206, p. 36-S)*

Senate Democrats tried and failed twice by wide margins to cut the money in the bill for Central America.

Sen. Christopher J. Dodd, D-Conn., first tried to cut the Central American money in the bill from $565.2 million to $178.9 million. Dodd's proposal was designed to prohibit Congress from spending more than was authorized in existing legislation.

Kasten acknowledged that Congress had not authorized the increased money to El Salvador and other Central American countries. But he said that the need for the money in the troubled region outweighed Dodd's procedural objections.

Dodd's amendment was rejected 37-62. *(Vote 200, p. 35-S)*

The Senate by a wider margin rejected an amendment by Inouye to delete all of the $117 million for El Salvador. Inouye said the money was unnecessary because there was "millions of dollars in the pipeline" that had not yet been spent by El Salvador. Inouye's amendment was defeated 29-69. *(Vote 201, p. 35-S)*

House-Senate Conference

House-Senate conferees immediately went to work on HR 6040, after Senate passage of the bill to pave the way for Congress to adjourn for the Republican national convention and for the Labor Day holiday.

Conferees spent more than five hours and several testy moments the evening of Aug. 9 slogging through the bill, but failed to agree on the Central American portion.

The crucial sticking point came over the $116.9 million in added military aid for El Salvador that the White House had requested and the Senate had added to HR 6040. The House had included no military funds for that country. An offer by Senate conferees to reduce the El Salvador aid to $90 million was rejected by House conferees.

Long adamantly refused to back away from his position against any further arms aid to El Salvador. Long said El Salvador still had $50 million in unspent U.S. military aid for the rest of fiscal 1984, which ended Sept. 30.

But Long's Senate counterpart, Kasten, said the El Salvadoran government's war against insurgents could not wait for new funds in a 1985 appropriation bill. "We need your help today, not in the '85 bill, which might not pass until December," said Kasten.

Twice during the conference, Kasten read a letter from Salvadoran President Duarte to Reagan appealing for the extra military and economic aid in the supplemental.

During an evening break, Kasten and Long met for about an hour with Inouye, the ranking Democrat on Kasten's subcommittee, and Kemp, the ranking Republican on Long's panel. While that meeting did nothing to break the impasse between Kasten and Long, it did give Kasten time to stitch together a new proposal to bring back to the conference with a significant convert — Inouye.

Kasten offered to reduce military aid to El Salvador to $90 million while also offering to drop $341 million from the Senate bill for U.S. contributions to international development banks, such as the World Bank. The House bill contained no funds for the banks.

Kasten said his revised spending levels provided the "minimum security assistance we can get away with" in Central America. The plan was endorsed by Inouye, who on the Senate floor had sponsored an amendment to cut all the military money for El Salvador. Inouye described the new proposal as "very reasonable."

The Senate conferees voted 14-2 for the Kasten plan. But Long immediately won a 12-8 vote from House conferees to stand firm on the House position. Rep. Jack Edwards, R-Ala., tried to coax some movement on the House side by proposing that military aid to El Salvador be reduced further to $70 million, but that also was rejected by House Democratic conferees.

The next day, Aug. 10, when the House approved the conference report (H Rept 98-977), Long and other Democrats sought to prevent an outright Reagan victory on El Salvador aid by proposing a $40 million increase — about a third of what the president wanted.

Acknowledging that Congress likely would vote more aid as an indication of support for Duarte, Long offered an amendment totaling $171 million in military and economic aid for Central America, of which $40 million would be for El Salvador. Republicans continued to push for $90 million but, to get backing from moderate Democrats, settled for $70 million for El Salvador. Offered by Kemp, this amendment totaled $498 million for Central America.

Long's amendment was rejected 57-340. He was deserted by conservatives who wanted more money for El Salvador, and by several liberals, who opposed any new funds. A disgruntled Rep. David R. Obey, D-Wis., said: "There are a hell of a lot of liberals who would rather pose for holy pictures than win." *(Vote 328, p. 100-H)*

The House then adopted Kemp's alternative 234-161. (*Vote 329, p. 100-H*)

Several hours later, the Senate adopted the conference report by a voice vote, clearing the $6.2 billion measure. Administration officials were delighted with the El Salvador military funds. "Obviously, we are very pleased. It's a very significant development," said Thomas R. Pickering, U.S. ambassador to El Salvador. Pickering had strategically placed himself directly off the House floor Aug. 10 along with other White House lobbyists while members of that chamber were voting on the military aid.

Fiscal 1985 Authorization

While the Appropriations committees were working on the bills which added the $62 million and $70 million in military aid for El Salvador for fiscal 1984, the House Foreign Affairs and Senate Foreign Relations committees were trying to reach agreement on fiscal 1985 authorization bills. However, for the third year in a row, Congress was unable to forge a consensus on foreign aid. The result was a continuing appropriations resolution (H J Res 648 — PL 98-473) which provided $18.2 billion for foreign aid for fiscal 1985, including $128.25 million in military aid and $195 million in economic aid for El Salvador. (*Continuing resolution, p. 444*)

Early in the year, it had appeared that the major stumbling block to the president's plans for El Salvador would come from the House Foreign Affairs Committee. On March 1, the Subcommittee on Western Hemisphere Affairs rejected increased military assistance for El Salvador in fiscal 1984 and imposed stiff human rights conditions and congressional controls on all economic and military aid to that country in fiscal 1985.

But by May 10, after the Duarte election, the House approved a bill (HR 5119) which not only authorized $178.7 million that Reagan had requested as a 1984 supplemental but also the $132.5 million military aid request for fiscal 1985.

But the Senate Foreign Relations Committee was so divided on the question of providing the president's requested funds for Central America that it had reported out a foreign aid authorization bill in April without any money for Central America. The committee tried to resolve the impasse over the Central American aid separately, but was not successful. By August, Senate Republican leaders gave up on any hope of getting a foreign aid authorization bill passed.

Faced with the impossibility of resolving the impasse over foreign aid, Congress added to the continuing appropriations resolution for fiscal 1985 (PL 98-473) $128.25 million for military assistance to El Salvador.

House Committee Action

When the House Foreign Affairs Subcommittee on Western Hemisphere Affairs debated the president's fiscal 1984-85 Central American aid package early in 1984, it appeared that the president's program for El Salvador faced the same opposition it had encountered for three years with House Democrats.

The panel March 1 dumped Reagan's request for $178.7 million in Salvadoran military aid for fiscal 1984. For fiscal 1985, the committee drafted a new requirement for conditions on military and economic aid to El Salvador. The provisions were part of the fiscal 1984-85 foreign aid authorization bill.

New Envoy Is Named

Richard Stone, President Reagan's special ambassador to Central America, resigned in February 1984, reportedly because of conflicts with a top State Department expert on Latin America.

He was succeeded by Harry W. Shlaudeman, former U.S. ambassador to Argentina, who had been executive director to the National Bipartisan Commission on Central America, chaired by former Secretary of State Henry A. Kissinger.

Stone, a Democrat who represented Florida in the Senate from 1975-80, was appointed to the ambassadorial post in March 1983. (*1983 Almanac p. 159*)

Although he traveled widely and arranged meetings between the government of El Salvador and its leftist opposition, Stone made little progress toward settling conflicts in the region.

Shlaudeman was confirmed by the Senate March 22.

For El Salvador to get the aid, the U.S. president would have to report to Congress that the Salvadoran government had achieved a list of human rights, judicial and other changes. Congress would approve the president's report by joint resolution. In effect, that procedure would have created a one-house veto of the aid, since both chambers would have to have approved such a resolution.

Stephen J. Solarz, D-N.Y., originally had proposed that the fiscal 1985 conditions apply only to military aid in excess of $64.9 million — the amount that up to that date had been approved by Congress for fiscal 1984. On an amendment by Gerry E. Studds, D-Mass., the subcommittee applied the restriction to all of Reagan's $132.5 million request for Salvadoran military aid for 1985. Later, the panel applied the restriction to all Economic Support Fund aid. Reagan had sought $210 million for that program and the panel approved half. Studds said the conditions were a blunt warning that Congress was demanding elimination of paramilitary death squads in El Salvador.

The full Foreign Affairs Committee completed work March 7 on the bill (HR 5119), except for provisions relating to Central America. Committee Democrats, after a series of meetings, on March 14 reached an uneasy agreement on a complicated proposal that rejected most of Reagan's requests and set tough new conditions on aid to El Salvador. Later on March 14, when the full committee met, outraged Republicans asked for a delay in considering the Central American portion of the aid bill until after the Salvadoran elections. Committee Democrats split over whether to delay action on Central America. Solarz said he feared the entire foreign aid bill would be held "hostage" to the Central American provisions. On his motion, the committee voted to delete the Central American aid proposals from HR 5119.

The Democrats' proposal was put by Chairman Dante B. Fascell, D-Fla., into a new bill, HR 5420. In a compromise between Democrats who differed over whether to approve some supplemental military aid for fiscal 1984, the members agreed to shift $56.8 million from Reagan's 1984 request to 1985 — resulting in a $189.3 million total for 1985. The Democrats did not establish a figure for economic aid.

Instead of imposing the strict conditions laid down by the subcommittee for all military and economic aid, the Democrats' plan in another compromise placed mild conditions on some of the aid and much stricter rules on the rest. The plan gave Reagan a free hand in fiscal 1985 to spend $64.8 million in military aid and half of his $210 million in military and economic aid in 1985 if both chambers of Congress passed a joint resolution, as the subcommittee bill had required, approving a presidential report stating that the Salvadoran government had achieved a series of human rights and other objectives.

House Floor Action

Divisions among Democratic leaders, however, enabled Reagan on May 10 to secure a victory on the Salvadoran aid issue for fiscal 1985.

By a dramatic 212-208 vote, the House approved a Republican-sponsored plan to give Reagan most of the military aid he sought for fiscal 1985, free of the stringent conditions set by the Democrats.

The Salvadoran aid was part of a $10.95 billion foreign aid authorization bill (HR 5119).

The House acted one day after Reagan made a nationally televised appeal for congressional support of El Salvador and other countries fighting leftist guerrillas in Central America. "If we do nothing or if we continue to provide too little help, our choice will be a communist Central America with additional communist military bases on the mainland of this hemisphere, and communist subversion spreading southward and northward," he said.

Majority Leader Jim Wright, D-Texas, splitting with Speaker Thomas P. O'Neill Jr., D-Mass., and other House leaders, led 55 Democrats in backing Reagan's plan. The May 10 vote demonstrated the sharp partisan divisions in the House and the cleavage between Southern and Northern Democrats on Central American issues. Democrats rejected Reagan's aid package 56-200, with all but seven of the 56 "yes" votes coming from the South. Republicans were nearly unanimous in supporting the president, 156-8.

The Republican substitute, offered by William S. Broomfield, R-Mich., was adopted on the key 212-208 vote. *(Vote 125, p. 42-H)*

The Broomfield amendment authorized $1.21 billion for military, economic, development and other aid programs to Central America in fiscal 1985.

The House took two other votes on Central American aid before passing the aid bill. First, by a 128-287 vote, it rejected an amendment by Studds that would have barred all military aid to El Salvador in 1985 unless that country had achieved a series of conditions on human rights and other issues. *(Vote 124, p. 42-H)*

Democrats demanded a second vote on the Broomfield substitute, in the futile hope that enough members would switch to defeat it. But the House ratified the earlier decision on a 211-208 vote. *(Vote 126, p. 42-H)*

With crossover support from some members who traditionally oppose foreign aid, such as Minority Whip Trent Lott, R-Miss., the House passed the bill 211-206. In a shift from normal practice on foreign aid bills, a majority of Democrats voted against the bill and a majority of Republicans for it. *(Vote 127, p. 42-H)*

The House never voted directly on the Democrats' version of the aid bill. The Broomfield substitute required presidential reports on El Salvador's progress on human rights but did not require achievement of the standards before the Salvadorans could receive arms aid.

The Broomfield amendment required the president to submit a report to Congress by Aug. 31, 1984, on El Salvador's "demonstrated progress" toward six objectives. The objectives included: ending unlawful violence, detention, abduction, torture and murder by military and security forces; establishing an effective judicial system; ensuring freedom of the press and freedom of association; participating in a dialogue with the opposition on involvement in future elections; complying with international agreements on protecting civilians in armed conflicts; and fully implementing the "land reform" program.

The president could spend one-half of El Salvador's 1985 military aid at the beginning of the fiscal year, on Oct. 1. To spend the rest, the president would have to send Congress another report by Jan. 31, 1985, saying that El Salvador had made "additional demonstrated progress" on the objectives.

If Congress did not pass a joint resolution rejecting those findings within 30 days, the remaining aid could go forward.

The Broomfield substitute also stated the sense of Congress, but did not require, that the number of U.S. military advisers in El Salvador should be limited to 55 unless Congress was consulted in advance. It required that the president, before sending economic aid to El Salvador, "be satisfied" that the Salvadoran Central Bank had implemented reforms recommended by Arthur Young & Co., a consulting firm, for the control of foreign exchange, especially U.S. aid.

Senate Committee Action

Divided along partisan and ideological lines, the Senate Foreign Relations Committee struggled in vain in early April to produce a compromise on Central American aid legislation. The committee attempted to reconcile two conflicting proposals.

One sponsored by Charles McC. Mathias Jr., R-Md., and other committee Republicans, implemented most of the recommendations of the Kissinger commission. A competing proposal, sponsored by Dodd and other Democrats, rejected many of the Kissinger recommendations and imposed tight conditions on economic and military aid to Central America, particularly El Salvador.

Of the two, the administration preferred the Mathias proposal, although State Department officials objected strongly to parts of it. The State Department opposed virtually every aspect of the Dodd amendment.

In drafting a foreign aid authorization bill for fiscal years 1984-85, the committee set formal working sessions on Central American issues for April 3-6. But each day the committee failed to make substantial progress because Mathias and Dodd were unable to bridge the gap between Republicans and Democrats on questions of how much aid the United States should give to El Salvador and under what conditions.

The Mathias and Dodd proposals differed on six major areas involving aid to Central America. Two involved aid to El Salvador:

● Mathias and Dodd proposed substantially different methods of setting conditions, such as respect for human rights and political reforms, that Central American countries would have to meet to receive aid. Mathias would have imposed the same conditions throughout the region and required only that the countries be making progress toward meeting those standards. Dodd would have banned all military and economic assistance to El Salvador until it had

U.S. Military Presence in Honduras

While playing down the extent of direct U.S. military involvement in Central America, the Reagan administration considerably expanded the U.S. presence in the region, especially in Honduras.

In a televised news conference in May 1984, President Reagan said that "security assistance is essential to all those who must protect themselves against the expanding export of subversion."

Although the administration was reluctant to disclose information about the buildup, two reports to Congress in 1984 provided details about U.S. military construction projects and troop levels in Honduras.

A Pentagon report, dated May 8, revealed "tentative plans" for U.S. military exercises in Honduras through 1988. The report also said the Pentagon would locate military equipment and supplies in Honduras in case U.S. troops were needed to defend U.S. allies in the region.

Democratic critics of Reagan's policies in Central America charged that the Pentagon used a continuous series of "exercises" as a facade for the establishment of a permanent military presence in Honduras. At any one time, 5,000 or more U.S. troops participated in two series of war games in Honduras, called Big Pine I and Big Pine II, that ran from March 1983 to February 1984. Those exercises involved construction of four airstrips, two radar stations and other military facilities such as a 13-mile tank trap near the border with Nicaragua. U.S. and Honduran forces also conducted combat maneuvers such as air strikes, artillery barrages and amphibious assault landings.

A State Department official said the exercises allowed U.S. and Honduran troops to work together in an atmosphere "realistic to an actual combat deployment." He noted that the U.S. Army's 101st Airborne artillery unit "made a rapid deployment and conducted live firing (along with) the Honduran army" on the north coast.

All the exercises in Honduras were accompanied by naval maneuvers in the region. From July to September 1983, the Navy conducted three maneuvers in waters near Central America. The largest exercise, called Ocean Venture '84, ran from late April to early May in the Caribbean; some 30,000 U.S. soldiers, sailors and airmen participated.

The administration had plans to build a large Regional Military Training Center in northern Honduras to replace a makeshift camp it had been using near Trujillo for training Honduran and Salvadoran soldiers. But the Honduran government announced it would no longer permit Salvadorans to be trained at the camp.

At the same time, Congress added a provision to a continuing resolution on appropriations (H J Res 648 — PL 98-473) for fiscal 1985 to bar the president from spending any money on the Honduran training facility until three things happened:

● The Honduran government provided a site for the camp.

● The president gave Congress a detailed plan and cost estimate.

● The Honduran government took steps to resolve a claim by a U.S. citizen whose property was confiscated for the center.

The Pentagon also was forced in 1984 to withdraw a request to Congress for $4.4 million for two construction projects at two bases in Honduras. The Pentagon pulled back the request June 8 to avert a floor fight over the Senate's military construction provisions in its version of the fiscal 1985 defense authorizations bill (PL 98-525). The General Accounting Office (GAO), an investigatory arm of Congress, reported that the Defense Department had used "improper" funding sources in building several military facilities, training Honduran troops and providing medical and other humanitarian services for Honduran civilians. *(Story, p. 37)*

The Senate had approved an additional $4.3 million for Honduran facilities for a U.S. Army air reconnaissance unit. In their report on the military construction bill (HR 5604 — H Rept 98-962) filed Aug. 7, House-Senate conferees approved the $4.3 million without comment.

The essence of the GAO's 28-page report was that the Defense Department used "operation and maintenance" funds to finance activities in Honduras that should have been expressly authorized by Congress under other categories.

---

met a series of rigorous conditions on human rights and other issues.

● Dodd would have prohibited the president from using his emergency powers to provide military aid to El Salvador. Mathias had no similar provision.

Unable to break the deadlock on Central American issues, the committee on April 11 approved an $11 billion foreign aid bill without any funding or provisions on Central America.

The committee approved its stripped-down aid bill on April 11 on a 16-2 vote, with Nancy Landon Kassebaum, R-Kan., and Richard G. Lugar, R-Ind., dissenting. But that vote masked deep divisions in the committee over how the Central American aid should be implemented. Earlier, on April 9, the committee rejected the Dodd plan by a vote of 8-9. The Mathias plan was rejected 9-9; Sen. Jesse Helms,

R-N.C., played the key role by joining the committee's eight Democrats to vote against it.

Dodd and Mathias continued negotiations and it was believed that a compromise had been reached in early May. All the Senate Foreign Relations Committee members but Helms had privately agreed to a compromise Central American aid package that would have been incorporated in an aid bill (S 2583) pending in the Senate. But that agreement fell apart on May 10 when Dodd insisted on reopening the question of how much aid each country in the region would get.

Senate Republican leaders, facing protracted debate and a losing race against the election-year calendar, decided Aug. 1 to give up trying to pass a full-scale foreign aid authorization bill for fiscal 1985. They considered putting the Central American authorizations on the omnibus supplemental appropriations bill (HR 6040) that was scheduled for floor debate the first week in August. Foreign Relations Chairman Charles H. Percy, R-Ill., told administration officials that he feared "15 filibusters," by liberals and conservatives, could doom the measure.

Fiscal 1985 Appropriations

Despite the deadlock which had developed over fiscal 1985 authorizing legislation for foreign aid, including funds for El Salvador, the Appropriations committees began moving aid bills forward in June.

Senate Committee Action

The Senate Appropriations Subcommittee on Foreign Operations on June 21, by voice vote and with little debate, adopted a $13.8 billion foreign aid bill that included about $1.4 billion for Central America. The full committee reported the bill (S 2793 — S Rept 98-531) on June 26.

The measure included $132.5 million in military aid for El Salvador in 1985 without any conditions on how the money could be spent. Kasten said the panel drafted the bill as a "benchmark" that later would be incorporated into an omnibus continuing appropriations resolution, as had been the case in the previous two years.

Kasten said approval of Reagan's requests for Central America was made possible by a new "bipartisan consensus" that had developed in Congress since the election and inauguration of Duarte as president of El Salvador.

While freeing the strings on military aid to El Salvador, the committee imposed several conditions on the $210 million in the bill for economic aid to that country. The conditions were aimed at ensuring that the money was not diverted illegally and that Congress was informed on how it was being used.

House Committee Action

The House Appropriations Subcommittee on Foreign Operations on Aug. 8 approved a 1985 foreign aid appropriations bill totaling $17.9 billion, which included $123.5 million in military aid for El Salvador — only $9.25 million less than the president's request. The $123.5 million was by far the biggest single amount of military aid the subcommittee had approved in one chunk.

Subcommittee Chairman Long said the reason for the panel's new receptivity to Reagan's Central American program was confidence in the new Salvadoran president. "We want to give Duarte a chance, and if that means more money, we're willing," Long said.

Adopted by voice vote, with most Democrats dissenting, the figure included: $106.75 million in Military Assistance Program grants (Reagan had requested $116 million), $15 million in foreign military guaranteed loans (Reagan's request) and $1.5 million in military training grants (the request).

The panel adopted a provision allowing the president to spend only half of the Military Assistance Program aid — $53.4 million — during the first half of the fiscal year, ending March 31, 1985. The remaining half could be spent any time during the second portion of the fiscal year. Long said the proposal would prevent the president from spending all of El Salvador's aid early in the fiscal year and then returning to Congress for more money later.

After extended debate, the subcommittee adopted a proposal by Mickey Edwards, R-Okla., allowing the president to speed up the second half of El Salvador's military

grants if he told Congress that an "emergency" existed and the House and Senate Appropriations committees gave "prior written approval."

By a 5-6 vote, the subcommittee rejected a plan by Matthew F. McHugh, D-N.Y., to cut the military aid grants to $72 million from the $106.75 million that Long had proposed. The net effect would have been to provide $89 million in total military aid to El Salvador: the $72 million in grants plus the other aid programs.

Long and Charles Wilson, D-Texas, joined four Republicans in rejecting that proposal, which was supported by five Democrats.

Without debate, the subcommittee approved $180 million of Reagan's $210 million request for economic aid to El Salvador.

The House Appropriations Committee approved the package on Sept. 12. Two days later, the Appropriations panel approved a Long amendment to insert the package into a catchall spending measure, the continuing resolution (H J Res 648 — H Rept 98-1030).

Continuing Resolution

The continuing resolution was passed by the House Sept. 25 and the Senate Oct. 4. The House adopted the conference report (H Rept 98-1159) Oct. 10, and the Senate cleared H J Res 648 (PL 98-473) Oct. 11. *(Details, p. 444)*

Depending on the course of the Salvadoran war, Reagan could ask for additional aid in 1985, claiming it was needed to make up for the $47 million that Congress pared from his fiscal 1984 request.

Congress put three major restrictions on El Salvador's military aid in fiscal 1985:

● Only half of the Military Assistance Program money could be spent before March 1, 1985, unless the president sought approval from the House and Senate Appropriations committees to spend it at a faster rate. Before he could spend the second half, the president must report to the committees that the Salvadoran government had made "substantial progress" in several areas, including curbing killings by so-called "death squads," eliminating government corruption, improving the performance of the military and conducting discussions with the leftist opposition about ending the civil war.

● $5 million was held in escrow until the Salvadoran government conducted a trial and obtained a verdict in the case of two Americans, Mark Pearlman and Michael Hammer, and a Salvadoran, José Rodolfo Viera, who were killed in January 1981. The three men worked for El Salvador's land reform program; no one had been charged with their murders, although U.S. officials said the Salvadoran government had solid evidence about who was responsible.

● All aid to El Salvador must be suspended if the elected president of El Salvador was deposed by a military coup or decree.

The continuing resolution also approved $195 million in Economic Support Fund aid to bolster El Salvador's overall economy, a slight cut from Reagan's $210 million request. But to guard against misuses, Congress insisted that the Central Bank of El Salvador keep that money in a separate account, and required the president to file specific reports on how it was spent.

An additional $6 million was included in the continuing resolution for improvements in the judicial system for El Salvador, including creation of investigative units, protection of key participants in pending cases and modernization of penal and evidentiary codes.

Congress Curtails Aid to Nicaraguan Rebels

After battling in 1983 and 1984 to end U.S. aid to anti-government rebels in Nicaragua, House Democrats succeeded in persuading Congress in 1984 to reject President Reagan's request for additional support for the guerrillas.

But while it halted U.S. aid to the Nicaraguan guerrillas, Congress reached a compromise that could allow some of the assistance to resume. In action on the fiscal 1985 continuing appropriations resolution (H J Res 648 — PL 98-473), Congress agreed in the last days of the session to allow the president to spend $14 million on the guerrilla operation after Feb. 28, 1985, provided both houses of Congress agreed. *(Continuing resolution, p. 444)*

That prospect seemed unlikely as the year ended because of events in 1984 that caused a gradual erosion of support for the covert effort, particularly among members of the Senate Intelligence Committee who had previously supported the president's policy.

In April, newspaper reports detailed participation by the CIA in the mining of Nicaraguan harbors. Key Senate Intelligence Committee members complained that they had not been informed about the CIA activities that the administration disputed, and both chambers voted to condemn the mining. *(Box, p. 88)*

The furor over the mining was followed in the fall by news stories about CIA involvement in the production of a manual that appeared to advocate the kidnapping and killing of Nicaraguan government officials by the guerrillas. Although the administration found low-level agency employees responsible for the manual, the findings and reports by the House and Senate Intelligence committees seemed to add to congressional doubts about continuing aid to the guerrillas. *(Box, p. 91)*

Aid Amounts

At the beginning of fiscal 1984, the administration had secured $24 million to continue aiding some 10,000 rebels, called "contras," who were battling Nicaragua's leftist government. The money was included in defense appropriation (HR 4185 — PL 98-212) and intelligence agencies authorization (HR 2968 — PL 98-215) bills, passed in November 1983. *(1983 Almanac p. 123)*

But Reagan apparently had planned to spend $35 million to $50 million to aid the contras. Saying that the $24 million would last only through May 1984, Reagan returned to Congress for another $21 million for fiscal 1984.

The administration attempted to gain the additional funds by having the Senate Appropriations Committee add the $21 million to House-passed supplemental appropriations legislation for fiscal 1984, which originally authorized an energy assistance program in the United States. *(Supplemental, p. 438)*

The Senate agreed to the $21 million in April, but when the bill went to a House-Senate conference, House conferees refused to accept the aid for the anti-government rebels. The dispute went on until June, when Senate conferees and the administration finally gave up trying for the funds. The stalemate was tying up final passage of H J Res 492, which also contained money for summer jobs programs for needy youths.

The administration sought $28 million for the contras in fiscal 1985 legislation, including defense authorization and intelligence agencies authorization bills. But the House

once again banned any aid to the contras Aug. 2 when it passed HR 5399 (PL 98-618), which authorized fiscal 1985 funds for the CIA and other intelligence agencies.

The issue continued to cause dispute in Congress and was one of the stumbling blocks to passage of the fiscal 1985 continuing resolution and adjournment. The administration, with the help of Senate conservatives, fought to gain some funds for the contras. A compromise was reached in the last days of the 98th Congress: $14 million was added to the spending bill and it was approved Oct. 11.

The $14 million could not be spent until after Feb. 28, 1985, and only if both chambers of Congress voted approval.

By cutting off U.S. involvement in the war in Nicaragua, which began when the Reagan administration took office, Congress for the first time in eight years halted an overseas "covert" activity by the CIA. In 1976, Congress had banned aid to anti-Marxist rebels in Angola. *(1976 Almanac p. 213, 1981 Almanac p. 165)*

Background

Nicaragua had been ruled by a one-family dictatorship until July 1979, when Anastasio Somoza was ousted in a broadly based revolution. The government was taken over by Sandinistas — leftists who took their name from Augusto Sandino, the national hero who battled the U.S. Marine occupation of Nicaragua in the early 1930s.

The anti-Sandinista rebels organized in Honduras under the banner of the Nicaraguan Democratic Force. U.S. involvement with the contras reportedly began in December 1981 with an executive order from Reagan authorizing covert actions by the CIA to disrupt arms shipments into Nicaragua and to harass what the order called the "Cuban-Sandinista support structure" in Nicaragua and elsewhere in Central America.

The CIA operations, based in Honduras, soon became an open secret through newspaper, magazine and television accounts. By the summer of 1983, guerrilla units were launching air and naval attacks that damaged major Nicaraguan oil storage installations.

Critics of administration policy to support the contras feared that the United States was expanding the scope of the Nicaraguan operation beyond the boundaries of U.S. and international law, aiming at the ouster of an internationally recognized government of a foreign country. Administration officials argued that they were not trying to overthrow the Sandinista government, merely trying to stop the flow of Soviet- and Cuban-supplied arms to leftists in El Salvador.

Congressional Disputes, Compromises

Congressional Democrats repeatedly tried to cut off the "covert" aid to the contras. In 1982, they succeeded in adding to a continuing appropriations resolution for fiscal 1983 (PL 97-377) an amendment prohibiting direct CIA efforts to overthrow the Nicaraguan government. The provision was known as the Boland amendment for its sponsor, House Intelligence Committee Chairman Edward P. Boland, D-Mass. *(1982 Almanac p. 238)*

Congress and the Reagan administration fought to a compromise in 1983 that gave Reagan $24 million to continue aiding the rebels, but only for nine months. Democrats led the House in voting twice in 1983 to stop the aid.

The fiscal 1984 defense appropriations bill (PL 98-212) and the intelligence agencies authorization bill (PL 98-215) both set a $24 million limit on the aid for the rebels. Both bills were cleared for the president Nov. 18 and signed Dec. 8 and Dec. 9, respectively.

Because the Nicaragua operation had begun in 1982 as a covert activity, its specific goals were never clearly stated in public, and congressional debate during 1983 did not clarify the issue. The operation had been conducted under the terms of two presidential "findings" that were not made public.

According to Capitol Hill sources, Congress authorized the CIA to provide just enough aid to the Nicaraguan insurgents to pressure the Sandinista-led government to drop its support for leftist guerrillas in El Salvador. The CIA was not allowed, under Reagan's findings, to aid the contras for the purpose of overthrowing the Nicaraguan government. However, leaders of the Nicaraguan Democratic Front had said they wanted to dismantle the Sandinista regime.

'Urgent' Supplemental: Senate

Reagan insisted early in 1984 that the $24 million appropriated by Congress late in 1983 would run out by May 1984. The president tried to get the normally friendly Senate Appropriations Committee to add $21 million in additional money for the contras to a supplemental 1984 appropriations bill (H J Res 493) providing $200 million for low-income energy assistance in the United States. The move was coupled with an attempt to add $93 million for El Salvador to a bill (H J Res 492) appropriating $150 million in food aid to Africa. Both bills were considered "must" legislation and had breezed to House passage March 6.

Added to the previously appropriated $24 million, the $21 million would have put CIA spending on the Nicaraguan operation in fiscal 1984 at $45 million — about $10 million more than the agency originally had requested for 1984 and $3 million more than it reportedly spent in fiscal 1983. Administration strategists reasoned that they could not get the aid through the House directly, but that House conferees would accept the Central American riders to H J Res 492 and H J Res 493 rather than jeopardize priority bills in a confrontation with Reagan.

Senate Committee Action

The tactic backfired at first when the committee rejected 14-15 a motion by Ted Stevens, R-Alaska, to attach the Nicaraguan money to the energy bill.

Reagan sent the CIA request to the Senate committee on March 8, just hours before the committee met. Chairman Mark O. Hatfield, R-Ore., said he had learned of Reagan's legislative strategy only a day earlier. A critic of U.S. military involvement in Central America, Hatfield warned that he would do everything possible to thwart the El Salvador and Nicaragua money. "I find it very difficult to comprehend that on March 8 we face a deadline, that I only heard about yesterday, on a problem in Nicaragua that will be in effect unless we act today," he said.

Stevens, majority whip and chairman of the Defense subcommittee, said he was "obligated" to push the Nicaragua proposal because Reagan had asked him to. But Hatfield wanted the committee to approve the energy bill

immediately, without amendments, and repeatedly ruled out of order Stevens' motions to raise the Nicaragua issue.

Stevens won the first test vote when the committee decided, 13-12, to delay action on the energy bill until March 13. But after a recess, the panel voted 13-12 to reconsider that action. After more procedural wrangling, the committee rejected 14-15 the Stevens motion.

But the vote was more a reflection of concern about the procedure rather than the substance of the issue for several senators. One week later, after the president had assured the Senate Intelligence Committee that it would not be bypassed on the issue, and after the Nicaraguan aid was stripped from H J Res 493, the energy assistance bill, the money was attached to H J Res 492.

On March 13, the Senate Intelligence Committee approved the $21 million in a slightly altered form proposed by Daniel K. Inouye, D-Hawaii. On a 14-0 vote, with Patrick J. Leahy, D-Vt., voting present, the panel approved $7 million in direct funding for the Nicaragua program and gave the CIA authority to draw up to $14 million more for the operation from the agency's contingency fund.

The next day, the Appropriations Committee approved the $21 million by voice vote with little debate.

Senators Raise Questions

Before the Senate voted on H J Res 492, however, Intelligence Committee members who had supported the aid began raising questions on the Senate floor. Daniel Patrick Moynihan, D-N.Y., vice chairman of the Intelligence Committee, in a March 29 speech focused attention on the ambiguous nature of the Nicaraguan operation. He said Reagan had implied in an interview in that morning's *New York Times* that the United States was seeking the overthrow of the Nicaraguan government.

The United States had told the Sandinistas, Reagan said, that covert action would stop when they "keep their promises and restore the democratic rule and have elections." Reagan said of Nicaragua's elections, set for November, "... There isn't anything yet to indicate that the election will be anything but the kind of rubber-stamp that we see in any totalitarian government."

In saying that, Moynihan told the Senate, Reagan "misstated his own policy," which was aimed at pressuring, not overthrowing, the Sandinistas. "If the government there cannot be changed by elections, how is it to be changed save by violent overthrow?" Moynihan asked. "That is a necessary if unintended conclusion to be drawn from the president's statement."

Committee member Dave Durenberger, R-Minn., made similar charges on March 29, after Moynihan's speech. Durenberger, while supporting the $21 million request, raised the sharpest criticisms of the Nicaragua operation that had come in public from a Republican on Capitol Hill.

"There is no real evidence that the covert action effort, itself, has brought about changes in Sandinista policy," he said. "There is no real evidence that it has lessened the flow of Cuban and Nicaraguan arms into El Salvador, although the contras are clearly striking at some targets that are part of the Sandinista support structure for Salvadoran guerrillas."

Senate Floor Action

The Senate April 5 passed H J Res 492 by a 76-19 vote. The bill included the $21 million in contra money despite attempts by Democrats to eliminate it. *(Vote 56, p. 12-S)*

CIA Role in Mining of Nicaraguan Ports . . .

Congressional support for U.S. aid to guerrillas, or "contras," fighting the leftist Nicaraguan government was significantly eroded in 1984 by public disclosures about CIA involvement in the mining of Nicaraguan harbors.

Unhappiness with the mining took the form of symbolic protest votes in both chambers on April 10 and April 12.

The Reagan administration defended the mining as an act of "collective self-defense," but refused to say publicly whether other countries asked for that form of defense.

The CIA's role in the mining was revealed April 6 in the *Wall Street Journal*. The operation was carried out by anti-Nicaraguan government commandos, supervised by CIA personnel.

One of the murkiest issues involved the timing and extent of administration consultation with Congress on the mining. Leaders in both chambers said the administration had failed to tell them of the mining until after it became public knowledge.

Two Senate committee chairmen who had supported Reagan's Central American policies raised that point.

Sen. Barry Goldwater, R-Ariz., chairman of the Intelligence Committee, which had jurisdiction over the CIA, wrote CIA Director William J. Casey a blistering letter. And Foreign Relations Committee Chairman Charles H. Percy, R-Ill., complained: "I just don't know where the sensitivity is."

In an April 10 statement, the administration said committees had been fully briefed on "all U.S. activities in the Central American region."

Goldwater insisted his committee had not been notified in advance about U.S. participation in the mining.

Edward P. Boland, D-Mass., chairman of the House Intelligence Committee, said his panel first learned of the mining on Jan. 31, when CIA officials "responded affirmatively" to a routine question about whether Nicaraguan harbors were being mined. The committee received further information in February and March, and had a full briefing on the subject on March 27, Boland said.

The Administration's Defense

The State Department gave a formal legal defense for the mining in classified and unclassified statements to the Senate Intelligence Committee. The one-page unclassified statement, entitled "Use of Naval Mines in the Exercise of Self-Defense," justified naval mining in theory, but did not discuss the Nicaraguan case.

The statement said a country that is attacked by another country, either by overt military means or by covert actions such as arms shipments to insurgent groups, can take "proportionate actions" in self-defense. The attacked country can appeal to "friendly third states" for support, it said.

"The use of naval mines is one legitimate means of exercising this right of individual and collective self-defense in appropriate circumstances," the statement said. "For example, the proportionate use of naval mines can be a legitimate means of interrupting a flow of arms destined for infiltration into the territory of the victim, or to disrupt the flow of military and other materials essential to the attack's over-all aggressive effort."

Incidents

According to a chronology in the April 4 *Congres-*

The task of defending the covert operation fell to Majority Whip Stevens, who said it was justified by Nicaragua's building its military up to 138,000 men. "Based on population, they have more commitment to arms than any other country in the world," he said.

Even so, he said, the United States was not seeking to overthrow the Sandinistas. "All this is doing is keeping pressure on them," he said, warning "that we will not allow them to attack their neighbors."

Stevens insisted that the covert operation had resulted in "substantial changes in policy" in Nicaragua. He said the Sandinistas had "significantly" cut back arms sent to Salvadoran guerrillas and stopped cross-border attacks on Honduras.

Kennedy Amendment

But Edward M. Kennedy, D-Mass., called administration policy in Nicaragua "illegal" and "indefensible." He sponsored an amendment to cut all $21 million from the bill. He said that despite U.S. assertions that the aim in aiding the contras was to pressure the Sandinista regime to change its policies, the aid was helping the guerrillas seize power.

Just before the vote on the Kennedy amendment on April 4, Majority Leader Howard H. Baker Jr., R-Tenn.,

read a letter from Reagan to the Senate in which Reagan asserted that no policy change had taken place. "The United States does not seek to destabilize or overthrow the government of Nicaragua; nor to impose or compel any particular form of government there," Reagan's letter said.

The Senate defeated the Kennedy amendment, 30-61. *(Vote 52, p. 12-S)*

Dodd, Levin Amendments

The Senate also killed two other attempts to restrict funds. One, offered by Christopher J. Dodd, D-Conn., barred the use of covert funds for "planning, directing, executing or supporting acts of sabotage or terrorism in, over or offshore from the territory of Nicaragua."

But Warren B. Rudman, R-N.H., said the line between terrorism and acts of war was vague and he was "uncertain" what Dodd meant by terrorism. The Senate tabled Dodd's amendment, 47-43. *(Vote 53, p. 12-S)*

On April 5, the Senate rejected an amendment by Carl Levin, D-Mich., which he said would put into law the policy Reagan had stated in his letter to Baker. The amendment barred the use of covert funds to support groups intending to overthrow the government of a country with which the United States had full diplomatic relations, such as Nicaragua.

. . . Erodes Hill Support for Aid to 'Contras'

sional Record by Sen. Jim Sasser, D-Tenn., U.S.-backed rebels were responsible for incidents in which:

• Feb. 25: Two fishing boats (of unidentified nationality) hit mines and sank at the Caribbean port of El Bluff. Two more vessels were damaged; two crew members were killed and seven were wounded.

• March 1: A Dutch dredging ship hit a mine at the Pacific port of Corinto. Five were injured; damages were assessed at $1 million.

• March 7: A Panamanian freighter was damaged by an explosion caused by mines at Corinto.

• March 20: A Soviet oil tanker was seriously damaged when it hit a mine at the Pacific port of Sandino; five crewmen were injured.

Nicaraguan officials also reported that a Liberian-registered vessel hit a mine at Corinto on March 28, causing light damage and no casualties.

House, Senate Votes

The Senate on April 10 and the House on April 12 adopted non-binding, "sense of the Congress" statements that no U.S. funds should be used to mine Nicaraguan waters. The two chambers acted after Reagan officials said the mining operation had been stopped.

The Senate approved its statement 84-12, with some of President Reagan's strongest backers voting for it. Sponsored by Edward M. Kennedy, D-Mass., it was adopted as an amendment to a tax bill (HR 2163). *(Vote 59, p. 13-S)*

Two days later, the House passed, 281-111, identical wording in a rush resolution (H Con Res 290). Unlike their Senate colleagues, House Republicans chose to fight the mining condemnation, which Minority Leader Robert H. Michel, R-Ill., called a "non-binding

media event." *(Vote 78, p. 28-H)*

CIA's Statement, World Court Ruling

In an unusual statement April 16, the CIA said Casey had kept a pledge to fully inform the Intelligence committees about operations. The CIA said the two panels had been briefed on Central American developments 22 times between Sept. 6, 1983, and April 2, 1984. The mining had been "discussed with members or staffers of the committees and other members of the Congress 11 times," the statement added.

Following closely on that statement were new reports that the CIA had failed to tell the committees of its role in supervising attacks on Nicaraguan oil facilities at the port of Corinto on Oct. 10, 1983.

CIA Director Casey on April 25-27 apologized to committee members for the CIA's failure to "fully inform" the committees about the agency's involvement in the mining. Sen. Daniel Patrick Moynihan, D-N.Y., who had resigned his vice chairmanship of the Senate Intelligence Committee because the committee had been "the victim of a breach of trust," retracted the resignation after Casey's apology.

Nicaragua protested the mining in April to the World Court at The Hague, Netherlands, but the administration declared it would not respect the tribunal's jurisdiction over U.S. actions in Central America.

On May 10, the court issued a preliminary ruling condemning the CIA's involvement in the mining of Nicaraguan ports. The court called on the United States to "immediately cease and refrain" from the mining, which the administration said it already had done. In January 1985, the administration said it would boycott further World Court proceedings on the matter.

But Stevens said that Levin's amendment would effectively cut off aid to the contras, since they had stated that they intended to overthrow the Sandinista regime in Nicaragua. The Senate agreed to Stevens' motion to table the Levin amendment, 51-44. *(Vote 54, p. 12-S)*

Conference Impasse

The next day, April 6, press reports began about CIA participation in the mining of Nicaraguan harbors, triggering recriminations on Capitol Hill by members who said they had not been notified in advance. On April 10, the Senate voted a non-binding, "sense of the Congress" condemnation of the bombing. On April 12, the House followed suit.

To regain lost ground, Reagan went on the offensive May 9 with a nationally televised address in which he portrayed Nicaragua's Sandinista government as a threat to the entire Western Hemisphere.

"The Sandinista rule is a communist reign of terror," he said, charging that the government had broken its 1979 promises of holding free elections, had repressed critics and tried to "wipe out an entire culture" — the Miskito Indians who live in northeastern Nicaragua.

With the backing of Cuba and the Soviet Union, Nica-

ragua was "supporting aggression and terrorism against El Salvador, Honduras and Guatemala," Reagan said.

Reagan said the United States had a "moral duty" to support the Nicaraguan guerrillas, whom he referred to as "freedom fighters." While he made no direct plea to Congress to approve his requests for $21 million for the contras, the overall thrust of the speech made it clear that Reagan aimed to generate congressional support for the contras.

Sticking Points

Despite the president's efforts, however, House and Senate conferees on the "urgent" supplemental could not reach agreement on the $21 million the Senate had added to H J Res 492.

After two days of meetings May 16-17, House conferees refused to accept the Senate-passed provision. Senate conferees continued to insist on their position.

Stevens at first seemed to acknowledge that the Senate would give in, but asked that a cap in existing law on covert aid to Nicaragua be lifted so that funds could be provided to wind the operation down.

But Boland refused to allow that. "They have sufficient funds now to wind the program down if they wanted to," he said.

House Floor Vote

The disagreement moved the debate to the House floor May 24 where the aid for the contras was rejected by a vote of 241-177. *(Vote 162, p. 54-H)*

Some House Democrats expressed a willingness to compromise by providing $4 million to $6 million to "wind down" the operation and pay off the CIA-hired guerrillas. But the administration refused to accept any compromise that would set a clear-cut termination date for the aid.

Intelligence Bills

While the House and Senate were arguing over the $21 million, work had begun on 1985 authorizing legislation, which presented the next opportunity for the administration to secure funds for the Nicaraguan rebels. The Senate bill contained $28 million for the contras, while the House version banned further aid.

House Version

The House Intelligence Committee inserted in its bill authorizing fiscal 1985 funds for the CIA and other intelligence agencies (HR 5399) a flat ban on further aid to the contras. The committee issued its report on HR 5399 on May 10 (H Rept 98-743, Part I). *(Intelligence bills, p. 119)*

Most of the House bill and report were secret; the House committee put its language on the ban on aid to the contras in the public part of its bill and report.

Section 107 of the House bill contained a strict prohibition on U.S. aid to the contras: "During fiscal year 1985, no funds available to the Central Intelligence Agency, the Department of Defense or any other agency or entity of the United States involved in intelligence activities may be obligated or expended for the purpose or which would have the effect of supporting directly or indirectly, military or paramilitary operations in Nicaragua by any nation, group, organization, movement or individual."

Senate Version

The Senate Intelligence Committee on May 24 reported S 2713 (S Rept 98-481) containing $28 million that the president had requested for fiscal 1984. The president could spend the $28 million only if he reported that the rebels were not trying to overthrow the Sandinista government.

One committee source said the restriction was intended to put into law the assurances that Reagan had given the Senate in the April 4 letter that Majority Leader Baker had read on the Senate floor during the vote on H J Res 492.

The Senate bill also required the CIA to report to the committee in writing whenever it or the contras began a new military campaign. The provision was intended to prevent a repetition of the agency's failure to inform the committee fully about the U.S. involvement in the mining of Nicaraguan harbors.

Shultz Trip to Managua

On June 1, Secretary of State George P. Shultz met with key Nicaraguan leaders in Managua, in part to show that congressional critics were wrong in saying that the administration was reluctant to negotiate with leftists in the region. The trip, while widely praised, produced no apparent political breakthroughs in Congress.

Republicans had hoped that Shultz' trip to Managua might produce additional support in both chambers for the administration request, but there were no signs to that effect. House Majority Leader Jim Wright, D-Texas, gave an interpretation opposite that intended by the administration; he said on June 4 that Congress should not vote funds for the rebels while Shultz was negotiating with Nicaraguan leaders.

The administration faced an additional problem when House Intelligence Committee aides produced evidence that the CIA had exceeded the $24 million spending limit for the Nicaraguan operation. Part of the evidence, sources said, was that the CIA charged to its overall operating budget the $1.2 million cost of a "mother ship" that was used to direct the mining of Nicaraguan harbors early in 1984.

Defense Authorization Bill

Support for the administration position on the covert aid for the contras continued to wane in June, in particular among Senate Democrats who had previously backed the president. On June 18, the Senate rejected an amendment to the fiscal 1985 defense authorization bill (S 2723) that would have prohibited U.S. assistance to the anti-government guerrillas in 1985.

But the vote of 58-38 disguised a sharp drop in support among key Democrats at a time when the administration was waging an uphill battle to continue subsidizing the contras. *(Vote 141, p. 26-S)*

Four Democrats on the Intelligence Committee who earlier had backed Reagan's policy of arming the Nicaraguan rebels bolted on the vote, depriving the administration of strong bipartisan support. The four were Inouye, Moynihan, Lloyd Bentsen, Texas, and Walter D. Huddleston, Ky. Republican committee member William S. Cohen, Maine, also voted against the aid.

The amendment, cosponsored by Kennedy and Jeff Bingaman, D-N.M., said that nothing in the defense bill should be "deemed to authorize the appropriation of any funds for the purpose of or which would have the effect of supporting, directly or indirectly, paramilitary operations in Nicaragua by any group, organization, movement or individual."

Inouye gave the most specific list of reasons for dropping his support: The program was no longer secret, the United States had lost control over the contras, the program had "gone beyond" its initial justification of stemming the flow of arms from Nicaragua to Salvadoran guerrillas, and the high visibility of the issue was "slowly but surely eroding whatever credibility" was left with the CIA.

In explaining his abandonment of the contra aid, Moynihan said the administration needed to concede the "elemental dictates of realism," especially in light of solid House opposition to the program.

'Urgent' Supplemental: Final Action

Worried that the politics of the situation were working to the administration's disadvantage, Senate Majority Leader Baker repeatedly warned Reagan in June that chances of winning the full $21 million for the contras was slim.

Domestic politics finally forced Senate Republicans and the president to give up the fight for the $21 million. The months-long dispute over the Nicaraguan issue had held up funds in the supplemental for several critical domestic programs, including summer jobs for youths. With

CIA-Approved Manual Sparks an Uproar

A CIA-approved manual that seemed to advocate the kidnapping and killing of Nicaraguan government officials by U.S.-backed guerrillas became a hot political issue in the closing weeks of the presidential campaign and sparked two congressional and two presidential investigations.

Democratic presidential candidate Walter F. Mondale and other Democrats cited the manual as evidence that President Reagan wanted to overthrow Nicaragua's leftist Sandinista government.

Mondale and House Speaker Thomas P. O'Neill Jr., D-Mass., demanded the resignation of CIA Director William J. Casey.

The Associated Press reported Oct. 14 that the CIA in 1983 had approved the 44-page manual, titled "Psychological Operations in Guerrilla Warfare."

The manual gave instructions on military and political means of battling the Sandinistas. Much of the manual described how to meet the practical needs of a guerrilla army.

But in one controversial section, the manual said the rebels should "neutralize" government officials.

Administration Inquiries

Reagan ordered two probes on Oct. 18. One investigation, by the CIA's inspector general, was completed on Oct. 30 and the results sent to the president's Intelligence Oversight Board. The three-member board conducted its own investigation and submitted both findings to Reagan.

Both investigations concluded that low-level CIA officials were responsible for the manual.

CIA Director Casey defended the manual in a letter dated Oct. 25 and delivered to the Intelligence committees on Oct. 31.

The manual was prepared by the guerrillas "with the help of an adviser provided by the CIA," he said. Complaining that press reports had distorted the manual's content, Casey said its purpose was not to train the guerrillas to kill government officials in Nicaragua.

The "emphasis is on education, avoiding combat if possible," Casey said.

Reagan and his aides disavowed any connection with political assassinations in Nicaragua, noting that a presidential order barred U.S. involvement in such killings.

Under orders issued in 1976 by President Ford and updated in 1981 by Reagan, U.S. agencies were barred from taking part in assassinations. *(1981 Almanac p. 150)*

The CIA in mid-November punished six officials for their part in the manual. Reportedly, three officials received official letters of reprimand, two officials were suspended from duty temporarily and a contract employee known by the pseudonym John Kirkpatrick was "allowed" to resign.

Uproar Over 'Neutralizing'

The section of the manual that caused the political uproar was entitled "Selective Use of Violence for Propagandistic Effects."

As translated by the Congressional Research Service, the section began: "It is possible to neutralize carefully selected and planned targets, such as court judges ... police and state security officials, CDA (Sandinista Defense Committee) chief, etc. For psychological purposes, it is necessary to take extreme precautions, and it is absolutely necessary to gather together the population affected, so that they will be present, take part in the act, and formulate accusations against the oppressor."

There were differing interpretations of what the work "neutralize" was meant to convey.

After an Oct. 22 CIA briefing, Senate Intelligence Committee member Sam Nunn, D-Ga., said use of the word "could lead one to the conclusion that the president's policy [barring assassinations] was being or could possibly be breached."

But Malcolm Wallop, R-Wyo., said the statement on neutralizing, when read in the context of the entire manual, advocated "restraint" and not necessarily assassinations.

House, Senate Reports

The House Intelligence Committee conducted a two-month inquiry and reported on its findings Dec. 5. The Senate Intelligence Committee also investigated the Nicaraguan program and issued its report (S Rept 98-665) at the end of 1984.

The House Intelligence Committee's informal report endorsed the results of the two administration findings that only low-level CIA employees were involved in production of the manual.

The committee said the CIA, in producing the manual, unintentionally violated a 1983 law that barred U.S. efforts to overthrow the Nicaraguan government.

That law, the "Boland amendment" barring aid to the guerrillas for the purpose of ousting the government, was in effect from December 1982 to December 1983, during the time when the manual was prepared. *(1983 Almanac p. 123)*

The House panel said that, while the manual was "repugnant to American values" and an "embarrassment to the United States," it did not violate the executive order prohibiting CIA involvement in assassinations.

The Senate committee, long the main source of congressional support for the administration's aid to the Nicaraguan rebels, joined the House panel in condemning the CIA's handling of the program.

The Senate panel faulted the CIA for "inadequate supervision and management" of the aid, and warned that such complaints "will surely affect congressional consideration of any request by the president to resume the Nicaraguan program."

As examples of mismanagement, the Senate committee emphasized the publication of the manual and the CIA's failure to notify Congress in advance of the mining of Nicaraguan harbors. *(CIA involvement in mining, p. 88)*

school letting out in major cities, even strong supporters of the covert aid were under great political pressure to drop the issue so the domestic programs could clear Congress.

On June 25, the Senate voted 88-1 to delete the $21 million from H J Res 492, with Paula Hawkins, R-Fla., casting the lone "nay" vote. *(Vote 156, p. 28-S)*

The House ratified the action the next day on a voice vote, clearing the bill for the president's signature (PL 98-332).

Compromise Sought

Although the administration could have tried to resurrect the aid in the so-called "regular" supplemental for fiscal 1984 (HR 6040 — PL 98-396), it was believed that such a move, with little time left in the session, would have created the same conflicts between the administration and Capitol Hill that had bogged down the urgent supplemental.

The two most widely discussed compromises were to provide just enough money to "wind down" the war in Nicaragua or to provide enough money to keep the war going, but with conditions that satisfied some congressional concerns.

House Intelligence Committee Chairman Boland said House conferees on the urgent supplemental had been willing in May to approve funds, if the money were restricted "solely for the safe and expeditious withdrawal" of the contras from Nicaragua. House conferees also had been willing, he said, to provide money for "humanitarian support" of contras who left Nicaragua and gave up their weapons.

But, Boland said, Senate conferees and the administration refused to accept those provisions. Boland said the offer of quickly phasing out the contra aid remained the only basis on which he thought the House would come to an agreement with the Senate.

Some Senate Republicans also floated the idea of approving aid for the contras in 1985 but with conditions, such as banning the mining of Nicaraguan harbors or attacks on fuel supplies and other economic targets.

But Boland rejected such a proposal, if it meant continuing the war in Nicaragua. "The only condition we're interested in is ending that war," he said.

House Votes Intelligence Bill

In a July 24 nationally televised news conference, Reagan said the United States had a "responsibility" to prevent Nicaragua from becoming a Soviet "base in the Western Hemisphere" similar to Cuba. With that statement, he appeared again to be expanding the goal of U.S. support for the contras beyond the limited mission — pressuring Nicaragua to live with its neighbors — that he had told Congress officially.

Nevertheless, the House again rejected the idea of continued support for the contras by approving a ban on such aid in the fiscal 1985 authorization for the CIA and other intelligence agencies (HR 5399). The House passed the measure Aug. 2 by a vote of 294-118, after Republican leaders decided not to mount a futile challenge to the Nicaraguan provision. *(Vote 306, p. 94-H)*

Sixty-five Republicans voted for the bill, although the aid to the contras had enjoyed wide GOP support on Capitol Hill. House aides said many of the Republicans voted for the bill because they supported the underlying intelli-

On MiGs, a War of Words

With Congress out of session and the presidential campaign over, the Reagan administration escalated its war of words with the leftist government of Nicaragua in early November.

Charging that the Sandinistas were engaging in an unnecessary military buildup and threatening neighboring pro-U.S. governments in Central America, the Reagan administration warned it might take military action.

The Nicaraguans, in turn, alleged that the United States was preparing to invade their country. Each side denied the other's charges.

On Nov. 6, the day of the U.S. elections, an unnamed administration official told CBS News that the United States had "credible evidence" that a Soviet freighter, the Bakuriani, might be carrying MiG-21 warplanes and was about to dock at the Nicaraguan port of Corinto, on the Pacific Ocean.

The ship docked the next day and unloaded crates apparently containing military equipment. Reagan officials said the United States had warned the Soviets not to deliver MiG fighters to Nicaragua. And in a press conference, Reagan said that for Nicaragua to receive such planes would "indicate that they are contemplating being a threat to their neighbors here in the Americas."

For three days, administration spokesmen seemed to encourage speculation that the United States would take military action should MiG fighters turn up on the docks of Corinto.

Nicaragua, meanwhile, lodged a formal protest and moved to mobilize its people. On Nov. 7, the Sandinista leaders said that the United States was "attempting to create conditions for a direct military action by the United States against Nicaragua that includes massive bombings of Nicaraguan territory and aggressive actions with the participation of U.S. troops." The Sandinistas on Nov. 12 declared a national alert, calling out thousands of militia members and rolling several of the army's Soviet-supplied tanks into the streets of Managua.

On Nov. 9, U.S. officials said it appeared that the Soviet ship had not unloaded MiG fighters, and the ship left Nicaragua on Nov. 11.

But the officials warned that several other Soviet ships were on their way to Nicaragua, and they charged that ships from Soviet-bloc countries in October had unloaded Mi-24 "Hind" attack helicopters "ideal" for use against the contras operating in the mountains of northern Nicaragua.

Few members of Congress were in Washington during the Nicaraguan flap, and the administration apparently made little effort to seek the advice of congressional leaders.

One Reagan critic, Rep. Michael D. Barnes, D-Md., said that if the administration considered Nicaragua a threat to other countries in Central America, there were "better solutions than unilateral military action by the United States." Barnes chaired the Western Hemisphere Affairs Subcommittee of the House Foreign Affairs Committee.

gence authorizations, not because they backed the ban on aiding the contras.

Attacking the contra aid ban, Minority Leader Robert H. Michel, R-Ill., said it was the Nicaraguan regime — not the U.S. government — that was making war in Central America.

"By denying the contras funding we are left, realistically speaking, with the alternatives of either an American invasion of a country or American evasion of responsibility," Michel said. "The United States according to this view must either be an interventionist bully or an isolationist wimp — there can be no middle ground."

But Boland said that "the secret war hasn't brought Central America closer to peace or Nicaragua closer to democracy. What it does is to provide the Sandinistas with the perfect excuse to foist unfair elections, a huge army, censorship and the draft on the Nicaraguan people."

Final Compromise

The companion Senate Intelligence bill (S 2713) contained the $28 million the president sought for the contras in fiscal 1985. The bill remained stymied for months until the last day of the session, Oct. 11, when it was incorporated into HR 5399 and cleared by Congress.

Paving the way for Senate action was a compromise on the Nicaraguan issue Oct. 10 through the vehicle of the 1985 continuing appropriations resolution (PL 98-473), which had become the catchall spending measure for every department and agency for which no regular authorization bill had yet been enacted.

The House had passed its version of the continuing resolution on Sept. 25; the Senate approved its companion measure on Oct. 4. But when House and Senate conferees tried to reconcile two versions, Nicaragua posed one of the biggest stumbling blocks.

Both sides tied the question to a related provision in the continuing resolution that would have prevented the president from using U.S. armed forces to fight in Central American wars.

Trade-Offs

The White House and Senate Republicans were willing to delete the $28 million from the bill — if the House agreed to drop a ban on the CIA's using its contingency fund to help the contras and also drop a prohibition on using U.S. forces in the region. Sen. J. Bennett Johnston, D-La., an administration supporter on the Nicaragua issue, also proposed approving half the $28 million, with no further aid to the contras to be provided after March 1, 1985, unless Congress approved.

But Rep. Boland refused to accept any compromise that would allow continued U.S. contra aid. "The House voted four times to stop this war in Nicaragua."

When the House conferees did compromise on the issue, it was by providing that the president could spend $14 million but only after Feb. 28, 1985. If he decided at that time that he wanted to spend the $14 million, he would have to submit a report to Congress after Feb. 28, certifying that the money was needed to combat Sandinista expansionism. Both houses of Congress would have to approve any request, effectively giving either chamber a veto.

Spending Measure, Intelligence Bill Clear

The House approved the conference report on Oct. 10 (H Rept 98-1159). The Senate cleared the measure on Oct. 11 (PL 98-473). The fiscal 1985 authorization for the CIA and other intelligence agencies also cleared on Oct. 11 (PL 98-618), containing the same provisions on the contra aid as in the continuing resolution.

There was some dispute in Congress about how serious a defeat Reagan had suffered on the issue.

Senate Majority Whip Stevens, the chief negotiator on the administration's behalf, called the result a "legitimate compromise" that merely postponed a decision until early in 1985.

Pete V. Domenici, R-N.M., chairman of the Senate Budget Committee and one of the most active senators on Central American issues, played down the significance of the decision: "I don't think it's going to cause that much damage in the interim."

But Moynihan said his fellow Democrats won a major victory over Reagan. "The program [of aid to the contras] has ended," he said. "The president's options in Central America have been closed." ∎

Hill Rejects Multi-Year Central America Aid

President Reagan, following the recommendations of a presidential commission headed by former Secretary of State Henry A. Kissinger, in 1984 proposed an $8 billion, six-year program of assistance to Central America. But Congress enacted only pieces of the package.

Congress approved most of the $1 billion-plus in economic and development aid that the commission recommended for fiscal 1985. But it rejected a plan to authorize follow-up aid for fiscal years 1986-89.

Reagan had appointed the commission in July 1983 in hopes of getting a broad consensus behind his program of supporting El Salvador against leftist guerrillas while pressuring Nicaragua to drop its pro-Soviet stance. The panel's formal title, "National Bipartisan Commission on Central America," reflected Reagan's search for such a political consensus. (*1983 Almanac p. 169*)

The Kissinger commission's report, which endorsed the thrust of Reagan's approach toward Central America, failed to quell the political debate in Washington about his policies. (*El Salvador, p. 73; Nicaragua, p. 86*)

The commission recommendations suffered their biggest setback in the Republican-controlled Senate, where liberal Democrats and Jesse Helms, R-N.C., joined in an unusual coalition to help block the 1985 foreign aid authorizations bill (S 2582).

The Kissinger panel reported to Reagan on Jan. 11, calling for more than $8 billion in economic aid to the region through 1989 and for firm U.S. resistance to the expansion of Soviet and Cuban influence. It endorsed a "substantial" increase in military aid for El Salvador and backed indirectly Reagan's program of "covert" aid to anti-government rebels, called "contras," fighting the Sandinista government in Nicaragua. The commission also called on Reagan and Central American leaders to meet to decide on a plan for long-range economic development in the region. (*Summary text, p. 29-A*)

The commission did not recommend using U.S. military forces to fight in Central America. But it said the

United States should consider force against the Nicaraguan government as a "last resort" if it refused to agree to stop supporting guerrilla movements in other countries.

Reflecting congressional initiatives, the commission recommended one major departure from Reagan's policy. It advised conditioning military aid to El Salvador and Guatemala on progress on such human rights concerns as curbing the activities of so-called "death squads." The recommendation for strictly enforced conditions on aid to El Salvador reflected a longstanding dispute. *(El Salvador conditions, pp. 73, 85; 1983 Almanac p. 156)*

Commission Report

In broad terms, the commission endorsed the Reagan view of why Central America was in turmoil and what should be done about it.

Reciting the region's long history of poverty and injustice, and the more recent history of stymied economic growth, the commission said "the roots of the crisis are both indigenous and foreign. Discontents are real, and for much of the population conditions of life are miserable," making the region "ripe for revolution."

But, the commission said, "these conditions have been exploited by hostile outside forces — specifically Cuba, backed by the Soviet Union and now operating through Nicaragua — which will turn any revolution they capture into a totalitarian state, threatening the region and robbing the people of their hopes for liberty."

The United States was not threatened by "indigenous reform, even indigenous revolution" in the region, the commission said. "But the intrusion of aggressive outside powers exploiting local grievances to expand their own political influence and military control is a serious threat to the United States, and to the entire hemisphere."

The report put the conflict in Central America squarely in the context of competition between the United States and the Soviet Union.

The Soviet-Cuban advance affected the global balance of power, the commission said. Forced to "defend against security threats near our borders," it said, the United States "would either have to assume a permanently increased defense burden, or see our capacity to defend distant trouble-spots reduced, and as a result have to reduce important commitments elsewhere in the world." The result would be a "strategic coup" for the Soviet Union.

Recommendations

The commission's major recommendations included:

Military Aid. Saying the current levels of U.S. military aid to El Salvador "are not sufficient to preserve even the existing military stalemate over a period of time," the commission called for "significantly increased levels of military aid as quickly as possible." The panel did not specify an amount, but noted that the Pentagon had estimated a need for $400 million over fiscal years 1984-85 to "break the military stalemate." Congress should approve the aid on a multi-year basis, the commission said.

In fiscal 1984, Congress had limited military aid to $64.8 million, and said 30 percent of that amount could not be spent until the government obtained a verdict in the cases of five former national guardsmen accused of murdering four American churchwomen in December 1980.

The commission also called for boosting military aid to Honduras and providing arms aid to Guatemala, with conditions.

Conditions. At the insistence of AFL-CIO President Lane Kirkland, the panel recommended making military aid to El Salvador and Guatemala contingent on social and political progress. "Death squads" tied to Salvadoran government security forces and right-wing factions had killed thousands of civilians, the commission said, and security forces in Guatemala had engaged in "brutal behavior."

The commission said Congress should force the president to make periodic reports, for each country, on: "demonstrated progress toward free elections; freedom of association; the establishment of the rule of law and an effective judicial system; and the termination of the activities of the so-called death squads, as well as vigorous action against those guilty of crimes and the prosecution to the extent possible of past offenders."

Those conditions "should be seriously enforced," the commission said.

In a dissent to that recommendation, Kissinger, Nicholas F. Brady and John Silber endorsed those objectives, but said the conditions should not be interpreted "in a manner that leads to a Marxist-Leninist victory in El Salvador, thereby damaging vital American interests and risking a larger war."

Nicaragua. Saying that "the consolidation of a Marxist-Leninist regime in Managua would be seen by its neighbors as a permanent security threat," most commission members indirectly endorsed Reagan's aid to rebels trying to overthrow the government. The report said the majority "believe that the efforts of the Nicaraguan insurgents represent one of the incentives working in favor of a negotiated settlement" in the region.

In dissents, commissioners Henry G. Cisneros said aid to the rebels should be suspended through 1985 to give Nicaragua a chance to hold elections, and Carlos F. Diaz-Alejandro said the aid "is likely to strengthen the most extremist sectors of the Sandinista leadership."

Negotiations. As had Reagan, the commission rejected steps leading to "power-sharing" between the Salvadoran government and leftist rebels as "only a prelude to a takeover by the insurgent forces." Instead, the panel said, El Salvador should hold its planned March 25 presidential vote and try to ensure that "all significant groups have a right to participate."

On a regional basis, the commission endorsed the 21-point plan outlined in October 1983 by the "Contadora group" of Mexico, Panama, Venezuela and Colombia.

Short-term Aid. The commission backed Reagan's policy of bolstering Central American economies with short-term aid. But it said the budget of $477 million in fiscal 1984 economic aid to Costa Rica, El Salvador, Guatemala, Honduras, Belize and Panama was not adequate, and it recommended a $400 million supplemental. Nicaragua should not be given aid until it dropped its pro-Soviet behavior, the commission said.

The additional money was aimed at creating jobs, reducing balance-of-payments deficits and bringing about economic stability.

Long-term Aid. The economies of Central America would not improve substantially until conflict in the region was ended, the commission said. Nevertheless, it called for a new program based on aid from outside the region, particularly the United States.

Citing estimates that Central America needed $24 million in outside loans and aid through 1990, the commission said about half should be provided by private banks, international development banks and other countries, and most of the rest must come from the United States.

To cover most of that need, the commission recommended an $8 billion aid program over fiscal years 1985-89. Annually, the program would have roughly doubled what the United States spent in fiscal 1983. Congress was to appropriate about $6 billion and the rest was to be loan guarantees and other programs that did not require appropriations.

The commission said Congress should authorize the full five-year program at once, with appropriations for individual years to follow.

About one-fourth of the U.S. aid would be channeled through a new multilateral body, which the panel called the Central American Development Organization.

Nicaragua would receive aid only if it permitted elections and guaranteed human rights, the commission said.

Throughout the region, economic aid would be tied to steps to improve tax laws, eliminate corruption and encourage private enterprise and investment, it added.

The commission set a modest goal for improving the Central American economies: a return, by 1990, to the region's 1980 standard of living. By 1983, the commission said, per capita income had fallen in every country in Central America from peak levels of the late 1970s.

Regional Efforts. The panel endorsed past regional economic efforts and said they should be revived and expanded. Specifically, it said the United States should provide loans and other incentives to revive the moribund Central American Common Market (a regional free-trade zone) and should join and contribute to the Central American Bank for Economic Integration, which made industrial development loans.

Trade Benefits. The panel recommended that the United States and other industrialized nations take further steps to encourage trade with Central America. It suggested that the United States review its non-tariff barriers (such as quotas on sugar) to imports from the region and that European countries follow the U.S. lead in dropping most tariffs on the region's products.

Partisan Reaction

Republican members of Congress embraced the report, predicting it would give Reagan new leverage on Capitol Hill. Democrats, for the most part, attacked the recommendations that supported Reagan's actions and praised those elements that challenged his policies.

Sen. Charles McC. Mathias Jr., R-Md., one of eight non-voting "senior counselors" to the panel, noted that the commission found aid was needed to avert pro-Soviet revolutions throughout the region. "The price tag, compared to the alternative, is going to look cheap," he said.

Another senior counselor, Rep. Michael D. Barnes, D-Md., complained that Reagan had "stacked" the panel with members receptive to his policies.

Kissinger defended the report, saying it demonstrated "a remarkable consensus." Of the recommendations, he said: "We do not guarantee success, but without a program of this kind, success is surely not attainable."

A middle view came from Rep. Charles E. Bennett, D-Fla., who said he had opposed most foreign aid but might vote for some commission proposals. The proposed $8 billion in economic aid in the 1980s would not be "overwhelming if it is properly handled," he said. "It is less than we would spend if we were headed for war."

However, Bennett said he was not convinced by the

commission's indirect endorsement of U.S. "covert" aid to anti-government rebels in Nicaragua. "I don't think our country has to stoop to that kind of activity."

Campaigning for the Plan

Before it was even submitted to Congress, the package faced delays because of its large aid increases. Military aid always provoked opposition among Democrats. And the proposal for about $1.5 billion annually in economic aid came at a time when the U.S. deficit was appproaching $200 billion a year.

Reagan launched his campaign for the aid package in his weekly Saturday radio speech on Jan. 14. Even as his aides were working on the details, Reagan labeled the proposal in two different ways. One, called the "Central American Democracy, Peace and Recovery Initiative," was meant to play down the military aspects of U.S. policy in the region. The other title, the "Jackson Plan," invoked the name of the late Sen. Henry M. Jackson, D-Wash. (1953-83), the original proponent of a commission to study Central America's problems.

Another feature of the administration campaign was the Jan. 16 release of a report on "the situation in El Salvador." Taking the place of semiannual human rights "certification" that Congress had demanded in 1982 and 1983, the report was intended to demonstrate that Reagan shared congressional concerns about human rights issues in El Salvador.

Committees' Scrutiny

At hearings Feb. 7 and 8, members of the Senate Foreign Relations and House Foreign Affairs committees expressed concern about the workability of the package and its $8 billion-plus price tag. However, few members came out against it.

Kissinger and other commission members insisted in their testimony that expanded assistance was needed to prevent a "crisis" from developing into a total takeover of Central America by leftists aligned with Cuba and the Soviet Union.

The commission recommended that military aid to El Salvador and Guatemala be conditioned on improved respect for human rights, but stopped short of calling for an aid cutoff. Some committee members wanted tougher restraints, arguing that Salvadoran rights abuses would stop only if the government there was threatened with losing aid.

The House on Feb. 7 passed a bill (HR 4656) reinstating a military aid ban unless the president certified to Congress twice yearly that the Salvadoran government was making progress on rights and other issues.

Senate Foreign Relations Chairman Charles H. Percy, R-Ill., while opposing an aid cutoff, said Feb. 7 that "conditionality is absolutely crucial and essential." Sen. Paul E. Tsongas, D-Mass., echoed many members' concern: "The problem is nobody believes conditionality . . . is acceptable to the administration."

Sen. Nancy Landon Kassebaum, R-Kan., said the panel's report was flawed: it would provide "an $8 billion carrot" in the form of aid, but a stick — conditionality — that was "a weak reed of the frailest kind." Congress, she said, would not be willing to halt aid to any Central American nation in danger of falling to Marxist rebels.

The ranking Democrat on the Senate panel, Claiborne Pell of Rhode Island, led the attack on the recommendation for boosts in military aid, saying it did not represent "the road to a peaceful solution" in El Salvador.

Several members of both committees voiced skepticism on two grounds: the countries of Central America could have trouble putting to good use such a rapid expansion of economic aid, and the assistance might be wasted unless turmoil in the region subsides.

Rep. Lee H. Hamilton, D-Ind., addressed both issues. The United States was "literally deluging these countries with money in a short period of time," he said. "I have a deep concern about the ability of these countries to absorb [the aid] and our ability to administer it." Noting that guerrillas had blown up bridges financed by U.S. tax dollars, Hamilton asked Kissinger: "How can we vote for $8 billion over a five-year period if we have no assurance that the security situation will improve?"

Helms Dissent

Sen. Helms registered the stiffest opposition to the commission report, labeling it "a mandate for socialism." Its recommendations, he said, were "a danger to our national security equal to those of the communist incursion" in the region.

Although the report was "liberally spiked with appeals to support the private sector, the actual mechanisms put foward run in . . . the direction of state intervention and control of the economy," Helms said.

Administration's Proposal

After resolving a last-minute question about constitutionality, the administration on Feb. 17 sent Congress suggested legislation to implement the commission's recommendations. It was introduced Feb. 21 as HR 4873 and HR 4874. *(Presidential message, p. 18-E)*

For the most part, Reagan's plan followed the outlines of the commission's recommendations, calling for expanded economic and military aid to the region and establishment of new economic, political and human rights guidelines for the aid. Most controversy centered around the administration's request for $311 million in additional military aid to El Salvador.

Constitutional Issue

The administration's package was delayed in early February, when Justice Department lawyers objected to a provision that gave a new agency, the Central American Development Organization (CADO), control over how some U.S. economic aid would be spent.

As proposed by the Kissinger panel, CADO would have been run by representatives of Central American countries. The commission proposed that one-fourth of U.S. development aid for the region be sent through CADO.

The Justice Department determined that giving a foreign-dominated board control over the expenditure of U.S. tax dollars would have been unconstitutional. But Kissinger commission member Kirkland insisted that the original recommendation be adhered to as much as possible. Negotiations on the issue produced a compromise under which Congress would encourage, but not mandate, that CADO have veto power over one-fourth of U.S. aid.

Aid Reports

Political prospects for the Kissinger recommendations were dealt a blow by revelations of difficulties in U.S. aid programs in El Salvador.

The Associated Press reported on Feb. 13 that a U.S.-financed consultant's study found mismanagement and corruption in the $100 million-plus economic aid program in El Salvador. The classified study said lax Salvadoran regulations allowed businessmen there to divert aid to private bank accounts in the United States.

Another investigation, by the inspector general of the U.S. Agency for International Development (AID) found that the U.S.-backed "land reform" program in El Salvador had encountered serious management problems and faced a "bleak" future without substantial amounts of additional aid.

However, AID itself said that finding was based on narrow technical grounds and ignored the positive benefits of land reform.

El Salvador Aid

The most controversial component of the package involved imposing human rights conditions on El Salvador. The administration was willing to require the Salvadoran government, in return for U.S. arms assistance, to curb human rights abuses by military and paramilitary groups.

But it opposed any law under which aid would have to be halted if the conditions were not met at any given moment.

Secretary of State George P. Shultz told the Foreign Relations Committee on Feb. 23 that the administration did not want to set "these periodic moments in time when . . . an all or nothing cutoff is called for."

Shultz and other officials said the Salvadoran government had taken steps, such as cracking down on "death squads," in response to U.S. administration pressure — not because of any threat that the aid would be stopped.

But some members of Congress contended that El Salvador's government and military would respond only when faced with a cutoff of aid.

Something for Everyone

Reagan's legislation offered something for each of the two opposing sides in the Central America debate.

For liberals who saw poverty as the root cause of the region's problems, Reagan requested a boost in economic development programs. He also met liberals part way on offering to impose human rights conditions on military aid to El Salvador.

For conservatives who said that defeating leftist insurgents was the foremost priority, Reagan asked an emergency infusion of military aid and insisted that he — not Congress — determine whether El Salvador met the human rights conditions.

Reagan requested money for four of the five countries in Central America: Costa Rica, El Salvador, Guatemala and Honduras. He excluded Nicaragua, where the leftist government was battling U.S.-backed guerrillas. Also included in the legislation, even though they technically were not part of Central America, were Belize (formerly British Honduras) and Panama.

The administration said it would try to ensure that Nicaragua would not get direct benefits from some regionwide efforts, such as loans to bolster the Central America Common Market, a free-trade zone of which Nicaragua was a member.

Reagan's bill sought to make authorizations for economic aid to Central America through 1989, and for military aid in fiscal years 1984-85. Congress would have had to enact separate appropriations to provide the money for each year.

Economic Aid

The legislation called for a six-year program of economic, development and related aid for Central America totaling $8.3 billion. Of that, $6.3 billion was to be in programs requiring direct appropriations by Congress and $2 billion was to be in loan guarantees and other credits that must be authorized by Congress but that, for technical reasons, did not count as budget authority in appropriations bills.

Reagan asked specific figures for only two years, fiscal 1984 and 1985. For 1984, he requested $400 million in supplemental economic and development aid; that would nearly double, to $830.1 million, the amount of aid Congress already had approved for the region. For 1985, Reagan requested $1.1 billion in direct appropriations and $600 million in non-appropriated guarantees.

For fiscal years 1986-89, Reagan requested $1.2 billion in each year for economic and development aid, and $40 million for each year in housing loan guarantees. Reagan also requested $200 million in fiscal 1984 for U.S. export guarantees. Those requests totaled $5.1 billion.

In other documents, the administration said its program for 1986-89 was expected to total $6.2 billion, including $4.8 billion in appropriated funds and $1.4 billion in guarantees.

The request for authorizations beyond fiscal year 1985 was one of the most controversial items in the aid package. Congress traditionally had authorized foreign aid funds for only one or two years at a time, and a longer-term authorization would cut into direct control over the aid programs by the two authorizing committees — House Foreign Affairs and Senate Foreign Relations.

In the early years of the administration's program, the biggest priority was to be pumping money directly into the economies of Central American countries, most of which had been declining since 1980.

Of the $2.1 billion budgeted for fiscal 1984-85, $931 million was earmarked for the Economic Support Fund (ESF), the main program the U.S. government used to shore up economies of friendly countries. Most ESF money was for financing exports to Central America of goods from the United States, such as seed for farmers and equipment and raw materials for manufacturers. Another $600 million was to be used by AID, the Export-Import Bank and other agencies to guarantee private loans that also would enable countries to buy U.S. supplies and equipment.

By comparison, Reagan budgeted $193 million over fiscal 1984-85 to finance long-term development projects, such as building schools, running health clinics and teaching new techniques to farmers. Another $145 million would finance U.S. food exports to the region; the remaining $89 million was to be spent on management and other programs.

Starting in 1986, the administration was to shift its focus to development projects, with main goals of restoring economic growth to a rate of at least 6 percent per year and increasing agricultural production by 4 percent annually.

The administration also set specific goals in health, education and other fields. Among them were: increasing primary school enrollment by 1989 to 95 percent of the school-age population from the current rate of 84 percent, reducing infant mortality to 55 per thousand by 1989 from 65 per thousand, providing family planning services to 600,000 couples and increasing low-income housing construction and water and sewer services 25 percent by 1989.

Reagan accepted the Kissinger panel's suggestion for scholarships to enable 10,000 Central American youths to attend colleges in the United States. Administration officials said that would cost about $290 million through 1989.

Development Agency

The most complicated part of Reagan's legislation was the proposal to set up a new agency that would lend a multilateral flavor to the U.S. assistance in the region.

The Kissinger panel had recommended that one-fourth of U.S. economic and development aid to the region be channeled through a Central American Development Organization. The agency, to be composed of representatives from Central America and the United States, would consider economic policies, political systems and respect for human rights in allocating money to countries.

Reagan altered the CADO proposal in two significant ways. First, his legislation did not establish the agency, but merely set out "a series of principles to guide the negotiations" among the United States and other countries that would lead to creating it. Second, his proposal did not give CADO direct control over any U.S. aid; instead, it was to allow CADO to make general recommendations on aid programs in the region, and veto up to 25 percent of the economic aid allocated by the United States for any country in the region.

One reason for the changes, officials said, was because of Justice Department objections that the original Kissinger commission plan was unconstitutional, because the United States could not give an outside agency control over taxpayer dollars.

Another reason was that the Reagan administration had been reluctant to rely on multilateral agencies for foreign aid programs, saying such agencies do not always reflect U.S. priorities. The administration had reduced contributions to the World Bank and similar agencies, while pumping more money into programs run directly by U.S. government agencies. As envisioned by the commission, CADO could have become the very kind of multilateral body the administration was seeking to de-emphasize.

One purpose of CADO, the Kissinger commission reported, would be to encourage Central American countries to drop economic policies that the Reagan administration blames for stifling economic growth. Among those policies were overvalued exchange rates, high tariff barriers to imports and interest rates that were "negative" in real terms because they were below the inflation rate.

Other Issues

Reagan asked for authority to use U.S. aid to compensate owners whose land was taken for a land reform program. Although couched in broad terms, the effect of that authority was to be limited to El Salvador, where a U.S.-promoted program to reallocate land faced severe political troubles caused in part by the government's inability to compensate landowners.

Reagan's proposal sought to waive a 1962 ban on the use of U.S. foreign aid to compensate any owners whose property was nationalized.

In this instance, the administration went somewhat beyond the Kissinger commission report, which did not recommend legislation on the issue and said only that Central American governments should allocate their resources "to ensure that former owners are effectively compensated" for their land.

Compensation put some liberals in a quandary. While

they supported the land reform program because it had broken up huge estates and had given land to thousands of peasants, liberals such as Gerry E. Studds, D-Mass., had objected to using U.S. funds to compensate wealthy Salvadoran landowners, some of whom had been accused of financing the right-wing "death squads" accused of killing hundreds of civilians, including employees of the land reform program.

Helms had led opposition by some conservatives to all phases of land reform programs, including owner compensation, as "socialism."

Another major proposal would have authorized $300 million in non-appropriated funds in fiscal 1985 to guarantee loans made by the Export-Import Bank for high-risk exports of U.S. goods to Central America.

Military Aid

Reagan requested an additional $259 million in military aid in fiscal 1984 and $256 million in 1985. The bulk of each year's amounts was to go to the government of El Salvador. Reagan said the military aid was "vital to shield progress on human rights and democratization against violence from extremes of both right and left."

Unlike his proposal for economic aid, Reagan's request for military aid did not include authorization for years after fiscal 1985. One administration official said the military situation in the region was so "uncertain" that it was impossible to determine how much aid would be needed in later years.

In addition to the direct aid to each country, Reagan requested $25 million in 1984 and $20 million in 1985 to train Salvadoran and Honduran troops at the new U.S. regional military training center in Honduras. An administration statement said training at that center emphasized "the more aggressive, highly mobile tactics needed for dealing effectively with insurgent forces."

By far the single most controversial proposal in Reagan's legislation dealt with human rights conditions on military aid to El Salvador.

Reagan's legislation would have required the president to send Congress a report every six months, starting no later than July 31, 1984, "fully describing the policies of the government of El Salvador for achieving political development, economic development and conditions of security." Specifically, the reports would cover human rights, elections and negotiations.

The president would be required "in every appropriate instance" to "impose conditions" on aid that would help the Salvadoran government achieve political, economic and security objectives.

But Reagan's legislation sidestepped the touchy issue of suspending the aid if the Salvadoran government failed to meet any of the conditions.

Administration officials insisted that Reagan's proposal followed the Kissinger commission recommendation that aid to El Salvador, "through legislation requiring periodic reports, be made contingent upon demonstrated progress" toward such goals as free elections, improvements in the judicial system, and the termination of killings by death squads. The commission said such conditions "should be seriously enforced."

Reagan also proposed resuming military aid to Guatemala. He requested $10 million in low-interest arms loans and $300,000 in military training aid for that country in fiscal 1984.

The United States had not given direct military aid to any of the right-wing governments in Guatemala since 1977. Congress in 1983 blocked Reagan's first request for such aid. In the 1984 continuing resolution (PL 98-151), it voted to ban all U.S. aid to Guatemala except for humanitarian aid administered by private organizations. *(1983 Almanac p. 137)*

The Kissinger commission had said that "the same policy approach" on human rights conditions it proposed for El Salvador also be applied to Guatemala.

Reagan also proposed a substantial increase in military aid to Costa Rica, the only country in Central America without an army. In recent years, the United States had given Costa Rica about $2 million annually to buy helicopters, patrol boats, ammunition and other supplies for that country's rural guard and civil guard.

Aid to Police Forces

Another controversial proposal would have allowed the administration to give up to $20 million each year directly to police departments in Central America, with the aim of strengthening the "administration of justice."

Section 660 of the foreign aid law prohibited any U.S. aid for foreign police; this ban was enacted in 1974 because of charges that U.S. money was being used by repressive police forces in Latin America. *(1974 Almanac p. 533)*

The administration's bill sought to leave the general ban intact, but waive it only for training, scholarships, and similar programs in Central America.

First House Test

The House Foreign Affairs Subcommittee on Western Hemisphere Affairs on March 1 gutted the key provisions of Reagan's Central America initiative.

On the more pressing issue of increasing military assistance to El Salvador, the subcommittee voted along party lines to reject Reagan's request for $178.7 million in additional aid in fiscal 1984 and to impose stiff human rights conditions and congressional controls on all economic and military aid to that country in fiscal 1985.

At the same time, the Democratic majority on the panel spurned Reagan's request for a five-year commitment of more than $8 billion in economic aid to Central America.

The subcommittee approved $243 million for 1984 and $621 million for 1985, but rejected Reagan's request for subsequent years. The subcommittee backed establishing a $500 million fund for reconstruction and development once countries in the region had signed a comprehensive peace agreement and settled on a regional development plan.

The subcommittee's action was the first formal congressional response to the Kissinger commission findings. But administration officials and Republicans insisted it was not a fair test because the subcommittee was dominated by liberal Democrats who never had accepted Reagan's policies toward Central America.

The administration launched an all-out assault on the subcommittee actions, bringing several U.S. ambassadors to Central American countries to Washington to lobby Congress. James H. Michel, deputy assistant secretary of state for inter-American affairs, said the panel would "seriously retard our efforts to achieve our national objectives in Central America."

The subcommittee rejected a series of amendments by Douglas K. Bereuter, R-Neb., that would have softened the

Commission Members

Following are the members of the National Bipartisan Commission on Central America, headed by former Secretary of State Henry A. Kissinger:

Nicholas F. Brady, a New Jersey businessman who served as an interim Republican senator for eight months in 1982; San Antonio Mayor Henry G. Cisneros; William P. Clements Jr., former GOP governor of Texas; Carlos F. Diaz-Alejandro, professor of economics at Yale University; Wilson S. Johnson, president of the National Federation of Independent Business; AFL-CIO President Lane Kirkland; Richard M. Scammon, a Washington political consultant; John Silber, president of Boston University; former Supreme Court Justice Potter Stewart; Robert S. Strauss, a Washington lawyer and Democratic Party operative; and William B. Walsh, president of Project Hope.

Sitting in on the panel's talks but not voting were 11 "senior counselors." Jeane J. Kirkpatrick, U.S. representative to the United Nations, was President Reagan's emissary. Kissinger appointed his former State Department aides Winston Lord, president of the Council on Foreign Relations, and William D. Rogers, a Washington lawyer. Congressional leaders named Sens. Lloyd Bentsen, D-Texas; Charles McC. Mathias Jr., R-Md.; Pete V. Domenici, R-N.M.; and Reps. Jim Wright, D-Texas; Michael D. Barnes, D-Md.; Jack F. Kemp, R-N.Y.; and William S. Broomfield, R-Mich. Sen. Daniel K. Inouye, D-Hawaii, succeeded an eighth member, Sen. Henry M. Jackson, D-Wash., who died on Sept. 1. Harry W. Shlaudeman, former U.S. ambassador to Argentina, was executive director.

impact of the Democrats' changes.

Barnes, the subcommittee chairman and a leading critic of Reagan's policies, admitted he had "reservations" about some of his panel's actions. But Barnes and other Democrats said they were warning Reagan that he must be more willing to compromise with members of Congress concerned about human rights and other issues in Central America.

El Salvador

For fiscal 1985, the panel drafted a new requirement for conditions on military and economic aid to El Salvador. For El Salvador to get the aid, the U.S. president would have to report to Congress that the Salvadoran government had "achieved" a list of human rights, judicial and other changes. Congress would approve the president's report by joint resolution. In effect, that procedure would have created a one-house veto of the aid, since both chambers would have to approve such a resolution.

Rep. Stephen J. Solarz, D-N.Y., originally had proposed that the fiscal 1985 conditions apply only to military aid in excess of $64.8 million — the amount provided in 1984. On an amendment by Studds, the subcommittee applied the restriction to all of Reagan's $132.5 million request for El Salvador in 1985. Later, the panel applied the restriction to all Economic Support Fund aid to El Salvador; Reagan had sought $210 million for that program and the panel approved half.

Studds said the conditions were a blunt warning that

Congress was demanding elimination of paramilitary "death squads" in El Salvador.

Other Issues

On other Central America issues, the panel recommended:

● An end to the large-scale military exercises the Reagan administration had conducted in Honduras since the summer of 1983. The subcommittee sought to require the withdrawal of all U.S. military personnel, except for a maximum of 300 people to guard the U.S. Embassy and to run military aid programs there. *(Honduras facilities, p. 84)*

● Rejection of Reagan's request for $45 million to equip and staff a U.S. camp in Honduras used to train Honduran and Salvadoran soldiers.

● Approval of Reagan's $10 million request for military aid to Guatemala in 1985 — if the money was used for "non-lethal" purposes, such as construction of mobile medical clinics.

● Limited approval of Reagan's request to waive, for Central America, a ban on aid to foreign police forces.

Committee Action

The full Foreign Affairs Committee moved with unaccustomed speed through the bulk of its fiscal 1984-85 foreign aid authorizations bill (HR 5119) Feb. 28 to March 7. But on March 14, after members were unable to agree on the broad Central America provisions, the committee severed the package from the bill. The committee approved its stripped-down, $9.5 billion measure on March 15, without the Kissinger commission proposals.

Committee Democrats had agreed informally to reject nearly all of Reagan's request for legislation to implement the commission's recommendations.

To buy time to lobby for its requests, the administration had sought postponement of committee action on Central America, threatening to oppose any aid bill that did not include a regional aid package to its liking.

The Foreign Affairs Committee was sharply divided, with most Democrats seeking to gut the key elements of Reagan's Central America policies, while Republicans and the administration warned that to do so would kill the entire aid measure.

Many members of both parties in Congress were leery of promising more aid to El Salvador until after that country's March 25 elections. They were concerned that the next president could be Roberto d'Aubuisson, a far-right president who had been linked in press reports to death squads.

Foreign Affairs Committee Democrats, after a series of meetings, on March 14 reached an uneasy agreement on a complicated proposal that rejected most of Reagan's requests and would set tough new conditions on aid to El Salvador.

Later that day, when the full committee met, outraged Republicans asked for a delay in considering the Central America portion of the aid bill until after the Salvadoran elections. The Democratic proposal "sends the worst possible signal at the worst possible time," said ranking Republican William S. Broomfield of Michigan. "Our action in this committee should not give cause for charges of interference or influence in that election. Committee action at this time could do precisely that." Adding the Democrats' conditions on Central America assistance doomed the foreign aid bill, he said.

Committee Democrats split over whether to delay action on Central America. Some, according to Barnes, wanted to wait until after the Salvadoran elections.

Solarz said he feared the entire foreign aid bill would be held "hostage" to the Central America provisions. On his motion, the committee voted to delete the Central America aid proposals from the bill.

James H. Michel, of the State Department, said the severing of Central America from the aid bill "simply defers" the committee's decisions.

House Democrats' Plan

The Democratic proposal represented a compromise on several Central America issues. Rejecting the bulk of the economic and military aid proposals made by the Kissinger commission, committee Democrats approved $250 million in aid, and only for fiscal 1985, beginning Oct. 1, 1984. And, after a series of compromises, they decided to impose new restrictions on several major aspects of Reagan's policies in the region.

Although the majority view prevailed, Committee Chairman Dante B. Fascell, D-Fla., managed to tone down some of the provisions that the administration most disliked. On April 11, Fascell introduced a new bill (HR 5420) including the plan. HR 5420 was not considered by the full committee and later was incorporated into HR 5119.

The cornerstone of the Democrats' plan was a series of conditions on economic and military aid to El Salvador in fiscal 1985. Reagan had sought $132.5 million in arms aid and $210 million in economic aid for El Salvador.

In a compromise between Democrats who differed over whether to approve some supplemental military aid for fiscal 1984, the members agreed to shift $56.8 million from Reagan's 1984 request to 1985 — resulting in a $189.3 million total for 1985. The Democrats did not establish a figure for economic aid.

The Democrats set conditions on all of El Salvador's military and economic aid in 1985, but in another compromise placed mild conditions on some of the aid and much stricter rules on the rest. Under the Democrats' plan, El Salvador could get $64.8 million in arms aid and half of its economic aid if the president certified to Congress that the Salvadorans were making "demonstrated progress" on human rights and other issues.

El Salvador would get the remaining $124.5 million in military aid and its remaining economic aid if:

● The president submitted a second report to Congress certifying that the government "has achieved" three goals: an end to the involvement of military forces in "death squads"; participation in negotiations with all opposition — including the guerrillas — unless the opposition refused; and compliance with international treaties on protecting civilians during civil wars.

● Congress enacted a joint resolution stating agreement with the president's second report. In effect, that condition would give either the House or Senate a veto over the remaining aid, since passage of the joint resolution by both chambers would be needed to free it up.

The Democrats' plan also would limit the number of U.S. military trainers at any one time to 55 (the administration's current self-imposed limit) and effectively would bar the president from using his emergency powers to provide aid to El Salvador without the approval of Congress.

Other major provisions of the plan would have:

● Prohibited introduction of U.S. military forces into Honduras except for protection of the U.S. Embassy and up to 300 personnel needed to train Honduran troops and to administer arms sales programs.

● Limited military aid to Honduras to $56 million in fiscal 1984 (Reagan had requested $77.5 million) and to $41 million in 1985 (Reagan requested $61.3 million).

● Prohibited all economic and military aid and arms sales to Guatemala, except for $10 million in aid over 1984-85 for engineering, construction and medical programs of the Guatemalan army.

● Established a Fund for Reconstruction and Development of Central America, with $250 million allocated for fiscal 1984 and "comparable" amounts promised for future years. The money would be available to countries if the president certified to Congress that they had signed a comprehensive peace agreement.

● Encouraged the president to join with other countries in setting up a Central American Development Organization, which would have had veto power over expenditure of 25 percent of U.S. regional economic aid.

Alternative Proposals

That proposal by Foreign Affairs Democrats represented the middle ground of three broad alternatives approved for floor action by the Rules Committee on May 3. None of the three alternatives was to be subject to amendment on the floor.

One of the other two options, to be offered by Broomfield, sought to provide nearly all the $1.2 billion Reagan requested for Central America aid in fiscal 1985 with few major restrictions on how it could be spent. The administration actively supported this amendment, and threatened to oppose the whole bill if it were defeated.

At the other end of the spectrum, an amendment to be offered by Studds would have made it almost impossible for Reagan to provide economic and military aid to El Salvador in fiscal 1985. Studds would have banned the aid unless El Salvador met conditions, such as disbanding the death squads, that the Reagan administration had said could not be fulfilled in the near future.

The Rules Committee deleted a key provision of the Foreign Affairs Democrats' plan that had been meant to guarantee rapid congressional consideration of follow-up legislation required to put most of El Salvador's aid into effect.

House Floor Action

Division among Democratic leaders helped Reagan gain on May 10 a victory on Central America aid. By a dramatic 212-208 vote, the House approved the Broomfield amendment to HR 5119. *(Vote 125, p. 42-H)*

The House acted one day after Reagan made a nationally televised appeal for congressional support of El Salvador and other countries fighting leftist guerrillas in Central America. "If we do nothing or if we continue to provide too little help, our choice will be a communist Central America with additional communist military bases on the mainland of this hemisphere, and communist subversion spreading southward and northward," he said.

The aid was part of a $1.3 billion 1985 request for all of Central America that would implement most of the Kissinger commission recommendations. The House action breathed some life into the commission's package.

The Democratic-controlled House long had been considered the main hurdle to Reagan's Central American policies. But Majority Leader Jim Wright, D-Texas, splitting with Speaker Thomas P. O'Neill Jr., D-Mass., and other House leaders, led 55 Democrats in backing Reagan's plan.

The House vote came four days after a runoff presidential election in El Salvador that the administration had portrayed to Congress as a victory for democracy. The May 6 Salvadoran balloting, eventually won by center-left candidate José Napoleón Duarte, weighed heavily on the House debate.

Much of the debate also demonstrated that members were torn between the imperatives of fighting communism in Central America and the desire to avoid too much involvement — especially a supporting combat role for U.S. troops — with a Salvadoran government that seemed incapable of protecting civilians from "death squads."

Partisan Divisions

The May 10 votes demonstrated the sharp partisan splits in the House, and the cleavage between Southern and Northern Democrats over Central America. Democrats rejected Reagan's package 56-200, with all but seven of the 56 "yes" votes coming from the South. Republicans were nearly unanimous in supporting Reagan, 156-8.

The House took two other votes on Central America aid before passing the aid bill. First, by 128 to 287, it rejected the Studds amendment, which would have barred military aid to El Salvador in 1985 unless that country achieved conditions on human rights and other issues. *(Vote 124, p. 42-H)*

The Broomfield substitute then was adopted on the key vote of 212-208.

Democrats demanded a second vote on the Broomfield substitute, in the hope that enough members would switch to defeat it. But the House ratified the earlier decision, 211-208. *(Vote 126, p. 42-H)*

With crossover support from some members who traditionally opposed foreign aid, such as Minority Whip Trent Lott, R-Miss., the House passed the bill 211-206. *(Vote 127, p. 42-H)*

Broomfield Amendment

The Broomfield amendment authorized $1.21 billion for military, economic, development and other aid programs to Central America in fiscal 1985.

But the amendment did not include authorizations for aid after 1985, a feature that Kissinger commission members had said was one of the most important of the initiative.

Broomfield's substitute also authorized $281 million in supplemental aid for fiscal 1984, with the bulk going for economic aid ($119 million) and military aid ($129.35 million). The amendment did not specify amounts for individual countries in either 1984 or 1985.

The Broomfield substitute required presidential reports on El Salvador's progress on human rights and other issues. But it did not require achievement of the standards before the Salvadoran government could receive arms aid.

The Broomfield amendment also:

● Required the president to notify Congress 30 days in advance of assigning U.S. military personnel to any Central American country for joint exercises.

● Banned all military aid for Guatemala in fiscal years 1984-85, except for $10 million over the two years to pay for the engineering and construction of mobile medical facilities to aid the poor.

● Encouraged the president to negotiate with other countries to establish a Central American Development Organization, which would make recommendations on political and economic matters in the region. The organization would be composed of representatives from other countries that donated aid to the region and of Central American countries that committed themselves to human rights, democracy and other reforms. It would have an informal veto power over the expenditure of 25 percent of U.S. economic aid to the region.

● Lifted, at the president's discretion, a legal ban on the use of U.S. foreign aid to compensate landowners in foreign countries whose land was taken in a land reform program. El Salvador, which was running a land reform program at the insistence of the U.S. government, would be the main beneficiary of this provision.

● Authorized $20 million in 1985 for scholarships, training and other programs to improve the justice systems in Central American countries. This provision did not include an administration request to waive a legal ban on U.S. aid to police forces in foreign countries.

● Approved an administration request that the Agency for International Development be allowed to guarantee up to $300 million worth of risky loans by the U.S. Export-Import Bank to finance exports to Central America.

Senate Committee

In early April 1984, the Senate Foreign Relations Committee split along partisan and ideological lines when it considered Central America provisions in marking up its fiscal 1984-85 foreign aid authorizations bill. The result was an impasse that helped doom the foreign aid bill in the Senate. There were two conflicting proposals:

One, sponsored by Mathias and other committee Republicans, sought to implement most of the Kissinger commission's recommendations.

The other proposal, sponsored by Christopher J. Dodd, D-Conn., and other Democrats, rejected many of the Kissinger recommendations and sought to impose tight conditions on economic and military aid to Central America, particularly El Salvador.

Of the two, the administration preferred the Mathias proposal, although State Department officials objected strongly to parts of it. The State Department opposed virtually every aspect of the Dodd amendment.

The committee set formal working sessions on Central American issues for April 3-6. But each day the committee failed to make substantial progress because Mathias and Dodd could not bridge the gap between Republicans and Democrats on questions of how much aid should the United States provide the Salvadoran military, and under what conditions, and how deeply should the United States get involved in the region's wars.

The Foreign Relations Committee's deliberations were overshadowed by the Senate's landmark debate in late March and early April on Central America aid in a supplemental appropriations bill (H J Res 492). *(Details, p. 75)*

Negotiations

After repeated false starts, the committee got down to serious talks on Central America on April 4 — the sixth day of its work on the foreign aid bill. Unable to agree on major issues, the committee turned over the task of hammering out details to staff aides.

The major areas of dispute:

● Mathias and Dodd proposed substantially different methods of setting conditions, such as respect for human rights and political reforms, that Central American countries would have to meet to receive aid. Mathias wanted to impose the same conditions throughout the region and require only that the countries be making "progress" toward meeting those standards. Dodd wanted to ban all military and economic assistance to El Salvador until it met a series of rigorous conditions on human rights and other issues.

● With differences in detail, Mathias and Dodd sought to block expenditure of any fiscal 1985 aid that had been authorized and appropriated for Central America unless Congress had passed joint resolutions releasing the funds. The administration preferred the Mathias provision; it would allow some money to be spent even if Congress had not passed the required resolutions. But State Department officials adamantly opposed any procedure that would result in authorized and appropriated money being contingent on a congressional joint resolution. Such a requirement would allow a "small minority" in Congress to use delaying tactics to halt aid to Central America, said Michel, of the State Department.

● Dodd wanted to ban military aid and arms sales to Guatemala, while Mathias wanted to allow such aid under the same conditions set for other Central American nations. Reagan had requested $35 million in economic aid and $10 million in military aid to Guatemala in 1985.

● Dodd wanted to ban U.S. military exercises in Honduras unless Congress authorized them in advance. Mathias had no similar provision.

● Dodd wanted to prohibit all "covert" aid to military and paramilitary groups in the region — in effect, stopping the current U.S. aid to guerrillas battling the government of Nicaragua. Mathias had no similar provision. *(Covert issue, p. 86)*

● Dodd wanted to prohibit the president from using his emergency powers to provide military aid to El Salvador. Mathias had no similar provision.

Another contentious issue was Reagan's proposal that the Agency for International Development guarantee up to $300 million in risky loans to Central American countries from the U.S. Export-Import Bank. Mathias supported that proposal; Dodd and an apparent majority opposed it.

Helms Sides With Democrats

On April 9, the committee rejected both the Mathias and Dodd proposals, by votes of 9-9 and 8-9. The tie came on the Mathias proposal; Helms played the key role by joining the committee's eight Democrats in voting against it.

Helms did not attend the April 9 session, but left his proxy with Percy and sent along a blistering three-page statement attacking the Kissinger commission plan.

"The economic aid will be wasted and the military aid will be too little, too late," the statement said. "In the context of the present struggle, military aid is the more humanitarian of the two."

Mathias said the administration "brought out the big guns" to lobby for the Kissinger commission plan. But committee aides said that lobbying was sporadic and had no effect on Helms or Democrats. Several administration officials also appeared to be ambivalent about the bill, saying that they wanted Congress to pass one but only if it did not include provisions they disliked.

On April 11, the deadlocked Senate committee followed the House committee's example and approved a foreign aid bill for fiscal 1985 with the Central America provisions stripped out. That action, by a panel widely seen as receptive to the Kissinger commission recommendations, was a major setback for the plan.

The committee approved its stripped-down aid bill on a 16-2 vote. Kassebaum dissented because the bill violated her proposal for a freeze on federal spending. Richard G. Lugar, R-Ind., also voted "no."

Final Action

On May 9, while the House was debating the foreign aid bill, all the Senate committee members but Helms reached private agreement on a compromise aid package that would have been incorporated into the Senate foreign aid bill (S 2582). But the agreement fell apart the next day; Dodd insisted on reopening the question of how much aid each country in the region would get.

Controversy over Central America aid and other issues continued to stall the Senate's foreign aid bill until early August, when Senate Republican leaders, mindful of the election-year calendar, gave up on the measure.

Proponents of the Kissinger commission plan hoped to attach the authorization to the omnibus continuing appropriations resolution (H J Res 648 — PL 98-473), which cleared Congress Oct. 11. But key components of the multi-year plan died in the struggle over the continuing resolution, the largest and most sweeping stopgap funding bill Congress had ever approved. *(Story, p. 390)*

Instead of giving Reagan the $1.2 billion a year he wanted for Central America through fiscal 1989, Congress approved $1.1 billion for fiscal 1985.

Among the specific regionwide items that Reagan requested, but Congress rejected, were: authority for the United States to participate in a new multinational agency, the Central American Development Organization, to oversee U.S. aid; a new $20 million program to improve the administration of justice in Central American countries; exemption of Central America from a 1974 law banning aid to foreign police forces; and authorization for a new program of scholarships to enable 10,000 Latin American students to attend U.S. colleges through 1989.

But the continuing resolution did include authorizations and appropriations for a new "trade credit insurance" program to guarantee $300 million worth of loans made by the Export-Import Bank for high-risk exports of goods to Central America. The program, opposed in the Senate by an unusual coalition led by conservative Helms and liberal Claiborne Pell, D-R.I., was slipped into the continuing resolution at the last minute by administration backers.

Congress also set a $225 million limit on development aid programs in Central America — a cut of $48 million from Reagan's requests. That limit was a compromise between the House Appropriations Committee, which had voted a $200 million limit, and the Senate Appropriations panel, which had approved Reagan's request.

El Salvador

Congress provided $128.25 million in military aid for El Salvador in fiscal 1985. Of that amount, $111.75 million was in Military Assistance Program grants, $15 million was in Foreign Military Sales low-interest loans, and $1.5 million was for military training.

Congress put three major restrictions on El Salvador's

military aid in fiscal 1985:

● Only half of the MAP money could be spent before March 1, 1985, unless the president sought approval from the House and Senate Appropriations committees to spend it faster. Before he could spend the second half, the president would have to report to the committees that the Salvadorans had made "substantial progress" in several areas, including curbing "death squads," eliminating government corruption and conducting discussions with leftist opposition.

● $5 million was held in escrow until the Salvadoran government conducted a trial and obtained a verdict in the case of three land reform workers, Americans Mark Pearlman and Michael Hammer and Salvadoran José Rodolfo Viera, who were killed in January 1981.

● All aid to El Salvador would be suspended if the elected president of that country were deposed by a military coup or decree.

The continuing resolution also approved $195 million in Economic Support Fund aid to bolster El Salvador's overall economy, a slight cut from Reagan's $210 million request. Congress insisted that the Central Bank of El Salvador keep that money in a separate account, and required the president to file specific reports on how it was spent.

An additional $6 million was included in the continuing resolution for improvements in El Salvador's judicial system.

Guatemala

For the second year in a row, Congress rejected Reagan's request to resume aid for Guatemala to buy weapons from the United States. President Carter had cut off all arms sales and military aid to Guatemala in 1977 because of human rights abuses by the government there. Reagan requested $10 million in Foreign Military Sales loans for Guatemala in fiscal years 1984 and 1985, but Congress had banned the aid because of continuing repression by the rightist government.

However, the continuing resolution lifted, for 1985, a related ban on aid to train Guatemalan military officers. Reagan requested, and Congress approved, $300,000 for that purpose.

House-Senate conferees on the continuing resolution also pared, to $12.5 million, Reagan's $35 million request for economic aid to Guatemala, and required that the money be spent on programs "aimed directly at improving the lives of the poor."

Reagan also had requested $40 million for development aid to Guatemala — an amount that would be subject to cuts resulting from the $225 million Central America limit imposed in the continuing resolution.

Regional Training Center

The continuing resolution cast further doubt on administration plans to build a large Regional Military Training Center in northern Honduras. The United States for two years had been training Honduran and Salvadoran soldiers at a makeshift camp near Trujillo, and Reagan sought $45 million from Congress, over fiscal 1984-85, for a permanent facility.

But the Honduran government announced that it would no longer permit Salvadorans to be trained at the camp.

At about the same time, Panama closed a large U.S. military training center in the former Panama Canal Zone.

Those events forced the administration to work on new plans for training troops from El Salvador and the rest of Central America; officials said no decision has been made.

In the meantime, conferees on the continuing resolution added a provision barring the president from spending any money on the Honduran training center until three things had happened: the Honduran government had provided a site for it; the president had given Congress a detailed plan and cost estimate; and the Honduran government had taken steps to resolve a claim by a U.S. citizen, Tenustickes Ramiraz, whose property was confiscated for the center.

Aside from El Salvador and Guatemala, the continuing resolution did not set specific aid levels for Central American countries. However, the measure provided enough military aid for the president to give Costa Rica and Honduras his full requests: $10 million and $62.5 million, respectively.

Another provision set aside $5 million to help Central American countries develop "energy self-sufficiency." ■

Hill Again Fails to Pass Authorizations Bill

For the third year in a row, Congress failed to enact regular authorizations and appropriations bills for foreign aid programs. Instead, $18 billion worth of foreign aid spending for fiscal 1985 was included in an omnibus continuing appropriations resolution (H J Res 648 — PL 98-473), which cleared Congress on Oct. 11.

The House passed an aid authorizations bill (HR 5119) on May 10. But the Senate never took up its companion measure (S 2582), because of disputes over aid to Central America and because neither the Reagan administration nor the Foreign Relations Committee was able to drum up enough support for the bill. *(Central America issues, p. 93)*

Also working against foreign aid legislation was the political unpopularity of such programs, especially in an election year.

The House and Senate committees reported foreign aid bills in 1982 and 1983, but those measures died before reaching the floor of either chamber. *(1983 Almanac p. 140; 1982 Almanac p. 156)*

A last-minute attempt to attach a full authorizations bill to the continuing resolution failed when several Senate Democrats complained that the move was being made behind their backs. Several provisions of the House-passed bill, however, were included in the resolution. *(Story, p. 390)*

Committee Reports

The House Foreign Affairs and Senate Foreign Relations committees were torn by partisan fighting over Central American aid. Unable to compromise, they reported their bills without funding or policy provisions on Central America.

Foreign Affairs filed its stripped-down bill, HR 5119, in March. But the committee's Democratic majority settled on a Central American aid package that Chairman Dante B. Fascell, D-Fla., later incorporated into an alternative bill, HR 5420. Portions of that measure were in turn incorporated into HR 5119 before the House took up the bill in early May. *(Details, p. 100)*

The House Foreign Affairs Committee did not issue a report on HR 5420, since it never formally considered it. The House panel filed its report on HR 5119 (H Rept 98-628) on March 21.

Senate Foreign Relations filed its report on S 2582 (S Rept 98-400) on April 18. Neither committee report included money for Central America.

The House committee, in an accounting maneuver, transferred about $2 billion in military aid to "off-budget" status, thereby showing an overall cut of about $1.7 billion from Reagan's non-Central America requests. In its bill, the Senate panel added about $360 million to the president's programs. But it held the net increase to $58 million by claiming that the administration had about $305 million in unused authorizations from fiscal 1984 that could be diverted to 1985.

Middle East

In keeping with past practice and political realities, both committees boosted aid to Israel. Among members of Congress, the Jewish state was by far the most popular recipient of U.S. aid. As in each year, especially election years, members of both parties vied for the honor of sponsoring amendments that raised aid to Israel above the president's request.

At the other end of the political spectrum, Egypt and Jordan, two "moderate" Arab nations, suffered rebukes at the hands of the House committee. The panel added to its bill a series of statements about and conditions on aid to those countries.

Israel. Reagan had sought $1.4 billion in military grants and $850 million in economic grants for Israel. The military aid would have been $300 million less than the fiscal 1984 amount, half of which was in loans, and the economic aid would have been $60 million less than the 1984 amount.

Both committees approved the military aid level as requested but increased the economic aid: the House committee to $1.1 billion and the Senate panel to $1.2 billion. In contrast to previous years, the administration did not oppose the add-on for Israel.

By putting funds for Israel and Egypt in a special "Camp David" account, the Senate panel said its add-on for Israel would not force Reagan to cut back economic aid for other countries.

But William Schneider Jr., under secretary of state for security assistance, noted that Congress would inevitably trim overall funds in subsequent action on foreign aid authorization and appropriations bills.

Because Israel's aid was to be politically protected from the congressional budget knife, he said, the panel's increases "in fact are going to have to be taken away from other countries. I'm not saying that the additions are at all unworthy, but the iron law of resources would simply make it likely that all the additions are going to have to come from somewhere."

By a 9-7 vote, Foreign Relations adopted an amendment by Alan Cranston, D-Calif., and Joseph R. Biden Jr., D-Del., decreeing that economic aid to Israel should always be sufficient to cover that country's annual payments to the United States on past debts. Cranston said Israel's yearly payments were not expected to exceed $1.2 billion through 1999. However, the Congressional Budget Office said this provision could cost at least $1.4 billion annually by 1990 and a total of $28 billion over 35 years.

The strongest opponent of the amendment was another of Israel's most vocal supporters on the Senate committee: Rudy Boschwitz, R-Minn. He said it might be interpreted in future years as setting a maximum level of economic aid, not the minimum level that Cranston and Biden intended.

In a further concession to Israel, the Senate panel adopted an amendment by John Glenn, D-Ohio, stipulating that Israel get its economic aid in the first quarter of each fiscal year.

Both committees also set aside $400 million of the military aid for work on Israel's new "Lavi" fighter plane. Of that amount, $150 million was to be spent on research and development in the United States and $250 million was to be spent buying equipment in Israel. Congress in 1983 set a precedent for funding the Lavi, appropriating $550 million. That action overrode a longstanding U.S. policy of not allowing countries to use aid funds to develop their own weapons systems. *(1983 Almanac p. 134)*

Egypt. The two committees took opposite approaches toward Egypt. The Senate panel approved more economic aid than Reagan had requested. The House panel, on the other hand, implicitly rebuked Egypt for its alleged failure to adhere to its 1979 peace treaty with Israel.

Both committees approved Reagan's $1.175 billion military aid request for Egypt, along with $2 million for military training and $243.3 million worth of food aid.

On an amendment by Charles McC. Mathias Jr., R-Md., the Senate panel added $65 million to Reagan's $750 million request for economic aid. Mathias said the money was needed to provide "some equivalence" between Egypt and Israel, since the committee already had boosted economic aid to Israel by $350 million. The administration agreed in supporting the boost.

Complaining about the "lack of progress in the normalization of relations between Egypt and Israel," the House committee held Egypt to blame. Egypt had not had an ambassador in Israel since September 1982, following the massacre of civilians at two Palestinian refugee camps in Israeli-held territory in Lebanon.

The House committee, in its bill, stated the sense of Congress that U.S. aid was provided to Egypt "in the expectation that the Egyptian government will support and fulfill" the provisions of the 1978 Camp David accord and the 1979 peace treaty between Egypt and Israel. In those documents, the two countries promised to maintain regular diplomatic relations.

The committees treated Jordan in much the same way they treated Egypt — approving aid but with the House panel adding provisions expressing displeasure at that country's failure to negotiate with Israel.

For Jordan, the committees approved Reagan's requested $95 million in military aid (half in low-interest loans and half in regular loans) and $20 million in economic aid.

The House committee provision, offered by Larry Smith, D-Fla., said Jordan could not buy from the United States, or receive aid to buy, certain advanced weapons systems unless the president certified to Congress that Jordan was "publicly committed to the recognition of Israel and to prompt entry into direct peace negotiations with Israel" under the terms of U.N. Security Council resolutions 242 and 338. Those resolutions recognized Israel's right to exist but called on Israel to return territory seized from its Arab neighbors. The amendment also said that aid was provided to Jordan "in the hope that Jordan will enter into direct negotiations with Israel" under the terms of the U.N. resolutions.

Smith said one purpose of the amendment was to block a sale to Jordan of "Stinger" anti-aircraft missiles. Reagan on March 21 withdrew a proposed Stinger sale in the wake of an uproar caused by statements by Jordan's King Hussein that the United States could no longer be trusted to mediate Arab-Israeli disputes. *(Story, p. 116)*

Both committees approved provisions that would put into law, and toughen, a longstanding U.S. policy banning recognition of and direct negotiations with the Palestine Liberation Organization (PLO) until that group recognized Israel's right to exist and accepted the U.N. resolutions.

The two provisions stated that "no officer or employee of the United States government and no agent or other individual acting on behalf" of the government might negotiate with the PLO until it met the conditions. The committees added a third condition: that the PLO had to renounce "the use of terrorism."

At the administration's request, the Senate panel added a loophole allowing PLO negotiations in an emergency or to meet humanitarian needs.

The committees acted in response to reports that the Reagan administration had conducted secret talks, through an intermediary, with the PLO for nine months in 1981-82. Administration officials said those talks did not violate U.S. policy because they were not negotiations.

Lebanon. While saying it hoped for progress toward peace in Lebanon, the Senate committee rejected Reagan's $20 million request for economic aid to that country. The House committee approved the $20 million, and both committees endorsed a $15 million military aid program for Lebanon. The administration had put military aid to Lebanon on hold pending an improvement in the security situation there.

In rejecting the economic aid, the Senate committee noted that the administration had been unable to spend all of the $150 million in emergency aid Congress had authorized for Lebanon in 1983. As the panel was working on its bill, the administration notified Capitol Hill that $40 million of economic aid for Lebanon was being transferred to Grenada, the Caribbean island that the United States invaded in October 1983. The committee expressed "regret" about the $40 million transfer but made no move to block it.

The Foreign Relations Committee itself dipped into Lebanon's economic aid pot, approving an amendment by Mathias that would use $50 million of leftover aid to establish a trust fund to help finance the American University of Beirut, a private institution that received U.S. government funds.

Philippines

Both panels made symbolic cuts in arms aid to the Philippines, in a statement about the dictatorship of President Ferdinand E. Marcos.

Reagan had sought $180 million in aid to the Philippines as the first installment on a five-year, $900 million program that amounted to rent for two huge U.S. military installations: Clark Air Field and Subic Bay Naval Base.

The request included $95 million in economic aid grants, $60 million in Foreign Military Sales (FMS) loans and $25 million in Military Assistance Program (MAP) grants.

The House committee, at the suggestion of Stephen J. Solarz, D-N.Y., eliminated the $60 million in FMS loans and shifted that amount to economic aid. Solarz said the Philippines needed economic aid, and a cut in military aid would put "distance" between the United States and Marcos.

Democrats on the Senate panel offered the same provision, but were outvoted, 10-7, by Republicans, who decided to shift $30 million from FMS loans to economic aid.

The Senate committee also incorporated in its bill the text of a resolution (S Con Res 71) introduced by Edward M. Kennedy, D-Mass., deploring the 1983 assassination of Philippine opposition leader Benigno S. Aquino Jr. and calling on the Marcos government to hold fair elections in May.

Pakistan

Responding to fresh reports that Pakistan was continuing to develop a nuclear bomb, the Senate unit first adopted, then under administration pressure watered down, an amendment threatening to cut off $525 million in U.S. aid to that country.

Restrictions on aid to Pakistan were imposed in 1979 because of that country's reported determination to build a nuclear bomb. In 1981, the restrictions were waived for six years to bolster support of Pakistan in the wake of the Soviets' occupation, in late 1979, of neighboring Afghanistan. *(1981 Almanac p. 161)*

The Senate committee adopted an amendment banning aid to Pakistan if it acquired a nuclear bomb. That provision replaced one voted earlier by the committee that would have banned aid if there was evidence that Pakistan was seeking to build a bomb — a provision the administration opposed because it was reported to have such evidence and would have been forced to stop aid to Pakistan.

The committee also adopted a Cranston amendment calling on Pakistan to hold free elections and to observe basic human rights. The panel said it was concerned that "prolonged military rule and continued human rights abuses in Pakistan could undermine" U.S.-Pakistani ties.

Military Aid

After deciding to postpone action on Central America, both committees approved the bulk of Reagan's requests for military aid. Reagan sought $6.05 billion for military assistance in fiscal 1985, not counting Central American programs. The Senate panel approved $6.25 billion and the House committee $5.73 billion.

The two biggest military aid programs were FMS loans and MAP grants. Both enabled foreign countries to buy U.S. weapons and military services. Another program, International Military Education and Training, provided direct grants so foreign military officers could receive training in the United States. The fourth military aid program, the Guarantee Reserve Fund, subsidized bad FMS debts.

Gritting its collective teeth, the Senate committee accepted Reagan's proposal to shift $2 billion in military aid on to the budget. But the House panel shied away from that step, which would have had the effect of making the foreign aid bill look some $2 billion bigger.

In the past, FMS-guaranteed loans were "off-budget": although they had to be authorized and appropriated, they did not show up in budget totals or count toward the total size of foreign aid bills because they did not directly result in spending by the U.S. Treasury. All other arms aid programs had been counted in budget totals because they involved grants and low-interest loans that did cause an immediate drain on the Treasury.

In a move it called honest budgeting, the administration in 1984 proposed making the entire FMS program count as part of the budget. Administration officials argued that FMS loans created potential liabilities against the U.S. Treasury, and so should be included in the budget.

The Foreign Relations and Foreign Affairs committees long had endorsed such a step. But in an election year, both panels were reluctant to add to the size of their aid bills, even through a technical change.

The Senate committee, which had been the strongest advocate of "on-budget" financing, accepted the full Reagan proposal. Not counting aid figures for Central American countries, that action had the effect of shifting about $2 billion in FMS guaranteed loans on to the budget.

At the recommendation of Chairman Fascell, the House committee rejected the on-budget request for fiscal 1985 but said it would approve the shift starting in fiscal 1986. The panel would write its fiscal 1986 bill in 1985, a non-election year when presumably it would face less political pressure.

Concessional Loans. Reagan had requested $538.5 million for a new "concessional" program enabling 16 countries to buy U.S. weapons and defense services with loans bearing a 5 percent interest rate. Standard U.S. FMS loans are at the market rate for Treasury securities, averaging 12 percent in recent years.

The House committee approved $358.5 million for concessional loans to 11 countries, excluding three countries in Central America (El Salvador, Guatemala and Panama). It rejected Reagan's requests for Pakistan ($100 million) and the Philippines ($30 million). The panel said it rejected the Pakistan request because that country, citing its "non-aligned" status, did not want to receive special low-interest loans and instead preferred the higher-rate guaranteed loans.

Foreign Affairs also cut concessional loan requests for Tunisia (from $25 million to $18 million) and Turkey (from $250 million to $237 million).

The Senate panel approved $478.5 million for concessional loans to 12 countries. Aside from failing to act on the requests for Central America, that panel's major change was to reject the $30 million request for the Philippines.

On an amendment by Frank H. Murkowski, R-Alaska, the Senate committee limited the concessional loan program to 10 percent of the annual total for FMS loans. Since the committee approved $5.01 billion in FMS loans, Murkowski's amendment would limit concessional loans to $501 million. The limit would not apply to forgiven loans for Israel and Egypt.

The Murkowski amendment also set a minimum interest rate: concessional loans would have to carry a minimum rate of 5 percent, or 7 percentage points below the prevailing market rates for the U.S. government, whichever was greater.

Arms Sales. In reaction to the Reagan administration's increasing use of arms sales as a foreign policy tool, both committees adopted amendments that sought to pressure the administration on the issue.

The Senate committee provision, sponsored by Paul S. Sarbanes, D-Md., stated the sense of Congress that the United States should begin negotiations with its NATO allies to limit the volume and level of sophistication of arms sold to developing countries.

The committee said "a collective policy among the Western democracies" was needed to ensure that competition for arms sales did not damage Western security interests and to prepare for potential East-West talks on limiting conventional arms sales.

President Carter's administration initiated negotiations with the Soviet Union on limiting arms sales, but those talks collapsed in 1978 without producing any agreements.

The House unit required the president to submit a report to Congress discussing arms sales issues and the prospects for international agreements to limit them. In its report, but not in the bill, the House committee also called on the president to begin arms sales discussions with U.S. allies.

In related provisions:

● The Senate panel sought to put into law its demand for veto authority over the "reprogramming," or transfer, of any foreign aid funds from one account or one country to another. The committee first declared that it had this power in 1983, when it insisted on a voice in the reprogramming of military aid to El Salvador. By tradition and law, apparently only the House and Senate Appropriations committees had such veto power.

● Both committees agreed to Reagan's request to add South Korea to a list of countries given special terms for repaying their guaranteed FMS loans. The Senate committee also voted to add Morocco and Tunisia to the list. Under those terms, selected countries had up to 30 years to pay off the loans — including a 10-year grace period to delay payments on the principal. Standard terms called for payment of all principal and interest within 12 years. Other recipients of the special terms were Greece, Portugal, Somalia, Spain, the Sudan and Turkey.

The Senate committee adopted an amendment by Murkowski stating that no more than 22 percent of all FMS loans could be made under the special repayment terms. The amendment also banned the special terms for countries in arrears on previous FMS loans. Neither provision would have a direct effect in fiscal 1985, but either provision could force the administration to curtail the use of special repayment terms in future years.

● Both committees agreed to allow additional U.S. military advisers in several countries. By law, the Pentagon was not allowed to station more than six military officials in any one country to supervise U.S. arms sales unless Congress gave advance approval. In the past, Congress had given such permission for 12 countries, and Reagan wanted to station more than six advisers in each of eight additional countries: El Salvador, Honduras, Lebanon, Pakistan, the Sudan, Tunisia, Venezuela and North Yemen. The Senate committee approved the request, but the House committee said no for El Salvador, Honduras and the Sudan.

● The House committee included a provision curbing the president's ability to use one of his special emergency powers: section 614 of the foreign aid laws, by which he was able to provide unlimited military aid and arms sales to other countries regardless of legal restrictions. The committee's provision sought to put a $750 million cap on section 614 sales to another country. The limit would be allowed to rise to $1 billion if the buying country received $250 million in foreign aid to pay for the arms. In 1981, administration officials threatened to use the section 614 authority to sell AWACS radar planes and other equipment to Saudi Arabia if Congress vetoed the sale. Congress allowed the $8.5 billion sale, but the administration's threat prompted the House committee to move to pre-empt such an action in the future. *(1981 Almanac p. 129)*

● On an amendment by Sen. Larry Pressler, R-S.D., the Senate unit voted to require the president to report to Congress whenever he approved arms sales to a country that were at least $100 million in excess of the military aid authorized for that country. This amendment was aimed at giving Congress information on the use of "cash flow financing," in which the administration made commitments for arms sales and then, citing those commitments, demanded that Congress approve aid to finance the sales.

● Both committees reduced to $114 million Reagan's request for $274 million for a reserve fund used to reimburse the U.S. government when foreign countries fall behind on their payments on military aid loans.

● Both committees rejected an administration proposal that would have set a single fee that foreign countries would pay for U.S. training of their military officers. The United States had several levels of charges, with U.S. military aid recipients paying the lowest fee and wealthy allies paying the highest. The proposed change would have reduced the fees paid by several wealthy nations such as Saudi Arabia and West Germany — a fact that Senate committee members cited in rejecting the change.

● On an amendment by Glenn, the Senate committee voted to require that the administration resubmit to Congress any foreign arms sale notice if "sensitive technology" was added after Congress had approved a sale. Glenn offered the amendment because the administration in 1982 refused to seek congressional approval to add sophisticated radar equipment to F-16 warplanes being sold to Pakistan.

● Both committees approved the administration request for increases in the maximum penalties for violations of the Arms Export Control Act (PL 94-329), which governed foreign military sales. The maximum criminal penalty would be increased to a fine of $1 million or 10 years' imprisonment, or both; the current maximums were a $100,000 fine and two years' imprisonment. The maximum civil penalty would be increased from a $100,000 fine to a $500,000 one.

● The Senate panel would ban use of FMS loans for purchases of weapons and other supplies outside the United States unless the president certified to Congress that doing so was important to the U.S. national interest. The committee said it did not want foreign countries to use U.S. aid to expand their arms industries or to buy weapons from U.S. competitors.

Africa

Reagan's "economic policy initiative" to bolster capitalist economies in Africa won approval from both committees — but with conditions.

As proposed by the administration, the new African aid program would reward countries that made economic "reforms" such as eliminating price controls that discouraged farm production.

Reagan requested $75 million for the program in fiscal 1985 and said he intended to ask a total of about $500 million over the fiscal years 1985-89.

Secretary of State George P. Shultz said in January that countries "that we think are on the right track" — and thus likely candidates to receive the aid — were Senegal, Zambia, Madagascar, Somalia and the Sudan.

The House committee added conditions meant to en-

hance the poverty-fighting aspect of the program, while the Senate committee added restrictions meant to ensure that aid provided under the program would not be diverted to other purposes.

The House panel required: that the administration consult with Congress before selecting recipients; that standard criteria for economic aid programs, such as an emphasis on funding imports to bolster agricultural production, be applied to projects funded by the initiative; and that the initiative be directed toward "growth with equity," not just economic growth.

The Senate committee agreed with the House panel's demand for advance consultation on the selection of countries to get the aid, but it did not include the other House requirements. Instead, the Senate panel added several other conditions, including: that aid be directed to countries that made "meaningful reforms" such as eliminating government monopolies that hindered production; that none of the program's aid be given to any country that had "historically misappropriated significant portions of its revenues for private purposes" (a provision that might affect such countries as Zaire and Nigeria); that the assistance not be used to pay African countries' debts to foreign banks or to meet economic conditions imposed by the International Monetary Fund; and that the United States would coordinate the new program with aid efforts of other donor governments and international agencies.

The House committee imposed conditions on regular U.S. economic and military aid programs to several African countries. But to avoid controversy the committee set less severe conditions than it had proposed in 1982 and 1983. *(Africa aid, p. 121)*

Among other African issues:

● For Zaire, the House committee cut military aid grants to $4 million, from Reagan's $15 million request, and cut economic aid to $5 million from Reagan's $15 million request. The committee also stipulated that all economic aid to Zaire must be spent through private agencies; Reagan had proposed using economic aid to subsidize U.S. exports to Zaire. The Senate committee limited Zaire's economic and military aid to $10 million each. Both committees had complained for years about corruption in Zaire.

● For Tunisia, the House panel cut military aid to $58 million, from Reagan's $65 million request, while boosting economic aid from $3 million to $10 million. The Senate panel approved the full arms aid request and raised economic aid to $15 million.

● For Morocco, both committees approved Reagan's requests for $50 million in military aid and $15 million in economic aid. But the House panel imposed conditions to reduce any U.S. involvement in Morocco's war against Algerian-backed guerrillas for control of the Western Sahara. The panel stated that U.S. policy must support a negotiated political solution to the war and that any U.S. military aid to Morocco must be consistent with that policy. That provision was in keeping with the House committee's long-standing opposition to sales of arms that Morocco might use in the war. The House bill also prohibited U.S. military advisers to Morocco from serving in the Western Sahara as long as the war continues.

● For regional economic programs in southern Africa, the Senate committee approved Reagan's $37 million request, but the House committee boosted the total to $60 million. In contrast to previous years, the House committee did not earmark funds for projects in Tanzania or in Mozambique. Tanzania was ineligible for U.S. aid because it had failed to keep up its payments on past U.S. loans. The Reagan administration — which in previous years opposed aid to the leftist government of Mozambique — recently had agreed to provide some aid because of that country's negotiation in March of a peace agreement with neighboring South Africa.

● For Zimbabwe, both committees accepted the administration's $15 million request for economic aid — a sharp cut from the $40 million that Congress appropriated for fiscal 1984. The House Foreign Affairs Subcommittee on Africa had said it wanted more aid for Zimbabwe but admitted that "it is not realistic" to get it over administration opposition. The administration had reduced the aid to protest Zimbabwe's votes in the United Nations in opposition to U.S. policy. Reagan also requested, and the committee approved, $15 million in development aid to Zimbabwe.

South America

Toughening a 1981 law, the House committee decided to ban military aid to Chile unless an elected civilian government was in power there and the Chilean government agreed to extradite alleged Nazi war criminal Walter Rauff to Israel.

Reagan had requested only $50,000 for military training aid to Chile in 1985 — a request that, if granted, would qualify that country for reduced rates on all its U.S. military training.

The House provision effectively would have banned the aid to Chile for some time, since the government of Augusto Pinochet had resisted all calls for elections.

Congress in 1981 had weakened restrictions on military aid and arms sales to Chile because Reagan said such an action would encourage political reforms. Foreign Affairs said it favored re-enacting tough aid curbs "as a signal to the executive branch" that Congress opposed restoring military ties to Chile until elections were held there. *(1981 Almanac p. 162)*

Foreign Affairs imposed similar conditions on military training aid to Paraguay and Uruguay. Paraguay could not receive the $50,000 in training aid until it extradited alleged Nazi war criminal Joseph Mengele to Israel; Uruguay would be denied its $60,000 in military training aid because of its refusal to conduct free elections.

At the request of Chairman Claude Pepper, D-Fla., and other members of the House Rules Committee, the Foreign Affairs panel added $90 million in special economic aid to three South American countries: $50 million for Peru, and $20 million each for Ecuador and Bolivia. Reagan requested no economic aid for those countries, although the United States had development and food aid programs in each of them.

Latin Scholarships

Expanding on a recommendation by the Kissinger commission on Central America, the House committee approved $50 million for a new program of scholarships at U.S. universities for disadvantaged students from Latin America and the Caribbean. Half the money would be administered by the U.S. Agency for International Development (AID) and the other half by the U.S. Information Agency.

The commission, chaired by former Secretary of State Henry A. Kissinger, had recommended a multi-year, $8 billion-plus aid package for Central America. *(Story, p. 93)*

Among its recommendations was a program of 10,000 scholarships over five years to students from Central America. But the House panel broadened it to include students from all of Latin America and the Caribbean.

The committee stipulated that at least 75 percent of the money had to finance undergraduate and technical education, and at least 15 percent had to be allocated to students from the Caribbean. At least 30 percent of the students receiving the scholarships had to be engaged in training programs in agriculture.

Haiti

The House committee, saying the human rights situation in Haiti had deteriorated, voted to impose tough conditions on aid to that country.

In a restatement of provisions in the fiscal 1984 continuing appropriations resolution (PL 98-151), the committee insisted that most of Haiti's $29 million in economic and development aid be provided through private organizations, rather than through the Haitian government.

The committee also said Haiti could receive economic, development and military training assistance if the president reported to Congress that Haiti was cooperating in stemming the flow of illegal immigrants to this country, was cooperating in implementing U.S. aid programs there, was complying with economic policy conditions imposed by the International Monetary Fund and was making human rights and political reforms such as allowing the establishment of free political parties.

The House committee also banned military aid grants and FMS loans to Haiti in fiscal 1984-85; Reagan had requested $300,000 in military grants in each of those years.

Economic Aid

Because of aid increases for Israel, both panels approved substantial boosts in Reagan's request for the Economic Support Fund (ESF), the multibillion-dollar program that was used to bolster the economies of countries friendly to the United States.

Reagan requested $2.797 billion for ESF aid in 1985 — more than half of it for Israel and Egypt. The House committee approved $3.236 billion and the Senate committee $3.071 billion. The Senate panel also said another $171 million authorized for ESF aid in fiscal 1984 was available to be spent in 1985 instead.

Both bills would authorize the president to use up to $75 million of each year's ESF account for emergency purposes — a provision originally enacted by Congress in 1981.

In several specific cases, especially for African countries, the House panel sought to force the administration to use ESF aid for economic development and anti-poverty programs, rather than for broad support of the economies in recipient nations.

The Senate committee took a more general approach to the issue of how ESF money should be used, adopting an amendment that sought to encourage the administration to use ESF aid for development projects.

Development Aid

In another skirmish in a long-running battle, the House committee voted to boost funds for two U.S.-run development programs above Reagan's request. House committee members had charged for three years that the administration had given short shrift to economic development programs, while favoring military aid.

The Senate unit took the opposite approach, cutting the requests for several development programs on the grounds that the administration already had $43.6 million in leftover authorizations from fiscal 1984.

The House panel's biggest boost was a $69.9 million increase, to $305 million, in population control programs run by AID. That was sponsored by Peter H. Kostmayer, D-Pa., who had advocated similar increases in previous years. The committee also added $16 million to Reagan's $698.7 million request for AID agricultural development programs.

In its only increase above Reagan's requests for AID programs, the Senate panel added $22 million for population programs. Both committees earmarked 16 percent of the population aid account for the U.S. contribution to the U.N. Fund for Population Activities.

Both committees approved a $25 million "child survival fund" that would finance efforts by private agencies and international groups such as the United Nations Children's Fund and the World Health Organization to improve health standards for children in developing countries. The administration had not requested the fund.

As in previous years, both committees boosted voluntary contributions to various U.N.-related organizations above Reagan's requests.

The House committee complained about the "executive branch game" of proposing cuts in those contributions, in the expectation that Congress would restore the money.

The Senate panel said its increases for the agencies "should have been no surprise" since it had done the same thing in previous years. In its report, Foreign Relations complained that Reagan's 1985 budget would have cut total contributions to the agencies by 28 percent below the 1984 amount.

Reagan proposed $191.8 million for 18 agencies affiliated with the United Nations, the Organization of American States and other international bodies. Playing their roles in the budget game, the House committee approved $279.1 million and the Senate committee $281.9 million.

The biggest boost was for the U.N. Development Program, which provided technical aid to developing countries. Reagan proposed a $120 million contribution for 1985, $40 million less than the 1984 level. The House panel approved $170 million and the Senate unit $175 million.

The development program was one of the most popular U.N. agencies among members of Congress; its administrator, former Rep. F. Bradford Morse, R-Mass. (1961-72), was known as one of the most effective lobbyists for any foreign aid agency.

Other Issues

Police Training. The House committee approved, but in a substantially watered-down form, Reagan's request for permission to supply direct aid to police forces in Central American and Caribbean countries.

Since 1975, section 660 of the foreign aid law had banned assistance to any law enforcement agencies in other countries. The ban was enacted because of charges that some U.S.-funded police agencies in Latin American countries systematically engaged in torture and other human rights violations.

In its bill, Foreign Affairs agreed to permit aid to police agencies in countries that had longstanding democratic traditions, that did not have standing armed forces and that did not consistently engage in gross violations of human rights standards. The committee said the only Cen-

tral American and Caribbean countries that would qualify under its standard were Costa Rica and several Caribbean islands. The Senate panel did not address the issue because it was part of Reagan's Central America package.

China. For the third year in a row, both panels threw back to the president the question of whether China should be removed from a list of communist countries prohibited from receiving U.S. aid.

Reagan had asked Congress each year since 1982 to take China off the no-aid list, although the United States had no plans to provide direct aid to China. In response, both committees had added provisions to their foreign aid bills allowing the president to remove China from the list if he determined and reported to Congress that doing so was "important to the national interest" of the United States.

Inter-American Foundation. Responding to a December 1983 decision by Reagan appointees to fire Peter D. Bell, president of the Inter-American Foundation, the House committee included in its bill a provision strengthening the powers of the agency president and requiring the foundation to devote its resources to serving poor people in Latin America.

UNESCO. The House panel asked the president to appoint a "bipartisan panel of experts" to study whether this country should withdraw from the United Nations Educational, Scientific and Cultural Organization as the administration had threatened to do at the end of 1984. The provision sought a report from the experts by Oct. 1, and asked the administration to consult with Congress before making its final decision on being in UNESCO. (The United States subsequently pulled out of UNESCO, in December 1984.)

Peace Corps. The House committee approved $125.5 million for Peace Corps operations in 1985 — $10.5 million above Reagan's request. Congress had boosted Peace Corps funds in each of the previous three fiscal years.

For the second year in a row, Foreign Affairs also called for a substantial increase in the number of Peace Corps volunteers — to at least 10,000 by the end of fiscal year 1988. The corps now had about 5,000 volunteers, one-third of its peak in 1966.

Development Agency. The Senate committee included in its aid bill Reagan's requested $2.25 billion three-year authorization for the U.S. contribution to the seventh replenishment of funds for the International Development Association, an arm of the World Bank. The fiscal 1985 contribution would be $750 million.

Foreign Relations added a provision, not requested by Reagan, authorizing an additional $500 million contribution in fiscal 1986 if the president determined that the money was needed because of economic deterioration in borrower countries.

The Foreign Affairs bill had no comparable provision because that committee did not have jurisdiction over international development banks. That jurisdiction was held by the House Banking Committee. *(Story, p. 124)*

Cuban Drug Smuggling. Both panels adopted amendments calling attention to alleged involvement by Cuba in international trafficking in narcotics. The committees asked the administration to raise the issue at the United Nations and in other international forums.

House Floor Action

The House approved its $10.95 billion foreign aid authorization bill, HR 5119, on May 10, after handing Reagan a very important victory in his three-year-long struggle for congressional backing of U.S. involvement in Central America.

The House approved a Republican-sponsored plan that would give Reagan most of the military aid he had requested for El Salvador, free of the stringent conditions sought by some Democrats.

The House later approved the bill 211-206. *(Vote 127, p. 42-H)*

The votes cleared the way for additional "emergency" aid for El Salvador in the 1984 fiscal year. *(Supplemental appropriations, p. 429)*

Passage of HR 5119 authorized Reagan's original $178.7 million supplemental request for El Salvador in 1984. *(Salvador aid, p. 76)*

The El Salvador aid was part of a $1.3 billion 1985 request for all of Central America that would implement most of the Kissinger commission's recommendations.

The Democratic-controlled House long had been considered the main hurdle to Reagan's Central American policies. But Majority Leader Jim Wright, D-Texas, splitting with Speaker Thomas P. O'Neill Jr., D-Mass., and other House leaders, led 55 Democrats in backing Reagan's plan.

Twice in 1983, the House had rejected aid to Nicaraguan guerrillas. But before May 10, it never had voted directly on aid to the government of El Salvador, which was fighting leftist rebels. The administration as well as Democrats had been hesitant to test the El Salvador issue in the House. And Congress had skirted politically unpopular foreign aid issues in 1982 and 1983, by handling aid funds in omnibus spending bills.

The House vote came four days after presidential elections in El Salvador that the administration had portrayed to Congress as a victory for democracy.

The May 10 votes demonstrated the sharp partisan divisions in the House, and the cleavage between Southern and Northern Democrats on Central American issues. Democrats rejected Reagan's aid package 56-200, with all but seven of the 56 "yes" votes coming from the South. Republicans were nearly unanimous in supporting the president, 156-8.

The Republican substitute, offered by William S. Broomfield, R-Mich., was adopted on the key 212-208 vote. *(Vote 125, p. 42-H)*

The House took two other votes on Central American aid before passing the aid bill. First, by a 128-287 vote, it rejected an amendment by Gerry E. Studds, D-Mass., that would have barred all military aid to El Salvador in 1985 unless that country had achieved a series of conditions on human rights and other issues. *(Vote 124, p. 42-H)*

Democrats demanded a second vote on the Broomfield substitute, in the futile hope that enough members would switch to defeat it. But the House ratified the earlier decision on a 211-208 vote. *(Vote 126, p. 42-H)*

Those votes, however, did not ensure passage of the bill, because many conservatives traditionally opposed foreign aid and some liberal Democrats could not swallow a vote that would affirm military aid to El Salvador.

The administration, in fact, had devoted nearly as much attention to lobbying for the full bill as for the Central American aid.

With crossover support from some members who traditionally opposed foreign aid, such as Minority Whip Trent Lott, R-Miss., the House passed the bill 211-206. In a shift from normal practice on foreign aid bills, a majority of

Democrats voted against the bill and a majority of Republicans for it.

The key question in House debate on the bill May 10 was to what extent should the United States place conditions on its military aid for El Salvador.

The two alternatives before the House took significantly different routes in answering that question.

The Republican substitute, offered by Broomfield and ultimately approved by the House, required presidential reports on El Salvador's progress on human rights and other issues. But it did not require achievement of the standards before the Salvadoran government could receive arms aid.

The Foreign Affairs Democrats' version, which the House never directly voted on, would have given El Salvador $64.8 million in military aid in fiscal 1985 virtually free of conditions. However, to provide more aid in 1985, Reagan would have been required to report to Congress that El Salvador "had achieved" several goals, such as eliminating the death squads and negotiating with its opposition.

Broomfield Amendment

The Broomfield amendment authorized $1.21 billion for military, economic, development and other aid programs to Central America in fiscal 1985.

But in its major departure from Reagan's request, the substitute did not include authorizations for aid after 1985.

Broomfield's substitute also authorized $281 million in supplemental aid for fiscal 1984, with the bulk going for economic aid ($119 million) and military aid ($129.35 million). The amendment did not specify amounts for individual countries in either 1984 or 1985.

The amendment required the president to submit a report to Congress by Aug. 31, 1984, on El Salvador's "demonstrated progress" toward six objectives. The objectives included: ending unlawful violence, detention, abduction, torture and murder by military and security forces; establishing an effective judicial system; ensuring freedom of the press and freedom of association; participating in a dialogue with the opposition on involvement in future elections; complying with international agreements on protecting civilians in armed conflicts; and fully implementing the "land reform" program.

The president could spend one-half of El Salvador's 1985 military aid at the beginning of the fiscal year, on Oct. 1. To spend the rest, the president would have to send Congress another report by Jan. 31, 1985, saying that El Salvador had made "additional demonstrated progress" on the objectives. If Congress did not pass a joint resolution rejecting those findings within 30 days, the remaining aid could go forward.

The Broomfield substitute also stated the sense of Congress, but did not require, that the number of U.S. military advisers in El Salvador should be limited to 55 unless Congress was consulted in advance. It required that the president, before sending economic aid to El Salvador, "be satisfied" that the Salvadoran Central Bank had implemented reforms recommended by Arthur Young & Co., a consulting firm, for the control of foreign exchange, especially U.S. aid.

On other issues, the Broomfield amendment:

● Required the president to notify Congress 30 days in advance of assigning U.S. military personnel to any Central American country for joint exercises.

● Banned all military aid for Guatemala in fiscal years 1984-85, except for $10 million over the two years to pay for the engineering and construction of mobile medical facilities to aid the poor.

● Encouraged the president to negotiate with other countries to establish a Central American Development Organization, which would make recommendations on political and economic matters in the region. The organization was to be composed of representatives from other countries that donated aid to the region and of Central American countries that committed themselves to human rights, democracy and other reforms. It was to have an informal veto power over the expenditure of 25 percent of U.S. economic aid to the region.

● Lifted, at the president's discretion, a legal ban on the use of U.S. foreign aid to compensate landowners in foreign countries whose land was taken in a land reform program. El Salvador, running a land reform program at the insistence of the U.S. government, was to be the main beneficiary of this provision.

● Authorized $20 million in 1985 for scholarships, training and other programs to improve the justice systems in Central American countries. This provision did not include an administration request to waive a legal ban on U.S. aid to police forces in foreign countries.

● Approved an administration request that the Agency for International Development be allowed to guarantee up to $300 million worth of risky loans by the U.S. Export-Import Bank to finance exports to Central American countries.

Turkey, Cyprus

A major administration concession helped head off House adoption of an amendment that would have sharply restricted arms aid to Turkey.

The concession, announced on May 8, was an agreement by the administration to provide $250 million in special economic aid to Cyprus, the Mediterranean island that was partially occupied by Turkey.

The $250 million spurred agreement by House members who had been negotiating how to avoid a bitter floor fight on the issue of aid to Turkey. With the White House support, those members produced an amendment giving Cyprus the $250 million and cutting $85 million from Reagan's request for $755 million in military aid for Turkey. The House adopted that amendment 376-27 on May 9. *(Vote 119, p. 40-H)*

Members of Congress friendly to Cyprus and Greece — Turkey's traditional rival in the region — had threatened greater trims.

Both Turkey and Greece were NATO allies, but Greece had strong political support in Congress and Turkey did not. Many members blamed Turkey and Turkish Cypriots for the repeated failure of negotiations to resolve the disputes on Cyprus.

Faced with a potential aid cut for Turkey, the administration accepted a suggestion by Larry Winn Jr., R-Kan., for an "incentive package" for Greece, Turkey and their allies on Cyprus to reach agreement on issues stemming from Turkey's 10-year occupation of the northern third of the island.

Winn originally proposed boosting economic aid for all three countries, but the administration and a bipartisan coalition in Congress settled on the $250 million fund for Cyprus if there was "substantial progress" toward a settlement on the issue.

Even with the additional aid for Cyprus, pro-Greek members insisted on cutting Turkey aid beyond the $39

million, and negotiations led by Winn and Lee H. Hamilton, D-Ind., chairman of the Europe and Middle East Subcommittee, produced agreement on the $85 million cut.

The amendment incorporating the additional aid for Cyprus and setting a $670 million limit on military aid for Turkey was offered by Edward F. Feighan, D-Ohio. He called the $670 million "a modest cap" that represented "a clear expression of congressional frustration over the deadlock on Cyprus."

Pro-Greek members won a clear-cut victory on a related amendment, offered by Broomfield. Adopted by voice vote, that measure stipulated that Greece should receive the same proportion of low-interest military loans that Turkey received.

Reagan had proposed giving Turkey about half of its military loans in the form of low-interest "concessional" credits, while forcing Greece to pay market interest rates on all its $500 million in military loans.

Philippines

Another effort to use military aid to extract concessions from a foreign country — this time the Philippines — failed by a wide margin May 9 because House leaders refused to break further from the administration.

Tony P. Hall, D-Ohio, proposed eliminating $25 million in military grants Reagan had requested for the Philippines as part of a $180 million-per-year package that served as unofficial "rent" for two U.S. bases there.

The amendment was rejected 149-259, although Hall managed to attract the support of a majority of Democrats. *(Vote 120, p. 40-H)*

The Foreign Affairs Committee had eliminated $60 million in military loans to the Philippines, and transferred that amount to economic aid. As a result, Hall's amendment would have had the effect of eliminating all military aid to the Philippines in 1985 — an action the administration argued would have been an implicit violation of a 1984 agreement allowing the United States to operate the two military bases. Hall called his amendment "a very modest reduction" that would show Capitol Hill concern about the authoritarian nature of the government of President Ferdinand E. Marcos.

Military Aid Freeze

On the closest vote of the May 9 session, the House rejected, 207-208, an amendment by Byron L. Dorgan, D-N.D., that would have frozen military grants in fiscal 1985 at 1984 levels to all countries except those in Central America. *(Vote 122, p. 40-H)*

Dorgan said the amendment would have cut $165 million from Reagan's $587 million request for non-Central America aid under the Military Assistance Program.

Dorgan called that grant program "one of the fastest growing items in the federal government."

But Fascell said the amendment would force sharp cuts in aid to some nations while leaving others unscathed — especially those that got aid in return for hosting U.S. military bases. "I simply characterize that as a disaster," Fascell said.

If the amendment had been adopted, according to Fascell, Reagan would have had only $48 million to aid 19 countries that did not have U.S. bases. One of those countries, the Sudan, had been budgeted for $69 million, and was under attack from Libya.

Dorgan's amendment attracted support from an unusual coalition of conservatives who opposed foreign aid as a general principle and liberals particularly critical of Reagan's increases in military aid.

When the 15 minutes for voting ran out, Dorgan's amendment appeared to be carrying. But a series of vote switches produced the one-vote margin against it.

Committee sources said the amendment was an example of anti-aid measures that, if adopted, might have prompted the administration to withdraw its support from the bill.

United Nations

A compromise offered by Mark D. Siljander, R-Mich., headed off an amendment by Robert S. Walker, R-Pa., that would have barred military aid to countries that voted against U.S. positions in the United Nations more than 15 percent of the time.

Adopted by voice vote, the Siljander compromise instructed the president to use votes in the U.N. General Assembly as "a major criterion" in deciding how to allocate foreign aid.

Walker said he offered his original amendment as a protest against the practice of aiding countries that consistently opposed U.S. foreign policy interests. "The kinds of nations we're talking about, I'm not sure are ones I want to be selling weapons to."

But several of Walker's prominent conservative colleagues said he was misjudging the purpose of the foreign aid program.

"I ask my colleagues to consider whether the foreign aid program . . . is a reward for good deportment in the United Nations," said Henry J. Hyde, R-Ill. Instead, he said, foreign aid programs "help us acquire allies when we need them."

Siljander said he, like Walker, was "very, very frustrated that we seem to be rewarding our enemies too often." But votes in the United Nations were not the only standard by which foreign aid recipients should be judged, Siljander said.

Siljander's amendment, adopted by voice vote, directed the president to consider U.N. votes when deciding on aid, but did not require those votes to be the deciding factor in determining whether countries got aid.

Middle East

On May 9, the House rejected, by voice vote, a rare attempt to impose conditions on U.S. aid to Israel. George W. Crockett Jr., D-Mich., offered an amendment declaring that U.S. aid to Israel was provided in the expectation that the Israeli government would fulfill the provisions of its 1979 peace treaty with Egypt. *(1979 Almanac p. 138)*

The text of the bill before the House called on Egypt to adhere to the treaty, and Crockett wanted to make the same demand of Israel. The bill authorized $2.5 billion in military and economic aid for Israel and $2.2 billion in aid for Egypt.

Crockett said Israel's annexation of the Golan Heights, its continued expansion of Jewish settlements in the occupied West Bank and its 1982 invasion of Lebanon "*in toto* constitute an infraction of the spirit if not the letter of the Camp David accords," on which the 1979 treaty was based.

By demanding Egyptian compliance with the treaty, but not Israeli compliance, he said, the bill "seeks to impose on the U.S. government the foreign policy goals and aims of the Israeli government."

Crockett said the administration did not, and should have, opposed the bill's provision when it was being drafted

by the House Foreign Affairs Subcommittee on the Middle East.

Larry Smith, D-Fla., led opposition to Crockett's amendment, saying the full committee had approved the provision because "there are many of us who share grave concerns about the commitment and the compliance" of Egypt to the Camp David accords.

Smith noted that Egypt recalled its ambassador to Israel in 1982 and had curtailed the trade and cultural arrangements with Israel that were called for in the peace treaty.

On a related matter, the House adopted, by voice vote, an amendment by Ed Zschau, R-Calif., directing the president to report to Congress by Jan. 15, 1985, on the extent to which each Middle East country receiving U.S. aid "is pursuing policies that enhance the peace process."

Zschau conceded that his amendment was not necessary, because Congress could obtain the requested information through routine hearings. But he said it might help the peace process by focusing attention on actions that the United States wanted each country in the region to take.

During Foreign Affairs action on the bill in March, Zschau had pushed an amendment stating that the United States was giving aid to Middle East countries in the expectation that they would pursue peace and would consider all peace initiatives offered by the president and others.

Pro-Israel members of the committee watered down the amendment because it could have been interpreted as calling on Israel to heed Reagan's September 1982 "peace initiative." Israel rejected that initiative because it called for Palestinians to assume eventual control of the West Bank in association with Jordan.

Other Major Amendments

In other action, the House:

● Rejected, 40-379, an amendment by Nick J. Rahall II, D-W.Va., that would have killed $400 million in U.S. aid for development of Israel's new "Lavi" warplane. Rahall said the Lavi would compete with U.S. planes and cost 6,000 jobs in the United States. But pro-Israel members pounced on Rahall's amendment as a threat to U.S.-Israeli security ties and said the Lavi would create 20,000-30,000 jobs in this country. *(Vote 121, p. 40-H)*

● Modified an amendment by Christopher H. Smith, R-N.J., that would have had the effect of banning U.S. aid to all population control programs run by the United Nations and other agencies in China. Instead, the House adopted by voice vote a milder alternative offered by Fascell that would have barred use of U.S. aid by any agency in China for coerced abortions.

● Adopted, by voice vote, an amendment by Mervyn M. Dymally, D-Calif., adding $15 million for operations of the American University in Beirut.

● Adopted, by voice vote, an amendment by Robert J. Lagomarsino, R-Calif., adding $75 million to Reagan's $45 million request for economic aid to the Dominican Republic. The extra money was in response to riots in that country early in May stemming from the imposition of economic austerity measures demanded by the International Monetary Fund. Jorge Blanco, president of the Dominican Republic, had asked Reagan during a visit to Washington in April for added economic aid but was refused.

● Adopted, by voice vote, an amendment by William H. Gray III, D-Pa., stipulating that 10 percent of all contracts awarded by the Agency for International Development should be reserved for "economically and socially disadvantaged" groups and enterprises, and for black colleges and similar agencies.

● Adopted, by voice vote, an amendment by Lagomarsino adding $15 million in military loans for Peru. Reagan had requested $10 million. The increase was proposed by Rules Committee Chairman Pepper, who visited Peru in late 1983.

In voice votes May 9, the House:

● Rejected an amendment by Ted Weiss, D-N.Y., that would have deleted from the bill an attack on Cuba over drug policy. The provision stated that involvement by Cuba's government in drug trafficking was "injurious to the world community" and violated international law. Weiss called the provision "a misguidedly zealous anti-Cuban, anti-communist anti-whatever kind of paranoia." But proponents said the provision was based on evidence that Cuba was "aiding and abetting" drug smugglers.

● Adopted an amendment by Gary L. Ackerman, D-N.Y., requiring that alleged Nazi war criminal Walter Rauff be "expelled" from Chile in order for that country to be eligible for U.S. military aid and arms sales. The bill had demanded that Rauff be extradited to Israel, which Chile refused to do. Rauff died in Chile on May 14.

● Adopted an amendment by Denny Smith, R-Ore., stating that "it should not be the policy of the United States government to protect the profits of financial institutions with loans outstanding to Argentina and other Latin American countries."

● Adopted an amendment by Earl Hutto, D-Fla., calling on U.S. agencies that run educational exchange programs to consider the possibility of planning for the establishment of U.S.-sponsored educational institutions in one or more nations in Latin America and the Caribbean.

● Adopted an amendment by Gerald B. H. Solomon, R-N.Y., requiring the president to report annually to Congress on the extent to which all countries belonging to the United Nations support U.S. foreign policy. The president also would be required, in allocating U.S. foreign aid, to consider whether recipient countries were "engaged in a consistent pattern of opposition" to U.S. foreign policy. Solomon said the amendment would continue a provision already in the law for fiscal 1984, under a continuing appropriations resolution (PL 98-151).

● Adopted an amendment by Hall calling on the president to encourage Indonesia to allow access to East Timor by international relief agencies, journalists and human rights organizations. The amendment also asked the president to work with Portugal, Australia and other countries to develop policies to end "the ongoing human suffering" in East Timor, which Indonesia invaded in 1975 and claimed as a province.

● Adopted an amendment by Douglas K. Bereuter, R-Neb., stating the sense of Congress that the Mexican government had adopted policies and actions that "constitute a significant impediment" to transport of commercial goods through its territory. The amendment directed the secretary of state to conduct negotiations with Mexican officials toward easing the barriers, and required him to report to Congress on the talks by Jan. 1, 1985.

● Adopted an amendment by Bill McCollum, R-Fla., condemning the alleged use of chemical weapons in the Iran-Iraq war and by the Soviet Union and its allies in Afghanistan and Southeast Asia. The amendment called for international investigations and negotiations over such weapons.

● Adopted an amendment by Ron Coleman, D-Texas, requiring the president to establish "appropriate accountability procedures" to ensure that foreign aid funds were used as intended by Congress. Without citing specifics, Coleman said some foreign aid funds might be wasted or diverted to improper uses. He did not say how the procedures to be established under his amendment would differ from accounting standards currently in use.

● Adopted an amendment by Jerry Lewis, R-Calif., stating U.S. objections to actions by the United Nations Educational, Scientific and Cultural Organization (UNESCO). The bill called on the president to establish a bipartisan panel to review the impact of the announced U.S. withdrawal from UNESCO. Lewis' amendment stated that the United States was considering its withdrawal because of "serious concerns" about how UNESCO was fulfilling its constitution, because of UNESCO's attacks on Israel and on Western institutions and values such as freedom of the press and because "there are vital questions" about how UNESCO had spent its funds.

● Adopted an amendment by Don Ritter, R-Pa., condemning the Soviets for occupying Afghanistan and stating that it should be U.S. policy "to secure the removal from Afghanistan of Soviet troops and return Afghan sovereignty to the Afghan people."

Bill Dies in Senate

While the House was debating its bill, members of the Senate Foreign Relations Committee tried without success to reach a compromise on Central America provisions for that chamber's foreign aid authorizations bill, S 2582. *(Details, p. 102)*

The stalemate continued until Aug. 1, when Senate Republican leaders, facing protracted debate on Central America and other controversial issues, as well as a losing race against the election-year calendar, gave up on trying to pass a full-scale authorizations bill.

The Senate had been scheduled to take up the foreign aid authorizations bill on Aug. 3. But at a meeting two days earlier, Majority Leader Howard H. Baker Jr., R-Tenn., Foreign Relations Committee Chairman Charles H. Percy, R-Ill., and others on the panel reportedly decided that debate on the bill would be too divisive to be ended before the Aug. 10 pre-Republican convention recess.

"The debate would have taken several days, and even so, final passage was not assured," said an informed Senate aide.

Baker told administration officials that he feared "15 filibusters," by liberals and conservatives, could doom the measure.

Percy informed other senators that he would miss most of the planned debate on Aug. 6-7 because he had commitments for his re-election campaign in Illinois. Percy for months had pressed for Senate action on the bill, the major work of his committee.

Appropriations Legislation

When Congress considered the omnibus continuing appropriations resolution (H J Res 648 — PL 98-473) in early October, leaders of the Foreign Relations and Foreign Affairs committees tried to insert a full-scale authorizations bill into that legislation.

On Oct. 4, aides of the committees drafted an authorizations bill, including the Kissinger commission plan for Central America, which was introduced the next day as S

3069 and HR 6409. Conferees on the continuing resolution initially agreed to incorporate the measure by referring to it in the text of their bill.

But Democrats objected, saying Congress should not enact into law a bill written entirely by staff. They also wanted to avoid giving Reagan a victory on the Kissinger plan.

Faced with that objection, the conferees deleted the staff-written authorizations. Ironically, the Democrats' objections had the effect of eliminating several Central America human rights and land reform provisions that Democrats had sought.

However, the continuing resolution included several specific items from the House-passed HR 5119 and from the Senate's companion bill, S 2582. *(Details, p. 390)*

The largest single authorization was for a $2.25 billion contribution, over three years, to the International Development Association, an arm of the World Bank. Neither chamber of Congress had considered that authorization prior to enactment of the continuing resolution. *(Story, p. 393)*

Lebanon, Embassy Security

Terrorist bombings caused turmoil throughout 1984 for U.S. policy in the Middle East, particularly in Lebanon.

At the beginning of the year, the United States was still reeling from the October 1983 bombing that killed more than 240 U.S. military personnel stationed at the Beirut airport as part of a multinational force. *(1983 Almanac p. 113)*

Some 1,600 Marines were hunkered down in bunkers at the airport, and President Reagan was refusing mounting calls in Congress to bring them home. But on Feb. 7, after radical Moslem armies stormed through West Beirut, Reagan suddenly announced he was "redeploying" the Marines to ships offshore.

With that, House Democrats dropped plans for action on a resolution (H Con Res 248) that called on Reagan to begin the "prompt and orderly withdrawal" of the Marines.

Reagan subsequently ordered the total withdrawal of Marines from the waters off Lebanon, and the issue died down, except for bursts of recrimination between Reagan and congressional Democrats.

But the Sept. 20, 1984, terrorist bombing of a U.S. Embassy annex near Beirut, killing two Americans and a dozen others, reopened the issue. Congress on Oct. 5 cleared an omnibus bill (HR 6311 — PL 98-533) authorizing $355.5 million to bolster security at U.S. embassies overseas.

Of that amount, $110.2 million was appropriated in the fiscal 1985 continuing resolution (H J Res 648 — PL 98-473). PL 98-533 also established a new program of rewards for persons providing conclusive information about terrorist acts committed in the United States or directed against U.S. property.

Anti-Terrorism Legislation

The bill to boost embassy security, the most important of four "anti-terrorism" bills Reagan had proposed in April 1984, remained in limbo until after the Sept. 20 embassy annex bombing.

Congress moved ahead on the bill in a bitter climate of bickering between Democrats and the administration over responsibility for security lapses at the embassy annex. Reagan infuriated Democrats with an off-the-cuff remark Sept. 23 in which he appeared to shrug off the failure to complete embassy security arrangements, saying that "anyone that's ever had their kitchen done over knows that it never gets done as soon as you wish it had."

House Speaker Thomas P. O'Neill Jr., D-Mass., called that statement a "blatantly stupid alibi" for security failures, and Senate Minority Leader Robert C. Byrd, D-W.Va., said it "trivializes the loss of American lives."

"There was bipartisan outrage that security was not appropriate," said Rep. Daniel A. Mica, D-Fla., following a closed-door meeting on Sept. 26 at which House Foreign Affairs Committee members questioned State Department officials. Those officials admitted that security was inadequate, but they said State decided to move into the building even before security arrangements were completed because it was safer for diplomats than the previous building in West Beirut.

Administration Funding Request

The administration on Sept. 26 formally sought congressional approval of $110.2 million, along with 172 new State Department personnel, to make "urgent" improvements in security at 35 to 50 embassies.

That request was for less than a third of the $356.3 million that administration officials, a day earlier, had privately told members of Congress was needed for a more comprehensive bolstering of embassy security in the coming two years. Congress had authorized $700 million for improved embassy security since 1979.

Ronald I. Spiers, under secretary of state for management, called the request a "direct and immediate response" to the Lebanon bombing, but insisted that the administration would have asked for the money anyway in 1985.

The Foreign Affairs Committee on Sept. 26 voted authorization for the full $356.3 million, including $351 million for the State Department and $5.3 million for the U.S. Information Agency (USIA).

The Senate Foreign Relations Committee, which had approved a companion bill (S 2625 — S Rept 98-618) on Sept. 25, also approved the full $356.3 million on Sept. 28. Earlier, on Sept. 18, the Senate Judiciary Committee had approved S 2625.

Democrats, and some Republicans, criticized the administration for presenting the stripped-down $110.2 million request instead of the $356.3 million. Spiers said the rest would be sought in 1985.

On Sept. 28, administration officials finally asked the Foreign Relations Committee to authorize the full $356.3 million. But that failed to satisfy panel members, who asked sharp questions about why Reagan was still seeking actual appropriations of only $110.2 million.

"If he wants the moon, have him ask for it, and I'll try to get it," said Joseph R. Biden Jr., D-Del.

House, Senate Passage

The administration said only $110.2 million could be spent before Congress acted on a supplemental spending bill in mid-1985.

The House authorized the full $355.3 million in passing HR 6311 on Oct. 1, and the Senate followed suit Oct. 5.

Congress included only the $110.2 million in fiscal 1985 continuing appropriations legislation (H J Res 648 — PL 98-473).

In addition to authorizing the money, PL 98-533 established the new $10 million program of rewards for information about terrorist activities in the United States and overseas.

Final Provisions

To counter terrorism, PL 98-533:

● Authorized the attorney general to pay rewards of up to $500,000 each to individuals who furnished information leading to the arrest or conviction, in any country, of persons for committing an act of terrorism against a U.S. person or U.S. property, or for conspiring or attempting to commit such a terrorist act. Rewards also could be paid for information leading to the prevention, frustration or favorable resolution of an act of terrorism against a U.S. person or property. A "U.S. person" was defined as anyone located in the United States.

● Authorized the attorney general to take steps to protect the identities of reward recipients and their families.

● Authorized $5 million, without fiscal year limitation, for rewards paid by the attorney general.

● Authorized the secretary of state to pay rewards of up to $500,000 each to individuals furnishing information leading to the arrest or conviction of any person for committing, conspiring or attempting to commit an act of terrorism overseas. Rewards also could be made for information leading to the prevention, frustration or favorable resolution of such a terrorist act, if the act was directed against a U.S. person or U.S. property and was outside the jurisdiction of the United States.

● Authorized the secretary of state to take steps to protect the identities of award recipients and their families.

● Authorized $5 million, without fiscal year limitation, for such rewards paid by the secretary of state.

● Urged the president to seek more effective international cooperation in combating terrorism.

● Called for high priority to be given to negotiations leading to the establishment of an international working group to combat terrorism.

● Called on the State Department to review its approach to providing security against terrorism, and directed the secretary to report to Congress by Feb. 1, 1985, on the findings of the Advisory Panel on Security of United States Missions Abroad.

● Authorized, without fiscal year limitation, $350,963,000 to the State Department and $5,315,000 to the U.S. Information Agency "security enhancement" at U.S. diplomatic missions overseas.

● Directed the secretary of state and the USIA director to report to Congress by Feb. 1, 1985, on how the security money was allocated.

Other Parts of the Package

The three other bills in Reagan's anti-terrorism package met with a mixed fate:

● One (S 2623, HR 5690) sought to implement a 1981 international agreement requiring countries to establish jurisdiction over sabotage of civil air flights. The bill established a fine of up to $100,000 and/or a prison sentence of up to 20 years for persons convicted of air sabotage. The Senate Judiciary Committee approved S 2623 (S Rept 98-619) on Sept. 19, and the House Judiciary Crime Subcommittee approved HR 5690 on Sept. 26.

● Another (S 2624, HR 5689) would have implemented a 1979 U.N. treaty against hostage-taking. The bill would have amended U.S. kidnapping law to cover cases in which a threat was made to kill, injure or continue to detain a kidnapping victim in order to force a third party to take some action. The House Crime Subcommittee approved that measure on Sept. 26.

Elements of this part of the package were folded into PL 98-473, the continuing resolution, which contained a large anti-crime section. (*Crime bill provisions, p. 215*)

● The remaining component of the package (S 2626, HR 5613) would have allowed the secretary of state to designate individuals, groups or countries as "terrorists" and would ban U.S. citizens, resident aliens or businesses from providing any training or support to designated terrorists.

This bill, however, sparked opposition from civil liberties groups and questions about its vague definition of terrorism. The bill died in committee in both chambers.■

Jerusalem Embassy

Two House Foreign Affairs subcommittees on Oct. 2 approved H Con Res 352, calling on the president to move the U.S. Embassy in Israel to Jerusalem from Tel Aviv. But the measure, which for months had been the subject of intense negotiations between its sponsors and the administration, died at that point because Congress ran out of time to consider it.

The resolution was a watered-down version of a bill (HR 4877, S 2031) that would have required the president to move the embassy to Jerusalem. The original legislation had the nominal support of more than half the members of Congress.

The administration adamantly opposed any congressional action on the issue because the status of Jerusalem was a sensitive issue in any negotiations between Israel and its Arab neighbors.

An Emotional Issue

Pro-Israel groups and members of Congress hailed the action by the House Foreign Affairs subcommittees on the Middle East and International Operations as the first step toward changing a longstanding U.S. policy of keeping the official embassy out of Jerusalem, parts of which were claimed by both Israel and Jordan.

By moving the embassy to Jerusalem, which Israel called its capital, "we will have obliterated an obnoxious, unseemly ... discriminatory standard," said Rep. Tom Lantos, D-Calif., a prime sponsor of the resolution. Rep. Benjamin A. Gilman, R-N.Y., was joint sponsor.

During subcommittee debate on the emotional issue, George W. Crockett Jr., D-Mich., charged that the panels acted because of "political pressure" exerted by "the strongest lobby — the Israeli lobby."

The Israeli government had never taken an official position on the congressional action. However, Israeli Ambassador Meir Rosenne in the summer of 1984 lobbied on Capitol Hill in favor of the Lantos-Gilman legislation after representatives of the Islamic Conference countries came to Washington to oppose it.

Subcommittees' Voting

Crockett, one of the most vocal opponents of the Jerusalem legislation, left before the subcommittees voted on the matter. Apparently, only four of the 13 members present answered "no" on the voice vote: Lee H. Hamilton, D-Ind., chairman of the Middle East subcommittee; Larry

Winn Jr., R-Kan., senior Republican on that panel; Ed Zschau, R-Calif.; and Mervyn M. Dymally, D-Calif.

Sporadic negotiations in 1984 between Lantos and Gilman and the administration failed to produce any agreement on the issue. The two House members late in September rejected the White House's final compromise offer, which was a proposed letter from President Reagan congratulating them for raising the issue but restating administration opposition to their legislation.

Rep. Daniel A. Mica, D-Fla., chairman of the International Operations Subcommittee, called the Jerusalem bill "a very, very delicate issue" — one that had caused the two panels to hold five open hearings with 27 witnesses, two closed hearings and "dozens" of informal meetings.

The United States put its embassy in Tel Aviv when Israel became a nation in 1948; since then Israel had moved most government offices to Jerusalem. Proponents of the embassy move argued that Israel was the only country where the United States refused to put its embassy in the city that the country called its administrative capital. ▪

Jordanian, Saudi Arms

Faced with overwhelming opposition in Congress, President Reagan on March 21 withdrew a proposal to sell Stinger anti-aircraft missiles to Jordan and Saudi Arabia.

But less than three months later, as the Iran-Iraq war escalated with shipping attacks in the Persian Gulf, Reagan sidestepped Congress and used his "emergency" authority to send the Saudis 400 of the missiles. Saudi Arabia became the first country outside the North Atlantic Treaty Organization ·or Japan to get Stingers.

Reagan had proposed on Feb. 29 and March 1 to sell Saudi Arabia 1,200 Stinger missiles and 400 launchers, at a cost of $141 million, and Jordan 1,613 Stinger missiles and 315 launchers, at a cost of $133 million.

Administration officials said both countries needed the missiles to reinforce their air defenses: Jordan against a threat from Syria and Saudi Arabia against a threat from Iran and other radical Arab states.

Opponents complained that the shoulder-fired missiles could be captured by extremists. Sen. Bob Packwood, R-Ore., said if Stingers were sold to any Arab nation, "some are going to fall into the hands of terrorists, and that means there is not going to be a plane outside any major airport in the civilized world that will be safe."

Israel and many of its Capitol Hill allies objected that the missiles could fall into the hands of the Palestine Liberation Organization.

Congress had never passed legislation blocking an overseas arms sale. The Jordanian sale marked the first time a president had withdrawn a proposed arms sale without the clear intention of resubmitting it at a later date. Jordan continued to want Stingers, but prospects for congressional acceptance of a sale in 1985 were doubtful.

Sale to Jordan Withdrawn

Reagan's March 21 decision to withdraw the Stinger sales to Jordan and Saudi Arabia came as a surprise.

Opponents voiced astonishment that Reagan surrendered, saying the president might have won a bruising political battle on Capitol Hill had he chosen to fight. Congressional sources said the administration made no

effort to head off opposition to the sales, which had been planned for nearly four years.

The Stinger decision was a blow to Reagan's Middle East policy, which focused on bolstering "moderate" Arab countries such as Jordan, Saudi Arabia and Lebanon in hopes that they would be willing to negotiate with Israel.

Hussein Statements

Congressional opposition to the sales was fed by anti-U.S. statements by Jordan's King Hussein. In an interview published March 15 in *The New York Times*, Hussein said the United States could no longer serve as a mediator between Israel and Arab neighbors. "You obviously have made your choice, and your choice is Israel," Hussein said. "Therefore, there is no hope of achieving anything."

In subsequent interviews with U.S. television networks, Hussein repeatedly attacked the United States as a major stumbling block to peace in the Middle East.

Hussein's statements were "the frosting on the cake" that convinced undecided members of Congress to oppose the Stinger sales, said Packwood.

Mounting Opposition

By March 21, Packwood had rounded up 55 signatures on a letter asking Reagan to withdraw the sales, and he voiced confidence that 75 senators would have voted to reject the sales had the issue reached the floor.

Packwood's list included 21 Republicans and 34 Democrats. Several GOP leaders who did not sign the letter were known to have urged Reagan to withdraw the sale.

In the House, Larry Smith, D-Fla., had gathered 65 cosponsors for a bill (HR 5140) to block the sales. Smith said the bill would have passed the House by an overwhelming majority had Reagan not withdrawn the sales.

A 1974 law (PL 93-559) gave Congress 30 days after receiving notice to block major arms sales by passing a concurrent resolution, which did not need presidential signature. But in 1983, the Supreme Court ruled such "legislative vetoes" unconstitutional. *(1983 Almanac p. 566)*

The Stinger issue did not come to a vote in either chamber. The only formal congressional action on the issue was the adoption by the House Foreign Affairs Committee, on Feb. 29, of an amendment to the 1984-85 foreign aid authorization bill (HR 5119) banning any sales of advanced arms to Jordan until that country agreed to negotiate with and recognize Israel. *(Foreign aid bill, p. 104)*

Bargaining Chip

The administration tried to use the Stinger sale withdrawal as a bargaining chip to thwart congressional action on two related issues: Reagan's proposal to spend $220 million creating a "rapid deployment force" for the Jordanian army, and mounting congressional support for legislation (HR 4877, S 2031) requiring the U.S. Embassy in Israel to be moved to Jerusalem from Tel Aviv.

The rapid deployment force proposal called for the United States to train and equip two brigades of the Jordanian army to respond to emergencies in the Middle East. Congress secretly authorized the program in 1983, but appropriations for it were held up after protests by pro-Israel senators, who feared Jordan could use the force against Israel. *(1983 Almanac p. 134)*

The administration renamed its proposal the "Joint Logistics Planning Program," and to dilute opposition dropped a plan to give Jordan 58 Stingers.

The efforts to salvage the rapid deployment force bore

some fruit, with several leading pro-Israel members of Congress, Packwood for one, saying they would not oppose it. But the administration backed away from the funding in late May 1984, at the same time that it announced it would resubmit its proposal to sell the Saudis 1,200 Stingers.

The administration made a more direct connection between the Stinger sales and the Jerusalem issue. On March 20, according to sources, Under Secretary of State Lawrence S. Eagleburger offered to withdraw the Stinger sales if the Israeli lobby would stop pressing for passage of the Jerusalem bills. The offer was rejected; Reagan withdrew the Stinger sales anyway. *(Jerusalem embassy, p. 115)*

Saudis Get Stingers

On May 24, as the Iran-Iraq war produced attacks on Persian Gulf shipping, the administration announced it would resubmit to Congress its proposal to sell the Saudis 1,200 Stingers.

Four days later, on May 28, Reagan sent 400 of the anti-aircraft missiles to Saudi Arabia.

Sale of the missiles through an "emergency" authority enabled Reagan to avoid a 30- to 50-day review by Congress. The portable missiles and 200 launchers for them, plus training and support equipment, was to cost the Saudis a total of $40 million.

Reagan on May 30 sent Congress a formal notification of the sale along with a justification for using his emergency powers, while administration officials sought to reassure Congress that safeguards would prevent terrorists from getting the missiles.

The president authorized the sale under the Arms Export Control Act (PL 90-629), which governed cash sales of military items overseas. In most cases, the president could not actually make the sale until 30 days after notifying Congress. The 30-day waiting period normally was preceded by an informal 20-day period, during which members of Congress had a chance to express objections to an arms sale before it was announced officially.

Reagan invoked a rarely-used part of section 36b(1) of the law, which allowed him to waive the requirement for the delay if he certified to Congress that "an emergency exists" that required an immediate sale "in the national security interests of the United States."

Concerns Deflected

Concerns over protecting shipping in the Persian Gulf apparently deflected opposition to the sale on Capitol Hill. Administration officials had consulted with congressional leaders before announcing the emergency sale, also helping to defuse potential opposition.

Congressional sources said some leaders agreed to support the emergency sale, or at least not actively oppose it, in return for what they viewed as a commitment by the administration not to press ahead with a larger sale until after the November elections.

Reagan also sent a U.S.-manned KC-10 tanker plane to Saudi Arabia for inflight refueling of 62 Saudi-owned F-15 warplanes and four U.S.-owned Airborne Warning and Control System (AWACS) radar planes operating over Saudi territory. Administration officials insisted the unarmed KC-10 tanker, a version of the DC-10 airliner, would be protected by the Saudi air force and would be safe from attack in the gulf war.

The KC-10 joined three KC-135 tankers — versions of the Boeing 707 airliner — that had been in Saudi Arabia along with the AWACS planes.

In addition, Reagan speeded up the delivery to Saudi Arabia of previously approved military equipment, including larger fuel tanks for the Saudi F-15s, ammunition and other unspecified items. However, Reagan reportedly rejected a Saudi request for special racks that would boost the number of bombs the F-15s could carry. Israel had vigorously opposed selling the bomb racks to any Arab nation.

U.S. Involvement

About 20 percent of the non-communist world's oil supplies were shipped through the Persian Gulf. The United States got less than 5 percent of its total oil from the region.

Reagan repeatedly said the United States would take the necessary steps to ensure that the gulf remained open to shipping. However he coupled that pledge with denials that the United States planned unilateral action.

In contrast to its response to some crises, such as the wars in Lebanon and Central America, the administration did not embark on a massive escalation of the U.S. naval presence in the Persian Gulf region.

According to Pentagon reports to Congress, the United States sold Saudi Arabia $2.6 billion in military equipment, weapons and services in fiscal 1983 and expected sales of about $3.6 billion in fiscal 1984 and $6.5 billion in fiscal 1985, which started Oct. 1, 1984.

On June 4, the United States sent to Saudi Arabia an advanced version of the AWACS radar plane, designed to be able to detect attacks on shipping.

A State Department spokesman said on June 6 that the administration had decided that the use of U.S. military personnel to monitor the gulf war did not come under the provisions of the War Powers Resolution (PL 93-148). Under that law, the president must notify Congress whenever he sent U.S. troops into hostilities, into situations where hostilities were imminent, or when the troops were sent overseas "equipped for combat."

Spokesman Alan D. Romberg said the manning of the four AWACS planes and accompanying fuel tanker planes did not come under the War Powers act because U.S. personnel themselves would not be engaged in combat.

Objections

Rep. Lee H. Hamilton, D-Ind., Middle East subcommittee chairman, questioned whether Reagan properly used his emergency power to send the missiles. "The president has a fairly hard time making the case that there is a threat to U.S. national security" justifying the use of such an "extraordinary" power, he said.

Words of caution also came from a handful of Reagan's conservative Republican allies on Capitol Hill on June 5, hours after the Saudis for the first time used U.S.-supplied weapons to defend its air space against Iranian attack.

During a hearing of the Senate Appropriations Subcommittee on Foreign Operations, a panel that included some of Congress' most vocal supporters of Israel, senators reflected the concerns of pro-Israel lobbyists that Stingers could fall into the hands of terrorists.

Subcommittee Chairman Bob Kasten, R-Wis., in a harsh opening statement, accused the administration of making "bizarre" decisions and of misusing the president's emergency powers to sidestep Congress in making foreign arms sales.

Kasten complained about two specific aspects of the Stinger incident: that the administration on May 23-25 consulted with congressional leaders about selling 200 missiles to Saudi Arabia, but then decided late on May 25 to send 400 missiles; and that the sale was made during Congress' Memorial Day recess.

"You have at the very least abused the consulting process and . . . I can tell you that such consultations will have little meaning to me in the future," Kasten said.

In response, Michael H. Armacost, under secretary of state for political affairs, said the administration had responded to "a genuine emergency."

In addition to protesting the manner in which the sale was handled, subcommittee members charged that recent administration actions risked involving the United States directly in the gulf war without measurably improving Saudi Arabia's defense against outside attacks.

Alfonse M. D'Amato, R-N.Y., said the United States was "taking sides" in the Iran-Iraq conflict by selling equipment that likely would be used only against Iran. "We're injecting ourselves into the situation needlessly," he said.

Reagan did not resubmit his proposal for sale of the remaining 800 Stingers to Saudi Arabia in 1984. ∎

Support for Afghan Rebels

Congress appropriated $50 million for aid to anti-Soviet rebels in Afghanistan in an omnibus spending bill for fiscal 1984. And there were indications that the CIA would spend far more to help Afghan rebels in fiscal 1985: as high as $250 million, *The Washington Post* reported on Jan. 13, 1985.

Precise amounts of the aid to the rebels, Moslem "mujahideen," were secret. Authorization for the CIA assistance was contained in the fiscal 1985 intelligence authorization bill (PL 98-618) and appropriations were in secret defense portions of the 1985 continuing resolution (PL 98-473). *(Intelligence bill, p. 119; continuing resolution, p. 444)*

And nearly three years after Sen. Paul E. Tsongas, D-Mass., publicly raised the issue, Congress on Oct. 3-4 completed action on an amended resolution (S Con Res 74) calling on the administration "to effectively support" the Afghan rebels. The administration had opposed the original version of the resolution on the grounds that it might focus attention on Pakistan, through which most supplies for the rebels flowed.

The mujahideen had inflicted heavy casualties on the 100,000-plus Soviet troops who had occupied Afghanistan since December 1979.

Covert Aid

After simmering for years on Washington's back burner, questions about the extent and purpose of U.S. involvement in Afghanistan surfaced July 26, when the House Appropriations Committee approved $50 million to aid the mujahideen. At the administration's request, that panel added the money to the omnibus supplemental appropriations bill (HR 6040 — PL 98-396). *(Supplemental, p. 439)*

The committee's action was supposed to be secret; the $50 million was inserted, on an amendment by Charles Wilson, D-Texas, under an account for "other procurement" by the Air Force, a frequent hiding place for the CIA budget. The committee briefly closed its doors when it considered the issue. But the secret leaked out within several hours, and the next day *The Wall Street Journal* published a report on the aid.

Meanwhile, sources said the United States already had provided $200 million to $300 million to the rebels since mid-1979 — months before the Soviets invaded to consolidate their control of the communist regime in Kabul.

In the past, all aid to the Afghans had been hidden deep within dozens of accounts in the "classified" portion of the Defense Department's regular budget. But for parliamentary reasons, Wilson had to add the money to the supplemental as a readily identifiable separate item, thus provoking reporters' curiosity.

A Popular Program

U.S. aid to the Afghans, said one intelligence source, "dwarfs in size and scope" the CIA's much more controversial aid to anti-government guerrillas in Nicaragua. *(Story, p. 86)*

And in contrast to the Nicaragua operation, the aid to anti-Soviet Afghans enjoyed wide support in Congress.

"I don't know anybody who wants to be against backing religious freedom fighters against the atheistic horde from the north," Wilson said. "You can't make a case against it."

The Afghan conflict represented a constant source of irritation to U.S.-Soviet relations.

Under President Carter, the United States imposed several sanctions on the Soviet Union, including a boycott of the 1980 summer Olympic Games in Moscow, to protest the invasion of Afghanistan. President Reagan kept up the rhetorical attack on the Soviet Union for its continued occupation of Afghanistan, but had dismantled Carter's sanctions.

Some Afghan rebels complained that the United States had provided just enough aid to cause discomfort to the Russians, but not enough to give the Afghans a chance of winning.

Tsongas Resolution

Tsongas first introduced his resolution (S Con Res 126) on Sept. 30, 1982, with every member of the Senate co-sponsoring it but one: Charles McC. Mathias Jr., R-Md.

Mathias objected to the measure as a "Tonkin Gulf-type resolution" that could give the administration a blank check to provide any kind of aid. He blocked action on it in the Foreign Relations Committee at the end of the 1982 lame-duck session.

Tsongas re-introduced the resolution in October 1983 as S Con Res 74, with 68 cosponsors.

Sources said the CIA opposed the resolution on grounds that any public discussion of the issue would endanger the supply lines for U.S. aid to the Afghans.

Tsongas in January agreed to several changes that watered down the tone of the resolution. But the administration repeated its opposition to the clause calling for direct aid to the Afghans, and at a closed committee briefing in January, State Department officials insisted that it be eliminated.

A companion resolution in the House (H Con Res 237) was sponsored by Don Ritter, R-Pa., with 168 co-sponsors; it remained bottled up in the House Foreign Affairs Committee.

The deadlock was broken Sept. 25, when the Senate

Foreign Relations Committee deleted the call for "effective material assistance," inserting wording that the administration should "effectively support" the rebels. The panel approved S Con Res 74, and the administration dropped its opposition to the watered-down resolution.

The Senate passed S Con Res 74 on Oct. 3 and the House approved the measure on Oct. 4. ∎

Vatican Ambassador

The Reagan administration announced Jan. 10 that it would establish full diplomatic ties with the Vatican. A day later, President Reagan nominated William A. Wilson, a California rancher and land developer who had been serving as his personal envoy to the Vatican, as the first U.S. ambassador to the Holy See since 1867.

The decision touched off vigorous drive against Senate confirmation of the nomination by non-Catholic religious groups; they said it would violate the separation of church and state in the United States. The administration said it would recognize the Vatican as an independent state and would not confer special status on the Roman Catholic Church.

On Feb. 2, Sen. Jesse Helms, R-N.C., succeeded in postponing a Senate Foreign Relations Committee vote on the Wilson nomination. But on Feb. 22, the committee approved the nomination, 16-1, with Helms casting the lone dissenting vote.

Voting on Ash Wednesday, March 7, the Senate confirmed the nomination by a vote of 81-13. *(Vote 31, p. 7-S)*

The State Department later reprogrammed $351,000 to pay for the ambassador and staff in the new diplomatic mission.

From 1797 to 1848, the United States maintained consular relations with the Vatican. From 1848 to 1867 it had full diplomatic ties, but in 1867 Congress prohibited the use of federal funds to continue those relations. Starting with Franklin D. Roosevelt, U.S. presidents sent personal representatives to the Holy See. In November 1983, Congress repealed the law barring funds for a Vatican mission. *(Background, 1983 Almanac p. 168)* ∎

Intelligence Agencies

Congress on Oct. 11 cleared HR 5399, making authorizations in fiscal 1985 for the CIA and other intelligence agencies. The bill was cleared one day after an agreement was reached on the major issue in the bill: CIA aid to antigovernment guerrillas in Nicaragua. President Reagan signed the bill into law (PL 98-618) on Nov. 8.

As passed by the House Aug. 2, the bill included a ban on all aid to the Nicaraguan guerrillas. The Senate did not consider its version (S 2713) until after the Nicaragua issue was settled.

The aid issue was resolved Oct. 10 by conferees on the fiscal 1985 continuing appropriations resolution (H J Res 648 — PL 98-473). The next day, the House and Senate Intelligence committees incorporated that accord into a compromise version of the intelligence bill, which both chambers then passed without debate.

Most major provisions of HR 5399 were secret, but intelligence sources said it authorized about $9 billion for the CIA and nine other agencies.

Nicaragua Issue

The House and Senate bills (HR 5399, S 2713) had contained directly conflicting provisions on the Nicaragua issue.

The House intelligence bill would have prohibited any U.S. aid to thousands of guerrillas, called "contras," who were battling the leftist Nicaraguan regime. The Senate bill allowed $28 million in aid to the contras in fiscal 1985, as long as the president reported that they were not trying to overthrow the government.

The Senate Intelligence Committee, which drafted S 2713, reaffirmed its position on June 13 by rejecting, 4-8, an amendment by Joseph R. Biden Jr., D-Del., that would have placed tight restrictions on aid to the contras. The panel originally had approved the $28 million on May 23, but was forced to reconsider the issue because of subsequent confusion among members and staff about what was decided.

The final compromise barred U.S. aid to the guerrillas before March 1, 1985; thereafter, the president could spend up to $14 million aiding the guerrillas, if both houses of Congress approved. *(Details, p. 92)*

Other Provisions

In other provisions, PL 98-618:

● Authorized CIA security personnel to perform such tasks as arresting trespassers at agency facilities, such as its headquarters in Langley, Va. Previously, agency employees were not allowed any police or law enforcement powers.

● Exempted the Defense Intelligence Agency, during fiscal years 1985-86, from standard civil service rules for classification of civilian employees. This provision allowed the agency to set its own salary schedules.

● Authorized $114.5 million to complete a $190 million two-year authorization for design and construction of a news building at CIA headquarters in Langley, Va. The first $75.5 million had been authorized by the fiscal 1984 intelligence authorization bill (PL 98-215). Intended to consolidate CIA offices that had been in several dozen locations in the Washington area, the new building would double the size of CIA facilities at Langley.

House, Senate Bills

The House Intelligence Committee issued its report on HR 5399 on May 10 (H Rept 98-743, Part I), and the Armed Services Committee issued Part II of the report under the same number on May 23.

The Senate Intelligence panel reported S 2713 on May 24 (S Rept 98-481).

As in previous years, nearly all major provisions of the two intelligence bills were classified. Members of Congress were allowed to inspect the secret provisions, but had to sign a statement promising not to reveal any of the information.

In addition to the CIA, the bills authorized funds for the National Security Agency, the Defense Intelligence Agency and the intelligence arms of the four military services.

Nicaragua Issue

Section 107 of the House bill contained a strict prohibition on U.S. aid to the contras: "During fiscal year 1985, no funds available to the Central Intelligence Agency, the Department of Defense or any other agency or entity of the United States involved in intelligence activities may be obligated or expended for the purpose or which would have the effect of supporting directly or indirectly, military or paramilitary operations in Nicaragua by any nation, group, organization, movement or individual."

The House Intelligence Committee put that language in the public part of its bill and report. During its deliberations on the issue, the panel defeated, on a party-line 4-7 vote, an attempt by Republicans to approve Reagan's request for $28 million to assist the contras in 1985.

The panel's wording was similar to the $24 million restriction on the contras aid contained in the fiscal 1984 defense funding bill (PL 98-212). *(1983 Almanac p. 123)*

The Senate Intelligence panel approved Reagan's request but placed new curbs on how the money could be used. That committee put its Nicaragua provisions in the secret part of the intelligence bill, and committee sources have revealed few details.

The Senate bill barred the use of covert aid for the purpose or effect of overthrowing the Nicaraguan government or to bring about a change in the makeup of that regime.

One committee source said the restriction was intended to put into law assurances that Reagan gave the Senate in an April 4 letter to Baker while that chamber was debating the Nicaragua issue.

In that letter, Reagan said: "The United States does not seek to destabilize or overthrow the government of Nicaragua; nor to impose or compel any particular form of government there."

Several committee members of both parties complained that the administration had not adhered to previous restrictions that were intended to prevent the use of CIA funds to overthrow the Nicaraguan regime. In the wake of Reagan's April 4 letter, Biden said he did not believe what the president said.

The Senate bill also required the CIA to report to the committee in writing whenever it or the contras began a new military campaign. The latter provision was intended to prevent a repetition of the agency's failure to inform the committee fully about U.S. involvement in the mining of Nicaraguan harbors. In that case, CIA Director William J. Casey reportedly mentioned the mining only in passing during a briefing on intelligence matters. *(Mining, p. 88)*

According to committee sources, Biden had offered a proposal, with restrictions, and the panel adopted it on May 23. Later, Biden disputed the exact wording drafted by the committee staff to implement his proposal.

When the committee reconsidered the issue on June 13, Biden offered a new proposal with two restrictions: The aid to the contras was to be limited to interrupting or stopping the flow of arms from Nicaragua to leftist guerrillas in El Salvador; and the committee was to be empowered to cut off the aid once it found that the arms flow had stopped.

Biden argued that the administration should be willing to accept the limits because it had used the Nicaraguan arms traffic as the justification for aiding the contras.

But a majority of committee members apparently found Biden's proposal too narrow, and it was rejected 4-8. William S. Cohen, R-Maine, joined Biden, Patrick J. Leahy, D-Vt., and Daniel Patrick Moynihan, D-N.Y., in the minority.

Soviet Spies

The Senate Intelligence Committee included in its bill a provision that called for the gradual reduction in the

---

Career Officers for CIA?

The chairman and vice chairman of the Senate Intelligence Committee on Sept. 25 proposed legislation that would require future directors of the Central Intelligence Agency to be career intelligence officers.

But Chairman Barry Goldwater, R-Ariz., and Vice Chairman Daniel Patrick Moynihan, D-N.Y., disagreed about whether their proposal reflected dissatisfaction with CIA Director William J. Casey.

Goldwater, who had tangled with Casey on several occasions, most recently over the mining of Nicaraguan harbors, insisted that the proposal was not directed at Casey. "Mr. Casey has done a superb job," Goldwater told the Senate on Sept. 27.

But Moynihan cited frequently raised charges about the role of Casey, Ronald Reagan's 1980 campaign chairman, in the "debategate" incident and questions about Casey's personal finances.

No action was taken on the bill (S 3019) before Congress adjourned Oct. 11. Aides said the senators hoped to stimulate debate in 1985 on whether the CIA chief should be a political appointee.

Moynihan authored S 3019, which would have required that the director of central intelligence and his deputy both be appointed "from among career civilian or military intelligence officers."

Existing law (PL 80-253) allowed the two top CIA officers to be military officers or civilians but did not stipulate that they needed intelligence experience. The only restriction was that both the director and his deputy could not be military officers.

Casey served in the CIA's predecessor agency in World War II (the Office of Strategic Services) but devoted most of his career to business, writing and service in other government agencies. Casey's deputy, John N. McMahon, was a career intelligence officer.

Moynihan and Goldwater said their bill would prohibit "political" appointments of future CIA directors and deputies.

---

diplomatic staff of any country that "engages in intelligence activities within the United States harmful to the national security of the United States." Although the provision did not cite a specific country, its sponsors, Walter D. Huddleston, D-Ky., and Leahy, said the Soviet Union and its satellites were the targets.

The committee report cited FBI estimates that about 40 percent of Soviet-bloc diplomatic representatives in the United States were intelligence officers. The Soviet Union had about 300 personnel stationed in the United States in mid-1984, compared with about 200 U.S. citizens stationed as diplomats in the Soviet Union.

The committee's bill would have required the president to eliminate "disparities" in the number of U.S. and Soviet diplomatic personnel, unless he determined that an "imbalance" was in the national interest of the United States.

In implementing that provision, the committee said, the president should not allow into the United States more diplomats from the Soviet Union and its allies than the number of U.S. diplomats those countries would admit.

The provision did not require the president to expel or

refuse to admit only Soviet diplomats suspected of intelligence activity. However, Huddleston and Leahy said that reducing the overall number of Soviet diplomats in the United States would force the Soviet Union to cut back the number of its intelligence agencies — perhaps by as much as 100.

The Huddleston-Leahy provision was referred jointly to the Foreign Relations Committee, which by voice vote on June 21 rejected it.

Responding to pressure from Secretary of State George P. Shultz, Foreign Relations adopted an alternative requiring the State Department to report to Congress each year on the number of diplomats in the United States from the Soviet Union and other hostile countries. Shultz said the original Huddleston-Leahy provision would invite retaliation against U.S. diplomats overseas.

The provision included in the bill, as enacted into law:

• Stated the sense of Congress that the numbers and treatment of diplomats in the United States from hostile countries should not exceed the numbers and treatment of U.S. diplomats in those countries.

• Required the president to submit an annual report to Congress, beginning in November 1985, stating the number and treatment of diplomats in the United States from hostile countries and the number of U.S. diplomats in those countries. The president also was required to report on any actions the United States might take to correct any "imbalance."

• Allowed either the director or the deputy director of the Office of Foreign Missions in the State Department to be either a foreign service officer or a representative of intelligence agencies. Previously, the director was required to be a foreign service officer. The office was responsible for ensuring that embassies and other diplomatic missions in the United States comply with U.S. laws.

House Floor Action

Affirming for the fourth time its opposition to aiding the contras, the House approved HR 5399 on Aug. 2.

The House passed the measure 294-118, after Republican leaders decided not to mount a futile challenge to the Nicaragua provision. *(Vote 306, p. 94-H)*

Sixty-five Republicans voted for the bill, although the aid to the contras had enjoyed wide GOP support on Capitol Hill. House aides said many of the Republicans voted for the bill because they supported the underlying intelligence authorizations, not because they backed the ban on aiding the contras.

Attacking the contra aid ban, Minority Leader Robert H. Michel, R-Ill., said it was the Nicaraguan regime — not the U.S. government — that was making war in Central America.

"By denying the contras funding we are left, realistically speaking, with the alternatives of either an American invasion of a country or American evasion of responsibility," Michel said. "The United States according to this view must either be an interventionist bully or an isolationist wimp — there can be no middle ground."

But Edward P. Boland, D-Mass., chairman of the Intelligence Committee, said that "the secret war hasn't brought Central America closer to peace or Nicaragua closer to democracy. What it does is to provide the Sandinistas with the perfect excuse to foist unfair elections, a huge army, censorship and the draft on the Nicaraguan people."

Previous House votes against the Nicaragua aid were taken May 24, 1984, Oct. 20, 1983, and July 28, 1983. *(1984 Almanac, vote 162, p. 54-H)*   ∎

Food Aid for Africa

Moved by starvation and death in Africa, the Reagan administration sent an unprecedented amount of emergency food assistance to drought-stricken countries on the continent in 1984.

But the food and logistical aid, however crucial, was less generous than some members of Congress and relief groups said was needed.

In fiscal 1984, the Agency for International Development (AID) approved some $172 million in emergency assistance for Africa.

With the famine spreading later in the year, the administration stepped up its response. In the first 45 days of fiscal 1985, which began Oct. 1, 1984, AID approved some $200 million in emergency aid for 16 African countries. Almost half of the aid, nearly $100 million, went to Ethiopia, most severely affected by the famine.

Other major recipients included Kenya, Sudan, Mauritania and Mozambique.

The U.S. response to Africa's crisis was "truly enormous," in the words of AID Administrator M. Peter McPherson. But to such longtime congressional proponents of Africa aid as Howard Wolpe, D-Mich., chairman of the House Foreign Affairs Subcommittee on Africa, it came "too late."

More than two dozen African countries were on the U.N. Food and Agriculture Organization's emergency list, with several others also facing severe hunger problems.

Many observers noted that the drought compounded a disturbing phenomenon throughout Africa: The continent's population was growing at an annual rate of 2.7 percent, while per capita food production had plummeted by 10 percent in a decade. Countries once self-sufficient in food now were on their way to becoming permanently dependent on other nations.

Governments, pressed by growing urban populations, had held food prices down. Farmers, unable to subsist on the land, moved to the cities. Because of poor land management and drought, the continent's deserts were spreading. Other recurring problems were pervasive poverty, war, civil strife and mass migrations of refugees.

Anticipating increased food needs, members of Congress sought in 1984 to boost appropriations for food aid to the continent, while the administration put forward a plan aimed at promoting capitalism in Africa.

The Wheat Reserve

On Nov. 28, the administration announced it intended, for the first time, to release wheat from the U.S. emergency reserve.

The Wheat Reserve Act of 1980 (PL 96-494) established a reserve of four million metric tons. It was only to be used to help needy countries if wheat was not available in domestic U.S. markets. But the president could release up to 300,000 tons to meet an "unanticipated" need. *(1980 Almanac p. 94)*

Proponents of using the wheat reserve argued that such action would streamline food aid by getting around the competitive bidding process. But the administration never before had used the reserve, contending that the U.S. government could buy wheat for foreign aid from U.S. farmers.

In a Nov. 15 meeting with Agriculture Secretary John R. Block, Sen. Robert Dole, R-Kan., urged that the wheat be sent to Africa, and others on Capitol Hill supported the idea. Two weeks later, on Nov. 28, an aide to Block said the secretary would release 300,000 tons of the reserve.

The Aid Process

U.S. efforts to respond to Africa's food problems focused on two approaches: emergency assistance — food and seeds, and trucks to deliver them — and long-term aid to help countries develop their economies to avert food shortages in the future. The fiscal 1985 omnibus continuing appropriations resolution (H J Res 648 — PL 98-473) provided about $1.2 billion for foreign aid and food assistance to Africa. The bulk of the money was for ongoing economic development programs. *(Story, p. 444)*

The prime food aid program was the Agriculture Department's Food for Peace program, launched in 1954 under PL 480 to help reduce U.S. grain surpluses and aid needy countries. Under Titles I and III of Food for Peace, the U.S. government underwrote food sales to Third World countries that could obtain low-interest loans from the U.S. government to buy U.S. farm products. Under Title II, the United States provided donations to countries that could not afford loans.

In fiscal 1984, appropriations for the worldwide PL 480 program of grants and loans totaled $1.6 billion, of which $740 million was Title II grants. Sub-Saharan Africa got $172 million in emergency Title II grants, $117 million in regular Title II, and $127 million in Titles I and III loans.

In fiscal 1985, Congress appropriated $1.9 billion for Food for Peace overall. But of that $710 million — $30 million less than in fiscal 1984 — was for Title II donations.

Decisions on who got the aid were made through an intricate bureaucratic process, involving representatives of four agencies: AID, the State Department, the Agriculture Department and the Office of Management and Budget. Each agency brought its own policy concern — foreign relations, marketing or fiscal.

Lead times for food shipments were as long as three months, much of it consumed by U.S. bureaucratic steps. First, a request would be received by AID and processed in Washington. A subcommittee including representatives of the four agencies would review and approve it, then the Agriculture Department would arrange for purchase and shipping of the food.

Distribution inside recipient countries was done through one of three channels: private voluntary organizations, such as Catholic Relief Service or World Vision; the World Food Program, a consortium of 20 donor nations; or directly from government to government.

The U.S. government tried in 1984 to cut the long lead time for food aid to Ethiopia by diverting shipments of ready-to-eat foods — bulgur wheat, processed sorghum, vegetable oil and non-fat dried milk — that had been headed for other countries, such as India.

1984 Supplemental Appropriations

Sen. John C. Danforth, R-Mo., after he visited Mozambique and seven other countries in January 1984, returned with graphic accounts of "emaciated bodies, sticklike limbs and distended bellies." His slides of starving Africans

prompted President Reagan in February to request $90 million in supplemental emergency food aid in fiscal 1984. Some members of Congress complained that amount was not enough.

The House Appropriations Committee, on an amendment by Matthew F. McHugh, D-N.Y., boosted the emergency aid to $150 million. "We should err, if we err at all, on the side of providing funds which will go to people in need, rather than err on the side of providing too little," McHugh said.

The bill also authorized the sale of up to $90 million in Commodity Credit Corporation (CCC) stocks to African nations or to countries helping them meet their emergency food needs.

The House passed the bill (H J Res 492) on March 6 by a vote of 374-29. *(Vote 32, p. 12-H)*

Members on both sides of the aisle spoke in support of the increased funding, calling it necessary in the face of extreme need.

"It is wise and moral to give what we can," said Rep. Virginia Smith, R-Neb., ranking minority member of the Agriculture Appropriations Subcommittee.

Rep. E. "Kika" de la Garza, D-Texas, chairman of the Agriculture Committee, said the United States should provide aid despite high budget deficits and hunger on its own shores.

"In spite of our problems," de la Garza said, "the American people are willing to sacrifice."

But a contentious battle delayed H J Res 492 on the Senate side, when the administration and Bob Kasten, R-Wis., chairman of the Senate Appropriations Subcommittee on Foreign Operations, tried to attach to the bill $93 million in military assistance to El Salvador. The Senate Appropriations Committee added the Central America funds to the bill on March 14.

Danforth eventually succeeded in getting conferees on a less controversial measure (H J Res 493 — PL 98-248) to tack $90 million in Africa money onto that measure. They also added on the House-passed provision making available $90 million from Commodity Credit Corporation food stocks for sale to Africa. H J Res 493 cleared Congress on March 27, by a voice vote in each chamber. *(Story, p. 438)*

Disputes over other efforts to supply military aid to El Salvador and covert aid to Nicaraguan guerrillas delayed until June 25 the passage of H J Res 492 (PL 98-332), containing the remaining $60 million in supplemental Africa aid. Because time was running out in fiscal 1984, the $60 million was programmed for fiscal 1985. *(Story, p. 429)*

Linkage of Africa aid to Central America assistance in these two bills angered many on Capitol Hill. House Speaker Thomas P. O'Neill Jr., D-Mass., charged that the administration had "shown it is ready to starve Africans so that it can kill Central Americans."

AID Administrator McPherson, in Capitol Hill hearings throughout the fall, sidestepped such criticism and maintained that the administration was sending all the aid it could get through the pipeline.

Trucks and Seeds. While aid proponents were pushing for more food assistance, they also sought more money to pay for other emergency needs — trucks, blankets and seeds. Annual funding for such aid was $25 million.

In fiscal 1984, an additional $16 million was approved in the regular supplemental appropriations measure (HR 6040 — PL 98-396), which cleared Congress on Aug. 10.

Economic Policy Initiative

Apart from increasing emergency food aid, the administration offered two approaches to bolster aid to Africa, and both had only limited success on Capitol Hill.

The first, called the Economic Policy Initiative, was a five-year, $500 million plan to provide extra aid to promote changes in African countries' economic systems. Assistance would have been directed toward nations that showed willingness to pursue policies that would promote economic growth through capitalism. In fiscal 1984, Reagan sought $75 million as a first installment for the plan.

But the extent to which aid should be used to entice less-developed countries to change internal policies stirred debate in the international community. Some on Capitol Hill suggested it could become a "slush fund" to reward U.S. allies.

The Senate Foreign Relations and House Foreign Affairs committees approved the $75 million as part of the foreign aid authorization (HR 5119, S 2582), although the Democratic-controlled House panel added conditions requiring AID to report to Congress on potential recipients before the agency decided how the money would be spent. The purpose was to ensure that the administration's efforts to promote capitalism did not come at the expense of the poorest nations.

The House Appropriations Committee also approved the program, but it was sidetracked in the Senate by Republican Kasten, who said the plan was not needed because the current Foreign Assistance Act already authorized programs to promote economic reform.

The program ultimately died. Conferees on the continuing appropriations resolution for fiscal 1985 diverted the $75 million into the Economic Support Fund, a program bolstering the economies of friendly countries.

Emergency Food Initiative

Reagan's second initiative was unveiled July 10, at a White House ceremony marking the 30-year anniversary of the Food for Peace program. The five-point food aid program, based on recommendations of a task force chaired by Robert Keating, ambassador to Madagascar, called for:

• Creation of a special $50 million presidential fund for severe food emergencies.

• Financing or payment of ocean and inland transportation costs for U.S. emergency food aid.

• "Pre-positioning" of grain in selected Third World areas.

• Creation of a government task force to provide better forecasts of food needs.

• Establishment of an advisory group of business leaders to share information on Third World hunger and food production.

The proposal, however, carried some hitches. The $50 million would not be new money; it would be reprogrammed from other AID accounts.

"Frankly, it's not clear to me why they don't increase the allocation for existing food accounts," Wolpe complained in August. "To some extent, this smacks of election-year publicity."

The proposal to finance inland transportation, however, drew widespread praise as a step toward alleviating difficulties in distribution. Previously, Title II only paid for ocean transportation, and many countries sold part of the food they received to pay for trucks, spare parts and other delivery expenses.

Those two elements of the plan required congressional action. With the foreign aid authorization bill dead in the Senate, the continuing resolution (H J Res 648 — PL 98-473) became the vehicle for the proposal. An amendment offered Oct. 2 by Sen. Nancy Landon Kassebaum, R-Kan., added the $50 million fund and provided for payment of inland transportation in the Senate's version of the continuing resolution. Conferees authorized both, but appropriated no new money.

The proposal to pre-position grain, aimed at cutting down on delivery time, began to be implemented. Some 15,000 tons of grain were earmarked for storage in Niger. But with that country undergoing severe feeding problems, AID donated the grain to Niger for immediate use.

1985 Supplemental Proposals

Anticipating increased needs in Africa, Rep. Ted Weiss, D-N.Y., with Wolpe as co-sponsor, introduced a supplemental appropriations bill (HR 6203) on Sept. 6. Weiss, a member of the Foreign Affairs Subcommittee on Africa, sought to boost fiscal 1985 food donations by $265 million. His bill also called for $185 million in added funding for health care, refugee assistance, disaster aid and outreach programs.

The measure, however, never got off the ground in the waning days of the 98th Congress.

By the end of 1984, the administration and Capitol Hill Democrats were setting the stage for a replay of debate over how much aid the United States should give Africa. On Jan. 3, 1985, the opening day of the 99th Congress, Weiss and Wolpe reintroduced their bill (HR 100), with the overall total increased to more than $1 billion.

The same day, administration officials announced an African Hunger Relief Initiative. They said it would provide $411 million in food and other aid in fiscal 1985, on top of $590 million the United States already had given African countries. ∎

Genocide Treaty

Despite overwhelming support among senators and the belated backing of President Reagan, a handful of conservatives blocked Senate approval of a United Nations treaty outlawing genocide.

In what had the same effect as a filibuster, Sen. Jesse Helms, R-N.C., and other conservatives used procedural tactics and the threat of amendments to thwart action on the treaty at the very end of the 98th Congress.

Drafted in 1947-48 with the help of the United States, the treaty (Exec O, 81st Cong, 1st sess) called on signatories to take steps to prevent and punish a number of acts described as genocide. The treaty had been stalled in the Senate for 35 years.

In lieu of the treaty, the Senate on Oct. 11 adopted, 87-2, a resolution (S Res 478) commending the treaty's principles and pledging to act "expeditiously" on it during the first session of the 99th Congress, in 1985.

That resolution was so broadly worded that it attracted the votes of two of the four senators who recently have spoken publicly against the genocide treaty: Helms and Orrin G. Hatch, R-Utah. Two other treaty opponents, John P. East, R-N.C., and Steven D. Symms, R-Idaho, cast the two "nay" votes on S Res 478. *(Vote 271, p. 47-S)*

Administration Support

The genocide treaty, negotiated in the late 1940s, defined genocide as the intentional destruction of any national, racial, ethnic or religious group by killing its members, causing them serious physical or mental harm, imposing living conditions intended to bring about their destruction, or preventing births.

Reagan, who had ordered a review of the treaty after taking office in 1981, announced his support on Sept. 5. Several Democrats privately voiced suspicion that Reagan backed the treaty just two months before the presidential election as a way of courting favor with Jewish groups. However, longtime treaty proponent Sen. William Proxmire, D-Wis., praised Reagan for giving the treaty the push that was needed to get it to the Senate floor.

In spite of Reagan's endorsement, however, the administration made little effort to overcome opposition to the treaty by conservatives in the Senate. On Oct. 10, when the Senate was debating the treaty, administration officials were directing their lobbying efforts toward House-Senate conference action on an omnibus continuing appropriations resolution (H J Res 648). *(Continuing resolution, p. 444)*

Committee Action

The Senate Foreign Relations Committee met Sept. 12, hoping for action to approve the treaty. But Helms stalled committee action, saying that he had constitutional doubts about the treaty. Helms said he wanted the Senate to attach to the treaty two "understandings":

● That legislation needed to implement the treaty not conflict with the Constitution.

● That the United States not accept the jurisdiction of the International Court of Justice in matters that the United States determined were strictly domestic.

Officials of the State and Justice departments told the committee they could not accept those conditions. They said the Helms proposals were unnecessary and incompatible with the treaty's purpose.

A week later, on Sept. 19, the committee met and approved the treaty, 17-0. Helms voted "present."

Floor Action

At the beginning of Senate action Oct. 10, Helms asked a series of parliamentary questions about rules for debating the treaty.

The answers, given by presiding officer Dave Durenberger, R-Minn., revealed that the Senate was required to take at least two days to give final approval to the treaty and an associated resolution of ratification — unless Senate rules were waived by unanimous consent.

Helms said that "nobody is trying to block approval" of the treaty. But through his questions, Helms signaled that he or his allies would object to waiving the rules, thus making it impossible for the Senate to act quickly at a time it was hoping to adjourn.

In a series of Senate speeches on Oct. 10, opponents of the treaty expressed support for the goal of preventing genocide but insisted that the treaty was flawed in several respects. They argued that the treaty would violate the U.S. Constitution by making international law superior to U.S. law and would be ineffective in stopping genocide by the Soviet Union and other communist countries.

Although the treaty had been before the Senate for more than three decades, the conservatives argued that few senators understood its terms or the consequences of its adoption.

Calling the treaty a "noble gesture," Helms said he and others were merely trying to ensure that "the sovereignty and independence of the United States are not in any way compromised through inadvertence." In approving the treaty, he said, the Senate "might unthinkingly, unwittingly commit this nation to be a subordinate to an international structure that in the long run would threaten our freedom and independence."

Symms complained that the treaty failed to prevent such acts of genocide as the Soviet Union's crushing of resistance in Afghanistan and the murder of millions of Cambodians by the government of Pol Pot in the 1970s.

But treaty supporters rejected such arguments. The treaty was one of many international accords that called on the United States to implement its own laws, said Claiborne Pell, D-R.I.

Proxmire and other treaty advocates also noted that the Soviet Union had ratified the treaty and had used the United States' failure to do so as a propaganda tool against U.S. human rights efforts overseas. "We have had 17 Congresses that have met and adjourned since President Truman first sent this to the Senate and asked for action on it — 17. None of them have acted on it," Proxmire noted.

Symms proposed, but did not have a chance to offer, an amendment that would have declared abortion to be a form of genocide. Senate leaders said adoption of such an amendment would prevent U.S. ratification of the treaty because any amendment would have to be accepted by all other nations that had ratified the treaty.

Under pressure from Majority Leader Howard H. Baker Jr., R-Tenn., Symms withdrew another amendment that called on the president to submit to Congress annual reports on the Soviet Union's violations of existing arms control treaties.

After S Res 478, the resolution commending the treaty's principles, was adopted, Baker said that was "the best possible result that can be obtained under the present circumstances" of Senate failure to ratify the treaty.

Proxmire, who had given several thousand Senate speeches in favor of the genocide treaty, said he counted more than 80 senators in favor of the treaty — well more than the two-thirds vote necessary to approve it and the 60 votes necessary to break a filibuster.

"It's going to pass some day," Proxmire said. "We've waited 35 years." ∎

Development Bank Funding

After months of dispute over levels of funding for the International Development Association (IDA), Congress approved $2.25 billion for fiscal years 1985 through 1987 for the World Bank affiliate.

As in 1981, Congress sidestepped separate votes on the program by authorizing and funding IDA programs in an omnibus continuing appropriations resolution (H J Res 648 — PL 98-473). The spending bill cleared Congress Oct. 11. *(1981 Almanac p. 142; continuing resolution, p. 444)*

In contrast to regular loans made by the World Bank at market interest rates, IDA loans were interest-free, 50-year grants with a 10-year grace period on repayment. Grants went to the poorest nations and were used for such projects as roads and hydroelectric plants.

Some members criticized IDA for making "giveaway" loans and questioned its effectiveness as a means of maintaining U.S. influence abroad. Members also shied away from contributing to multilateral development banks because Congress had little control over how such funds are spent.

The $2.25 billion commitment as the U.S. share of the IDA's lending pool was 31 percent lower than the previous U.S. pledge. It brought the total IDA pool to $9 billion, $7 billion less than the World Bank originally had sought.

The continuing resolution contained a $750 million appropriation for the first year of the three-year commitment to IDA and $150 million for the final installment of the U.S. previous pledge.

Earlier in 1984, it appeared that the $150 million installment might fail to win congressional approval. It was cut Aug. 10 during a House-Senate conference on a fiscal 1984 supplemental appropriation bill (HR 6040 — PL 98-396). *(Supplemental, p. 439)*

But the money was restored by the House Appropriations Committee Sept. 12 during consideration of the fiscal 1985 foreign assistance funding package that was incorporated into the continuing resolution.

Administration Proposal

IDA had requested $1 billion a year from the United States for fiscal 1985-87. But the administration was committed to a contribution of $750 million a year.

The administration portrayed Congress as the stumbling block to a higher IDA donation, citing cutbacks in Reagan's requested appropriations over 1981-84. In 1984, for example, the president asked for $1.095 billion for IDA, and Congress appropriated $945 million.

The administration sent to Capitol Hill legislation March 8 proposing its $2.25 billion authorization for fiscal 1985-88.

The several weeks' delay in sending the legislation to the two authorizing committees, House Banking and Senate Foreign Relations, sparked speculation that the administration was holding up the bill because of differences with Japan over a plan to boost that country's share of funding for the World Bank.

A Treasury spokesman said the delay resulted from personnel changes within the department, not from any dispute involving the World Bank.

In 1981 Congress passed a three-year authorization bill for IDA. It pushed the authorization through that year by coupling it to the Omnibus Budget Reconciliation Act. When that authorization expired, decisions on U.S. contributions to IDA incorporated into continuing appropriations resolutions.

Senate Committee Action

Sen. Charles McC. Mathias Jr., R-Md., called the administration's proposed 25 percent cut in IDA funding "disturbing," noting that over 40 percent of U.S. foreign aid was military assistance, while contributions to development banks had dropped to less than 10 percent of the total aid package.

To put some pressure on the administration the Foreign Relations Committee on March 29 approved by voice vote an amendment to an IDA funding bill (S 2416). It authorized the president to boost U.S. contributions by $500 million in fiscal 1986 if he decided that economic conditions in recipient nations, especially those in Africa, had deteriorated and an increase was necessary. Increases would be subject to congressional appropriation. The plan was backed by Mathias and John C. Danforth, R-Mo.

The White House opposed the amendment. In a March 28 letter to the Foreign Relations Committee, George R. Hoguet, acting assistant Treasury secretary for international affairs, said an IDA contingency fund was unnecessary and would "introduce an element of uncertainty in the U.S. position."

The committee's action was designed to refute the administration's argument that Congress would not authorize a larger IDA contribution and put the ball back in the administration's court.

On April 11, the committee included the Mathias-Danforth provision in its $11 billion foreign-aid package (S 2346). The panel approved the package 16-2.

Both S 2416 and S 2346 also contained the $2.25 billion in three-year IDA funding. Neither bill saw floor action; the IDA provisions were incorporated into a new bill (S 2582 — S Rept 98-400) reported on April 18. That bill, stripped of controversial Central America provisions, in turn never received Senate floor consideration. Foreign aid authorizations were contained in the continuing appropriations resolution (PL 98-473). *(Foreign aid authorization bill, p. 103)*

House Committee Action

The House Banking Subcommittee on International Development Institutions on May 2 unanimously approved the $2.25 billion three-year funding authorization for IDA.

Despite the vote of 11-0, the bill (HR 5336) provoked sharp criticism from Sander M. Levin, D-Mich., who said the administration's request was inadequate.

Levin had planned to offer the Mathias-Danforth language as an amendment, but decided against it. An amendment-free bill had the best hope of passing in the House, Levin said.

Full committee action on the IDA authorization was delayed as Chairman Fernand J. St Germain, D-R.I., held it hostage. St Germain wanted the Department of Housing and Urban Development to agree to rewrite regulations for a housing aid program. *(Story, p. 415)*

After HUD complied, the committee returned to the IDA bill, reporting HR 5336 on Aug. 10 (H Rept 98-981). The bill did not receive floor consideration, and IDA provisions were among the foreign aid authorizations and appropriations incorporated into the continuing resolution. ∎

Economic Policy

Despite generally healthy economic developments throughout the year, Congress directed much of its time and attention in 1984 to reducing future federal deficits.

Defying conventional wisdom, which held that Congress would not have the political will power to raise taxes and cut spending in an election year, legislators cast aside President Reagan's "holding action" fiscal 1985 budget and approved a three-year, $149.2 billion deficit "down payment" package that included $50 billion in tax increases.

Although the package barely put a dent in deficits projected to total about $600 billion through fiscal 1987, most economists agreed that it helped stabilize the growth of deficits and gave the economy some breathing room.

"Obviously a lot more remains to be done," Dan Rostenkowksi, D-Ill., chairman of the House Ways and Means Committee said. "But we have made a start — a down payment."

To achieve these deficit reductions, however, Congress turned its budget process inside out. Deadlines were missed and legislative action to cut spending, raise taxes and appropriate money preceded adoption of the budget resolution, which is supposed to be Congress' annual spending and tax blueprint.

"We knew from the start," said Senate Budget Committee Chairman Pete V. Domenici, R-N.M., "that this was going to be an impossible year" in terms of using the traditional budget process. Despite the convoluted strategy, the congressional budget process continued to provide the framework for the deficit debate.

The Economy

The final economic growth figures for 1984 showed just how strong the recovery was. Even with a slight lull in the summer, the gross national product for 1984 was 6.8 percent larger than the previous year, making it the biggest gain since 1951.

This strong rebound was accompanied by steadily declining inflation. The year-end figure for 1984 showed that inflation grew at 3.7 percent, the lowest rate since 1967.

Civilian unemployment continued a steady drop from its high of 10.7 percent in December 1982 during the first six months of 1984. It reached 7.2 percent in June, and then, after rising to 7.5 percent in July and August, hit 7.1 in November and ended the year at 7.2 percent.

The sole major bleak spot on the economic scene was an unprecedented trade deficit, which was caused in part by the unusually strong dollar. The gap between U.S. exports and goods shipped to the United States soared to $123.3 billion in 1984, the Commerce Department estimated. The figure was nearly double the record $69.4 billion trade deficit registered in 1983.

The Budget and Taxes

For the third year in a row, President Reagan's annual budget submission was "dead on arrival" on Capitol Hill. And again, the chief congressional concern was that the fiscal 1985 fiscal blueprint did not go far enough to reduce ballooning federal deficits.

Although the administration proposed three-year spending reductions and cost savings of $73 billion and tax increases of $33.5 billion, the projected deficits would have hovered around $180 billion for each year through fiscal 1987.

Reagan's commitment to increase defense spending dramatically while refusing to raise substantial new revenues generated criticism from members of both political parties.

After bipartisan deficit-reduction negotiations with the White House failed, each chamber moved ahead with its own budget strategy.

House Democrats developed and speedily adopted a $182 billion deficit-reduction plan that was envisioned as a "pay-as-you-go" budget. This new concept made increases for defense and certain social programs dependent on offsetting increases in taxes.

Senate budget manuevering took much longer. After weeks of prodding, GOP Senate leaders eventually hammered out a three-pronged package that won the president's blessing. It was designed to reduce deficits by $149.5 billion over fiscal years 1985-87.

This "Rose Garden Plan," so-named because Reagan announced support for the deficit down payment at a White House Rose Garden ceremony, called for almost equal amounts of defense spending reductions, domestic program savings and tax increases.

Turning the budget process on its head, the Senate first approved a deficit reduction package (HR 4170) and then adopted a budget resolution that set out spending and revenue targets. It took the Senate more than a month of debate to pass the spending cut/tax increase package, which for the first time called for legislated spending "caps" on discretionary and defense appropriations.

Conferees worked out the differences between the tax components of each chamber's deficit-reduction measure and many of the spending reductions with dispatch. Reagan signed the legislation (PL 98-369) on July 18. The bill included tax loophole closers and other provisions to beef up tax compliance; it also called for spending reductions in Medicare.

But the conference to work out discrepancies on both the budget resolution and the Senate's spending caps deadlocked over defense spending.

It took the intervention of Senate Majority Leader Howard H. Baker Jr., R-Tenn., and House Speaker Thomas P. O'Neill Jr., D-Mass., to resolve the defense issue. Once the two arrived at a compromise allowing for military spending to rise 5 percent above inflation, the budget resolution was adopted without delay.

Monetary Policy

The Federal Reserve Board steered a restrained, yet sufficiently accommodative course to keep the economy humming through the year.

At several junctures administration officials, intent on sustaining a robust economy through the election, engaged in a round of "Fed bashing." The Fed was accused of keeping the money supply unnecessarily tight, given the low rate of inflation.

After the economy began to slow noticeably in late summer and early fall, the Fed began easing its rein on the money supply.

Major banks lowered the prime rate — the interest rate given to their best customers — to 10.75 percent, the lowest level since the start of 1983.

—By Dale Tate

Reagan Budget for Fiscal 1985

Large Deficits Projected:

President's Fiscal 1985 Budget Faces Election-Year Pressures

Early reviews of President Reagan's fiscal 1985 budget proposal indicate that it may encounter in Congress the same intense, election-year partisanship that helped shape it initially.

When the White House Feb. 1 unveiled a plan marked by a huge projected deficit for the fiscal year beginning Oct. 1, 1984, members of Congress reacted largely along party lines. Many Republicans called it "realistic," and most Democrats branded it "irresponsible."

The president has "wasted an opportunity," charged the ranking Democrat on the Senate Budget Committee, Lawton Chiles of Florida. Chiles accused Reagan of ducking the deficit issue and "bowing to the old political wisdom which dictates that hard issues cannot be faced squarely in an election year."

In his budget message, however, Reagan credited his policies of the past three years with putting the United States "well on our way to sustained long term prosperity." *(Text, p. 8-E)*

Urging deficit reductions, he nevertheless proposed a budget in which outlays of $925.5 billion would greatly outweigh projected revenues of $745.1 billion. *(Budget totals, box, this page)*

White House officials acknowledged that election-year pressures played a role in framing a budget that avoided major tax-increase or spending-cut proposals. They portrayed the budget's proposed $180.4 billion deficit for fiscal 1985 as tentative, depending on the response to President Reagan's call Jan. 25 for negotiations with congressional leaders toward $100 billion in deficit reductions over three years. *(Deficit reduction, p. 143)*

In a quick Democratic riposte to the president's offer, House Majority Leader Jim Wright of Texas promised an initiative from his party that would produce budget savings of $200 billion

—As published in the Feb. 4, 1984, Weekly Report

between fiscal 1985 and 1987.

This flurry of eleventh-hour maneuvering by the president and Democratic congressional leaders added a new dimension to a comprehensive proposal prepared by the administration and released Feb. 1 as the president's official budget message.

In that budget large deficits were envisioned through 1987, though they were expected to decline to $180 billion in that year. The deficit figures compare to a 1983 level of $195.4 billion, a record.

With a few exceptions, the basic

The Budget Totals

(Fiscal years, in billions of dollars)

	1983 actual	1984 estimate	1985 estimate	1986 estimate	1987 estimate
Budget authority	$866.7	$912.5	$1,006.5	$1,100.3	$1,181.2
Outlays	796.0	853.8	925.5	992.1	1,068.3
Revenues	600.6	670.1	745.1	814.9	887.8
Deficit	—195.4	—183.7	—180.4	—177.1	—180.5

outlines of Reagan's fiscal 1985 budget look familiar: massive military increases, a freeze on domestic spending programs, and minor tax increases with no retreat from the big tax cut he pushed through Congress in 1981. *(1981 Almanac p. 91)*

Reagan called for continued buildup of U.S. military forces, proposing $305 billion in budget authority, or a 13 percent rise in inflation-adjusted dollars. Budgets for the Defense Department that the president has submitted to Congress over the past three years have called for inflation-adjusted increases of more than 10 percent. In the fiscal 1984 budget, Congress scaled that back to 5 percent,

and much the same is expected to happen this year. *(Defense, p. 399)*

Besides the sharply higher defense budget, more money is slated in 1985 for a number of select programs. In a concession to environmentalists, Reagan has proposed a major effort to attack the problem of acid rain. There also would be more dollars for a crackdown on drug peddling by organized crime.

The spending plan seeks to achieve deficit reductions of $106 billion over the next three years by cutting Medicare and other programs and imposing modest tax hikes.

And the president proposed adoption of two constitutional amendments intended to aid in limiting federal spending.

Several Republican leaders responded favorably to the broad outlines of Reagan's budget. "It's a budget free of obscurities and asterisks," said Senate Majority Leader Howard H. Baker Jr., R-Tenn.

David A. Stockman, director of the Office of Management and Budget (OMB), characterized the budget as a "fiscal stabilizing action."

The administration's rationale for offering only modest deficit reductions, according to Stockman, is a political climate regarded as not conducive to major reductions. Stockman said that "it is fairly clear that big, sweeping changes are not feasible or likely to happen this Congress."

Democrats Decry Deficits

That reasoning did not sit well with the Democrats. When Martin S. Feldstein, chairman of the president's Council of Economic Advisers, offered

Budget Highlights

Following are the highlights of President Reagan's fiscal 1985 budget, which he submitted to Congress on Feb. 1:

Continuing High Deficits. President Reagan's fiscal 1985 budget projects a $180.4 billion deficit, only marginally smaller than the projected deficit of $183.7 in the current year. He did propose a modest, three-year plan to save $73.6 billion from tax increases, spending cuts and interest-cost reductions.

Defense Buildup. The administration's request for $305 billion in budget authority for military spending represents a 13 percent inflation-adjusted increase over fiscal 1984 spending and continues the massive defense buildup begun by Reagan in 1981. Several other national security programs, including foreign aid, were designated for increased funds in fiscal 1985.

Holding the Line on Taxes. The president's proposal for raising $8 billion in new forms of revenue in fiscal 1985 reflects his continued opposition to substantial new taxes. The hikes would mainly involve closing of loopholes and levying of taxes on health insurance premiums.

Minor Spending Initiatives. Other than defense and foreign aid, the spending increases proposed by the administration for fiscal 1985 are modest. They include higher funding for research and development, the United States Information Agency, veterans' programs, and law enforcement, as well as money for a permanent space station.

Optimistic Economic Forecast. The administration's economic scenario, which White House officials acknowledge is premised on enactment of sizable deficit reductions, envisions the economy growing at a 4.5 percent rate in 1984. The figure is slightly higher than the traditional second-year recovery rate.

---

it at a hearing of the Joint Economic Committee Feb. 2, Sen. William Proxmire, D-Wis., shot back, "Regardless of what happened last year," when there was a stalemate between the president and Congress over a deficit reduction plan, "the president has to come back and propose a program."

After their initial skepticism, the Democrats reacted to Reagan's offer to sit down at the negotiating table and find $100 billion in deficit reductions over the next three years, by upping the ante.

Wright told reporters Feb. 1 that the president's deficit-reduction proposals were "cosmetic." He added that Democrats intend to put together a plan for "at least $200 billion" in deficit reductions.

No details were available. But Wright suggested that the Democrats would concentrate on defense spending, large entitlement programs and new taxes, possibly including a delay in the indexing of taxes to offset inflation, due to begin in 1985.

In the Senate, Minority Leader Robert C. Byrd, D-W.Va., said he was setting up a working group that would develop proposals to cut the deficit.

Republican reaction to the Reagan budget plan was more subdued. Rep. Barber B. Conable Jr., R-N.Y., said the budget was "realistic," but admitted, "It's not a happy budget."

What happens next is in doubt.

There is sentiment in Congress among both Republicans and Democrats, including many of those who serve on the Budget or tax-writing committees, to put politics aside and hammer out a deficit-reducing "down payment." Thus far, the congressional leadership of both parties has been cautious about how to approach the negotiations and guarded about the prospects for success.

Some members of Congress have expressed a bittersweet optimism that the talks will be fruitful. Sen. Joseph R. Biden Jr., D-Del., Feb. 2 told a Budget Committee hearing: "Things that start off as politics, sometimes

turn out with substantive results."

More of the Same

In a continuing attempt to curb domestic spending growth, Reagan proposed a freeze of domestic discretionary spending. The administration tried the freeze approach last year and was successful in maintaining overall domestic spending levels.

In addition to the proposed hikes for the Pentagon, other so-called "national interest" programs, such as a major expansion of international broadcasting activities, would receive sizable budget increases. But many members have said that they continue to have the same reservations this year that they had in 1983 about the president's spending and tax priorities.

In a remark echoed by other Democrats, Chiles labeled the budget "an election-year document which dodges the serious issues which would help insure a strong and viable economy for the country's future." And Chiles contended that the budget contains a number of "election year policy shifts."

Among the changes from previous budgets, Reagan proposed to:
● Increase operating funds for the Environmental Protection Agency 8.5 percent after proposing to cut it $1.3 billion in fiscal 1984;
● Increase funds for low-income energy assistance; and
● Increase funds for block grants to states for primary and secondary education after proposing to decrease or freeze funding for these programs in earlier budgets.

Reagan also shied away from an earlier idea to cut Medicare costs by about $2 billion in fiscal 1985, because Republican House members signaled that the effort would be rebuffed immediately. The budget calls for Medicare savings of $1.05 billion or about half the amount originally discussed.

The fiscal 1985 budget, however, does contain some cuts in programs that benefit the poor and elderly. Included in this category are reductions in housing for the elderly; food and nutrition programs; Aid to Families with Dependent Children; Medicaid; and aid to low-income college students.

Deficit Reduction Plan

In his budget message, Reagan said: "The long winter of transition from the misguided policies of the past, with their inflationary and growth-deadening side effects, is now

White House Officials See Risks in Budget

"Does this budget have your stamp of approval?" Sen. Donald W. Riegle Jr., R-Mich., asked budget director David A. Stockman at a hearing on Feb 2.

After several attempts at avoiding a direct answer, Stockman finally pounded his hand on the table and said, "There, it's stamped."

Stockman's gesture underscored the less than enthusiastic support administration officials have expressed for President Reagan's fiscal 1985 budget during appearances on Capitol Hill.

Stockman and Martin S. Feldstein, chairman of the president's Council of Economic Advisers, began edging away from the budget document 24 hours after it was sent to Congress and warned that, if Congress did not enact some deficit-reducing measure this year beyond the president's budget, the economy was in jeopardy.

Reagan Jan. 25 called on congressional leaders to negotiate with the administration on deficit reductions.

In testimony before the Senate Budget, Finance and Joint Economic committees, Stockman, Feldstein and Treasury Secretary Donald T. Regan agreed that at least a $100 billion package of spending cuts and tax increases would be necessary to keep the economy on the right track.

"The 1985 budget is driven by the economy of 1984," Stockman told the Senate Budget Committee Feb. 2. "Beyond that, much more needs to be done. The whole path in this budget is dependent on a down payment this year and major improvements next year and the year after."

Stockman and Feldstein both acknowledged that the administration's fiscal 1985 spending blueprint would not produce a deficit as low as the projected $180.4 billion.

On Feb. 2 Feldstein said, "This budget is not what we want to see happen. My sense is that these negotiations supersede completely the budget that has been sent up." He added, "We're going to have to have additional tax revenues; we're going to have to trim back on the size of the defense authorization; and we're going to have to have domestic spending cuts."

Absent these deficit reductions, Feldstein said, "I think there is something to worry about."

One thing that became evident after several days of hearings on the fiscal 1985 budget is the divergence in economic philosophy between Regan and Feldstein.

During Regan's testimony before the Senate Budget Committee Feb. 3, Lawton Chiles, D-Fla., asked how important deficits really are. He cited the Economic Report, in which Feldstein makes a very strong case that deficits have a significant impact on the economy.

Regan shot back that the president had written the first eight pages of the Economic Report, and added, "As far as I'm concerned, you can throw the rest away."

Riegle responded to the Treasury secretary's pointed disavowal of Feldstein's work: "You have created an impossible situation here. Who are we to believe?"

Later at the hearing, Feldstein brushed aside the Treasury secretary's comments, saying Regan's differences with him involve "technical questions." (*Economic report, p. 14-E*)

Everything on the Table

Despite the differences, there does seem to be a consensus within the administration that much of the budget is open to negotiation.

When Senate Budget Committee Chairman Pete V. Domenici, R-N.M., asked Stockman Feb. 2 if everything was on the table, Stockman replied, "Yes."

When Domenici asked about restraint in defense spending, Stockman said, "We'd be willing to look at it."

On taxes, Stockman said, "Initiatives raising revenues through closing loopholes are appropriate items for consideration."

At a Senate Finance Committee hearing Feb. 2, Regan qualified Stockman's statement, spelling out which tax increases the president would accept. He said the president would oppose any major tax increase and would insist on retaining provisions of a 1981 law to take effect in 1985 that would index individual income taxes to offset the effects of inflation.

Regan said, flatly: "The president does want and will insist upon indexing staying in."

---

yielding to a springtime of hope for America."

But to continue the recovery, Reagan cautioned, "there must be substantial reductions in spending and strictly limited increases in receipts."

The president proposed reductions and cost savings totaling $73 billion, and tax increases totaling $33.5 billion, over the next three years.

A $32 billion portion of the spending reductions, however, is an accounting adjustment in defense spending. Another $14 billion is attributable to debt service savings. Actual proposed spending cuts amount to only $5 billion in fiscal 1985; $10 billion in fiscal 1986; and $12 billion in fiscal 1987. In the fiscal 1984 budget Reagan proposed $43 billion in savings, and $558 billion over five years.

The breakdown for revenue increases is: $7.8 billion in fiscal 1985; $11.6 billion in fiscal 1986; and $14.1 billion in fiscal 1987.

The president rebuffed the advice of several administration officials to resubmit last year's contingency tax plan, which would have kicked in if deficits were too high and spending cuts had been made. Since the proposal was rejected out-of-hand last year, the president decided there was no point in resubmitting it to Congress in the budget for fiscal year 1985.

Instead, he directed the Treasury Department to complete a study and make recommendations by the end of 1984 on how to make the tax system simpler and fairer.

Further, he urged Congress to enact this year constitutional amendments requiring a balanced budget and permitting a president to veto line items in appropriations bills.

He added, "Where Congress lacks the will to enforce upon itself the strict fiscal diet that is now necessary,

Reagan Administration Economic Assumptions

(Calendar years; dollar amounts in billions)

	Actual 1982	FORECAST 1983[1]	FORECAST 1984	FORECAST 1985	ASSUMPTIONS 1986	ASSUMPTIONS 1987	ASSUMPTIONS 1988	ASSUMPTIONS 1989
Major Economic Indicators:								
Gross national product (percent change, fourth quarter over fourth quarter):								
Current dollars	2.6	10.4	9.8	8.9	8.6	8.3	8.0	7.4
Constant (1972) dollars	−1.7	6.1	4.5	4.0	4.0	4.0	4.0	3.8
GNP deflator (percent change, fourth quarter over fourth quarter)	4.4	4.1	5.0	4.7	4.4	4.1	3.8	3.5
Consumer Price Index (percent change, fourth quarter over fourth quarter) [2]	4.5	2.9	4.5	4.7	4.4	4.1	3.8	3.5
Unemployment rate (percent, fourth quarter) [3]	10.5	8.4	7.7	7.5	7.2	6.5	5.8	5.7
Annual Economic Assumptions:								
Gross national product:								
Current dollars:								
Amount	3,073	3,309	3,642	3,974	4,319	4,681	5,059	5,445
Percent change, year over year	4.0	7.7	10.1	9.1	8.7	8.4	8.1	7.6
Constant (1972) dollars:								
Amount	1,485	1,535	1,616	1,682	1,750	1,820	1,892	1,966
Percent change, year over year	−1.9	3.3	5.3	4.1	4.0	4.0	4.0	3.9
Incomes:								
Personal income in dollars	2,579	2,742	2,978	3,224	3,503	3,782	4,055	4,358
Wages and salaries in dollars	1,568	1,664	1,802	1,946	2,109	2,296	2,496	2,708
Corporate profits in dollars	174	205	255	292	318	355	377	391
Price level:								
GNP deflator:								
Level (1972 = 100), annual average	206.9	215.6	225.4	236.2	246.9	257.3	267.4	277.0
Percent change, year over year	6.0	4.2	4.5	4.8	4.5	4.2	3.9	3.6
Consumer Price Index: [2]								
Level (1967 = 100), annual average	288.6	297.4	310.4	324.6	339.3	353.6	367.4	380.6
Percent change, year over year	6.0	3.0	4.4	4.6	4.5	4.2	3.9	3.6
Unemployment rates:								
Total, annual average [3]	9.5	9.5	7.8	7.6	7.3	6.8	6.1	5.7
Insured, annual average [4]	4.7	3.8	3.3	3.3	3.2	2.8	2.4	2.2
Federal pay raise (percent) [5]	4.0	—	3.5	3.5	5.8	5.5	5.3	5.1
Interest rate, 91-day Treasury bills (percent) [6]	10.7	8.6	8.5	7.7	7.1	6.2	5.5	5.0
Interest rate, 10-year Treasury notes (percent)	13.0	11.1	10.3	9.2	8.6	7.2	6.1	5.5

[1] *Preliminary actual data.*

[2] *CPI for urban wage earners and clerical workers. Two versions of the CPI are now published. The index shown here is that currently used, as required by law, in calculating automatic cost-of-living increases for indexed federal programs. The manner in which this index measures housing costs will change significantly in 1985.*

[3] *Percent of total labor force, including armed forces residing in the United States.*

[4] *This indicator measures unemployment under state regular unemployment insurance as a percentage of covered employment under that program. It does not include recipients of extended benefits under that program.*

[5] *In 1984 and 1985, general schedule and military pay raises occur in January. The military pay raises are 4.0% and 5.5%, respectively. An October 1985 pay raise of 5.6% (military and general schedule) is projected. General schedule pay raises normally become effective in October — the first month of the fiscal year. Thus, the October 1986 pay raise will set new pay scales that will be in effect during fiscal year 1987.*

[6] *Average rate on new issues within period on a bank discount basis. These projections assume, by convention, that interest rates decline with the rate of inflation. They do not represent a forecast of interest rates.*

SOURCE: Fiscal 1985 Budget

it needs the help of the executive branch.

"We need a constitutional amendment granting the president the power to veto individual items in appropriations bills," he said.

But neither proposal is expected to fare well in Congress.

In any event, the procedure for adopting a constitutional amendment is so torpid that it is highly unlikely that Reagan could have either the line-item veto or the balanced budget mandate at his disposal in time to affect the 1985 budget.

Consequences of the Deficit

If no deficit-cutting tonic is forthcoming, some believe the nation's economic health may be in jeopardy.

Differences exist within the administration and among politicians and economists as to what the economic consequences will be if Congress does not enact major deficit-reducing measures this year.

The administration is apparently counting on the economy being healthy and robust enough to withstand any possible ill effects that the deficit might cause. Yet many economists believe that large federal borrowing eventually puts pressure on the credit markets, crowding out private investment. This ultimately leads to higher interest rates, and a slowdown in economic activity.

Commenting upon the significance of the budget, Stockman said the administration hopes that the elections will be "a way for the American people to give some direction and guidance to the administration and Congress as to how this deficit problem could be resolved."

Meanwhile, Democrats have countered that the president, by failing to address the deficit issue now, is "mortgaging our children's future."

"Our children are going to have to pay for the results of the administration's 'spend and borrow' economic philosophy," said Minority Leader Byrd. "This check-kiting cannot last forever."

Chiles added, "By refusing once again to face the deficit issue, the president is almost insuring that the increasing federal deficits will not only halt the economic recovery, but will erode the vitality of the national economy, continue the overpricing of American goods abroad, keep interest rates high at home and leave us vulnerable to a renewed and perhaps devastating recession."

Also, there is some dispute about whether the administration's deficit projections — as bleak as they are — are bleak enough.

Proxmire predicted that the deficits will be about $250 billion instead of $180.4 billion as forecast by the administration.

The deficit will be higher, Proxmire said, because the administration's economic forecasts have been "monumentally wrong."

"The administration is predicting continued robust economic growth through 1985," he added. "But the warning signs are already up. These large deficits are going to push up inflation and interest rates or both."

Feldstein told reporters Feb. 2: "If this [the president's] budget is enacted and nothing more, we have no forecast for what the deficits would be. They would be higher than what we've predicted here."

Legislative Agenda

Now that the budget is on Capitol Hill, Congress will spend the next few weeks listening to scores of administration officials, witnesses from the Congressional Budget Office, the General Accounting Office, public interest groups, and others.

According to Senate Budget Committee Chairman Pete V. Domenici, R-N.M., his panel "will pursue a schedule that will allow us to complete action on the first budget resolution for fiscal 1985 by the end of March in committee and allow the Senate leadership to complete action on the

budget by the April recess."

Domenici said he hoped to incorporate in the budget any suggestions the bipartisan negotiating team might come up with. In addition, the Budget chairman said he planned to incorporate the $28 billion in deficit savings included in the fiscal 1984 reconciliation bill (S 2062) still pending in the Senate.

According to a House Budget Committee aide, the House will also try to move expeditiously on the budget, although there is some doubt it can complete work as early as last year when the budget resolution was approved March 23. The one potential problem is the high-powered bipartisan negotiations, he said. If those talks bog down, it could slow the whole process.

Economic Outlook

In assessing the economic results of the past year and looking ahead to the next year, the administration struck a note at times congratulatory, at others optimistic.

According to the budget, 1983 was "one of the best years in the postwar period...." The budget document adds, "Although the magnitude of the recovery was somewhat surprising, the eventual reversal of the economic trends of the previous decade was expected. Indeed, it has been the goal of the administration's economic policies from its first days in office."

The administration singled out the "unwinding of inflation" as its most important economic accomplish-

---

Administration Cuts Deficit Estimate

Citing stronger than expected economic growth plus congressional actions to curb spending and raise taxes, the Reagan administration Aug. 15 lowered its fiscal 1984 deficit estimate to $174.3 billion.

The new estimate was in line with the $172 billion deficit projection released by the Congressional Budget Office (CBO) Aug. 6. But the two offices varied widely in their future, or "outyear," deficit projections.

OMB's mid-session budget review showed deficits steadily declining, so that by 1989 the budget shortfall would drop to $139.3 billion. CBO estimated that in 1989 the deficit would be $263 billion unless additional tax increases and spending cuts were made. The disparity was due largely to differing estimates of interest costs. The OMB deficit estimates also assumed adoption of a number of legislative changes proposed by the administration. But many of these proposals were rejected by Congress.

OMB's economic outlook assumed the economy will grow at 6.5 percent, measured from the fourth quarter of 1983 to the fourth quarter of 1984. Inflation, as measured by the Consumer Price Index, would increase 3.8 percent over the same period and unemployment would drop to 6.8 percent by the end of the year, the agency projected.

ment. But it acknowledged the role played by the Federal Reserve Board in this success.

"A foundation for recovery" — built on low inflation, curtailed spending, an incentive-oriented tax system, and a reduction in regulatory interference — "is now in place," the budget document says.

"If the new policies are maintained consistently," it continues, "the recent favorable economic trends are likely to strengthen and persist in the years ahead."

The administration's economic outlook reflects a cooling down of the economy, with all the major indexes continuing to improve, but at a slower pace.

Specifically, the administration estimates that real output as measured by the gross national product (GNP) will grow 4.5 percent beginning with the fourth quarter of 1983 to the fourth quarter of 1984. The growth rate would be slightly higher than usual for the second year of a recovery. Output would grow 4 percent in 1985.

The administration expects the inflation rate to increase slightly to 5 percent from the fourth quarter of 1983 to the fourth quarter of 1984, and somewhat again in 1985 to 4.7 percent.

The unemployment rate, which dropped sharply at the end of 1983, would continue to decline, but more slowly. It would average 7.8 percent in 1984 and 7.6 percent in 1985.

Interest costs, measured in relation to three-month Treasury bills, are projected to drop almost imperceptibly in 1984, averaging 8.5 percent in 1984 and, more significantly, 7.7 percent in 1985.

Council of Economic Advisers Chairman Feldstein acknowledged Feb. 1 that the budget's economic outlook assumes the adoption of $100 billion in deficit reductions plus unspecified "further significant actions in 1985."

If those things happen, Feldstein said, "then I think we can have the preconditions for the kind of small real growth, favorable inflation, and interest rates that are the underlying assumptions in these calculations."

If those things do not happen, Feldstein added, "it would not be the kind of healthy recovery with low inflation we would like to have."

Fiscal Policy

In the realm of fiscal policy, Reagan's fiscal 1985 budget provides few

Budget Terminology

The federal budget is the president's financial plan for the federal government. It accounts for how government funds have been raised and spent, and it proposes financial policies. It covers the **fiscal year**. Fiscal year 1985 begins Oct. 1, 1984, and ends Sept. 30, 1985.

The budget discusses **receipts**, amounts the government expects to raise in taxes; **budget authority**, amounts agencies are allowed to obligate or lend; and **outlays**, amounts actually paid out by the government in cash or checks during the year. Examples of outlays are funds spent to buy equipment or property, to meet the government's liability under a contract or to pay the salaries of employees. Outlays also include net lending — the difference between disbursements and repayments under government lending programs.

The budget has a twofold purpose: to establish governmental priorities among federal programs and to chart U.S. **fiscal policy**, which is the coordinated use of taxes and expenditures to affect the economy.

Congress adopts its own budget in the form of **budget resolutions**. The **first budget resolution**, which is supposed to be adopted by May 15, sets overall goals for taxes and spending, broken down among major budget categories called **functions**. The **second budget resolution**, to be adopted by Sept. 15, sets binding budget figures.

An **authorization** is an act of Congress that establishes government programs. It defines the scope of programs and sets a ceiling for how much can be spent on them. Authorizations do not actually provide the money. In the case of authority to enter contractual obligations, though, Congress authorizes the administration to make firm commitments for which funds must later be provided. Congress also occasionally includes mandatory spending requirements in an authorization in order to ensure spending at a certain level.

An **appropriation** provides money for programs — within the limits established in authorizations. An appropriation may be for a single year, a specified period of years, or an indefinite number of years, according to the restrictions Congress wishes to place on spending for particular purposes.

Appropriations generally take the form of **budget authority**. Budget authority often differs from actual outlays. That is because, in practice, funds actually spent or obligated during a year may be drawn partly from the budget authority conferred in the year in question and partly from budget authority conferred in previous years.

surprises or departures in policy.

The budget outlines four major elements of the administration's fiscal plan, most of them carryovers from last year's budget:

● a continued freeze on real domestic spending growth;

● continued increases in defense, international security, and "other core purposes of government";

● domestic spending cuts totaling $62 billion over fiscal 1985-89; and

● a total federal spending burden that is a declining percentage of the gross national product, but which the administration called "still too high and which defines the spending control challenges for 1985 and beyond."

The $925 billion in proposed outlays for fiscal 1985 represents an 8.4 percent or $71.8 billion increase over the comparable figure in fiscal 1984. The lion's share of the increase would

go to the Defense Department.

The budget deals at length with the administration's record in curbing domestic spending. "After an era in which the real cost of government doubled three times in less than three decades," it says, "the shift in national policy inaugurated by the Reagan administration will result in a decade-long domestic real spending freeze."

The goal of the administration's fiscal policy is a restoration of the "1971 *status quo ante*" — meaning a return to the ratio that existed between domestic spending and the GNP. The target is a level of domestic spending below 11.6 percent of GNP by 1989. It is currently 14 percent of GNP.

The budget discusses the potential problem of a growing structural deficit — one that is built into the budget and not the result of a recession. The administration blamed what it regards as long-term excessive domestic spending and the need to compensate in coming years for the inadequate defense spending of the decade preceding Reagan's election.

"If no policy actions were taken to reduce them, these large current services deficits would pose serious economic problems," the budget message says.

It theorizes that structural deficits would cause inflation if either the debt is monetized by the creation of more money or if government borrowing should crowd out private investment by driving interest rates higher and inhibiting economic growth.

The budget also highlights the potential ill effects of mounting debt-service costs. In 1971 the cost of financing the debt was $37 billion; in 1984 it will be $113.6 billion.

But the budget document predicts that, if the fiscal 1985 budget as proposed is adopted, the debt service claim on GNP will decline.

1984 Revisions

The administration's revised projections of fiscal 1984 budget figures show outlays at $853.76 billion, revenues at $670.07 billion and a deficit of $183.68 billion. The spending increases would be offset by higher revenues, resulting in a slightly lower deficit than the administration originally projected.

Now proposed is a total of $388.54 million in fiscal 1984 rescissions, the largest being $331.4 million for public and Indian housing programs.

On the other side of the ledger, Reagan's fiscal 1985 spending blueprint also includes a request for $2.77 billion for fiscal 1984 supplemental appropriations, and $2.24 billion for pay supplementals. Agriculture would receive the biggest share of the supplemental request. Its slice would total $1.17 billion. The money would be earmarked for the Federal Crop Insurance Corporation, food stamps, child nutrition programs and special supplemental feeding programs.

The net effect of the supplemental appropriations budgets, based on OMB's figures, would be an increase in the fiscal 1984 spending authority of $4.713 billion.

Credit Budget

The president's fiscal 1985 proposal contains a credit budget covering all direct loan obligations and loan guarantee commitments of federal

The Budget Dollar
Fiscal Year 1985 Estimate

Where It Comes From ...

Borrowing	Individual Income Taxes	Social Insurance Receipts	Corporate Income Taxes	Excise Taxes	Other
20¢	36¢	29¢	8¢	4¢	3¢

Where It Goes ...

Direct Benefit Payments for Individuals	National Defense	Net Interest	Other Federal Operations	Grants to States and Localities
42¢	29¢	13¢	5¢	11¢

agencies. The credit budget totals in both areas have been declining since 1982.

According to the budget, however, the composition of the direct loan portion "is expected to remain relatively constant," with agricultural and business loans making up about one-third of all new loan obligations.

For fiscal 1985, the administration requested a $4.8 billion decrease in the credit budget to $130.5 billion.

New direct loan obligations in 1985 would total $31.7 billion; loan guarantee commitments would be $98.8 billion.

The major reductions in the credit budget would occur in the Farmers Home Administration because of a decrease in agricultural credit insurance fund activities. There

also would be large cutbacks in Rural Electrification Administration loan guarantees. *(Rural electrification, p. 364)*

Increases, however, were sought for foreign military sales, the Federal Housing Administration and guaranteed student loans.

Current Services

The 1974 Congressional Budget Act (PL 93-344) required the president to report to Congress his estimates of outlays and budget authority needed to maintain current government services at the same level as those of the fiscal year in progress, with no changes in policy. These figures, known as the "Current Services Estimates," are a baseline to measure the budget's proposed program

Fiscal 1985 Budget by Function: $925.5 Billion in . . .

(in millions of dollars†)

	BUDGET AUTHORITY‡			OUTLAYS		
	1983	1984 est.	1985 est.	1983	1984 est.	1985 est.
NATIONAL DEFENSE						
Military Defense	$239,474	$258,151	$305,000	$205,012	$231,000	$264,400
Atomic Energy Defense Activities	5,718	6,712	7,806	5,171	6,002	7,133
Defense-related Activities	642	452	569	301	546	507
TOTAL	$245,835	$265,316	$313,375	$210,484	$237,548	$272,040
INTERNATIONAL AFFAIRS						
Foreign Economic and Financial Assistance	$ 4,711	$ 4,960	$ 5,198	$ 3,960	$ 4,601	$ 5,170
International Security Assistance	4,589	5,267	10,004	3,755	5,516	7,775
Conduct of Foreign Affairs	1,837	2,014	2,259	1,766	2,054	2,204
Foreign Information and Exchange Activities	681	787	952	602	770	911
International Financial Programs	−4,632	9,931	3,925	−1,089	561	1,432
TOTAL	$ 7,186	$ 22,959	$ 22,338	$ 8,995	$ 13,502	$ 17,492
GENERAL SCIENCE, SPACE AND TECHNOLOGY						
General Science and Basic Research	$ 1,638	$ 1,965	$ 2,253	$ 1,644	$ 1,864	$ 2,141
Space Flight	4,085	4,048	3,821	4,053	4,091	3,884
Space Science, Applications and Technology	1,596	1,735	2,019	1,486	1,590	1,899
Supporting Space Activities	647	808	964	562	746	894
TOTAL	$ 7,966	$ 8,555	$ 9,057	$ 7,745	$ 8,291	$ 8,818
ENERGY						
Energy Supply	$ 2,552	$ 2,034	$ 1,583	$ 2,421	$ 2,032	$ 1,606
Energy Conservation	449	456	382	477	490	410
Emergency Energy Preparedness	242	159	447	215	203	357
Energy Information, Policy and Regulation	878	764	735	886	737	771
TOTAL	$ 4,121	$ 3,413	$ 3,148	$ 3,999	$ 3,463	$ 3,144
NATURAL RESOURCES AND ENVIRONMENT						
Water Resources	$ 4,605	$ 3,716	$ 3,605	$ 3,901	$ 4,207	$ 3,830
Conservation and Land Management	1,883	801	285	1,503	862	323
Recreational Resources	1,581	1,394	1,298	1,454	1,608	1,502
Pollution Control and Abatement	3,677	3,976	4,175	4,263	3,937	4,171
Other Natural Resources	1,547	1,603	1,473	1,548	1,689	1,521
TOTAL	$ 13,294	$ 11,489	$ 10,837	$ 12,669	$ 12,302	$ 11,346
AGRICULTURE						
Farm Income Stabilization	$ 29,330	$ 2,442	$ 10,363	$ 20,628	$ 8,927	$ 12,599
Agricultural Research and Services	1,698	1,786	1,717	1,578	1,766	1,720
TOTAL	$ 31,028	$ 4,227	$ 12,080	$ 22,206	$ 10,693	$ 14,319
COMMERCE AND HOUSING CREDIT						
Mortgage Credit and Thrift Insurance	$ 2,787	$ 2,998	$ 2,749	$ 2,125	$ 1,063	$ −1,177
Postal Service	789	879	692	789	879	692
Other Advancement of Commerce	1,694	1,619	1,631	1,508	1,863	1,613
TOTAL	$ 5,270	$ 5,496	$ 5,071	$ 4,422	$ 3,805	$ 1,127
TRANSPORTATION						
Ground Transportation	$ 19,159	$ 20,761	$ 19,920	$ 14,316	$ 18,116	$ 18,631
Air Transportation	4,850	5,314	6,389	4,000	4,768	5,149
Water Transportation	2,912	3,237	3,032	2,969	3,092	3,143
Other Transportation	110	115	116	99	147	137
TOTAL	$ 27,031	$ 29,427	$ 29,457	$ 21,385	$ 26,123	$ 27,061
COMMUNITY AND REGIONAL DEVELOPMENT						
Community Development	$ 5,281	$ 4,793	$ 4,177	$ 4,293	$ 4,682	$ 4,788
Area and Regional Development	2,950	2,205	1,884	2,644	2,769	2,618
Disaster Relief and Insurance	480	234	308	−1	143	179
TOTAL	$ 8,712	$ 7,232	$ 6,369	$ 6,936	$ 7,594	$ 7,586

... Expenditures, $1.01 Trillion in Spending Authority

(in millions of dollars†)

	BUDGET AUTHORITY‡			OUTLAYS		
	1983	1984 est.	1985 est.	1983	1984 est.	1985 est.
EDUCATION, TRAINING, EMPLOYMENT, SOCIAL SERVICES						
Elementary, Secondary and Vocational Education	$ 6,854	$ 7,266	$ 7,331	$ 6,294	$ 6,959	$ 7,144
Higher Education	7,418	6,931	7,006	7,231	7,766	7,188
Research and General Education Aids	1,147	1,115	1,017	1,055	1,176	1,163
Training and Employment	5,515	8,388	4,845	5,295	5,085	4,910
Other Labor Services	640	687	707	599	673	703
Social Services	6,604	6,838	6,604	6,133	7,025	6,785
TOTAL	$ 28,178	$ 31,225	$ 27,510	$ 26,606	$ 28,683	$ 27,893
HEALTH						
Health Care Services	$ 19,230	$ 25,242	$ 25,446	$ 23,037	$ 24,647	$ 26,550
Health Research	4,252	4,759	4,850	3,973	4,434	4,787
Education and Training of Health Care Work Force	491	458	349	578	442	410
Consumer and Occupational Health and Safety	1,068	1,134	1,158	1,066	1,143	1,168
TOTAL	$ 25,041	$ 31,593	$ 31,802	$ 28,655	$ 30,665	$ 32,916
SOCIAL SECURITY AND MEDICARE						
Social Security	$184,133	$175,900	$198,467	$170,724	$179,161	$190,639
Medicare	46,403	62,778	70,203	52,588	61,064	69,683
TOTAL	$230,536	$238,678	$268,670	$223,311	$240,225	$260,321
INCOME SECURITY						
General Retirement and Disability Insurance	$ 5,043	$ 8,031	$ 6,682	$ 5,581	$ 5,496	$ 5,670
Federal Employee Retirement and Disability	35,190	37,026	67,513	20,563	21,569	40,017
Unemployment Compensation	29,348	26,406	21,903	31,464	20,727	20,069
Housing Assistance	10,025	8,022	5,582	9,556	10,041	10,908
Food and Nutrition Assistance	18,154	17,657	17,167	17,952	17,622	17,090
Other Income Security	20,989	20,435	20,341	21,096	20,503	20,605
TOTAL	$118,748	$117,578	$139,187	$106,211	$ 95,957	$114,360
VETERANS BENEFITS AND SERVICES						
Income Security	$ 14,216	$ 14,970	$ 15,386	$ 14,250	$ 14,611	$ 15,056
Education, Training and Rehabilitation	1,667	1,573	1,270	1,625	1,410	1,325
Hospital and Medical Care	8,816	9,039	9,890	8,272	8,972	9,597
Housing	−78	−67	−75	3	19	−72
Other Benefits and Services	743	788	825	696	787	817
TOTAL	$ 25,364	$ 26,303	$ 27,297	$ 24,846	$ 25,799	$ 26,723
ADMINISTRATION OF JUSTICE						
Federal Law Enforcement Activities	$ 3,061	$ 3,417	$ 3,505	$ 2,887	$ 3,407	$ 3,515
Federal Litigative and Judicial Activities	1,702	1,920	1,854	1,627	1,921	1,847
Federal Correctional Activities	468	489	568	418	500	574
Criminal Justice Assistance	137	211	146	167	193	203
TOTAL	$ 5,367	$ 6,038	$ 6,074	$ 5,099	$ 6,021	$ 6,140
GENERAL GOVERNMENT						
Legislative Functions	$ 1,418	$ 1,463	$ 1,412	$ 1,196	$ 1,354	$ 1,447
Executive Direction and Management	103	113	122	96	114	121
Central Fiscal Operations	3,246	3,520	3,717	3,045	3,467	3,642
General Property and Records Management	476	255	237	200	399	238
Central Personnel Management	142	149	153	115	155	155
Other General Government	794	478	569	768	597	565
Deductions for Offsetting Receipts	−636	−424	−425	−636	−424	−425
TOTAL	$ 5,544	$ 5,553	$ 5,786	$ 4,784	$ 5,652	$ 5,744
GENERAL PURPOSE FISCAL ASSISTANCE						
General Revenue Sharing	$ 4,574	$ 4,574	$ 4,575	$ 4,620	$ 4,574	$ 4,574
Other General Purpose Fiscal Assistance	1,790	2,167	2,084	1,834	2,167	2,084
TOTAL	$ 6,364	$ 6,741	$ 6,658	$ 6,454	$ 6,741	$ 6,658
NET INTEREST						
Interest on the Public Debt	$128,619	$149,500	$164,700	$128,619	$149,500	$164,700
Interest Received by Trust Funds	−17,102	−19,396	−22,587	−17,102	−19,396	−22,587
Other Interest	−21,742	−21,865	−25,974	−21,743	−21,865	−25,974
TOTAL	$ 89,775	$108,239	$116,138	$ 89,774	$108,239	$116,138
CIVILIAN AGENCY PAY RAISES	—	—	$ 446	—	—	$ 430
CONTINGENCIES	—	—	—	—	—	—
INCREASED EMPLOYING AGENCY RETIREMENT PAYMENTS	—	—	$ 509	—	—	$ 509
UNDISTRIBUTED OFFSETTING RECEIPTS	$ −18,614	$ −17,544	$ −35,273	$ −18,614	$ −17,544	$ −35,273
GRAND TOTAL	$866,745	$912,517	$1,006,538	$795,969	$853,760	$925,492

† Figures may not add to totals due to rounding. ‡ Primarily appropriations.

SOURCE: Fiscal 1985 Budget

changes and year-to-year growth.

The current services figures for the Defense Department, however, are computed differently. According to OMB, the defense figures are drawn from the administration's 1984 mid-session review budget request.

Current services outlays for fiscal 1985 were estimated to be $944.9 billion, or 10.6 percent higher than in fiscal 1984.

Budget authority was estimated to be $1,030.8 billion, an increase of 13.1 percent over fiscal 1984.

Revenues are projected to increase from $666.6 billion in fiscal 1984 to $737.3 billion in fiscal 1985.

The current services deficit resulting from these figures is estimated at $207.6 billion in fiscal 1985 — $20.1 billion higher than the $187.5 billion deficit in fiscal 1984. If only current services were budgeted, the deficit would drop to $193 billion by fiscal 1989.

Program Highlights

Taxes. The Reagan budget calls for tax increases of $7.8 billion in fiscal 1985, $11.6 billion in fiscal 1986, and $14.1 billion in fiscal 1987.

These include a new "women's initiative" that would expand individual retirement accounts (IRAs) so that a homemaker and her husband could contribute up to $4,000 to an IRA. The tax proposals also call for structural reforms, such as restrictions on tax-exempt leasing, the taxation of life insurance companies and restrictions on industrial development bonds.

The biggest increase in revenues would come from a proposal offered last year and rejected by Congress — the taxation of health insurance premiums.

The administration also resubmitted certain tax breaks including tuition tax credits, enterprise zone tax incentives and a higher education tax incentive.

National Defense. Reagan's fiscal 1985 defense budget request follows the pattern of sizable increases started three years ago.

The Pentagon's request for $305 billion in budget authority was $47 billion higher than the amount appropriated for the Defense Department in fiscal 1984. This represented an inflation-adjusted increase of 13 percent. For fiscal 1985 total defense outlays were projected at $272 billion, of which $264 billion was in Pentagon

accounts — all but $8 billion.

The defense spending plan reflects a strong emphasis on investment-oriented spending, such as procurement, research and development, and military construction.

The budget also indicates a strong commitment to improving all three legs of the so-called nuclear "triad." This includes the production of the MX missile and development of an-

other land-based missile; production of B-1 bombers and development of a successor; and production of a 12th Trident missile submarine, with development of a new, more accurate missile to go with it.

The request also includes a 5.5 percent pay hike for military personnel, and a 3.5 percent raise for Pentagon civilians.

In addition to the Pentagon's budget, other defense-related programs bring the total fiscal 1985 request for the "national security function" to $313.4 billion.

The biggest share of the non-Pentagon defense funds would go to the Energy Department for the development and manufacture of nuclear weapons.

International Affairs. One of the single largest proposed increases in the fiscal 1985 budget is for foreign aid.

Reagan asked for a 50 percent increase in the foreign aid budget, from $10.2 billion in fiscal 1984 to $15.2 billion in fiscal 1985. Most of the increase is in the $5 billion Foreign Military Sales program, which Reagan would include in the budget for the first time. Until now most of that

money was not counted in budget authority totals because it consisted of loans that were guaranteed by the Federal Financing Bank.

Reagan also proposed a new program of military and economic aid to Central America, in line with the Kissinger commission's recommendations. The budget includes planning figures of about $500 million in fiscal 1984 and $750 million in 1985, for additional aid to the region. But Reagan's actual recommendations are expected to be about $695 million in fiscal 1984 and $656 million in 1985.

Other major aid increases would go to Israel, Egypt, Lebanon, Africa and the Philippines. In a classified annex to the defense budget, Reagan also requested about $200 million to equip and train two brigades of the Jordanian army as a rapid deployment force in the Middle East.

In addition, the administration requested a much smaller contribution to the International Development Association (IDA), a World Bank affiliate that makes "soft" loans mostly to Third World countries.

The fiscal 1985 budget request for the IDA was $750 million, compared to $945 million authorized in fiscal 1984.

Funding levels for the Export-Import Bank's direct loan, loan guarantee, and insurance programs remained at fiscal 1984's relatively high level.

Labor. The Department of Labor's budget would retain employment and training programs at about their fiscal 1984 level. This would include $3.6 billion for the Job Training Partnership Act, the principal federal training program.

The administration resubmitted two job-related proposals that went nowhere in Congress last year: a youth subminimum wage of $2.50 an hour for summer months; and elimination of the work incentive program known as WIN to help welfare recipients get jobs.

The budget also contained a request to extend the Targeted Jobs Tax Credit program, which gives employers tax credits for part of the wages paid if they hire disadvantaged workers. The program expires Dec. 31, 1984.

Although there were no policy changes proposed for the regular unemployment program, the administration asked that state and federal employment insurance be extended to rail employees. Currently rail workers are covered by their own unemploy-

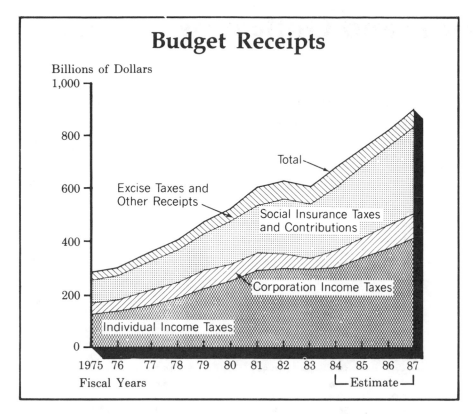

Budget Receipts

Billions of Dollars

Total

Excise Taxes and
Other Receipts

Social Insurance Taxes
and Contributions

Corporation Income Taxes

Individual Income Taxes

1975 76 77 78 79 80 81 82 83 84 85 86 87
Fiscal Years

Estimate

poses new, mandatory cost-sharing so that beneficiaries would pay nominal fees for hospitalization.

The budget declares biomedical research a top priority and requests an $89 million funding increase in fiscal 1985 for the National Institutes of Health.

Energy. For the first time, the administration proposes funding for conservation, solar energy and other renewable energy resources that is somewhat in line with what Congress has appropriated.

Rather than attempting to slash spending in those areas, it called for fiscal 1985 funding levels totaling $591 million for weatherization of schools, hospitals and low-income homes, conservation research and solar-energy renewables research. In fiscal 1984 Congress appropriated $646 million for these purposes; Reagan had requested only $176 million.

The administration proposed to continue to fill the Strategic Petroleum Reserve at a rate of 145,000 barrels per day.

Natural Resources and Environment. The environment and natural resources budget makes some prominent concessions to environmentalists, but not as many as they sought.

The Environmental Protection Agency's fiscal 1985 budget was $4.2 billion, up from $3.9 billion appropriated for fiscal 1984.

The budget proposes to increase greatly spending for research into the politically volatile subject of acid rain. Governmentwide funding for research into acid rain would top $120 million in fiscal 1985.

Another concession to environmentalists is Reagan's request for $157.5 million for federal acquisition of park and recreation lands in the Department of Interior.

The budget includes funds to start construction of five new water projects by the Bureau of Reclamation in the Western states of Wyoming, Arizona, California, Nevada and Idaho.

Transportation. The administration requested $28.6 billion in budget authority for transportation programs in fiscal 1985 — up $1.2 billion over fiscal 1984.

Seventy-two percent of the money would come from various user fees — such as the gas tax and airline passenger fees.

Rather than eliminating mass transit operating subsidies in 1985, as

ment program financed with payroll contributions from railroad employees. The program has been seriously under-funded recently because of high unemployment.

Welfare. The administration recycled last year's proposals for reforming Aid to Families with Dependent Children. The plan includes a "workfare" proposal to require states to set up mandatory work programs for welfare recipients. The Department of Health and Human Services estimates this would reduce outlays by $633 million in fiscal 1985.

The budget includes proposals to strengthen child-support enforcement. The administration's position has already been set in legislation pending in Congress.

After failing to cut energy assistance to low-income people for the last two years, the administration proposed budget authority for the program at its fiscal 1984 level of $1.87 billion. It would pay for part of the program from a new source: revenues collected in settlements of lawsuits against oil companies for overcharging.

Agriculture. The Agriculture Department's budget revives familiar money-saving proposals that appear no more likely to pass Congress this year than before.

For federal food programs such as

food stamps and school lunches, the administration requests nearly $1 billion in supplemental funds to cover the rest of fiscal 1984. Anticipated higher employment and proposed revisions in the food stamp program are expected to reduce food stamp spending to $10.8 billion in fiscal 1985, down from the fiscal 1984 total of $11.3 billion.

Reagan favors deep cuts in federal programs that help pay farmers' costs for controlling erosion, and severely reduced funds for water projects.

For the third year in a row, the budget calls for slashing federally guaranteed lending to rural electric and telephone systems.

Among other new items in the proposed Agriculture budget: a $2 million investment in improving black land-grant colleges and a $28.5 million biotechnology research initiative.

Health. The final health budget includes only about half the Medicare spending reductions that had appeared in earlier versions.

What remains is a one-year freeze on physician fees, and increases in the premiums that Medicare beneficiaries pay. These changes would save approximately $1.05 billion in fiscal 1985.

For Medicaid the budget pro-

Budget Authority and Outlays by Agency

(in billions of dollars†)

DEPARTMENT OR OTHER UNIT	BUDGET AUTHORITY			OUTLAYS		
	1983 actual	1984 estimate	1985 estimate	1983 actual	1984 estimate	1985 estimate
Legislative branch	$ 1.7	$ 1.7	$ 1.7	$ 1.4	$ 1.7	$ 1.7
The Judiciary	.8	.9	1.0	.8	.9	1.0
Executive Office of the President	.1	.1	.1	.1	.1	.1
Funds appropriated to the President	3.3	16.5	13.1	5.5	8.1	11.1
Agriculture	56.4	27.8	35.0	46.4	34.8	37.7
Commerce	1.9	2.0	1.6	1.9	2.2	2.0
Defense — Military [1]						
Including accruals [2]	*(238.7)*	*(258.1)*	305.0	*(204.4)*	*(231.0)*	264.4
Excluding accruals	239.5	258.2	—	205.0	231.0	—
Defense — Civil						
Including military retirees[2]	*(19.6)*	*(19.2)*	29.9	*(18.9)*	*(19.6)*	20.0
Excluding military retirees	3.4	2.7	—	2.9	3.1	—
Education	15.4	15.4	15.4	14.6	16.1	15.5
Energy	9.3	9.7	10.8	8.4	8.8	9.9
Health and Human Services	280.2	295.0	324.8	276.6	296.0	318.1
Housing and Urban Development	16.0	13.7	10.5	15.3	15.9	15.2
Interior	5.0	4.6	4.3	4.6	4.9	4.4
Justice	3.0	3.4	3.7	2.8	3.4	3.7
Labor	36.4	36.2	28.0	38.1	27.1	26.4
State	2.8	2.9	3.4	2.3	2.6	3.1
Transportation	26.3	28.6	28.6	20.6	25.3	26.2
Treasury	117.1	137.9	149.7	116.4	137.7	149.5
Environmental Protection Agency	3.7	4.0	4.2	4.3	4.0	4.2
General Services Administration	.7	.3	.3	.2	.5	.3
National Aeronautics and Space Administration	6.9	7.2	7.5	6.7	7.1	7.4
Office of Personnel Management	35.7	37.8	40.9	21.3	22.6	23.7
Small Business Administration	1.0	.6	.6	.5	.4	.4
Veterans Administration	25.3	26.3	27.2	24.8	25.8	26.7
Other agencies	10.7	16.0	16.5	10.3	10.8	10.1
Allowances [3]	—	—	1.0	—	—	.9
Undistributed offsetting receipts:						
Interest received from trust funds	−17.1	−19.4	−22.6	−17.1	−19.4	−22.6
Interest received from Outer Continental Shelf escrow account	—	—	−.4	—	—	−.4
Employer share, employee retirement:						
Including accrual offset	*(−23.5)*	*(−25.3)*	−27.9	*(−23.5)*	*(−25.3)*	−27.9
Excluding accrual offset	−8.1	−8.8	—	−8.1	−8.8	—
Rents and royalties on the Outer Continental Shelf	−10.5	−8.7	−7.4	−10.5	−8.7	−7.4
Total undistributed offsetting receipts:						
Including accrual offset[2]	*(−51.1)*	*(−53.4)*	−58.3	*(−51.1)*	*(−53.4)*	−58.3
Excluding accrual offset	−35.7	−36.9	—	−35.7	−36.9	—
Total budget authority and outlays	**$866.7**	**$912.5**	**$1,006.5**	**$796.0**	**$853.8**	**$925.5**

[1] *Includes allowances for civilian and military pay raises for Department of Defense.*
[2] *Beginning in 1985, the budget reflects establishment of a military retirement trust fund. Entries in parentheses show amounts for 1983 and 1984 on a comparable basis.*
[3] *Includes allowances for civilian agency pay raises and increased employing agency payments for employee retirement.*
† *Figures may not add to totals due to rounding.*

SOURCE: Fiscal 1985 Budget

OMB initially wanted, the budget calls for phasing the subsidies out over four years.

The big winner in the transportation budget is the Federal Aviation Administration, with a $1 billion increase over last year.

Housing. President Reagan's fiscal 1985 budget proposes 100,000 additional units of assisted housing. However, 87,500 of them would be in the form of cash vouchers to the poor. This is a program Congress has been reluctant to embrace in the past two years.

The Department of Housing and Urban Development would have total fiscal 1985 budget authority of $10.5 billion, a decrease of $3.2 billion from the fiscal 1984 level of $13.7 billion. Most of the decrease would affect assisted housing programs. But the administration proposed 10,000 units for elderly and handicapped housing and 2,500 units of housing on Indian reservations.

Law Enforcement. Budget authority for the administration of justice would continue to increase under Reagan's fiscal 1985 budget plan. The president asked for $6.1 billion for justice-related programs with the bulk of that amount, $3.7 billion, going to the Justice Department.

The major initiative in the law enforcement budget is a $63.9 million hike for the Immigration and Naturalization Service. Most of the amount is for 1,000 new positions to crack down on illegal aliens trying to enter the United States.

The department would add 150 new positions and receive $8.3 million for increased tax enforcement, primarily to combat the recent growth in tax shelter abuses and to improve collection of delinquent taxes.

Education. After proposing cuts that were repeatedly rebuffed by Congress since it has been in office, the administration now is calling for a $15.5 billion Education Department budget — just slightly over this year's appropriations level.

The administration requested an additional $250 million for the education block grant to states. The block grants are extra money that the states may spend on educational improvements as they see fit.

While keeping the agency's overall budget at fiscal 1984 levels, the administration proposes cuts in and elimination of a number of smaller education programs. Also included in the budget is a proposal recycled from last year to revamp aid to college students so as to emphasize "self help."

Faced with congressional opposition, the administration dropped a plan to consolidate vocational and adult education programs into a block grant.

Veterans. The budget request for a wide array of veterans' programs — including disability compensation, health care and housing — is close to the fiscal 1984 level adjusted for inflation.

However, a 15 percent increase in education readjustment benefit levels is included. No such increase has been granted since 1980. Hospital construction funding for fiscal 1985 was increased to $600 million, providing money for four major design projects.

Total fiscal 1985 spending for veterans' programs would amount to $26 billion.

Research and Development, Space. The administration requested $150 million to begin research and development on a permanent manned space station, expected to be fully in operation by 1992. The total cost is expected to be $8 billion.

Funding for the National Aeronautics and Space Administration would increase by 4 percent, from $7.2 billion this year to $7.5 billion in fiscal 1985.

Reagan also proposed an increase in governmentwide funding for basic research by more than 10 percent, to $8 billion.

Federal Employees. Under Reagan's plan, federal civilian employees would receive a 3.5 percent pay raise on Jan. 1, 1985. Military personnel would receive a 5.5 percent boost on the same date as an incentive to stay in the service.

Further, the budget calls for changes in the civil service retirement system. Federal employee and agency contributions to the pension fund would increase from the current 7 percent to 9 percent in 1986. Cost-of-living increase payments to retired workers would be delayed from June 1984 to January 1985.

Legislative. The $1.7 billion slated for Congress in the 1985 budget to cover its operating expenses is approximately the same amount Congress and its agencies will receive in 1984. The budget includes a supplemental 1984 request for Congress of $194 million.

The budget also proposes increases for the House and Senate leadership offices, and a nearly 50 percent increase in funding for the attending physician's office in the Capitol. ∎

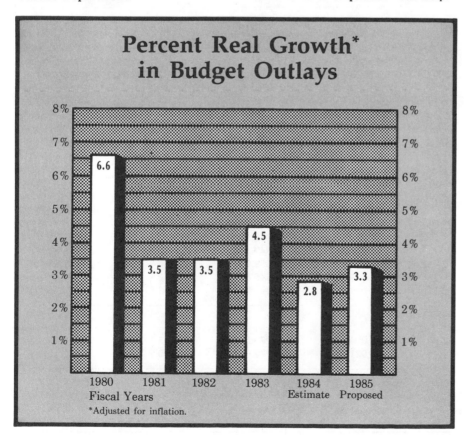

Percent Real Growth*
in Budget Outlays

Fiscal Years	
1980	6.6
1981	3.5
1982	3.5
1983	4.5
1984 Estimate	2.8
1985 Proposed	3.3

*Adjusted for inflation.

Presidents, Congress and the Budget, 1979-85

(in billions of dollars)

	Budget Authority	Outlays	Revenues	Deficit
Fiscal Year 1979				
Carter Budget	568.2	500.2	439.6	−60.6
First Resolution	568.85	498.8	447.9	−50.9
Second Resolution	555.65	487.5	448.7	−38.8
Revised Second Resolution	559.2	494.45	461.0	−33.45
Actual	556.7	493.6	465.9	−27.7
Fiscal Year 1980				
Carter Budget	615.5	531.6	502.6	−29.0
First Resolution	604.4	532.0	509.0	−23.0
Second Resolution	638.0	547.6	517.8	−29.8
Revised Second Resolution	658.9	572.65	525.7	−46.95
Actual	658.8	579.6	520.0	−59.6
Fiscal Year 1981				
Carter Budget	696.1	615.8	600.0	−15.8
Carter Revisions	691.3	611.5	628.0	+16.5
First Resolution	697.2	613.6	613.8	+ 0.2
Second Resolution	694.6	632.4	605.0	−27.4
Revised Second Resolution	717.5	661.35	603.3	−58.05
Actual	718.4	657.2	599.3	−57.9
Fiscal Year 1982				
Carter Budget	809.8	739.3	711.8	−27.5
Reagan Revision	772.4	695.3	650.3	−45.0
First Resolution[1]	770.9	695.45	657.8	−37.65
Revised Second Resolution	777.67	734.10	628.4	−105.7
Actual	779.9	728.4	617.8	−110.6
Fiscal Year 1983				
Reagan Budget	801.9	757.6	666.1	−91.5
First Resolution[2]	822.39	769.82	665.9	−103.92
Revised Resolution	877.2 } *	807.4 } *	604.3	−203.1 } *
	883.36 }	812.85 }		−208.55 }
Actual	866.7	795.97	600.56	−195.4
Fiscal Year 1984				
Reagan Budget	900.1	848.5	659.7	−188.8
First Resolution[2]	919.5 }	849.5 }	679.6	−169.9 }
	928.73 } *	858.93 } *		−179.33 } *
Revised Resolution	918.9	845.6	672.9	−172.7
Actual	927.4	841.8	666.5	−175.36
Fiscal Year 1985				
Reagan Budget	1,006.5	925.5	745.1	−180.4
First Resolution[2]	1,021.35	932.05	750.9	−181.15

[1] *Second resolution merely reaffirmed figures in first resolution.*
[2] *First resolution became binding at beginning of fiscal year Oct. 1.*

* *Larger figure assumed enactment of 10 programs included in a special $8.5 billion reserve fund.*

$149.2 Billion Deficit-Cutting Plan Approved

Efforts to cut federal budget deficits, estimated to remain near $200 billion annually through 1989, occupied legislators for most of 1984. After months of negotiations among administration officials, Democratic leaders in the House and Republican leaders in the Senate, lawmakers in October finally agreed to cut deficits by $149.2 billion through fiscal year 1987.

The deficit reduction plan had three elements: increased taxes, reduced spending on domestic programs and a slowdown in defense funding. The House and Senate were able to agree on a tax increase/domestic spending cut bill in late June. But a stalemate on the Pentagon budget continued until the final weeks of the session.

The final elements of the deficit-reducing measures Congress agreed to were incorporated in its fiscal 1985 budget: $50.8 billion in increased tax revenues; $58.3 billion from smaller increases in the defense budget; $12.2 billion in savings from entitlements and other mandatory benefit programs; $3.9 billion from reductions in non-defense discretionary spending; $18.3 billion from net interest savings; and $5.7 billion from offsetting receipts.

As a first installment on its deficit reduction plan, Congress June 27 cleared a bill (HR 4170 — PL 98-369) providing $50 billion in tax increases and $13 billion in spending cuts through fiscal 1987.

In 1983 controversy and confusion over the budget prevented both chambers from passing much smaller revenue-raising bills. But the threat of $200 billion annual deficits and fears that Congress could pay for its inaction at the polls in November pushed members to act. The budget cuts enacted in 1984 included reductions in a bill (HR 4169) approved by the House in October 1983 and by the Senate in April 1984. *(Story, p. 160; 1983 deficit reduction action, 1983 Almanac p. 231)*

House, Senate Plans

Congress' annual fiscal argument was complicated by the strategy adopted by the administration and GOP leaders in the Senate. Reversing the procedures established by the Congressional Budget and Impoundment Control Act of 1974 (PL 93-344), the Senate refused to consider a fiscal 1985 budget resolution, Congress' non-binding spending and taxing guideline, before it enacted legislation mandating deficit reductions. *(Budget resolution, p. 155; Budget Act, 1974 Almanac p. 145)*

The House followed the traditional route outlined in the Budget Act. First it approved a budget resolution (H Con Res 280) that set overall spending and revenue goals. And then it passed two separate bills — a tax increase in HR 4170 and spending cuts in HR 5394 — designed to implement its budget.

H Con Res 280 laid out a program to cut the deficit by $182 billion in fiscal years 1985-87. The plan called for a $49.8 billion tax increase, a $95.6 billion defense-spending slowdown and $15 billion in domestic spending cuts, among other savings.

The Senate, on the other hand, instead of establishing a fiscal framework with a budget resolution, spent many weeks debating, and eventually approving, the "Rose Garden" deficit-reduction plan of tax increases and spending cuts. A budget resolution conforming to the deficit package was routinely approved the next day.

Legislative Summary

April 5. The House adopts its fiscal 1985 budget resolution (H Con Res 280) setting overall spending and revenue goals. The resolution calls for deficit reductions totaling $182 billion over fiscal 1985-87.

April 11. The House passes a bill (HR 4170) to raise $49.2 billion in new revenues through fiscal 1987.

April 12. The House passes a separate bill (HR 5394) to trim $3.9 billion from entitlement programs through fiscal 1987. The spending cut provisions subsequently are incorporated in HR 4170.

April 13. Before considering a budget resolution, the Senate approves a deficit reduction package consisting of $47 billion in tax increases and $15 billion in Medicare and Medicaid spending cuts. The package, which is attached to a minor House-passed tariff bill (HR 2163), is part of the "Rose Garden" plan that has been agreed to by President Reagan and GOP Senate leaders. The plan calls for $140 billion in deficit reductions through fiscal 1987, consisting of tax increases, limits on increases in military spending, and cuts in federal benefit and other non-defense programs.

May 17. After weeks of haggling, the Senate approves the remaining elements of the Rose Garden plan. It then passes HR 4170, first substituting its own deficit reduction provisions.

May 18. After substituting its counterpart (S Con Res 106), the Senate adopts H Con Res 280, which conforms to the legislation passed a day earlier.

June 27. Congress approves a compromise version of HR 4170, providing $50 billion in tax increases and $13 billion in spending cuts through fiscal 1987.

Oct. 1. Congress completes action on H Con Res 280. By assuming tax increases, spending cuts and savings from lower interest rates, the final version of the budget resolution shows deficit reductions totaling $149.2 billion through fiscal 1987.

The Senate's Rose Garden plan, so named because President Reagan endorsed it March 15 at a ceremony in the White House Rose Garden, envisioned deficit reductions worth $140 billion through fiscal 1987. The $140 billion was spread in roughly equal amounts among tax increases, defense spending curbs and domestic spending cuts.

At the center of the Senate's deficit-cutting plan were two spending caps — one for defense and one for all non-military discretionary spending. The administration and the GOP leadership insisted on putting the caps in the deficit reduction bill. By incorporating them in the legislation, the caps would have established, in law, Congress' spending plan for three fiscal years. As part of a budget resolution, the caps would have been only recommendations, because budget resolutions are congressional documents that are not signed into law.

The caps were employed to convince both Reagan and conservative Republicans that they could count on long-term efforts to increase military spending and restrain domestic spending. In exchange, Reagan and the conservatives supported a relatively modest tax hike.

But many members of Congress, including the chairman of the Senate Appropriations Committee, Mark O. Hatfield, R-Ore., acknowledged that the caps were not enforceable because one Congress cannot bind another by its actions. Congress would be free to approve an appropriations bill above a cap level — subject to a possible presidential veto.

House refusal to abide by the Senate caps led to a compromise in the House-Senate conference on the deficit-reduction legislation that substituted non-binding language for the spending ceilings.

Deficit 'Down Payment'

The search for deficit cutbacks began in earnest after the budget submitted by President Reagan in early February was rejected out of hand by both political parties because it did not go far enough to reduce anticipated deficits. The administration budget forecast a $180.4 billion deficit for fiscal 1985; deficits thereafter would eventually drop. Many members also objected to the budget's proposed 13 percent inflation-adjusted increase for defense programs. *(Reagan budget, p. 129)*

The Congressional Budget Office (CBO) presented a bleak deficit picture when it released its review of the administration's fiscal 1985 budget Feb. 22. The CBO report showed deficits climbing steadily over five years to $248 billion in fiscal 1989 instead of the $123 billion estimate claimed by the administration.

In advance of the release of his budget and the CBO analysis and in response to calls from congressional leaders, the president had used his Jan. 25 State of the Union address to ask Congress to join him in a bipartisan effort to craft a deficit "down payment" that would reduce the federal deficit by $100 billion through fiscal 1987. *(State of the Union, text, p. 5-E)*

Democratic leaders appointed Majority Leader Jim Wright, D-Texas, to represent House Democrats, and Democratic Conference Secretary Daniel K. Inouye, D-Hawaii, to speak for Senate Democrats. Senate Majority Leader Howard H. Baker Jr., R-Tenn., asked Sen. Paul Laxalt, R-Nev., to be his representative, and House Minority Leader Robert H. Michel, R-Ill., appointed House Minority Whip Trent Lott, R-Miss., as his chief spokesman. Baker and Michel also asked the senior Republicans on the Budget, Appropriations, Senate Finance and House Ways and Means committees to participate.

The negotiations stalled over defense spending almost immediately. Democrats continued to push a proposal to "stretch out" a five-year plan for weapons research, development and procurement and troop increases into six years.

As the talks continued, the House moved ahead with its budget resolution to slash deficits by $182 billion. And the Senate GOP leadership concocted the Rose Garden plan, which contained $150 billion in deficit reductions — later reduced to $140 billion. The rate of growth for defense in the Republican plan was held at 5.1 percent.

At the same time, House and Senate tax-writing committees made headway on revenue-raising legislation to curb federal budget deficits. And the regular appropriations process moved ahead with work toward deficit cuts without waiting for a breakthrough in the down payment negotiations.

Spending Cuts, Tax Increases

With relative ease and little fanfare, Congress gave final approval June 27 to the first installment of the president's down payment on the deficit, a package of spending cuts and tax increases to reduce the deficit by $63 billion through fiscal 1987.

The bill (HR 4170 — PL 98-369) formed the core of deficit-cutting legislation enacted in 1984. President Reagan signed the measure July 18.

Although the president had warned earlier that he would not accept tax hikes until more spending restraints were in place, Reagan changed course and sent a letter to members before the final vote pledging to sign HR 4170 (H Rept 98-861).

The final version of HR 4170 — hammered out by House-Senate conferees after almost three weeks of negotiations that ended June 23 — was adopted in the House by a vote of 268-155. *(Vote 245, p. 76-H)*

The Senate adopted the conference report several hours later on an 83-15 vote after rejecting a motion to table (kill) the measure by a vote of 22-76. *(Votes 161, 160, p. 28-S)*

The first installment was expected to generate approximately $50 billion in new taxes and cut government spending by about $13 billion through fiscal 1987.

Most of the tax increases were contained in a host of provisions designed to shut down a wide range of tax loopholes and shelters. But liquor and telephone taxes were increased, and tax breaks on real estate investment were restricted.

A few sweeteners were hidden in the package, including a tax break for investors and an increase in the earned income tax credit for poor working families.

The largest spending reductions were made in Medicare, the nation's health care program for the elderly and disabled. The legislation increased out-of-pocket costs for beneficiaries and imposed a 15-month freeze on physician fees reimbursed by Medicare.

Changes also were made in cost-of-living increases for military retirees, and salaries of federal judges were increased 4 percent.

Final Provisions

Figures for amounts expected to be saved or lost by provisions of HR 4170 are estimates for fiscal years 1984-87, unless otherwise noted.

The final version of the deficit reduction measure:

Individual Taxes

Liquor. Increased the $10.50 tax on a gallon of 100 proof liquor to $12.50, effective Oct. 1, 1985. The change meant about a 32-cent increase in the cost of a fifth of 80 proof liquor. Beer and wine were not affected. The change was expected to raise about $1 billion through fiscal 1987.

Telephones. Extended for two years the 3 percent telephone excise tax, due to expire at the end of 1985, raising $3.2 billion.

Income Averaging. Restricted the use of income averaging, a tax-calculating technique that lowers taxes for individuals who have large increases in income from one year to the next.

The bill required that a taxpayer's income increase 40 percent above his average annual income in the previous three years to qualify for income averaging. Previously, income 20 percent above the previous four years was eligible for averaging. The provision, effective for the taxable year 1984, was expected to generate about $6 billion through fiscal 1987.

Interest Exclusion. Repealed a provision in existing law allowing taxpayers, after 1984, to exclude from taxes 15 percent of their net interest income, with a maximum allowable exclusion of $450 for individuals and $900 for couples. Net interest is interest income above the amount of interest payments deducted by the taxpayer. The repeal was expected to raise almost $7 billion.

Estate and Gift. Delayed for three years a scheduled reduction in the maximum estate and gift tax. The maximum rate would be 55 percent through 1987 and 50 percent thereafter, instead of 55 percent in 1984 and 50 percent afterward. Revenue raised: $580 million.

The bill also closed a loophole that allowed housing bonds issued under the Housing Act of 1937 to be exempt from estate and gift taxes. Conferees agreed that such bonds purchased after June 19, 1984, would be subject to the taxes.

Foreign Income. Froze for four years the $80,000 maximum exclusion for income earned abroad. The exclusion had been scheduled to increase to $85,000 in 1984, $90,000 in 1985 and $95,000 in 1986. Under the bill, the exclusion would increase to $95,000 by 1990.

Capital Gains. Reduced from one year to six months the length of time an asset had to have been held before proceeds from its sale could qualify for special capital gains tax treatment. Under existing law, the top tax rate on capital gains was 20 percent, compared with 50 percent for ordinary income. The change was effective for assets acquired between June 22, 1984, and Jan. 1, 1988; it was expected to cost the Treasury $547 million.

Conferees did not agree to a Senate proposal to limit deductions for capital losses.

Earned Income Tax Credit. Increased from $500 to $550 the maximum credit allowed for low-income wage earners with dependent children, effective Jan. 1, 1985. The credit was completely phased out for those earning more than $11,000 per year, instead of the existing $10,000 limit.

Mileage Deduction. Raised from 9 cents to 12 cents the mileage tax deduction allowed for individuals who used their automobiles while performing charitable work, effective Jan. 1, 1985.

Tax Benefit. Eliminated a quirk in existing law that allowed individuals to receive a tax break when calculating the proper deduction for state income tax payments, effective Jan. 1, 1984. Estimated revenue gain: $756 million.

Estimated Tax. Required that individuals liable for the alternative minimum tax — usually those who take large deductions — make quarterly estimated tax payments during the course of the tax year, effective Jan. 1, 1985. Revenue gain: $700 million.

Business Taxes

'Luxury' Cars. Limited business tax deductions for automobiles that cost more than $16,000. Previously, individuals received a 6 percent investment tax credit in the first year the car was in operation and could write off the cost of the car over three years. The bill limited the tax credit to $1,000 and the write-off period was stretched out over a longer period of time, depending on the car's value.

The tax breaks were reduced proportionally for cars that were used for business less than 100 percent of the time. The provision generally applied to property purchased after June 18, 1984.

Personal-Use Equipment. Restricted business tax breaks for equipment, such as home computers, boats and airplanes, that was used for business 50 percent or less of the time. Taxpayers were required to keep a detailed log of business use of such equipment, including automobiles. In addition, use of such property had to be a requirement of employment, not a convenience for the employee, to qualify for a deduction.

The provision applied generally to equipment put into service after June 18, 1984. This change, plus the "luxury" car provision, was expected to raise approximately $750 million.

Sale/Leaseback. Clamped down on the use of so-called "sale/leaseback" arrangements used by non-profit organizations and governmental entities to benefit indirectly from tax breaks they could not use directly. The bill prevented those involved in such leasing plans from benefiting from the generous business tax breaks that made such arrangements worthwhile. However, a number of exceptions were made for ongoing projects. The provision was expected to raise $5.5 billion and was applied generally to property placed in service after May 23, 1983.

Truck Taxes. Reduced scheduled tax hikes on heavy trucks enacted in 1982 and effective July 1, 1984. Under the bill, trucks that weighed less than 55,000 pounds were exempted from the highway use tax. Those weighing more than 55,000 would pay $100, plus $22 for every 1,000 pounds above 55,000 pounds. Trucks weighing more than 75,000 pounds would pay a maximum tax of $550, compared with $1,600 required by the 1982 bill. *(1982 Almanac p. 320)*

House/Senate/Final Deficit-Reduction Packages

The following totals are for deficit reductions, in billions of dollars, from fiscal year 1984 through fiscal 1987.

	House	Senate	Final
Tax increases	$49.8	$47.7	$50.8
Spending cuts			
Military	$95.6	$40.2	$58.3
Non-military discretionary spending	4.6	13.4	3.9
Entitlement benefits	10.2	18.4	12.2
Other *	2.0	3.5	5.7
Net interest	20.2	17.2	18.3
TOTALS	**$182.4**	**$140.1****	**$149.2**

* Includes Grace commission savings in the House budget and offsetting receipts in the Senate plan.
** Total may not add due to rounding.

SOURCES: House and Senate Budget committees

To pay for the truck tax change, the excise tax on diesel fuel was increased from 9 cents to 15 cents a gallon, effective Aug. 1, 1984. Owners of small diesel trucks and cars would receive a one-time tax rebate to compensate them for the fuel tax increase.

Leasing. Delayed for four years, until 1988, the effective date of liberalized rules governing business leasing of equipment. The rules, designed primarily to help unprofitable firms, were enacted in 1982 to replace so-called "safe-harbor" leasing that allowed firms to sell unused tax breaks. Widely recognized as a tax giveaway, safe harbor leasing helped profitable and unprofitable firms alike. The delay was expected to save $2.7 billion. *(1982 Almanac p. 29)*

Life Insurance. Overhauled taxation of the life insurance industry to eliminate different treatment of two segments of the industry, the mutual insurance companies and the stock companies. One of the main changes gave firms a 20 percent reduction in their tax liability. The entire package lowered the industry's taxes $1.4 billion through fiscal year 1987, and was generally effective on Jan. 1, 1984.

Corporate Tax Rates. Phased out benefits of graduated corporate tax rates for companies with taxable income in excess of $1 million, effective Jan. 1, 1984. Estimated revenue gain: $600 million.

Golden Parachutes. Clamped down on the use of so-called "golden parachute" agreements, generous severance payments to executives displaced by a corporate merger. The bill imposed a 20 percent excise tax on payments in excess of 300 percent of the executive's usual annual salary, and prevented the business from taking a deduction for the excess payment. The provision was generally effective for contracts entered into after June 14, 1984.

Windfall Profits. Delayed a scheduled reduction in the top tax rate on newly discovered oil. The bill kept the existing 22.5 percent tax, which was scheduled to drop to 15 percent by 1986, through 1987; it would then drop to 20 percent in 1988 and 15 percent thereafter.

Small Business. Froze for four years a law allowing small businesses to write off, in one year, assets worth less than $5,000, instead of depreciating them over a longer period. The $5,000 limit was scheduled to rise to $7,500 in 1984 and 1985 and $10,000 thereafter. Estimated revenue gain: $1.4 billion.

Corporate 'Preferences.' Reduced from 85 percent to 80 percent the value of certain business tax deductions, called "preference items" — such as some accelerated depreciation benefits, effective Jan. 1, 1985. Revenue raised: $993 million.

Tax Straddles. Restricted a tax avoidance scheme involving stock options "straddles" through which investors defer income from one year to the next, effective Jan 1, 1984. However, the top tax rate on such transactions was lowered from about 50 percent to 32 percent. Revenue raised: $700 million.

A provision was added to the bill by House Ways and Means Committee Chairman Dan Rostenkowski, D-Ill., making it more difficult for the Internal Revenue Service to collect taxes from commodity traders — many of whom are located in Rostenkowski's Chicago district — for use of a similar tax avoidance scheme prior to 1981.

Foreign Withholding. Repealed the existing 30 percent withholding tax on interest paid to foreign investors, applicable to obligations issued after the date of enactment. The change was made to eliminate a tax haven in the Netherlands Antilles, but also opened the door to more foreign investment in the United States.

Foreign Sales Corporations. Set up, at the administration's request, a new export subsidy program involving Foreign Sales Corporations to replace existing Domestic International Sales Corporations (DISCs). Under the plan, approximately $12 billion in taxes on export income deferred under DISCs was to have been forgiven. The change was made because of objections raised by U.S. trading partners about the DISC subsidy. The provision was generally effective Jan. 1, 1985.

Foreign Tax Shelter. Prevented firms from sheltering income from the sale of foreign trade receivables (promises to pay for goods), generally effective after March 1, 1984. Estimated revenue raised: $1.4 billion.

Accounting. Made several accounting changes primarily aimed at preventing companies or individuals from taking deductions before expenses were required to be paid. Firms using the accrual method of accounting could not take deductions until closer to the time the expense was actually incurred. Exceptions were made for future decommissioning costs of nuclear plants and for mine reclamation. The bill also eliminated certain tax shelters that used such early-deductions techniques.

Freddie Mac. Repealed a tax exemption for the Federal Home Loan Bank Mortgage Corporation, or Freddie Mac, a federally backed corporation that buys and sells mortgages and mortgage-backed securities. Removal of the exemption, effective Jan. 1, 1985, put Freddie Mac on a more competitive footing with private mortgage firms.

Other Changes

Fringe Benefits. Exempted from taxes most common employee fringe benefits, such as parking spaces, airline tickets, employee discounts and college tuition. To qualify for the exemption such benefits had to be available to all employees on a non-discriminatory basis, with the exception of parking spaces. The provision generally was made effective on Jan. 1, 1985.

Faculty Housing. Extended for two years a moratorium on the issuance of regulations by the Treasury Department on taxation of on-campus housing benefits for faculty members, that had been set to expire at the end of 1983.

Industrial Development Bonds (IDBs). Limited the amount of IDBs and student loan bonds that could be issued annually within a state to the greater of $150 per capita or $200 million (for less populous states). The provision was generally effective for bonds issued after Dec. 31, 1983. The $150 per capita limit was to be lowered to $100 in 1986.

Exceptions were made for bonds used to finance multifamily housing and publicly owned airports, docks, wharves, mass transit facilities and convention or trade show facilities. Exceptions also were made for hundreds of specific projects already in the works. The changes were expected to raise approximately $400 million.

Taxable Bonds. Closed a number of loopholes used by investors in taxable bonds, such as savings bonds and Treasury bills, to reduce their tax liability.

Mortgage Revenue Bonds. Allowed state and local governments to issue tax-exempt mortgage revenue bonds, through 1987, to help finance low- and moderate-income housing. The authority had expired Dec. 31, 1983.

The extension was expected to cost about $1.6 billion.

Real Estate. Increased from 15 years to 18 years the length of time over which a building could be depreciated. Exceptions were made for low-income housing. Critics had charged that the shorter depreciation period, enacted in 1981, was too generous. The provision applied to property placed in service after March 15, 1984. Revenue gain: $2.6 billion.

Welfare Benefit Plans. Restricted several potential tax abuses involving voluntary employees beneficiary associations, trusts used to fund employee health and welfare benefits.

'Cafeteria Plans.' Restricted the use of new benefit plans that the Internal Revenue Service (IRS) feared were used to avoid taxes. The plans offered employees a choice of fringe benefits. The bill permitted the plans to offer only non-taxable fringe benefits, starting Jan. 1, 1985.

Employee Stock Ownership Plans (ESOPs). Delayed for three years a scheduled increase in a tax credit for employer contributions to ESOPs, while making a number of other changes, generally effective Jan. 1, 1985, to encourage the use of such plans. The changes were expected to raise approximately $1.7 billion. ESOPs are stock bonus plans often used to encourage employee interest in a company's success.

Tax Shelters. Made a number of changes to eliminate tax shelters involving partnerships. The bill also required registrations of tax shelters with the IRS and higher penalties for promotion of "abusive" tax shelters.

Charitable Deductions. Required individuals who claim a deduction for a charitable contribution of property worth more than $5,000 to have the property appraised to determine its value, effective for contributions made after Dec. 31, 1984.

Interest-Free Loans. Provided guidelines for taxing benefits from interest-free loans or below-market interest rate loans, including those between family members. The lender would pay income taxes on the interest forgone, but the borrower could deduct the same amount. The provision generally did not apply to loans under $100,000 unless they were made solely to avoid taxes. The provision generally applied to loans made after June 6, 1984. Revenue raised: about $500 million.

Targeted Jobs. Extended for one year the 1978 targeted jobs tax credit, due to expire at the end of 1984. The credit was designed to encourage employment of disadvantaged youth, the handicapped and Vietnam veterans. *(1978 Almanac p. 221)*

Social Security. Allowed churches a one-time option to drop out of the retirement system. If they did so, the churches' employees were required to pay higher payroll taxes, as though they were self-employed.

Church Audits. Imposed restrictions on IRS investigations of churches' tax liability, effective Jan. 1, 1985.

Special Tax Breaks. Allowed a number of tax breaks for special interests and individuals — as was common in any large tax bill — ranging from a $16 million tax break for the Allis-Chalmers Corp. to tax relief for a woman whose handicapped foster child won a house in a radio contest.

Studies. Required the Treasury Department to conduct a study of alternative tax systems and tax shelters by Dec. 31, 1984.

Medicare

Physician Fee Freeze. Barred for 15 months, beginning July 1, 1984, increases in the amounts the Medicare

system reimbursed doctors for services performed for Medicare patients.

Doctors were not required to accept Medicare "assignment," that is, agree to accept Medicare reimbursement as full payment for services, except for required beneficiary deductibles and co-payments. But those who did accept assignment for all their Medicare patients would have an advantage when new Medicare reimbursement fees were calculated after the freeze was lifted.

Doctors who accepted Medicare patients, but did not abide by the freeze, were subject to stiff penalties.

Assignment. Established a voluntary assignment program in which doctors committed themselves in advance, for a year, to accept assignment for all their Medicare patients. Participation was encouraged by publishing lists and otherwise informing the elderly about which doctors take assignment, and by offering expedited payment procedures for physicians in the voluntary program.

Estimated savings for this provision and the fee freeze: $2.2 billion.

Premiums. Extended for two years a requirement, due to expire at the end of 1985, that beneficiaries' premium payments for coverage of non-hospital services ("Part B" Medicare coverage) be calculated so that altogether, these payments yielded 25 percent of Part B program costs. The provision increased the 1986 monthly premium from an estimated $17.70 to $19.10 and from $18.60 to $21.30 in 1987. Estimated savings: $1.2 billion.

Working Aged. Permitted non-working wives and husbands, aged 65 to 69, to make the employment-based health coverage of their spouses their primary medical plan, rendering Medicare a supplementary, "secondary payer." The choice could be made even if the working spouse had not yet reached 65. Also, required employers to offer to these older spouses the same medical coverage they provided to spouses of younger employees. Estimated savings: $1 billion.

Hospital Reimbursement. Limited for fiscal 1985 and 1986 the rate of increase in Medicare payments to hospitals. The provision applied both to the limits, passed by Congress in 1982, for increases in Medicare payments to hospitals for overall costs of caring for beneficiaries and to a new system, passed in 1983, of flat rates of payment per illness. The latter system, based on "diagnosis related groups," was being phased in to replace the older, "cost-based" payment system. Estimated savings: $1.1 billion. *(1983 Almanac p. 391)*

Laboratory Fees. Established a schedule of fixed fees for Medicare payments for tests conducted by independent laboratories for outpatients. The schedule set fees at 60 percent of the charges (or 62 percent for hospital laboratory work on outpatients) prevailing in the year beginning July 1, 1984.

Medicare would pay 100 percent of the scheduled fee to laboratories or doctors accepting assignment for laboratory tests. (This meant waiver of required out-of-pocket payments by patients for coinsurance or deductibles.) Those not accepting assignment would, as under existing law, receive 80 percent of the scheduled fee, with no waiver of patients' payments. Laboratories were required to bill Medicare directly.

Estimated savings: $963 million.

Hospital Assets. Revised rules for revaluing, for purposes of calculating certain Medicare payments, a hospital's capital-related costs, such as depreciation and interest. The revised rules were meant to limit increases in the value of such capital costs when hospital ownership changed.

Skilled Nursing Facilities. Restored the use of separate limits on Medicare payments to hospital-based and free-standing nursing facilities, with a somewhat higher rate for hospital-based units in recognition of their higher costs. Estimated cost: $125 million.

Inpatient/Outpatient Costs. Required the secretary of health and human services to issue regulations barring hospitals from including, in certain claims for outpatient services, costly expenses relating to inpatient services. Estimated savings: $165 million.

Medicare Coverage. Authorized Medicare to pay for immunization against viral hepatitis for Medicare-covered kidney disease patients on dialysis and to pay for supplies needed by hemophiliacs for treating themselves with a substance that promoted blood clotting.

Durable Medical Equipment. Authorized 20 percent co-payments by beneficiaries for durable medical equipment provided by home health care services. Estimated savings: $75 million.

Medicaid, Other Health Aid

Children and Pregnant Women. Required states to provide Medicaid assistance to certain needy women and children not receiving coverage in some states. Medicaid was the nation's health-care program for the poor.

The Child Health Assurance Programs (CHAP) was established to assist poor, first-time pregnant women once their pregnancy had been verified, pregnant women in two-parent families in which the principal breadwinner was unemployed and poor children born on or after Oct. 1, 1983, up to age 5 in two-parent families. Estimated cost: $270 million. The provision was generally effective Oct. 1, 1984.

Federal Matching. Increased annual limits on Medicaid matching payments to Puerto Rico, the Virgin Islands, Guam, the Northern Mariana Islands and American Samoa. Estimated four-year cost: $80 million.

Assignment of Rights. Mandated that states require Medicaid beneficiaries to assign to the states any right they had to other health benefits programs (so that states could collect from such programs any available payments for medical care of the covered beneficiaries). Existing law permitted, but did not require, states to take this step. The provision generally was made effective on Oct. 1, 1984. Estimated savings: $22 million.

Nursing Care. Relaxed certain requirements, on which Medicaid payments were contingent, for periodic certification by doctors that a beneficiary still needed care in a nursing facility.

Maternal and Child Health. Raised the annual authorization for the maternal and child health block grant program from $373 million to a permanent level of $478 million — the level appropriated in 1983, beginning in fiscal year 1984.

Public Assistance

Supplemental Security Income (SSI). Raised the assets a needy aged, blind or disabled person could have and still qualify for SSI benefits. The existing $1,500 limit ($2,250 for couples) was gradually increased to $2,000 ($3,000 for couples) by 1989, at a cost of $65 million.

The bill also limited, in some cases substantially, the amount an individual's SSI payments could be reduced by the government in an effort to recoup past overpayments.

Aid to Families With Dependent Children (AFDC). Made several changes in the AFDC program to help families who were thrown off the rolls, or were subject to removal from the rolls, as a result of changes made to the program in 1981. These included allowing up to 15 months of additional Medicaid coverage to those who lost AFDC benefits because they had taken low-paying jobs.

The bill also expanded AFDC eligibility to families with higher incomes than existing law allowed.

Additional Spending Cuts

Grace Commission. Implemented several recommendations of the President's Private Sector Survey on Cost Control, also known as the Grace commission, for an estimated savings of $3.2 billion.

The changes:

● Accelerated the deposit and collection of federal non-tax receipts, such as customs duties.

● Allowed the Treasury Department, in limited cases, to deduct from an individual's tax refund uncollected government debts — such as student loan repayments.

● Increased the use of tax returns and other government records to verify an individual's eligibility for public assistance. *(Grace commission, p. 184)*

Puerto Rican Rum. Eliminated by the end of 1984 a scheme used by the Puerto Rican government to collect a tax rebate from the Treasury for liquor diverted from the U.S. mainland to the island for redistribution in the United States. The bill also limited repayments to Puerto Rico for taxes collected on liquor distilled on the island to $10.50 for a gallon of 100 proof liquor. Estimated savings: $757 million.

Other Provisions

HR 4170 also:

Cost-of-Living. Moved the date for payment of cost-of-living adjustments for federal military retirees from Dec. 1, 1985, to Jan. 1, 1986. Estimated reduction in expected outlays from this one-time bookkeeping change: $1.6 billion.

Judges' Raise. Provided a 4 percent pay raise for federal judges retroactive to Jan. 1, 1984, costing $1.7 million over one year.

Credit Unions. Increased the contributions credit unions must make to the federal agency that insured them, saving about $1 billion.

Procurement. Imposed more stringent requirements on federal procurement procedures and established a legal requirement for "full and open" competition for all contracts. *(Story, p. 197)*

Farm Loans. Extended provisions of the 1983 reconciliation bill requiring farmers to seek disaster loans from the Farmers Home Administration before they could be considered eligible for Small Business Administration loans. Estimated savings: about $200 million through 1987. *(1983 Almanac p. 233)*

Veterans. Eliminated retroactive awards of veterans' non-service-connected disability pensions for the period between the date of disability and the date of application for a pension unless the veteran's disability prevented him from applying for a pension for at least 30 days, beginning on the date of the disability. Also increased the fee for veterans' home loans. Combined savings: about $721 million through fiscal 1987.

Synthetic Fuels Rescission. Rescinded $2 billion from the spending authority of the Synthetic Fuels Corporation. This rescission allowed overall budget authority for domestic spending programs to increase by that amount.

Committee Action

Working in the shadow of the deficit down payment negotiations, the two congressional tax-writing committees, the House Ways and Means Committee and the Senate Finance Committee, forged ahead on their own, drafting legislation to reduce the budget gap.

Ways and Means March 1 approved a package of tax increases that totaled an estimated $49.2 billion for fiscal 1984-87. The package (H Rept 98-432, Part II) was attached to HR 4170, which the committee initially had reported in 1983.

Senate Finance began work on a bill Feb. 23. At the outset, Chairman Robert Dole, R-Kan., said, "We may be able to do more than the deficit reduction task force is able to do in the next 30 to 40 days." The committee March 21 approved a package to increase taxes $48 billion through fiscal 1987.

The Senate committee also agreed to $25.8 billion in spending savings. And the package included $21.4 billion in tax increases and $3.8 billion in funding cuts that also were in a budget reconciliation bill (S 2062) pending on the Senate floor.

Despite the heated dispute over the broad outlines of the federal budget, there were surprisingly few differences over how to raise taxes. In 1984, unlike past years, a consensus emerged among the House, the Senate and the administration on how much revenue to raise and, for the most part, on who should pay. The Rose Garden plan included $48 billion in specific tax hikes culled from the House and Senate bills.

Both packages included proposals from the administration's fiscal 1985 budget to curtail a wide range of tax shelters. Both also raised liquor and telephone excise taxes, revamped taxation of the life insurance industry, restricted the use of tax-exempt industrial development bonds and reduced scheduled tax hikes for large trucks.

In part, the consensus on taxes formed because both committees steered clear of proposals that would threaten what was most dear to the Reagan administration: across-the-board income tax cuts enacted in 1981 and indexing of tax brackets to offset inflation, scheduled to go into effect in 1985. *(1981 Almanac p. 91)*

Comparison of Bills

As approved by the two committees, the Ways and Means and Finance packages made the following changes:

Individual Taxes

Individual Retirement Accounts (IRAs). The House bill permitted IRA holders to contribute an extra $1,750 to their accounts each year without penalty. The contribution would be taxed as regular income, but tax on the interest it earned would be deferred. Under existing law, IRA holders could contribute up to $2,250 a year tax-free.

The Senate bill expanded the amount of tax-free contributions to an IRA allowed for a non-working spouse from $250 a year to $2,000 by 1990. The limit was to be increased to $750 in 1985 and 1986, to $1,250 in 1987 and 1988, to $1,750 in 1989 and to $2,000 after 1989.

Cigarettes and Liquor. The House bill imposed a 12-cents-per-pack excise tax on cigarettes through 1987. The current tax, 16 cents per pack, was scheduled to drop to 8 cents Oct. 1, 1985. The bill also raised the $10.50-per-gallon tax on distilled liquor to $14.25.

The Senate bill raised the tax on distilled liquor by $2 per gallon.

Telephones. Both committees agreed to continue for two years the 3 percent telephone excise tax due to expire at the end of 1985.

Income Averaging. Both bills restricted the use of income averaging to lower taxes for individuals who had large increases in income from one year to the next. The bills increased, from 20 percent to 40 percent, the amount a taxpayer's annual income must rise above average income over a base period to use income averaging. In addition, the base period was reduced from the four previous years to the three previous years.

Interest Exclusion. The House bill repealed a provision in current law that allowed taxpayers to exclude from taxes 15 percent of their net interest income, with a maximum allowable exclusion of $450 for individuals and $900 for couples. The Senate bill delayed the change, set to go into effect in 1985, until 1988.

Foreign Income. Both bills froze, through 1988, the maximum amount of tax-free income an individual can earn abroad at $80,000 a year. The amount was scheduled to increase to $95,000 by 1986.

Capital Gains. The Senate bill reduced from one year to six months the amount of time an asset must be held before the proceeds could qualify for preferred tax treatment. It also reduced from $3,000 to $1,000 the amount of capital losses that could be offset against ordinary income. The House bill contained no such provision.

Fringe Benefits. HR 4170 gave statutory authority to the tax-free status of most employee fringe benefits, such as free airplane tickets, tuition and parking spaces. The Senate bill extended for two years a moratorium on Treasury Department issuance of regulations on the taxation of fringe benefits. That moratorium, originally enacted in 1978, expired at the end of 1983. However, the Treasury Department had agreed on its own not to issue such regulations in anticipation of congressional action on the issue.

Dividend Reinvestment. The Senate bill repealed a tax break enacted in 1981 for public utilities shareholders who received dividends in the form of additional utility stock instead of cash. Such shareholders were allowed to receive up to $750 a year ($1,500 for couples) in tax-free dividends in the form of stock. There was no similar provision in HR 4170.

Earned Income Tax Credit. The Senate bill increased from $500 to $525 the maximum credit allowed for low-income wage earners with dependent children. The House bill did not address the issue.

Business Tax Changes

Tax-Exempt Bonds. Both bills renewed a tax exemption for mortgage subsidy bonds, which state and local governments issue to raise money to lend to home buyers at below-market interest rates. The House bill extended the exemption through 1988, while the Senate bill extended it through 1987. The mortgage-bond tax exemption expired at the end of 1983.

Both bills also restricted the use of tax-exempt industrial development bonds by state and local governments.

The House version set a $150 per capita limit on the amount of IDBs that could be issued annually in any state to finance construction of private projects. The Senate bill included no cap, but restricted other tax breaks that were available to private projects funded by the bonds.

'Luxury' Cars. The Ways and Means Committee restricted business tax deductions for automobiles costing more than $21,000. Under intense lobbying pressure from automobile manufacturers, the Finance Committee rejected a similar proposal and instead curbed business tax deductions for autos, yachts, airplanes, computers and similar equipment that also was used personally. Only individuals who could show they used the equipment for business more than 90 percent of the time were eligible for a full tax break.

Real Estate. The Senate bill increased the tax depreciation period for all buildings, except low-income housing, from 15 years to 20 years. It also tightened procedures used by Treasury to recapture some of the tax break when a building was sold before the end of the depreciation period. The House bill included no similar provisions.

Sale/Leasebacks. Both bills clamped down on the use of leasing plans by non-profit organizations and governments that transferred tax breaks they could not use to private investors. They prevented those involved in such leasing plans from benefiting from other business tax breaks, such as the investment tax credit and accelerated depreciation.

Life Insurance. Both bills revamped taxation of the life insurance industry to redistribute the tax burden between different segments of the industry. A stopgap insurance tax plan enacted in 1982 expired at the end of 1983, returning taxation of the industry to a system that required mutual insurance companies to pay more taxes than their competitors, the stock companies.

Small Business. Both bills froze for four years a law that allowed small businesses to write off, in one year, personal property costing less than $5,000 instead of depreciating it over a longer period.

Leasing. Both packages delayed for four years the effective date of liberalized rules, scheduled to take effect in 1984, that governed business leasing of equipment. The new rules were enacted in 1982 to replace so-called safe-harbor leasing tax breaks.

Foreign Trade. The Senate bill revamped a tax break for U.S. exporters through the use of Domestic International Sales Corporations.

Research and Development. The Senate bill made permanent a 25 percent tax credit allowed businesses for new expenditures on research and development. The credit was set to expire at the end of 1985. The House bill did not extend the credit.

Other Tax Changes

Abusive Tax Shelters. Both bills included Reagan administration budget proposals to clamp down on a number of abusive tax shelters and other tax loopholes.

Also restricted were partnerships, often formed to invest in real estate, that reaped tax benefits by allocating income and expenses among the partners.

Both bills also eliminated a tax scheme by the Puerto Rican government to collect a rebate from the Treasury for liquor diverted from the U.S. mainland to the island for redistillation. The Senate bill ended the tax break June 30, 1984. The House bill extended it for an additional year because of the island government's dependence on the tax rebate to balance its budget.

Income Tax Offset. The Senate bill allowed the Treasury to deduct from an individual's income tax refund an amount sufficient to pay other government debts — such as a student or small business loan — owed by the individual. The offset could only be used as a last resort. The House bill had no similar provision.

Olympic Checkoff. The Senate bill allowed individuals to indicate on their income tax returns if they wanted to contribute $1 to support the U.S. Olympic team.

Private Foundations. Both bills made several changes in law to ease taxation of private foundations.

Other Tax Breaks. The Senate bill called for several other tax breaks not dealt with in the House measure. These included the administration's enterprise zone plan to offer tax breaks to businesses that set up shop in 75 economically distressed areas. The bill also called for a three-year extension of a program called the targeted jobs tax credit, which encouraged employment of disadvantaged youth and Vietnam veterans.

The Senate package also extended a number of business and individual energy tax credits that were due to expire. To pay for some of the extensions, the bill repealed a tax credit for taxpayers who made their homes more energy efficient.

Spending Cuts

The Senate bill called for a wide range of Medicare and Medicaid cuts not included in the House bill.

The Ways and Means Committee originally approved a package of approximately $1.8 billion in Medicare spending cuts through fiscal 1987 as part of HR 4170. But that section of the bill was later detached and was included in HR 5394, the House budget reconcilation bill approved April 12. During floor consideration of HR 5394, about $1 billion in Medicare savings was rejected, including provisions to impose a one-year freeze on physicians' fees paid by Medicare and to require doctors to accept set fees for hospital services.

The Senate committee package went much further, calling for approximately $12 billion in Medicare and Medicaid savings through fiscal 1987, including a hike in premiums paid by Medicare beneficiaries. The Finance Committee also agreed to a freeze on doctors' fees in Medicare cases and penalties for physicians who refuse to accept "assignment" of Medicare fees.

Under the bill, premiums paid by Medicare beneficiaries would increase from $14.60 a month in 1984 to $27.80 a month by 1989. Under existing law premiums were scheduled to rise to $20.40 a month by that year.

The committee agreed to raise the premium to $36 by 1989, but reversed itself because of concern the hike would be too severe for elderly beneficiaries.

In addition, the Senate legislation restricted Medicare reimbursements to hospitals and rounded off premium payments to the next lowest dollar.

Tax Floor Action

The tax measures aimed at generating nearly $50 billion in revenues through fiscal year 1987 were approved in both houses with little argument. The House passed HR 4170, raising $49.2 billion, April 11 on a 318-97 vote after little more than three hours of debate. *(Vote 71, p. 24-H)*

The Senate adopted its $47 billion tax increase package by a 76-5 vote taken during the session that began

April 12. The measure, which had been attached to a minor House-passed tariff bill (HR 2163), also cut Medicare and Medicaid spending by almost $15 billion through fiscal 1987. *(Vote 77, p. 15-S)*

House Debate

The House passed its tax package quickly and uneventfully, in sharp contrast to the drawn-out and acrimonious discussion in 1983 over a similar but smaller revenue-raising bill. That measure — raising $8 billion over three years — was blocked from floor consideration because of objections to IDB restrictions and controversy over Medicare spending cuts. *(1983 Almanac p. 231)*

In 1984 both Republicans and Democrats spoke out in favor of the bill and urged passage as a necessary first step toward reducing the deficit. House Minority Leader Michel allayed GOP fears about voting to raise taxes before the House acted to cut spending by referring to an April 11 letter from President Reagan. In the letter Reagan promised Michel he would use his veto power to ensure that House spending bills were in line with the Rose Garden plan.

The bill, considered under a rule that prohibited floor amendments, was unchanged from the package approved March 1 by the Ways and Means Committee.

Senate Action

Debate did not progress as smoothly in the Senate as it did in the House, but when the dust settled the original Finance Committee bill remained largely intact.

Alterations to the bill amounted to a $1 billion cut, through fiscal year 1987, from the $48 billion in taxes in the bill as offered by the Finance Committee. And provisions to restrict the use of IDBs and increase taxes on real estate were severely weakened.

Action on the tax package began April 9 but was quickly stalled by an amendment offered by Sen. Edward M. Kennedy, D-Mass., expressing the sense of Congress that U.S. funds should not be used to mine Nicaraguan ports or territorial waters and that the United States should accept World Court jurisdiction over the matter. A modified version of the amendment was adopted. *(Nicaragua, p. 86)*

IDBs. The IDB controversy was provoked by Alfonse M. D'Amato, R-N.Y., who had threatened to tie up Senate consideration of the bill if the committee's IDB restrictions were not eased. A compromise worked out between D'Amato and Dole, approved by voice vote shortly before adoption of the tax package April 13, lowered the amount the package was projected to raise by approximately $200 million. It restricted the use of tax-exempt bonds for parking lots, professional office buildings and health clubs and exempted from other restrictions in the bill certain manufacturing projects and projects that received federal matching grants in distressed urban areas.

Depreciation. The Senate also agreed by a vote of 62-19 to replace the committee proposal to increase from 15 years to 20 years the minimum time period over which a building could be depreciated. The measure was opposed strongly by the real estate lobby, which argued it would restrict investment.

Instead, the Senate agreed to a depreciation life of 20 years in 1984, 19 years in 1985 and 18 years thereafter. To make up for the loss in expected revenues incurred by the change, the Senate voted to reduce tax credits available for the rehabilitation of old buildings. *(Vote 74, p. 15-S)*

Other Amendments. A proposal by Sen. John H. Chafee, R-R.I., to delay tax indexing for three years was tabled (killed), 57-38. *(Vote 61, p. 13-S)*

Also defeated were efforts by Sen. Wendell H. Ford, D-Ky., to delete provisions increasing the federal excise tax on distilled liquor from $10.50 per gallon to $12.50 a gallon.

A Ford amendment to delete the tax increase and make up the resulting $1.3 billion revenue loss by eliminating the enterprise zone provision was defeated 15-76. Another Ford amendment to cut the liquor tax hike in half and increase taxes on wine was tabled (killed), 62-32. *(Votes 67, 68, p. 14-S)*

Adopted during the course of the Senate debate was a proposal by D'Amato to revise a 1983 law (PL 98-21) requiring taxation of certain Social Security benefits.

The law, part of the plan to restore the financial integrity of the Social Security system, required individuals to include tax-exempt interest income when calculating whether they were wealthy enough to have taxes levied against their benefits. Retirees whose incomes (including half of their Social Security benefits) exceeded $25,000 were required to pay income taxes on half their Social Security benefits. *(1983 Almanac p. 219)*

D'Amato's amendment deleted tax-exempt income from the calculation and was agreed to by voice vote after a tabling motion failed 32-63. The change was expected to cost $141 million through fiscal 1987. *(Vote 66, p. 14-S)*

The Senate also agreed to:

● An amendment by Sen. William S. Cohen, R-Maine, to continue through 1985 a credit available to taxpayers who made energy-saving home improvements. The committee package would have ended the credit on the date of enactment.

A motion to table (kill) the Cohen amendment was defeated 38-55. The change was expected to cost $400 million through fiscal year 1987. *(Vote 69, p. 14-S)*

● A Max Baucus, D-Mont., amendment limiting business tax deductions for cars that cost more than $15,000. An identical provision, originally part of the Finance Committee package, was deleted in committee after the automobile industry mounted an intense lobbying campaign against it.

● An amendment by Dan Quayle, R-Ind., allowing individuals who had exhausted state unemployment benefits to withdraw funds from their IRAs without penalty.

● An amendment to delete a provision in the bill to strengthen the alternative minimum tax levied against taxpayers who employ a large number of tax breaks.

● An amendment postponing until Jan. 1, 1986, the effective date of a ruling by the Internal Revenue Service that the clergy and military personnel cannot take home mortgage deductions if they use tax-free compensation to pay the mortgage.

● An amendment increasing the authorization for the Maternal and Child Health block grant program by $97 million through fiscal 1987. The effect would be to raise the funding to a permanent level of $478 million per year.

Spending Cuts Floor Action

After approving revenue-raising measures, the chambers proceeded to consider spending-cut measures to bring federal funding into line with their respective fiscal plans, either the budget resolution approved by the House or the budget resolution, patterned after the Rose Garden plan, that had been approved by the Senate Budget Committee.

House

The House passed its budget reconcilation bill (HR 5394) April 12 on a 261-152 vote. The bill cut a total of $3.9 billion from entitlement programs. *(Vote 75, p. 26-H)*

As HR 5394 was presented to the House, including the Medicare provisions stripped from HR 4170 during the Ways and Means Committee consideration of the tax legislation, the measure shaved about $4.8 billion from 1985-87 deficits by cuts in a variety of domestic programs. But bowing to pressure from the American Medical Association, the House refused to agree to a one-year freeze on physicians' fees paid by Medicare and a requirement forcing doctors to accept set fees for hospital services. Elimination of those provisions cut the savings in HR 5394 to $3.9 billion.

Although most members supported that portion of the Medicare amendment affecting physicians' fees, Republicans and rural Democrats balked at the related "assignment" provisions that required doctors to bill the Medicare program directly for hospital services and to accept program reimbursement as payment in full for these services. A Republican motion to send the reconciliation package back to House committees with instructions to change the Medicare provisions and eliminate all spending increases in the bill was defeated 172-242. *(Vote 74, p. 26-H)*

Included in the House-passed reconciliation package, nonetheless, were changes in Medicare fee schedules covering reimbursement for clinical laboratory services. The revised fee schedules were expected to save $974 million in 1984-87.

Other three-year savings in HR 5394 included:

● $981 million from changes in benefits for federal retirees. Federal civilian and military personnel who retired before age 62 would receive one-half the retirement cost-of-living adjustment scheduled for fiscal 1986 and 1987.

● $212 million by extending a provision of the 1983 reconciliation bill requiring farmers to seek disaster loans from the Farmers Home Administration before they could qualify for Small Business Administration loans.

● $800 million from changes in the veterans' pensions programs and the veterans' home loan guaranty program.

● $107 million from revamped management of welfare programs.

● $1.6 billion from accelerated handling of non-tax federal receipts, such as loan repayments.

Despite the deficit-reduction aim of the reconciliation package, it also called for new spending in several areas: on welfare and agriculture programs and on the proposed Child Health Assurance Program, which expanded Medicaid coverage for maternal and pediatric care. *(CHAP, 1983 Almanac p. 419)*

Senate

The Senate spent four weeks debating various deficit-reduction plans as amendments to HR 2163 before approving the Rose Garden plan May 17. Though the critical spending part of the plan passed on a 65-32 vote, the wide margin belied the misgivings that Democrats and some Republicans expressed toward it. *(Vote 100, p. 19-S)*

Before Majority Leader Baker succeeded in obtaining a majority to support the proposal, he had to thwart challenges led by members of both parties to refashion drastically the Rose Garden plan. The breakthrough came on the eve of the bill's passage. Baker joined with other Republican leaders and White House officials in striking a deal with GOP dissidents on a $2 billion increase over three years in domestic spending programs.

The compromise preserved the defense-spending level that Baker had described as essential for Reagan's continued support.

Under the three-year spending caps in the plan, military spending authority totaled $299 billion in fiscal 1985; $333.7 billion in fiscal 1986; and $372 billion in fiscal 1987, while the budget for other discretionary spending was $139.8 billion in fiscal 1985; $144.3 billion in fiscal 1986; and $151.5 billion in fiscal 1987. The tax portion increased revenues by $47.7 billion, about the same amount as in the House budget.

The Senate May 17 passed HR 4170 on a 74-23 vote after substituting the entire Rose Garden package, including the tax and spending portions, for the House-passed provisions. The next day, in what was a mere formality, it adopted the House budget resolution, 41-34, after substituting its counterpart (S Con Res 106). Unlike the budget resolutions, which were fiscal targets that Congress set for itself, HR 4170 would be binding legislation if signed by the president. *(Votes 101, 102, pp. 19-S, 20-S)*

The caps were one of the most divisive factors during the Senate debate. The defense spending authority cap allowed an average 7 percent, inflation-adjusted growth rate through fiscal 1987. Under the other cap, all remaining discretionary spending was held to a 2 percent growth rate in fiscal 1985 and a slightly higher increase in fiscal 1986 and 1987. The Republican leadership narrowly fended off an attempt by GOP moderates to merge the two caps, which would have given the Appropriations Committee the leeway to take money from defense, if it felt other programs warranted additional money.

Leadership Plan. The GOP leadership broke the logjam and cleared the way for final passage of the Rose Garden plan when it convinced five moderate Republicans to support an amendment adding $2 billion to the non-defense appropriations cap. These Republicans were: Mark Andrews, N.D.; Charles McC. Mathias Jr., Md.; Robert T. Stafford, Vt.; Lowell P. Weicker Jr., Conn.; and Chafee. A plan backed by the moderates to combine the defense and non-military spending authority caps, setting defense spending at $37 billion less than the leadership plan and domestic spending at $20.3 billion more, was killed May 10.

But the vote on the moderates' plan was very close, forcing Baker and Senate Budget Committee Chairman Pete V. Domenici, R-N.M., to take the group's demands seriously. The Synthetic Fuels Corporation provided the bargaining chip the leadership was looking for. On May 14 the administration announced that it intended to rescind $9.5 billion in spending authority for the Synthetic Fuels Corporation. The next day Domenici and Sen. James A. McClure, R-Idaho, chairman of the Senate Energy and Natural Resources Committee, came up with the notion of using $2 billion of that money to increase the spending authority cap for non-defense programs. The Senate voted to approve the switch, 62-37. *(Vote 96, p. 19-S)*

The five moderates said after the vote that they accepted the leadership-administration offer because it was the best they were likely to get. "I think it's a matter of what you can get," Weicker said. "You don't have a majority, and by that I mean a majority of Democrats or Republicans, for any significant decrease in defense spending or for any meaningful increase in education and health programs."

Start of Debate. The Senate's consideration of various deficit-cutting plans began during the week of April 23.

The Senate April 25 rejected a plan sponsored by Jesse Helms, R-N.C., on a 27-68 vote. A budget outline offered by Steven D. Symms, R-Idaho, was voted down, 11-84, on April 26. The Senate, also on April 26, accepted by voice vote an amendment by Sen. Dennis DeConcini, D-Ariz., to save $4.4 billion in fiscal 1985 by cutting administrative costs such as consultant fees and travel costs. *(Votes 78, 80, p. 16-S)*

K-G-B Freeze. The deficit-reduction plan believed to have had the best chance of replacing the leadership's measure was a bipartisan package known as the K-G-B plan after its sponsors, Nancy Landon Kassebaum, R-Kan., Charles E. Grassley, R-Iowa, and Joseph R. Biden Jr., D-Del. The original sponsors were later joined by Baucus. The plan froze 1985 defense and non-defense discretionary programs and cost-of-living adjustments for benefit programs at 1984 levels, and achieved three-year deficit reductions of $260 billion, including the $48 billion tax increase already approved by the Senate.

But during floor debate May 2, John Tower, R-Texas, chairman of the Senate Armed Services Committee, and Ted Stevens, R-Alaska, chairman of the Senate Appropriations Subcommittee on Defense, warned of dire results from freezing defense spending at $265 billion, the level for fiscal 1984. The plan's supporters were unable to muster sufficiently persuasive rebuttals. Their plan was defeated, 33-65, on May 2. *(Vote 85, p. 17-S)*

Democrats' Alternative. A Democratic proposal, offered by Lawton Chiles, D-Fla., the senior Democrat on the Budget Committee, to reduce the deficit $204 billion drew six Republican defectors, but failed May 8 on a 49-49 vote. The six Republicans were Chafee, Andrews, Mathias, Weicker, Larry Pressler, S.D., and John Heinz, Pa. *(Vote 88, p. 18-S)*

The Democratic alternative saved $204 billion from 1984-87. Instead of the 7 percent inflation-adjusted growth proposed for defense in the Republican leaders' plan, the Democrats sought a 4 percent rise. Revenues in the Democrats' package increased by $81.3 billion, compared to the $48.3 billion in the GOP-leadership plan. The revenue increase was predicated on a two-year delay in tax indexing scheduled to take effect in 1985.

However, low-income taxpayers were protected by retaining personal-exemption indexing and the zero bracket amount, the threshold below which people owed no taxes.

And the Democratic alternative reduced non-defense spending by $17.4 billion.

Also rejected were:

● Another deficit reduction plan offered by Slade Gorton, R-Wash., that reduced deficits by $234.3 billion from fiscal 1984-87 in part by capping cost-of-living adjustments for federal workers and retirees and recipients of Social Security and federal workers' compensation at the Consumer Price Index (CPI) minus 3 percent. The plan also capped the indexing of personal income taxes for inflation at CPI minus 3 percent. The amendment was defeated 23-72. *(Vote 92, p. 18-S)*

● An amendment by Bill Bradley, D-N.J., to cut the proposed inflation-adjusted growth rate for defense in the GOP-leadership plan from 7 percent to 5 percent and use part of that money to restore funds for "priority" domestic programs such as education, medical research and environmental protection. Bradley's package also restored $6 billion of the $9 billion in Medicare cuts. The amendment was tabled (killed), 51-43. *(Vote 89, p. 18-S)*

● Two amendments offered by Kennedy to restore cuts

in the Medicare program. *(Votes 90, 91, p. 18-S)*

Moderate Republicans. As the Senate neared a vote on the leadership plan, it became clear that the support of the moderate Republicans was crucial to approval of any deficit-cutting proposal. Four moderates — Chafee, Weicker, Andrews and Stafford — talked with the GOP leadership and the administration May 9 about possible changes in the Rose Garden package. Office of Management and Budget Director David A. Stockman offered to add a minimal amount to the levels for non-defense discretionary spending. But he was adamant that the two spending caps be preserved.

The moderates wanted to combine the caps, providing the Appropriations Committee with the flexibility to transfer some money from defense to other programs.

The dissident Republicans met with Baker and Domenici before the vote on their amendment. But when no further significant concessions were offered, they decided to test their strength on the Senate floor. Their plan was tabled (killed) May 10 on a 48-46 vote. *(Vote 93, p. 18-S)*

An amendment offered by Chafee limited all discretionary spending authority to $434.5 billion in 1985, $472.3 billion in 1986, and $514.6 billion in 1987. The figures presumed a $37 billion drop in defense spending below the GOP leadership plan and a $20.3 billion addition to domestic programs.

The often tense floor debate centered on the caps. Referring to them, Weicker said, "This irrationality, this weed that springs out of the Rose Garden — like any weed, it deserves to be plucked and discarded."

In closing the debate, Baker said merging the caps would "destroy the foundation" of the plan. The GOP-leadership plan was a three-legged stool, Baker added, referring to defense curbs, domestic cuts and tax increases. "If one of those legs is removed it would cause the collapse of the whole package," he warned.

Despite Baker's strong words, eight Republicans voted against tabling the amendment: Andrews, Chafee, Weicker, Stafford, Cohen, Heinz, Pressler and Grassley. Illinois Republican Charles H. Percy initially voted with the moderate Republicans. But after some jawboning by Baker, Percy switched his vote. This changed the result from a tie, which would have defeated the tabling motion, to a majority to table the amendment.

Hollings Freeze. A plan offered by Ernest F. Hollings, D-S.C., J. James Exon, D-Neb., and Andrews sought $315.9 billion in deficit reductions over four years by allowing a modest increase in defense, but freezing spending in fiscal 1985 with modest increases later in other programs. It was rejected, 38-57. *(Vote 84, p. 17-S)*

Line-Item Veto. Taking another tack to cut deficits, Mack Mattingly, R-Ga., May 3 proposed the line-item veto as a two-year experiment rather than wait for Congress to approve a constitutional amendment authorizing the president to reject funds for specific programs in an appropriations bill. In his State of the Union address Jan. 25, Reagan called for a line-item amendment.

The line-item veto was attacked by Appropriations Committee Chairman Hatfield as "not a mechanism to achieve meaningful reductions of the federal deficit." Others argued that a statutory line-item veto would be contrary to the Constitution, which required a two-thirds vote of Congress to override a presidential veto. The Mattingly proposal would have allowed a majority vote.

The Senate never voted on the desirability of the line-item veto, but only on procedural issues related to the question of whether Congress would have the power to legislate such a device without a constitutional amendment. Chiles raised a point of order, arguing that Mattingly's amendment would violate the Constitution. Mattingly moved to table Chiles' motion, but lost on a 45-46 vote. Then the Senate voted 56-34 to uphold the point of order. *(Votes 86, 87, p. 17-S)*

Judges' Salaries. The Senate May 1 approved an amendment to increase federal judges' salaries 3.5 percent retroactive to Jan. 1, 1984. The pay raise would cost $1.7 million over one year, according to an estimate of the Congressional Budget Office. The amendment by Sen. George J. Mitchell, D-Maine, was approved on a 67-28 vote. *(Vote 83, p. 17-S)*

HR 4170 Conference

The House-Senate conference on HR 4170 began June 6. The conferees were split into 12 subconferences, each assigned a specific section of the bill. Conferees on the tax provisions made rapid progress, approving items to raise about $40 billion in three short sessions June 6-8. Reaching agreement on the remaining tax provisions and sensitive spending issues dragged on for more than two weeks.

Conferees from the House Ways and Means and Senate Finance committees reached final agreement on the bulk of the deficit reduction package after a marathon session that started at 8:30 a.m. June 22 and ended at 5:15 a.m. the following day. The conference report (H Rept 98-861) was filed June 23.

In early sessions, conferees had resolved most of the minor differences between the House and Senate versions of the bill. The most difficult issues were postponed until the final hours, when members and staffers, exhausted by the lengthy talks, moved swiftly through the remaining provisions.

Conferees overcame a major stumbling block when administration and Republican Senate leaders the week of June 18 compromised on the cap proposal to preset spending levels for three fiscal years. The administration's insistence that the bill contain mandatory spending caps through fiscal 1987 on domestic and defense spending was finessed when negotiators agreed to substitute non-binding language for the ceilings.

The final version of HR 4170 contained "sense of the House" language calling for a $182 billion deficit reduction through fiscal 1987. It also contained "sense of the Senate" language that said the Senate would abide by its domestic and military caps in fashioning appropriations bills for fiscal 1985. Neither chamber was bound by the other's "sense" language.

Provisions Eliminated

In the end, conferees agreed to drop several contentious provisions, including a proposed increase in the cigarette excise tax passed by the House and the administration's plan to set up so-called "enterprise zones" to encourage development of economically distressed areas. *(Story, p. 168)*

Dole said that the White House had to be convinced to sacrifice its enterprise zone initiative to keep the entire conference agreement from falling apart. The House would agree to drop its cigarette excise tax hike only if the zone proposal, opposed by Rostenkowski, was withdrawn, he said. If retained in the final conference report, the cigarette provision likely would have run into stiff opposition from Helms of North Carolina, who was up for re-election in his tobacco-growing state.

Conferees also:

● Rejected a provision in the Senate bill to expand the use of IRAs for non-working spouses and in the House bill to allow higher non-deductible contributions for all IRA holders.

● Retained existing law allowing certain tax credits for the rehabilitation of old and historic buildings.

● Retained existing law allowing energy tax credits for residences and businesses to expire at the end of 1985.

● Allowed the 25 percent tax credit for new research and development expenses to expire at the end of 1985.

● Dropped a Senate provision that allowed retirees to exclude tax-exempt income in calculating whether their Social Security benefits were subject to tax.

● Dropped the Senate provision permitting individuals to reduce their tax refund or increase their tax payment by $1 to help fund the U.S. Olympic Committee.

● Rejected Senate proposals to delay Medicare eligibility for all beneficiaries by one month, to round Medicare benefits down to the next lowest dollar and to increase the Part B deductible.

● Retained existing law allowing a reduction in federal Medicaid matching funds to states to expire after fiscal 1984.

Capital Gains, IDBs, Real Estate

The House also accepted, in a surprise move, a Senate provision to reduce from one year to six months the length of time an asset must be held before the proceeds from its sale can qualify for preferred capital gains tax treatment. The move was unexpected because Rostenkowski had rejected identical Senate provisions in conferences on two previous tax bills.

In exchange, the maximum tax credit available to working-poor families was increased from $500 to $550.

The conferees also reached last-minute agreement on restrictions on the use by state and local governments of IDBs and changes in real estate depreciation.

They resolved the IDB issue by crafting a compromise to give states the option of choosing the greater of a $150 per capita limit or an overall $200 million ceiling on the amount of IDBs issued annually within a state. And they agreed to increase from 15 years to 18 years the write-off period for new investment in real estate. The House had instructed its conferees not to accept any lengthening of the write-off period, but neither Dole nor Rostenkowski was thought to have any great affection for the real estate industry, which was fighting the change.

An impasse over spending cuts affecting the poor and tax breaks for the wealthy and the middle class was broken after the House agreed to the physician fee freeze and the Senate, after getting the go-ahead from the White House, dropped approximately $5 billion in tax breaks included in its version of the deficit-reduction plan. These included the tax credits to promote energy conservation and business research and an administration proposal to expand the use of IRAs for non-working spouses.

Final Action

Opposition in the House to the conference report on HR 4170 was muted, but a number of senators spoke out strongly against it.

Sen. D'Amato, backed by several conservatives concerned that the measure did not do enough to reduce the deficit, charged that spending cuts in the package were "illusory."

But in the end rhetoric lost out to fears that defeat of the legislation would send a harmful message to financial markets and to the electorate. D'Amato's motion to table (kill) the conference report was opposed by all but 13 Republicans and 9 Democrats. *(Vote 160, p. 28-S)*

Imputed Interest. Slightly more troublesome was a last-minute flap over a provision in the bill to penalize those who helped finance the sale of their homes or businesses by offering loans at below-market interest rates.

The National Association of Realtors had objected strongly to the "imputed interest" language, and the House June 27 passed a separate measure (H Con Res 328) mak-

ing "technical" corrections in HR 4170 exempting most residences and small farms from the interest rate provision.

But in the Senate, the resolution was held up by some Democrats, led by John Melcher, D-Mont., who wanted to expand the exemptions to include larger farms and small businesses. After hours of negotiations June 29, the Senate tabled (killed) a Melcher amendment to exempt some small businesses but agreed by voice vote to a proposal offered by Dole to exempt all farms. The revised resolution was then sent back to the House where it received final approval. *(Vote 174, p. 30-S).*

Debate over imputed interest also held up passage of a debt limit extension in the closing hours of the session. *(Story, p. 165)*　　　　■

Budget Process Reversed During '84 Session

Congress, led by the Republican-controlled Senate, wrote a new chapter in the budget process in 1984 by turning the decade-old procedure on its head.

Faced with $200 billion annual deficits projected through fiscal year 1989, GOP leaders in the Senate and Reagan administration officials opted for a strategy that would commit Congress to deficit-cutting legislation before it adopted a fiscal 1985 budget resolution.

Under the terms of the 1974 Congressional Budget and Impoundment Control Act (PL 93-344), lawmakers were supposed to adopt a non-binding fiscal plan setting out spending and taxing targets before appropriations committees acted on the funding bills for that year. In 1984, however, Republicans insisted that Congress first agree to legislation (HR 4170) mandating deficit-reducing tax increases and spending cuts. The administration and the Senate leaders agreed on a fiscal plan in mid-March, the "Rose Garden" plan, so named because President Reagan endorsed it at a ceremony in the White House Rose Garden. It was then translated into legislation.

Once Congress approved all of the deficit reductions in HR 4170 — spending cuts, a tax increase and slowdown of the growth of defense spending — agreement was reached on the fiscal 1985 budget resolution (H Con Res 280), which simply reflected the revenue increases and funding reductions included in HR 4170. *(Deficit reduction, p. 143; Budget Act, 1974 Almanac p. 145)*

House Committee Action

The leaders of the Democratic-controlled House spent several weeks in February and March forging a consensus among their colleagues on the shape of the fiscal 1985 budget. The leadership, working with House Budget Committee Chairman James R. Jones, D-Okla., eventually endorsed a proposal based on a so-called "pay-as-you-go" concept, which required any new spending to be offset by either increases in taxes or spending cuts in other areas.

Several factions on the House Budget Committee struggled to take the lead on a framework for writing the fiscal 1985 budget resolution. There were those on the panel who called for something "dramatic," as one aide put it. This group favored reducing the deficit by $200 billion instead of by the $100 billion President Reagan suggested when he asked in his State of the Union message for a deficit-cutting "down payment." *(Text, p. 5-E)*

Others supported a budget "freeze," continuing taxes

and spending at fiscal 1984 levels. When it came to defining a freeze, however, members had varying ideas. Some said the freeze should include defense spending. Others wanted exceptions for sensitive domestic programs.

Another faction supported the pay-as-you-go approach. That approach won out, approved by the Democratic leadership in mid-March.

The House Budget Committee reported two budget resolutions on March 28. H Con Res 280 included the pay-as-you-go amendment, and H Con Res 282 (H Rept 98-645) did not. H Con Res 280 was adopted on a party-line 19-9 vote by the committee. The committee approved the second version to appease junior Democrats who wanted to force a floor vote on pay-as-you-go as an amendment to the budget resolution. They had argued it would be a difficult choice for anti-tax members who supported higher defense spending. But the Democratic leadership decided to use H Con Res 280 as their vehicle.

H Con Res 280 envisioned deficit reductions of $182 billion during fiscal years 1985-87. Under the House Democratic plan, defense was limited to a 3.5 percent increase after adjustment for inflation. On the domestic spending side, House Democrats reduced spending about $15 billion through 1987. The House budget called for $49.8 billion in tax hikes.

The basic fiscal 1985 budget resolution called for a 3.5 percent increase in all programs except for Social Security, defense, social programs for which people qualify on the basis of low income and a limited number of discretionary domestic programs for the poor. The percentage was lower than the expected rate of inflation in fiscal 1985 of 5 percent.

Funding for the exempted categories would increase at the rate of inflation. But the committee also agreed to the pay-as-you-go additions as a committee amendment.

Under the pay-as-you-go proposal, the exempted categories could grow 3.5 percent above inflation. But to finance the increases, $49.8 billion in taxes would be needed, slightly more than the amount included in the House version of HR 4170.

The resolution called for budget authority of $1,002.1 billion in fiscal 1985, outlays of $918.1 billion and revenues totaling $742.45 billion.

The three-year deficit reduction totals in the Democratic budget plan broke down as follows: $31.35 billion in 1985; $63.35 billion in 1986; and $87.65 billion in 1987. The budget would be in deficit $174.45 billion in 1985; $172.3

billion in 1986; and $182 billion in 1987.

During committee action, Rep. Bill Frenzel, R-Minn., offered an amendment to the pay-as-you-go provision that required any tax increase to be used to lower federal deficits. The amendment was defeated by voice vote.

The committee's budget resolution allowed higher revenues not only to reduce the deficit, but also to pay for certain programs, such as employment for disadvantaged youth, public works jobs for community renewal and increased funds for Aid to Families with Dependent Children.

In addition to setting spending levels for fiscal 1985, the House budget resolution called on eight committees to make specific deficit reductions. These reconciliation savings were to be reported by the committees before May 1.

The Budget Committee planned to then package all the deficit reductions into one spending reconciliation bill. The resolution required $12.35 billion in entitlement savings over the three years. However, some of this amount was already approved as part of the 1984 reconciliation bill (HR 4169) approved by the House in October 1983. *(1984 reconciliation bill, p. 160)*

The committee's resolution provided for a public debt limit, which crossed the $1 trillion mark in 1981, of more than $2 trillion in fiscal 1986.

Liberals Push for 'Pay-As-You-Go'

A group of liberals new to the Budget Committee provided the impetus behind the resolution approved by the committee. Rep. George Miller, D-Calif., a member of House Budget, began championing the pay-as-you-go scheme in 1982, when he offered it as an alternative to the fiscal 1983 budget. *(1982 Almanac p. 194)*

Liberal Democrats such as Miller supported pay-as-you-go because they felt it would force members to decide on the government's priorities. They pointed out, for instance, that in the Budget Committee's resolution, if the pay-as-you-go amendment was adopted and defense and means-tested entitlement programs were allowed 3.5 percent inflation-adjusted increases, defense would rise $45 billion while social spending would rise only about $5 billion.

These liberals believed that military spending had been too generous in relationship to funding for domestic programs. And they contended members who supported hefty increases in the defense budget should be willing to pay for them.

House GOP Plan

The Budget Committee's Republicans, such as Rep. Phil Gramm of Texas, made light of the pay-as-you-go proposal. "It's kind of crazy to talk about pay-as-you-go when you have a $175 billion deficit," he said.

The three-year deficit reduction plan endorsed by the House GOP leadership called for the same defense cuts and tax increases contained in the Senate Rose Garden package, but froze discretionary spending for three years rather than one. The plan also included greater administrative savings from the so-called Grace commission, a business group that made recommendations in January on ways to eliminate fiscal waste in the federal government. *(Grace commission, p. 184)*

House Floor Action

The House April 5 adopted its "pay-as-you-go" budget

resolution on a vote of 250-168. Before that vote, the House rejected a Republican plan and six other alternative budgets. *(Vote 65, p. 22-H)*

The alternative fiscal plans came from both ends of the Democratic Party spectrum — and from several points in between. The two GOP proposals were from the party's mainstream and from its conservative wing.

The chief challenge was not from the Republicans' deficit reduction package, but from a modified freeze proposal offered by Florida Democrats Buddy MacKay and Bill Nelson that would have reduced deficits $234 billion over fiscal 1985-87.

The plan had the appeal of being simple and straightforward. It provided for a defense increase only to the extent of inflation, and a 3.5 percent increase in most discretionary spending. Means-tested entitlement programs and Social Security would be fully funded under current law. But programs for low-income persons were not protected, as they were under the pay-as-you-go budget. The plan also called for $47.2 billion in new taxes. Despite heavy support from freshman Democrats, the plan was defeated 108-310. *(Vote 63, p. 22-H)*

The $205 billion GOP deficit reduction plan that included the Grace commission savings was rejected on a similar vote, 107-311. *(Vote 64, p. 22-H)*

The House also rejected:

● A three-year, $261 billion deficit package offered by the liberal Democratic Study Group (DSG) to limit the growth in discretionary spending and hold defense increases to adjustments for inflation. However, the DSG plan called for $76.2 billion in additional revenues. Rejected 132-284. *(Vote 62, p. 22-H)*

● The Congressional Black Caucus' $324 billion plan — the largest of all the deficit reduction packages — to increase domestic spending $99 billion but make $203 billion in defense cuts, while raising $181 billion in taxes. Rejected 76-333. *(Vote 61, p. 22-H)*

● The president's original February budget, which called for $925.5 billion in spending and a $180.4 billion deficit. Rejected 1-401. *(Vote 58, p. 20-H)*

● A plan offered by William E. Dannemeyer, R-Calif., on behalf of the conservative Republican Study Committee to reduce deficits $206 billion over three years. More than half the spending reductions would have resulted from Grace commission savings. The plan called for only $7 billion in tax increases. Rejected 51-354. *(Vote 59, p. 20-H)*

● A proposal of the Conservative Democratic Forum — or "Boll Weevils" — offered by Buddy Roemer, D-La., to cut deficits over three years by $225 billion. Their so-called "2 percent solution" would have trimmed 2 percentage points off future inflation adjustments for benefit programs and off indexing income taxes, due to begin in 1985. Rejected 59-338. *(Vote 60, p. 20-H)*

Senate Committee Action

As the full Senate was debating a deficit-reducing tax-increase package, the Senate Budget Committee April 11 endorsed by a single vote a budget plan (S Con Res 106 — S Rept 98-399), backed by the GOP leadership and President Reagan, to slice $143.7 billion off the deficit through fiscal 1987. The budget-cutting plan received no Democratic votes. Though only one Republican defected from the party's ranks to vote against it — Mark Andrews, N.D. — a number of others expressed misgivings.

The committee settled for the Reagan-backed plan

Final Budget Totals Compared

(Fiscal years, in billion of dollars)

	1984	1985	1986	1987
Budget Authority				
Reagan mid-session budget review	916.1	1006.9	1105.2	1199.4
House resolution	918.9	1013.9	1088.9	1176
Senate resolution	918.6	1023.4	1108.5	1208.8
Conference agreement	918.9	1021.3	1103.8	1200.2
Outlays				
Reagan mid-session budget review	858.1	930.6	997.3	1076.6
House resolution	845.6	923	988.1	1069.3
Senate resolution	845.5	933.1	1004.7	1093.5
Conference agreement	845.6	932	1033.5	1088.6
Revenues				
Reagan mid-session budget review	670.7	763.8	831.8	904.1
House resolution	672.9	750.9	810.8	881
Senate resolution	672.9	750.9	810.8	881
Conference agreement	672.9	750.9	810.8	881
Deficit				
Reagan mid-session budget review	−172.4	−174.2	−184.8	−176
House resolution	−172.7	−172.1	−177.3	−188.3
Senate resolution	−172.6	−182.2	−193.9	−212.5
Conference agreement	−172.7	−181.1	−192.7	−207.6

only after five other plans that would have achieved larger deficit reductions failed to attract a majority. The biggest challenge came from a bipartisan proposal sponsored by Sens. Nancy Landon Kassebaum, R-Kan., Charles E. Grassley, R-Iowa, and Joseph R. Biden Jr., D-Del.

The plan called for a one-year spending freeze on all federal programs, achieving deficit reductions over the three years of $241.8 billion.

At one point the "K-G-B" plan, as it was dubbed, had a majority of votes. But then Sen. Bob Kasten, R-Wis., switched from yes to no, and after a number of changes the plan failed on a 7-13 vote.

Besides simplicity, the plan's strongest selling point was its promise of bigger deficit reductions in 1985 than either the Republican leadership's plan or the Democratic alternative sponsored chiefly by ranking committee member Lawton Chiles of Florida.

The most vociferous opponent of the plan was Armed Services Chairman John Tower, R-Texas, who also was a member of the Budget panel. The freeze on defense spending, Tower charged, would "almost be tantamount to unilateral disarmament."

Senate Budget Committee Chairman Pete V. Domenici, R-N.M., cautioned committee members that if they voted for the plan they were voting against such things as Social Security increases scheduled for January. Although the plan had a great deal of appeal, it was highly unlikely it would ever be implemented, he said.

The Democratic alternative, which would have cut deficits $150 billion over fiscal years 1985-87, was defeated 10-11. Andrews was the only Republican who voted for the Democrats' plan.

Senate Committee's Plan

Despite the dissatisfaction with the GOP leadership plan, the Senate budget panel left intact the details hammered out in March by Republicans and the administration. As re-estimated by the Congressional Budget Office, the resolution adopted by the Senate Budget Committee would save $143.7 billion over 1985-87, compared to an earlier projection of $149.5 billion.

The savings reflected a lower estimate of the outlays that would result from a "freeze" on discretionary spending, lower interest cost on the national debt and lower cost-savings from Medicare reforms.

The deficit reduction package included: $48.3 billion in tax increases; $40.2 billion in cutbacks in Reagan's defense buildup; $37.4 billion in reductions in non-defense spending programs; and $17.8 billion in savings from lower interest payments on the national debt.

Military spending would rise at an inflation-adjusted rate of slightly more than 7 percent over three years, compared to the 3.5 percent rate assumed in the House-passed budget resolution. Seven percent growth translated into a $56.8 billion three-year reduction in budget authority, and a $40.2 billion cut from the president's February defense request.

Further reductions came from holding 1985 non-defense discretionary spending at the 1984 level. In 1986 and 1987, these programs would grow at the rate of inflation.

Also factored into the domestic spending cuts were: savings from the 1984 spending reconciliation package (HR 4169) cleared by Congress April 5; provisions of the Senate's 1983 reconciliation bill (S 2062) that were not part of HR 4169, including changes in veterans' benefits and military retirement procedures; the Agricultural Programs Adjustment Act; and a Senate Banking Committee bill (S 2522) to increase the capitalization of the National Credit Union Insurance Fund that was included in deficit reduction legislation (HR 4170). *(Reconciliation, p. 160; farm bill, p. 361; HR 4170, p. 143)*

Senate Floor Action

Following the dictates of the Republican leadership's schedule, the Senate waited until it had passed HR 4170, the administration-backed deficit reduction legislation, and then, in what was a mere formality, endorsed H Con Res 280 after inserting the text of its counterpart (S Con Res 106). The vote on the budget resolution was 41-34. *(Vote 103, p. 19-S)*

Conference

The conference on the fiscal 1985 budget resolution was marked by the conflict that characterized the budget process throughout 1984 — the Senate's determination to force agreement on deficit reduction legislation before adopting a final budget guideline. The key obstacle was the Senate's insistence on including spending "caps" in the deficit reduction measure that would set funding levels for defense and non-defense spending for three years. House and Senate budget conferees met during the week of June 11. At the same time, conferees from other committees were ironing out differences between the House and Senate versions of HR 4170, the deficit down payment bill.

HR 4170 cleared Congress June 27, after Senate conferees agreed to non-binding language that allowed each chamber to follow its own budget in setting appropriation levels.

Budget conferees ironed out differences on most of the spending targets — including an update of the fiscal 1984 spending and revenue figures. The conference report called for fiscal 1984 targets of $672.9 billion in revenues; $918.9 billion in budget authority; $845.6 billion in outlays; and a deficit of $172.6 billion.

But the budget resolution negotiations deadlocked as the focus of the debate shifted to the level of defense spending. Following marching orders issued by the White House, Senate Republicans refused to budge from the average 7 percent inflation-adjusted growth rate through fiscal 1987 agreed to by the president in the Rose Garden plan.

An attempt to block an increase in the debt limit June 28 was made by House Democrats, led by Budget Committee Chairman Jones, as a way to force Republicans back to the bargaining table. But the GOP conferees failed to respond and refused to meet. A debt limit measure was approved the next day. *(Debt limit, p. 165)*

Defense Spending 'Range' Proposal

At a June 26 meeting of the budget conference, Senate Republicans stressed they would insist on the $299 billion in budget authority their budget resolution called for. The next day, Domenici and Tower, chairman of the Senate Armed Services Committee, offered House conferees a proposed military spending "range" to be included in the budget resolution instead of a specific spending ceiling. The high end of the range would be the Senate's $299 billion in budget authority for fiscal 1985, and the low point would be the $285.7 billion level included in the House budget.

Domenici and Tower both argued that the defense spending level would ultimately be decided through the appropriations process, and that it would be wrong to prejudge that decision by establishing a specific number in the budget resolution.

House Democrats argued that the final defense number would almost certainly be lower than the $299 billion figure. And, they said, it was the purpose of the budget process to weigh priorities for all government programs as part of the overall fiscal plan.

After refusing the Senate's range offer, House Democrats proposed to "split the difference" and set the defense spending level at a 5 percent inflation-adjusted growth rate, about the level of growth agreed to in the 1983 budget resolution. The 5 percent rate would provide $292.2 billion in spending authority and $261 billion in outlays for fiscal 1985. Republicans declined the offer.

Compromise, But Only Once

The Senate Republican game plan, according to budget and leadership aides, was to postpone a decision on defense spending until the last possible moment. The theory was that if a compromise was reached as part of the budget resolution, that number would be subject to negotiation — and possible reduction — once again during the give-and-take of the appropriations process.

Initially, it appeared that the Republicans wanted to use the conference on the defense authorization bill (HR 5167) as the basis for the budget agreement. The defense level in the House bill — assuming a 6 percent real growth rate — was significantly higher than the 3.5 percent inflation-adjusted growth rate assumed in the House budget resolution. The Senate's authorization measure provided a 7.8 percent inflation-adjusted growth rate for military programs. But the conference on the defense authorization bill also was stalled — at least in part because Senate Republicans did not want any specific defense number that could be used to lower the final defense appropriations level. *(Defense authorization, p. 37)*

Senate Democrats' Pressure

During the week of July 30, determined not to let Republican leaders forget that Congress had not adopted a fiscal 1985 budget resolution, a band of Democrats used rhetoric and procedure to block action on the 1985 agriculture appropriations bill (HR 5743). Led by Chiles and backed by the Senate Democratic leadership, Democrats objected to a Budget Act waiver that had to be approved before the agriculture bill could be debated.

Technically, under the 1974 Budget Act, a first budget resolution setting spending and revenue targets for the coming fiscal year must be in place before appropriations bills could be considered. Without a budget resolution, a waiver must be granted. The House May 22 had approved a blanket waiver for all fiscal 1985 appropriations bills.

The Senate had routinely agreed to waive the Budget Act in debating 1985 funding bills. But on Aug. 1, when Baker asked for a waiver on the agriculture bill, Chiles objected.

"What we are doing ... is trying to wipe out the mandate of the Budget Act and take us back to the old days when we went ahead, passed appropriations bills, and then just added up the total ... ," Chiles said.

The Senate Aug. 8 voted 68-30 to invoke cloture, cutting off debate on Chiles' objection to the budget waiver. *(Vote 198, p. 35-S)*

Detailed Comparison of Fiscal 1985 Budget Targets

(in billions of dollars)

Category	Reagan Budget	August Revisions	House Target	Senate Target	Conference Agreement
National Defense					
Budget Authority	$313.4	$298.9	$285.7	$299.0	$292.9
Outlays	272.0	266.2	255.9	266.0	262.9
International Affairs					
Budget Authority	22.3	22.1	18.0	15.25	20.8
Outlays	17.5	17.2	14.55	4.1	16.5
Science & Space					
Budget Authority	9.1	9.0	8.75	8.5	8.75
Outlays	8.8	8.7	8.6	8.45	8.6
Energy					
Budget Authority	3.1	−4.2	4.45	4.2	4.2
Outlays	3.1	2.8	4.2	4.05	4.05
Natural Resources					
Budget Authority	10.8	11.1	11.85	12.10	11.85
Outlays	11.3	11.6	12.0	12.15	12.0
Agriculture					
Budget Authority	12.1	12.1	17.15	17.1	17.1
Outlays	14.3	15.1	16.5	16.4	16.4
Commerce & Housing					
Budget Authority	5.1	5.0	6.5	6.4	6.45
Outlays	1.1	0.3	2.0	2.0	2.0
Transportation					
Budget Authority	29.5	29.4	29.1	28.85	30.05
Outlays	27.1	26.9	27.1	27.0	27.1
Community Development					
Budget Authority	6.4	6.5	7.0	6.9	6.9
Outlays	7.6	7.7	8.2	8.2	8.2
Education & Social Services					
Budget Authority	27.5	28.6	30.5	30.8	30.8
Outlays	27.9	29.4	29.85	29.9	29.9
Health					
Budget Authority	31.8	32.6	33.0	33.35	33.15
Outlays	32.9	33.8	34.15	34.2	34.15
Medicare					
Budget Authority	70.2	71.7	269.75*	70.3	70.3
Outlays	69.7	68.7	253.75*	65.35	65.35
Income Security					
Budget Authority	139.2	142.1	146.15	144.6	143.6
Outlays	114.4	110.3	111.15	110.95	111.7
Social Security					
Budget Authority	198.5	199.0	—*	199.4	199.45
Outlays	190.6	189.3	—*	188.4	188.75
Veterans' Benefits					
Budget Authority	27.3	27.1	26.85	26.85	26.85
Outlays	26.7	26.7	26.3	26.35	26.35
Justice					
Budget Authority	6.1	6.1	6.15	6.1	6.15
Outlays	6.1	6.2	6.1	6.0	6.1
General Government					
Budget Authority	5.8	5.7	5.7	5.65	5.7
Outlays	5.7	5.6	5.65	5.5	5.6
Fiscal Assistance					
Budget Authority	6.7	6.5	6.45	6.45	6.45
Outlays	6.7	6.5	6.45	6.45	6.45
Net Interest					
Budget Authority	116.1	130.2	133.25	133.8	133.8
Outlays	116.1	130.2	133.25	133.8	133.8
Allowances					
Budget Authority	1.0	1.0	0.75	0.95	−0.75
Outlays	.9	1.0	0.40	1.0	−0.70
Offsetting Receipts					
Budget Authority	−35.3	−33.8	−33.1	−33.15	−33.15
Outlays	−35.3	−33.8	−33.1	−33.15	−33.15

* House combined Medicare and Social Security.

The next day, at a meeting of the budget conferees, Chiles suggested that the Republican and Democratic leadership and the chairman of the Budget and defense authorizing committees and the Defense Appropriations subcommittees convene a budgetary "summit" meeting to hammer out a defense spending compromise. Senate Majority Leader Howard H. Baker Jr., R-Tenn., gave his support to the idea Aug. 10, but not before Chiles threatened to again attempt to filibuster appropriations bills on the Senate floor. After Baker agreed to the summit, Chiles withdrew his threat.

Negotiating sessions between Baker and O'Neill centered on the MX missile. A compromise reached Sept. 20 set fiscal 1985 defense spending at about 5 percent over 1984 levels, after taking inflation into account. The agreement also set conditions on MX spending. *(Story, p. 59)*

Final Action

Once the defense logjam was broken, conferees moved quickly to approve the budget resolution. Conferees finished work Sept. 25. The next day, the Senate approved the conference report on the budget resolution (H Rept 98-1079) by voice vote. The House approved the report Oct. 1 on a 232-162 vote. *(Vote 374, p. 116-H)* ∎

Fiscal 1984 Reconciliation

Congress in early April cleared a budget reconciliation bill left hanging from 1983.

By a 67-26 vote, the Senate April 5 passed a measure (HR 4169 — PL 98-270) providing $8.2 billion in budget savings over fiscal 1984-87. The Senate made no changes in the bill, which the House had passed in October 1983. However, the delay in enactment trimmed $2.1 billion from the $10.3 billion House-approved savings figure. The savings were mandated by the fiscal 1984 budget resolution (H Con Res 91). *(Vote 57, p. 12-S; 1983 Almanac p. 233)*

Most of the savings in HR 4169 came from delaying cost-of-living adjustments (COLAs) for federal retirees. COLAs for military retirees were put off from May until December. Pension increases for civilian retirees were delayed until January 1985.

Other provisions of HR 4169 extended for three years, until Sept. 30, 1986, a requirement that farmers seek disaster loans from the Farmers Home Administration before seeking more favorable loans from the Small Business Administration (SBA). The bill reduced interest rates on SBA disaster loans, imposing ceilings of 4 percent on loans to homeowners and businesses who could not find credit elsewhere, 8 percent on loans to those who could. It made eligible for SBA disaster assistance businesses adversely affected by the Payment-in-Kind (PIK) farm acreage reduction program and by the devaluation of the Mexican peso. Direct loans for physical disasters were limited to $500 million annually, non-physical disasters to $100 million annually in fiscal 1984-86.

HR 4169 also gave white-collar federal employees and members of Congress a 4 percent pay raise in 1984 instead of the 3.5 percent increase that took effect in January. The increase, retroactive to January, cost $249 million in 1984.

Although several senators were unhappy about the backdoor pay raise for themselves, Budget Committee Chairman Pete V. Domenici, R-N.M., said he did not want to change the House-passed version of HR 4169, go to conference and risk missing an April 30 deadline necessary to achieve the federal retiree savings.

The Senate passed a separate bill (S 2539) to hold the pay increase to 3.5 percent, but the House did not act and the 4 percent raise was awarded. This boosted congressional salaries to $72,600 a year. *(Story, p. 203)*

Before sending the reconciliation bill to the president, the Senate and House approved a concurrent resolution (S Con Res 102) striking provisions that would have given disabled veterans a 4.1 percent COLA in April. Congress had approved a 3.5 percent COLA in a separate bill (S 1388) cleared Feb. 9. *(Story, p. 501)* ∎

Bill Revising Social Security Disability Clears

A bill (HR 3755 — PL 98-460) to protect the disabled from being unfairly dropped from the Social Security disability rolls was cleared Sept. 19 by unanimous votes in both the House and the Senate.

The approval marked the end of more than three years of controversy over the administration's efforts to rid the disability insurance program of ineligible recipients through periodic reviews.

It also brought to a close a lengthy, convoluted and sometimes emotional legislative debate. The passions the issue sometimes evoked were not reflected in the overwhelming congressional support of the final package. *(Background, 1983 Almanac p. 273)*

The Senate adopted the conference report on the bill (H Rept 98-1039) by a vote of 99-0. House approval came several hours later by a vote of 402-0. *(Senate vote 226, p. 39-S; House vote 358, p. 110-H)*

President Reagan signed the legislation Oct. 9.

Background

The administration undertook the controversial disability reviews in March 1981 in response to a 1980 con-

gressional mandate to clean up an estimated $2 billion in program waste.

But disability groups and their allies in Congress complained that the administration undertook the reviews with unnecessary zeal. They charged the administration with attempting to trim the $18-billion-a-year program, which provided benefits to workers too disabled to hold a job, as part of its overall effort to reduce the size of government.

Almost half of the 1.2 million individuals whose cases came under review were told they no longer qualified for benefits. But about 200,000 were reinstated to the program after appealing their cases to independent administrative law judges.

Critics charged that many had been dropped from the rolls even though their medical condition had remained stable or worsened since they first were declared eligible for benefits. They charged the administration often based its decisions on flimsy and incomplete evidence, resulting in the loss of benefits for many individuals who were clearly unable to work.

As approved by Congress, the legislation made it more difficult for the 3.8 million individuals on the rolls to have their benefits taken away.

The administration was required to show that an individual's medical condition had improved since the person was first placed on the rolls, and that he or she was able to work, before benefits could be cut. Many who had already been taken off the rolls were to have their cases reconsidered under the new review standard.

The legislation also allowed those thrown off the rolls to continue receiving payments while they appealed their cases.

Flood of Complaints

The final package received bipartisan praise from members of Congress, relieved that the complicated and politically embarrassing issue had been resolved.

Members' offices had been flooded with constituent complaints almost since the reviews began. And news stories of thousands of disabled workers losing benefits, homes and, in some cases, their lives as a result of the reviews had plagued politicians, many of whom were up for re-election in 1984.

Although there was broad support in Congress to do something about the program as early as 1983, there was tremendous conflict over just what should be done.

A number of senators, including Senate Finance Committee Chairman Robert Dole, R-Kan., and Russell B. Long, D-La., ranking minority member on the Finance Committee, were reluctant to make changes pushed by disability lobby groups that they said would counteract Congress' original directive to clean up the program.

The Social Security Administration also fought the legislation, claiming that it could correct most problems administratively.

But attempts by Health and Human Services (HHS) Secretary Richard S. Schweiker and his successor, Margaret M. Heckler, to address problems with the program failed to quell the criticism.

By early 1984, the disability reviews had all but collapsed, with half of the states either refusing or under court order not to administer the program. While the program was run by the federal government, the actual reviews were conducted by state agencies.

In addition, the administration routinely was losing disability cases in the federal courts, including a number of class action suits in which thousands of recipients were ordered back on the rolls. In an internal review of its litigation process, the Social Security Administration acknowledged that the "agency's credibility before the federal courts is at an all-time low."

In March, the House passed its version of HR 3755 by an overwhelming 410-1 vote, despite the administration's continued opposition to the legislation.

Two weeks later, HHS Secretary Heckler did an about-face and announced a nationwide moratorium on the disability review program, pending the enactment of a bill.

Final Provisions

As cleared by Congress, HR 3755:

Medical Improvement. Allowed the secretary of health and human services to terminate benefits only if there was substantial evidence that an individual's medical condition had improved since first being placed on the rolls and that the individual was able to work.

Benefits could also be cut if there was substantial evidence that:

● The individual had benefited from vocational therapy

or advances in medical or vocational therapy or technology, and was able to work.

● An individual's impairment was not as disabling as originally thought, based on new or improved diagnostic techniques or evaluations.

● The original decision had been made in error or fraudulently obtained.

● The individual was unlawfully working, could not be located or failed to cooperate in the review process.

The new regulations were to go into effect within six months of enactment.

Eligibility. Applied the new medical improvement standard to all cases that came up for review after enactment, to cases still pending in the disability program's appeals process, to most cases pending in federal court and to cases in which a request for judicial review was made between March 15, 1984, and 60 days after enactment.

Congressional aides estimated that between 120,000 and 130,000 cases on appeal would be remanded to the secretary for reconsideration under this provision.

Benefits During Appeals. Allowed individuals who appealed their cases to continue collecting benefits until they had taken their appeal to an administrative law judge, one of the final steps of the appeals process. If the individual lost the case, the benefits had to be repaid.

Individuals whose cases were remanded to the secretary for reconsideration under the new medical improvement standard were allowed to collect benefits until a new decision was made.

The provision was effective through 1987 for Social Security disability recipients and was made permanent for disabled recipients of Supplemental Security Income.

Mental Impairments. Required, within 120 days of enactment, publication of new standards for evaluating mental disabilities. A moratorium on reviews of mentally impaired beneficiaries, in place since June 7, 1983, was to end with publication of the new standards.

The bill also required that efforts be made to have a qualified psychiatrist or psychologist participate in the determination of whether an individual was mentally disabled. Previously, only a physician and a state disability examiner had to review the case.

Review Standards. Made a number of changes in existing standards used to determine if an individual was disabled. Included in these changes was a requirement that the combined effects of an individual's multiple impairments be weighed in determining if there was a disability, even if each of the impairments alone would be insufficient for such a determination. Under prior law, the combined effects of multiple impairments could not be considered.

The bill continued through 1986 the existing practice of rejecting as conclusive evidence of disability an individual's claim that he or she was in pain. It required, however, that the Department of Health and Human Services complete a study by Dec. 31, 1985, on the role of pain in determining disability.

Monitoring of "Payees." Increased monitoring of unrelated individuals allowed to collect Social Security and Supplemental Security Income benefits for elderly, disabled or poor beneficiaries unable to cash checks on their own. Penalties for misuse of such funds were raised.

Uniform Standards. Made changes to ensure that the standards and procedures used for determining an individual's eligibility for disability benefits were more clear-cut and uniform throughout the program.

State Compliance. Required the secretary of health

and human services to take over disability operations in states that failed to comply with federal law.

Since the 1981 clampdown on the program, 10 states had refused to carry out the reviews under the new federal standards. But the federal government took no steps to take over administration of the program in those states.

Advisory Council. Required the appointment by June 1, 1985, of a 10-member panel of medical and vocational experts to advise the health and human services secretary on disability policies, standards and procedures.

Review Frequency. Required the secretary to issue regulations on how often those on the rolls should have their cases reviewed.

House Action

Handing the Reagan administration one of its most resounding defeats, the House voted 410-1 March 27 to ease the administration's tough, new reviews of the Social Security disability rolls.

Philip M. Crane, R-Ill., cast the lone dissenting vote. *(Vote 47, p. 18-H)*

The bill was reported (H Rept 98-618) by the House Ways and Means Committee March 14, although actual markup of the legislation had occurred in 1983.

The House bill required the administration to show that an individual's medical condition had improved before he or she could be taken off the rolls. It also made permanent a provision allowing individuals to collect benefits while appealing an adverse decision.

During an hour of debate on the House floor, member after member spoke in favor of the legislation, many lambasting the administration's review process as "cruel" and "insensitive."

But some Republicans cautioned that the legislation would prove to be only a temporary solution and that other steps would have to be taken to keep a tight rein on the program. Barber B. Conable Jr., R-N.Y., noted a wide disparity in the estimated cost of the bill. The Congressional Budget Office said it would cost $1.5 billion over five years, compared with a $3.4 billion estimate by the Social Security Administration.

But Conable implored the administration to drop its opposition to the legislation and to work with Congress on fashioning an acceptable compromise.

Senate Action

Stunned by the overwhelming House vote and warnings of retribution at the polls, administration officials announced April 13 the White House would drop opposition to the disability bill. And a moratorium on all further reviews was imposed until the legislation could be enacted.

This sudden reversal opened the way for approval May 16 by the Senate Finance Committee of legislation (S 476 — S Rept 98-466) similar to the House measure. Like HR 3755, the bill allowed individuals to continue collecting benefits if their medical condition had not improved since they had been placed on the rolls.

However, the Senate measure required the individual beneficiary to prove that his or her medical condition was the same or had worsened to continue collecting payments. The House measure shifted the burden of proof onto the Social Security Administration, requiring it to show an individual's condition had improved before benefits could be stopped.

Under S 476, the "medical improvement" provision would expire no later than three and a half years after enactment. The House version contained no expiration date.

The Senate bill also required lower cost-of-living increases in disability payments if the Social Security Disability Insurance trust fund — which financed the program — was expected to have less than 20 percent of the funds at the beginning of a year that it would need to pay the year's benefits, and if Congress took no corrective action.

According to Social Security actuaries, such a benefit cut could have come as early as 1988 under the most pessimistic economic assumptions.

While disability groups were not pleased with this and some of the other provisions of the Senate measure, spokesmen expressed satisfaction that the committee had finally acted, allowing the legislation to go to the Senate floor and be subject to revision in conference with the more favorable House measure.

Following the House's lead, the full Senate May 22 adopted the disability bill by a lopsided 96-0 vote. It passed the measure (HR 3755) after substituting the text of the Finance Committee bill (S 476) for the House version. *(Vote 109, p. 20-S)*

Conference Agreement

House and Senate conferees reached an informal agreement on the legislation Sept. 14 after lengthy behind-the-scenes negotiations.

Running through the discussions was the same conflict that had characterized much of the disability debate: discovering a way to protect the truly disabled from losing their benefits while trimming the program of ineligible recipients.

One of the biggest issues in disagreement was the medical improvement standard.

The final agreement more closely resembled the House provision, which placed on the administration the burden of proving an individual's medical condition had improved before benefits could be stopped. Language was added, however, to provide the administration with some flexibility in cases where an individual was clearly ineligible for disability payments.

Conferees also agreed to drop two of the most controversial items in disagreement which could have threatened final passage.

They rejected a House provision that would have required the administration to apply a decision by a circuit court of appeals on a disability review case to all disability review cases within the circuit, or to appeal the case to the Supreme Court.

The administration routinely recognized such court decisions as applicable only to the individual case decided by the court. It had steadfastly opposed the kind of change mandated by the legislation.

However, conferees agreed to include language in their final report raising questions about the constitutionality of the administration's practice and urging the administration to have the issue resolved in the Supreme Court.

They also encouraged the administration to pursue its policy of "non-acquiescence" to court decisions only when it intended to appeal a decision all the way to the Supreme Court.

Also dropped from the final conference agreement was the Senate provision to reduce annual cost-of-living increases for disability recipients if reserves in the Disability Insurance trust fund fell too low, and if Congress failed to take action to correct the shortfall. ∎

Social Security COLAs

The Senate Oct. 11 approved by voice vote a measure (HR 6299 — PL 98-604) that assured Social Security recipients a cost-of-living allowance (COLA) on Jan. 1, 1985, clearing the bill to the president. The House passed HR 6299 Oct. 2 by a vote of 417-4. President Reagan signed the bill Oct. 30. *(Vote 377, p. 116-H)*

Reagan requested the legislation in July, when it appeared that the inflation rate for 1984 would be less than 3 percent. Under existing law, the COLA payment was delayed one year when inflation was that low.

By the time the bill was enacted, however, it was clear that fiscal 1984 inflation had exceeded the 3 percent mark, making the legislation unnecessary. But neither members of Congress nor the administration were willing to sacrifice the political credit associated with approval of the popular measure, guaranteeing its enactment.

The House Ways and Means Committee had approved the bill (H Rept 98-1099) Sept. 26. The Senate had originally passed Reagan's proposal July 26 by a vote of 87-3. But the House bill differed from the Senate measure — in addition to the inflation waiver, the House bill also called for a Social Security Administration study of permanent changes in the COLA — requiring a second Senate vote on the bill. *(Vote 185, p. 32-S)* ∎

Congress Approves Pension 'Equity' Measure

As part of an election-year effort to prove its commitment to women's issues, Congress passed a bill that attempted to free pension law of sex discrimination. The Senate approved "The Retirement Equity Act" (HR 4280 — PL 98-397) Aug. 6 by voice vote, and the House cleared the bill Aug. 9.

President Reagan signed the bill Aug. 23.

The bill expanded pension coverage for employees who left and subsequently returned to a job. HR 4280 also ensured the pension rights of homemakers whose working spouses died before reaching retirement age. And it lowered the age at which young workers could start building up pension credits. Although the pension changes applied to both men and women, HR 4280 was particularly helpful to women whose careers were interrupted or who depended on the pension of their spouses.

Both the president and members of Congress hoped to reap political benefits from the measure. The bill, part of a legislative package designed to end economic bias toward women, has been championed by Democratic vice presidential nominee Geraldine A. Ferraro, D-N.Y.

The Reagan administration, although it initially offered only lukewarm support for the measure, endorsed pension equity to combat charges that it was insensitive to women's rights issues.

Congress also completed action on another "economic equity" measure, a child support enforcement bill, Aug. 9. *(Child support, p. 463)*

Ferraro heralded approval of the legislation, calling it a "great day for American women and a great day for every American who is working to provide old age security for him or herself or their family."

Republicans also wanted a share of the glory. During brief Senate debate, Robert Dole, R-Kan., chairman of the Finance Committee and sponsor of the legislation, called it "an excellent measure to protect the retirement income of all Americans."

The Senate passed its version of the measure in November 1983. A House measure, which provided broader coverage, was approved May 22. House and Senate committee staffs worked out a compromise that was approved July 31 by the Senate Finance Committee. *(1983 Almanac p. 276)*

Background

HR 4280 revised the 1974 Employee Retirement Income Security Act (ERISA), as well as provisions of the Internal Revenue Code that regulated pension plans, a key source of income for retired persons. *(1974 Almanac p. 244)*

Under ERISA, employers were not required to offer pension plans, but those who did had to comply with certain minimum standards. ERISA, for example, mandated the maximum length of time employees could be required to work before they were "vested," or had a permanent right to employer-financed benefits even if they changed jobs before retirement.

Most employees had to work 10 years under a pension plan to become vested, and interruptions in a career could result in the loss of pension credits. Before enactment of HR 4280, employers were allowed to exclude workers from participating in a pension plan until they turned 25.

The sponsors of HR 4280 argued that women and others who entered the work force relatively early and interrupted their careers to raise families were penalized by provisions of current pension law.

Major Provisions

As signed by the president, HR 4280:

● Mandated that employees be permitted to participate in pension plans when they turned 21. Previously, employers did not have to enroll employees as plan participants until they reached 25.

● Required pension plans to count the years of employees' service from the time wage earners turned 18 in calculating when they had worked long enough to be vested. The minimum vesting age under existing pension law was 22.

● Permitted employees to leave a job and return without sacrificing the pension credit built up unless the "break in service" exceeded five consecutive years or the amount of time the employee worked at the job before leaving, whichever was greater. Under current law, unvested workers lost pension credits if their "break in service" exceeded the number of years they had worked under the pension plan.

● Barred pension plans from counting a one-year maternity or paternity leave as a break in service.

● Required pension plans to provide survivor benefits for the spouses of employees who died after they were vested regardless of the worker's age. Under current law, a spouse could be denied survivor benefits if the wage earner died before reaching minimum retirement age.

● Prohibited pension plan participants from waiving

survivor coverage without the written consent of their spouses.

● Assured that employees who had accrued retirement benefits would not lose those benefits when an employer changed or terminated a pension plan.

● Clarified the authority of state courts to divide up pension benefits between spouses in divorce proceedings.

● Increased from $1,750 to $3,500 the mandatory amount that an employer could provide as a lump sum when closing out a plan without the participant's request.

● Strengthened disclosure requirements for participants' pre-retirement survivor benefits and other pension rules. Generally, the provisions would apply to pension plans starting in 1985.

House Committee Action

The House Ways and Means Committee approved HR 4280 March 27.

The Ways and Means Committee made some liberalizing changes in the version of HR 4280 that had been approved in November 1983 by the Education and Labor Committee, which also had jurisdiction over pension matters. A compromise version (H Rept 98-655, Part II) of the two committees' bills was reported by Ways and Means May 17.

A key provision of the Ways and Means bill protected spouses from being denied survivor benefits if a worker died before retirement. Under existing law, those benefits could have been lost even if the worker had been employed long enough to be vested.

House Committee Provisions

As approved by Ways and Means, HR 4280 required most pension plans to provide benefits to a spouse if a vested employee died before reaching retirement age. The Education and Labor bill had provided automatic joint and survivor benefits only after an employee had worked for a company 10 years.

Other provisions of the House bill, designed to accommodate the career patterns of women, whose participation in the labor force is highest when they are relatively young, also would benefit younger workers.

HR 4280 required pension plans to begin counting service toward vesting after employees turned 18. In existing law, the minimum age for vesting calculations was 22. The Ways and Means bill also lowered the minimum age for enrollment in pension plans from 25 to 21. The committee dropped a provision of the Education and Labor bill that allowed certain pension plans to continue using the 25-year-old enrollment age, provided they granted retroactive credits when a worker turned 25.

As approved by Ways and Means, HR 4280 also:

● Allowed workers to take up to five years off before returning to a job without losing pension credits.

● Prohibited pension plans from counting maternity or paternity leave as a break in service. However, the bill did not include provisions sought by women's rights advocates that would have allowed partial credits toward vesting to accumulate while a worker was on maternity or paternity leave.

● Required spouses' consent if workers decided to forgo joint and survivor benefits. Current law allowed employees to decline such coverage without their spouse's knowledge. A worker who forfeited survivor benefits collected a higher pension payment after retirement. But the payments continued only as long as the wage earner lived; survivor benefits, though smaller, continued after the worker's death.

● Repealed a provision of current law that allowed survivor benefits to be denied to a spouse if a worker died of non-accidental causes within two years after choosing joint and survivor coverage.

● Allowed state courts to divide up pension benefits in divorce cases.

House Floor Action

The House May 22 unanimously approved HR 4280. The vote was 413-0. *(Vote 138, p. 48-H)*

The politically popular bill breezed through the House under expedited legislative procedures that permitted no amendments and required a two-thirds majority vote for passage. With time for debate limited by the "suspension" procedure, floor managers were hard pressed to accommodate all the members who wanted to speak in support of the measure.

House Panel Compromise

HR 4280 was brought to the House floor after members resolved relatively small differences between the Education and Labor Committee and the Ways and Means Committee versions of the bill.

Provisions

As approved by the House, HR 4280 would:

● Bar employers from excluding workers aged 21 or over from pension plans.

● Require pension plans to count the years of employees' service from the time they turn 18, in calculating when they have worked long enough to be vested.

● Allow employees who have worked fewer than five years to take five years off without losing pension credit for earlier service.

● Bar pension plans from counting a one-year maternity or paternity leave as a break in service.

● Require pension plans to provide survivor benefits for the spouses of employees who died after they were vested regardless of the worker's age.

● Prohibit employees from waiving survivor coverage without the written consent of their spouses.

● Specify that decisions to waive pre-retirement survivor benefits be made after workers turn 35, and that decisions to forgo post-retirement survivor benefits be made within 90 days before pension payments begin.

● Repeal a provision of current law that allowed pension plans to deny survivor benefits to a spouse if a worker died of natural causes within two years after choosing survivor coverage.

● Clarify the authority of state courts to divide up pension benefits between spouses in divorce proceedings.

Senate Action

The Senate had taken the lead in pension "equity" legislation, passing a bill (HR 2769) in November 1983. The measure provided survivors' benefits if an employee had worked at the same firm for 10 years and died after reaching age 45. And it permitted up to a five-year break in service.

After the House approved its version of the legislation, three committee staffs ironed out differences between the

House- and Senate-approved versions of the bill and the Senate Finance Committee July 31 approved the revised model.

The modified version passed by the Finance Committee July 31 emerged from negotiations among the staffs of three congressional committees with pension jurisdiction: the Finance panel, the House Education and Labor Committee and the House Ways and Means Committee.

The compromise was then approved by the Senate Aug. 6 and by the House Aug. 9.   ∎

Debt Limit Hikes Linked to Deficit Cutting

Congressional action to increase the public debt limit — the government's authority to borrow for funding government programs — was linked to efforts to reduce the federal deficit throughout 1984.

Almost from the start of the session, members of Congress in both political parties warned President Reagan that they might vote against an increase in the ceiling on the public debt unless he participated in bipartisan deficit-reduction talks. As the year progressed, they held to their pledges, stalling on the must-do legislation to pressure administration action on budget cutting.

For many fiscal conservatives, raising the debt limit had become a litmus-test vote. Over the years, a vote to increase the ceiling had been used by conservatives to campaign against more liberal opponents. House defeat of many debt bills led in 1979 to adoption of a new procedure whereby the House voted on debt ceiling increases as part of the budget resolution. *(1979 Almanac p. 305)*

First Round

Congress' first deadline to increase the public debt limit came at the end of May. Because a conference report on the budget resolution had not been adopted, the House was forced to vote on a separate debt ceiling bill.

On the first vote May 22, the House rejected, 150-262, a bill (HR 5665 — H Rept 98-785) lifting the ceiling from $1.49 trillion to $1.52 trillion through June 22. *(Vote 142, p. 48-H)*

The tally came as a surprise to House leaders of both parties. They mistakenly had expected members would not recoil at the $30 billion short-term increase.

Conservative Republicans urged their colleagues to vote against the measure, arguing that refusing to extend the debt ceiling would force action on substantial deficit cuts. When a majority of GOP members voted against the bill, some House Democrats sat on their hands or also voted no.

On a second vote May 24, the House passed another measure (HR 5692) providing a $30 billion debt ceiling increase through June 22. The vote was 211-198. *(Vote 159, p. 52-H)*

By May 24, the government had reached the limit of its borrowing authority, according to the Treasury Department. What persuaded a majority of House members to act was the specter of too little money in the till for Social Security recipients to cash their checks, as well as the members' desire to leave Washington for the Memorial Day recess, which began May 24.

A majority of Republicans refused to back the bill. Only 69 voted with 142 Democrats for the measure.

House leaders had proposed the June 22 expiration, hoping the date would dovetail with conference action on a tax-increase measure (HR 4170). They planned to include a larger and longer-term debt hike in the tax bill, insulating the increase from political byplay and creating a deadline for passage of the revenue increases. *(HR 4170, p. 143)*

Before approving the debt bill by voice vote later May 24, the Senate deleted the June 22 expiration date and converted the increase from "temporary" to "permanent."

In 1983, lawmakers had eliminated an earlier distinction between "permanent" and "temporary" debt ceilings that had caused the ceiling to drop to a permanent level of $400 billion barring periodic action by Congress. During Senate debate on HR 5692, ranking Finance Committee Democrat Russell B. Long, La., argued that while the temporary ceiling had been viewed as a "restraint on spending," the United States "is more deeply in debt as a result." *(1983 legislation, 1983 Almanac p. 239)*

One hour after the Senate action, the House agreed, by voice vote, to the Senate amendment. Reagan signed HR 5692 (PL 98-302) May 25.

In addition to increasing the debt ceiling by $30 billion, HR 5692 raised by $50 billion the amount of long-term bonds that could be issued at interest rates higher than the statutory limit of 4.25 percent. Under the bill the limit was increased to $200 billion.

Second Round

In late June, an attempt led by House Democrats to force action on the military budget by refusing to raise the public debt ceiling proved futile. After defeating two debt-limit bills June 28, enough Democrats backed off to allow approval of a debt measure (HR 5953 — PL 98-342) the next day. Following the 208-202 House vote, the measure breezed through the Senate on a voice vote, clearing the measure for the president. He signed it July 6. *(Vote 270, p. 84-H)*

The bill increased the government's authority to borrow money from $1.52 trillion to $1.573 trillion.

The Democrats hoped that by holding the debt limit increase hostage, Senate Republicans would agree to negotiate on military spending in the pending congressional budget resolution. The House budget resolution called for 3.5 percent inflation-adjusted growth rate for Pentagon spending. The Senate plan, crafted by the Republican leadership and the White House, set defense spending at 7 percent. Failure to agree on a growth rate had stalled the budget process. *(Budget resolution, p. 155)*

House Democrats responded in force to exhortations to kill the measure (HR 5927) as a means to get a budget resolution. At the urging of House Budget Committee Chairman James R. Jones, D-Okla., the House June 28 defeated two debt-limit increases (HR 5927) as a ploy to coerce Senate Republicans to the bargaining table. Jones said defeating the debt hike was a "means of forcing action" on the budget conference. But the GOP conferees failed to respond and refused to meet.

First, a Ways and Means Committee amendment to

increase the government's borrowing authority by $232 billion — setting the new ceiling at $1.753 trillion — was defeated 87-332. Then the House turned down, 138-282, the underlying bill to raise the ceiling by $53 billion to $1.573 trillion. *(Votes 256, 257, p. 80-H)*

Later that day the Ways and Means Committee reported HR 5953, which was an exact duplicate of the earlier debt limit hike, including the committee amendment. By the time the House took it up June 29, Jones had softened his position. Again, the House defeated the long-term committee amendment, but this time it approved the short-term extension. About one hour later, the Senate approved it by voice vote.

Third Round

The final congressional action on the debt limit in 1984 was a cliffhanger, with the Senate finally agreeing Oct. 12 to raise the public debt limit, clearing the way for the 98th Congress to adjourn. The approval came on a 37-30 Senate vote. Just 14 hours earlier, members had rejected the measure (H J Res 654) by a vote of 14-46, throwing into doubt when Congress would go home. *(Votes 275, 273, p. 48-S)*

In fact, some senators, weary from more than two weeks of often contentious debate on the debt ceiling bill, a continuing spending resolution and other last-minute measures, had already left Washington and had to be flown back to ensure final passage. *(Continuing resolution, p. 444)*

As approved (PL 98-475), the bill raised the $1.573 trillion limit on federal borrowing authority to $1.824 trillion, which was expected to provide sufficient credit for the government through Sept. 30, 1985. The Treasury Department had announced earlier in the week of Oct. 8 that the federal government had already borrowed to within $25 million of the existing ceiling.

After the initial defeat, a frustrated majority leader, Howard H. Baker Jr., R-Tenn., moved to reconsider the vote and promptly called for a recess to give him time to line up enough votes to pass the measure.

The House had approved the increase Oct. 1 as part of its agreement to a fiscal 1985 budget resolution.

Because of congressional delay in approving the debt-limit hike, the Treasury Department postponed an Oct. 10 auction of $5.5 billion in seven-year notes and an Oct. 11 auction of $4 billion in 20-year bonds, both needed to raise cash for the government. Treasury Secretary Donald T. Regan wrote in a letter to members that the postponements could cost the government $400 million in higher interest costs.

Imputed Interest

Much of the congressional foot-dragging on the debt limit was due not to objections over the measure itself, but to a dispute over an arcane real estate tax provision enacted earlier in 1984 as part of HR 4170, the tax increase/spending cut measure. *(Story, p. 143)*

Intended to limit tax-avoiding real estate schemes, the so-called "imputed interest" provision imposed a tax penalty on sellers who financed certain sales at below-market interest rates. The imputed interest penalty was strongly opposed by the real estate industry, and their allies in Congress threatened to tie up the debt limit bill unless the tax provision were repealed, delayed or weakened.

House Ways and Means Committee Chairman Dan Rostenkowski, D-Ill., said he would refuse to entertain any

amendments on the debt measure that would require the House to take a potentially troublesome vote.

The issue was resolved by amending a separate, unrelated bill, following extensive negotiations among the House, the Senate, real estate lobbyists and the administration. Both houses agreed Oct. 11 to delay the effective date of the imputed interest penalty for six months — until July 1, 1985. The delaying provision was attached to a bill (HR 5361) to extend for one year the tax-free status of employer-provided group legal services benefits, which both houses cleared by voice vote. *(HR 5361, p. 176)*

The way to final agreement was cleared when the Senate Oct. 11 agreed by a vote of 57-26 to table a Steven D. Symms, R-Idaho, amendment to the debt limit bill that called for total repeal of the imputed interest penalty. *(Vote 272, p. 47-S)*

Symms said the new restrictions were too complex and would hamper business activity. He argued that seller-financing with below-market interest rates was often the only way some sales could go forward, given the existing high interest rates in the open market.

But apparently more convincing was a threat by Howard M. Metzenbaum, D-Ohio, to filibuster the amendment. Metzenbaum argued that repeal would open the way to excessive tax abuse. He said an earlier compromise to limit the imputed interest penalty, which was added to the debt limit by an 81-0 vote, would go a long way toward meeting members' objections. *(Vote 269, p. 47-S)*

After the tabling vote, the Senate agreed to strip the compromise plan from the debt limit measure and to attach it to the legal services fringe benefit bill. Senate leaders agreed not to clear the debt limit bill until the House had acted on HR 5361.

The compromise, forged over a five-week period by Senate Finance Committee Chairman Robert Dole, R-Kan., John Melcher, D-Mont., and real estate representatives, exempted from the new law sales of a primary residence or vacation home for $250,000 or less, a farm or ranch with a purchase price of $2 million or less and small businesses with a sales price of $1 million or less. Some residence sales and farm sales were already exempt.

House Amendment

But when the measure was sent to the House Oct. 11, it was rejected by Ways and Means Committee Chairman Rostenkowski. Instead he proposed a three-month delay of the Jan. 1 effective date, for sales involving mortgages of $2 million or less.

The House agreed to the amendment, and returned the legal assistance benefits measure to the Senate.

When it became apparent that the three-month delay would not pass the Senate, negotiators from the House and Senate met behind closed doors for more than three hours to hammer out an acceptable plan.

At nearly 11 p.m. Oct. 11, Dole returned to the Senate floor with the proposed six-month delay — also only for loans of $2 million or less — which was approved by voice vote.

Shortly afterwards, Rostenkowski warned House members that rejection of the proposal would "kill the bill" and possibly require members — eager to depart to begin campaigning in earnest — to delay adjournment even longer. He promised to take up the imputed interest issue again early next year and the amended bill was agreed to, clearing the legal services fringe benefit measure for the president.

Spending, Nuclear Freeze Amendments

Lost in the shuffle over imputed interest was an amendment offered by Sen. Paul E. Tsongas, D-Mass., to the debt limit bill that would have shortened the borrowing extension to six months and required Congress to vote on a one-year freeze of government spending before it could expand the government's borrowing authority again.

The Senate Oct. 5 refused on a 30-61 vote to table (kill) the amendment, and it was clear the measure had the votes to pass. But as part of the agreement to keep the debt limit uncluttered, Tsongas agreed to withdraw his amendment and attach it to the legal services measure along with the first imputed interest compromise. However, the House stripped the Tsongas amendment from the measure before it was sent back to the Senate with the new imputed interest proposal. *(Vote 267, p. 46-S)*

The Senate Oct. 5 tabled (killed), by a vote of 55-42, an amendment by Edward M. Kennedy, D-Mass., and Mark O. Hatfield, R-Ore., calling for a U.S.-Soviet freeze on the testing, production and development of nuclear weapons. A similar nuclear freeze proposal was tabled Oct. 31, 1983, when it was offered to another measure to increase the public debt limit. *(Vote 266, p. 46-S; 1983 Almanac p. 213)* ∎

Balanced Budget Measure

The House voted overwhelmingly Oct. 2 for a bill to require the president to submit a balanced budget to Congress. The vote was 411-11. The measure was not considered by the Senate. *(Vote 381, p. 118-H)*

Republicans rebuked their Democratic colleagues for bringing up what they called a political "gimmick" while failing to schedule a vote on a constitutional amendment to balance the budget. *(Balanced budget amendment, p. 261)*

But in the end, 155 GOP members joined with 256 Democrats and voted for the bill (HR 6300) introduced by House Budget Committee Chairman James R. Jones, D-Okla.

In the Senate, Dave Durenberger, R-Minn., introduced a bill to require the president to submit annual budgets that would include proposals aimed at balancing the budget by 1989. Like the Jones bill, Durenberger's measure also would permit the submission of unbalanced budgets.

The Jones bill passed by the House required, for fiscal 1986 and thereafter, that the president submit a balanced budget plan. The bill also permitted the president to submit a revenue and spending plan that was not in balance, provided that it was accompanied by a balanced plan.

Similar provisions would apply to the House and Senate Budget committees. Under the bill, the congressional panels would have to report a balanced budget proposal for each fiscal year. The committees also could approve unbalanced budgets. ∎

Line-Item Veto

President Reagan's call for a constitutional amendment permitting line-item vetoes went nowhere in Congress in 1984.

Line-item veto authority would allow a president to reject spending for specific programs in an appropriations bill without having to veto the entire measure. It would take a two-thirds vote of each chamber to override the veto.

In his State of the Union address Jan. 25, Reagan said he had found this authority to be a "powerful tool" against wasteful spending when he was governor of California. Forty-three of the nation's governors had line-item veto power, according to the president's Feb. 1 budget message. *(State of the Union text, p. 5-E; budget message, p. 8-E)*

The line-item veto proposal was one of two constitutional amendments Reagan requested to help cut federal deficits. His other proposal, a constitutional amendment to require a balanced federal budget, also failed to win Congress' endorsement. *(Story, p. 261)*

Unlike bills, which need only a simple majority to pass, constitutional amendments require approval by a two-thirds majority in each chamber and ratification by three-fourths (38) of the states.

Supporters said the president needed line-item veto authority if he were to succeed in rooting waste from the federal budget and bringing government spending under control.

Opponents argued that the veto would usurp the powers of Congress and, in any event, would have limited impact on the deficit. Since the veto would affect only actual appropriations, some of the largest components of the federal budget would be beyond its reach. These included entitlement programs, such as Social Security, Medicare and Medicaid, for which mandatory spending was cemented in law, and net interest, or the cost of financing the federal debt.

The line-item veto proposal gained substantial support in 1983, when Congress' failure to achieve its deficit reduction goals intensified demands for additional presidential authority to control federal spending. *(Background, 1983 Almanac p. 238)*

Floor Votes

Although the line-item veto amendment never emerged from committee in either chamber, there were several floor votes on the spending issue in 1984.

Early in the session, House Republicans offered two proposals that stopped short of a constitutional amendment. Both failed by wide margins:

● The House Jan. 24 rejected by a 131-245 vote an amendment offered by Phil Gramm, R-Texas, that would have permitted the president, by executive order, to eliminate or reduce funding items under the low-income weatherization program (HR 2615). *(Vote 4, p. 2-H; weatherization, p. 354)*

● A week later, during consideration of a library aid authorization bill (HR 2878), the House rejected 144-248 an amendment offered by Newt Gingrich, R-Ga., that would have given the president line-item veto authority over money appropriated under the bill. *(Vote 11, p. 6-H; library aid, p. 461)*

In the Senate, the issue arose May 3 during consideration of deficit reduction legislation (HR 4170), but was turned aside on procedural grounds.

On a 56-34 vote, the Senate sustained a point of order against an amendment offered by Mack Mattingly, R-Ga., that would have given the president authority to veto line items in appropriations bills. At issue was Congress' power to legislate such a device without a constitutional amendment. The Senate never voted on the substance of the Mattingly proposal. *(Votes 86, 87, p. 17-S; deficit reduction, p. 143)* ∎

Donovan Indictment

In court documents made public Oct. 2, a Bronx County, N.Y., grand jury named Labor Secretary Raymond J. Donovan in an indictment concerning financial dealings of the Schiavone Construction Co. while Donovan was the firm's executive vice president. Donovan left Schiavone when he joined the Reagan Cabinet in 1981.

At an Oct. 2 arraignment, Donovan pleaded not guilty to the 137-count indictment. Donovan claimed that the grand jury investigation that gave rise to the indictment was a politically motivated "inquisition."

Democrats, however, contended that the indictment was further proof that the administration had paid insufficient attention to ethical questions raised about some of President Reagan's appointees.

Immediately after learning that he had been named in the indictment, Donovan said he asked the president to grant him a leave of absence without pay "to assure that this matter does not become part of the current election campaign" and to allow him to devote his full attention to fighting the charges. In Donovan's absence, Labor Undersecretary Ford B. Ford took over the helm of the Labor Department.

The indictment accused Donovan and nine other individuals of one count of grand larceny, 125 counts of falsifying business records and 11 counts of filing false documents in connection with a $186 million New York City subway-tunnel construction project for which Schiavone received a contract in 1978.

Donovan contended the investigation was a rehash of a 1982 probe of his activities by a federal special prosecutor, Leon Silverman. After his nine-month investigation, Silverman concluded that there was "insufficient credible evidence" to warrant bringing federal charges against Donovan. *(1982 Almanac p. 67)*

Questions about the Schiavone firm delayed Donovan's confirmation as labor secretary. He was the last member of Reagan's original Cabinet to win Senate approval. *(1981 Almanac p. 17-A)*

The Donovan indictment was made public less than two weeks after an investigation of the financial dealings of Edwin Meese III, Reagan's nominee for attorney general, found no evidence of criminal conduct. *(Meese nomination, p. 248)* ∎

Enterprise Zones Fail

President Reagan's proposal to provide tax breaks for businesses that located in designated "enterprise zones" in inner cities and rural areas failed to become law for the third year in a row.

The plan, intended to bring jobs and development to decaying areas, had been included by the Senate in its version of the 1984 deficit reduction act (HR 4170 — PL 98-369). It was dropped in conference with the House. The proposal would have authorized the secretary of housing and urban development to name up to 25 zones for three years; businesses locating in the zones would be eligible for various tax and regulatory relief. *(Story, p. 143)*

Sen. Robert Dole, R-Kan., reintroduced the proposal as a separate bill (S 2914), but it did not reach the floor before adjournment.

Reagan, charging that House Democrats had refused to consider the plan, wrote House Minority Whip Trent Lott, R-Miss., in September, asking the House to consider enterprise zones. Lott, however, was unable to bring it to the House floor.

Although he first proposed creating an enterprise zone program in 1982, Reagan had been unable to persuade Congress to enact it. The Senate twice before had approved legislation. In 1983, it attached the plan to an interest withholding bill, but the provision was dropped in conference with the House. In 1982, the Senate included it in a tax bill that died. *(1983 Almanac p. 23; 1982 Almanac p. 69)*

Some majority members of the key Ways and Means Committee and its chairman remained opposed. The panel held hearings but had never acted on the proposal.

Critics doubted that the tax incentives would create new jobs in the zones, a point also raised by a Congressional Research Service evaluation of the proposal.

And they questioned the propriety of giving businesses tax breaks that would reduce federal revenues at a time of high deficits. According to the Senate Finance Committee, the tax breaks would cost $1.3 billion in lost revenues over three years.

While the proposal faltered in Washington, state and local governments moved ahead. Some states already allowed tax relief in specific areas, and 24 states since 1981 had enacted enterprise zone legislation or created zones administratively. By 1984, zone programs were under way in almost 300 cities.

Early returns indicated that they were drawing new activity and jobs to decaying areas. For example, the Sabre Foundation, a Washington-based organization, reported that the diverse state and local programs had created 4,601 jobs so far.

British Import

To the president, enterprise zones represented a break with the old-line federal programs of heavy subsidies and central planning. It was the ideal urban program, entailing minimum federal involvement and maximum private sector incentives.

Many urban groups backed the plan. However, they warned that it would not make up for administration cuts in housing, job and economic development programs.

The Senate-passed plan would have required potential sites to be nominated by state and local governments according to criteria of economic distress and population. Also, local governments would be required to make a commitment to remove impediments to economic development, such as cutting red tape or making street improvements.

Businesses that located in zones would be eligible for tax relief, including extra investment credit for capital costs. ∎

Conservation Corps Vetoed

A popular proposal (HR 999) to set up an American Conservation Corps (ACC) was pocket-vetoed by President Reagan Oct. 30.

The measure, which authorized $225 million over three years to establish a program to give thousands of young people conservation jobs on public and Indian lands, cleared Congress in the closing days of the session with House approval Oct. 9. The vote was 296-75. The bill had

. *(Vote*

e even
rsion of
h 1983.
ver four

rvation
e. *(1982*

sistently
obs pro-
mbodied
ent that
eto text,*

0 million
n in 1987
e Depres-

he House
deral per-
9 that was
the gov-
vided, 25
r Depart-
nt and 35
upport In-
dian programs and the remainder was to be used for special
projects.

In its first year, the program would have provided about 18,500 jobs on conservation and rehabilitation projects, providing both year-round and summer employment. Sponsors estimated that more than 37,000 jobs could be created if the program were fully funded at $100 million in 1987.

Unemployed youths aged 16 to 25 would be eligible for the year-round jobs program, while those aged 15 to 21 would qualify for the summer jobs.

The bill required "special efforts" to recruit and enroll disadvantaged young people, but did not exclude others from participating in the program. Although the Senate had been under some pressure to limit the program exclusively to the disadvantaged, some supporters argued that part of the benefit of the program would come from bringing together participants from diverse social and economic backgrounds. ∎

Industrial Policy Falters

Legislation to establish a national industrial policy was approved by two House committees but went no further in the 98th Congress.

A measure (HR 4360) to establish a Bank for Industrial Competitiveness, a Council for Industrial Competitiveness and a Federal Industrial Mortgage Association (FIMA) won the approval of both the House Banking Committee and the House Energy and Commerce Committee. The legislation had been the subject of hearings held in November 1983. *(1983 Almanac p. 251)*

The bank was designed to make loan guarantees and purchase stock to help finance industrial modernization. It was slated to receive $8.5 billion in federal funds over 10 years. The council was to have been a board of government, business and labor leaders to coordinate government industrial policy, while FIMA would establish a wider market for industrial mortgages to help small and medium-size firms that needed capital. HR 4360 was approved by the Banking Committee April 24 (H Rept 98-697, Part I). It was reported by Energy and Commerce June 6 (H Rept 98-697, Part II).

A second industrial policy measure (HR 4361 — H Rept 98-693, Part I) was reported by the Banking Committee, also on April 24. It called for a $500 million authorization over four years for an Advanced Technology Foundation to fund applied scientific research. ∎

Export Reauthorization Fails

Congress Oct. 11 failed to extend the Export Administration Act, forcing the president to continue to rely indefinitely on emergency powers to control U.S. shipments abroad.

Because of a standoff between the two chambers, hard-won agreements reached during six months of stop-and-start House-Senate conferences were scrapped. And government controls over exports remained largely under the umbrella of the International Emergency Economic Powers Act of 1977 (PL 95-223).

The controls expired Sept. 30, 1983. The House had approved a two-year extension (HR 3231) Oct. 27, 1983, but the Senate did not act on the reauthorization until March 1, 1984, when it approved a six-year extension by voice vote. As Congress considered reauthorizing the measure, the executive branch relied on the emergency powers and temporary extensions of the act. The last extension expired at the end of March. *(Background, 1983 Almanac p. 253)*

The export act authorized restrictions on U.S. shipments overseas to protect national security, promote foreign policy and prevent shortages of important commodities. The act also was meant to promote exports and provided the legal basis for the existing ban on exports of Alaskan oil.

Lengthy Conference

House and Senate conferees tried to meld the two bills during 14 conference sessions and countless hours of informal negotiations between April and October 1984. Especially hard-fought were a Senate plan to boost Defense Department controls on licenses for certain high-technology exports and a House-backed proposal to ban new U.S. commercial bank loans to the South African government.

Sen. Jake Garn, R-Utah, chairman of the Senate Banking Committee, which had jurisdiction over the bill, for months had insisted on stronger Defense Department controls to prevent technology with potential military use from being diverted to communist countries. House conferees had objected equally strongly to increased Defense Department monitoring, arguing that it would hamstring business. The administration also opposed Garn's plan to expand Pentagon controls, preferring discretionary arrangements to legislation.

Garn wanted to see the proposed ban on South Africa bank loans dropped to prevent an encroachment on the jurisdiction of the Senate Banking Committee, aides said.

The Senate bill included milder potential sanctions against U.S. companies in South Africa.

Final Reauthorization Attempt

In a last-ditch attempt to renew the act, Senate backers, led by Garn, Oct. 10 offered a five-year extension of controls (HR 4230) that included many of the compromises that had been reached in the conference. The bill, which excluded the increased Pentagon controls and the South African loan ban, was passed by voice vote.

In making his offer, Garn said the tougher controls were no longer necessary because a presidential directive, issued in March, outlined ways the Defense and Commerce departments could jointly control licensing, although neither department had signed a memorandum of understanding making the power-sharing agreement official.

The next day, the House approved, 269-62, the bulk of the Senate bill, with one important change: reinstatement of the bank loan ban. *(Vote 406, p. 124-H)*

Rep. Stephen J. Solarz, D-N.Y., who had fought in conference for sanctions against South Africa, argued that the ban on bank loans belonged in the final bill because conferees had agreed to it.

The proposal was opposed as too strong by some House Republicans and too weak by the Congressional Black Caucus. However, under the rule on the bill, members could not vote on alternative sanctions.

On the final House vote, many caucus members voted "present" to protest what Rep. Parren J. Mitchell, D-Md., called "the weak-kneed, go-along policy" of the United States on South African racial segregation.

The revised House bill was dismissed as "very flawed" by Sen. John Heinz, R-Pa., chairman of the Banking Subcommittee on International Finance and Monetary Policy, who had guided the original Senate bill on its long course through Congress. Late Oct. 11, with senators growing restive to adjourn, the Senate indefinitely postponed action on the issue. ∎

Mortgage Bill Cleared

Despite some objections from the banking industry, the Senate Sept. 26 cleared a bill removing some regulatory impediments private companies faced in trying to buy mortgages from banks and to sell securities backed by them.

The Senate by voice vote approved the bill (S 2040) as amended by the House Sept. 11. It was signed into law Oct. 3 (PL 98-440).

The American Bankers Association and the U.S. League of Savings Institutions asked Senate Banking Committee Chairman Jake Garn, R-Utah, to hold up Senate acceptance of the House changes because the bill did not permit banks to underwrite mortgage-backed securities. That authority was being considered in conjunction with another bill on banking deregulation (S 2851). *(Banking, p. 271)*

The purpose of S 2040 was to increase the amount of money available for mortgages by removing impediments private companies had encountered in dealing with mortgage-backed securities.

The bill had been reported (S Rept 98-293) Nov. 2, 1983, by the Senate Banking, Housing and Urban Affairs Committee. It was passed by the Senate Nov. 17, 1983, but the action was vitiated the next day because of a technical error. The Senate approved it again Feb. 9, 1984.

Before passing the measure Sept. 11, the House amended the bill to permit the Federal National Mortgage Association (Fannie Mae) and the Federal Home Loan Mortgage Corporation (Freddie Mac) to buy second mortgages up to $57,000 and allow Fannie Mae to buy mortgages on manufactured homes. A similar provision had been included in a bill reported Sept. 6 by the Energy and Commerce Committee (HR 4557 — H Rept 98-994). ∎

Housing Act Corrections

Congress completed action Oct. 3 on legislation (S 2819 — PL 98-479) to correct technical problems that had arisen in implementing the 1983 Housing and Rural Recovery Act (PL 98-181). *(1983 Almanac p. 277)*

It was signed by President Reagan Oct. 17.

The Senate Banking, Housing and Urban Affairs Committee reported the bill June 28 (no written report). The Senate approved the legislation June 29 by voice vote. The House passed S 2819 with minor amendments Sept. 11.

The House approved the conference report (H Rept 98-1103) by voice vote Oct. 2 and the Senate by voice vote Oct. 3.

S 2819 clarified that a community could qualify for community development grants even if it had relatively few low- and moderate-income residents.

The measure permitted Baltimore and Denver to use revenue from urban renewal projects for activities financed by federal community development grants. The bill also clarified that very-low-income families could receive vouchers to be used toward rent in buildings renovated under the rental rehabilitation program created by PL 98-181.

Conferees agreed to require the Solar Energy and Energy Conservation Bank to issue regulations establishing criteria for assistance from the bank for various projects.

In addition, the final legislation required the Department of Housing and Urban Development to develop regulations providing for insurance from the Federal Housing Administration on mortgages on public hospitals. ∎

Longshore Compensation

Congress Sept. 20 cleared legislation (S 38 — PL 98-426) to revamp a special federal workers' compensation law for longshoremen. The House approved the conference report on the bill (H Rept 98-1027) by voice vote Sept. 18. The Senate, also by voice vote, approved the conference report two days later. President Reagan signed the measure Sept. 28.

The bill overhauled the Longshoremen's and Harbor Workers' Compensation Act to curb abuses and limit benefit increases under the program, which guaranteed compensation to dockworkers and other maritime employees for job-related injuries or death. It also scaled back coverage of the act to exclude certain kinds of employees who were not directly exposed to the hazards of maritime work, such as office clerical workers in maritime firms.

However, the bill was designed to broaden coverage for workers with occupational diseases. It eased certain procedural requirements that critics of the current system said had made it difficult for workers to get compensation for diseases with long latency periods.

The House passed its version of S 38 April 10. The Senate had approved the bill in June 1983; its version went somewhat further than the House's in scaling back coverage and curbing benefits. Conferees from the House and Senate finished work on the bill Sept. 11.

Background

Congress established the federally regulated system to compensate disabled longshoremen in 1927, after the Supreme Court ruled that state compensation programs could not cover dockworkers working over navigable waters.

The cost of providing compensation was borne principally by employers, who generally took out insurance policies to cover the benefits. As under state workers' compensation laws, employees covered by the Longshoremen's Act were barred from suing their employers for damages.

In 1972, Congress boosted benefits and expanded the law's scope to include not only people who actually worked over water, but also a variety of onshore employees of maritime firms. Since then, employers had complained about the cost of providing increased benefits and the difficulty of obtaining insurance to cover them.

Criticism of the act was further fueled in 1981, when a Senate investigation found the program had been manipulated by organized crime and unscrupulous doctors and workers.

A bill intended to respond to those concerns, sponsored by Sen. Don Nickles, R-Okla., was passed by the Senate in 1982. It died in the House, but the legislation was revived by Nickles in the 98th Congress. *(1982 Almanac p. 65; 1983 Almanac p. 271)*

Provisions to make it easier for workers to receive compensation for occupational diseases were added to the bill in the House.

Critics of existing law argued that victims of occupational disease faced procedural obstacles in obtaining compensation under a system designed to handle typical work injuries. For example, they said deadlines for filing notice

of injury and claims were unrealistically short for occupational diseases because the first signs of harm from exposure to a toxic substance might not be immediately disabling — or could emerge so long after exposure that their cause might not be immediately apparent.

To meet such concerns, conferees extended deadlines for occupational disease victims to file notices and claims. Deadlines would be measured from the time a disease manifested itself and a worker knew, or should have known, the disability was job-related.

Provisions

Major provisions of S 38:

● Excluded from coverage under the Longshoremen's Act certain kinds of employees, such as office clerical workers, builders of small recreational boats and certain marina employees. Workers were excluded only if they were eligible for coverage by state workers' compensation programs.

● Repealed death benefits that currently were provided when workers receiving compensation died of causes unrelated to their occupational injuries.

● Limited death benefits, which had been unrestricted, to 200 percent of the national average weekly wage.

● Imposed a 5 percent limit on annual benefit increases. Increases were tied to increases in the national average weekly wage.

● Imposed new limits on workers' freedom to switch doctors, and required the Labor Department to compile a list of physicians not qualified to provide medical care under the act. Doctors would be placed on the list, and no reimbursement for their services would be paid for at least three years, if they had submitted false statements or charged excess fees.

● Extended the deadline for filing notice of a job-related injury to one year, from 30 days, for victims of occupational disease. The deadline for filing a claim was extended to two years, from one year.

● Authorized benefits for victims of occupational disease in cases where workers discovered their disability — or died — in retirement.

● Increased penalties for filing fraudulent claims. ∎

Wide-Ranging Trade Package Clears Congress

Congress Oct. 9 cleared an omnibus trade bill (HR 3398 — PL 98-573) that was an amalgam of more than 100 measures. President Reagan signed the bill Oct. 30.

HR 3398's most controversial provisions included authority for the administration to initiate free-trade talks with Israel, preferred treatment of exports from developing nations and import relief for the steel and wine industries.

Work on the bill began early in the 98th Congress. It ended just three days before Congress adjourned.

The push for more extensive laws against unfair trade practices came on the heels of a record-high U.S. trade deficit in 1983 of $70 billion. Backers of trade remedy legislation contended that new kinds of unfair trade practices accounted partly for the surge in imports and thus contributed to soaring trade deficits.

The vast majority of the bill's provisions were requests for import relief for particular products.

The measure also extended the president's authority to retaliate against unfair trade practices and to expand

trade in services and broadened the definitions of unfair trade subsidies. And it contained fiscal 1985 authorizations for the U.S. Customs Service, the International Trade Commission and the Office of the U.S. Trade Representative.

The House adopted the conference report on HR 3398 (H Rept 98-1156) on a 386-1 vote. The Senate then approved it by voice vote. *(Vote 399, p. 122-H)*

Administration Priorities

As cleared by Congress HR 3398 contained three administration priorities: extension of the generalized system of preferences (GSP), authority to enter negotiations aimed at establishing a U.S.-Israel free-trade area and expansion of administration authority to respond to other nations' trade practices.

The GSP, a program that allowed certain exports from some developing countries to enter the United States duty free, was renewed for eight and one-half years. The administration's position, which was reflected in the Senate version of HR 3398, would have extended GSP for 10 years; the House bill would have continued the program for five years.

The administration sought the GSP extension for symbolic as much as economic and philosophical reasons. The concessions could be used to induce recipients to lower trade barriers. Benefits also reassured developing nations that the United States was committed to multilateral arrangements to promote free trade.

The program, which applied to about 3 percent of U.S. imports, had been criticized by labor groups and some lawmakers as a "giveaway" in the face of mounting trade deficits.

The administration sought the provision to go ahead with a U.S.-Israel free trade arrangement to strengthen economic and strategic ties with Israel, promote Israel's long-term economic self-sufficiency and expand U.S. and Israeli trade. The authority to negotiate U.S.-Israel free trade also allowed the Office of the U.S. Trade Representative to pursue similar arrangements with other nations.

The third administration priority, the trade "reciprocity" provisions, authorized talks to lower or eliminate barriers to trade in high-technology products, U.S. investment abroad and trade in services, such as banking. It also permitted the elimination of duties on some high-tech items for up to five years.

The trade reciprocity provision was a leftover from previous Senate action. The original measure (S 144) was approved by the Senate in April 1983 after getting caught up in a legislative wrangle over withholding taxes on interest and dividend income. *(1983 Almanac p. 259)*

Wine, Steel

The bill also gave grape growers the right to file unfair-trade complaints about wine imports. The International Trade Commission earlier in 1984, in denying the wine industry's petition for import relief, decided that grape growers were not part of the domestic wine industry, and therefore excluded grape data from the wine injury claim. European wine producers objected to the bill and threatened to retaliate by cutting back on millions of dollars' worth of purchases of U.S. soybeans and other farm products.

The bill also clarified the application of trade remedies, enjoyed by goods, to the service industries.

The measure also contained provisions designed to offer some help for the import-beleaguered steel and copper industries. In September the president rejected the recommendations of the International Trade Commission (ITC) and declined to impose quotas on steel and copper imports to the United States. *(Box, p. 173)*

House

In June 1983, the House passed HR 3398, an omnibus tariff bill that made 23 minor changes in tariff and customs law. It had been reported from the House Ways and Means Committee June 24 (H Rept 98-267).

The House Ways and Means Committee April 10 approved a "trade remedies" bill (HR 4784 — H Rept 98-725) that outlawed new kinds of export subsidies, which provided an edge to foreign products in U.S. markets.

The measure was opposed by the Reagan administration as inconsistent with international trade agreements. Among the subsidies the bill sought to counteract: dis-

counts on supplies of natural resources that foreign companies used in manufacturing exports, and "targeting," a government practice to coordinate antitrust, tax and other policies to bolster selected industries.

Under current U.S. law the president was empowered to retaliate with import tariffs, or countervailing duties, against a range of traditional subsidies such as direct loans or grants.

The administration contended that HR 4784 would contravene several rules of the General Agreement on Tariffs and Trade, the international trade pact between the United States and other industrialized nations.

Reflecting the administration's concerns, Rep. Barber B. Conable Jr., R-N.Y., the senior Republican on the panel, offered two amendments, both unsuccessful, to delete provisions of the bill that he said would invite other nations' retaliation against U.S. agricultural exports.

One of the provisions allowed the United States to impose countervailing duties against imports manufactured with natural resources acquired at discounted prices.

Conable also tried to weaken a targeting provision by requiring proof of a foreign government's intent to subsidize an industry.

An amendment by Marty Russo, D-Ill., adopted by voice vote, preserved the Commerce Department's power to impose import quotas instead of tariffs as a trade weapon. As reported by the Ways and Means Trade Subcommittee, HR 4784 shifted that power to the president.

Other amendments approved included those by:

● Dan Rostenkowski, D-Ill., requiring the Commerce Department to monitor imports of related products when one instance of "dumping" imports at artificially low prices is found.

● Richard T. Schulze, R-Pa., to strike provisions changing anti-dumping rules applied to communist countries.

Retaliation

The House July 26 approved HR 4784. The vote was 259-95. *(Vote 294, p. 90-H)*

The bill strengthened the Commerce Department's power to act against several foreign practices not currently defined by international agreement as export subsidies or unfair trade practices.

Designated eligible for U.S. retaliation were government support for natural resource and energy prices and imports made with subsidized components.

The measure also addressed "downstream dumping," the practice of adding subsidized components made in one country to exports assembled in another country. Under HR 4784, proof of downstream dumping would trigger anti-dumping duties.

The bill also required an in-depth study of trading partners' methods of targeting. The bill originally had called for protection against targeting. But Trade Representative William E. Brock III argued that trading partners could claim that the U.S. computer, semiconductor and other industries received unfair help from Washington, and, bowing to industry and administration pressure, the bill's supporters agreed to modify the legislation to call for a study.

Paperwork Bill

The House Sept. 18 passed an omnibus tariff bill (HR 6064 — H Rept 98-1015) that also reduced paperwork for the U.S. Customs Service. It later was attached to HR 3398.

HR 6064 raised from $250 to $1,250 the limit on items

Steel, Copper Quotas

The administration announced Sept. 18 that President Reagan had rejected tariffs and quotas on steel imports but had endorsed negotiations to limit shipments of steel to the United States. The president Sept. 6 had decided against imposing quotas or tariffs on copper imports.

Reagan's decisions on copper and steel were provoked by International Trade Commission recommendation to set quotas and tariffs to aid domestic producers.

While turning down a proposal to impose tariffs and quotas on imported carbon steel, Reagan pledged to enter negotiations with major foreign steel suppliers on "voluntary" agreements to keep their exports to about 20 percent of the domestic market.

Steel imports equaled about 25 percent of the U.S. market in 1984. By January 1985, the administration had reached agreements with major steel exporting nations that would come close to meeting its objective of reducing steel imports by about 25 percent over five years, when coupled with an existing curb on European steel and arrangements with other foreign steel makers.

The decision managed to defuse some political pressure from steel interests and lawmakers in steel-producing states, potentially increase the president's leverage to extract trade concessions from foreign suppliers and maintain the appearance of the administration's commitment to free trade.

The administration chose "voluntary restraints" rather than the unilateral imposition of quotas in part to reduce the risk of retaliation by foreign nations. Retaliation could harm U.S. agriculture and other export-dependent industries. Sen. Pete Wilson, R-Calif., and other farm-state lawmakers had argued against quotas.

that importers and U.S. travelers returning from overseas had to declare in writing with the Customs Service. It also incorporated 62 minor changes in tariff and trade laws, many to ease imports of chemicals not readily available from U.S. manufacturers.

The bill also established a new customs district in the Pacific Northwest to consolidate customs jurisdiction in that part of the country and to improve handling of the growing volume of trade in the Pacific Rim.

On the issue of possible European restrictions on U.S. farm exports, including profitable soybean and animal feed shipments, HR 6064 requested the president to oppose any limits and to respond immediately if restrictions were imposed. The bill passed by voice vote under suspension of the rules, the procedure that barred amendments and required a two-thirds majority for approval.

House Package

The core of the House version of HR 3398 was approved Sept. 26 by the House Ways and Means Committee. The measures included the Democrats' response (HR 6301) to President Reagan's steel import decision, as well as measures on U.S.-Israel free trade (HR 5377), expanded import relief for domestic wine makers (HR 3795) and a five-year extension of the GSP (HR 6023).

The steel plan added to the bill conformed to a program backed by Democratic presidential candidate Walter F. Mondale. The plan asked the president to work to keep steel imports to 17 percent of the U.S. market — lower than the 20 percent figure favored by the president and closer to the 15 percent target contained in steel quota legislation backed by the steel industry and several committee Democrats.

The Ways and Means measure also tied import relief to steel producers' steps to modernize plants and aid unemployed or laid-off workers. With the plan, the committee edged closer to a national industrial policy to coordinate government and business activities.

In addition, the bill sought to extend for two years the Trade Adjustment Assistance Program, which targeted government aid to workers who lost their jobs because of foreign competition. *(1983 Almanac p. 251)*

The steel plan, introduced by Chairman Rostenkowski shortly before the committee met, was passed by voice vote after only a few minutes of debate.

GSP. Committee members approved, 12-8, an amendment by Rep. Russo to extend for five years the GSP. To overcome objections by organized labor and some lawmakers that the program cost U.S. jobs and sales, the committee approved several conditions to tighten eligibility requirements and distribute benefits to the poorest developing countries.

The committee version required that countries, in order to receive benefits, demonstrate that they honored U.S. patents and other intellectual property rights, reduced barriers to U.S. investment and trade in services and protected worker rights. The measure also automatically cut off benefits to the wealthiest developing countries within two years after they had achieved an average annual per capita income of $9,000.

Moreover, it gave the United States more options to deny or reduce benefits to less wealthy developing countries that were competing vigorously against U.S. goods and services, unfairly protecting their markets or violating worker rights.

However, the committee rejected an amendment by Richard A. Gephardt, D-Mo., to cut off GSP benefits to the top three exporters in the program, Taiwan, Hong Kong and Korea.

Israel. The committee unanimously approved a provision authorizing negotiations to lower or remove most trade barriers with Israel. The provision also narrowly expanded a few of the powers that the Office of the U.S. Trade Representative had sought to counteract trade barriers.

However, members qualified the original version of the U.S.-Israel plan on the recommendation of the Ways and Means Trade Subcommittee and the urging of the textile industry and producers of specialized products and crops such as chemical salts and tomatoes.

Some textile interests, including longtime Israel supporters in the AFL-CIO and the International Ladies' Garment Workers' Union, argued that a free-trade arrangement with Israel would cost U.S. jobs and make other countries' requests for lower trade barriers hard to resist.

Some producers of specialized products and crops also argued that their sales would be hurt by increased Israeli imports.

The committee also adapted from the 1983 Caribbean Trade Initiative several trade safeguards and applied them to U.S.-Israel trade. In particular, the modifications retained duties on products shipped through Israel from one country to another simply to take advantage of Israel's duty-free status with the United States. *(Caribbean trade plan, 1983 Almanac p. 252)*

In response to concerns of farm interests, members agreed to fast-track reviews of requests to grant temporary duties on Israeli imports of perishable agricultural goods while injury claims were reviewed.

Wine. The committee also approved a watered-down version of wine "equity" legislation. The bill required the U.S. trade representative to consult with major foreign wine producers to reduce or eliminate wine trade barriers, work to correct trade barriers the trade representative's office determined should be counteracted and report to Congress on progress made.

The bill also gave grape growers the right to file unfair-trade complaints about wine imports. To ensure that the provision would not be misinterpreted to let producers of other types of raw materials also file certain trade complaints, the committee accepted an amendment offered by Bill Frenzel, R-Minn., limiting the provision to grape growers.

House Floor Action

The House Oct. 3 gathered the parts of its trade package into one piece of legislation. All of the various components — some of which were approved the same day — were attached to HR 3398.

Approved by the House Oct. 3 were HR 5377, the U.S.-Israel free-trade arrangement, on a 416-6 vote; HR 6301, steel import stabilization, on 285-134 vote; HR 3795, wine equity, by voice vote; HR 6023, GSP, by voice vote; and HR 2848, service industries commercial development, by voice vote. *(Votes 385, 386, p. 118-H)*

Ater they were approved, the bills were attached to HR 3398. The House also agreed to amend HR 3398 with HR 4784, the trade remedies bill passed July 26; HR 4901, the customs forfeiture provisions of HR 4901, which would give the Customs Service greater power to confiscate property and make arrests in drug cases; HR 5188, the fiscal 1985 authorization for the Customs Service, the International Trade Commission and the Office of the U.S. Trade Representative; and HR 6064, the omnibus tariff bill passed Sept. 18.

Senate

The Senate March 2 began debate on HR 3398, but failed to make much progress. The bill was put aside until other trade components were ready for floor action in September.

As first considered on the floor, the bill was a combination of a routine tariff adjustment bill and the provisions of S 144, which gave the president and his trade representative more authority to negotiate tariffs and retaliate against unfair trading practices.

Senate Committee

Senate action on the trade bill switched back to the committee level in late July, with the Senate Finance Committee fashioning amendments to HR 3398. The catchall measure was loaded up July 31 with additional amendments, including provisions to expand the president's authority to retaliate against unfair trading practices and to encourage freer trade with Israel and Canada.

The free-trade arrangements provision was contained in a bill (S 2746 — S Rept 98-510) reported by the Senate Finance Committee June 12.

The committee also approved a 10-year extension of the GSP and about 80 miscellaneous tariff and trade items. The GSP bill (S 1718 — S Rept 98-485) was reported by the Finance Committee May 24.

All of the additional items added to the bill were incorporated into a massive committee amendment that was attached to HR 3398 on the Senate floor.

Senate Floor

The Senate Sept. 20 unanimously approved HR 3398 after its managers were able to fend off strongly protectionist amendments aimed at aiding import-sensitive domestic industries. The vote on passage was 96-0. *(Vote 228, p. 40-S)*

During four days of stop-and-start debate Sept. 17-20, floor managers John C. Danforth, R-Mo., and Lloyd Bentsen, D-Texas, headed off controversial amendments that could have killed the bill by building upon carefully negotiated agreements with the Finance Committee, the U.S. trade representative and the administration. U.S. Trade Representative Brock appeared on the floor to buttonhole senators, using his floor privilege as a former senator (R-Tenn., 1971-77).

The Senate bill tightened GSP eligibility requirements and established stricter standards to gain support for the program.

The U.S.-Israel free-trade arrangement was designed to reduce most restrictions on the $3 billion in annual trade between Israel and the United States. To win the support of some senators concerned that freer trade with Israel could hurt U.S. sales of specialized products, such as jewelry and cirtus fruits, the administration issued assurances that free-trade arrangements for import-sensitive products would be introduced gradually.

The bill also authorized talks with Canada to lower or eliminate some trade barriers on some products and industries. HR 3398 also extended the administration's authority to negotiate free-trade arrangements.

The trade reciprocity provision left over from S 144 directed the executive branch to seek new international agreements to promote trade in services, U.S. investment abroad and high technology. It also provided for yearly accounting of major barriers to trade in goods, services and U.S. foreign investment and expanded the president's authority to counteract other countries' unfair trade practices.

Domestic Content. Some trade issues were noticeable by their absence in the Senate version of HR 3398. Advocates of domestic content legislation, which required that a certain percentage of cars imported to the United States contain fixed amounts of U.S. parts and labor, dropped plans to add their bill to the trade package. *(Domestic content, 1983 Almanac p. 257)*

Steel, Copper, Shoes. The trade package also managed to elude strictly protectionist measures for the steel industry, although the president's Sept. 18 decision to deny tariffs and quotas on steel had upset some steel-state senators.

John Heinz, R-Pa., chairman of the Senate Steel Caucus, added a provision to expand the U.S. Customs Service's authority to monitor steel imports from countries agreeing to the voluntary restraints favored by the president.

In response to Reagan's Sept. 6 rejection of the ITC recommendation to grant import relief to the copper industry, the Senate accepted an amendment by Pete V. Domenici, R-N.M., calling for negotiations on voluntary export restraints with major foreign copper-producing nations.

And the shoe industry won a chance to reopen its petition for import relief denied by the ITC in June.

Trade Practices. Many textile and other industry and labor concerns were addressed by provisions strengthening the Commerce Department's power to counteract several foreign-trade practices not currently defined by international accords as unfair trade actions.

Amendments. The Senate Sept. 17 adopted by voice vote two amendments by Frank R. Lautenberg, D-N.J., to consider as trade barriers countries' refusal to honor patents, trademarks and copyrights, and directed the United States to negotiate to protect intellectual property rights.

The Senate also:

● Adopted by voice vote Sept. 18 an amendment offered by Heinz to devise firmer standards for judging the trade-distorting practices of countries whose economies are government-controlled, and procedures for relief from those practices.

● Adopted Sept. 19 by voice vote an amendment offered by Pete Wilson, R-Calif., directing the U.S. trade representative to work to lower or reduce trade barriers to the domestic wine industry.

● Approved Sept. 18 by voice vote an amendment by George J. Mitchell, D-Maine, to establish an office in the Commerce Department to assist small businesses in trade matters.

● Approved Sept. 19 by voice vote an amendment offered by Wilson that would make "emergency relief" available to U.S. farmers if the Israel free-trade agreement resulted in a flood of imports of selected agricultural products.

Conference

House and Senate conferees moved quickly as adjournment neared. Although major components of the package — free trade with Israel, aid to domestic steel producers, import relief procedures for domestic wine-makers and the GSP extension — threatened to hang up the conference, conferees finished work Oct. 5.

After painstaking negotiations, most provisions opposed by the Reagan administration were dropped or softened by the conference.

Conferees agreed to authorize the president to negotiate a free-trade agreement with Israel. But the final agreement included additional, more restrictive, language authorizing free-trade negotiations with other countries.

The conference agreement also instructed the president to work to reduce steel imports to 17-20 percent of the domestic market. His enforcement of any negotiated limit was tied to the industry's efforts to reinvest earnings to modernize their operations. Most domestic steel producers also were required to spend 1 percent of net cash-flow for worker retraining.

A House provision extending for two years the Trade Adjustment Assistance Act, which aided workers who lost their jobs when imports caused domestic plant closings, was dropped.

The final version of HR 3398 excluded three intricate proposals that would have extended the range of foreign actions eligible for trade remedies. Lawmakers cut a provision, strongly opposed by the administration because it feared retaliation, to allow duties on imports made with natural resources heavily subsidized by foreign governments.

Also removed from the bill was a controversial provision to assess duties on unfairly priced exports from countries, such as China, whose economies are government-controlled. The administration strongly opposed the provision, which would have set a new standard for judging whether government-set prices were fair.

In addition, lawmakers dropped a proposal that would extend protection to U.S. producers against illegally priced exports shipped from one country but manufactured with another country's unfairly subsidized or priced parts.

In other major action, conferees:

● Extended the generalized system of preferences for 8.5 years. The conference tightened eligibility requirements for GSP privileges, but less severely than the House bill would have done.

● Adopted a watered-down wine equity provision instructing the U.S. trade representative to consult with major foreign wine producers to promote U.S. wine trade. Conferees also agreed to allow grape growers to join wine makers in bringing unfair trade practices cases.

● Asked the president to negotiate voluntary import restraints with leading foreign copper producers.

● Granted the president authority to negotiate reduced barriers to trade in services and investments abroad.

● Voted to extend to service industries the same remedies for some unfair foreign trade practices as already applied to goods.

Provisions

As cleared by Congress, HR 3398:

● Extended the GSP for eight and one-half years. For the first time, Congress tied GSP benefits to countries' steps to open markets to exports from the United States, honor patents and other intellectual property rights and respect workers' rights.

The bill denied GSP benefits to countries with annual per capita incomes of more than $8,500.

● Permitted administration officials to pursue talks with Israel on the establishment of a free-trade agreement between the two nations.

HR 3398 also approved a limited version of powers, long desired by the Office of the U.S. Trade Representative, to negotiate free-trade area agreements with other countries.

The administration had sought to lower or remove trade barriers on some Canadian products, but opposition from members, including some representing Canadian border states, scotched the plan. However, the administration could proceed with talks with Canada under the broader negotiating authority contained in HR 3398.

● Expanded administration authority to respond to other nations' trade practices. The trade reciprocity provisions authorized negotiations to reduce or remove barriers against trade in high-technology products, U.S. investment abroad and trade in services, such as banking. It also permitted the elimination of duties on some high-tech items for up to five years.

● Clarified the application of trade remedies enjoyed by goods to the service industries.

● Permitted the government to charge duties on unfairly priced goods exported to the United States made with various kinds of government-subsidized assistance, such as financing.

● Requested the administration to remove or reduce barriers to U.S. wine trade. Wine equity provisions in earlier versions of the bill had required the administration to ease obstacles impeding export of U.S. wine.

At the prompting of California grape growers, members also approved a proposal, opposed by the administration, to let grape growers join wine makers in filing unfair-trade complaints. The provision allowing growers to ask for relief expired in 1986.

● Instructed the president to negotiate voluntary copper import reductions with major foreign copper producers.

● Broadened the criteria by which the ITC could assess some kinds of import damage. The provision was designed with an eye toward reversing an ITC recommendation against relief for the shoe industry.

● Gave the president authority to enforce the voluntary restraints on steel imports he recommended Sept. 18. That authority was to be linked to steelmakers' commitment to modernizing operations and retraining workers.

Lawmakers also merged House and administration steel proposals, asking the president to reduce steel imports to between 17 percent and 20.2 percent of the U.S. market.

● Granted the U.S. Customs Service more power to confiscate property during drug-smuggling investigations. And authorized $729 million in fiscal 1985 for the Customs Service, the ITC and the Office of the U.S. Trade Representative. ∎

Energy Trade

Congress cleared legislation designed to help domestic manufacturers of renewable energy technology compete in the international market.

HR 3169 (H Rept 98-537, S Rept 98-508) had passed the House by voice vote Nov. 16, 1983. After approving a technical amendment, the Senate passed the measure, also by voice vote, on June 28. The House accepted the Senate amendment the next day and the measure was signed by the president July 18 (PL 98-370).

As enacted, HR 3169 required the commerce secretary to establish a government program aimed at promoting the export of U.S.-made renewable energy products. The measure also directed the commerce secretary to evaluate the status of the domestic renewable energy industry and its ability to compete in international markets and report his findings to Congress before May 31, 1985. And the legislation also established a federal interagency working group, chaired by the secretary of energy, to recommend government actions.

The House version had the commerce secretary heading the interagency working group, the Senate amendment made the Energy Department the lead agency.

Sponsored by Rep. Ron Wyden, D-Ore., the legislation was in response to growing international competition in the renewable energy technology business.

Such technology included photovoltaics (solar energy cells) and wind energy turbines. Because foreign governments actively promoted and subsidized the export of renewable energy products made in their countries, the share of the international market held by United States firms declined. ∎

Defense Production

Congress April 10 cleared for the president a bill (S 1852 — PL 98-265) reauthorizing the Defense Production Act, a 1950 law that gave the president various powers to guarantee the economic health of defense-related industries. The president signed the bill April 17.

The House approved the conference report on the bill (H Rept 98-651) by voice April 10. The Senate approved the conference report April 5. The House passed its version of S 1852 on Oct. 6, 1983. The Senate had acted Sept. 30, 1983. *(1983 Almanac p. 265)*

The bill reauthorized the Defense Production Act, which expired March 30, through Sept. 30, 1986. Under the act, the president had the power to offer financial incentives to ensure adequate supplies of materials and minerals vital to defense production.

S 1852 gave Congress new oversight authority over the president's powers to authorize loans and loan guarantees to defense-related industries. And for the first time since the law was enacted, the president was required to determine that defense projects covered by the act were essential to national defense. In addition, the legislation gave Congress 60 days' notice before new projects went forward.

The administration had sought a five-year extension of the existing law without the added restrictions.

The Defense Production Act had been granted temporary, six-month extensions since September 1982. ∎

Miscellaneous Tax Measures

In the rush of last-minute business before adjournment, the Senate Oct. 11 cleared for the president's signature several miscellaneous tax measures, including one (HR 2568 — PL 98-611) to continue through 1985 the tax-free status of employer-provided educational fringe benefits.

The Senate agreed to HR 2568 by voice vote. The president signed it Oct. 31.

The existing law that allowed for tax-free educational aid expired at the end of 1983. The new measure made the tax exclusion retroactive to Jan. 1, 1984, but it also imposed a new $5,000 limit on the amount of such benefits an individual could receive tax-free in a year.

The Senate also agreed to a House-passed measure (HR 5361 — PL 98-612) extending through 1985 the tax-free status of employer contributions to group legal service plans. The president signed it Oct. 31.

HR 5361 included a compromise agreement on a disputed real estate tax law that had threatened to hold up passage of a measure to increase the public debt limit. *(Debt limit, p. 165)*

Also cleared by voice vote in both chambers was a measure (HR 6112 — PL 98-601) to provide unemployment insurance tax relief to small businesses in Illinois. The president signed HR 6112 Oct. 30.

The Senate also used a stripped-down House tariff bill (HR 2163) as a vehicle for a number of special-interest tax proposals, which traditionally popped up in the final hours of a congressional session. But the House failed to act on the bill before the Oct. 12 adjournment. The measure included provisions to ease taxes for firms in West Virginia and South Carolina and another provision to allow taxpayers to help retire the federal debt with contributions on their federal tax returns.

Background

Many in Congress and the administration were concerned that the growth of fringe benefits in place of direct employee compensation was eroding the income tax base, leading to a loss of potential tax revenues.

Some restrictions on the tax-free status of fringe benefits were enacted earlier in 1984 as part of the Deficit Reduction Act of 1984 (PL 98-369), but agreement could not be reached on the educational assistance benefits during that debate because of disagreement over whether the benefits should be subject to Social Security payroll taxes. *(Deficit reduction, p. 143)*

House Action

The House approved the three tax measures — HR 5361, HR 2568 and HR 6112 — on Oct. 1, under suspension of the rules, which required a two-thirds majority for passage and prohibited all amendments.

By a vote of 300-87, the House approved HR 5361, extending the tax-free status of employer contributions to group legal service plans. *(Vote 375, p. 116-H)*

By voice vote, the House approved HR 2568 excluding from taxes employer-provided educational benefits. Also adopted by voice vote was the measure (HR 6112) providing small Illinois businesses with temporary relief from a January 1985 hike in federal unemployment taxes. The business owners had complained that a quirk in Illinois law prevented them from receiving the full credit allowed businesses in other states to offset the federal tax hike. The tax bills were approved by the House Ways and Means Committee Sept. 19 (HR 2568 — H Rept 98-1049; HR 5361 — H Rept 98-1050; and HR 6112 — H Rept 98-1043). ∎

Congress and Government

Although there were no changes in the House and Senate power structure in 1984, the way was paved for several key leadership changes in succeeding years.

In the Senate, there was a five-way contest to replace Majority Leader Howard H. Baker Jr., R-Tenn., who retired at the end of the 98th Congress. After a campaign of several months, Republican senators Nov. 28 chose Kansan Robert Dole as the new majority leader, starting in the 99th Congress. In addition, Senate Republicans put new people into five other GOP leadership slots for the 99th Congress.

In the House, Speaker Thomas P. O'Neill Jr., D-Mass., declared that he would retire in January 1987 at the end of the 99th Congress. O'Neill's announcement March 1 set off internal maneuvering for the top slots in the House Democratic leadership.

Neither of these changes directly affected business in 1984. But they both gave a sense of transition to the second session of the 98th Congress, as members prepared to usher in a new set of leaders in coming years.

Rumblings of discontent were heard in both parties in both chambers. Conservative House Republicans, frustrated by their minority status and their inability to get their legislative priorities on the House agenda, turned to confrontational tactics — a strategy occasionally at odds with that of their leaders.

Meanwhile, conservative House Democrats demanded a "voice at the table" in making party policy decisions, while a group of mid-level Democrats sought a broader role for themselves in leadership councils. And in the Senate, besides the changes in the GOP management scheduled for the 99th Congress, Democrats debated the need for new party leaders, even though they ultimately backed Robert C. Byrd, D-W.Va., when he was challenged by Lawton Chiles, D-Fla., for the minority leader's job in the 99th Congress.

Besides searching for new faces in their leadership, senators also examined changes in their rules to help the Senate function more effectively. A 12-member Temporary Select Committee to Study the Senate Committee System was appointed in June to recommend ways to streamline the unwieldy committee structure.

The special committee, headed by Dan Quayle, R-Ind., Nov. 29 suggested several changes, including rigorous enforcement of the rule allowing senators to serve on only three committees. The Quayle panel also proposed some alterations in Senate procedures to reduce the parliamentary tangles that often ensnarled the Senate. The panel's proposals were to be introduced as a resolution in the 99th Congress, to be considered by the Rules Committee.

Television Dispute

Broadcasts of congressional business were a volatile issue in both chambers in 1984.

Wth his Senate term about to run out, Baker in September tried one last time to convince his colleagues to allow gavel-to-gavel television and radio broadcasts of Senate proceedings.

But even though such broadcasts were Baker's pet project, the Senate refused to enter the television age. After a weeklong filibuster against a bill authorizing the broadcasts, Baker acknowledged that opposition was too strong, and he pulled the proposal from the floor.

It was a different story in the House, where live broadcasts of daily House proceedings have been under way since 1979.

The House broadcasts came of age in 1984 when a group of Young Turk Republicans began using them to promote their conservative agenda. The Republicans, organized under the banner of the Conservative Opportunity Society, reserved blocks of floor time in the evening to deliver speeches on conservative issues and attacks on Democratic policies to the growing TV audience. Some 17 million homes nationwide were wired to receive the broadcasts via C-SPAN, the Cable Satellite Public Affairs Network.

After months of needling by the junior Republicans, Democrats began to protest. The gloves came off in the "TV war" on May 15, when O'Neill and Georgia's Newt Gingrich, a leader of the Young Turk Republicans, got into a shouting match on the House floor — a fight that led to the official chastisement of O'Neill for using derogatory words about another member.

The catalyst for the blowup was O'Neill's unilateral decision to have TV cameras pan the chamber during the end-of-the-day speeches, to show viewers that the room was often empty. Previously, the camera focused only on the member speaking.

After the angry clash between O'Neill and Gingrich — a symbol of the polarization between Democrats and Republicans that lasted all year — members considered ways to revamp TV broadcasts of House proceedings. Republicans wanted to bar the use of funds to pan the House chamber unless it was done uniformly from gavel to gavel, while some Democrats favored pulling the plug on the broadcasts altogether.

At their caucus meeting in early December, House Democrats considered limiting the time reserved for "special order" speeches at the end of each day. But the plan was shelved after Republicans protested that the change was a "gag rule" and liberal Democrats voiced concern about restraints on free speech.

Balance of Power

Despite a 1983 Supreme Court decision that declared the legislative veto unconstitutional, there were no signs in 1984 that the balance of power between Congress and the executive branch had tilted toward the executive branch.

Instead, Congress continued to include legislative-veto

provisions in bills it passed in 1984, while also adjusting existing statutes to make them conform to the Supreme Court's ruling. The legislative veto — a tool by which a single congressional committee, one house of Congress or both the House and Senate could overturn an executive branch regulation or order — still was inserted into at least 11 different bills, according to one study.

In another court case in 1984, Congress scored a victory over the executive branch when a federal appeals court ruled that President Reagan acted unconstitutionally when he used a pocket veto in November 1983 to reject legislation involving aid to El Salvador. The court indicated that the president did not have the authority to veto a bill by "pocketing" it — taking no action — between the first and second sessions of the same Congress.

Yet in its own internal affairs, Congress lost a round when the Supreme Court Nov. 26 left intact a lower court ruling that members of Congress may be sued for job bias by Capitol Hill employees who are not involved in the legislative process. The decision reinstated a sex discrimination suit against Rep. Ed Jones, D-Tenn., by a House food service manager he had fired in 1982.

Even though members of Congress have immunity in lawsuits related to official actions they take in Congress, by allowing this case to proceed, the Supreme Court opened the door to further challenges to congressional immunity.

Ethical Problems

Two House members and one senator came under the scrutiny of congressional ethics committees during 1984, largely for alleged misdeeds involving their spouses' financial dealings.

Rep. Geraldine A. Ferraro of New York, the 1984 Democratic vice presidential nominee, came under investigation by the House Committee on Standards of Official Conduct after allegations were made that she violated the 1978 Ethics in Government Act by failing to adequately disclose her husband's financial holdings. In December, the ethics panel voted that Ferraro technically had violated the ethics law about 10 times through errors or insufficient information on her financial disclosure forms from 1978 to 1983.

In another financial disclosure case, the House July 31 reprimanded George Hansen, R-Idaho, for failing to reveal various financial dealings that must be disclosed under the Ethics in Government Act. The House action followed Hansen's federal court conviction on a charge of filing false disclosure statements concerning nearly $334,000 in loans and profits involving himself and his wife.

On the Senate side, Mark O. Hatfield, R-Ore., came under investigation by the Senate Ethics Committee because of questions about the propriety of a $55,000 payment by Greek entrepreneur Basil A. Tsakos to Hatfield's wife, Antoinette. Hatfield, who helped Tsakos promote a trans-African pipeline, said his wife earned the money for real estate work she performed for Tsakos. In late September, the ethics panel voted to drop its staff review of Hatfield's dealings with the Greek businessman after concluding there was insufficient evidence of wrongdoing.

Pay Controversy

The Senate wanted to rescind a congressional pay raise in 1984, but the House never went along. In January, the Senate voted to revoke the $2,400 cost-of-living increase members automatically received Jan. 1. But the House ignored the Senate's symbolic sign of budget austerity, and buried the salary rollback in committee. As a result, the raise stayed in effect all year for members of both chambers. Combined with another slight increase in April, members earned $72,600 in 1984.

For federal employees, Congress passed legislation changing the merit pay system for managers in civil service grades 13-15. For these employees, who were given raises based on performance evaluations, the bill established a uniform five-tiered rating system for employees, and allowed cash awards for exceptional performers.

Congress set aside, however, a proposed study of possible sex discrimination in the federal work force. The pay equity study was dropped from the merit pay bill after a commitment was made to its proponents that the issue would be considered in 1985.

—By Diane Granat

One FOIA Bill Clears, But Overhaul Bill Stalls

Congress cleared one bill in 1984 granting the Central Intelligence Agency (CIA) an exemption from some provisions of the 18-year-old Freedom of Information Act (FOIA). But a major revision of the law that passed the Senate in February — the first such revision in a decade — was never reported out of House committee.

President Reagan signed HR 5164 (PL 98-477) on Oct. 15, authorizing the CIA director to close certain operational files from FOIA review. Although the files themselves were usually found to be exempt from disclosure, the CIA had requested, and under the new law received, a waiver from FOIA search and review requirements for those files.

A second, much more inclusive bill (S 774), passed the Senate by voice vote Feb. 27 after minimal debate, incorporating a number of administration-requested changes in FOIA to make it easier for agencies to close files from public view. The bill also incorporated changes sought by news organizations, including financial incentives for agencies to comply with the act's deadlines for responding to FOIA requests.

Although that bill, which was the result of three years of compromise and negotiations, passed the Senate with relative ease, it was quickly bottled up in the House Government Operations Committee, where it died.

Background

The FOIA, originally enacted in 1966 (PL 89-487), required the federal government and its agencies to make available to citizens, upon request, all documents and records except those that fell into specified exempt categories.

In 1974, over President Ford's veto, Congress strengthened the law, imposing deadlines for agencies to respond to requests and permitting federal judges to review agency decisions to classify certain material. *(1974 Almanac p. 648)*

Upon taking office, President Reagan began an effort to curtail the availability of access to government information in several ways.

The proposed wholesale revision of FOIA and the proposal to tighten access to CIA files were part of that effort. The administration also proposed to expand the use of polygraphs and require lifetime pre-publication review of everything written by some 120,000 federal workers. A bill (HR 4681) to prevent that action failed. *(Story, p. 183)*

CIA Exemption

The Senate Sept. 28 by voice vote cleared and sent to the president HR 5164, authorizing the CIA director to close certain operational files from review under the FOIA.

The House had passed the bill Sept. 19, by a 369-36 vote. The Senate, which had passed a similar bill (S 1324) in November 1983, accepted the House version, which gave courts more latitude to review challenges to agency decisions. *(Vote 356, p. 108-H)*

Background

The Freedom of Information Act applied to the CIA as it did to any other federal agency. In response to any request for records, the agency had to search its files for applicable material, review it to see what portions might be disclosed and what portions were exempt, and disclose all parts that were not exempt and could be separated from exempt matter.

The CIA argued that its operational files were almost always found to be exempt, and that search and review requirements were an unproductive and unnecessary burden on the agency. The CIA also argued that if it were relieved of some of its search and review requirements, it could respond in a more timely manner to other FOIA requests.

As cleared, the bill defined operational files to include records relating to the identities of sources and methods, and to the routine administration and management of intelligence activities.

HR 5164 continued to require the agency to search files in response to FOIA requests by individuals about themselves, or requests for information regarding covert actions or suspected CIA improprieties. And the bill reversed a ruling by the Justice Department and the Office of Management and Budget that invoked the Privacy Act to deny individuals FOIA access to information about themselves. Despite that provision, the Reagan administration supported the bill.

The measure also required the agency to report to Congress on its implementation of the bill.

Joining the CIA in support of the bill was the American Civil Liberties Union (ACLU), primarily because of expectations that the agency would be more prompt in releasing files that were not exempt. Because of objections by its Southern California chapter, the ACLU general counsel reviewed the group's position on the bill, but it did not withdraw its support.

Nevertheless, HR 5164 faced opposition from some press organizations, who argued that it would give the CIA director too much latitude in closing files that might otherwise be available under FOIA.

Ted Weiss, D-N.Y., who led the opposition in Congress, said the bill "would dangerously intrude on the power of courts to review the actions of the CIA and would likely limit legitimate public access to CIA documents." Weiss noted cases of CIA activities revealed through FOIA requests, and said HR 5164 would make similar discoveries more difficult.

Weiss also said that the bill would restrict judicial review of documents that the agency had withheld, by allowing the agency to send the court a written summary of documents in their place. But, if a plaintiff had personal knowledge that files should not be withheld, a court would have to order the CIA to search and review the files.

Legislative History

A Senate bill (S 1324), which was very similar to HR 5164, was reported unanimously by the Senate Select Committee on Intelligence Nov. 9, 1983 (S Rept 98-305). By voice vote, the Senate passed the bill Nov. 17, 1983.

The House bill was reported May 1 by the House Select Committee on Intelligence (H Rept 98-726, Part I).

The House Government Operations Subcommittee on Government Information July 25 voted in favor of HR 5164, after adding several amendments to the House Intelligence Committee version.

One amendment was designed to ensure greater oversight of the bill, by requiring the CIA to submit four semiannual public reports on its implementation of and compliance with the bill. The second amendment was designed to eliminate use of the Privacy Act to deny individuals FOIA access to information about themselves.

Over the objections of Weiss, the House Government Operations Committee July 31 approved HR 5164. The bill was reported by the committee Sept. 10 (H Rept 98-726, Part II).

FOIA Overhaul

As reported by the Senate Judiciary Committee Sept. 12, 1983, the more sweeping rewrite of the information act (S 774 — S Rept 98-221) was nearly identical to a bill reported by the panel in the 97th Congress. That bill never made it to the floor. *(1982 Almanac p. 521)*

S 774 would have allowed the attorney general to withhold information about law enforcement and investigations of organized crime, given agencies more time to release records and made it more difficult to obtain information submitted by businesses to the government.

It also would have imposed uniform fees, based on the actual cost of processing FOIA requests, to search for, process and copy requested government information. It would have waived those fees automatically for journalists, scholars and non-profit groups.

Before passing the bill, the Senate deleted one provision contained in the committee version, and amended another.

One provision, inserted by the committee at the request of the Department of Defense, would have exempted from disclosure technical data that could not legally be exported outside the United States. After the Judiciary Committee approved S 774, however, Congress passed the fiscal 1984 defense authorization bill (S 675 — PL 98-94), including the technical data exemption. The Senate struck that section from the bill.

A second floor amendment clarified that fees to be assessed for processing requests for commercially valuable technical information would be user fees, not royalties. The word "royalty" led some senators to question if S 774 was allowing the government to claim a copyright, which it was forbidden to do.

Orrin G. Hatch, R-Utah, chief sponsor of S 774, said the bill represented a compromise between those who wanted broad exemptions to FOIA and those who wanted to expand the flow of information. It "eliminates many of the current problems of the act without weakening its effectiveness as a valuable means of keeping the public informed about government activities," Hatch said.

Similarly, Patrick J. Leahy, D-Vt., who fought administration efforts to weaken the act, said S 774 "recognizes the legitimate complaints of some agencies and submitters, while maintaining FOIA's major premises and all of its principal features."

Rep. Glenn English, D-Okla., chairman of the House Government Operations Subcommittee on Government Information, was skeptical of claims that the basic law needed revision, and moved slowly on S 774. His subcommittee held hearings on the bill, but never took a vote.

"I don't think there's much question" that the administration has pursued a policy of keeping information from the public, English said. One Justice Department official called his subcommittee the "black hole of freedom of information reform."

Major Provisions

As passed by the Senate, S 774 would have:

Fees and Waivers

• Authorized the Office of Management and Budget to promulgate guidelines to all federal agencies to establish a uniform schedule of fees.

• Permitted agency fee schedules to provide for recovery of the costs of reviewing records to determine what material should be released and what should be withheld.

• Permitted agencies to assess a "fair value fee," in addition to other processing fees, in the case of a request for records containing commercially valuable technical information generated or procured by the government at substantial cost to the public.

• Required agencies to waive fees for scholars, representatives of the news media and non-profit groups; prohibited fee waivers if the material was for commercial use.

• Permitted agencies to retain one-half of the fees they collected, if they were in substantial compliance with the time limits in the act; required agencies to apply that money to offset their own costs of complying with FOIA disclosure requirements.

Time Limits

• Provided for an extension of 30 working days for agencies to respond to requests and appeals, in addition to the existing deadline of 10 working days for a response to an initial request and 20 working days for response to an appeal. The total period for responding should not exceed 60 working days, except under "exceptional circumstances."

• Permitted extensions where the head of an agency specified in writing that processing a request would interfere with the timely performance of a statutory agency function; where an agency must notify submitters of information in order to consider objections to disclosure; and where an agency had "an unusually large" volume of requests or appeals.

• Required agencies to promulgate regulations to enable a requester who demonstrated a compelling need for expedited processing to be given priority over other requesters.

Business Confidentiality

• Required agencies to promulgate regulations specifying procedures by which submitters of trade secrets or confidential commercial or financial information could present claims of confidentiality; required agencies to notify submitters when they planned to release such information; permitted the submitter to object in writing.

• Waived the notification requirement when an agency decided a request should be denied; if the submitter failed to substantially comply with the confidentiality rule, or if a law enforcement agency acquired the information in the course of a lawful criminal investigation.

Judicial Review

• Required that suits by requesters to release information denied to them be brought within 180 days of the agency's final administrative action.

• Required agencies to notify requesters and submitters whenever a suit was brought concerning a particular request or submission, and required equal treatment for both sides in the action.

• Allowed district courts to enjoin an agency from disclosing information if a submitter objected to disclosure. Submitter actions must be brought before the documents were released.

● Provided that a court may require a submitter to pay the attorneys' fees of a requester who has substantially prevailed in the litigation. Under existing case law, courts may award attorneys' fees against agencies.

Law Enforcement Records

● Broadened the exemption of law enforcement records and information regarding law enforcement techniques to include all law enforcement records and techniques, investigatory or non-investigatory.

● Broadened exemptions for protection of enforcement proceedings, personal privacy, identities of confidential sources and the life and physical safety of persons.

● Expanded the definition of confidential sources that could be protected to include state, local and foreign agencies and private institutions; exempted all information furnished by confidential sources, whether or not it was available elsewhere.

● Excluded from the requirements of the act information and records maintained by a law enforcement agency under an informant's name or other identifying name, if the requester was a third party seeking access by those names.

Other Provisions

Public Record Requests. Permitted an agency, where a portion of the records requested consisted of public record, to furnish an index of the publicly available materials instead of the materials themselves, or provide the materials at the reasonable standard charge or, at the agency's discretion, at no charge.

Internal Manuals, Examination Materials. Exempted from disclosure materials related to an agency's internal personnel rules and practices; required agencies to demonstrate that disclosure could reasonably be expected to jeopardize its investigations, inspections or audits.

Privacy. Clarified that information about an individual would be exempt from the act whether or not it was filed under personnel or medical files; expanded the exemption to include information that could reasonably be expected to constitute an invasion of privacy or that could be used for solicitation purposes.

Secret Service. Exempted from the act information or records maintained by the Secret Service if the agency determined that disclosure could be expected to harm its ability to perform its protective functions.

'Jigsaw Puzzle' Problem. Permitted an agency, in deciding whether the release of particular information would be harmful, to take into account other information it knew or believed to be available to the requester.

Request Restrictions. Prohibited FOIA requests by foreign nationals; also authorized the attorney general to prescribe limitations or conditions on the use of the act by convicted felons.

Discovery. Prohibited a party to a judicial proceeding in which the government was also a party from using FOIA to obtain records that could be sought through the discovery procedure.

Organized Crime. Exempted from the act documents generated or acquired by a law enforcement authority in the course of an organized crime investigation within five years of the date of the request; provided that no document subject to this exclusion could be destroyed until

the document had been available for disclosure for a period of at least 10 years.

Agency Reports. Required agencies to report to Congress by March 1 each year on their Freedom of Information activities during the previous calendar year.

Statutory Exemptions. Required agencies, within 270 days of enactment, to compile a list of laws other than FOIA that exempted information from disclosure under FOIA.

Polygraph Curb Fails to Pass

A bill to curb the federal government's use of lie detector tests was reported by two House committees, but did not get to the House floor in 1984.

The House Post Office and Civil Service Committee Aug. 6 reported the bill (HR 4681 — H Rept 98-961, Part I). And the House Armed Services Committee Sept. 21 became the second panel to report the bill (H Rept 98-961, Part II).

The Judiciary Committee and the Permanent Select Committee on Intelligence also shared jurisdiction over the measure, but the two panels did not file reports. There was no similar bill introduced in the Senate.

HR 4681, as approved by the House Post Office and Civil Service Committee June 27, would have prohibited agencies from requiring employees or applicants for employment to submit to polygraphs, except for criminal investigations.

The bill also would have cancelled any existing contracts granting the government pre-publication review over writings of federal employees who were authorized to deal with sensitive materials. It would have banned such contracts in the future.

The bill exempted the Central Intelligence Agency and the National Security Agency. Other agencies, such as the FBI, planned to seek exemptions.

The House Armed Services Committee unanimously approved HR 4681, after endorsing the recommendation of its Investigations Subcommittee to give a partial exemption to the Department of Defense.

The subcommittee amendment would have allowed the use of polygraphs for seven specific purposes, primarily to clear individuals for access to high-level security information. Bill Nichols, D-Ala., chairman of the Investigations Subcommittee and author of the amendment, said that polygraphs had been useful in detecting and deterring espionage.

In 1983, according to Armed Services staff, the Pentagon conducted about 3,500 polygraph tests. A provision in the Senate version of the fiscal 1985 defense authorization bill (HR 5167) limited the department to 3,500 tests in fiscal 1985. That provision was included in the defense authorization conference report (H Rept 98-1080) and became law (PL 98-525). *(Story, p. 37)*

Background

HR 4681 was introduced in response to a proposed Reagan administration initiative, contained in National Security Decision Directive 84, that would have required about 120,000 employees with access to sensitive classified information to submit their writings for review.

The directive, issued in March 1983, also would have stepped up the government's use of polygraphs and imposed penalties on employees who refused to submit to polygraphs.

The proposed directive was aimed at curbing leaks of classified information, but it provoked an outcry in Congress. In response, the administration announced in February that it had suspended the directive for the rest of 1984.

Supporters of the bill said that despite that assurance,

agencies continued to use polygraphs and to require employees to sign contracts agreeing that they would submit their writings for pre-publication review. The General Accounting Office reported in June that 156,000 military and civilian employees had been required to sign pre-publication review agreements, and that the Defense Department planned to expand greatly its use of polygraphs. ∎

Few Grace Commission Budget Cuts Adopted

During his re-election campaign in 1984, Ronald Reagan regularly held up as his blueprint for second-term budget cuts a 47-volume report issued in January 1984 by the President's Private Sector Survey on Cost Control.

Better known as the Grace commission, after its chairman, industrialist J. Peter Grace, the panel listed 2,478 recommendations that it claimed would save $424 billion over three years. The commission recommended changes in management and programs in 36 areas in the federal government, ranging from civil service pensions to data processing to entitlement programs.

The commission, composed of 161 top business and organization executives, emphasized a shift to what it called sound business practices to eliminate waste. It predicted that the government's multibillion-dollar deficits could be virtually wiped out by the year 2000 "without raising taxes, without weakening America's needed defense build-up, and without harming in any way necessary social welfare programs."

Almost a year after the report was issued, however, fewer than a fifth of the recommendations had been implemented, according to the White House. Most of those were management reforms within the administration.

In the face of objections that the anticipated savings were overstated and that many recommendations would require controversial changes of policy, Congress showed little inclination to follow the commission's lead. Only a handful of the commission's proposals that required Congress' approval were enacted, with projected savings of just over $3 billion.

Claims Disputed

In February, an analysis done jointly by the non-partisan Congressional Budget Office (CBO) and the General Accounting Office (GAO) disputed the claims of the Grace commission. CBO and GAO examined many of the commission's recommendations, representing 89 percent of the anticipated savings, and estimated that they would save $98 billion over three years, a third of the amount estimated by Grace.

Noting that the biggest savings could only come from changes in federal programs enacted by Congress — not through administrative action — the CBO-GAO report said that most of the recommendations should be characterized as policy changes, not as improvements in efficiency or elimination of waste.

Among the anticipated three-year savings that would require major policy adjustments, the commission proposed:

● Requiring a means test to determine if recipients of federal social welfare payments, such as Social Security, food stamps and Medicare, really needed these benefits. Savings: $59 billion.

● Scaling down civil service and military retirement benefits, which the Grace panel claimed were three to six times higher than the best private plans. Savings: $61 billion.

● Repealing the Davis-Bacon Act, which required federal contractors to pay higher wages than they otherwise would in certain areas. Savings: $5 billion.

● "Privatizing" the agencies that sold federally generated electricity, an action that was predicted to approximately triple the price of hydroelectric power in the Northwest. Savings: $20 billion.

Such changes "represent tough decisions with difficult trade-offs," CBO and GAO observed.

One key recommendation that Congress repeatedly refused to accept was that the president be given item veto power. That would have allowed him to knock out particular items to which he objected, without vetoing large bills — particularly appropriations bills — in their entirety.

As sound as the commission's recommendations might have seemed to the business world, many of them proved politically treacherous over the past two decades.

For example, President Carter had little success convincing Congress to cut questionable water projects, as suggested by the Grace commission. President Ford had even less success getting Congress to cut the subsidy for commissaries, the military's grocery stores.

Some Savings Implemented

In a report issued July 18, the White House Office of Cabinet Affairs noted that $40.9 billion, or 9.6 percent of the total projected Grace commission savings, had been implemented.

Included in the total already saved was $2.4 billion from increasing contributions and reducing benefits under the railroad retirement system, as provided by legislation (PL 98-76) restoring the solvency of the system. *(1983 Almanac p. 272)*

The total also included $2.7 billion saved from reducing the backlog in collecting delinquent taxes, $2.6 billion saved by paying bills on time, $2.1 billion saved by speeding up the deposit of funds received by the government, and $1.1 billion by adjusting the fill rate and construction schedule of the Strategic Petroleum Reserve.

Another $62.6 billion in savings was proposed in the administration's fiscal 1985 budget, the White House report said. Most of the fiscal 1985 budget proposals drawn from the commission report were ignored or rejected by Congress, including savings of $5.2 billion from reducing the grades of 31,000 federal employees, and $1.3 billion from charging user fees for deep port and inland navigation.

Several recommendations of the Grace commission were included as provisions of the deficit reduction act (HR

4170 — PL 98-369). These were expected to save $3.2 billion. *(Story, p. 143)*

One, which allowed the Treasury Department in limited cases to deduct from an individual's tax refund uncollected government debts, such as student loan repayments, was expected to save $800 million. Other Grace debt collection recommendations had been previously incorporated in the Debt Collection Act of 1982 (PL 97-365). *(1982 Almanac p. 520)*

Another provision of the deficit reduction act was acceleration of the collection and deposit of non-tax receipts, such as customs duties. That provision was expected to save $1.6 billion over three years.

A third provision improved the procedures for verifying an applicant's income in determining eligibility for means-tested programs, such as food stamps. The act authorized the Internal Revenue Service to disclose information about an applicant's unearned income, such as interest and dividends, to state and federal agencies administering the programs, and required states to implement a system for verifying income and eligibility for the programs. This provision was expected to save $800 million over three years.

Other provisions of HR 4170 implemented Grace recommendations, but the exact amount of their savings was unclear. One such provision required the Social Security Administration to obtain earnings reports from beneficiaries several months earlier than in prior law, in order to improve enforcement of restrictions on the amount Social Security recipients could earn without having their benefits reduced.

And the act required agencies to reduce spending on federal travel, consulting fees, printing and motor vehicle costs by an unspecified amount.

Congress Criticized

One of the 47 volumes of the Grace commission report — "The Cost of Congressional Encroachment" — claimed that a large chunk of federal waste stemmed from members' efforts to bring water projects, military bases and federal offices to their districts, and to keep them there.

In addition to pork-barreling, it charged Congress with interfering in day-to-day executive agency decisions on pay scales, employee reorganizations and contracting.

The report pinned responsibility on Congress for approximately 100 examples of what the commission considered wasteful spending. An end to congressional interference in day-to-day agency management could save $7.8 billion in costs and snag $1.1 billion in new revenues over three years, the report said.

While it cited a litany of examples, the "Congressional Encroachment" report left gaping blanks where the names of Congress members, projects, states and communities had been deleted from earlier staff drafts.

Grace explained the deletions by saying: "We wanted to expose the system and not attack individuals, who are merely a product, and the innocent tools, of a failed culture." The report further explained that Congress' support was needed to carry out the Grace panel's recommendations. ∎

Whistleblower Awards

Congress refused — under pressure from the Reagan administration — to renew a program that authorized cash awards to federal employees who blew the whistle on waste, fraud and mismanagement in the government, and to extend existing legal protections for whistleblowers.

House sponsors promised to try to revive the awards program in early 1985.

Both the House and Senate passed a bill (HR 5646) that would have extended for three years the grants program, which began in 1981 and expired Sept. 30, 1984.

The administration had not opposed continuing the awards program, but objected to a last-minute Senate amendment that would have given federal courts jurisdiction over complaints that whistleblowers had been harassed on the job for reporting waste or fraud. The bill died in the closing hours of the session, when the House refused to accept the Senate amendment.

House Action. The House Post Office and Civil Service Committee Sept. 19 unanimously approved the bill (H Rept 98-1053). The House then passed the bill by voice vote Sept. 24.

Under the bill, as passed by the House:

● Agency inspectors general could have handed out awards totaling $10,000 or 1 percent of the cost-saving to federal employees who disclosed waste or fraud, and the president could give up to 50 awards of $20,000 each a year.

● At the request of the Department of Defense, the bill would have allowed the Pentagon's inspector general to grant cash awards to whistleblowers who were members of the armed services.

● The General Accounting Office (GAO) would have been asked to review the program by March 16, 1987.

● The GAO also would have been asked to make a cost-benefit study of a day-care system for the children of federal employees.

Senate Action. After three amendments — one substantive, two non-controversial — were added on the floor, the bill passed the Senate by voice vote Oct. 11.

The troublesome amendment, sponsored by Sen. Charles E. Grassley, R-Iowa, and supported by Merit System Protection Board Special Counsel K. William O'Connor, would have permitted the special counsel to appeal complaints of retribution or harassment of whistleblowers by their superiors to federal court.

When the merit board was created in 1978 (PL 95-454), the special counsel was authorized to investigate allegations of illegal personnel practices, such as retribution or harassment. Under existing law, the merit board had final jurisdiction to rule on such complaints. *(1978 Almanac p. 818)*

House Objections. Reps. Bill Frenzel, R-Minn., and George C. Wortley, R-N.Y., who were acting for the administration, objected to the substantive Senate amendment, and the bill died.

The Justice Department complained that confusion and bad precedent could come from having its lawyers defend an agency accused of intimidating a whistleblower, while the merit board's attorneys defended the board's actions and the special counsel represented the employee. All the attorneys involved in such a case would be paid by the government.

The whistleblower awards program was created by the Omnibus Budget Reconciliation Act of 1981 (PL 97-35), as a trial program to expire in 1984. *(1981 Almanac p. 396)*

Over the three years of the program's existence, inspectors general gave awards totaling $8,800, for cost-savings estimated at more than $1 million. The president gave no awards. ∎

Reagan Vetoes First Comprehensive NOAA Bill

President Reagan Oct. 19 pocket-vetoed a bill (S 1097) authorizing programs for the National Oceanic and Atmospheric Administration (NOAA) for fiscal 1985-86. Reagan said several provisions of the NOAA authorization would have hampered the agency's management ability. *(Veto message, p. 24-E)*

Both House and Senate on Oct. 3 adopted the conference report on the bill (H Rept 98-1093), which authorized $852 million in fiscal 1984, $929 million in fiscal 1985 and $258 million in fiscal 1986 for atmospheric, satellite and oceanic programs of the National Oceanic and Atmospheric Administration, clearing the measure for the president.

The fiscal 1984 authorization was identical to the agency's appropriation for that year, but by the time the conference report was adopted, fiscal 1985 had begun. Money for NOAA was included in the Commerce Department's fiscal 1985 appropriations bill. *(Story, p. 373)*

The conference report authorized $246 million more in fiscal 1985 than the amount approved by the House, and $28 million less than approved by the Senate. The final authorization was identical to the spending level in the fiscal 1985 Commerce Department appropriations bill (HR 5712 — PL 98-411), which included NOAA.

Members of both houses characterized the bill as part of the first comprehensive authorization for the agency since it was created by executive order in 1970. Previous NOAA authorizations had been included in a variety of bills covering programs relating to the environment, and weather and ocean research.

A companion bill (S 1098), which included authorizations for sea-grant college programs and some ocean research, passed both houses in different forms in 1983. The different versions were never resolved, however, and the bill died. Provisions of a second companion bill (S 1100) were included in the final version of S 1097. A third companion bill (S 1099), which only covered fiscal 1984, was enacted in 1983.

President's Objections

The provisions in S 1097 to which Reagan objected were those:

● Requiring the secretary of commerce to provide 60 days' notice and hold public hearings before closing or consolidating weather service or weather service forecast offices. Reagan said that would virtually preclude closing or consolidating those offices.

● Requiring 30 days' notice before NOAA could seek bids from the private sector to contract out services, such as nautical chart-making. That, Reagan said, would result in "excessive and unjustifiable delays."

● Limiting transfer to the Navy of a weather satellite, known as NOAA-D. Reagan said that would "require the inefficient use of a government asset."

Similar, but less restrictive, language governing transfer of the satellite had been included earlier in PL 98-411, NOAA's fiscal 1985 appropriation. *(Story, p. 373)*

Reagan rejected the NOAA authorization with a "pocket veto," which occurred when the president did not sign the bill and Congress was not in session. If the president had not signed the bill within 10 days of receiving it, excluding Sundays, and Congress had been in session, it would have become law.

Legislative Action

The Senate Committee on Commerce, Science and Transportation reported S 1097 in May 1983 (S Rept 98-109) as one of a package of authorization bills for NOAA.

Also in May 1983, the House Committee on Science and Technology reported HR 2900, a similar authorization for NOAA (H Rept 98-135, Part I).

In addition to authorizing spending levels for various NOAA operations, the House bill and S 1097 contained provisions prohibiting NOAA from selling the nation's weather satellites to private firms. Strong congressional opposition to such a sale developed following the March 1983 administration announcement that it wished to sell the satellites separately or as a package. Under the plan, the government would have bought back data from the satellites' new owners, distributing some free and some at a charge. *(1983 Almanac p. 587)*

Floor Action

The Senate by voice vote passed S 1097 and its three companion bills — S 1098, S 1099 and S 1100 — in June 1983.

The House by voice vote Jan. 26, 1984, passed its version of the authorization bill (HR 2900), after first substituting the language of a separate NOAA authorization bill (HR 3597), which had not been reported by committee.

The House then substituted the revised language of HR 2900 for the language of S 1097 and returned that bill to the Senate.

The House version of the bill authorized $650.9 million in fiscal 1984, the same amount as the fiscal 1984 appropriations for the agency (HR 3222 — PL 98-166), and $683.4 million in fiscal 1985.

The total spending level for fiscal 1984 was $104 million more than the Reagan administration requested, and included money for programs that the administration wanted to eliminate, such as the Great Lakes Environmental Research Laboratory.

Michael A. Andrews, D-Texas, offered an amendment requiring the agency to notify Congress 45 legislative days before contracting out to the private sector any services such as mapping and charting. Although Raymond J. McGrath, R-N.Y., said contracting out would reduce costs and "make the government more efficient," the House adopted Andrews' amendment by a 257-124 vote. *(Vote 10, p. 4-H)*

In addition, the House agreed by voice vote to an amendment offered by Norman E. D'Amours, D-N.H., requiring the National Weather Service, as part of its daily reporting service, to report on acid rain.

The Senate by unanimous consent April 12 substituted its own revised language for S 1097, and sent the bill to conference committee.

The Senate bill authorized $852 million in fiscal 1984, $957 million in fiscal 1985 and $258 million in fiscal 1986.

Satellite Sales. The question of selling government satellites continued to concern members of both houses during consideration of the NOAA authorization. The final House- and Senate-passed versions of S 1097 that went to conference had deleted provisions prohibiting sale of weather satellites. Similar provisions had been included in a variety of laws enacted in 1983.

But Congress was meanwhile considering a similar proposal to sell the government's Landsat satellites, which later passed. *(Story, p. 195)*

The proposed Landsat deal caused both the House and Senate to include a provision authorizing $4 million to plan for continuing a civil land-surveying satellite system, should problems develop after Landsat was sold.

And the Senate bill noted that NOAA was planning to sell one of its polar-orbiting weather satellites, known as NOAA-D, to the Navy for the Navy Remote Ocean Sensing System. The bill ordered NOAA to transfer the satellite to the Navy, but to ensure that data from it was made available for civilian navigation.

Companion Bills. S 1098 (S Rept 98-107), authorizing sea-grant college programs and some ocean research, was amended by the House and passed by voice vote in August 1983. It was reconsidered by the Senate in November 1983, amended further and passed again by voice vote. And on March 15, 1984, the House by unanimous consent amended the bill yet again and passed it. It was never again considered by the Senate and it died at the end of the 98th Congress.

S 1099 (S Rept 98-80), authorizing NOAA's marine fisheries program for fiscal 1984 only, was amended and passed the House Nov. 16, 1983. Two days later the Senate agreed to the House amendment, clearing the bill. The president signed S 1099 into law Dec. 6, 1983 (PL 98-210).

S 1100 (S Rept 98-105), authorizing NOAA's administrative functions, marine services and aircraft services, was never considered separately by the House. The programs covered by the bill were authorized in the final version of S 1097, however.

Conference Action

Conferees agreed to retain the Senate bill's spending figures for fiscal 1984 and 1986. For fiscal 1985, conferees compromised on spending.

Since the House bill made no mention of the NOAA-D satellite transfer and cautioning that the state of the weather satellite fleet was "precarious," conferees wrote new language making sale of the satellite contingent on a successful launch of a new satellite, NOAA-F. The conference report also required the Navy to reimburse NOAA for use of the satellite.

The satellite-sale language in S 1097 was written to supersede a similar restriction included in NOAA's appropriations bill (HR 5712 — PL 98-411). Language in the appropriations conference report (H Rept 98-952) said that NOAA-D could not be sold unless the secretary of commerce decided that NOAA did not need it, and the Navy paid for it and promised civil data from the satellite to NOAA.

Conferees also compromised on a provision restricting NOAA's plans to contract out some of its services. The House version had required NOAA to give Congress 45-days' notice before seeking bids to contract out services, but the final version required 30-days' notice. The Senate version required a 30-day notice before the issuance of a contract, rather than before bids were solicited.

Conferees agreed to drop Rep. D'Amours amendment requiring the weather service to report daily on acid rain. Rep. Don Fuqua, D-Fla., chairman of the House science committee said a hold had been placed on the bill in the Senate because of the provision. In order to pass the bill, Fuqua said, the provision must be dropped. ∎

Inspectors General

The House by voice vote Feb. 6 passed a bill (HR 3625) that would have established offices of inspector general in the departments of Treasury and Justice — the only Cabinet departments without them. The bill would have provided a uniform salary level for inspectors general, and authorized personnel in the offices of inspector general to administer oaths, affirmations and affidavits.

According to the Congressional Budget Office, the bill would have cost $110,000 in fiscal 1984, and $1.85 million over five years. Rep. Frank Horton, R-N.Y., citing a report by the President's Council on Integrity and Efficiency, said inspectors general saved $30.8 billion from March 1981 to February 1984.

The bill was reported by the House Government Operations Committee Dec. 7, 1983 (H Rept 98-586). After passing the House, it was referred to the Senate Governmental Affairs Committee, where it died. ∎

Federal Debt Collection

To help collect some of the estimated $40 billion in bad debts owed to the federal government, the Senate July 25 passed a bill (S 1668) authorizing the Justice Department to contract with private attorneys to litigate debt-collection cases. Sponsors Alfonse M. D'Amato, R-N.Y., and Charles H. Percy, R-Ill., said U.S. attorneys' offices were ill-equipped to handle the large volume of such cases.

The Committee on Governmental Affairs reported the bill June 12 (S Rept 98-511), noting that in 1984 the federal government was owed $40 billion in defaulted debts, including $25 billion in loans.

The Senate passed the bill 96-1 after adopting, 95-1, three amendments offered by Howard M. Metzenbaum, D-Ohio, aimed at keeping the costs of the private attorneys down. The amendments required the Justice Department to seek competitive bids and the attorney general to set limits on contingency fees for successful cases. *(Votes 178, 179, p. 31-S)*

The House Judiciary Committee, to which S 1668 was referred, did not report the Senate bill or a similar House bill (HR 5196). ∎

Earthquake Hazard Reduction

President Reagan signed into law March 22 a bill (S 820 — PL 98-241) reauthorizing federal earthquake hazards reduction and fire prevention programs.

The bill authorized $65.5 million in fiscal 1984 and $72.6 million in fiscal 1985 for four agencies to conduct research and set housing construction standards to prevent or ready the nation for future earthquakes.

The multiagency authorization involved programs conducted by the Federal Emergency Management Administration (FEMA), U.S. Geological Survey (USGS), the National Science Foundation (NSF) and the National Bureau of Standards.

The bill also authorized $15.7 million in fiscal 1984 and $21 million in fiscal 1985 for fire prevention and control programs of the U.S. Fire Administration, an agency of FEMA.

As cleared, the bill followed the House version (HR 2465), passed by voice vote Feb. 1. The House substituted the language of HR 2465 as an amendment to S 820. On March 8, the Senate by voice vote concurred in the House amendment, clearing the bill for the president. The Senate had passed S 820 by voice vote in April 1983. *(1983 Almanac p. 591)*

As reported in May 1983 by the House Interior and Science and Technology committees (H Rept 98-99, Parts I and II), HR 2465 authorized $67 million in fiscal 1984 for earthquake programs and $17.7 million for fire prevention, but the House adopted an amendment cutting money for NSF earthquake programs and FEMA fire programs to meet the levels contained in the 1984 Department of Housing and Urban Development/Independent Agencies appropriations bill (PL 98-45).

In addition, the House agreed to add money for fiscal 1985 for FEMA earthquake and fire programs, to meet the administration's recommendations. The House rejected an attempt to cut fiscal 1985 budgets for the USGS and NSF.

The Senate version of the bill, as reported in March 1983 by the Senate Commerce, Science and Transportation Committee (S Rept 98-42), authorized $61 million for earthquake programs in fiscal 1984, $65.7 million in fiscal 1985 and $70.7 million in fiscal 1986. The administration had requested only $60.5 million for fiscal 1984.

The Senate had passed a separate bill (S 809) in April 1983 authorizing fire prevention programs. That bill, reported by the Senate Commerce Committee in March 1983 (S Rept 98-41), authorized $14.7 million for fiscal 1984 and $15.5 million for fiscal 1985. ∎

Indian Aid Bill

President Reagan Oct. 4 signed into law a bill (S 2614 — PL 98-449) extending grants and loan guarantees for Indian economic development.

The reauthorization increased the amount that could be guaranteed to individuals from $100,000 to $250,000, and authorized up to $5.5 million in fiscal 1985 and thereafter for interest subsidies on guaranteed loans.

In addition, the law authorized up to $10 million in fiscal 1986 and thereafter for Indian business development grants, and increased the amount of grants from $50,000 to $100,000 to individuals and from $50,000 to $250,000 to tribes.

The Senate Committee on Indian Affairs reported the bill May 18 (S Rept 98-459) and the Senate passed the bill by voice vote June 8.

A similar House bill (HR 5519) was reported Sept. 5 by the House Committee on Interior and Insular Affairs (H Rept 98-991). The House passed HR 5519 by voice vote Sept. 11, and substituted the language of that bill for that of S 2614. The Senate by voice vote adopted the House version with a minor amendment Sept. 21. The House accepted the Senate amendment Sept. 24, clearing the bill for the president. ∎

Indian Reimbursement Bill

Citing a 22-year-old decision by the Indian Claims Commission, President Reagan Oct. 17 pocket-vetoed a bill (S 1967) that would have reimbursed the Gros Ventre and Assiniboine Tribes of the Fort Belknap Indian Community in Montana for irrigation construction between 1895 and 1913. *(Veto text, p. 24-E)*

When Congress is in session, a bill becomes law if the president does not sign it within 10 days of receiving it, excluding Sundays. If Congress has adjourned within that 10-day period, the president may pocket-veto the bill by not acting upon it.

S 1967 would have required the Treasury to pay the community nearly $107,760, plus 4 percent annual interest, for a total of $457,000. A claim for the same reimbursement was dismissed by the Indian Claims Commission on Nov. 20, 1962.

The bill was reported by the Senate Committee on Indian Affairs April 18 (S Rept 98-406) and passed the Senate by voice vote June 26.

The House Committee on Interior and Insular Affairs reported the bill Sept. 28 (H Rept 98-1094). S 1967 passed the House by voice vote Oct. 2 under suspension of the rules, which required a two-thirds majority, thus clearing the bill for the president. ∎

Indian Health Care

President Reagan Oct. 19 pocket-vetoed a bill (S 2166) reauthorizing Indian health care programs for four years. In his veto message, Reagan did not object to the spending levels authorized in the bill. Instead, he criticized a new demonstration program that would have made Indians in Montana who were eligible for state and local health services for the indigent also eligible for Indian Health Service (IHS) programs. *(Veto text, p. 25-E)*

Reagan said the new program would reduce access to health services by making Montana's Indians ineligible for state and local services unless IHS services were exhausted.

He also criticized as unconstitutional a provision changing the status of the IHS.

Money for the Indian Health Service was contained in the continuing resolution that made appropriations for fiscal 1985 (H J Res 648 — PL 98-473).

Legislative History

Sponsors of the bill, which was two years in the making, claimed it would raise Indian health care to national standards by increasing manpower, upgrading health facilities, and providing modern water and sanitation systems to many Indian communities.

S 2166 would have authorized training of health-care professionals, programs to alleviate deficiencies in Indian health, and services for Indians in urban areas. The bill also would have established a new $12 million catastrophic health emergency fund, and authorized reimbursement to the IHS for services provided to Indians eligible for Medicaid and Medicare.

The bill would have elevated the IHS to the same level as the Health Resources and Services Administration under the Public Health Service; the IHS was a component of the Health Resources Administration. The reorganization was to be delayed while a blue-ribbon panel determined if the change would improve the delivery of health care. If the panel found the change would not work, an additional six-month delay would have been allowed to give Congress time to repeal the reorganization.

The bill also would have authorized a National Academy of Sciences' study of nuclear resource development and associated health hazards for miners and Indian communities near uranium mines.

The Senate Committee on Indian Affairs reported S 2166 on May 22 (S Rept 98-471). By voice vote Sept. 12, the Senate passed the bill, with its four-year reauthorization.

Also in May, the House Interior and Commerce committees reported a companion bill to S 2166 (HR 4567 — H Rept 98-763, Parts I and II). The House passed HR 4567, which contained a three-year reauthorization, by voice vote Sept. 14, and substituted it for the Senate bill.

A conference report on S 2166 (H Rept 98-1126) was filed Oct. 2, authorizing spending at $368.7 million over four years.

Conferees retained House-passed provisions establishing an emergency fund for catastrophic health care, set at $12 million in fiscal 1985, and elevating the Indian Health Service to the same level as the Health Resources and Services Administration. As reported by the Senate Indian Affairs Committee, S 2166 made the same change, but an amendment on the Senate floor deleted the provision from the bill.

Conferees accepted a limited version of a Senate provision allowing Indians eligible for state and local health services for the indigent to be eligible for Indian Health Service programs as well. Conferees also agreed to a Senate provision authorizing the reimbursement of the Indian Health Service for services provided to Indians eligible for Medicaid and Medicare.

By voice vote, the Senate adopted the conference report Oct. 3. Also by voice vote, the House adopted the conference report and cleared the bill for the president the following day.　　■

King, Columbus Holidays

President Reagan signed two bills in August creating commissions to prepare for national celebrations.

One bill, appropriately numbered HR 1492 (PL 98-375), set aside $2 million to celebrate the 500th anniversary of Christopher Columbus' first voyage to the New World. The other bill (HR 5890 — PL 98-399) required a commission set up to observe the Rev. Dr. Martin Luther King Jr.'s birthday in 1986 to pay its own way.

Columbus Quincentenary

The House Post Office and Civil Service Committee reported HR 1492 in May 1983 (H Rept 98-150). The bill created an unpaid 30-person commission to plan for the 1992 Columbus quincentenary celebration.

The bill also authorized creation of a 20-person staff for the commission with expenses of up to $220,000 a year — to a maximum of $2 million.

The House June 21, 1983, passed HR 1492 under suspension of the rules, a procedure that required a two-thirds majority but allowed no amendments. The vote was 288-123.

The Senate Judiciary Committee reported a nearly identical bill (S 500 — S Rept 98-194) in July 1983.

By a 67-23 vote, the Senate Feb. 1 passed HR 1492, substituting the language of S 500. *(Vote 4, p. 3-S)*

The Senate also adopted an amendment offered by Charles McC. Mathias Jr., R-Md., removing the secretary of the Smithsonian Institution from the commission to conform to constitutional requirements, and reducing the membership to 29.

The conference report on the bill (H Rept 98-876) reestablished the commission at 30 members. The Senate adopted the conference report by voice vote June 27.

The House voted 279-130 on July 25 to adopt the conference report, clearing the bill for the president. *(Vote 284, p. 86-H)*

King Holiday

The House Post Office and Civil Service Committee July 23 reported a bill (HR 5890 — H Rept 98-893) establishing a non-paid commission to assist in the first observance of the legal holiday honoring King.

The King holiday commission was to encourage ceremonies to celebrate the first observance of the holiday, established by Congress in 1983 (PL 98-144) to take place on the third Monday in January 1986. Unlike the bill creating the holiday, which was passed after a bitter battle, the bill establishing the commission sailed through Congress. *(1983 Almanac p. 600)*

The commission was to consist of 31 members, who could appoint a director and a staff of up to five persons. The bill required that all expenditures of the commission be paid by donated funds.

The House passed the bill by voice vote July 24, and the Senate passed the bill by voice vote Aug. 1, adding a technical amendment. The House by unanimous consent accepted the Senate amendment Aug. 8, clearing the bill for the president.　　■

National Party Conventions

President Reagan July 11 signed a bill authorizing increased federal payments to the Democratic and Republican parties for nominating convention costs. The bill (HR 5950 — PL 98-355) raised from $6 million to $8 million the ceiling on payments to each party out of the presidential election income-tax-checkoff fund.

The bill was reported by the House Ways and Means Committee June 28 (H Rept 98-877, Part I). By a 226-169 vote, the House passed the bill June 29, the last day Congress was in session before recessing for the Democratic convention. *(Vote 271, p. 84-H)*

The Senate by voice vote passed the bill the same day, clearing it for the president.

The bill had been requested by the leaders of both parties, particularly to cover increased security costs. No restrictions were placed on use of the money, however. Sponsors of the bill said that the national party conventions had received money from the Law Enforcement Assistance Administration (LEAA) in prior years. The LEAA went out of business in 1982. *(1982 Almanac p. 378)*

A provision similar to HR 5950 had been added to the deficit reduction bill (HR 4170) by the Senate, but dropped in conference. *(Story, p. 143)*　　■

Polling Place Accessibility

President Reagan signed a bill Sept. 28 (HR 1250 — PL 98-435) designed to make it easier for the elderly and handicapped to participate in federal elections. The bill required that polling places for federal elections in all states be accessible to handicapped and elderly voters, after Dec. 31, 1985. If no accessible facility were available, such voters could be reassigned, upon request, to the nearest accessible polling place, or state elections officials would have to provide alternate means of accommodating them.

States without mail or door-to-door voter registration also were required to provide a reasonable number of accessible registration sites. States had to provide registration and voting aids for the handicapped and elderly, and absentee ballots with no requirement for notarization or medical certification unless required by state law.

The House Administration Committee reported the bill June 21 (H Rept 98-852) and the House passed the bill by voice vote June 25.

The Senate Rules Committee reported the bill Aug. 9 (S Rept 98-590), with amendments clarifying that states had an option of accommodating handicapped or elderly voters whose home precincts were not accessible. The committee also added a sunset provision to the bill that would terminate its effects after 10 years, unless Congress voted to retain the law.

The Senate, by voice vote Aug. 10, passed HR 1250, including the committee amendments. The House, by unanimous consent Sept. 12, accepted the Senate amendments, clearing the bill for the president. ∎

D.C. Home Rule, Judges

Congress approved a major revision to the District of Columbia Home Rule Act (PL 93-198) governing congressional review of laws enacted by the D.C. government, but another bill died that would have given the D.C. mayor authority to appoint judges for D.C. courts.

The congressional-review bill (HR 3932) had been passed by the House in 1983, but languished in the Senate because of administration objections. Its provisions were included, however, in the closing days of the 98th Congress as part of the continuing resolution that made appropriations for fiscal 1985 (H J Res 648 — PL 98-473).

The House also passed the bill (HR 5951) that would have shifted judicial appointment authority to the D.C. mayor, but it was never considered in Senate committee.

Home Rule

The District's Home Rule Act and a provision in it that allowed Congress to reject District-government-passed laws became an issue after a June 1983 ruling of the Supreme Court. The court's decision declared unconstitutional legislative-veto provisions contained in more than 200 laws. *(Legislative veto, 1983 Almanac p. 565; Home Rule Act, 1973 Almanac p. 734)*

Legislative-veto provisions allowed all or part of Congress, with or without the president's approval, to block executive action. In ruling them unconstitutional, the court not only altered the balance of power between Congress and the president, but also threw into doubt the constitutionality of entire laws, such as the District Home Rule Act, of which legislative veto provisions were only a part. As a result, Congress scrambled in 1984 to find ways to remedy the confusion created by the ruling, including consideration of bills such as HR 3932. *(Story, p. 192)*

Of particular concern to supporters of HR 3932 was the District's authority to borrow, which they feared might be jeopardized if the entire home-rule charter were invalidated because of the legislative-veto ruling.

The House District of Columbia Committee reported HR 3932 Sept. 28, 1983 (H Rept 98-393). By voice vote, the House passed the bill Oct. 4, 1983.

To replace the suspect legislative veto and settle the issue, the House-passed bill required Congress to pass — and the president to sign — a joint resolution in order to disapprove any law enacted by the District government. Existing law had allowed a simple resolution of either house to disapprove a District law.

The administration, however, wanted to keep a tighter control over the District's criminal laws, by requiring Congress to pass a joint resolution to approve — not reject — changes in the District's criminal code.

Administration objections kept the Senate from considering the bill for much of 1984. The administration eventually dropped its objections, however, because of a provision in the bill that extended the congressional review period for criminal laws from 30 days to 60 days.

The Senate Governmental Affairs Committee reported the bill Sept. 13 (S Rept 98-635), but the full Senate did not have time to consider the bill before adjournment. The House then added the provisions of HR 3932 to the continuing appropriations resolution (H J Res 648) and they survived in the conference report (H Rept 98-1159), which was adopted Oct. 10 in the House and Oct. 11 in the Senate. *(Stories, pp. 428, 444)*

D.C. Judges

The House by voice vote July 30 passed HR 5951, which would have amended the District Home Rule Act to transfer from the president to the mayor authority to appoint local judges.

The mayor's appointments to appellate and trial courts would have been subject to confirmation by the District council. Under existing law, the president's nominations were subject to confirmation by the Senate.

The Reagan administration strongly opposed the bill. A statement issued by the White House argued that the existing appointment procedure "is efficient, effective and one that recognizes the unique character of, and the interests of the United States government in, the federal district."

Sponsors countered that local officials should be solely responsible for local judges.

The bill also would have changed the procedure for nominating judges in the District, eliminating two federally appointed members of a judicial nomination commission.

And HR 5951 would have raised the statutory limit on claims filed in D.C. Small Claims Court from $750 to $2,000 — a provision aimed at reducing a backlog in D.C. Superior Court.

The House District of Columbia Committee reported HR 5951 July 25 (H Rept 98-909). By voice vote July 30, the House passed the bill.

The Senate Governmental Affairs subcommittee on the District of Columbia, which was more concerned with HR 3932, the bill concerning congressional review of D.C. laws, did not take action on the judges bill in 1984. ∎

Olympic Tax Checkoff

Efforts in both the House and Senate to help collect private contributions for the U.S. Olympic Committee (USOC) through an income-tax-form checkoff failed.

A House bill (HR 1984), was reported April 26 by the Judiciary Committee (H Rept 98-711, Part I). But the Ways and Means Committee, to which the bill had been jointly referred, did not report the bill, and the House never voted on it.

A similar provision was added to the comprehensive 1984 deficit reduction bill (HR 4170) by the Senate Finance Committee. Although that provision survived on the Senate floor, it was stricken from the bill in conference.

Background

Because U.S. Olympic teams survived almost entirely on private financing while teams from other nations received hefty subsidies from their governments, the USOC appealed to Congress for help.

Specifically, the group wanted a way for taxpayers to contribute to the USOC by checking off a box on their federal income tax forms, similar to the way existing law permitted taxpayers to contribute to presidential election campaign matching funds.

The presidential campaign-fund checkoff raised an estimated $287.4 million from 1972 to 1984. Supporters of HR 1984 predicted that the Olympic checkoff could raise $40 million a year. The USOC's four-year budget for the 1981-84 period was $88.7 million.

Despite a policy of private financing for the Olympics, the U.S. government did provide some public support for the 1984 Los Angeles Games. The fiscal 1984 appropriation for the Customs Service included $3.7 million for 31 positions "for coping with the large influx of foreign participants and visitors that will be arriving for the Summer Olympics," according to the Senate Appropriations Committee report (S 1646 — S Rept 98-186).

Legislative History

By voice vote March 27, the House Judiciary Committee approved HR 1984, to permit a tax checkoff for the USOC. The bill would have allowed a $1 checkoff from any refund due a taxpayer ($2 for joint returns) and also would have allowed taxpayers to send a cash contribution to the Olympic Committee with their returns. Unlike the presidential campaign checkoff, it would not permit diversion of taxes due the federal government.

HR 1984 also would have established a U.S. Olympic Trust Fund to collect the receipts, which would have been paid out by the Treasury Department.

The Judiciary Committee, which does not normally handle tax matters, was given jurisdiction over the bill because the USOC was a federally chartered organization, and Judiciary handled federal charters.

The Treasury Department and some members of Congress opposed HR 1984, fearing that allowing the Olympic checkoff would set a precedent and open the floodgates to other charities. The Olympic Committee was not the only private organization that indicated interest in a federal income tax checkoff.

For example, Sen. Dave Durenberger, R-Minn., introduced a bill that would have permitted a checkoff on federal income tax returns for wildlife conservation efforts.

Although the presidential campaign-fund checkoff was the only one allowed in existing law, such devices were becoming common in the states. As of 1984, 31 states allowed taxpayers to check off a box on their state tax forms to contribute refund payments to wildlife conservation. In six years, according to Defenders of Wildlife, states with such checkoffs raised more than $13 million.

Many members of the House Ways and Means Committee, which shared jurisdiction over the bill with Judiciary, opposed it, for reasons similar to Treasury's. The panel did not report it to the House.

In the Senate Finance Committee, however, the Olympic checkoff provision was included March 21 in the deficit-reduction package (HR 4170). The provision stayed in the bill through Senate floor action May 17, but opposition from House conferees caused it to be dropped from the conference report on HR 4170 (H Rept 98-861). *(Deficit reduction, p. 143)* ∎

National Archives

In a move creating the first independent agency since he took office, President Reagan signed on Oct. 19 a bill (S 905 — PL 98-497) making the National Archives and Records Administration a separate agency within the executive branch. The conference report (H Rept 98-1124) on the bill was cleared by Congress Oct. 4.

The National Archives — charged with handling, preserving and disseminating federal records — was independent from its creation in 1934 until 1949, when it was placed under the then-newly created General Services Administration (GSA).

S 905 made the archivist a presidential appointee, subject to confirmation by the Senate. Conferees on the measure dropped a Senate provision that would have set the archivist's term at 10 years, in an effort to make the appointment non-political; instead, conferees accepted House language allowing the president to remove the archivist, but requiring that notice of the reasons be given to Congress.

And in response to concern over a 1983 Supreme Court decision that struck down one-house legislative vetoes of regulations issued by the administration, conferees accepted a House provision concerning protection of tape recordings made by former President Richard M. Nixon and retained by the Archives. *(Background, 1974 Almanac p. 654)*

Existing law had given either house of Congress authority to reject regulations governing release of those tapes by passing a simple resolution — not a law subject to presidential signature. The high court ruled such authority unconstitutional, however. *(1983 Almanac p. 565)*

The Senate bill merely struck the unconstitutional provision, but the House version required any future regulations to be submitted to Congress and not take effect for 60 days to give Congress the opportunity to pass a law rejecting them.

The bill also required federal agencies to report to the archivist on the planned disposal of federal records, and to allow the Archives to request the attorney general to initiate legal action if an agency failed to prevent or act on the illegal removal of records.

The Senate Governmental Affairs Committee reported S 905 April 3 (S Rept 98-373) and the Senate passed the bill by voice vote June 21.

The House Government Operations Committee reported a similar bill April 25 (HR 3987 — H Rept 98-707). The House passed the bill by voice vote Aug. 2 and substituted the House bill language for that of S 905. The House first rejected an amendment that would have left the Archives as an agency within the GSA, but with enhanced stature. ∎

Presidential Libraries

The House June 25 passed a bill (HR 5584) requiring private donors to pay part of the cost of maintaining presidential libraries. The Senate never considered that bill, or a more far-reaching bill reported out of Senate committee (S 563) that would have curtailed federal payments to former presidents, as well as limited federal support for libraries.

Under existing law, presidential libraries were built with private contributions and then donated to the federal government, which paid to maintain them. In fiscal 1983, for example, the federal government paid $13 million to operate seven libraries.

HR 5584 would have required that an endowment be set aside for the library's maintenance at the time it was turned over to the government. The endowment would have to be created from private contributions and equal 20 percent or more of the cost of building a presidential library. The earnings from the endowment would be used to pay part of the operating costs.

The Reagan administration supported the bill, which would have affected libraries for presidents taking office after Reagan.

The bill was reported June 21 by the House Government Operations Committee (H Rept 98-856). The House passed the bill June 25 by voice vote.

Presidents' Benefits

The Senate Governmental Affairs Committee May 9 reported a bill (S 563 — S Rept 98-637) that would have limited benefits to former presidents, including Secret Service protection, libraries and office staff. According to Lawton Chiles, D-Fla., sponsor of the bill, benefits to the three living former presidents (Richard M. Nixon, Gerald R. Ford and Jimmy Carter), for presidential widow Lady Bird Johnson, and for presidential libraries cost the taxpayers $29 million in fiscal 1984, up from $64,000 in 1955.

The bill would have halted Secret Service protection to former presidents after five years. And a spouse and children would have been entitled to protection only if they were residing with the former president or were traveling with him.

Under existing law, former presidents were entitled to full Secret Service protection, 24 hours a day for life. An amendment to keep lifetime protection was defeated. In addition, their spouses received full protection for life or until they remarried, and their children received protection until they reached age 18.

Libraries would have been limited in size to 60,000 square feet for a one-term president and 70,000 square feet for a two-term president. Existing libraries ranged from less than 30,000 square feet for President Hoover's library in Stanford, Calif., to more than 110,000 square feet for President Johnson's in Austin, Texas. Chiles' bill, like the House bill, would only have applied to presidents after Reagan.

Office staff allowances would have been limited to $300,000 a year, gradually reduced to $200,000. To prevent the use of federal money for the personal or political gain of a former president, the bill would have prohibited the use of staff allowances for partisan political activities or income-generating activities. If a former president were to use federally paid staff in writing his memoirs, the bill would have required the book to be printed and sold by the Government Printing Office, with proceeds going to the federal Treasury. ∎

Infrastructure Study

The president Oct. 19 signed a bill (S 1330 — PL 98-501) requiring an annual survey of the nation's infrastructure — roads, bridges, dams, water and sewer systems and the like — and requiring that the president's annual budget submission to Congress include a detailed summary of federal civilian and military construction projects.

The bill established a National Council on Public Works Improvement, which was required to submit reports in 1986, 1987 and 1988 on the age, condition, costs and needs for future construction of public works improvements.

The bill authorized a five-member council, three of whom were to be appointed by the president, and one each by the president pro tempore of the Senate and the Speaker of the House. For staff, printing and other costs, the bill authorized annual expenditures of about $3.5 million. The council was to go out of business in April 1988, after issuing its final report.

Beginning in 1985, the president's annual budget message to Congress was to contain in a separate report projections for military and civilian construction projects and an assessment of needs over 10 years for new civilian public works construction projects.

S 1330 was reported in November 1983 by the Senate Committee on Environment and Public Works (S Rept 98-341), establishing the National Council on Public Works Improvement and requiring the president's budget request to report on civilian public works projects.

The Senate passed the bill Feb. 9 by voice vote.

HR 1244, a companion bill to S 1330 that required only that a civilian public works construction program be a part of the president's budget request, was reported by the House Committee on Public Works and Transportation in May 1983 (H Rept 98-153, Part I). The House Government Operations Committee reported the bill April 25 (H Rept 98-153, Part II), adding military construction projects — bases as well as weapons system platforms, but not including the weapons themselves — to the required budget report.

The House passed the bill May 15 by a voice vote.

Conferees retained the basic provisions of the Senate bill creating the public works council and the House provisions regarding reporting in the budget on civilian and military construction projects.

The House adopted the conference report on S 1330 (H Rept 98-1134) Oct. 4 and the Senate adopted the conference report Oct. 5, clearing the measure for the president. ∎

Government Reorganization

Two bills enacted in 1984 extended the president's authority to make limited changes in the organization of Cabinet departments and federal agencies, and ratified past government reorganizations, dating back 50 years.

Both bills were passed in response to a 1983 Supreme Court decision that declared unconstitutional the legislative veto, a provision by which one house of Congress could reject an action of the administration. *(1983 Almanac p. 565)*

Previous laws authorizing the president to reorganize executive branch agencies, dating to 1932, contained legislative-veto provisions. Concern that prior reorganizations might be declared illegal, because the laws under which they were effected might be declared unconstitutional, prompted Congress to ratify past reorganizations and to change the procedure by which Congress could object to a future reorganization plan.

Ratification Bill

The first of the reorganization bills (HR 6225 — PL 98-532) simply ratified all previous reorganizations of federal agencies and departments implemented under the various laws that had authorized presidents to shift agency responsibilities.

All but two of the 16 laws enacted from 1932 through 1983 to give presidents reorganization authority contained some sort of provision giving Congress a one-house veto of reorganization plans.

But, in *Immigration and Naturalization Service v. Chada*, the Supreme Court in 1983 ruled a similar one-house veto unconstitutional.

Immediately following *Chada*, more than 100 lawsuits were filed challenging a 1978 reorganization that transferred enforcement authority of the Equal Pay Act and the Age Discrimination in Employment Act from the Labor Department to the Equal Employment Opportunity Commission (EEOC).

In 1984, the 2nd U.S. Circuit Court of Appeals ruled in *EEOC v. CBS Inc.* that the EEOC reorganization — implemented under the Reorganization Act of 1977 (PL 95-17) — was illegal. And, in at least four cases other than *EEOC v. CBS*, federal district courts ruled the transfer of enforcement authority to have been illegal.

The 2nd Circuit, however, stayed the effect of its decision until Dec. 31, 1984, to give Congress time to act to ratify the EEOC reorganization.

HR 6225 was reported by the House Government Operations Committee Sept. 28 (H Rept 98-1104) and passed the House Oct. 1 by voice vote, with little debate and without amendment.

The Senate, by voice vote Oct. 4, passed the bill unchanged. The president signed it Oct. 19.

1984 Reorganization Act

The second of two reorganization bills passed in 1984 (HR 1314 — PL 98-614) restored through Dec. 31, 1984, the president's authority to restructure government agencies without having to ask Congress to pass a law making the changes.

Previous authority to reorganize the government was contained in the Reorganization Act of 1949 (PL 81-109), as revised by the Reorganization Act of 1977 (PL 95-17). Before 1984, the act's authority had been extended eight times, and had lapsed five times. It had last been renewed for one year in 1980 by PL 96-230. That renewal expired April 7, 1981. *(Background, 1980 Almanac p. 543)*

Under the 1977 version of the law, the president was required to submit to Congress a proposed reorganization plan, which would automatically take effect in 60 days unless either house passed a resolution to disapprove it.

Such reorganization plans were prohibited from creating new Cabinet-level departments, abolishing existing departments, transferring an entire department or regulatory agency to another department or agency, or combining two or more departments or regulatory agencies.

Beyond renewing the president's authority to reorganize agencies, HR 1314 added a prohibition to the law, preventing the president from renaming Cabinet-level departments.

The key provision of HR 1314, however, altered the procedure for congressional approval of proposed reorganizations, eliminating the one-house veto, which had been part of various laws enacted since 1932 to allow agency reorganizations, and which was ruled unconstitutional in the 1983 *Chada* decision.

In its place, HR 1314 required that reorganization plans would take effect only if both House and Senate passed a joint resolution approving the plan, and the president signed the resolution. Congress had to act within 90 days of receiving the plan from the president, or the plan would be deemed disapproved.

HR 1314 was reported by the House Government Operations Committee May 16, 1983 (H Rept 98-128, Part I). Except for minor technical changes, the bill was reported intact March 30, 1984, by the House Rules Committee (H Rept 98-128, Part II). With minimal debate and without amendment, the House passed the bill by voice vote April 10. With similar dispatch, the Senate passed the bill by voice vote Oct. 11, in the closing hours of the 98th Congress.

The bill became law Nov. 8, immediately upon the president signing it, but actually President Reagan never had authority to propose a reorganization. The law required reorganization plans to be submitted only while Congress was in session. Congress had adjourned Oct. 12 and did not reconvene before the reorganization authority expired Dec. 31.   ∎

President Signs NASA Authorization Measure

Inaugurating a new era in manned space exploration, President Reagan July 16 signed into law the fiscal 1985 authorization bill for the National Aeronautics and Space Administration (NASA).

The $7.5 billion measure (HR 5154 — PL 98-361), cleared June 28, authorized the agency to begin research and development on a permanent manned space station, which Reagan proposed in his State of the Union message. *(Text, p. 5-E)*

NASA planned to put the station into space in 1992. It would allow commercial manufacturing of critical materials and pharmaceuticals that could not be produced economically on Earth, and could make possible more ambitious

space travel. However, some scientists, while recognizing the advantages of a space station, questioned the need for a permanent human presence in space.

NASA officials estimated the cost of the space station at about $8 billion by the time of launch.

HR 5154 also created a National Commission on Space to study space activities and formulate an agenda for the nation's civilian space program. The commission would include a non-voting representative of the Department of Defense (DOD) on its advisory board, but the bill stated that the space program should be separate from any military space program.

The emphasis on the civilian space program grew out

of the concerns of several members that the program might become overwhelmed or taken over by the military uses of space. During consideration of the bill, the House Science and Technology Committee voted to drop the DOD representative from the advisory board, but that action was reversed on the House floor.

Provisions

As signed into law, HR 5154 authorized a total of $7,526,400,000 for NASA, including $2.48 billion for research and development.

Manned Space Station. The research budget included $150 million to begin work on the manned space station. The bill emphasized that the station "may be used only for peaceful purposes," and may not be used to carry into space any nuclear weapons.

New Space Programs. HR 5154 also authorized funding for two other new programs requested by the administration:

• $16 million for a vehicle to study the climatic and geologic evolution of Mars. The vehicle, expected to cost between $300 million and $375 million, was scheduled for launch in 1990.

• $55.7 million for a satellite to put into space instruments to measure the upper atmosphere.

Ongoing Programs. HR 5154 authorized $3.6 billion for space flight, control and data communications, the ongoing programs of NASA. That was $190 million below the fiscal 1984 figure, in part because NASA expected an increase in reimbursements from other countries, private companies and federal agencies that used the space shuttle, and because most of the construction of shuttle vehicles was complete.

The bill authorized more than the president requested for certain NASA programs, including an added $40 million to continue flight demonstrations of an advanced communications satellite expected to lower the cost of satellite communications for rural and remote areas.

Commission on Space. HR 5154 created a National Commission on Space to study existing and proposed space activities and formulate an agenda for the nation's civilian space program. The bill directed the 15-member commission to identify long-range goals, opportunities and policy options for the civilian space program for the next 20 years, and authorized $1 million for its activities in fiscal 1985.

The commission would have non-voting, ex officio advisers from various government departments and agencies, including the Department of Defense. However, the bill declared that "the separation of the civilian and military space programs is essential to ensure the continued health and vitality of both."

House Committee Action

The House Science and Technology Committee approved HR 5154 March 20 by a vote of 31-7 and filed its report March 21 (H Rept 98-629).

The principal disagreements in committee were over funding levels and over whether to include a Defense Department representative on the new space commission's advisory board.

The $7.5 billion authorization approved by the committee was $40 million over the amount requested by the president, and several members, led by ranking Republican Larry Winn Jr., Kan., voted against it for that reason.

However, others, including George E. Brown Jr., D-Calif., argued for even higher funding.

The committee rejected two attempts by Brown to add funds for particular projects.

Brown first offered an amendment to add $10 million for a solar optical telescope, which would be used on the space shuttle to perform experiments.

The Space Science and Applications Subcommittee already had added $4 million to the $105.4 million budget request for the solar optical telescope and an infrared telescope facility in space. Brown said the additional $10 million would permit construction to begin on the project.

Subcommittee Chairman Harold L. Volkmer, D-Mo., said that while he was "not averse" to adding the money, putting the bill even further over the budget would threaten its passage.

The committee rejected Brown's amendment, 7-27.

Brown then sought to add $5 million that the subcommittee had cut from the $60.7 million request for a proposed upper-atmosphere research satellite. Volkmer again argued that budgetary constraints necessitated the cut, and the committee rejected Brown's proposal by voice vote.

The committee also rejected, 10-26, an amendment by Manuel Lujan Jr., R-N.M., to allow the NASA administrator to cut from the authorization the $40 million the subcommittee had added to Reagan's request.

Brown and Volkmer argued that that would give the administrator too much authority.

Space Commission Debate

Another debate erupted over Volkmer's amendment to remove the DOD from the advisory committee of the proposed space commission.

Volkmer said the job of the commission was to plan for the civilian space program, and that DOD, which conducts a space program of its own, should not be involved.

Others argued that the two programs should be linked. Moreover, said Herbert H. Bateman, R-Va., the DOD representative would be only one, non-voting member of the board. "We have no reason to fear that we're somehow going to prostitute the civilian space program," he said.

Dan Glickman, D-Kan., agreed, noting that the Pentagon's space program gave it expertise that would be desirable on the board.

Lujan proposed a substitute to Volkmer's amendment that, among other things, would have put DOD back on the commission's advisory board. Although Glickman and Ralph M. Hall, D-Texas, joined most Republicans in voting for Lujan's substitute, it failed, 17-18. Volkmer's amendment then passed by voice vote.

Committee Amendments

The committee also approved amendments:

• By Glickman, to shift $5 million of the $347 million available for aeronautics research and technology to high-speed aeronautics research.

• By Robert S. Walker, R-Pa., to authorize NASA to seek financial contributions from space agencies of other countries for a possible fifth shuttle vehicle.

House Floor Action

The House passed HR 5154 March 28 by a vote of 389-11, after adopting an amendment to cut every item in the bill by .55 percent. *(Vote 49, p. 18-H)*

The amendment, offered by Walker and adopted by

voice vote, cut $40 million from the $7.5 billion authorization reported by the Science and Technology Committee and brought the bill back in line with the president's $7.49 billion budget request.

By voice vote, the House also voted to reverse the Science Committee and put a representative of the Defense Department back on the advisory board of the National Commission on Space.

Senate Action

Committee. The Senate Commerce, Science and Transportation Committee approved HR 5154 May 8, and filed its report May 17 (S Rept 98-455).

The Senate version of the bill authorized $7.58 billion, $91 million more than the amount requested by Reagan. It included the requested $150 million for the manned space station and enthusiastically endorsed the project. It also included $1.47 billion for the space shuttle program — enough to complete production of the fourth space shuttle orbiter, *Atlantis,* and to maintain production readiness for a fifth orbiter if needed, the committee said.

Like the House, the Senate panel also upped Reagan's request for spare parts for the space shuttle fleet.

The committee also agreed to establish a National Commission on Space.

Floor. The Senate passed HR 5154 by voice vote on June 21.

Final Action

The conference report on the bill, filed June 27 (H Rept 98-873), authorized $7.526 billion for NASA.

The Senate adopted the conference report by voice vote June 27, but there was considerable opposition to it in the House because the bill contained $35 million more than the House-passed version of the bill. It also was $35 million higher than the fiscal 1985 appropriation for NASA, cleared by Congress the same day (HR 5713 — PL 98-371).

The House finally approved the conference report on HR 5154 June 28 by a 298-119 vote, clearing it for the president. *(Vote 258, p. 80-H)* ∎

Landsat Sale

President Reagan July 17 signed into law legislation paving the way for the federal government to sell to the private sector satellites that take pictures of the Earth and the data from such satellites.

Reagan said the bill (HR 5155 — PL 98-365) was a step toward "returning to the private sector those activities which it can best perform."

Provisions. The legislation established guidelines for the gradual sale of the satellites, known as land-remote sensing satellites (Landsat). The Commerce Department would license the private owners and maintain an archive of the data produced by them. The data is used in such activities as mineral exploration, agriculture and cartography.

The bill also prohibited the government from selling its weather satellites, which Reagan had proposed to do in 1983. That plan met with strong opposition from Congress, which voted several times in 1983 to prohibit it. *(1983 Almanac p. 588)*

Legislative History. HR 5155 was reported by the House Science and Technology Committee April 3 (H Rept 98-647) and passed the House by voice vote April 9 under suspension of the rules.

The Senate Commerce, Science and Transportation Committee reported the bill May 17 (S Rept 98-458) after adopting an amendment by Larry Pressler, R-S.D., preserving a role for the EROS Data Center in Sioux Falls, S.D., by making it the permanent national archive for Landsat and any future satellite data.

The Senate passed the bill by voice vote June 8.

The House approved the Senate version June 28, after adding provisions clarifying the authority of the Federal Communications Commission in the licensing of commercial remote sensing systems. The Senate agreed to the amended version June 29, clearing it for the president. ∎

Space Launch Licensing

President Reagan Oct. 30 signed into law a bill (HR 3942 — PL 98-575) designed to encourage and facilitate commercial space launches.

The bill prohibited anyone from launching satellites or other space objects from the United States without a license and gave the Department of Transportation (DOT) authority to issue such licenses.

The legislation also authorized the sale or leasing of government property, such as launch pads, to private firms.

The bill reflected Reagan's space policy, which designated the reusable space shuttle as the government's primary space launch system and encouraged commercial launches of expendable launch vehicles.

To help monitor compliance with federal interests, the bill authorized DOT to place federal officials at launch sites, production facilities or assembly sites used by licensees. DOT was required to consult with the State and Defense Departments on licensing matters affecting foreign policy or national security.

The bill required liability insurance coverage for commercial space launch activities.

HR 3942 was reported by the House Science and Technology Committee May 31 (H Rept 98-816) and passed the House June 5 by voice vote under suspension of the rules. The committee said the existing regulatory structure for space launches was too complex, involving as many as 18 federal agencies and 22 different statutes and sets of regulations, thus inhibiting private involvement in the field.

The Senate Commerce, Science and Transportation Committee reported its version of the bill Oct. 3 (S Rept 98-656), and the Senate passed it on Oct. 9. The House agreed to the Senate version the same day, clearing it for the president. ∎

Bureau of Standards Bill Veto

President Reagan Oct. 30 pocket-vetoed the National Bureau of Standards (NBS) fiscal 1985 authorization bill (HR 5172), because of provisions aimed at improving manufacturing technology in the United States, particularly in the areas of robotics and automation.

As cleared, HR 5172 authorized nearly $126 million for the NBS for fiscal 1985, approximately the spending level requested by the president. The bill included authorizations of $5.8 million for the Fire Research Center, and $3.1 million for the Building Research Center, both of which Reagan had proposed to eliminate.

In his veto message, the president said the robotics and automation provisions constituted an "unwarranted role" for the federal government in investment decisions that were best left to industry. *(Veto message, p. 26-E)*

The president charged that providing federal support for research, development, education and training into new manufacturing technologies, as contemplated by the robotics provisions, might have served "as the basis for a federal industrial policy," which the administration "steadfastly opposed." He also expressed doubts that the programs and expenditures proposed would have improved the competitiveness of U.S. manufacturing.

Although the fiscal 1985 NBS authorization bill died with Reagan's veto, Congress included almost $124 million for the agency in the Commerce Department appropriation bill (PL 98-411). *(Story, p. 373)*

House Action

The House Science and Technology Committee reported HR 5172 April 4 (H Rept 98-650), authorizing $132.8 million for NBS activities in fiscal 1985, nearly $7 million more than the president's budget request and $17 million above the fiscal 1984 appropriation. The committee objected to the president's plan to eliminate NBS fire research and building research programs, and included specific authorizations for both programs.

The bill came to the House floor April 26, where Republicans succeeded through a series of roll-call votes in cutting the total authorization to about $126 million. *(Votes 87-92, p. 32-H)*

The votes came late on a Thursday afternoon, after many members had already left town, and amid much heated parliamentary wrangling. First, members voted 164-151 to limit to $2.5 million a proposed $6 million cut in the committee-passed authorization.

Members then voted 185-126 in favor of the $6 million cut and voted a second time on the $2.5 million cut, rejecting it by a 123-172 vote.

Then, by a 146-143 vote, the House eliminated a $500,000 study of the conversion to the metric system by private industry.

Finally, by a 159-129 vote, the House voted to postpone final passage of the bill.

On May 2, with little of the debate and parliamentary wrangling that characterized consideration of the bill on April 26, the House passed HR 5172 by voice vote.

Senate Action

The Senate Committee on Commerce, Science and Transportation reported on May 2 a companion NBS authorization bill (S 2458 — S Rept 98-423) for fiscal 1985. The Senate bill authorized $131.6 million in total spending for the NBS, slightly less than the House bill, as reported, but like the House bill, continued the authorizations for fire research and building research.

By voice vote, and with minimal debate, the Senate passed S 2458 on June 26.

The House did not take action on S 2458. The Senate Commerce Committee, however, reported HR 5172 to the floor Aug. 27, including the authorization levels from S 2458, but without a written report.

On Sept. 21, the Senate by voice vote passed HR 5172, after adopting by voice vote a substitute amendment. The substitute incorporated the House-passed authorization levels for NBS, but added provisions from a separate, Senate-passed and House committee-reported bill (S 1286) designed to enhance manufacturing technology, especially through research into robotics and automation.

Robotics Provisions. Ultimately the cause for Reagan's veto of the NBS authorization, S 1286, the robotics bill was reported May 8 by the Senate Commerce Committee, and passed the Senate June 8 by voice vote and without a word of debate.

The House Science and Technology Committee, after adopting several amendments that narrowed the focus of some research programs and created a center for robotics research at NBS, reported it Sept. 25 (H Rept 98-1078). The bill passed by the Senate was very similar in most respects to the version later reported by the House committee.

The key provisions would have established a program in the Office of Productivity, Technology and Innovation in the Department of Commerce to conduct research and development for improved manufacturing technologies, including computer-assisted design; automated handling, processing, assembly and testing of products; integrated manufacturing systems; and new metallurgical technology.

The program would have supported basic and applied research through grants and cooperative agreements in universities, non-profit institutions, industry associations and other firms.

The Senate-passed bill authorized spending totaling $218 million for fiscal 1985-88. The House committee version contained a total authorization for the same period of $250 million. As included in the NBS authorization bill (HR 5172), the provisions of S 1286 were essentially those taken from the House committee version.

Final Action

After limited debate, including concerns expressed by some members that the bill would be subject to a veto because of the robotics provisions, the House Oct. 4 accepted the Senate amendments to HR 5172 by voice vote, clearing the bill for the president.   ∎

Small Business Programs

Congress failed in 1984 to reauthorize Small Business Administration (SBA) programs through 1985 or 1986, despite the fact that both houses passed bills to do so.

A separate bill to increase the fiscal 1984 authorization for three SBA loan programs to match spending levels in the fiscal 1984 SBA appropriation bill passed both houses in slightly different form, but it, too, failed to clear.

SBA Reauthorization

Reagan administration objections to several House-passed provisions — including disaster aid for commercial fishing businesses adversely affected by severe weather patterns on the West Coast — blocked a conference agreement on S 1323, a bill reauthorizing the SBA through fiscal 1986.

Senate Action. The bill was reported in May 1983 by the Senate Small Business Committee (S Rept 98-129). It passed the Senate by voice vote Oct. 7, 1983, with only a minor amendment allowing loan guarantees for purchases of new property — land, buildings or equipment — when the owners of the business would not be identical to the owners of the new property.

As passed by the Senate, S 1323 authorized SBA expenditures of $1.07 billion in fiscal 1984 and $896 million in fiscal 1985. In line with administration requests, the Senate bill would have eliminated direct federal loans to small businesses, except for those that were minority-owned. A vote in committee to restore the direct loan program failed on an 8-10 vote.

House Action. In May 1983, the House Small Business Committee also reported a reauthorization bill for the SBA through fiscal 1985 (HR 3020 — H Rept 98-182).

The committee bill included total SBA authorization levels for fiscal 1984 of $1.44 billion and for fiscal 1985 of $1.35 billion.

The House committee agreed to continue the direct loan program, and resurrected a provision repealed in the 1981 budget reconciliation act (PL 97-35), allowing loan assistance to firms whose economic base was harmed by fluctuations in the value of the Mexican peso.

The committee bill also expressly required the SBA to guarantee loans for purchase of pollution control equipment, when part of the construction money came from tax-exempt bonds. The SBA had been refusing to guarantee such loans since 1982 and the administration opposed the provision.

The House passed HR 3020 on March 15, 1984, by a 386-11 vote. Then, by voice voice, the House substituted the language of HR 3020 for that of S 1323 and passed the Senate bill. *(Vote 39, p. 14-H)*

A House floor amendment passed by voice vote cut the total committee-passed authorization levels for direct loans and other SBA programs to $986 million in fiscal 1984, and $1.08 billion in fiscal 1985. A second floor amendment, passed by voice vote, added to the bill fiscal 1986 authorization levels equal to those for fiscal 1985, plus a 4 percent inflation factor.

An attempt to eliminate the direct-loan program for all but minority-owned firms was rejected 72-331 in the House. *(Vote 38, p. 14-H)*

The House also adopted amendments by voice vote extending disaster loan assistance to fishing businesses harmed by "El Niño," an unusual and severe pattern of ocean currents off the West Coast in 1982 and 1983, and to

agricultural businesses adversely affected by the 1983 drought, which was also attributed to El Niño.

Members rejected by voice vote an amendment to delete the provision providing assistance to businesses hurt by the devaluation of the Mexican peso.

Conference Committee. Both the House and Senate appointed conferees on the bill, but administration threats to veto any bill that contained the El Niño provision, and other disagreements, prevented conferees from meeting. The bill died at the end of the session.

Fiscal 1984 Loan Programs

A bill (HR 6013) raising the fiscal 1984 authorizations for three SBA programs to levels already provided in the agency's fiscal 1984 appropriations bill (PL 98-166) also did not reach conference.

Because those programs were previously authorized for fiscal 1984 in the 1981 budget reconciliation act (PL 97-35) at levels lower than the fiscal 1984 appropriation, and because a new SBA authorization (S 1323, HR 3020) was stalled in conference for unrelated reasons, the General Accounting Office determined that passage of HR 6013 was necessary to allow the spending ceilings to rise.

The bill would have raised authorizations for the handicapped loan program from $15 million to $20 million, the Small Business Investment Corporations from $160 million to $250 million, and the Minority Enterprise Small Business Investment Corporations from $35 million to $41 million.

The bill was reported by the House Small Business Committee July 27 (H Rept 98-914), including a provision similar to that in HR 3020, requiring the SBA to guarantee loans for purchase of pollution control equipment, when money from tax-exempt bonds was involved. That provision was opposed by the Reagan administration.

The House passed the bill by voice vote July 30, without amendment.

The Senate passed the bill by voice vote Sept. 17, after agreeing by voice vote to drop the House-passed provision concerning pollution control equipment.

The House insisted on its provision and the Senate failed to respond to the House's request for a conference. The bill died at the end of the session. ∎

Procurement Bills Aimed at Cutting Costs

President Reagan Oct. 30 signed a comprehensive bill (HR 4209 — PL 98-577) aimed at reducing the cost to all government agencies of buying spare parts and supplies. The bill sought to increase competition, limit overhead charges and special prices for commercially available goods, and boost small business participation in federal procurement.

Some provisions similar to those contained in HR 4209, as cleared, as well as provisions from two other procurement bills (HR 5084, HR 2133) were included in the Defense Authorization Act of 1984 (HR 5167 — PL 98-525). Those provisions primarily applied to Pentagon purchases. *(Defense authorization, p. 37)*

And Congress included in the Deficit Reduction Act of 1984 (HR 4170 — PL 98-369) most provisions of a second bill (S 338), designed to increase competition primarily in non-defense contracting. *(Deficit reduction, p. 143)*

Both the deficit reduction and defense authorization bills cleared earlier than the final procurement bill, HR 4209.

Enactment of the various procurement provisions culminated a two-year effort by six congressional committees to cut procurement costs. In 1983, Congress had cleared a bill (HR 2293 — PL 98-191) reauthorizing and strenghtening the Office of Federal Procurement Policy, an agency within the Office of Management and Budget. That bill restored the agency's responsibility for writing governmentwide regulations on procurement. *(1983 Almanac p. 589)*

Congress also cleared in 1983 a bill (S 272 — PL 98-72) designed to increase competition for contracts, particularly by small businesses, by requiring advance notice of bidding. *(1983 Almanac p. 587)*

More than a half-dozen other major bills in both

chambers were considered in the 98th Congress to improve competition or otherwise cut procurement costs, sparked by reports that the Defense Department (DOD) had paid seemingly exorbitant prices for routine, commercially available parts — including a notorious $435 hammer. Much of the blame for government overpayment was laid to the Pentagon's practice of buying goods from one contractor instead of requiring competitive bids — so-called sole-source contracting. The Pentagon bought 80 percent of all goods and services used by the federal government.

Major Bills Considered

The most significant procurement bills considered in 1984 included:

● **S 338, Competition in Contracting Act of 1983.** Reported unanimously in March 1983 by the Governmental Affairs Committee (S Rept 98-50) and unanimously in June 1983 by the Armed Services Committee (S Rept 98-297), S 338 passed the Senate by voice vote Nov. 11, 1983. *(1983 Almanac p. 590)*

The provisions of S 338 were incorporated on the Senate floor into the Senate-passed version (S 2163) of HR 4170, the Deficit Reduction Act. In conference on the deficit bill, the major provisions of S 338 were left largely intact.

● **HR 5184, Competition in Contracting Act of 1984.** The Government Operations Committee approved the bill May 9, but it was not reported until Oct. 10 (H Rept 98-1157). The bill did not see floor action, but some of its provisions were considered by conferees in drafting a compromise procurement section for the cleared version of HR 4170, the Deficit Reduction Act.

● **HR 5064, Defense Spare Parts Procurement Reform Act.** Reported April 18 by the Armed Services Committee (H Rept 98-690), the bill did not see floor action, but some of its major provisions were incorporated on the House floor into the House-passed version of HR 5167, the defense authorization.

● **HR 2133, Small Business Competition for Federal Procurements.** Reported Nov. 12, 1983, by the Small Business Committee (H Rept 98-541), the bill did not see floor action, but some of its major provisions were also incorporated on the House floor into the House-passed version of the defense authorization.

● **S 2489, Small Business Competition Enhancement Act of 1984.** Reported May 11, 1984, by the Small Business Committee (no written report) and June 14, 1984, by the Armed Services Committee (S Rept 98-523), the bill passed the Senate Aug. 7, and was substituted for the language of HR 4209. Several of the spare-parts provisions of S 2489 were also included in the Senate-passed version of the defense authorization.

● **HR 4209, Small Business Breakouts.** Reported Nov. 10, 1983, by the Small Business Committee (H Rept 98-528), the bill passed the House May 21. A related bill — S 2489 — passed the Senate Aug. 7. A compromise version of HR 4209, worked out informally among six House and Senate committees and drawn heavily from the provisions in S 2489, was agreed to in the House Oct. 2 and the Senate Oct. 4, clearing the bill for the president.

Small-Business Breakouts

HR 4209 and S 2489 were designed to promote small business participation in the contracting process. The Senate bill was far more comprehensive in its approach to cost-cutting and encouraging small-business participation. Both bills, however, contained a key provision requiring that a Small Business Administration (SBA) representative be placed in each major federal procurement center to "break out" parts of larger contracts for bidding by small businesses.

That provision grew out of a pilot program in which four Air Force procurement centers had similar "break-out" officers. The General Accounting Office (GAO) found that the four centers saved $7.4 million through bidding in 1982 on parts previously bought through sole-source contracts. In 1983, the GAO reported, the four procurement centers saved $36 million through competitive bidding.

In 1984, there were between 15 and 20 major procurement centers, each of which had an annual contract volume of over $150 million for spare parts.

Provisions

As cleared, HR 4209 provided that:

● SBA representatives — whose jobs would be to "break out" contracts for competition — would be located in each Defense Department procurement center, and the SBA could choose to put representatives in non-military centers. SBA representatives could allow agencies to buy goods direct from manufacturers, eliminating "pass-through" charges assessed by contractors.

● Small-business participation in procurement would be enhanced by sharply limiting the use of "prequalification requirements." Agencies must justify the use of prequalification requirements, and allow potential contractors to show their ability to qualify for a contract.

● Agencies must plan for future competitive procurement of spare parts by encouraging the use of goods already available in the government's supply system and the competitive re-procurement of spare parts.

● Notices, following consistent standards, must specify details of bidding opportunities and must be listed in *Commerce Business Daily*, a Department of Commerce publication.

● Notices of proposed procurement regulations must be published in the *Federal Register*, with an opportunity for public comment.

● Regulations must be written specifying the amount of overhead charges allowed in a contract, and prohibiting the purchase of commercially available goods at a price higher than the commercial price.

● Contractors could not restrict sales by their subcontractors directly to the government.

● Contracts would have to spell out the contractor's responsibility for providing the government technical data.

● Regulations must be written defining the legitimate proprietary interests of the government and contractors. The government would have proprietary rights over information produced at public expense, and contractors could claim proprietary rights over data produced at private expense. A procedure would be set up to review contractors' claims of proprietary rights.

Legislative History

House Action. HR 4209, reported in November 1983, passed the House by voice vote and without amendment May 21. As passed, the bill required the SBA to assign a "break-out" procurement officer to each major federal procurement center, to identify purchasing contracts that could be broken out for competitive bidding.

Senate Action. As reported by the Senate Small

Business and Armed Services committees, S 2489 in many respects paralleled the procurement sections of the Senate defense authorization bill (S 2723), reported by the Armed Services Committee May 31 (S Rept 98-500). The provisions of S 2489, however, applied governmentwide, not just to Pentagon purchases.

S 2489, as reported, offered incentives to major contractors to anticipate future competitive procurement of spare parts in major systems' designs. And prequalification requirements for contracts, such as the use of "qualified bidders lists," were severely limited under the bill.

The bill required agencies to include information on technical data in contracts, and that major contractors provide the data.

Penalties, including cancellation of contracts, were specified for contractors, who, claiming they were protecting trade secrets, were found to have unjustly withheld information. Some small businesses had said that they could not bid on contracts because they lacked the necessary technical information.

On the floor, the Senate through a series of voice votes added as amendments to S 2489 several other provisions that were included in the Senate defense authorization bill.

Provisions added on the floor included:

● A requirement that if a contractor sold goods to the government, which the contractor also sold commercially, the contractor must charge the government the lowest commercial price.

● Rewards for procurement officials who saved the government money.

● A requirement that procurement regulations be published.

● Limits on overhead charges added by defense contractors.

● A requirement of at least four years of tenure for program managers responsible for procurement of major defense weapons systems.

● A requirement that the Pentagon's computer spare parts procurement be improved.

● Establishment of an Office of Competition Advocate General in the armed services and in the National Aeronautics and Space Administration, who must be a flag officer and must review every non-competitive contract over $100,000.

● A requirement that the General Accounting Office report on the extent the bill increased the opportunity for small business access to government contracts.

The text of S 2489, as amended, was then substituted for that of the more limited House bill, HR 4209. The amended version of HR 4209 then passed the Senate Aug. 7 by a vote of 94-0. *(Vote 197, p. 35-S)*

Final Action. A compromise version of HR 4209 was worked out informally over several months among the members of the House Armed Services, Government Operations and Small Business committees, and the Senate Armed Services, Governmental Affairs and Small Business committees.

The compromise agreement eliminated some provisions that had been duplicated in the cleared version of the defense authorization, but in final form closely followed the Senate version of the bill.

By a 416-0 vote, the House Oct. 2 adopted a resolution (H Res 599), agreeing to the compromise, and sent it to the Senate. *(Vote 383, p. 118-H)*

Two days later, the Senate agreed to the compromise by voice vote, clearing the bill for the president.

Defense Authorization Act

Both House- and Senate-passed versions of the defense authorization contained provisions — many of them similar — aimed at increasing competition for Pentagon contracts, particularly for purchase of spare parts, in hopes that seemingly exorbitant prices for common items might be reduced.

Provisions

As cleared, the procurement sections of HR 5167 provided that:

● Procurement regulations with a significant impact beyond internal Defense Department operations must be published.

● Supplies available through a standard contract should not be bought through a special order.

● Contractors should incorporate commercially available items into major systems designs and plan for future purchase of replacement parts for major systems through competitive bidding.

● Approval of sole-source contracts would be delegated to flag officers, senior civilian employees or the heads of contracting offices.

● "Competition advocates" would be placed in each military department.

● Bids from suppliers who were not "prequalified" could not be rejected, if suppliers could meet bidding standards before contracts were awarded.

● Contracts should be written to allow for release of technical data, and under no circumstances could a contractor limit the government's use of technical data beyond seven years.

● Commercially available parts must be sold to the government at the lowest commercial price.

● Manufacturers must be identified by contractors, to allow for direct purchase of parts from the manufacturer.

● Parts should be purchased in economically advantageous quantities.

● Contractors could not prohibit their subcontractors from doing business directly with the government.

● Pricing procedures must ensure that an item's cost reflected its intrinsic value, and must disallow extra overhead costs.

Legislative History

House Action. The House defense authorization bill, HR 5167, was amended on the floor to include provisions from two other House procurement bills that did not see floor action — HR 5084 and HR 2133.

Rep. Bill Nichols, D-Ala., during floor debate May 30, offered provisions adapted from HR 5064. As reported by the Armed Services Committee April 18, the bill sought to identify direct suppliers and allow direct sales to the government from subcontractors to reduce "pass-through" costs from prime contractors.

The bill also sought to grant the government more rights to technical data, create competition advocates in military departments and require publication of significant procurement regulations.

Rep. Berkley Bedell, D-Iowa, chairman of the Small Business Subcommittee on General Oversight and the Economy, then offered an amendment to the Nichols amendment that incorporated major portions of HR 2133.

Bedell's amendment would have eliminated qualified bidders lists; required competitive bidding for spare parts, unless certain specified criteria are met; required negotiations for proprietary rights to technical information; and specified that commercially available parts be sold to the government at the lowest commercial price.

Rep. Parren J. Mitchell, D-Md., Small Business Committee chairman, had tried unsuccessfully to bring HR 2133 to the House floor earlier in May, but it was opposed by Government Operations Committee Chairman Rep. Jack Brooks, D-Texas.

HR 2133, as reported by the Small Business Committee in November 1983, would have required federal contracts of between $25,000 and $2 million to be set aside for small businesses if certain criteria were met. It also would have eliminated the requirement that firms be on a "qualified bidders list" in order to bid for defense contracts.

HR 2133, as reported, also would require DOD to give special preference to small firms "in or near" areas of high unemployment. Civilian agencies were required by existing law to give preference to small firms located in areas of high unemployment.

To win over opponents of the measure, Bedell struck the unemployment provision and excluded certain contracts from the set-aside provision, when he offered parts of HR 2133 as his amendment to the defense authorization.

Brooks and Nichols, however, continued to oppose the Bedell amendment — particularly the elimination of qualified bidders' lists and the limitations on proprietary information — on the grounds that the provisions would go too far and harm suppliers and the Pentagon's procurement processes.

Despite the opposition, Bedell's motion to add provisions from HR 2133 to Nichols' original amendment passed on a 324-75 vote. The amended Nichols amendment was then added to the House defense authorization bill by a 396-0 vote. *(Votes 169, 170, pp. 54-H, 56-H)*

Senate Action. The Senate defense authorization bill, S 2723, as reported from the Armed Services Committee, included a number of provisions adapted from S 2489, the procurement bill that formed the core of the cleared version of HR 4209.

During Senate floor debate June 13, Carl Levin, D-Mich., offered an amendment that he said was in essence a technical correction to the provisions added in committee. His amendment, accepted by voice vote, focused chiefly on efforts to encourage acquisition of replacement parts to major systems through competitive bidding and on granting proprietary rights to the government for some technical data.

Then, during floor debate June 20, Charles E. Grassley, R-Iowa, offered an amendment — also accepted by voice vote — further defining the government's rights to technical data and limiting the exclusion of bidders through use of qualified bidders lists.

Final Action. The conference report on HR 5167, filed Sept. 26 (H Rept 98-1080) drew from provisions contained in both versions of the defense authorization.

Deficit Reduction Act

The provisions of S 338, which passed the Senate in November 1983, were incorporated intact on the Senate floor into the deficit reduction bill (HR 2163, which was later substituted for the text of the House deficit reduction bill, HR 4170).

Those provisions survived largely intact through conference on HR 4170, but were altered somewhat, including

some provisions of HR 5184, as approved by the House Government Operations Committee.

Provisions

As cleared, the procurement sections of HR 4170 provided that:

● Generally all federal contracts should be awarded following a standard of "full and open" competition.

● Agencies could maintain alternative sources of supply for parts or services, and establish those "dual sources" through competitive bidding.

● Specific set-asides in existing law for small or minority-owned firms would be exempted from the competition requirements, or that competition would be limited to small businesses for contracts granted under those set-aside programs.

● Under four general and two qualified exemptions, sole-source contract awards would be authorized. Among the exempted cases for sole-source awards were instances where only one contractor would be capable of rendering a service or providing a part. Conferees specified that the exemption was not to be used as a "loophole" to evade the general competition requirement.

● Competition was required but limited for small contracts.

● A "competition advocate" would be established in each executive agency.

● Any actual or prospective bidder whose direct economic interest would be affected by the award of a procurement contract could file a protest with the Comptroller General, who would, within specified time limits, review the protest and recommend corrective action to the agency if a violation were found. In most cases, a contract could not be awarded if a protest had been filed and not resolved.

Legislative History

Senate Action. During floor consideration of HR 2163, which was the Senate version of the deficit reduction bill, provisions from S 338, which had passed the Senate in November 1983, were added by voice vote and with virtually no debate.

S 338, as passed the Senate, and as offered to the deficit bill, sought to require the use of competitive bids for most federal procurement, defense and domestic. It set the standard of "effective competition" for contracts, and required published notices of bidding for domestic contracts of greater than $10,000, and limited occasions for sole-source defense contracts.

Final Action. There were no parallel provisions in the House version of the deficit reduction bill, HR 4170, but a similar bill to S 338 — HR 5184 — was approved by the House Government Operations Committee May 9.

HR 5184 was not reported to the House until Oct. 10, however, and never saw floor action, largely because of opposition from small-business advocates who believed the bill did not adequately protect contract set-asides in existing law for small and minority-owned firms.

Key provisions in HR 5184 were that government contracting should be "full and open," as contrasted with "effective," as required by S 338 and the provisions in the deficit reduction bill, and that the General Accounting Office would have the authority to review bid protests within specified time limits, with contracts suspended in most cases while a protest was filed. Conferees accepted the House bill's language on those two points in the conference report on HR 4170.

When President Reagan signed HR 4170, the only provision he mentioned was that concerning bid protests, which he said was unconstitutional, since GAO, a legislative branch agency, was given authority that should properly belong to the executive branch.

Conferees also specified that existing set-asides for small and minority-owned firms should not be jeopardized by increasing competitive procedures generally in the government. ∎

U.S. Mint Authorization

The House May 15 passed a $47.8 million authorization (HR 5371) for the U.S. Mint for fiscal 1985, but the bill was not acted on by the Senate, and died with adjournment. It was the second year that the Mint's authorization did not clear.

The authorized spending level in the House bill was identical to the amount requested by the administration, and was slightly less than the $52 million appropriated in fiscal 1984.

The bill would have limited expenditures from the Mint's off-budget "coinage metal fund," which covered the costs of making coins, to $200 million per year.

Prior to 1982, the Mint operated under a permanent authorization, but the House Banking Committee wanted one-year authorizations to give it an opportunity to evaluate regularly the Mint's operations. In 1983, Congress failed to pass an authorization bill, and funds for the Mint were deleted from the Treasury, Postal Service appropriations bill by a point of order on the House floor. However, the money later was added to the fiscal 1984 continuing appropriations resolution (H J Res 413 — PL 98-151) by conferees. *(1983 Almanac p. 531)*

The fiscal 1985 Treasury, Postal Service appropriations bill, which contained appropriations for the Mint, failed to clear, but its provisions were included in the fiscal 1985 continuing appropriations resolution (H J Res 648 — PL 98-473). The bill appropriated $47.6 million for the Mint in fiscal 1985. *(Continuing resolution, p. 444; Treasury, Postal Service appropriation, p. 425)* ∎

Merit Pay, Pay Equity

President Reagan Nov. 8 signed a bill (HR 2300 — PL 98-615) that made changes in the merit pay system affecting managers in civil service grades 13-15, and in the Senior Executive Service.

The merit-pay provisions were taken from a separate bill (S 958) and added on the Senate floor to HR 2300, which granted survivor and health care benefits to some former spouses of federal civil servants. *(Former spouses benefits, p. 202)*

S 958 had passed both Senate and House in differing forms, but never went to conference because the House version contained a controversial provision requiring a study of possible sex discrimination in the pay scales of the federal work force.

Merit Pay

As cleared, HR 2300 made several changes in the merit pay system affecting federal managers in civil service grades 13-15. Under the 1978 Civil Service Reform Act (PL

95-454), these 110,000 employees were given raises based on performance evaluations. *(1978 Almanac p. 818)*

Since that law went into effect, managers had complained that some good performers had been receiving smaller raises than those they supervised, who received automatic raises, and that the performance evaluations varied from agency to agency. A March study by the General Accounting Office (GAO), which examined the merit pay system in four agencies, corroborated that view.

Reps. Frank R. Wolf, R-Va., and Steny H. Hoyer, D-Md., whose suburban Washington districts contained many workers affected by the program, sponsored legislation in the House to overhaul the system. Virginia Republicans John W. Warner and Paul S. Trible Jr. sponsored a similar proposal in the Senate.

The provisions contained in HR 2300 would establish a uniform five-tiered rating system, and would grant raises to employees who rated highly, and deny raises to those who rated poorly. The bill would also allow cash awards for exceptional performers.

In addition, the bill would establish minimum and maximum levels for performance awards, and would require agencies to spend at least 1.15 percent of their aggregate base pay on performance awards after five years.

Provisions in the earlier House bill would have permitted an employee to appeal to the Merit Systems Protection Board, if the employee received a low performance rating, but that provision was dropped.

Senior Executive Service

HR 2300 also made changes in the Senior Executive Service (SES), the highest levels of the civil service.

The SES also was established by the 1978 civil service act, and that measure permitted Congress to abolish the SES after five years, which ended in July. According to the House Post Office and Civil Service Committee report on HR 5680 (H Rept 98-832), the committee heard of problems with the system, but did not hear any recommendations to scrap it.

HR 2300 established minimum and maximum performance bonuses, and eliminated the existing cap on the number of employees who received bonuses.

In addition, the bill extended the notification period for transferring a career employee outside his or her commuting area. It also guaranteed most employees civil service positions, if they were removed from the SES by reductions in force.

At the insistence of the Senate and the administration, a House provision capping the number of political appointees in the SES was dropped.

Pay Equity

Sen. Alan Cranston, D-Calif., agreed to let HR 2300 come to the floor only after he reached an agreement with opponents of the proposed pay-equity study to consider the question again in 1985. Cranston had tried to add a similar pay equity provision to the continuing appropriations resolution (H J Res 648). That effort failed Oct. 3 on a 41-57 vote. *(Vote 256, p. 45-S)*

The agreement called for GAO to study the costs, methodology and scope of a pay equity survey, and to report back to Congress by March 1, 1985. Ted Stevens, R-Alaska, chairman of the Senate Governmental Affairs Civil Service Subcommittee and an opponent of the pay equity provision, promised to hold hearings on the GAO study.

Rep. Mary Rose Oakar, D-Ohio, chief House sponsor

of the pay equity provision, which was contained in the House-passed version of S 958, said she was "very greatly disappointed that the Senate refused to act on this very important provision."

Legislative History

The Senate Governmental Affairs Committee Feb. 3 reported S 958, containing merit pay and Senior Executive Service provisions (S Rept 98-351).

The Senate passed the bill by voice vote March 1, after accepting by voice vote an amendment from William Proxmire, D-Wis., prohibiting government dining rooms used exclusively by senior military or civilian officials or U.S. senators from charging less for meals than they cost to prepare.

The House Post Office and Civil Service Committee June 11 reported HR 5680 (H Rept 98-832), a bill that included merit pay, Senior Executive Service and pay equity provisions.

The House rejected an amendment from Daniel B. Crane, R-Ill., that would have altered the pay equity provision. Crane's amendment would have focused the study not on jobs with "comparable duties" and "comparable working conditions," but instead on jobs with "substantially equal duties" and "substantially equal working conditions." Crane's amendment was defeated by a 22-395 vote. *(Vote 264, p. 82-H)*

The House then defeated by voice vote an amendment by Rep. William E. Dannemeyer, R-Calif., that would prohibit the use of a federal pay equity study in any lawsuit charging sex discrimination in federal pay scales.

The House passed HR 5680 on June 28 by a 413-6 vote. By voice vote, it then substituted the language of HR 5680 for that of S 958 and returned the bill to the Senate. *(Vote 265, p. 82-H)*

HR 2300, as reported by the Post Office and Civil Service Committee Sept. 24 (H Rept 98-1054), and as passed the House by voice vote the same day, only contained provisions relating to benefits for former spouses.

After much parliamentary wrangling over the pay equity provision, the Senate by voice vote Oct. 10 added the language of the Senate-passed version of S 958 to HR 2300. The Senate then passed the bill by voice vote. The House accepted the Senate amendments by voice vote the same day, clearing the bill for the president. ∎

Former Spouse Benefits

After attaching provisions to make changes in the merit pay system for some federal employees, Congress Oct. 10 cleared for President Reagan's signature a bill (HR 2300 — PL 98-615) allowing former spouses of federal workers to receive survivor benefits.

The House had passed the bill Sept. 24. The Senate Oct. 10 added the merit-pay provisions from a separate bill (S 958) to the pension bill. The House then accepted the Senate amendments the same day, clearing the bill for the president. *(Merit pay, p. 201)*

Alan Cranston, D-Calif., held up Senate consideration of HR 2300 until he reached an agreement with Ted Stevens, R-Alaska, chairman of the Governmental Affairs Subcommittee on Civil Service, to consider in 1985 the separate issue of sex discrimination in federal pay scales. As cleared by Congress, HR 2300 permitted the Office of Personnel Management (OPM) to recognize court orders granting survivor benefits to former spouses of federal employees and retirees. The bill also permitted federal employees to elect to provide survivor benefits for former spouses.

Under a 1978 change in the civil service retirement system (PL 95-366), OPM was required to recognize court orders granting annuities to former spouses of federal employees. A separate bill enacted in 1984 (HR 4280 — PL 98-397) gave state courts the authority to divide private pension benefits in divorce proceedings.

HR 2300 extended that authority to civil service survivor benefits. The bill also permitted certain former spouses to participate in the federal employee health benefits program. That provision only applied to former spouses of employees who had not remarried and who had obtained court orders requiring survivor annuities. The spouses had to pay both the employees' and the government's share of the premiums.

The bill granted retroactive survivor benefits to certain former spouses.

The House Post Office and Civil Service Committee Sept. 24 unanimously reported HR 2300 (H Rept 98-1054). By voice vote and without amendment, the House passed the bill the same day.

The Senate Governmental Affairs Committee had under consideration a similar bill (S 2821), but did not act on it. The Senate Oct. 10, however, took up HR 2300, and after adding the merit pay provisions from S 958, passed the bill by voice vote, clearing it for the president. ∎

Postal Service Pay

A midsummer contract dispute between the U.S. Postal Service and postal workers' unions went to arbitration after Congress stepped in and barred the Postal Service from cutting pay and benefits for new employees.

An amendment to the fiscal 1984 supplemental appropriations bill (HR 6040 — PL 98-396), cleared by Congress Aug. 10 and signed into law Aug. 22, prohibited the Postal Service from changing pay scales before contract negotiations were completed.

Rep. Silvio O. Conte, R-Mass., offered the amendment on the House floor, arguing that he was trying to restore bargaining balance between the Postal Service and its unions.

The House adopted Conte's amendment by voice vote Aug. 1, but the Senate Appropriations Committee reported the bill Aug. 2 without the provision (S Rept 98-570). It became an issue in conference, where Senate conferees refused to accept the House position, arguing that Congress should not get involved in the dispute.

During the conference, Sen. Ted Stevens, R-Alaska, proposed a compromise making the provision non-binding, but House conferees stuck by their provision. The House voted 378-1 Aug. 10 to insist on its position, and the Senate accepted it. *(Vote 330, p. 100-H)*

Background

More than 600,000 postal employees began working without a contract July 20, when their three-year-old contract expired.

The unions argued for a 10 percent wage and benefit increase the first year. Management, on the other hand, backed a three-year wage freeze, and proposed that new workers be paid 23 percent less than current employees. The lower wage, the Postal Service argued, was what private-sector employees in comparable jobs were paid. The two-tiered system, the service explained, would institute the comparable wage without harming current employees.

In addition, the Postal Service maintained that the wage increase the unions sought would cause the price of a first-class stamp, then 20 cents, to rise to as much as 28 cents within three years.

On July 25, after talks broke down, Postmaster General William F. Bolger announced that the service would impose its final bargaining position. Supporters of the unions cried foul. "There is no doubt that this move was an attempt by the postmaster general to bust the postal unions," said Rep. Patricia Schroeder, D-Colo.

Others argued that the move was illegal under the Postal Reorganization Act of 1970 (PL 91-375). "This unilateral restructuring of the employee compensation system undermines the entire collective bargaining procedure set up by the Congress," said Rep. Gerald D. Kleczka, D-Wis.

Under private-sector labor law, an employer was allowed to impose one of its bargaining positions after a contract expired; if the union objected, it was allowed to strike. Postal workers, however, were barred from striking.

The Postal Reorganization Act, enacted after a weeklong postal workers' strike, required that if a contract expired and the two sides had not reached agreement, a federal fact-finding panel would begin a 45-day investigation. If the issues were still unresolved, the matter would be referred to a three-person arbitration board to conclude a binding agreement. *(1970 Almanac p. 341)*

Arbitrators were appointed to review the postal workers' contract, for the first time under the reorganization act. They decided Dec. 24 to award postal workers a 2.7 percent annual raise over three years, cut starting pay in some jobs by as much as $5,000 or 25 percent, and raise maximum pay by 5 percent. ∎

Federal, Congressional Pay

President Reagan Aug. 30 proposed a 3.5 percent pay raise for white-collar federal workers, effective Jan. 1, 1985. Members of Congress received an identical raise under a law that gave them the same salary increases as other white-collar federal employees. The extra money boosted congressional salaries from $72,600 a year to $75,100.

The raise was guaranteed to take effect — federal white-collar pay hikes were automatic — when Congress failed to vote otherwise before adjourning.

The raise scheduled for 1985 came on top of a 4 percent raise that federal white-collar employees and members of Congress received in 1984.

President Reagan in August 1983 had recommended a 3.5 percent raise for federal workers, effective Jan. 1, 1984.

In late 1983, the Senate blocked an attempt to increase the raise to 4 percent. And on Jan. 26 the Senate passed a bill (S 2211) to rescind the 3.5 percent raise. That measure was buried in the House Post Office and Civil Service Committee, leaving the raise in effect.

In April, however, as part of the 1983 Budget Reconciliation Act (HR 4169 — PL 98-270), Congress increased the 3.5 percent salary hike by one-half percentage point, for a total 1984 pay raise of 4 percent. That action in-creased members' salaries to $72,600. *(1983 Almanac pp. 576, 577; story, p. 160)*

On Sept. 5, the first day Congress was in session after Reagan's announcement of the scheduled 1985 raise, Rep. Stan Parris, R-Va., introduced a bill (HR 6191) to give federal workers and members of Congress a 4 percent raise effective Oct. 1, 1984. That measure was never acted upon.

Background

Since 1971, under the Federal Pay Comparability Act (PL 91-656), federal white-collar employees had received automatic raises set by the president, based on the recommendations of his appointed "pay agent." Those raises took effect automatically, unless Congress voted otherwise.

In 1975, Congress rushed through an amendment to a minor Postal Service bill (PL 94-82) tying its own raises to the white-collar raises the president set, but retaining a requirement that the raises be voted on annually. In 1983, raises for members of Congress also became automatic under a provision contained in a continuing appropriations bill enacted in 1981 (PL 97-51). *(1981 Almanac p. 286; 1975 Almanac p. 703)*

The president's pay agent — the director of the Office of Personnel Management, the secretary of labor and the director of the Office of Management and Budget — was created by PL 91-656 to recommend raises to bring federal salaries in line with those of comparable private-sector jobs.

The raise proposed by the president for 1985 was far short of the 18.28 percent increase deemed necessary by the pay agent to make federal salaries comparable.

As had happened in each of the previous six years, the president rejected the pay agent's recommendations, citing budget considerations. ∎

Pay Raise Repeal Effort Fails

Despite an overwhelming Senate vote to repeal a pay raise for members of Congress, the House ignored the Senate's move and members kept the extra money.

The Senate voted 66-19 Jan. 26 to revoke the $2,400 cost-of-living increase lawmakers automatically received Jan. 1, 1984, boosting members' annual salaries from $69,800 to $72,200. *(Vote 2, p. 2-S)*

But House leaders sent the bill (S 2211) to the Post Office and Civil Service Committee, which took no action, and the bill died at the end of the 98th Congress. Similar House bills (HR 4594, HR 4600) to repeal the pay raise also died in the committee without hearings.

The salary rollback required House approval to take effect.

Recognizing members' personal financial needs and the fact that they began paying about $2,500 in Social Security taxes in 1984, House leaders from both parties wanted to protect members from an election-year vote on the politically difficult subject by simply keeping it off the floor.

"I would think it is extraordinarily unwise for us to follow the action of the Senate and interrupt the cost-of-living adjustment," said Majority Whip Thomas S. Foley, D-Wash. And an aide to House Speaker Thomas P. O'Neill Jr., D-Mass., said O'Neill "believes in the pay raise." (On Jan. 1, 1985, members of Congress received an additional 4 percent raise, bringing their salaries to $75,100 a year.)

Repeal Effort

The 3.5 percent pay raise was granted under a 1975 law that gave members of Congress the same cost-of-living increases received by white-collar federal employees. No vote was necessary because a 1981 law provided an automatic appropriation that insulated members from a vote each year. *(Federal, congressional pay, p. 203)*

Several Republican senators objected to the "backdoor" pay hike, arguing that House members had received a 15 percent increase in 1982 and senators had taken the same raise in 1983. *(1982 Almanac p. 544)*

Senate Majority Leader Howard H. Baker Jr., R-Tenn., promised Don Nickles, R-Okla., that he would bring Nickles' pay repeal bill (S 2211) to the floor as soon as Congress returned from its nine-week winter vacation.

The bill was brought up the day after President Reagan's State of the Union message calling for budget austerity, and many senators said the pay rollback was a symbolic sign of their concern about the budget deficit.

During the Senate debate, Nickles said, "We are in hard times. The country is going broke with deficits. It is hard for those of us who like to see cuts in every area, including defense, to accept a raise."

"We are going to have to do some belt tightening of our own here as members of the Senate to set an example for the belt tightening we must do" in the federal budget, said J. James Exon, D-Neb.

S 2211 would have repealed the 3.5 percent raise for members of Congress, but would not have affected other federal employees. The pay cut would not have been retroactive.

The Jan. 1 increase went into effect without any legislative action by members, and without the agonizing, acrimonious debate that typically preceded votes on the politically sensitive issue. Fearing voter backlash, members were generally reluctant to approve pay hikes for themselves, particularly in an election year.

Critics contended the boost was unwarranted because the House in 1982 and the Senate in 1983 had given themselves a 15 percent pay raise. Other critics said members' salaries should not be set through backdoor increases.

"If Congress wants a pay raise, they ought to be willing to have it up on the floor for everyone to see and vote up or down," said Jake Garn, R-Utah, a cosponsor of S 2211. "We have had sneaky ones over the years, but this is the worst one."

Nickles and Garn had tried to block the cost-of-living hike in November 1983 through an amendment to the fiscal 1984 defense appropriations bill (HR 4185). The amendment was withdrawn because of procedural problems, but Majority Leader Baker then pledged to address the issue early in 1984. *(1983 Almanac p. 577)*

Making good on that promise, Baker cosponsored Nickles' repeal bill and brought it to the floor just three days after it was introduced.

Opponents of the bill argued that the salary rollback — which would save about $1.3 million in 1984 — was a feeble gesture at budget austerity in the face of $200 billion budget deficits.

"If we really want to get down to the core, we will get into the areas where we are really spending money," said Barry Goldwater, R-Ariz. "Take a look at the welfare state."

Others warned that if salaries were not adequate to cover the high cost of maintaining homes both in their states and in Washington, members would be forced to rely more heavily on honoraria and other outside earnings.

A Senate leadership aide said the Senate could have taken up a bill that rescinded the pay raise for senators only. But such a measure probably would have sailed through the House, and senators would have suffered the pay repeal alone. So the bill was written to affect both chambers, he said.

If the pay repeal was to die in the House, "there won't be . . . tears over it here," the Senate aide said.

Even Nickles, who said he would be "disappointed" if the House did not pass the measure, conceded that most senators would be relieved if the House killed the bill.

Pay Commission Proposal

In the spring, the Senate Judiciary Committee sent the full Senate a proposed constitutional amendment to establish an independent commission to set the salaries of members of Congress.

The Senate, however, never debated the resolution, and it, too, died at the end of the 98th Congress.

The measure (S J Res 1 — S Rept 98-655) was ordered reported by voice vote March 22 without a recommendation for or against its passage. To be enacted, a constitutional amendment required approval by a two-thirds majority of the House and Senate, and ratification by three-fourths of the states.

Under existing law, Congress could raise or lower the pay of its members. Members automatically received the same annual pay raises the president awarded to white-collar federal employees.

Under S J Res 1, the president would have appointed a nine-member commission that would set congressional salaries on July 1 of each even-numbered year. The salaries would take effect when the members of a newly elected Congress took office the following January and would stay in effect for that two-year Congress.

The idea was not dissimilar from a plan already in existence. In 1967, Congress established a Commission on Executive, Legislative and Judicial Salaries to be appointed every four years by the president to recommend salaries for federal officials. Initially, the president could modify or simply pass along the commission's recommendations and they would go into effect unless Congress vetoed them. However, in 1977, Congress changed the law to require congressional votes on the recommendations, and the commission's findings subsequently decreased in political value. *(1982 Almanac p. 546; Congress and the Nation Vol. V, p. 889)* ∎

Court Restricts President's Pocket-Veto Power

A federal appeals court ruled Aug. 29 that President Reagan acted unconstitutionally when he used a pocket veto in November 1983 to reject legislation linking aid to El Salvador with human rights progress there.

In a 2-1 decision, a panel of the U.S. Court of Appeals for the District of Columbia ruled that Reagan did not have the authority to veto the bill (HR 4042) by "pocketing" it — taking no action — between two sessions of Congress.

The decision came in a lawsuit filed by Rep. Michael D. Barnes, D-Md., and 32 other Democratic House members. The full House and Senate later joined the case as plaintiffs.

"I'm very pleased. But I am not surprised by the decision," said Barnes, chairman of the Foreign Affairs Subcommittee on Western Hemisphere Affairs and sponsor of HR 4042.

"Our position is well-founded in the law. And it is one that is supported by the leadership of both houses of the Congress, Republican and Democratic," Barnes said.

The three-judge appeals panel issued a one-page order reversing a lower court decision handed down in March. A longer opinion was expected but had not been issued by year's end.

Justice Department attorneys said they would not decide whether to ask the Supreme Court to review the case until they saw the detailed opinion from the appeals court.

"It's a little hard to analyze the decision until we see what the basis for it was," said Justice attorney Richard K. Willard. Attorneys for both sides, though, had said earlier that they expected the case to reach the Supreme Court.

The appeals court decision was supported by Judges Spottswood W. Robinson 3d and Carl McGowan. Judge Robert H. Bork dissented on the grounds that members of Congress did not have the legal standing to bring the lawsuit.

The decision overturned a ruling March 9 by U.S. District Court Judge Thomas P. Jackson, who held that a president may exercise a pocket veto when Congress is between sessions, as Reagan did in 1983 when he refused to sign HR 4042 during the Thanksgiving-Christmas recess between the first and second sessions of the 98th Congress. (1983 Almanac p. 156)

Presidential Options

At issue in the case was whether the president can pocket-veto a bill between the first and second session of a two-year term of Congress or during other intra-session recesses, or whether the pocket veto may be used only after Congress had adjourned at the end of a full two-year term.

The question involved a president's options after Congress had sent him a bill for his signature. When the legislature is in session, the president has 10 working days to sign a bill or veto it; a vetoed bill is returned to Congress with an explanation detailing the reasons for rejecting it. If the president neither signs nor vetoes a measure for 10 days while Congress is in session, it automatically becomes law.

However, Article I, Section 7 of the U.S. Constitution provides that a bill "shall not be a law" if "Congress by their adjournment prevent its return." With Congress not meeting, the president can, by declining to act, pocket-veto the bill because he does not have an opportunity to return it to Congress with his objections.

Attorneys for the members of Congress argued that Reagan should have used a normal veto procedure, which gives Congress a chance to override a veto by a two-thirds majority vote in both houses. They said a pocket veto may be used only if the return of a bill is "prevented" by Congress' final adjournment.

With HR 4042, congressional attorneys said, return was not prevented because both chambers appointed officers to receive presidential messages while Congress was away, and it was possible to reconvene members at the call of the leadership.

"The original purpose of the pocket veto clause was not to be the principal mechanism by which the president and Congress resolve an issue. It's an emergency backstop mechanism," said House counsel Steven Ross.

"If the president did not like the El Salvador bill, he was not without remedy. All he had to do was take 10 seconds to sign a veto message," Ross said.

In asserting that Reagan's veto of HR 4042 was invalid, members claimed that the measure had become law.

But the court's ruling did not appear to have an immediate influence on aid to El Salvador and human rights reporting requirements, although it could resolve a long-standing dispute between the executive and legislative branches over pocket vetoes.

"There is no immediate substantive effect, but the long-term procedural effect of this decision is significant," Barnes said.

"Resolving this issue in favor of the Congress does shift some power to the legislative branch. It will make it more difficult in the future for the president to avoid a direct confrontation with the Congress on issues he finds troublesome," he said.

Without a detailed court opinion, congressional officials were uncertain whether HR 4042's El Salvador reporting requirements would take effect.

The bill, passed by voice vote in both chambers in late 1983, would have reinstated during fiscal 1984 a requirement that the president certify to Congress every 180 days that El Salvador was making sufficient progress on human rights and other issues to merit continued U.S. assistance. Without such certifications, military aid to El Salvador would be cut off.

The certification requirement was first enacted in 1981 in PL 97-113. It was in effect for fiscal years 1982 and 1983, and expired Sept. 30, 1983. The semiannual reports had been used by congressional Democrats to challenge the Reagan administration's support of the Salvadoran government.

Even if HR 4042 had taken effect immediately after the ruling, its duration would have been short-lived because fiscal 1984 ended Sept. 30.

In addition, new El Salvador reporting requirements were included in a fiscal 1984 supplemental appropriations bill (H J Res 492 — PL 98-332) approved by Congress June 26. (Story, p. 429)

The supplemental spending bill required the president to report every 60 days, during the remainder of fiscal 1984, on various issues in El Salvador, including elections, the administration of justice, government actions to curtail so-called death squads, the training of the armed forces and land reform.

Under this law, the State Department issued a report to Congress July 12 that said the government of El Salvador had made significant progress in ending killings of civilians by death squads alleged to be aligned with the country's military.

Legal Background

From 1789 to 1980, presidents vetoed 2,391 bills, 1,011 by pocket veto. President James Madison issued the first pocket veto in 1812.

Reagan had pocket-vetoed seven bills, but other than the El Salvador measure, only one was during a congressional intersession. That veto was in December 1981, on a bankruptcy bill. (1981 Almanac p. 436)

The precedent in this area of law was set by a 1929

Supreme Court decision. In that case, based on President Calvin Coolidge's veto of an Indian claims bill during a four-month congressional recess, the court upheld the president's authority to pocket-veto a bill between sessions of the same Congress. The justices held that the term "adjournment" applied to any congressional break preventing the return of a bill within a 10-day period.

Questions arose in the early 1970s about what kind of a congressional adjournment "prevents" the return of a bill by the president. Court decisions in 1974 and 1976 specified that a president's power to use the pocket veto was restricted to final adjournments of Congresses.

The 1974 decision by the U.S. Court of Appeals for the District of Columbia stemmed from a lawsuit by Sen. Edward M. Kennedy, D-Mass., challenging President Nixon's use of a pocket veto during a six-day recess. The bill involved was a medical training measure. The appeals court upheld Kennedy's challenge and ruled that Nixon had improperly used his pocket-veto power.

Two years later, in another suit brought by Kennedy, the U.S. District Court for the District of Columbia broadened the first ruling. The court said pocket vetoes could not be used during adjournments between sessions of Congress or within a session if both chambers appointed agents to receive presidential messages. President Ford agreed not to use the pocket veto when Congress had appointed people to receive veto messages. President Carter did not use any intersession pocket vetoes.   ∎

Televised Partisan Skirmishes Erupt in House

Junior Republicans, frustrated by their inability to debate conservative legislative goals in the House, took their case directly to the public in 1984 via cable television.

Almost every day the House was in session, at the close of legislative business, they attacked Democrats in speeches called "special orders."

Gavel-to-gavel coverage of the House was beamed to about 17 million homes nationwide by the Cable Satellite Public Affairs Network, best known as C-SPAN. And, according to estimates by Newt Gingrich, R-Ga., some 200,000 people might be watching the House on TV at any moment.

"That's not a bad crowd," boasted Gingrich, a leader of the self-styled Republican guerrillas. "This is the beginning of the ability to have a nationwide town hall meeting."

The stated aim of Gingrich and about a dozen other junior Republicans was to bring up their conservative agenda. But behind that, their goal was to embarrass Democrats on volatile issues such as school prayer and abortion. To do so, they relied on television, one of the most powerful political tools around.

Although their strategy was tailored for a television audience, it took its toll on the day-to-day operation of the House. No one expected the 1984 election year to be friendly, but few thought the House's veneer of courtesy would shatter so easily.

Members who at first were mildly annoyed by the barrage of partisan speeches and parliamentary challenges became impatient, especially when the name-calling reached a nasty level. Republicans called the Democrats "dictators" and "cheaters." Democrats retorted that the GOP agitators — whom one staffer called "the simian caucus" — were "obnoxious" and "phony."

In mid-spring the Democrats retaliated. Speaker Thomas P. O'Neill Jr., D-Mass., ordered the cameras that broadcast the proceedings to pan the House chamber during special orders to show viewers that the room was often empty. Previously, the cameras had focused only on the member speaking.

At year's end, Democrats debated but could not agree on a limit on special orders to prevent Republicans from using the free air time unchecked.

Conservative Opportunists

The main actors in this daily drama were young Republicans frustrated because Democratic leaders refused to schedule debate on any part of their conservative program.

Their goals, which they said matched President Reagan's, were to get votes on constitutional amendments to allow school prayer, outlaw abortion, require a balanced federal budget and permit the president to veto individual items in an appropriations bill. None of these issues was on the agenda of the Democratic leadership, which generally did not believe there was broad public support for them.

"The policy of going along to get along has been singularly unproductive in forcing to the floor issues that are important to the president and the American people," Gingrich said.

So the group, which called itself the Conservative Opportunity Society (COS), started meeting in Gingrich's office in early 1983 to figure out how to accomplish their objectives.

Vin Weber of Minnesota was the operation's coordinator. Gingrich, a former history professor, was viewed as the philosopher-in-residence. Robert S. Walker, Pa., a self-appointed parliamentary monitor, was the front man on the floor. Other key players were Dan Coats, Ind., Judd Gregg, N.H., Dan Lungren, Calif., Connie Mack, Fla., and Barbara F. Vucanovich, Nev.

Although the group started without the official sanction of House GOP leaders, Weber, Coats and Gregg worked with the Republican Policy and Research committees on their legislative agenda. This was to satisfy Minority Leader Robert H. Michel, Ill., who asked them to reach for a broader base.

Guerrilla Tactics

The group's pesky floor tactics started Jan. 23, the day the second session of the 98th Congress convened.

Their first step was to seek unanimous consent to call up bills on school prayer, a balanced budget, line-item veto and abortion. Several Democrats rose to object and, while this kept the issues from the floor, the Democrats walked into a new problem.

The National Republican Campaign Committee (NRCC), waiting in the wings, noted, for example, that freshman Democrat Ron Coleman of Texas objected to the school prayer amendment. The NRCC quickly sent a press release to newspapers in Coleman's conservative district proclaiming that Coleman was responsible for keeping a school prayer bill from the floor. Similar releases were sent attacking other Democrats.

To blunt future such attacks on individual Democrats, O'Neill invoked a rule Jan. 25 requiring that unanimous consent requests be cleared by the leadership in both parties. Lacking such approval, O'Neill said, the chair may deny recognition for such requests. O'Neill's action stifled this tactic for the time being.

Also on Jan. 23, the COS crew tried to reserve four hours a day through Congress' planned Oct. 4 adjournment for special orders, the speeches given at the end of each legislative day, usually to an empty chamber. But their request, which took up five pages in the *Congressional Record*, was denied by Democratic leaders, who said the Republicans wanted to monopolize the time.

Reaction

The initial Democratic response to the tactics used by Gingrich, Walker and others was to laugh them off as silly and pointless.

O'Neill said the young Republicans' "crustiness and ruthlessness" helped Democrats by turning off the public.

Coleman, the Texas Democrat hit with one of their attacks, said he thought the ploy would backfire. He said a newspaper in his district quickly editorialized against the "dirty tricks" the Republicans used in pouncing on Coleman on the school prayer issue.

"I think it did them more damage than it did me," Coleman said.

As the elected Republican leader, Michel was in a difficult position. Some of the floor tactics started without his knowledge or approval. Also, he felt pressure from older and more moderate Republicans who thought the young conservatives were seizing the party's stage in the House. As one moderate put it, "It looks like they're running the show, not Michel."

At the same time, though, Michel was sensitive to the frustrations of younger members in a minority, and he urged them to work within the system.

"I told this small coterie that you're only going to be effective if you broaden the base and bring more members into it," Michel said.

"To get things done you have to have support of members on your own side," Michel said. "I told them to be mindful of that, or you'll be cast in the role of being obstructionists or hell-raising types."

Michel also warned the group that their conservative agenda might not be every Republican's "cup of tea."

Gloves Come Off

In mid-May, all vestiges of congressional comity disappeared in the fight over the partisan use of House television broadcasts.

The dispute reached the boiling point May 15 when Speaker O'Neill was officially chastised for using derogatory words about a member. Congressional researchers said he was the first Speaker since 1797 to be rebuked for his language.

O'Neill's outburst occurred in a shouting match with Gingrich. O'Neill said Gingrich's behavior was "the lowest thing" he had seen in the House.

The catalyst for the blowup was O'Neill's unilateral decision May 10 to have TV cameras pan the chamber during special orders to show that the room was often empty.

The rousing fight between O'Neill and Gingrich May 15 was the most venomous floor exchange observers had seen in years. And it signaled a polarization between Democrats and Republicans that lasted for the remainder of the year.

"I would not be buying any stock in bipartisanship if I were you," said Thomas J. Downey, D-N.Y.

"No good can come out of this. Just a lot of bitterness and a lot of hatred," said Silvio O. Conte, R-Mass., a 25-year House veteran.

Michel May 17 introduced a resolution (H Res 500) calling for a rules change to require cameras to pan the chamber during all business, not just special orders, and also show members voting, which was not broadcast. The resolution was endorsed by the House Republican Conference but never came to a floor vote.

Televising the entire chamber during all working hours would have shown that few members were on the floor for most debates. Televising the voting would show viewers "the arm twisting and vote switching that goes on," an aide to Michel said.

One indirect effect of the House uproar may have been a further delay in efforts to televise the Senate. "The House having to hang its laundry in public is going to have a chilling effect with the members," a Senate leadership aide said. *(Story, p. 209)*

The House events during the week of May 14 stemmed from months of tension between the group of junior Republicans and the Democrats they were attacking.

"The blowup was inevitable," said Byron L. Dorgan, D-N.D. "We had special orders night after night after night that painted Democrats as irresponsible, as liberals not interested in the federal deficit and not interested in foreign policy."

At first most Democrats ignored the speeches. But, Dorgan said, "in the past few weeks there has been concern that the public might be buying some of these things."

On May 8, Gingrich and Walker used a special order to read into the *Congressional Record* a study critical of Democrats' foreign policy statements over the past 15 years. The report by the conservative Republican Study Committee named about 50 House Democrats, some of whom later charged that it contained innuendoes that smacked of McCarthyism.

Several Democrats complained to O'Neill that they had no chance to defend themselves during the special order, which started at about 7:30 p.m. Gingrich later said he sent letters alerting each Democrat named in the report that it would be read, but several said they never received notice.

O'Neill, who under House rules controlled the television cameras, retaliated May 10 by ordering that a wide-angle lens show the television audience what gallery observers already knew: that the chamber usually was occupied by as few as one or two members during special orders. Until May 10 the cameras never strayed from the member speaking because lawmakers feared the reaction of viewers wondering why their representative was not in the chamber during every debate.

Many viewers were surprised by the empty seats. "I didn't realize until . . . they made that pan that there was nobody in the whole place, and that was one of the best acting jobs I've ever seen," said a C-SPAN viewer from Salinas, Calif.

The first to receive the panning treatment was Walker, who was enraged when he discovered during a special order May 10 the TV screen was showing an almost empty room.

In Walker's defense, Michel wrote to O'Neill May 11 charging that the Speaker singled out Walker for "public ridicule" and that O'Neill made the decision to show the empty seats "without prior consultation."

O'Neill explained his decision the following Monday, May 14. In an unusual floor speech and in comments to reporters, he said the GOP speechmaking was "a sham" and that the public should know "when it's after hours, it's for home consumption."

O'Neill said he would continue using the wide-angle lens during special orders, but not during regular legislative business. He also announced that, as of that day, type would crawl across the bottom of the screen at regular intervals during special orders announcing that "the House has completed its scheduled legislative business and is proceeding with special orders."

O'Neill's speech brought Gingrich to the floor the next day, May 15, to answer him. As Gingrich defended the Republicans' foreign policy paper, O'Neill, who was listening from the floor, lost his temper.

O'Neill charged that Gingrich had challenged "the Americanism" of Democrats named in the study, and said, "It is the lowest thing that I have ever seen in my 32 years in Congress."

At that point, Minority Whip Trent Lott, R-Miss., demanded that "the Speaker's words be taken down," a phrase used when members want remarks repeated by a clerk and a ruling from the chair on their propriety.

Massachusetts Democrat Joe Moakley, a close friend of O'Neill, was in the chair at the time. But after learning from the parliamentarian that the words violated House rules against personal insults, Moakley said "that type of characterization should not be used in debate."

Normally a member deemed out of order was barred from debate for the rest of the day. But in a conciliatory move, Lott asked that O'Neill be allowed to continue speaking.

When he resumed, O'Neill said he was not questioning Gingrich's patriotism, but his judgment.

"I was expressing my opinion," O'Neill said. "As a matter of fact, I was expressing my opinion very mildly, because I think much worse than what I said."

Things became even more bitter on May 30, when the National Republican Congressional Committee began airing two 30-second television commercials that accused O'Neill of breaking House rules, falsifying congressional records and bottling up legislation.

"Is this the way our Founding Fathers meant for things to be?" an announcer asked in one ad, as the camera focused on a portrait of George Washington, a tear welling up in his eye.

Guy Vander Jagt, R-Mich., chairman of the GOP campaign committee, said the $17,000 ad program was designed to show the public that "something is very wrong" in the House.

"It's not just the Speaker. It's the whole House that is out of order," Vander Jagt said.

Democrats replied that the GOP "lie and buy campaign" would only make O'Neill a national folk hero. "Go for it, make my day," declared Tony Coelho, D-Calif., chairman of the Democratic Congressional Campaign Committee.

Appropriations Vote

Besides raising concern about the decline of civility in the House, the partisan events in May also intensified debate about how the House should televise its proceedings.

One forum was the Appropriations Subcommittee on the Legislative Branch. In work on a fiscal 1985 spending bill (HR 5753) for congressional operations, Jerry Lewis, R-Calif., offered an amendment barring the use of funds to pan the House chamber unless it was done uniformly from gavel to gavel.

The subcommittee May 16 rejected Lewis' amendment by voice vote. When the bill came before the full committee May 31, Lewis proposed the amendment but withdrew it before a vote was taken. When the bill came before the House June 6, Lewis offered it again, and argued, "If we are going to pan the floor, then we should pan the floor with regularity and with a sense of fairness."

Because of a complicated House rule making it difficult for members to attach "riders," or limitations on the use of specific funds, to appropriations bills, the House never debated Lewis' amendment. Instead, the vote occurred on a procedural motion on whether to allow Lewis to offer it.

On that vote, House Democrats almost solidly lined up behind O'Neill, shelving the GOP amendment 234-147. Only four Democrats joined the 143 Republicans who supported the proposal. *(Vote 191, p. 60-H)*

Campaign Use

Also in the spring, with the elections approaching, additional partisan warfare erupted over campaign use of videotapes of daily House sessions.

Coelho, chairman of the Democratic Congressional Campaign Committee, said May 9 that the Democrats were starting a library of House television tapes for challengers to use in campaigns against Republican incumbents. The Republicans already were stockpiling tapes.

House rules prohibited members from using tapes of floor proceedings for political or commercial purposes. But there was nothing to stop a challenger from using the tapes against an incumbent.

House Republicans, meanwhile, were ready to endorse free access to House videotapes by all political candidates.

Acknowledging that there was no simple way to control the use of floor tapes by challengers, Vander Jagt, chairman of the National Republican Congressional Committee, said the way to "even up" the situation was to allow incumbents also to use the tapes in campaign advertising.

Problems first arose in 1980, when former Rep. Raphael Musto, D-Pa., was accused of violating the House rule barring the use of tapes in campaign ads when he ran a TV spot using films of his swearing-in ceremony that year. The House Committee on Standards of Official Conduct did not discipline Musto, who was defeated for re-election later that year.

The issue arose again in 1982, when Democratic candidate G. Douglas Stephens ran an ad using taped parts of a floor speech by his opponent, House Minority Leader Michel. Stephens narrowly lost to Michel in the November race.

Shortly after that incident, Vander Jagt asked Coelho to join him in withholding party support from any candidate who used videotapes in campaign commercials.

Coelho's reply came early in 1984, when he offered a House rules change to penalize challengers who use taped debate in ads. Upon taking office, the new member could be subject to censure or reprimand after an investigation.

The House Democratic Caucus was to consider a modified version of Coelho's plan May 9. But Coelho said he withdrew it because Vander Jagt refused to go along with it, and Democratic leaders were not interested in changing the rules without bipartisan support.

Instead, Coelho said he would offer the proposal in December as part of the package of rules changes the caucus would consider for the next Congress. But in December, Coelho offered no rules changes. The issue of using tapes did not arise in the fall elections.

Caucus Consideration

One of the most volatile issues before the Democratic Caucus in December was a plan to curb the time devoted to special-order speeches.

The caucus committee on organization, study and review Nov. 19 recommended that special orders at the end of the day should be limited to one hour for Democrats and one hour for Republicans, to be controlled by leaders of each party.

Existing rules allowed unlimited time on these speeches by members of either party.

Still angry about the after-hours attacks of Republicans throughout 1984, many Democrats called for restrictions on the speeches or a policy change so they would not be broadcast. In addition, some complained that it was expensive for the House to continue in session long after regular legislative business was completed. One estimate set the cost of the speeches at $10,000 an hour, to cover employee salaries, utilities and other expenses.

Despite this grumbling, there was heavy opposition to the proposed restrictions when the caucus considered them Dec. 4. After two days of negotiations between Democrats and Republicans and among the Democrats themselves, the proposal was shelved.

"We have not come to an agreement about how to prevent the abuses we have seen this year, and at the same time guarantee everyone the right to express their point of view," said Rep. Bill Alexander, Ark., Democratic chief deputy whip.

Don Edwards, D-Calif., a civil libertarian, led the caucus fight against the special-order restrictions.

"There's an element of a gag rule in it," Edwards said. "Instead of each of us having an unrestricted right to speak, we would have to go hat in hand to the Speaker or minority leader to ask for time to speak."

Edwards suggested instead that the Speaker and Democratic Caucus should be given additional staff, such as speech writers, to make sure Democratic speeches are competitive with the Republicans.

"My idea is to professionalize our viewpoint and beat them at their own game," Edwards said.

House Republicans, who were adamantly opposed to the new restrictions, were relieved that the Democrats could not reach an agreement.

"The challenge to the Democrats in the post-Mondale era is not to strangle us in debate, but to join us," Gingrich said. ∎

Senate TV Plan Fails Again

The Senate Sept. 21 denied Majority Leader Howard H. Baker Jr., R-Tenn., his dream of bringing the Senate into the television age.

On Sept. 21 senators refused to end a week-long filibuster against a resolution (S Res 66) to allow gavel-to-gavel television and radio coverage of the Senate. Baker's motion to end debate was rejected 37-44. *(Vote 230, p. 41-S)*

Although Baker lost, two procedural votes earlier that

week indicated that most senators were willing to at least discuss the proposal. *(Votes 223, 224, p. 39-S)*

The resolution's critics said there was considerable support for limited television coverage of the Senate, but not gavel-to-gavel broadcasts. Baker said there was not enough time left in the session to negotiate a compromise.

In his last opportunity to plead the case for televising the Senate before his retirement, Baker told his colleagues Sept. 17 that admitting TV cameras to the Senate chamber would restore "vigorous and well-informed debate" in the Senate.

Complaining that Senate debate "is stilted, truncated, ritualized, canned and read into the record with the conviction of a talking computer," Baker said that senators "file into the chamber only to ratify in public what we have decided in private.

"Television could help change that," he said. "Any honest senator will concede that when the television lights are on in our committee hearing rooms, attendance is high and political competition is keen."

Baker's proposal would have cost about $3.5 million for equipment and $900,000 in annual operating costs.

Opposition to the Senate broadcasts was led by Russell B. Long, D-La., and Wendell H. Ford, D-Ky. Long successfully filibustered a similar measure in 1982. *(1982 Almanac p. 540)*

He argued that senators would posture in front of the cameras and television would attract senators to the floor when they should be attending committee meetings.

Long said some senators thought they needed to be televised in order to compete with their House colleagues. But he warned that if cameras entered the chamber, senators would turn to elocution coaches and makeup experts to prepare them for television.

William Proxmire, D-Wis., another TV opponent, argued that television would make it harder for senators to reach compromises in private because "senators will find that the positions they took in their opening statements have been engraved in film."

Moreover, Proxmire said, "television thrives on the dramatic," and "any additional incentives to confrontation can only mean more argument — and probably worse legislation." Still other opponents contended that the broadcasts would be too costly.

Ford offered a substitute to allow radio, but not television, broadcasts. He argued that radio coverage would be less expensive, reach more people and would be less disruptive of Senate proceedings. Baker refused to accept Ford's proposal.

Compromise proposals to restrict coverage to major legislative debates were discussed but never offered as amendments.

An aide to Long said the senator's opposition to the broadcasts stiffened after watching the 1984 uproar over televised proceedings in the House.

The House began televising its proceedings in 1979. By 1984, about 17 million homes nationwide had been hooked up to the broadcasts via C-SPAN, the Cable Satellite Public Affairs Network.

The House broadcasts created little controversy until the second session of the 98th Congress, when a group of conservative Republicans started delivering speeches, geared to the television audience, attacking Democrats and promoting their own political agenda. Their strategy generated partisan clashes about how television should be used in the House. *(Story, p. 206)*

Background

The only time television had been permitted in the Senate chamber was in 1974 to cover the swearing-in ceremony of Vice President Nelson A. Rockefeller. In 1978, radio broadcasts were permitted for the debate on the Panama Canal treaties.

When Baker became majority leader in January 1981, he made television and radio coverage of the Senate his top priority, calling for an electronic extension of the public gallery. But Baker was unable to persuade his colleagues to go along. *(1981 Almanac p. 391)*

In February 1982 the Senate debated a proposal to allow continuous coverage by television cameras and radio microphones. Baker failed to cut off Long's filibuster, and the proposal eventually died with the end of the 97th Congress.

In 1983, the Rules and Administration Committee voted 6-3 to report, without recommendation, a new resolution (S Res 66) authorizing Senate broadcasts. *(1983 Almanac p. 595)*

S Res 66 would have allowed unedited, gavel-to-gavel television and radio coverage of Senate deliberations. It would have permitted the camera only to focus on the senator who was recognized to speak, rather than pan the chamber.

The House followed that policy of camera coverage until spring 1984, when Speaker Thomas P. O'Neill Jr., D-Mass., ordered the cameras to scan the chamber during speeches at the end of the day, showing viewers that the room often was empty.

The Senate resolution would have prohibited the political or commercial use of tapes, but would have provided them free to news organizations. House rules prohibited members from using tapes in their campaigns, but there were no restrictions on their use by non-incumbents. ∎

Three Members Face Charges

Three members of Congress faced investigations by ethics committees in 1984.

● Rep. George Hansen, R-Idaho, was reprimanded by the House after he was convicted of violating the 1978 Ethics in Government Act.

● Rep. Geraldine A. Ferraro, D-N.Y., was found by the House Committee on Standards of Official Conduct (ethics) to have technically violated the same law.

● Sen. Mark O. Hatfield, R-Ore., was investigated by the Senate Ethics Committee staff over his dealings with a Greek businessman. However, the committee found there was insufficient evidence of wrongdoing against Hatfield to justify a full-scale inquiry.

Hansen

The House July 31 reprimanded Hansen for failing to reveal various financial dealings required to be disclosed under the 1978 Ethics in Government Act (PL 95-521). *(Background, 1978 Almanac p. 835)*

Hansen, a seven-term conservative, was sentenced June 15 to between five and 15 months in prison and a $40,000 fine following his April 2 federal felony conviction on the disclosure charges. Hansen was appealing his conviction, the first ever under the 1978 law.

Hansen was narrowly defeated in his re-election bid Nov. 6.

In reprimanding Hansen, the House handed down its mildest form of punishment. It also could have censured him or expelled him from office. The vote for a reprimand was 354-52 with six members voting present. *(Vote 295, p. 90-H)*

Leaders of the House ethics committee, which had recommended the reprimand, used a parliamentary tactic to block a House vote on either increasing the penalty to censure or involving other House members.

During the debate, a defiant Hansen maintained his innocence, insisting that Reagan administration officials and other members of Congress had been caught in questionable financial reporting snags similar to his.

Among those Hansen named was Ferraro, the Democratic vice presidential nominee, whose financial disclosure reports had omitted information about her husband's real estate business in which she was an officer. Ferraro said she would provide complete details about her own finances and those of her husband, John Zaccaro.

Hansen's reference to Ferraro brought a rebuke from Rep. Barber B. Conable Jr., R-N.Y. Conable said that citing other examples before any charges had been brought against anyone else "is both unfair to that member and to the House."

It was Conable who provided the parliamentary tactic to prevent a vote on increasing the penalty or on considering sanctions on the same resolution for other House members, such as Ferraro. By moving to recommit the Hansen resolution (H Res 558) to the ethics committee, Conable precluded any other motion to recommit the bill with specific instructions to increase the penalty or name Ferraro. Conable's motion was rejected by voice vote without debate.

It was such a recommittal motion in 1983 by which the House censured Reps. Gerry E. Studds, D-Mass., and Daniel B. Crane, R-Ill., after the ethics committee had recommended only a reprimand. *(1983 Almanac p. 580)*

A Conable aide, Harry K. Nicholas, said Conable was asked to make the motion by ethics committee Chairman Louis Stokes, D-Ohio. By making the motion, Conable had to vote against Hansen's reprimand, even though he would have voted for it, according to Nicholas. Conable retired after the 98th Congress.

After the House voted to reprimand him, Hansen denied that he tried to link Ferraro with his case. "I don't think I raised the Ferraro issue. I think the Ferraro issue kind of raised itself," he told reporters.

During his House speech, Hansen also referred to Attorney General William French Smith and presidential counselor Edwin Meese III, both of whom had had questions raised about their own financial transactions.

In the case of Ferraro, she had indicated on disclosure forms that she believed she was exempt from including her husband's assets because she was not involved with them and did not expect to derive any benefit from them.

By comparison, Hansen did not claim the same spousal exemption on his disclosure forms even though he had claimed that the financial transactions prompting his legal problems involved his wife and did not benefit him. Hansen's conviction and reprimand stemmed from his failure to report nearly $334,000 in loans and profits between 1978 and 1981.

"It's the difference between disclosing and trying to hide something," Rep. Nick J. Rahall II, D-W.Va., told reporters after the House vote, referring to distinctions between the Ferraro matter and Hansen's case. Rahall was a member of the ethics committee that voted 11-1 to reprimand Hansen.

Hansen, who maintained that he was the victim of an overzealous Justice Department and a biased ethics committee staff, presented a spirited 35-minute defense with a typically flamboyant speech.

Calling himself a "victim of a horrendously unfair process," Hansen warned that a vote to punish him on disclosure charges could come back to haunt other members. "If you reprimand me, you may also harm yourselves," he said.

Hansen was indicted April 7, 1983, in U.S. District Court for the District of Columbia. Before the case went to trial, Hansen was allowed to appeal all the way to the U.S. Supreme Court, arguing that the 1978 law could not result in criminal prosecution because it was a legislative activity protected by the Constitution's speech and debate clause. The Supreme Court, however, rejected his appeal on Jan. 9, 1984, and the trial began March 21. *(1983 Almanac p. 592)*

Hansen's 1984 conviction was not his first legal problem. In 1975, Hansen pleaded guilty to two misdemeanor charges of filing late and false campaign finance reports from his 1974 House primary. He received a two-month prison sentence that was suspended and instead paid a $2,000 fine. *(1975 Almanac p. 698)*

Ferraro

The House ethics committee voted Dec. 3 that Ferraro had technically violated government ethics laws about 10 times in failing to report or reporting incorrectly a number of items on her financial disclosure forms from 1978 through 1983.

Because Ferraro — who gave up her seat to run for vice president — was not returning to Congress when it reconvened in January 1985, the committee decided that the House would not be able to act on the complaint while Ferraro was still a member. The panel vote, reportedly 8-2, was taken in secret.

Ferraro told reporters she felt "completely vindicated" by the ethics committee's report.

The 46-page report also concluded that Ferraro failed to meet the standards necessary for claiming to exempt her husband's financial interests from her financial disclosure forms. But the panel did not investigate that question.

Rep. Hank Brown, R-Colo., in a dissenting statement, urged the committee to conduct a hearing on the question. Noting that Hansen was reprimanded by the House for failing to disclose his wife's financial interests, Brown said not looking further into Ferraro's claims would set a "double standard."

The ethics probe came about because of a complaint by the Washington Legal Foundation, a conservative public interest law firm. The foundation alleged that Ferraro committed 12 violations of financial disclosure laws from 1978 through 1983. The committee concluded that "approximately 10" of the allegations were sustained.

Questions about her finances dogged Ferraro almost from the moment in July when she got the vice presidential nod from Walter F. Mondale, the Democratic presidential nominee. She tried to quell the controversy with an extraordinary press conference Aug. 21, producing a stack of documents detailing her finances for the past several years.

The documents showed that Ferraro and her husband paid about 40 percent of their income in taxes during the past six years, and that their net worth totaled about $3.8 million.

In releasing the materials, the couple also sent a check for $53,459 to the Internal Revenue Service in back taxes and interest to cover an underpayment on their 1978 taxes. The underpayment, attributed to an error by their accountant at the time, was discovered by accountants for Arthur Young & Co., who were hired by Ferraro and Zaccaro to review their financial records.

At the news conference in New York City, Ferraro denied any wrongdoing or impropriety by herself or her husband. She asserted that the materials distributed were "probably more financial disclosures than you have from any other candidate in the history of the United States and from any other spouse."

Still in question after the disclosures, however, was whether Ferraro was eligible during her six years in the House to omit information about her husband's finances on her congressional financial disclosure forms.

The ethics law required a member of Congress to disclose the financial interests and liabilities of a spouse unless the member could show he or she did not know about, contribute to or benefit from the spouse's income. Ferraro claimed she met those criteria for an exemption. But because she was an officer and stockholder in her husband's real estate company, it was not clear that she was entitled to the exemption.

During her news conference, Ferraro said she believed it was appropriate to claim the exemption on her congressional forms for the past six years.

Although she owned one of the only three shares of stock in P. Zaccaro Co., and had been listed as either vice president or secretary-treasurer of the family business, she claimed no knowledge of its operations. Her stock ownership and title, she said, were to enable her to take over the company in case of her husband's death.

"I have never participated in the workings of that business, despite the title," Ferraro said. During her six years in Congress, she kept her finances separate from her husband's because, "I did not want to know his business then and I do not want to know it now."

Hatfield

Hatfield similarly had problems with his spouse's finances, but the Senate Ethics Committee voted unanimously Sept. 25 that there was not enough evidence to conduct a full-scale investigation.

In late July, news reports linked Hatfield's aid to Greek entrepreneur Basil A. Tsakos with Tsakos' $55,000 payment to Hatfield's wife Antoinette.

Hatfield, the chairman of the Senate Appropriations Committee, was subsequently investigated to determine whether there was any improper connection between his support of a trans-African oil pipeline promoted by Tsakos and the money Tsakos paid Mrs. Hatfield.

The senator insisted his wife legitimately earned the $55,000 for real estate work she did for Tsakos, including finding and overseeing the decorating of an apartment. But according to sworn testimony to the Ethics panel by two former Tsakos employees, Mrs. Hatfield did not perform those services.

In a Portland, Ore., news conference Aug. 13, Hatfield said it was a "mistake" for his wife to accept the money at a time when he publicly supported Tsakos' trans-African pipeline. But Hatfield maintained there was "nothing unethical or illegal" about his support for the pipeline and that his wife's real estate business was separate from his work as a senator.

At the press conference, the Hatfields said they had donated $55,000 — an amount equal to the fees — to the Shriners Hospital for Crippled Children in Portland.

Stating that he had "no regrets" about his support of the project as an alternative oil route, Hatfield said, "I would have supported the concept of a trans-African pipeline in exactly the same way and with exactly the same degree of enthusiasm had I been single, or married to a fan dancer."

Although Hatfield denied that his endorsement of the pipeline was influenced by the fees his wife received from Tsakos, he added that "my insensitivity to the appearance of impropriety was a mistake." Hatfield was easily re-elected in November to the seat he first won in 1966. ∎

Law Enforcement/Judiciary

Congress in 1984 approved major changes in federal criminal laws after struggling with revisions for more than a decade. It also took important steps to adapt other areas of the law to changes brought on by new technology.

The House and Senate Judiciary committees had an unusually active and productive year, with significant legislative achievements offset by two major setbacks.

In addition to the comprehensive anti-crime package, Congress cleared a law revising the federal bankruptcy court system to overcome constitutional problems identified by the Supreme Court in 1982. The law also made substantive changes in the bankruptcy code and created 85 new federal district and appeals court judgeships. The new judicial positions made it highly probable that President Reagan's judicial appointments in his second term would give him control of the entire federal judiciary.

Seeking to address problems created by technological change, Congress gave copyright-style protection to the semiconductor chips that lay at the heart of the computer revolution. It also revamped some aspects of patent law and granted certain antitrust exemptions to joint research and development projects by two or more companies.

On the other side of the ledger, Congress for the third year in a row failed to clear a major immigration reform bill, although the legislation had passed both chambers. And civil rights advocates suffered a bitter defeat when the Senate shelved a House-passed bill to overturn a Supreme Court decision narrowing the scope of key anti-discrimination laws.

The Reagan Record

Although enactment of the anti-crime package was a major victory for Reagan, who had lobbied for it vigorously, the president did not fare as well with two other items on his agenda.

He had championed a constitutional amendment to allow organized, recited prayer in the public schools. But the Senate decisively rejected the proposal and an alternative that would have allowed silent prayer or meditation in public schools. Four months after the prayer amendment was rejected, Congress passed a bill to allow student religious groups to meet in public schools during non-class hours under the same terms as other student groups.

Reagan's other setback came when he nominated his longtime adviser, Edwin Meese III, to replace William French Smith as attorney general.

Meese's nomination ran into trouble in the Senate Judiciary Committee when questions arose about possible links between personal financial help he received from several individuals and the federal appointments those individuals subsequently received. A report by an independent counsel cleared Meese of any criminal wrongdoing, but no action was taken on the nomination in 1984. Reagan resubmitted it early in 1985.

Anti-Crime Package

The House and Senate Judiciary Committees had been working on a revision of the federal criminal code since 1973. Congress had approved relatively minor piecemeal changes in the law in the preceding three years, and had even cleared a less sweeping omnibus bill in 1982. But Reagan vetoed that measure because of objections to one provision dealing with drug-law enforcement.

The 1984 anti-crime package overhauled federal sentencing procedures to reduce disparities in the punishment of defendants who committed similar crimes, and allowed pretrial detention of suspects considered dangerous to the community. It redefined insanity and shifted the burden of proof to the defense in establishing such claims. It prohibited computer tampering, unauthorized use of credit cards or bank-account access numbers, and trafficking in counterfeit trademarked goods. Other provisions increased penalties for major drug offenses and gave officials new authority to seize the assets and profits of drug traffickers.

In addition, the law set up a grant program for state anti-crime projects, although one far more modest than the defunct Law Enforcement Assistance Administration.

The bill did not include a provision restoring the death penalty for federal crimes, even though the Senate passed such legislation as a separate measure. Lack of a federal death penalty had no bearing on state criminal justice, however. In 1984, there were more people executed under state laws — 21 — than in any year since 1963.

The Senate passed its crime package in February, while the House Judiciary Committee worked on separate bills covering much the same ground. Prior to 1984, the House had resisted major changes in sentencing and bail procedures. While Democrats on the House Judiciary Committee conceded something had to be done, they disagreed with the Republican-controlled Senate on the approach.

Reagan and House Republicans turned up the heat on the issue. In several Saturday afternoon radio speeches, the president castigated the House for dragging its feet on the Senate-passed crime package. And as the November elections drew nearer, House Democrats — fearing they would be labeled "soft on crime" — grew more and more concerned about Reagan's attacks.

A group of House Republicans sensed an opportunity and won a floor vote attaching the Senate crime package to the fiscal 1985 continuing appropriations resolution. The Senate quickly agreed to the maneuver, and the crime package cleared as part of the funding bill.

New Technology, Old Laws

As part of another end-of-the-session package, Congress cleared legislation granting the makers of semiconductor chips 10 years of protection from illegal copying of their chips. The law gave copyright-style protection to "mask works fixed in a semiconductor chip." A mask work was the intricate design pattern on a chip that routed electrical signals so they would perform specific tasks.

Responding to the concerns of various elements of high-technology industry, Congress also eased antitrust restrictions for companies that combined forces for research and development. Industry spokesman said that fears over antitrust lawsuits had blocked joint research efforts, leading to wasteful duplication that dulled the competitive edge of U.S. companies in world markets.

To protect the copyright interests of record companies and songwriters, Congress barred commercial rentals of most phonograph records unless the copyright holder granted permission and received royalties. Industry officials had testified that too many records were being rented for home tape-recording, threatening their livelihood.

Bankruptcy

The House and Senate, mired in disagreement over bankruptcy policy and politics, struggled for two years to rewrite a 1978 law that overhauled bankruptcy laws and created a separate bankruptcy court system. The 1978 law sought to streamline what had been a cumbersome process. But the Supreme Court in 1982 said Congress went too far, giving bankruptcy judges broad legal authority but not enough independence.

Some House members, led by Judiciary Chairman Peter W. Rodino Jr., D-N.J., contended that the only way to ensure a constitutional and efficient system was to put the bankruptcy judges on the same footing as federal district judges by giving them lifetime appointments and irreducible salaries. But the Senate did not want to approve a new layer of life-tenured judges, and the U.S. Judicial Conference, which set policy for the federal courts, fought the proposal relentlessly. The final bill gave overall authority for bankruptcy matters to federal district court judges and made bankruptcy judges adjuncts of those courts.

From a legal standpoint, the legislation was urgently needed to comply with the Supreme Court's ruling on the bankruptcy court structure. But what really propelled it through Congress was a head of political steam built up by two disparate interest groups — organized labor and the consumer credit industry.

The Supreme Court Feb. 22 galvanized organized labor when it ruled 5-4 that any company that had filed for bankruptcy could unilaterally abrogate its collective bargaining agreement. Labor leaders contended that the decision would wreak havoc on unions, and they gave top priority to persuading Congress to reverse the ruling.

The credit industry, meanwhile, was lobbying just as hard for changes in the law that would make it harder for individuals to escape their debts by declaring bankruptcy.

In the end, the House and Senate put together a multifaceted bill that revamped the bankruptcy court system, reversed the Supreme Court's labor ruling, and authorized bankruptcy judges to deny protection to a debtor if it would be a "substantial abuse" of the bankruptcy law to allow the person to cancel his debts.

Judicial Appointments

Reagan in his first term began an ideological transformation of the federal judiciary. When he took office, he found a federal bench dominated by the appointees of Democratic presidents. In his first term, the president appointed 167 judges — approximately one-fourth of all sitting federal jurists. By the end of his second term, it appeared virtually certain that Reagan would have appointed a clear majority of the lower federal court judges.

The majority of Reagan's appointments were white males. But he did appoint 17 women to the federal bench, including Sandra Day O'Connor, the first woman on the Supreme Court. Reagan named one black to a district court seat and elevated a black district court judge to a seat on the 2nd U.S. Curcuit Court of Appeals. Eight Hispanics were appointed, one to the 1st U.S. Circuit Court of Appeals and the remaining seven to district court positions.

Immigration Reform

Interest group pressures and election-year politics played a large role in derailing the immigration reform bill. The legislation would have penalized employers who knowingly hired illegal aliens, while authorizing millions of illegal aliens already in this country to legalize their status. It also would have expanded an existing program allowing foreign workers to enter the United States temporarily to work in agriculture.

The measure passed the Senate by a wide margin in 1983, but it barely squeaked through the House in 1984. The margin of victory was only 216-211.

Hispanic members and their liberal Democratic allies opposed the employer sanction provisions, contending they would lead to discrimination against workers who looked or sounded foreign. Conservatives and members from states bordering Mexico opposed the amnesty provisions. Organized labor disliked the temporary worker program.

A House-Senate conference committee managed to resolve all of the issues but one — how the federal government should indemnify the states against the anticipated costs of providing social services to newly legalized aliens. Members from California and Florida, in particular, were concerned about the cost issue. They wanted full federal reimbursement to the states, while the Reagan administration insisted on a cap for federal expenditures. Unable to resolve the dispute, the conference broke up in disagreement in the waning days of the session.

Civil Rights

A group of conservative senators led by Orrin G. Hatch, R-Utah, and backed by the administration caused the defeat of the year's major civil rights bill.

The bill would have overturned the Supreme Court's Feb. 28 decision in *Grove City College v. Bell*. The court ruled that Title IX of the 1972 Education Act Amendments banned sex discrimination only in a "program or activity" receiving federal aid, not in the entire institution. Three other laws barred discrimination based on race, age or handicap in any "program or activity" receiving federal funds, and civil rights lawyers warned that the *Grove City* ruling would restrict enforcement of these statutes as well.

The House easily passed a bill amending all four statutes to make clear that any "recipient" of aid, not simply any "program or activity," would be required to conform to anti-bias laws. The House bill was held at the Senate desk, where Majority Leader Howard H. Baker Jr., R-Tenn., could have called it up for consideration at any time. He did not, and a companion Senate bill stalled in the Labor and Human Resources Committee, chaired by Hatch.

Supporters of the bill tried to attach it as an amendment to the fiscal 1985 continuing appropriations resolution, touching off parliamentary gridlock in the Senate for four days. With no agreement in sight, the Senate finally voted Oct. 2 to table, and thus kill, the amendment.

—By Nadine Cohodas

Major Crime Package Cleared by Congress

President Reagan Oct. 12 signed into law a sweeping anti-crime package that represented the culmination of an 11-year effort to make major changes in the federal criminal code.

The crime provisions were attached to the fiscal 1985 continuing appropriations resolution (H J Res 648 — PL 98-473) cleared by Congress Oct. 11. *(Funding bill, p. 444)*

The package was not quite as comprehensive as earlier criminal code reform proposals. But the new law incorporated many major elements of the earlier proposals, and it was the most far-reaching anti-crime measure enacted since the 1968 Omnibus Crime Control and Safe Streets Act. *(Code reform history, 1979 Almanac p. 363; Safe Streets Act, 1968 Almanac p. 225)*

Major Elements

The new law overhauled federal sentencing procedures to reduce the disparity in punishment for defendants who commit similar crimes, and allowed pretrial detention of defendants considered dangerous to the community.

Other provisions prohibited tampering with computers, unauthorized use of credit cards or bank-account access numbers, and trafficking in counterfeit trademarked goods. Still others substantially increased penalties for major drug offenses and gave federal prosecutors new authority to seize the assets and profits of drug traffickers.

In addition, the law re-established a grant program for state anti-crime projects, although one substantially more modest than the defunct Law Enforcement Assistance Administration.

Further, it tightened the legal definition of insanity and made it harder for criminal suspects to employ such a defense successfully. This section was largely an outgrowth of concern over the acquittal based on insanity of John W. Hinckley Jr., who shot President Reagan and three other people in a March 30, 1981, assassination attempt. *(1981 Almanac p. 6)*

Pressure From Reagan

President Reagan could claim a large share of credit for getting the crime package enacted. Beginning with his 1983 State of the Union address, he made it one of his top domestic priorities.

"It is high time that we make our cities safe again," the president declared in that Jan. 25 message. "This administration hereby declares an all-out war on big-time organized crime and the drug racketeers who are poisoning our young people." *(Text, 1983 Almanac p. 3-E)*

On March 16, 1983, Reagan sent to Capitol Hill an anti-crime proposal that contained a number of provisions ultimately included in the legislation that cleared Congress. *(Text, 1983 Almanac p. 19-E)*

The Senate on Feb. 2, 1984, passed by 91-1 a comprehensive crime bill (S 1762) containing most of Reagan's proposals. *(Vote 6, p. 3-S)*

At his next televised press conference, on Feb. 22, the president opened his remarks by declaring the legislation "long overdue," and urging the Democratic-controlled House "to stop dragging its feet and to act promptly." He returned to the theme repeatedly in the months thereafter.

Throughout the year, House Republicans also hammered away at the crime issue, denouncing the Democratic leadership in general and the House Judiciary leadership in particular for failing to act on the Senate-passed package.

The criticism greatly annoyed House Democrats, but they never found an effective way to counteract it. The House Judiciary Committee, which disliked omnibus bills, approved several important elements of the Senate package as separate pieces of legislation, and the full House passed those bills. Sentencing reform and pretrial detention legislation, however, lagged behind other provisions, and these were considered to be the most important sections of the crime package.

Legislative Maneuvering

On Sept. 25, House Republicans employed an end run to get the Senate crime bill passed. Rep. Dan Lungren, R-Calif., a Judiciary Committee member, made a motion to send the "must-pass" fiscal 1985 continuing appropriations resolution (H J Res 648) back to the Appropriations Committee with instructions to attach a House bill (HR 5963) identical to the Senate crime package and return the measure to the full House.

Lungren's motion was agreed to 243-166, with 89 Democrats joining 154 Republicans in supporting the maneuver. *(Vote 370, p. 112-H)*

The funding bill, with the crime package attached, promptly returned to the House floor and was passed the same day, 316-91. *(Vote 371, p. 114-H)*

On Oct. 2, House Democrats countered by consolidating various Judiciary Committee proposals into one bill (HR 5690) and proposing it for passage under suspension of the rules, which requires a two-thirds majority. The bill passed 406-16. *(Vote 382, 118-H)*

When the funding bill (H J Res 648) got to the Senate, members decided to retain the crime provisions, even though most other riders were eventually stripped from the measure. A few amendments were made to the crime section, and a number of new provisions were added. Nearly all of the new provisions had been approved as separate bills by one chamber or the other. They dealt with such issues as terrorism, trademark counterfeiting, computer and credit card fraud, and victim compensation.

The Senate decision assured that major crime legislation would be enacted in 1984. And the House Democrats' Oct. 2 move to pass their own bill did have some effect on the final product. When appropriations conferees met Oct. 10, they called in House and Senate Judiciary members to advise them on the crime section of H J Res 648.

During a lengthy and somewhat testy meeting, a final compromise crime package was worked out. Senators resisted efforts to alter the pretrial detention and sentencing provisions. But House Judiciary members succeeded in tailoring the measure's drug enforcement provisions more to their liking.

Criticisms of the Bill

While most lawmakers hailed passage of the anti-crime measure, representatives of the American Civil Liberties Union (ACLU) expressed deep concern about the preventive detention, insanity and computer crime provisions. They said these provisions infringed on individual liberties, and Jerry Berman, of the ACLU's Washington, D.C., office, contended that it was "fraudulent" to claim "that this bill will reduce violence ... or make this a safer society."

Berman said one of the computer crime provisions was so broad that it amounted to a "government secrecy" law. He was referring to a provision that made it a crime for a person who was authorized to use a government computer to use it in a manner beyond the scope of his authorization and subsequently disclose the information he obtained.

The Senate passed a bill (HR 5616) Oct. 11 to revise this provision in PL 98-473, but the House did not act on it.

The sentencing provisions caused some concern in the federal judiciary, because they reduced the historically broad discretion of judges to impose punishment. Under the new law, federal judges were required to stay within specific sentencing guidelines, to be written within 18 months, or justify in writing why they had departed from those guidelines. Judges were given three of the seven slots on a special commission that was to draft the sentencing guidelines.

The U.S. Judicial Conference, the policy-making arm of the federal judiciary, had supported a House Judiciary Committee version of the sentencing bill (HR 6012), which gave judges greater authority over the creation of the sentencing guidelines.

The federal judiciary "recognizes the need to have a commission and guidelines," said conference spokesman William James Weller, "but judges have been apprehensive about the process being controlled by people who aren't in the business every day of actually sitting there and making the difficult sentencing decisions."

Final Provisions

As cleared by Congress, the crime sections of PL 98-473 included the following major provisions:

Bail, Preventive Detention

● Authorized federal judges to consider whether a defendant posed a danger to the community in deciding whether to release him before trial.

● Authorized judges to detain a suspect before trial upon a determination that no conditions for release would assure both the defendant's appearance at trial and the safety of the community. Existing law required pretrial release under the minimal conditions required to assure the defendant's appearance for trial.

● Established a presumption that a defendant was not entitled to pretrial release if there was enough evidence to charge him with a major drug offense or specified other serious crimes. The defendant could seek to rebut the presumption.

● Required detention after conviction pending sentencing or appeal, unless a judge found by clear and convincing evidence that the defendant was not likely to flee or pose a danger to the community.

Previously, there was a presumption in favor of release on bail, even after conviction.

● Increased penalties for bail jumping from a maximum of five years in prison and a $5,000 fine to 10 years in prison and a $25,000 fine.

● Required revocation of bail of a person arrested for a crime committed while on pretrial or post-conviction release, and set up procedures for such revocation.

● Permitted an appeal of release and detention orders by both the government and the defendant. Under the law prior to PL 98-473, only the defendant could appeal.

Sentencing

● Established four general purposes of sentencing and specified that individuals could be sentenced to probation, a fine, a prison term or a combination of those sentences. An organization could be put on probation, fined or a combination of the two.

● Created a grading system for crimes, ranking them according to their seriousness.

● Established a seven-member commission to write guidelines for sentencing, which were to be completed within 18 months of enactment. Panel members, to be appointed by the president and confirmed by the Senate, must include three federal judges.

● Required judges to follow sentencing guidelines produced by the commission, although a judge could deviate from them if he stated in writing the mitigating and aggravating factors that led him to do so.

● Authorized a defendant to appeal a sentence that was harsher than the guidelines and authorized the government to appeal a sentence more lenient than the guidelines.

● Barred parole for prisoners incarcerated after the guidelines went into effect. Phased out parole over five years for prisoners incarcerated before the guidelines took effect.

● Provided that a sentence of more than one year could be shortened at the end of each year by 15 percent for good behavior.

● Gave a judge authority to modify a term of imprisonment if certain conditions specified in the bill were met.

● Gave a judge authority, when imposing a sentence, to order supervision of a defendant after his prison term ended. Existing law provided varying degrees of supervision when defendants were put on parole, but not after completion of a prison term.

Forfeiture: Seizure of Assets

● Expanded the government's authority to require forfeiture of profits and proceeds from organized crime enterprises and narcotics trafficking.

● Established revolving funds in the Justice and Treasury departments for a number of purposes, including maintenance of equipment seized through forfeiture proceedings, payment of rewards for information leading to seizure, purchase of drugs pursuant to an undercover operation, and rebuilding seized equipment so it could be used for drug enforcement.

● Increased the value of goods that could be forfeited to federal agents without a full-scale court proceeding. Prior to enactment of the law, goods valued at up to $10,000 could be forfeited through default proceedings, when no one showed up to claim the goods. The new law raised the value for most cases to $100,000.

Insanity Defense

● Modified the definition of insanity to require a defendant to prove that as a result of a severe mental disease or defect, he was unable to appreciate the nature and wrongfulness of his acts. Existing law required proof that a defendant suffered from a mental disease or defect that left him unable to appreciate the criminality of his conduct or conform his conduct to the law.

● Shifted the burden of proof for establishing insanity to the defendant, who had to show by clear and convincing evidence that he met the legal test. Under existing law, the prosecutor had to show beyond a reasonable doubt that the defendant did not meet the insanity test.

● Limited psychiatric testimony to the presentation and explanation of a diagnosis of mental disease or defect; no testimony would be allowed on whether the defendant had the mental state or condition constituting an element of the crime, such as intent, or a defense to it, such as the inability to understand the wrongfulness of his actions.

● Provided for commitment to a mental hospital or other suitable facility of anyone found not guilty by reason of insanity until such time as a court determined that the person had recovered sufficiently so that his release would not endanger other people or their property. Under the previous law, there was no federal procedure for commitment of those acquitted on insanity grounds.

Drug Enforcement

● Increased maximum fines for most serious drug offenses from $25,000 to $125,000 for individuals. For trafficking in large quantities of specified drugs, including heroin and cocaine, the maximum fine was set at $250,000, and the maximum prison term at 20 years. Under current law, the maximum prison term was 15 years.

● Authorized judges to fine a drug offender up to twice the gross profits from his enterprise instead of imposing the fine specified for the crime in question.

● Increased the first-offense penalty for illegally distributing or making certain drugs from a maximum of five years to 15 years.

● Gave the attorney general emergency authority to require tight control, similar to that already in effect for heroin, of new chemical substances when he determined such action was "necessary to avoid an imminent hazard to the public safety." Required 30 days' notice before the attorney general could place a substance on "Schedule I" status, the most restrictive for controlled substances. The emergency listing would expire after one year, although the attorney general could extend it for up to six months.

● Required anyone who manufactured or distributed any controlled substance to obtain an annual registration from the attorney general.

● Required anyone dispensing or proposing to dispense any controlled substance to obtain a registration from the attorney general for a term of not less than one nor more than three years.

● Required the attorney general to register a physician or pharmacy to dispense and conduct research with controlled substances if an applicant was authorized to do so under the laws of the state in which he practiced, and no circumstances existed that would make such registration "inconsistent with the public interest." Such circumstances would include, among others, a prior criminal record involving drug offenses, or an adverse recommendation by a state licensing board or professional disciplinary authority.

● Expanded the authority of the attorney general to deny or revoke a registration upon a finding that the registration was inconsistent with the public interest, as determined according to specified factors.

● Required the attorney general to present the applicant or registrant with a document stating the basis of the denial or revocation and to give the person an opportunity to respond.

● Authorized the attorney general to suspend any registration on an emergency basis upon finding that there was "imminent danger to the public health and safety." Previously, a practitioner could be stripped of his registration only upon criminal conviction, upon proof that the application for registration was false, or upon revocation of a license to practice medicine by an appropriate licensing board.

● Authorized the attorney general to seize or place under seal any controlled substances owned or possessed by a registrant whose registration had expired or who had ceased to practice or do business in the manner contemplated by his registration.

● Authorized the attorney general to establish programs, including investigations, collection of information and grants, to help states reduce the amount of drugs diverted from medical channels to the black market.

Justice Assistance

● Created an Office of Justice Programs within the Department of Justice, headed by an assistant attorney general appointed by the president and confirmed by the Senate.

● Authorized the assistant attorney general to publish and disseminate information on the progress of criminal justice systems, and maintain liaison with the executive and judicial branches of the state and federal governments, public and private research and educational institutions.

● Gave the assistant attorney general authority to coordinate programs of the National Institute of Justice and Bureau of Justice Statistics.

● Created a Bureau of Justice Assistance within the Justice Department, headed by a director appointed by the attorney general.

● Authorized the director to provide funds to eligible states, local governments and private, non-profit organizations for criminal justice projects through a block grant program.

● Provided "such sums as may be necessary" to carry out the block grant program.

● Provided that of the amount appropriated each year, 80 percent was to be set aside to give each participating state at least $250,000. Any remaining amount would be allocated based on population.

● Established that the purpose of the block grant program was to provide funds for anti-crime programs of proven effectiveness, with special emphasis on combating violent crime and dealing with serious offenders. The measure specified 18 types of programs that could be funded.

● Limited federal grants to 50 percent of program costs.

● Required applicants to make a detailed request for funds covering the type of program the funds would be used for and providing assurance that state and local officials and members of the public had been apprised of the application and given an opportunity to comment upon it.

● Provided an applicant the opportunity to seek a reconsideration of any grant proposal that was rejected.

● Required each state to designate a "state office" to prepare applications and administer grants.

● Provided that 20 percent of the funds appropriated would be for "discretionary" grants to public agencies and non-profit organizations for training of criminal justice personnel, technical assistance to state and local governments, multi-state projects and demonstration projects.

● Created a pilot program of grants to help states and localities build new prisons to relieve overcrowding and improve substandard facilities.

● Limited grants to no more than 20 percent of the cost of constructing a correctional facility.

● Authorized the director of justice assistance to establish a clearinghouse of information on the construction and modernization of prisons.

● Authorized $25 million annually for fiscal years 1984-88 to carry out the pilot program and set up the clearing-house.

● Authorized the head of the FBI to conduct training programs for state and local officials at the FBI's National Academy in Quantico, Va.

● Required annual reports to Congress on the various programs set up under this title.

● Provided for $50,000 in benefits to the survivors of law enforcement officers and firefighters who died as the result of injuries sustained in the line of duty.

● Permitted immediate payment, upon a showing of need, of up to $3,000 to a survivor expected to qualify for full benefits. Any interim sum would be deducted from the $50,000.

Surplus Property

● Authorized the donation of surplus federal property for the construction and modernization of state prison or jail facilities.

Violent Crime Amendments

● Made murder-for-hire a federal crime when interstate commerce was involved; made violent crimes such as murder, kidnapping and assaults federal offenses if they were in aid of racketeering activities.

● Prohibited "solicitation" to commit a crime of violence, which covered a person who tried to persuade another to commit a crime of violence.

● Revised and strengthened existing requirements of minimum mandatory sentences for use of a firearm in the commission of federal crimes, setting a minimum sentence of five years in addition to whatever sentence was imposed for the underlying crime.

● Provided new penalties for kidnapping specified federal officials and for crimes directed at the family members of specified federal officials.

● Prohibited carrying or using in a crime of violence a handgun loaded with armor-piercing ammunition, and set a mandatory five-year prison term as the minimum penalty.

● Made it a federal offense to damage willfully energy facilities such as electrical transmission towers if the damage exceeded $100,000 or resulted in a significant interruption of the facility; the maximum penalty was set at 10 years in prison and a $50,000 fine.

Non-Violent Crime

● Created a new obstruction-of-justice offense for impairing an authorized search by moving, concealing or destroying the property that was the object of the search.

● Created a new offense to cover theft, fraud and bribery involving federal money disbursed to private organizations or to state and local governments under a federal program.

● Created a new offense for counterfeiting the securities of state and local governments or of corporations.

● Clarified the law covering receipt of stolen bank property to cover situations in which a defendant knew property was stolen even though he did not know it was stolen from a bank.

● Revised the law covering bank bribery to broaden the types of institutions, such as credit unions and the Federal Home Loan Bank System, not currently covered and to cover indirect as well as direct bribes.

● Created a new bank fraud offense to cover anyone who knowingly executed or attempted to execute a scheme to defraud a federally chartered or insured financial institution or to obtain any assets of such institution through false or fraudulent pretenses. A prison term of up to five years and a fine of up to $10,000 was established.

● Made possession of contraband in prison a criminal offense. Under previous law, bringing contraband into a prison or moving it around was a federal offense, while possessing such material was not.

● Revised current law barring theft and fraud involving "cattle" to cover theft and fraud involving "livestock."

● Prohibited anyone from obtaining or using without permission another's livestock worth $10,000 or more, and set a penalty of up to five years in prison and a fine of up to $10,000.

Juvenile Justice

● Reauthorized the Office of Juvenile Justice and Delinquency Prevention for fiscal 1985-88, to be funded by "such sums as may be necessary" for each of the years. The office was to help states develop alternatives to incarceration of juveniles and to develop programs to combat juvenile delinquency.

● Reauthorized the Runaway and Homeless Youth Act of 1974 (PL 93-415) for fiscal 1985-88. This law, administered by the Department of Health and Human Services, authorized assistance to state and local facilities that provided emergency shelter care for runaways.

● Authorized such sums as necessary to carry out these programs for fiscal 1985-88.

● Emphasized in both the juvenile justice and runaway youth programs that the family of the children involved should be made part of any counseling and treatment program.

● Continued the two mandates of the original 1974 law — removal of juveniles from adult jails and the creation of institutions, such as group homes, for juveniles who committed no crimes but who were runaways or truants.

● Required for the first time that grants from the administrator's discretionary pool of funds be made on a competitive basis. Previously, there were no statutory requirements for awarding these grants.

Missing Children

● Required for the first time federal assistance in locating missing children and providing treatment for such children and their families. The programs were to be run by the administrator of the juvenile justice office.

● Required establishment of a national toll-free hotline that members of the public could use to report information about missing children aged 13 or under.

● Established a national clearinghouse to provide technical assistance to public and private agencies involved in locating missing children; coordinate public and private missing-children programs, and disseminate information about such programs.

● Required periodic studies to determine how many children were reported missing each year, how many were abducted by strangers, how many were the victims of parental kidnappings, and how many were recovered.

● Authorized the administrator to award grants to public agencies and non-profit organizations for research, demonstration projects or service programs related to the problem of missing children and sexual exploitation of children.

● Created an advisory board on missing children to make recommendations for federally assisted missing-children programs.

● Provided $10 million for fiscal 1985 for the program and such sums as might be necessary for the remaining fiscal years.

Procedural Changes

● Allowed federal prosecution as adults of certain juvenile defendants charged with serious federal drug offenses or crimes of violence. Under previous law, most cases involving juveniles were transferred to the states unless the attorney general determined that the state could not handle the case.

● Authorized emergency wiretaps without a court order in situations involving immediate danger of death or serious physical injury to any person. Emergency wiretaps also were authorized in cases involving child pornography, illegal currency transactions and offenses against crime victims and witnesses.

● Gave the attorney general new authority to seek a court order to bar a mail-fraud, wire-fraud or bank-fraud scheme once he had sufficient evidence of a violation of anti-fraud laws.

Labor Racketeering

● Raised from a misdemeanor to a felony willful violation of the Taft-Hartley Act provisions involving labor bribery or payoffs in excess of $1,000. Increased penalties to a maximum of five years in prison and a $15,000 fine, from one year in prison and a $10,000 maximum.

● Barred union officials from holding union or trust fund positions for a minimum of three years and a maximum of 13 years after conviction on corruption charges. Under previous law, the maximum disqualification was five years.

● Provided disqualification only for those union officials who used their position in a labor union to seek or obtain an illegal gain.

● Made clear that federal labor racketeering provisions did not bar states from enacting their own laws to deal with labor racketeering.

Foreign Currency Transactions

● Increased civil and criminal penalties for violating record-keeping and reporting requirements involving the transport of currency in and out of the United States.

● Authorized customs officers to stop and search, without a warrant, any vehicle, vessel or person entering or leaving the United States if the officer had reasonable cause to suspect a violation of currency transaction laws.

● Authorized rewards of 25 percent, up to a $150,000 maximum, to anyone who provided information leading to recovery of more than $50,000 through a penalty, fine or forfeiture.

Witness Protection

● Authorized relocation and protection of federal or specified state witnesses and potential witnesses when the attorney general determined that a crime of violence was likely to be committed against those individuals.

● Authorized relocation and protection for the immediate family of the witness, or another person closely associated with the witness, if those individuals might also be endangered.

● Required the attorney general to issue guidelines on the types of cases in which witnesses could be protected.

● Gave U.S. officials and employees immunity from civil liability for their decisions to protect or not to protect a witness.

● Gave the attorney general discretion to determine how long to protect a witness, and authorized the attorney general to provide the witness with identity documents, housing, transportation to a new home, a payment to meet basic living expenses, and help in obtaining a job.

● Required deductions from living-expense payments to a protected witness to cover court-ordered family support payments.

● Gave the attorney general discretion to disclose or withhold information on the identity or location of a protected witness. Required disclosure of such information to state and local law enforcement officials when the person in question was sought for a crime of violence or an offense punishable by more than one year in prison.

● Provided for a $5,000 fine, five-year prison term or both for anyone convicted of illegally disclosing information about the identity and location of a protected witness.

● Required the attorney general, "to the extent practicable," to obtain information about the suitability of a person for protection and relocation. Such information was to include a criminal history, if any, and a psychological evaluation of the person.

● Required the attorney general to determine whether the need for a person's testimony outweighed the risk of endangering people and property in the community where a witness was to be relocated, and barred relocation if the risk to the public outweighed the need for the person's testimony.

● Required the attorney general to issue a written "memorandum of understanding" to the protected witness specifying the person's responsibilities under the program. These required no criminal conduct, payment of all legal obligations and civil judgments, agreement to testify and provide information to law enforcement officials, and agreement to take the necessary steps to avoid detection.

● Provided for emergency protection in specified circumstances without the written memorandum.

● Allowed the attorney general to terminate protection of a witness for a substantial breach of the memorandum of understanding.

● Specified procedures for notifying a protected witness of a civil proceeding against him and set out elaborate procedures for enforcing the rights of any litigant who had a judgment against a protected witness. Authorized disclosure to the plaintiff of the identity and location of a protected person who failed to comply with a civil judgment against him. If the attorney general did not make such disclosure upon request, the plaintiff could seek a federal court hearing on the issue.

● Barred the attorney general from relocating any child in connection with protecting a witness if it appeared that a person other than the witness had legal custody of that child.

● Provided detailed procedures for safeguarding custody and visitation arrangements involving a protected witness who had legal custody of a child, and required the parent being relocated to seek and abide by modifications in the existing court-ordered custody arrangements if compliance with a visitation order was not possible.

● Specified that the custody and visitation rights of the non-relocated parent could not be infringed if a child was relocated as part of the program.

● Required the Justice Department to pay transportation and security costs necessary to ensure up to 12 visits per year, or up to 30 days, between parents and children.

● Provided for arbitration if no agreement on modifying

a custody arrangement was reached within 60 days of a legal action to alter the arrangement.

● Authorized the attorney general to pay restitution or, in the case of death, compensation to any victim injured or killed by a person protected under the federal program.

● Authorized $1 million annually for this compensation program.

● Limited compensation in cases involving death to a maximum of $50,000, and prohibited payments to victims receiving restitution or compensation through other programs or through insurance.

Foreign Business Records

● Permitted the use of foreign business records as evidence in criminal proceedings if the custodian of those records provided a certification setting forth specified information about how the records were compiled and kept.

● Allowed a defendant to challenge the admission of the records into evidence under certain circumstances.

● Transferred from the State Department to the Justice Department responsibility for administering the Foreign Agents Registration Act, but required the attorney general to inform the State Department of foreign registrations it had received.

● Made clear that the United States had jurisdiction over any offense committed by or against a national of the United States any place outside the jurisdiction of another country. This provision was intended to cover crimes that might occur on Antarctica, an ice floe or the moon. (A "national" was a U.S. citizen or a person whose principal place of residence was the United States.)

Drug Policy Board

● Created a National Drug Enforcement Policy Board, a high-level interagency council to coordinate federal drug enforcement activities.

● Designated the attorney general as chairman and included on the board the secretaries of state, Treasury, defense, health and human services, the director of the Office of Management and Budget, the director of the Central Intelligence Agency and any other officials the president wanted to appoint.

● Authorized the board to develop and coordinate all U.S. efforts to halt national and international drug trafficking.

● Authorized the chairman to make recommendations to the board for coordination of drug enforcement activities, to be the primary adviser to the president on drug enforcement issues, and to review and approve the reprogramming of funds relating to drug enforcement.

● Specified that neither the new drug board nor its chairman could "interfere with the routine law enforcement or intelligence decisions of any agency" or undertake activities "inconsistent with" the authority and responsibilities of the director of central intelligence.

● Required the chairman to submit a report to Congress within nine months of enactment on drug enforcement policy. After the first report, others would be required every two years.

Victim Compensation

● Created a Crime Victims Fund in the Treasury Department financed through fines collected from persons convicted of federal offenses, with specified exceptions, plus forfeited bonds and collateral.

● Set a $100 million maximum for the fund and required

any excess money to go to the Treasury.

● Barred deposits in the fund after Sept. 30, 1988.

● Specified that half the amount in the fund each year would be available for grants to existing state victim-compensation programs to meet claims, and half to states to provide victim assistance programs such as rape counseling.

● Allowed the attorney general to deduct up to 5 percent of the total in the fund for services to victims of federal crimes. This money would come out of the share allotted to states for victim services.

● Authorized the attorney general, in making annual grants to state victim-compensation programs, to provide funds equal to 35 percent of the amounts awarded to crime victims by the state program during the previous fiscal year, other than awards for property damage.

● Defined an "eligible" program as one that was operated by a state and offered compensation to victims or their survivors for medical expenses, loss of wages and funeral expenses.

● Authorized the attorney general to make grants to states, subject to available funds, for crime victim-assistance programs run by public agencies or non-profit organizations.

● Provided that each state should receive $100,000 under the grant and that any remaining money should be distributed among the states on the basis of population. If there was less than $100,000 per state available, then the money would be distributed to the states equally.

● Authorized a federal court, upon request by a U.S. attorney, to ensure that someone convicted of a crime causing physical harm to an individual did not profit from that crime. A court could order forfeiture of all or part of the proceeds the defendant or his designee received from a contract relating to depiction of the crime in a movie, book, newspaper, magazine, drama, radio or television production.

● Authorized a judge to order the person who contracted with the defendant to pay the specified amount to the attorney general.

● Provided that proceeds paid to the attorney general through forfeiture be held in the Crime Victims Fund for five years, but allowed payment for specified purposes, including a fine or monetary award to the victim. At the end of the five-year period, a court could require all or part of forfeited proceeds to be released for use by the Crime Victims Fund.

Trademark Counterfeiting

● Prohibited trafficking in goods or services using a counterfeit trademark and set a fine of up to $250,000, a prison term of up to five years, or both for a first offense by an individual. A corporation could be fined up to $1 million. A second offense by an individual would carry a maximum $1 million fine and 15-year prison term, while an organization could be fined up to $5 million.

● Authorized a judge to order the destruction of goods in the possession of a defendant that were determined to be counterfeit.

● Increased civil penalties for counterfeiting by allowing a judge to impose triple damages or three times the profits from counterfeiting, whichever was greater. A judge could decline to award triple damages if he found "extenuating circumstances."

● Authorized a plaintiff to seek a court order — without prior notice to the opposing party — directing federal authorities to seize counterfeit goods, the equipment and documents used to make and sell them.

• Required, before such an "ex parte" order was issued, that the plaintiff post bond covering the costs of the goods in question, and that the judge find factual evidence indicating that only such an order would assure that the goods in question remained intact for further legal proceedings.

• Required a court hearing on the seizure within 15 days.

• Authorized an award of damages and attorneys' fees to anyone whose goods had been wrongfully seized.

Credit Card Fraud

• Provided a maximum fine of $10,000 or twice the value obtained, and a prison term of up to 10 years, for anyone who used or trafficked in one or more unauthorized credit cards or other "access devices," such as bank card numbers, and obtained at least $1,000 in value in any one-year period.

• Set the same penalties for anyone who possessed with intent to defraud 15 or more counterfeit or unauthorized cards or code numbers.

• Set a maximum $50,000 fine or twice the value obtained and a maximum 15-year prison term for anyone who produced, used or trafficked in counterfeit access devices or who trafficked in equipment to make such devices.

• Provided a maximum $100,000 fine, or twice the value obtained and a maximum 20-year prison term for a second offense of the above crimes.

Computer Fraud

• Made it a felony to gain unauthorized entry into a computer for purposes of obtaining classified information with intent or reason to believe the information would be used to the injury of the United States or advantage of another country. Unauthorized use of classified information by someone authorized to have access to the computer was also banned.

• Made it a felony to attempt to commit the above crime.

• Provided a maximum penalty on the first offense of $10,000 or twice the value obtained, and a maximum prison term of 10 years. A second offense would carry a maximum $100,000 fine or twice the value obtained, and a maximum 20-year prison term.

• Made it a misdemeanor to enter a computer illegally and obtain information covered by federal laws protecting privacy of financial and credit information.

• Made it a misdemeanor to enter a government computer illegally and affect the computer's operations.

• Made it a misdemeanor to use a government computer for purposes other than the authorized use and then modify, destroy or disclose information obtained, or prevent authorized use of the computer.

• Set a maximum $5,000 penalty or twice the value obtained, and a maximum one-year prison term, for the first misdemeanor offense. A second offense would carry a maximum fine of $10,000 or twice the value obtained, and a maximum 10-year prison term.

Armed Career Criminals

• Allowed federal prosecution of specified repeat state offenders.

• Provided a mandatory 15-year prison term and $25,000 fine for any defendant with three previous state convictions for robbery or burglary who possessed a firearm that had traveled in interstate commerce. The sentence

could not be suspended nor could the defendant be paroled.

Terrorism

• Required imprisonment for up to life for taking hostages either inside the United States or outside the country in order to compel a third person or government to do or abstain from doing a particular act as a condition for releasing the hostages.

• Barred prosecution under this section unless the offender or person detained was a U.S. national, the offender was found in the United States, or the U.S. government was the one the offender sought to influence.

• Set a fine of up to $100,000, imprisonment of up to 20 years, or both for anyone who destroyed or damaged aircraft or aircraft facilities in the United States, or acted violently toward any person on such an aircraft, or knowingly provided false information that could endanger an aircraft in flight. The same penalties were established for anyone attempting to commit the above crimes.

• Provided the same penalties for anyone who performed an act of violence against a "civil" aircraft of another country or placed a dangerous device aboard such aircraft, if that offender was later found in the United States.

• Provided a maximum $25,000 fine and maximum five-year prison term for anyone who willfully threatened to commit any of the above offenses.

• Provided a civil penalty of up to $10,000 for anyone who knowingly conveyed false information that was likely to be believed concerning an attempt or alleged attempt to violate specified regulations governing aircraft licensing and safety.

• Provided a civil penalty of up to $10,000 for anyone, other than law enforcement officers and certain authorized personnel, who boarded or attempted to board an aircraft while carrying a concealed dangerous weapon.

• Raised the fine for carrying concealed weapons or explosives aboard an aircraft from $1,000 to $10,000. The offense also carried a maximum one-year prison term.

• Raised the fine for committing an act with a weapon or explosive aboard an aircraft from $5,000 to $25,000. The offense also carried a maximum five-year prison term.

• Set a maximum $25,000 fine and five-year prison term for anyone who willfully and maliciously, or with reckless disregard for human life, knowingly conveyed false information about committing a crime on board an aircraft, interfering with flight crews, or carrying weapons or explosives aboard.

• Provided a maximum $25,000 fine and five-year prison term for anyone who threatened to commit such acts.

U.S. Attorneys' Salaries

• Authorized the attorney general to fix the salaries of U.S. attorneys and their assistants at a level not to exceed the maximum paid to employees in the Senior Executive Service. The maximum salary was thereby raised to $69,900 per year, up from a current maximum of $66,400.

Defense Attorneys' Fees

• Raised the current rate for court-appointed defense lawyers from $20 per hour for out-of-court work and $30 per hour for in-court work to $40 and $60 respectively. The pay rates for these attorneys had not been changed since 1970.

• Raised the maximum payment for a felony case and

for an appeal from $1,000 for each to $2,000 for each.
  ● Raised the maximum payment for a misdemeanor case from $400 to $800.
  ● Raised the maximum for other proceedings, such as a parole revocation, from $250 to $500.
  ● Maintained current law allowing the maximums to be exceeded through a request to the chief judge of the federal district where the case in question resided.

Background

Criminal Code Reform History

The effort to revise the federal criminal code dated back to 1966, when, at the instigation of Congress, a National Commission on Reform of Criminal Laws was created. Headed by Gov. Edmund G. Brown of California (1959-67), the commission produced a report that led to the introduction on Jan. 4, 1973, of the first omnibus crime bill, S 1. That proposal drew swift and steady fire from civil liberties groups, who claimed it was harmful to individual rights. *(1973 Almanac p. 374)*

Although numerous hearings were held on the legislation, the Senate Judiciary Committee did not act on either S 1 or on a successor version introduced Jan. 15, 1975, at the start of the 94th Congress.

In 1977, however, Sens. Edward M. Kennedy, D-Mass., and John L. McClellan, D-Ark. (1943-77; House, 1935-39), introduced S 1437, a revised criminal code reform that omitted some of the more controversial provisions of earlier versions. That bill was passed by the Senate on Jan. 30, 1978, but died in the House.

Kennedy tried again in the 96th Congress, supported by Sens. Strom Thurmond, R-S.C., and Orrin G. Hatch, R-Utah. A criminal code bill (S 1722) was reported from the Senate Judiciary Committee Jan. 17, 1980, but Kennedy became so deeply involved in his unsuccessful bid to wrest the Democratic presidential nomination from President Carter that the bill was sidetracked. The House Judiciary Committee also approved a criminal code bill, HR 6915, but that measure went no further.

Work resumed in the 97th Congress, as the Senate Judiciary Committee approved yet another criminal code package (S 1630) Nov. 18, 1981, formally reporting the measure Jan. 25, 1982 (S Rept 97-307).

Although that measure, like its predecessors, proved too hot for the Senate to handle in an election year, some of its non-controversial provisions were passed separately (S 2572) on Sept. 30, 1982, and then attached to a minor House-passed bill (HR 3963) that was cleared by Congress in the session that began Dec. 20. However, Reagan objected to certain portions of the bill, most notably a section creating a new, centralized Cabinet-level office to combat drug trafficking, dubbed the "drug czar." He pocket-vetoed the measure Jan. 14, 1983. *(1982 Almanac p. 419)*

Senate Committee Action

With Reagan insisting that he placed a high priority on anti-crime legislation, despite his veto of the 1982 bill, Kennedy and Thurmond started over in the 98th Congress. Along with Paul Laxalt, R-Nev., and Joseph R. Biden Jr., D-Del., they introduced another omnibus anti-crime package (S 1762) that was approved by the Judiciary Committee July 21, 1983, and formally reported Aug. 4, 1983 (S

Rept 98-225). Sen. Charles McC. Mathias Jr., R-Md., cast the lone vote against the measure in committee.

Controversial Items Split Off

To minimize the prospect that the crime package would get bogged down on the Senate floor in fights over emotional issues, the committee split off into separate bills provisions it knew would generate controversy. These included a revised drug czar proposal and measures to re-institute the federal death penalty, restrict use of *habeas corpus* claims by state prisoners and modify the exclusionary rule, which barred use at trials of illegally seized evidence.

The drug czar plan was later incorporated into the final crime package (H J Res 648). The other three bills (S 1765, S 1763, S 1764) were passed by the Senate, but died in the House. *(Stories, pp. 227, 228)*

Senate Floor Action

The Senate began work on S 1762 on Jan. 27. Because the bill included only provisions with bipartisan support, it was expected to sail through the Senate.

That hope faded Jan. 31, however, when Sens. Howard M. Metzenbaum, D-Ohio, and Dale Bumpers, D-Ark., offered an amendment to make it a federal felony for any government official or employee to record a phone conversation without the other party's consent. Exemptions were provided for law enforcement, national security, and foreign intelligence and counterintelligence personnel.

Telephone Taping

Metzenbaum and Bumpers said their amendment was prompted by disclosures that Charles Z. Wick, head of the United States Information Agency, had recorded dozens of telephone conversations without the other party's consent.

The amendment drew vehement protests from Senate Republicans, and representatives from the Justice Department and the government's intelligence agencies rushed to the Capitol to urge senators to block the amendment. Justice also sent over two long letters identifying possible problems with the proposals.

Bumpers and Metzenbaum said they were amazed at the opposition. They said that they had provided exemptions in the areas of concern, and Metzenbaum said repeatedly that he had asked Justice and the intelligence agencies to bring him proposed language for the exemptions.

None had been forthcoming, Metzenbaum said. "I'm starting to think that what this whole thing is about is that a lot more secret taping is going on than a lot of us imagined."

Some Republicans said the amendment was nothing but a slap at Reagan, a close friend of Wick, an allegation Bumpers called "misinformation." He said the amendment was designed to bar "peeping Tomism."

"Does this mean the president wants to go out and campaign that he was violently opposed to a law that in effect stopped peeping Toms?" Bumpers asked.

After considerable debate, the amendment was finally rejected 41-51. *(Vote 5, p. 3-S)*

Final Passage, Backup Steps

With the phone taping issue out of the way, the Senate passed S 1762 on Feb. 2 by a 91-1 vote. As in committee, Mathias cast the lone "nay." *(Vote 6, p. 3-S)*

Mathias expressed strong reservations about the bill's

sentencing provisions, which he unsuccessfully sought to amend.

In a move designed to facilitate House passage of at least portions of S 1762, the Senate Feb. 2-3 passed three of the most important sections of the measure as separate bills.

A sentencing bill (S 668 — S Rept 98-223) was passed 85-3 on Feb. 2. Mark Hatfield, R-Ore., and Howell Heflin, D-Ala., joined Mathias in voting "nay." *(Vote 7, p. 3-S)*

On Feb. 3, the Senate by 84-0 passed as a separate bill (S 215 — S Rept 98-147) provisions that permitted pretrial detention of criminal suspects deemed dangerous to the community. *(Vote 9, p. 4-S)*

Also passed separately Feb. 3, this time by voice vote, was legislation (S 948 — S Rept 98-224) to expand the federal government's authority to require forfeiture of profits and proceeds from organized crime and drug trafficking.

House Action

The House Judiciary Committee, and the House itself, dealt with crime bills in a piecemeal fashion until the very end of the session.

The effort was to little avail; the Senate simply ignored most of these House-passed measures. Senate provisions on the subjects addressed by the House ultimately became law after being attached en masse to the continuing appropriations resolution.

Crime bills that were passed by the House, only to be incorporated in H J Res 648 along lines approved by the Senate, included:

Pay for Defense Lawyers

This bill (HR 4307 — H Rept 98-764), passed by voice vote May 21, raised the hourly pay for defense lawyers appointed in federal criminal cases from a maximum of $30 an hour to $50 an hour. In special circumstances, the rate could be $75 an hour.

The hourly rate had not been changed since 1970. Since then, there had been a different pay rate for in-court time ($30 per hour) and out-of-court time ($20 per hour). HR 4307 would have ended this distinction.

Federal Witness Protection

By 376-41, the House May 22 suspended the rules and passed a bill (HR 4249 — H Rept 98-767) to tighten controls on a Justice Department program that gave new identities, relocation and other protection to federal witnesses in exchange for their testimony in criminal cases. *(Vote 141, p. 48-H)*

The legislation was prompted by criticism over the years that stemmed from crimes committed by witnesses who were given new identities and relocated.

The bill also established a victim compensation fund for innocent persons injured by individuals admitted to the witness protection program. A $2 million maximum was authorized for yearly appropriations for the fund.

Missing Children

The House June 4 passed by voice vote a bill (HR 4971 — H Rept 98-741) to create a national clearinghouse to coordinate efforts to locate missing children and to set up a toll-free hotline to receive tips about their whereabouts.

The program was included in legislation reauthorizing juvenile justice programs of the Department of Justice.

Computer, Credit Card Fraud

The House July 24 passed a bill (HR 5616 — H Rept 98-894) that for the first time would make it a crime to obtain unauthorized access to computers and obtain classified information, protected financial information, or something of value. The measure, which also made it a felony to use a credit or bank card, or their code numbers, without authorization, was passed by 395-0. *(Vote 281, p. 86-H)*

Criminal Fines

On July 30, the House by voice vote approved a bill (HR 5846 — H Rept 98-906) to make criminal fines more severe and improve the government's ability to collect them.

The House and Senate Judiciary committees had studied federal criminal fine levels over the last decade in connection with efforts to revamp the entire criminal code. Both committees concluded that current fine levels were too low to be effective.

HR 5846 substantially increased maximum fine levels for all federal crimes. The bill provided that an individual could be fined the greatest of the amount specified for the crime in question, twice the gain or loss resulting from the crime, or in the case of any felony or of a misdemeanor resulting in death, $250,000.

A similar scheme was established for corporations, except that if a corporation were convicted of a felony or a misdemeanor resulting in death, the fine could be the greater of $1,000,000 or twice the gain or loss resulting from the crime.

Foreign Business Records

A bill (HR 5919 — H Rept 98-907) to make it easier to use foreign-kept business records at criminal trials in the United States was passed July 30 by voice vote. The bill permitted the admission into evidence of foreign business records if the custodian of those records provided a certification setting forth specified information about the records and how they were kept. A defendant would have the right to challenge the admission of the documents under certain circumstances.

Bribery and Fraud

Also July 30, the House by voice vote approved a bill (HR 5872 — H Rept 98-901) to close loopholes in current laws prohibiting bribery and fraud involving financial institutions. The bill barred all payments intended to influence an officer or employee of a financial institution in making a discretionary decision. However, to avoid making a crime out of trivial actions, such as taking a loan officer to dinner following a successful transaction, the bill required that the payment in money or its equivalent be more than $100.

Escape From Custody

By voice vote July 30, the House passed a bill (HR 5526 — H Rept 98-902) to make it a federal crime to escape from federal custody or confinement that resulted from specified civil or criminal proceedings.

Contraband in Prison

A bill (HR 5910 — H Rept 98-908) to make it a crime to possess any contraband in prison was passed by voice vote July 30. Current law provided penalties for bringing contraband into a prison or removing it, but not for mere possession. The bill also amended the current law covering prison riots by adding a definition of "riot" and providing a

$250,000 fine for conviction. Currently, there was only a 10-year prison term.

Drug Penalties

This bill (HR 4901 — H Rept 98-845, Parts I and II), passed Sept. 11 by voice vote, allowed forfeiture of assets of those convicted of certain drug offenses and substantially increased penalties for drug offenses.

HR 4901 increased maximum fines for the most serious drug offenses from $25,000 to $250,000 for individuals, and from $25,000 to $1 million for entities convicted of drug offenses. The measure also gave judges the option of fining a defendant twice the profits or gross proceeds from the trafficking.

Drug 'Czar'

This measure (HR 4028 — H Rept 98-1008) was also approved Sept. 11 by voice vote. In contrast to a 1982 proposal that provoked Reagan's veto, HR 4028 did not create any centralized new drug enforcement office. Instead, it increased the authority of the director of the existing Office of Drug Abuse Policy, created when the Drug Abuse Office and Treatment Act (PL 92-255) was enacted in 1972. *(1972 Almanac p. 162)*

Trademark Counterfeiting

Passed by a 403-0 vote on Sept. 12, this bill (HR 6071 — H Rept 98-997) created new criminal penalties for making and selling products with counterfeit trademarks. It also expanded and stiffened existing civil penalties. *(Vote 344, p. 106-H)*

The measure was intended to stem what sponsors and government experts said was a booming $6 billion business of passing off shoddy and sometimes hazardous goods as popular brand-name products.

HR 6071 provided a maximum fine of $250,000, a five-year prison term or both for a person convicted of counterfeiting goods or services. A corporation could be fined up to $1 million.

Money-Laundering

This bill (HR 6031 — H Rept 98-984), passed Sept. 10 by voice vote, increased civil and criminal penalties for illicit financial transactions, generally known as "money-laundering." The measure amended the Currency and Foreign Transactions Reporting Act, which set reporting and record-keeping rules for financial transactions.

Customs agents were authorized to conduct warrantless searches when they had "reasonable grounds to believe" that currency laws were being violated.

Drug Diversion

On Sept. 18, the House by voice vote passed a bill (HR 5656 — H Rept 98-835) to help control the diversion of prescription drugs from medical channels into the black market. It allowed the Drug Enforcement Administration to revoke or deny a physician's registration to write prescriptions if the attorney general found that registration inconsistent with the public interest.

Omnibus Bill

On Oct. 2, reacting to the parliamentary coup pulled by House Republicans in getting the Senate-passed crime package attached to the continuing resolution, House Democratic leaders put on the floor an omnibus crime bill (HR 5690) of their own.

This measure, which contained provisions generally paralleling those of the Senate bill, was passed 406-16 under suspension of the rules. *(Vote 382, p. 118-H)*

The greatest differences between HR 5690 and the Senate bill (S 1762) involved sentencing procedures, the insanity defense and drug laws. ∎

Pharmacy Robberies

Congress May 17 cleared for President Reagan a bill (S 422 — PL 98-305) creating a new federal crime covering the robbery or burglary of controlled substances.

The measure was aimed primarily at thefts from drug stores, and pharmacists had been pressing for the legislation for years. They contended that as dispensers of powerful drugs with a street value far above their actual cost, they were vulnerable to attacks by those interested in making money on the black market.

Final action came when the Senate by voice vote accepted House amendments to S 422. The House had passed a compromise version of the measure by voice vote May 8.

The compromise, worked out through informal negotiations between the chambers, was essentially the same as the version reported March 30 by the House Judiciary Committee (HR 5222 — H Rept 98-644).

The Senate had passed S 422 in February, both separately (S Rept 98-353) and as part of a larger anti-crime package (S 1762 — S Rept 98-225). *(Crime package, p. 215)*

Background

The Justice Department already had authority under broad federal robbery and burglary statutes to prosecute crimes involving controlled substances. However, the department had told Congress in past years that it was not interested in investigating these types of crimes, which could be handled by state authorities.

Justice officials changed their minds in late 1983, however, and said they could live with legislation such as S 422 if requirements for federal jurisdiction were carefully worked out.

Rep. William J. Hughes, D-N.J., chairman of the House Judiciary Subcommittee on Crime, said there was merit to providing a federal "backup" to state prosecutions of drug robberies and burglaries.

Hughes said there were 6,000 robberies and burglaries of controlled substances between 1977 and 1981. Such crimes had "terrorized the community of dispensing pharmacists," he said.

"This legislation is an important step forward in controlling the diversion of large quantities of dangerous drugs from the legitimate channels of commerce to the streets and the black market," said Rep. Peter W. Rodino Jr., D-N.J., chairman of the House Judiciary Committee.

Major Provisions

As cleared, S 422 included the following major provisions:

● Provided for federal prosecutions in any one of three instances — when the value of the substances taken was at least $500; when the offender traveled in interstate or foreign commerce or used a facility of interstate commerce in the offense; or when a person other than the offender was killed or suffered "significant" bodily injury.

The original House bill provided for jurisdiction when

there was "serious" bodily injury, but at the request of the Senate, the language was changed.

The Senate bill did not spell out the conditions of jurisdiction but required the attorney general's approval for any prosecution under the legislation unless state or local authorities requested assistance.

● Provided for a fine of up to $25,000 and prison terms of up to 20 years for robberies or burglaries involving controlled substances.

● Provided a maximum prison sentence of 25 years and a fine of up to $35,000 if the offense was committed with a dangerous weapon.

● Provided a maximum fine of $50,000 and life imprisonment if a death occurred during a robbery or burglary covered by the bill.

Child Pornography Bill

Amid growing public concern about sexual abuse of children, Congress May 8 cleared a bill (HR 3635 — PL 98-292) to strengthen federal laws against production and distribution of pornographic materials involving children.

Final action came when the House by voice vote accepted a compromise version that had been approved by the Senate March 30. The legislation had begun moving in 1983, but it snagged in the closing days of the session that year. *(1983 Almanac p. 318)*

Among other things, the measure removed a requirement in existing law that child pornography be proven "obscene" before convictions could be obtained. It also raised the age of children protected under the law and authorized law enforcement agents to seize the assets and equipment of pornographers.

"This legislation will close loopholes and provide prosecutors with new tools they need to strengthen our enforcement efforts against those who produce or traffic in such smut," Rep. William J. Hughes, D-N.J., chairman of the House Judiciary Subcommittee on Crime, told the House May 8.

In signing the bill May 21, President Reagan announced the creation of a national commission to study the effects of pornography on society. Another presidential commission had made such a study in 1970 and found that pornography had no significant effect on behavior. But Reagan said, "I think the evidence that has come out since that time plus the tendency of pornography to become more extreme shows that it is time to take a new look at this conclusion. And it's time to stop pretending that extreme pornography is a victimless crime."

Major Provisions

As cleared, HR 3635 included the following major provisions:

● Raised from 16 to 18 the maximum age of children protected.

● Removed an existing requirement that sexually explicit materials depicting children be "obscene" before they may be banned.

● Barred the production and distribution of child pornography regardless of whether it was commercially disseminated.

● Raised the fine for a first offense from $10,000 to a maximum of $100,000, and raised the fine for a second offense from $15,000 to $200,000.

● Provided for a fine of $250,000 against organizations

that were found to have violated the law.

● Required anyone convicted of sexually exploiting children to forfeit the assets used in producing the pornographic material and the profits accumulated from it.

● Authorized court-approved wiretapping to combat child pornography.

The House bill had included a provision excluding from coverage simulations of sexual activity if there was "no possibility of harm to the minor taking into account the nature and circumstances of the simulation, and if there is redeeming social, literary, educational, scientific or artistic value." At the insistence of the Senate, this provision was stricken.

Drug Abuse Monitoring

President Reagan March 20 signed into law a bill (HR 2173 — PL 98-236) that reauthorized funding for drug abuse programs for federal offenders.

The measure was cleared by Congress March 8, when the Senate passed it. The House had approved HR 2173 May 9, 1983. *(1983 Almanac p. 314)*

The program reauthorized by the legislation provided drug abuse testing, monitoring and treatment to convicted federal offenders released on parole or probation.

The measure authorized $5 million for fiscal 1984, $5.5 million for fiscal 1985 and $6 million for fiscal 1986.

The drug monitoring program was first authorized by Congress in 1966 (PL 89-793) and had been extended periodically since then. *(Background, 1978 Almanac p. 210)*

Criminal Fine Collection

Congress Oct. 11 cleared legislation (HR 5846 — PL 98-596) designed to improve the collection of fines in federal criminal cases.

Final action came when the House by voice vote approved a compromise version of the measure, which the Senate had passed earlier in the day.

The House originally had passed the bill July 30 by voice vote under suspension of the rules, which required a two-thirds majority.

Provisions

As cleared by Congress, HR 5846 included the following major provisions:

● Set forth three alternative fines and gave judges the option of choosing the greatest of the following: (1) the amount specified in the applicable law; or (2) twice the gain derived by a defendant or the pecuniary loss inflicted on the victim; or (3) for misdemeanors punishable by six months or more, $100,000; for misdemeanors resulting in loss of life or for any felony, $250,000 if the defendant was an individual or $500,000 if the defendant was an organization.

● Imposed an interest rate of 1.5 percent per month on delinquent fines, and if a fine was more than 90 days delinquent, imposed a penalty of 25 percent of the amount past due.

● Required the U.S. Parole Commission, when it paroled a prisoner who owed a fine, to set as a condition of parole that the prisoner make a diligent effort to pay the fine.

● Gave the U.S. government a new type of lien to help collect fines.

• Gave federal judges new authority to impose conditions to help ensure later payment of a fine when an order requiring payment was stayed.

• Permitted the Justice Department, when a fine was to be paid in installments, to declare the entire unpaid balance of the fine to be due and payable if a scheduled installment was missed. ∎

Aviation Drug Trafficking

Legislation designed to curb the use of airplanes in illegal drug trafficking was sent to President Reagan by Congress Oct. 4 (S 1146 — PL 98-499).

The measure amended the Federal Aviation Act of 1958 to provide for revocation of the airman and registration certificates of the pilots and owners of aircraft used in drug trafficking.

Final action came when the Senate on Oct. 2 and the House on Oct. 4 adopted a conference report (H Rept 98-1085) on the bill.

The legislation had initially been reported by the Senate Commerce Committee on Sept. 15, 1983 (S Rept 98-228) and passed by the Senate on Sept. 27, 1983. A companion bill (HR 1580 — H Rept 883) was reported by the House Public Works and Transportation Committee on June 29, 1984, and passed by the full House on July 24.

The president signed the drug trafficking bill into law on Oct. 19.

Final Provisions

Under S 1146 as cleared, the administrator of the Federal Aviation Administration (FAA) was required to revoke the airman's certificate of any pilot convicted of a state or federal drug-related felony who was flying or was on board an airplane involved in the offense. Offenses involving simple possession of an illegal drug did not trigger revocation.

The FAA administrator was required to take the same action against any pilot who "knowingly engaged in" an illicit drug transaction involving his aircraft, even if that person had not been prosecuted for the offense. But no airman's certificate could be revoked if the pilot in question had been charged with a drug offense and then acquitted.

An airman whose certificate was revoked by the FAA could appeal to the National Transportation Safety Board, which was required to conduct a hearing on the case before affirming or reversing the FAA order.

S 1146 also required the FAA administrator to revoke the certificate of registration of the owner of any aircraft used in drug trafficking if the owner knew the plane would be used in such a manner. The same appeals process as for pilots was established.

A pilot or aircraft owner whose certificate was revoked would have to wait five years to obtain a new one, unless the FAA determined that the five-year period was excessive, given the nature of the offense in question.

Finally, the bill stiffened existing penalties for operating an aircraft without a valid airman's certificate. Under current law, such an offense carried a $1,000 civil penalty. S 1146 provided that anyone who knowingly piloted an aircraft without a certificate and violated state or federal drug laws was subject to a fine of up to $25,000 and a prison term of up to five years. ∎

Bullet Bill, Gun Legislation

Responding to election-year jitters of members, House leaders Sept. 26 abruptly shelved a bill (HR 6067) to ban the import, manufacture and sale of armor-piercing bullets that could penetrate protective vests worn by police.

The move came after the politically powerful National Rifle Association (NRA) made clear that it would oppose the bill approved Aug. 8 and reported Sept. 6 (H Rept 98-996) by the House Judiciary Committee.

Rep. Jack Brooks, D-Texas, had planned to offer a substitute version as a floor amendment. It would have barred import and manufacture, but not sales, of the so-called "cop-killer" bullets. But some police organizations backing HR 6067 denounced this as essentially useless.

With many House members fearful of offending either the NRA or police groups pressing for strong legislation, the bill was simply pulled from the calendar.

Background

Law enforcement agencies had urged Congress for years to enact a law to protect officers from armor-piercing bullets. Legislation on the subject had been circulating in Congress since 1980, but it ran into difficulty because of opposition from the NRA. The NRA contended that such bills were a "foot in the door" to gun control.

Leading advocates of the bullet legislation included Rep. Mario Biaggi, D-N.Y., a 23-year police veteran who was shot 10 times in the line of duty, and Sen. Daniel Patrick Moynihan, D-N.Y.

Biaggi expressed frustration at the attacks on the legislation by the NRA, labeling the gun group's opposition as "nothing but a knee-jerk reaction based more on paranoia than on any semblance of reason."

The key part of HR 6067 was the section defining the bullets to be covered. This proved difficult because of concerns that ammunition with legitimate purposes, such as hunting, might be inadvertently banned.

As approved by the committee, the bill applied to bullets that were constructed entirely from one or a combination of seven specified metals and that were designed for use in handguns.

The measure did not cover "shotgun shot" generally used for hunting. Nor did it affect certain target-shooting ammunition or ammunition the secretary of the Treasury determined was used primarily for sporting purposes.

William J. Hughes, D-N.J., chairman of the Crime Subcommittee, told colleagues that the bill would cover only about 1 percent of the armor-piercing bullets available. Hughes said this was the case because 99 percent of the bullets manufactured were for long guns and many of those could be fired by a handgun and could pierce armor.

Senate Gun Legislation

In the Senate, foes of gun controls succeeded in winning Judiciary Committee approval of a bill (S 914) easing restrictions on the sale of shotguns, rifles and some handguns. The gun bill was approved May 10 and reported (S Rept 98-583) Aug. 8, but it went no further.

During committee debate April 12, Sen. Edward M. Kennedy, D-Mass., offered an amendment to bar production and import of cop-killer bullets. Sen. Orrin G. Hatch, R-Utah, promptly offered a substitute amendment that required instead a mandatory sentence for any crime committed with an armor-piercing bullet. Hatch's substitute was adopted 14-1.

As approved by the committee, S 914 retained existing controls banning interstate sales of small, concealable handguns, but it lifted controls on sales of other guns. It allowed a person from one state to buy a gun over the counter from a licensed dealer in another state so long as the sale did not violate the laws of either the seller's or buyer's state. ∎

Senate Death Penalty Bill

The Senate Feb. 22 passed a bill (S 1765) re-establishing a federal death penalty for specified crimes, but the measure went nowhere in the House.

The Senate debate on the death penalty bill marked the first time in a decade that either chamber had discussed the issue. The Supreme Court in 1972 invalidated all existing death penalty statutes, although the justices did not find capital punishment per se unconstitutional. *(CQ Guide to the Supreme Court, p. 575)*

Since 1972, 38 states had rewritten their death penalty statutes to conform with that year's court decision and later rulings on the subject.

After a hiatus of many years, executions in the United States began again in 1977. Since then, dozens of prisoners had been executed, and the pace was accelerating throughout 1984.

In 1974, the Senate passed a death penalty bill to meet guidelines set out by the Supreme Court, but the measure languished in the House. *(1974 Almanac p. 298)*

In 1984, the only federal law carrying a legally enforceable death penalty was one prohibiting homicide during an aircraft hijacking. The air piracy law was enacted in 1974. *(1974 Almanac p. 275)*

In the past, the federal death penalty was imposed only sparingly. Between 1953 — the year of the highly publicized executions of Ethel and Julius Rosenberg for espionage — and 1963, when the last federal execution took place, there were seven federal prisoners put to death, according to the U.S. Bureau of Prisons.

The Senate Bill

S 1765, which was reported Aug. 4, 1983, by the Senate Judiciary Committee (S Rept 98-251), authorized death sentences for treason, espionage, federal crimes that resulted in the death of another person and, in specified instances, attempts to kill the president.

The attempt provision called for the death penalty when a person seriously injured or came "dangerously close" to killing the president. This provision grew out of the March 30, 1981, shooting that wounded President Reagan and three other persons. *(1981 Almanac p. 6)*

To comply with Supreme Court guidelines, S 1765 required a two-stage trial. The first part was to determine the defendant's guilt or innocence. A defendant found guilty would then face a separate hearing on the issue of punishment. The jury or, in specified instances, a judge could consider "aggravating" factors, such as a prior conviction for a state or federal capital offense, or committing the crime "in an especially heinous, cruel or depraved manner."

The jury or judge also would be required to consider any "mitigating" factors, such as the young age of a defen-

dant or the fact that the defendant was under substantial duress.

Before imposing the death penalty, the jury or judge would have to determine that aggravating factors outweighed any mitigating factors.

Senate Debate

During debate Feb. 8, 9 and 22, senators on both sides of the issue presented one grisly story after another to illustrate their points of view. Proponents sought to show why the death penalty was justified, while foes recounted tragic mistakes made when the wrong defendants were convicted.

Senate Judiciary Chairman Strom Thurmond, R-S.C., who sent four men to their executions as a South Carolina judge four decades earlier, contended that "society demands the death penalty for the most aggravated murders to send a signal that innocent life is precious indeed and cannot be violated without like consequence to the killer."

People who commit heinous crimes, he said, "have forfeited their own right to life.... I am convinced that the death penalty is a deterrent for the crimes for which it is consistently imposed."

Sen. Carl Levin, D-Mich., was in sharp disagreement with Thurmond on that point. He said the death penalty was not a deterrent, noting that a Library of Congress study covering 1977-82 showed that states with capital punishment had a murder rate nearly twice that of states without the death penalty.

Levin, like other opponents, said the criminal justice system was not error proof.

"You can't cure your mistake," he said, "if you put people to death." ∎

Exclusionary Rule Change

Legislation to relax the so-called "exclusionary rule" to permit use of certain illegally obtained evidence in criminal trials was passed by the Senate Feb. 7, but it died in the House.

The bill (S 1764 — S Rept 98-350) was passed by the Senate by 63-24. *(Vote 12, p. 4-S)*

The Supreme Court July 5 took much of the heat out of the congressional debate when it approved modifications in the rule similar to those in S 1764.

The exclusionary rule was first developed by the Supreme Court in 1914 for use in federal trials, then applied to state trials in 1961. Intended to deter unlawful police conduct, the rule barred the introduction at trial of evidence that was obtained in violation of the law or a suspect's constitutional rights. *(CQ Guide to the Supreme Court, p. 548)*

Federal and state prosecutors across the country had long sought elimination or modification of the rule, contending that it interfered with effective law enforcement and led to the release on "technicalities" of clearly guilty criminals.

The American Civil Liberties Union and the American Bar Association strongly opposed changing the rule, arguing that to do so would erode the Fourth Amendment's prohibition on unreasonable searches and other constitutional protections.

Senate Bill

S 1764 created an exception to the exclusionary rule to allow use of evidence obtained by officers acting with a reasonable, good-faith belief that their conduct was legal. A presumption that an officer acted in good faith would exist if the evidence was seized within the scope of a search warrant. The bill affected only federal criminal cases.

Sen. Charles McC. Mathias Jr., R-Md., a leading opponent of S 1764, contended the bill sent a "message" to "weaken the Fourth Amendment.... We ought to think long and hard before we send that message."

Sen. Dale Bumpers, D-Ark., said the bill changed an "objective evaluation" of an officer's conduct to a "subjective good faith" standard. "You do not have to worry about what was on the officer's mind under present law," he said.

Sen. Strom Thurmond, R-S.C., who guided the bill through the Judiciary Committee, countered that the exclusionary rule "illustrates much of what is wrong within our present system of criminal justice. Instead of a system of criminal law in which the search for truth, the search for guilt or innocence, is the principal guiding objective, we have seen our system increasingly degraded into one in which procedures and details and form are elevated above all else."

The House Judiciary Subcommittee on Criminal Justice held oversight hearings in March 1983 on the exclusionary rule in general. However, the panel did not move any legislation concerning the rule.

The Court Ruling

The 6-3 court ruling July 5 recognizing a "good faith" exception to the exclusionary rule marked the most significant relaxation of the evidentiary rule in the 70 years since it was first enunciated by the high court. The decision came in the case of *United States v. Leon. (Decision, p. 5-A)*

A few weeks earlier, on June 11, the court by 7-2 had carved out a more limited "inevitable discovery" exception to the rule, permitting use of evidence collected through police misconduct if that evidence would inevitably have been discovered anyway. *(Nix v. Williams, p. 7-A)*

The Reagan administration had urged the court to endorse a good-faith exception.

Writing for the court, Justice Byron R. White justified a good-faith exception by a simple cost-benefit analysis and limited it to situations in which police obtained a warrant and executed a search in accord with it, only to have that warrant later found to be defective.

The rule had no deterrent effect on police in this situation, White explained, and simply "cannot pay its way."

Justices William J. Brennan Jr., Thurgood Marshall and John Paul Stevens dissented. "The court's victory over the Fourth Amendment is complete," Brennan declared for himself and Marshall. He called the ruling the climax of the "court's gradual but determined strangulation of the rule" over the last decade, and predicted that the majority would soon relax the exclusionary rule even in cases where police acted without a warrant.

Stevens, in a separate dissent, said the court was on the verge of converting "the Bill of Rights into an unenforced honor code that police may follow in their discretion."

Although he concurred with the majority, Justice Harry A. Blackmun sounded a cautionary note. "If it should emerge from experience that, contrary to our expec-

tations, the good faith exception ... results in a material change in police compliance with the Fourth Amendment, we shall have to reconsider what we have undertaken here," he said.

The court reversed a 9th U.S. Circuit Court of Appeals decision excluding evidence in a federal narcotics case because the search warrant used to seize it was later found to be based on insufficient information.

The majority described the exclusionary rule as a judicial remedy intended to deter police from violating the Fourth Amendment guarantee against unreasonable search and seizure by denying them the use of evidence obtained in violation of that guarantee.

White explained that "when an officer acting with objective good faith has obtained a search warrant ... and acted within its scope ... there is no police illegality and thus nothing to deter."

Nor did the rule deter judges and magistrates from issuing invalid search warrants, the court majority said. "Judges and magistrates are not adjuncts to the law-enforcement team; as neutral judicial officers, they have no stake in the outcome of particular criminal prosecutions. The threat of exclusion thus cannot be expected significantly to deter them."

White said it cost society too much — in terms of weakened prosecutions — to apply the rule rigidly. "Particularly when law enforcement officers have acted in objective good faith or their transgressions have been minor, the magnitude of the benefit conferred on such guilty defendants offends basic concepts of the criminal justice system," he wrote.

"We conclude that the marginal or nonexistent benefits produced by suppressing evidence obtained in objectively reasonable reliance on a subsequently invalidated search warrant cannot justify the substantial costs of exclusion," White said.

The dissenters took a far broader view of the exclusionary rule's purpose. For them, the use of illegally obtained evidence in court inflicted a second constitutional injury upon a defendant, and destroyed the integrity of the judicial system that permitted its use.

"The majority," wrote Brennan, "ignores the fundamental constitutional importance of what is at stake here.... The task of combating crime and convicting the guilty will in every era seem of such critical and pressing concern that we may be lured by the temptations of expediency into forsaking our commitment to protecting individual liberty and privacy. It was for that very reason that the framers of the Bill of Rights insisted that law enforcement efforts be permanently and unambiguously restricted in order to preserve personal freedoms." ∎

Habeas Corpus Revisions

A bill (S 1763 — S Rept 98-226) revising federal court procedures for handling writs of *habeas corpus* was approved by the Senate Feb. 6.

The measure was designed to relieve some of the growing workload of the federal courts. It was passed by a 67-9 vote. *(Vote 11, p. 4-S)*

Habeas corpus writs were petitions filed by prisoners claiming they had been incarcerated in violation of their constitutional rights. Generally, prisoners filed them after they had exhausted all of their available appeals in state courts.

Supporters of the bill in and out of Congress contended that prisoner claims were often frivolous and tied up valuable federal court resources. A treatise on federal court procedure, cited in the Judiciary Committee report, noted that *habeas* claims were "the most controversial and friction-producing issue in the relation between the federal courts and the states. . . . Federal judges are unhappy at the burden of thousands of mostly frivolous petitions, state courts resent having their decisions re-examined by a single federal district judge, and the Supreme Court in recent terms has shown a strong inclination to limit its availability."

Senators who opposed S 1763 agreed there was a problem, but suggested the bill was too restrictive in its efforts to limit state prisoner suits.

The bill made several modifications of current law, including the following:

●Changed the standard of review for *habeas* cases, requiring federal courts to give deference to state adjudications that were "full and fair." Currently, federal judges were not required to hold new fact-finding hearings, but they were required to make determinations on questions of law and then reapply the facts to the law, regardless of the scope of the state proceedings.

●Barred a defendant from raising in federal court claims that were not raised in state court unless very specific conditions were met.

●Established a one-year time limit for filing *habeas* petitions, with the time running from the point at which state remedies were exhausted.

Max Baucus, D-Mont., offered an amendment to delete the provision requiring federal court deference to state adjudication. It was tabled, and thus killed, 59-17. *(Vote 10, p. 4-S)* ∎

Immigration Reform Dies at Session's End

For the third year in a row, a sweeping immigration reform measure died in Congress, the victim of swirling interest-group pressures and election-year political qualms.

Supporters worked into the final days of the 98th Congress, hoping that a House-Senate conference committee could agree on a compromise version of the legislation (S 529) in time for approval by both chambers. The effort failed Oct. 11, a day before adjournment.

In 1982, a similar immigration bill (S 2222) passed the Senate but died on the House floor in the last days of a lame-duck session. *(1982 Almanac p. 405)*

In 1983, S 529 passed the Senate by a 76-18 vote, but a companion bill (HR 1510 — H Rept 98-115, Parts I-IV) was blocked in the House by Speaker Thomas P. O'Neill Jr., D-Mass. *(1983 Almanac p. 287)*

The House finally passed its version of the immigration bill by a razor-thin 216-211 vote June 20, 1984. *(Vote 226, p. 72-H)*

Congress was in recess much of the summer for the Democratic and Republican National Conventions, and the conference committee did not begin work on the immigration bill until Sept. 13. The delay proved fatal, given the complexity of the legislation and the intense feelings it provoked.

S 529 was designed to curb the growing flow of illegal aliens into the United States. It set up penalties for employers who knowingly hired illegal aliens, while authorizing millions of illegal aliens who had entered the United States prior to Jan. 1, 1981, to obtain legalization of their status.

It also expanded an existing program that allowed foreign workers to enter the country temporarily for work in agriculture, and it overhauled exclusion, asylum and deportation procedures.

Like predecessor legislation in 1981-82, the bill was sponsored by Sen. Alan K. Simpson, R-Wyo., and Rep. Romano L. Mazzoli, D-Ky., chairmen of the Senate and House Judiciary subcommittees on immigration.

Fire From All Sides

President Reagan generally supported S 529, but he did not make it a priority issue. And it was his reservations about the cost of the proposed legalization program that proved the final sticking point for the House-Senate conferees.

Hispanic lobbyists contended that the employer-sanction provisions would result in discrimination against anyone who looked or sounded foreign, and they fought the bill vigorously. They found an ally in Democratic presidential nominee Walter F. Mondale, who said that he would never support a sanctions program.

Many conservatives in both parties flatly opposed the bill's amnesty provisions. Most members from Southwestern border states — California, Arizona, New Mexico and Texas — also opposed the measure, fearing that the legalization program would drive up social service costs in their states.

Neither organized labor nor big Western growers were satisfied with the final provisions on the temporary worker program. And business groups were opposed to the employer sanction provisions of the final version.

1983 Background

After watching immigration legislation die in the waning hours of the 97th Congress, Simpson and Mazzoli made sure their bills got off to a fast start in the 98th. Their respective subcommittees began markups the week of April 4, 1983, completing work within three days.

Senate Action

The full Senate Judiciary Committee approved S 529 on April 19, 1983, and reported the bill (S Rept 98-62) two days later. The Senate passed the measure 76-18 on May 18 after four days of debate.

The Senate bill prohibited employment of illegal aliens. It required employers of at least four workers to check documents of job applicants, such as a driver's license and Social Security card, and to keep records of those they hired. It set a fine of $1,000 per alien for the first violation and $2,000 per alien for the second, and called for criminal penalties if a "pattern or practice" of hiring illegal aliens was found.

As approved by the Senate, S 529 made permanent resident status available to illegal aliens who had arrived in the United States prior to Jan. 1, 1977, and had resided here continuously since then. It permitted aliens to apply for temporary resident status if they had been in the country before Jan. 1, 1980.

S 529 authorized a four-year block grant program of $1.1 billion to $1.4 billion to help states meet costs associated with the legalization program. The funds were designed to cover such things as educational and health services for newly legalized aliens.

House Committee Actions

In the House, HR 1510 had to clear far more hurdles than its Senate counterpart.

The full Judiciary Committee approved the measure May 5, 1983, after making a number of changes in the version produced by Mazzoli's subcommittee.

Thereafter, the bill underwent further modifications in the Agriculture, Education and Labor, and Energy and Commerce committees, which finished their work the week of June 20, 1983.

All four versions of the legislation were sent to the House Rules Committee. Chairman Claude Pepper, D-Fla., told the chairmen of the four committees he wanted them to work out a compromise version before Rules took up the bill. But negotiations failed to produce any agreement.

With Hispanic groups stepping up their opposition to the legislation, and with no sign of an accord among the four House committees, O'Neill announced Oct. 4 that he would not attempt to bring the bill to the floor in 1983.

House Rules Committee Action

The House Rules Committee finally began hearings on HR 1510 on April 5, 1984. The panel was seeking a way to accommodate the amendments proposed by the three committees that marked up the bill after Judiciary had finished with it, and by some representatives — including Hispanic members — who were not on any of the panels.

The House Judiciary Committee in 1982 reported a similar immigration bill, which went to the floor under a rule allowing unlimited amendments. Opponents led by Edward R. Roybal, D-Calif., then chairman of the Hispanic Caucus, had prepared hundreds of amendments. The bill was not considered until late in the session, and time ran out before the House acted on it.

Pepper and other Rules Committee members conceded that an open rule would not be feasible in 1984. They told witnesses that some kind of limit on amendments and on the time for debate would be required.

More than three dozen House members testified at the Rules hearings, and many criticized HR 1510.

On June 8 the Rules Committee granted a rule for the bill setting boundaries for floor consideration. The rule (H Res 519) used the Judiciary Committee version of HR 1510 as the basis for floor debate and permitted 69 amendments to be offered.

Among those were the amendments voted by the Agriculture, Education and Labor, and Energy and Commerce committees. Also in order were amendments proposed by Roybal.

During the week of June 4, lobbyists in Washington worked the House to drum up opposition to HR 1510, while their supporters outside the capital wrote letters and called members to express their concerns about the legislation.

Opponents of the bill forced a Democratic Party caucus on the issue June 7 that was attended by 140 members. Majority Leader Jim Wright, D-Texas, characterized the

caucus debate as "vigorous." Roybal and some of his allies had hoped for a caucus vote instructing the Rules Committee not to grant a rule for the bill, but under pressure from O'Neill, Roybal did not press this tactic.

House Floor Action

The House took up HR 1510 on June 11, adopting the rule for its consideration by a comfortable 291-111 margin. *(Vote 204, p. 64-H)*

But that vote was no clue to the bitter debate that was to follow.

For seven days, House members slogged through dozens of amendments, arguing heatedly about almost every section of the complex bill.

The cornerstone of the bill — penalties for employers who knowingly hired illegal aliens — remained intact despite several challenges. But a second pivotal title, creating a program to grant legal status, or amnesty, to millions of illegals already in the country, was modified somewhat. And a hotly disputed proposal to create a flexible foreign guest worker program for growers was adopted.

Employer Sanctions

Amendments Adopted. The House adopted six amendments June 12-13 that altered the employer sanctions provisions, although the basic thrust of this title remained intact. They were:

● By 321-97, an amendment offered by Dan Lungren, R-Calif., to require an employer to keep records of everyone hired and attest to the fact he had checked documents, such as a Social Security card or driver's license, to verify each employee's eligibility to work in the United States. *(Vote 206, p. 64-H)*

The amendment replaced Judiciary Committee language inserted by Thomas N. Kindness, R-Ohio, that barred record-keeping and screening requirements until federal immigration officials investigated an employer and found an undocumented worker on the payroll.

The Lungren amendment made the bill substantially in line with the Senate measure.

● By voice vote, an amendment of Sam B. Hall Jr., D-Texas, exempting employers of three or fewer workers from the sanctions. The Senate bill contained a similar exemption.

● By a 14-12 division vote, an amendment by Ron Coleman, D-Texas, eliminating criminal penalties for employers, leaving a civil fine of $1,000 per illegal alien hired. As approved by the Judiciary Committee, HR 1510 provided for a criminal fine of up to $3,000 and imprisonment for up to a year for each illegal alien hired after the third violation of the law.

The Senate bill provided for a fine of $1,000 and imprisonment of up to six months for each violation when a "pattern or practice" of hiring illegal aliens was found.

● By 242-155, a Hall amendment requiring the government to set up a system to allow employers to verify workers' Social Security identification numbers by telephone to determine whether the employee was eligible to work. *(Vote 208, p. 66-H)*

Hall said his proposed system would work just like credit card verification systems, which handled some 70 million transactions each month.

Opponents charged it would be too expensive and could create serious invasion-of-privacy problems.

J. J. Pickle, D-Texas, chairman of the Ways and

Means Subcommittee on Social Security, said the Hall proposal would cost $1 billion. To give the Social Security Administration responsibility for revising the card to make it more secure, reissuing it to millions of citizens and then verifying the numbers would cause "chaos," he charged.

Don Edwards, D-Calif., said the proposal would be "the beginning of a national surveillance system."

● By a 57-51 division vote, a Roybal amendment striking language in the bill calling for a presidential study of a "secure system" to determine employment eligibility.

The amendment produced emotional debate among members who said they had suffered discrimination. In highly personal terms, they argued that the study could be the first step toward a national identification card, which they said was reprehensible.

"I was born in Europe and I am an immigrant," said Sala Burton, D-Calif. "Obviously, I am an American citizen or I could not serve in this body. However, the most detestable thing in the world is to have an ID card," she said. "The Jews in Europe, in Poland, where I was born, were wearing yellow stars. Is that what we really want?"

Norman Y. Mineta, D-Calif., told members that he and his family were incarcerated in the United States during World War II simply because they were of Japanese origin. He said the government abused its authority once and could abuse it again if some national identity system were created.

Barney Frank, D-Mass., took issue with these remarks, pointing out that the bill sought only a study of a secure identification and expressly ruled out creation of a national ID card.

● By 404-9, a Frank amendment making it an "unfair employment-related immigration practice" to discriminate on the basis of national origin or alienage. This was designed to prevent employers from using the sanctions provisions of the bill as an excuse to avoid hiring foreign-sounding workers. The amendment set up a "special counsel" in the newly created U.S. Immigration Board to investigate allegations of discrimination. Under the bill, the board also was to handle appeals of immigration matters from administrative law judges. *(Vote 207, p. 66-H)*

Amendments Rejected. The House rejected several amendments applicable to the sanctions title of the bill, including:

● By 120-304, an amendment by Roybal, a leading Hispanic member, to replace employer sanctions with beefed up enforcement of existing labor laws on wages, hours and working conditions. Some 140 Republicans — all but 20 of those voting — joined 164 Democrats to block the proposal, while 100 Democrats voted for it. *(Vote 210, p. 66-H)*

● By 166-253, an amendment by Augustus F. Hawkins, D-Calif., for the Education and Labor Committee, that restructured the employer sanction provisions and included the anti-discrimination language in the Frank amendment. (The amendment was defeated prior to the vote on the Frank language.) *(Vote 205, p. 64-H)*

● By 137-274 the House rejected an amendment by Patricia Schroeder, D-Colo., putting a three-year limit on the employer sanction provisions. *(Vote 209, p. 66-H)*

Legalization

Amendments Rejected. The bill's amnesty provisions precipitated two full days of debate before the issue was resolved. The key vote came on June 20, when members by 195-233 rejected an amendment of Bill McCollum, R-Fla., to delete the amnesty program from the bill. *(Vote 224, p. 70-H)*

As approved by the House Judiciary Committee, HR 1510 provided permanent resident status for any illegal alien who could prove he was in the United States prior to Jan. 1, 1982, and had lived in the country continuously since then. The alien was barred from most forms of federal and state assistance for five years, although certain exceptions were provided.

(Neither the House bill nor the Senate version changed provisions of current law that allowed a permanent resident to seek U.S. citizenship after five years. Permanent residents enjoyed virtually all the rights of a citizen, except that they could not vote, hold public office or hold military office.)

The Senate bill, with its stricter, two-tiered timetable for legalization, barred temporary residents from most forms of assistance for six years, while permanent residents would be barred from aid for three years.

On June 19, Lungren offered an amendment to make the House bill conform to the Senate legalization provisions. He said the committee bill was too broad and amounted to blanket amnesty for aliens. Lungren also contended that the Judiciary provisions would cost $6.6 billion between 1985 and 1989, compared with $3.4 billion for his proposal. (Even though the bill provided a five-year ban on most forms of federal aid, there were exceptions that could have been costly.)

Frank, who had proposed the Judiciary Committee's Jan. 1, 1982, cutoff date, argued that Lungren's amendment simply made a bad situation worse. Frank said there were already millions of illegal aliens who lived as "an underclass." To make the amnesty provisions as restrictive as Lungren proposed would simply perpetuate "a large class of potentially desperate people," he claimed.

Kent Hance, D-Texas, who had based his unsuccessful bid for the Democratic nomination to the U.S. Senate on his opposition to amnesty, contended that legalization was a jobs issue. "Amnesty costs jobs for American citizens. It legalizes the theft of American jobs," he declared.

The Reagan administration strongly supported the Lungren amendment, and mounted a concentrated campaign of phone calls in its behalf. The effort failed, however, as Democrats largely stuck together to defeat the proposal 181-245. *(Vote 220, p. 70-H)*

After this vote, E. Clay Shaw Jr., R-Fla., offered an amendment to grant permanent resident status to aliens who could prove they were in the country before Jan. 1, 1980. His amendment was rejected by 177-246 on another generally party-line vote. *(Vote 221, p. 70-H)*

Amendments Adopted. Immediately after the Shaw vote, Majority Leader Wright offered what he said was a "sensible, reasonable, middle ground that most Americans would support." His proposal authorized temporary resident status to aliens who could prove they were in the United States before Jan. 1, 1982. After two years, these aliens could apply for permanent resident status. They had to show that they had at least a minimal understanding of English and knew something about the American government system or were "pursuing a course of study" to learn these subjects.

"I am not one of those who believe that we must homogenize America. I do not think we have to pour all these great strains into one great melting pot and come out with a single stream of sameness," Wright said. "But I do not believe either that we want to create the temptations to a Balkanization of American society into little subcultures," he said. "Language is the thread, the common thread, that ties us all together."

Roybal asserted that Wright's provision would discourage people from seeking legalization. "The moment you say to working people throughout this country that unless you start learning English you will not be able to become a legal resident, then there is a reservation in his mind," Roybal said. "For it is most difficult for those who work long hours to be able to go to school at night."

The Wright amendment was adopted 247-170. *(Vote 222, p. 70-H)*

Guest Workers

Amendments Adopted. In addition to sanctions and the amnesty program, HR 1510 included a title expanding an existing temporary foreign worker program known as the "H-2" program. (The name came from a section in the 1952 immigration law that allowed foreign workers into the United States on a temporary basis.)

An Agriculture Committee amendment offered by Leon E. Panetta, D-Calif., and cosponsored by Sid Morrison, R-Wash., was an addition to this section of HR 1510. Panetta and Morrison, whose districts included large agricultural sectors, said that even though the bill expanded the current H-2 program, it still was insufficient to meet growers' needs.

Their amendment was designed to ameliorate the effects of the employer penalty title of the bill. Growers acknowledged their dependence on illegal aliens, or undocumented workers, and warned that if such workers were barred in the future — the goal of the bill — they would have to be guaranteed a supply of labor through legal channels to harvest crops.

The bill originally required employers to apply for temporary foreign workers 50 days before they needed them. Panetta's amendment allowed growers, but not other types of employers, to apply for workers just 72 hours in advance of anticipated need.

The attorney general was authorized to allow these workers to stay in the United States for up to 11 months. The workers were not restricted to just one employer but could move from grower to grower within a specified "agricultural region" to be defined by the attorney general. (The H-2 program restricted the worker to the employer who requested him.)

Panetta said his proposal included safeguards against abuses in wages and working conditions. He denounced opponents who claimed his proposal amounted to another "bracero" program, a controversial program that brought nearly five million Mexican laborers into the United States from 1942-54, primarily to do agricultural work.

But opponents charged that the new program would open the way for exploitation. Bill Richardson, D-N.M., called it "inhumane." Henry B. Gonzalez, D-Texas, said it amounted to "rent-a-slave." And Frank called the proposal "an extraordinary set of exemptions for the agricultural sector."

Despite such protests, the House adopted the amendment by 228-172. *(Vote 216, p. 68-H)*

The vote was a surprise to several of the bill's supporters who opposed the new guest worker program. It was a bitter defeat for the AFL-CIO, which had lobbied intensely against the proposal.

"This Congress has just performed an outrageous act," said Jane O'Grady, one of the labor organization's top lobbyists. "They have just abandoned U.S. farm workers."

After the vote, Mazzoli predicted the provision would be modified in conference with the Senate to provide more protections for workers.

Amendments Rejected. Prior to debating the Panetta amendment, the House rejected two proposals that would have changed the H-2 program outlined in the bill:

● By voice vote, an amendment by John N. Erlenborn, R-Ill., to alter some of the restrictions on employers in the bill as well as in current law.

● By 164-256, an Education Committee amendment offered by George Miller, D-Calif., to retain much of current law regarding regulation of the H-2 program. *(Vote 215, p. 68-H)*

Asylum Procedures

● By 208-192, the House adopted an amendment by McCollum further streamlining procedures for handling asylum, deportation and exclusion cases. *(Vote 212, p. 66-H)*

The amendment deleted a provision requiring an immigration officer to inform aliens caught at the border of their rights to a lawyer and to have an administrative law judge review the facts of their case before they could be excluded from the country. Another key feature deleted a provision allowing "class action" lawsuits involving a pattern or practice of constitutional violations in asylum adjudications.

Enforcement

By voice vote, the House adopted a Roybal amendment increasing funding for the Immigration and Naturalization Service (INS) through fiscal 1986, covering, among other things, increased border patrol, training for INS personnel and creation of an anti-smuggling program with Canada and Mexico.

By 133-285 the House rejected an amendment by Hamilton Fish Jr., R-N.Y., to strike language requiring immigration officials to obtain a search warrant before going into "open fields" to look for undocumented workers. S 529 included a similar provision. *(Vote 211, p. 66-H)*

Legal Immigration

By 168-231, the House rejected an amendment by Carlos J. Moorhead, R-Calif., to set a yearly cap of 450,000 on legal immigration. The cap did not include refugees, defined as those persons fleeing their homeland because of a well-founded fear of persecution. *(Vote 213, p. 68-H)*

The Senate bill included an annual immigration cap of 425,000 persons.

By 411-4, the House adopted a Roybal amendment to clarify the meaning of "continuous physical presence" in the United States when the issue arises in deportation cases. The amendment was designed to ensure that no alien would be deported because of a brief, emergency trip out of the country. *(Vote 214, p. 68-H)*

Final Passage Vote

When the House vote on passage of HR 1510 finally came June 20, it proved to be the most dramatic of the entire year.

The outcome was in doubt until the last seconds of the 15-minute tally. Throughout the roll call, the balance teetered back and forth — more often favoring foes than supporters of the bill.

At the very end, however, sponsors managed to round up enough support to push the bill over the top, 216-211.

"I begged those guys. I said, 'For God's sake, don't let us come up empty-handed,' " said Mazzoli at a press conference after the vote.

Mazzoli and Lungren, principal floor manager for the Republicans, agreed that the legalization issue was the main reason for the close final vote — closer than the margins on 18 other roll calls between June 11 and June 20. They said that a number of members who had voted for amendments during the debate ended up opposing the bill because they believed its legalization provisions were too lenient.

Indeed, members from Southwestern border states — California, Arizona, New Mexico and Texas — voted 15-64 against the bill.

A number of liberal Democrats also opposed the bill, siding with Hispanic members who led a futile crusade against the measure because of the employer penalties. The Hispanics argued repeatedly that the provisions would result in discrimination because employers, anxious to avoid the sanctions, would not hire anyone who looked foreign, spoke with an accent or had a foreign-sounding surname.

A tired Robert Garcia, D-N.Y., chairman of the Hispanic Caucus, said simply, "The tide was against us."

House Provisions

As passed by the House, HR 1510 contained the following major provisions:

Employer Sanctions

● Prohibited employment of illegal aliens by any employer of four or more persons and provided for a civil fine of $1,000 per alien for each violation. On a second violation, an employer could be fined $2,000 per alien.

● Authorized the attorney general to seek an injunction or restraining order against any person or entity engaged in a "pattern or practice" of employing or recruiting illegal aliens.

● Required an employer of four or more persons to sign a form attesting, under penalty of perjury, that he had verified that each newly hired worker was eligible for employment in the United States. Such forms had to be retained, available for inspection by the Immigration and Naturalization Service or Labor Department, for three years after hiring or one year after the worker's termination, whichever was later.

● Authorized a fine of $500 per alien against employers who failed to keep records concerning verification of an employee's work eligibility.

● Specified that in determining a worker's employment eligibility, an employer had to examine any of the following documents: U.S. passport, Social Security card, birth certificate, alien documentation or registration card, driver's license with photograph, or any other identification permitted under regulations to be developed by the Justice Department.

● Required the attorney general, in cooperation with the secretaries of labor and of health and human services, to establish a method to validate the Social Security account numbers of job applicants, and required employers to submit the Social Security numbers of prospective employees for validation.

● Provided that compliance with these validation procedures constituted a complete defense against charges of hiring an illegal alien.

● Provided a one-year period of public education on the

sanctions. During the first six months, the penalties would not apply, although the prohibition on hiring illegals would be in effect.

● Provided that an employer be given notice of an alleged violation and the right to a hearing before an administrative law judge. The hearing had to be held within 200 miles of the place where the employer resided or the place where the alleged violation occurred.

● Gave an employer the right to appeal any fine imposed by an administrative law judge to a federal appeals court.

● Prohibited discrimination against any job applicant because of national origin or alienage, except for positions that must, by law, be filled by U.S. citizens.

● Provided that any victim of alleged discrimination, or any INS officer, could file charges with a special counsel of the U.S. Immigration Board established under the bill, who was to investigate the charges, or with the board itself if the special counsel failed to act within 30 days.

● Required the U.S. Immigration Board to designate administrative law judges to hear complaints of discrimination and recommend action to the board.

● Authorized the board, based on "the preponderance of the testimony taken," to issue cease-and-desist orders to any employer judged guilty of discrimination based on national origin or alienage, to require hiring and the award of back pay to anyone adversely affected by such discrimination, and to impose a civil penalty of $2,000 for each individual discriminated against. On the second violation, the fine would increase to $3,000 for each individual discriminated against. The fine would be $4,000 per individual when the employer was found to have engaged in a pattern or practice of discrimination.

Enforcement and Fees

● Set the authorization for the INS at $700 million for fiscal 1985 and $715 million for fiscal 1986.

The Senate, in the fiscal 1985 Department of Justice authorization bill (S 2606) recommended $574.54 million, the administration's request. The House Judiciary Committee provided $595.16 million in its version of the bill. *(Related story, p. 253)*

● Authorized an extra $80 million in fiscal 1984 for increased patrols along U.S. borders, to remain available in fiscal 1985.

● Authorized $6 million annually in fiscal 1984-86 for a task force to monitor employer sanctions provisions.

● Required the attorney general to submit a plan to Congress within two months of enactment of the bill specifying the steps taken to assure adequate border patrol, including personnel, equipment training and support services. The attorney general would be required to submit similar plans for the two succeeding fiscal years.

● Required the attorney general to develop a plan for immigration "emergencies" to cover resettlement of immigrants and assistance to states and localities adversely affected by such emergencies.

● Required the attorney general to submit the emergency plan to the House and Senate Judiciary committees within four months of enactment.

● Required the attorney general to initiate talks with Mexico and Canada to establish a program to discourage smuggling of illegal aliens into the United States and to report back to Congress on the progress of such a plan within a year of enactment of the bill.

● Made it a crime to bring or attempt to bring an unauthorized alien into the United States either directly or indirectly, for commercial advantage or private profit, when the smuggling was undertaken knowingly or with "reckless disregard" of the fact that the alien was not authorized to enter the United States.

● Set a fine of up to $10,000, a prison term of up to five years or both for a violation of the anti-smuggling provisions of the bill, regardless of the number of aliens involved.

● Authorized the attorney general, in consultation with the secretary of state, to impose fees on aliens for their use of border facilities or INS services.

● Required INS officials to obtain warrants before searching farms or "other outdoor operations" for undocumented workers. This provision effectively overturned, as far as immigration law was concerned, an April 17 Supreme Court ruling in the cases of *Oliver v. United States* and *Maine v. Thornton*. By 6-3, the justices ruled that no warrants were needed for open-field searches. *(Court ruling, p. 5-A)*

Exclusion, Asylum, Deportation

● Provided expedited procedures for stopping illegal aliens at the border and barring them from the United States. An alien could be excluded from the United States, without a hearing, when an immigration officer determined that the person did not have the documentation required to enter the country, did not have "any reasonable basis" for legal entry into the United States and did not indicate an intention to apply for asylum.

● Provided for a hearing before a Justice Department administrative law judge on the exclusion of an alien when there was doubt about the alien's status.

● Allowed one immigration officer to challenge another officer's determination that an alien could be admitted to the United States, and provided for a hearing before an administrative law judge in this instance.

● Required the attorney general to establish procedures to ensure that aliens were not summarily excluded without being asked why they sought to enter the United States.

● Provided a hearing when an alien claims asylum, but restricted the hearing to issues raised in connection with the asylum claim.

● Gave administrative law judges within the Department of Justice authority to hear and decide cases involving exclusion from the United States, deportations, rescinding an alien's adjustment to legal status, certain asylum cases and cases involving the assessment of fines under the employer sanctions provisions.

● Created a U.S. Immigration Board in the Justice Department as a separate agency, composed of a chairman and six other members appointed by the president and confirmed by the Senate. Board members were given six-year terms, except that the first board would serve staggered terms.

● Gave the board authority to hear appeals from decisions of the administrative law judges on a number of matters, including deportation, exclusion and asylum cases, cases involving administrative fines and those involving revocation of visas.

(The board was to replace the existing Board of Immigration Appeals, which was created entirely by regulation and operated under the direct supervision of the attorney general. Under current law, the attorney general had the authority to reverse the immigration board's decision.)

● Gave the board chairman authority to appoint the administrative law judges in accordance with the competi-

tive merit system used for such appointments by the Office of Personnel Management.

● Provided special consideration for current immigration judges in the selection of new administrative law judges.

● Provided judicial review in the federal appeals courts of final U.S. Immigration Board orders in exclusion, deportation and asylum cases. (Currently, judicial review of exclusion orders was possible only through *habeas corpus* proceedings, which required that an individual be in detention.)

● Provided that any alien physically present in the United States or any alien at a land border or port of entry could seek asylum.

● Created special requirements for aliens seeking asylum against whom exclusion or deportation proceedings had begun. Applications from such aliens could not be considered unless the individual had served notice of intention to seek asylum within 14 days of the exclusion or deportation proceedings and had actually filed the application within 30 days of the proceedings. Time restrictions could be waived if an administrative law judge deemed such action to be in the interests of justice.

● Barred an alien whose asylum application was rejected from applying again unless the alien could show changed circumstances.

● Required that asylum applications be considered before administrative law judges specially trained in international relations and international law.

● Set time limits for hearing the asylum application.

● Required all asylum hearings to be open unless an applicant requested a closed hearing.

● Required an asylum applicant to be advised of his right to a lawyer and the availability of legal services, and to be allowed to present evidence and witnesses in his own behalf, to examine and object to evidence against him, and to cross-examine government witnesses.

● Required a complete record of the hearing to be kept.

● Required administrative law judges to decide all asylum cases not later than 30 days after completion of hearings.

● Put the burden of proof on the applicant to prove that he met the required test for being given asylum.

● Barred the reopening of an asylum proceeding unless the applicant could show changed circumstances that would result "in a change in the basis for the alien's claim for asylum."

● Required the attorney general to report to Congress annually on the status of asylum cases.

● Required the president to study the advisability of proposing to Mexico the creation of a "people-to-people" program between Mexico and the United States designed to help improve the Mexican economy.

● Required the president to submit study results to Congress within one year after enactment of the bill.

Legal Immigration

● Allowed 20,000 extra immigrant visas annually for citizens of Canada and Mexico.

● Provided that if citizens of either border country failed to use all of their allotted extra immigrant visas in one fiscal year, citizens of the other nation could use the surplus the following fiscal year.

● Required the president, starting in 1987, to report to Congress every three years on the number of aliens admitted to the country and their impact on the economy, labor market, housing market, educational systems, social services, foreign policy, environmental quality, resources and population growth of the United States.

● Made it possible for the children or spouses of long-time employees of international organizations living in the United States to obtain "special immigrant" status in specified circumstances, allowing them to remain in the United States even if the employee died or retired.

● Clarified the standard for "continuous physical presence" in the United States to be used in cases involving suspension of deportation. The clarification was intended to bar the deportation of someone who had to leave the country for a brief period in an emergency.

Temporary Foreign Workers

● Expanded and revised an existing "H-2" program allowing aliens to be admitted into the country for temporary work, primarily in agriculture.

● Gave the secretary of labor overall authority for issuing regulations governing the H-2 program, in consultation with the attorney general and secretary of agriculture.

● Gave the labor secretary authority to allow temporary workers to remain in the country for up to 11 months each year.

● Required applications for temporary foreign workers to be filed 50 days before the anticipated need. (Current law required such applications 80 days before anticipated need.)

● Required an agricultural employer to certify that there were not sufficient able, willing, qualified and available workers at the time and place needed to perform the labor required, and that the employment of foreign workers would not adversely affect wages and working conditions of similarly employed domestic workers.

● Required the employer to provide housing for foreign workers or a housing allowance if housing in the area was available.

● Provided that an employer could be denied certification for up to three years for a substantial violation of a material term or condition of the labor certification.

● Required the attorney general, in consultation with the labor and agriculture secretaries, to establish a three-year transitional program to phase out the use of undocumented workers in the agriculture industry.

● Created a new, foreign guest worker program for the growers of perishable crops, allowing growers to apply for workers 72 hours in advance of need.

● Gave the attorney general authority to set the numerical limit for such workers each month and each year.

● Allowed the workers to remain in the country up to 11 months and to go from grower to grower within a specified "agricultural region," which would be defined by the attorney general.

● Required a grower, before seeking foreign workers, to make a "good-faith effort to recruit in the area of intended employment willing and qualified domestic agricultural workers."

● Required growers to provide wages and working conditions that did not adversely affect the wages and working conditions of workers in the United States similarly employed.

● Provided civil fines for growers who violated program regulations.

● Required non-immigrant foreign students entering the United States after the effective date of the bill to leave the country after completing their studies. The bill provided waivers for students with advanced degrees who were offered faculty positions, students with degrees in the natural sciences, mathematics, computer science or engineering who were offered a research or technical position by an employer in the field of their degrees, and students who obtained advanced degrees in business or economics, had exceptional ability and had been offered employment because of such ability. The provision was to expire in 1989.

● Created a pilot program to waive visa requirements for certain non-immigrant visitors from designated "low-risk" countries who entered the United States for a business or pleasure trip of not more than 90 days. Aliens covered by this program had to meet certain specifications set out in the bill.

Legalization

● Authorized the attorney general to grant temporary resident status to any alien who could prove he entered the United States prior to Jan. 1, 1982, and resided here continuously since then in "unlawful" status. The alien had to apply for legalization within one year after enactment of the bill.

● Required applicants for legalization to show that they had not been convicted of a felony or three misdemeanors committed in the United States; had not assisted in the persecution of any person because of race, religion, nationality, membership in a particular social group or political opinion; and had registered for the military draft if eligible.

● Permitted Cubans and Haitian "boat people," who entered the United States during the 1980 Mariel "boatlift," to apply for temporary resident status.

● Provided that 13 months after being granted temporary resident status, an alien could apply for permanent resident status, but such status could not be granted until the alien was a temporary resident for two years.

● Required an alien seeking permanent resident status to establish that he had resided in the United States continuously since receiving temporary resident status; had not been convicted of any felony or of three or more misdemeanors; had "a minimal understanding of ordinary English" and knowledge of U.S. history and government or was "satisfactorily pursuing a course of study" in these subjects; and that any dependent children were enrolled, or the parent was pursuing enrollment, in a school "or other course of instruction" to learn these subjects. The language and related requirements could be waived for aliens age 65 and over.

● Specified that "continuous residence" would not be lost because of brief and casual trips away from the United States under specified circumstances.

● Allowed those granted temporary resident status to work legally in the United States.

● Allowed the attorney general to rescind temporary resident status upon determining that an alien in fact was not eligible for such status, or if the alien committed an act that made him inadmissible, or if after 25 months in the country, the alien failed to seek permanent resident status.

● Provided criminal penalties for aliens who knowingly and willfully made false statements in applying for legal status.

● Barred temporary residents from receiving most forms of federal financial assistance for five years. Exceptions were provided for aid to the blind, aged and disabled, children under 18, specified emergencies, and pregnant women.

● Exempted Cuban and Haitian "entrants" from the

financial aid restrictions.

● Allowed states to bar legalized aliens from most forms of state financial assistance.

● Provided that an alien whose application for permanent resident status was denied could seek a hearing and appellate review by an administrative law judge.

● Barred judicial review except when an order of deportation was being appealed.

● Required the president to send Congress a report on the impact of legalization 18 months after the date of enactment.

● Authorized the attorney general to grant permanent resident status to any Cuban or Haitian who arrived in the United States before Jan. 1, 1982, or received an immigration designation of "Cuban/Haitian entrant" prior to the date of enactment of the bill. Affected aliens had to apply for status adjustment within two years after enactment.

● Gave the attorney general discretion to grant legal status to aliens who could show they had been in the United States prior to Jan. 1, 1973, and had lived in the country continuously since then. Under existing law, the attorney general could grant legal status to those who could show they had been in the country since June 30, 1948. This provision was not in the Senate bill.

Legalization Aid

● Authorized the appropriation of such sums as necessary for fiscal 1984-87 to reimburse states 100 percent for costs associated with legalization.

● Specifically authorized payments to states to assist local agencies in educating newly legalized aliens. The amount of payment was to be based on the number of such aliens enrolled in the elementary and secondary public schools under the jurisdiction of state educational agencies.

Conference/Final.

Political Problems

S 529 remained plagued by political problems even after it squeaked through the House.

During the Democratic National Convention in San Francisco July 16-19, Hispanic delegates and lobbyists mounted a strong campaign against the bill.

While a threatened first-ballot boycott by Hispanic delegates failed to materialize, those delegates did press presidential candidate Walter F. Mondale and his running mate, Rep. Geraldine A. Ferraro, D-N.Y., to renew and intensify their opposition to the immigration measure. Mondale promised to do whatever he could to kill it.

Simpson criticized the "partisan hysteria, hoopla and hype against this legislation that sprang from the Democratic convention," saying it was forcing delays in convening a conference committee.

The Reagan administration created another problem for the bill. On July 25, White House press spokesman Larry Speakes said the House version "was unacceptable," primarily because it would be too costly. The measure authorized 100 percent reimbursement to states for costs associated with the amnesty program. The Senate bill provided a block grant to states for amnesty costs.

Also on July 25, Hance and Schroeder announced formation of a new coalition to block any immigration bill that came back to the House. The coalition included Hispanic and civil liberties groups, plus business groups such as the Chamber of Commerce of the United States and Associated Builders & Contractors.

Conference Commences

Seven Senate conferees were finally appointed Aug. 7, and 29 House conferees were named Sept. 6. The House group was so large because it included members of all four committees that had worked on the bill.

The conference got under way Sept. 13, and members spent most of the first two sessions ironing out differences over the sanctions provisions.

On Sept. 14, conferees settled an important, unrelated issue. They agreed to drop a Senate provision setting a strict yearly cap of 425,000 on legal immigration to the United States. Currently, there was a yearly cap of 270,000, but immediate relatives of U.S. citizens were not counted against the cap, which meant the actual total was flexible — and much higher.

Sanctions, Identity Issue

On Sept. 13, conferees agreed to a Senate provision providing a criminal fine and a prison term of up to six months for each employer violation when a "pattern or practice" of hiring illegal aliens was found.

After extended debate, conferees agreed to drop a Senate requirement for a presidential study of a "secure system" to check employment eligibility. They also accepted House language stating that nothing in the bill "shall be construed to authorize, directly or indirectly, the issuance or use of national identification cards or the establishment or administration of a national identification card."

Although it was not part of the conference agreement or statement of managers, conferees at Simpson's urging agreed that the chairmen of the House and Senate Judiciary committees would set up a special panel to monitor employment verification.

Conferees also agreed to establish a three-year demonstration project to determine whether a telephone verification system, similar to that used for credit cards, could be used in checking the validity of Social Security cards. This was a modification of a House provision, sponsored by Hall, requiring the attorney general, in consultation with other federal officials, to establish a telephone verification system for Social Security cards within two years of enactment of the bill.

Conferees agreed to bar all employers from knowingly hiring illegal aliens. But those employing only three or four workers were exempted from keeping documents attesting that they had checked an employee's eligibility to work. The House bill had exempted small employers from all sanctions coverage.

Legalization

On Sept. 17, conferees reached agreement on the legalization program. The compromise provided that aliens who could prove they entered the United States prior to Jan. 1, 1977, and resided here continuously since then could apply for permanent resident status. After five years, they could seek to become U.S. citizens.

Illegal aliens who could prove they were in the country prior to Jan. 1, 1981, could apply for temporary resident status. Within two years, they could seek to adjust their status to permanent resident. They had to show a "minimal understanding of ordinary English" and knowledge of U.S. history and government, or be "satisfactorily pursuing a course" to gain such knowledge.

The Senate bill, which was passed in May 1983, had the same 1977 eligibility date for permanent residence, but it set the eligibility date for temporary resident status at Jan. 1, 1980. Temporary residents would have had to wait three years before seeking permanent resident status.

The House bill allowed aliens in the country prior to Jan. 1, 1982, to seek temporary resident status, adjusting to permanent resident status after two years.

Conferees also reached a compromise Sept. 17 on the appeals process for an alien denied legal status.

Conferees agreed Sept. 20 that newly legalized permanent residents would be barred from most forms of public assistance for three years. Temporary residents would be barred from such assistance for five years — two years as temporary residents and another three after they achieved permanent resident status. This was basically a modification of the House provision; the Senate bill had been slightly more restrictive.

On Sept. 21, conferees carved out a number of exceptions to the prohibitions against federal aid. Newly legalized aliens were permitted to receive emergency medical aid, assistance for the aged, blind and disabled, and aid for pregnant women, for instance.

Guest Worker Program

On Sept. 21, conferees agreed to scuttle the House provision creating an open-ended program to allow foreign workers in the country for up to 11 months each year to harvest "perishable crops."

Instead, conferees revamped an existing temporary-worker program known as "H-2" to make it easier for growers to get foreign workers on short notice. One important provision allowed a grower to get a review within 72 hours of a Labor Department denial of his request to use foreign workers.

While any foreign worker would be under contract to a particular grower or growers' association, the worker could move from one producer to another within the association.

All efforts by liberal House Democratic conferees to tighten protections for workers were rejected, as they had been on the House floor.

Patrick Quinn, who represented the National Council of Agricultural Employers, said many growers considered the compromise too restrictive. "A significant portion of Western agriculture will oppose this," he said.

Morrison and Panetta claimed the expedited procedures simply put current regulations into the bill. However, representatives of organized labor, the Labor Department, and the House Education and Labor Committee contended the compromise eased current restrictions.

Anti-Bias Provisions

Despite hours of negotiations, conferees had difficulty resolving differences over the House provision barring employment discrimination based on national origin or alienage. Frank, who sponsored the anti-bias section when it was added on the House floor, insisted that except for jobs where the law required employment of a citizen — such as in certain defense contracting — citizenship should not be a factor in hiring.

Although the Frank amendment had been adopted on June 12 by a 404-9 vote, with little debate, House GOP conferees claimed that many members did not fully understand what they were voting on. They and the Senate conferees warned the Frank amendment would lead to lawsuits against employers who hired U.S. citizens over

aliens, and they refused to accept the provision.

Fish said it was "a tragedy that this issue of alienage discrimination has been blown way out of proportion. Alienage is a temporary situation. It is not an immutable one," such as race, he said, and should not receive special treatment in the law without proof that discrimination existed.

Almost no one had expected the Frank amendment to snag the bill, especially after conferees had managed to resolve issues thought to be far more difficult. But House Judiciary Chairman Peter W. Rodino Jr., D-N.J., recessed the conference Sept. 26 and said he would not call another meeting unless there was a new proposal that might break the logjam.

That breakthrough finally came the week of Oct. 1, when Rep. Charles E. Schumer, D-N.Y., put together a compromise on the discrimination issue that was approved Oct. 9 by the conference committee.

The compromise dropped the ban against discrimination based on alienage, but allowed aliens who signed a document affirming their intent to become U.S. citizens to seek administrative remedies for alleged employment discrimination.

Funding Snag

The House bill had authorized 100 percent reimbursement to the states for costs associated with legalization, with funds subject to appropriations by Congress each year. The Senate bill created a block grant program, with money distributed to the states according to a formula based primarily on the number of legalized aliens in a state.

Conferees from border states with large illegal alien populations opposed the Senate approach. They argued that it would fall far short of reimbursing their states for the costs of such things as educational and health services for the newly legalized population.

Rep. Larry Smith, D-Fla., said that despite federal promises, his state still had not been reimbursed by the federal government for costs resulting from the flood of Cubans who came to the country during the Mariel "boatlift" of 1980. "My state has suffered enough," the Florida Democrat said in arguing for a generous reimbursement program.

On Sept. 20, conferees agreed to an informal $1 billion yearly cap over four years for the alien legalization program. The cap was to be part of a statement of managers to accompany the conference report.

Simpson believed that the Sept. 20 action would satisfy administration concerns about the costs of legalization, but he subsequently discovered that Reagan would not accept the informal cap.

Rescue Efforts Fail

During the week of Oct. 1, Schumer tried to put together a compromise on the funding issue as well as the anti-discrimination provision. Part of his proposal involved making the $1 billion cap a formal part of the legislation, as the administration had wanted.

When conferees convened Oct. 9, the anti-bias provision was accepted. But House conferees voted 13-15 to reject the $1 billion yearly cap as part of the bill. Seven members who had voted for the cap in the statement of managers switched their votes and voted against the cap as part of the bill.

Conferees from states with large illegal alien populations contended that the $1 billion would be insufficient to cover the anticipated costs of legalization, leaving the states with a heavy financial burden.

Schumer started a new round of negotiations with Smith and Panetta, who had voted against the cap. By the evening of Oct. 10, Schumer had worked out a new compromise with Simpson that drew Panetta's support. But Schumer was unable to convince any other House conferee to switch, and time ran out on the 98th Congress.

"We exhausted our potential for compromise," Mazzoli said Oct. 11. "Pretty soon you don't have any tools to split hairs any finer." ∎

Refugee Entries Up in 1984

After a two-year decline, the number of refugees admitted into the United States rose in fiscal 1984, according to the State Department. But admissions were still less than half the total when President Reagan took office.

Under the law, refugees are defined as people fleeing persecution in their own countries. In fiscal 1984, 71,113 refugees were admitted, up 9,432 from the previous year's 61,681 total. In fiscal 1981, the total number of refugees admitted to the United States was 159,252. *(Chart, below; background, 1983 Almanac p. 305)*

The 1984 increase over the fiscal 1983 level was attributable largely to refugees coming from East Asia, especially Vietnam. In fiscal 1983, 39,408 such refugees were admitted, down from 73,522 the year before. In fiscal 1984, the number jumped to 51,960.

The big 1983 drop resulted from two factors, according to immigration specialists. First, a refugee-processing center began operations at Bataan in the Philippines, delaying the arrival in the United States of several thousand refugees. They were getting cultural and language training at the center, and while they had been approved for admission to the United States in fiscal 1983, they did not arrive until after the end of the fiscal year.

The other factor was a temporary dispute between the Immigration and Naturalization Service and the State Department over whether certain people fleeing Cambodia qualified as refugees. That dispute was subsequently resolved.

Fiscal 1985 Levels Set

For fiscal 1985, the Reagan administration authorized a total of 70,000 refugee admissions, 50,000 of them from East Asia.

In testimony before the House and Senate Judiciary committees Sept. 11, Secretary of State George P. Shultz for the first time proposed earmarking slots in the quota for East Asia for political prisoners in Vietnam and "Amerasian" children, who were Asian children fathered by U.S. servicemen. The secretary proposed that 10,000 of the 50,000 slots for East Asia be reserved for these two groups.

Although a 1982 law (PL 97-359) allowed Amerasian children to come to the United States as immigrants, key provisions had proved unworkable for those in Vietnam. The law had principally aided the entry of Korean children. *(1982 Almanac p. 410)*

Shultz said that "current and former political prisoners are of particular humanitarian concern to the United States." He added that although spokesmen for the communist regime in Vietnam had claimed they would be willing to release political prisoners for resettlement, only a handful had been set free over the previous two years.

The committees concurred in the Shultz earmarking proposal. One congressional staffer said that it was "now up to the Vietnamese" to release the people the United States said it would take.

Shultz' remarks came during annual consultations with Congress, which have been a regular feature of refugee policy since enactment of a 1980 law (PL 96-212) revising the refugee admissions process. *(1980 Almanac p. 378)* ∎

Refugee Resettlement Funds

Although the House passed a bill in 1983 reauthorizing refugee resettlement programs for three years, the measure (HR 3729) failed to pass the Senate. The legislation became snarled in a dispute over proposals to reduce the number of refugees on welfare. States with large refugee populations, such as California and Florida, were concerned about the cost of supporting jobless refugees.

Money for resettlement programs ultimately was included in the fiscal 1985 continuing appropriations resolution (H J Res 648 — PL 98-473). The amount available for fiscal 1985 was between $410 million and $460 million, with the bulk of that amount — perhaps $270 million — used for cash and medical assistance for refugees. *(Continuing resolution, p. 444)*

U.S. Refugee Admissions, Fiscal 1981-85

	Actual Admissions Fiscal 1981	Actual Admissions Fiscal 1982	Actual Admissions Fiscal 1983	Actual Admissions Fiscal 1984	Authorized Admissions Fiscal 1985
Asia	131,139	73,522	39,408	51,960	50,000
Soviet Union/ Eastern Europe	20,148	13,536	13,492	11,000	9,000
Near East	3,829	6,304	5,465	5,246	5,000
Africa	2,119	3,356	2,648	2,747	3,000
Latin America/ Caribbean	2,017	579	668	160	3,000
TOTAL	**159,252**	**97,297**	**61,681**	**71,113**	**70,000**

SOURCE: State Department

HR 3729 (H Rept 98-404), as passed by the House Nov. 14, 1983, reauthorized resettlement and assistance programs established under a 1980 law (PL 96-212) overhauling the process for admitting refugees into the United States. *(1983 Almanac p. 304; 1980 Almanac p. 378)*

Senate Committee Action

The Senate Judiciary Committee approved the House-passed bill by voice vote June 14, 1984, and formally reported it (S Rept 98-564) on July 24.

The committee acted after deleting from the bill a number of program changes endorsed by the House. The House passed its version of the measure in 1983. *(1983 Almanac p. 304)*

Neither version of the bill set overall funding limits for refugee programs. The House bill, however, earmarked $100 million annually for social services for refugees, plus $14 million to screen refugees for health problems and $50 million for "targeted assistance" to areas with heavy refugee populations.

The Senate committee deleted the $50 million for targeted assistance. Staffers on the Immigration and Refugee Policy Subcommittee said that the Office of Refugee Resettlement — part of the Department of Health and Human Services — already had authority to target assistance.

The House bill included a provision making all refugees presumptively eligible for Medicaid, the federal-state medical program for the poor, for the first year they were in the country. This was intended to encourage refugees to take jobs, even ones that did not provide health benefits, instead of trying to qualify for welfare programs that entitled them to Medicaid.

The Reagan administration strongly opposed this language, contending that medical assistance should not be provided without regard to need. The Senate committee rejected the House provision. Subcommittee staffers said the House proposal was an "unproven and inequitable" solution to refugee unemployment.

The House bill moved the Office of Refugee Resettlement from the Social Security Administration to the Office of the Secretary of Health and Human Services. The Senate bill deleted this language.

The Senate committee also amended a House provision requiring voluntary agencies that helped resettle refugees to be "legally and financially responsible" for the basic needs of refugees during their first 90 days in the United States. The committee softened that language, requiring that agencies "develop and submit a resettlement plan for the early employment of each refugee" and monitor implementation for up to one year after the refugee's arrival. ■

'Grove City' Rights Bill Shelved by Senate

The major civil rights bill of the year died Oct. 2 when the Senate shelved the proposal after last-minute negotiations failed to produce a compromise acceptable to all parties.

By 53-45, senators voted to table the measure. *(Vote 245, p. 44-S)*

The House had passed the bill (HR 5490) on June 26, but a Senate version (S 2568) remained bottled up in the Labor and Human Resources Committee. Its supporters in late September offered the bill as an amendment to the continuing appropriations resolution (H J Res 648) required to keep many government agencies running in fiscal 1985, and it was this amendment that was tabled Oct. 2. *(Funding bill, p. 444)*

The demise of the legislation was a blow to civil rights groups and their Capitol Hill supporters, who had prevailed in every other civil rights battle in Congress since 1981. Civil rights activists vowed that they would be back in the 99th Congress with a similar bill.

The legislation was designed to overturn the Supreme Court's Feb. 28 ruling in *Grove City College v. Bell*, which narrowed the reach of one major anti-discrimination law and was expected to affect three others as well. *(Court ruling, p. 9-A)*

The death of the bill was a victory for the Reagan administration and for Sen. Orrin G. Hatch, R-Utah, who had opposed the measure with unusual vigor. They claimed it would have gone beyond a simple reversal of the court decision to expand significantly federal authority to enforce anti-discrimination laws.

Sen. Edward M. Kennedy, D-Mass., a key sponsor of the measure, chastised the Senate for its action.

"Shame on this body," he said. "Shame on this body.... If we table this civil rights amendment, we are saying we will tuck discrimination under the mattress until next year."

The Court Decision

In deciding the *Grove City* case, the Supreme Court sharply curtailed the sweep of a ban on sex discrimination by federally aided schools and colleges. The court ruled 6-3 that Title IX of the 1972 Education Amendments did not apply to all programs at a recipient institution, but only to the particular program receiving aid. *(Title IX, 1972 Almanac p. 385)*

With its decision, the court placed its stamp of approval on the Reagan administration's reversal of earlier federal policy. Until 1983, the executive branch had consistently interpreted the law as covering an entire affected institution, not just particular programs at each school or college. But the Reagan administration opted for the more narrow reading.

Civil rights lawyers warned that the court's narrow interpretation of Title IX could lead to rulings that would similarly limit the scope of federal laws prohibiting discrimination based on race, age or handicap.

Broad Reach, Narrow Coverage

The court ruled on two major questions about Title IX. The *Grove City* decision expanded the reach of the law to virtually every school and college in the country, while limiting its effect within each institution.

The court rejected the argument of the Pennsylvania college that it was not subject to Title IX because it received no federal aid directly. Federal dollars did find their way onto the campus as individual students received federal basic educational opportunity grants, also known as Pell grants. The justices ruled unanimously that such indirect aid was sufficient to bring Grove City College within the reach of Title IX. The administration had urged such a ruling on this point.

The effect was to make every college and university in

the country subject to Title IX; few, if any, had remained as independent of federal aid as Grove City College.

However, the court's ruling on the second point — applying Title IX only to particular programs receiving federal aid — sharply limited the law's effectiveness. On this issue, the college and the administration successfully joined forces to urge the justices to reverse the 3rd U.S. Circuit Court of Appeals — and a decade of administrative interpretation of the law.

The majority read the language of Title IX as confining its scope to particular programs. The critical provision prohibited sex discrimination in "any education program or activity receiving federal financial assistance."

Only by ignoring that language could the justices conclude that federal student aid funds paid to the college as tuition represented federal aid to the entire institution, wrote Justice Byron R. White. "The fact that federal funds eventually reach the college's general operating budget cannot subject Grove City to institution-wide coverage," he said.

Under the broad view taken by the appeals court in this case, an entire school would become subject to Title IX if only one of its students received federal aid. "This result cannot be squared with Congress' intent," White declared.

In Grove City's case, the grants to students represented aid to the college's financial aid program, and only that program was subject to Title IX, the court held.

Although they concurred in the outcome, Justice Lewis F. Powell Jr., Chief Justice Warren E. Burger and Justice Sandra Day O'Connor described this case as "an unedifying example of overzealousness on the part of the federal government." Pointing out that Grove City had never been charged with sex discrimination but simply with refusing to sign forms certifying its compliance with Title IX, the three justices criticized the government for choosing to litigate this case at all.

Justice John Paul Stevens criticized the majority for issuing an unnecessary advisory opinion on the breadth of Title IX coverage within an institution. All the court was required to decide in this case was whether Grove City was a recipient of federal aid subject to Title IX, he contended.

Justices William J. Brennan Jr. and Thurgood Marshall dissented from the majority's narrow view of Title IX's reach within a school or college. The majority "ignores the primary purposes for which Congress enacted Title IX," wrote Brennan.

"The absurdity of the court's decision" is clear when one examines its practical effect, Brennan continued. Grove City College's financial aid program cannot discriminate on the basis of sex due to Title IX, but the admissions, athletic or academic departments were under no such restriction, he noted.

Protests in Congress

The decision generated immediate protest on Capitol Hill. In November 1983 the House had voted 414-8 to oppose a narrow interpretation of Title IX. Fifty members of the 98th Congress reiterated that view in a friend-of-the-court brief filed in the *Grove City* case.

Rep. Patricia Schroeder, D-Colo., said that House vote had sent a clear message that Congress intended Title IX to be construed broadly, "but the Supreme Court must have had their earmuffs on."

Sen. Bob Packwood, R-Ore., said, "It is . . . of little use to bar discrimination in any specific program in the institution if a woman cannot gain admittance to or participate in

the institution because of its discriminatory policies."

Legislation Introduced

Bills (HR 5490, S 2568) to overturn the *Grove City* decision were introduced in both chambers April 12. The legislation made clear that any "recipient" of federal aid — rather than any "program or activity" receiving aid — would be required to conform to non-discrimination laws. The word "recipient" was defined to cover an entire institution.

In addition to Title IX, the other major civil rights laws amended by the legislation included:

● Title VI of the Civil Rights Act of 1964, which prohibited discrimination based on race, color or national origin in all federally assisted programs or activities.

● Section 504 of the Rehabilitation Act of 1973, which barred discrimination against the handicapped in programs or activities receiving federal assistance.

● Age Discrimination Act of 1975, which prohibited discrimination based on age in programs or activities receiving federal aid.

House Committee Action

Moving with unusual dispatch, two House committees — Judiciary and Education and Labor — approved HR 5490 (H Rept 98-829, Parts I and II) by voice vote May 23. The action followed six days of joint hearings on the measure.

William Bradford Reynolds, head of the Justice Department's civil rights division, testified May 22 that the department opposed the legislation. He said it was drafted in such a vague manner that it would substantially broaden the federal government's power to penalize institutions and state and local governments for discriminating on the basis of race, sex, age or handicap.

At a news conference May 22, President Reagan was asked about the legislation and indicated he might veto it because it was too broad.

However, at a briefing May 23, Education Secretary T. H. Bell said he could support, with modification, the basic House bill.

Education Markup

During the Education Committee markup, Howard C. Nielson, R-Utah, offered an amendment that would have reversed the part of the *Grove City* decision holding that federal grants and loans to students constituted federal aid for purposes of Title IX coverage. However, his amendment was rejected 4-27.

The committee also rejected an amendment by Steve Bartlett, R-Texas, that would have brought members of Congress within the scope of the anti-bias laws that applied to federal aid recipients.

The Bartlett amendment was rejected 14-19 after Paul Simon, D-Ill., chief sponsor of HR 5490 and chairman of the Postsecondary Education Subcommittee, argued that the issue should not be addressed as part of the bill.

House Floor Action

The House June 26 approved HR 5490 by 375-32. (*Vote 243, p. 76-H*)

Advocates of the bill contended the court ruling changed what had been the standard interpretation of existing law and that HR 5490 simply restored the law to its pre-*Grove City* status.

Hamilton Fish Jr., N.Y., a Republican floor manager of the bill, asserted during debate June 25 that "this legislation does not make any substantive changes in the law. It would not result in any changes in the status quo as to the type or number of recipients [of federal aid]."

Sponsors of HR 5490 wanted to keep the bill from being amended and they nearly succeeded. Seven amendments were rejected or derailed on procedural points.

Amendment on Congress Adopted

Adopted was one amendment by Bartlett, stating that Congress and the federal judiciary could be considered "recipients" under the bill to the extent that other federal "entities" were covered by anti-bias laws. The amendment was adopted by a 133-54 standing vote.

After the vote, members and lobbyists said they were unclear about the meaning or effect of the amendment because virtually no federal entities were covered by the statutes referred to in the bill.

Fish and Democratic floor managers Simon and Don Edwards, Calif., said they supported Bartlett's position that Congress should be covered, but added that they did not want to expand the coverage of existing law in this legislation.

Another Bartlett amendment on the same subject was rejected earlier when it was ruled out of order for going beyond the scope of the legislation. That amendment mandated that members of Congress be deemed recipients of federal financial assistance in order to extend coverage of civil rights laws referred to in the bill. A point of order against the amendment was sustained 277-125. *(Vote 241, p. 76-H)*

Another amendment was adopted to make clear that the bill would not change the status of black colleges or universities in the country.

Amendments Rejected

The following amendments were rejected:

● By Bartlett, requiring a finding of discrimination before federal assistance could be terminated, by voice vote.

● By Nielson, to exempt from coverage higher education institutions whose only federal aid was loans or grants to students, by voice vote.

● By Mark D. Siljander, R-Mich., to define the term "person" under the bill to include unborn children from the moment of conception, by 186-219. *(Vote 242, p. 76-H)*

● By Siljander, to make provisions of the Age Discrimination Act of 1975 applicable to unborn children from the moment of conception, ruled out of order.

Senate Committee Action

No Markups

S 2568, companion bill to HR 5490, stayed bottled up in the Senate Labor and Human Resources Committee.

Backers of the bill accused its Republican opponents of using delaying tactics to block it. Hatch, the committee chairman, denied charges of obstructionism, but said he would oppose the bill "with every ounce of my capacity" if its scope was not narrowed.

On Aug. 7, Hatch introduced a competing proposal (S 2910), which was not as broad as S 2568. It would have covered only Title IX and would have barred discrimination by any "institution" receiving federal funds, not just any "program or activity."

Civil rights lawyers asserted that this legislation was inadequate. They maintained that all forms of discrimination that could be affected by the Supreme Court decision had to be barred, not just sex bias at schools.

Senate Action

Baker Role

Backers of the civil rights bill had foreseen the likelihood that Hatch's committee would be a stumbling block, and they succeeded in getting the House-passed HR 5490 put directly on the Senate calendar.

This meant that Senate Majority Leader Howard H. Baker Jr., R-Tenn., could have called up the measure for debate at any time. Baker and Majority Whip Ted Stevens, R-Alaska, were among the bill's 63 Senate cosponsors.

Sponsors said they had a promise from Baker that he would bring up the civil rights legislation for debate. On Sept. 5, Baker publicly said the legislation "will be considered on the floor," but he did not say in what context.

As the month wore on, however, Baker shifted his position. He told the bill's advocates he would not call it up unless they were able to reach a compromise with the Reagan administration over the scope of the measure.

The opposing parties had negotiated all summer, with most of the debate centering on the definition of "recipient." Hatch and Reynolds argued that it had to be narrowed or current law would be vastly expanded. For instance, they said, small grocery stores could be considered "recipients" of U.S. aid if the stores had customers who received food stamps.

Advocates of the bill contended that Reynolds and Hatch were simply conjuring up a parade of horribles. But they worked out a package of amendments they said clarified the scope of "recipient."

Despite intense negotiations in September — including one all-night session — no agreement was reached.

At a Sept. 20 news conference, Sens. Kennedy and Packwood said compromise talks had broken down. They said that unless Baker relented and called up HR 5490, they would force a floor vote on the *Grove City* bill by offering it as an amendment to other legislation.

The Continuing Resolution

As it happened, Senate Minority Leader Robert C. Byrd, D-W.Va., took the lead in forcing a showdown on the civil rights issue.

On Sept. 27, Byrd offered the text of the civil rights bill as an amendment to the fiscal 1985 continuing appropriations resolution (H J Res 648).

GOP leaders immediately challenged the amendment on grounds that it was non-germane to the appropriations bill, a point sustained by the presiding officer. But the Senate brushed aside such objections, voting 51-48 to allow the amendment. Thirty-nine Democrats and 12 Republicans voted in favor of debating the issue on the continuing resolution. *(Vote 236, p. 42-S)*

Baker, acting for Hatch, promptly put forward controversial proposals on school busing, gun control and tuition tax credits as additional amendments to the stopgap appropriations measure. A four-day parliamentary snarl ensued that continued through a rare Saturday session. *(Story, p. 242)*

On Sept. 29, civil rights advocates won another test vote as the Senate voted 92-4 to invoke cloture, thus limiting debate, on their amendment. *(Vote 238, p. 43-S)*

Senate Rules Barely Survive Rights Fight

Efforts to attach a major civil rights bill to the fiscal 1985 continuing appropriations resolution (H J Res 648) touched off a parliamentary war that threatened to turn Senate rules and traditions into battlefield casualties.

The Senate eventually fought its way clear, but only after Sen. Bob Packwood, R-Ore., a leading advocate of the rights legislation, effectively surrendered Oct. 2 in order to stop the Senate from "horribly disregarding our procedures."

The civil rights bill sought to overturn a Feb. 28 Supreme Court decision in *Grove City College v. Bell* that narrowed the reach of an anti-discrimination law.

Because Majority Leader Howard H. Baker Jr., R-Tenn., refused to allow the House-passed bill (HR 5490) to be debated on its own, backers sought to attach it to other legislation. The vehicle they chose was the stopgap funding bill, whose passage was required to keep the government running. (*H J Res 648, p. 444*)

Each side had its procedural wizard. For the civil rights advocates, it was Minority Leader Robert C. Byrd, D-W.Va., a widely acknowledged parliamentary master. For the opposition, it was Labor and Human Resources Chairman Orrin G. Hatch, R-Utah, helped by aide Steven J. Markman.

In the middle was Baker, relying on advice from Senate Parliamentarian Robert B. Dove.

It all started Sept. 27 when Byrd, acting for Edward M. Kennedy, D-Mass., offered the text of the civil rights bill as a substitute for language the Appropriations Committee proposed to delete from the funding bill.

Byrd then offered a second amendment, substituting new language for his first amendment. The second amendment, although basically the text of the civil rights bill, was just different enough from the first amendment to qualify as a substitute.

The effect of Byrd's moves was to guarantee that there could be a vote on the civil rights language as he proposed it. Bills could be amended only twice, or "in the second degree," which Byrd proposed.

All opponents could do was offer "perfecting" amendments to the original Byrd substitute and to the language the Appropriations panel proposed to strike. A perfecting amendment was one that altered a portion of the language of a bill or amendment. It had to be voted on before a substitute amendment.

Baker, acting for Hatch, offered a perfecting amendment on tuition tax credits to Byrd's first amendment on civil rights. Even if adopted, this would have fallen if the second Byrd amendment had been adopted, because the second Byrd amendment was a substitute for the entire first proposal.

Baker, acting for Hatch, also offered perfecting amendments to the language proposed to be stricken by the Appropriations Committee. One of these amendments would have eased current gun control regulations. Because it was an amendment "in the first degree," Hatch could offer a second one. Baker, again acting for his Utah colleague, then offered a "second-degree amendment" to restrict federal judges' authority to order school busing.

At that point, no other amendments could be added by either side. Amendments in the second degree had been offered to both the Byrd civil rights substitute and the original Appropriations Committee proposal.

The first step toward disposing of all these amendments came Sept. 27, when Byrd asked the Senate to decide whether his civil rights amendment, a legislative proposal, was germane to a funding bill. By a 51-48 vote, the Senate judged the amendment germane. (*Vote 236, 42-S*)

Backers of Byrd's amendment then filed a motion to invoke cloture, or limit debate. If three-fifths of the Senate, 60 members, voted to invoke cloture, debate was limited to one hour per senator and the measure under consideration had to come to a vote within 100 hours.

On Sept. 29, the Senate voted 92-4 to cut off debate on the first Byrd amendment. (*Vote 238, p. 43-S*)

Once cloture was invoked, all amendments had to pertain to the subject matter on which cloture had been invoked. Under cloture, germaneness rulings were made by the chair. But a ruling could be appealed and overturned by a majority vote of the Senate — a step that was rarely taken.

On Sept. 29, Hatch appealed the ruling of the chair that his busing amendment was non-germane. Baker moved to table, or kill, Hatch's appeal, and his motion was agreed to, 55-39. (*Vote 239, p. 43-S*)

James A. McClure, R-Idaho, then appealed a ruling that the gun provisions were non-germane. Baker moved to table that appeal. But his motion was rejected, 31-63. (*Vote 240, p. 43-S*)

That vote meant the Senate was primed to overturn its own rules restricting debate after cloture was invoked. Baker and Byrd warned that senators were heading down a dangerous path that could cause legislative chaos.

For two days, Baker's pleas fell on deaf ears. In fact, several senators expressed concern about the political impact of their vote supporting Baker's motion to kill the busing amendment. They worried that constituents would see the tabling vote as an endorsement of court-ordered busing.

Baker heeded their concerns. On Oct. 1, he gave senators another chance to vote on the busing measure. He offered a motion to reconsider his own tabling vote of Sept. 29. The reconsideration motion was agreed to, 60-37, and when the Senate voted the second time on a motion to table Hatch's appeal, the motion was rejected 41-56. (*Votes 241, 242, p. 43-S*)

A subsequent motion to reconsider the Baker tabling motion on the gun provisions also was rejected, 20-77. (*Vote 243, p. 43-S*)

At this point, the Senate was in a position to overturn the chair's ruling on the germaneness of the busing and gun amendments.

Those tallies, however, never took place. Instead, the Senate voted to table the initial Byrd civil rights amendment. The tuition tax credit proposal fell with it. The gun amendment then was tabled by voice vote, taking the busing proposal with it.

But on Oct. 2, in an effort to extricate the Senate from its procedural tangle and smooth the way for adjournment, Packwood finally moved to table, and thus kill, the *Grove City* amendment. Hatch's three amendments were dropped moments later.

Packwood's Switch

Packwood's move was unusual and surprising; he and Kennedy were the chief sponsors of the bill and had pressed Baker for three months to put the measure before the Senate.

During the session Sept. 29, Packwood heatedly defended his efforts to get the bill to the floor. "When you cannot get a bill up — a bill that is the most important bill for the civil rights of millions of Americans in this country — in any other way than attaching it to another measure," Packwood said, "we will do it and we need to bear no shame."

By Oct. 2, Packwood had changed his tune. The Senate was still immersed in procedural quicksand, and Packwood said he feared the chamber was about to do violence to its rules because of the parliamentary maneuvering unless somebody yielded.

The senator said he was willing to kill the civil rights bill for the year "so that we might get on with the public's business, but also so that we can get on with the procedures by which we govern ourselves."

Civil rights lobbyists were dismayed and stunned. William L. Taylor, a leading negotiator on the bill for the civil rights groups, called Packwood's move "absolutely stupefying." In fact, rights lobbyists had asked Packwood not to offer the motion. They said that if the bill was going to die,

it should be Hatch or Baker who delivered the final blow.

"We had the votes until one of our sponsors gave away the ball game," said Althea T. L. Simmons, head of the NAACP's Washington office.

Temporary Reprieve

Packwood made his tabling motion at about 4 p.m. Oct. 2. Just before the vote was to occur, Robert Dole, R-Kan., waving a piece of paper, stood up and said he had a compromise proposal that might resolve matters.

After a brief consultation, Baker agreed to postpone the tabling vote to allow the parties to talk yet another time. For nearly five hours, shuttle diplomacy ensued, as key senators and staff carried proposals between Baker's office, where administration officials and Hatch were huddled, and a room off the Senate chamber, where the civil rights groups had gathered.

Dole's proposed compromise would have covered all four statutes, but would have applied only to money going to educational institutions. A second section of his proposal stated that federal courts should ignore the Supreme Court's *Grove City* interpretation of "program or activity" if challenges arose over discrimination in other entities, such as hospitals.

While the administration and the civil rights groups were willing to accept this, Hatch would not, according to negotiators from both sides. He offered a subsequent proposal that was considerably narrower and unacceptable to the civil rights groups.

When the negotiations failed to produce a solution, the Senate went forward with the tabling vote. ∎

Reagan Gaining Control of Federal Judiciary

Through his appointments to the federal district and appeals courts, President Reagan in his first term began an ideological transformation of the federal judiciary.

In filling vacancies and newly created judgeships, the president by late 1987 was expected to have appointed a majority of the lower federal court judges, completing a shift from a predominantly Democratic to a conservative Republican bench.

Although less publicized than Supreme Court appointments, the president's selections to the lower federal courts had their own significance. The 571 authorized district court judges handled civil and criminal cases every day, affecting the lives of citizens far more directly than the nine justices. The 156 authorized appellate judges had an opportunity to review these cases, and the majority of their decisions were final. Only a fraction of all appeals court rulings ever were considered by the high court and eventually decided by the justices.

Reagan's Appointments

In his first term, President Reagan appointed 167 judges, including Sandra Day O'Connor, his historic selection as the first woman on the Supreme Court. *(1981 Almanac p. 409)*

The president appointed 130 district court judges (26 percent of the 506 sitting judges) and 31 judges to the 12 regional appeals courts (23 percent of the 133 sitting judges). In addition he made two appointments to the U.S. Court of Appeals for the Federal Circuit, which primarily

handled trademark and patent cases, and three appointments to the U.S. Court of International Trade. These were lifetime appointments with a salary equal to that of a district court judge.

In 1985 alone, the president could fill at least another 100 lifetime judicial appointments — most as a result of a 1984 bankruptcy reform law (HR 5174 — PL 98-353), which included provisions adding 61 judgeships to the district courts and 24 to the appeals courts. Only 10 of those positions had been filled by the end of 1984. *(Bankruptcy law, p. 263)*

Reagan was likely to gain considerably more appointments through resignations or deaths of sitting judges. He also could get more appointments if some older judges decided to take "senior status," a form of semi-retirement that created an official vacancy even though the judge continued to handle cases. The only distinction between senior status and active status was that a senior judge had a right to decline to hear cases, although relative few did so each year. Any judge age 65 or older was eligible for senior status after 15 years on the bench.

A Justice Department official said that based on historical trends, it was "a definite possibility" enough vacancies of one type or another would occur to make Reagan's appointees a majority of all federal judges.

Although Reagan put a sizable number of judges on the bench in his first term, he fell short of his predecessor, Jimmy Carter. Aided by the 1978 Omnibus Judgeship Act (PL 95-486), which created 152 new federal judgeships,

Judicial Appointments

U.S. Court of Appeals

	Women	Blacks	Hispanics
Johnson	2.5%	5.0%	Not available
Nixon	0	0	Not available
Ford	0	0	Not available
Carter	19.6	16.1	3.6
Reagan	9.1	3.0	3.0

U.S. District Court

	Women	Blacks	Hispanics
Johnson	1.6%	3.3%	2.5%
Nixon	0.6	2.8	1.1
Ford	1.9	5.8	1.9
Carter	14.1	14.1	6.8
Reagan	9.2	.8	5.4

SOURCES: The Johnson, Nixon and Ford statistics are from a study by Sheldon Goldman of the University of Massachusetts at Amherst. The Carter and Reagan statistics were compiled by Congressional Quarterly based on figures from the Justice Department.

Carter ended his presidency having appointed 262 federal judges. *(1978 Almanac p. 173)*

He did not name anyone to the Supreme Court, however, because no vacancies occurred during his term.

Few Women, Minorities

Carter was publicly committed to increasing the number of blacks, women and Hispanics on the federal bench. And when he left office in 1980, he had appointed 40 women, 38 blacks and 16 Hispanics to the lower courts — more than any other president.

Groups representing minorities and women were buoyed by their gains under Carter, but their progress showed considerably under Reagan. *(Chart, above)*

At the end of his first term, Reagan — who made no similar commitment to affirmative action — had appointed 17 women to the federal bench, including O'Connor.

Most of the women, 12, were put on the district courts; one was given a seat on the 9th U.S. Circuit Court of Appeals, another was put on the trade court, and the remaining two were given positions on the Court of Appeals for the Federal Circuit.

Reagan appointed one black to a district court seat and elevated a black district court judge to a seat on the 2nd U.S. Circuit Court of Appeals. Eight Hispanics were appointed, one to the 1st U.S. Circuit Court of Appeals and the remaining seven to district court positions. Three of those appointments were to the traditionally Hispanic district court in Puerto Rico.

Next to Carter, Reagan put more women and Hispanics on the bench than any other president. But his record of black judicial appointments "is the worst record since [President] Eisenhower," according to political scientist Sheldon Goldman, of the University of Massachusetts.

Goldman noted that the number of women appointed to judgeships increased when politicians and pollsters started to talk about the "gender gap" — polling informa-

tion showing that women were less likely to vote for Reagan than men. Nine of the 17 women judges were appointed in the last 18 months of Reagan's first term, he pointed out.

On the other hand, he said, the administration had "no political commitment to blacks. They feel they owe nothing to blacks."

Jane Wilcox, the Justice Department's special counsel for judicial selection, had no apologies for the Reagan appointments. "We're pretty proud of our record, really," she said. "I think in the last four years we were very successful as far as putting on the bench judges we believe were qualified, as well as being believers in judicial restraint." (In this usage, "judicial restraint" means narrow reading of the law to avoid intrusion into the legislative and executive functions.)

Acknowledging that there were few black appointees, Wilcox said part of the problem was senators' failure to bring names forward. While the president had virtually a free hand in selecting appeals court judges, senators traditionally had significant influence over nominations for district court positions.

"We have sent the message to senators that we would like to see the names of qualified minorities," Wilcox said, adding that there were "just not that many" black Republicans who were "excited about the president's emphasis on judicial restraint."

Wilcox said that the administration was "committed to a position of no preference given to anybody on the basis of race or gender."

Efforts had been made to find qualified women and minorities, she said, but "we would find it repugnant to the Constitution to put anybody ahead of or behind anyone else based on their race or gender."

Although women did better than blacks and Hispanics in winning federal court appointments under Reagan, representatives of some women's groups were still dissatisfied. They said there were more qualified women available for the federal bench than had been appointed.

To Althea T. L. Simmons, head of the NAACP's Washington office, Reagan's record of black judicial appointments "says blacks are not being considered an integral part of society."

"The administration is not listening to people who disagree with them," said Arnold Torres, executive director of the League of United Latin American Citizens.

A positive assessment of the Reagan record came from Daniel J. Popeo, founder and general counsel of the Washington Legal Foundation, a business-oriented law and research organization. He called Reagan's selections "the most qualified judicial candidates going on the bench in history ... who will shy away from judicial activism."

ABA Ratings, Wilkinson Nomination

Assessments of a judicial nominee's abilities were difficult, with the only constant provided by the ratings of the American Bar Association (ABA), which had reviewed the qualifications of nominees for 36 years.

However, with changes in personnel and philosophy over time, even the ABA's ratings were subject to debate. Indeed, in 1984, ABA officials were called before the Senate Judiciary Committee to defend their process during the controversial nomination of J. Harvie Wilkinson III, a University of Virginia law professor, to be a federal appeals court judge.

Wilkinson, 39, received a "qualified" rating from the bar group, although opponents contended that he was not qualified for the appeals position and did not meet the ABA's own requirements. Wilkinson was a law clerk for Supreme Court Justice Lewis F. Powell Jr. in 1972-73, taught at the university from 1973-78, was editorial page editor at the *Virginian-Pilot* in Norfolk from 1978-81, worked at the Justice Department from 1982-83 and then returned to the university.

Critics also contended that Wilkinson improperly lobbied the ABA to secure the rating, a charge that Wilkinson denied.

After months of controversy, Wilkinson was confirmed by the Senate Aug. 9 by a vote of 58-39. *(Vote 209, p. 37-S)*

That vote came minutes after the Senate voted 65-32 to invoke cloture and cut off a filibuster against the nomi-

nation led by Sens. Edward M. Kennedy, D-Mass., and Howard M. Metzenbaum, D-Ohio. *(Vote 208, p. 37-S)*

Of all Reagan's appointees, 9.6 percent were given the highest ABA rating, "exceptionally well qualified."

The rating of "well qualified" was given to 40.7 percent of the nominees, and 49.7 percent of the nominees were rated "qualified."

Of all Carter's appointees, 6.1 percent were rated "exceptionally well qualified," 49.6 percent were rated "well qualified" and 43.1 percent were rated "qualified."

An "unqualified" rating was given to 1.1 percent of Carter's appointees but to none of Reagan's confirmed selections. (The numbers do not equal 100 percent because of rounding.) ∎

School Prayer Issue Flares in Many Guises

Congress in 1984 rebuffed efforts to permit organized, recited prayers in the public schools, but members agreed to a more limited measure aimed at relaxing current strictures on any type of religious activity in the schools.

The Senate March 20 dealt a sharp blow to President Reagan and his conservative religious supporters by rejecting a proposed constitutional amendment to permit organized, recited prayers in public schools. The 56-44 vote was 11 votes short of the two-thirds majority needed to pass the prayer measure, S J Res 73. *(Vote 34, p. 9-S)*

But four months later, on July 25, Congress cleared for the president a bill (HR 1310 — PL 98-377) allowing student religious groups to meet in public high schools before or after school on the same terms as other student groups. *(Story, p. 488)*

And a day after that, on July 26, the House passed an omnibus education bill (HR 11) that included a provision requiring schools receiving federal aid to permit students to participate in "moments of silent prayer." The prayer provision was added on the House floor by votes of 378-29 and 356-50. *(Votes 288, 289, p. 88-H)*

Before agreeing to the silent prayer proposal, members had rejected by 194-215 a stronger amendment that would have cut off federal funds to schools that prohibited either silent or spoken prayer. *(Vote 287, p. 88-H)*

Although other elements of HR 11 were eventually enacted (S 2496 — PL 98-511), the silent prayer amendment was scrubbed in conference with the Senate. *(Education bill, p. 493)*

At year's end, the silent prayer issue was pending before the Supreme Court, which was expected to decide in 1985 on the constitutionality of an Alabama law authorizing public schools to begin each day with a moment of silent prayer or meditation.

Background

Religious freedom in the United States is protected under the First Amendment to the Constitution, which states: "Congress shall make no law respecting an establishment of religion, or prohibiting the free exercise thereof. . . ."

Supreme Court Rulings, 1962-63

In 1962, the Supreme Court ruled in the New York case of *Engel v. Vitale* that state officials could not require public school students to recite a particular prayer each

day. To do so, the justices said, violated the "establishment" clause of the First Amendment.

The next year, in a Pennsylvania case, *School District of Abington Township v. Schempp,* the court declared unconstitutional the practice of daily Bible readings in the public schools. There was only one dissenting vote in each case. *(CQ Guide to the Supreme Court, p. 462)*

No other modern court ruling generated as much controversy for as long a period. "The Supreme Court has made God unconstitutional," thundered Sen. Sam J. Ervin Jr., D-N.C. (1954-74). "Why should the majority be so severely penalized by the protests of a handful?" asked evangelist Billy Graham.

Congressional Proposals

In the decades following the court's rulings, advocates of school prayer worked tirelessly — but fruitlessly — to persuade Congress to pass a constitutional amendment overturning the decisions.

In 1966, a proposed prayer amendment fell nine votes short of winning the necessary two-thirds majority in the Senate. It was the first time either chamber had voted on such a proposal since the court's rulings.

In 1971, the House failed to muster a two-thirds majority in support of another prayer amendment. The final tally was 240-163, 29 votes shy of the margin needed.

That measure was brought to the House floor through a discharge petition, prying it out of a hostile House Judiciary Committee. After a majority (218) of House members sign such a petition, the committee is discharged from further consideration of a measure, which can then be brought directly to the floor.

Stymied in their frontal assaults, advocates of prayer in the schools next tried stripping the federal courts of their jurisdiction to hear challenges to such practices. In 1976, the Senate rejected a proposal that would have eliminated the jurisdiction of the federal courts over all cases involving the public schools, including prayer cases.

Prayer advocates fared better in 1979, when the Senate by 47-37 adopted a proposal barring Supreme Court review of any state law related to "voluntary prayers in public schools." The proposal was an amendment by Jesse Helms, R-N.C., to legislation creating a Department of Education. It was subsequently stripped off the Education Department bill and attached to a separate bill intended to give the Supreme Court greater control over which appeals from the lower courts it would hear. That measure died in the

House. *(Congress and the Nation Vol. V, p. 803)*

In 1980, in a continuing appropriations resolution funding parts of the government for fiscal 1981, Congress prohibited use of any Education Department funds to prevent the implementation of voluntary prayer and meditation in public schools. *(1980 Almanac p. 219)*

In 1981, in its version of the fiscal 1982 State, Justice, Commerce appropriations bill, the House approved an amendment barring the Justice Department from using any funds in the bill to obstruct programs of voluntary prayer in the schools. But a Senate filibuster over the prayer issue ultimately led to the demise of the entire bill. *(1981 Almanac p. 364)*

In 1982, Helms tried to attach to a debt-ceiling bill a rider that would have barred the Supreme Court and lower federal courts from handling cases involving "voluntary" school prayer. But he was unable, on four tries, to muster the 60 votes needed to break a filibuster against the amendment. *(1980 Almanac p. 403)*

Senate Action

Judiciary Committee Action

In 1983, the Senate Judiciary Committee decided to let the full Senate choose between two alternative constitutional amendments allowing some form of prayer in public schools. By 14-3, the committee sent to the floor without recommendation two resolutions.

The first (S J Res 73), strongly supported by Reagan and conservative religious groups, would have allowed organized, recited prayer in the schools.

The second (S J Res 212), sponsored by Sen. Orrin G. Hatch, R-Utah, permitted silent prayer or meditation and assured student religious groups the same access to public school facilities during non-class hours as other voluntary student groups.

The Senate took no action on either proposal in 1983, and there was no substantive action on the prayer issue in the House that year. *(1983 Almanac p. 301)*

Reagan Support, Other Lobbying

The chief lobbyist for S J Res 73, the vocal prayer amendment, was none other than Reagan himself. During his political career, the president had been a frequent critic of the Supreme Court rulings.

He vigorously supported a constitutional amendment to overturn those decisions, declaring in his 1983 State of the Union address that "God should never have been expelled from America's classrooms in the first place."

Throughout 1984, Reagan continued to speak in favor of a prayer amendment, devoting a Feb. 25 radio address to the subject and a March 6 speech to the National Association of Evangelicals.

He lobbied a number of senators directly, either in person or by telephone, in the days and hours before the March 20 vote in the Senate.

The issue also was the subject of intensive lobbying by interest groups, religious organizations and various celebrities arrayed for or against the prayer amendment. Conservative groups such as Moral Majority and Christian Voice lobbied hard in support of S J Res 73, while leaders of mainline religions — Methodists, Lutherans and Jews, among others — opposed it.

For weeks before the vote, senators were inundated with mail and telephone calls, many of them generated by

TV religious personalities using their electronic pulpits to rally support for the amendment.

The Proposed Amendment

The text of S J Res 73 read: "Nothing in this Constitution shall be construed to prohibit individual or group prayer in public schools or other public institutions. No person shall be required by the United States or any state to participate in prayer. Neither the United States nor any state shall compose the words of any prayer to be said in public schools."

The last sentence had been added in the Judiciary Committee at the insistence of Chairman Strom Thurmond, R-S.C.

The Senate Debate

The Senate began its debate on the prayer issue the week of March 5, creating the atmosphere of a revival meeting around much of the Capitol.

A 12-hour vigil in support of school prayer was held in a congressional office building March 5, a human chain for prayer stretched from the Capitol to the Supreme Court for a few hours March 7, and members of the clergy on both sides of the issue held informal meetings with reporters and senators to press their views.

Although the House had no prayer proposal before it, some members favoring S J Res 73 kept the House in session for an all-night talkathon on the subject March 5 to lend support to their allies in the Senate.

Debate in the Senate itself was largely desultory, broken by occasional spirited exchanges between Hatch, a prayer amendment advocate, and Sen. Lowell P. Weicker Jr., R-Conn., leader of the opposition to S J Res 73.

Silent Prayer Alternative

Before voting on the vocal-prayer amendment, the Senate March 15 decisively rejected the principal alternative to S J Res 73.

By 81-15, senators voted to table, and thus kill, an amendment offered by Sen. Alan J. Dixon, D-Ill., that would have allowed silent prayer or meditation in the schools. *(Vote 33, p. 8-S)*

Dixon's proposal was offered as an amendment to S J Res 73 because Majority Leader Howard H. Baker Jr., R-Tenn., would not agree to allow him to call it up on its own.

A number of senators said they voted against the Dixon alternative because they wanted to give Reagan a vote on the original language of S J Res 73. Also, the president's supporters feared that S J Res 73 might lose votes if senators knew they could fall back on a silent-prayer alternative.

Hatch, who had sponsored S J Res 212, a silent-prayer amendment similar to Dixon's, voted against the Dixon amendment. He said it was uncomfortable to vote against what amounted to his own proposal, but explained that he wanted to give the president a "clean" vote on the vocal prayer amendment.

Vocal Prayer Rejected

With Vice President George Bush in the presiding officer's chair to demonstrate the administration's support for school prayer, the Senate March 20 finally voted on S J Res 73.

The 56-44 vote fell 11 votes short of the two-thirds majority needed for passage of a constitutional amendment. Eighteen Republicans joined 26 Democrats in voting against the amendment. Voting for it were 37 Republicans and 19 Democrats.

Opponents led by Weicker warned that children holding minority religious views — or none at all — would feel uncomfortable participating in a prayer alien to their beliefs and stigmatized if they refused to participate.

"The issue really is not prayer in schools for our children," said Weicker. "They have that right today. No court case, no law, no Supreme Court ruling prevents any individual child or any adult in this nation from praying wherever or whenever they wish."

Prayer supporters, meanwhile, vowed to press their cause anew.

"Round one is over, but so long as I am in the U.S. Senate, there will be many more rounds to come," said Helms.

"The issue of free religious speech is not dead as a result of this vote," Reagan said March 21. "We have suffered a setback, but we have not been defeated. Our struggle will go on."

Although the president spoke with some senators at the White House and called others before the vote, he failed to persuade some of them to back the prayer amendment.

One of those senators, Arlen Specter, R-Pa., who was Jewish, told Reagan of feeling uncomfortable attending elementary school in Wichita, Kan., where Christian prayers were recited.

Specter, who said he was still undecided after speaking to Reagan March 16, ultimately voted against the prayer amendment despite the fact that 90 percent of the letters and phone calls received by his office during the two weeks preceding the vote were in favor of prayer.

"This was a very difficult vote to protect minority rights. It was a tough vote," said Specter.

For conservative religious groups, the Senate's prayer vote was greeted with a vow to retaliate at the polls.

"Politically, we've got something that we can take to the polls this November, in 1986 and 1988," said Gary Jarmin, a lobbyist for the pro-prayer group Christian Voice.

Election-year concerns were evident in the vote. Of the 33 senators whose terms expired in 1984, 23 (70 percent) voted in favor of the prayer amendment. Eighteen of the 34 senators (53 percent) up for re-election in 1986 voted "yea," but just 15 of the 33 members (45 percent) whose terms expired in 1988 did so.

Silent Prayer Court Case

Less than two weeks after the Senate vote, on April 2, the Supreme Court reiterated its opposition to organized school prayer, summarily affirming an appeals court decision that struck down as unconstitutional an Alabama law that permitted teachers to lead willing students in prayer at the beginning of class.

But the court agreed to review the constitutionality of a second Alabama law permitting a moment of silence for prayer or meditation at the start of each school day.

The Reagan administration, which had lobbied for restoration of vocal prayer in the schools, urged the justices at least to permit silent prayer.

"To hold that the moment of silence is unconstitutional is to insist that any opportunity for religious practice, even in the unspoken thoughts of schoolchildren, be extirpated from the public sphere," the administration declared in a brief urging the court to review and uphold the Alabama law.

Moment-of-Silence Case

On Dec. 4, the justices heard arguments in *Wallace v. Jaffree*, the most closely church-state case in years.

At issue was an Alabama law, first approved in 1978 and amended in 1982, which stated:

"At the commencement of the first class of each day in all grades in all public schools, the teacher in charge of the room in which each such class is held may announce that a period of silence not to exceed one minute in duration shall be observed for meditation or voluntary prayer, and during any such period no other activities shall be engaged in."

Twenty-two states had similar laws.

The Alabama law was challenged by Ishmael Jaffree, a father of five, who argued that Alabama had "put its official seal of approval on state-sponsored organized group prayer in its public schools," in clear violation of the "establishment clause" of the First Amendment.

In January 1983, a federal district judge in Alabama dismissed Jaffree's case, declaring that the First Amendment did not apply to limit state action — notwithstanding a 50-year line of Supreme Court decisions to the contrary.

Four months later, that decision was overturned by the 11th U.S. Circuit Court of Appeals, which held the moment-of-silence law unconstitutional.

The Arguments

In a brief defending its law, Alabama argued that nothing in the court's earlier school prayer rulings indicated "that providing a period of silence for public school children in which they may meditate, pray or — if they choose — daydream in any way offends the Constitution."

By failing to read the "free exercise" and "establishment" clauses of the First Amendment together, the state said, lower courts had created "unnecessary tension" between the two. When they are read together, the First Amendment "affirmatively mandates accommodation, not merely tolerance, of all religions," Alabama said.

The Reagan administration, in a friend-of-the-court brief, supported that argument. "Permitting school children to maintain a moment of silence in the public schools presents no threat to the values protected by the establishment clause," the solicitor general said. "It evinces a 'benevolent neutrality' in keeping with the libertarian spirit of both religion clauses."

Failure "to accommodate the religious needs of students" in the years since the 1962-63 court rulings "has contributed to the exodus of many religious students ... from the public schools," the administration said.

"The values of pluralism and diversity in our public schools suffer needlessly from a reading of the establishment clause that destroys the possibility of accommodating, in a spirit of toleration, voluntary religious practices of the sort involved in this case," the administration said.

But Jaffree, in challenging the Alabama law, contended that the accommodation argument "falls from its own weight." There was nothing to accommodate, he said, because even without the state-enforced moment of silence, "students have complete freedom to offer a personal, private prayer during any of the other 23 hours and 59 minutes of the day...."

The First Amendment, he said, "prohibits the state from transforming an individual's right to silently pray, at any time, into a formal act of group worship in a tax-supported public institution attended by individuals of all faiths and beliefs, including non-believers." ∎

Probe of Finances Stalls Meese Nomination

White House counselor Edwin Meese III was named Jan. 23 to succeed William French Smith as attorney general. However, questions about his personal financial dealings touched off a prolonged investigation that kept his nomination on hold throughout 1984.

As a result, Smith remained in office all year despite a professed desire to "return to private life."

Meese, one of President Reagan's closest advisers, was cleared of any criminal wrongdoing by an independent counsel, or special prosecutor, appointed by Smith at the nominee's own request. The prosecutor conducted a five-month probe of allegations against Meese.

In a 385-page report issued Sept. 20, independent counsel Jacob A. Stein concluded, "We find no basis with respect to any of the 11 allegations for the bringing of a prosecution against Mr. Meese for the violation of a criminal statute."

However, Stein made "no comment on Mr. Meese's ethics and the propriety of his conduct or an evaluation of Mr. Meese's fitness for office."

Stein's report came too late to salvage Meese's nomination in 1984. With the 98th Congress drawing to a close, Senate Judiciary Chairman Strom Thurmond, R-S.C., had said Sept. 7 that regardless of what Stein's report concluded, he would not resume confirmation hearings on Meese's nomination before adjournment.

In a statement released by the White House, Reagan said he would resubmit Meese's nomination in 1985. He predicted his aide would become "a truly distinguished attorney general." *(Nomination, p. 21-A)*

The Nomination

Meese's nomination was announced Jan. 23, the same day that Smith resigned as attorney general, effective upon the confirmation of a successor.

Smith Resignation, Record

Smith, formerly a member of a large, prestigious Los Angeles law firm and Reagan's personal lawyer, said he wanted to return to his law practice. He also said he wanted to be available to help Reagan's re-election campaign and that "this would not be possible in my present position."

At a news conference Jan. 23, Smith said he was "not aware of any previous administration that has made as many changes in policy and organization at the Justice Department as we have in the last three years."

He cited as accomplishments bringing the FBI into the fight against illegal drugs, setting up nationwide drug task forces, opposing court-ordered school busing and hiring quotas as remedies for racial discrimination, and stepping up collection of debts owed the federal government.

Smith said he was most disappointed by the failure of Congress to approve three major pieces of legislation sought by the administration — an anti-crime package, an immigration reform measure and a bill to restructure the bankruptcy courts. By the end of the year, two of the three had passed — the crime bill and a bankruptcy reform package. *(Stories, pp. 215, 263)*

And the immigration bill had come close, dying in a House-Senate conference committee in the final days of the 98th Congress. *(Story, p. 229)*

Meese Background, Role

Meese's background was entirely different from that of Smith, who was a corporate lawyer before becoming attorney general. Starting in 1959, Meese spent eight years as deputy district attorney in Alameda County, Calif. He was named Reagan's legal affairs secretary in 1967, when Reagan became governor of California, and then served as Reagan's chief of staff until 1974.

Meese practiced corporate law from 1974-77, then became a law professor at the University of San Diego, where he also served as director of the law school's Center for Criminal Justice Policy and Management.

Reagan's campaign adviser in 1980, he was named counselor to the president after Reagan took office. He was one of three to four men in the president's inner circle.

In his White House role, Meese helped shape administration policy on justice-related issues.

In 1983, he was the prime force behind Reagan's successful effort to remake the supposedly independent Civil Rights Commission into an agency more in tune with the president's views. Reagan ultimately achieved his goal, after a protracted, bitter fight. *(1983 Almanac p. 292)*

Meese was behind unsuccessful administration efforts to abolish the Legal Services Corporation, which provided civil legal assistance to the poor. *(Story, p. 262)*

And he was reported to be a major force behind the administration's short-lived attempt to change government policy barring tax breaks for private schools that discriminate. *(1982 Almanac p. 297)*

Meese was given credit for helping influence the Justice Department's decision to seek a narrow interpretation of the law barring sex discrimination in federally financed education programs. The administration's position prevailed in a Supreme Court decision in the case of *Grove City College v. Bell*, touching off a move in Congress to rewrite the law. *(Story, p. 239)*

Meese provoked a storm of controversy in December 1983 when he said there was little, if any, proof of hunger in the country. Critics branded him as insensitive to the plight of the impoverished.

Senate Hearings

Civil rights groups opposed the Meese nomination, and initially it appeared that Senate Judiciary Committee confirmation hearings would focus on their concerns.

Benjamin Hooks, executive director of the NAACP, labeled Meese "an anti-civil rights devil" and said his nomination was "bad news for black Americans, women and other minorities."

The Judiciary Committee opened confirmation hearings March 1-2. As expected, Democrats questioned Meese about his involvement in the civil rights policies of the Reagan administration. And they asked whether Meese, a longtime associate of President Reagan, could maintain his independence as attorney general.

Committee Republicans praised Meese as a qualified candidate whose legal background suited his new post. Thurmond called Meese a "highly principled man committed to the fair administration of justice." Other Republicans generally tried to draw Meese out about his views on justice issues.

Civil Rights Concerns

Meese tried to defuse concerns about his civil rights stance, telling committee members, "My policy is to have vigorous enforcement of the civil rights laws . . . and a great deal of communication with affected parties."

But Edward M. Kennedy, D-Mass., called the Reagan administration's civil rights record "a disgrace" and contended that Meese had been "the architect of most, if not all, of the administration policies in this area."

Kennedy said he was concerned about whether Meese would be the attorney general "for all Americans," and whether he would "stand for the elimination of discrimination."

"I clearly stand for the elimination of discrimination and prejudice wherever it can be found . . . ," Meese replied.

Sen. Joseph R. Biden Jr., D-Del., ranking Democrat on Judiciary, questioned Meese about the administration's contention that the Internal Revenue Service (IRS) lacked authority to continue a longtime practice of barring tax exemptions to racially discriminatory private schools. The Supreme Court in May 1983 rebuffed that claim 8-1, declaring firmly that "racial discrimination in education is contrary to public policy." *(1983 Almanac pp. 3-A, 10-A)*

Meese said he had not been intimately involved in administration decisions on the matter and contended the case was not about changing the law on discrimination but about proper regulation of the IRS.

Asked if racially discriminatory schools should receive tax breaks, Meese replied "absolutely not."

Independence From Reagan?

Several Democratic senators and Republican Charles McC. Mathias Jr., Md., questioned Meese, chief of staff of the 1980 Reagan campaign, about his independence from the president. They recalled that the Senate, in approving its version of the existing Ethics in Government Act, had adopted a floor amendment barring any top campaign official from serving as attorney general. The amendment was dropped the following year in a House-Senate conference. *(1977 Almanac p. 578)*

Meese maintained that he was not a political operative. "Aren't you a major political adviser?" Biden asked.

"I would say I am a major policy adviser, if you can distinguish that from being a political adviser," Meese replied, adding that he would continue to advise Reagan, but not on politics.

Mathias said he was concerned about communications from the White House that could pressure the Justice Department to shift its position on pending court cases.

Meese assured the committee that he could exercise "independent judgment" if a conflict arose between the White House and Justice.

Financial Questions

In the first hint of troubles to come, some Democrats March 1-2 also questioned Meese about financial transactions surrounding the sale of his home in California.

The questions about Meese's financial dealings concerned loans he obtained to cover payments on a home in La Mesa, Calif., which he eventually sold, and payments on a new house in Virginia.

Meese maintained that he had nothing to do with a federal appointment given to a man who had helped him obtain $60,000 in loans.

Howard M. Metzenbaum, D-Ohio, noted that when Meese was 15 months in arrears on two California bank loans, instead of foreclosing or threatening to foreclose, the bank gave Meese a new loan.

Meese contended the loans were properly secured by his La Mesa home and were to be paid off as soon as the house was sold.

During additional hearings March 5-6, and in press accounts thereafter, attention was focused more intensively on Meese's financial transactions and the help given him by individuals later appointed to federal jobs.

California House Deal

Metzenbaum questioned Meese and two California businessmen extensively about their connections.

One of the men, Thomas J. Barrack, a real estate developer, put together a deal to buy Meese's home in La Mesa, Calif., in August 1982. The house had been on the market for 20 months and Meese was more than a year behind in mortgage payments when it finally was sold.

Barrack, whose name did not appear on any legal documents involving the house, said he loaned $70,000 to a business associate to make up part of the buyer's down payment for the Meese house. The rest of the $307,500 sale price was covered by a bank note. Barrack said he later forgave the $70,000 loan — in essence contributing that amount to Meese's profit from sale of the house.

Just weeks after putting together the house deal, Barrack flew to Washington to discuss a federal job. In December 1982 he obtained a position as an assistant secretary in the Interior Department. He was in line for a new position at the Commerce Department in 1983 but decided instead to return to his business ventures in California.

Meese said in testimony March 1-2 that he did not know Barrack, although they had talked by telephone about the house deal. He said he had had nothing to do with Barrack's appointment. Barrack also said that he did not know Meese. He said he got involved in the house deal because former White House personnel director Pendleton James, a close friend, asked him to help.

Barrack said it was James who talked to him about coming to work for the federal government. Barrack said he never talked to Meese about getting a federal position and that Meese never knew he had put up the $70,000 down payment for the La Mesa home.

On March 6, Metzenbaum delved into $60,000 in loans Meese obtained through his tax adviser, John R. McKean. McKean, a San Francisco accountant, later was named chairman of the U.S. Postal Service Board of Governors.

McKean discussed the possibility of a seat on the board with White House adviser Michael K. Deaver a month after arranging the Meese loans. He was nominated for the seat four months later, and subsequently was elected board chairman.

McKean said he also did tax work for Deaver, who introduced him to Meese. McKean said he arranged a $58,000 loan for Deaver so that Deaver could become part of a tax shelter enterprise.

McKean told Metzenbaum he believed Meese and Deaver recommended him for the Postal Service position, although he was not clear about Meese's role.

Meese said March 1 he knew McKean was under consideration for the position and he "knew of no reason then and know of no reason now" that McKean should not be on the board. He said he did not recommend McKean for the position.

In response to questions from Metzenbaum, McKean

said that after he reviewed Meese's financial situation in June 1981, he determined Meese would need about $60,000 during 1981 to meet his financial obligations. Most of these, McKean said, were payments on his unsold California house and payments for a new house in Virginia.

McKean said Meese, who then made $60,000 a year, had a yearly liability of $51,216 on the two houses.

McKean said he arranged a $40,000 loan for Meese in June and a $20,000 loan six months later. Meese paid 21 percent interest in the first three months on the $40,000 loan and 18 percent or the prime rate, whichever was higher, thereafter. The interest on the $20,000 loan was 18 percent or the prime rate, whichever was higher.

Meese repaid the loans in full and also paid interest totaling $23,440, McKean said. The final payment of $3,340.12 was made just three weeks before Meese's confirmation hearings began.

Loan to Meese's Wife

By March 15, more allegations had come to light. *The Washington Post* disclosed March 14 that Meese's wife, Ursula, in December 1980 received a $15,000 loan from Edwin Thomas, who served as Meese's deputy in the White House and later as a regional director of the General Services Administration (GSA) in San Francisco.

Meese failed to report the loan on his financial disclosure statement. After the news story, he wrote Thurmond and apologized for "inadvertently" leaving it off.

The Ethics in Government Act of 1978 required senior government officials to disclose all outstanding loans of more than $10,000 each and covered loans to their family members. *(1978 Almanac p. 835)*

Documents subsequently released to the committee showed that Mrs. Meese used the Thomas loan to buy stock for the couple's children in Biotech Capital Corp., a venture capital firm. She sold the stock for a $3,398 loss in May 1983.

A subsidiary of Biotech received an exemption from the Small Business Administration in early 1981 that permitted the firm to participate in an SBA loan guarantee program.

A House subcommittee March 16 asked the Securities and Exchange Commission (SEC) to look into possible insider trading activities in connection with the $15,000 loan to Mrs. Meese.

The request came March 16 from Rep. John D. Dingell, D-Mich., chairman of the Energy and Commerce Subcommittee on Oversight and Investigations.

"It would be highly inappropriate for Mr. Meese to be confirmed as the nation's premier lawyer and later have it revealed that he had violated the very laws he had sworn to uphold," Dingell wrote to SEC Chairman John Shad.

John Fedders, director of the SEC's division of enforcement, replied that the commission needed more information before it would consider a probe.

Ethics Proposal

In another development related to the Meese nomination, Senate Minority Leader Robert C. Byrd, D-W.Va., introduced legislation March 19 to alter the way top presidential appointments were handled.

Byrd's bill (S 2446) sought to give the Office of Government Ethics, which was created under the 1978 ethics law, the responsibility for conducting background investigations of appointees who had to be confirmed by the Senate.

The bill also required a president re-elected to a second term to resubmit for renewed Senate confirmation the nominations of Cabinet officers and other top-level officials he wanted to keep in his second administration.

Byrd called this a "fail-safe" procedure. He said it would give the Senate a chance to judge the "track record" of the presidential appointee and to weigh "new information which may have surfaced subsequent to the original confirmation proceedings."

His legislation was referred to the Governmental Affairs Committee, but went no further in 1984.

Campaign Papers

Metzenbaum and Sen. Carl Levin, D-Mich., raised questions about Meese's knowledge of 1980 Democratic campaign strategy papers that found their way to the Reagan campaign and wound up in administration files.

Levin charged March 15 that Meese had "misled" a House subcommittee in July when he said in a letter that he had no knowledge of any use of, or transactions involving, President Carter's campaign documents by members of Reagan's election team.

The Human Resources Subcommittee of the House Post Office and Civil Service Committee was investigating how the Reagan campaign got hold of the Democratic papers. On March 14 the panel voted to release documents it had collected to Levin and to Metzenbaum, who was leading Judiciary Committee Democrats in questioning Meese.

The documents released included 1980 memos sent to Meese referring to information in the Democratic campaign papers. Levin noted that when Meese was shown the documents, he said he "recalled seeing these kinds of documents at the time," apparently contradicting his July 1983 letter.

On March 14, Metzenbaum's office released other documents showing that Meese told the House subcommittee at one point that he recalled seeing a memo on the Carter campaign but could not remember what was done with it. In a subsequent statement, Meese said he could not recall seeing the document, according to Metzenbaum's office.

Special Prosecutor Probe

With prospects for his confirmation as attorney general increasingly uncertain, Meese on March 22 asked the Justice Department to seek a special prosecutor to investigate the mounting allegations against him.

"Because of unsubstantiated charges that have been widely publicized by those who oppose my nomination to be attorney general, I feel that there must be a comprehensive inquiry that will examine the facts and make public the truth," Meese said in a letter asking Attorney General Smith to seek appointment of a special prosecutor by a three-judge panel.

That request came five days after the Justice Department launched a preliminary investigation as a first step toward such an appointment.

The post-Watergate Ethics in Government Act of 1978 created a mechanism for the appointment of a special prosecutor whenever serious allegations involving top federal officials arise. The law was amended in 1982 to spell out more precisely the circumstances that would trigger such an appointment and to change the investigator's name from "special prosecutor" to "independent counsel." *(Special prosecutor history, p. 251)*

Sensitive Cases Draw Special Prosecutors

The position of "special prosecutor" was almost as old as questions about the ability of the executive branch to investigate itself.

While special prosecutors reached a peak of prominence during the Watergate scandal of 1973-74, demands for independent investigators to look into allegations of high-level wrongdoing dated back much further.

In the 19th century, during the Grant administration, a special prosecutor was called in to investigate whether the president's personal secretary was involved in a ring of tax-evading whiskey distillers.

In the wake of the "Teapot Dome" scandal in the 1920s, Congress passed a joint resolution calling for a special prosecutor to probe charges of corrupt leasing of oil reserves by Harding administration officials. Members were spurred by concern that the Justice Department was lackadaisical in its pursuit of the matter.

During the Truman administration, officials from the Justice Department and the old Bureau of Revenue were accused of fixing tax cases. President Truman appointed his own former attorney general, J. Howard McGrath, to conduct a cleanup campaign, but the House Judiciary Committee objected. Members claimed conflict of interest, pointing out that McGrath was attorney general when the alleged improprieties occurred.

Truman then appointed a new independent prosecutor, a liberal Republican from New York with no ties to the president. McGrath tried to fire the new lawyer but instead ended up resigning in disgrace.

Watergate and Its Aftermath

The idea of a special prosecutor to investigate the June 17, 1972, burglary of Democratic National Committee headquarters by men with ties to President Nixon's re-election committee emerged in the spring of 1973. Nixon had nominated Elliot L. Richardson as attorney general, but the Senate Judiciary Committee blocked his confirmation until Richardson promised to appoint a special prosecutor to probe Watergate. He subsequently selected Harvard law Professor Archibald Cox and promised him complete independence.

Within five months, Cox was demanding secret tape recordings Nixon had made of his White House conversations. Cox refused to accept transcript summaries Nixon was offering, and the president ordered Richardson to fire Cox. Richardson balked and resigned. His deputy, William D. Ruckelshaus, was fired after refusing to carry out Nixon's order. Solicitor General Robert H. Bork finally fired Cox, setting off the public outcry and House impeachment probe that eventually led to Nixon's Aug. 9, 1974, resignation.

Five years later, Congress passed the Ethics in Government Act of 1978, which among other things set up a mechanism for court appointment of a temporary special prosecutor to probe allegations against high government or campaign officials. *(1978 Almanac p. 835)*

The attorney general was required to seek such an appointment unless, after a preliminary investigation, he determined the allegations were "so unsubstantiated that no further investigation is warranted."

The Reagan administration opposed reauthorization of the law in 1981-82, contending it unconstitutionally involved the judiciary — through the appointment of a special prosecutor — in the enforcement of laws, an executive branch function.

However, Congress in late 1982 cleared a five-year reauthorization of the special prosecutor law. It tightened the standards triggering the appointment of a prosecutor, shortened the list of officials covered by the law (as well as the length of time they would be covered after leaving office), provided for reimbursement of legal fees incurred by those under investigation who were not indicted, and changed the name of the special prosecutor to "independent counsel." *(1982 Almanac p. 386)*

Recent Experience

As of 1984, there had been at least a dozen investigations under the law, but only four special prosecutors were appointed. Two probed alleged drug abuse by top Carter aides Hamilton Jordan and Tim Kraft. A third investigated alleged racketeering ties of President Reagan's secretary of labor, Raymond J. Donovan. The fourth probed allegations involving the personal finances of Reagan's counselor and nominee for attorney general, Edwin Meese III. None of the probes led to criminal indictments. (A special prosecutor also was appointed by Attorney General Griffin B. Bell in 1979 to look into possible loan improprieties by the Carter family's peanut warehouse. Bell said a special prosecutor was not obligatory because the alleged improprieties occurred before the law was enacted. No evidence of wrongdoing was uncovered.)

Of the cases in which the preliminary investigation found insufficient evidence to warrant a special prosecutor, only three were made public. These involved charges that President Carter and Vice President Walter F. Mondale illegally solicited political contributions at a White House luncheon, that Reagan national security adviser Richard V. Allen had taken bribes from foreigners, and that Reagan-era CIA Director William J. Casey had violated the foreign agents registration law when he represented Indonesia in a case before the federal government.

The Reagan administration won an important victory June 25, 1984, when the U.S. Appeals Court for the District of Columbia, sitting *en banc*, unanimously ruled that courts cannot order the appointment of a special prosecutor over the objections of the attorney general.

The appeals court reversed a May 14 lower court order directing the Justice Department to name an independent counsel to investigate how Carter campaign papers in 1980 came into possession of the Reagan campaign.

It was the second appeals court ruling in less than a month turning aside demands from private citizens for appointment of an independent counsel. A June 5 ruling by a three-judge panel of the same court had rebuffed demands for an independent probe of a 1979 melee in Greensboro, N.C., involving the Ku Klux Klan and Communist Party demonstrators.

Reagan, who supported Meese's request, said the inquiry would "demonstrate the high level of integrity and dedication which have marked Ed's long career of public service." The president stood behind the nomination and said that Meese would remain in his White House post "until confirmed" as attorney general.

The Senate Judiciary Committee postponed further confirmation hearings while the issue of naming a special prosecutor was resolved. As it turned out, the suspension lasted the rest of the year.

Smith Seeks Independent Counsel

Smith on March 27 heeded Meese's request and asked a special federal court to appoint an independent counsel to investigate a range of allegations involving Meese. He acted five days after the Justice Department began a preliminary investigation as a first step toward seeking a special prosecutor. The ethics act, enacted in the wake of Watergate, created a process for appointing a special prosecutor whenever serious allegations arose involving top federal officials. The 1982 amendments spelled out more precisely the circumstances that would trigger such an appointment and changed the investigator's title to "independent counsel." *(1982 Almanac p. 386)*

In his application for an independent counsel, Smith said his request was prompted by information gleaned March 15 "from public sources" that Meese had failed to list on his financial disclosure form a $15,000 loan to his wife, Ursula, from Edwin Thomas.

"During the time that this loan was outstanding, Mr. Thomas and members of his family obtained appointive federal jobs with the executive branch of government," Smith said.

A false statement or omission on a financial disclosure form could be a violation of law if it was knowing or willful. Smith noted that Meese had said the omission was inadvertent and that there was no connection between the loan and the government jobs.

Resolving questions about the failure to report the loan and about any relationship between the loan and the jobs required "careful investigation," Smith said.

Meese retained three attorneys to help him work with the prosecutor: Meese's close friend, E. Robert Wallach, a San Francisco trial attorney; Washington lawyer Leonard Garment, who helped defend President Nixon during the Watergate scandal; and Max Kampelman, another Washington lawyer and one-time associate of the late Hubert H. Humphrey.

Under 1982 revisions to the 1978 Ethics in Government Act, which created a mechanism for appointment of special prosecutors, the subject of an investigation could be reimbursed for attorneys' fees if no indictment resulted from the probe and the costs would not have been incurred by a private citizen in similar circumstances.

Broad Inquiry

Smith recommended that the independent counsel's investigation be broad enough to cover several other areas, including the following:

● Meese's financial transactions with four other individuals, in addition to the Thomases, who received federal jobs after helping Meese.

● The Meese family's purchase and subsequent sale, at a loss, of stock in Biotech Capital Corp., a venture capital firm.

● Special treatment for business entities in which Meese

had a financial interest. A Biotech subsidiary received an exemption from the Small Business Administration (SBA) in 1981 permitting the firm to participate in an SBA loan guarantee program.

● Meese's promotion in the military reserve. A report by the Army inspector general's office found that Meese was improperly transferred from retired to active reserve status and then promoted to colonel. The report said Meese was unaware of the improper actions and was not to blame. To quiet the controversy, Meese asked in February to return to retired status.

● Meese's statements to the House Post Office and Civil Service Committee and the Senate Judiciary Committee about Carter campaign materials. Meese had said in affidavits that he did not recall seeing information addressed to him that contained or referred to documents and information from the Carter campaign.

● On March 29, a White House spokesman acknowledged that Meese and nine other White House officials had kept $375 cufflinks given to them during a 1983 visit to South Korea. Federal law required gifts worth more than $140 to be turned over to the government or reported within 60 days.

Meese returned his cufflinks March 28, the spokesman said.

Stein Appointed Counsel

Stein, a Washington, D.C., trial lawyer, was named April 2 as "independent counsel" to investigate the allegations swirling around Meese.

A day later, Smith, who had hoped to return to private law practice by this time, met with Reagan and at the president's behest agreed to remain in office until his successor was confirmed.

The appointment of Stein, 59, a past president of the District of Columbia Bar Association, was made by a special panel of three federal appeals court judges under provisions of the ethics law.

The three-judge panel gave Stein authority to investigate and prosecute "any allegation or evidence of violation of any federal criminal law by Mr. Meese." The panel specifically asked Stein, a former Watergate defense lawyer, to look into questions about Meese's financial dealings and whether he helped obtain federal jobs for seven persons who had assisted him financially.

The special prosecutor was also expected to probe Meese's knowledge of Jimmy Carter campaign materials obtained by Reagan campaign officials in 1980, and his status in the military reserve.

After Stein's appointment, Reagan said he had "instructed all members of the administration to cooperate fully with the independent counsel" and added that the White House would have "no further comment on this matter" pending completion of the inquiry.

Stein had been in private practice in Washington since 1948. He had taught at the law schools of three universities, Harvard, George Washington and Georgetown.

During Watergate, Stein defended Kenneth Parkinson, a lawyer for President Nixon's Committee to Re-elect the President, on charges related to the Watergate cover-up. Parkinson was the only Watergate defendant acquitted.

Stein also represented White House press secretary James S. Brady, who was seriously injured March 30, 1981, when a gunman attempted to kill Reagan. Stein was asking $100 million in damages for Brady from companies that manufactured and distributed the handgun used to wound

Reagan and others in the shooting. *(1981 Almanac p. 6)*

Meese Loans Repaid

On Aug. 13, Meese filed his annual financial disclosure statement, reporting that he had paid off two of the loans under scrutiny by the special prosecutor and had taken out a second mortgage on his McLean, Va., home to cover the third.

Listed as "paid in full" was the previously undisclosed $15,000 loan from Thomas to Meese's wife and the $60,000 in loans from McKean, which had been the subject of Senate testimony.

A personal loan in the range of $50,000 to $100,000 from the National Bank of Commerce of Washington, D.C., was paid by Meese taking out a second mortgage on his home.

Probe Concluded

After a five-month probe, Stein issued his report Sept. 20, finding no evidence of criminal conduct by Meese.

Meese promptly said that the report "cleared the air and affirmed what my family and I have always known: that we have lived honorable lives, that we have paid our debts with our own money, and that we have never taken advantage of our official position to obtain private gain."

Stein and his five deputies investigated 11 charges against Meese. Six were listed in the order appointing the independent counsel. Five more came to Stein's attention during the course of his probe.

Most allegations centered around Meese's financial dealings, and whether there was a relationship between certain loans made to Meese or his wife, Ursula, and the appointment to federal jobs of persons who helped him financially.

Other inquiries included Meese's return to active status in the Army Reserve and his subsequent promotion; his knowledge of how President Carter's 1980 campaign materials ended up in the Reagan campaign; his receipt of funds from the Presidential Transition Fund and Foundation; his receipt of cuff links from the government of South Korea; and his connection with federal grants to Pepperdine University and American University.

Stein found no evidence that Meese was responsible for giving a federal job to Thomas, to Thomas' wife, Gretchen, attorney-examiner in the San Francisco office of the Merit Systems Protection Board; or Thomas' son, Tad, who worked for the Department of Labor. Thomas had lent $15,000 to Ursula Meese.

Stein also found no evidence that Meese willfully omitted the loan, or stock his wife purchased with the loan, from his financial disclosure form.

Others who lent money to the Meeses and later received federal appointments included four former officers of the Great American Savings Bank of California, which made three home loans to the Meeses: Edwin J. Gray, later chairman of the Federal Home Loan Bank Board; Clarence M. Pendleton Jr., later chairman of the Civil Rights Commission; Gordon Luce, named to the President's Commission on Housing and appointed an alternate delegate to the United Nations General Assembly in 1982; and Marc Sandstrom, named in 1981 to the Board of Directors of the Legal Services Corporation.

"Despite the various degrees of support Mr. Meese gave to the appointments of Messrs. Luce, Gray, Sandstrom and Pendleton," the report said, "the evidence does not warrant the finding that such support was con-

nected with the bank's treatment of the Meeses."

The independent counsel also found no evidence that John R. McKean, who lent Meese $60,000, received his appointment as a member of the Board of Governors of the U.S. Postal Service in return for the loan.

Other Charges

Stein did find that "applicable laws and regulations were misapplied, violated or ignored in transferring Mr. Meese to active status" in the Army Reserve, supporting an earlier conclusion by the inspector general of the Army. However, Stein concluded that the evidence did not justify a criminal charge against Meese.

Regarding the Carter campaign materials, Stein found no evidence that Meese violated criminal law, either in obtaining the materials or in statements made to congressional investigators.

Stein also concluded that Meese's payments from the Presidential Transition Fund and Foundation were proper, and properly reported.

Despite allegations that the Meeses intervened on behalf of Pepperdine and American universities, the report concluded that neither of the Meeses had any role in securing federal grants for the schools.

Although federal law required federal employees to surrender tangible gifts from a foreign government if those gifts had a retail value greater than $140, and although the cuff links Meese received from the government of South Korea were valued at $375, the report said, "Meese's failure to return the cuff links was based on his good faith that the value of the cuff links was within acceptable limits. There is no basis for criminal prosecution." ∎

Justice Authorization Dies

The Senate passed a fiscal 1985 authorization bill for the Justice Department, approving a total of $3.49 billion for department programs, but the House failed to act on its version of the measure.

The Senate bill (S 2606 — S Rept 98-498), which passed June 15 by voice vote, authorized about $10 million less than a bill reported May 15 by the House Judiciary Committee (HR 5468 — H Rept 98-759). The administration requested $3.67 billion in its fiscal 1985 budget request submitted to Congress in February.

The department had not had a regular authorization since fiscal 1980; it had been operating since then on temporary authorizations.

Permanent Authority

Department officials were seeking permanent authority for some of their operations, particularly those involving certain investigatory functions. Congress refused to go along with such a sweeping proposal, but the Senate bill did include permanent authorization for "routine, noncontroversial activities," according to Judiciary Chairman Strom Thurmond, R-S.C.

For example, permanent authority was granted for payment of witness expenses, the purchase of firearms for some agencies, routine FBI criminal investigations, FBI protection of the president and the attorney general, cooperative agreements with the states for support of U.S. prisoners in non-federal institutions, and payment of translators for the Immigration and Naturalization Service.

In remarks on the bill June 15, Thurmond noted that the committee retained annual oversight authority for "sensitive department activities and any new requested functions." It also retained power to set annual dollar levels for all department functions.

House Committee Bill

The bill (HR 5468) approved by voice vote May 1 by the House Judiciary Committee authorized $3.586 billion in fiscal 1985 for the Justice Department.

The committee made additions to the Reagan request in selected areas. It added $20 million for the Immigration and Naturalization Service, putting its total at $595.16 million.

By voice vote, the panel adopted an amendment by Hamilton Fish Jr., R-N.Y., to add funding for 40 additional immigration judges. These judges handled, among other things, cases involving individuals who were being excluded from the United States or who were being deported from the country. Fish said there currently was authorization for 60 judges but that this number was insufficient to keep up with the caseload.

An additional $15.7 million over the administration's request was provided for the federal prison system, bringing its total to $595.99 million. Of that, $5.5 million would be for the National Institute of Corrections to provide for technical assistance and training to state and local correctional authorities. Another $4 million was provided for 200 new corrections officers at existing facilities.

Provisions Compared

The bills passed by the Senate and approved by the House Judiciary Committee included the following major provisions:

Immigration and Naturalization Service. The Senate bill authorized $574.54 million, the administration request. The House bill provided $595.16 million. Within the Senate authorization was $43.6 million requested by the administration for a major Southern border enforcement initiative.

FBI. The Senate bill authorized $1.12 billion for the FBI, while the House provided $1.16 billion, about the administration request.

Drug Enforcement Administration. The Senate provided $300.85 million, down from the $334.65 million requested by the administration. The House version provided Reagan's request. Also authorized in the Senate bill was $96.9 million for organized crime drug enforcement activities.

Federal Prisons. The Senate bill authorized $580.22 million for operations of the federal prison system and support of U.S. prisoners in state institutions. ∎

Semiconductor Chips Win Legal Protection

Congress Oct. 9 cleared a legislative package (HR 6163 — PL 98-620) that gave the makers of semiconductor chips 10 years of protection against illegal copying of their chips.

The omnibus bill, which was pasted together in the closing days of the 98th Congress, also clarified trademark laws, modified patent law, sharply reduced the civil cases entitled to speedy federal court consideration and created a new institute to help state judicial systems.

The vehicle for all this legislation was a federal court housekeeping bill that established new sites for holding sessions of selected federal courts.

Legislative History: Putting Package Together

All but the patent and judicial institute sections of HR 6163 had been passed by the House as separate measures.

The patent provisions were reported Aug. 15 in somewhat different form by the House Science and Technology Committee (HR 5003 — H Rept 98-983). They modified a 1980 patent law (PL 96-517) designed to establish a uniform policy for inventions arising from contracts between the government and small businesses or non-profit organizations, including universities. *(1980 Almanac p. 405)*

The institute section received a 243-176 majority when it was considered as a separate bill (HR 4145 — H Rept 98-685) by the House May 22, but it failed to get the two-thirds required under suspension of the House rules. *(Vote 140, p. 48-H)*

The Senate May 16 passed a bill on computer chip protection (S 1201 — S Rept 98-425) and on June 21 passed a measure to create a state justice institute (S 384 — S Rept 98-480). The House passed its chip bill (HR 5525 — H Rept 98-781) on June 11 by 388-0. *(Vote 199, p. 64-H)*

The House approved by voice vote Sept. 11 provisions of HR 6163 involving priority treatment of civil cases by the federal courts (HR 5645 — H Rept 98-985). The trademark section (HR 6285) of the legislation was passed by the House Oct. 1 by voice vote.

On Oct. 3, the Senate by voice vote tacked all of the legislation onto HR 6163 (H Rept 98-1062), the court housekeeping bill reported Sept. 24 by the House Judiciary Committee and passed by the House the same day under suspension of the rules.

Final action on the package came Oct. 9, when the House by 363-0 agreed to the Senate's amendment. *(Vote 396, p. 120-H)*

Chip Protection

The most important part of the package was the section providing copyright-style protection to the makers of the tiny silicon chips that lay at the heart of the microcomputer revolution.

Testimony before House and Senate committees showed that manufacturers of semiconductor chips were vulnerable to piracy by firms that could photograph a chip, analyze and duplicate it. These "pirate" firms could then sell the chip more cheaply than the original maker because they had been been spared the millions of dollars in research expenditures usually required to develop a chip.

Rep. Carlos J. Moorhead, R-Calif., noted one government study found that "the R&D costs for a single complex chip could reach $4 million, while the costs of copying such a chip could be less than $100,000."

Unless chip makers received protection from copying, supporters of the bill said, innovation could be stifled as companies became increasingly leery of sinking resources into the development of new, more sophisticated chips only to see them copied and sold cheaply by pirate companies.

"This vote occurs not a minute too soon," said Rep. Don Edwards, D-Calif., who, with Rep. Norman Y. Mineta, D-Calif., first introduced the semiconductor chip bill in

1978. "With this measure," Edwards said, "innovating firms finally will be able to combat the unfair chip piracy that is sapping their strength and destroying their incentive to continue to invest in the crucial but very expensive creative endeavors necessary to maintain American leadership in this field."

The most troublesome issue surrounding chip protection was defining what a chip actually was and then fitting it into existing law.

A semiconductor chip was something like a scientific Dagwood sandwich. It was made up of a system of intricate layers of material with unique designs etched on them. The designs routed electrical signals so they would perform specific tasks, and chips ran computers and other products.

Under existing law, copyright protection was not available for the imprinted design patterns on the semiconductor chips, known as "mask works."

As cleared, HR 6163 gave the mask works 10 years of what was essentially copyright protection, but it created a new section of law specifically designed for the computer chips. This approach, the brainchild of Rep. Robert W. Kastenmeier, D-Wis., did not attempt to fit chip protection into existing copyright law, which covered more traditional "writings" such as books and plays.

Kastenmeier noted that the bill constituted "the first new intellectual property law in nearly 100 years."

The Senate's chip bill provided for criminal penalties for infringement, but the House bill and the final compromise version provided only civil remedies.

"It seems that every day we are creating a new penal statute of some sort with little thought given to investigative and evidentiary problems, to the burdens on judges and juries, and to the goals of and pressures on the correctional system," Kastenmeier said Oct. 9. "I am pleased we have not so erred in this act."

When the Senate approved the compromise Sept. 27, Sen. Charles McC. Mathias Jr., R-Md., said the Senate "with some reluctance" would yield to the House. Mathias said he believed that criminal sanctions did play "a limited but important role" in copyright enforcement, and added that he would seek to reopen the issue of criminal sanctions for mask work infringement if the civil remedies proved inadequate.

Trademark Issue

The trademark section of HR 6163 overturned a year-old federal appeals court decision redefining when a trademarked product became "generic" and no longer entitled to protection. The court case involved a clash between Parker Brothers, makers of the game "Monopoly," and Anti-Monopoly Inc., makers of "Anti-Monopoly: the 'Bust-the-Trust' Game."

The 9th U.S. Circuit Court of Appeals used a new "motivational" test for deciding when a trademarked item had become generic. Focusing on whether a majority of the relevant public could identify the producer of the game, the court decided that "monopoly" had become generic because a majority of the consumers surveyed simply wanted to play the game and were not motivated by the fact that Parker Brothers produced Monopoly.

The decision produced immediate outcries from businesses that claimed the new test would be unworkable and would dilute the protections offered by many existing trademarks.

HR 6163 made clear that the only test for determining whether a registered trademark had become generic was

whether the "relevant public" recognized a trademark as a way of identifying and distinguishing one specific product or service from others, regardless of who the maker was.

Final Provisions

As cleared by Congress, HR 6163 included these major provisions:

Trademark Clarification

● Revised the definition of a trademark to make clear that a mark could not be considered the "common descriptive name" of goods, and thus not entitled to protection, solely because it was also used as a name of or to identify a unique product or service.

● Provided that the test for determining whether a registered mark had become "generic" was whether the relevant public recognized a trademark as a way of identifying a specific product or service, and not whether the public could identify the producer of the item or service.

● Made clear that "purchaser motivation" could not be a test for deciding whether a trademark had become a common descriptive name of a product or service, and therefore not entitled to protection.

● Provided that the legislation should not provide a basis for reopening any final judgment in a case when the judgment was entered prior to the date of enactment.

State Justice Institute

● Established a private, non-profit corporation, the State Justice Institute, to help improve judicial administration in state court systems.

● Established an 11-member board of directors appointed by the president and confirmed by the Senate, and provided that the board include six judges, one state court administrator and four members from the public sector. No more than two of the public-sector directors could be of the same political party.

● Authorized the institute to award grants and enter into contracts to conduct research and demonstration projects, to serve as a clearinghouse for information and participate in joint projects with other agencies.

● Barred the institute from participating in litigation unless the institute was a party, from interfering with the operations of any state judicial system, and from lobbying of any kind.

● Barred institute funds and personnel from involvement in political party activities, campaigns of any candidate, or campaigns for ballot initiatives or referendums.

● Authorized $13 million for fiscal 1986, $15 million for fiscal 1987 and $15 million for fiscal 1988.

Computer Chips

● Created a new chapter of Title 17 of the U.S. Code (the copyright title) to protect semiconductor chips from unauthorized copying.

● Provided 10 years of copyright-style protection for "mask works fixed in a semiconductor chip."

● Defined a mask work as a series of related images fixed or encoded on a piece of semiconductor material, such as silicon, that were arranged in a pattern to perform a specific function.

● Provided that a mask work was considered "fixed" when it was part of an actual semiconductor chip product, such as a computer, not just a plan or drawing of such product. The definition was worded so that a mask work could also be considered to be fixed when it was put on a magnetic tape that could be reproduced.

● Allowed the owner of a mask work to apply to the Register of Copyrights for registration of a claim of protection, and directed the register to issue a certificate of registration if he determined that the mask work met the specified requirements.

● Allowed an owner of a mask work to seek federal district court review of a refusal to register a mask work, provided the appeal was filed within 60 days of the refusal.

● Provided that a mask work was entitled to protection if the owner was a national or domiciliary of the United States, a national or domiciliary or sovereign authority of a foreign nation that was a party to a treaty affording protection to mask works to which the United States was also a party, or a stateless person, wherever that person was domiciled.

● Provided protection for a mask work that was first "commercially exploited" in the United States. "Commercially exploited" was defined to mean the distribution to the public of a semiconductor chip product embodying the mask work in question. The term covered an offer to sell or transfer such a product only when the offer was in writing and occurred after the mask work was "fixed" in the semiconductor chip product.

● Provided protection for mask works that came within the scope of a presidential proclamation covering protection afforded to mask works by foreign nations.

● Barred protection for mask works that were not original or consisted of designs that were staple, commonplace, or familiar in the semiconductor industry, or that were combinations of designs in a manner not considered as a whole to be original.

● Provided the owner of a mask work protection for 10 years, beginning on the date on which the mask work was registered or first commercially exploited anywhere in the world, whichever occurred first.

● Granted the owner of a mask work exclusive rights to reproduce the mask work by optical, electronic or any other means, to import or distribute a semiconductor chip product embodying the mask work, and to have another person reproduce, import or distribute such product.

● Allowed "reverse engineering" of protected mask works, which covered the reproduction of the mask work "solely" for the purpose of teaching, analyzing or evaluating the concepts or techniques embodied in the mask work or its components.

● Protected an innocent purchaser of a pirated semiconductor chip product from liability for using the chip but required the user to pay a "reasonable royalty" on each unit of the infringing product that the purchaser imported or distributed after being notified that the mask work involved was protected.

● Made liable for infringement any person who violated any exclusive rights of the owner of a protected mask work.

● Entitled the owner of a registered mask work to file a civil action for infringement.

● Entitled the owner of a mask work that was denied protection to file a suit for infringement under specified circumstances and gave the Register of Copyrights the discretion to join the suit on the issue of whether the mask work was eligible for protection.

● Gave the secretary of the Treasury and the U.S. Postal Service authority to write regulations concerning the exclusion of products from the United States that might infringe on a protected mask work.

● Gave federal district courts the authority, in an infringement suit, to grant temporary restraining orders and permanent injunctions to restrain infringement of a mask work owner's exclusive rights.

● Allowed an owner who prevails in an infringement suit to be awarded actual damages and the infringer's profits attributable to the infringement under terms specified in the legislation.

● Allowed a prevailing mask work owner to elect to receive a flat damage award covering all infringements of one mask work instead of actual damages and profits. The award could not be greater than $250,000.

● Required any action for infringement to be initiated within three years after the claim arises.

● Authorized a judge, while an action was pending, to impound any products, drawings or tapes that were claimed to have been made, imported or used in violation of the mask work owner's exclusive rights.

● Authorized a judge, as part of a final judgment, to order the destruction of any infringing semiconductor chip products.

● Barred a civil action for infringement of a mask work until 60 days after enactment of the law.

● Provided protection for a mask work first commercially exploited on or after July 1, 1983, and before the date of enactment, if a claim of protection was registered with the Copyright Office before July 1, 1985.

● Authorized the secretary of commerce to provide protection for mask works of nationals, domiciliaries and sovereign authorities of a foreign nation under specified conditions set out in the legislation.

Civil Case Priorities

● Deleted from federal law about 80 provisions granting expedited U.S. court treatment for specified types of civil cases.

● Retained requirements for expedited treatment of cases involving personal liberty, such as a *habeas corpus* claim that one was imprisoned in violation of the Constitution; cases involving requests for a temporary restraining order or preliminary injunction; or cases where "good cause" had been shown. Good cause would be shown when a claimant could demonstrate that the factual setting of the case made clear that a right under the Constitution or a federal statute would be maintained through prompt judicial action.

Court Sites

● Created three new places for holding federal courts, realigned the boundaries of divisions in three federal districts and changed the place of holding court in one federal district.

● Made technical corrections in a 1982 law creating a U.S. Court of Appeals for the Federal Circuit, primarily to handle appeals in patent cases. *(1982 Almanac p. 396)*

Research and Patent Policy

● Put new limits on a 1980 law that allowed small business, universities and non-profit organizations to retain the title to patents resulting from federally funded research.

The bill also modified a 1980 patent law (PL 96-517) that was designed to establish a uniform policy for inventions arising from contracts between the government and small businesses or non-profit organizations, including universities. *(1980 Almanac p. 405)*

● Allowed federal agencies to limit patent ownership by

small business or non-profit organizations that were not located or did not have a place of business in the United States.

• Repealed a provision in the 1980 law allowing government agencies to retain ownership of inventions produced by non-profit organizations operating government-owned laboratories or facilities.

• Provided specific authority for the Energy Department to own inventions relating to its naval nuclear propulsion or weapons-related programs made by the non-profit operators of its government-owned labs.

• Imposed a limit on the amount of royalties a contract operator of a government-owned laboratory could retain after paying patent administrative expenses and a share of the royalties to the inventor. The limit was based upon 5 percent of the annual budget of the laboratory, but contained certain incentive provisions aimed at stimulating continued efforts to transfer technology if and when royalties reached the 5 percent cap.

• Removed a provision in the 1980 law that limited the time period for which non-profit organizations could grant exclusive licenses without approval of the funding agency.

• Consolidated in the Commerce Department all authority to issue regulations under the 1980 law.

• Codified invention-reporting and ownership-election procedures established administratively by the Office of Management and Budget (OMB). These were to expire Feb. 1, 1985.

Record Rentals/Copyright

In an effort to curb unauthorized taping, Congress Sept. 21 cleared a bill (S 32) to bar commercial rentals of most phonograph records unless the copyright owner had granted permission.

The measure, which President Reagan signed Oct. 4 (PL 98-450), granted exceptions for non-profit libraries and educational institutions.

Final action came when the Senate by voice vote accepted House amendments to the bill.

The House had passed its version of the legislation (HR 5938 — H Rept 98-987) Sept. 11. The Senate originally had passed S 32 in 1983. *(1983 Almanac p. 313)*

Provisions

As cleared by Congress, S 32 modified the "first sale" doctrine, which terminated some rights of copyright owners at the point of the first sale at the retail or wholesale level.

The bill barred rentals of "non-dramatic" musical recordings unless the record maker granted a licensed distributor the right to rent its records and was paid a special royalty fee each time a record was rented. Songwriters who held a copyright on the music would share proportionally in any royalties.

The bill was spurred by concerns among songwriters and record companies that the record rental market — which currently consisted of about 200 outlets — was growing, damaging record sales. These copyright holders contended that records were rented almost exclusively to tape. In testimony before Congress, they noted that some record rental outlets included a blank tape in the price for renting a record.

S 32 provided only civil remedies for violating the new anti-rental provision. The Senate version had provided

criminal penalties as well, but senators yielded on that point.

Sen. Charles McC. Mathias Jr., R-Md., sponsor of the Senate bill, told the Senate that the bar to criminal penalties applied only to the "mere unauthorized rental or lending of copyrighted sound recordings," and not to egregious "independent violations" of the copyright laws.

"Thus," he said, "to take a dramatic example, one whose role in a massive record piracy conspiracy consisted of lending records to the operation, knowing that they would be used as masters to create thousands of illegal copies, would not be exempt from criminal liability merely because his or her activity consisted of lending the recordings to his or her confederates."

The ban on record rentals did not apply to the existing inventory of stores now in business.

The prohibition would lapse in five years unless renewed by Congress. This was the position of the House. The Senate bill called for a permanent ban on unauthorized rentals.

Mathias said the Senate believed permanent legislation was appropriate, but was willing to yield because "this disagreement should not hold up enactment of this bill."

However, the senator said that no precedent had been set for "sunset" provisions in other copyright legislation.

Municipal Antitrust Shield

Congress Oct. 11 cleared a bill (HR 6027 — PL 98-544) to protect local governments from monetary damage awards in antitrust suits.

Courts still could grant injunctions against cities and counties ordering them to stop anti-competitive practices.

The bill also restored the authority of the Federal Trade Commission (FTC) to seek injunctions against local governments for alleged anti-competitive practices. A provision in the fiscal 1985 Commerce, Justice, State appropriations law (PL 98-411) that covered the FTC had restricted the agency's authority to bring such suits. *(Story, p. 373)*

HR 6027 cleared when the Senate adopted a conference report on it by voice vote. The House had approved the report hours earlier, 318-0. *(Vote 408, p. 124-H)*

Background

HR 6027 was prompted by a 1982 Supreme Court decision, *Community Communications Inc. v. City of Boulder, Colo.,* that left local governments vulnerable to triple-damage suits.

In that case, the court ruled 5-3 that a Boulder ordinance imposing a three-month moratorium on expansion of cable television systems within the city limits — a period within which the city invited competing systems to enter the market — was not immune from federal antitrust challenges. *(1982 Almanac p. 11-A)*

Warning that the decision opened the way for huge antitrust damage awards against cities and counties, local government officials asked Congress to bar such recoveries.

Senate Judiciary Action

The Senate Judiciary Committee approved its version of the antitrust shield (S 1578) by voice vote June 14 and formally reported the measure (S Rept 98-593) a day later.

S 1578, sponsored by Judiciary Committee Chairman Strom Thurmond, R-S.C., provided that local governments could not be sued for triple damages. However, the government still could file a lawsuit against a local entity seeking an injunction against anti-competitive activity.

The bill granted similar protection to private parties, such as ambulance companies, when they were acting under the direction of local governments.

The Senate bill was silent on the issue of whether it was applicable to antitrust cases already proceeding through the courts. There were differences of opinion on what that silence meant. Some lawyers said retroactive coverage was implied, while others said the issue would be handled case by case, based on the equities of the litigation in question.

House Judiciary Committee

The House Judiciary Committee approved HR 6027 on Aug. 1 and reported it Aug. 8 (H Rept 98-965).

The bill, approved by voice vote, protected municipalities from monetary damages in antitrust cases but still allowed courts to grant injunctions against cities and counties ordering them to stop anti-competitive practices.

After lengthy debate, the committee by 17-14 adopted an amendment by Henry J. Hyde, R-Ill., that in effect barred damage recoveries in pending antitrust cases against municipalities. In some of these cases, plaintiffs had been awarded millions of dollars, although the litigation was still in the appeals process.

While the original bill provided retroactive immunity against treble damages, the usual penalty for antitrust violations, it did allow plaintiffs in cases pending as of July 1, 1984, to collect actual damages. The Hyde amendment struck this language, leaving the bill silent on pending cases.

Jack Brooks, D-Texas, offered an amendment to allow antitrust plaintiffs to collect actual damages against municipalities. But his proposal was rejected by voice vote.

In addition to granting municipalities immunity from damage awards, the Senate bill also gave such immunity to third parties, such as ambulance companies, operating under the direction of local governments. The House committee accepted an amendment by Don Edwards, D-Calif., to include a similar provision in HR 6027.

The committee rejected, by voice vote, an amendment by Harold S. Sawyer, R-Mich., that would have allowed either a prevailing defendant or a prevailing plaintiff to collect attorneys' fees in municipal antitrust suits. Under current law, which would be carried forward in HR 6027, only a prevailing plaintiff could collect attorneys' fees.

House, Senate Floor Action

The House passed HR 6027 Aug. 8 by a 414-5 vote. *(Vote 318, p. 96-H)*

The Senate amended the measure Oct. 4 and returned it to the House.

The House Oct. 9 tried to suspend the rules to further amend and pass the bill, a step requiring a two-thirds majority. The vote was 220-160, 34 short of the 254 required. *(Vote 401, p. 122-H)*

Stymied in that effort, the House then agreed Oct. 10 to a conference with the Senate, and negotiators reached an accord later that day (H Rept 98-1158).

Conference: Pending-Case Issue

Snagging the bill was the issue of whether and how it should apply to pending cases. Since the *Boulder* ruling, some 200 antitrust suits had been filed against localities. In

one case, a jury awarded a developer $28 million in damages against two Illinois local governments, Lake County and Grays Lake Village. The developer contended that local bans on new sewer hookups were anti-competitive and prevented him from building new housing.

HR 6027 was originally silent on the subject of pending cases. But in later versions of the legislation, each chamber barred retroactive application except in narrow circumstances. There were differences in the House and Senate versions, however, that required a conference.

Conferees met Oct. 10 in a raucous two-hour session to iron out their differences. They agreed on compromise language that made the legislation generally inapplicable to pending cases. But the bar to a damage award could be applied if a defendant government could convince a judge that "in light of all the circumstances," it would be unfair not to protect the government from paying damages.

The legislation specified that a jury verdict, a district court judgment or "any stage of litigation" subsequent to a verdict or judgment would be considered presumptive evidence that the bill was inapplicable to a pending case.

A local government could seek to overcome this evidence, but a statement of managers accompanying the conference report stated that if a case had gone beyond a jury verdict or court judgment, a government would need "compelling equities" on its side to justify barring a damage award.

Proponents of retroactive application of the bill claimed that it would be unfair to leave 200 local governments vulnerable to triple-damage awards. They noted that prior to the *Boulder* ruling, no local government ever had been sued for damages, and that once HR 6027 was enacted, none could be.

Opponents said that laws rarely, if ever, were made retroactive, and that to do so would set a bad precedent. ∎

Joint Research Ventures

Congress Oct. 1 cleared for the president a bill (S 1841 — PL 98-462) easing antitrust obstacles for companies that cooperated in joint research and development ventures.

The measure, which enjoyed strong support from the Reagan administration, was designed to encourage technological innovation. During hearings in 1983, industry representatives told the House and Senate Judiciary committees that there was wasteful duplication of research in some fields because companies feared they would run afoul of the antitrust laws if they pooled their efforts.

Among other things, the legislation made clear that it was not an automatic antitrust violation if two or more companies combined for specified research purposes. If such a joint venture were challenged, a court would apply a "rule of reason" in determining whether there was an antitrust violation, weighing the venture's effects on competition.

Final action on S 1841 came when the House, by voice vote, adopted the conference report on the measure (H Rept 98-1044). The Senate approved the conference report Sept. 26, also by voice vote.

Provisions

As cleared by Congress, S 1841 included the following major provisions:

● Required participants in a joint venture to report their

identities and the objectives of their research to the attorney general and the Federal Trade Commission (FTC) within 90 days of setting up such a venture.

● Required the attorney general or the FTC to publish within 30 days a notice in the *Federal Register* of the parties involved and, "in general terms, the area of planned activity."

● Provided that once such notice was filed, the parties were protected against triple damages in any antitrust suit that might be filed challenging the venture. Only actual damages could be awarded if violations were found.

● Directed a court to use the "rule of reason" in determining whether a venture was anti-competitive. The bill stated that factors to be considered included the "effects on competition in properly defined, relevant markets and development markets."

● Provided attorneys' fees to defendants in a suit challenging a joint venture if the judge determined the plaintiff's claim or conduct was "frivolous, unreasonable, without foundation, or in bad faith."

● Provided attorneys' fees to a plaintiff who "substantially" prevailed on a particular claim. The award would be the cost "attributable to such claim."

● Allowed a judge to offset any award of attorneys' fees for one claim in a lawsuit with a deduction for another claim determined to be frivolous or brought in bad faith.

Legislative History

The House Judiciary Committee moved first on the joint research legislation, approving its version (HR 5041) on March 20 and reporting it (H Rept 98-656) on April 6.

Judiciary Chairman Peter W. Rodino Jr., D-N.J., said that there was "little evidence to support the notion that our antitrust laws actually prevent formation of R&D joint ventures. But business apprehension about potential antitrust violations can hinder such activity."

The House passed HR 5041 by 417-0 on May 1. *(Vote 95, p. 34-H)*

On March 22, the Senate Judiciary Committee approved S 1841, which was formally reported (S Rept 98-427) on May 3. The legislation was passed 97-0 by the full Senate on July 31. *(Vote 194, p. 34-S)*

Following a conference to iron out minor differences between the two bills, the Senate agreed to the conference report (H Rept 98-1044) on Sept. 26 and the House followed suit Oct. 1, sending S 1841 to President Reagan. ■

President Vetoes Fee Bill

President Reagan Nov. 8 pocket-vetoed a bill (HR 5479) making permanent a 1980 law that allowed the award of attorneys' fees to individuals and small businesses that prevailed in legal disputes with the government.

As under current law, the government would not have had to pay attorneys' fees if it proved that its position was "substantially justified."

Congress cleared the bill Oct. 11. Final action came when the Senate by voice vote accepted a compromise version of the bill that had earlier been accepted by the House.

The 1980 law, the "Equal Access to Justice Act" (PL 96-481), expired Oct. 1, and congressional action was required to extend its provisions. *(1980 Almanac p. 550)*

According to the Administrative Office of the U.S. Courts, a total of $2.47 million was paid out in fiscal 1982

and 1983 in 64 court cases. In fiscal 1983, awards totaling $35,934 were made in eight administrative proceedings.

Reagan Veto Message

Reagan said that although he supported the thrust of the bill, he objected to a provision requiring the government to justify an agency's underlying action in addition to its position during administrative or court litigation. "In effect," the president said, "every step of the agency decision-making process, at whatever level, could become the subject of litigation discovery." *(Veto text, p. 28-E)*

Reagan also objected to a provision of HR 5479 requiring the federal government to pay interest on any awarded attorneys' fees that had not actually been paid within 60 days of the award. This provision, he said, "would give lawyers who have received awards under the act more favorable treatment than any other group entitled to interest payments from the United States."

The president said he would make "the permanent and retroactive reauthorization of the act a high legislative priority of the administration in the next Congress."

In the meantime, he said, he was issuing a memorandum to all agency heads urging them to ensure that agency positions in litigation continued to be substantially justified.

Bill's Provisions

As cleared by Congress, HR 5479 included these major provisions.:

● Made permanent the 1980 law.

● Added local government units to the category of parties potentially entitled to seek attorneys' fees in adversary adjudications involving the federal government.

● Restricted eligibility for awards to individuals whose net worth did not exceed $2 million at the time the adversary adjudication was initiated, and to businesses or local government units with a net worth of $7 million or less and a total work force of 500 or fewer employees. The old limits had been $1 million net worth for individuals and $5 million for businesses.

● Specified that no award of attorneys' fees or other expenses could be made until the underlying merits of the case had been finally determined and court appeals of that ruling had been exhausted.

● Permitted the U.S. government, as well as the opposing party, to appeal an attorneys' fee award. Under current law, only the non-federal party could appeal.

● Required payment of interest by the government to any prevailing party who did not receive complete payment of attorneys' fees and other expenses within 60 days after final award of such fees and expenses.

● Made clear that the government's position included the "underlying action" that led to the adversary proceeding, and not simply the government's conduct on a particular issue in the case while in court.

House Committee, Floor Action

The House Judiciary Committee approved HR 5479 May 22 but did not formally report it (H Rept 98-992) until Sept. 6.

The measure was approved by voice vote after the committee rejected an amendment by Bruce A. Morrison, D-Conn., that sought to permit the award of attorneys' fees to individuals who prevailed in administrative hearings in Social Security cases.

Social Security Cases

The original law exempted the Social Security Administration from being sued for attorneys' fees in an administrative proceeding, but allowed fee recovery for Social Security cases that went into federal court.

Morrison's amendment would have applied the bill to administrative proceedings. Morrison noted that Social Security and Supplemental Security Income recipients who challenged the agency had a better than 50 percent success rate. That record, Morrison said, "indicates substantial failure on the part of the secretary to exercise sufficient care when making initial determinations. Availability of [attorneys' fees] will provide an incentive to the secretary to take whatever steps are necessary to improve the initial process for determining eligibility in these cases."

But Robert W. Kastenmeier, D-Wis., chief sponsor of the bill, urged defeat of the amendment. He told Morrison that House Ways and Means Committee members said they would assert jurisdiction over the bill if the amendment was adopted, and probably would delay its consideration by the full House.

Morrison urged his colleagues to disregard the Ways and Means threat, adopt his amendment and negotiate with the other committee to move the bill. However, his amendment failed on a 10-11 vote.

The debate over the amendment was just the latest display of congressional concern about the Social Security system's administrative procedures. The day the Judiciary Committee voted, the Senate joined the House in approving a bill (HR 3755) aimed at making it harder for the Reagan administration to throw beneficiaries off the Social Security disability rolls. *(Story, p. 160)*

Other Amendments

By voice vote, the committee adopted an amendment of Hamilton Fish Jr., R-N.Y., to clarify that local governments could be eligible under the bill to receive an award of attorneys' fees. The Fish amendment defined a local government to include, among other things, cities, counties, villages, Indian tribes, school districts and sewer districts. However, these entities would have to meet eligibility standards set out in the original law requiring a net worth of no more than $5 million and a maximum of 500 employees.

By voice vote, the committee adopted an amendment by Thomas N. Kindness, R-Ohio, to give the government a right to appeal any attorneys' fee award. Currently, the law allowed only the non-government party to appeal. The bill as originally drafted gave the government a discretionary appeal, but Kindness said the government should have automatic right to appeal.

The House passed HR 5479 on Sept. 11, without amendment. The measure was approved by voice vote, under suspension of the rules.

Senate Committee, Floor Action

The Senate Judiciary Committee approved its version (S 919) of the fee bill by voice vote June 7 and reported it to the full Senate Aug. 8 (S Rept 98-586).

Unlike the House measure, S 919 included a provision to allow attorneys' fees to be awarded in administrative proceedings involving Social Security cases. However, this provision was to expire after three years unless renewed by Congress.

The Senate bill had been delayed for weeks because of a fight over unrelated provisions that would have allowed appeals from administrative actions to be heard in federal courts all over the country instead of only in Washington D.C., as current law required.

Sen. Alan K. Simpson, R-Wyo., chief proponent of the proposal, wanted to attach it to S 919. But after encountering opposition, he agreed June 7 to let the matter come to the floor as a separate measure.

The provisions of S 919 were substituted for the text of HR 5479 when that bill reached the Senate floor Oct. 4, and a week later the two chambers approved the final, compromise version of the legislation. ∎

Mandatory Jurisdiction Bill

By voice vote Sept. 11, the House passed legislation designed to lighten the workload of the Supreme Court. But the measure (HR 5644) died in the Senate.

The bill would have wiped out the Supreme Court's "mandatory" jurisdiction, a class of cases the court had to review even if the justices dismissed them without fullblown consideration. HR 5644 would have allowed the court to select which of these cases it wanted to hear, just as it did with most other cases.

The House had passed a similar bill in the 97th Congress but that measure, too, died in the Senate. *(1982 Almanac p. 395)*

All nine justices had urged Congress to enact the bill as one means of easing the Supreme Court's workload. The court's caseload peaked in the 1981-82 term, when 5,311 cases were docketed, an increase from 4,781 in the preceding term. Since then, however, the caseload at the court had leveled off. There were 5,079 cases docketed in the 1982-83 term and 5,100 cases in the 1983-84 term that ended July 5.

The cases covered by the bill included appeals of state court rulings involving federal laws, and appeals of rulings involving certain federal agencies. The House Judiciary Committee report on the bill (H Rept 98-986) said there was no reason that important questions of law in these areas could not be handled through the high court's selection of cases on a discretionary basis. ∎

Patent Law Revisions

The Senate Oct. 11 cleared non-controversial patent legislation (HR 6286 — PL 98-622) after dropping sections opposed by the makers of generic drugs.

As cleared, the measure tightened existing law to prevent manufacturers from evading U.S. patent restrictions by making components of a patented product within the United States and then shipping the parts abroad for assembly. To be liable for patent infringement, a company had to supply "all or a substantial part" of the components of a patented invention in such a way as to "actively induce" their combination into the product protected by a patent.

Dropped from the final bill was a provision that would have made liable for patent infringement any company that imported, sold or used within the United States a product made abroad with a process that was patented here. So-called "process patents" were important in the telecommunications, drug and biotechnology industries, among others.

Makers of generic drugs, inexpensive copies of brand-name pharmaceuticals, charged that the provision opened the door to frivolous, time-consuming lawsuits against them by brand-name drug makers seeking to block them from importing bulk pharmaceuticals on which the generic drug industry depended.

Statutory Invention Registration

A second major provision of the bill created a procedure for "statutory invention registration" that offered limited, defensive protection to inventors. The expedited new procedure, which was optional, gave protection against infringement lawsuits claiming that another person was the first with the discovery in question. However, the inventor was given none of the exclusive rights to use or market the item that went with the more traditional form of patent.

Sen. Charles McC. Mathias Jr., R-Md., chief sponsor of the Senate version of the bill (S 1535), said the new procedure was especially well suited for inventors who worked for the government, because in many cases all they needed was "protection from suits for infringement. They are not interested in exclusive rights to the work."

The government currently held some 28,000 patents, and federal agency applications for new ones contributed significantly to the workload of the Patent and Trademark Office. HR 6286 ordered the secretary of commerce to report to Congress annually on the use of the new procedure and any cost savings attributable to it.

The new protection also was available to private inventors. At a hearing on the legislation July 20, 1983, Donald W. Banner, president of the Intellectual Property Owners Inc., testified that many private sector inventors would use the new patent procedure to make public inventions they might otherwise keep private as trade secrets.

The Reagan administration supported the bill. Representatives of the Patent and Trademark Office said the legislation would help ease their workload because a full-fledged patent examination, which sometimes could take years, would not be required under the statutory invention registration procedure.

Patent Interference Proceedings

To improve administrative proceedings in the Patent and Trademark Office of the Department of Commerce, HR 6286 created a new administrative board to handle disputes over who was the first inventor of a given patentable invention. Currently, these "interference" proceedings were conducted by the Board of Patent Interferences. However, this board did not have authority to address all questions that could arise over a patent.

The bill combined the interference board with the Board of Appeals of the Patent and Trademark Office, a unit that currently could decide whether a product or process was patentable but could not decide which inventor had priority. The new entity could decide both questions.

Employed Inventors

HR 6286 also created a National Commission on Innovation and Productivity to study the rights of inventors employed by government and private industry. A recurring issue was who received compensation for new creations — the employee who worked on the invention, or the company or individual employing him.

The commission also was to seek to determine why there had been a decline in the number of patents issued to U.S. inventors while there was an increase in the percentage of patents issued to foreign inventors.

Legislative History

HR 6286 went to the House floor Oct. 1 without ever receiving full Judiciary Committee approval, although this was done with the approval of committee Chairman Peter W. Rodino Jr., D-N.J.

The House approved the measure by voice vote.

In the Senate, the Judiciary Committee reported S 1535 on Oct. 5 (S Rept 98-663).

Final action on HR 6286 came Oct. 11 when the Senate accepted House amendments to a substitute version incorporating most of S 1535 that the Senate had approved earlier in the day. ∎

State Lottery Advertising

By voice vote June 14 the Senate Judiciary Committee approved a bill (S 1876 — S Rept 98-537) to modify an antiquated federal law barring interstate advertising for most lotteries and gaming activities. But the measure advanced no further.

The bill was sponsored by Sen. Paul Laxalt, the Nevada Republican who chaired Judiciary's Criminal Law Subcommittee. The other chief sponsor was Laxalt's home-state colleague, Sen. Chic Hecht, R-Nev.

Under existing law, which was more than 100 years old, it was illegal to broadcast or mail information concerning almost all wagering activities even though such activities were perfectly legal. The only exception was for state-run lotteries, which could be advertised in the state holding the game and in adjacent states that also ran lotteries.

The bill expanded this exception to allow advertising for all wagering enterprises that were authorized, licensed and regulated by the states. Laxalt emphasized that the bill covered only lawful, state-supervised or state conducted activities. The ban on advertising for illegal or unregulated lotteries remained in effect.

Seventeen states and the District of Columbia currently raised funds through lotteries, and voters in four more states — California, Missouri, Oregon and West Virginia — approved lottery initiatives or referendums in the Nov. 6 elections.

State lotteries grossed $5.2 billion in fiscal 1983, a ninefold increase over a decade earlier, and their take was expected to triple in five more years. ∎

Balanced Budget Amendment

Despite pressure from President Reagan and the states, Congress took no action in 1984 on proposals for an amendment to the Constitution requiring a balanced federal budget.

The Senate Judiciary Committee reported such an amendment (S J Res 5 — S Rept 98-628) Sept. 20, but the measure went no further. A companion House proposal (H J Res 243) remained bottled up in the Judiciary Committee, although the Democratic-controlled House — in an election-year maneuver — on Oct. 2 passed a bill requiring the president to submit a balanced budget. The Republican-controlled Senate ignored that measure. *(Story, p. 167)*

State Drive Stalled

Since 1975, 32 states had passed resolutions demanding that Congress convene a constitutional convention to consider a budget amendment. If 34 states had acted, Congress would have been required to call a convention.

But Congress won at least a temporary reprieve through court action in two states. In August and October, respectively, the top state courts in California and Montana declared unconstitutional ballot initiatives aimed at forcing the legislatures in those states to petition for a constitutional convention. In both states, the courts ruled that the U.S. Constitution required conventions to be called at the petition of legislatures, not by voters.

The twin court actions effectively took the steam out of efforts by supporters of a balanced budget amendment to force House and Senate votes on the proposal. Once members were assured that there was no way the tally of state convention calls could reach 34, they proved less than eager to confront the issue.

Convention Procedures

No procedures existed for determining what was a valid state call for a constitutional convention, nor for actually running one. There had been no such convention since the Founding Fathers met to draft the present Constitution.

The Senate Judiciary Committee approved a bill (S 119 — S Rept 98-594) May 17 establishing procedures for holding a constitutional convention. The bill provided that the president pro tempore of the Senate and the Speaker of the House would convene the convention. Delegates would have to adopt convention rules by a three-fifths majority vote.

The same subject was under discussion in the Civil and Constitutional Rights Subcommittee of the House Judiciary Committee, although no legislation moved.

Subcommittee Chairman Don Edwards, D-Calif., wrote Judiciary Chairman Peter W. Rodino Jr., D-N.J., July 17 to tell him that the panel had begun to collect information on a constitutional convention.

Constitutional Convention Requests

Following is a list of the states that had called for a constitutional convention to consider an amendment requiring a balanced U.S. budget.

Alabama	Nebraska
Alaska	Nevada
Arizona	New Hampshire
Arkansas	New Mexico
Colorado	North Carolina
Delaware	North Dakota
Florida	Oklahoma
Georgia	Oregon
Idaho	Pennsylvania
Indiana	South Carolina
Iowa	South Dakota
Kansas	Tennessee
Louisiana	Texas
Maryland	Utah
Mississippi	Virginia
Missouri	Wyoming

Many members believed a constitutional convention would be disastrous and could range far beyond the balanced budget issue to other areas such as abortion and school busing. Sen. Orrin G. Hatch, R-Utah, who sponsored S 119, said that the bill ensured that a convention would be limited to a specific subject. The National Taxpayers Union, which had been pushing for a constitutional convention on the budget issue, agreed.

But the Citizens to Protect the Constitution, a private, non-partisan organization formed around the budget issue, maintained that a constitutional convention would be calamitous. "Any attempt by Congress, the courts or the executive branch to limit a constitutional convention to a pre-arranged agenda would be problematical at best, and probably unenforceable," said the committee's statement of principles. "Thus the risk of a 'runaway' convention, which would seek to impose its own political, social and economic agenda, is great indeed."

Old Issue

A proposed balanced budget amendment had been floating around Congress for at least a decade, but while the Democrats controlled both chambers, it remained buried in the Judiciary committees.

When the Republicans took over the Senate in January 1981, all that changed. Senate Judiciary Chairman Strom Thurmond, R-S.C., and Hatch, chairman of the Constitution Subcommittee, made the proposal a priority item. In August 1982, a proposed constitutional amendment passed the Senate by a vote of 69-31, two votes more than the required two-thirds.

Much of the Senate debate focused on whether the president should be required to submit a balanced budget to Congress. A Democratic amendment to include such a requirement was rejected.

The House considered a balanced budget measure Oct. 1, 1982, after supporters gathered 218 signatures on a discharge petition forcing the proposal out of the Judiciary Committee. The amendment failed 236-187, 46 short of the necessary two-thirds. *(1982 Almanac p. 391)*

The proposals before the House and Senate Judiciary Committees in 1984 were nearly identical to the legislation considered in 1982. In general, they required Congress to adopt a balanced federal budget every year unless a three-fifths majority voted to allow a deficit, or unless there was a declaration of war in effect. ∎

Legal Services Corporation

For the first time since taking office, President Reagan put before the Senate a full slate of proposed directors for the Legal Services Corporation (LSC). But none of the nominees was confirmed, so Reagan waited until Congress adjourned and then gave them all recess appointments.

From December 1981 through December 1984, Reagan made a total of 30 recess appointments to the LSC board. Not a single board member was confirmed, but those given recess appointments were able to sit until the end of the session of Congress following their appointments.

Throughout his first term, Reagan sought to abolish the LSC, which was established in 1974 to fund civil legal services for the poor. Congress consistently refused to go along, although it did reduce LSC funding and imposed new restrictions on the corporation's activities. *(Background, 1983 Almanac p. 476)*

The corporation had to scale back operations since 1981, largely because its budget was reduced. In fiscal 1981, its appropriation was $321 million. Its funding was cut to $241 million in fiscal 1982 and 1983, while the fiscal 1984 Commerce, Justice, State appropriations bill (PL 98-166) set the corporation's funding at $275 million. *(1983 Almanac p. 322)*

For fiscal 1985, Congress voted $305 million for the LSC as part of the Commerce, Justice, State appropriations bill (HR 5712 — PL 98-411). *(Story, p. 373)*

The 1984 Appointments

On May 2, the Senate Labor and Human Resources Committee recommended confirmation of 10 of Reagan's 11 nominees to the LSC.

The final nomination, that of Michael B. Wallace, a Mississippi lawyer who formerly was an aide to House Minority Whip Trent Lott, R-Miss., was sent to the Senate without recommendation.

The committee had tied 9-9 on a motion to approve the nomination, which meant that the motion failed. But Chairman Orrin G. Hatch, R-Utah, then asked the panel to send Wallace's name to the full Senate without recommendation as a courtesy to Reagan.

Jennings Randolph, D-W.Va., who had voted against Wallace initially, switched his vote on the second tally. He said he agreed that the president deserved a vote on Wallace, given the committee deadlock. "But I shall vote against this nominee in the Senate," Randolph declared.

Controversy Over Nominees

Wallace's nomination was controversial because of work he did as an aide to Lott in 1981-83. During that time, Wallace took an active role in opposing key elements of a bill to extend and strengthen enforcement sections of the 1965 Voting Rights Act. In addition, congressional sources said that Wallace and Lott encouraged the administration to change a longstanding Internal Revenue Service policy of denying tax exemptions to private schools that practiced racial discrimination. The administration's attempt to do so was repudiated by the Supreme Court in 1983. *(1983 Almanac p. 10-A)*

"I think this is a dreadful nomination," said Sen. Thomas F. Eagleton, D-Mo. "It is totally out of sympathy with the role, scope and purpose of the Legal Services Corporation."

Hatch defended the nominee, saying that Wallace had "intellectual disagreements" with some people on civil rights matters but was "a person who feels deeply on some of these issues."

The nomination of attorney LeaAnne Bernstein, an aide to LSC President Donald P. Bogard, also was controversial but was approved 10-8.

Eagleton contended that Bernstein was an "activist" within the LSC and not simply a clerical aide to Bogard. He said she helped develop a strategy to hold national board meetings in far-off places, such as Window Rock, Ariz., that discouraged public participation at the meetings.

One of the other nominees, lawyer Robert A. Valois of Raleigh, N.C., had stirred controversy during confirmation hearings in 1983 because of his labor law activities. Critics charged that he helped companies develop "union-busting" strategies, but he denied the charge.

Valois was approved by voice vote along with eight other nominees: William C. Durant III, a Detroit lawyer; Claude G. Swafford, a lawyer from South Pittsburg, Tenn., who was active in Republican Party politics; Pepe J. Mendez, a Denver lawyer who worked in Reagan's 1980 campaign; Paul Eaglin, a Fayetteville, N.C., lawyer who worked for two years as a legal aid attorney; Thomas F. Smegal Jr., a San Francisco attorney with ties to the Republican Party; Basile J. Uddo, a law professor at New Orleans' Loyola Law School and an anti-abortion activist; Lorain Miller of Detroit; and Hortencia Benavidez of El Paso.

On Nov. 23, after the 98th Congress had adjourned, Reagan used his recess appointment power to put all 11 of his nominees on the LSC board. They could serve until the end of the 1985 session. ∎

Congress Revamps Bankruptcy Laws, Courts

Congress June 29 cleared legislation that made significant changes in U.S. bankruptcy laws and also sought to put the nation's bankruptcy courts back on a sound legal footing. The action came two years and one day after the Supreme Court had invalidated a bankruptcy court structure established in a 1978 law.

President Reagan signed the new bankruptcy bill into law July 10 (HR 5174 — PL 98-353).

Final congressional action on HR 5174 came when first the House and then the Senate adopted a conference report (H Rept 98-882) on the bill. The House passed the measure March 21, while the Senate approved an amended version June 19.

In addition to restructuring the bankruptcy courts, HR 5174 made a number of substantive changes in bankruptcy law.

It gave labor contracts higher standing than other creditors when ailing companies sought relief in bankruptcy; made it more difficult for individuals to declare bankruptcy and escape their debts; granted priority to grain farmers and fishermen in disputes over bankrupt grain elevators and fish processing plants; gave shopping centers more control over the disposal of a bankrupt tenant's lease; and barred discharge through bankruptcy of debts incurred as a result of drunken driving.

The bill also authorized the president to appoint 85 new federal district and appeals court judges, but specified that no more than 40 could be appointed prior to Jan. 21, 1985. *(Reagan judicial appointments, p. 243)*

Final Provisions

As cleared by Congress, HR 5174 included the following provisions:

Bankruptcy Courts

● Gave U.S. district courts original jurisdiction over all bankruptcy proceedings arising under or related to Title 11 of the U.S. Code (bankruptcy law).

● Allowed a district court judge "in the interests of justice" or out of "respect for state law" to abstain from hearing a bankruptcy proceeding or one related to a bankruptcy case when that case involved state law.

● Required a federal judge to abstain, upon a motion by a party to a bankruptcy proceeding based on a state law claim, if the judge determined that the case could be "commenced and timely adjudicated" in state courts. No federal court review was available on the abstention decision.

● Retained current law on the venue of bankruptcy proceedings.

● Authorized the regional federal appeals courts to appoint bankruptcy judges for each of the 93 federal judicial districts, with a total of 232 such judges to be designated. The judges, who were considered adjuncts of the district courts, were given 14-year terms.

● Allowed bankruptcy judges to be transferred temporarily to judicial districts other than their own.

● Authorized the district judges to refer to bankruptcy judges all proceedings arising under or related to a case stemming from Title 11.

● Authorized bankruptcy judges to hear and determine all cases under Title 11 and all "core proceedings," as defined in the law, under Title 11.

● Defined core proceedings to include administration of estates, allowance or disallowance of claims against an estate, property exemptions of the estate, counterclaims against an estate, orders for obtaining credit, orders to turn over property of the state, motions to terminate, annul or modify automatic stays that prevented a creditor from closing out a transaction with the debtor, determining the priority and validity of liens, confirmation of reorganization plans, and other proceedings affecting the liquidation of assets.

● Authorized the bankruptcy judge to determine whether a particular proceeding was a "core proceeding."

● Required a district court judge to order that a personal injury or wrongful death claim related to Title 11 be tried in the federal district court in which the bankruptcy case was pending or in the district court in the district in which the claim arose.

● Allowed a bankruptcy judge to hear a proceeding that was not a "core proceeding." In such a case, the bankruptcy judge would submit proposed findings of fact and conclusions of law to the district judge, who would make the final decision based on the bankruptcy judge's findings. Any party could request a new hearing on specified issues before the district judge.

● Allowed the district court judge, with the consent of the parties, to refer a proceeding related to a case under Title 11 to a bankruptcy judge, subject to district court review.

● Authorized the district court to withdraw, in whole or in part, any case or proceeding referred to a bankruptcy judge on its own motion or on the timely motion of any party. The district judge must withdraw a proceeding from bankruptcy court if the judge determined that resolution of the proceeding required consideration of both Title 11 and other federal laws regulating organizations or activities affecting interstate commerce.

● Authorized appeals in the district court of final decrees and certain specified interim orders of bankruptcy judges. Authorized, in lieu of district court appeals, appeals to a special appellate panel of bankruptcy judges. Such panels would be established by the judicial councils of the regional federal circuits.

● Provided that the salary of a bankruptcy judge in effect on June 27, 1984, $66,100 per year, remain in effect until changed by Congress

● Specified that the term of office of any bankruptcy judge serving on June 27, 1984, be extended until this bill was signed into law despite Congress' failure to act before the June 27 deadline that ended the transitional phase of the bankruptcy system established April 1, 1979.

● Expressed the "sense of Congress" that the regional appeals courts should consider appointing to full 14-year terms the individuals serving as bankruptcy judges at the time of enactment.

Federal Judgeships

● Authorized a total of 24 new federal appeals court judgeships.

● Provided that no more than 11 appeals court judgeships could be filled before Jan. 21, 1985 — one day after the inauguration of the president elected Nov. 6, 1984.

● Authorized a total of 61 new U.S. district court judgeships.

● Provided that no more than 29 district court judgeships could be filled prior to Jan. 21, 1985.

Consumer Bankruptcies

● Allowed a judge to dismiss a consumer bankruptcy petition if the judge determined that granting the request would result in a "substantial abuse" of the bankruptcy code.

● Required that the judge make such a ruling on his own and not at the request or suggestion of any party.

● Allowed a bankruptcy judge to consider a debtor's current income and expenditures in determining whether an alternative to bankruptcy was feasible. (Under existing law, only assets and liabilities, not income, could be considered.)

● Required that a debtor filing for bankruptcy be told what options existed for resolving his financial problems.

● Barred a debtor from discharging debts owed to a single creditor and aggregating more than $500 for "luxury goods," as defined in the law; services incurred on or within 40 days before an order for relief; or cash advances aggregating more than $1,000 that were extensions of consumer credit under an open-end credit plan obtained 20 days before an order for relief.

● Barred a private employer from terminating the employment of or discriminating against an individual who was or had been a debtor or gone bankrupt, or who was "associated with" a debtor or bankrupt person.

Grain Elevator Bankruptcies

● Required bankruptcy judges, upon request in a case involving grain storage facilities, to set up a timetable for disposing of grain stored there and the proceeds from it.

● Required the court to distribute the grain or proceeds from it first to producers who had stored their grain in such a facility pursuant to a contract.

● Mandated the distribution of grain within 120 days of the bankruptcy filing except when special circumstances required more time.

● Authorized a judge to grant a lien against the assets of elevators to farmers who had sold grain to the elevator but had not received payment at the time of the bankruptcy filing.

● Provided the same expedited proceedings and distribution to fishermen who sold their fish to processors who subsequently went bankrupt.

● Required the judge, in grain cases, to allow state or federal agencies with responsibility of liquidating farm pro duce storage facilities to participate in the distribution process.

Shopping Center Bankruptcies

● Set a time limit of 60 days for a trustee for a bankrupt shopping center tenant to assume or reject the shopping center lease. A judge could extend the time under certain circumstances.

● Required the debtor's trustee "timely" to pay the rent and any other charges owed the shopping center owner, although the court could grant up to 60 days for payment of obligations.

● Required the trustee, when assigning the lease to another party, to conform with requirements in the lease pertaining to such things as the use of the property.

Drunken Driving/Bankruptcy

● Barred the discharge in bankruptcy of debts incurred as the result of drunken driving. (Under current law, such a debt was dischargeable unless it resulted from "willful and malicious injury" to person or property. In most states, drunken driving was considered merely negligent conduct, not willful and malicious.)

Referees' Salaries

● Corrected errors in the 1978 bankruptcy reform act pertaining to payment of expenses from each case to help cover costs of operating the bankruptcy system.

Repurchase Agreements

● Established new procedures designed to protect those who deal in "repurchase agreements," which are a principal means of financing U.S. government securities and money market instruments. A repurchase agreement is a transfer of a financial instrument — often government securities — by one party to another for payment, with a simultaneous agreement by the second party to transfer the instrument back to the first party on demand or on a date certain for payment that reflects a rate of interest set by the parties.

● Expanded the definition of repurchase agreement to clarify the financial instruments covered and added a new definition of repurchase "participant" to cover those who dealt in repurchase agreements and had an outstanding repurchase agreement with a person 90 days before the person filed for bankruptcy.

● Barred repurchase agreements from the automatic stay provisions of bankruptcy law, which barred a creditor from closing out a transaction with the debtor without court approval.

Timeshares and Bankruptcy

● Revised current bankruptcy law to make clear that timeshare agreements for use of property were to be treated in the same manner as a lease of property. This would mean that if the entity holding the timeshare lease went bankrupt, the tenant would have the right to keep the lease under a reorganization plan or seek damages if the timeshare contract were abrogated by the debtor. (Bankruptcy judges previously had interpreted the law not to cover timeshare agreements in the same manner as property leases.)

Labor Contracts

● Provided that a debtor company or the debtor's trustee could take over or break a collective bargaining agreement only in accordance with this section's provisions.

● Required a debtor company, after filing for bankruptcy but before applying to break its contract, to meet with employee representatives to propose changes in the contract necessary to allow the company's reorganization. The company was required to provide the employee representative with sufficient information to evaluate the proposed contract changes.

● Required the company's representative to bargain in good faith with the employee representative (union) to reach "mutually satisfactory" modifications to the labor contract.

● Allowed a company to file an application to reject (abrogate) the collective bargaining agreement.

● Required the judge to schedule a hearing not later than 14 days after the application was filed, although the time could be extended seven days in special circumstances. All interested parties had the right to be present and heard at the hearing.

● Required the judge to rule on the application for rejection within 30 days after the hearing began, although the time could be extended if both sides agreed.

● Allowed the company to terminate or alter any provisions of the collective bargaining agreement if the judge did not rule within 30 days, or by the agreed upon time, pending the judge's ruling on the application for rejection.

● Authorized a judge to approve an application for rejecting a contract only if the court found that the trustee had, prior to the hearing, made a proposal that conformed to the law, the employee representative refused to accept such proposal "without good cause" and that the "balance of the equities" in the case clearly favored rejection of the agreement.

● Authorized the judge to allow the company to implement interim changes in the terms, conditions and benefits of the labor contract if they were deemed essential to the continuation of the debtor's business.

● Stated that no provisions in this section should be interpreted to allow a company unilaterally to terminate or alter any labor contract provisions without following the procedures set forth.

● Made the section effective on the date of enactment but exempted cases filed under Chapter 11 of the bankruptcy code that had been initiated before the date of enactment.

Effective Dates

● Specified that the bill applied to cases filed 90 days after enactment except for cases involving collective bargaining disputes and involuntary bankruptcies.

Background

Court Ruling: The Marathon Case

HR 5174 made the first major changes in the nation's bankruptcy procedures since 1978, when Congress overhauled a system that had been essentially untouched since 1938. The 1978 law (PL 95-598) abolished bankruptcy referees, who were subordinate to federal district courts, and created an independent bankruptcy court system to be run by judges appointed by the president for 14-year terms. The law allowed a transition period until March 31, 1974, to phase in the new system. *(1978 Almanac p. 179)*

The 1978 law gave bankruptcy judges power to resolve not only straightforward bankruptcy issues, but also a myriad of other legal disputes in which a bankrupt individual or company might be involved.

On June 28, 1982, the Supreme Court ruled in *Northern Pipeline Construction Co. v. Marathon Pipeline Co.* that Congress had given bankruptcy judges too much authority over a range of legal issues and not enough independence from the other branches of government. Unlike federal district and appeals court judges, who were appointed for life under Article III of the Constitution, bankruptcy judges were to be appointed under Article I for fixed terms.

The court gave Congress until Dec. 24, 1982, to come up with a new plan. When Congress failed to meet that deadline, the U.S. Judicial Conference issued an interim rule for handling bankruptcy matters through the federal district courts, which could refer matters to bankruptcy judges. *(1982 Almanac p. 389)*

Throughout 1983, the House and Senate remained deadlocked on how to restructure the bankruptcy courts to remedy the constitutional defect identified by the justices, and on what other changes to make in bankruptcy law.

The House Judiciary Committee in February 1983 reported a bill (HR 3 — H Rept 98-9, Part I) that would have given bankruptcy judges the same lifetime tenure as other federal judges. But this bill stalled at the House Rules Committee, which was under pressure from 200 some House members to allow a floor amendment making it harder for individuals to declare bankruptcy and escape their debts. House Judiciary Chairman Peter W. Rodino Jr., D-N.J., chief advocate of HR 3, opposed such an amendment.

The U.S. Judicial Conference, policy-making arm of the federal judiciary, opposed the Article III approach of the House bill. It wanted bankruptcy judges to be appointed by the 12 regional federal appeals courts and to act as adjuncts of the district courts, their power circumscribed.

The Senate passed a bankruptcy bill (S 1013) in April 1983 that was considerably closer to the Judicial Conference's proposal than to HR 3. That measure made bankruptcy judges adjuncts of the U.S. district courts, appointed by the president for 14-year terms. The legislation also created scores of new federal district and appeals court judgeships, tightened consumer bankruptcy standards and made a number of other substantive changes in bankruptcy laws. *(1983 Almanac p. 318)*

Court Ruling: The Bildisco Case

Bankruptcy legislation gained new urgency in 1984, as the March 31 end of the transition period provided in the 1978 law loomed.

But the Supreme Court threw a political wild card into the game when it ruled 5-4 on Feb. 22 that companies filing for reorganization under Chapter 11 of the federal bankruptcy law could abrogate their collective bargaining agreements, even before receiving court approval to do so. The justices ruled 9-0 that courts could permit companies to toss out their labor contracts upon a finding that the contract was burdensome and that on balance, the best interests of the company, its creditors and its employees favored such a move. *(National Labor Relations Board v. Bildisco & Bildisco, p. 13-A)*

The ruling appalled organized labor, and touched off a massive lobbying effort to persuade Congress to overturn the court's decision. House Judiciary Chairman Rodino introduced such a bill (HR 4908) within hours of the decision, but the real maneuvering on the issue occurred in the

context of the larger, multi-faceted bankruptcy legislation already moving through the legislative mills.

Labor, like Rodino, opposed changes in consumer bankruptcy standards. But its top priority was reversing the *Bildisco* decision, and pressure for a package deal rapidly began to mount.

House Committee Action

When it became clear in February that HR 3, the bill passed by the House in 1983, was still in trouble, Rodino started compromise talks with Rep. Mike Synar, D-Okla., chief sponsor of the bill (HR 1800) to make it tougher for individuals to escape their debts by declaring bankruptcy.

By March 9, according to congressional sources, the two had reached agreement on language preserving the substance of HR 1800, which permitted a judge to bar individual declarations of bankruptcy if the judge determined this would be "a substantial abuse" of the bankruptcy laws because the debtor could in fact pay off his debts. Rodino was able to add a provision giving the debtor a presumption of being entitled to go into bankruptcy. That presumption would have to be overcome by evidence showing that the debtor could pay his debts over time.

After further negotiations, Rodino on March 19 introduced HR 5174. It included the provisions of HR 3 creating independent bankruptcy judges with lifetime appointments; the compromise provisions on consumer bankruptcy; protections for union contracts with companies that filed for bankruptcy; provisions to help farmers affected by grain elevator bankruptcies; and a section creating a total of 75 new federal district and appeals court judgeships.

Rules Committee Action

The House Rules Committee took up HR 5174 on March 20. At the direction of Speaker Thomas P. O'Neill Jr., D-Mass., the panel struck from the bill the provisions creating new federal judgeships. Democrats, hoping to defeat Reagan in November, did not want to give him a host of new lifetime appointments in an election year.

The committee approved a rule (H Res 465) for floor consideration that permitted only one amendment to be offered — an alternative proposal for restructuring the bankruptcy courts.

The alternative, put forward by Rep. Robert W. Kastenmeier, D-Wis., reflected the preferences of the Judicial Conference. It gave overall authority for bankruptcy matters to federal district judges. Bankruptcy judges, appointed by the 12 regional federal appeals courts, were made adjuncts to the district courts and authorized to handle clear-cut bankruptcy issues. Cases that involved other legal matters, such as an antitrust claim, were to go to the district courts.

The Kastenmeier proposal was similar to the bankruptcy bill passed by the Senate, except that under the Senate bill, the bankruptcy judges would have been appointed by the president.

House Floor Action

The House passed HR 5174 on March 21 after adopting the Kastenmeier amendment as a substitute for the Rodino-backed plan for independent bankruptcy court judges with life tenure.

Bankruptcy Court Scheme Modified

The vote on the substitute making bankruptcy courts an adjunct of federal district courts was 250-161. *(Vote 44, p. 16-H)*

Proponents of the Kastenmeier approach said it avoided the confusion and expense of establishing a separate system of bankruptcy judges with life tenure and higher salaries.

Kastenmeier said his amendment minimized disruption of the current bankruptcy system because it essentially incorporated the interim rule that the courts had been operating under since 1982. The Judicial Conference, which crafted the interim rule, supported the amendment.

However, the amendment's opponents, who had the backing of the Reagan administration, said the only sure way to address the constitutional problems identified by the Supreme Court was to give bankruptcy judges life tenure.

Rodino and his allies contended that parceling out cases between bankruptcy and district court judges invited litigation over jurisdictional questions and left bankruptcy courts on the same shaky legal grounds that led to the system's invalidation by the Supreme Court in June 1982.

"Why risk another unconstitutional system when a constitutional one is a simple matter of changing the term of office [of the judges]?" asked Rodino.

Labor Contracts

The strategy of linking the stronger protections for union contracts to the urgently needed courts bill angered Republicans, who charged that the labor proposal was being "railroaded" through the House without adequate consideration.

"The committee record [on the labor provision] is an absolute blank," said Hamilton Fish Jr. of New York, the ranking Republican on the Judiciary Committee. "And yet, it reverses a 9-0 decision of the U.S. Supreme Court."

Although a similar proposal (HR 4908) to nullify the Supreme Court decision had been introduced by Rodino Feb. 22, no hearings on the measure had been held.

Charging that the omnibus bankruptcy bill was to be considered under a "gag rule," Republicans assailed the terms of debate that permitted only one amendment to be offered — on the court issue — and barred separate votes on the labor provisions. But they lost on the procedural question, as this rule for debate was adopted, 242-166. *(Vote 43, p. 16-H)*

Provisions affecting labor contracts reversed the Supreme Court's 5-4 ruling that a company could abrogate its union contract as soon as it filed for bankruptcy, without waiting for court approval.

The high court had also ruled unanimously that judges need not give extra weight to collective bargaining agreements in dealing with bankruptcy cases. But HR 5174 required courts to find that a company was on the verge of collapse before allowing a contract to be voided.

The labor provisions applied only to bankruptcy cases initiated after the bill was enacted. Pending cases that had stirred wide controversy — such as the scuttling of union contracts by Continental Airlines after it filed for bankruptcy in 1983 — were not affected by the bill.

Barney Frank, D-Mass., said the new language merely reflected how Congress had intended the 1978 bankruptcy law to apply in cases involving labor contracts.

"I do not believe that members thought, when they voted in 1978, that they were drastically changing labor law," Frank said.

But critics said the bill's standards were too harsh, and would force ailing companies into insolvency when reorganization under bankruptcy court protection might keep them in business.

Stalemate

As time ran out on the transition period provided under the 1978 law, Congress March 30 cleared a bill (S 2507 — PL 98-249) giving itself one month's breathing room to come up with a final version of HR 5174.

Without congressional action or some interim move by the U.S. Judicial Conference, the country technically would have been without functioning bankruptcy courts April 1.

The one-month extension of the transition period cleared March 30 proved to be a harbinger of things to come. As a stalemate between the House and Senate dragged on, Congress passed three more short-term bills over the next two months (S 2570 — PL 98-271; HR 2174 — PL 98-299; S 2776 — PL 98-325).

The Senate, prodded by business organizations, was resisting the House-passed labor contract provisions, contending that they went too far in protecting unions. Sen. Orrin G. Hatch, R-Utah, and his staff led negotiations the week of March 26 among other senators and representatives of business and organized labor, but no agreement was reached.

The House, on the other hand, objected to the breadth of the Senate bill, which included provisions on all of the issues addressed by HR 5174 plus a section to change procedures for handling bankruptcies in shopping centers; a section to expedite procedures for dealing with fish processing plants that went bankrupt; a section to bar a person from discharging through bankruptcy proceedings debts incurred as a result of a drunken driving accident; a section designed to protect persons who bought time-shared units in developments that later went bankrupt; and a section that exempted certain short-term securities from bankruptcy proceedings.

The Senate bill also included a section creating 85 new federal judgeships — 61 district court positions and 24 federal appeals court slots.

Final Action

On June 19, the Senate finally passed HR 5174 after amending it to conform with the provisions of the bill it had passed in 1983. This step paved the way for a House-Senate conference on the legislation.

After it became clear that a number of members would object to any further short-term extensions of the transition period, conferees finally met June 26-28 to reconcile the differences between the two versions of the bill.

The Senate bill did not address the labor issue, but the House insisted on some language to alleviate the effect of the court decision. In return, the House accepted a number of other changes in the bankruptcy code and agreed to create 85 new federal court judgeships.

Final action on HR 5174 came June 29 when first the House and then the Senate adopted the conference report. The vote in the House was 394-0; the Senate action came on a voice vote. *(Vote 272, p. 84-H)*

Status of Sitting Judges

Before Congress acted, the existing bankruptcy courts

technically went out of business. At midnight June 27, the authority of the courts to do business expired.

To cover the gap, Congress wrote into HR 5174 a provision retroactively allowing all existing bankruptcy judges to continue serving for up to 15 months longer without having to be reappointed under the new system.

Both the Justice Department and the Administrative Office of the U.S. Courts said this provision was unconstitutional because it amounted to a congressional appoint-

ment of judges. Under the Constitution, only the president and the federal judiciary could appoint federal judges.

When he signed HR 5174 into law July 10, Reagan expressed his concern about constitutionality of this provision.

However, three separate federal district courts ruled later in the year that the congressional action was valid.

At the end of 1984, the Justice Department had not decided whether to appeal any of the cases.∎

Transportation/Commerce/Consumers

Not since the Great Depression has the nation's financial system posed such crises for Congress' consideration as it did in 1984.

The industry, battered by a decade of back-to-back recessions, high inflation and spiraling interest rates, struggled to recover while confronting an increasingly competitive financial environment.

Clouding the year was concern that the nation's largest banks faced defaults on billions of dollars in loans to developing countries, many of them victims of global recession or falling oil export prices. Though international crisis was avoided when loans were renegotiated and interest rates dipped, major banks' earnings were down, and the banks remained vulnerable to their borrowers' economic and political upheavals.

At home, depression in the oil and gas industries bankrupted producers and suppliers, and their defaults on once-profitable loans threatened banks throughout the Southwest. Midwestern banks with agricultural loans were dragged down with the falling fortunes of U.S. farmers, who were clobbered by high interest rates, low crop prices, reduced land values and a strong dollar that inflated the prices of farm exports.

Meanwhile, banks and savings and loan (S&L) institutions faced growing competition from non-traditional rivals — securities, retail, insurance and real estate firms that used loopholes in federal law and newly liberalized state laws to enter the banking business. Banks and S&Ls, in turn, continued to press Congress for deregulation — an easing of the federal regulations and laws that prevented them from entering the other businesses.

Failures and Problem Banks

By year's end, 828 banks were on the government's "problem list," nearly four times the number on the roster when the decade began. Seventy-nine banks failed — breaking 1983's post-Depression record by 31.

But as alarmed as Congress was by the record failures, its debate over banking deregulation was most affected by a bank that did not close. Continental Illinois National Bank & Trust Co. of Chicago, the nation's eighth-largest bank, stayed open only after U.S. regulators intervened with a multibillion-dollar rescue package that included unprecedented financial guarantees for big depositors.

The package generally was accepted on the Hill as unavoidable. Had Continental collapsed under the weight of its bad energy and farm loans, it likely could have pulled down some of its biggest customers — including major U.S. businesses, foreign investors and 2,000 smaller banks with millions of dollars on deposit at the bank.

But even among supporters, the Continental rescue raised questions:

● Had regulators created a two-tier system, with one tier for small banks that the country could afford to let close and another for those that some members of Congress dubbed "TBTF" — Too Big To Fail?

● Should Congress have had some say in the regulators' rescue plans?

● Did the 50-year-old system of deposit insurance need reforming? Under law, the government insured all customers' deposits up to $100,000. Was that too high for a system designed to protect average savers? Or was it too low to prevent the kind of run on deposits by major customers that imperiled Continental?

● And, finally, how could Congress grant further decontrol of banks at a time when more regulation, rather than less, seemed to be demanded by the perilous financial condition of so many banks?

Fernand J. St Germain, D-R.I., chairman of the House Banking, Finance and Urban Affairs Committee, seized on the last question to press his fight against administration and Senate proposals that would have freed banks to compete in the securities, real estate and insurance fields.

But his Senate counterpart, Banking Chairman Jake Garn, R-Utah, repeatedly countered that deregulating banks to compete in other fields would help many banks avoid ruin by increasing their sources of assets.

The impasse between Garn and St Germain over expanded banking powers prevented enactment of a major banking bill, despite the sense of crisis in the financial industry. The germ for a compromise was a desire on all sides to close what was called the non-bank bank loophole, but the House-Senate split proved too great to bridge.

A non-bank bank is a financial firm that either offers demand deposits, such as checking accounts, or makes commercial loans, but does not do both. It thus escapes the legal definition of a bank in the 1956 Bank Holding Company Act, and avoids the ban on interstate banking.

Under congressional pressure, Comptroller of the Currency C. Todd Conover, who shared responsibility for approving non-bank bank charters with the Federal Reserve Board, reluctantly agreed to a moratorium on the hundreds of applications pending before him. But when Congress adjourned in October without action, Conover carried out his vow to immediately begin approving charters.

Corporate Mergers

In other matters of commerce, major corporate mergers sparked legislative activity. Numerous committees considered measures to restrict combinations of big oil companies in the wake of several mergers — including the largest in U.S. history, Standard Oil of California's $13.2 billion purchase of Gulf Corp. No laws were enacted.

Corporate takeovers, and takeover attempts, in other industries also caused widespread concern that entrepreneurial capital and energy were being expended on unproductive ends.

Also, the business tactics used to achieve or to fend off

an unwanted takeover aroused criticism. Perhaps the most controversial was "greenmail" — a sort of corporate blackmail whereby a firm targeted for an unwanted takeover buys back its stock from a raider, but at a premium price that is not offered to other stockholders.

Congress considered legislation to limit greenmail and other corporate strategies, but no bills passed.

Bell Breakup Aftermath

The historic breakup of the Bell telephone companies from American Telephone & Telegraph Co. (AT&T) took effect Jan. 1. Complaints about higher local rates and service delays dogged the transition, but Congress took a wait-and-see stance. In January, the Federal Communications Commission bowed to members' pressure and delayed until June 1985 its proposed "access charges" for residential and small business customers. The charges, which local phone companies would add to monthly bills, were intended to offset the loss of long-distance revenues that the companies previously shared with AT&T.

Transportation

Congress' major opportunity to shore up the nation's "infrastructure" — the network of roads, bridges, mass transit, dams and water and sewer facilities — was caught in a political crossfire in the last days of the 98th Congress. House and Senate conferees could not agree on legislation to release approximately $7.2 billion from the Highway Trust Fund for work on the Interstate Highway System.

It was the second consecutive year that the states failed to get expected funds, and highway officials said it might keep the Interstate system from being completed by its target date of 1990.

More than 96 percent of the planned 42,500-mile system was open to traffic. But the stalemate left 43 states with less than $10 million available for construction, and some projects had to be suspended for lack of funds.

Despite complaints from the American Association of State Highway and Transportation Officials and others that the federal government was collecting $3 million to $4 million per day in fuel taxes that the states needed, Congress was unable to act to free the funds. The primary impediment was disagreement over how much federal money should be spent on special highway projects in members' districts.

Mass Transit

The 1-cent-per-gallon gas tax earmarked for mass transit construction in the 1982 Surface Transit Assistance Act (PL 97-424) brought in approximately $400 million more than expected annually. But attempts by James J. Howard, D-N.J., chairman of the House Public Works and Transportation Committee, to free the money as part of the Interstate highway construction bill were thwarted by the administration and by the Senate Banking, Housing and Urban Affairs Committee.

The administration contended that the money was not yet available to be spent. The Senate panel, which had jurisdiction over mass transit, objected to transit's being included in a highway bill that had not been considered by the committee.

In a separate issue, the Urban Mass Transportation Administration (UMTA) tried to impose discipline on the funding of new mass transit systems financed by the new tax. UMTA, saying new systems were being started far faster than federal funds could support, wanted to use cost-effectiveness criteria to decide which programs would be funded. But Congress disagreed with the criteria, particularly with the weight given to the amount of funding offered by local communities, and earmarked $422.5 million for 12 cities it selected.

Highway Safety

Highway fatalities rose about 2.9 percent in 1984, according to the National Highway Traffic Safety Administration (NHTSA). That marked the first increase since 1979, when rising gas prices forced drivers to curtail driving, and reflected increased vehicle usage in 1984.

But NHTSA attributed half of all traffic fatalities to drunk driving. A nationwide crusade against drunk driving led 26 states to strengthen their enforcement measures, and it put Congress in the spotlight in June when momentum gathered behind a measure to pressure states to raise their minimum drinking age to 21.

The bill, which would withhold certain highway funds from states with lower drinking ages, passed quickly after President Reagan decided to support it. He originally had objected that establishing the drinking age was a matter best left to the states.

Air Travel

A ceremony Dec. 31 marked the end of the Civil Aeronautics Board (CAB), which had regulated the airline industry since 1938. The target date for its dissolution had been set in 1978 in airline deregulation legislation (PL 95-504). Both the administration and Congress agreed to transfer CAB consumer protection authority, such as making rules to regulate smoking on flights, to the Department of Transportation (DOT). And although the administration wanted to give jurisdiction over mergers and antitrust exemptions to the Department of Justice, Congress gave all remaining functions to DOT.

Railroads

1984 was a good year for an industry that had been declining for decades until the fuel-consciousness of the energy crisis and the railroad deregulation act of 1980 (PL 96-448) revived its fortunes. Profits were approximately $2.5 billion; freight traffic was up 10.6 percent over 1983. Part of that increase, however, was attributed to heavy coal shipments made in anticipation of a miners' strike that never materialized.

One of the most successful railroads, Conrail, made close to $500 million but found itself on the auction block. The administration tried to fulfill its longstanding wish to sell the railroad back to the private sector. But, partially because of Conrail's profitability, it could not accomplish the sale.

At year's end, DOT was considering three bidders, each of which offered approximately $1.2 billion in cash. However, DOT made no recommendation on the preferred bidder, and a skeptical Congress adjourned without considering legislation needed to implement the sale. Members of Congress from the Northeast were particularly wary because of the importance of Conrail to their states' economies.

—By Jacqueline Calmes and Stephen Gettinger

Standoff Blocks Banking Deregulation Bill

A House-Senate standoff over banking reforms blocked enactment in 1984 of a major deregulation bill that the Reagan administration had favored.

In a joint statement Oct. 4, the rival chairmen of the House and Senate Banking committees said that "legislation addressing the competitive and regulatory framework of the financial system would be the first priority" of their panels in 1985.

For two years, Senate Banking Chairman Jake Garn, R-Utah, had labored for an administration-backed bill (S 2181) to close legal loopholes and to free banks to engage in securities, real estate, insurance and other financial services that had been off-limits to them. The Senate overwhelmingly approved a pared-down version (S 2851 — S Rept 98-560) Sept. 13.

But Garn's House counterpart, Fernand J. St Germain, D-R.I., steadfastly opposed bank deregulation and pushed his own bill (HR 5916 — H Rept 98-889) that only closed loopholes that permitted some firms to evade the federal ban on interstate banking. On Sept. 21, St Germain abruptly dropped the fight without taking his bill to the House floor, saying it was pointless to proceed, given the differences with the Senate.

Non-Bank Banks Proliferate

The absence of banking legislation had a quick and significant impact on the industry. A major impetus for banking legislation had been concern over the proliferation of "non-bank banks" that legally avoided the ban on interstate banking by limiting their services.

The 1956 Bank Holding Company Act (PL 84-511) defined a bank as an institution that both accepts demand deposits, such as checking accounts, and makes commercial loans. A firm performing only one of the functions was called a "non-bank bank."

Such a firm was not subject to the Bank Holding Company Act, including the ban on interstate banking. However, it was eligible for U.S. deposit insurance.

After banks and other firms discovered the loophole, banking regulator C. Todd Conover, comptroller of the currency, in 1983 began granting charters for non-bank bank offices nationwide. But under pressure from Congress and other regulators who argued he was creating a separate system of unregulated banks, Conover imposed a moratorium, saying he would wait until the end of the 98th Congress to give members time to approve banking legislation.

With no legislation enacted, immediately after Congress adjourned Conover starting approving the backlog of several hundred non-bank bank applications.

Background

In recent years, members of Congress had watched with chagrin as federal regulators, courts, states, businesses and financial institutions chipped away at longstanding banking laws. Members became increasingly concerned that the actions of the states, federal regulators or the private sector would erode congressional control over the financial system.

Banks continued to press for relief from Depression era laws that barred them from such commercial activities as insurance and securities, while non-bank firms were free to offer competing bank services. The non-banking industry — investment firms, insurance agents, Realtors and retail chains such as Sears, Roebuck and Co. and J. C. Penney Co. — fiercely opposed relaxing the laws.

Commercial firms and major banks aggressively took advantage of loopholes in federal law to engage in forms of interstate banking, reviving fears that community banks could be crushed by big city banks and that local funds would be siphoned for loans to Third World countries and New York developers. The differences between the big banks and smaller institutions split the industry on the issue of banking legislation.

Finally, congressional nerves were strained by the threatened collapse of some of the nation's financial institutions. Most notably, the eighth-largest U.S. bank, Continental Illinois National Bank & Trust Co. of Chicago, received an unprecedented $4.5 billion rescue package from the federal government to keep it afloat.

Meanwhile, the number of banks on the government's "problem list" continued to multiply, exceeding 800 banks by 1984's end. Many were smaller institutions, particularly in the Midwest and Southwest, with outstanding loans in the hard-hit agricultural and energy-producing fields. *(Box, p. 273)*

New Banking Powers

Since the 1970s, when high interest rates and new technologies made it possible and profitable, securities and retail firms, insurance companies and a new breed of conglomerate began offering banking-style financial services along with their non-financial products.

The prototype conglomerate was Sears, Roebuck and Co., the largest retail merchandise chain in the country. A customer who came to Sears for a garden hose also could buy insurance, buy and sell real estate or stocks and bonds, open a money market fund account or, through automated teller machines, conduct ordinary banking transactions.

Alarmed at the competition from firms not governed by the tight regulations they have to satisfy, banks searched out ways — and demanded the right — to enter fields traditionally denied them. The campaign to revise the nation's financial system lasted for most of the decade. *(1980 Almanac p. 275)*

Although Congress responded in 1980 with the Depository Institutions Deregulation and Monetary Control Act (PL 96-221) phasing out interest rate ceilings, it did not include the broad, sweeping reforms sought by the industry.

In 1982, the Reagan administration proposed that Congress broaden banks' powers to allow them to deal in securities, insurance and real estate. Instead, Congress enacted the Garn-St Germain Act (PL 97-320) that bolstered the ailing savings and loan industry and gave S&Ls and banks a new tool, the Money Market Deposit Account, to compete with money market mutual funds. *(1982 Almanac p. 45)*

The administration continued to argue that banks needed new authority to compete in other financial services areas. Garn, who had been pushing for broader powers for banks for years, pressed the deregulation fight. But, given the united opposition of the non-banking industries, Garn got no further than hearings.

South Dakota Loophole

With deregulation legislation stymied, big banks found a way to move into other states to participate in otherwise forbidden business. One way was through the "non-bank bank loophole."

Another was to take advantage of the more liberal laws some states were enacting for state-chartered financial institutions, as a way to attract business. Thus, through a state-chartered subsidiary, national banks were able to go into other states and exercise financial powers that federal law precluded.

The most notable example was the "South Dakota loophole," named after two laws passed in that state in 1983 at the urging of New York-based Citicorp. The term came to refer to the ability of financial institutions to acquire new powers — such as insurance marketing — by buying or forming a state-chartered bank.

One South Dakota law authorized out-of-state bank holding companies such as Citicorp to acquire or charter a state bank in South Dakota, a move permissible under federal law with specific state approval. The second law gave any state-chartered South Dakota bank authority to own an insurance firm if the insurance arm operated only out of state.

Soon afterwards, Citicorp announced that it would seek to acquire the American State Bank of Rapid City, S.D., and use the state-chartered bank to enter the insurance business.

The insurance industry was outraged and various others — including Federal Reserve Chairman Paul A. Volcker — were profoundly disturbed by what they saw as a bald circumvention of federal law.

Regional Compacts

States also were forming regional banking compacts, which allowed local banks to open interstate offices within the compact's borders. The Bank Holding Company Act permitted interstate banking if the affected states authorized it but, until 1984, only Maine and Alaska had done so.

States began considering compacts as a way to keep major New York and California banks from moving in alongside their smaller, local institutions. Critics in Congress lamented what some called the financial "Balkanization" of the country.

Three New England states, including St Germain's home of Rhode Island, banded together. Garn's state of Utah invited Western states to form a compact. Southeast, Southwest, Mid-Atlantic and Midwest states also discussed compacts.

Volcker Urges Action

To help restore order to the banking system, Volcker urged Congress to act. On March 27 he told the Senate Banking Committee:

"I can well visualize the day, if we don't act and all the states go their own way and all the loopholes are exploited, that in a few years, we'll be back here and we will have a great crisis and you're going to say, 'Where was the Federal Reserve?' And we're going to say, 'Well, we didn't have any authority or power to deal with this situation.'"

Three deregulation bills awaited Senate action. They were Garn's S 2181, S 2134 by William Proxmire, Wis., ranking Democrat on the Senate Banking Committee, and S 1609, the administration bill on which the others were based.

All three bills attempted to close the non-bank bank loophole, although Garn's bill permitted non-bank banks, with limits, to offer consumer accounts and loans. Also, all three allowed bank holding companies to underwrite local and state revenue bonds, and market mutual funds.

The Garn and administration bills freed banks to become insurance and real estate brokers. Proxmire's bill would not.

The Continental Caper

The federally funded rescue of the nation's eighth largest bank fueled the debate, giving opponents of banking deregulation a real-life argument against Garn's proposal to free financial institutions to compete in the insurance, real estate and securities fields.

In May, a week of rumors of imminent collapse ignited a run on Continental that threatened international finance. On May 17, federal regulators stepped in with a $7.5 billion tourniquet: The Federal Deposit Insurance Corp. (FDIC) loaned $1.5 billion, and other banks provided the rest to shore up Continental.

More important, the FDIC threw out the existing $100,000-per-account legal limit for deposit insurance, assuring even multimillion-dollar depositors of the safety of their money. And the Federal Reserve Board said Continental would have unlimited access to low-interest loans from its reserves.

Finally, when the emergency actions did not seem to be helping, the federal regulators engineered a permanent $4.5 billion plan under which the government effectively took control of the bank, infusing it with $1 billion in new capital and assuming $3.5 billion of its worst loans.

The government's rush to save Continental widened the fissure between large and small banks. Even supporters of the rescue bemoaned what they saw as a *de facto* two-class banking system, with an underclass of smaller institutions that could be allowed to fail, and an upper class of major money-center banks that could not.

And in Congress, Continental's rescue immediately colored the debate over deregulation.

"People are saying, 'What are we doing offering new powers to these lunatics when they can't handle the powers they've got?'" said a Senate committee aide.

Garn argued that Continental's plight was irrelevant to his bill and was being exploited by opponents. One foe was St Germain, who blasted the bailout and noted that smaller banks had been forced to close or merge with healthy institutions.

The dilemma for members of Congress over the rescue of Continental was evident at a May 24 hearing of the House Banking Committee. One after another, members criticized the action as unfair to smaller institutions and a violation of free-market principles. But in turn, they acknowledged the potentially disastrous repercussions had a bank with $41 billion in assets been left to die.

Continental's situation was unique, rather than indicative of banking generally, Stewart B. McKinney, R-Conn., said. First, it was well-known for several years that the bank held too many bad energy loans. Second, since Illinois prohibited branch banking, Continental was limited primarily to its Chicago base in trying to attract funds. That, McKinney and others said, led the bank to make bad loans.

Bills Begin to Move

After months of glacial movement, three panels acted within a week of each other to approve separate bills re-

Financial Industry Ups and Downs

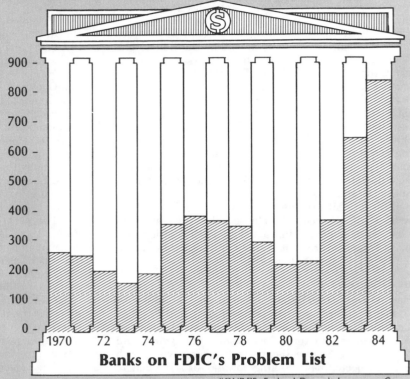

Banks and savings and loan (S&L) institutions have been buffeted by changing economic conditions in recent years. After World War II and until the 1970s, prosperity and bankers' conservatism combined to keep failure rates negligible.

Then came years of high inflation mixed with recessions. Institutions began taking more risks and opening more branches, helped along by liberalized state laws. Competitive pressures increased.

In the 1980s, Congress phased out the caps on interest rates for savers' deposits. Increasingly, banks and S&Ls competed not only among themselves but also with non-banking firms that offered alternative, high-interest investments.

As these charts show, many financial institutions did not weather the recession of 1973-75, and failure rates went up in 1975 and 1976.

Several relatively stable years followed. Then, as the 1970s closed, spiraling interest rates and the recession of 1981-82 doomed record numbers of banks and S&Ls. S&Ls were hit especially hard, since they held long-term mortgage loans with low interest but had to pay high interest to draw deposits.

Congressional aid in 1982 helped some S&Ls survive until interest rates briefly came back down. But when interest rates again inched upward, their futures were back in doubt again.

Banks on FDIC's Problem List

SOURCE: Federal Deposit Insurance Corp.

The Federal Deposit Insurance Corp.'s (FDIC) "problem bank" list told much the same story. The identities of those banks, whose finances merited regulators' extra attention, were guarded carefully because disclosure could ignite a run by depositors. By Dec. 31, 828 banks were on the list — almost four times the total (217) of 1980.

Insured Bank Failures

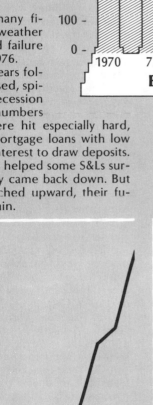

The last bank failure of 1984 occurred Dec. 22, when the First Security Bank of Sandwich, Ill., with $10.4 million in deposits, closed. The bank was reopened Dec. 24 as the First National Bank of Sandwich, a subsidiary of Union Bankcorp in Illinois. There were 79 failures in 1984.

SOURCE: Federal Deposit Insurance Corp.

Savings and Loan Casualties

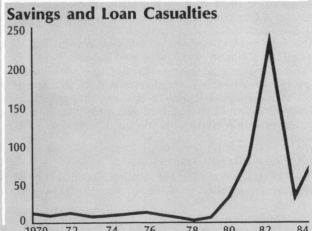

The total of 70 includes troubled S&Ls that did not close but merged with healthy institutions, with or without FLIC financial assistance. Regulators do not consider such supervised mergers as failures, though industry analysts do.

SOURCE: Federal Home Loan Bank Board

defining the legal boundaries between banking and commerce.

All three bills (HR 5916, HR 5881 and S 2181) would have plugged the loopholes that permitted firms to evade the ban on interstate banking by redefining a "bank." Companies would have to divest properties that did not comply.

The bills, using similar language, would have closed the non-bank bank loophole by amending the Bank Holding Company Act's definition of bank.

First, the current definition of a bank as an institution that both makes commercial loans and takes demand deposits would be expanded. Demand deposits would include not only checking accounts but also similar transaction services, specifically the popular NOW accounts that allow customers to write third-party checks from an interest-bearing account. NOW accounts had not been considered demand deposits, so some non-bank banks were able to offer a full-line of banking services, including both commercial loans and NOW accounts.

Second, the bills further defined banks as institutions that were FDIC-insured. The House bills went a step further than Garn's Senate bill, to include in the definition of a bank not only insured institutions but also those banks eligible for FDIC membership.

Major Differences

Beyond the shared desire to rein in the limited-service banks, major differences divided the House and Senate.

The much broader Senate bill sponsored by Garn would free banks and thrift institutions like savings and loans to compete in the securities business, while both House bills rejected new banking powers. Also, the Senate bill would sanction limited interstate banking, while the House bills did not.

In the race to act before the July 4 recess, the last to finish was the Senate Banking Committee, where the debate over deregulation had begun more than a year ago. On June 27, Garn shepherded a pared-down S 2181 through a daylong markup to approval by voice vote. (Afterward, it was renumbered S 2851.)

The day before, on June 26, the House Banking Committee voted 32-16 to approve HR 5916, sponsored by St Germain and Chalmers P. Wylie, R-Ohio, the ranking minority member.

Beating the two Banking committees to a vote June 21 was the House Energy and Commerce Subcommittee on Telecommunications, Consumer Protection and Finance. The panel, which handled securities-related legislation, approved by voice vote HR 5881, a measure that Chairman Timothy E. Wirth, D-Colo., modeled largely on the St Germain-Wylie bill. Wirth's bill was never acted on by the full committee.

House Committees' Action

While Garn and the Reagan administration continued to press for deregulation, St Germain would not hear of it — literally.

In hearings, he had told pro-deregulation witnesses, including Treasury Secretary Donald T. Regan, that they could not testify on the subject. And at the June 26 markup, St Germain ruled that amendments for expanded bank powers were not germane and could not be considered. Instead, he said, HR 5916 would be simply "a loophole closer."

Like the other bills, it would close the "non-bank bank

loophole" by redefining bank. But doing so raised a controversial question of which of the scores of non-bank banks must be divested. St Germain originally would have forced all to be divested within two years. Before the markup, he agreed that parent firms could keep non-bank banks if charter applications had been filed with U.S. regulators by Jan. 1, 1983.

In close votes, St Germain fended off several proposals to change the cutoff date, criticizing them as benefiting firms whose holdings would have to be divested under the bill. He named J. C. Penney Co. Inc., Sears, Roebuck and Co., Control Data Corp., Prudential-Bache Securities Inc., and Dimension Financial Corp.

But when one amendment finally was approved, St Germain switched his vote to the majority side so he could move to reconsider the vote later. After a lunch break, he did so, and this time the amendment lost on a 23-23 tie.

Finally the panel voted 25-22 for a proposal by Douglas K. Bereuter, R-Neb., to exempt from the new definition non-bank banks approved by regulators by June 30, 1983.

The panel also approved, 29-18, a proposal by Doug Barnard Jr., D-Ga., preserving banks' ability to provide discount brokerage services — taking customers' orders to buy stock without giving investment advice.

The last major threat to the bill came from Democrats who often collided with the chairman, notably Stephen L. Neal, N.C.; John J. LaFalce, N.Y.; and Stan Lundine, N.Y.

Neal proposed a substitute bill providing a moratorium until June 30, 1985, on non-bank bank expansions while Congress considered the issue further. No holdings would have to be divested. It failed, 17-31.

The vote flipped on approval of HR 5916. The tally was 32-16, with almost all those who supported the moratorium voting against the bill.

Senate Committee Action

For Garn, the pro-deregulation argument had long been summed up by his oft-used phrase, "the level playing field." He complained that firms such as Sears and Merrill Lynch increasingly entered the banking business but banks were prevented from competing in the non-banks' areas.

"It boils down to an issue of fairness within the financial services industry," he said June 27.

Thirty-five amendments had been prepared for the markup, but the major changes in the bill were made beforehand by Garn himself. To forge consensus, he removed provisions allowing bank and thrift holding firms to deal in real estate and insurance.

Of the broad banking deregulation he first proposed, Garn kept only provisions allowing banks to deal, through affiliates, in securities — mutual funds, mortgage-backed securities, municipal revenue bonds and commercial paper. (Mortgage-backed securities are investments of home loans that are pooled together. Commercial paper is a kind of corporate IOU that major companies issue to raise funds instead of taking out a bank loan. And municipal revenue bonds are securities issued by state and local governments to pay for projects — bridges or roads, for example. They are repaid with proceeds, such as tolls, generated by the project.)

Still, it was an uphill fight, given the intense lobbying by interests protecting their turf and members' concern for big banks' health in the wake of the federal bailout of Continental Illinois.

Three Republicans — John Heinz, Pa.; Chic Hecht,

Nev.; and Alfonse M. D'Amato, N.Y. — invoked Continental's example in arguing that banks should not be permitted to enter risky ventures.

Garn argued that Continental was "irrelevant ... a convenient plum dropped into the hands of those who oppose additional powers."

But the committee agreed with Hecht that allowing banks to sponsor and sell their own mutual funds "is a risk that we cannot afford to take at this time." Members voted 11-7 for his amendment to strike the provision.

Garn won the next two votes. Members voted 10-8 to retain the mortgage-backed securities provision and 12-6 for municipal revenue bond powers.

He lost — and insurance lobbyists won — on another amendment to restrict state regulation of banks.

The issue was the South Dakota loophole, which permitted bank holding companies to market insurance nationwide by acquiring state-chartered subsidiaries in states with liberal bank laws such as South Dakota's.

Garn's bill would have limited such activities to the chartering state. For the insurance industry, that did not go far enough to keep banks out of their business. Christopher J. Dodd, D-Conn., whose state was home to major insurance corporations, offered an amendment providing that even within a state, a bank holding company and its state-chartered subsidiary were subject to federal law restricting banks' marketing of insurance.

It first failed on a 9-9 tie, but, after a lunch break, Paul S. Trible Jr., R-Va., switched his vote to back Dodd and the amendment was approved 10-8. Garn, a former insurance agent, condemned the insurance lobby as "wrong and greedy" to push the amendment.

The panel voted 11-7 to retain a requirement that the Federal Reserve Board pay banks interest on certain reserves they must deposit with the board. Proxmire unsuccessfully moved to strike the proposal, saying the interest would be a "gift" to banks that would cost the government up to $1 billion annually by 1988.

By a 12-5 vote, D'Amato lost his fight against a section authorizing states' regional banking compacts. Citicorp, headquartered in D'Amato's New York, had challenged a New England compact in federal court.

Two controversial amendments to prohibit corporate "greenmail" and "golden parachutes" were added by voice vote, despite Garn's complaint that they were not germane.

Greenmail referred to the practice of corporate directors buying back company stock, at a premium, from large shareholders who threatened a takeover. Golden parachutes was a term for any bonuses that directors or officers arranged for themselves if a takeover threatened their jobs.

The committee report (S Rept 98-560) was filed July 17.

Senate Floor Action

The Senate, returning to work Sept. 5 after a three-week Labor Day recess, immediately came to a stop as New York's senators filibustered Garn's bill.

Citicorp and the Chase Manhattan Bank wanted to kill the bill primarily because it sanctioned compacts formed by states to keep big New York and California banks from opening branches in their regions to compete with local banks.

For three days, New York Sens. Daniel Patrick Moynihan, D, and D'Amato blocked approval of a procedural motion by Majority Leader Howard H. Baker Jr., R-Tenn.,

to consider the bill.

A frustrated Garn condemned the "greed, greed, greed" of lobbyists and what he termed the insincerity of senators who urged him to delay for further study, despite two years of hearings on his bill.

Garn also repeated his pledge, made in an Aug. 7 floor speech, that he would not support a narrower bill like St Germain's that only closed loopholes without providing new powers for banks.

"That is so narrow as to be totally unacceptable to this senator," he said.

Garn insisted his bill was "95 percent non-controversial." He said the stumbling blocks were the compacts provision, the securities powers and a provision to close the South Dakota loophole.

Passage of the Bill

After considering the bill Sept. 11 and 12, the Senate Sept. 13 gave it overwhelming approval by a vote of 89-5. Passage came after opponents abruptly dropped delaying tactics that had thwarted its progress for seven days. *(Vote 221, p. 38-S)*

Late on Sept. 13, Heinz closed four hours of arguments on his amendment to remove the securities provisions from the bill by announcing he would withdraw the amendment. He said its defeat would only mean senators did not have a "full and complete understanding of the issues."

And D'Amato, after leading a week of protest that required two cloture votes to stifle, conceded that he had no more than a half dozen supporters and would not press for action on more than 40 amendments against the regional banking provision.

The lack of support had been signaled Sept. 10 when the Senate by 89-3 agreed to invoke cloture and cut off debate. The vote gave the first indication of the weakness of the D'Amato-Moynihan position. *(Vote 215, p. 38-S)*

The vote on the motion to proceed, taken Sept. 11, was a lopsided 95-2, with D'Amato and James Abdnor, R-S.D., the sole "no" votes. Baker and Garn filed a second cloture petition after it became clear D'Amato, Heinz and several others would continue their attempts to filibuster. *(Vote 216, p. 38-S)*

On Sept. 13, the vote for cloture on the bill was 92-6. The six votes represented "a high-water mark" for opponents, D'Amato joked afterward, and, having at least stalled the bill's progress for a week, the small group of dissenters decided not to prolong the debate into another week. *(Vote 219, p. 38-S)*

"We'd come to a point where all I could do is build up hostility," D'Amato said.

Though D'Amato took up the big New York banks' cause on the regional compacts issue, he teamed with Heinz in opposing the banking industry on the securities provisions. D'Amato, chairman of the Banking Subcommittee on Securities, said about 40 senators would have voted for Heinz' amendment to bar banks from entering the securities business.

Both D'Amato and Heinz argued that banks should remain separate from the securities industry, as provided by the 1933 Banking Act, to prevent the kind of risk-taking that had caused many Depression-era bank failures.

Heinz, chairman of the Banking Subcommittee on International Finance and Monetary Policy, objected that bank affiliates, which were government-regulated and insured, would have an advantage competing against securities firms. He referred to the near-collapse of Continental

The Regulators: More Than One Watchdog

There were a number of agencies regulating the banking industry as Congress considered major banking legislation in 1984.

In addition to regulatory agencies in all 50 states for state-chartered financial institutions, there were three federal regulatory agencies for banks and one for the savings and loan (S&L) industry.

And when it came to their main supervisor, banks and S&Ls could shop around for the agency they preferred — a tactic one former regulator described as "divide and conquer." For example, a state-chartered bank could choose between the Federal Deposit Insurance Corp. and the Federal Reserve Board. Also, institutions could choose either a federal or state charter.

The following is a brief description of the federal regulatory agencies for financial institutions:

The Office of the Comptroller of the Currency had primary responsibility for regulating 4,800 federally chartered national banks. The comptroller's office, a quasi-independent arm of the U.S. Treasury, was headed by C. Todd Conover, an appointee of President Reagan. The office approved all applications for bank charters, branch offices, mergers and new services, such as discount brokerages.

The Federal Reserve Board was the primary regulator for bank holding companies, which were organizations with controlling stock interests in one or more commercial banks. The seven-member board of governors, chaired by Paul A. Volcker, also regulated 1,000 state-chartered banks that were voluntary members of the Federal Reserve System, and had some jurisdiction over national banks. The regulatory function was in addition to the Fed's better-known responsibility for the nation's monetary policy. There were 12 regional Federal Reserve banks, which were the superbanks for Fed members.

The Federal Deposit Insurance Corp. (FDIC), formed in 1933, was chief regulator for state-chartered banks that were not members of the Fed but whose deposits were insured, up to a certain amount, by the FDIC's insurance fund. Also, the FDIC was the receiver, handling the property settlements, for national banks and some state banks that failed. Both the FDIC and the Federal Home Loan Bank Board supervised federal savings banks. The FDIC had a three-member board: Chairman William M. Isaac, Director Irvine H. Sprague, and Comptroller Conover, all presidential appointees.

FDIC insurance, from a fund financed through assessments on banks, was required for federally chartered institutions but voluntary for state banks that were not Fed members.

The Federal Home Loan Bank Board, headed by Chairman Edwin J. Gray, regulated more than 3,000 federally and state-chartered savings and loan associations. Formed in 1932, it supervised Federal Home Loan Banks in 12 districts, from which the thrift institutions could borrow money to finance residential mortgages, much as commercial banks drew from the Federal Reserve System's 12 district banks. Also, the board operated the Federal Savings and Loan Insurance Corp., which was similar to the banks' FDIC but was not independent.

Illinois Bank & Trust Co.

"Right now the securities industry is free from government support," Heinz said. "We don't subsidize them. We don't bail them out.... But the same can't be said of the banking industry."

But Garn repeatedly countered that "greedy" securities firms were trying to protect their monopoly and keep banks from providing financial services closely related to banking.

Insurance Lobby Victory

The insurance lobby won a victory in a controversy over the South Dakota loophole.

S 2851 originally provided that a bank holding company's state-chartered affiliate could market insurance only in the state that granted the charter. But in committee, Dodd won approval of his amendment to prohibit holding companies or their state affiliates from marketing insurance interstate or intrastate.

South Dakota's Abdnor, with Garn and Banking Committee member Slade Gorton, R-Wash., complained that the Dodd amendment violated states' rights to regulate banking within their borders.

Dodd countered that bank holding companies were creations of federal law, set up for tax advantages, and so their affiliates should be regulated by federal law.

With jubilant insurance lobbyists watching, the Senate voted 38-56 against Gorton's amendment allowing state-chartered bank subsidiaries to sell insurance in their home states. *(Vote 220, p. 38-S)*

Other Provisions

Several other amendments were approved during debate on S 2851. One, by Proxmire, removed a provision that would have obliged the Federal Reserve to pay banks interest on certain funds that they were required to keep on reserve with the Fed. Proxmire said the payment would be "a $4 billion bonanza" for banks over six years, and was inappropriate when Congress was trying to cut the budget deficit. The vote Sept. 12 was 76-20. *(Vote 217, p. 38-S)*

An amendment by Howard M. Metzenbaum, D-Ohio, to prohibit lenders from raising the interest on adjustable-rate mortgages by more than 5 percentage points over the life of the loan, passed by voice vote Sept. 12.

A second Metzenbaum amendment, also adopted by voice vote Sept. 12, would require banks to disclose fees charged to customers.

Other major provisions of the 131-page bill:

• Provided protections for consumers who acquired property under lease plans that have an option to buy.

• Required banks to disclose how long they waited to credit a customer's account while a check cleared.

• Imposed a $10,000 fine and/or 10 years in prison for fraudulent use of credit cards.

• Prohibited corporate "greenmail" and "golden parachutes." ∎

Ocean Shippers' Antitrust Measure Clears

The U.S. international shipping industry achieved a long-sought goal in 1984 with the final passage of a bill broadening antitrust immunity and revising federal regulation.

The Shipping Act of 1984 had been passed by both chambers in 1983, but Congress adjourned before completing the conference to reconcile differences in the two versions. *(1983 Almanac p. 554)*

Final congressional action came March 6, 1984, when the House by voice vote adopted the conference agreement (S 47 — H Rept 98-600). The Senate had adopted it by a vote of 74-12 Feb. 23. President Reagan signed the measure into law (PL 98-237) March 20. *(Vote 17, p. 5-S)*

The measure gave shipowners virtual antitrust immunity to meet in conferences — or cartels — to set prices and take other collective action to limit competition in international shipping. While opponents argued that the grant of immunity was too broad, supporters said it was needed to allow U.S. firms to compete with foreign companies.

"Most other nations with whom we trade either sanction or support the cartel system," Rep. Peter W. Rodino Jr., D-N.J., said. "Carriers that serve the U.S. trades must be given a clear set of rules that allows them to function in this international environment." Rodino was chairman of the Judiciary Committee, which along with the Merchant Marine and Fisheries Committee, crafted the bill.

Supporters argued that the basic regulatory law that granted limited immunity to shipping cartels serving foreign trade routes had become clouded by court and federal regulatory decisions. They said S 47 clarified that law — the Shipping Act of 1916 — while placing limits on shipping firms to protect shippers and consumers. The bill, for example, expanded the powers of shippers to bargain with conferences for the best rates.

The bill's backers also contended the proposal would simplify and speed approval of conference agreements by the Federal Maritime Commission (FMC). They charged that the current standards the agency was required to use to approve an agreement, including finding that the pact met a "public interest standard," was vague. The conference agreement eliminated the need for time-consuming reviews of the agreements and generally required the FMC to approve agreements within a specified time period unless they failed to meet the specific requirements of the new law.

In the past, opponents were successful in blocking maritime antitrust bills. The Senate passed a bill in 1980, but a more complex measure was held up in the House. In 1982, a House-passed bill was tied up in the Senate by a filibuster threat. *(1980 Almanac p. 259; 1982 Almanac p. 343)*

However, such foes as Sen. Howard M. Metzenbaum, D-Ohio, spoke against the conference agreement but did not try to stymie it. "I have a basic concept," Metzenbaum said, "a basic feeling that when there is price fixing, when there is a dividing of markets, it is not in the best interests of the country."

Provisions

As cleared by Congress, the Shipping Act of 1984:
- Made the act effective 90 days after enactment.

- Specified that all joint agreements among ocean common carriers to fix rates; pool or apportion traffic revenues, earnings or losses; regulate sailings and cargo volume; engage in exclusive or cooperative working arrangements; and control, regulate or prevent competition in international ocean transportation were covered by the act. Common carriers transported packaged goods between U.S. and foreign ports; bulk carriers, which transported grain and oil, were not covered.

- Stipulated that agreements involving international transportation by U.S. marine terminal operators, which furnished dock or other facilities, were covered by the act.

- Defined "shippers association" as a group of shippers that consolidated or distributed freight on a non-profit basis for the members of the group to secure carload, truckload or other volume rates or contracts. The association could negotiate rates on behalf of its members, and shipowners were prohibited from refusing to negotiate with the association.

- Required that all joint agreements be filed with the FMC but exempted from the filing requirements certain bulk cargoes and forest products, as well as recyclable metal scrap and wastepaper products that competed with them.

- Mandated that all agreements conform to detailed requirements, including allowing free entry or exit from conference membership to any carrier and permitting carriers after 10 days' notice to independently offer a different rate or service other than agreed on by the conference. In addition, each agreement must at the request of any conference member require an independent neutral body to police the obligations of the conference and its members.

- Directed the FMC to reject any agreement that did not meet the requirements enumerated in the law and to give the reasons for the rejection.

- Specified that, unless rejected by the FMC, agreements became effective 45 days after filing or 30 days after being published in the *Federal Register*, whichever was later.

- Authorized the FMC to request additional information and justification for the agreement. In that case, unless rejected by the FMC, agreements would become effective 45 days after receipt of the additional information or a statement explaining why the request was not heeded.

- Allowed the FMC to honor a request to act on an agreement in an expedited period of time of no less than 14 days.

- Authorized the FMC to seek a federal court injunction barring the implementation of an agreement, even if the agreement did not violate prohibited acts listed in the law. An injunction could be sought if the FMC determined that the agreement violated a general standard stating that "the agreement is likely, by a reduction in competition, to produce an unreasonable reduction in transportation service or an unreasonable increase in transportation cost." The burden of proof would be on the FMC, and third parties would not be allowed to intervene in court.

Antitrust Exemption

- Exempted from antitrust laws all agreements filed and approved by the FMC under the provisions of the act, and activities undertaken by carriers "with a reasonable basis to conclude" that the activity was pursuant to an agreement that would be acceptable to the FMC.

● Authorized the FMC to exempt any class of agreements or activities from the requirements of the act and from antitrust laws if it determined they would not be discriminatory, substantially reduce competition or be detrimental to commerce.

● Exempted from antitrust laws certain agreements involving foreign inland shipments (intermodal agreements) and foreign storage and handling. This allowed liner conferences to set rates on a shipment from its origin to its destination, even if non-waterborne modes were to be used.

● Eliminated existing law that permitted private antitrust suits for treble damages when the alleged violation involved an infraction of the shipping act.

Tariffs

● Required that each common carrier and conference subject to the act file all tariffs, or schedules, showing rates, charges, classifications, rules and practices with the FMC. Tariffs covering bulk cargo, forest products, recycled metal scrap and wastepaper were exempted.

● Permitted different rates for shipments of a specified volume of goods over a specified period of time.

● Authorized common carriers or conferences to enter into service contracts with shippers or shippers' associations in which the carrier agreed to provide a certain amount of space and shippers agreed to ship a certain amount of cargo over a period of time.

● Prohibited rate increases from becoming effective earlier than 30 days after filing with the FMC, unless the FMC approved. Rate decreases would be effective upon filing.

Government-Owned Carriers

● Continued current law governing carriers owned or controlled by foreign governments, including prohibiting "unjust or unreasonable" low rates or other conditions of service.

● Exempted carriers of nations with most-favored-nation treaties with the United States and exempted rates of foreign carriers for shipments between their home country and the United States.

● Authorized the FMC to suspend the rates of foreign government-owned carriers, on 60 days' notice, if it believed they were unjust and unreasonable, and limited the suspension to no more than 180 days while the FMC investigated the issue.

● Required the FMC to notify the president of a suspension or disapproval order within 10 days.

● Authorized the president to request the FMC to delay its order if he found that it was in the interests of foreign policy or national defense.

Prohibited Acts

In addition to specific acts barred by previous laws, the 1984 act:

● Prohibited false billing, classification, weighing or measurement in order to obtain lower rates.

● Prohibited common carriers from discriminating against shippers in rates or service, or rebates or refunds.

● Barred carriers from refusing to negotiate with a shippers' association, or retaliating against a shipper by refusing cargo space because the shipper had patronized another carrier or filed a complaint.

● Prohibited a conference or group of two or more common carriers from boycotting shippers, restricting use of intermodal services or technological innovations, allocating shippers among specific carriers or engaging in any predatory practice aimed at denying entry or eliminating participation in a particular route to a common carrier not a member of the conference.

● Barred loyalty contracts, except when they met antitrust laws for exclusive contracts that govern other industries. Loyalty contracts were agreements by which a shipper received a lower rate by committing all or a portion of its cargo to a carrier or conference.

Complaints

● Authorized any person to file a complaint with the FMC and seek reparations. However, only the FMC could allege that agreements were substantially anti-competitive.

● Authorized the FMC to investigate any matter that might involve a violation of the act and impose sanctions, including fines of up to twice the amount of injury shown, within three years of the alleged violation. The FMC or the complainant could seek a federal court injunction against a continuation of the activity in question.

Penalties

● Authorized the FMC to levy a civil penalty of up to $25,000 for each knowing violation of the act and a penalty of up to $5,000 for other violations.

● Authorized the FMC to suspend for up to 12 months any and all tariffs of a common carrier violating the act.

● Permitted the FMC to levy a penalty of up to $50,000 for each shipment made by a common carrier under a tariff that had been suspended.

● Required the FMC to notify the president of any punitive action within 10 days.

● Required the FMC to notify the president of any order under this section and authorized him to overturn that action within 10 days if it was determined to be in the interest of national defense or foreign policy.

● Permitted alleged violators to appeal through the courts and authorized the attorney general at the request of the FMC to obtain court-ordered payment of penalties.

Study and Advisory Commission

● Required the FMC, during the five years after enactment, to collect and analyze information on the impact of the act on international shipping, including changes in price and service, time involved in regulatory proceedings and the general status of independent carriers.

Within six months after the end of the five-year period, the FMC must report to the departments of Justice and Transportation, the Federal Trade Commission and a newly created Advisory Commission on Conferences in Ocean Shipping.

● Established, five and one-half years after enactment, a 17-member Advisory Commission on Conferences in Ocean Shipping to include a Cabinet-level officer and eight members of the private sector appointed by the president, four members of the Senate and four members of the House.

● Authorized $500,000 to carry out the commission's activities.

● Required the commission to conduct a comprehensive study of conferences in ocean shipping and recommend whether the national interest would be best served by prohibiting conferences, or by permitting conferences with open or closed membership, with a report to be submitted to the president and Congress within a year of the establishment of the commission.

Conference Action

The agreement reached by conferees Feb. 22 included the following major compromises:

● **Shippers' Association.** The House bill did not address the issue of whether shippers could form councils to negotiate with shipowners. The Senate bill provided for joint ventures by small shippers. The agreement provided for shippers' associations but did not extend antitrust immunity to them.

● **Independent Action.** Both bills called for a continuation of the right of a member of a conference to take independent action — for example, to offer a rate different from that set by the conference. But the House would have allowed independent action after just two days' notice to the conference, while the Senate limited independent action to certain rates. The compromise called for 10 days' notice.

● **Public Interest Standard.** While both bills removed the cartel's burden of showing that an agreement met a "public interest standard," they differed in the manner in which the FMC could act to prevent an agreement from being implemented.

The Senate version permitted the FMC to seek an injunction against an agreement only if it violated specific requirements enumerated in the bill. The House version authorized FMC intervention against substantially anticompetitive agreements — a variation on the public interest standard — even if they did not violate specific prohibitions of the bill.

The compromise allowed the FMC to seek an injunction if it found that an agreement would reduce competition and lead to an "unreasonable" increase in cost or reduction in service.

In addition, the compromise included specific guidelines governing agreements. It continued the prohibition against such actions as predatory pricing and boycotts.

● **Long-Range Study.** The House version established a 22-member commission to study the ocean-liner industry and make recommendations on deregulation within a year after its first meeting. The Senate called for the General Accounting Office to conduct a comprehensive two-year study of federal regulation of the industry.

The compromise established, five and a half years after enactment, a 17-member Advisory Commission on Conferences in Ocean Shipping to study the role of conferences in international shipping. Funding of $500,000 was authorized. The panel was to examine whether conferences should be prohibited, or whether conference membership should be open to all — as current U.S. law required — or closed.

In the five-year interim, the FMC was to study the impact of the 1984 act and report to the commission. ∎

Insider Trading Curbs

Congress July 25 cleared a bill (HR 559 — PL 98-376) toughening penalties for the misuse of confidential information to profit in the stock market.

Passage marked a successful end to the Securities and Exchange Commission's (SEC) two-year effort to toughen the punishment for insider trading — the misuse of nonpublic material information to profit from buying and selling securities.

Under existing law, the SEC had been able to go to court to seek an injunction barring a person from future violations, and an order forcing the person to forfeit any profits gained or losses avoided through insider transactions.

HR 559 added a third remedy: The SEC could ask a court for a civil penalty of up to three times the benefit to the violator. For instance, a trader who earned $100,000 from buying stock in a company, on a tip that the firm was about to merge with another, could be fined $400,000 — the sum of the profit and treble damages.

In addition, HR 559 increased the maximum criminal penalty for "willful violation" of the 1934 Securities Exchange Act to $100,000, from the $10,000 ceiling set 50 years earlier.

The final version also included a Senate amendment clarifying that the bill applied to trading not only in stocks but also in stock options. (An option permited a person to buy a specified number of shares of stock at a specific time for a specific price.)

Another provision added by the Senate allowed the SEC to bar or suspend dealers from the securities market if they had been disciplined by the Commodity Futures Trading Commission for violating the Commodity Exchange Act.

Final action on HR 559 came when the House by voice vote July 25 accepted the Senate version. The Senate had approved HR 559 by voice vote June 29, after substituting the text of its bill (S 910) for the version passed by the House Sept. 19, 1983. *(1983 Almanac p. 265)*

Background

Insider trading was covered under the anti-fraud provisions of federal securities laws. The term could include advance tips on such matters as corporate earnings reports, lucrative contracts, oil strikes, mergers, news reports or product failures.

Violators could be corporate officers, directors and controlling stockholders, as well as underwriters, investment analysts, lawyers, accountants, government officials, journalists and printers who sometimes received inside information before it was available to the public.

Abuses had multiplied with the increase in corporate mergers and takeovers — news of which caused stock prices to rise and fall dramatically. The SEC had initiated more cases against insider trading in the previous six years than in all the 44 years of its history, according to the House Energy and Commerce Committee's 1983 report (H Rept 98-355).

"Despite these vigorous enforcement efforts," SEC Chairman John S. R. Shad wrote in a 1982 letter to Congress, "insider trading continues because it presents the opportunity to reap huge profits with little risk."

The SEC tried to define insider trading in 1982, when it drew up its legislative proposal. It failed. In 1983 the House Energy and Commerce Subcommittee on Telecommunications, Consumer Protection and Finance likewise attempted and gave up.

Both decided to rely on past precedent. To write a definition into law, they agreed, would invite new litigation and open loopholes.

Nevertheless, Sen. Alfonse M. D'Amato, R-N.Y., insisted a definition could be found. His Senate Banking Subcommittee on Securities went to work and, at his behest, so did the SEC, for more than six months.

D'Amato offered a draft that would have prohibited "unfair use" of privileged information that violated a person's "contractual or fiduciary obligations." The definition would not have required the SEC to show, as it had to under existing law, that an individual personally benefited from giving or receiving a tip.

This proof of personal benefit had figured in two widely publicized SEC investigations. In both — one involving former Deputy Secretary of Defense Paul Thayer, and another implicating a *Wall Street Journal* reporter — the SEC had given details of the men's romantic ties with other defendants, to whom they allegedly gave confidential information.

Some securities industry spokesmen supported D'Amato's draft, saying it would end the SEC's need to release "salacious" information.

But the SEC and others objected. Finally, D'Amato relented. On June 25, the Banking Committee unanimously approved S 910, without the definition. S 910 was reported June 26, but no written report was filed. ∎

Unisex Insurance

Legislation to bar insurance companies from using gender as an actuarial factor for computing insurance rates and benefits was drastically revised before it was approved by the House Energy and Commerce Committee March 28.

Supporters of equal insurance rates and benefits for men and women promptly abandoned the revised version. There was no further action on the bill (HR 100), and no report was filed.

The committee action was a slap to a coalition of women's and civil rights groups and to the bill's cosponsors — Committee Chairman John D. Dingell, D-Mich., James J. Florio, D-N.J., and Barbara A. Mikulski, D-Md.

Victory went to the insurance industry, which had mounted a multimillion-dollar effort that included TV ads warning that "unisex insurance" would force women to pay higher premiums for life, auto, health, annuity and pension insurance. Industry supporters contended that sex characteristics were legitimate factors for risk calculations because women generally lived longer, had fewer accidents and were healthier.

But opponents said women received pension and annuity payments up to 15 percent lower than men's because of the assumption a woman would live longer to collect. Conversely, they said, health-conscious men and men who drove safely were penalized on the basis of their sex. They said insurance rates should be based instead on such factors as lifestyle, smoking and drinking habits, and driving record.

As introduced, HR 100, "The Nondiscrimination in Insurance Act," had applied to both individual and group insurance plans. It would have required all health plans to provide maternity and abortion coverage. Auto and health plans would have been revised on a unisex basis at renewal. For pension plans, it called for benefits after the effective date to be paid without regard to sex, even though the customer's previous contributions to the plan were made under sex-based rates.

The substitute approved by the committee after a contentious five-hour markup would have extended protections only to group employee plans and not to individual insurance programs — thus exempting most auto and many life and health insurance plans. It would have required health plans with abortion coverage to be higher priced and made maternity coverage optional for individual health insurance.

It would have allowed states to police insurance discrimination if they enacted similar laws and would not have required pension payments to be equal for both sexes after the effective date unless contributions had been made on a unisex basis. Insurance companies would have been given two years to comply with the bill.

Concession Attempt

HR 100 had won subcommittee approval in April 1983, but full committee action was delayed for nearly a year because many members remained undecided on the bill. *(1983 Almanac p. 558)*

In the week before full committee markup, the sponsors offered several concessions aimed at two industry complaints — that the bill would force retroactive and costly revision of existing life insurance and retirement plans, and that it required "topping off" — equalizing benefits by bringing women's payments up to men's.

The sponsors agreed to exempt life insurance policies bought before the bill's effective date; extended the date for compliance from 90 days after passage to one year; and permitted insurers to decide how to equalize benefits, possibly by bringing men's and women's payments to some midpoint.

The changes did not satisfy foes. Norman F. Lent, R-N.Y., and Wayne Dowdy, D-Miss., sponsors of the substitute to HR 100, said the bill would cost the industry billions of dollars, and add more than $1 billion to women's auto and life insurance premiums.

As for pensions, they pointed out that 21 states prohibited any reduced benefits for government employees, meaning payments to women would have to be raised to men's levels since men's benefits could not be reduced to some middle figure. Taxpayers would bear the cost, they warned.

But Florio countered that any higher costs for group employee plans would not be the result of his bill, but rather the consequence of employers' compliance with a 1983 U.S. Supreme Court decision, *Arizona Governing Committee v. Norris*. That ruling, and a 1978 decision, *City of Los Angeles v. Manhart*, held that Title VII of the 1964 Civil Rights Act forbade employers with more than 15 employees from offering group insurance plans with rates or benefits that differed for men and women. *(1983 Almanac p. 10-A)*

Amendments Approved

During the markup, the committee adopted by voice vote two anti-abortion amendments.

One amendment would have required insurance coverage for abortions to be voluntary, and the other amendment would have required any insurer who offered abortion coverage to provide identical plans without the coverage, at lower cost.

In perhaps the biggest blow to women's groups, the panel approved by a 24-18 vote an amendment by W. J. "Billy" Tauzin, D-La., to apply non-discriminatory ratemaking only to group employee plans. The Tauzin amendment would have created a commission to study whether anti-discrimination legislation was needed for individual plans.

The committee then by voice votes substituted the amended Dowdy-Lent bill for the original bill and ordered it reported. ∎

CAB Sunset Law Approved

Legislation to transfer consumer protection powers of the Civil Aeronautics Board (CAB) to the Department of Transportation (DOT) when the CAB went out of business Jan. 1, 1985, was signed by President Reagan Oct. 4 (HR 5297 — PL 98-443).

The 1978 airline deregulation law (PL 95-504) required the CAB to go out of existence but made no provision to transfer to another agency such consumer and regulatory activities as controlling smoking on flights and bumping passengers to other flights. HR 5297 did not affect the deregulation of routes and fares established by the 1978 legislation. *(1978 Almanac p. 496)*

The measure was cleared for the president Sept. 20 when the Senate adopted the conference report (H Rept 98-1025) by voice vote. The House had adopted the conference report by voice vote the day before.

Provisions

As cleared, the Civil Aeronautics Board Sunset Act of 1984:

● Transferred from the CAB to DOT authority to continue consumer protection rules such as those regulating smoking on flights, baggage damage and bumping of passengers to other flights.

● Transferred from the CAB to DOT the authority to approve consolidations, mergers and antitrust exemptions for airlines.

● Transferred from the CAB to DOT authority to deal with competitive abuses, preserving a controversial recent ruling by the CAB governing computer reservation systems.

● Gave DOT authority to certify an air carrier's fitness.

● Allowed DOT to collect information on civil air travel.

● Required DOT to study the feasibility of a high-speed rail line between West Falls Church, Va., and Dulles International Airport.

● Allowed current CAB employees to be transferred to other agencies.

● Gave DOT, rather than the Postal Service, authority to set rates for transportation of mail for the state of Alaska until 1989.

● Directed the Postal Service, in contracting for transportation of mail in Alaska, to use established, year-round carriers.

● Preserved the current level of air service between Cordova, Yakutat, Gustavus, Petersburg and Wrangell, Alaska, until 1987, with a cap of $3.6 million per year for compensation under a program in which the government subsidized service in small communities, without which service might not be provided.

● Required DOT to consider the question of access for the handicapped to airports in issuing rules or orders.

Legislative History

House. The House passed HR 5297 (H Rept 98-793) by voice vote June 5. The measure was reported May 21 by the Public Works and Transportation Committee.

The Reagan administration opposed the bill, which transferred CAB functions to the Transportation Department. The administration wanted the Federal Trade Commission to take over consumer-related functions and the Justice Department to absorb antitrust matters such as approval of airline mergers and granting of antitrust exemptions.

Antitrust waivers had been required for some key industry practices, including the system that allowed airlines to use standardized tickets and to check baggage through to a final destination.

Senate. A similar bill was unanimously reported July 25 by the Senate Commerce, Science and Transportation Committee (S 2796 — S Rept 98-565).

But by 11-5, the panel added a controversial amendment to give individuals and communities the right to petition DOT to redress grievances — a provision toward possible re-regulation of the airline industry that Transportation Secretary Elizabeth Hanford Dole warned could trigger a veto of the bill.

The Senate passed an amended version of HR 5297 by voice vote Aug. 8.

The Senate-passed measure encompassed the provisions of S 2796 with one exception: Senators approved an amendment by Bob Packwood, R-Ore., chairman of the Commerce Committee, giving the Justice Department authority over certain antitrust matters. As reported by the Commerce Committee, the Senate measure had corresponded with HR 5297 on the antitrust issue — giving the authority to DOT — but Packwood agreed to change that provision when the measure came to the Senate floor.

Conference. Senate-House conferees Sept. 13 reached agreement on the differences between the two bills. They accepted the House position on transferring antitrust authority to the Transportation Department, and they dropped a Senate provision giving DOT the power to hear grievances against airlines. Conferees agreed to require DOT to consider the access needs of handicapped passengers. ■

Puerto Rico Cruises

American travelers would be able to go by ship between the mainland and Puerto Rico under legislation cleared by Congress Oct. 11 (HR 89 — PL 98-563).

The bill, sought by Puerto Rico's tourist industry but opposed by U.S. shipping interests, was cleared for the president when the House by voice vote agreed to minor changes in HR 89 adopted by the Senate earlier that day. The House had passed the bill by a vote of 390-25 May 15. *(Vote 130, p. 44-H)*

The measure permitted foreign-flag ships to carry passengers between Puerto Rico and the U.S. mainland. Under current law, ship travel between points in the U.S. was restricted to U.S.-flag ships, but regular service to Puerto Rico on such ships had not been available since 1953. There were only two U.S.-registered cruise ships, and both served the Hawaiian Islands.

Foreign-flag cruise ships were allowed to dock in Puerto Rico, but customs regulations forbade passengers from disembarking for more than 24 hours. Cruise ships had not been able to offer fly-cruise packages in which tourists could travel by ship from a U.S. port and fly back from Puerto Rico.

Supporters of the legislation said it would boost the island's tourist-oriented economy. Opponents, including maritime unions and U.S. shipping companies, said it would discourage U.S. ship operators from trying to revive coastal service. The exemption would be phased out if U.S.-flag carriers offered service in the future.

The bill was reported by the Merchant Marine and Fisheries Committee on May 3 (H Rept 98-733) and by the

Senate Commerce, Science and Transportation Committee on Oct. 4 (S Rept 98-658).

In 1982, the Senate blocked a similar bill that had passed the House by a vote of 387-0. In 1984, several senators voiced opposition, but they did not attempt to hold up the legislation, which the Senate passed by voice vote Oct. 11.   ∎

Telephone Access Fees

The Senate Jan. 26 shelved legislation that would have postponed a controversial Federal Communications Commission (FCC) plan to impose new monthly charges on residential and small business telephone users.

After four days of debate, the Senate by a 44-40 vote rejected a motion to take up the bill (S 1660). The Senate vote came one day after the FCC reaffirmed its decision to delay the new fees. *(Vote 1, p. 2-S)*

S 1660 had been reported by the Senate Commerce Committee Oct. 7, 1983 (S Rept 98-270). The House Nov. 10, 1983, had passed a tougher bill (HR 4102) that would have banned the fees altogether. *(1983 Almanac p. 545)*

The Senate vote was seen as a major victory for the Reagan administration and American Telephone & Telegraph Co. (AT&T) and a defeat for a coalition of consumer groups and labor unions, led by Ralph Nader's Public Citizen.

Commerce Committee Chairman Bob Packwood, R-Ore., chief sponsor of S 1660, said the key to the bill's defeat was not the $4 million lobbying campaign waged against the legislation by AT&T but the fact that the FCC had changed its position and agreed to defer imposition of the fees.

The day before the vote, the FCC affirmed its Jan. 16 decision not to impose the so-called "access charges" in April 1984 and to put them off until at least June 1985. S 1660 would have blocked the charge through 1985. The FCC acted after 32 senators wrote requesting the delay.

The FCC had proposed the access charge to replace the longstanding system of cross-subsidies that had been helping to keep local rates artificially low at the expense of overpriced long-distance rates. The FCC and AT&T said the charges were essential to the success of the court-ordered breakup of AT&T, which took effect Jan. 1. They would enable AT&T to cut long-distance rates and better compete with other long-distance companies.

Under the FCC's revised plan, the access charge for residential users and small businesses with one line would go into effect no sooner than June 1985 and would be capped at $4 per month until 1980.

Opponents of S 1660 said that the FCC, by revising its original plan, had done what the bill wanted the agency to do. "I thought our goal all along was to change the commission's course, and change it we have," said Frank R. Lautenberg, D-N.J., who originally proposed the moratorium on residential access charges.

Although AT&T had criticized the FCC for postponing the charges, it had feared that Congress might take even stronger steps. AT&T Executive Vice President Kenneth J. Whalen said, "We are glad to see the issues returned to the FCC for resolution."

Fourth Delay

Robert Dole, R-Kan., who was among the senators asking the FCC to delay the fees, commended Packwood for drawing attention to the issue and forcing the FCC to modify its plan.

But Packwood did not claim victory. He said the FCC had "ducked, bobbed and weaved in the hope of finessing itself to a position where either this issue loses its head of steam or perhaps we will get to a point where we have a long adjournment and forget about it."

Packwood insisted all along that the FCC still could change its position. "If Congress wants to make sure that what we want to achieve is going to be achieved," he said, "we had best do it by statute rather than leaving it to the vagaries of the FCC. They have already proven that it will be impossible to predict what they might do."

The latest FCC plan was its fourth proposal on access charges. In December 1982, the agency proposed a $2-a-month charge on residential users beginning Jan. 1, 1984, gradually rising to about $8 to $12 per month by 1990. In 1983 and 1984, the FCC revised its plan, slowing the increase in residential fees.

(On Dec. 19, the FCC voted for a $1 monthly charge, effective in June. It would increase to $2 monthly in 1986 and be capped at that, pending FCC hearings in 1986.)

Business Fees Delayed

Large businesses and long-distance telephone companies won a brief reprieve from paying their new access charges. The FCC, under pressure from congressional opponents of the charges, on March 20 moved the effective date for the charges from April 3 to June 13, 1984.

The FCC had delayed the charges once before, from Jan. 1 to April 3. At the time of the second delay, the FCC said more time was needed to review the rates proposed by the seven local Bell companies.   ∎

Recall of Dangerous Toys

A loophole in federal law that prevented products hazardous to children from being recalled as quickly as other dangerous goods was closed by Congress in 1984.

The House Oct. 3 cleared the bill (HR 5818) for the president, who signed it Oct. 17 (PL 98-491).

The legislation allowed the Consumer Product Safety Commission (CPSC) to order that toys, furniture or clothes for children be pulled from the market immediately — just as other faulty products were — if the commission found "substantial risk of injury." The CPSC could publish notice of the defect, order a recall and require a retailer to repair, replace or refund a purchase.

Previously, children's products were regulated under the Federal Hazardous Substances Act, rather than the later Consumer Product Safety Act that created the commission. The earlier law required the CPSC to go through a time-consuming administrative process before it could order a recall of children's goods. *(Congress and the Nation Vol. II, p. 797)*

Legislative History. HR 5818 was reported by the House Energy and Commerce Committee on July 24 (H Rept 98-895) and was passed by the House by voice vote on Aug. 6. A companion measure was reported Aug. 9 by the Senate Commerce, Science and Transportation Committee (S 2650 — S Rept 98-591) and passed by the Senate by voice vote Sept. 12.

On Oct. 3 the Senate by voice vote approved HR 5818 with minor changes. Later that day the House accepted the Senate changes, clearing the measure for the president.   ∎

Congress Encourages 21-Year Drinking Age

In response to growing pressure to curb drunken driving, Congress July 28 cleared legislation to encourage states to raise the minimum drinking age to 21.

The Senate June 26 added the drinking age and other drunken-driving provisions to a non-controversial House-passed bill (HR 4616 — H Rept 98-641) that required states to spend federal funds to promote the use of children's car seats. The House by voice vote cleared the bill June 28 for the president, who signed it July 17 (PL 98-363).

The legislation took a "carrot and stick" approach. For the "stick," it required withholding a portion of federal highway funds from states that by 1987 had not enacted laws prohibiting the purchase or possession of alcohol by persons under the age of 21. The "carrot" provided financial incentives for states to institute mandatory minimum sentences for drunken drivers.

In the past, federal action had focused only on establishing financial incentives to encourage states to crack down on drunken driving. A 1982 law (HR 6170 — PL 97-364) authorized an extra $125 million in highway safety funds in fiscal 1983-85 for states that established tough drunken-driving laws. A 21-year-old drinking age was one of several suggested remedies. *(1982 Almanac p. 339)*

Impetus for a stronger approach came from a number of groups, including Mothers Against Drunk Drivers (MADD), a grass-roots group claiming a half-million members in 44 states. Largely composed of victims of drunken drivers, and victims' relatives, MADD campaigned in state after state using their own tragic stories to dramatize the problem.

MADD said federal action was needed to establish a uniform drinking age because states with a minimum drinking age of 21 found that their teenagers drove to neighboring states where it was legal to drink. That created what MADD called "blood borders" as teenagers drove home drunk.

Opposition to a national minimum drinking age came from student groups, restaurant owners, retail sellers of alcohol and the Distilled Spirits Council of the United States. Conservatives argued that requiring a national minimum age was an infringement of states' rights and constituted age discrimination.

While President Reagan supported a 21-year drinking age, he initially opposed the legislation on the grounds it violated states' rights but later supported it.

Legislative Summary

The House moved first on the drunken driving issue. On June 7 it added to a controversial highway funding bill (HR 5504) an amendment withholding certain highway aid from states that failed to raise the drinking age to 21. *(Highway funding, p. 290)*

The Senate's highway aid bill (S 2527) was mired in controversy of its own, and advocates of tougher drunken driving laws chose as the vehicle for their efforts HR 4616, a non-controversial child-restraint bill passed by the House April 30.

Several key senators held up action, however, until a compromise was reached that permitted them to add amendments providing incentives to states to strengthen penalties for drunk drivers of any age.

The compromise amendment, offered June 26 by Frank R. Lautenberg, D-N.J., was adopted by a vote of 81-16, and the bill passed by voice vote. *(Vote 158, p. 28-S)*

With the pre-July 4 recess jam of legislation, it appeared the House might not act on the Senate amendment. But Rep. James J. Howard, D-N.J., chairman of the Public Works and Transportation Committee and chief sponsor of the House measure, squeezed the bill onto the calendar.

Early in the morning of June 28, with only a score of members left on the floor, the House agreed to the measure by voice vote, clearing it for the president.

Provisions

As cleared by Congress, HR 4616:

● Authorized $126.5 million in fiscal 1985 and $132 million in fiscal 1986 for grants to the states for highway safety programs.

● Required states to spend at least 8 percent of their highway safety funds for programs to promote the use of child safety restraints in automobiles.

● Added state-sponsored programs to combat driving under the influence of drugs to the criteria under which states could receive incentive grants under PL 97-364 to combat drunk driving.

● Authorized a total of $23.5 million in fiscal 1985 and 1986 to help states computerize their traffic records to pinpoint places where traffic accidents occurred most frequently.

● Penalized states with a drinking age under 21 by withholding 5 percent of their federal highway funds (not including highway safety funds) in fiscal 1987 and 10 percent in 1988; those funds could be restored if a state subsequently raised its drinking age to 21.

● Provided incentive grants, up to 5 percent of current highway safety funds, for states that enacted mandatory minimum sentences for those convicted of drunken driving.

'Fire-Safe' Cigarettes

Congress Oct. 4 cleared legislation (HR 1880 — H Rept 98-917) authorizing a study of the feasibility of developing "fire-safe" cigarettes that would be less likely to ignite household furnishings.

The final version delegated the lead role in the study to the Consumer Product Safety Commission, with prominent roles for the U.S. Fire Administration and the Department of Health and Human Services.

The bill was reported July 30 (H Rept 98-917) by the House Energy and Commerce Committee. The House passed the measure by voice vote Aug. 6. Both chambers subsequently added minor amendments, with the Senate finally accepting the House-amended version on Oct. 4. The president signed the measure Oct. 30 (PL 98-567).

The legislation, developed in cooperation with the Tobacco Institute, created a 15-member group, including four members from the institute, to advise Congress within two and a half years whether a fire-safe cigarette was feasible.

The sentences could include the following: for first offenders, two days in jail or 100 hours of community service and a 90-day license suspension; for second offenders, 10 days and a one-year suspension; for third offenders, 120 days and a three-year suspension. Those convicted of driving while their licenses were suspended for drunken driving would get at least 30 days.

Background

Through the efforts of MADD and other groups, increasing national attention focused on alcohol-related traffic accidents. Supporters of national legislation argued that 50 percent of the 45,000 annual traffic deaths were caused by drunk drivers, with between 5,000 and 10,000 of the fatalities being under 21.

Alcohol-related accidents were the leading cause of death among youths 15-24 years old, they said.

They cited several studies that noted that youths were involved in proportionately far more automobile accidents than adults and recommended raising the legal drinking age as an effective means of lowering traffic fatalities.

A minimum national drinking age was one of the recommendations made in 1982 by the Presidential Commission on Drunk Driving. The commission also called for withholding 100 percent of federal highway aid from any state that did not have a 21-year minimum drinking age.

While 24 states between 1970 and 1973 lowered the drinking age from 21, more than a dozen states had raised the legal limit since 1974. Currently, 22 states had a minimum drinking age of 21, and Arizona was to join them Jan. 1, 1985. Nine states permitted people younger than 21 to drink beer or wine.

A National Transportation Safety Board (NTSB) study found that in the first year after Michigan raised its drinking age from 18 to 21, there was a 21 percent decline in alcohol-related deaths among drivers 18 to 20. NTSB, like the presidential commission, favored a nationwide drinking age of 21, but NTSB advocated that the states pass their own laws.

House Action

The first signal that Congress was ready to enact stiffer drunk driving laws came Feb. 7 when the House Energy and Commerce Committee approved a bill (HR 3870 — H Rept 98-606) making it a federal crime to sell to anyone under 21 alcoholic beverages manufactured in another state, transported in interstate commerce or sold in an establishment that was in or affected interstate commerce. Violators would be assessed a $5000 fine.

A companion bill (S 1948) was then pending in the Senate Commerce, Science and Transportation Committee.

However, HR 3870 never reached the floor, and on June 7, Howard opened a different legislative avenue by offering a drinking age amendment to HR 5504, a bill to release over $7 billion in Interstate highway funds.

Howard's amendment would have withheld 15 percent of federal highway construction aid over two years, beginning in 1987, if states with lower ages at which individuals were permitted to buy liquor failed to raise the minimum age to 21.

The amendment passed by voice vote after more than two dozen members spoke up for it. The House subsequently passed HR 5504 on June 7 by a 297-73 vote. *(Vote 198, p. 62-H)*

Senate Action

After the House acted, momentum to enact tough drunken driving legislation quickened, with Reagan announcing his support for the legislation June 13.

However, floor action on the Senate's version of the highway funding bill (S 2527) was blocked by disputes over the addition of special highway projects and mass transit funding.

Senators turned to HR 4616 as a vehicle for drunken driving legislation. But floor action was delayed because Sen. Lowell P. Weicker Jr., R-Conn., and other senators protested that the amendment being discussed focused only on age and did not provide incentives for the states to strengthen other laws, such as providing stiffer penalities and sentences for violations of all age groups.

The path for Senate action was cleared June 21 when key senators reached a compromise offering both incentives and punishments.

The most controversial portion of the compromise amendment offered by Lautenberg was a provision withholding 5 percent of federal highway funds in fiscal 1987 and 10 percent in fiscal 1988 from states that failed to raise their drinking age to 21. Conservatives fought it as an infringement on states' rights and as age discrimination.

A substitute amendment was offered by Gordon J. Humphrey, R-N.H., which would have provided incentives rather than punishments to the states for such action.

Opponents of Humprhey's proposal pointed to the 1982 federal law, which offered extra funds to states that enacted 21-year-old drinking ages. They said only four states had done so.

"It is time to use the stick — sparingly, but effectively," Lautenberg said.

Humphrey and Steven D. Symms, R-Idaho, argued that Lautenberg's plan infringed on states' rights by pressuring them on a matter traditionally under state control.

Symms also suggested that "raising the legal drinking age has no effect on the actual drinking age," citing statistics from states where alcohol-related fatalities among teenagers had risen after the drinking age had been raised.

Several senators said the move constituted age discrimination, especially since, statistically, teenagers were no worse offenders than those in the 21-to-25 age group, and the peak age for drunk driving was 37.

"Why the magic age of 21?" asked Sen. Patrick J. Leahy, D-Vt. "Why not 25? How about 30, 35, 40?"

In the end, however, members believed it was, in Lautenberg's words, "a rare opportunity to take action to save young lives." The Humphrey amendment failed by a 35-62 vote after four hours of debate, and the Lautenberg proposal was approved. *(Vote 157, p. 28-S)*

The amendment also provided incentives for states to beef up laws penalizing driving while under the influence of drugs and to computerize records. It also raised the House-passed authorizations for grants to states for highway safety programs from $115 million in fiscal 1985 to $126.5 million, and from $120 million in fiscal 1986 to $132 million. ∎

Sports Team Moves

The Senate Commerce, Science and Transportation Committee Aug. 9 reported a bill (S 2505 — S Rept 98-952) designed to block professional sports teams from making sudden breaks away from their hometowns. There was no further action, however, in the 98th Congress.

After committee approval of the bill June 13 by a 9-8 vote, Sen. Slade Gorton, R-Wash., conceded that it was too late in the session to expect further action on his bill. But he said the committee vote laid the groundwork for action in 1985 on several questions involving major-league sports — not only concerning teams that abandoned their hometowns, but also major-league expansions, revenue sharing and antitrust exemptions.

By coincidence, Gorton filed his bill March 29 — the same day the Baltimore Colts football team left that city, literally in the dark of night, for Indianapolis. The furor that the team owner spawned in the Washington area gave a major boost to what became known as "the Colts' bill."

Provisions

Under the bill, a local community would have had a "right of first refusal" before its professional football, baseball, basketball or hockey team could have relocated. S 2505 would have established procedures for a local stadium authority, along with a team's league, to determine whether a planned move was justified, based on factors such as fan support, team finances and stadium condition.

One controversial provision of Gorton's bill would have required the National Football League (NFL) to add two new teams, one of which must be located in Baltimore.

The NFL would have been exempted from the relocation procedures if the league had agreed, by Jan. 31, 1985, to add two new teams. But Gorton said he would push for a bill applicable to the NFL as soon as there was resolution in a related lawsuit pitting the NFL against the Los Angeles Raiders, formerly the Oakland Raiders.

Objections Raised

Several senators objected to the bill. John C. Danforth, R-Mo., asked, "Why does the government of the United States want to get into this?"

Gorton countered that major-league teams received more public subsidies — through taxpayer-financed stadiums, "sweetheart leases" and local tax breaks — than most local businesses. He said fans deserved protection from "the absolutely arbitrary movement of teams ... simply because an individual owner wishes to move." ∎

Efforts to Deregulate Broadcasting Collapse

Efforts in the House to reach agreement on the deregulation of the broadcasting industry broke down in April 1984, and a Senate-passed measure died when Congress adjourned.

After nearly a year of on-and-off negotiations, members of the House Energy and Commerce Subcommittee on Telecommunications failed to agree on the legislation.

The Senate had passed a deregulation bill (S 55) in 1983, but Rep. Timothy E. Wirth, D-Colo., subcommittee chairman, had blocked action on a similar House bill (HR 2382). By 1984, HR 2382 had 232 sponsors in the House.

Wirth had promised to submit deregulation legislation to the full Energy and Commerce Committee by Oct. 15, 1983, after allies of the broadcasting industry had threatened to bypass his panel and take the issue before the full committee. But no agreement was reached by October, and the negotiations continued in the next session. *(1983 Almanac p. 551)*

The debate within the panel broke along a philosophical divide. Deregulation supporters said broadcasters should enjoy the same First Amendment freedoms as other media. Opponents countered that, despite the growth of cable television and other technological innovations, the public airwaves were limited and so licensees should continue to be regulated.

Senate attempts in 1981 and 1982 to deregulate the broadcasting industry also had been stymied by House opponents. *(1981 Almanac p. 569; 1982 Almanac p. 341)*

Background

The National Association of Broadcasters (NAB), the radio and television trade organization, had been pushing hard for deregulation.

Additional pressure was put on Congress when the Federal Communications Commission (FCC) announced in June 1983 that it planned to deregulate the television industry on its own administratively. One major reason the FCC cited for its move was to put over-the-air broadcasters on a more equal footing with cable TV stations, which operated under different and less restrictive standards.

Under proposed FCC rules, the commission was to give up many of its controls over program content and licensing of the 862 commercial TV stations in the United States. The action was the latest of several steps initiated by FCC Chairman Mark S. Fowler to get the government out of regulating the broadcast industry. The FCC was expected to take a year or more to implement its new rules, depending on court challenges.

In 1981, the FCC had moved to eliminate most regulations governing the nation's 8,260 commercial radio stations. That action was upheld May 1983 in a ruling by the U.S. Court of Appeals for the District of Columbia.

One of the most significant rule changes proposed by the FCC was eliminating the "5-5-10" guideline for news and public service programming. The regulation suggested TV broadcasters devote at least 5 percent of their air time to news and public affairs; 5 percent to local programs; and 10 percent to non-entertainment shows. That was to be replaced by a more general requirement for programming that "addresses issues of concern" to viewers.

Other proposed changes included ending the regulations that required a station to provide rebuttal time to persons whose integrity was attacked on the air and to opponents of political candidates endorsed by station editorials; lifting the existing limit of 16 minutes of commercials per hour; dropping most requirements for stations to maintain logs of their programs; and eliminating the ascertainment rule that forced stations to survey their audiences to find out what kinds of programs were desired.

Philosophical Differences

Behind the battle over deregulation was a basic philosophical difference about the federal role in setting standards governing the content of what might be broadcast.

Existing law, based on the Federal Communications Act of 1934, required broadcasters to serve the public interest. Regulations developed over the years had defined what public interest meant and how broadcasters were expected to serve it, such as through the 5-5-10 guideline and the existing process of license renewal, in which a broadcaster's past performance was compared to the services promised by a new applicant (called "comparative renewal").

Proponents of deregulation contended the industry had reached the point at which government controls over program content were no longer necessary because competition in the open market would see that most viewers' needs were met.

The FCC's Fowler pointed out that radio stations were so diverse and competitive that listeners were assured a full choice of programming, and that cable technology was providing much the same choice in television.

The FCC also argued that broadcasters spent vast amounts of time complying with federal regulations — up to 2.5 million working hours a year, by one estimate. Removing unnecessary federal rules would allow "marketplace forces to operate more cheaply and efficiently," in the words of Sen. Barry Goldwater, R-Ariz., chairman of the Commerce, Science and Transportation Subcommittee on Communications.

But critics did not believe the broadcasting business had become all that diverse, especially in rural areas where there were over-the-air broadcast stations or cable TV systems.

Even though existing FCC regulations seldom had been used to deny a broadcaster's license, the critics said the government should retain its regulatory power to make sure broadcasters paid attention to their audience. As they saw it, the industry's deregulation proposals would allow broadcasters to save a lot of money, enjoy permanent licensing and escape responsibility for local coverage.

The major umbrella organization fighting broadcast deregulation was the Telecommunications Research and Action Council (TRAC), which included 120 labor, civil rights, church and consumer groups.

Legislative Proposals

The key deregulation bills in the Senate and House — S 55 and HR 2382 — would have codified the FCC's radio and TV deregulation efforts.

S 55 would have ended the comparative renewal process for licenses. For radio, the bill would have eliminated news and public affairs requirements, limits on commercials, and rules that required stations to survey the needs and interests of their audience. Broadcasters would have had to pay fees to help cover the cost of FCC regulation.

HR 2382, proposed by Tom Tauke, R-Iowa, and W. J. "Billy" Tauzin, D-La., went even further than S 55 in deregulation. It not only codified the FCC's deregulation of radio and TV, but also eliminated any fee broadcasters would pay.

Negotiations Collapse

During the Telecommunications Subcommittee negotiations, Wirth dropped his insistence on two issues that had doomed past deregulation efforts — comparative license renewal for television and radio stations, and spectrum fees that radio stations would pay for the use of the public airwaves.

But, in return, Wirth and his allies insisted the bill had to have public-interest safeguards, such as requirements that TV broadcasters air minimum amounts of news, public affairs and educational children's programming. Other regulations proposed by Wirth had included guarantees for rebuttal of political criticism and for minority licenses.

The broadcasting industry would not accept Wirth's demands. Convinced that any bill would be more "regulatory than deregulatory," the NAB broke with the subcommittee March 9.

The NAB asked John D. Dingell, D-Mich., Energy and Commerce Committee chairman, to take the matter out of Wirth's grip, a tactic that had failed in 1983. Again, on March 22, Dingell refused.

The talks finally broke down the next month. Wirth on April 27 released a memo in which he said the recent stance taken by subcommittee members Tauke and Tauzin "comes very close to evidencing bad faith."

On April 30, Tauke told a broadcasters' convention that he and Tauzin had broken off talks because of "basic philosophical differences" with Wirth.   ∎

Cable Deregulation Passed

One day before adjournment, Congress passed a bill to deregulate cable television, culminating a four-year effort to balance the rights of the industry against those of the cities that granted franchises.

Cable companies had pushed for a national policy to protect them from what they considered to be a hodgepodge of local regulations that restricted the growth of the industry. Cities wanted to retain some control through the franchising process and in 1984 sought to counter rulings by the Federal Communications Commission (FCC) and U.S. Supreme Court that permitted federal regulation to supersede local or state actions.

Attempts to strike a balance had failed since 1981, and the 1984 outcome was in question up until the closing days of the session.

The measure that was cleared by the House by voice vote Oct. 11 (S 66 — PL 98-549) was the fourth version of the legislation to surface in the 98th Congress. Two earlier compromises failed to reach the floor because of differences between the National Cable Television Association (NCTA) and groups representing cities, such as the U.S. Conference of Mayors and National League of Cities.

The two sides agreed on a third version, which the House approved by voice vote Oct. 1. But several senators blocked floor action because of objections to the House's affirmative action requirements, and key members privately pronounced the measure dead.

When Congress continued in session past the expected adjournment date of Oct. 4, negotiations resumed. A compromise that included dropping what some senators regarded as minority hiring quotas led to the Senate's passing the bill by voice vote Oct. 11.

The final legislation was considerably different from the original S 66 (S Rept 98-67) passed by the Senate June 14, 1983. Some cities had backed away from that bill, declaring it too lenient to the industry. *(Senate passage, 1983 Almanac p. 552; previous action, 1982 Almanac p. 341; 1981 Almanac p. 557)*

As cleared by Congress, S 66 recognized cities' power to grant and renew franchises but outlined standard procedures to be followed so that cable companies would be less vulnerable to local decisions. The bill limited cities' control over cable programming, allowed cities to regulate rates for only two years except under limited circumstances and capped the franchise fees cities could charge companies at 5 percent of local revenues. The bill also contained provisions to protect the privacy of subscribers.

Provisions

As cleared, the Cable Telecommunications Act (S 66):

● Stipulated that cities could regulate cable rates only for basic service — the transmission of signals from local broadcast stations — and only for two years after enactment. After that, rates would not be regulated.

● Permitted cable companies to raise subscription rates by up to 5 percent a year, without prior approval, during the two years that rates were locally regulated.

● Stated that cities had the power to grant and renew franchises for local cable systems.

● Replaced the current jumble of state and local renewal procedures with national standards, which included optional hearings, criteria for local officials' decisions, a court appeals process and compensation for firms forced to sell property when franchises were revoked.

● Required that all parts of a city be served, to guard against bypassing low-income areas.

● Capped the franchise fees that a city could charge a cable TV company at 5 percent of the company's local gross revenues.

● Exempted from regulation one-way cable services such as videotex, teletext, computer software and dial-a-movie, but provided that two-way services such as data and voice transmission would continue to be regulated by state utility commissions, as telephone companies were.

● Permitted cities to require that cable companies reserve channels for public, educational and government use.

● Precluded cities from demanding specific video or information programs, although broad categories — such as news or children's shows — could be requested.

● Allowed cities to ban programs they judged to be obscene and required companies to provide "lock box" devices to subscribers who wanted to prevent their children from watching objectionable shows.

● Provided that cable operators could drop or change promised services but only after negotiations with local officials.

● Required channels to be available for lease by commercial interests with programs to air, free of editorial control of the cable company.

● Prohibited local television or telephone companies from also owning an area's cable franchise, unless the purchase was made before July 1, 1984, or unless the FCC permitted a telephone company to provide cable service to a rural area that otherwise might not attract other cable companies.

Privacy

● Protected subscribers' privacy by requiring their prior approval before cable companies could disclose any "personally identifiable information," such as their program choices or viewing habits.

● Set civil and criminal penalties for the theft of cable services, such as tapping neighbors' wires or using converters, satellite dishes or other devices to receive cable signals without paying the company.

● Strengthened FCC power to enforce anti-discrimination regulations.

● Lengthened the time allowed for public comment on cable licensing matters, giving interested parties a better chance to participate.

● Established a congressional commission to study telecommunications policies.

House Action

A cable television bill (HR 4103) approved in November 1983 by the House Energy and Commerce Subcommittee on Telecommunications remained in limbo because of disagreement by some cities and cable system operators.

In May 1984, the NCTA, the National League of Cities and the U.S. Conference of Mayors announced they had reached a compromise. The revised bill (HR 4103 — H Rept 98-934) was approved June 26 by the House Energy and Commerce Committee, with some additional changes. But the industry, citing court and agency rulings handed down only days before the markup, almost immediately called for revisions easing local control of subscriber rates, license renewal and fees, to bring the bill in line with the rulings.

On June 18, the Supreme Court in *Capital Cities Cable Inc. et al. v. Crisp* struck down Oklahoma's ban on cable transmission of wine ads and reaffirmed the authority of the FCC to pre-empt state and local regulation of cable TV.

In the wake of the ruling, some cable TV operators were anxious to shuck HR 4103, with its limited decontrol, and rush to the FCC for full deregulation.

The NCTA board of directors July 17 agreed to seek revisions, including greater easing of local control of subscriber rates, assurance of franchise renewal, restrictions on franchise fees and freer access to apartment buildings.

Most of all, NCTA wanted the House to reconsider language that would end cities' authority to regulate subscriber rates after four years. Given the Supreme Court's action, some operators did not want to wait that long to be freed from city control.

The National League of Cities, however, objected to the proposed changes and called for passage of the bill as reported by the committee.

Another Compromise

Members in both chambers prodded the industry and city to reach another compromise.

The Senate's chief sponsor of S 66, Barry Goldwater, R-Ariz., repeatedly warned the cities against intransigence. From the House side, John D. Dingell, D-Mich., Energy and Commerce chairman, in a letter Sept. 21 castigated the industry for "greed and arrogance" and threatened, "The ultimate victim will be the cable industry itself."

Dingell's letter was timed for a Sept. 24 emergency meeting of the NCTA board. The board agreed to send its negotiators back to the cities with a new proposal.

The two sides Sept. 26 announced they had reached another compromise on HR 4103. The pact would end cities' control over cable rates after two years, instead of four years as the committee bill provided. Cable operators had wanted city control of rates to end immediately.

The compromise also created a standard process for franchise renewals.

In addition, Rep. Timothy E. Wirth, D-Colo., chairman of the Subcommittee on Telecommunications, agreed to drop an amendment he had added in markup permitting apartment dwellers to order any cable service, even if alternative service was provided to the building. Cable operators had complained that would benefit their competitors in the satellite master antenna television business, who provided private systems serving only multi-unit residential dwellings.

After accepting a series of amendments offered by

Wirth incorporating the compromise, the House approved HR 4103 by voice vote Oct. 1 and amended the text to S 66.

Final Action

The appointment of Senate conferees was blocked by several members, led by Orrin G. Hatch, R-Utah, and Jesse Helms, R-N.C.

They objected to a House provision requiring cable companies to hire women and minorities for top-level jobs in partial proportion to their percentage of the local work force. Companies with fewer than five employees were exempted. The guidelines were similar to existing regulations of the FCC, but the Senate Republicans objected to what they regarded as "quotas."

Late on Oct. 5, the Senate appeared ready to act after the bill's sponsors — Goldwater and Bob Packwood, R-Ore., chairman of the Commerce, Science and Transportation Committee — agreed to strike the affirmative action section.

But that prompted Howard M. Metzenbaum, D-Ohio, a supporter of the provision, to block floor action.

On Oct. 11, key House members agreed to drop all references to the percentages of jobs to be filled by women and minorities. The same day, the Senate by voice vote adopted a Hatch amendment strengthening the FCC's power to enforce its current regulations. As modified, the bill required the FCC to certify annually that companies complied with the regulations, to make on-site audits every five years and to assess fines of $200 a day for violations.

Also adopted were amendments by Goldwater clarifying technical sections of the bill and creating a congressional commission to review telecommunications policies; and by Metzenbaum, ensuring public participation in franchise proceedings.

Members also agreed to delete House language prohibiting a newspaper from owning a cable system in its city. ∎

Public Broadcast Vetoes

President Reagan twice slapped down a bipartisan effort to restore administration budget cuts for public broadcasting and vetoed two bills that would have authorized three times his funding request.

In both cases, the president said the increases could not be justified in light of the need to exercise spending restraint to lower the budget deficit.

The vetoed bills were:

● S 2436, which authorized $761 million for fiscal 1987-89 for the Corporation for Public Broadcasting (CPB) and $159 million for fiscal 1985-87 for the Public Telecommunications Facilities Program, which provided grants for broadcast equipment. The president vetoed the measure Aug. 29. *(Veto text, p. 24-E)*

● S 607, which authorized $675 million over three years for CPB and $100 million over three years for the facilities program. Reagan pocket-vetoed the measure on Oct. 19, after Congress had adjourned *sine die.* (When Congress is in session, a bill becomes law without the president's signature if he does not act upon it within 10 days, excluding Sundays. When Congress has adjourned within the 10-day period, the president may pocket-veto the bill by not acting upon it.) *(Veto text, p. 25-E)*

The administration had proposed a total of $255 million for CPB and sought no funds for the facilities program.

The second veto came in spite of efforts by Sen. Barry Goldwater, R-Ariz., to reach a compromise with the administration. But the president said the proposed funding level was still too high and told Congress in his veto message that "unrestrained increases of this magnitude — no matter how worthy the programs — are unacceptable."

Goldwater, chairman of the Senate Commerce, Science and Transportation Committee Subcommittee on Communications, was the chief Senate sponsor of both bills.

Failure to enact the reauthorization bills did not immediately affect funding for the two programs.

Congress had included $200 million for fiscal 1987 for CPB in the Labor, Health and Human Services, Education appropriations bill (HR 6028 — PL 98-619). CPB funds were appropriated two years in advance in an effort to insulate the corporation from political pressures. *(Appropriations, p. 421)*

Earlier, $24 million for the facilities program was included in the Commerce, Justice, State and the Judiciary appropriations bill (HR 5712 — PL 98-411). *(Appropriations, p. 373)*

CPB, a non-profit corporation that administered funding for public television and radio stations and for special, non-commercial programming, depended on federal funds for about 20 percent of its budget. Previously, Congress had appropriated $130 million for each of fiscal years 1984-86. *(1983 Almanac p. 505; 1982 Almanac p. 252; 1981 Almanac p. 567)*

The administration contended that the corporation catered to a cultural and intellectual elite and should be privately supported by its audience. *(1982 Almanac p. 340)*

The First Measure

Senate Action. The Senate Commerce, Science and Transportation Committee unanimously approved S 2436 on April 10. Its report (S Rept 98-432) was filed May 8, and the Senate passed the bill by voice vote June 15.

The measure authorized $238 million in fiscal 1987, $253 million in fiscal 1988 and $270 million in fiscal 1989 — a total of $761 million for CPB.

A previously enacted authorization called for fiscal 1984 funding of $145 million, $153 million in fiscal 1985, and $162 million in fiscal 1986.

The bill also authorized $159 million for fiscal years 1985 through 1987 for the Public Telecommunications Facilities Program.

House Action. The House Energy and Commerce Committee May 8 unanimously voted to report a companion measure (HR 5541 — H Rept 98-772) with the same funding levels as S 2436. The report was filed May 15.

The House July 24 passed the bill by a vote of 302-91, although some conservative Republicans nearly short-circuited it with parliamentary maneuvers. Like the administration, they said entertainment programs should be supported by private sources. *(Vote 279, p. 86-H)*

Timothy E. Wirth, D-Colo., chairman of the Energy and Commerce Subcommittee on Telecommunications, argued that the big increase in authorized funding levels was justified because the authorization had been slashed 40 percent in 1981. Private sources of funds did not fill the gap, Wirth said.

He criticized the administration contention that the facilities program had fulfilled its mission and should be dropped. He said 30 percent of the country could not receive radio signals and 10 percent could not receive public television.

The House rejected, 176-217, an amendment by Mike Oxley, R-Ohio, to cut CPB funds to $186 million for 1987, $214 million for 1988 and $246 million for 1989; and for the facilities program to $14 million for 1985, $16 million for 1986 and $18 million for 1987. *(Vote 278, p. 86-H)*

It also rejected, 95-298, an amendment by William E. Dannemeyer, R-Calif., to freeze CPB funds at $130 million in each fiscal year. *(Vote 277, p. 86-H)*

After the House approved its bill, Dannemeyer objected to a routine motion to attach the text to the Senate-passed bill, stalling final House action for two weeks.

On Aug. 8, the House agreed 324-89 to a rule allowing the substitution, and members by voice vote passed the amended S 2436. *(Vote 320, p. 98-H)*

The Senate Aug. 9 cleared the measure for the president.

After the Veto

In the veto message on S 2436, Reagan indicated he could support the "more reasonable" increases of 25 percent that Oxley had proposed on the House floor.

Although Democratic House proponents of the bill prodded the Republican Senate to override the veto, Goldwater picked up what one CPB spokesman called "an olive branch" in Reagan's message — the reference to Oxley's proposal. He decided to work for a compromise rather than push for an override.

However, Goldwater's negotiations were unsuccessful and, at his urgings, the Senate Sept. 20 by voice vote passed the second bill (S 607) authorizing only slightly less money for public broadcasting than S 2436.

S 607, approved by voice vote, authorized $200 million in fiscal 1987, $225 million in fiscal 1988 and $250 million in fiscal 1989 for CPB. It also authorized $25 million for fiscal 1985, $35 million for fiscal 1986 and $40 million for fiscal 1987 for facilities grants.

The total of $775 million was $145 million less than contained in S 2436. The new total was $520 million more than Reagan requested, and $81 million more than the sum he indicated in his veto message that he could accept.

The House Oct. 5 passed the second bill by a vote of 308-86, after members by 167-233 defeated an Oxley substitute cutting the funding levels to those endorsed by Reagan in his Aug. 29 message. *(Votes 394, 395, p. 120-H)*

The House also voted 68-328 to defeat an amendment by Dannemeyer that would have limited public broadcasting to a 5 percent annual increase. *(Vote 393, p. 120-H)*∎

Election Projections

Congress approved a non-binding resolution (H Con Res 321) calling on the news media to refrain from characterizing or predicting the outcome of an election until the polls had closed.

However, all the major networks ignored the request during the 1984 presidential election and before the polls had closed on the West Coast projected that President Reagan had won re-election.

The resolution, adopted by 352-65 by the House June 26 and by voice vote by the Senate Sept. 21, was spawned by complaints about early projections of the outcome of the 1980 presidential election. *(Vote 239, p. 74-H)*

It was one of several measures introduced by members angry that television networks, using exit polls of voters as they left polling places, declared Reagan the 1980 winner long before polls closed in many states.

Members complained that such early projections discouraged late voter turnout. Many Democrats blamed the networks for the hair-thin losses in 1980 of two members of Congress (Al Ullman, D-Ore., 1957-81; and James C. Corman, D-Calif., 1961-81) and uncounted local elections in the West.

Network representatives said the resolution infringed on their First Amendment rights and argued there was little evidence that voter turnout was impaired by their projections.

Legislative History. The House Administration Committee reported a resolution (H Con Res 227 — H Rept 98-671) April 10 that asked news organizations only to refrain from making projections.

Before the measure went to the floor, Rep. Al Swift, D-Wash., introduced H Con Res 321, which also requested the news media to hold off on making "characterizations" about an election before the polls closed.

The House and Senate did not resolve a difference in their interpretation of the resolution. Swift said he believed the resolution asked news organizations to refrain from projecting any presidential election results until the polls closed on the West Coast. Sen. Bob Packwood, R-Ore., chairman of the Commerce, Science and Transportation Committee, which reported the resolution Sept. 12 (S Rept 98-600), said he believed it sought to delay presidential election projections about a state only until the polls had closed in that state. ∎

Broadcast Freedom Bill

An effort to win what proponents called "full First Amendment rights" for broadcasters failed when the chairman of the Commerce, Science and Transportation Committee was unable to obtain the panel's support for his bill (S 1917).

The committee June 13 voted 6-11 against approving the bill, even though Chairman Bob Packwood, R-Ore., had revised it to apply only to radio and not to television. The defeat doomed the issue for the 98th Congress, but a spokesman for the National Association of Broadcasters said he expected the effort to be renewed in 1985.

As originally filed, Packwood's bill would have repealed several sections of the 1934 Communications Act, which regulated broadcasting on the grounds that the airwaves were a scarce resource that belonged to the public.

One regulation, the Fairness Doctrine, required radio and TV broadcasters to air significant issues and to give time to those who complained that their views were omitted. Another, the equal time rule, held that if any political candidate received air time, rivals could claim the same.

Also, the original bill would have repealed the "reasonable access rule," which held that federal candidates could demand that stations accept their political advertising at any time, and the "lowest unit rate" rule, which allowed candidates to pay for their ads at the cheapest rate available.

In 1982, Packwood unsuccessfully pushed for a constitutional amendment to guarantee broadcasters freedom of expression. In 1983, he filed S 1917. However, even if it had passed the Senate, key House members opposed any change in the Communications Act.

To win committee support for his bill, Packwood revised the bill to apply only to radio, and only for a five-year experimental period. It also made no changes in the reasonable access and low-rate rules. "Radio is so diverse and so numerous that you can barely call it scarce in the normal sense of that term," Packwood argued.

However, Ernest F. Hollings, D-S.C., argued that the First Amendment was not meant to protect the broadcaster's speech as much as it was intended to uphold the public's right to hear diverse views.   ∎

Highway Funding Stalled for Second Year

For the second consecutive year, Congress in 1984 failed to meet a deadline for releasing money to the states for Interstate highway construction.

Both chambers passed measures to permit the allocation of about $7.2 billion from the Highway Trust Fund for fiscal years 1984 and 1985. But procedural snarls and disagreements over how many special "demonstration" highway projects to include prevented the Senate from acting until Oct. 4, just a week before adjournment.

In the final days of the session, House-Senate conferees failed to agree on the extent of funding for members' special demonstration highway and bridge projects, and the measure died. The version passed by the House June 7 (HR 5504) contained 52 special projects that could eventually cost $2.45 billion, while the bill passed by the Senate Oct. 4 (S 3024) contained 16 projects with a price tag of $178.6 million.

There was no controversy regarding the main provision of the legislation — approval of cost estimates of future spending needs for Interstate highway projects and transit projects substituted for canceled Interstate projects. Involved were $5.3 million for Interstate construction, plus approximately $1.9 billion in other funds.

The money was to be distributed Oct. 1, 1983, but Congress had been unable to act because of the disagreement. An emergency bill releasing six months' worth of fiscal 1984 funds (HR 4957 — PL 98-229) was cleared March 2. *(1983 impasse, 1983 Almanac p. 559)*

Distribution of the remainder of fiscal 1984 funds was to have come with enactment of the fiscal 1985 legislation.

But, because a bill was not enacted, states received only about a quarter of the money they should have gotten over the last two years, leaving most states virtually out of cash for Interstate construction and raising the possibility that the Interstate Highway System might not be completed by the 1990 target date.

The impasse did not go unnoticed by the states and other interested parties.

The National Governors' Association adopted a resolution at its annual meeting July 31 suggesting that governors lobby for release of highway funds. According to the governors' group, 33 states each had less than $15 million in Interstate funds, while the average cost of building one mile of highway was $12 million.

Others who pled for action included Federal Highway Administration (FHWA) Administrator Ray A. Barnhart, the Associated General Contractors and the American Road and Transportation Builders Association.

Controversies

The money, raised from gas and diesel taxes and other road-related fees that made up the Highway Trust Fund, was to be distributed to the states according to formula but could not be allocated without congressional approval of an Interstate Cost Estimate and Interstate Substitute Cost Estimate. *(1982 Almanac p. 317)*

The supposedly routine approval had, in recent years, become controversial as members sought to tinker with the formulas or to add extra highway projects for their constituents, beyond the projects covered by their state's formula allocations.

Originally intended to fund innovative programs, the demonstration projects had grown from three in 1973-74 to 12 in 1982, according to the FHWA's Barnhart. The bills passed by the two chambers in 1984 included a total of 68.

The demonstration projects were particularly attractive because they were 100 percent federally financed, while regular federal Interstate construction funds allocated by formula pay for only 90 percent.

"I don't call these boondoggles because some are very legitimate projects, but I think national commitments should be met first," Barnhart said.

Other controversies besides the special projects delayed action on the bill.

The House's insistence that the bill cover mass transit as well as highways delayed a conference until one day before adjournment.

Sen. Jake Garn, R-Utah, chairman of the Banking, Housing and Urban Affairs Committee, which had jurisdiction over mass transit, told his colleagues he would not allow discussions on mass transit construction funding because the bill had not been considered by his committee. The House Public Works Committee, which had handled the House highway funding bill, had jurisdiction over mass transit, but the Senate Environment and Public Works Committee, which originated the Senate version, did not.

House members finally agreed to go to conference without discussing the mass transit issue, but the conference broke up over the insistence of Senate conferees that a cap be placed on funding for special highway and bridge projects.

The final Senate proposal would have required states to pick up one-third of the cost of the demonstration projects, which were currently 100 percent federally funded, and placed a $30 million cap on each project. In addition, the Senate proposal would have allowed only preliminary planning on a major Boston project supported by House Speaker Thomas P. O'Neill Jr., D-Mass.

House Action

The Public Works Works and Transportation Committee reported its highway funding measure (HR 5504 — H Rept 98-768) May 15.

During the markup May 9, several members defended the practice of adding demonstration projects to the bill. Noting that Transportation Secretary Elizabeth Hanford Dole had recommended a veto if projects were added to the bill, Gene Snyder, R-Ky., ranking minority member, said, "That doesn't mean we should all pack up and go home."

By voice vote and without opposition, the committee added seven new projects to the 31 already in the bill. The additional $37 million included $24 million for four projects in Cook County, Ill. The rest were for work in Harney County, Ore.; Wayne County, Mich.; and Erie County, N.Y. In addition, the bill made eligible for federal aid a Boston highway and tunnel project supported by Speaker O'Neill.

Several more projects were added on the floor before the House approved the bill June 7 by a vote of 297-73. Included were demonstrations in New Jersey, Virginia, Ohio and New York. *(Vote 198, p. 62-H)*

A key floor amendment, approved by voice vote, blocked distribution of certain highway funds to states unless they enacted a minimum drinking age of 21. That provision, which supporters hoped would cut down on drunken driving among teenagers, was subsequently enacted into law as an amendment to HR 4616 (PL 98-363), which established a child safety restraint seat program. *(Story, p. 283)*

Repair Funds. The bill also changed the formula for allocating highway repair funds to the states. Under the bill, the funds would be allocated solely on the basis of highway use, measured by vehicle miles traveled and gasoline and diesel consumption. Previous formulas had included the length of roads in the state. Members from sparsely populated states opposed the new formula, which would shift a larger proportion of funds to more populous states.

James F. McNulty Jr., D-Ariz., was unsuccessful in offering an amendment to block the formula change. The amendment was rejected, 93-315. *(Vote 197, p. 62-H)*

Mass Transit. HR 5504 also increased Urban Mass Transit Administration (UMTA) funding for mass transit capital projects, from $1.1 billion to $1.5 billion annually through fiscal 1987.

House staff members said the 1-cent of the gasoline tax dedicated to mass transit trust was raising more money than had been expected; UMTA opposed the increase, saying the extra funds would not be available until 1986.

Senate Action

Committee. The issue of whether to add new highway projects to the bill delayed approval by the Senate Environment and Public Works Committee.

A bill approved by the Subcommittee on Transportation April 24 (S 2527) contained no demonstration add-ons. A May 1 markup by the full panel was cut short when it became clear that several senators — including Majority Leader Howard H. Baker Jr., R-Tenn. — wanted funding for special projects.

The full committee June 6 failed to curb the addition of special projects but did impose a $25 million cap on the amount for each demonstration project and required states to pay half the cost. As reported June 15 (S Rept 98-524), the bill included 10 demonstration projects with an estimated cost of $106 million.

The bill also contained a provision aimed at avoiding future deadlocks and guaranteeing a stable source of funding for the states. It required FHWA to apportion congressionally authorized funds based on the latest available cost estimate, unless Congress passed a law overriding it. Current law required Congress to act before the money could be apportioned.

Another provision changed the method for calculating the distribution of funds. The 1982 law guaranteed states they would get at least 85 percent of the gas taxes raised in their states.

An amendment to S 2527 by Lloyd Bentsen, D-Texas, adopted by the committee, changed the way the minimum allocation was computed. While it would apply to all states, Texas would be the big winner, with $64.5 million added to its allocation in fiscal 1985, according to Bentsen. The only state to be seriously hurt under the change would be Illinois, which would lose $30 million the first year.

The Senate committee bill did not address the issue of mass transit funding.

Floor. Floor action on S 2527 stalled several times, partly because of controversial items in the measure itself and partly because the bill became enmeshed in other disputes. In the closing days of the session, some senators were determined to bring a controversial civil rights measure to the floor and tried to attach it to the highway bill, which led to a gridlock of filibusters and procedural maneuvers. *(Civil rights, p. 239)*

When S 2527 was brought up Sept. 20, it was greeted by a surprise filibuster mounted by the two Illinois senators, Republican Charles H. Percy and Democrat Alan J. Dixon.

They protested the change in the formula for calculating the minimum allocation. They argued that the change would cost Illinois $30 million in fiscal 1985 and $27 million in fiscal 1986.

On Sept. 24, the Senate voted 70-12 to shut off debate. But Dixon persisted in using parliamentary maneuvers to make it clear that he still could stall the legislation. After further jockeying, a compromise was reached that would guarantee Illinois the extra $30 million for one year, with an opportunity for a second year of full funding. *(Vote 232, p. 41-S)*

In an effort to free the cost allocations from procedural and other controversies, the Environment and Public Works Committee met Sept. 26 to approve a replacement, S 3024 (no written report). The new measure incorporated the text of S 2527 and added several amendments, including another five special "demonstration projects."

The substitute aroused little debate in committee. In addition to the five new demonstration projects, the bill included provisions to satisfy the Illinois senators and a series of amendments to the Uniform Relocation Assistance and Land Acquisition Policies Act (PL 91-646). *(1970 Almanac p. 761)*

The relocation provisions updated the procedures under which individuals and businesses were compensated for being displaced by federal and federally assisted projects. The changes, which were requested by the administration, had passed the Senate May 20, 1983, as S 531 (S Rept 98-71) and were contained in the House version of the highway bill. *(1983 action, 1983 Almanac p. 587)*

Senate Passage. The Senate Oct. 4 approved S 3024 by voice vote.

Heeding the urgings of Jennings Randolph, D-W.Va., and other supporters of the legislation, several members agreed to drop potentially divisive amendments. The jettisoned amendments included proposed changes in mass transit construction funding that would have divided urban and rural states, a provision to allow states to shift funds between categories, and several unrelated pieces of legislation.

The only substantial controversy came on an amendment by Arlen Specter, R-Pa., to change the formula for distributing highway repair money to the states. His formula would have considered the length of highways, bridge repair needs and diesel fuel consumption. A similar formula change was contained in the House bill.

Specter's proposal was hotly opposed by members from Western states. The Senate voted to table (kill) Specter's amendment by a vote of 75-21. *(Vote 265, p. 46-S)*

Only one demonstration project, for South Carolina, was added on the floor. That brought the total number of special projects to 16, with a federal price tag of approximately $178.6 million.

Earlier Extension

To provide time to settle controversies surrounding the allocation of Interstate highway funds, Congress cleared legislation (HR 4957 — PL 98-229) releasing about half of the money for a one-year period to the states.

The House by voice vote Feb. 29 passed the bill, and the Senate by voice vote March 2 cleared the measure for the president. There was no committee action in either chamber.

The bill released about half of the $4 billion earmarked for fiscal 1985 Interstate construction. Construction funds are allocated a year in advance. It also provided half of the $700 million earmarked for fiscal 1984 projects approved by local authorities as substitutes for once-planned Interstate highways.

HR 4957 also authorized an additional $150 million from the Highway Trust Fund for road repairs of damage caused by unusually bad weather in 1983. It removed a $30 million limit for emergency repair funds for each state.

HR 4957 was a relatively stripped-down version of a bill passed by the House in 1983 (HR 3103) that was burdened with a number of controversial provisions that the Senate would not accept. *(1983 Almanac p. 559)*

As cleared, HR 4957:

● Authorized an additional $150 million for emergency road repair, bringing the total to $250 million.

● Removed the $30 million limit that any state could receive for emergency road repair.

● Made a highway in the Devils Slide, Calif., area and a culvert in Louisiana eligible for emergency funds.

● Permitted Maryland to transfer $100 million from one highway construction account to another.

● Authorized the use of 4R (resurfacing, restoring, rehabilitating and reconstructing) funds to upgrade highways newly designated as part of the Interstate system.

● Authorized the use of federal funds for a bridge in Illinois that had been the subject of a court dispute.

● Removed cement from road construction materials required by law to be made in the United States. ∎

Truck Safety

States could ask the Department of Transportation (DOT) to ban large tandem trucks from unsafe portions of the Interstate Highway System under legislation (S 2217 — PL 98-554) signed by the president Oct. 30.

The bill also improved the uniformity of truck safety laws and broadened the power of DOT to enforce truck safety regulations.

Some older portions of the Interstate system did not meet standards for lane width, but in 1982 and 1983, states lost the power to ban from Interstate highways single-trailer trucks 48 or more feet long, tandem rigs with 28-foot or more trailers or trucks less than 102 inches wide. *(1982 Almanac p. 318)*

But state officials and auto safety groups continued to complain that the big rigs were a hazard on many older Interstate segments. Those roads, particularly in the Northeast, did not meet current federal standards for curves, lane widths, ramp lengths, shoulders and bridge clearances.

Some states tried to ban tandem trailers from certain highways, but the U.S. Supreme Court held that the action infringed on the federal right to regulate interstate commerce.

The Senate Commerce, Science and Transportation Committee reported the bill June 6 (S Rept 98-505). The legislation as approved by the Senate by voice vote Oct. 2, incorporated provisions of S 2174, a safety bill reported by the Commerce Committee in May (S Rept 98-424).

The House, which had passed a more limited bill (HR 5568 — H Rept 98-926) Aug. 6, approved S 2217 with minor amendments by voice vote Oct. 11. Final action came later the same day when the Senate by voice vote concurred in the House amendments, clearing the measure for the president. ∎

Maritime Authorization

Congress by voice vote Oct. 11 cleared a $468.6 million fiscal 1985 authorization (S 2499 — PL 98-556) for the Maritime Administration in the Department of Transportation. The president signed the bill Oct. 30.

The path to final action was cleared when the Senate Oct. 11 by voice vote amended its committee bill to include provisions included by the House in the version (HR 4706) it had passed in April. The House by voice vote later Oct. 11 agreed to send the bill to the president.

The final bill authorized about $8 million more than President Reagan requested. The fiscal 1984 appropriation was $485.96 million.

Legislative Action

The House Merchant Marine and Fisheries Committee reported HR 4706 (H Rept 98-635) March 26, and the full House approved it by voice vote April 3. The $468.6 million authorization included $377.8 million to subsidize operations of a fleet of about 142 U.S.-flag ships in foreign trade and $10 million for research and development. The $80.8 million for operations and training included $5 million to convert the *Santa Mercedes* to a training vessel for delivery to the state of Massachusetts.

The administration opposed authorizing funding for the training ship and also for $3 million for fuel oil aid to state maritime academies.

The Senate bill, as approved by the Commerce, Science and Transportation Committee April 10 and reported May 14 (S Rept 98-445), matched the House operating subsidy and research and development figures. However, it called for $75.8 million in operations and training funds and authorized $12.3 million for fiscal 1985 for the Federal Maritime Commission. The House version had not authorized funding for the commission.

Neither bill contained controversial policy changes, such as subsidies for ship construction, which had blocked the maritime authorizations for two years. *(1983 Almanac p. 549)*

The final measure accepted the House operations and training figures, including $5 million for the training ship conversion. It also included $12.3 million for the Federal Maritime Commission, as the Senate wanted. ∎

Coast Guard Authorization

Operating a boat while drunk could bring a penalty of a $5,000 fine and/or a year in jail under the Coast Guard authorization (S 2526 — PL 98-557) cleared by Congress Oct. 9.

Current law had set penalties for operating a boat in a negligent manner that endangered safety but did not specifically penalize intoxication.

The Senate Commerce, Science and Transportation Committee reported the bill May 17 (S Rept 98-454). The Senate passed it by voice vote Oct. 5, and the House gave its approval by voice vote Oct. 9. The president signed the legislation Oct. 30.

The measure authorized Coast Guard funding of about $2.4 billion for fiscal 1985 and $2.6 billion for fiscal 1986. The 1985 funding was about 10 percent more than the president sought but only about 1 percent more than fiscal 1984 spending.

The measure also set minimum personnel levels of 39,150 active military employees and 5,484 civilian employees. The administration had sought a slight reduction in personnel. The bill updated language in Coast Guard administrative statutes that had referred only to one sex, and prohibited the sale of recreational boats with known safety defects.

The House had considered a slightly different authorization bill reported by the Merchant Marine and Fisheries Committee March 22 (HR 4841 — H Rept 98-631). The House passed the measure March 29 by a vote of 348-38. *(Vote 53, p. 18-H)* ∎

Auto Theft Bill Passed

President Reagan Oct. 25 signed into law a bill (HR 6257 — PL 98-547) to blunt the illegal "chop shop" market in stolen auto parts by requiring identification marks on major auto components, such as doors and fenders.

The legislation required automakers to mark parts on car lines with high theft rates. But to soften the opposition of the auto industry, the final measure required fewer auto lines to be marked than originally proposed and provided a way for automakers to win exemptions from the requirement of marking parts.

The bill, reported Sept. 26 by the House Energy and Commerce Committee (H Rept 98-1087, Part I), was approved by the House by voice vote Oct. 1. The Senate, whose similar bill (S 1400 — S Rept 98-478) was tied up in another controversy involving bumper standards, accepted the House version Oct. 4 by voice vote, clearing the measure for the president.

Impetus for the legislation came from reports that auto theft had risen dramatically — one car was stolen every 31 seconds — and that thieves were more likely to be members of organized crime than individual "joy riders."

Crime rings, through chop shops, dismantled stolen autos and resold parts. Loss of property and higher insurance costs drove the price of auto theft as high as $5 billion a year nationwide, according to bill supporters.

Similar proposals had failed in past sessions because automakers objected to the added cost of marking parts.

The bill required domestic and foreign auto manufacturers to mark a vehicle identification number (VIN) on 14 parts, to be chosen by the secretary of transportation. Only car lines with higher-than-average theft rates would have

to be marked, but no firm would have to mark more than 14 lines. (A "line" was defined as a group of automobiles distributed by a manufacturer; for example, Ford's Mustang and Thunderbird would be "lines.")

Also the law established criminal penalties for trafficking in stolen parts and for removing VINs.

The bill allowed car makers to avoid VIN requirements if car models included anti-theft devices known as "black boxes." General Motors was the only automaker to have the black boxes under development, congressional staff aides said.

The device was expected to cost several hundred dollars, a GM spokesman said. In contrast, the cost of marking parts was limited by the bill to $15 a car.

Major Provisions

As cleared, major provisions of the Motor Vehicle Theft Law Enforcement Act of 1984:

● Required auto manufacturers to place identification numbers on the 14 major parts of vehicle lines that had a higher than average rate of theft.

● Defined "major part" to include the engine; transmission; doors; hood; grille; bumpers; fenders; deck lid, tailgate or hatchback; rear quarter panels; trunk floor pan; and frame or supporting structure.

● Limited to 14 the number of car lines any single manufacturer would be required to mark.

● Stipulated that if the manufacturer and secretary disagreed on which lines or parts to mark, the secretary would make the selection after proper notice to the manufacturer.

● Required the selection of lines and parts to be made at least six months prior to the beginning of a model year.

● Allowed a manufacturer to petition the secretary for an exemption if a line of vehicles was equipped with an anti-theft device that was standard equipment and was determined by the secretary to be effective.

● Stipulated that the cost of identification not exceed $15 per vehicle.

● Established civil penalties for violation by manufacturers of $1,000 for each violation, up to a maximum of $250,000.

● Established penalties for trafficking in, importing or exporting stolen motor vehicles and their parts. Persons convicted of removing or altering an identification number would be subject to a fine of up to $5,000 and/or a maximum of five years in prison. Persons convicted of trafficking in stolen motor vehicles would be subject to a $25,000 fine, and/or a maximum 10-year prison sentence. Those who knowingly imported or exported stolen vehicles and parts would be subject to a $10,000 fine and/or up to five years in prison.

● Required the secretary to prepare certain studies, including within three years of enactment, an assessment of the benefits of a similar anti-theft program for trucks, multipurpose passenger vehicles and motorcycles, and, within four years of enactment, a determination of the cost-effectiveness of the program.

House Committee Action

The House Energy and Commerce Committee approved the bill Sept. 18 by voice vote, shelving the original measure (HR 3999) sponsored by Timothy E. Wirth, D-Colo. The new version was the product of long negotiations between Wirth and Chairman John D. Dingell, D-Mich., whose state was home to the auto manufacturers.

A change engineered by Dingell provided the exemption from the requirement to mark parts on car lines with high theft rates if a manufacturer could instead install an anti-theft device, commonly called a "black box."

Congressional aides and lobbyists dubbed the provision "the GM black box amendment" since only General Motors Corp. was said to have such a device under development.

Originally, the bill would have mandated that all 119 domestic and foreign lines be marked. But earlier compromises limited the requirement to an estimated 47 car lines that had higher-than-average theft rates. For example, Ford's Escort would not have to be marked, but its Thunderbird probably would.

Regardless of theft rates, no manufacturer would have to mark more than 14 lines — another concession to GM since it was the only firm with more than 14 high-theft lines, aides said.

Senate Committee

A companion Senate bill (S 1400) had hit a snag since its April 10 markup in the Senate Commerce, Science and Transportation Committee.

Donald W. Riegle Jr., D-Mich., and Wendell H. Ford, D-Ky., invoked a Senate tradition of putting a "hold" on the bill and blocking action, because they opposed a provision reinstating a federal requirement that auto bumpers be built to withstand a 5-mph collision. The National Highway Traffic Safety Administration had set a 5 mph standard in 1971 but halved it to 2.5 mph in 1982 as part of a Reagan administration drive to reduce industry regulations and costs.

John C. Danforth, R-Mo., who had sponsored the amendment reinstating the tougher standard, reluctantly agreed to drop the bumper provision. But that prompted a counter-hold by Howard M. Metzenbaum, D-Ohio, a supporter of a stronger bumper requirement.   ∎

Park Ride Inspections

The House Oct. 2 passed legislation (HR 5790) to restore some federal oversight of amusement rides at fixed-park sites. However, there was no further action on the bill before adjournment.

The bill, reported by Energy and Commerce Sept. 25 (H Rept 98-1072), passed by a vote of 300-119. *(Vote 378, p. 116-H)*

In 1981, Congress rescinded the Consumer Product Safety Commission's authority over rides at permanent sites, leaving the commission the authority only to inspect rides or order repairs for traveling carnivals. *(1981 Almanac p. 573)*

HR 5790 would have reinstated the commission's power to inspect fixed rides, but only in states — 20 at the time of consideration — that had no inspection laws or in cases where a ride had caused injury or death.

The bill also would have required park operators to report dangerous rides to the commission, so it could act as a national clearinghouse for such information. Sponsors were Paul Simon, D, and Henry J. Hyde, R, both of Illinois, where several people had been hurt and one man killed in park accidents during 1984.   ∎

TV Rerun Rule Forestalled

Congressional action to bar proposed rules allowing television networks to have a financial interest in the pro-

grams they aired was forestalled by the failure of networks and independent producers to reach agreement.

In November 1983, the Senate Commerce, Science and Transportation Committee postponed action until after March 15 on a House-passed bill (HR 2250) that would have delayed a Federal Communications Commission (FCC) proposed rules change until June 1. The FCC agreed to delay the rules to give the networks and their opponents — Hollywood studios, producers and stars — time to compromise.

Current rules barred networks from the lucrative syndication and rerun markets.

But talks between the two sides broke down in January, with both alleging bad faith. A Senate Commerce Committee aide said "nothing is anticipated to happen legislatively," and no committee action was taken on the House bill.

The House had passed its bill Nov. 8 after the FCC proposed dropping 1970 rules limiting networks from controlling or profiting from reruns of shows. FCC Chairman Mark Fowler had agreed to delay action until May 10 after President Reagan said he would support a two-year moratorium on the proposed changes. *(1983 Almanac p. 560)* ∎

Amtrak, Rail Issues

Various disputes blocked congressional action on legislation reauthorizing funding for Amtrak, the federally subsidized passenger railroad, and the Federal Railroad Administration (FRA).

Fiscal 1985 funding for the two entities was included in the continuing appropriations reesolution signed by the president Oct. 12 (H J Res 648 — PL 98-473). *(Story, p. 444)*

Congress had failed to enact an Amtrak reauthorization in 1983, partly because of concerns about how government debts owed by the railroad might be repaid. *(1983 Almanac p. 561)*

The House passed three separate bills to reauthorize Amtrak, the FRA and the Railroad Accounting Principles Board (HR 3648, HR 5585 and HR 4439). The Senate Commerce, Science and Transportation Committee included all three in a bill it reported May 17 (S 2537 — S Rept 98-457), but that bill did not reach the floor.

Amtrak Reauthorization

House. The Amtrak bill (HR 3648 — H Rept 98-371) the House approved by voice vote March 6 contained controversial provisions allowing Congress to veto any sale of Conrail.

The House rejected by 147-254 an amendment by James T. Broyhill, R-N.C., to eliminate the requirement. Broyhill was ranking minority member of the Energy and Commerce Committee, which had reported the bill Sept. 21, 1983. *(Vote 33, p. 12-H)*

Opponents, led by James J. Florio, D-N.J., chairman of the Subcommittee on Transportation, argued that congressional review was needed to prevent the Department of Transportation (DOT) from making a bad sale. But Broyhill said the prospect of congressional rejection of a proposed sale would have a chilling effect on negotiations, a position shared by DOT.

A 1981 law (PL 97-35) permitted DOT to sell portions or all of Conrail to private enterprise but also allowed Congress, without presidential review, to veto any DOT plan. Some members feared that the administration might sell the railroad in such a way that vital freight service to the Northeast would be lost. *(1981 Almanac p. 561)*

However, the Supreme Court invalidated legislative vetoes not presented to the president for his signature. The Commerce Committee in its report on the bill (H Rept 98-371) contended that the court also wiped out the authority to sell the railroad and new procedures were necessary to provide for congressional review.

Broyhill's amendment would have permitted a sale, unless Congress passed a resolution of disapproval.

DOT continued to negotiate with several potential buyers of Conrail but made no recommendation before Congress adjourned. *(Conrail, p. 298)*

Other Issues. The House-passed bill authorized $730 million in operating and capital subsidies for Amtrak for fiscal 1984 and $724 million in fiscal 1985.

The House agreed to drop a section dealing with Amtrak's debt, an issue that had blocked action when the bill came to the floor Oct. 6, 1983. Although Amtrak was technically in default Oct. 1 on about $800 million in principal and $200 million in interest owed to the Federal Financing Bank, administrative steps were taken to repay the debt.

It also adopted a package of amendments offered by Florio to authorize $2.1 million for the U.S. Railway Association and $11.1 million for the Federal Railroad Administration Office of Administrator, in fiscal 1985.

Besides the funding levels, the amendments also required Amtrak to reinstate rail passenger service between Tampa and St. Petersburg, Fla., and delete a proposed authorization for rail service improvements of the Maitland Line in Pennsylvania.

The amendments delayed until the second year of operation the imposition of performance criteria for certain passenger trains jointly funded by Amtrak and the states.

Senate. The bill ordered reported April 10 by the Senate Commerce, Science and Transportation Committee was a broader measure covering Amtrak, the FRA safety programs and the Railroad Accounting Board.

For Amtrak, the legislation would have authorized $716.4 million in fiscal 1984 and $720 million in 1985. It did not contain language pertaining to the Conrail sale and omitted provisions pertaining to the debt repayment.

Rail Safety

The Senate Committee's Amtrak bill also would have authorized $26.7 million and $28.4 million in fiscal 1985 and 1986 respectively for the safety functions of the FRA.

While the committee urged FRA to complete proposed rules involving drug and alcohol abuse among railroad workers, a separate bill passed by voice vote by the House Sept. 20 (HR 5585 — H Rept 98-795) gave the Transportation Department 60 days to issue rules. The bill had been reported by the Energy and Commerce Committee May 21.

The House-passed bill also authorized $55.4 million in fiscal 1985 and $57.7 million in 1986 for the safety programs of the FRA.

The administration strongly objected to a House provision that gave railroad employees the right to sue DOT for enforcement of safety standards. The Senate committee proposal contained no similar language.

Railroad Accounting Board

The Senate committee's Amtrak bill also authorized appropriations of $1 million each year for fiscal 1984-86 for the Railroad Accounting Principles Board, an independent

---

Odometer Fraud Bill

A bill designed to ensure used-car buyers of the accuracy of a vehicle's mileage meter was passed Oct. 10 by the Senate, but there was no further action on the measure.

The odometer anti-fraud bill (S 1407) was intended to close a gap in the current law, which banned rolling back mileage but lacked record-keeping requirements, according to backers.

The bill, reported by the Commerce, Science and Transportation Committee June 6 (S Rept 98-504), would have required states to print a car's mileage on both the title and on the owner's annual registration card. Under the bill, if the car were sold, the application to transfer a title would have been required to include the previous owner's most recent registration card showing the mileage.

Sponsors said the paperwork not only guaranteed the mileage reading but also provided a paper trail to trace fraud. To guard against forgery, the bill called for titles to be printed by a process that made tampering detectable.

The National Automobile Dealers Association supported the bill, arguing that its members sometimes purchased used cars without knowing the mileage had been changed. One out of seven of the 20 million used cars sold annually had had its odometer rolled back, the National Highway Traffic Safety Administration estimated.

---

group that was to develop accounting methods to help the Interstate Commerce Commission evaluate the financial condition of railroads.

The board was authorized by the Staggers Rail Act of 1980 (PL 96-448), which eased federal regulation of the railroad industry. But the board had never been funded, and its authorization expired Sept. 30, 1983.

The House handled the issue in a bill separate from its Amtrak legislation. By voice vote Feb. 7 it passed a bill (HR 4439 — H Rept 98-594) reauthorizing the board for the same period and at the same funding level as the Senate panel. The bill had been reported by the Energy and Commerce Committee Feb. 6. ∎

Air Bag Rule Issued

Congressional attempts to require automakers to put air bags in some automobiles were largely superseded by the announcement July 11 of a final rule on the issue by Transportation Secretary Elizabeth Hanford Dole.

The new rule required automakers to phase in crash protection — air bags, automatically closing seat belts or "crashproof" interiors — between 1986 and 1989. It left a loophole for manufacturers, however: if states representing two-thirds of the U.S. population passed laws by April 1, 1989, making seat-belt use mandatory, the regulation would not apply.

New York enacted the first such law in June, and

automakers were expected to press other states to follow. They said consumers would object to the extra cost of safety devices, which Dole estimated at $320 per vehicle for air bags and $45 for passive safety belts.

The action by the Department of Transportation (DOT) might bring a cease-fire, at least in Washington, in what Supreme Court Justice Byron R. White had called "the regulatory equivalent of war" between auto dealers and manufacturers, on one side, and insurance companies and auto safety advocates on the other. *(1983 Almanac p. 14-A)*

The air-bag issue had bounced between Congress, DOT and the courts since 1969, when the government first tried to require them. *(Congress and the Nation Vol. V, p. 296)*

One of the most current bills was reported by the Senate Commerce, Science and Transportation Committee Oct. 27, 1983 (S 1108 — S Rept 98-283). It would have applied to only one line of cars from each major manufacturer; however, it did not reach the floor. *(1983 Almanac p. 544)*

Dole's decision reflected a significant switch for the Reagan administration, which in 1981 rescinded a Carter administration rule that would have required passive restraints on all cars by 1984. The Supreme Court termed the rescission "arbitrary and capricious" in June 1983 in a suit brought by insurance companies, and required DOT to reconsider.

The new rule required manufacturers to provide crash protection in 10 percent of their cars after Sept. 1, 1986, 25 percent in 1987, 40 percent in 1988 and 100 percent by 1989. Manufacturers must decide what kind of equipment to provide in order to protect occupants in a 30 mph crash.

To encourage innovation in developing air bags and other technologies, automakers could protect a smaller percentage of their fleets in the phase-in period if they used devices other than seat belts.

Consumer groups were not pleased by the regulation.

Joan Claybrook, who as administrator of the National Highway Traffic Safety Administration had formulated the Carter administration's air-bag requirements, said the decision "assures another long delay before the public is able to buy air bags."

Consumer advocate Ralph Nader denounced the new regulation as "a snare and a delusion" that would "gladden the evil hearts of the executives of General Motors." ∎

Hazardous Materials

Legislation (S 2706) reauthorizing funding for programs regulating shipments of hazardous materials was cleared by Congress Oct. 11 and signed by President Reagan Oct. 30 (PL 98-559).

The measure authorized $7.5 million for fiscal 1985 and $8 million for fiscal 1986 for Department of Transportation (DOT) programs under the Hazardous Materials Transportation Act. The legislation also authorized the transportation secretary to enter into agreements with private entities to participate in a central system to report hazardous material transportation accidents.

In addition, the bill required the secretary and the director of the Federal Emergency Management Agency (FEMA) jointly to evaluate training and planning for responding to incidents involving the transportation of haz-

ardous materials and to report their findings to Congress within five months.

Legislative History

The Reagan administration had sought a one-year funding authorization of $7.3 million.

On May 15 the House Public Works and Transportation Committee reported HR 5530 (H Rept 98-774, Part I), authorizing $7.4 million for fiscal 1985, adding $100,000 for training state and local personnel.

The bill mandated a study, to be conducted jointly by DOT and FEMA, of emergency response training and planning for hazardous materials transportation accidents.

It also required a feasibility study of a system by which state and local governments would be notified in advance of a shipment of hazardous materials through their jurisdictions. The secretary was authorized to contract with a private entity to use a central reporting system on accidents involving the transport of hazardous materials.

On May 21 the House Energy and Commerce Committee reported its own one-year authorization bill (HR 5642 — H Rept 98-794, Part I) similar to HR 5530.

Two days later, the Senate Commerce, Science and Transportation Committee reported a two-year measure (S 2706 — S Rept 98-479) authorizing $7.5 million for fiscal 1985 and $8 million for 1986. The Senate measure also authorized the secretary to use a private central reporting system for hazardous materials transportation accidents.

The Senate passed S 2706 by voice vote June 15. The House Oct. 11 passed the Senate bill with an amendment requiring the joint Transportation Department-FEMA study of emergency response planning. On Oct. 11 the Senate accepted the House amendment, clearing the measure for the president. ∎

Product Liability Dies

A potent coalition of businesses failed again to win passage of a national law that would pre-empt state laws regarding victims' lawsuits against defective products.

As in two previous Congresses, the industry-backed product liability bill (S 44) got no further than the Senate Commerce, Science and Transportation Committee, where it was approved 11-5 March 27. *(1982 Almanac p. 330)*

Though the proposed law was a top priority of lobby groups for hundreds of manufacturers, another formidable alliance — consumer groups, trial lawyers, labor and state officials — opposed it. Democratic senators' threats of a filibuster blocked a floor vote late in the 98th Congress. Meanwhile, the House took no action on a companion measure (HR 2927).

Manufacturers argued that current laws in the 50 states and the District of Columbia had resulted in what one lobbyist called "a garden variety" of confusing and sometimes contradictory provisions. But those laws had one thing in common that businesses wanted to change: a legal standard holding firms to "strict liability" for injuries caused by their products, even if a manufacturer was innocent of negligent or reckless behavior in making a good.

Businesses sought not just a uniform federal law but one requiring victims to meet a greater burden of proof. S 44, sponsored by Bob Kasten, R-Wis., chairman of the Commerce Subcommittee on Consumers, would replace the strict liability standard in many cases with one demanding proof of a manufacturer's negligence.

Consumers, Labor, Lawyers Opposed

Consumer groups, labor and trial lawyers strongly resisted, arguing that the bill would make it difficult — impossible, in some cases — for victims to recover damages.

State officials adamantly opposed the bill as an unprecedented intrusion on states' rights. For the first time, a federal statute would be binding on states, but — in contrast with civil-rights cases, for instance — access to federal courts would be prohibited except in cases where the plaintiff and defendant were from different states.

Perhaps most controversial was a provision that would allow only one victim to receive punitive damages from a firm facing multiple claims. Punitive damages were granted to punish a firm that acted with reckless disregard for safety, and were awarded in addition to "compensatory damages" covering victims' actual losses.

The punitive damages limit was included at the request of Paul S. Trible Jr., R-Va., and Richmond-based A. H. Robins Co. The pharmaceutical maker had been the target of more than 11,000 lawsuits by women alleging injuries from its Dalkon Shield intrauterine contraceptive device.

Widespread news accounts of Robins' legal problems tarred S 44, given its Robins-inspired limit on damages. A Senate source called the link "our biggest problem."

Committee Action

The Commerce Committee approved a product liability bill by voice vote at the end of 1982, too late for further consideration in the 97th Congress. Kasten introduced S 44 at the start of the 98th Congress.

Hearings were held in early 1983, followed by months of redrafting to suit consumers, labor, the Reagan administration and senators. A final hearing was held in March 1984.

On March 27, the committee approved the bill 11-5. It was reported May 23 (S Rept 98-476). Of nine Republicans, only Chairman Bob Packwood of Oregon voted against the bill.

By a 13-2 vote, the committee amended S 44 to create a panel of experts, charged with proposing a way to compensate some victims who otherwise would not recover damages under the bill. Such victims would include those who could not identify a firm that made a faulty product, and those with injuries caused by dangers — from drugs or chemicals, for example — that were unknown to the makers.

Ernest F. Hollings, D-S.C., a former trial lawyer, condemned the bill as the worst he had seen in an 18-year Senate career. He protested that S 44 would cause legal chaos — not end it — as courts struggled to interpret the new law. He also argued that the bill would "further injure the injured" by impeding their chances of winning legal relief.

But Kasten insisted, "We are trying to pinpoint responsibility in a fair way." He said his bill would restore a legal balance between business and consumers, reducing firms' legal costs and the price of U.S. goods.

Filibuster Threats

A crowded Senate calendar, and the summer recesses for the political parties' presidential-nominating conventions, kept S 44 from the floor for months. On Sept. 17, the bill received a boost when Reagan sent Kasten a letter of endorsement, thus quieting two years of internal administration debate over whether his administration should back a bill that appeared to contradict its drive to return power to states.

Majority Leader Howard H. Baker Jr., R-Tenn., supported S 44 and repeatedly included it on his tentative floor agenda through Congress' final days in October. But, short of the 60 votes needed to invoke cloture and end the certain filibusters, he and Kasten never brought S 44 to the floor.

In the House, Henry A. Waxman, D-Calif., chairman of the House Energy and Commerce Subcommittee on Health and the Environment, refused to consider product-liability legislation until the Senate approved a bill.

Though Waxman supported the concept of a national law, he said that he opposed the Senate bill because "I don't think we ought to shift the burden to the injured party." ∎

Credit Card Surcharges

The House and Senate failed to resolve an impasse over whether to continue a federal ban on surcharges added to credit-card purchases. The ban, extended three times over 10 years, expired Feb. 27.

Supporters of surcharges said they were needed to offset retailers' costs of processing credit-card transactions. A Federal Reserve Board study found that the costs added an average 3.1 percent to prices, forcing cash customers to subsidize credit customers' purchases.

The Senate followed the lead of Jake Garn, R-Utah, chairman of the Banking, Housing and Urban Affairs Committee, and William Proxmire of Wisconsin, its senior Democrat, in favoring a bill (S 2336) to permit surcharges of up to 5 percent.

The House, led by Frank Annunzio, D-Ill., chairman of the Banking Subcommittee on Consumer Affairs, supported a permanent prohibition on surcharges. In 1983, the House voted 349-73 to extend the ban until July 31, 1984, but the Senate did not act on the measure. *(1983 Almanac p. 267)*

On Feb. 22, less than a week before the ban was to end, the Senate Banking Committee approved S 2336 (no written report) to allow the extra fees. But to provide time for the House and Senate to settle their differences, the panel also approved a second bill (S 2335 — no written report) to prolong the ban until May 15, 1984.

On Feb. 28, the Senate voted 84-0 for S 2335 to continue the ban into May. It approved S 2336, allowing surcharges, by voice vote. *(Vote 20, p. 6-S)*

The next day, Feb. 29, the House agreed to the time extension, passing S 2335 by voice vote. However, members added the text of a separate bill passed by the House in 1983 (HR 3622 — H Rept 98-426) providing penalties for credit card fraud. The tactic riled senators pursuing their own anti-fraud legislation and further tangled the knot over credit-card surcharges. *(1983 Almanac p. 267)*

Impasse Continues

Through March, the Senate refused to take up the House-amended S 2335. And the Senate-passed S 2336 allowing surcharges appeared dead in Annunzio's subcommittee as Annunzio began pushing a new bill (HR 5026) to ban surcharges permanently.

The split seemed bridged on March 27. Midway through a subcommittee hearing, Annunzio and Garn (reached by phone) agreed to another temporary proposal, this time extending a ban until May 31, 1985.

HR 5026 was amended to reflect the arrangement, and the subcommittee approved it by voice vote. Annunzio steered quickly past the full Banking Committee, and the House by 355-34 passed the bill April 3. *(Vote 56, p. 20-H)*

The compromise dissolved in the Senate. Garn never was able to bring HR 5026 to a vote in the face of threats from a bipartisan group of senators, led by Alfonse M. D'Amato, R-N.Y., to offer an amendment calling for a permanent ban. D'Amato's cause got a boost when American Express Co. rallied hundreds of thousands of its eight million cardholders to write members of Congress in opposition to surcharges.

No further action was taken in either house. Despite Congress' inaction, most merchants did not begin imposing surcharges for fear of violating federal truth-in-lending or state usury laws.

Consumers Split

Supporting surcharges were the National Retail Merchants Association and the Service Station Dealers of America. The Consumer Federation of America, a former opponent, decided to back the surcharge proposals in the face of arguments that cash customers were paying higher prices to make up for credit-card paperwork costs.

Other consumer groups opposed surcharges, contending that merchants would not lower prices if the extra fees were permitted. Along with American Express, Visa and Mastercard, companies battled the surcharge proposals out of concern that, if enacted, customers would use their cards less. ∎

Business Merger Tactics

Amid bipartisan concern about corporate takeover battles, a House panel endorsed a bill intended to halt some of the more controversial business tactics used. The measure was not taken up by the full House.

The bill (HR 5693 — H Rept 98-1028) was approved by the Energy and Commerce Committee by voice vote Aug. 2 and reported Sept. 17. The measure would have restricted offensive moves by a bidder and the defenses of its target company. Both Republican and Democratic supporters said the changes would have benefited stockholders, whose shares often lost value in the skirmishing.

The Reagan administration opposed the bill, saying it was unnecessary and an intrusion on states' rights to regulate commerce.

The legislation would have limited two widely questioned practices: "golden parachutes," the lucrative severance packages given to executives whose jobs were jeopardized by possible takeovers, and "greenmail," the premium price that a company paid a would-be raider to buy back its stock.

The bill, sponsored by Timothy E. Wirth, D-Colo., was the product of more than a year of work in his Subcommittee on Telecommunications, Consumer Protection and Finance. It also reflected recommendations of a 1983 advisory committee to the Securities and Exchange Commission (SEC).

Highlights of Bill

Among the highlights of the bill:

● It would have closed what was known as the "13(d) window."

A section of the 1934 Securities Exchange Act required any person who bought more than 5 percent of a firm's stock to notify the SEC and the firm within 10 days. Meanwhile, the bidder could continue to accumulate stock, with officers and stockholders unaware a takeover was under way. The bill would have required a bidder to reveal a stock acquisition of more than 5 percent within 24 hours. Purchase of additional shares would have been prohibited for two business days.

● Golden parachutes would have been banned once a tender offer — a public invitation to buy stockholders' shares — had been made.

● Greenmail would have been subject to stockholder approval.

● A company would not have been able to issue new stock to dilute the raider's control.

● The minimum period for a tender offer for more than 5 percent of a company's stock would have been lengthened from 20 days to 40 days. ∎

Conrail Sale Fails to Materialize

The Reagan administration's long-held dream of selling Conrail to the private sector failed to materialize in 1984.

Congress was skeptical of the negotiations between the Department of Transportation (DOT) and potential buyers of the newly profitable freight railroad. As adjournment approached and DOT failed to recommend a preferred buyer, Congress ignored DOT's draft of the legislation required to ease any sale.

Earlier in the year, there was concern in Congress that the administration might be able to sell Conrail without consulting Congress. In March, in passing an Amtrak authorization (HR 3648), the House approved language that would have allowed Congress to veto any Conrail sale. *(Story, p. 294)*

But by June, it was clear that such a step was not needed. The administration conceded that no sale could occur unless Congress acted to forgive Conrail's $3.2 billion debt to the federal government and to remove constraints on management that had been imposed when Conrail was first created.

As DOT's talks with prospective buyers continued, pressure built in the House for a full-scale inquiry, especially from members from the Northeast who wanted to mitigate any potential adverse impact of a sale on their states' economies.

A letter urging a one-year moratorium to study the sale was circulated July 26 by Rep. Bob Edgar, D-Pa., a member of the Public Works and Transportation Committee. It was signed by several key House members, including James J. Howard, D-N.J., chairman of the Public Works and Transportation Committee; James L. Oberstar, D-

Minn., and Frank Horton, R-N.Y., co-chairmen of the Northeast-Midwest Congressional Coalition; and Jack F. Kemp, R-N.Y., who had close ties to the administration.

The letter was sent to Rep. James J. Florio, D-N.J., chairman of the Energy and Commerce Subcommittee on Commerce, Transportation and Tourism, which had jurisdiction over legislation relating to the Conrail sale. Florio said he was in no hurry to approve a sale and would conduct a full-scale inquiry into both DOT's recommendation and other competing offers.

Resurgence of Conrail

While the rest of the U.S. economy rebounded after World War II, the railroads went into serious decline. That was due largely to the rise of long-distance trucking, but it was exacerbated by featherbedding and other expensive labor protections, and by inflexible government regulation.

A series of mergers and bankruptcies ensued, the most serious of which was the failure of the Penn Central in 1970.

After several years of study and attempts to reorganize the troubled railroads, Congress in 1975 created the Consolidated Rail Corporation, or Conrail, to take over service from the bankrupt Penn Central and six other failing railroads. Stretching from Chicago and St. Louis in the West to Washington and Boston in the East, it was the nation's second-largest railroad in terms of freight revenue. *(1975 Almanac p. 757)*

The railroad operated like any other railroad but was subject to some legislative restrictions. Policy was set by an independent board of directors whose members were appointed by DOT and the U.S. Railway Association (USRA), an agency set up by Congress to restructure the bankrupt railroads. USRA oversaw Conrail's operations but neither agency was controlled by DOT or by the Federal Railroad Administration within DOT.

At first, Conrail was a sinkhole for federal funds. The government paid approximately $3.4 billion to buy the assets and settle claims of the failed railroads and poured another $3.2 billion into federal operating subsidies.

But by 1981, Conrail had experienced a remarkable turnaround. By slicing its work force from 100,000 employees in 1976 to fewer than 40,000 in 1984, and cutting its trackage from 17,700 miles to 14,200, its balance sheet turned from red ink to black.

In 1980 it suffered a net loss of $244 million, but it took its last federal subsidies in June 1981. It made profits of $39 million in 1981, $174 million in 1982 and $313 million in 1983. The expected 1984 profit of $500 million was among the best in the industry.

Administration's Remedy

When the Reagan administration took office, it quickly determined that the government's involvement in Conrail threatened the budget and also violated Reagan's principles forbidding government interference in the private sector.

In April 1981, Transportation Secretary Drew Lewis, saying that Conrail would soak up another $4 billion in subsidies by 1985, proposed that the government sell Conrail piecemeal. *(1981 Almanac p. 561)*

Some 15,000 rail workers marched on Washington, and the plan aroused fierce opposition in the Northeast. Congressional opposition blocked the administration's plans, but the sale proposal spurred Congress, which had been concerned principally with protecting rail service and jobs,

to pay new attention to Conrail's economic efficiency.

An alternative plan was developed that would let Conrail strip off unprofitable baggage and give it time to prove itself. As part of the package, labor made wage concessions that left Conrail employees earning 12 percent less than the industry standard.

The Northeast Rail Service Act (NERSA), contained in budget reconciliation legislation enacted by Congress later in 1981 (PL 97-35), allowed Conrail to divest itself of money-losing commuter railroads and made it easier to eliminate little-used routes and lay off employees. The law stated that Conrail could eventually be sold to private enterprise, but it forbade DOT to sell it piece by piece if Conrail became profitable.

Technical legal changes, such as those giving the General Accounting Office access to the company's books and requiring that its headquarters be in Philadelphia, also would be expected by any purchaser, staff aides said.

Question of Priorities

In 1982, DOT hired the New York investment house of Goldman, Sachs & Co. to advise it on what some called "the largest privatization in the history of the country."

DOT scoured the country for buyers. At first there was little interest, except for an offer by Conrail's employees to take it over. But in April 1984, the Alleghany Corp. of New York, a cash-rich firm that previously had been involved with railroads, offered $1 billion in cash, plus other considerations.

The Alleghany offer aroused interest and controversy. But Goldman, Sachs said it was "within the range of fair compensation," and DOT said it would wait two months for other bids.

When the deadline expired June 19, DOT had received 15 bids. Some were insubstantial — an Indiana warehousing company offered $1 cash — but most offered terms on a par with Alleghany's bid.

DOT had announced that its first priority in evaluating bids was to leave Conrail in a strong financial position, so it would not revert to government ownership again. Other considerations were to continue service to as much of the system as possible and to recoup some of the $7.6 billion the government had invested in Conrail in capital costs, operation subsidies and labor settlements.

DOT Picks Finalists

By fall, DOT maintained that only three offers culled from the original 15 bids — Alleghany Corp., a group headed by J. Willard Marriott Jr. and Norfolk Southern Corp. — would be considered.

Details of the three surviving offers were:

● Alleghany Corp. of New York was a firm that owned the Chesapeake and Ohio Railway until 1954, and then took over the New York Central, which was merged in 1962 with the Pennsylvania Railroad to create Penn Central. Alleghany pulled out of the Penn Central and currently operated only a small steel company.

It had almost $800 million in its coffers, the proceeds of the sale of its major subsidiary in January. Alleghany said it had to invest much of this cash by January 1985 or face major tax liability.

Alleghany's original offer was for $1 billion in cash plus giving up a major portion of the tax benefits that could accrue to a new owner. Alleghany also offered to buy out labor's interest in Conrail.

In October, Alleghany announced that it had added

$200 million in cash and the sacrifice of another $150 million in potential tax credits. It also offered labor shares of Alleghany stock and seats on the boards of both Alleghany and Conrail.

● J. Willard Marriott Jr. of Washington, D.C., the head of the hotel chain and a major GOP contributor, led an investment group seeking to acquire Conrail. Its offer was understood to be similar to Alleghany's.

● Norfolk Southern Corp. of Norfolk, Va., which owned two railroads, the Southern and the Norfolk and Western. Its lines competed with Conrail lines in some parts of the Northeast, and the company wanted to reduce duplication of services. It, too, was understood to offer about the same amount of cash, $1.2 billion, plus provisions to buy labor's share.

Congressional Concerns

Each of the plans, however, seemed capable of generating significant opposition in Congress.

There were congressional suspicions about how well all of the major bidders would meet DOT's priorities: Competing railroads might buy Conrail to consolidate lines, thereby cutting jobs and competition; investment groups might sell off the railroad in chunks or cut back service to smaller communities; smaller owners might not have the experience or financial backing to weather a downturn in the economy.

The two groups with the most clout on Capitol Hill, Conrail labor and management, did not back any of the offers. In 1978, legislation gave labor 15 percent of the railroad, and labor's cooperation in keeping wages down was considered essential to profitability. *(1978 Almanac p. 491)*

Management, which had great credibility in Congress because of its success in making the railroad solvent, opposed all three bidders and called for a public offering.

What's It Worth?

While members of Congress from the Northeast were primarily concerned with protecting rail service in their region, they also expressed a growing fear that the sale would become a giveaway.

No one suggested that the government would be able to recoup its $7 billion investment. But the question of how much Conrail was worth drew attention.

Conrail was expected to end the year with approximately $800 million in cash, which did not include a half-billion dollars being put into capital projects. In addition, the company had overpaid its employee pension assets by another $250 million.

A Conrail vice president for finance estimated that the firm needed only $250 million to $300 million in cash.

Thus, $750 million could be available immediately to a purchaser to put toward the purchase.

The value of Conrail's assets, such as track, buildings, equipment and real estate, were estimated at between $3.5 billion and $4 billion. Conrail's assets gave it substantial borrowing power, which could be attractive to a purchaser of the company.

The greatest value of all, however, might lie in Conrail's tax status.

While the bidders offered to forgo some advantages from Conrail's years of losses, the company still could provide substantial tax benefits that would be valuable to an owner. ∎

Pipeline Safety Bill

Legislation authorizing $8.6 million in fiscal 1985 for pipeline safety programs supervised by the Department of Transportation (DOT) was cleared by Congress.

The Senate passed the bill (S 2688) by voice vote Sept. 21, and the House cleared it by voice vote Sept. 26. Both chambers had approved pipeline bills in June, and the final bill was a compromise reached by key members without a formal conference. The president signed the measure Oct. 11 (PL 98-464).

The compromise accepted the House-passed one-year authorization period instead of the two years approved by the Senate and requested by the Reagan administration. The shorter time period was to provide impetus for DOT to make improvements in the pipeline inspection program in 1985 before the one-year authorization expired. The improvements were recommended by the General Accounting Office.

The final bill also provided for a one-time survey of interstate pipeline facilities built before 1940 and a study of the feasibility of shipping methanol through existing pipelines.

The compromise reduced the House-passed funding level by $110,000.

Legislative Action. On May 15, the House Public Works and Transportation and the Energy and Commerce committees reported HR 5313 (H Rept 98-780, Parts I and II). The bill authorized $8.7 million in fiscal 1985 for programs authorized by the Natural Gas Pipeline Safety Act of 1968 (PL 90-481) and the Hazardous Liquid Pipeline Safety Act of 1979 (PL 96-129). *(1968 Almanac p. 339; 1979 Almanac p. 352)*

On June 25, the House passed the bill by voice vote and substituted its text for that of S 2688, which the Senate had passed by voice vote June 21.

The Senate version, reported May 17 (S Rept 98-456) by the Commerce, Science and Transportation Committee, had authorized $8.6 million for fiscal 1985 and $9.2 million for fiscal 1986. ∎

Shipbuilding Subsidies

Senate and administration opposition prevented enactment of a House-passed bill (HR 5220) to revive subsidies for commercial shipbuilding.

The National Defense Shipyard Protection Act of 1984 would have authorized $250 million for fiscal 1985. Of that, $50 million would have been for a longstanding government program to buy used vessels for the national Defense Reserve Fleet and $200 million was for the first year of a new Shipyard Incentive Program.

Proponents, particularly members of the House Merchant Marine and Fisheries Committee, argued that idle U.S. shipyards had deteriorated or closed as a result of subsidy cuts during the Reagan administration.

Hoping to win support for the merchant marine and commercial shipping with a pro-defense argument, bill proponents contended that without peacetime subsidies, the yards would be hard pressed to mobilize for production in case of war.

The Reagan administration, with Congress' backing, had not funded shipbuilding programs and had bought out many existing federal contracts. Administration officials said private yards were adequately subsidized by Navy contracts. *(1981 Almanac p. 570)*

"The administration seems to have conceded commercial shipbuilding to foreign yards while indicating that the shipbuilding program for the Navy will be sufficient to maintain our shipbuilding base," Mario Biaggi, D-N.Y., chairman of the House Merchant Marine Subcommittee, said at a subcommittee markup. "The Congress, at the same time, has done little to change that impression."

The subcommittee approved the bill May 2 by voice vote, as did the full committee on May 10. It was reported (H Rept 98-757) May 15.

Before the committee vote, Joel Pritchard, R-Wash., a supporter, warned that the bill not only faced administration opposition, but also "very bad sledding over in the Senate."

The House passed HR 5220 by voice vote on Sept. 5. On Sept. 11, it was referred to the Senate Commerce, Science and Transportation Committee, which, as expected, never acted on the legislation.

The proposed Shipyard Incentive Program differed markedly from the current system, unfunded since 1980, that paid shipbuilders a sum based on the difference between their costs and the much lower costs of foreign yards. Under the proposed program, a shipbuilder could have been paid up to 50 percent of construction costs, without regard to foreign prices. Also, payment would have been in full, instead of in increments during construction. To be eligible, a yard would have to be capable of building three ships simultaneously, and its ship design and bid would have to be accepted by the secretaries of transportation and of the Navy.

The bill also would have allowed a U.S. ship operator to receive a subsidy for ships built in foreign yards, but only if the operator spent an equal amount in a U.S. yard since Jan. 1, 1984. ∎

Environment/Energy

Despite election-year political maneuvering, Congress in 1984 managed to chalk up several significant accomplishments in the fields of environmental protection and energy development.

It overhauled and strengthened one major law regulating hazardous wastes.

It set aside more acreage as federally protected wilderness in the lower 48 states than at any time since the 1964 Wilderness Act created a national system for preserving roadless forest lands from development.

It cleared several important Western water development bills, approved a Nuclear Regulatory Commission reauthorization and revived the Synthetic Fuels Corporation after slashing its funding.

The list of things Congress did not do in 1984 was considerably longer, however.

Legislation to overhaul the law controlling natural gas pricing proved too hot to handle. An $18 billion package of Eastern water projects stalled in the closing days of the session. Also falling short of enactment were bills to renew the "superfund" program for cleanup of abandoned hazardous-waste dumps, to rewrite the Clean Air Act and to revise the Clean Water Act.

As the year ended, most of the major environmental laws enacted during the 1970s were ready or overdue for reauthorization. Among them were the Clean Water Act, the Clean Air Act, Safe Drinking Water Act, Ocean Dumping Act, and laws governing the use of pesticides and the marketing of toxic chemicals.

Quiet Restored at the Agencies

During the first two years of his administration, President Reagan was constantly on the defensive over environmental issues — largely because of controversies created by his top appointees in the field, Interior Secretary James G. Watt and Environmental Protection Agency (EPA) Administrator Anne M. Burford.

By the end of 1983, however, both Watt and Burford had been forced to resign. And with new and respected leadership at Interior and EPA, congressional committees did not hold the multitude of oversight hearings they had in 1983, when the administration's environmental policies and management came under heavy fire.

At the Interior Department, Secretary William P. Clark put off until 1985 many decisions on controversial issues, such as revision of the government's coal-leasing program, and he moderated a number of positions taken by Watt.

EPA's operating budget began to climb again after several years of decline. William D. Ruckelshaus, who replaced Burford as administrator, by most accounts restored public confidence in the agency, taking actions that often were aggressively protective of the environment.

Clark and Ruckelshaus were essentially firefighters, called in to douse the flames of controversy that had been fanned by Watt and Burford. By year's end, their work successfully completed, both men announced they were leaving government service.

Electioneering and the Environment

Environmental and conservation groups critical of the Reagan administration's record campaigned against the president, but failed miserably in their ultimate goal of dislodging him.

The administration spent a good deal of time in the 18 months before the election seeking to defuse the environment as a campaign liability, and it largely succeeded. But during those 18 months, the environmentalists managed to change the administration's behavior significantly from what it had been during the Watt-Burford era.

Congressional inaction on major environmental reauthorizations obscured, in many cases, the fact that environmentalists held the high ground. Reagan had come into office in 1981 on a platform that called for amending laws such as the Clean Air Act to ease the burden on industry. Environmentalists, fearing Reagan had enough support in Congress to succeed, fought the administration to a standstill on the changes during 1981-83.

By 1984, environmentalists were usually on the offensive, seeking to tighten existing laws. Rep. Henry A. Waxman, D-Calif., for example, launched a drive in his House Energy subcommittee to add new controls on acid rain to the Clean Air Act. He came within one vote of succeeding. Likewise, even though failure to enact a new superfund law was a major disappointment for environmentalists, the debate centered not on whether to weaken existing law but on how much to strengthen it.

The scantiness of legislative output was not simply the result of the shortness of the election-year session. It was also a sign of profound and intense disagreement over what environmental laws ought to do.

Election years sometimes prompt Congress to avoid controversial issues. In the Senate, where acid rain and natural gas pricing pitted members of the same party against each other, that effect could be seen in 1984. Senate rules made it easy for a few members to stop a bill.

But in the House, environmentalists and Democrats took the election as a signal to push hard for what they wanted. Chief sponsor James J. Florio, D-N.J., for example, decided to seek renewal of the superfund a year before it was to expire, aware that Reagan would not want to veto a strong bill before the election. Members seeking federal water projects in their districts wanted action in 1984 as well, hoping to campaign on benefits they had brought to their constituents.

Although the House passed those bills and others by large margins, the measures never made it to the Senate floor.

Toxic Waste Law

The most significant pollution-control legislation enacted in 1984 was a reauthorization of the law on handling, storage and disposal of hazardous wastes — the Resource Conservation and Recovery Act (RCRA).

Congress dramatically tightened the 1976 law, taking away from EPA the enforcement discretion that some members claimed the agency had abused. The 1984 law, for example, banned the disposal of hazardous liquids in landfills, from which they could leak and pollute well water. EPA in February 1982 had suspended a rule against liquids in landfills, reinstating it only after a public and congressional outcry.

The new law also brought tens of thousands of small businesses, from dry cleaners to gas stations, under requirements for safe disposal of the hazardous wastes they produce. EPA had set the cut-off point for enforcement of the law at quantities less than 2,200 pounds per month, but Congress dropped the threshold to 220 pounds per month.

The process of passing the four-year reauthorization bill was studded with obstacles, and conferees did not reach final agreement until just days before the 98th Congress adjourned. While the House first passed the bill in November 1983, the legislation did not win approval in the Senate until July 1984.

The bill's enactment seemed to reflect the potency of toxic waste as a political issue. Democrats made clear at their July 1984 convention that they intended to use Reagan's record on the control and cleanup of such wastes against him. The logjam of objections that had stalled the bill short of the Senate floor finally broke after the Democratic convention, when the administration signaled it wanted an environmental bill to sign.

Wilderness Protection

The biggest step Congress took on natural resources was setting aside more than 8.3 million acres of national forest land in 20 states as federally protected wilderness. Those pristine lands were permanently shielded from roadbuilding, logging, mining and other development.

The 1984 wilderness legislation went a long way toward settling a debate that had raged since at least 1977, when President Carter sent Congress his recommendations for wilderness designations. The state-by-state decision process meant in most cases that local loggers, miners and environmentalists had to reach a consensus, then win support from most members of a state delegation.

The outpouring of bills resulted from a key compromise on the issue of how to "release" for other uses the lands considered but not finally named as wilderness. That nationwide compromise was negotiated by Sen. James A. McClure, R-Idaho, chairman of the Senate Energy Committee, and Rep. John F. Seiberling, D-Ohio, chairman of the House Interior Subcommittee on Public Lands. More than 14.6 million acres were released under the year's legislation.

Wilderness protection became a national controversy early in the Reagan administration when Interior Secretary Watt seemed poised to allow new oil and gas leasing in areas already declared wilderness. The 1964 Wilderness Act allowed such leasing until Jan. 1, 1984, although few such leases had been granted. In the face of Watt's threat, Congress blocked wilderness leasing through a variety of measures from 1981 through 1983.

Water Projects

By far the most expensive resource bill of the year was the $18 billion omnibus authorization for Army Corps of Engineers water projects, mainly in the East: ocean ports, navigation works for inland rivers and canals, and flood control. The House passed it 259-33 in a frenzied evening session before recessing for the Democratic convention. Bills such as that one, with over 300 individual projects in nearly as many congressional districts, had in earlier decades been a pre-election tradition.

In the Senate, however, budgetary reality prevailed. A Senate committee reported a scaled-down $11 billion omnibus bill, but the Senate never took it up for consideration.

East-West conflict over water policy was another issue that stalled the Corps of Engineers omnibus bill in the Senate. Sponsors wanted to include a title creating a national water policy board to replace one Congress abolished at Reagan's request in 1982. Western senators objected to the panel, which could have put under one umbrella both the Interior Department's Bureau of Reclamation, which served the West, and the Corps of Engineers.

Western water interests got more done in Congress than Eastern ones. The bureau once again increased its share of the total available water appropriations at the expense of the corps. Westerners also got a $650 million dam safety bill, a reaffirmation of below-market pricing for federal hydroelectric power from the Hoover Dam, new projects for controlling salinity in the Colorado River, and a demonstration of ways to recharge an aquifer that is slowly being pumped dry beneath the high plains states.

Inaction on Energy Issues

With one notable exception, Congress took little significant action on energy issues in 1984. A flurry of concern over the mergers of several huge oil companies came to nothing. Plentiful oil and gas supplies undermined legislative efforts to improve the nation's preparedness for future energy shortages. And natural gas pricing was simply too controversial to tackle in an election year.

Congress did find itself forced to decide the fate of the U.S. Synthetic Fuels Corporation (SFC), which was created in 1980 after a decade of energy supply disruptions to stimulate development of so-called "synthetic fuels" from tar sands, oil shale, coal and other underutilized resources.

The SFC had been plagued by management troubles almost since its inception, and these reached crisis proportions by early 1984 as resignations left the SFC board without the quorum it needed to conduct business. With a worldwide oil glut making energy cheap and plentiful, few companies had any interest in pursuing costly synfuels development. Congress lost patience with the fumbling SFC, and began eyeing its rich cache of funds for possible savings in an era of high deficits.

By year's end, Congress had stripped the agency of some $7 billion, leaving it with about that much still to spend — under strict new conditions. Reagan then made enough recess appointments to give the board a quorum and put the SFC back in business.

—By Joseph A. Davis

Congress Tightens Hazardous Waste Controls

Legislation to renew and tighten the law regulating handling and disposal of hazardous wastes was cleared by Congress Oct. 5, but President Reagan waited until Nov. 8 to sign it into law (HR 2867 — PL 98-616).

A second major hazardous-waste proposal (HR 5640), which would have extended and strengthened the 1980 law creating a "superfund" for the cleanup of abandoned toxic-waste dumps, died in the Senate in the waning days of the session. *(Story, p. 309)*

The two measures — and the hazardous-waste problem they were designed to address — dominated the environmental agenda before Congress in 1984.

Final action on HR 2867 came when the Senate adopted a conference report on the bill (H Rept 98-1133). The House had adopted the report Oct. 3. Conferees reached agreement on the bill Sept. 28.

The House passed HR 2867 Nov. 3, 1983; the Senate followed suit July 25, 1984. *(1983 Almanac p. 335)*

The legislation reauthorized and strengthened the Resource Conservation and Recovery Act (RCRA — PL 94-580) of 1976, which governed "cradle-to-grave" handling of hazardous wastes. Under the law, the Environmental Protection Agency (EPA) issued and enforced rules on the generation, storage, treatment and disposal of such wastes. *(1976 Almanac p. 199)*

Provisions

As cleared by Congress, HR 2867 included the following major provisions:

Authorizations

● Authorized appropriations for four years to carry out programs under RCRA, totaling $233.74 million for fiscal 1985, $253.90 million for 1986, $250.02 million for 1987 and $249.52 million for 1988. The bill included specific authorizations for general administration, enforcement grants for states, state waste-site inventories, state solid-waste programs, state recycled-oil programs, state underground tank regulation programs, EPA criminal investigators and other activities.

Liquids in Landfills

● Banned the disposal of any bulk or non-containerized liquid hazardous waste in any landfill, effective six months after enactment.

● Required EPA to issue, within 15 months, regulations minimizing to the extent technologically feasible the landfill disposal of containerized liquid hazardous waste.

● Banned disposal of non-hazardous liquids in hazardous-waste landfills beginning 12 months after enactment, unless it was the only available alternative and posed no threat to an underground source of drinking water.

Land Disposal

● Banned land disposal (except for underground injection) of certain highly hazardous wastes listed in California's program, unless EPA issued regulations within 32 months finding that prohibiting disposal of specific wastes on that list in specific types of facilities was not necessary to protect human health and the environment. The burden of detailed proof was on those trying to show such disposal

to be safe. Extensions for up to 54 months were allowed in certain cases if insufficient alternate disposal capacity was available.

● Banned land disposal of solvents and dioxins if EPA did not within 24 months issue regulations finding specific disposal practices safe. Extensions of up to 54 months in certain cases were allowed if no other disposal capacity was available.

● Required EPA to publish, within 24 months, a schedule for determining whether to ban land disposal of all other hazardous wastes listed under RCRA, considering first those presenting the greatest hazard. EPA had to issue those decisions for one-third of the remaining wastes within 45 months, two-thirds within 55 months, and for all within 66 months.

● Banned land disposal of any of those wastes for which EPA failed to meet the 66-month deadline, but allowed for variances if EPA failed to meet the earlier deadlines.

● Banned disposal of liquid and other hazardous wastes in any salt dome, salt-bed formation, underground mine or cave. The ban began with enactment, but such disposal could be allowed if EPA later issued standards and, for a specific facility, found no environmental threat and issued a permit.

Small-Quantity Generators

● Required EPA to issue by March 31, 1986, standards for handling hazardous wastes from generators of between 100 kilograms (kg) and 1,000 kg (220 to 2,200 pounds) per month. The standards could be less stringent than those for wastes from larger generators, but had to protect human health and the environment. EPA could regulate generators of less than 100 kg per month if necessary to protect human health and the environment.

● Required shipments of hazardous waste generated in quantities between 100 kg and 1,000 kg per month to be accompanied by a uniform manifest, starting within 270 days of enactment.

● Required EPA standards to allow on-site storage of hazardous wastes without a permit for up to 180 days. Storage of up to 6,000 kg for up to 270 days was allowed if the generator had to ship wastes more than 200 miles.

Underground Storage Tanks

● Required owners to notify state agencies of underground tanks used to store hazardous substances and petroleum products such as gasoline.

● Required EPA to issue regulations for detecting leaks from such underground tanks, record-keeping, reporting and correction of leaks, taking tanks out of operation, evidence of financial responsibility, and performance standards for new tanks.

● Allowed states to manage their own underground tank regulatory programs if those were no less stringent than the federal one, had adequate enforcement and had EPA approval.

Waste Facility Standards

● Required all new or expanded land disposal facilities for hazardous wastes, in order to qualify for permits, to have at least two liners, to have leachate collection systems above the top liner and between the two liners, functioning in part as a leak detection system, and to have groundwater monitoring. The requirement applied to all landfills and surface impoundments — new facilities or units, replacement units or lateral expansions of existing facilities — applying for permits after the date of enactment. Some requirements could be waived for certain foundry and mining wastes.

● Required incinerators receiving a permit after enactment to destroy and remove at least 99.99 percent of the hazardous substances they burned, as EPA rules currently required.

Surface Impoundments

● Prohibited existing surface impoundments not meeting minimum technological requirements from receiving, storing, or treating any hazardous waste listed under RCRA. The ban was to take effect in four years for most existing hazardous-waste impoundments. The minimum technological requirements were those for new impoundments (double liners and leak detection, or the equivalent, and groundwater monitoring).

● Allowed exemptions from that prohibition under certain conditions for impoundments that were not within one-quarter of a mile of an underground source of drinking water and had at least one non-leaking liner, or that contained partially treated wastewater subject to other EPA permitting authorities.

Burning and Blending

● Required producers, burners, distributors and marketers of fuels produced from hazardous waste (including used oil) to notify EPA of their operations within 15 months unless specifically exempted by EPA. Single-family or two-family residences were exempt.

● Required EPA, within 15 months, to issue record-keeping requirements for such facilities.

● Required EPA, within two years, to issue technical standards for such operations.

● Required a warning label to appear on the invoice or bill of sale accompanying waste-derived fuels, beginning in 90 days and continuing until EPA issued regulations superseding the requirement.

Listing of Wastes

● Required EPA to list chlorinated dioxins and chlorinated dibenzofurans as hazardous wastes under the law, where appropriate, within six months and to list other halogenated dioxins and dibenzofurans where appropriate within one year. Within 15 months EPA had to decide whether or not to list 17 specified wastes. EPA was to identify or list wastes that contained hazardous constituents at concentrations that endangered health or the environment.

● Required EPA, in considering petitions to remove from the list a specific waste, to consider factors (including additional constituents) other than those for which the waste was listed if EPA had reason to believe the additional factors could cause the waste to be hazardous.

Inspections

● Required EPA to inspect each federal hazardous-waste facility annually, beginning 12 months after enactment. States with authorized RCRA programs could also inspect the facilities. Each federal agency had to submit to EPA and authorized states a continuing inventory of the hazardous-waste sites it had ever owned or operated. If an agency

failed to do so, EPA was to conduct the inventory.

● Required EPA to inspect annually all hazardous-waste facilities operated by state or local governments and to make the results available to the public.

● Required EPA or authorized states to inspect hazardous-waste handling facilities at least every two years, beginning 12 months after enactment.

Permits

● Required EPA to process all applications for land disposal permits within four years, for incinerator permits within five years, and for all other permits within eight years.

● Provided that permits under RCRA for land disposal, incineration and treatment facilities for hazardous wastes be of fixed terms not exceeding 10 years. EPA was to review land disposal permits after five years to ensure compliance with currently applicable requirements. EPA could review and modify a permit at any time. When renewing permits, EPA was to consider new technology and regulations.

● Terminated 12 months after enactment, unless certain conditions were met, the "interim status" of existing land disposal facilities (a status given to facilities already in operation when RCRA was enacted in 1976, under which they did not have to comply with all the law's requirements while their application for a permit was pending at EPA). Facilities had to apply for a final permit and certify that they were complying with groundwater monitoring and financial responsibility requirements.

● Required EPA to issue rules within 30 months for monitoring and control of air emissions at hazardous-waste treatment, storage and disposal facilities.

● Required owners or operators of hazardous-waste landfills or surface impoundments to submit, with their permit applications, information about the potential for public exposure to hazardous substances in connection with the facility. The information was to be transmitted to the Agency for Toxic Substances and Disease Registry (ATSDR), which could perform a health assessment if it judged the risk to be substantial. The public could also submit relevant information to EPA, ATSDR or the state. Whenever such a facility posed a substantial potential risk to human health, the EPA administrator or an authorized state (with EPA's concurrence) could request ATSDR to perform an assessment of the health risks. EPA had to pay for the studies it requested.

● Authorized EPA to issue permits for experimental facilities without first issuing permit standards. EPA could modify or waive requirements for permit application or issuance, except for requirements for public participation and financial responsibility. Such permits were for one year, renewable for up to three one-year terms.

Enforcement

● Required the attorney general, at EPA's request, to deputize qualified EPA employees to act as special marshals in RCRA criminal investigations.

● Expanded the list of actions constituting crimes under RCRA and raised maximum penalties. The severest penalty, for persons convicted of handling hazardous waste with knowledge that they were violating the law and were endangering other persons, was a fine of up to $250,000 ($1 million for an organization) and imprisonment for up to 15 years.

● Authorized EPA to issue orders requiring corrective

action, or to bring a civil suit, when there was a release of hazardous wastes from an interim-status facility. Set civil penalties of up to $25,000 per day for non-compliance.

● Made the RCRA ban on open dumping of hazardous wastes enforceable by citizen suits.

● Required EPA, upon receiving information of an imminent hazard at a hazardous-waste site, to provide immediate notice to the appropriate local government and post a notice at the site.

● Required EPA to provide for public notice and comment before entering into a settlement of any imminent-hazard action it brings.

● Under certain circumstances, authorized claims to be made directly against insurance companies or others who had guaranteed the financial responsibility of the owner or operator of a hazardous-waste facility who declared bankruptcy.

Other Provisions

● Banned the use of dioxin-contaminated wastes or any other hazardous waste as a dust suppressant, unless the waste was hazardous solely because of its ignitability.

● Required EPA to decide within one year whether to list used motor oil as a hazardous waste under RCRA and to issue standards for recycling it within two years. Generators of used oil who recycled it according to EPA standards were exempt from manifest, record-keeping and reporting requirements.

● Banned underground injection of hazardous wastes into or above any formation that contained, within one-quarter mile of the well, an underground source of drinking water. Variances were allowed in certain cases where it could be shown the waste would not endanger drinking water.

● Established a 19-member National Groundwater Commission to assess groundwater issues and to report to Congress on groundwater contamination from hazardous wastes.

The bill authorized $7 million for the commission. The commission was to focus on the quality rather than the quantity of groundwater and to avoid infringing on state water rights. Ten of the 19 commissioners were to be members of Congress.

● Prohibited exports of hazardous waste, beginning in 24 months, unless EPA was notified that the receiving country had consented to accept the waste, a copy of that consent was attached to the manifest and the shipment conformed to the terms of the consent. An international agreement could substitute for specific consent.

● Required each generator of more than 1,000 kg of hazardous waste per month to certify that he was undertaking a program to reduce the amount of waste to the extent economically practical and that the proposed method of treatment, storage or disposal was the one currently available to him that minimized the threat to health and the environment.

Certifications were to be based solely on the judgment of the generator, and the bill established no mechanism for verifying them and no penalties for false certification.

● Created an ombudsman's office within EPA to answer complaints and requests from the public for information about matters within EPA's purview.

● Stipulated that nothing in this act should be construed to affect, modify or amend the Uranium Mill Tailings Radiation Control Act of 1978. *(PL 95-604, 1978 Almanac p. 750)*

Background

RCRA, enacted in 1976, established stricter standards for the transport, storage, treatment and disposal of hazardous wastes than for ordinary household and municipal wastes. EPA defined hazardous wastes generally as those that were toxic, flammable, corrosive or explosive.

From the outset, EPA had difficulty administering RCRA. It did not finish issuing the principal regulations for the program until 1982, six years after enactment of the law. And even then, the agency came under criticism from some in Congress who thought the regulations were too lax.

The law was designed to regulate the disposal of hazardous wastes from the time of enactment forward. The task of cleaning up existing toxic-waste dumps was left to the superfund program.

Under RCRA, all facilities handling hazardous wastes had to have either federal permits or state permits issued under a federally approved program.

The law set up a system for "cradle-to-grave" tracking of hazardous wastes, with a standard EPA manifest to accompany such wastes at each stage of shipment, storage, treatment, recycling and final disposal.

1983 Action

The House passed HR 2867 on Nov. 3, 1983. The Senate Environment and Public Works Committee approved its own RCRA reauthorization bill July 28, 1983, and reported it Oct. 28 (S 757 — S Rept 98-284). But that measure did not reach the Senate floor before the 1983 session ended.

Both bills were designed to close loopholes in the original law that allowed as much as half of the nation's hazardous wastes to escape regulation.

For example, current regulations exempted generators of less than 1,000 kilograms (kg) per month of hazardous waste — 2,000 pounds. At least 20 states already regulated small-quantity generators more stringently than the federal government.

Senate Action

Although the Environment Committee had approved its version of the RCRA reauthorization in July 1983, almost a full year passed before the legislation reached the Senate floor.

Action was delayed by the objections of several senators to particular aspects of the bill. Majority Leader Howard H. Baker Jr., R-Tenn., said that when the bill first came out of the Environment Committee, "I had a string of 'notifies' and 'holds' and carryings-on like that that stretched halfway down the page."

But by June 7, 1984, a letter circulated by Sen. Frank R. Lautenberg, D-N.J., and signed by 52 senators from both parties was delivered to Baker urging him to bring the bill to the floor.

Even though Baker never succeeded in winning a specific time agreement from members opposed to the measure, he called it up July 25.

The Senate passed HR 2867 the same day by a 93-0 vote, after substituting the provisions of S 757 for those contained in the House version. *(Vote 181, p. 31-S)*

The Senate's RCRA bill reauthorized funding for the hazardous waste program through fiscal 1989, applied regulations for the first time to businesses that generated small quantities of hazardous wastes and restricted disposal of some hazardous wastes in landfills.

It also restricted the blending of hazardous wastes with used oil and their burning as fuel, beefed up EPA's enforcement authority, gave citizens the right to sue polluters when EPA failed to do so, and required EPA to regulate underground storage tanks for petroleum.

The Reagan administration's position on the RCRA bill was unclear.

"The administration supports enactment of S 757 only if it is amended to delete or modify inflexible and unnecessary regulatory mandates which could impose from $10 billion to $20 billion per year in added costs on the economy, while providing limited environmental benefits," said a July 25 statement from the Office of Management and Budget (OMB). The statement detailed provisions the administration did not like, many of which remained in the final Senate bill.

But other officials, including certain White House staffers and EPA Administrator William D. Ruckelshaus, reportedly took a more positive view of the legislation, seeing it as a bill President Reagan would be well advised to sign in an election year.

Amendments

Before final passage of the bill, the Senate adopted some 21 amendments or blocks of amendments, all by voice vote, granting concessions to members who had problems with specific provisions or wanted something added.

Chief among the changes were concessions made by Dave Durenberger, R-Minn., to Steven D. Symms, R-Idaho, on provisions aimed at controlling leakages from underground storage tanks, and modifications sought by Alan K. Simpson, R-Wyo., broadening an exemption for mining wastes from tougher standards for land disposal of hazardous wastes.

Conference/Final

House-Senate conferees began meeting Sept. 18 in an effort to work out a compromise version of HR 2867. After several days of sometimes difficult negotiations, they reached an accord Sept. 28 on a four-year RCRA reauthorization. The conference report (H Rept 98-1133) was filed Oct. 3.

The House bill authorized RCRA appropriations of $162.2 million for fiscal 1984, $170.4 million for 1985, and $175.5 million for 1986. The Senate bill authorized $125 million for fiscal 1985 and $140 million annually for fiscal 1986-89. Conferees adopted the Senate spending levels for fiscal 1985-88.

At meetings Sept. 18, 25, 26 and 28, RCRA conferees hammered out compromise language for the complex bill. Most provisions were aimed at closing loopholes in existing law, and House-Senate differences were minor. Conferees spent much of their time resolving three of the four most controversial issues before them: how to regulate generators of small quantities of hazardous wastes, limit disposal of hazardous wastes in landfills and regulate underground tanks for the storage of petroleum and other hazardous substances.

The Superfund Snarl

A fourth issue almost derailed the negotiations entirely. Until mid-afternoon Sept. 28, conferees battled over what to do with a set of amendments to the superfund law that the Senate had tacked onto its RCRA bill.

The superfund amendments had been loaded onto the RCRA bill in the Senate because their sponsors felt that measure had a better chance of enactment than a separate bill (S 2892) extending and strengthing the 1980 superfund law.

But House conferees, at the urging of Rep. James J. Florio, D-N.J., the key House sponsor of both the superfund and RCRA bills, balked at attaching those amendments to the RCRA bill before the Senate passed its superfund bill. Florio and House Energy Committee Chairman John D. Dingell, D-Mich., had abandoned earlier efforts to link the two bills on the House floor when they said they received assurances from Senate leaders that the Senate would act on a superfund bill.

House conferees insisted on deferring action on the superfund amendments to RCRA until the Senate acted on its more comprehensive superfund bill. Senate conferees finally agreed to strip the disputed amendments from the RCRA bill.

Issues Resolved

The provision on small-quantity generators agreed to by the conferees Sept. 25 was a blend of House and Senate versions. It gave the Environmental Protection Agency (EPA) until March 31, 1986, to issue rules for businesses and institutions that generated between 100 and 1,000 kilograms (220 and 2,200 pounds) of hazardous waste per month. The rules had to be sufficient to protect human health and the environment.

The bill gave EPA the option of issuing rules for generators of quantities smaller than 100 kilograms per month.

On Sept. 26, conferees agreed on most of the provisions limiting the disposal of hazardous wastes on land. That included an immediate ban on hazardous wastes in underground mines and salt formations until EPA took certain regulatory actions to protect the environment. Effective six months after enactment, there was to be a statutory ban on placement of bulk or non-containerized hazardous liquids in any landfill.

Furthermore, specified wastes were banned entirely from land disposal, with an effective date extension if no alternative disposal capacity was immediately available.

On Sept. 28, conferees approved provisions to regulate underground tanks for storage of petroleum and other hazardous substances. The House RCRA bill contained no such provisions, because the House had dealt with this problem in its superfund bill (HR 5640).

Provisions adopted by the conference required tank owners to notify state agencies of the location of their tanks.

The bill also required EPA to issue rules for leak-detection systems adequate to protect human health and the environment. Within 35 months, EPA was required to issue performance standards for new tanks.

States could manage the regulatory programs, but state programs could be "no less stringent" than EPA's national standards.

One of the last issues to be settled was how to regulate PCBs, a toxic material used in electrical transformers and for other industrial purposes. PCBs were currently regulated under the Toxic Substances Control Act, but the House bill sought to list them as hazardous wastes subject to RCRA controls.

The House finally dropped its bid to bring PCBs under RCRA, thus resolving the issue.　　■

Superfund Reauthorization Passed by House

Legislation (HR 5640) to extend and expand the "superfund" program for the cleanup of abandoned hazardous-waste dumps moved through the House in 1984 but died in the Senate.

President Reagan opposed renewal of the program until 1985, when authority for the taxes that financed it was scheduled to expire. Democrats pushing for an expanded cleanup effort excoriated the president for his position and charged that the Republican-controlled Senate had "caved in" to administration pressure.

The $1.6 billion superfund was created in 1980 when Congress, at the urging of President Carter, cleared the Comprehensive Environmental Response, Compensation and Liability Act (PL 96-510). The program was funded by a tax on crude oil and raw chemicals ("feedstocks"), plus appropriations from Congress. *(1980 Almanac p. 584)*

The bill passed by the House in 1984 would have renewed the 1980 law for five years and increased the size of the Hazardous Substance Response Trust Fund (the superfund) to $10.2 billion.

The Senate Environment and Public Works Committee approved its own $7.5 billion, five-year superfund reauthorization bill (S 2892 — S Rept 98-631) on Sept. 13, but that measure was referred to the Finance Committee, which did not act on it.

The problem of hazardous-waste disposal, and legislation to address it, preoccupied environmentalists and their allies in Congress during 1984. Although the superfund reauthorization died in the closing days of the session, Congress did clear legislation (HR 2867 — PL 98-616) renewing and strengthening the nation's other major law dealing with hazardous wastes, the Resource Conservation and Recovery Act (RCRA). *(Story, p. 305)*

Background

Before the federal government started to regulate hazardous-waste disposal under RCRA in 1976, toxic, corrosive, explosive and flammable materials could be legally jettisoned just about anywhere. By then, decades of abuse had left thousands of hazardous sites scattered across the countryside. *(1976 Almanac p. 199)*

The superfund was created primarily to deal with abandoned dump sites, where no one was willing to take responsibility for cleaning up properly. For these sites, the law allowed the Environmental Protection Agency (EPA) to go after whoever caused the problem — generators or transporters of waste, owners or operators of dumps.

If dump owners had disappeared, EPA could hold completely responsible the companies whose wastes ended up in the dump — even if they acted in good faith, believing the waste haulers and dump operators would do their jobs properly. Legally, the liability was divided among all the parties the government could locate.

EPA could order those responsible for a dump to clean it up. If they did not cooperate, EPA could do the cleanup itself, and then sue them later for up to three times the actual costs.

If EPA could not recover the cleanup costs, it paid them directly out of the superfund. The fund came from two sources: 12.5 percent from the general Treasury, and 87.5 percent from a tax on petroleum and on the raw materials that go into the making of chemical products.

EPA estimated that 71 percent of the nation's hazardous waste came from the chemical industry.

In 1984, the Environmental Protection Agency, which administered both RCRA and the superfund law, estimated there were at least 22,000 dangerous waste dumps in the United States. As many as 2,200 of the sites required urgent cleanup at a cost EPA estimated to be between $8.4 billion and $16 billion.

The size of those numbers, a quantum leap from EPA's thinking only a year before, caused consternation at the White House and the Office of Management and Budget, which insisted the figures not be released. They were made public in late January by Rep. James J. Florio, D-N.J., who was leading the congressional fight to get the superfund reauthorized and strengthened.

Past Mismanagement

The superfund law, and complaints about how EPA carried it out, were the focus of congressional investigations in 1983 that shook EPA to its foundations. Among the casualties were Administrator Anne M. Burford and Rita Lavelle, the Reagan appointee who was in charge of the superfund. *(1983 Almanac p. 332)*

Among the problems Congress found was that EPA was slow in setting up procedures needed to get the program started and slow in spending the money in the fund.

Another finding was that EPA preferred to negotiate rather than litigate against dumpers to collect costs, a preference that was delaying cleanup, recovering less than full costs, and settling for inadequate cleanups at many sites. EPA was charged with making "sweetheart deals" with industry.

While Burford headed EPA, the Reagan administration opposed reauthorization of the superfund law. But seeking to blunt some environmental criticism in an election year, Reagan announced a policy shift in January 1984 in his State of the Union message, saying he would support reauthorization of superfund. *(Text, p. 5-E)*

Burford's successor, EPA Administrator William D. Ruckelshaus, said March 15 that the administration would wait until 1985 to propose a reauthorization bill. He said EPA needed time to complete legally required reports to Congress that were not due until December 1984.

House Committee Action

Superfund legislation got off to a rocky start in 1984 as it ran into unexpected trouble April 4 in a House Energy and Commerce subcommittee.

Florio, chairman of the Subcommittee on Commerce, Transportation and Tourism, abruptly adjourned a panel markup session after opponents dealt a blow to the strong bill he wanted. By a 5-4 margin, the subcommittee substituted a simple five-year reauthorization of the present $1.6 billion fund for the $11.25 billion measure Florio and environmentalists were proposing in its place.

Compromise Proposed

After the setback, Florio began negotiations with key members of the panel to seek a compromise. On May 10, a compromise bill (HR 5640) was introduced by Florio and cosponsored by Reps. John D. Dingell, D-Mich., chairman of the House Energy Committee, James J. Howard, D-N.J., chairman of the House Public Works Committee, and 32 other members of both parties.

Two key Republicans, Reps. Norman F. Lent, N.Y., and Don Ritter, Pa., announced their support for the bill and urged quick action. Lent was the ranking GOP member of Florio's subcommittee, which had primary jurisdiction on the bill. Ritter, also on that panel, had often championed chemical industry positions on toxic waste bills.

The compromise split some of the differences between a bill (HR 4915) introduced by Lent and the more ambitious one (HR 4813) originally proposed by Florio. It called for a cleanup fund of approximately $9 billion for fiscal 1986-90, to be funded by a $1.45 billion annual tax on petroleum and chemical feedstocks and a $600 million annual tax on disposal of hazardous wastes. The current superfund totaled $1.6 billion for fiscal 1981-85.

The compromise dropped most of the provisions Florio sought for compensating victims of toxic waste dumps, but kept "emergency relief" consisting of health studies and mitigation of victim exposure. In addition, the bill still authorized private lawsuits in federal court seeking compensation for injuries caused by toxic dumping.

On May 23, Florio's subcommittee approved HR 5640.

Energy Committee Approval

The full Energy and Commerce Committee approved the superfund reauthorization June 20 by a vote of 38-3. The measure was formally reported July 16 (H Rept 98-890, Part I), with Reps. James T. Broyhill, R-N.C., Tom Corcoran, R-Ill., and Mike Oxley, R-Ohio, filing dissenting views.

While the committee adopted more than two dozen amendments to the bill before ordering it reported, the changes mostly fine-tuned and clarified the bill and did not change the broad outlines of the compromise approved in subcommittee May 23.

The only roll-call vote on an amendment came when W. J. "Billy" Tauzin, D-La., moved to recommend to the Ways and Means Committee that it exempt zinc, nickel and aluminum, as well as certain compounds of those metals, from a tax on raw materials (or "feedstocks") that helped finance the superfund. His motion was rejected by a 14-24 vote.

Tax provisions of the superfund bill were under the jurisdiction of the Ways and Means Committee. Energy Chairman Dingell ruled that his committee could not amend the section of the bill dealing with tax revenue.

That obstacle did not stop the Energy Committee from expressing its will on the tax provisions. The panel simply put its ideas into its report as recommendations to the Ways and Means Committee.

Approval by Other House Committees

Two other House committees approved HR 5640 before the measure went to the floor. Public Works and Transportation acted on July 31, and Ways and Means followed suit on Aug. 2.

Florio's bill survived intact the stormy late-night July 31 markup by Public Works.

That panel first rejected, 21-28, a substitute offered by John B. Breaux, D-La., that would have pegged the fund at $6.2 billion over five years. Then it accepted, one-by-one, a long series of amendments that included much of what Breaux sought. Finally, at 10:15 p.m., it rejected the entire package of changes by a 23-26 vote and adjourned — leaving Florio's bill essentially unchanged.

Chairman Howard said the action would send a message to the House that "the Public Works Committee does not want to have a weaker bill than what came to us from the Energy Committee."

Ways and Means Aug. 2 overhauled the revenue-producing part of the bill (Title V), partially shifting the burden from chemical companies and hazardous-waste generators to oil companies and the general fund of the Treasury. By a 27-5 vote, the committee adopted a package of amendments to be offered as a substitute to Title V of the Florio bill.

The Ways and Means substitute was designed to generate $10.2 billion from fiscal 1986-90, slightly more than Florio's bill, which was to produce an estimated $8.8 billion to $9.7 billion.

The Ways and Means substitute doubled the amount to be collected through a tax on crude oil, from the $1.2 billion Florio figure to $2.4 billion over five years. While Florio authorized $1.1 billion in superfund appropriations from general tax revenues, the Ways and Means substitute authorized $2.3 billion.

Ways and Means nearly halved the $4.6 billion the Florio bill sought to collect from petroleum-based raw chemicals (or "feedstocks"), dropping that to $2.5 billion. But it dramatically raised the tax on inorganic feedstocks, from Florio's $1 billion to $1.8 billion.

Ways and Means dropped the Florio bill's $1.8 billion "waste-end" tax on the disposal of wastes until the Treasury Department studied such a tax. If Congress did not enact a waste-end tax by July 1, 1986, the petroleum and feedstock taxes would be raised to generate another $1.2 billion.

House Floor Action

The House passed the superfund reauthorization Aug. 10 by a 323-33 vote, after Democrats abandoned plans to link the measure to a separate hazardous-waste bill that had already passed the Senate. *(Vote 333, p. 102-H)*

The linkage maneuver was an effort to pressure the Senate into acting on its own superfund bill, which at the time was still in the Environment and Public Works Committee. It involved a scheme to attach HR 5640 to a separate bill (HR 2867) already passed by both chambers and awaiting conference. HR 2867 reauthorized the Resource Conservation and Recovery Act of 1976 (PL 94-580), which regulated disposal of hazardous wastes.

House Energy Chairman Dingell argued that the superfund-RCRA hookup was a fair procedure because the two bills were "integrally related." The Senate-passed RCRA bill contained at least six provisions that amended the superfund law.

But Lent, a key architect of the House superfund bill, called the hookup move "a partisan strategy" and "a politically motivated crapshoot which will result in no hazardous-waste legislation being enacted this year."

"By sending RCRA and superfund over as one, we would be trying to force the Senate to act on a legislative package, the major portion of which has not been reviewed by the appropriate Senate committees," he said.

Ritter said the maneuver was "designed to embarrass the Republican administration and ... Republican members of Congress," by allowing Democrats to say Republicans were "not dealing with hazardous-waste problems."

Sen. Robert T. Stafford, R-Vt., chairman of the Senate Environment Committee called Florio "to express the very strong hope" that he would not attempt the superfund-RCRA hookup, which Stafford said would hurt the chances for both bills.

House Democrats finally decided not to push for the linkup, for fear of jeopardizing enactment of the RCRA bill.

Partisan Sniping

Floor debate on the superfund bill was marked by partisan sniping, with some Republicans adopting the Reagan administration's stance that no action was needed in 1984. "I don't know why it is necessary to deliberate in such haste," said Barber B. Conable Jr., R-N.Y., Aug. 9. "I don't know the genesis of this measure, but I suspect it was the San Francisco Democratic convention."

But Thomas J. Downey, D-N.Y., countered that the bill was needed to prod the EPA into cleaning up more toxic waste sites. During the Reagan administration, Downey said, the EPA had cleaned up only six of the 546 priority superfund sites.

"Over the last four years it seems that study is all the EPA has done about this problem," Downey said.

The political emphasis the Democrats placed on the superfund bill was evident in the comments of Rep. Geraldine A. Ferraro of New York, the Democratic vice presidential nominee.

Referring to "the sorry performance of the EPA" in running the superfund, Ferraro told the House: "The American people demand action. They clearly will not tolerate further delay." She repeated her remarks before banks of TV cameras in a press conference on the House lawn, flanked by environmentalists and Florio, the bill's chief sponsor.

Rules Battle

The biggest superfund issue — who should pay the $10 billion tab for cleanup of thousands of abandoned toxic dumps — was largely settled Aug. 8, before the House even took up the bill.

In an unusual all-day battle, the Rules Committee blocked virtually any funding proposals other than that approved Aug. 2 by the Ways and Means Committee. The Ways and Means version put the major burden for the cleanup costs on oil companies, chemical companies and the general Treasury.

The only amendment the rule (H Res 570) allowed to those tax provisions was one offered by Conable to end the tax Sept. 30, 1986, after one year, instead of after five years as provided by Ways and Means.

Minority Whip Trent Lott, R-Miss., a member of the Rules Committee, said: "I don't think I've ever seen the Rules Committee labor more over a rule." The panel heard more than 25 House members as witnesses and cast several razor-thin votes on allowing certain amendments on the floor.

The Rules Committee was caught not only in the partisan cross fire between Democrats and Republicans, but in jurisdictional wrangling between two of the three powerful committees with claims on the bill.

By granting what was in effect a modified closed rule on the tax part of the bill, the Rules panel upheld Ways and Means and rejected the tax provisions sought by the Energy panel. Energy Chairman Dingell had asked Rules to allow consideration of five tax provisions, but all were rejected.

The closed tax section and the RCRA-superfund hookup engendered serious opposition to the rule on the House floor. But it was adopted, by a 218-199 vote. *(Vote 323, p. 98-H)*

Citizens' Suits, Victims' Compensation

The other major issue was settled on the House floor Aug. 9, when members knocked out of the bill a section that, for the first time, would have given citizens the right to sue polluters in federal court for damages caused by hazardous-waste dumping.

The vote went to the heart of one of the most controversial superfund issues — whether and how to compensate the victims of incidents such as the one at Love Canal in New York, where residents were faced with medical problems and homes they could not live in.

The Energy Committee language would have allowed citizens to sue dumpers for compensation in such cases. Currently, citizens could sue under liability laws in most states, but standards of proof and other legal obstacles made such suits very hard to win.

After heated debate, the House by 208-200 adopted an amendment by Harold S. Sawyer, R-Mich., that deleted the citizens' suit provision from HR 5640. *(Vote 324, p. 100-H)*

Sawyer then tried to delete from the bill a separate provision giving citizens the right to sue in federal court to compel a federal, state or local agency to perform a duty required under the superfund law. This amendment was rejected 141-248. *(Vote 325, p. 100-H)*

Rep. Elliott H. Levitas, D-Ga., offered an amendment to create an administrative mechanism for compensating individuals harmed by exposure to hazardous wastes and to set aside 12 percent of the superfund for that purpose. But his proposal was rejected 159-200. *(Vote 331, p. 100-H)*

Bill Highlights

As passed by the House, HR 5640 included the following highlights:

● Increased the size of the superfund program from the current $1.6 billion (fiscal 1981-85) to an estimated $10.2 billion for fiscal 1986 through 1990.

● Authorized appropriations of $2.3 billion from the general Treasury during fiscal 1986-90 to finance the Hazardous Substance Response Trust Fund ("superfund"). The current law authorized $220 million in general appropriations over five years. The Florio version would have authorized $1.1 billion.

● Imposed taxes on crude oil and raw chemicals ("feedstocks") estimated to yield $7.9 billion during fiscal 1986-90. The current law generated $1.38 billion and the Florio bill would have generated $6.8 billion.

● Imposed a tax on crude oil received at U.S. refineries of 7.86 cents per barrel, for an estimated tax yield of $2.4 billion. The current tax was 0.79 cents per barrel and the Florio version would have put the tax at 4.5 cents per barrel.

● Increased from 42 to 66 the number of raw chemicals subject to the "feedstock" tax and raised the rates at which they were taxed, a move designed to yield an estimated $2.5 billion from petroleum-based chemicals and $1.8 billion from inorganic chemicals over five years.

● Established a mandatory schedule for the EPA to clean up priority superfund sites. EPA was to begin studies on all sites on its National Priority List within two years of the bill's enactment. EPA was to begin actual cleanup work on 150 sites per year beginning in fiscal 1987, and finish work on all 546 sites currently on the list within five years. EPA was to list 1,600 sites by Jan. 1, 1988.

● Established uniform national standards for waste-site cleanup, dictating "how clean is clean." Remedial actions were to meet standards necessary to protect human health and the environment. Where relevant, pollution at a site could not exceed the most stringent standard for a particular pollutant set under other environmental laws. EPA could waive the standards under certain circumstances.

● Held the persons or companies responsible for the toxic wastes at a superfund site to be *strictly* liable and *jointly and severally* liable for cleanup costs. Under strict liability, companies were liable even if they had not been negligent. Under joint and several liability, each company contributing wastes to a site could be held liable for the entire cleanup cost. Companies had certain defenses against these doctrines under the bill and under common law.

● Gave citizens the right to sue EPA or any state or local agency to compel it to perform any duty under the superfund law which it had failed to perform. They could also sue the federal, state or local agency, or a private company, to force it to clean up pollutants for which it was responsible.

● Eased financial burdens on the states related to superfund cleanup programs. It required, for example, the federal government to pay 90 percent of the costs of operating and maintaining a superfund site once it was cleaned up. Under current law, states paid 100 percent of those long-term costs.

● Authorized individuals exposed to hazardous substances to petition EPA to conduct a health effects study at that site and to provide emergency relief. If the study found a significant risk to human health, EPA had to take emergency steps to end the risk, such as provision of alternative drinking water supplies and relocation of individuals.

● Established a new program to clean up groundwater contamination caused by leaks from underground tanks used to store certain petroleum products or hazardous liquids. It required EPA to set up a regulatory program to prevent such leaks within 27 months after enactment. States could assume responsibility for the program. It also set aside a special $850 million account within the superfund, financed by the crude oil tax, to clean up such contamination.

● Stated that it was the goal of Congress to develop a mechanism for taxing disposal of hazardous wastes — the so-called "waste-end tax." The bill instructed the Treasury secretary to submit by April 1, 1985, various legislative proposals for such a tax. The proposals were to be designed to discourage environmentally unsound disposal of hazardous wastes and they had to be administratively feasible. If Congress did not enact a waste-end tax by July 1, 1986, the petroleum and feedstock tax rates were to be increased to produce an additional $1.2 billion. The original Florio version included a waste-end tax.

Senate Committee Action

The Senate Environment and Public Works Committee got a slow start the first two weeks of August on marking up a superfund bill of its own (S 2892) introduced by Chairman Stafford and Jennings Randolph, D-W.Va., ranking minority member of the panel.

Although the committee spent several days on the bill,

it did not act before Congress broke for a three-week recess Aug. 10.

Following that recess, however, the pace picked up and on Sept. 13, the Environment Committee approved S 2892 (S Rept 98-631) by a 17-1 vote. Steven D. Symms, R-Idaho, was the lone dissenter.

The committee's "bare-bones" $7.5 billion, five-year reauthorization was far less ambitious than the $10.2 billion measure passed by the House Aug. 10. While the House bill set tight new deadlines and standards for cleanup of toxic waste sites, the Senate Environment bill was basically a renewal of the existing law.

Political Heat

Lobbying on the superfund bill reached a fever pitch before the Senate Environment Committee action. As the panel was meeting Sept. 13, a grass-roots coalition supporting the bill held a press conference before a bank of TV cameras. Residents from areas near toxic dump sites in 10 states told of their children getting sick or dying and blamed the toxic wastes.

The group, assembled by the National Campaign Against Toxic Hazards, said that they had sought to meet with Senate Majority Leader Howard H. Baker Jr., R-Tenn., to urge him to schedule floor action on the superfund bill, but Baker had refused to meet with them.

Chemical and oil companies, which faced the possibility of a major tax increase if the superfund was enlarged, also were lobbying hard. Public Citizen, a Ralph Nader group, released a study Sept. 6 that said the 25 biggest chemical companies had contributed $2.2 million to congressional campaigns since the superfund law was passed in 1980.

On Sept. 12, EPA announced final action to add 128 sites to its National Priority List, qualifying them for federal cleanup money and bringing the total on the list to 538 sites. Lee M. Thomas, EPA's superfund chief, said action would be taken within a month to add up to 250 more sites.

But Florio, the key architect of the House-passed superfund bill, discounted the announcement, saying EPA had already announced the 128 sites a year ago. "It's obviously an effort to fool people into thinking something is being done," Florio said.

EPA had estimated that the current $1.6 billion superfund could pay for cleanup of only about 200 sites.

Committee Bill

The foundation of S 2892 was a reauthorization of current law that Stafford proposed as a compromise when progress stalled on a more ambitious version he had introduced July 31.

The bare-bones substitute authorized $206 million annually in appropriations from the general fund of the Treasury for fiscal 1986-90. It also set a $6.47 billion cap on federal authority to tax petroleum and raw chemicals to pay for the superfund, to expire Sept. 30, 1990.

Environment Committee members left to the Finance Committee the job of setting the tax rates for specific chemicals and of making sure revenue would be adequate to meet cleanup needs.

The committee rejected, 3-13, an amendment by Alan K. Simpson, R-Wyo., that would have cut the bill back to a one-year, $1 billion reauthorization.

Amendments Adopted

By voice votes, members approved 21 amendments,

most of which made relatively minor adjustments in the existing law. Among the more significant of those were the following:

● An amendment by George J. Mitchell, D-Maine, to set up a five-state demonstration program for assistance to victims of toxic waste incidents. The program, whose funding would be limited to $30 million annually, would take a group-insurance approach, paying medical and burial costs only. Claimants would not have to prove a dumper's negligence, but would still have to prove that a toxic dump had caused their illness.

● An amendment by Frank R. Lautenberg, D-N.J., that would make household water, not just drinking water, available to residents of a toxic area where EPA was providing alternative water supplies.

● An amendment by Lautenberg redefining "remedial action" (permanent cleanup) so that the superfund could pay 90 percent of operating costs, at EPA's discretion, for up to five years instead of the current one year. When groundwater pollution required cleanup, pumping and treatment of water could go on for decades, a cost states currently picked up after a year.

● An amendment by John H. Chafee, R-R.I., disqualifying a state from getting funds for remedial action unless it had capacity to handle 20 years' worth of hazardous waste legally under the provisions of RCRA. A contract with another state willing to take the waste would satisfy the requirement.

● An amendment by Gordon J. Humphrey, R-N.H.,

codifying into law the current practice for performance of health and toxicological studies at superfund and other sites.

Finance Committee

After the Environment Committee completed action on S 2892, the bill went to the Senate Finance Committee for action on tax measures that could raise the $7.5 billion the bill was expected to cost.

Finance held public hearings on the measure in mid-September, but it took no action on the legislation in 1984.

Senate Floor Action

Stymied in their efforts to win a floor vote on S 2892, backers of the superfund bill sought to attach its provisions to the fiscal 1985 continuing appropriations resolution (H J Res 648), a must-pass measure funding numerous government agencies whose regular appropriations bills had not passed.

New Jersey Democrats Bill Bradley and Lautenberg offered a superfund amendment to H J Res 648 on Oct. 2, but the Senate by 38-59 held their amendment to be non-germane. *(Vote 247, p. 44-S)*

Most Republicans opposed the amendment, viewing the vote as a matter of party discipline on the procedural issue of halting add-ons to the embattled continuing resolution. ∎

Millions of Acres Win Wilderness Protection

Congress cleared more wilderness legislation in 1984 than in any other year since the 1964 Wilderness Act set up a national system for preserving pristine federal lands from drilling, logging, mining, road building and other development.

Twenty separate bills were sent to President Reagan during the year, providing wilderness protection to lands in Arizona, Arkansas, California, Florida, Georgia, Mississippi, Missouri, New Hampshire, New Mexico, North Carolina, Oregon, Pennsylvania, Tennessee, Texas, Utah, Vermont, Virginia, Washington, Wisconsin and Wyoming.

The total amount of land set aside was more than 8.3 million acres — an area larger than the state of Maryland. Most of that land henceforth could be used only for hiking, fishing, hunting, canoeing, nature study and other activities that leave no permanent marks of man.

The 20 bills were the product of arduous negotiations between developers and environmentalists that in many cases had lasted for years. All but a handful of them were achieved through consensus, winning the support of both sides and usually of the entire state congressional delegation.

An important part of the legislation from the developers' viewpoint was the release for logging and drilling of a total of 13.5 million acres in the affected states, acreage previously protected as potential wilderness.

The year's action brought to about 88.6 million acres the total amount of federally designated wilderness. Most of that, some 56.4 million acres, was in Alaska, with only 32.2 million acres in the lower 48 states. Alaska's wilderness was designated in a 1980 law after years of bitter arguments. *(1980 Almanac p. 575)*

Wilderness bills for Colorado and Idaho were considered by the 98th Congress but those measures never cleared.

Background

The 1964 Wilderness Act (PL 88-577) allowed Congress to protect from all development federally owned lands that were still largely untouched by man. *(Congress and the Nation Vol. I, p. 1061)*

Since 1979, Congress had been sifting through recommendations made after the second Roadless Area Review and Evaluation (RARE II). The RARE II study looked at about 46.1 million acres in the lower 48 states and recommended about 9.9 million acres for designation as wilderness, 28.5 million acres for non-wilderness, and 7.7 million for further planning. These were executive branch recommendations, but only Congress could officially designate wilderness areas.

Until Congress acted, the law required the affected lands to be managed in a way that would preserve their wilderness characteristics. All 46 million acres became, in effect, temporary de facto wilderness.

The 96th Congress set aside as wilderness 4.2 million acres in seven states. The 97th Congress set aside 132,011 acres in six states, but President Reagan vetoed one of those bills, involving 49,150 acres in Florida. *(1980 Almanac p. 617; 1982 Almanac p. 464)*

In 1983, Congress added only one state — Montana — to its list, designating 259,000 acres there as wilderness. But it began work on 10 other bills, most of which cleared in 1984. *(1983 Almanac p. 342)*

Impetus for Action

The flurry of action in 1984 could be attributed to several factors. One was that the election year provided a window of political opportunity — a tacit guarantee that any bills sent to the president in 1984 would be signed, as they might not have been in past or coming years.

Another was impatience. Decisions on the status of most of the national forest lands Congress acted on had been pending since at least 1977, when the Carter administration began the RARE II study. While timber companies often opposed big new wilderness set-asides, they chafed even more at the larger amounts of land put on indefinite hold by the decision process.

"It was in everybody's interest to end the uncertainty," said Rep. John F. Seiberling, D-Ohio, the quarterback for wilderness legislation in the House. "That fact finally dawned on most of the hard-liners on the industry side as well as the environmentalists' side."

Seiberling chaired the Interior and Insular Affairs Subcommittee on Public Lands and National Parks, the panel with wilderness jurisdiction in the House.

Environmentalists in March launched a $100,000 grass-roots lobbying campaign to bring local conservation leaders from 28 states to Washington, D.C., to meet with over 300 individual members of Congress and press for wilderness legislation.

"I'm sure the election year was a factor," Seiberling said shortly after the 20th bill cleared. "That is where public opinion can be felt."

Sources in some delegations, such as Washington's, said they had assurances Reagan would sign any wilderness bill they sent him in 1984 — but not necessarily in 1985.

RARE III Threat?

Seiberling discounted the significance of the Reagan administration's proposed "RARE III" study in prompting action. The U.S. Forest Service had announced in February 1983 that it would throw out the Carter-era RARE II recommendations and start over.

The announcement came in response to an October 1982 federal appeals court decision finding defects in RARE II. But although the Forest Service planned to issue new recommendations as early as 1985, Seiberling said the likelihood of new court challenges to RARE III promised the forest industries only further delay.

Release Issue Settled

A key issue thwarting settlement of individual wilderness bills in previous years was the terms under which lands studied under RARE II but not named as wilderness were "released" for other uses.

The logjam was effectively broken May 2 when an accord on the release issue was reached between Seiberling and his Senate counterpart, James A. McClure, R-Idaho, chairman of the Senate Energy and Natural Resources Committee.

Seiberling and environmentalists had favored a "soft" release formula that left the released lands available for reconsideration as wilderness relatively soon. McClure, the Reagan administration and the forest industry had favored various "hard" release formulas that delayed reconsideration for decades or longer and encouraged development in the meantime.

The McClure-Seiberling release compromise, which required wilderness reviews every 15 years, was made part of most of the bills Congress cleared.

Administration Positions

In his televised Oct. 7 debate with Walter F. Mondale, the Democratic presidential nominee, Reagan claimed credit for the year's legislative output, saying, "We have added millions of acres to the wilderness lands." *(Debate text, p. 107-B)*

Conservationists could scarcely contain their irritation with Reagan's claim. "Congress and conservationists across the country are responsible for this magnificent achievement," said William A. Turnage, president of the Wilderness Society. "Although the Reagan administration likes to take the credit, the truth is that many of these bills passed in spite of the administration, not because of it."

"The administration threw up numerous roadblocks during the past four years, making the campaign to preserve wilderness exceedingly more difficult than usual," Turnage said.

Turnage and other conservationists pointed to the administration's backing for hard release provisions in many of the bills that passed with the compromise formula.

Also, Reagan's first interior secretary, James G. Watt, had sought to open up existing wilderness areas to oil and gas leasing. In 1981-82, Watt endorsed legislative proposals that would have allowed wilderness leasing for up to 20 years. Congress expressed its displeasure in a series of votes during 1981 and 1982 that culminated in a flat ban on oil and gas leasing in wilderness areas. *(1982 Almanac p. 461)*

Reagan vetoed one wilderness bill, for Florida, on Jan. 14, 1983. He opposed provisions in the measure compensating phosphate companies for mining claims put aside by the bill. *(1982 Almanac p. 464)*

And while Congress, in the major wilderness bills passed in 1984, usually voted to preserve more acres than the Carter RARE II study had recommended, the Reagan administration often supported less acreage than RARE II.

State-by-State List

Arkansas

The Arkansas bill (S 2125 — PL 98-508), in its final compromise version, designated 91,100 acres, down from the 117,000 acres in the version originally passed by the Senate. It designated eight wilderness areas and one wilderness addition in the Ouachita and the Ozark-Saint Francis national forests.

Under the legislation, some 93,000 acres of forest land were released from further consideration as wilderness.

The bill was reported May 18 by the Senate Energy and Natural Resources Committee (S Rept 98-462), and passed by the Senate Aug. 9.

In the House, it was reported Sept. 28 by the Interior and Insular Affairs Committee (H Rept 98-1097) and passed with amendments Oct. 2. The Senate agreed to the House amendments Oct. 4, clearing the bill for the president.

Arizona

The Arizona bill (HR 4707 — PL 98-406) granted federal wilderness status to more than one million acres, including some lands under the management of the Interior Department's Bureau of Land Management (BLM).

The largest protected area encompassed some 658,580 acres of national forest lands south of the Grand Canyon. Also designated as wilderness was 6,670 acres of BLM land in the Aravaipa Canyon and about 396,000 acres of BLM and Forest Service land on the "Arizona Strip" in the northern part of the state.

The bill also designated a 39.5-mile segment of the Verde River as part of the National Wild and Scenic Rivers System. *(Story, p. 319)*

It released almost 1,125,000 acres of national forest land from further wilderness consideration. And it added 850 acres to the existing Chiricahua National Monument.

HR 4707 was reported March 30 from the Interior and Insular Affairs Committee (H Rept 98-643) and passed April 3 by the House. The vote under suspension of the rules was 335-56. *(Vote 55, p. 20-H)*

In the Senate, the measure was placed directly on the calendar and it passed with amendments Aug. 9. The House agreed to the Senate amendment Aug. 10, clearing the bill for Reagan.

California

The California bill (HR 1437 — PL 98-425) was the year's largest, and possibly most controversial, wilderness bill. It designated as wilderness 39 national forest areas totaling some 1.8 million acres. The bill also designated 1.4 million acres of national park land as wilderness, increasing protection for parts of Yosemite National Park and Sequoia-Kings Canyon National Park.

And it made 83 miles of the Tuolumne River part of the National Wild and Scenic Rivers System. That stretch of the river had been studied for a possible hydroelectric project. *(Story, p. 319)*

The bill also established a 66,000-acre national scenic area around Mono Lake, Calif., to be administered by the U.S. Forest Service.

It released from further wilderness consideration some 2.4 million acres.

The House passed an earlier version of HR 1437 on April 12, 1983, two days after the death of Rep. Phillip Burton, D-Calif., a feisty conservationist who had personally crafted that 2.33 million-acre version of the bill. The Reagan administration recommended only 1.2 million acres of wilderness and opposed the Burton version.

The House bill languished in the Senate until June 29, 1984, when a compromise version was announced by Sens. Alan Cranston, D-Calif., and Pete Wilson, R-Calif., drawing support from at least 32 members of the state's 45-member House delegation. The compromise was approved Aug. 1 by the Senate Energy Committee (S Rept 98-582) and passed by the Senate Aug. 9.

The House cleared HR 1437 for the president Sept. 12, by a 368-41 vote on a motion to agree to Senate amendments to the bill. Eleven California Republicans voted "no," and all California Democrats who cast votes voted "yes." *(Vote 342, p. 106-H)*

The real test had come earlier, when the House by 295-112 adopted the rule (H Res 573) for consideration of the motion without any further amendments. Three California Republicans, Charles Pashayan Jr., Gene Chappie and Norman D. Shumway, had urged defeat of what they called a "gag rule" in a Sept. 11 letter to their colleagues. *(Vote 341, p. 104-H)*

Florida

The Florida bill (HR 9 — PL 98-430) gave wilderness protection to seven areas totaling 49,150 acres in the Apalachicola, Ocala and Osceola national forests. It also named two wilderness areas comprising another 10,000 acres. And it prohibited phosphate mining in the Osceola National

Forest. Some 68,500 acres were released from further wilderness consideration.

Reagan in 1982 vetoed an earlier version of HR 9 that included provisions he opposed for compensating holders of phosphate mining claims in the Osceola forest. The compensation language was removed from the bill cleared by the 98th Congress. *(1983 Almanac p. 464)*

The House Interior Committee reported HR 9 on May 11, 1983 (H Rept 98-102, Part I) and the Agriculture Committee reported it June 1 (H Rept 98-102, Part II). The bill was passed by the House June 6, 1983.

The Senate Energy Committee reported the measure Aug. 6, 1984 (S Rept 98-580), and the full Senate passed it with amendments Aug. 9. The House agreed to the Senate amendments Sept. 12, clearing the bill for the president.

Georgia

The Georgia bill (S 2773 — PL 98-514) designated two areas in the Chattahoochee National Forest totaling approximately 14,439 acres, the Ellicot Rock Wilderness Addition and the Southern Nantahala Wilderness.

Some 68,424 acres were released from further wilderness consideration.

S 2773 was reported Sept. 18 by the Senate Agriculture Committee (S Rept 98-611). It was passed by the Senate Oct. 2 and cleared by the House Oct. 4.

Mississippi

The Mississippi bill (S 2808 — PL 98-515) was one of the last to be introduced and set aside the smallest amount of land of any wilderness bill enacted in 1984 — some 5,500 acres in two areas of the De Soto National Forest.

It released another 2,400 acres from further wilderness consideration.

The bill was reported Sept. 18 by the Senate Agriculture Committee (S Rept 98-613). It was passed by the Senate Oct. 2 and cleared by the House Oct. 4.

Missouri

The first wilderness bill to clear in 1984 (S 64 — PL 98-289) set aside 16,500 acres of national forest land in Missouri as the Irish Wilderness.

Slightly different versions of the bill had been passed by both the Senate and House in 1983, but it was not until April 9, 1984, that House-Senate conferees reached agreement on a compromise measure (H Rept 98-663).

The House adopted the conference report May 2 by a 254-142 vote, and the Senate cleared the measure by voice vote a day later. *(Vote 112, p. 38-H)*

New Hampshire

The New Hampshire bill (HR 3921 — PL 98-323) set aside more land as wilderness — 77,000 acres — than any other East Coast wilderness legislation in 1984. All of the land was in the White Mountain National Forest.

The bill also ordered a study of Wildcat Brook for protection under the National Wild and Scenic Rivers Act.

The bill was passed by the House in 1983. It was reported April 26, 1984, by the Senate Agriculture Committee (S Rept 98-414) and passed by the Senate with amendments on May 24. The House agreed to the Senate amendments June 6, clearing the bill for the president.

New Mexico

The New Mexico bill (HR 6296 — PL 98-603) was a compromise version designating in the San Juan Basin the

3,968-acre Bisti Wilderness and the 23,872-acre De-na-zin Wilderness. It protected a 2,720-acre area known as the Fossil Forest from mineral development, but dropped a proposed Ah-shi-sle-pah wilderness area.

Like the Arizona bill, HR 6296 protected some BLM land as well as land managed by the Forest Service.

The measure was passed by the House Oct. 3, amended and passed by the Senate on Oct. 5 and cleared the same day when the House accepted the Senate amendments.

North Carolina

The North Carolina bill (HR 3960 — PL 98-324) designated a total of about 68,750 acres as wilderness — including 53,590 acres in seven new areas and 15,160 acres expanding four existing areas — in all four of the state's national forests.

It also named five areas totalling about 25,816 acres for study as potential wilderness, and released another 114,000 acres from further wilderness consideration.

The House originally passed the bill Nov. 16, 1983. The Senate Agriculture Committee reported the legislation April 26 (S Rept 98-415) and the Senate passed it with amendments May 24. The House cleared the bill June 4 when it agreed by unanimous consent to the Senate amendments.

Oregon

The Oregon bill (HR 1149 — PL 98-328) set aside as wilderness some 930,400 acres in 13 national forests within the state, while releasing 2.1 million acres from further wilderness consideration. It also created a 156,900-acre Oregon Cascades Recreation Area within four national forests in the state.

The wilderness issue had caused emotional debate for several years in Oregon, where environmentalism and the logging industry were both strong forces. Sen. Mark O. Hatfield, R-Ore., key author of the version of the bill finally enacted, pictured it as a compromise among conflicting interest groups and geographic areas.

House opponents, however, said it was not a compromise. "This compromise is being settled between the environmentalists — the environmentalists here and the environmentalists there," said Robert F. Smith, R-Ore., during House debate June 4. "I have not been a part of the compromise nor has anybody been a part of the compromise that is opposed to this bill, in the beginning or even now."

Hatfield's proposal was the last in a series going back to the RARE II study. As a result of that Forest Service study, the Carter administration in 1979 proposed about 416,000 acres in Oregon for wilderness. The House Interior Committee in late 1982 reported a one million-acre bill, but it failed to pass the House under suspension of the rules, a procedure requiring a two-thirds majority vote. The House passed a larger Oregon wilderness bill of about 1.13 million acres in March 1983, on a 252-93 vote. That bill, HR 1149, made no progress in the Senate until Hatfield came up with his compromise substitute, which was reported May 18 by the Energy and Natural Resources Committee (S Rept 98-465) and passed May 24 by the Senate.

Opposing the Hatfield bill were Robert Smith, whose district included about 65 percent of the land in the bill, and Denny Smith, R-Ore., whose district contained about 10 percent. Three other House members from Oregon, and both of the state's Republican senators, supported it.

"This legislation is going to do away with a number of jobs," said Denny Smith. "We have some 130,000 Oregonians who are unemployed. Many of those who are unemployed are in the timber industry."

But Les AuCoin, D-Ore., disagreed: "I am surprised the gentleman would make the argument that this somehow steals jobs from Oregonians." He said the bill brought the total amount of wilderness in the state to about 2 million acres, while 15 million acres in the state were available for commercial logging.

James Weaver, D-Ore., also denied the bill would affect jobs, saying the bill set aside only 150 million board feet of usable timber, while 18 billion board feet were currently under contract and unharvested because they could not be sold.

On June 6, the House sided with the majority of the Oregon delegation, voting 281-99 to concur in the Senate amendments to HR 1149, thereby clearing the bill for the president. *(Vote 194, p. 62-H)*

Pennsylvania

The bill (HR 5076 — PL 98-585) designated two wilderness areas: the 368-acre Allegheny Islands Wilderness and the 9,337-acre Hickory Creek Wilderness, both in the Allegheny National Forest. It also established a 23,100-acre Allegheny National Recreation Area there.

Released from further wilderness consideration were 1,600 acres.

HR 5076 was reported April 26 by the House Interior Committee (H Rept 98-713) and passed May 1 under suspension of the rules. The vote on passage was 387-28. *(Vote 103, p. 36-H)*

In the Senate, the measure was reported Sept. 18 by the Agriculture Committee (S Rept 98-616) and passed with amendments Oct. 2. The House agreed to the Senate amendments Oct. 4, clearing the bill for the president.

Tennessee

The Tennessee bill (HR 4263 — PL 98-578) designated three areas in the Cherokee National Forest totaling almost 25,000 acres — the Big Frog, Citico Creek and Bald River Gorge wildernesses. It also designated two areas totaling 8,257 acres for further study, and released 20,076 acres from further wilderness consideration.

HR 4263 was reported April 26 by the House Interior Committee (H Rept 98-714) and passed May 1. The vote on passage was 404-12. *(Vote 104, p. 36-H)*

The legislation was reported Sept. 18 by the Senate Agriculture Committee (S Rept 98-615) and passed Oct. 2 with amendments by the Senate. The House accepted the Senate amendments Oct. 4, clearing the bill.

Texas

The Texas bill (HR 3788 — PL 98-574) designated national forest areas totaling approximately 34,346 acres and encouraged the exchange of private and federal lands to consolidate two of the areas. The areas were the Turkey Hill, Upland Island, Big Slough, Indian Mounds, and Little Lake Creek Wildernesses. They were located in the Angelina, Davy Crockett, Sabine and Sam Houston national forests.

Released from further wilderness consideration were 44,600 acres.

The bill as cleared represented a compromise between an 8,000-acre wilderness proposal supported by the Reagan administration and a 63,000-acre version pushed by conservationists.

HR 3788 was reported May 2 by the House Interior Committee (H Rept 98-730) and passed by voice vote on May 8.

In the Senate, it was reported Sept. 18 by the Agriculture Committee (S Rept 98-614) and passed by voice vote Oct. 2. The House agreed to Senate amendments Oct. 4, clearing the measure.

Utah

The Utah bill (S 2155 — PL 98-428) designated as wilderness 12 areas totaling about 750,000 acres in the Wasatch-Cache, Ashley, Uinta, Dixie and Manti-LaSal national forests. It released some three million acres of national forest land from further wilderness consideration.

The bill was reported Aug. 6 by the Senate Energy Committee (S Rept 98-581) and passed Aug. 9 by the Senate.

In the House, it was reported Sept. 13 by the Interior Committee (H Rept 98-1019) and passed Sept. 17 under suspension of the rules.

Vermont

The Vermont bill (HR 4198 — PL 98-322) designated 41,260 acres in the Green Mountain National Forest as wilderness and another 22,000 acres as a national recreation area. The bill created four new wilderness areas and expanded an existing one.

HR 4198 was passed by the House in 1983. In the Senate, it was reported April 26, 1984, by the Agriculture Committee (S Rept 98-416) and passed May 24.

Final action came June 4, when the House agreed to the Senate amendments.

Virginia

The Virginia bill (HR 5121 — PL 98-586) designated 55,984 acres in the Jefferson and George Washington national forests as wilderness, releasing another 157,000 acres from further consideration for that status.

HR 5121 was reported April 25 by the House Interior Committee (H Rept 98-712) and passed May 8. The vote was 376-20. *(Vote 116, p. 40-H)*

In the Senate, the bill was placed on the calendar Oct. 2 and passed with amendments Oct. 4. The House agreed

to the Senate amendments Oct. 9, clearing the bill for the president.

Washington

The Washington bill (S 837 — PL 98-339) designated a total of 1,038,878 acres of wilderness in the state, while releasing another 1.4 million acres for other uses.

It also established an 8,600-acre Mt. Baker National Recreation Area and an 87,757-acre North Cascades Scenic Highway Corridor.

S 837 was reported May 18 by the Senate Energy Committee (S Rept 98-461) and passed May 24 by the Senate.

In the House, it was passed June 18 under suspension of the rules, clearing it for the president.

Wisconsin

The Wisconsin bill (HR 3578 — PL 98-321) added 24,339 acres of new wilderness in the Chequamegon and Nicolet National Forests and provided special protective management for two other areas not named as wilderness.

Some 69,000 acres were released from further consideration as wilderness.

The House originally passed the bill Nov. 16, 1983.

In the Senate, it was reported April 26 by the Agriculture Committee (S Rept 98-413) and passed with amendments May 24.

The House June 4 agreed by unanimous consent to the Senate amendments, clearing the measure for the president.

Wyoming

The Wyoming bill (S 543 — PL 98-550) designated about 884,049 acres in 14 national forest areas as wilderness and about 180,540 acres for further wilderness study.

It released 2.7 million additional acres from further wilderness consideration.

S 543 was passed by the Senate in 1983, but remained lodged in the House Interior Committee for most of 1984. After last-minute negotiations between the Wyoming delegation and the House Interior Committee, the bill was discharged from that panel and sent to the floor, where it was passed with amendments Oct. 2.

The Senate concurred in the amendments Oct. 4, clearing the bill. ∎

Wild and Scenic Rivers System Expanded

For the first time since President Reagan took office in 1981, Congress enlarged the National Wild and Scenic Rivers System. Five new rivers were added to the system in 1984 and thus given protection from dams and development that could spoil them for boating and fishing.

The action brought the number of rivers or river segments in the system to 65, totaling about 7,200 miles.

The National Park Service had inventoried some 1,500 river segments totaling 61,000 miles that it thought might be eligible for wild and scenic status. There were almost 3.5 million miles of river in the United States, according to the American Rivers Conservation Council.

An Orphan Program

Since Congress created it in 1968, the Wild and Scenic Rivers System had been the "orphan child" among the

bigger federal conservation programs such as the park system, the wilderness system, and the forest system.

The wild and scenic rivers program had no fixed bureaucratic address. Rivers designated for protection were managed by different federal agencies, depending on whose lands they traversed.

Although Congress began the system with eight rivers, it was slow to follow up; only four more rivers were added in the next six years.

But if the program was already an orphan when it showed up on the Reagan administration's doorstep, conservationists claimed that Reagan did little to feed and care for it.

"The administration has not simply been passive on river issues," said Chris Brown, conservation director of the American Rivers Conservation Council. "They have tried to drown the whole program through funding cuts, changed recommendations, reorganizations, management plans and court cases."

Former Interior Secretary James G. Watt sent a signal when he described a raft trip he took down the Colorado River in the Grand Canyon in the summer of 1981. He told a group of national park concessionaires that while the first day of the trip was "thrilling," the second was "a little tedious," and by the fourth day he was "praying for helicopters" to take him out of the canyon. "I don't like to paddle and I don't like to walk," he said.

Within weeks of taking office, Watt abolished the Interior Department's Heritage Conservation and Recreation Service, which managed the wild and scenic rivers program at the national level. The remnants of the national bureaucracy, reduced in size, were by 1984 in a minor office of the National Park Service. The administration consistently proposed deep cuts in funding for the program, but Congress refused to go along.

Prior to 1984, the last additions to the system came not through congressional action, but through administrative action in the waning hours of the Carter administration. Interior Secretary Cecil D. Andrus on Jan. 19, 1981, designated five northern California rivers — the Klamath, Trinity, Eel, North Fork of the American, and Smith rivers — totaling 1,235 river miles, or almost 18 percent of the miles then in the system.

Water districts elsewhere in the state, joined by timber companies, went into federal court seeking to cancel the designations, and the Reagan administration found itself having to defend designations it apparently was not sure it supported.

When U.S. District Judge William Ingram nullified the designations in February 1983, the Environmental Defense Fund (EDF) appealed. The Justice Department filed a motion to dismiss EDF's appeal, but when its motion was denied, Justice turned around and came back into the case on the side of the environmentalists. In May 1984, the 9th U.S. Circuit Court of Appeals reversed the lower court's decision, reviving the designations. The timber and water interests appealed to the U.S. Supreme Court.

Wild and Scenic Rivers Act

The Wild and Scenic Rivers Act of 1968 (PL 90-542) authorized a federal-state system for river preservation, similar in some ways to the national park and wilderness systems. *(1968 Almanac p. 487)*

Once a river was put into the system, it could be protected through federal acquisition of some surrounding land and a prohibition on federal dam-building. The main instrument, however, was planning.

There were two basic ways for a river to get into the system: by an act of Congress or by a state request and the interior secretary's approval. In most cases, a lengthy period of study came first, during which all parties had a chance to say why they thought a river segment should or should not be included. Afterwards, there was still more debate on a management plan.

Three kinds of protection were available under the law. *Wild rivers* were unpolluted, free of dams and accessible only by trail. *Scenic rivers* were also free of dams and ran through areas that were still largely primitive, but they could be reached in places by roads. *Recreational rivers* could have been dammed already, were readily accessible by road and could have some development along their banks.

Many wild rivers were surrounded by federal land, giving the government control over development.

When the river corridor included private land, the law authorized the government to acquire a limited amount of it, in some cases by condemnation. Federal acquisition often consisted of buying a "scenic easement," an agreement by the landowner not to use the land in ways that would spoil the river.

Objections from private landowners proved a key obstacle to designation of many river segments studied for inclusion in the system.

The law prohibited the Federal Energy Regulatory Commission from licensing any hydroelectric project on rivers designated as wild and scenic or under study for such treatment. It also prohibited the federal government from giving licenses, financial aid, or other help to water projects that would adversely affect the wild and scenic qualities of such rivers.

Durenberger Bill

There were 27 state wild and scenic river programs, which taken together were larger than the federal program. They protected some 317 river segments totaling 11,400 miles, over and above the 7,200 miles in the federal system.

A major legislative initiative on wild rivers came in August 1983 with the introduction of a bill (S 1756) by Sen. Dave Durenberger, R-Minn., that would have beefed up state river programs. The 98th Congress took no action on the Durenberger bill, but the Senate Energy Subcommittee on Public Lands and Reserved Water, chaired by Malcolm Wallop, R-Wyo., did hold hearings on it March 6, 1984, and it was expected to be reintroduced in 1985.

Environmentalists applauded the Durenberger bill — indeed, they helped write it. The Reagan administration opposed some of its major features. Negotiations in 1984 partly reconciled the different views.

The Durenberger bill authorized $5 million yearly in federal grants to support state river programs. The grants were to be matched by the state, and half of the money was to be passed through to local governments or private organizations for use in river conservation activities.

The bill authorized another $2 million annually in federal grants for up to 75 percent of the costs of statewide river studies.

To encourage volunteers to do more of the work of river conservation, the bill authorized federal agencies to recruit and train volunteers, pay incidental expenses and make equipment available to them.

The bill also tried to encourage voluntary donations of land or easements to both federal and state river programs by explicitly recognizing their tax deductible status.

The most controversial part of the bill was its so-called "consistency" requirement. As introduced, the bill prohibited federal agencies from granting licenses or permits that could affect state-designated rivers unless the state approved. Durenberger and the Interior Department later agreed on softer consistency language, requiring the federal agencies to "accommodate the views" of state and local governments.

The administration also objected to creation of a new federal grant program. Negotiations failed to settle that issue.

Reagan Bill

One of the Reagan administration's few legislative initiatives on the environment was a bill (S 1084) to add eight new river segments to the wild and scenic system.

The proposal, first unveiled in the fall of 1982, was introduced on April 19, 1983. The 98th Congress took no action on the bill itself, although it designated two of the eight rivers.

Environmentalists opposed the Reagan bill, saying it took away from the river system more than it gave. The segments proposed for designation in S 1084 were "drastically chopped down," they said, from those the Forest Service had recommended during the Carter era.

The Reagan bill also proposed amendments to the 1968 law that would have made it harder to designate rivers, easier to develop them, and easier to remove them from the system.

The rivers Reagan proposed designating were segments of Clarks Fork in Wyoming; the Elk, the Conejos and the Los Pinos in Colorado; the Verde in Arizona; the Au Sable in Michigan; the Snake in Wyoming and the Piedra in Colorado.

Designations

Congress added the following rivers to the system in 1984:

Tuolumne River

Language designating 83 miles of the Tuolumne as a wild and scenic river was enacted as part of a California wilderness bill (HR 1437 — PL 98-425). *(Story, p. 315)*

For the better part of a century, people had fought over the Tuolumne ("Too-wal-um-ee") River, which tumbled from a Yosemite National Park glacier down toward Modesto in California's fertile, thirsty Central Valley.

The river was a prize contested by farmers, electric utilities, kayakers, fishermen and campers.

Congress in 1975 ordered a study of the Tuolumne for possible designation as a wild and scenic river, and in 1978, the Interior and Agriculture departments recommended such designation for 83 miles of the river.

But also in 1978, two Central Valley irrigation districts applied to the Federal Power Commission, currently the Federal Energy Regulatory Commission (FERC), for a preliminary permit to study the feasibility of building a massive hydroelectric project, the Ponderosa project, on the main stem of the Tuolumne.

Tuolumne County, hoping to get a hammerlock on some of the power Ponderosa would produce, applied for small hydro projects upstream of it.

FERC finally granted a preliminary permit to the Modesto and Turlock irrigation districts in October 1982, but reminded them of the 1978 recommendation for wild and scenic designation. The districts went ahead at their own risk, sinking some $7 million into a study expected to cost $15 million in all.

The districts, whose function as suppliers of electric power overshadowed their role as providers of water to their service areas, said that additional hydroelectric capacity was needed to meet the demand that would accompany economic and residential development.

When the districts shifted their studies into high gear, the conservationists did the same with their decade-old effort to have the Tuolumne named a wild and scenic river. One bill (HR 2474) to designate the river was introduced by California Democrats Ronald V. Dellums and Don Edwards, who represented Berkeley and San Jose. Another (HR 5083) came from Richard H. Lehman, D-Calif.

Lehman's support for designation was critical, because it was in his district that the 83-mile segment of the Tuolumne actually lay. Another supporter was Ed Zschau, R-Calif., who represented the Turlock district. By the time the smoke had cleared in February 1984, many major California newspapers had editorialized in favor of designation and about two-thirds of the state's 45-member House delegation had signed on as cosponsors.

However, Tony Coelho, D-Calif., who represented Modesto, wanted the Ponderosa project to have a chance for construction. Coelho was chairman of the Democratic Congressional Campaign Committee, which provided funds and other support to members needing help in re-election. He introduced his own bill (HR 5291), which would have designated the river, at least in name, but allowed the Ponderosa project anyway.

The House Interior Subcommittee on Public Lands held hearings May 3-4 on the Tuolumne issue. And at those hearings, Coelho had a new ally — the Reagan administration. The administration asked Congress to delay any action on designating the river until the dam studies were finished. Its stand was identical to that of Coelho, who never flatly and publicly said he opposed designation or supported the dams.

The Senate Energy Committee, however, attached the Tuolumne designation to the California wilderness bill, which was passed by the Senate Aug. 9. Adding the Tuolumne to the wilderness bill, and doing so in the Senate, proved to be a strategic move. Wild-river advocates had bypassed the House Interior Committee, where Coelho — a panel member — would have had the most leverage.

The last chance to stop the Tuolumne designation evaporated when its supporters asked for and got a closed rule for floor debate on the Senate-amended bill. The rule permitted only a motion that the House agree to the Senate amendments; no further amendments were in order.

The House approved the rule 295-112, and it approved the bill by an even larger margin, 368-41, sending it to the president Sept. 12. *(Votes 341, 342, pp. 104-H, 106-H)*

Verde River

Flowing down from the central highlands of Arizona, the Verde River was a rare "desert river" that attracted and supported wildlife from miles around. Apart from recreation, it provided nesting grounds for bald eagles and other unique species. The Verde was a favorite of Morris K. Udall, D-Ariz., who chaired the House Interior Committee. The 41-mile segment designated by Congress ran through the Prescott, Coconino and Tonto national forests. Management of the river as wild and scenic required accommodation with flood control and livestock grazing activities.

The Forest Service had originally found 78 miles of the river eligible for wild and scenic status. Compromise language designating 39.5 miles was made part of statewide Arizona wilderness legislation (HR 4707 — PL 98-406) cleared Aug. 10. *(Story, p. 314)*

Au Sable/Pere Marquette

The Au Sable and the Pere Marquette were two popular canoeing and fishing rivers in Michigan's lower peninsula.

Part of the Pere Marquette was designated wild and scenic by Congress in November 1978 (PL 95-625).

The river, however, was a major spawning ground for the lamprey eel, a saltwater species that invaded the Great Lakes basin through the St. Lawrence Seaway. Lampreys were destroying valuable sport and commercial fish in much of the Great Lakes system. As an alternative to chemical pesticides, which harm other aquatic species, the state wanted to build a small dam to block the eels from their spawning grounds. Since wild and scenic status banned dam-building, legislation was needed to allow the lamprey control.

A House bill (HR 3472) to allow the lamprey control was reported from the Interior Committee on April 26 (H Rept 98-717), and passed by the House on May 1.

The Senate Energy Committee, rather than acting on the House bill, reported out its own bill (S 2732) on Aug. 3 (S Rept 98-574). That bill added to the Pere Marquette lamprey-control provisions a wild and scenic designation for 23 miles of the Au Sable River.

The Forest Service had originally recommended 74 miles of the Au Sable for designation, but the Reagan administration proposed cutting that to 23 miles, in response to concerns from private landowners along the river. Conservationists agreed, hoping to add more of the river later. The designated corridor included more than 6,000 acres, most of it part of the Huron National Forest. Some 600 acres of the land was privately owned.

The Senate passed S 2732 on Aug. 9 and the House passed it in the same form Sept. 24. The president signed it into law on Oct. 4 (PL 98-444).

Three Oregon Rivers

Another bill (S 416) cleared by Congress gave varying degrees of protection to three rivers in Oregon: the Illinois, the Owyhee, and the North Umpqua.

A tributary of the Rogue River in Southwest Oregon, the Illinois River drained from the Siskiyou National Forest in the Coastal Range. Chinook and coho salmon were abundant there, as well as steelhead and cutthroat trout. It was also used for whitewater boating. The Coos-Curry Electric Cooperative had proposed to build a hydroelectric dam on the river.

The Owyhee River ran through steep canyons in the desolate high desert of southeast Oregon. Kayakers and rafters used the river when it was high from spring runoff, and during the rest of the year fishermen sought rainbow trout there. Pronghorn antelope, bighorn sheep and other wildlife were found nearby.

The North Umpqua River descended from the Umpqua National Forest in Oregon's Cascade Range, not far from Crater Lake National Park in the southwest part of the state. Although used for hiking and boating, it was renowned mainly for its steelhead, an oceangoing relative of the trout that returned to inland streams to spawn. Conservationists sought to protect the river from road-building, logging and other development.

As cleared, S 416 designated 112 miles of the Owyhee and 50 miles of the Illinois as wild and scenic. The bill also gave protective study status to 33 miles of the North Umpqua.

S 416 was reported by the Senate Energy Committee on May 18 (S Rept 98-460), and passed by the Senate on May 24. House Interior reported the bill Sept. 24 (H Rept 98-1068), and the House passed it under suspension of the rules the same day. The Senate agreed to the House amendments Oct. 3, and the president signed the bill Oct. 19 (PL 98-494).

Wildcat River

The Wildcat River, flowing out of the White Mountain National Forest in northern New Hampshire, formed a 120-foot waterfall at the town of Jackson. An electric utility was studying a hydroelectric project there that would "de-water" the falls, a tourist attraction important to the area's economy.

Congress designated a 14-mile stretch of the river, including the falls, for wild and scenic study, protecting it from development during a six-year period for completion of the study.

The study provision became part of a New Hampshire wilderness bill (HR 3921), which was cleared June 6 and signed into law (PL 98-323) June 19. *(Story, p. 315)*

Horsepasture River

The small Horsepasture River dropped steeply out of the Blue Ridge Mountains in western North Carolina. With five major waterfalls, it dropped some 1,700 feet in four miles. Found to be eligible for "natural and scenic" designation under the state's protective system, it was used by canoeists, campers, hikers and fishermen. An electric utility was seeking a permit for a hydroelectric project that would divert water around the falls.

Congress designated for a three-year wild and scenic study the four-mile section of the river being eyed for the hydro project. Those provisions were added to an unrelated national forest bill (HR 3601) at the urging of the House member from that area, James McClure Clarke, D-N.C. Reagan signed the measure into law Oct. 17 (PL 98-484). ∎

Omnibus Water Project Bill Dies in Senate

For the first time since 1976, Congress came close to passing an omnibus water resources authorization, but the bill died in the closing days of the session.

Efforts to get new water projects started through appropriations measures also failed. The House tacked funding for some "new starts" onto the continuing appropriations resolution (H J Res 648) that provided fiscal 1985 funding for a number of government agencies, but at the insistence of the Reagan administration, the money was later stripped out in conference with the Senate.

The House June 29 passed an $18 billion omnibus bill (HR 3678 — H Rept 98-616, Parts I-IV) authorizing construction of more than 300 dams, harbors, locks, levees and other water development and conservation projects.

An $11 billion Senate water projects bill (S 1739) was reported April 2 by the Senate Environment and Public Works Committee (S Rept 98-340), April 26 by the Energy and Natural Resources Committee (S Rept 98-418), and June 8 by the Senate Finance Committee (S Rept 98-509).

However, differences among the three committees on the bill's provisions thwarted a time agreement for floor consideration of S 1739.

The House tacked HR 3678 onto the continuing appropriations resolution, but a last-ditch effort to do the same in the Senate failed when the authorizing proposal was ruled non-germane by a 36-60 vote taken in the session that began Oct. 3. *(Vote 263, 46-S)*

The authorizing measure was later removed from the

funding bill by House-Senate conferees — again under pressure from the administration. *(Story, p. 444)*

Background

Congress had not passed an omnibus water projects bill since 1976. *(1976 Almanac p. 202)*

Funding continued, however, for projects already authorized and under construction and for operation of projects already built. In fact, water spending rose in nominal dollars, from an annual level of $2.6 billion or less in 1973-75 to a peak of $4.1 billion in 1980-81, before falling back to about $3.7 billion in 1983. *(1983 Almanac p. 354)*

For fiscal 1985, Congress cleared an energy and water appropriations bill (HR 5653 — PL 98-360) that gave $3.8 billion to the U.S. Army Corps of Engineers and the Interior Department's Bureau of Reclamation. *(Story, p. 369)*

Although funding did not suffer over the decade, what it went for changed dramatically. Historically, the corps' construction budget was far larger than its budget for operations and maintenance. In the 1980s, however, operations spending caught up with construction funding and for fiscal 1985, actually surpassed it, $1.3 billion to $890 million.

The shift was only partly a result of congressional and presidential austerity measures. It also reflected the needs of a maturing public works program and an aging infrastructure — where maintenance costs took up an ever-larger share of a fixed-size pie.

And it signaled a shift of funds from the Eastern-oriented corps to the Western-oriented Bureau of Reclamation. The corps' 1985 funding stood at $2.791 billion — almost unchanged from fiscal 1980, when it was $2.796 billion. But the bureau's funding climbed from $607 million in fiscal 1980 to $1.053 billion for fiscal 1985.

Administration Position

Although the administration in 1983 appeared to embrace stiff new requirements for greater cost-sharing by local beneficiaries of water projects, President Reagan himself backed away from such moves in the 1984 election year.

Reagan's decision seemed to resolve three years of feuding among administration officials — some of whom wanted to reduce the water-project drain on the Treasury, and some of whom wanted to prevent mutiny among the president's supporters in water-poor Western states.

But it left high and dry members of Congress who had been pushing for greater local cost-sharing on federally sponsored water projects. One of these, Sen. Howard M. Metzenbaum, D-Ohio, called the move "a cheap political ploy."

Fifteen Western GOP senators had warned Reagan in an April 1983 letter that his and their 1984 election chances could be hurt by policies that appeared "anti-West" and "anti-water."

The threat, as they perceived it, was a proposal to impose uniform cost-sharing requirements on all federal water agencies, including both the Bureau of Reclamation, which operated only in the West, and the Army Corps of Engineers, which concentrated on the East. Assistant Army Secretary William R. Gianelli, who headed corps civil works programs, had joined in June 1983 with the Office of Management and Budget (OMB) in claiming such a plan was administration policy.

But former Interior Secretary James G. Watt, a West-

erner who headed the Cabinet council dealing with water resources, promptly disavowed Gianelli's formula.

Watt emphasized that the Interior Department, which housed the Bureau of Reclamation, would decide cost-sharing questions on a case-by-case basis, with special concern for the local sponsor's ability to pay.

The 1983 letter to Reagan from Western senators was engineered by Sen. Paul Laxalt, R-Nev., Reagan's closest friend in the Senate and general chairman of the president's 1984 campaign organization.

Laxalt finally got the answer he wanted at a dramatic, impromptu ceremony Jan. 24, when Watt's successor, Interior Secretary William P. Clark, personally delivered a letter from Reagan rejecting any fixed formula for splitting the cost of dams, locks and other water projects between the federal government and local beneficiaries.

House Committee Action

The omnibus House authorization bill (HR 3678) was reported March 8 by the Public Works and Transportation Committee and moved through four other committees the week of April 9 (H Rept 98-616, Parts I-IV).

The word "omnibus" translated roughly as "something for everybody." HR 3678, the creation of Rep. Robert A. Roe, D-N.J., chairman of the Public Works Subcommittee on Water Resources, offered something to environmentalists, water policy reformers and administration budget-cutters. And it brought the urban Northeast into a fraternity controlled by Sun Belt committee chairmen by setting up a new $800 million yearly loan program for rehabilitating aging municipal water supply systems.

The greatest changes made in Roe's version of the bill by the other committees came on seven amendments approved by the Merchant Marine and Fisheries Committee on April 11.

Adopting an amendment offered by Mario Biaggi, D-N.Y., Merchant Marine approved a "fast track" permit process for federal port development projects and set up limited federal loan guarantees for the non-federal share of costs for such projects.

Michigan and Minnesota members of the Merchant Marine panel successfully offered an amendment to delete a section of the bill that would have authorized year-round extension of the navigation season on the annually ice-locked Great Lakes and the St. Lawrence Seaway. The project, estimated to cost more than $600 million, would have used icebreakers, air bubblers, floating booms, and other methods to help combat ice.

The Great Lakes winter navigation project was backed by Arlan Stangeland, R-Minn., ranking minority member on the Public Works Subcommittee on Water Resources. However, environmentalists and several Great Lakes states opposed the project and said it was not cost-effective.

House Floor Action

The House passed HR 3678 on June 29 by a 259-33 vote. *(Vote 276, p. 84-H)*

Action was slowed by amendments offered by members wanting to add or adjust projects in their districts. The night of June 28, intense debate broke out over an amendment by E. Clay Shaw Jr., R-Fla., to de-authorize the 110-mile Cross-Florida Barge Canal. No construction money had been appropriated for the project, which was one-third built, for nearly a decade.

The issue sparked more than an hour of debate as members from Florida thronged to the floor to speak, and it left House members with a tough decision in the face of a divided delegation. Shaw's amendment was finally rejected on a cliffhanger 201-204 vote. Six of the 19 members from Florida, all Democrats, opposed it. Among them was Claude Pepper, D-Fla., who had first proposed the project back in 1942. *(Vote 266, p. 82-H)*

The committee bill imposed heavier cost-sharing requirements on local users and sponsors than had been seen for decades. Nonetheless, Rep. Thomas E. Petri, R-Wis., supported by environmentalists and the Reagan administration, tried to toughen those provisions by requiring local beneficiaries to contribute part of their share of project costs "up front" — during construction. But his amendment was rejected, 85-213. *(Vote 275, p. 84-H)*

Provisions of HR 3678

As passed by the House, HR 3678 contained the following major provisions:

Ports

● Authorized six deep-draft superports at depths of more than 45 feet: Norfolk Harbor, Mobile Harbor, Mississippi River Ship Channel, Texas City Channel, New York Harbor and Los Angeles-Long Beach Harbor.

● Authorized construction of some 27 projects for the improvement of general cargo ports (those with an authorized depth of 45 feet or less).

● Maintained current policy authorizing the federal government to pay 100 percent of the costs of designing, building and operating the navigation features of general cargo ports.

● Set the non-federal share of costs for deep-draft ports at 50 percent of the incremental costs associated with that part of a project deeper than 45 feet.

● Prohibited non-federal interests that imposed fees on vessels in order to pay their share of costs for deep-draft ports from imposing those fees on any vessels other than commercial vessels requiring a channel depth greater than 45 feet.

The bill neither authorized nor required collection of such fees.

● Established a Port Infrastructure Development and Improvement Trust Fund of up to $2 billion to be collected from customs revenues. The funds would be used for port development.

Inland Waterways

● Authorized seven lock and dam projects on the inland waterway system:

Oliver Lock and Dam, Ala.; Gallipolis Locks and Dam, Ohio and W.Va.; Winfield Locks and Dam, W.Va.; Lock and Dam 7 Replacement, Monongahela River, Pa.; Lock and Dam 8 Replacement, Monongahela River, Pa.; Lock and Dam 26 Replacement, Ill.; Bonneville Lock and Dam, Ore. and Wash.

● Imposed no new user charges on inland waterway users beyond a 1978 fuel tax (The Inland Waterways Revenue Act of 1978 — PL 95-502), which was deposited in the Inland Waterways Trust Fund.

● Provided that one-third of the cost of new lock and dam projects be paid for out of the Inland Waterways Trust Fund, and the remainder from the general fund of the Treasury.

Flood Control

● Authorized some 72 flood control projects.

● Set at 25 percent the basic non-federal share of costs for projects authorized in the bill and for previously authorized projects for which construction contracts had not been signed as of the date of enactment. Under current law and traditional policies, the non-federal share for such projects could range from less than 5 percent to more than 50 percent.

● Placed a cap of 30 percent on the non-federal share when the costs of land, easements, rights-of-way and relocations exceeded 25 percent of total costs. Current law (the 1936 Flood Control Act) required non-federal interests to contribute the lands, easements, rights-of-way and relocations necessary for local flood control projects.

● Authorized the secretary of the Army to pay the additional amount if the cost of necessary lands, easements, rights of ways and relocations exceeded 30 percent.

● Provided for non-federal interests to pay the cash portion of their share (when the in-kind contribution was less than 25 percent of project costs), with interest, over a 15-year period beginning after completion of the project.

Other Water Projects

● Authorized some 15 projects for protection of shorelines.

● Authorized some 55 projects for water resources conservation and development, including mitigation of damages to fish and wildlife, water supply, hydroelectric power, stream bank erosion control, navigation and other purposes.

● Deauthorized more than 300 projects or portions of projects that had potential costs estimated at $17 billion in cumulative outlays by fiscal 1996.

Water Supply

● Created an $800 million annual loan program for improving public water supply systems, a financial responsibility that the federal government had previously left to local governments.

● Authorized the secretary of the Army to make loans to operators of water supply systems for the purpose of repairing, rehabilitating, expanding or improving them, including costs of engineering and real property as well as construction.

● Made eligible as borrowers those operators of public water supply systems who were either state or local governmental units or private borrowers whose rates and services were subject to state regulation.

● Limited the amount of any such loan to 80 percent of project costs, except in remote rural areas or cases where the secretary found a larger loan appropriate for economic reasons.

● Prohibited the lending of more than $40 million to any single operator and prohibited the lending of more than $80 million annually for projects in any single state.

● Prohibited loans for projects intended solely to increase the number of persons served by a water supply system.

● Required a resolution of approval of individual loans by the House Public Works and Transportation Committee and the Senate Environment and Public Works Committee before the secretary could make such loans.

● Listed some 16 loans to water supply systems authorized by the bill and not subject to further congressional approval.

● Required loan recipients to show the secretary they would carry out locally suitable water conservation programs before such loans could be made.

● Empowered the Treasury secretary to set the interest rate for each such loan, as of the beginning of the fiscal year in which construction starts, on the basis of the average interest rate payable by the Treasury upon its outstanding marketable 15-year public obligations.

● Required non-federal interests to provide necessary lands, easements and rights of way for such projects. Where the value of those lands was less than 20 percent of project costs allocable to water supply, the difference had to be paid by the non-federal interest before construction. Where the value exceeded 20 percent, the Army secretary had to acquire, on request of the non-federal sponsor, lands equal in value to the difference.

● Authorized for the loan program $800 million annually for fiscal 1984 through 1987 and such sums as may be necessary for each fiscal year thereafter. Loan repayments, including interest, would be deposited in the general fund of the Treasury.

General Provisions

● Defined planning objectives for Army Corps of Engineers water projects to include enhancement of regional economic development, quality of the total environment, social well-being and quality of life, prevention of loss of life, and national economic development. Required the corps to evaluate all benefits and costs, both quantifiable and unquantifiable, related to these objectives in planning future projects.

● Required the Army secretary to consider, for project planning purposes, the benefits attributable to project features improving environmental quality to be at least equal to the costs of such features.

● Established a $35 million Environmental Protection and Mitigation Fund to be available in advance of construction for environmental protection or mitigation measures authorized as part of Corps projects, including acquisition of lands to offset loss of fish and wildlife habitat. The Army secretary was to reimburse the fund from the first appropriations made for each project.

● Authorized the Army secretary, in consultation with appropriate federal, state and local agencies, to study the water resources needs of river basins and regions in the United States and report to Congress by Oct. 1, 1987.

● Authorized the Army secretary to restore to a safe condition dams, owned by state or local governments, found to be hazardous by the corps. The state or local government had to repay the cost of the work over a period of up to 50 years, with interest.

● Extended indefinitely the existing authorization for appropriations for the corps to remove drift and debris from navigable U.S. waters, and raised from $5 million to $12 million the annual authorization for removal of obnoxious aquatic plant growths.

● Authorized $5 million for fiscal 1984 through 1986 for the corps' program to control river and harbor ice.

● Authorized the corps to seek appropriations for preservation and interpretation of properties at corps projects that are on the National Register of Historic Places.

● Directed the corps to extend the navigation season on the Great Lakes and St. Lawrence Seaway by means of ice booms, air bubblers, lock modifications, dredging and other measures, in accordance with the recommendations of an October 1979 corps report.

● Directed the corps, when lands were to be acquired for recreation or for fish and wildlife habitat to offset losses from a water project, to acquire those lands before construction or at the same time as other lands acquired for the project.

● Directed the Army secretary to establish in the Directorate of Civil Works of the Office of the Chief of Engineers an Office of Environmental Policy.

● Included a "sunset" provision deauthorizing any project authorized in the bill unless funds had been obligated for planning, design or construction by five years after enactment.

● Required the Army secretary, to the extent he determined feasible, to provide for employment of local residents in construction of projects.

● Required the corps to contract out at least 30 percent of the architectural and engineering services required for water projects.

● Increased the dollars-per-project ceiling for various kinds of small projects that the corps had authority to undertake without specific authorization from Congress.

Water Policy Board

● Created a National Board on Water Resources Policy, replacing the now-abolished Water Resources Council. The board was to consist of seven members: the secretaries of interior, agriculture, and the Army, the administrator of the Environmental Protection Agency, two members appointed by the president and confirmed by the Senate (one nominated by the Speaker of the House and one by the president pro tempore of the Senate), and a chairman appointed by the president and confirmed by the Senate.

● Gave the board responsibility for performing regional and national water resource studies, helping coordinate federal water resources research, and establishing principles, standards, and procedures for the formulation and evaluation of federal water and related land resource projects.

● Provided that the principles and standards set by the old Water Resources Council and in effect on March 9, 1983, remained in effect until new ones were established by the board.

● Established a State Water Resources Advisory Committee, with a member appointed by the board from each major U.S. water region. The committee would submit recommendations to the board, and through it, to the president and Congress.

● Authorized the board to make grants to states and territories to assist them in water resource planning and management, to be matched in cash or in kind. Authorized for such grants $20 million annually for fiscal 1984 through 1988, to be allocated among the states on the basis of population, land area, financial need and need for the grant, providing that each state received at least $100,000.

Senate Committee Action

The Senate Environment and Public Works Committee reported its own $11 billion omnibus water-projects bill (S 1739 — S Rept 98-340) on Nov. 17, 1983.

The Energy and Natural Resources Committee approved the bill (S Rept 98-418) April 26 after stripping from it key reforms sought by the Environment Committee.

The Energy Committee voted 10-8 to remove water projects of the Interior Department's Bureau of Reclamation from the jursidiction of a proposed National Board on Water Resources Policy.

Members also approved by voice vote an amendment exempting Bureau of Reclamation water projects from the bill's requirements that local users and beneficiaries pay certain portions of a project's costs.

The committee's action emphasized the fundamental differences over water policy of the two committees. The Environment Committee sought to impose uniform cost-sharing guidelines on most federally financed water projects, while the Energy Committee effectively sought a separate policy for the arid Western states under the Bureau of Reclamation's jurisdiction.

The Energy Committee only got referral of those portions of the bill that dealt with the Bureau of Reclamation, over which it had jurisdiction. The Environment Committee had jurisdiction over Army Corps of Engineers' water projects, most of which were in the East.

Appropriations

The largest water measure cleared during the year was the fiscal 1985 energy and water appropriations bill (HR 5653 — PL 98-360), which gave $3.8 billion to the U.S. Army Corps of Engineers and the Interior Department's Bureau of Reclamation. This funding was mostly for projects already authorized and under construction, or for operation of projects already built.

The Appropriations committees in both chambers very carefully took a stand of "no new starts" in the regular fiscal 1985 bill, as they had for several years. The chairmen said they wanted to wait until an authorization bill had been approved.

While waiting for action on an authorization bill, the Appropriations committees in 1983 packaged some proposed new starts into a supplemental funding bill. The House passed its version (HR 3958), providing $119 million for 43 new projects, and the Senate Appropriations Committee approved a $78 million version for 27 projects. *(1983 Almanac p. 520)*

The Reagan administration had proposed 19 new starts for about $50 million. Its proposed new starts favored projects where local beneficiaries were ready to share costs, but this ranking bothered the congressional committees. The Appropriations panels wanted to protect their role as gatekeepers. And the authorizing panels felt that cost-sharing policy was *their* jurisdiction.

After waiting nearly three years for an authorizing bill to settle the cost-sharing issue, the House Appropriations Committee Sept. 14 finally added the House-passed new-starts bill (by then worth $139 million) to the fiscal 1985 continuing resolution, H J Res 648.

After signals of a likely veto from OMB, the House Rules Committee tried to strip the new-starts package from the continuing resolution. But the House defeated that rule Sept. 20, and the Rules Committee not only put the new starts back in, but opened the bill up to other riders, including the authorizing measure, HR 3678.

Silvio O. Conte, R-Mass., ranking Republican on the Appropriations Committee who was famous for criticizing what he considered pork-barrel bills, said: "It's going to make the Chicago stockyards look anemic."

In passing H J Res 648 on Sept. 25, the full House approved both the new starts and the big water-projects authorization. The Senate Appropriations Committee the same day approved $82.9 million in new starts as part of the continuing resolution, but no authorization package.

When the continuing resolution came out of Senate Appropriations without any water authorization, House Public Works Chairman James J. Howard, D-N.J., and Sen. James Abdnor, R-S.D., chairman of the Senate Environment Subcommittee on Water Resources, tried to negotiate a compromise authorizing bill. By late Oct. 3, they had largely agreed on one that melded the two earlier bills.

At about 6 a.m. on Oct. 4, after the Senate had been in session all night, Abdnor moved to add a modified version of S 1739 to the continuing resolution, a version reflecting a compromise with the other Senate committees and with the House. But the Senate rejected that amendment as non-germane by a 36-60 vote. *(Vote 263, p. 46-S)*

Senate Appropriations Chairman Mark O. Hatfield, R-Ore., up for re-election, then tried desperately to negotiate an agreement with the White House that would save funding for some of the new starts, including the work at the Bonneville Lock and Dam on the Columbia River in his state. House-Senate conferees tentatively agreed on a $100 million compromise for new-starts funding.

But an Oct. 5 letter from OMB Director David A. Stockman to Hatfield made clear that the administration would oppose a bill that had *any* water projects in it unless Congress approved basic cost-sharing reforms. Reluctantly, the conferees dropped all new starts and authorizations from the bill.

Before throwing in the towel, Hatfield complained bitterly to fellow conferees, charging that the Reagan administration showed "no limitation in its lust" for defense spending, while refusing to go along with water spending that did not add up to "even the petty cash fund for the Pentagon." ∎

Dam Safety Repairs Voted

The House Aug. 10 cleared for President Reagan's signature a compromise bill (HR 1652 — PL 98-404) authorizing $650 million in new spending for safety-related dam repairs in Western states.

The bill settled a four-year controversy over whether local beneficiaries of those water projects should share the costs of repairs by requiring some beneficiaries to repay 15 percent of those costs at market interest rates.

The House had narrowly opposed a cost-sharing requirement, but it bowed to the Senate's position on the issue.

Background

HR 1652 authorized funding to repair about 40 Western dams administered by the Interior Department's Bureau of Reclamation. Some were built as long ago as 1911. They were judged unsafe because of faulty or obsolete engineering, new flooding and earthquake forecasts, or simple rusting and crumbling of old age.

When such dams failed, the results could be catastrophic. The 1976 failure of the Teton Dam in Idaho killed 11 people and caused some $400 million in damages. Because most such dams were designed and built by the federal government, the Treasury could end up paying significant damage claims, bill sponsors said. So far it had paid out $350 million in claims from the Teton Dam disaster alone.

Congress in 1978 authorized $100 million for safety repairs to federal dams (PL 95-578), but the need had grown since then. *(1978 Almanac p. 723)*

The House and Senate in 1983 reported legislation (HR 1652 — H Rept 98-168; S 672 — S Rept 98-258) adding $650 million to the old $100 million authorization, but neither chamber brought a bill to the floor. *(1983 Almanac p. 349)*

Arizona Concerns

One place the dam safety issue hit home was Phoenix, Ariz., built on the Salt River. Six upstream dams — all on the unsafe list — restrained the flash floods the river was prone to. The Bureau of Reclamation estimated that if only one of them burst, damages to the city could amount to $630 million. During bad rains in February 1982, the dams looked so shaky that officials prepared to evacuate Phoenix residents in the flood plain.

Repairs or replacements of those six dams could cost as much as $380 million — well over half the amount authorized in HR 1652. A chief sponsor of the bill was Morris K. Udall, D-Ariz., whose House Interior and Insular Affairs Committee reported the bill May 16, 1983 (H Rept 98-168).

Udall told House colleagues that because the dams were mostly designed and built by the federal government, the Treasury should take responsibility for safety repairs. He argued that the buyer of a defective automobile would not expect to pay to have the defect fixed, but would expect the repairs to be the responsibility of the manufacturer.

Cost-Sharing Switch

The House passed its version of the bill — without cost-sharing — by voice vote on March 20, 1984.

By a razor-thin 194-192 margin, members chose a government-pays formula over a user-pays formula that was favored by environmentalists and taxpayers' groups. Most representatives from Western states opposed user cost-sharing. *(Vote 42, p. 16-H)*

That was a switch for the House, which had taken the opposite stand in an April 1982 vote on a similar bill. *(1982 Almanac p. 449)*

A total of 43 House members who had supported a tough cost-sharing amendment in 1982 voted for a much weaker substitute this time. Nineteen members switched the other way.

The House was following the lead of the Reagan administration, which did its own about-face on water project cost-sharing. In 1982, the administration supported cost-sharing. In a Jan. 24 policy statement, Reagan reversed direction and said the cost of dam safety repairs should be borne entirely by the federal government.

Rep. Gerald B. H. Solomon, R-N.Y., one of the leading advocates of cost-sharing, lambasted the administration's change of heart. Noting he was "a longstanding supporter of President Reagan," Solomon said he was "very sorry" that Reagan had switched positions, attributing the change to election-year concern for Western sensitivities.

"For political reasons, and solely for political reasons, these born-again dam builders at the Interior Department have sold out any conservative principles that they have had ... and I resent it, as my colleagues can tell," Solomon said.

The chief advocates of cost-sharing on the House floor were Bob Edgar, D-Pa., and Solomon. Edgar, an environmentalist, referred to himself and Solomon, a fiscal conservative, as "ideological bookends."

They offered a pair of amendments that would have

required irrigators, municipal water users and other local beneficiaries to repay some repair costs over a 50-year period — on terms similar to those for new reclamation dams, which Solomon called "already quite generous."

The bill reported to the floor by the Interior Committee called for the federal Treasury to pay all safety repair costs apart from expenditures needed to counteract normal wear and tear. As under existing law, such maintenance outlays had to be paid by local beneficiaries.

Solomon moved to amend the committee bill by requiring local users and beneficiaries to reimburse the government for some additional costs.

Then Abraham Kazen Jr., D-Texas, chairman of the Interior Subcommittee on Water and Power Resources, offered a substitute to Solomon's amendment, saying it was a compromise version that had the support of the Reagan administration. The Kazen amendment required local cost-sharing if the repair projects produced new economic benefits. Solomon, however, said almost none of the projects involved new economic benefits and hence, the government would recoup little if any of its $650 million commitment.

Edgar then offered an amendment to Solomon's proposal that changed it only slightly. He explained this was a tactic to get a vote on cost-sharing first. But Edgar's and Solomon's opponents all voted with them, knowing it was a "free vote" that could be undone by voting "yea" on the Kazen substitute. Edgar's amendment was adopted 382-0. *(Vote 41, p. 16-H)*

The vote on Kazen was close, with the "nay" votes (supporting Solomon) pulling ahead during the final seconds. But last-minute vote-switching put Kazen out ahead, 194-192.

Senate Action

The bill's chances of passage in the Senate, however, were jeopardized by objections from Howard M. Metzenbaum, D-Ohio.

Senate Energy Committee Chairman James A. McClure, R-Idaho, and others finally negotiated an agreement with Metzenbaum for partial cost-sharing.

Under the compromise, 15 percent of the safety costs would be allocated to the various users of a dam, who had to pay it back at market rates of interest. Irrigation users, however, could pay back without interest, subject to their ability to pay. Under present law, most users paid back costs at rates lower than market rates, resulting in a significant government subsidy.

Only safety-related work was eligible for funding under the bill; work to offset normal aging and wear of a dam facility, or work that would create additional benefits to users, was not eligible.

Without further committee-level action, the Senate brought up the House bill Aug. 9, adopted a Metzenbaum amendment that embodied the compromise, and passed the bill by voice vote.

Malcolm Wallop, R-Wyo., arguing the viewpoint of many Western states, said that even though safety costs were part of the capital investments reclamation dam users had originally agreed to help pay, "the bargain originally made never included paying for the same service twice."

"Local users are not responsible for safety defects at federal dams. The federal government is," Wallop said, adding that he did not want to delay any further legislation that could save lives.

Metzenbaum argued that it was unfair to shift the Western dam repair costs to the taxpayers of all states, but he hailed the agreement on some cost-sharing as an important precedent.

In adopting the plan, Metzenbaum said, "I believe we establish the principle that virtually no federal water investment shall be immune from cost-sharing."

Final Action

Final action on HR 1652 came one day later, as the House Aug. 10 agreed to the Senate amendments to the bill.

President Reagan signed the legislation into law on Aug. 28.   ■

Hoover Dam Power Pricing

The Senate July 31 sent to the president a bill (S 268 — PL 98-381) to preserve until 2017 the bargain rates charged for power generated by the Hoover Dam.

The Senate cleared the measure by a vote of 64-34, a day after voting 60-28 to invoke cloture and close off debate on the measure. Sen. Howard M. Metzenbaum, D-Ohio, had been waging a one-man stand against the bill. *(Votes 192, 187, p. 33-S)*

The Senate had originally passed S 268 (S Rept 98-137) in 1983.

The House passed its own version of the measure (HR 4275) May 3, 1984, by a vote of 279-95. It then amended S 268 to conform to the provisions of HR 4275 and passed the Senate bill by voice vote. *(Vote 115, p. 38-H)*

Final action came when the Senate agreed to the amendments of the House.

Provisions

As cleared by Congress, S 268:

● Authorized the secretary of the interior to add equipment to increase the generating capacity of Hoover Dam by 500 megawatts, more than a third of present capacity.

● Provided for improved access to the dam for visitors, who numbered one million each year.

● Required that improvements to the dam, estimated to cost $77 million, be paid for by customers of Hoover Dam power.

● Added surcharges to be used for salinity control and for the Central Arizona Project, a large water project.

● Allocated the power from Hoover Dam among utilities for the states of Arizona and Nevada, the city of Los Angeles, the Southern California Edison Co., and three Southern California cities.

● Required that parties to a pending lawsuit over allocation of Hoover power withdraw their claims in order to be eligible for power under the new contracts. Otherwise, the allocation would be divided among other utilities in the same state.

● Extended contracts for allocation and pricing of Hoover Dam power until Sept. 30, 2017.

● Provided for disposition of surplus power from the Navajo Generating Station in Page, Ariz., with first preference going to Arizona utilities.

● Required the secretary of energy to report to committees of the House and Senate on all Colorado River Storage Project power resources.

● Authorized the secretary of the interior to build fish passage facilities within the Yakima River Basin in the state of Washington.

● Required contracts with the Western Area Power Administration, one of the six power marketing groups of the Department of Energy, to contain conservation programs.

● Placed a one-year limitation on the period during which lawsuits over the allocation of power from Hoover Dam could be filed.

Background

The Hoover was one of the world's largest dams, established by the Boulder Canyon Project of 1928. *(Congress and the Nation Vol. I, p. 812)*

With a price based on construction and interest costs from the 1930s, the Hoover Dam's electricity was one of the greatest energy bargains in the world — four-tenths of 1 cent per kilowatt hour. The national average was 6.5 cents, according to the Congressional Research Service, and power from a nuclear plant could cost far more.

An Important Precedent

S 268 extended for 30 years the arrangements under which power from the Hoover Dam on the Colorado River had been allocated and priced since 1937. Those contracts were scheduled to expire May 31, 1987.

By extending the formula, Congress kept intact the policy of pricing power at what it cost to produce it, rather than what it was worth on the open market. The Senate had inserted language in four appropriations bills in the preceding two years to protect that principle from re-examination.

The Hoover Dam bill was a crucial test, because the dam was one of the first major federal power projects to make it through its original 50-year payback period. If the pricing formula for this dam had been changed, it would have set a precedent of great potential impact on the West, which depended heavily on federal power and water projects.

Members from California, Arizona and Nevada, the three states that drew power from Hoover Dam, pushed hard for the bill, and they were backed by members from other Western states with projects that would face similar tests in the future.

House Action

The House May 3 scotched efforts to change the pricing formula for electricity from the Hoover Dam.

By a 176-214 vote, the House rejected an amendment by Barbara Boxer, D-Calif., that would have auctioned the power off to any utility wishing to bid on it at market rates. *(Vote 114, p. 38-H)*

It then passed the bill by a 279-95 vote. *(Vote 115, p. 38-H)*

By voice vote, the House dropped Title I of the bill, which authorized $258 million for increasing generating capacity at seven other Bureau of Reclamation power plants in California, Montana, California, Idaho and Wyoming.

As passed, the measure ratified an agreement between the Energy Department and California, Nevada and Arizona on how the power would be allocated until the year 2017.

The original contracts reserved most of the power for the Los Angeles area, with small shares allotted to Arizona and Nevada, which were underdeveloped at the time. Nevada sued in 1981 to get more power, with other parties joining in, but an out-of-court settlement was reached that was reflected in S 268.

Boxer represented the San Francisco area, which was frozen out of the arrangement along with San Diego. She argued in vain that it was time to break up "the exclusive Hoover club" and share the power with Utah, Colorado, New Mexico and the rest of California.

The House-passed bill set the price of Hoover power at the level agreed to in 1937 — about one-half cent per kilowatt-hour.

Boxer said the bill set "Depression-era prices for a 21st-century resource." She argued that her amendment would help lower deficits by bringing in $3.5 billion during the first 10 years. "These valuable resources are squandered," Boxer said, "by a pricing policy which is older than most members of this chamber."

Morris K. Udall, D-Ariz., chairman of the House Interior Committee, opposed Boxer's amendment, saying it would not only hurt 11 million ratepayers now using Hoover power, but would upset pricing arrangements for other federal hydroelectric projects around the country — including those on the Niagara and Columbia rivers and in the Tennessee valley.

Senate Action

When S 268 returned to the Senate in late July, opponents of the bill, led by Metzenbaum, charged that low rates for Hoover Dam's power discouraged conservation, encouraged industry to relocate in the Southwest and amounted to a subsidy that could cost the Treasury $6 billion in the next 10 years.

"This is a giveaway," said Metzenbaum. "It is a throwaway. It is illogical. It is absurd."

Western senators said consumers were receiving no bargains, since the costs cited by Metzenbaum did not include transmission or distribution and since Hoover Dam supplied such a low percentage of power to utilities that their rates to consumers were near or above the national average.

The Westerners insisted that the principle of basing power rates on the cost of producing that power was the only fair one — and the only one allowed private utilities. Sen. Daniel J. Evans, R-Wash., said that if the concept of market-based rates was extended to other federal projects, the result would be "to literally auction off the infrastructure of the United States to the highest bidder."

Amendments offered by Metzenbaum would not have based rates on market value, but would have shortened the period for which contracts were extended in order to force study and debate on the policy. Westerners said a decision on the Hoover Dam's contracts could not be put off, since utilities needed to be able to sell long-term bonds to finance improvements to the dam. Metzenbaum's amendments were either ruled out of order or tabled.

Cloture Invoked

Metzenbaum had barely begun his fight before he was faced, after only four hours, with a cloture petition to shut off debate. The cloture vote July 30 went down to the wire. After the regular 15-minute voting period expired, Metzenbaum stood at the front of the chamber, calling for "regular order." As a delaying tactic to enable the leadership to round up more votes, several senators repeatedly switched their votes back and forth until 60, the minimum required to invoke cloture, had been obtained. The final tally was 60-28. *(Vote 187, p. 33-S)*

The next day, Metzenbaum gave up the fight even though he had plenty of ammunition, in the form of amendments and parliamentary procedure, to drag out the contest.

He sat down, however, only after a bitter parting shot against the tactics his opponents had used against him. "Yesterday, our integrity — and our reputation as the world's greatest deliberative body — took repeated body blows," he said.

Metzenbaum was joined in protest by Dale Bumpers, D-Ark., who objected to the strategy even though he planned to vote against Metzenbaum on the bill itself. "I thought the conduct of the Senate yesterday was deplorable," he said.

Final approval of S 268 came on a motion by Majority Leader Howard H. Baker Jr., R-Tenn., to concur in the House amendments. The motion was agreed to 64-34. *(Vote 192, p. 33-S)* ∎

Colorado Salinity Control

The House Oct. 9 cleared for the president a bill (HR 2790 — PL 98-569) authorizing new projects for controlling salt content in the Colorado River.

Dissolved salts and minerals were a major pollution problem for the Colorado, and the United States had a treaty obligation to Mexico, where the river ended, to keep salinity at certain levels.

Irrigated agriculture was both a cause and a victim of salinity in the Colorado and its tributaries. Too much irrigation washed salts from the soil and caused downstream farmers trouble when the salt levels exceeded what their crops would tolerate.

In a 1974 law (PL 93-320), Congress authorized a desalting plant near the Mexican border and four upstream control units. *(1974 Almanac p. 827)*

Provisions

HR 2790 amended the 1974 law to authorize one new salinity control unit and part of a second.

It also authorized an upgraded program by the Department of Agriculture for helping farmers use irrigation water more efficiently, thus reducing salinity.

The bill increased to 30 percent, or higher in some cases, the share of project costs to be borne by farmers and other local beneficiaries. It did not raise current spending authorizations, which amounted to about $300 million.

Legislative Action

HR 2790 was reported Sept. 13 by the House Interior and Insular Affairs Committee (H Rept 98-1018) and passed Oct. 2 under suspension of the House rules.

It passed the Senate with minor amendments Oct. 5, and the House accepted the Senate amendments Oct. 9, clearing the measure for the president. ∎

High Plains Groundwater

The House Sept. 14 cleared for the president a bill (HR 71 — PL 98-434) calling for study and demonstration projects exploring the potential for groundwater recharge in the high plains states.

Heavy pumping from wells in those states, primarily for irrigation, had badly depleted the Ogallala Aquifer, which lay under parts of New Mexico, Oklahoma, Colorado, Kansas, Nebraska and Texas.

Much of that water was not being replenished naturally.

HR 71 authorized $500,000 for a study of the problem, and another $20 million to demonstrate technologies (such as high-pressure injection of water from surface sources) for recharging the aquifers.

That $20 million, however, had to be matched by some $5 million in local funds, a 25 percent cost-sharing figure that disarmed objections from potential critics of the bill.

The legislation was reported in May 1983 from the House Interior and Insular Affairs Committee (H Rept 98-167) and passed June 20, 1983.

The Senate Energy and Natural Resources Committee reported it March 29, 1984 (S Rept 98-372) and it passed the Senate with amendments Aug. 10. The House agreed to those amendments Sept. 14, clearing the bill. ∎

Water Bill Veto Overridden

Congress March 22 overrode President Reagan's veto of a bill (S 684) to authorize $36 million annually for water resources research. As a result, the measure became law (PL 98-242) without his signature.

The Senate acted first, on March 21, and its 86-12 vote gave the House the impetus it needed to override by 309-81 the next day. *(Vote 35, p. 9-S; vote 45, p. 16-H)*

Reagan had vetoed the bill Feb. 21. The veto, his eighth of the 98th Congress and 23rd of his presidency, was only his fourth to be overridden.

S 684 authorized Interior Department grants for water research projects and programs at land grant colleges in 50 states and some U.S. territories. That program had been operating since 1964, and the bill reauthorized it for fiscal years 1985-89.

The president had argued that federal support was no longer necessary. "I believe that these state institutes are now at a point where further federal involvement in their research activities is not necessary," Reagan said in his Feb. 21 veto message. "They can stand and continue to succeed on their own." *(Text, p. 19-E)*

Final Provisions

As enacted over President Reagan's veto, S 684 included the following provisions:

● Reauthorized water resources research institutes in each state, and authorized $10 million in federal matching grants to them annually for fiscal 1985 through 1989.

● Set the number of non-federal dollars needed to match each federal dollar at one for fiscal 1985 and 1986, one and one-half for 1987 and 1988, and two for 1989.

● Authorized $20 million annually for five years for 50-50 matching grants to water research projects in the national interest. These were to be awarded by the interior secretary on the basis of merit.

● Authorized $6 million annually for five years for grants or contracts for development of water-related technology of national importance.

● Conveyed to the towns of Wrightsville Beach, N.C., and Roswell, N.M., certain lands no longer needed by the federal government for desalinization demonstration projects.

Background

Water research institutes were established at land grant colleges in 50 states and Puerto Rico under PL 88-379, enacted in 1964, and had operated for 19 years with a mix of federal and state funding. *(Congress and the Nation Vol. I, p. 890)*

Although they supported basic research, the individual institutes most often focused on problems unique to a given state or region. For example, Massachusetts had studied acid rain, Pennsylvania had studied acid mine drainage, and New Mexico had studied desalinization technology.

Supporters said federal funding helped build the states' problem-solving capability, but Reagan said the program should be state-financed. His budgets for fiscal 1982 through 1985 requested an end to federal funding of the water research program.

Although authorizing legislation for the program expired at the end of fiscal 1982, Congress kept it alive with year-to-year appropriations in 1983 and 1984.

Legislative History

The bill as originally passed by the Senate on May 25, 1983, authorized $21.1 million yearly for water research. As passed by the House on Oct. 31, 1983, the measure called for $60 million yearly. There was no opposition in either chamber. *(1983 Almanac p. 349)*

The Senate on Nov. 18, 1983, approved a compromise version authorizing $36 million annually, and the House agreed to those changes Feb. 7, 1984, by unanimous consent, clearing the bill.

The final version made several concessions to the Reagan position. Besides lowering the authorization ceiling from the $60 million originally called for by the House, it required state funds to match the federal grants — tapering off the federal share to one dollar for every two non-federal dollars by 1988.

After those and other changes, the Interior Department dropped its objections to the bill, but the Office of Management and Budget still recommended a veto.

Reagan vetoed the bill Feb. 21, saying that the water research program was "not an appropriate federal activity."

"If we are truly to succeed in reducing federal spending," Reagan said, "we must sort out those responsibilities which are appropriately federal from those which can be more effectively and fairly implemented at the state and local level."

Hill strategists supporting S 684 took their time before mounting the override attempt, methodically seeking support on an issue they admitted excited little political passion and giving state university officials time to contact their members.

During the first weeks after Reagan's veto, House sponsors were non-committal about an override attempt, watching and waiting for developments in the Senate.

Some House supporters of S 684 believed that an override would be easier in the Senate, where each member had a direct interest in the bill, than in the House, where most members did not have a water research institute in their own districts.

The Override

The Republican-controlled Senate voted first because the bill originated there. During the vote March 21, all but one of the votes against the override came from Republicans — William L. Armstrong, Colo.; Howard H. Baker Jr., Tenn.; Thad Cochran, Miss.; John C. Danforth, Mo.; Robert Dole, Kan.; Pete V. Domenici, N.M.; Daniel J. Evans, Wash.; Richard G. Lugar, Ind.; Don Nickles, Okla.; Arlen

Specter, Pa.; and John Tower, Texas.

William Proxmire of Wisconsin was the lone Democrat opposing the override.

Evans was the sole speaker to defend the veto in the Senate. He emphasized the need for deficit reduction and said, "Now is the time to start."

Although the House vote on March 22 showed a comfortable 309-81 margin, backers of the override did not leave success to chance. Democratic leaders worked the doors during the voting, urging an override.

During the House debate, fiscal conservative Robert S. Walker, R-Pa., argued for budgetary restraint.

Minority Leader Robert H. Michel, R-Ill., confessed to "mixed emotions" about the "difficult choice" on a bill that brought funds to his district. But he said, "I have to say I agree with the president's intent."

They were overwhelmed, however, by both Democrats and Republicans who said the bill already met Reagan more than half way. Even Dick Cheney, R-Wyo., chairman of the Republican Policy Committee, urged an override. ∎

House Approves Revision of Clean Water Act

The House June 26 passed a compromise Clean Water Act revision (HR 3282), but the Senate failed to act on its own, less costly, version of the legislation (S 431).

The 405-11 House vote reflected a compromise that offered concessions to most of the interest groups contending over the bill. *(Vote 240, p. 74-H)*

But some of those groups remained dissatisfied, and the Reagan administration objected to the funding levels authorized in the bill — more than $24 billion in new authorizations, according to the Congressional Budget Office.

Among other things, the House bill more than doubled the current $2.4 billion annual authorization for sewage treatment plant construction grants — a program that Reagan sought to reduce or possibly eliminate.

Overdue for Action

The Clean Water Act, last overhauled in 1977 (PL 95-217), gave the Environmental Protection Agency (EPA) power to regulate discharges of industrial waste water into lakes and streams. It also provided federal funds to help cities and counties build sewage systems. *(1977 Almanac p. 697)*

Authorization for spending to carry out parts of the Clean Water Act lapsed in 1982, but Congress had funded enforcement through annual appropriations bills while it considered how to revise the law.

The House bill more than doubled authorized spending levels for the water pollution control program. For fiscal 1985, it set the total spending ceiling at more than $6.2 billion, compared with about $2.6 billion under existing law.

S 431, reported Sept. 21, 1983, by the Senate Environment and Public Works Committee (S Rept 98-233), set spending ceilings only slightly above current levels. *(1983 Almanac p. 360)*

House Committee Action

The House Public Works and Transportation Committee approved HR 3282 by voice vote May 10.

Before doing so, the panel stripped from the bill several provisions sought by environmentalists, studded it with local exemptions and grants for specific sewage treatment plants, took the sharp edges off of some regulatory provisions and added federal grants for sewers that could speed new housing construction.

Environmentalists called the final product "a bad bill, heavily laden with pork and special-interest bonuses," while industry groups called it "a very good bill."

Committee Changes

The Public Works Subcommittee on Water Resources on May 1 had approved a virtual doubling of federal funds available in grants and loans for local sewage system construction.

Ed Hopkins, a lobbyist for the Clean Water Action Project, an environmental group, said more sewage treatment was necessary, but that the committee had in effect reversed a number of reforms Congress made in the construction grants program in 1981. *(PL 97-117, 1981 Almanac p. 515)*

Among other things, the full committee made new "collector" sewers eligible for federal construction grants under the act. Collectors, the smallest local sewer lines, ran under residential streets. Environmentalists and budget-cutters had argued that federal money should go first to building plants to treat sewage already coming from existing lines. They said the collector grants amounted to a subsidy for new residential housing development that could further overload existing systems.

The committee also approved an amendment by Chairman James J. Howard, D-N.J., that imposed a ban on new sewer hookups in New York City if the city increased the amount of raw sewage it dumped into the Hudson River after March 15, 1986. New Jersey, downstream from the city's discharge, bore much of its brunt. New York was currently building new sewage treatment plants to alleviate the problem.

New York officials vehemently opposed Howard's amendment, but Rep. Geraldine A. Ferraro, D-N.Y., lost on a voice vote when she sought to strike it.

Among more than 20 specific amendments adopted by the committee was an extension of up to one year for the electroplating industry in meeting the stringent "best available technology" treatment requirements scheduled to take effect July 1, 1984.

House Floor Action

Before it passed HR 3282, the House adopted a substitute offered by Robert A. Roe, D-N.J., and 10 other amendments, all of which were approved by the floor managers for both the majority and the minority. Roe chaired the Public Works Subcommittee on Water Resources.

Roe's substitute embodied a compromise with environmentalists that headed off a planned barrage of amendments and averted a floor fight. The compromise, concluded June 20, defused most of the environmentalists' objections to the bill as reported June 6 by Public Works (H Rept 98-827).

New York Sewage

The only real debate in the House came on an amendment offered by Ferraro, which revisited the committee's dispute between the members of the New York delegation and their New Jersey neighbors across the Hudson River.

Ferraro wanted to delete language in the committee bill that set a March 15, 1986, deadline for New York City to limit the amount of raw sewage it discharged into the Hudson.

The committee's deadline was strongly backed by Roe and Howard, who complained that New York's untreated sewage washed up on the seashore beaches of their state.

Ferraro, however, noted that the city was building new sewage treatment plants to correct the problem, and complained New York was being singled out for "punitive" measures that could have a "chilling effect" on construction of new buildings there.

Ferraro's amendment was rejected by voice vote, but the New York sewage limit prompted Sen. Alfonse M. D'Amato, R-N.Y., to place a "hold" on any time agreement for floor action on the Senate bill, which contained no such provision.

Provisions

Major provisions of HR 3282 as passed by the House included the following:

● Authorized annual appropriations for fiscal 1985-88 for various water pollution control programs, including $160 million for general administration of the program by the EPA, $75 million for grants to state pollution control programs, $100 million for areawide (Section 208) water quality management, $100 million for the rural clean water program, $100 million to carry out interagency agreements and $30 million for the clean lakes program.

● Authorized appropriations eventually totaling more than $5 billion yearly to support construction of municipal sewage treatment systems. The authorized ceiling on direct construction grants was raised from the present $2.4 billion yearly to $2.9 billion in fiscal 1985 and to $3.4 billion for fiscal 1986-88. Another $1.6 billion yearly was authorized to create a new state-run revolving loan fund to support municipal sewage system construction.

● Raised the federal share of costs covered by municipal construction grants to 65 percent, from 55 percent, beginning Oct. 1, 1984.

● Raised to $500 million annually, from $200 million, the amount (beyond the total for construction grants) that could be spent correcting problems caused by overflows from combined storm-sanitary sewers into bays and estuaries.

● Extended the July 1, 1984, deadline for industries to comply with stricter wastewater treatment requirements — called Best Available Technology (BAT) and Best Conventional Technology (BCT). BAT controls for toxic pollutants would have to be in place 3½ years after EPA set guidelines for each particular industry. BCT controls for non-toxic pollutants were to be in place by July 1, 1987.

● Required EPA, in cooperation with the states, to list all "toxic hot spots" — waters where water-quality standards would not be achieved even with BAT and BCT pollution controls, and to issue a mandatory plan for achieving those standards within five years.

● Raised the maximum civil penalty for certain violations of the Clean Water Act from $10,000 to $20,000 per day.

● Toughened penalties for the worst criminal violations of the Clean Water Act, raising the maximum penalties from $50,000 per day and two years in jail to $100,000 per day and four years in jail, or both.

● Created a new program of federal grants to states to help them carry out EPA-approved plans for controlling "non-point source" pollution — that is, runoff from a broad area of land rather than discharges from individual pipes. The bill authorized $150 million yearly for fiscal 1985 through 1989 for grants covering 50 percent of state costs.

● Allowed companies that re-mine old coal mines to be legally responsible only for new pollution. Drainage from such old mines often contained acid, iron and manganese. The bill allowed EPA to issue discharge permits less stringent than for a new mining operation — but not to allow any more pollution than existed before the re-mining began.

● Authorized EPA to set a single compliance date for pre-treatment by "integrated facilities." Current law required EPA to set standards for pre-treatment of each category of industrial wastes before they were discharged into municipal sewage systems. "Integrated facilities" were those discharging two or more categories of wastes — and thus possibly subject to different deadlines.

● Extended the deadline for compliance with pre-treatment standards for the electroplating industry from June 30, 1984, to Dec. 31, 1984.

● Made saltwater lakes, as well as freshwater lakes, eligible for funding to reverse pollution under the clean lakes program. The bill also authorized $100 million yearly for fiscal 1985 through 1989 for federal grants to the states to control non-point source pollution under this program. When the old authorization expired at the end of fiscal 1982, the ceiling was $30 million yearly.

● Authorized grants to the states of up to $25 million yearly for fiscal 1985 through 1989 for restoring the quality of acid lakes.

● Extended the term of permits for industrial wastewater discharges from five years, the current term after which dischargers had to apply for new permits, to 10 years. But permits had to be modified promptly to ensure compliance with any new toxic pollution discharge limits set by EPA or water-quality standards set by states.

● Exempted from permit requirements the unpolluted discharges from ditches designed to channel stormwater around petroleum and mining operations, but required such operations to monitor the quality of such discharges yearly and report to EPA.

● Authorized $150 million yearly for fiscal 1985 through 1987 for grants by EPA to provide up to 50 percent of the costs of providing alternative drinking water supplies to communities whose groundwater had been contaminated.

● Tightened slightly the conditions under which EPA could grant a waiver of the requirement for secondary treatment of municipal wastewater discharged into deep ocean waters or estuaries with strong tidal currents.

● Authorized the EPA administrator to convene a federal-state-local "management conference" to develop plans for solving pollution problems in estuaries with multi-state drainage. Authorized federal grants for half the cost of carrying out such plans — with ceilings of $10 million for fiscal 1984, $30 million for 1985, $50 million for 1986, and $75 million for 1987 and 1988. Authorized $10 million annually for fiscal 1984-88 for administration and studies related to such plans.

● Re-established a special state-federal cleanup program for the Chesapeake Bay, authorizing $3 million for EPA and $10 million for grants to the states annually for fiscal 1985-88 to carry it out. Authorized $1.5 million annually for fiscal 1985-88 for grants to states to study pollution problems in Narragansett Bay.

● Directed EPA to make a grant to San Diego, Calif., of such sums as were needed to build treatment works for 60 million gallons per day of municipal sewage and industrial wastes emanating from Tijuana, Mexico, as well as wastewater from San Diego.

● Authorized $10 million annually from fiscal 1985-88 for a federal-state cleanup program for the New York and New Jersey Harbor area.

● Re-established a special office within EPA for Great Lakes studies and cleanup, with authority for carrying out cleanup plans under the U.S.-Canadian Great Lakes Water Quality Agreement of 1978. Authorized for this purpose various appropriations averaging $10 million annually for fiscal 1985 through 1990.

● Authorized $25 million, beginning in fiscal 1985, for a program to demonstrate the effectiveness of liming in restoring the quality of acidified lakes and watersheds, conducted by EPA with the U.S. Fish and Wildlife Service.

● Authorized $250 million, beginning in fiscal 1985, for a federal grant to pay 75 percent of the cost of building works to provide secondary treatment for the metropolitan Seattle, Wash., area.

● Authorized $7.5 million annually for fiscal 1985-89 for grants to states for 50 percent of the costs of carrying out groundwater quality protection programs.

● Established a National Groundwater Commission to study groundwater quality and quantity problems. The 19-member commission was to be made up of six members from the House, four members from the Senate, eight members appointed by the president, and the director of the Office of Technology Assessment. The commission's chairman was to be a House member appointed by the Speaker. After reporting to the president and Congress, the commission was to go out of existence on Jan. 1, 1987. For its work, $7 million was authorized. ∎

Drinking Water Bill Dies

The House Sept. 18 approved legislation overhauling the 1974 Safe Drinking Water Act, but attempts at reaching a compromise with the Senate failed and the bill died at adjournment.

Sponsors had drafted a compromise Oct. 5, hoping it could be accepted by the Senate as a substitute for a bill (S 2649) approved Sept. 26 by the Senate Environment and Public Works Committee.

But for differing reasons, Sens. Max Baucus, D-Mont., Alan K. Simpson, R-Wyo., and Steven D. Symms, R-Idaho, found the compromise unacceptable, while Henry A. Waxman, D-Calif., principal House negotiator, found Simpson's and Symms' proposals equally unacceptable.

Background

The Safe Drinking Water Act (PL 93-523) empowered the Environmental Protection Agency (EPA) to set national purity standards for drinking-water systems, to be enforced by the states or directly by the agency if states did not do so. The national standards were to be based on recommendations by the National Academy of Sciences about what levels of pollution were acceptable if human health were the only consideration. The EPA was to adjust these ideal levels to take feasibility and cost into account.

For several reasons, implementation of this ambitious scheme lagged. The academy, in 1977, declined to say how much of any given contaminant could be considered safe. The modestly funded water program was not always a top EPA priority, and agency efforts during the Carter administration to move ahead aggressively on several fronts were battered in court actions.

Rep. Dennis E. Eckart, D-Ohio, a cosponsor of the 1984 legislation, said he had learned that "you can lead the EPA to water but you can't make them regulate it." The bill, he added, "will make them do it."

Key sections of the House legislation set deadlines for EPA standard-setting; failure to meet the deadlines would expose the agency to lawsuits.

Other important sections barred many underground deposits of toxic wastes near underground sources of drinking water, and provided matching funds to protect these water sources. Rep. Edward R. Madigan, R-Ill., cosponsor of the bill, said it was expensive and often impossible to clean up pollution of these underground sources, and that prevention was much less costly.

The bill was a compromise measure, worked out by Eckart, Madigan, and environmental and industry groups.

House Committee, Floor Action

By voice vote, the House Energy and Commerce Committee approved the bill (HR 5959 — H Rept 98-1034) Sept. 13 after rejecting amendments to lower its funding levels and drop new programs to protect underground sources of drinking water from pollution.

The Reagan administration opposed the measure. In a Sept. 14 letter to House members, the Office of Management and Budget (OMB) objected to the bill's requirements for federal approval of state groundwater plans, its expansion of the basic drinking water regulatory program and its expense — 300 percent more than the president's fiscal 1985 budget request for the program, according to OMB.

Despite such objections, the House passed the legislation Sept. 18 by 366-27. *(Vote 353, p. 108-H)*

House Bill: Major Provisions

As passed by the House, HR 5959 included the following major provisions:

● Required EPA, within 12 months of enactment, to set standards (maximum contaminant levels or MCLs) for 14 volatile organic chemicals listed in a 1982 EPA notice as potentially subject to regulation. Also required EPA, within 36 months, to set MCLs for 50 organic, inorganic, microbial and radionuclide contaminants of drinking water listed in September 1983. Also required EPA, within 36 months, to set MCLs for other substances that the EPA administrator believed could be hazardous to health. EPA could decline to set a standard by the deadline if it did not find enough evidence to suggest an adverse health effect from a contaminant.

● Changed the designation of the health-related, ideal contaminant "levels" to "goals." (The change was meant to reduce public confusion between the goals and MCLs.)

● Specified that an MCL be as close to the health goal as "feasible," defining feasible as using the "best available technology" or other means, as determined by EPA. The bill cited granular activated carbon technology (GAC) as an example of best available technology. This language was considered a more demanding standard than existing law, which defined feasible as using generally available technology. (A 1978 EPA plan to require large water systems to use GAC, which removed a range of organic chemical contaminants, failed because of industry opposition.)

● Directed the EPA, with the advice of its Science Advisory Board, to establish the recommended, health-related contaminant levels (goals), on which the MCLs were based.

● Required the EPA to require public water systems to monitor water for unregulated contaminants at least once every five years; required systems to make test results available to customers.

● Revised authorities for enforcing water standards, by setting deadlines for EPA action, permitting EPA to use administrative instead of court orders for enforcement, permitting more flexibility in requirements that systems notify customers of violations, and making other changes.

● Made tampering or threatening to tamper with a public water system a federal crime, punishable with fines and imprisonment.

● Barred underground disposal of hazardous waste above or into a formation containing a source of drinking water. The prohibition applied to disposal in toxic waste "injection wells" whose metal-lined bores were within one-quarter mile of the water source.

● Permitted injection of contaminated groundwater into the aquifer (a type of underground water source) from which it came, if the EPA found the injection to be part of an acceptable cleanup of toxic materials as mandated by federal statute.

● Required, within 18 months of enactment, that EPA require regular monitoring of underground drinking water sources; required a cooperative EPA-state survey of all hazardous waste injection wells in the United States.

● Required states to adopt plans, approved by EPA, to protect underground sources of drinking water from contamination that was harmful to health. Defines "underground source of drinking water" as one that could supply drinking water to a public water system using economically feasible and advanced treatment methods.

● Authorized a federal-state-local program to protect aquifers that were sole sources of drinking water, with matching funds for planning and implementation, and new enforcement authorities. Among other things, a polluter of a sole-source aquifer could be required to provide another source of drinking water.

● Authorized a total of $216 million annually for fiscal years 1986-89 for various safe drinking water programs. The total included funding for a new $10 million-a-year program to finance technical assistance to small water systems, and new authorizations totaling $35 million a year in matching funds for planning and implementation of programs designed to protect sole-source aquifers.

Senate Committee Action

Eight days after the House passed HR 5959, the Senate Environment and Public Works Committee on Sept. 26 agreed unanimously to report its own version (S 2649 — S Rept 98-641) of the legislation.

Sen. Dave Durenberger, R-Minn., sponsor of the Senate version, warned that a single member could easily sink the bill in the short time before Congress adjourned. "We should not ask which politician can stand behind the toughest bill for the next two weeks. . . . Our job is to fix a law that is central to human health but which works poorly

as currently structured," Durenberger told his Senate Environment and Public Works Subcommittee on Toxic Substances and Environmental Oversight at its Sept. 24 markup of the bill.

But Waxman, a key House figure, said he would not accept the Senate plan, which skirted some of OMB's objections. "I'd rather have no bill at all," said Waxman, who chaired the House Energy and Commerce Health Subcommittee, which had jurisdiction over the legislation.

Both Waxman and Eckart, a cosponsor of the House bill, said that OMB's attack on the bill surprised them, because officials of EPA, which administered the law, had not raised strong objections to the House legislation.

The House version was worked out in private sessions among environmentalist and water industry officials, Eckart, Madigan and Waxman. EPA officials were consulted on technical questions and, according to Waxman, were "quite sympathetic to our position."

"What you're seeing," Eckart said, "is part of a fallout between Stockman and Ruckelshaus over who calls the shots in the administration on environmental policy." (David A. Stockman was OMB director; William D. Ruckelshaus was EPA administrator.) An OMB spokesman declined to comment on this interpretation.

What Both Bills Did

Both bills for the first time set specific deadlines for EPA to establish national standards on contaminants. Both empowered EPA to order compliance directly; existing law authorized only the more cumbersome process of suing violators. Both bills required more checking of drinking water sources for contamination, and both provided new funding for technical assistance to small water systems.

The bills made tampering with public water systems a federal crime, barred injection of hazardous wastes into underground sources of drinking water, except in certain circumstances, and authorized new protection programs for one type of underground drinking water source, aquifers that were sole sources of water for a community or region.

The Major Differences

The bills were far from identical, however.

The House bill, for instance, would create a $50 million-a-year program to protect underground sources of drinking water, with state planning and local implementation. There was growing evidence of pollution of these underground water formations, which provide about half the nation's drinking water. Cleansing them was considered impossible, or inordinately expensive.

The House groundwater plan drew a special OMB objection, and Durenberger indicated that it could not win a majority of votes in the Environment Committee. There was no equivalent in the Senate bill. Durenberger stressed his personal support for a groundwater plan, but he said that it "would mean the end of the drinking water amendments . . . and that seems to me too high a price."

While both bills included a special protection program for sole-source aquifers, Waxman said the $15 million-a-year Senate demonstration program was too little compared with the $35-million-a-year House plan.

Some of the fiercest disagreements were over bill language on such matters as EPA standard-setting, the water-cleansing technology that EPA could require, the underground injection ban, and the agency's use of administrative orders for compliance — the new alternative to lawsuits provided by the bill. Waxman said the Senate bill was no better than existing law, although environmentalist groups who disliked the Senate plan said that overstated the case.

The House trigger for standard-setting on specific contaminants was "sufficient evidence to constitute a rational basis to believe" the substance could harm human health. The Senate bill relied on the wording in existing law, which also referred to health effects but appeared to require much stronger proof to support agency action. Durenberger said he was still trying to construe the special meaning of the House language.

Another difference was that the House bill required EPA to use its power to issue administrative orders in specified circumstances, while the Senate bill gave the agency discretion — as EPA preferred — to decide when to issue such orders.

Durenberger said that EPA wanted enforcement flexibility so that it did not have to respond to minor violations by the nation's 60,000 public water systems.

Still, Sen. George J. Mitchell, D-Maine, said he found it "somewhat disconcerting to hear someone charged with enforcing the law ask that they not be required to do so."

Compromise Efforts Fail

By Oct. 4, House and Senate negotiators had informally worked out most of their differences, but some sticking points remained.

Negotiators agreed to omit from a final bill an ambitious new program to protect underground sources of drinking water from pollution. The underground water plan, part of the House-passed bill, drew objections from the Reagan administration and a number of members of the Senate Environment Committee.

Retained was a smaller program, approved by both chambers, for protecting one type of underground source, sole-source aquifers.

The negotiators kept relatively high program funding levels that had drawn administration objections, and they ironed out most differences on regulatory language.

The major remaining difference was a Simpson amendment in the Senate bill that permitted appeals from cases involving the law's national regulations to be brought in U.S. appeals courts around the nation, instead of restricting these cases to the federal appeals court in Washington, D.C., as existing law required.

Simpson, according to an aide, believed that the appeals should be heard in the regions affected by a given dispute.

Another disagreement was on the stronger health-related language for setting water purity standards that appeared in the House bill and the proposed compromise. Waxman and Baucus wanted that language, while Symms wanted to retain language in existing law, according to aides.

Lobbyists for environmentalists expressed regret at losing the legislation, but claimed that both the judicial-review amendment and existing health standards would cause lengthy delays in setting national drinking water standards. Such delays, they said, would defeat the basic purpose of the legislation, which was to force quick standard-setting by EPA.

Advocates of legislation to strengthen the Safe Drinking Water Act vowed that they would introduce their proposals again in 1985, after the 99th Congress got under way. ∎

Ocean Dumping Bill Dies

For the third year in a row, the House passed a bill to overhaul the program regulating the dumping of wastes in the ocean, but the Senate failed to act on the legislation.

The House Oct. 1 suspended the rules and passed a bill (HR 4829 — H Rept 98-766, Parts I and II) that revised the ocean dumping permit program and called for an end to the dumping of municipal sludge on a blighted sea-bottom just 12 miles off the New York-New Jersey coast.

As passed by the House, HR 4829 reauthorized Title I ("The Ocean Dumping Act") of the Marine Protection, Research and Sanctuaries Act of 1972 (PL 92-532) for fiscal 1985-87 at spending levels of $4.25 million annually. *(Congress and the Nation Vol. III, p. 798)*

That law set up procedures for the Environmental Protection Agency (EPA) to regulate the dumping of waste in the ocean and prohibited the dumping of "harmful" municipal sludge. HR 4829 amended the Ocean Dumping Act to tighten its requirements and set new schedules for EPA to carry them out.

The House passed similar bills in 1983 and 1982, but the Senate did not act on them. The Senate held no hearings in 1984 on the legislation. *(1983 Almanac p. 360)*

The dump site affected by HR 4829, the New York Bight apex, was only about 90 feet deep and annually received millions of tons of the solids (sludge) removed from the sewage of New York City and other municipalities. The bill outlawed dumping there in 18 months or whenever another site became available.

Because of this provision, New York senators put a "hold" on the bill when it reached the Senate, and the legislation died in the adjournment rush.

The EPA was already in the process of designating a new dumping site 106 miles offshore, a move some municipalities had resisted because it was more expensive to barge the sludge that far offshore. The House bill authorized federal funds to reimburse the municipalities for the excess costs of moving to the farther site — 100 percent of the excess cost for fiscal 1986, and 50 percent of the excess cost for 1987. ∎

Striped Bass Bill Cleared

The House Oct. 11 cleared for the president a bill (HR 5492 — PL 98-613) to conserve dwindling stocks of Atlantic striped bass.

The bill encouraged states to carry out a plan adopted by the Atlantic States Marine Fisheries Commission, which set a 24-inch minimum size for striped bass caught in the ocean and a 14-inch limit for fish caught in state waters. If a state did not reduce its annual catch by 55 percent, the secretary of commerce could declare a moratorium on striped bass fishing in that state.

HR 5492 affected all Atlantic coastal states north of South Carolina.

Recreational landings of the popular fish had dropped from about 9.3 million pounds in 1960 to less than 556,000 pounds in 1980. Overfishing and pollution were suspected as causes.

Legislative Action

HR 5492 was reported Sept. 17 from the House Merchant Marine and Fisheries Committee (H Rept 98-1029) and passed by the House Oct. 4.

The House adopted amendments putting an 18-month sunset on the bill's provisions and authorizing $1.04 million for the Ohio National Wildlife Conservation Area.

It rejected, 98-307, an amendment offered by Herbert H. Bateman, R-Va., that would have made discretionary, rather than mandatory, the moratorium to be imposed on states failing to reduce their catch by the required percentages. *(Vote 390, p. 120-H)*

In the Senate, the bill was amended and passed Oct. 11. Final action came when the House agreed to the Senate amendment, which deleted language requiring study of acid rain as a possible cause of striped bass population decline.

That amendment was offered by Sen. John H. Chafee, R-R.I., chairman of the Environment Subcommittee on Environmental Pollution, after Minority Leader Robert C. Byrd, D-W.Va., objected to the acid rain language. Byrd's state was a major producer of high-sulfur coal, the burning of which was believed to be a principal cause of acid rain. ∎

Marine Mammal Protection

In the session that began June 27, Congress cleared for the president's signature a bill (HR 4997 — PL 98-364) to reauthorize the Marine Mammal Protection Act for four years and renew limits on the accidental killing of porpoises in tuna fishing.

Final action came when the House agreed to amendments the Senate made when it passed the bill earlier that day. House had originally passed the bill June 5.

The Marine Mammal Protection Act (PL 92-522) was originally enacted in 1972. It set up a management, research and regulatory program to protect saltwater animals such as whales, porpoises, seals, polar bears and walruses. Congress had last reauthorized the law (PL 97-58) in 1981. *(1981 Almanac p. 523)*

The law gave the Commerce Department responsibility for preventing depletion of whales, dolphins, porpoises, sea lions and seals, and the Interior Department responsibility for polar bears, walruses, sea otters, manatees and dugongs.

Provisions

As cleared, HR 4997 authorized funding for fiscal 1985-88 for the Commmerce Department, the Interior Department, and the Marine Mammal Commission, which carried out the law to keep populations of marine mammals from being depleted.

It also froze the current 20,500-animal limit on porpoises that could be accidentally taken by U.S. fishermen in the eastern Pacific, and banned import of fish products from nations whose standards were less protective.

Because of improvements in fishing gear and techniques, the actual annual take of porpoises by tuna fishermen was well below the limit. It dropped from an estimated 386,000 in 1972 to some 8,258 in 1983.

The bill renewed for 18 months, until Dec. 31, 1985, fishing agreements with the Soviet Union and Poland.

The Senate amendments added an extension of the existing fishing agreement with the European Economic Community, until a new agreement was reached or until Sept. 30, 1984, whichever was sooner.

Other Senate amendments incorporated into the final version authorized $5 million a year to establish a Coastal

Resources Research and Development Institute in Oregon, adjusted a flood insurance dispute in Cameron Parish, La., clarified laws providing compensation to U.S. fishermen whose vessels were seized by foreign governments under laws not recognized by the United States, regularized safety-related inspection and manning requirements for U.S. fish processing and fish tender vessels, and provided for transportation of cargo to remote communities in Alaska.

Legislative History

The House Merchant Marine and Fisheries Committee approved HR 4997 by voice vote May (H Rept 98-758).

The House passed it June 5, and the Senate amended it and passed it June 27. ∎

Coastal Revenue Sharing

Legislation (S 2463) to give states a share of revenues from federal offshore oil and gas drilling leases fell victim to Senate opposition the week of Oct. 8.

A conference report (H Rept 98-1006) on the measure to set up a $300 million fund for grants to coastal states and territories was adopted by the House Sept. 13 by a vote of 312-94. *(Vote 347, p. 106-H)*

But when the report was brought to the Senate floor Oct. 9, Sens. John C. Danforth, R-Mo., and Dave Durenberger, R-Minn., indicated they were prepared to block it, by filibuster if necessary. With Congress in a hurry to adjourn, there was no time to overcome their opposition.

Background

A major source of federal revenue, offshore oil and gas leasing, exploration and production was expected to bring some $6 billion into the Treasury in fiscal 1985.

Although states shared 50-50 with the federal government the revenue produced as a result of energy and mineral leasing on federal lands within their borders, they received nothing from leases located more than three miles off their shores — a discrepancy that coastal states considered unfair.

The states contended that offshore drilling imposed expensive burdens on them, and that the federal government should help pay those costs.

But the Reagan administration strongly opposed the revenue-sharing proposal, calling it an unwarranted drain on the Treasury. It also criticized the suggested allocation formula for providing "windfall payments" to states that had no offshore leasing activity or that opposed offshore leasing.

The House passed a similar revenue-sharing bill in 1982, but that measure also died in the Senate. *(1982 Almanac p. 448)*

Legislative History

The House passed its version of the revenue-sharing bill (HR 5 — H Rept 98-206) on Sept. 14, 1983, by a comfortable 301-93 margin. *(1983 Almanac p. 359)*

The Senate Commerce Committee approved its own revenue-sharing measure (S 800 — S Rept 98-112) on April 21, 1983, but that bill never reached the floor.

Instead, on June 21, 1984, the Senate passed S 2463 (S Rept 98-391), a fisheries bill having nothing to do with offshore leasing revenues.

The House June 26 attached the revenue-sharing provisions to S 2463, passed the amended bill and asked for a conference with the Senate. On June 28, the Senate agreed to go to conference.

Conferees reached an accord Aug. 8 on a compromise version of the legislation, which would have divided about $300 million annually among 30 states, four territories and Puerto Rico.

Provisions

Under the conference plan, 4 percent of revenues from federal drilling leases, up to a maximum of $300 million the first year, was to be distributed to the states as block grants. Small increases were allowed in future years, based on a three-year average of revenues to smooth out year-to-year variations.

Funds were to be allocated according to a five-part formula based on shoreline mileage, population and energy activities. The largest recipients would have been Louisiana, with $45 million; Alaska, with $36.3 million; and California, with $23.4 million.

States bordering the Great Lakes were made eligible as well as those along the coasts. Each state could receive a minimum of 1.62 percent and a maximum of 15 percent of the total.

States could lose a portion of their share, however, if they did not have a federally approved Coastal Zone Management plan, a provision that currently would have penalized Texas $4.77 million, Illinois $4.26 million, Ohio $5.3 million, Georgia $2.46 million, Indiana $4.56 million and Minnesota $4.56 million.

Administration Objections

No sooner had conferees reached an agreement than the administration denounced the bill and threatened a veto — a move that irritated those involved in the conference, since it came only hours after members agreed to delay filing their report until September in hopes that the White House would compromise.

Sen. Ted Stevens, R-Alaska, said he had a draft of the administration letter in his pocket at the conference but did not show it to other members because it would only have angered them.

Stevens himself seemed irked by the letter to conference leaders. Although it was on the stationery of Interior Secretary William P. Clark and also was signed by Energy Secretary Donald P. Hodel and Treasury Secretary Donald T. Regan, Stevens put the blame for it on the fourth signer, Office of Management and Budget Director David A. Stockman.

"Stockman is totally unrealistic," said Stevens. "He seems to believe the federal government will get all the revenues without any sharing."

Senate Inaction

As it developed, the administration had enough support in the Senate to block final action on S 2463.

Even though the House easily adopted the conference report, the threat of a filibuster sank the legislation in the Senate.

"The smell of pork is in the air," said Durenberger, who called the measure "a brand new entitlement program that will actually increase the deficit by over $300 million in perpetuity."

Danforth criticized the bill's managers for trying to pass a conference report on a subject that had never been considered on the Senate floor. ∎

Control of Offshore Leasing

Legislation to give states more control over oil and gas leasing off their shores won approval in a Senate committee in 1984 but failed to reach the floor of either chamber.

The Senate bill (S 2324) and a companion House measure (HR 4589) were designed to overturn a Jan. 11 Supreme Court ruling that effectively denied any role to states in the process leading to awards of federal offshore oil and gas drilling leases.

S 2324 was approved by a 9-7 vote May 8 and reported June 13 by the Senate Commerce Committee (S Rept 98-512), but it went no further.

In the House, the Merchant Marine Subcommittee on Oceanography approved HR 4589 by an 8-2 vote on May 3, but the full committee never acted on the legislation.

The Reagan administration vigorously opposed both versions of the legislation.

The Court Ruling

By a 5-4 vote, the high court ruled in the case of *Secretary of the Interior v. California* that states could not block federal offshore lease sales by arguing that the sales were inconsistent with state plans for protecting their coastal areas. *(Court ruling, p. 15-A)*

The ruling removed a major obstacle to the aggressive offshore leasing program initiated by former Interior Secretary James G. Watt, despite the protests of environmentalists and objections from several coastal states.

But Watt's successor, William P. Clark, during the remainder of the year backed off considerably from Watt's oft-criticized leasing program, slowing its pace and smoothing relationships with the states.

The court case involved a clash between two federal laws. The 1972 Coastal Zone Management Act (CZMA) assured states that once they won federal approval for plans for managing and protecting their coastal areas, any federal action "directly affecting" those coastal zones would have to be consistent with the state plans insofar as possible. *(1972 Almanac p. 970)*

Six years later, Congress amended the Outer Continental Shelf (OCS) Lands Act to overhaul federal programs for leasing OCS lands for development of oil and gas resources. *(1978 Almanac p. 668)*

But the 1978 amendments did not end the frequent conflict between the federal interest in producing more energy and the state interest in protecting fishing and recreation industries along local shores.

While he did not start the conflict, Watt fueled the flames by proposing in April 1981 a five-year plan to offer up to one billion offshore acres, nearly the entire OCS, for oil and gas leasing. Watt submitted that plan to Congress for a 60-day review on May 11, 1982, and when Congress took no action to block it, put it into effect on July 21, 1982. *(1982 Almanac p. 449)*

When the administration moved in 1981 to sell leases on 115 tracts in the Santa Maria basin off California, the state invoked the provision of CZMA requiring federal actions to be consistent with an adopted state management plan. Both a federal district court and a federal appeals court sided with the state, blocking the lease sale.

Six other states filed separate court challenges to offshore leasing off their coasts — Alaska, Maine, Massachusetts, New Jersey, New York and North Carolina.

However, the Supreme Court ruled that the Interior

Department did not have to make any "consistency" finding under CZMA before selling offshore oil and gas leases. Such determinations were required only at later stages of the development process, when exploration drilling and production began, the court said.

Justice Sandra Day O'Connor wrote the opinion, joined by Justices Lewis F. Powell Jr., William H. Rehnquist, Byron R. White and Chief Justice Warren E. Burger.

O'Connor said OCS lease sales were not actions "directly affecting" a state's coastal zone, adding that states did retain "considerable authority to veto inconsistent exploration or development and production plans."

Justices John Paul Stevens, William J. Brennan Jr., Thurgood Marshall and Harry A. Blackmun dissented sharply. The "activities" of offshore leasing and actual development could not be neatly separated, Stevens wrote, because "development is the expected consequence of leasing; if it were not, purchasers would never commit millions of dollars to the acquisition of leases."

Stevens said that it was "directly contrary to the legislative scheme not to make a consistency determination at the earliest possible point. If exploration and development of the leased tracts cannot be squared with the requirements of the CZMA, it would be in everyone's interest to determine that as early as possible."

States such as Louisiana, Alaska and Texas had largely welcomed drilling off their shores, because petroleum plays a major role in their economies. But others had shunned it to some degree — including California, Massachusetts, Florida and Oregon, where petroleum was not as large a portion of the economy, where fishing and recreation were also economically important, and where population was often dense.

Although Congress did not block Watt's five-year OCS plan, it was clearly unhappy with the administration's policies and for the third year in a row included language in the annual Interior Department appropriations bill banning offshore lease sales in specific tracts. *(Interior appropriations; p. 378)*

House Subcommittee Action

The House Merchant Marine and Fisheries Subcommittee on Oceanography approved HR 4589 on May 3 by an 8-2 vote.

The subcommittee sent the measure to the full committee after adopting a substitute offered by Norman E. D'Amours, D-N.H., the bill's sponsor and chairman of the subcommittee.

As approved, the bill required federal agencies conducting activities "significantly affecting" a state's coastal zone to do so in a manner consistent with policies of an approved state coastal zone management program.

Senate Committee Action

The Senate Commerce, Science, and Transportation Committee approved S 2324 on May 8.

The 9-7 vote for the bill came over the strenuous objections of oil-state Sens. Russell B. Long, D-La., and Ted Stevens, R-Alaska, and flew in the face of veto threats from the Reagan administration.

Committee Chairman Bob Packwood, R-Ore., a primary sponsor of S 2324, substituted an amended version he hoped would soften the opposition. But the administration only stepped up its fight against the bill in the days before the Senate markup.

As approved by the Senate committee, S 2324 required federal agencies conducting activities "significantly affecting" a state's coastal zone to do so in a manner consistent with "enforceable mandatory policies" of an approved state coastal zone management program. Sponsors said the covered federal activities included offshore petroleum leasing.

Packwood's amendment excluded from second-guessing by the states those federal actions affecting economic, social and aesthetic conditions in the coastal zone. The bill applied only to federal actions affecting coastal "natural resources or land or water uses."

Interior Secretary Clark said the administration opposed both the House and Senate versions of the legislation. He told House committee leaders in an April 25 letter that "if it is enrolled, we will recommend to the president that he disapprove the bill."

Clark argued that the bill was "unnecessary" and that it had "the potential for adversely affecting the activities conducted by virtually every agency of the federal government."

Packwood insisted the bill would have no drastic effects — that it would simply return the legal situation to what it was before the Supreme Court's decision. "Civilization didn't end" under the previous legal interpretation, he reminded the committee.

Moreover, Packwood said, "this in no way gives states any veto authority," because under the Coastal Zone Management Act, the secretary of commerce had to approve state coastal plans or any change in them.

"The principal objections I have heard have been from the oil and gas industry," Packwood said.

Long, more sympathetic to the petroleum industry, said the measure might produce an energy shortage: "Until we can feel more certain that this measure won't impede energy development, I won't be able to vote for it," he said.

Stevens said the bill "uses litigation to hold up development.... There won't be any leasing in California or Florida or Delaware — and what does that mean? It means that they'll do it all up my way."

Sen. Slade Gorton, R-Wash., gave Packwood the key vote needed to report the bill. Gorton said he could not support the measure unless it was amended to exempt from the consistency requirement all federal actions under the Magnuson Act (the Fishery Conservation and Management Act of 1976 — PL 94-265, as later amended). *(1976 Almanac p. 234)*

That law set up regional Fishery Management Councils comprised of state, fishing industry and other representatives, whose plans, once approved by the commerce secretary, would have had status as federal actions.

Gorton insisted on exempting all activities under the Magnuson Act, which authorized international agreements on commercial fishing quotas and territories. He called the agreements "vitally important to the fishing community in my state," and fretted that the coastal zone consistency requirement could allow a single state to upset the precarious balance of interests in the international agreements.

Packwood somewhat reluctantly allowed Gorton's amendment to be adopted without objection. ∎

Wetlands Loan Extended

Congress Oct. 4 cleared for the president a bill (HR 5271 — PL 98-548) extending for 10 years the Wetlands Loan Act, which helped fund preservation of waterfowl breeding and feeding grounds.

The bill was cleared when agreement looked unlikely on a more ambitious wetlands protection measure (HR 3082) that had been passed by the House but not the Senate. *(Story, this page)*

Facing an impasse on HR 3082 in 1983, Congress had enacted a one-year extension (HR 2395 — PL 98-200) of the Wetlands Loan Act. *(1983 Almanac p. 349)*

HR 5271 extended until Sept. 30, 1994, the authorization for appropriations under the Wetlands Loan Act, which was originally passed in 1961 (PL 87-383). As later amended, that law authorized $200 million in appropriations for federal acquisition of wetlands to preserve them from draining, filling and subsequent development. *(Congress and the Nation Vol. I, p. 1067)*

Approximately $46 million of that authorization, which was to expire Sept. 30, 1984, remained unappropriated. Under the law, the appropriations were considered a "loan" against future revenues from the federal "duck stamps" that hunters had to buy. The duck stamp funds currently went directly for wetlands conservation. Once the loan expired, however, 75 percent of duck stamp receipts had to go into the Treasury to repay the loan.

HR 5271 delayed the beginning of repayment until Oct. 1, 1994.

HR 3082 (H Rept 98-440, Parts I-IV), passed by the House Sept. 20, would have forgiven the loan altogether. Because it was more controversial and the Senate's schedule was crowded, the House Merchant Marine and Fisheries Committee put forward HR 5271 (H Rept 98-705) as a fallback position.

The House passed the bill Sept. 24, the Senate amended it in the session that began Oct. 3 and the House agreed to the Senate amendments Oct. 4, clearing the bill.

One of the Senate amendments was technical, while the others established a Connecticut Coastal National Wildlife Refuge and an Atchafalaya National Wildlife Refuge in Louisiana. ∎

Wetlands Protection Bill

The House Sept. 20 passed a bill (HR 3082) that expanded funding for protection of the nation's dwindling wetlands, but the bill died — largely because of controversy over an unrelated provision involving jetties at Oregon Inlet in North Carolina.

Instead, Congress cleared a separate, simpler bill (HR 5271 — PL 98-548) that extended for 10 years the Wetlands Loan Act, which helped fund preservation of wetlands. *(Story, p. 336)*

Background

For more than 20 years, Congress had financed federal purchase of wetlands through the Wetlands Loan Act of 1961 (PL 87-383). As later amended, the loan act authorized $200 million in appropriations for federal acquisition of wetlands to preserve them from draining, filling and subsequent development. The money had to be repaid to the Treasury with revenues from Migratory Bird Conservation Stamps ("duck stamps") that waterfowl hunters were required to purchase. *(Congress and the Nation Vol. I, p. 1067)*

Without action by Congress, the loan act would have expired Sept. 30, 1983. Facing an impasse on HR 3082 in 1983, Congress enacted a one-year extension (HR 2395 — PL 98-200) of the law. *(1983 Almanac p. 349)*

HR 5271, cleared in 1984, extended until Sept. 30, 1994, the authorization for appropriations under that law.

Senate Committee Action

Two Senate committees in 1984 approved legislation (S 1329) that would have forgiven the wetlands loan entirely. But the measure never reached the Senate floor.

The Environment and Public Works Committee reported the bill Jan. 26 (S Rept 98-349) and the Energy and Natural Resources Committee followed suit April 6 (S Rept 98-383).

Before ordering its version reported by 15-2, Senate Energy adopted two amendments offered by Malcolm Wallop, R-Wyo.

One of them, adopted 10-4, deleted provisions setting up new entrance fees at federal wildlife refuges.

The other, adopted by voice vote, authorized $75 million annually for wetlands acquisition, subject to appropriation by Congress. The Environment Committee had wanted to take that amount from the billions in offshore oil revenues pumped each year into the Land and Water Conservation Fund, and to transfer it automatically into the Migratory Bird Conservation Fund, which is a permanent appropriation.

House Action

The House Merchant Marine and Fisheries Committee reported HR 3082 in 1983, but the bill was referred to two other committees — Interior and Insular Affairs, and Public Works and Transportation. They did not complete work on it until March 6, 1984, and Merchant Marine then filed a supplemental report Sept. 11 (H Rept 98-440, Parts I-IV).

The bill reached the House floor later that month, and it was passed Sept. 20 by a vote of 351-45. *(Vote 360, p. 110-H)*

Oregon Inlet: N.C. Jetties

The House rejected, 194-203, an amendment by John F. Seiberling, D-Ohio, to strip off a rider authorizing the use of lands from the Cape Hatteras National Seashore and the Pea Island National Wildlife Refuge to build jetties along the Oregon Inlet, N.C. The jetties were meant to keep the inlet, which ran between two barrier islands, from filling up with sand. *(Vote 359, p. 110-H)*

The Oregon Inlet project was backed by Walter B. Jones, D-N.C., chairman of the Merchant Marine Committee, and by other members from North Carolina. The project was meant to help fishermen who needed year-round access to fishing grounds in the open sea. It was authorized by Congress in 1970, but the Interior Department had blocked use of adjacent land for the project.

The jetty project was expected to cost at least $94.5 million to build and another $4 million annually to maintain.

Environmentalists said costs would be even higher — as much as $600 million over the project's 50-year life. They argued the jetties could disrupt natural currents along that part of the coast, causing destruction of other parts of the barrier islands. They preferred to continue the current program of dredging the channel in Oregon Inlet.

The House vote keeping the rider on HR 3082 complicated the measure's chances for approval in the Senate, where objections from environmentalist allies could block action in the waning days of the session. That was why the separate loan act extension was moved instead.

Provisions

As passed by the House, HR 3082:

● Authorized the interior secretary to establish admission fees at certain national wildlife refuges to augment the Migratory Bird Conservation Fund, which was used for wetlands conservation.

● Increased the price of Migratory Bird Conservation Stamps ("duck stamps") in steps from $7.50 to $15.00 by fiscal 1988.

● Established a new Wetlands Conservation Fund to receive $75 million annually in fiscal 1985-94. The money was to be transferred from the Land and Water Conservation Fund, which was derived mainly from offshore oil and gas revenues.

● Authorized the Interior Department, subject to annual appropriations, to allocate up to two-thirds of the funds from the Wetlands Conservation Fund to the states for conservation and acquisition of wetlands.

● Authorized the Interior Department to use the remainder for acquisition of wetlands to be included in the national wildlife refuge system.

● Required states, to be eligible for money from the fund, to have a wetlands conservation plan or project approved by the Interior Department.

● Required the Interior Department to develop a national plan, in consultation with the states, ranking wetlands conservation projects in order of priority.

● Set a timetable for the Interior Department to finish its national wetlands inventory and mapping program. For that purpose, it authorized annual appropriations of $15.4 million for fiscal 1984-87, $7.65 million for fiscal 1988-94, and $900,000 for fiscal 1995-96.

● Required the Interior Department to submit to Congress by Sept. 30, 1985, a report on the causes of destruction of wetlands and ways to preserve them.

● Forgave the obligation of the Migratory Bird Conservation Fund to repay about $150 million in "advance" appropriations authorized under the Wetlands Loan Act.

● Authorized the use of national park and refuge land for a jetty project at Oregon Inlet, N.C. ■

EPA Research Authorization

The House Feb. 9 passed a bill (HR 2899) authorizing Environmental Protection Agency (EPA) research programs for fiscal 1984-85, but the legislation died in the Senate.

Instead, the research programs and the rest of EPA's activities were continued through provisions in the fiscal 1985 appropriations bill (HR 5713 — PL 98-371) for the Department of Housing and Urban Development and independent agencies. *(Story, p. 415)*

The vote on House passage of HR 2899 was 362-9. *(Vote 23, p. 8-H)*

The Reagan administration Feb. 2 expressed opposition to the bill, objecting that it contained too much money with too many strings attached. President Reagan in October 1982 vetoed on similar grounds an EPA authorization bill for fiscal 1983-84. *(1982 Almanac p. 440)*

There was some confusion over the administration's position prior to the House vote — with differing versions coming from EPA and the Office of Management and Budget (OMB).

This fueled charges by a key House Democrat that OMB had undercut the position EPA had taken in discussions with the Science and Technology Committee. The committee reported HR 2899 (H Rept 98-212) in 1983 and later developed certain amendments to it after negotiations with EPA.

"We thought we had an understanding in good faith on both sides," said James H. Scheuer, D-N.Y., who chaired the Science subcommittee that handled the bill. "But EPA had the rug pulled out from under them by the real environmental policy makers in this administration — OMB."

OMB never told the Science Committee of its opposition, according to staff, but instead notified the Rules Committee in a statement dated Feb. 2.

Many at EPA were surprised at the OMB move. OMB had not, according to one source, consulted EPA about the bill and had not informed EPA before it took its position.

White House and OMB officials denied that. "EPA very definitely was consulted," said OMB spokesman Edwin L. Dale.

One EPA source later said OMB had notified the agency but the notice had not been forwarded properly once it reached the agency.

Amendments Approved

Before final passage, the House adopted by voice vote nine amendments to the bill, five of which were offered by Science Committee Chairman Don Fuqua, D-Fla.

One of those amendments dropped from the committee-approved bill a requirement aimed at balancing out the interest groups represented on the EPA Science Advisory Board, which critics feared would tilt toward industry. This provision was the only one opposed by the administration that was deleted before the House passed the bill.

Other adopted amendments adjusted authorizations for individual research programs without changing overall funding totals.

Also adopted was an amendment by Dan Glickman, D-Kan., earmarking not less than 25 percent of hazardous waste research funds for study of feasible alternatives to land disposal.

Funding Levels

As passed by the House, HR 2899 authorized total appropriations of $283.5 million for fiscal 1984 and $297.7 million for fiscal 1985.

Reagan had asked $205.5 million for fiscal 1984 and $278.0 million for fiscal 1985.

The House rejected, in a 4-10 standing vote, an amendment offered by Larry Winn Jr., R-Kan., to cut the fiscal 1985 authorization to the level requested in Reagan's budget.

Even the House-approved authorization represented a big drop since the Carter years; the agency's actual fiscal 1981 research appropriation was $355.6 million.

Other Provisions

Other significant provisions of the bill included ones that would have:

● Authorized EPA to pay for review by outside scientists of research proposals being considered for funding.

● Permitted EPA to transfer no more than 10 percent of authorized funds between research programs without congressional approval. The administration opposed this provision as an "unconstitutional" legislative veto.

● Prohibited reductions-in-force in EPA research programs without congressional approval.

● Earmarked 20 percent of the funding total for long-term basic research. OMB opposed this provision.

● Authorized a research program dealing with the health and ecological effects of pollution from energy production and with technologies for controlling it.

● Authorized a Senior Environmental Assistance Program to employ older Americans in EPA research. Congress cleared somewhat similar separate legislation in this area (S 518 — PL 98-313). *(Story, this page)*

● Established a research program on indoor air pollution. The administration opposed this provision as "not an appropriate federal responsibility." ∎

Senior Citizens, EPA Jobs

Congress May 24 cleared for the president a bill (S 518 — PL 98-313) authorizing the Environmental Protection Agency (EPA) to employ senior citizens in its pollution-control programs.

The measure made permanent a pilot program called the Senior Environmental Employment project that began in 1976. It authorized EPA to make grants to, or enter into agreements with, private non-profit organizations to employ citizens 55 and older in pollution abatement, prevention and control activities of federal, state or local environmental agencies.

S 518 was passed by the Senate March 26, then amended and passed by the House on May 23. The Senate agreed to the House amendments May 24, clearing the bill for the president. ∎

Arctic Research Program

Congress June 26 cleared for President Reagan a bill (S 373 — PL 98-373) that set up new panels to oversee federal Arctic research and the development of materials critical to high technology.

Final action came when the House, which had passed the bill April 24, agreed to Senate amendments to it. The Senate had originally passed S 373 on June 27, 1983, but without the title on critical materials.

Provisions

Title I of the bill established a five-member Arctic Research Commission appointed by the president for staggered four-year terms. The commission was to "develop and recommend an integrated national Arctic research policy" and cooperate with a second body set up by the bill in implementing that policy.

The second body, the Interagency Arctic Research Policy Committee, was composed of representatives of the National Science Foundation and selected other federal agencies. It would take the lead in developing a five-year plan for federal Arctic research efforts, and in coordinating the activities of various other agencies. At least 12 federal agencies currently spent a combined total of $100 million a year on research in the Arctic.

Title II established a National Critical Materials Council made up of three presidential appointees. The council was to advise the president on coordination of federal programs involving critical materials, and make recommendations to Congress.

"Critical materials" were non-fuel materials, including minerals, vital to the nation's economy or security. For many of them, the United States was dependent on other countries of questionable political stability. For example, Zaire provided about 40 percent of U.S. imports of cobalt, a metal used in jet engine parts but not mined in the United States.

Reagan opposed the House bill's more sweeping provisions creating the new panel, and wanted to keep authority for materials policy in his Cabinet Council on Natural Resources. The Senate amendments diluted the council's authority, making it almost exclusively an advisory body.

House Action

Before passing S 373 on April 24, the House amended it by voice vote with a substitute text worked out by the two committees with jurisdiction over it, Science and Technology and Merchant Marine and Fisheries (H Rept 98-593, Parts I and II).

The vote for passage was 253-1, with one member voting "present." *(Vote 79, p. 30-H)* ∎

Clean Air Bill Stalled by Acid Rain Dispute

Legislation to reauthorize the Clean Air Act stalled in the 98th Congress, largely because both Congress and the Reagan administration remained deeply divided over how to combat acid rain.

Early in 1984, the Senate Environment and Public Works Committee approved a clean-air bill (S 768) with new controls on acid rain, but the measure never reached the floor, where it faced stiff opposition.

In the House, Rep. Henry A. Waxman, D-Calif., chairman of the Energy and Commerce Subcommittee on Health and the Environment, shelved a clean-air bill in May after his panel voted 10-9 to strip acid-rain controls from the legislation.

Within the administration, William D. Ruckelshaus, administrator of the Environmental Protection Agency (EPA), was pressing for acid-rain controls — although more modest ones than either the Senate or House bill contained.

But Ruckelshaus lost out to the Office of Management and Budget (OMB), which opposed any controls on acid rain because of their cost. President Reagan urged more research instead, saying not enough was known about acid rain to justify an expensive control program. His position was roundly condemned by virtually all of the Democratic contenders for president, who made it an issue during early primaries in New England — the area of the United States that suffered the most from acid rain.

Background

1984 was the fourth year in a row that Congress had wrestled unsuccessfully with proposals to rewrite the Clean Air Act, the nation's most complex and far-reaching environmental law.

The air pollution control law was enacted in 1970 (PL 91-604) and amended significantly in 1977 (PL 95-95). *(Congress and the Nation Vol. III, p. 757; 1977 Almanac p. 627)*

The original law required EPA to establish safe concentrations for seven major air pollutants and set a 1975 standard for states to meet those standards. When it appeared that most states would not meet the deadline, Congress extended it to 1982, or, for areas with severe auto-related pollution, to 1987. *(Clean Air Act summary, 1981 Almanac p. 425)*

Funding authorizations under the law expired Sept. 30, 1981, but Congress provided money for its enforcement through annual appropriations bills, and the law's regulatory provisions remained on the books.

To protect hundreds of cities and counties from sanctions required by the law against jurisdictions that failed to meet the Dec. 31, 1982, deadline for compliance with national air quality standards, Congress in 1983 imposed a moratorium on action against any community that was actively trying to implement an EPA-approved cleanup plan. That moratorium effectively removed the one compelling impetus for action on a clean air bill in the 98th Congress. *(1983 Almanac p. 339)*

Senate Committee Action

The Senate Environment and Public Works Committee March 13 approved and May 3 formally reported a bill (S 768 — S Rept 98-426) to renew the Clean Air Act and add new controls on acid rain.

Despite the comfortable 16-2 margin in the committee, which was dominated by senators from the Northeast and the West, the bill was expected to face stiff floor opposition from some senators representing Midwestern and Appalachian states. The key issue was control of sulfur dioxide emissions from coal-burning utilities — thought to be the main cause of acid rain.

Voting against the motion to report S 768 were Jennings Randolph, D-W.Va., the committee's ranking minority member, and Steven D. Symms, R-Idaho. Randolph's opposition was based on the acid rain provisions.

The Senate committee's bill followed a "polluter pays" formula for acid rain control, which would have put the major cost burden on Midwestern and Ohio Valley states. Midwesterners had called for either delaying any controls or spreading the cost nationwide.

Before approving the bill, the committee headed off an amendment offered by Max Baucus, D-Mont., to repeal the current law's requirement that utilities use smokestack "scrubbers" no matter whether they were burning clean or dirty coal.

But members adopted an amendment that would, for the first time, make it illegal for an ordinary citizen to disconnect the pollution control device on his automobile or put leaded gasoline in a car designed for unleaded. This amendment was offered by Dave Durenberger, R-Minn., and cosponsored by committee Chairman Robert T. Stafford, R-Vt.

"It has become evident that some people are willing to endanger the health of all of us in order to save a few cents at the gas pumps," Stafford said. "That is unacceptable and it must be stopped."

Otherwise, the bill was similar to one reported out of the committee in 1982 that died at the end of the 97th Congress before reaching the Senate floor.

Auto Pollution Controls

As approved, the bill retained existing standards limiting passenger auto emissions to no more than 3.4 grams per mile for carbon monoxide, 1.0 grams per mile for nitrogen oxides, and 0.41 grams per mile for hydrocarbons. Most

new cars already met those standards.

Auto pollution controls had brought major gains in air quality for most parts of the country since Congress first passed the Clean Air Act in 1970.

But EPA reported that auto misfueling and tampering with pollution control devices remained serious causes of pollution.

Under current law, it was illegal for auto manufacturers or dealers to remove or disconnect any of the pollution control devices on a car. Durenberger's amendment made such actions illegal for "any person." It also newly prohibited sale or manufacture of devices designed to defeat the pollution controls.

Courts could impose civil fines on violators of the present auto emissions law and regulations.

Durenberger's amendment allowed the EPA to impose the fines administratively, subject to appeal in court.

Individual car owners were made subject to maximum fines of $2,500; others, such as dealers, mechanics, fleet managers, manufacturers and refiners, could be fined up to $10,000 per violation.

Leaded Gasoline

The amendment also made it illegal for any person to put leaded gasoline into a car designed for unleaded fuel. Such misfueling was not now illegal for individual car owners.

One of the chief pollution control devices on modern passenger cars was called a catalytic converter. Most U.S. cars made in the last 10 years had one. Attached to the exhaust pipe, it chemically converted pollutants into harmless substances. The reaction was triggered by a platinum catalyst, which remained chemically unchanged itself. Lead from gasoline, however, could quickly ruin the catalyst, leaving pollutants to pass through in the exhaust. Cars with converters were designed to use unleaded gas.

Besides damaging the catalyst, lead was also a pollutant in its own right. Scientists had established that lead poisoning caused brain damage, lower IQ scores and other health problems, especially in children. Most of the lead going into the atmosphere cames from cars, they said.

Lead was added to gasoline to cure performance problems, primarily engine knock, caused by gasoline containing less octane than a car required. It was less costly for refiners to mix additives with low-octane gasoline than to produce high-octane gasoline. As a result, leaded gasoline cost less than unleaded gasoline with the same "octane rating."

EPA surveyed cars from the model years 1975 and later, and it found that about 18 percent of the cars on the road had been tampered with and 13 percent of converter-equipped cars had been misfueled. People did this, EPA said, because they believed they would save on gasoline or get better performance.

EPA officials said, however, that car owners neither saved money nor improved performance by misfueling and tampering. They said performance problems that cars built in the mid-1970s experienced with no-lead gas had been solved with better engineering on more recent models and new anti-knock additives. In fact, they said, lead gummed up an engine, necessitating more frequent tuneups and oil changes.

In a turnabout from policies under his predecessor, Anne M. Burford, EPA Administrator Ruckelshaus began mounting an attack on the problem, by slapping large penalties on some highly visible violators, including the

Supreme Court Upholds 'Bubble Concept'

President Reagan's campaign to lighten the regulatory burden on business and industry took a big step forward June 25 when the Supreme Court reinstated controversial clean air regulations that environmentalists had challenged as too permissive.

The court held that a 1981 decision by the Environmental Protection Agency (EPA) to permit states to use the "bubble concept" for enforcing the Clean Air Act in areas that had not yet met clean air standards was "a reasonable accommodation of manifestly competing interests."

Use of this concept permitted existing plants to make major changes in their facilities without complying with all of the law's standards governing new sources of pollution. As long as pollution from a new source in one part of a plant was offset by reductions in emissions from another part, the plant as a whole could be treated as though it were a single unit enclosed in a bubble.

The Case: Background

The Carter administration rejected use of the bubble concept, but the Reagan EPA adopted it.

In 1982 the U.S. Court of Appeals for the District of Columbia, acting in a suit brought by the Natural Resources Defense Council (NRDC), blocked EPA's clean air regulations, finding them inconsistent with the purpose of the Clean Air Act — to improve the quality of the nation's air.

The administration and industry representatives appealed, asking the justices to find that the appeals court had overstepped its proper role in blocking the regulations.

The court's decision in the three cases, *Environmental Protection Agency v. Natural Resources Defense Council, Chevron USA Inc. v. NRDC, American Iron and Steel Institute v. NRDC*, came by a vote of 6-0. *(Court ruling, p. 15-A)*

Supporting the administration were Chief Justice Warren E. Burger and Justices Harry A. Blackmun, William J. Brennan Jr., Lewis F. Powell Jr., John Paul Stevens and Byron R. White.

Justices Sandra Day O'Connor, William H. Rehnquist and Thurgood Marshall took no part in the decision.

Easing Regulations

Underlying the clean air issue in the case were a number of larger questions closely related to the administration's efforts to ease the burden of federal regulation on business.

This case, focusing on the power of an agency to redefine key terms as it implements regulatory legislation, was seen as the administration's second line of attack on federal regulation.

Its first, frontal assault — directly rescinding certain regulations — resulted in a major defeat in June 1983, when the court rejected as arbitrary and capricious the administration's attempt to rescind a requirement that all cars be equipped with passive safety restraints — automatic seat belts or air bags. *(1983 Almanac p. 3-A)*

In that case, the court told the administration it had to provide reasoned justification for rescinding regulations. With rescission made considerably more difficult, the use of redefintion as an alternative route to deregulation became more important.

Agency Discretion Upheld

Finding the "bubble concept" a reasonable policy choice for EPA to make, Justice Stevens emphasized the agency's broad power to make such decisions and the courts' limited role in reviewing them. "A court may not substitute its own construction of a statutory provision for a reasonable interpretation made by the administrator of an agency," he wrote.

Since Congress did not define "major stationary source," the key term at issue in this case, the court looked to the purposes of the permit program used to enforce the Clean Air Act. In that program, Stevens wrote, "Congress sought to accommodate the conflict between the economic interest in permitting capital improvements to continue and the environmental interest in improving air quality."

EPA, he said, was well within its authority when it decided that in areas where air quality standards had not yet been met, an entire plant could be considered a single source. As long as total emissions from that source did not increase, changes in various components of the plant could be made without undergoing full-scale EPA review as a new pollution source.

In amending the Clean Air Act in 1977, Congress did not expressly address this definitional issue, Stevens noted. *(1977 Almanac p. 627)*

For the court's purposes, Stevens said, the reason for congressional inaction was irrelevant. "Judges are not experts in the field, and are not part of either political branch of the government. Courts must, in some cases, reconcile competing political interests, but not on the basis of the judges' personal policy preferences.

"In contrast, an agency to which Congress has delegated policy-making responsibilities may, within the limits of that delegation, properly rely upon the incumbent administration's views of wise policy to inform its judgments.

"While agencies are not directly accountable to the people," Stevens said, "the chief executive is, and it is entirely appropriate for this political branch of the government to make such policy choices — resolving the competing interests which Congress itself either inadvertently did not resolve, or intentionally left to be resolved by the agency charged with the administration of the statute in light of everyday realities."

When an agency's interpretation of a law was challenged by those who argued primarily that it reflected an unwise policy, the challenge had to fail, Stevens said. "In such a case, federal judges — who have no constituency — have a duty to respect legitimate policy choices made by those who do."

Philadelphia Police Department.

Ruckelshaus reportedly believed that banning lead in gas altogether might be an easier way to get at the problem than trying to enforce the law against millions of individual motorists.

Some 40 states had laws against misfueling and tampering, but only a few were enforcing those laws with much vigor.

The easiest way for states to enforce such laws was with inspection and maintenance programs, which some states used for annual safety checks. Twenty states had working pollution inspection programs in early 1984, and EPA expected another seven or eight states where the air was dirtier than federal health standards to get such programs going.

Acid Rain

The acid rain controls in S 768 were stronger than those the Environment Committee approved in 1982. The panel increased from eight million tons to 10 million tons the annual reductions required in utility emissions of sulfur dioxide.

Those would be reductions below actual emissions in 1980, chosen as a base year, of approximately 24 million tons. They went well beyond what was needed to meet the health-based standards in current law.

Acid rain politics were sometimes partisan — but always regional. New England and the rest of the Northeast suffered the most from acid rain because they were downwind of its major sources — coal-burning electric utilities in the Ohio River Valley and industrial Midwest, where ratepayers would be required to shoulder the highest cleanup costs under S 768.

Coal from Appalachia and the Midwest, where many miners were unemployed, contained more sulfur than the cheap, abundant coal from the West. Utilities could reduce sulfur dioxide emissions cheaply by burning low-sulfur coal.

But the 1970 law helped Eastern coal compete with Western coal by requiring all utilities to reduce the amount of sulfur dioxide in their smokestack gas — no matter how clean it was to start with. This so-called "percentage reduction" requirement in effect mandated expensive stack gas scrubbers for all coal-burning utilities, neutralizing the cost advantages of Western coal.

Members of Congress representing Appalachian and Midwestern states had defended the percentage reduction requirement as zealously as Westerners had opposed it.

S 768 kept the scrubber requirement for meeting health standards in existing law but abandoned it for achieving further reductions to control acid rain.

House Subcommittee Action

The House Energy and Commerce Subcommittee on Health and the Environment on May 2 voted 10-9 to strike the entire acid rain section from a clean air bill (HR 5314) proposed by Waxman, its chairman.

The California Democrat promptly called the vote "a likely death knell" to chances for legislation in 1984, as indeed it proved to be.

The subcommittee began marking up HR 5314 the week of April 23 but quickly became snagged on the acid rain section.

Waxman's proposal would have required installation of expensive scrubbers on the country's 50 dirtiest utility plants and imposed a nationwide tax on electric bills to spread the cost burden beyond local utility ratepayers.

But this approach was opposed by most Western members of Congress, who said it was not fair for their region to pay for pollution it neither created nor suffered from.

The members voting to strike the acid rain controls included all six Republicans on the 19-member panel and three Midwestern Democrats: Dennis E. Eckart, Ohio; John D. Dingell, Mich., and Thomas A. Luken, Ohio. Also voting to strike was Richard C. Shelby, D-Ala. Edward R. Madigan, R-Ill., the ranking minority member, offered the motion to strike.

Madigan's motion followed adoption of several Waxman amendments intended to make the bill more acceptable to Eckart — who normally sided with environmentalists but represented a district with high unemployment and two of the 50 targeted power plants.

Waxman said he had no warning that Eckart would vote against him on the motion to strike the acid-rain section, while Eckart said he had.

"He brought it all down," Waxman said. "We have done all that we could do for Ohio, and that's not enough."

Eckart, asked about Waxman's statements, said: "This bill did not come down from Mt. Sinai carved on two tablets of stone." ∎

Coal Leasing Suspended

Interior Secretary William P. Clark largely defused congressional criticism of the federal coal-leasing program in 1984, as he voluntarily suspended all leasing during the year and set about overhauling the program.

Clark told Congress early in the year that he was adopting nearly all of the recommendations of a blue-ribbon commission created by Congress and appointed by his predecessor, James G. Watt, after charges of mismanagement arose in 1983.

The administration's critics had charged that Watt's aggressive energy development policies resulted in the sale of too much federal coal at a time when coal companies already had massive reserves and could not sell what they had. Watt stoutly defended his program, arguing it would increase the nation's independence from foreign energy sources and lower energy costs to the consumer.

With Watt gone and Clark moving to meet the concerns of program critics, Congress did not renew a moratorium on leasing it had imposed as part of the fiscal 1984 Interior Appropriations bill (PL 98-146). The moratorium expired May 17. *(1983 Almanac p. 462)*

Background

Watt had engaged in a yearlong tussle with Congress following the 1982 sale of coal leases on federal lands in the Powder River Basin in Wyoming and Montana.

The largest single coal lease sale in the nation's history, with 1.6 billion tons of coal offered, it came after a decade when there had been little or no leasing as a result of various legal and administrative moratoriums.

The Interior Department accepted bids totaling $54.7 million, but the General Accounting Office, watchdog arm of Congress, said the fair market value of the tracts leased was $165.3 million.

The Powder River sale touched off widespread criticism in Congress, with members charging that Watt was peddling federal coal at "fire-sale prices."

In a fiscal 1983 supplemental appropriations measure (PL 98-63) cleared July 29, Congress ordered Watt to appoint an independent commission to review the coal-leasing program, and it gave the commission six months to complete its study and report back to Congress. Named to chair the panel was David F. Linowes, a professor at the University of Illinois, who had previously chaired a Watt-appointed commission studying the government's oil and gas royalty program. *(Background, 1983 Almanac pp. 350, 509)*

Linowes Commission Report

The Linowes commission, in a report sent to Congress Feb. 17, found that Watt had accepted lease prices that were too low, and it recommended a number of changes in the federal program.

The commission made 30 recommendations for administrative action by the department and six suggestions for legislative changes.

Secretary Clark told the Senate Energy and Natural Resources Committee April 5 that he would adopt all but one of the 30 administrative recommendations made by the commission. (The exception involved a recommendation that coal companies give the federal government information on private coal transactions for use in analyzing market pricing.)

An Interior spokesman said Clark also supported the commission's legislative recommendations.

But Clark's concessions did not satisfy environmentalists. Sierra Club representative Brooks B. Yeager said Clark's official response to the commission report, dated March 19, was "too narrow in scope, too vague in detail, and far too reluctant to recognize and remedy the flaws in Secretary Watt's approach."

Legislative Changes

The following six of the Linowes commission's 36 recommendations involved possible changes in law:

● Congress should keep in place the "diligent development" requirement of the Coal Leasing Act Amendments of 1976. (Aimed at keeping companies from buying leases simply to speculate on rising coal prices, it required lessees to begin mining within 10 years or lose the lease.) But Congress should consider allowing 10-year extensions of leases with advance payment of escalating royalties, which would stimulate timely development.

● For undeveloped pre-1976 leases, the lessee should begin paying advance royalties with the next lease adjustment, on the same escalating schedule applied to extensions of post-1976 leases.

● Congress should keep a requirement that qualified surface owners consent before coal rights beneath their land are leased. But Congress should consider limits on payments allowable for surface owner consent.

● Congress should consider giving the interior secretary authority to reduce federal royalty rates for coal tracts before a lease sale, where current rates would adversely affect production.

● The base for calculating federal royalty payments should be the freight-on-board price minus all state and local taxes such as severance taxes.

● Congress should study whether shippers of federal coal were adequately protected from anti-competitive or discriminatory practices when slurry pipelines or other forms of transportation competition were insufficient.

Administrative Changes

Other key commission recommendations, which could be carried out by Interior without new legislation, included the following:

● "The government should establish and announce in a timely fashion a coal leasing schedule to promote predictability and stability of federal leasing actions. In doing so, the government should have the flexibility to change the timing of lease sales and the quantity of coal offered based on its assessment of market conditions."

● "To maintain a responsive and orderly coal leasing program, the states, through their participation in the Regional Coal Teams and the Federal-State Coal Advisory Board, should continue to play a significant role both in establishing leasing levels and in setting leasing schedules. The inclusion of state personnel in providing staff support to the Regional Coal Teams is encouraged."

● "The government should not seek to raise the price above the competitive market level by limiting the amount of coal that federal leasing policies make available to the market. But neither should it lease so much as to flood a depressed market."

● "The quantity of coal leased should be determined so the government will receive a fair return consistent with the achievement of other public policy objectives, such as promoting efficient land use and environmental planning and conserving appropriate amounts of coal for the future."

● "In deciding on the appropriate level of future coal leasing, the amount that might be provided through preference right leasing should be taken into account." Because the Interior Department had acted "very slowly" on pending preference right lease applications, "review of these applications should be rapidly completed, preferably within the next two years. Stress should be on those areas in which a lease sale is scheduled in the next year or so."

● Tracts should be selected for coal leasing "in such a manner that their characteristics will enhance the attainment of fair market value."

● "The Interior Department should sponsor more drilling for use in tract delineation and it should encourage cooperative drilling in which any additional firms could participate by paying a pro-rated charge."

● "Cooperative leasing procedures are desirable to obtain logical mining units that may be reasonably expected to receive greater bidding competition than fragmented coal holdings."

● "The exchange of federal and non-federal coal tracts should be pursued more vigorously, but in a careful and prudent manner, to consolidate federal and non-federal coal lease holdings of equivalent value into logical mining units."

● "The government should have leasing policies that distinguish between new production tracts on the one hand and maintenance and bypass tracts on the other."

● "In the conduct of lease sales, the government should continue to rely on bonus bidding."

● "To promote more competitive bidding, the government should test the feasibility of and experiment with a variety of auction techniques."

● "Minimum submissible bids should be established on a regional basis. This minimum should be expressed as an amount per ton."

● "Wherever possible, leases should be sold on a competitive basis. However, where reasonable efforts to obtain competitive bids have failed, the government should have authority to negotiate a fair price."

• "The industry bids received on tracts in a lease sale on which there was extensive competition, along with the government's pre-sale appraisals, can constitute appropriate and important sources of information for post-bid acceptance and rejection decisions."

• "The Interior Department employs basic methodologies for estimating fair market value that are widely accepted in the conduct of appraisals by industry and government. However, model design, input data and analysis should be improved."

• "Where a federal tract is of use to only one party and no competition is expected, estimates of tract value should be based on the value of the tract to the adjoining mine or coal owner, rather than the 'competitive' or 'stand alone' value."

• "The inspector general should be directed to conduct periodic audits of the federal coal program and necessary expertise should be contracted from the private sector where appropriate." ∎

Timber Contract Relief

The House Oct. 1 cleared and sent to the president a bill (HR 2838 — PL 98-478) allowing logging companies to get out of high-cost contracts to buy timber grown on federally owned lands.

Although David A. Stockman, director of the Office of Management and Budget (OMB), urged defeat of the legislation the very day the House acted, President Reagan somewhat reluctantly signed the bill into law Oct. 16.

The measure particularly benefited logging companies in the Pacific Northwest — a Republican stronghold that Reagan was reluctant to offend in an election year.

"It now appears," Reagan said in signing the bill, "that our successful efforts to control inflation mean that market prices for wood products will not rise enough to prevent severe economic hardship to many forest-dependent communities unless the provisions of this new law are implemented."

The Senate had added the timber contract relief language to a House-passed bill authorizing government aid to groups volunteering to plant seedlings on public lands, then passed the measure Sept. 26.

Final action on HR 2838 came when the House by voice vote suspended the rules and concurred in the Senate amendments to the bill.

Background

Under existing law, timber companies contracted with the federal government to buy and cut timber on publicly owned land. Contracts were usually awarded to the highest bidder, with proceeds going to the Treasury.

In the late 1970s, inflation and heavy demand led companies to bid up contract prices for timber. But a subsequent collapse of the housing market coupled with sharp reductions in inflation left many firms stuck with contracts to buy timber at prices well above its current market value. A number of smaller companies faced possible bankruptcy unless relief was granted.

A threatened filibuster by Sen. Howard M. Metzenbaum, D-Ohio, killed an earlier timber bill in 1982. In 1984, however, the Senate adopted a number of amendments to HR 2838 that were designed to allay Metzenbaum's concerns. *(1982 Almanac p. 458)*

The changes in the bill were insufficient to satisfy the administration, however.

OMB Director Stockman, in an Oct. 1 letter to House Minority Leader Robert H. Michel, R-Ill., said, "I strongly urge you to help defeat this effort to force taxpayers to provide a small number of corporations with $400 million worth of special relief," Stockman said.

Provisions

As cleared by Congress, HR 2838 included the following major provisions:

• Allowed logging companies to "buy out" of their purchase obligations for up to 55 percent of timber contracted for prior to Jan. 1, 1982, if they still held the contract.

• Set a maximum of 200 million board feet on the amount of timber subject to buy-out.

• Established a formula for determining how much companies had to pay to buy out of existing contracts.

• Specified that when a potential net loss was more than a company's net worth, the firm had to pay $10 per thousand board feet.

• Required companies facing a potential loss between 50 percent and 100 percent of net worth to pay 10 percent of the contract overbid.

• Required companies facing a loss of less than 50 percent of their net worth to pay 15 percent of the overbid for the first 125 million board feet, 20 percent of the overbid between 125 million and 150 million board feet, 25 percent between 150 million and 175 million board feet, and 30 percent between 175 million and 200 million board feet.

• Required buy-out payments to go directly to the U.S. Treasury.

• Allowed companies to finance their buy-out payments by borrowing from the federal government at market interest rates.

• Effective Jan. 1, 1985, required cash down payments at the time any timber contract was executed and periodic payments over the remaining life of the contract.

• Limited to no more than 5.2 billion board feet the net amount of "merchantable sawtimber" that could be sold annually in Oregon and Washington through fiscal 1991.

• Authorized the agriculture secretary to waive annually all or part of the fees required for use of national forest lands for camping by the Boy Scouts of America and other non-profit organizations that agreed to perform certain services in return.

Senate Action

The Senate Energy and Natural Resources Committee attached the timber-relief provisions to HR 2838 before reporting the bill to the Senate Aug. 27 (S Rept 98-596).

The Senate passed the compromise legislation on Sept. 26 by a vote of 94-2. *(Vote 235, p. 41-S)*

Before approving the bill, the Senate adopted by voice vote a series of four amendments by Metzenbaum, one of the measure's chief critics.

With relief legislation stalled in 1983, the Reagan administration administratively allowed companies to extend the term of their contracts for five years without paying interest. That took some immediate pressure off of the companies, but many kept pressing for a longer-term solution.

"The government cannot collect its damages from bankrupt companies, workers will lose their jobs, and communities already in precarious situations will be thrust into chaos — all to prove an abstract legal principle that 'a contract is a contract'," said Sen. Mark O. Hatfield, R-Ore.

The Senate-passed bill allowed companies to partially

"buy out" of their contracts according to a specific formula. Companies could buy out of their obligation to purchase up to 55 percent of timber contracted for prior to Jan. 1, 1982, if they still held the contract. The maximum buy-out allowed would be 200 million board feet.

The amount companies paid for the buy-out was calculated by comparing a company's net worth to the damages it would have to pay under the contract. When the potential net loss was more than a company's net worth, it would have to pay $10 per thousand board feet. When the loss was between 50 and 100 percent of the company's worth, it would have to pay 10 percent of the contract overbid. Companies whose loss was less than 50 percent would, under the bill brought to the floor, have had to pay 15

percent of the overbid.

A key Metzenbaum amendment altered this formula to shift some of the burden of payment off smaller companies and onto larger companies. For companies losing less than 50 percent of their worth, it set the buy-out price at 15 percent of the overbid for the first 125 million board feet, 20 percent of the overbid between 125 million and 150 million board feet, 25 percent between 150 million and 175 million board feet, and 30 percent between 175 million board feet and the ceiling of 200 million board feet.

Other Metzenbaum amendments required buy-out payments to go directly to the Treasury and allowed companies to finance their buy-out penalties by borrowing from the federal government at market interest rates. ∎

Ruckelshaus, Clark Depart; Hodel Shifts Jobs

Just weeks before President Reagan was inaugurated for his second term, all three of his top environment and energy officials announced their resignations.

The first to depart was William D. Ruckelshaus, administrator of the Environmental Protection Agency (EPA), whose resignation was announced Nov. 28, 1984, and took effect Jan. 5, 1985. One of his top assistants, Lee M. Thomas, head of EPA's toxic-waste programs, was nominated to succeed him.

Interior Secretary William P. Clark announced on Jan. 1, 1985, that he would leave his post by spring. After 18 years serving Reagan in state and federal governments, Clark said he wanted to return to his California ranch.

And on Jan. 10, the White House revealed that Energy Secretary Donald P. Hodel would shift to the Interior Department to succeed Clark. To replace Hodel, Reagan nominated White House personnel director John S. Herrington as secretary of energy.

The changes paved the way for a possible new phase in Reagan's policies on natural resources and the environment — an area where the president encountered considerable opposition from Congress during his first term.

The Firefighters

Both Ruckelshaus and Clark were "firefighters" called in by the president before the 1984 election to quell political brushfires touched off by their predecessors. And by all accounts, both succeeded at that task.

Ruckelshaus replaced Anne M. Burford, who headed EPA from 1981 until she resigned March 9, 1983, under a barrage of criticism of her management of EPA in general and its enforcement of the "superfund" hazardous-waste cleanup law in particular. More than a dozen of Burford's top aides either resigned or were fired as well, as the agency went through its worst crisis since it was created in 1970. (*Background, 1983 Almanac p. 332; related story, p. 346*)

Clark took over from James G. Watt, Reagan's combative first secretary of the interior, whose penchant for politically damaging remarks led to his downfall. Watt resigned Oct. 9, 1983, nine months to the day after Burford left EPA. (*1983 Almanac p. 327*)

Energy-Interior Merger?

The shift of Hodel from the Department of Energy (DOE) to Interior came amid year-end reports that Reagan was considering an effort to persuade Congress to merge the two departments.

Hodel had served at Interior under Watt, so he had unique expertise at both departments.

Thomas to Head EPA

Reagan on Nov. 29 announced the selection of EPA Assistant Administrator Thomas, 40, to succeed Ruckelshaus. Thomas currently headed the agency's hazardous-waste programs. He was generally well regarded in Congress, but some members feared he lacked the authority and independence within the administration that Ruckelshaus enjoyed.

Thomas had been at EPA since early 1983, when he was named to succeed Rita M. Lavelle, fired Feb. 7 of that year in the midst of the controversy over management of the superfund program.

He had served from 1981-83 as associate director of the Federal Emergency Management Agency. In that post, he headed a task force to deal with dioxin contamination at Times Beach, Mo.

The Ruckelshaus Record

Ruckelshaus smoothed EPA's relations with Congress after the frequent and bitter confrontations that marked Burford's tenure.

He had served as the agency's first chief in 1970-73, so he needed little introduction to the administrator's post.

Equally important to Congress, he had established during the Watergate era that he would stand up to anyone — including the president of the United States — on matters of conscience. Ruckelshaus in October 1973 was serving as deputy attorney general when President Nixon ordered Attorney General Elliot L. Richardson to fire Watergate special prosecutor Archibald Cox, who was pressing for tape recordings of Nixon's White House conservations. Richardson refused, and resigned. Ruckelshaus, next in line, likewise refused and was dismissed in that "Saturday night massacre." (*1973 Almanac p. 1009*)

During his EPA tenure the second time around, Ruckelshaus sometimes found his policy objectives frustrated — but he publicly defended Reagan's positions on key environmental issues.

He unsuccessfully pressed Reagan to take action against acid rain, which had become the major air-quality issue of the 1980s. But the president insisted on seeking more research instead. (*Clear air, p. 339*)

Ruckelshaus succeeded in obtaining tougher EPA restrictions on lead in gasoline, and he imposed mandatory controls in 1984 on use of the pesticide ethylene dibromide (EDB).

In his resignation letter to Reagan, Ruckelshaus said, "The ship called EPA is righted and is now steering a steady course. I am convinced, Mr. President, that properly led, the dedicated people of EPA will continue to serve well your administration and this country."

Reagan, in a letter accepting the resignation, said Ruckelshaus had "established a firm foundation on which your successor can continue to build and in which Americans can have complete confidence."

Ruckelshaus had earlier told reporters that he expected to work with the 99th Congress for at least a few months on reauthorizing environmental laws, but he had left open the question of how long he would stay on. The White House announcement of his resignation came sooner than had been expected — the same day that David A. Stockman, director of the Office of Management and Budget (OMB), presented Reagan with proposals for deep cuts in domestic spending, including EPA programs, as part of a deficit reduction plan.

Rep. James J. Florio, D-N.J., chairman of a House subcommittee that handled toxic-waste legislation, said he understood from "sources inside the agency" that Ruckelshaus' resignation was prompted by the proposed cuts and his inability to get them reversed.

In a Nov. 29 appearance on NBC-TV's "Today" show, Ruckelshaus denied that he left the agency because of cuts proposed by OMB. Despite previous OMB pressure for EPA spending reductions, Congress had generally shielded the agency from deep cuts.

Rep. John D. Dingell, D-Mich., chairman of the House Energy and Commerce Committee, said Nov. 29 that he viewed Ruckelshaus' departure with "deep foreboding."

"There are two overriding concerns," Dingell said. "First, the extent to which the administration's intended cuts in EPA's budget will bring about a retreat in environmental protection, and second, the degree to which the White House and OMB are committed to gutting our environmental laws during reauthorization in the new Congress." Dingell's committee wrote many environmental laws and oversaw EPA's enforcement of them.

In the Senate, Robert T. Stafford, R-Vt., chairman of the Environment and Public Works Committee, said, "I regret very much that Bill Ruckelshaus is leaving the EPA. He came when it was in deep trouble. He has restored its morale and brought many able administrators back into the agency to serve with him. He will be difficult to replace."

Predicting that Thomas "will be a good steward" of EPA programs, Stafford said he would be readily confirmed by the Senate.

Hodel Replaces Clark

Hodel, 49, was confirmed as energy secretary in December 1982. During the first two years of the Reagan administration, he had served with Watt as under secretary of interior.

Hodel won praise from members of Congress for his management of DOE, even from Democrats who opposed his policies. House Energy and Commerce Chairman Dingell said he and Hodel "enjoyed a pretty good relationship." And House Interior Committee Chairman Morris K. Udall, D-Ariz., said he had worked effectively with Hodel

---

Burford Resigns — Again

Faced with House and Senate resolutions opposing her appointment, Anne M. Burford resigned as chairman of a government advisory committee on Aug. 1, the day before she was to be sworn in to a job she had characterized as "a joke."

President Reagan accepted her resignation as chairman of the National Advisory Committee on Oceans and Administration. He had named her to the post July 2.

Burford in 1983 had resigned as administrator of the Environmental Protection Agency amid allegations of mismanagement, political manipulation and possible conflicts of interest. Her appointment to a new environmental post brought a barrage of criticism. *(1983 Almanac p. 332)*

Burford's resignation from the advisory committee came after the House July 31 passed a resolution disapproving of her appointment and urging Reagan to withdraw it. The vote was 363-51. *(Vote 296, p. 90-H)*

The Senate had passed a similar resolution July 24 as an amendment to the fiscal 1985 Treasury, Postal Service appropriations bill (HR 5798). The vote was 74-19. *(Vote 177, p. 31-S)*

Before the House voted, Burford touched off a new round of criticism when she called the advisory committee "a nothing-burger" and "a joke" in July 28 remarks in Vail, Colo. The 18-member panel provided policy reviews and program advice to the secretary of commerce on programs of the National Oceanic and Atmospheric Administration.

---

on a 1982 nuclear-waste disposal bill. *(1982 Almanac p. 304)*

Some environmentalists were skeptical of Hodel's commitment to conservation, however, because of his work under Watt. A Sierra Club spokeswoman criticized Hodel's support for nuclear power and his management at Interior of coal-leasing programs.

As administrator of the Bonneville Power Administration from 1972 to 1977, Hodel pushed for rapid construction of new power plants through the Washington Public Power Supply Service (WPPSS), nicknamed "Whoops." Cancellation of two nuclear plants led to the default of $2.25 billion in WPPSS bonds in July 1983. *(1983 Almanac p. 466)*

Clark Record

During his tenure at Interior, Watt shifted its policies away from resource conservation and toward energy development. Although Clark never disowned Watt's policies, he defused outside criticism of Interior's activities. He softened many of Watt's hard-line stands, improved relations with Congress and opened dialogue with environmental groups.

Clark resumed acquisition of new lands for national parks, after Congress had repeatedly ignored Watt's requests for a halt to such purchases. Clark also slowed controversial sales of offshore oil and gas leases.

Clark was chief of staff during Reagan's first term as California governor. In 1969, Reagan appointed him to the first of several judicial posts in the state, culminating in a

1973 appointment to the state Supreme Court.

Clark left the bench in 1981 to serve as deputy secretary of state, then moved to the White House as national security adviser in 1982. He was confirmed as interior secretary on Nov. 18, 1983. *(1983 Almanac p. 330)*

Interior saw an unusual number of other top-level departures in 1984, and the new secretary was expected to have a say in filling those vacancies.

Announcing their resignations in the fall of 1984 were three assistant secretaries at Interior: Garrey E. Carruthers, G. Ray Arnett and Kenneth L. Smith. Carruthers' domain included energy and minerals, Smith managed Indian affairs, and Arnett had been responsible for fish, wildlife and parks. Also announcing retirement in the fall was Russell E. Dickenson, director of the National Park Service.

Richard Mulberry resigned as inspector general in the summer of 1984, after he had come under congressional criticism for the way he handled investigations of alleged improper actions in a coal lease sale. Pending a permanent appointment, Arthur J. Dellinger was serving as acting inspector general. *(Coal leasing program, p. 342)*

The top post at the Bureau of Reclamation also was being filled on an acting basis, by Robert A. Olson.

Herrington to Head DOE

Herrington, 45, arrived at DOE as a relative unknown. "As far as I am aware, he doesn't have any experience in energy matters," Dingell said.

Herrington was a veteran of past Reagan campaigns. In 1981, he worked as White House personnel director before becoming assistant secretary of the Navy for manpower and Reserve affairs in October of that year. He returned to the White House in June 1983 as assistant to the president for personnel.

A graduate of Stanford University, Herrington received a law degree from the University of California's Hastings College of Law.

Like Dingell, Ed Rothschild of the Citizen/Labor Energy Coalition, a lobbying group, criticized Herrington's lack of experience in energy. "It means he'll be learning on the job, and we don't need that again," he said, referring to two previous energy secretaries, Charles W. Duncan Jr. in the Carter administration and James B. Edwards, Reagan's first energy secretary.

Merging the Departments?

Hodel's shift back to Interior fueled talk that DOE might be abolished and its functions folded into the Interior Department. Such a plan fit with the Reagan administration's desire to limit sharply government's role in setting energy policy.

White House spokesman Larry Speakes said Reagan, who had endorsed DOE's dissolution since 1980, asked Hodel and Herrington to study consolidation of their two departments. A 1982 attempt to merge Energy with the Commerce Department was generally ignored by Congress. *(1982 Almanac p. 303)*

In the 1982 attempt to abolish DOE, the administration proposed transferring most of its functions to the Department of Commerce. But the administration had trouble finding congressional sponsors, and leaders of the House and Senate Energy committees opposed the plan.

Sen. J. Bennett Johnston, D-La., who opposed the 1982 attempt, said he thought highly of Hodel. "Because he is going [to Interior], I am not adverse at this point to the merger of Energy and Interior."

But, Johnston added, it was essential that the nuclear weapons program go to Interior as well.

The question of what to do with the Energy Department's nuclear weapons program was a major problem with the previous plan. Control over development and production of nuclear weapons was put under civilian control in 1946, under the Atomic Energy Commission, and given to DOE when the department was created in 1977. Proposals to shift nuclear weapons programs to the Defense Department met with strong congressional opposition.

The nuclear weapons program accounted for about 55 percent of Energy's $13.8 billion 1985 appropriation, DOE officials said.

Senate Energy and Natural Resources Committee Chairman James A. McClure, R-Idaho, who also opposed the 1982 proposal, had no immediate reaction to the new suggestion, saying only that he would have to be convinced that a merger would save a significant amount of money and be administratively efficient.

Dingell said that merging the two departments was "just as silly and misguided an idea as it was when first proposed."

He was skeptical, he said, because DOE's efforts to enhance energy production sometimes conflicted with Interior's efforts to protect the environment. ∎

Congress Slashes Funding of Synfuels Program

The U.S. Synthetic Fuels Corporation (SFC), under attack from a wide spectrum of critics, saw its appropriations sharply reduced by Congress in 1984, but it survived moves by some members to abolish it altogether.

In June Congress took away $2 billion from the SFC as part of a deficit-reduction package (HR 4170 — PL 98-369). *(Story, p. 143)*

As part of the Interior Department's portion of the fiscal 1985 continuing appropriations resolution (H J Res 648 — PL 98-473), Congress rescinded another $5.375 billion in previously approved SFC funds. *(Interior appropriations, p. 378)*

That was less than the $9 billion Reagan had asked Congress to rescind in May, but under the terms of a compromise reached in September with congressional leaders, the administration agreed to accept a smaller cut and

to revitalize the SFC board by proposing nominees to fill five vacancies. The corporation had been stalled since April for lack of a quorum on its seven-member board.

By year's end, Reagan had made three recess appointments to the board — thus allowing it to resume operations. Named to the SFC were lame-duck Rep. Tom Corcoran, R-Ill., who had lost a primary bid to oust GOP Sen. Charles H. Percy; Paul W. MacAvoy, a former member of the Council of Economic Advisers under President Ford; and Eric H. Reichl, a synfuels technologist. Two vacancies remained unfilled.

Background

Launched by Congress and the Carter administration in 1980 after a decade of energy disruptions, the ambitious synfuels program was meant to stimulate the development of synthetic fuels in an effort to promote U.S. energy independence. The SFC provided price supports and loan guarantees to business ventures trying to make synfuels production commercially viable. *(1980 Almanac p. 477)*

Synthetic fuels were produced from such underused raw materials as coal, tar sands, oil shale and heavy sands, which together accounted for 85-90 percent of U.S. fossil fuel reserves.

Under the terms of the 1980 Energy Security Act (PL 96-294), the initial $14.9 billion authorized by Congress was to take the corporation through fiscal 1984. At that point, the SFC was to submit a detailed report on its future strategy. Thereafter, Congress could make additional authorizations, subject to annual appropriations.

Experts expected oil prices to continue soaring, reaching $42.50 a barrel, at which point synfuels supposedly could compete commercially.

Instead, world oil demand collapsed, and a barrel of oil sold for less than $30 a barrel in 1984. Many potential synfuels project sponsors backed off.

In early 1984 the SFC had been able to find only one small project to support and had committed just $120 million of the almost $15 billion made available four years before. Staunch backers of the SFC concept such as House Majority Leader Jim Wright, D-Texas, complained the SFC board was moving too slowly.

Internal Problems

Adding fuel to the congressional doubts about the SFC were a series of embarrassing revelations of internal problems at the corporation.

In August 1983 SFC President Victor A. Schroeder resigned amid conflict-of-interest charges. On April 26, 1984, his successor to the $135,000-a-year post, Victor M. Thompson, also resigned under fire for failing to disclose, when he was appointed, that his actions as head of a Tulsa, Okla., bank were being investigated by the Securities and Exchange Commission.

Thompson's departure left the SFC board with only three members, one shy of a quorum. But just before he quit, the board approved $1.4 billion in subsidies for two controversial synfuels projects.

Another SFC board member quit May 16, leaving just two directors on the seven-member panel.

Administration Seeks Cut

On May 14 the White House announced that President Reagan would make nominations to fill the SFC board vacancies, but at the same time the president proposed to cancel $9 billion in synfuels spending. Energy Secretary Donald P. Hodel suggested that the new nominations would not come unless Congress acted on the spending cuts.

The administration urged that funds remaining in the SFC account after the rescission be committed only to projects that met a "market test." By restricting SFC support to projects producing fuels that "will not cost significantly more than the projected market price of competing fuels," the White House's proposed market test would have ruled out most synfuels projects then under consideration.

Other Legislation

Sen. William Proxmire, D-Wis., in early 1984 introduced a bill (S 2358) to place a moratorium on further funding of synfuels projects until Congress re-examined the program. A companion measure, HR 4098, sponsored by Rep. Howard Wolpe, D-Mich., garnered more than half the members of the House as cosponsors.

In February 1984, in a letter to Reagan, 12 members of congressional Budget committees — six from the House and six from the Senate — had urged the president to defer obligation of any more SFC funds until Congress approved a comprehensive strategy for the program. The Office of Management and Budget (OMB), however, advised the president he did not have the necessary authority to impound SFC money.

Reagan's May 14, 1984, proposal effectively pre-empted congressional attempts to scale back or kill the SFC. Even so, his plan did not go far enough for some congressional critics. For example, Proxmire complained, "Instead of cutting two-thirds of the corporation's budget, he should have gone all the way and shut it down."

Legislative Action

The $2 Billion Rescission

The first move to cut back SFC funding came in the Senate, just two days after Reagan proposed a $9 billion rescission.

On May 16, the Senate voted to rescind $2 billion in synfuels money as part of its deficit-reduction bill (HR 4170). GOP leaders persuaded five moderate Republicans to go along with the spending-cut legislation only after agreeing to use the $2 billion savings from the synfuels program for non-defense spending allotments.

The five were Mark Andrews, N.D.; John H. Chafee, R.I.; Charles McC. Mathias Jr., Md.; Robert T. Stafford, Vt., and Lowell P. Weicker Jr., Conn.

An amendment to increase spending authority levels by $2 billion for non-defense discretionary programs was approved 62-37. *(Vote 96, p. 19-S)*

Although the House version of HR 4170 had contained no synfuels rescission, the $2 billion cut was accepted by House-Senate conferees and included in the final legislation cleared June 27 and signed into law by the president on July 18 (PL 98-369).

$5 Billion Rescission: Interior Bill

The House Aug. 2 cut $5 billion from the budget of the SFC as it approved the Interior appropriations bill (HR 5973) for fiscal 1985.

The $5 billion cut struck a compromise between the program's defenders, who had tried to protect its already appropriated funds from any cuts, and its opponents, who had hoped to rescind most or all of its remaining funds.

Rule Defeated. One of SFC's stoutest defenders, House Majority Leader Wright, had fought for a rule to keep any SFC funding cut from coming to the floor. The Rules Committee obliged on July 24, approving by 7-4 a rule (H Res 551) that did not waive points of order against anticipated amendments rescinding all or part of the SFC's existing funding.

But the House July 25 rejected that rule, 148-261, thus ensuring a showdown on the synfuels funding. *(Vote 285, p. 88-H)*

The vote was a victory for the administration. OMB Director David A. Stockman called some members personally before the vote, asking them to oppose the rule.

However, the vote was not a partisan one. House Democrats split right down the middle, 127-126, on adoption of the rule. Republicans generally opposed it, 21-135.

The July 25 action was only the second time a rule granted by the Rules Committee had been rejected by the House during the 98th Congress, according to committee staff. The other was a rule on a tax increase bill (H Res 376 — HR 4170) that was defeated on Nov. 17, 1983. *(1983 Almanac p. 231)*

Rescission Vote. The Aug. 2 vote on the $5 billion rescission offered by William R. Ratchford, D-Conn., was 236-177, drawing support from both factions. Wright voted for the amendment. *(Vote 308, p. 94-H)*

Democrats, who had split evenly on whether to adopt the rule, supported the Ratchford amendment 169-83. Republicans, many of whom were holding out for a larger, $10 billion cut, opposed it 67-94; they had gone against the rule 21-135.

Ratchford's $5 billion cut was offered as an alternative to a $10 billion cut proposed by Silvio O. Conte, R-Mass., and backed by the Reagan administration. Since Ratchford's proposal was offered as an amendment to Conte's amendment, the House would have voted on a $10 billion cut if Ratchford had been defeated.

Some supporters of bigger cuts were drawn to the Ratchford proposal as a result of a surprise amendment offered by Sidney R. Yates, D-Ill., chairman of the Appropriations Subcommittee on Interior. Yates' amendment, adopted by voice vote, barred any SFC funds for price and loan guarantees to two Colorado oil shale projects that critics had called too big and too expensive — Union II ($2.7 billion) and Cathedral Bluffs ($2.19 billion).

House Debate. SFC critics argued that the nation could not afford to spend billions to develop synthetic fuels, likely to be far more expensive than natural oil and gas, at a time when it was cutting social programs to cure the deficit.

But SFC supporters insisted the nation should push forward with development of technologies for making oil and gas from its abundant domestic reserves of coal and oil shale, technologies that promised to lessen U.S. energy dependence on foreign sources such as Persian Gulf nations.

Conte, in arguing for his amendment Aug. 2, told the House: "The question here is not one of Democrats vs. Republicans or Congress vs. the administration. The only question before us today is whether we will vote in favor of the taxpaying workers of this country, or whether we will vote to bail out the pet projects of the fat cat oil barons. Will we prevent the waste of $10 billion on environmentally unsound projects, or will we continue to add on to the deficit with little to show except lavish offices and charges of scandal?"

Wright, who ended debate on the Ratchford amendment, argued: "The first question is this: How shall we expect the United States ever really to be taken seriously in the world if, only five years after the second Arab embargo brought our nation to its economic knees for the second time in a decade, we abandon the goal of energy independence by doing away with the one long-term program . . . to achieve that goal? What kind of message does that send to the Khomeinis and Qaddafis of this world? Does it not invite yet another Arab oil embargo?"

Senate Action. The Senate Appropriations Committee approved its $8.13 billion version of the Interior appropriations bill by voice vote on Aug. 1. That version contained no synfuels rescission, although critics of the SFC planned to offer one as a floor amendment.

$5 Billion Cut: Continuing Resolution

Because the Senate failed to act on the Interior funding bill, appropriations for programs covered by that measure were rolled into a fiscal continuing appropriations resolution (H J Res 648).

In dealing with the continuing resolution, the Senate Appropriations Committee recommended a $5.2 billion rescission that reflected the compromise worked out in September with the administration. This would have returned less money to the Treasury than the House version, since $750 million of the Senate amount was to be set aside in a special account reserved for projects to demonstrate cleaner ways to burn coal. The Senate passed its version of the continuing resolution Oct. 4.

During debate on H J Res 648, the Senate Oct. 3 rejected, 37-60, an amendment offered by Bill Bradley, D-N.J., to rescind $9 billion in synfuels funds. *(Vote 262, p. 46-S)*

Provisions. House-Senate conferees on H J Res 648 agreed to strip $5.375 billion from the synfuels program, with $750 million of that amount to go to the Senate's coal program.

The rescission left the SFC with about $8 billion to spend. Of that, $5.7 billion was earmarked for projects that had already received letters of intent from the SFC. Half of any money not spent on those projects was to revert to the Treasury.

Conferees dropped a House provision that would have denied funding to two Colorado projects, Union II and Cathedral Bluffs. Those projects, which had drawn objections on economic and environmental grounds, together could cost about $5 billion.

An amendment by Sen. Howard M. Metzenbaum, D-Ohio, to impose financial disclosure and conflict-of-interest restrictions on SFC board members, was adopted by the Senate and the conference. Two SFC presidents stepped down amid conflict-of-interest charges. ∎

IEA Antitrust Exemption

Congress March 15 cleared for the president a bill (HR 4194 — PL 98-239) to extend until June 30, 1985, an antitrust exemption for major U.S. oil companies that participated in international oil-sharing arrangements during times of crisis.

Final action came when both chambers adopted a conference report (H Rept 98-620) on the legislation.

The path for enactment was cleared when Senate conferees agreed to drop a provision that tied the extension to passage of a law giving the president authority to control domestic oil prices and supplies in an international energy crisis. *(Related story, p. 356)*

U.S. oil companies participated in the International Energy Agency (IEA), formed in 1974 as a mechanism for allocating oil to the United States and its allies in the event of a worldwide shortage, only upon guarantees that they would not be subject to antitrust prosecution for passing marketing data to the IEA for use in planning for an oil supply disruption.

Standby Allocation Issue

In November 1983, with the antitrust exemption due to expire Dec. 31, both chambers passed the extension bill.

The House acted Nov. 7, passing a simple extension

bill that had been reported Nov. 2 by the Energy and Commerce Committee (H Rept 98-472).

The Senate passed the measure Nov. 17, after it had adopted an amendment by Howard M. Metzenbaum, D-Ohio, ending the exemption as of June 30, 1984, unless a law was enacted before then empowering the president to control oil supplies and prices during an emergency. *(Background, 1983 Almanac p. 371)*

President Reagan had vetoed a standby allocation measure in 1982, arguing the market should allocate prices and supplies. *(1982 Almanac p. 301)*

The House refused to accept the Senate version, with the Metzenbaum amendment attached, and the antitrust exemption expired Dec. 31, 1983.

The impasse continued until March 1984. In a House-Senate conference March 14, Metzenbaum, who was a conferee, agreed to give up his amendment since it was clear that it did not have the strong support of Senate leaders.

Metzenbaum reiterated his dislike of an international oil allocation mechanism in the absence of any means of allocating oil domesticly in a crisis. But he agreed to pursue the issue in another context.   ■

Divisive Natural Gas Bill Scrapped in House

Congress failed to act in 1984 on legislation changing federal controls on natural gas. Energy experts on both sides of Capitol Hill worked on the controversial issue for months, but they could not develop a consensus measure.

The end of the effort was signaled Sept. 26 when House Speaker Thomas P. O'Neill Jr., D-Mass., told a press conference, "There will be no natural gas bill [this session]. There will be no time for that. It's just too controversial."

O'Neill's words were the formal death sentence for a measure (HR 4277) that attempted to iron out problems in the natural gas marketplace but threatened to divide both parties in a bitter regional fight. That bill had been reported May 31 (H Rept 98-814) by the House Energy and Commerce Committee.

The Senate also took no floor action in 1984, although Senate Energy Committee Chairman James A. McClure, R-Idaho, and 11 other interested senators met informally about a half dozen times from February to May in an unsuccessful effort to develop a consensus bill.

Besides McClure, the group included Sens. David L. Boren, D-Okla., Bill Bradley, D-N.J., John C. Danforth, R-Mo., Pete V. Domenici, R-N.M., Wendell H. Ford, D-Ky., John Heinz, R-Pa., Roger W. Jepsen, R-Iowa, J. Bennett Johnston, D-La., Nancy Landon Kassebaum, R-Kan., Don Nickles, R-Okla., and Malcolm Wallop, R-Wyo.

The lack of congressional action meant that price controls on approximately half of all U.S. gas supplies expired Jan. 1, 1985, the date set by the 1978 Natural Gas Policy Act (NGPA — PL 95-621). That law put a permanent lid on prices for "old" gas, that from wells drilled before April 20, 1977. But it permitted decontrol of "new" gas beginning in 1985. *(1978 Almanac p. 639)*

Background

Skyrocketing consumer gas bills in 1982 and 1983 caused intense pressure on Congress to relieve the plight of ratepayers, especially those on low or fixed incomes facing a choice of "heat or eat."

Despite a glut of gas, market forces had not pushed prices down. After severe gas shortages in the winter of 1976-77, pipeline companies had rushed to sign contracts with producers assuring themselves and their customers an adequate supply — at almost any price.

But as consumer gas bills surged in subsequent years, many in Congress began to question the automatic price increases written into the contracts signed in the late 1970s. Their fears of future price increases were merely exacerbated in February 1983, when President Reagan sent

Congress a plan for eventual decontrol of all natural gas — "old" as well as "new."

Intensive efforts to tackle natural gas pricing issues in the 1983 session of Congress ended in stalemate. The Senate on Nov. 15, 1983, rejected by lopsided margins two competing alternatives — a consumer-oriented bill keeping controls on old gas and a producer-oriented bill removing them.

House Energy Committee action also ended inconclusively in 1983, when Chairman John D. Dingell, D-Mich., on Nov. 17 suspended markup on HR 4277 after losing a 23-19 test vote on a consumer-oriented proposal. *(1983 Almanac p. 366)*

House Committee Action

HR 4277 (H Rept 98-814) squeaked through the Energy and Commerce Committee April 12 during a bitter session in which opponents failed, on votes on 16 amendments, to crack the fragile coalition supporting the bill.

The committee by 22-20 adopted a substitute text that drew votes from representatives of consumer states and some gas pipeline supporters, but was bitterly opposed by representatives of gas-producing states.

As approved, the bill allowed pipelines and distributors to force renegotiations with natural gas producers on certain contract clauses that could force prices up. It also allowed other changes in contracts that governed the marketing of natural gas.

The complex measure represented a shaky compromise among various interest groups, and few members were enthusiastic about it. Representatives from gas-producing states in the Southwest vigorously opposed it, while many from gas-consuming states in the Midwest and the Northeast wanted stronger action to protect consumers.

Fragile Support Coalition

The substitute, offered by Edward R. Madigan, R-Ill., drew support from three other committee Republicans, as well as 18 Democrats. That 22-vote coalition barely controlled the balance of power in the 42-member committee, defeating producer-state Democrats and the majority of Republicans, who remained loyal to Reagan's call for price decontrol. The administration, in an April 9 letter from Energy Secretary Donald P. Hodel, strenuously opposed the proposal.

Although offered by Madigan, both the substitute and the coalition supporting it were put together under the leadership of Rep. Philip R. Sharp, D-Ind. Support from Dingell was crucial.

But even Dingell had reservations about the measure; in May, he told gas industry representatives, "I am not completely happy with that bill." He invited them to suggest changes.

The substitute reflected a compromise in which Sharp agreed to drop price rollbacks and an extension of controls in return for the support of several Republicans on provisions to adjust contracts that governed the gas business.

In grueling markup sessions April 10-12, producer-state Democrats and the Republicans opposing the Madigan substitute hoped to peel away at least one of the votes Madigan's proponents needed to report out the bill. In the end, however, they failed to make even that tiny dent in the coalition.

W. J. "Billy" Tauzin, D-La., and other opponents charged that the "brotherhood of 22" had "taken an unholy blood oath" to accept no amendments, however meritorious, to their substitute.

Sharp denied that, but said Madigan's supporters needed to protect their slim majority in order to move the bill at all. He said they had agreed to accept no amendment unless it was acceptable to each of the 22.

Tauzin and his allies offered amendment after amendment, 16 in all, crafted to be as enticing and inoffensive as possible. But each was defeated, usually by the same 22 "no" votes.

Near the end of the second day of the markup, Madigan's opponents began voicing their frustration. Bob Whittaker, R-Kan., said: "This is not a legitimate markup." Mike Synar, D-Okla, said he could no longer "believe this thing is fair in any way, shape or form."

But Chairman Dingell, who had until then stayed aloof from the fracas except to vote, spoke up to say the markup was "part of a proper process," and that opponents had been assured "full opportunity to have their say" and offer amendments.

He observed, however, that "one thing indispensable to success on this committee is having the votes."

Tauzin rejoined that the assurances were "a little like telling a condemned man he can say something before you shoot him." He walked out of the markup after the 13th vote.

The Tauzin group saved until almost the end what they hoped would be their "killer" amendment, the one that would finally crack the hardened coalition. Offered by Bill Richardson, D-N.M., it would have strengthened the substitute's "contract carriage" provisions, which allowed gas distributors to buy directly from producers and force pipelines to transport the gas if they had unused capacity.

But even the contract carriage amendment failed to break the "blood oath" coalition. One member some thought would be vulnerable to the appeal, Tom Tauke, R-Iowa, had said ahead of time he would stick to Madigan's language although he wanted more. The amendment failed 20-22.

With the coalition's strength proven, Sharp moved the previous question — a bid to cut off further debate. The committee agreed to the motion 20-11. After two intervening procedural votes, the bill as amended by Madigan was ordered reported 22-20.

Provisions of HR 4277

As approved by the committee, HR 4277 contained the following major provisions:
- Left largely intact the permanent NGPA freeze on the wellhead price of old gas.

- Froze prices for new gas and for high-cost "stripper" and "tight sands" gas at the NGPA ceiling levels as of the date of enactment of HR 4277. The NGPA otherwise allowed those ceiling prices to rise each month until Dec. 31, 1984, after which all ceilings were removed under NGPA.
- Retained an NGPA schedule that decontrolled as of Jan. 1, 1985, the prices of some categories of new and other gas.
- Allowed pipelines to force gas producers to renegotiate existing contracts for certain high-priced gas. If pipeline and producer did not agree within six months, the question was to be settled by an arbitrator. Once the pipeline sought renegotiation, the producer could within 60 days terminate the contract and sell the gas to another customer.
- Tightened restrictions on the ability of the Federal Energy Regulatory Commission (FERC) to raise the price of old interstate gas by use of its rulemaking authority. FERC could do so only on a case-by-case basis.
- Limited the enforceability of "take-or-pay" requirements in existing gas contracts to 50 percent of the contracted volume for three years after enactment. The limit applied to new and high-cost gas under contract to both interstate and intrastate pipelines. Gas not taken could be resold by the producer. The limitation did not apply to contracts renegotiated after April 2, 1984. The seller could seek a financial hardship adjustment from FERC.
- Capped price escalator clauses in existing contracts at their levels as of Dec. 31, 1984. The cap was to stay in effect for two years, beginning on Jan. 1, 1985. If the producer and pipeline had not renegotiated the contract price after those two years, a new fair market value would be set through binding arbitration.
- Prohibited pipelines from enforcing "minimum commodity bill" requirements in contracts with their customers. These requirements, similar to take-or-pay clauses, forced local distributors to pay certain costs to the pipeline if they did not take a minimum quantity of gas.
- Imposed a new "prudency" standard on pipelines in their purchase of gas from producers, aimed at keeping them from paying too much.

Under the standard, FERC could deny a pipeline the chance to charge its customers for gas on which it overpaid, reducing the pipeline's profits.
- Prohibited pipelines from giving preferential transportation to gas they owned or to gas owned by their affiliated producing companies.
- Gave FERC authority to order "contract carriage" — that is, to order a pipeline to carry gas purchased directly by a distributor from a producer, when the pipeline had available capacity, and when such carriage was in the "public convenience and necessity" or the pipeline had been discriminatory in refusing.
- Repealed certain restraints on natural gas demand contained in the 1978 Industrial Powerplant and Fuel Use Act, and repealed the incremental pricing program set by the NGPA.
- Prohibited importation of Algerian liquefied natural gas by one pipeline at Lake Charles, La., without renegotiation of its high price — but imposed no new controls on gas imports from Mexico and Canada.
- Required FERC to do an 18-month study to determine whether regulations were needed to ensure that residential and small business consumers did not subsidize the lower "preferential prices" given to large industrial customers. FERC was also given authority to issue such rules.

Too Hot to Handle

For months, HR 4277 appeared moribund. Then, shortly before the August recess, Speaker O'Neill asked the Rules Committee to consider the measure. A majority of the House, 218 members, had signed a June 29 letter to O'Neill urging him to move the bill.

During the week of Sept. 10 word went out that the natural gas bill had been put on the Rules agenda for the following week, and staffers and lobbyists mobilized for a bitter fight. Members began to barrage the committee with requests to offer amendments.

But at a Democratic caucus meeting that week, some members complained that they would be forced to vote on a no-win issue, one that would hurt the Democratic presidential ticket in the Southwest. When the next Rules Committee agenda was published on Sept. 14, natural gas was nowhere to be found.

Sources said O'Neill would not promise floor time even if the bill made it through Rules, and a head count of Rules Committee members showed a 6-7 vote against bringing it to the floor.

On Sept. 26, O'Neill formally declared the measure dead.

"What happened was that the opposition backed us up to the point where there was so little time left we couldn't do it," said Sharp.   ∎

NRC Reauthorization Clears

After reaching a compromise on the controversial issue of emergency evacuation planning for nuclear power plants, Congress on Oct. 11 cleared a Nuclear Regulatory Commission (NRC) reauthorization bill for fiscal 1984-85 (S 1291 — PL 98-553). The president signed the bill Oct. 30.

The Senate passed the bill by voice vote on Oct. 10 and the House followed suit the next day.

Although the measure did not clear until 11 days after the start of fiscal 1985 — more than a year after the previous NRC authorization (PL 97-415) had expired — funding for the NRC for fiscal 1984 and 1985 was not in jeopardy. Appropriations at close to the levels requested by the administration were included in both the fiscal 1984 and 1985 energy and water development appropriations bills (PL 98-50, PL 98-360). *(1983 Almanac p. 500; fiscal 1985 bill, p. 369)*

Emergency Evacuation Issue

The issue of emergency evacuation planning was of particular concern to New York, where the Long Island Lighting Company had been prevented from opening its Shoreham nuclear power plant, in part because Suffolk County authorities refused to draw up an emergency evacuation plan. Such plans were required for the NRC to issue an operating license after the Three Mile Island, Pa., nuclear power plant accident in 1979. Suffolk County argued that population density on Long Island made evacuation impossible. *(1980 Almanac p. 502)*

Senate action in the Environment and Public Works Committee was stalled for several months while Sens. Alan K. Simpson, R-Wyo., chairman of the Nuclear Regulation Subcommittee, and Daniel Patrick Moynihan, D-N.Y., attempted to resolve the matter.

They finally reached a compromise that specified that even if state or local officials refused to participate in developing an emergency preparedness plan, the NRC could issue an operating license for a nuclear power plant if it determined that the utility itself had prepared an acceptable emergency preparedness plan. The NRC was required to evaluate whether a plan submitted by a utility would work.

Previously, the NRC had accepted utility emergency plans only when state or local officials were working on an emergency plan but it was delayed.

Provisions

As cleared, S 1291 embraced the text of S 2846 (S Rept 98-546). Its major provisions authorized:

● $466.8 million for fiscal 1984 and $460 million for fiscal 1985 for NRC salaries and expenses, including:

$91.49 million in fiscal 1984 and $87.14 million in fiscal 1985 for the Office of Nuclear Reactor Regulation;

$70.91 million in fiscal 1984 and $74.77 million in fiscal 1985 for the Office of Inspection and Enforcement;

$36.28 million in fiscal 1984 and $35.71 million in fiscal 1985 for the Office of Nuclear Material Safety and Safeguards;

$199.74 million in fiscal 1984 and $193.29 million in fiscal 1985 for the Office of Nuclear Regulatory Research;

$27.52 million in fiscal 1984 and $27.47 million in fiscal 1985 for Program Technical Support;

$40.86 million in fiscal 1984 and $41.62 million in fiscal 1985 for Program Direction and Administration.

● A pilot program to assess the merits of relocating certain NRC personnel to regional offices. The effect of the pilot program requirement was to slow down an NRC effort to decentralize its licensing procedures.

● Continued work toward the establishment of a "nuclear data link," which would give the NRC direct computer access to data from nuclear reactors.

The House Interior Committee, which also considered the bill, had rejected such a program during markup in 1983, because it feared that the NRC was moving to take over control of reactors in case of an accident.

Senators, however, said that serious information problems surfaced in the Three Mile Island accident, and S 1291 authorized a prototype program to address the problem.

● Transfer of an operating license from a U.S. corporation to a U.S. subsidiary of a foreign corporation, provided certain conditions were satisfied.

Legislative History

Both the House and Senate reported NRC reauthorization bills in 1983 (S 1291, HR 2510), but neither measure came to the floor.

The Senate Environment and Public Works Committee on May 16, 1983, reported S 1291 as a simple funding reauthorization bill (S Rept 98-118), never intending for it to come to the floor in that form. The committee hoped to resolve a number of legislative issues, including whether to continue NRC's authority to grant temporary operating licenses and whether to reform the entire licensing process, and consider those issues as amendments to S 1291. But the committee made no headway on licensing reform and bogged down in a dispute over emergency planning requirements.

The committee dropped an extension of the temporary licensing authority from the bill during markup.

The House Interior and Energy committees both reported HR 2510 (H Rept 98-103, Parts I and II) in 1983. The Energy Committee version would have continued NRC's authority to grant temporary licenses; the Interior Committee version would have discontinued it. The dispute was not reconciled and the bill did not reach the floor. The temporary licensing authority died on Dec. 31, 1983. *(1983 Almanac p. 370)*

After Simpson and Moynihan reached agreement on emergency planning, the Senate Environment Committee June 19 voted 13-0 to report S 2846 (S Rept 98-546), which reflected the decisions made by the committee during the previous 13 months.

The Senate Energy Committee, which had a limited referral, deleted a portion of the bill dealing with nuclear waste and reported the bill (S Rept 98-579) on Aug. 6. The dropped provision attempted to clarify the rights of states under a 1982 law (PL 97-425) governing disposal of nuclear wastes. *(1982 Almanac p. 304)*

In testimony July 31 before the Senate Energy Subcommittee on Energy Research and Development, spokesmen for the Department of Energy, the Texas governor's office and an environmental group asked that the provision be deleted. They all said it was so ambiguously worded that it could end up hindering the waste disposal process, rather than facilitating it.

The Senate on Oct. 10 passed S 1291, after amending it to incorporate the text of S 2846. The House passed S 1291 without amendment on Oct. 11, clearing the bill. ∎

Oil Company Mergers

Three corporate mergers involving some of the nation's largest oil companies sparked a brief congressional effort to impose a moratorium on such combinations until the long-range effect of the actions could be determined.

But the effort faded when Senate supporters failed to attach an 11-month moratorium as a rider to a fiscal 1984 supplemental appropriations bill (H J Res 492 — PL 98-332) during debate on the measure in March.

Instead, the Senate voted for a congressional study of mergers — and even that watered-down plan was dropped when the supplemental appropriations bill reached a House-Senate conference committee several weeks later. *(Supplemental, p. 429)*

A number of other merger moratorium proposals were introduced on both sides of Capitol Hill and several committees held hearings, but none of the bills got past the hearing stage.

President Reagan had no "concern . . . or opposition" to the oil mergers, according to White House press spokesman Larry Speakes.

And Energy Secretary Donald P. Hodel said the industry concentration would not hurt the nation's future energy supplies.

Six-Month Moratorium Plan

The move to impose a moratorium on mergers was led by Sens. J. Bennett Johnston, D-La., Howard M. Metzenbaum, D-Ohio, and Warren B. Rudman, R-N.H., who were concerned about large oil companies "drilling for oil in Wall Street" rather than in the ground. They argued that the mergers left the companies deeply in debt and unable to spend much money looking for new oil and gas reserves.

Johnston's first moratorium proposal came in February, after Texaco Inc., the nation's third largest oil com-

pany, offered $10.1 billion for Getty Oil Corp., the No. 13 company.

Johnston proposed a six-month moratorium on oil company mergers involving the top 150 companies — those with reserves of more than 10 million barrels. He offered the moratorium as an amendment to a bill (S 979) reauthorizing the Export Administration Act, but the Senate Feb. 29 tabled the amendment, 52-42. *(Vote 24, p. 6-S)*

Within weeks, two other mergers were announced: Standard Oil of California (SoCal), the No. 5 oil company, bid $13.2 billion for No. 4 Gulf Corp., and Mobil Corp., the nation's second largest oil company, offered $5.7 billion for Superior Oil Co.

11-Month Moratorium

On March 12, Johnston circulated a new moratorium proposal, this one affecting only the top 50 oil companies — those with worldwide reserves of more than 100 million barrels. The proposal, which exempted the three large takeovers already under way, called for creation of a commission to study mergers while the moratorium was in place and to report to Congress.

Johnston offered the proposal as an amendment to a fiscal 1984 supplemental appropriations bill (H J Res 492). At the request of John C. Danforth, R-Mo., Johnston extended the moratorium expiration date from Sept. 21, 1984, to March 1, 1985, with the report due Jan. 1, 1985, to give Congress time to consider any legislative changes.

On March 28, however, the Senate effectively killed the proposal by adopting a substitute requiring Congress to study the issue, but putting no constraints on mergers in the meantime. The vote came as a surprise, since it appeared that a majority of senators favored the moratorium.

Majority Leader Howard H. Baker Jr., R-Tenn., on behalf of Robert Dole, R-Kan., and other moratorium foes, offered the substitute amendment. It called for the Senate Finance, Energy and Judiciary committees to study the merger question and to report to the Senate by July 1, 1984. Further, the amendment stipulated that any legislative changes recommended by the committees be retroactive to March 27, 1984.

Rudman's motion to table the substitute failed by a vote of 39-57, and it subsequently was adopted by voice vote. *(Vote 40, p. 10-S)*

The provision was dropped by House-Senate conferees on H J Res 492 before they filed their report (H Rept 98-792) on the measure May 17. ∎

CWIP Bill Dies in Senate

For the second year in a row, Congress failed to pass legislation that limited the ability of federally regulated utilities to charge consumers of electricity for construction costs before new power plants were placed in service.

The legislation (HR 555) was prompted by a 1983 ruling of the Federal Energy Regulatory Commission (FERC) that permitted federally regulated utilities to include in their rate base up to 50 percent of the interest costs of borrowing for plants under construction (called CWIP — Construction Work in Progress), without having to show need. The rates paid by customers were determined by the size of the rate base and the percentage rate of return on the rate base permitted by regulators. (Direct costs of construction were recovered through a depreciation component in utility rates after facilities went into service.)

The FERC rule, which became effective July 1, 1983, followed similar decisions by many state utility regulatory agencies. It was generally supported by Energy Secretary Donald P. Hodel and investor-owned utilities, although the utilities would have preferred authority to include 100 percent of interest costs in the rate base. About 10 percent of the nation's electricity sales were regulated by FERC; the remainder were subject to state regulation.

The legislation (HR 555) limited the ability of utilities to charge consumers of electricity sold under FERC jurisdiction for construction costs before new power plants were placed in service. *(Background, 1983 Almanac p. 372)*

Legislative History

HR 555 was reported Aug. 9, 1983, by the House Energy and Commerce Committee (H Rept 98-350). It was passed by the House Feb. 8, 1984, by a 288-113 vote. *(Vote 19, p. 8-H)*

As passed, the bill restricted the use of CWIP charges to financially pressed utilities unable to generate more than 40 percent of planned construction expenditures internally.

To qualify for inclusion of CWIP costs in its rate base and a consequent hike in rates charged to consumers, a utility had to demonstrate to FERC that the facility to be constructed was necessary to meet customer demand and that the utility could not borrow the construction funds except at costs significantly above the national average.

Floor debate was divided largely along partisan lines, with each side arguing that its position would save consumers money.

Advocates of the bill (mostly Democrats) said it would save consumers money and encourage utilities to look at alternatives to building expensive new power plants.

Opponents (mostly Republicans) claimed the bill would discourage utilities from making needed investments and lead to "rate shocks" once new facilities began operation and their construction costs were factored into utility rate bases.

Rep. Carlos J. Moorhead, Calif., ranking Republican on the Energy and Commerce Subcommittee on Energy Conservation and Power, which reported the bill, offered the language of the FERC rule as an amendment to HR 555. That amendment was defeated on a largely party-line vote of 135-266. *(Vote 18, p. 8-H)*

Two CWIP bills were introduced in the Senate, S 817 by Howard M. Metzenbaum, D-Ohio, and S 1069 by John H. Chafee, R-R.I. The Senate Energy Subcommittee on Energy Regulation held three days of hearings but no markup session was held. ∎

Weatherization Program

Congress turned down an effort to greatly increase authorized funding levels for home "weatherization" work for low-income families.

But members did clear a Head Start and human services measure (S 2565 — PL 98-558) that contained provisions revamping the Energy Department's weatherization program, liberalizing some aspects of it. *(Head Start bill, p. 485)*

Background

The weatherization program was first authorized by a 1976 law (PL 94-385). It helped low-income families pay for

work such as insulation, weather-stripping and repairs that could cut their energy costs. An estimated one million homes had benefited from the program by 1984. *(1976 Almanac p. 95)*

Fiscal 1983 funds for the program totaled $245 million, including $100 million from a one-time emergency jobs bill (PL 98-8). Fiscal 1984 funds, provided in the Interior appropriations bill (PL 98-146), totaled some $190 million. Also, some weatherization funds were provided in other programs.

The main weatherization program received a $191 million appropriation for fiscal 1985 in the Interior portion of the continuing appropriations resolution (H J Res 648 — PL 98-473). *(Story, p. 444)*

The Reagan administration's fiscal 1985 budget submission had asked Congress to shift funding for the weatherization program from the Treasury to a proposed new Petroleum Overcharge Restitution Fund.

The fund was to be supported by fines paid by oil companies for overcharging their customers. The fund also was to be used to support the Low-Income Energy Assistance Program run by the Department of Health and Human Services, according to the administration proposal.

The Energy Department requested a fiscal 1985 appropriation of $238 million for its weatherization program, but only on the condition that the special fund be established.

Rep. James T. Broyhill, R-N.C., ranking Republican on the House Energy Committee and Commerce Committee, introduced such a bill (HR 4972), but Congress took no action on the proposal.

Reauthorization Bill: HR 2615

In drafting legislation (HR 2615) to reauthorize the weatherization program, the House Energy Committee approved a $500 million funding level for fiscal 1985. The committee reported its version of the bill May 12, 1983 (H Rept 98-108).

But the full House, at the urging of freshman Democrat Thomas R. Carper of Delaware, on Jan. 24, 1984, cut the authorization to $200 million, leaving the Energy Department program at roughly current levels. The vote on Carper's amendment was 233-142. *(Vote 5, p. 2-H)*

The House then passed HR 2615 by a 222-157 vote. *(Vote 6, p. 2-H)*

Deficit Concerns

Debate on HR 2615, the first legislation considered by the House in 1984, served as a forum for arguments about the federal budget deficit.

Republicans complained that the bill as reported by the Energy Committee was a "budget-buster," calling for a $310 million increase over fiscal 1984 spending.

Supporters of the program, including some Republicans from Northern states, argued that the weatherization program was cost-effective and accused opponents of trying to balance the budget "on the backs of the poor and homeless."

Debate was largely along partisan lines, but it was a freshman Democrat — Carper — who offered the successful amendment to reduce the authorized spending level. His amendment also called for a five-year reauthorization, rather than 10 years as in the original proposal.

The amendment caused some confusion since all time for debate had expired before Carper could explain it. Although Democrats as a group opposed it by a 108-124 margin, freshman Democrats backed Carper 32-23.

Carper said in an interview that he began drafting his amendment late in the floor debate after discussions with a number of colleagues, including several other freshman Democrats. He said those talks left him with the impression that the bill could not pass in its original form because of widespread concern about the deficit.

Three Republican amendments were rejected before Carper offered his amendment:

● By George W. Gekas, R-Pa., to prohibit use of funds unless the secretary of the Treasury certified to Congress that such expenditures would not add to the national debt. Rejected, 168-205. *(Vote 3, p. 2-H)*

● By William E. Dannemeyer, R-Calif., to prohibit the appropriation of funds until the relevant recommendations made by the president's Private Sector Survey on Cost Control (the Grace commission) had been implemented. Ruled out of order. *(Grace commission report, p. 184)*

● By Phil Gramm, R-Texas, to give the president a line-item veto of any funds authorized or appropriated by the bill. Congress would have 60 days to override the veto. Rejected 131-245. *(Vote 4, p. 2-H)*

Second Try: S 2565

The Senate did not consider HR 2615, but it approved certain changes in the weatherization program through an amendment to a measure (S 2565) that cleared Congress in the last week of the session. That measure reauthorized the Head Start, Community Services Block Grant and Low Income Energy Assistance programs. *(Story, p. 485)*

S 2565 was reported May 24 by the Senate Labor and Human Resources Committee (S Rept 98-484). A much-revised version was offered as a committee substitute amendment by Chairman Orrin G. Hatch, R-Utah, when the bill reached the Senate floor Oct. 4. It had been hammered out by key members of the Senate panel and two House committees — Education and Labor, and Energy and Commerce.

By voice votes, the committee substitute was adopted and S 2565 was passed by the Senate Oct. 4.

The House approved the legislation Oct. 9 by a 376-6 vote, clearing it for the president. *(Vote 398, p. 122-H)*

Provisions

As cleared, the weatherization portion of S 2565:

● Liberalized weatherization eligibility requirements to conform with standards for eligibility in the Low Income Energy Assistance Program, which helped poor families pay their energy bills.

● Authorized use of weatherization funds to pay for furnace modifications.

● Struck down the requirement that the Energy Department follow a time-consuming rulemaking process before making new energy-saving measures eligible for weatherization funds.

● Changed the $1,600 per house maximum expenditure cap to allow individual expenditures of more than that as long as the average statewide expenditure was no more than $1,600 per house.

● Authorized homes that participated in pre-1979 weatherization programs to receive further weatherization assistance to meet new program guidelines.

● Authorized the energy secretary, beginning in fiscal 1986, to earmark between 5 and 15 percent of each year's funds for allocation to states that have done the best job providing weatherization assistance during the previous year. ∎

Energy Conservation

By failing to agree on a single approach to reform, the House and Senate ensured that an unpopular energy conservation program went into effect Jan. 1, 1985, while a broadly supported one was allowed to lapse.

The House and Senate failed to reconcile their respective versions of legislation (HR 5946) to renew the popular Residential Conservation Service (RCS), which required utilities to offer "energy audits" to homeowners. The bill also sought to block the Jan. 1, 1985, implementation of a similar Commercial and Apartment Conservation Service (CACS) that was widely opposed.

Background

The RCS program was established in 1978 as part of a larger energy package (PL 95-619). It was under fire because it reached a tiny proportion of homes, most of them affluent, and because most of the cost of energy audits was passed along to consumers by utilities.

The president had proposed no funding for the program's administration in fiscal years 1982-84, but Congress voted funding of approximately $3 million each year. *(1978 Almanac p. 645)*

The Commercial and Apartment Conservation Service was established in 1980, but preliminary administrative actions were delayed and steps toward implementation did not begin until late in 1984. At year's end, most states had not yet received approval of their CACS implementation plans. *(1980 Almanac p. 480)*

House Action

The House version of HR 5946 (H Rept 98-903) would have reformed and extended the RCS for five years while killing the CACS, under a compromise supported by the utilities and conservationists. But the Senate balked at the comprehensive approach, insisting instead on a one-year freeze in the status quo — extending the RCS and delaying the CACS (S Rept 98-625).

The House bill would not have forced the utilities to perform residential energy audits. Instead, the bill would have allowed utilities to achieve conservation through methods such as financing programs for energy-saving repairs, measures to reduce peak-hour demand, or rebates for energy-efficient equipment. It also would have added protection for small businessmen, who complained that having utilities make referrals for repairs froze small contractors out of the market.

Senate Action

The House passed HR 5946 by voice vote July 30, and the Senate substituted its version by voice vote Oct. 3. Later that day, the House accepted the Senate's one-year delay in any program changes, but insisted that the reforms embodied in HR 5946 go into effect after a year if there was no congressional action. The Senate Oct. 5 refused to agree to that approach, and the House never reconsidered the matter.

A spokesman for the Edison Electric Institute, a lobbying group representing utilities, said the stalemate "will make nobody happy." Utilities strongly opposed CACS, saying the business and apartment audits would be costly and unlikely to lead to significant conservation. They were willing to go along with a reformed RCS program, strongly supported by conservationists. ∎

Energy Research Bill

A bill to reauthorize the Department of Energy's research activities for fiscal 1985-87 snagged in the House over an attempt to divert $2 billion from the U.S. Synthetic Fuels Corporation (SFC) into other energy research.

However, research funding was provided in the fiscal 1985 energy and water development appropriations bill (HR 5653 — PL 98-360). *(Story, p. 369)*

The research authorization bill HR 5244 (H Rept 98-686) was reported April 12 by the House Science and Technology Committee.

It was scheduled for floor action Aug. 8, but Science Committee Chairman Don Fuqua, D-Fla., wanted to offer an amendment to authorize a transfer of funds from the troubled SFC. Problems arose in drafting the language, and House leaders pulled the bill off the schedule. *(Synfuels program, p. 347)*

The Senate did not take up an energy research authorization.

HR 5244 provided a three-year authorization, beginning at $3.34 billion for fiscal 1985, for civilian research and development activities of the Energy Department. ∎

Emergency Preparedness

Congress took only a few minor actions on energy emergency preparedness legislation, a topic that many members had hoped would be the subject of major legislation in 1984.

At the start of the year, key members of the Energy committees on both sides of Capitol Hill were drafting bills designed to strengthen U.S. preparations for an energy shortage such as occurred in 1973 or 1979.

But in the face of administration opposition to some proposals and only lukewarm support for others, no comprehensive legislation was enacted.

Congress did clear one minor measure (HR 4194 — PL 98-239) extending an antitrust exemption for major U.S. oil companies that participated in an international energy supply-sharing program. *(Story, p. 349)*

Senate Preparedness Bill

Senate Energy Committee Chairman James A. McClure, R-Idaho, sponsored legislation (S 1678) that attempted to set forth a comprehensive program for meeting any future energy shortages.

He introduced the measure in 1983 and sought administration backing for the bill, promising in exchange to support the administration's plan to slow the purchase of oil to fill the Strategic Petroleum Reserve (SPR).

S 1678 required the administration to provide a specific plan for use of SPR oil, granted antitrust and conflict-of-interest exemptions to Executive Reserves (private industry experts who would assist government agencies in a crisis), provided federal pre-emption of state laws allocating supplies and setting prices, encouraged private industry to develop voluntary plans to cope with shortages and authorized a test drawdown of SPR.

During Senate Energy hearings early in 1984, administration witnesses were lukewarm in their support for the bill and recommended a number of changes.

McClure abruptly broke off markup of the measure after a June 20 session in which Sen. Bill Bradley, D-N.J.,

to McClure's surprise, was able to add provisions calling for the federal government to set up a program of block grants to state governors to lessen the impact of higher energy prices during a shortage.

The Bradley amendment also would have required the president to recommend modifications in existing financial assistance programs to meet the needs arising from big increases in energy prices.

SPR Test Sale

The only other emergency preparedness bill to receive much attention was a measure requiring the government to conduct a test sale of SPR oil.

HR 3880 (H Rept 98-1003), requiring a test sale of 1.1 million barrels of oil, passed the House by voice vote Sept. 18. But the Senate did not consider the measure.

Supporters of the bill argued that a test sale was needed to boost public confidence in the reserve and to work out technical problems in the paperwork and actual transfer of the oil from underground storage in Louisiana and Texas to refineries.

The administration did not oppose the bill, but said a test sale in times of an oil surplus would be of little help in predicting problems that could arise in using SPR oil in times of an energy crisis. ∎

Nuclear Waste Sites

Three sites in Nevada, Texas and Washington were targeted Dec. 19 by the Department of Energy (DOE) for geologic exploration to determine which should house the nation's first repository for high-level radioactive waste.

The naming of the sites was a major step in the procedure set up by a 1982 law (PL 97-425) to establish a deep, underground permanent storage area for highly radioactive nuclear waste by 1998. *(1982 Almanac p. 304)*

The three sites were Yucca Mountain in Nye County, Nev.; Deaf Smith County, Texas; and Hanford, Wash.

Two other sites (Richton Dome in Perry County, Miss., and Davis Canyon in San Juan County, Utah) were named as possible substitutes, should one of the current three be rejected after a three-month period for public comment.

DOE planned to submit its final recommendations to the president in the summer of 1985. He was to recommend a single site in 1990.

The state selected could veto the waste repository, but such a veto could be overridden by both houses of Congress.

Three environmental groups went into federal court Dec. 18 contesting the DOE site-selection process. Texas and Nevada did likewise on Dec. 19 and Dec. 14, respectively. ∎

Hydropower Fee Scale

Legislation limiting how much the government could charge hydroelectric projects each year for the use of water stored by federal dams died in the waning days of the 98th Congress.

The bill (S 1132), which was meant to encourage the development of hydropower, was aimed at assisting public utilities or private companies that wanted to build generators to take advantage of water stored behind federal dams.

The Senate passed the bill (S 1132) by voice vote March 30, but the House amended it before returning the bill to the Senate Oct. 1. The Senate accepted some House amendments but added others of its own Oct. 10, and the House had no time to consider the bill again prior to the Oct. 12 adjournment of Congress.

The bill set a sliding scale for annual charges by the Federal Energy Regulatory Commission for use of water stored by federal dams. The size of the fee depended on the amount of energy generated.

Although the fee provision was acceptable to both the House and Senate, the Senate deleted from the House-passed bill a separate section aimed at clarifying the authorities of the National Marine Fisheries Service — an issue that was in litigation at the time. Sen. James A. McClure, R-Idaho, chairman of the Senate Energy and Natural Resources Committee, said it would be "unwise to prejudge" a matter before the courts.

S 1132 was reported March 12 by the Senate Energy and Natural Resources Committee (S Rept 98-363).

It passed the Senate March 30 by voice vote.

In the House it was referred to the Energy and Commerce Committee, which reported the legislation Sept. 24 (H Rept 98-1052).

Agriculture

Fifty years after the federal government first paid farmers to plow under crops and slaughter surplus livestock, the Reagan administration launched a drive to end many Depression-era farm programs and eliminate the assumption that the federal government was directly responsible for farmers' well-being.

In 1934 Agriculture Secretary Henry A. Wallace had written that federal efforts to manage the farm economy were "but a temporary method for dealing with an emergency." Such interventions, Wallace warned, "seriously disturb . . . the farm economy." But since then the notion that Washington would guarantee minimum prices for commodities, supplement farmers' incomes and compensate farmers for efforts to cut back on surpluses had become embedded in the rural economy. Over time, Congress had changed many of the specifics of the federal farm programs but left their basic shape intact.

However, by late 1984, Agriculture Secretary John R. Block, Senate Agriculture Committee Chairman Jesse Helms, R-N.C., and portions of the farm community were saying that the programs had, in fact, destabilized American agriculture and had to be changed radically.

"America's farm policies aren't working — it's time to change them," Helms announced in a post-election press release.

Agriculture Secretary Block, acknowledging that much of American agriculture was sunk in a multi-year recession, told a farm policy conference in December that farms had been failing for nearly 50 years "with almost the same intensity, regardless of farm policies pursued. It's time to start something different."

Joining the assault were business and environmental leaders alarmed at the chronic economic and environmental problems of American agriculture and convinced that federal programs were making those problems worse.

The White House attempted earlier in 1984 to trim drastically a fundamental farm subsidy, the target price. It eventually got what it wanted, but only after making concessions to every major farming interest.

Debating Modifications

The administration waited until after the November elections to publicize its startlingly austere plan for farm programs. But for much of the year a broad debate on future farm programs had ranged from congressional chambers to an Oklahoma food bank, where debt-pressed farmers showed up to collect charity groceries and protest their economic plight.

The House Agriculture Committee held hearings looking forward to 1985 when Congress was scheduled to review expiring farm programs and write another omnibus agriculture bill. The Senate Agriculture and Budget committees, the Congressional Budget Office, the Agriculture Department (USDA) and privately funded groups published lengthy analyses of farm programs. Former secretaries of agriculture, Washington-based farm consultants and lobbyists and academic farm experts were on the road, speaking at what they said was an unprecedented number of conferences on agriculture policy during 1984.

These activities revealed a pervasive dissatisfaction with the status quo. A major Congressional Budget Office (CBO) report, issued in February, reflected much of current thinking when it observed that the programs' twin goals — enhancing farm incomes during periods of surplus and stabilizing farm prices and incomes — were in conflict. And, the report observed, "Current farm programs have been progressively less able to achieve these conflicting objectives" left over from the 1930s.

When the programs began, nearly a fourth of the nation's population lived on farms and depended heavily on farm income; but by 1984, CBO reported, only 3 percent lived on farms and only "300,000 farms, or 12 percent of all farms, produce nearly 70 percent of farm output." Moreover, incomes of families living on these farms were, on an average, "well above average non-farm levels."

Probably the most significant change from the 1930s was the integration of farms into the domestic and international economies. By 1984, two of every five acres was grown for export, and exports accounted for about a quarter of gross farm income. Farm prices had become highly sensitive to a number of factors beyond the reach of domestic farm programs: currency exchange rates, changes in weather and crop production, trade and farm policies of foreign governments.

Trouble Signs

There were compelling signs of trouble in the farm economy that drew the attention of the administration and other program critics: severe financial problems for a signficant number of farmers; reversals in such businesses as seed and fertilizer and equipment suppliers and bankers whose economic health depended on farm prosperity; growing problems with erosion, depletion of water sources and contamination of water and food with agricultural chemicals; and very high costs of federal aid to farmers.

When Congress wrote a multi-year "omnibus" agriculture bill in 1981, the estimated four-year cost of price support, loan, subsidy and other aid programs for farmers was about $11 billion.

But the programs swiftly soaked up a billion dollars more than that amount in 1982 alone, and costs soared to $18.9 billion in 1983, when the administration also dispensed an additional $9 billion worth of surplus commodities to farmers through the PIK (Payment-in-Kind) program, which paid farmers for idling crop land. By 1984, USDA officials were putting four-year costs of the programs above $50 billion, a figure considered untenable by the Office of Management and Budget.

Like welfare and food stamps and other "entitlements," the basic farm programs cost more in hard times, because more people sought more help from them. The high program costs clearly signaled financial stress in American agriculture, particularly the "mid-size" commercial farms of such "heartland" states as Iowa, Illinois and Kansas.

Banking experts reported that 15 percent of these commercial farms — those with annual sales of more than $40,000 — had precarious debt-to-asset ratios of 70 percent. Farms with that level of debt were thought unable to survive in current market conditions.

Yet the economic status of individual farmers was far from uniform, meaning that help desperately needed by some was a windfall for others. Farms that managed to stay free of expensive debt were likely to be quietly holding their own. A tiny minority of highly capitalized, high-tech spreads dominated markets while scooping in million-dollar subsidies from Washington.

Downward Adjustment

The problem to be solved — surplus production — was as old as the Depression that spawned the programs. One congressional aide neatly summed up the current problem when he remarked that "We've now got 93 million acres of wheat production — and 60 to 70 million acres of market." With differing numbers, the same was true of corn, rice, cotton, dairy goods and even honey. USDA reckoned that the overall productive capacity exceeded agricultural markets by about 10 percent.

The surplus reflected agriculture's painful downward adjustment from the export boom of the 1970s, a decade of dizzying growth in farm exports, farm productivity, farm-land values — and farmers' debt. In that period, exports had grown at what CBO called "the extraordinary rate of 20 percent per year, from about $7 billion in 1970 to nearly $41 billion in 1980."

By 1984 farm exports, instead of growing, were entering their fourth year of decline, with USDA predicting that export levels for the year would register a 15 percent drop from 1980. U.S. commodities were being crowded in global markets by expanding agricultural production of other nations, which was often buttressed with hefty subsidies.

The situation left those farmers that had borrowed heavily to expand in the 1970s, and to keep going in the early 1980s, unable to keep up loan payments. Their problems, by 1984, were beginning to sink the country bankers that had kept them going through two or three or four profitless years. In the first half of 1984, three agricultural banks failed; in the second six months, 22 went under, according to the Independent Bankers Association of America, which expected the pace to accelerate in 1985. Some analysts estimated that as much as 20 percent of the

nation's $215 billion farm debt would have to be written off.

The Federal Deposit Insurance Corporation's June 30 list of banks with more problem loans than capital included more than 200 farm banks — twice the number reported a year earlier.

What made the debt problem acute was a dramatic deflation in the value of land, farmers' prime asset. In Iowa, for instance, farm land values plummeted 37 percent since 1981.

Program Changes

As the year ended, the administration and its supporters, including Helms and much of the "agribusiness" community, were saying that such drastic problems called for drastic solutions. They blamed much of the problem on farm price supports and subsidies and production controls, saying these programs were perversely inflating the price of U.S. commodities to foreign buyers. They also argued that under the "umbrella" of high U.S. farm prices, other nations were able to expand production and aggressively grab global markets, leaving the United States as a residual supplier.

The administration's stark solution to the problem was to ask Congress to cut farm program spending in half and radically revise the policies underlying the programs. Such changes would, Block argued, put agriculture in fighting trim to compete in tight world markets.

Much of what the administration wanted could have been predicted from nearly four years' worth of speeches by Block and other USDA officials, who consistently argued that government programs had destabilized agriculture. Their anti-government stance, however, had been tempered by decisions during Reagan's first term to run the enormous PIK program — the largest acreage reduction program in the history of such federal efforts; to launch the first payments ever to dairymen for cutting back on production, and to otherwise employ the very programs at which Block scoffed.

Farm-state members who had spent the year listening to farmers' woes found the administration's less-government solution improbable. There were those, such as Sen. Thad Cochran, R-Miss., who agreed in principle but thought that the current economic problems of farming ruled out immediate action. There were others, such as House Agriculture Committee Chairman E. "Kika" de la Garza, D-Texas, who disputed the basic assumption that Depression-era farm programs were inherently bad. According to de la Garza, the only thing wrong with the programs was mismanagement by an administration philosophically opposed to government intervention in agriculture.

—By Elizabeth Wehr

Reagan 'Freeze' on Farm Aid Clears Congress

Congress April 3 approved an overhaul of federal farm programs that partly satisfied the administration's long-standing objections to the target price program, which made cash payments to farmers when market prices for crops fell below specified levels. The bill imposed a "freeze" on — and for one crop a cut in — scheduled increases in the "targets" used to determine payment levels. But to win passage of the measure (HR 4072 — PL 98-258), the administration had to give ground on other farm issues.

The Senate approved the conference report (H Rept 98-646) on the bill April 2 by voice vote. The House passed the measure April 3 on a 379-11 vote. President Reagan signed HR 4072 April 10. *(Vote 54, p. 20-H)*

In return for the freeze, the administration agreed to give farmers early cash payments in 1984 for not growing wheat, corn, cotton and rice in 1985. The bill also liberalized terms for federal loans to farmers and spelled out administration commitments to boost farm exports and food donations abroad.

What began as an administration-backed thrift measure appeared to many members an election-year wish list by the time Congress cleared it.

The freeze on target price increases was, nevertheless, a notable achievement for the administration because it meant that bidding on future levels for the price support began at much lower levels in 1985, when Congress was scheduled to reauthorize farm programs in an omnibus agriculture bill. In 1981, the last time Congress considered omnibus farm legislation, the Reagan administration proposed to do away with the target price program altogether. *(1981 Almanac p. 535)*

The target price program supplemented farmers' incomes by paying them the difference between market prices and targets set by law when prices dropped below the targets.

Background

Creation of the 1984 bill began in November 1982 when the Reagan administration proposed to offer its huge 1983 acreage reduction (Payment-in-Kind or PIK) program "in exchange for congressional approval of a freeze on target prices at 1983 levels," Sen. Robert Dole, R-Kan., told the Senate April 2. PIK used surplus commodities to pay farmers who agreed to scale back on the crops they raised. *(1983 Almanac p. 380)*

Farmers got the PIK program, but Congress did little with the target price freeze until November 1983, when the House passed HR 4072. That version, however, modified only wheat target prices and added incentives to draw wheat farmers into the stringent 1984 wheat acreage reduction program. The Senate added the broader freeze and the payments for idling crop land to that bill. *(1983 Almanac p. 386)*

In early March, administration officials, faced with a meager sign-up for the wheat program, renewed negotiations. These stretched out over weeks as farm-state members sought concessions from the administration.

Provisions

As cleared, HR 4072:
- Set the wheat target price at $4.38 per bushel for 1984

and 1985 crops (instead of $4.45 and $4.65, respectively, as in existing law). It also authorized 1984 and 1985 wheat acreage reduction programs in which farmers who reduced their wheat harvest by 30 percent qualified for basic farm program benefits such as price supports. For a third of that amount — 10 percent of his base — a farmer would be paid $2.70 a bushel.

The administration's 1984 wheat program had called for a 30 percent reduction in a farmer's total acreage devoted to wheat as a condition for receiving farm program benefits, with no payments. It also permitted farmers to set aside up to 20 percent more land and receive a payment-in-kind of surplus wheat for doing so. HR 4072 raised the PIK payment rate to 85 percent of expected yield from the administration's 75 percent.

- Permitted farmers to graze livestock or harvest hay on idled wheat acreage in states where this practice had been approved by the state committees of farmers that helped administer federal price supports and other programs.
- Kept 1985 target prices at 1984 levels of $3.03 a bushel for corn, 81 cents per pound for cotton and $11.90 per hundred pounds (cwt) for rice. If current law had not been modified, target prices for these commodities would have risen in 1985 to $3.18 for corn, 86 cents for cotton and $12.40 for rice. Also required the Agriculture Department to offer 1985 crop reduction programs if the "carryovers" of surplus commodities at the end of the year exceeded specified levels.

For each crop, the bill spelled out various combinations of paid and unpaid participation levels and set payment rates at $1.50 a bushel for corn and 35 cents a pound for cotton and a minimum rate of $3.50 per cwt for rice. The rice payment increased with the size of the surplus.

- Authorized loans to farmers who harvested 1984 or 1985 corn before it matured, for silage. The collateral was not the silage, however, but corn a producer would buy for purposes of securing the loan.
- Permitted farmers to sign up in 1984 for 1985 programs and receive half the set-aside payment when they enlisted; farmers in the 1984 wheat program also received early payments.

Export Aid

- Stated that it was the sense of Congress that the administration should make the following increases, above current spending levels, to expand farm exports: in fiscal 1984, $150 million for the Food for Peace (PL 480) program, in addition to the $90 million PL 480 supplemental appropriation for African food aid, and $500 million in guaranteed export loans from the Commodity Credit Corporation (CCC), the agency that administered price support programs. In fiscal 1985, $175 million for PL 480; $1.1 billion in CCC funds for export credit guarantees and $100 million in direct export loans from the CCC. Also provided in 1985 another $50 million either for PL 480 or for the CCC export credits. *(African food aid supplemental, p. 429)*
- Authorized a two-year pilot project in which the CCC acquired through barter or exchange 40,000 tons of milk processed by the ultra-high temperature method for donation to needy nations. Milk sterilized by ultra-high temperature treatment needed no refrigeration and had a shelf life of five months.

• Permitted donation overseas of CCC-owned surplus wheat through a program that currently donated CCC dairy goods.

Domestic Credit

• Mandated that applications for disaster loans be filed within eight months after a disaster. Previously, deadlines were set administratively and ranged from six months to a year after a county was designated a disaster area.

• Stipulated that farm assets used as collateral for emergency disaster loans would carry the value they had a year before a disaster declaration rather than the value they had at the time the loan was negotiated.

• Required that $250 million in economic emergency direct loans be made available in fiscal 1984 and mandated that $310 million be available for insured loans in the program; authorized additional insured loans.

• Required the secretary of agriculture to make emergency disaster loans available to farmers in counties contiguous to those designated eligible for disaster assistance, with these loans based on individual losses.

• Raised the ceiling on Farmers Home Administration (FmHA) farm operating loans to individuals to $200,000 and on guaranteed operating loans to $400,000. Limits currently were $100,000 and $200,000, respectively.

• Required that the interest rate for FmHA loans that had been rescheduled — renegotiated because farmers could not make payments — be the lower of either the rate of the original loan or the rate prevailing at the time of the rescheduling. Also extended to 15 years, from 7 years, the maximum repayment period for rescheduled loans.

• Required at least 20 percent of farm ownership and operating direct loans in fiscal 1984 to be reserved for low-income farmers with limited resources. These borrowers qualified for lower interest rates on the loans.

• Authorized rescheduling of FmHA loans for borrowers who agreed to plant timber on crop or pasture land and use proceeds from timber sales to repay the loan.

• Prohibited FmHA personnel from buying farm land for which an FmHA loan had been denied for three years after a loan refusal.

House Action

The House in November 1983, reacting to fears of a massive wheat crop in the spring of 1984, passed HR 4072 in the hopes of attracting more farmers to the government program to reduce wheat production. Its consideration in 1983 was blocked in the Senate.

House Provisions

As passed in the House on a voice vote, HR 4072:

• Set the target price for 1984 and 1985 wheat crops at $4.38 a bushel, instead of $4.45 and $4.65 respectively.

• Authorized a 1984 acreage reduction program under which farmers would have to take 20 percent of their customary acreage out of production to qualify for federal farm program benefits like price supports. If they took out an additional 10 percent, they would be paid at least $3 per bushel on the estimated yield of the idled land — or less under certain circumstances. The administration had specified a 30 percent acreage reduction to qualify for federal programs, without cash payments.

• Raised to 85 percent of yield, from 75 percent, the rate of PIK payments to farmers. The administration had offered PIK payments for 75 percent of yield for farmers

idling up to 20 percent more acreage, in addition to the basic 30 percent required for program eligibility.

Senate Action

The Senate Agriculture Committee, rushing to beat spring plantings, approved the farm bill March 8.

The committee bill partly met the goal of the administration, which sought the target price freeze. And it partly met demands of farm groups that said they needed more aid to recover from the 1983 drought.

And it responded to complaints of wheat producers about the wheat acreage reduction program established for the 1984 crop. Wheat farmers' low rate of participation in the program had raised the specter of a massive surplus in 1984 and continuing low prices for the crop.

The bill was negotiated in private sessions by Dole, budget director David A. Stockman and other senators with strong interests in the affected crops — wheat, corn and feed grains, cotton and rice. As part of the bargain, the administration offered to boost funding for the Food for Peace program, which sent surplus food overseas to needy nations, and for guaranteed loans for farm exports.

Only wheat interests — and not all of them — were satisfied with the package when it came before the committee. The panel went ahead, assuming that negotiations would continue and that further changes would be made on the Senate floor.

The Agriculture Department estimated that the target price cut, and improved participation in acreage reduction programs, would lower farm program spending by about $3 billion in 1984-87. But members were skeptical about the savings. When Sen. Roger W. Jepsen, R-Iowa, asked whether the amount was $3 billion, Dole shot back, "I wouldn't want to bet on it."

Senate Floor Action

The negotiations with farm-state senators continued as the bill's backers tried to move the bill to the Senate floor. Two attempts — March 15 and March 20 — to start floor action on HR 4072 were blocked by Sens. Howell Heflin, D-Ala., and John Melcher, D-Mont. Both had heard complaints from constituents that they were not getting enough in return for giving up target price increases.

Melcher failed to win concessions, but Heflin had more luck. He negotiated an amendment with administration officials to sweeten the terms for cotton by making a paid-diversion program more likely in 1985.

The Senate finally passed the legislation March 22 after concessions by the administration overcame most obstacles. The vote was 78-10. *(Vote 39, p. 9-S)*

Passage of the bill was almost hung up at the last minute over its treatment of rice. While senators and staffers negotiated an amendment offered by David Pryor, D-Ark., Pryor and Dale Bumpers, D-Ark., conducted a minor filibuster. Agreement was reached, and the Pryor amendment was adopted by voice vote. It improved payments to rice farmers if surplus commodities triggered an acreage reduction program in 1985. The Senate also adopted by voice vote a Melcher amendment to establish a program to channel surplus dairy products and wheat to needy nations.

The Senate approved several other amendments by voice vote, including:

• By Sam Nunn, D-Ga., to reschedule delinquent FmHA loans if borrowers planted timber on crop or pasture land.

Proceeds from timber sales would be used to pay off the loan.

● By Edward Zorinsky, D-Neb., to authorize a two-year pilot project in which the Commodity Credit Corp. would acquire through barter or exchange 40,000 tons of milk processed by the ultra-high temperature method for donation to needy nations.

● By Zorinsky, to prohibit for three years FmHA personnel from buying farm land for which the agency had denied a loan.

Senate Provisions

As passed by the Senate March 22, HR 4072:

● Set the wheat target price at $4.38 per bushel for 1984 and 1985 crops. It also authorized a 1984 and 1985 wheat acreage reduction program in which a farmer would not plant 20 percent of his wheat acreage to qualify for basic farm program benefits. In addition, a farmer could be compensated for retiring another 10 percent of his land.

● Permitted farmers to receive half of the payments for both 1984 and 1985 at the time they signed up in 1984.

● Kept 1985 target prices at 1984 levels of $3.03 a bushel for corn, 81 cents per cwt for cotton and $11.90 per cwt for rice. It also required the Agriculture Department to offer in 1985 acreage reduction programs of at least 25 percent of the acreage for each crop, if the carryover of surplus stocks at the end of the year exceeded certain levels. At least 5 percent of the land retired would qualify for reduction payments. Acreage reduction programs had to be offered if the following carryover levels were reached: corn, at least 1.1 billion bushels; cotton, at least 3.7 million bales; rice, at least 25 million cwt. If the rice carryover exceeded 42.5 million cwt, the paid diversion rate would be raised.

● Stated that it was the sense of Congress that the administration make the following increases, above current spending levels, to expand farm exports: in fiscal 1984, request that Congress appropriate $150 million more for the Food for Peace (PL 480) program; in fiscal 1984, provide at least $500 million more in guaranteed export loans from the CCC; in fiscal 1985, request that Congress appropriate at least $175 million more for PL 480; in fiscal 1985, provide at least $1.1 billion more in CCC funds for export credit guarantees, and at least $100 million more in direct export loans from the CCC. Also, either ask Congress to appropriate or provide from the CCC, in 1985, another $50 million either for PL 480 or for CCC export credits.

● Stipulated that farm assets used as collateral for emergency disaster loans would carry the value they had a year before a disaster declaration, rather than the value they had at the time the loan was negotiated.

● Authorized $250 million in economic emergency direct loans for fiscal 1984, for a total of $600 million (of which $310 million would be direct loans and $290 million would be guaranteed loans).

● Required the secretary of agriculture to make emergency disaster loans available to farmers in counties touching those that had been designated as eligible for disaster assistance, with these loans based on individual losses.

● Raised the ceiling on FmHA farm operating loans to individuals to $200,000 and to $400,000 for guaranteed operating loans. Limits currently in place were $100,000 and $200,000, respectively.

● Required that the interest rate for the balance of rescheduled FmHA loans be the lower of either the rate of the original loan or the rate prevailing at the time of the rescheduling. Also, extended to 15 years, from 7 years, the maximum repayment period for rescheduled loans.

● Required that at least 20 percent of farm ownership and operating direct loans in fiscal 1984 be reserved for low-income farmers with limited resources.

Conference

The conference on HR 4072 was marked by attempts by House members to leave their imprint on a rewrite of farm programs that had been crafted by the Senate and the Reagan administration.

House members won modest changes in the bill's cotton and rice provisions and authority for new loans for farmers based on corn raised to feed livestock. But Senate conferees — backed by Agriculture Department officials — rejected more costly cotton and rice plans.

Conference Decisions

Major decisions made by conferees:

● Eliminated House-approved early target price "deficiency payments" to wheat farmers. The bill, however, did provide early payments to farmers for reducing their crops.

● Added to the new rice program an additional, intermediate level of surplus that would trigger a paid acreage reduction program in 1985.

● Revised the new cotton program to expand the paid acreage reduction program under certain circumstances.

● Authorized, but did not require, federal loans to farmers that would be based, indirectly, on the corn they harvested before maturity to use as silage to feed livestock.

● Rejected a conservation package proposed by Rep. Ed Jones, D-Tenn. Even so, most of the conferees appeared to back the package, which combined "sodbuster" language with financial incentives for conservation. It was the financial incentives that drew opposition from GOP senators and administration representatives. *(Sodbuster, p. 364)* ∎

Agricultural Credit Expanded

After two years of opposing legislation to relax repayment terms on loans to financially strapped farmers, the Reagan administration reversed course Sept. 18 and offered farmers a new, billion-dollar program of debt forgiveness and loan guarantees.

A total of $650 million for federal guarantees for private farm loans, one part of the administration plan, was included in the fiscal 1984 supplemental appropriations bill (HR 6040 — PL 98-396). The president had not requested this money; legislators had added it earlier in 1984 after the Independent Bankers Association lobbied for a billion-dollar farm loan guarantee plan. *(Supplemental, p. 439)*

As much as $700 million from a fund set up by the Farmers Home Administration (FmHA) could be spent on another part of the plan, deferral of principal repayments with interest forgiveness, on troubled FmHA loans to farmers.

In 1982 and 1983, both the House and Senate voted to let farmers postpone federal loan repayments and restructure their debts, but failed to complete action on the legislation. Agriculture Department officials insisted then that such measures were unneeded because they already were working with individual farmers experiencing credit problems. The department repeatedly had been sued for not using existing authority to defer loan repayments for debt-ridden farmers. *(1983 Almanac p. 384)*

The credit plan was unveiled by President Reagan the day before he left on a re-election campaign tour through financially troubled Midwestern farm states. Farm debt, probably the most painful political issue in the farm community, stood at a record high of $215 billion, up from $166 billion in 1980.

Reagan Plan

The administration plan:

● Authorized FmHA to defer interest payments on 25 percent of the principal of a loan, up to $100,000, for up to five years. The interest that would have been charged on that portion of the principal, for that period, would never have to be paid. Agriculture Secretary John R. Block said the outer limit for the program was $700 million.

● Authorized FmHA to guarantee repayment of private and farm credit system loans to farmers under special terms, applying only to so-called "non-performing" or "classified" loans (which borrowers could not pay). These guarantees were available if the private lender agreed to lower by at least 10 percent the principal owed by a farm borrower; the guarantee covered 90 percent of the reduced loan.

● Established two-person county teams, with expertise in farm management and lending, to work out financial plans with farmers and their creditors.

● Authorized the Agriculture Department to pay private lending institutions to process FmHA loan applications.

Other Farm Aid

The credit plan was the last of a series of administration actions taken in 1984 to aid farmers. On Sept. 14, the Agriculture Department announced its 1985 price support programs for feed grains, cotton and rice, authorizing cash payments to growers of upland cotton and rice for cutting back harvests.

Growers of feed grains, cotton, rice and wheat also were offered an estimated $2 billion worth of "advance deficiency payments" when they signed up for participation in 1985 federal crop programs. Deficiency payments were made when market prices for a crop fell below a legally established "target" figure; the amount paid to a farmer was the difference between the target price and a lower market price.

The administration sought, without success, to end the target price program in 1981. In 1984 it persuaded Congress to freeze scheduled increases in the crop target prices. *(Story, p. 361)*

The administration also requested an International Trade Commission investigation of tobacco imports, and the administration announced new U.S. grain sales to the Soviet Union, together with a presidential pledge to sell the Russians even more. ∎

Senate Critics Block REA Bill

Popular legislation (S 1300, HR 3050) to shore up the federal fund that lent money to rural electric and telephone systems failed to clear Congress. Last-minute attempts to win a Senate vote were blocked Oct. 10 when Howard M. Metzenbaum, D-Ohio, and Alan K. Simpson, R-Wyo., objected to Senate debate on the bill.

The measure would have revised loan repayment terms for both utilities borrowing from the Rural Electrification Administration (REA) and for REA's substantial debts to the U.S. Treasury. REA supporters claimed the agency's major lending fund would run out of money in the next decade, and that a rescue was essential to preserve rural electric and telephone systems. The fund had been lending money to rural utilities at 5 percent interest or lower, while paying much higher interest rates to borrow it.

The bill passed the House (H Rept 98-588, Part I) March 1 by a vote of 283-111. *(Vote 31, p. 12-H)*

It had been approved by the House Agriculture Committee in October 1983. *(Background, 1983 Almanac p. 388)*

The measure ran into trouble in May when Simpson objected to its costs, to sales of REA-subsidized power to wealthy corporations, and to REA involvement in the financially troubled nuclear power industry.

When Simpson announced his objections in a blunt letter sent May 3 to his Senate colleagues, the legislation was moving along nicely, buoyed by skillful lobbying by the electric and telephone cooperatives and independent telephone systems that rely on REA. The bill had rolled through the House despite isolated warnings the plan was neither as cheap nor as effective as advocates said. Some 46 senators had signed on as sponsors.

Despite Simpson's misgivings, the Senate Agriculture Committee approved the legislation (S Rept 98-545) June 7, adopting several amendments to the bill as passed by the House. The Senate panel changed a formula for setting interest rates on REA loans to electric and telephone utilities to ensure that utilities' interest payments would cover REA's interest payments on the money it borrowed. A second amendment required approval by the Federal Financing Bank for refinancing of one type of REA debt. Another would have required special low-interest loans to utilities facing financial problems, an amendment that greatly reduced the number of utilities eligible for loans.

Had the bill cleared Congress, President Reagan likely would have vetoed it. The administration objected to the plan's cost but was unable to find a member to introduce a stringent, alternative REA bill that Reagan sent to Congress in early April.

The intricacies of S 1300 confused debate, masking an underlying conflict between the administration and the utilities. S 1300 would have effectively locked in the size of the agency — and some of its key policies that the Reagan administration sought to change. Administration officials wanted to reduce the amount of money lent by REA, raise loan rates to what it cost the government to get the money, and target the loans to utilities with intractable financial problems. ∎

'Sodbuster' Conservation Bill

Landmark legislation to discourage farming on easily erodible land stalled in conference over penalties for plowing up erosion-prone land.

The Senate passed "sodbuster" legislation (S 663) in November 1983 to deny federal farm program benefits to crops grown on fragile land. The House May 8 passed by voice vote a more restrictive bill: while S 663 barred farm benefits only for the crop or crops planted on erodible land, the House bill (HR 3457 — H Rept 98-696) denied benefits for all of a farmer's crops if any part were grown on fragile land. *(Background, 1983 Almanac p. 387)*

Both bills made farmers who plow fragile land ineligible for farm aid — federal price support programs, federally subsidized crop insurance, Farmers Home Administration loans and disaster payments. With certain exceptions, the prohibition applied to the year in which the erodible land was plowed.

But conferees were unable to resolve a major disagreement over cutting the aid just for crops planted on erodible land or for all a farmer's crop. Senate conferees also refused to accept an additional conservation "reserve" program in the House bill that would pay farmers for retiring overused crop land for extended periods of time. As in the "soil bank" program begun in the 1950s, the land would have been planted with crops that prevented erosion, such as hay or timber, for several years.

The Reagan administration supported a sodbuster provision halfway between the Senate and House versions — one that would have barred program benefits to all of a specific crop if a part of it were produced on erodible land. But the administration objected strongly to the long-term conservation plan in the House bill. ∎

Agricultural Trade Group

Legislation (H J Res 600 — PL 98-412) to create an industry-financed commission to recommend steps to improve U.S. agricultural trade was signed by President Reagan Aug. 30. The measure authorizing the 35-member panel passed by voice votes in the House Aug. 6 and the Senate Aug. 10.

The commission, scheduled to make preliminary recommendations to Congress by March 1985, was designed to study problems contributing to a three-year decline in U.S. farm exports. The recommendations were to serve as the basis for omnibus farm legislation. A final commission report was scheduled for July 1985.

The legislation permitted the federal government to accept private contributions to fund the commission's work, and authorized back-up funding of up to $1 million from the Commodity Credit Corp., if contributions failed to cover the commission's costs.

The panel was made up of members of congressional agriculture and trade committees, and executive branch and industry officials. ∎

Honey Promotion

A bill (HR 5358 — PL 98-590) empowering honey producers and importers to establish a self-financed program to advertise and otherwise promote the consumption of honey was signed by President Reagan Oct. 30.

The House approved its version of the bill (H Rept 98-892) by voice vote July 24. The Senate passed the measure by voice vote on Oct. 4.

The program, subject to a vote of approval by a majority of the industry, was to be financed by assessments levied against producers and importers. Participation was voluntary. The legislation did not authorize production controls or any other type of limitation on honey marketing. ∎

Farm Chemical Patents Stalled

Legislation giving makers of pesticides, animal drugs and other agricultural chemicals longer patent protection to compensate for regulatory delays won the approval of the House Judiciary Committee but died without further action.

The bill, reported Oct. 1 (HR 6034 — H Rept 98-1122), had been approved Aug. 8 in a 20-8 vote by the committee. The provisions for patent extensions were meant to encourage companies to invest in the research and development of new and improved products.

The bill ran into trouble when a staff draft of amendments approved by the Judiciary Subcommittee on Courts, Civil Liberties and the Administration of Justice was reported to overturn an important Supreme Court decision on pesticide regulation. The June 26 court decision upheld the 1978 Fungicide, Insecticide and Rodenticide Act amendments that authorized public disclosure of health and safety data submitted by a pesticide manufacturer to the federal government. Submission of such data was required in applications for federal registration of pesticides; registration was required prior to marketing. *(Court decision, p. 14-A; 1978 Almanac p. 697)*

Sponsor Dan Glickman, D-Kan., said committee staff members had inadvertently made the troublesome change, and in full committee the bill was amended to restore the intent of the subcommittee action. But by then, environmental groups had raised other objections and were demanding that agricultural chemical makers make concessions on unrelated legislation (HR 5495) tightening limits on pesticide residues in food. ∎

Grain, Cotton Inspection

Two bills to continue programs that required grain and cotton producers to pay for the federal services that established the quality of their crops cleared the 98th Congress.

One measure (HR 5221 — PL 98-469) extended, through Sept. 30, 1988, so-called user fees that financed the Department of Agriculture's Federal Grain Inspection Service. The service was responsible for inspecting and weighing grain and supervised comparable state agencies that carried out these functions.

The House approved its version (H Rept 98-756) May 21 by voice vote. The Senate measure (S Rept 98-617) cleared by voice vote Sept. 28. The bill was signed by the president Oct. 11.

The second bill (S 2085 — PL 98-403) continued, through the same date, authorization for fees paid by cotton producers for Agriculture Department classification and grading. The measure won voice vote approval in the Senate (S Rept 98-395) on May 2. The House passed its version May 21 after adding technical amendments. The Senate concurred in the amendments by voice vote, clearing the measure to the president Aug. 10. It was signed Aug. 28.

The user fees were authorized in 1981 in response to the Reagan administration's broad policy of shifting the cost of certain federal agricultural services to those who used them. Authority for both fees expired in September. *(Background, 1983 Almanac p. 549)*

The grain measure made non-controversial changes

related to short-term investment of producers' fees by the federal government and the cap on the portion of fees that could be used for administrative costs. The cotton bill also revised certain terms of the fee program. ∎

Organic Farming

Organic farming — use of crop rotation, biological pest control and similar agricultural practices — was promoted by a bill (HR 2714 — H Rept 98-587) that passed the House by a 206-184 vote Jan. 26. The measure was not considered by the Senate. *(Vote 9, p. 4-H)*

The bill authorized $10.5 million in fiscal years 1985-89 for study and pilot research projects on individual farms. It also specified that farmers could receive federal conservation cost-sharing payments for using a specific practice ("intercropping") that retarded erosion while enhancing the nitrogen content of soil. The administration opposed the bill; similar legislation was defeated by the House in 1982. ∎

Central Kitchen Inspections

President Reagan Oct. 17 signed a non-controversial bill (HR 5223 — PL 98-487) that exempted certain central restaurant kitchens from inspection requirements of federal meat and poultry laws. The bill passed the House (H Rept 98-885) July 24 by voice vote. The Senate approved its version of the bill Oct. 2 by voice vote after adding an amendment requiring central kitchens to continue to keep records mandated by the meat and poultry laws and permitting the Agriculture Department to examine central kitchens' facilities, inventories and records. The House accepted the Senate amendment and cleared the bill by voice vote the next day.

The legislation put central kitchens on the same footing as individual restaurants, which already were exempt from those requirements. Central kitchens, which prepare ready-to-eat food served in branch restaurants, were still subject to health and safety inspections by state and local authorities. Meat prepared in those kitchens was subject to federal inspection elsewhere. ∎

Appropriations

Caught in a nettle of budget and election-year politics, the regular appropriations process ground to a halt two months before the Oct. 1 start of fiscal year 1985. As a result, most funding for the new fiscal year was enacted as part of the largest catchall continuing appropriations bill ever adopted by Congress.

The mammoth $470 billion funding bill (H J Res 648 — PL 98-473), which cleared Congress Oct. 11, contained money for programs in nine of the 13 regular appropriations measures Congress considers each year. H J Res 648 also included an omnibus crime package. *(Crime bill, p. 215)*

Despite the scope of the continuing appropriations resolution, Congress approved less spending than the administration had originally requested for discretionary programs. According to the Office of Management and Budget, total budget authority for fiscal 1985 was $563.5 billion, compared with $572.9 billion requested by President Reagan in his February 1984 budget submission. *(Reagan budget, p. 129)*

Congress imposed this appropriations austerity in response to demands to reduce federal deficits, which were projected to remain near $200 billion annually through the end of the decade. The lower funding levels were achieved, in part, by limiting the increase in spending for most programs to 2 percent. Senate Republicans agreed to this formula as part of the "Rose Garden" budget negotiations, and later the full Senate endorsed it. And on the House floor, Republicans successfully pushed through across-the-board percentage cuts in five appropriations bills. *(Deficit reduction, p. 143)*

Following a time-honored course, the omnibus spending bill became the vehicle for dozens of legislative orphans as it worked its way through the legislative process. Both the House and Senate attached authorizations worth billions of dollars in "pork barrel" water projects. And the House affixed the foreign aid authorization and an omnibus crime package to the resolution.

But by the time the ladened continuing appropriations resolution went to conference, Election Day was less than a month away. Veto pressures from Reagan, coupled with the desire to return home for campaigning, provided the incentive to forgo most of the extras attached to the bill. In the end, the catchall funding bill was stripped — with the exception of the crime package — to its essentials.

Budget Battle Breeds Delay

A provision of the 1974 Congressional Budget and Impoundment Control Act (PL 93-344) stated that Congress could not approve appropriations measures until the conference report on the first budget resolution was adopted.

Over the years each chamber had waived that provision for individual appropriations measures — but sparingly. 1984, however, proved to be a unique year.

The House Democratic leadership started the appropriations cycle with the intention of meeting or exceeding its 1983 record of approving 10 money bills before the new fiscal year began. The House passed its budget resolution (H Con Res 280) in early April. And the House Appropriations Committee was set to begin drafting annual appropriations measures as soon as it had the final numbers from the House-Senate conference on the budget resolution.

But the Senate spent over a month on its deficit-reduction plan. And it did not approve a budget resolution until May 18. In addition, resistance by House members to legislated spending "caps" that were an essential part of the Senate's deficit-reduction measure guaranteed a protracted budget conference.

Reluctant to wait until the budget resolution was in place, in late May the House Appropriations Committee began to draft its 1985 spending bills, using the House-passed budget resolution as its benchmark.

Because the conference report on the budget had not been adopted, the House had to approve a budget waiver when it took up its first appropriations bill May 22. But rather than approve an exemption for the Energy and Water bill (HR 5653) alone, the House agreed to a blanket waiver (H Res 501) allowing all appropriations measures to be considered even though the budget was not in place.

The House began churning out appropriations measures, and by the Independence Day recess had approved eight of the 13 appropriations bills.

The Senate was working its way through appropriations bills as well, waiving the Budget Act bill by bill. That practice continued until the Senate took up the agriculture funding bill (HR 5743) Aug. 1, when Sen. Lawton Chiles, D-Fla., decided to take a stand for the congressional budget process by fighting the waiver. Chiles' goal was to force final action on the fiscal 1985 budget resolution, which had been suspended in limbo because of a dispute over defense spending.

His talkathon lasted about a week before the Senate voted to impose cloture. But when the next appropriations bill was scheduled to be debated, Chiles threatened another filibuster. It was then that Senate Majority Leader Howard H. Baker Jr., R-Tenn., agreed to Chiles' suggestion, made on Aug. 9, that a high-level summit on defense spending be convened.

The defense impasse was resolved, but not until Sept. 20, 11 days before the start of the fiscal year.

By then Congress had little choice but to lump the nine remaining appropriations bills in a continuing resolution. It took days for conferees to resolve the key issues in the omnibus bill — aid to rebels fighting the leftist government in Nicaragua, the level of funding for specific defense programs, and the water project money. In the interim Congress was forced to pass four temporary stopgap funding bills before it gave final approval to H J Res 648.

—By Dale Tate

Fiscal 1985
Status of Appropriations
98th Congress, Second Session

Appropriation Bills	House	Senate	Final	Almanac Page
Agriculture and related agencies (HR 5743)	Passed 6/6/84	Passed 8/10/84	Funding included in PL 98-473	383
Commerce, Justice, State, Judiciary (HR 5712)	Passed 5/31/84	Passed 6/28/84	PL 98-411 signed 8/30/84	373
Defense (HR 6329, S 3026)	Committee reported 9/26/84	Committee reported 9/26/84	Funding included in PL 98-473	399
District of Columbia (HR 5899)	Passed 6/28/84	Passed 8/10/84	Funding included in PL 98-473	428
Energy and Water Development (HR 5653)	Passed 5/22/84	Passed 6/21/84	PL 98-360 signed 7/16/84	369
Foreign Aid (HR 6237, S 2793)	Committee reported 9/13/84	Committee reported 6/26/84	Funding included in PL 98-473	390
Housing and Urban Development, Independent Agencies (HR 5713)	Passed 5/30/84	Passed 6/21/84	PL 98-371 signed 7/18/84	415
Interior and related agencies (HR 5973)	Passed 8/2/84	Committee reported 8/6/84	Funding included in PL 98-473	378
Labor, Health and Human Services, Education (HR 6028)	Passed 8/1/84	Passed 9/25/84	Funding included in PL 98-473	421
Legislative Branch (HR 5753)	Passed 6/6/84	Passed 6/21/84	PL 98-367 signed 7/17/84	387
Military Construction (HR 5898)	Passed 6/28/84	Committee reported 7/26/84	Funding included in PL 98-473	407
Transportation and related agencies (HR 5921, S 2852)	Committee reported 6/22/84	Committee reported 7/17/84	Funding included in PL 98-473	410
Treasury, Postal Service, General Government (HR 5798)	Passed 6/27/84	Passed 7/25/84	Funding included in PL 98-473	425
Continuing Appropriations, Fiscal 1985 (H J Res 648)	Passed 9/25/84	Passed 11/4/84	PL 98-473 signed 10/12/84	444

Energy/Water Spending Bill is First to Clear

The first fiscal 1985 appropriations bill to be cleared by Congress was a $15.37 billion energy and water development package (HR 5653) funding politically popular projects in most congressional districts.

President Reagan signed the bill into law (PL 98-360) on July 16. Congress cleared it in the early morning hours of a session that began June 27.

Passage was sped by a compromise on the perennially controversial Garrison Diversion project in North Dakota. The bill provided $53.6 million toward construction of that $1.1 billion system of aqueducts and irrigation canals, but it set up a 12-member commission to study ways of redesigning the project to meet objections from environmentalists, Canadians and other opponents.

The bill also cleared the way legislatively for construction of a high-voltage electric transmission line from the power-rich Pacific Northwest to the power-hungry cities of central and Southern California. As signed, it left largely intact House-passed language on the 500-kilovolt Pacific power line. Controversy over the transmission facility had threatened to thwart Senate passage of the bill June 21.

The bill funded construction and operation of hundreds of dams, harbors, canals and irrigation systems by the U.S. Army Corps of Engineers and the Interior Department's Bureau of Reclamation — plus various Energy Department activities, including the production of nuclear warheads and other defense-related projects.

Missing from the bill were several large spending items that had caused controversy in previous years, including the Clinch River Breeder Reactor in Tennessee and the Tennessee-Tombigbee Waterway in Alabama and Mississippi.

Traditional adversaries of those big projects, such as Reps. Silvio O. Conte, R-Mass., and Bob Edgar, D-Pa., gave the bill at least lukewarm support.

"This is a responsible bill," Conte said during House floor debate. But he chided, "Even though these controversial projects are not in the bill, I do not want to hear anyone up here asking, 'Where's the pork?' There are enough projects in this bill for just about everyone to bring home a little piece of the bacon."

The Reagan administration, which had advocated austerity in domestic spending, did not oppose the bill.

Final Provisions

Funding Levels

As cleared, the bill appropriated $15.37 billion in net new budget authority — down from the $15.87 billion the president had originally requested. The bill passed by the House May 22 weighed in at $15.47 billion, while the Senate bill passed June 21 totaled $15.32 billion. The fiscal 1984 appropriation was $14.5 billion. *(Fiscal 1985 funding chart, p. 371)*

Congress' biggest cut in the Reagan budget came in the area of atomic energy defense activities, which accounted for roughly half of the funds in the bill. Reagan had asked for $7.8 billion, while Congress gave him $7.3 billion. But the bill still gave Reagan almost two-thirds of the $1.2 billion increase over fiscal 1984 levels he sought for nuclear weapons.

Garrison Diversion

Although the House version of HR 5653 provided no funding for the Garrison Diversion project, the Senate approved $53.6 million, and conferees went along with that sum. The action came after a compromise between environmentalists and Sen. Mark Andrews, R-N.D., disarmed potential objections to the funding.

The project, diverting water from the Garrison Dam reservoir into the Red River basin, was expected to irrigate some 250,000 acres in North Dakota at a total cost of about $1.1 billion. Andrews and other supporters said the project was promised to North Dakota in 1944, when the federal government flooded 500,000 acres in the state to build the Pick-Sloan project for flood control downstream in the Missouri River basin.

Under the compromise, a 12-member commission appointed by the interior secretary was to report by Dec. 31, 1984, on possible changes in project design that could meet the state's water needs while minimizing damage to waterfowl, wetlands and fisheries. If eight of the 12 commissioners agreed on an alternative design, that version would be funded. Otherwise, the money in the bill was to be released for the project as it was previously designed.

No New Water Projects

Missing from the final bill was any money to start construction of new federal water projects. The Reagan administration had asked for $46 million for new projects by the Army Corps of Engineers and the Interior Department's Bureau of Reclamation.

Rep. Tom Bevill, D-Ala., chairman of the House Appropriations Subcommittee on Energy and Water Development, said the panel omitted funds for new construction because it was waiting for enactment of authorizing legislation (HR 3678, S 1739). *(Story, p. 320)*

House Committee Action

The House Appropriations Committee approved its $15.47 billion version of the bill (H Rept 98-755) on May 15. The measure had been approved by the Energy and Water Development Subcommittee on May 3.

The committee bill had no funding for any "new starts" on construction of water projects. It also lacked funding for the once-controversial Clinch River Breeder Reactor and the Tennessee-Tombigbee Waterway. Construction funding for the Tenn-Tom had been essentially completed in fiscal 1984 by carrying over unspent funds from the fiscal 1983 bill. The Senate had decisively killed the Clinch River reactor in 1983. *(1983 Almanac pp. 500, 538)*

The panel also omitted funds for the still-alive and controversial Garrison Diversion; proponents were counting on the Senate to add the project, as it had in 1983 after the House had left it out.

Reagan Requests Trimmed

The $15.47 billion total in the committee's bill was $404 million below the Reagan administration's budget request of $15.87 billion. But both figures were still well above fiscal 1984 appropriations, which were $14.5 billion.

Roughly half the funds in the bill, about $7.4 billion,

were related to national security, according to Rep. Bevill, chairman of the Subcommittee on Energy and Water Development. The Department of Energy was responsible for building nuclear warheads and for a number of other defense-related atomic energy activities.

For the Energy Department as a whole, the committee approved 1985 appropriations of $10.85 billion — substantially above the 1984 appropriation of $10.18 billion, but still far less than the $11.42 billion Reagan wanted.

The committee cut spending significantly below 1984 levels for the research program into magnetic nuclear fusion and other nuclear energy. The Nuclear Regulatory Commission (NRC) sustained a $30 million cut from the level of $468 million requested by Reagan.

The committee's report said the NRC cut was a response to a "significant decline in future licensing and inspection requirements," noting there had not been a license sought for a new nuclear power plant in eight years, and no new plants were being planned.

The committee kept alive at 1984 levels the Appalachian Regional Commission (ARC) development programs, which the administration wanted to cut by nearly half. The committee funded ARC highway construction and economic development programs at $157 million, up slightly from the $150 million appropriated for 1984. Reagan had requested only $80 million.

Water Projects

For the Army Corps of Engineers, which built and maintained most water projects in the East, the committee voted $2.87 billion — more than Reagan's $2.71 billion request and 1984's $2.64 billion appropriation.

That sum included $152 million for general investigations, $933 million for general construction, $326 million for Mississippi River system flood control, $10 million for flood control and coastal emergencies, $1.34 billion for general operations and maintenance, and $113 million for general expenses.

For the Interior Department's Bureau of Reclamation, which was responsible for most water projects in the West, the committee approved $1.03 billion — up from $963 million in fiscal 1984, but slightly below Reagan's $1.08 billion request.

House Floor Action

The House passed HR 5653 May 22 after turning back all amendments — leaving unchanged the $15.47 billion funding level set by the Appropriations Committee.

Before the bill finally passed, 349-46, two matters aroused controversy. *(Vote 145, p. 48-H)*

First, the House rejected an effort to shift research money from nuclear breeder reactors to solar energy. Second, an effort to cap the price the federal government charged to enrich uranium was stricken from the bill on a point of order.

Solar Energy Amendment

The House rejected, 171-229, an amendment offered by Richard L. Ottinger, D-N.Y., that would have shifted funds from nuclear breeder reactor research into solar energy research and other programs. *(Vote 144, p. 48-H)*

Ottinger, chairman of the Energy and Commerce Subcommittee on Energy Conservation and Power, proposed to take $43.1 million out of the $298 million breeder reactor research budget. Of that, $23.9 million would have gone to

various solar research and development programs. Another $8 million would have gone to a program to demonstrate technology for "extended burnup" of nuclear reactor fuel, and $1.25 million to 25 university research reactors. The remaining $10 million savings would not have been spent.

Ottinger argued that before Reagan took office, "we had a very balanced energy budget — spending was spread reasonably among all energy technologies."

During Reagan's tenure in the White House, "this balance was destroyed," Ottinger claimed. "Since 1981, solar energy programs have been cut by 70 percent. Conservation programs have been cut by 50 percent. Fossil energy was cut by over 80 percent. Meanwhile, nuclear fission (including waste) and nuclear fusion have remained about the same.

"The net result," he argued, was a "shift toward an all-nuclear budget."

Leading the speakers in opposition to Ottinger's amendment was Marilyn Lloyd, D-Tenn., chairman of the House Science and Technology Subcommittee on Energy Research and Production. Lloyd represented the district containing Oak Ridge, a center of breeder research.

Lloyd called the amendment "mischievous at best, because it is intended to savage a technology program which the Department of Energy is now restructuring to support a number of advanced breeder designs. A strong technology effort is needed here to allow the department and industry to develop low-cost liquid metal breeders, which also have very attractive safety features."

Also arguing against the amendment was Sid Morrison, R-Wash., whose district contained the Hanford Nuclear Reservation.

"At a time when threats to the Persian Gulf oil supply again dominate the news headlines," Morrison argued, it would be unwise "to cut funds for a technology which holds the promise of an essentially inexhaustible supply of energy. . . ."

Uranium Enrichment Price

Ottinger succeeded in knocking out of the bill a ceiling on the price the Energy Department could charge utilities and other customers for enriched uranium that fueled nuclear reactors. The Appropriations Committee had set the price cap at $135 per "separative work unit."

The New York Democrat lodged a point of order against that ceiling, under a House rule that prohibited making changes in existing law in an appropriations bill.

Ottinger claimed, and Bevill conceded, that such a price cap was not authorized in any existing law, and actually was contravened by the Atomic Energy Act of 1954. That law required the government to recover its costs for enrichment work, and the government did so as of 1984.

Ottinger said the committee-backed cap could cost the government billions of dollars, "fundamentally changing the nature of the program from one that pays its own way to another taxpayer-subsidized nuclear program."

Arguing for the cap was John T. Myers, R-Ind., ranking minority member on the Energy and Water Subcommittee. He said that the United States in 1974 was producing virtually all the nuclear fuel for peaceful use in the world. Because of price increases, he claimed, the nation's share of the world market by 1984 had dropped to about 40 percent.

Myers said the price cap could help control nuclear proliferation. "If we have lost 60 percent of production of uranium enrichment in the world, we lost absolute control

Fiscal 1985 Energy/Water Appropriations

Following are the fiscal 1985 appropriations in budget authority for energy and water development contained in HR 5653. The chart shows the administration request, the amounts approved by the House and Senate, and the final amount cleared by Congress (*in thousands of dollars*):

	Administration Request	House- Passed Amount	Senate- Passed Amount	Final Amount
Army Corps of Engineers				
Construction	$ 874,000	$ 933,014	$ 871,780	$ 890,000
Operation & maintenance	1,297,000	1,339,683	1,317,557	1,305,000
Flood control, Mississippi River & tributaries	304,000	326,309	310,300	321,000
Other flood control, coastal emergencies	10,000	10,000	30,000	25,000
Other	231,000	264,851	233,789	250,000
Subtotal	2,716,000	2,873,857	2,763,426	2,791,000
Bureau of Reclamation				
Construction	764,137	707,817	752,397	740,000
Operation & maintenance	149,689	149,689	149,689	149,689
Other	163,105	167,520	155,910	163,020
Subtotal	1,076,931	1,025,026	1,057,996	1,052,709
Department of Energy (DOE)				
Energy Supply, Research & Development	2,042,113	1,926,149	1,990,168	1,958,165
Uranium Enrichment	1,675,300	1,650,300	1,675,300	1,650,300
(Gross Revenues)	(1,675,300)	(1,650,300)	(1,675,300)	(1,650,300)
General Science & Research	746,105	726,905	726,905	726,905
Nuclear Waste Disposal Fund	327,669	327,669	327,669	327,669
Atomic Energy Defense Activities	7,805,825	7,404,901	7,272,925	7,333,701
Administration	358,034	356,034	356,034	356,034
(Misc. revenues)	(219,459)	(219,459)	(219,459)	(219,459)
Power Marketing Administrations				
Alaska Power Administration	3,233	3,233	3,233	3,233
Bonneville Power Administration				
(Limitation on Direct Loans)	(40,000)	(40,000)	(40,000)	(40,000)
Southeastern Power Administration	35,744	35,744	35,744	35,744
Southwestern Power Administration	29,208	31,208	31,208	31,208
Western Area Power Administration	248,230	218,230	248,230	218,230
Subtotal, Power Marketing Administrations	316,415	288,415	318,415	288,415
Federal Energy Regulatory Commission (FERC)	100,677	95,677	95,677	95,677
(Revenues applied)	(60,000)	(60,000)	(60,000)	(60,000)
Subtotal, FERC	40,677	35,677	35,677	35,677
Geothermal Resource Development Fund	121	121	121	121
(Limitation on guaranteed Loans)	(500,000)	(500,000)	(500,000)	(500,000)
Subtotal, DOE	11,417,500	10,846,412	10,808,455	10,807,228
Independent Agencies				
Nuclear Regulatory Commission	468,200	438,200	458,200	448,200
Tennessee Valley Authority	115,308	126,308	115,308	120,000
Appalachian Regional Commission				
Salaries & expenses	0	2,700	1,700	2,300
Funds appropriated to the president				
Regional development programs	0	57,300	38,000	49,000
Appalachian highway system	80,000	100,000	80,000	100,000
Delaware River Basin Commission	455	455	455	455
Interstate Commission on the Potomac River Basin	0	70	70	70
Susquehanna River Basin Commission	397	397	397	397
Subtotal, Independent Agencies	664,360	725,430	694,130	720,422
GRAND TOTAL	**$15,874,791**	**$15,470,725**	**$15,324,007**	**$15,371,359**

to make sure some of that power, that energy, does not go into weapons," he said.

But Myers conceded Ottinger's point of order was technically correct, and the chair sustained it.

Senate Committee Action

The Senate Appropriations Committee June 5 approved by voice vote and reported its own $15.37 billion version of the energy and water appropriations bill (S Rept 98-502).

The committee's amendments were based on recommendations approved by the Subcommittee on Energy and Water Development by voice vote on May 24.

Neither panel made major changes in the $15.47 billion version of the bill the House passed May 22.

The Senate committee increased by $51 million the amount given to a magnetic fusion program by the House, bringing the total to $470 million — still $13 million below Reagan's request.

It also reversed a House rider that sought to keep the Energy Department from moving a uranium mill tailings pile in Salt Lake City, Utah. The committee's report cited health threats and supported moving the pile.

The committee let stand the House floor action removing the price cap on uranium enrichment services. It also held the line against funding for any new construction starts for water projects.

Water Projects: East to West

For the construction and operation of water projects, the Senate committee shifted funds from the Army Corps of Engineers, which worked mostly in Eastern and coastal states, to the Interior Department's Bureau of Reclamation, which worked in the Western states.

Compared to House levels, it cut the corps' budget by about $110 million and boosted the bureau's by nearly $33 million. Western states were more strongly represented in the Senate than in the House. The Senate committee gave the corps $2.76 billion and the bureau about $1.06 billion.

Garrison Compromise

The perennial controversy over Garrison Diversion was defused during the days before the Senate committee's markup by a compromise between environmentalists and the North Dakota delegation. While the House bill contained no money for the project, the Senate subcommittee had included Reagan's full request of nearly $53.6 million.

The Garrison Diversion, a $1.1 billion system of aqueducts and irrigation canals, was to deliver water from the massive lake behind Garrison Dam in North Dakota, irrigating some 250,000 acres.

Fiscal conservatives had opposed the Garrison project, claiming it was too expensive for the benefits it would yield. Environmentalists claimed it would destroy waterfowl breeding grounds. Canadians feared that the project's transfer of water from the Missouri River basin into the Red River basin would introduce harmful fish species into their ecosystem. For years, those groups had fought to slow or stop the project, which in 1984 was under construction.

Under the compromise, a special commission was to report by Dec. 31, 1984, on ways to meet the state's water needs while minimizing harm to waterfowl, wetlands and Canadian fisheries. The 12-member panel was to be appointed by the interior secretary. If eight of 12 commission-

ers agreed on a redesign, that version would be funded. Otherwise, funding was to be released for the project as it had previously been designed and authorized.

Energy Funding

The Senate committee gave the Energy Department $10.85 billion — very close to the House total but below the Reagan request of $11.4 billion.

Most of those funds went to the building of nuclear warheads and other atomic energy defense activities. Reagan had asked for $7.8 billion in that category. The House cut the amount to $7.4 billion, and the Senate committee cut it further to $7.3 billion. But all of those figures amounted to a hefty increase from the fiscal 1984 appropriation of $6.6 billion.

Included was full funding for pre-production work on warheads for the MX missile, a subject of heated controversy, and for the Trident II missile warhead.

Senate Floor Action

The Senate passed HR 5653 by voice vote on June 21, endorsing the compromise on the Garrison Diversion that had been worked out earlier but not added to the bill in committee.

The Senate-passed bill was about $100 million below the $15.47 billion version passed May 22 by the House.

The Senate by voice vote adopted a compromise amendment offered by Andrews that barred spending of the $53.6 million appropriated in HR 5653 for Garrison until Dec. 31, 1984. That was the date that recommendations were due from a new commission established under the amendment to study possible changes in the project's design that could satisfy all parties.

The only Senate roll call on HR 5653 came June 21 on an amendment by Dennis DeConcini, D-Ariz., to add $5 million to the funding for solar energy research. That amendment was tabled by 60-33. *(Vote 153, p. 27-S)*

Before passing the bill by voice vote, the Senate accepted 15 amendments, changing it little overall from the version approved June 5 by the Senate Appropriations Committee.

Pacific Power Transmission

Controversy over a House-approved 500-kilovolt Pacific power transmission facility briefly threatened to thwart Senate passage of the bill June 21.

Construction of such power lines had been authorized in a 1964 law (PL 88-552), but Congress had reserved the authority to approve specific projects. HR 5653 authorized the energy secretary to build whatever additional facilities he deemed necessary, and to accept funds contributed by area utilities to help build them.

Just before the bill was ready for Senate passage, Pete Wilson, R-Calif., offered an amendment instructing the secretary to proceed "taking into account all the interests involved," saying it was a compromise that had been agreed to by California utilities.

But Senate Appropriations Chairman Mark O. Hatfield, R-Ore., objected, saying the language "may provide lawyers with a hook to hang their hat on in channeling or delaying construction of these lines." His state was anxious to sell the power.

Project advocates feared it could be delayed by a dispute between California's investor-owned utilities such as Pacific Gas & Electric Co. (PG&E) that had about 80 percent of the state's electric customers and the smaller, publicly owned utilities, mostly municipal, that had about 20 percent of the customers. A group of about 20 municipalities had offered to put up much of the money for the new line and was eager to go forward with it. The municipalities were dependent on PG&E for peak power, and feared that PG&E would try to thwart their bid for independence.

After a hasty cloakroom huddle, the Senate agreed to keep the House language largely intact, adding report language directing the secretary to proceed promptly with the new 500-kilovolt line, dropping from participation any utilities seeking to delay construction. The conference committee later added language calling for negotiations with all interested parties.

Conference/Final Action

The House, on June 27, and then the Senate, in the early morning hours of the session that began the same day, adopted without change a conference report (H Rept 98-866) worked out June 26.

The conference committee for the most part split the difference on the comparatively few items in disagreement. The $15.37 billion total recommended by the conferees fell between the House's $15.47 billion and the Senate's $15.32 billion.

For the Corps of Engineers, the final bill appropriated $2.79 billion, less than the House figure of $2.87 billion but more than the Senate figure of $2.76 billion. The final appropriation of $1.052 billion for the Bureau of Reclamation came out closer to the Senate's $1.057 billion total than the House's $1.025 billion mark.

For magnetic fusion research, the final bill allotted $440 million, a compromise between the House's $419 million funding and the $470 million figure set by the Senate.

On the question of the uranium mill tailings at Salt Lake City, the final bill supported relocation of the tailings, but specified a cost-sharing arrangement. Up to $42 million (the cost of stabilizing the tailings in place), 90 percent of costs would be borne by the federal government and 10 percent by the state; beyond that, the federal government would pay 75 percent and the state 25 percent. ∎

Funding for Commerce, Justice, State Clears

Congress Aug. 9 cleared an $11.5 billion fiscal 1985 appropriations bill for the Commerce, Justice and State departments, the federal judiciary and 17 related agencies that included funding for a number of programs President Reagan had sought to abolish.

The measure (HR 5712 — PL 98-411) was signed into law Aug. 30.

The final bill contained about $79 million more than the version approved by the Senate June 28, and $771 million more than the House approved May 31. About $1 billion had been stripped from the House version on the floor on procedural points and amendments. *(House, Senate bills compared, p. 377)*

The spending bill contained $375.1 million more than the administration's request of $11.1 billion.

Since 1981, Congress routinely had funded several programs Reagan sought to eliminate or drastically reduce, and the fiscal 1985 bill was no exception. *(Background, 1983 Almanac p. 472)*

Congress provided funds for the Economic Development Administration (EDA), the Legal Services Corporation (LSC) and programs designed to help states combat juvenile delinquency — all of which the administration sought to abolish.

The EDA was designed to spur community development, and the LSC provided funding for legal aid in civil cases for the nation's poor. The corporation, which submitted its budget directly to Congress, requested $325.3 million.

The Reagan administration had tried to abolish the LSC since 1981, but Congress consistently refused to go along. However, the agency's budget had been trimmed from its levels in the Carter administration, and President Reagan, through appointments to the LSC board of directors, altered the direction of the corporation.

The appropriations bill included $18.5 million for the National Endowment for Democracy, a little more than half of what the administration had requested. The endowment, authorized in 1983, provided grants to private organizations such as the AFL-CIO and the U.S. Chamber of Commerce to establish programs in foreign countries to teach people about the U.S. political system and to promote democracy. *(1983 Almanac p. 148)*

In addition, the legislation included $64.3 million for the Federal Trade Commission (FTC), which was the subject of a prolonged dispute over authorizing legislation. The measure barred the FTC from bringing antitrust suits against local governments unless the committees with oversight jurisdiction over the agency specifically allowed such suits in the FTC's authorization bill. *(Related story, p. 257)*

Final Provisions

As cleared by Congress, HR 5712 appropriated the following amounts in budget authority for fiscal 1985 *(in thousands of dollars)*:

	Final Request	Final Amount
Commerce Department		
General Administration	$ 40,890	$ 36,490
Bureau of the Census	174,599	166,500
Economic and Statistical Analysis	31,622	31,085
Economic Development Administration	22,476	228,500
International Trade Administration	172,948	192,418
Minority Business Development Agency	49,885	49,885
U.S. Travel and Tourism	8,583	12,000
National Oceanic and Atmospheric Administration	881,400	1,149,116
Patent and Trademark Office	101,631	101,631
National Bureau of Standards	126,062	123,985
National Telecommunications and Information Administration	13,944	37,694
Subtotal, Commerce Department	1,624,040	2,129,304

Related Agencies

Federal Communications Commission	92,611	93,611
Federal Maritime Commission	12,292	12,292
Federal Trade Commission	66,231	64,311
International Trade Commission	28,410	24,830
Marine Mammal Commission	648	929
Maritime Administration	75,730	80,367
Office of the U.S. Trade Representative	14,179	13,582
Securities and Exchange Commission	104,683	105,337
Small Business Administration	569,100	700,250
Subtotal, Related Agencies	**963,884**	**1,095,509**

Department of Justice

General Administration	73,584	74,150
U.S. Parole Commission	8,778	8,913
Legal Activities	808,558	805,565
Interagency Law Enforcement	2,559	1,500
Federal Bureau of Investigation	1,157,223	1,147,123
Drug Enforcement Administration	334,654	329,988
Immigration and Naturalization Service	574,539	576,417
Federal Prison System	595,193	603,506
Office of Justice Assistance, Research and Statistics	133,739	145,551
Subtotal, Justice Department	**3,688,827**	**3,692,713**

Related Agencies

Civil Rights Commission	12,747	12,747
Equal Employment Opportunity Commission	161,155	160,755
Legal Services Corporation	325,253 [1]	305,000
Subtotal, Related Agencies	**499,155**	**478,502**

State Department

Administration of Foreign Affairs	1,705,273	1,631,721
International Organizations and Conferences	589,165	558,667
International Commissions	27,513	26,785
U.S. Bilateral Science and Technology Agreements	2,000	—
The Asia Foundation	10,000	9,600
Soviet-East European research and training	5,000	4,800
Subtotal, State Department	**2,338,951**	**2,231,573**

Related Agencies

Arms Control and Disarmament Agency	19,468	19,468
Board for International Broadcasting	100,498	97,498
Commission for Security and Cooperation for Europe	550	550
Japan-United States Friendship Commission	1,600	1,600
U.S. Information Agency	885,424	796,356
Subtotal, Related Agencies	**1,007,540**	**915,472**

The Judiciary

Supreme Court of the United States	16,385	16,385
U.S. Court of Appeals for the Federal Circuit	6,414	5,150
U.S. Court of International Trade	6,096	6,070
Courts of Appeals, District Courts and other judicial services	955,635	912,718
Administrative Office of the U.S. Courts	29,360	28,250
Federal Judicial Center	9,631	9,330
Subtotal, the Judiciary	**1,023,521** [1]	**977,903**
Grand Total	**$11,145,918**	**$11,520,976**

[1] *Submitted to Congress directly.*

House Committee Action

The House Appropriations Committee May 23 reported an $11.89 billion version of HR 5712 (H Rept 98-802). The total spending was $759.93 million more than Reagan had requested and $1.39 billion more than Congress had appropriated to date for the affected agencies and departments.

Reagan Proposals Ignored

The committee recommended funding for several programs Reagan sought to eliminate:

● $278.6 million in new budget authority and $150 million in loan guarantee authority for the Economic Development Administration.

● $325.3 million — $50.3 million more than was appropriated in fiscal 1984 — for the Legal Services Corporation. The committee report stated that the funds were to be spent in accordance with language in the fiscal 1984 appropriations bill, which set out certain restrictions on Legal Services lawyers and members of the corporation's board of directors. *(1983 Almanac p. 322)*

● The committee provided $70.2 million, approximately the same as the fiscal 1984 appropriation, for programs designed to help states combat juvenile delinquency.

As approved by the Appropriations Committee, the bill included the following provisions:

Commerce Department

The committee provided $2.19 billion for Commerce, $567.9 million above the administration request of $1.62 billion and $222.7 million above the fiscal 1984 funding. The bulk of the increase over the Reagan proposal was the money for the EDA and funding for the National Oceanic and Atmospheric Administration (NOAA).

The committee recommended $1.51 billion in new budget authority for NOAA, an increase of $269.7 million over the president's request and $130.5 million over fiscal 1984 spending. Of the total appropriation, $1.1 billion was for fisheries, marine, weather, environmental and satellite programs.

U.S. Travel and Tourism Administration. The committee recommended $8.6 million for the agency, the president's request. That was a decrease of $3.4 million from the 1984 appropriation. The reductions in part came from decreases in brochure publication and advertising funding, and elimination of research and marketing programs, and of funding for trade shows and special market activities.

International Trade Administration. The committee recommended $198.9 million for the trade administration, almost $26 million above the budget request and $31.5 million above the fiscal 1984 funding level. Of the total, $30 million was earmarked for the Trade Adjustment Assistance program, designed to provide special unemployment benefits to workers who lost their jobs because of foreign competition.

Public Telecommunication Facilities, Planning and Construction. The committee provided $25 million for planning and construction grants for public radio, television and non-broadcast facilities. Reagan asked no money for these items.

The report made clear the committee's continuing support for the grant program, despite the administration's lack of enthusiasm.

Commerce-Related Agencies

Maritime Administration. The full budget request of $83.8 million in new budget authority was provided for the Maritime Administration. In addition, the committee provided $377.8 million, the administration request, for payment of operating subsidies to operators of U.S.-flag vessels, to help them compete with foreign-operated vessels. That was $23.5 million below the amount made available in fiscal 1984. It was the second consecutive year in which the operating subsidies were cut. In fiscal 1984, the subsidy was trimmed $52.7 million from the 1983 level.

Federal Communications Commission (FCC). The committee recommended $94.1 million for the FCC — $1.5 million above the budget request and $7.7 million above the fiscal 1984 appropriation.

Federal Trade Commission. The bill included $65.2 million for the FTC, $1.7 million more than the Reagan request but $1.2 million less than the fiscal 1984 funding.

By a vote of 21-16, the committee adopted an amendment by Martin Olav Sabo, D-Minn., barring the use of any funds appropriated under the bill to bring antitrust actions against a municipality or any unit of local government.

Sabo said the provision was prompted by FTC complaints lodged against Minneapolis and New Orleans contending that those cities' taxicab regulations violated antitrust laws.

Small Business Administration (SBA). The committee recommended $805.3 million for the SBA, $236.2 million more than the administration requested and $209.3 million above the fiscal 1984 funding level.

It gave this explanation for the hike: "Since more repayments on outstanding loans to the Small Business Administration and to banks who made guaranteed loans have not been made when due, the increased amounts are necessary to fund the same level of activities as in fiscal 1984."

Justice Department

The total for the Justice Department was $3.74 billion in new budget authority, $64.9 million more than the Reagan request and $365.9 million more than the fiscal 1984 appropriation.

The increase over the budget request resulted primarily from funds for juvenile justice programs, and for state and local grants for drug enforcement.

Organized Crime Drug Enforcement. The committee recommended $2.5 million for this program — $59,000 less than the budget request and $86.6 million below the fiscal 1984 appropriation. The committee noted that the reduction was the result of the administration's

decision to transfer some functions of the enforcement program to other Justice Department agencies.

FBI. The bill included $1.15 billion for the FBI — a reduction of $9.9 million from the budget request but an increase of almost $100.4 million over the 1984 funding level. The report said the reduction from the budget request was the result of disallowing a restoration of a 1 percent cut made in the fiscal 1984 appropriation act and disallowing a requested increase in rent to the General Services Administration (GSA) in excess of 7 percent.

Drug Enforcement Administration (DEA). The committee recommended $333.3 million for the DEA, $1.4 million less than the budget request but $47.1 million more than the fiscal 1984 appropriation. The report said the reduction from the budget request resulted solely from disallowing an increase beyond 7 percent in rent to the GSA.

Immigration and Naturalization Service. The agency was given $591 million — $16.5 million above the budget request and $89.8 million above the fiscal 1984 appropriation. The committee said all non-discretionary cost increases and all requests for program increases were funded.

Justice-Related Agencies

Civil Rights Commission. Although the administration recommended funding for the U.S. Commission on Civil Rights, civil rights advocates and some members of Congress expressed concern about the agency's operations and independence.

Reagan effectively seized control of the panel in December 1983 after Congress expanded its membership from six to eight. Reagan appointed four members and ensured that a fifth — chosen by House Minority Leader Robert H. Michel, R-Ill. — agreed with his views. *(1983 Almanac p. 292)*

At Appropriations hearings in 1984, some members suggested that funding for the commission be eliminated. But the committee decided to recommend funding at the administration-requested level, $12.8 million, and sought to address the issue of the panel's operations in report language.

The panel earmarked $2.3 million for reports, studies and monitoring of federal programs; almost $5 million for field operations; and $1.2 million for "liaison and public information dissemination."

The committee made clear that although the commission was reconstituted, its basic fact-finding mission and jurisdiction were unchanged.

The committee said it believed "specifically that [the commission's] consideration of issues related to civil rights implications of budget and appropriations decisions remains useful and important for the deliberations of this committee and Congress."

Legal Services Corporation. The committee recommended $325.3 million for the LSC, the amount sought by the corporation, which by law submitted its request directly to Congress. Reagan had again sought to abolish the agency.

Federal Judiciary

The committee recommended $985.1 million for the federal judiciary, which included the Supreme Court, the appeals and district courts, and several specialized courts. The amount was $38.4 million under the budget request, which was submitted to Congress directly by the judiciary.

However, the recommended funding was $102.1 million over the fiscal 1984 appropriation.

State Department

The bill provided $2.31 billion for State, $27.8 million less than the budget request and $241.2 million above fiscal 1984 appropriations to date. The committee included a new $13 million appropriation for protection of foreign missions and officials, $3.5 million more than the budget request.

The recommended funding would provide for reimbursement of state and local governments in cases of extraordinary need for protection of foreign missions and officials throughout the United States ($6 million), and protection of foreign missions and officials accredited to the United Nations and to other international organizations ($7 million).

As it did in the fiscal 1984 spending bill, the committee included $10 million for the Asia Foundation, a three-decade-old private foundation whose board of trustees included several prominent Washington residents.

State-Related Agencies

Arms Control and Disarmament Agency. The bill provided $19.5 million, the same as the administration request and $968,000 above the fiscal 1984 appropriation.

United States Information Agency (USIA). The committee recommended $834.7 million for the USIA, $50.7 million less than the budget request but $175 million more than fiscal 1984 appropriations.

Included in the total was $8.5 million for radio broadcasting to Cuba through the Voice of America Radio Marti program. That was $2.7 million below the administration request and $1.5 million less than the fiscal 1984 funding level.

The USIA funding also included $31.3 million for the National Endowment for Democracy, established in 1983 to encourage "free and democratic institutions throughout the world through private sector initiatives."

House Floor Action

The House May 31 passed a $10.7 billion fiscal 1985 appropriations bill for four departments and assorted agencies after knocking out $31.3 million for a year-old program to encourage U.S.-style democracy in foreign countries.

Charging that the endowment program could lead to meddling in foreign elections, Richard L. Ottinger, D-N.Y., offered the amendment to delete its funding. His amendment was adopted 226-173. *(Vote 174, p. 56-H)*

As passed by the House 303-98, the measure (HR 5712) provided $380 million less than the $11.13 billion proposed by the Reagan administration. *(Vote 176, p. 56-H)*

Funding Cuts

The bill reported by the Appropriations Committee had provided $11.89 billion. But $1.14 billion was trimmed on the House floor through procedural moves and amendments.

Of the total reduction, $438 million was cut as the result of a proposal by Clarence E. Miller, R-Ohio, to make a 4 percent cut in all discretionary funding. His motion to recommit the bill to the Appropriations Committee with instructions to make the cut was agreed to 208-194. *(Vote 175, p. 56-H)*

More than $700 million was stricken from the measure

for programs that were not yet authorized. Authorizations set out the broad policy guidelines and funding maximums for programs, and appropriations had to fit within the authorizations.

Often, authorization bills for programs had not been passed when their appropriations measures were considered, but the House adopted a rule waiving points of order that could be lodged against such funding because of the lack of authorization.

For the second year in a row, however, Neal Smith, D-Iowa, chairman of the Appropriations Subcommittee on Commerce, Justice, State and Judiciary, brought his bill to the floor without a rule. It was thus subject to points of order. Smith declined to seek a rule because he was convinced that he could not get one that met his specifications.

As a result of the lack of authorizations and the lack of a rule, $65.2 million in funding for the FTC was deleted from the measure on a point of order. Another $325.3 million for the LSC and $278.6 million for the EDA were likewise deleted because they had not been authorized.

Federal Trade Commission

Members got a chance to vent their frustrations with the FTC when Silvio O. Conte, R-Mass., the ranking member of the full Appropriations Committee, offered an amendment to delete language from the bill that barred the agency from using any funds in the bill to bring antitrust suits against municipalities.

The language was inserted in committee by Sabo and Lindy (Mrs. Hale) Boggs, D-La., who were angered by suits the FTC had brought against Minneapolis and New Orleans contending that those cities' taxicab regulations violated antitrust laws.

Sabo, arguing for retention of the language, said it was merely a device to hold the line until Congress could look at the issue of antitrust liability of municipalities.

The Conte amendment was defeated and the language remained in the bill.

Senate Committee Action

The Senate Appropriations Committee June 12 approved an $11.47 billion version of HR 5712. The committee made only minor changes from the bill as approved June 7 by its Subcommittee on Commerce, Justice, State and Judiciary.

Endowment for Democracy

The Senate subcommittee by a 6-5 vote had restored the funding for the National Endowment for Democracy. At the full committee June 12, Lowell P. Weicker Jr., R-Conn., sought to strike the money, but his amendment was rejected 10-14. Six Republicans joined four Democrats in opposing the program, while seven Republicans and seven Democrats voted to keep the money in.

Warren B. Rudman, R-N.H., then tried to cut the endowment's appropriation by $10 million and to bar money from going to either the Republican or Democratic parties. His proposal was rejected 12-16.

Rudman said funding for the political parties was "a radical departure from what this government has ever done before."

Ted Stevens, R-Alaska, agreed, but did not want the endowment funding cut. "This is little enough in comparison with the billions spent on the other side to foster the growth of communism," he said.

LSC Funding

The Senate committee provided $297.55 million for the LSC, the same as the subcommittee recommendation.

However, the committee June 12 added a new provision at Rudman's request barring travel by the president of the LSC, members of its board of directors, and employees until the corporation answered questions about its proposed fiscal 1985 budget. Rudman told the committee he had been waiting a month for the answers and said his amendment was intended to make LSC personnel "stay in Washington and do some work."

Senate Floor Action

The Senate June 28 passed an $11.45 billion version of HR 5712, after trimming $10 million from the National Endowment for Democracy. The vote was 79-15. *(Vote 173, p. 30-S)*

Democracy Program Trimmed

By a 62-30 vote, the Senate adopted a Rudman amendment stripping $10 million from the endowment budget for grants to international institutes run by the

Comparing House and Senate Funding

Following are fiscal 1985 appropriations in budget authority requested by President Reagan and approved by the House and Senate in HR 5712 for the departments of State, Justice and Commerce, their related agencies and the federal judiciary *(in thousands of dollars):*

	Administration Request	House-Passed Bill	Senate-Passed Bill
Department of Commerce	$ 1,668,981	$ 1,835,210	$ 2,137,758
Related Agencies			
Federal Communications Commission	92,611	90,347	94,111
Federal Maritime Commission	12,292	11,800	12,292
Federal Trade Commission	66,231	— [1]	64,311
International Trade Commission	28,410	25,044	24,030
Marine Mammal Commission	648	892	929
Maritime Administration	75,730	80,455	75,467
Office of the United States Trade Representative	14,179	13,231	13,782
Securities and Exchange Commission	104,683	102,468	105,337
Small Business Administration	569,100	773,085	626,410
Department of Justice	3,673,852	3,590,836	3,675,564
Related Agencies			
Commission on Civil Rights	12,747	12,237	12,747
Equal Employment Opportunity Commission	161,155	153,845	161,155
Legal Services Corporation	325,253 [2]	— [1]	297,550
Department of State	2,338,951	2,222,936	2,228,879
Related Agencies			
Arms Control and Disarmament Agency	19,468	18,689	19,468
Board for International Broadcasting	100,498	96,478	100,498
Commission on Security and Cooperation in Europe	550	528	550
Japan-United States Friendship Commission	1,600	1,536	1,600
United States Information Agency	885,424	771,273	805,656
The Judiciary	1,023,521 [2]	948,675	983,741
TOTAL	$11,175,884	$10,749,565	$11,441,835

[1] *Some or all funds deleted by House because programs were unauthorized.*
[2] *Submitted to Congress directly.*

Republican and Democratic parties. *(Vote 168, p. 29-S)*

The Senate defeated two other efforts to kill the entire endowment. By a 42-51 vote, it rejected an amendment by Weicker deleting the entire $31.3 million budgeted for the endowment. *(Vote 167, p. 29-S)*

Then, by a 44-49 vote, it rejected an amendment by Ernest F. Hollings, D-S.C., allocating the money instead for scholarships to students from Latin America. *(Vote 169, p. 30-S)*

FTC Antitrust Authority Restored

By voice vote, the Senate adopted a Rudman amendment restoring the authority of the Federal Trade Commission to bring antitrust suits against local governments. The FTC could seek only injunctive relief — not triple damages, a usual remedy in antitrust suits.

Hollings tried to delete funding authority for all local-government FTC suits, but his proposal was rejected 36-63. *(Vote 166, p. 29-S)*

LSC. Jesse Helms, R-N.C., tried to delete $297.55 million for the Legal Services Corporation, but his proposal was rejected. Helms contended that the LSC appropriation was out of order because language attached to it was legislation on an appropriations bill. The presiding officer ruled that Helms was correct. However, the Senate overruled the chair 27-72. *(Vote 164, p. 29-S)*

Conference/Final Action

Conference

House and Senate conferees agreed Aug. 2 on an $11.52 billion bill (H Rept 98-952).

With just a smattering of debate, conferees agreed to provide $18.5 million for the National Endowment for Democracy and retained Senate language barring money for either political party.

After nearly two hours of discussion, conferees agreed on compromise language to bar the FTC from bringing antitrust suits against local governments unless the committees with oversight jurisdiction over the FTC specifically allowed such suits in the agency's authorization. The

FTC operated without an authorization in fiscal 1983 and 1984, using funds provided in appropriations measures.

The compromise language was similar to a provision inserted in the original House bill at the request of members angered by FTC suits challenging taxicab regulations in Minneapolis and New Orleans. The Senate had replaced the House provision with language restoring the FTC's authority to seek court orders against local governments to stop anti-competitive practices. The Senate language also had barred private parties from collecting monetary damages against local governments in antitrust suits.

Conferees provided $305 million for the LSC, $7.45 million more than the $297.55 million in the Senate bill. The House had struck the funding for the LSC on a point of order.

Conferees retained language in the Senate bill that barred LSC officials from promulgating, enforcing or implementing new regulations unless both the Senate and House Appropriations committees had been notified.

Final Action

Final action on the conference report came Aug. 9 when the Senate adopted the measure by voice vote after five minutes' discussion.

The House adopted the report a day earlier after debating and voting on three controversial issues. The House vote to adopt the report was 277-135. *(Vote 312, p. 96-H)*

In separate votes, the House endorsed three agreements reached by conferees:

● The Federal Trade Commission compromise was agreed to, 226-193. *(Vote 313, p. 96-H)*

Rep. Elliott H. Levitas, D-Ga., had suggested that the FTC funding should be approved but that the commission should be barred from making final rules until reauthorization legislation had been enacted. His suggestion was rebuffed, however.

● Fiscal 1985 funding of $305 million for the LSC was agreed to when the House adopted the conference committee agreement, 278-138. *(Vote 314, p. 96-H)*

● By 237-181, members accepted the conference compromise on funding for the National Endowment for Democracy. *(Vote 315, p. 96-H)* ∎

Interior Funding Rolled Into Catchall Measure

For the fourth year in row, Congress banned offshore oil and gas leasing in selected areas as it approved $8.1 billion in fiscal 1985 appropriations for the Interior Department and related agencies.

The Interior funding was rolled into the yearlong fiscal 1985 continuing appropriations resolution (H J Res 648 — PL 98-473) signed Oct. 12 by President Reagan. *(Continuing resolution, p. 444)*

The House passed a regular fiscal 1985 Interior spending bill (HR 5973 — H Rept 98-886) on Aug. 2, and the Senate briefly considered its own version of the measure on Sept. 26. But with time running out in the 98th Congress, the Senate ultimately decided to add Interior funding provisions to the continuing resolution instead of trying to complete work on HR 5973.

The final funding was slightly below the amount provided under both the House and Senate versions, but still

well above Reagan's $7.7 billion budget request. *(Chart, p. 382)*

Fiscal 1984 Interior appropriations totaled $8.02 billion.

As cleared, H J Res 648 reflected several important policy decisions made in conjunction with the Interior appropriations.

Offshore Leasing Ban

The one-year offshore leasing ban applied to several areas off California and to the productive Georges Bank fishing grounds off New England.

The bill also banned leasing of oil, gas, mineral and geothermal resources on roughly 30 million acres under study for possible wilderness designation in the future.

Congress had included similar provisions in the fiscal 1982-84 Interior funding bills, expressing its objections to the administration's accelerated energy development policies. *(1981 Almanac p. 369; 1982 Almanac p. 262; 1983 Almanac p. 462)*

Legislation to give states greater control over leasing through the Coastal Zone Management program died when Congress adjourned. A bill (S 2324 — S Rept 98-512) approved by the Senate Commerce Committee never made it to the Senate floor, and a House version (HR 4589) never achieved markup in the Merchant Marine Committee. The administration opposed the legislation. *(Story, p. 335)*

House-Senate conferees on the Interior portion of the continuing resolution, led by Rep. Sidney R. Yates, D-Ill., and Sen. James A. McClure, R-Idaho, voiced hope that this would be the last time Congress felt a need to impose leasing bans. "The managers will not continue such blanket moratoria in the future," they said, unless the Interior Department's administrative process failed to ensure resource protection.

"The department is urged to pursue a resolution of the long-term leasing status of these areas through continuing negotiations with the appropriate congressional, state and local officials," they said.

Synthetic Fuels Corporation

The most controversial policy issue, the fate of the trouble-plagued U.S. Synthetic Fuels Corporation (SFC), was settled when conferees agreed to rescind $5.375 billion in funds previously appropriated for grants and loans to businesses seeking to make synfuels production commercially viable. An additional $2 billion was rescinded earlier in the year. Reagan in May had asked for a $9.5 billion rescission. *(Synfuels, p. 347)*

Conferees accepted a Senate provision directing that $750 million of the amount rescinded go to a special account reserved for projects to demonstrate cleaner ways to burn coal.

Conferees dropped a House provision that would have denied funding to two Colorado projects, Union II and Cathedral Bluffs. Those projects, which some opposed on economic and environmental grounds, together could cost about $5 billion.

An amendment by Sen. Howard M. Metzenbaum, D-Ohio, to impose financial disclosure and conflict-of-interest restrictions on SFC board members, was adopted by the Senate and by the conference. Two SFC presidents stepped down amid conflict-of-interest charges.

The SFC, set up in 1980 after a decade of energy disruptions, was meant to encourage commercialization of fuels made from coal, shale and tar sands through a program of price supports and loan guarantees to private businesses. *(1980 Almanac p. 477)*

The corporation was slow to spend $20 billion Congress gave it in 1980, and resignations of most of its board of directors under charges of mismanagement left it paralyzed during much of 1984.

Strategic Petroleum Reserve

Not counted against budget totals was $2.05 billion in the final bill to buy oil for the Strategic Petroleum Reserve, which was meant to give the nation a cushion against disruptions of oil imports.

Reagan had asked for $1.89 billion, which would have allowed the pumping of about 145,000 barrels per day into storage. The final appropriation, less than originally approved by either the House or the Senate, allowed a fill rate of about 159,000 barrels per day. This was more than

Reagan wanted, but it was a cutback from the fiscal 1984 rate of 186,000 barrels per day.

Conservation, Parks

Congress appropriated $4.32 billion for the Interior Department, less than either the House or Senate versions of the bill, but still well above the Reagan administration request of $3.98 billion.

Much of the extra spending went to resource conservation agencies whose budgets Reagan wanted to hold down, including the National Park Service, the Fish and Wildlife Service and the Bureau of Land Management (BLM).

Congress provided more than Reagan sought for acquisition of lands for federal and state parks, refuges and recreation areas under the Land and Water Conservation Fund. The $256.7 million provided was far above Reagan's request of $174.6 million. The House had voted $304 million and the Senate committee $242 million.

Still, all those amounts represented a drastic decline in park land acquisition, which peaked during the Carter administration, when appropriations averaged more than $500 million annually.

Congress sharply boosted the BLM's budget for removing wild horses and burros from federal land — from $4.9 million in fiscal 1984 to $16.7 million for fiscal 1985. The wild mustangs, seen as a nuisance by ranchers and a cause by animal lovers, were adopted or sold.

Timber Sales, Energy Programs

The Interior segment of PL 98-473 included funds for a number of other agencies.

The bill gave $1.31 billion to the U.S. Forest Service, allowing preparation for sale of 11.2 billion board feet of timber, not considering effects of a timber contract relief bill (HR 2838 — PL 98-478) signed Oct. 16. *(Timber bailout, p. 344)*

Congress again gave Reagan unwanted funds for two large Energy Department programs that he had tried for four years to cut back.

It approved $275 million for fossil energy research and development, well above Reagan's $200 million request. These programs sought to squeeze more out of the nation's energy resources through techniques such as coal liquefaction and enhanced oil recovery.

Congress provided $459 million for energy conservation programs, although Reagan requested only $390 million. Much of that money went to state and local grant programs that were especially popular with members from the Northeast and Midwest, including the home weatherization program, funded at $191 million.

House Committee Action

Funding Levels

The House Appropriations Committee June 28 approved HR 5973 by voice vote, endorsing a funding level of about $8.3 billion.

Panel members defeated a move by committee Republicans to trim spending in the bill across the board.

As approved by the Appropriations Committee, the bill provided $4.34 billion for the Interior Department, $1.56 billion for the Agriculture Department's U.S. Forest Service, $806 million for the Energy Department and $1.6 billion for other agencies.

Not included in the total were off-budget funds to buy

oil for the Strategic Petroleum Reserve. The bill appropriated $2.35 billion for that oil, while the administration requested $1.89 billion. The committee set the fill rate for the reserve at 186,000 barrels per day, the fiscal 1984 level, while the administration asked for 145,000 barrels per day.

As in previous years, the panel gave Reagan more than he requested for government acquisition of park, recreation and wildlife refuge lands under the Land and Water Conservation Fund. The committee approved $302 million for the fund ($75 million of which was to go to the states), while Reagan asked $175 million ($7.5 million of which was for the states). The fiscal 1984 appropriation was $256 million, including $75 million for the states.

The committee also gave Reagan more than he wanted for fossil energy research and development. The panel approved $268 million, the same as 1984 spending, while Reagan asked just under $200 million.

The committee approved $485 million for energy conservation programs, well above the Reagan request of $390 million and the 1984 appropriation of $431 million.

Spending for Indian programs in the bill totaled $2.07 billion — about $242 million more than Reagan had requested and $182 million more than the 1984 appropriation. Included in the committee total were $1.07 billion for Interior's Bureau of Indian Affairs, $914 million for Indian health programs and $69 million for Indian education programs.

Yates, chairman of the Interior subcommittee, backed off from a subcommittee-approved transfer of $200 million from the general Treasury to the Petroleum Overcharge Restitution Fund to pay for the low-income home weatherization program.

The full committee dropped that transfer because the restitution fund proposed by the Reagan administration had not been authorized by Congress. As approved, the bill retained weatherization spending at $200 million from Treasury funds.

Republicans, however, still voiced concern over the bill's spending total of nearly $8.31 billion. That was more than President Reagan's request of $7.68 billion and fiscal 1984 appropriations of $8.02 billion.

Joseph M. McDade, R-Pa., ranking minority member on Yates' subcommittee, moved to cut 6 percent from each spending category in the bill across the board, but his proposal was defeated on a 15-24 show of hands.

Leasing Bans

As approved, the bill banned offshore oil and gas leasing sales in the Georges Bank area off New England and in three large areas off California. The committee narrowly rejected, 20-21, a proposal by McDade to delete those leasing bans.

At Yates' urging, the committee removed a moratorium approved by the subcommittee June 19 on leasing in Bristol Bay off the coast of Alaska. Yates said Interior Secretary William P. Clark had agreed to seek further environmental data on the sale, which was expected to be delayed until fiscal 1986.

Yates had originally recommended two more offshore bans — in the St. George Basin off Alaska and in the Atlantic off eastern Florida. But on a motion by Tom Loeffler, R-Texas, those two bans were stricken in subcommittee.

The subcommittee's version of the bill would have halted an Interior Department leasing program intended to encourage exploration on federal lands without known oil and gas potential. That program replaced competitive bidding with a lottery system, on the assumption that oil companies would not pay much for the right to drill in unpromising areas. Lease winners who struck oil still had to pay royalties to the Treasury, just as competitive lease-holders did.

The program came in for congressional criticism during the initial years of the Reagan administration, when areas likely to contain oil were found to have been raffled off as well — possibly costing the government leasing revenue. Yates, in urging an end to the lottery, charged there had been fraud and abuse in the program. But Loeffler said Clark had reformed the program after temporarily suspending it in October 1983.

At the full committee, Yates recommended that the ban on the award of leases by lottery be removed from the bill after Morris K. Udall, D-Ariz., chairman of the Interior and Insular Affairs Committee, promised to hold hearings on the oil lottery. The Appropriations Committee accepted Yates' recommendation.

Synfuels

The most intensely debated issue during the markup was a Reagan administration proposal to rescind $9 billion in funds already appropriated to the U.S. Synthetic Fuels Corporation.

Silvio O. Conte, R-Mass., ranking Republican on the full committee, moved to rescind the SFC funds — as he had done unsuccessfully in subcommittee. He did not propose the so-called "market test" urged by Reagan, which would have required remaining SFC funds to be used only for projects producing synfuels at close to the cost of conventional fuels.

Conte's amendment was rejected 17-23, in a vote that divided the panel's leadership. McDade voted against his Republican colleague, while Democrat Yates voted for the amendment and against Appropriations Chairman Jamie L. Whitten, D-Miss. Conte tried again, offering a $5 billion rescission. That amendment was rejected 19-22.

Coal Leasing

Subcommittee Chairman Yates said Interior Secretary Clark had partially satisfied him that adequate reforms were under way in the troubled federal coal leasing program. As a result, Yates withdrew his panel's recommendation for a new moratorium on such leasing.

That recommendation had been made May 22, when the subcommittee approved a fiscal 1984 supplemental spending measure.

Criticism from Congress over the speed with which the department was leasing coal on federal lands resulted in the attachment of a leasing ban to the fiscal 1984 Interior appropriations bill. That ban expired May 17.

Clark seemed to have disarmed some Capitol Hill critics when he promised no leasing until the end of 1984 and said he would adopt almost all recommendations of a blue-ribbon commission set up to study whether the Treasury was getting fair market value for coal leases on federal lands. *(Story, p. 342; background, 1983 Almanac p. 350)*

House Floor Action

Spending Cut

The House Aug. 2 cut $5 billion from the budget of the troubled U.S. Synthetic Fuels Corporation as it approved the Interior appropriations bill (HR 5973 — H Rept 98-886) for fiscal 1985.

Before passing the bill, the House adopted a Republican-sponsored amendment trimming spending totals 3 percent across-the-board to bring the bill close to the ceilings in the so-called Rose Garden deficit reduction plan. *(Story, p. 143)*

The 212-181 vote to cut the spending totals came on an amendment offered by McDade, which was resisted in vain by the bill's manager, Yates. *(Vote 310, p. 94-H)*

The 3 percent cut and other changes brought the bill's total to about $8.03 billion. The committee deducted the $5 billion SFC rescission from that and claimed a net appropriation of $3,033,865,000.

Synfuels Rescission

The $5 billion cut in SFC's funding struck a compromise between the program's defenders, who had tried to protect its already appropriated funds from any cuts, and opponents, who had hoped to rescind most or all of its remaining funds.

The Reagan administration had asked for a $9 billion cut, but one of SFC's stoutest defenders, House Majority Leader Jim Wright, D-Texas, had fought for a rule to keep any SFC funding cut from coming to the floor. The House demanded a vote July 25 by defeating the rule proposed to govern floor action. The vote was 148-261. *(Vote 285, p. 88-H)*

That rule, approved July 24 by the Rules Committee, would have allowed points of order to be lodged against amendments to rescind SFC money.

House rejection of the rule was a victory for the administration. David A. Stockman, director of the Office of Management and Budget, called some House members personally before the vote, asking them to oppose the rule.

But while it pitted the White House against House Democratic leaders, the vote was not a particularly partisan one. House Democrats split right down the middle, 127-126, on adoption of the rule. Republicans generally voted against adoption, 21-135.

Meeting again on July 26, the Rules Committee approved by voice vote a rule (H Res 557) waiving points of order against an amendment to be offered by Conte, seeking a $10 billion rescission. Perfecting amendments to the Conte amendment, seeking only to change the dollar amount, also were made in order.

The key vote on the $5 billion rescission offered by William R. Ratchford, D-Conn., was 236-177, drawing support from both factions. Wright voted for the amendment. *(Vote 308, p. 94-H)*

Democrats supported the Ratchford amendment 169-83. Republicans, many of whom were holding out for the larger $10 billion cut, opposed it 67-94.

Ratchford's $5 billion cut was offered as an alternative to a $10 billion cut proposed by Conte. Since Ratchford's proposal was offered as an amendment to Conte's amendment, the House would have voted on a $10 billion cut if Ratchford's amendment had been defeated.

Some supporters of bigger cuts were drawn to the Ratchford proposal as a result of a surprise amendment offered by Yates.

The amendment, adopted by voice vote, barred any SFC funds for price and loan guarantees to two Colorado oil shale projects that critics called too big and too expensive — Union II ($2.7 billion) and Cathedral Bluffs ($2.19 billion).

Amendments Adopted

Among the amendments adopted by the House before it passed the bill was one prohibiting the use of Fish and Wildlife Service funds to conduct deer hunting in the Loxahatchee National Wildlife Refuge. It was offered by Larry Smith, D-Fla., and adopted by voice vote. Hunts held there for population control in previous years had aroused protests from some wildlife groups.

The House also adopted by voice vote an amendment to raise by $3 million the amount for research on how air pollution affected forest growth. Offered by James Weaver, D-Ore., this amendment reflected a concern over tree die-offs in Germany's Black Forest and some Appalachian areas in the United States that tentatively were blamed on acid rain and other air pollution. The money was taken from the Forest Service's road construction account.

The House July 31 also adopted by voice vote a Yates amendment rescinding $226 million in unused funds previously appropriated for timber purchaser road credits. Logging companies could deduct from the price they paid the government for federal timber the costs of building roads into a forest to cut and haul the timber.

Senate Committee Action

The Senate Appropriations Committee reported its $8.15 billion appropriation (S Rept 98-578) on Aug. 6. The bill made no attempt to rescind funds of the Synthetic Fuels Corporation.

The Senate committee cut some $380 million from the House committee's bill, but its version was $12 million above the total passed by the House.

Highlights of the bill included:

• $4.32 billion for the Interior Department.

• $1.33 billion for the U.S. Forest Service in the Department of Agriculture.

• $973 million for the Department of Energy.

• $2.35 billion (off budget) to purchase crude oil for the Strategic Petroleum Reserve, setting the fill rate at 186,000 barrels per day. The administration had sought a fill rate of 145,000 barrels per day.

The Senate committee's bill appropriated some $240 million for purchase of park, wildlife refuge, and recreation lands under the Land and Water Conservation Fund. President Reagan had requested only $176 million and the House had appropriated about $304 million.

The Senate panel also struck provisions of the House bill banning offshore oil and gas leases sales for three areas off California and in the Georges Bank area off the New England coast.

In addition, the panel deleted a House rider barring land exchanges that would change the boundaries of parks and other conservation units set up in the Alaska National Interest Lands Act of 1980. *(1980 Almanac p. 575)*

Final Action

Although the Senate began consideration of the Interior bill on Sept. 26, members soon set it aside. The provisions of the committee-approved bill were rolled into the continuing appropriations resolution (H J Res 648), which was passed by the Senate Oct. 4.

House-Senate conferees resolved differences between the House and Senate versions of the Interior bill as part of their negotiations over the larger spending measure.

In addition to settling such issues as the offshore leas-

Final Fiscal 1985 Interior Appropriations

Following is the budget authority requested by President Reagan and appropriated under H J Res 648 (PL 98-473) for the Interior Department and related agencies in fiscal 1985 *(in thousands of dollars):*

	Budget Request	House Bill	Senate Bill	Final Appropriation
Department of the Interior				
Bureau of Land Management	$ 538,309	$ 546,824	$ 592,088	$ 577,327
U.S. Fish and Wildlife Service	364,237	398,724	414,516	419,565
National Park Service	823,087	963,755	918,313	918,834
U.S. Geological Survey	382,312	417,448	412,230	412,251
Minerals Management Service	167,381	167,207	166,992	163,482
Bureau of Mines	117,634	123,049	138,184	135,959
Office of Surface Mining	361,390	382,070	372,726	372,033
Bureau of Indian Affairs	992,696	1,066,311	1,054,360	1,057,738
Territorial & International Affairs	149,961	195,179	174,781	174,352
Departmental Offices	85,581	81,597	92,271	84,373
Subtotal	3,982,588	4,342,164	4,336,461	4,315,914
Related Agencies				
Forest Service	$1,433,624	$1,340,044	$1,339,014	$1,310,073
Department of Energy				
Fossil Energy	199,881	267,558	275,633	274,947
Naval Petroleum & Oil Shale Reserves	223,804	159,855	164,216	156,874
Energy Conservation	390,077	485,494	449,844	458,610
Economic Regulatory Administration	27,157	31,037	23,397	24,742
Strategic Petroleum Reserve (SPR) & Emergency Preparedness	0	0	6,220	6,096
SPR Petroleum Account [1]	(1,889,550)	(2,351,400)	(2,349,550)	(2,049,550)
Energy Information Administration	57,863	62,057	61,563	60,424
Indian Health	741,950	914,129	839,778	855,362
Indian Education	68,780	68,780	68,780	67,404
Smithsonian	196,932	198,599	187,971	189,561
National Endowment for the Arts	143,875	175,000	162,000	163,660
National Endowment for the Humanities	125,475	145,000	139,975	139,478
Other Agencies	87,330	97,139	97,714	95,288
Subtotal	$3,696,748	$3,944,692	$3,816,105	$3,802,519
Total: Interior, Related Agencies	7,679,336	8,286,856	$8,152,566	$8,118,433
Treasury Department (Synfuels Rescission)	−9,500,000	−5,000,000	−5,200,000	−5,375,000
General Reduction		−252,991		
GRAND TOTAL (Net Budget Authority)	−$1,820,664	$3,033,865	$2,952,566	$2,743,433

[1] *Off budget.*

ing bans and the synfuels rescission, conferees resolved several other disputes.

Like the Senate, the conferees deleted a House-passed prohibition against land exchanges affecting Alaska park lands.

The conference committee adopted the House-passed ban on the use of Fish and Wildlife Service funds to conduct deer hunting on the Loxahatchee National Wildlife Refuge, and added $3 million, as the House had wanted, for research on the effects of acid rain on forest growth.

Conferees overruled both chambers' rescission of $226 million in unused credits that had been available to logging companies that built roads into timber areas. Instead, the conferees transferred those funds to the Forest Service road construction fund. ∎

Farm Program Funds Included In Stopgap Bill

Congress cleared legislation Oct. 11 making $34.5 billion in appropriations for farm and food programs. Agriculture funding for fiscal year 1985 was included in a $470 billion stopgap spending bill (H J Res 648 — PL 98-473) that had held up adjournment for a week.

President Reagan signed the measure Oct. 12. *(Stopgap bill, p. 444)*

The agriculture appropriations bill included in H J Res 648 was largely the same measure agreed to Sept. 19 by House-Senate conferees working on the regular farm appropriation (HR 5743 — H Rept 98-1071).

Negotiators had dropped a "sodbuster" conservation plan and other policy-changing amendments added by the Senate. And they had added $500 million in guaranteed loan authority for the Farmers Home Administration (FmHA) to finance a Reagan administration farm credit initiative.

The bill included nearly $1 billion in funds for three food programs that would become available only when formally requested by the administration. The extra money reflected estimates of costs of carrying the programs at current caseload levels through all of fiscal 1985; the president's budget, assuming money-saving changes in the programs that had not been authorized, had requested less.

Funding added to the stopgap bill included $1 million for agricultural research, $3.2 million for administrative costs incurred by a new generic drugs program and an extra $8.3 million, if the administration formally requested it, for research on acquired immune deficiency syndrome (AIDS). *(Generic drugs, p. 451)*

Provisions

As signed into law, H J Res 648 provided the following amounts for the Department of Agriculture and related programs:

	Budget Request	Final Amount
Agriculture Programs		
Office of the Secretary	$ 5,240,000	$ 5,240,000
Standard Level User Charges	67,254,000	67,254,000
Advisory Committees	1,398,000	1,385,000
Departmental Administration	28,697,000	24,697,000
Governmental and Public Affairs	7,691,000	7,615,000
Inspector General	30,142,000	30,142,000
General Counsel	15,142,000	14,929,000

	Budget Request	Final Amount
Federal Grain Inspection Service	6,936,000	6,936,000
Agricultural Research Service	488,040,000	520,072,000
Cooperative State Research Service	266,785,000	284,276,000
Extension Service	299,377,000	343,727,000
National Agricultural Library	11,661,000	11,400,000
Animal and Plant Health Inspection Service	224,524,000	279,402,000
Food Safety and Inspection Service	356,067,000	353,239,000
Economic Research Service	47,480,000	46,159,000
Statistical Reporting Service	57,534,000	56,289,000
Agricultural Cooperative Service	3,565,000	4,639,000
World Agricultural Outlook Board	1,677,000	1,642,000
Agricultural Marketing Service	30,461,000	32,969,000
Packers and Stockyards Administration	9,035,000	9,035,000
Agricultural Stabilization & Conservation Service	50,857,000	50,957,000
Federal Crop Insurance Corporation	368,234,000	310,000,000
Commodity Credit Corporation	8,698,269,000	8,350,000,000
Subtotal	**$11,076,066,000**	**$10,812,004,000**
Rural Development Programs		
Office of Rural Development Policy	2,423,000	2,345,000
Farmers Home Administration	4,027,126,000	4,018,126,000
Rural Electrification Administration	31,181,000	31,181,000
Soil Conservation Service	475,036,000	609,383,000
Agricultural Stabilization & Conservation Service	92,550,000	211,300,000
Subtotal	**$ 4,628,316,000**	**$ 4,872,335,000**

	Budget Request	Final Amount
Domestic Food Programs		
Child Nutrition Programs	1,454,147,000	1,426,161,000*
Special Milk Program	17,600,000	17,600,000
Women, Infants & Children (WIC) Program	1,254,288,000	1,254,288,000*
Commodity Supplemental Food Program	23,004,000	24,918,000
Food Stamps	10,797,573,000	10,797,573,000*
Nutrition Assistance for Puerto Rico	825,000,000	825,000,000
Food Donations Programs	139,546,000	139,546,000
Temporary Emergency Food Assistance	50,000,000	50,000,000
Food Program Administration	83,187,000	83,187,000
Nutrition Information	7,496,000	7,496,000
Subtotal	$14,651,841,000	$14,625,769,000
International Programs		
Foreign Agricultural Service	83,291,000	83,448,000
Food for Peace (PL 480)	1,355,000,000	1,355,000,000
Office of International Cooperation and Development	4,074,000	5,038,000
Subtotal	$ 1,442,365,000	$ 1,443,486,000
Other Agencies		
Food and Drug Administration	394,004,000	402,794,000
Commodity Futures Trading Commission	27,292,000	27,292,000
Subtotal	$ 421,296,000	$ 430,086,000
TOTAL	$32,219,884,000	$32,183,680,000
Section 32 Transfers	2,301,833,000	2,335,814,000
TOTAL OBLIGATIONAL AUTHORITY	**$34,521,717,000**	**$34,519,494,000**

Loan Authorization: HR 5743 also provided the following loan authorizations:
- $8,474,000,000 in direct and insured loans (budget request: $6,844,000,000).
- $2,031,000,000 in guaranteed loans (budget request: $1,531,000,000).

These additional funds would be available upon submission of budget requests for them: Child Nutrition, $48,700,000; WIC, $245,712,000; Food Stamps, $652,427,000.

House Committee Action

The House Appropriations Committee reported HR 5743 (H Rept 98-809) May 30. As approved by the committee, the bill set aside $32,181,945,000 for farm and food programs administered by the Agriculture Department (USDA) and related agencies. It also provided $2,335,814,000 in so-called "Section 32" funds, customs receipts earmarked by law for USDA programs.

The bill's $34,517,759,000 total was $3,958,000 less than the president's budget request and $430,550,000 more than the total amount of food and nutrition funding voted for fiscal 1984.

The Reagan administration did not strongly object to the committee-approved bill, although the measure repeated fiscal maneuvers that Office of Management and Budget (OMB) Director David A. Stockman fought in 1983 as budget-busting, "scorekeeping gimmicks." *(1983 Almanac p. 516)*

Partial-Year Financing

As it had done in the past, the House committee greatly exceeded the administration's budget requests for programs with high visibility in the countryside — including the Rural Electrification Administration (REA), soil conservation and watersheds, rural housing and rural water purification and waste disposal systems.

And as in earlier years, the panel found money to finance these increases and still managed to come in under the president's budget by providing less than requested for the Commodity Credit Corporation (CCC), crop insurance and certain other programs.

Another tactic was to appropriate less than full-year funding for food programs. The Appropriations Committee chairman, Rep. Jamie L. Whitten, D-Miss., said supplemental appropriations would make up the difference.

In 1983 these tactics brought a stinging rebuke and a threat of a presidential veto from Stockman. However, less money was involved in 1984, and a spokesman for OMB said that the committee had largely stayed within spending levels for non-defense, discretionary spending that were agreed to by the president and reflected in a deficit-reduction plan (HR 4170) that the Senate had approved May 17. *(Deficit reduction, p. 143)*

Agriculture Programs

For price supports, research, crop insurance and other farm programs, the committee-approved bill provided $10.9 billion, about $180 million less than the budget request. The panel sliced $17.5 million from the administration's request for competitive research — research grants that are awarded on a competitive basis.

The committee appropriated $54.9 million more than requested for the Animal and Plant Health Inspection Service, saying more was essential to combat hundreds of millions of dollars' worth of agricultural damage by pests and diseases.

For the Federal Crop Insurance Program, the bill set aside $328 million, $40 million less than requested. For the CCC, which managed farm price support programs, the bill provided $8.5 billion, which was $198 million less than the budget request. In 1983 the committee chopped $500 million from the CCC request.

Rural Development

For financing individual farmers, rural housing, water, electrification and conservation and other programs, the bill provided $822 million, some $254 million more than requested. However, many rural programs used "off-budget" loan authorizations that were not counted in the $822 million appropriation, and it was in these programs that the House committee bill departed markedly from administration requests.

For instance, the bill appropriated $1.1 billion in authority for REA loans for rural telephone and electric services; the budget request was $575 million. The $3.3 billion total for rural housing included a $983 million boost over the budget.

Another addition was $200 million for business and

industrial development loans, for which the budget requested nothing. In a conciliatory gesture, the committee agreed to pare $100 million from the higher figure suggested by its agriculture subcommittee.

The panel's $135.7 million increase for the Soil Conservation Service, which funded watershed and flood prevention programs, brought the service's total to $610.8 million. The Agricultural Stabilization and Conservation Service, whose projects included cost-sharing, erosion-control projects on farms, received a $118.7 million increase for a $211 million total.

Food Programs

For domestic food programs, the bill provided $14.7 billion, which was $22.7 million more than requested and $809.9 million more than spending for fiscal 1984.

The committee report said that budget requests were not enough to fund current services for a full year for food stamps, child nutrition programs (including school lunches) and the food program, known as WIC, for low-income women, infants and children. And it pointed out that Congress had approved none of the budget's money-saving policy changes that would make cuts.

For the child nutrition program, the committee bill provided a total of $3.8 billion in appropriated and Section 32 funds. That amount, $48.7 million more than the budget request, was enough to complete the year. But the bill would bar the use of the extra money until the administration formally requested it.

For WIC, the panel provided $1.3 billion through Aug. 1, 1985.

For food stamps, the bill approved $10.8 billion through Sept. 7, 1985. The report said the program would need an extra $374 million.

Other Programs

The committee's $1.2 billion appropriation for the Food for Peace program (PL 480) was $150 million less than the president requested. The $399 million appropriation for the Food and Drug Administration included $5.5 million more than requested; the administration had expected to collect that amount in new "user fees" from applicants for approval of new drugs, but the committee rejected the fee policy.

House Floor Action

The House passed its $34.2 billion version of HR 5743 June 6 after taking a 1 percent bite out of the measure's spending levels.

By a 232-164 vote, the House approved an amendment by Rep. Robert S. Walker, R-Pa., providing an across-the-board reduction of 1 percent in all programs funded by the bill. The House then passed the bill by voice vote. *(Vote 187, p. 60-H)*

As passed by the House, the bill provided a total of $34.2 billion, which was about $85 million more than total fiscal 1984 appropriations and nearly $350 million less than the presidential budget request.

The Walker amendment cut about $340 million from the bill reported by the Appropriations Committee. The 1 percent cut applied to the bill's $31.86 billion in direct appropriations and the $2.31 billion in Section 32 funds.

For a time in 1984, across-the-board reductions became a regular feature of the House's treatment of funding bills. The legislative branch appropriations measure (HR

5753) was cut by 2 percent June 6. On May 31, the House approved a 4 percent cut in the Commerce, Justice and State fiscal 1985 appropriations bill (HR 5712). *(Legislative branch, p. 387; Commerce, Justice, State, p. 373)*

Obey Amendment

A broader debate on spending reduction was set off when Rep. David R. Obey, D-Wis., offered an amendment that would have cut 64 percent from all the programs in the bill that were not entitlements. (Food stamps and a number of the farm support programs were generally considered to work like entitlements because their benefits must be provided to individuals who met eligibility criteria.)

Obey suggested that members substitute his amendment for Walker's, which he called merely symbolic. He argued that few of his colleagues would address what he considered the real budget issues — expensive defense and entitlement programs and an inadequate revenue base. That left only discretionary programs, he said; a 64 percent cut in all of them would balance the budget.

Obey's move prompted charges and countercharges that neither Congress nor Reagan was serious about resolving budget deficits. The House June 6 rejected Obey's amendment by a 6-388 vote. *(Vote 186, p. 60-H)*

Senate Committee Action

The Senate Appropriations Committee added $1 billion to HR 5743 before agreeing July 26 to report the $36 billion measure (S Rept 98-566).

The committee bill also sharply nudged the Department of Agriculture to revise a controversial change in its rules for marketing orders. The orders permitted growers of specialty crops, such as oranges, to engage in certain joint practices, including advertising or restricting market access.

Most of the extra money added by the committee was for food stamps and WIC. Sen. Thad Cochran, R-Miss., chairman of the panel's Subcommittee on Agriculture, Rural Development and Related Agencies, said the extra money would not enlarge the programs but would let them continue at their current size through the end of fiscal 1985.

Because the Senate panel chose to provide full-year funding for the food programs, instead of partial-year funding as the House had done, its bill exceeded the president's budget by about $1.3 billion.

Cochran said that because Congress had not enacted money-saving changes assumed by the budget, the panel provided enough "over-budget" money to maintain the programs at current levels. He also noted that the bill did not exceed the ceiling set by the Senate-passed fiscal 1985 budget resolution (H Con Res 280).

As approved by the Senate committee, HR 5743 appropriated $33,414,901,710 for farm and food programs administered by the Agriculture Department and related agencies for fiscal 1985. It also provided $2,335,814,000 in Section 32 funds.

The bill's $35,750,715,710 total was $758 million more than the fiscal 1984 appropriation and $1.6 billion above the House's fiscal 1985 total.

Marketing Order Changes

The Senate committee adopted a marketing-order amendment offered by Sen. Dennis DeConcini, D-Ariz., aimed at a June Agriculture Department proposal for navel and Valencia oranges. Prior to that proposal, the department had permitted growers to vote separately on each proposed change in a marketing order. But the orange proposal called for a single vote on a package of 23 changes, and further specified that rejection of the package would also terminate the marketing order itself.

Strong opposition came from Sunkist, the Arizona-California cooperative. DeConcini's amendment and similar language in a House supplemental appropriations bill effectively required the department to go back to separate votes on the orders. On July 27 congressional sources reported that USDA had backed down, but department spokesmen said they could not confirm any changes in the orange order. *(Supplemental appropriations, p. 439)*

Senate-House Differences

The Senate bill also provided for:
● Some $283 million more than the House bill for the CCC, for a total of $8.7 billion.
● A $310 million total for the federal crop insurance program, compared with $325 million approved by the House and $368 million requested by the administration.
● A $162 million addition for the Food for Peace (PL 480) program.

The Senate bill also boosted off-budget loan authorizations for the popular REA and certain other credit programs. And it exceeded the administration's budget, and in some cases the House bill, in funding for popular conservation and water projects. Some of these reflected spending levels approved by the House Appropriations Committee but reduced by the House-adopted 1 percent across-the-board spending cut.

Senate Floor Action

Senate floor consideration of the agriculture appropriations bill was temporarily held up by a band of Democrats upset that lawmakers had failed to adopt a budget resolution that would lay out the terms of Congress' deficit-cutting efforts.

During the week of July 30, Democrats used rhetoric and procedure to block action on HR 5743. It was the latest in a series of maneuvers designed to force Republicans back to the bargaining table on defense spending, the sole issue thwarting a final budget agreement.

The Democratic blockade was dismantled Aug. 8. Two days later, however, Senate Republicans agreed to negotiate defense spending.

Before it passed its $36 billion version of the agriculture appropriations bill Aug. 10 on a 71-11 vote, the Senate approved, for the third time, a "sodbuster" plan to withhold federal farm program benefits from farmers who plow up easily erodible land. *(Vote 214, p. 37-S)*

During consideration of the bill the Senate sent the Treasury Department a strong message objecting to a proposal permitting foreign investors to purchase anonymously U.S. government securities, so-called "bearer bonds." Treasury officials assured senators the department would not adopt the selling practice.

Before passing the bill Aug. 10, the Senate approved, 83-4, an amendment offered by Sen. Edward M. Kennedy, D-Mass., increasing WIC spending by $29 million. Kennedy said the additional money was needed in light of recent Census Bureau figures that showed that one million more Americans fell below the poverty line in 1983. *(Vote 212, p. 37-S)*

Bearer Bonds

Opposition to bearer bonds arose Aug. 9, when Sen. Howard M. Metzenbaum, D-Ohio, argued on the floor that the securities encouraged tax evasion because overseas purchasers did not have to identify themselves. Bearer bonds could not be sold in the United States.

Metzenbaum said that because these bonds would not be subject to U.S. registration requirements, Americans could evade tax payments on their earnings from them. Nothing, Metzenbaum claimed, would prevent Americans from buying these bonds in the European market.

The following day, it was learned that a consortium of U.S. investment banks purchased $1.7 billion worth of Treasury bonds with the announced intention of repackaging them as bearer bonds for sale in the European market. And Metzenbaum told the Senate that, although Treasury had promised not to sell the securities, other government agencies were "planning to do so on their own."

His sense of the Senate amendment expressing the Senate's disapproval of Treasury and other government agencies' bonds that could be repackaged and sold overseas as bearer bonds was approved by voice vote.

But before the conference on the agriculture bill was completed, the Treasury Department announced it would not issue bearer bonds and other government agencies followed suit. Instead, a special registered security was designed to allow foreign investors to maintain a degree of anonymity. Metzenbaum's bearer bond amendment was dropped in conference.

Sodbuster

The sodbuster language attached to the bill would have barred price supports, loans and other federal subsidies for a crop if part of it were grown on erosion-prone land. A weaker version, barring benefits only to that part of a crop produced on fragile land, passed the Senate in 1982 and again in 1984. *(Sodbuster, p. 364; 1982 Almanac p. 255)*

Senate adoption of the language came Aug. 9 on a 62-34 vote to adopt an amendment by Sen. John Melcher, D-Mont., to substitute the stronger language for an amendment by Sen. William L. Armstrong, R-Colo. Armstrong, the original sponsor of sodbuster legislation, proposed the weaker version. *(Vote 210, p. 37-S)*

Other Amendments

Other amendments approved Aug. 9 added $1.1 million for boll-weevil control in California and Arizona, and reiterated a longstanding prohibition on trading by new firms in leverage contracts and dealer options. These two types of financial transactions, under the jurisdiction of the Commodity Futures Trading Commission (CFTC), had been subject to abuses, and Congress had wanted to bar growth in this type of business until the CFTC showed itself capable of regulating it.

The boll-weevil funding amendment was sponsored by Sen. Pete Wilson, R-Calif., and the CFTC leverage amendment by Sen. Richard G. Lugar, R-Ind., with an amendment by Sen. Walter D. Huddleston, D-Ky., to include dealer options.

The Senate Aug. 9 tabled (killed) on a 66-25 vote an amendment by Sen. J. James Exon, D-Neb., to allow target prices to rise to levels they would have reached before Congress imposed a freeze on the subsidy program. *(Vote 211, p. 37-S; target price freeze, p. 361)*

On Aug. 10, the Senate by voice vote approved an

amendment by Sen. James A. McClure, R-Idaho, adding $500,000 for grasshopper control.

Conference

House-Senate conferees agreed Sept. 19 on a $34.5 billion fiscal 1985 agriculture appropriations bill, and decided that an extra $1 billion would become automatically available for food stamps and the WIC program if the administration requested the money.

Conferees also approved $500 million for a special Farmers Home Administration loan guarantee program, announced by President Reagan, for farmers who could not pay their debts. An earlier supplemental appropriations bill had provided an additional $150 million for the guarantees. *(Farm credit, p. 363)*

In another farm credit decision, conferees directed the Agriculture Department to issue, within 60 days of enactment of the appropriations bill, rules for farmers to request deferrals of FmHA loans. FmHA had, for years, the authority to defer loan repayments for farmers in temporary financial difficulty. But the agency's apparent reluctance to use this authority provoked lawsuits and court orders instructing the department to issue the rules. The suggestion for the deadline came from Sen. Thomas F. Eagleton, D-Mo.

To resolve the House bill's provisions of partial-year funding for food stamps and WIC, conferees agreed to use the full-year, Senate levels for the two programs, but specified that $1 billion of that amount could not be spent until budget requests were received.

In other decisions, conferees generally split the difference between House and Senate versions in the numerous farm program accounts, and dropped all policy changes — including authority for the sodbuster conservation initiative added on the floor to the Senate bill. The DeConcini amendment concerning marketing orders survived, however. ∎

$1.55 Billion Legislative Appropriation Cleared

Congress June 28 cleared a $1.55 billion legislative branch appropriations bill (HR 5753 — PL 98-367) for fiscal 1985. *(Details, chart p. 389)*

The conference report on HR 5753 (H Rept 98-870) was adopted by the House on a 253-157 vote June 28. The Senate cleared the bill later that day by voice vote. *(Vote 259, p. 80-H)*

President Reagan signed the bill July 17. The White House by tradition does not interfere with appropriations for congressional operations.

HR 5753 contained $77 million more than the fiscal 1984 spending level and $46 million less than Reagan proposed in his 1985 budget.

Although the president makes a legislative branch budget request, Congress writes the figures and the administration includes them in the budget without comment.

The bill provided funds for the House, Senate and legislative agencies such as the Library of Congress, Government Printing Office and General Accounting Office (GAO).

House Committee

The House Appropriations Subcommittee on the Legislative Branch May 16 included $1.273 billion for fiscal 1985 in the spending bill that eventually was numbered HR 5753. The total did not include any funds for operation of the Senate. By tradition, that money is added to the bill by the Senate.

The full House Appropriations Committee May 31 approved the bill (H Rept 98-811) by voice vote.

House Television. Although the bill breezed through the committee, controversy over the House television system arose briefly when Jerry Lewis, R-Calif., presented an amendment barring the use of funds for television cameras to pan the House chamber unless it was done uniformly from gavel to gavel.

Lewis' proposal stemmed from a decision May 10 by House Speaker Thomas P. O'Neill Jr., D-Mass., to have a wide-angle lens sweep the chamber during "special order" speeches delivered at the end of the legislative day. Until then, the cameras focused on the member speaking, and television viewers never saw that most of the seats in the chamber were empty. *(Story, p. 206)*

House Republicans, who had been using the special-order speeches to blast Democrats, were angry about O'Neill's decision and called for a rules change to require cameras to pan the chamber during all business, not just special orders.

"The public does have a right to know. If we're going to show certain levels of attendance at some times, we should show it all the time," Lewis said.

The television question had become a highly partisan dispute, and committee Democrats jeered when Lewis proposed his amendment. Rather than ask for a vote, Lewis withdrew the amendment. But he promised to discuss it when the bill reached the House floor.

Funding. The bill was roughly $62 million, or 5 percent, more than the sum appropriated in fiscal 1984 for the same programs.

Vic Fazio, D-Calif., chairman of the Appropriations Legislative Subcommittee, said the measure contained about $30 million less than the 1985 budget request for the items the bill covered.

The committee report estimated an additional $288 million appropriation would be needed for Senate activities.

House and joint congressional offices would receive $728 million under the bill, while $545 million would go to related agencies, such as the Library of Congress, General Accounting Office and Government Printing Office.

Fazio said the bill contained a net reduction of 72 employees in the legislative branch. "I think we have a tight bill here," he said.

Most of the increase over 1984 stemmed from projected pay raises for congressional employees, and higher costs because of inflation.

The committee bill contained $425 million for the House, up from $384 million in 1984. This included $47 million for salaries for House supporting officers, such as the doorkeepers and chaplain; $38 million for committee employees; and $164 million for members' personal staffs. For members' official expenses, the committee included $68 million.

For official mail costs, the bill provided $74 million, down from $107 million in 1984. Congressional mailing costs traditionally are lower during a non-election year.

The committee bill also included:

- $65 million for the Architect of the Capitol to manage congressional buildings and grounds.
- $15 million for the Office of Technology Assessment, a congressional advisory body.
- $17 million for the Congressional Budget Office.
- $186 million for the Library of Congress, and $40 million for its Congressional Research Service.
- $42 million for the Government Printing Office, and an additional $81 million for congressional printing.
- $308 million for the General Accounting Office, an agency that monitors government efficiency.

House Floor

The main issues when the bill came to the House floor June 6 were televising the House and an across-the-board cut in HR 5753. The bill was approved 247-138. *(Vote 193, p. 62-H)*

The House decided to continue giving television viewers a selective picture of its proceedings by allowing cameras to pan the chamber only after regular legislative business had ended for the day.

But the House bowed to public criticism of congressional costs by trimming its own budget 2 percent for the new fiscal year beginning Oct. 1. As a result of the cut, the bill contained $1.25 billion for House offices and legislative agencies, such as the Library of Congress and Government Printing Office.

The debate on HR 5753 was introspective, touching briefly on the volatile question of House television procedures. While the House never actually voted on the television coverage rule, it declined in a procedural vote to consider an amendment that would have required cameras to sweep the House chamber throughout the legislative day.

The decision to cut legislative branch funds by 2 percent followed a trend in other 1985 money bills. Earlier on June 6, the House approved a 1 percent across-the-board cut in fiscal 1985 agriculture appropriations (HR 5743). The week before, the House slashed funding for the Commerce, Justice and State departments (HR 5712) by 4 percent. *(Agriculture, p. 383; Commerce, p. 373)*

With the precedent set in the other spending bills, most debate on HR 5753 focused on GOP demands that the House tighten its own belt as a symbolic gesture of fiscal austerity.

The House took two votes on an amendment by Bill Frenzel, R-Minn., to cut the measure by roughly $25 million. The first time, the amendment was adopted 201-175. Later, when Democrats thought they had found enough votes to defeat the amendment and used a procedural maneuver to get another roll call, it was approved again 193-190. *(Votes 190, 192, p. 60-H)*

"The vote was cast with a political eye on the campaign this fall," complained Fazio.

"They can't resist the temptation to succumb to voting against themselves and their own institution. This is the way they go back to their constituents and say, 'We agree with our challengers and their criticisms of Congress,'" Fazio said.

Lewis, the ranking Republican on Fazio's subcommittee, said the bill was one of the few outlets for Republicans to try to influence House operations.

"This bill, because it is the legislative appropriations bill, has become a vehicle whereby a sizable number of minority members develop amendments to vent their frus-

trations about the way the House is run," Lewis said.

Although Lewis did not join his GOP colleagues in voting to cut the bill's funding, he did propose a strictly partisan amendment on House broadcasting procedures.

Lewis' proposal, backed by the Republican leadership, would have barred the use of funds for television cameras to pan the House chamber unless it was done uniformly from gavel to gavel.

Republicans were furious about O'Neill's May 10 decision to show the vacant seats. But if he insisted, they said, it should also be done during legislative business, when most members also were away from the chamber.

"If we are going to pan the floor, then we should pan the floor with regularity and with a sense of fairness," Lewis argued June 6. He urged "a uniform and neutral camera coverage policy ... that will not be subject to charges of political or partisan manipulation or retribution."

Because of a complicated House rule making it difficult for members to attach "riders," or limitations on the use of specific funds, to appropriations bills, the House never debated Lewis' amendment. Instead, the vote occurred on a procedural motion on whether to allow Lewis to offer it.

On that vote, House Democrats solidly lined up behind O'Neill, shelving the GOP amendment 234-147. Only four Democrats joined the 143 Republicans who supported the proposal. *(Vote 191, p. 60-H)*

The party-line vote reflected escalating partisanship in the House in 1984. The squabbles over TV coverage were part of a deeper split over House procedure.

Although Fazio repeatedly argued that HR 5753 was "a tight bill" with no room for cuts, Republicans Hank Brown of Colorado and Frenzel offered several amendments to reduce its funding.

"I believe that every member of the House will want to show to his or her constituents that he or she is willing to make a little bit of sacrifice out of the moneys spent for us," Frenzel said.

Before twice adopting his 2 percent across-the-board cut, the House rejected another Frenzel amendment to trim funds for House operations by $13 million. The amendment was defeated 191-201. *(Vote 188, p. 60-H)*

After a lengthy discussion of the merits of hiring people to run automatic elevators in House office buildings, the House rejected, 176-205, an amendment by Brown to cut $88,354 for elevator operators' salaries. *(Vote 189, p. 60-H)*

Senate Committee

When the Senate Appropriations Committee considered HR 5753 June 12, it restored the House-passed 2 percent cut. The committee's report (S Rept 98-515) was filed June 14.

The committee's additions brought the funding in the bill to $1.55 billion, $46 million below the president's request. It added $270 million for Senate operations and $21 million for Senate office buildings. The House version totaled $1.25 billion.

Alfonse M. D'Amato, R-N.Y., chairman of the legislative branch subcommittee, said his panel deleted the 2 percent cut at the request of congressional support agencies, such as the Congressional Budget Office and the General Accounting Office.

Before agreeing to report HR 5753, the committee added $93,000 to the accounts of the senators from Ari-

Legislative Branch Appropriations

Following are the amounts contained in the House version of the fiscal 1985 legislative branch appropria- tions bill (HR 5753), the Senate version and the conference agreement that cleared June 28:

	House Bill	Senate Bill	Final Amount
Congressional Operations			
Senate	$ 0	$ 269,955,000	$ 269,955,000
House	425,207,000	425,207,000	425,207,000
Joint Items	84,559,000	84,369,188	84,418,188
Office of Technology Assessment	15,362,000	15,924,000	15,549,000
Congressional Budget Office	17,418,000	17,418,000	17,418,000
Architect of the Capitol	65,110,000	86,187,850	86,215,850
Congressional Research Service	39,833,000	39,887,860	39,833,000
Government Printing Office (congressional printing)	80,879,000	80,800,000	80,800,000
Subtotal	$ 728,368,000	$1,019,748,898	$1,019,396,038
Related Agencies			
Botanic Garden	2,044,000	2,044,000	2,044,000
Library of Congress	185,877,000	185,877,000	185,877,000
Architect of the Capitol (library buildings)	5,709,000	5,709,000	5,709,000
Copyright Royalty Tribunal	217,000	217,000	217,000
Government Printing Office (non-congressional printing)	42,137,000	42,068,000	42,068,000
General Accounting Office	307,557,000	294,704,000	294,704,000
Railroad Accounting Principles Board	1,000,000	1,000,000	1,000,000
Subtotal	$ 544,541,000	$ 531,619,000	$531,619,000
less 2 percent general reduction	−$25,476,457		
Total	$1,247,432,543	$1,551,367,898	$1,551,015,038

zona, to reflect the fact that the state moved above three million in population, based on the latest census figures.

The bill also added $562,000 for the Office of Technology Assessment, which provides information and analysis to Congress on the effects of technologies, for an additional six positions. Nine new positions were added in fiscal 1984. The bill reduced the appropriation for GAO from $308 million to $295 million. The administration requested $329 million.

The administration had requested 500 new positions at GAO, for a total of 5,500, but the committee said the increased staffing should occur at a slower pace and provided funds for an additional 50 positions.

Senate Floor

When the full Senate considered HR 5753 June 21, it narrowly voted to restore the money cut by the House for legislative branch expenditures. In a 39-36 vote, the Senate refused to accept the 2 percent across-the-board cut. The Senate then quickly approved the bill by voice vote. *(Vote 154, p. 28-S)*

In the brief debate over the appropriations bill, Don Nickles, R-Okla., argued that the Senate should follow the House's lead in applying fiscal austerity to its own affairs.

"For crying out loud," Nickles said, "people have been telling us to get our house in order. I think we have to make some sacrifice ourselves if we are going to ask others to make sacrifices as well."

But other senators argued that the House cut was applied indiscriminately. "I generally object to across-the-board cuts," said Jake Garn, R-Utah, "because where you have multi-department budgets some may be able to absorb much more than 2 percent; some may not or should not have any cut."

Garn, who was not even a member of the Legislative Branch Subcommittee, managed the bill on the floor for the subcommittee chairman, Alphonse M. D'Amato, R-N.Y., who was absent.

After rejecting the 2 percent cut, the Senate agreed to two minor amendments by Dale Bumpers, D-Ark., the senior Democrat on the subcommittee. Both amendments dealt only with the Senate and were retained in conference.

The first moved from Oct. 1 to Aug. 1 the annual date when senators could transfer funds from their clerk-hire accounts for paying staff to their office expense accounts.

The second amendment lifted salary restrictions on mid-level Senate staffers. It did not give senators any additional funds, but allowed them to pay personal and committee staffers whatever they chose. The upper limit of approximately $70,000 on staff salaries was retained.

Conference

Conferees agreed on a common version of the bill June 27 after striking the 2 percent across-the-board cut the House had approved June 6.

While the House-approved reduction would have saved about $25 million, conferees instead agreed on about $13 million in savings in a few categories.

"We made a number of savings without going across the board. To get a 1 percent cut, we needed to save $12.7 million, and we're over $13 million. We've clearly gone over the halfway mark," said Fazio. ∎

Reagan Gets Most of '85 Foreign Aid Wish List

In spite of election-year politics and disputes over Central America, Congress approved the bulk of President Reagan's requests for foreign aid programs in fiscal 1985.

The continuing appropriations resolution (H J Res 648 — PL 98-473), which cleared Congress Oct. 11, included a record $18.2 billion for foreign aid, just $81 million less than Reagan had wanted. *(Charts, pp. 391, 397; continuing resolution story, p. 444)*

Congress rejected only one major Reagan request: a five-year, $8 billion authorization for economic and development aid to Central American countries. That was a major proposal of a presidential commission headed by former Secretary of State Henry A. Kissinger. However, Congress did give Reagan most of the Central America aid he wanted just for fiscal 1985. *(Final provisions, p. 394)*

Key parts of the Kissinger commission plan died as Congress for the third year in a row failed to enact a full-scale authorization bill for foreign aid. Instead, Congress tacked onto the continuing resolution a handful of authorizations for foreign aid programs. In theory, Congress each year is supposed to enact separate foreign aid authorizations and appropriations bills. *(1981 Almanac pp. 161, 339; 1982 Almanac pp. 156, 242; 1983 Almanac pp. 140, 521)*

In general, the foreign aid provisions of the continuing resolution caused little controversy — largely because El Salvador was no longer a major political issue in Congress. Congress approved most of Reagan's requests for aid to help that country's government fight leftist guerrillas after José Napoleón Duarte, a centrist, was elected president in May. *(Story, p. 73; background, 1983 Almanac p. 154)*

The $18.2 billion foreign aid total in the continuing resolution was $4.7 billion above the total foreign aid appropriated for fiscal 1984 in a continuing resolution (PL 98-151) and two supplementals (PL 98-332 and PL 98-396). But because of a bookkeeping change in the way military aid was counted in 1985, the actual increase in spending for programs was only $311 million.

Senate Committee Bill

Recognizing that Congress was likely to stick to its recent pattern of lumping the two types of legislation together in an omnibus spending bill, the Senate Appropriations Committee drafted what Bob Kasten, R-Wis., chairman of the Foreign Operations Subcommittee, called a "benchmark" bill, to be incorporated later into a continuing resolution.

The Senate panel approved its appropriations bill (S 2793 — S Rept 98-531) on June 26. It contained $13.8 billion in foreign aid spending for fiscal 1985 that the Subcommittee on Foreign Operations had approved on June 21.

Reagan had requested $132.5 million in military aid for El Salvador, and the Senate measure contained the full amount, without the conditions on how the money could be spent that Congress had imposed in the past.

As approved by the full committee, S 2793 gave Reagan all but about $91.4 million of his foreign aid requests for fiscal 1985. In addition to the funding for Central America, the bill provided direct U.S. economic, military and development aid to about 70 countries; it also gave indirect aid to several dozen countries through international agencies such as the World Bank. *(Banks' funding, box, p. 393)*

S 2793 included $1.2 billion for Central America in fiscal 1985: $962.6 million in economic development and related aid, and $255.9 million in military aid.

The panel made no changes from Reagan's request, which included such controversial issues as military aid to El Salvador, the beginning of a new guarantee program for Export-Import Bank loans to the region and the resumption of military aid to the military dictatorship in Guatemala.

While freeing the strings on military aid to El Salvador, the committee imposed several conditions on the $210 million in the bill for economic aid to that country. The conditions were aimed at ensuring that the money was not diverted illegally and that Congress would be informed how it was being used.

On other issues, the Appropriations Committee:

● Sidestepped the hotly contested issue of military aid to Turkey. Daniel K. Inouye, D-Hawaii, had threatened to offer an amendment barring $230 million in military grants for Turkey unless it gave up control of the formerly Greek Cypriot city of Famagusta (also known as Varosha) on Cyprus. Turkey had occupied the northern third of Cyprus since 1974. The Famagusta amendment had been approved by the Foreign Relations Committee, but was vigorously opposed by the administration. Inouye said he dropped his amendment because Turkish Cypriot leader Rauf Denktash had offered new proposals to the United Nations on the future of Famagusta.

● Approved most of Reagan's requests for U.S. contributions to international development banks, including a $750 million payment to the International Development Association, an arm of the World Bank.

● Rejected Reagan's request for $75 million as the first installment on a new five-year "economic policy initiative" for Africa. Reagan wanted the money to reward African countries that made economic "reforms," such as reducing the role of government in the marketplace. *(Africa aid, pp. 121, 395, 429, 438)*

● Approved Reagan's request to count all military aid programs in the federal budget; in previous years, about $4 billion annually in military loan guarantees had not been counted as part of the budget.

● Barred U.S. aid for population control programs to any country or international agency "which includes as part of its population planning programs forced or coerced abortion."

The ban was aimed at China, which was alleged to require abortions in some cases. The United States did not provide direct aid to China, but proponents of the ban wanted to ensure that U.S. population aid did not reach China through other agencies.

● Approved Reagan's full request for $85 million in military aid to the Philippines to implement a new agreement for operation of U.S. bases there. The Senate Foreign Relations and House Foreign Affairs committees had both agreed to shift some of the military aid to economic aid as a symbolic protest against the authoritarian rule of President Ferdinand E. Marcos.

● Stated the sense of the Senate that annual U.S. economic aid to Israel should never be less than Israel's annual

Foreign Aid Appropriations, Fiscal 1985

The following chart shows President Reagan's request, the House- and Senate-approved amounts, and the final amounts, in new budget authority, for foreign aid appropriations in fiscal 1985. Foreign aid programs were included in a continuing resolution, PL 98-473.

(The figures in parentheses show program limitations; except for part of the Export-Import Bank loans, these limitations do not count as new budget authority. The figures for individual development banks include only paid-in capital.)

Program	Request	House-Passed Amount	Senate-Passed Amount	Final Amount
Inter-American Development Bank	$ 223,000,983	$ 223,000,983	$ 110,500,983	$ 110,500,983
Inter-American Investment Corp.	13,000,000	10,000,000	13,000,000	10,000,000
International Bank for Reconstruction and Development	139,720,549	139,720,549	109,721,549	109,721,549
International Development Association	900,000,000	900,000,000	750,000,000	900,000,000
Asian Development Bank and Fund	204,465,016	160,348,846	157,348,846	113,232,676
African Development Fund	50,000,000	50,000,000	50,000,000	50,000,000
African Development Bank	17,986,678	17,986,678	17,987,678	17,987,678
Total callable capital for development banks	(3,684,012,169)	(3,684,012,169)	(2,465,011,934)	(2,465,011,934)
International Organizations and Programs	241,800,000	323,228,000	347,414,000	358,676,500
Subtotal, Multilateral Aid	**$ 1,789,973,226**	**$ 1,824,285,056**	**$ 1,555,973,056**	**$ 1,670,119,386**
Agriculture aid	752,551,000	745,551,000	749,800,000	755,551,000
Population aid	250,002,000	290,000,000	250,000,000	290,000,000
Health aid	158,138,000	173,138,000	155,000,000	223,138,000
Special health, agriculture aid	0	0	75,000,000	0
Child Survival Fund	0	25,000,000	25,000,000	25,000,000
Education, human resources aid	188,833,000	188,833,000	184,000,000	188,833,000
Energy, selected development aid	226,175,000	168,000,000	214,000,000	190,000,000
Science and technology aid	10,000,000	10,000,000	10,000,000	10,000,000
Private sector revolving fund	(20,000,000)	(20,000,000)	(20,000,000)	(20,000,000)
American schools and hospitals abroad	10,000,000	30,000,000	30,000,000	30,000,000
International disaster aid	25,000,000	25,000,000	25,000,000	25,000,000
Sahel development	97,500,000	97,500,000	50,000,000	97,500,000
African Economic Policy Initiative	75,000,000	75,000,000	0	0
Foreign Service retirement and disability	40,562,000	40,562,000	40,562,000	40,562,000
Economic Support Fund	3,438,100,000	3,664,000,000	3,838,100,000	3,826,000,000
Peacekeeping	49,000,000	47,000,000	44,000,000	44,000,000
Agency for International Development (AID) operating expenses	404,113,000	391,533,250	395,016,000	391,533,250
Trade and Development program	21,000,000	21,000,000	21,000,000	21,000,000
AID reappropriation	0	0	25,000,000	25,000,000
International narcotics control	50,217,000	50,217,000	50,217,000	50,217,000
Inter-American Foundation	11,992,000	11,992,000	11,992,000	11,992,000
African Development Foundation	3,000,000	1,000,000	1,000,000	1,000,000
Peace Corps	124,000,000	124,000,000	133,200,000	128,600,000
Migration, refugee aid	341,450,000	323,000,000	340,000,000	325,500,000
Anti-terrorism program	5,000,000	2,500,000	5,000,000	5,000,000
Subtotal, bilateral aid	**$ 6,281,633,000**	**$ 6,504,826,250**	**$ 6,672,887,000**	**$ 6,705,426,250**
Military assistance program grants	924,500,000	653,100,000	917,000,000	805,100,000
International military education and training	60,910,000	51,532,000	60,910,000	56,221,000
Foreign military sales: forgiven loans and direct credits [1]	5,100,000,000	4,809,000,000	5,100,000,000	4,939,500,000
Defense acquisition fund limitation	(325,000,000)	(225,000,000)	(325,000,000)	(325,000,000)
Guarantee Reserve Fund	274,000,000	104,000,000	274,000,000	109,000,000
Subtotal, military aid	**$ 6,359,410,000**	**$ 5,617,632,000**	**$ 6,351,910,000**	**$ 5,909,821,000**
Housing guaranty program limitation	(160,000,000)	(150,000,000)	(160,000,000)	(160,000,000)
Housing guaranty program reserve	10,000,000	40,000,000	10,000,000	40,000,000
Overseas Private Investment Corporation	(165,000,000)	(165,000,000)	(165,000,000)	(165,000,000)
Export-Import Bank total limitation	(13,848,930,000)	(13,882,930,000)	(13,883,930,000)	(13,883,900,000)
Budget authority effect of Ex-Im Bank limitations	3,830,000,000	3,865,000,000	3,865,000,000	3,865,000,000
Two-percent cut	0	−279,734,866	0	0
Grand Total	**$18,271,016,226**	**$17,572,008,440**	**$18,455,770,056**	**$18,190,366,636**

[1] *For fiscal 1985, all foreign military sales credit programs were counted as new budget authority; previously, only about one-fourth of the money in those programs was counted as new budget authority.*

payments to the United States on past loans and grants. The Congressional Budget Office had said such a requirement could boost Israel's economic aid to $1.4 billion by 1990. The committee approved $1.2 billion for Israel in 1985, $350 million above Reagan's request. The panel also boosted economic aid to Egypt to $815 million, from Reagan's $750 million request.

House Committee Bill

On Aug. 8, the House Appropriations Subcommittee on Foreign Operations approved a $17.49 billion foreign aid appropriations bill containing $123.5 million in military aid for El Salvador. The House panel voted conditions on how the money could be spent.

The panel also approved $180 million of Reagan's $210 million request for economic aid to El Salvador. The subcommittee also made cuts in development aid to Central America that, if applied across the board, would have limited El Salvador's development aid to $58 million; Reagan had requested $80 million.

The subcommittee pared military aid for Central America but did not specify cuts for countries other than El Salvador. Reagan's major requests were $62.5 million for Honduras, $20 million for Panama and $10 million for Costa Rica.

The subcommittee "deferred" Reagan's request for $18 million to run a center, in Honduras, where the United States trained Honduran and Salvadoran troops. The panel demanded that Honduras resolve a claim by a U.S. citizen whose land was expropriated for the training center.

The panel also cut more than $200 million in economic and development aid for Central American countries other than El Salvador. The biggest cut eliminated a $136.6 million request for regional economic programs, most of which had been earmarked for reviving the Central American Common Market, a free-trade zone.

The panel also eliminated a $35 million economic aid request for Guatemala. Other economic aid amounts approved by the panel were: $160 million for Costa Rica (Reagan's request), $70 million for Honduras (Reagan requested $75 million), $10 million for Panama and $4 million for Belize.

The subcommittee set a $200 million limit — $73 million below Reagan's request for development aid programs for Central America.

Reagan's requests for long-term aid to Central America, in fiscal years 1986-89, were not before the subcommittee. If the president had succeeded in getting multi-year authorizations for that aid, Congress would have had to appropriate the funds on an annual basis.

Greece, Turkey

On the politically sensitive issue of aid to Greece and Turkey, the House subcommittee walked a tightrope. Reagan had requested $755 million in military aid for Turkey in fiscal 1985 — largely to help it buy U.S.-built F-16 fighter planes. Reagan also had requested $500 million in military aid to Greece.

The Foreign Operations Subcommittee slashed the Turkey figure to $540 million, making deep cuts in grants and loans. But as part of its balancing act on the issue, the subcommittee chose to reduce Turkey's aid, rather than impose tough conditions on it.

The panel approved Reagan's full $175 million request for economic aid to Turkey, and the $500 million military

aid for Greece. However, the panel did not consider a widely supported proposal to reduce the interest rate on military loans to Greece.

Full Committee Action

When the full Appropriations Committee met Sept. 12 to approve the foreign aid package, it showed no desire to pick a fight with the administration over El Salvador aid. The committee's $17.8 billion package (HR 6237 — H Rept 98-1021) made one significant change from the subcommittee version: it added $319.6 million in U.S. grants to international financial institutions, such as the World Bank.

Rep. Silvio O. Conte, R-Mass., who sought the additional money, said it was necessary to bring the United States up to date in past obligations to the banks.

The committee also approved an amendment by Rep. Jack Hightower, D-Texas, requiring that at least 5 percent of economic aid to foreign countries be spent on health care for their citizens. Hightower said that only about 1 percent of economic aid went to health care.

Continuing Resolution

On Sept. 14, the day after reporting its bill, the House Appropriations panel inserted the package into the continuing resolution in lieu of language that would have funded foreign aid at the level of the budget estimate or the previous year's continuing resolution, whichever was lower. *(1983 Almanac p. 528)*

By late September, other foreign aid questions were among the many issues shaping both chambers' versions of the continuing resolution. The Senate Appropriations Committee incorporated the foreign aid appropriations bill in its version of the resolution on Sept. 25, but made some changes. It approved an amendment guaranteeing for five years that economic support provided to Israel would not drop below the annual debt repayments Israel made to the United States.

The panel also approved an amendment reducing the administration's request for $755 million in aid to Turkey by $40 million.

On Sept. 25, members debating the continuing resolution on the House floor added the foreign aid authorizations bill (HR 5119) by voice vote. They also voted a 2 percent cut in all foreign aid, with the exception of assistance earmarked for Egypt and Israel. *(Vote 367, p. 112-H)*

A major foreign policy issue that surfaced in debate over the continuing resolution in the Senate was military aid to guerrillas, or "contras," fighting the leftist government of Nicaragua. The House bill included language barring any military aid to the guerrillas; the Senate version included $28 million. *(Story, p. 86)*

On Oct. 3, under intense pressure from the administration, the Senate stuck to its position by rejecting, 42-57, an Inouye amendment that sought to "wind down" the Nicaraguan war. Inouye's proposal would have barred further military aid to help the rebels fight but would have provided $2 million to help them get out of Nicaragua and $4 million to resettle them elsewhere. *(Vote 252, p. 44-S)*

The Senate also rejected, 45-53, an amendment by Christopher J. Dodd, D-Conn., that would have barred the contras from using U.S. money to engage in "terrorist" activities. *(Vote 254, p. 45-S)*

The administration also headed off two major challenges to its overseas military aid program.

Late in the session that began Oct. 3, the Senate tabled

(killed), 51-46, an amendment by Larry Pressler, R-S.D., that would have deprived Turkey of $215 million of the $715 million in military grants in the military aid program. *(Vote 261, p. 46-S)*

Pressler's amendment, adopted by the Foreign Relations Committee in the spring, would have barred the grants unless Turkey relinquished control of the town of Varosha on Cyprus. Administration officials were concerned because the Pressler amendment was backed by the politically influential "Greek lobby," and State Department officials argued that the amendment would disrupt Turkey's military modernization. Pressler countered that foreign aid should be used to pressure Turkey to pull its troops off Cyprus.

On Oct. 3, the Senate turned back, 46-54, an amendment sponsored by David Pryor, D-Ark., that would have cut the Military Assistance Program by $211.5 million, to $705.5 million. The program helped foreign countries buy U.S. arms. *(Vote 251, p. 44-S)*

Conference Action

Aid to the Nicaraguan contras was one of the issues contributing to the logjam over the continuing resolution. In talks Oct. 4-5, House-Senate conferees settled all issues relating to the actual expenditure of foreign aid funds.

In negotiations the evening of Oct. 4, conferees agreed to a compromise figure of $700 million for military aid to Turkey — $15 million less than that country got in fiscal 1984. *(Details, p. 396)*

But attempts to compromise the Nicaragua funds failed during the Oct. 4-5 talks. Both sides tied the question to a related provision in the continuing resolution that would prevent the president from using U.S. armed forces to fight in Central America.

The White House and Senate Republicans were willing to delete the $28 million from the bill — if the House agreed to drop a ban on the CIA's using its contingency fund to help the contras and also drop the prohibition on using U.S. forces in the region.

The conferees eventually reached a compromise by which the aid was cut to $14 million, and none of it could be given before Feb. 28, 1985. To spend the $14 million, the president would have to submit a report to Congress after Feb. 28, certifying that the money was needed to combat expansionism by the Nicaraguan regime. Both houses would have to approve any request, effectively giving either chamber a veto. Congress accepted the compromise on Oct. 10.

Authorizations

An attempt by leaders of the Senate Foreign Relations and House Foreign Affairs committees to insert a full-scale authorizations bill into the continuing resolution was blocked by Senate Democrats. *(Authorization bill, p. 103)*

On Oct. 4, aides of the committees drafted an authorizations bill, including the Kissinger plan, which was introduced the next day as S 3069 and HR 6409. Conferees on the continuing resolution initially agreed to incorporate the measure by referring to it in the text of their bill.

But Democrats objected, saying Congress should not enact into law a bill written entirely by staff. They also wanted to avoid giving Reagan a victory on the Kissinger plan.

"I realize that the staff views us as a constitutional

Most International Bank Money Survives

After months of struggle that threatened to scuttle some funds earmarked for the World Bank's affiliates, Congress accepted most but not all of the administration's requests for funds for international financial institutions.

The massive continuing resolution (H J Res 648 — PL 98-473) approved Oct. 11 included $1.3 billion for the multilateral banks as part of the foreign aid appropriation.

Especially hard fought was funding for the International Development Association (IDA), which lends to the poorest developing nations. Some members criticized IDA for its "giveaway," no-interest loans and questioned its effectiveness as a means of maintaining U.S. influence abroad. *(Story, p. 124)*

As in 1981, lengthy debate on the politically unpopular program was skirted by approving IDA programs through an omnibus bill, thereby avoiding a separate vote in each chamber. The fiscal 1985 continuing resolution authorized the administration's request of $2.25 billion for fiscal 1985-87 as the U.S. share of IDA's international lending pool. *(1981 Almanac p. 142)*

The $2.25 billion commitment was 31 percent lower than the previous U.S. pledge and brought the total IDA pool to $9 billion, $7 billion less than the World Bank had originally requested.

The emergency spending bill also contained a $750 million appropriation for the first year of the three-year commitment to IDA and $150 million for the final installment of the previous pledge. *(1983 Almanac p. 525)*

Earlier in the year, it appeared that the final installment might fail to win congressional approval. It was cut Aug. 10 during a House-Senate conference on a fiscal 1984 supplemental appropriation bill (HR 6040 — PL 98-396). But the money was restored by the House Appropriations Committee Sept. 12 during consideration of the fiscal 1985 foreign assistance funding bill that was later tacked onto the continuing resolution. *(House committee action, p. 392; supplemental, p. 439)*

To hold down the total fiscal 1985 appropriation for the banks in the continuing resolution, Congress cut $44 million from the Asian Development Fund's proposed $144 million appropriation. The direct contribution to the Inter-American Development Bank was reduced by $20 million, to $38 million.

For other institutions, the continuing resolution contained $109.7 million for the World Bank, $72.5 million for the Inter-American Development Bank's Fund for Special Operations, which lent at below-market interest rates, $113.2 million for direct contributions to the Asian Development Bank, $50 million for the African Development Fund and $17.9 million for the African Development Bank. *(African aid, box, p. 395)*

impediment, but this is going a little bit too far," said Sen. Patrick J. Leahy, D-Vt. "I've asked for an explanation of what's in the bill, and nobody can give me one. I might support it, if I knew what was in it. I doubt if any elected member of Congress knows what's in it."

Faced with that objection, the conferees deleted the staff-written authorizations. Ironically, the Democrats' objections had the effect of eliminating several Central America human rights and land reform provisions that Democrats had sought.

Major Provisions

However, the continuing resolution did include several specific items from an authorizations bill (HR 5119) passed by the House on May 10 and from a companion bill (S 2582) approved in April by the Senate Foreign Relations Committee.

The largest single authorization was for a $2.25 billion contribution, over three years, to the International Development Association, an arm of the World Bank. Neither chamber of Congress had considered that authorization prior to enactment of the continuing resolution. *(Box, p. 393)*

Military Aid

Since taking office, Reagan placed a premium on military assistance as needed to help friendly foreign governments defend themselves against real and potential threats by the Soviet Union and its allies.

With Reagan pushing it, military aid shot up dramatically in recent years. In fiscal 1981, the last budget year for which the administration of President Carter was largely responsible, the United States provided $3.2 billion to foreign governments through the major military aid programs. Under Reagan, the figures were: $4.3 billion in 1982, $5.6 billion in 1983 and $6.5 billion in 1984.

The fiscal 1985 continuing resolution provided $5.9 billion. Some of the drop-off from 1984 to 1985 resulted from the introduction of a new program giving about 16 countries smaller loans in 1985 than in the past, but under better terms. Interest rates for those countries were projected to be about 5 percent, compared with the 10-12 percent charged for standard military aid loans. For example, Indonesia was to receive $45 million in 1985, a cut of $5 million from 1984, but half of its 1984 aid would be at the reduced interest rate.

Another $300 million was pared from the overall aid total by reducing military aid to Israel to $1.4 billion in fiscal 1985, from $1.7 billion in 1984. But Israel was to get all its 1985 aid as a grant, whereas it had to pay back half of its previous aid.

In a step toward what they called "honest budgeting," Congress and the administration also agreed to count all foreign military aid as part of the federal budget, starting in 1985. In the past, only about one-fourth of all military aid dollars showed up in the budget as actual appropriations; the rest was in Foreign Military Sales guaranteed loans that were counted as "off-budget."

The fastest growing part of the aid budget was the Military Assistance Program, which provided grants to help foreign countries buy U.S. weapons and military services. That program soared from $110 million in fiscal 1981 to $805 million in fiscal 1985.

El Salvador

Of Reagan's request for $132.5 million in military aid in fiscal 1985 for El Salvador, Congress provided $128.25 million in the continuing resolution. Of the approved amount, $111.75 million was in Military Assistance Program grants, $15 million was in Foreign Military Sales low-interest loans, and $1.5 million was for military training.

Congress put three major restrictions on El Salvador's military aid in fiscal 1985:

• Only half of the Military Assistance Program money could be spent before March 1, 1985, unless the president sought approval from the House and Senate Appropriations committees to spend it at a faster rate. Before he could spend the second half, the president would have to report to the committees that the Salvadoran government had made "substantial progress" in several areas, including curbing killings by so-called "death squads," eliminating government corruption, improving the performance of the military and conducting discussions with the leftist opposition about ending the civil war.

• $5 million was held in escrow until the Salvadoran government conducted a trial and obtained a verdict in the case of two Americans, Mark Pearlman and Michael Hammer, and a Salvadoran, José Rodolfo Viera, who were killed in January 1981. The three men worked for El Salvador's land reform program; no one had been prosecuted for their murders, although U.S. officials said the Salvadoran government had solid evidence about who was responsible.

• All aid to El Salvador would have to be suspended if the elected president of El Salvador was deposed by a military coup or decree.

The continuing resolution also approved $195 million in Economic Support Fund aid to bolster El Salvador's overall economy, a slight cut from Reagan's $210 million request. But to guard against misuse, Congress insisted that the Central Bank of El Salvador keep that money in a separate account, and required the president to file specific reports on how it was spent.

An additional $6 million was included in the continuing resolution for improvements in the judicial system in El Salvador, including creation of investigative units, protection of key participants in pending cases and modernization of penal and evidentiary codes.

Central America

Reagan had asked for $1.2 billion in appropriations for economic, development and military aid to Central America in fiscal 1985. He also requested authorizations for at least $1.2 billion annually in fiscal years 1986-89, in accordance with the Kissinger commission's recommendations for multi-year aid to the region. Congress approved about $1.1 billion for 1985, but rejected the request for follow-up authorizations.

Among the specific regionwide items that Reagan requested, but Congress rejected, were: authority for the United States to participate in a new multinational agency, the Central American Development Organization, to oversee U.S. aid; a new $20 million program to improve the administration of justice in Central American countries; exemption of Central America from a 1974 law banning aid to foreign police forces; and authorization for a new program of scholarships to enable 10,000 Latin American students to attend U.S. colleges through 1989.

But the continuing resolution included authorizations and appropriations for a new "trade credit insurance" program to guarantee $300 million worth of loans made by the

Export-Import Bank for high-risk exports of goods to Central America.

That program drew opposition in the Senate by an unusual coalition led by conservative Jesse Helms, R-N.C., and liberal Claiborne Pell, D-R.I., but was slipped into the continuing resolution at the last minute by administration backers.

Congress also set a $225 million limit on development aid programs in Central America — a cut of $48 million from Reagan's requests.

That limit was a compromise between the House Appropriations Committee, which had voted a $200 million limit, and the Senate Appropriations panel, which had approved Reagan's request.

For the second year in a row, Congress rejected Reagan's request to resume aid for Guatemala to buy weapons from the United States. President Carter had cut off all arms sales and military aid to Guatemala in 1977 because of human rights abuses by the government there. Reagan requested $10 million in Foreign Military Sales loans for Guatemala in fiscal years 1984 and 1985, but Congress banned the aid because of continuing repression by the rightist government.

However, the continuing resolution lifted, for 1985, a related ban on aid to train Guatemalan military officers. Reagan requested, and Congress approved, $300,000 for that purpose.

House-Senate conferees on the continuing resolution also pared, to $12.5 million, Reagan's $35 million request for economic aid to Guatemala, and required that the money be spent on programs "aimed directly at improving the lives of the poor."

Reagan also had requested $40 million for development aid to Guatemala — an amount that would be subject to cuts resulting from the $225 million Central America limit imposed in the continuing resolution.

The continuing resolution cast further doubt on administration plans to build a large Regional Military Training Center in northern Honduras. The United States for two years trained Honduran and Salvadoran soldiers at a makeshift camp near Trujillo, and Reagan sought $45 million from Congress, over fiscal 1984-85, for a permanent facility.

But the Honduran government announced that it would no longer permit Salvadorans to be trained at the camp. At about the same time, Panama closed a large U.S. military training center in the former Panama Canal Zone. Those events forced the administration to work on new plans for training troops from El Salvador and the rest of Central America.

In the meantime, conferees on the continuing resolution added a provision barring the president from spending any money on the Honduran training center until three things happened: the Honduran government had provided a site for it; the president had given Congress a detailed plan and cost estimate; and the Honduran government had taken steps to resolve a claim by a U.S. citizen, Tenustickes Ramiraz, whose property was confiscated for the center.

Aside from El Salvador and Guatemala, the continuing resolution did not set specific aid levels for Central American countries. However, the measure provided enough military aid for the president to give Costa Rica and Honduras his full requests: $10 million and $62.5 million, respectively.

Another provision set aside $5 million to help Central American countries develop "energy self-sufficiency."

Middle East

Israel, faced with severe economic problems, won a bonanza of aid concessions from the administration and Congress — and the promise of more in the future.

Among the concessions enacted into law by the continuing resolution:

● A shift under which Israel was to receive all of its military aid as a grant, rather than half-grant, half-loan, as in the past. In 1985, Israel was to get a $1.4 billion grant — worth more, administration aides said, than the $1.7 billion grant and loan it got in fiscal 1984.

● Israel would be able to use $400 million of its arms aid

'Status Quo' on Africa Aid

The omnibus continuing appropriations resolution (H J Res 648 — PL 98-473) provided most of the $1.2 billion in various aid programs that President Reagan sought for Africa in fiscal 1985. But that amount fell short of what some private groups and members of Congress said was needed to combat widespread poverty and famine on the continent.

"It's basically status quo," said Rep. Howard Wolpe, D-Mich., chairman of the Foreign Affairs Subcommittee on Africa. *(Story, p. 121)*

The administration requested about $90 million more in African aid for fiscal 1985 than Congress approved for fiscal 1984, according to Senate figures. Congress accepted most of the administration's recommendations as part of the continuing resolution, but made two major changes. Lawmakers:

● Killed, at least for the time being, the administration's request for a new program, called the Economic Policy Initiative, intended to reward African countries that moved away from socialistic policies toward private enterprise. Reagan asked for $75 million for the program in fiscal 1985 as the first installment of a five-year, $500 million commitment.

Instead, Congress diverted the $75 million into the Economic Support Fund, a government program that bolsters the economies of friendly countries.

● Specified that Africa should get at least as much in no-interest loans from the International Development Association (IDA) during the next three years as it did during the previous three years.

The move was made to protect Africa from the administration's decision to cut the U.S. contribution to IDA, which contributed to a projected drop in IDA's lending pool from $12 billion to $9 billion in fiscal 1985 through 1988. *(Box, p. 393)*

Congress also earmarked $42 million for health and development assistance, approved $97.5 million for the Sahel Development Fund, a program that since the mid-1970s had helped drought-stricken western Africa, and gave about $68 million in direct contributions to the African Development Bank and Fund, the same levels as fiscal 1984.

Earlier in 1984, in supplemental appropriations bills for fiscal 1984, Congress provided $150 million in emergency food aid to Africa, more than the administration sought, but only about half as much as the United Nations' Food and Agriculture Organization said was needed. *(Supplementals, pp. 429, 438)*

to develop and build its new warplane, the Lavi. Of that amount, $150 million would have to be spent in the United States and $250 million in Israel. Congress had approved $550 million for the plane in fiscal 1984, setting a precedent for allowing Israel to spend U.S. aid on the Lavi.

● Israel was to get $1.2 billion in Economic Support Fund grants in fiscal 1985 — an increase of $290 million over fiscal 1984 and of $350 million over Reagan's 1985 request.

● In a concession with long-term implications, the continuing resolution stated that it was U.S. "policy and intention" to give Israel at least as much economic aid each year as Israel owed the United States annually on past loans. Section 534 of the continuing resolution said that guarantee was being made because "an economically and militarily secure Israel serves the security interests of the United States." At the end of 1984, Israel owed the United States about $9.6 billion, on which it was making annual interest and principal payments of about $1.1 billion. According to the Congressional Budget Office, Israel's annual payments were expected to rise to about $1.4 billion by fiscal 1990. The aid guarantee originally was proposed in 1983 by Sen. Alan Cranston, D-Calif.

● The continuing resolution exempted Israel — and possibly Lebanon and Turkey — from a 1980 law (PL 96-533, section 705b) that banned construction and engineering firms in "advanced developing countries" from competing for work on U.S. foreign aid-financed projects. Under this exemption, Israeli firms could compete on U.S. aid projects anywhere.

● $2 million under the Agency for International Development's energy aid program was set aside for overseas development programs carried out in cooperation between the United States and Israel. Israel, a provider of technical aid to several countries, mostly in Africa, had sought $20 million in U.S. support for those efforts.

Congress also awarded increased aid to Egypt under the continuing resolution: $1.175 billion in military aid and $815 million in economic aid, all as a grant. The arms aid was the same as Reagan's request, but Congress added $65 million to the economic aid request as a partial balance to its much bigger boost in Israel aid.

In fiscal 1984, Egypt received $1.365 billion in military aid, of which it had to repay $900 million, and $750 million in economic aid grants.

In addition, $100 million of the 1985 economic aid was to be provided as a no-strings-attached cash transfer to the Egyptian government, instead of the normal procedure under which all economic aid funds were allocated for specific programs that must be approved by the United States.

In a mild rebuke to Egypt, the continuing resolution stated that U.S. aid was based "in great measure upon the continued participation of Egypt" in the 1978 Camp David accords and the 1979 Egyptian-Israeli peace treaty. Egypt recalled its ambassador to Israel in 1982, to protest the Israeli invasion of Lebanon. Some members of Congress charged that Egypt's refusal to return an envoy violated its treaty commitments to Israel.

Enshrining in law a U.S. policy in effect since 1975, the continuing resolution barred any official of the U.S. government from recognizing or negotiating with the Palestine Liberation Organization (PLO) as long as that group continued to refuse to recognize Israel's right to exist, refused to accept U.N. resolutions 242 and 338 on the Middle East and failed to renounce terrorism.

Then-Secretary of State Kissinger had promised Israel in 1975 that the United States would not negotiate with the PLO. Some members of Congress complained that the Reagan administration skirted that pledge in 1981-82 by conducting secret talks with the PLO.

On a related matter, the continuing resolution stated the sense of Congress that the United States should not sell "sophisticated weaponry" to Jordan until that country had committed itself to recognize Israel and to begin "serious peace negotiations" with Israel.

Sophisticated weaponry was defined as advanced aircraft, new air defense weapons or "other new advanced weapons." Reagan in March proposed to sell Jordan 1,613 "Stinger" anti-aircraft missiles, but withdrew the sale after it prompted a storm of protest in Congress.

A formal ban on advanced arms sales to Jordan had been included in the foreign aid authorization bill (HR 5119) passed by the House on May 10. But Reagan, in a letter to continuing resolution conferees, threatened to veto any measure that included such a prohibition. In the face of that threat, the conferees watered the Jordan language down to a non-binding sense of Congress statement.

Greece, Turkey

Reagan had requested $755 million for Turkey, an increase of $40 million over the previous fiscal year. But 1984 was an especially sensitive year for Congress to consider aid to Turkey because it was the 10th anniversary of Turkey's invasion and occupation of the northern third of Cyprus, an island in the eastern Mediterranean populated by rival Greeks and Turks.

Pressured by pro-Greek lobbying, the House Foreign Affairs, Senate Foreign Relations and House Appropriations committees all recommended major cuts or restrictions on Turkey's aid. The administration vigorously opposed such efforts, saying they would damage U.S. ties with a country that was an important member of NATO and that hosted several U.S. military and intelligence installations.

In the final days of negotiations on the continuing resolution, on Oct. 4, House and Senate foreign aid conferees were $45 million apart on Turkish aid: House members refusing to approve more than $670 million and Senate members refusing to settle for less than $715 million. With that deadlock, the four foreign aid negotiators took the issue to the full 44-member conference committee. There, Conte suggested a compromise of $700 million, and it was readily approved.

The $700 million included $215 million in Military Assistance Program grants ($15 million below Reagan's request) and $485 million in Foreign Military Sales loans ($40 million below the request). Turkey also was to receive $175 million in economic aid, which was not controversial.

Greece was to get $500 million in arms aid. Both Greece and Turkey were to get special loans at 5 percent interest.

As in past years, the continuing resolution also included $15 million in economic aid for Cyprus — five times Reagan's request.

AID Programs

In approving $1.7 billion for development programs run by the Agency for International Development, Congress took two new steps to boost health care in poor countries, especially for children.

It added $60 million for health and nutrition education

'Security Aid' Totals, Fiscal 1984-85

Following are amounts for major "security assistance" programs for key countries. Security assistance includes Foreign Military Sales (FMS) loans, Military Assistance Program (MAP) grants and Economic Support Fund (ESF) loans and grants. Not included in the chart are such programs as military training, development aid, food aid, and contributions from international organizations.

The fiscal 1984 final figures include President Reagan's regular and supplemental requests and amounts appropriated by Congress in a continuing resolution (PL 98-151) and two supplementals (PL 98-332 and PL 98-396).

The fiscal 1985 "preliminary" amounts were allocated by the administration under a continuing resolution (PL 98-473) signed into law Oct. 12. *(Figures are in millions of dollars; country totals are in bold type; fiscal 1983 figures, 1983 Almanac p. 514)*

Country	Fiscal 1984		Fiscal 1985	
	Request	Final	Request	Preliminary
Egypt	**$ 2,050**	**$ 2,115**	**$ 1,925**	**$ 1,990**
FMS[1]	1,300	1,365	1,175	1,175
ESF	750	750	750	815
Israel	**2,485**	**2,610**	**2,250**	**2,600**
FMS[2]	1,700	1,700	1,400	1,400
ESF	785	910	850	1,200
Jordan [3]	**135**	**135**	**115**	**110**
FMS	115	115	95	90
ESF	20	20	20	20
Lebanon	**65**	**15**	**35**	**10**
FMS	15	15	15	5
ESF	50	0	20	5
Pakistan	**525**	**525**	**525**	**525**
FMS	300	300	325	325
ESF	225	225	200	200
Turkey [3]	**930**	**853.5**	**930**	**875**
FMS	525	585	525	485
MAP	230	130	230	215
ESF	175	138.5	175	175
Greece [3]	**280**	**500**	**500**	**500**
FMS	280 [4]	500	500	500
Cyprus	**3**	**15**	**3**	**15**
ESF	3	15	3	15
Spain	**412**	**412**	**412**	**412**
FMS	400	400	400	300
ESF	12	12	12	12
Portugal	**145**	**145**	**205**	**205**
FMS	45	45	55	55
MAP	60	60	70	70
ESF	40	40	80	80
South Korea	**230**	**230**	**230**	**220**
FMS	230	230	230	220

Country	Fiscal 1984		Fiscal 1985	
	Request	Final	Request	Preliminary
Philippines [3]	**$ 100**	**$ 100**	**$ 180**	**$ 180**
FMS	50	50	60	15
MAP	0	0	25	25
ESF	50	50	95	140
Tunisia [3]	**140**	**111.5**	**68**	**85**
FMS	90	92	50	50
MAP	50	18	15	15
ESF	0	1.5	3	20
Somalia	**75**	**67**	**75**	**63**
MAP	40	32	40	33
ESF	35	35	35	30
Morocco [3]	**97**	**75.75**	**65**	**58**
FMS	60	38.75	10	3
MAP	30	30	40	40
ESF	7	7	15	15
Sudan	**180**	**165**	**189**	**159**
MAP	60	45	69	45
ESF	120	120	120	114
Zaire	**20**	**17**	**30**	**17**
MAP	10	7	15	7
ESF	10	10	15	10
Costa Rica	**140**	**139**	**169.8**	**169**
MAP	10	9	9.8	9
ESF	130	130	160	160
El Salvador [3]	**452.2**	**405.5**	**341**	**321.75**
FMS	18.5	18.5	15	15
MAP	223.7	176.5	116	111.75
ESF	210	210.5	210	195
Guatemala	**50**	**0**	**45**	**12.5**
FMS	10	0	10	0
ESF	40	0	35	12.5
Honduras	**190**	**189**	**136.3**	**136.3**
MAP	77.5	76.5	61.3	61.3
ESF	112.5	112.5	75	75

[1] *In fiscal 1984, $465 million of Egypt's FMS was in forgiven loans; in fiscal 1985, all of it was in forgiven loans.*
[2] *In fiscal 1984, $850 million of Israel's FMS was in forgiven loans; in fiscal 1985, all of it was in forgiven loans.*

[3] *In fiscal 1985, these countries were to receive part of their FMS loans at below-market interest rates.*
[4] *Reagan originally requested $280 million for Greece, but under pressure from Congress later revised his request to $500 million.*

programs, primarily for efforts to combat measles, dehydration and starvation.

And it established a new $25 million Child Survival Fund, which would support programs by UNICEF and other agencies to reduce mortality rates among infants and children in poor countries.

Neither program was requested by the Reagan administration.

Of the $25 million for the Child Survival Fund, $1 million was set aside for studies by Johns Hopkins University in Baltimore — the former employer of Rep. Clarence D. Long, D-Md., who was the chief House foreign aid conferee.

The conferees resolved, for the time being, a potentially bitter dispute over U.S. population aid.

On the one hand, conferees approved $290 million for overseas family planning programs, including those run by the U.S. government and several run by the United Nations and other international agencies. That was $40 million over Reagan's request.

But the conferees also rejected an attempt by House members to put Congress on record as opposing a new Reagan administration policy that played down the need for family planning programs and emphasized the role of economic growth in stemming population increases. Instead, the continuing resolution stated the sense of the House that the administration should stand by previous U.S. policies that strongly advocated family planning programs.

On a related matter, the continuing resolution included a House-passed provision barring U.S. population aid to any country or organization that used "involuntary abortion" in its family planning programs. Previous U.S. law barred aid to countries that practiced "forced or coerced abortion."

Some anti-abortion groups had said "involuntary" was a broader term than "forced or coerced," and therefore would constitute a tighter ban.

The continuing resolution also required the administration to give at least $46 million, or 16 percent of its family planning funds, to the U.N. Fund for Population Activities.

The administration had threatened to cut off aid to that agency unless it promised not to pay for abortions.

The bill did not take a position on the issue of the International Planned Parenthood Federation, also threatened with suspension of U.S. contributions unless it renounced all abortion-related activities. On Dec. 11, the administration decided on a strict interpretation of its anti-abortion policy, with the result that Planned Parenthood would be cut off from U.S. assistance. The federation, which received $13.5 million from the United States in 1984, had said it could not accept the administration's conditions.

Other Provisions

In other foreign aid provisions, the continuing resolution:

● **Philippines Aid.** Shifted $45 million in military aid to the Philippines to economic aid, as a symbolic congressional protest against the authoritarian regime of President Marcos.

Reagan had requested $180 million for the Philippines, in connection with a new agreement for the operation of U.S. military bases there. He sought $60 million in military aid loans, $25 million in military aid grants and $95 million in economic aid. The continuing resolution allowed the full $180 million, but shifted the mix to $15 million in military aid loans, $25 million in military grants and $140 million in economic aid.

● **Emergency Food Relief.** Established a $50 million fund for the president to provide emergency aid to relieve "severe food shortages" overseas. President Reagan had requested it.

● **Haiti Aid Restrictions.** Barred all military aid to Haiti, and permitted economic and development aid to that country only if the president reported to Congress every six months that the Haitian government was continuing to cooperate with efforts to halt illegal emigration to the United States, was cooperating with U.S. efforts to improve the management of aid programs there, and was making progress toward respecting human rights and reforming its political system.

Reagan had requested $5 million in economic aid and $49.7 million in development and food aid for Haiti in fiscal 1985.

● **Narcotic Drugs.** Barred U.S. aid to any country found by the president to be "failing to take adequate measures" to prevent narcotic drugs produced in its territory from entering the United States.

● **Aid to Polish Farmers.** Appropriated $10 million in fiscal years 1985-86 for aid to farmers in Poland under a new foundation run by the Polish Catholic Church.

Reagan had proposed the contribution in August, shortly after the Polish government agreed to allow the church to establish a foundation to buy supplies and equipment for farmers.

● **Defaults.** Barred U.S. aid to any country more than one year in default on past obligations to the United States. Conferees also directed the administration to prepare plans for making such a cutoff.

● **Zaire Aid.** Pared both economic and military aid to Zaire. Economic aid was set at $10 million, $5 million below Reagan's request, and arms aid was set at $4 million, $6 million below the request.

Congress had trimmed aid to Zaire annually for several years to protest government corruption and authoritarian rule by President Mobuto Sese Seko.

● **Development Aid for Minorities.** Set aside 10 percent of all development aid funds for the use of colleges, universities, businesses and other organizations owned or controlled by minorities, including blacks, Hispanics, other disadvantaged persons and women.

The administrator of AID could waive this requirement.

● **Reports to Congress.** Directed the president to report to Congress on the extent to which countries receiving U.S. aid supported U.S. foreign policies. Any country found by the president to be engaged in "a consistent pattern of opposition" to U.S. policies would be prohibited from receiving aid.

● **American Universities.** Directed the secretary of state to conduct a study of the best way to continue U.S. backing for the American University of Beirut and the American University of Cairo. Both institutions received money under the foreign aid program, but both had encountered financial difficulties in recent years.

The Senate Foreign Relations Committee had recommended establishment of a $50 million trust fund for the American University of Beirut, but the final continuing resolution merely suggested a trust fund as one alternative. ∎

For Defense, $274.4 Billion in Fiscal 1985

An omnibus continuing resolution (H J Res 648 — PL 98-473), cleared for President Reagan Oct. 11, included a $274.4 billion defense appropriation for fiscal 1985.

The defense spending portion of the bill came as something of an anticlimax, since the contentious issues of the defense budget total and the immediate future of the MX missile had been settled earlier in negotiations between the White House, Senate Majority Leader Howard H. Baker Jr., R-Tenn., and House Speaker Thomas P. O'Neill Jr., D-Mass. The agreement, announced Sept. 20, broke a months-long impasse over the fiscal 1985 defense authorization bill. *(Story, p. 444)*

Under the agreement, the total defense appropriation for the year was set at $292.9 billion, of which the $274.4 billion that would normally have been included in the main defense appropriations bill was incorporated into the continuing resolution. The continuing resolution deferred a decision on continued production of the controversial missile. *(Charts, pp. 400, 403)*

That amount did not include $1.5 billion for production of a second batch of 21 MX missiles (in addition to the 21 MXs already paid for by the fiscal 1984 budget). As part of the September agreement, the 1985 money for MX could be spent only if Congress adopted two resolutions in the spring of 1985.

The appropriations conferees agreed that the $1.5 billion would not consist of new appropriations. Instead, it was to come from funds that had been appropriated for various defense projects over the last two years, but had not been spent because of changing prices or production plans.

The new limitations on the MX represented a potential setback for Reagan, who had made the missile the centerpiece of his nuclear weapons program. In the final version of the appropriations measure, Reagan also lost a little ground, compared with the outcome of the companion defense authorization bill (HR 5167 — PL 98-525). *(Authorization bill, p. 37)*

Some examples:

● Tests of the anti-satellite (ASAT) missile would be delayed until March 1, 1985, at the earliest with no more than three allowed during fiscal 1985. The provision marked a novel action by Congress: imposing a test moratorium on a new weapon.

● The $1.63 billion approved by the Senate for development of a space-based anti-missile defense — a program liberal arms-control advocates had ridiculed as "Star Wars" — was trimmed to $1.40 billion. Reagan had requested $1.78 billion and the House had appropriated $1.09 billion.

● The defense portion of the bill also included new limitations on funding for rebels, or "contras," who were battling the leftist government of Nicaragua. *(Details, pp. 86, 88)*

ASAT Test Limits. As a practical matter, it was unclear whether the moratorium on ASAT tests until March 1, 1985, would delay the ASAT test schedule, which was secret. The missile had been tested once and was expected to be tested again before, in a third test, it would be aimed at a target satellite.

The limitation to three ASAT target tests came on top of the defense authorization bill's limitation to two "suc-cessful" tests. Authorization conferees had warned the Pentagon against trying to circumvent that limit by aiming an ASAT to miss its target narrowly and then claiming that the test did not succeed.

Several anti-ASAT lobbyists credited Joseph P. Addabbo, D-N.Y., chairman of the House Appropriations Subcommittee on Defense, with extracting White House concessions beyond those in the authorization bill.

Committee Action

The Appropriations panels' markup of the defense appropriations measure fell into the political deadlock that stalled the conference committee on the annual defense authorization bill — which typically precedes the appropriations measure — all summer.

In the authorization process, Reagan and his congressional allies were unwilling to compromise with House Democrats over the size of the defense budget and the future of the MX missile. The administration feared that if they compromised on these issues in the authorization bill, they would then have to renegotiate them with the House a second time in the appropriations bill, leading to a lower budget and tighter restrictions on MX production.

As a result, the authorization conference and the appropriations markups were delayed until the White House, Baker and O'Neill negotiated an agreement on the budget level and MX issues.

By the time that deal was struck Sept. 20, all unfinished appropriations measures were being incorporated into an omnibus bill — a so-called continuing resolution — so that Congress could complete its work quickly and adjourn by early October.

On Sept. 26, the two Appropriations panels reported separate versions of a defense appropriations bill (HR 6329 — H Rept 98-1086, S 3026 — S Rept 98-636). However, those provisions were considered on the floor of each house only as part of a continuing resolution.

Senate Committee

The Republican-controlled Senate panel's bill, as usual, was the higher of the two, appropriating $278 billion out of an overall defense budget of $297 billion.

The Senate Appropriations Committee made a sweeping cut in funds for the DIVAD — or Sergeant York — that was unusual but not unprecedented.

Though the congressional defense panels rarely had acted so forcefully against a major weapon already in production, the Senate Armed Services Committee had taken similar steps in 1982. That panel then refused to authorize continued production of the AH-64 Apache anti-tank helicopter, citing escalating price estimates. But the Armed Services Committee later agreed to a conference report authorizing purchase after the Army and the helicopter manufacturer reached agreement on a lower price for the Apache. *(1982 Almanac p. 77)*

The DIVAD (division air defense) tank, armed with two radar-guided 40mm cannons, was designed to protect front-line Army units against helicopters firing anti-tank guided missiles.

When prototype DIVADs began undergoing tests in the early 1980s, they experienced a series of failures. The

Fiscal 1985 Appropriations for Defense

	Administration Request	House-Passed	Senate-Passed	Final Appropriation
	(in thousands of dollars)			
Military Personnel	$ 67,831,600	$ 66,989,691	$ 67,015,104	$ 66,895,639
Operations and Maintenance	80,927,042	76,599,129	78,201,727	77,521,356
Procurement	107,586,341	93,167,871	99,314,304	97,111,404
Research and Development	33,985,037	29,779,538	31,897,567	31,187,071
Revolving Funds	1,762,056	1,627,156	1,553,656	1,553,956
Other Programs	129,747	128,247	129,747	128,747
Total, new budget authority	292,221,823	268,291,632	278,112,105	274,398,173
Transfer from unspent, earlier appropriations	0	1,771,800	1,280,000	0
Total funding available	$292,221,823	$270,063,432	$279,392,105	$274,398,173

problems were serious enough that the 1982 decision to begin production of the weapon came under review by Defense Secretary Caspar W. Weinberger.

Meanwhile, DIVAD production funds had been appropriated in each year since fiscal 1982. The fiscal 1985 budget request was for 130 of the tanks ($515.8 million), reduced in May to 117 ($451 million).

The authorization conference report approved the revised fiscal 1985 request, but barred use of the funds until production-line DIVADs passed realistic field tests.

Similar provisions were contained in the House-reported version of the defense appropriations bill and in the Senate Defense Subcommittee's appropriations measure.

But as the full Senate Appropriations panel finished its review of the defense bill Sept. 26, subcommittee Chairman Ted Stevens, R-Alaska, recommended that only $50 million be appropriated for DIVAD procurement, to be used only to keep the production line "warm," that is, ready to resume production if Congress became convinced that it had passed its tests.

The amendment, deleting some $558 million from various accounts associated with DIVAD production, was agreed to by voice vote.

House Committee

The $268 billion bill reported to the House would have brought the overall defense budget to about $290 billion.

By a vote of 24-21, the House committee cut to $1.09 billion the budget for developing space-based anti-missile weapons, a program that arms control activists criticized as "Star Wars."

Reagan called for the program to make nuclear weapons "impotent and obsolete." But traditional arms control lobbyists maintained that a "leak-proof" defense would be technically impossible and would simply extend the arms race to outer space.

Before Congress recessed in August, these activists canvassed the committee for support of an amendment

that would have cut the program to $1.1 billion. They assumed that the Defense Subcommittee would recommend a $1.37 billion appropriation, the amount approved by the House version of the authorization bill.

To the lobbyists' pleasant surprise, the subcommittee recommended a figure $200 million lower than the House-passed authorization. The "Star Wars" opponents then decided to seek a further reduction to $1.09 billion, which would amount to a real increase for the program of 5 percent over the fiscal 1984 budget, the same increase as was allowed for the overall defense budget.

This was the first vote taken in the House on Reagan's "Star Wars" proposal. Arms control lobbyists had decided not to try to reduce the program during the authorization debate in May. Instead, they concentrated their political resources on slowing down development of the ASAT missile.

Senate, House Bills

After being reported by the House Appropriations Committee Sept. 26, the defense bill (HR 6329 — H Rept 98-1086) was incorporated into the continuing resolution being considered by the House. Similarly, the Senate version of the resolution contained S 3026, the defense bill reported by the Senate Appropriations Committee Sept. 26 (S Rept 98-636).

The only issue from the defense part of the continuing resolution that provoked spirited floor debate in either house was the administration's request to fund guerrillas opposed to Nicaragua's leftist government. *(Story, p. 444)*

Nuclear Warfare

The Sept. 20 White House-Capitol Hill compromise approved $2.5 billion for MX procurement. However, unless Congress passed two resolutions in March 1985 approving MX production, $1.5 billion of the funds could not be spent — nor could any missiles be built beyond the 21 approved in fiscal 1984.

To continue development of MX and a new, small ICBM intended to complement it and to test new missile-basing methods that would better survive Soviet attack, the two bills approved similar amounts: $2.34 billion in the Senate and $50 million less in the House.

Much of the public discussion about a small missile — informally dubbed "Midgetman" — had assumed that it would be deployed in armored, mobile launchers. But the Senate Appropriations Committee insisted that the Pentagon conduct a "full and fair evaluation" of both that approach and the option of moving each missile at random among dozens of alternative launch sites.

This latter notion — called "Multiple Protective Shelters" — was the MX basing method favored by the Air Force in the late 1970s, but it was scrubbed by the Reagan administration. The Senate panel suggested that it might be much cheaper than the mobile-launcher approach.

Bombers. The House bill trimmed $590 million from the $7.7 billion requested to buy 34 B-1 bombers plus their spare parts and some components that would be used in additional B-1s to be requested in next year's budget. In the past, Congress had not tampered with Reagan's B-1 production requests, in return for an administration pledge to keep the total cost of the planned 100 B-1s down to $20.5 billion (in fiscal 1981 dollars). Members feared that the administration could use congressional cutbacks as a justification for breaching that cost ceiling.

But the House Appropriations panel insisted that cuts could be made in areas that would not affect the Pentagon's administration of the B-1 contract. These cuts took account of lower-than-anticipated bids from B-1 subcontractors and a reduction in the program manager's contingency fund, which the committee deemed too large.

The Senate's bill approved the entire $7.7 billion request. Its Appropriations panel ordered the Air Force to use any contracting windfalls to pay for part of the fiscal 1986 B-1 budget.

According to subcommittee Chairman Stevens, the conferees agreed to $150 million of the House B-1 reduction.

The amounts appropriated in the two versions of the bill for the so-called "stealth" bomber, designed to evade enemy detection, were secret — as was the amount requested for the project.

Mirroring their respective versions of the authorization bill, the two houses differed considerably in their appropriation to modernize the existing fleet of B-52 bombers: The Senate approved $527 million and the House $336 million of $574 million requested.

In a perennial congressional adjustment to the Pentagon budget, both bills reduced the amount appropriated to replace the engines of KC-135 tankers, used to refuel bombers and other planes in midair. The bills ordered the Air Force to put cheaper, secondhand engines in some tankers flown by reserve units.

The appropriation for buying new engine kits was cut to $705 million by the House and $616 million by the Senate, compared with an initial request for $934 million. The cuts were partly offset in each bill by an addition of $73.2 million to pay for engine replacement on the reserve planes.

Submarine Missiles. The appropriations bills differed only slightly from the budget in funding a 12th submarine to launch Trident missiles ($1.5 billion).

Only minor reductions were made in the $2.1 billion request to develop a new, more accurate version of the Trident missile, the Trident II. The Senate pared $16 million and the House cut $40 million. For components that would be used in the first production-line versions of the Trident II, the Senate approved the $163 million request while the House trimmed $15 million.

Both houses had appropriated the $106 million Reagan had requested to develop the E-6 communications plane, designed to serve as an airborne command post for submerged missile subs, sending signals over a trailing antenna several miles long. The plane, a version of the Boeing 707 jetliner, would replace the current fleet of C-130 transport planes.

Ground Combat

Assuming that production costs for the M-1 tank would continue to run lower than estimated, both bills told the Army to buy more tanks than it had requested, and for less money. Both appropriated funds for 840 tanks — compared with the 720 requested — but trimmed the $1.5 billion request by $96 million. Unspent money from the previous fiscal year would be used to help pay for the increase.

However, the Senate renewed one of the previous year's battles by proposing that the Army seek a second source for the tank's gas turbine engine. The Army had proposed selection of a second engine maker in 1983, to put competitive pressure on Avco Corp., the original supplier of M-1 engines.

At the insistence of the House, selection of a second manufacturer was barred in 1983, but the Senate version of the new defense bill would have repealed that ban. The Senate Appropriations Committee argued that only the threat of competition had forced Avco to reduce its price for the engines in the last year and to offer a warranty on their performance.

Both houses trimmed from 710 to 655 the number of Bradley fighting vehicles — armored infantry carriers equipped with anti-tank missiles. However, there were slight differences in how much money would be available to pay for them. The House trimmed the $997 million request by $74 million, the Senate by $46 million.

Anti-Tank Weapons. The Senate approved the full amounts requested to buy the Army's current tank-hunting helicopters: $1.2 billion for 144 Apache helicopters which carry laser-guided missiles; $217 million to modify existing small helicopters to scout out targets for the larger Apaches and spotlight them with lasers for the Apache's missiles to home in on.

The House, citing budgetary limits, reduced the Apache program by $80 million (14 helicopters) and trimmed $13 million from the "scout" program.

On the other hand, the House approved the full $75 million requested to develop a new, small helicopter (called LHX) that would replace some 5,000 older helicopters currently used for scouting and other missions. The Senate cut $10 million from the request, contending that the Army was unduly rushing development of the new plane.

Even after making hefty reductions in the administration's January request, each bill appropriated more than $1 billion for various guided missiles designed chiefly to knock out tanks and other heavily armored targets:

● Of $296 million requested in January for nearly 22,000 TOW missiles to be carried by helicopters, jeeps and other vehicles, the House approved $294 million (18,500 missiles) and the Senate approved $168 million (6,000 missiles). The

Senate figure reflected the budget reduction proposed by the president in May, as part of an overall deficit-reduction effort.

• The budget requested $260 million for nearly 6,500 laser-guided Hellfires, to be carried by attack helicopters. The Senate trimmed only $10 million while the House cut $21 million and 1,000 missiles from the request.

• Both bills approved 3,200 Maverick, air-launched anti-tank missiles rather than the nearly 5,300 requested ($705 million). The House appropriated $454 million, the Senate $485 million.

• The budget funded more than 2,200 Copperhead, laser-guided artillery shells ($103 million). Both bills increased the number of shells by nearly 50 percent, the Senate approving $145 million, the House $143 million. But both bills concurred in the administration's decision in May to defer initial production of the Aquila — a tiny, remote-controlled airplane designed, in part, to shine a laser on Copperhead targets. This amounted to a reduction of $114 million.

Future Tank Killers. Both Appropriations committees slammed the Pentagon for failing to coordinate the numerous research programs working on futuristic anti-tank weapons.

As the committees had insisted in 1983, the Defense Department had submitted an "anti-armor master plan." However, the House panel dismissed the document as "essentially a compendium of all existing programs and an affirmation that all are needed," noting that the budgets and schedules for several anti-tank programs were substantially changed after the so-called master plan was submitted.

"The nation faces too severe financial problems to allow continued development of many systems to accomplish the same ends," the committee argued.

The Senate committee complained that the Army's anti-tank research programs were so uncoordinated that when one of them was canceled in the summer of 1984, the service could not tell the Senate committee what other anti-tank programs should receive funds previously budgeted for the defunct project.

Each of the bills slashed well over half of the $338 million requested to develop a method to attack tank columns more than a hundred miles behind enemy lines. Congress had insisted that the Army and Air Force collaborate on a common program to develop an airborne radar (called JSTARS) that would locate tank columns and a missile (called JTACMS) that would be guided to the spot by the radar and would rain anti-tank warheads onto the vehicles below.

Both Appropriations committees, criticizing the services for going their separate ways, approved funds only for Army work on the missile ($79 million) and for Air Force work on the radar ($50 million by the House and $69 million by the Senate).

To develop four additional kinds of anti-tank weapons, the administration had requested last January a total of $110 million. The Senate approved the vast bulk of that amount, but the House allowed only $30 million and specified one of the four.

Anti-Aircraft Weapons. The Senate bill included $50 million to keep the production line for DIVAD anti-aircraft guns "warm," so it could be easily restarted if the weapon passed some tests it had hitherto failed. The Army had requested $516 million in January to build 132 guns but Defense Secretary Weinberger trimmed that to $100

million Sept. 29, after suspending production of the weapon. The House bill approved 117 guns ($430 million), contingent on the weapon's passing its tests.

Reflecting the earlier authorization measure, both houses trimmed the $1.1 billion request for long-range Patriot anti-aircraft missiles: the Senate to $970 million, the House to $976 million. They also agreed to defer a $33 million request to modernize existing Vulcan anti-aircraft guns. In each case, program delays had been cited as the reason.

Both bills also added to the budget $32 million to accelerate purchase of Chaparral, short-range anti-aircraft missiles for Army Reserve and National Guard units.

Neither bill included the $250 million that the defense authorization conference report had added to the fiscal 1985 budget to beef up anti-aircraft defenses around U.S. bases in Europe. The money was earmarked for missile defenses that would be manned by U.S. allies. Congress had added $250 million for this purpose to the fiscal 1984 defense budget and it had not yet been spent.

The House Appropriations Committee argued that additional money could not be spent in fiscal 1985 because of the timing of the bilateral agreements governing these joint ventures. The Senate committee added that it would approve no additional funds for the European base defense project until the Pentagon started building the project into its own budget requests.

Tactical Air Combat

Because of funding adjustments in the wake of a competition for Air Force engine contracts, both houses made whopping reductions in the budget request for Air Force fighters, without substantially reducing the number of planes paid for.

The budget had requested 48 F-15s and 150 smaller F-16s for a combined total of $4.48 billion. The House approved 40 F-15s and 150 F-16s for $4 billion; the Senate backed 42 F-15s and 150 F-16s for $4.3 billion, with various funding transfers accounting for much of the discrepancy between the two bodies.

Similar minor issues accounted for the small changes made in the request for combat planes for Navy aircraft carriers. Both houses approved the requested number:

• 24 F-14 fighters, budgeted and approved by the House for $787 million, but funded by the Senate at $742 million.

• 84 smaller F-18s, designed to double as fighters and light bombers. The budget and the Senate put their price at $2.35 billion; the House at $2.26 billion.

• Six A-6E medium bombers packed with electronic gear to find ground targets at night or in bad weather. The budget was $215 million, the House appropriation $199 million, the Senate figure $198 million.

• 32 AV-8B Harriers, light bombers used by the Marine Corps with swiveling jet nozzles that permit vertical take-offs and landings. Of the $742 million requested, $736 million was approved by the House and $737 million by the Senate.

The Senate Appropriations Committee also lauded the Navy and Air Force for planning to improve current combat types rather than developing new planes for service in the 1990s. Both houses added $70 million to the budget to develop an updated A-6E with new engines and electronics. The Senate also added $15 million to give F-18s some electronic equipment like that used by the larger A-6Es to find targets at night.

The Senate also added $74 million to test more power-

Funding for Major Defense Programs, Fiscal 1985

Following is a comparison of the amounts Congress authorized and appropriated for major defense programs in fiscal 1985. Amounts for weapons procurement included some funds for components of items to be bought in future budgets.

(amounts in millions of dollars)

	Reagan Request		Enacted Authorization (HR 5167)		Enacted Appropriation (H J Res 648)	
	Number	Amount	Number	Amount	Number	Amount
Strategic Weapons						
MX missile	40	$2,939	21	$2,352	21	$2,352[1]
B-1 bomber	34	7,103	34	7,103	34	7,071
Trident submarine	1	1,755	1	1,706	1	1,748
Trident II missile R&D		2,091		2,075		2,063
Strategic defense initiative ("star wars")		1,777		1,527		1,400
Intermediate-Range Missiles						
Pershing II missile	93	456	70	375	70	370
Ground-launched cruise missile (GLCM)	120	571	120	571	120	569
Ground Combat						
M-1 tank	720	1,759	840	1,702	840	1,859
Bradley troop carrier	710	1,056	680	992	680	962
Apache anti-tank helicopter	144	1,290	144	1,290	144	1,247
'Deep Strike' weapons (JTACMS and JSTARS)		318		234		113
Sergeant York anti-aircraft gun (DIVAD)	132	529	117	449	0	100
Patriot anti-aircraft missile	585	1,096	440	976	440	976
Naval Warfare						
Aircraft carrier rebuilding	1	764	1	764	1	714
Battleship modernization	1	423	1	0[2]	1	0[2]
Aegis cruiser	3	3,150	3	3,150	3	2,985
Aegis destroyer (DDG-51)	1	1,173	1	1,174	1	1,050
Sub-hunting submarine	4	2,880	4	2,880	4	2,665
Anti-submarine helicopters (LAMPS I and LAMPS III)	24	452	30	524	30	499
Tactical Air Combat						
F-15 fighter	48	2,053	42	1,953	42	1,955
F-16 fighter	150	3,748	150	3,119	150	3,033
F-14 carrier fighter	24	977	24	968	24	956
F-18 carrier fighter	84	2,686	84	2,626	84	2,501
A-6E carrier bomber	6	215	6	215	6	214
AV-8B vertical takeoff bomber	32	823	32	807	32	797
Airlift and Sealift						
LSD amphibious ship	2	490	2	490	2	490
purchase of commercial ships for reserve cargo fleet		31		31		31
C-5 transport plane	10	2,099	8	1,782	8	1,682
KC-10 tanker-cargo plane	8	647	8	566	8	565
C-17 cargo plane R&D		129		129		123

[1] MX production funds included $852 million in new appropriations and $1.5 billion in unspent funds from earlier years.

[2] Renovation of the battleship *Missouri* was to be paid for entirely from defense funds appropriated in earlier years but not spent.

ful versions of the two jet engines powering Air Force fighters and $12 million to develop a larger version of the F-16 using one of those modified engines.

Aerial Missiles. The budget requested $407 million for 400 of the hundred-mile-range Phoenix missiles carried by the Navy's F-14 fighters. Both houses approved only 265 missiles ($310 million in the House; $317 million in the Senate). The committees observed that the Navy had halted Phoenix production and was looking for a second contractor to make future Phoenix contracts competitive.

Both houses cited technical problems besetting the AMRAAM missile and scaled back from 174 to 20 the number funded. This radar-guided weapon, with a range of several tens of miles, would be the first missile that could be used by F-16 fighters at night or in bad weather. The $348 million budget request was trimmed to $74 million in the House and $73 million in the Senate.

Largely because of the slippage in AMRAAM funding, the Senate increased from the 1,250 budgeted (for $258 million) to 2,020 (for $388 million) the number of Sparrow radar-guided missiles that AMRAAM was intended to replace. The House committee warned that increasing the number of Sparrows would reduce the number of AMRAAMs ultimately produced, thus making it harder to keep the new missile's price down through competitive bidding.

Both houses approved the 1,000 short-range Sidewinder missiles requested, with the House trimming $10 million from the $69 million budgeted.

Naval Warfare

Both houses approved all of the major combat vessels requested by the Navy. There were, however, minor disagreements over funding adjustments, including reductions of several hundred million dollars in the January budget request.

The $423 million requested to modernize the battleship *Missouri* no longer was needed, since the money was available from surplus funds appropriated for shipbuilding in earlier years but not spent.

To rebuild the 25-year-old aircraft carrier *Independence*, the $583 million requested was approved. The Senate trimmed $50 million from the $181 million requested for equipment that would be used in the future overhaul of the carrier *Kitty Hawk*.

Approved as requested was $532 million for 180 Tomahawk, long-range cruise missiles that would be used to arm battleships and most modern cruisers and destroyers. The House bill included a prohibition on deployment of the nuclear-armed version of Tomahawk, but that was dropped in conference.

Both houses approved three cruisers and the first of a new class of destroyers, all equipped with the Aegis antimissile defense system. But their assumptions about how much could safely be trimmed from the $4.3 billion budgeted for those ships differed to the tune of some $800 million.

The $3.1 billion budgeted for the cruisers was trimmed $207 million by the Senate and $326 million by the House. The Senate approved the entire $1.2 billion budgeted for the destroyer. However, the House insisted that the ship could be built for $940 million and that only $490 million of that amount was needed in new appropriations, with the remaining $450 million coming from unspent funds from prior years.

The positions of the two houses were reversed in the case of the four sub-hunting submarines for which the administration requested $2.3 billion. In this instance, the Senate made the more optimistic assumption about how much money would be left over from earlier budgets. The Senate cut $450 million from the request, arguing that $290 million of the amount could be made up from prior appropriations. The House cut $178 million and transferred to the account $50 million from earlier budgets.

Citing projected savings from a more rapid production rate, both houses increased the number of LAMPS III anti-submarine helicopters — the type carried by most modern warships — from the 18 budgeted ($333 million) to 24 ($375 million). Both approved the request for six smaller LAMPS I helicopters used by older anti-submarine ships. The House added $3 million and the Senate $10 million to test installation of a more powerful engine in the LAMPS I.

Moving the Forces Abroad

Both houses approved the same production rates for large, long-range cargo planes, but differed over money.

For eight more of the huge C-5s, the Senate approved $1.45 billion and the House $1.36 billion. The budget requested 10 planes for $1.77 billion. Part of the larger House reduction reflected the House Appropriations Committee's complaint that the C-5 and several other Air Force plane requests included too much money to pay for changes in the design of the airplane.

Eight KC-10 tanker planes — versions of the DC-10 jetliner intended to refuel fighters and cargo planes in mid-flight — had been requested for $243 million. The House pared the appropriation to $186 million, the Senate to $190 million.

The $129 million request to continue development of the C-17 transport, intended to carry tanks and other heavy equipment to small, primitive airstrips, had been cut to $123 million in May. Both houses approved the lower level.

The House added $100 million to the $129 million request, approved by the Senate, for so-called Civil Reserve Air Fleet (CRAF) modifications. These changes would permit civilian jetliners to be quickly converted to haul military cargo.

Sealift. The House approved $15 million of the $31 million requested by Reagan — and approved by the Senate — to continue buying existing commercial ships to enlarge the fleet of cargo vessels the Navy keeps in reserve, but ready to sail on short notice. Unspent funds from earlier budgets were being allocated to the program, according to the House committee.

Both houses added $7.7 million to the Navy's operations account because the ready reserve cargo fleet was expanding more rapidly than had been foreseen toward the goal of 77 ships.

Also moving more rapidly than the budget had assumed was the conversion of commercial ships to serve as floating storage depots that could haul the weapons and supplies of Marine Corps units to potential trouble spots. Four more of these ships would be ready for service in fiscal 1985 than had been budgeted, so both houses added $27 million to pay for loading them.

Overseas Storage. Both bills reiterated the current law limiting the storage of tanks, trucks and other heavy Army equipment in so-called POMCUS depots in Europe. The point of the program was to let reinforcements be flown quickly from the United States aboard commandeered airliners in case war threatened, thus saving the weeks it would take to ship the heavy equipment by sea.

With four divisions' worth of equipment already in POMCUS storage, the two Appropriations committees had resisted efforts to send two more divisions' worth to Europe. The Air Force and Marine Corps bought extra equipment to pre-position in areas of likely deployment, but the Army drew its POMCUS stocks from U.S.-based forces — including politically influential reserve and National Guard units. The Appropriations panels complained that this inhibited training by home-based units and rendered them useless in any region other than in Europe.

Under the limitation imposed the previous year and reaffirmed in the fiscal 1985 bills, the POMCUS program could not be expanded beyond four divisions' worth if it would result in active-duty forces' having less than 70 percent of their regular equipment stocks or if reserve forces would have less than 50 percent of their authorized equipment.

Operations and Readiness

The January request for $80.9 billion in operations and maintenance funds was cut $4.3 billion by the House and $2.7 billion by the Senate.

However, in each case, the reduction included more than $2 billion in what amounted to fact-of-life changes in the cost of Pentagon operations: lower-than-budgeted prices for fuel and other supplies and the continued strengthening of the dollar against foreign currencies.

Reflecting the strong political support for increasing the "readiness" of U.S. forces, both houses added funds to the budget for maintenance-related projects.

The House gave the Army an additional $300 million to boost its readiness in the near-term, of which $50 million was earmarked to hike the number of hours Army pilots would fly each month. House Appropriations complained that the 9.5 hours per month averaged by Army pilots was less than half the flying time of Navy and Air Force pilots.

The Senate also added $50 million to boost Army flying time. It also added $15 million to reduce the backlog of Army equipment overdue for scheduled maintenance.

The House assumed that the Navy could save $100 million in carrying out its $2.8 billion program to overhaul nearly 60 ships. But it also rejected an administration proposal in May to defer the overhaul of two nuclear-powered ships for a savings of $320 million. And it added $71 million to the overhaul schedule of two amphibious landing ships.

The Senate cut $88 million from the request, but also turned down the proposed $320 million reduction.

Personnel Policies

Both houses approved only part of the proposed increase of nearly 30,000 in the number of active-duty military personnel (which would bring the services' total to 2,165,800 members). The House reduced the proposed total by 16,400 members ($218 million), the Senate by 10,260 ($189 million).

Both also sliced the $612 million request for re-enlistment bonuses. Complaining that the Army and Navy were overlooking cheaper ways to fill critical job specialties, the House cut $59 million and the Senate $61 million from their requests.

The nearly $1.1 billion requested for the so-called variable housing allowance (VHA) also was whacked by both houses. The allowance was created in 1981 to help low-paid personnel in case they were stationed in areas with high housing costs. The Senate Appropriations Committee had been particularly critical of the program's administration, charging that it had become a general supplement to military pay.

In its report on S 3026, the Senate panel estimated that 97-99 percent of all domestically stationed military personnel living outside of military bases received VHA payments, in addition to the housing allowance that long has been a part of military pay.

The House cut $116 million from the request, the Senate $156 million.

Troops in Europe. The Senate bill reflected Senate Appropriations' two-year-old campaign to block increases in the number of U.S. troops in Europe unless other NATO members paid more of the cost of the alliance's defense. The Senate bill barred an increase in the number of Air Force personnel in Europe above the current ceiling of 89,900 and cut $13.5 million from the budget for personnel transfers.

Preparing the Reserves for Combat

As usual, both the House and Senate added funds to the defense appropriations measure to beef up the reserve and National Guard forces. The House added $783 million, the Senate $918 million.

The politically influential reserve community always had been able to count on congressional largess. But in recent years, the Pentagon appeared to have taken the reserves more seriously in planning wartime assignments. This fact, and budgetary constraints on the size of the active-duty military, had won broad political support for modernizing the reserves' combat gear and giving them more realistic training.

Major additions by the House included $300 million for 16 C-130 transport planes, $73 million to replace the engines on reserve-operated tanker planes, $68 million to refurbish F-14 fighters that would be assigned to Naval Reserve squadrons and $60 million to equip attack helicopters with anti-tank missiles.

The Senate added 10 C-130s ($179 million) and only half as much to modify attack helicopters ($30 million). But it also added $431 million to be used at the discretion of reserve and Guard commanders for equipment that would improve their combat readiness.

Conference Action

Both the Senate and House versions of the defense appropriations bill had drawn on prior-year funds to pay part of the cost of various projects in the fiscal 1985 budget. For example, the House bill provided $940 million (of $1.2 billion requested) for a new Navy destroyer, but appropriated only $490 million in new funds: the remaining $450 million would be unspent, prior-year money, the House Appropriations Committee decreed.

By shifting all of the unspent prior-year money into the MX account — and funding all other programs with new appropriations — the conferees were able to blur the lines of a major disagreement. According to one source, Joseph P. Addabbo, D-N.Y., chairman of the House Appropriations Subcommittee on Defense, wanted to count against the $292.9 billion ceiling any prior-year funds used to pay for fiscal 1985 programs. His Senate counterpart, Ted Stevens, R-Alaska, insisted that only new appropriations be counted toward the ceiling.

Since the $1.5 billion in MX funds would not be available to the Pentagon unless Congress approved them in 1985, conferees agreed that the prior-year funds earmarked for that purpose — the only prior-year funds used in the conference report (H Rept 98-1159) — would not be counted as part of the continuing resolution.

Other Nuclear Warfare

The House had voted to cut $431 million from President Reagan's $7.7 billion request to buy 34 B-1 bombers and associated parts. The continuing resolution conferees rejected most of that cutback.

Nearly half of the House reduction came from the request for so-called "management reserves" — contingency funds to cover unforeseen problems. The conferees approved the reserves requested for the B-1, but insisted that those funds be accounted for at year's end.

Of the total House cut, the conferees approved a small part: $67.2 million, of which $31.6 million had been earmarked for a new missile-launcher for the B-1's bomb bay.

The same missile-launcher accounted for $80 million of the $108 million cut by conferees from the president's $574 million request for modernization of existing B-52 bombers. According to the conference report, the $80 million was unnecessary since tests of the new launcher would not be completed until mid-1986.

To replace the engines on 43 tanker planes used to refuel bombers in midair, the conferees approved the $826 million recommended by the House. The Senate had trimmed the appropriation by $89.3 million, arguing that a like amount of prior-year money could be used to make up the difference.

Anti-Satellite Missile. Opponents of the anti-satellite (ASAT) missile decided to try limiting tests of the weapon rather than trying to block its production.

That strategy's partial success was embodied in a conference agreement that barred until March 1985 any ASAT tests against a target in space and allowed only three such tests for the rest of fiscal 1985.

Both houses had approved the $65.2 million requested to begin full-scale ASAT production.

However, the House denied an additional $38.7 million scattered through various accounts to prepare for continued ASAT production and eventual deployment. The Senate had approved this request.

The House approved $157.4 million of the $195.5 million request for research and development associated with ASAT. The Senate had approved the entire request.

In each case, the two houses split the difference, approving $18.5 million for procurement and $170.4 million for research and development related to ASAT.

Ground Combat

Both houses had increased the number of M-1 tanks from the 720 in the budget to 840, while reducing the appropriation of new money from $1.47 billion to less than $1.39 billion. More than $170 million in unspent prior-year money made up the difference, in each case. Because the conferees decided to recycle unspent money from prior-year appropriations only into the MX missile account, they had to appropriate $1.54 billion to pay for the 840 tanks.

The conferees trimmed $40 million from the $1.2 billion request — approved by both houses — for 144 Apache tank-hunting helicopters.

For 655 Bradley armored troop carriers, the conferees approved $937 million. In May, the administration had trimmed its request for 710 Bradleys ($997 million) to 655

($952 million), the amount approved by the Senate.

The administration's May budget revision included a proposal to buy only 6,000 TOW anti-tank guided missiles, instead of the 18,000 requested in January. The conferees agreed, appropriating $132 million, instead of the original $240 million request.

DIVAD Gun. The conferees agreed to Defense Secretary Weinberger's Sept. 29 request that no DIVAD anti-aircraft guns be purchased in fiscal 1985, pending further tests of the weapon. The $516 million requested for 132 of the guns was trimmed to $100 million to be used only to keep the DIVAD production line intact, in case further production was approved in fiscal 1986.

The $100 million could not be spent until 30 days after Congress had received a report on realistic tests of the DIVAD.

According to the Army, reports of the DIVAD's failure in past tests were misleading: The gun was developed — with full congressional approval — under a schedule that called for taking risks and cutting corners in order to save time. Shortcomings revealed by tests were being remedied, Army officials insisted.

Nevertheless, the appropriations conferees expressed their "strong concern" over past DIVAD tests and warned the Army that they would "take an avid interest in the conduct and evaluation of forthcoming tests."

Tactical Air Combat

Both defense appropriations bills had trimmed several hundred million dollars from the January budget request for Air Force fighter planes. The cut reflected the choice of a new engine for the F-16, not any change in the number of planes bought.

The combat airplane decisions facing conferees involved only modest amounts — compared with sums being appropriated — and turned mostly on financial assumptions. The number of planes was not a major issue.

The amounts agreed to for the principal types of combat aircraft:

- $1.8 billion for 42 Air Force F-15s.
- $2.4 billion for 150 smaller Air Force F-16s.
- $771 million for 24 F-14 Navy fighters.
- $2.3 billion for 84 Navy F-18s, which double as fighters and small bombers.

The conferees compromised on $314 million to build more of the 100-mile-range Phoenix missiles used by the Navy's F-14s. In fiscal 1984, Congress had appropriated $30 million to let Hughes Aircraft Corp., which builds the Phoenix, increase its production rate from 40 missiles per month to 55. But the conferees on the 1985 resolution told the Navy to use the $30 million to enable another contractor to set up a competing Phoenix production line.

Naval Warfare

Differences over appropriations for major warships also had turned largely on budgeting techniques — including the use of prior-year funds — rather than on issues of military policy.

The conferees agreed on $2.1 billion for three, nuclear-powered sub-hunting submarines, $2.9 billion for three cruisers equipped with the Aegis anti-missile defense system and $1.05 billion for the first of a new class of destroyers equipped with a smaller version of Aegis.

The House Appropriations Committee earlier had lauded the Navy for driving down warship prices through the use of competitive bidding for ship contracts. In fiscal

1984, the service saved a total of $228 million on three cruisers and $108 million on three submarines, according to the panel.

The conferees ordered the Navy to extend its use of competitive bidding by finding manufacturers to bid against the current builders of certain equipment on the cruisers and destroyers. A case in point was the complex and expensive Aegis radar system on the cruisers, which accounted for about half the cost of those ships.

They also insisted that the Navy prepare a second shipyard to bid for future destroyer contracts against whichever yard won the contract for the first destroyer.

Airlift and Sealift

On the two largest cargo plane projects, conferees had only to resolve relatively minor budget questions. They approved $1.39 billion for eight huge C-5 transports and $375 million toward future C-5 purchases. For eight KC-10 midair refueling tankers, $190 million was appropriated along with $375 million for parts to be used in similar planes bought with future budgets.

For the Civil Reserve Air Fleet — a program to modify civilian jetliners so they could be easily converted to haul military cargo in wartime — $129 million was approved, as requested. But the conferees also transferred to that program $145 million that Congress had added to the fiscal 1983 budget, over strenuous Air Force objections, to buy three Boeing 747 cargo planes.

The earlier congressional initiative was to placate members who wanted the Air Force to buy a fleet of 747s instead of resuming production of Lockheed-built C-5s. Stuck with the Boeings, the Air Force announced they would be assigned to a reserve unit in New York. But early in 1984, the service proposed instead to cancel the Boeing purchase and give C-5s to the New York reservists.

Personnel Costs

The companion authorization bill (HR 5167) had trimmed the active-duty manpower ceiling to 2,152,470, which was 13,330 less than the budget request. The conferees translated this into a reduction of $209 million in the military personnel account and $26 million in the operations and maintenance account.

The conferees also trimmed $14.5 million from Air Force travel costs, in keeping with the Senate's opposition to increasing the number of Air Force personnel stationed in Europe.

A total of $156 million was trimmed from the so-called "variable housing allowance," paid to personnel who lived off military bases. The congressional defense committees had complained that the services had been much too generous in paying a benefit that was intended to cover personnel assigned to areas with especially high living costs.

Principally because of reserve strength limits set in the authorization bill, the conferees cut $241 million from the budget request for reserve personnel costs. But they retained many of the initiatives by which each house had added funds to the bill to beef up the reserve and National Guard forces. Among these initiatives was a pool of $380 million parceled out among the reserve branches to use at their discretion to buy equipment that would improve their combat readiness. The Senate had added $431 million for this purpose.

Maintenance and Readiness

The $98.6 billion request for operations and mainte-

nance funds was cut by $3.4 billion, much of which would come from price decreases rather than any reduction in Pentagon programs.

For instance, according to the conference report, declining fuel prices accounted for $1.3 billion of the cutback and a drop in the price of various other supplies accounted for nearly $500 million more of the reduction.

Even counting those essentially bookkeeping reductions, operations and maintenance was reduced far less, proportionally, than the $107.6 billion procurement request, which was cut by $10.5 billion.

That reflected the political popularity of funding for "combat readiness," which also was evident in certain congressional additions to the appropriations measure.

The Army was the big winner in this department with conferees approving the following increases to the Army budget:

● $300 million to be used at the Army's discretion for readiness improvement, a proposal incorporated into the House bill.

● $118 million to increase the number of hours Army pilots fly each month (including $68 million in additional spare parts), another House idea.

● $402 million to increase stockpiles of ammunition for wartime use, similar to a provision of the Senate bill. This increase brought the Army ammunition appropriation to $2.65 billion, which was $152 million over the budget request. ∎

Military Construction

Congress voted to give the Defense Department $8.4 billion for its construction projects in fiscal 1985. This just about split the difference between the $8.26 billion that the House had appropriated and the $8.54 billion appropriated by the Senate. President Reagan had requested $10.3 billion.

The House passed its version of the military construction spending bill (HR 5898) June 28. But the Senate's version was one of the appropriations packages that was incorporated into an omnibus spending resolution (H J Res 648 — PL 98-473), which cleared Congress on Oct. 11. *(Continuing resolution, p. 444)*

A companion military construction authorization bill (HR 5604 — PL 98-407) cleared Congress Aug. 9. It contained authorizations totaling $9.13 billion, compared with the president's request of $10.5 billion. *(Story, p. 64)*

NATO Burden-Sharing

An issue in the military construction bills, as it had been since 1977, was congressional dissatisfaction with burden-sharing between the United States and its chief allies in Western Europe and Japan. Allies were not paying a fair share of the cost, some members complained, and the administration was not trying hard enough to make them pay more. *(1983 Almanac p. 469)*

Citing the loss of U.S. jobs to foreign manufacturers, many members complained that allied economies — particularly Japan's — had a competitive edge because of their much lower defense expenditures.

Governments in those countries and many Pentagon officials, however, contended that critics were ignoring many of the burdens — such as land costs and utilities — borne by the allies in the name of the common defense.

NATO's 1978 agreement to seek annual defense budget increases, after inflation, of 3 percent exacerbated the burden-sharing issue on Capitol Hill.

It provided a simple benchmark against which most NATO members had fallen short in most years, except for the United States.

With Congress confronting the options of higher taxes, higher deficits, stark reductions in domestic programs or a slowdown in Reagan's proposed defense buildup, the argument that allies should do more offered a way for members to seek lower defense spending without seeming to endorse a weaker overall military position.

Just how far congressional sentiment had come was underscored June 20, when Sen. Sam Nunn, D-Ga., offered an amendment to the defense authorization bill that would have trimmed U.S. troops in Europe by almost 30 percent unless the other NATO members began following through on certain agreed-to defense improvements. The amendment was rejected 55-41, but only after a very heavy lobbying effort by the White House. *(Vote 149, p. 27-S; story, p. 37)*

House Action

Congressional frustration over the burden-sharing issue was underscored in the fiscal 1985 military construction appropriations bill passed by the House June 28. Most of the $2 billion in cuts the House bill made in Reagan's request were imposed by the House Appropriations Committee, and at least $140 million in cuts came from projects the panel said should be paid for by U.S. allies.

Committee Report

In its report on the appropriations bill (H Rept 98-850), filed June 20, the House Appropriations Committee slammed the Pentagon for "going it alone" to meet military threats, regardless of whether U.S. allies with equal or greater immediate stakes at issue were willing to do more.

The committee said unilateral U.S. efforts have a pernicious side effect. "As the trend toward U.S. willingness to proceed unilaterally continues, our allies have shown less and less willingness to contribute a fair share."

Projects in Europe that the committee insisted should be paid for by the NATO alliance (or by the country hosting the facilities) included:

- $38 million for improvements to an Army airfield at Ansbach, West Germany.
- $29 million to support equipment of Army units in West Germany with the DIVAD anti-aircraft tank.
- $13 million for improvements to existing facilities so Air Force units could continue operating in the event of attack by chemical weapons.

Airbase Improvements. The panel refused to provide U.S. funds to build ammunition and fuel dumps and maintenance shops at non-U.S. airbases in Europe that would be used by the 1,500 U.S. fighter planes scheduled to fly to the continent as reinforcements in the first 10 days of a NATO mobilization.

Improvement of these so-called "co-located operating bases," or COBs, for reinforcing U.S. squadrons was one goal of Sen. Nunn's amendment to the defense authorization bill.

The committee dropped from the bill $16.7 million for COB improvements in Britain and $24.5 million earmarked for such facilities at a single airfield in Turkey.

In each case, the panel insisted that NATO pay for the projects through its Infrastructure fund — the common fund for projects of mutual benefit.

Asian Allies. The committee also demanded that U.S. allies outside NATO pay for some U.S. facilities that would improve their defenses. The committee refused $15.8 million for a fuel storage facility in South Korea and $7.2 million for facilities at Misawa airfield in Japan, which was to house U.S. F-16 fighter planes.

The panel also rejected $9.3 million requested for two schools for the children of U.S. military personnel stationed in Japan, noting that Japan previously had paid for such schools.

Honduras Facilities. The panel dropped $8.7 million requested for three projects in Honduras, on grounds they had not been authorized in HR 5604. *(Honduras bases, p. 84)*

It also added to the bill a provision requiring the secretary of defense to inform the Appropriations Committees of any military exercise in which more than $100,000 was expected to be spent on construction efforts, whether they were intended to be temporary or not.

The committee complained that it had not been informed of construction plans associated with prior U.S. training exercises in Honduras.

Floor Action

The House passed the appropriations bill by a 347-52 vote shortly after midnight on June 28. *(Vote 255, p. 80-H)*

It first adopted 218-180 an amendment by James F. McNulty Jr., D-Ariz., that cut the bill by $25 million. According to McNulty, this was the amount that could be saved if the Pentagon contracted for buildings using performance standards — defining what a building should do — rather than standards defining how a building should be built. *(Vote 254, p. 80-H)*

Senate Committee Action

The Senate Appropriations Committee reported its version of the military construction spending bill July 26 (S Rept 98-567).

The Senate committee's version of the bill reflected concern that the House went too far in denying funds for overseas projects in hopes that U.S. allies would pay instead.

Compared with Reagan's budget request for construction, the Senate panel's version of the bill would have trimmed $1.8 billion — $200 million less than was cut by the House.

Of the $2 billion reduction made by the House, at least $140 million came from projects that the House Appropriations Committee had argued should be paid for by allies who would reap security benefits.

In its report, the Senate committee echoed the House panel's complaint that U.S. allies were not paying a fair share of the cost of common defense.

However, the Senate committee restored $114 million of the House cuts. Allied funding for some of the disputed projects was infeasible for various reasons, the panel said. Other projects were too vital to let them become hostage to dickering among allies, it maintained.

In its report on HR 5898, the Senate Appropriations panel expressed "deep concern that many of our allies are not contributing to defense initiatives that provide for mutual security."

It included in the bill a provision expressing the sense

Military Construction Appropriations, Fiscal 1985

Following are the amounts requested by President Reagan and appropriated by the fiscal 1985 omnibus continuing resolution (H J Res 648 — PL 98-473) for military construction projects. *(Fiscal 1984 amounts, 1983 Almanac p. 470)*

	Administration Request	House-Passed	Senate-Passed	Final Appropriation
	(in thousands of dollars)			
Army	$1,900,000	$1,606,350	$1,640,177	$1,593,137
Navy	1,945,300	1,449,442	1,551,742	1,534,592
Air Force	2,165,400	1,543,225	1,635,818	1,572,655
Defense Agencies	459,500	309,108	351,010	302,198
NATO Infrastructure	296,700	131,700	107,200	107,200
Guard and Reserve	390,800	402,223	406,600	407,709
Family Housing	3,160,500 [1]	2,841,273 [1]	2,843,417 [1]	2,887,715 [1]
Miscellaneous	—	−24,850	—	—
Total	**$10,318,200**	**$8,258,471**	**$8,535,964**	**$8,405,206**

[1] *Does not include $71,272,000 requested and appropriated without change for application to debt reduction.*

of Congress that allies should follow through on the 1978 agreement to boost defense budgets at an annual rate of 3 percent.

NATO Construction

Among the nearly $2 billion worth of projects approved for Europe, the Senate committee included the following funds that had been denied by the House:

● $48.51 million for facilities in Ansbach, West Germany, including $31 million to house Apache tank-hunting helicopters that were being added to the U.S. force there. The House Appropriations Committee had insisted that NATO should pay for the helicopter installations. The Senate panel agreed but pointed out that such facilities did not meet current guidelines for NATO funding.

● $29.1 million for barracks, a maintenance shop and headquarters building in Giessen, West Germany, to be used in connection with deployment of the DIVAD anti-aircraft tank. A plan to move several large Army units from their quarters near the Rhine to Giessen — much closer to the defensive positions the units would occupy in a war — had stalled. Congress had insisted that the German government pay for the new installations. The Senate committee said that the buildings it funded would be needed whether or not the restationing plan was implemented.

● $13.4 million to protect various Air Force facilities against attack by chemical weapons. Under NATO rules, these projects were not eligible for funding by the alliance.

● $24.5 million to improve a Turkish airfield at Mus, so it could be used by U.S. units in case of war. Though NATO planned to pay for the project, the panel agreed with the Pentagon that it was needed so urgently that the United States needed to pay for it immediately and be reimbursed later by the alliance. The House had rejected this argument.

The Senate "paid" for the Mus project by deducting $24.5 million from the $131.7 million requested in the Pentagon's revised budget for the annual U.S. contribution to NATO's so-called Infrastructure fund — the alliance's pool for funding construction projects.

Asian Allies

The committee also approved $15.8 million for underground fuel storage tanks in South Korea; the House had wanted the Korean government to pay for them. The Senate panel said that Korea already contributed "substantially" to the cost of U.S. facilities in the country and that the tanks were urgently needed.

In addition, the panel approved the entire $18 million requested to build quarters for a U.S. squadron of F-16 jet fighters at Japan's Misawa air base. The House had insisted that Japan build fuel storage tanks and runway aprons for which $7.2 million was requested.

However, the Senate panel said Japan already was kicking in its fair share of the cost of basing the U.S. planes at Misawa.

Oman Reduction

However, the Senate committee agreed with the House to deny a $37.9 million request for Air Force facilities in Oman, at the mouth of the Persian Gulf. Some of the proposed items — a laundry, for example — seemed superfluous at a base that would be occupied only if U.S. forces were dispatched to war in the region, the committee said.

Other items in the package — including bombproof airplane hangars — should be paid for either by NATO or by Oman, which would have the use of them unless U.S. forces arrive, according to the panel.

Conference Action

The Senate committee's bill was incorporated into the omnibus continuing resolution, and final provisions on military construction were negotiated by House-Senate conferees on the spending resolution.

The conference report (H Rept 98-1159) on the continuing resolution, which cleared Congress Oct. 11, funded some, but not all of the major construction projects in NATO and Japan that had become issues in the 1985 burden-sharing fight.

Conferees approved $19 million for a maintenance building in Ansbach, West Germany, saying it was urgently needed. But they denied $12 million the administration had requested for an aircraft parking apron at Ansbach. The conferees argued that the parking apron could await expected funding by the alliance.

They refused the $13 million requested to buy an unused rug factory in Rheinburg, West Germany, for conversion to a supply headquarters. The Pentagon should approach "the highest level" of the West German government to seek German funding, they said.

The conferees also dropped the embargo they had placed on spending $23.5 million appropriated in 1982 for projects at Vilseck, West Germany. The projects were part of the Army's so-called "master restationing plan" under which three U.S. battalions in West Germany would be moved to new facilities 100 miles closer to the positions they were assigned to defend in case of Soviet attack.

Congress had insisted that the West German government pay for most of the new construction that would be involved, arguing that the move would leave West Germany better defended. The conferees said that the Vilseck projects were needed regardless of the restationing plan's fate, to accommodate new equipment being assigned to the Army in Europe. A go-ahead for these facilities marked no retreat from their insistence that West Germany pay for any wholesale troop shift, they insisted.

NATO should provide the $24.5 million requested to improve an air base in Turkey that would be used by U.S. fighters in time of war, the conferees said. But they agreed to provide $8.5 million of $13.4 million requested to protect several facilities in Europe against chemical attack.

For a fuel storage dump at Japan's Misawa air base, site of a planned wing of U.S. F-16 fighter planes, $4.4 million was approved. But the conferees insisted that under the U.S.-Japan cost-sharing arrangement for Misawa, the host country would make improvements in airport parking pavements for which $2.8 million had been requested.

On the other hand, a $15.8 million request to build a fuel storage tank in Korea was turned down. The Pentagon was told to seek Korean funding for the work.

MX Missile Program

Of the $29.3 million Reagan had requested for construction related to MX missile deployment at Warren Air Force Base near Cheyenne, Wyo., the conference committee approved $16.6 million. This would be enough to deploy the first 10 MXs, according to the committee.

Conferees deferred the $5.9 million the Senate added to the budget for community impact assistance to the Warren area. They wanted a formal request from the executive branch before appropriating the funds.

Construction related to another controversial weapon — the anti-satellite (ASAT) missile — also was placed on hold. The Air Force had requested $16.5 million for facilities at Langley Air Force Base near Newport News, Va., where the weapons first would be deployed. ∎

Transportation Funding Set at $11.6 Billion

Funding of $11.6 billion for the Department of Transportation (DOT) and related agencies for fiscal 1985 was included in the $470 billion continuing appropriations resolution signed by the president Oct. 12 (H J Res 648 — PL 98-473).

House and Senate Appropriations committees had approved separate transportation funding bills (HR 5921, S 2852), but both measures were threatened with vetoes because Reagan administration officials opposed "excesses" in various programs, particularly mass transit. The bills' totals, however, were slightly lower than the president's $11.8 billion request.

The continuing resolution provided $188.8 million less than the president had sought for transportation programs. The total was $503.3 million higher than fiscal 1984 funding.

The conference report on the resolution (H Rept 98-1159) was adopted by the House Oct. 10 and cleared by the Senate Oct. 11. *(Story, p. 444)*

Conferees had before them the Senate committee's appropriations bill and a new proposal from House members that called for funding at existing levels or at the amounts requested by President Reagan, whichever were lower. *(Chart, p. 412)*

The House committee bill had become snarled in a turf fight between the Appropriations and Public Works and Transportation committees that stymied further action. The House leadership was not able to arbitrate the dispute, and it became necessary to include funding for transportation programs in the continuing resolution.

Transportation Funding

Following are highlights for fiscal 1985 transportation funding:

● **Highway Programs.** A limit of $13.25 billion was set on contract obligations for highway development from the Highway Trust Fund, which was financed from taxes on fuel and vehicle parts.

The bill provided a ceiling of $126.5 million on obligations for grants from the trust fund for state and local highway safety programs.

● **Mass Transit.** The bill provided $2.4 billion for formula grants from the Highway Trust Fund to subsidize the construction and operation of local bus and railway systems. As in past years, Congress rejected the administration's attempt to end operating subsidies.

For discretionary grants to finance a variety of repair and expansion projects, the bill set a limit of $1.12 billion on obligations from the trust fund. It earmarked $422.5 million for new construction projects in 12 cities: Portland (light rail), $19 million; Seattle (bus tunnel) $20 million; Detroit (automated system) $5 million; Miami (rail construction and circulator) $49 million; Santa Clara (light rail) $64.8 million; Atlanta (rail construction) $95 million; Los Angeles (rail construction) $117.2 million; Houston (busways) $35 million; Jacksonville (people mover) $1.8 million; St. Louis (engineering) $10 million; Buffalo (light rail) $2.7 million; and San Diego (light rail) $3 million.

But the conference report noted that "the total cost of these projects far exceeds what can reasonably be expected to be available" in the long term. The report signaled Congress' intent to turn over more financial responsibility to state and local governments:

"The conferees expect the federal role in mass transit to shift increasingly to promoting and planning sound fixed guideway transit projects and to leveraging state, local and private resources to construct these projects. In this regard, it is essential that significant new non-federal financial sources be developed if the projects currently being planned are to be constructed."

The bill applauded recent efforts of the Urban Mass Transportation Administration to develop criteria for evaluating proposals for new systems.

Also, it required DOT to tell Congress in March 1985 whether it would be feasible to develop standards for reviewing requests for operating subsidies.

Such standards, the report said, should satisfy critics — like those in the administration — who opposed operating assistance for mass transit because the federal government had no control over local expenses and revenues.

● **Aviation.** The Federal Aviation Administration (FAA) received $4.4 billion in new budget authority. That included $1.4 billion from the Airport and Airway Trust Fund to update air traffic control operations, an 82.7 percent increase over fiscal 1984. The trust fund was supported by taxes on plane tickets and fuel.

Grants from the fund for local airport development were capped at $925 million. The administration and both committee bills had proposed $987 million.

Exemptions from federal standards for aircraft noise were granted for airports in Miami, Fla., and Bangor, Maine. Senators from the two states argued that the airports were frequented by foreign carriers that could not comply with standards due to take effect Jan. 1. Airport jobs would be lost without the exemptions, they said.

The continuing resolution prohibited the use of any funds to develop a rule reducing passenger traffic at busy Washington National Airport, a favorite with members of Congress because of its proximity to the Capitol.

● **Coast Guard.** New budget authority totaled $2.5 billion. For the first time, the transportation secretary was directed to demand warranties from contractors for major equipment purchases, a requirement that paralleled one imposed on the Defense Department in its fiscal 1984 appropriations. *(Story, p. 399)*

● **Railroads.** The bill provided $802.3 million for the Federal Railroad Administration (FRA), including $684 million for Amtrak, the federally subsidized passenger railroad.

Also, $27.8 million was allocated for improvements to the Northeast Corridor route between Washington, D.C., and Boston. The administration opposed funding for the corridor, which had received $2.2 billion, but House conferees had proposed $100 million and Senate conferees, $10 million.

● **Interstate Commerce Commission.** Congress adopted the Senate's lower figure of $48 million, but some members suggested a supplemental appropriation might be required later.

● **U.S. Railway Association.** This agency, which oversaw the federally subsidized freight railroad, Conrail, received $2.1 million.

House Committee Action

The House Appropriations Committee on June 7 approved $11.8 billion for transportation programs in fiscal 1985, or $851.6 million more than the current level. The bill was reported (HR 5921 — H Rept 98-859) June 22.

Though the total of the bill was $64,000 less than the administration's request, the bill faced a veto because of what budget director David A. Stockman called "excesses" in funding for individual programs, particularly mass transit.

"Due to the numerous problems in these areas, it would be difficult to recommend that [the president] sign the bill in its present form," Stockman said in a memo to the panel.

However, Lawrence Coughlin, R-Pa., ranking minority member of the Appropriations Subcommittee on Transportation, said changes in the Reagan budget were "within the right of the committee to make." Coughlin's district in suburban Philadelphia was heavily reliant on mass transit.

The bill, based on recommendations from a closed meeting of the transportation subcommittee May 15, included $11.2 billion for DOT and $621.1 million for related agencies.

Highlights included $2.4 billion for the Coast Guard but with a cut of nearly 800 personnel; a $13.3 billion cap on spending from the Highway Trust Fund for the Interstate Highway System and other roadway projects; $1.5 billion to continue modernization of the air traffic control system; a $2.55 billion cap on formula grants for mass transit construction and operations; and a $1.125 billion ceiling on grants from the Highway Trust Fund for mass transit capital expenses, including construction and new equipment.

Though the bill provided $11.8 billion for transportation programs in fiscal 1985, another $16.9 billion from highway, mass transit and aviation trust funds was available without congressional appropriation. Including those funds, the total program level for transportation was $28.7 billion.

Few Amendments

On June 6, most of the panel's discussion involved members' opposition to a provision of a separate highway funding bill (HR 5504). It would, they claimed, omit the Appropriations Committee from the process of determining which cities would receive funds to build new mass transit systems. The bill left the decision to the secretary of transportation, along with the House and Senate Public Works committees.

"This is not just a turf battle; this is bad public policy," Coughlin said.

(The House passed HR 5504 on June 7, with no debate on the controversial provision. *(Story, p. 290)*)

The committee also debated funding for the Washington, D.C., area's subway, "Metro." At issue was an amendment by Steny H. Hoyer, D-Md., to allow construction on any part of the unfinished 26 miles of the 101-mile system — even if the segment was not hooked to an operating leg.

Many members objected that Metro would build in outlying areas to be assured of money later for connections.

Fiscal 1985 Transportation Funds

Separate appropriations bills for the Department of Transportation and related agencies were reported by the House and Senate Appropriations committees (HR 5921 — H Rept 98-859; S 2852 — S Rept 98-561). However, neither bill reached the floor.

The conference committee on H J Res 648 considered the Senate committee's appropriations bill and a new proposal from the House members that called for funding at existing levels or at the amounts requested by the administration, whichever was lower.

	Budget Request	House Proposal	Senate Committee	Final Appropriation
Department of Transportation				
Office of the Secretary	$ 48,945,000	$ 46,153,000	$ 57,346,000	$ 55,700,000
Coast Guard	2,500,261,139	2,446,297,456	2,504,630,139	2,506,130,139
Federal Aviation Administration	4,697,635,500	3,648,409,000	4,498,431,500	4,373,431,500
Federal Highway Administration	40,391,000	44,520,000	88,716,000	89,466,000
National Highway Traffic Safety Administration	90,157,000	78,300,000	84,850,000	82,350,000
Federal Railroad Administration	756,752,000	871,752,000	800,486,000	802,286,000
Urban Mass Transportation Administration	2,965,787,000	2,962,592,200	2,975,700,000	3,031,500,000
Research and Special Programs Administration	18,623,000	18,623,000	20,394,000	18,900,000
Office of the Inspector General	27,306,000	26,795,000	27,956,000	27,900,000
Subtotal	11,145,857,639	10,143,441,656	11,058,509,639	10,987,663,639
Related Agencies				
Architectural and Transportation Barriers Compliance Board	2,000,000	1,900,000	2,000,000	2,000,000
National Transportation Safety Board	20,845,000	20,845,000	21,700,000	21,700,000
Civil Aeronautics Board	71,046,000	69,846,000	57,600,000	57,600,000
Interstate Commerce Commission	53,966,000	53,966,000	48,000,000	48,000,000
Panama Canal Commission	443,946,000	413,725,000	434,246,000	429,846,000
U.S. Railway Association	0	2,100,000	2,000,000	2,100,000
Washington Metropolitan Area Transit Authority	46,175,945	46,175,945	46,175,945	46,175,945
Subtotal	637,978,945	608,557,945	611,721,945	607,421,945
GRAND TOTAL	$11,783,836,584	$10,751,999,601	$11,670,231,584	$11,595,085,584

But Hoyer, whose district included planned routes, had lobbied fellow Democrats and won on a party-line 24-14 vote.

Major Provisions

For DOT, the bill included:

● **Office of the Secretary.** The bill increased the administration's request by $4.3 million, to $53.2 million, primarily for the transfer of some employees from the Civil Aeronautics Board (CAB) and the Research and Special Programs Administration. The two agencies were to be phased out in fiscal 1985.

The Democratic-controlled panel took several slaps at the Republican-headed department. The travel budget was cut by $200,000, and the report admonished the department "to exercise more prudence in approving overseas travel requests." A $500,000 cut was made "in response to the tardiness and quality of the reports" that the department made to the panel.

Also, the bill limited the department to 60 political employees — the 1980 level. The report criticized the department for increasing its political staff to 78 while reducing overall employment nearly 10 percent.

● **Coast Guard.** The bill provided $2.4 billion in new budget authority, $125.8 million less than the request and $79.7 million below the current level. Of the total, $1.8 billion was for operations, such as search and rescue efforts. That was $40.7 million above the request and $98.6 million more than the current figure. Also, the bill directed the secretary to issue regulations requiring warranties for major purchases.

The panel accepted the administration's plan to drop nearly 800 employees and provided for 37,202 military positions and 4,798 civilian jobs.

● **Federal Aviation Administration.** The FAA received $4.5 billion, $191.1 million under the request and $887.4 million above the current level.

The committee doubled the existing $750 million expenditure for facilities and equipment to $1.5 billion, as part of a long-term $9.1 billion effort to upgrade the national air traffic control system. The administration wanted nearly $1.7 billion.

For FAA operations, including air traffic control and oversight for travel safety, the bill provided $2.6 billion — $27.2 million less than requested and $122.6 million more than fiscal 1984. The funds included $1.5 million from the Airport and Airway Trust Fund.

The bill capped grants from the trust fund for airport planning and development at $987 million — the same as the request and $187 million above the fiscal 1984 funding. The committee said priority should go to 16 airports — most of them in districts of members from the Appropriations and Public Works committees.

● **Federal Highway Administration (FHWA).** The bill allowed $71.3 million for the FHWA — $60.9 million more than the administration's budget and $16.7 million more than the current figure.

Also, the bill set a $13.3 billion ceiling on spending from the Highway Trust Fund. That was $615 million less than the administration's proposal and $660 million more than the present ceiling.

The administration requested no funds for demonstration projects intended to reroute rail lines away from central cities, or to construct overpasses and underpasses. The bill raised the current $15 million appropriation to $48 million.

● **National Highway Traffic Safety Administration (NHTSA).** The committee approved $108.9 million for motor vehicle and driver safety programs — $11.3 million less than requested and $9.9 million above fiscal 1984. The total included $28 million for the Bureau of Motor Carrier Safety, which the panel wanted to transfer to NHTSA from the FHWA to decrease duplication in safety programs. The administration requested $30 million for the bureau in the FHWA budget.

Also, the bill set a cap of $110 million on grants from the trust fund for highway safety to state and local governments and of $44 million on grants for programs to discourage drunken driving.

The bill report scored NHTSA for not requiring that autos have pre-drilled holes suitable for installing tether straps for child-restraint seats. The committee wanted to withhold $10 million until a rule, which NHTSA had been considering for nearly four years, was issued.

● **Federal Railroad Administration.** The committee allowed $807.5 million — $50.7 million more than requested but $141.8 million below the current level.

The administration proposed to end funding to upgrade the Boston-to-Washington "Northeast Corridor." But the committee approved $54 million for the project under Amtrak's appropriation. The bill permitted $734 million for Amtrak, with an additional $4 million transferred from the Coast Guard for a bridge project. The administration proposed $680 million for Amtrak, which currently received $716.4 million.

● **Urban Mass Transportation Administration.** The committee approved $3.2 billion in new budget authority, $233.6 million more than the administration and $181.4 million more than at present.

The administration's top objection, of the 13 specified in Stockman's memo, was to the bill's $2.55 billion for mass transit formula grants — $160.5 million above the Reagan budget. The grants, which were funded through proceeds from increased gas taxes enacted in 1982, financed both construction of new mass transit projects and operations of existing systems. *(1982 Almanac p. 317)*

The administration opposed operating subsidies. But the committee, as in past years, rebuffed its efforts to limit such grants.

The administration also complained that a $1.125 billion cap on discretionary grants, which financed capital expenses for bus and rail systems, was $25 million too high.

Related Agencies

Proposals for related agencies included:

● **National Transportation Safety Board.** $21.7 million, or $855,000 more than the administration request and $842,000 above the current budget.

● **Civil Aeronautics Board.** $5.6 million for salaries and expenses, or $13.4 million less than requested.

● **Interstate Commerce Commission.** $54.5 million for salaries and expenses, or $584,000 above the request and $5.4 million less than current funding. Deregulation had decreased the agency's responsibilities, and thus its budget.

● **U.S. Railway Association.** $2.1 million to continue monitoring the Conrail system through fiscal 1985. The administration wanted no funds.

House Action Blocked

An old-fashioned turf fight to determine which House members set funding levels for transportation blocked action on the fiscal 1985 appropriations bill.

The House leadership tried and failed to mediate the dispute between James J. Howard, D-N.J., chairman of the Public Works and Transportation Committee, and members of the House Appropriations Committee.

Beginning in early June, Howard blocked a floor vote on the appropriations bill. He objected that the measure earmarked funds and set obligation ceilings for highway, mass transit and aviation programs, a job he said belonged to his committee, not to Appropriations.

But Appropriations Committee members, led by William Lehman, D-Fla., chairman of the Appropriations Subcommittee on Transportation, countered that they had followed the practice of the past eight years.

Howard complained that the bill was "so egregious" that it threatened "the integrity of the United States House of Representatives."

The complaint came in a July 26 letter to House members that was signed by Howard; Glenn M. Anderson, D-Calif., chairman of the Public Works Subcommittee on Surface Transportation; Gene Snyder, R-Ky., the committee's ranking minority member; and Bud Shuster, R-Pa., ranking minority member on the subcommittee.

They complained that the Rules Committee had granted a waiver of points of order against new authorizations contained in HR 5921. They urged defeat of the rule and the bill.

Appropriations Committee members likewise lobbied their colleagues for support.

Lehman and his subcommittee's ranking Republican, Coughlin, argued that of 20 items that the Public Works Committee objected to, only 11 were protected from points of order by the rule. Of the 11, they added, most were agreed to by Public Works subcommittee heads, or were identical to authorization bills already passed by the House.

The key to the dispute appeared to be the Appropriations Committee's treatment of Section 3 grants for mass transit. Each committee claimed authority to earmark funds and impose caps on obligations.

The Appropriations Committee had included a number of mass transit programs in HR 5921 that Howard said should be handled solely by his panel. The programs included rail modernization money for eight cities including Boston and New York, and rail and bus construction money for eight cities including Atlanta, Los Angeles and Portland, Ore.

The groundwork for the battle was laid in 1982, during House debate of the landmark Surface Transportation Assistance Act (PL 97-424), which raised gasoline taxes 5 cents a gallon, with 4 cents going to highway projects and 1 cent to mass transit.

That law provided that the Public Works Committee could create new budget authority for mass transit grants, committee members and aides pointed out. Silvio O. Conte, R-Mass., ranking minority member of the Appropriations Committee, tried to delete the provision but, as a Howard aide recalled, "he was drubbed," 305-96.

Senate Committee Action

With the House bill tied up in the jurisdictional dispute, the Senate Appropriations Committee approved its own measure (S 2852 — S Rept 98-561) on June 28. The report was filed July 17.

The bill provided a total of $11.7 billion — $125 million less than the administration and House amounts and $726 million above fiscal 1984.

Highlights included:

● **Office of the Secretary:** $57.3 million. That was $11.2 million more than in fiscal 1984, $8.4 million more than the administration's request and $4.1 million more than the House bill. Much of the raise was for salaries and expenses that the office would incur when it assumed some duties of the CAB.

● **Coast Guard:** $2.5 billion in new budget authority, $50.4 million more than in fiscal 1984, $4.4 million more than the administration's estimate, and $130.2 million more than the House bill.

The panel rejected a House proposal to rescind $107.5 million in contract authority for assistance to state boating safety programs for fiscal years 1983-1985. Also, the committee provided $41.5 million more than the House bill to acquire and upgrade vessels, aircraft and navigation aids.

● **Federal Aviation Administration:** $4.5 billion in new budget authority, an $879.3 million increase over fiscal 1984, $199.2 million less than the request and $8.1 million below the House proposal.

Like the House and administration proposals, the committee bill set a $987 million cap on airport development grants from the Airport and Airway Trust Fund.

The Senate bill, like the House measure, called for $2.6 billion for FAA operations, including air traffic control. Of that, $1.4 billion would come from the aviation trust fund.

As reported, the bill nearly doubled the current $750 million budget for facilities and equipment, to $1.492 billion — $8 million less than the House bill and $165 million below the administration request.

● **Federal Highway Administration:** $76.7 million, $1.1 million more than the current spending, and $36.3 million more than the administration's request, but $22.6 million less than the House proposal.

S 2852 also set a cap of $13.55 billion on contract obligations from the Highway Trust Fund.

● **National Highway Traffic Safety Administration:** $84.9 million, $6.9 million more than the current level, $4 million more than the House proposal, but $5.3 million below the request.

The Senate bill imposed a $100 million ceiling on grants for state and local highway safety programs. The amount equaled the 1984 cap but was $1.9 million more than the administration level and $10 million less than the House limit.

Committee members echoed House criticism of NHTSA for failing, after almost four years, to implement a rule requiring autos to have anchorages suitable for the straps on child-restraint seats. But senators rejected a House penalty withholding $10 million until a rule was final.

● **Federal Railroad Administration:** $800.5 million. That was $148.8 million less than the current budget, $43.7 million more than the request and $7 million less than the House appropriation.

Of that, Amtrak was to receive $700 million — $16.4 million less than fiscal 1984 and $34 million less than the House proposal, but $20 million more than the administration would like. The Senate committee provided $10 million for improvements to the Washington, D.C.-to-Boston "Northeast Corridor" route.

● **Urban Mass Transportation Administration:** $3 billion in new budget authority, $42.3 million below 1984 spending levels, $9.9 million more than the administration's request and $223.7 million less than the House proposal.

Both the Senate committee and the administration differed significantly from the House bill in two programs for mass transit grants.

One program — formula grants that funded both capital and operating expenses for mass transit projects — totaled $2.4 billion under the committee and administration plans, $160.5 million more than the House sum. But the Senate panel joined the House in rejecting an administration effort to devote grants solely to capital costs and to withhold funding for operating subsidies.

For a second type of grant, which transferred funds from Interstate highway projects to mass transit, the Senate and administration proposals both provided $250 million — $70 million less than the House.

The Senate bill capped obligations for mass transit discretionary grants, which financed a variety of construction, repair and expansion projects, at $1.12 billion — $20 million more than the administration request and $5 million less than the House provided.

Related Agencies

● **National Transportation Safety Board:** $21.7 million, which was equal to the House bill, $842,000 more than the current budget and $855,000 below the administration estimate.

● **Civil Aeronautics Board:** $5.6 million for salaries and expenses, identical to the House proposal but $12.8 million below 1984 funding and $13.4 million less than the administration's request.

● **Interstate Commerce Commission:** $48 million for salaries and expenses, $12 million less than current funding, $6 million below the administration proposal and $6.6 million less than the House bill.

● **U.S. Railway Association:** $2 million to oversee the Conrail system, $100,000 less than the House proposal.■

$56.5 Billion Approved for HUD, Agencies

A $56.5 billion fiscal 1985 appropriations bill for the Department of Housing and Urban Development (HUD) and several independent agencies was signed into law July 18 (HR 5713 — PL 98-371).

The measure was $1.87 billion more than President Reagan had requested, $253 million more than the version passed by the Senate June 21 and $1.89 billion less than the version passed by the House May 30. (Provisions, p. 417)

The fiscal 1984 appropriation was $56.1 billion.

On major housing programs, the bill reversed many of the administration's proposed policies. The final bill provided for the 100,000 additional units of housing the president requested, but Congress rejected administration proposals on the kinds of housing that would receive assistance.

Major spending items in the final version included $12.1 billion for HUD, with $8 billion earmarked for subsidized housing programs; $25.8 billion for the Veterans Administration (VA); $4.4 billion for the Environmental Protection Agency (EPA); and $7.5 billion for the National Aeronautics and Space Administration (NASA).

The Senate adopted the conference report (H Rept 98-867) by voice vote June 27, clearing the measure for the president. The House by voice vote had adopted the conference report earlier that day.

House Committee Action

The House Appropriations Committee May 23 approved a $58.4 billion fiscal 1985 spending bill.

The measure, ordered reported by voice vote, included $14 billion for HUD, $25.8 billion for the VA, $4.4 billion for the EPA and $4.6 billion for general revenue sharing grants to local governments.

The report (H Rept 98-803) was filed May 23. The committee made no change to the bill as approved by the HUD/Independent Agencies Subcommittee May 15.

The bill was $2.3 billion over the fiscal 1984 appropriation and $3.8 billion over the administration's request.

Most of the increase over the request was for subsidized housing. The president had asked for $6.2 billion for assisted housing; the committee approved $10 billion in new budget authority, and assumed $2.1 billion in recaptures of previously obligated funds and funds carried over from the previous year.

The panel balked at the administration plan to provide cash vouchers for 91,000 units. Vouchers could be used by qualified recipients like cash to rent housing on their own. The administration wanted to substitute them for the current subsidy system in which payments were made to owners of private housing to make up the difference between the tenant's income and the market rent.

But the committee decided to fund only 38,500 vouchers and to provide the traditional subsidies for 36,500 housing units under the Section 8 program of rental assistance in existing housing. The Section 8 program was more expensive than vouchers because it committed funds over 15 years, while the vouchers required a commitment of funds for only five years.

Subcommittee Chairman Edward P. Boland, D-Mass., said the administration's voucher request was too high.

"The request is far and away and beyond what the administration can actually utilize in fiscal 1985," he said.

He added that the 1983 HUD authorization (HR 3959 — PL 98-181) called for a small pilot voucher program that had not yet been started. "There ought to be a further test of that demonstration program," Boland said. (1983 Almanac p. 277)

(Funds for the demonstration voucher program and for a new construction/rehabilitation program were provided in a supplemental appropriations bill (H J Res 517) that at the time of committee action was pending in the Senate. It later was folded into the HUD appropriation bill by conferees.)

Other Departments

The committee bill also added $105 million to the president's request for the operating budget of the EPA, while reducing the request for the "superfund" hazardous waste cleanup program from $640 million to $600 million.

It added $1 million for the Consumer Product Safety Commission (CPSC), $40 million for veterans' health care and $800,000 for the General Services Administration Consumer Information Center.

The bill also reduced by $75 million the budget request for the Federal Emergency Management Agency (FEMA), mostly by cutting civil defense programs, and cut $2 million from the president's budget for the National Science Foundation (NSF). However, the bill added $20 million to the NSF budget for advanced computers, known as "supercomputers."

HUD Programs

The committee recommended $14 billion for HUD, up from $13.5 billion appropriated in fiscal 1984. Major elements included:

● **Assisted Housing.** While providing the 100,000 units of additional subsidized housing units for the poor sought by Reagan, the committee offered its own plan for what kind of housing would be funded. (Programs, box, p. 416)

It added $1.9 billion for 10,000 units of public housing for very low-income families; the administration requested no funds for new public housing.

Partly to offset the addition of the public housing, the panel reduced from 2,500 to 1,000 the number of units of Indian housing, cutting the request by $235 million.

The committee also cut $920 million from the $1.6 billion requested for the 91,000 vouchers the administration wanted, leaving funds for 38,500 instead. It set aside $2.55 billion for 36,500 units of existing housing in the Section 8 rental program for low-income persons. In addition, it provided $629 million for 7,500 units of Section 8 housing that had undergone moderate rehabilitation, the same as the 1984 level. However, the panel agreed to the budget request of $1.4 billion for 10,000 housing units for the elderly and handicapped.

The committee charged that HUD overestimated the amount of money it would recapture from unspent appropriations and reduced the estimate from $2.8 billion to $1.3 billion. But the panel accepted the administration's recommendation to rescind up to $81.6 million in contract authority, which permitted obligations in advance of appro-

Housing Glossary

Following are brief descriptions of some of the major federally assisted housing programs. In most cases, tenants paid as rent the highest of 30 percent of their adjusted income, 10 percent of gross income or the portion of welfare assistance designated to meet housing costs.

Vouchers. Tenants received certificates that they used much like food stamps to apply towards rent in housing they selected on their own. If the rent was below the amount of the certificate, the tenant pocketed it; it if was over, the tenant was responsible for paying it. Commitments for vouchers were for five years, and could be renewed twice. The federal government also paid the local public housing authority (PHA) a fee to administer the program.

Section 8 Rental Assistance. This was the primary program providing housing aid for new and existing housing, and substantially or moderately rehabilitated dwellings. Although some Section 8 aid was in the form of vouchers, in most instances the government paid the landlord the difference between what the tenant could pay and the market rent. To be eligible for aid, a tenant's income could not exceed 50 percent of the median income for the area. The government contract with the landlord for the subsidies was generally for 15 years. As with vouchers, the federal government paid the local PHA an administrative fee, although the fee was higher for the Section 8 program.

Rent Supplements. In this program, the government made partial rent payments to landlords of privately owned, operated and financed multi-family housing. Tenants had to be eligible for the Section 8 program. Although state-aided, non-federally insured projects continued to be funded under the rent supplement program, most existing contracts were being shifted to the Section 8 program.

Public Housing. The federal government made payments to local or state public housing agencies to develop, own and operate low-income housing projects. Tenant eligibility was determined by state law, but tenant rent, set by the federal government, was a percentage of income.

Indian Housing. The federal government provided aid to help Indian housing authorities to develop and operate rental and homeownership units. Eligibility was determined by tribal or state law.

Elderly or Handicapped. The government provided long-term direct loans to eligible sponsors to finance rental housing for persons over 62-years old or to the handicapped. Section 8 subsidies also were available to lower the rent.

up to $7.6 million in contract authority and $165 million in budget authority.

● **Housing Payments.** The bill agreed to the request of $11.7 billion for annual subsidized housing payments mandated by existing contracts. Included were the Section 8 low-income rent subsidy, rent supplement, low-income public housing and college housing. (The amount was contract authority and not part of the bill's total new budget authority.)

● **Elderly or Handicapped.** The bill endorsed the administration's request for a limit of $500 million for loans to build approximately 10,000 units of housing for the elderly and handicapped.

● **Operating Subsidies.** The committee met the budget request of $1.1 billion for payments to local public housing authorities to help finance the operation of public housing projects. That was $240 million less than appropriated in fiscal 1984, but the committee expected that $250 million in fiscal 1984 funds would carry over into fiscal 1985. The administration had wanted to rescind those funds.

● **Counseling Assistance.** Although the president again requested no funds, the committee recommended $4 million for housing counseling aid, $500,000 over the amount appropriated in fiscal 1984. The money was intended to support agencies that would provide counseling to help at least 50,000 clients cope with housing problems, including default.

● **Federal Housing Administration (FHA).** As requested, the committee approved $388 million to make up losses in FHA programs, a $135 million increase over fiscal 1984. The losses were caused by mortgage defaults on FHA insured loans and the sale of HUD-owned properties. The panel also agreed to limit temporary mortgage aid to financially strapped homeowners to $65.4 million in fiscal 1985.

● **Solar Bank.** The panel again rescued the Solar Energy and Conservation Bank, which the administration had tried to eliminate for four years. It approved $25 million for fiscal 1985 for grants to encourage energy conservation and solar technology. *(1983 Almanac p. 497)*

● **Community Development Block Grants.** The bill matched the request for $3.5 billion for grants to states and local governments for community development programs. Urban Development Action Grants, which provided matching grants to distressed urban areas to stimulate economic activity, were funded at $440 million, the same as the request and the fiscal 1984 appropriation.

● **Fair Housing and Equal Opportunity.** The committee agreed to the request of $6.7 million for grants to state and local fair housing agencies, and to support community housing review boards, $2 million more than the fiscal 1984 appropriation.

Environmental Protection

To help the beleaguered EPA rebuild after experiencing severe budget cuts and management problems, the committee provided $1.3 billion for the EPA's operating program budget, an increase of $105 million over Reagan's request of $1.2 billion. Total EPA funding was set at $4.4 billion, up $360 million over current funding.

The largest increase was $40 million for abatement control and compliance, including air and water pollution controls and grants to states to manage hazardous waste. The panel approved $436 million, compared with a request of $396 million.

It also increased the request for research and develop-

priations, and $1.83 billion in budget authority for rent supplements on behalf of needy tenants.

The panel also decided to convert 3,023 units in a rent subsidy program for the very-low-income to the existing Section 8 rent subsidy program, resulting in a rescission of

Fiscal 1985 HUD/Agency Funds

Congress June 27 cleared a fiscal 1985 spending bill (HR 5713) for the Department of Housing and Urban Development (HUD) and several independent agencies.

Following are the amounts requested by the president, approved by the House and the Senate and the appropriation agreed to by conferees.

	Administration Request	House-passed	Senate-passed	Final Appropriation
Department of Housing and Urban Development				
Housing Programs	$ 6,039,849,000	$ 9,769,539,500	$ 7,667,738,000	$ 7,923,825,775
Community Development	3,920,000,000	3,920,000,000	3,926,000,000	3,924,000,000
Policy Development & Research	20,900,000	15,900,000	20,000,000	16,900,000
Fair Housing Assistance	6,700,000	6,700,000	6,700,000	6,700,000
Management & Administration	295,235,000	295,235,000	298,135,000	295,235,000
Solar Energy Bank	0	25,000,000	0	15,000,000
Total, HUD	$10,282,684,000	$14,032,374,500	$11,918,573,000	$12,181,660,775
Independent Agencies				
American Battle Monuments Commission	11,065,000	11,065,000	11,065,000	11,065,000
Consumer Product Safety Commission	35,000,000	36,000,000	35,000,000	36,000,000
Cemeterial Expenses, Army	7,759,000	7,759,000	7,759,000	7,759,000
Environmental Protection Agency	4,293,254,000	4,385,275,000	4,380,354,000	4,372,775,000
Council on Environmental Quality	700,000	700,000	700,000	700,000
Office of Science and Technology Policy	2,194,000	2,194,000	2,194,000	2,194,000
Federal Emergency Management Agency	630,072,000	554,909,000	559,868,000	561,368,000
GSA Consumer Information Center	349,000	1,149,000	1,149,000	1,149,000
HHS Office of Consumer Affairs	2,096,000	2,096,000	2,096,000	2,096,000
National Aeronautics and Space Administration	7,491,400,000	7,491,400,000	7,491,400,000	7,491,400,000
National Science Foundation	1,501,792,000	1,499,792,000	1,501,792,000	1,501,792,000
Neighborhood Reinvestment Corporation	15,271,000	15,271,000	15,512,000	15,512,000
Selective Service System	28,130,000	27,780,000	27,780,000	27,780,000
Treasury Department				
General Revenue Sharing	4,566,700,000	4,566,700,000	4,566,700,000	4,566,700,000
Salaries and Expenses	7,941,000	7,941,000	7,941,000	7,941,000
Veterans Administration	25,792,091,000	25,821,091,000	25,760,040,000	25,755,408,000
Grand Total	$54,668,498,000	$58,436,496,500	$56,289,923,000	$56,543,299,775

ment from $163 million to $193 million, adding funds for research into acid rain and indoor air pollution.

To prepare for the increases, the committee added funds to the $639 million requested for salaries and expenses, for a total of $672 million.

The panel cut the request for the hazardous waste cleanup fund, or "superfund," from $640 million to $600 million. It argued that its total was the largest amount that could feasibly be spent in fiscal 1985, noting that the $600 million and the 1,357 personnel provided for represented a tripling of funding and doubling of staff in two years.

It agreed to Reagan's request for $2.4 billion in construction grants to states and municipalities.

Veterans Administration

For the VA, the committee recommended $25.8 billion, an increase of $29 million over the request and $832 million over the fiscal 1984 appropriation.

To help the VA prepare for an expected onslaught of demand brought by an aging veteran population, the panel increased medical care funds by $40 million, from $8.77 billion requested to $8.81 billion.

That total also included $33 million for readjustment counseling for Vietnam veterans.

The committee also matched the request of $14 billion for compensation and pensions, which did not include any money for a cost-of-living increase. The panel noted supplemental funding might be necessary.

Also, it agreed to $620 million for construction projects and reiterated its opposition to congressional decisions about where to place hospitals.

Space Program

The committee approved $150 million for NASA to begin planning for a permanent manned space station expected to be in operation in the early 1990s, in accordance with a request made by Reagan in his State of the Union address. However, it earmarked $15 million of those funds for the parallel development of a "man-tended" station, one which astronauts would visit from time to time, rather than inhabit. *(Text, p. 5-E)*

It agreed to the request for a total budget of $7.5 billion for NASA. However, it rearranged funds within that total, adding $40 million for an advanced communications satellite and allowing the agency to cut corresponding funds at its discretion.

Other Agencies

● **Consumer Product Safety Commission.** The committee added $1 million to Reagan's $35 million request for the CPSC, targeting the increase to emerging hazard programs.

● **Selective Service System.** Although recommending a $3.28 million increase over fiscal 1984, the panel cut the request for the Selective Service System by $350,000, to $27.8 million. It continued a ban on the use of funds to induct any person into the armed services.

● **Consumer Information Center.** The committee rejected the administration's proposed change in the role of the General Services Administration's Consumer Information Center, and added $800,000 to the president's $349,000 request. The administration proposed redirecting half the staff from traditional information activities to undertake new marketing programs financed by fees.

House Floor Action

The House May 30 passed the bill, leaving the funding levels unchanged from those approved by the committee. It was passed by a 282-110 vote. *(Vote 168, p. 54-H)*

Bill Green, R-N.Y., ranking minority member of the Appropriations Subcommittee on HUD/Independent Agencies, told the House that budget director David A. Stockman had said the bill was "generally consistent" with the administration's request.

Some members argued that it was still too expensive. Bill Frenzel, R-Minn., said that the House budget resolution assumed a 3.5 percent increase over fiscal 1984 for domestic programs, but HR 5713 was 4.7 percent over last year. "We aren't under the budget," he said.

Robert S. Walker, R-Pa., offered an amendment authorizing the president to cut an item in the bill by up to 10 percent, a power the president had sought. That could, he said, save up to $5.8 billion.

"Should we not be doing something to reduce deficits in real terms?" Walker asked. "The place where we can do that is on appropriations bills."

But Boland said the amendment might exceed the president's constitutional authority. "This is a line-item veto," he told members as they entered the chamber to vote.

Walker's amendment was defeated, 133-258. *(Vote*

167, p. 54-H)

The House adopted an amendment by John D. Dingell, D-Mich., barring the move of a VA hospital from Allen Park, Mich., to Detroit until after a General Accounting Office audit.

Space Station

Walker also tried unsuccessfully to remove the requirement that NASA begin development of a man-tended space station, in addition to a permanently manned station. The bill earmarked 10 percent of the development funds, or $15 million, for the complementary development of a space station that astronauts would visit.

Walker said that the bill sent "mixed signals" to potential investors, who would provide capital for the development of industry in space.

But Green was concerned that a commitment to a manned station, expected to cost at least $8 billion by 1992, might jeopardize other NASA programs in the future. He said the committee would prefer a manned station, but he wanted to leave options open. "This will assure that this House and this Congress will have choices," he said.

Walker's amendment was defeated on a voice vote.

Senate Committee Action

The Senate Appropriations Committee June 7 approved a $56.28 billion fiscal 1985 appropriation bill by voice vote. It was $2.2 billion less than the House-passed version and $1.6 billion above President Reagan's request. It also was $172 million more than the fiscal 1984 appropriation.

The bill included $11.7 billion for HUD, $25.8 billion for the VA, $4.4 billion for the EPA and $4.6 billion for general revenue sharing grants to local governments.

The committee made one substantive change to the bill as approved the day before by the Subcommittee on HUD/Independent Agencies. The panel adopted an amendment by Walter D. Huddleston of Kentucky, ranking Democrat on the subcommittee, adding $850,000 for FEMA hurricane and dam safety programs.

The biggest difference between the House and Senate committee versions of the bill was in subsidized housing. The House approved $10 billion for assisted housing; the Senate panel recommended $7.7 billion in new budget authority. In addition, it assumed no recaptures of previously obligated funds; instead, the committee added another $2.8 billion in new budget authority, and rescinded the president's proposed deobligations of that amount.

Although the committee reduced the House level of funding for assisted housing, it provided for more units by rearranging the types of subsidized housing within that total and including more of the less expensive housing. Its bill funded 113,000 new units, compared with the 100,000 provided for by the House and requested by the president.

Other Agencies

The committee recommended $18 million less than the House's $1.3 billion for the EPA operating budget, but the total EPA funding of $4.38 billion was $87 million over the president's request and $22.2 million more than the House bill. The panel approved the full $640 million request for the "superfund" hazardous waste cleanup program; the House had cut the request by $40 million.

For the VA, the full committee cut $61 million from the House version, mostly by reducing construction projects. Subcommittee Chairman Jake Garn, R-Utah, said he was dissatisfied with the VA for failing to provide the committee with a list of priorities for construction.

The committee bill also added $241,000 to the House version and the administration request for the Neighborhood Reinvestment Program, and added $5 million to the House version for FEMA, bringing the total for that agency to $559 million, $71 million below the request.

HUD Programs

The $11.9 billion the panel provided for HUD was $2.1 billion below the House amount. Major elements included:

● **Assisted Housing.** The bill provided $7.7 billion in new budget authority for 113,000 more units of subsidized housing. The rearranged mix of housing included the following:

● 14,000 units for the elderly and handicapped, compared with 10,000 set by the House and requested by the administration.

● 2,500 for Indian housing, the same as the request, but 1,500 more than the House.

● 20,000 15-year rent subsidies under the Section 8 program, compared with 36,500 in the House bill and none requested.

● 38,500 cash vouchers for the poor, the same as the House, but 52,500 less than requested.

The committee also called for 38,500 new five-year rent subsidies under the Section 8 rental assistance program, which were not in the House bill. The panel did not include any funds for new public housing or for moderate rehabilitation of existing rental housing.

Rather than anticipate the $2.8 billion the president expected to recapture from unspent prior appropriations, the panel recommended rescinding those funds and provided an equal amount in new budget authority.

The bill increased funds for public housing modernization from the $1.55 billion approved by the House, to $1.9 billion. The major difference was $250 million added by the committee by taking funds earmarked for potential development and making them available to modernize current public housing.

● **Elderly or Handicapped.** The committee added $200 million to the administration's $500 million request for a limit on loans for the construction of housing for the elderly and handicapped. The increase was expected to support an additional 4,000 units.

● **Operating Subsidies.** To help public housing authorities finance the operation of low-income housing projects, the panel recommended $1.15 billion, $25 million over the amount passed by the House and requested by the administration. The extra $25 million was targeted for advanced architectural and engineering work for the comprehensive improvement assistance program for physical and management improvements.

● **Counseling Aid.** The panel recommended $3.5 million for grants to local agencies to provide counseling on housing problems for tenants and homeowners. The president requested zero; the House included $4 million.

● **Solar Bank.** The committee accepted the administration recommendation the Solar Energy and Energy Conservation Bank get no money. The House provided $25 million.

● **Community Development Block Grants.** For grants to state and local governments for community development programs, the committee recommended $3.47 billion, $4 million more than requested and approved by the House. The committee added the excess to the secretary's discretionary fund for special projects involving community and infrastructure needs.

● **Policy Development and Research.** The panel provided $20 million, $900,000 less than the request and $4.1 million more than the House bill, for research programs in HUD. It added $500,000 for an ongoing public housing modernization study and $500,000 to begin an evaluation of the housing voucher program.

Environmental Protection

Within the $4.38 billion for the EPA, the committee recommended a 17.2 percent increase over fiscal 1984 for abatement control and compliance. It approved $462 million, $66 million more than the request and $26 million more than the House bill. The largest increase was $32 million for grants to states to increase levels of enforcement.

In matching the administration's request of $640 million for the "superfund," the committee said that cutting expenditures, as the House did, would reduce the number of cleanup projects already in the pipeline.

Veterans Administration

The $25.8 billion recommended for the VA was $32 million below the president's request and $61 million below the House. The total was $771 million over fiscal 1984 funding.

The biggest increase over fiscal 1984 was for medical care. The committee recommended $8.79 billion, $25 million over the request but $15 million below the House level. The committee added 500 additional medical care personnel, including 220 for in-house readjustment counseling centers.

Space Program

The committee matched the House's $150 million for research on a proposed space station in its $7.5 billion recommendation for the National Aeronautics and Space Administration. But it dropped the earmarking of funds toward the development of a man-tended station. Instead, it prohibited the funding of manned components of the station until April 1, 1985, when a congressionally mandated study on automation was to be completed.

The panel also added $50 million for structural and engine spares for the space shuttle, to prepare for a possible fifth shuttle vehicle.

The committee recommended that NASA use its discretion to cut $50 million from the account to offset that increase.

Senate Floor Action

The Senate June 21 by voice vote approved $56.289 billion for HUD and the agencies, adding some $6 million to the committee bill. The total was $178 million above the fiscal 1984 funding level and more than $2.1 billion below the fiscal 1985 House-passed measure.

Amendments included the following by:

● John Heinz, R-Pa., to add $4.144 million over an 18-month period to fund 29 congregate housing services programs that were scheduled to expire in 1985. Under the program, HUD awarded three- to five-year grants to local public housing agencies or non-profit sponsors to provide meals and other supportive services to the elderly, who might otherwise require nursing home or other institutional care. Under the 1978 act setting up the program, HUD was to evaluate the program and report to Congress in June 1985. Adopted by voice vote.

● Heinz, to add $2 million for the second year of the Neighborhood Development Program, authorized in the housing provisions of a fiscal 1984 funding bill (PL 98-181) to stimulate revitalization of economically distressed neighborhoods by local, non-profit groups. Adopted by voice vote.

● Robert T. Stafford, R-Vt., to earmark $5.125 million appropriated by the bill for toxicological tests by the Department of Health and Human Services on chemicals found in superfund sites. Adopted by voice vote.

● Garn for Jennings Randolph, D-W.Va., to delete a provision that prevented EPA from funding certain solid wastes management activities. Adopted by voice vote.

Larry Pressler, R-S.D., offered but then withdrew an amendment to require that one-half of the $2.5 million to provide technical assistance to cities that had not received Urban Development Action Grants go to cities with populations under 30,000.

Garn, chairman of the Senate Banking Committee, said he favored the intent of the measure but asked that members of Congress be allowed first to work with HUD to increase the number of small cities receiving grants.

Conference Action

Conferees reached agreement on the bill June 26 and filed the report the same day.

Major items included:

Assisted Housing

Conferees agreed to allocate $8 billion for assisted housing, and limited the new voucher program to 38,500 units.

Also the final bill provided funds for 37,500 Section 8 rental assistance units. In addition, the legislation set aside funding for 5,000 public housing apartments, as the House proposed, cut the administration request for 2,500 units of Indian housing by 500 and upped the number of units for the elderly and handicapped by 2,000, to 12,000.

Also, $3.5 million was provided, as proposed by the Senate, for counseling assistance.

About $5 billion was included for HUD activities that did not involve subsidized housing. That included $440 million for the Urban Development Action Grants, to spur private development in economically distressed areas. Conferees accepted a Senate proposal to earmark $2.5 million for technical assistance to small cities. They also included $3.47 billion for Community Development Block Grants.

Funding for the Solar Energy and Energy Conservation Bank was set at $15 million.

Conferees also accepted two amendments that had been approved on the Senate floor. One added $4.1 million to extend a pilot "congregate services" program providing services to the elderly where they lived, reducing the need for institutionalization. The other added $2 million for grants to promote neighborhood development.

EPA, Other Agencies

For the beleaguered EPA, conferees exceeded the administration request by $79.5 million, for a total of $4.4 billion. The operating budget was set at $1.3 billion, an increase of $99.5 billion over the budget request.

Conferees split the difference between the House and

Senate versions on the "superfund" hazardous waste cleanup program, settling on $620 million for the program, cutting the administration request by $20 million. Some $14.6 million was earmarked for the Department of Health and Human Services activities in conjunction with the superfund, including $5.1 million for a toxicology study.

It added to the $639.3 million sought for salaries to reach a total of $656.3 million, which would support 278 additional positions.

The final bill raised Reagan's request for research and development from $163.4 million to $193 million and matched the $2.4 billion sought for construction grants to states and municipalities. For abatement, control and compliance, the conferees agreed to $447.5 million, a $51 million increase over the request.

In agreeing to $25.8 billion for the VA, less than was originally approved by both the House and Senate, conferees accepted the lower Senate figure for VA major construction projects, which was about $50 million below the House level.

Although the conference report did not name any projects to be built, it did eliminate several from the administration's request, including a 60-bed nursing home in Providence, R.I., and an addition to a parking garage in San Francisco.

Both chambers wanted the VA to submit a revised list of 1985 projects by Sept. 1, 1984. The final bill included an increase of $24.7 million above the budget request for medical care.

The conference agreement also retained the thrust of a House floor amendment barring the move of a VA hospital from Allen Park, Mich., to Detroit until after a General Accounting Office audit.

For NASA, the total of $7.5 billion was the same as the administration requested and as provided by the House and Senate.

Conferees compromised on the approach sought by the House to develop space stations that would be tended by humans and the Senate preference for automation. They included $150 million to begin research on a space station, as provided by both chambers. However, conferees agreed that NASA should consider both a station that would be occasionally tended by humans and one using robotics, in addition to a permanently manned station, without mandating that a certain portion of funds be used to study the other options.

The bill met the budget request of $1.5 billion for the National Science Foundation, but conferees adjusted items within the total. The largest increase was $20 million for additional work on so-called "supercomputers."

Supplemental Added

In addition to the housing and agency provisions, conferees added the provisions of a fiscal 1984 HUD supplemental appropriations bill (H J Res 517) that had passed the House March 29 but had been stalled in the Senate. That measure released $1.5 billion in new budget authority that had been approved in 1983 and $1 billion in unused budget authority appropriated in prior years. *(1983 Almanac p. 495)*

The $1.5 billion in new budget authority included $615 million for grants to local governments to build new rental housing and to repair existing housing, and $242 million to provide cash vouchers for 15,000 poor families to use for housing they found on their own. The balance was allocated to the Section 8 rental assistance program.

H J Res 517 had been reported by the House Appropriations Committee March 21 (H Rept 98-630) and passed by the House March 29 by a vote of 340-55. *(Vote 50, p. 18-H)*

The measure bypassed the Senate Appropriations panel, but floor action was stalled, partly because of the displeasure of some members with HUD's regulations determining which cities would be eligible for the new rental and repair grants.

The program, authorized in 1983 (PL 98-181), would provide grants to developers to be matched by private funds, to build rental housing in areas where the market was tight. At least 20 percent of the dwellings were to be reserved for low-income tenants and the developer could not convert the units to condominiums for 20 years. *(1983 Almanac p. 277)*

But HUD's proposed regulations would have allowed only 41 large cities — 7 percent of those over 50,000 population — to qualify for the grants, and 25 of them were in New Jersey and California. The list omitted many large cities, including Cleveland, Washington, D.C., and Detroit.

When HUD in June agreed to expand to 133 the number of large cities eligible for the funds, Sen. Donald W. Riegle Jr., D-Mich., withdrew the hold he had placed on H J Res 517. The Senate by that time had begun moving its version of the HUD fiscal 1985 appropriation bill, and key members decided to fold H J Res 517 into the larger legislation.

$104 Billion Labor-HHS Funding Bill Clears

President Reagan Nov. 8 signed into law a bill (HR 6028 — PL 98-619) providing $104.6 billion for the Departments of Health and Human Services (HHS), Labor, Education and related agencies.

Technically, Labor-HHS programs were financed from the Oct. 1 start of the fiscal year until Nov. 8 under a series of short-term continuing appropriations measures and the massive continuing appropriations resolution (H J Res 648 — PL 98-473) cleared by Congress Oct. 11 and signed by the president Oct. 12. The text of the regular Labor-HHS appropriation was removed from the continuing resolution when the president signed HR 6028. *(Continuing resolution, p. 444)*

The House Appropriations Committee reported HR 6028 July 26. The House passed the bill Aug. 1. The Senate Appropriations Committee discharged its version of the measure Sept. 5. The full Senate approved the bill Sept. 25.

Disputes over abortion funding and prayer in public schools temporarily stalled the measure, but lawmakers were able to resolve differences that in the recent past had blocked enactment of the bill. House-Senate conferees on HR 6028 failed to reconcile the differences between House and Senate positions on abortion funding and school prayer. But the Senate, in the waning days of the congressional session, agreed to the House positions. *(Background, 1983 Almanac p. 504)*

Provisions

As signed into law, HR 6028 contained the following funding for the Departments of Labor, HHS, Education and related agencies:

	Budget Request	Final Amount
Labor Department		
Employment and Training Administration		
Program administration	$ 65,922,000	$ 67,625,000
Training and employment services	3,610,624,000	3,769,545,000
Community service employment for older Americans	317,300,000	326,000,000
Federal unemployment benefits	56,000,000	75,000,000

	Budget Request	Final Amount
Grants to states for unemployment insurance and employment services	23,500,000	23,500,000
Labor-Management Services Administration	61,186,000	60,211,000
Employment Standards Administration	1,353,382,000	1,353,982,000
Occupational Safety and Health Administration	217,752,000	219,652,000
Mine Safety and Health Administration	150,550,000	150,550,000
Bureau of Labor Statistics	146,860,000	152,860,000
Departmental Management	139,395,000	141,720,000
Total, Labor Department	6,142,471,000	6,340,645,000
Health and Human Services		
Health resources and services	1,187,119,000	1,427,694,000
Medical facilities guarantee and loan fund	26,500,000	26,500,000
Centers for Disease Control	369,864,000	410,530,000
National Institutes of Health		
Cancer	1,101,069,000	1,183,806,000
Heart, Lung and Blood	718,852,000	805,269,000
Dental Research	91,096,000	100,688,000
Arthritis, Diabetes, and Digestive and Kidney Diseases	475,324,000	543,576,000
Neurological and Communicative Disorders and Stroke	344,601,000	396,885,000
Allergy and Infectious Diseases	325,379,000	370,965,000
General Medical Sciences	423,853,000	482,260,000
Child Health and Human Development	280,178,000	313,295,000
Eye	157,873,000	181,678,000

	Budget Request	Final Amount
Environmental Health Sciences	183,755,000	194,819,000
Aging	117,390,000	144,521,000
Research resources	245,728,000	304,025,000
John E. Fogarty Center	11,426,000	11,728,000
National Library of Medicine	51,320,000	52,410,000
Director	27,509,000	38,304,000
Buildings and facilities	11,100,000	21,730,000
Alcohol, Drug Abuse and Mental Health Administration	845,455,000	922,621,000
St. Elizabeths Hospital	48,595,000	48,595,000
Assistant secretary for health	193,001,000	180,392,000
Health Care Financing Administration	35,661,247,000	35,141,638,000
(Fiscal 1986 advance)	(5,980,000,000)	(5,980,000,000)
Social Security Administration		
Payments to Social Security trust funds	512,722,000	512,722,000
Black lung payments	1,024,131,000	1,024,131,000
(Fiscal 1986 advance)	(270,000,000)	(270,000,000)
Supplemental Security Income	9,346,290,000	9,325,000,000
(Fiscal 1986 advance)	(2,345,769,000)	(2,345,769,000)
Assistance payments	$ 4,871,025,000	$5,794,000,000
(Fiscal 1986 advance)	(1,812,840,000)	(2,095,000,000)
Child support enforcement	425,411,000	480,000,000
(Fiscal 1986 advance)	(160,000,000)	(160,000,000)
Low-income energy assistance	1,875,000,000	2,100,000,000
Refugee resettlement	359,512,000	(deferred)
Assistant secretary for human development	5,171,901,000	5,653,816,000
Community services	8,679,000	372,435,000
Departmental management	217,341,000	213,991,000
Total, HHS	66,710,246,000	68,780,024,000
(Fiscal 1986 advance)	(10,568,609,000)	(10,850,769,000)

Education Department

	Budget Request	Final Amount
Compensatory education	3,480,000,000	3,695,663,000
Special programs	778,879,000	748,109,000
Impact aid	506,630,000	695,000,000
Bilingual education	139,245,000	142,951,000
Handicapped education	1,214,445,000	1,321,270,000
Rehabilitation services	1,091,660,000	1,233,300,000
Vocational and adult education	831,314,000	831,314,000
College student assistance	3,654,000,000	4,621,000,000
Guaranteed student loans	2,840,677,000	3,079,477,000
Higher and continuing education	252,071,000	479,083,000
Higher education facilities loans	14,194,000	14,194,000
Education research and statistics	62,978,000	59,978,000

	Budget Request	Final Amount
Libraries	——	125,000,000
Special institutions	241,465,000	253,830,000
Departmental management	300,950,000	301,387,000
Total, Education Department	15,408,508,000	17,601,556,000

Related agencies

	Budget Request	Final Amount
ACTION	120,217,000	150,164,000
Corporation for Public Broadcasting (Fiscal 1987 advance)	(100,000,000)	(200,000,000)
Federal Mediation and Conciliation Service	22,451,000	23,611,000
Federal Mine Safety and Health Review Commission	3,837,000	3,837,000
National Commission on Libraries and Information Science	690,000	720,000
National Council on the Handicapped	500,000	750,000
National Labor Relations Board	137,964,000	137,964,000
National Mediation Board	6,358,000	6,358,000
Occupational Safety and Health Review Commission	6,143,000	6,143,000
Railroad Retirement Board	420,000,000	420,000,000
Soldiers' and Airmen's Home	37,352,000	42,352,000
Total, related agencies	755,512,000	791,899,000
(Fiscal 1987 advance)	(100,000,000)	(200,000,000)
Total, Fiscal 1985	$89,016,737,000	$93,514,124,000
(Fiscal 1986 advance)	(10,568,609,000)	(10,850,769,000)
(Fiscal 1987 advance)	(100,000,000)	(200,000,000)
GRAND TOTAL	$99,685,346,000	$104,564,893,000

House Committee

The House Appropriations Committee July 26 reported a $96.1 billion appropriation for the Departments of Labor, HHS, Education and various independent agencies (H Rept 98-911).

For fiscal year 1985, the bill provided $6.1 billion for the Department of Labor, $61.5 billion for HHS and $17.2 billion for the Education Department. For the independent agencies covered by the bill, including ACTION, the National Labor Relations Board and the National Council on the Handicapped, it provided $788 million. The committee bill also contained $10.6 billion in fiscal 1986 spending for health and human services.

Mandatory spending for entitlement programs such as Medicaid was set at $71 billion. Spending for discretionary programs, which were controlled by annual appropriations, totaled $25.2 billion, $3.5 billion more than President Reagan had requested.

The House committee did not provide funds — $7.2

billion worth — for several programs that had not yet been authorized by Congress. These included the Corporation for Public Broadcasting, the Labor Department's community service employment program for the elderly, the Centers for Disease Control in HHS, and the Education Department's "impact aid" program, which provided money to school districts with large populations of children of federal employees.

House Floor

The House Aug. 1 passed HR 6028 by a 329-91 vote. The measure called for spending of $96.1 billion for the Departments of Labor, HHS, Education and related agencies. *(Vote 299, p. 90-H)*

Controversy over spending increases marked debate on the bill. Discretionary spending, for which levels were set annually, was $25.2 billion, about $3.5 billion over the administration request. About $70.9 billion in the bill was earmarked for mandatory entitlement progams such as Medicare, Medicaid and Social Security, over which the Appropriations Committee had no control.

A number of attempts to reduce spending in the bill were fought back on the floor. Some members charged that the measure was too costly and would become even costlier in conference with the Senate version, which included about $7.5 billion in additional funding for unauthorized programs.

Reagan's budget director, David A. Stockman, warned in a letter to the Appropriations Committee that the House bill, along with the Senate additions, would be $479 million above the March deficit "down payment" plan agreed to by the White House and congressional Republicans and would be unacceptable to the administration. *(Deficit reduction, p. 143)*

The House approved proposed increases over the budget for student aid, job training and the National Institutes of Health. The biggest hike was for loans and grants to college students, which the House increased $1.4 billion over the administration's $3.7 billion request.

The only spending increase approved on the floor was an amendment by John N. Erlenborn, R-Ill., to raise appropriations for the HHS Office of Civil Rights by $1.1 million to $18.9 million. The amendment was accepted by voice vote.

Limits in the bill on the use of funds for abortion, busing and to prevent voluntary school prayer were not mentioned on the floor.

Labor

The bill provided $6.1 billion for the Department of Labor, $300 million over the president's budget request, but $9.6 billion less than was appropriated in fiscal 1984.

The difference from the fiscal 1984 appropriation was due primarily to a $7.1 billion advance to the unemployment trust fund and other funds that had been approved the previous year. The change from the fiscal 1984 bill also resulted from a special one-time advanced funding appropriation of $2.9 billion to cover a transition in funding methods for job training and employment services under the Job Training Partnership Act. *(1982 Almanac p. 39)*

The fiscal 1985 bill approved by the House provided $3.8 billion for job programs, $214 million over the comparable 1984 level and $238 million over the president's budget. During consideration of the measure, members agreed to provide $100 million more than the $725 million

requested for youth employment programs for the summer of 1985.

Health and Human Services

The House bill called for $72 billion in new funds for the Department of Health and Human Services, $5.4 billion above the fiscal 1984 budget and $1 billion over the president's request for authorized programs. Most of the increase over the 1984 level was in federal payments to the Medicare trust fund and to a new advance appropriation for Supplemental Security Income for the aged, blind and disabled poor.

Major items included:

National Institutes of Health. $4.8 billion for the National Institutes of Health, $599 million above fiscal 1984 funding and $505 million above the administration's request.

Alcohol, Drug Abuse, Mental Health. $405 million for alcohol, drug abuse and mental health programs, $50 million more than requested in the budget.

Medicaid. $21.2 billion for the mandatory federal share of state Medicaid costs, the same amount requested by the president.

Medicare. $19.8 billion for federal payments to the Medicare trust fund to help pay for physicians' services used by beneficiaries. The amount was $2.1 billion above the fiscal 1984 level. It was also $97 million less than the president requested because of updated estimates of Medicare's fiscal 1985 funding requirements.

Supplemental Security Income. $9.3 billion for aid to 4 million aged, blind and disabled poor. The amount was almost $1 billion over the fiscal 1984 amount, primarily because of a one-month forward shift in funding, required by the 1983 Social Security legislation. *(1983 Almanac p. 219)*

Welfare. $4.9 billion, in addition to $2.1 billion left over from fiscal 1984, for federal matching payments to states for basic welfare programs, including Aid to Families with Dependent Children.

Child Support Enforcement. $425 million, the administration's request, for child support enforcement.

Human Development. $2.7 billion, the administration's request, for the social services block grant to the states. The bill also included $652 million for family social services and $267 million for the Work Incentive (WIN) program to help welfare recipients achieve independence from federal aid, a program the administration had proposed to eliminate.

Community Services Block Grants. $362 million for the community services block grant program for state anti-poverty efforts, which the administration had proposed eliminating.

Education

The House approved $17.2 billion for the Department of Education, $2.3 billion over the administration's authorized request and $2.5 billion over fiscal 1984 spending.

Major items included:

Compensatory Aid. $3.7 billion for the basic program of federal elementary and secondary school aid for the disadvantaged. The amount was $200 million over fiscal 1984 and $207 million over the administration's request.

Block Grants. $679 million for state block grants for elementary and secondary schools, a cut of $50 million from the administration's request.

Handicapped. $1.3 billion in education for the

handicapped, mostly distributed through state grants. The appropriation was $84 million over the administration's request. The bill also provided $1.2 billion, $124 million over the budget, for vocational rehabilitation and handicapped research.

Student Aid. $5.1 billion for student financial assistance, $1.4 billion over the budget and $1.1 billion over fiscal 1984 spending. The bill included $3.8 billion for Pell grants, which provided financial assistance to needy college students, $425 million for supplemental educational opportunity grants, $600 million for college work-study programs and $225 million for direct student loans. The House rejected an administration plan to restructure student aid programs by placing more emphasis on work study.

The bill also included $3 billion for guaranteed student loans, $205 million over the administration's request.

Higher Education. $459 million, $207 million over the budget request, for higher education programs, including assistance for the disadvantaged.

Senate Committee

Moving on a faster track than its House counterpart to set spending for social programs, the Appropriations Committee June 26 approved a $94.3 billion version of HR 6028. By custom and by the House's interpretation of the U.S. Constitution, appropriations measures originated in the House.

The Senate Appropriations Committee was discharged from further consideration of HR 6028 on Sept. 5. The bill then was placed on the calendar. The Senate bill (S 2836) to appropriate fiscal 1985 funds for Labor-HHS-Education was reported by the Appropriations Committee June 29 (S Rept 98-544).

The committee asked for fiscal 1985 spending of $6.4 billion for the Labor Department, $70 billion for HHS, $17.2 billion for the Education Department and $793 million for independent agencies.

Mandatory spending for entitlements was set at $62.8 billion. The bill also included $31.5 billion for discretionary programs — about $3.6 billion more than the Reagan budget request and $2.4 billion more than was provided in fiscal 1984.

Abortion, School Prayer

The Senate bill, as approved by the Senate Appropriations Subcommittee on Labor, HHS, Education and Related Agencies June 19, had not included language restricting the use of federal funds to pay for abortions.

Debate on the issue was sparked when Thomas F. Eagleton, D-Mo., a longtime foe of abortion, proposed an amendment to restore language that had been a standard feature of the law since 1977, allowing the use of Medicaid funds for abortions only when the mother's life was threatened.

But the committee voted 15-11 to broaden the Eagleton amendment to allow funding in cases involving rape and incest under language proposed by Subcommittee Chairman Lowell P. Weicker, Jr., R-Conn.

The committee bill did not include a provision that had been part of the law for the previous four years, barring the use of funds to prevent "the implementation of programs of voluntary prayer and meditation" in public schools.

Senate Floor

The Senate Sept. 25 approved HR 6028 by a 71-20 vote. *(Vote 234, p. 41-S)*

Floor debate on the bill began on Sept. 21 but, with heated controversy expected, the Senate postponed consideration of the abortion provision. Before cutting off debate on the bill Sept. 21, the Senate approved several non-controversial amendments, including $200 million for improving mathematics and science education.

As approved by the Senate, HR 6028 included fiscal 1985 funding of $6.4 billion for the Labor Department, $70.1 billion for HHS, $17.6 billion for the Education Department, and $793 million for related agencies.

It also included $11.1 billion in fiscal 1986-87 funding for certain programs, including the Corporation for Public Broadcasting.

Overall — for fiscal 1985-87 — the Senate bill provided about $105.9 billion, while the House had included $96.1 billion in its version of HR 6028.

However, the House did not earmark money for several unauthorized programs that were funded under the Senate bill. In a comparison of the bills, based on programs funded by both, it was estimated that the Senate bill provided about $1.8 billion more than the House measure.

Social Issues

When debate on the bill resumed Sept. 25 there was virtually no discussion of abortion. Opponents of the less restrictive language said they did not challenge the committee amendment because they were confident the narrower abortion restriction would be restored in conference with the House.

Jesse Helms, R-N.C., offered an amendment that would have restored limits on the use of funds to prevent school prayer and brought the Senate bill in line with the House's. Weicker threatened to torpedo the entire bill if the school prayer language were restored. He said that the amendment would be acceptable if it limited only the use of funds for preventing "individual" voluntary prayer. After intensive behind-the-scenes wrangling, the watered-down prayer language was accepted by Helms who offered it as a substitute for his original amendment. The amendment was adopted by voice vote.

Conference

Conferees Oct. 2 approved a compromise bill (H Rept 98-1132) to provide $93.5 billion in fiscal 1985 funding for the Departments of Labor, Education and HHS, but negotiators failed to reconcile differences over abortion funding and funding to prevent prayer in public schools.

Rather than haggle over those touchy subjects, the conferees reported the compromise funding bill with the abortion and school prayer issues in dispute, leaving their resolution to floor action.

The conference version of HR 6028 provided about $6.3 billion for the Labor Department, $68.8 billion for HHS, $17.6 billion for the Education Department and $792 million for related agencies in fiscal 1985.

It also provided $11 billion in fiscal 1986-87 appropriations for such programs as the Corporation for Public Broadcasting and Aid to Families with Dependent Children.

Of the funds provided under the compromise bill, about $72 billion was for mandatory spending for entitlement programs. Some $32.5 billion was provided for discretionary programs — about $3.8 billion more than the president requested.

Major items of the compromise bill included:

Employment Training. Funding for job training programs was set at $3.7 billion, compared with the $3.6 billion provided in fiscal 1984.

Biomedical Research. The $5.15 billion provided for the National Institutes of Health was about 15 percent more than was appropriated in 1984.

Medicaid. The $16.3 billion for the mandatory federal share of state Medicaid costs was about $700 million more than the cost of the entitlement program in 1984.

Medicare. $18.8 billion was included for federal payments to the Medicare trust fund to help pay for physicians' services for beneficiaries.

Welfare. $6.17 billion was provided for federal matching payments to states for welfare programs, including Aid to Families with Dependent Children, in addition

to the $2.1 billion left over from fiscal 1984.

Energy Assistance. $2.1 billion was provided for aid to the poor to help pay their fuel bills, up only slightly from $2.08 billion in 1984.

Compensatory Education. Aid for the education of disadvantaged schoolchildren was set at $3.7 billion, compared with the $3.5 billion appropriated in 1984.

College Student Aid. $3.6 billion was included for Pell Grants to help low-income students pay college tuition, enough to allow the maximum award to increase from $1,900 to $2,100. About $2.8 billion was appropriated in 1984.

Education Block Grant. $500 million was provided for block grants for elementary and secondary education, a $50 million increase over the amount set aside for 1984. But conferees refused to accept the House level of $638 million or the administration's request of $650 million — larger increases that had been proposed to help schools meet growing public demand for education reform. ∎

Treasury-Postal Funding Placed in Stopgap Bill

For the fifth year in a row, the regular funding bill for the Treasury Department, Postal Service and other agencies failed to win congressional approval. As in the recent past, funding was provided by a catchall continuing resolution (H J Res 648 — PL 98-473). The continuing appropriation resolution providing fiscal 1985 funding was signed by the president Oct. 12. *(Continuing resolution, p. 444; background on Treasury-Postal appropriations, 1983 Almanac p. 531)*

Conferees on H J Res 648 had few differences to resolve because conferees on the regular Treasury-Postal Service funding bill (HR 5798) had reached almost complete agreement Aug. 9. The House adopted the conference agreement (H Rept 98-993) on HR 5798 Sept. 12, but its rejection of several Senate amendments stalled further action.

The continuing resolution provided the same funding amounts that House and Senate conferees on HR 5798 had agreed to. Funding was set at $12.8 billion — $417 million above the president's request — for the Treasury Department, Postal Service and other independent agencies, including the Executive Office of the President.

The main difference with the administration's request was Congress' approval of a $349 million increase in funds for the U.S. Postal Service to subsidize free and reduced-rate mail for newspaper, book and magazine publishers and non-profit groups.

The House-Senate dispute on HR 5798 centered on a Senate provision to require new forfeiture proceedings for drug-smuggling equipment confiscated by the government. The provision was adopted as part of a larger anti-crime package attached to the continuing resolution. *(Crime bill, p. 215)*

Provisions

As signed into law, H J Res 648 provided the following amounts:

Agency	Budget Request	Final Amount
Treasury Department		
Office of the Secretary	$ 84,242,000	$ 56,474,000

Agency	Budget Request	Final Amount
International Affairs	——	22,768,000
Federal Law Enforcement		
Training Center	16,964,000	18,314,000
Bureau of Government		
Financial Operations	239,908,000	235,994,000
Bureau of Alcohol,		
Tobacco and Firearms	161,771,000	169,271,000
U.S. Customs Service	617,405,000	687,890,000
Bureau of the Mint	47,758,000	47,758,000
Bureau of the Public		
Debt	197,955,000	197,955,000
Internal Revenue Service	3,516,859,000	3,511,200,000
Payment where energy		
credit exceeds		
liability for tax	100,000	100,000
Secret Service	275,731,000	286,500,000
Subtotal	$ 5,158,693,000	$ 5,234,224,000
U.S. Postal Service		
Payment to the Postal		
Service Fund	$ 691,556,000	$ 1,040,509,000
Subtotal	$ 691,556,000	$ 1,040,509,000
Executive Office of the President		
President's Compensation	250,000	250,000
Office of Administration	16,172,000	16,172,000
The White House Office	24,985,000	24,985,000
Executive Residence	4,601,000	4,601,000
Official Residence of		
the Vice President	219,000	219,000
Special Assistance to		
the President	1,663,000	1,663,000
Council of Economic		
Advisers	2,560,000	2,560,000
Office of Policy		
Development	3,020,000	3,020,000
National Security Council	4,605,000	4,605,000

Agency	Budget Request	Final Amount
Office of Management and Budget	40,005,000	38,500,000
Office of Federal Procurement Policy	1,615,000	1,615,000
Unanticipated Needs	1,000,000	1,000,000
Subtotal	$ 100,695,000	$ 99,190,000
Independent Agencies		
Administrative Conference of the United States	$ 1,468,000	$ 1,468,000
Advisory Commission on Intergovernmental Relations	2,131,000	2,131,000
Advisory Committee on Federal Pay	220,000	220,000
Commission on Executive, Legislative and Judicial Salaries	160,000	160,000
Committee for Purchase from the Blind and Other Severely Handicapped	710,000	710,000
Federal Election Commission	10,230,000	12,900,000
General Services Administration	499,849,000	495,089,000
Office of Personnel Management	5,819,374,000	5,815,074,000
Merit Systems Protection Board	25,060,000	25,060,000
Federal Labor Relations Authority	17,197,000	17,197,000
U.S. Tax Court	22,344,000	22,344,000
Subtotal	$ 6,398,743,000	$ 6,392,353,000
Grand Total	$12,349,687,000	$12,766,276,000

House Committee

The House Appropriations Committee June 7 approved HR 5798 (H Rept 98-830). The bill as reported by the committee called for total spending of $12.8 billion. The fiscal 1985 appropriation was $43 million less than the House-passed budget resolution (H Con Res 280) allocated for the agencies. *(Budget resolution, p. 155)*

Several committee Democrats gave notice, however, that when the measure reached the House floor they intended to call for an across-the-board cut in executive office programs in retaliation for the 2 percent overall reduction the House had approved in its legislative branch appropriations bill (HR 5753). *(Legislative funding, p. 387)*

The committee agreed to a subcommittee proposal to add $36 million for the U.S. Customs Service in order to maintain fiscal 1984 employment levels, preserving 923 customs employees' jobs. The full committee also voted to increase the number of Customs Service personnel by an additional 650 positions when it approved an amendment by Rep. John P. Murtha, D-Pa., adding $29 million for the agency. Murtha argued that additional agents were required to protect ailing industries — such as the steel business in his district — against illegal imports.

The committee bill contained several controversial

provisions that were in the Treasury-Postal bill in 1983. One provision prohibited the use of federal employee health benefit funds to pay for abortions except to save the life of the expectant mother. Similar language was part of the fiscal 1984 continuing resolution (PL 98-151), which funded agencies covered by the Treasury-Postal Service bill and other appropriations measures that had not cleared Congress by the end of the session. *(1983 Almanac p. 528)*

The bill also contained language banning the Office of Personnel Management from implementing regulations that would tie federal pay raises and job security to job performance for white-collar employees. The administration objected when similar language was included in 1983. *(1983 Almanac p. 602)*

House Floor

By a 313-98 vote, the House passed HR 5798 June 27, setting spending at $11,896,587,701. The bill was about $453 million less than the amount requested by the administration and $885 million below the total recommended by the House Appropriations Committee. *(Vote 252, p. 78-H)*

Anti- and pro-abortion forces clashed on the House floor over the ban on the use of federal employee health benefits to fund abortions. Opponents argued the prohibition placed an unfair restriction on benefits that federal workers had earned as a term of their employment. But proponents said tax dollars should not be used in such a "life and death" issue. An amendment to delete the provision from the bill was rejected by a vote of 156-261. *(Vote 247, p. 78-H)*

The House, by a 347-59 vote, cut $147,100 from the $1.17 million fund used to pay for the pensions, staffs and other expenses of former presidents. An earlier proposal to cut $890,000 from the fund was rejected, 180-232. *(Votes 251, 250, p. 78-H)*

The House voted 345-66 to accept a 1 percent across-the-board reduction in all spending recommended by the committee, except in the Executive Office of the President. Funds for that office were cut by some $4.8 million — about a 5 percent reduction — in House floor action June 21. *(Vote 248, p. 78-H)*

Funding was deleted entirely for the U.S. Customs Service and the Bureau of the Mint after members raised points of order objecting that legislation authorizing the spending had not been enacted.

The House accepted the committee's recommendation to raise by $349 million President Reagan's $452 million request for postal subsidies for free and reduced-rate mail sent by non-profit organizations, and newspaper, book and magazine publishers. The amount requested by Reagan would have meant a 50 percent increase in rates for such mailers.

Other Provisions

Treasury Department. Besides deleting funds for the Customs Service and the Bureau of the Mint, the House agreed June 21 to cut $13.3 million from the $239.9 million committee recommendation for Treasury's Bureau of Government Financial Operations, which oversaw federal cash management.

The total appropriation for the Treasury Department was $4.5 billion, and included funding for approximately 500 Internal Revenue Service positions for investigations, tax collection and taxpayer service that the administration had wanted to eliminate.

Office of Personnel Management (OPM). The House agreed to a $4.3 million savings in the $5.8 billion OPM budget, to be achieved by consolidation of certain instructional activities. It retained language, opposed by the administration, to prevent OPM from implementing regulations linking pay raises and job security with job performance for white-collar federal employees.

Executive Office of the President. The House June 21 adopted amendments by Elliott H. Levitas, D-Ga., to cut funding for the Office of Administration by $1.5 million and salaries and expenses for the White House and the Office of Management and Budget (OMB) by $3.3 million. The first amendment was adopted 326-74, the others by voice vote. *(Vote 229, p. 72-H)*

General Services Administration (GSA). The House agreed to cut approximately $13 million from the $492 million GSA appropriation recommended by the committee. The savings were to be achieved through more efficient use of computers and better contracting techniques.

Senate Committee

The Senate Appropriations Committee reported its version of HR 5798 (S 2853 — S Rept 98-562) July 17. The Senate bill called for fiscal 1985 Treasury-Postal Service appropriations of $12,738,652,000 — approximately $389 million above the administration's request and $795 million above the House bill.

The differences between it and the House-passed legislation were due largely to the House's 1 percent across-the-board cut and the deletion of Customs Service and Bureau of the Mint funds on the House floor.

The Senate measure exceeded the administration's budget request mainly because it, like the House bill, included a $349 million increase in the postal subsidy for free and reduced-rate mail. It also increased funds for the U.S. Customs Service by allowing for 923 positions the administration had proposed eliminating and by funding 100 new positions.

The Senate committee also agreed to a $12.4 million increase in funding for the Customs Service's air interdiction program to clamp down on illegal drug trafficking and other smuggling.

Instead of requesting reduced funding for former presidents, as the House had done, committee members decided to order a General Accounting Office study of the spending.

To pay for the additional Customs Service funding and the postal subsidy increase, the committee agreed to cut funding for the Internal Revenue Service by $32.4 million, to $3.484 billion. It also reduced funding for the GSA by $5.5 million and for OMB by about $1 million.

Senate Floor

With very little of the controversy that marked debate on Treasury-Postal appropriations bills in previous years, the Senate July 25 passed HR 5798 by a vote of 78-15. *(Vote 180, p. 31-S)*

The $12.7 billion bill was $842 million over the funding level approved by the House. Senate approval marked the first time since 1979 that the chamber had passed a Treasury-Postal Service funding bill.

Potential floor fights over abortion aid for federal em-

ployees and allowances for former presidents were averted during the debate. The only controversy was over an unrelated amendment by Edward M. Kennedy, D-Mass., urging the president to withdraw his controversial appointment of Anne M. Burford, former administrator of the Environmental Protection Agency, to head an advisory commission on national oceanic and atmospheric policy.

The Senate July 24 approved the non-binding "sense of the Senate" amendment by a vote of 74-19, after rejecting, 18-75, a motion to table (kill) the proposal. *(Votes 177, 176, p. 31-S; Burford story, p. 346)*

Abortion

Passage of the bill was eased considerably when Bob Packwood, R-Ore., decided not to bring up a proposed amendment to delete the provision in the bill forbidding the use of federal employee health benefits to fund abortions, except when the life of the mother was in danger. Packwood said he had insufficient votes to win. In 1983, a similar effort in the Senate failed by only one vote. Packwood said that with three of his supporters absent, he could have lost by as many as five votes.

Past Presidents

Also averted was a fight over a proposal by Lawton Chiles, D-Fla., to phase out allowances and Secret Service protection provided to former presidents. Chiles had sponsored separate legislation (S 563) calling for the cuts, but White House opposition had blocked its consideration by the Senate. Senate Appropriations Committee Chairman Mark O. Hatfield, R-Ore., agreed during debate on the Treasury-Postal Service funding bill to drop his "hold" on the bill. *(Former presidents' benefits, p. 192)*

A separate amendment by John H. Chafee, R-R.I., to limit federal funding for presidential libraries, was adopted by voice vote after Chafee modified it to apply only to future presidents. He originally had called for limits on federal funding for seven existing presidential libraries and libraries planned for former Presidents Richard M. Nixon and Jimmy Carter and for President Reagan.

As adopted, the amendment forbade the use of federal funds only for the operation of "non-archival" library activities such as displays of presidential memorabilia.

Other Amendments

The Senate also agreed to an amendment to deny funds for the office of the secretary of the Treasury unless the administration appointed two public members to the Social Security Board of Trustees as required by legislation enacted in 1983 to save the Social Security system from insolvency. *(1983 Almanac p. 219)*

And the Senate approved a Chiles amendment to streamline the procedures used to dispose of airplanes, ships and other property seized by the federal government from smugglers and illegal aliens. Chiles charged that existing procedures lost the federal government money because, under them, it took too long to sell the seized property.

Conference

House and Senate conferees agreed Aug. 9 to a $12.8 billion version of HR 5798. The House, on a 276-110 vote, adopted the conference report (H Rept 98-993) Sept. 12 but rejected several Senate amendments, blocking further action. *(Vote 339, p. 104-H)*

In meetings Aug. 8 and 9, conferees quickly resolved

most differences over funding levels in the House and Senate versions of the bill. Conferees rejected a number of savings approved on the House floor June 27, including a 1 percent across-the-board cut totaling $119 million. Also dropped was the House provision cutting the former presidents' appropriation for pensions, salaries and staffs by $147,100.

They rejected a $1.3 million cut in the White House budget approved on the House floor, but they agreed to cut the OMB budget by $1.5 million. Funds were restored for the U.S. Customs Service and the Bureau of the Mint. These had been dropped on the House floor because of objections that the programs had not yet been authorized.

Special Interest Provisions

Most of the conference haggling revolved around a number of special-interest provisions.

Much controversy centered on a provision added in the Senate to increase from $120 million to $250 million the cap on the funds that could be spent on the national defense stockpile. In a compromise that involved some complex horse trading, conferees agreed to raise the stockpile spending cap to $185 million.

In exchange, Senate conferees agreed to House-passed provisions to spend $5 million on improvements to the John F. Kennedy Library in Boston and to allow construction and repair of a number of other federal buildings in House members' districts around the country.

Conferees also agreed to a compromise plan to continue until July 1, 1985, a congressional directive that prevented the Office of Personnel Management from implementing the regulations linking pay raises and job security to job performance for white-collar federal employees.

Issues Unresolved

Conferees were unable to resolve differences on several issues. The major dispute concerned Senate provisions to facilitate the disposal of airplanes, ships and other property seized by the federal government from smugglers and drug traffickers. The provision was later adopted as part of an anti-crime package attached to H J Res 648.

Another Senate amendment in disagreement, limiting federal funding of new presidential libraries, was dropped in the conference on H J Res 648.   ∎

D.C. Appropriation

Congress cleared the fiscal 1985 appropriation for the District of Columbia as part of the omnibus continuing appropriations resolution (H J Res 648 — PL 98-473) only after settling a yearlong dispute with the administration about the District government's home-rule authority. *(Continuing resolution, p. 444; home rule, p. 190)*

A separate bill making appropriations for the District (HR 5899) had passed both chambers and its details had been worked out in conference. It was the provisions contained in the conference report on HR 5899 (H Rept 98-1088), filed Sept. 26, that were added to the continuing resolution, which cleared Oct. 11.

The measure provided $533 million in federal funds, including a $425 million federal payment to the District as compensation for lost property-tax revenue and costs incurred in its role as the nation's capital.

The total federal appropriation was identical to the

Senate-passed version of the bill and $106 million less than the amount approved by the House. It exceeded the president's budget request by $29.9 million.

In addition, the bill provided $2.36 billion for the District in locally collected revenue, which was $21 million more than Reagan requested and $45 million more than the House approved.

Other Provisions

As part of the money bill, conferees on HR 5899 approved a provision aimed at correcting a major defect in the city's home-rule charter that concerned the ability of Congress to overturn District government-passed laws.

A 1983 Supreme Court decision that struck down similar so-called "legislative veto" provisions enacted by Congress was seen as a threat to the District's home-rule charter. *(1983 Almanac p. 565)*

The House feared that the District's authority to borrow might be jeopardized if the entire charter were invalidated because of the legislative-veto ruling. As a result, the House included in its version of the appropriation bill $155 million for long-term capital loans.

For similar reasons, the Senate version of HR 5899 contained a provision allowing the District to borrow against the full faith and credit of the U.S. Treasury, if federal courts should rule that the entire home-rule charter was unconstitutional.

To replace the suspect legislative veto and settle the issue, the House passed a bill (HR 3932) in October 1983 requiring Congress to pass — and the president to sign — a joint resolution in order to disapprove any law enacted by the District government.

On the eve of the House-Senate conference on HR 5899, the administration dropped its opposition to that approach, and conferees added the bill's provisions to HR 5899.

Conferees on HR 5899 also accepted a Senate provision that would change the mailing address of the Soviet Embassy in Washington, D.C., to "1 Andrei Sakharov Plaza." Sakharov, a Soviet citizen and Nobel Prize-winning physicist, had reportedly been on a hunger strike to protest the Soviet government's treatment of his wife, Yelena Bonner.

The House report on the bill (H Rept 98-851) urged the city to change the name of the street to "Andrei Sakharov Avenue," instead of naming the building.

Conferees also accepted Senate language adding $9.9 million for criminal justice programs, including vocational education and salaries for new judges, and a House provision adding $55.2 million for reimbursements to St. Elizabeths Hospital, including a $20 million one-time payment to cover a shortfall in the city's budget.

On Oct. 9, the House cleared for the president a related bill (HR 6224), paving the way for the transfer of the hospital from the federal government to the District by 1987, and ending federal assistance by 1991. The Reagan administration had proposed ending federal assistance to the hospital in fiscal 1984, and HR 6224 authorized less in annual payments than a previous version. *(1983 Almanac p. 494)*

Legislative History

The House Appropriations Committee reported HR 5899 June 20 (H Rept 98-851), including a total federal appropriation of $639.5 million, and an appropriation of District-collected revenue of $2.32 billion.

During floor action on the bill June 28, Rep. Robert S. Walker, R-Pa., offered an amendment that would cut the federal and District appropriations in the bill by 2 percent. Rep. Thomas A. Daschle, D-S.D., moved to amend the Walker amendment, and cut the appropriations by 1 percent. On a vote of 138-286, Daschle's amendment failed; Walker's amendment then passed on a 239-186 vote. *(Votes 260, 261, p. 80-H)*

Later the same day, the House reversed itself, and on a 151-273 vote, Walker's amendment was defeated. The House then passed the bill by a vote of 308-116. *(Votes 262, 263, p. 82-H)*

The Senate Appropriations Committee reported the bill Aug. 1 (S Rept 98-568), including a total federal appropriation of $533 million and a District appropriation of $2.63 billion.

After accepting by voice vote a "sense of the Congress" amendment that the District should be more aggressive in combating drug trafficking, the Senate passed the bill by voice vote. ∎

Supplemental, Stripped of Latin Aid, Clears

Congress June 26 broke a monthlong deadlock over military and covert aid to Central America and cleared a $1.1 billion fiscal 1984 supplemental appropriations measure (H J Res 492 — PL 98-332).

The final bill included $61.75 million in emergency military aid for El Salvador, down from the $92.75 million requested by the administration. But it dropped the $21 million sought for covert aid to Nicaraguan rebel "contras."

As originally passed by the House March 6, the measure (H Rept 98-604) simply provided $150 million in emergency food aid for famine-stricken Africa.

But the Reagan administration, in an attempt to avoid unfriendly committees, sent its request for Central America directly to the Senate Appropriations Committee, provoking a bitter confrontation over jurisdiction and foreign policy. *(El Salvador policy, p. 73; Nicaragua, p. 86)*

After nine days of often emotional debate, the Senate April 5 passed a $1.15 billion version (S Rept 98-365) containing the funds for Central America and a host of programs ranging from food for Africa to summer jobs for American youth.

For almost a month, the chambers searched in vain for an agreement on a level of covert aid that congressional leaders and the administration could accept. The House adamantly objected to the $21 million to continue CIA support for anti-government guerrillas in Nicaragua.

However, with summer under way, attention focused on a Senate-added item, $100 million for youth summer jobs. Almost daily, Democrats, led by House Speaker Thomas P. O'Neill Jr., D-Mass., chastised the Senate Republican leadership and the administration for insisting on the aid for the contras, holding up the summer job program.

While most issues were resolved easily in two days of meeting, conferees broke up in disagreement May 17 over the Central American issues. House members refused to accept the provisions on El Salvador and Nicaraguan contras, while the Senate insisted upon them.

The House adopted the conference report (H Rept 98-792) May 24 by a vote of 376-36, with the Central America provisions being the only ones in dispute. When the items in disagreement were put to a vote, administration lobbying paid off with the House agreeing 267-154 to the El Salvador funds. However, the House rejected the $21 million for the contras by 241-177. *(Votes 160, 161, p. 52-H; vote 162, p. 54-H)*

The Senate June 25 adopted the conference report by a vote of 79-2 and then voted 88-1 to strip from the bill the controversial $21 million provision. The next day the House cleared the measure for the president. *(Votes 155, 156, p. 28-S)*

As signed into law July 2, the bill provided $60 million in emergency food aid for Africa, down from the $90 million requested by the administration.

In an effort to protect the food aid from being held hostage by the Central American funding flap, Congress provided another $90 million in emergency food aid to another urgent supplemental for fiscal 1984 (H J Res 493 — PL 98-248). *(Story, p. 438)*

H J Res 492 also included $845.5 million in domestic food programs, $25 million for the Customs Service for the purchase of up to eight drug interceptor aircraft, $21 million for the purchase of flooded land in Tug Fork, W.Va., and $2 million to pay the salaries of Civil Aeronautics Board employees for the rest of the fiscal year.

Provisions

As cleared, H J Res 492 contained the following funding for fiscal 1984:

	Administration Request	Final Amount
Food for Peace (PL 480) for Africa	$ 90,000,000	$ 60,000,000*
Child Nutrition Programs	545,544,000	545,544,000
Women, Infants and Children (WIC) Food Program	166,986,000	300,000,000
United States Information Agency, Nassau County, N.Y.	0	850,000
Civil Aeronautics Board Salaries and Expenses	0	2,000,000
Corps of Engineers Tug Fork, W.Va.	0	21,000,000
El Salvador		
Juror Protection	0	500,000
Refugee Assistance	0	7,000,000
Emergency Military Aid	92,750,000	61,750,000
Covert Aid	21,000,000	0
Summer Youth Employment	0	100,000,000
Senate Expenses	0	61,000
Customs Service	0	25,000,000
TOTAL	$916,280,000	$1,123,705,000

* Another urgent supplemental appropriation for fiscal 1984 (H J Res 493 — PL 98-248) provided $90 million in emergency food aid for Africa and $200 million for low-income energy assistance.

General Provisions

Besides the funding levels, H J Res 492 also:

● Required the Office of Surface Mining to release $1 million from Montana's state share for cleanup of the Colorado Tailings site near Butte.

● Required the immediate termination of fiscal 1984 military aid to Panama if the May 6, 1984, elections were disrupted by the Panamanian armed forces. (They were not.)

● Disapproved the administration's deferral of $14 million for construction of the Cumberland Gap tunnel.

● Required the president to submit a report to Congress on the whereabouts of military equipment sent since 1980 to El Salvador, and the location of military personnel trained with U.S. funds.

● Required the immediate cutoff of military aid to El Salvador in the event of a military coup in that country.

● Stated the sense of Congress that the United States should provide military equipment to El Salvador to suppress guerrilla terrorism.

● Provided $1.6 billion in rural housing loans to low-income families, and $690 million to very-low-income borrowers, and allowed up to $230 million to be transferred from low-income to very-low-income accounts.

● Provided $25 million to the Commodity Credit Corporation (CCC) revolving fund to finance exports of U.S. agricultural commodities and provided not less than $5 million in short-term agricultural export credits.

● Barred the National Park Service or the U.S. Fish and Wildlife Service from contracting out services until the agencies completed, and Congress reviewed, a study supporting the contract.

● Maintained a Customs district at Bridgeport, Conn., through Oct. 1.

Background

Representatives of international relief agencies said some 24 countries in Africa suffered food shortages, caused largely by the worst drought on the continent in the century. Inadequate distribution systems, civil wars and a 20-year pattern of declining food production also contributed to the famine.

Food shortages reportedly were most severe in Ethiopia, Ghana, Mauritania and Mozambique. According to Bread for the World, a relief and lobbying group in Washington, D.C., as many as 100,000 persons died of starvation during 1982-83 in Mozambique in southeast Africa. That group said 100 million-150 million Africans eventually could be affected by shortages.

Several members of Congress who visited Africa returned with grim stories of death and starvation.

Sen. John C. Danforth, R-Mo., who visited eight African countries in January, said he found the "classic symptoms" of starvation, especially in rural areas: "emaciated bodies, sticklike limbs and distended bellies." In Mozambique, he said, "I saw what people look like when they're eating leaves off the trees."

Rep. Mickey Leland, D-Texas, said he learned that people traveled hundreds of miles in search of food.

Danforth showed pictures of starving Africans to Reagan, who responded Feb. 9 by requesting the $90 million in additional food aid.

But Danforth said he was worried that any U.S. aid might not arrive in time. "We have to act and we have to

act quickly," he said at a Feb. 21 press conference. If Congress delayed approving additional aid, he added, "hundreds of thousands will die."

House Committee Action

The House Agriculture Appropriations Subcommittee on Feb. 23 approved Reagan's request for $90 million in emergency free food for Africa, and added an authorization for another $90 million in food sales to Africa, at prices the stricken nations could afford.

Relief officials had said much more food than Reagan requested was needed in Africa before the June harvests, which were expected to be meager; it was estimated that it would take three months from the time Congress approved aid until food could be loaded on ships.

The $90 million in aid would provide 245,000 tons of free milk, corn and other grains, under the PL 480 "Food for Peace" program. It would be in addition to 218,000 tons, valued at $85 million, already provided by the United States on an emergency basis. Another $10 million in aid was announced on Jan. 30, and $10 million more was to be announced on Feb. 27.

Although the additional $90 million in sales would allow African countries to buy U.S. food at prices those nations could afford to pay, some relief officials said most of those countries could not afford to pay at all.

Full Committee Action

The House Appropriations Committee Feb. 29 almost doubled the subcommittee's recommendations, raising the donated food for Africa to $150 million. It accepted the additional $90 million in food sales.

Matthew F. McHugh, D-N.Y., offered the amendment to increase the aid from $90 million, saying, "We should err, if we err at all, on the side of providing funds which will go to people in need, rather than err on the side of providing too little."

McHugh's language made it clear that the funds should be spent only if the Agency for International Development was certain it would go to people who needed it.

That provision satisfied members who feared the food would rot on docks because the recipient nations could not or would not distribute it, or that the food would disappear into the black market while thousands starved.

The $150 million in donated food would come from surplus stocks held by the CCC. In addition, the CCC was authorized to sell up to $90 million worth of food to the African nations, or to others that would send the food to Africa.

House Floor Action

The measure was approved by the House March 6 by a 374-29 vote after members on both sides of the aisle spoke in support of increasing the funding over the $90 million requested by the administration. *(Vote 32, p. 12-H)*

"It is wise and moral to give what we can," said Virginia Smith, R-Neb., ranking minority member of the Agriculture Appropriations Subcommittee.

E. "Kika" de la Garza, D-Texas, chairman of the Agriculture Committee, said the United States should provide aid despite high budget deficits and hunger on its own shores. "In spite of our problems," de la Garza said, "the American people are willing to sacrifice."

The only objection came from Bill Frenzel, R-Minn., who argued that permitting sales of CCC stocks could violate international trade agreements. Nevertheless, he said, "the severity of the drought and the testimony of my colleagues convinced me that this is a necessary gesture."

Senate Committee Action

The food aid measure almost immediately became entangled in a bold attempt by the administration to bypass House Democrats and get emergency funding for its operations in El Salvador and Nicaragua.

Reagan Strategy

As devised on March 5 and 6, the administration strategy was to get the normally friendly Senate Appropriations Committee to add the $21 million for the CIA-backed war in Nicaragua to a bill (H J Res 493) providing $200 million for low-income energy assistance in the United States. The $92.75 million for El Salvador was to be added to H J Res 492 appropriating $150 million in food aid to Africa.

The energy and Africa bills were considered "must" measures in the House. Administration strategists had hoped the House would accept the Central America riders rather than jeopardize the bills in a confrontation with Reagan.

The administration also theorized that House Democrats might go along with more money for Central America rather than risk being blamed for "losing" friendly countries to communism.

But that effort failed March 8 in the Republican-controlled Senate Appropriations Committee. The committee rejected, 14-15, Reagan's request to add to H J Res 493 $21 million to continue helping guerrillas who were fighting Nicaragua's leftist government.

Stunned by the rebuff, administration allies on the committee postponed action on a companion Reagan request to include $92.75 million in military aid to the Salvadoran government.

The administration power play was widely viewed on Capitol Hill as a major political blunder that could jeopardize Reagan's entire $8 billion-plus Central America aid program.

Several key leaders were angered because the administration failed to notify them of its request to add Central America funding to the House-passed supplemental appropriations measure. They said they learned of the plan only after word leaked out to reporters. More seriously, by seeking an end run around the House and some Senate committees it considered unfriendly, the administration violated jurisdictional boundaries, which were sacrosanct in Congress.

Senate Budget Committee Chairman Pete V. Domenici, R-N.M., complained about the "extemporaneous, under-the-gun" administration lobbying: "If the State Department is going to manage the remaining activity in the way they have managed this so far, I guarantee them and I guarantee the president, they are going to fail."

While the administration directed its efforts to the Senate, Democrats on the House Foreign Affairs Committee struggled to develop an alternative to Reagan's Central America plan. After four days of private talks, the Democrats on March 8 tentatively agreed to reject any extra military aid for El Salvador in fiscal 1984 and to place tough conditions on military aid for 1985. They were to discuss the issue again on March 14.

Also, on March 7-8 the Senate Intelligence Committee insisted that Reagan seek its approval for the Nicaragua money before taking the request to the Appropriations Committee. The Intelligence panel oversaw "covert" activities, and Chairman Barry Goldwater, R-Ariz., reportedly was furious that the administration was planning to bypass it.

Committee Action on Nicaragua

But the administration's scheme to pre-empt the House failed by a one-vote margin March 8 when the Senate Appropriations Committee voted 14-15 to reject the request to attach $21 million in covert aid for Nicaragua guerrillas to H J Res 493.

Two senators who normally supported Reagan on Central America — Warren B. Rudman, R-N.H., and Lawton Chiles, D-Fla. — deserted him on key votes that led to rejection of the CIA money.

Rudman said he feared the Nicaragua rider would kill or delay the energy bill. "There are people in my state who are cold," he said.

Chiles objected to the procedure and said he wanted more information about CIA activities in Nicaragua.

The Appropriations Committee's session was one of its most acrimonious in years. For more than two hours, senators squabbled about procedure and personal privilege. Sitting with an aide between them, Chairman Mark O. Hatfield, R-Ore., and Majority Whip Ted Stevens, R-Alaska, battled throughout the meeting.

A critic of U.S. military involvement in Central America, Hatfield warned that he would do everything possible to thwart the money for El Salvador and Nicaragua. "I find it very difficult to comprehend that on March 8 we face a deadline, that I only heard about yesterday, on a problem in Nicaragua that will be in effect unless we act today," he said.

Stevens, chairman of the Subcommittee on Defense, said he was "obligated" to push the Nicaragua proposal because Reagan asked him to do so.

Both men struggled to control their tempers as the meeting dragged on under the television lights. Hatfield fiddled nervously with his chairman's gavel. Stevens squirmed in his chair and, during a recess, paced the floor as some of his colleagues went to an adjoining room to be lobbied by administration officials.

Hatfield wanted the committee to approve the energy bill immediately, without amendments. Stevens wanted to attach the administration amendment providing $21 million for Nicaragua — or at least to delay action to give the administration more time to lobby.

Hatfield repeatedly ruled out of order Stevens' motions to raise the Nicaragua issue, and at one point, Stevens exploded: "Somewhere there must be some concept of fairness."

Stevens won the first test vote, when the committee decided, 13-12, to delay action on the energy bill until March 13. But after a recess, the panel voted 13-12 to reconsider that action.

After more procedural wrangling, and little debate on the substance of the issue, the committee rejected, 14-15, Stevens' motion to attach the Nicaragua money to the energy bill.

All Republicans except Hatfield, Rudman and Lowell P. Weicker Jr., Conn., supported Stevens, and all Democrats except Dennis DeConcini, Ariz., and J. Bennett Johnston, La., opposed him.

El Salvador Aid

Left unresolved by the committee's March 8 action was Reagan's request to boost aid to El Salvador.

Reagan had sent a $178.7 million request for additional military aid for El Salvador to Congress on Feb. 17, and it was pending in several committees. Since early February there were reports that Reagan would use emergency powers to provide some of the aid without approval of Congress.

Members were outraged, and the State Department decided not to use the emergency powers. Instead, it would seek the money from the Senate Appropriations Committee, which had approved all of Reagan's previous requests for such aid.

When the Appropriations Committee met again March 14, it quickly added the $21 million for Nicaragua to H J Res 492, but the El Salvador funds took more time.

After rejecting, 13-16, an effort to delay action, the panel approved the El Salvador funds by voice vote and included a requirement that the aid be contingent on reports from the president that human rights concerns were being met.

Bob Kasten, R-Wis., offered the amendment containing the administration funding request, saying it was necessary to ensure that the March 25 elections in that country proceeded peacefully. "Without the funds," Kasten said, "the armed forces will collapse."

But Daniel K. Inouye, D-Hawaii, said the administration failed to provide documents justifying the urgency of the aid and offered a motion to defer action until the administration proved it was crucial. Inouye argued that Congress should wait to see who won the Salvadoran election. One presidential candidate, Roberto d'Aubuisson, had been linked to right-wing "death squads."

"We have no knowledge about who will use the funds," Inouye said. "It is of some consequence."

But Stevens said, "It is incumbent on this committee to respond to need. We should send a signal during the election period that we're not going to walk away and wash our hands," referring to an earlier comment by an administration official that compared the committee with Pontius Pilate.

Deferring action could send the wrong message to Central America, Mark Andrews, R-N.D., agreed. But he said the administration, not Congress, should bear the burden. "We're not bringing this on. The administration did," he said.

Andrews also argued that the African food aid should be passed without any riders. "I hope we don't louse up the Food for Peace bill with this," he said.

Even though Andrews, Chairman Hatfield and Weicker voted with most of the committee Democrats to defer the El Salvador request, the Inouye motion failed, 13-16.

Inouye said he would offer a floor amendment to reduce the aid to about $50 million, the amount that Pentagon documents indicated was necessary to continue existing activities.

Human Rights

Kasten's proposal included an attempt to guarantee that the aid would be contingent on El Salvador's making progress in human rights.

Based on the recommendations of the commission on Central America headed by former Secretary of State Henry A. Kissinger, Kasten's amendment required that the administration certify to Congress that El Salvador had made progress toward free elections, freedom of association, the establishment of a rule of law and an effective judicial system, termination of killings by death squads and prosecution of those guilty of crimes. *(Kissinger commission, p. 93)*

At the suggestion of DeConcini, Kasten modified his proposal to require a certification every 60 days, instead of making only one certification.

But Patrick J. Leahy, D-Vt., said the conditions still were not enough to guarantee progress. "We can wrap this in all kinds of language, as we have in the past," Leahy said, "but let's not kid ourselves into thinking this will make any kind of change."

Arlen Specter, R-Pa., offered a stiffer plan requiring El Salvador to establish a special investigative prosecuting unit to expedite bringing alleged death squad members to justice. Aid would be cut 50 percent until the Reagan administration certified after 60 days that the prosecuting unit was working.

But that might violate the Salvadoran Constitution, Kasten suggested.

Saying that "we should not be writing foreign policy in this committee," Domenici submitted a motion to table (kill) Specter's amendment. It carried, 21-3.

Other Amendments

As reported by the panel, the resolution included $959 million more than the House-passed $150 million.

Child Nutrition. The committee adopted Thomas F. Eagleton's, D-Mo., proposal to add an administration request for a fiscal 1984 supplemental appropriation of $545 million for child nutrition programs, including school lunches, school breakfasts and meals in child-care centers.

According to Eagleton, the Agriculture Department would run out of funds in mid-May.

In addition, the panel agreed to add $300 million for the Women, Infants and Children (WIC) program, $133 million more than the administration requested. Eagleton said that the administration's request would result in 400,000 recipients being cut from the program.

Federal Magistrates. The panel also approved an amendment by DeConcini to set the top salary of federal magistrates at $65,800 a year. DeConcini said a 1978 law that linked the salaries of magistrates and bankruptcy judges would expire April 1. He said that an oversight in the drafting of that law would result in magistrates' salaries reverting to the 1978 level of $51,000.

Panama. Concerned that the May 6 elections in Panama remained free, the committee agreed to an Inouye amendment to withhold military aid to that country if the military disrupted the elections.

Cumberland Gap. The committee also agreed to disapprove an administration deferral of funds for construction of the Cumberland Gap tunnel. That left the funds — $14 million — available to be spent.

Senate Floor Action

After decisively rejecting Democratic efforts to cut or sharply restrict funding, the Senate by a 76-19 vote April 5 passed H J Res 492 providing $61.75 million for El Salvador and $21 million for covert aid to Nicaraguan rebels. *(Vote 56, p. 12-S)*

Administration supporters prevailed on most votes during the nine days of debate. Consideration began March

22 and continued on March 26-30 and April 2-5.

On passage, 53 Republicans voted with 23 Democrats to support the package, while Weicker of Connecticut was the only Republican voting against it.

Democratic critics got the full-scale debate they sought on Reagan's policy but won only partial victories. They succeeded with an amendment requiring funds to El Salvador to be cut off if there were a military coup there, and they secured a pledge from the Intelligence Committee to probe possible Central Intelligence Agency involvement in Salvadoran death squad activity.

Mostly, though, critics could muster only 20 to 30 votes for each of their 12 amendments, revealing a deep division within the Democratic Party on Central American policy. A key amendment requiring congressional authorization for the introduction of troops in El Salvador was aimed at presenting a united Democratic front; but 10 Democrats joined most Republicans in casting their votes against the proposal.

Other votes indicated, however, there were cracks in Senate support for administration Central American policy. For the first time, members of the Intelligence Committee publicly expressed doubts about continued covert aid there.

Funding by the measure totaled $1.15 billion. Besides the Central American funds, the bill included $545 million for child nutrition aid, $100 million for summer youth jobs and $300 million for the WIC food program.

Initial Debate Postponed

Majority Leader Howard H. Baker Jr., R-Tenn., had hoped to bring up the Central American aid package March 21 but withdrew it to proceed with another measure.

Edward M. Kennedy, D-Mass., warned later that he would object to any attempt to bring it up before the Salvadoran election March 25.

"I just wish to indicate to the majority leader my opinion," Kennedy said, "and that of a number of other members of this body, that the March 25 presidential election should take place without the Senate interfering in any way by adopting a position on the emergency aid supplemental."

But Baker said the Senate should act immediately. "I think it is a very positive interference or at least a very positive signal to the people who will participate in the election in El Salvador," he said.

Baker March 22 said he intended to bring up the supplemental. But after late-night consultations with other key senators and administration officials, he announced an agreement with the administration to cut its proposed $92.75 million in military aid to El Salvador by one-third and to postpone a vote until after the election.

Under the terms of the agreement, which Baker said he supported, Inouye would offer an amendment to cut the El Salvador aid to $61.75 million.

Inouye originally had intended to offer an amendment to cut the figure to $49.2 million, the amount the Pentagon had indicated was necessary to carry on existing activities through the end of fiscal 1984. Inouye agreed to add $12.5 million more to provide necessary medical supplies and training.

March 28: Oil Mergers

Although debate continued sporadically March 26-27, no substantive action occurred until March 28, when the Senate took up the issue of oil mergers before turning to the Central America controversies.

In a surprise move, senators killed a proposed 11-month moratorium on mergers involving the 50 largest oil firms, adopting instead a substitute requiring Congress to study the issue. It had appeared that a majority of senators favored the moratorium.

Johnston had revised an earlier moratorium plan and exempted three large takeovers already under way: SoCal-Gulf, Texaco-Getty and Mobil-Superior. Also, Johnston had cut the number of firms affected from 150 — those with reserves of more than 10 million barrels — to 50 companies with worldwide reserves of more than 100 million barrels.

Although he and some of his supporters still favored a retroactive moratorium, Johnston said he recognized that "the votes are on the side of these [future] mergers."

While admitting that "we don't know all of the results" of the mergers, Johnston said he suspected that they could be harmful to the economy, draining money from credit markets and exploration budgets.

His proposal would have created a commission to study mergers while the moratorium was in place, and to report to Congress. At the request of Missouri's Danforth, Johnston extended the moratorium expiration date from Sept. 21, 1984, to March 1, 1985, with the report due Jan. 1, 1985, to give Congress time to consider any legislative changes.

Others argued that the merger of large energy firms would not harm the economy or consumers. Johnston's proposal "seeks to protect the American people from non-existent dangers," said Lloyd Bentsen, D-Texas.

Noting that "the market is self-correcting," Bentsen cautioned Congress to keep its hands off the marketplace. "I don't believe the Congress should be in the business of legislating moratoriums on economic activities, especially when the public interest is not being harmed."

Orrin G. Hatch, R-Utah, agreed, but suggested that Congress did not know enough about the issue. He proposed a substitute requiring the president to appoint a commission to study the merger question, without imposing a halt.

Moratorium backers called Hatch's plan a "hollow substitute." "One thing we cannot do," said Rudman, "is simply sit by and do nothing."

In response, Baker, on behalf of Robert Dole, R-Kan., and other moratorium foes, proposed that Congress, rather than a presidential commission, look into the problem, without calling a halt to the mergers. The plan called on the Finance, Energy and Judiciary committees to study the merger question and to report to the Senate by July 1, 1984.

Further, Dole's amendment stipulated that any legislative changes recommended by the committees take effect March 27, 1984.

With that provision, Dole said, oil companies rushing into mergers were "put on notice" that any tax or antitrust laws they wanted to take advantage of may be swept out from under them.

But Johnston called Dole's plan a "killer amendment," saying that Congress would not have time to deal with all the changes that needed to be considered. "The clock would catch everything that comes under the Dole amendment," Johnston said.

Rudman's motion to table Dole's plan failed by a vote of 39-57, and it subsequently passed by voice vote. *(Vote 40, p. 10-S)*

March 29: Central America

In delving into the Central America controversy March 29, the Senate rejected two efforts to limit U.S. involvement in Central America and agreed to the compromise cutting emergency funds for El Salvador by one-third, to $61.75 million.

Critics of administration policies in Central America, led by Kennedy and Christopher J. Dodd, D-Conn., resisted pleas by GOP leaders for quick action on the aid package. The critics had been pushing for an extended debate on Central American policy since the measure came to the floor March 26.

But late March 29, after two Kennedy amendments to curtail U.S. activities in the region were rejected, Dodd and Kennedy agreed to limit debate. In return, Republican leaders agreed not to press for a roll-call vote on the administration-backed amendment cutting funds for El Salvador to $61.7 million. The reduced amount was approved by voice vote.

Part of the agreement included putting off additional Central America amendments until floor consideration resumed the week of April 2. Kennedy and others indicated they then would offer more than 20 amendments to keep the debate focused on foreign policy.

The two nearly identical Kennedy proposals that failed would have required congressional authorization to send combat forces to Central America. The first, barring troops in El Salvador, Nicaragua and Honduras, was in response to a report in *The Washington Post* that American planes were used in reconnaissance missions over El Salvador.

Although Kennedy hoped for prolonged discussion of the amendment, Baker quickly moved to table it as Kennedy started to leave to attend a committee meeting. The motion carried, 71-20. *(Vote 41, p. 10-S)*

Kennedy then introduced an almost identical amendment, except for the deletion of the word "Honduras," and demanded a debate. "You can table the amendment," Kennedy said, "but you cannot table the issue."

Kennedy and others evoked the memory of the Vietnam War. Dodd contrasted Kennedy's amendment to the Gulf of Tonkin Resolution passed by Congress, which authorized President Johnson to send combat troops to Vietnam. He warned that the Senate should not make the same mistake again.

Donald W. Riegle Jr., D-Mich., agreed. "The people who brought us Vietnam, who brought us the Vietnam War policy, are in the process of bringing us the same kind of policy in Central America," he said.

John P. East, R-N.C., reached further back in history to defend American involvement in the region. Calling the Kennedy approach "no policy at all," East said, "It is basically the old isolationism of the 1930s; we simply wash our hands of what is occurring in Central America. I think we do that at great risk."

After almost three hours of debate, Kennedy's second amendment failed, 23-72. *(Vote 42, p. 10-S)*

April 2: El Salvador Cut Fails

Kennedy offered an amendment April 2 to cut El Salvador funding from $61.75 million to $21 million. He said that amount would last through the runoff presidential election, which he warned could be won by second-place d'Aubuisson.

Inouye, who had convinced the administration to agree to cut its original request of $92.75 million to $61.75 mil-

lion, said he was sympathetic to Kennedy's aims. But he said he wanted a compromise that would pass. "I could be on your side and voting against all military assistance," said Inouye. "I know that we would lose."

Another proposal by John Melcher, D-Mont., would have cut funding from $61.75 million to $35.4 million, but it would have sliced more deeply into military aid than Kennedy's plan. Melcher included $7.9 million in military aid, while all of the $21 million in Kennedy's plan was military aid. Melcher also proposed $13.5 million in medical aid and $14 million in food aid.

Melcher's sharp cut in military aid concerned several senators. It would result in a "bloodbath," said Inouye. It is a "catastrophic signal to send to the Salvadorans," said Kasten.

East accused the two Democrats of stalling. "The real effect of this is to gut any real genuine military assistance to the army of El Salvador," said East. "To me, that would be a real tragedy."

Kennedy's amendment failed by a 25-63 vote, and Melcher's, by 24-63. *(Votes 46, 47, p. 11-S)*

Two other Kennedy amendments were adopted by voice vote. One provided $7 million for displaced persons in El Salvador and the second required progress on land reform as a condition for military aid.

April 3: Conditions Rejected

Besides rejecting efforts to cut the funds provided to El Salvador, the Senate turned down several attempts to put conditions on the funding.

Kennedy April 3 proposed withholding 15 percent of the funds, or $9.26 million, until the Salvadoran government obtained a verdict in the 1981 murders of two U.S. labor advisers in that country.

Opponents argued that since the case was far from resolution, the amendment amounted to a 15 percent cut. Inouye noted that in the United States in 1982, out of 100 arrests for murder, 32 of those arrested were not prosecuted. "How can we hold El Salvador to a higher standard?" he asked.

Kennedy, his voice rising, shot back, "We are not talking about unsolved murders. We are talking about organized assassination squads."

The Senate tabled Kennedy's amendment, 69-24. *(Vote 48, p. 11-S)*

Specter then proposed withholding 30 percent of the money, or $18.5 million, until the 1980 deaths of four U.S. churchwomen were solved. That case was expected to come to trial soon. A similar Specter amendment had been added to the fiscal 1984 foreign aid appropriation, and as a result, $19 million in military aid to El Salvador had not yet been spent.

Specter argued that the Salvadoran government should be pressured to bring the case to trial. But Vermont's Leahy said that Specter's 1983 amendment should preclude any new Salvadoran aid at all. He proposed, as a substitute, that no more money be sent until the murders were resolved.

Specter, arguing a total ban went too far, said, "It is unwise to tie the hands of the administration totally."

Kasten's motion to table Specter's amendment carried, 54-39, which also had the effect of killing Leahy's substitute. *(Vote 49, p. 11-S)*

The Senate later adopted by voice vote an amendment by Daniel Patrick Moynihan, D-N.Y., adding $500,000 to protect jurors and witnesses in the trial of the alleged killers of the churchwomen.

Kennedy proposed a further restriction, to prohibit military aid after May 31, 1984, unless the administration certified by June 30, 1984, that the Salvadoran government had agreed to participate in unconditional negotiations with all parties in the conflict in that country, including the leftist guerrillas. The amendment was tabled, 63-26. *(Vote 50, p. 11-S)*

An amendment he offered to require the president to report to Congress within 120 days of enactment on the location of U.S. equipment sent to El Salvador since 1980 was adopted by voice vote.

A proposal by Pete Wilson, R-Calif., stating that it was U.S. policy to povide military aid to El Salvador to protect the people and to suppress guerrilla activity to allow economic revival also was adopted by voice vote.

April 4: Combat Troops

After a heated two-hour debate, the Senate April 4 voted for the third time against requiring congressional authorization for the introduction of combat troops in or over Central America.

On March 29, the Senate had rejected two Kennedy amendments on the subject.

The third effort, initiated by Leahy, differed from Kennedy's in several respects. It was limited to El Salvador and did not supersede the War Powers act, which required the president to withdraw troops 60 days after their introduction unless Congress passed a joint resolution authorizing their presence.

Inouye cosponsored Leahy's amendment but had spoken against Kennedy's proposals, because, he said, they weakened the War Powers act.

Leahy's plan was an attempt by Senate Democrats to present a unified front on a Central American issue. It was drafted by a task force set up by the leadership and chaired by Inouye.

Supporters evoked the memory of the Vietnam era. "We're finding ourselves slip-sliding into the Americanization of this war," Leahy warned.

Joseph R. Biden Jr., D-Del., bet Nancy Landon Kassebaum, R-Kan., a month's salary that Reagan, if re-elected, would send troops into El Salvador the day after Election Day.

Leahy likened his amendment to a referendum on the introduction of troops. "Are you in favor of American armed forces fighting in El Salvador or are you not?" he asked.

But others argued that Leahy's plan would tie the hands of the president, perhaps beyond the Constitution's limits. "We would be way off base entirely," said John C. Stennis, D-Miss., "to give this much of a limitation to the executive."

The amendment was tabled, 59-36. *(Vote 51, p. 12-S)*

Also on April 4, the Senate adopted by voice vote an amendment, opposed by the administration, to cut off funds to El Salvador in the event of a military coup against the newly elected government. Sponsor Dale Bumpers, D-Ark., said he had heard reports that a coup was possible by right-wing forces if moderate José Napoleón Duarte won the runoff.

Senate critics also failed to limit aid to Nicaraguan rebels.

Kennedy called administration policy in Nicaragua "illegal [and] ... indefensible" and called for cutting all $21 million from the bill.

He said that despite U.S. assertions that the aim in aiding the anti-government guerrillas was to pressure the Sandinista regime to change its policies, the aid was helping the guerrillas, or "contras," seize power.

"There are very, very few people in this world who really believe that our aid to the contras is not an attempt to overthrow the government of Nicaragua," Kennedy said.

But Majority Whip Stevens argued that the Sandinistas were so well armed, "it would be ludicrous to think that we could possibly overthrow that government with even $21 million."

But the issue of precisely what the stated purpose was had become clouded March 29, when Reagan, in an interview with *The New York Times*, said the covert aid was aimed at overthrowing the Nicaraguan government, contrary to previously stated administration policy.

Just before the vote on the Kennedy amendment on April 4, Majority Leader Baker read a letter from Reagan asserting that no policy change had taken place. The Senate defeated the amendment, 30-61. *(Vote 52, p. 12-S)*

The Senate also killed two other attempts to restrict funds. One, offered by Dodd, barred the use of covert funds for "planning, directing, executing or supporting acts of sabotage or terrorism in, over or offshore from the territory of Nicaragua."

But Rudman said the line between terrorism and acts of war was vague and he was "uncertain" what Dodd meant by terrorism. The Senate tabled Dodd's amendment, 47-43. *(Vote 53, p. 12-S)*

April 5: Honduras

On April 5, the Senate rejected an amendment by Carl Levin, D-Mich., which he said would put into law the policy Reagan had stated in his letter to Baker. The amendment barred the use of covert funds to support groups intending to overthrow the government of a country with which the United States had full diplomatic relations, such as Nicaragua.

"We cannot very innocently provide money knowing that the money will be illegally spent," said Inouye, a cosponsor of the amendment.

But Stevens said that Levin's amendment would effectively cut off aid to the contras, since they had stated that they intended to overthrow the Sandinista regime in Nicaragua. The Senate agreed to Stevens' motion to table the Levin amendment, 51-44. *(Vote 54, p. 12-S)*

Jim Sasser, D-Tenn., tried to prohibit the Department of Defense from using operation and maintenance funds to convert temporary facilities used for military exercises in Honduras to permanent use.

He said that the administration had built "a military infrastructure capable of supporting a major armed intervention by U.S. troops in the region" without explaining what it was doing. He said that congressional authorization should be required before construction of permanent military facilities in Honduras.

But Stevens, saying the facilities were temporary, proposed a substitute to permit their upgrading. It also retained a provision in the committee bill allowing the president to use operations and maintenance funds if he determined that an emergency existed that required construction, modification or improvement.

Sasser countered with a plan allowing upgrading but leaving out the president's emergency authority.

Stevens' motion to table Sasser's original amendment was agreed to, 50-44, leaving in place the language barring the expenditure of operations and maintenance funds for other than temporary facilities. *(Vote 55, p. 12-S)*

Non-Central America Amendments

Other amendments adopted during debate — by voice vote, unless otherwise indicated — included the following:

● **March 29:** By DeConcini, adding $25 million for the purchase of eight drug interceptor aircraft for use by the Customs Service against airborne drug smugglers.

● By Alfonse M. D'Amato, R-N.Y., providing $850,000 for the U.S. Information Agency for payment to Nassau County, N.Y., as reimbursement for activities carried out by the county during the 1984 International Games for the Disabled.

● By DeConcini and Strom Thurmond, R-S.C., setting the maximum salary for federal magistrates at $67,500 a year and requiring congressional authorization for any pay increase.

● **March 30:** By Thad Cochran, R-Miss., requiring guaranteed export credits for agricultural commodities for fiscal 1985 to be at a level of $5 billion, instead of $3 billion as requested.

● By Cochran, adding $175 million for the PL 480 "Food for Peace" credit program, and cutting direct food aid to Africa from $150 million to $60 million in fiscal 1984. Adopted 71-2. *(Vote 43, p. 11-S)*

● By Cochran, making available $1.38 billion for low-income families and $920 million for very-low-income families, from the Farmers Home Administration rural housing loan fund.

● By Melcher, providing $5 million in emergency food aid to the Philippines. Adopted 57-19. *(Vote 44, p. 11-S)*

● By Cochran, permitting the Federal Crop Insurance Corporation to borrow from the Treasury up to $50 million to pay for damages resulting from the 1983 drought.

● By Max Baucus, D-Mont., and Cochran, requiring the Office of Surface Mining to release $1 million from Montana's state share for cleanup of the Colorado Tailings site near Butte.

● By Specter, providing $3.4 million for construction and renovation of academic facilities in Philadelphia.

● By David L. Boren, D-Okla., eliminating the June 30, 1984, deadline for new state participation in the Work Incentive demonstration program, and striking the three-year limit on participation in the program.

● **April 5:** By Melcher, requiring the Department of Education to distribute appropriated impact aid funds, which assisted school districts having heavy concentrations of dependents of federal employees.

● By Alan J. Dixon, D-Ill., providing $100 million for summer youth employment programs to assure that areas received at least 90 percent of their 1983 funding.

● By Stevens, providing $15 million for the Corporation for Public Broadcasting in fiscal 1984, $23 million for 1985 and $32 million in 1986; and to prohibit the use of funds for entertainment of government officials and discrimination on the basis of sex, race, color, national origin or religion.

● By Hatfield, earmarking $61,000 from the Senate contingency fund to print and sell "A History of the Senate."

● By Hatfield and Minority Leader Robert C. Byrd, D-W.Va., authorizing construction of the Bonneville lock and dam in Oregon and Washington, and the Gallipolis lock and dam in Ohio and West Virginia.

● By Baucus, barring the National Park Service from contracting out services until it completed, and Congress reviewed, a study supporting the contract.

● By Spark M. Matsunaga, D-Hawaii, urging that Naval Civil Engineer Corps officers, or Seabees, provide aid and training for African rural projects.

● By Melcher, urging that surplus wheat and dairy products be sent to aid Guatemalan refugees in Mexico.

Provisions

As passed by the Senate, H J Res 492 appropriated for fiscal 1984:

Central America

● $61.75 million for El Salvador, including $49.25 million in military aid and $12.5 million in medical aid. Funds would be cut off in the event of a military coup in that country. The president must certify to Congress within 60 days after enactment, and every 60 days thereafter, that the government of El Salvador had demonstrated progress toward free elections, freedom of association, establishment of an effective judicial system, land reform and the termination of activities of so-called death squads.

● $7 million for refugee assistance to El Salvador.

● $500,000 for witness and juror protection in the case of four murdered U.S. churchwomen in El Salvador.

● $21 million in covert aid to rebels in Nicaragua.

Food Aid, Other Programs

● $60 million for PL 480 "Food for Peace" emergency food donations to Africa and $175 million in credits.

● $545.5 million for child nutrition programs, including school lunches, school breakfasts and meals in child-care centers.

● $300 million for the Women, Infants and Children program, providing food to poor women who are pregnant or nursing, and impoverished young children.

● $5 million for PL 480 "Food for Peace" emergency food aid to the Philippines.

● $3.4 million for the historically black Lincoln University and Cheyney State College in Philadelphia, Pa.

● $850,000 for the U.S. Information Agency for payment to Nassau County, N.Y., for county activities involving the 1984 International Games for the Disabled.

● $25 million for the purchase of eight drug interceptor aircraft for use by the Customs Service against airborne drug smugglers.

● $100 million for the summer youth employment program, requiring that local areas received at least 90 percent of their 1983 funding.

● $15 million for the Corporation for Public Broadcasting in fiscal 1984, $23 million for fiscal 1985, and $32 million in fiscal 1986; and prohibited the use of funds for entertainment of government officials, and discrimination on the basis of sex, race, color, national origin or religion.

● $61,000 for the contingency fund of the Senate for printing and selling "A History of the Senate."

Miscellaneous Provisions

● Made available $1.38 billion for low-income families, and $920 million for very-low-income families, from the Farmers Home Administration rural housing loan fund.

● Permitted the Federal Crop Insurance Corporation to borrow from the Treasury up to $50 million to pay for damages resulting from the 1983 drought.

● Required the secretary of agriculture to make available $5 million in short-term export credits.

● Required the Office of Surface Mining to release $1 million from Montana's state share for cleanup of the Colorado Tailings site near Butte.

● Eliminated the June 30, 1984, deadline for new state participation in the Work Incentive demonstration program, and struck the three-year limit on participation in the program.

● Set the maximum salary for federal magistrates at $67,500 a year and required congressional authorization for any pay increase.

● Required the immediate termination of military aid to Panama if the Panamanian military disrupted the May 6 national election.

● Disapproved the administration's deferral of $14 million for construction of the Cumberland Gap tunnel.

● Required the Senate Judiciary, Energy and Natural Resources, and Finance committees to study oil company mergers, and report to the Senate by July 1, 1984. Any recommendations enacted would be effective March 27, 1984.

● Barred the National Park Service from contracting out services until it completed, and Congress reviewed, a study supporting the contract.

● Required the Department of Education to distribute appropriated impact aid funds, which assisted school districts having heavy concentrations of dependents of federal employees.

● Authorized construction of the Bonneville lock and dam in Oregon and Washington, and the Gallipolis lock and dam in Ohio and West Virginia.

● Urged that Naval Civil Engineer Corps officers, or Seabees, provide aid and training for African rural projects.

● Urged that surplus wheat and dairy products be sent to aid Guatemalan refugees in Mexico.

● Required the president to report to Congress within 120 days of enactment on the location of U.S. equipment sent to El Salvador since 1980.

● Stated that it was U.S. policy to provide military aid to El Salvador to protect the people and to suppress guerrilla activity to allow economic revival.

Conference Action Stalled

O'Neill and Baker agreed April 12 to send Congress on its Easter recess without resolving the issue of aid to Central America, allowing the Reagan administration to use its emergency powers to send money to El Salvador.

The leaders had hoped to reach agreement before the recess, but congressional anger over U.S. policies in Central America and sharp divisions over funding levels made it clear that they would not be able to complete a House-Senate conference on the emergency supplemental appropriation.

The Senate's $21 million in covert aid to Nicaraguan rebels drew increased opposition in the wake of reports that the CIA was responsible for mining Nicaraguan harbors.

Both chambers overwhelmingly adopted non-binding resolutions condemning the mining, throwing the question of aid to Nicaraguan rebels in doubt. "There is no question in my mind," said O'Neill, "that the $21 million in covert aid hasn't got a chance in the House."

But Baker said he thought the covert aid was "salvageable" and said there was a "clear distinction between disapproval of the mining of the harbor and continued support for the program."

On El Salvador, House Democratic leaders agreed to support a total of $32.5 million, whether the administration sent it or Congress appropriated it.

Other Issues In Dispute

Jamie L. Whitten, D-Miss., House Appropriations Committee chairman, also objected to the array of Senate amendments. He said some were legislative provisions that did not belong on an appropriations bill, especially so early in the year.

"At the end of a session, if it's the last train going, you jump on," Whitten said.

Whitten April 11 introduced a separate supplemental appropriations bill (HR 5419), which included elements of the Senate version that he said he thought the House would accept.

It contained the Senate levels of $100 million for summer youth jobs and $60 million in food aid to Africa. But it cut child nutrition programs from $545.5 million to $401.5 million and the Women, Infants and Children nutritional program from $300 million to $66 million.

In addition, HR 5419 kept a Senate provision separating rural housing loans for low-income and very-low-income families. It also permitted military aid for El Salvador at present levels for 30 days, from unobligated military assistance and included $25 million in agricultural export credits.

Setback for President

The president's El Salvador proposal received two setbacks May 2 when the House Appropriations Committee approved Whitten's new bill that did not contain an aid provision and the full House voted against going to conference on H J Res 492.

The Appropriations Committee by voice vote reported a renumbered version of Whitten's scaled-down supplemental appropriations measure (HR 5564 — H Rept 98-729) after a controversial provision — allowing the president to send aid to El Salvador at existing levels for 30 days from unused military assistance funds — was removed.

By reporting a new bill, committee leaders hoped to move ahead with non-controversial funding provisions while trying to resolve the Central American issue.

Whitten said he had inserted the 30-day provision in HR 5564 before Reagan April 13 invoked executive authority to sell security-related equipment to El Salvador to help safeguard presidential elections there.

As reported, HR 5564 included $60 million for food aid to drought-stricken Africa, $100 million for summer youth jobs, $401.5 million for child nutrition and $66 million for the WIC program, the nutrition program for low-income pregnant and nursing women and preschool children.

In addition, HR 5564 contained a provision creating separate accounts for rural housing loans for low-income and very-low-income families, and included $25 million in agricultural export credits.

Most of those provisions, though some at different funding levels, had been added by the Senate to H J Res 492.

House Rejects Conference

Silvio O. Conte, R-Mass., complained about the "comic opera" that he said Whitten was conducting in his effort to skirt a conference with the Senate on H J Res 492. "We've faced them [the Senate]," said Conte. "We're not afraid of those guys. . . . Let's not take this devious route," he said.

But Whitten called H J Res 492 a "Sears, Roebuck catalog" because of all the amendments that were added by the Senate.

Conte, the senior Republican on the committee, then moved to postpone indefinitely consideration of Whitten's bill and instead to instruct the House conferees to meet with the Senate on H J Res 492. That motion was defeated by the committee on a party-line 16-26 vote.

Later that day, Conte offered a similar motion on the floor of the House but lost by a party-line 159-245 vote. Conte said that, as far as he knew, a motion to instruct conferees simply to meet was "unique in the history of the House." *(Vote 111, p. 38-H)*

Conference Action

With increasing pressure to move ahead on the summer jobs program and other non-Central America aid issues, conferees met May 16-17.

Some issues in the two-day conference were resolved easily. Without debate, conferees dropped the Senate provisions concerning military facilities in Honduras and oil company mergers.

But it was the Central American funding that produced the deadlock.

"This side of the table is not under any circumstances going to recede" on the Nicaraguan aid, Rep. Edward P. Boland, D-Mass., said.

Stevens at first seemed to acknowledge that the Senate would give in, but asked that a cap in existing law on covert aid to Nicaragua be lifted so that funds could be provided to wind·the operation down.

But Boland, chairman of the House Select Committee on Intelligence, refused to allow that. "They have sufficient funds now to wind the program down if they wanted to," Boland said.

Stevens said that a detailed discussion of the issue would require a closed session, and conferees put off the matter until May 17.

When they met again, Stevens held fast to the Senate position to provide the $21 million in covert aid. "At this point, the Senate has spoken," Stevens said. "We would like the House to address the issue."

Senate conferees voted 5-3 to insist on the Senate position. Inouye, Stennis, Kasten and Cochran joined Stevens in favor. Hatfield, Weicker and William Proxmire, D-Wis., voted against.

Stevens said later that pressure from Southern and Southwestern members might force the House to change its position. "If we indicate a lessening of our resolve in Central America, we've got to prepare ourselves for a wave of three to five million immigrants," he said.

El Salvador

Most of the negotiations on El Salvador went on behind closed doors, but hopes for a quick resolution soon faded. "Right now, the House is not willing to negotiate with us on this," said Kasten, chairman of the Senate Appropriations Subcommittee on Foreign Operations.

Rep. Clarence D. Long, D-Md., said their difference was one of "psychology," noting that both sides wanted to help the newly elected Duarte regime win the support of the armed forces. In his view, Long said, "The best way to get their cooperation is to withhold military aid."

But Kasten said, "Frankly, if they [the House] vote it down, I'm concerned about the ability of the Duarte gov-

ernment to maintain its leadership of the government and the army."

House conferees did accept Senate provisions appropriating $7 million for assistance for Salvadoran refugees, and $500,000 for witness and juror protection in the forthcoming case of Salvadoran national guardsmen accused of murdering four U.S. churchwomen. Conferees also accepted Senate provisions placing conditions on aid to that country.

Other Provisions

Conferees added two new provisions to the bill. One added $2 million for the Civil Aeronautics Board, to pay for salaries and expenses from Aug. 1 through Sept. 30. The other provided $21 million for the Army Corps of Engineers to buy land flooded by the Tug Fork water project in West Virginia.

House conferees accepted Senate provisions that added:

● $60 million for PL 480 "Food for Peace" emergency food aid to Africa.

● $545.5 million for child nutrition programs, including school lunches, school breakfasts, and meals in child-care centers.

● $300 million for the WIC program, providing food for poor women who are pregnant or nursing, and impoverished young children.

● $850,000 for the U.S. Information Agency for payment to New York for activities involving the 1984 International Games for the Disabled.

● $25 million for the purchase of up to eight drug interceptor aircraft for use by the Customs Service against airborne drug smugglers.

● $100 million for the summer youth employment program. ▮

Energy Aid Funds

A measure (H J Res 493 — PL 98-248) providing $200 million in low-income energy aid and $90 million in food aid to Africa for fiscal 1984 was cleared by Congress March 27.

The legislation originally contained only funds for the energy program. But when another measure (H J Res 492) providing $150 million in food aid for famine-stricken Africa became embroiled in foreign policy controversy, Congress added some food aid funds to the energy-aid legislation. *(Story, p. 429)*

House Action. The resolution containing only the energy aid funds was reported (H Rept 98-605) Feb. 29 by the House Appropriations Committee.

Because of the extreme U.S. winter, the administration requested an additional $200 million for energy assistance for the poor to be administered by the Department of Health and Human Services.

The program had been funded at $1.9 billion. During debate on the second continuing resolution for fiscal 1984, the House in 1983 approved an additional $195 million. However, that amount was dropped in conference after administration officials said the extra money would not be needed because they expected to meet any increased demand for aid with funds from the settlement of a pending oil overcharge lawsuit against the Exxon Corp.

However, they promised they would request more money if it became clear the Exxon funds would not be available. The litigation was still pending in February 1984.

The measure was passed by the House by voice vote March 6.

Senate Action. The Senate Appropriations Committee reported H J Res 493 on March 8 (no written report). When the energy aid bill reached the floor March 15, Sen. John C. Danforth, R-Mo., in an effort to free the African food-aid from the foreign policy controversy, offered an amendment to provide $80 million in food assistance. The amendment was adopted by voice vote.

Conference Action. Conferees agreed to raise the amount to $90 million for emergency food donations and allowed another $90 million in food to be made available by the Commodity Credit Corporation for sale or barter.

The House adopted the conference report (H Rept 98-632) by voice vote March 27, and the Senate later that day cleared the measure by voice vote. It was signed into law March 30. ∎

2nd FY '84 Supplemental Hikes El Salvador Aid

The Reagan administration won a major foreign policy victory when Congress Aug. 10 cleared a supplemental appropriations bill containing $70 million in military aid to the U.S.-backed government in El Salvador.

The $6.2 billion measure (HR 6040 — PL 98-396) moved through Congress in two weeks. Its passage paved the way for Congress to adjourn for the Republican National Convention and the Labor Day holiday.

The bill funded an assortment of government programs for the remainder of the 1984 fiscal year, which ended Sept. 30. Aside from the El Salvador money, which the administration viewed as critical, the bill included $700 million for the federal food stamp program, which would have run out of money before Congress returned Sept. 5, and $486 million for three veterans' benefits programs that also were close to running out of funds.

Also included in the bill were funds to pay the costs of the invasion of Grenada in October 1983 and of the U.S. "peacekeeping" mission in Lebanon, which ended in February 1984, and to build a new oil repository in Texas for the Strategic Petroleum Reserve.

The largest single item in the bill provided $2.1 billion for federal pay raises that went into effect in January 1984. *(Provisions, box, p. 441)*

The final version of the bill contained slightly less than the $6.3 billion originally requested by the administration, which sought more foreign aid money but less for domestic programs. The House-passed version of the legislation contained about $5.4 billion, the Senate bill nearly $7 billion.

Final Action

Final action on HR 6040 came a little after 6 p.m. on Aug. 10 when the Senate adopted the conference report on the bill by voice vote. The House had adopted the report (H Rept 98-977) a few hours earlier by a vote of 312-85. *(House vote 327, p. 100-H)*

The key was House agreement to provide the $70 million for El Salvador. Administration officials were delighted with the El Salvador military funds even though the White House and Republican-controlled Senate originally had sought $116.9 million. Overall, Congress during the year gave Reagan most of the money he requested for military aid for El Salvador for fiscal 1984-85. *(El Salvador roundup, p. 73)*

"Obviously we are very pleased. It's a very significant development," said Thomas R. Pickering, U.S. ambassador to El Salvador, of the House decision. Pickering strategically placed himself directly off the House floor Aug. 10, along with other White House lobbyists, while the House was voting on the military aid to El Salvador.

Late the night before, a House-Senate conference committee deadlocked on Central America when Senate conferees proposed $90 million in El Salvador military aid and their House counterparts stuck to a position of no further money for fiscal 1984. The conferees, however, agreed to send the matter back to the House floor.

Rep. Clarence D. Long, D-Md., tried to stave off a higher military aid level by proposing $40 million for El Salvador. Long, chairman of the Appropriations Subcommittee on Foreign Operations, had led the effort to stop any additional military money from going to El Salvador in 1984.

But Long was deserted by conservatives, who wanted more money for El Salvador, and by several liberals, who did not want to approve any new funds. His amendment was rejected 57-340. *(Vote 328, p. 100-H)*

"There are a hell of a lot of liberals who would rather pose for holy pictures than win," said a disgruntled David R. Obey, D-Wis., after the vote.

Moments later, the House voted 234-161 for an amendment by Jack F. Kemp, R-N.Y., that included the $70 million in military aid for El Salvador. Kemp's amendment contained a total of $498 million in combined economic and military assistance to all of Central America, as opposed to $171 million in Long's rejected package. *(Vote 329, p. 100-H)*

This supplemental was the so-called "regular" one, used every year to finance items such as annual federal pay raises that were not included in the routine appropriations bills.

Congress on June 26 cleared the first omnibus supplemental spending bill of 1984 (H J Res 492 — PL 98-332). It included $1.1 billion for a variety of programs, all of which were labeled "urgent" either by the administration or by their congressional sponsors. That measure was delayed for weeks because of a dispute over Reagan's request for aid to anti-government guerrillas, called "contras," in Nicaragua. *(Nicaragua, p. 86; first supplemental, p. 429)*

House Committee Action

The House Appropriations Committee reported HR 6040 (H Rept 98-916) July 27, providing $5.4 billion in supplemental fiscal 1984 funding.

The committee originally had intended to begin work on the measure in mid-June. But it postponed its action at that time because the bill had become loaded down by special interest items, with members ready to offer some 25 amendments adding at least $1 billion to its cost. Chairman Jamie L. Whitten, D-Miss., used the intervening weeks to pare back the proposals that had been drafted by the panel's subcommittees.

When the full committee finally took up the measure on July 26, after less than 24 hours' notice to members, Whitten was able to report that the subcommittees had squeezed out $290 million from the bill that was to have been considered in June. Just as important, he said, the committee averted most of the amendments that would have added more spending to the measure.

Whitten said the measure was $931 million less than Reagan's various requests. But more than one-third of the cut came in aid to Central America.

Ranking Republican Silvio O. Conte, Mass., predicted the bill would be "unacceptable" to the White House because it added millions of dollars above Reagan's requests for several domestic programs while cutting aid to Central America.

"This bill, I hate to say it, smells of veto bait," Conte told his colleagues.

In its only sharply contested action on the bill, the Appropriations panel rejected, 13-21, an effort by Republicans to add $648 million for foreign aid programs requested by Reagan, of which $359 million was for Central America. The vote was largely along party lines: only two Democrats, Charles Wilson and Jack Hightower, both of Texas, joined Republicans in supporting the aid request.

In an unusual move, the committee also approved $50 million in additional aid to Moslem rebels, called the *mujahideen*, who were battling the Soviet Union's occupation of Afghanistan. The $50 million was included in an amendment, sponsored by Wilson, that officially was described as "procurement" for the U.S. Air Force. Defense Department accounts are used to fund "covert" operations by the CIA, such as aid to the Afghan rebels. The committee discussed the amendment briefly in a closed session near the end of its deliberations on the supplemental.

According to sources, the CIA secretly had provided the Afghan rebels about $100 million in the last two years.

Highlights

The bill's largest appropriation was $2.1 billion for pay raises to federal workers, of which approximately $1.6 billion went to Defense Department employees.

The bill did not include pay raises for members of Congress because that money was appropriated automatically each year. Members received the same cost-of-living raises as most federal white-collar workers. *(1981 Almanac p. 286)*

Other major items in the bill included:
- $700 million, the same as Reagan's request, to keep the food stamp program running through the end of the fiscal year.
- $485.7 million for various benefit programs administered by the Veterans Administration.
- $459.2 million to build a new facility at Big Hill, Texas, for the Strategic Petroleum Reserve.
- $284 million for operations and maintenance programs of the Defense Department; most of the money went to pay for the invasion of Grenada in October 1983 and the U.S. "peacekeeping" mission in Lebanon, which ended in February when Reagan withdrew most of the 1,200 Marines from Lebanon.
- $175 million for the PL 480 "Food for Peace" program, which provided loans and grants for foreign countries to receive U.S. surplus food.
- $150 million, not requested by the administration, for home mortgage loan guarantee programs.

- $150 million for operating loans for farmers, guaranteed by the Farmers Home Administration, and $25 million for farm ownership loans. Also, $50.2 million for land acquisition, equipment and improvements for facilities used by the Agricultural Research Service, and $25 million for the federal crop insurance program.
- $50 million for the "superfund" hazardous waste cleanup program.
- $170 million for foreign economic aid and $24.75 million for foreign military aid.
- $60 million, not requested by Reagan, for the Federal Emergency Management Agency for emergency food and shelter programs for the homeless.
- $52.4 million for various congressional operating expenses and new programs run by Congress.
- $34.65 million for operation of Indian programs by the Bureau of Indian Affairs, along with $17 million for construction programs.
- $25 million for repairs at various Job Corps training centers.

The full committee voted to cut only one item that had been recommended by a subcommittee. By a 17-14 vote, the panel adopted an amendment by Steny H. Hoyer, D-Md., paring $12.5 million over three years from the amount provided for the Corporation for Public Broadcasting. As drafted by the subcommittee on Labor-Health and Human Services-Education, the bill had included $70 million. *(Public broadcasting, p. 288)*

The measure included several policy provisions, directing the administration to take certain actions or not to take other ones. That was in spite of Whitten's efforts to strip from the bill any "legislation" that might be subject to a point of order. In theory, appropriations bills are not supposed to include provisions on policy, which is the province of the authorizing committees.

The committee stripped from the bill a legislative provision, drafted by the Interior subcommittee, banning the sale or lease of coal on public lands before Oct. 1, 1985. Subcommittee Chairman Sidney R. Yates, D-Ill., said the ban was no longer necessary because Interior Secretary William P. Clark had started reforms in the troubled federal coal leasing program.

But the committee added another provision, sponsored by Jerry Lewis, R-Calif., prohibiting the Agriculture Department from changing regulations relating to marketing orders, which permitted growers of certain crops jointly to advertise, limit access to markets or take certain other actions. Similar language was added to the fiscal 1985 Agriculture appropriations bill (HR 5743). *(Story, p. 383)*

Other special interest items added to the bill included: $300,000 for a special payment to the school district near the West Point, N.Y., military academy; $10 million for an outpatient facility in Kraków, Poland, named for the late Rep. Clement J. Zablocki, D-Wis. (1949-83), who chaired the House Foreign Affairs Committee; a ban on Defense Department use of petroleum storage ships not built in the United States; and $570,000 to establish a model retraining program for displaced workers in Johnstown, Pa., in the district of committee member John P. Murtha, D-Pa.

Central America

As approved by the committee, the bill included $106 million in economic aid and $24.75 million in military aid to Central American nations.

Reagan's pending 1984 requests for the region totaled

Fiscal 1984 Supplemental Appropriations

Following are the provisions of the fiscal 1984 supplemental appropriations bill cleared by Congress Aug. 10 (HR 6040 — PL 98-396) *(in new budget authority)*:

	Revised Administration Request	House-Passed Amount	Senate-Passed Amount	Final Amount
Title I				
General Supplementals				
Agriculture	$ 1,000,000,000	$ 978,567,000	$ 1,100,367,000	$ 1,029,567,000
Commerce, Justice, State and Judiciary	73,380,000	61,731,000	113,438,000	120,340,000
Defense	356,900,000	329,900,000	331,900,000	331,900,000
Energy and Water Development	157,600,000	——	23,500,000	23,500,000
Housing and Urban Development, Independent Agencies	186,918,000	401,618,000	383,368,000	481,868,000
Interior and Related Agencies	129,951,000	633,026,000	652,527,000	662,828,000
Labor, Health and Human Services, Education	58,200,000	227,969,000	627,798,000	260,848,000
Legislative Branch	183,291,000	52,345,400	143,610,900	143,459,000
Military Construction	85,000,000	58,000,000	79,000,000	74,000,000
Transportation	143,475,000	118,100,000	116,900,000	118,100,000
Treasury, Postal Service, General Government	239,711,000	239,481,000	239,481,000	239,481,000
Foreign Operations	1,012,774,170	230,495,000	1,039,388,170	602,922,000
Title II				
Increased Pay Costs	2,326,140,000	2,053,392,000	2,131,950,000	2,087,932,000
Total	**$5,953,340,170**	**$5,384,624,400**	**$6,983,228,070**	**$6,176,745,000**

$565.3 million; that money was supposed to implement the recommendations of his "bipartisan" commission on Central America, headed by former Secretary of State Henry A. Kissinger. *(Story, p. 93)*

But Democrats on the Foreign Operations Subcommittee slashed Reagan's request, saying they did not see an emergency situation that justified such a rapid aid boost.

As in previous years, the most controversial aid recipient in the region was El Salvador. The bill included $25 million in economic aid but no military aid for El Salvador.

For other Central American countries, the bill included: Costa Rica, $60 million in economic aid and $7.85 million in military aid; Honduras, $20 million in economic aid and $10 million in military aid; Panama, $2.5 million in military aid; and $3.1 million for military training of Salvadoran and Honduran troops at a camp in Honduras.

The bill also banned aid to Guatemala, except for projects to help Indians there or for economic development projects run by private agencies.

Kemp proposed the amendment in full committee that would have provided Reagan's full requests for El Salvador and the other countries in Central America. The recommendation of the Foreign Operations Subcommittee "emasculates security assistance to Central America," he said.

Kemp acknowledged that he lacked the votes to get his amendment adopted by the committee, but he said he was offering it anyway, because "I want the record to be clear that many of us in the minority think this is too important an issue for us to turn our backs on."

Administration officials said they made little effort to press the committee on the issue because of the difficulty of getting Democrats to vote for money to implement a controversial foreign policy at the same time they were being urged to cut back on spending for domestic programs.

Immediately after Kemp made his impassioned plea for aid to Central America, Wes Watkins, D-Okla., summed up the administration's political problem.

"We've zeroed rural America" in the bill, Watkins angrily shouted at Kemp, to the applause and cheers of his colleagues.

House Floor Action

The House passed HR 6040 Aug. 1 by a 304-116 vote. *(Vote 301, p. 92-H)*

An effort by Kemp to add an additional $359 million for military and economic assistance to Central America was ruled out of order. The bill, as passed, included $106 million in economic aid and nearly $25 million in military aid to Central American countries. None of the military assistance, however, was destined for El Salvador, which would have been the principal beneficiary of Kemp's amendment.

Kemp argued that the United States needed to strengthen its support of the government of President José Napoleón Duarte of El Salvador. "I think each and every one of us wants to do something to help implement the democratic reforms that not only are coming, but must continue to come in El Salvador."

But Long said more U.S. money would go to Central America in fiscal 1985, obviating the need for additional funds in the last two months of the current fiscal year.

"This administration, which stresses that throwing money at a problem is no solution, is proposing to do precisely that in Central America," said Long.

Long raised a point of order against the Kemp amendment on the grounds that it would have provided funds not authorized by legislation.

Jack Brooks, D-Texas, who was presiding over the House during the debate, wasted no time in sustaining Long's objection. "It's not authorized and everybody knows it," said Brooks.

Brooks' blunt language was reported more diplomatically in that day's *Congressional Record*. "Failing any citation to laws authorizing the appropriations contained in the amendment, the chair sustains the point of order," the Record quoted Brooks in a polite alteration of what he actually said.

Before passing the supplemental, the House defeated an amendment by Robert S. Walker, R-Pa., to make a 1 percent across-the-board cut in the measure. Walker's amendment lost by an 184-238 vote. *(Vote 300, p. 90-H)*

Although Appropriations Committee leaders calculated the bill as being well below Reagan's request, Bill Frenzel, R-Minn., called it a "budget buster" laden with less-than-urgent special projects.

"This bill is rife with such chauvinistic projects, which, while worthy, are by no means urgent. It ought to be defeated. If not, it ought to be vetoed," said Frenzel.

But Conte, who had opposed the bill in committee, nonetheless urged the full House to approve it. "We should have, and could have, done a better job in cutting unrequested supplementals. But we are past that point now. The recess is only eight days away. We do not have time to go back to our subcommittees and construct another bill," said Conte.

The only money added to the bill on the House floor came on an amendment by Mario Biaggi, D-N.Y., that was adopted on a voice vote. Biaggi's amendment added $10 million for senior citizen centers and $5 million for providing meals to the elderly.

Senate Committee Action

The Senate Appropriations Committee approved its $6.8 billion version of the bill Aug. 2 (S Rept 98-570).

House Appropriations Committee leaders had said the House bill was about $915 million less than the amount requested by Reagan, a total they put at $6.3 billion. The Senate Appropriations Committee, however, calculated the Reagan request at $5.9 billion, thus putting its version of HR 6040 about $859 million above the president's.

The difference between what the two committees considered to be the right figure for the president's request was approximately $450 million that both panels included in the bill. The Senate panel said the money was requested for fiscal 1985, not 1984; the House considered it part of the 1984 request.

The Senate version of the bill contained $565 million in economic and military assistance to Central American countries as opposed to only $131 million in the House bill.

Bob Kasten, R-Wis., chairman of the Appropriations Subcommittee on Foreign Operations, called the Central America funding a "down payment" on the Kissinger commission's recommendations for combined military and economic assistance to U.S. allies in that region.

Although the Senate bill included the Central America money requested by the White House, the measure's overall price tag had the administration "quite concerned," Appropriations Committee Chairman Mark O. Hatfield, R-Ore., told the panel as it began marking up the bill.

Aside from the Central America money, the Senate committee's version of HR 6040 was $1.4 billion larger than the House-passed bill because of money added for financial aid for college students, veterans' assistance and other programs.

For example, the Senate bill included $353 million for Pell grants to needy college students. The House did not include any additional 1984 funds for the program. The Senate's figure for veterans' programs was $130 million more than the figure in the House bill.

The Senate's higher numbers prompted a plea from Hatfield to hold the line on amendments adding even more to the bill.

Despite that, Walter D. Huddleston, D-Ky., won approval of an amendment adding $50 million to combat asbestos hazards in schools. And Alfonse M. D'Amato, R-N.Y., secured $8.5 million to buy a training vessel for the New York State Maritime College. Both changes were made by voice vote.

The Senate bill also contained a provision designed to stall a July decision by the Federal Communications Commission (FCC) to increase the number of television stations that could be owned by companies.

The existing limit of seven TV stations, seven AM and seven FM radio stations that could be owned by any one company would rise to 12 of each and eventually be phased out altogether, under the FCC decision.

Critics of the decision feared it would permit a greater concentration of ownership of stations and cut down on diversity of programming.

The amendment offered by Warren B. Rudman, R-N.H., would prevent the FCC from implementing the television part of its decision until June 30, 1985. The amendment was approved by an 18-7 vote.

Senate Floor Action

The Senate passed its version of the supplemental bill shortly after midnight, some 10 hours after the chamber began debating the measure Aug. 8. The vote on final passage was 62-32. *(Vote 206, p. 36-S)*

The bill, which started on the Senate floor with a $6.8 billion price tag, swelled to nearly $7 billion before the night was over, not including $650 million added in farm loan guarantees, which, as guarantees, were not counted in the bill's total spending.

Democrats tried and failed twice by wide margins to cut the money in the bill for Central America.

Christopher J. Dodd, D-Conn., first tried to cut the Central America allotment from $565.2 million to $178.9 million. Dodd's proposal was designed to prohibit Congress from spending more than was authorized in existing legislation.

"I'm saying you shouldn't spend taxpayers' money on something that you haven't authorized," said Dodd.

Kasten acknowledged that Congress had not authorized the increased money to El Salvador and other Central American countries. But he said that the need for the money in the troubled region outweighed Dodd's procedural objections.

"It's not the right way to do it but it's the only way to do it," said Kasten. Dodd's amendment was rejected 37-62. *(Vote 200, p. 35-S)*

The Senate by a wider margin rejected an amendment by Daniel K. Inouye, D-Hawaii, to delete all of the $116.9 million in military aid for El Salvador contained in the Senate bill. Inouye said the money was unnecessary because there were "millions of dollars in the pipeline" that had not yet been spent by El Salvador. Inouye's amendment was defeated 29-69. *(Vote 201, p. 35-S)*

The Central America money provided most of the controversy during the Senate's debate on the supplemental, offering a showcase for supporters and critics of the administration's policies toward the region.

The measure, however, also offered a convenient vehicle for senators to add special projects or take potshots at other White House activities.

As evening wore on into night Aug. 8, the Senate devoted nearly two hours to an amendment by Max Baucus, D-Mont., that called on Reagan to withdraw his temporary appointment of Martha Seger to the Federal Reserve Board. Seger, whose nomination to a 14-year term on the Fed was pending before the Senate, was given a temporary recess appointment by the president on July 2.

After a spirited debate, the Senate voted 53-43 to table Baucus' amendment. *(Vote 205, p. 36-S; Seger, p. 21-A)*

Earlier, senators considered an amendment by Bob Packwood, R-Ore., designed to place the Senate on record in opposition to the White House's views on a worldwide population conference in Mexico City. The administration had sparked a controversy by recommending that the federal government withhold money from groups such as Planned Parenthood that used private funds to promote abortions in foreign countries with overpopulation problems.

Packwood's plan was derailed when Jesse Helms, R-N.C., proposed that the population amendment include a statement commending Reagan for his anti-abortion stance. When a motion to table the Helms add-on amendment was rejected, 43-52, Packwood withdrew the entire proposal. *(Vote 202, p. 35-S)*

The Senate adopted, 57-40, an amendment by Alan J. Dixon, D-Ill., to add $60 million to the $60 million already in the bill for emergency shelters and food programs for the nation's homeless. *(Vote 203, p. 35-S)*

The Senate, by a 23-69 vote, ruled non-germane an amendment by Claiborne Pell, D-R.I., dealing with U.S. policy regarding Taiwan. *(Vote 204, p. 36-S)*

Conference Action

Conferees worked more than five hours the evening of Aug. 9 but were unable to reach agreement on the bill's Central America provisions. Those differences were left to be resolved by the full House and Senate the following day.

The crucial sticking point came over the $116.9 million in additional military aid for El Salvador that the White House had requested and the Senate had added to HR 6040. The House had included no military funds for that country. An offer by Senate conferees to reduce the El Salvador aid to $90 million was rejected by House conferees.

Long adamantly refused to back away from his position against any further military aid to El Salvador. Long said El Salvador still had $50 million in unspent U.S.

military aid for the remainder of fiscal 1984.

But Kasten, Long's Senate counterpart, said the El Salvador government's war against insurgents could not wait for new funds in a 1985 appropriation bill. "We need your help today, not in the '85 bill, which might not pass until December," said Kasten.

Twice during the conference, Kasten read a letter from El Salvador President Duarte to President Reagan appealing for the extra military and economic assistance in the supplemental.

During an evening break, Kasten and Long met for about an hour with Inouye, the ranking Democrat on Kasten's subcommittee, and Kemp, the ranking Republican on Long's subcommittee.

While that meeting did nothing to break the impasse between Kasten and Long, it did give Kasten time to stitch together a new proposal to bring back to the conference with a significant convert — Inouye.

Kasten offered to reduce military aid to El Salvador to $90 million while also offering to drop $341 million from the Senate bill for U.S. contributions to international development banks, such as the World Bank. The House bill contained no funds for the banks.

Kasten said his revised spending levels provided the "minimum security assistance we can get away with" in Central America. The plan was endorsed by Inouye, who on the Senate floor had sponsored an amendment to cut all the military money for El Salvador. Inouye described the new proposal as "very reasonable."

The Senate conferees voted 14-2 for the Kasten plan. But Long immediately won a 12-8 vote from House conferees to stand firm on the House position. Rep. Jack Edwards, R-Ala., tried to coax some movement on the House side by proposing that military aid to El Salvador be reduced further to $70 million, but that also was rejected by House Democratic conferees.

Senate conferees agreed to drop a provision for $353 million in Pell grants for needy college students. The House had included the funding in a fiscal 1985 appropriations bill (HR 6028), but Senate sponsors said the money was needed to make up a shortfall in the current fiscal year.

The Senate also backed down partly on its attempt to double the House allotment for an emergency food and shelter program. The House bill contained $60 million as opposed to the Senate's $120 million figure. Conferees agreed to $70 million. Earlier, House conferees agreed to a Senate addition of $50 million to eliminate asbestos hazards in schools.

A Senate provision to delay an FCC decision on ownership of television stations became moot when the FCC itself decided Aug. 9 to delay its ruling. To ensure that the FCC lived up to its latest action, the conferees included language from the FCC delay announcement in the bill.

In some instances, each side won conference approval of pet projects. For example, the House had included $2.5 million to restore Franklin D. Roosevelt's presidential yacht, the *Potomac*. The Senate did not include any money for the yacht's restoration but added $8.5 million to the same part of the bill to buy a training vessel for a maritime academy in New York, a project pushed vigorously by D'Amato.

In the spirit of compromise, conferees agreed both to restore FDR's craft and purchase the ship D'Amato sought. "When it gets that late you end up solving a lot of problems by giving everybody what they want," quipped a Senate aide afterward. ∎

Last-Minute Money Bill Was Largest Ever

Congress Oct. 11 — more than a week after the start of the new fiscal year — cleared a $470 billion continuing appropriations resolution for fiscal 1985, the largest and most sweeping stopgap funding bill ever approved. Controversy over the massive bill closed part of the government for a few hours and delayed Congress' scheduled Oct. 4 adjournment.

The omnibus spending bill (H J Res 648 — PL 98-473) was approved by the Senate Oct. 11 on a 78-11 vote. The House had agreed the night before, on a 252-60 standing vote, to adopt the conference report (H Rept 98-1159). *(Senate vote 270, p. 47-S)*

President Reagan signed H J Res 648 on Oct. 12.

The measure was needed because only four of the 13 regular fiscal 1985 appropriations bills had been enacted by the Oct. 1 start of the 1985 fiscal year.

The size of the bill and its timing — it was one of the last major legislative vehicles considered before Congress adjourned Oct. 12 — made enactment a struggle.

As the measure made its way through Congress, it picked up a major overhaul of the criminal code, and dropped off an $18 billion water project authorization, more than $100 million in appropriations for water projects, the foreign aid authorization bill and dozens of extraneous provisions.

The bill contained the entire texts of five regular fiscal 1985 appropriations bills: Defense, Foreign Assistance, Interior, Military Construction and Transportation. The House had approved the Military Construction and Interior bills, but the Senate had not acted. The other bills had been approved by House and Senate committees but, because of turf battles or controversial issues, had not been voted on by either chamber. The differences between the House and Senate versions of these measures were resolved during the conference on H J Res 648.

The continuing resolution also incorporated the provisions of the conference reports on appropriations for Agriculture, Labor-Health and Human Services (HHS) and Education, Treasury-Postal Service and the District of Columbia. The original versions of these bills were approved in both chambers, and negotiators settled most House-Senate differences in conference. With the exception of Labor-HHS, however, the final versions of the bills had not been voted on. The remaining items in dispute were resolved in the continuing resolution.

Congress Oct. 10 cleared the conference report on the Labor-HHS bill, and its provisions were removed from the continuing resolution when the president signed the regular appropriation into law.

Because it was late in approving H J Res 648, Congress was forced to pass four interim funding bills to finance the government between Oct. 1 and midnight Oct. 11. The first interim measure (H J Res 653 — PL 98-441) was cleared Oct. 1. The second interim funding bill (H J Res 656 — PL 98-453) was cleared Oct. 4, but it came too late to stop Reagan from sending home thousands of government workers. The third bill (H J Res 659 — PL 98-455) cleared Oct. 5. The final interim appropriation (H J Res 663 — PL 98-461) passed Oct. 9.

Reagan ordered the shutdown of eight Cabinet-level departments and several independent federal agencies Oct. 4, 10 hours after part of the federal government technically ran out of money. An estimated 500,000 "non-essential" federal workers were sent home at midday. House-Senate conferees on H J Res 648 agreed to pay federal workers for the brief time they were off Oct. 4.

An impasse over a continuing spending resolution caused a partial closing of the federal bureaucracy once before, on Nov. 23, 1981. In a more limited case, the Federal Trade Commission briefly closed on May 1, 1980, when its funding ran out. *(1981 Almanac p. 298; 1980 Almanac p. 233)*

Major Provisions

As enacted, H J Res 648 contained:

● **Agriculture:** $32.2 billion in fiscal 1985 for agriculture programs, rural development, food assistance and related agencies. *(Story, p. 383)*

● **Interior:** $8.1 billion for Interior and related agencies. Also included was a $5.38 billion rescission of existing funds for the Synthetic Fuels Corporation. *(Story, p. 378)*

● **Labor-HHS:** $104.56 billion. This provision was removed when the regular Labor-HHS bill (HR 6028 — PL 98-619) was signed into law. The bill continued the existing prohibition against Medicaid funding for abortions, except when the mother's life was at risk. *(Story, p. 421)*

● **Military Construction:** $8.4 billion in military construction appropriations, including $85 million for construction related to the deployment and testing of 10 MX missiles. *(Story, p. 407)*

● **Treasury-Postal Service:** $12.8 billion for the Treasury Department, U.S. Postal Service, Executive Office of the President and other independent agencies. *(Story, p. 425)*

● **Transportation:** $11.6 billion. An obligation ceiling of $13.2 billion was set for programs funded by the Highway Trust Fund. *(Story, p. 410)*

● **D.C. Appropriations:** $533.3 million in federal funds and approval of the expenditure of $2.36 billion from the D.C. treasury in fiscal 1985. *(Story, p. 428)*

● **Foreign Aid:** $18.2 billion for foreign aid programs. The agreement contained $700 million in military aid for Turkey and $500 million for Greece. El Salvador received $128.3 million in military aid, $275 million in economic and development assistance. *(Story, p. 390)*

● **Defense:** $274.4 billion. When money for nuclear warheads, contained in the Energy Department appropriations bill, and for military construction was added, the total amounted to $292.9 billion. That figure reflected an inflation-adjusted 5 percent growth rate for defense over fiscal 1984 spending. *(Story, p. 399)*

● **Crime:** The major anti-crime package contained in the continuing resolution generally reflected a measure passed by the Senate in February (S 1762 — S Rept 98-225). The provisions in the crime section of the bill included: bail and sentencing reform; restrictions on the use of the insanity defense; aid to crime victims; and the establishment of a "drug czar." *(Story, p. 215)*

General Provisions

In addition to the nine fiscal 1985 appropriations bills and the crime measure, the continuing resolution contained several "general provisions" that added, deleted or shifted significant amounts of money and reshaped federal policy.

Among the general provisions were items to:

• Provide $110.2 million for the initial phase of a program to increase security at U.S. embassies and missions abroad. The total cost of the two-year program was estimated to be $366.3 million, with the remainder to be requested as an urgent supplemental in January 1985.

• Provide $306.6 million requested by the administration for the Veterans Administration's loan guarantee revolving fund.

• Provide $4 million for the U.S. Institute of Peace included in the defense authorization bill.

• Rescind up to $4.3 million in annual Department of Housing and Urban Development contract authority and $69.1 million in budget authority.

Conferees added $300 million to continue public housing programs to compensate for a provision in the deficit reduction package (HR 4170 — PL 98-369) passed in June that could have prohibited public housing agencies from issuing tax-exempt notes for development and modernization.

The $300 million would offset the higher interest costs for taxable bonds compared with tax-exempt bonds. *(Deficit reduction, p. 143)*

• Allow the Small Business Administration to provide disaster loans to parts of the fishing industry harmed by "El-Niño," the 1982-83 wind conditions that caused unusually warm currents in the Pacific Ocean, disrupting fishing harvests.

• Provide $3.6 million for work on Blair House, the nation's official guest house used by visiting heads of state and other dignitaries.

• Provide $3.2 million for the Food and Drug Administration to implement the Drug Price Competition and Patent Term Restoration Act (S 1538). *(Story, p. 451)*

• Provide $2 million to rebuild a lighthouse on Nantucket Island, Mass.

• Provide $400,000 to establish a commission to study the 1932-33 Ukranian famine. Before these funds could be spent, the operating budget of the commission had to be submitted to the House and Senate Appropriations committees for approval.

• Provide $8.4 million to the Food and Drug Administration for activities related to acquired immune deficiency syndrome (AIDS).

• Overhaul procedures for congressional review of District of Columbia laws. Under the Home Rule Act governing Washington, D.C., Congress could overturn legislation approved by local authorities without any action by the president. However, that provision was ruled unconstitutional by the Supreme Court in 1983, throwing into doubt the District's home rule authority and its ability to borrow money. The provision in the continuing resolution required Congress to pass, and the president to sign, a joint resolution in order to disapprove any District law. *(Details of home rule action, p. 190)*

• Provide $1 million to two Florida research centers for emergency research on citrus canker, a plant disease that in August and September threatened Florida's citrus industry.

• Provide additional funding — $25 million — for three Small Business Administration programs unable to spend as much as had been appropriated in fiscal 1984.

Both chambers had passed a bill (HR 6013) raising fiscal 1984 authorizations to the levels provided in the appropriations bill, but the measure died at the end of the session.

House Committee Action

The House Appropriations Committee Sept. 14 approved the omnibus funding bill. Before approving the bill by voice vote, the committee rejected, 23-24, an amendment to force two votes in 1985 on the MX missile, instead of the one vote called for in the defense authorization bill (HR 5167).

The committee agreed to an amendment offered by Rep. Tom Bevill, D-Ala., chairman of the Appropriations Subcommittee on Energy and Water Development, to provide $139 million for water and flood control projects. According to Bevill, these projects were approved by the House in HR 3958. *(1983 Almanac p. 520)*

As approved by the Appropriations panel, the continuing resolution contained funding for Agriculture, the District of Columbia, Interior, Labor, Health and Human Services, and Military Construction at the House-passed appropriations level. Foreign aid funding equaled the amount approved by the Appropriations Committee Sept. 12. Defense spending continued at the current rate until the regular Defense Department appropriations bill was reported by the Appropriations Committee. The continuing resolution did, however, contain restrictions on the MX missile and other weapons systems contained in the defense authorization bill.

Transportation programs were funded at the current rate. Treasury-Postal Service funding was equal to the amount in the conference report on the regular appropriation.

Rules Action. The administration had warned that a bill encumbered by costly new programs would be vetoed. Despite pressure from members to include their programs in the stopgap bill, the House Rules Committee, on an 11-1 vote, Sept. 20 sent to the House floor a stripped-down version of the continuing resolution. The panel ignored the pleas of colleagues to permit additional amendments to the bill, and it dropped from the measure the $139 million the Appropriations Committee had added for water projects. The Sept. 20 procedural rule simply funded programs and agencies included in the nine fiscal 1985 appropriations bills that had not been signed into law.

After spirited debate, the House defeated the rule, 168-225. *(Vote 362, p. 110-H)*

The next day, the panel did an about-face, and voted to give the House the chance to vote on 11 amendments to the bill, including an $18 billion water projects bill and the entire $11 billion foreign aid authorization.

House Floor Action

On the House floor, H J Res 648 became a potential vehicle for nearly every major stalled legislative initiative of the 98th Congress once the rule allowing consideration of 11 amendments was adopted, 257-135. *(Vote 364, p. 112-H)*

As approved by the House Sept. 25 on a 316-91 vote, the catchall money bill included water projects, the foreign aid authorization and the Senate-passed omnibus crime package President Reagan strongly supported (S 1762, HR 5963). It also contained new money for child-care abuse prevention programs and increased food stamp benefits. *(Vote 371, p. 114-H)*

Rep. Jamie L. Whitten, D-Miss., chairman of the House Appropriations Committee, made the case for additional spending Sept. 25. Over the past four years, Whitten said, "We have held the line on this side to a greater degree than I ever thought possible. But on the Senate side, they have added amendment after amendment." Sanctioning the addition of the authorization bills to the appropriations measure, Whitten noted, "We bring you what we feel we have to do to give equal treatment to our colleagues in the House."

Authorizations. The addition of the water projects and foreign aid bill to the continuing resolution was a bipartisan affair that reflected the House's frustration with Senate inaction on major authorization measures.

The water resources package, which authorized funding for construction of 300 projects including dams, harbors, locks and levees and other water development and conservation projects, had been approved by the House in June, but the Senate did not act on companion legislation (S 1739). Supporters argued that if it were not attached to the continuing resolution, it was unlikely that it would be enacted in 1984.

No one spoke out against the addition of these "pork-barrel" projects, which would fund projects across the country, and the amendment was agreed to 336-64. *(Vote 365, p. 112-H)*

The debate on the foreign aid package also was brief. The House approved HR 5119 on May 10, but as with the water bill, the Senate had not passed its version. Rep. Dante B. Fascell, D-Fla., chairman of the House Foreign Affairs Committee, said including the bill in the continuing resolution "simply gives us an opportunity to enact an authorization bill." The amendment was approved by voice vote.

But following its adoption, the House approved another amendment affecting foreign aid. By a vote of 273-134, the House agreed to a 2 percent reduction in all foreign aid, with the exception of assistance earmarked for Egypt and Israel. *(Vote 367, p. 112-H)*

Other Amendments. During floor consideration, the House:

● Adopted by voice vote an amendment by Rep. Silvio O. Conte, R-Mass., to provide $159.5 million in fiscal 1987 forward funding for the Corporation for Public Broadcasting. *(Story, p. 288)*

● Adopted by voice vote an amendment by Rep. Leon E. Panetta, D-Calif., to restore the basis of benefits in the food stamp program from 99 percent to 100 percent of a nutritionally adequate low-cost diet known as the "Thrifty Food Plan." The amendment was part of a hunger relief bill (HR 5151) approved by the House Aug. 1. *(Story, p. 469)*

● Adopted, 369-37, an amendment by Rep. George Miller, D-Calif., to provide $50 million to states to train child-care facility staff and parents of attending children in the prevention of child abuse. *(Vote 369, p. 112-H)*

● Adopted by voice vote an amendment by Rep. Julian C. Dixon, D-Calif., to make provisions of the Washington, D.C., Home Rule Act consistent with the Supreme Court's decision on legislative vetoes. The change permitted Congress to reverse District laws by enacting a joint resolution, which the president must sign. Under existing law, congressional disapproval generally was expressed in a concurrent resolution, which did not require the president's signature. *(Legislative veto, 1983 Almanac p. 565; home rule provision, p. 190)*

Senate Committee Action

The Senate Appropriations Committee, meeting Sept. 25, followed the pattern set by its House counterpart and included $82.9 million for water and flood control projects. The biggest controversies in the committee's deliberations,

however, were over foreign aid issues.

After a lengthy debate, the panel agreed to an amendment guaranteeing for five years that economic support provided to Israel would not drop below the annual debt repayments Israel made to the United States.

The committee also approved an amendment reducing the administration's request for $755 million in aid to Turkey by $40 million. The House had cut aid to Turkey to $540 million.

Although Congress had hotly debated military aid to El Salvador, the president was guaranteed most of the money he requested in both the House and Senate continuing resolutions. *(El Salvador, p. 73)*

The level of defense spending in the Senate's interim funding bill equaled the amount approved in the defense appropriations bill reported by the full committee.

In domestic areas, the committee agreed to rescind $5.2 billion of the Synthetic Fuels Corporation's spending authority. The House had proposed a $5 billion rescission.

Medicaid Abortions. The committee reversed a decision on Medicaid-funded abortions made by the full Senate the same day. The Labor-Health and Human Services appropriations bill approved by the Senate Sept. 25 allowed Medicaid payments for abortions performed as a result of rape or incest. The committee approved a provision in the continuing resolution that would return to current law, which permitted Medicaid abortions only when the mother's life was endangered. Medicaid was the nation's health-care program for the poor.

Abortion opponents avoided a floor fight over abortion during consideration of the regular appropriations bill because they were confident they would prevail on the continuing resolution.

The committee agreed to provide $35 million to states for training in child care and child abuse prevention techniques. The House continuing resolution set aside $50 million for the program.

Senate Floor Action

The Senate approved H J Res 648 Oct. 4 by voice vote after a series of lengthy sessions and a procedural snarl over civil rights legislation.

The Senate took up its bill Sept. 27, but efforts to move ahead on the floor were unsuccessful, and private negotiations were inconclusive. Oct. 1 fell on a Monday, so a session was set for Saturday, Sept. 29.

Less than 15 minutes after it began work on the continuing resolution Sept. 27, it became evident that the Senate had no intention of being any more restrained than the House. Senate Minority Leader Robert C. Byrd, D-W.Va., offered as an amendment a major civil rights bill (S 2568) designed to overturn the Supreme Court's *Grove City College v. Bell* decision.

The move tied up Senate action for four days. The Senate extricated itself from the procedural maze it constructed over the Grove City amendment Oct. 2, voting 53-45 to table the amendment. *(Vote 245, p. 44-S; Grove City story, p. 239)*

The Senate then worked for more than 22 hours straight, debating such sensitive issues as federal funding for abortions and foreign aid to Turkey and less controversial topics like relief for poultry farmers. Most attempts to amend the bill were turned back.

Nicaragua, Military Aid. On Oct. 3, the Senate began debate over funding for rebels fighting the left-wing government of Nicaragua. The House bill had a flat prohibition on any U.S. support for paramilitary activities in Nicaragua, while the Senate bill approved Reagan's full $28 million request for the guerrillas. Under intense pressure from the administration, the Senate stuck to its position by rejecting, 42-57, an amendment by Daniel K. Inouye, D-Hawaii, that sought to "wind down" the Nicaraguan war. *(Vote 252, p. 44-S; story, p. 86)*

In the wake of the Sept. 20 bombing of the U.S. Embassy in Beirut, the Senate approved the administration request for $110.2 million to strengthen security in U.S. embassies around the world. But an amendment by Sen. Joseph R. Biden Jr., D-Del., that would have released the funds only after the president certified they were sufficient to ensure adequate security, was tabled (killed), 61-37. *(Vote 258, p. 45-S)*

Conference

House-Senate negotiators deadlocked over issues ranging from military aid for Nicaragua to "pork-barrel" water projects during the conference on H J Res 648, forcing a delay in the scheduled congressional adjournment.

Many minor differences were resolved quickly. But the same issues that plagued Congress throughout the year — the defense budget and U.S. policy in Central America — immediately tripped up the conference. At the heart of the dispute, at least over money issues, was a difference in interpretation of the defense agreement reached by House Speaker Thomas P. O'Neill Jr., D-Mass., and Senate Majority Leader Howard H. Baker Jr., R-Tenn., on Sept. 20. *(Defense, p. 399)*

After months of stalemate over defense spending issues, the two congressional leaders had agreed on a compromise military spending figure that approximately split the difference between the House and Senate positions and resolved differences over the MX missile. Conferees finally agreed to essentially abide by the O'Neill-Baker agreement.

The question of aid to rebels fighting the leftist Sandinista government of Nicaragua was resolved in a compromise that required the approval of both chambers in early 1985 to release additional funds.

Water Projects. Both sides had decided to include about $100 million in new construction or "starts" for water resource, port dredging and flood control projects. Conferees' determination to hold on to some of the water

funds in the bill concerned the administration, which via a letter signed by budget director David A. Stockman, threatened a Reagan veto of the continuing resolution if it contained any new water money.

Shortly after the conference session began, Whitten proposed that the negotiators approve the conference report and allow him to take the measure back to the House with the major defense issues as amendments in disagreement. The House would take separate votes on the resolution and the unresolved amendments and send the measures to the Senate. The Senate would then vote on the amendments in disagreement, or could amend them, raising the possibility that the conferees would reconvene.

But Stevens balked, recalling how in 1979 the House passed a conference report with amendments in disagreement, adjourned and went home, leaving the Senate with no option other than to accept the House position. *(1979 Almanac p. 277)*

Whitten Oct. 10 told his Senate counterparts that the House leadership had decided the only way to get the administration to sign the continuing resolution and get Congress out of town was to remove all money for water projects from the measure. With that offer, the impasse on the continuing resolution began to break. Reagan's threat to veto the bill containing water project money lost its impact. And the onus was put on the Senate to give ground on the outstanding defense issues.

Final Action

In the House, the floor debate on the continuing resolution was swift and uneventful.

But two Republican senators Oct. 11 engaged in a spirited debate about Nicaragua, and whether the water projects were traded away for freedom in Central America.

". . . We have relinquished on those [national security issues] and in exchange the House has relinquished on water projects," John P. East, R-N.C., charged.

But Ted Stevens, R-Alaska, who was managing the bill on the floor, said there was no "connection between the water resource action and the defense action."

It was up to Congress, East said, to explain to the public what was at stake in Nicaragua. "The average American doesn't know the difference between a contra and a caterpillar, and a Sandinista and a sardine," East said. ∎

Health/Education/Welfare

Although inflation in health care costs moderated in 1984, the nation's total medical bill of $355 billion was a record 10.8 percent of the gross national product (GNP), the overall production of goods and services.

An Oct. 10 report by the Department of Health and Human Services (HHS) showed that health spending rose 10.3 percent in 1983, compared with the previous year. In 1982, the rate had been 12.5 percent. The 1983 figure was the slowest rate of increase in a decade, although still above the 7.7 rise in the GNP. (The October report provided the most timely health spending figures available; data on health spending typically lags a year or more because of reporting methods.)

About $1,459 per person had been spent on health care in 1983, compared with $1,337 in 1982.

In July, when Consumer Price Index figures also showed a decline in medical care inflation, HHS Secretary Margaret M. Heckler had credited the slowdown in inflation to the president's "bold new approach" that had "broken the back of the health care inflation monster that has plagued us for more than two decades."

She appeared to be referring to new controls on hospital payments by Medicare, the federal health program for the elderly and disabled. They had been sent by the administration to Congress late in 1982 in response to a congressional request. The controls — flat rates of payment for treating specific illnesses — were only partly in place when Heckler spoke.

A second major Reagan-era control, temporarily freezing Medicare payment rates to doctors, passed Congress after being amended to prevent doctors from raising their fees during the freeze and passing higher costs on directly to their patients.

When the October cost figures were released, Heckler took a view more common in the health care industry, that the downward trend resulted from cost-control pressures from many sources, including state and local governments and private businesses striving to hold down the expense of employee health care benefits, as well as federal actions.

A key factor in the slowdown appeared to be changes in the way hospitals were being used. The American Hospital Association (AHA) reported declines in 1984 in key indicators of hospital growth. Admissions, lengths of stay, number of beds in use and number of surgical procedures had all increased less rapidly or stopped growing since 1983, according to AHA data.

One AHA official explained that there were no definitive analyses yet of the trend, but he speculated that hospitals were responding to three or four years of stiff cost-control pressure coming from many directions, including state Medicaid programs and private insurers negotiating tough contracts with the hospitals.

The official predicted that the downward trend would continue because many hospitals appeared to be making permanent changes, such as reducing staff size and closing wings. Hospitals also were diversifying, offering satellite clinics, nursing and home-care services as less expensive alternatives to acute inpatient care.

Medicare Survival

The October figures showed that Medicare remained the largest federal health program, costing $57.4 billion. The survival of the program was about the only health policy issue to be raised in the presidential campaign.

Walter F. Mondale, the Democratic presidential candidate, called for a national cap on all health care expenditures, with states taking the lead in regulating or otherwise controlling health care expenditures. Mondale campaign officials said the plan could save $12 billion by 1989 and would put Medicare on firm financial footing while also protecting all Americans from rapidly escalating health care costs.

Mondale's plan was similar to legislation proposed by Rep. Richard A. Gephardt, D-Mo., and Sen. Edward M. Kennedy, D-Mass., that was largely ignored by Congress.

President Reagan did not offer a health cost control plan, although he observed in an Oct. 7 debate that "something is going to have to be done in the next several years to make [Medicare] fiscally sound."

The year had begun with forecasts that the Medicare fund that paid for hospitalization of beneficiaries would run out of money in five to 10 years. Members of Congress expressed concern but showed little inclination to move swiftly. Hearings were held and some money-saving measures enacted as part of a broad deficit-reduction package. But neither those changes nor Medicare savings measures enacted in previous years were considered adequate to stave off bankruptcy.

Most members considered the actions required to save the plan — deep benefit cuts, large tax increases or both — too difficult to address during an election year.

Moreover, Sen. Dave Durenberger, R-Minn., chairman of the Finance Subcommittee on Health, said he thought the U.S. health care system was changing so rapidly that it might be impossible to know in 1984 what might cure the bankruptcy problem 10 years later.

The Medicare situation was simple and grim: The Hospital Insurance Trust Fund was paying money out faster than it was coming in.

The mathematics of the problem were laid out in a March report by the Federal Advisory Council on Social Security. According to the report, the number of elderly enrollees in Medicare had grown from 19.1 million in 1966 to 26.8 million in 1983 and the number of disabled enrollees also had grown significantly.

Between 1980 and 2030, the council noted, the total U.S. population would grow by 40 percent, but the elderly population would more than double, and the older people were expected to live longer.

Meanwhile, medical costs had risen 192 percent from 1970 through the end of 1983, compared with a 157 percent rise in the Consumer Price Index.

Finally, the ratio of taxpayers to elderly beneficiaries dropped from 4-to-1 in 1965 to 3.31-to-1 in 1980, and was expected to be 2.7-to-1 by 2015. That ratio was considered disastrous because Medicare was a "pay-as-you-go" plan, meaning that current payroll taxes paid for current benefits.

The council recommendations included raising the age of eligibility, reworking the benefit package, and providing vouchers to beneficiaries who wanted to drop out of the federal program and buy private health plan coverage instead. It opposed any new taxes to shore up the failing fund, except that it did back an administration plan to tax part of the value of employment-based health insurance plans, and also called for increases in federal alcohol and tobacco taxes, with the revenues devoted to Medicare.

Education

A continuing groundswell of interest in upgrading the quality of U.S. schools formed the backdrop for education legislation in 1984. The clamor for school reform provided grist for the rhetorical mills of lawmakers, but most of the substantive action took place off Capitol Hill.

According to the Education Commission of the States, 18 states in 1984 increased high school graduation requirements. Another 18 had done so in 1983. Since 1980, some 16 states — including four in 1984 — had imposed new testing requirements for teachers seeking certification.

With much of the impetus for change coming from state legislatures, the education reform movement was accompanied in many places by a marked shift of influence from local school districts to the state level.

Congress responded cautiously, and constructed no ambitious, broad-based new school aid programs. Facing a tight budget and a public seen as not supportive of federal initiative, what new programs Congress did enact were modest, low-cost and carefully targeted.

Some education analysts saw Congress' relatively low profile in the reform movement as one of its most striking features. By contrast, Congress had a strong hand in setting national priorities when it enacted the landmark laws of the 1960s that promoted equal educational opportunity for the poor and minority groups.

There was some concern that increased emphasis on raising educational standards would be accompanied by a retreat from a commitment to equal opportunity for the poor and others at a disadvantage in education. But at the federal level, the bulk of the education budget continued to promote opportunities for the disadvantaged.

In December, the Department of Education cited rising standardized test scores and declining dropout rates in some states as signs of academic gains. The department found that students' average score on college entrance exams increased in 32 states between 1982 and 1984, while the scores dropped in 10 states. That record "provides tangible evidence of the academic turnaround that has resulted from the higher standards and expectations we have set for ourselves over the past few years," said Education Secretary T. H. Bell.

It also reported that 14 states had enacted merit pay or other forms of performance-based pay plans for teachers. Such schemes for rewarding the best teachers were heavily promoted by Bell.

Bell, announcing his resignation just two days after President Reagan's landslide re-election victory, became the first Cabinet member to say he would not stay around for a second Reagan term.

At year's end, a replacement had not yet been named. Reagan said he was delaying the nomination of a successor because the department's future was still in question. During the administration's budget deliberations late in the year, Reagan's unfulfilled promise to abolish the Department of Education resurfaced. *(Successor named, p. 21-A)*

Some of Reagan's conservative supporters were glad to see Bell go because they regarded him as insufficiently committed to key items on the conservative agenda, including the abolition of the department.

But some interest groups viewed Bell's departure with trepidation because they saw him as a moderating influence on the administration's efforts to cut the education budget. The administration's fiscal 1985 budget request was the first since Reagan took office that did not recommend cutting the Education Department's budget.

During the presidential campaign, Democratic challenger Mondale tried to make an issue out of Reagan's efforts to cut education funding. But Reagan managed to steer clear of dollars-and-cents issues. Instead, he emphasized education themes with broad popular appeal — higher academic standards, stricter discipline and school prayer.

There was a change in federal education leadership in Congress in 1984. The chairmanship of the House Education and Labor Committee changed hands for the first time since 1967, after the Aug. 3 death of Carl D. Perkins, D-Ky. An 18-term congressional veteran, Perkins played a key role in creating major federal education and job training programs. He was succeeded as chairman by another veteran of the War on Poverty, Augustus F. Hawkins, D-Calif.

Welfare

The number of people in poverty increased to 35.3 million in 1983, bringing the poverty rate up to 15.2 percent from 15 percent in 1982.

Analysts continued to disagree over who should be counted as poor. Administration officials said that the incidence of poverty was overstated by the way the Census Bureau set the poverty rate, because it did not count as income the value of "in-kind" benefits such as food stamps and medical care subsidies for the poor.

Budget Director David A. Stockman had said in late 1983 that the poverty rate would drop by one-third if the measurement of income included in-kind benefits — a prediction that was borne out when the Census Bureau in February issued an analysis taking account of in-kind benefits. But however poverty was measured, the bureau found, the poverty rate increased from 1979 to 1982.

In the presidential campaign, the administration's critics tried to pin part of the blame for the increase in poverty on cuts in aid to the needy under Reagan. They cited, for example, a study by the Congressional Research Service that showed that some 560,000 people had fallen below the poverty line in 1982 because of changes in federal social programs for the poor.

But Reagan and his supporters insisted that the social safety net remained intact, and that the poor were better off because of economic improvements and lower inflation.

—By Janet Hook and Elizabeth Wehr

Generic Drug Legislation Cleared by Congress

Congress completed a landmark drug bill intended to make cheaper versions of many widely prescribed drugs available to consumers while giving manufacturers extra-long patents for new brand-name pharmaceuticals.

The last time Congress passed a drug law of such magnitude was 1962, when it adopted the requirement that manufacturers demonstrate efficacy — as well as safety — of new drugs. *(Congress and the Nation, Vol. I, p. 1181)*

Final action came Sept. 12 when the Senate accepted House amendments to the bill (S 1538 — PL 98-417) by voice vote. The House had unanimously passed the measure Sept. 6. It was signed into law Sept. 24.

The Food and Drug Administration (FDA) estimated that under the bill, more than 150 drugs could be offered in cheaper generic forms — saving consumers $1 billion over the next 12 years. Publicly funded programs such as Medicaid and veterans' health services also were expected to save substantial amounts on drug purchases.

Passage of the bill concluded nearly a year of intense and difficult negotiations among the research-based companies that created new, brand-name drugs, generic-drug makers and representatives of consumers, the elderly and organized labor.

In 1982 a broad patent term restoration measure had died after failing to pass the House, in large part because of objections that it made too many concessions to drug makers without any offsetting benefits in the form of more inexpensive drugs for consumers. *(1982 Almanac p. 400)*

Those interests were merged in the basic compromise, revealed at a June press conference by sponsors Rep. Henry A. Waxman, D-Calif., and Sen. Orrin G. Hatch, R-Utah. But throughout the legislative process nearly a dozen research-based firms doggedly insisted on further concessions.

Until just before final passage the "dissident" firms, as they were termed, fought against their trade association, the Pharmaceutical Manufacturers Association (PMA), which had led compromise negotiations. The fight was so bitter that top PMA officials resigned abruptly.

Long-Running Battles

The 1984 dispute was the tail-end of exceptionally long-running battles over public policy and drugs. In 1960 and 1961, Estes Kefauver, D-Tenn. (House, 1939-43; Senate, 1949-63), criticizing the economic concentration of multinational drug firms, had begun pressing for cheaper drugs. But Kefauver's controversial drug price provisions were not included in the 1962 drug law overhaul. *(Congress and the Nation Vol. I, pp. 1754-55)*

Meanwhile, by the mid-1970s, pharmaceutical firms were pressing for changes in federal drug regulations, arguing that lengthy mandatory procedures robbed them of patent protection and, accordingly, profits from exclusive markets. The Carter administration had proposed major revisions in drug regulation in 1978; the Senate passed a somewhat different version in 1979, but that bill died without further action. *(1979 Almanac p. 485)*

One key section of the 1984 measure directed the FDA to expand its use of a special fast-track procedure for approving generic drugs. Those duplicates of expensive brand-name drugs, sold by their chemical names, retailed for 50 percent to 80 percent less.

The agency had been using the expedited procedure only for drugs it had approved before 1962. That meant that so-called "post 1962" drugs still enjoyed exclusive marketing, free of competition, even after their patents expired. The expense of going through the regular FDA approval procedures generally discouraged generic versions of post-1962 drugs.

A second section, intended to create more financial incentives for the development of new drugs, gave drug companies up to five more years of patent protection for new drugs, as well as certain other exclusive marketing rights. Companies had complained that a significant part of the standard 17-year patent was lost to regulatory reviews. A patent for a new drug usually was obtained shortly after discovery, but subsequent testing and FDA approval took up to $70 million and 10 years, according to the firms.

Passage of the bill marked a successful alliance between sponsors Hatch, a conservative, and Waxman, a liberal, who also had worked together in 1984 on bills relating to cigarette labeling and organ transplants. *(Cigarettes, p. 478; transplants, p. 476)*

The bill also included an unrelated textile labeling section, added in the House to gain some political advantage during technical procedural maneuvers.

Provisions

As signed into law, S 1538:

● **Drug Approval.** Directed the FDA to make broader use of its expedited approval procedure for generic copies of patented drugs, upon expiration of the patent. The procedure waived requirements for testing to show that a drug was safe and effective; it required only that a generic drug be shown to be the chemical duplicate of the original (which had undergone safety and effectiveness tests). Existing FDA practice was to allow the expedited procedure, known as an abbreviated new drug application (ANDA), only for generic copies of drugs that had received FDA marketing approval prior to 1962.

Generic copies of drugs that had been approved by the FDA between 1962 and 1982 would qualify for ANDA approval upon expiration of the patents. Copies of drugs approved between 1982 and the date of enactment of S 1538 would qualify for ANDA approval only after a 10-year period of exclusive marketing, authorized by the bill. Generic versions of drugs approved after enactment would be eligible for the ANDA procedure after the expiration of the patents, including any extension of the patents authorized by the bill.

● Directed the FDA to withhold ANDA approval of a generic drug in cases where a generic maker had legally challenged the validity of the patent for the drug to be copied. In such cases, the FDA must withhold approval of a generic drug until a court decision on the challenge, but no longer than 30 months.

● Provided an additional exclusive marketing right, apart from a patent extension, for new drugs approved by the FDA after enactment of the bill. The exclusive marketing would be available only for drugs that did not have active patents. For drugs that were new chemical entities, no generic copies could be marketed for five years after FDA approval of the original. For drugs that were not new chemical entities but required extensive clinical testing — generally over-the-counter versions of prescription drugs

— no generic versions could be marketed for three years after approval. In both cases, a generic company could begin the required testing in anticipation of expiration of the exclusive marketing date.

For drugs approved between 1982 and the date of enactment, no generic versions could be marketed for two years after approval.

No legal challenges to a patent could be filed until the end of the exclusive marketing period, except for drugs protected for five years. For them, a challenge could be filed at the end of the fourth year, meaning that the 30-month delay for litigation would begin at that time.

● **Patents.** Authorized a single extension of a patent on a new drug for humans, a medical device, or a food or color additive, subject to FDA approval. The extension would add up to two years of patent protection for drugs awaiting FDA approval at the time of enactment, or up to five years for drugs submitted for approval after enactment.

● Permitted an applicant for an extension of a product with several patents to select the patent on which to seek the extension.

● Provided that the total time of patent protection left to a product after FDA approval, plus any extension, could not exceed 14 years. (Currently, drug patents could have only eight or 10 years remaining after FDA marketing approval.)

● Permitted testing of a patented drug, prior to expiration of the patent, for purposes of securing FDA approval to market a generic version of the drug after expiration of its patent.

● **Textiles.** Required that clothing sold in the United States be conspicuously labeled to show country of origin and that mail-order and other catalogs indicate whether clothing was manufactured in this country or imported.

House Committees' Action

Waxman, chairman of the Energy and Commerce Subcommittee on Health, in 1983 had won subcommittee approval of a one-page bill dealing only with approval of generic drugs. By June 1984, a 44-page compromise combining generic drug and patent provisions (HR 3605, S 2748) had been introduced by Waxman and Hatch.

In the House, two committees reviewed the bill.

The first panel to act, the Energy and Commerce Committee, reported (H Rept 98-857, Part I) the bill June 21 after having approved it by voice vote in a June 12 meeting. The second panel, the Judiciary Committee, filed its report (H Rept 98-857, Part II) on Aug. 1.

Waxman and Hatch had revealed the compromise legislation in a press conference held to hail the measure's broad support. However, eight major drug firms immediately let it be known that they opposed the plan. The eight were Bristol-Myers Co., Johnson & Johnson, Squibb Corp., American Home Products Corp., Merck & Co. Inc., Hoffmann-La Roche Inc., Schering-Plough Corp. and Procter & Gamble Co.

"In my opinion, they oppose this legislation because they don't want lower-cost generic drugs on the market, even though their patents have expired," Waxman said.

The eight dissenting firms, which later grew to 11, were for the most part makers of profitable drugs that would become newly eligible for generic versions, because their patents had or were about to expire.

Among the more than 150 drugs with expiring patents were Valium, Hoffmann-La Roche's popular tranquilizer

with 1983 sales of $250 million; Inderal, a cardiovascular medicine from American Home Products Corp. with 1983 sales of $300 million; and Merck's Aldomet, another cardiovascular drug with 1983 sales of $175 million.

The dissident companies sought a number of concessions, such as the right to get extensions on each of several patents that might apply to a single drug. A manufacturer might secure separate patents on, for instance, liquid or tablet versions of a drug, and certain manufacturing procedures.

At the June 12 Energy and Commerce markup, no members spoke against the bill. But Thomas A. Luken, D-Ohio, whose district included Procter & Gamble, unsuccessfully tried to raise a point of order that Waxman's 44-page compromise bill was not germane. Committee Chairman John D. Dingell, D-Mich., ruled against him.

After certain revisions were accepted, the bill was reported by voice vote, with only Thomas J. Bliley Jr., R-Va., whose district included A.H. Robins Co. Inc., shouting "no."

Judiciary Committee

The next stop for the legislation was the Judiciary Committee, which agreed July 31 to report the bill after rejecting amendments that appeared to address the interests of the dissenting companies. Sponsors of the amendments said, however, that they were nothing more than "simplifying" changes requested by the U.S. Patent Office.

William J. Hughes, D-N.J., offered changes that he said would clarify the bill's patent procedures. Among other things, the changes would have let a drug company apply for multiple patent extensions. Opponents, led by Robert W. Kastenmeier, D-Wis., argued that the firms could use the multiple extensions to stretch out their exclusive marketing rights. Kastenmeier's Judiciary Subcommittee on Courts, Civil Liberties and the Administration of Justice had previously approved the bill.

Another argument occurred over whether firms making generic drugs should be able to start federally required testing on a drug before the patent on the original expired. Early testing enabled a generic manufacturer quickly to market its version of a drug once the patent ran out. The bill explicitly allowed such early testing, which had been a common practice until a 1984 court decision ruled it out.

The committee rejected an amendment by Carlos J. Moorhead, R-Calif., that would have permitted the tests only in limited circumstances. Kastenmeier said that the amendment also would delay the availability of generic drugs.

The committee also agreed to a Kastenmeier amendment knocking out of the bill a new, patent-like exclusive marketing right for drugs that were not eligible for patents.

Senate, House Floor Action

A new, somewhat different version (S 2926) of the bill reflecting further negotiations went directly to the Senate floor Aug. 10, bypassing committee consideration and winning Senate approval. The new version reflected relatively modest additional concessions by Hatch and Waxman to the dissenting companies.

Only Sen. Howard M. Metzenbaum, D-Ohio, who registered last-minute objections to new exclusive marketing rights for the firms included in the latest version, voted against passage.

By delaying Senate action until late in the last day

before the August recess, Metzenbaum thwarted sponsors' plans to win a quick House vote and thereby clear the measure for the president before the recess. However, Senate passage had been considered the most difficult hurdle because there a single member could have blocked the bill.

New Changes Made

The new round of negotiations made these changes in the basic compromise:

● The original bill directed the FDA to postpone approval of a generic drug under court challenge for patent infringement until the court ruled, but limited the postponement to no longer than 18 months. The compromise extended that to 30 months.

● The Hatch compromise provided an extra measure of marketing protection, separate from the patent extension, for new drugs approved by the FDA after enactment of the bill.

The extra protection applied only to drugs that did not have active patents. For drugs that were new chemical entities, no copies could be marketed for five years after FDA approval of the original. For those that were not new chemical entities and required extensive clinical testing, no copies could be marketed for three years after approval.

In both cases, a generic company could begin the required testing in anticipation of expiration of the exclusive marketing date.

The compromise also provided for two years of exclusive marketing for drugs approved between 1982 and the date of enactment.

The compromise did not disturb a 10-year exclusive marketing period for drugs approved between 1962 and enactment.

● The original bill specified that a patent extension would be available only for a first patent on a new drug. The dissenters argued that often the first of several patents on a new drug was not the most meaningful. They wanted extra patent time for new uses of drugs, new formulations or similar changes.

The compromise preserved the bill's principle of one patent extension per drug but permitted a manufacturer some latitude to choose which patent he wanted to extend.

The non-patent marketing rights excised by Kastenmeier and added back by Hatch continued to be controversial enough to threaten survival of the bill up to the last minute. Kastenmeier and Metzenbaum complained that Hatch and Waxman had given too much monopoly power to well-heeled drug companies. Metzenbaum was particularly concerned that a five-year exclusive marketing right, combined with an additional 30-month delay to accommodate litigation, was too much protection from competition.

Overwhelming House Passage

Waxman brought the House bill (HR 3605) to the House floor Sept. 6, winning a series of amendments bringing it into line with the Senate-passed bill. Among Waxman's amendments, however, was one substantive change from the Senate bill, reflecting a concession to Metzenbaum and others in his camp. It shortened the time a drug would be protected by the provision relating to marketing rights and delay for litigation.

House passage was by an overwhelming 362-0 vote. The House then substituted its amended bill for the text of an unrelated Senate-passed patent measure (S 1538 — S Rept 98-547), returning it to the Senate for final approval. *(Vote 337, p. 104-H; patent bill, p. 260)*

The House had rejected, by huge margins, several amendments that would have upset the bill's delicate balance between consumer and generic drug interests and those of companies making brand-name products.

One amendment, rejected 66-304, would have shortened the time during which a drug could be protected from competition because of legal challenges. The second, rejected 24-347, would have excluded over-the-counter, nonprescription drugs from the bill. *(Votes 334, 335, p. 104-H)*

In other action, the House added an unrelated textile-labeling amendment, which Waxman had agreed to earlier as part of a complex procedural strategy. The textile section, sponsored by Butler Derrick, D-S.C., required textiles and clothing to be conspicuously labeled to show country of origin, and required catalogs to indicate whether such merchandise was made in the U.S. or abroad. ∎

House Rejects Heroin Bill

Emotional pleas for cancer patients dying in terrible pain did not convince the House to let doctors use heroin, under controlled circumstances, to relieve the suffering.

The House Sept. 19 rejected, by a 55-355 vote, the bill (HR 5290) permitting the federal government to provide hospital and hospice pharmacies with diacetylmorphine, commonly known as heroin. *(Vote 355, p. 108-H)*

The measure had been reported April 12 by the House Energy and Commerce Committee (H Rept 98-689).

Heroin was banned from medical use in the United States in the 1920s because of concern about its addictive properties. The temporary program would have let doctors use the drug in treating dying patients whose severe pain did not respond to other medications.

A group representing families of cancer patients, the National Committee on the Treatment of Intractable Pain, had sought the legislation since the 1970s.

Heroin had been used as a painkiller in England for a number of years and in this country in research programs sponsored by the National Cancer Institute.

Before rejecting the bill, the House also turned down, by a 178-232 vote, an amendment by William J. Hughes, D-N.J., to increase penalties for illegal diversion of the drug, and strengthen controls on its medical use. *(Vote 354, p. 108-H)*

Debate was unusually impassioned. Opponents, citing the nation's immense drug abuse problems, said that pharmacies would be robbed and the heroin diverted to illegal use.

Charles B. Rangel, D-N.Y., said that legitimizing any heroin use would send a terrible message, both to drug abusers at home and to foreign nations under pressure from the United States to stop producing abused drugs.

Opponents also argued that doctors, trained to avoid causing addiction in patients, tended to underuse existing pain medications that could work if properly used. And they claimed that a highly potent version of the analgesic Dilaudid, approved in 1984, gave doctors a drug with the same benefits of swift action and small dosages as heroin.

J. Roy Rowland, D-Ga., a physician, told the House, "I have been in this situation many times with families who had members who were dying with terminal cancer, and I have always been able to give relief of the pain."

Lined up against the measure were the Reagan administration, the American Medical Association and other medical and pharmacists' groups. The administration's opposition was so active that John D. Dingell, D-Mich., Energy and Commerce Committee chairman, complained of violations of statutory prohibitions against executive branch lobbying.

Sponsor Henry A. Waxman, D-Calif., and other supporters said the amount of heroin that would be used in the program — perhaps 15 pounds a year — was minuscule compared to the tons of illegal heroin flooding the nation. ∎

Arts, Humanities Funding

Congress May 17 cleared legislation (HR 2751 — PL 98-306) that increased authorizations for cultural support agencies to bring them in line with actual appropriations of recent years.

HR 2751 was approved by the House by voice vote Feb. 21 and by the Senate by voice vote April 5. It was cleared after the House by voice vote accepted a minor Senate amendment. The president signed the bill May 31.

The bill lifted spending ceilings set by the 1981 budget reconciliation act (PL 97-35). Previous fiscal 1984 authorizations set by the reconciliation act were $119.3 million for the National Endowment for the Arts, $113.7 million for the Endowment for the Humanities and $9.6 million for the Institute of Museum Services (IMS). *(1981 Almanac p. 399)*

HR 2751 authorized $166.5 million for the arts endowment, $158.8 million for the humanities and $20.2 million for IMS in fiscal 1984. For fiscal 1985, it authorized "such sums" as Congress considered necessary. Appropriations for those three agencies for fiscal 1982-84 each year exceeded authorizations in the 1981 act.

The bill also officially transferred IMS from the Education Department to the National Foundation for the Arts and Humanities. That change had been made in Interior Department appropriations riders since fiscal 1982.

Legislative History. The House passed HR 2751 on Feb. 21 after dropping a provision approved by the Education and Labor Committee earmarking $500,000 for arts organizations in Washington, D.C.

The set-aside, which would have come from funds for the National Endowment for the Arts, was opposed by arts advocates who objected to earmarking funds for some groups while others had to vie for grants.

The elimination of the set-aside for Washington arts groups was approved by voice vote under an amendment by Paul Simon, D-Ill., chairman of the Education Postsecondary Education Subcommittee.

The bill had been reported by the Education and Labor Committee May 16, 1983 (H Rept 98-163), with a supplemental report filed Oct. 26, 1983 (H Rept 98-163, Part II).

On April 5, the Senate approved HR 2751 by voice vote with minor changes that were accepted by the House. ∎

NSF Authorization Blocked

For the fourth straight year, the National Science Foundation (NSF) was left without an authorization when the Senate Labor and Commerce committees failed to resolve a jurisdictional dispute.

As in 1983, funding was provided, however, in the

appropriations bill for the Department of Housing and Urban Development and various independent agencies (HR 5713 — PL 98-371). *(1983 Almanac p. 604; fiscal 1985 HUD appropriations, story, p. 415)*

The money bill included $1.5 billion for NSF, exactly the same amount requested by the administration. The total included $40 million for advanced scientific computing (supercomputers) — $20 million more than the administration requested.

The NSF supported non-medical scientific research through grants and contracts with colleges, universities and research organizations.

Legislative Background. The House April 25 passed HR 4974 (H Rept 98-642), authorizing $1.56 billion for the NSF in fiscal 1985. Most of the $58 million increase over the administration request was for supercomputers.

HR 4974 was reported by the House Science and Technology Committee March 30.

The House rejected, 175-180, an amendment by Judd Gregg, R-N.H., to cut the $60 million authorization for supercomputers back to the level sought by the president. Gregg said that NSF would not be able to use the $40 million that the committee added to the request for the advanced computers. *(Vote 80, p. 30-H)*

The House also rejected an amendment by Robert S. Walker, R-Pa., to reduce every authorization in the bill by 3.9 percent to bring the total to the president's request. That vote was 170-183. *(Vote 81, p. 30-H)*

After defeating the two Republican-backed amendments, the House passed the authorization bill, 252-99. *(Vote 82, p. 30-H)*

In the Senate, two authorization bills were reported, but neither was brought to the floor because the Labor and Human Resources and Commerce, Science and Transportation committees both claimed jurisdiction and could not resolve their dispute.

Senate Commerce April 26 reported S 2601 (S Rept 98-412) authorizing $1.53 billion for the NSF in fiscal 1985.

On May 25, Senate Labor reported S 2521 (S Rept 98-495) authorizing $1.5 billion. ∎

Vocational Rehabilitation

A three-year reauthorization of federal vocational training programs for the handicapped cleared Congress Feb. 9, putting an end to months of controversy.

The conference report (S 1340 — H Rept 98-595) extending the Rehabilitation Act of 1973 (PL 93-112) was approved Feb. 9 by the House, 384-3, and the Senate by voice vote cleared the measure. The president signed it Feb. 22 (PL 98-221). *(Vote 21, p. 8-H)*

The measure authorized $1.038 billion for state grants in fiscal 1984, with the spending ceiling rising 7.7 percent in 1985 and in 1986. It also extended through fiscal 1986 several smaller vocational rehabilitation programs, including research and training.

The House Education and Labor Committee estimated the total cost of the bill at $1.158 billion in fiscal 1984, $1.251 billion in 1985 and $1.349 billion in 1986.

Conferees reached agreement on S 1340 after House negotiators Feb. 1 agreed to drop controversial amendments that would have authorized additional spending for 11 unrelated education and social programs.

The inclusion of the extraneous programs had held up action on the vocational rehabilitation bill in 1983. When it became apparent the dispute would not be resolved before the end of 1983, Congress included a simple fiscal 1984 funding authorization for the rehabilitation program as an amendment to a measure reauthorizing education programs for the handicapped (S 1341 — PL 98-199). *(1983 Almanac p. 402)*

When conferees finally met in February 1984 on S 1340 — a more detailed rehabilitation reauthorization measure — House negotiators also agreed to drop amendments that would have provided aid to school districts with a large influx of immigrants and revised the allocation of low-income energy assistance.

As cleared, S 1340:

● Authorized $1.038 billion for state grants in fiscal 1984, $1.118 billion in 1985 and $1.203 billion in 1986.

● Authorized $121 million for discretionary programs in fiscal 1984, $134 million in 1985 and $145 million in 1986.

● Required states to set up programs to advise and protect the rights of the disabled. Many states had such programs, but they were not mandated.

Bill Shifts Vocational Education Emphasis

A five-year extension of federal aid to vocational education that put more emphasis on improving and modernizing vocational training was cleared in the final month of the 98th Congress.

The measure, which overhauled vocational education programs for the first time since 1976, was agreed to by the Senate by voice vote Oct. 3. The House cleared the conference report (HR 4164 — H Rept 98-1129) by voice vote Oct. 4.

Although the bill rejected the Reagan administration's proposal to simplify the program and increase states' discretion, he signed it into law Oct. 19 (PL 98-524). For three years, the administration had proposed turning federal aid to vocational education into a simplified block grant to states.

But the bill cleared by Congress continued to funnel funds through the states and expanded current requirements that states set aside proportions of their grants to improve access to vocational programs for groups that traditionally had been poorly served, such as the handicapped. The rest would be used to upgrade vocational programs and initiate new ones.

The final bill authorized $950 million in fiscal 1985 — 28 percent more than the president requested — and set no specific spending caps for 1986-89.

A thorny issue for conferees was whether to continue to allow federal funds to be used for basic maintenance of existing vocational programs — a provision of current law retained in modified form in the bill approved by the House March 8 (H Rept 98-612).

The version approved by the Senate Aug. 8 omitted the provision on the theory that the limited federal funds — which constituted only about 10 percent of nationwide expenditures on vocational programs — should be targeted on national priorities of stimulating innovation and expanding access to training.

But House conferees argued that such a limitation would be particularly harmful to poor, rural school districts that depended heavily on federal aid, and would lead to schools' tailoring their applications to seem "new and improved" simply to qualify for federal aid.

Conferees agreed to allow only part of the basic state grants — those funds earmarked for special groups — to be used for basic maintenance.

Under the compromise, states were required to use 10 percent of their grants for serving the handicapped, as under current law, and 22 percent for the disadvantaged, up from 20 percent.

New "set-aside" provisions earmarked 3.5 percent of state grants for eliminating sex stereotyping in vocational training, 1 percent for serving prison inmates and 20.5 percent for training adults, including single parents and homemakers.

In an effort to bring vocational programs more in line with changing times, the bill provided for increased coordination with the private sector and for special attention to the training needs of women and workers looking for new job skills.

Provisions

As signed into law, HR 4164:

● **Authorizations.** Set funding at $950 million in fiscal 1985, and such sums as Congress considered necessary in 1986-89.

The authorization included:

● $835.3 million for basic grants to states. Of the total, 2 percent was held in reserve by the Education Department for national programs, including research and data collection, and an additional 1.5 percent was earmarked for programs serving Indians and native Hawaiians.

● $15 million for training projects run jointly by schools and community organizations.

● $32 million for consumer and homemaking education.

● $35 million for adult training, coordinating with programs for retraining dislocated workers under the Job Training Partnership Act (JTPA). *(1982 Almanac p. 39)*

● $1 million for guidance and counseling services.

● $20 million for joint projects with industry for high-technology training, limiting federal aid to no more than half the cost of such projects.

● $8 million for state councils on vocational education.

● $3.7 million for bilingual vocational education.

● **State Grants.** Allocated funds to states under a formula based on the population in various age groups and per capita income.

● Stipulated that states spend 43 percent of their federal funds for upgrading and modernizing training programs or starting new ones.

The remaining 57 percent was earmarked for expanding access to training for members of specified groups that had been poorly served by vocational programs. Of those funds, states were required to spend: 10 percent for the handicapped; 22 percent for the disadvantaged and for students with limited proficiency in English; 3.5 percent for eliminating sex stereotyping in vocational education; 12 percent for training and retraining adults; 8.5 percent for single parents and homemakers; and 1 percent for prison inmates.

● Specified that states could use only part of their grants

— funds earmarked for special populations — for basic maintenance of existing programs.

● **Miscellaneous.** Barred states from spending more than 7 percent of their federal money for administrative expenses.

● Required states to assign at least one employee full time to administer programs to serve women.

● Directed state boards of vocational education to establish technical committees of representatives of industry, trade groups and labor to provide advice on tailoring programs to meet labor market needs.

● Required states to submit an initial three-year plan, to be updated every two years, assessing how to meet the needs of the job market and students. The plans must be reviewed by state councils that oversaw JTPA programs.

● Required states to allocate at least 80 percent of their funds to local programs, including all of the money earmarked for the handicapped and disadvantaged.

● Mandated that federal funds for disadvantaged and handicapped students cover no more than 50 percent of the extra cost of serving them.

● Required funds both for the disadvantaged and the handicapped to be allocated to localities based not only on the number of such students served in the previous year, but also on the number of economically disadvantaged students enrolled. The new formula was designed to channel more money into low-income areas.

● Barred the use of funds for the purchase of equipment if the purchase would result in financial gain to a professional organization representing the interests of the purchaser or its employees.

● **National Programs.** Established a 17-member National Council on Vocational Education to advise the president and Congress on vocational education needs, with particular emphasis on cooperating with private industry to ensure that job training corresponded with job openings.

● Earmarked national program funds in the following manner: 35 percent to support research, with at least $6 million a year for a National Center for Research in Vocational Education; 35 percent for demonstration projects, including projects for dislocated and older workers; and 30 percent for data collection.

● **Education Summit.** Retained a Senate amendment authorizing $500,000 for a national summit conference on ways to improve education. *(1983 Almanac p. 400)*

Background

The Vocational Education Act of 1963 (PL 88-210) was due to expire at the end of fiscal 1984. The congressional review came on the heels of deep funding cuts for vocational education, which dropped from $779 million in fiscal 1980 to $656 million in fiscal 1982. Spending since then had been restored but only to $739 million in fiscal 1984. *(1981 Almanac p. 499)*

The budget squeeze spurred some members to recommend narrowing the focus of vocational aid and sent interest groups scrambling to ensure that their constituents were not given short shrift in the overhaul.

Vocational education programs — where students learned job skills in areas ranging from agriculture to business, from upholstering to tool and die making — had been primarily financed with state and local money. The federal program provided only about 10 percent of the $7.3 billion spent on vocational programs in fiscal 1981, the most recent year for which figures were available.

Although federal aid accounted for only a small share of the total spent, support for vocational training was one of the oldest forms of federal aid to education. Long before the Great Society programs of the 1960s to promote equal educational opportunity, the federal government was helping states finance occupational training.

The Smith-Hughes Act of 1917 (PL 64-347) authorized matching grants to states for secondary school programs in agriculture, home economics, trade and industrial subjects.

With the enactment of the Vocational Education Act of 1963, Congress moved away from funding programs in specific occupations and expanded the goal of federal aid to include helping those with "special educational handicaps." *(Congress and the Nation Vol. I, p. 1220)*

Although most federal aid continued to be used for basic maintenance of vocational programs, Congress put more emphasis on meeting the special needs of the disadvantaged and handicapped in later revisions of the act.

As amended in 1976, the act required states to use 20 percent of their basic grants to serve disadvantaged students — including those with limited proficiency in English — and 10 percent for the handicapped. The 1976 law also required states to take steps to eliminate sex-role stereotyping in vocational education. *(Congress and the Nation Vol. IV, p. 393)*

The Vocational Education Act had not undergone substantial revision since 1976, but in the interim, an exhaustive study of the program was submitted to Congress by the National Institute of Education.

A key conclusion of that 1981 report was that the act "attempts to accomplish too much with too few resources." While Congress over the years had added an increasing number of federal goals to the legislation, the report said, the "resources available under the [act] are insufficient to help states realize all of them."

Serving the 'Under-Served'

As Congress reassessed federal goals in vocational education, one of the most controversial issues was the treatment of the handicapped, disadvantaged and other "under-served" groups.

Some members, especially in the Senate, wanted to reduce or eliminate funds for basic maintenance of vocational programs and give priority to the under-served groups. However, vocational education officials argued that higher priority should be given to program improvement.

Other issues included:

Modernization. Members generally agreed that it would be self defeating to promote access to vocational programs without also addressing the need to upgrade equipment and curricula to meet the changing demands of the labor market.

Simplification. Debate over how to improve access for under-served groups was tied closely to questions about how far the federal government should go in detailing how states should use their grants.

State officials had long complained about the Vocational Education Act's complex system of programs and sub-programs, regulations and set-asides, and called for simplification of the law to give them greater discretion in using federal money to meet local needs.

But federal prescriptions were defended by members who believed they were necessary to ensure that the money was used to promote national priorities.

The Reagan administration wanted to simplify the act by consolidating the various vocational programs into a block grant to states. (In its fiscal 1985 budget, however, the administration backed away from its past proposal to consolidate both vocational and adult education programs into a single block grant.)

The administration's proposal would have required states to use at least 10 percent of the block grant for the handicapped and 20 percent for the disadvantaged.

Industry Involvement. Many members and business leaders, seeking to make vocational training more responsive to labor market needs, wanted to give employers a greater role in planning and evaluating programs.

But some members and educators were wary of forging too close a link with business, warning that the general educational purpose of vocational programs might be lost by gearing them too narrowly to the immediate needs of employers.

House Committee Action

As endorsed Feb. 23 by the House Education and Labor Subcommittee on Elementary, Secondary and Vocational Education, HR 4164 permanently reauthorized the vocational education act.

It authorized about $1.5 billion for vocational education in fiscal 1985, including $1 billion for state grants. That was almost twice as much as appropriated for fiscal 1984. The total included $50 million for joint projects with industry to train high-technology workers and $275 million to retrain adults.

Before voting 20-1 in favor of the bill, the panel during two days of markup dropped a proposal that critics charged would undermine support for the handicapped and disadvantaged.

As originally drafted, HR 4164 would have authorized $325 million in fiscal 1985 for a separate program for students with "special needs" — dropping current provisions that set aside 20 percent of the state grant for serving the disadvantaged, including students with limited proficiency in English, and 10 percent for the handicapped.

Critics contended that Congress would be unlikely to fund the new program and that earmarking funds was the best way to ensure that federal money was used to improve access to vocational education.

The panel approved by voice vote an amendment by subcommittee Chairman Carl D. Perkins, D-Ky., retaining the current law setting aside funds for the disadvantaged and handicapped. The amendment also required states to use another 5 percent of their grants on sex equity programs.

The separate $325 million program was dropped and that amount was added to the $725 million authorization for state grants.

Other Amendments. The subcommittee also approved amendments by the following:

● Perkins, to allow states to continue using federal money for basic maintenance of vocational programs. HR 4164 originally would have limited the use of federal funds for maintenance of programs, focusing instead on expansion, improvement and innovation.

● Baltasar Corrada, New Prog.-Puerto Rico, to continue a program of aid to bilingual vocational education, which had been dropped under the original version of HR 4164.

● Bill Goodling, R-Pa., to drop a provision authorizing $3 million for 10 new vocational education research institutes, using the money instead for grants to states to set up a pool of modern high-technology equipment that could be loaned to local programs.

Full Committee. The Education and Labor Committee by a vote of 32-4 ordered HR 4164 reported Feb. 29 after turning back a GOP effort to increase aid for adult vocational training geared to the needs of the job market. The report (H Rept 98-612) was filed March 5.

The GOP proposal, introduced by Marge Roukema, R-N.J., would have increased from 15 percent to 20 percent the amount earmarked for such programs. It was rejected 11-24.

Supporters argued that more federal aid should be focused on programs that trained adults in job skills needed to enter or re-enter the work force.

Perkins opposed it, saying it would unravel the subcommittee compromise under which advocates for the handicapped and disadvantaged agreed to drop proposals to increase the amount earmarked for those groups. If the set-aside for adult programs were increased, Perkins said, the panel would be under pressure to boost allotments for other groups.

As approved, the bill retained the compromise by maintaining current law that earmarked 30 percent of state grants for serving disadvantaged and handicapped students, and 15 percent for postsecondary and adult vocational programs.

The bill continued to permanently reauthorize the Vocational Education Act. But to win the support of budget-conscious Republicans, the committee agreed to drop the $1.5 billion authorization level for fiscal 1985 and to authorize "such sums" as Congress deemed necessary.

Other Amendments. The committee approved, 19-17, an amendment by Gary L. Ackerman, D-N.Y., allowing states to use federal funds to support secondary school programs that integrated academic and vocational training.

It rejected, 15-19, a Roukema amendment to prohibit the use of funds to buy equipment, if the purchase benefited an organization representing the purchaser or its employees. Her amendment was prompted by controversy over a new catalog of educational computer software endorsed by the National Education Association (NEA), based on evaluations by teachers. Part of the profits from the sale of the software was to go to a foundation established by the NEA, leading some members to question whether the union would benefit.

House Floor Action

The House March 8 passed the bill by an overwhelming 373-4, despite some Republicans' criticism that it made only "cosmetic" changes in current law. *(Vote 37, p. 14-H)*

As approved after two days of debate, the bill extended vocational education programs through fiscal 1989 at funding levels to be determined by Congress. The language permanently authorizing the programs was dropped and the extension was limited to five years in an amendment by Steve Bartlett, R-Texas, that was adopted by voice vote.

GOP critics maintained that the bill perpetuated an inadequate status quo and failed to focus enough on what they called top priorities — the need to modernize vocational programs and to retrain workers.

To remedy what he saw as a basic flaw in the bill, Bartlett proposed eliminating language that allowed federal funds to be used for basic maintenance of vocational programs. His amendment would have limited funding to new or upgraded programs, allowing support for existing programs only in exceptional cases.

But Perkins argued that many programs in economically depressed areas could not continue without federal maintenance funds, and Bartlett's amendment was rejected 60-313. *(Vote 36, p. 14-H)*

Roukema's efforts to increase aid for training geared to the job market failed, as it had in committee. But she succeeded in reoffering her proposal to discourage arrangements in which a professional education organization reaped financial profit from its endorsement of educational equipment, such as computer software. The amendment, approved 205-173, prohibited federal vocational funds from being used to buy equipment if the purchase would result in financial gain to a professional organization that represented the purchaser or its employees. *(Vote 35, p. 12-H)*

The House also by voice vote dropped provisions that would have allowed states to use federal funds to support programs that integrated vocational and academic training.

Other Major Provisions

As approved by the House, HR 4164:

● Reauthorized the Vocational Education Act through fiscal 1989, allowing Congress to appropriate such sums as necessary. The Congressional Budget Office estimated the bill authorized $1.1 billion in fiscal 1985.

● Earmarked 5 percent of appropriations for national programs administered by the secretary of education, including: at least $3.56 million a year for the National Occupational Information Coordinating Committee; at least $6 million a year for the National Center for Research in Vocational Education; and at least $3 million a year for grants to help states set up pools of high-technology equipment that could be loaned to local programs.

● Maintained current provisions for allocating funds to states under a formula based on the population in various age groups and per capita income.

● Continued grants for homemaking and consumer education, requiring states to spend at least one-third of the funds in economically depressed or high unemployment areas.

● Dropped requirements that each state spend at least 20 percent of the money it used for program improvement on guidance and counseling services. Instead, separate grants for such services were authorized.

● Authorized grants to states for joint projects with industry to provide training in high-technology fields, limiting federal aid to no more than half the cost of such projects.

● Authorized grants to states for training adults, including the unemployed and those needing new skills.

● Continued requirements to earmark at least 20 percent of each state's basic grant for serving disadvantaged students, including those with limited proficiency in English, at least 10 percent for serving the handicapped, and 15 percent for postsecondary and adult programs.

● Continued the current mandate that federal funds for the disadvantaged and handicapped cover no more than 50 percent of the extra cost of serving such students.

● Stipulated that states spend up to 5 percent of their basic grants on programs to eliminate sex bias in vocational education and to provide services for women participating in vocational programs such as child care.

● Dropped current requirements that each state spend at least 80 percent of its basic grant on instruction and no more than 20 percent on support services and improvement of programs. The bill required states to allocate at least 80 percent of their funds to local programs.

● Required the allocation of funds to localities under formulas to be devised by states, but required that the states ensure that more money go to economically depressed regions or areas with high unemployment.

Senate Committee Action

While the House bill made few major policy changes, the bill (S 2341) approved by the Senate Labor and Human Resources Subcommittee on Education March 1 sharply narrowed the focus of federal aid and gave priority to serving the handicapped and disadvantaged.

As approved by a vote of 11-0, S 2341 required states, after reserving money for administrative costs, to use two-thirds of their grants for special services for the handicapped, disadvantaged, and three other targeted groups. The rest would be used for general program improvement.

Dan Quayle, R-Ind., strongly objected to earmarking funds for specific groups and introduced an amendment that would give states more flexibility in spending the money. A vote on the amendment was put off until full committee, but the subcommittee approved other Quayle amendments to drop set-asides for home economics and counseling.

Full Committee. Two months later, the full Labor and Human Resources rejected Quayle's effort to give states more flexibility and unanimously reported S 2341 (S Rept 98-507) May 23.

The committee accepted a package of amendments offered by Education Subcommittee Chairman Robert T. Stafford, R-Vt., and others to win support of vocational education groups that had objected to mandating how states should allocate funds.

The package revised a formula in the subcommittee bill determining how states should allocate funds for serving the disadvantaged and the disabled. The subcommittee plan was designed to shift money from wealthier schools to urban areas and other regions with heavy concentrations of low-income students.

Responding to complaints that the formula was too rigid and could deny funds to existing vocational programs that served handicapped and disadvantaged students, the Stafford amendment set broader criteria for allocating funds.

Kennedy Amendments. The committee also approved an amendment by Edward M. Kennedy, D-Mass., to reauthorize $3.7 million for bilingual vocational training.

Kennedy agreed to draft language to accommodate the concerns that bilingual training should be only an "interim step" while students learn English.

The committee also adopted two Kennedy amendments that:

● Authorized $500,000 to convene a national summit conference on education.

● Extended the Women's Educational Equity Act, which supported projects for eliminating sex bias from education programs. The bill authorized $6.2 million in fiscal 1985 and such sums as Congress considered necessary in 1986-89.

As approved, the bill authorized about $900 million for fiscal 1985. It dropped current provisions allowing states to use grants for the basic maintenance of vocational programs, while the House-passed bill retained operating support.

The bill earmarked roughly half the funds going to

states for expanding training opportunities for groups, including women, the poor and the disabled, that had limited access to vocational programs.

Of that money — almost $400 million — states would be required to use 25 percent for serving the handicapped, 50 percent for the disadvantaged, 2 percent for prison inmates and 23 percent for sex equity programs to help homemakers and single parents enter the work force. Current law earmarked funds only for the disadvantaged and handicapped.

The other $400 million would be used for improving and modernizing vocational programs — for example, for the purchase of up-to-date equipment. Ten percent would be earmarked for joint projects with industry for high-technology training and 30 percent would be used for adults in need of training and retraining.

Senate Floor Action

The Senate Aug. 8 passed HR 4164 by voice vote after substituting the text of S 2341. The Senate made no major changes in the committee bill. Among the amendments approved were the following, all adopted by voice vote:

● To require states to allocate at least 80 percent of their funds to local programs but specified that states could withhold funds to school districts that qualified for less than $1,000. All funds earmarked for the handicapped and disadvantaged would have to be passed on to the local level.

● To strengthen state assessment of vocational education, and the development and contents of the state plan.

● To authorize $20 million in fiscal 1985 for state grants for joint projects between schools and community-based organizations to enroll severely economically and educationally disadvantaged youth in vocational training and other education programs.

● To authorize state grants to community-based organizations with records of effectiveness to provide vocational education services to single parents and homemakers.

Other Major Provisions

As passed by the Senate, the bill:

● Authorized $923.7 million for vocational education in fiscal 1985 and such sums as Congress considered necessary in fiscal 1986-89.

The 1985 total included: $20 million for consumer and homemaking education; $3.7 million for bilingual vocational training; $20 million for training programs run jointly by schools and community organizations; and $880 million for basic vocational programs at the state and national level.

● Earmarked 2 percent of vocational education appropriations for national programs, including research and statistics-gathering, and another 2 percent for programs serving Indians.

. ● Barred states from spending more than 6 percent of their federal money for administrative expenses.

● Required about half of each state's grant — a total of almost $400 million nationally — to be used for expanding training opportunities for groups that had had limited access to vocational education. Of that amount, states were required to use 50 percent for serving the disadvantaged, 25 percent for the handicapped, 2 percent for prison inmates and 23 percent to help homemakers and single parents enter the work force.

● Specified that the remaining half of state grants be used for improving and modernizing vocational programs. Of that amount, 10 percent was earmarked for joint projects with industry for high-technology training and 30 percent would be used for training programs for adults.

● Extended for five years the Women's Education Equity Act, authorizing $6.2 million in fiscal 1985.

● Authorized $500,000 for the Education Department to hold a national summit conference on school improvement.

Conference Action

House and Senate conferees began meeting in mid-September and were able to quickly decide how much money to authorize. More difficult to resolve were specific issues about the grants, including how much money should be earmarked for particular purposes and how much each set-aside should be.

Conferees agreed to continue support for a national research center on vocational education, after the Senate backed down from its proposal to spread research funding more broadly. At least $6 million a year would be provided for the research center, operated by Ohio State University under a federal contract.

Handicapped, Disadvantaged Set-Aside. Conferees compromised on a set-aside of 32 percent of state grant funds earmarked for serving the needs of handicapped and disadvantaged students. The House version left unchanged the previous requirement that states set aside 30 percent of their grants for those two groups. The Senate bill increased the set-aside to about 35 percent and stated more explicitly what kinds of services should be provided.

Sex Stereotypes. Conferees also locked horns over improving vocational training for women. The House allotted 5 percent of the state grants for eliminating sex stereotyping in vocational training at all levels. The Senate set aside twice as much money for its women's programs but targeted it on training for a more narrowly defined group — single parents and homemakers.

The negotiators agreed to earmark 3.5 percent of state grants for eliminating sex stereotyping and 8.5 percent for single parents and homemakers.

Women's Equity. Conferees dropped a Senate provision extending the Women's Educational Equity Act, which was reauthorized in another bill. *(Story, p. 494)*

Equipment Purchase. The compromise also included a House provision barring the use of funds to buy equipment, including computer software, if the purchase would result in financial gain to a professional group representing the interests of the buyer or its employees.

Summit Conference. Conferees accepted the Senate proposal to authorize $500,000 for a national summit on school improvement. The House in 1983 had passed a similar bill (HR 3245) but the Senate had not acted on separate summit legislation. ∎

VISTA Bill Cleared

Congress May 8 cleared legislation extending the life of Volunteers in Service to America (VISTA), a remnant of the War on Poverty that the Reagan administration had proposed abolishing three years in a row.

The conference report on S 1129 (H Rept 98-679),

which reauthorized VISTA and several popular volunteer programs for the elderly, was adopted by the Senate by voice vote April 11 and by the House May 8. President Reagan signed the measure May 21 (PL 98-288).

The House adopted the conference report by a vote of 369-25, despite some Republicans' objections that it would give priority to funding VISTA over other volunteer anti-poverty programs. *(Vote 117, p. 40-H)*

The bill extended federally sponsored volunteer programs run by ACTION through fiscal 1986, authorizing $158.4 million in fiscal 1984, $166.1 million in 1985 and $175.2 million in 1986. Most of the money was earmarked for Older American Volunteer programs.

Funding Compromise

The final provisions for financing VISTA were designed to strike a balance between S 1129 as passed by the Senate in September 1983 and by the House in October 1983. The bills differed sharply on the funding mechanism.

The Senate version of S 1129 (S Rept 98-182) set spending ceilings for VISTA beginning with $15 million in fiscal 1984. But the House bill (HR 2655 — H Rept 98-161) had set a "funding floor" of $25 million in 1984 — and more in subsequent years — to prevent funds from being diverted to other programs. *(1983 Almanac p. 398)*

The compromise set spending ceilings for VISTA of $17 million in fiscal 1984, $20 million in fiscal 1985 and $25 million in fiscal 1986. But the measure specified minimum levels of VISTA service that had to be provided — a "floor" measured in volunteer service time rather than dollars. Congressional aides said about $14 million would have to be spent to support the required levels of service.

Provisions

As cleared by Congress, S 1129:

Anti-Poverty Programs

● Authorized funding for VISTA at $17 million in fiscal 1984, $20 million in fiscal 1985 and $25 million in fiscal 1986; and specified minimum levels of volunteer service time to be funded each year.

● Required at least 20 percent of all VISTA volunteers to be older than 55.

● Expanded the list of possible assignments for VISTA volunteers to include addressing the problems of the homeless, unemployed, illiterate, hungry, and people with drug and alcohol problems.

● Provided for VISTA volunteers to be given training before and during their participation in a project.

● Prohibited the use of VISTA funds for projects that were not directed toward anti-poverty goals.

● Authorized $1.8 million a year through fiscal 1986 for Service Learning Programs, in which high school and college students worked in anti-poverty projects, and $1.984 million a year for Special Volunteer Programs for encouraging participation in volunteer services.

Older American Volunteers

● Authorized $111.8 million in fiscal 1984, $115.3 million in 1985 and $118.4 million in 1986 for Retired Senior Volunteer, Senior Companion and Foster Grandparent programs.

● Increased the stipend for Senior Companions and Foster Grandparents from $2 to $2.20 an hour.

● Authorized a $12 million increase in the Senior Com-

panion program for training volunteers to provide home-care services for the elderly.

● Stated that localities could not be required to contribute more than 30 percent of the cost of Retired Senior Volunteer projects, although larger contributions could be encouraged.

General Provisions

● Authorized $25.8 million in fiscal 1984, $27 million in 1985 and $28 million in 1986 for administration of ACTION programs.

● Limited the number of consultants, outside experts and employees in certain non-civil-service positions that could be hired by ACTION.

● Required ACTION to give grant recipients at least 75 days' notice that their renewal might be denied.   ∎

Older Americans Act

Congress Sept. 26 cleared legislation authorizing about $4 billion over three years for popular nutrition and social service programs for the elderly.

The measure (S 2603 — H Rept 98-1037) established a new program to promote health education for the elderly and extended, without major changes, existing programs under the Older Americans Act (PL 89-73). The measure was last extended in 1981. *(1981 Almanac p. 496)*

The House Sept. 26 cleared the measure by voting 393-2 to adopt the conference report. The measure had been approved by the Senate by voice vote earlier in the day. *(Vote 372, p. 114-H)*

The president signed the legislation Oct. 9 (PL 98-459).

Final action came after congressional negotiators resolved the relatively minor differences between the versions of S 2603 passed May 24 by the Senate and Aug. 8 by the House.

Under the Older Americans Act, aid was distributed to state and regional agencies to provide meals, transportation and other services for the elderly. Most of the programs, for which about $1.1 billion was appropriated in fiscal 1984, were run by the Department of Health and Human Services. The bill also reauthorized food aid administered by the Agriculture Department and a Labor Department community jobs program for the elderly.

Neither the House nor Senate versions of S 2603 had incorporated the Reagan administration's proposal to consolidate aid to the elderly into a block grant to the states. The bill, however, liberalized current provisions that allowed states to transfer federal funds between their social service and nutrition programs.

The bill included two changes to the Age Discrimination in Employment Act that had been included by the Senate affecting business executives and Americans working abroad. The anti-bias law protected most workers from being forced to retire before they turned 70. *(Background, 1978 Almanac p. 265)*

Major Provisions

As cleared by Congress, major provisions of S 2603:

● Authorized $1.26 billion in fiscal 1985, $1.3 billion in 1986 and $1.37 billion in 1987 for Older Americans Act programs. The total included $8.55 million in fiscal 1985 for new grants to universities to develop health education programs for the elderly. No spending ceiling was set for the new program in 1986 and 1987.

● Modified the manner in which the members of the Federal Council on the Aging were appointed. The president, the Senate and the House each would appoint five members; previously, the entire membership was appointed by the president.

● Put new emphasis on meeting the needs of minorities, aiding elderly victims of violence and abuse, and serving victims of Alzheimer's disease and their families.

● Allowed states receiving aid for nutrition and support service programs to use up to 5 percent of their allocations or $500,000, whichever was greater, for administrative costs.

● Increased the proportion of funds states could transfer between nutrition and social service programs from the current 20 percent limit to 27 percent in fiscal 1985, 29 percent in 1986 and 30 percent in 1987.

● Modified the Community Service Employment program, which subsidized part-time jobs for low-income elderly people, to lower the cap on administrative expenses to 13.5 percent in fiscal 1986 and 12 percent in 1987. Labor Department regulations previously barred project sponsors from using more than 15 percent of their funds for administration.

● Modified a provision of the age discrimination act that allowed firms to force executives and other high-level professionals to retire after age 65 if they were entitled to retirement benefits of at least $27,000. The threshold was raised to $44,000.

● Extended coverage of the age law to American citizens who were working for U.S. companies abroad.

Legislative Action

Senate. The Senate May 24 passed S 2603 by voice vote. The bill authorized modest spending increases in Older Americans programs: $1.16 billion in fiscal 1985, $1.21 billion in 1986 and $1.28 billion in 1987 for nutrition and social service programs for the elderly.

The bill was brought to the floor with the understanding that no amendments would be offered to the version reported May 18 by the Labor and Human Resources Committee (S Rept 98-467).

Going along with the agreement to speed consideration of the bill, John Heinz, R-Pa., dropped plans to introduce an amendment to improve housing and services to help the elderly to live independently.

The Senate bill allowed states more latitude in transferring funds between nutrition and social service programs. It would increase from 20 percent to 35 percent the proportion of funds that could be transferred.

House. The House Aug. 8 approved HR 4785 by a vote of 406-12 as reported May 9 by the Education and Labor Committee (H Rept 98-737). It then substituted its text for that of S 2603. *(Vote 317, p. 96-H)*

The House bill set funding levels at $1.34 billion for fiscal 1985, $1.4 billion in 1986 and $1.47 billion in 1987. Those funding levels, higher than either the administration had requested or than were provided in the Senate-passed S 2603, drew opposition from the administration. The executive branch objected that the bill's three-year authorization total was $860 million more than the budget request.

The House version also included an authorization of $8.5 million in fiscal 1985 for a demonstration program to promote health education for the elderly. The bill increased the funds that could be transferred by states from 20 percent to 25 percent.

Conference. House and Senate negotiators split the difference on authorized funding levels and compromised on how big a portion of each state's federal funds could be transferred from nutrition to social services programs.

Conferees accepted a number of Senate provisions that were not included in the House version, including:

● The changes in the Age Discrimination in Employment Act affecting high-level business executives and Americans working abroad.

● The added emphasis placed on serving victims of Alzheimer's disease.

● The change in the authority for appointing members of the Federal Council on the Aging.

Conferees accepted the House provision adding $8.55 million for grants to universities to develop health education programs for the elderly. ∎

Library Aid Reauthorized

After trying for nearly three years to eliminate federal aid to libraries, President Reagan Oct. 17 signed legislation (HR 2878 — PL 98-480) reauthorizing the Library Services and Construction Act (PL 84-597) through fiscal 1989.

The administration had maintained that the act already had accomplished its purpose of improving access to public libraries. But the continuation of the popular programs faced little opposition on Capitol Hill.

The House adopted the conference report on the measure (H Rept 98-1075) by voice vote Oct. 2, and the Senate followed suit the next day, clearing the legislation.

The final measure authorized a total of $839 million for grants to improve and build libraries: $151 million in fiscal 1985, $161 million in 1986, $171 million in 1987, $181 million in 1988 and $175 million in 1989.

It included new grants for libraries to buy foreign-language materials and to coordinate literacy programs and authorized $2 million for an endowment fund at Howard University.

The bill also included riders authorizing $22 million for projects at four universities in the home states of key lawmakers. The grants were:

● $6.5 million for construction of a library addition at the University of Hartford, an amount sought by Sen. Lowell P. Weicker Jr., R-Conn.

● $9 million to build a handicapped research and training center at the University of Kansas, money sought by Sen. Robert Dole, R-Kan.

● $3.5 million for a facility to house the Carl Vinson Institute of Government at the University of Georgia, a project backed by Sen. Mack Mattingly, R-Ga.

● $3 million for a John W. McCormack Institute of Public Affairs at the University of Massachusetts at Boston. Rep. Joe Moakley, D-Mass. — whose House seat was once occupied by former Speaker of the House McCormack — helped secure the money.

House, Senate Action

By a vote of 357-39, the House Jan. 31 approved the bill, authorizing $156 million in 1985, with funding rising $10 million each year to $186 million in 1988. The bill had been reported by the Education and Labor Committee on May 16, 1983 (H Rept 98-165). *(Vote 12, p. 6-H)*

The House rejected 144-248 an amendment by Newt Gingrich, R-Ga., to allow a presidential line-item veto over money appropriated under the bill. He said the proposal was a "tiny little experiment" in the line-item veto requested by President Reagan. *(Vote 11, p. 6-H; line-item veto, p. 167)*

The Senate Labor and Human Resources Committee by a vote of 17-1 reported a companion measure (S 2490 — S Rept 98-486) May 23. The bill extended federal aid to libraries for five years, authorizing $143 million in fiscal 1985, rising $8 million each year to $175 million in 1989.

It also reauthorized funding through fiscal 1989 for the National Center for Education Statistics and the National Assessment for Educational Progress, a project that periodically evaluated the academic achievement of school children. And, the bill authorized up to $2 million to establish an endowment at Howard University in Washington, D.C.

The Senate by voice vote approved S 2490 June 21 after adding an amendment authorizing an additional $19 million earmarked for three university construction projects. The Senate passed HR 2878 after substituting the text of its bill.

Additional Action. Before sending the bill on to conference, the House Aug. 8 amended HR 2878 to add a pet project of its own: $3 million for the John W. McCormack Institute of Public Affairs at the University of Massachusetts. That authorization had been the subject of a separate measure, HR 4066, reported by the Education and Labor Committee on the same day (H Rept 98-963).

Conference

Conferees accepted the Senate's five-year authorization but tilted slightly toward the House-passed funding totals for fiscal 1985-88. For each of the first four years, the authorized funding level was $5 million below the House total.

Conferees agreed to retain all four special university construction grants and the endowment fund for Howard University.

They dropped the Senate authorization for the National Center for Educational Statistics and the National Assessment for Educational Progress. Funds for those programs were authorized in an omnibus social services measure (S 2496 — PL 98-511). *(Story, p. 493)* ∎

Education Bills Cleared

Congress May 23 cleared legislation (HR 5287) that kept alive several small education programs that the Reagan administration had wanted to eliminate. The reauthorization bill, signed by the president June 12 (PL 98-312), also prevented the inadvertent cutoff of aid to certain colleges that would have been caused by 1983 legislation.

As signed into law, HR 5287:

● Extended the Department of Education's law school clinical experience program, authorizing $1.5 million in fiscal 1985, $2 million in 1986, $2 million in 1987, $2.5 million in 1988 and $3 million in 1989.

● Authorized funds for the Allen J. Ellender Fellowship program, which helped low-income students participate in a week-long program in Washington, D.C., sponsored by the Close Up Foundation. The bill authorized $1.5 million annually in fiscal 1984 and 1985, $2 million each year in fiscal 1986 and 1987, and $2.5 million in both fiscal 1988 and 1989.

The administration requested no money for either program in its fiscal 1985 budget.

Other major provisions of the bill:

● Earmarked $1 million in the education secretary's discretionary fund for a law-related education program. That program had been folded into an education block grant created in 1981.

● Authorized $3.4 million for grants to the Urban Education Foundation of Pennsylvania Inc., to renovate facilities at its urban research park in Philadelphia.

● Made technical changes in a law passed in 1983 to prevent the inadvertent cutoff of federal funds to an endowment assistance program for small colleges. The 1983 legislation (PL 98-95) authorized additional funds for challenge grants, which must be matched dollar-for-dollar in non-federal funds. The added funds were aimed primarily at predominantly black colleges. *(1983 Almanac p. 397)*

Background

As cleared, the bill's law-related education and Ellender fellowship provisions were similar to those in HR 3324 (H Rept 98-286), which passed the House Oct. 21, 1983, but was not considered by the Senate. *(1983 Almanac p. 405)*

But HR 5287 started out in the House simply as a measure to make technical corrections in the 1983 endowment legislation. The House passed the bill in that form by voice vote on May 1, with no committee action.

The Senate considered the measure on May 16 and, at the behest of Sen. Robert T. Stafford, R-Vt., added the other provisions. The expanded bill was passed by voice vote.

On May 23 the House accepted the Senate amendments, clearing the bill for the president. ∎

Foreign Language Aid

The House passed legislation aimed at improving foreign language education in 1984, but the bill died when the Senate did not consider it.

The measure (HR 2708 — H Rept 98-162) would have authorized $50 million each year in fiscal 1984-86 to support model school programs and for grants to colleges based on the number of students enrolled in foreign language courses.

The bill was passed by the House Feb. 23 by 265-120. In the Senate, the legislation did not emerge from the Labor and Human Resources Committee. *(Vote 27, p. 10)*

During House debate, supporters of the bill noted that only 15 percent of all high school students were enrolled in foreign language courses and argued that the measure would provide incentives to expand and improve programs.

The House rejected an amendment stipulating that money for the foreign-language program could be provided only in a separate appropriation bill. Supporters said the financing restriction would allow the president to evaluate funding for the new program on its own merits, without giving him line-item veto authority. The amendment, by George W. Gekas, R-Pa., was rejected 145-243. *(Vote 26, p. 10-H)*

The House also rejected, on a division vote of 35-67, an amendment by Robert S. Walker, R-Pa., to cut authorization levels by 10 percent. ∎

Child Support Enforcement

The president Aug. 16 signed legislation (HR 4325 — PL 98-378) to require the withholding of money from the paychecks of parents delinquent in court-ordered child support payments.

The bill was cleared Aug. 8 when the House adopted the conference report (H Rept 98-925) by a vote of 413-0. The Senate had adopted the measure Aug. 1 by a vote of 99-0. *(Vote 319, p. 98-H; vote 195, p. 34-S)*

In addition to withholding past-due support payments from wages, the bill required states to pass laws allowing liens to be placed against a parent's property and to intercept federal and state income tax refunds on behalf of a child. Also, it extended child support assistance to all families, not just welfare families, who were already covered by federal child support law.

The bill was designed to help up to two million children who were entitled to an estimated $4 billion in support payments. It was part of the Economic Equity Act, a package of legislative proposals aimed at improving the treatment of women in such areas as tax law, insurance and pensions. *(1983 Almanac, p. 298)*

The House had originally passed the measure Nov. 16, 1983. The Senate passed its version April 25 by a vote of 94-0. *(1983 Almanac p. 418; vote 79, p. 16-S)*

The two bills were substantially similar. In addition to requiring states to withhold past-due support payments from wages, both bills agreed on placing liens against a parent's property and diverting tax refunds on behalf of a child. In addition, they provided incentives to reward states with effective child support enforcement programs.

Also, both bills required states to extend child support assistance to non-welfare families. States that failed to meet the new child support assistance provisions would lose substantial federal funds including federal welfare payments in the form of Aid to Families with Dependent Children (AFDC).

Conference Action

However, there were differences. The House required states to continue for four months Medicaid coverage for families that would have lost AFDC eligibility because their income rose with the child support payments, while the Senate version made no similar provision. Conferees accepted the House language.

Conferees also included a Senate provision extending to non-welfare families a program that intercepted federal income tax refunds for parents behind on payments. The House bill had no similar provision.

A compromise was reached on federal contributions to help cover state administrative costs. The House bill continued current law, which stated that the U.S. government would pay 70 percent of the administrative costs states incurred in enforcing child support payments, while the Senate wanted to cut that to 65 percent over five years, beginning in fiscal 1987. Conferees agreed to continue the 70 percent level but to drop it to 66 percent by 1990.

Provisions

As signed by the president, the Child Support Enforcement Amendments of 1984 (HR 4325) stated that aid in obtaining court-ordered child support payments must be extended to all families.

Procedures

The bill required states to enact laws by Oct. 1, 1985, establishing the following:

● Employer withholding of wages, if support payments were delinquent in an amount equal to one month's support or if the parent owing support requested withholding earlier.

● Imposition of liens against real and personal property for amounts of overdue support.

● Requiring parents who had a record of non-payment to post bonds or other financial guarantees to secure payment of overdue child support.

● Establishing expedited court or administrative procedures to obtain and enforce child support orders.

● Notifying individual AFDC recipients at least once a year of the amount of child support collected for them by the state.

● Permitting the establishment of paternity anytime before a child's 18th birthday.

● Making information available to credit agencies if the arrearage was $1,000 or more, and permitting states to provide information involving smaller amounts.

Withholding

The bill also:

● Limited the amount that could be withheld from a parent's paycheck to 55 percent of disposable income in the case of an absent parent — one who did not have custody of the child — with a second family, and 65 percent for an absent parent without a second family.

● Required states to follow legal procedures before withholding income, including notifying persons of withholding and of procedures to contest the withholding.

● Required employers of absent parents, upon proper notice, to withhold the stipulated amount from the parent's wages, to be forwarded to the proper state agency, and permitted states to reimburse employers for their costs of withholding.

● Directed states to levy fines against employers who fired, refused to employ or otherwise disciplined a parent whose wages must be withheld.

● Permitted states to extend withholding to income other than wages, such as pensions, bonuses and commissions, or dividends.

● Required states to withhold child support payments from state tax refunds and, through the Internal Revenue Service, to tap federal tax refunds.

Federal Funds

● Required the federal government to pay 70 percent of state and local administrative costs for child support enforcement for fiscal years 1984-87, 68 percent in 1988-89 and 66 percent in 1990.

● Established a new system of incentive grants to reward states with good child support collection programs. Each state received as an incentive at least 6 percent of the amount it collected in child support. States with good records of child support assistance received up to 10 percent.

● Authorized special grants to promote improvements in interstate enforcement at $7 million in fiscal 1985, $12 million in 1986 and $15 million in 1987.

● Required the secretary of Health and Human Services to issue regulations mandating states to petition courts to include medical support as part of a child support order whenever health care coverage was available to the parent without custody at reasonable cost.

● Stipulated that if a family lost AFDC benefits as a result of its income increasing from child support payments, the state must continue Medicaid health care coverage for four calendar months, effective upon the date of enactment.

● Required state child support agencies to undertake support collections on behalf of certain children receiving foster care effective Oct. 1, 1984. Those children were not specifically covered by previous law.

Legislative History

The federal-state child support program was established in 1975 to help families, most of them headed by women, locate absent parents, establish paternity and collect support payments. Legislation to strengthen the program was fueled by congressional concern about the growing number of parents who failed to make good on their child support promises.

Efforts to reduce such delinquencies drew support from both sides of the aisle and from the Reagan administration.

After House passage of the bill, advocates of strengthening child support early in 1984 took the Senate Finance Committee to task for "stalling" on the bill. In two separate letters, members of the Congressional Caucus on Women's Issues and nine Republican congresswomen urged committee Chairman Robert Dole, R-Kan., to speed consideration of the bill.

Dole said he hoped to act on the bill before the February recess, but the measure took a back seat to a package of spending cuts and tax increases. The bill (HR 4325) was approved by the panel March 23, and the report (S Rept 98-387) was filed April 9.

Controversy over the financing of child support services had been generated by an administration proposal to cut federal matching payments for state administrative costs. Critics charged that the plan would defeat the purpose of the child support bill.

While the House had voted to maintain current levels of federal aid, the Senate committee voted to trim the federal match gradually over five years.

Under pressure from Dole, the panel narrowly rejected some proposals that would have increased the cost of the bill — including an amendment to liberalize Medicaid coverage for families who dropped off the welfare rolls as a result of receiving more child support. ∎

Family-Life Programs

Congress Oct. 9 cleared a one-year reauthorization of federal grant programs for family planning and adolescent family-life projects to aid pregnant teenagers.

The bill (S 2616) authorized $162.6 million for family-planning grants and $30 million for family-life projects for fiscal 1985. The family-life projects provided teenagers with job and adoption services, counseling and other alternatives to abortion, and discouraged teen sexual activity.

The Senate adopted the conference report (H Rept 98-1154) by voice vote Oct. 9, and the House by voice vote cleared it for the president later in the day. The president signed the bill Oct. 19 (PL 98-512).

Both chambers had passed multi-year reauthorizations, but reconciling differences was delayed by disagree-

ment on whether to require federally funded family-planning services to notify parents of teenagers seeking contraceptives.

The Reagan administration unsuccessfully sought to require the notification, while the House Energy and Commerce Committee report (HR 5600 — H Rept 98-804) pointedly restated existing law, which directed agencies to encourage parent-child communication about teenagers' use of the agency's services, to the extent practicable.

The final bill, worked out in informal negotiations, made no major policy changes in either program. Negotiators agreed to limit the authorization to one year with the intention of dealing with the issue in 1985.

Legislative Action

House. The House Energy and Commerce Committee reported HR 5600 on May 23 as a three-year reauthorization of federal funding for family-planning clinics and for programs to aid pregnant teens and teenage parents. It also included the text of HR 5601, which authorized preventive health block grants. The measure authorized total funding of $906.5 million.

The committee rejected an amendment by William E. Dannemeyer, R-Calif., to require notification of parents of teenagers who seek aid from family planning agencies that receive funding from the federal government.

On June 11 the House passed HR 5600 by a vote of 290-102. The bill made no changes in the family planning or adolescent life program, despite the Reagan administration's request to fold it into a block grant. The administration also objected to earmarking funds for rape crisis programs and to the total funding level. *(Vote 201, p. 64-H)*

As passed, HR 5600:

● Reauthorized grants and other support for family-planning services by state and local governments, clinics and non-profit groups at $162.6 million, $171.8 million, and $181.4 million respectively in fiscal years 1985-87.

● Reauthorized the adolescent family-life program at $30 million, $31.7 million and $33.5 million respectively in fiscal years 1985-87.

● Reauthorized preventive health services block grants at $98.5 million annually for fiscal years 1985-87. The money could be used for rat control; fluoridation; hypertension screening and treatment; community-based programs to combat smoking, alcohol use by children and teenagers, and other problems; public health services; establishing home health agencies; emergency medical services; and rape crisis services. The provision added a requirement that the U.S. government collect data on the impact of the funds.

● Increased the authorization for rape crisis services from $3 million to $3.5 million in any year.

● Required states to spend 65 percent of their fiscal 1981 expenditures for hypertension control.

Senate. On May 25 the Senate Labor and Human Resources Committee reported S 2616 (S Rept 98-496). The measure dealt solely with the adolescent family-life program, authorizing $30 million annually for fiscal 1985-87. The Senate passed the measure by voice vote June 29.

Final Action. The House passed S 2616 on Aug. 10 after substituting the text of HR 5600. House and Senate negotiators agreed to retain the family-planning and adolescent family-life provisions, but the other House provisions were dropped. Those issues were later addressed in S 2301 (PL 98-555). *(Story, p. 473)* ∎

Federal Abortion Alternatives Cut by Reagan

In his 1984 State of the Union address, President Reagan called on Americans to "come together in a spirit of understanding and helping" and find "positive solutions to the tragedy of abortion."

Throughout his first term, the president championed a constitutional amendment and bills to outlaw abortion, none of which passed. But Reagan gave little encouragement to federal programs to deter unwanted pregnancies or provide pregnant women alternatives to abortion.

As soon as he took office in 1981, the president sought cuts in the government's three main programs related to pregnancy prevention and assistance for pregnant women.

Aside from a desire to reduce the budget, part of the reason, according to administration officials, was profound discomfort with government involvement in family planning programs. Some of Reagan's staunchest supporters believed the government should have no role in providing services or information on sex education or contraception.

Congress refused to go along with Reagan's cuts in two of the three programs that provided alternatives to abortion. But the president in 1981 was successful in cutting by almost one-fourth the money available for the government's major family planning program, Title X of the Public Health Service Act of 1970. *(Chart, p. 466)*

While funding for Title X increased following that 1981 cut, it had not yet reached the level in 1984 that it was at in President Carter's last year in office.

Although programs to help pregnant women enjoyed considerable congressional support, they were scattered throughout the government. This prevented a direct vote on any comprehensive package of alternatives to abortion.

Almost all funding for the existing alternatives was contained in the annual appropriations bill for the Departments of Labor, Health and Human Services (HHS) and Education. But many conservative members opposed to abortion who might have supported increased funding for the individual alternatives would not vote for the larger spending bill, which funded most of the government's social programs.

New Initiatives

There were two new federal initiatives related to abortion alternatives since 1981, neither proposed by the administration. One was the Adolescent Family Life Program proposed by Sen. Jeremiah Denton, R-Ala.

Established in 1981, the program was spending nearly $15 million in fiscal 1985 on 59 demonstration projects to discourage teenagers from engaging in sexual activity, while encouraging those who did become pregnant to carry their pregnancies to term.

No abortion counseling was allowed. But this provision, along with another that encouraged religious organizations to apply for grants, resulted in a lawsuit challenging the constitutionality of the entire program.

The other initiative, enacted in 1984, was a modification of Medicaid, the federal-state health program for the poor, to require state coverage for first-time pregnant women. Known as the Child Health Assurance Program (CHAP), it was the result of a compromise between congressional opponents and supporters of abortion.

One defender of legalized abortion was Henry A. Waxman, D-Calif., chairman of the House Energy and Commerce Subcommittee on Health and the Environment, which had jurisdiction over family planning and maternal and child health programs. Waxman supported Denton's program and worked with some abortion opponents for the Medicaid change.

"I respect the anti-abortion position that many people hold," he said. "But what I can't understand is why they wouldn't support at least some family planning counseling and contraceptive programs and why they wouldn't be strongly for those programs that can offer a better chance for a fetus to develop into a healthy baby and for that baby to have an opportunity to succeed in life because the baby's health needs have been met.

"I have always found it incredible," Waxman added, "that an administration opposed to abortion would also oppose family planning — which is the only federal program that could directly help reduce the number of unwanted pregnancies."

Administration officials disagreed. Marjory Mecklenburg, who oversaw federal family planning programs as a deputy assistant secretary at HHS, said Reagan had a commendable record on the issues related to abortion.

"Not only does the president favor protection of the unborn, but he is also concerned about alternatives to abortion," she said. "Because an administration proposes some changes in a program does not necessarily mean they are opposed to it. It may mean they see ways to improve the program. That has been the position of this administration regarding family planning services.

"It is the administration's view that some categorical service programs such as family planning and maternal-child health programs are best administered by the states through block grants," Mecklenburg said.

Abortion Status

Abortion became legal nationwide in the United States with the Supreme Court's 1973 *Roe v. Wade* decision. In that ruling, the court established the right of a woman to have an abortion based on an implied right of privacy in the Constitution. The court reaffirmed its basic position in a set of rulings in 1983. *(1983 Almanac p. 306)*

Since 1973, the number of abortions reported each year had averaged about 1.5 million. About one-third of those abortions were performed on teenagers, according to the Alan Guttmacher Institute, an affiliate of Planned Parenthood Federation of America that conducted research on family planning and reproductive health.

Since 1976 Congress had barred federal funding for most abortions for poor women, although court challenges delayed the ban until August 1977. In 1984, federal funds were available for abortions only to save the life of the pregnant woman.

The funding ban was upheld by the Supreme Court, as were state laws that barred state funding for abortions. However, 15 states and the District of Columbia still provided abortion funding for poor women in 1984. The states were Alaska, California, Colorado, Connecticut, Hawaii, Maryland, Massachusetts, Michigan, New Jersey, New York, North Carolina, Oregon, Pennsylvania, Washington and West Virginia.

Defining Alternatives

Defining alternatives to abortion proved to be almost as controversial as the debate over abortion itself. At bot-

Federal Money for Abortion Alternatives . . .

	FY '81		FY '82	
	Request	**Actual**	**Request**	**Actual**
FAMILY PLANNING SERVICES [1] Primarily funds family planning clinics that offer contraceptives, family planning services and abortion counseling.	$ 162,047,000	$ 161,671,000	$ 124,800,000	$ 124,176,000
ADOLESCENT FAMILY LIFE PROGRAM [2] Funds demonstration projects providing services to pregnant teenagers; no abortion counseling permitted.	—	—	11,033,000	11,033,000
POPULATION AND CONTRACEPTIVE RESEARCH [3] National Institute of Child Health and Human Development. Conducts research on fertility and contraception.	76,830,000	77,371,000	82,594,000	80,277,000
MATERNAL AND CHILD HEALTH BLOCK GRANT [1] Funds state programs to provide health care, including prenatal services, to low-income families.	391,543,000	454,393,000	331,000,000	373,750,000
SPECIAL SUPPLEMENTAL FOOD PROGRAM FOR WOMEN, INFANTS & CHILDREN (WIC) [4] Food program for low-income women and children with emphasis on pregnant women.	924,540,000	927,040,000	652,608,000	934,080,000

SOURCES: [1] *Senate Appropriations Subcommittee on Labor/Health and Human Services/Education.* [2] *Department of Health and*

tom were questions of the proper role of government, religious tenets and the country's shifting morality.

The continuum of possibilities ranged from preventing an unwanted pregnancy to providing services to the children of unwanted pregnancies.

Some in the anti-abortion, or "pro-life," movement had reservations about the federal government's efforts to reduce the number of abortions.

Judie Brown, president of the American Life Lobby, for example, said the federal government should have no role in family planning. Her group and others, such as United Families of America, opposed the basic family planning program, Title X, arguing that it did little to prevent

unwanted pregnancies and actually encouraged sexual promiscuity and abortion, particularly among adolescents.

The Roman Catholic Church, another major element of the anti-abortion movement, saw the issue as part of a larger social problem. In an Oct. 25 speech, Joseph Cardinal Bernardin of Chicago said, "The Catholic position on abortion requires — by the law of logic and the law of love — a social vision which joins the right to life to the promotion of a range of other rights: nutrition, health care, employment and housing."

The U.S. Catholic Conference, the public policy arm of the nation's bishops, actively supported the CHAP legislation. The conference also supported increased funding for

. . . Counseling, Contraception and Nutrition

FY '83		FY '84		FY '85	
Request	Actual	Request	Actual	Request	Actual
— 0 — proposed health block grant for states	$ 124,088,000	— 0 — proposed block grant	$ 140,000,000	— 0 — proposed block grant	$ 142,500,000
16,000,000	13,404,000	16,318,000	14,918,000	14,716,000	14,716,000
85,676,000	86,209,000	90,725,000	90,776,000	93,777,000	104,950,000 (tentative)
350,000,000	478,000,000	336,190,000	399,000,000	407,300,000	478,000,000
1,060,000,000	1,160,000,000	1,060,000,000	1,360,000,000	1,254,288,000	1,500,000,000

Human Services.   [3] *National Institute of Child Health and Human Development.*   [4] *Senate Appropriations Subcommittee on Agriculture.*

child nutrition programs and those providing health services for low-income mothers.

Federal Programs

At the federal level there were seven programs, including the new adolescent pilot project and CHAP, that provided funds to help prevent unwanted pregnancies or provide services to women carrying their pregnancies to term.

● **Family Planning, Title X of the Public Health Service Act.** This title authorized funding for clinics that disseminated information on family planning and contraceptives. While abortion counseling and referral were permitted, no funds could be used to perform abortions.

● **Population and Contraceptive Research.** Congress provided money to the National Institute of Child Health and Human Development (NICHD), one of the National Institutes of Health, for research on fertility and new contraceptives.

Funding for these programs rose during Reagan's first term from about $83 million in fiscal 1982 to about $105 million in 1985. The bulk of the money, however, went for fertility research. Only about 9 percent was used for contraceptive research.

Apart from the government's funding of contraceptive research, international support for such research was declining, as was private research by companies that made contraceptives, according to Jeannie I. Rosoff, president of the Guttmacher Institute.

● **Maternal and Child Health Block Grants.** This program provided grants to states for health care, including prenatal services, to low-income families. It was created in 1935 as part of the Social Security Act, but it changed form over the years. By the mid-1970s there were seven categorical programs designed to aid mothers and children. They were rolled into a single block grant in 1981.

In President Carter's last year, these programs received $454 million. In his first year, Reagan requested only $331 million, although Congress provided $374 million. By fiscal 1985, the administration requested $407 million, while Congress provided $478 million.

The administration argued that states could administer the program more efficiently so that less money overall resulted in the same level of services.

But health advocates said less federal money resulted in fewer people served. They noted that the program was started in the first place because states had declined to provide sufficient health services to needy women and infants.

● **Women, Infants and Children (WIC) Program.** This food program, run by the Agriculture Department, provided food to low-income women, with emphasis on pregnant women and women with infants. It fed approximately three million people annually.

The program was popular with members of Congress, who regularly cited studies showing that WIC helped produce healthier children.

In Carter's last year, the program received $927 million. Reagan tried to cut it to $653 million in fiscal 1982, but Congress provided $934 million. WIC's fiscal 1985 appropriation was $1.5 billion.

● **CHAP.** Enactment of the CHAP provisions in 1984 ended a five-year on-again, off-again effort to require states to provide Medicaid coverage to poor women pregnant for the first time and to women and young children in families where the principal wage earner was unemployed.

Previously, states could cover first-time pregnant women, but Congress did not require it.

Federal matching funds available to states totaled about $270 million for fiscal 1985.

The new program was largely the result of an agreement between liberal and conservative members, including a number who were strong abortion foes. They felt it was both fiscally and morally desirable to assure prenatal and infant care, arguing that early care would prevent more expensive medical and social problems later in life.

● **Title XX of the Social Security Act.** This program provided funds to states for an array of social services, including family planning.

From 1972 to 1981, states could get 90 percent federal reimbursement under Title XX for any money they used for family planning services. The 90 percent match was eliminated in 1981 when Reagan revised the program as part of overall budget changes.

Only a small portion of the program, which totaled $2.7 billion in fiscal 1985, had been used for family planning, according to the Guttmacher Institute.

In fiscal 1981, the last year in which the 90 percent match was available, $60 million was used for family planning by 33 states.

In fiscal 1982, the first year of the Reagan administration, the amount dropped to $46 million distributed among 28 states, and preliminary indications for fiscal 1983 showed the funding dropped below $39 million.

Family Planning

The most controversial of all these programs was the family planning program, created by Congress in 1970. The program was the major source of support for more than 5,000 family planning clinics run by hospitals, health departments, Planned Parenthood affiliates and other agencies.

The program's first appropriation in 1971 was $6 million. By the end of the Carter administration in fiscal 1981, it was getting $162 million.

In fiscal 1982, Reagan proposed $125 million for family planning — a 23 percent cut. Congress went along, appropriating $124 million. In the next three years, the administration did not request any money expressly for the program but rather proposed to give states a "primary health care" block grant they could use for a variety of purposes, including family planning.

Congress refused to go along and continued to provide earmarked funding. For fiscal 1985 the program was given $143 million.

Shortly after Reagan took office, he made clear he opposed Title X.

"I regret we do not have the votes to defeat the Family Planning Program," he wrote in a letter to Sen. Orrin G. Hatch, R-Utah, who had just become chairman of the Labor and Human Resources Committee, which had jurisdiction over family planning programs.

Anti-abortion groups, led by Brown's American Life Lobby, stepped up their drive to kill the program, claiming federal family planning money had been used improperly to lobby Congress on abortion.

While the administration was not able to kill the Title X program, it did reorganize it in a way that critics charged reduced its effectiveness. Instead of being run by career public health officials in HHS, the program was put under Mecklenburg, a former president of American Citizens Concerned for Life, headquartered in Minneapolis.

Despite widespread criticism from family planning advocates, the administration in January 1983 published a regulation requiring parental notification for adolescents receiving prescription contraceptives through a Title X program. But two federal district courts found the rule to be in violation of Title X and barred its use.

Critics contended the Title X program was not working. Even though it spent almost $1.6 billion since 1970, Brown noted that "illegitimacy, venereal disease and teenage pregnancy rates have continually climbed." The program "is a marked and repeated failure, and thereby a total waste of federal tax dollars," she said.

Asta Kenney, a specialist on teenage pregnancy for the Guttmacher Institute, conceded teenage pregnancy had gone up, but she said the rate would have been much higher without family planning programs.

"We don't know what has caused the increase in sexual activity among teenagers," Kenney said. "We do have some reason to believe that family planning is not causing teenagers to be sexually active inasmuch as most teenagers only come to a family planning clinic when they have been sexually active for a year."

According to Faye Wattleton, president of Planned Parenthood, more than 800,000 pregnancies were averted in 1981, about half of them among teenagers, as a result of family planning programs. Had the pregnancies occurred, Wattleton said, there would have been an estimated

282,000 additional births and 433,000 more abortions. The remaining pregnancies would have ended in miscarriages.

While Title X money went to a variety of public and non-profit organizations, funds generally did not go to organizations prominent in the anti-abortion movement. The reason, according to Douglas Johnson, legislative director for the National Right to Life Committee, was that the program required a grantee to offer a full range of counseling, including referrals for abortion. Anti-abortion groups that offered services for pregnant women, such as the nationwide Birthright, did not apply for funding because they refused "to become accomplices" in abortions, Johnson said.

There were efforts in at least four states to establish state-funded family planning programs that barred abortion counseling. But these were thrown out by the courts as a violation of constitutional free speech provisions, according to a spokesman for the American Civil Liberties Union (ACLU), which participated in all of the lawsuits.

Discouraging Sex

The three-year-old Adolescent Family Life Program barred abortion counseling and encouraged teenagers to postpone sexual activity.

By comparison with the Title X program, it was tiny. The first appropriation in fiscal 1982 was $11 million, and its fiscal 1985 funding was $14.7 million.

Of its 59 demonstration projects, 44 were in state health and social service agencies, six in hospitals and nine in universities or schools, according to Mecklenburg.

The main emphasis was on postponement of sexual activity by teenagers. Teenage girls already pregnant were encouraged to put their babies up for adoption.

The program was challenged in a lawsuit brought by Protestant clergymen, the American Jewish Congress and several individuals. They were represented by the ACLU.

They contended the program created an impermissible entanglement of government and religion. ACLU lawyer Tina Sanchez said that by encouraging religious groups to apply for grants and by barring any counseling or referrals

for abortion, the program benefited some religions, such as Catholicism, but discriminated against religious groups that did not have clear anti-abortion tenets.

Some of the program money went to Catholic organizations that used it to put on "family life" and sex education classes in parochial schools.

Johnson of the National Right to Life Committee contended the lawsuit was a harassment by advocates of legalized abortion.

Despite the program's current legal problems, Denton said he believed it was a workable option that could lead to greater state efforts. "I hope the results of the demonstration programs will encourage states to be interested," Denton said.

Waxman, who supported the Adolescent Family Life Program, said Denton deserved "a great deal of credit for trying to think of some other approach that may be helpful. I have supported his pilot project because I thought we ought to give it a chance." But, Waxman added, "I don't think for the overwhelming majority of adolescents this particular approach will be successful."

Part of the program was designed to make sure that pregnant teenagers were told about the option of putting their babies up for adoption.

Adoption counseling was supposed to be available through programs funded by the Title X family planning program. But William L. Pierce, president of the National Committee for Adoption, said most publicly funded programs were not discussing adoption with pregnant women. "There isn't much that local, state or federal agencies are doing in providing information about the adoption option," said Pierce, whose privately financed organization was formed in 1980 and grew to 118 affiliates in 45 states and the District of Columbia.

Aside from the Adolescent Family Life Program, Congress appropriated $12.8 million for adoption assistance in fiscal 1985, about $8 million more than 1984. HHS sent this money to states to assist them in finding homes for children who were hard to place because of their age, minority status or handicap.   ∎

Stalemate Blocks Expansion of Food Aid

Because of a stalemate between advocates of more food aid to the poor and those seeking program reductions, Congress did not complete action on legislation partially restoring some Reagan-era cuts in food stamps, school lunch and other federal food aid programs.

Two House-passed bills to liberalize child nutrition programs (HR 7) and food stamps (HR 5151) died at the end of the session, as did a Senate Agriculture Committee bill (S 2722) that would have continued certain child nutrition programs at current funding levels.

The expiring child nutrition programs were extended by the continuing resolution (H J Res 648), which also made one change in food stamps. The change restored food stamp benefit levels to 100 percent, from 99 percent, of the thrifty food plan. The government used the plan to measure the cost of an inexpensive diet and, in turn, to calculate food stamp benefit levels. *(Continuing resolution, p. 444)*

The House also created a new, non-legislating committee to call attention to hunger in America and abroad. But it rejected a proposal to provide more timely statistics on

the nutritional status of Americans (HR 4684).

The House bills and the new committee were the House response to reports from emergency food services and the press, beginning in late 1981, that the recession and food program spending restraints had made it increasingly difficult for the poorest of Americans, and those who had lost their jobs, to eat properly.

The Reagan administration and its allies such as Sen. Jesse Helms, R-N.C., tended to discount the hunger reports and said that the food programs needed further tightening to prevent their abuse by those who could buy their own food. Helms chaired the Senate Agriculture Committee, which had jurisdiction over food programs.

Advocates of program increases pointed out that a special commission appointed by President Reagan in 1983 to investigate the hunger reports had declared, early in 1984, that indeed there were hungry Americans — although it could not say how many, or how bad the problem was. There was, according to the commission, no overall monitoring of the nutritional status of Americans that could show whether the status of the poor had worsened.

Commission Report

On Jan. 9, 1984, the 13-member President's Task Force on Food Assistance found that "allegations of rampant hunger simply cannot be documented." The panel had been appointed by Reagan in August 1983, when he ordered a "no-holds-barred" study of the hunger reports. *(1983 Almanac p. 412)*

The task force declared that recent money-saving changes in food stamps and other federal food programs had not reduced access of the poor to food aid, as critics of the changes claimed. It found "no evidence that widespread undernutrition is a major health problem in the United States."

Yet, given the testimony it had heard, "We cannot doubt that there is hunger in America," it said. Certain groups, the task force suggested, probably could not get enough to eat all the time — such as children whose parents could not provide a full diet, the homeless and people whose limited resources were depleted by rent, utility and other bills.

The group said that major increases or changes in federal food programs were not needed, but it made a number of recommendations. The most controversial was a proposal for an optional block grant program for food aid instead of the specifically targeted federally designed programs.

States choosing block grant funding would decide how to distribute assistance to individuals and institutions. That would have meant an end to uniform national eligibility and benefit standards — meaning that where an individual or family lived would determine whether they got food stamps or other aid, and how much they would get.

Other task force recommendations included stiffer financial penalties for states failing to bring their food stamp error rates down to levels mandated by law, more timely collection of data on nutrition, and modest increases in assets a food stamp recipient could own.

New Hunger Committee

The new 17-member Select Committee on Hunger, chaired by Rep. Mickey Leland, D-Texas, was authorized by a 309-78 vote on Feb. 22 on a resolution (H Res 15 — H Rept 98-568) sketching out its duties. *(Vote 25, p. 10-H)*

A similar Senate select committee, chaired by George S. McGovern, D-S.D. (House 1957-61; Senate 1963-81), created in 1968, had effectively focused national attention on hunger problems and was credited with building political support for major expansions of the federal food programs during the 1970s.

Leland's committee held hearings both on domestic hunger problems and on the severe famine in Ethiopia. Although its authorization expired with the end of the 98th Congress, there was little doubt that it would be continued in the following session.

Nutrition Update Rejected

The House on Oct. 2 by a 265-157 vote rejected a bill (HR 4684 — H Rept 98-1076) that would have created a coordinated 10-year program to track the nutritional status of Americans and set priorities for research on food and health. Because the bill was brought up under suspension of the rules, a two-thirds majority — 282 in this case — was required to pass the measure. *(Vote 380, p. 116-H)*

The bill would have authorized $5 million in fiscal 1985 and $3 million thereafter. It reflected six years of committee hearings on poor coordination and time lags in current federal research on nutrition by the Agriculture Department (USDA) and the Department of Health and Human Services (HHS).

Sponsors Buddy MacKay, D-Fla., and George E. Brown Jr., D-Calif., said that the results from current programs were poorly coordinated and obsolete by the time they were analyzed and published. MacKay pointd out that a comprehensive nutritional status monitoring system, ordered by Congress in 1977, still did not exist.

However, opponents argued that the measure would duplicate existing efforts and was not needed. The bill, reported Sept. 25 by the Science and Technology Committee, drew objections from both USDA and HHS.

House Child Nutrition Bill

The House by a 343-72 vote May 1 passed a bill (HR 7 — H Rept 98-633) that liberalized eligibility standards for subsidized school meals and boosted government contributions for school breakfasts. *(Vote 94, p. 32-H)*

It also would have lowered the prices paid by students for reduced-price school lunches and breakfasts, and funded extra meals and snacks for children in home-based child-care facilities.

The changes partly reversed cuts enacted in the 1981 reconciliation bill (PL 97-35); children of the working poor had been particularly hard hit by the cuts, according to advocates of HR 7. *(1981 Almanac p. 256)*

The changes already had passed the House as another bill (HR 4091) by a 306-114 vote in 1983. Backers sought a second vote because the Senate had ignored the bill. *(1983 Almanac p. 417)*

When the child nutrition measure returned to the House floor in 1984, it was as part of a four-year $9 billion reauthorization of expiring child nutrition programs. For one program, serving pregnant women, infants and children (WIC), the bill nearly doubled authorized spending levels in the next four years, to $2 billion.

Other expiring programs provided funds for nutrition education and training, summer food service for children, state administration expenses and food service equipment purchases.

The bill, reported by the Education and Labor Committee on March 23, was brought to the floor April 11, although scheduling problems halted work before the bill was completed.

Action on amendments April 11 reflected the major themes of debate that had begun in the Education and Labor Committee, between liberal Democrats such as Chairman Carl D. Perkins, D-Ky., who wanted more aid for the poor, and moderate Republicans who wanted to support the bill but in a less expensive form.

Amendments accepted by the House included those by:

● Perkins, to let private schools charging tuitions of $2,500 or less participate in school breakfast and administrative expense programs, as well as in school lunches. The committee bill raised the tuition limit to that level — a $1,000 increase — for school lunches.

● Perkins, to limit to two years a permanent committee ban against changes in the method of determining eligibility for free or reduced-price lunches according to family income. The ban was intended to prevent the Agriculture

Department from counting "in-kind" benefits such as food stamps as part of a family's income when determining eligibility.

● Bill Goodling, R-Pa., to restrict the use of "tiering" in the home child-care food program, to facilities where specified percentages of children were poor enough to qualify for free or reduced-price meals.

Tiering, eliminated in 1981 but restored by the committee bill, permitted a day-care program to receive federal subsidies for free or reduced-price meals for all children if a majority of its children qualified for the meals.

● George Miller, D-Calif., to eliminate a new "capped entitlement" status for WIC. Committee language would have required that the full amount authorized for WIC be appropriated and spent each year.

● Goodling, to specify that federal reimbursement authorized for the costs of verifying student eligibility for subsidized meals be limited to the direct costs of such verification.

Later Action

When the bill came up again May 1, Goodling and Steve Bartlett, R-Texas, withdrew pending amendments that would have required states to match federal spending for their administrative expenses. Goodling said Perkins had promised to reconsider the issue in the spring of 1985, when an Agriculture Department report was due.

The House adopted an amendment by Pat Williams, D-Mont., making children from families receiving food stamps automatically eligible for free breakfasts. The committee bill had made those children automatically eligible for free lunches.

Before voting to pass HR 7, the House by a 136-270 vote rejected a substitute by Bartlett that would have reauthorized the expiring programs for three years at current spending levels and with no policy changes. *(Vote 93, p. 32-H)*

Provisions

Major provisions of HR 7, as passed by the House:

● Authorized funding for WIC of $1.36 billion for fiscal 1984, $1.55 billion for 1985, $1.7 billion for 1986, $1.85 billion for 1987 and $2 billion for 1988, and reauthorized, at current levels for four years, nutrition education and training, summer food service for children and state administrative cost programs.

● Lowered the price for students of reduced-price lunches and raised the income eligibility standard for such meals to $19,305 for a family of four, up from $18,315, for the year ending June 30.

● Increased the existing federal subsidy for each child for school breakfasts and established new federal regulations to improve the nutritional quality of the meals.

● Made children in families receiving Aid to Families with Dependent Children (AFDC) or food stamps automatically eligible for free breakfasts and lunches.

● Allowed private schools charging annual tuitions of $2,500 or less to participate in the school lunch and breakfast and administrative expenses programs. Existing law limited eligibility to schools charging $1,500 or less.

● Authorized funds for an additional daily meal and snack for eligible children in day-care centers, restoring the daily total to three meals and two snacks.

● Reinstated a deduction for high medical expenses used in determining school meal eligibility and repealed a re-

quirement that the income standard for free meals be the same as for food stamps.

● Ended a ban on the use of the special milk program in schools also participating in a federally subsidized meal program, for kindergarten children only.

● Restored "tiering" in the child-care food program, with certain limits. The changes reversed, in part or in full, program changes made in 1981.

● Authorized $10 million a year to help states or local areas buy food service equipment for schools with a high percentage of low-income students.

● Required the Agriculture Department to dispense WIC money evenly throughout the year to avoid giving states so much near the end of the year that they could not use it all.

● Required the Agriculture Department to study the feasibility of operating a free school lunch program for all children that would pay for itself.

● Barred the Agriculture Department from changing in the next two years the method of determining eligibility for free or reduced-price lunches according to family cash income.

Senate Child Nutrition Bill

The Senate Agriculture Committee on May 25 reported legislation (S 2722 — S Rept 98-489) continuing expiring child nutrition programs for two years, including WIC, which would be maintained at the current caseload level of about three million persons.

The committee had agreed informally May 16 to report the bill and to continue private negotiations on whether to expand the bill on the Senate floor to include some restorations in food stamps, school lunch and other food aid programs.

No further action was taken, however. Committee Chairman Helms insisted that any program expansions be coupled with equivalent spending reductions. Although a bipartisan majority of the committee reportedly supported some liberalizations in the programs, similar to those going through the House, Republican committee members did not want to force the issue in public.

The committee had met briefly May 2 to vote on a somewhat different version (S 1913) of HR 7 and on alternatives sponsored by Helms and Robert Dole, R-Kan. A 12-member majority of the panel had sponsored S 1913, but even so, the committee postponed a decision until May 16.

Dole, chairman of the nutrition subcommittee, urged the two-week delay. He suggested limiting action to WIC and other expiring programs, which would mean no action on either the child nutrition programs addressed in HR 7, or on food stamps.

Food stamps were an issue because Walter D. Huddleston, D-Ky., author of S 1913, also had introduced a broader version (S 2607) with some food stamp changes, and a House subcommittee had scheduled a May 8 markup of "anti-hunger" legislation (HR 5151) liberalizing certain features of food stamps.

Helms, who favored tightening food programs to combat fraud, reminded members that he had his "own ideas" on those matters. When Dole asked if members were ready to rule out food stamp action in 1984, there was no response. Dole noted that the fiscal 1985 budget resolution was being debated in the Senate, so the panel did not know how much food program spending would be allowed.

He also argued that uncompleted budget and tax legislation, and election-year incursions on congressional schedules left little time to consider non-essential matters.

"I would hope we can forget about food stamps this year, forget about child nutrition," said Dole. "All these people are around here, pushing hot buttons, saying 'Oh, you've got to do this. You've got to do that.' This will be around next year."

Mark Andrews, R-N.D., protested that delay would make members look "awfully damn ridiculous." He urged getting "on about the work and let the amendments fall where they may."

House Food Stamp Bill

With the virtual certainty that it would not become law in 1984, the House Aug. 1 approved a hunger relief bill by a nine-to-one margin.

The billion-dollar food stamp bill (HR 5151) was passed by a 364-39 vote after members agreed to several changes in the version reported (H Rept 98-782) May 15 by the House Agriculture Committee. Debate had begun July 27. *(Vote 305, p. 92-H)*

Key sections of the bill made modest increases in food stamp eligibility and benefit levels, while beefing up federal penalties for states that failed to lower their program errors to specified levels. Other sections raised federal funding for state-run job-search programs for the poor and explicitly specified that "street people" without fixed addresses could qualify for food stamps if they met other program eligibility standards.

There was little outright opposition to the bill, which had strong, bipartisan support. However, members also knew there was little likelihood of Senate action because of the stalemate between Helms and Agriculture Committee members backing more food aid. Moreover, budget director David A. Stockman, in a June 24 letter to Republican members, had warned of a presidential veto.

Many of the bill's provisions, such as those relating to homeless persons and assets and eligibility tests, had been recommended in January by the presidential task force on hunger. The bill was silent on that panel's major and most controversial recommendation, for an optional food aid block grant for states. And the House rejected by voice vote an amendment by Rep. Robert S. Walker, R-Pa., to authorize such block grants.

Leon E. Panetta, D-Calif., author of the bill and chairman of the Agriculture subcommittee with jurisdiction over food stamps, said subcommittee hearings in 1983 and 1984 "disclosed a tremendous need for food assistance on the part of those segments of our people whom economic recovery has simply passed by."

Panetta also said the bill did not exceed budget allowances in the House-passed 1985 budget resolution.

Before passing the bill, the House took the following actions:

● Rejected, by 120-293, an amendment by Bill Emerson, R-Mo., that would have affirmed an existing mandate that states require food stamp recipients to submit monthly financial reports. The bill, responding to complaints of bureaucratic "paper-shuffling," made such monthly reporting programs optional for states. *(Vote 302, p. 92-H)*

● Adopted, by 384-25, a Panetta amendment that authorized cost-of-living increases in the car values used to calculate eligibility for food stamps. The bill, following a task force recommendation, had increased the maximum car

value to $5,500 from $4,500, but E. Thomas Coleman, R-Mo., complained that even the existing maximum $4,500 value meant that food stamp recipients could drive more valuable cars than average taxpayers. Coleman sought to strike the increase from the bill, and Panetta countered with the substitute amendment, which was adopted. *(Vote 304, p. 92-H)*

● Adopted, by voice vote, a Panetta amendment permitting states to apply whatever they recovered in erroneously issued food stamps against the new error-rate penalty imposed by the bill. The bill required that states repay the federal government, dollar for dollar, for all erroneously issued stamps in excess of a 5 percent error rate.

● Adopted, by voice vote, an amendment by Bruce A. Morrison, D-Conn., revising the medical deduction used to calculate eligibility and benefits for elderly and disabled persons. Existing law permitted the deduction of medical expenses exceeding $35 monthly. Morrison, arguing that many elderly and disabled persons had very low incomes, proposed deductions based either on $35 or on 5 percent of income, whichever was lower.

Provisions

Major provisions of HR 5151, as passed Aug. 1 by the House, would have:

● Affirmed that individuals without fixed addresses could qualify for food stamps.

● Permitted state agencies to stagger issuance of food stamps throughout a month and required them to evaluate the need for evening and weekend hours at food stamp offices.

● Specified that the Oct. 1, 1984, adjustment of food stamp benefits be based on 100 percent of the "thrifty food plan," instead of 99 percent as under existing law. The plan was used to establish the current cost of a minimally adequate diet, which in turn was used to determine benefit levels. The changes were all recommended by the presidential task force.

● Revised the definition of "disabled" to make Supplemental Security Income (SSI) and Railroad Retirement Act beneficiaries and others eligible for food stamps.

● Made beneficiaries of AFDC or SSI automatically eligible for food stamps.

● Raised to 20 percent, from 18 percent, the amount of earned income deducted from a household's income in determining eligibility and benefits.

● Raised to $155 a month, from $130 a month, the maximum combined deduction for dependent care and shelter expenses.

● Specified that the medical deduction used to calculate eligibility and benefits for elderly and disabled persons would apply to expenses exceeding $35 a month (as under existing law) or 5 percent of income, whichever was lower.

● Raised to $2,250, from $1,500, the maximum assets permitted for food stamp eligibility (or $3,500, up from $3,000, for the elderly and disabled). Raised to $5,500, from $4,500, the maximum value of a car or other vehicle excluded from calculating a household's assets.

● Required state agencies to use Internal Revenue Service information on unearned income to verify eligibility; required verification of such information from other sources if it were to be used as a basis for reducing, ending or denying benefits.

● Increased funding for state-run job search programs for beneficiaries and required the federal government to match state costs for running the programs and an individual's costs in meeting the requirement to search for a job. Provided a 60-day disqualification for households including a member subject to job search requirements who failed to meet those requirements.

● Established a four-year pilot food assistance program, through fiscal 1989, for low-income residents of rural Alaska.

● Barred banks or other financial institutions from charging fees to food stores for redeeming food stamps.

● Required states to repay the federal government the full costs of erroneously issued stamps in excess of a 5 percent error rate, beginning in fiscal 1986. Permitted states to apply whatever they recovered in erroneously issued stamps to their penalty. Existing law required states to cut error rates to 5 percent by fiscal 1985, with partial loss of administrative funds for those that did not.

● Repealed a provision that states require food stamp households to submit monthly income reports to retain eligibility; instead, made such monthly reporting optional for states.

● Authorized the use of the commodity supplemental food program to assist the low-income elderly if such use did not deny benefits to the low-income women, infants and children for whom the program was authorized.

● Required the Agriculture Department to include a representative sample of low-income households in a proposed national continuous survey of food consumption and in any other national food survey it conducted.

● Authorized a total of $30 million in fiscal 1985-88 to promote consumer and nutrition education, targeted on low-income households. ∎

Preventive Health

The House Oct. 9 cleared a three-year, $707 million reauthorization (S 2301 — PL 98-555) of funding for childhood immunization, tuberculosis control and other preventive health programs.

The final bill authorized the following funding:

● $98.5 million each year for fiscal 1985-87 for block grants for such programs as rape prevention, hypertension, fluoridation and urban rat control.

● For childhood immunization programs, $52 million for fiscal 1985, $59 million in 1986 and $65 million in 1987.

● For tuberculosis control, $8 million in fiscal 1985, $9 million in 1986 and $10 million in 1987.

● For venereal disease programs, including programs designed to prevent acquired immune deficiency syndrome, $57 million in fiscal 1985, $62.5 million in 1986 and $68 million in 1987.

● $5 million per year for state planning and $2 million per year for new demonstration projects on emergency medical services for children.

Legislative History. The Senate by voice vote Sept. 28 approved its bill (S 2301 — S Rept 98-393), which had been reported April 12 by the Labor and Human Resources Committee.

The House Oct. 1 by a vote of 368-18 passed its bill (HR 5538 — H Rept 98-1063), reported Sept. 24 by the Energy and Commerce Committee. The House substituted the text of its bill for the Senate version. *(Vote 376, p. 116-H)*

Differences were settled by informal negotiation, with

both chambers accepting the compromise Oct. 9.

The final bill omitted a new home health care program that the Senate had included. The Senate had dropped that provision earlier at the request of sponsor Orrin G. Hatch, R-Utah, who noted there were objections to the expense of the program. ∎

Health Promotion

The Senate Oct. 11 cleared a three-year, $269 million reauthorization (S 771 — PL 98-551) of two federal centers that collected health statistics and studied health care services, and a third office that coordinated health promotion and disease prevention research and other projects.

The bill, passed by the House Oct. 9, also authorized new health promotion and disease prevention research centers at universities. It expanded the mission of the health care services office within the Department of Health and Human Services to include assessments of medical technology and created a new federal advisory council on health care technology, with representatives from federal agencies and private industry. The bill also provided federal funds for a second health technology panel associated with the National Academy of Sciences.

The House version also included a clarification of the definition of an orphan drug. Those drugs, developed for rare diseases, qualified for special regulatory and tax treatment. The Senate accepted the House change. *(Orphan drugs, 1982 Almanac p. 490)*

S 771 first passed the Senate in 1983; portions of the final version had passed the House and Senate in 1983 and 1984 as sections of other bills (HR 2350, HR 5496, S 540). *(1983 Almanac p. 409)* ∎

Hospice Payments Raised

A bill designed to encourage hospices to participate in the Medicare program was cleared by Congress Oct. 11.

The measure (HR 5386 — PL 98-617) raised the Medicare payment rate for routine home patient care by hospices and extended for one year two expiring provisions of federal aid to states for foster care.

Hospices offered terminal patients a less expensive form of treatment than hospitals and provided social support for the patients and their families. The payment rate was raised from $46.25 per day to $53.17, subject to annual review by the secretary of health and human services. *(1983 Almanac p. 398)*

The bill, reported Sept. 28 by the House Ways and Means Committee (H Rept 98-1100), was passed by the House Oct. 1 by voice vote.

The Senate Oct. 11 added to the bill an amendment that extended for one year certain provisions of the Adoption Assistance and Child Welfare Act of 1980, including a provision allowing states to use certain federal foster care funds for child welfare services. It also allowed states for another year to claim federal matching payments for children whose parents voluntarily placed them in foster care. *(1980 Almanac p. 417)*

The House accepted the Senate changes Oct. 11, clearing the measure for the president. The two foster care provisions had been included in a bill (HR 6266 — H Rept 98-1048) approved by the House Oct. 1. ∎

Reagan Vetoes Two Major Health Bills

President Reagan vetoed two major health bills Oct. 30 that had been cleared in the final days of the 98th Congress.

One bill would have created an arthritis research institute and reauthorized selected medical research programs (S 540), and the second would have continued community health programs and subsidies for training health professionals (S 2574).

In his veto messages, Reagan said "adequate authority" to continue the health programs was provided by the continuing appropriations resolution (H J Res 648 — PL 98-473). *(Veto messages, pp. 26-E, 27-E)*

Although the president cited cost, he stressed policy disagreements with Congress as reasons for the vetoes.

Arthritis, Nursing Institutes

Reagan termed the new arthritis institute and a new federal research institute on nursing authorized by S 540 "unnecessary" and "premature." He noted a study of the organizational structure of the National Institutes of Health (NIH) was to be released by the Institute of Medicine, part of the National Academy of Sciences.

He also objected to "overly specific requirements for the management of research that place undue constraints on executive branch authorities and functions."

Legislative History. The bill had been discharged May 22 from the Senate Labor and Human Resources Committee. The panel had reported an NIH bill (S 773) in 1983 that created the arthritis institute. But disagreements over whether that measure should become a vehicle for language relating to fetal research held it up, and sponsors decided to move ahead with the arthritis institute. *(1983 Almanac p. 409)*

The Senate approved the bill by voice vote May 24. In addition to creating the new National Institute of Arthritis and Musculoskeletal and Skin Diseases, the bill authorized $68.6 million for fiscal 1985-88 for a national data base and grants for research centers and related activities on those diseases. An amendment broadening the mandate of the Office of Technology Assessment to include work on biomedical ethics was adopted.

The Senate-passed bill acquired a lengthy reauthorization of other major NIH programs and a new nursing institute when it reached the House. By voice vote, the House passed S 540 after amending the text of its $7.6 billion reauthorization (HR 2350) of research institutes. That bill had passed the House in 1983.

Final Action. The final bill imposed a three-year moratorium on rare federally funded medical research involving human fetuses and authorized a biomedical ethics commission to study questions raised by the research.

The $4.7 billion bill compared with a $3.9 billion budget request for the National Cancer Institute and the National Institute of Heart, Lung and Blood Disease.

The Senate by voice vote Oct. 9 adopted the conference report (H Rept 98-1155), and the House by voice vote later that day cleared it for the president.

House NIH bills in earlier years had provoked sharp objections that they exposed the respected research institutes to undue political pressure. Conferees agreed, the day before final action, on fetal research guidelines that gener-

ally followed those of the House version, with one exception. They decided that NIH could not grant a little-used waiver from the rules for three years, until the new bioethics commission could make recommendations.

Provisions

As cleared by Congress, S 540 would have:

● Established a National Institute of Arthritis and Musculoskeletal and Skin Diseases, and a National Institute on Nursing. Funding levels would be determined by appropriations.

● Established a bipartisan congressional biomedical ethics advisory board which would appoint a bioethics commission to study such issues as genetic engineering and fetal research.

● Authorized $2 million for fiscal 1985, $2.5 million for 1986 and $3 million for 1987 for commission activities.

● Specified that NIH-funded research using human fetuses may be conducted under the following conditions: for non-viable living human fetuses outside the womb, the research must enhance the well-being of the fetus, increase its chances of survival or develop important biomedical information that could not otherwise be obtained and that did not increase the risk of suffering or injury or death to the fetus. For fetuses in the womb, the research must enhance the well-being of the fetus and present only minimal risk, whether the fetus is intended for abortion or is to be carried to term.

Those were essentially the same guidelines currently used by NIH. However, NIH also permitted rarely-used waivers of the "minimal risk" standard in certain circumstances.

The bill barred use of the waivers for three years until the new bioethics panel study reported.

● Reauthorized the National Cancer Institute research and cancer control programs at $1.2 billion for fiscal 1985 and $1.3 billion for 1986.

● Reauthorized the National Heart, Lung and Blood Institute disease control and related programs at $820 million in fiscal 1985 and $870 million in 1986.

● Reauthorized the medical library assistance program at $11 million and $12 million respectively in fiscal 1985 and 1986, and for the National Research Awards program, $220 million and $238 million respectively.

● Authorized special research programs on spinal cord injury and regeneration, Alzheimer's disease, bioengineering to overcome paralysis and mental retardation.

● Provided explicit authority for various institutes and their directors, authorizing the NIH director to reorganize or abolish institutes, and making certain other changes.

● Spelled out procedures for investigations of scientific misconduct in NIH-funded research and for assuring proper care of research animals; also required an 18-month study of such animal research.

● Authorized new associate directors of prevention research in the Cancer and Child Health Institutes and in the office of the NIH director.

● Authorized funding of $2 million a year for an independent research center to study health effects of nuclear energy; also authorized a cancer screening center for persons exposed to radioactive fallout from nuclear-bomb tests in Nevada.

Health Professions

In vetoing the health professions measure, Reagan noted that the bill (S 2574) authorized 41 percent more in spending than he had requested.

He said the legislation took "the wrong approach" by continuing "obsolete federal subsidies" at a time of anticipated surpluses of doctors and nurses, and by maintaining "a static and rigid categorical framework" for such aid.

Reagan objected to continuing National Health Service Corps scholarships, which required recipients to practice in health shortage areas. He contended that new scholarships were no longer needed.

He also protested the bill's repeal of "a key reform" proposed by his administration and approved by Congress in 1981 — a little-used block grant program for community health centers serving indigent populations in areas with few medical resources. States had virtually ignored the optional grant program, which would have saddled them with new spending and administrative responsibilities. *(1981 Almanac p. 463)*

Legislative History. The Senate June 28 passed S 2574 and three other bills whose provisions later were incorporated into the final health professions bill:

● S 2574, reported May 25 by the Labor and Human Resources Committee (S Rept 98-492), reauthorized aid to nursing schools and their students, emphasizing advanced training of nurse practitioners, anesthetists and midwives. Funding was set at $223.8 million for fiscal 1985-87.

● S 2308, reported May 25 (S Rept 98-490), authorized $1.3 billion for fiscal 1985-87 for community and migrant health care programs but did not renew the block grant authority.

● S 2311, reported April 18 (S Rept 98-401), authorized $400,000 annually for fiscal 1985-87 for training and technical assistance for Health Maintenance Organizations (HMO). The bill also ended or phased out other federal aid, such as loans, to HMOs.

● S 2559, reported May 25 (S Rept 98-491), authorized $886.8 million for fiscal 1985-89 for scholarships, loans and loan insurance for students pursuing health careers. It also included a four-year $70.35 million reauthorization of the National Center for Health Services Research and a four-year $178 million reauthorization of the National Center for Health Statistics.

House. The House passed HR 5602 by voice vote Sept. 6. The $2.9 billion measure was approved after the House agreed by voice vote to trim $218.6 million from the $3.1 billion version reported June 4 (H Rept 98-817) by the Energy and Commerce Committee.

The House rejected, by a 78-236 vote, an amendment by William E. Dannemeyer, R-Calif., that would have further reduced authorization levels. *(Vote 338, p. 104-H)*

After finishing the bill, the House substituted it for the text of S 2574. The bill included a $363 million reauthorization for loans and grants to medical and other schools for fiscal 1985-86; a three-year, $243.6 million reauthorization of aid to schools of nursing and their students; and a four-year, $375 million reauthorization for the National Health Service Corps.

It provided a four-year reauthorization, at levels as needed, for HMOs and a four-year reauthorization for community and migrant health centers, providing $1.7 billion and $220 million respectively.

Final Action. The Senate adopted the conference report (H Rept 98-1143) by voice vote Oct. 4, and the House cleared it Oct. 9 by a vote of 363-13. *(Vote 400, p. 122-H)*

The final bill effectively ended the little-used state block grant for community health centers and created a smaller block grant to support primary-care programs run by states. It also ended most aid to HMO programs.

Provisions

As cleared, S 2574 would have:

● Reauthorized loans and grants to medical and other schools and financial aid for their students, with funding set at $487.3 million for fiscal 1985-87. Half the funds were earmarked for loans for disadvantaged students.

● Reauthorized aid to nursing schools and their students at $226.2 million for fiscal 1985-87, targeting funds on advanced specialized nursing.

● Reauthorized the National Health Service Corps, providing scholarship funds as needed in fiscal years 1985-87.

● Reauthorized community and migrant health centers at $1.7 billion and $213 million respectively for fiscal 1985-88.

● Authorized for fiscal 1985-88 $76 million for a new primary-care state block grant to states and a new technical assistance program.

● Reauthorized $400,000 annually for fiscal 1985-88 for HMO training and technical aid, plus funds as needed through fiscal 1988 for the program's loan default fund. The bill phased out or canceled other HMO grant, loan and loan guarantee programs.

● Authorized $3 million for fiscal 1985-87 for plague prevention and control. ∎

Drug Dumping Examined

Congress was asked to repeal a stringent federal ban against exporting American-made drugs that had not met the standards of safety and effectiveness required for sale in the United States.

But the bill got no further than House and Senate hearings, where it became embroiled in controversy about corporate "dumping" of inappropriate drugs in Third World nations. The bill (S 2878) was introduced by Sen. Orrin G. Hatch, R-Utah, chairman of the Labor and Human Resources Committee.

Rep. Henry A. Waxman, D-Calif., chairman of the House Health subcommittee with jurisdiction over the bill, did not express an opinion on the measure. Waxman, according to aides, was sympathetic to arguments of genetic engineering firms that they needed foreign markets for their pharmaceutical products. But he was said to be concerned about other aspects of the bill.

Hatch and other supporters, including drug companies, the Food and Drug Administration (FDA) and the World Health Organization argued that the ban had not kept drugs lacking FDA approval from being sold abroad. Multinational firms, they said, evaded the limit by arranging for the drugs to be manufactured abroad, or for competing foreign firms to supply them.

Repeal of the ban long had been sought by drug firms; they renewed their drive in 1984 in conjunction with a prominent genetic engineering firm, Genentech, which had specialized in pharmaceutical products. Officials of that company said that they and other genetic engineering firms could not afford to make their products abroad and that unique U.S. "biotechnologies" would be shipped to foreign competitors if the ban on exporting medical products made by those technologies continued.

Advocates apparently hoped to include repeal language in landmark legislation (HR 3605, S 1306) coupling changes in drug patent rules with easing of limits on inexpensive, "generic" copies of pharmaceuticals. One preliminary Senate Labor and Human Resources committee version of that bill included the repeal, but it was excised, in part because of objections by Sen. Edward M. Kennedy, D-Mass., and Sen. Howard M. Metzenbaum, D-Ohio.

Amendments to federal drug law in 1983 had had the effect of barring commercial exports of U.S.-made drugs, except for antibiotics, that had not been approved by the FDA for domestic sales. The House in 1976 had included a repeal of the ban in a regulatory bill (PL 94-295) for medical devices, such as pace makers. The Senate in 1979 also had approved repeal as part of a massive overhaul of drug laws that died when the House failed to act on it. *(1976 Almanac p. 535; 1979 Almanac p. 485)*

Hatch's bill would have permitted U.S. drug companies to export a drug that had not met FDA standards, if it had been approved for marketing by another nation with a drug regulatory process deemed effective by the agency. Hatch said his plan would mean more protection for underdeveloped nations without adequate means of evaluating drugs themselves. He and other advocates also said the ban had inappropriately withheld drugs that were, for various reasons, inappropriate for the United States but useful in certain conditions elsewhere.

Opponents cited examples of U.S. companies minimizing side effects of antibiotics, and bribing drug regulators abroad. They also criticized as inadequate the foreign drug regulations that would have substituted for FDA approval.■

Compromise Organ Transplant Bill Passed

Congress completed action in 1984 on a bill (S 2048 — PL 98-507) to ease the difficulties of mortally ill patients and their families in seeking organ transplant surgery.

The Senate on Oct. 4 by voice vote adopted the conference report (H Rept 98-1127) on the bill, clearing it for the president, who signed it Oct. 19. The House had adopted the agreement by voice vote Oct. 3.

Key members had worked out a compromise, without a formal conference, between the version passed by the Senate April 11 and the bill (HR 5580) passed by the House June 21.

The legislation established a national computerized network to match transplant patients with organs, and it provided funds to upgrade and coordinate local and regional agencies that procured human organs for transplantation. It made selling organs for transplantation a federal crime.

It also created a task force to evaluate the ethical, legal, economic and other difficult issues raised by the expensive lifesaving surgery.

Those steps were designed to ease the problems that had driven families of some transplant patients to enlist the aid of the White House, prominent politicians and the media in appeals for organs and for funds to finance the operations.

Medical developments, especially the approval of a powerful new immunosuppressive drug called cyclosporine, made organ transplant surgery more feasible. Immunosuppressive drugs helped prevent the rejection by a patient of a transplanted organ.

But the operations and especially the post-surgical care cost tens of thousands of dollars. The federal government and private insurers generally had resisted paying for the transplant procedures except under pressure from the press and politicians. Moreover, there were shortages of organs and uneven success in matching patients with those that were available.

Dispute Over Drug

The final bill omitted a $30 million House provision that for two years would have financed cyclosporine for transplant patients who could not otherwise afford the drug.

Sen. Orrin G. Hatch, R-Utah, and the Reagan adminis-

tration opposed the drug funding. They argued that the long-term effects of the new drug were unknown and that the precedent of singling out one very expensive drug for federal financing was unwise. The administration also predicted much higher costs for the drug coverage. Hatch, chairman of the Labor and Human Resources Committee, was the Senate sponsor of the bill.

The drug-funding issue held up agreement on the bill for months because House sponsor Albert Gore Jr., D-Tenn., was reluctant to yield on the funding. However, Hatch's position was strengthened in September when the *New England Journal of Medicine* reported that cyclosporine had caused fatal kidney failure in two heart transplant patients.

The drug's potential for causing high blood pressure and kidney damage had been previously known, but the *Journal* article highlighted continuing discussions within the medical community about the relative benefits and risks of cyclosporine.

Gore agreed to drop the drug funding and instead made the medical and policy questions raised by immunosuppressive therapy the top priority for the new task force.

Conferees also reduced the authorization for grants for organ procurement agencies from the House-passed six years, to three years, and reduced the authorized funding from $40 million to $25 million.

Major Provisions

As signed into law, the Organ Procurement and Transplantation Act:

● Created a task force to study and report on ethical, legal, financial and other questions associated with organ transplant surgery. Among the issues before the task force would be the allocation of the surgery and the limited supply of human organs, extent of insurance coverage, establishment of a national voluntary registry of volunteer organ donors and, as the first priority, the medical value of immunosuppressive therapy and payments for such therapy.

● Authorized $2 million annually to support a national computerized system for matching patients with scarce organs.

● Authorized $5 million in fiscal year 1985, $8 million in

1986 and $12 million in 1987 for grants to create or upgrade local and regional agencies that procured human organs for transplantation and that participated in the national matching network. Specified that task force recommendations should be taken into account but that agency funding was not contingent on the recommendations.

• Prohibited the purchase or sale of human organs for transplantation and authorized fines of up to $50,000 and/or imprisonment for up to five years for knowingly violating the prohibition.

• Directed the secretary of health and human services (HHS) to assign responsibility for administering organ transplant programs to the Public Health Service or to some other unit.

• Provided for a national registry of transplant patients to facilitate scientific evaluations of procedures.

House Action

Although the House Energy and Commerce Committee on Nov. 18, 1983, reported an organ transplant bill (HR 4080 — H Rept 98-575, Part I), the legislation went through several revisions before reaching the floor.

As reported in 1983, HR 4080:

• Authorized grants to start or improve local or regional organ procurement organizations that met certain standards, including participation in a new national transplantation network. Provided for $4 million in fiscal 1984, $8 million in 1985, $12 million in 1986 and $16 million in 1987.

• Required the secretary of health and human services to establish by contract a computerized national transplantation network to help match organs with persons needing them.

• Required the secretary to maintain a national registry of transplant patients, with data necessary to evaluate the effectiveness of transplantation.

• Established a new office in the Public Health Service to encourage organ donation and to assist organ procurement organizations and the national network.

• Required the establishment of a task force to report on medical, legal, ethical and other issues relating to human organ procurement and transplantation.

• Made the sale of human organs a federal crime with penalties of fines of up to $50,000 and imprisonment for up to five years.

• Authorized the secretary, with the advice of medical experts, to provide selective Medicare funding for transplants and other new procedures. Medicare could designate the conditions for which it would fund a procedure, and could pay for treatments only at medical centers with records of excellence.

• Required state Medicaid programs to adopt written policies covering transplants and require states without such policies to follow Medicare policy.

• Authorized Medicare payments for immunosuppressive drugs, such as cyclosporine, that patients take after leaving the hospital. Medicare currently paid only for drugs administered during hospital stays.

The provisions on Medicare and on federal funding for immunosuppressive drugs were to prove especially controversial.

On March 6, 1984, the Ways and Means Subcommittee on Health, which had jurisdiction over Medicare and Medicaid, approved the major provisions of HR 4080 but refused to authorize government payments for immunosuppressive drugs, such as cyclosporine.

Transplant surgeons said that cyclosporine, first used in 1979, improved the survival rates without the harsh, immediate side effects of alternative drugs. The drug cost about $5,000 per year per patient.

Charles B. Rangel, D-N.Y., supported the drug payments on the grounds that Congress long ago had decided that Medicare should assist persons with kidney failure. In 1972 Congress declared such persons eligible for Medicare, and the program had paid routinely for kidney transplants, but not the cyclosporine.

"Let's not say, 'Have a successful operation, but we're not going to pay for life-sustaining drugs afterward,' " Rangel said.

But Henson Moore, R-La., said that the Food and Drug Administration found no difference between survival rates of transplant patients treated with cyclosporine and those of individuals who used other drugs. Moore also said that lobbyists for the elderly told him that other life-saving drugs taken by elderly beneficiaries of Medicare should be funded for outpatient use.

Far-Reaching Change

The most far-reaching change proposed by the bill — accepted by both committees — was the provision allowing Medicare to limit payments for transplants or other sophisticated procedures to medical centers with proven records of success and, possibly, to patients who had been diagnosed as suffering certain ailments.

Current Medicare practice was an "all-or-nothing" policy of financing difficult, expensive medical procedures everywhere, or nowhere.

Except for kidneys, Medicare generally had designated organ transplants as "experimental" and refused to pay for them. Because Medicaid, the federal-state medical program for the poor, and private insurers patterned their coverage on Medicare, the proposed change could have a wide impact.

Spokesmen for the private insurance industry, which faced enormous pressure to pay for the operations, urged even more restrictions than those proposed by the bill. Without them, they said, they could not keep the expensive surgery from distorting the nation's medical expenditures.

However, the provision was vehemently opposed by the American Medical Association and the Reagan administration.

Gore agreed to drop the Medicare and Medicaid provisions, and a new bill (HR 4474) was approved May 1 by the Energy and Commerce Subcommittee on Health.

However, HR 4474 continued to authorize federal financing of immunosuppressive drugs. But the drug financing would be handled by the secretary of health and human services instead of Medicare, as in HR 4080. The new bill authorized the drug funding for two years only.

Removing Medicare and Medicaid references meant that the bill would not go to the House Ways and Means or Senate Finance committees, which also had jurisdiction over these programs. According to staff, there was a real possibility that the full committee would reject much of the bill and substitute a simple authorization for a task force to study organ transplant issues. Also, the issue was not a high priority for the Finance Committee, which might have delayed action.

House Floor Action

A renumbered version of HR 4474 was reported by the Energy and Commerce Committee May 15 (HR 5580 — H Rept 98-769) and reached the floor June 20. It was approved June 21 by a vote of 396-6. *(Vote 228, p. 72-H)*

Before passing HR 5580, the House rejected an amendment by William E. Dannemeyer, R-Calif., that would have brought the measure in line with a leaner transplant bill (S 2048) approved April 11 by the Senate.

The amendment, rejected 25-379, would have reduced the total amount authorized by the bill from $78 million to $21 million. In addition to dropping the authorization for $30 million for immunosuppressive drugs, it would have scaled back new grants for local organ procurement agencies from $40 million over four years to $15 million over three years. (*Vote 227, p. 72-H*)

Provisions. After approving HR 5580, the House substituted its text for the Senate bill's and passed S 2048. As passed by the House, S 2048:

● Authorized $4 million in fiscal 1985, $8 million in 1986, $12 million in 1987, $16 million in 1988, and such sums as Congress considered necessary in 1989 and 1990 for grants to set up and improve local organ procurement organizations.

● Authorized $2 million annually for four years for HHS to establish a national computerized system for matching organ donors and patients.

● Established a national registry of organ transplant patients.

● Authorized $10 million in fiscal 1985 and $20 million in 1986 for federal financing of immunosuppressive drugs.

● Barred the sale of human organs for transplantation.

● Established an administrative unit within the Public Health Service to coordinate federal transplant policies and programs.

● Provided for a task force to study medical, ethical and other issues raised by organ transplantation.

Senate Action

A more limited Senate bill (S 2048) was approved by Hatch's Labor and Human Resources Committee March 21. The report (S Rept 98-382) was filed April 6.

The bill was approved by the Senate April 11. There were no objections to the measure, which passed by voice vote.

Hatch told his colleagues that while highly publicized appeals might help some patients, "we need something better" to provide equitable access to lifesaving surgery.

The legislation set up a task force to evaluate efforts to develop an organ procurement system and to establish a plan for a coordinated national donor network. The task force was to report six months after enactment of the bill.

The legislation authorized $2 million annually to fund a private registry of donors and individuals needing organ transplants.

In addition, $5 million was authorized annually for fiscal 1985-87 to aid non-profit organ procurement organizations, subject to recommendation by the task force. To qualify for the funds, the agencies would have to coordinate their activities with transplant centers and participate in the new national matching system.

Other sections barred the sale of human organs for transplantation and created a task force to study and report on ethical, legal, financial and other issues associated with the surgery. The task force was to deal with the most painful issue raised by transplant surgery: allocation of the lifesaving but exceptionally expensive procedures, and the limited supply of human organs. Distribution of the grants to transplant agencies would be governed by the findings of the task force.   ∎

New Cigarette Labels

Legislation (HR 3979 — PL 98-474) requiring sharp new warnings for cigarette packages and advertisements identifying such smoking risks as cancer and harm to unborn children was cleared by Congress in 1984.

The House-passed bill mandating new rotating warnings was approved Sept. 26 by the Senate with minor amendments. The House the same day by voice vote cleared the amended version for President Reagan.

The four new labels, to be rotated periodically, warned of cancer, heart disease and other health problems, and advised smokers that cigarette smoke contained carbon monoxide. Health groups sought the new labels after the Federal Trade Commission (FTC) in 1981 reported that the current, general health warning had lost impact. That warning read: "Warning: The Surgeon General Has Determined That Cigarette Smoking Is Dangerous To Your Health."

The four new warning statements to be required on the packages and advertising of all cigarette brands sold in the United States one year after enactment of HR 3979 were:

SURGEON GENERAL'S WARNING: Smoking Causes Lung Cancer, Heart Disease, Emphysema, and May Complicate Pregnancy.

SURGEON GENERAL'S WARNING: Quitting Smoking Now Greatly Reduces Serious Risks to Your Health.

SURGEON GENERAL'S WARNING: Smoking by Pregnant Women May Result in Fetal Injury, Premature Birth and Low Birth Weight.

SURGEON GENERAL'S WARNING: Cigarette Smoke Contains Carbon Monoxide.

Until 1984, tobacco interests fiercely had fought any change in the current general warning label. But growing pressure in Congress, including strong support for higher cigarette taxes, prompted industry officials to negotiate a labeling compromise, according to members working on the bill. Tobacco officials refused publicly to acknowledge their participation.

The compromise bill, passed by the House Sept. 10, came to the Senate floor after sponsors agreed to several other changes sought by Sen. Wendell H. Ford, D-Ky. A series of very negative findings on cigarettes and health were dropped from the bill text and were to appear in expanded form in the committee report (H Rept 98-805).

The findings included, for example, a statement that the surgeon general had found cigarette smoking to be the "largest preventable cause of illness and premature death in the United States," associated with "the unnecessary deaths of over 300,000 Americans annually."

Also, the Senate added language to make clear that cigarette distributors or retailers could not be held responsible for the rotation system. Ford also said that health groups backing the bill had agreed to fight for new restraints on imported tobacco.

Provisions

As cleared by Congress, HR 3979:

● Directed the secretary of health and human services to support research and public information programs on the dangers to human health of smoking and to report annually to Congress on these activities, with any recommendations for change.

● Required packages of and advertisements for cigarettes sold in the United States to bear one of four new labels, with the texts to be rotated quarterly by each company under plans approved by the Federal Trade Commission. The size of the labels was to be 50 percent larger than the existing labels. Texts for outdoor billboard ads were to be slightly shorter.

● Required makers and importers of cigarettes to disclose annually to the secretary all ingredients added to tobacco in cigarettes. The information could be transmitted through a third party, without identifying either the brand or maker of a cigarette. Authorized the secretary to report to Congress on any health hazards posed by such ingredients.

● Stated that the bill neither limited nor expanded existing FTC authority over cigarette advertising.

House Committee Action

The bill was approved May 17 by the Energy and Commerce Committee after it was told that the tobacco industry, in a remarkable about-face, would not object. The report was filed May 23.

The committee approved the bill by voice vote after accepting, 22-0, a substitute offered by Albert Gore Jr., D-Tenn., who said that tobacco industry representatives had agreed to the substitute less than 24 hours before.

Gore, who had led months-long negotiations to reach a compromise acceptable to health groups and tobacco interests, said that cigarette makers realized that pressure was building for even harsher "punitive" anti-tobacco legislation next year.

Henry A. Waxman, D-Calif., sponsor of an earlier version of the labeling bill that was stalled by controversy, suggested that the industry saw even more alarming battles ahead on federal cigarette taxes and that it wanted to gain some good will by compromising. *(1983 Almanac p. 408)*

Gore also said that cigarette executives could not publicly support the new labels because of their belief that any industry statement linking smoking to cancer or other illnesses might invite liability suits.

One sign of the strength of the compromise effort was the involvement in the industry negotiations of Rep. Charlie Rose, D-N.C., and Rep. Thomas J. Bliley Jr., a Republican from the tobacco-growing state of Virginia. Neither Bliley nor James T. Broyhill, R-N.C., raised objections to the measure in the Energy and Commerce Committee, as they had done before.

In the past, Rose and other representatives of tobacco-growing regions secured the help of both the House Democratic leadership and the Senate Republican leadership to defend the controversial crop. Asked whether he was pleased with the committee vote for the labeling bill, Rose said, "No. I'm just glad it's over."

The New Labels

Under the committee bill, the current warning language was to be replaced by four different statements, to be rotated four times a year. The new warnings would be printed in a heavily bordered rectangle, 50 percent larger than the existing warning.

Slightly different, compressed versions of the language would be used in cigarette advertisements on billboards.

The bill also required cigarette makers to inform the Department of Health and Human Services (HHS) of all chemicals added to cigarette tobacco. Under a voluntary

agreement, the manufacturers currently informed HHS of the most commonly used additives, but no federal agency had full information on what chemicals were used in cigarettes and what their effect was on human health, either separately or in combination with other additives.

HHS would transmit information on the additives — without identifying either a manufacturer or a brand name — to Congress.

The federal government currently had no authority to regulate the ingredients of cigarettes. But should disclosure reveal any hazardous additives in cigarettes, Gore said, Congress could publicize the dangers of the additive or pass new regulatory legislation.

The bill also established statutory authority for federal research and public information programs on smoking and health.

What Was Changed

Matthew L. Myers, a lobbyist for the coalition of health groups, said that the compromise meant the loss of important features of the Waxman bill, which was approved in September 1983 by the Energy and Commerce Subcommittee on Health. But the compromise appeared to retain most of the force of that bill.

The warning texts in the Waxman bill flatly stated that smoking causes cancer and may cause other health problems. The addition of the phrase "Surgeon General's Warning" helped shield cigarette makers from liability suits, according to Bliley.

The final bill omitted a section stating that the warning labels did not relieve cigarette makers of legal liability for their product. And it added some protections against improper disclosure of manufacturers' trade secret additives.

House Floor Action

Floor action on the bill had been expected almost immediately after committee approval but was delayed several times.

One reason was to allow members and industry representatives to discuss the bill's impact on FTC authority to regulate cigarette advertising.

Also, Sen. Jesse Helms, R-N.C., a strong defender of tobacco interests, disputed press reports that he had been persuaded by Sen. Orrin G. Hatch, R-Utah, to let the bill go forward.

Hatch was chairman of the Labor and Human Resources Committee, which reported a strong labeling bill (S 772 — S Rept 97-177) in July 1983. Helms, chairman of the Agriculture Committee, and several other tobacco-state senators put "holds" on S 772, preventing floor action.

After several scheduled floor votes were canceled, Commerce Committee Chairman John D. Dingell, D-Mich., set a June 22 deadline for the industry to secure Helms' support and met with Helms as the deadline approached. He called off a June 26 vote but indicated through aides that Helms had agreed to let the bill go forward eventually, if cigarette makers would agree to buy more American-grown tobacco.

The manufacturers' growing reliance on foreign tobacco had been a sore political issue in tobacco-growing states. Rose and certain state farm organization officials already had been working for a year to secure similar purchase commitments.

The House Sept. 10 approved the bill by voice vote.

Senate Action

After the House vote, plans to speed the bill directly to the Senate floor went awry when it became known that several tobacco-state senators wanted referral of the bill to the Commerce, Science and Transportation Committee because of its advertising sections. The labeling bill reported in 1983 by the Labor and Human Resources Committee (S 772) contained no advertising provisions, and some Commerce members wanted to reclaim jurisdiction over the issue.

On Sept. 12, however, Commerce Committee Chairman Bob Packwood, R-Ore., a supporter of the new legislation, took the first steps in a procedure to bypass his committee and go directly to a floor vote.

But Ford's objections halted action temporarily until agreement was reached on dropping the negative findings on health and making it clear that distributors or retailers were not responsible for the rotation system. ∎

Medicare Changes

Having imposed new out-of-pocket costs on Medicare beneficiaries and clamped new spending controls on hospitals in previous years, Congress in 1984 ordered a temporary halt to increases in Medicare payment rates for doctors.

The fee freeze and other changes in Medicare, the nation's health program for the elderly and disabled, made up the largest spending reductions included in a multi-part deficit reduction package (HR 4170 — PL 98-369) cleared by Congress in June. *(Deficit reduction detail, p. 143)*

The fee freeze extended to October 1985. In addition, the bill established a controversial "assignment" program intended to keep doctors from simply passing on cost increases to patients during the freeze. Participation in the program was to be voluntary but Congress enacted financial penalties for doctors who stayed out of the program.

Those two provisions were estimated to make savings of $2.2 billion.

Another $1.2 billion in savings was expected from the bill's provisions increasing out-of-pocket costs for beneficiaries of Medicare.

The legislation also limited the rate of increase in Medicare payments to hospitals for fiscal 1985 and 1986. The provision applied both to the limits passed by Congress in 1982 to increase payments to hospitals for overall costs of caring for beneficiaries and to the 1983 system that established flat rates of payment per illness. The estimated savings were $1.1 billion. *(1983 Almanac p. 391)*

The deficit reduction bill included a new Child Health Assurance Plan requiring states to broaden their Medicaid coverage to cover more low-income women during pregnancy and more young children. *(Background, 1983 Almanac p. 419)*

Conferees approved additional public assistance spending worth an estimated $500 million to $600 million involving Aid to Families with Dependent Children and Supplemental Security Income.

Alcohol, Mental Health

Congress completed action Oct. 4 on a multi-year reauthorization (S 2303) of federal research, prevention and treatment programs for alcohol and drug abuse and mental health problems. The measure authorized $1.95 billion for the programs in fiscal 1985-87.

The House adopted the conference agreement (H Rept 98-1123) on the bill by voice vote Oct. 4, clearing the measure for the president. The Senate had adopted the agreement earlier in the day. The president signed the measure Oct. 19 (PL 98-509).

As signed, S 2303:

● Authorized $515 million in fiscal 1985, $545 million in 1986 and $576 million in 1987 for block grants to states for alcohol, drug abuse and mental health services.

● Authorized $52 million in fiscal 1985 and $61 million in 1986 for research by the National Institute on Alcohol Abuse and Alcoholism.

● Authorized $68 million in fiscal 1985 and $74 million in 1986 for research by the National Institute on Drug Abuse.

● Authorized $20 million annually in fiscal years 1985-87 for mental health community services grants administered by the National Institute of Mental Health.

● Established an Alcohol, Drug Abuse and Mental Health Advisory Council to assess national needs and advise Congress and the Alcohol and Drug Abuse and Mental Health Administration on how those needs were being met by current programs.

● Required the secretary of health and human services to prepare a comprehensive national plan to combat alcoholism and alcohol abuse to be presented to Congress by Oct. 1, 1985.

● Required states to allocate not less than 5 percent of their block grants to initiate and expand treatment of substance abuse among women, and 10 percent of the grants for mental health services for disturbed children and adolescents.

Senate Action

The Senate authorized the block grants and research funds in separate bills.

Block Grants. S 2303 (S Rept 98-381) authorized nearly $1.6 billion in block grants. It was reported by the Labor and Human Resources Committee April 6 and passed by voice vote April 26.

The bill authorized $490 million in fiscal 1985, $518 million in 1986 and $547 million in 1987 for the Alcohol, Drug Abuse and Mental Health state block grant programs. It included $7 million annually over three years for demonstration projects on preventing and treating alcohol and drug problems of women.

The bill also authorized funds for a new grant program to support halfway houses, day-care programs and other services to aid "deinstitutionalized" mental patients — individuals with chronic mental illness who required continuing support services to live outside hospitals.

For the new grant program to aid mental patients, the bill allowed $5 million annually in fiscal years 1985-87 for planning and $20 million annually in the last two fiscal years to pay for services, such as halfway houses, day care or supervised work.

Research Funds. The Senate June 28 passed by voice vote S 2615 (S Rept 98-477) authorizing a total of

$419.5 million in fiscal 1985-87 for the National Institute on Drug Abuse, the National Institute on Alcohol Abuse and Alcoholism, and research and demonstration programs. The bill, reported May 23 by the Senate Labor and Human Resources Committee, specifically authorized research on alcohol and drug problems among women, and prime-time television advertisements to combat alcoholism and drug abuse.

House Action

Both state grant and research funds for alcohol and drug abuse and mental health were authorized by HR 5603, which the House passed on June 11 by a vote of 360-33. *(Vote 202, p. 64-H)*

On June 28 the House passed S 2303 by voice vote after substituting the text of HR 5603.

Key alcohol and drug abuse and mental health provisions of HR 5603:

● Authorized $532 million in fiscal 1985, $564 million in 1986 and $598 million in 1987 for grants for alcohol, drug abuse and mental health services.

● Revised the allocation formula for state block grants. However, it guaranteed that no state would get less under the new formula than it did in fiscal 1984. The new formula, to be phased in over three fiscal years, more closely reflected state population and per capita income.

● Increased from 15 percent to 25 percent the maximum amount of the grants that states could allocate between substance abuse and mental health.

● Required states to allocate at least 10 percent of the funds for alcohol and drug abuse services for women and mental health services for severely disturbed children.

● Required the Alcohol, Drug Abuse and Mental Health Administration to administer the program and expanded its non-research responsibilities, rejecting the administration plan to shift the program to the Office of the Assistant Secretary for Health.

● Authorized for alcohol abuse research $48 million in fiscal 1985 and $55 million in 1986; for drug abuse research, $64 million and $72 million respectively.

Conference

As part of a previous agreement, House conferees agreed to drop their provisions not related to alcohol and drug abuse and mental health. Those provisions, authorizing funds for programs dealing with individuals with developmental disabilities, were addressed in another conference. *(Story, this page)*

On other major provisions, conferees:

● Accepted the House-passed two-year authorization for research funds, rather than the Senate's three-year authorization.

● Compromised on authorized funding levels for the state block grants.

● Accepted the Senate's authorization for mental health grants, with minor amendments.

● Agreed to the House's revision in the block grant allocation formula, with minor modifications. Under the block grant allocation compromise, no state would receive less than it did in fiscal 1984.

● Accepted the House provision that increased from 15 percent to 25 percent the maximum amount of the grants that states could allocate between substance abuse and mental health.

● Conferees required states to allocate at least 5 percent of the funds for alcohol and drug abuse services for women

and 10 percent of the funds for mental health services for severely disturbed children. The House-passed bill had required a 10 percent allocation for each category.

● Rejected a House provision requiring the Alcohol, Drug Abuse and Mental Health Administration to continue to administer the block grant program, instead stressing that any transfer of management responsibility should be done only if the administration could show concrete evidence that the shift would improve the program. ▮

Developmental Disabilities

Significant spending increases for developmental disabilities programs were authorized under a three-year bill (HR 5603 — H Rept 98-1074) cleared by Congress Oct. 4.

The conference report on HR 5603 was adopted by voice vote by the House Oct. 3 and by the Senate Oct. 4. The president signed the bill Oct. 19 (PL 98-527).

The compromise bill authorized $75.7 million in fiscal 1985, $80.4 million in 1986 and $85.2 million in 1987 for the programs. Some $62 million had been appropriated for the programs in fiscal 1984.

Most of the money was for grants to states to provide and coordinate services for the mentally retarded and severely handicapped.

The measure put increased emphasis on states' providing job-related services for the disabled. The version of HR 5603 approved by the Senate June 28 would have required states to provide such programs.

But House members feared that the requirement would force states to discontinue existing programs in order to comply. Under the compromise bill, states were required to provide employment-related services after fiscal 1986 only if annual appropriations for state grants reached $50.25 million.

Provisions

As cleared, the bill authorized funds in four categories:

● $50.25 million in fiscal 1985, $53.4 million in 1986 and $56.5 million in 1987 for state grants. About $44 million had been provided for the grants in fiscal 1984.

● $13.75 million in fiscal 1985, $14.6 million in 1986 and $15.5 million in 1987 for agencies that provided advocacy and protective services for the disabled. In fiscal 1984, $8.4 million was appropriated.

● $9 million in fiscal 1985, $9.6 million in 1986 and $10.1 million in 1987 for university-affiliated training facilities. That represented a modest increase in the authorization.

● $2.7 million in fiscal 1985, $2.8 million in 1986 and $3.1 million in 1987 for special project grants for assessment and demonstration projects, a slight increase in the authorized funding level.

Legislative Action

House. The Energy and Commerce Committee on June 6 reported an initial version of HR 5603 (H Rept 98-826) that included not only the developmental disabilities authorization but state grants and research funds for alcohol and drug abuse and mental health programs. The bill, passed by the House by a 360-33 vote June 11, authorized $2.3 billion in fiscal 1985-88. *(Vote 202, p. 64-H)*

The alcohol and drug abuse and mental health programs were addressed in another bill (S 2303). *(Story, p. 480)*

For the developmental disabilities programs, the bill authorized $69.2 million in fiscal 1985, $75.2 million in 1986, $81.6 million in 1987 and $87.8 million in 1988.

Edward R. Madigan of Illinois, ranking Republican on the Subcommittee on Health and the Environment, said the fiscal 1985 authorization was 11 percent over current funding but an increase of only 8 percent over the funding request by the president.

Senate. The Senate provided its developmental disabilities authorizations in S 2573. The bill, passed by voice vote June 26, authorized $82.1 million in 1985, $88.2 million in 1986 and $94.4 million in 1987. It was reported by Senate Labor and Human Resources May 25 (S Rept 98-493). On June 28, the Senate passed HR 5603 after substituting the text of S 2573.

Conference

Key members in the House and Senate had decided that only developmental disabilities would be addressed in the conference on HR 5603.

The House on June 28 took steps to permit consideration of the alcohol and drug abuse and mental health portions of its original version of HR 5603 during the conference on S 2303.

Conferees accepted the Senate-passed three-year authorization of developmental disabilities programs rather than the four-year House-passed measure.

Negotiators generally agreed on funding levels about midway between the House- and Senate-passed totals, although conferees approved almost exactly the lower levels authorized by the House for special programs. ■

Child Abuse, 'Baby Doe' Legislation Cleared

Legislation (HR 1904 — PL 98-457) designed to ensure that severely handicapped infants received appropriate medical care was signed into law Oct. 9 by the president.

The conference report on the bill (HR 1904 — H Rept 98-1038) was filed Sept. 19 in the House. The so-called "Baby Doe" provisions responded to concerns about cases in which parents and doctors had withheld treatment from handicapped infants.

The bill was cleared Sept. 28 by voice vote by the Senate. The House had adopted the conference report two days earlier.

The Reagan administration strongly supported the bill's provisions to protect severely handicapped infants. However, it objected to the increased funding authorizations and to a new program to prevent family violence.

The bill reauthorized through fiscal 1987 aid for child-abuse prevention and adoption programs. Some $18 million was provided for those programs in fiscal 1984, but HR 1904 allowed spending of up to $45 million in 1985, rising to $48.1 million in 1987.

As a condition of receiving federal child-abuse aid, state child protection agencies would be required to have procedures for responding to reports of medical neglect of handicapped infants who were denied treatment for life-threatening conditions.

Both the version of the bill passed by the House Feb. 2 and by the Senate July 26 included provisions sparked largely by the so-called "Baby Doe" case, in which a Bloomington, Ind., infant born with Down's syndrome and an incomplete esophagus was allowed to die.

The Department of Health and Human Services (HHS) had responded in 1983 by issuing regulations requiring hospitals to post notices saying it was illegal to withhold care from infants because of their disabilities, and providing a toll-free "hot line" for reporting cases of neglect. The regulations were struck down by a federal judge and reissued in modified form Jan. 12. *(1983 Almanac, p. 390)*

The conference bill drew heavily on the Senate version, which had been backed by a coalition of medical, disability and right-to-life groups. Conferees were concerned that the House version of HR 1904 would have required doctors to make heroic efforts to keep handicapped babies alive, even when treatment was futile.

The compromise language specified that withholding care did not constitute medical neglect in certain circumstances, such as when an infant was "irreversibly comatose."

In an effort to address another emotionally charged social problem, the new family-violence program provided matching grants to help states provide shelter and services for battered wives and other victims of domestic abuse. HHS would administer the program.

The measure authorized $158.1 million in fiscal years 1984-87 to aid child-abuse prevention programs. It also included $5 million a year for promoting the adoption of hard-to-place children, including severely handicapped infants. It authorized $63 million over three years for a new program to prevent family violence and aid state efforts to provide shelter to victims of domestic abuse.

Major Provisions

As signed into law, the Child Abuse Amendments of 1984:

● **Child Abuse.** Authorized $33.5 million in fiscal 1984, $40 million in 1985, $41.5 million in 1986 and $43.1 million in 1987 for the prevention and treatment of child abuse. If total appropriations in any year exceeded $30 million, the bill specified that $5 million be used for the prevention of sexual abuse and $5 million for grants to help states meet the "Baby Doe" requirements of the bill.

● Specified that at least $9 million of the total appropriated each year be used for grants to states and $11 million for research, demonstration projects, training and technical aid.

● **Handicapped Infants.** Required states, to qualify for federal child protection grants, to establish procedures for responding to cases of medical neglect, including the withholding of treatment from disabled infants with life-threatening conditions. States must provide for coordination and consultation with hospital officials.

● Specified that withholding life-saving treatment from disabled infants would not constitute medical neglect in certain circumstances, such as when treatment would be futile, simply prolong dying or fail to correct all the life-threatening conditions.

● Authorized grants to help states set up procedures for preventing medical neglect of severely handicapped infants, education and training programs for parents and hospital officials who deal with such babies, and services to promote their adoption.

- ● **Adoption Opportunities.** Authorized $5 million a year through fiscal 1987 for grants to encourage adoption of handicapped or other hard-to-place children.
- ● **Family Violence.** Authorized $11 million in fiscal 1985, $26 million in 1986 and $26 million in 1987 for matching grants to states to provide shelter and other services for the victims of domestic violence and for programs to prevent such abuse.
- ● Specified that at least 60 percent of funds distributed in the grant program be used for emergency shelters and other services.
- ● Authorized HHS to transfer up to $2 million each year to the attorney general for grants to train police to handle cases of domestic violence.

House Action

The House passed HR 1904 by a vote of 396-4, despite appeals from opponents who argued that the federal government should not get involved in sensitive medical decisions about whether or not a severely handicapped infant should be allowed to die. *(Vote 15, p. 6-H)*

The bill had been reported (H Rept 98-159) by the Education and Labor Committee May 16, 1983, amid controversy over the HHS regulations.

The House rejected, 182-231, an amendment backed by the American Medical Association (AMA) and several other medical groups that would have dropped the infant protection provisions. *(Vote 13, p. 6-H)*

The bill reauthorized through fiscal 1987 the Child Abuse Prevention and Treatment Act (PL 95-266), which provided grants to states to fight child abuse, spur adoption and combat sexual abuse of children.

It authorized $30.5 million for child-protection programs in fiscal 1984, rising to $34.9 million in fiscal 1987. It also provided $65 million over three years for the prevention of family violence.

HR 1904 expanded the definition of child abuse to include cases in which medical aid or other life-saving procedures were withheld from infants because they were handicapped.

To qualify for federal child-protection grants under the bill, states must establish procedures for reporting and investigating cases of medical neglect of handicapped infants. Cases in which care was withheld from such infants automatically would be referred to a child-protection agency, to ensure that the decision was medically justified and not based on judgments about the future quality of life.

"Who among us will say, 'I do not want to lead that life, therefore, that life should not be led,'" said Austin J. Murphy, D-Pa., the principal sponsor of the bill and chairman of the Select Education Subcommittee that drafted the measure.

Echoing arguments made against the HHS "Baby Doe" regulations, critics of HR 1904 contended that the bill constituted an unwarranted federal intrusion in the decisions of doctors and families. Others said that the bill's infant-care provisions were unnecessary because new rules established by HHS provided adequate protection.

But supporters said the provisions established a firmer basis for the rules and argued that the government had a responsibility to save the lives of handicapped infants where it was "medically reasonable" to do so — whether or not the infant's parents agreed with their doctor's judgment.

Before passing the bill, the House approved by voice vote a Murphy amendment that dropped provisions requiring states to set up local medical boards to review decisions on the treatment of handicapped infants. The amendment also made clear that states did not have to set up new procedures, such as a hot line to handle reports of infant neglect, but could use existing child-protection programs to comply with the bill's requirements.

The amendment to drop all "Baby Doe" language, introduced by Rod Chandler, R-Wash., would have established a national commission to study the issue and required HHS to issue guidelines for hospitals that wanted to establish advisory panels on the treatment of handicapped babies.

The House approved, 367-31, an amendment by George Miller, D-Calif., that authorized $65 million over three years for projects to prevent family violence. *(Vote 14, p. 6-H)*

Senate Action

Moving to break a yearlong logjam that had stalled a child protection bill (S 1003), lawmakers of widely divergent political views endorsed a compromise amendment to ensure that handicapped babies received adequate medical care for life-threatening conditions.

The compromise made clear that doctors would not be required to take extraordinary steps to keep handicapped babies alive under certain circumstances — if, for example, the treatment would only prolong the process of dying.

The amendment's sponsors included conservative Republican Orrin G. Hatch of Utah and liberal Democrat Alan Cranston of California. Other sponsors were Jeremiah Denton, R-Ala., Christopher J. Dodd, D-Conn., Nancy Landon Kassebaum, R-Kan., and Don Nickles, R-Okla.

Controversy over how the "Baby Doe" issue should be handled had prevented S 1003 from coming to the Senate floor ever since it was approved by the Labor and Human Resources Committee in May 1983 (S Rept 98-246).

As approved by the committee, S 1003 differed from the House approach of requiring states to ensure treatment for handicapped infants. The Senate committee wanted to create a panel to study the issue and, if it was deemed appropriate, authorize HHS to issue rules requiring hospitals to set up procedures to handle "Baby Doe" cases.

But the bill left both sides of the issue dissatisfied. Some critics wanted stronger protections for the infant, and others were wary of HHS's dictating hospital procedures.

Under the compromise, hospitals were encouraged but not required to set up committees to review "Baby Doe" cases.

Responsibility for responding to reports of alleged neglect were given to existing state child-protection agencies as part of their responsibility for handling cases of medical neglect. Federal funds for child protection programs would be cut off to states that do not have procedures for handling "Baby Doe" cases.

Responding to concerns that state agencies might lack the resources to handle such cases, the proposal added $5 million a year to funding authorized in the committee bill and provided training and technical aid.

While the House bill also was designed to ensure that handicapped infants got "medically indicated treatment," that key phrase was left undefined. Some feared the omission would leave the matter open to varying interpretations in different states that might go beyond, or fall short of, what Congress intended.

Careful Definition

Under the compromise, "medically indicated treatment" was carefully defined as treatment that physicians judged to be most likely to be effective in correcting the conditions that threatened an infant's life.

But the proposal also specified situations in which withholding treatment would not constitute medical neglect, such as when an infant was irreversibly comatose or when treatment would be "virtually futile" in saving the infant's life, and treatment itself would be "inhumane."

The exceptions were "painstakingly negotiated in an attempt to meet some of the concerns of the medical community," said one Senate aide. But the changes were not enough to win the support of the AMA.

An AMA spokesman said that the bill's infant-care guidelines left no room for consideration of the "quality of life" severely handicapped infants would face if they could be kept alive indefinitely.

The compromise, however, was backed by other medical groups that opposed past "Baby Doe" proposals, including the American Hospital Association and the American Academy of Pediatrics. It also was backed by such groups as the Disability Rights Center, the Association for Retarded Citizens and the American Life Lobby.

The Senate July 26 easily approved the compromise by voice vote and by a vote of 89-0, substituted the text of S 1003 for HR 1904. *(Vote 184, p. 32-S)*

As approved by the Senate, HR 1904 authorized $37.5 million in fiscal 1984, $44 million in 1985, $45.5 million in 1986 and $47 million in 1987 for child protection and adoption programs, and $35 million through 1987 for family violence protection. ∎

Child Abuse Funds

Faced with a rash of shocking reports of child abuse in day-care centers, Congress in 1984 moved to encourage states to step up training and screening of child-care workers.

The stopgap appropriations bill for fiscal 1985 signed by President Reagan Oct. 12 (H J Res 648 — PL 98-473) provided an additional $25 million for states for training child-care workers. *(Story, p. 444)*

But states would get their full share of the extra money only if they established procedures for checking the employment history and criminal records of people who took care of children.

The measure also authorized a new program of matching grants for states that set up special funds for the prevention of child abuse.

'Shocked and Angered'

"We all have been shocked and angered by the tragic incidents of child abuse in day-care settings," said Rep. George Miller, D-Calif., whose amendment adding training funds to the stopgap bill was adopted by the House Sept. 25. He referred to news reports of charges alleging child abuse that had been filed against the staff of some child care facilities.

"We have a three-alarm fire going out there, and this is the only way in which we can get the money to the states

immediately through an existing process," he said.

Miller's proposal would have provided $50 million for training child-care workers. Conferees on the bill, however, accepted the version of the amendment approved by the Senate Oct. 2, which set spending at $25 million and authorized the new matching grants for child abuse prevention.

The $25 million was added to the $2.7 billion appropriated for the Social Services Block Grant, which provided aid for day care, counseling and other activities. The extra funds were earmarked for training child-care workers, state licensing officials and parents, with emphasis on helping them prevent and recognize the signs of child abuse.

Although the measure provided incentives for states to set up procedures to screen child-care workers, backers of the amendment said that background checks alone were not enough to improve the quality and safety of child care. They argued that poor training of day-care personnel was a key shortcoming that demanded federal attention. Miller cited estimates that 75 percent of child-care workers had had no training.

Sen. Dennis DeConcini, D-Ariz., a sponsor of the amendment, said more training money was needed to make up for ground lost since 1981, when Congress dropped provisions of the social services grant that earmarked about $75 million a year for training programs. *(1981 Almanac p. 488)*

As a result, DeConcini said, 24 states used none of their federal social service funds for training.

The DeConcini amendment incorporated a proposal by Sen. Christopher J. Dodd, D-Conn., to authorize federal matching grants for states that set up a trust fund or some other special financing mechanism for child abuse prevention. Dodd said that 20 states currently had set up such special funds.

Congress Sept. 28 cleared legislation (HR 1904 — PL 98-457) reauthorizing established programs for child abuse prevention and treatment. *(Story, p. 482)*

But Dodd said that most of the limited funds available under those programs were used by states for treatment of victims of abuse, leaving little for prevention efforts. Although the matching grants were authorized for five years under the stopgap money bill for fiscal 1985, no funds were appropriated for them.

Provisions

As cleared by Congress, the child care provisions of H J Res 648:

● **Training.** Appropriated an additional $25 million for the Social Services Block Grant in fiscal 1985.

● Specified that the extra money be allotted to states for training child-care providers, licensing and enforcement officials and parents, particularly in the area of preventing abuse in child-care programs.

● Required states to use the extra money to supplement, not supplant, the funds they otherwise would spend on training.

● Required the secretary of health and human services (HHS) to draft model standards for day-care centers, to provide guidance in such areas as staff training and evaluation, staff-child ratios, probation periods and background checks for new employees and visitation by parents. The guidelines, which were to be drafted by HHS within three months, would be distributed to states, but their adoption would not be mandatory.

● Required states receiving the child-care training funds to establish, by Sept. 30, 1985, state laws requiring a nationwide check of criminal records and procedures for checking the employment history of child-care personnel and employees of juvenile correctional and detention facilities. States that failed to comply would, in effect, have to repay half the training money they received by having future allotments under the Social Services Block Grant reduced.

● **Matching Grants.** Authorized grants to states that established a trust fund or other special financing mechanism for child abuse prevention programs, such as public

information campaigns and support for community prevention programs.

● Authorized Congress to appropriate such funding as it considered necessary for the new grants in fiscal years 1985-89.

● Limited federal grants to 25 percent of the money a state spent in the previous year for child abuse prevention — or an amount equaling 50 cents per child in the state, whichever was less.   ∎

New Programs Added to Head Start Bill

Congress Oct. 9 approved an omnibus social services bill (S 2565 — PL 98-558) to extend the popular Head Start program, after members broke a logjam over a politically divisive formula for allocating energy aid for the poor.

The House, voting 376-6, cleared the bill, which reauthorized Head Start and low-income energy aid for two years. The president signed it Oct. 30. *(Vote 398, p. 122-H)*

The final bill, which had been approved by the Senate Oct. 4, revised the formula for allocating energy aid to channel more funds to warm-weather states — although not as much as members from those regions had wanted.

The pressure to clear the Head Start bill before adjournment also provided an opportunity for members to make a last-minute push for their favorite legislative proposals. S 2565 incorporated several new education and social programs including block grants to expand child care services, teacher scholarships and research grants for universities in the home states of key members — add-ons that led one critic to dub the measure a social services "Christmas tree."

Head Start provided educational, health, nutrition and other social services for disadvantaged preschool children. The program had been widely hailed by both Republicans and Democrats and was one of the few major anti-poverty programs that had escaped the budget-cutting rigors of the Reagan administration.

The House overwhelmingly approved a two-year extension of Head Start June 26 as part of legislation (HR 5885) that also reauthorized the Community Services Block Grant and other social services.

Separate House bills (HR 2439 — H Rept 98-139, Parts I and II; HR 5620 — H Rept 98-747, Part I) extending the low-income energy assistance program never made it to the House floor.

Energy Aid Formula

In the Senate, action had stalled after the Labor and Human Resources Committee May 9 approved S 2565 to extend Head Start, community services grants and the energy aid program. The report (S Rept 98-484) was filed May 24.

A key obstacle was the formula for allocating low-income energy assistance, which would have remained unchanged in the version of the bill approved by the Labor Committee.

Members from warm-weather regions complained that the current allocation formula shortchanged their constituents because it did not take account of the cost of cooling as well as heating the homes of poor families.

Sen. J. Bennett Johnston, D-La., had planned to introduce an amendment during floor debate changing the formula to channel more money to Southern states.

But with time for consideration of the bill running short, Senate and House negotiators worked out a compromise on the energy aid formula and other elements of S 2565 that they thought could be approved by the Senate without a floor fight and by the House without a formal conference.

The revised energy aid formula was greatly simplified from its current form and was expected to shift more money to warm-weather states. But the compromise did not result in as drastic a shift as would have been the case under changes considered by Johnston and other critics of the current program.

The compromise based state allocations on total energy expenditures, including both heating and cooling, by low-income families. But it guaranteed that no state would receive less in fiscal 1985 than it did in 1984, and it protected states from sharp reductions in funds in fiscal 1986.

Those protections did not go far enough to satisfy Rep. Silvio O. Conte, R-Mass., who said the formula change meant that "some people who have been kept out of the cold will no longer receive assistance with their high New England heating bills."

Child Care Compromise

The bill also resolved differences over new programs to expand child care services. The House May 14 had approved legislation (HR 4193 — H Rept 98-745) authorizing federal aid to help communities set up child care programs in school facilities before and after school hours. *(Story, p. 487)*

A similar measure reported by the Senate Labor and Human Resources Committee May 25 (S 1531 — S Rept 98-494) was opposed by committee Chairman Orrin G. Hatch, R-Utah, who argued that the federal government should not be directly involved in the funding of child care.

The compromise incorporated in the Head Start bill provided state block grants to help set up child care programs in school facilities. The state grants also supported efforts to disseminate information about the availability of care for children, the elderly and the handicapped — an approach favored by Hatch. A similar information-referral program had been included in the House Head Start bill.

Education Add-Ons

Most of the education add-ons had been introduced in response to the spate of commission reports issued in 1983 recommending improvements in U.S. schools — including scholarships to lure bright students into teaching and to keep good teachers in the profession. It was a scaled-down version of a measure (HR 4477 — H Rept 98-964) that had been approved by the House Aug. 8. *(Story, p. 488)*

Many House members were pleased that the omnibus

bill, when it came over from the Senate, included education initiatives they had backed. But other members were dismayed that the bill carried proposals that had not been formally considered by education committees in either the House or Senate — including funds for two university research centers.

Provisions

As signed into law, S 2565:

• **Head Start.** Authorized $1.09 billion in fiscal 1985 and $1.22 billion in 1986.

• Required the Department of Health and Human Services (HHS) to spend at least as much on Head Start training and technical assistance as was spent in fiscal 1982 — about $25 million.

• Barred HHS from changing the method for measuring income to prescribe eligibility for Head Start for two years, unless expressly approved by Congress.

• **Child Care.** Authorized $20 million a year in fiscal 1985-86 for state block grants to help expand the availability of dependent-care services.

• Specified that states use 40 percent of their allotments for grants to organizations to provide information about services for the care of children, the elderly and the handicapped.

• Specified that the remaining 60 percent of states' funds be used to help establish before- and after-school child care programs in community centers and unused school facilities.

• **Community Services Block Grant.** Authorized $400 million in fiscal 1985 and $415 million in 1986 for the block grants, which supported community anti-poverty programs.

• Reduced from 90 percent to 83 percent the proportion of block grant funds that states were required to give to community agencies that were receiving aid under anti-poverty programs that were abolished when the block grant was created in 1981.

• Authorized $2.5 million each year for fiscal 1985 and 1986 for community food and nutrition programs.

• **Follow Through.** Authorized $10 million in fiscal 1985 and $7.5 million in 1986 for the Follow Through program, which provided services for disadvantaged children after they left preschool programs like Head Start.

• **Weatherization Aid.** Modified a program that helped low-income families pay for home weatherization work that could cut energy costs, to bar states from imposing stricter eligibility standards than were applied under the low-income energy assistance program.

• Limited expenditures to a statewide average of $1,600 per dwelling. *(Story, p. 354)*

• **Special Projects.** Authorized $6 million to build a Center for Excellence in Education at Indiana University, which would conduct research and training for people who wanted to be schoolteachers and administrators.

• Authorized $4 million for the construction of a research center at the University of Utah to conduct research on the health effects of nuclear energy and other new energy technologies, and $6 million for cancer screening and research in a city in Utah that was affected by fallout from nuclear-weapons testing.

• **Low-Income Energy Assistance.** Authorized $2.14 billion in fiscal 1985 and $2.28 billion in 1986.

• Required states to reserve a portion of their funds at least until March 15 each year to handle energy crises.

• Specified that states' allocations be based on total energy expenditures by low-income households, including heating and cooling costs.

• Specified that, under the revised allocation formula, no state would receive less in fiscal 1985 than it did in 1984. Other protections were included for small states and to limit the reductions that could be imposed on states in fiscal 1986.

• Dropped from 25 percent to 15 percent the proportion of energy aid that states are allowed to carry over to the next fiscal year.

• **Teacher Scholarships.** Authorized $20 million in fiscal 1986, $21 million in 1987, $22 million in 1988 and $23 million in 1989 for scholarships of up to $5,000 a year for students who plan to become schoolteachers.

• Authorized $1 million in 1986, $2 million in 1987, $3 million in 1988 and $4 million in 1989 in one-year fellowships for outstanding teachers to take sabbaticals or pursue other projects.

• **Merit Scholarships.** Authorized $8 million a year in fiscal 1986-88 for merit scholarships of up to $1,500 for outstanding college students.

• **Educational Administrators.** Authorized $20 million a year in fiscal 1985-89 for establishing training centers for elementary and secondary school administrators.

• **Native Americans.** Extended through fiscal 1986 a program designed to promote economic and social self-sufficiency among Native Americans, authorizing the appropriation of such sums as Congress considered necessary.

House Action

Efforts to put the omnibus social services bill on a legislative fast track were defeated in the House June 7 after Republicans bitterly objected to procedures one said made a "farce of the legislative process."

The bill (HR 5145 — H Rept 98-740), which extended Head Start along with several other anti-poverty programs, failed to receive the two-thirds vote needed for passage under suspension of the rules. That procedure, often used for non-controversial bills, limited debate and barred amendments, allowing only an up-or-down vote on the version approved April 26 by the Education and Labor Committee.

The 261-156 vote was 17 short of the two-thirds needed, handing a victory to Republicans who said the bill was too costly and complex to be considered under the procedure. *(Vote 196, p. 62-H)*

Democratic backers of the bill said that speedy action was needed to ensure that the programs were reauthorized during the year's short congressional session.

But Republicans complained that closer scrutiny should be applied to a bill as broad as HR 5145, which authorized a total of $1.2 billion in fiscal 1985 and more in later years for five social service programs.

They also objected to the reauthorization of the Community Services Block Grant, an anti-poverty program that the Reagan administration repeatedly proposed abolishing, and pointed out that it did not expire until 1986.

The administration had argued that the Community Services Block Grant duplicated activities of the Social Services Block Grant. Both were created by the 1981 budget reconciliation act to replace other programs. *(1981 Almanac pp. 488, 490)*

But defenders of the block grant said it was the only

federal program expressly directed at combating the causes of poverty at the community level. Supporters feared that the president would veto separate block grant legislation.

As approved by the committee, HR 5145 authorized $1.1 billion in fiscal 1985, rising to $1.35 billion in 1989 for Head Start. Almost $1 billion had been appropriated for fiscal 1984.

It also extended the block grant through fiscal 1989, with an authorization of $434.5 million in 1985, increasing to $527 million in 1989. Current appropriations were $352 million.

Second Attempt Succeeds

Sponsors agreed to scale back the reauthorization period from five years to two years and to drop the language allowing additional years of funding for the Community Services Block Grant.

The House June 26 by a vote of 409-10 agreed to suspend the rules and passed the revised bill (HR 5885). *(Vote 238, p. 74-H)*

To defuse the issue of the block grant, the compromise did not extend the block grant beyond its expiration date of 1986, although it did let spending increase by 5 percent in fiscal 1985 and 1986.

By limiting the bill to two years, sponsors said they had cut its total cost from about $8 billion to about $2.5 billion.

Provisions

As approved by the House, HR 5885:
- **Head Start.** Authorized $1.11 billion in fiscal 1985 and $1.3 billion in fiscal 1986.
- Required the Department of Health and Human Services to spend at least as much on Head Start training and technical assistance as was spent in fiscal 1982 — about $25 million.
- Barred HHS from changing the method for measuring income to prescribe eligibility for Head Start for two years, unless expressly approved by Congress. The provision was included to head off possible administration efforts to count non-cash benefits such as food stamps as part of a family's income in determining eligibility.
- **Community Services Block Grant.** Authorized $409 million in fiscal 1985 and $429 million in 1986. An additional authorization of $5 million was included for community food and nutrition programs.
- Required states to allocate 85 percent of their block grants to local community action agencies.
- **Follow Through.** Authorized $22.15 million in fiscal 1985 and $23 million in 1986 for the Follow Through program, which provided services for disadvantaged children after they left preschool programs like Head Start. Under the 1981 budget reconciliation act, Follow Through was to be phased out at the end of fiscal 1984 and its functions transferred to a block grant program. *(1981 Almanac p. 499)*
- **Child Care.** Authorized $8 million in fiscal 1985 and $8.4 million in 1986 for grants to organizations that provided information and referrals about child care services.
- **Native Americans.** Extended through fiscal 1986 a program designed to promote economic and social self-sufficiency among Native Americans.
- Prohibited the Reagan administration from transferring the Administration for Native Americans from the Department of Health and Human Services to the Interior Department.

Senate Action

The Senate Labor and Human Resources Committee May 9 approved its omnibus social services bill (S 2565 — S Rept 98-484), after key members reached a compromise that included limiting spending increases for Head Start, the community services block grant and a program that helped poor families pay their fuel bills.

The panel thought it had averted a potentially divisive issue in the low-income energy assistance program by considering no changes in the formula for allocating funds to states. However, they did not succeed because the bill as later revised made changes to the formula that became a key point during Senate floor consideration.

As approved by the committee, S 2565 included a three-year extension of low-income energy assistance and Head Start and added one year to the current authorization of the Community Services Block Grant.

The measure approved by the committee also represented a compromise between conservatives who wanted to give states and the Department of Health and Human Services more leeway in administering the programs, and backers of a competing bill (S 2374) who wanted to apply certain restrictions on how federal funds were used.

For example, S 2374 would have required a state to reserve at least 5 percent of its energy assistance funds for emergencies, which could not be used for other purposes until after March 15. The compromise would require states to reserve an emergency fund, but would not mandate a specific amount.

The compromise also dropped a provision governing the Community Services Block Grant that would have continued to guarantee funding to community action agencies and other groups that had received aid under the anti-poverty programs replaced by the block grant.

Other provisions of S 2565:
- **Community Services Block Grant.** Authorized $400 million in fiscal 1987.
- **Head Start.** Authorized $1.075 billion in fiscal 1985, $1.142 billion in 1986 and $1.213 billion in 1987.
- Required HHS to spend at least as much on Head Start training and technical assistance as was spent in fiscal 1982 — about $25 million. However, the requirement would not apply if overall appropriations for Head Start dropped below fiscal 1984 levels.
- **Low-Income Energy Assistance.** Authorized $2.2 billion for energy aid in fiscal 1985, rising to $2.575 billion in 1987.
- Dropped from 25 percent to 20 percent the proportion of energy aid that states were allowed to carry over to the next fiscal year. That cap would be set at 15 percent for states that took advantage of another option that allowed them to shift some of their energy aid to other federal block grant programs. ∎

Aid for Latch-Key Children

The House May 14 approved legislation designed to address the needs of so-called "latch-key" children who have to fend for themselves because their working parents cannot find affordable day care.

The bill (HR 4193 — H Rept 98-745) encouraged communities to set up after-school child-care programs in unused school facilities. While the Senate did not act on a similar bill awaiting floor action, block grants to help set up programs in school facilities were authorized in an omnibus social services bill (S 2565) enacted in 1984. *(Story, p. 485)*

The House bill would have authorized $30 million a year for fiscal 1985-87 for grants for local programs to address the needs of latch-key children. The grants would have been awarded by the Department of Health and Human Services to public and private agencies to provide before- and after-school child-care services in unused public school facilities or community centers. Priority was to be given to projects in areas where there was a shortage of child-care services.

It also would have established a national clearinghouse for social services information and required grant recipients to base fees on family income.

The bill sailed through the House on fast-track legislative procedures, clearing the floor within a week of its approval May 8 by the Education and Labor Committee.

Administration, Senate Objections

The measure was opposed by the Reagan administration, which argued that a new program was unnecessary because the federal government already subsidized child care through other programs — such as the tax credit allowed for child-care expenses.

The bill reported by the Senate Labor and Human Resources Committee May 25 (S 1531 — S Rept 98-494) authorized $15 million a year for fiscal 1984-86. It was opposed by committee Chairman Orrin G. Hatch, R-Utah. ∎

Teacher Scholarships

Scholarships to draw bright students into teaching — and to keep good teachers in the profession — were authorized by a bill passed by the House Aug. 8.

Although there was no Senate action on the measure, the House bill was similar to a scholarship program that later was included in an omnibus social services bill (S 2565) cleared by Congress. *(Story, p. 485)*

The House bill (HR 4477 — H Rept 98-964), approved by voice vote, would have authorized four-year college scholarships named in honor of Carl D. Perkins, D-Ky., chairman of the Education and Labor Committee, who died Aug. 3. The committee had approved the bill June 20.

Scholarships of up to $5,000 a year would have been awarded to students who graduated in the top 10 percent of their high school classes and intended to become teachers. Some 10,000 scholarships were to be available over fiscal 1986-90. Grantees would have been required to teach two years for every year they received aid or else repay the money, plus interest and fees.

To help retain good teachers, the bill also authorized one-year fellowships or sabbaticals for two teachers in each congressional district for fiscal 1986-90.

Although no ceiling on appropriations for the student scholarships was included, the program was estimated to cost $200 million over four years. The teachers' program would have cost about $18 million a year. ∎

Bill Allows School Religious Meetings

President Reagan Aug. 11 signed legislation (HR 1310 — PL 98-377) allowing student religious organizations to meet in public high schools on the same terms as other student groups.

The measure was cleared by the House July 25 after months of elaborate parliamentary maneuvering and controversy over religion in the public schools.

Final action came when the House voted overwhelmingly to accept without change a bill passed by the Senate June 27 that required federally funded high schools to allow all voluntary student groups — including religious ones — to meet in school facilities before and after class hours, if other extracurricular groups were given such access.

The so-called "equal access" proposal was cleared as an amendment to a popular education bill designed to improve science and mathematics instruction. The House had passed its version of the math-science bill in 1983. *(Story, p. 491; 1983 Almanac p. 396)*

While the final school access measure applied to all student groups that wanted to meet on high school premises, an earlier equal access bill (HR 5345 — H Rept 98-710) that protected only religious groups was narrowly defeated in the House May 15.

The school access proposals were prompted by concern among religious organizations that student religious groups had been barred from using school facilities while other student organizations were permitted to meet there. The legislation was strongly supported by President Reagan, whose 1984 re-election campaign emphasized support for religious and other "traditional" values.

One bill (S 1059 — S Rept 98-357) designed to ensure

religious groups' access to elementary and secondary school facilities was approved in 1983 by the Senate Judiciary Committee. *(1983 Almanac p. 301)*

The issue gathered momentum after the Senate March 20 handily rejected a proposed constitutional amendment (S J Res 73) to permit organized, recited prayer in the public schools. The vote was 56-44, 11 short of the required two-thirds majority. *(Vote 34, p. 9-S; story, p. 245)*

The access bill was viewed by many in Congress as a political safety net that might protect them from the ire of constituents angered by the defeat of the school prayer amendment.

While critics charged that the legislation represented a "backdoor" effort to bring religion into public schools, the access bills drew support from many members who had opposed the school prayer amendment.

Leading House Democrats were divided over the issue. Advocates of the school access measure had a key ally in Rep. Carl D. Perkins, D-Ky., chairman of the Education and Labor Committee, who pushed the issue through elaborate legislative channels.

Opponents, including influential members of the House Judiciary Committee, hoped the school access legislation was dead after they blocked passage of HR 5345 on May 15. Although the bill garnered a majority vote, it fell 11 votes short of the two-thirds majority needed to pass because it had been brought up under special legislative procedures.

But the issue was revived when a companion school access measure was introduced in the Senate as an amendment to the math-science education bill. But faced with the threat of a filibuster, sponsors revised the access amendment to address some of the criticisms made during House debate on HR 5345.

Final action on HR 1310, including the equal access amendment, came the day after Reagan, in a July 24 news conference, criticized the Democrat-controlled House for keeping the access bill "bottled up" along with several other items on the administration's legislative agenda.

Provisions

As signed into law, the school-access provisions of HR 1310:

● Made it unlawful for a secondary school receiving federal funds to deny use of its buildings to religious, political and other student groups before and after school while granting such access to other "non-curriculum related" groups. Schools that allowed only curriculum-related groups to meet did not have to comply with the equal access requirements.

● Specified that the meetings be voluntary and student-initiated, with no sponsorship by the school or government, and that they not be controlled or regularly attended by outsiders.

● Stipulated that school officials could be present at religious meetings only as monitors, not as participants.

● Barred states and school districts from requiring any person to participate in religious activity or from expending public funds beyond the cost of providing space for student meetings.

● Specified that the measure did not permit states and school districts to discriminate against small student groups.

● Stipulated that schools found in violation of the law not be penalized by the cutoff of federal funds.

● Specified that the law did not restrict the right of schools to maintain order and discipline and protect the well-being of students and faculty.

House Committee Action

"Equal access" legislation was put on a fast track in the House by Education and Labor Committee Chairman Perkins, who cosponsored HR 5345 with Rep. Don Bonker, D-Wash.

The Education Committee voted 30-3 to approve HR 5345 on April 5, just one day after the measure was approved by the Education and Labor Subcommittee on Elementary, Secondary and Vocational Education, which also was chaired by Perkins.

The three members voting against the bill were Gary L. Ackerman, D-N.Y., Sala Burton, D-Calif., and Paul Simon, D-Ill.

As approved by the committee, HR 5345 required public secondary schools to permit students to meet in school facilities for religious purposes during non-instructional hours if they had a general policy of letting other student groups meet in the building. The penalty for failing to provide equal access for religious groups would be the loss of federal education aid.

However, the penalty would apply only for denying access to religious groups and not if schools refused to let other groups — such as unpopular political organizations — use their buildings.

The protections applied only to voluntary meetings that were initiated by students. The bill stipulated that school officials could be present at religious meetings only

as monitors, not as participants.

Before approving the bill, the committee rejected several amendments by Ackerman, a vocal opponent of the bill. One amendment would have barred outside religious officials from participating in students' meetings.

Critics charged that the bill was an unconstitutional effort to bring religion into the public schools and would interject the federal government into the decisions of local school districts. But supporters said HR 5345 was designed only to protect the free speech rights of student religious groups.

Supporters also said HR 5345 was intended to extend to high schools the principle of a 1981 Supreme Court decision that permitted religious groups to meet on college campuses. That case involved the University of Missouri's refusal to allow a student religious group to meet in campus buildings on the same terms as non-religious groups. *(1982 Almanac p. 10-A)*

The court ruled that because the university had an "open forum" policy allowing a variety of student groups to use its facilities, that policy had to be applied neutrally, even if a religious group wanted to use the buildings.

The committee bill would apply only to secondary schools. Both elementary and secondary schools were covered by the access bill (S 1059) approved by the Senate Judiciary Committee in September 1983.

In another key difference, S 1059 would have provided legal remedies for those whose rights were violated, while the House bill would have cut off federal education aid as an enforcement tool.

Sponsors of HR 5345 included the funding cutoff rather than judicial remedies to keep the measure from being reviewed by the House Judiciary Committee, where key members were opposed to the access bill and were likely to bury it.

House Floor Action

Proponents of the access bill sought quick House floor action, while critics tried to stall and drum up enough opposition to block HR 5345.

With the lopsided committee vote of 30-3 under his arm, Perkins immediately went to House Speaker Thomas P. O'Neill Jr., D-Mass., and asked for a quick vote on the "suspension" calendar. That procedure, while requiring a two-thirds majority to pass a bill, limited debate and prohibited amendments.

Don Edwards, D-Calif., chairman of the House Judiciary Subcommittee on Civil and Constitutional Rights, opposed the bill and said he believed that some members who supported the bill in committee did not understand what they were voting on. But because HR 5345 provided only administrative rather than judicial remedies, it went straight to the floor without being reviewed by Edwards' subcommittee.

After the Education Committee acted, Edwards urged O'Neill to put off a floor vote. The Speaker acceded to Edwards' initial request for delay, putting off a vote until May 7. Afraid that Perkins would prevail on the floor, Edwards came up with a new delaying tactic.

The week of May 1 he rounded up signatures from about 80 Democrats requesting a party caucus on the access issue May 9. Under party rules, such a request required a delay in the scheduled floor vote. Perkins eventually got a promise from the Speaker for a May 15 House floor vote.

Sponsors deliberately chose the "suspension" procedure for bringing the bill to the floor because it prevented opponents from offering amendments. The one drawback was the requirement of a two-thirds majority to pass.

The May 15 vote on the motion to suspend the rules and pass HR 5345 was 270-151, 11 short of the two-thirds majority required to pass the bill. *(Vote 129, p. 44-H)*

Barry Lynn of the American Civil Liberties Union (ACLU), which opposed HR 5345, said the bill's defeat was "a bigger victory for the First Amendment" than defeating the school prayer proposal. "As a practical matter, this would have blurred the distinction between school and church far more than a minute of prayer," Lynn said.

Senate Action

In the wake of the House's failure to approve HR 5345, it was considered unlikely that the Senate would act on its companion bill. Nonetheless, the issue resurfaced on the Senate floor June 6, during debate on a bill to improve mathematics and science education (S 1285 — S Rept 98-151). S 1285 was the Senate companion to HR 1310 (H Rept 98-6, Parts I and II), a math-science education bill approved by the House in 1983.

Sen. Jeremiah Denton, R-Ala., introduced an amendment to S 1285 to make it unlawful for secondary schools receiving federal funds to bar student religious groups from meeting in schools during non-class hours if other student groups were allowed to use school facilities. The amendment, which was cosponsored by Mark O. Hatfield, R-Ore., specified that religious meetings would have to be voluntary and student-initiated.

Introduction of the equal access amendment to the math-science bill took many by surprise, including Majority Leader Howard H. Baker Jr., R-Tenn. In deference to absent members who wanted to address the issue — including Lowell P. Weicker Jr., R-Conn., a fierce opponent of the school access legislation — Baker cut debate on the amendment short. Several other less-controversial amendments to the math-science bill were approved June 6, but no vote was taken on the access proposal and no firm date was set for continuing debate.

Faced with the threat of a filibuster, Hatfield and others redrafted the school access amendment before S 1285 was brought back to the Senate floor June 27.

Hatfield's compromise amendment, which was approved 88-11, included changes intended to address some criticisms raised to earlier equal access proposals. *(Vote 159, p. 28-S)*

Both HR 5345 and the original Denton amendment would have protected only religious student groups against being denied equal access to school facilities.

Critics raised questions about giving special legal protection to religious meetings, saying that would give them preferential treatment while allowing access to be denied to unpopular political groups, for example.

To accommodate that objection, the compromise amendment introduced by Hatfield June 27 extended the "equal access" principle to all student groups by making it unlawful for a high school receiving federal funds to deny use of its buildings to religious, political and other student groups while granting such access to other extracurricular groups before and after school.

Hatfield said that change in the amendment underscored the "freedom of speech" issues at stake. Once a school provided a forum for extracurricular student meetings, Hatfield said, officials should not be able to deny access to groups based on the subject of their meetings.

The revised version also strengthened protections against student meetings being controlled by outsiders and required meetings to be held before or after school.

The Hatfield amendment also defined more narrowly which schools had to comply with the "equal access" policy. It would apply only to schools that received federal funds and allowed their facilities to be used by groups whose activities were not related to an educational curriculum — a category that Hatfield said would include groups like the Young Democrats or a chess club.

But if a school allowed only "curriculum related" groups — such as a French or Spanish club — to meet, it would not be required to offer the same access to religious, political and other extracurricular groups.

The Senate measure did not include specific sanctions to be applied to schools that failed to comply, but backers said there would be remedies through the federal courts. The amendment did make clear, however, that schools should not be penalized by cutting off federal education funds, as was the case under the House school access bill.

The ACLU did not endorse the Hatfield amendment but said it was a "very significant improvement" over earlier proposals.

Nonetheless, the measure drew harsh words during Senate floor debate from critics who saw it as a last-ditch effort to allow prayer in the schools.

Critics such as Howard M. Metzenbaum, D-Ohio, charged that the measure also would force schools to open their doors to cults as well as to mainstream religions.

Hatfield emphasized the measure protected the rights only of student-initiated meetings and that schools would still have the authority to deny the use of facilities to groups that would be disruptive or engaged in unlawful practices.

Slade Gorton, R-Wash., objected to extending the measure's scope to include political and other extracurricular groups. While he supported efforts to eliminate barriers to religious groups' meeting on school premises, Gorton said the broader proposal would undermine schools' authority to bar meetings of extremist groups such as the Ku Klux Klan.

Hatfield said he would have preferred the narrower version that focused on protecting religious groups from being denied access but backed the broader version as "the best we can get."

Hailing passage of the bill, Denton said the "sealed door" that has kept student religious groups out of the schools "has had its seal broken."

After tacking on the access amendment and approving S 1285 by voice vote, the Senate substituted its bill for the text of HR 1310.

Final Action

The school access amendment was given a good chance of surviving in conference with the House because a leading supporter of the amendment — Perkins — would be playing a key role in the conference.

However, the measure was cleared for the president without going to conference. In a two-part vote July 25, the House agreed to accept without change the Senate-passed version of the math-science bill, including the school access amendment.

But those votes came only after another round of

legislative maneuvering by proponents and opponents of the school access bill.

The day after the Senate approved HR 1310, advocates of the school access amendment were confronted by an unexpected roadblock. Speaker O'Neill June 28 denied a routine request by Perkins to go to conference on HR 1310.

Instead, O'Neill sent the Senate version of HR 1310 both to Perkins' Education and Labor Committee and the Judiciary Committee, where opponents hoped it would die quietly. The committees were given until Aug. 6 to consider the school access provisions.

Outraged by the move, Perkins laid plans for bringing the issue back to the floor July 25 under an obscure legislative process known as "Calendar Wednesday." The procedure allows committee chairmen to bypass the House leadership and bring to the floor any bill that has been reported by their committees.

But rather than resort to that tactic, Perkins worked out an agreement with O'Neill and Edwards to bring the Senate math-science bill to the floor under suspension of the rules. The unusual arrangement allowed separate up-or-down votes on the equal access amendment and then on the remaining provisions of the math-science bill. The process also barred amendments and limited debate.

The procedure drew harsh words from Hamilton Fish Jr., R-N.Y., ranking minority member of the Judiciary Committee, who accused sponsors of "ramrodding" the bill through the House.

The changes in the school access proposal made by the Senate helped sway the votes of some members who had opposed the earlier House bill. That part of the Senate bill was approved by the House 337-77. *(Vote 282, p. 86-H)*

The House then voted 393-15 to adopt the other Senate provisions of HR 1310 authorizing new aid for math and science education, clearing the measure for the president. *(Vote 283, p. 86-H)* ∎

Math-Science Bill Cleared

A new two-year program to bolster the quality of mathematics and science education was authorized under legislation (HR 1310 — PL 98-377) signed by President Reagan Aug. 11.

The measure cleared Congress July 25 when the House voted to accept without change the version of HR 1310 approved by the Senate June 27.

The bill authorized $965 million over fiscal 1984-85 for new programs in the Education Department and National Science Foundation (NSF) to upgrade math and science instruction, primarily through teacher training and retraining.

Under miscellaneous amendments tacked on along the way, HR 1310 also authorized $857 million for unrelated education programs — aid to magnet schools involved in desegregation plans, grants for education reform projects and funds for removing hazardous asbestos from schools.

The principal impetus behind the math-science education proposal was congressional concern over the shortage of qualified math and science teachers and evidence of declining science knowledge among students.

The House had approved HR 1310 (H Rept 98-6, Parts I and II) in March 1983 and the Senate Labor and Human Resources Committee had approved its companion version (S 1285 — S Rept 98-151) in May 1983. *(1983 Almanac p. 396)*

However, the final stages of congressional action were slowed by efforts to use the politically popular bill as a vehicle for controversial amendments.

By the time the measure cleared, the basic education provisions of HR 1310 were overshadowed by heated debate over religion in the schools. The Senate added to the math-science bill a much-disputed proposal allowing student religious groups to meet in public high schools on the same terms as other student groups. *(Story, p. 488)*

The House eliminated the need for a conference on HR 1310 by accepting the Senate version, including the amendment affecting religious meetings.

Although the bill authorized $425 million in fiscal 1984 and $540 million in fiscal 1985 for the new math-science programs, actual appropriations fell far short of those spending ceilings. No funds were appropriated for fiscal 1984 and $100 million was provided in fiscal 1985. *(Appropriations, p. 421)*

Nonetheless, some education advocates believed enactment of HR 1310 carried important symbolic weight. They saw it as the first significant step the federal government had taken to address the recent wave of public concern about the need to shore up the quality of U.S. schools.

However, some critics argued that the new program, with its emphasis on teacher training, would not deal with what many saw as the root of the teacher-shortage problem — the temptation for math and science teachers to leave the profession for higher paying jobs.

Provisions

Following are the education provisions of HR 1310:

● **Math and Science Education.** Authorized $350 million in fiscal 1984 and $400 million in 1985 for Education Department grants to states for training and retraining of math and science teachers. However, 10 percent of the funds were earmarked for grants to be distributed at the discretion of the secretary of education.

● Required states to use 70 percent of their allocations for improving instruction at the elementary and secondary level and 30 percent for higher education.

● Allowed states to approve the use of funds for improving foreign language and computer instruction in cases where a school district had no need to bolster its math and science programs.

● Authorized $45 million in fiscal 1984 and $80 million in 1985 for additional programs to be administered by the NSF, including grants for teacher training institutes and for the development of instructional materials, awards to recognize outstanding teachers and merit scholarships for college students who planned to become math or science teachers.

● Authorized $30 million in fiscal 1984 and $60 million in 1985 to support joint projects involving educational institutions and the private sector in improving math, science and engineering education.

● **Magnet Schools.** Authorized $75 million a year in fiscal years 1984-86 for magnet schools, which provided special programs in such subjects as music or science to attract students of diverse racial, social and ethnic backgrounds.

● Specified that a school district would be eligible for aid if it was carrying out a voluntary or court-ordered desegregation plan or if it lost at least $1 million as a result of the elimination of a previous desegregation aid program in 1981.

● **School Asbestos.** Authorized aid for removing asbestos from school buildings, to be administered by the Environmental Protection Agency (EPA). A similar program had been authorized in 1980 to be run by the Education Department, but Congress never appropriated money for it.

● Authorized funding for the EPA program at $50 million a year in fiscal 1984 and 1985 and $100 million in each of the next five years for grants or 20-year interest-free loans to remove asbestos from schools.

● **Educational Excellence.** Authorized $16 million in fiscal 1984 and 1985 for awards to school districts to carry out education improvement projects.

Senate Action

S 1285 was approved in May 1983 by the Senate Labor and Human Resources Committee. Like the companion math-science bill approved by the House in 1983, S 1285 enjoyed broad bipartisan support that was fueled by a spate of highly publicized reports calling for broad reforms to bolster the quality of U.S. schools.

But the bill was not brought to the Senate floor for almost a year after it was approved by the committee.

A principal obstacle to floor action was a planned amendment to set up a new $100 million program of aid to schools undergoing desegregation.

The amendment, whose prime backers were Daniel Patrick Moynihan, D-N.Y., and Thomas F. Eagleton, D-Mo., was drafted to succeed the Emergency School Aid Act (ESAA), a desegregation aid program that was abolished in 1981 when Congress created an education block grant replacing a number of categorical programs. *(1981 Almanac p. 499)*

Many school districts, particularly in large urban areas, that had received ESAA funds got less money under the state block grants.

The House in 1983 approved legislation (HR 2207 — H Rept 98-136) to establish a new version of the ESAA program, authorizing $100 million a year in competitive grants. *(1983 Almanac p. 404)*

But plans to introduce a similar proposal as an amendment to S 1285 drew strong objections from Sen. Orrin G. Hatch, R-Utah, chairman of the Labor and Human Resources Committee, who opposed resurrection of broad desegregation aid.

Desegregation Compromise

When S 1285 was brought to the Senate floor June 6, key members backed a desegregation compromise that targeted aid more narrowly than the ESAA program.

The compromise authorized $75 million a year through fiscal 1986 for magnet schools that were part of a desegregation plan. The Reagan administration had endorsed magnet schools as a way of achieving voluntary racial integration without mandatory busing.

Introduced by Hatch, the compromise amendment was approved 86-3. It specified that school districts qualified for aid if they lost at least $1 million in aid after ESAA was abolished. The grants also were made available to other school districts that were under court-ordered desegregation plans or voluntary plans approved by civil rights officials in the Education Department. *(Vote 112, p. 22-S)*

Asbestos, Educational Excellence

The Senate also approved by voice vote an amendment

by James Abdnor, R-S.D., revamping and extending a program of aid to schools for the removal of hazardous asbestos. An asbestos program had been in place in the Department of Education since 1980, but Congress never provided money for it.

The Abdnor amendment transferred the program from the Education Department to the EPA and authorized $600 million over fiscal years 1984-90.

In the wake of enactment of HR 1310, a House-passed proposal to reauthorize the Education Department's program for five years was dropped from S 2496, an omnibus education bill. *(Story, p. 493)*

The Senate also approved by voice vote an amendment by John Heinz, R-Pa., authorizing $16 million in fiscal 1984 and 1985 for grants to school districts for education reform projects.

But another roadblock was thrown in the way of final action on the math-science bill June 6 when Jeremiah Denton, R-Ala., introduced an amendment to allow student religious groups to meet in public schools.

Debate on the controversial amendment was cut short June 6 and the bill was laid aside with no firm date set for continuing its consideration.

Logjam Broken

The bill was brought back to the floor June 27 after a compromise school-access amendment was drafted. Introduced by Mark O. Hatfield, R-Ore., the compromise was approved 88-11. *(Vote 159, p. 28-S)*

The Senate managed to avoid another flare-up over the math-science bill when the White House and its Senate allies dropped plans to push a contested amendment to lower the minimum wage for teenagers during the summer months.

Charles H. Percy, R-Ill., had been encouraged by the White House to introduce the youth subminimum wage proposal — a plan bitterly opposed by organized labor.

But the White House backed down from that strategy, an aide to the Senate Republican leadership said, because an expected filibuster of the subminimum wage proposal would have jeopardized passage of the entire bill, including the administration-backed school access provision.

Donald W. Riegle Jr., D-Mich., tried to add $15 million a year to establish after-school day care centers — a plan opposed by the administration as an unnecessary and duplicative use of federal money. The amendment was tabled by a vote of 51-42. *(Vote 162, p. 29-S)*

Although a bill (S 1531 — S Rept 98-494) incorporating a similar proposal was reported by the Senate Labor and Human Resources Committee May 25, it was strongly opposed by Hatch. But in later congressional action, a compromise proposal for providing grants to states for establishing after-school day care centers was included in an omnibus social-services bill (S 2565 — PL 98-558). *(Story, p. 485)*

After approving S 1285 by voice vote, the Senate substituted its bill for the text of HR 1310.

House Action

HR 1310 was cleared for the president July 25, when the House voted overwhelmingly to accept without change the Senate-passed bill.

The bill was brought to the House floor only after elaborate parliamentary maneuvering by proponents and opponents of the Senate school-access amendment.

The Senate bill was considered under unusual procedures that allowed separate up-or-down votes on the school-access amendment, which was approved 337-77, and on the remaining provisions of the math-science bill. The measure was cleared for the president after the House voted 393-15 to accept the education provisions of the Senate bill. *(Votes 282, 283, p. 86-H)*

Carl D. Perkins, D-Ky., chairman of the House Education and Labor Committee, urged his colleagues to adopt the Senate version of the math-science bill, saying that it contained only "minor differences" from the version approved by the House in 1983. ∎

Education Bill Extending 10 Programs Signed

Legislation to revamp and extend 10 education programs was signed by President Reagan Oct. 19, despite his administration's reservations about several elements of the omnibus school-aid bill (S 2496 — PL 98-511).

The measure was cleared after the conference report on S 2496 (H Rept 98-1128) was adopted by voice vote by the Senate Oct. 3 and by the House Oct. 4.

The bill reauthorized for four years or more: bilingual education grants; "impact aid" for school districts that educated the children of federal employees; aid for the education of adults, Indians and immigrants; the Women's Educational Equity Act; the National Center for Education Statistics; the National Assessment of Educational Progress; and aid for education in the Virgin Islands and teacher training in U.S. territories.

A conference committee paved the way for final action when negotiators Oct. 1 agreed to drop a controversial rider to the House version of S 2496 that required schools to allow moments of silent prayer.

As approved by the Senate June 28, S 2496 (S Rept 98-503) included only a five-year reauthorization of aid to adult education. But the House version (HR 11 — H Rept 98-748), approved July 26, was an omnibus bill that tied the renewal of adult education aid to an overhaul of bilingual education grants and the extension of other programs whose authorizations lapsed Sept. 30, 1984.

The most significant changes made by S 2496 were in federal aid to bilingual education, even though the Senate had considered no legislation on the politically sensitive subject.

The final bill included the major elements of a compromise, included in the House-passed bill, that had been crafted amid controversy over the effectiveness of bilingual methods, which provided non-English-speaking students with academic instruction in their native languages while they were learning English.

The compromise, drafted by the House Education and Labor Committee, attempted to strike a middle ground between bilingual advocates who wanted to continue focussing federal aid on dual language instruction and others who wanted to provide support for alternatives to bilingual methods.

The changes did not go as far as the Reagan administration and some members wanted, but they were enough to avert a major confrontation with critics of bilingual education when the bill went to the House floor.

However, floor consideration of the omnibus bill was marked by controversy over another hotly contested election-year issue — prayer in public schools.

During debate on the omnibus bill June 26, the House rejected a proposal that would have cut off funds to schools that prohibited voluntary silent or spoken prayer. Instead, the House approved a watered down version that required schools to permit students to participate in moments of silent prayer.

Faced with the threat of a filibuster by Senate school-prayer opponents, the silent-prayer amendment was dropped from the final version of S 2496 by House and Senate conferees.

Other elements of the compromise bill fell into place relatively quickly when the conference committee met Oct. 1, as negotiators patched together elements of House and Senate versions of S 2496 that differed widely in scope.

The final measure's adult education provisions came, with only minor revisions, from the Senate-passed bill. For other programs, conferees accepted the major elements of the House-passed bill. The concessions on both sides had to do principally with funding levels and the duration of each program's authorization.

Provisions

The programs reauthorized under the bill were extended for either four or five years. Authorizations for fiscal 1985 totaled some $1.2 billion. Except where noted, the conference report set no specific spending ceilings for fiscal years after 1985.

As cleared, S 2496:

● **Adult Education.** Extended through fiscal 1988 grants to states for adult education programs to teach individuals basic literacy skills, authorizing $140 million in fiscal 1985.

● Earmarked 5 percent of adult education funds for the secretary of education to use for research and other special projects, stipulating that the discretionary fund not be established unless total appropriations exceeded $112 million.

● Allowed states to use funds at for-profit institutions if they could provide services not available at public schools or could provide equivalent training for less cost. Profit-making organizations also were made eligible for grants from the secretary's discretionary fund.

● **Bilingual Education.** Authorized a revised program of aid to bilingual education through fiscal 1988, setting a $176 million spending ceiling for 1985.

● Earmarked 60 percent of funds for grants to local programs. Of that, 75 percent was earmarked for "transitional" bilingual programs, which provided some academic instruction in students' native languages while they learned English.

● Earmarked up to 10 percent of total funding for alternatives to transitional bilingual instruction, such as English-as-a-second-language classes. Alternative programs would get 4 percent of appropriations up to $140 million and half of any additional funds, but no more than 10 percent of the total.

● Set aside 25 percent of total appropriations for teacher training.

● Required "transitional" bilingual programs receiving aid to provide structured English-language instruction and classes in the students' native language "to the extent necessary" for a child to learn English.

● Mandated that programs receiving aid, whether they used bilingual or alternative methods, be designed so that students could meet promotion and graduation standards.

● Authorized new grants to school districts for bilingual classes comprised of both English-speaking and limited-English-speaking students; programs of proven academic excellence; English instruction for students' families; preschool and other special bilingual programs; and development of teaching materials.

● Authorized grants to state education agencies, universities and other groups for bilingual education data collection, evaluation and research.

● **Impact Aid.** Authorized $740 million in fiscal 1985, rising $20 million a year to $800 million in 1988, for impact aid, including Category B payments that continued to be limited, as they were in 1984, to no more than one-third the amount to which districts were entitled under the formula set in law.

● Extended through fiscal 1988 other forms of impact aid, including school building funds and disaster aid.

● Eliminated the requirement that a school district enroll at least 10 eligible children in order to receive impact aid payments.

● Limited the amount of money the Education Department could collect in one fiscal year from school districts that received overpayments under the impact aid program that reimbursed districts for revenues lost from federally owned, non-taxable property.

● **Women's Education.** Authorized $10 million in fiscal 1985, $12 million in 1986, $14 million in 1987, $16 million in 1988 and $20 million in 1989 for the Women's Educational Equity Act, which supported projects to promote equitable treatment of women in education.

● Dropped from $15 million to $6 million the amount of money that must be appropriated before local projects could be funded. Below that "trigger," only projects of national significance could be financed.

● Clarified the purposes of small grants for innovative sex-equity projects and increased the limit on awards from $25,000 to $40,000.

● Specified that the National Advisory Council on Women's Educational Programs should include men as well as women, and members with expertise in education and in student financial assistance.

● **Indian Education.** Required the Bureau of Indian Affairs, before closing any schools it operated, to notify and consult with affected Indian tribes and school boards, and to make a study to ensure that adequate alternative services were available for each child.

● Provided for consultation with Indian tribes and communities when boundaries were drawn for attendance at schools operated by the Bureau of Indian Affairs.

● Permitted funds to be distributed in advance of the fiscal year for which they were appropriated for schools operated or financed by the Bureau of Indian Affairs.

● Authorized Education Department aid to school districts that educated Indian children through fiscal 1986, setting a $100 million spending ceiling in 1985, and provided for three automatic one-year extensions of the program after fiscal 1986.

● Eliminated the current ceiling on the number of fellowships awarded to Indians for graduate study, which were limited to 200 a year.

● **Immigrant Education.** Authorized $30 million in

fiscal 1985 and $40 million a year in 1986-89 for aid to school districts that educated large numbers of immigrant children.

● Specified that a school district was eligible for aid if it enrolled at least 500 immigrant children or if such children made up at least 3 percent of total enrollment.

● **General Provisions.** Required the Education Department to establish within the Office of Elementary and Secondary Education an office to administer aid for the education of migrant workers.

● Authorized $8 million in fiscal 1985 and $10.8 million a year in 1986-89 for the National Assessment of Educational Progress, a project to evaluate children's academic achievement, and provided for the project to make data available on a state-by-state basis.

● Authorized $10 million in fiscal 1985, rising $2 million a year to $18 million in 1989 for grants and contracts by the National Center for Education Statistics.

● Barred state and local education agencies from using Education Department funds to buy equipment when the purchase would result in financial gain to a professional organization that represented the interest of the purchaser or its employees.

● Authorized $5 million in fiscal 1985 and $7 million a year in 1986-89 in education aid to the Virgin Islands and for teacher training in U.S. territories.

● **College Student Aid.** Required the Education Department to continue using existing eligibility rules for Pell grants for needy college students through academic year 1986-87, including rules for determining whether applicants were self-supporting or dependent upon their parents.

Background

Congress faced a long list of education programs that were to expire at the end of fiscal 1984. Debate over new funding levels for education was pulled in different directions by two key themes of 1984 congressional election campaigns. Many lawmakers felt under pressure, on one hand, to portray themselves as fiscally responsible, and on the other, to demonstrate their support for education.

Spending for many of the programs up for reauthorization had been curtailed by the 1981 budget reconciliation law (PL 97-35) through fiscal 1984. *(1981 Almanac p. 499)*

House Democrats had tried to raise the ceilings for several education programs in 1983 under an amendment to a vocational rehabilitation bill (HR 3520 — H Rept 98-298), but the amendment was dropped in conference. *(Story, p. 454; 1983 Almanac p. 402)*

Another provision of the 1981 law called for elimination of a portion of the impact aid program known as "Category B" payments, which were for the education of children whose parents either lived or worked on federal property. "B" payments were to be dropped at the end of fiscal 1984, but there was wide congressional support for continuing them.

One of the most controversial programs due for reauthorization was federal aid to bilingual education. It was up for renewal amid debate about the effectiveness of traditional bilingual programs, which provided some native language instruction while students are learning English.

Growing numbers of schools were using alternative methods to help non-English-speaking students gain language proficiency, such as "immersing" students in a structured English program that did not include separate instruction in their mother tongues. But such programs generally had not been eligible for federal aid under the Education Department's program of aid to bilingual education.

The Reagan administration proposed breaking with past policy and allowing federal funds to be used to support alternative methods as well as traditional bilingual courses.

Critics said that bilingual courses, in some cases, fostered students' dependence on their native tongue rather than speeding entry into regular English classes.

But supporters saw bilingual education as a key tool to protect language-minority children against educational neglect and discrimination. They said native-language instruction ensured that students kept up scholastically while they were learning English.

Senate Action

As approved by the Senate by voice vote June 28, S 2496 extended federal aid to adult education through fiscal 1989 with few major changes. Considered amid growing concern about adult illiteracy, the measure had been approved May 2 by the Labor and Human Resources Committee.

The bill authorized $140 million for adult education in fiscal 1985 — $40 million more than President Reagan had requested — and set no specific spending ceilings for the next four years.

Backing down from earlier efforts to merge vocational and adult education into a state block grant, the administration in 1984 endorsed keeping a separate adult education program to help combat adult illiteracy.

As requested by the administration, S 2496 set aside 5 percent of the program's funds for the education secretary to use for research and other special programs. However, the bill stipulated that the secretary's discretionary funds could not be provided unless total appropriations exceeded $112 million.

The Senate refused to go along with the administration's proposal to allow profit-making organizations to receive adult education aid, but S 2496 allowed the secretary to use his discretionary funds to support such institutions.

House Committee Action

A five-year extension of adult education aid was just one part of the omnibus education bill (HR 11) approved April 25 by the House Education and Labor Subcommittee on Elementary, Secondary and Vocational Education. The bill also extended through fiscal 1989 aid for the education of immigrants, impact aid, the Women's Educational Equity Act, aid to schools for the removal of asbestos, Indian education programs and others whose authorization expired at the end of fiscal 1984.

Bilingual education aid was the main focus of controversy in the subcommittee debate. The central issue was whether the $139 million Education Department program should continue to require that schools, to qualify for grants, provide some native language instruction while children are learning English.

The panel maintained the requirement by approving, 10-8, an amendment by Dale E. Kildee, D-Mich. The amendment, based on a bill (HR 5231) Kildee introduced with Baltasar Corrada, New Prog.-Puerto Rico, also increased the share of bilingual funds earmarked for teacher training and authorized new grants for teaching the fam-

ilies of children with limited proficiency in English.

The subcommittee turned back GOP efforts to revamp the program to give more latitude to schools that wanted to use other methods for teaching non-English-speaking students.

The Kildee-Corrada amendment was approved along party lines, but Kildee said after the markup that some committee Democrats were sympathetic to the view that "we should allow some flexibility for alternative methods" if it did not drain support for traditional bilingual programs.

Full Committee Approval

The House Education and Labor Committee approved HR 11 May 2, after key members moved to defuse controversy over bilingual education.

The panel adopted a compromise amendment that attempted to strike a middle ground between bilingual education advocates who wanted to continue focusing federal aid on dual language instruction and other members who wanted to provide support for alternatives to bilingual methods.

Under the compromise, a portion of the money appropriated for bilingual grants would be earmarked for alternative methods. The portion set aside would range from 4 percent to 10 percent, depending on whether Congress increased spending for bilingual aid.

The compromise did not go far enough to satisfy some Republicans who wanted to eliminate any requirement that grant recipients provide native-language instruction to non-English-speaking students. But supporters said the compromise would allow testing of alternative methods without substantially reducing support for traditional bilingual approaches.

In other areas of the bill, the committee:

Impact Aid. Rejected an amendment by Bill Goodling, R-Pa., that would have curtailed impact aid by narrowing the focus of "B" payments to school districts with the heaviest concentrations of federal employees.

Asbestos Removal. Rejected a Goodling amendment that would have allowed school districts to use up to 1 percent of the money they received under other federal education programs to pay for the removal of asbestos.

Women's Education. Rejected an amendment by Howard C. Nielson, R-Utah, to earmark half of the budget for the Women's Educational Equity Act for local sex-equity projects, rather than continuing to finance only projects of "national significance."

Existing law focused funds on national projects unless appropriations for the act exceeded $15 million. In 1984, only $5.76 million was provided. Nielson's opponents argued that his amendment would spread limited resources too thinly.

Adult Education. Adopted an amendment by Pat Williams, D-Mont., to extend adult education aid, without change, for two years, although most programs included in HR 11 were extended for five years. Williams had drafted an amendment revamping the program that, among other things, would have required more coordination between adult education and job training programs.

Faced with opposition to overhauling the program without closer scrutiny, Williams proposed the simple two-year extension to allow time for consideration of broader changes.

General Provisions. Adopted an amendment by Marge Roukema, R-N.J., to bar the use of federal education aid for buying instructional equipment, such as computer software, when the purchase would result in financial gain to a professional organization that represented the interests of the purchaser or its employees.

The provision expanded the scope of a similar ban the House tacked onto a vocational education bill, which was intended to discourage arrangements for selling and purchasing equipment that some members said involved a potential for conflict of interest. *(Vocational education, p. 455)*

House Floor Action

The House began consideration of HR 11 July 25, and approved it 307-85 on July 26, after floor debate dominated largely by the issue of prayer in public schools. *(Vote 292, p. 88-H)*

School Prayer. The House July 26 approved an amendment to require schools receiving federal money to permit students to participate in moments of silent prayer.

Before agreeing to the proposal, the House rejected a stronger amendment pushed by conservatives that would have allowed spoken prayer in schools. The conservatives' plan, rejected by a 194-215 vote, would have cut off federal funds to schools that prohibited silent or spoken prayer. *(Vote 287, p. 88-H)*

Then, in two roll-call votes of 378-29 and 356-50, members adopted the silent prayer language. *(Votes 288, 289, p. 88-H)*

The initial impetus behind bringing up the prayer issue came from conservative Republicans who had relentlessly criticized House Democrats for refusing to allow debate on school prayer legislation.

Debate was instigated by Dan Coats, R-Ind., who introduced the conservative-backed amendment to cut off federal aid to schools and states that had a policy of barring voluntary prayer in school.

Noting that it had been 13 years since the House last squarely addressed the school prayer issue, Coats said that "every school prayer amendment has been bottled up" since then.

The Coats amendment was considered just one day after the House cleared for the president "equal access" legislation (HR 1310 — PL 98-377) that gave student religious groups the same right to meet in school buildings before and after school on the same terms as other student groups. *(Equal access, p. 488)*

Some critics of the "equal access" bill regarded it as a backdoor effort to bring prayer into the schools. But Coats said the access bill left a "gaping hole" because it allowed students to meet for religious purposes in school facilities only before and after class hours.

Supporters of the Coats amendment contended that it would not sanction organized group prayer but was intended only to guarantee the rights of individual students to freedom of speech and the exercise of religion.

But opponents objected that Coats' proposal also would allow spoken prayer in the classroom. They maintained that students in religious minorities would feel ostracized or coerced into participating in prayers alien to their beliefs.

Silent Prayer Alternative

Members were offered an alternative when Steve Gunderson, R-Wis., introduced an amendment that one Democrat described as giving political "cover" to members

who opposed allowing vocal prayer in schools but wanted "to show people they believe in prayer."

The Gunderson amendment barred states and school districts from denying "individuals in public schools the opportunity to participate in moments of silent prayer." It also stated that no person could be required to participate in prayer and that federal, state and local officials could not "influence the form or content of any prayer" in public schools.

Many members — both critics and supporters — maintained that the Gunderson amendment would have little effect because students already were able to engage in silent voluntary prayer. As a practical matter, it was argued, there was no way school authorities could stop it.

But Don Edwards, D-Calif., a leading House civil libertarian, argued that the measure was "not as innocuous as people would like us to believe." He maintained that nothing in the bill would preclude organized moments of silent prayer supervised by teachers and school officials.

At year's end, a case challenging the silent prayer issue was pending before the Supreme Court, which was expected to rule in 1985 on the constitutionality of an Alabama law authorizing public schools to begin each day with a moment of silent prayer or meditation.

Education Funding

After the school prayer controversy was settled, the House turned back to the basic provisions of HR 11.

Debate over the spending levels proposed in the bill sparked another round of partisan controversy, with Republicans and Democrats jockeying for position over the election-year issues of fiscal responsibility and support for education.

Republicans characterized the bill as a "budget buster" that would take the lid off spending ceilings that had been imposed by the 1981 budget reconciliation bill. They challenged Democrats to live up to promises of fiscal restraint that presidential candidate Walter F. Mondale made at the Democratic convention.

The Congressional Budget Office estimated that the bill, as reported by the Education and Labor Committee, would authorize a total of $2.7 billion in fiscal 1985 for the 11 education programs, rising to $3.1 billion in 1989.

Republicans said the 1985 authorizations were more than double the current spending levels and would have exceeded by $1.7 billion the amount that had been envisioned under the House-passed budget resolution.

About $1 billion of the excess was the result of a technicality unintended by the bill's sponsors and was corrected by an amendment adopted when HR 11 was first brought to the House floor July 25.

But Goodling still objected to the remaining $700 million exceeding the House budget resolution. He introduced an amendment to scale back the authorizations to about $974 million — about $33.6 million over fiscal 1984 levels. The amendment was rejected, 169-233. *(Vote 290, p. 88-H)*

The Democrats introduced their own amendment to scale back the 1985 spending levels in the bill, though not as far as Goodling had proposed. Their plan, approved 397-0, trimmed the overall authorization from about $1.7 billion to $1.32 billion. *(Vote 291, p. 88-H)*

Although there was no comparable omnibus education bill pending in the Senate, the House paved the way for a conference by substituting the text of HR 11 for S 2496, the Senate's adult education bill.

Although the Senate version of S 2496 did not include

most of the programs covered by the House version, the Senate had taken action on several education programs in other legislation:

● A five-year extension of the Women's Educational Equity Act was approved by the Senate under an amendment to a vocational education bill (HR 4164). *(Story, p. 455)*

● The Senate-passed version of a library-aid bill (HR 2878) included amendments to reauthorize the National Center for Education Statistics and the National Assessment for Educational Progress. *(Story, p. 461)*

● The Senate voted to extend impact aid as an amendment to the fiscal 1985 defense authorization bill (HR 5167). *(Story, p. 37)*

Conference Action

A conference committee reached agreement Oct. 1 on the omnibus education bill after House negotiators agreed to drop the provision requiring schools to allow moments of silent prayer.

Orrin G. Hatch, R-Utah, the head of Senate conferees and a leading advocate of school prayer, found himself in the unlikely position of asking House negotiators to eliminate the prayer language because he expected it would provoke a filibuster in the Senate.

Some House negotiators were eager to drop the amendment because they had opposed it on the House floor. But Rep. Steve Bartlett, R-Texas, said it was a "shame" to kill the amendment and predicted that the issue would resurface in 1985.

In a key step toward agreement on other elements of the bill, Senate conferees accepted the major elements of the House's rewrite of bilingual education aid.

House negotiators granted concessions considered important to blunting administration opposition to the bill. Conferees modified a House proposal requiring the Education Department to undo a controversial reorganization that took effect in 1983. The House bill had called for the agency to restore three small programs to more prominent positions, but the compromise required the reinstatement of only one of them — aid for the education of migrant workers.

The other two programs that were not included involved aid for desegregation projects and women's educational equity.

House negotiators also agreed to drop a proposed overhaul in the Education Department's audit procedures that would have put the burden of proof on the department when audit findings were appealed, a provision opposed so strongly by the administration that Hatch warned that it could provoke a presidential veto.

In other areas, the conference committee:

● Accepted virtually all of the provisions of the Senate's adult education bill, but scaled back the authorization from four to five years.

● Accepted the House bill's major provisions for extending impact aid, including the continuation of "Category B" payments. However, the compromise authorized somewhat less than had been proposed by the House, setting funding ceilings at $740 million in fiscal 1985, rising to $800 million in 1988.

● Authorized $30 million in fiscal 1985 and $40 million a year in 1986-89 to aid school districts that educated large numbers of immigrant children. The House bill had authorized $70 million in fiscal 1985.

● Dropped provisions of the House bill that extended aid

for school asbestos removal. The Education Department's asbestos program had been revised and transferred to the Environmental Protection Agency under another education bill (HR 1310 — PL 98-377) signed into law Aug. 11. *(Story, p. 488)*

Final Action

The conference report on S 2496 was adopted by voice vote by the Senate Oct. 3 and by the House Oct. 4, clearing the measure for the White House.

The Reagan administration apparently was divided over whether the president should sign the measure. Administration officials had objected to the bill's price tag and other aspects of the bill, and Goodling said Oct. 4 he had been told that the Office of Management and Budget would urge a veto. However, Goodling said he also had learned Education Secretary T. H. Bell would recommend that the measure be signed.

Reagan signed the measure Oct. 19, although he said he still objected to portions of the bill including the extension of impact aid "B" payments.

"If item veto authority were available to me, I would eliminate this portion of the bill," said Reagan.

Reagan also said, in signing the bill, that he would continue to seek broader reforms in the bilingual education program.   ∎

School Aid Bill Dies

A bill (HR 5609) that would have set up a broad new program of school-improvement aid died on the House floor Sept. 13 without having been brought to a vote.

Republican plans to introduce amendments on school prayer and other controversial issues spoiled Democrats' appetite for further action on the measure. Although heavily lobbied by the National Education Association, HR 5609 was not brought back to the floor after general debate was completed Sept. 13.

Republicans charged that the bill, which would have authorized an estimated $8.6 billion over three years for school-improvement projects, was an election-year ploy by Democrats.

"HR 5609 is being brought before the House not because it has a realistic chance of being enacted into law," said John N. Erlenborn, R-Ill., "but because the NEA [National Education Association] and some of the bill's proponents feel that it makes good politics in this election year."

The measure was a top legislative priority of the NEA, the nation's largest teachers' union and a prominent backer of Democrat Walter F. Mondale's bid for the presidency.

By the time the bill had been brought to a vote in the House Education and Labor Committee May 10, more than half the members of the House had signed on as cosponsors. The report (H Rept 98-754) was filed May 15.

Paying for Quality

The bill would have authorized a new program of aid to school districts for improving instruction in science, mathematics, foreign languages, communications and technology.

As approved by the Education Committee, the bill set no specific spending limits, but the Congressional Budget

Office estimated that it would have taken $2.7 billion in fiscal 1985, $2.9 billion in 1986 and $3 billion in 1987 to fully fund the program.

Supporters of the measure said a major infusion of federal aid was needed to help schools respond to the public clamor for shoring up educational quality. Some Democrats took shots at President Reagan for calling attention to problems in schools while seeking cuts in federal education aid.

Maintaining that improving schools required more of the federal government than "cheerleading and slogans," William D. Ford, D-Mich., said, "If you want quality, you have to pay for quality."

Opponents of the bill charged it would duplicate existing programs and that Democrats' support for the expensive measure did not square with their agitation for reducing the federal deficit.

GOP Amendments

Republicans also were prepared to press their own agenda of issues through amendments to HR 5609.

Robert S. Walker, R-Pa., filed an amendment that would require schools receiving aid to allow voluntary prayer in schools.

A similar proposal had been rejected during July 26 floor debate on an omnibus education bill (HR 11). The House instead approved a watered-down alternative that required schools to allow moments of silent prayer. *(Story, p. 493)*

Walker also planned to propose a variation on tuition tax credits. His amendment would allow money under the bill to be used to reimburse parents for part of their private-school tuition.

Members had advance notice of the controversial amendments to be offered because, under the terms for floor debate approved by the Rules Committee, all amendments had to be filed the day before HR 5609 was brought to the floor. Despite GOP objections to the restriction, the rule was adopted, 311-89. *(Vote 348, p. 106-H)* ∎

Computer Tampering

A bill to impose sizable fines and jail sentences on computer "hackers" if, for the fun of it, they tapped into or changed computerized medical records was passed Sept. 17 by the House, but the Senate did not act on the measure.

The bill (HR 5831 — H Rept 98-918), passed by voice vote in the House, authorized fines of up to $5,000 or prison sentences of up to a year for unauthorized access to computerized medical records. For unauthorized altering of the records, the fine was up to $25,000, the prison term up to 5 years.

Sponsor Ron Wyden, D-Ore., believed that the medical records problem warranted a very specific measure, an aide said. Penalties for computer tampering were included in an omnibus crime bill enacted in 1984. *(Story, p. 215)*

Wyden's bill responded to a well-publicized incident in 1983 in which teenage computer enthusiasts, using a home computer, broke into the computerized records of cancer patients at Memorial Sloan-Kettering Cancer Center in New York. Wyden told the House that the youngsters had gained access to the radiation treatment records of some 6,000 past and present patients at the center "and had at their fingertips the ability to control the radiation levels that every patient received.

"Luckily," Wyden added, "no one was hurt this time," but such computer "hacking has become a popular pastime among thousands of people. . . . Many of these people take pride in their ability to break into computer files, to beat the odds. . . . For them, it's a game."

Wyden also said that no federal statute outlawed such unauthorized entry and tampering with computerized medical records, and few state laws did so. The youngsters who broke into the Sloan-Kettering files received, Wyden said, "a slap on the wrist, two years' probation for putting so many vulnerable patients at great risk."

Howard C. Nielson, R-Utah, said he supported the intent of the measure but that it was too narrow in addressing only medical records, and too broad in its assertion of federal authority over misuse of "telecommunications" devices, including telephones. ∎

Peace Institute

After years of effort by Sen. Jennings Randolph, D-W.Va., and other members to set up a federal institution dedicated to the study of peace and conflict resolution, Congress in 1984 authorized the establishment of a U.S. Institute for Peace.

Some $6 million in fiscal 1985 and $10 million in 1986 were authorized to establish the U.S. Institute of Peace as part of the fiscal 1985 defense authorization bill (HR 5167 — PL 98-525) that cleared Congress Sept. 27. *(Story, p. 37)*

Background

The peace institute provisions of HR 5167 were similar to a bill (S 564 — S Rept 98-244) to establish a U.S. Academy of Peace that was reported in September 1983 by the Senate Labor and Human Resources Committee. That measure never reached the floor. *(1983 Almanac p. 399)*

The measure called for a federally sponsored facility to "conduct research . . . into the causes of war . . . and the elements of peace" and to develop skill in peace and conflict resolution.

It would have authorized $7.5 million for an academy site and $16 million for the first two years of operations. After initial federal funding, the academy would establish a private endowment and operate independently.

Critics contended that the plan was idealistic and fraught with danger.

1984 Action

The proposal was added to the 1984 defense authorization bill by an amendment sponsored by Sens. Mark O. Hatfield, R-Ore., Spark M. Matsunaga, D-Hawaii, and Randolph, who was retiring at the end of the session. The three had sponsored the 1983 bill as well.

The amendment, adopted by voice vote June 20, authorized $23.5 million over two years to acquire and operate a peace academy in Washington, D.C.

Conferees on the defense authorization, however, modified the proposal, dropping the Senate-passed $7.5 million capitalization fund and making the "academy" a research institute that would neither acquire property nor operate as a school. An institute grants program was named after Randolph. ∎

Agent Orange Compensation Measure Signed

President Reagan Oct. 24 signed into law a bill (HR 1961 — PL 98-542) that for the first time mandated compensation payments to some veterans who were exposed to Agent Orange, a defoliant used in Vietnam that was contaminated with a highly toxic chemical.

The new law, which required the Veterans Administration (VA) to establish a system for review of compensation claims by the Veterans Administration, based on advice from a panel of scientific experts, also acknowledged for the first time that exposure of Vietnam veterans to Agent Orange resulted in their contracting disease.

The new law also required the VA to establish a second review system, with its own scientific panel, for compensation claims by veterans who participated in atmospheric atomic weapons tests or served in occupied Hiroshima and Nagasaki, Japan. Some of these veterans said they suffered from diseases resulting from exposure to low-level ionizing radiation.

The law generally reflected the Senate version of the bill, which passed May 22. The House version, which passed Jan. 30, presumed that three specific diseases were caused by exposure to Agent Orange and three others were caused by exposure to low-level radiation.

Senators, however, were reluctant to put into law — absent conclusive scientific evidence — a presumption that all six diseases were caused by exposure to the herbicide or radiation.

Creation of the scientific advisory panels was designed to aid in determining which claims of Agent Orange- or radiation-induced death or disability had merit, and particularly to review the results of several major studies of the adverse health effects of exposure to Agent Orange and low-level radiation.

The temporary benefits mandated under the law were set to expire just before one major scientific review, being conducted by the federal Centers for Disease Control (CDC), was due to be completed. The temporary payments would be extended or terminated, depending on the results of the study.

Provisions

As signed into law, HR 1961 (PL 98-542):

● Required the administrator of the Veterans Administration to set guidelines for deciding claims for compensation due to disability or death brought by veterans exposed to Agent Orange, an herbicide known to be contaminated with dioxin, a highly toxic chemical. The exposure must have occurred in Vietnam between Aug. 5, 1964, and May 7, 1975.

● Provided disability payments from Oct. 1, 1984, until Sept. 30, 1986, for veterans suffering from chloracne, a skin disease, or porphyria cutanea tarda (PCT), a liver disorder, two diseases believed to be caused by exposure to Agent Orange.

● Required the VA to set guidelines for deciding compensation claims brought by veterans exposed to low-level ionizing radiation during atmospheric atomic tests or the U.S. occupation of Hiroshima and Nagasaki, Japan, prior to July 1, 1946.

● Required the VA to create and consult with two eight-member scientific advisory committees, whose specialties were to be the adverse health effects of dioxin exposure and low-level radiation exposure.

● Directed the VA administrator, when writing guidelines or settling claims, to give veterans the benefit of the doubt where "there is an approximate balance of positive and negative evidence regarding the merits of an issue."

● Required that final regulations establishing the guidelines for review of disability claims be published in the *Federal Register* within 300 days of enactment of the law.

Background

Passage of the new law capped a decade-long effort to obtain health care and compensation for veterans exposed to Agent Orange. In 1979, Congress first ordered a study by the VA of the health effects of Agent Orange on veterans (PL 96-151). *(1979 Almanac p. 518)*

And in 1981, veterans won a long fight to get the VA to provide medical treatment for ailments attributed to Agent Orange exposure, with passage of a law (PL 97-72) that also granted medical care to veterans who were exposed to low-level radiation. The law also expanded the Agent Orange health-effects study that was ordered in 1979. Conduct of that study was eventually transferred from the VA to the CDC. *(1981 Almanac p. 481)*

Just before adjourning in November 1983, Congress in a major veterans' health-care bill (PL 98-160) asked the VA to conduct a study of the long-term health effects of exposure to low-level radiation, and agreed in a supplemental appropriations bill (PL 98-181) to spend $54 million on the CDC Agent Orange study. *(1983 Almanac pp. 410, 536)*

But, until enactment of HR 1961, Congress had set no policy on disability payments to veterans who claimed injury in the line of duty from radiation or Agent Orange exposure, and the VA had handled claims brought by veterans one by one.

Vietnam veterans blamed a variety of diseases, as well as birth defects in their children, on Agent Orange exposure. Specifically, such exposure was believed by some to cause chloracne, a skin rash; porphyria cutanea tarda, a liver condition that could affect up to 150,000 Vietnam veterans; and a cancer known as soft-tissue sarcoma, an often fatal disease that could affect about 30 Vietnam veterans a year.

Some veterans exposed to low-level ionizing radiation claimed the exposure caused cancer of the thyroid; polycythemia vera, a rare disease of the bone marrow; and leukemia.

Numbers Affected

At the time of final passage of HR 1961, Sen. Alan Cranston, D-Calif., ranking member of the Committee on Veterans' Affairs, said that about 200,000 veterans had been exposed to radiation during atmospheric tests and another 110,000 had been exposed in Hiroshima and Nagasaki, according to figures from the Defense Nuclear Agency.

Cranston said the VA had received 2,566 claims relating to radiation exposure, including 985 involving malignancies, and 21,693 claims relating to Agent Orange exposure. Only 30 veterans had received compensation for diseases believed to be caused by exposure to radiation and 25 had been compensated for exposure to Agent Orange, Cranston said.

History of Agent Orange

Code-named Agent Orange because of the color of the drums in which it was stored, an estimated 52 million pounds of the herbicide — a combination of 2,4-D and 2,4,5-T — were sprayed in South Vietnam between 1961 and 1971 to defoliate trees and destroy crops. The herbicide contained varying quantities of dioxin, a contaminant created in the manufacturing process of 2,4,5-T and one of the most toxic substances known.

Dozens of studies on the health effects of Agent Orange were begun, the largest being the one conducted by the CDC, expected to be completed by 1987 or 1988.

Preliminary findings from the CDC study, released in August 1984, revealed that veterans exposed to Agent Orange generally had no increased risk of fathering children with birth defects; however, the study found that the risk of fathering babies with certain specific birth defects — spina bifida, cleft lip and certain tumors — was higher for veterans exposed to Agent Orange, than for the population at large.

But studies by the Office of Technology Assessment and other groups, conducted at Cranston's request, showed that the risk to veterans of fathering children with those particular birth defects was not as great as the CDC had presumed.

Enactment of HR 1961 granted the second major disability package to Agent Orange victims in a matter of weeks. On Sept. 25, Judge Jack B. Weinstein of the U.S. District Court for the Eastern District of New York gave formal approval to an agreement reached in May between lawyers for Vietnam veterans and lawyers for seven major chemical companies that produced the defoliant.

The agreement established a fund of $180 million, which was expected to reach $250 million by 1986 to 1990, when veterans would be able to draw on it. The chemical companies were to pay into the fund to compensate those exposed to Agent Orange. Details of who would be eligible to receive money from the fund and the amount of payments were unresolved in late 1984.

One party not named in the suit was the federal government, which contracted with the chemical companies to produce the herbicide during the Vietnam War. Veterans were prohibited by law from suing the government for actions committed during wartime, but spouses and children of Vietnam veterans had a suit pending against the federal government. The chemical companies also sued the federal government to reimburse them for the $180 million. These suits remained unresolved in late 1984.

Legislative Action

House Action

In July 1983, the House Veterans' Affairs Subcommittee on Compensation, Pensions and Insurance approved HR 1961. The House Committee on Veterans' Affairs amended the bill Nov. 3, 1983, to extend coverage to veterans exposed to radiation, and then approved HR 1961 the same day by a 30-0 vote. The committee reported the bill Jan. 25, 1984 (H Rept 98-592).

The committee bill represented a compromise between members who wanted to compensate veterans for a number of diseases they blamed on their exposure to Agent Orange and radiation, and those who wanted to delay action until the CDC study was finished. The compromise authorized payments to veterans until one year after completion of the study, at which time payments could be continued, if deemed warranted by the study results.

Payments under the bill would have been made to veterans exposed to Agent Orange who, within 20 years of their service in Southeast Asia, contracted soft-tissue sarcoma, or within one year contracted PCT or chloracne.

Disability payments also would have been made to veterans exposed to radiation at atomic tests or in Hiroshima and Nagasaki, if within 20 years of the exposure they contracted cancer of the thyroid, polycythemia veta or leukemia.

The committee bill also authorized death benefits for these veterans' survivors.

The VA and several veterans' advocacy groups opposed the bill, arguing that it presumed that any veteran who served in Southeast Asia during the Vietnam era had been exposed to Agent Orange, and noting that scientific evidence linking Agent Orange with the diseases named in the bill was uncertain.

The Congressional Budget Office estimated the bill would cost $4.7 million in fiscal 1984 and $25.5 million over five years.

By voice vote, the House passed the bill Jan. 30 under suspension of the rules, a procedure that allowed no amendments and required a two-thirds majority for passage.

Senate Action

The Senate Committee on Veterans' Affairs, headed by Alan K. Simpson, R-Wyo., in 1983 had before it — but did not act on — a Cranston-sponsored bill (S 1651) that would have required the VA to set guidelines for compensating veterans who contracted diseases they claimed were caused by exposure to Agent Orange, or to low-level radiation.

In April 1984, Simpson sponsored a non-binding resolution (S Res 372), that simply urged the VA to set guidelines for reviewing scientific studies and for resolving claims relating to Agent Orange and radiation exposure.

Although Simpson said he secured a pledge from the VA to abide by his resolution, several veterans' groups — including The American Legion, the Disabled American Veterans, the Veterans of Foreign Wars and the Vietnam Veterans of America — insisted that the VA be required by law to set compensation guidelines.

In addition, the veterans' organizations preferred Cranston's approach, which would have allowed judicial review of agency decisions on compensation claims.

The Senate committee did not take action on Cranston's bill in 1983, but Cranston tried and failed on a 6-6 committee vote to attach the provisions of S 1651 to a separate veterans' compensation bill (S 1388).

Cranston then threatened to try to attach the Agent Orange and radiation disability provisions to S 1388 when it came to the floor. He withdrew his amendment, however, when the Senate agreed to consider S 1651 in early 1984. *(1983 Almanac p. 27; compensation bill, p. 501)*

After Simpson introduced his resolution, he and Cranston negotiated a compromise version of S 1651, retaining the key provisions of Cranston's bill that required the VA to write guidelines for settling claims and allowed judicial review. The two senators reached agreement on the final version of the bill hours before Senate consideration, winning support from major veterans' groups and the administration.

The Senate by voice vote May 22 adopted amendments to the Cranston-Simpson compromise defining the makeup of a scientific advisory committee created by the bill to review studies relating to Agent Orange and radiation exposure, limiting the amount of evidence a veteran would have had to submit to prove exposure, and stressing the link between malignant cancer and radiation exposure.

The Senate then adopted by a 95-0 vote the Cranston-Simpson compromise as a substitute amendment to S 1651. *(Vote 107, p. 20-S)*

By unanimous consent the Senate then substituted the language of S 1651 for the language of HR 1961, and requested a conference with the House on HR 1961.

Final Action

There were two major differences between the Senate and House versions of the bill. One was the House version's presumption that specific diseases were caused by exposure to Agent Orange and radiation; Cranston preferred to require the VA to write guidelines for reviewing claims of disability. The second difference was Cranston's judicial review provision; there was nothing like it in the House bill.

House and Senate conferees informally worked out a compromise between the two.

The compromise, which accepted the Senate approach of requiring the VA to write guidelines, also allowed temporary disability payments to veterans who suffered from two diseases believed to be caused by Agent Orange. Only veterans who served in Vietnam, not all of Southeast Asia, were covered by that provision, unlike in the earlier House version.

The compromise dropped the Senate provision that allowed judicial review of VA guidelines and claims decisions.

The House, by unanimous consent Oct. 3, adopted the compromise as a House amendment to HR 1961.

By voice vote Oct. 4, the Senate also adopted the House amendment, clearing the bill for the president. ∎

Disabled Veterans' COLA

Congress Feb. 9 cleared legislation (S 1388 — PL 98-223) authorizing a 3.5 percent cost-of-living adjustment (COLA) in disabled veterans' compensation benefits.

The increase, effective April 1, 1984, affected benefits paid to some 2.25 million disabled veterans and their families, as well as to about 300,000 survivors of veterans who died of service-connected causes.

S 1388, which also made a number of other changes in veterans' programs, was the first of two veterans' COLA bills approved by Congress in 1984. HR 5688 (PL 98-543), cleared Oct. 9, provided another 3.2 percent increase, effective Dec. 1, 1984. That bill also increased G.I. Bill and other veterans' educational benefits. *(Story, p. 502)*

In passing S 1388, Congress endorsed one of President Reagan's fiscal 1985 budget recommendations — a 3.5 percent COLA for disabled veterans, their families and survivors, effective April 1, 1984. However, it also expressed the sense of Congress that the next COLA should take effect Dec. 1, 1984 — not April 1, 1985, as Reagan had requested.

Legislative History

As cleared, S 1388 was a compromise containing provisions from several bills passed by the House and Senate.

The Senate had passed its version of the bill Nov. 18,

1983. It authorized a 3.5 percent COLA and contained a number of provisions from two House-passed veterans' bills (HR 2936, HR 2948), which expanded the Board of Veterans Appeals and made changes in the Veterans Administration (VA) home loan guaranty program. *(1983 Almanac p. 604)*

Also in 1983, the House Veterans' Affairs Committee reported a bill (HR 2937) authorizing a 4.1 percent COLA for disabled veterans. That bill became part of the budget reconciliation bill (HR 4169) passed by the House Oct. 25, 1983. The veterans' provisions were deleted when HR 4169 cleared in April 1984. *(Story, p. 160)*

Staffs of the House and Senate Veterans' Affairs committees worked out a compromise version of S 1388, which the House accepted by voice vote Feb. 8, the Senate Feb. 9.

Provisions

As cleared, S 1388 (PL 98-223):

● Increased disability benefits for veterans, dependents and survivors, and increased clothing allowances for certain disabled veterans, by 3.5 percent, effective April 1, 1984.

● Expressed the sense of Congress that future increases for veterans, dependents and survivors take effect on Dec. 1 of the fiscal year involved.

● Provided service-connected disability payments for former prisoners of war suffering from dysthymic disorder, or depressive neurosis.

● Increased benefits for blinded veterans who also suffered hearing loss from service-connected injuries.

● Provided that when a veteran received hospital care in excess of 21 days in one month for a service-connected disability, the period for payment of increased compensation on account of such care would begin the first day of that month.

● Permitted an adopted child to receive benefits even though the child was 18 or over at the time of adoption, if the child was incapable of self-support at age 18 and was a member of the veteran's household.

● Extended through fiscal 1989 authority to provide matching-fund grants to states for establishing, expanding or improving state veterans' cemeteries.

● Permitted certain Vietnam-era veterans ineligible for the Post-Vietnam Era Educational Assistance Program (VEAP), to elect to participate in VEAP in lieu of G.I. Bill benefits.

● Conformed the level of survivors' educational assistance benefits for high school training to the level of Vietnam-era veterans' G.I. Bill benefits for such training.

● Barred concurrent receipt of benefits under more than one educational assistance program administered by the VA for pursuit of one program of education.

● Allowed restoration of VA home loan guaranty entitlement when a property was sold by a veteran-purchaser to a non-veteran and subsequently resold to an eligible veteran, if the new veteran-purchaser substituted his entitlement.

● Provided for the guaranty of a loan to a veteran for the purchase of a manufactured home if the lot on which the home was permanently affixed was owned or being purchased by the veteran, and the home, as affixed, was regarded as real property by the state.

● Expanded eligibility for veterans' employment and training programs to veterans with 10 or 20 percent disability, if the veteran was determined to have a serious employment handicap.

● Authorized the VA to permit VA-appointed fiduciaries to deduct from beneficiaries' estates certain limited commissions for services at the administrator's discretion.

• Expanded from 50 to 65 the number of members of the Board of Veterans Appeals.

• Expanded the membership of the Special Medical Advisory Group to include individuals, other than members of health and allied professionals specified in current law, who had experience pertinent to the missions of the VA's Department of Medicine and Surgery.

• Expedited certain medical facility construction by authorizing the administrator to obligate up to $25 million in fiscal 1985 for working drawings.

• Provided that the Springfield, Mo., Confederate Cemetery become the Springfield National Cemetery, and removed the restriction that permitted the burial of only Confederate veterans there.

• Authorized benefits for Senior Reserve Officers Training Corps members who incurred disabilities before Oct. 1, 1982.   ∎

COLA, Education Benefits

Congress Oct. 9 cleared a bill (HR 5688 — PL 98-543) authorizing a 3.2 percent increase in disabled veterans' compensation benefits, effective Dec. 1, 1984.

The bill also provided a 10 percent increase in G.I. Bill and other veterans' education and rehabilitation benefits, effective Oct. 1, 1984.

President Reagan had requested a 4.3 percent cost-of-living adjustment (COLA) for disabled veterans, their families and survivors, to take effect April 1, 1985. Both the Senate and the House approved COLAs exceeding that level, but based on Congressional Budget Office (CBO) projections of lower inflation, in October Congress agreed to the 3.2 percent figure. It refused to delay the increase to April, however.

Provisions of HR 5688 affecting the G.I. Bill and other veterans' education and employment programs originally were part of a separate measure (HR 5398) that passed the House Aug. 6. Also included in HR 5688 were provisions of a bill passed by the House May 21 (HR 5617 — H Rept 98-776) that increased grants for specially adapted housing for disabled veterans.

HR 5688 was the second veterans' COLA bill enacted in 1984. An earlier bill (S 1388 — PL 98-223), cleared in February, authorized a 3.5 percent increase effective April 1, 1984, and stated that the next COLA should take effect on Dec. 1, 1984. *(Story, p. 501)*

Provisions

As cleared, HR 5688 (PL 98-543):

• Authorized a 3.2 percent cost-of-living increase in compensation benefits for disabled veterans, their dependents and survivors, effective Dec. 1, 1984.

• Authorized a 10 percent increase in veterans' education assistance benefits, including the G.I. Bill and vocational rehabilitation benefits, effective Oct. 1, 1984.

• Extended for two years, until Sept. 30, 1986, the veterans readjustment appointment program, which helped handicapped veterans get non-competitive appointments to federal jobs.

• Established a four-year pilot program providing education and vocational training for veterans under age 50 who were eligible for disability pensions.

• Established a four-year trial work period for 100 percent service-connected disabled veterans who might, with additional education and training, be able to work. Veterans would not lose their disabled rating while in the program.

• Extended certain provisions of the emergency veterans' job training program enacted in 1983 (PL 98-77). The bill gave veterans an additional three months (to Feb. 29, 1985) to sign up for the program and an extra six months (to Sept. 1, 1985) to begin their training. It also extended the availability of appropriated funds under the program for one year. *(1983 bill, 1983 Almanac p. 599)*

• Increased the limit on grants to severely disabled veterans for specially adapted housing to $35,500, from $32,500, and for automotive adaptive equipment to $5,000, from $4,400, effective Jan. 1, 1985.

Legislative History

HR 5688 was reported by the House Veterans' Affairs Committee June 7 (H Rept 98-828) and passed the House by voice vote under suspension of the rules on June 18.

The bill provided for a 4.3 percent cost-of-living increase in disabled veterans' compensation benefits, effective Dec. 1, 1984. It also called for establishment within the Veterans Administration of an advisory committee on "atomic veterans" — those exposed to ionizing radiation from atomic weapons testing or during the occupation of Hiroshima and Nagasaki after World War II.

The bill also contained provisions to add systemic lupus erythematosus to the list of diseases presumed to be service-connected, if contracted within a year after leaving the service; increase the automobile allowance for certain disabled veterans; increase the maximum servicemen's group life insurance benefit; and establish a pilot program of vocational training assistance for certain disabled veterans under age 50.

The CBO estimated outlays under the bill at $331.5 million in fiscal 1985, and $2.1 billion over fiscal 1985-89.

HR 5398

The House Veterans' Affairs Committee had reported HR 5398, the Veterans' Education and Employment Amendments of 1984, on May 15 (H Rept 98-775). The House passed the measure by voice vote under suspension of the rules on Aug. 6.

As passed by the House, the bill authorized a 15 percent increase in veterans' education benefits, effective Jan. 1, 1985; extended the veterans' readjustment appointment program, known as VRA, which was to expire Sept. 30, 1984; and extended certain provisions of the 1983 emergency veterans' job training act.

The increases in G.I. Bill benefits and vocational rehabilitation subsistence allowances were the first since 1981, Rep. Marvin Leath, D-Texas, told the House. The benefits were increased then by PL 96-466, enacted in 1980. *(1980 Almanac p. 438)*

About 461,200 Vietnam-era veterans were expected to receive G.I. Bill benefits in 1985, Leath said, while about 33,000 disabled veterans would receive vocational training. Under the VRA program, established in 1970, more than 200,000 disabled and educationally disadvantaged Vietnam-era veterans had been placed in federal jobs.

Senate Action

Committee. The Senate Veterans' Affairs Committee

July 25 approved a 4.7 percent COLA for disabled veterans, to take effect Dec. 1 even if the Consumer Price Index were below 4.7 percent. The committee reported its bill Sept. 17 (S 2736 — S Rept 98-604).

The bill also authorized a 10 percent increase in veterans' education and vocational rehabilitation benefits; established a pilot work program for totally disabled veterans; extended the VRA program and the sign-up period for the emergency job training program; and increased housing and automobile assistance grants for disabled veterans.

The CBO estimated outlays under the bill at $510.9 million in fiscal 1985 and $679 million in fiscal 1986.

Floor. The Senate passed the bill by voice vote Oct. 2, after adopting several amendments, including one raising servicemen's life insurance benefits to $50,000, from $35,000.

Final Action

The House Oct. 5 accepted the Senate version of HR 5688 with amendments reflecting bill sponsors' agreement on a 3.2 percent COLA and compromises between the two versions of the legislation.

The Senate agreed to the House amendments Oct. 9, clearing the bill for the president.

The final version did not include a House provision adding lupus to the list of service-connected diseases, nor did it contain an increase in servicemen's life insurance benefits approved by both chambers.

The House provision to establish an advisory committee on "atomic veterans" also was not included in HR 5688 but became part of another bill (HR 1961 — PL 98-542) instead. *(Story, p. 499)* ∎

Veterans' Health Care

Congress Oct. 3 cleared a bill (HR 5618 — PL 98-528) authorizing special programs for the treatment of veterans suffering from post-traumatic stress disorder, a condition affecting many Vietnam veterans.

The measure also directed the Veterans Administration (VA) to set up guidelines for treatment of veterans for drug and alcohol abuse and dependency, and made other changes in veterans' health care programs.

Although the administration had opposed the provision calling for the establishment of treatment units for veterans suffering from post-traumatic stress disorder, President Reagan signed the bill into law.

The administration also opposed a House-passed provision that would have allowed the VA to fill prescriptions written by private physicians for treatment of veterans' service-connected disabilities. That provision was dropped from the final version of the bill.

Provisions

As signed into law, HR 5618 (PL 98-528):

● Authorized the VA to establish special programs for the treatment of veterans suffering from post-traumatic stress disorder.

● Authorized special programs for training health care personnel in the treatment of post-traumatic stress disorder.

● Directed the VA, after consulting with the attorney general, to issue regulations for security in VA facilities, including rules for conduct on VA property and penalties for violations of the rules. The VA could also set rules for enforcement and arrest authority of VA police officers.

● Directed the VA to provide guidelines for treatment of veterans for drug and alcohol abuse and dependency.

● Provided permanent authorization for the research and education activities of VA Geriatric Research, Education and Clinical Centers, which were to expire Sept. 30, 1984, and authorized "such sums as may be necessary" for the programs.

● Authorized grants to states for acquiring existing buildings to be used as health care facilities. Existing law had allowed grants only for new buildings.

● Required the VA to coordinate its health care programs with state, local and private programs, and to place special emphasis on veterans 65 or older.

● Authorized the VA to provide devices, including telecaptioning television decoders, to deaf disabled veterans.

● Required the VA to report by Sept. 30, 1985, on its programs for terminally ill veterans; also required a study of health-care services for veterans living in areas far from VA health-care facilities.

Legislative History

House. The House Veterans' Affairs Committee reported HR 5618 on May 15 (H Rept 98-779). The House passed the measure May 21 by voice vote under suspension of the rules, despite administration opposition to several major provisions.

The VA opposed provisions calling for the establishment of treatment units for veterans suffering from post-traumatic stress disorder, and allowing the VA to fill prescriptions written by private physicians for treatment of veterans' service-connected disabilities.

Under existing law, the VA could fill prescriptions only for veterans permanently housebound or in need of regular aid and attendance. VA Deputy Administrator Everett Alvarez Jr. said the provision in HR 5618 would significantly increase the potential for abuse and would require unwieldy administrative procedures.

Senate, Final Action. The Senate Veterans' Affairs Committee reported a similar veterans' health care bill on May 25 (S 2514 — S Rept 98-487). The Senate passed the legislation Aug. 8.

The House and Senate Veterans' Affairs Committees subsequently worked out a compromise between the two versions. The Senate panel objected to the prescription provision, and it was dropped from the bill. Also dropped was a Senate provision extending for two years, through Sept. 30, 1987, the VA's authority to contract with non-VA half-way houses and other community-based programs to provide drug and alcohol abuse treatment for veterans. The House committee said it planned to hold hearings on the issue in 1985.

The House accepted the compromise version Oct. 2; the Senate, Oct. 3. ∎

Veterans' Job Preference

The House July 30 passed a bill (HR 5799) providing job security for veterans employed by the federal government as guards, custodians, elevator operators and messengers. However, the Senate took no action on the measure so it did not become law.

The bill was reported by the Post Office and Civil Service Committee July 27 (H Rept 98-915). It passed the House by voice vote under suspension of the rules.

The Reagan administration strongly opposed the bill, arguing that it tied the government's hands in trying to contract out services, which the administration said saved money. The Congressional Budget Office estimated the bill would result in $5 million in lost savings in fiscal 1985.

Under existing law, the four positions were reserved for veterans, unless no veterans were available. HR 5799 would have prohibited agencies from contracting out those positions if the contract would result in the veterans losing their jobs; it would have allowed agencies to reassign or transfer the veterans, if certain conditions were met.

The bill also would have required federal agencies, in contracting out services, to consider first hiring workers from sheltered workshops for the blind and severely handicapped.

Veterans' Group Charter

Despite opposition from the Veterans of Foreign Wars (VFW), the House voted 295-96 June 11 to grant a federal charter to the Vietnam Veterans of America Inc. (VVA). However, the Senate did not act on the bill. *(Vote 200, p. 64-H)*

The House bill (HR 4772) was reported by the Judiciary Committee June 6 (H Rept 98-822).

The VFW objected to granting a federal charter for the 16,000-member organization because of differences it had with VVA President Robert E. Muller. In a letter to VFW officials, Cooper T. Holt, executive director of the VFW's Washington office, called Muller "a propaganda conduit for the communist government of Vietnam." Muller had visited Hanoi, and on one occasion, laid a wreath on the tomb of North Vietnam's former president, Ho Chi Minh.

SPECIAL REPORTS

CQ

Court Swings to Right, Reagan Wins Victories

President Reagan was the big winner of the Supreme Court's 1983-84 term.

In a series of major decisions, the high court put its stamp of approval on the administration's proposals for significant changes in national policy on questions of civil and individual rights, business, environmental and criminal law.

The string of victories marked a dramatic comeback for the White House. During Reagan's first three years in office, the high court repeatedly rebuffed administration arguments that it was time to rethink the court's position on matters ranging from abortion and busing to tax policy and affirmative action.

In 1984, however, the court found the administration's arguments — presented by Solicitor General Rex E. Lee and his office — considerably more persuasive.

A Conservative Court

Reagan's victories were only the most visible aspect of the most conservative court term in decades.

The 1983-84 term — the 15th since Warren E. Burger took over the chief justice's post from Earl Warren — looked like a watershed term, one in which the Supreme Court turned firmly away from judicial activism aimed at enlarging individual rights to a new posture of committed conservativism.

In virtually every area of the law, the court swung its weight to the side of the government, deferring to the authority of Congress, the executive branch, states and cities. Of all the groups whose rights were argued before the court this term, only women came away with notable victories. And even they could not claim a clean sweep.

The court this term declared laws or government practices in violation of the Constitution in only 17 of the more than 150 cases it decided. Fifteen of those involved state laws or practices; only two concerned federal laws. Those two were the law barring editorializing by public broadcast stations and part of a law limiting photographic depictions of U.S. currency.

Time and again, the court reversed rulings by the 12 regional U.S. circuit courts of appeals, which were dominated by relatively liberal judges named by Democratic presidents, particularly President Jimmy Carter. The court reversed lower courts in 93 cases, affirming them in only 38 — a clear contrast with the 1982-83 term, when it reversed 80, but affirmed 55.

Two appeals courts on which appointees of Democratic presidents decisively outnumbered those of GOP executives chalked up the worst win-loss records before the Supreme Court. The justices reversed all eight of the decisions they reviewed from the U.S. Court of Appeals for the District of Columbia, long a bastion of liberalism. Seven of that court's 11 judges were Democratic appointees. But even this record was outdone by the frequency with which the high court reversed decisions of the 9th U.S. Circuit Court of Appeals, the nation's largest with 23 judges — 16 of them Democratic appointees. The court reviewed 27

decisions of this appeals court, which is based in San Francisco. It found only one to affirm without qualification; 23 were reversed outright.

Election-year concern about the effect of a second term for Reagan, in which he might appoint additional conservative justices, seemed almost irrelevant for the short term. By replacing the moderate Potter Stewart with the conservative Sandra Day O'Connor in 1981, Reagan had already tipped the balance of the court to the right. Additional Reagan justices would merely reinforce that trend — and ensure that it continued into the future.

In criminal law, the court's record in the 1980s turned decidedly conservative, favoring the arguments of prosecutors and police three or four times as often as those of defendants. That trend continued and intensified in 1984, as the justices carved out major new exceptions to key evidentiary rules aimed at protecting the rights of suspects.

Despite its conservative views on criminal law, until this term the court had continued the Warren court's tradition of enlarging the Constitution's protection for individual rights and civil rights, and expanding the scope of First Amendment guarantees.

In the 1983-84 term, however, the court breached that tradition as often as it honored it. The justices voted to limit the reach of affirmative action, to narrow the scope of the ban on sex discrimination by federally aided colleges, and to make clear that the Constitution provides little protection for the privacy or property of prison inmates. The court also found no constitutional problems in Congress' decision to deny federal education aid to young men who failed to register for the draft, or in a city's move to ban political signs on public property.

Blackmun, White Swing to Right

The court was unanimous or nearly so in an unusually high percentage of its cases. Almost 70 percent of its decisions came without dissent or by votes of 8-1 or 7-2, up from 60 percent in the last term.

When only one member of the court dissented, it was usually Justice John Paul Stevens, maintaining his maverick reputation. When two justices dissented, they were Thurgood Marshall and William J. Brennan Jr. And in well over half of the cases decided by 6-3 votes, the three were Stevens, Brennan and Marshall.

Justices Byron R. White and Harry A. Blackmun cast the key votes defining the term's conservative character.

As in the 1982-83 term, White was the swing vote in a number of cases, and this term, he swung more often to the conservative than to the liberal side. When the court divided 6-3 or 5-4, White voted with the liberals in only one of every four cases, a definite change from the previous term, when he had joined the liberals — Brennan, Marshall, Stevens and Blackmun — on one of every three close cases.

Justice Blackmun, a reliable new ally of the court's liberals during the 1982-83 term, pulled away from them this time around. He voted with the conservative majority on most of the major issues of the term — particularly in the field of criminal law, but also to narrow the reach of affirmative action and of the law banning sex discrimination. Altogether, Blackmun sided with the liberals only half as often on close cases this term as last.

The Reagan Record

Although the administration fared far better than in 1982-83, when it sometimes commanded the vote of no more than one justice, President Reagan won many of his legal victories by narrow 5-4 and 6-3 margins.

Reagan's success was due in part to the choice of issues upon which the administration took a position. Last term's major setbacks came on abortion, tax exemptions for discriminatory private schools, and rescission of auto seat-belt and air-bag regulations.

In all three, the solicitor general was asking the court to approve major changes in settled areas of law and public policy, changes sought primarily by conservative activists or by big business.

This time, the administration took its stand on less explosive issues, endorsing positions supported by a broader constituency in the nation at large.

Arguing that the primary goal of Warren court rulings separating church and state or guaranteeing fair treatment for criminal suspects had been attained, the solicitor general told the justices that lower courts were taking the precedents one step too far — a trend the court should halt.

Voluntarily joining pending cases as a "friend of the court," Solicitor General Lee successfully urged the justices to permit more public use of religious symbols, to curtail the reach of affirmative action, and to approve new exceptions to the controversial exclusionary rule, which barred use in criminal trials of illegally obtained evidence.

In the major policy-change cases in which the government was itself a party, administration attorneys skillfully tailored their arguments to the justices' inclination to take a literal, restrictive view on questions of statutory law.

The justices approved a narrow reading of key sections of the Clean Air Act and of Title IX of the 1972 Education Amendments, the ban on sex discrimination by federally funded education programs. And in so doing, the high court contributed to a major goal of the Reagan administration: easing the burden of federal regulation of American life.

Judicial Restraint

Reagan's representatives capitalized on the fact that he and a majority of the justices shared the belief that the role of the federal judiciary was a limited one — that judges had no business making policy, but should defer to the judgment of Congress and the executive unless a constitutional breach or clear abuse of administrative discretion was involved.

The administration sounded this theme repeatedly in its arguments, and the justices responded in the same key. Time and again, the nation's most powerful judges curtailed the authority of other federal judges to enforce federal and state laws, insisting that the judiciary should generally defer to the "political" branches of government.

"Federal judges — who have no constituency — have a duty to respect legitimate policy choices made by those who do," the court declared June 25 in a case involving interpretation of the Clean Air Act.

Upholding the administration's power to restrict travel to Cuba, the court June 28 reiterated an earlier dictate that matters relating to the conduct of foreign relations "are so exclusively entrusted to the political branches of government as to be largely immune from judicial inquiry or interference."

And a day later, as it upheld the administration's rule banning overnight sleeping by demonstrators in Lafayette Park, White declared that nothing in the court's precedents "assign to the judiciary the authority to replace the Park Service as the manager of the nation's parks or endow the judiciary with the competence to judge how much protection of park lands is wise. . . ."

The Close Calls

When the intent of Congress was difficult to discern, a divided court sometimes invited it to clarify matters. On Jan. 17, for example, the justices split 5-4 in declaring that home videotape recording does not violate copyright laws as presently written.

"One may search the Copyright Act in vain for any sign that the elected representatives of the millions of people who watch television every day have made it unlawful to copy a program for later viewing at home, or have enacted a flat prohibition against the sale of machines that make such copying possible," wrote Justice Stevens for the majority.

The four dissenters claimed that neither had Congress included home video recording in the category of activities expressly exempted from copyright coverage. "Like so many other problems created by the interaction of copyright law with a new technology, there can be no really satisfactory solution to the problem presented here until Congress acts," said Justice Blackmun.

In the case of video recorders and copyright law, Congress ducked the invitation to act. Although several bills on the subject were considered during the 98th Congress, none advanced beyond the hearing stage.

However, Congress did respond vigorously to other controversial court decisions. It flatly reversed a 5-4 ruling that permitted companies filing for bankruptcy to abrogate unilaterally their collective bargaining agreements, and modified a 9-0 ruling in the same case that set forth standards a bankruptcy judge must use in reviewing company requests to scrap their labor contracts.

Seeking to overturn another 5-4 decision, the House overwhelmingly passed legislation to make clear that if any part of an institution received federal funds, the entire institution was subject to federal bans on discrimination based on sex, race, age or handicap. The court had ruled that only the particular program receiving funds was subject to anti-bias coverage. Although Senate backers of the House civil rights bill won a test vote, they were unable to break through a procedural snarl at the end of the session in time to act on the legislation.

That legislation seemed certain to reappear in the 99th Congress, which convened in January 1985, along with bills to overturn at least two other 1984 Supreme Court decisions — one curbing state involvement in offshore oil leasing and another denying attorneys' fees to parents who prevail in suits aimed at forcing local schools to provide services to their handicapped children, as required by federal law.

—By Elder Witt

Major Decisions, 1983-1984 Term

CRIMINAL LAW

Search and Seizure

Michigan v. Clifford, decided by a 5-4 vote, Jan. 11, 1984. Powell announced the decision in an opinion joined by three other justices; Stevens concurred; Rehnquist, Burger, Burger, Blackmun and O'Connor dissented.

The warrantless entry and search of a burned residence five hours after the fire was extinguished, without notice to the absent residents of the dwelling, was a violation of the Fourth Amendment guarantee against unreasonable search and seizure.

Colorado v. Nunez, decided by a 9-0 vote, Feb. 21, 1984. *Per curiam* (unsigned) opinion.

The court dismissed this case after hearing arguments by state prosecutors challenging a state court's decision to suppress evidence because it had been obtained with a search warrant issued on the basis of an informer's tip and the state would not disclose the identity of the informer. The justices decided that the state court's decision was based on state law, not federal law, and thus should be left intact.

United States v. Jacobsen, decided by a 7-2 vote, April 2, 1984. Stevens wrote the opinion; Brennan and Marshall dissented.

A federal narcotics agent is not required to obtain a warrant before conducting a chemical test on the contents of a damaged package handed over to the federal agent by a private company. A test that merely determines the identity of a substance does not compromise any legitimate privacy interest and thus need not be authorized by a warrant.

Oliver v. United States, Maine v. Thornton, decided by a 6-3 vote, April 17, 1984. Powell wrote the opinion; Marshall, Brennan and Stevens dissented.

Police need not obtain search warrants before searching privately owned open fields, even if the fields are marked by "no trespassing" signs and enclosed by gates and fences. One cannot legitimately expect that activities conducted outdoors in fields will remain private.

Immigration and Naturalization Service v. Delgado, decided by a 7-2 vote, April 17, 1984. Rehnquist wrote the opinion; Brennan and Marshall dissented.

Immigration agents need not obtain warrants, or have evidence that some workers at a particular factory are illegal aliens, before they move into a factory and "sweep" through it questioning workers about their citizenship. Such a "sweep" is not a seizure of the work force, since employees are free to move about and to leave as long as they answer questions about their citizenship to the satisfaction of the federal agents.

Welsh v. Wisconsin, decided by a 7-2 vote, May 15, 1984. Brennan wrote the opinion; White and Rehnquist dissented.

Police violated the Fourth Amendment's guarantee of privacy and security when they entered a home at night without a warrant in order to arrest the occupant for drunken driving. An immediate arrest was not justified by any special circumstances; the police should have obtained a warrant.

United States v. Karo, decided by a 6-3 vote, July 3, 1984. White wrote the opinion; Brennan, Marshall and Stevens dissented.

Federal agents did not violate the guarantee against unreasonable searches when they installed a beeper inside a can of ether purchased by suspected drug dealers and then followed the dealers by monitoring the beeper.

Warrantless use of the beeper to verify that the can was taken into a private home and use of that information as the basis for a search warrant for the home was a violation of the Fourth Amendment rights of the occupants of the house, but the warrant was justified on the basis of other untainted information.

Hudson v. Palmer, decided by votes of 9-0 and 5-4, July 3, 1984. Burger wrote the opinion; Stevens, Brennan, Blackmun and Marshall dissented.

The Fourth Amendment guarantee against unreasonable search and seizure does not apply in prison cells. Prisoners have no reasonable expectation of privacy in their cells and are subject to random searches at any time.

As long as state law provides a remedy for a guard's intentional destruction of an inmate's personal property, such destruction does not deny the inmate due process of law.

United States v. Leon, decided by a 6-3 vote, July 5, 1984. White wrote the opinion; Brennan, Marshall and Stevens dissented.

Illegally obtained evidence may be used at a trial if the police who seized it had obtained a search warrant and thought they were acting legally. The court approved this "good faith" exception to the exclusionary rule it had adopted 70 years earlier forbidding the use of such evidence at a trial. Prosecutors had long been urging such an exception.

The court's decision in this case was limited to a situation in which police obtained a warrant and executed a search in accord with it, only to have the warrant later found to be defective. In such an instance, excluding valid evidence found in the search has no deterrent effect on police misconduct and exacts too high a price from society, the court held.

Massachusetts v. Sheppard, decided by a 7-2 vote, July 5, 1984. White wrote the opinion; Brennan and Marshall dissented.

The exclusionary rule need not be applied to exclude evidence obtained in a search authorized by a warrant that subsequently was held invalid because of a technical mistake on the part of the judge issuing it. This was the court's first application of the "good faith" exception to the rule adopted in *United States v. Leon* (above).

Segura v. United States, decided by a 5-4 vote, July 5, 1984. Burger wrote the opinion; Stevens, Brennan, Marshall and Blackmun dissented.

An illegal entry by police into an apartment, without a warrant, for the purpose of securing the premises does not require the exclusion of evidence taken later from that residence pursuant to a search authorized by a valid search warrant based upon information possessed by police before their illegal entry.

Self-Incrimination

Minnesota v. Murphy, decided by a 6-3 vote, Feb. 22, 1984. White wrote the opinion; Marshall, Stevens and Brennan dissented.

A probationer's statements to his probation officer are admissible in court. A probationer is not "in custody" when he is talking with his probation officer, and *Miranda v. Arizona* (1966) thus does not require that he be warned of his rights before being asked about crimes.

United States v. Doe, decided by votes of 9-0 and 6-3, Feb. 28, 1984. Powell wrote the opinion; Marshall, Brennan and Stevens dissented in part.

The Fifth Amendment guarantee against compelled self-incrimination cannot be claimed by a businessman to avoid disclosure of voluntarily prepared business records of a sole proprietorship, the court held 6-3.

However, the court unanimously agreed that the government is required to grant at least a limited immunity from prosecution to a businessman producing such records under subpoena if it appears that his compliance — tacit admission that the records exist and are in his possession — may be incriminating.

New York v. Quarles, decided by votes of 5-4 and 6-3, June 12, 1984. Rehnquist wrote the opinion; O'Connor, Stevens, Marshall and Brennan dissented.

The court recognized a "public safety" exception to the rule set out in *Miranda v. Arizona* (1966), which denies prosecutors use of evidence obtained from a suspect not advised of his constitutional rights. This was the first exception the court had permitted to this rule.

In some situations, "concern for public safety" dictates that police ask a suspect a particular question immediately, such as "Where's the gun?" In these cases, the suspect's reply and any evidence it leads to may be used against him.

Berkemer v. McCarty, decided by a 9-0 vote, July 2, 1984. Marshall wrote the opinion.

Drivers stopped by police for questioning about traffic offenses do not have to be advised of their constitutional rights until they are taken into custody.

Anyone who has been arrested for any reason, however, must be warned of his right to remain silent and his right to have an attorney before he is questioned by police.

Double Jeopardy

Justices of Boston Municipal Court v. Lydon, decided by a 9-0 vote, April 18, 1984. White wrote the opinion.

Federal courts can entertain petitions for habeas corpus relief from persons who are free on personal recognizance. The guarantee against double jeopardy was not violated by Massachusetts' system, under which a defendant who elected a bench trial and was convicted was, upon appeal, entitled to a new trial before a jury.

Arizona v. Rumsey, decided by a 7-2 vote, May 29, 1984. O'Connor wrote the opinion; Rehnquist and White dissented.

Once a judge or jury has decided not to impose a death sentence on a convicted criminal, the double jeopardy guarantee forbids the state to argue for the death penalty in a second sentencing proceeding.

This applies even when the first sentence has been set aside by a higher court because it found that the sentencing judge misinterpreted the law.

Ohio v. Johnson, decided by votes of 7-2 and 6-3, June 11, 1984. Rehnquist wrote the opinion; Stevens and Marshall dissented; Brennan dissented in part.

A defendant who pleads guilty to the lesser two of four criminal charges, all related to the same criminal incident, cannot invoke the double jeopardy guarantee in order to avoid being tried on the two greater charges.

Richardson v. United States, decided by votes of 8-1 and 7-2, June 29, 1984. Rehnquist wrote the opinion; Brennan, Marshall and Stevens dissented.

When a jury deadlocks and a mistrial is declared, it is no violation of the double jeopardy guarantee for the defendant to be retried on the unresolved charges. The double jeopardy guarantee applies only when some event, such as an acquittal, terminates the original jeopardy.

A Fair and Public Trial

Koehler v. Engle, affirmed by a 4-4 vote, March 26, 1984. *Per curiam* (unsigned) opinion; Marshall did not participate.

The court left intact an appeals court ruling that a trial judge improperly shifted the burden of proof to a defendant charged with murder when he instructed the jury that malice can be implied from any deliberate and cruel act, and that a person is presumed to intend the natural consequences of his actions.

James v. Kentucky, decided by a 7-1 vote, April 18, 1984. White wrote the opinion; Rehnquist dissented. Marshall did not participate in the decision.

A defendant whose lawyer asked the judge to admonish the jury not to draw any adverse inference from his failure to testify in his own behalf was, by the denial of that request, deprived of his right to have the jury so instructed to protect his right to remain silent.

Waller v. Georgia, Cole v. Georgia, decided by a 9-0 vote, May 21, 1984. Powell wrote the opinion.

A defendant's right to a public trial extends to pretrial hearings concerning the suppression of evidence. Such a hearing may be closed over a defendant's objection only if there is an overriding interest likely to be prejudiced by an open hearing. Even then, only as much of the hearing as is required to serve that interest may be closed, and the judge must consider reasonable alternatives to closure and make findings to support closure.

The court held that a Georgia judge erred in closing an entire seven-day hearing to protect evidence aired during several hours of the hearing.

Patton v. Yount, decided by a 6-2 vote, June 26, 1984. Powell wrote the opinion; Marshall did not participate; Brennan and Stevens dissented.

A murder defendant's second trial, four years after his first, was not prejudiced by excessive publicity. The record showed that publicity about the case diminished between the first and second trials and thus did not support his challenge to his conviction on these grounds.

Reed v. Ross, decided by a 5-4 vote, June 27, 1984. Powell wrote the opinion; Rehnquist, Brennan, Stevens and O'Connor dissented.

Where a constitutional claim is so novel that its legal basis is not reasonably available to an attorney, a defendant has cause for failing to raise that claim during his trial or appeal. Such claim may then serve as a basis for a request for a federal writ of habeas corpus.

A man convicted of murder in 1969 had valid cause not to challenge on appeal jury instructions requiring him to prove lack of malice in his actions. The Supreme Court did not rule such instructions improper until 1975.

Right to Counsel

McKaskle v. Wiggins, decided by a 6-3 vote, Jan. 23, 1984. O'Connor wrote the opinion; White, Brennan and Marshall dissented.

So long as a defendant who wishes to act as his own attorney retains control over the organization and conduct of his defense and his role in that defense, some participation of standby appointed counsel does not deny him his right to act as his own attorney.

Flanagan v. United States, decided by a 9-0 vote, Feb. 21, 1984. O'Connor wrote the opinion.

A federal judge's decision to disqualify a single defense counsel who is representing all four defendants in a criminal case is not an immediately appealable order. Such an order may be reviewed by an appeals court only after trial.

Solem v. Stumes, decided by a 6-3 vote, Feb. 29, 1984. White wrote the opinion; Stevens, Brennan and Marshall dissented.

The Supreme Court's decision in *Edwards v. Arizona* (1981), which held that once a suspect has invoked his right to counsel, any subsequent conversation between him and police must be initiated by the suspect, should not be applied retroactively to events occurring before it was announced.

Strickland v. Washington, decided by an 8-1 vote, May 14, 1984. O'Connor wrote the opinion; Marshall dissented.

A defendant who claims his attorney was so ineffective that he was denied his constitutional right to the aid of counsel must show that the lawyer made errors at the trial so serious that they resulted in the defendant's being denied a fair trial. Without such a showing, this claim cannot succeed.

United States v. Cronic, decided by a 9-0 vote, May 14, 1984. Stevens wrote the opinion.

An appeals court erred when it inferred from an appointed attorney's lack of criminal law experience, and the brief period he was given to prepare for trial, that a defendant was denied the right to the effective aid of counsel. Such a conclusion must be supported by evidence of serious errors by counsel that so prejudiced the trial that the defendant was denied a fair trial.

United States v. Gouveia, decided by an 8-1 vote, May 29, 1984. Rehnquist wrote the decision; Marshall dissented.

Prison inmates, placed in administrative detention under suspicion of murdering a fellow inmate, are not entitled to have attorneys appointed to aid them until they are formally charged with a crime.

Nix v. Williams, decided by a 7-2 vote, June 11, 1984. Burger wrote the opinion; Brennan and Marshall dissented.

The court approved an "inevitable discovery" exception to the exclusionary rule, which bars the use at trial of evidence obtained in violation of a defendant's rights. Under this exception, such evidence may be used if the prosecution can prove by a preponderance of the evidence that it ultimately would have been discovered by lawful means.

The ruling came in the case of a man twice convicted of murder. In 1977, the justices reversed the first conviction because they found that the defendant had been denied his right to counsel by police who had persuaded him, by their conversation with each other during a long car trip without defendant's counsel, to lead them to the body of his victim (*Brewer v. Williams*).

In 1984, however, the court upheld the man's second conviction, rejecting arguments that any evidence related to the body of the victim was inadmissible as the "fruit" of police misconduct. The court held that because the body would inevitably have been discovered by a search then under way, the evidence could be used.

Capital Punishment

Pulley v. Harris, decided by a 7-2 vote, Jan. 23, 1984. White wrote the opinion; Brennan and Marshall dissented.

The Constitution does not require state courts to review a death sentence to ensure that it is proportional to the punishment imposed on others convicted of similar crimes. Such proportionality review is permitted, but not required, by the constitutional guarantee of due process.

Spaziano v. Florida, decided by a 6-3 vote, July 2, 1984. Blackmun wrote the opinion; Stevens, Brennan and Marshall dissented.

A judge may disregard a jury's recommendation of a life sentence and impose a sentence of death instead.

Nothing in the Constitution requires that only juries decide to sentence someone to die. A judge may be given sole responsibility for imposing sentence and thus is free to override a jury's recommendation.

False Statements

United States v. Rodgers, decided by a 9-0 vote, April 30, 1984. Rehnquist wrote the opinion.

The law that prohibits knowing and willful false statements in any matter "within the jurisdiction of any department or agency of the United States" applies to statements made to the Federal Bureau of Investigation and U.S. Secret Service concerning a fictitious plot to assassinate the president.

United States v. Yermian, decided by a 5-4 vote, June 27, 1984. Powell wrote the opinion; Rehnquist, Brennan, Stevens and O'Connor dissented.

An individual may be convicted of making false statements in a "matter within the jurisdiction of any department or agency of the United States" without the prosecution proving that he knew that the false statement came within federal jurisdiction.

Due Process

Schall v. Martin, Abrams v. Martin, decided by a 6-3 vote, June 4, 1984. Rehnquist wrote the opinion; Brennan, Marshall and Stevens dissented.

For the first time, the court upheld a preventive detention law as constitutional. The justices ruled that New York's law permitting pretrial detention of juveniles when there is a serious risk that the juvenile may commit a serious crime before trial falls within the bounds set by the constitutional guarantee of due process.

Detention in such a case protects both the juvenile and society, the court said, and the law contains sufficient procedural safeguards against violation of a juvenile's rights.

California v. Trombetta, decided by a 9-0 vote, June 11, 1984. Marshall wrote the opinion.

The due process guarantee does not require state police to preserve, for use by drunken driving defendants at trial, samples of a driver's breath at the time he or she was tested on an instrument measuring alcohol levels.

Thigpen v. Roberts, decided by a 7-2 vote, June 27, 1984. White wrote the opinion; O'Connor and Powell dissented.

Prosecutorial vindictiveness denied due process to a man who was charged with manslaughter while he was appealing his conviction on misdemeanor traffic offenses arising out of the fatal auto accident.

Hobby v. United States, decided by a 6-3 vote, July 2, 1984. Burger wrote the opinion; Marshall, Brennan and Stevens dissented.

Claims that blacks and women are discriminated against in the selection of federal grand jury foremen — who perform essentially ministerial functions — are not sufficient reason to conclude that a white male defendant indicted by a grand jury has been denied his due process right to fair treatment.

Wasman v. United States, decided by a 9-0 vote, July 3, 1984. Burger wrote the opinion.

When a defendant is retried on a charge after winning a reversal of his first conviction on appeal, the judge may impose a more severe sentence following a new conviction if he can cite conduct or events that occurred subsequent to the first sentencing that justify a harsher sentence the second time around.

Plea Bargains

Mabry v. Johnson, decided by a 9-0 vote, June 11, 1984. Stevens wrote the opinion.

A defendant's acceptance of a plea bargain does not give him any constitutional right to have that bargain enforced. Withdrawal of the bargain by a prosecutor, before entry of plea, is no basis for challenging a later guilty plea entered in keeping with another less favorable plea bargain.

General

Russello v. United States, decided by a 9-0 vote, Nov. 1, 1983. Blackmun wrote the opinion.

Under the 1970 Racketeer Influenced and Corrupt Organizations Act, federal prosecutors may force organized crime figures to forfeit all profits and proceeds from racketeering activity, as well as their share in the business itself.

Dixson v. United States, Hinton v. United States, decided by a 5-4 vote, Feb. 22, 1984. Marshall wrote the opinion; O'Connor, Brennan, Rehnquist and Stevens dissented.

Officials of a community-based private social service corporation that administers federal grant funds for a city are "public officials" subject to prosecution for bribery under the federal law barring bribery of public officials.

United States v. One Assortment of 89 Firearms, decided by a 9-0 vote, Feb. 22, 1984. Burger wrote the opinion.

The acquittal of a gun owner on charges of dealing in firearms without a license, in violation of federal law, does not bar a subsequent action by the government seeking forfeiture of his firearms.

New York v. Uplinger, dismissed by a 5-4 vote as improvidently granted, May 29, 1984. *Per curiam* (unsigned) opinion; Burger, White, O'Connor and Rehnquist dissented.

After argument, the court dismissed New York's appeal of a state court decision holding unconstitutional a state law that prohibited loitering "in a public place for the purpose of engaging, or soliciting another person to engage, in deviate sexual intercourse or other sexual behavior of a deviate nature."

INDIVIDUAL, CIVIL RIGHTS

Affirmative Action

Firefighters Local Union #1784 v. Stotts, decided by a 6-3 vote, June 11, 1984. White wrote the opinion; Brennan, Marshall and Stevens dissented.

Federal judges may not override a valid seniority system to preserve the jobs of black workers hired under an affirmative action plan.

The court overturned a federal court order directing the Memphis, Tenn., fire department to ignore its usual rule of "last hired, first fired" in carrying out budget-dictated layoffs.

The court held that the lower court lacked the authority to issue an order modifying the city's good-faith seniority system, the sort of system the Civil Rights Act of 1964 expressly immunized from challenge.

Job Discrimination

Equal Employment Opportunity Commission (EEOC) v. Shell Oil Co., decided by votes of 9-0 and 5-4, April 2, 1984. Marshall wrote the opinion; O'Connor, Burger, Powell and Rehnquist dissented in part.

The court ruled unanimously that a lower court should enforce a subpoena issued by the EEOC to Shell, seeking the company's records as an initial step in investigating charges that the company discriminated against black and female employees.

By 5-4, the court upheld the EEOC procedures in filing such a complaint, rejecting Shell's argument that such a complaint should include specific dates and other details of the allegedly discriminatory actions.

Westinghouse Electric Corp. v. Vaughn, April 30, 1984. *Per curiam* (unsigned) opinion.

The court dismissed without comment the company's appeal of a federal district court finding that a black employee, who admittedly had some work-related problems, was disqualified as a machine operator primarily because of her race.

Cooper v. Federal Reserve Bank of Richmond, decided by an 8-0 vote, June 25, 1984. Stevens wrote the opinion.

Individual workers who charge that they were the victims of illegal discrimination by their employer can pursue those claims in separate lawsuits even though a group of employees of which they were a part failed to prove that the employer systematically discriminated against them.

Burnett v. Grattan, decided by a 9-0 vote, June 27, 1984. Marshall wrote the opinion.

Federal courts may "borrow" statutes of limitations from state laws for actions under the Civil Rights Acts. However, a federal court erred in applying a strict limitation from a state law providing for administrative resolution of job bias claims to a job bias suit brought under the century-old civil rights acts permitting such suits. The longer period permitted by state law for filing civil suits would have been a more appropriate choice.

Sex Discrimination

Grove City College v. Bell, decided by votes of 6-3 and 9-0, Feb. 28, 1984. White wrote the opinion; Brennan, Marshall and Stevens dissented.

Title IX of the 1972 Education Amendments, which bars sex discrimination in any "program or activity" receiving federal aid, does not apply to all programs at an institution. By 6-3, the court said the ban on sex bias applies only to the particular program receiving the aid.

Title IX does apply to schools or colleges that receive federal aid only indirectly, through federal grants or loans to their students, the court ruled unanimously.

Hishon v. King & Spalding, decided by a 9-0 vote, May 22, 1984. Burger wrote the opinion.

Title VII of the 1964 Civil Rights Act applies to law firms, like other employers, forbidding them to discriminate among their employees on the basis of race or sex.

A woman who charged that she was denied fair consideration for partnership by a law firm because of her sex should have a chance to prove those charges in court.

Rights of the Handicapped

Consolidated Rail Corp. v. Darrone, decided by a 9-0 vote, Feb. 28, 1984. Powell wrote the opinion.

Persons denied jobs because of a handicap may sue to enforce Section 504 of the Rehabilitation Act of 1973, which forbids discrimination against otherwise qualified individuals because of a handicap "under any program or activity receiving federal financial assistance."

Section 504 can be used to contest job bias against handicapped persons whether or not the primary purpose of the federal aid received by the employer was to create jobs.

Irving Independent School District v. Tatro, decided by votes of 9-0 and 6-3, July 5, 1984. Burger wrote the

opinion; Brennan, Marshall and Stevens dissented.

Under the Education for All Handicapped Children Act (PL 94-142), a school district is obligated to provide catheterization to a child with spina bifida who requires the procedure every three or four hours to relieve her bladder. This is a "related supportive service" necessary to enable the child to remain in school and can be provided by an instructed lay person.

Nothing in the law, however, permits a court to award attorneys' fees to the parents of the child who won this case or to other parents who successfully sue to force schools to provide services to their children under PL 94-142.

Smith v. Robinson, decided by a 6-3 vote, July 5, 1984. Blackmun wrote the opinion; Brennan, Stevens and Marshall dissented.

Parents who sue to compel the state to provide their handicapped child with the free appropriate public education they are guaranteed by the Education for All Handicapped Children Act may not be awarded their attorneys' fees by a lower court, because that law does not provide for such awards. Related laws permitting fee awards may not be used as the basis for fee awards in PL 94-142 cases.

Draft Registration

Selective Service System v. Minnesota Public Interest Research Group, decided by a 6-2 vote, July 5, 1984. Burger wrote the opinion; Brennan and Marshall dissented; Blackmun did not take part in the decision.

Congress did not violate the constitutional ban on bills of attainder when it approved a 1982 law (PL 97-252) denying federal student aid to male college students who fail to register for the military draft. A bill of attainder is a legislative measure imposing punishment upon an identifiable group without trial.

Congress acted not to punish non-registrants, but to encourage draft registration. Denial of a government benefit does not constitute punishment. Non-registrants are given a 30-day grace period within which to register after they are notified that they will otherwise be ineligible for federal student aid.

Travel Curbs

Regan v. Wald, decided by a 5-4 vote, June 28, 1984. Rehnquist wrote the opinion; Brennan, Blackmun, Marshall and Powell dissented.

The court upheld the Reagan administration's 1982 restrictions on travel to Cuba, which a lower court had held unconstitutional because they had not been promulgated in keeping with procedures outlined by the 1977 International Emergency Economic Powers Act (PL 95-223).

A grandfather clause in that law, which limited executive power to impose economic sanctions on foreign countries in peacetime, preserved the president's authority to impose such restrictions on countries then subject to restrictions. That included travel to Cuba, because property transactions with Cuba were restricted in 1977.

Attorneys' Fees

Blum v. Stenson, decided by a 9-0 vote, March 21, 1984. Powell wrote the opinion.

The court ruled that Congress, in passing the Civil Rights Attorneys' Fee Awards Act of 1976, did not intend judges to grant higher awards to attorneys in private law firms than to those in public-interest firms. The court rejected arguments that awards to public-interest firms should be based on costs, instead of on market rates charged by attorneys in private practice.

The court upheld an award of $79,000 to the Legal Aid Society of New York, which successfully represented a class of Medicaid recipients suing New York over an issue of eligibility. That fee was based on the market rate charged by New York attorneys for their services. The court reversed an additional fee award of almost $40,000, a bonus that it found unjustified by the facts of the situation.

Damage Suits

McDonald v. City of West Branch, Mich., decided by a 9-0 vote, April 18, 1984. Brennan wrote the opinion.

A discharged city policeman may seek damages in federal court for violations of his First Amendment rights, even though an arbitrator declared his firing to be for just cause. Arbitration decisions made pursuant to a collective bargaining agreement do not foreclose federal civil rights damage suits.

Board of Education of Paris Union School District No. 95 v. Vail, affirmed by a 4-4 vote, April 23, 1984. Marshall did not take part in the decision.

By an equally divided vote, the court affirmed an appeals court ruling that a public school teacher whose contract was not renewed had a constitutionally protected interest in continued employment and could sue the school board for depriving him of that interest without due process of law. The school had assured the teacher that he would continue to be employed and gave no explanation for failing to renew the contract.

Tower v. Glover, decided by a 9-0 vote, June 25, 1984. O'Connor wrote the opinion.

Public defenders are not immune from damage suits brought by defendants who claim that they conspired with state officials to violate their clients' constitutional rights.

Anytime a private individual conspires with state officials to deprive another of his federal constitutional rights, he acts "under color of" state law and comes within the reach of the civil rights law permitting damage suits protesting such violations.

Davis v. Scherer, decided by votes of 9-0 and 5-4, June 28, 1984. Powell wrote the opinion; Brennan, Marshall, Blackmun and Stevens dissented.

Although state officials violated administrative regulations in discharging a state employee, they retain qualified immunity from a civil rights damage suit brought by the employee, who argued that he was discharged in violation of his constitutional rights.

Equal Protection

Palmore v. Sidoti, decided by a 9-0 vote, April 25, 1984. Burger wrote the opinion.

A state court offends the guarantee of equal protection when it takes custody of a child from the natural mother because of her remarriage to someone of a different race. "Private biases may be outside the reach of the law, but the law cannot, directly or indirectly, give them effect," the court ruled.

Tax Exemptions for Private Schools

Allen v. Wright, decided by a 5-3 vote, July 3, 1984. O'Connor wrote the opinion; Brennan, Stevens and Blackmun dissented; Marshall did not participate.

Parents of black public school students who had not suffered any specific, personal injury as a result of existing federal policy concerning tax-exempt status for private schools lack legal standing to sue the Internal Revenue Service for being too lenient in enforcing that policy.

Aliens

Immigration and Naturalization Service v. Phinpathya, decided by a 9-0 vote, Jan. 10, 1984. O'Connor wrote the opinion.

A deportable alien, absent from the United States for a three-month period during eight years of residence here, cannot avoid deportation by invoking a law authorizing suspension of deportation for an alien "who has been physically present in the United States for a continuous period of not less than seven years."

Bernal v. Fainter, decided by an 8-1 vote, May 30, 1984. Marshall wrote the opinion; Rehnquist dissented.

States may not deny resident aliens the right to become notaries public. The Constitution's guarantee of equal protection strictly limits the power of states to require that certain posts be held only by citizens.

In striking down a Texas law, the court ruled that the duties of a notary are not so closely bound up with self-government that the state is justified in reserving such jobs for U.S. citizens.

Immigration and Naturalization Service v. Stevic, decided by a 9-0 vote, June 5, 1984. Stevens wrote the opinion.

The Refugee Act of 1980 did not relax the standard of proof for persons who seek to avoid deportation by arguing that they will be subject to persecution in their homeland. Such persons still must prove that there is "a clear probability" of persecution in order to avoid deportation.

Sure-Tan v. National Labor Relations Board (NLRB), decided by votes of 7-2 and 5-4, June 25, 1984. O'Connor wrote the opinion; Rehnquist and Powell dissented in part; Brennan, Marshall, Stevens and Blackmun dissented in part.

Illegal aliens working in the United States are protected by federal labor law from reprisals for their efforts to organize a union, the court held, 7-2. The NLRB correctly held an employer guilty of an unfair labor practice when he retaliated against employees organizing a union by reporting some of them to immigration authorities as illegal aliens.

But the court ruled, 5-4, that the appeals court reviewing the NLRB order exceeded its power when it ordered a minimum of six months' back pay for each of the alien workers. Such orders are properly tailored by the NLRB to each individual case.

Immigration and Naturalization Service v. Lopez-Mendoza, decided by a 5-4 vote, July 5, 1984. O'Connor wrote the opinion; Brennan, White, Marshall and Stevens dissented.

The exclusionary rule — which forbids the government

to use evidence obtained in violation of a defendant's rights — cannot be invoked in civil deportation proceedings.

Prison Inmates

Block v. Rutherford, decided by a 6-3 vote, July 3, 1984. Burger wrote the opinion; Marshall, Brennan and Stevens dissented.

Nothing in the Constitution grants prison inmates or pretrial detainees the right to "contact visits" with friends or family members. These are visits at which the inmate is permitted to embrace or touch the visitors.

FIRST AMENDMENT

Church and State

Lynch v. Donnelly, decided by a 5-4 vote, March 5, 1984. Burger wrote the opinion; Brennan, Marshall, Blackmun and Stevens dissented.

The inclusion of a Nativity scene in a municipally sponsored Christmas holiday display in Pawtucket, R.I., did not violate the First Amendment ban on establishment of religion, the court ruled.

The Constitution "affirmatively mandates accommodation, not merely tolerance, of all religions, and forbids hostility toward any," the court majority declared.

"There is an unbroken history of official acknowledgement by all three branches of government of the role of religion in American life from at least 1789," the justices noted.

Freedom of Speech

Minnesota State Board for Community Colleges v. Knight, decided by a 6-3 vote, Feb. 21, 1984. O'Connor wrote the opinion; Stevens, Brennan and Powell dissented.

Minnesota law did not deny state employees First Amendment rights of free speech and freedom of association by authorizing only selected employee representatives to confer with their employers on policy and employment matters outside the scope of mandatory bargaining.

"The Constitution does not grant to members of the public generally a right to be heard by public bodies making decisions of policy," declared the court. "To recognize a constitutional right to participate directly in goverment policymaking would work a revolution in existing government practices."

Los Angeles City Council v. Taxpayers for Vincent, decided by a 6-3 vote, May 15, 1984. Stevens wrote the opinion; Brennan, Marshall and Blackmun dissented.

Cities concerned about "visual clutter" may constitutionally ban the posting of signs on public property. A Los Angeles posting ban was an appropriate and constitutional means of minimizing such clutter. There was no hint of bias or censorship in passage or implementation of the ban, which applied to all posted signs, regardless of content. Also, there were alternative means of conveying the messages to be presented by posters.

Secretary of State of Maryland v. Munson, decided by a 5-4 vote, June 26, 1984. Blackmun wrote the opinion; Burger, Rehnquist, Powell and O'Connor dissented.

Charitable solicitations are "so intertwined with speech that they are entitled to the protections of the First Amendment," the court declared in striking down a Maryland law limiting to 25 percent of gross income the amount a charity could spend on fundraising.

Clark v. Community for Creative Non-Violence, decided by a 7-2 vote, June 29, 1984. White wrote the opinion; Brennan and Marshall dissented.

The Reagan administration's ban on camping — defined to include sleeping — in certain national parks did not unconstitutionally burden freedom of expression.

Without deciding whether sleeping may in some situations constitute protected expression under the First Amendment, the court ruled that the ban in question was a reasonable restriction on the time, place and manner in which First Amendment rights may be exercised. The sleeping ban, applied in this case to Lafayette Park across from the White House, was a reasonable way for the government to try to maintain the good condition of the national parks for all visitors, the court ruled.

Federal Communications Commission v. League of Women Voters of California, decided by a 5-4 vote, July 2, 1984. Brennan wrote the opinion; Rehnquist, Burger, White and Stevens dissented.

Congress violated the First Amendment when it prohibited editorials on public radio and television stations that accepted grants from the Corporation for Public Broadcasting. The government presented no justification sufficient to support such a sweeping ban, which was aimed at "precisely that form of speech which the framers of the Bill of Rights were most anxious to protect — speech that is 'indispensable to the discovery and spread of political truth.' . . . "

Free Press

Press-Enterprise Co. v. Superior Court of California, Riverside County, decided by a 9-0 vote, Jan. 18, 1984. Burger wrote the opinion.

Jury selection proceedings in criminal trials should be open to the press and public unless the judge finds an overriding interest requires that these proceedings be closed, the court ruled.

A California judge violated that right of access by excluding press and public from all but three days of a six-week jury selection process prior to a rape-murder trial. The judge presented no findings to support closure and did not consider alternatives.

Keeton v. Hustler Magazine Inc., decided by a 9-0 vote, March 20, 1984. Rehnquist wrote the opinion.

Nationally circulated newspapers and magazines can be sued in any state in which they have substantial circulation. The court held that a New York resident could sue Hustler, an Ohio corporation, for libel in a federal court in New Hampshire, because Hustler sold 10,000 to 15,000 copies of its magazine in that state each month.

Calder v. Jones, decided by a 9-0 vote, March 20, 1984. Rehnquist wrote the opinion.

California courts had jurisdiction over a libel case brought by actress Shirley Jones, a California resident, against an editor and writer of an article in the *National Enquirer,* which was published by a Florida corporation, even though the writer and the editor were in Florida and had little or no contact with the state of California.

The target of the article was California and a California resident; therefore, California courts could exercise jurisdiction over those responsible for the article.

Bose Corp. v. Consumers Union of the United States, decided by a 6-3 vote, April 30, 1984. Stevens wrote the opinion; White, Rehnquist and O'Connor dissented.

Federal appeals courts reviewing libel damage awards won by public figures must independently review the evidence to determine whether it was sufficient to prove actual malice on the part of the press defendant. In such a review, appeals courts are not restricted by the federal rules of procedure, which permit appeals courts to overturn a trial court's finding of fact only if that finding was "clearly erroneous."

Seattle Times Co. v. Rhinehart, decided by a 9-0 vote, May 21, 1984. Powell wrote the opinion.

Freedom of the press is not violated by a court order restraining the publication of information about the members and supporters of a religious organization when that information was obtained through pre-trial discovery compelled by the court.

Regan v. Time Inc., decided by votes of 5-4 and 8-1, July 3, 1984. White wrote the opinion; Brennan, Marshall, Blackmun, Powell and Stevens dissented.

Congress violated the First Amendment in 1958 when it amended a century-old law severely restricting the publication of photographs of U.S. currency to permit photographs for "philatelic, numismatic, newsworthy, historical and educational purposes." This provision unconstitutionally distinguished among publications on the basis of content. Only Justice Stevens voted to uphold this aspect of the law.

The court upheld a portion of the law requiring that all illustrations be in black and white, be undersized or oversized, and that the negative and plates used be destroyed. Brennan, Marshall, Blackmun and Powell dissented.

Freedom of Association

Roberts v. U.S. Jaycees, decided by a 7-0 vote, July 3, 1984. Brennan wrote the opinion; Burger and Blackmun did not participate.

Minnesota may invoke its public accommodations law to require the U.S. Jaycees, a large non-exclusive membership organization, to admit women as full members. A state's interest in ensuring equal treatment for its women citizens outweighs any First Amendment freedom of speech or association the Jaycees asserted.

The First Amendment protects a freedom of intimate association in family and other personal relationships — and a freedom of expressive association among larger groups. But the latter is not absolute, and in this case the state's compelling interest in ensuring women equal access to public accommodations outweighed that interest.

ELECTION LAW

Voting Rights

McCain v. Lybrand, decided by a 9-0 vote, Feb. 21, 1984. Stevens wrote the opinion.

The attorney general's approval of 1971 changes in procedures for electing members of a county council, submitted for clearance as required by Section 5 of the Voting Rights Act, could not to be interpreted as approval of 1966 election procedure changes that had not been submitted for such clearance.

Escambia County, Fla. v. McMillan, decided by an 8-1 vote, March 27, 1984. *Per curiam* (unsigned) opinion; Marshall dissented.

The court sent back to a federal appeals court a case in which an at-large system of electing county commissioners was challenged as unconstitutional, directing the appeals court to decide whether the Voting Rights Act provided a basis for upholding the district court decision that the at-large system violated the rights of black voters in the county.

BUSINESS LAW

Agriculture: Milk Marketing

Block v. Community Nutrition Institute, decided by an 8-0 vote, June 4, 1984. O'Connor wrote the opinion; Stevens did not participate.

Congress did not give consumers any role in the development or enforcement of milk marketing orders under the Agricultural Marketing Agreement Act. Consumers thus have no authority to challenge those orders; the system providing for such orders is a closed one, limited to producers, handlers and the agriculture secretary.

Antitrust

Monsanto Co. v. Spray-Rite Service Corp., decided by an 8-0 vote, March 20, 1984. Powell wrote the opinion; White did not participate in the decision.

The court upheld a $10.5 million antitrust judgment assessed against Monsanto after a jury found it had terminated Spray-Rite's distributorship of its products because the distributor consistently undercut the prices charged by other distributors.

Something more than evidence of complaints from other distributors about discount pricing must be presented to justify such a finding; there must be direct or circumstantial evidence that reasonably tends to prove that the manufacturer and others had a conscious intent to maintain resale price levels. Such evidence was presented in this case, and the judgment was upheld.

Jefferson Parish Hospital District No. 2 v. Hyde, decided by a 9-0 vote, March 27, 1984. Stevens wrote the opinion.

A hospital that is one of many in a large metropolitan area does not violate federal antitrust law by entering into an exclusive contract with one firm of anesthesiologists under which that firm provides all the anesthesia services for all surgery at that hospital. There is no evidence that this sort of arrangement, tying the provision of anesthesia by one firm to surgery at that hospital, is per se illegal or that it operates to restrain competition in the market.

Copperweld Corp. v. Independence Tube Corp., decided by a 5-3 vote, June 19, 1984. Burger wrote the opinion; White did not participate; Stevens, Brennan and Marshall dissented.

A corporation and its wholly owned subsidiary are not capable of conspiring to restrain trade in violation of Section 1 of the Sherman Antitrust Act.

The court overturned a $7.5 million damage award to Independence that had been based on a finding that Copperweld and its wholly owned subsidiary, Regal Tube, conspired to urge suppliers not to deal with Independence, a new competitor.

National Collegiate Athletic Association (NCAA) v. Board of Regents of the University of Oklahoma, decided by a 7-2 vote, June 27, 1984. Stevens wrote the opinion; White and Rehnquist dissented.

An NCAA plan that limited the number of college football games that could be televised, limited the number of televised games in which any one school could appear, prohibited all members from selling television rights to football games except in accord with the NCAA plan, and fixed the minimum aggregate price to be paid for these rights by the networks violated federal antitrust laws.

This television package plan unreasonably restrained trade in violation of Section 1 of the Sherman Act.

Banking

Securities Industry Association v. Board of Governors of the Federal Reserve System, decided by a 6-3 vote, June 28, 1984. Blackmun wrote the opinion; O'Connor, Brennan and Stevens dissented.

Congress in 1933 drew a line separating commercial banking from investment banking; the Federal Reserve Board blurred that line when it approved a commercial bank's marketing of commercial paper for some of its corporate customers.

Section 16 of the Glass-Steagall Act forbids commercial banks to underwrite or market stocks, bonds, notes, or other securities. Commercial paper falls in this category and cannot be marketed under Section 16.

Securities Industry Association v. Board of Governors of the Federal Reserve System, decided by a 9-0 vote, June 28, 1984. Powell wrote the opinion.

The Federal Reserve Board was within its authority when it permitted a bank holding company to acquire a discount securities brokerage firm.

Approving BankAmerica's acquisition of Charles Schwab & Co., the court held that the operation of a discount brokerage firm — basically the execution of buy and sell orders for customers, without investment advice — was similar to the business of many bank trust departments. Thus, the acquisition did not violate the Glass-Steagall Act of 1933, which forbids banks to underwrite or market securities.

Bankruptcy and Labor Contracts

National Labor Relations Board v. Bildisco & Bildisco, decided by votes of 9-0 and 5-4, Feb. 22, 1984. Rehnquist wrote the opinion; Brennan, White, Marshall and Blackmun dissented in part.

A company attempting to reorganize its affairs under federal bankruptcy laws may, with a bankruptcy judge's permission, abrogate its collective bargaining contract upon a showing that the contract is burdensome and on balance, the best interests of the company, its creditors and

its employees favor such a step. It is not necessary to show that the company will go out of business if it does not reject its contract.

By a 5-4 vote, the court also held that a failing company that has filed for bankruptcy is not guilty of an unfair labor practice if it unilaterally rejects or modifies certain provisions of its collective bargaining contract.

Copyright Law and Video Recorders

Sony Corporation of America v. Universal Studios Inc., decided by a 5-4 vote, Jan. 17, 1984. Stevens wrote the opinion; Blackmun, Marshall, Powell and Rehnquist dissented.

Home taping of copyrighted television programs for personal, non-commercial use does not violate copyright laws. The court overturned a 1981 appeals court decision holding the Sony Corp., some of its retailers and its advertising agency liable for damages for contributing to copyright infringement by selling Sony's Betamax video recorders.

The primary use of these machines is "time-shift" recording, taping programs for later viewing at a more convenient time. This is a fair use of the machines, not a violation of copyright laws, the court held.

Eminent Domain

Kirby Forest Industries v. United States, decided by a 9-0 vote, May 21, 1984. Marshall wrote the opinion.

When government uses "straight-condemnation" proceedings to take privately owned timberland for a national preserve, the date of the taking of the land is the date that the government tenders payment to the landowner, not the date it institutes the proceedings. No interest is due for period between date of complaint and date of payment.

Air Cargo Liability Limits

Trans World Airlines Inc. v. Franklin Mint Corp., Franklin Mint Corp. v. Trans World Airlines Inc., decided by an 8-1 vote, April 17, 1984. O'Connor wrote the opinion; Stevens dissented.

Although Congress in 1978 repealed the official price for gold, the standard used under the Warsaw Convention to determine the limits of airline liability for lost cargo, the international limits set under that convention are still in effect for U.S. airlines.

Multi-Employer Pension Funds

Schneider Moving & Storage Co. v. Robbins, Prosser's Moving & Storage Co. v. Robbins, decided by a 9-0 vote, April 18, 1984. Powell wrote the opinion.

Trustees of a multi-employer trust fund may sue an employer directly for failing to make required contributions to the fund, without first submitting to arbitration a basic disagreement with that employer over the meaning of a term in the agreement setting up the fund.

Pension Benefit Guaranty Corp. v. R. A. Gray & Co., decided by a 9-0 vote, June 18, 1984. Brennan wrote the opinion.

Congress did not deny affected employers due process of law in making certain liability provisions of the Multiemployer Pension Plan Amendments Act of 1980 (PL 96-

364) applicable to employers withdrawing from such plans in the five months prior to enactment. The contested provision required such employers to make a contribution to the plan to cover future payments to employees.

This provision was a rational means of furthering a legitimate legislative purpose, the court held.

Securities

Daily Income Fund Inc. v. Fox, decided by a 9-0 vote, Jan. 18, 1984. Brennan wrote the opinion.

Shareholders suing a mutual fund to recover allegedly excessive fees paid to fund advisers are not required by the federal rules of civil procedure to demand, before bringing suit, that the fund's directors recover the fees.

Securities and Exchange Commission v. O'Brien, decided by a 9-0 vote, June 18, 1984. Marshall wrote the opinion.

The Securities and Exchange Commission is not required to notify the persons who are the subject of non-public investigations when it issues subpoenas to third parties as part of such investigations.

Relocation Aid

Norfolk Redevelopment and Housing Authority v. C & P Telephone Company of Virginia, decided by an 8-0 vote, Nov. 1, 1983. Rehnquist wrote the opinion; Powell did not participate.

Public utilities are not eligible for relocation aid as "displaced persons" under the Uniform Relocation Act of 1970 when their transmission lines are displaced by federally funded projects. That law did not change the common law principle that a utility forced to relocate from a public right-of-way does so at its own expense.

Trucking Regulation

Interstate Commerce Commission (ICC) v. American Trucking Association Inc., decided by a 5-4 vote, June 5, 1984. Marshall wrote the opinion; O'Connor, Blackmun, Powell and Stevens dissented.

The ICC has inherent authority to reject a tariff setting trucking rates, even if the rates are already in effect, if it finds that the tariff violates motor-carrier rate-bureau agreements under the Motor Carrier Act of 1980. The ICC can order trucking companies to refund overcharges collected under the rate schedule while it was in effect.

Taxation

Aloha Airlines Inc. v. Director of Taxation of Hawaii, decided by a 9-0 vote, Nov. 1, 1983. Marshall wrote the opinion.

The Airport Development Acceleration Act of 1973 prohibited state taxes on air travel and pre-empted Hawaii law imposing a tax on the annual gross income of airlines operating entirely within that state.

Commissioner of Internal Revenue v. Engle, Farmar v. United States, decided by a 5-4 vote, Jan. 10, 1984. O'Connor wrote the opinion; Blackmun, Brennan, White and Marshall dissented.

Taxpayers who own oil and gas wells may take a depletion deduction on part of the income they receive from leaseholders, even in years when the wells do not produce oil or gas.

Badaracco v. Commissioner of Internal Revenue, Deleet Merchandising Corp. v. United States, decided by an 8-1 vote, Jan. 17, 1984. Blackmun wrote the opinion; Stevens dissented.

A taxpayer who files a false or fraudulent return and later files a correct amended return may still be assessed the appropriate tax and penalties from the first return at any time; the three-year limitation on assessment of federal income taxes does not apply in such circumstances.

Dickman v. Commissioner of Internal Revenue, decided by a 7-2 vote, Feb. 22, 1984. Burger wrote the opinion; Powell and Rehnquist dissented.

Intrafamily interest-free loans are subject to federal gift taxes. The tax is assessed against the donor on the value of the use of the money lent.

United States v. Arthur Young & Co., decided by a 9-0 vote, March 21, 1984. Burger wrote the opinion.

There is no immunity protecting the tax accrual workpapers of a company's independent auditor from a summons by the Internal Revenue Service.

Limbach v. The Hooven & Allison Co., decided by a 9-0 vote, April 18, 1984. Blackmun wrote the opinion.

Ohio's state tax commissioner may argue again, against the same company as earlier, in defense of a state property tax on certain imported goods held unconstitutional by the court in 1945, because in 1976 the court overruled the precedent upon which the 1945 decision was based (*Michelin Tire Corp. v. Wages* overruling *Low v. Austin,* 1872).

Westinghouse Electric Corp. v. Tully, decided by a 9-0 vote, April 24, 1984. Blackmun wrote the opinion.

New York discriminated against exports from other states in violation of the Commerce Clause when it permitted corporations to claim a tax credit on the accumulated income of their subsidiary Domestic International Sales Corporations only for gross receipts attributable to export shipments from New York.

Trade Secrets/Pesticide Law

Ruckelshaus v. Monsanto Co., decided by votes of 8-0 and 7-1, June 26, 1984. Blackmun wrote the opinion; White did not participate; O'Connor dissented.

The court found "no constitutional infirmity" in two key provisions of the Federal Insecticide, Fungicide and Rodenticide Act as amended in 1978.

The two provisions permit the Environmental Protection Agency (EPA) to disclose to the public health and safety data submitted to it by a company applying to register a pesticide, and to use that data to evaluate a second company's application for a license for a similar pesticide.

Both provisions had been held unconstitutional by a lower court judge who upheld Monsanto's contention that they permitted the government to take trade secrets, private property, without just compensation. The court held that Monsanto knew that EPA could make such disclosure when it submitted the data, and thus could not claim that disclosure was a taking.

LABOR LAW

Bureau of Alcohol, Tobacco and Firearms v. Federal Labor Relations Authority, decided by a 9-0 vote, Nov. 29, 1983. Brennan wrote the opinion.

The Civil Service Reform Act of 1978 does not require federal agencies to pay a daily allowance and travel expenses to employees who must travel in order to act as negotiators for unions representing government employees. Employees receive their salary for days spent in such labor negotiations, but no additional allowance.

Donovan v. Lone Steer Inc., decided by a 9-0 vote, Jan. 17, 1984. Rehnquist wrote the opinion.

Federal wage and hour inspectors are not required to obtain a warrant before they issue administrative subpoenas ordering businesses to produce payroll records for inspection for compliance with federal wage and hour laws.

National Labor Relations Board v. City Disposal Systems Inc., decided by a 5-4 vote, March 21, 1984. Brennan wrote the opinion; O'Connor, Burger, Powell and Rehnquist dissented.

Under federal labor law, an employee covered by a collective bargaining agreement specifying that workers should not be required to drive unsafe vehicles is protected from reprisals if he refuses to drive a vehicle on grounds that he believes it to be unsafe.

Ellis v. Brotherhood of Railway, Airline and Steamship Clerks, decided by votes of 9-0 and 8-1, April 25, 1984. White wrote the opinion; Powell dissented in part.

Under a Railway Labor Act provision authorizing union shops, a union may use dues collected from objecting employees to finance its conventions, social activities and publications, but not to pay for organization, litigation or death benefits. The union's use of dues for permissible purposes does not violate the First Amendment rights of objecting employees.

The union's plan to reimburse objecting employees a portion of the dues spent on impermissible purposes does not adequately remedy the improper use of these funds.

Local #82, Furniture & Piano Moving, Furniture Store Drivers, Helpers, Warehousemen & Packers v. Crowley, decided by an 8-1 vote, June 12, 1984. Brennan wrote the opinion; Stevens dissented.

A federal judge exceeded his authority under Title I of the Labor-Management Reporting and Disclosure Act when he declared a union election already under way to be in violation of members' rights and spelled out procedures for a new court-supervised election.

Washington Metropolitan Area Transit Authority v. Johnson, decided by a 6-3 vote, June 26, 1984. Marshall wrote the opinion; Rehnquist, Brennan and Stevens dissented.

A general contractor subject to the provisions of the Longshoremen's and Harbor Workers' Compensation Act is immune from negligence damage suits by employees claiming they suffered respiratory ailments as a result of exposure to dust and other pollutants in the course of their work, because the employer saw to it that those employees were covered by workmen's compensation insurance.

The immunity provisions of federal workmen's compensation law apply to general contractors as well as sub-contractors, who in this case, were the actual employers of the plaintiff workmen.

ENERGY

Silkwood v. Kerr-McGee Corp., decided by a 5-4 vote, Jan. 11, 1984. White wrote the opinion; Powell, Burger, Marshall and Blackmun dissented.

The Atomic Energy Act, which asserts exclusive federal jurisdiction over nuclear safety, does not deny states the power to punish egregious violations of nuclear safety regulations through liability laws.

The court reinstated a $10 million punitive damages award made by an Oklahoma jury to the family of Karen Silkwood, a Kerr-McGee employee who died in an accident in 1974 after she was found to be contaminated with plutonium. Plutonium, a highly radioactive substance, was made into fuel pins for nuclear reactors at the Kerr-McGee plant at which Silkwood worked.

Escondido Mutual Water Co. v. La Jolla, Rincon, San Pasqual, Pauma and Pala Bands of Mission Indians, decided by a 9-0 vote, May 15, 1984. White wrote the opinion.

The Federal Power Act requires the Federal Energy Regulatory Commission (FERC) to accept, as part of a license for a hydroelectric project on an Indian reservation, any conditions imposed by the interior secretary (who has jurisdiction over the reservation). This requirement applies only to reservations within which projects are located, not to nearby affected reservations.

The Mission Indian Relief Act of 1891 does not give Mission Indians veto power over FERC decisions to license hydroelectric projects.

Aluminum Company of America v. Central Lincoln Peoples' Utility District, decided by an 8-1 vote, June 5, 1984. Blackmun wrote the opinion; Stevens dissented.

The Bonneville Power Administration acted within its legal authority under the Pacific Northwest Electric Power Planning and Conservation Act of 1980 when it allocated power among its customers in a way challenged by public utilities as shortchanging them in favor of industrial and private utility companies.

ENVIRONMENT

Secretary of the Interior v. California, Western Oil and Gas Association v. California, California v. Secretary of the Interior, decided by a 5-4 vote, Jan. 11, 1984. O'Connor wrote the opinion; Stevens, Brennan, Marshall and Blackmun dissented.

States may not block federal offshore lease sales by arguing that the sales are inconsistent with state plans for protecting coastal areas. The 1972 Coastal Zone Management Act does not require the interior secretary to find lease sales on the Outer Continental Shelf consistent with the coastal management plans of adjacent states. Such consistency determinations are required by law only at later stages of oil and gas development.

Environmental Protection Agency v. Natural Resources Defense Council (NRDC), Chevron USA Inc. v. NRDC, American Iron and Steel Institute v. NRDC, decided by a 6-0 vote, June 25, 1984. Stevens wrote the opinion;

Marshall, Rehnquist and O'Connor did not participate.

An Environmental Protection Agency decision to adopt the "bubble concept" for enforcing the Clean Air Act was a reasonable policy choice, well within the agency's authority under the law. Under that concept, an entire plant may be considered one source of air pollution, and changes in portions of the plant may be made without a full-scale environmental review if total emissions from the plant do not increase.

SOCIAL SECURITY

Heckler v. Mathews, decided by a 9-0 vote, March 5, 1984. Brennan wrote the opinion.

Congress acted within constitutional limits in 1977 when it decided, for a limited time and purpose, to reinstate the use of a provision of the Social Security Act that had been held unconstitutional by the Supreme Court.

The court approved continued use, for persons retiring before December 1982 and eligible for a government pension, of a dependency test that required husbands, but not wives, to prove dependence on their spouses before receiving spousal benefits under the law.

This provision was an exception to a pension offset provision approved in 1977 that required retired government workers receiving pensions to have their Social Security spousal benefits reduced by the amount of their pension. The exception was intended to protect those workers, mostly women, who planned for retirement expecting to receive both the full spousal benefits and their pensions.

Heckler v. Ringer, decided by a 6-3 vote, May 14, 1984. Rehnquist wrote the opinion; Stevens, Brennan and Marshall dissented.

Challenges to government rules denying Medicare reimbursement for certain surgical procedures may be brought in federal court only after all administrative remedies for such claims have been exhausted.

Heckler v. Community Health Services of Crawford County Inc., decided by a 9-0 vote, May 21, 1984. Stevens wrote the opinion.

A health care provider is obligated to reimburse the government for excess Medicare payments that the provider received as a result of an erroneous interpretation of government regulations by a government agent.

Heckler v. Day, decided by a 5-4 vote, May 22, 1984. Powell wrote the opinion; Marshall, Brennan, Blackmun and Stevens dissented.

Federal courts must not set deadlines for the government to meet in reviewing contested Social Security disability claims. In light of the awareness of Congress of the problem of delay in this process, and its express rejection of mandatory deadlines, it would be "an unwarranted judicial intrusion into this pervasively regulated area for federal courts to issue injunctions imposing deadlines."

STATE POWERS

Boundary Dispute

Louisiana v. Mississippi, decided by a 9-0 vote, April 2, 1984. Blackmun wrote the opinion, confirming the report of the Special Master.

The bottom hole of an oil well in reach of the Mississippi River, which serves as the boundary between Louisiana and Mississippi, was throughout the disputed period west of the boundary line and within Louisiana.

Eminent Domain

Hawaii Housing Authority v. Midkiff, decided by an 8-0 vote, May 30, 1984. O'Connor wrote the opinion; Marshall did not participate in the decision.

The state government may use its power of eminent domain to take land from a few large landowners, through condemnation with compensation, in order to transfer ownership to many smaller landowners. This use of government power for a public purpose is well within the "police power" government has traditionally exercised to promote the public welfare.

The court upheld Hawaii's 1967 Land Reform Act, which had been challenged as an unconstitutional taking of private property for private purposes.

Land Claims

Summa Corp. v. California, decided by an 8-0 vote, April 17, 1984. Rehnquist wrote the opinion; Marshall did not participate in the decision.

California, which did not claim any interest in Ballona Lagoon during 1852 proceedings that resulted in the issuance of a federal patent confirming the interest of private citizens, cannot more than a century later claim that it held an easement in the lagoon for commerce, navigation, fishing or other such public purposes.

Pre-Emption

Southland Corp. v. Keating, decided by votes of 7-2 and 6-3, Jan. 23, 1984. Burger wrote the opinion; O'Connor, Rehnquist and Stevens dissented.

The Federal Arbitration Act's guarantee of a right to arbitrate in commercial contracts containing arbitration clauses pre-empts California law which requires judicial consideration of claims brought under state franchise investment law and thereby renders unenforceable arbitration provisions in franchise contracts.

Michigan Canners & Freezers Association Inc. v. Agricultural Marketing and Bargaining Board, decided by a 9-0 vote, June 11, 1984. Brennan wrote the opinion.

The Federal Agricultural Fair Practices Act, enacted to enable the development of voluntary agricultural cooperatives as counterparts to large agricultural processors, pre-empts the Michigan Agricultural Marketing and Bargaining Act insofar as the state law requires that all producers of a commodity abide by contracts negotiated by the association, which the state accredited as the bargaining unit for that commodity.

Hayfield Northern Railroad Co. Inc. v. Chicago & Northwestern Transportation Co., decided by a 9-0 vote, June 12, 1984. Marshall wrote the opinion.

The Staggers Rail Act of 1980, governing abandonment of certain rail lines and providing that shippers may obtain continued service by purchasing or subsidizing continued operation, did not pre-empt a state's use of its eminent domain powers to condemn abandoned rail property.

Brown v. Hotel & Restaurant Employees & Bartenders International Union Local #54, decided by a 4-3 vote, July 2, 1984. O'Connor wrote the opinion; Brennan and Marshall did not participate; White, Powell and Stevens dissented.

The National Labor Relations Act does not pre-empt New Jersey's law, which disqualifies persons who have been convicted of certain offenses or who associate with criminal offenders from holding offices in the union representing employees of the Atlantic City, N.J., casinos. Congress has recognized that some states find it necessary to impose such additional restrictions on the qualifications for union posts.

Privileges and Immunities

United Building and Construction Trades Council of Camden County v. Mayor and Council of City of Camden, decided by an 8-1 vote, Feb. 21, 1984. Rehnquist wrote the opinion; Blackmun dissented.

A city ordinance requiring at least 40 percent of the employees on municipal public works projects to be city residents can be challenged as a violation of the constitutional requirement that each state extend to citizens of the other states all the privileges and immunities of its own citizens.

Hoover v. Ronwin, decided by a 4-3 vote, May 14, 1984. Powell wrote the opinion; Stevens, White and Blackmun dissented. Rehnquist and O'Connor did not participate.

The grading policies of the state bar examination committee, an agency of the Arizona Supreme Court, come within the category of "state action" immune from challenge under federal antitrust laws.

Pulliam v. Allen, decided by a 5-4 vote, May 14, 1984. Blackmun wrote the opinion; Powell, Burger, Rehnquist and O'Connor dissented.

Judges are not immune from prospective injunctions issued under the Civil Rights Act of 1871 forbidding them to act, in the future, in a way that infringes on the civil rights of individuals. Judges are not immune, under the 1976 Civil Rights Attorneys' Fee Awards Act, from orders to pay the attorneys' fees of persons who successfully sue them for such unconstitutional actions.

Regulation

South-Central Timber Development Inc. v. Wunnicke, decided by a 6-2 vote, May 22, 1984. White wrote the opinion; Rehnquist and O'Connor dissented; Marshall did not participate.

A state law specifying that timber from state lands may not be shipped out of state without partial processing in state unconstitutionally burdens interstate commerce and cannot be defended by the argument that Congress imposed a similar requirement on timber taken from federal land in the state. Such an argument can protect a similar state regulation only when congressional intent to sanction such regulations is unmistakable, which was not the case here.

Capital Cities Cable Inc. v. Crisp, decided by a 9-0 vote, June 18, 1984. Brennan wrote the opinion.

The court struck down Oklahoma's ban on the broadcasting of liquor ads, as applied to cable television systems operating within the state. This state regulation of the content of the cable programs, requiring deletion of such ads from out-of-state programs broadcast in-state, was in irreconcilable conflict with federal regulations governing cable television and requiring that cable operators carry broadcast signals "in full, without deletion or alteration."

Federal regulation of the entire array of signals carried by cable television systems pre-empts any state or local regulation of such signals, the court held.

Full Faith and Credit

Migra v. Warren City School District Board of Education, decided by a 9-0 vote, Jan. 23, 1984. Blackmun wrote the decision.

The Constitution's "full faith and credit" clause applies to make final a state court judgment in a breach-of-contract case, and to preclude later federal civil rights damage suits based on the same situation and raising issues already resolved by state court.

Jurisdiction

Solem v. Bartlett, decided by a 9-0 vote, Feb. 22, 1984. Marshall wrote the opinion.

South Dakota has no criminal jurisdiction over an Indian who committed a crime on part of the Cheyenne River Sioux Reservation, which was opened to homesteading by non-Indians in 1908. The federal law opening this land to homesteading did not diminish the boundaries of the reservation.

Helicopteros Nacionales de Colombia, S. A. v. Hall, decided by an 8-1 vote, April 24, 1984. Blackmun wrote the opinion; Brennan dissented.

A Colombian corporation that contracted to provide transportation by helicopter for a joint venture headquartered in Houston — during that company's construction of a pipeline in Peru — has insufficient contact with Texas to permit a Texas court to assert jurisdiction over it in a lawsuit arising from a helicopter crash in Peru in which several U.S. citizens were killed.

Three Affiliated Tribes of the Fort Berthold Reservation v. Wold Engineering, P. C., decided by a 7-2 vote, May 29, 1984. Blackmun wrote the opinion; Rehnquist and Stevens dissented.

State trial courts may have jurisdiction over cases brought by Indian tribes against non-Indian defendants regarding matters arising within the reservation.

State Taxation

South Carolina v. Regan, decided by votes of 9-0 and 8-1, Feb. 22, 1984. Brennan wrote the opinion; Stevens dissented in part.

The court agreed to exercise its original jurisdiction to consider fully this case between a state and the U.S. government. South Carolina challenged as unconstitutional provisions of the Tax Equity and Fiscal Responsibility Act of 1982 (PL 97-248) denying tax exemptions to interest paid on unregistered bonds. The state, backed by 23 other states, argued that forcing states to issue registered bonds burdened their powers to borrow money.

The court rejected the Reagan administration's argument that this case could not be brought in federal court because of the Anti-Injunction Act, which denied federal courts jurisdiction over cases to restrain the assessment or collection of taxes. The justices reasoned that Congress did not intend this ban to apply to cases such as this one, in which South Carolina had no alternative forum in which to pursue its claim.

Armco Inc. v. Hardesty, decided by an 8-1 vote, June 12, 1984. Powell wrote the opinion; Rehnquist dissented.

West Virginia unconstitutionally discriminated against interstate commerce by imposing a gross receipts tax on businesses selling property at wholesale and exempting local manufacturers, who pay a higher manufacturing tax, from it.

Bacchus Imports Ltd. v. Dias, decided by a 5-3 vote, June 29, 1984. White wrote the opinion; Brennan did not participate; Stevens, Rehnquist and O'Connor dissented.

Hawaii's exemption of a local brandy and fruit wine from its 20 percent tax on wholesale liquor sales violated the Constitution by discriminating against interstate commerce in favor of local products.

Water Rights

Colorado v. New Mexico, decided by an 8-1 vote, June 4, 1984. O'Connor wrote the opinion; Stevens dissented.

Colorado failed to meet its burden of proving that water should be diverted — for use in Colorado — from the Vermejo River, which originates in Colorado, flows into New Mexico and has historically been used entirely by New Mexicans.

FEDERAL COURTS

United States v. Mendoza, decided by a 9-0 vote, Jan. 10, 1984. Rehnquist wrote the opinion.

The United States is not foreclosed from litigating a constitutional question raised by a Filipino national seeking naturalization by the fact that the issue had been decided against the government in a similar earlier case.

In general, once a court has decided a matter of law or fact, that decision governs any later case arising out of a different situation but involving one of the parties to the earlier decision. The court held that this doctrine, called collateral estoppel, applied differently to the government than to private litigants, and would operate only when both parties were the same as those in the earlier case.

United States v. Stauffer Chemical Co., decided by a 9-0 vote, Jan. 10, 1984. Rehnquist wrote the opinion.

The government may not relitigate an issue in a case in which the parties are the same as a similar case in which the issue has already been decided. The court held that this doctrine of collateral estoppel prevented the United States from contesting a company's challenge to its use of private contractors as clean air inspectors, because another federal court, acting in another case between the United States and the company, had forbidden the government to use private contractors for this purpose.

McDonough Power Equipment Inc. v. Greenwood, decided by a 9-0 vote, Jan. 18, 1984. Rehnquist wrote the opinion.

The failure of one juror to disclose relevant informa-

tion during the jury selection process in a civil case is not sufficient reason for an appeals court to order a new trial unless there is evidence that the juror's dishonesty threatens the fairness of the trial.

Pennhurst State School and Hospital v. Halderman, decided by a 5-4 vote, Jan. 23, 1984. Powell wrote the opinion; Stevens, Brennan, Marshall and Blackmun dissented.

Federal judges may not order state officials to comply with state laws. The 11th Amendment denies federal courts jurisdiction over cases brought by citizens against a state without its consent; federal courts therefore lack the power to hear cases in which citizens charge state officials with failing to carry out state law.

The court reversed a federal court order directing Pennsylvania officials to relocate mentally retarded residents of state schools in less restrictive environments. That order was based on a Pennsylvania law.

Heckler v. Edwards, decided by a 9-0 vote, March 21, 1984. Marshall wrote the opinion.

The law permitting a direct appeal to the Supreme Court from a U.S. district court ruling that a federal law is unconstitutional does not permit such a direct appeal when the constitutionality of the statute is not the issue on appeal.

MISCELLANEOUS

Access to Information

United States v. Weber Aircraft Corp., decided by a 9-0 vote, March 20, 1984. Stevens wrote the opinion.

The Freedom of Information Act does not require disclosure of witness statements given in the course of a safety investigation of an Air Force plane crash. These statements are exempt as "inter-agency or intra-agency memorandums or letters, which would not be available by law to a party other than an agency in litigation with the agency."

Federal Communications Commission (FCC) v. ITT World Communications, decided by a 9-0 vote, April 30, 1984. Powell wrote the opinion.

The Government in the Sunshine Act does not require public access to informal consultations between members of the FCC and foreign communications officials. Such consultations are not "meetings" within the scope of the law's requirements.

Damage Suits Against United States

Kosak v. United States, decided by an 8-1 vote, March 21, 1984. Marshall wrote the opinion; Stevens dissented.

The U.S. government cannot be sued for alleged damage to private property that occurs while the property is in the custody of the U.S. Customs Service.

United States v. S. A. Empresa de Viacao Aerea Rio Grandense (VARIG Airlines), decided by a 9-0 vote, June 19, 1984. Burger wrote the opinion.

The U.S. government cannot be sued for damages by persons injured in an air crash involving an aircraft that the federal government certified as airworthy years earlier.

Federal inspections of this type fall within the discretionary-function exception to the Federal Tort Claims Act, which allows some damage suits against the government based on the negligence of its employees.

Wage Compensation, Garnishment

United States v. Lorenzetti, decided by a 9-0 vote, May 29, 1984. Blackmun wrote the opinion.

A federal employee compensated for medical expenses and lost wages incurred as a result of a work-related accident, as provided for under the Federal Employees' Compensation Act, is obligated by that law to reimburse the government if he receives "pain and suffering" compensation under state law from those who caused his injury.

Franchise Tax Board of California v. United States Postal Service, decided by a 9-0 vote, June 11, 1984. Stevens wrote the opinion.

Upon request, the U.S. Postal Service or other federal employer must garnish, or withhold from, a worker's wages to help a state collect overdue state income tax payments. No court order is needed for such action.

United States v. Morton, decided by a 9-0 vote, June 19, 1984. Stevens wrote the opinion.

The United States is not liable to a serviceman, whose wages it garnished subject to a state court order to collect alimony and child support from him, even though a reviewing court later held that the state court lacked jurisdiction over the serviceman necessary to issue the order. ∎

Nominations and Confirmations

Yearlong Dispute Stalls Meese Nomination

A yearlong controversy stalled Senate action on President Reagan's only 1984 Cabinet nomination — that of presidential adviser Edwin Meese III to head the Justice Department.

Reagan resubmitted the nomination early in 1985. He also proposed a number of other Cabinet changes in the wake of his 1984 re-election victory.

Meese was nominated to succeed Attorney General William French Smith, who wished to return to private law practice in California. The nomination, originally submitted Jan. 23, 1984, ran into trouble over questions about Meese's financial dealings. Inquiries centered on whether Meese had helped to get federal jobs for people who provided financial assistance for him and his wife.

Meese denied any impropriety, but his nomination was put on hold pending an investigation of the allegations. An independent counsel's report, issued Sept. 20, cleared Meese of any criminal wrongdoing. But the Senate did not act on the Meese nomination during the remainder of the session. *(Story, p. 248)*

Other major 1984 appointment controversies involved nominations to the Federal Reserve Board and an appellate court judgeship. Several nominations to foreign policy posts ran into opposition from Sen. Jesse Helms, R-N.C. Disputes continued over the board of directors of the Legal Services Corporation, which Reagan wanted to abolish.

Second-Term Shuffles

The long-planned change of command at the Justice Department was one of several top-level job shuffles in prospect as President Reagan began his second term:

● The president announced Jan. 8, 1985, that Treasury Secretary Donald T. Regan would switch jobs with White House Chief of Staff James A. Baker III.

● The administration announced that Energy Secretary Donald P. Hodel would replace Interior Secretary William P. Clark, who said he wished to return to his California ranch. John S. Herrington, White House personnel director, was nominated to succeed Hodel. *(Story, p. 345)*

● William D. Ruckelshaus resigned as administrator of the Environmental Protection Agency, and Reagan nominated Lee M. Thomas, a top Ruckelshaus assistant, to succeed him. *(Story, p. 345)*

● The president nominated William J. Bennett, chairman of the National Endowment for the Humanities, to succeed Education Secretary T. H. Bell, who resigned.

Economic Advisers: Vacancy

One key post remained vacant as Reagan began his second term. No successor had been named for Martin S. Feldstein, who resigned as chairman of the president's Council of Economic Advisers July 10. Another seat on the three-member council also was vacant.

Feldstein, whose outspoken calls for deficit reduction measures had angered other administration officials, returned to Harvard University and resumed the presidency of the National Bureau of Economic Research.

Federal Reserve: Seger

Another key economic post was filled July 2 when Martha Seger, a finance professor at Central Michigan University, was named to the Federal Reserve Board on a controversial recess appointment. The Senate Banking Committee had approved the Seger nomination June 28 on a 10-8 party-line vote, but committee Democrats belittled her qualifications and vowed to continue their attack when the nomination reached the Senate floor.

Reagan made the recess appointment, which permitted Seger to sit on the board through the 1985 session of Congress, during a three-week recess that began the day after the committee vote. The president's action permitted Seger to participate in a key Federal Reserve meeting scheduled July 16-17 to set preliminary monetary growth targets for 1985.

Senators objecting to Seger's temporary appointment offered an amendment Aug. 8 to a supplemental appropriations bill (HR 6040) urging the president to withdraw her appointment. After a spirited debate, the Senate killed the amendment on a 53-43 vote. *(Vote 205, p. 36-S; supplemental story, p. 439)*

Seger was one of several controversial recess appointees named by Reagan in 1984. Others included appointees to the Legal Services Corporation and the National Council on the Humanities. *(Below)*

Vatican Envoy: Wilson

The Senate March 7 approved, by an 81-13 vote, the nomination of William A. Wilson to be the first U.S. ambassador to the Vatican since 1867. Wilson, a Southern California rancher and land developer, had been President Reagan's personal envoy to the Vatican since February 1981. *(Vote 31, p. 7-S; story, p. 119)*

The administration announced Jan. 10 that it intended to establish full diplomatic ties with the Vatican. On Jan. 11 Reagan nominated Wilson to the new diplomatic post. The Senate Foreign Relations Committee Feb. 22 approved the nomination by a 9-1 vote. Helms cast the sole dissenting vote.

State Department: Armacost

The Senate by voice vote May 16 confirmed the nomination of Michael H. Armacost as under secretary of state for political affairs, the No. 3 post at the State Department. The Senate Foreign Relations Committee approved the nomination May 15, 17-0; Helms was the only committee member who did not vote. The North Carolina senator had raised questions about Armacost's role in several Carter administration policy decisions affecting Asia, but had said he was satisfied by Armacost's written responses to a series of questions.

USIA: Lenkowsky

The Foreign Relations Committee May 15 killed the nomination of Leslie Lenkowsky to the No. 2 post at the U.S. Information Agency (USIA). A motion to report his

Membership of Federal Regulatory Agencies, 1984

Civil Aeronautics Board

(Five members appointed for six-year terms; not more than three members from one political party; agency due to expire Jan. 1, 1985.)

Member	Party	Term Expires	Confirmed by Senate
Dan McKinnon (C)	R	12/31/84	10/26/81
Gloria Schaffer	D	12/31/84	9/13/78
James R. Smith	I	12/31/84	8/27/80
Diane Kay Morales	R	12/31/84	12/16/82
Barbara E. McConnell	R	12/31/84	9/21/83

Commodity Futures Trading Commission

(Five members appointed for five-year terms; not more than three members from one political party.)

Member	Party	Term Expires	Confirmed by Senate
Susan M. Phillips (C)	R	4/13/85	10/27/81
Kalo A. Hineman	R	6/19/86	12/16/81
Fowler C. West	D	4/13/87	10/1/82
William E. Seale	D	4/13/88	11/15/83
Robert R. Davis	R	4/13/89	9/28/84

Consumer Product Safety Commission

(Five members appointed for seven-year terms; not more than three members from one political party.)

Member	Party	Term Expires	Confirmed by Senate
Nancy Harvey Steorts (C)	R	10/26/84	7/27/81
Stuart M. Statler	R	10/26/86	7/26/79
Terrence M. Scanlon	D	10/26/89	3/23/83
Saundra B. Armstrong	D	10/26/90	11/18/83
Carol G. Dawson	R	10/26/85	*

* Member sitting on commission pending Senate confirmation.

Federal Communications Commission

(Five members appointed for seven-year terms; not more than three members from one political party.)

Member	Party	Term Expires	Confirmed by Senate
Mark S. Fowler (C)	R	6/30/86	5/14/81
James H. Quello	D	6/30/91	6/15/84
Henry M. Rivera	D	6/30/87	7/31/81
Mary Ann Weyforth-Dawson	R	6/30/88	6/4/81
Dennis Patrick	R	6/30/85	3/30/84

Federal Election Commission

(Six members appointed for six-year terms; not more than three members from one political party.)

Member	Party	Term Expires	Confirmed by Senate
Lee Ann Elliott (C)	R	4/30/87	7/1/82
Danny Lee McDonald	D	4/30/87	7/1/82
Frank P. Reiche	R	4/30/85	7/25/79
John W. McGarry	D	4/30/89	7/29/83
Joan D. Aikens	R	4/30/89	7/29/83
Thomas E. Harris	D	4/30/85	6/19/79

Federal Energy Regulatory Commission

(Five members appointed to staggered four-year terms; not more than three members from one political party.)

Member	Party	Term Expires	Confirmed by Senate
Raymond J. O'Connor (C)	R	10/20/87	10/28/83
Georgiana Sheldon	R	10/20/84	6/4/81
Anthony G. Sousa	R	10/20/84	7/27/81
Oliver G. Richard III	D	10/20/85	8/19/82
Charles G. Stalon	D	10/20/87	6/21/84

Federal Reserve System Governors

(Seven members appointed for 14-year terms; no statutory limitation on political party membership.)

Member	Party	Term Expires	Confirmed by Senate
Paul A. Volcker (C)	D	1/31/92	8/2/79
J. Charles Partee	I	1/31/86	12/19/75
Henry C. Wallich	R	1/31/88	2/8/74
Emmett J. Rice	D	1/31/90	6/12/79
Lyle E. Gramley	D	1/31/94	5/15/80
Preston Martin	R	1/31/96	3/30/82
Martha Seger	R	1/31/98	*

* Member sitting on board pending Senate confirmation.

Federal Trade Commission

(Five members appointed for seven-year terms; not more than three members from one political party.)

Member	Party	Term Expires	Confirmed by Senate
James C. Miller III (C)	R	9/25/88	9/21/81
Patricia P. Bailey	R	9/25/87	6/26/80
George W. Douglas	D	9/25/89	12/16/82
Terry Calvani	R	9/25/90	11/16/83
Mary L. Azcuenaga	I	9/25/91	*

* Member sitting on commission pending Senate confirmation.

Interstate Commerce Commission

(Membership is being reduced gradually under a 1982 law, PL 97-253. As of Jan. 1, 1986, the ICC will have five members; not more than three from one political party. Members will serve five-year terms.)

Member	Party	Term Expires	Confirmed by Senate
Reese H. Taylor Jr. (C)	R	12/31/83 * †	6/16/81
Frederic N. Andre	R	12/31/87	3/16/82
Malcolm M. B. Sterrett	R	12/31/87	2/9/82
Heather J. Gradison	R	12/31/88	6/16/82
Andrew J. Strenio	D	12/31/85 †	9/6/84
J. J. Simmons III	D	12/31/85	9/6/84
Paul H. Lamboley	D	12/31/84	9/6/84

* Member sitting on commission pending Senate confirmation for term ending Dec. 31, 1985.
† Position to be eliminated Dec. 31, 1985.

Nuclear Regulatory Commission

(Five members appointed for five-year terms; not more than three members from one political party.)

Member	Party	Term Expires	Confirmed by Senate
Nunzio J. Palladino (C)	R	6/30/86	6/19/81
Thomas M. Roberts	R	6/30/85	7/31/81
James K. Asselstine	I	6/30/87	5/13/82
Frederick M. Bernthal	R	6/30/88	8/4/83
Lando W. Zech Jr.	I	6/30/89	*

* Member sitting on commission pending Senate confirmation.

Securities and Exchange Commission

(Five members appointed for five-year terms; not more than three members from one political party.)

Member	Party	Term Expires	Confirmed by Senate
John S. R. Shad (C)	R	6/5/86	4/8/81
James C. Treadway Jr.	R	6/5/87	8/19/82
Charles C. Cox	R	6/5/88	11/18/83
Aulana L. Peters	D	6/5/89	5/22/84
Charles L. Marinaccio	D	6/5/85	5/22/84

nomination favorably failed 6-11.

The agency operated overseas cultural and exchange programs, among them an overseas speakers' program. Questions about the speakers' program arose early in the year in the wake of news reports that the agency was keeping a list of people it did not consider fit as speakers because of differences with the administration. Among the more than 90 individuals on the "blacklist" were presidential aspirant Sen. Gary Hart, D-Colo., civil rights activist Coretta Scott King and television journalist Walter Cronkite. During hearings, witnesses disagreed over Lenkowsky's knowledge of the list. Lenkowsky had been acting deputy director of the agency since December 1983.

Appeals Court: Wilkinson

J. Harvie Wilkinson III was confirmed Aug. 9 as a judge on the 4th U.S. Circuit Court of Appeals. The 58-39 vote came after the Senate voted 65-32 to invoke cloture and cut off a filibuster against the nomination led by Sens. Edward M. Kennedy, D-Mass., and Howard M. Metzenbaum, D-Ohio. *(Votes 208, 209, p. 37-S)*

An earlier cloture vote had failed by a 57-39 vote July 31. Cloture required the votes of 60 senators, three-fifths of the entire membership. *(Vote 193, p. 33-S)*

Kennedy and Metzenbaum contended that Wilkinson, 39, was not qualified for the post and that he waged an improper lobbying campaign to get an American Bar Association (ABA) committee to give him a rating of "qualified." The ABA panel regularly reviewed the qualifications of federal judicial nominees.

Wilkinson, a University of Virginia law professor, had served as a clerk for U.S. Supreme Court Justice Lewis F. Powell Jr. in 1972-73, taught at the university in 1973-78, was editorial page editor of the *Virginian Pilot* in 1978-81 and a deputy assistant attorney general in the civil rights division of the Justice Department in 1982-83.

The Judiciary Committee approved the nomination 11-5 on March 15, but subsequently information surfaced suggesting that Wilkinson had encouraged the lobbying effort after learning that his nomination was in trouble with the ABA panel. At a Judiciary hearing Aug. 7, ABA committee Chairman Frederick B. Buesser Jr. said several panel members had complained about calls on Wilkinson's behalf. One of them was made by Powell.

Legal Services Corporation

President Reagan used his recess appointment power Nov. 23 to name 11 individuals to the board of the Legal Services Corporation (LSC). The move bypassed temporarily Senate confirmation for the appointees, who could serve until the end of the first session of the 99th Congress. Reagan appointed the same people he had nominated for the 11-member board in 1984. *(Story, p. 262)*

Ten of 11 nominees had been approved by the Senate Labor and Human Resources Committee on May 2. The nomination of Michael B. Wallace, a Mississippi lawyer who was formerly an aide to House Minority Whip Trent Lott, R-Miss., was sent to the Senate without recommendation.

Wallace's confirmation was controversial because of work he did as an aide to Lott in 1981-83.

During that time, Wallace took an active role in opposing key elements of a bill to extend and strengthen the enforcement sections of the 1965 Voting Rights Act. In addition, Wallace and Lott encouraged the administration to change a longstanding Internal Revenue Service policy of denying tax exemptions to private schools that practiced racial discrimination.

Humanities Council

Reagan gave recess appointments July 2 to seven persons who had been nominated previously to the National Council on the Humanities. The 26-member council advised the chairman of the National Endowment for the Humanities on funding proposals submitted to it.

Reagan's use of his recess appointment power during Congress' three-week July break angered critics of some of the seven council nominees and led to charges that the president had acted to circumvent Senate scrutiny of his choices.

A common argument raised against several of the nominees was that they lacked sufficient academic credentials or background in the humanities to qualify them for seats on the council.

1984 Confirmations

The president sent 4,127 civilian nominations to the Senate in 1984. The Senate confirmed 4,001 and two were withdrawn.

Listed below are 115 persons appointed by President Reagan to major federal posts and confirmed by the Senate in 1984. Information is given in the following order: name of office, salary (as of confirmation date), appointee, legal residence, last occupation before appointment, selected political, public policy or other posts held, date of birth, party affiliation (where available) and confirmation date.

EXECUTIVE OFFICE OF THE PRESIDENT

Council on Environmental Quality

Member, $69,900 — **Jacqueline E. Schafer;** New York City; regional administrator, Region II, Environmental Protection Agency (1982-84); professional staff member, U.S. Senate Environment and Public Works Committee (1977-82); legislative assistant to U.S. Sen. James L. Buckley (1971-76); Oct. 12, 1945; Republican; May 24.

Office of Science and Technology Policy

Deputy director, $71,100 — **Bernadine Healy Bulkley;** Baltimore; director, coronary care unit (1977-84) and active staff member, medicine and pathology (1976-84), The Johns Hopkins Hospital; various positions leading to associate professor of medicine, The Johns Hopkins School of Medicine (1974-82); Aug. 2, 1944; Republican; June 15.

Deputy director, $71,100 — **John P. McTague;** Long Island, N.Y.; chairman, national synchrotron light source department, Brookhaven National Laboratory (1982-84); adjunct professor, chemistry department, Columbia University (1982-84); professor, chemistry department, and member, Institute of Geophysics and Planetary Physics, University of California at Los Angeles (1970-82); Nov. 28, 1938; Republican; June 15.

CABINET DEPARTMENTS

Department of Commerce

Under secretary for economic affairs, $70,800 — **Sidney L. Jones;** Potomac, Md.; research scholar, American Enterprise Institute (1979-83); assistant to Board of Governors, Federal Reserve System (1978-79); fellow, Woodrow Wilson International Center for Scholars (1977-78); counselor to the secretary, Treasury Department (1975); assistant secretary for economic policy, Treasury

Department (1974-77); Sept. 23, 1933; Republican; March 13.

Under secretary for travel and tourism, $70,800 — **Donna F. Tuttle;** Los Angeles; chairman or finance director of various state, local and national political campaigns (1979-84); founder, owner and manager, Frame Interiors (1975-79); April 21, 1947; Republican; March 5.

Assistant secretary for economic development, Economic Development Administration, $69,600 — **J. Bonnie Newman;** Durham, N.H.; associate director for presidential personnel, Executive Office of the President (1982-84); administrative assistant to U.S. Rep. Judd Gregg (1981-82); director, Judd Gregg for Congress Committee (1980-81); executive director, Forum on New Hampshire's Future (1978-80); dean of students, University of New Hampshire (1972-78); June 2, 1945; Republican; Feb. 9.

General counsel, $69,600 — **Irving P. Margulies;** Gaithersburg, Md.; deputy general counsel and then acting general counsel, Commerce Department (1981-84); associate general counsel, Housing and Urban Development Department (1977-81); June 9, 1925; Republican; March 26.

Assistant secretary for international economic policy, $69,900 — **Joseph F. Dennin;** Washington, D.C.; deputy assistant secretary for Africa, the Near East and South Asia, International Trade Administration, Commerce Department (1982-84); deputy assistant secretary for finance, investment and services, Commerce Department (1981-82); deputy associate attorney general, Justice Department (1979-81); June 9, 1943; Republican; May 16.

Assistant secretary for trade development, $69,900 — **Harold P. Goldfield;** New York City; deputy assistant secretary for trade development, Commerce Department (1983-84); associate counsel to the president, Executive Office of the President (1981-83); associate, Schulte Roth & Zabel (1980-81); associate, Cadwalader, Wickersham & Taft (1978-80); Aug. 5, 1951; Republican; May 10.

Assistant secretary for administration, $69,900 — **Katherine M. Bulow;** Bowie, Md.; special assistant to the assistant secretary for administration and then deputy assistant secretary for administration, Commerce Department (1981-84); director, building management division, Republican National Committee (1977-81); administrator, Petrochemical Energy Group (1973-75); Oct. 4, 1943; Aug. 9.

Department of Defense

Deputy secretary, $72,200 — **William H. Taft IV;** Lorton, Va.; general counsel, Defense Department (1981-84); associate, Leva, Hawes, Symington, Martin and Oppenheimer (1977-81); executive assistant to the secretary and then general counsel, Health, Education and Welfare Department (1973-77); principal assistant to the deputy director and then principal assistant to the director, Office of Management and Budget (1970-73); Sept. 13, 1945; Republican; Feb. 2.

General counsel, $69,900 — **Chapman B. Cox;** Arlington, Va.; deputy assistant secretary for logistics and then assistant secretary for manpower and reserve affairs, Navy Department (1981-84); associate, partner and then managing partner, Sherman & Howard (1972-81); associate, Adams, Duque & Hazeltine (1968-72); July 31, 1940; Republican; May 1.

Assistant secretary for command, control, communications and intelligence, $69,900 — **Donald C. Latham;** McLean, Va.; deputy under secretary for communications, command, control and intelligence, Office of the Under Secretary for Research and Engineering, Defense Department (1981-84); consultant, Riverside Research Institute (1981); division vice president for engineering, government systems division in Moorestown, N.J., RCA Corp. (1978-80); director of engineering, Orlando, Fla., division, Martin Marietta Aerospace (1977-78); Dec. 22, 1932; Republican; Aug. 2.

Assistant secretary-comptroller, $69,900 — **Robert W. Helm;** Arlington, Va.; director of defense programs and national security telecommunications policy, National Security Council, Executive Office of the President (1982-84); senior analyst for defense and international affairs, minority staff (1979), and then senior defense analyst, majority staff (1980-82), Senate Budget Committee; professional staff member, Los Alamos Scientific Lab-

oratory (1975-78); Aug. 19, 1951; Republican; Aug. 2.

Assistant secretary for development and support, $69,900 — **James P. Wade Jr.;** Reston, Va.; principal deputy under secretary for research and engineering, Defense Department (1981-84); assistant to the secretary for atomic energy, and chairman, military liaison committee to the Energy Department, Defense Department (1978-81); deputy assistant secretary for policy plans and National Security Council affairs, and director, Strategic Arms Limitation Talks Task Force, Defense Department (1974-77); Dec. 26, 1930; Aug. 2.

Assistant secretary for research and technology, $69,900 — **Robert S. Cooper;** Washington, D.C.; director, Defense Advanced Research Projects Agency, Defense Department (1981-84); vice president for engineering, Satellite Business Systems Inc. (1979-81); director, Goddard Space Flight Center, National Aeronautics and Space Administration (1975-79); assistant director of defense research and engineering, Defense Department (1972-75); Feb. 8, 1932; Republican; Aug. 2.

Air Force

Assistant secretary for financial management, $69,900 — **Richard E. Carver;** Peoria, Ill.; mayor, Peoria, Ill. (1973-84); president, Carver Lumber Co. (1959-84); Aug. 28, 1937; Republican; Sept. 26.

Army

Assistant secretary for financial management, $69,600 — **Pringle P. Hillier;** Fairfax, Va.; principal deputy assistant secretary and then acting assistant secretary for installations, logistics and financial management, Department of the Army (1981-84); principal analyst for ground forces, Congressional Budget Office (1978-81); May 20, 1939; Republican; Feb. 29.

Navy

Assistant secretary for financial management and comptroller, $69,600 — **Robert H. Conn;** Kilmarnock, Va.; deputy under secretary for financial management and comptroller, Department of the Navy (1981-84); manager, federal liaison division, Arthur Andersen & Co. (1972-81); June 8, 1925; Republican; Feb. 29.

Assistant secretary for manpower and reserve affairs, $69,900 — **Charles G. Untermeyer;** Washington, D.C.; deputy assistant secretary for installations and facilities, Department of the Navy (1983-84); executive assistant to the vice president, Executive Office of the President (1981-83); member, Texas House of Representatives (1977-81); March 7, 1946; Republican; Aug. 2.

Assistant secretary for shipbuilding and logistics, $69,900 — **Everett Pyatt;** Arlington, Va.; principal deputy assistant secretary for shipbuilding and logistics, Department of the Navy (1981-84); deputy chief financial officer for project and business management, Energy Department (1980-81); principal deputy assistant secretary for logistics, Department of the Navy (1977-80); July 22, 1939; Aug. 2.

Department of Education

General counsel, $69,600 — **Maureen E. Corcoran;** San Francisco; associate, Weissburg and Aronson (1983-84); special assistant to the U.S. attorney in Washington, D.C., Justice Department (1983); special assistant to the general counsel, Health and Human Services Department (1981-83); member, Hassard, Bonnington, Rogers & Huber (1979-81); Feb. 4, 1944; Republican; Feb. 29.

Department of Energy

Director, Office of Civilian Radioactive Waste Management, $69,900 — **Benjamin C. Rusche;** Columbia, S.C.; president, Management and Technical Resources Inc. (1984); vice president, Management Analysis Co. (1982-84); special assistant for policy and programs, Office of the Secretary, Energy Department (1981-82); corporate director for health and safety, E. I. du Pont de Nemours Co. (1977-78); director, Office of Nuclear Reactor Regulation, Nuclear Regulatory Commission (1975-77); Feb. 18, 1931; Republican; May 24.

Assistant secretary for defense programs, $69,900 — **William W. Hoover;** McLean, Va.; deputy assistant secretary for military application and director of military application, Energy Department (1979-84); various active duty positions leading to commander of the Lowry Technical Training Center, Lowry Air Force Base, Department of the Air Force (1955-84); March 30, 1932; Republican; Aug. 9.

Federal Energy Regulatory Commission

Member for term expiring Oct. 20, 1987, $69,900 — **Charles G. Stalon;** Carbondale, Ill.; commissioner, Illinois Commerce Commission (1977-84); research economist, Federal Power Commission (1969-70); associate professor, economics department, Southern Illinois University (1963-77); Oct. 26, 1929; Democrat; June 21.

Department of Health and Human Services

Assistant secretary for public affairs, $69,600 — **Stephanie Lee-Miller;** Los Angeles; public information officer, Office of Public Affairs, Commerce Department (1981-84); owner and partner, Contact California (1979-81); administrative director, NAACP Legal Defense and Educational Fund (1979); public affairs community programs director, The Coro Foundation (1971-77); March 7, 1950; Republican; March 15.

Assistant secretary for legislation, $69,900 — **John F. Scruggs;** Alexandria, Va.; special assistant to the president for legislative affairs, Executive Office of the President (1982-84); floor assistant to the minority whip, U.S. House of Representatives (1981-82); minority counsel, Rules of the House Subcommittee, U.S. House of Representatives Rules Committee (1980-81); staff assistant, U.S. House of Representatives Rules Committee (1978-80); Jan. 14, 1955; Republican; June 8.

Under secretary, $71,100 — **Charles D. Baker;** Rockport, Mass.; various positions leading to vice chairman and director, Harbridge House (1965-84); deputy under secretary and then assistant secretary for policy and international affairs, Transportation Department (1969-71); June 21, 1928; Republican; Aug. 9.

Department of Housing and Urban Development

Assistant secretary for housing and federal housing commissioner, $69,600 — **Maurice L. Barksdale;** Fort Worth, Texas; deputy assistant secretary for multifamily housing programs, Housing and Urban Development Department (1982-83); regional vice president, Essex and Union Mortgage Co. (1976-82); president, HMB Management Co. (1975-82); vice president, Citizens Trust Bank (1974-75); Jan. 7, 1939; Republican; Feb. 9.

Assistant secretary for policy development and research, $69,900 — **June Q. Koch;** Potomac, Md.; deputy under secretary for intergovernmental relations, Housing and Urban Development Department (1981-84); vice president, Koch & Associates (1976-80); director of federal liaison, Philadelphia Bicentennial Corp. (1973-75); Jan. 18, 1933; Republican; June 29.

Department of the Interior

Under secretary, $70,800 — **Ann Dore McLaughlin;** Washington, D.C.; assistant secretary for public affairs, Treasury Department (1981-84); president, McLaughlin & Co. (1977-81); Washington, D.C., manager, Braun and Co. (1977-81); director of state and local government relations, Union Carbide Corp. (1974-77); director, Office of Public Affairs, Environmental Protection Agency (1973-74); Nov. 16, 1941; Republican; Feb. 22.

Assistant secretary for territorial and international affairs, $69,600 — **Richard T. Montoya;** Austin, Texas; deputy assistant secretary for territorial and international affairs, Interior Depart-

ment (1983-84); director, Governor's Office of Regional Development, state of Texas (1979-83); deputy secretarial representative, Commerce Department (1976-79); assistant regional director for the U.S. small business administrator, Dallas (1971-76); May 5, 1947; Republican; Feb. 21.

Assistant secretary for water and science, $69,900 — **Robert N. Broadbent;** Boulder City, Nev.; commissioner, Bureau of Reclamation, Interior Department (1981-84); trustee, Federal Bankruptcy Court, Las Vegas, Nev. (1975-81); owner, partner and manager, Boulder City Drug (1950-75); June 19, 1926; Republican; Aug. 10.

Solicitor, $69,900 — **Frank K. Richardson;** Sacramento, Calif.; professor, Pepperdine Law School (1983-84); associate justice, California Supreme Court (1974-83); presiding justice, Court of Appeals, Third District (Sacramento), state of California (1971-74); private law practice (1939-71); Feb. 13, 1914; Republican; June 28.

Department of Justice

Deputy attorney general, $72,600 — **Carol E. Dinkins;** Houston; associate (1973-80) and then partner (1980-81, 1983-84), Vinson & Elkins; assistant attorney general, Land and Natural Resources Division, Justice Department (1981-83); Nov. 9, 1945; Republican; May 18.

Assistant attorney general for legal policy and counselor to the attorney general, $69,900 — **Harold J. Lezar Jr.;** Houston; special counsel and then counselor to the attorney general, Justice Department (1981-84); private law practice (1980-81); general counsel to the secretary of state, state of Texas (1979-80); staff assistant and speechwriter to the president, Executive Office of the President (1971-74); Sept. 30, 1948; Republican; Aug. 6.

Department of Labor

Assistant secretary for employment and training, $69,900 — **Frank C. Casillas;** Downers Grove, Ill.; director, Casillas Associates (1983-84); various positions leading to vice president of business development and technology, Bunker Ramo-Eltra Corp. (1968-83); April 19, 1926; Republican; June 15.

Department of State

Assistant secretary for international narcotics matters, $69,900 — **Jon R. Thomas;** Memphis, Tenn.; deputy assistant secretary for international narcotics matters, State Department (1982-84); senior staff member, policy planning staff, State Department (1980-82); political officer, Spain and then Switzerland, State Department (1971-77); Jan. 7, 1946; Republican; Oct. 4.

Ambassadors

Ireland, $69,600 — **Robert F. Kane;** San Mateo, Calif.; senior director, Ropers, Majeski, Kohn, Bentley, Wagner & Kane (1979-84); justice, California Courts of Appeal, Division Two (1971-79); judge, Superior Court of San Mateo County, state of California (1969-71); March 15, 1926; Republican; Feb. 27.

Peru, $70,800 — **David C. Jordan;** Charlottesville, Va.; assistant professor, associate professor and then professor, government and foreign affairs department, University of Virginia (1965-84); visiting professor, University of Chile (1982); visiting professor, University of La Plata and University of the Savior (1975); April 30, 1925; Feb. 29.

Republic of Malawi, $69,900 — **Weston Adams;** Columbia, S.C.; private law practice (1972-84); member, South Carolina House of Representatives (1972-74); associate, Albert Watson law office (1971-72); Sept. 16, 1938; Republican; June 8.

Guatemala, $71,100 — **Alberto Martinez Piedra;** Bethesda, Md.; senior policy adviser to the ambassador, permanent mission of the U.S. to the Organization of American States, State Department (1982-84); professor, economics department, Catholic University (1964-82); Jan. 29, 1926; June 28.

Nepal, $69,900 — **Leon J. Weil;** New York City; general

partner and then senior vice president, Herzfeld & Stern (1974-84); various positions leading to chief executive officer, Steiner Rouse and Co. (1950-74); June 15, 1927; Republican; Aug. 9.

Norway, $69,900 — **Robert D. Stuart Jr.;** Lake Forest, Ill.; various positions leading to chairman of the finance committee, Quaker Oats Co. (1947-84); April 26, 1916; Republican; Sept. 17.

Department of Transportation

Assistant secretary for governmental affairs, $69,600 — **Charles G. Hardin;** Annapolis, Md.; chief clerk and then majority staff director, Transportation and Related Agencies Subcommittee, U.S. Senate Appropriations Committee (1981-84); professional staff member, U.S. House of Representatives Appropriations Committee (1973-80); April 10, 1947; Republican; Feb. 29.

General counsel, $69,600 — **Jim J. Marquez;** Lawrence, Kan.; U.S. attorney, District of Kansas (1981-84); private law practice (1979-81); secretary, Department of Corrections, state of Kansas (1977-79); March 10, 1941; Republican; Feb. 29.

Department of Treasury

Assistant secretary for international affairs, $69,600 — **David C. Mulford;** Rockford, Ill.; senior investment adviser, Saudi Arabian Monetary Agency (1975-84); director, Merrill Lynch, Pierce, Fenner and Smith (1978-84); managing director, Merrill Lynch White Weld Capital Markets Group (1966-78); June 27, 1937; Republican; March 15.

Assistant secretary for policy planning and communications, $69,600 — **Alfred H. Kingon;** Chevy Chase, Md.; assistant secretary for international economic policy, Commerce Department (1983-84); editor in chief, *Saturday Review* (1980-82); editor in chief, *Financial World* (1973-83); editor, *Money & Credit* (1970-73); May 11, 1931; Republican; March 15.

Assistant secretary for legislative affairs, $69,900 — **Bruce E. Thompson Jr.;** Chevy Chase, Md.; deputy assistant secretary for legislative affairs and then assistant secretary for business and consumer affairs, Treasury Department (1981-84); legislative assistant to U.S. Sen. William V. Roth Jr. (1974-81); June 5, 1949; Republican; May 3.

INDEPENDENT AGENCIES

Agency for International Development

Assistant administrator, Bureau for Latin America and the Caribbean, $71,100 — **Victor M. Rivera;** Vienna, Va.; director, Minority Business Development Agency, Commerce Department (1981-84); senior advocate, Office of Chief Council for Advocacy, Small Business Administration (1977-81); district director and then regional director, Small Business Administration (1973-77); July 27, 1937; Republican; Aug. 9.

Assistant administrator for Africa, $69,900 — **Mark L. Edelman;** St. Louis County, Mo.; senior adviser to the administrator and executive secretary, Agency for International Development (1983-84); deputy assistant secretary for international management and budgetary analysis, State Department (1981-83); program analyst, Agency for International Development (1981); legislative assistant to Sen. John C. Danforth (1977-81); June 27, 1943; Republican; Oct. 4.

Assistant administrator, Bureau for External Affairs, $69,900 — **Cathryn L. Semerad;** Kensington, Md.; executive director, Advisory Committee on Voluntary Foreign Aid, and then associate deputy administrator, Bureau for External Relations, Agency for International Development (1981-84); specialist, Office of Presidential Personnel, Executive Office of the President (1979-81); Jan. 16, 1943; Republican; Oct. 4.

Assistant administrator for program and policy coordination, $69,900 — **Richard A. Derham;** Seattle; general counsel and then acting assistant administrator for program and policy coordination, Agency for International Development (1983-84); various positions leading to managing partner, Davis, Wright, Todd, Riese & Jones (1965-83); May 29, 1940; Republican; Oct. 11.

Asian Development Bank

Director, with the rank of ambassador, $69,900 — **Joe O. Rogers;** Arlington, Va.; executive director, House Republican Conference (1981-84); economic counsel to Sen. William L. Armstrong (1980-81); director, Task Force on Economic Policy, House Republican Research Committee (1979-80); economist, experimental technology incentives program, National Bureau of Standards (1978-79); assistant professor, economics department, Wake Forest University (1977-78); Dec. 4, 1948; Republican; Oct. 5.

Commodity Futures Trading Commission

Commissioner for term expiring April 13, 1989, $69,900 — **Robert R. Davis;** Fairfax, Va.; economist, Joint Economic Committee (1984); various positions leading to vice president and economist, Harris Trust and Savings Bank of Chicago (1979-84); financial economist, Federal Deposit Insurance Corporation (1977-79); April 3, 1949; Republican; Sept. 28.

Equal Employment Opportunity Commission

Member for term expiring July 1, 1988, $69,900 — **Fred W. Alvarez;** Albuquerque, N.M.; member, Sutin, Thayer & Browne (1980-84); trial attorney, National Labor Relations Board, Oakland, Calif., and San Francisco (1976-80); law clerk to Chief Justice LaFel E. Oman, New Mexico Supreme Court (1975-76); June 1, 1949; Democrat; May 11.

Member for term expiring July 1, 1989, $69,900 — **Tony E. Gallegos;** Pico Rivera, Calif.; commissioner, Equal Employment Opportunity Commission (1982-84); various positions leading to manager, Douglas Aircraft Co., division of McDonnell Douglas Corp. (1952-82); Feb. 13, 1924; Democrat; Sept. 26.

Export-Import Bank

First vice president and vice chairman, $69,600 — **John A. Bohn Jr.;** Oakland, Calif.; U.S. director, Asian Development Bank (1981-84); various positions leading to vice president of correspondent banking division and manager of international personal banking department, Wells Fargo International Banking Group (1972-81); Oct. 31, 1937; Republican; March 13.

Federal Communications Commission

Member for term expiring June 30, 1991, $69,900 — **James H. Quello;** Alexandria, Va.; member, Federal Communications Commission (1974-84); consultant, Storer Broadcasting (1972-73); vice president and station manager, Goodwill Stations Inc. (1947-72); April 21, 1914; Democrat; June 15.

Federal Emergency Management Agency

Administrator, U.S. Fire Administration, $69,900 — **Clyde A. Bragdon Jr.;** Newhall, Calif.; various positions leading to county forester and fire warden-fire chief, Los Angeles County Fire Department, state of California (1956-84); July 20, 1929; Republican; June 15.

Federal Home Loan Bank Board

Member for term expiring June 30, 1986, $69,600 — **Mary A. Grigsby;** Houston; vice chairman, United Savings of Texas (1983-84); various positions leading to director and president, Houston First American Savings (1941-80); July 25, 1916; Democrat; Feb. 3.

Interstate Commerce Commission

Member for term expiring Dec. 31, 1984, $69,900 — **Paul H. Lamboley;** Reno, Nev.; private law practice (1969-84); associate, Woodburn, Foreman, Wedge, Blakey, Folsom & Hug (1968-69); July 17, 1940; Democrat; Sept. 6.

Member for term expiring Dec. 31, 1985, $69,900 — **J. J. Simmons III;** Washington, D.C.; under secretary, Interior Department (1983-84); commissioner, Interstate Commerce Commission (1982-83); vice president, government relations, Amerada Hess Corp. (1970-82); March 26, 1925; Democrat; Sept. 6.

Member for term expiring Dec. 31, 1985, $69,900 — **Andrew J. Strenio;** Bethesda, Md.; assistant director for regulatory evaluation, Bureau of Consumer Protection, Federal Trade Commission (1982-84); staff economist, Council of Economic Advisers, Executive Office of the President (1980-81); member, Wald, Harkrader & Ross (1980); research associate, Huron Institute (1978-79); April 3, 1952; Democrat; Sept. 6.

National Credit Union Administration

Member of the board for term expiring Aug. 2, 1989, $69,900 — **P. A. Mack Jr.;** Washington, D.C.; member, National Credit Union Administration (1979-84); owner and manager, Mack Farms (1955-84); administrative assistant to Sen. Birch Bayh (1971-79); Sept. 8, 1930; Democrat; Sept. 28.

National Science Foundation

Director, $72,600 — **Erich Bloch;** South Salem, N.Y.; various positions leading to vice president for technical personnel development, IBM Corp. (1953-84); Jan. 9, 1925; Aug. 6.

National Transportation Safety Board

Chairman for term expiring April 30, 1985, $71,100 — **James E. Burnett Jr.;** Clinton, Ark.; member and then chairman, National Transportation Safety Board (1981-84); special associate justice, Arkansas Supreme Court (1981); city judge, Damascus, Ark. (1979-81); private law practice and juvenile judge, Van Buren County, state of Arkansas (1973-81); Sept. 20, 1947; Republican; May 18.

Member for term expiring Dec. 31, 1988, $69,900 — **Patricia A. Goldman;** Washington, D.C.; member and then vice chairman, National Transportation Safety Board (1979-84); executive director, Wednesday Group, U.S. House of Representatives (1972-79); legislative counsel, National League of Cities and U.S. Conference of Mayors (1971-72); March 22, 1942; Republican; May 18.

Securities and Exchange Commission

Member for term expiring June 5, 1985, $69,900 — **Charles L. Marinaccio;** Crofton, Md.; general counsel and then minority general counsel, U.S. Senate Banking, Housing and Urban Affairs Committee (1975-84); director, Executive Secretariat, Law Enforcement Assistance Administration, Justice Department (1973-75); adviser to the Division of Supervision and Regulation and senior attorney, Federal Reserve Board (1969-73); Dec. 10, 1933; Democrat; May 22.

Member for term expiring June 5, 1989, $69,900 — **Aulana L. Peters;** Los Angeles; associate and then partner, Gibson, Dunn & Crutcher (1973-84); administrative assistant, Organization for Economic Cooperation and Development (1966-67); Nov. 30, 1941; Democrat; May 22.

Tennessee Valley Authority

Member of board of directors for term expiring May 18, 1993, $69,900 — **John B. Waters;** Sevierville, Tenn.; member, Tennessee-Tombigbee Waterway Authority (1978-84); various positions leading to senior partner, Hailey, Waters, Sykes & Sharp (1959-84); federal co-chairman, Appalachian Regional Commission (1969-71); July 15, 1929; Republican; Aug. 3.

United States Information Agency

Associate director for management, $69,600 — **Woodward Kingman;** San Francisco; executive vice president, Crocker National Bank (1974-83); president and chief executive officer, Government National Mortgage Association, Housing and Urban Development Department (1969-74); Sept. 5, 1925; Feb. 27.

U.S. International Trade Commission

Member for term expiring Dec. 16, 1988, $69,600 — **Susan Wittenberg Liebeler;** Malibu, Calif.; law professor, Loyola Law School (1973-84); special counsel to the chairman, Securities and Exchange Commission (1981-82); July 3, 1942; Independent; March 15.

Member for term expiring Dec. 16, 1985, $69,600 — **David B. Rohr;** Laurel, Md.; professional staff member and then staff director, Trade Subcommittee, U.S. House of Representatives Ways and Means Committee (1974-84); various positions leading to director, Trade Negotiations and Agreements Division, Office of International Trade Policy, Commerce Department (1961-74); April 18, 1933; Democrat; March 15.

JUDICIARY

U.S. Circuit Courts

Judge, Federal Circuit, $77,300 — **Pauline Newman;** Philadelphia; various positions leading to director, patent and licensing department, FMC Corp. (1954-84); June 20, 1927; Republican; Feb. 27.

Judge, 9th Circuit, $77,300 — **Robert R. Beezer;** Seattle; law clerk, associate and then partner, Schweppe, Doolittle, Krug, Tausend & Beezer law firm (1956-84); July 21, 1928; Republican; March 27.

Judge, Federal Circuit, $77,300 — **Jean G. Bissell;** Columbia, S.C.; general counsel and various positions leading to vice chairman and chief administrative officer, South Carolina National Corp. (1976-84); general counsel (1976-84), executive vice president (1980-81) and senior vice president (1976-80), The South Carolina National Bank; partner, McKay, Sherrill, Walker, Townsend & Wilkins (1971-76); June 9, 1936; June 8.

Judge, Fourth Circuit, $77,300 — **J. Harvie Wilkinson III;** Charlottesville, Va.; assistant, associate and then full professor, University of Virginia Law School (1973-84); deputy assistant attorney general, civil rights division, Justice Department (1982-83); editorial page editor, *Virginian-Pilot*, Landmark Communications Inc. (1978-81); law clerk to Justice Lewis F. Powell Jr., U.S. Supreme Court (1972-73); Sept. 29, 1944; Aug. 9.

Judge, Fifth Circuit, $77,300 — **Robert M. Hill;** Dallas; judge, U.S. District Court for the Northern District of Texas (1970-84); member, Woodruff, Hill, Kendall & Smith (1959-70); Jan. 13, 1928; June 15.

Judge, First Circuit, $77,300 — **Juan R. Torruella del Valle;** Isla Verde, Carolina, Puerto Rico; judge, U.S. District Court for the District of Puerto Rico (1975-84); partner, Pieras & Torruella (1969-74); June 7, 1933; Oct. 3.

Judge, Fourth Circuit, $77,300 — **Emory M. Sneeden;** Columbia, S.C.; counsel and then shareholder, McNair Glenn Konduros Corley Singletary Porter & Dibble (1981-84); associate dean and lecturer, University of South Carolina School of Law (1978-82); chief counsel, U.S. Senate Judiciary Committee (1980-81); member, Randall, Bangert & Thelen (1978-79); May 30, 1927; Republican; Oct. 3.

Judge, Sixth Circuit, $77,300 — **H. Ted Milburn;** Chattanooga, Tenn.; judge, U.S. District Court for the Eastern District of Tennessee (1983-84); judge, Sixth Judicial Circuit, state of Tennessee (1973-83); member, Bishop, Thomas, Leitner, Mann and Milburn (1959-73); May 26, 1931; Republican; Oct. 3.

Judge, Ninth Circuit, $77,300 — **Cynthia Holcomb Hall;** Pasadena, Calif.; judge, U.S. District Court for the Central District of California (1981-84); judge, U.S. Tax Court (1972-81); Feb. 19, 1929; Oct. 3.

Judge, Ninth Circuit, $77,300 — **Charles E. Wiggins;** San Francisco; counsel, Pillsbury, Madison & Sutro (1984); member, Pierson, Ball & Dowd (1982-84); member, Musick, Peeler & Garrett (1979-82); U.S. representative, 39th Congressional District, California (1967-79); Dec. 3, 1927; Republican; Oct. 3.

U.S. District Courts

Judge, District of Alaska, $73,100 — **H. Russel Holland;** Anchorage, Alaska; various partnerships leading to partner, Holland & Trefry (1966-68 and 1970-84); private law practice (1968-70); assistant U.S. attorney, District of Alaska (1963-65); Sept. 18, 1936; March 26.

Judge, Central District of California, $73,100 — **Harry L. Hupp;** Los Angeles; judge, Superior Court of California, Los Angeles County (1972-84); member, Beardsley, Hufstedler and Kemble (1955-72); April 5, 1929; Republican; March 20.

Judge, Eastern District of California, $73,100 — **Edward J. Garcia;** Sacramento, Calif; judge, Sacramento Municipal Court, Sacramento County, state of California (1972-84); deputy district attorney and then chief deputy district attorney, Sacramento County, state of California (1959-72); Nov. 24, 1928; Republican; March 13.

Judge, Southern District of Indiana, $73,100 — **Sarah E. Barker;** Morgantown, Ind.; U.S. attorney, Southern District of Indiana (1981-84); associate and then partner, Bose McKinney & Evans (1977-81); assistant U.S. attorney and then first assistant U.S. attorney, Southern District of Indiana (1972-77); June 10, 1943; Republican; March 13.

Judge, District of Maryland, $73,100 — **John R. Hargrove;** Baltimore; associate judge, Maryland Circuit Court, 8th Judicial Circuit (1974-84); administrative judge, District Court of Baltimore City (1971-74); associate judge, Municipal Court of Baltimore City (1968-71); Oct. 25, 1923; Democrat; Feb. 9.

Judge, Northern District of Mississippi, $73,100 — **Neal B. Biggers;** Corinth, Miss.; judge, Mississippi Circuit Court, 1st Circuit (1975-84); visiting assistant instructor, judicial education, University of Mississippi (1974); district attorney, Mississippi Circuit Court, 1st Circuit (1968-74); July 1, 1935; Democrat; March 27.

Judge, District of Arizona, $73,100 — **Paul G. Rosenblatt;** Prescott, Ariz.; presiding judge, Division One, Yavapai County Superior Court, state of Arizona (1973-84); private law practice (1971-73); administrative assistant to U.S. Rep. Sam Steiger (1967-72); April 4, 1928; Republican; June 8.

Judge, Central District of California, $73,100 — **Alicemarie H. Stotler;** Newport Beach, Calif.; partner, Stotler & Stotler (1983-84); judge, Orange County Superior Court, state of California (1978-83); judge, Orange County Municipal Court, state of California (1976-78); private law practice (1973-76); May 29, 1942; Republican; May 1.

Judge, Western District of Louisiana, $73,100 — **John M. Duhe Jr.;** Iberia Parish, La.; judge, 16th Judicial Circuit, state of Louisiana (1979-84); private law practice (1957-79); April 7, 1933; Republican; June 8.

Judge, Southern District of Mississippi, $73,100 — **Tom S. Lee;** Forest, Miss.; private law practice (1965-84); April 8, 1941; June 8.

Judge, Central District of California, $73,100 — **James M. Ideman;** Rolling Hills Estates, Calif.; judge, Los Angeles Superior Court, state of California (1979-84); deputy district attorney, office of the district attorney for Los Angeles County, state of California (1964-79); April 2, 1931; Republican; June 15.

Judge, Central District of California, $73,100 — **William J. Rea;** Pacific Palisades, Calif.; judge, Los Angeles Superior Court, state of California (1968-84); partner, Moore, Graves, Madory & Rea (1964-68); Feb. 21, 1920; Republican; June 15.

Judge, Southern District of California, $73,100 — **Rudi M. Brewster;** San Diego; member, Gray, Cary, Ames & Frye (1960-84); May 18, 1932; June 15.

Judge, Southern District of New York, $73,100 — **Peter K. Leisure;** New York City; litigation partner, Whitman & Ransom (1978-84); associate and litigation partner, Curtis, Mallet-Prevost, Colt & Mosle (1966-78); March 21, 1929; June 15.

Judge, District of Vermont, $73,100 — **Franklin S. Billings Jr.;** Woodstock, Vt.; associate justice and then chief justice, Supreme Court, state of Vermont (1975-84); judge, Superior Court, state of Vermont (1966-75); June 5, 1922; June 15.

Judge, Central District of California, $73,100 — **William D. Keller;** Los Angeles; member, Hahn & Cazier (1981-84); private law practice (1978-81); member, Rosenfeld, Meyer & Susman (1977-78); U.S. attorney for the Central District of California (1972-77); Oct. 29, 1934; Republican; Oct. 3.

Judge, Northern District of California, $73,100 — **Charles A. Legge;** Orinda, Calif.; various positions leading to chairman, Bronson, Bronson & McKinnon (1956-84); Aug. 24, 1930; Republican; Sept. 17.

Judge, Northern District of Illinois, $73,100 — **Charles R. Norgle Sr.;** Elmhurst, Ill.; associate judge (1973-78 and 1980-81) and judge (1978-79 and 1981-84), 18th Judicial Circuit, state of Illinois; March 6, 1937; Republican; Oct. 3.

Judge, Northern District of Illinois, $73,100 — **Ilana D. Rovner;** Chicago; deputy governor for Chicago and legal counsel to the governor, state of Illinois (1977-84); assistant U.S. attorney for the Northern District of Illinois (1973-77); Aug. 21, 1938; Republican; Sept. 12.

Judge, Eastern District of Louisiana, $73,100 — **Marcel Livaudais Jr.;** Orleans Parish, La; U.S. magistrate for the Eastern District of Louisiana (1977-84); partner, Loeb & Livaudais (1971-77); March 3, 1925; Republican; Sept. 17.

Judge, Western District of Louisiana, $73,100 — **F. A. Little Jr.;** Alexandria, La.; various positions leading to president, Gold, Little, Simon, Weems & Bruser (1966-84); Oct. 26, 1936; Republican; Oct. 11.

Judge, Eastern District of Michigan, $73,100 — **Richard F. Suhrheinrich;** Grosse Pointe Farms, Mich.; senior partner, Kitch, Suhrheinrich, Saurbier & Drutchas (1969-84); Aug. 15, 1936; Republican; Oct. 3.

Judge, District of Nevada, $73,100 — **Howard D. McKibben;** Minden, Nev.; judge, Ninth Judicial District, state of Nevada (1977-84); deputy district attorney and then district attorney for Douglas County, state of Nevada (1969-77); April 1, 1940; Republican; Oct. 3.

Judge, Eastern District of Pennsylvania, $73,100 — **Anthony J. Scirica;** Conshohocken, Pa.; judge, Court of Common Pleas, Montgomery County, state of Pennsylvania (1980-84); partner, McGrory, Scirica, Wentz and Fernandez (1966-80); member, Pennsylvania General Assembly (1971-79); Dec. 16, 1940; Republican; Sept. 17.

Judge, Eastern District of Tennessee, $73,100 — **James H. Jarvis II;** Maryville, Tenn.; judge, 30th Judicial Circuit, state of Tennessee (1977-84); judge, Law and Equity Court, Blount County, state of Tennessee (1972-77); Feb. 28, 1937; Oct. 11.

Judge, Middle District of Tennessee, $73,100 — **Thomas A. Higgins;** Nashville, Tenn.; member, Cornelius, Collins, Higgins & White (1961-84); Aug. 15, 1932; Republican; Oct. 3.

Judge, Western District of Texas, $73,100 — **Walter S. Smith Jr.;** Waco, Texas; partner, Vaughn, Terrell, Lynn & Crowden (1984); member, Sleeper, Johnston, Helm & Fontaine (1983-84); judge, 54th Judicial District, state of Texas (1980-82); associate, Fulbright, Winniford, Bice & Marable (1978-80); Oct. 26, 1940; Republican; Oct. 3.

U.S. Court of International Trade

Judge, $73,100 — **Dominick L. DiCarlo;** Brooklyn, N.Y.; assistant secretary, international narcotics matters, State Department (1981-84); member, New York State Assembly (1965-81); private law practice (1962-81); March 11, 1928; Republican; June 8.

U.S. Tax Court

Judge, $73,100 — **Julian I. Jacobs;** Bethesda, Md.; associate and then partner, Gordon, Feinblatt, Rothman, Hoffberger & Hollander (1972-84); associate, Hoffberger & Hollander (1969-72); Aug. 13, 1937; March 15.

Judge, $73,100 — **Joel Gerber;** Arlington, Va.; various positions leading to acting chief counsel, Internal Revenue Service, Treasury Department (1972-84); July 16, 1940; May 10.

Judge, $73,100 — **Lawrence A. Wright;** South Burlington, Vt.; associate and then senior partner, Gravel, Shea & Wright (1971-84); state tax commissioner, Department of Taxes, state of Vermont (1969-71); Dec. 25, 1927; Republican; Sept. 28. ∎

Kissinger Commission Report

Kissinger Panel Recommends Major Aid Package

In July 1983, President Reagan appointed a commission in hopes of getting a broad consensus behind his program of supporting El Salvador against leftist guerrillas while pressuring Nicaragua to drop its pro-Soviet stance.

The panel's formal title, "National Bipartisan Commission on Central America," reflected Reagan's search for a political consensus. (1983 Almanac p. 169)

Chaired by former Secretary of State Henry A. Kissinger, the panel reported to Reagan on Jan. 11, 1984. The commission called for more than $8 billion in economic aid to the region through 1989 and for firm U.S. resistance to the expansion of Soviet and Cuban influence. (Story, p. 93; members, p. 99)

It endorsed a "substantial" increase in military aid for El Salvador and backed indirectly Reagan's program of "covert" aid to anti-government rebels in Nicaragua. It also called on Reagan and Central American leaders to meet to decide on a plan for long-range economic development in the region.

Following is the text of an information sheet issued Jan. 11 on the commission's report:

Outline

The report, which is dedicated to [the late] Sen. Henry Jackson [D-Wash., (1953-83), who first proposed the commission], consists of the following chapters:

1. Introduction and basic themes.
2. Places crisis in larger hemispheric context.
3. Provides historical perspective.
4. Examines prospects for economic and political development; presents recommendations.
5. Discusses social issues — health and education particularly — and makes recommendations.
6. Explores security issues and recommends U.S. action.
7. Looks at diplomatic aspects and offers recommendations on pursuing negotiated settlements.
8. Conclusion.

On security and diplomatic issues, the report deals with El Salvador, Honduras, Nicaragua, Guatemala and Costa Rica.

Panama and Belize are included for discussion of development programs.

Major Themes

● The crisis in Central America is acute. Its roots are indigenous — in poverty, injustice and closed political systems. But world economic recession and Cuban-Soviet-Nicaraguan intervention brought it to a head.

● The crisis will not wait. It must be addressed at once and simultaneously in all its aspects. Ultimate resolutions depend on economic progress, social and political reform. But insurgencies must be checked if lasting progress is to be made on these fronts.

● Indigenous reform, even indigenous revolution, is no threat to the U.S. But the intrusion of outside powers exploiting local grievances for political and strategic advantage is a serious threat. Objective of U.S. policy should be to reduce Central American conflicts to Central American dimensions.

● United States has fundamental interests at stake: Soviet-Cuban success and resulting collapse of Central America would compel substantial increase in our security burden or redeployment of forces to detriment of vital interests elsewhere.

● As a nation we have deep and historic interest in promotion and preservation of democracy. Report concludes that pluralistic societies are what Central Americans want and are essential to lasting solutions. In this case our strategic interests and our ideals coincide.

● Central Americans desperately need our help and we have a moral obligation to provide it. The U.S. and other nations can make a difference. But in the end solutions will depend on the efforts of Central Americans themselves.

● Although there is urgent need for action, no quick solutions can be expected. U.S. must make a long-term commitment and stick to a coherent policy.

● That policy can and should be bipartisan. Commission found wide consensus on principles and objectives.

Political and Economic Development

● Central American economies grew substantially during the 60s and early 70s. But income distribution was highly inequitable, except in Costa Rica and Panama.

● Trend toward more pluralistic political

systems in El Salvador, Guatemala and Nicaragua reversed in early 70s.

● World recession and rising political violence had catastrophic effect on region's economies in late 70s, early 80s. All have declined dramatically. El Salvador's gross domestic product is off 25% since 1978.

● Even with successful stabilization programs and restored political stability, per capita wealth in 1990 would only be three-quarters of what it was in 1980.

● There must be substantial increase in outside assistance.

● Commission believes economic development cannot be separated from political and social reform. Objective must be parallel development of pluralistic societies and strong economies with far more equitable distribution of wealth.

● We propose a program of U.S. assistance designed to promote economic growth, democratization and greater social equity.

● We encourage the greatest possible involvement of the U.S. private sector in the stabilization effort. Recommend the formation of an emergency action committee of private sector personalities to provide advice on new private-public initiatives to spur growth and employment.

Recommendations: An Emergency Stabilization Program

● Leaders of U.S. and Central America should meet to initiate a comprehensive approach to economic development of the region and reinvigoration of the Central American Common Market.

● A $400 million supplemental in FY84 over and above the $477 million now in the budget for the seven countries. There is urgent need to stabilize economies now going downhill very fast.

● Focus this assistance on labor-intensive infrastructure projects and housing. Unemployment is a critical problem — politically and economically.

● Establish a program to provide U.S. Government guarantees for short-term trade credits. External credit has dried up. Without it economies cannot be reactivated.

● Provide an emergency loan to the Central American Common Market to permit the reactivation of this vital organization. Lack of resources in the market to settle trade accounts among the countries has stalled it.

● U.S. Government should take an active role in the efforts to resolve the external debt problems of Central America and should encourage the countries that have not done so to seek multilateral rescheduling.

● Also encourage commercial banks to renegotiate at the lowest possible interest rates.

Recommendations:
Medium and Long-term

● Commission estimates $24 billion in net external exchange inflows needed to 1990 to foster a growth rate of 3 percent per capita, returning these countries to pre-recession levels of per capita wealth. About half — $12 billion — is expected to come from international institutions, other donor countries and loans and investments from private sector sources.

● U.S. Government will have to provide as much as $12 billion if these financing needs are to be met.

● We propose in this context a program of $8 billion over next five fiscal years (FY85-89) in USG assistance. This would be divided very roughly into about $6 billion in appropriated funds and about $2 billion in contingent liabilities covering guarantees, insurance and the like.

● Compared with current projections for FY85-89, these contributions would constitute an increase of about $2.8 billion in appropriated funds and $.7 billion in contingent liabilities over the five-year period.

● Urge that Congress authorize multiyear funding of this program. Commission believes firm, long-term commitment is essential.

● To give form and structure to the development effort suggest establishment of the Central American Development Organization (CADO). Perhaps ¼ of U.S. aid could be channelled through CADO.

● CADO would consist of the United States and those countries of the seven willing to commit themselves to internal democracy and reform. Continued membership would depend on demonstrated progress toward those goals. Adherence to regional security pact also required.

● Nicaragua could participate by meeting these conditions.

● CADO's principal body would be a Development Council with tripartite, ILO-style representation. Would assess program and progress toward economic growth, democratization, reform and preservation of human rights.

● Other democracies would be invited to join.

Additional Recommendations

● Expanded assistance from the U.S. Government for democratic institutions and leadership training — neighborhood groups, cooperatives, binational centers and visitor programs for leaders of labor unions, local governments and other organizations.

● Require a firm commitment by the Central Americans to economic policies, including reforms in tax systems, to encourage private enterprise and individual initiative, to create favorable investment climates, to curb corruption where it exists, and to spur balanced trade.

● Urge extension of duty-free trade to Central America by other major trading nations.

● Review non-tariff barriers to imports from Central America with a view toward using whatever flexibility that exists within the framework of multilateral agreements, to favor Central American products.

● Establishment of the Central American Development Corporation — a privately owned venture-capital company which could initially be financed by a loan from the U.S. Government.

● Recommend that the United States join the Central American Bank for Economic Integration.

● Technical and financial support for export promotion and a U.S. Government review of non-tariff barriers to Central American imports.

● Expanded availability of insurance guarantees for new investments from the U.S. Government's Overseas Private Investment Corporation.

● Increased focus in assistance programs on small business and accelerated agricultural development — particularly in production of food for domestic consumption.

Health and Education

● Democracy and prosperity in the region require accelerated human development. Hunger, disease and illiteracy sap a people's vitality and impede the growth of viable democratic institutions.

● Literacy rates are unacceptably low in several countries (e.g., Guatemala 45%, El Salvador 63%, Honduras 60%) handicapping education efforts seriously.

● Widespread malnutrition also handicaps education by sending physically and mentally underdeveloped children to school.

● Goals should include a reduction of malnutrition, elimination of illiteracy, expanded education, health, and housing opportunities.

● Initial efforts must be to increase food assistance to Central America through the PL 480 programs.

● Commission calls for formation, under direction of the Peace Corps, of a Literacy Corps and a Central American Teachers Corps.

● To meet needs in higher education, U.S. government scholarships should be raised to approximately 10,000 over 4-6 years, a level comparable to Cuban and Soviet Union efforts.

● Educational reform can also be encouraged in the areas of technical and vocational education, through the expansion of the International Executive Service Corps, and through closer cooperation with Central American universities to improve the quality of education.

● Judicial systems in Central America can be strengthened by providing resources for training judges, judicial staff, and public prosecutors.

● Continuation and expansion of existing programs for disease control and eradica-

tion, as well as immunization and oral rehydration.

● Training of primary health workers, especially nurses, should be expanded and the means developed to integrate private and public financing of health services.

● Assistance programs should target the area's severe housing shortage.

● Training of public administrators required to improve public service.

● U.S. Government should provide more resources to meet critical problem of refugees and displaced persons — more than one million of them need help.

Security Issues

● In El Salvador there are two separate conflicts: (1) between those seeking democratic reform and those seeking to retain their privileges; (2) between Marxist-Leninist guerrillas and those who oppose Marxism-Leninism.

● In discussing the latter we identify three general propositions about such guerrilla movements:

(1) They depend on external support. Without it they are unlikely to succeed.

(2) They develop their own momentum which reform alone cannot stop.

(3) Victorious, they create totalitarian regimes, even though they have enlisted support of democratic elements in order to project democratic, reformist image.

● External support comes from Soviet Union, Cuba and now Nicaragua. Cuba has developed into a leading military power through Soviet assistance. Since Sandinista victory, Soviets have come around to support Cuban strategy of armed road to power in Central America.

● There are serious strategic implications for the United States in Soviet-Cuban support for armed insurgency in the region.

● Triumph of hostile forces there could require us to devote large resources to defend our southern approaches.

● This could mean either substantially increased defense burden for the United States, or a redeployment of forces to the detriment of our interests elsewhere.

● Threat to our shipping lanes in the Caribbean.

● Increased violence and dislocation in the area from which we could not isolate ourselves.

● Erosion of our power to influence events worldwide as we are perceived as unable to influence events close to home.

El Salvador

● The war is stalemated, a condition to the ultimate advantage of the guerrillas.

● U.S. military assistance is inadequate to permit modern, humane and successful counter-insurgency.

● Commission recommends that U.S. provide significantly increased levels of military assistance for greater mobility, more training, higher force levels and more equipment.

● Assistance is to be conditioned through legislation on terminating death squads, progress toward democracy and establishment of the rule of law.

● In Guatemala, such assistance should only be provided if the same terms are met.

● Increased military assistance also needed for Honduras to build a credible deterrent and to meet renewed efforts at insurgency.

● Commission concludes that U.S. security interests are importantly engaged in Central America. Larger program of military assistance needed, as well as expanded support for economic growth and social reform.

● Success will depend on an end to massive violations of human rights and the neutralization of external support for the insurgencies.

The Search for Peace

● A successful U.S. political strategy in Central America requires resources to promote economic growth, vigorous efforts to advance democracy and reform; other inducements and penalties.

● General strategic objective of U.S. diplomacy in Central America should be to reduce the civil wars, national conflicts and military preparations to Central American dimension.

● Specifically, we should seek to stop the war and killing in El Salvador. Create conditions under which Nicaragua becomes a peaceful and democratic member of the Central American community. And open the way for democratic development in all countries.

● Commission calls for negotiations in El Salvador between guerrillas and the government to be elected in March to establish conditions for later legislative and municipal elections in which all could participate: electoral commission with FMLN-FDR

representation, cease-fire and end to all violence; international observation of elections.

● Adequate economic and military assistance from U.S. can help to achieve such a settlement.

● Commission believes military stalemate works against rather than for a political settlement based on the popular will.

● In Nicaragua, consolidation of a Marxist-Leninist regime would create a permanent security threat. Nicaragua's mainland location makes it a crucial steppingstone to promote armed insurgency in Central America. Cuban personnel (2,000 military advisers and 6,000 civilian officials), several hundred Soviet, East European, Libyan and PLO advisers, extensive arms deliveries (13,000 tons in 1983) add an external dimension to the threat posed by Nicaragua to its neighbors.

● What gives the current situation its special urgency is the external threat posed by the Sandinista regime in Nicaragua, supported by Cuban military strength, backed by Soviet weapons, guidance and diplomacy, and integrated into the Cuban network of intelligence and subversion.

● Central American leaders believe pluralistic political orders are essential to long-term security.

● An alternative would be an attempt at containment. But that would threaten militarization of the isthmus — the creation of garrison states. Democracy would wither. And the U.S. could find itself as surrogate policeman.

● Commission proposes comprehensive regional settlement based on:

(1) Respect for sovereignty and non-intervention.

(2) Verifiable commitments to non-aggression and an end to all attempts at subversion — covert or overt.

(3) Limitations on arms and sizes of armed forces. Prohibition of foreign forces, bases and advisers.

(4) No military forces, bases or advisers of non-Central American countries would be permitted.

(5) Commitment to internal pluralism and free elections in all countries.

(6) Provision for verification of all agreements.

(7) Establishment of an inter-government council to meet regularly to review compliance.

(8) Adherence to the overall agreement would be required for membership in the Central American Development Organization.

● U.S. would support the agreement and provide assistance; and would commit itself to respect results of elections within countries as long as principles of pluralism at home and restraint abroad observed.

● Commission's proposal based on and amplifies 21 points of the Contadora Group.

● Commission fully endorses Contadora efforts.

● Finally, majority of Commission opposes dismantling existing incentives and pressures for the regime in Managua to negotiate seriously.

● As for Cuba, Commission sees little possibility of separating it from Soviet Union. But U.S. should be prepared to negotiate seriously if Cuba were to show itself prepared for genuine coexistence, dropping support for insurgency in Central America and revolutionary violence elsewhere in the world.

● As for Soviet Union, establishment of Soviet military base in Nicaragua is not the major concern. Before that could have happened the crisis would have reached proportions not containable in Central American dimensions.

● There is little promise in negotiating with the Soviet Union over Central America. Soviets would seek [to] cast such negotiations in terms of sphere of influence, an unacceptable concept for the U.S. ∎

POLITICAL REPORT

CQ

Presidential Election

Carries 49 States:

Landslide Victory by Reagan Underscores Democratic Ills

Walter F. Mondale frequently asked during the primary season, "Where's the beef?" But many Democrats may be wondering after his lopsided loss to President Reagan Nov. 6, 1984, "Where's the base?"

Reagan's win was about as sweeping as they come, exposing again the Democrats' limited appeal in presidential voting. Reagan drew 59 percent of the popular vote — just shy of the 61 percent standard established by President Lyndon B. Johnson in 1964. He won all but one state, a feat performed previously only by Richard M. Nixon in 1972, and won a record 525 electoral votes. That left 13 electoral votes for Mondale, who carried the District of Columbia and his home state of Minnesota. *(Past landslides, p. 4-B)*

In spite of the magnitude of Reagan's victory, hardly anyone was surprised. The pollsters had been predicting a massive Reagan sweep since late summer, with final election-eve surveys showing him far ahead. Unlike the 1980 presidential race, which had a volatile finish that propelled Reagan to a decisive victory over President Jimmy Carter, most voters seemed to have had their minds made up in 1984 long before Election Day.

By early November, the only question was whether Reagan would become the first presidential candidate to sweep every state since the national popular vote tally was instituted in the early 1800s. He just missed achieving that distinction; despite a late campaign stop in Mondale's home state, Reagan lost Minnesota — but only by less than 35,000 votes. *(Results, p. 6-B)*

For the Democrats, the 1984 election was another in their growing string of presidential election drubbings. At no time in this century has a major party gone through a series of

electoral debacles as one-sided as the Democrats have experienced in the last 12 years. In two of the last four contests they have carried only one state. In three of the last four races, they have carried no more than six states.

In recent years it has taken unusual circumstances for the Democratic presidential ticket to be competitive. Carter capitalized on public disfavor with the Republicans generated by the Watergate scandal to win in 1976. Yet even then his victory margin was just 2 percentage points. In the other three elections since 1968, the Democrats have lost by margins of 23, 10 and now 18 percentage points.

1984 was not a particularly auspicious year for the Democrats to break the GOP's recent White House dominance. Reagan is one of the most popular of recent presidents, and the perceived economic upswing served to underscore his themes of peace and

prosperity. Adding to the Republican advantage was Mondale's relative unpopularity even within his own party. In the Democratic primaries, more than three out of every five voters cast ballots for a candidate other than the former vice president.

Yet 1984 probably offered a more legitimate test of the Democrats' national appeal than any presidential campaign in the last two decades. There was no major independent or third-party candidate on the ballot to divert votes as in 1968 and 1980. There was no party "outsider" atop the ticket, like George McGovern in 1972 and Carter in 1976. And with both Mondale and Reagan assured more than $40 million in federal funds to conduct their fall campaigns, there was no shortage of money.

Democrats were hopeful that Reagan, the "great communicator" of the early 1980s, would be the "great polarizer" of 1984, helping to galvanize millions of voters who were hurt by his cutbacks in spending for social programs or objected to his redirection of the federal government. The outline of a massive anti-Reagan vote was evident in 1982, when a surge in the number of black, blue-collar and unemployed voters helped propel Democrats to some major gains.

—Adapted from the Nov. 10, 1984, Weekly Report

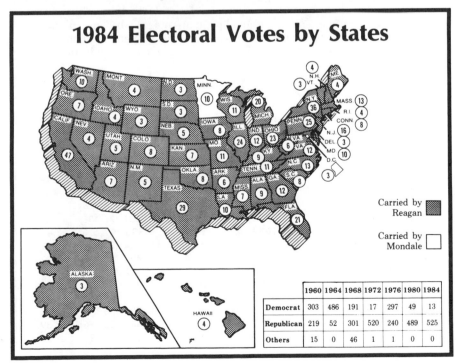

1984 Electoral Votes by States

	1960	1964	1968	1972	1976	1980	1984
Democrat	303	486	191	17	297	49	13
Republican	219	52	301	520	240	489	525
Others	15	0	46	1	1	0	0

But Democratic hopes of building a class-oriented anti-Reagan majority in 1984 evaporated with the economic upswing. The party did help register millions of new voters, many of them black.

But Democratic efforts to dramatically expand and refashion the electorate were blunted, first by the Republicans, who mounted a well-financed registration effort of their own, and then by the common perception that developed in late summer that the race was not even close.

Instead of 100 million voters participating in the presidential election, as the Democrats had hoped, unofficial vote totals indicated that about 90 million people voted. That figure increased to nearly 93 million when absentee ballots and third-party and write-in votes were tabulated. That vote total was large enough to end the 20-year decline in the presidential-year voter turnout rate, which slumped to 52.6 percent of the voting-age population in 1980.

But the turnout increase was not large enough to do Mondale much good. While his national popular vote total was about 1 million votes higher than Carter's in 1980, Reagan's soared upward by nearly 10 million votes. Reagan became the first candidate to win more than 50 million votes in a presidential election.

Watershed or Silver Lining?

Reagan's landslide win has encouraged some observers to talk of 1984 as a "watershed" election similar to Franklin D. Roosevelt's 1936 landslide triumph, which cemented for a generation the Democrats' New Deal majority. Still, history may ultimately show the 1984 presidential contest to be something else — possibly a "silver lining" election like 1928, when new Democratic voting patterns were evident even though their candidate, Alfred E. Smith, lost badly. Or the election may be simply another slap in the face for the Democrats, a stunning rebuke without any new vote patterns of consequence emerging to aid either party in the future.

Several factors encourage the "watershed" hypothesis. For one, Reagan ran unusually well among young voters (aged 18 to 29). He won more than 55 percent of their ballots, according to an ABC News-*Washington Post* poll. Youth has been a weak link for the GOP in the past, supporting Democratic presidential candidates in recent elections more loyally than any other age group. But for whatever reason — economic self-interest,

attraction to Reagan and his strong, "grandfatherly" qualities or distaste for the Democrats as the party of malaise and Carter — the youth vote broke overwhelmingly for Reagan.

There was no corresponding swing to the Democrats among older voters. Although polls showed Mondale running more strongly than Carter did in 1980 among voters over 30, the Democrats were hardly drawing a large enough share of their vote to scare GOP strategists.

The 1984 results also showed the GOP reclaiming "Wallace country," the conservative white South that deserted the Democratic Party with Alabama Gov. George C. Wallace in 1968, returned briefly to support Carter in 1976 and was up for grabs in 1984. Reagan won it decisively. An example is the vote from Coffee County, Alabama, a Wallace stronghold in 1968 and a county that Reagan carried by just 4 percentage points over Carter in 1980. But in this election, Reagan beat Mondale in Coffee County by 39 percentage points.

By holding a significant share of the white vote in 1980, Carter won Georgia and finished within 3 percentage points of Reagan in seven Southern states. But with Reagan winning overwhelming white support in 1984, the votes from an enlarged and almost unanimously Democratic black community made little difference. Reagan carried every Southern state by at least 18 percentage points.

While Reagan made significant inroads among white Southerners and the young, he also was able to reclaim the support of many moderate Republicans, who showed signs of drifting away from the GOP in 1980. Yankee Republicans, in particular, seem to have returned to the fold. Many of them supported former GOP Rep. John B. Anderson's independent candidacy in 1980 and Anderson was encouraging them this election to vote for Mondale. But few appeared to have followed his lead. Reagan increased his vote percentage by at least 10 points from 1980 in five of the six New England states, all of which gave Anderson at least 10 percent of the vote four years ago.

Evidence that 1984 could be a "silver lining" election for the Democrats is less obvious. In 1928, there was a tangible demonstration of the Democrats' growing appeal to urban ethnic voters as Alfred E. Smith won Massachusetts and Rhode Island, the first time a Democratic presidential candi-

Reagan and Past Landslides

Landslides are not unusual in presidential contests. In nearly one out of every three elections since a national popular-vote tally became commonplace around 1824, the winner has received at least 55 percent of the total vote. Most of the big winners, like President Reagan, have been incumbents seeking re-election.

In the following chart, incumbents are indicated with an asterisk (*). The number in parentheses is the winning candidate's percentage of the electoral vote. Reagan and his 1984 totals, which are based on nearly complete but unofficial returns, are highlighted in bold type.

	Year	Percentage of Popular Vote	Electoral Vote	States Won
Lyndon B. Johnson (D) *	1964	61.1	486 (90.3%)	44
Franklin D. Roosevelt (D) *	1936	60.8	523 (98.5%)	46
Richard M. Nixon (R) *	1972	60.7	520 (96.7%)	49
Warren G. Harding (R)	1920	60.3	404 (76.1%)	37
Ronald Reagan (R) *	**1984**	**58.9**	**525 (97.6%)**	**49**
Herbert Hoover (R)	1928	58.2	444 (83.6%)	40
Franklin D. Roosevelt (D)	1932	57.4	472 (88.9%)	42
Dwight D. Eisenhower (R) *	1956	57.4	457 (86.1%)	41
Theodore Roosevelt (R) *	1904	56.4	336 (70.6%)	33
Andrew Jackson (D)	1828	56.0	178 (68.2%)	14
Ulysses S. Grant (R) *	1872	55.6	286 (78.1%)	31
Dwight D. Eisenhower (R)	1952	55.1	442 (83.2%)	39
Abraham Lincoln (R) *	1864	55.0	212 (90.6%)	22

Ronald and Nancy Reagan wave to supporters celebrating his 49-state re-election victory, while Democratic candidates Walter F. Mondale and Rep. Geraldine A. Ferraro ponder their defeat at a Nov. 7, 1984, press conference.

date had accomplished that in years.

But this election, there were no obvious Democratic breakthroughs. Efforts to exploit the gender gap failed. Even with New York Rep. Geraldine A. Ferraro on the Democratic ticket, women preferred Reagan over Mondale by a margin of 8 percentage points, according to the ABC-*Washington Post* poll. The same survey found that men favored Reagan by 24 percentage points.

And the extensive campaigning by Mondale and Ferraro on the West Coast produced no victories. The Democrats drew no more than 45 percent of the vote in Oregon, Washington and California.

Regional Strengths, Weaknesses

The best news for the Democrats may be that in most states Mondale was able to draw about 35 to 40 percent of the vote. There was no region where the party's presidential vote consistently collapsed below 30 percent, as it did for McGovern in the South in 1972 and for Carter in much of the West in 1980.

Yet while Mondale was able to tap a respectable vote, he was strong hardly anywhere. Carter came within 5 percentage points of carrying a dozen states in 1980; Mondale finished within 5 percentage points of winning just three more states — Maryland, Massachusetts and Rhode Island.

Mondale was unable to reach out beyond the traditional Democratic base. According to the ABC News-*Washington Post* poll, he won nine out of every 10 black votes, while winning with smaller majorities the sup-

port of Jews, union households, the unemployed and least educated. Although GOP voters were nearly unanimous in their support for Reagan, nearly one out of every four Democrats deserted Mondale to back the incumbent. Among them were a large share of blue-collar, ethnic voters.

One of the few highlights for the Democrats was their strong showing in the large Frost Belt urban centers. Not only did Mondale draw massive majorities in New York City (61 percent of the vote), Chicago (65 percent), Philadelphia (65 percent), Baltimore (71 percent) and Washington, D.C. (87 percent), but also there were significantly more votes cast in most of the large cities than in 1980.

But in no case was the urban vote large enough to swing the state to Mondale. The result is a party still struggling to find a reliable base. While Republican candidates have been able to count on rolling up huge majorities in most states in the western half of the country, Democratic strength often varies with their candidates. Carter tended to be strongest in the South; McGovern ran well in states with large numbers of young voters and high-tech industries, such as Massachusetts, Wisconsin, California and Oregon; Hubert H. Humphrey was particularly strong in the Northeastern industrial states.

The 10 states in which Mondale drew his highest percentages in 1984 are clustered in the Northeast Corridor (the District of Columbia, Maryland, Pennsylvania, New York, Massachusetts and Rhode Island) and the upper Midwest (Minnesota, Iowa and

Wisconsin). West Virginia rounds out the list.

Reagan's top 10 are scattered all over the country. Six are in his native West, including his two best states, Utah (75 percent of the vote) and Idaho (73 percent). Other leading Reagan states in the region are Alaska, Arizona, Nevada and Wyoming. Two of the others (Kansas and Nebraska) are in the agricultural Midwest. New Hampshire and Oklahoma complete Reagan's top 10.

But speaking of Republican strength this election is a relative term. Reagan received at least 60 percent of the vote in nearly two-thirds of the states, including three of the largest electoral vote prizes — Florida, New Jersey and Texas.

After looking at these numbers, the best thing the Democrats might do is hope that history repeats itself in 1988. The last three presidents who won landslide re-election victories have seen their own party lose the next presidential election. Four years after Republican Dwight D. Eisenhower won a second term in 1956, Democrat John F. Kennedy was elected. Four years after Johnson scored his landslide win in 1964, Nixon was swept into the White House. And four years after Nixon's big win over McGovern in 1972, Carter was on his way to Washington.

Presidents can take credit for any successes during their first term and blame the problems on their predecessors. But in their second terms, the blame is all theirs and their party's next standard-bearer hears the criticism. ∎

Official 1984 Presidential Election Results

(Based on reports from the secretaries of state for the 50 states and the District of Columbia) *

Total Popular Vote: 92,666,758   **Reagan Plurality: 16,887,762**

	RONALD REAGAN (Republican)		WALTER F. MONDALE (Democrat)		ELECTORAL VOTES	
	Votes	%	Votes	%	Reagan	Mondale
Alabama	872,849	61	551,899	38	9	
Alaska	138,377	67	62,007	30	3	
Arizona	681,416	66	333,854	33	7	
Arkansas	534,774	60	338,646	38	6	
California	5,467,009	58	3,922,519	41	47	
Colorado	821,817	63	454,975	35	8	
Connecticut	890,877	61	569,597	39	8	
Delaware	152,190	60	101,656	40	3	
District of Columbia	29,009	14	180,408	85		3
Florida	2,730,350	65	1,448,816	35	21	
Georgia	1,068,722	60	706,628	40	12	
Hawaii	185,050	55	147,154	44	4	
Idaho	297,523	72	108,510	26	4	
Illinois	2,707,103	56	2,086,499	43	24	
Indiana	1,377,230	62	841,481	38	12	
Iowa	703,088	53	605,620	46	8	
Kansas	677,296	66	333,149	33	7	
Kentucky	821,702	60	539,539	40	9	
Louisiana	1,037,299	61	651,586	38	10	
Maine	336,500	61	214,515	39	4	
Maryland	879,918	53	787,935	47	10	
Massachusetts	1,310,936	51	1,239,606	48	13	
Michigan	2,251,571	59	1,529,638	40	20	
Minnesota	1,032,603	50	1,036,364	50		10
Mississippi	582,377	62	352,192	37	7	
Missouri	1,274,188	60	848,583	40	11	
Montana	232,450	60	146,742	38	4	
Nebraska	460,054	71	187,866	29	5	
Nevada	188,770	66	91,655	32	4	
New Hampshire	267,050	69	120,347	31	4	
New Jersey	1,933,630	60	1,261,323	39	16	
New Mexico	307,101	60	201,769	39	5	
New York	3,664,763	54	3,119,609	46	36	
North Carolina	1,346,481	62	824,287	38	13	
North Dakota	200,336	65	104,429	34	3	
Ohio	2,678,559	59	1,825,440	40	23	
Oklahoma	861,530	69	385,080	31	8	
Oregon	685,700	56	536,479	44	7	
Pennsylvania	2,584,323	53	2,228,131	46	25	
Rhode Island	212,100	52	196,300	48	4	
South Carolina	615,539	64	344,459	36	8	
South Dakota	200,267	63	116,113	37	3	
Tennessee	990,212	58	711,714	42	11	
Texas	3,433,428	64	1,949,276	36	29	
Utah	469,105	75	155,369	25	5	
Vermont	135,865	58	95,730	41	3	
Virginia	1,337,078	62	796,250	37	12	
Washington	1,051,670	56	798,352	43	10	
West Virginia	405,483	55	328,125	45	6	
Wisconsin	1,198,584	54	995,740	45	11	
Wyoming	133,241	71	53,370	28	3	
Total	54,455,093	59	37,567,331	41	525	13

* *Minor-party candidates are not included.*

 Senate Elections

Democrats Have Net Gain of Two Senate Seats

Neither the Republicans nor the Democrats came away with quite what they wanted from the 1984 struggle for control of the Senate.

Republicans hoped that President Reagan's march to re-election would bring about a modest reprise of 1980, when the GOP defeated nine Democratic senators and attained a Senate majority for the first time since the 1954 elections.

But this election, Reagan was no trailblazer: Democrats retained 13 of the 14 seats they were defending, and a trio of Democratic House members captured Republican seats: Illinois Rep. Paul Simon edged out three-term veteran Sen. Charles H. Percy, chairman of the Foreign Relations Committee; Iowa Rep. Tom Harkin defeated Sen. Roger W. Jepsen; and Tennessee Rep. Albert Gore Jr. crushed state Sen. Victor Ashe to take the seat being vacated by Senate Majority Leader Howard H. Baker Jr.

Countering that good news for the Democrats was an unexpected outcome in Kentucky — the defeat of two-term Democratic Sen. Walter D. Huddleston at the hands of Jefferson Country (Louisville) Judge Mitch McConnell.

McConnell's advantage was slim — about 5,100 votes according to complete, but unofficial returns. Huddleston requested a recanvass, but the result did not change. *(Election results, p. 25-B; switches, newcomers, box, p. 9-B)*

Since McConnell's victory stood up, Democrats had to settle for a net gain of two Senate seats, shifting the party ratio to 53 Republicans and 47 Democrats.

That standing is an improvement over the pre-election ratio of 55-45, but it is a comedown from the Democrats' 1983 prediction that the party could recapture Senate control this year by picking up a number of Republican seats Democrats regarded as shaky. *(Senate control map, p. 8-B; membership list, p. 11-B)*

As it turned out, Democrats failed to win most of the GOP seats in the "at risk" category. The biggest Democratic disappointment came in North Carolina, where GOP incumbent Jesse

U.S. Senate

98th Congress		99th Congress	
Democrats	45	Democrats	47
Republicans	55	Republicans	53

Democrats

Freshmen	5
Incumbents re-elected	11
Incumbent defeated	1
(Walter D. Huddleston, Ky.)	

Republicans

Freshmen	2
Incumbents re-elected	15
Incumbents defeated	2
(Roger W. Jepsen, Iowa;	
Charles H. Percy, Ill.)	

Helms narrowly won his bitter battle with Democratic Gov. James B. Hunt Jr. It was the most expensive Senate contest ever, with the campaigns spending a total of about $22 million, eclipsing the $12.5 million spent in the 1982 California Senate contest.

In four other key states where

Democrats had hoped to pull upsets, Republicans prevailed easily: Mississippi Sen. Thad Cochran, who was elected with only 45 percent in 1978, won 61 percent against former Gov. William Winter; Sen. Gordon J. Humphrey, once regarded as a staunch conservative, moderated his image and won a second term with 59 percent in New Hampshire; Texas Rep. Phil Gramm, who switched parties in 1983, also polled 59 percent to earn the right to replace retiring GOP Sen. John Tower; and Sen. Rudy Boschwitz took 58 percent in Minnesota, encountering no problems with Walter F. Mondale's coattails because the Democratic presidential nominee barely carried his home state.

Looking Ahead to 1986

Ever since Democrats lost control of the Senate in 1980, they have assumed that vengeance will be theirs in the 1986 elections. Republicans must defend 22 of the 34 Senate seats at stake then, including 16 seats held by freshmen, many of whom rode in on Reagan's coattails in 1980. *(Expiration dates of Senate terms, p. 12-B)*

Sen. Jesse Helms, R-N.C., and his wife, Dot, celebrate his re-election victory over Democratic Gov. James B. Hunt Jr. in the most expensive Senate battle in history.

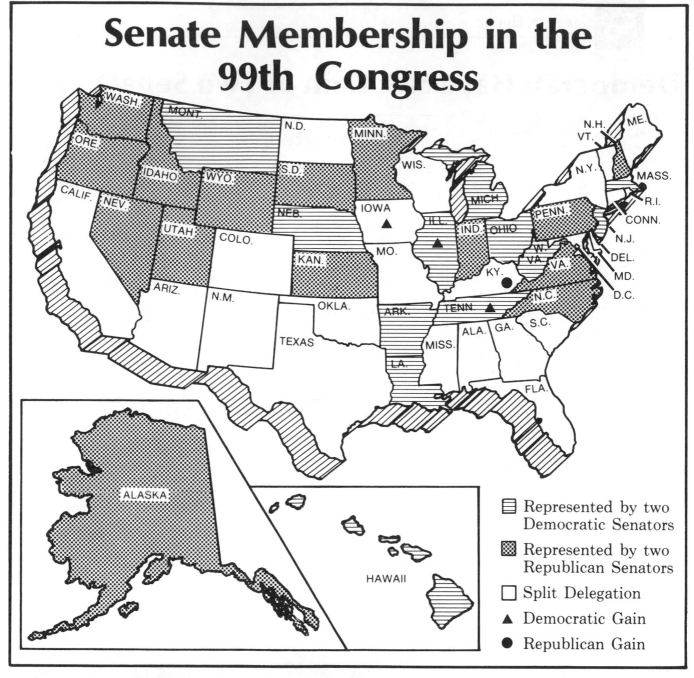

Senate Membership in the 99th Congress

Legend:
- ▤ Represented by two Democratic Senators
- ▦ Represented by two Republican Senators
- ☐ Split Delegation
- ▲ Democratic Gain
- ● Republican Gain

There is ample recent precedent for the type of wholesale turnover Democrats hope for in 1986. In Senate elections of 1976, 1978 and 1980, high turnover was the norm; the average number of freshmen elected in each of those years was 19. *(Chart, p. 10-B)*

Furthermore, a party occupying the White House for two consecutive terms generally suffers Senate losses at the six-year point of its reign; the question is not "if," but "how many?" Republicans lost three seats in 1974, Democrats lost three in 1966, and the GOP dropped 13 in 1958.

The past two Senate elections, however, suggest the GOP may have a chance to retain Senate control in 1986. In 1982 and again in 1984, there was very little volatility in Senate elections. Two years earlier, only five newcomers were elected to the Senate — the smallest group in the history of popular Senate elections. This election, of the 29 senators who sought another term (four retired), 26 won. In only six Senate contests did the winner receive less than 55 percent of the vote.

The stability present in the past two Senate elections could mean that voters are looking more at individuals than party labels in making choices for the Senate. In 1982, when the Republican administration was being blamed for the economic recession, only one GOP senator failed to win re-election. In 1984, even though Reagan easily carried many of the states with Senate races, there was no sweep-out of Democratic senators. In Arkansas, for example, Reagan's 61 percent tally did not impede Democratic Sen. David Pryor, who won 58 percent against GOP Rep. Ed Bethune.

In Nebraska — one of three states that gave Reagan more than 70 percent — enough voters responded well to the homespun, conservative style of Democratic Sen. J. James Exon to help him stave off a vigorous challenge from Republican Nancy Hoch, a University of Nebraska regent. The national Republican Party made a concerted effort to boost Hoch, and early returns on election night showed the race very tight. But Exon, who like Pryor is a former governor with many allies in his state, won with 53 percent.

Also contributing to stability in the Senate is the heightened political alertness of incumbents. Many senators first elected in 1976 and 1978 have been more aggressive campaigners and more closely attuned to their constituents than the Washington-oriented veterans they replaced.

This election, Michigan Democratic Sen. Carl Levin was sharply criticized for frequently opposing Reagan administration policies. But Levin spent about $3 million, more than twice the amount spent by his Republican opponent, former astronaut Jack Lousma. And Levin ran a commercial featuring a film clip of Lousma speaking before a group of workers in Japan; Lousma told the group that he owned a Toyota automobile — a remark that did not go over well in Michigan's "buy American" environment. Though Reagan carried nearly 60 percent of the Michigan vote, Levin won with 53 percent, slightly higher than the percentage he posted when he first took the seat in 1978.

Yet even if the Republican-dominated class of 1980 proves to be adept at campaigning, Republicans will have a tough time holding Senate control in 1986. Precedent argues against continued division of control in Congress after 1986; never in the nation's history have voters kept the chambers of Con-

Following in the footsteps of his father, lower left, Rep. Albert Gore Jr., D-Tenn., has claimed a seat in the Senate.

gress divided between the parties for longer than six years.

The Newcomers

Although the Senate freshman class of 1984 is not large, it is a politically experienced group of activists likely to make a mark in Senate affairs quickly. The average age of the class is 44, so the impact of these freshmen may well be felt for years to come.

Each of the four representatives who won promotion — Simon, Harkin, Gore and Gramm — has served three terms or more in Congress; McConnell was in his eighth year as county executive in Kentucky's most populous county; Democrat John D. "Jay" Rockefeller IV of West Virginia, who won the seat of retiring Democratic Sen. Jennings Randolph, was finishing

his second term as governor. Democrat John F. Kerry of Massachusetts, who succeeds retiring Democratic Sen. Paul E. Tsongas, was in his first term as lieutenant governor.

The dean of the group is Simon, 55, whose earnest manner and trademark bow tie have made him unique in the hurly-burly world of Illinois politics for three decades. Percy tried to portray Simon as an "ultraliberal," but a narrow majority of voters saw the challenger as a Democrat seeking "practical answers to practical problems," as Simon described himself.

Simon's victory by a single percentage point was one of four Democratic successes in close Senate elections. The Democrats' ability to win four of the six races decided by less than 55 percent was a significant

Senate Newcomers, Switched Seats, Losers

State	98th	99th	Winner	Loser	Incumbent
Illinois	R	D	Paul Simon (D)	Charles H. Percy (R)	Percy
Iowa	R	D	Tom Harkin (D)	Roger W. Jepsen (R)	Jepsen
Kentucky	D	R	Mitch McConnell (R)	Walter D. Huddleston (D)	Huddleston
Massachusetts	D	D	John F. Kerry (D)	Raymond Shamie (R)	Paul E. Tsongas (D)*
Tennessee	R	D	Albert Gore Jr. (D)	Victor Ashe (R)	Howard H. Baker Jr. (R)*
Texas	R	R	Phil Gramm (R)	Lloyd Doggett (D)	John Tower (R)*
West Virginia	D	D	John D. "Jay" Rockefeller IV (D)	John R. Raese (R)	Jennings Randolph (D)*

Retiring

Senate Freshmen, 1914-1984

Year	Freshmen Senators	Democrats	Republicans	Others
1914	10	7	3	
1916	19	8	11	
1918	17	6	11	
1920	17	4	13	
1922	19	12	6	1
1924	13	3	10	
1926	15	8	7	
1928	11	1	10	
1930	19	14	5	
1932	16	16	0	
1934	13	13	0	
1936	16	13	2	1
1938	13	5	8	
1940	12	5	7	
1942	13	3	10	
1944	14	8	6	
1946	23	6	17	
1948	18	14	4	
1950	14	6	8	
1952	16	6	10	
1954	14	7	7	
1956	10	6	4	
1958	18	15	3	
1960	9	7	2	
1962	12	9	3	
1964	8	6	2	
1966	7	2	5	
1968	15	5	10	
1970	11	5	5	1
1972	13	8	5	
1974	11	9	2	
1976	18	10	8	
1978	20	9	11	
1980	18	2	16	
1982	5	2	3	
1984	7	5	2	

accomplishment; in 1982, Republicans won nine of 12 races in the closely contested category. This election, the Democratic Senatorial Campaign Committee held back money to pump into close races late in the campaign, and that strategy helped candidates such as Simon and Levin to prevail.

Harkin, like Simon, is a member of the Class of 1974 in the House, the so-called "Watergate babies." Unlike some of his colleagues, he has never moved to the right with the national political mood. He does, however, present his liberal views in a populist package.

Throughout the campaign, Harkin, 44, was regarded as at least an even-money bet to defeat Jepsen, who was saddled with an undistinguished legislative record and various personal controversies, including a flurry of publicity in June that he had applied for membership in 1977 to a Des Moines "health spa" that was later closed for prostitution.

In Tennessee, Gore proved himself adept at tailoring his message to suit his electorate. He claimed support beyond the normal Democratic constituency with his work on toxic-waste cleanup, a matter of concern in traditionally Republican East Tennessee, and he enhanced his stature as a pragmatist by agreeing to support the MX missile in 1983 in exchange for shifts in the Reagan administration's bargaining position in arms control talks.

Although Reagan carried Tennessee with 59 percent, Gore's bipartisan appeal buried Republican Ashe, whose 34 percent tally was the poorest showing of any GOP Senate candidate in the state in almost a quarter-century.

In spite of a huge financial advantage, Rockefeller won in West Virginia with an unimpressive 52 percent. The state's economy is still struggling after his eight years as governor; that fact and Reagan's victory in the traditionally Democratic state helped boost John R. Raese, an error-prone political neophyte who struggled to put up $1 million against Rockefeller's $9 million-plus.

The West Virginia contest demonstrated that money can compensate for many weaknesses; without such a wide lead in spending, Rockefeller might have lost. Overall, big spending was a good guarantee of success. Of the 12 Senate candidates who through mid-October 1984 reported spending more than $2.5 million each, nine won.

Massachusetts stayed true to its Democratic history in electing Kerry, 40, over conservative GOP businessman Raymond Shamie. Republicans had hoped to provoke a realignment in the state by pulling to their side the conservative, working-class ethnic Democrats who often clash with issue-oriented liberal Democrats. Reagan managed to carry Massachusetts narrowly, but most Democrats united behind Kerry to give him a comfortable victory with 55 percent. Kerry's politics are liberal — he criticized Shamie for supporting Reagan's arms buildup and Central America policies — but his Irish-Catholic background helped him appeal to many ethnic voters.

Gramm's easy victory was part of a banner Republican year in Texas; Reagan won the state with 64 percent and the GOP gained four House seats. With the state in a conservative mood, Gramm, 42, a champion of free enterprise economics, was well-positioned to defeat Democratic state Sen. Lloyd Doggett, whose liberalism was highlighted by conservative Democratic opponents who campaigned against him for the nomination.

In Kentucky, McConnell clearly benefited from Reagan's coattails. The president carried Kentucky with 60 percent, pulling McConnell ahead of Huddleston by about 5,100 votes. Also contributing to the outcome was the fuzzy image many voters had of Huddleston, an easygoing mainstream Democrat who mostly worked behind the scenes on state-related matters.

McConnell, the first Republican to win statewide in Kentucky since 1968, labeled Huddleston a "shadow senator," and the incumbent, lacking a strong personal following, could not overcome the criticism. ∎

Senate Membership in the 99th Congress

Democrats 47   Republicans 53
Freshman Senators - 7

Seats Switched Parties D to R - 1   Seats Switched Parties R to D - 3

> ### Senators elected in 1984 are *italicized*
> ### # Freshman Senators
> ### ✔ Seat Switched Parties

ALABAMA
Jeremiah Denton (R)
Howell Heflin (D)

ALASKA
Frank H. Murkowski (R)
Ted Stevens (R)

ARIZONA
Barry Goldwater (R)
Dennis DeConcini (D)

ARKANSAS
Dale Bumpers (D)
David Pryor (D)

CALIFORNIA
Pete Wilson (R)
Alan Cranston (D)

COLORADO
William L. Armstrong (R)
Gary Hart (D)

CONNECTICUT
Lowell P. Weicker Jr. (R)
Christopher J. Dodd (D)

DELAWARE
William V. Roth Jr. (R)
Joseph R. Biden Jr. (D)

FLORIDA
Paula Hawkins (R)
Lawton Chiles (D)

GEORGIA
Mack Mattingly (R)
Sam Nunn (D)

HAWAII
Daniel K. Inouye (D)
Spark M. Matsunaga (D)

IDAHO
James A. McClure (R)
Steven D. Symms (R)

ILLINOIS
Alan J. Dixon (D)
✔ *Paul Simon (D)#*

INDIANA
Richard G. Lugar (R)
Dan Quayle (R)

IOWA
Charles E. Grassley (R)
✔ *Tom Harkin (D)#*

KANSAS
Robert Dole (R)
Nancy Landon Kassebaum (R)

KENTUCKY
✔ *Mitch McConnell (R)#*
Wendell H. Ford (D)

LOUISIANA
J. Bennett Johnston (D)
Russell B. Long (D)

MAINE
William S. Cohen (R)
George J. Mitchell (D)

MARYLAND
Charles McC. Mathias Jr. (R)
Paul S. Sarbanes (D)

MASSACHUSETTS
Edward M. Kennedy (D)
John F. Kerry (D)#

MICHIGAN
Carl Levin (D)
Donald W. Riegle Jr. (D)

MINNESOTA
Rudy Boschwitz (R)
Dave Durenberger (R)

MISSISSIPPI
Thad Cochran (R)
John C. Stennis (D)

MISSOURI
John C. Danforth (R)
Thomas F. Eagleton (D)

MONTANA
Max Baucus (D)
John Melcher (D)

NEBRASKA
J. James Exon (D)
Edward Zorinsky (D)

NEVADA
Chic Hecht (R)
Paul Laxalt (R)

NEW HAMPSHIRE
Gordon J. Humphrey (R)
Warren B. Rudman (R)

NEW JERSEY
Bill Bradley (D)
Frank R. Lautenberg (D)

NEW MEXICO
Pete V. Domenici (R)
Jeff Bingaman (D)

NEW YORK
Alfonse M. D'Amato (R)
Daniel Patrick Moynihan (D)

NORTH CAROLINA
John P. East (R)
Jesse Helms (R)

NORTH DAKOTA
Mark Andrews (R)
Quentin N. Burdick (D)

OHIO
John Glenn (D)
Howard M. Metzenbaum (D)

OKLAHOMA
Don Nickles (R)
David L. Boren (D)

OREGON
Mark O. Hatfield (R)
Bob Packwood (R)

PENNSYLVANIA
John Heinz (R)
Arlen Specter (R)

RHODE ISLAND
John H. Chafee (R)
Claiborne Pell (D)

SOUTH CAROLINA
Strom Thurmond (R)
Ernest F. Hollings (D)

SOUTH DAKOTA
James Abdnor (R)
Larry Pressler (R)

TENNESSEE
✔ *Albert Gore Jr. (D)#*
Jim Sasser (D)

TEXAS
Phil Gramm (R)#
Lloyd Bentsen (D)

UTAH
Jake Garn (R)
Orrin G. Hatch (R)

VERMONT
Robert T. Stafford (R)
Patrick J. Leahy (D)

VIRGINIA
Paul S. Trible Jr. (R)
John W. Warner (R)

WASHINGTON
Daniel J. Evans (R)
Slade Gorton (R)

WEST VIRGINIA
Robert C. Byrd (D)
John D. "Jay" Rockefeller IV (D)#

WISCONSIN
Bob Kasten (R)
William Proxmire (D)

WYOMING
Alan K. Simpson (R)
Malcolm Wallop (R)

Years of Expiration of Senate Terms

— 1986 —

(34 Senators: 22 Republicans, 12 Democrats)

Abdnor, James, R-S.D.	Garn, Jake, R-Utah	Leahy, Patrick J., D-Vt.
Andrews, Mark, R-N.D.	Glenn, John, D-Ohio	Long, Russell B., D-La.
Bumpers, Dale, D-Ark.	Goldwater, Barry, R-Ariz.	Mathias, Charles McC. Jr., R-Md.
Cranston, Alan, D-Calif.	Gorton, Slade, R-Wash.	Mattingly, Mack, R-Ga.
D'Amato, Alfonse M., R-N.Y.	Grassley, Charles E., R-Iowa	Murkowski, Frank H., R-Alaska
Denton, Jeremiah, R-Ala.	Hart, Gary, D-Colo.	Nickles, Don, R-Okla.
Dixon, Alan J., D-Ill.	Hawkins, Paula, R-Fla.	Packwood, Bob, R-Ore.
Dodd, Christopher J., D-Conn.	Hollings, Ernest F., D-S.C.	Quayle, Dan, R-Ind.
Dole, Robert, R-Kan.	Inouye, Daniel K., D-Hawaii	Rudman, Warren B., R-N.H.
Eagleton, Thomas F., D-Mo.	Kasten, Bob, R-Wis.	Specter, Arlen, R-Pa.
East, John P., R-N.C.	Laxalt, Paul, R-Nev.	Symms, Steven D., R-Idaho
Ford, Wendell H., D-Ky.		

— 1988 —

(33 Senators: 14 Republicans, 19 Democrats)

Bentsen, Lloyd, D-Texas	Hecht, Chic, R-Nev.	Riegle, Donald W. Jr., D-Mich.
Bingaman, Jeff, D-N.M.	Heinz, John, R-Pa.	Roth, William V. Jr., R-Del.
Burdick, Quentin N., D-N.D.	Kennedy, Edward M., D-Mass.	Sarbanes, Paul S., D-Md.
Byrd, Robert C., D-W.Va.	Lautenberg, Frank R., D-N.J.	Sasser, Jim, D-Tenn.
Chafee, John H., R-R.I.	Lugar, Richard G., R-Ind.	Stafford, Robert T., R-Vt.
Chiles, Lawton, D-Fla.	Matsunaga, Spark M., D-Hawaii	Stennis, John C., D-Miss.
Danforth, John C., R-Mo.	Melcher, John, D-Mont.	Trible, Paul S. Jr., R-Va.
DeConcini, Dennis, D-Ariz.	Metzenbaum, Howard M., D-Ohio	Wallop, Malcolm, R-Wyo.
Durenberger, Dave, R-Minn.	Mitchell, George J., D-Maine	Weicker, Lowell P. Jr., R-Conn.
Evans, Daniel J., R-Wash.	Moynihan, Daniel Patrick, D-N.Y.	Wilson, Pete, R-Calif.
Hatch, Orrin G., R-Utah	Proxmire, William, D-Wis.	Zorinsky, Edward, D-Neb.

— 1990 —

(33 Senators: 17 Republicans, 16 Democrats)

Armstrong, William L., R-Colo.	Gramm, Phil, R-Texas	McConnell, Mitch, R-Ky.
Baucus, Max, D-Mont.	Harkin, Tom, D-Iowa	Nunn, Sam, D-Ga.
Biden, Joseph R. Jr., D-Del.	Hatfield, Mark O., R-Ore.	Pell, Claiborne, D-R.I.
Boren, David L., D-Okla.	Heflin, Howell, D-Ala.	Pressler, Larry, R-S.D.
Boschwitz, Rudy, R-Minn.	Helms, Jesse, R-N.C.	Pryor, David, D-Ark.
Bradley, Bill, D-N.J.	Humphrey, Gordon J., R-N.H.	Rockefeller, John D. "Jay" IV, D-W.Va.
Cochran, Thad, R-Miss.	Johnston, J. Bennett, D-La.	Simon, Paul, D-Ill.
Cohen, William S., R-Maine	Kassebaum, Nancy Landon, R-Kan.	Simpson, Alan K., R-Wyo.
Domenici, Pete V., R-N.M.	Kerry, John F., D-Mass.	Stevens, Ted, R-Alaska
Exon, J. James, D-Neb.	Levin, Carl, D-Mich.	Thurmond, Strom, R-S.C.
Gore, Albert Jr., D-Tenn.	McClure, James A., R-Idaho	Warner, John W., R-Va.

GOP Disappointed With Gains in the House

For the second time in a little over a decade, Republicans have watched with disappointment as their presidential standard-bearer swept triumphantly across the nation followed by a threadbare retinue of new U.S. House members.

The Nov. 6, 1984, elections revealed considerable hesitation nationwide over an all-out endorsement of Republican policies, as voters in district after district stopped short of backing GOP challengers who campaigned on their loyalty to Ronald Reagan.

After several closely contested battles were decided, Republicans had gained at least 14 seats, falling well short of making up the 26 seats they lost in the 1982 midterm elections. One race was still undecided at year's end. *(House results, p. 25-B)*

The results in 1984 are reminiscent of the 1972 elections, when Richard M. Nixon racked up overwhelming margins around the country, but carried only 12 fellow Republicans into the House behind him. Similarly skimpy coattails accompanied a strong re-election showing by Republican Dwight D. Eisenhower in 1956, when he won a second term by a stunning margin but the GOP lost two seats in the House.

The GOP's House results could pose problems for enactment of President Reagan's second term legislative agenda. Republican stratelists had estimated that 22-25 new members were required to reawaken the coalition of Republicans and conservative Democrats that gave the GOP effective control of the House in the two years following the 1980 elections.

Although several newly elected Democrats are expected to side generally with House conservatives, the net ideological shift may be less dramatic than the Republican pickups would indicate, since at least four of the defeated Democrats voted consistently with the conservative coalition of Republicans and Southern Democrats.

The Republicans' modest gains could also leave them in an uncomfortable position as 1986 and the second half of Reagan's term approach.

Elections in the sixth year of an administration historically have decimated the House ranks of the party controlling the White House.

No Major Shift

Returns from the 435 congressional districts indicated that Democrats would control the House with 252 members to the GOP's 182 when the 99th Congress convened Jan. 3, 1985. Under the new totals, Democrats would have at least nine seats more than they had after the banner GOP election year in 1980.

Going into the election, Democrats held 266 seats and Republicans 167, with vacancies in a New Jersey district previously held by a Republican and in a Kentucky district held by a Democrat. Those seats stayed in their respective parties' hands Nov. 6, and were filled for the remainder of the term in special elections.

There will be at least 43 House freshmen in 1985, a small class, due mostly to the relatively low number of open seats in 1984. There were 81 freshmen after the 1982 election.

Of the members elected in 1982, at least four Democrats went down to defeat Nov. 6, a figure fairly close to the norm for freshmen. On average, their Democratic colleagues in the

class of 1982 ran 3.9 percentage points ahead of their showings two years ago, while Republicans seeking their first re-election surged a full 10 points.

In similarly adverse conditions for Republicans two years earlier, GOP freshmen ran only 2 percentage points better than their 1980 scores, while Democrats jumped 12.3 points.

Although Reagan's strength in the election was crucial to Republican victories in most of the districts the GOP took from the Democrats, his coattails proved half as strong against Democratic incumbents as they were four years ago, when the GOP lost three incumbents but unseated 28 Democratic members.

In 1984, three Republicans were defeated, but only 13 or 14 Democrats lost their seats. Among the defeated Democrats were six subcommittee chairmen: California's Jerry M. Patterson, Maryland's Clarence D. Long, Donald J. Albosta of Michigan, Georgia's Elliott H. Levitas, Joseph G. Minish of New Jersey, and North Carolina's Ike Andrews.

Democrats got some welcome news in California, where voters rejected by a 10-point margin an initiative pushed by Republican Gov. George Deukmejian that would have redrawn the state's congressional districts. The current map heavily favors Democrats, and party leaders feared that a new one would cut severely into their House delegation.

Republicans scored a net gain of four in the 27 districts left open by the retirement, primary defeat or death of an incumbent, winning five formerly Democratic seats but losing an Arkansas district to the opposition.

Close Contests

The outcomes in several districts were especially close. The closest was in Indiana's 8th District, where Democratic incumbent Frank McCloskey faced a challenge from Republican Richard D. McIntyre. McIntyre was certified the winner by the Indiana secretary of state, but McCloskey claimed the seat was his on the basis of a later recount. The House early in 1985 declared the seat vacant, pending

U.S. House

98th Congress		99th Congress	
Democrats	267	Democrats	252
Republicans	168	Republicans	182
		Vacant	1
Democrats			
Net Loss		14*	
Freshmen		12	
Incumbents re-elected		240*	
Incumbents defeated		13*	
Republicans			
Net Gain		14*	
Freshmen		31*	
Incumbents re-elected		151	
Incumbents defeated		3	

Does not include result of Indiana 8th contest.

an investigation.

In Illinois, the successor to 22nd District Democrat Paul Simon, who gave up his seat for a successful Senate bid, was former Democratic Rep. Kenneth J. Gray (1955-74), although his 1,200-vote margin prompted his opponent to consider requesting a recount.

Three Republican-held seats also were in doubt for days after the election.

Embattled incumbent George Hansen trailed challenger Richard Stallings by 133 votes in Idaho's 2nd District, after a county-by-county vote check.

In North Carolina's open 9th Congressional District, Republican J. Alex McMillan led attorney D. G. Martin by 371 votes.

And in Utah's 2nd District, which GOP Rep. Dan Marriott gave up in an unsuccessful bid for the governorship, Democratic state Sen. Frances Farley trailed Lt. Gov. David S. Monson by 472 votes once 2,500 absentee ballots were counted.

Short Coattails

The modest nature of the GOP's House gains came despite a vigorous pre-election effort by the party's national election apparatus to give Reagan as much company on Capitol Hill as possible. In the days before the election, Vice President George Bush campaigned for Republican challengers, and the GOP's House campaign committee aired advertisements and sent out mailings encouraging voters to cast straight Republican ballots.

The failure of these efforts to boost party-line voting perhaps was due in part to voters' unwillingness to give Reagan the sweeping mandate heavy gains in the House would have signaled. Democratic leaders were quick to interpret the House results as demonstrating that "voters wanted a 'check' or a 'balance' against Mr. Reagan," in the words of California Democratic Rep. Tony Coelho, chairman of the Democratic Congressional Campaign Committee.

Some Republicans, including House Minority Leader Robert H. Michel, Ill., contended that, had Reagan

---

U. S. House Members Defeated

	Terms		Terms
James F. McNulty Jr., D-Ariz.	1	Joseph G. Minish, D-N.J.	11
Jerry M. Patterson, D-Calif.	5	Ike Andrews, D-N.C.	6
William R. Ratchford, D-Conn.	3	Robin Britt, D-N.C.	1
Elliott H. Levitas, D-Ga.	5	James McClure Clarke, D-N.C.	1
George Hansen, R-Idaho	7	Lyle Williams, R-Ohio	3
Daniel B. Crane, R-Ill.	3	Jack Hightower, D-Texas	5
Clarence D. Long, D-Md.	11	Bill Patman, D-Texas	2
Donald J. Albosta, D-Mich.	3	Tom Vandergriff, D-Texas	1

---

paid more attention to close contests, his popularity would have helped GOP candidates over the top.

Still, in many cases Republicans were aiming at Democratic candidates who were able to separate themselves from the national ticket, making their assiduous attention to local affairs the dominant issue.

In Connecticut, for example, where a Republican gale unseated Democrat William R. Ratchford in the 5th District and put both houses of the state Legislature in GOP hands, Democratic freshman Bruce A. Morrison survived by playing up his work on local projects in the New Haven-area 3rd District.

Similarly, freshman Democrat Lane Evans, who took Illinois' 17th District out of Republican hands in 1982, held on despite the conservative nature of his district. Since entering office, Evans had established a reputation for tireless constituent service. His work paid off handsomely in 1984, when he carried not only traditionally Democratic parts of the district, but also several heavily Republican rural counties.

Several Democrats also demonstrated the value of intensive early preparation. Oklahoma's James R. Jones, who, because of his position as chairman of the House Budget Committee, was a top Republican target, began early to prepare for his re-election. He built up a huge treasury, topping the list of House candidates nationally in campaign receipts, and was ready with material buttressing his claims of independence when his opponent tried to tie him to liberal Democratic leaders in Washington.

In California, Democrat George E. Brown Jr. for the third time fought off a challenge from insurance broker John Paul Stark in his 36th District. After their last face-off, in which Stark held Brown to 54 percent of the

---

vote, Brown kept his organization ready for a rematch and made sure to keep in close touch with the local business and religious communities, where much of Stark's potential strength lay. Brown won with 57 percent.

Brown's preparation contrasted with the more laid-back attitude of fellow-Democrat Patterson, the subcommittee chairman who lost his Orange County 38th District to former Rep. Robert K. Dornan (1977-83). While Dornan blanketed the district with mailings and campaigned energetically, Patterson stayed in Washington until Congress adjourned, and was slow to gear up his counterattack.

Reagan's were not the only coattails available Nov. 6. In states such as Alabama and Oklahoma, strong showings by incumbent Democratic senators helped House Democrats beat back strong challenges. In Indiana, a close gubernatorial contest between Republican Gov. Robert D. Orr and Democratic state Sen. W. Wayne Townsend proved crucial to Democrats, breaking the Republican vote and helping incumbent Philip R. Sharp survive a contest that many expected him to lose. Townsend also helped boost McCloskey's vote.

Encouragement for the GOP

But if the House results failed to satisfy Republicans hoping for a major congressional realignment to match their recent presidential strength, they still gave some signs that the party is picking up steam in traditionally Democratic territory.

Regionally, the GOP made most of its gains where Democrats historically have been strongest — the South, where eight Democratic seats went Republican, and the East, where five shifted into the GOP column. Equally important, the party picked up at least three heavily blue-collar seats and showed enough potency in others to mark them as potential future battlegrounds.

The Republicans' best gains came in Texas and North Carolina, where bitterly fought Senate contests brought out huge numbers of voters whose unalloyed loyalty to Reagan proved devastating to Democrats lower down on the ticket.

The results were especially striking in Texas, where the GOP will control 10 of 27 seats — its best showing ever and a sign of remarkable growth for a party that a scant 10 years earlier controlled only a trio of seats.

Three of the seat switches came where conservative Democratic incumbents lost to Republicans who based their challenges on linking opponents to the national Democratic ticket.

In the Amarillo-area 13th District, five-term veteran Jack Hightower took only 47 percent of the vote against lawyer Beau Boulter in a contest Hightower had been expected to survive. Although Hightower had compiled one of the more conservative records in the Democratic delegation and had spurned Walter F. Mondale at the Democratic National Convention by voting for Ohio Sen. John Glenn, Boulter successfully portrayed him as a national liberal.

In the Gulf Coast 14th District, Bill Patman narrowly missed winning a third term, losing to a hard-charging 29-year-old former White House aide, Mac Sweeney. Patman voted against a majority of Democrats in the House 53 percent of the time in 1984, but Sweeney was able to link him to national Democratic Party figures.

While Democrats may be able to regain those districts in a good Democratic year, they will probably not get the chance in the suburban Fort Worth 26th District, where Democrat Tom Vandergriff lost despite redistricting changes that should have helped him. The conservative Vandergriff was unable to raise his head above the GOP tide that lifted political newcomer Richard Armey into his seat.

The GOP also managed to pick up two historically Democratic open seats. In Democratic Rep. Kent Hance's 19th District, which Hance gave up in an unsuccessful Senate primary bid, Republican Larry Combest won an easy victory to replace the conservative Hance.

A more striking GOP victory came in a district Republicans already held, the 6th. Until Republican Rep. Phil Gramm left the Democratic Party in 1983, the seat had never been out of Democratic hands. The 6th backed Gramm in a special election held after he switched parties, but Democrats expected it to revert to their column once Gramm surrendered it to make

his successful Senate bid in 1984. However, hanging tightly to Reagan's and Gramm's coattails, Republican engineering consultant Joe Barton defeated former state Rep. Dan Kubiak.

Black, White Voting Patterns

Elsewhere in the South, the Democratic Party's growing reliance on black voters was brought home with special force. In districts with sizable black populations where Democratic incumbents faced credible Republican challengers — such as South Carolina's 6th and Mississippi's 4th — they overcame them with little trouble.

But in North Carolina, where voter turnout was unusually high, three incumbent Democrats with relatively small numbers of black voters in their districts were defeated, and two others almost lost to weak opponents. Democrats in the more heavily black eastern districts of the state had little trouble in the election.

After narrowly missing in 1982, Republican William Cobey Jr. managed this time to knock off six-term incumbent Ike Andrews in the 4th District. Andrews fought off Cobey two years ago despite a last-minute arrest for drunken driving, and Cobey went into this contest still lacking much of a natural base in the generally Democratic district. But the huge numbers of conservative voters turning out for Reagan and Republican Sen. Jesse Helms proved too much for Andrews, and Cobey emerged with about 51 percent of the vote.

Similar problems beset freshman Democrats Robin Britt, who lost to Republican state Rep. Howard Coble in the 6th District, and James McClure Clarke, who was beaten by the Republican he had unseated in 1982, Bill Hendon. With Reagan and Helms encouraging a disproportionate number of white Democrats to cross party lines this year, a heavy turnout in Britt's and Clarke's predominantly white districts was bound to hurt.

Republicans also scored a significant gain in Georgia, where Patrick Lynn Swindall's defeat of Elliott Levitas in the suburban Atlanta 4th District gave the GOP its second district in the state. A 1982 redistricting plan pushed by black and Republican legislators had taken most of the 4th's black population to shore up the vote in a neighboring district, and the result was a suburban district that was ready to fall into the GOP column.

Blue-Collar

The GOP's pickups in the East included three districts where blue-collar voters make up much of the population. In New Hampshire's 1st District, Republican Robert C. Smith carried industrial Manchester with 61 percent of the vote.

In Connecticut's 5th District, where state Rep. John G. Rowland unseated William Ratchford, Naugatuck Valley factory towns gave Ratchford only slim margins, and Naugatuck went for Rowland. And in Maryland's 2nd District, Republican Helen Delich Bentley succeeded in knocking off longtime Rep. Clarence Long, in part on the strength of her showing in the blue-collar towns surrounding Baltimore.

In all three cases, the Republican challengers benefited from Reagan's presence at the top of the ticket, but they also campaigned as decidedly local candidates, stressing their ties to the district more than their allegiance to the national GOP.

The Republicans' other two gains in the region came in the New Jersey 11th, where veteran Democrat Minish was unable to overcome the handicap placed on him by new district lines that gave him massive numbers of new suburban voters, and in the 20th District of New York. There, Westchester County territory given up by retiring Democratic Rep. Richard L. Ottinger fell to Scarsdale accountant Joseph J. DioGuardi.

Democratic Gains

The Democrats' three apparent pickups included two in districts where the Republican incumbents had been weakened by scandal. In Idaho's 2nd District, Republican George Hansen has suffered recurring electoral difficulties since allegations concerning false campaign finance reports and questionable personal debts first surfaced in 1975. This election, after his conviction for filing false financial disclosure statements, his constituents seem to have had enough, giving challenger Richard Stallings a paper-thin lead over the incumbent.

In Illinois' 19th District, Republican Daniel B. Crane, censured by the House in 1983 for sexual misconduct with a female congressional page, lost his seat to state Sen. Terry L. Bruce. Bruce put together an overwhelming margin in Champaign County, where Crane has never been popular, and matched Crane in the usually Republican rural counties to the south. ∎

House Membership in the 99th Congress

ALABAMA
1. H.L. "Sonny" Callahan (R)#
2. William L. Dickinson (R)
3. Bill Nichols (D)
4. Tom Bevill (D)
5. Ronnie G. Flippo (D)
6. Ben Erdreich (D)
7. Richard C. Shelby (D)

ALASKA
AL Don Young (R)

ARIZONA
1. John McCain (R)
2. Morris K. Udall (D)
3. Bob Stump (R)
4. Eldon Rudd (R)
5. Jim Kolbe (R)#

ARKANSAS
1. Bill Alexander (D)
2. Tommy Robinson (D)#
3. John Paul Hammerschmidt (R)
4. Beryl Anthony Jr. (D)

CALIFORNIA
1. Douglas H. Bosco (D)
2. Gene Chappie (R)
3. Robert T. Matsui (D)
4. Vic Fazio (D)
5. Sala Burton (D)
6. Barbara Boxer (D)
7. George Miller (D)
8. Ronald V. Dellums (D)
9. Fortney H. "Pete" Stark (D)
10. Don Edwards (D)
11. Tom Lantos (D)
12. Ed Zschau (R)
13. Norman Y. Mineta (D)
14. Norman D. Shumway (R)
15. Tony Coelho (D)
16. Leon E. Panetta (D)
17. Charles Pashayan Jr. (R)
18. Richard H. Lehman (D)
19. Robert J. Lagomarsino (R)
20. William M. Thomas (R)
21. Bobbi Fiedler (R)
22. Carlos J. Moorhead (R)
23. Anthony C. Beilenson (D)
24. Henry A. Waxman (D)
25. Edward R. Roybal (D)
26. Howard L. Berman (D)
27. Mel Levine (D)
28. Julian C. Dixon (D)
29. Augustus F. Hawkins (D)
30. Matthew G. Martinez (D)
31. Mervyn M. Dymally (D)
32. Glenn M. Anderson (D)
33. David Dreier (R)
34. Esteban Edward Torres (D)
35. Jerry Lewis (R)
36. George E. Brown Jr. (D)
37. Al McCandless (R)
38. Robert K. Dornan (R)†#
39. William E. Dannemeyer (R)
40. Robert E. Badham (R)
41. Bill Lowery (R)
42. Dan Lungren (R)
43. Ron Packard (R)

44. Jim Bates (D)
45. Duncan L. Hunter (R)

COLORADO
1. Patricia Schroeder (D)
2. Timothy E. Wirth (D)
3. Michael L. Strang (R)#
4. Hank Brown (R)
5. Ken Kramer (R)
6. Daniel L. Schaefer (R)

CONNECTICUT
1. Barbara B. Kennelly (D)
2. Sam Gejdenson (D)
3. Bruce A. Morrison (D)
4. Stewart B. McKinney (R)
5. John G. Rowland (R)#
6. Nancy L. Johnson (R)

DELAWARE
AL Thomas R. Carper (D)

FLORIDA
1. Earl Hutto (D)
2. Don Fuqua (D)
3. Charles E. Bennett (D)
4. Bill Chappell Jr. (D)
5. Bill McCollum (R)
6. Buddy MacKay (D)
7. Sam Gibbons (D)
8. C.W. Bill Young (R)
9. Michael Bilirakis (R)
10. Andy Ireland (R)
11. Bill Nelson (D)
12. Tom Lewis (R)
13. Connie Mack (R)
14. Daniel A. Mica (D)
15. E. Clay Shaw Jr. (R)
16. Larry Smith (D)
17. William Lehman (D)
18. Claude Pepper (D)
19. Dante B. Fascell (D)

GEORGIA
1. Lindsay Thomas (D)
2. Charles Hatcher (D)
3. Richard Ray (D)
4. Patrick L. Swindall (R)#
5. Wyche Fowler Jr. (D)
6. Newt Gingrich (R)
7. George W. "Buddy" Darden (D)
8. J. Roy Rowland (D)
9. Ed Jenkins (D)
10. Doug Barnard Jr. (D)

HAWAII
1. Cecil Heftel (D)
2. Daniel K. Akaka (D)

House Lineup †

Democrats 252
Freshman Democrats - 12
#Freshman Representative

Republicans 182
Freshman Republicans - 31
†Former Representative

† Does not include result from Indiana 8th District.

IDAHO
1. Larry E. Craig (R)
2. Richard Stallings (D)#

ILLINOIS
1. Charles A. Hayes (D)
2. Gus Savage (D)
3. Marty Russo (D)
4. George M. O'Brien (R)
5. William O. Lipinski (D)
6. Henry J. Hyde (R)
7. Cardiss Collins (D)
8. Dan Rostenkowski (D)
9. Sidney R. Yates (D)
10. John Edward Porter (R)
11. Frank Annunzio (D)
12. Philip M. Crane (R)
13. Harris W. Fawell (R)#
14. John E. Grotberg (R)#
15. Edward R. Madigan (R)
16. Lynn Martin (R)
17. Lane Evans (D)
18. Robert H. Michel (R)
19. Terry L. Bruce (D)#
20. Dick Durbin (D)
21. Melvin Price (D)
22. Kenneth J. Gray (D)†#

INDIANA
1. Peter J. Visclosky (D)#
2. Philip R. Sharp (D)
3. John Hiler (R)
4. Dan Coats (R)
5. Elwood Hillis (R)
6. Dan Burton (R)
7. John T. Myers (R)
8. Vacant
9. Lee H. Hamilton (D)
10. Andrew Jacobs Jr. (D)

IOWA
1. Jim Leach (R)
2. Tom Tauke (R)
3. Cooper Evans (R)
4. Neal Smith (D)
5. Jim Ross Lightfoot (R)#
6. Berkley Bedell (D)

KANSAS
1. Pat Roberts (R)
2. Jim Slattery (D)
3. Jan Meyers (R)#
4. Dan Glickman (D)
5. Bob Whittaker (R)

KENTUCKY
1. Carroll Hubbard Jr. (D)
2. William H. Natcher (D)
3. Romano L. Mazzoli (D)

4. Gene Snyder (R)
5. Harold Rogers (R)
6. Larry J. Hopkins (R)
7. Carl C. "Chris" Perkins (D)#

LOUISIANA
1. Bob Livingston (R)
2. Lindy (Mrs. Hale) Boggs (D)
3. W. J. "Billy" Tauzin (D)
4. Buddy Roemer (D)
5. Jerry Huckaby (D)
6. Henson Moore (R)
7. John B. Breaux (D)
8. Gillis W. Long (D)

MAINE
1. John R. McKernan Jr. (R)
2. Olympia J. Snowe (R)

MARYLAND
1. Roy Dyson (D)
2. Helen Delich Bentley (R)#
3. Barbara A. Mikulski (D)
4. Marjorie S. Holt (R)
5. Steny H. Hoyer (D)
6. Beverly B. Byron (D)
7. Parren J. Mitchell (D)
8. Michael D. Barnes (D)

MASSACHUSETTS
1. Silvio O. Conte (R)
2. Edward P. Boland (D)
3. Joseph D. Early (D)
4. Barney Frank (D)
5. Chester G. Atkins (D)#
6. Nicholas Mavroules (D)
7. Edward J. Markey (D)
8. Thomas P. O'Neill Jr. (D)
9. Joe Moakley (D)
10. Gerry E. Studds (D)
11. Brian J. Donnelly (D)

MICHIGAN
1. John Conyers Jr. (D)
2. Carl D. Pursell (R)
3. Howard Wolpe (D)
4. Mark D. Siljander (R)
5. Paul B. Henry (R)#
6. Bob Carr (D)
7. Dale E. Kildee (D)
8. Bob Traxler (D)
9. Guy Vander Jagt (R)
10. Bill Schuette (R)#
11. Robert W. Davis (R)
12. David E. Bonior (D)
13. George W. Crockett Jr. (D)
14. Dennis M. Hertel (D)
15. William D. Ford (D)
16. John D. Dingell (D)
17. Sander M. Levin (D)
18. William S. Broomfield (R)

MINNESOTA
1. Timothy J. Penny (D)
2. Vin Weber (R)
3. Bill Frenzel (R)
4. Bruce F. Vento (D)
5. Martin Olav Sabo (D)
6. Gerry Sikorski (D)

House Membership in the 99th Congress

7. Arlan Stangeland (R)
8. James L. Oberstar (D)

MISSISSIPPI
1. Jamie L. Whitten (D)
2. Webb Franklin (R)
3. G. V. "Sonny" Montgomery (D)
4. Wayne Dowdy (D)
5. Trent Lott (R)

MISSOURI
1. William Clay (D)
2. Robert A. Young (D)
3. Richard A. Gephardt (D)
4. Ike Skelton (D)
5. Alan Wheat (D)
6. E. Thomas Coleman (R)
7. Gene Taylor (R)
8. Bill Emerson (R)
9. Harold L. Volkmer (D)

MONTANA
1. Pat Williams (D)
2. Ron Marlenee (R)

NEBRASKA
1. Douglas K. Bereuter (R)
2. Hal Daub (R)
3. Virginia Smith (R)

NEVADA
1. Harry Reid (D)
2. Barbara F. Vucanovich (R)

NEW HAMPSHIRE
1. Robert C. Smith (R)#
2. Judd Gregg (R)

NEW JERSEY
1. James J. Florio (D)
2. William J. Hughes (D)
3. James J. Howard (D)
4. Christopher H. Smith (R)
5. Marge Roukema (R)
6. Bernard J. Dwyer (D)
7. Matthew J. Rinaldo (R)
8. Robert A. Roe (D)
9. Robert G. Torricelli (D)
10. Peter W. Rodino Jr. (D)
11. Dean A. Gallo (R)#
12. Jim Courter (R)
13. H. James Saxton (R)#
14. Frank J. Guarini (D)

NEW MEXICO
1. Manuel Lujan Jr. (R)
2. Joe Skeen (R)
3. Bill Richardson (D)

NEW YORK
1. William Carney (R)
2. Thomas J. Downey (D)
3. Robert J. Mrazek (D)
4. Norman F. Lent (R)
5. Raymond J. McGrath (R)
6. Joseph P. Addabbo (D)
7. Gary L. Ackerman (D)
8. James H. Scheuer (D)
9. Thomas J. Manton (D)#
10. Charles E. Schumer (D)

11. Edolphus Towns (D)
12. Major R. Owens (D)
13. Stephen J. Solarz (D)
14. Guy V. Molinari (R)
15. Bill Green (R)
16. Charles B. Rangel (D)
17. Ted Weiss (D)
18. Robert Garcia (D)
19. Mario Biaggi (D)
20. Joseph J. DioGuardi (R)#
21. Hamilton Fish Jr. (R)
22. Benjamin A. Gilman (R)
23. Samuel S. Stratton (D)
24. Gerald B. H. Solomon (R)
25. Sherwood L. Boehlert (R)
26. David O'B. Martin (R)
27. George C. Wortley (R)
28. Matthew F. McHugh (D)
29. Frank Horton (R)
30. Fred J. Eckert (R)#
31. Jack F. Kemp (R)
32. John J. LaFalce (D)
33. Henry J. Nowak (D)
34. Stanley N. Lundine (D)

NORTH CAROLINA
1. Walter B. Jones (D)
2. Tim Valentine Jr. (D)
3. Charles Whitley (D)
4. William W. Cobey Jr. (R)#
5. Stephen L. Neal (D)
6. Howard Coble (R)#
7. Charlie Rose (D)
8. W. G. "Bill" Hefner (D)
9. J. Alex McMillan (R)#
10. James T. Broyhill (R)
11. Bill Hendon (R)†#

NORTH DAKOTA
AL Byron L. Dorgan (D)

OHIO
1. Thomas A. Luken (D)
2. Bill Gradison (R)
3. Tony P. Hall (D)
4. Mike Oxley (R)
5. Delbert L. Latta (R)
6. Bob McEwen (R)
7. Michael DeWine (R)
8. Thomas N. Kindness (R)
9. Marcy Kaptur (D)
10. Clarence E. Miller (R)
11. Dennis E. Eckart (D)
12. John R. Kasich (R)
13. Don J. Pease (D)
14. John F. Seiberling (D)
15. Chalmers P. Wylie (R)
16. Ralph Regula (R)
17. James A. Traficant Jr. (D)#
18. Douglas Applegate (D)
19. Edward F. Feighan (D)
20. Mary Rose Oakar (D)
21. Louis Stokes (D)

OKLAHOMA
1. James R. Jones (D)
2. Mike Synar (D)
3. Wes Watkins (D)

4. Dave McCurdy (D)
5. Mickey Edwards (R)
6. Glenn English (D)

OREGON
1. Les AuCoin (D)
2. Bob Smith (R)
3. Ron Wyden (D)
4. James Weaver (D)
5. Denny Smith (R)

PENNSYLVANIA
1. Thomas M. Foglietta (D)
2. William H. Gray III (D)
3. Robert A. Borski (D)
4. Joe Kolter (D)
5. Richard T. Schulze (R)
6. Gus Yatron (D)
7. Bob Edgar (D)
8. Peter H. Kostmayer (D)
9. Bud Shuster (R)
10. Joseph M. McDade (R)
11. Paul E. Kanjorski (D)#
12. John P. Murtha (D)
13. Lawrence Coughlin (R)
14. William J. Coyne (D)
15. Don Ritter (R)
16. Robert S. Walker (R)
17. George W. Gekas (R)
18. Doug Walgren (D)
19. Bill Goodling (R)
20. Joseph M. Gaydos (D)
21. Tom Ridge (R)
22. Austin J. Murphy (D)
23. William F. Clinger Jr. (R)

RHODE ISLAND
1. Fernand J. St Germain (D)
2. Claudine Schneider (R)

SOUTH CAROLINA
1. Thomas F. Hartnett (R)
2. Floyd Spence (R)
3. Butler Derrick (D)
4. Carroll A. Campbell Jr. (R)
5. John M. Spratt Jr. (D)
6. Robert Tallon (D)

SOUTH DAKOTA
AL Thomas A. Daschle (D)

TENNESSEE
1. James H. Quillen (R)
2. John J. Duncan (R)
3. Marilyn Lloyd (D)
4. Jim Cooper (D)
5. Bill Boner (D)
6. Bart Gordon (D)#
7. Don Sundquist (R)
8. Ed Jones (D)
9. Harold E. Ford (D)

TEXAS
1. Sam B. Hall Jr. (D)
2. Charles Wilson (D)
3. Steve Bartlett (R)
4. Ralph M. Hall (D)
5. John Bryant (D)
6. Joe Barton (R)#
7. Bill Archer (R)

8. Jack Fields (R)
9. Jack Brooks (D)
10. J. J. Pickle (D)
11. Marvin Leath (D)
12. Jim Wright (D)
13. Beau Boulter (R)#
14. Mac Sweeny (R)#
15. E. "Kika" de la Garza (D)
16. Ronald Coleman (D)
17. Charles W. Stenholm (D)
18. Mickey Leland (D)
19. Larry Combest (R)#
20. Henry B. Gonzalez (D)
21. Tom Loeffler (R)
22. Tom DeLay (R)#
23. Albert G. Bustamante (D)#
24. Martin Frost (D)
25. Michael A. Andrews (D)
26. Richard Armey (R)#
27. Solomon P. Ortiz (D)

UTAH
1. James V. Hansen (R)
2. David S. Monson (R)#
3. Howard C. Nielson (R)

VERMONT
AL James M. Jeffords (R)

VIRGINIA
1. Herbert H. Bateman (R)
2. G. William Whitehurst (R)
3. Thomas J. Bliley Jr. (R)
4. Norman Sisisky (D)
5. Dan Daniel (D)
6. James R. Olin (D)
7. D. French Slaughter (R)#
8. Stan Parris (R)
9. Frederick C. Boucher (D)
10. Frank R. Wolf (R)

WASHINGTON
1. John Miller (R)#
2. Al Swift (D)
3. Don Bonker (D)
4. Sid Morrison (R)
5. Thomas S. Foley (D)
6. Norman D. Dicks (D)
7. Mike Lowry (D)
8. Rod Chandler (R)

WEST VIRGINIA
1. Alan B. Mollohan (D)
2. Harley O. Staggers Jr. (D)
3. Bob Wise (D)
4. Nick J. Rahall II (D)

WISCONSIN
1. Les Aspin (D)
2. Robert W. Kastenmeier (D)
3. Steve Gunderson (R)
4. Gerald D. Kleczka (D)
5. Jim Moody (D)
6. Thomas E. Petri (R)
7. David R. Obey (D)
8. Toby Roth (R)
9. F. James Sensenbrenner Jr. (R)

WYOMING
AL Dick Cheney (R)

House Newcomers, Switched Seats and Losers

State	District	Old	New	Winner	Loser	Incumbent
Alabama	1	R	R	H. L. "Sonny" Callahan (R)	Frank McRight (D)	Jack Edwards (R) [1]
Arizona	5	D	R	Jim Kolbe (R)	James F. McNulty Jr. (D)	McNulty
Arkansas	2	R	D	Tommy Robinson (D)	Judy Petty (R)	Ed Bethune (R) [2]
California	38	D	R	Robert K. Dornan (R)	Jerry M. Patterson (D)	Patterson
Colorado	3	D	R	Michael L. Strang (R)	W Mitchell (D)	Ray Kogovsek(D) [1]
Connecticut	5	D	R	John G. Rowland (R)	William R. Ratchford (D)	Ratchford
Georgia	4	D	R	Patrick Lynn Swindall (R)	Elliott H. Levitas (D)	Levitas
Idaho	2	R	D	Richard Stallings (D)	George Hansen (R)	Hansen
Illinois	13	R	R	Harris W. Fawell (R)	Michael J. Donohue (D)	John N. Erlenborn (R) [1]
	14	R	R	John E. Grotberg (R)	Dan McGrath (D)	Tom Corcoran (R) [3]
	19	R	D	Terry L. Bruce (D)	Daniel B. Crane (R)	Crane
	22	D	D	Kenneth J. Gray (D)	Randy Patchett (R)	Paul Simon (D) [2]
Indiana*	1	D	D	Peter J. Visclosky (D)	Joseph B. Grenchik (R)	Katie Hall (D) [4]
Iowa	5	D	R	Jim Ross Lightfoot (R)	Jerome D. Fitzgerald (D)	Tom Harkin (D) [2]
Kansas	3	R	R	Jan Meyers (R)	John E. Reardon (D)	Larry Winn Jr. (R) [1]
Kentucky	7	D	D	Carl C. "Chris" Perkins (D)	Aubrey Russell (R)	Carl D. Perkins (D) [5]
Maryland	2	D	R	Helen Delich Bentley (R)	Clarence D. Long (D)	Long
Massachusetts	5	D	D	Chester G. Atkins (D)	Gregory S. Hyatt (R)	James M. Shannon (D) [3]
Michigan	5	R	R	Paul B. Henry (R)	Gary J. McInerney (D)	Harold S. Sawyer (R) [1]
	10	D	R	Bill Schuette (R)	Donald J. Albosta (D)	Albosta
New Hampshire	1	D	R	Robert C. Smith (R)	Dudley Dudley (D)	Norman E. D'Amours (D) [2]
New Jersey	11	D	R	Dean A. Gallo (R)	Joseph G. Minish (D)	Minish
	13	R	R	H. James Saxton (R)	James B. Smith (D)	Edwin B. Forsythe (R) [6]
New York	9	D	D	Thomas J. Manton (D)	Serphin R. Maltese (R)	Geraldine A. Ferraro (D) [7]
	20	D	R	Joseph J. DioGuardi (R)	Oren J. Teicher (D)	Richard L. Ottinger (D) [1]
	30	R	R	Fred J. Eckert (R)	W. Douglas Call (D)	Barber B. Conable Jr. (R) [1]
North Carolina	4	D	R	William W. Cobey Jr. (R)	Ike Andrews (D)	Andrews
	6	D	R	Howard Coble (R)	Robin Britt (D)	Britt
	9	R	R	J. Alex McMillan (R)	D. G. Martin (D)	James G. Martin (R) [8]
	11	D	R	Bill Hendon (R)	James McClure Clarke (D)	Clarke
Ohio	17	R	D	James A. Traficant Jr. (D)	Lyle Williams (R)	Williams
Pennsylvania	11	D	D	Paul E. Kanjorski (D)	Robert P. Hudock (R)	Frank Harrison (D) [4]
Tennessee	6	D	D	Bart Gordon (D)	Joe Simpkins (R)	Albert Gore Jr. (D) [2]
Texas	6	R	R	Joe Barton (R)	Dan Kubiak (D)	Phil Gramm (R) [2]
	13	D	R	Beau Boulter (R)	Jack Hightower (D)	Hightower
	14	D	R	Mac Sweeney (R)	Bill Patman (D)	Patman
	19	D	R	Larry Combest (R)	Don R. Richards (D)	Kent Hance (D) [3]
	22	R	R	Tom DeLay (R)	Doug Williams (D)	Ron Paul (R) [3]
	23	D	D	Albert G. Bustamante (D)	unopposed	Abraham Kazen Jr. (D) [4]
	26	D	R	Richard Armey (R)	Tom Vandergriff (D)	Vandergriff
Utah	2	R	R	David S. Monson (R)	Frances Farley (D)	Dan Marriott (R) [9]
Virginia	7	R	R	D. French Slaughter (R)	Lewis M. Costello (D)	J. Kenneth Robinson (R) [1]
Washington	1	R	R	John Miller (R)	Brock Evans (D)	Joel Pritchard (R) [1]

* Does not include result from Indiana 8th District.

[1] *Retired.*
[2] *Ran for Senate.*
[3] *Defeated in Senate primary.*
[4] *Defeated in primary.*
[5] *Died Aug. 3, 1984.*
[6] *Died March 29, 1984.*
[7] *Ran for vice president.*
[8] *Ran for governor.*
[9] *Defeated in gubernatorial primary.*

 State Elections

Republicans Pick Up One Governorship

The 13 gubernatorial elections held Nov. 6, 1984, did little to dent the 2-1 advantage the Democratic Party has in governorships it controls.

Republicans notched victories in North Carolina, Rhode Island, Utah and West Virginia, where the statehouses were left vacant in 1984 by departing Democratic incumbents.

But the Democrats managed to capture three new seats, toppling Republican incumbents in North Dakota and Washington and picking up the seat left open by retiring GOP Gov. Richard A. Snelling in Vermont.

Republicans thus scored a net gain of one seat, boosting the total governorships under their control from 15 to 16 and reducing the number of states in the Democratic column from 35 to 34. *(Results, p. 25-B; map, p. 22-B; list of governors, p. 23-B)*

Republicans also scored gains in state legislatures. *(Chart, p. 20-B; story, p. 24-B)*

The GOP's showing represents an improvement over 1982, when the party suffered a net loss of seven seats. Republicans still remain a long way, however, from capturing a majority of governorships — a feat they last accomplished in 1969.

A single-seat Republican gubernatorial gain may seem meager in a year when President Reagan romped to a 49-state re-election victory. But presidential landslides seldom have had much effect on gubernatorial elections in recent years.

While Democrat Lyndon B. Johnson swept to victory with 61 percent of the vote nationwide in 1964, his party slid back one seat at the statehouse level. GOP President Richard M. Nixon's landslide victory in 1972 had a similarly negligible effect.

Even in 1980, when Reagan's strong victory was accompanied by a Republican gain of four governorships, there was no strong link between the two. The GOP gubernatorial nominees ran ahead of Reagan in three of those four states.

Significant swings in party control of governorships are more likely in midterm elections than in a presidential year. As John F. Bibby, a political

No 'Coattail' Effect Seen in Statehouses

scientist at the University of Wisconsin-Milwaukee, has pointed out, the sitting president's party has suffered setbacks at the gubernatorial level in every midterm election but one since 1950.

That phenomenon is due in part to the fact that over the last two decades, many states have moved their gubernatorial elections to the presidential midterm year.

Making History

The newly elected Republican governors range in style and spirit from North Carolina's James G. Martin, a soft-spoken and restrained chemistry professor and six-term member of the U.S. House, to West Virginia's Arch A. Moore Jr., a blunt and sometimes blustery politician who previously served two terms as the state's governor (1969-1977).

Of the two, Martin had the rougher road to victory. Although his 12-year tenure as representative of North Carolina's 9th District gave him a solid base in the city of Charlotte, he had to begin from scratch in building

Governorships

Current lineup		1985	
Democrats	35	Democrats	34
Republicans	15	Republicans	16

Democrats

Net Loss	1
Incumbents re-elected	2
Incumbents defeated	0

Republicans

Net Gain	1
Incumbents re-elected	2
Incumbents defeated	2
(Allen I. Olson, N.D.; John Spellman, Wash.)	

beyond it.

Martin's task was somewhat complicated by the concurrent campaign of Republican U.S. Sen. Jesse Helms, whose re-election bid riveted the state's attention and sapped much of its GOP resources.

Martin needed strong support from Helms' hard-core conservative enthusiasts, even though he always had stood apart from the powerful National Congressional Club organization allied with Helms.

But Martin improved his name recognition with a series of statewide "Jim Martin Listens" tours and attracted conservative attention by reminding voters of his ardent advocacy of supply-side economics and his loyalty to Reagan.

Martin rolled up 54 percent of the statewide vote to defeat Attorney General Rufus Edmisten, becoming only the second Republican in this century to win the North Carolina Statehouse. (The first, James E. Holhouser, served from 1973-1977.)

Unprecedented Third Term

Moore was favored to return to the West Virginia governorship from the outset of the 1984 campaign.

The controversial Republican had suffered some setbacks in the mid- and late-1970s, including a 1975 indictment on extortion charges, on which he was acquitted the following year. He ran unsuccessful campaigns for the Senate in 1978 and the governorship in 1980.

Nevertheless, Moore was considered far and away the most credible statewide Republican candidate in West Virginia in the last 20 years and became the clear front-runner as soon as he announced his interest in winning back his old job.

Moore's previous exposure and superior financing gave him advantages over his Democratic opponent, state House Speaker Clyde M. See Jr. See's rocky relations with organized labor further benefited Moore.

The Republican's 53 percentage point victory brought him to an unprecedented third term in the West Virginia Statehouse.

Partisan Lineups of State Legislatures . . .

State	Governor	1985 Legislature	October 1984 Upper House			January 1985 Upper House		
Alabama	D	D	28D	4R	3I	28D	4R	3I
Alaska	D	● X	9D	11R		9D	11R	
Arizona	D	R	12D	18R		12D	18R	
Arkansas	D	D	32D	3R		31D	4R	
California	R	D	25D	14R	1I	25D	15R	
Colorado	D	R	14D	21R		11D	24R	
Connecticut	D	● R	23D	13R		12D	24R	
Delaware	R	● X	13D	8R		13D	8R	
Florida	D	D	32D	8R		32D	8R	
Georgia	D	D	49D	7R		47D	9R	
Hawaii	D	D	20D	5R		21D	4R	
Idaho	D	R	14D	21R		14D	28R	
Illinois	R	D	33D	26R		31D	28R	
Indiana	R	R	18D	32R		20D	30R	
Iowa	R	D	28D	22R		29D	21R	
Kansas	D	R	16D	24R		16D	24R	
Kentucky	D	D	28D	10R		28D	10R	
Louisiana	D	D	38D	1R		38D	1R	
Maine	D	D	23D	10R		24D	11R	
Maryland	D	D	41D	6R		41D	6R	
Massachusetts	D	D	33D	7R		32D	8R	
Michigan	D	X	18D	20R		18D	20R	
Minnesota	D	● X	42D	25R		42D	25R	
Mississippi	D	D	49D	3R		49D	3R	
Missouri	R	D	23D	11R		22D	12R	
Montana	D	● D	24D	26R		27D	23R	
Nebraska	D		49-seat Non-partisan Unicameral Legislature					
Nevada	D	● X	17D	4R		13D	8R	
New Hampshire	R	R	7D	15R	2V	6D	18R	
New Jersey	R	D	23D	17R		23D	17R	
New Mexico	D	● X	23D	19R		21D	21R	
New York	D	X	26D	35R		26D	35R	
North Carolina	● R	D	44D	6R		38D	12R	
North Dakota	● D	● R	21D	32R		24D	29R	
Ohio	D	● X	17D	16R		15D	18R	
Oklahoma	D	D	34D	14R		34D	14R	
Oregon	R	D	21D	9R		17D	10R	3U
Pennsylvania	R	X	23D	27R		23D	27R	
Rhode Island	● R	D	29D	21R		39D	11R	
South Carolina	D	D	40D	6R		37D	9R	
South Dakota	R	R	9D	26R		10D	25R	
Tennessee	R	D	22D	11R		23D	10R	
Texas	D	D	26D	5R		25D	6R	
Utah	● R	R	5D	24R		6D	23R	
Vermont	● D	● X	13D	17R		17D	13R	
Virginia	D	D	32D	8R		32D	8R	
Washington	● D	D	26D	23R		26D	21R	2U
West Virginia	● R	D	31D	3R		29D	5R	
Wisconsin	D	D	19D	14R		19D	14R	
Wyoming	D	R	11D	19R		11D	19R	

TOTAL PARTY CONTROL:
Democrats: 28
Republicans: 11
Split: 10

October 1984 Upper House:
Democrats: 1,204
Republicans: 727
Independents: 4
Vacancies: 2

October 1984 Lower House:
Democrats: 3,421
Republicans: 2,008
Independents: 13
Vacancies: 9

SOURCE: National Conference of State Legislatures

. . . and Governorships for 1985 Sessions

October 1984 Lower House			January 1985 Lower House			Upper House Gains †	Lower House Gains †	State
88D	12R	5I	88D	12R	5I	No change	No change	Alabama
19D	21R		21D	17R	1L, 1U	No change	Undecided	Alaska
21D	39R		21D	38R	1U	No change	Undecided	Arizona
93D	7R		90D	10R		+1 R	+3 R	Arkansas
48D	32R		47D	33R		+1 R	+1 R	California
25D	40R		18D	47R		+3 R	+7 R	Colorado
87D	64R		64D	87R		+11 R	+23 R	Connecticut
25D	16R		20D	21R		No change	+5 R	Delaware
84D	36R		78D	42R		No change	+6 R	Florida
156D	24R		154D	26R		+2 R	+2 R	Georgia
43D	8R		40D	11R		+1 D	+3 R	Hawaii
19D	51R		17D	67R		+7 R	+16 R	Idaho
70D	48R		67D	51R		+2 R	+3 R	Illinois
43D	57R		39D	61R		+2 D	+4 R	Indiana
60D	40R		60D	40R		+1 D	No change	Iowa
53D	72R		49D	76R		No change	+4 R	Kansas
77D	23R		73D	25R	2U	No change	Undecided	Kentucky
90D	14R	1I	90D	14R	1I	No change	No change	Louisiana
92D	58R	1V	84D	67R		+1 R	+9 R	Maine
124D	17R		124D	17R		No change	No change	Maryland
131D	29R		126D	34R		+1 R	+5 R	Massachusetts
63D	47R		58D	52R		No change	+5 R	Michigan
77D	57R		64D	70R		No change	+13 R	Minnesota
115D	5R	1I	115D	5R	1I	No change	No change	Mississippi
110D	53R		108D	55R		+1 R	+2 R	Missouri
55D	45R		50D	50R		+3 D	+5 R	Montana
								Nebraska
23D	19R		17D	25R		+4 R	+6 R	Nevada
158D	234R	2I, 6V	108D	292R		+3 R	+58 R	New Hampshire
44D	36R		44D	36R		No change	No change	New Jersey
45D	25R		43D	27R		+2 R	+2 R	New Mexico
98D	52R		94D	56R		No change	+4 R	New York
102D	18R		83D	37R		+6 R	+19 R	North Carolina
55D	51R		41D	64R	1T	+3 D	Undecided	North Dakota
62D	37R		59D	40R		+2 R	+3 R	Ohio
76D	25R		69D	32R		No change	+7 R	Oklahoma
36D	24R		33D	24R	3U	Undecided	Undecided	Oregon
103D	99R	1V	103D	100R		No change	+1 R	Pennsylvania
85D	15R		78D	22R		+10 D	+7 R	Rhode Island
103D	20R	1V	95D	26R	3U	+3 R	Undecided	South Carolina
16D	54R		13D	57R		+1 D	+3 R	South Dakota
60D	38R	1I	62D	37R		+1 D	+2 D	Tennessee
113D	37R		97D	53R		+1 R	+16 R	Texas
17D	58R		16D	59R		+1 D	+1 R	Utah
65D	84R	1I	72D	78R		+4 D	+7 D	Vermont
65D	34R	1I	65D	34R	1I	No change	No change	Virginia
56D	42R		49D	39R	9U	Undecided	Undecided	Washington
88D	12R		76D	24R		+2 R	+12 R	West Virginia
58D	41R		52D	47R		No change	+6 R	Wisconsin
25D	38R	1I	18D	46R		No change	+8 R	Wyoming

January 1985 Upper House:
Democrats: 1,186
Republicans: 752
Independents: 3
Undecided: 5

January 1985 Lower House:
Democrats: 3,152
Republicans: 2,283
Libertarians: 1
Independents: 8
Undecided: 19
Tie: 1

SYMBOLS

D = Democrat	T = Tie
R = Republican	U = Undecided contests as of Nov. 15.
L = Libertarian	
I = Independent	● = Change in party control
V = Vacancy	X = Party control split

† Due to the addition of seats through redistricting, one party's gains may not equal the other's losses.

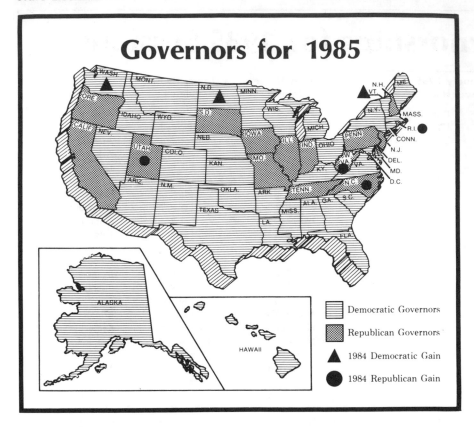

Governors for 1985

Democratic Governors

Republican Governors

▲ 1984 Democratic Gain

● 1984 Republican Gain

Democrats Break Records

The Democrats also broke records in 1984.

In Vermont, former Lt. Gov. Madeleine M. Kunin eked out a narrow victory to become the first woman governor of the state. The Swiss-born former journalist joins Democratic Gov. Martha Layne Collins of Kentucky as one of only two female governors nationwide.

Kunin's successful effort to break the gender barrier is not her only distinction. In replacing retiring Republican Gov. Snelling, she has become only the third Democrat to capture the state's governorship in the last 130 years.

Kunin's victory came on her second attempt. In 1982, she entered the gubernatorial race on the assumption that Snelling was retiring only to find herself face-to-face with the feisty incumbent after he reversed the announcement that he would step down. Kunin's showing — she polled 44 percent of the vote — helped make her an early front-runner this election.

Attorney General John J. Easton Jr., the GOP nominee, closed quickly on her, capitalizing on a costly television ad campaign. But Kunin's argument that she would be a more activist governor than the Republican, cou-

pled with her highly personal grassroots campaign style, helped keep her in the running.

Kunin finished with a 3,661-vote edge in complete but unofficial returns, just clearing the 50 percent mark. Under state law, a lesser percentage would have required the GOP-controlled state Legislature to decide the election.

Party Domination

In two gubernatorial races, party domination became a key campaign theme.

Rhode Island Republican Edward DiPrete won a convincing victory over state Treasurer Anthony J. Solomon, in part by blaming the state's wobbly economy on the Democrats' one-party rule. DiPrete, the mayor of Cranston, is the first Republican governor in Rhode Island since John H. Chafee, now a U.S. senator, held the office from 1963-69.

In Utah, state House Speaker Norman H. Bangerter broke a Democratic lock on the Statehouse to become the first Republican governor of the Beehive State in 20 years.

His victory came despite warnings from his Democratic opponent, former U.S. Rep. Wayne Owens, that Bangerter's election would further

move GOP-minded Utah down the path to becoming a one-party state.

Unexpected Victory

The most unexpected victory came in North Dakota, where state Rep. George Sinner cut GOP Gov. Allen I. Olson's tenure short after just one term. Olson and Washington's GOP Gov. John Spellman were the only two incumbent governors defeated on Election Day.

A wealthy sugar beet farmer from the Red River Valley, Sinner surprised some North Dakotans by winning his own party's nod. Although he had served as a state senator for four years in the early 1960s and won a seat in the state House in 1982, Sinner was considered the underdog against a better-known Democratic hopeful, former Gov. Arthur Link. But Sinner cleared his first hurdle by winning the state Democratic Party's endorsement at the party's 1984 convention.

Against Olson, Sinner faced even longer odds. The incumbent Republican had failed to arouse a fervent following, but his superior name recognition and the state's enthusiasm for the national GOP ticket appeared to give him a comfortable edge.

Sinner scored points by complaining that the incumbent had dragged his heels on pushing completion of the Garrison Diversion water project, and by running television ads that used a picture of a farmer pitching manure as a metaphor for some of the statements made in Olson's campaign.

In the end, it was not even close. Sinner finished with 56 percent of the vote, running 22 percentage points ahead of Democratic presidential nominee Walter F. Mondale in the state. Sinner's victory avenges the Democrats, who controlled the North Dakota Statehouse for two decades before Olson pulled it away in 1980.

Pierce County Executive Booth Gardner ousted Spellman for the Washington governorship, a job that is proving increasingly difficult to hold for more than four years. Spellman and his predecessor, Democrat Dixy Lee Ray, each served only one term. Washington has not re-elected a governor since 1972.

An heir to the Weyerhaeuser lumber fortune, Gardner benefited from a businessman-turned-politician appeal. Ironically, it was the same sort of image that helped Spellman win election four years earlier.

But Spellman failed to ignite the Washington electorate during his term

1985 Occupants of the Nation's Statehouses

Here is a list of the governors and governors-elect of the 50 states, and the years in which each office is next up for election. The names of governors elected in 1984 are *italicized*. Asterisks (*) denote incumbents re-elected.

Alabama — George C. Wallace (D) 1986
Alaska — Bill Sheffield (D) 1986
Arizona — Bruce Babbitt (D) 1986
Arkansas — *Bill Clinton (D) 1986**
California — George Deukmejian (R) 1986
Colorado — Richard D. Lamm (D) 1986
Connecticut — William A. O'Neill (D) 1986
Delaware — *Michael N. Castle (R) 1988*
Florida — Robert Graham (D) 1986
Georgia — Joe Frank Harris (D) 1986
Hawaii — George Ariyoshi (D) 1986
Idaho — John V. Evans (D) 1986
Illinois — James R. Thompson (R) 1986
Indiana — *Robert D. Orr (R) 1988**
Iowa — Terry Branstad (R) 1986
Kansas — John Carlin (D) 1986
Kentucky — Martha Layne Collins (D) 1987
Louisiana — Edwin W. Edwards (D) 1987
Maine — Joseph E. Brennan (D) 1986
Maryland — Harry R. Hughes (D) 1986
Massachusetts — Michael S. Dukakis (D) 1986
Michigan — James J. Blanchard (D) 1986
Minnesota — Rudy Perpich (D) 1986
Mississippi — Bill Allain (D) 1987
Missouri — *John Ashcroft (R) 1988*

Montana — *Ted Schwinden (D) 1988**
Nebraska — Bob Kerrey (D) 1986
Nevada — Richard H. Bryan (D) 1986
New Hampshire — *John H. Sununu (R) 1986**
New Jersey — Thomas H. Kean (R) 1985
New Mexico — Toney Anaya (D) 1986
New York — Mario M. Cuomo (D) 1986
North Carolina — *James G. Martin (R) 1988*
North Dakota — *George Sinner (D) 1988*
Ohio — Richard F. Celeste (D) 1986
Oklahoma — George Nigh (D) 1986
Oregon — Victor G. Atiyeh (R) 1986
Pennsylvania — Richard L. Thornburgh (R) 1986
Rhode Island — *Edward DiPrete (R) 1986*
South Carolina — Richard W. Riley (D) 1986
South Dakota — William J. Janklow (R) 1986
Tennessee — Lamar Alexander (R) 1986
Texas — Mark White (D) 1986
Utah — *Norman H. Bangerter (R) 1988*
Vermont — *Madeleine M. Kunin (D) 1986*
Virginia — Charles S. Robb (D) 1985
Washington — *Booth Gardner (D) 1988*
West Virginia — *Arch A. Moore Jr. (R) 1988*
Wisconsin — Anthony S. Earl (D) 1986
Wyoming — Ed Herschler (D) 1986

and suffered credibility problems when he raised taxes after promising not to in 1980.

Although Gardner was hampered himself by a shy and unexciting style, he gained ground by claiming he could run the state government like a business and branding Spellman an ineffective manager. Gardner finished with a 53-47 percentage point win.

A Close Call

Republicans came dangerously close to losing a third statehouse. The comfortable lead Indiana Gov. Robert D. Orr enjoyed in polls a month before the contest almost disappeared on Election Day.

State Sen. W. Wayne Townsend, the Democratic nominee, accused Orr of misrepresenting Indiana's financial status. He reminded voters that Orr had said before the 1982 election that the state had no major financial problems — but announced a heavy deficit and called for a hefty tax increase afterward. The Democrat also complained that Orr had perpetuated patronage politics in the state's vehicle licensing system.

Orr held on to clinch a 52-48 per-

centage point victory, but Townsend's strong showing appears to have helped bolster other Democrats on the ticket.

In other GOP victories, Delaware Lt. Gov. Michael N. Castle, a tall and personable man whose looks were once likened to a clean-shaven Abraham Lincoln, won a comfortable victory in his bid to succeed his political mentor, GOP Gov. Pierre S. "Pete" du Pont IV.

Castle defeated former state Supreme Court Justice William T. Quillen with 55 percent of the vote.

Missourians selected Attorney General John Ashcroft, a gospel-singing lawyer with a conservative political base, to succeed departing GOP Gov. Christopher S. "Kit" Bond. Ashcroft garnered 57 percent of the vote statewide to defeat Lt. Gov. Kenneth J. Rothman.

At 42, Ashcroft is the youngest member of the 1984 gubernatorial class, while West Virginia's Moore, 61, is the oldest.

Incumbents Re-elected

In each of the three remaining states that held gubernatorial contests in 1984, incumbents were re-elected to

the Statehouse with ease.

Republican John H. Sununu tightened his hold on the New Hampshire Statehouse, racking up 67 percent of the vote against state House Minority Leader Chris Spirou in winning a second two-year term.

Democratic Gov. Bill Clinton of Arkansas coasted to his third two-year term, turning back contractor Woody Freeman and overcoming the re-election hurdle that tripped him up once before.

Clinton, initially elected governor in 1978, was defeated in 1980, a victim in part of his own overconfidence. But Clinton successfully mended fences in his comeback attempt, vowing no longer to "lead without listening." The result was a comfortable Clinton victory in 1982.

In Montana, Democratic incumbent Ted Schwinden was so confident of victory over state Sen. Pat Goodover that he spent most of his time helping his party's state legislative candidates. Bolstered by a record of fiscal prudence that has enabled him to win Republican support, Schwinden finished with 70 percent of the vote. ∎

Pick Up 300 Seats:

Republicans Score Gains in State Legislatures

Although President Reagan's landslide re-election was accompanied by only modest congressional and gubernatorial gains for the Republican Party, the GOP scored an impressive string of victories in state legislative contests Nov. 6.

The election results did not dramatically affect the overall legislative dominance of the Democrats, who now control both chambers in 28 states. But further Republican advances in several states could pose a long-range danger to the Democratic majority in the U.S. House, since the legislatures will control the congressional redistricting process following the 1990 census.

Republicans next year will control both chambers in just 11 states, the same number as before the election. But they achieved a net gain of five states in which they control one chamber, bringing to 10 the number of legislatures where party control is divided.

Overall, Democrats will control 66 legislative chambers next year, compared with 32 for the Republicans. One state, Nebraska, has a non-partisan, unicameral Legislature.

Many of the Republican pickups were in states with heavy Democratic majorities, particularly in the South, so the figures on party control do not fully reflect Republican gains. The partisan breakdown of the individual seats gives a clearer picture: Republicans added nearly 300 seats nationwide.

The 49 partisan state Senates — upper chambers — will have a total of 1,186 Democrats and 752 Republicans next year. The state Houses — lower chambers — will have 3,152 Democrats and 2,283 Republicans. The totals, estimated by the National Conference of State Legislatures, do not include the results of a handful of undecided legislative races.

Only one other party, the Libertarian, will be represented in a state legislature.

The Libertarians won a single seat in the Alaska House, regaining one of two seats they had held in 1980 and lost in 1982.

Women and blacks made small legislative gains nationwide. United Press International surveys found that there will be 000 female state legisla-

tors next year, up from 911 in 1984, and 373 black legislators, compared with 372 this year.

State Party Gains

By far the most striking legislative change came in Connecticut, where Republicans took control of both chambers from the Democrats. Aided by a Reagan landslide in the state and divisions within the Democratic Party, Connecticut Republicans won an additional 11 seats in the Senate and 23 seats in the House.

In absolute numbers, though, the Connecticut GOP gains were not the biggest in the country. New Hampshire Republicans picked up 58 seats in the 400-member House. One of the losing candidates was Democrat Endicott Peabody, who was seeking a state House seat to resurrect a political career that included one term as governor of Massachusetts in the 1960s and a campaign for the Democratic vice presidential nomination in 1972.

Republicans also picked up control of one legislative chamber each in Delaware, Minnesota, Nevada, New Mexico and Ohio. Idaho Republicans added significantly to their existing majorities, gaining enough votes to override any future vetoes by Democratic Gov. John V. Evans.

Perhaps more important in the long run, however, were the Republican gains in traditionally Democratic Southern states. Significant GOP pickups came in Florida (six seats in the two chambers combined), North Carolina (25 seats), South Carolina (9) and Texas (17).

Democrats were not without some offsetting gains of their own, however. In Alaska, the party ended Republican legislative dominance by winning a bare majority in the House. Vermont Democrats pulled off a similar feat, taking control of the Senate by a four-seat margin.

There were 13 states that had gubernatorial elections in 1984, and in most cases the party that won the governorship also scored legislative gains. But there were a few cases where legislators swam against the gubernatorial tide. Despite the victory of Republican gubernatorial candidate Edward DiPrete, Rhode Island Democrats gained 10 seats in the Senate, reversing the major gains made by the GOP in a 1983 special election. And a Republican takeover of the North Dakota House came despite the defeat of incumbent Gov. Allen I. Olson at the hands of Democrat George Sinner.

A summary of state legislative results appears on pages 20-B—21-B. ∎

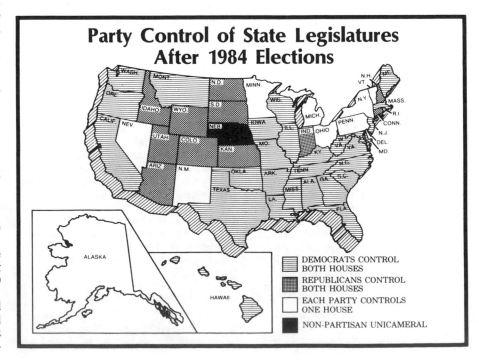

Party Control of State Legislatures After 1984 Elections

DEMOCRATS CONTROL BOTH HOUSES

REPUBLICANS CONTROL BOTH HOUSES

EACH PARTY CONTROLS ONE HOUSE

NON-PARTISAN UNICAMERAL

Election Results

Returns for Governor, Senate and House

Here are nearly complete unofficial 1984 vote returns compiled by Congressional Quarterly from various sources, including the News Election Service, as of Nov. 9, 1984. In some cases, there will be significant changes in final, official returns.

The box below shows party designation symbols. Because

percentages are rounded, they do not all equal 100.

* indicates incumbents.

X denotes candidates without major-party opposition.

— denotes minor parties for which the vote was not available.

● denotes race undecided at the end of 1984.

ALABAMA

	Vote Total	Percent
Senate		
Howell Heflin (D)*	780,931	62
Albert Lee Smith Jr. (R)	464,384	37
S. D. "Yana" Davis (LIBERT)	12,146	1
House		
1 Frank McRight (D)	81,228	49
H. L. Callahan (R)	85,520	51
2 Larry Lee (D)	71,981	39
William L. Dickinson (R)*	113,005	60
Frank Tipler III (LIBERT)	2,048	1
3 Bill Nichols (D)*	111,785	96
Mark Thornton (LIBERT)	4,302	4
4 Tom Bevill (D)*	X	X
5 Ronnie G. Flippo (D)*	138,692	96
D. M. Samsil (LIBERT)	5,883	4
6 Ben Erdreich (D)*	128,323	60
J. T. "Jabo" Waggoner (R)	86,549	40
Steve Smith (LIBERT)	1,026	0
Mark Curtis (SOC WORK)	—	—
7 Richard C. Shelby (D)*	129,686	97
Charles A. Ewing (LIBERT)	4,110	3

ALASKA

	Vote Total	Percent
Senate		
John E. Havelock (D)	49,237	29
Ted Stevens (R)*	121,879	71
House		
AL Pegge Begich (D)	72,442	44
Don Young (R)*	93,846	56

ARIZONA

	Vote Total	Percent
House		
1 Harry W. Braun III (D)	45,505	22
John McCain (R)*	162,002	78
2 Morris K. Udall (D)*	X	X
3 Bob Schuster (D)	55,451	26
Bob Stump (R)*	149,664	72
Lorraina M. Valencia (LIBERT)	3,762	2
4 Eldon Rudd (R)*	X	X
5 James F. McNulty Jr. (D)*	108,205	48
Jim Kolbe (R)	113,754	51
Herb Johnson (LIBERT)	1,958	1

ARKANSAS

	Vote Total	Percent
Governor		
Bill Clinton (D)*	527,364	63
Woody Freeman (R)	312,089	37
	Vote Total	Percent
Senate		
David Pryor (D)*	481,943	58
Ed Bethune (R)	354,147	42
House		
1 Bill Alexander (D)*	X	X
2 Tommy Robinson (D)	99,067	47
Judy Petty (R)	86,632	41
Jim Taylor (I)	24,281	12
3 John Paul Hammerschmidt (R)*	X	X
4 Beryl Anthony Jr. (D)*	X	X

CALIFORNIA

	Vote Total	Percent
House		
1 Douglas H. Bosco (D)*	149,575	62
David Redick (R)	90,470	38
2 Harry Cozad (D)	69,324	30
Gene Chappie (R)*	158,224	70
3 Robert T. Matsui (D)*	X	X
4 Vic Fazio (D)*	126,872	62
Roger Canfield (R)	75,269	36
Roger C. Pope (LIBERT)	3,924	2
5 Sala Burton (D)*	137,067	74
Tom Spinosa (R)	44,796	24

Abbreviations for Party Designations

AE	—American Eagle	*LAB F*	—Labor and Farm
AM	—American	*LU*	—Liberty Union
AMI	—American Independent	*NF*	—Nuclear Freeze
C	—Conservative	*NU*	—New Union
CIT	—Citizens	*P*	—Prohibition
COM	—Communist	*PFP*	—Peace and Freedom
CST	—Constitution	*POP*	—Populist
CWP	—Communist Workers	*POPU*	—Popular
D	—Democratic	*R*	—Republican
DFL	—Democratic Farmer-Labor	*RC*	—Rainbow Coalition
I	—Independent	*RP*	—Rate Payers Against LILCO
IL	—Independent for LaRouche	*RTL*	—Right to Life
IP	—Independence	*SOC*	—Socialist
I-R	—Independent-Republican	*SOC LAB*	—Socialist Labor
IV	—Independent Vote	*SOC WORK*	—Socialist Workers
KP	—Key	*TICP*	—Tisch Independent Citizens
L	—Liberal	*WL*	—Workers League
LIBERT	—Libertarian	*WWP*	—Workers World

		Vote Total	Percent
	Joseph Fuhrig (LIBERT)	3,927	2
	Henry Clark (PFP)	—	—
6	Barbara Boxer (D)*	158,955	68
	Douglas Binderup (R)	69,217	30
	Howard Creighton (LIBERT)	5,462	2
7	George Miller (D)*	148,221	67
	Rosemary Thakar (R)	74,074	33
8	Ronald V. Dellums (D)*	141,245	60
	Charles Connor (R)	92,687	40
9	Fortney H. "Pete" Stark (D)*	134,270	70
	J. T. Eager Beaver (R)	50,331	26
	Martha Fuhrig (LIBERT)	7,255	4
10	Don Edwards (D)*	100,368	63
	Robert P. Herriott (R)	55,238	35
	Edmon V. Kaiser (AMI)	—	—
	Perr Cardestam (LIBERT)	2,717	2
11	Tom Lantos (D)*	146,131	71
	John J. Hickey (R)	59,125	29
	Nicholas W. Kudrovzeff (AMI)	—	—
12	Martin Carnoy (D)	88,368	36
	Ed Zschau (R)*	150,144	62
	Bill White (LIBERT)	5,663	2
13	Norman Y. Mineta (D)*	136,936	65
	John D. Williams (R)	69,180	33
	John R. Redding (LIBERT)	3,740	2
14	Ruth "Paula" Carlson (D)	57,325	24
	Norman D. Shumway (R)*	176,840	73
	Fred W. Colburn (LIBERT)	6,727	3
15	Tony Coelho (D)*	99,287	66
	Carol Harner (R)	49,357	32
	Richard M. Harris (LIBERT)	2,897	2
16	Leon E. Panetta (D)*	149,252	71
	Patricia Smith Ramsey (R)	58,385	28
	Bill Anderson (LIBERT)	3,231	1
17	Simon Lakritz (D)	43,813	27
	Charles Pashayan Jr. (R)*	121,153	73
18	Richard H. Lehman (D)*	125,577	67
	Dale L. Ewen (R)	60,774	33
19	James C. Carey Jr. (D)	67,938	32
	Robert J. Lagomarsino (R)*	146,161	68
	Charles J. Zekan (PFP)	—	—
20	Mike LeSage (D)	50,185	29
	William M. Thomas (R)*	122,586	71
21	Charles Davis (D)	60,655	26
	Bobbi Fiedler (R)*	168,765	72
	Robert T. Leet (LIBERT)	4,250	2
22	Carlos J. Moorhead (R)*	178,782	85
	Michael B. Yauch (LIBERT)	30,988	15
23	Anthony C. Beilenson (D)*	135,926	62
	Claude Parrish (R)	80,394	37
	Larry Leathers (LIBERT)	3,367	1
24	Henry A. Waxman (D)*	93,811	65
	Jerry Zerg (R)	48,751	34
	James Green (PFP)	—	—
	Tim Custer (LIBERT)	2,355	1
25	Edward R. Roybal (D)*	71,756	72
	Roy D. "Bill" Bloxom (R)	23,717	24
	Anthony G. Bajada (LIBERT)	4,224	4
26	Howard L. Berman (D)*	113,722	63
	Miriam Ojeda (R)	66,896	37
27	Mel Levine (D)*	101,128	54
	Robert B. Scribner (R)	83,210	44
	Jeff Avrech (LIBERT)	2,840	2
	Thomas L. O'Connor Jr. (PFP)	—	—
28	Julian C. Dixon (D)*	109,252	76
	Beatrice M. Jett (R)	32,001	22
	Don Federick (LIBERT)	2,797	2
29	Augustus F. Hawkins (D)*	106,494	87
	Echo Y. Goto (R)	16,289	13
30	Matthew G. Martinez (D)*	62,837	55
	Richard Gomez (R)	52,205	45

		Vote Total	Percent
	Houston A. Myers (AMI)	—	—
31	Mervyn M. Dymally (D)*	97,972	71
	Henry C. Minturn (R)	40,440	29
32	Glenn M. Anderson (D)*	99,472	61
	Roger E. Fiola (R)	59,860	37
	Marc F. Denny (LIBERT)	2,430	2
	Patrick J. McCoy (PFP)	—	—
33	Claire K. McDonald (D)	52,799	27
	David Dreier (R)*	142,501	71
	Gail Lightfoot (LIBERT)	4,591	2
	Mike Noonan (PFP)	—	—
34	Esteban Edward Torres (D)*	85,033	60
	Paul R. Jackson (R)	56,786	40
35	Jerry Lewis (R)*	X	X
	Kevin Akin (PFP)	—	—
36	George E. Brown Jr. (D)*	103,076	57
	John Paul Stark (R)	78,904	43
37	David E. Skinner (D)	83,932	36
	Al McCandless (R)*	146,196	64
38	Jerry M. Patterson (D)*	71,288	46
	Robert K. Dornan (R)	84,131	54
	Michael S. Bright (PFP)	—	—
39	Robert E. Ward (D)	53,546	24
	William E. Dannemeyer (R)*	170,250	76
40	Carol Ann Bradford (D)	84,622	35
	Robert E. Badham (R)*	158,455	65
	Maxine Bell Quirk (PFP)	—	—
41	Robert L. Simmons (D)	83,552	34
	Bill Lowery (R)*	156,554	63
	Sara Baase (LIBERT)	7,114	3
42	Mary Lou Brophy (D)	58,161	25
	Dan Lungren (R)*	171,142	75
	John S. Donohue (PFP)	—	—
43	Lois E. Humphreys (D)	49,525	23
	Ron Packard (R)*	159,315	74
	Phyllis Avery (LIBERT)	6,608	3
44	Jim Bates (D)*	97,467	70
	Neill Campbell (R)	38,961	28
	Jim Conole (LIBERT)	3,130	2
45	David W. Guthrie (D)	44,420	23
	Duncan L. Hunter (R)*	145,014	75
	Patrick Wright (LIBERT)	3,857	2

COLORADO

		Vote Total	Percent
Senate			
	Nancy Dick (D)	428,803	35
	William L. Armstrong (R)*	780,554	64
	Craig Green (LIBERT)	10,593	1
	Earl Higgerson (P)	—	—
	David Martin (SOC WORK)	—	—
House			
1	Patricia Schroeder (D)*	126,166	62
	Mary Downs (R)	73,900	37
	Dwight Filley (LIBERT)	1,683	1
	Kathy Emminizer (SOC WORK)	—	—
2	Timothy E. Wirth (D)*	112,756	54
	Michael J. Norton (R)	95,503	45
	Jerry Van Sickle (LIBERT)	2,668	1
3	W Mitchell (D)	84,036	43
	Michael L. Strang (R)*	110,837	57
	Robert Jalehka (LIBERT)	1,148	0
	Henry John Olshaw (I)	—	—
4	Mary Fagan Bates (D)	53,866	28
	Hank Brown (R)*	136,343	71
	Randy Fitzgerald (LIBERT)	2,824	1
5	William Geffen (D)	41,556	22
	Ken Kramer (R)*	150,472	78
6	Daniel L. Schaefer (R)*	X	X
	John Heckman (I)	—	—

CONNECTICUT

		Vote Total	Percent
House			
1	Barbara B. Kennelly (D)*	147,108	62
	Herschel A. Klein (R)	90,513	38
	Charles F. Sundblade (LIBERT)	785	0
2	Sam Gejdenson (D)*	123,122	55
	Roberta F. Koontz (R)	102,210	45
	Donald Wood (LIBERT)	984	0
3	Bruce A. Morrison (D)*	123,506	52
	Lawrence J. DeNardis (R)	114,669	48
	Michael R. Cohen (LIBERT)	377	0
	James J. Valenti (I)	—	—
4	John M. Ormon (D)	69,666	30
	Stewart B. McKinney (R)*	165,657	70
5	William R. Ratchford (D)*	109,882	46
	John G. Rowland (R)	130,568	54
	James P. Peron (LIBERT)	479	0
6	Arthur H. House (D)	85,254	36
	Nancy L. Johnson (R)*	150,890	64

DELAWARE

		Vote Total	Percent
Governor			
	William T. Quillen (D)	107,736	45
	Michael N. Castle (R)	133,892	55
Senate			
	Joseph R. Biden Jr. (D)*	147,056	60
	John M. Burris (R)	97,903	40
House			
AL	Thomas R. Carper (D)*	141,472	59
	Elise R. W. du Pont (R)	100,142	41
	G. Luther Etzel (LIBERT)	286	0

FLORIDA

		Vote Total	Percent
House			
1	Earl Hutto (D)*	X	X
2	Don Fuqua (D)*	X	X
3	Charles E. Bennett (D)*	X	X
4	Bill Chappell Jr. (D)*	127,665	65
	Alton H. "Bill" Starling (R)	67,635	35
5	Bill McCollum (R)*	X	X
6	Buddy MacKay (D)*	X	X
7	Sam Gibbons (D)*	95,320	59
	Michael N. Kavouklis (R)	65,889	41
8	Robert Kent (D)	45,340	20
	C. W. Bill Young (R)*	184,421	80
9	Jack Wilson (D)	50,511	21
	Michael Bilirakis (R)*	185,900	79
10	Patricia M. Glass (D)	60,071	39
	Andy Ireland (R)*	94,954	61
11	Bill Nelson (D)*	102,282	61
	Rob Quartel (R)	66,629	39
12	Tom Lewis (R)*	X	X
13	Connie Mack (R)*	X	X
14	Daniel A. Mica (D)*	151,424	55
	Don Ross (R)	122,550	45
15	Bill Humphrey (D)	62,834	35
	E. Clay Shaw Jr. (R)*	118,170	65
16	Larry Smith (D)*	102,660	56
	Tom Bush (R)	79,681	44
17	William Lehman (D)*	X	X
18	Claude Pepper (D)*	71,744	60
	Ricardo Nunez (R)	47,365	40
19	Dante B. Fascell (D)*	109,033	65
	Bill Flanagan (R)	59,012	35

GEORGIA

		Vote Total	Percent
Senate			
	Sam Nunn (D)*	1,316,545	80
	Jon Michael Hicks (R)	327,695	20

House

		Vote Total	Percent
1	Lindsay Thomas (D)*	120,505	82
	Erie Lee Downing (R)	27,018	18
2	Charles Hatcher (D)*	X	X
3	Richard Ray (D)*	106,422	81
	Mitchell Cantu (R)	24,321	19
4	Elliott H. Levitas (D)*	106,336	47
	Patrick L. Swindall (R)	120,441	53
5	Wyche Fowler Jr. (D)*	X	X
6	Gerald Johnson (D)	52,046	31
	Newt Gingrich (R)*	116,592	69
7	George "Buddy" Darden (D)*	101,814	55
	William E. Bronson (R)	83,851	45
8	J. Roy Rowland (D)*	X	X
9	Ed Jenkins (D)*	102,777	67
	Frank H. Cofer Jr. (R)	50,096	33
10	Doug Barnard Jr. (D)*	X	X

HAWAII

House

		Vote Total	Percent
1	Cecil Heftel (D)*	113,978	83
	Willard F. Beard (R)	20,376	15
	Christopher Winter (LIBERT)	3,349	2
2	Daniel K. Akaka (D)*	112,086	82
	A. D. Shipley (R)	19,908	15
	Amelia Fritts (LIBERT)	4,354	3

IDAHO

Senate

	Vote Total	Percent
Peter M. Busch (D)	105,487	26
James A. McClure (R)*	293,416	72
Donald B. Billings (LIBERT)	7,366	2

House

		Vote Total	Percent
1	Bill Hellar (D)	63,567	31
	Larry E. Craig (R)*	139,021	69
2	Richard Stallings (D)	101,099	50
	George Hansen (R)*	101,032	50

ILLINOIS

Senate

	Vote Total	Percent
Paul Simon (D)	2,334,580	50
Charles H. Percy (R)*	2,273,043	49
Marjorie H. Pries (CIT)	—	—
Ishmael Flory (COM)	—	—
Steven I. Givot (LIBERT)	58,120	1
Nelson Gonzalez (SOC WORK)	—	—

House

		Vote Total	Percent
1	Charles A. Hayes (D)*	X	X
	Eddie L. Warren (SOC WORK)	—	—
2	Gus Savage (D)*	140,307	82
	Dale F. Harman (R)	30,870	18
3	Marty Russo (D)*	140,046	64
	Richard D. Murphy (R)	78,060	36
4	Dennis E. Marlow (D)	68,435	36
	George M. O'Brien (R)*	121,325	64
5	William O. Lipinski (D)*	104,373	63
	John M. Paczkowski (R)	60,588	37
6	Robert H. Renshaw (D)	51,922	25
	Henry J. Hyde (R)*	156,523	75
7	Cardiss Collins (D)*	130,177	78
	James L. Bevel (R)	36,699	22
8	Dan Rostenkowski (D)*	110,945	71
	Spiro F. Georgeson (R)	44,895	29
9	Sidney R. Yates (D)*	138,013	67
	Herbert Sohn (R)	66,812	33
10	Ruth C. Braver (D)	56,908	28
	John Edward Porter (R)*	149,997	72
11	Frank Annunzio (D)*	135,015	63
	Charles J. Theusch (R)	80,820	37
12	Edward J. LaFlamme (D)	45,285	22
	Philip M. Crane (R)*	158,853	78
13	Michael J. Donohue (D)	76,951	33
	Harris W. Fawell (R)	156,639	67
14	Dan McGrath (D)	81,768	38
	John E. Grotberg (R)	133,584	62
15	John M. Hoffman (D)	50,459	27
	Edward R. Madigan (R)*	135,780	73
16	Carl R. Schwerdtfeger (D)	90,673	42
	Lynn Martin (R)*	127,239	58
17	Lane Evans (D)*	128,266	57
	Kenneth G. McMillan (R)	98,065	43
18	Gerald A. Bradley (D)	86,839	39
	Robert H. Michel (R)*	135,938	61
19	Terry L. Bruce (D)	118,185	52
	Daniel B. Crane (R)*	108,304	48
20	Dick Durbin (D)*	145,088	61
	Richard G. Austin (R)	91,820	39
21	Melvin Price (D)*	123,584	69
	Robert H. Gaffner (R)	54,773	31
22	Kenneth J. Gray (D)	116,948	50
	Randy Patchett (R)	115,710	50

INDIANA

Governor

	Vote Total	Percent
W. Wayne Townsend (D)	994,966	48
Robert D. Orr (R)*	1,097,879	52
Rockland Snyder (AM)	—	—
James A. Ridenour (LIBERT)	6,745	0

House

		Vote Total	Percent
1	Peter J. Visclosky (D)	147,035	71
	Joseph B. Grenchik (R)	59,986	29
	James E. Willis (LIBERT)	943	0
2	Philip R. Sharp (D)*	118,426	54
	Ken MacKenzie (R)	102,236	46
	Cecil Bohanon (LIBERT)	625	0
3	Michael P. Barnes (D)	102,312	47
	John Hiler (R)*	113,898	53
	Robert A. Lutton (LIBERT)	645	0
4	Michael H. Barnard (D)	79,660	39
	Dan Coats (R)*	124,692	61
	John B. Cameron Jr. (AM)	—	—
	Joseph F. Laiacona (LIBERT)	467	0
5	Allen B. Maxwell (D)	66,486	32
	Elwood Hillis (R)*	142,878	68
	David E. Osterfeld (LIBERT)	1,151	0
6	Howard O. Campbell (D)	64,806	28
	Dan L. Burton (R)*	165,026	71
	Linda Dilk (LIBERT)	1,255	1
7	Arthur E. Smith (D)	52,555	30
	John T. Myers (R)*	117,899	68
	Barbara L. J. Bourland (LIBERT)	2,441	2
8	Frank McCloskey (D)* ●	116,843	50
	Richard D. McIntyre (R)	116,770	50
	Michael J. Fallahay (LIBERT)	759	0
9	Lee H. Hamilton (D)*	139,216	65
	Floyd E. Coates (R)	74,261	35
	Douglas S. Boggs (LIBERT)	673	0
10	Andrew Jacobs Jr. (D)*	110,836	59
	Joseph P. Watkins (R)	75,780	41
	Bradford L. Warren (LIBERT)	889	0

IOWA

Senate

	Vote Total	Percent
Tom Harkin (D)	713,286	56
Roger W. Jepsen (R)*	559,176	44
Garry DeYoung (I)	—	—

House

		Vote Total	Percent
1	Kevin Ready (D)	64,224	33
	Jim Leach (R)*	131,101	67
2	Joe Welsh (D)	76,930	36
	Tom Tauke (R)*	136,364	64
3	Joe Johnston (D)	84,950	40
	Cooper Evans (R)*	130,081	60
4	Neal Smith (D)*	136,500	61
	Robert R. Lockard (R)	87,985	39
5	Jerome D. Fitzgerald (D)	101,087	49
	Jim Ross Lightfoot (R)	104,247	51
6	Berkley Bedell (D)*	128,689	62
	Darrel Rensink (R)	77,839	38

KANSAS

Senate

	Vote Total	Percent
James R. Maher (D)	206,187	22
Nancy Landon Kassebaum (R)*	735,080	77
Marian Ruck Jackson (AM)	—	—
Lucille Bieder (C)	—	—
Douglas N. Merritt (LIBERT)	6,815	1
Freda H. Steele (P)	—	—

House

		Vote Total	Percent
1	Darrell Ringer (D)	47,689	24
	Pat Roberts (R)*	154,567	76
	Clement N. Scoggin (P)	—	—
2	Jim Slattery (D)*	107,903	61
	Jim Van Slyke (R)	68,440	39
	Kenneth C. Peterson Sr. (P)	—	—
3	John E. Reardon (D)	84,838	42
	Jan Meyers (R)	116,060	58
	John S. Ralph Jr. (I)	—	—
4	Dan Glickman (D)*	138,619	75
	William V. Krause (R)	47,355	25
5	John A. Barnes (D)	46,229	26
	Bob Whittaker (R)*	133,728	74
	Vearl A. Bacon (P)	—	—

KENTUCKY

Senate

	Vote Total	Percent
Walter D. Huddleston (D)*	635,441	50
Mitch McConnell (R)	638,816	50
Dave Welters (SOC WORK)	7,427	0

House

		Vote Total	Percent
1	Carroll Hubbard Jr. (D)*	X	X
2	William H. Natcher (D)*	91,500	62
	Timothy A. Morrison (R)	56,056	38
3	Romano L. Mazzoli (D)*	143,931	68
	Suzanne M. Warner (R)	67,409	32
	Peggy Kreiner (SOC WORK)	1,260	0
4	William P. Mulloy II (D)	92,043	47
	Gene Snyder (R)*	102,608	53
5	Sherman W. McIntosh (D)	40,015	24
	Harold Rogers (R)*	124,478	76
6	Jerry Hammond (D)	47,339	27
	Larry J. Hopkins (R)*	125,972	72
	Tony Suruda (LIBERT)	953	1
7	Carl C. Perkins (D)	122,072	74
	Aubrey Russell (R)	43,612	26

LOUISIANA

Senate

	Vote Total	Percent
J. Bennett Johnston (D)*	X	X

House

		Vote Total	Percent
1	Bob Livingston (R)*	X	X
2	Lindy (Mrs. Hale) Boggs (D)*	X	X
3	W. J. "Billy" Tauzin (D)*	X	X

	Vote Total	Percent
4 Buddy Roemer (D)*	X	X
5 Jerry Huckaby (D)*	X	X
6 Henson Moore (R)*	X	X
7 John B. Breaux (D)*	X	X
8 Gillis W. Long (D)*	X	X

MAINE

Senate

Elizabeth H. Mitchell (D)	142,312	26
William S. Cohen (R)*	400,953	74
P. Anne Stoddard (CST)	—	—

House

1 Barry J. Hobbins (D)	102,588	36
John R. McKernan Jr. (R)*	180,702	64
2 Chipman C. Bull (D)	57,220	23
Olympia J. Snowe (R)*	192,231	77
Kenneth E. Stoddard (CST)	—	—

MARYLAND

House

1 Roy Dyson (D)*	91,045	58
Harlan C. Williams (R)	64,758	42
2 Clarence D. Long (D)*	102,325	49
Helen Delich Bentley (R)	108,077	51
3 Barbara A. Mikulski (D)*	126,459	68
Ross Z. Pierpont (R)	59,567	32
Lawrence K. Freeman (I)	—	—
4 Howard M. Greenebaum (D)	56,418	34
Marjorie S. Holt (R)*	108,857	66
5 Steny H. Hoyer (D)*	112,390	72
John E. Ritchie (R)	42,945	28
6 Beverly B. Byron (D)*	117,116	65
Robin Ficker (R)	62,746	35
7 Parren J. Mitchell (D)*	X	X
8 Michael D. Barnes (D)*	170,890	71
Albert Ceccone (R)	66,238	28
Samuel K. Grove (LIBERT)	1,813	1

MASSACHUSETTS

Senate

John F. Kerry (D)	1,369,295	55
Raymond Shamie (R)	1,123,235	45

House

1 Mary L. Wentworth (D)	63,091	28
Silvio O. Conte (R)*	158,864	72
2 Edward P. Boland (D)*	140,773	70
Thomas P. Swank (R)	60,059	30
3 Joseph D. Early (D)*	146,497	67
Kenneth J. Redding (R)	71,369	33
4 Barney Frank (D)*	172,396	74
Jim Forte (R)	60,096	26
5 Chester G. Atkins (D)	120,224	54
Gregory S. Hyatt (R)	103,731	46
6 Nicholas Mavroules (D)*	167,206	73
Frederick S. Leber (R)	63,330	27
Donald P. Bachelder (RC)	—	—
7 Edward J. Markey (D)*	149,379	71
S. Lester Ralph (R)	61,954	29
8 Thomas P. O'Neill Jr. (D)*	X	X
Laura Ross (COM)	—	—
9 Joe Moakley (D)*	X	X
10 Gerry E. Studds (D)*	142,914	56
Lewis Crampton (R)	113,619	44
11 Brian J. Donnelly (D)*	X	X

MICHIGAN

Senate

Carl Levin (D)*	1,856,659	53
Jack Lousma (R)	1,661,198	47
Samuel L. Webb (CWP)	—	—
Lynn Johnston (LIBERT)	9,112	0
Arthur R. Tisch (TICP)	—	—
Fred Mazelis (WL)	—	—
William Roundtree (WWP)	—	—
Max Dean (I)	—	—

House

1 John Conyers Jr. (D)*	147,763	90
Edward J. Mack (R)	16,832	10
Andrew Pulley (SOC WORK)	—	—
2 Mike McCauley (D)	60,747	31
Carl D. Pursell (R)*	136,527	69
James L. Hudler (LIBERT)	923	0
Greg Severance (TICP)	—	—
3 Howard Wolpe (D)*	106,634	53
Jackie McGregor (R)	93,334	47
4 Charles S. Rodebaugh (D)	72,615	37
Mark D. Siljander (R)*	126,052	63
5 Gary J. McInerney (D)	85,192	38
Paul B. Henry (R)	139,969	62
Richard Whitelock (LIBERT)	1,312	0
6 Bob Carr (D)*	106,292	53
Tom Ritter (R)	94,915	47
James E. Hurrell (LIBERT)	606	0
Russel Severance (TICP)	—	—
7 Dale E. Kildee (D)*	X	X
Samuel Johnston (I)	—	—
8 Bob Traxler (D)*	104,452	63
John Heussner (R)	61,384	37
9 John M. Senger (D)	61,101	29
Guy Vander Jagt (R)*	150,181	71
Nicholas Hamilton (LIBERT)	635	0
10 Donald J. Albosta (D)*	100,984	49
Bill Schuette (R)	102,553	50
George Leet (LIBERT)	1,042	1
11 Tom Stewart (D)	86,993	42
Robert W. Davis (R)*	122,494	58
12 David E. Bonior (D)*	65,598	59
Eugene J. Tyza (R)	44,759	40
Keith P. Edwards (LIBERT)	557	1
13 George W. Crockett Jr. (D)*	130,403	87
Robert Murphy (R)	20,299	13
14 Dennis M. Hertel (D)*	113,277	59
John Lauve (R)	77,779	40
Virginia L. Cropsey (LIBERT)	1,087	1
15 William D. Ford (D)*	93,272	60
Gerald R. Carlson (R)	61,852	40
16 John D. Dingell (D)*	120,399	64
Frank Grzywacki (R)	67,621	36
Donald Kostyu (LIBERT)	1,018	0
17 Sander M. Levin (D)*	X	X
18 Vivian H. Smargon (D)	44,602	20
William S. Broomfield (R)*	179,760	79
Timothy O'Brien (LIBERT)	1,545	1

MINNESOTA

Senate

Joan Anderson Growe (DFL)	792,910	42
Rudy Boschwitz (I-R)*	1,101,075	58
Richard Putman (LIBERT)	4,000	0
Jeffrey N. Miller (NU)	—	—
Eleanor Garcia (SOC WORK)	—	—

House

1 Timothy J. Penny (DFL)*	133,767	57
Keith Spicer (I-R)	100,117	43
2 Todd Lundquist (DFL)	87,831	37
Vin Weber (I-R)*	149,349	63
3 Dave Peterson (DFL)	64,418	27
Bill Frenzel (I-R)*	176,085	73
4 Bruce F. Vento (DFL)*	166,341	75
Mary Jane Rachner (I-R)	56,657	25
Peter Brandli (SOC WORK)	—	—
5 Martin Olav Sabo (DFL)*	156,532	74
Richard D. Wieblen (I-R)	53,823	26
Kathryn Anderson (CIT)	—	—
6 Gerry Sikorski (DFL)*	121,318	63
Patrick Trueman (I-R)	72,213	37
7 Collin C. Peterson (DFL)	97,956	43
Arlan Stangeland (I-R)*	129,779	57
8 James L. Oberstar (DFL)*	156,872	68
Dave Rued (I-R)	75,147	32
David Salner (SOC WORK)	—	—

MISSISSIPPI

Senate

William F. Winter (D)	369,962	39
Thad Cochran (R)*	575,963	61

House

1 Jamie L. Whitten (D)*	135,956	88
John Hargett (I)	17,824	12
2 Robert G. Clark (D)	87,049	49
Webb Franklin (R)*	91,390	51
Hardy Caraway (I)	798	0
3 G. V. "Sonny" Montgomery (D)*	X	X
4 Wayne Dowdy (D)*	112,969	56
David Armstrong (R)	89,757	44
5 Arlon "Blackie" Coate (D)	25,814	15
Trent Lott (R)*	142,224	85

MISSOURI

Governor

Kenneth J. Rothman (D)	870,604	43
John Ashcroft (R)	1,164,893	57

House

1 William Clay (D)*	124,539	65
Eric Rathbone (R)	66,331	35
2 Robert A. Young (D)*	137,044	52
John Buechner (R)	125,878	47
Chad G. Colopy (LIBERT)	1,669	1
3 Richard A. Gephardt (D)*	X	X
4 Ike Skelton (D)*	147,666	67
Carl D. Russell (R)	73,508	33
5 Alan Wheat (D)*	150,841	66
Jim Kenworthy (R)	72,477	32
Mike Roberts (LIBERT)	5,069	2
6 Kenneth C. Hensley (D)	79,704	35
E. Thomas Coleman (R)*	146,023	65
7 Ken Young (D)	72,548	31
Gene Taylor (R)*	162,867	69
8 Bill Blue (D)	70,126	34
Bill Emerson (R)*	133,218	66
9 Harold L. Volkmer (D)*	121,386	53
Carrie Francke (R)	108,695	47

MONTANA

Governor

Ted Schwinden (D)*	239,568	70
Pat M. Goodover (R)	90,128	27
Larry Dodge (LIBERT)	11,060	3

Senate

Max Baucus (D)*	193,061	57
Chuck Cozzens (R)	139,121	41
Neil Halprin (LIBERT)	8,042	2

	Vote Total	Percent

House

1 Pat Williams (D)*	110,836	66
Gary K. Carlson (R)	53,251	32
Royer G. Warren (LIBERT)	4,100	2
2 Chet Blaylock (D)	56,275	34
Ron Marlenee (R)*	108,360	66

NEBRASKA

Senate

| J. James Exon (D)* | 334,278 | 53 |
| Nancy Hoch (R) | 299,787 | 47 |

House

1 Monica Bauer (D)	54,955	26
Douglas K. Bereuter (R)*	157,088	74
2 Thomas F. Cavanaugh (D)	72,818	35
Hal Daub (R)*	133,704	65
3 Tom Vickers (D)	35,892	17
Virginia Smith (R)*	179,570	83

NEVADA

House

1 Harry Reid (D)*	73,242	56
Peggy Cavnar (R)	55,391	43
Joe Morris (LIBERT)	1,885	1
2 Andrew Barbano (D)	36,130	26
Barbara F. Vucanovich (R)*	99,675	71
Dan Becan (LIBERT)	4,201	3

NEW HAMPSHIRE

Governor

| Chris Spirou (D) | 115,850 | 33 |
| John H. Sununu (R)* | 234,714 | 67 |

Senate

Norman E. D'Amours (D)	142,314	41
Gordon J. Humphrey (R)*	208,433	59
Saunder H. Primack (LIBERT)	1,138	0

House

1 Dudley Dudley (D)	63,625	40
Robert C. Smith (R)	93,500	60
Arne B. Erickson (LIBERT)	492	0
John G. H. Muelhke Jr. (I)	—	—
2 Larry Converse (D)	42,556	23
Judd Gregg (R)*	138,900	76
Alan Groupe (LIBERT)	1,154	1

NEW JERSEY

Senate

Bill Bradley (D)*	1,917,391	65
Mary V. Mochary (R)	1,043,984	35
Harold F. Leinendecker (LIBERT)	6,412	0
Julius Levin (SOC LAB)	—	—
Priscilla Schenk (SOC WORK)	—	—
Jasper C. Gould (I)	—	—
James T. Hagen (I)	—	—

House

1 James J. Florio (D)*	148,818	72
Frederick A. Busch Jr. (R)	57,228	28
Jerry Zeldin (LIBERT)	781	0
2 William J. Hughes (D)*	127,194	63
Raymond G. Massie (R)	74,048	37
3 James J. Howard (D)*	120,072	59
Brian T. Kennedy (R)	82,019	41
Lawrence D. Erickson (I)	—	—
Frank Krushinski Jr. (I)	—	—

4 James C. Hedden (D)	86,291	40
Christopher H. Smith (R)*	130,852	60
5 Rose Brunetto (D)	66,863	29
Marge Roukema (R)*	163,905	71
6 Bernard J. Dwyer (D)*	127,228	58
Dennis Adams (R)	89,274	41
Stephen Friedlander (LIBERT)	2,648	1
7 John F. Feeley (D)	56,637	26
Matthew J. Rinaldo (R)*	165,220	74
Paul Nelson (LIBERT)	785	0
8 Robert A. Roe (D)*	112,922	63
Marguerite A. Page (R)	66,431	37
Daniel A. Maiullo Jr. (LIBERT)	566	0
9 Robert G. Torricelli (D)*	148,521	63
Neil Romano (R)	85,753	37
10 Peter W. Rodino Jr. (D)*	104,999	84
Howard E. Berkeley (R)	19,725	16
11 Joseph G. Minish (D)*	91,353	43
Dean A. Gallo (R)	120,146	57
12 Peter Bearse (D)	76,819	34
Jim Courter (R)*	144,785	65
Joseph R. Kerr III (LIBERT)	1,593	1
13 James B. Smith (D)	86,613	39
H. James Saxton (R)	133,093	61
Bernardo S. Doganiero (SOC LAB)	—	—
Don Smith (I)	—	—
14 Frank J. Guarini (D)*	111,713	66
Edward T. Magee (R)	56,642	34
Herbert H. Shaw (I)	—	—

NEW MEXICO

Senate

Judith A. Pratt (D)	140,252	28
Pete V. Domenici (R)*	357,987	72
Orlin G. Cole (write-in)	—	—

House

1 Charles Ted Asbury (D)	60,016	34
Manuel Lujan Jr. (R)*	114,740	65
Steven P. Curtis (LIBERT)	2,022	1
2 Peter R. York (D)	40,255	26
Joe Skeen (R)*	115,221	74
3 Bill Richardson (D)*	99,729	62
Louis H. Gallegos (R)	59,191	37
Shirley Jones (LIBERT)	2,425	1

NEW YORK

House

1 George J. Hochbrueckner (D,RP)	91,533	47
William Carney (R, C, RTL)*	103,489	53
2 Thomas J. Downey (D, IP)*	94,651	54
Paul Aniboli (R, C, RTL)	81,378	46
3 Robert J. Mrazek (D)*	116,667	51
Robert P. Quinn (R, C)	110,226	48
Elizabeth E. Capazzi (RTL)	2,663	1
4 Sheldon Engelhard (D, L)	65,065	29
Norman F. Lent (R, C)*	152,669	69
John J. Dunkle (RTL)	4,155	2
5 Michael d'Innocenzo (D,IV)	78,033	35
Raymond J. McGrath (R,C)*	137,755	62
Jack Olchin (L)	1,632	1
Paul F. Callahan (RTL)	3,715	2
6 Joseph P. Addabbo (D,L)*	118,389	84
Philip J. Veltre (R, C, RTL)	21,661	16
7 Gary L. Ackerman (D, L)	94,527	69
Gustave A. Reifenkugel (R, C)	42,060	31
8 James H. Scheuer (D, L)*	99,948	62
Robert L. Brandofino (R, C)	59,980	38
9 Thomas J. Manton (D)	68,920	53

Serphin R. Maltese (R, C, RTL)	61,967	47
10 Charles E. Schumer (D, L)*	112,187	72
John H. Fox (R, C)	43,209	27
Alfred F. Donohue Jr. (RTL)	2,152	1
11 Edolphus Towns (D, L)*	78,448	85
Nathaniel Hendricks (R)	12,035	13
Alfred Hamel (C)	1,671	2
12 Major R. Owens (D, L)*	78,640	90
Joseph N. O. Caesar (R, C, RTL)	8,613	10
13 Stephen J. Solarz (D, L)*	80,215	66
Lew Y. Levin (R, C, RTL)	42,789	34
14 Kevin L. Sheehy (D)	48,054	30
Guy V. Molinari (R, C, RTL)*	112,485	70
Terence H. Benbow (L)	—	—
15 Andrew J. Stein (D, L)	78,748	44
Bill Green (R, I)*	100,372	56
16 Charles B. Rangel (D, R)*	114,487	98
Michael T. Berns (C)	2,560	2
Marshall England (KP)	—	—
Nan Bailey (SOC WORK)	—	—
17 Ted Weiss (D, L)*	152,641	81
Kenneth Katzman (R)	31,114	17
Leonard Steinman (C)	3,508	2
Judah Rubenstein (IL)	—	—
18 Robert Garcia (D, L)*	82,700	89
Curtis Johnson (R)	9,008	10
John W. Farrell (C)	1,350	1
Rafael Perez (POPU)	—	—
19 Mario Biaggi (D, R, L, RTL)*	147,616	95
Alice Farrell (C)	8,420	5
20 Oren J. Teicher (D)	91,068	48
Joseph J. DioGuardi (R, C)	97,208	50
Florence T. O'Grady (RTL)	3,432	2
21 Lawrence W. Grunberger (D)	39,786	21
Hamilton Fish Jr. (R, C, RTL)*	152,668	79
22 Bruce M. Levine (D, L)	53,666	27
Benjamin A. Gilman (R)*	133,357	69
Robert DeMaggio (RTL)	7,896	4
23 Samuel S. Stratton (D)*	176,839	78
Frank Wicks (R, NF)	50,323	22
Richard Ariza (SOC WORK)	—	—
24 Edward J. Bloch (D)	60,463	28
Gerald B. H. Solomon (R, C, RTL)*	157,555	72
25 James J. Ball (D)	49,116	28
Sherwood L. Boehlert (R)*	129,348	72
Michael J. Fahy (RTL)	—	—
26 Bernard J. Lammers (D)	55,253	30
David O'B. Martin (R, C)*	126,466	70
27 Thomas C. Buckel Jr. (D,L)	90,709	44
George C. Wortley (R, C)*	116,112	56
John B. Carroll (RTL)	—	—
28 Matthew F. McHugh (D)*	115,012	57
Constance E. Cook (R)	84,386	41
Mark R. Masterson (RTL)	4,261	2
29 James R. Toole (D)	47,716	26
Frank Horton (R)*	127,970	68
James L. Hale (C)	7,639	4
Erskine Nero (WWP)	—	—
Donald M. Peters (RTL)	3,798	2
30 W. Douglas Call (D)	96,760	45
Fred J. Eckert (R, C, RTL)	117,265	55
31 Peter J. Martinelli (D, L)	55,511	25
Jack F. Kemp (R, C, RTL)*	163,653	75
32 John J. LaFalce (D, L)*	137,690	70
Anthony J. Murty (R, C, RTL)	61,359	30
33 Henry J. Nowak (D, L)*	151,691	78
David S. Lewandowski (R, C, RTL)	43,915	22

	Vote Total	Percent
34 Stan Lundine (D)*	111,422	56
Jill Houghton Emery (R, C)	87,165	43
Carol L. Fisher (RTL)	2,382	1

NORTH CAROLINA

Governor

	Vote Total	Percent
Rufus Edmisten (D)	994,675	46
James G. Martin (R)	1,177,816	54
H. Fritz Prochnow (LIBERT)	4,500	0
Gregory McCartan (SOC WORK)	—	—

Senate

James B. Hunt Jr. (D)	1,050,470	48
Jesse Helms (R)*	1,133,315	52
Bobby Yates Emory (LIBERT)	9,321	0
Kate Daher (SOC WORK)	—	—

House

1 Walter B. Jones (D)*	120,920	67
Herbert W. Lee (R)	59,413	33
2 Tim Valentine (D)*	121,932	68
Frank H. Hill (R)	58,153	32
3 Charles Whitley (D)*	99,529	64
Danny G. Moody (R)	54,817	36
4 Ike Andrews (D)*	109,478	49
William W. Cobey Jr. (R)	111,748	51
5 Stephen L. Neal (D)*	105,302	51
Stuart Epperson (R)	101,620	49
6 Robin Britt (D)*	100,061	49
Howard Coble (R)	103,912	51
Meryl Lynn Farber (SOC·WORK)	—	—
7 Charlie Rose (D)*	89,504	59
S. Thomas Rhodes (R)	61,130	41
8 W. G. "Bill" Hefner (D)*	99,816	51
Harris D. Blake (R)	95,813	49
9 D. G. Martin (D)	108,972	50
J. Alex McMillan (R)	109,258	50
10 Ied A. Poovey (D)	50,736	27
James T. Broyhill (R)*	138,498	73
11 James McClure Clarke (D)*	107,828	49
William M. Hendon (R)	112,006	51

NORTH DAKOTA

Governor

George Sinner (D)	137,065	56
Allen I. Olson (R)*	108,078	44

House

AL Byron L. Dorgan (D)*	190,275	79
Lois Ivers Altenburg (R)	50,193	21

OHIO

House

1 Thomas A. Luken (D)*	121,392	58
Norman A. Murdock (R)	88,713	42
2 Thomas D. Porter (D)	68,251	31
Bill Gradison (R)*	149,603	69
3 Tony P. Hall (D)*	X	X
4 William O. Sutton (D)	47,062	23
Mike Oxley (R)*	161,267	77
5 James R. Sherck (D)	78,636	37
Delbert L. Latta (R)*	132,218	63
6 Bob Smith (D)	52,648	26
Bob McEwen (R)*	149,985	74
7 Donald E. Scott (D)	45,908	24
Michael DeWine (R)*	141,678	76
8 John T. Francis (D)	46,610	23
Thomas N. Kindness (R)*	154,972	77

	Vote Total	Percent
9 Marcy Kaptur (D)*	117,536	56
Frank Venner (R)	92,605	44
10 John M. Buchanan (D)	54,538	27
Clarence E. Miller (R)*	144,556	73
11 Dennis E. Eckart (D)*	133,019	67
Dean Beagle (R)	66,240	33
12 Richard Sloan (D)	65,105	31
John R. Kasich (R)*	148,083	69
13 Don J. Pease (D)*	130,523	66
William G. Schaffner (R)	58,830	30
James S. Patton (I)	7,922	4
14 John F. Seiberling (D)*	136,129	72
Jean E. Bender (R)	54,136	28
15 Duane Jager (D)	59,180	29
Chalmers P. Wylie (R)*	147,647	71
16 James Gwin (D)	58,149	28
Ralph Regula (R)*	152,134	72
17 James A. Traficant Jr. (D)	122,426	54
Lyle Williams (R)*	104,861	46
Reynold J. Johnjulio (I)	—	—
18 Douglas Applegate (D)*	155,223	76
Kenneth P. Burt Jr. (R)	49,255	24
19 Edward F. Feighan (D)*	139,413	56
Matthew J. Hatchadorian (R)	107,844	44
Arnold Gleisser (I)	—	—
20 Mary Rose Oakar (D)*	X	X
Bill Smith (I)		
21 Louis Stokes (D)*	164,714	83
Robert L. Woodall (R)	29,442	15
Omari Musa (I)	—	—
Milton R. Norris (I)	4,351	2

OKLAHOMA

Senate

David L. Boren (D)*	846,244	76
Will E. Crozier (R)	258,876	23
Robert T. Murphy (LIBERT)	10,560	1

House

1 James R. Jones (D)*	93,815	52
Frank Keating (R)	85,227	47
D. Lynn Neal (LIBERT)	1,137	1
2 Mike Synar (D)*	135,511	74
Gary K. Rice (R)	47,716	26
3 Wes Watkins (D)*	129,136	78
Patrick K. Miller (R)	36,695	22
4 Dave McCurdy (D)*	107,409	64
Jerry Smith (R)	58,884	35
Gordon E. Mobley (LIBERT)	1,718	1
5 Allen Greeson (D)	36,328	22
Mickey Edwards (R)*	124,069	75
D. Frank Robinson (LIBERT)	4,597	3
6 Glenn English (D)*	94,361	59
Craig Dodd (R)	65,699	41

OREGON

Senate

Margie Hendriksen (D)	382,121	34
Mark O. Hatfield (R)*	748,952	66

House

1 Les AuCoin (D)*	131,812	54
Bill Moshofsky (R)	114,145	46
2 Larryann C. Willis (D)	89,185	43
Robert F. Smith (R)*	116,415	57
3 Ron Wyden (D)*	161,815	73
Drew Davis (R)	60,625	27
4 James Weaver (D)*	127,611	58
Bruce Long (R)	91,316	42

	Vote Total	Percent
5 Ruth McFarland (D)	104,206	46
Denny Smith (R)*	124,005	54

PENNSYLVANIA

House

1 Thomas M. Foglietta (D)*	145,166	74
Carmine DiBiase (R)	49,865	26
2 William H. Gray III (D)*	177,225	91
Ronald J. Sharper (R)	17,375	9
Katherine L. Karlin (SOC WORK)	—	—
3 Robert A. Borski (D)*	143,175	64
Flora L. Becker (R)	80,505	36
John J. Hughes (I)	—	—
4 Joe Kolter (D)*	112,354	57
James Kunder (R)	85,055	43
5 Louis J. Fanti (D)	53,092	27
Richard T. Schulze (R)*	141,636	73
6 Gus Yatron (D)*	X	X
7 Bob Edgar (D)*	124,054	50
Curt Weldon (R)	123,573	50
8 Peter H. Kostmayer (D)*	112,435	51
David A. Christian (R)	108,651	49
9 Nancy Kulp (D)	60,969	34
Bud Shuster (R)*	117,070	66
10 Gene Basalyga (D)	44,465	23
Joseph M. McDade (R)*	145,086	77
11 Paul E. Kanjorski (D)	110,737	59
Robert P. Hudock (R)	77,163	41
12 John P. Murtha (D)*	133,149	70
Thomas J. Fullard III (R)	56,626	30
Joseph E. Krill (AE)	—	—
13 Joseph M. Hoeffel (D)	103,840	44
Lawrence Coughlin (R)*	133,642	56
14 William J. Coyne (D)*	162,468	77
John Robert Clark (R)	42,540	20
Richard E. Caligiuri (LIBERT)	6,273	3
Alfred Duncan Jr. (SOC WORK)	—	—
15 Jane Wells-Schooley (D)	79,110	42
Don Ritter (R)*	109,336	58
16 Martin L. Bard (D)	43,488	24
Robert S. Walker (R)*	138,323	76
17 Stephen A. Anderson (D)	48,470	27
George W. Gekas (R)*	129,348	73
18 Doug Walgren (D)*	149,172	63
John G. Maxwell (R)	87,240	37
Daniel M. Mulholland (LIBERT)	1,328	0
19 F. John Rarig (D)	43,468	24
Bill Goodling (R)*	138,989	75
Gary M. Shoemaker (LIBERT)	1,629	1
20 Joseph M. Gaydos (D)*	157,999	76
Daniel Lloyd (R)	50,055	24
21 James A. Young (D)	68,099	36
Tom Ridge (R)*	122,006	64
Edward J. Hammer (I)	—	—
22 Austin J. Murphy (D)*	151,958	79
Nancy S. Pryor (R)	40,557	21
Clare M. Fraenzl (SOC WORK)	—	—
23 Bill Wachob (D)	88,655	48
William F. Clinger Jr. (R)*	94,976	52

RHODE ISLAND

Governor

Anthony J. Solomon (D)	157,814	40
Edward DiPrete (R)	237,160	60

Senate

Claiborne Pell (D)*	277,022	73
Barbara Leonard (R)	104,074	27

	Vote Total	Percent
House		
1 Fernand J. St Germain (D)*	126,510	69
Alfred Rego Jr. (R)	57,694	31
2 Richard Sinapi (D)	61,837	32
Claudine Schneider (R)*	130,274	68

SOUTH CAROLINA

	Vote Total	Percent
Senate		
Melvin Purvis Jr. (D)	271,820	32
Strom Thurmond (R)*	577,587	67
Stephen Davis (LIBERT)	12,852	1
House		
1 Ed Pendarvis (D)	51,529	38
Thomas F. Hartnett (R)*	83,924	62
2 Ken Mosely (D)	63,321	37
Floyd Spence (R)*	107,389	62
Cynthia E. Sullivan (LIBERT)	1,915	1
3 Butler Derrick (D)*	68,505	60
Clarence E. Taylor (R)	43,949	39
Robert Madden (LIBERT)	1,155	1
4 Jeff Smith (D)	56,362	35
Carroll A. Campbell Jr. (R)*	102,966	64
William Ray Pike (LIBERT)	1,436	1
5 John M. Spratt Jr. (D)*	81,345	92
Dick Winchester (AM)	4,043	4
Linda Blezins (LIBERT)	3,265	4
6 Robin Tallon (D)*	97,054	59
Lois Eargle (R)	64,532	40
Hugh Thompson (LIBERT)	2,016	1

SOUTH DAKOTA

	Vote Total	Percent
Senate		
George V. Cunningham (D)	79,680	26
Larry Pressler (R)*	232,356	74
House		
AL Thomas A. Daschle (D)*	179,244	57
Dale Bell (R)	133,200	43

TENNESSEE

	Vote Total	Percent
Senate		
Albert Gore Jr. (D)	991,212	61
Victor Ashe (R)	553,331	34
Khalil-Ullah Al-Muhaymin (I)	—	—
Ed McAteer (I)	85,745	5
House		
1 James H. Quillen (R)*	X	X
2 John F. Bowen (D)	38,779	23
John J. Duncan (R)*	132,153	77
3 Marilyn Lloyd (D)*	99,306	52
John Davis (R)	90,116	48
4 Jim Cooper (D)*	95,449	75
James Beau Seigneur (R)	31,193	25
5 Bill Boner (D)*	X	X
6 Bart Gordon (D)	101,628	63
Joe Simpkins (R)	60,406	37
7 Don Sundquist (R)*	X	X
8 Ed Jones (D)*	X	X
9 Harold E. Ford (D)*	132,814	71
William B. Thompson Jr. (R)	53,072	29

TEXAS

	Vote Total	Percent
Senate		
Lloyd Doggett (D)	2,110,834	41
Phil Gramm (R)	2,988,346	59

	Vote Total	Percent
House		
1 Sam B. Hall Jr. (D)*	X	X
2 Charles Wilson (D)*	110,628	59
Louis Dugas Jr. (R)	76,145	41
3 Jim Westbrook (D)	46,890	17
Steve Bartlett (R)*	228,819	83
4 Ralph M. Hall (D)*	114,458	58
Thomas Blow (R)	84,367	42
5 John Bryant (D)*	X	X
6 Dan Kubiak (D)	96,579	44
Joe Barton (R)	124,472	56
7 Billy Willibey (D)	32,365	13
Bill Archer (R)*	210,545	87
8 Don Buford (D)	62,259	35
Jack Fields (R)*	114,845	65
9 Jack Brooks (D)*	116,200	59
Jim Mahan (R)	81,336	41
10 J. J. Pickle (D)*	X	X
11 Marvin Leath (D)*	X	X
12 Jim Wright (D)*	X	X
13 Jack Hightower (D)*	95,316	47
Beau Boulter (R)	107,564	53
14 Bill Patman (D)*	86,507	49
Mac Sweeney (R)	89,341	51
15 E. "Kika" de la Garza (D)*	X	X
16 Ron Coleman (D)*	54,274	56
Jack Hammond (R)	42,638	44
17 Charles W. Stenholm (D)*	X	X
18 Mickey Leland (D)*	108,819	80
Glen E. Beaman (R)	26,379	20
Jose Alvarado (I)	—	—
19 Don R. Richards (D)	73,499	42
Larry Combest (R)	102,844	58
20 Henry B. Gonzalez (D)*	X	X
21 Joe Sullivan (D)	46,901	19
Tom Loeffler (R)*	199,320	81
22 Doug Williams (D)	67,539	36
Tom DeLay (R)	122,660	64
23 Albert G. Bustamante (D)	X	X
24 Martin Frost (D)*	150,210	68
Bob Burk (R)	71,703	32
25 Michael A. Andrews (D)*	112,145	63
Jerry Patterson (R)	64,679	37
26 Tom Vandergriff (D)*	109,697	48
Richard Armey (R)	119,384	52
27 Solomon P. Ortiz (D)*	103,278	64
Richard Moore (R)	57,141	36

UTAH

	Vote Total	Percent
Governor		
Wayne Owens (D)	273,307	44
Norman H. Bangerter (R)	348,585	56
L. S. Brown (AM)	—	—
House		
1 Milton C. Abrams (D)	55,702	28
James V. Hansen (R)*	141,203	71
Willy Marshall (LIBERT)	1,136	1
2 Frances Farley (D)	104,704	50
David S. Monson (R)	104,847	50
Hugh Butler (I)	1,451	0
3 Bruce R. Baird (D)	46,016	25
Howard C. Nielson (R)*	136,950	74
D. W. Crosby (LIBERT)	1,068	1

VERMONT

	Vote Total	Percent
Governor		
Madeleine M. Kunin (D)	115,500	50
John J. Easton Jr. (R)	111,809	49
Marian Wagner (CIT)	—	—

	Vote Total	Percent
William Wicher (LIBERT)	1,904	1
Richard Gottlieb (LU)	681	0
House		
AL Anthony Pollina (D)	59,686	27
James M. Jeffords (R)*	146,091	67
James Hedbor (LIBERT)	9,274	4
Peter Diamondstone (LU)	4,662	2
Morris Earle (I)	—	—

VIRGINIA

	Vote Total	Percent
Senate		
Edythe C. Harrison (D)	599,849	30
John W. Warner (R)*	1,387,473	70
House		
1 John McGlennon (D)	79,024	40
Herbert H. Bateman (R)*	117,146	59
E. J. Green (I)	2,172	1
2 G. William Whitehurst (R)*	X	X
3 Thomas J. Bliley Jr. (R)*	X	X
Roger L. Coffey (I)	—	—
4 Norman Sisisky (D)*	X	X
5 Dan Daniel (D)*	X	X
6 James R. Olin (D)*	103,388	52
Ray Garland (R)	96,185	48
7 Lewis M. Costello (D)	76,569	42
D. French Slaughter (R)	107,393	58
R. E. Frazier Sr. (I)	—	—
8 Richard L. Saslaw (D)	95,900	44
Stan Parris (R)*	122,185	55
Donald W. Carpenter (I)	1,800	1
9 Frederick C. Boucher (D)*	102,366	52
Jefferson Stafford (R)	93,562	48
10 John P. Flannery II (D)	98,742	38
Frank R. Wolf (R)*	163,853	62

WASHINGTON

	Vote Total	Percent
Governor		
Booth Gardner (D)	906,928	53
John Spellman (R)*	792,547	47
Mark Calney (I)	—	—
Bob LeRoy (POP)	—	—
Cheryll Hidalgo (SOC WORK)	—	—
House		
1 Brock Evans (D)	106,989	44
John Miller (R)	136,712	56
2 Al Swift (D)*	128,278	60
Jim Klauder (R)	84,540	40
Gary Franco (POP)	—	—
3 Don Bonker (D)*	137,254	71
Herb Elder (R)	55,415	29
4 Mark Epperson (D)	40,316	24
Sid Morrison (R)*	128,320	76
5 Thomas S. Foley (D)*	142,997	70
Jack Hebner (R)	61,922	30
6 Norman D. Dicks (D)*	99,352	66
Mike Lonergan (R)	47,713	32
Dan Blachly (LIBERT)	2,544	2
7 Mike Lowry (D)*	163,059	71
Robert O. Dorse (R)	65,838	29
Mark Manning (SOC WORK)	—	—
8 Bob Lamson (D)	82,985	38
Rod Chandler (R)*	136,206	62

WEST VIRGINIA

	Vote Total	Percent
Governor		
Clyde M. See Jr. (D)	342,317	47
Arch A. Moore Jr. (R)	385,573	53

	Vote Total	Percent
Senate		
John D. "Jay" Rockefeller IV (D)	368,483	52
John R. Raese (R)	337,097	48
Mary E. (Joan) Radin (SOC WORK)	—	—
House		
1 Alan B. Mollohan (D)*	104,252	55
James Altmeyer (R)	86,927	45
2 Harley O. Staggers Jr. (D)*	96,728	56
Cleve Benedict (R)	74,712	44
3 Bob Wise (D)*	122,933	69
Margaret Miller (R)	55,964	31
4 Nick J. Rahall II (D)*	98,490	67
Jess T. Shumate (R)	49,221	33

WISCONSIN

	Vote Total	Percent
House		
1 Les Aspin (D)*	127,105	56
Pete Jansson (R)	99,105	44
2 Robert W. Kastenmeier (D)*	159,919	64
Albert E. Wiley Jr. (R)	91,334	36
3 Charles F. Dahl (D)	74,416	32
Steve Gunderson (R)*	160,376	68
4 Gerald D. Kleczka (D)*	156,767	67
Robert V. Nolan (R)	77,705	33
K. Rick Kissell (LAB F)	—	—
5 Jim Moody (D)*	X	X
William C. Breihan (SOC WORK)	—	—
6 David L. Iaquinta (D)	54,522	24
Thomas E. Petri (R)*	170,216	76
7 David R. Obey (D)*	145,659	61

	Vote Total	Percent
Mark G. Michaelsen (R)	92,637	39
8 Paul Willems (D)	72,623	31
Toby Roth (R)*	159,728	68
Gary L. Barnes (LIBERT)	1,958	1
Cornelius D. Van Handel (LAB F)	—	—
9 John Krause (D)	65,441	27
F. James Sensenbrenner Jr. (R)*	179,518	73
Stephen K. Hauser (CST)	—	—

WYOMING

	Vote Total	Percent
Senate		
Victor A. Ryan (D)	40,246	22
Alan K. Simpson (R)*	145,527	78
House		
AL Hugh B. McFadden Jr. (D)	45,570	24
Dick Cheney (R)*	136,662	74
Craig A. McCune (LIBERT)	3,808	2

Republican Convention

GOP Celebrates Reagan-Bush Renomination

Brimming with confidence that President Reagan and Vice President Bush would be "the winning team" in November, a jubilant Republican Party held its convention in Dallas Aug. 20-23.

With the ticket's renomination certain beforehand, the 33rd Republican National Convention was more a celebration for GOP activists than a business meeting. Criticisms from the party's shrinking band of moderates, worried by the strongly conservative tone of the platform, did little to dispel the optimistic mood of delegates, who looked forward with confidence to Reagan's easy re-election victory.

Along with showering praise on Reagan and his administration, Republican leaders also sought to use the convention to advance a long-range goal — persuading conservative Democrats to shift to the GOP. Throughout the week, speakers made attacks on the current leadership of the Democratic Party a key theme of the convention.

Reagan, too, emphasized criticisms of the Democrats in his 55-minute acceptance speech Aug. 23. "The choices this year are not just between two different personalities or between two political parties," Reagan said. "They are between two different visions of the future, two fundamentally different ways of governing — their government of pessimism, fear and limits ... or ours of hope, confidence and growth." *(Text, p. 36-B)*

Convention speakers also sought repeatedly to link Democratic presidential nominee Walter F. Mondale with the Carter administration, in which he served as vice president. "Carter-Mondale" became their shorthand for a list of evils: inflation, high interest rates, foreign policy failures and sagging national spirit.

To underline their contention that the Democratic ticket and the party's leadership was out of step with most Democrats, GOP officials gave the convention spotlight to a number of Democrats-turned-Republicans, such as Rep. Phil Gramm of Texas, who mounted a successful 1984 campaign for the Senate. Another Democrat given a prominent place in the proceedings was Jeane J. Kirkpatrick, the U.S. representative to the United Nations. Kirkpatrick, whom one party leader referred to as "an enlightened Democrat," delivered a strongly worded foreign policy speech during the opening session Aug. 20.

In response to the candidacy of Rep. Geraldine A. Ferraro, D-N.Y., Mondale's running mate, party leaders made clear they were making a pitch for women voters this year. Several women, including keynote speaker Katherine D. Ortega, the U.S. treasurer, gave speeches.

Aug. 20: Opening Day

The Republican National Convention officially came to order Aug. 20 at 10:04 a.m. CDT in the main exhibit hall of the Dallas Convention Center.

The opening speakers set the themes of the four-day gathering, singing the praises of their party and criticizing the Democrats.

Republican National Committee Chairman Frank J. Fahrenkopf Jr., introduced by a short film shown on television screens suspended from the ceiling, declared that the GOP is "the party of America's future."

The Democrats, he charged, caved in to "an orgy of pressure groups" at their convention in San Francisco July 16-19. And he labeled Mondale as "just a man who can't say no. He made so many promises to so many pressure groups that it's clear Mr. Mondale left more than his heart in San Francisco."

Ladies' Night

The evening session Aug. 20 was the GOP's "ladies' night." Four of the six speakers were women — Ortega, Kirkpatrick, Health and Human Services Secretary Margaret M. Heckler and Dr. Virginia Boyack, who gave a salute to senior citizens.

Although Ortega was billed as the keynote speaker, it was Democrat Kirkpatrick who received the most sustained and vigorous applause from the delegates.

Kirkpatrick began by saying she was "grateful that you should invite me, a lifelong Democrat" to the convention. "On the other hand," she added, "I realize you are inviting many lifelong Democrats to join our common cause."

She had harsh words for her fellow Democrats, charging that they "treat foreign affairs as an afterthought." She asserted that the Carter administration "did not seem to notice much, care much, or do much" about a host of international problems.

"The Carter administration's motives were good," she said, "but their policies were inadequate, uninformed and mistaken."

Kirkpatrick concluded on a confident note, declaring that Reagan's election signaled to the world that "we have the necessary energy and conviction to defend ourselves, as well as a deep commitment to peace. And now, the American people, proud of our country, proud of our freedom, proud of ourselves, will reject the San Francisco Democrats and send Ronald Reagan back to the White House."

In her speech, the last of the evening, Ortega echoed one of Kirkpatrick's themes — that the Democrats in San Francisco did not represent the real Democratic Party. She contended that "mainstream Democrats" have been "shut out of their traditional party home by the narrow interest groups in charge of last month's Democratic convention."

Then she issued an invitation to "those millions of Democrats abandoned by their national leadership in San Francisco" to join the GOP. "We Republicans here in Dallas say we welcome you to our home. Nuestra casa es su casa. Our home is your home. Join us now."

Earlier, before Rep. Guy Vander Jagt, Mich., gave a brief address, delegates were shown a five-minute film critical of congressional Democrats. As graphics flashed on the screen, a narrator listed several issues, such as tuition tax credits and an anti-crime bill, that have "popular support" but have been either "killed" or "bottled up" in the House. "Democrats in Congress," the narration concluded. "They're hurting America."

Senate Majority Leader Howard H. Baker Jr. of Tennessee also addressed the delegates that night. "Fifty million people said 'no' to Walter Mondale four years ago, and they can't wait to say 'no' again to him in 1984," said Baker, who did not seek re-election to the Senate.

Aug. 21: Day Two

During the morning session Aug. 21, delegates tended to some procedural duties. In a matter of minutes, they adopted party rules that were to cover the 1988 nominating process, and approved the report of the credentials committee. Conservatives in the panel prevailed over moderates on the formula for allocation of delegates.

With no debate, the party also adopted the platform for the 1984 campaign. During the week of Aug. 13, the 106-member platform committee had worked over the campaign document and delivered to delegates a statement that conformed to the themes Reagan had stressed in his first term.

There had been spirited fights over language in the platform, principally over tax increases, criticism of the independent Federal Reserve Board, the refusal to endorse the Equal Rights Amendment (ERA) and opposition to abortion.

Despite heavy White House lobbying, the platform contained strong language opposing tax boosts — stronger than administration officials wanted. Reagan's operatives also were unable to soften the language critical of the Federal Reserve Board, but they declined to press the issue for fear of producing a backlash that would have made the language harsher. *(Platform text, p. 41-B)*

Some moderate delegates had considered trying to offer a minority plank on the ERA stating respect for differing Republican views on the issue. But moderates determined that they lacked support to bring a floor challenge. To receive consideration by the full convention, party rules require that a minority plank have the backing of 25 percent of the platform committee members or a majority of six state delegations.

Ford, Kemp, Dole Speeches

The highlight of the evening session Aug. 21 was a speech by former President Gerald R. Ford. Ford wasted no time attacking the Democratic nominee, telling delegates: "Mondale wants this election to be a 'referendum on the future.' I can't blame him for wanting to forget the past, the four years of Carter-Mondale from 1977 through 1980. Who wants to remember four years of roaring inflation, skyrocketing interest rates and so-called 'malaise?' "

Ford zeroed in on Mondale's claim to be campaigning for a "new realism" that would combine strong though conciliatory foreign policies with tough economic initiatives and widespread sacrifice to reduce the federal deficit. Mondale is "just peddling fear," Ford charged. "Americans aren't about to buy Vice President Mondale's 'new realism.' There's only one kind of realism. You don't get it by crossing Jimmy Carter's innocence with George McGovern's pie in the sky."

The evening session also proved to be something of a candidates' night, with 1988 presidential hopefuls getting an opportunity to address the audience. The first was New York Rep. Jack F. Kemp.

In his speech, which focused on the platform's foreign policy plank, Kemp declared, "Our economy is expanding again without inflation. The United States is respected.

Our adversaries are on the defensive. America is once again a model for other nations. . . . Isn't it good to have a president who doesn't apologize for America?" he asked to applause. "Today," he continued, "Mr. Mondale and his party's platform have nothing to offer but fear. Fear of the future. Fear of growth. Fear of global leadership. . . ."

Senate Finance Committee Chairman Robert Dole of Kansas also addressed the convention. Dole, whose name was on most lists of presidential contenders, told delegates that during the Carter administration, Americans lacked hope.

"All of us wondered — no one more than the young — is America still what she had been — a country of the future? The four years of Ronald Reagan are answering that question. And it is that we celebrate," Dole said.

During the Reagan administration, the senator said, the GOP has "displayed a capacity to convert that guiding light of American identity from the stuff of dreams to the substance of daily living. It's that vision for which we seek your support."

He was followed to the rostrum by his wife, Elizabeth Hanford Dole, secretary of transportation. She, too, has been mentioned for one of the spots on the ticket in 1988.

Her speech was devoted to the role of women in the coming election. She contended that women "are not a voting block. We're individuals and we won't fall lock-step in line."

Defending Reagan's record on women's issues, Dole asserted that "this president has backed up his words with deeds." She noted his appointments — her own, plus the selection of the first woman Supreme Court justice and women to fill two other Cabinet positions.

Earlier in the evening, House Minority Leader Robert H. Michel, Ill., the convention's permanent chair, addressed the delegates. Quoting a line from one of the Democratic presidential candidates, Michel said, "As Jesse Jackson might say, 'Mr. Mondale, your time has come' and gone. Someone else whose time has come and gone is House Speaker 'Tip' O'Neill," Michel said to sustained cheers.

"Tip O'Neill and the Democrats have had an iron grip on the House of Representatives for almost 30 years. We've seen that great deliberative body degenerate into a wasteland of inefficiency and neglect," he declared.

Michel reminded delegates that, at the time, House Democrats outnumbered Republicans by 99 votes. "The Democratic leadership dictates the rules, dictates the ratios on committees, dictates the legislative agenda and dictates the schedule," he charged. "They must not dictate our future."

Aug. 22: Day Three

On the evening of Aug. 22, delegates renominated Reagan and Bush, following first lady Nancy Reagan's appeal to "make it one more for the Gipper."

Although the outcome came as no surprise, there was a state-by-state roll call on the nominations. On an unusual joint roll call, Reagan received 2,233 votes, with two delegates, from Illinois and Pennsylvania, abstaining.

Bush received 2,231 votes. In addition to the two abstentions, U.N. Representative Kirkpatrick received one vote from a delegate in Alabama, and Kemp got one vote from Nebraska.

Nevadan Paul Laxalt, the president's closest friend in the Senate, put Reagan's name in nomination. He delivered a rousing speech, emphasizing the problems of the "Carter-

Mondale" administration and highlighting successes under Reagan.

Laxalt, who reminded delegates that he had nominated Reagan in 1980, said, "When I stood before you then, America was a shaken nation — humbled at home, humiliated abroad. After an unprecedented string of domestic and foreign policy failures, President Carter and his handpicked vice president, Walter Mondale, had this nation on its knees.

"In four short years, President Reagan has helped rebuild the confidence of the American people — confidence in themselves, their country, and confidence in our president."

Laxalt launched a bruising attack on Mondale, saying the Democrats turned for their "standard bearer to the public official that Jimmy Carter's own attorney general said was the most liberal thinker in that administration; the public official that Jimmy Carter's attorney general said was most responsible for leading the administration astray and into the quicksand of Washington liberalism. He was the vice president. The name is Mondale and the cause is malaise."

Laxalt also criticized the Democratic platform as "a return to the days of tax and tax, spend and spend — big government, higher taxes and weakness at home and abroad."

Republicans, Laxalt said, were "lucky to have a different choice — Ronald Reagan." Laxalt said he is often asked what is the key to Reagan — "what makes him tick?

"The answer is a simple one," he said. "Ronald Reagan is a leader who's not afraid to lead. That's what it's all about."

After Laxalt's speech, the convention hall erupted in a 25-minute demonstration.

Rep. Bobbi Fiedler, Calif., delivered a brief speech seconding the nomination.

California Gov. George Deukmejian placed Bush's name in nomination. Deukmejian, too, took aim at the Democrats. Their message, he asserted, is "a message of fear. Fear that the prosperity they couldn't produce will end if we re-elect the team that produced it, Ronald Reagan and George Bush.... We're not afraid. We're not scared. We're confident."

Deukmejian extolled Bush as "businessman, congressman, naval officer, ambassador, diplomat, director of intelligence, and vice president. No one, no one in the United States can match that experience."

Earlier in the evening, Sen. Barry Goldwater, R-Ariz., addressed the convention. Goldwater, the party's presidential nominee in 1964, said he wanted to talk to the delegates about "freedom." He opened his speech with a slogan from his unsuccessful campaign 20 years before: "Let me remind you," he said, "extremism in the defense of liberty is no vice."

He charged that the Democrats at their convention "turned their backs on our own heritage. Indeed, they would have us ashamed of our freedom and our ability to defend it. To me, the worst part was that they said nicer things about the Soviet Union than about our own military services."

Goldwater lashed out at the Democrats' conduct of foreign policy. "Every war in this century began and was fought under Democratic administrations," he said. "You doubt me?" he asked, reeling off a list of five wars and the Democratic presidents who were in office when they were fought.

Aug. 23: Closing Day

On the final night of the convention, Reagan and Bush came to the hall to claim their nominations.

Bush launched an attack on the Democrats, charging that "for over half a century, the liberal Democrats have pursued a philosophy of tax and spend, tax and spend."

He reminded delegates that in his July 19 acceptance speech, Mondale promised to raise taxes: "Mr. Mondale calls this promise to raise taxes an act of courage. But it wasn't courage — it was just habit, because Mr. Mondale is a gold medal winner when it comes to increasing the tax burden of the American people....

"The message the American people got from San Francisco was, 'We'll raise your taxes.' Our message from Dallas is: The American people want less spending and less regulation, not more taxes. They want to keep America's dynamic economy growing."

To Democrats embracing their party's platform adopted in July, Bush said, "No matter how your rhetoric tries to move away from your voting records; no matter how hard you try to turn your back on Jimmy Carter; no matter how much you now talk about family values, this country will not retreat. You've had your chance. Your time has passed." *(Text, p. 39-B)*

After Bush's speech, the hall was darkened, and for 18 minutes, a film on Reagan's accomplishments was shown. With testimonials, footage of foreign trips, and voice-over narrative by Reagan, it sought to portray the president as a concerned leader and statesman. The film had been the focus of controversy when television networks hesitated to show all of it; in the end, two — NBC and the Cable News Network — did.

When the film was over, Reagan came to the podium amid a thunderous ovation.

"America is on the move again, and expanding towards new eras of opportunity for everyone," Reagan declared. "We're accused of having a secret," he added, referring to Mondale's charge that the administration has a "secret plan" to raise taxes in 1985. "Well, if we have one it is that we're going to keep the mighty engine of this nation revved up. And that means a future of sustained economic growth without inflation that's going to create for our children and grandchildren a prosperity that finally will last."

The United States' place in the world has been restored from a low point during the Carter years, he asserted, adding, "We are not the cause of all the ills of this world. We are a patient and generous people. But for the sake of our freedom and that of others, we cannot permit our reserve to be confused with a lack of resolve."

Reagan also sought to portray himself as a man of peace. "There are only two nations who by their agreement can rid the world of these doomsday weapons, the United States of America and the Soviet Union," he said. "For the sake of our children and the safety of this earth, we ask the Soviets — who have walked out of our negotiations — to join us in reducing and, yes, ridding the earth of this awful threat."

Reagan concluded with a bid for support from disaffected Democrats, reminding them that he, too, was once a Democrat. He said he did not leave the party; the party left him. "As Democratic leaders have taken their party further and further away from its first principles, it's no surprise that so many responsible Democrats feel that our platform is closer to their views," he said, "and we welcome them to our side." ∎

Text of Reagan Acceptance Speech

Following is the Associated Press text of President Reagan's Aug. 23 speech accepting the Republican presidential nomination as delivered at the Republican National Convention, in Dallas.

Thank you very much. Mr. Chairman, Mr. Vice President, delegates to this convention, and fellow citizens:

In 75 days, I hope we enjoy a victory that is the size of the heart of Texas.

Nancy and I extend our deep thanks to the Lone Star State and the "Big D" — the city of Dallas — for all their warmth and hospitality.

Four years ago, I didn't know precisely every duty of this office, and not too long ago, I learned about some new ones from the first-graders of Corpus Christi School in Chambersburg, Pa.

Little Leah Kline was asked by her teacher to describe my duties.

She said: "The president goes to meetings. He helps the animals. The president gets frustrated. He talks to other presidents."

How does wisdom begin at such an early age?

Clear Political Choice

Tonight, with a full heart and deep gratitude for your trust, I accept your nomination for the presidency of the United States.

I will campaign on behalf of the principles of our party which lift America confidently into the future.

America is presented with the clearest political choice of half a century.

The distinction between our two parties and the different philosophy of our political opponents are at the heart of this campaign and America's future.

I've been campaigning long enough to know that a political party and its leadership can't change their colors in four days.

We won't, and no matter how hard they tried, our opponents didn't in San Francisco.

We didn't discover our values in a poll taken a week before the convention.

And we didn't set a weathervane on top of the Golden Gate Bridge before we started talking about the American family.

The choices this year are not just between two different personalities, or between two political parties.

They are between two different visions of the future, two fundamentally different ways of governing — their government of pessimism, fear and limits — or ours of hope, confidence, and growth.

Their government sees people only as members of groups; ours serves all the people of America as individuals.

Theirs lives in the past, seeking to apply the old and failed policies to an era that has passed them by; ours learns from the past and strives to change by boldly charting a new course for the future.

Theirs lives by promises, the bigger, the better. We offer proven, workable answers.

Inflation and Interest Rates

Our opponents began this campaign hoping that America has a poor memory.

Well, let's take them on a little stroll down memory lane.

Let's remind them of how a 4.8 percent inflation rate in 1976 became back-to-back years of double-digit inflation — the worst since World War I — punishing the poor and the elderly, young couples striving to start their new lives, and working people struggling to make ends meet.

Inflation was not some plague borne on the wind.

It was a deliberate part of their official economic policy needed, they said, to maintain prosperity.

They didn't tell us that with it would come the highest interest rates since the Civil War.

As average monthly mortgage payments more than doubled, home building nearly ground to a halt, tens of thousands of carpenters and others were thrown out of work.

And who controlled both houses of Congress and the executive branch at the time?

Not us. Not us.

Campaigning across America in 1980, we saw evidence everywhere of industrial decline.

And in rural America, farmers' costs were driven up by inflation; they were devastated by a wrongheaded grain embargo, and were forced to borrow money at exorbitant interest rates just to get by, and many of them didn't get by.

Farmers have to fight insects, weather, and the marketplace — they shouldn't have to fight their own government.

The high interest rates of 1980 were not talked about in San Francisco.

Taxes

But how about taxes?

They were talked about in San Francisco.

Will Rogers once said he never met a man he didn't like.

But if I could paraphrase Will, our friends in the other party have never met a tax they didn't like — they didn't like, or hike.

Under their policies, tax rates have gone up three times as much for families with children as they have for everyone else over these past three decades.

In just the five years before we came into office, taxes roughly doubled.

Some who spoke so loudly in San Francisco of fairness were among those who brought about the biggest, single, individual tax increase in our history in 1977, calling for a series of increases in the Social Security payroll tax and in the amount of pay subject to the tax.

The bill they passed called for two additional increases between now and 1990, increases that bear down hardest on those at the lower income levels.

The Census Bureau confirms that, because of the tax laws we inherited, the number of households at or below the poverty level paying federal income tax more than doubled between 1980 and 1982.

Well, they received some relief in 1983 when our across-the-board tax cut was fully in place, and they'll get more help when indexing goes into effect this January.

Our opponents have repeatedly advocated eliminating indexing.

Would that really hurt the rich?

No, because the rich are already in the top brackets.

But those working men and women who depend on a cost-of-living adjustment just to keep abreast of inflation would find themselves pushed into a higher tax bracket and wouldn't even be able to keep even with inflation because they'd be paying a higher income tax.

That's "bracket creep" and our opponents are for it; and we're against it.

It's up to us to see that all our fellow citizens understand that confiscatory taxes, costly social experiments and economic tinkering were not just the policies of a single administration.

For the 26 years prior to January of 1981, the opposition party controlled both houses of Congress.

Every spending bill and every tax for more than a quarter of a century has been of their doing.

About a decade ago, they said federal spending was out of control, so they passed a budget control act, and, in the next five years, ran up deficits of $260 billion. Some control.

In 1981, we gained control of the Senate and executive branch. With the help of some concerned Democrats in the House we started a policy of tightening the federal budget instead of the family budget.

A task force chaired by Vice President George Bush — the finest vice president this country has ever had — it eliminated unnecessary regulations that had been strangling business and industry.

Misery Index

And while we have our friends down memory lane, maybe they'd like to recall a gimmick they designed for their 1976 campaign.

As President Ford told us the night before last, adding the unemployment and inflation rates, they got what they called a Misery Index — in '76 it came to 12½ percent.

And they declared the incumbent had no right to seek re-election with that kind of Misery Index.

Four years ago in the 1980 election, they didn't mention the Misery Index.

Possibly because it was then over 20 percent.

And do you know something?

They won't mention it in this election either; it's down to 11.6, and dropping.

Poor Americans

By nearly every measure, the position of poor Americans worsened under the leadership of our opponents.

Teenage drug use, out-of-wedlock births, and crime increased dramatically.

Urban neighborhoods and schools deteriorated.

Those whom government intended to help discovered a cycle of dependency that could not be broken.

Government became a drug — providing temporary relief, but addiction as well.

And let's get some facts on the table that our opponents don't want to hear.

The biggest annual increase in poverty took place between 1978 and 1981 — over 9 percent each year in the first two years of our administration. Well, I should — pardon me, I didn't put a period in there.

In the first two years of our administration, that annual increase fell to 5.3 percent.

And 1983 was the first year since 1978 that there was no appreciable increase in poverty at all.

Pouring hundreds of billions of dollars into programs in order to make people worse off was irrational and unfair.

Faith in the Human Process

It was time we ended this reliance on the government process and renewed our faith in the human process.

In 1980, the people decided with us that the economic crisis was not caused by the fact that they lived too well. Government lived too well.

It was time for tax increases to be an act of last resort, not of first resort.

The people told the liberal leadership in Washington, "Try shrinking the size of government before you shrink the size of our paychecks."

Our government was also in serious trouble abroad.

We had aircraft that couldn't fly and ships that couldn't leave port.

Many of our military were on food stamps because of meager earnings, and re-enlistments were down.

Ammunition was low, and spare parts were in short supply.

Many of our allies mistrusted us.

In the four years before we took office, country after country fell under the Soviet yoke.

Since Jan. 20, 1981, not one inch of soil has fallen to the communists.

But worst of all, worst of all, Americans were losing the confidence and optimism about the future that has made us unique in the world.

Parents were beginning to doubt that their children would have the better life that has been the dream of every American generation.

We can all be proud that pessimism is ended.

Confident About the Future

America is coming back and is more confident than ever about the future.

Tonight, we thank the citizens of the United States — whose faith, and unwillingness to give up on themselves or this country saved us all.

Together, we began the task of controlling the size and activities of the government by reducing the growth of its spending while passing a tax program to provide incentives to increase productivity for both workers and industry.

Today, a working family earning $25,000 has about $2,900 more in purchasing power than if tax and inflation rates were still at the 1980 level.

Today, of all the major industrial nations of the world, America has the strongest economic growth; one of the lowest inflation rates; the fastest rate of job creation — 6½ million jobs in the last year and a half; a record 600,000 business incorporations in 1983; and the largest increase in real, after-tax personal income since World War II.

We're enjoying the highest level of business investment in history, and America has renewed its leadership in developing the vast new opportunities in science and high technology.

America is on the move again, and expanding toward new areas of opportunity for everyone.

Now, we're accused of having a secret.

Well, if we have, it is that we're going to keep the mighty engine of this nation revved up.

And that means a future of sustained economic growth without inflation that's going to create for our children and grandchildren a prosperity that finally will last.

Defense and Foreign Policy

Today, our troops have newer and better equipment, their morale is higher.

The better armed they are, the less

likely it is they will have to use that equipment.

But if, heaven forbid, they are ever called upon to defend this nation, nothing would be more immoral than asking them to do so with weapons inferior to those of any possible opponent.

We have also begun to repair our valuable alliances, especially our historic NATO alliance.

Extensive discussions in Asia have enabled us to start a new round of diplomatic progress there.

In the Middle East, it remains difficult to bring an end to historic conflicts — but we're not discouraged.

And we shall always maintain our pledge never to sell out one of our closest friends — the state of Israel.

Closer to home, there remains a struggle for survival for free Latin American states — allies of ours, they valiantly struggle to prevent communist takeovers fueled massively by the Soviet Union and Cuba.

Our policy is simple: We are not going to betray our friends, reward the enemies of freedom or permit fear and retreat to become American policies — especially in this hemisphere.

None of the four wars in my lifetime came about because we were too strong.

It is weakness that invites adventurous adversaries to make mistaken judgments.

America is the most peaceful, least warlike nation in modern history.

We are not the cause of all the ills of the world.

We are a patient and generous people.

But for the sake of our freedom and that of others, we cannot permit our reserve to be confused with a lack of resolve.

"New Realism"

When we talk of the plight of our cities, what would help more than our enterprise zones bill which provides tax incentives for private industry to help rebuild and restore decayed areas in 75 sites all across America?

If they really wanted a future of boundless new opportunities for our citizens, why have they buried enterprise zones, over the years, in committee?

Our opponents are openly committed to increasing your tax burden.

We are committed to stopping them, and we will.

They call their policy the "new realism."

But their "new realism" is just the "old liberalism."

They will place higher and higher taxes on small businesses, on family farms and every working family so that government may once again grow at the people's expense.

You know, we could say they spend money like drunken sailors but that would be unfair to drunken sailors.

(Cheers from crowd, chants of "four more years.")

All right, I agree. All right. I was going to say it would be unfair because the sailors are spending their own money.

Our tax policies are and will remain pro-work, pro-growth, and pro-family.

We intend to simplify the entire tax system; to make taxes more fair, easier to understand, and, most important, to bring the tax rates of every American further down, not up.

Now, if we bring them down far enough, growth will continue strong; the underground economy will shrink; the world will beat a path to our door; and no one will be able to hold America back; and the future will be ours.

Reduce Risk of Nuclear War

Another part of our future, the greatest challenge of all, is to reduce the risk of nuclear war by reducing the levels of nuclear arms.

I have addressed parliaments, have spoken to parliaments in Europe and Asia during these last 3½ years declaring that a nuclear war cannot be won and must never be fought.

And those words in those assemblies were greeted with spontaneous applause.

There are only two nations who by their agreement can rid the world of those doomsday weapons, the United States of America and the Soviet Union.

For the sake of our children and the safety of this earth, we ask the Soviets — who have walked out of our negotiations — to join us in reducing and, yes, ridding the earth of this awful threat.

If Democrats Win in November

When we leave this hall tonight, we begin to place those clear choices before our fellow citizens.

We must not let them be confused by those who still think that G.N.P. stands for Gross National Promises.

But after the debates, the position papers, the speeches, the conventions, the television commercials, primaries, caucuses, and slogans — after all this, is there really any doubt at all about what will happen if we let them win this November?

Is there any doubt that they will raise our taxes?

That they will send inflation into orbit again?

That they will make government bigger than ever, and deficits even worse?

Raise unemployment?

Cut back our defense preparedness?

Raise interest rates?

Make unilateral and unwise concessions to the Soviet Union?

And they'll do all that in the name of compassion.

It's what they've done to America in the past, but if we do our job right, they won't be able to do it again.

(Cheers and chants from crowd.)

Renew the Mandate of 1980

In 1980 —

It's getting late.

(Cheers and chants from crowd.)

In 1980, we asked the people of America: Are you better off than you were four years ago?

Well, the people answered by choosing us to bring about a change.

We have every reason now, four years later, to ask that same question again, for we have made a change, the American people joined and helped us.

Let us ask for their help again to renew the mandate of 1980, to move us further forward on the road we presently travel.

The road of common sense, of people in control of their own destiny; the road leading to prosperity and economic expansion in a world at peace.

As we ask for their help, we should also answer the central question of public service: Why are we here? What do we believe in?

Well, for one thing, we're here to see that government continues to serve the people and not the other way around.

Yes, government should do all that is necessary, but only that which is necessary.

We don't lump people by groups or special interests, and let me add, in the party of Lincoln, there is no room for intolerance, and, not even a small corner for anti-Semitism or bigotry of any kind.

Many people are welcome in our house, but not the bigots.

We believe in the uniqueness of each individual.

We believe in the sacredness of human life.

For some time now we've all fallen into a pattern of describing our choice as left or right.

It has become standard rhetoric in discussions of political philosophy.

But is that really an accurate description of the choice before us?

Go back a few years to the origin of the terms and see where left or right would take us if we continued far enough in either direction.

Stalin. Hitler. One would take us to communist totalitarianism and the other to the totalitarianism of Hitler.

Isn't our choice really not one of left or right, but of up or down: down through the welfare state to statism, to more and more government largesse, accompanied always by more government authority, less individual liberty and ultimately totalitarianism, always advanced as for our own good.

The alternative is the dream conceived by our founding fathers, up to the ultimate in individual freedom consistent with an orderly society.

We don't celebrate Dependence Day on the Fourth of July.

We celebrate Independence Day.

We celebrate the right of each individual to be recognized as unique, possessed of dignity and the sacred right to life, liberty and the pursuit of happiness.

At the same time, with our independence goes a generosity of spirit more evident here than in almost any other part of the world.

Recognizing the equality of all men and women, we're willing and able to lift the weak, cradle those who hurt, and nurture the bonds that tie us together as one nation under God.

Finally, we are here to shield our liberties, not just for now or for a few years, but forever.

Leaving the Democratic Party

Could I share a personal thought with you tonight?

Because tonight is kind of special for me.

It is the last time, of course, that I will address you under these circumstances.

I hope you'll invite me back to future conventions.

Nancy and I will be forever grateful for the honor you've done us, for the opportunity to serve, and for your friendship and trust.

I began political life as a Democrat, casting my first vote in 1932 for Franklin Delano Roosevelt.

That year, the Democrats called for a 25 percent reduction in the cost of government by abolishing useless commissions and offices and consolidating departments and bureaus, and giving more authority to state governments.

As the years went by and those promises were forgotten, did I leave the Democratic Party, or did the leadership of that party leave not just me but millions of patriotic Democrats who believed in the principles and philosophy of that platform?

One of the first to declare this was a former Democratic nominee for president — Al Smith, the happy warrior — who went before the nation in 1936 to say on television — on radio — that he could no longer follow his party's leadership, and that he was "taking a walk."

As Democrat leaders have taken their party further and further away from its first principles, it's no surprise that so many responsible Democrats feel that our platform is closer to their views, and we welcome them to our side.

Four years ago we raised a banner of bold colors — no pale pastels.

"A Shining City on a Hill"

We proclaimed a dream of an America that would be "a shining city on a hill."

We promised that we'd reduce the growth of the federal government, and we have.

We said we intended to reduce interest rates and inflation, and we have.

We said we would reduce taxes to provide incentives for individuals and business to get our economy moving again. We said — and we have.

We said there must be jobs with a future for our people, not government make-work programs, and, in the last 19 months, as I've said, 6½ million new jobs in the private sector have been created.

We said we would once again be respected throughout the world, and we are.

We said we would restore our ability to

protect our freedom on land, sea, and in the air, and we have.

We bring to the American citizens in this election year a record of accomplishment and the promise of continuation.

We came together in a "national crusade to make America great again," and to make "a new beginning."

Well, now, it's all coming together.

Springtime of Hope

With our beloved nation at peace, we are in the midst of a springtime of hope for America.

Greatness lies ahead of us.

Holding the Olympic Games here in the United States began defining the promise of this season.

All through the spring and summer, we marveled at the journey of the Olympic Torch as it made its passage, east to west.

Over 9,000 miles, by some 4,000 runners, that flame crossed a portrait of our nation.

From our Gotham City, New York, to the cradle of liberty, Boston, across the Appalachian springtime, to the city of the big shoulders, Chicago.

Moving south toward Atlanta, over to St. Louis past its Gateway Arch, across wheat fields into the stark beauty of the Southwest and then up into the still snow-capped Rockies.

And after circling the greening Northwest, it came down to California, across the Golden Gate, and finally into Los Angeles.

(Cheers for every area he mentioned.)

And all along the way, that torch became a celebration of America. And, we all became participants in the celebration.

Each new story was typical of this land of ours.

There was Ansel Stubbs, a youngster of 99, who passed the torch in Kansas to a 4-year-old, Katie Johnson.

In Pineville, Ky., it came at 1 a.m., so hundreds of people lined the streets with candles.

At Tupelo, Miss., at 7 a.m. on a Sunday morning, a robed church choir sang "God Bless America" as the torch went by.

The torch went through the Cumberland Gap, past the Martin Luther King Jr. Memorial, down the Santa Fe Trail and alongside Billy the Kid's grave.

In Richardson, Texas, it was carried by a 14-year-old boy in a special wheelchair.

In West Virginia, the runner came across a line of deaf children and let each one pass the torch for a few feet, and at the end those youngsters' hands talked excitedly in their sign language.

Crowds spontaneously began singing "America the Beautiful" or "The Battle Hymn of the Republic."

And then, in San Francisco, a Vietnamese immigrant, his little son held on his shoulders, dodged photographers and policemen to cheer a 19-year-old black man pushing an 88-year-old white woman in a wheelchair as she carried the torch.

My friends, that's America.

We cheered in Los Angeles as the flame was carried in and the giant Olympic torch burst into a billowing fire in front of the teams.

The youth of 140 nations assembled on the floor of the coliseum.

And in that moment, maybe you were struck as I was with the uniqueness of what was taking place before 100,000 people in the stadium, most of them citizens of our country, and over a billion worldwide watching on television.

There were athletes representing 140 countries here to compete in the one country in all the world whose people carry the bloodlines of all those 140 countries and more.

Only in the United States is there such a rich mixture of races, creeds, and nationalities — only in our melting pot.

Liberty

And that brings to mind another torch, the one that greeted so many of our parents and grandparents.

Just this past Fourth of July, the torch atop the Statue of Liberty was hoisted down for replacement.

We can be forgiven for thinking maybe it was just worn out from lighting the way to freedom for 17 million new Americans.

So now we'll put up a new one.

The poet called Miss Liberty's torch the "lamp beside the golden door."

Well, that was the entrance to America and it still is.

And now you really know why we are here tonight.

The glistening hope of that lamp is still ours.

Every promise, every opportunity is still golden in this land.

And through that golden door our children can walk into tomorrow with the knowledge that no one can be denied the promise that is America.

Her heart is full; her door is still golden, her future bright.

She has arms big enough to comfort and strong enough to support.

For the strength in her arms is the strength of her people.

She will carry on in the eighties unafraid, unashamed, and unsurpassed.

In this springtime of hope, some lights seem eternal.

America's is.

Thank you, God bless you, and God bless America. ∎

Delivered Aug. 23:

Bush Acceptance Speech

Following is the Associated Press text of Vice President George Bush's Aug. 23 speech accepting the Republican vice presidential nomination as delivered at the Republican National Convention, in Dallas.

Thank you very much.

Mr. Chairman, madam chairman, and my fellow Republicans, and my fellow Americans.

I accept your nomination and the honor and challenge it represents.

Four years ago in Detroit, I pledged my total dedication and energies to support our president. And that has been a very easy pledge to keep. Tonight, I pledge again my every effort to support President Reagan as he leads this nation into four more years of prosperity, opportunity and peace.

In 1980, America needed Governor Reagan in the White House to restore power to the grassroots and to give the American people fresh hope and a new beginning.

In 1984, America needs President Reagan in the White House for a second term to finish the job — to keep this country moving forward.

But we can't move forward, we can't move forward, if we have a majority in Congress that wants to go back.

With your all-out effort, we will maintain control of the Senate — and we'll get a House of Representatives that will move forward with President Reagan and the party of the future — not backward with Tip O'Neill and the party of the past.

Taxes

For over half a century, the liberal Democrats have pursued this philosophy of tax and spend, tax and spend.

And, sure enough, out of that Moscone Center in San Francisco, that temple of doom, came Mr. Mondales's first promise — a solemn promise to raise everyone's taxes.

Well, Mr. Mondale calls this promise to raise taxes a lot of courage, an act of courage. But it wasn't courage — it was just habit, because he is a gold medal winner when it comes to increasing the tax burden of the American people.

Well, President Reagan, with strong support in Congress, cut tax rates across the board for every single American — and he'll keep those rates cut.

And the message the American people got from San Francisco was, "We'll raise your taxes."

But our message from Dallas is: The American people want less spending, less regulation, and not more taxes.

They want to keep America's dynamic economy strong.

They want to reduce the deficits by making government more efficient, holding the line on spending, and through economic growth.

And as for a balanced budget, our message is this: Let the big spenders in Congress step aside. Give us the balanced budget amendment.

Give us the line-item veto and watch what this president can do.

Time for Democrats Has Passed

I heard that speaker in San Francisco last month exhorting his fellow Democrats with the cry, "Our time has come; our time has come."

The American people have a message for the tax raisers, the free spenders, the excess regulators — the government-knows-best handwringers, those who would promise every special interest group everything — and that message is this: "Your time has passed; your time has passed."

No matter how your rhetoric tries to move away from your voting records, no matter how hard you try to turn your back on Jimmy Carter, no matter how much you now talk about family values, this country will not retreat. You've had your chance. Your time has passed.

President's Accomplishments

This president has turned this country's economy around. Since we came into office, productivity is up; personal savings are up; consumer spending is up; housing starts are up; take-home pay is up; inflation — the cruelest tax of all — is down, and more Americans are at work than at any time in the history of the United States.

More Americans are enjoying our country because our parks are cleaner and our air is purer. Under this president, more lands have been acquired for parks, more for wilderness. The quality of life is better. And that's a fact.

You know more Americans are giving to help others. Private contributions in the great tradition of neighbor helping neighbor are up. And that's a fact.

And at the same time, government help for the truly needy is up. The Social Security system has been strengthened and saved by our president's leadership and a truly bipartisan effort in Congress.

More Americans now have a chance for quality education. Test scores are up in our schools. In striving for excellence, we have re-emphasized fundamentals. We believe in teaching kids to read, and to write, to add and to subtract. We believe in classroom discipline and in merit pay for teachers. We believe in local control of schools. And we believe kids should not be prohibited from prayer. And that's a fact.

We're waging all-out war against narcotics in our schools, in our neighborhoods, and across the land. We will not rest until American society is free from the threat of drug pushers and that's a fact.

More Americans are safe. Crime is down, and that's a fact.

President Reagan and I think it's time that we worried less about the criminals and more about the victims of crime.

As for our judicial system, it's always been my view that the Supreme Court should not be all caught up and involved in the political arena. But, since the Democrats made this an issue in San Francisco, let me say that the American people want a Supreme Court that will interpret the Constitution, and not legislate.

We heard that liberal convention in San Francisco attack the president regarding the Supreme Court. But the record shows that President Reagan's sole appointment to the court, Sandra Day O'Connor, is an outstanding justice. And that's a fact.

And, one more fact, and let this be heard loud and clear: Ronald Reagan has protected and will continue to protect the rights of all Americans. Discrimination based on race, religion, sex or age will never be tolerated by this president nor this vice president. And, furthermore, we condemn the vicious anti-Semitism of Louis Farrakhan and the ugly bigotry of the Ku Klux Klan.

Problems Remain

Of course, problems remain. Of course, problems remain. And, yes, there's still much to be done to provide opportunity for those Americans that truly need help. But the answer doesn't lie in going back to the "malaise" days of Carter and Mondale.

The answer doesn't lie in Mr. Mondale's new spending programs — programs that John Glenn estimated would cost up to $170 billion more; or in Mondale deficits that Fritz Holling estimated at $400 billion. It doesn't lie in the programs of a man that Gary Hart called "mush."

Instead, the answer lies in a dynamic private sector that provides jobs, jobs with dignity. The answer lies in limited government and unlimited confidence in the American people.

New Confidence in U.S. Leadership

Just as there's a new confidence — a new optimism — there is new confidence in U.S. leadership around the world. Since becoming vice president, I've gone to 59 countries. Talked to the leaders of those countries and to many other foreign leaders who have come here.

Forgotten is the Carter-Mondale era of vacillation — of weakness — of lecturing to our friends and then letting them down. In this hemisphere, when 1,000 American lives were threatened and when four small Caribbean countries called out for U.S. support to give democracy a chance, President Reagan acted.

And I don't care what Walter Mondale says about it or what Tip O'Neill says about it. Grenada was a proud moment in the history of the United States of America.

Because our president stood firm in

defense of freedom, America has regained respect throughout the world. And, because President Reagan has made America stronger, chances for world peace — true, lasting peace — are stronger.

Our European alliance has never been more solid. More countries in Central and South America have turned to democracy since Ronald Reagan became president. Thirteen Latin American countries have held democratic elections since 1980.

We have strengthened our friendships with countries in the Pacific. We are doing more to foster democratic change and to help the hungry in Africa. We are reaching out to more countries in the Middle East and our strategic relations with Israel have never been stronger.

And, one last point on foreign affairs.

I am proud to serve with a president who is working for peace and I am proud to serve with a president who doesn't go around apologizing for the United States of America.

Message of Optimism, Hope

As vice president, I've had the opportunity to watch this president in action. I've seen a real leader make tough decisions. No longer do we read and hear stories about the job of president being too big for any one person. Gone are the days of blaming the American people for what was really a failure not of the people, but of our national leadership.

Four years ago, we came into office to restore our economy, expand opportunity for all Americans and secure a lasting peace.

Much has been done. Much remains to be done. But this we know: more Americans today believe we have strong, principled, firm leadership in the White House.

This is the message we will take from this convention — a message of optimism, a message of hope.

Three decades ago, a great American president stood on the Capitol steps and made his second inaugural address.

"May we pursue the right without self-righteousness," said Dwight Eisenhower.

"May we know unity without conformity."

"May we grow in strength without pride in self."

"May we, in our dealings with all the people of the Earth, ever speak truth and serve justice."

And, finally, said President Eisenhower, "May the light of freedom . . . flame brightly, until at last the darkness is no more."

Now, as in President Eisenhower's day, these words reflect the true spirit and aspirations of the American people.

May we continue to keep the light of freedom burning. And may we continue to move forward in the next four years — on the high road to peace, prosperity and opportunity — united behind a great president, Ronald Reagan.

Thank you all, very, very much. ∎

Text of 1984 Republican Party Platform

Following is the text of the 1984 Republican Party platform, as adopted Aug. 21 at the party's national convention in Dallas.

PREAMBLE

This year, the American people will choose between two diametrically opposed visions of what America should be.

The Republican Party looks at our people and sees a new dawn of the American spirit.

The Democratic Party looks at our nation and sees the twilight of the American soul.

Republicans affirm that now, as throughout history, the spiritual and intellectual genius of the American people will create a better nation and maintain a just peace. To Republicans, creativity and growth are imperatives for a new era of opportunity for all.

The Republican Party's vision of America's future, the heart of our 1984 Platform, begins with a basic premise:

> From freedom comes opportunity; from opportunity comes growth; from growth comes progress.

This is not some abstract formula. It is the vibrant, beating heart of the American experience. No matter how complex our problems, no matter how difficult our tasks, it is *freedom* that inspires and guides the American Dream.

If everything depends on freedom — and it does — then securing freedom, at home and around the world, is one of the most important endeavors a free people can undertake.

Thus, the title of our Platform, "America's Future: Free and Secure," is more than a summary of our Platform's message. It is the essence.

The Democratic Party understands none of this. It thinks our country has passed its peak. It offers Americans redistribution instead of expansion, contraction instead of growth, and despair instead of hope. In foreign policy it asserts the rhetoric of freedom, but in practice it follows a policy of withdrawal and isolation.

The Democratic Party, in its 1984 Platform, has tried to expropriate the optimism and vision that marked the 1980 Republican Platform.

Rhetorical pilfering of Republican ideals cannot disguise one of history's major ironies: the party whose 1932 standard-

bearer told the American people, as president, that all we have to fear is fear itself has itself become the party of fear.

Today we declare ourselves the Party of Hope — not for some but for all.

It has been said that mercy must have a human heart and pity a human face. We agree. Democrats measure social programs in terms of government activity alone. But the divine command to help our neighbor is directed to each individual and not to a bureaucratic machine. Not every problem cries out for a federal solution.

We must help the poor *escape* poverty by building an economy which creates more jobs, the greatest poverty fighter of them all. Not to help the poor is to abandon them and demean our society; but to help the poor without offering them a chance to escape poverty is ultimately to degrade us all.

The great tasks of compassion must be accomplished both by people who care and by policies which foster economic growth to enhance all human development.

In all these areas, at home and abroad, Ronald Reagan has demonstrated the boldness of vision, the optimism for our future, and the confidence in the American people that can transform human lives and the life of a nation. That is what we expect from a President who, wounded by an assassin, walked his way into a hospital and cheerfully assured the world that he and his country would not be deterred from their destiny.

His example has shaped the 1984 Republican Platform, given it meaning and inspired its vision. We stand with President Reagan and with Vice President Bush to make it a reality.

ECONOMIC FREEDOM AND PROSPERITY

Free Enterprise, Democracy, and the Role of Government

Free enterprise is fundamental to the American way of life. It is inseparable from the social, religious, political, and judicial institutions which form the bedrock of a nation dedicated to individual freedom and human rights.

Economic growth enables all citizens to share in the nation's great physical and spiritual wealth, and it is maximized by giving them the fullest opportunity to engage in economic activities and to retain the rewards of their labor.

Our society provides both a ladder of opportunity on which all can climb to suc-

cess and a safety net of assistance for those who need it. To safeguard both, government must protect property rights, provide a sound currency, and minimize its intrusions into individual decisions to work, save, invest, and take risks.

The role of the federal government should be limited. We reaffirm our conviction that State and local governments closest to the people are the best and most efficient. While President Reagan has done much to alleviate federal regulatory and bureaucratic burdens on individuals and businesses, Congress has failed to act. The size and scope of the federal government remains much too large and must be reduced.

During the Carter-Mondale Administration, no group of Americans was spared from the impact of a failing economy. Family budgets were stretched to the limit to keep pace with increases in taxes and costs of food, energy, and housing. For the first time, owning a home slipped out of reach for millions. Working people saw their wage increases outpaced by inflation. Older Americans saw their savings and retirement incomes consumed by basic living costs. Young people found job opportunities narrowing. Disadvantaged Americans faced an inefficient and wasteful bureaucracy which perpetuated programs of dependency. American business and industry faced recession, unemployment, and upheaval, as high interest rates, inflation, government regulation, and foreign competition combined to smother all enterprise and strike at our basic industries.

When President Reagan took office in 1981, our economy was in a disastrous state. Inflation raged at 12.4 percent. The cost of living had jumped 45 percent in the Carter-Mondale years. The prime rate was 21.5 percent. Federal spending increases of 17 percent per year, massive tax rate increases due to inflation, and a monetary policy debasing the dollar had destroyed our economic stability.

We brought about a new beginning. Americans are better off than they were four years ago, and they're still improving. Almost six and one-half million have found jobs since the recovery began, the largest increase in our history. One and one-half million have come in manufacturing — a part of our economy designated for stagnation and government control by Democrats. More than 107 million Americans, more than ever before, are working. Their industry proves that policies which increase incentives for work, saving, and investment do lead to economic growth, while the redistributionist policies of the past did cause unemployment, declining incomes, and idle industries.

We will therefore continue to return control over the economy to the people. Our policies will maximize the role of the individual and build on the success of the past four years: (a) the most rapid decline in unemployment of any post-World War II recovery; (b) inflation dramatically reduced; (c) interest rates significantly cut; (d) a 25 percent cut in federal tax rates; (e) automatic tax increases eliminated by indexing tax rates; (f) the financial holdings of American families increased by over $1.8 trillion; (g) oil prices down 35 percent in real terms; and (h) 300 million hours once devoted to government paperwork returned to individuals and business.

Our most important economic goal is to expand and continue the economic recovery and move the nation to full employment without inflation. We therefore oppose any attempts to increase taxes, which would harm the recovery and reverse the trend to restoring control of the economy to individual Americans. We favor reducing deficits by continuing and expanding the strong economic recovery brought about by the policies of this Administration and by eliminating wasteful and unnecessary government spending. Mondale-Ferraro, by contrast, boast that they will raise taxes, with ruinous effects on the economy.

To assure workers and entrepreneurs the capital required to provide jobs and growth, we will further expand incentives for personal saving. We will expand coverage of the Individual Retirement Account, especially to homemakers, and increase and index the annual limits on IRA contributions. We will increase the incentives for savings by moving toward the reduction of taxation of interest income. We will work for indexation of capital assets and elimination of the double taxation of dividends to increase the attractiveness of equity investments for small investors.

We oppose withholding on dividend and interest income. It would discourage saving and investment, create needless paperwork, and rob savers of their due benefits. A higher personal savings rate is key to deficit control. We therefore oppose any disincentives to thrift.

History has proven again and again that wage and price controls will not stop inflation. Such controls only cause shortages, inequities, and ultimately high prices. We remain firmly opposed to the imposition of wage and price controls.

We are committed to bringing the benefits of economic growth to all Americans. Therefore, we support policies which will increase opportunities for the poorest in our society to climb the economic ladder. We will work to establish enterprise zones in urban and rural America; we will work to enable those living in government-owned or subsidized housing to purchase their homes.

As part of our effort to reform the tax system, we will reduce disincentives to employment which too often result in a poverty trap for poor American families.

Fiscal and Monetary Policy

Taxation

A major goal of all Republicans in 1980 was to reduce the oppressive tax rates strangling Americans. The tax burden, which had increased steadily during the Carter-Mondale Administration, was at a record high and scheduled to go even higher. Taxes as a percentage of GNP rose from 18.2 percent in 1976 to 21 percent in 1981 and would have reached 24 percent by 1984. The tax bill for the median-income family of four had risen from $1,713 in 1976 to $2,778 in 1980 and would have reached $3,943 in 1984.

Double-digit inflation had pushed individuals into ever higher marginal tax brackets. High marginal tax rates reduced the incentive for work, saving, and investment, and retarded economic growth, productivity, and job creation.

With the Economic Recovery Tax Act of 1981, we carried out the first phase of tax reduction and reform by cutting marginal tax rates by 25 percent. Tax brackets were indexed to prevent tax hikes through bracket creep. In addition, families received further relief by reducing the marriage penalty and lowering estate and gift taxes.

Businesses and workers benefitted when we replaced outdated depreciation systems with the accelerated cost recovery system, reduced capital gains tax rates, and lowered the pressures which high tax rates place on wage demands. Investment in plants and equipment has increased 16.5 percent since 1982, resulting in 6.3 million new jobs.

In 1980, we promised the American people a tax cut which would be progressive and fair, reducing tax rates across-the-board. Despite Democrat opposition we succeeded in reducing the tax rates of all taxpayers by about 25 percent with low-income taxpayers receiving a slightly larger percentage tax reduction than high-income taxpayers. These sound economic policies have succeeded. We will continue our efforts to further reduce tax rates and now foresee no economic circumstances which would call for increased taxation.

The bulk of the tax cut goes to those who pay most of the taxes: middle-income taxpayers. Nearly three-fourths of its benefits go to taxpayers earning less than $50,000. In fact, these taxpayers now pay a smaller percentage of total income taxes than they did in 1980; and those earning more than $50,000 pay a larger percentage of total income taxes than they did in 1980.

As a result, the income tax system is fairer now than it was under Carter-Mondale. To keep it fair, Republicans indexed the tax code: starting in 1985, individual tax brackets, the zero bracket amount, and the personal exemption will be adjusted annually for inflation. As a result, cost of living raises will no longer push taxpayers into higher brackets.

For years, congressional big spenders used inflation as a silent partner to raise taxes without taking the heat for passing tax increases. With indexing, taxpayers will be protected against that theft. Low- and moderate-income taxpayers benefit the most from indexing and would bear the brunt of the hidden tax increases if it were repealed.

Nearly 80 percent of the tax increase from the repeal of indexing would fall on taxpayers earning less than $50,000. For a family of four earning $10,000, repeal of indexing would result in a staggering 40 percent tax increase over the next five years. We pledge to preserve tax indexing. We will fight any attempt to repeal, modify, or defer it.

The Republican Party pledges to continue our efforts to lower tax rates, change and modernize the tax system, and eliminate the incentive-destroying effects of graduated tax rates. We therefore support tax reform that will lead to a fair and simple tax system and believe a modified flat tax — with specific exemptions for such items as mortgage interest — is a most promising approach.

For families, we will restore the value of personal exemptions, raising it to a minimum of $2,000 and indexing to prevent further erosion. We will preserve the deduction for mortgage interest payments. We will propose an employment income exclusion to assure that tax burdens are not shifted to the poor. Tax reform must not be a guise for tax increases. We believe such an approach will enhance the income and opportunities of families and low- and middle-income Americans.

We oppose taxation of churches, religious schools, or any other religious institutions. However, we do believe that any business income unrelated to the religious function of the institution should be subject to the same taxes paid by competing businesses.

We oppose the setting of artificially high interest rates which would drastically curtail the ability of sellers to finance sales of their own property. Rather, we encourage marketplace transfer of homes, farms, and smaller commercial properties.

Spending and Budget

The Republican Party believes the federal budget must be balanced. We are committed to eliminating deficits and the excessive spending that causes them. In 1980, federal spending was out of control, increasing at a rate of over 17 percent. We have cut that growth rate by almost two-thirds.

But Congress ignored many of the President's budget reforms. It scaled back and delayed the tax cuts. As a result, we began to pay the price for the irresponsible spending and tax policies of the Carter-Mondale Administration. The resulting recession dramatically increased the deficit, and government spending continues at an unacceptable level.

Democrats claim deficits are caused by Americans' paying too little in taxes. Nonsense. We categorically reject proposals to increase taxes in a misguided effort to balance the budget. Tax and spending increases would reduce incentives for economic activity and threaten the recovery.

Even when we achieve full employment and with robust economic growth, federal spending — including credit programs and other off-budget items — will remain too high. As a percentage of GNP, it must be reduced.

The congressional budget process is bankrupt. Its implementation has not brought spending under control, and it must be thoroughly reformed. We will work for the constitutional amendment requiring a balanced federal budget passed by the Republican Senate but blocked by the Democrat-controlled House and denounced by the Democrat Platform. If Congress fails to act on this issue, a constitutional convention should be convened to address only this issue in order to bring deficit spending under control.

The President is denied proper control over the federal budget. To remedy this, we support enhanced authority to prevent wasteful spending, including a line-item veto.

Monetary Policy

Our 1980 Platform promised to bring inflation under control. We did it. This cruelest tax — hitting hardest at the poor, the aged, and those on fixed incomes — raged up to 13.3 percent under Carter-Mondale. We have brought it down to about 4 percent and we strive for lower levels.

The effects of our program have been dramatic. Real, after-tax incomes are rising. Food prices are stable. Interest rates have fallen dramatically, leading to a resurgence in home building, auto purchases, and capital investment.

Just as our tax policy has only laid the groundwork for a new era of prosperity, reducing inflation is only the first step in restoring a stable currency. A dollar now should be worth a dollar in the future. This allows real economic growth without inflation and is the primary goal of our monetary policy.

The Federal Reserve Board's destabilizing actions must therefore stop. We need coordination between fiscal and monetary policy, timely information about Fed decisions, and an end to the uncertainties people face in obtaining money and credit. The Gold Standard may be a useful mechanism for realizing the Federal Reserve's determination to adopt monetary policies needed to sustain price stability.

Domestically, a stable dollar will mean lower interest rates, rising real wages, guaranteed value for retirement and education savings, growth of assets through productive investment, affordable housing, and greater job security.

Internationally, a stable dollar will mean stable exchange rates, protection for contract prices, commodity prices which change only when real production changes, greater resources devoted to job-creating

investment, less protectionist pressure, and increased trade and income for all nations.

Regulatory Reform

Our 1980 Platform declared that "excessive regulation remains a major component of our nations's spiraling inflation and continues to stifle private initiatives, individual freedom, and State and local government autonomy." President Reagan's regulatory reform program contributed significantly to economic recovery by removing bureaucratic roadblocks and encouraging efficiency. In many fields, government regulation either did not achieve its goals or made limited improvements at exorbitant cost. We have worked with industry and labor to get better results through cooperation rather than coercion.

The flood of regulation has stopped. The number of new regulations has been halved. Unrestrained growth in the size and spending of the regulatory workforce has stopped. Some $150 billion will thereby be saved over the next decade by consumers and businesses. In the past four years alone, 300 million hours of government-mandated paperwork were eliminated. We have reduced the regulatory burden on Americans by making government rules as cost-effective as possible. We must maintain this progress through comprehensive regulatory reform legislation and a constitutional procedure which will enable Congress to properly oversee executive branch rules by reviewing and, if necessary, overturning them.

So consumers can have the widest choice of services at the lowest possible prices, Republicans commit themselves to breaking down artificial barriers to entry created by antiquated regulations. With the explosion of computer technologies just beginning to enhance our way of life, we will encourage rather than hinder innovative competition in telecommunications and financial services.

There are still federal statutes that keep Americans out of the workforce. Arbitrary minimum wage rates, for example, have eliminated hundreds of thousands of jobs and, with them, the opportunity for young people to get productive skills, good work habits, and a weekly paycheck. We encourage the adoption of a youth opportunity wage to encourage employers to hire and train inexperienced workers.

We demand repeal of prohibitions against household manufacturing. Restrictions on work in the home are intolerable intrusions into our private lives and limit economic opportunity, especially for women and the homebound.

Support For Small Business

America's small business entrepreneurs have led the way in fueling economic recovery. Almost all the 11 million non-farm businesses in the United States are small, but they provide over 50 million jobs. We must keep them strong to ensure

lasting prosperity. Republicans reaffirm our historic ties with independent business people and pledge continued efforts to help this energetic segment of our economy.

We have created a climate conducive to small business growth. Our tax rate reductions increased incentives for entrepreneurial activity and provided investment capital through incentives to save. Reduced capital gains taxes further stimulated capital formation and increased the return on small business investment. Greater depreciation allowances encouraged modernization. Estate tax changes will allow families to keep the rewards of their labors.

We have insisted on less federal interference with small business. As a result, burdensome regulations were reduced, and runaway agencies like OSHA were reined in. We have ensured that the federal government pays its bills on time or pays interest penalties.

Presidential action has focused needed attention on increased government procurement from small and minority businesses. In FY 1983 the Small Business Administration directed $2.3 billion in federal sole-source contracts to minority firms through its 8(a) program — a 45 percent increase over 1980. This record amount was achieved along with management improvements that eliminated past abuses in that program.

Three million women business owners are generating $40 billion in annual receipts and creating many new jobs. Yet, their enterprises face barriers in credit, access to capital, and technical assistance. They lag far behind in federal procurement contracts. We are dedicated to helping them become full partners in the economic mainstream of small business.

To them and to all who make America grow, we reaffirm our commitment to reduce marginal tax rates further. We oppose any scheme to roll back the estate tax cuts and will seek further reductions for family businesses. Moreover, we support lower capital gains tax rates and indexation of asset values to protect investors from inflation.

We will create enterprise zones to revitalize economically depressed areas by offering simplified regulation and lower taxes for small businesses that relocate there.

We will make it easier for small businesses to compete for government contracts, not only to assist the private sector but also to provide competition and greater cost control in federal purchases.

In a continuing effort to offset our balance of trade, we reaffirm our strong support for this nation's tourism industry.

Science and Technology

We pledge to continue the Reagan Administration's science and technology policies, which have enhanced economic recovery and our nation's research capability.

We have refocused federal research and development spending on basic research, and it has increased more than 50 percent.

We propose to extend the incremental research and development tax credit to stimulate greater activity in the private sector.

To allow U.S. firms to compete on an equal footing with foreign companies, we will permit U.S. firms to cooperate in joint research and development projects.

Energy

In 1980, energy prices were at all-time highs and rising rapidly. The OPEC cartel had an iron grip on free world economies. Oil imports rose, and domestic production fell under Carter-Mondale price controls and allocations. Competition in energy markets declined.

We have all but eliminated those disastrous policies. President Reagan's immediate decontrol of oil prices precipitated a decline in real oil prices and increased competition in all energy markets. Oil price decontrol crippled the OPEC cartel.

The results have been dramatic. Imported oil prices are down 35 percent in real terms. The real price of gasoline is at a five-year low. Energy consumption has declined relative to economic growth. Energy efficiency increased by 12 percent since 1980, with lower costs to businesses and families. The Strategic Petroleum Reserve is now four times larger than in 1980, providing significant protection against any disruption in imports.

We will complete America's energy agenda. Natural gas should be responsibly decontrolled as rapidly as possible so that families and businesses can enjoy the full benefits of lower prices and greater production, as with decontrolled oil. We are committed to the repeal of the confiscatory windfall profits tax, which has forced the American consumer to pay more for less and left us vulnerable to the energy and economic stranglehold of foreign producers.

While protecting the environment, we should permit abundant American coal to be mined and consumed. Environmentally sound development of oil and natural gas on federal properties (which has brought the taxpayers $20 billion in revenue in the last four years) should continue. We believe that as controls have been lifted from the energy marketplace, conservation and alternative sources of energy, such as solar, wind, and geothermal, have become increasingly cost-effective. We further take pride in the fact that Reagan Administration economic policies have created an environment most favorable to the small businesses that pioneer these alternative technologies.

We now have a sound, long-term program for disposal of nuclear waste. We will work to eliminate unnecessary regulatory procedures so that nuclear plants can be brought on line quickly, efficiently, and safely. We call for an energy policy, the stability and continuity of which will restore and encourage public confidence in the fiscal stability of the nuclear industry.

We are committed to the termination of the Department of Energy. President Reagan has succeeded in abolishing that part which was telling Americans what to buy, where to buy it, and at what price — the regulatory part of DOE. Then he reduced the number of bureaucrats by 25 percent. Now is the time to complete the job.

Agriculture

Securing a Prosperous Rural America

The Republican Party is thankful for, and proud of, the ability of American farmers and ranchers to provide abundant, high quality, and nutritious food and fiber for all our citizens and millions more throughout the world. This unmatched ability to produce is basic to this country's high standard of living. We recognize that a prosperous agriculture is essential to the future of America and to the health and welfare of its people. We have set the stage for securing prosperity in rural America. In 1979, farm and ranch production costs increased 19 percent, in 1983 they actually declined by almost 3 percent. The prime interest rate has been brought down from 21.5 percent to 13 percent. Our reputation as a reliable world food and fiber supplier has been restored. Despite that remarkable beginning, much remains to be done.

We believe well managed, efficient American farm and ranch operations are the most cost-effective and productive food and fiber suppliers in the world, and therefore have the inherent economic capability and right to make a profit from their labor, management, and investments. The primary responsibility of government with respect to agriculture is to create the opportunity for a free and competitive economic and policy environment supportive of the American farmers' and ranchers' industrious and independent spirit and innovative talent. We further believe that, to the extent some well-managed and efficient farms and ranches are temporarily unable to make a profit in the marketplace, it is in the public interest to provide reasonable and targeted assistance.

The Carter-Mondale Administration, and 28 years of a Congress rigidly controlled by the Democrats and out of touch with the people, brought farmers and ranchers to the hardest times since the Great Depression. Farm and ranch incomes fell to disastrous levels. Uncontrolled inflation and the highest interest rates in over a century prevented farmers from operating at a profit, and 300,000 of them went out of business under Carter-Mondale.

In the span of but four devastating years, the Carter-Mondale Administration managed to jeopardize this country's agricultural heritage by putting America's farmers $78 billion further in debt (a 75 percent increase) and inflating farmers' annual food and fiber production costs by $46 billion (55 percent increase). These irresponsible inflationary policies led to spiraling land values and to the illusion of enhanced debt-bearing wealth. This paper wealth was converted into very real and unavoidable debt. Debt payments, combined with record cost of production levels, have presented many farmers and ranchers with severe cash flow problems. On top of all that came the Carter-Mondale grain embargo of 1980. Thus, one begins to understand the origins of the financial stress farmers and ranchers are experiencing today. Adding insult to injury, farmers and ranchers found themselves blamed as Carter-Mondale inflation ballooned consumer food costs by $115 billion, a 50 percent increase in four years.

Republicans support a sound agricultural credit policy, including the Farm Credit System, to meet agriculture's expanding credit needs. We support an extensive examination of agricultural and rural credit and crop insurance programs to assure they are adequately serving our farmers and rural residents.

Interest Rates and Farm and Ranch Indebtedness

The magnitude of indebtedness and the level of interest rates significantly influence farm and ranch profitability. The interrelationship between high interest rates and the high value of the dollar has caused an erosion in our competitive position in export markets. Republicans recognize that lower interest rates are vital to a healthy farm and ranch economy and pledge that an economic priority of the first order will be the further lowering of interest rates by intensifying our efforts to cut federal spending to achieve a balanced budget and reform Federal Reserve policy.

Republicans are very much aware of the devastating impact which high interest rates have had, and continue to have, on the viability of America's farmers and ranchers. We also realize that, unless interest rates decline significantly in the near future, the character of American agriculture and rural life will be tragically changed. For these reasons, we pledge to pursue every possible course of action, including the consideration of temporary interest rate reductions, to ensure the American farmer or rancher is not a patient that dies in the course of a successful economic operation.

Republicans are cognizant that there are many well-managed, efficient, farm and ranch operations which face bankruptcy and foreclosure. The foreclosures and resulting land sales will jeopardize the equity positions of neighboring farms and ranches, compounding financial problems in agriculture. Republicans pledge to implement comprehensive Farmers Home Administration and commercial farm and ranch debt restructuring procedures, including the establishment of local community farm and ranch finance committees, which shall advise borrowers, lenders, and government officials regarding debt restructuring alternatives and farmer and rancher eligibility.

Setting the Stage for Farm and Ranch Recovery

Sensitive to the needs of farmers and ranchers, we have made the best of the tools available to deal with the Carter-Mondale failure. Among the many specific accomplishments of the Reagan Administration in agriculture, Republicans are proud to have:

● Lifted the Carter-Mondale grain embargo and demonstrated by word and deed that farm and ranch product embargoes will not be used as a tool of foreign policy, negotiated a long term agreement with the Soviet Union, and strengthened our credibility as a reliable supplier by enacting contract sanctity legislation.

● Increased food assistance and agricultural export financing programs to over $7 billion, a record level.

● Challenged unfair export subsidy practices and aggressively countered them with "blended credit" and other export expansion programs.

● Achieved major breakthroughs in Japan's beef and citrus quotas, allowing our exports to double over four years.

● Resisted protectionist efforts by other industries, such as domestic content legislation, that would cause a backlash against U.S. farm and ranch exports.

● Developed and implemented the PIK program to draw down burdensome reserve stocks of major commodities created by the Carter-Mondale embargo.

● Reformed bankruptcy law to provide for accelerated distribution of farm products in bankrupt elevators, acceptance of warehouse receipts and scale tickets as proof of ownership, and allowing a lien against elevator assets for unpaid farmers.

● Eliminated the marriage penalty for a surviving spouse and protected family farms and ranches by exempting, by 1987, up to $600,000 from estate taxes.

● Accelerated depreciation of farm and ranch equipment and buildings and increased the exemption for agricultural vehicles from the heavy vehicle use tax.

● Increased the gasoline tax exemption by 50 percent for alcohol fuels, stimulating demand for domestic grain production and reducing dependency on foreign oil.

● Worked with rural credit and farm and ranch lending institutions to assure adequate capital at the lowest possible interest rates.

● Responded to the emergency financial needs of farmers and ranchers stricken by drought and flood.

We want real profits for farmers and ranchers. We have begun the turnaround on farm and ranch incomes. Sound fiscal, monetary, and growth-oriented tax policies are essential if farmers are to realize sufficient and enduring profits. We support legislation to permit farmers, ranchers, and other self-employed individuals to deduct from their gross income up to one-half of the cost of their personal hospitalization insurance premiums.

Government policies should strengthen the ability of farmers and ranchers to provide quality products at reasonable rates of return in an expanding economy. We believe that federal farm programs should be tailored to meet economic needs and requirements of today's structurally diverse and internationally oriented agriculture. These programs must be sensitive to potential impacts on all agriculture, especially non-program commodities, livestock, agribusiness and rural communities.

Republicans believe that the future of American agriculture lies in the utilization of our rich farmland, advanced technology, and hard working farm and ranch people, to supply food and fiber to the world. Traditional farm programs have threatened the confidence of America's farmers and ranchers and exhausted the patience of American taxpayers. We reject the policy of more of the same, and we further reject the Democrats' public utility vision of agriculture which views it as a problem to be minimized by further political and bureaucratic management. Our new programs will bring the flexibility to adjust to rapidly changing export market conditions and opportunities, and, in a timely and effective manner, respond to the inherent, uncontrollable risks of farming and ranching.

Rural Americans impart a special strength to our national character, important to us all. Whether farmers or not, all rural citizens should have the same consideration as those who live in towns and cities in economic development, energy, credit, transportation availability, and employment. Opportunities for non-farm jobs have become increasingly important to farm and ranch families, enhancing life and work in rural America.

Toward Fair and Expanded Markets and Responding to Hunger

Agriculture is an international advantage for the United States. But a successful farm and ranch policy demands earnest attention to building on the strength of our domestic production capacity and to developing world markets, for American agriculture cannot be prosperous without exports.

Our farmers and ranchers must have full access to world markets and should not have to face unfair export subsidies and predatory dumping by other producing nations without redress. Republicans believe that unfair trade practices and non-tariff barriers are so serious that a comprehensive renegotiation of multilateral trade arrangements must be undertaken to revitalize the free, fair, and open trade critical to worldwide economic growth.

The Republican Party is unalterably opposed to the use of embargoes of grain or other agricultural products as a tool of foreign policy. The Carter-Mondale grain embargo is still — more than any other factor — the cause of the present difficulties in American agriculture and possibly the irretrievable loss of foreign markets. Republicans say "Never again." The Democratic Platform says nothing.

America has a long history of helping those in need, and the responsibility for food assistance has been shared by federal and State governments and neighborhood volunteers. Federal expenditures in this area exceeded $19 billion in 1983, the highest amount ever. Numerous private and public efforts assure that adequate food is available. This expresses faith in our future and reflects our people's goodness.

We will provide adequate resources in programs ranging from food stamps to school lunches for the truly needy. We also recognize that fraud and abuse must be eliminated from those programs. We stress maximum local control consistent with national objectives.

Reducing Excessive Regulation in Agriculture

Excessive federal regulations, many imposed by the Carter-Mondale Administration, have been a crushing burden.

In 1980, we pledged to make sensible reductions in regulations that drained the profitability from farming, ranching, and commercial fishing. We did just that. We restored balance to the Interior Department's ineffective predator-control policies, and we moderated the EPA's and the FDA's excessive adherence to "zero risk" standards concerning the use of pesticides, antibiotics, food additives, and preservatives.

Republicans favor modernizing our food-safety laws, providing guidelines for risk-benefit assessment, peer review, and regulatory flexibility consistent with other health and safety policies.

Soil and Water Conservation

Agriculture must be both economically and environmentally sustainable. The soil and water stewardship of our farmers, ranchers, watermen, and rural people is commendable. Republicans believe that long-term soil, water, and other conservation policies, emphasizing environmentally sound agricultural productivity, rangeland protection, fish and wildlife habitat, and balanced forestry management, must be a top priority. Conservation practices must be intensified and integrated with farm programs to safeguard our most valuable resources. Volunteer participation, emphasizing State and local control and adequate incentives, is essential to effective conservation.

Water Policy

In 1980, we pledged a water policy which addressed our national diversity in climate, geography, reclamation needs, and patterns of land ownership. We promised a partnership between the States and federal government which would not destroy traditional State supremacy in water law, and which would avert a water crisis in the coming decades. That partnership is now working to meet these challenges.

The Future of Farming

American agriculture is the world's most successful because of the hard work and creativity of family farmers and ranchers. They have benefitted immensely from agricultural research, extension, and teaching, unequalled in the world. Cooperative extension, operating in every county, brings the results of USDA and Land Grant University research to rural America. We support these programs, with special attention to marketing efficiencies, reduced production costs, and new uses for farm and ranch commodities. We also encourage the establishment of regional international research and export trade centers.

Our agricultural people have developed the ideals of free enterprise and have based their enterprise on our culture's basic element, the family. The family farm and ranch is defined as a unit of agriculture production managed as an enterprise where labor and management have an equity interest in the business and a direct gain or loss from its operation. Family farms and ranches are the heart, soul, and backbone of American agriculture; it is the family farm that makes our system work better than any other.

Our rural and coastal people developed a great diversity of support organizations. They organized farm and ranch cooperatives, and rural electric and telephone cooperatives to provide essential services. They established farm and ranch organizations to work for better farm policies and to improve the quality of rural life. Republicans note with particular pride and enthusiasm the vital impact women have always had in American farming and ranching, and we support efforts to increase their role.

American agriculture has always relied upon the hardworking people who harvest seasonal and perishable crops. Republicans support comprehensive farm-labor legislation, fair to workers *and* employers, to protect consumers from work stoppages which disrupt the flow of food.

Republicans also recognize the tremendous efforts of commercial fishers to bring nutritious seafood products to market, thus strengthening America's food base.

Our agriculture is both a global resource and a tremendous opportunity. Only America possesses the natural, technological, management, and labor resources to commercially develop agriculture's next frontier.

We are encouraged by innovation in agriculture, and applaud its diversity, creativity, and enterprise. Commercial applications of new technology and marketing and management innovations are creating additional opportunities for farming and ranching. Republicans have set the stage for building a new prosperity into our fundamentally strong agricultural system. We renew our national commitment to American farmers and ranchers.

International Economic Policy

The recent tremendous expansion of international trade has increased the standard of living worldwide. Our strong economy is attracting investment in the United States, which is providing capital needed for new jobs, technology, higher wages, and more competitive products.

We are committed to a free and open international trading system. All Americans benefit from the free flow of goods, services and capital, and the efficiencies of a vigorous international market. We will work with all of our international trading partners to eliminate barriers to trade, both tariff and non-tariff. As a first step, we call on our trading partners to join in a new round of trade negotiations to revise the General Agreement on Tariffs and Trade in order to strengthen it. And we further call on our trading partners to join us in reviewing trade with totalitarian regimes.

But free trade must be fair trade. It works only when all trading partners accept open markets for goods, services, and investments. We will review existing trade agreements and vigorously enforce trade laws including assurance of access to all markets for our service industries. We will pursue domestic and international policies that will allow our American manufacturing and agricultural industries to compete in international markets. We will not tolerate the loss of American jobs to nationalized, subsidized, protected foreign industries, particularly in steel, automobiles, mining, footwear, textiles, and other basic industries. This production is sometimes financed with our own tax dollars through international institutions. We will work to stop funding of such projects that are detrimental to our own economy.

The greatest danger today to our international trade is a growing protectionist sentiment. Tremendous fluctuations in exchange rates have rendered long-term international contracts virtually useless. We therefore urge our trading partners to join us in evaluating and correcting the structural problems of the international monetary system, to base it on more stable exchange rates and free capital markets.

Further, we support reorganization of trade responsibilities in order to reduce overlap, duplication, and waste in the conduct of international trade and industry.

Revisions in that system will stabilize trade relations so that debtor nations can repay their debts. These debts are the direct result of their domestic policies, often mandated by multilateral institutions, combined with the breakdown of the international monetary system. Slower economic growth, reduced imports, and higher taxes will not relieve debt burdens, but worsen them. The only way to repay the debts is to create productive capacity to generate new wealth through economic expansion, as America has done.

Austerity should be imposed not on people, but on governments. Debtor nations seeking our assistance must increase incentives for growth by encouraging private investment, reducing taxes, and eliminating subsidies, price controls, and politically motivated development projects.

SECURITY FOR THE INDIVIDUAL

America was built on the institutions of home, family, religion, and neighborhood. From these basic building blocks came self-reliant individuals, prepared to exercise both rights and responsibilities.

In the community of individuals and families, every generation has relearned the art of self-government. In our neighborhoods, Americans have traditionally taken care of their needs and aided the less fortunate. In the process we developed, independent of government, the remarkable network of "mediating institutions" — religious groups, unions, community, and professional associations. Prominent among them have been innumerable volunteer groups, from fire departments and neighborhood-watch patrols to meals-on-wheels and the little leagues.

Public policy long ignored these foundations of American life. Especially during the two decades preceding Ronald Reagan's election, the federal government eroded their authority, ignored their rights, and attempted to supplant their functions with programs at once intrusive and ineffectual. It thereby disrupted our traditional patterns of caring, sharing, and helping. It elbowed out the voluntary providers of services and aid instead of working through them.

By centralizing responsibility for social programs in Washington, liberal experimenters destroyed the sense of community that sustains local institutions. In many cases, they literally broke up neighborhoods and devastated rural communities.

Washington's governing elite thought they knew better than the people how to spend the people's money. They played fast and loose with our schools, with law enforcement, with welfare, with housing. The results were declining literacy and learning, an epidemic of crime, a massive increase in dependency, and the slumming of our cities.

Worst of all, they tried to build their brave new world by assaulting our basic values. They mocked the work ethic. They scorned frugality. They attacked the integrity of the family and parental rights. They ignored traditional morality. And they still do.

Our 1980 Republican Platform offered a renewed vision. We based it upon home, family, and community as the surest guarantees of both individual rights and national greatness. We asserted, as we do now, the ethical dimension of public policy: the need to return to enduring principles of conduct and firm standards of judgment.

The American people responded with enthusiasm. They knew that our roots, in family, home, and neighborhood, do not tie us down. They give us strength. Once more we call upon our people to assert their supervision over government, to affirm their rights against government, to uphold their interests within government.

Housing and Homeownership

Homeownership is part of the American Dream. For the last two decades, that dream has been endangered by bad public policy. Government unleashed a dreadful inflation upon homebuyers, driving mortgage rates beyond the reach of average families, as the prime rate rose more than 300 percent (from 6.5 percent to 21.5 percent). The American worker's purchasing power fell every year from 1977 through 1980.

No wonder the housing industry was crippled. Its workers faced recurrent recessions. The boom-and-bust cycle made saving foolish, investment risky, and housing scarce.

Federal housing blighted stable low-income neighborhoods, disrupting communities which people had held together for generations. Only government could have wasted billions of dollars to create the instant slums which disgrace our cities.

In our 1980 Platform, we pledged to reverse this situation. We have begun to do so, despite obstructionism from those who believe that the taxpayer's home is government's castle.

We attacked the basic problem, not the symptoms. We cut tax rates and reduced inflation to a fraction of the Carter-Mondale years. The median price house that would cost $94,800 if Carter-Mondale inflation had continued now costs $74,200. The average monthly mortgage payment, which rose by $342 during the Carter-Mondale years, has increased just $24 since January 1981. The American Dream has made a comeback.

To sustain it, we must finish the people's agenda.

We reaffirm our commitment to the federal-tax deductibility of mortgage interest payments. In the States, we stand with those working to lower property taxes that strike hardest at the poor, the elderly, and large families. We stand, as well, with Americans earning possession of their homes through "sweat-equity" programs.

We will, over time, replace subsidies and welfare projects with a voucher system, returning public housing to the free market.

Despite billions of dollars poured into public housing developments, conditions remain deplorable for many low-income Americans who live in them. These projects have become breeding grounds for the very problems they were meant to eliminate. Their dilapidated and crumbling structures testify to decades of corrupt or incompetent management by poverty bureaucrats.

Some residents of public housing developments have reversed these conditions by successfully managing their own housing units through creative self-help efforts. It is abundantly clear that their pride of ownership has been the most important factor contributing to the efficiency of operation, enhancing the quality of housing, improving community morale, and providing incentives for their self-improvement.

The Republican Party therefore supports the development of programs which will lead to homeownership of public housing developments by current residents.

We strongly believe in open housing. We will vigorously enforce all fair housing laws and will not tolerate their distortion into quotas and controls.

Rent controls promise housing below its market cost but inevitably result in a shortage of decent homes. Our people should not have to underwrite any community which erodes its own housing supply by rent control.

Sound economic policy is good housing policy. In our expanding economy, where people are free to work and save, they will shelter their families without government intrusion.

Welfare

Helping the less fortunate is one of America's noblest endeavors, made possible by the abundance of our free and competitive economy. Aid should be swift and adequate to ensure the necessities of a decent life.

Over the past two decades, welfare became a nightmare for the taxpayer and the poor alike. Fraud and abuse were rampant. The costs of public assistance are astronomical, in large part because resources often benefit the welfare industry rather than the poor.

During the 1970s, the number of people receiving federal assistance increased by almost 300 percent, from 9 million to 35 million, while our population increased by only 11.4 percent. This was a fantastic and unsustainable universalization of welfare.

Welfare's indirect effects were equally bad. It became a substitute for urgently needed economic reforms to create more entry-level jobs. Government created a hellish cycle of dependency. Family cohesion was shattered, both by providing economic incentives to set up maternal households and by usurping the breadwinner's economic role in intact families.

The cruelest result was the maternalization of poverty, worsened by the breakdown of the family and accelerated by destructive patterns of conduct too long tolerated by permissive liberals. We endorse programs to assist female-headed households to build self-sufficiency, such as efforts by localities to enable participants to achieve permanent employment.

We have begun to clean up the welfare mess. We have dramatically reduced the poor's worst enemy — inflation — thereby protecting their purchasing power. Our resurgent economy has created over six million new jobs and reduced unemployment by 30 percent.

We have launched real welfare reforms. We have targeted benefits to the needy through tighter eligibility standards, enforced child-support laws, and encouraged "workfare" in the States. We gave States more leeway in managing welfare programs, more assistance with fraud con-

trol, and more incentives to hold down costs.

Only sustained economic growth, continuing our vigorous recovery, can give credible hope to those at the bottom of the opportunity ladder.

The working poor deserve special consideration, as do low-income families struggling to provide for their children. As part of comprehensive simplification of the federal tax code, we will restore the real value of their personal tax exemptions so that families, particularly young families, can establish their economic independence.

Federal administration of welfare is the worst possible, detached from community needs and careless with the public's money. Our long tradition of State and local administration of aid programs must be restored. Programs and resources must be returned to State and local governments and not merely exchanged with them. We will support block grants to combine duplicative programs under State administration.

We must also recognize and stimulate the talents and energy of low-income neighborhoods. We must provide new incentives for self-help activities that flow naturally when people realize they *can* make a difference. This is especially critical in foster care and adoption.

Because there are different reasons for poverty, our programs address different needs and must never be replaced with a unitary income guarantee. That would betray the interest of the poor and the taxpayers alike.

We will employ the latest technology to combat welfare fraud in order to protect the needy from the greedy.

Whenever possible, public assistance must be a transition to the world of work, except in cases, particularly with the aged and disabled, where that is not appropriate. In other cases, it is long overdue.

Remedying poverty requires that we sustain and broaden economic recovery, hold families together, get government's hand out of their pocketbooks, and restore the work ethic.

Health

Our tremendous investment in health care has brought us almost miraculous advances. Although costs are still too high, we have dramatically enhanced the length and quality of life for all.

Faced with Medicare and Medicaid mismanagement, government tried to ration health care through arbitrary cuts in eligibility and benefits. Meanwhile, inflation drove up medical bills for us all. Economic incentives were backwards, with little awareness of costs by individual patients. Reimbursement mechanisms were based on expenses incurred, rather than set prospectively. Conspicuously absent were free-market incentives to respond to consumer wishes. Instead, government's heavy hand was everywhere.

We narrowly averted disaster. We

moved creatively and carefully to restructure incentives, to free competition, to encourage flexible new approaches in the States, and to identify better means of health-care delivery. Applying these principles, we will preserve Medicare and Medicaid. We will eliminate the excesses and inefficiencies which drove costs unacceptably high in those programs. In order to assure their solvency and to avoid placing undue burdens on beneficiaries, reform must be a priority. The Republican Party reaffirms its commitment to assure a basic level of high quality health care for all Americans. We reaffirm as well our opposition to any proposals for compulsory national health insurance.

While Republicans held the line against government takeover of health care, the American people found private ways to meet new challenges. There has been a laudable surge in preventive health care and an emphasis upon personal responsibility for maintaining one's health. Compassionate innovation has developed insurance against catastrophic illness, and capitated "at risk" plans are encouraging innovation and creativity.

We will maintain our commitment to health excellence by fostering research into yet-unconquered diseases. There is no better investment we as a nation can make than in programs which hold the promise of sounder health and longer life. For every dollar we spend on health research, we save many more in health care costs. Thus, what we invest in medical research today will yield billions of dollars in individual productivity as well as savings in Medicare and Medicaid. The federal government has been the major source of support for biomedical research since 1945. That research effort holds great promise for combatting cancer, heart disease, brain disorders, mental illness, diabetes, Alzheimer's disease, sickle cell anemia and numerous other illnesses which threaten our nation's welfare. We commit to its continuance.

Many health problems arise within the family and should be dealt with there. We affirm the right and responsibility of parents to participate in decisions about the treatment of children. We will not tolerate the use of federal funds, taxed away from parents, to abrogate their role in family health care.

Republicans have secured for the hospice movement an important role in federal health programs. We must do more to enable persons to remain within the unbroken family circle. For those elderly confined to nursing homes or hospitals, we insist that they be treated with dignity and full medical assistance.

Discrimination in health care is unacceptable; we guarantee, especially for the handicapped, non-discrimination in the compassionate healing that marks American medicine.

Government must not impose cumbersome health planning that causes major delays, increases construction costs, and stifles competition. It should not unduly delay the approval of new medicines, nor adhere to outdated safety standards hindering rapidly advancing technology.

We must address ailments, not symptoms, in health-care policy. Drug and alcohol abuse costs thousands of lives and billions of dollars every year. We reaffirm our vigorous commitment to alcohol and drug abuse prevention and education efforts. We salute the citizens' campaign, launched from America's grassroots, against drunk driving. We applaud those States which raised the legal drinking age.

Much illness, especially among the elderly, is related to poor nutrition. The reasons are more often social than economic: isolation, separation from family, and often a mismatch between nutritional needs and available assistance. This reinforces our efforts to protect federal nutrition programs from fraud and abuse, so that their benefits can be concentrated upon the truly needy.

A supportive environment linking family, home, neighborhood, and workplace is essential to sound health policy. The other essential step is to encourage the individual responsibility and group assistance that are uniquely American.

Environment

It is part of the Republican philosophy to preserve the best of our heritage, including our natural resources. The environment is not just a scientific or technological issue; it is a human one. Republicans put the needs of people at the center of environmental concerns. We assert the people's stewardship of our God-given natural resources. We pledge to meet the challenges of environmental protection, economic growth, regulatory reform, enhancement of our scenic and recreational areas, conservation of our non-renewable resources, and preservation of our irreplaceable natural heritage.

Americans were environmentalists long before it became fashionable. Our farmers cared for the earth and made it the world's most bountiful. Our families cared for their neighborhoods as an investment in our children's future. We pioneered the conservation that replenished our forests, preserved our wildlife, and created our national park system.

The American people have joined together in a great national effort to protect the promise of our future by conserving the rich beauty and bounty of our heritage. As a result, by almost any measure, the air is cleaner than it was 10 years ago, and fish are returning to rivers where they had not been seen for generations.

Within the last four years, dramatic progress has been made in protecting coastal barrier islands, and we began the Park Preservation and Restoration Program to restore the most celebrated symbols of our heritage. We support programs to restore and protect the nation's estuaries, wetland resources, and beaches.

The Republican Party endorses a strong effort to control and clean up toxic wastes. We have already tripled funding to clean up hazardous waste dumps, quadrupled funding for acid rain research, and launched the rebirth of the Chesapeake Bay.

The environmental policy of our nation originated with the Republican Party under the inspiration of Theodore Roosevelt. We hold it a privilege to build upon the foundation which we have laid. The Republican Party supports the continued commitment to clean air and clean water. This support includes the implementation of meaningful clean air and clean water acts. We will continue to offer leadership to reduce the threat to our environment and our economy from acid rain, while at the same time preventing economic dislocation.

Even as many environmental problems have been brought under control, new ones have been detected. And all the while, the growth and shifts of population and economic expansion, as well as the development of new industries, will further intensify the competing demands on our national resources.

Continued progress will be much more difficult. The environmental challenges of the 1980s are much more complex than the ones we tried to address in the 1970s, and they will not yield quickly to our efforts. As the science and administration of environmental protection have become more sophisticated, we have learned of many subtle and potentially more dangerous threats to public health and the environment.

In setting out to find solutions to the environmental issues of the 1980s and 1990s, we start with a healthy appreciation of difficulties involved. Detecting contamination, assessing the threat, correcting the damage, setting up preventive measures, all raise questions of science, technology, and public policy that are as difficult as they are important. However, the health and well being of our citizens must be a high priority.

The number of people served by waste water treatment systems has nearly doubled just since 1970. The federal government should offer assistance to State and local governments in planning for the disposal of solid and liquid wastes. A top priority nationwide should be to eliminate the dumping of raw sewage.

We encourage recycling of materials and support programs which will allow our economic system to reward resource conservation.

We also commit ourselves to the development of renewable and efficient energy sources and to the protection of endangered or threatened species of plants and wildlife.

We will be responsible to future generations, but at the same time, we must remember that quality of life means more than protection and preservation. As Teddy Roosevelt put it, "Conservation means development as much as it does protection." Quality of life also means a good job, a decent place to live, accommodation for a growing population, and the continued economic and technological development essential to our standard of living, which is the envy of the whole world.

Transportation

America's overall transportation system is unequalled. Generating over 20 percent of our GNP and employing one of every nine people in the work force, it promotes the unity amid diversity that uniquely characterizes our country. We travel widely, and we move the products of field and factory more efficiently and economically than any other people on earth.

And yet, four years ago, the future of American transportation was threatened. Over several decades, its vigor and creativity had been stunted by the intrusion of government regulation. The results were terribly expensive, and consumers paid the price. Our skies and highways were becoming dangerous and congested. With the same vision that marked President Eisenhower's beginning of the Interstate Highway System, the Reagan Administration launched a massive modernization of America's transport systems.

An expanded highway program is rebuilding the nation's roads and bridges and creating several hundred thousand jobs in construction and related fields. Driving mileage has increased by 8 percent, but greater attention to safety has led to a 17 percent reduction in fatalities, saving more than 8,000 lives yearly.

In public transit, we have redefined the federal role to emphasize support for capital investment, while restoring day-to-day responsibility to local authorities.

Our National Airspace Plan is revolutionizing air traffic control. It will improve flight safety and double the nation's flight capacity, providing better air service and stimulating economic growth.

Regulatory reform is revitalizing American transportation. Federal agencies had protected monopolies by erecting regulatory barriers that hindered the entry of new competitors. Small businesses and minority enterprises were virtually excluded. Prices were set, not by the public through free exchange, but by Washington clerks through green eyeshades.

Republicans led the successful fight to break government's stranglehold. The deregulation of airline economics (not their safety!) will be completed on December 30, 1984, when the Civil Aeronautics Board closes its doors forever. Through our regulatory reform efforts, the rail and trucking industries are now allowed to compete in both price and service. We also led the fight to deregulate interstate bus operations by enacting the Bus Regulatory Reform Act of 1982. While returning to a more free and competitive marketplace, we have ensured that small communities in rural America will retain necessary services through transitional assistance like the Essential Air Service Program, which will continue for four more years.

The Shipping Act of 1984 secured the first major reform of maritime law, as it applies to the U.S. liner trade, since 1916.

This major step introduces genuine competition to the maritime industry, while enhancing our ability to compete against international cartels. Important in peacetime, critical in times of conflict, one of our proudest industries had long been neglected. We have expanded employment and brought hope of a future worthy of its past. The Reagan defense program now provides more work for our shipyards than at any time since World War II. We seek to halt the decline of our commercial fleet and restore it to economic strength and strategic capacity to fulfill its national obligations. We also seek to maximize the use of our nation's existing port facilities and shipbuilding and repair capability as a vital transportation resource that should be preserved in the best long-term interest of this country.

The American people benefit from regulatory reform. Air travelers now have a remarkable range of options, and flight is within reach of the average family budget. In the trucking business, increased competition has lowered prices and improved service.

The future of America's freight rail system is again bright. As a result of our reforms, the major private railroads have climbed back to profitability. Government red tape caused their red ink; by cutting the former, we are wiping out the latter. In addition, we transformed Conrail from a multi-billion dollar drain on the taxpayers into an efficient, competitive freight railroad. Returning Conrail as a financially sound single entity to private ownership, with service and jobs secure, will provide the nation with an improved rail freight system to promote economic growth. It will also return to the Treasury a significant portion of the taxpayers' investment, virtually unheard of for a federal project. We support improved passenger rail service where economically justified. We have made substantial progress in reducing the taxpayers' subsidy to Amtrak while maintaining services for which there is genuine demand. The Reagan Administration is selling the Alaska Railroad to the State of Alaska and transferring Conrail's commuter lines to the jurisdictions they serve.

The Republican Party believes that the nation's long-term economic growth will depend heavily on the adequacy of its public works infrastructure. We will continue to work to reverse the long-term decline that has occurred. We should foster development of better information on the magnitude and effectiveness of current federal, State and local government capital expenditures and innovative financing mechanisms which would improve our capacity to leverage limited federal funds more effectively.

America's leadership in space depends upon the vitality of free enterprise. That is why we encourage a commercial space-transportation industry. We share President Reagan's vision of a permanent manned space station within a decade, viewing it as the first stepping stone toward creating a multi-billion dollar private

economy in space. The permanent presence of man in space is crucial both to developing a visionary program of space commercialization and to creating an opportunity society on Earth of benefit to all mankind. We are, after all, the people who hewed roads out of the wilderness. Our families crossed ocean, prairie, and desert no less dangerous than today's space frontier to reach a new world of opportunity. And every route they took became a highway of liberty. Like them, we know where we are going: forward, toward a future in our hands. Because of them, and because of us, our children's children will use space transportation to build both prosperity and peace on earth.

Education and Youth

Our children are our hope and our future. For their sake, President Reagan has led a national renewal to get back to the "basics" and excellence in education. Young people have turned away from the rebellion of the 1960s and the pessimism of the 1970s. Their hopeful enthusiasm speaks better for a bright future than any government program.

During the Reagan Administration, we restored education to prominence in public policy. This change will clearly benefit our youth and our country. By using the spotlight of the Oval office, the Reagan Administration turned the nation's attention to the quality of education and gave its support to local and State improvement efforts. Parents and all segments of American society responded overwhelmingly to the findings of the National Commission on Excellence in Education, appointed by President Reagan. Its report, along with others from prominent experts and foundations, provided the impetus for educational reform.

Ronald Reagan's significant and innovative leadership has encouraged and sustained the reform movement. He catapulted education to the forefront of the national agenda and will be remembered as a president who improved education.

Unlike the Carter-Mondale Democrats, Republicans have levelled with parents and students about the problems we face together. We find remedies to these problems in the common sense of those most concerned: parents and local leaders. We support the decentralization necessary to put education back on the right track. We urge local school communities, including parents, teachers, students, administrators, and business and civic leaders, to evaluate school curricula — including extra-curricular activities and the time spent in them — and their ultimate effect upon students and the learning process. We recognize the need to get "back to basics" and applaud the dramatic improvements that this approach has already made in some jurisdictions.

In schools, school districts, and States throughout our land, the past year and one-half has been marked by unprecedented response to identified education deficiencies. *The Nation Responds*, a recent report by the Reagan Administration, referred to a "tidalwave of school reform which promises to renew American education." According to that report:

● Forty-eight States are considering new high school graduation requirements and 35 have approved changes.

● Twenty-one States report initiatives to improve textbooks and instructional material.

● Eight States have approved lengthening the school day, seven are lengthening the school year, and 18 have mandates affecting the amount of time for instruction.

● Twenty-four States are examining master teacher or career ladder programs, and six have begun statewide or pilot programs.

● Thirteen States are considering changes in academic requirements for extra-curricular and athletic programs, and five have already adopted more rigorous standards.

Education is a matter of choice, and choice in education is inevitably political. All of education is a passing on of ideas from one generation to another. Since the storehouse of knowledge is vast, a selection must be made of what to pass on. Those doing the selecting bring with them their own politics. Therefore, the more centralized the selection process, the greater the threat of tyranny. The more diversified the selection process, the greater the chance for a thriving free marketplace of ideas as the best insurance for excellence in education.

We believe that education is a local function, a State responsibility, and a federal concern. The federal role in education should be limited. It includes helping parents and local authorities ensure high standards, protecting civil rights, and ensuring family rights. Ignoring that principle, from 1965 to 1980, the United States indulged in a disastrous experiment with centralized direction of our schools. During the Carter-Mondale Administration, spending continued to increase, but test scores steadily declined.

This decline was not limited to academic matters. Many schools lost sight of their traditional task of developing good character and moral discernment. The result for many was a decline in personal responsibility.

The key to the success of educational reform lies in accountability: for students, parents, educators, school boards, and all governmental units. All must be held accountable in order to achieve excellence in education. Restoring local control of education will allow parents to resume the exercise of their responsibility for the basic education, discipline, and moral guidance of their children.

Parents have the primary right and responsibility for the education of their children; and States, localities, and private institutions have the primary responsibility for supporting that parental role. America has been a land of opportunity because America has been a land of learning. It has

given us the most prosperous and dynamic society in the world.

The Republican Party recognizes the importance of good teachers, and we acknowledge the great effort many put forth to achieve excellence in the classroom. We applaud their numerous contributions and achievements in education. Unfortunately, many teachers are exhausted by their efforts to support excellence and elect to leave the classroom setting. Our best teachers have been frustrated by lowered standards, widespread indifference, and compensation below the true value of their contribution to society. In 1980-81 alone, 4 percent of the nation's math and science teachers quit the classroom. To keep the best possible teachers for our children, we support those education reforms which will result in increased student learning, including appropriate class sizes, appropriate and adequate learning and teaching materials, appropriate and consistent grading practices, and proper teacher compensation, including rewarding exceptional efforts and results in the classroom.

Classroom materials should be developed and produced by the private sector in the public marketplace, and then selections should be made at the State, local, and school levels.

We commend those States and local governments that have initiated challenging and rigorous high school programs, and we encourage all States to take initiatives that address the special educational needs of the gifted and talented.

We have enacted legislation to guarantee equal access to school facilities by student religious groups. Mindful of our religious diversity, we reaffirm our commitment to the freedoms of religion and speech guaranteed by the Constitution of the United States and firmly support the rights of students to openly practice the same, including the right to engage in voluntary prayer in schools.

While much has been accomplished, the agenda is only begun. We must complete the block-grant process begun in 1981. We will return revenue sources to State and local governments to make them independent of federal funds and of the control that inevitably follows.

The Republican Party believes that developing the individual dignity and potential of disabled Americans is an urgent responsibility. To this end, the Republican Party commits itself to prompt and vigorous enforcement of the rights of disabled citizens, particularly those rights established under the Education for All Handicapped Children Act, Section 504 of the Rehabilitation Act of 1973, and the Civil Rights of Institutionalized Persons Act. We insist on the highest standards of quality for services supported with federal funds.

In addition, government should seek out disabled persons and their parents to make them knowledgeable of their rights. We will work toward providing federal funds to State and local governments sufficient to meet the degree of fiscal participation already promised in law.

We are committed to excellence in education for all our children within their own communities and neighborhoods. No child should be assigned to, or barred from, a school because of race.

In education, as in other activities, competition fosters excellence. We therefore support the President's proposal for tuition tax credits. We will convert the Chapter One grants to vouchers, thereby giving poor parents the ability to choose the best schooling available. Discrimination cannot be condoned, nor may public policies encourage its practice. Civil rights enforcement must not be twisted into excessive interference in the education process.

Teachers cannot teach and students cannot learn in an undisciplined environment. We applaud the President's promise to provide protection to teachers and administrators against suits from the unruly few who seek to disrupt the education of the overwhelming majority of students.

We urge the aggressive enforcement of the Protection of Pupil Rights amendment (also known as the Hatch Amendment, 20 U.S.C. 1232h) in order to protect pupils' and parents' rights. The amendment prohibits requiring any pupil to reveal personal or family information as part of any federally supported program, test, treatment, or psychological examination unless the school first obtains written consent of the pupil's parents.

The recent Grove City and Hillsdale College cases have raised questions about the extension of federal interference with private colleges, universities, and schools. Since federal aid, no matter how indirect, is now being linked to nearly every aspect of American life, great care must be taken in defining such terms as "federal financial assistance," "indirect" assistance, and "recipient" of assistance. We are deeply concerned that this kind of federal involvement in the affairs of some of the nation's fine private universities, colleges, and schools, many of which have remained stubbornly free of federal entanglements, can only bring with it unintended results. As the historical party of Lincoln and individual rights, we support enactment of legislation which would ensure protection of those covered under Title IX.

We urge States to establish partnerships with the scientific and business worlds to increase the number of teachers in these critical areas of learning. We also recognize a vast reservoir of talent and experience among retirees and other Americans competent to teach in these areas and ready to be tapped.

We endorse experiments with education such as enterprise zones and Cities-in-Schools. We reaffirm our commitment to wipe out illiteracy in our society. Further, we encourage the Congress and the States to reassess the process for aiding education, awarding funds on the basis of academic improvement rather than on daily attendance.

We are aware that good intentions do not always produce the desired results. We therefore urge our schools to evaluate their sex education programs to determine their impact on escalating teenage pregnancy rates. We urge that school officials take appropriate action to ensure parent involvement and responsibility in finding solutions to this national dilemma.

We support and encourage volunteerism in the schools. President Reagan's Adopt-a-School program is an example of how private initiative can revitalize our schools, particularly inner-city schools, and we commend him for his example.

Our emphasis on excellence includes the nation's colleges and universities. Although their achievements are unequalled in the world — in research, in proportion of citizens enrolled, in their contribution to our democratic society — we call upon them for accountability in good teaching and quality curricula that will ensure competent graduates in the world of work.

We pledge to keep our colleges and universities strong. They have been far too dependent on federal assistance and thus have been tied up in federal red tape. Their independence is an essential part of our liberty. Through regulatory reform, we are holding down the costs of higher education and reestablishing academic freedom from government. This is especially important for small schools, religious institutions, and the historically black colleges, for which President Reagan's Executive Order 12320 has meant new hope and vigor. We further reaffirm and support a regular Black College Day which honors a vital part of our educational community.

Republicans applaud the information explosion. This literacy-based knowledge revolution, made possible by computers, tapes, television, satellites, and other high technology innovations, buttressed by training programs through the business sector and foundations, is a tribute to American ingenuity. We urge our schools to educate for the ever-changing demands of our society and to resist using these innovations as substitutes for reasoning, logic, and mastery of basic skills.

We encourage excellence in the vocational and technical education that has contributed to the self-esteem and productivity of millions. We believe the best vocational and technical education programs are rooted in strong academic fundamentals. Business and industry stand ready to establish training partnerships with our schools. Their leadership is essential to keep America competitive in the future.

In an age when individuals may have four or five different jobs in their working career, vocational education and opportunities for adult learning will be more important than ever. The challenge of learning for citizenship and for work in an age of change will require new adaptations and innovations in the process of education. We urge the teaching profession and educational institutions at all levels to develop the maximum use of new learning opportu-

nities available through learning-focused high technology. This technology in education and in the workplace is making possible, and necessary, the continuing education of our adult population. The participation by adults in educational offerings within their communities will strengthen the linkages among the places where Americans live, work, and study.

Important as technology is, by itself it is inadequate for a free society. The arts and humanities flourish in the private sector, where a free market in ideas is the best guarantee of vigorous creativity. Private support for the arts and humanities has increased over the last four years, and we encourage its growth.

We support the National Endowments for the Arts and Humanities in their efforts to correct past abuses and focus on developing the cultural values that are the foundation of our free society. We must ensure that these programs bring the arts and humanities to people in rural areas, the inner city poor, and other underserved populations.

Crime

One of the major responsibilities of government is to ensure the safety of its citizens. Their security is vital to their health and to the well-being of their neighborhoods and communities. The Reagan Administration is committed to making America safe for families and individuals. And Republican programs are paying dividends.

For the first time in the history of recorded federal crime statistics, rates of serious crime have dropped for two consecutive years. In 1983, the overall crime rate dropped 7 percent; and in 1982, the overall crime rate dropped 3 percent. In 1982 (the latest year for which figures are available), the murder rate dropped 5 percent, the robbery rate was down 6 percent, and forcible rape dropped 5 percent. Property crimes also declined: burglary decreased 9 percent, auto theft declined 2 percent, and theft dropped 1 percent.

Republicans believe that individuals are responsible for their actions. Those who commit crimes should be held strictly accountable by our system of justice. The primary objective of the criminal law is public safety; and those convicted of serious offenses must be jailed swiftly, surely, and long enough to assure public safety.

Republicans respect the authority of State and local law enforcement officials. The proper federal role is to provide strong support and coordination for their efforts and to vigorously enforce federal criminal laws. By concentrating on repeat offenders, we are determined to take career criminals off the street.

Additionally, the federal law enforcement budget has been increased by nearly 50 percent. We added 1,900 new investigators and prosecutors to the federal fight against crime. We arrested more offenders and sent more of them to prison. Convic-

tions in organized crime cases have tripled under the Reagan Administration. We set up task forces to strike at organized crime and narcotics. In the year since, 3,000 major drug traffickers have been indicted, and nearly 1,000 have already been convicted. We are helping local authorities search for missing children. We have a tough new law against child pornography. Republicans initiated a system for pooling information from local, State and federal law enforcement agencies: the Violent Criminal Apprehension Program (VI-CAP). Under this program, State and local agencies have the primary law enforcement responsibility, but cross-jurisdictional information is shared rapidly so that serial murderers and other violent criminals can be identified quickly and then apprehended.

Under the outstanding leadership of President Reagan and Vice President Bush's Task Force on Organized Crime, the Administration established the National Narcotics Border Interdiction System. We set up an aggressive Marijuana Eradication and Suppression Program, gave the FBI authority to investigate drugs, and coordinated FBI and DEA efforts. We reaffirm that the eradication of illegal drug traffic is a top national priority.

We have levelled with the American people about the involvement of foreign governments, especially Communist dictators, in narcotics traffic: Cuba, the Soviet Union, Bulgaria — and now the Sandinistas in Nicaragua — are international "pushers," selling slow death to young Americans in an effort to undermine our free society.

The Republican Party has deep concern about gratuitous sex and violence in the entertainment media, both of which contribute to the problem of crime against children and women. To the victims of such crimes who need protection, we gladly offer it.

We have begun to restore confidence in the criminal justice system. The Carter-Mondale legal policy had more concern for abstract criminal rights than for the victims of crime. It hurt those least able to defend themselves: the poor, the elderly, school children, and minorities. Republican leadership has redressed that imbalance. We have advanced such reforms as restitution by convicted criminals to their victims; providing victims with full explanations of what will occur before, during, and after trial; and assuring that they may testify at both trial and sentencing.

The Republican Senate has twice passed, with one dissenting vote, a comprehensive federal anti-crime package which would:

● Establish uniform, predictable and fair sentencing procedures, while abolishing the inconsistencies and anomalies of the current parole system;

● Strengthen the current bail procedures to allow the detention of dangerous criminals, who under current law are allowed to roam the streets pending trial;

● Increase dramatically the penalties for narcotic traffickers and enhance the ability of society to recoup ill-gotten gains from drug trafficking;

- Narrow the overly broad insanity defense; and
- Provide limited assistance to states and localities for the implementation of anti-crime programs of proven effectiveness.

In addition, the Republican Senate has overwhelmingly passed Administration-backed legislation which would:

- Restore a federal constitutionally valid federal death penalty;
- Modify the exclusionary rule in a way recently approved by the Supreme Court; and
- Curtail abuses by prisoners of federal *habeas corpus* procedures.

The Democrat bosses of the House of Representatives have refused to allow a vote on our initiatives by the House Judiciary Committee, perennial graveyard for effective anti-crime legislation, or by the full House despite our pressure and the public's demand.

The best way to deter crime is to increase the probability of detection and to make punishment certain and swift. As a matter of basic philosophy, we advocate preventive rather than merely corrective measures. Republicans advocate sentencing reform and secure, adequate prison construction. We concur with the American people's approval of capital punishment where appropriate and will ensure that it is carried out humanely.

Republicans will continue to defend the constitutional right to keep and bear arms. When this right is abused and armed felonies are committed, we believe in stiff, mandatory sentencing. Law-abiding citizens exercising their constitutional rights must not be blamed for crime. Republicans will continue to seek repeal of legislation that restrains innocent citizens more than violent criminals.

Older Americans

We reaffirm our commitment to the financial security, physical well-being, and quality of life of older Americans. Valuing them as a treasure of wisdom and experience, we pledge to utilize their unique talents to the fullest.

During the Carter-Mondale years, the silent thief of inflation ruthlessly preyed on the elderly's savings and benefits, robbing them of their retirement dollars and making many dependent on government handouts.

No more. Due to the success of Reaganomics, a retiree's private pension benefits are worth almost $1,000 more than if the 1980 inflation rate had continued. Average monthly Social Security benefits have increased by about $180 for a couple and by $100 a month for an individual. Because President Reagan forged a hard-won solution to the Social Security crisis, our elderly will not be repeatedly threatened with the program's impending bankruptcy as they were under the irresponsible policies of the Carter-Mondale Administra-

tion. We will work to repeal the Democrats' Social Security earnings-limitation, which penalizes the elderly by taking one dollar of their income for every two dollars earned.

Older Americans are vital contributors to society. We will continue to remove artificial barriers which discourage their participation in community life. We reaffirm our traditional opposition to mandatory retirement.

For those who are unable to care for themselves, we favor incentives to encourage home-based care.

We are combatting insidious crime against the elderly, many of whom are virtual prisoners in their own homes for fear of violence. We demand passage of the President's Comprehensive Crime Control package, stalled by the Democrat-controlled House Judiciary Committee. We support local initiatives to fight crime against the elderly.

Older Americans want to contribute, to live with the dignity and respect they have earned, and to have their special needs recognized. The Republican Party must never turn its back on our elderly, and we ensure that we will adequately provide for them during their golden years so they can continue to enjoy our country's high standard of living, which their labors have helped provide.

Advancing Opportunity

Throughout this Platform are initiatives to provide an opportunity ladder for the poor, particularly among minorities, in both urban and rural areas. Unlike the Carter-Mondale Administration that locked them into the welfare trap, Republicans believe compassion dictates our offering real opportunities to minorities and the urban poor to achieve the American Dream.

We have begun that effort; and as a pledge of its continuance, this Platform commits us, not to a war of class against class, but to a crusade for prosperity for all.

For far too long, the poor have been trapped by the policies of the Democratic Party which treat those in the ghetto as if their interests were somehow different from our own. That is unfair to us all and an insult to the needy. Their goals are ours; their aspirations we share.

To emphasize our common bond, we have addressed their needs in virtually every section of this Platform, rather than segregating them in a token plank. To those who would see the Republican future for urban America, and for those who deserve a better break, we offer the commitments that make up the sinew of this Platform.

Congress must pass enterprise zones, to draw a green line of prosperity around the red-lined areas of our cities and to help create jobs and entrepreneurial opportunities.

We offer the boldest breakthrough in housing policy since VA mortgages: we offer opportunities for private ownership of housing projects by the poor themselves.

We pledge comprehensive tax reform

that will give America back what was its post-war glory: a pro-family tax code with a dramatic work incentive for low-income and welfare families.

We offer hope, not despair; more opportunities for education through vouchers and tuition tax relief; and increased participation in the private enterprise system through the reform of counterproductive taxes and regulations.

Together with our emphatic commitment to civil rights, Republican programs will achieve, for those who feel left out of our society's progress, what President Reagan has already secured for our country: a new beginning to move America to full employment and honest money for all.

A FREE AND JUST SOCIETY

In 1980, the Republican Party offered a vision of America's future that applied our traditions to today's problems. It is the vision of a society more free and more just than any in history. It required a break with the worn-out past, to redefine the role of government and its relationship with individuals and their institutions. Under President Reagan's leadership, the American people are making that vision a reality.

The American people want an opportunity society, not a welfare state. They want government to foster an environment in which individuals can develop their potential without hindrance.

The Constitution is the ultimate safeguard of individual rights. As we approach the Constitutional Bicentennial in 1987, Republicans are restoring its vitality, which had been transgressed by Democrats in Congress, the executive, and in the courts.

We are renewing the federal system, strengthening the States, and returning power to the people. That is the surest course to our common goal: a free and just society.

Individual Rights

The Republican Party is the party of equal rights. From its founding in 1854, we have promoted equality of opportunity.

The Republican Party reaffirms its support of the pluralism and freedom that have been part and parcel of this great country. In so doing, it repudiates and completely disassociates itself from people, organizations, publications, and entities which promulgate the practice of any form of bigotry, racism, anti-semitism, or religious intolerance.

Americans demand a civil rights policy premised on the letter of the Civil Rights Act of 1964. That law requires equal rights; and it is our policy to end discrimination on account of sex, race, color, creed, or national origin. We have vigorously enforced civil rights statutes. The Equal Employment Opportunity Commission has recovered record amounts of back pay and other compensation for victims of employment discrimination.

Just as we must guarantee opportunity, we oppose attempts to dictate results. We will resist efforts to replace equal rights with discriminatory quota systems and preferential treatment. Quotas are the most insidious form of discrimination: reverse discrimination against the innocent. We must always remember that, in a free society, different individual goals will yield different results.

The Republican Party has an historic commitment to equal rights for women. Republicans pioneered the right of women to vote, and our party was the first major party to advocate equal pay for equal work, regardless of sex.

President Reagan believes, as do we, that all members of our party are free to work individually for women's progress. As a party, we demand that there be no detriment to that progress or inhibition of women's rights to full opportunity and advancement within this society.

Participation by women in policy-making is a strong commitment by the Republican Party and by President Reagan. He pledged to appoint a woman to the United States Supreme Court. His promise was not made lightly; and when a vacancy occurred, he quickly filled it with the eminently qualified Sandra Day O'Connor of Arizona.

His Administration has also sought the largest number of women in history to serve in appointive positions within the executive branch of government. Three women serve at Cabinet level, the most ever in history. Jeane Kirkpatrick, the U.S. Representative to the United Nations, Elizabeth Dole, Secretary of Transportation, and Margaret Heckler, Secretary of Health and Human Services, head a list of over 1,600 women who direct policy and operations of the federal government.

The Republican Party continues to search for interested and qualified women for all government positions. We will continue to increase the number of first-time appointments for women serving in government at all levels.

Our record of economic recovery and growth is an additional important accomplishment for women. It provides a stark contrast to the Carter-Mondale legacy to women: a shrinking economy, limited job opportunities, and a declining standard of living.

Whether working in or outside the home, women have benefitted enormously from the economic progress of the past four years. The Republican economic expansion added over six million new jobs to the economy. It increased labor force participation by women to historic highs. Women's employment has risen by almost four and one-half million since the last Carter-Mondale year. They obtained almost one million more new jobs than men did. Economic growth due to Republican economic policies has produced a record number of jobs so that women who want to work outside the home now have unmatched opportunity. In fact, more than 50 percent of all women now have jobs outside the home.

The spectacular decline in inflation has immeasurably benefitted women working both in and outside the home. Under President Reagan, the cost increase in everyday essentials — food, clothing, housing, utilities — has been cut from the Carter-Mondale highs of over 10 percent a year to just over 4 percent today. We have ushered in an era of price stability that is stretching take-home pay hundreds of dollars farther. In 1982, for the first time in 10 years, women experienced a real increase in wages over inflation.

Lower interest rates have made it possible for more women, single and married, to own their homes and to buy their own automobiles and other consumer goods.

Our 25 percent reduction in marginal tax rates provided important benefits to women, as did the virtual elimination of the "widow's tax" which had jeopardized retirement savings of senior women. At the same time, we raised the maximum child care tax credit from $400 to $720 per family. We will continue to actively seek the elimination of discrimination against homemakers with regard to Individual Retirement Accounts so that single-income couples can invest the same amount in IRAs as two-income couples.

In addition, President Reagan has won enactment of the Retirement Equity Act of 1984. That legislation, strongly supported by congressional Republicans, makes a comprehensive reform of private pension plans to recognize the special needs of women.

Our record of accomplishment during the last four years is clear, but we intend to do even better over the next four.

We will further reduce the "marriage penalty," a burden upon two-income, working families. We will work to remove artificial impediments in business and industry, such as occupational licensing laws, that limit job opportunities for women, minorities, and youth or prevent them from entering the labor force in the first place.

For low-income women, the Reagan Administration has already given States and localities the authority, through the Job Training Partnership Act, to train more recipients of Aid to Families with Dependent Children for permanent, not make-work, jobs. We have increased child support collections from $1.5 billion to $2.4 billion and enacted a strong child support enforcement law. We will continue to stress welfare reforms which promote individual initiative, the real solution to breaking the cycle of welfare dependency.

With women comprising an increasing share of the work force, it is essential that the employment opportunities created by our free market system be open to individuals without regard to their sex, race, religion, or ethnic origin. We firmly support an equal opportunity approach which gives women and minorities equal access to all jobs — including the traditionally higher-paying technical, managerial, and professional positions — and which guarantees that workers in those jobs will be compensated in accord with the laws requiring

equal pay for equal work under Title VII of the Civil Rights Act.

We are creating an environment in which individual talents and creativity can be tapped to the fullest, while assuring that women have equal opportunity, security, and real choices for the promising future. For all Americans, we demand equal pay for equal work. With equal emphasis, we oppose the concept of "comparable worth." We believe that the free market system can determine the value of jobs better than any government authority.

The Department of Justice has identified 140 federal statutes with gender-based distinctions. Proposed legislation will correct all but 18; six are still under study; the rest, which actually favor women, will remain as is. President Reagan's Fifty States Project, designed to identify State laws discriminating against women, has encouraged 42 States to start searches, and 26 have begun amending their laws. The Department has filed more cases dealing with sex discrimination in employment than were filed during a comparable period in the Carter-Mondale Administration.

Working with Republicans in Congress, President Reagan has declared 1983-1992 the Decade of Disabled Persons. All Americans stand to gain when disabled citizens are assured equal opportunity.

The Reagan Administration has an outstanding record in achieving accessibility for the handicapped. During the past two years, minimum guidelines have at last been adopted, and the Uniform Federal Accessibility Standard has become fact.

The Republican Party realizes the great potential of members of the disabled community in this country. We support all efforts being made at the federal level to remove artificial barriers from our society so that disabled individuals may reach their potential and participate at the maximum level of their abilities in education, employment, and recreation. This includes the removal, in so far as practicable, of architectural, transportation, communication and attitudinal barriers. We also support efforts to provide disabled Americans full access to voting facilities.

We deplore discrimination because of handicap. The Reagan Administration was the first to combat the insidious practice of denying medical care or even food and water to disabled infants. This issue has vast implications for medical ethics, family autonomy, and civil rights. But we find no basis, whether in law or medicine or ethics, for denying necessities to an infant because of the child's handicap.

We are committed to enforcing statutory prohibitions barring discrimination against any otherwise qualified handicapped individuals, in any program receiving federal financial assistance, solely by reason of their handicap.

We recognize the need for watchful care regarding the procedural due process rights of persons with handicaps both to prevent their placement into inappropriate programs or settings and to ensure that their rights are represented by guardians or other advocates, if necessary.

For handicapped persons who need care, we favor family-based care where possible, supported by appropriate and adequate incentives. We increased the tax credit for caring for dependents or spouses physically or mentally unable to care for themselves. We also provided a deduction of up to $1,500 per year for adopting a child with special needs that may otherwise make adoption difficult.

We are committed to seeking out gifted children and their parents to make them knowledgeable of their educational rights.

We reaffirm the right of all individuals freely to form, join, or assist labor organizations to bargain collectively, consistent with State laws and free from unnecessary government involvement. We support the fundamental principle of fairness in labor relations. We will continue the Reagan Administration's "open door" policy toward organized labor and its leaders. We reaffirm our long-standing support for the right of States to enact "Right-to-Work" laws under section 14(b) of the Taft-Hartley Act.

The political freedom of every worker must be protected. Therefore, we strongly oppose the practice of using compulsory dues and fees for partisan political purposes. Also, the protection of all workers must be secured. Therefore, no worker should be coerced by violence or intimidation by any party to a labor dispute.

The healthy mix of America's ethnic, cultural, and social heritage has always been the backbone of our nation and its progress throughout our history. Without the contributions of innumerable ethnic and cultural groups, our country would not be where it is today.

For millions of black Americans, Hispanic Americans, Asian Americans, and members of other minority groups, the past four years have seen a dramatic improvement in their ability to secure for themselves and for their children a better tomorrow.

That is the American Dream. The policies of the Reagan Administration have opened literally millions of doors of opportunity for these Americans, doors which either did not exist or were rapidly being slammed shut by the no-growth policies of the Carter-Mondale Administration.

We Republicans are proud of our efforts on behalf of all minority groups, and we pledge to do even more during the next four years.

We will continue to press for enactment of economic and social policies that promote growth and stress individual initiative of minority Americans. Our tax system will continue to be overhauled and reformed by making it fairer and simpler, enabling the families of minorities to work and save for their future. We will continue to push for passage of enterprise zone legislation, now bottled up in the Democrat-controlled House of Representatives. That bill, discussed elsewhere in this platform, will help minority Americans living in cities and urban areas to get jobs, to start their own businesses, and to reap the fruits of entrepreneurship by tapping their individual initiative, energy, and creativity.

We honor and respect the contributions of minority Americans and will do all we can to see that our diversity is enhanced during the next four years. Active contributions by minorities are the threads that weave the fabric that is America and make us stronger as a nation. We recognize these individuals and their contributions and will continue to promote the kinds of policies that will make their dreams for a better America a reality. The party of Lincoln will remain the party of equal rights for all.

We continue to favor whatever legislation may be necessary to permit American citizens residing in the Virgin Islands, Guam, and Puerto Rico to vote for president and vice president in national elections.

We support the right of Indian Tribes to manage their own affairs and resources. Recognizing the government-to-government trust responsibility, we are equally committed to working towards the elimination of the conditions of dependency produced by federal control. The social and economic advancement of Native Americans depends upon changes they will chart for themselves. Recognizing their diversity, we support the President's policy of responsibly removing impediments to their self-sufficiency. We urge the nations of the Americas to learn from our past mistakes and to protect native populations from exploitation and abuse.

Native Hawaiians are the only indigenous people of our country who are not officially designated as Native Americans. They should share that honored title. We endorse efforts to preserve their culture as a unique element in the human tapestry that is America.

Family Protection

Republicans affirm the family as the natural and indispensable institution for human development. A society is only as strong as its families, for they nurture those qualities necessary to maintain and advance civilization.

Healthy families inculcate values — integrity, responsibility, concern for others — in our youth and build social cohesion. We give high priority to their well-being. During the 1970s, America's families were ravaged by worsening economic conditions and a Washington elite unconcerned with them.

We support the concept of creating Family Education Accounts which would allow tax-deferred savings for investment in America's most crucial asset, our children, to assist low- and middle-income families in becoming self-reliant in meeting the costs of higher education.

In addition, to further assist the young families of America in securing the dream of homeownership, we would like to review the concept of Family Housing Accounts which would allow tax-exempt savings for a family's first home.

Preventing family dissolution, a leading cause of poverty, is vital. It has had a particularly tragic impact on the elderly, women, and minorities. Welfare programs have devastated low-income families and induced single parenthood among teens. We will review legislation and regulations to examine their impact on families and on parental rights and responsibilities. We seek to eliminate incentives for family break-up and to reverse the alarming rate of pregnancy outside marriage. Meanwhile, the Republican Party believes that society must do all that is possible to guarantee those young parents the opportunity to achieve their full educational and parental potential.

Because of Republican tax cuts, single people and married people without dependents will have in 1984 basically the same average tax rates they had in 1960. The marriage penalty has been reduced. However, a couple with dependents still pays a greater portion of their income in taxes than in 1960. We reaffirm that the personal exemption for children be no less than for adults, and we will at least double its current level. The President's tax program also increased tax credits for child care expenses. We will encourage private sector initiatives to expand on-site child care facilities and options for working parents.

The problem of physical and sexual abuse of children and spouses requires careful consideration of its causes. In particular, gratuitous sex and violence in entertainment media contribute to this sad development.

We and the vast majority of Americans are repulsed by pornography. We will vigorously enforce constitutional laws to control obscene materials which degrade everyone, particularly women, and depict the exploitation of children. We commend the Reagan Administration for creating a commission on pornography and the President for signing the new law to eliminate child pornography. We stand with our President in his determination to solve the problem.

We call upon the Federal Communications Commission, and all other federal, State, and local agencies with proper authority, to strictly enforce the law regarding cable pornography and to implement rules and regulations to clean up cable pornography and the abuse of telephone service for obscene purposes.

Immigration

Our history is a story about immigrants. We are proud that America still symbolizes hope and promise to the world. We have shown unparalleled generosity to the persecuted and to those seeking a better life. In return, they have helped to make a great land greater still.

We affirm our country's absolute right to control its borders. Those desiring to enter must comply with our immigration laws. Failure to do so not only is an offense to the American people but it is fundamentally unjust to those in foreign lands patiently waiting for legal entry. We will preserve the principle of family reunification.

With the estimates of the number of illegal aliens in the United States ranging as high as 12 million and better than one million more entering each year, we believe it is critical that responsible reforms of our immigration laws be made to enable us to regain control of our borders.

The flight of oppressed people in search of freedom has created pressures beyond the capacity of any one nation. The refugee problem is global and requires the cooperation of all democratic nations. We commend the President for encouraging other countries to assume greater refugee responsibilities.

Our Constitutional System

Our Constitution, now almost 200 years old, provides for a federal system, with a separation of powers among the three branches of the national government. In that system, judicial power must be exercised with deference towards State and local officials; it must not expand at the expense of our representative institutions. It is not a judicial function to reorder the economic, political, and social priorities of our nation. The intrusion of the courts into such areas undermines the stature of the judiciary and erodes respect for the rule of law. Where appropriate, we support congressional efforts to restrict the jurisdiction of federal courts.

We commend the President for appointing federal judges committed to the rights of law-abiding citizens and traditional family values. We share the public's dissatisfaction with an elitist and unresponsive federal judiciary. If our legal institutions are to regain respect, they must respect the people's legitimate interests in a stable, orderly society. In his second term, President Reagan will continue to appoint Supreme Court and other federal judges who share our commitment to judicial restraint.

The Republican Party firmly believes that the best governments are those most accountable to the people. We heed Thomas Jefferson's warning: "When all government, in little as in great things, shall be drawn to Washington as the center of all power, it will render powerless the checks provided of one government on another."

For more responsible government, non-essential federal functions should be returned to the States and localities wherever prudent. They have the capability, knowledge, and sensitivity to local needs required to better administer and deliver public services. Their diverse problems require local understanding. The transfer of rights, responsibilities, and revenues to the "home front" will recognize the abilities of local government and the limitations of a distant federal government.

We commend the President for the bold initiatives of his "New Federalism." The enacted block grants discussed else-where in this Platform are a positive step. But the job of making government more accountable to the people has just begun. We strongly favor the expansion of block-grant funding and other means to restore our nation's federal foundation.

More than 40 years ago, a grave injustice was done to many Americans of Japanese ancestry. Uprooted from their homes in a time of crisis, loyal citizens and residents were treated in a way which contravened the fundamental principles of our people. We join them and their descendants in assuring that the deprivation of rights they suffered shall never again be permitted in this land of liberty.

To benefit all Americans, we support the privatization of government services whenever possible. This maximizes consumer freedom and choice. It reduces the size and cost of government, thus lessening the burden on taxpayers. It stimulates the private sector, increases prosperity, and creates jobs. It demonstrates the primacy of individual action which, within a free market economy, can address human needs most effectively.

Within the executive branch, the Reagan Administration has made government work more efficiently. Under the direction of the Office of Personnel Management, non-defense government employment was reduced by over 100,000. The overwhelming majority of federal employees are dedicated and hard-working. Indeed, we have proposed to base their pay and retention upon performance so that outstanding federal employees may be properly rewarded.

The federal government owns almost a third of our nation's land. With due recognition of the needs of the federal government and mindful of environmental, recreational, and national defense needs, we believe the sale of some surplus land will increase productivity and increase State and local tax bases. It will also unleash the creative talents of free enterprise in defense of resource and environmental protection.

The expression of individual political views is guaranteed by the First Amendment; government should protect, not impinge upon First Amendment rights. Free individuals must have unrestricted access to the process of self-government. We deplore the growing labyrinth of bewildering regulations and obstacles which have increased the power of political professionals and discouraged the participation of average Americans. Even well-intentioned restrictions on campaign activity stifle free speech and have a chilling effect on spontaneous political involvement by our citizens.

The holding of public office in our country demands the highest degree of commitment to integrity, openness, and honesty by candidates running for all elective offices. Without such a commitment, public confidence rapidly erodes. Republicans, therefore, reaffirm our commitment to the fair and consistent application of financial disclosure laws. We will continue our support for full disclosure by all high officials of the government and candidates in positions of public trust. This extends to the financial holdings of spouses or dependents, of which the official has knowledge, financial interest, or benefit. We will continue to hold all public officials to the highest ethical standards and will oppose the inconsistent application of those standards on the basis of gender.

Republicans want to encourage, not restrict, free discourse and association. The interplay of concerned individuals, sometimes acting collectively to pursue their goals, has led to healthy and vigorous debate and better understanding of complex issues. We will remove obstacles to grass-roots participation in federal elections and will reduce, not increase, the federal role.

Republicans believe that strong, competitive political parties contribute mightily to coherent national policies, effective representation, and responsive government. Forced taxpayer financing of campaign activities is political tyranny. We oppose it.

In light of the inhibiting role federal election laws and regulations have had, Congress should consider abolishing the Federal Election Commission.

We are the party of limited government. We are deeply suspicious of the amount of information which governments collect. Governments limited in size and scope best ensure our people's privacy. Particularly in the computer age, we must ensure that no unnecessary information is demanded and that no disclosure is made which is not approved. We oppose national identification cards.

We support reasonable methods to fight those who undermine national security, prevent crosschecks of government benefit records to conceal welfare fraud, or misuse financial secrecy laws to hide their narcotics profits under the guise of a right to privacy.

Private property is the cornerstone of our liberty and the free enterprise system. The right of property safeguards for citizens all things of value: their land, merchandise and money, their religious convictions, their safety and liberty, and their right of contract to produce and sell goods and services. Republicans reaffirm this God-given and inalienable right.

The unborn child has a fundamental individual right to life which cannot be infringed. We therefore reaffirm our support for a human life amendment to the Constitution, and we endorse legislation to make clear that the Fourteenth Amendment's protections apply to unborn children. We oppose the use of public revenues for abortion and will eliminate funding for organizations which advocate or support abortions. We commend the efforts of those individuals and religious and private organizations that are providing positive alternatives to abortion by meeting the physical, emotional, and financial needs of pregnant women and offering adoption services where needed.

We applaud President Reagan's fine record of judicial appointments, and we reaffirm our support for the appointment of judges at all levels of the judiciary who respect traditional family values and the sanctity of innocent human life.

AMERICA SECURE AND THE WORLD AT PEACE

The Future of Our Foreign Policy

President Reagan has restored the American people's faith in the principles of liberal democracy. Today, we have more confidence in the self-evident truths of democracy than at any time since World War II.

The first principle of that faith is that all human beings are created equal in the natural human right to govern themselves.

Just as we assert the right of self-government, it follows that all people throughout the world should enjoy that same human right. This moral principle must be the ideal by which our policy toward other nations is directed.

We Republicans emphasize that there is a profound moral difference between the actions and ideals of Marxist-Leninist regimes and those of democratic governments, and we reject the notions of guilt and apology which animate so much of the foreign policy of the Democratic Party. We believe American foreign policy can only succeed when it is based on unquestioned faith in a single idea: the idea that all human beings are created equal, the founding idea of democracy.

The supreme purpose of our foreign policy must be to maintain our freedom in a peaceful international environment in which the United States and our allies and friends are secure against military threats, and democratic governments are flourishing in a world of increasing prosperity.

This we pledge to our people and to future generations: we shall keep the peace by keeping our country stronger than any potential adversary.

The Americas

Our future is intimately tied to the future of the Americas. Family, language, culture, and trade link us closely with both Canada, our largest trading partner, and our southern neighbors.

The people of both Mexico and Canada are of fundamental importance to the people of the United States of America, not just because we share a common border, but because we are neighbors who share both history and a common interest for the present and future. Under President Reagan, our relations with both countries are being carried out in a serious, straight-forward manner in a climate of mutual respect. As our countries seek solutions to common problems on the basis of our mutual interests, we recognize that each country has a unique contribution to make in working together to resolve mutual problems.

The security and freedom of Central America are indispensable to our own. In addition to our concern for the freedom and overall welfare of our neighbors to the south, two-thirds of our foreign trade passes through the Caribbean and the Panama Canal. The entire region, however, is gravely threatened by Communist expansion, inspired and supported by the Soviet Union and Cuba. We endorse the principles of the Monroe Doctrine as the strongest foundation for United States policy throughout the hemisphere.

We encourage even closer ties with the countries of South America and consider the strengthening of representative governments there as a contribution to the peace and security of us all. We applaud the Organization of American States for its efforts to bring peace and freedom to the entire hemisphere.

Republicans have no illusions about Castro's brutal dictatorship in Cuba. Only our firmness will thwart his attempts to export terrorism and subversion, to destroy democracy, and to smuggle narcotics into the United States. But we also extend a constructive, hopeful policy toward the Cuban people. Castro resents and resists their desire for freedom. He fears Radio Marti, President Reagan's initiative to bring truth to our Cuban neighbors. He is humiliated by the example of Cuban-born Americans, whose spiritual and material accomplishments contrast starkly with Communist failures in their birthplace. We believe in friendship between the Cuban and the American peoples, and we envision a genuine democracy in Cuba's future.

We support the President in following the unanimous findings of the Bipartisan Commission on Central America, first proposed by the late Senator Henry "Scoop" Jackson of Washington.

Today, democracy is under assault throughout the hemisphere. Marxist Nicaragua threatens not only Costa Rica and Honduras, but also El Salvador and Guatemala. The Sandinista regime is building the largest military force in Central America, importing Soviet equipment, Eastern bloc and PLO advisers, and thousands of Cuban mercenaries. The Sandinista government has been increasingly brazen in its embrace of Marxism-Leninism. The Sandinistas have systematically persecuted free institutions, including synagogue and church, schools, the private sector, the free press, minorities, and families and tribes throughout Nicaragua. We support continued assistance to the democratic freedom fighters in Nicaragua. Nicaragua cannot be allowed to remain a Communist sanctuary, exporting terror and arms throughout the region. We condemn the Sandinista government's smuggling of illegal drugs into the United States as a crime against American society and international law.

The heroic effort to build democracy in El Salvador has been brutally attacked by Communist guerrillas supported by Cuba and the Sandinistas. Their violence jeopardizes improvements in human rights, delays economic growth, and impedes the consolidation of democracy. El Salvador is nearer to Texas than Texas is to New England, and we cannot be indifferent to its fate. In the tradition of President Truman's postwar aid to Europe, President Reagan has helped the people of El Salvador defend themselves. Our opponents object to that assistance, citing concern for human rights. We share that concern, and more than that, we have taken steps to help curb abuses. We have firmly and actively encouraged human rights reform, and results have been achieved. In judicial reform, the murderers of the American nuns in 1980 have been convicted and sentenced; and in political reform, the right to vote has been exercised by 80 percent of the voters in the fair, open elections of 1982 and 1984. Most important, if the Communists seize power there, human rights will be extinguished, and tens of thousands will be driven from their homes. We, therefore, support the President in his determination that the Salvadoran people will shape their own future.

We affirm President Reagan's declaration at Normandy: there is a profound moral difference between the use of force for liberation and the use of force for conquest and territorial expansion. We applaud the liberation of man and mind from oppression everywhere.

We applaud the liberation of Grenada, and we honor those who took part in it. Grenada is small, and its people few; but we believe the principle established there, that freedom is worth defending, is of monumental importance. It challenges the Brezhnev doctrine. It is an example to the world.

The Caribbean Basin Initiative is a sound program for the strengthening of democratic institutions through economic development based on free people and free market principles. The Republican Party strongly supports this program of integrated, mutually reinforcing measures in the fields of trade, investment, and financial assistance.

We recognize our special-valued relationship with Puerto Rico and the Virgin Islands; and we will support special measures to ensure that they will benefit and prosper from the Caribbean Basin Initiative, thereby reinforcing a stronghold of democracy and free enterprise in the Caribbean. The Republican Party reaffirms its support of the right of Puerto Rico to be admitted into the Union after it freely so determines, through the passage of an admission bill which will provide for a smooth fiscal transition, recognize the concept of a multicultural society for its citizens, and secure the opportunity to retain their Spanish language and traditions.

The Soviet Union

Stable and peaceful relations with the Soviet Union are possible and desirable, but they depend upon the credibility of American strength and determination. As our power waned in the 1970s, our very weakness was provocative. The Soviets exploited it in Afghanistan, the Middle East, Africa, Southeast Asia, and the Western Hemisphere. Our policy of peace through strength encourages freedom-loving people everywhere and provides hope for those who look forward one day to enjoying the fruits of self-government.

We hold a sober view of the Soviet Union. Its globalist ideology and its leadership obsessed with military power make it a threat to freedom and peace on every continent. The Carter-Mondale Administration ignored that threat, and the Democratic candidates underestimate it today. The Carter-Mondale illusion that the Soviet leaders share our ideals and aspirations is not only false but a profound danger to world peace.

Republicans reaffirm our belief that Soviet behavior at the negotiating table cannot be divorced from Soviet behavior elsewhere. Over-eagerness to sign agreements with the Soviets at any price, fashionable in the Carter-Mondale Administration, should never blind us to this reality. Any future agreement with the Soviets must require full compliance, be fully verifiable, and contain suitable sanctions for non-compliance. Carter-Mondale efforts to cover up Soviet violations of the 1972 Strategic Arms Limitations agreement and Anti-ballistic Missile Treaty emboldened the Soviets to strengthen their military posture. We condemn these violations, as well as recent violations of chemical and toxic weapons treaties in Afghanistan, Southeast Asia, and the Iran-Iraq war. We insist on full Soviet compliance with all treaties and executive agreements.

We seek to deflect Soviet policy away from aggression and toward peaceful international conduct. To that end, we will seek substantial reductions in nuclear weapons, rather than merely freezing nuclear weapons at their present dangerous level. We will continue multilateral efforts to deny advanced Western technology to the Soviet war machine.

We will press for Soviet compliance with all international agreements, including the 1975 Helsinki Final Act and the U.N. Declaration on Human Rights. We will continue to protest Soviet anti-semitism and human rights violations. We admire the courage of such people as Andrei Sakharov, his wife Yelena Bonner, Anatole Shcharansky, Ida Nudel and Josef Begun, whose defiance of Soviet repression stands as a testament to the greatness of the human spirit. We will press the Soviet Union to permit free emigration of Jews, Christians, and oppressed national minorities. Finally, because the peoples of the Soviet empire share our hope for the future, we will strengthen our information channels to encourage them in their struggle for individual freedom, national self-determination, and peace.

Europe

Forty years after D-Day, our troops remain in Europe. It has been a long watch, but a successful one. For four decades, we have kept the peace where, twice before, our valiant fought and died. We learned from their sacrifice.

We would be in mortal danger were Western Europe to come under Soviet domination. Fragmenting NATO is the immediate objective of the Soviet military buildup and Soviet subversion. During the Carter-Mondale years, the Soviets gained a substantial military and diplomatic advantage in Europe. They now have three times as many tanks as we do and almost a monopoly on long-range theater nuclear forces. To keep the peace, the Reagan-Bush Administration is offsetting the Soviet military threat with the defensive power of the Alliance. We are deploying Pershing II and Cruise missiles. Remembering the Nazi Reich, informed voters on both sides of the Atlantic know they cannot accept Soviet military superiority in Europe. That is why the British, Italian, and West German parliaments have approved Euromissile deployments, and why new NATO base agreements were concluded successfully in Portugal, Spain, Turkey, and Greece. This is a victory for the Reagan-Bush Administration and our European friends.

The United States again leads the Alliance by offering hope of a safer future. As America's strength is restored, so is our allies' confidence in the future of freedom. We will encourage them to increase their contributions to our common defense.

To strengthen NATO's Southern Flank, we place the highest priority on resolving the Cyprus dispute and maintaining our support for both Greece and Turkey, with non-recognition of regimes imposed in occupied territory. We share a deep concern for peace and justice in Northern Ireland and condemn all violence and terrorism in that strife-torn land.

We stand in solidarity with the peoples of Eastern Europe: the Poles, Hungarians, East Germans, Czechs, Rumanians, Yugoslavs, Bulgarians, Ukrainians, Baltic peoples, Armenians, and all captive nations who struggle daily against their Soviet masters. The heroic efforts of Lech Walesa and the Solidarity movement in Poland are an inspiration to all people yearning to be free. We are not neutral in their struggle, wherever the flame of liberty brightens the black night of Soviet oppression.

The tragic repression of the Polish people by the Soviet-inspired military dictatorship in Poland has touched the American people. We support policies to provide relief for Polish nationals seeking asylum and refuge in the United States.

The Middle East

President Reagan's Middle East policy has been flexible enough to adapt to rapidly changing circumstances, yet consistent and credible so that all nations recognize our determination to protect our vital interests. The President's skillful crisis management throughout the Iran-Iraq war has kept that conflict from damaging our vital interests. His peace efforts have won strong bipartisan support and international applause. And his willingness to stand up to Libya has made peace-loving states in the region feel more secure.

The 1979 Soviet invasion of Afghanistan, which surprised the Carter-Mondale Administration, brought Soviet forces less than 400 miles from the strategic Straits of Hormuz. The seizure of American hostages in Iran that year caught the United States unprepared and unable to respond. Lebanon is still in turmoil, despite our best efforts to foster stability in that unhappy country. With the Syrian leadership increasingly subject to Soviet influence, and the Palestine Liberation Organization and its homicidal subsidiaries taking up residence in Syria, U.S. policy toward the region must remain vigilant and strong. Republicans reaffirm that the United States should not recognize or negotiate with the PLO so long as that organization continues to promote terrorism, rejects Israel's right to exist, and refuses to accept U.N. Resolutions 242 and 338.

The bedrock of that protection remains, as it has for over three decades, our moral and strategic relationship with Israel. We are allies in the defense of freedom. Israel's strength, coupled with United States assistance, is the main obstacle to Soviet domination of the region. The sovereignty, security, and integrity of the state of Israel are moral imperatives. We pledge to help maintain Israel's qualitative military edge over its adversaries.

Today, relations between the United States and Israel are closer than ever before. Under President Reagan, we have moved beyond mere words to extensive political, military, and diplomatic cooperation. U.S.-Israeli strategic planning groups are coordinating our joint defense efforts, and we are directly supporting projects to augment Israel's defense industrial base. We support the legislation pending for an Israel-U.S. free trade area.

We recognize that attacks in the U.N. against Israel are but thinly disguised attacks against the United States, for it is our shared ideals and democratic way of life that are their true target. Thus, when a U.N. agency denied Israel's right to participate, we withheld our financial support until that action was corrected. And we have worked behind the scenes and in public in other international organizations to defeat discriminatory attacks against our ally.

Our determination to participate actively in the peace process begun at Camp David has won us support over the past four years from moderate Arab states. Israel's partner in the Camp David accords, Egypt, with American support, has been a constructive force for stability. We pledge continued support to Egypt and other moderate regimes against Soviet and Libyan subversion, and we look to them to contribute to our efforts for a long-term settlement of the region's destructive disputes.

We believe that Jerusalem should remain an undivided city with free and unimpeded access to all holy places by people of all faiths.

Asia and the Pacific

Free Asia is a tremendous success. Emulating the United States economically and politically, our friends in East Asia have had the world's highest economic growth rates. Their economies represent the dynamism of free markets and free people, in stark contrast to the dreary rigidity and economic failures of centrally planned socialism. U.S. investments in Asia now exceed $30 billion, and our annual trade surpasses that with any other region.

Unable to match this progress, the Soviet Union, North Korea, and Vietnam threaten the region with military aggression and political intimidation. The Soviet rape of Afghanistan, the criminal destruction of the KAL airliner, the genocide in Vietnam, Cambodia and Laos, the steady growth of Soviet SS-20 forces in East Asia, the rapid increase of the Soviet Pacific Fleet, the continuing build-up of North Korean forces and the brutal bombing of South Korean leaders in Rangoon, the recent deployment of Soviet forces at Cam Ranh Bay, the continued occupation of Cambodia by the Vietnamese, and chemical and biological weapons attacks against defenseless civilian populations in Afghanistan and Southeast Asia are some of the more obvious threats to the peace of Asia and to America's friends there.

Republicans salute the brave people of Afghanistan, struggling to regain their freedom and independence. We will continue to support the freedom fighters and pledge our continuing humanitarian aid to the thousands of Afghan refugees who have sought sanctuary in Pakistan and elsewhere.

To preserve free Asia's economic gains and enhance our security, we will continue economic and security assistance programs with the frontline states of Korea, Thailand, and Pakistan. We will maintain defense facilities in Korea, Japan, the Philippines, and the Indian Ocean to protect vital sea lanes.

We will promote economic growth while we strengthen human rights and the commitment to both democracy and free markets. We will help friendly nations deal with refugees and secure their help against drug cultivation and trafficking.

Our relations with Japan are central to America's role in the Far East, and they have never been better. The world's second-largest industrial power can make an increasingly important contribution to peace and economic development over much of Asia. We applaud Japan's commitment to defend its territory, air space, and sea lanes. We are heartened by its increases in defense spending and urge Japan to further expand its contribution to the region's defense. We have made progress in our trade relations and affirm that, with good will on both sides, broader agreement is likely.

In keeping with the pledge of the 1980 Platform, President Reagan has continued the process of developing our relationship with the People's Republic of China. We commend the President's initiatives to build a solid foundation for the long-term relations between the United States and the People's Republic, emphasizing peace-

ful trade and other policies to promote regional peace. Despite fundamental differences in many areas, both nations share an important common objective: opposition to Soviet expansionism.

At the same time, we specifically reaffirm our concern for, and our moral commitment to, the safety and security of the 18 million people on Taiwan. We pledge that this concern will be constant, and we will continue to regard any attempt to alter Taiwan's status by force as a threat to regional peace. We endorse, with enthusiasm, President Reagan's affirmation that it is the policy of the United States to support and fully implement the provisions of the Taiwan Relations Act. In addition, we fully support self determination for the people of Hong Kong.

The Republic of Korea is a stalwart ally. To deter aggression, we will maintain our forces there which contribute to our common defense. Our growing economic relations are good for both countries and enhance our influence to foster a democratic evolution there.

We prize our special relationship with the Philippines. We will make every effort to promote the economic development and democratic principles they seek. Because the Clark and Subic Bay bases are vital to American interests in the Western Pacific, we are committed to their continued security.

We recognize the close and special ties we have maintained with Thailand since the days of Abraham Lincoln. Thailand stands tall against the imperialist aggression of Vietnam and the Soviet Union in Southeast Asia.

We hail the economic achievements of the Association of Southeast Asian Nations. We will strengthen economic and political ties to them and support their opposition to the Vietnamese occupation of Cambodia.

Almost a decade after our withdrawal from Vietnam, thousands of Americans still do not know the fate of their fathers, brothers, and sons missing in action. Our united people call upon Vietnam and Laos with one voice: return our men, end the grief of the innocent, and give a full accounting of our POW-MIAs. We will press for access to investigate crash sites throughout Indochina. We support the efforts of our private citizens who have worked tirelessly for many years on this issue.

Africa

Africa faces a new colonialism. The tripartite axis of the Soviet Union, Cuba, and Libya has unleashed war and privation upon the continent. We are committed to democracy in Africa and to the economic development that will help it flourish. That is why we will foster free-market, growth-oriented, and liberalized trading policies.

As part of reforming the policies of the International Development Association, we have assisted in directing a larger proportion of its resources to sub-Saharan Africa. To nurture the spirit of individual initia-

tive in Africa, our newly created African Development Foundation will work with African entrepreneurs at the village level. In addition, through our rejection of the austerity programs of international organizations, we are bringing new hope to the people of Africa that they will join in the benefits of the growing, dynamic world economy.

We will continue to provide necessary security and economic assistance to African nations with which we maintain good relations to help them develop the infrastructure of democratic capitalism so essential to economic growth and individual accomplishment. We will encourage our allies in Europe and east Asia to coordinate their assistance efforts so that the industrialized countries will be able to contribute effectively to the economic development of the continent. We believe that, if given the choice, the nations of Africa will reject the model of Marxist state-controlled economies in favor of the prosperity and quality of life that free economies and free people can achieve.

We will continue to assist threatened African governments to protect themselves and will work with them to protect their continent from subversion and to safeguard their strategic minerals. The Reagan-Bush Administration will continue its vigorous efforts to achieve Namibian independence and the expulsion of Cubans from occupied Angola.

We reaffirm our commitment to the rights of all South Africans. Apartheid is repugnant. In South Africa, as elsewhere on the continent, we support well-conceived efforts to foster peace, prosperity, and stability.

Foreign Assistance and Regional Security

Developing nations look to the United States for counsel and guidance in achieving economic opportunity, prosperity, and political freedom. Democratic capitalism has demonstrated, in the United States and elsewhere, an unparalleled ability to achieve political and civil rights and long-term prosperity for ever-growing numbers of people. We are confident that democracy and free enterprise can succeed everywhere. A central element in our programs of economic assistance should be to share with others the beneficial ideas of democratic capitalism, which have led the United States to economic prosperity and political freedom.

Our bilateral economic assistance program should be directed at promoting economic growth and prosperity in developing nations. Therefore, we support recently enacted legislation untying our programs from the policies of austerity of international organizations such as the International Monetary Fund.

We have changed the Carter-Mondale policy of channeling increasing proportions of U.S. assistance through multinational institutions beyond our control. We strongly support President Reagan's decision not to increase funding for the International Development Association because of its predilection for nations with state-dominated economic systems. Our contribution to the International Fund for Agricultural Development will be eliminated due to its consistent bias toward non-market economies. And the anti-American bureaucracy of the U.N.'s Educational, Scientific and Cultural Organization (UNESCO) will no longer be supported by U.S. taxpayers. We will not support international organizations inconsistent with our interests. In particular, we will work to eliminate their funding of Communist states.

Prominent among American ideals is the sanctity of the family. Decisions on family size should be made freely by each family. We support efforts to enhance the freedom of such family decisions. We will endeavor to assure that those who are responsible for our programs are more sensitive to the cultural needs of the countries to which we give assistance.

As part of our commitment to the family and our opposition to abortion, we will eliminate all U.S. funding for organizations which in any way support abortion or research on abortion methods.

To strengthen bilateral foreign assistance, we will reduce or eliminate assistance to nations with foreign policies contrary to our interests and strengthen the Secretary of State's hand by ensuring his direct control over assistance programs.

Foreign military assistance strengthens our security by enabling friendly nations to provide for their own defense, including defense against terrorism.

Terrorism is a new form of warfare against the democracies. Supported by the Soviet Union and others, it ranges from PLO murder to the attempted assassination of the Pope. Combatting it requires an integrated effort of our diplomacy, armed forces, intelligence services, and law-enforcement organizations. Legislative obstacles to international cooperation against terrorism must be repealed, followed by a vigorous program to enhance friendly nations' counter-terrorist forces. In particular, we seek the cooperation of our hemispheric neighbors to deal comprehensively with the Soviet and Cuban terrorism now afflicting us.

International Organizations

Americans cannot count on the international organizations to guarantee our security or adequately protect our interests. The United States hosts the headquarters of the United Nations, pays a fourth of its budget, and is proportionally the largest contributor to most international organizations; but many members consistently vote against us. As Soviet influence in these organizations has grown, cynicism and the double standard have become their way of life.

This is why President Reagan announced that we will leave the worst of these organizations, UNESCO. He has put the U.N. on notice that the U.S. will strongly oppose the use of the U.N. to foster anti-semitism, Soviet espionage, and hostility to the United States. The President decisively rejected the U.N. Convention on the Law of the Sea and embarked instead on a dynamic national oceans policy, animated by our traditional commitment to freedom of the seas. That pattern will be followed with regard to U.N. meddling in Antarctica and outer space. Enthusiastically endorsing those steps, we will apply the same standards to all international organizations. We will monitor their votes and activities, and particularly the votes of member states which receive U.S. aid. Americans will no longer silently suffer the hypocrisy of many of these organizations.

Human Rights

The American people believe that United States foreign policy should be animated by the cause of human rights for all the world's peoples.

A well-rounded human rights policy is concerned with specific individuals whose rights are denied by governments of the right or left, and with entire peoples whose Communist governments deny their claim to human rights as individuals and acknowledge only the "rights" derived from membership in an economic class. Republicans support a human rights policy which includes both these concerns.

Republican concern for human rights also extends to the institutions of free societies — political parties, the free press, business and labor organizations — which embody and protect the exercise of individual rights. The National Endowment for Democracy and other instruments of U.S. diplomacy foster the growth of these vital institutions.

By focusing solely on the shortcomings of non-Communist governments, Democrats have missed the forest for the trees, failing to recognize that the greatest threat to human rights is the Communist system itself.

Republicans understand that the East-West struggle has profound human rights implications. We know that Communist nations, which profess dedication to human rights, actually use their totalitarian systems to violate human rights in an organized, systematic fashion.

The Reagan-Bush Administration has worked for positive human rights changes worldwide. Our efforts have ranged from support for the Helsinki Accords to our support of judicial and political reform in El Salvador.

The Republican Party commends President Reagan for accepting the Honorary Chairmanship of the campaign to erect a U.S. Holocaust Memorial in Washington, D.C. and supports the efforts of the U.S. Holocaust Council in erecting such a museum and educational center. The museum will bear witness to the victims and survivors of the Holocaust.

For Republicans, the struggle for human freedom is more than an end in itself. It is part of a policy that builds a foundation for peace. When people are free to express themselves and choose democratic governments, their free private institutions and electoral power constitute a constraint against the excesses of autocratic rulers. We agree with President Truman, who said: "In the long run our security and the world's hopes for peace lie not in measures of defense or in the control of weapons, but in the growth and expansion of freedom and self-government."

To this end, we pledge our continued effort to secure for all people the inherent, God-given rights that Americans have been privileged to enjoy for two centuries.

Advocacy for Democracy

To promote and sustain the cause of democracy, America must be an active participant in the political competition between the principles of Communism and of democracy.

To do this, America needs a strong voice and active instruments of public diplomacy to counter the Communist bloc's massive effort to disinform and deceive world public opinion. Republicans believe that truth is America's most powerful weapon.

The Reagan-Bush Administration has elevated the stature of public diplomacy in the councils of government and increased the United States Information Agency budget by 44 percent in four years. New programs have been launched in television, citizen exchanges, and dissemination of written information. The National Endowment for Democracy has enlisted the talent of private American institutions, including the AFL-CIO and the U.S. Chamber of Commerce, to educate our friends overseas in the ways of democratic institutions. A sustained billion-dollar effort is modernizing and expanding the Voice of America, strengthening the Voice's signal, lengthening its broadcasts, improving its content, adding new language services and replacing antiquated equipment. Radio Marti, the new broadcast service to Cuba, will begin to broadcast the truth about Cuba to the Cuban people.

Initial steps have been taken to improve the capabilities of Radio Free Europe and Radio Liberty, which serve the captive nations of the Soviet bloc. We pledge to carry out a thorough improvement program for these radios, including new transmitters and other means of penetrating the jamming which denies the RFE/RL signal to millions of captive people, including the increasingly discontented Soviet minorities, behind the Iron Curtain.

Because of the importance we place on people-to-people exchange programs, Republicans support the dedicated work of Peace Corps volunteers. America must nurture good relations not only with foreign governments but with other peoples as well. By encouraging the free flow of ideas and information, America is helping to build the infrastructure of democracy and demonstrating the strength of our belief in the democratic example. The United States

Peace Corps, reflecting traditional American values, will follow the White House initiative promoting free enterprise development overseas in third world countries.

The tradition of addressing the world's peoples, advocating the principles and goals of democracy and freedom, is as old as our Republic. Thomas Jefferson wrote the Declaration of Independence "with a decent respect to the opinions of mankind." This popular advocacy is even more important today in the global struggle between totalitarianism and freedom.

The Future of Our National Security

Republicans look to the future with confidence that we have the will, the weapons, and the technology to preserve America as the land of the free and the home of the brave. We stand united with President Reagan in his hope that American scientists and engineers can produce the technology and the hardware to make nuclear war obsolete.

The prospect for peace is excellent because America is strong again. America's defenses have only one purpose: to assure that our people and free institutions survive and flourish.

Our security requires both the capability to defend against aggression and the will to do so. Together, will and capability deter aggression. That is why the danger of war has grown more remote under President Reagan.

When he took office, defense policy was in disarray. The Carter-Mondale Administration had diminished our military capability and had confused the pursuit of peace with accommodating totalitarianism. It could not respond to the determined growth of Soviet military power and a more aggressive Soviet foreign policy.

We are proud of a strong America. Our military strength exists for the high moral purpose of deterring conflict, not initiating war. The deterrence of aggression is ethically imperative. That is why we have restored America's defense capability and renewed our country's will. Americans are again proud to serve in the Armed Forces and proud of those who serve.

We reaffirm the principle that the national security policy of the United States should be based upon a strategy of peace through strength, a goal of the 1980 Republican Platform.

Maintaining a technological superiority, the historical foundation of our policy of deterrence, remains essential. In other areas, such as our maritime forces, we should continue to strive for qualitative superiority.

President Reagan committed our nation to a modernized strategic and theater nuclear force sufficient to deter attack against the United States and our allies, while pursuing negotiations for balanced, verifiable reductions of nuclear weapons under arms control agreements.

In order to deter, we must be sufficiently strong to convince a potential adversary that under no circumstances would it be to its advantage to initiate conflict at any level.

We pledge to do everything necessary so that, in case of conflict, the United States would clearly prevail.

We will continue to modernize our deterrent capability while negotiating for verifiable arms control. We will continue the policies that have given fresh confidence and new hope to freedom-loving people everywhere.

Arms Control for the Future

Americans, while caring deeply about arms control, realize that it is not an end in itself, but can be a major component of a foreign and defense policy which keeps America free, strong, and independent.

Sharing the American people's realistic view of the Soviet Union, the Reagan Administration has pursued arms control agreements that would reduce the level of nuclear weaponry possessed by the superpowers. President Reagan has negotiated with flexibility, and always from a position of strength.

In the European theater, President Reagan proposed the complete elimination of intermediate-range nuclear missiles. In the START talks with the Soviet Union, he proposed the "build-down" which would eliminate from the U.S. and Soviet arsenals two existing nuclear warheads for each new warhead.

The Soviet Union has rejected every invitation by President Reagan to resume talks, refusing to return unless we remove the Pershing II and Cruise missiles which we have placed in Europe at the request of our NATO allies. Soviet intransigence is designed to force concessions from the United States even before negotiations begin. We will not succumb to this strategy. The Soviet Union will return to the bargaining table only when it recognizes that the United States will not make unilateral concessions or allow the Soviet Union to achieve nuclear superiority.

The Soviet Union, by engaging in a sustained pattern of violations of arms control agreements, has cast severe doubt on its own willingness to negotiate and comply with new agreements in a spirit of good faith. Agreements violated by the Soviet Union include SALT, the Anti-Ballistic Missile Treaty of 1972, the Helsinki Accords, and the Biological and Toxin Weapons Convention of 1972. This pattern of Soviet behavior is clearly designed to obtain a Soviet strategic advantage.

To deter Soviet violations of arms control agreements, the United States must maintain the capability to verify, display a willingness to respond to Soviet violations which have military significance, and adopt a policy whereby the defense of the United States is not constrained by arms control agreements violated by the Soviet Union.

We support the President's efforts to curb the spread of nuclear weapons and to improve international controls and safeguards over sensitive nuclear technologies.

The President's non-proliferation policy has emphasized results, rather than rhetoric, as symbolized by the successful meeting of nuclear supplier states in Luxembourg in July of this year. We endorse the President's initiative on comprehensive safeguards and his efforts to encourage other supplier states to support such measures.

Defense Resources

The first duty of government is to provide for the common defense. That solemn responsibility was neglected during the Carter-Mondale years. At the end of the Eisenhower era, nearly 48 percent of the federal budget was devoted to defense programs, representing 9.1 percent of our gross national product. By 1980, under Carter-Mondale, defense spending had fallen to only 5 percent of gross national product and represented only 24 percent of the federal budget. The Reagan Administration has begun to correct the weaknesses caused by that situation by prudently increasing defense resources. We must continue to devote the resources essential to deter a Soviet threat — a threat which has grown and should be met by an improved and modernized U.S. defense capability. Even so, the percentage of the Reagan Administration budget spent on defense is only about half that of the Eisenhower-Kennedy era.

Readiness

In 1980, our military forces were not ready to perform their missions in the event of emergency. Many planes could not fly for lack of spare parts; ships could not sail for lack of skilled personnel; supplies were insufficient for essential training or sustained combat. Today, readiness and sustainability have improved dramatically. We not only have more equipment, but it is in operating condition. Our military personnel have better training, pride, and confidence. We have improved their pay and benefits. Recruiting and retaining competent personnel is no longer a problem.

Under the Democrats, the All-Volunteer Force was headed for disastrous failure. Because of the Carter-Mondale intransigence on military pay and benefits, we saw the shameful spectacle of patriotic service families being forced below the poverty level, relying on food stamps and other welfare programs. The quality of life for our military has been substantially improved under the Reagan Administration. We wholeheartedly support the all-volunteer armed force and are proud of our historic initiative to bring it to pass.

From the worst levels of retention and recruiting in post-war history in 1979, we have moved to the highest ever recorded. We are meeting 100 percent of our recruiting needs, and 92 percent of our recruits are high school graduates capable of mastering the skills needed in the modern armed services. In 1980, 13 percent of our ships and 25 percent of our aircraft squadrons reported themselves not combat ready because of personnel shortages. Today, those figures have dropped to less than 1 percent and 4 percent respectively.

Today, the United States leads the world in integrating women into the military. They serve in a variety of non-combat assignments. We have made significant strides in numbers of women and their level of responsibility. Female officer strength has grown by 24 percent under the Reagan Administration and is projected to increase, with even greater increases for non-commissioned officers.

Conventional and Strategic Modernization

In 1980, we had a "hollow Army," a Navy half its numbers of a decade earlier, and an Air Force badly in need of upgrading. The Army is now receiving the most modern tanks, fighting vehicles, and artillery. The Navy has grown to 513 ships with 79 more under construction this year, well on its way toward the 600-ship, 15-carrier force necessary for our maritime strategy. The Air Force has procured advanced tactical aircraft. By decade's end, our intertheater lift capacity will have increased by 75 percent. We pledge to rescue a shipbuilding industry consigned to extinction by the Carter-Mondale team.

Since the end of World War II, America's nuclear arsenal has caused the Soviet Union to exercise caution to avoid direct military confrontation with us and our close allies.

Our nuclear arms are a vital element of the Free World's security system.

Throughout the 1970s and up to the present, the Soviet Union has engaged in a vast buildup of nuclear arms. In the naive hope that unilateral restraint by the United States would cause the Soviet Union to reverse course, the Carter-Mondale Administration delayed significant major features of the strategic modernization our country needed. There was no arms race because only the Soviet Union was racing, determined to achieve an intimidating advantage over the Free World. As a result, in 1980, America was moving toward a position of clear nuclear inferiority to the Soviets.

President Reagan moved swiftly to reverse this alarming situation and to re-establish an effective margin of safety before 1990. Despite obstruction from many congressional Democrats, we have restored the credibility of our deterrent.

Reserve and Guard Forces

We salute the men and women of the National Guard and the Reserves. The Carter-Mondale team completely neglected our vital Reserve and Guard forces, leaving them with obsolete equipment, frozen pay, and thousands of vacancies.

The Reagan Administration has transformed our Reserve and National Guard. The Naval Reserve will ultimately operate 40 of the fleet's 600 ships. Navy and Marine Air Reserve units now receive the most modern aircraft, as do the Air Force Reserve and Guard. Army Reserve and Guard

units now receive the latest tanks, infantry fighting vehicles, and artillery. Reserve pay has increased 30 percent, and reserve components are having record success in filling their positions. Our country counts on the Reserves and the Guard, and they can count on us.

Management Reform

The Republican Party advocates a strong defense and fiscal responsibility at the same time. This Administration has already made major advances in eliminating the deep-rooted procurement problems we inherited. Republicans have changed the way the Pentagon does business, encouraging greater economy and efficiency, stretching the taxpayer's dollar.

Learning nothing from past mistakes, the Carter-Mondale Administration returned to centralized defense management. The predictable result: competition fell to only 15 percent of Pentagon procurement; programs were mired in disastrous cost overruns and disputes; outrageous and exorbitant prices were paid for spare parts; and the taxpayers' money was wasted on a grand scale.

We have tackled this problem head-on. We returned management to the Services and began far-reaching reforms. To hold down costs, we more than doubled competition in Pentagon procurement. We appointed Competition Advocate Generals in each Service and an overall Inspector General for the Pentagon. We increased incentives for excellent performance by contractors, and we have applied immediate penalty for poor performance. Our innovative approaches have already saved the taxpayers billions of dollars.

Spare parts acquisition has undergone thorough reform. Improving spare parts management, involving a Department of Defense inventory of almost four million items, is a complex and massive management challenge. The Pentagon's new 10-point program is already working. Old contracts are being revamped to allow competition, high prices are being challenged, and rigorous audits are continuing. As an example, a stool cap for a navigator's chair, once priced at $1,100, was challenged by an alert Air Force Sergeant. It now costs us 31 cents. The Pentagon obtained a full refund and gave the Sergeant a cash reward.

Our men and women in uniform deserve the best and most reliable weapons that this country can offer. We must improve the reliability and performance of our weapons systems, and warranties can be a very positive contribution to defense procurement practices, as can be the independent office of operational testing and evaluation, which was another positive Republican initiative.

The acquisition improvement program now includes program stability, multi-year procurement, economic production rates, realistic budgeting, and increased competition. The B-1B bomber, replacing our aging B-52 force, is ahead of schedule and

under cost. We support our anti-submarine warfare effort and urge its funding at its current level. For the last two years, the Navy has received nearly 50 ships more than three years ahead of schedule and nearly $1 billion under budget. The U.S.S. Theodore Roosevelt, our newest aircraft carrier, is 17 months ahead of schedule and almost $74 million under cost.

We have reformed inefficient procurement practices established decades ago, and we will continue to ensure the most gain from each defense dollar.

The Tasks Ahead

The damage to our defenses through unilateral disarmament cannot be repaired quickly. The hollow Army of the Carter-Mondale Administration is hollow no more, and our Navy is moving toward a 600-ship force.

We share President Reagan's determination to restore credible security for our country. Our choice is not between a strong defense or a strong economy; we must succeed in both, or we will succeed in neither.

Our forces must be second to none, and we condemn the notion that one-sided military reduction will induce the Soviets to seek peace. Our military strength not only provides the deterrent necessary for a more peaceful world, but it is also the best incentive for the Soviets to agree to arms reduction.

Veterans

America is free because of its veterans. We owe them more than thanks. After answering the call to arms, they brought leadership and patriotism back to their communities. They are a continuing resource for America. Through their membership in veterans' service activities, they have strongly supported President Reagan's defense policy. Knowing firsthand the sacrifices of war, they have spoken out frequently for a strong national defense.

Veterans have earned their benefits; these must not be taken away. The help we give them is an investment which pays our nation unlimited dividends.

We have accomplished a great deal. We are meeting the needs of women veterans and ensuring them equal treatment. We must prepare to meet the needs of aging veterans.

We are addressing the unique readjustment problems of Vietnam veterans by expanding the store-front readjustment counseling program, extending vocational training and job placement assistance, and targeting research toward understanding delayed stress reaction in combat veterans. We have moved to alleviate the uncertainty of veterans exposed to Agent Orange by providing nearly 129,000 medical exams and by launching an all-out, government-wide research effort.

We are making major strides in improving health care for veterans. VA hospital construction has expanded to meet community needs, and benefits for disabled veterans have been improved.

We will maintain the veterans' preferences for federal hiring and will improve health, education, and other benefits. We support the Reagan Administration's actions to make home ownership attainable by more veterans, as well as our program to help veterans in small business compete for government contracts. We will extend to all veterans of recent conflicts, such as Lebanon and Grenada, the same assistance.

In recognition of the unique commitment and personal sacrifices of military spouses, President Reagan has called upon the nation to honor them and proclaimed a day of tribute. We will remember them and advance their interests.

National Intelligence

Knowing our adversaries' capabilities and intentions is our first line of defense. A strong intelligence community focuses our diplomacy and saves billions of defense dollars. This critical asset was gravely weakened during the Carter-Mondale years.

We will continue to strengthen our intelligence services. We will remove statutory obstacles to the effective management, performance, and security of intelligence sources and methods. We will further improve our ability to influence international events in support of our foreign policy objectives, and we will strengthen our counterintelligence facilities.

Strategic Trade

By encouraging commerce in militarily significant technology, the Carter-Mondale Administration actually improved Soviet military power. Because of that terrible error, we are now exposed to significant risk and must spend billions of defense dollars that would otherwise have been unnecessary.

The Reagan Administration halted the Carter-Mondale folly. We have strengthened cooperative efforts with our allies to restrict diversion of militarily critical technologies. We will increase law-enforcement and counterintelligence efforts to halt Soviet commercial espionage and illegal exploitation of our technology.

Terrorism

International terrorism is not a random phenomenon but a new form of warfare waged by the forces of totalitarianism against the democracies.

In recent years, certain states have sponsored terrorist actions in pursuit of their strategic goals. The international links among terrorist groups are now clearly understood; and the Soviet link, direct and indirect, is also clearly understood. The Soviets use terrorist groups to weaken democracy and undermine world stability.

Purely passive measures do not deter terrorists. It is time to think about appropriate preventive or pre-emptive actions against terrorist groups before they strike.

Terrorism is an international problem. No one country can successfully combat it. We must lead the free nations in a concerted effort to pressure members of the League of Terror to cease their sponsorship and support of terrorism.

A Secure Future

During the Carter-Mondale Administration, the Soviets built more weapons, and more modern ones, than the United States. President Reagan has begun to reverse this dangerous trend. More important, he has begun a process that, over time, will gradually but dramatically reduce the Soviet Union's ability to threaten our lives with nuclear arms.

His leadership came none too soon. The combined damage of a decade of neglect and of relentless Soviet buildup, despite treaties and our restraint, will not be undone easily.

Today, the Soviet Union possesses over 5,000 intercontinental nuclear warheads powerful and accurate enough to destroy hard military targets, and it is flight-testing a whole new generation of missiles. The Carter-Mondale Administration left this country at a decided disadvantage, without a credible deterrent. That is why President Reagan embarked on a modernization program covering all three legs of the strategic triad.

Republicans understood that our nuclear deterrent forces are the ultimate military guarantor of America's security and that of our allies. That is why we will continue to support the programs necessary to modernize our strategic forces and reduce the vulnerabilities. This includes the earliest possible deployment of a new small mobile ICBM.

While the Carter-Mondale team hid beneath an umbrella of wishful thinking, the Soviet Union made every effort to protect itself in case of conflict. It has an operational anti-satellite system; the United States does not. A network of huge ultramodern radars, new anti-missile interceptors, new surface-to-air missiles, all evidence the Soviet commitment to self-protection.

President Reagan has launched a bold new Strategic Defense Initiative to defend against nuclear attack. We enthusiastically support President Reagan's Strategic Defense Initiative. We enthusiastically support the development of non-nuclear, space-based defensive systems to protect the United States by destroying incoming missiles.

Recognizing the need for close consultation with our allies, we support a comprehensive and intensive effort to render obsolete the doctrine of Mutual Assured Destruction (MAD). The Democratic Party embraces Mutual Assured Destruction. The Republican Party rejects the strategy of despair and supports instead the strategy of hope and survival.

We will begin to eliminate the threat posed by strategic nuclear missiles as soon as possible. Our only purpose (one all people share) is to reduce the danger of nuclear war. To that end, we will use superior American technology to achieve space-based and ground-based defensive systems as soon as possible to protect the lives of the American people and our allies.

President Reagan has asked, "Would it not be better to save lives than to avenge them?" The Republican Party answers, "Yes!" ∎

Democratic Convention

Democrats Nominate Mondale and Ferraro

Democrats concluded a long and difficult campaign for their presidential nomination with a display of party unity and a historic vice presidential choice.

The Democratic National Convention, held July 16-19 in San Francisco, picked former Vice President Walter F. Mondale to be the party standardbearer against President Reagan.

Mondale's victory, however, was almost overshadowed by the attention generated by his selection of Rep. Geraldine A. Ferraro to be his running mate. Ferraro, a three-term House member from Queens, New York, was the first woman ever chosen for the national ticket by a major party.

The relatively harmonious convention was an important achievement for the Democratic Party, which had been torn by an acrimonious contest for the nomination. By the end of the convention, Mondale and his chief rivals for the nomination — Colorado Sen. Gary Hart and the Rev. Jesse Jackson — seemed to have put aside their most visible differences.

Mondale finished the convention balloting with nearly 1,000 votes more than Hart, his closest competitor, yet he was by no means the overwhelming choice. He polled 2,191 votes — about 55 percent of a possible 3,933.

Although the convention ended on a unified note, it did not begin that way. A last-minute imbroglio over Mondale's attempt to oust California lawyer Charles T. Manatt as chairman of the Democratic National Committee (DNC) proved embarrassing to the Mondale campaign.

While the candidate's decision to name Georgia state party Chairman Bert Lance to replace Manatt never seriously jeopardized Mondale's chances of nomination, it raised doubts about his political judgment. Just before the convention began, Mondale agreed under pressure to retain Manatt and named Lance as general campaign chairman. Lance, who was President Carter's budget director, had resigned under fire over his banking practices in Georgia.

Despite fears that radical and homosexual elements in San Francisco would stage confrontations in the streets outside the convention center — evoking memories of the party's 1968 catastrophe in Chicago — there were no violent incidents.

July 16: Opening Day

The opening of the Democrats' 39th convention July 16 had been preceded by two days of very public squabbling after Mondale unsuccessfully attempted to remove Manatt as chairman of the Democratic National Committee.

But as delegates took their seats in the subterranean Moscone Center, a jovial Manatt presided, and the party seemed to put aside its differences. An amiable atmosphere prevailed even though the long and narrow confines of the convention hall afforded a good view of the podium to only some of the 3,933 delegates and 1,313 alternates.

Pre-convention accommodations helped prevent any fights over the reports from the credentials and party rules committees. Although Hart initially had threatened to challenge the status of some Mondale delegates, he changed his mind well before the convention. The credentials committee report, presented by California Assemblyman Richard Alatorre, was adopted by voice vote.

An agreement on future party rules changes, worked out between candidates in June, headed off a floor fight on that potentially divisive topic. The proposals would be considered by a new rules review commission that would meet after the election. If adopted, the changes could significantly alter the way the party chooses its presidential candidate in 1988 and could diminish the role of party officials in future conventions. Presented by Rules Committee Chairman Julian C. Dixon, a three-term House member from California, the proposals were adopted by voice vote.

Former President Carter addressed the delegates and received a warm reception, even though affection from the party had mostly eluded him since leaving office. "For this generation, our generation, life is nuclear survival, liberty is human rights, the pursuit of happiness is equal opportunity," Carter said, sounding themes reminiscent of his administration.

Cuomo Speech

But the emotional highlight of the first night clearly belonged to New York Gov. Mario M. Cuomo, who gave the convention's keynote address. Cuomo's eloquent appeal for Democratic unity, family values and compassion for the poor helped set the tone for the rest of the convention.

Speaking forcefully but without dramatic oratorical flourishes, Cuomo showed the straightforward speaking skill that earned him the title "Albany's Great Communicator." His speech combined an appeal to Democratic traditions with specific attacks on the domestic and foreign policies of the Reagan administration.

Noting Reagan's recent reference to America as "a shining city on a hill," Cuomo said that "the hard truth is that not everyone is sharing in this city's splendor and glory."

"There is despair, Mr. President," Cuomo continued, "in the faces that you don't see, in the places that you don't visit in your shining city."

The theme of family unity was a major thread running throughout Cuomo's speech. Democrats, he said, were united by "a single fundamental idea that describes better than most text books and any speech that I could write what a proper government should be. The idea of family. Mutuality. The sharing of benefits and burdens for the good of all." In one of the speech's most emotional moments, Cuomo referred to his own father, who had arrived from Italy more than 50 years before. "I learned about our kind of democracy from my father. And, I learned about our obligation to each other from him and from my mother," Cuomo said.

Turning to the administration's record, Cuomo told delegates that "we must get the American public to look past the glitter ... to the hard substance of things." He focused particularly on the administration's budget deficit, which he said was "the largest in the history of this universe." He warned, "It is a mortgage on our children's future that can only be paid in pain and that could bring this nation to its knees."

Cuomo was equally critical of the administration's foreign policy, which he said "drifts with no real direction, other than an hysterical commitment to an arms race that leads nowhere — if we're lucky. And if we're not, it could lead us to bankruptcy or war."

He also focused on the administration's military involvements in the Middle East and Central America, speaking of "the loss of 279 young Americans in Lebanon in pursuit of a plan and a policy that no one can find or describe." And he charged that "we give money to Latin American governments that murder nuns, and then lie about it."

July 17: Day Two

Aided by a last-minute compromise among the major candidates, the convention avoided a divisive floor battle over the party platform July 17. But fireworks were supplied later in abundance by Jackson, who brought delegates to their feet with a rousing speech.

The basis for a relatively amicable solution to platform disputes had been laid in June, when the party's platform-writing panel had approved a document fashioned by Mondale backers, but acceptable in most regards to Jackson and Hart. Only five minority planks emerged from the June meetings — four backed by Jackson and one by Hart. *(Platform text, p. 73-B)*

But the continuing disputes over the five minority proposals left Democrats worried that Mondale could be weakened by divisive floor fights. After a meeting among the three major candidates on July 16, a compromise package eventually was worked out.

In general, the proposals approved by the convention gave something to both the Hart and Jackson camps, but showed Mondale forces in solid control on key points.

The first two minority proposals generated little heated debate and were easily defeated by the Mondale forces. The first, proposed by Jackson, called on the United States to adopt a policy against the "first use" of nuclear weapons. It was rejected by 1,405.7 to 2,216.3, with some delegates casting less than a full vote.

The second, also proposed by Jackson, called for major reductions in defense spending. The majority plank, by contrast, called for slowing, but not reversing, the defense spending increases of the Reagan administration. The proposal lost on a vote of 1,127.6 to 2,591.6.

Jackson's third proposal generated more emotional debate, giving rise to an angry confrontation among black delegates over the use of runoff primary elections in Southern states. Jackson had made the runoff question a major issue, arguing that runoffs discriminated against black and other minority candidates. "Runoff primaries deny the political empowerment of minorities," New York Assemblyman Albert Vann intoned from the podium. The Mondale-backed majority plank was critical of runoffs as impediments to full voting rights, but it did not go so far as Jackson's proposal, which called for elimination of the procedure.

The most dramatic moment in the runoff debate came when Atlanta Mayor Andrew Young took the rostrum to support the majority position. Young, who had angered many blacks by declining to throw his support to Jackson, was almost drowned out by a chorus of boos from the floor. The minority plank was defeated by a vote of 1,253.2 to 2,500.8.

Jackson fared better on his proposal to strengthen the party's stance on affirmative action programs to overcome discrimination against minorities in employment and education. His original proposal would have committed the party to back quotas, except those that were "inconsistent with the principles of our country." Mondale's forces, reluctant to include the controversial concept of quotas in the platform, favored a more general affirmative action commitment.

Before debate could begin, however, District of Columbia Del. Walter E. Fauntroy, Jackson's platform spokesman, announced from the podium that all camps had agreed to new language leaving out the quota concept. Instead, the minority plank was altered to pledge support for "verifiable measurements" of progress toward equal opportunity, but did not spell out what those measurements might be. The compromise language was approved without opposition.

Hart's sole minority plank outlined conditions for the use of U.S. military force. Mondale backers originally had opposed the plank, fearing it might hinder a president's flexibility in a crisis, but they finally agreed to back the proposal. It was adopted, 3,271.8 to 351.2.

Jackson's Call

Memory of the platform debate faded quickly as the stage was set for Jackson's appearance. At first Jackson spoke almost haltingly, his voice cracking with emotion or exhaustion. But as he went on his tone became more forceful, encouraged by the repeated call-and-response chanting from black delegates.

By the end, Jackson had virtually abandoned his prepared text, slipping into the rhyming couplets — "hope in their brains, not dope in their veins" — for which he has become famous. "It's time for a change," and "Our time has come," he repeated.

Some of Jackson's speech represented the standard Democratic litany against Reagan, attacking the administration for its economic and foreign policies. Even there, however, Jackson showed his gift for catchy phrasing — "I would rather have [President Franklin D.] Roosevelt in a wheelchair than Reagan on a horse," he said at one point, generating another standing ovation from the increasingly enthusiastic delegates.

But other themes also emerged and seemed to represent a kind of emotional catharsis for the candidate and his supporters. One was a pledge to support the Democratic nominee, ending speculation that Jackson might refuse to back the ticket if he did not get what he wanted from the party.

Jackson coupled his unity pledge with a plea for forgiveness for any mistakes he had made during the campaign. He sought to reach out to Jewish voters, many of whom had been disenchanted with Jackson because of his ties to Black Muslim leader Louis Farrakhan.

"Our communities, black and Jewish, are in anguish, anger and pain," Jackson said. "Feelings have been hurt on both sides. But we cannot afford to lose our way.... We must bring back civility to the tensions. We must turn to each other and not on each other, and choose higher ground."

July 18: Day Three

The third session of the convention was given over to the formal selection of a presidential nominee. But before the actual balloting began, Hart took one last gamble to try and reverse his fortunes.

For weeks before the convention, it had seemed clear that Mondale controlled a majority of convention delegates. But Hart hoped that a dramatic speech on the night of balloting would sway enough Mondale delegates to deny the Minnesotan a first-ballot majority.

By that measure Hart's speech was not a success. Few, if any, Mondale delegates switched after hearing it. Nor did it attain the oratorical heights reached by Cuomo and Jackson. But the speech did serve as an emotional outlet for Hart delegates, who demonstrated at length before and after it, and the address symbolized his efforts to make peace with the party majority.

One of the main themes of Hart's speech was his call for Democratic unity in opposition to the Reagan administration. The nominating campaign, he said, was just a "family tussle," one that was dwarfed by the party's differences with Reagan.

But Hart went on to say that the party could not just concentrate on attacking Reagan, but also had to put forth its own proposals — the "new ideas" on which he had built his campaign. "What counts is not so much what we are against, as what we are for," Hart said, quoting former Democratic presidential candidate Adlai E. Stevenson.

To develop new solutions to current problems, Hart said that the party and nation had to "disenthrall themselves from the policies of the comfortable past that do not answer the challenges of tomorrow." He added, "The times change — and we must change with them."

Hart then outlined a series of efforts that the party should push as a "blueprint for a new democracy." He called for adoption of an industrial policy to rebuild the country's manufacturing base, expanded efforts to train workers for jobs in the technology of the future, a stepped-up campaign against environmental pollution and a foreign policy in which "conflicts and crisis between East and West are resolved, not on the battlefield, but at the bargaining table."

Finally, Hart stressed one of the key concepts of his campaign — his identification with the huge generation of Americans born since World War II. "A new generation of Americans is coming of age," he said, one that formed the core of the civil rights, peace and environmental movements, and "will make history yet again.... We will never give up.... We will prevail."

Nomination Balloting

Balloting for the presidential nomination followed Hart's speech. Once it got started, the actual nomination process went forward without prolonged demonstrations.

Four candidates were nominated and seconded. The first was former South Dakota Sen. George McGovern, the party's nominee in 1972, who had mounted a small-scale effort in 1984 before dropping out after the March 13 Massachusetts primary. Although he had not been in the race for months, McGovern had his name placed in nomination — by Massachusetts delegate James McGovern (no relation) — so that he could address the convention.

After calling for an end to U.S. military involvement in Central America and urging a nuclear arms freeze and expanded programs against hunger, McGovern withdrew

his name in favor of Mondale.

Jackson was nominated by Washington, D.C., Mayor Marion Barry, who said that Jackson "has changed the course of American politics." Former Rep. Shirley A. Chisholm of New York (1969-83), who in 1972 had become the first major black presidential candidate, seconded the nomination.

Hart was nominated by Connecticut Sen. Christopher J. Dodd, who repeated many of the themes Hart had used in an earlier address to the delegates. Dodd stressed that, while the party could not abandon its heritage, it had to move to fresh approaches to problems.

Los Angeles Mayor Tom Bradley gave the nominating speech for Mondale. "Who do we trust to make the tough decisions that face our country?" he asked delegates. "Mondale!" they responded to that and a series of similar questions.

Mondale quickly moved into a solid lead over Hart and Jackson in the balloting. But because some large states passed when their names were first called, Mondale had not reached the required 1,967 votes by the time all delegations had been recognized. New Jersey cast its strategic 115 votes for Mondale as the second round was called.

The final vote was 2,191 for Mondale, 1,200.5 for Hart and 465.5 for Jackson. There were 40 abstentions. *(State-by-state breakdown, p. 68-B)*

July 19: Closing Day

Ferraro's nomination for vice president on July 19 provided the convention with one of its most emotional moments. If male delegates seemed pleased by the possible political benefits to be gained by having a woman on the ticket, women seemed filled with joy and pride by the chance that one of their sisters might attain the nation's second-highest office.

Mondale had announced his selection of Ferraro July 12, and approval of her by the party was never in doubt. Her formal nomination was accomplished with dispatch. Her name was placed in nomination by fellow House member Barbara B. Kennelly of Connecticut, who said that Democrats were "breaking down another barrier to full equality and justice" with her selection.

Seconding the nomination were New Mexico Gov. Toney Anaya and Barbara Roberts Mason, a member of the Michigan Board of Education.

Although Ferraro was the only person nominated for vice president, party officials began a formal roll call of the states. One delegate from Alaska abstained, prompting a chorus of boos from other delegates. Arkansas quickly deferred to New York, which moved that the nomination be passed by acclamation. The motion carried with thundering cheers.

Ferraro was then introduced by House Majority Leader Jim Wright of Texas. Confronting one criticism leveled at Ferraro — her relatively short career in politics — Wright said Ferraro "has learned through the experience of living."

Ferraro emphasized the symbolic importance of her selection with her speech's first sentence: "I stand before you to proclaim tonight: America is the land where dreams can come true for all of us."

Ferraro stressed her belief in the importance of living by the rules: "The promise of our country is that the rules are fair. And if you work hard and play by the rules, you can earn your share of America's blessings." Under Reagan's administration, she said, "the rules are rigged against too many of our people."

As had the string of convention speakers before her, Ferraro criticized the administration's foreign and defense policies and called for a freeze on nuclear weapons.

She concluded her speech with a ringing promise: "To all the children of America, I say: The generation before ours kept faith with us, and like them, we will pass on to you a stronger, more just America."

Mondale Acceptance Speech

The product of weeks of intensive work by the candidate and a team of advisers, Mondale's acceptance speech July 19 was a carefully drawn outline for his campaign against Reagan. Although the former vice president had been criticized for lacking speech-making flair during the nomination campaign, he repeatedly brought delegates to their feet during his address.

To introduce Mondale, the party turned to Kennedy, one of its most effective practitioners of rousing oratory. Kennedy's booming voice filled the hall with denunciations of Reagan and the Republican Party, which he called a "cold citadel of privilege."

"By his choice of Geraldine Ferraro, Walter Mondale has already done more for this country in one short day than Ronald Reagan has done in four long years in office," he said.

Shortly before Mondale's address, aides had passed out thousands of small American flags to delegates, so the crowd was a sea of red, white and blue when the former vice president arrived on the podium.

Early in his address, Mondale conceded his greatest political failure — the crushing defeat he and President Carter received from Reagan in 1980. "Ronald Reagan beat the pants off us," he said, admitting that defeat was due at least in part to the Carter administration's mistakes.

He argued that the party's program in 1984 reflected an understanding of those mistakes, by containing "no defense cuts that weaken our security; no business taxes that weaken our economy; no laundry lists that raid our Treasury."

Mondale blasted the record budget deficits under the Reagan administration, which he said "hike interest rates, clobber exports, stunt investment, kill jobs, undermine growth, cheat our kids and shrink our future."

He promised that as president he would cut those deficits, currently nearing $200 billion a year, by two-thirds by the end of his term. To do that, he said, a president would have to raise taxes.

"Let's tell the truth.... Mr. Reagan will raise taxes, and so will I," Mondale said. "He won't tell you. I just did." Reagan would "sock it to average-income families" with the boosts, Mondale said; he would not.

Turning to the issue of nuclear weapons, Mondale recalled a recent visit to a Texas school, where children expressed fears of nuclear war. While acknowledging "deep differences with the Soviets," Mondale promised to meet annually with Soviet leaders and to seek to negotiate a nuclear freeze.

Mondale concluded his speech with his vision of America in the 1990s. After one term of the Mondale-Ferraro administration, he said, he hoped children would not worry about nuclear war, bright students would aspire to be teachers, there would be no hungry children, U.S.-made goods would be the best on the market, women and members of minority groups would be more represented among business leaders, and the Equal Rights Amendment would be part of the Constitution. ∎

Key Ballots at the 1984 Democratic Convention

These are the votes on the four platform planks voted on July 17.

State	Totals	Vote #1 No first use of nuclear weapons			Vote #2 Defense spending			Vote #3 Dual primaries			Vote #4 Military force restrictions		
		Y	N	A*	Y	N	A*	Y	N	A*	Y	N	A*
Alabama	62	15	46	1	11	49	2	13	49	0	61	1	0
Alaska	14	7	7	0	1	13	0	2	12	0	13	1	0
Arizona	40	20	19	0	18	21	0	20	19	0	39	0	0
Arkansas	42	13	29	0	12	30	0	7	33	2	39	2	1
California	345	149	84	0	99	170	0	129	128	0	285	31	0
Colorado	51	31	16	4	5	45	1	26	24	1	51	0	0
Connecticut	60	28	24	8	32	27	1	27	33	0	60	0	0
Delaware	18	1	17	0	1	17	0	1	17	0	18	0	0
D.C.	19	15	4	0	17	2	0	14	5	0	6	12	0
Florida	143	47	76	20	42	81	20	27	110	6	95	25	23
Georgia	84	40	33	0	38	45	0	39	42	0	67	1	2
Hawaii	27	1	26	0	0	27	0	0	27	0	0	0	0
Idaho	22	9	0	0	10	11	0	9	13	0	22	0	0
Illinois	194	42	145	0	40	147	0	48	143	0	191	0	3
Indiana	88	31	46	0	18	64	0	23	64	0	88	0	0
Iowa	58	22	36	0	7	51	0	5	53	0	58	0	0
Kansas	44	14	29	1	6	38	0	10	34	0	44	0	0
Kentucky	63	14	48	0	10	52	0	15	47	0	55	8	0
Louisiana	69	24	32	0	30	39	0	44	22	0	44	22	0
Maine	27	7	16	0	3	23	0	10	16	0	23	1	0
Maryland	74	20	51	3	20	54	0	18	56	0	51	19	4
Massachusetts	116	89	24	0	69	43	1	82	31	1	112	0	0
Michigan	155	43	105	7	32	118	5	37	111	7	137	0	18
Minnesota	86	37	41	8	30	48	8	25	57	4	73	2	11
Mississippi	43	15	26	2	16	26	1	13	29	1	33	8	2
Missouri	86	20	62	4	22	62	2	24	61	1	70	0	16
Montana	25	8	15	2	4	21	0	5	20	0	25	0	0
Nebraska	30	2	25	3	2	25	3	10	17	3	24	0	6
Nevada	20	6	14	0	3	17	0	5	15	0	19	0	0
New Hampshire	22	10	12	0	5	17	0	1	21	0	22	0	0
New Jersey	122	9	113	0	9	113	0	7	115	0	116	6	0
New Mexico	28	7	19	2	2	26	0	3	25	0	27	1	0
New York	285	134	140	0	131	139	7	125	146	3	196	57	0
North Carolina	88	28	56	0	19	66	0	32	55	0	73	3	0
North Dakota	18	13	5	0	8	10	0	8	10	0	18	0	0
Ohio	175	71	103	0	47	122	6	40	133	2	173	0	2
Oklahoma	53	16	35	2	3	47	3	3	49	1	49	3	1
Oregon	50	32	13	5	26	21	3	24	24	2	49	0	1
Pennsylvania	195	42	153	0	39	156	0	53	142	0	195	0	0
Puerto Rico	53	0	53	0	0	53	0	0	53	0	10	43	0
Rhode Island	27	11	15	1	11	15	1	8	18	1	24	0	2
South Carolina	48	21	23	4	23	19	6	21	25	2	21	19	8
South Dakota	19	7	12	0	7	12	0	7	12	0	0	6	0
Tennessee	76	31	41	4	29	41	6	34	39	3	72	1	3
Texas	200	53	137	10	47	141	12	39	150	11	152	38	10
Utah	27	17	10	0	11	15	1	13	14	0	19	7	1
Vermont	17	11	4	0	10	4	0	10	4	0	12	3	0
Virginia	78	29	48	0	29	48	0	33	43	0	50	23	4
Washington	70	49	18	0	29	39	1	35	35	0	67	0	0
West Virginia	44	12	27	5	12	29	3	17	24	3	0	0	0
Wisconsin	89	28	45	16	26	57	6	31	54	4	83	6	0
Wyoming	15	2	12	0	2	12	0	13	1	0	13	1	0
Latin America	5	0	5	0	.5	4.5	0	0	5	0	5	0	0
Democrats Abroad	5	1.5	3.5	0	1.5	3.5	0	0	5	0	5	0	0
Virgin Islands	6	1.2	4.8	0	2.6	2.6	.6	1.2	4.8	0	4.8	1.2	0
American Samoa	6	0	6	0	0	6	0	0	6	0	6	0	0
Guam	7	0	7	0	0	7	0	7	0	0	7	0	0
TOTALS:		1,405.7	2,216.3	112	1,127.6	2,591.6	99.6	1,253.2	2,500.8	58	3,271.8	351.2	118

*Abstentions

Presidential Balloting at the 1984 Democratic Convention

State	Totals	Mondale	Hart	Jackson	Other*	Abstained**
Alabama	62	39	13	9	1	0
Alaska	14	9	4	1	0	0
Arizona	40	20	16	2	0	2
Arkansas	42	26	9	7	0	0
California	345	95	190	33	0	27
Colorado	51	1	42	1	0	7
Connecticut	60	23	36	1	0	0
Delaware	18	13	5	0	0	0
District of Columbia	19	5	0	14	0	0
Florida	143	82	55	3	0	2
Georgia	84	40	24	20	0	0
Hawaii	27	27	0	0	0	0
Idaho	22	10	12	0	0	0
Illinois	194	114	41	39	0	0
Indiana	88	42	38	8	0	0
Iowa	58	37	18	2	1	0
Kansas	44	25	16	3	0	0
Kentucky	63	51	5	7	0	0
Louisiana	69	26	19	24	0	0
Maine	27	13	13	0	1	0
Maryland	74	54	3	17	0	0
Massachusetts	116	59	49	5	3	0
Michigan	155	96	49	10	0	0
Minnesota	86	63	3	4	16	0
Mississippi	43	26	4	13	0	0
Missouri	86	55	14	16	0	0
Montana	25	11	13	1	0	0
Nebraska	30	12	17	1	0	0
Nevada	20	9	10	1	0	0
New Hampshire	22	12	10	0	0	0
New Jersey	122	115	0	7	0	0
New Mexico	28	13	13	2	0	0
New York	285	156	75	52	0	0
North Carolina	88	53	19	16	0	0
North Dakota	18	10	5	1	2	0
Ohio	175	84	80	11	0	0
Oklahoma	53	24	26	3	0	0
Oregon	50	16	31	2	0	0
Pennsylvania	195	177	0	18	0	0
Puerto Rico	53	53	0	0	0	0
Rhode Island	27	14	12	0	0	0
South Carolina	48	16	13	19	0	0
South Dakota	19	9	10	0	0	0
Tennessee	76	39	20	17	0	0
Texas	200	119	40	36	2	0
Utah	27	8	19	0	0	0
Vermont	17	5	8	3	0	1
Virginia	78	34	18	25	0	1
Washington	70	31	36	3	0	0
West Virginia	44	30	14	0	0	0
Wisconsin	89	58	25	6	0	0
Wyoming	15	7	7	0	0	1
Latin America	5	5	0	0	0	0
Democrats Abroad	5	3	1.5	.5	0	0
Virgin Islands	6	4	0	2	0	0
American Samoa	6	6	0	0	0	0
Guam	7	7	0	0	0	0
	2,191	**1,200.5**	**465.5**	**26**	**40**	

*Here are the details on the votes for other candidates on the first ballot: Alabama: Martha Kirkland (mother of Reo Kirkland, a delegate from Alabama), 1; Iowa: former Sen. George McGovern, D-S.D., 1; Maine: Sen. Joseph R. Biden Jr., D-Del., 1; Massachusetts: McGovern, 3; Minnesota: Sen. Thomas F. Eagleton, D-Mo., 16; North Dakota: Eagleton, 2 (the votes for Eagleton, a staunch foe of abortion, were intended to express delegates' unhappiness with the platform's and the Mondale/Ferraro ticket's support for abortion rights); Texas: Sen. John Glenn, D-Ohio, 2.

** This figure does not include the following absences: Florida, 1; Missouri, 1; New York, 2; Oregon, 1; Rhode Island, 1; Texas, 3; Virginia, 1.

Democratic Acceptance Speeches

Text of Mondale Acceptance Speech

Following is the Associated Press text of former Vice President Walter F. Mondale's July 19 speech accepting the Democratic presidential nomination as delivered at the Democratic National Convention, in San Francisco.

My fellow Democrats, my fellow Americans:

I accept your nomination. Behind us now is the most wide open race in political history.

It was noisy — but our voices were heard. It was long — but our stamina was tested. It was hot — but the heat was passion, and not anger. It was a roller coaster — but it made me a better candidate, and it will make me a stronger president of the United States.

I do not envy the drowsy harmony of the Republican Party. They squelch debate; we welcome it. They deny differences; we bridge them. The are uniform; we are united. They are a portrait of privilege; we are a mirror of America.

Just look at us at here tonight: Black and white, Asian and Hispanic, Native and immigrant, young and old, urban and rural, male and female — from yuppie to lunchpail, from sea to shining sea. We're all here tonight in this convention speaking for America. And when we in this hall speak for America, it is America speaking.

When we speak of family, the voice is Mario Cuomo's.

When we speak of change, the words are Gary Hart's.

When we speak of hope, the fire is Jesse Jackson's.

When we speak of caring, the spirit is Ted Kennedy's.

When we speak of patriotism, the strength is John Glenn's.

When we speak of the future, the message is Geraldine Ferraro.

And now we leave San Francisco — together.

Future of America

And over the next hundred days, in every word we say, and every life we touch, we will be fighting for the future of America.

Joan and I are parents of three wonderful children who will live much of their lives in the twenty-first century. This election is a referendum on their future — and on ours. So tonight I'd like to speak to the young people of America — and to their parents and to their grandparents.

I'm Walter Mondale. You may have heard of me — but you may not really know me. I grew up in the farm towns of southern Minnesota. My dad was a preacher, and my mom was a music teacher. We never had a dime. But we were rich in the values that were important; and I've carried those values with me ever since.

They taught me to work hard; to stand on my own; to play by the rules; to tell the truth; to obey the law; to care for others; to love our country; to cherish our faith.

My story isn't unique.

In the last few weeks, I've deepened my admiration for someone who shares those same values. Her immigrant father loved our country. Her widowed mother sacrificed for her family. And her own career is an American classic: Doing your work. Earning your way. Paying your dues. Rising on merit.

My presidency will be about those values. My vice president will be Geraldine Ferraro.

Tonight, we open a new door to the future. Mr. Reagan calls it "tokenism." We call it America.

Ever since I graduated from Elmore High, I've been a Democrat. I was attorney general of my state; then a U.S. senator. Then, an honest, caring man — Jimmy Carter — picked me as his running mate and in 1976 I was elected vice president. And in 1980, Ronald Reagan beat the pants off us.

So tonight, I want to say something to those of you across our country who voted for Mr. Reagan — Republicans, Independents, and yes, some Democrats: I heard you. And our party heard you.

After we lost we didn't tell the American people that they were wrong. Instead, we began asking you what our mistakes had been. And for four years, I listened to all of the people of our country. I traveled everywhere. It seemed like I had visited every acre of America.

It wasn't easy. I remember late one night, as I headed from a speech in one city to a hotel a thousand miles away, someone said to me, "Fritz, I saw you on TV. Are those bags under your eyes natural?" And I said, "No, I got them the old-fashioned way. I earned them."

To the thousands of Americans who welcomed me into your homes and into your businesses, your churches and synagogues: I thank you.

You confirmed my belief in our country's values. And you helped me learn and grow.

New Realism

So, tonight we come to you with a new realism: Ready for the future, and recapturing the best in our tradition.

We know that America must have a strong defense, and a sober view of the Soviets.

We know that government must be as well-managed as it is well-meaning.

We know that a healthy, growing private economy is the key to the future.

We know that Harry Truman spoke the truth when he said: "A President . . . has to be able to say *yes* and *no*, but mostly no."

Look at our platform. There are no defense cuts that weaken our security; no business taxes that weaken our economy; no laundry lists that raid our Treasury.

We are wiser, stronger, and focused on the future. If Mr. Reagan wants to re-run the 1980 campaign: Fine. Let them fight over the past. We're fighting for the American future — and that's why we're going to win this campaign.

One last word to those who voted for Mr. Reagan.

I know what you were saying. But I also know what you were not saying.

You did not vote for a $200 billion deficit.

You did not vote for an arms race.

You did not vote to turn the heavens into a battleground.

You did not vote to savage Social Security and Medicare.

You did not vote to destroy family farming.

You did not vote to trash the civil rights laws.

You did not vote to poison the environment.

You did not vote to assault the poor, the sick, and the disabled.

And you did not vote to pay fifty bucks for a fifty-cent light bulb.

Four years ago, many of you voted for Mr. Reagan because he promised you'd be better off. And today, the rich are better off. But working Americans are worse off, and the middle class is standing on a trap door.

Lincoln once said that ours is to be a government of the people, by the people, and for the people. What we have today is a government of the rich, by the rich, and for the rich. And we're going to make a change in November. Look at the record.

Reagan Record

First, there was Mr. Reagan's tax program. What happened was, he gave each of his rich friends enough tax relief to buy a Rolls Royce — and then he asked your family to pay for the hub caps.

Then they looked the other way at the rip-offs, soaring utility bills, phone bills, medical bills.

Then they crimped our future. They let us be routed in international competition, and now the help-wanted ads are full of listings for executives, and for dishwashers — but not much in between.

Then they socked it to workers. They encouraged executives to vote themselves huge bonuses — while using King Kong tactics to make workers take Hong Kong wages.

Mr. Reagan believes that the genius of America is in the boardrooms and exclusive country clubs. I believe that the greatness can be found in the men and women who built our nation; do its work; and defend our freedom.

Truth About The Future

If this administration has a plan for a better future, they're keeping it a secret.

Here is the truth about the future: We are living on borrowed money and borrowed time. These deficits hike interest rates, clobber exports, stunt investment, kill jobs, undermine growth, cheat our kids, and shrink our future.

Whoever is inaugurated in January, the American people will have to pay Mr. Reagan's bills. The budget will be squeezed. Taxes will go up. And anyone who says they won't is not telling the truth to the American people.

I mean business. By the end of my first term, I will reduce the Reagan budget deficit by two-thirds.

Let's tell the truth. It must be done, it must be done. Mr. Reagan will raise taxes, and so will I. He won't tell you. I just did.

There's another difference. When he raises taxes, it won't be done fairly. He will sock it to average-income families again, and leave his rich friends alone. And I won't stand for it. And neither will you and neither will the American people.

To the corporations and freeloaders who play the loopholes or pay no taxes, my message is: Your free ride is over.

To the Congress, my message is: We must cut spending and pay as we go. If you don't hold the line, I will: That's what the veto is for.

Now that's my plan to cut the deficit. Mr. Reagan is keeping his plan secret until after the election. That's not leadership; that's salesmanship. And I think the American people know the difference.

I challenge tonight, I challenge Mr. Reagan to put his plan on the table next to mine — and then let's debate it on national television before the American people.

Americans want the truth about the future — not after the election.

When the American economy leads the world, the jobs are here, the prosperity is here for our children. But that's not what's happening today. This is the worst trade year in American history. Three million of our best jobs have gone overseas.

Mr. Reagan has done nothing about it. They have no plan to get our competitive edge back. But we do. We will cut the deficits, reduce interest rates, make our exports affordable, and make America number one again in the world economy.

We will launch a renaissance in education, in science, and learning. A mind is a terrible thing to waste. And this must be the best-educated, best-trained generation in American history. And I will lead our nation forward to the best system that this nation has ever seen. We must do it, we must do it.

It is time for America to have a season of excellence. Parents must turn off that television; students must do their homework; teachers must teach; and America compete. We'll be number one if we follow those rules; let's get with it in America again.

To big companies that send our jobs overseas, my message is: We need those

Democratic presidential nominee Walter F. Mondale and running mate Geraldine A. Ferraro

jobs here at home. And our country won't help your business — unless your business helps our country.

To countries that close their markets to us, my message is: We will not be pushed around any more. We will have a president who stands up for American workers and American businesses and American farmers in international trade.

When I grew up, and people asked us to imagine the future we were full of dreams. But a few months ago, when I visited a grade school class in Texas and asked the children to imagine the future, they talked to me about nuclear war.

As we've neared the election, this administration has begun to talk about a safer world. But there's a big difference: As president, I will work for peace from my first day in office — and not from my first day campaigning for re-election.

As president, I will reassert American values. I'll press for human rights in Central America, and for the removal of all foreign forces from the region. And in my first hundred days, I will stop the illegal war in Nicaragua.

We know the deep differences with the Soviets. And America condemns their repression of dissidents and Jews; their suppression of Solidarity; their invasion of Afghanistan; their meddling around the world.

But the truth is that between us, we have the capacity to destroy the planet. Every president since the bomb went off understood that and talked with the Soviets and negotiated arms control. Why has this administration failed? Why haven't they tried? Why can't they understand the cry of Americans and human beings for sense and sanity in control of these God awful weapons? Why, why?

Why can't we meet in summit conferences with the Soviet Union at least once a year? Why can't we reach agreements to save this earth? The truth is, we can. President Kennedy was right when he said: We must never negotiate out of fear. But we must never fear to negotiate. For the sake of civilization we must negotiate a mutual, verifiable nuclear freeze before those weapons destroy us all.

A Second Mondale Term

The second term of the Mondale-Ferraro Administration will begin in 1989.

By the start of the next decade, I want to ask our children their dreams, and hear not one word about nuclear nightmares.

By the start of the next decade, I want to walk into any classroom in America and hear some of the brightest students say, "I want to be a teacher."

By the start of the next decade, I want to walk into any public health clinic in America and hear the doctor say, "We haven't seen a hungry child this year."

By the start of the next decade, I want to walk into any store in America and pick up the best product, of the best quality, at the best price; and turn it over; and read, "Made in the U.S.A."

By the start of the next decade, I want to meet with the most successful business leaders anywhere in America, and see as many minorities and women in that room as I see here in this room tonight.

By the start of the next decade, I want to point to the Supreme Court and say, "Justice is in good hands."

Before the start of the next decade, I want to go to my second Inaugural, and raise my right hand, and swear to "preserve, protect, and defend" a Constitution that includes the Equal Rights Amendment.

My friends, America is a future each generation must enlarge; a door each generation must open; a promise each generation must keep.

For the rest of my life, I want to talk to young people about their future.

And whatever their race, whatever their religion, whatever their sex, I want to hear some of them say what I say — with joy and reverence — tonight: "I want to be president of the United States."

Thank you very much.   ∎

Delivered July 19:

Ferraro Acceptance Speech

Following is the Associated Press text of New York Rep. Geraldine A. Ferraro's July 19 speech accepting the Democratic vice presidential nomination as delivered at the Democratic National Convention, in San Francisco.

Ladies and gentlemen of the convention: My name is Geraldine Ferraro. I stand before you to proclaim tonight: America is the land where dreams can come true for all of us.

As I stand before the American people and think of the honor this great convention has bestowed upon me, I recall the words of Dr. Martin Luther King Jr., who made America stronger by making America more free.

He said: "Occasionally in life there are moments which cannot be completely explained by words. Their meaning can only be articulated by the inaudible language of the heart."

Tonight is such a moment for me.

My heart is filled with pride.

My fellow citizens, I proudly accept your nomination for vice president of the United States.

And I am proud to run with a man who will be one of the great presidents of this century, Walter F. Mondale.

The Future

Tonight, the daughter of a woman whose highest goal was a future for her children talks to our nation's oldest party about a future for us all.

Tonight, the daughter of working Americans tells all Americans that the future is within our reach — if we're willing to reach for it.

Tonight, the daughter of an immigrant from Italy has been chosen to run for [vice] president in the new land my father came to love.

Our faith that we can shape a better future is what the American dream is all about. The promise of our country is that the rules are fair. If you work hard and play by the rules, you can earn your share of America's blessings.

Those are the beliefs I learned from my parents. And those are the values I taught my students as a teacher in the public schools of New York City.

At night, I went to law school. I became an assistant district attorney, and I put my share of criminals behind bars. I believe: If you obey the law, you should be protected. But if you break the law, you should pay for your crime.

When I first ran for Congress, all the political experts said a Democrat could not win in my home district of Queens. But I put my faith in the people and the values that we shared. And together, we proved the political experts wrong.

In this campaign, Fritz Mondale and I have put our faith in the people. And we are going to prove the experts wrong again.

We are going to win, because Americans across this country believe in the same basic dream.

Elmore, Minn., and Queens

Last week, I visited Elmore, Minn., the small town where Fritz Mondale was raised. And soon Fritz and Joan will visit our family in Queens.

Nine hundred people live in Elmore. In Queens, there are 2,000 people on one block. You would think we would be different, but we're not.

Children walk to school in Elmore past grain elevators; in Queens, they pass by subway stops. But, no matter where they live, their future depends on education — and their parents are willing to do their part to make those schools as good as they can be.

In Elmore, there are family farms; in Queens, small businesses. But the men and women who run them all take pride in supporting their families through hard work and initiative.

On the Fourth of July in Elmore, they hang flags out on Main Street; in Queens, they fly them over Grand Avenue. But all of us love our country, and stand ready to defend the freedom that it represents.

Playing By The Rules

Americans want to live by the same set

of rules. But under this administration, the rules are rigged against too many of our people.

It isn't right that every year, the share of taxes paid by individual citizens is going up, while the share paid by large corporations is getting smaller and smaller. The rules say: Everyone in our society should contribute their fair share.

It isn't right that this year Ronald Reagan will hand the American people a bill for interest on the national debt larger than the entire cost of the federal government under John F. Kennedy.

Our parents left us a growing economy. The rules say: We must not leave our kids a mountain of debt.

It isn't right that a woman should get paid 59 cents on the dollar for the same work as a man. If you play by the rules, you deserve a fair day's pay for a fair day's work.

It isn't right that — that if trends continue — by the year 2000 nearly all of the poor people in America will be women and children. The rules of a decent society say, when you distribute sacrifice in times of austerity, you don't put women and children first.

It isn't right that young people today fear they won't get the Social Security they paid for, and that older Americans fear that they will lose what they have already earned. Social Security is a contract between the last generation and the next, and the rules say: You don't break contracts. We're going to keep faith with older Americans.

We hammered out a fair compromise in the Congress to save Social Security. Every group sacrificed to keep the system sound. It is time Ronald Reagan stopped scaring our senior citizens.

It isn't right that young couples question whether to bring children into a world of 50,000 nuclear warheads.

That isn't the vision for which Americans have struggled for more than two centuries. And our future doesn't have to be that way.

Changes In The Air

Change is in the air, just as surely as when John Kennedy beckoned America to a new frontier; when Sally Ride rocketed into space and when Rev. Jesse Jackson ran for the office of president of the United States.

By choosing a woman to run for our nation's second highest office, you sent a powerful signal to all Americans. There are no doors we cannot unlock. We will place no limits on achievement.

If we can do this, we can do anything.

Tonight, we reclaim our dream. We're going to make the rules of American life work fairly for all Americans again.

To an Administration that would have us debate all over again whether the Voting Rights Act should be renewed and whether segregated schools should be tax exempt, we say, Mr. President: Those debates are over.

On the issue of civil, voting rights and affirmative action for minorities, we must not go backwards. We must — and we will — move forward to open the doors of opportunity.

To those who understand that our country cannot prosper unless we draw on the talents of all Americans, we say: We will pass the Equal Rights Amendment. The issue is not what America can do for women, but what women can do for America.

To the Americans who will lead our country into the 21st century, we say: We will not have a Supreme Court that turns the clock back to the 19th century.

To those concerned about the strength of American family values, as I am, I say: We are going to restore those values — love, caring, partnership — by including, and not excluding, those whose beliefs differ from our own. Because our own faith is strong, we will fight to preserve the freedom of faith for others.

To those working Americans who fear that banks, utilities, and large special interests have a lock on the White House, we say: Join us; let's elect a people's president; and let's have government by and for the American people again.

To an Administration that would savage student loans and education at the dawn of a new technological age, we say: You fit the classic definition of a cynic; you know the price of everything, but the value of nothing.

To our students and their parents, we say: We will insist on the highest standards of excellence because the jobs of the future require skilled minds.

To young Americans who may be called to our country's service, we say: We know your generation of Americans will proudly answer our country's call, as each generation before you.

This past year, we remembered the bravery and sacrifice of Americans at Normandy. And we finally paid tribute — as we should have done years ago — to that unknown soldier who represents all the brave young Americans who died in Vietnam.

Let no one doubt, we will defend America's security and the cause of freedom around the world. But we want a president who tells us what America is fighting for, not just what we are fighting against. We want a president who will defend human rights — not just where it is convenient — but wherever freedom is at risk — from Chile to Afghanistan, from Poland to South Africa.

To those who have watched this administration's confusion in the Middle East, as it has tilted first toward one and then another of Israel's long-time enemies and wondered. "Will America stand by her friends and sister democracy?" We say: America knows who her friends are in the Middle East and around the world.

America will stand with Israel always.

Finally, we want a President who will keep America strong, but use that strength to keep America and the world at peace. A nuclear freeze is not a slogan: It is a tool for survival in the nuclear age. If we leave our children nothing else, let us leave them this Earth as we found it — whole and green and full of life.

I know in my heart that Walter Mondale will be that president.

The Gift of Life

A wise man once said, "Every one of us is given the gift of life, and what a strange gift it is. If it is preserved jealously and selfishly, it impoverishes and saddens. But if it is spent for others, it enriches and beautifies."

My fellow Americans: We can debate policies and programs. But in the end what separates the two parties in this election campaign is whether we use the gift of life — for others or only ourselves.

Tonight, my husband, John, and our three children are in this hall with me. To my daughters, Donna and Laura, and my son, John Jr., I say: My mother did not break faith with me . . . and I will not break faith with you. To all the children of America, I say: The generation before ours kept faith with us, and like them, we will pass on to you a stronger, more just America.

Thank you. ∎

Text of 1984 Democratic Party Platform

Following is the text of the 1984 Democratic Party platform, as adopted July 17 at the party's national convention in San Francisco.

PREAMBLE

A fundamental choice awaits America — a choice between two futures.

It is a choice between solving our problems, and pretending they don't exist; between the spirit of community, and the corrosion of selfishness; between justice for all, and advantage for some; between social decency and social Darwinism; between expanding opportunity and contracting horizons; between diplomacy and conflict; between arms control and an arms race; between leadership and alibis.

America stands at a crossroads.

Move in one direction, and the President who appointed James Watt will appoint the Supreme Court majority for the rest of the century. The President who proposed deep cuts in Social Security will be charged with rescuing Medicare. The President who destroyed the Environmental Protection Agency will decide whether toxic dumps get cleaned up. The President who fought the Equal Rights Amendment will decide whether women get fair pay for their work. The President who launched a covert war in Central America will determine our human rights policy. The President who abandoned the Camp David process will oversee Middle East policy. The President who opposed every nuclear arms control agreement since the bomb went off will be entrusted with the fate of the earth.

We offer a different direction.

For the economy, the Democratic Party is committed to economic growth, prosperity, and jobs. For the individual, we are committed to justice, decency, and opportunity. For the nation, we are committed to peace, strength, and freedom.

In the future we propose, young families will be able to buy and keep new homes — instead of fearing the explosion of their adjustable-rate mortgages. Workers will feel secure in their jobs — instead of fearing layoffs and lower wages. Seniors will look forward to retirement — instead of fearing it. Farmers will get a decent return on their investment — instead of fearing bankruptcy and foreclosure.

Small businesses will have the capital they need — instead of credit they can't afford. People will master technology — instead of being mastered or displaced by it. Industries will be revitalized — not abandoned. Students will attend the best colleges and vocational schools for which they qualify — instead of trimming their expectations. Minorities will rise in the mainstream of economic life — instead of waiting on the sidelines. Children will dream of better days ahead — and not of nuclear holocaust.

Our Party is built on a profound belief in America and Americans.

We believe in the inspiration of American dreams, and the power of progressive ideals. We believe in the dignity of the individual, and the enormous potential of collective action. We believe in building, not wrecking. We believe in bridging our differences, not deepening them. We believe in a fair society for working Americans of average income; an opportunity society for enterprising Americans; a caring society for Americans in need through no fault of their own — the sick, the disabled, the hungry, the elderly, the unemployed; and a safe, decent and prosperous society for all Americans.

We are the Party of American values — the worth of every human being; the striving toward excellence; the freedom to innovate; the inviolability of law; the sharing of sacrifice; the struggle toward justice; the pursuit of happiness.

We are the Party of American progress — the calling to explore; the challenge to invent; the imperative to improve; the importance of courage; the perennial need for fresh thinking, sharp minds, and ambitious goals.

We are the Party of American strength — the security of our defenses; the power of our moral values; the necessity of diplomacy; the pursuit of peace; the imperative of survival.

We are the Party of American vision — the trustees of a better future. This platform is our road map toward that future.

Chapter I. Economic Growth, Prosperity, and Jobs

Introduction

Building a prosperous America in a changing world: that is the Democratic agenda for the future. To build that America, we must meet the challenge of long-term, sustainable, noninflationary economic growth. Our future depends on it.

To a child, economic growth means the promise of quality education. To a new graduate, it means landing a good first job.

To a young family, growth means the opportunity to own a home or a car. To an unemployed worker, it means the chance to live in dignity again. To a farmer, growth means expanding markets, fair prices, and new customers. To an entrepreneur, it means a shot at a new business. To our nation, it means the ability to compete in a dramatically changing world economy. And to all in our society, growth — and the prosperity it brings — means security, opportunity, and hope. Democrats want an economy that works for everyone — not just the favored few.

For our party and our country, it is vital that 1984 be a year of new departures.

We have a proud legacy to build upon: the Democratic tradition of caring, and the Democratic commitment to an activist government that understands and accepts its responsibilities.

Our history has been proudest when we have taken up the challenges of our times, the challenges we accept once again in 1984 — to find new ways, in times of accelerating change, to fulfill our historic commitments. We will continue to be the party of justice. And we will foster the productivity and growth on which justice depends.

For the 1980s, the Democratic Party will emphasize two fundamental economic goals. We will restore rising living standards in our country. And we will offer every American the opportunity for secure and productive employment.

Our program will be bold and comprehensive. It will ask restraint and cooperation from all sectors of the economy. It will rely heavily on the private sector as the prime source of expanding employment. And it will treat every individual with decency and respect.

A Democratic Administration will take four key steps to secure a bright future of long-term economic growth and opportunity for every American:

● Instead of runaway deficits, a Democratic Administration will pursue overall economic policies that sharply reduce deficits, bring down interest rates, free savings for private investment, prevent another explosion of inflation and put the dollar on a competitive footing.

● Instead of government by neglect, a Democratic Administration will establish a framework that will support growth and productivity and assure opportunity.

● In place of conflict, a Democratic Administration will pursue cooperation, backed by trade, tax and financial regulations that will serve the long-term growth of the American economy and the broad national interest.

● Instead of ignoring America's future, a Democratic Administration will make a series of long-term investments in research, infrastructure, and above all in people. Education, training and retraining will become a central focus in an economy built on change.

THE FUTURE IF REAGAN IS REELECTED

"Since the Reagan Administration took office, my wife and I have lost half our net worth. Took us 20 years to build that up, and about three to lose it. That is hard to deal with...."

David Sprague, Farmer, Colorado (Democratic Platform Committee Hearing, Springfield, Illinois, April 27, 1984)

"There's got to be something wrong with our government's policy when it's cheaper to shut a plant down than it is to operate it.... The Houston Works plant sits right in the middle of the energy capital of the world and 85 percent of our steel went directly into the energy-related market, yet Japan could sit their products on our docks cheaper than we can make it and roll it there."

Early Clowers, President, Steel Workers Local 2708 (Democratic Platform Committee Hearing, Houston, Texas, May 29, 1984).

A Democratic future of growth and opportunity, of mastering change rather than hiding from it, of promoting fairness instead of widening inequality, stands in stark contrast to another four years of Ronald Reagan. Staying the course with Ronald Reagan raises a series of hard questions about a bleak future.

What would be the impact of the Republican deficit if Mr. Reagan is reelected?

A second Reagan term would bring federal budget deficits larger than any in American history — indeed, any in world history. Under the Republican's policies, the deficit will continue to mount. Interest rates, already rising sharply, will start to soar. Investments in the future will be slowed, then stopped. The Reagan deficits mortgage the future and threaten the present.

Mr. Reagan has already conceded that these problems exist. But as he said in his 1984 Economic Report to the Congress, he prefers to wait until after the election to deal with them. And then, he plans "to enact spending reductions coupled with tax simplification that will eventually eliminate our budget deficit."

What will Mr. Reagan's plan for "tax simplification" mean to average Americans if he is reelected?

Ronald Reagan's tax "reforms" were a bonanza for the very wealthy, and a disaster for poor and middle-class Americans. If reelected, Mr. Reagan will have more of the same in store. For him, tax simplification will mean a further freeing of the wealthy from their obligation to pay their fair share

of taxes and an increasing burden on the average American.

How will Mr. Reagan's "spending reductions" affect average Americans if he is reelected?

If he gets a second term, Mr. Reagan will use the deficit to justify his policy of government by subtraction. The deficits he created will become his excuse for destroying programs he never supported. Medicare, Social Security, federal pensions, farm price supports and dozens of other people-oriented programs will be in danger.

If Mr. Reagan is reelected, will our students have the skills to work in a changing economy?

If we are to compete and grow, the next generation of Americans must be the best-trained, best-educated in history. While our competitors invest in educating their children, Mr. Reagan cuts the national commitment to our schools. While our competitors spend greater and greater percentages of their GNP on civilian research and development, this President has diverted increasing portions of ours into military weaponry. These policies are short-sighted and destructive.

If Mr. Reagan is reelected, will basic industries and the workers they employ be brought into the future?

The Republican Administration has turned its back on basic industries and their communities. Instead of putting forward policies to help revitalize and adjust, Mr. Reagan tells blameless, anxious, displaced workers to abandon their neighborhoods and homes and "vote with their feet."

America's economic strength was built on basic industries. Today, in a changing economy, they are no less important. Strong basic industries are vital to our economic health and essential to our national security. And as major consumers of high technology, they are catalysts for growth in newly emerging fields. We need new approaches to ensure strong American basic industries for the remainder of this century and beyond.

Can the road to the future be paved with potholes?

Adequate roads and bridges, mass transit, water supply and sewage treatment facilities, and ports and harbors are essential to economic growth. For four years, the Reagan Administration has refused to confront adequately the growing problems in our infrastructure. Another term will bring four more years of negligence and neglect.

If Mr. Reagan is reelected, how many children will join the millions already growing up at risk?

Between 1980 and 1982, more than two million younger Americans joined the ranks of the poor: the sharpest increase on record.

With the Reagan Administration's cutbacks in prenatal care and supplemental food programs have come infant mortality rates in parts of our cities rivaling those of the poorest Latin American nations. Black infants are now twice as likely as white

infants to die during the first year of life.

Cuts in school lunch and child nutrition programs have left far too many children hungry and unable to focus on their lessons.

Teenage prostitution, alcohol and drug abuse, depression, and suicide have all been linked to child abuse. The Administration has abandoned most avenues to breaking the cycle of abuse. Funding to prevent and treat child physical abuse has been cut in half. And funds to help private groups set up shelters for runaway youth are being diverted elsewhere.

If Mr. Reagan is reelected, will we ensure that our children are able to enjoy a clean, healthy environment?

Protecting our natural heritage — its beauty and its richness — is not a partisan issue. For eighty years, every American President has understood the importance of protecting our air, our water, and our health. Today, a growing population puts more demands on our environment. Chemicals which are unsafe or disposed of improperly threaten neighborhoods and families. And as our knowledge expands, we learn again and again how fragile life and health — human and animal — truly are.

Ensuring the environmental heritage of future generations demands action now. But the Reagan Administration continues to develop, lease, and sell irreplaceable wilderness lands. While thousands of toxic waste sites already exist, and more and more are being created constantly, the Reagan Administration is cleaning them up at a rate of only 1.5 per year. The environmental legacy of Ronald Reagan will be long-lasting damage that can *never* truly be undone.

If Mr. Reagan is reelected, will we be able to heat our homes and run our factories?

Twice in the past, our country has endured the high costs of dependence on foreign oil. Yet the Reagan Administration is leaving us vulnerable to another embargo or an interruption in oil supply. By failing adequately to fill the Strategic Petroleum Reserve, and trusting blindly to the market to "muddle through" in a crisis this Administration has wagered our national security on its economic ideology. One rude shock from abroad or just one "market failure," and our country could find itself plunged into another energy crisis.

The New Economic Reality: Five Reagan Myths

Underlying the Reagan approach to the economy are five key myths; myths that determine and distort the Reagan economic policy, and ensure that it is not the basis for long-term growth.

The world has changed, but Ronald Reagan does not understand.

First, and most fundamental, the Reagan Administration continues to act as if the United States were an economic island unto itself. But we have changed from a relatively isolated economy to an economy of international interdependence. In fact, the importance of international trade to the U.S. economy has roughly doubled in a decade. Exports now account for almost 10 percent of GNP — and roughly 20 percent of U.S. manufactured goods. One in six manufacturing jobs now depends on exports, and one in three acres is now planted for the overseas market. Imports have also doubled in importance.

Financial markets are also closely linked. U.S. direct investments and commercial loans overseas now amount to hundreds of billions of dollars. A debt crisis in Mexico will affect balance sheets in San Francisco. A recession in Europe will limit the profits of U.S. subsidiaries operating in the European market. Lower overseas profits will limit the flow of earnings back to the United States — one important way the U.S. has found to help pay for the rising tide of imports. Hundreds of billions of dollars in foreign short-term capital invested here are sensitive to small shifts in interest rates or the appearance of added risk. It is only partly bad loans that brought Continental Illinois to the brink of bankruptcy. Heavily dependent on short-term foreign deposits, Continental Illinois was particularly vulnerable. Rumors that were false at the time were enough to set off a run on the bank.

The strength of American steel, the competitiveness of the U.S. machine tool industry, and the long-term potential of U.S. agriculture are no longer matters decided exclusively in Washington or by the American market. America must look to Tokyo, Paris, and the money markets in Singapore and Switzerland. Policy based on the myth that America is independent of the world around us is bound to fail.

Second, this Administration has ignored the enormous changes sweeping through the American work force.

The maturing of the baby boom generation, the sharp increase in the percentage of women seeking work, and the aging of the work force all have to be taken into account.

Decade by decade, more and more women have moved into the work force. This large-scale movement is already changing the nature of professions, altering the patterns of child care and breaking down sex-based distinctions that have existed in many types of employment.

In Ronald Reagan's vision of America, there are no single parent families; women only stay at home and care for children. Reagan's families do not worry about the effects of unemployment on family stability; they do not worry about decent housing and health care; they do not need child care. But in the real world, most Americans do. Providing adequate child care for the millions of American children who need it, and for their parents, is surely not a responsibility which belongs solely to the federal government. But, like the responsibility for decent housing and health care, it is one where federal leadership and support are essential.

The work force is also aging. For the first time in this century, the average American is 31 years of age. Coupled with greater longevity and the gradual elimination of mandatory retirement rules, older workers can be expected to increase steadily their share of the total work force.

Moreover, the kinds of jobs available in our economy are changing rapidly. The combined pressures of new products, new process technology, and foreign competition are changing the face of American industry.

New technologies, shifting economics and deregulation have opened up dozens of new careers both in traditional industrial concerns and in new businesses. Many of them did not exist at all only a few years ago.

And the change is far from over. In setting national policy, a government that ignores that change is bound to fail. In setting national policy, a government that ignores the future is short-changing the American people.

Third, the Reagan program has ignored the fundamental changes that are sweeping through the structure of American industry, the diversity of the economy and the challenges various sectors face. New products and new ways of manufacturing are part of the change. High technology is creating new competitive industries, and holding out the promise of making older industries competitive once again. Foreign competition has also had a major impact. But the tide runs much deeper than that.

In the past decade, small business and new entrepreneurs have become more and more of a driving force in the American economy. Small businesses are a growing force in innovation, employment, and the long-term strength of the American economy.

Technology itself appears to be changing the optimal size of American businesses. And unlike the conglomerate mergers of the 1960s, renewed emphasis on quality and efficient production has shifted the focus back to industry-specific experience.

An Administration that sets tax policy, spending priorities, and an overall growth program without understanding the new dynamics and the diversity of American industry is weakening, rather than strengthening the American economy.

Reaganomics is based on the theory that blanket tax cuts for business and the rich would turn directly into higher productivity, that private investors and industry would use the money saved to restore our edge in innovation and competitiveness.

In practice, the theory failed because it did not take into account the diversity within our economy. The economy is composed of a set of complex public and private institutions which are intricately interrelated and increasingly influenced by the pressures of international competition. In the international economy, multina-

tional companies and governments cooperate to win trade advantage, often at American expense.

We are coming to understand that in an expanding number of markets, industrial strategies, rather than just the energies of individual firms, influence competitive success. Indeed, success in marketing a product may depend more on the quality and productivity of the relationship between government and business than on the quality of the product. While several foreign industrial strategies have failed, foreign governments are becoming more sophisticated in the design and conduct of their industrial strategies. The Reagan Administration is not.

Fourth, the Reagan Administration has acted as if deficits do not count. The deficits are huge and are expected to get larger — and they are a major negative factor in everything from high interest rates to the third world debt crisis.

— Because of the huge tax cuts to benefit the wealthy, and an enormous military buildup bought on credit, the federal deficit in 1983 was equivalent to 6% of our GNP. In dollars it amounted to almost 200 billion — more than three times larger than the deficit Ronald Reagan campaigned against in 1980.

— Under the budget Reagan proposed to Congress earlier this year, the annual deficit would grow to $248 billion by 1989, and unless he makes major changes in current policy, it will exceed $300 billion. Reagan doubled the national debt during his first term. Given eight years, he will have tripled it. According to the proposed budget, at the end of his second term Reagan *by himself* will have put this country *three times deeper* into debt than *all our other Presidents combined*.

— As the Reagan debt hangs over us, more and more of our tax dollars are going nowhere. By 1989, the percentage of federal revenues to be spent on deficit interest payments alone will have doubled. *These unproductive payments will claim a staggering 42¢ on every personal income tax dollar we pay.* This huge allocation will do nothing to reduce the principal of the debt; it will only finance the interest payments.

— The interest payments on Reagan's debt are grossly out of line with historical spending patterns. Since 1981, more money has been squandered on *interest payments* on the Reagan-created debt alone than has been saved by all of Reagan's cuts in domestic spending. Nondefense discretionary spending, to be productively invested in programs to benefit the poor and middle class, and to build our social capital, is being overwhelmed by the enormous sums of money wasted on interest payments. By 1989, the annual payment will account for twice the percentage of federal revenue that we have ever set aside for such discretionary programs.

— Interest payments on the debt are rising

at an alarming rate. Today the annual payment has already reached $110 billion — twice what it was four years ago. During a second Reagan term, it will double *again*, reaching $207 billion by 1989.

— The consequences for the individual taxpayer are enormous. Deficit increases under Reagan so far are equivalent to $2,387 levied from every woman, man and child alive in the United States today.

— The consequences for the nation as a whole are also enormous. The massive government borrowing necessary to service the debt will amount to about three-quarters of the entire nation's net savings between 1983 and 1986.

The pressure of the deficits on interest rates has sucked in a wave of overseas investment. Some of those investments have been made in manufacturing plants or other commercial enterprises. Much of the foreign money, however, is in the form of portfolio holdings or even more liquid short-term bank deposits. It is an uncertain source of savings for a long-term investment program. To a limited degree, it puts the country in the same risky position as Continental Illinois Bank which relied heavily on short-term foreign deposits to make long-term domestic loans.

High interest rates will eventually take their toll on domestic investment, make their own contribution to inflationary pressure (while eventually slowing growth and inflation), and increase the tensions in the domestic banking system. They will also have a potentially devastating impact on the international economy. Each percentage point rise in U.S. interest rates adds $3-5 billion to the annual debt payments of the developing world. High American interest rates have also put added pressure on interest rates in the industrial democracies, dampening their own prospects for growth, and their ability to buy our goods.

Fifth, and finally, the Reagan Administration has virtually wished away the role of government. When it comes to the economy, *its view is that the government that governs best is one that governs not at all.*

A Democratic Administration must answer this challenge by reaffirming the principle that government must both "provide for the common defense" *and* "promote the general welfare" as coequal responsibilities under the Constitution. If the Democratic Party can succeed in correcting the present imbalance, it will reverse the cycle of pain and despair, and recapture the initiative in the area of social and economic progress.

The Reagan Administration succeeded in shifting massive resources from human needs functions of the Federal budget to military-related functions and created unprecedented deficits, based on the assumption that government should have a diminished responsibility for social progress, and thus, for the welfare of the needy and disadvantaged in society. The resulting Reagan-induced recession caused tremendous

suffering, threw millions of people out of work, terminated or reduced benefits, and raised the national misery index.

Mr. Reagan denies government's critical role in our economy. Government cannot, and should not, dominate our free enterprise economy. But American prosperity has been most pronounced when the government played a supportive or catalytic role in the nation's economic fortunes. There are a wide variety of examples stretching back through our entire history: government investments in roads and research, in education and training; government initiatives in opening up new economic possibilities, initiatives that started with the decision to protect domestic markets shortly after the Revolution to the ongoing commercial development of space.

Agriculture is a clear example of government cooperation with a highly competitive private sector that has yielded a harvest of economic results that is the envy of the world. The government helps fund the research, helps spread it through the economy, educates the modern farmer, influences production levels, and helps develop new markets overseas. It is America's most conspicuous example of a successful industrial strategy — combining the cooperative efforts of business, government and our universities.

Reagan's Recession and A Recovery Built on Debt

The Economic Roller Coaster — Following the first oil shock in 1973, the United States embarked on a ten year economic roller coaster. The up and down performance of the economy was paralleled by erratic macro-economic policy. There were wide swings from stimulative fiscal and monetary policies causing raging inflation, to government-engineered recessions.

The frequency of the cycles created a climate of uncertainty that was tailor-made to discourage and distort investment. Each cycle left the economy weaker than the one before. At the end of each recession the level of inflation was higher, and at the end of each recovery the level of unemployment had risen.

Even more disturbing was the decline in the rate of growth of productivity. By the end of the 1970s, productivity growth first stopped and then fell. Productivity growth has finally resumed — but the rate of growth remains disappointing compared both to our own economic past and the performance of other industrial economies.

Reaganomics and an Election Year Recovery — Ronald Reagan swept into office on the promise of a smaller government and a bigger private sector, of higher GNP and lower inflation, and of the elimination of federal deficits.

First, he proposed huge tax cuts. Mr. Reagan went so far as to suggest that the growth caused by his tax cuts would be so rapid that total tax revenues would actually rise even while tax rates were cut.

Second, he promised a huge defense build-up.

Third, he promised stable prices. How was he going to contain prices while stimulating rapid growth? His answer was tight money.

Fourth, the supply-siders promised growth and stable prices without the intervening pain of a recession. In effect, Reagan promised tight money without tears.

Cut taxes but raise more revenues. Arm to the teeth. Growth with stable prices. Tight money and no hard times. It just did not work out that way. Worse, there was never any reason to expect that it would. Reagan's kind of tax cuts were based neither on rational economic theory nor on any empirical evidence. And wishing simply did not make it so. George Bush was right when he called Reaganomics "voodoo economics."

Instead of growth, the country had plunging production and record unemployment. Instead of increased savings and investment, the country had bankruptcy and economic decline. The Reagan policies, which were supposed to break the cycle of inflation and recession, only made it worse.

Reagan cut domestic programs, but more than offset those cuts with vastly increased defense spending. The Government significantly reduced the growth of the money supply and kept real interest rates high. For a recession, real interest rates reached record highs. These interest rates brought an added problem. They attracted foreign funds and helped drive up the international value of the dollar. American business was faced with a double whammy — empty order books and high interest rates. For the increasingly large part of American business that either sells overseas or competes with imports at home, the over-valued dollar abroad meant their products cost far more compared to the foreign competition.

Reagan effectively created a tax on exports and a subsidy for imports. It was a climate that forced record bankruptcies, enormous unemployment, plant closings, and major corporate reorganizations. It was the largest and most severe economic collapse since the Great Depression.

The Reagan Administration then prepared for the election year by "staying the course" in fiscal policy (pumping up demand with huge deficits) and sharply reversing the course in monetary policy.

The Federal Reserve Board rapidly expanded the supply of money and the economy ceased to decline and began to recover.

The Millions Left Behind — But millions of Americans were left behind. Over the last two years, 1.8 million men and women became discouraged workers and more than 5.4 million have fallen into poverty. Nearly half of all minority youth are unemployed, and Black males have effectively lost 13 percent of their labor force participation in the last two decades. Unemployment on Indian reservations continues to be among the highest in the nation.

The U.S.-Mexico border has been devastated by the currency devaluations and economic crisis in Mexico. Small businesses have closed; American families are suffering hunger and poor health, as unemployment exceeds depression rates. Women continue to receive less than 60 percent of the wages that men receive, with minority women receiving far less. Millions of other Americans, including the growing number of women heading poor households or those who have been hard-hit by plant closings or obsolescent skills, avidly seek training or retraining in occupations that hold real promise for sustained employment opportunities in the future.

Millions of Americans, including those in the industrial and agricultural heartland, have been severely affected by the recent recession and the transformation in American industry that accompanied it. Furthermore, the changes seem to have come very quickly, and they do not seem to be over. Many Americans worked in auto, steel, machine tool, textile, agriculture and small business and related industries. Today for many of them, the recovery is a fiction, or seems very fragile. Plant closings have hit hard and job security and loss of health and pension benefits evoke memories from the past.

Investment in jobs for all Americans constitutes the key investment for the future of the nation. For every one million workers who go back to work, our country produces an additional $60-70 billion in goods and adds $25 billion to the Federal treasury. The Democratic Party will work aggressively to stimulate employment, rebuild trade and encourage labor-intensive industrialization.

Seven Threats to the Recovery

The current election year recovery is in serious jeopardy, threatened by a series of major economic problems:

● Unless corrective action is taken soon, the current $180 billion deficit will balloon even larger by the end of the decade.

● Interest rates are high and rising. The prime rate has jumped one and one half percentage points. A credit crunch is rapidly approaching in which federal borrowing for the deficit will overwhelm private demand for funds to fuel the recovery. Mortgage rates have risen to a point where home sales and housing starts are beginning to fall. The variable rate mortgage that buffers the thrift industry against high interest rates may, in the near future, put the entire industry under pressure as steadily rising rates put mortgage payments beyond the reach of the average homeowner.

● The Federal Reserve Board faces a deficit dilemma. By expanding the money supply to help finance the deficit, the Federal Reserve runs the risk of runaway inflation. But if it limits growth by restricting the money supply, high interest rates will distort growth or tip the economy back into recession.

● The Reagan Administration has done nothing to solve America's repeated problem of reconciling steady growth with stable prices, except by causing a deep recession. Continuing high levels of unemployment still exist in various communities across the country. Many jobs have disappeared. The Reagan Administration is not interested in new forms of fighting inflation — its anti-inflation program amounts to little more than unemployment, tight money and union busting. It is a highly cynical economic selective service that drafts only the poor and the middle class to fight the war against inflation. Unrestrained by the demands of another election, a second Reagan Administration will be even less concerned about the impact of deep recession on the average working American.

● Our trade deficit is a looming disaster for the national economy. An overvalued dollar, itself the product of high interest rates, helped create a nearly $70 billion trade deficit in 1983. It will be almost twice as large in 1984. Borrowing to support the deficits and buying abroad to maintain a recovery tilted toward consumption are eroding America's position as a creditor nation.

● America is very much a part of the international economy. And the recovery overseas has been slow to catch hold. European economies are strained by the impact of high American interest rates on their own economies. For many developing countries, growth has been slowed or even reversed by the overhang of an enormous burden of commercial and official debt. If they cannot buy our products, our economy must slow.

● The sheer size of the international debt burden is itself a threat to the recovery. It is not only a question of falling exports to Latin America. The American and international financial system has been put in peril by the weakening of debtor nations' ability to repay their debt to U.S. banks as interest rates rise.

Howard Baker called Mr. Reagan's policies a "riverboat gamble." We now know the outcome. The very wealthiest in our society have been big winners — but future generations of Americans will be the losers.

The Americans coming of age today face a future less secure and less prosperous than their parents did — unless we change course. We have an obligation to our children and to their children. We Democrats have a different vision of our future.

THE DEMOCRATIC ALTERNATIVE: A PROSPEROUS AMERICA IN A CHANGING WORLD

"There's a lot of people out there only making $3.35 an hour, and that's been since '81. That's a long time to be making $3.35 an hour.... Costs of living have gone up considerably. The insurance has gone up, gas, lights, water. It's a whole lot different now, it's not the same as '81. I know times have changed, but why can't the $3.35 change with them? I would like to know if anybody can answer. I urge the Democratic Party to develop policies and protect working people."

Doris Smith, Steward, SEIU Local 706 (Democratic Platform Committee Hearing, Houston, Texas, May 29, 1984)

"We do not have a surplus as long as one member of my family is hungry. He may live next door or on the other side of the world. However, it should not be the producer's responsibility to provide cheap food at the expense of his own children."

Roberta Archer, Farmer, Springfield, Illinois (Democratic Platform Committee Hearing, Springfield, Illinois, April 27, 1984)

"In the four years prior to Mr. Reagan taking over, I was fortunate to have four good years of employment, and I was able to put money aside in savings accounts which since have been exhausted. My unemployment benefits are exhausted too.... I may not qualify for any type of public assistance and the standard of living I was accustomed to for my wife and myself and my family has drastically changed.... But we as Democrats can join together in harmony and unison and we decide what is the future or the fate of our people and what is good for all of us. So I am very proud to be a Democrat."

James Price, unemployed mine worker (Democratic Platform Committee Hearing, Birmingham, Alabama, April 24, 1984)

Democratic growth is not just a matter of good numbers, but of opportunities for people. Jobs and employment are at the center of Democratic thinking. It is not only a question of legislation or appropriations. Rather, it is a philosophy that views employment as the ongoing concern of the country. Work in America is not an idle concept — but a definition of self, a door to future opportunity, and the key step in securing the economic necessities of the present.

An America at work is a moral obligation as well as the most effective way to return our economy to a high growth path. Employed people stimulate the economy, their taxes pay for the expenses of government and their production adds to our national wealth. Moreover, the social and economic fabric of the nation will be strengthened as millions of Americans who presently are frozen out of productive and dignified employment become contributing citizens.

The potential for America is unlimited. It is within our means to put America back on a long-term path that will assure both growth and broad-based economic opportunity. That is what the next Democratic Administration will do. First, we will adopt overall economic policies that will bring interest rates down, free savings for private investment, prevent another explosion of inflation, and put the dollar on a competitive basis. Second, we will invest for our future — in our people, and in our infrastructure. Third, we will promote new partnerships and participation by all levels of government, by business and labor, to support growth and productivity. Finally, government will work with the private sector to assure that American businesses and American workers can compete fully and fairly in a changing world economy.

Overall Economic Policies: A Firm Ground For Growth

A Democratic Administration will pursue economic policies which provide the basis for long-term economic growth and will allow us to fulfill our commitment to jobs for all Americans who want to work. A key part of the effort will be reducing and eventually eliminating the deficits that currently form a dark cloud over the nation's future. In addition, monetary policy must be set with an eye to stability and to the strengths or weaknesses of the economy. Finally, we will pursue policies that will promote price stability and prevent inflation from breaking out again.

Reducing the Reagan Budget Deficits

After plunging the nation into a deficit crisis, President Reagan refuses to take part in efforts to solve it. He postpones hard decisions until after the Presidential election, refusing to compromise, refusing to address revenues and defense spending seriously, refusing all but a "down payment" on the deficit. The President continues to stand apart from serious, comprehensive efforts to cut the deficit. There must be statesmanship and compromise here, not ideological rigidity or election year politics.

The Democratic Party is pledged to reducing these intolerable deficits. We will reassess defense expenditures; create a tax system that is both adequate and fair; control skyrocketing health costs without sacrificing quality of care; and eliminate other unnecessary expenditures. Through efficiency and toughness, we will restore sanity to our fiscal house.

We oppose the artificial and rigid Constitutional restraint of a balanced budget amendment. Further we oppose efforts to call a federal constitutional convention for this purpose.

Rational Defense Spending — In the last three years, the Defense Department was told by this Administration that it could have anything it wanted, and at any price. As Democrats, we believe in devoting the needed resources to ensure our national security. But military might cannot be measured solely by dollars spent. American military strength must be secured at an affordable cost. We will reduce the rate of increase in defense spending. Through careful reevaluation of proposed and existing weapons, we will stop throwing away

money on unworkable or unnecessary systems; through military reform we will focus defense expenditure on the most cost-effective military policies. We will insist that our allies contribute fairly to our collective security, and that the Department of Defense reduces its scandalous procurement waste.

And above all else, we will seek sensible arms control agreements as a means of assuring that there will be a future for our children and that we as a nation will have the resources we need to invest for the future.

Tax Reform — America needs a tax system that encourages growth and produces adequate revenues in a fair, progressive fashion. The Democratic Party is committed to a tax policy that embodies these basic values.

The present system is unfair, complex, and encourages people to use a wide range of loopholes to avoid paying their fair share of taxes. The combination of loopholes for the few and high rates for the many is both unfair and anti-growth. It distorts investment, diverting creative energies into tax avoidance. And it makes the tax code even less comprehensible to the average American.

Our tax code must produce sufficient revenue to finance our defense and allow for investment in our future, and we will ask every American to pay his or her fair share. But by broadening the tax base, simplifying the tax code, lowering rates, and eliminating unnecessary, unfair and unproductive deductions and tax expenditures, we can raise the revenues we need and promote growth without increasing the burden on average taxpayers.

Ronald Reagan's tax program gave huge breaks to wealthy individuals and to large corporations while shifting the burden to low and moderate income families. The Democratic Party is pledged to reverse these unsound policies. We will cap the effect of the Reagan tax cuts for wealthy Americans and enhance the progressivity of our personal income tax code, limiting the benefits of the third year of the Reagan tax cuts to the level of those with incomes of less than $60,000. We will partially defer indexation while protecting average Americans. We will close loopholes, eliminate the preferences and write-offs, exemptions, and deductions which skew the code toward the rich and toward unproductive tax shelters. Given the fact that there has been a veritable hemorrhage of capital out of the federal budget, reflected in part by the huge budget deficit, there must be a return to a fair tax on corporate income. Under the Reagan Administration, the rate of taxation on corporations has been so substantially reduced that they are not contributing their fair share to federal revenues. We believe there should be a 15% minimum corporate tax. In addition, our tax code has facilitated the transfer of capital from the United States to investments abroad, contributing to plant closing without notice in many communities and loss of millions of jobs. We will toughen compliance proce-

dures to reduce the $100 billion annual tax evasion.

Our country must move to a simpler, more equitable, and more progressive tax system. Our tax code can let the market put our country's savings to the best use. There must be a fair balance between corporate and personal tax increases. Wealthier taxpayers will have to shoulder a greater share of the new tax burdens. Economic distortions must be eliminated.

Controlling Domestic Spending — A balanced program for reducing Republican megadeficits must also deal with the growing costs of domestic programs. But this must be done in a way that is fair to average Americans.

Social Security is one of the most important and successful initiatives in the history of our country, and it is an essential element of the social compact that binds us together as a community. There is no excuse — as the Reagan Administration has repeatedly suggested — for slashing Social Security to pay for excesses in other areas of the budget. We will steadfastly oppose such efforts, now and in the future.

It is rather in the area of health care costs that reform is urgently needed. By 1988, Medicare costs will rise to $106 billion; by the turn of the century, the debt of the trust fund may be as great as $1 trillion. In the Republican view, the problem is the level of benefits which senior citizens and the needy receive. As Democrats, we will protect the interests of health care beneficiaries. The real problem is the growing cost of health care services.

We propose to control these costs, and to demand that the health care industry become more efficient in providing care to all Americans, both young and old. We will limit what health care providers can receive as reimbursement, and spur innovation and competition in health care delivery. The growth of alternative health care delivery systems such as HMOs, PPOs and alternatives to long-term care such as home care and social HMOs should be fostered so that high quality care will be available at a lower cost. We must learn the difference between health care and sick care.

Unlike the Republicans, we recognize that investing in preventive health care saves dollars as well as lives, and we will make the needed investment. The states must be the cornerstone of our health care policies, but a Democratic Administration will provide the leadership at the federal level to assure that health care is available to all who need help at a cost we can afford. In addition, we pledge to scour the budget for other areas of wasteful or unnecessary spending.

Monetary Policy for Growth

Reducing the deficit is the first step toward lowering interest rates and establishing the basis for fair tax and budget policies. But even with a Democratic fiscal policy reining in the deficit, the task of the Federal Reserve Board will be critical. Monetary policy must work to achieve stable real interest rates, the availability of capital for long-term investments, predictable long-term policy and stable prices. We reject the rigid adherence to monetary targets that has frequently characterized the Reagan monetary policy. Whatever targeting approach the Federal Reserve Board adopts, it must be leavened with a pragmatic appraisal of what is happening in the harsh world of the real economy, particularly the impact on unemployment, interest rates, and the international value of the dollar.

An Anti-Inflation Program

We have learned that sustained economic growth is impossible in a climate of high inflation or of inflationary expectations. The Reagan Administration's only prescription for inflation is recession — deliberate high unemployment — coupled with a relentless assault on the collective bargaining power and rights of working men and women. The Democratic Party believes that these tactics are both unacceptable and ineffective.

We will develop the following five-step program to stabilize prices:
— Growth — full order books encourage investments in new plants and equipment and research and development. The productivity growth that comes in tandem with new investment will help offset — point for point — any increase in cost.
— Increased flexibility in the marketplace — will also help keep inflationary pressures under control. There is no single policy that will make the U.S. economy more adaptable. Rather, there is a series of smaller steps which will help keep prices stable. In general, competitive markets are more likely to restrain sudden surges of prices than are markets dominated by a few large firms. No Democratic Administration will forget the use of old fashioned antitrust policy to keep markets competitive and prices down.
— Trade policy — is also an important component of any effective anti-inflation program. Expanding world markets for American goods increase the gains from large scale production and stimulate research and development on new products and processes.
— The price-wage spiral — as part of any effective anti-inflation program, serious policies to address the price-wage spirals and other inflationary pressures we have experienced in the past must be developed.
— We believe that an attack on sectoral sources of inflation — in food, fuel, utilities, health care, and elsewhere — is essential without economic distortions. Our agriculture, energy, and health programs will all promote sectoral price stability while assuring fair treatment for average Americans, including working men and women and family farmers. For example, the Strategic Petroleum Reserve is one clear response to reducing

the chance of another oil shock. The very presence of reserves in the U.S., Japan, and elsewhere reduces the likelihood of panic buying to replace suddenly threatened oil supplies. In this context, a far-reaching energy policy that emphasizes conservation and the development of alternative energy supplies will also help stabilize energy prices. And lower interest rates from reduced budget deficits will reduce upward pressure on housing costs and bring housing back within the reach of millions of Americans now excluded from the market.

Investing in People

America's greatest resource is our people. As Democrats, we affirm the need for both public and private investment — in our children; in our educational institutions and our students; in jobs, training, and transitional assistance for our workers — to build America's future. If we choose wisely, these investments will be returned to our country many times over. They are essential if we are to create an America with high-quality jobs and rising opportunities for all. And they are vital if we are to safeguard our competitive position in the world economy.

Investing in Children

Simple decency demands that we make children one of our highest national priorities. But the argument for so acting goes well beyond that. Programs for children represent the most critical investment we can make in our ability to compete in future world markets and maintain a strong national defense in the decades ahead.

Above all else, the Democratic Party stands for making the proper investment in coming generations of Americans.

Preventive efforts must be at the heart of the broad range of health, child care, and support programs for children. Helping these children makes good moral sense — and sound economic sense. Measles vaccine alone has saved $1.3 billion in medical costs in just ten years. Supplemental food programs for low-income pregnant women and infants save $3 for every dollar spent.

By improving access to medical care before and after birth, we can promote a generation of healthy mothers and healthy babies. Seeing that supplemental food programs for low-income pregnant women and infants reach all those eligible will do more than save the $40,000 now spent to treat one low birth weight infant in a neo-natal ward. It will also reduce the risk of birth defects for such infants.

We recognize that a hungry child is a child who cannot learn. Restoring school breakfast and school lunches for millions of children will improve their alertness and concentration in school.

Child care must also be a top priority. Helping communities establish afterschool

care programs will remove millions of American children from the serious risks they now face of injury, abuse and alienation by staying at home alone. Encouraging employers, churches, public centers, and private groups to provide quality, affordable child care will give millions of children whose parents must work the kind of adult supervision necessary to thrive. And setting up centers for child care information and referral will assist parents wherever they reside to locate quality care for their children.

Preventing child abuse must be at the forefront of Democratic Party concern. Local, community-based child abuse prevention programs must be strengthened and expanded. A child who learns first about the risks of sexual abuse in school will be less likely to become the target of repeated victimization. Federal challenge grants could encourage states to make local prevention efforts a real priority.

Prompt intervention efforts must also be provided for children in crisis. If we are to make any headway in breaking the cycle of child abuse, both victims and offenders must have access to treatment programs.

Juvenile offenders must not be left in adult jails where the only skills they acquire are those of the career criminal. Safe shelter and assistance must be available for the hundreds of thousands of runaway children at risk of exploitation in our cities. Local, state, and federal law enforcement agencies must refine ways to locate children who have been abducted. And children in foster care must not be allowed to graduate to the streets at age 18 without ever having known a permanent home.

We must ensure that essential surveys on children's health and welfare status are reinstated. We know more about the number of matches sold than about the number of children across the country who die in fires while alone at home. Likewise, we know less about hunger and malnutrition among children than we do about the health of the nation's poultry stock.

The Democratic Party affirms its commitment to protecting the health and safety of children in the United States. Existing laws mandating the use of automobile child restraints must be enforced, and child safety seat loaner or rental programs and public education programs must be encouraged, in order to reduce significantly the leading cause of death and serious injury among children between the ages of six months and five years — motor vehicle crashes.

The crises devastating many of our nation's youth is nowhere more dramatically evidenced than in the alarming rate of increase in teenage suicide. Over 6,000 young people took their lives in 1983, and for each actual suicide 50 to 100 other youths attempted suicide. The underlying causes of teenage suicide, as well as its full scope, are not adequately researched or understood. We must commit ourselves to seek out the causes, formulate a national policy of prevention, and provide guidance to our state and local governments in developing means to stem this devastating tide of self-destruction. We support the creation of a national panel on teenage suicide to respond to this challenge.

A Democratic Administration which establishes these priorities can reduce the risks for our young people and improve the odds. By so doing, it will serve their future ... and ours.

Investing in Education

No public investment is more important than the one we make in the minds, skills and discipline of our people. Whether we are talking about a strong economy, a strong defense or a strong system of justice, we cannot achieve it without a strong educational system. Our very future in international economic competition depends on skilled workers and on first-rate scientists, engineers, and managers.

We Democrats are committed to equity in education. We will insist on excellence, discipline, and high standards. Quality education depends on students, teachers and parents performing at the highest levels of achievement.

Today, education in America needs help. But, the Reagan Administration offers misleading homilies about the importance of education while aggressively slashing education programs.

This is intolerable. We know that every dollar we invest in education is ultimately returned to us six-fold. We know that the education of our citizens is critical to our democracy.

There are four key goals that a Democratic program for educational excellence must address: strengthening local capacity to innovate and progress in public education and encourage parental involvement; renewing our efforts to ensure that all children, whatever their race, income, or sex have a fair and equal chance to learn; attracting the most talented young people into teaching and enabling them to remain and develop in their profession; and ensuring that all American families can send their children on to college or advanced training.

Primary and Secondary Education — While education is the responsibility of local government, local governments already strapped for funds by this Administration cannot be expected to bear alone the burden of undertaking the efforts we need for quality education — from teacher training, to the salaries needed to attract and retain able teachers, to new labs, to new programs to motivate talented and gifted students, to new ties between businesses and schools — without leadership at the federal level.

Democrats will provide that leadership. We call for the immediate restoration of the cuts in funding of education programs by the Reagan Administration, and for a major new commitment to education. We will create a partnership for excellence among federal, state and local governments. We will provide incentives to local

school districts to concentrate on science, math, communications and computer literacy; to provide access to advanced technology. In all of these fields, but particularly in computers, there is a growing danger of a two-tier education system. The more affluent districts have adequate hardware and teachers prepared to use it. Many districts are left completely behind or saddled with a modern machine but no provision for faculty training. Every American child should have the basic education that makes computer literacy possible and useful. Major attention must be given to recruiting the finest young people into teaching careers, and to providing adequate staff development programs that enable educators to increase their effectiveness in meeting the needs of all students.

Vocational education should be overhauled to bring instructional materials, equipment, and staff up to date with the technology and practices for the workplace and target assistance to areas with large numbers of disadvantaged youth. We will insist that every child be afforded an equal opportunity to fulfill his or her potential. We will pay special attention to the needs of the handicapped.

Education is an important key to the upward mobility of all citizens and especially the disadvantaged, despite the fact that racial discrimination and other prejudices have set limits to such achievement.

The Reagan Administration has singled out for extinction the proven most successful education program — compensatory education for disadvantaged children. The Democratic Party will reverse this malicious onslaught and dramatically strengthen support in order to provide educational equity for all children.

Bilingual education enables children to achieve full competence in the English language and the academic success necessary to their full participation in the life of our nation. We reject the Reagan double-talk on bilingual education and commit ourselves to expanding and increasing its effectiveness.

We will emphasize the importance of preventing one-third of our student body nationwide from dropping out of school in the first place. And, we will supplement community-based programs encouraging students who have left school due to teenage parenthood, alcohol and drug abuse, or economic difficulties at home to complete their educations.

Recognizing that young people who are never given an opportunity for a job will be less likely to hold one in adulthood, we will also emphasize training and employment opportunities for youth. In so doing, we need to establish a genuine working partnership with the private sector.

Private schools, particularly parochial schools, are also an important part of our diverse educational system. Consistent with our tradition, the Democratic Party accepts its commitment to constitutionally acceptable methods of supporting the education of all pupils in schools which do not

racially discriminate, and excluding so-called segregation academies. The Party will continue to support federal education legislation which provides for the equitable participation in federal programs of all low and moderate income pupils.

For its part, when added to the traditional educational institutions of family, school and church, television has enormous promise as a teacher. When children spend more time in front of the television set than they do in the classroom, we must ask how television can help children, and why commercial broadcasters do so little programming for children today despite their legal responsibility as "public trustees" of the airwaves granted to them. The National Science Board, for instance, has recommended that commercial television stations be required to air a certain amount of information/educational programming for children each week. Properly developed, television can be an enormously efficient and effective supplemental teaching tool.

Higher Education — We will make certain that higher education does not become a luxury affordable only by the children of the rich. That is Ronald Reagan's America. In our America, no qualified student should be deprived of the ability to go on to college because of financial circumstance.

The Democratic Party reaffirms the importance of historically Black colleges. Today the survival of many of these colleges is threatened. The programs that assist them, which have been severely weakened in recent years, must be greatly strengthened with funding targeted toward Black and Hispanic institutions.

An explosion in demand for certain types of engineers, scientists and other technical specialists is creating a shortage of faculty and PhD candidates. We must encourage colleges and universities to train more scientists and engineers. More than one hundred years ago the Morrill Land Grant Act provided for agricultural colleges and programs that today still help keep American agriculture the world leader. We need a similar program today to encourage the training of scientists and engineers. At the same time, we must not neglect the arts and humanities, which enrich our spirit. The private sector must also recognize its responsibility to join partnerships which strengthen our diverse public and private higher education system.

Finally, all our educational institutions must adapt to growing numbers of adults returning to school to upgrade their skills, acquire new skills, prepare themselves for entirely new occupations, and enrich their lives.

Investing in the Arts

America is truly growing and prosperous when its spirit flourishes. The arts and humanities are at the core of our national experience. Creativity and the life of the mind have defined us at our best throughout our history. As scholars or artists, the museum-goers or students, craftsmen and craftswomen or the millions who use our libraries, countless Americans have a stake in a nation that honors and rejoices in intelligence and imagination.

The Democratic Party will set a new national tone of respect for learning and artistic achievement. Not only will the federal agencies that support them be strengthened and freed from political intimidation, but the White House itself will once again be a place where American cultural and intellectual life — in all its rich diversity — is honored. Excellence must start at the top.

Finally, the Democratic Party is also committed to the survival of public television and radio stations, which allow all Americans, regardless of ability to pay, to appreciate high quality, alternative programming. We oppose the efforts of the Reagan Administration to enact draconian cuts which would totally undermine the viability of this nation's excellent public broadcasting system, a broadcasting system which has given the country Sesame Street, 3-2-1 Contact, and other superb children's as well as cultural and public affairs programming.

Jobs, Training and Transitional Assistance

We must have a growing economy if we are to have jobs for all Americans who seek work. But even in a growing economy, the pressures of competition and the pace of change ensure that while jobs are being created, others are being destroyed. Prosperity will not be evenly distributed among regions and communities. We must make special efforts to help families in economic transition who are faced with loss of homes, health benefits, and pensions. And far too many of our young people, especially minorities, do not have the training and skills they need to get their first job. Democrats believe that it is a national responsibility to ensure that the burdens of change are fairly shared and that every young American can take the first step up the ladder of economic opportunity.

Of the 8.5 million Americans still out of work, 40 percent are under 25. Unemployment among teenagers stands at almost 20 percent. Less than three percent of the jobs created in the last three and a half years have gone to young people. Black and Hispanic youth have a double burden. Unemployment for black teenagers stands at 44 percent — a 20 percent increase in the last three years. Hispanic teens face a 26 percent unemployment rate.

As disturbing as these figures are, they do not tell the whole story. The unemployment rate measures only those teenagers who were actively looking for work, not those who have given up, completely discouraged by the lack of opportunity. Again the burden falls disproportionately on minority youth.

The Reagan Administration has dismantled virtually all of the successful programs to train and employ young people. Today, we are spending less to put young people to work than we were even under the last *Republican* Administration — 70 percent less, when inflation is taken into account. Youth unemployment has skyrocketed, while government efforts to combat it have dwindled to a trickle.

Unless we address this problem now, half of an entire generation may never know what it means to work. America cannot successfully compete in the world economy if a significant portion of our future work force is illiterate, unskilled, and unemployable.

The Democratic Party must give our young people new skills and new hope; we must work hand in hand with the private sector if job training is to lead to jobs. Specifically, targeted efforts are needed to address the urgent problem of unemployment among minority teenagers. We must provide job training for those who have dropped out of school, and take every step to expand educational opportunity for those still in school. We must recognize the special needs of the over-age 50 worker and the displaced homemaker. Through education, training and retraining we must reduce these dangerously high levels of unemployment.

We must provide an opportunity for workers, including those dislocated by changing technologies, to adapt to new opportunities; we must provide workers with choices as to which skills they wish to acquire. We know that Americans want to work. We are committed to ensuring that meaningful job training is available — for our students, for housewives returning to the workplace, and for those displaced by changing patterns of technology or trade.

— The federal government will develop a major comprehensive national job skills development policy that is targeted on the chronically unemployed and underemployed. We must train and place these Americans in high-demand labor shortage occupations, working with the private sector so that maximum employment and job creation can be achieved.

— We will overhaul the currently antiquated unemployment compensation system, and adequately fund job search listings of local employment agencies.

— We will also launch meaningful training programs that lead to job placement for women who receive public assistance, in order to break the cycle of dependence and to raise their standard of living. Instead of punitive reductions in AFDC and other benefits for women who seek training and employment while receiving such assistance, beneficiaries should be given a transition period during which they are permitted to earn income in a formal training program while receiving full benefits.

— We will seriously examine new approaches to training and retraining programs that could be financed directly by government, by labor and management, or by tax free contributions.

— If cancellations of specific weapons systems result in significant economic dislocations and job loss, it is a national responsibility to address the human consequences of national policy.

Investing in Infrastructure

Economic growth requires that America invest in our infrastructure as well as in our people. Investing in infrastructure means rebuilding our bridges and roads and sewers, and we are committed to doing that. But it also means investing in our cities, in decent housing and public transportation, and in regulatory systems for finance and telecommunication that will provide a sound basis for future economic growth.

Investing in our Cities

The Democratic Party recognizes the value of prosperous local government, and within that context we recognize that a healthy city is essential to the well-being of the nation, state, county and surrounding local governments.

Our nation's economic life depends on the economic growth of our cities. Our cities are not only the treasuries from which the nation draws its wealth; they are the centers of industry, the centers of art and culture, the breeding ground for economic innovation, and home to the majority of the American people. Our cities are among this country's greatest achievements, and they can be our country's greatest engine of economic growth.

Cities can be active partners with the federal government and private enterprises for creating new growth. They can be a dynamic entrepreneurial force — by encouraging education and research, by incubating promising new industries, by steering resources toward those most in need, and by fostering new cooperative arrangements among public agencies and private business. Cities can be a leading force for rebuilding the nation's economy.

But to do this, cities need state and national leadership which values the role of city and county government. Cities need a President willing to work and consult with mayors and county executives. They need an Administration which puts the needs of urban America on the top of the national agenda — because no plan for economic strength will survive when our cities are left behind.

Today, the Reagan Administration has turned its back on the cities. By sapping our cities' strength, this Administration is sapping our country's strength. Only the intervention of the Congress has prevented further and more devastating cuts in city-oriented programs. The Democratic Party believes in making our cities' needs a federal priority once again. We want to see again cities where people have jobs and adequate housing, cities whose bridges and mass transit are being maintained, and whose neighborhoods are safe to live in. And that will take a commitment by our federal government to help our cities again.

Toward that end, the Democratic Party pledges:

— a commitment to full employment. We believe the federal government must develop a major, comprehensive national job skills development policy targeted on the chronically unemployed and underemployed. We must launch special training programs for women who receive public assistance. We need to increase government procurement opportunities for small and minority firms and to encourage deposits of federal funds in minority-owned financial institutions. And to build for the future, the Democratic Party calls for a new national commitment to education, which must include raising standards, insisting on excellence, and giving all children a chance to learn, regardless of race, income or sex.

— a commitment to rebuilding the infrastructure of America. We need to inventory facility needs, set priorities and establish policies for the repair, maintenance, and replacement of public works by all levels of government. We need to create a federal capital budget to separate operating and capital outlays. We will consult local governments in decisions affecting the design and performance standards of facilities constructed under federal programs. And we need to create a national reconstruction fund to provide affordable loans to states and localities for infrastructure projects. .This will not only rebuild the infrastructure of our cities but provide badly needed employment for people who live there.

— a commitment to housing. We must restore government's positive role in helping all Americans find adequate and affordable housing. We reaffirm our commitment to public housing for the most disadvantaged members of our society. We must strengthen our commitment to the operation and rehabilitation of current government-assisted housing. We must maintain and expand the flow of mortgage capital, and bring interest rates down with sensible economic policies. We must pull together the patchwork of housing programs and cut through the red tape to make it easier for cities to receive the assistance to meet their own unique needs. We must upgrade and replenish housing in minority communities and create more units for poor and low-income people. And we must enforce fair housing standards to prohibit discrimination in the housing market.

Our Party must be a vehicle for realizing the hopes, the aspirations, and the dreams of the people of this country. And that includes the people who live in cities.

Physical Infrastructure

This nation's physical infrastructure — our bridges and roads, our ports, our railroads, our sewers, our public transit and water supply systems — is deteriorating faster than we can repair it. The gap between the necessary improvements and available resources grows every year. State and local governments, strapped by Reaganomics, have been forced repeatedly to defer maintenance, and to abandon plans for construction.

As Democrats, we recognize that infrastructure is the basis for efficient commerce and industry. If our older industrial cities are to grow, if our expanding regions are to continue to expand, then we must work with state and local governments to target our investment to our most important infrastructure. There is work to be done in rebuilding and maintaining our infrastructure, and there are millions of American men and women in need of work. The federal government must take the lead in putting them back to work, and in doing so, providing the basis for private sector investment and economic growth. We need to inventory facility needs, set priorities, and establish policies for the repair, maintenance and replacement of the public works by all levels of government. We need a capital budget to separate paying for these long-term investments from regular expenditures. Futhermore, we need a national reconstruction fund to provide affordable loans to states and localities for infrastructure projects.

Finance Infrastructure

At the heart of our economy is the financial infrastructure: a set of diverse interdependent institutions and markets which are the envy of the world. We must preserve their strengths. Until very recently, the United States operated with a domestic financial system that was built in response to the stock market crash of 1929, the massive series of bank failures that accompanied the Great Depression, and the speculative excesses of the stock market. There was an emphasis on placing different types of financial activities in different institutions. Commercial banks were not to float stock market issues. Investment bankers could. Neither took equity positions in individual companies. Separate savings and credit institutions were established to support housing and consumer durables. Soundness of the system, liquidity, investor and depositor protection, neutrality of credit and capital decisions, and a wide variety of financial institutions to serve the varying needs of business and consumers have been the fundamental goals.

Bit by bit, the American financial system began to change. The domestic financial market became closely tied to the international market, which in turn had become larger, more competitive, and more volatile. Inflation, technology, the growth of foreign competition, and institutional innovation all combined to create strong pressures for change. The 1980s brought a deregulation of interest rates and a wave of deregulatory decisions by financial regulators.

These changes raise serious threats to our traditional financial goals. Before leaping into a highly uncertain financial future, the country should take a careful look at the direction deregulation is taking, and what it means to our financial system and the economy.

Telecommunications

Telecommunications is the infrastructure of the information age. The last decade has seen an explosion in new technologies, expanded competition, and growing dependence on high quality telecommunications.

Nationwide access to those networks is becoming crucial to full participation in a society and economy that are increasingly dependent upon the rapid exchange of information. Electronically-delivered messages, and not the written word, are becoming the dominant form of communication. A citizen without access to telecommunications is in danger of fading into isolation. Therefore, the proper regulation of telecommunications is critical. We must encourage competition while preventing regulatory decisions which substantially increase basic telephone rates and which threaten to throw large numbers of low-income, elderly, or rural people off the telecommunications networks. We must also insure that workers in the telecommunications industry do not find their retirement or other earned benefits jeopardized by the consequences of divestiture.

This electronic marketplace is so fundamental to our future as a democracy (as well as to our economy) that social and cultural principles must be as much a part of communications policy as a commitment to efficiency, innovation, and competition. Those principles are diversity, the availability of a wide choice of information services and sources; access, the ability of all Americans, not just a privileged few, to take advantage of this growing array of information services and sources; and opportunity, a commitment to education and diverse ownership, particularly by minorities and women, that will give every American the ability to take advantage of the computer and the telecommunications revolution. We support the Fairness Doctrine and Equal Time requirements, along with other laws and regulations to the electronic media which encourage or require responsiveness to community needs and a diversity of viewpoints.

Housing

Decent, affordable housing has been a goal of national public policy for almost half a century, since the United States Housing Act of 1937. The Democratic Party has repeatedly reaffirmed the belief that American citizens should be able to find adequate shelter at reasonable cost. And we have been unwavering in our support of the premise that government has a positive role to play in ensuring housing opportunities for less fortunate Americans, including the elderly and the handicapped, not served by the private market.

In the last four years this long-standing commitment to decent shelter has been crippled by the underfunding, insensitivity, high interest rates, and distorted priorities of the Reagan Administration.

The Democratic Party has always accorded housing the high priority it deserves. One essential quality will characterize this commitment in the future. It must and will be comprehensive.

By advocating a comprehensive policy which addresses the totality of our housing needs, we do not mean to suggest that all concerns have an equal claim on resources or require the same level of governmental intervention. The bulk of our resources will be concentrated on those most in need, and government must take a leadership role where others cannot or will not participate.

Within a comprehensive framework for policy development and constituency building, we will establish priorities according to principles of compassion and equity. We would like to see a special effort in two areas in the first years of a new Democratic Administration.

First, we must intensify our commitment to the adequate operation, management, and rehabilitation of the current inventory of government-assisted housing. This housing stock is not one, but the only option for the least fortunate among our lower income families and senior citizens. It is the right thing to do and it makes economic sense to preserve our own economic investment.

Second, we must maintain and expand the flow of mortgage capital. The American dream of home ownership will fall beyond the reach of this generation and future ones if government fails to help attract new sources of capital for housing.

We will draw on our historic commitment to housing, and the best insights and energies of today's Democratic Party, to address the future housing needs of all the American people. The Democratic Party will develop short-range emergency responses to the problem of homelessness as well as long-range solutions to its causes. The Democratic Party will support upgrading and replenishment of the housing stock in minority communities, with more affordable units available so that poor and low income people can buy units with low interest loans. Also, fair housing standards need to be vigorously enforced by the federal, state and local governments in order to deal with persistent discrimination in the housing market for buyers and renters. Finally, the expansion of public housing and other publicly-assisted housing programs is a necessity due to the growth in the homeless population and in the high cost of commercially available units.

Transportation

Democrats vigorously support the concept of promoting competition in transportation and the elimination of unnecessary and inefficient regulation of the railroad industry. Democrats also insist on insuring a fair rate for captive shippers. It was the Democratic Party which was primarily re-

sponsible for the passage of the Staggers Rail Act of 1980, which was designed to accomplish these objectives.

The Democratic Party is committed to a policy of administering the transportation laws in a manner which will encourage competition and provide protection for captive shippers.

A comprehensive maritime policy that is tailored to the realities of today's international shipping world and to the economic, political, and military needs of the United States is a necessity. Such a policy should address all facets of our maritime industry — from shipping to shipbuilding and related activities — in an integrated manner.

A Framework for Growth

The American economy is a complex mix, incorporating any number of different actors and entities — private businesses, professional societies, charitable institutions, labor unions, regional development councils, and local school boards. The economy is driven by millions of individual decisions on spending and saving, on investing and wages. Government is only one force among many woven into the fabric of American economic life. Just as the wrong overall economic policy can disrupt the best private decisions, the best government economic policies will not put us on a path to long-term growth unless business, labor, and other private institutions meet their responsibilities and rise to the competitive challenge of a new era.

Private Sector Responsibilities

In many cases, the private sector is already playing a major role in laying the basis for future growth and meeting broad community responsibilities. In other cases, however, short-term considerations have been allowed to predominate at the expense of the long-term needs of the national economy.

A recent wave of mergers has been particularly troubling. Any number of large corporations have focused their energies arranging the next merger or defending against the latest takeover bid.

Many of our major competitors have targeted their efforts on investments in new methods of producing cheaper, high-quality products. To respond to the growing pressure of foreign competition, America's private sector must meet several challenges:

— Investing strategically — the more U.S. companies focus on long-term strategies to improve their competitive positions, the better off the entire economy will be.
— Managing cost and quality — U.S. companies will have to place similar emphasis on controlling costs and quality to effectively meet the best of the foreign competition.
— Competing internationally — U.S. business like other institutions in the country need to pay greater attention to the international market place.

Partnership, Cooperation and Participation

Partnership, cooperation and participation are central to economic growth. We need new cooperative institutions, and a steady redefinition of how labor and management, universities, the private sector, and state and local governments can work together.

— National cooperation — In developing a long-term growth strategy, there are several particularly important functions that today are poorly performed or poorly coordinated by the government: coordination and policy coherence; developing and disseminating useful economic information; anticipating economic problems; and developing long-term consensus between public and private sectors. To better accomplish these tasks, it is time that a national Economic Cooperation Council was created. Its charter would be simple and basic: (1) to collect, analyze, and disseminate economic data; (2) to create a forum where the gap between business, labor, and government is bridged, where all three develop the trust, understanding, and cooperation necessary to improve productivity; and, (3) to identify national priorities, make recommendations on how best to reach those goals, and help build consensus for action.
— State involvement — Under the guise of increasing the power of state government, the Reagan Administration has actually given the states only the power to decide what programs to cut or eliminate, because of the substantially decreased funding it has made available to the states. Should it be baby clinics, child immunization against disease, day care, maternal health, or youth services? The Democratic Party believes a strong partnership of federal, state and local governments is basic to effective and efficient decision-making, problem-solving, and provision of adequate services. We must also encourage cooperation between states and the private sector. State development agencies are already seeking closer ties to both business and universities. And universities are increasingly looking to the private sector in setting their research agendas.
— Local and community involvement — Citizen involvement in governance should be as great as possible. The responsibility for general governance, the delivery of programs and services, and the resolution of problems should be with the level of government that is closest to the citizenry and that can still discharge those responsibilities effectively and efficiently. These levels of government must assure basic civil liberties and justice for all citizens. They must not be abrogated by any local jurisdiction. The federal government should focus on the importance of local initiatives. For example, vocational education is an area where local schools and local business will increasingly be

brought together. Financial stability and adequate authority are essential prerequisites to developing successful public-private partnerships and maximizing citizen involvement in governance.

Government financial and technical assistance programs should give preference to viable worker and/or community-owned or -run businesses, especially as a response to plant shutdowns.

Broadening Labor-Management Cooperation

We support greater employee participation in the workplace. Employees should have an opportunity to make a greater contribution to workplace productivity and quality through actual ownership of the company, employee representation on corporate boards, quality work circles, and greater worker participation in management decisions. The government should encourage employee participation and ownership, particularly as an alternative to plant shutdowns. It is destructive of labor-management relations when concessions extracted from labor to preserve jobs are converted, after the restoration of profitability, into management bonuses, rather than restoring the concessions that the workers made. Such practices offend our sense of fairness, as does the Reagan Administration-inspired union-busting. Essential to fairness in the workplace is the basic right of workers to organize collectively.

Consumer Protection

The Democratic Party strongly reaffirms its commitment to federal programs which are designed to enhance and protect the health and safety of all Americans. Under the Reagan Administration, the critical missions of agencies such as the Consumer Product Safety Commission (CPSC), the National Highway Traffic Safety Administration (NHTSA), the Food and Drug Administration (FDA), the Occupational Safety and Health Administration (OSHA), the Mine Safety and Health Administration (MSHA), and the Federal Trade Commission (FTC) have been ignored and subverted.

The Reagan Administration proposed abolishing the CPSC, which has recalled over 300 million dangerous and defective products in its 10 year history. When it failed to accomplish this, the Administration attempted to submerge CPSC in the Department of Commerce. Also failing in this attempt, the Reagan Administration inflicted massive budget and personnel cuts on the Commission. The impact has been far reaching: recalls declined 66%, inspections were cut in half and over half of CPSC's regional offices have been closed. The result has been a paralysis of mission and an America more susceptible to dangerous products.

The record at the NHTSA, the agency mandated to reduce the appalling annual highway deaths of more than 50,000 Ameri-

cans, is just as shameful. The President has appointed administrators with no safety background and even less commitment to the public health mission of the agency. Critical lifesaving safety standards, such as one requiring automatic crash protection in cars, have been revoked. The enforcement of defect and recall programs, designed to remove dangerous vehicles from our roads, has been cut back. Recalls are at an all-time low and only one safety standard has been proposed in four years.

At OSHA and MSHA, we have witnessed a retreat from agency mandates to provide safe and healthful working conditions for this nation's working men and women. Existing standards have been weakened or revoked and not one single new standard has been implemented. Similarly, at the FDA there has been an important shift away from removing dangerous and ineffective drugs in favor of weakening standards for products. The FTC has run roughshod over the nation's antitrust laws, allowing 9 of the 10 largest mergers in history to occur.

The dangerous trends in all these areas must be immediately reversed to allow these vital health and safety agencies to pursue their missions aggressively, to protect and enhance the health and safety of all Americans.

Individual Empowerment

The Democratic Party's commitment to full equality is as much a part of providing individual opportunity as it is part of a program of social justice. At the heart of our values as a nation is our belief in independence. Anyone who has brought home a paycheck, bought a car, or paid off a mortgage knows the pride that economic self-sufficiency brings. And anyone who has lost a job, watched one's children go hungry, or been denied a chance at success knows the terrible indignity that comes with dependence.

As Democrats, we share that belief in independence. Our goal is to allow the greatest number of people the greatest opportunity for self-sufficiency.

As a Party, we are committed to preparing people to stand on their own; that is why we insist on adequate nutrition for our children and good educations for our young people. We are committed to permitting independence; that's why we believe discrimination on any basis must come to an end. We believe that independence should be prolonged for as long as possible; to ensure it continues even after retirement, we support Social Security and Medicare. And we believe we must preserve the self-respect of those who are unable to be completely self-sufficient — the very young, the unskilled, the disabled, the very old — and to help them toward as much independence as possible. As much as it is a strategy for long run economic growth, individual empowerment must itself be an operating philosophy. In the welfare system, in education, and in the laws affecting everyone from shareholders to the average

voter, the Democratic Party will ask if the individual is being made stronger and more independent.

America in a World Economy

The reality of international competition in the 1980s requires government policies which will assure the competitiveness of American industry and American workers. Democrats will support and encourage innovation and research and development in both the private and public sector. We will seek to strengthen America's small businesses. And we will pursue trade policies and industrial strategies to ensure that our workers and our businesses can compete fully and fairly in the international arena.

Innovation

Innovation — in process and product technology — is at the heart of our ability to compete in a world economy and produce sustained economic growth at home. And research and development, critical as it is for our growing high technology industries, is no less important for our basic industries. In the past generation, our world leadership in innovation has been increasingly jeopardized. We have not invested enough — or widely enough — to match our major competitors.

Research and Development — Since the mid-1960s, all the other major industrial nations have increased their expenditures for research and development more rapidly than we have. Over the past decade, manufacturing productivity rose more than four times faster in Japan, more than three times faster in France, and more than twice as fast in both West Germany and the United Kingdom than in the United States. And the number of patents granted to Americans each year has plunged by 40 percent.

The United States should revise its downward trend and increase the percentage of GNP devoted to commercially-rated R&D as a long-term spending goal. We must be at the cutting edge, and we will not get there without cooperation between the government and the private sector. As Democrats, our goal is to increase civilian research and development in this country, to expand its commercial application, and to provide more industries with the opportunity to take advantage of it.

At the national level, this means enhanced support for undergraduate and graduate training in science, mathematics, and engineering; increased support to refurbish and modernize university research laboratories; increased support for the National Science Foundation and similar efforts; and a commitment to civilian research and development.

Centers of Excellence — In the past generation, scientists and engineers, together with educators and business leaders throughout the United States, have begun countless new, high technology businesses such as those in Boston, Massachusetts,

California's Silicon Valley, North Carolina's Research Triangle, greater Denver, Colorado, and Austin, Texas to establish this country as a leader in the next generation of high technology industries — biotechnology, polymer sciences, robotics, photovoltaics, marine sciences, microelectronics. The Democratic Party will encourage and support centers that provide for cooperation of academic and entrepreneurial excellence, thereby strengthening our scientific and technological resources and creating tomorrow's jobs.

Small and Minority Business

The Democratic Party recognizes that small businesses create many, if not most of the new jobs in our country, and are responsible for much of the innovation. They are thus our greatest hope for the future. Our capacity as a nation to create an environment that encourages and nurtures innovative new businesses will determine our success in providing jobs for our people. In the private sector, spurring innovation means paying special attention to the needs of small, including minority and women-owned, and rapidly growing businesses on the cutting edge of our economy.

This will require incentives for research and development and for employee education and training, including relaxing certain restrictions on pension fund investment; targeted reform that stimulates the flow of capital into new and smaller businesses; a tax code that is no longer biased against small and rapidly growing firms; vigorous enforcement of our antitrust laws, coupled with antitrust policies that permit clearly legitimate joint research and development ventures; expanded small business access to the Export-Import Bank and other agencies involved in export promotion; and targeted reform that provides for the delivery of community-based, community-supported management assistance, and innovative means of making seed capital available for companies in our large cities, as well as our rural communities.

Rules and regulations should not weigh more heavily on new firms or small businesses than they do on the large, well-established enterprise. Risk taking is a key to economic growth in a modern industrial society. If anything, rules and regulations should encourage it.

The Small Business Administration must once again be responsive to the needs of entrepreneurs, including minorities and women. In addition, the heads of the Small Business Administration, the Minority Business Development Administration and other government agencies must ensure that the needs of smaller minority businesses are met at the regional and local levels. To further meet the needs of smaller minority businesses, we favor increasing government procurement, opportunities for smaller minority firms, encouraging deposits of federal funds in minority-owned financial institutions, and vigorously implementing all set-aside provisions for minority businesses.

The Democratic Party pledges to bring about these reforms and create a new era of opportunity for the entrepreneurs who have always led the way in our economy.

Meeting the Challenge of Economic Competition

Thirty years ago, half of all goods produced in the world were made in the United States. While we have greatly expanded our output of services, our share of manufactured products is now just one-fifth of the world's total. Once dominant U.S.-industries are now hard-pressed. In April, our trade deficit reached a stunning $12.2 billion for one month. At that rate, we would lose two million or more jobs this year alone. We will not allow our workers and our industries to be displaced by either unfair import competition, or irrational fiscal and monetary policies.

Some of these difficulties we have brought on ourselves, with shortsighted strategies, inadequate investment in plant, equipment, and innovation, and fiscal and monetary policies that have impaired our international competitiveness by distorting the value of the dollar against foreign currencies. But other difficulties have been thrust upon us by foreign nations.

The reality of the 1980s is that the international economy is the arena in which we must compete. The world economy is an integrated economy; the challenge for our political leadership is to assure that the new arena is in fact a fair playing field for American businesses and consumers. We are committed to pursuing industrial strategies that effectively and imaginatively blend the genius of the free market with vital government partnership and leadership. As Democrats, we will be guided by the following principles and policies.

— We need a vigorous, open and fair trade policy that builds America's competitive strength and that allows our nation to remain an advanced, diversified economy while promoting full employment and raising living standards in the United States and other countries of the world; opens overseas markets for American products; strengthens the international economic system; assists adjustment to foreign competition; and recognizes the legitimate interests of American workers, farmers and businesses.

— We will pursue international negotiations to open markets and eliminate trade restrictions, recognizing that the growth and stability of the Third World depends on its ability to sell its products in international markets. High technology, agriculture and other industries should be brought under the General Agreement on Trade and Tariffs. Moreover, the developing world is a major market for U.S. exports, particularly capital goods. As a result, the U.S. has a major stake in international economic institutions that support growth in the developing world.

— We recognize that the growth and development of the Third World is vital both to global stability and to the continuing expansion of world trade. The U.S. presently sells more to the Third World than to the European Community and Japan combined. If we do not buy their goods, they cannot buy ours, nor can they service their debt. Consequently, it is important to be responsive to the issues of the North/South dialogue such as volatile commodity prices, inequities in the functioning of the international financial and monetary markets, and removal of barriers to the export of Third World goods.

— If trade has become big business for the country, exports have become critical to the economic health of a growing list of American industries. In the future, national economic policy will have to be set with an eye to its impact on U.S. exports. The strength of the dollar, the nature of the U.S. tax system, and the adequacy of export finance all play a role in making U.S. exports internationally competitive.

— The United States continues to struggle with trade barriers that affect its areas of international strength. Subsidized export financing on the part of Europe and Japan has also created problems for the United States, as has the use of industrial policies in Europe and Japan. In some cases, foreign governments target areas of America's competitive strength. In other cases, industrial targeting has been used to maintain industries that cannot meet international competition — often diverting exports to the American market and increasing the burden of adjustment for America's import-competing industries. We will ensure that timely and effective financing can be obtained by American businesses through the Export-Import Bank, so that they can compete effectively against subsidized competitors from abroad.

— A healthy U.S. auto industry is essential to a strong trade balance and economy. That industry generates a large number of American jobs and both develops and consumes new technology needed for economic vitality. We believe it is a sound principle of international trade for foreign automakers which enjoy substantial sales in the United States to invest here and create jobs where their markets are. This can promote improved trade relations and a stronger American and world economy. We also believe U.S. automakers need to maintain high volume small car production in the U.S. With the U.S. auto companies' return to profitability (despite continued unemployment in the auto sector), we urge expanded domestic investment to supply consumers with a full range of competitive vehicles. We support efforts by management and labor to improve auto quality and productivity, and to restrain prices.

— Where foreign competition is fair,

American industry should compete without government assistance. Where competition is unfair, we must respond powerfully. We will use trade law and international negotiations to aid U.S. workers, farmers, and business injured by unfair trade practices.

— We need industrial strategies to create a cooperative partnership of labor, capital, and management to increase productivity and to make America competitive once more. Our keystone industries must be modernized and rebuilt, through industry-wide agreements. Where necessary, through Presidential leadership, we must negotiate industrial modernization and growth agreements that commit management to new domestic investment, higher levels of employment and worker training, as well as commit labor to ease the introduction of new technologies.

— There must be a broad consensus and commitment among labor, business and financial institutions that industry should and can be assisted, and in a particular way. We believe that all parties to modernization agreements must contribute to their success and that the government must be prepared to use a range of tools — including tax, import, and regulatory relief, and appropriate financing mechanisms — to assist this revitalization. There should be a primary emphasis on private capital in any such agreements.

— The problems of individual industries, rather than industry as a whole, is another area in which an Economic Co-operation Council will be effective. In the case of a particular industry, the Council would select sub-councils to solve specific problems. Key members of the interested businesses and unions, financial institutions, academic specialists and other concerned and knowledgeable parties would meet to hammer out proposed strategies and agreements. It is not a question of picking winners and losers. Nor is it even always a question of some industries being more important than others. Rather, it is an opportunity for government and the private sector to forge a consensus to capture new markets, to restore an industry to competitive health, or to smooth the transition of workers and firms to new opportunities.

— We want industries to modernize so as to restore competitiveness where it is flagging. If temporary trade relief is granted, the *quid pro quo* for relief will be a realistic, hardheaded modernization plan which will restore competitiveness involving commitments by all affected parties. The public is entitled to receive a fair return on its investment. Where government initiatives are necessary to save an industry like steel, auto or textiles, we must see that those initiatives meet the needs of the whole community — workers as well as executives, taxpayers and consumers as well as stockholders.

— To facilitate the efforts of workers and communities to keep plants open and operating and, in cases which closings are unavoidable, to help workers and communities to adapt, we support a requirement that companies give advance notification of plant closings or large-scale layoffs to their employees, surrounding communities and local governments. Where plants are nonetheless closed, we will help workers and communities to adapt.

— Finally, we need a vigorous effort to redress the currency distortions that are undermining our international competitiveness. In addition to reducing our budget deficit, we will press for improved economic coordination with the major industrialized nations; work with Japan and other countries to further liberalize currency and investment regulations; and negotiate toward agreements that will blunt speculative currency swings and restore stability and predictability to the international monetary system.

Agriculture

Agriculture — America's largest, most fundamental industry — has been plunged into its worst depression since Herbert Hoover presided over the farm economy's collapse half a century ago. During President Reagan's stewardship of our nation's agriculture economy: real prices paid to farmers for their commodities have plummeted by twenty-one percent; real interest rates paid by farmers have increased by as much as 1,200 percent; real farm income has fallen to its lowest level since 1933; debt owed by U.S. farmers and ranchers has swelled to $215 billion; and farm foreclosures and forced sales have tripled.

Ronald Reagan has hung a "for sale" sign on America's independent, family-based system of agricultural production. While these farmers have raised their production efficiency to record highs, Reagan's policies have forced down their prices, income, and financial worth.

The Reagan Administration has been unwilling to take sensible, fiscally responsible action needed to halt this accelerating downward cycle in agriculture. Because of this failure of leadership, nearly 200,000 good farmers and ranchers, including minority farmers, have gone out of business since he took office in 1981. This is a rate of more than 1,000 families pushed off their land every week, the equivalent of all the farms and ranches in California and Iowa, our two largest agricultural states. Hundreds of thousands of the remaining enterprises teeter on the brink of bankruptcy and cannot survive another four years of this Administration's agricultural mismanagement.

This collapse is happening despite the fact that Ronald Reagan has squandered taxpayers' money on his farm policies, spending $31 billion on his programs last year alone. That is *six times more* than any other President in history has spent on farm programs, and it is *$9 billion more* than was spent on farm programs *in all eight years* of President Kennedy's and President Johnson's Administrations combined.

Like 1932 and 1960, this election year represents a watershed for American agriculture. At stake is the survival of the family farm. Under President Reagan's policies of high costs and low prices, these family farmers cannot survive. They will continue to go out of business at a historic pace, to be replaced by an industrialized structure of agriculture that is dominated by conglomerates, giant farm combinations, and tax loss ventures. Already, under Reagan, 65 percent of net farm income has been concentrated in the hands of the largest 1 percent of farms, up from 42 percent just three years ago.

The Democratic Party renews its commitment to the family farm structure of American agriculture. We believe that the public need for a reliable supply of high-quality, reasonably priced food and fiber is best met by family farm enterprises whose primary business is farming or ranching. It is from hundreds of thousands of those competitive, diverse, decentralized, entrepreneurial families that the public gains superior agricultural efficiency and productivity. Accordingly, it is in these farming families that the public finds its most sensible investment. In addition, these farmers are the ones who show greatest concern for good conservation practices, quality of food, and rural values. We need more of these farmers, not fewer.

The Democratic Party pledges action. We must solve the immediate farm crisis through a combination of humanitarian aid programs abroad, aggressive promotion of farm exports, and a fair moratorium on farm debt and foreclosure by federal credit agencies to family farm borrowers being forced out of business through no fault of their own, until a long-term program addressing the farm credit crisis can be put into place. Beginning next January with the writing of a new long-term farm bill, the Democratic Party pledges to rebuild a prosperous system of family farms and ranches. We will forge a new agreement on a farm and food policy that assures a fair deal for family farmers, consumers, taxpayers, conservationists, and others with a direct stake in the organizational structure of the food economy.

Our goal is to restore the faith of family farmers that their hard work, ingenuity, efficiency, and good stewardship will be rewarded with profit, rather than debt. We seek a program that is focused specifically on the true family farm, that encourages long-term financial planning, that is tied to locally-approved soil conservation programs, and that reduces federal budget costs for farm programs.

We will target federal assistance toward true family-sized and beginning farmers' operations. We will stop good, efficient farmers from being thrown off their farms, while structuring incentives so as to achieve maximum participation in farm commodity programs. We will bring farm credit interest rates down and set supports at levels that at least enable farmers to recover actual production costs. We will use the full range of programs to reduce excess production when necessary to assure fair prices to farmers. As the overall economy improves, we will gradually adjust price supports toward a firm goal of parity of income. We will give new emphasis to producer-controlled marketing arrangements. We will revitalize the farmer-owned commodity reserve system. We will put in place tax policies that are fair to farmers, while removing unproductive incentives for investors seeking to avoid taxes. We must protect family farmers from land speculators and we must protect both farmers and consumers from income losses resulting from exorbitant pricing of middlemen. We will renew our country's historic commitment to agricultural science and education, to rural services such as cooperative electrification and telephones. We oppose Reagan Administration proposals that would more than double interest rates to rural cooperatives, and sharply reduce rural electric loan levels.

The Democratic Party reaffirms its commitment to soil and water conservation. We will actively promote the production of ethanol and other biomass sources of renewable energy and encourage conversion to energy self-sufficient farming operations.

Finally, we must reverse the annual decrease in the value and volume of U.S. farm exports which has occurred in each year of Ronald Reagan's term. Our farm exports are vital to the nation's prosperity and provide a major part of total farm income. We must restore the ability of U.S. farm products to compete in world markets, and increase world-wide demand for American agricultural products. To do this, we must make major changes in Ronald Reagan's economic policies, and correct his grossly distorted currency exchange rates, which have caused American competitiveness in international trade to decline. We must also resist efforts to lower commodity price supports; such action would only lower farm income without addressing the economic policies which are the root cause of declining competitiveness of U.S. farm products in world markets.

Critical to the recovery of farm income and exports will be the pursuit of economic policies that contribute to worldwide economic recovery. Flexible export credit programs and assurances of long-term availability of U.S. farm products will also be necessary to restore America's preeminence as an agricultural exporter and end the destruction of the family farm brought on by Ronald Reagan.

Managing Our Natural Resources

Our economy, the quality of our lives, and the kind of opportunities that we leave to our children all depend on how well we manage our wealth of natural resources. We must harvest enough timber and food, produce enough minerals, coal, oil and gas, and provide enough electric power to keep our economy growing. We must be prepared to avoid severe dislocations when conflicts in other parts of the world force energy prices to climb. At the same time that we encourage enhanced energy production, we must recognize that conserving irreplaceable resources, using energy efficiently instead of wasting it, and protecting our environment help guarantee a better life for twenty-first century America.

Protecting Our National Security

President Reagan has reduced our ability to defend our economy from the disruptions that would come if conflicts in other countries interrupt the world's oil supply. While the percentage of our oil imports from the Middle East has dropped, U.S. oil imports from other countries have increased. If war in the Middle East cuts back oil supplies from that region, Europe and Japan will pay higher prices to get replacement oil; a bidding war among oil-importing nations means that the price of oil all over the world, including the United States, will rise dangerously.

Ronald Reagan has refused to prepare us for that day. He has refused to fill the Strategic Petroleum Reserve as quickly as authorized by law, and in case of emergency, he has made clear that his policy will be simply to allow those who can pay the most to buy whatever supplies are available.

Our Party must spell out a comprehensive program for energy security. We should accelerate the filling of the Strategic Petroleum Reserve, so that it can play its intended role as a temporary national oil supply during future energy emergencies. And in an oil crisis, a Democratic President will make every effort to ensure that essential users — schools, farmers, hospitals, local bus and rail systems — have the supplies they need at reasonable prices. The Democratic Party will ensure that the especially vulnerable — the unemployed, the elderly, the poor — will not be unfairly forced to share the burden of rising oil prices.

Developing U.S. Energy Supplies

In today's complex world, no industrial nation can be fully self-sufficient. The United States and all countries in the free world depend on each other for resources, as markets, or as economic and political allies. But the strength of our own economy and the influence we exercise in the rest of the world are sure to be increased if we are capable of supplying more, not less, of our own energy.

America is blessed with abundant coal and natural gas, substantial supplies of oil, and plentiful reserves of uranium. Although very costly to process, vast supplies of oil shales and tar sands represent future energy sources. Significant contributions to our energy supply can be made by utilizing renewable resources and indigenous energy, such as active and passive solar systems, windpower, geothermal and ocean thermal power, and the recovery of gas from agricultural waste, coal mines, and garbage dumps. These proven energy sources, as well as more experimental energy systems, should be encouraged for the positive environmental and economic contribution they can make to our energy security.

The Democratic Party supports the aggressive promotion of coal exports, research and development into better technologies for using coal, and assurances that rates for transporting coal are fair and reasonable. To ensure that the environment and worker safety are fully protected as coal production increases to meet our national energy needs, we will vigorously implement and strictly enforce laws governing worker safety, land reclamation, air and water quality, and the protection of agriculture, fish, and wildlife.

The Democratic Party will support research and development for solar energy and other renewable energy systems, and will provide incentives for use of solar and other emerging energy systems. We will vigorously pursue our solar energy efforts and dramatically increase funding for the Solar Energy and Energy Conservation Bank and low-income weatherization, which could put hundreds of thousands of unemployed people to work weatherizing and installing solar energy systems in millions of American homes, especially the homes of low-income Americans. We oppose the Reagan Administration's efforts to fund these programs through petroleum price overcharge refunds from the oil companies.

We will support the federal research and development efforts slashed by the Reagan Administration, to promote the discovery of new energy supplies and energy use technologies.

The Democratic Party strongly opposes the Reagan Administration's policy of aggressively promoting and further subsidizing nuclear power. Today, millions of Americans are concerned about the safety of nuclear power plants and their radioactive waste. We recognize the safety and economic factors which bring into question the viability of this energy source.

We will insist on the highest possible standards of safety and protection of public health with respect to nuclear power, including siting, design, operation, evacuation plans, and waste disposal procedures. We will require nuclear power to compete fairly in the marketplace. We will reexamine and review all federal subsidies to the nuclear industry, including the Price-Anderson Act's limits on the liability of the industry which will be considered for reauthorization in the next Congress. A Democratic Administration will give the Nuclear Regulatory Commission the integrity, competence, and credibility it needs to carry out its mandate to protect the public health and safety. We will expand the role of the public in NRC procedures.

The Democratic Party believes high-level radioactive waste and other hazardous materials should be transported only when absolutely necessary. We will guarantee states full participatory rights in all decisions affecting the movement of high-level radioactive waste within their borders. We will require radioactive waste and hazardous materials emergency response plans along transportation routes, similar to those required for nuclear power plants. The Democratic Party will act swiftly to ensure states' authority to regulate routes and schedules for radioactive and other hazardous shipments.

We will ensure that no offshore oil and gas exploration will be taken up that is inconsistent with the protection of our fisheries and coastal resources. The leasing of public lands, both onshore and offshore, will be based on present demand and land use planning processes, and will be undertaken in ways that assure fair economic return to the public, protection of the environment and full participation by state and local governments. The Coastal Zone Management Act should be amended to require initial leasing decisions to be consistent with federally approved state and territorial coastal zone management plans. Interior states should be given consultation and concurrence rights with respect to onshore leases comparable to the rights afforded coastal states with respect to offshore leases.

We believe that synthetic fuels research and development support should emphasize environmental protection technologies and standards and hold out reasonable hope of long-term economic viability. The Democratic Party proposes to reevaluate the Synthetic Fuels Corporation.

Energy Conservation

The high cost of producing and using energy now constitutes a substantial share of U.S. capital spending. Energy conservation has become essential to our economy as well as our national security.

Strict standards of energy efficiency for home appliances, for example, could save enough money in the next 15 years to avoid the need for 40 new power plants. Better insulated houses and apartments can sharply reduce power and heating bills for families throughout America, and help utilities avoid the high cost of building more expensive powerplants.

Ronald Reagan sees no role for government in conserving energy, and he has gutted promising conservation efforts. The Democratic Party supports extension of the existing tax credits for business and residential energy conservation and renewable energy use, and expansion of those tax credits to include the incorporation of passive solar designs in new housing. The Democratic Party also supports faithful implementation of existing programs for energy efficiency standards for new appliances; upgrading of fuel efficiency stan-

dards for new automobiles; establishment of comparable fuel efficiency standards for new light trucks and vans; and development of an energy efficiency rating system to be used to advise homebuyers at the time of sale of the likely future energy costs of houses.

Lifeline Utility Rates

Recognizing that the elderly and the poor suffer most from high energy costs, the Democratic Party supports special, lower electricity and natural gas rates for senior citizens and low-income Americans.

Recycling

The Democratic Party recognizes that recovering and recycling new materials can conserve energy and natural resources, create additional jobs, reduce the costs of material goods, eliminate solid waste and litter, and avoid pollution. We will increase efforts to recover and recycle useful materials from municipal waste.

Protecting Our Environment

Americans know that industrial production and economic development do not have to mean ruined land or polluted air and water. Sound resource management, careful planning, and strict pollution control enforcement will allow us to have a prosperous economy and a healthy environment. For the last four years the Reagan Administration has assumed a radical position, working to eliminate the environmental protections forged through years of bipartisan cooperation.

Ronald Reagan's first appointees to key environmental positions have already been forced to resign. But the American people are entitled to more than the absence of scandal — they demand real action to protect the health and safety of our families and communities. The Democratic Party supports revitalizing the Environmental Protection Agency by providing it with a budget increase adequate to allow it to carry out its substantially increased responsibility to protect the people and enforce the law.

Hazardous Wastes

Thousands of dump sites across America contain highly dangerous poisons that can threaten the health and safety of families who live nearby or who depend on water supplies that could be contaminated by the poisons. Although Congress has established the Superfund for emergency cleanup of these dangerous sites, President Reagan refuses to use it vigorously. The Democratic Party is committed to enforcing existing laws, to dramatically increasing Superfund resources to clean up all sites that threaten public health, and to assuring that everyone whose health or property is damaged has a fair opportunity to force the polluters to pay for the damage. This increased support should be financed at least in part through new taxes

on the generation of hazardous wastes, so companies have an economic incentive to reduce the volume and toxicity of their dangerous wastes.

The Resource Conservation and Recovery Act should be expanded to include major new requirements for safer management of newly generated toxic waste. High priority must be given to establishing and implementing a program to phase out the land disposal of untreated hazardous waste, requiring instead that it be treated by chemical, biological, or thermal processes that render it harmless and safe for disposal. The Environmental Protection Agency also should adopt standards to ensure that the safest possible methods of managing particular wastes are used, and that available methods are used to reduce the volume and toxicity of waste produced by industry.

Clean Air and Water

The Democratic Party supports a reauthorized and strengthened Clean Air Act. Statutory requirements for the control of toxic air pollutants should be strengthened, with the environmental agency required to identify and regulate within three years priority air pollutants known or anticipated to cause cancer and other serious diseases. The Democratic Party calls for an immediate program to reduce sulfur dioxide emissions by 50% from 1980 levels within the next decade; this program shall include interim reductions within five years of its enactment. Our effort should be designed to reduce environmental and economic damage from acid rain while assuring such efforts do not cause regional economic dislocations. Every effort should be made to mitigate any job losses associated with any national acid rain program.

The Democratic Party is committed to strengthening the Clean Water Act to curb both direct and indirect discharge of toxic pollutants into our nation's waters, and supports a strengthened Environmental Protection Agency to assure help to American cities in providing adequate supplies of drinking water free of toxic chemicals and other contaminants.

Workplace Safety

The Democratic Party believes all Americans, in their workplaces and communities, have the right to know what hazardous materials and chemicals they may have been exposed to and how they may protect their health from such exposure. The Democratic Party supports appropriate funding levels for the Occupational Safety and Health Administration, reversing the Reagan budget cuts in that agency; vigorous enforcement of occupational safety and health standards; and worker right-to-know requirements.

Pesticides and Herbicides

The Democratic Party is committed to establishing standards and deadlines requiring all pesticides and herbicides to be thoroughly tested to ensure they do not cause cancer, birth defects, or other adverse health effects. We support rigorous research and information programs to develop and assist farmers with the use of integrated pest management and non-chemical pest control methods to reduce the health risk of controlling agricultural pests, and the establishment of strict deadlines to ensure that pesticides are fully tested and in compliance with health and safety standards. The Democratic Party is committed to ensuring that our nation's food supply is free of pesticides whose danger to health has been demonstrated, and believes it is irresponsible to allow the export to other nations of herbicides and pesticides banned for use in the U.S. and will act swiftly to halt such exports.

EPA Budget

The Democratic Party opposes the Reagan Administration's budget cuts, which have severely hampered the effectiveness of our environmental programs. The Environmental Protection Agency should receive a budget that exceeds in real dollars the agency's purchasing power when President Reagan took office, since the agency's workload has almost doubled in recent years.

Managing our Public Lands

The Democratic Party believes in retaining ownership and control of our public lands, and in managing those lands according to the principles of multiple use and sustained yield, with appropriate environmental standards and mitigation requirements to protect the public interest. The Democratic Party supports the substantial expansion of the National Wilderness Preservation System, with designations of all types of ecosystems, including coastal areas, deserts, and prairies as well as forest and alpine areas. Congressional decisions to designate wilderness should include evaluations of mineral resources and other potential land values.

The Democratic Party supports adequate funding of and restoration of federal programs to protect fully national parks, wildlife refuges, and wilderness areas from external and internal threats. Development activities within national wildlife refuges which are not compatible with the purposes for which the refuges were designated should not be allowed. The letter and the spirit of the Alaska National Interest Lands Conservation Act of 1980 should be followed, with an end to unsound land exchanges and other efforts to circumvent the law.

A new Democratic Party will provide adequate appropriations for the Land and Water Conservation Fund.

Wetlands — The Democratic Party supports coherent and coordinated federal policies to protect our nation's valuable and disappearing wetlands, which are critical nurseries for commercial fisheries and vital ecological, scenic, and recreational sources. These policies will include more active efforts to acquire threatened wetland areas, consideration of new tax incentives to encourage private efforts to preserve instead of develop wetlands, and elimination of current incentives that encourage wetlands destruction.

Wildlife — Fishing, hunting, and enjoyment of America's wildlife can continue to be an important part of our natural heritage only through active programs to maintain the diversity and abundance of plants, animals, and natural habitats. The Democratic Party supports protection of endangered species, land management to maintain healthy populations of wildlife, and full United States participation to implement international wildlife treaties.

Water Policy — The Democratic Party recognizes that finite and diminishing quantities of water, and often antiquated, inadequate, or inefficient water supply systems, threaten economic growth and the quality of life in all regions of the country. New water project starts, in the West by the Bureau of Reclamation, and in the rest of the country by the Corps of Engineers, are critical. We recognize that strong federal leadership is necessary to meet these needs, and to do so in environmentally sound ways.

The Democratic Party supports the creation of a national water resources planning board and a comprehensive review of the nation's water needs. We support major new water policy efforts addressing several national needs:

— We will help meet our nation's infrastructure needs, including the construction of new projects which are economically and environmentally sound. In the West, new reclamation water project starts are critical. In all cases, we will consider innovative and nonstructural alternatives on an equal basis.

— We will examine the water quantity and water quality issues associated with providing adequate water supply.

— We will help meet navigation, flood control, and municipal water supply system needs, with new assistance.

Federal water policy efforts must be carefully coordinated with affected state governments, making possible not only cooperative financing of water investments but a commensurate sharing of decision-making authority and responsibility.

Chapter II. Justice, Dignity and Opportunity

Introduction

Fulfilling America's highest promise, equal justice for all: that is the Democratic agenda for a just future.

For many of our citizens, it is only in the last two decades that the efforts of a broad, bipartisan coalition have begun to give real meaning to the dream of freedom and equality. During that time Democrats, spurred by the Civil Rights Movement, have enacted landmark legislation in areas including voting, education, housing and employment.

A nation is only as strong as its commitment to justice and equality. Today, a corrosive unfairness eats at the underpinnings of our society. Civil rights laws and guarantees — only recently achieved after hardfought battles, personal sacrifice and loss of life — are imperiled by an Administration that consciously seeks to turn the clock back to an era when second-class citizenship for women and minorities, disenfranchisement, and *de jure* and *de facto* segregation were very much the facts of life for well over half of America's population. Moreover, justice encompasses more than our nation's laws. The poor, the female, the minority — many of them just like boats stuck on the bottom — have come to experience an implacable and intractable foe in the Reagan Administration.

A new Democratic Administration will understand that the age-old scourge of discrimination and prejudice against many groups in American society is still rampant and very much a part of the reason for the debilitating circumstances in which disadvantaged peoples are forced to live. Although strides have been made in combatting discrimination and defamation against Americans of various ethnic groups, much remains to be done. Therefore, we pledge an end to the Reagan Administration's punitive policy toward women, minorities, and the poor and support the reaffirmation of the principle that the government is still responsible for protecting the civil rights of all citizens. Government has a special responsibility to those whom society has historically prevented from enjoying the benefits of full citizenship for reasons of race, religion, sex, age, national origin and ethnic heritage, sexual orientation, or disability.

The goal for the coming decades is not only full justice under the law, but *economic* justice as well. In the recent past, we have put our nation on the road toward achieving equal protection of all our citizens' human rights. The challenge now is to continue to press that cause, while joining a new battle — to assure justice and opportunity in the workplace, and in the economy.

Justice for all in today's America and the America of tomorrow demands not one, but two broad guarantees. First, we must guarantee that our nation will reinforce and extend its commitment to human rights and equal opportunity. And second, we must guarantee progress on the new frontier for the future: economic and social justice.

We are determined to enforce the laws guaranteeing equal opportunity, and to complete the civil rights agenda cast aside by the Reagan Administration. No President has the right to do what this Administration has done: to read selectively from the United States Code and simply ignore the laws ensuring basic rights and opportunities because they conflict with this Administration's ideology. As Democrats, we pledge to reverse the trend towards lawlessness which has characterized this Administration, and to keep our commitments to all in our community who look to the government for defense of their rights.

But we recognize that while a first step toward a just society is to guarantee the right of all workers to compete equally for a job, the next step is assuring that enough new jobs are created to give meaningful employment to all our workers for the future.

If in past decades we won the right for minorities to ride at the front of the bus, in coming years we must assure that minorities have the opportunity to own the bus company.

It will not be enough to say that our nation must offer equal access to health care — we must put comprehensive health care within the reach of all of our citizens, at a price all can afford.

It will not do simply to guarantee women a place in the work force — women deserve an equal chance at a career leading to the board of directors.

As Democrats, we believe that human rights and an economy of opportunity are two sides of the same coin of justice. No economic program can be considered just unless it advances the opportunity of all to live a better, more dignified life. No American is afforded economic justice when he or she is denied an opportunity to reap the rewards of economic growth.

Economic justice is also economic common sense. Any who doubt that should consider the toll of welfare, crime, prisons, public housing and urban squalor on our national wealth. We will pay a high price for all the disadvantaged or disenfranchised if we fail to include them in the new economic revolution.

As Democrats, therefore, we pledge to pursue a new definition of justice that meets the new demands of our time. Under a Democratic Administration, equality and fairness under the law will be matched by justice in the economy and in the workplace.

THE FUTURE IF REAGAN IS REELECTED

"Twenty years after the Equal Pay Act should have eradicated the last vestige of economic discrimination against women, employers have made little progress in integrating their work force.... It is the Republican governor of Washington State, and the Republican County Executive of Nassau County, New York, who are committing public resources to mount a legal defense for their jurisdictions' blatant sex discrimination practices.... The Reagan Administration from the outset has made it abundantly clear that civil rights and economic justice are to be sacrificed on the altar of corporate greed...."

Diana Rock, Director of Women's Rights, American Federation of State, County, and Municipal Em-

ployees (Democratic Platform Committee Hearing, Cleveland, Ohio, May 21, 1984)

"The Reagan Administration, upon taking office in 1981, set upon a concerted effort to roll back civil rights protections. This attack is underway in agency enforcement, court litigation, legislative initiative, and nominations of federal appointees."

Virna M. Canson, Regional Director, West Coast Region, NAACP (Democratic Platform Committee Hearing, Los Angeles, California, May 14, 1984)

The neglect of our historic human rights commitment will already be recorded as the first legacy of Ronald Reagan's years in the White House. But suppose Mr. Reagan is reelected.

What would become of America's commitment to equal justice and opportunity if Mr. Reagan is reelected?

The hard truth is that if Mr. Reagan is reelected our most vigorous defender of the rule of law — the United States Supreme Court — could be lost to the cause of equal justice for another generation. Today, five of the nine members of the Court are over 75. Our next President will likely have the opportunity to shape that Court, not just for his own term — or even for his own lifetime — but for the rest of ours, and for our children's too.

There can be little doubt that a Supreme Court chosen by Ronald Reagan would radically restrict constitutional rights and drastically reinterpret existing laws. Today, the fundamental right of a woman to reproduction freedom rests on the votes of six members of the Supreme Court — five of whom are over 75. That right could easily disappear during a second Reagan term. Already, the protections against employment discrimination have been restricted by the Court; a Reagan Court surely would reduce them further. The same is true for the right of workers to have a healthy and safe workplace, and to organize collectively in unions. Although the statute protecting voting rights has been extended through a massive bipartisan effort, opposed by the Reagan Administration, a Reagan Supreme Court could still effectively nullify it simply by erecting impossible standards of proof. Not long ago, the Court decided it should hire independent counsel to argue that tax exemptions for racially discriminatory schools were unlawful because the Justice Department refused to do so. Can anyone imagine a Reagan Court doing that? How much easier it would be for a Reagan Court simply to agree with a Reagan Department of Justice.

If Mr. Reagan is reelected, who would protect women and minorities against discrimination?

In the first year after the Reagan Administration assumed office, the number of cases involving charges of employment discrimination filed in court by the EEOC dropped by more than 70 percent. During

this Administration, the EEOC has refused to process a single comparable worth case filed by a woman. Meanwhile, the Reagan Justice Department has sought to destroy effective affirmative action remedies, and even to undermine *private* plans to reduce discrimination in employment. The actions of the Reagan Administration serve only to delay the day when fairness is achieved and such remedial measures are, therefore, no longer needed.

It is now clear that if Mr. Reagan is reelected, women and minorities seeking protection of their rights would be forced to contend not only with their employers, but with a hostile government. Equal employment opportunity and equity would remain elusive dreams.

If Mr. Reagan is reelected, who would assure access to justice?

Since the day of its inauguration, the Reagan Administration has conducted a continuous, full-scale war against the federal Legal Services Corporation, whose only job is to ensure that the poor are fairly heard in court, and that they get equal access to our system of justice. Thirty percent of the Corporation's lawyers have been laid off, and the Administration has used every means it could find to stack its Board with people hostile to the very concept of equal justice for the poor.

In the America of Ronald Reagan, you will only get as much justice as you pay for.

If Mr. Reagan is reelected, who would protect the rights of workers?

The Republican Administration has consistently viewed the dollar costs to businesses of providing a safe workplace as more important than the impact of injury and disease on working men and women. It has appointed officials to the National Labor Relations Board who openly oppose the rights of workers to organize and bargain collectively. The Department of Labor has ignored its mandate to enforce fair labor standards and has sought to reverse hardwon gains in protections for worker health and safety.

What would happen if Mr. Reagan is reelected? Will the right to bargain collectively be eviscerated through Republican-approved abuses of the bankruptcy laws? Will the National Labor Relations Act be converted into a tool that limits working men and women and empowers only their employers? Who will ensure that our next generation does not suffer the effects of toxic substances in the workplace — substances whose existence is not even revealed to the worker?

If Mr. Reagan is reelected, who would protect the rights of senior citizens?

Speaking at Philadelphia in 1980 during his campaign, Ronald Reagan vowed to a large audience of senior citizens his strong support for Social Security. He assured thousands of senior citizens on that occasion that as President he would see to it that every commitment made by the federal government to the senior citizens was faithfully kept.

Ronald Reagan violated that promise shortly after he became President. In 1981, speaking to a joint session of Congress, President Reagan said, "We will not cut Medicare." In a matter of weeks thereafter President Reagan asked the Congress of the United States to cut $88 billion in 1981 and the following four years from Social Security programs. He proposed to reduce by a third the number of people protected by the disability insurance program. He proposed to reduce by a third the benefits a senior citizen would receive if he or she retired at 62. He proposed to cut out the burial program for recipients of Social Security.

He proposed to cut millions from programs that Democratic Administrations had provided for the education of the children of the elderly covered by Social Security, slashing the list of beneficiaries of these programs by hundreds of thousands of sons and daughters of men and women covered by Social Security. And he called for the abolition of the $122-a-month minimum benefit program, which would have dropped over three million people from Social Security altogether.

The American people then revolted, and so did the Congress. The Democratic Party put a stop to the decimation of the Social Security program, but not before President Reagan had cut $19 billion from Social Security benefits in 1981 and the ensuing four years. Democrats in Congress forced the restoration of the $122-a-month minimum benefit program to those who were covered before the Reagan cuts, but never succeeded in extending coverage to the additional 7,000 people a month who would have become eligible after the Reagan cuts.

Instead of keeping his word that he would not cut Medicare, Reagan forced Congress every year beginning in 1981 to cut billions from the Medicare program. When Social Security developed financial problems due to massive unemployment in 1982, the Reagan Administration moved to "solve" them by cutting benefits further. Only the Democrats on the Social Security Commission prevented him from doing that.

If Mr. Reagan is reelected, how would we teach our children to respect the law?

We cannot teach our children to respect the law when they see the highest officials of government flaunting it at their will. Lawlessness has been a pattern in this Administration — and it is a pattern that is unlikely to be altered if Reagan and the Republicans stay in the White House.

More than forty top Republican officials have already been implicated in all kinds of wrongdoing. Murky transactions on the fringe of organized crime, accepting gifts from foreign journalists and governments, misusing government funds, lying under oath, stock manipulations, taking interest-free loans from wealthy businessmen who later receive federal jobs — all of these are part of business as usual with Ronald

Reagan's appointees.

The Republicans profess to stand for "law and order." But this is the same Administration that vetoed the bipartisan anti-crime bill in 1982. And when it comes to laws they do not like — whether they concern toxic wastes, pure food and drugs, or worker health and safety — this Administration simply makes believe they do not exist. The same is true overseas: this Administration is just as willing to ignore international law as domestic law. When we finally learned of its illegal mining of Nicaragua's harbors, the Reagan Administration hastily attempted, the night before Nicaragua sued us, to withdraw jurisdiction over the question from the World Court. But even this maneuver was carried out in an illegal fashion that the World Court later set aside.

This Republican Administration has been unprecedentedly eager to limit public debate by instituting "security agreements" that censor ex-officials, "revising" the Freedom of Information Act, refusing visas to foreign visitors who might provide another perspective on American policies overseas, and denying our war correspondents their historic position alongside our troops. This comes as no surprise: in the first term the Reagan Administration had a lot to hide. What would happen in a second?

If Mr. Reagan is reelected, what would happen to our unfinished civil rights agenda?

The answer is clear: an Administration which refuses to enforce the laws that are on the books can hardly be expected to respect — or even recognize — the rights of those who are not already specifically protected by existing law.

Nowhere is this Administration's hostility to equal rights and equal justice more apparent than in its attitude to the Equal Rights Amendment. As soon as the Reagan faction took control of the Republican Party at its convention in 1980, it ended that Party's forty-year commitment to passage of the Equal Rights Amendment. So long as this Administration remains in office, the proponents of unamended ERA have nothing less than an enemy in the White House. And if this is true for the women of America, it is equally true for disadvantaged minorities who must depend on this government's sense of justice to secure their rights and lead independent lives.

Since assuming office, the Reagan Administration has shown more hostility — indeed, more outright and implacable aggression — toward the American ideal of equal justice for all than even its harshest critics would have predicted in 1980. Given its first-term record, even our most pessimistic forecasts for four more Republican years may well fall short of the mark. No one knows the full extent of the damage Reagan could wreak on this country in another term. But we do know one thing: we cannot afford to find out.

THE DEMOCRATIC ALTERNATIVE: EQUAL JUSTICE FOR ALL

"The Democratic Party is challenged as never before to redirect the present dangerous course of our nation and our world, and to provide meaningful work at adequate pay for all our citizens and justice for all Americans.

"The dream of a nation fully committed to peace, jobs, and justice has fast become a nightmare under this Administration....

"Our choice today is to become just a new party in power in November with new faces and new pledges — or a truly great party with the courage to develop a new vision and a new direction for the sake of our nation and our world."

Coretta Scott King (Democratic Platform Committee Hearing, Washington, D.C., June 11, 1984)

"The Equal Rights Amendment is the only guarantee of full equality the women of this nation can trust and count on. We have seen in the past three and one-half years an administration that has gone out of its way to prove that laws, court decisions, executive orders, and regulations are not enough — they can be changed by a new majority, overturned, swept aside, underfunded, or rescinded. Only when the legislative protections against such discrimination are grounded in the bedrock of the Constitution can we feel that the vagaries of changing political climates or a hostile administration will not wipe out those protections."

Judy Goldsmith, President, National Organization for Women (Democratic Platform Committee Hearing, Washington, D.C., June 12, 1984)

Equal justice for all, in a Democratic future, means that every individual must have a fair and equal opportunity to fulfill his or her potential, and to be an independent, working member of our society — and it is the commitment of our Party to secure that opportunity.

We are determined to build an America of self-sufficient, independent people. We will enforce the laws guaranteeing equal opportunity and human rights, and complete the unfinished civil rights agenda. We will keep our commitments to all of the members of our community who rely upon our word to stay, or to become, independent — our senior citizens, those who served in the Armed Forces, the handicapped and disabled, the members of our American family who are trapped in poverty, and all Americans who look to government to protect them from the pain, expense, and dislocation caused by crime. And in fulfilling these and all the duties of government, a Democratic Administration will stand as an example to all of integrity and justice.

Equal Justice Under Law

Many have suffered from historical patterns of discrimination and others, because of their recent immigration in sizeable numbers, are subject to new forms of discrimination. Over the years, the Democratic Party has voiced a commitment to eradicating these injustices. In 1948, the Democratic Platform for the first time contained a plank committing this Party to the cause of civil rights. For almost forty years, we have fought proudly for that cause. In 1964, a Democratic President and a Democratic Congress enacted the landmark legislation prohibiting discrimination in employment and public accommodations. And for nearly two decades, a bipartisan commitment has existed in Congress and in the White House to expand and enforce those laws. Until Ronald Reagan.

This Administration has sought to erode the force and meaning of constitutionally-mandated and court-sanctioned remedies for long-standing patterns of discriminatory conduct. It has attempted to create new standards under each of our nation's civil rights laws by requiring a showing of intent to discriminate, and case-by-case litigation of class-wide violations. Its interpretation of two recent Supreme Court decisions attempts to sound the death knell for equal opportunity and affirmative action. In one case, the Administration interpreted the Court's decision as requiring that equal opportunity mandates associated with the receipt of *all* federal monies apply only to the specific program receiving federal funds. In the other, the Administration is using a ruling in favor of a *bona fide* seniority system to assault all affirmative action plans. As Democrats, we disagree. Instead, we reaffirm our long-standing commitment to civil rights for all and we pledge to enforce the laws guaranteeing equal opportunity for all Americans. The next Democratic Administration will offer unwavering support for the following:

A Strong, Independent Civil Rights Commission — A Democratic Administration will return the Commission on Civil Rights to an independent status and increase its funding. The Commission must be restored to its original mission of ensuring the enforcement of civil rights by those federal agencies charged with the task.

Strengthened Civil Rights Enforcement — We will restore a strong Equal Employment Opportunity Commission and renew the commitment of the Department of Justice and the Department of Labor to enforce civil rights laws and executive orders. A Democratic Administration will, by vigorously enforcing laws and strengthening education and training opportunities, increase minority participation in the workplace and eliminate wage inequities which leave minorities at the bottom of the pay scale.

Equal Educational Opportunity — The Democratic Party pledges to do all it can, beginning this year, to reverse the decision of the United States Supreme Court in the Grove City College case, and to restore as the law of the land the prohibition of any use of federal financial assistance to subsidize discrimination because of race, national origin, sex, age, or disability. Fulfilling this commitment means that every institution which receives government funds must guarantee equality and equal opportunity in all of its programs.

Religious Liberty and Church/State Separation — The current Administration has consistently sought to reverse in the courts or overrule by constitutional amendment a long line of Supreme Court decisions that preserve our historic commitment to religious tolerance and church/state separation. The Democratic Platform affirms its support of the principles of religious liberty, religious tolerance and church/state separation and of the Supreme Court decisions forbidding violation of those principles. We pledge to resist all efforts to weaken those decisions.

Ensure Fair Housing — We will enhance the authority of the Department of Housing and Urban Development to enforce our fair housing laws. A Democratic Administration will work to provide the Department with the resources and the power to seek cease and desist orders to prevent housing discrimination against minorities, women and families with children.

Affirmative Action — The Democratic Party firmly commits itself to protect the civil rights of every citizen and to pursue justice and equal treatment under the law for all citizens. The Party reaffirms its longstanding commitment to the eradication of discrimination in all aspects of American life through the use of affirmative action, goals, timetables, and other verifiable measurements to overturn historic patterns and historic burdens of discrimination in hiring, training, promotions, contract procurement, education, and the administration of all Federal programs. A Democratic Administration will resist any efforts to undermine the progress made under previous Democratic administrations and shall strongly enforce Federal civil rights standards such as equal opportunity, affirmative action in employment, contract procurement, education, and training. The Federal Government must set an example and be a model for private employers, making special efforts in both recruitment, training, and promotion to aid minority Americans in overcoming both the historic patterns and the historic burdens of discrimination. We will reverse the regressive trend of the Reagan Administration by making a commitment to increase recruitment, hiring, training, retraining, procurement, and promotional opportunity at the Federal level to aid minority Americans and women. We call on the public and private sectors to live up to and enforce all civil rights laws and regulations, i.e., Equal Employment Opportunity Programs, Title VI and Title VII of the Civil Rights Act, the Fair Housing Laws, and affirmative action requirements.

Eliminate Ethnic-Stereotyping and

Recognize Ethnic Diversity — While strides have been made in combatting discrimination and defamation against Americans of various ethnic groups, ethnic stereotyping continues. We support cooperation and understanding between racial, ethnic, and cultural groups and reject those who promote division based on fear or stereotyping which have their basis in social and economic inequity. We encourage respect for America's ethnic diversity.

Equal Access to Justice — Democrats believe that all our government processes should be open to all Americans, and that no essential right should be denied based on wealth or status. We therefore strongly support a well-funded, unrestricted Legal Services Corporation to ensure that none of our citizens is denied the full benefits of our judicial system. No American should suffer illegality or abuse simply because he or she is poor. And lawyers for the poor must not be prevented from acting in accordance with the same ethical canons as apply to lawyers for the rich: to represent their clients with all the zeal, devotion, energy, and creativity that the law allows.

Equal Rights for Women — A top priority of a Democratic Administration will be ratification of the unamended Equal Rights Amendment. In a Democratic America, the Constitution will be amended to provide:

Section 1. Equality of rights under the law shall not be denied or abridged by the United States or by any State on account of sex.

Section 2. The Congress shall have the power to enforce, by appropriate legislation, the provisions of this article.

Section 3. This article shall take effect two years after the date of ratification.

We will insist on pay equity for women. Today, white women who can find work earn, on average, only 62 cents for every dollar earned by white men. Black women earn only 58 cents for every dollar earned by white men, and Hispanic women only 56 cents. The earnings gap — and the occupational segregation of women which it reflects — extends to all women at every educational level, but is most pronounced among black and other women of color who are confronted by historical and contemporary racial barriers which transcend sex. The Democratic Party defines nondiscrimination to encompass both equal pay for equal work *and* equal pay for work of comparable worth, and we pledge to take every step, including enforcement of current law and amending the Constitution to include the unamended ERA, to close the wage gap. We also support efforts to reform private and civil service pension rules to ensure equal treatment for women, prohibit discrimination in insurance practices, and improve enforcement of child-support obligations. Our Party also recognizes that women cannot compete equally with men so long as they are expected to choose between having a job and having a family. The Democratic Party calls for universally available day-care with federal or business funding, for meaningful part-time work, and for flex-time on the job so that women — and men — can shape even full-time jobs around their family schedules.

Political Empowerment for Minorities and Women — The Democratic Party is committed to placing women as well as minorities in positions of power in government. We establish the goal of doubling the number of minorities and women in Congress by 1988. We will create and fund a talent bank of minorities and women to fill policy positions in the next Administration. We will recruit women and minorities to run for Governorships and all state and local offices. The Democratic Party (through all of its campaign committees) will commit to spending maximum resources to elect women and minority candidates and offer these candidates in-kind services, including political organizing and strategic advice. And the bulk of all voter registration funds will be spent on targeted efforts to register minorities and women.

Reproductive Freedom — The Democratic Party recognizes reproductive freedom as a fundamental human right. We therefore oppose government interference in the reproductive decisions of Americans, especially government interference which denies poor Americans their right to privacy by funding or advocating one or a limited number of reproductive choices only. We fully recognize the religious and ethical concerns which many Americans have about abortion. But we also recognize the belief of many Americans that a woman has a right to choose whether and when to have a child. The Democratic Party supports the 1973 Supreme Court decision on abortion rights as the law of the land and opposes any constitutional amendment to restrict or overturn that decision. We deplore violence and harassment against health providers and women seeking services, and will work to end such acts. We support a continuing federal interest in developing strong local family planning and family life education programs and medical research aimed at reducing the need for abortion.

The Rights of Workers — This nation established a labor policy more than a generation ago whose purpose is to encourage collective bargaining and the right of workers to organize to obtain this goal. The Democratic Party is committed to extending the benefit of this policy to all workers and to removing the barriers to its administration. To accomplish this, the Democratic Party supports: the repeal of Section 14B of the National Labor Relations Act; labor law reform legislation; a prohibition on the misuse of federal bankruptcy law to prevent the circumvention of the collective bargaining process and the destruction of labor-management contracts; and legislation to allow building trades workers the same peaceful picketing rights currently afforded industrial workers. We support the right of public employees and agricultural workers to organize and bargain collectively, and we will act to assure that right.

Inasmuch as farm workers are excluded from coverage under the National Labor Relations Act, the Democratic Party recognizes the heroic efforts of farm workers to gain contracts and their right under the law to use boycotts as an effective tool to achieve such ends. We must restore to federal workers their First Amendment rights by reforming the Hatch Act. We must also protect federal and private sector workers from invasions of their privacy by prohibiting the use of polygraphs and other "Truth Test" devices. In addition, the Mine Health Safety Act and the Occupational Health and Safety Act must be properly administered, with the concern of the worker being the highest priority. All efforts to weaken or undermine OSHA's basic worker protection provisions, or to shirk the duty to enforce them, are unacceptable and intolerable. For the victims of occupational disease, we insist on legislation to assure just compensation and adequate health care for these workers as well as vigorous enforcement action by OSHA to eradicate the causes of occupational disease. All fair labor standards acts, such as the minimum wage and Davis-Bacon protections, must be effectively enforced. We reject the so-called "sub-minimum wage" as an appropriate tool of social or economic policy. We strongly oppose workfare which penalizes welfare recipients and undercuts the basic principle of equal pay for equal work. Workfare is not a substitute for a jobs program.

The Responsibility of Economic Institutions — The Democratic Party continues to support the struggle of all citizens to secure economic equality. Therefore, we support policies calling for increased involvement of minorities and women in job training and apprenticeship programs. The Democratic Party encourages all economic institutions, including business and labor, to work actively to ensure that leadership at all levels of decision-making reflects the ethnic and gender diversity of the relevant work force by expanding opportunities for training and advancement.

Enforcing The Voting Rights Act — The right to vote — and to have one's vote counted fully and fairly — is the most important civil right of every American citizen. For without it, no other social, economic, or political rights can be fully realized.

Nothing is more shameful in the record of the Reagan Administration than its willful refusal to fulfill its responsibility to guarantee the voting rights of every American. Instead of moving America forward by expanding voting rights and by eliminating barriers to voting by minority citizens, the Reagan Administration fought a year-long, rear-guard action against efforts to strengthen the Voting Rights Act.

The Democratic Party commits itself to a wholly different course than that of the Reagan Administration. For while we are proud of our record of commitment to civil rights in the past, we recognize that the test of our commitment is what a Democratic Administration will do in the fu-

ture. Despite the great progress in securing voting rights for minority Americans in the past, there remain throughout our nation voting rules, practices, and procedures that have been and are used to discriminate against many citizens to discourage or deny their right to register and to vote, or dilute their vote when they do. A Democratic President and Administration pledge to eliminate any and all discriminatory barriers to full voting rights, whether they be at-large requirements, second-primaries, gerrymandering, annexation, dual registration, dual voting or other practices. Whatever law, practice, or regulation discriminates against the voting rights of minority citizens, a Democratic President and Administration will move to strike it down.

This is more than a verbal pledge. For minority citizens have waited far too long already to realize their full voting rights.

To prevent any further delay, the Democratic Party pledges to fund a serious, in-depth study of the use of second primaries and other practices throughout the nation that may discriminate against voting rights. This study shall be completed in ample time prior to the 1986 elections for the Party to act. The Democratic Party commits to use its full resources to eliminate any second primary, gerrymandering, at-large requirements, annexation, dual registration, dual voting or other voting practices that discriminate or act to dilute votes of minority citizens.

Wherever a runoff primary or other voting practice is found to be discriminatory, the State Party shall take provable, positive steps to achieve the necessary legislative or party rules changes.

Provable positive steps shall be taken in a timely fashion and shall include the drafting of corrective legislation, public endorsement by the state Party of such legislation, efforts to educate the public on the need for such legislation, active support for the legislation by the state Party lobbying state legislators, other public officials, Party officials and Party members, and encouraging consideration of the legislation by the appropriate legislative committees and bodies.

A Democratic Administration pledges also that the Justice Department shall initiate a similar study, and use the full resources of the law to eliminate any voting practice, such as second primaries, gerrymandering, annexation, dual registration, dual voting, or any other practice that discriminates or acts to dilute votes of minority citizens.

A Democratic President and Administration will use the full resources of the Voting Rights Act of 1982, with its strengthened enforcement powers, to investigate and root out any and all discriminatory voting barriers. A Democratic President will appoint as Attorney General, as Assistant Attorney General for Civil Rights, and throughout the Justice Department individuals with a proven record of commitment to enforcing civil rights and voting rights for all our citizens. The full resources of the Justice Department shall be used to investigate fully and speedily all alleged instances of discriminatory barriers. And a Democratic Administration shall use the full resources of the law, the power of government, and shall seek new legislation, if needed, to end discrimination in voting wherever it exists.

We are committed to a massive, nationwide campaign to increase registration and voting participation by women and minorities, including blacks, Asian Americans, native Americans, and Hispanics. Moreover, our Party must call for the creation of a new program to strengthen our democracy and remove existing obstacles to full participation in the electoral process. We should allow registration and voting on the same day (same day plans have worked well in several states) and we should provide mail-in registration forms throughout our communities. We should consider holding our elections on weekends or holidays, instituting 24-hour voting days, staggering voting times, and closing all polling places across the country at the same time.

We call on the television networks and all other media in the case of presidential elections to refrain from projecting winners of national races, either implicitly or explicitly, while any polls are still open in the continental United States; in the case of state elections, to refrain from projecting winners within a state, either implicitly or explicitly, while any polls in that state are still open.

Voting Rights for the District of Columbia — The Democratic Party supports self-determination for the District of Columbia that guarantees local control over local affairs and full voting representation in Congress. Towards this end, the Democratic Party supports the attainment of statehood for New Columbia; ratification of the District of Columbia Voting Rights Amendment; legislative, judicial, and fiscal autonomy; and a formula-based federal payment.

Puerto Rico — We continue to support Puerto Rico's right to enjoy full self-determination and a relationship that can evolve in ways that will most benefit U.S. citizens in Puerto Rico. The Democratic Party respects and supports the desire of the people of Puerto Rico, by their own will freely-expressed in a peaceful and democratic process, to associate in permanent union with the United States either as a commonwealth or as a state or to become an independent nation. We are also committed to respecting the cultural heritage of the people of Puerto Rico and to the elimination of the discriminatory or unfair treatment of Puerto Ricans as U.S. citizens under federal programs.

A Fair and Humane Immigration Policy — Our nation's outdated immigration laws require comprehensive reform that reflects our national interests and our immigrant heritage. Our first priority must be to protect the fundamental human rights of American citizens and aliens. We will oppose any "reforms" that violate

these rights or that will create new incentives for discrimination against Hispanic Americans and other minorities arising from the discriminatory use of employer sanctions. Specifically, we oppose employer sanctions designed to penalize employers who hire undocumented workers. Such sanctions inevitably will increase discrimination against minority Americans. We oppose identification procedures that threaten civil liberties, as well as any changes that subvert the basic principle of family unification. And we will put an end to this Administration's policies of barring foreign visitors from our country for political or ideological reasons. We strongly oppose "bracero" or guest-worker programs as a form of legalized exploitation. We firmly support a one-tiered legalization program with a 1982 cut-off date.

The Democratic Party will implement a balanced, fair, and non-discriminatory immigration and refugee policy consistent with the principle of affording all applications for admission equal protection under the law. It will work for improved performance by the Immigration and Naturalization Service in adjudicating petitions for permanent residence and naturalization. The Party will also advocate reform within the INS to improve the enforcement operations of the Service consistent with civil liberties protection. The correction of past and present bias in the allocation of slots for refugee admissions will be a top priority. Additionally, it will work to ensure that the Refugee Act of 1980, which prohibits discrimination on the basis of ideology and race in adjudicating asylum claims, is complied with. The Party will provide the necessary oversight of the Department of State and the Immigration and Naturalization Service so as to ensure that the unjustifiable treatment visited upon the Haitian refugees will never again be repeated.

The Democratic Party will formulate foreign policies which alleviate, not aggravate, the root causes of poverty, war, and human rights violations and instability which compel people to flee their homelands.

We support the creation of an international body on immigration to address the economic development problems affecting Mexico and Latin American countries which contribute to unauthorized immigration to the U.S. and to respond to the backlog of approved immigrant visas.

To pursue these and other goals, the Democratic Party nominee upon election shall establish the following national advisory committees to the President and the national Democratic Party: civil rights and justice; fair housing; affirmative action; equal rights for women; rights for workers; immigration policy; and voting rights. These committees shall be representative on the basis of geography, race, sex, and ethnicity.

Dignity for All — As Democrats, we take pride in our accomplishments of the past decades in enacting legislation to assure quality and in fighting the current

efforts of this Administration to turn its back on equal opportunity. But we also recognize that so long as any Americans are subject to unfair discrimination, our agenda remains unfinished. We pledge to complete the agenda, and to afford dignity for all.

— We reaffirm the dignity of all people and the right of each individual to have equal access to and participation in the institutions and services of our society. To ensure that government is accessible to those Americans for whom English is a second language, we call for federal hiring and training initiatives to increase the number of government employees skilled in more than one language. All groups must be protected from discrimination based on race, color, sex, religion, national origin, language, age, or sexual orientation. We will support legislation to prohibit discrimination in the workplace based on sexual orientation. We will assure that sexual orientation *per se* does not serve as a bar to participation in the military. We will support an enhanced effort to learn the cause and cure of AIDS, and to provide treatment for people with AIDS. And we will ensure that foreign citizens are not excluded from this country on the basis of their sexual orientation.

— We have long failed to treat the original inhabitants of this land with the dignity they deserve. A Democratic Administration will work in partnership with Indian nations to target assistance to address the twin problems of unemployment and poverty, recognizing appropriate Native American rights to self-determination and the federal government's fiduciary responsibility to the Native American nations. We will take the lead in efforts to resolve water and other natural resource claims of Native Americans. We must also reevaluate the mission of the Bureau of Indian Affairs in light of its troubled record.

— We owe history and ourselves a formal apology and a promise of redress to Japanese Americans who suffered unjust internment during World War II. No commitment to civil liberties could be complete without a formal apology, restitution of position, status or entitlements and reparations to those who suffered deprivation of rights and property without due process forty years ago.

— The Democratic Party strongly condemns the Ku Klux Klan, the American Nazi Party, and other hate groups. We pledge vigorous federal prosecution of actions by the Klan and American Nazi Party that violate federal law, including the enactment of such laws in jurisdictions where they do not exist. We further condemn those acts, symbols, and rituals, including cross-burnings, associated with anti-civil rights activities. We urge every state and local government to pursue vigorous protection of actions by the Klan and Nazi Party and other such groups that violate state or local law.

Americans Abroad — Americans abroad play a vital role in promoting the ideals, culture, and economic well-being of the United States. They are entitled to equitable treatment by their government and greater participation in decisions which directly affect them.

The Democratic Party will work to remedy the unique problems that U.S. citizens encounter abroad. In particular, we will consider ways to: protect their rights; eliminate citizenship inequities; make it easier for them to vote; have their interests actively represented in the federal government; provide them with fair coverage in federal social programs; honor the principles of residency in taxation; and ensure the adequate education of federal dependents abroad.

Insular Areas — The territories are in spirit full partners in the American political family; they should always be so treated. Their unique circumstances require the sensitive application of federal policy and special assistance. Their self-determination, along with that of the Trust Territory of the Pacific Islands, is an American commitment.

Democrats will work with the territories to improve their relationship with the rest of the United States and obtain equal rights for their citizens, including the right to vote for President. A Democratic President and Congress will coordinate their interests as foreign and domestic policy is made. We are committed to providing territorial America with essential assistance and equitable participation in federal programs. We will promote the growth and ensure the competitive position of territorial private sectors. It is Democratic policy that, together with the territories, the United States should strive to assist and develop closer relations with the territories' neighbors in the Caribbean and Pacific regions.

Economic Justice: Keeping Our Commitments

For some, the goal of independence requires greater support and assistance from government. We pledge to provide that support. Justice demands that we keep our commitments and display our compassion to those who most need our help — to veterans and seniors, to disadvantaged minorities, to the disabled and the poor — and we will.

A Healthy America — As Democrats we believe that quality health care is a necessity for everyone. We reaffirm our commitment to the long-term goal of comprehensive national health insurance and view effective health care cost containment as an essential step toward that goal. Health cost containment must be based on a strong commitment to quality of service delivery and care. We also pledge to return to a proper emphasis on basic scientific research and meeting the need for health professionals — areas devastated by the Reagan Administration.

Sickle Cell Anemia — Sickle Cell disease is a catastrophic illness that affects thousands of persons annually. Its victims include, but are not limited to, blacks, Hispanics, and persons of Mediterranean ancestry including Turks, Greeks, and Italians. Its morbidity rate is particularly high among infants, women and children.

Despite the compelling need for a national policy of sickle cell disease prevention and control, the present Administration has dramatically reduced the federal commitment to research and funding. The Democratic Party, on the other hand, pledges to make sickle cell a national health priority because we believe that only the federal government can adequately focus the necessary resources to combat such a major public health problem. Specifically, we pledge that a Democratic Administration will restore the National Sickle Cell Anemia Control Act to provide health parity to those individuals and families whose lives are threatened by this chronic and debilitating disorder.

Opportunities for the Elderly — There are more than 26 million Americans over the age of 65, and their numbers are growing rapidly. Most have spent a lifetime building America and raising the next generation, and when they choose to retire — and it should be their choice — they deserve to retire with dignity and security. Yet for millions of Americans, particularly women, minorities, and ethnic Americans, old age means poverty, insecurity, and desperation.

Beginning with President Franklin D. Roosevelt, the Democratic Party has been dedicated to the well-being of the senior citizens of America. President Roosevelt gave to the elderly Social Security. The following Democratic Administrations provided the elderly with Medicare, the Older Americans Act, the nutrition program, low-cost housing, elderly employment programs and many others to make lives longer, healthier and happier for senior citizens, those who have done so much to make America the great nation it is today. This Reagan Republican Administration is the first administration to stop the progress of aid to the elderly and to cut back on every helpful program which Democratic Administrations had enacted for our elders.

Now we have a crisis facing the country with respect to Medicare. Funds will be short in four years. Again, the Reagan Republican Administration, speaking recently through the Social Security Advisory Council, proposed that the way to meet this financial crisis was to make the people already paying into Medicare pay more and to cut benefits by raising the age of eligibility from 65 to 67.

Too many elderly people covered by Medicare are not able to pay the deductible now required by Medicare. We Democrats will never add more to the burdens of the people now covered by Medicare. Nor will we Democrats allow benefits to be cut under Medicare by raising the age of eligibility, for we know that Medicare, which

Democratic leadership established in 1964, is the only chance that millions of senior citizens have to get the health care they need.

To date, the needs of America's ethnic elderly have not been met. Ethnic American elderly number over seven million persons, or approximately one quarter of the total population of people over 65. A close examination of data from the U.S. Census reveals that nearly one-half of this ethnic population who are 65 years of age or older do not speak English. To assure the well-being of ethnic seniors who comprise a large segment of our elderly population, we should promote programs to strengthen family life, care for the elderly, and spur neighborhood revitalization and development of "language barrier-free" social and health services.

We also know that the number of senior citizens as a percentage of the population is rapidly growing. The Democratic Party is committed to the principle of forbidding any discrimination on account of age against the elderly, either in holding a job or obtaining one. We offer to the elderly an opportunity for additional training or retraining that will enable them to do better at the jobs they have or to turn to other jobs which they would like better.

In short, the Democratic Party, which for so long has been the champion of the elderly, assures the senior citizens of America that it will maintain its longstanding good faith with them. Whatever is right and good for the senior citizen shall always be close to the heart of the Democratic Party and ever a primary dedication of our Party.

It is the cherished aim and high purpose of the Democratic Party to make the last part of the long journey of life for our senior citizens as long, as healthy and as happy as may be.

As Democrats, we are proud of the programs we have created — Social Security and Medicare — to allow our senior citizens to live their lives independently and with dignity, and we will fight to preserve and protect those programs. We will work for decent housing and adequate nutrition for our senior citizens, and we will enforce the laws prohibiting age discrimination. We will not break faith with those who built America.

The Social Security Administration long had a reputation for administrative efficiency and high quality public service. Problems which have emerged under the current Administration — the financing crises, a deteriorating computer system, and arbitrary terminations of benefits to hundreds of thousands of disabled Americans — threaten the agency's ability to carry out its mission. The current Administration's policies have shaken people's confidence in the entire Social Security system.

The policies and operations of the Social Security Administration must be carefully and fully investigated to reform its operations so that the elderly and disabled receive the services and treatment to which they are entitled. In particular, we should explore the recommendation that the Social Security Administration become an independent agency.

Opportunities for Disabled Americans — There are nearly 36 million people with disabilities in the United States, who look to our government for justice. As Democrats, we have long recognized that a disability need not be an obstacle to a productive, independent life and we have fought to guarantee access to facilities, and adequate training and support to meet the special needs of the disabled. This Administration has closed its eyes to those needs, and in so doing, violated a fundamental trust by seeking to condemn millions of disabled Americans to dependency. We will honor our commitments. We will insist that those who receive federal funds accommodate disabled employees — a requirement this Administration sought to eliminate. We will insist that benefits be available for those who cannot work, and that training is available for those who need help to find work.

The Democratic Party will safeguard the rights of the elderly and disabled to remain free from institutionalization except where medically indicated. The rights of the disabled within institutions should be protected from violations of the integrity of their person. Also, we will promote accessible public transportation, buildings, make voting booths accessible, and strictly enforce laws such as the entire Rehabilitation Act of 1973.

Opportunities for Veterans — This country has a proud tradition of honoring and supporting those who have defended us. Millions of Americans in the years after World War II went to college and bought their homes thanks to GI benefits. But for the latest generation of American veterans, needed support and assistance have been missing.

The nation has begun to welcome home with pride its Vietnam veterans, as reflected in the extraordinary Vietnam Veterans Memorial which was built through public contributions. The Democratic Party shares the nation's commitment to Vietnam veterans.

No President since the beginning of the Vietnam War has been so persistently hostile to Vietnam veterans programs as Ronald Reagan. He has sought to dismantle the Readjustment Counseling Centers, opposed employment and Agent Orange benefits, as well as basic due process at the Veterans Administration, including judicial review.

The Vietnam War divided our nation. Many of the rifts remain, but all agree on the respect due Vietnam veterans for their distinguished service during a troubled time. The Democratic Party pledges to reverse Ronald Reagan's Vietnam veteran policies, helping our nation come together as one people. And we believe it is especially important that we end discrimination against women and minority veterans,

particularly in health and education programs.

We believe that the government has a special obligation to all of this nation's veterans, and we are committed to fulfilling it — to providing the highest quality health care, improving education and training, providing the assistance they need to live independent and productive lives.

Opportunities for the Poor — For the past four years, this Administration has callously pursued policies which have further impoverished those at the bottom of the economic ladder and pushed millions of Americans, particularly women and children, below the poverty line. Thanks to the Reagan budget cuts, many of the programs upon which the poor rely have been gutted — from education to housing to child nutrition. Far from encouraging independence, the Administration has penalized those seeking to escape poverty through work, by conditioning assistance on nonparticipation in the workplace. The figures tell part of the story:

— Today, 15 percent of all Americans live below the poverty line;

— Over three million more children are in poverty today than there were in 1979;

— Over half of all black children under age three live in poverty;

— More than one-third of all female-headed households are below the poverty line, and for non-white families headed by women with more than one child, the figure is 70 percent.

But the numbers tell only part of the story; numbers do not convey the frustration and suffering of women seeking a future for themselves and their children, with no support from anyone; numbers do not recount the pain of growing numbers of homeless men and women with no place to sleep, or of increasing infant mortality rates among children born to poor mothers. Numbers do not convey the human effects of unemployment on a once stable and strong family.

As Democrats, we call upon the American people to join with us in a renewed commitment to combat the feminization of poverty in our nation so that every American can be a productive, contributing member of our society. In that effort, our goal is to strengthen families and to reverse the existing incentives for their destruction. We therefore oppose laws requiring an unemployed parent to leave the family or drop out of the work force in order to qualify for assistance and health care. We recognize the special need to increase the labor force participation of minority males, and we are committed to expanding their opportunities through education and training and to enforcing the laws which guarantee them equal opportunities. The plight of young mothers must be separately addressed as well: they too need education and training, and quality child care must be available if they are to participate in such programs. Only through a nation that cares and a government that acts can those Americans trapped in poverty move toward

meaningful independence.

The Hungry and the Homeless — In the late 1960s, the nation discovered widespread hunger and malnutrition in America, especially among poor children and the elderly. The country responded with a national effort, of which Americans should be justly proud. By the late 1970s, medical researchers found that hunger had nearly been eliminated.

Since 1980, however, hunger has returned. High unemployment, coupled with deep cutbacks in food assistance and other basic support programs for poor families have led to conditions not seen in this country for years. Studies in hospitals and health departments document increases in numbers of malnourished children. Increasing numbers of homeless wander our cities' streets in search of food and shelter. Religious organizations, charities and other agencies report record numbers of persons standing in line for food at soup kitchens and emergency food pantries.

Strong action is needed to address this issue and to end the resurgence of hunger in America. The Democratic Party is committed to reversing regressive Reagan policies and to providing more adequate food aid for poor families, infants, children, elderly and handicapped persons. It is time to resume the national effort, jettisoned in 1980, to ensure that less fortunate Americans do not go without adequate food because they are too poor to secure a decent diet. As Democrats, we call upon the American people to join with us in a renewed commitment to fight hunger and homelessness so that every American can be a productive, contributing member of our society.

Hunger is an international problem as well. In many countries it threatens peace and stability. The United States should take the lead in working with our allies and other countries to help wipe hunger from the face of the earth.

A Democratic President will ensure that the needs of the world's children are given priority in all U.S. foreign assistance programs and that international assistance programs are geared toward increasing self-reliance of local populations and self-sufficiency in food production.

Integrity in Government

As Democrats, we believe that the American people are entitled to a government that is honest, that is open, and that is fully representative of this nation and its people, and we are committed to providing it.

After four years in which the roll of dishonor in the Administration has grown weekly and monthly — from Richard Allen to Rita Lavelle, from Thomas Reed to James Watt — it is time for an end to the embarrassment of Republican cronyism and malfeasance. Our appointments will be ones of which Americans can be proud. Our selection process in staffing the government will be severe. We will not tolerate impropriety in a Democratic Administration.

We must work to end political action committee funding of federal political campaigns. To achieve that, we must enact a system of public financing of federal campaigns. At the same time, our Party should assure that a system of public financing be responsive to the problem of underrepresentation of women and minorities in elective offices.

We Democrats are not afraid to govern in public and to let the American people know and understand the basis for our decisions. We will reverse current Administration policies that permit the widespread overclassification of documents lacking a relationship to our national security. We will rescind Reagan Administration directives imposing undue burdens on citizens seeking information about their government through the Freedom of Information Act.

We will insist that the government, in its relations with its own employees, set a standard of fairness which is a model for the private sector. We believe, moreover, that an Administration that cannot run its own house fairly cannot serve the American people fairly. We will ensure that government's number one priority is the performance of its mission under the law, and not the implementation of the narrow political agenda of a single Party. Sound management and fair government cannot be administered by a politicized work force. Neither can it be accomplished by a demoralized work force. A Democratic Administration will not devalue the pay, benefits, and retirement rights of federal workers guaranteed under the law. We will work to reverse personnel policies, including the contracting out of work traditionally performed by public employees, that have made it impossible for current federal employees to recommend a career in federal service to our nation's young people.

Our judicial system must be one in which excellence and access are the foundations. It is essential to recruit people of high integrity, outstanding competence, and high quality of judgment to serve in our nation's judiciary. And we oppose efforts to strip the federal courts of their historic jurisdiction to adjudicate cases involving questions of federal law and constitutional right.

Crime

No problem has worried Americans more persistently over the past 20 years than the problem of crime. Crime and the fear of crime affect us all, but the impact is greatest on poor Americans who live in our cities. Neither a permissive liberalism nor a static conservatism is the answer to reducing crime. While we must eliminate those elements — like unemployment and poverty — that foster the criminal atmosphere, we must never let them be used as an excuse.

Although the primary responsibility for law enforcement rests at the local level, Democrats believe the federal government can play an important role by encouraging local innovation and the implementation of new crime control methods as their effectiveness is shown. And when crime spills across state borders, the federal government must take the lead, and assume responsibility for enforcing the law. This Administration has done neither. It has talked "law and order" while cutting law enforcement budgets. It has decried the influence of drugs, while cutting back on customs enforcement.

As a result, drug trafficking and abuse have risen to crisis proportions in the United States. In 1983, an estimated 60 tons of cocaine, 15,000 tons of marijuana, and 10 tons of heroin entered the United States, clear evidence that we are losing the effort overseas to control the production and transshipment of these and other dangerous drugs. Domestically, the illicit trafficking in drugs is a $100 billion per year business; the economic and social costs to our society are far higher.

Today, in our country, there are 25 million regular abusers of marijuana, close to 12 million abusers of cocaine, and half a million heroin addicts. Since 1979, hospital emergency room incidents — including deaths — related to cocaine have soared 300 percent; incidents related to heroin have climbed 80 percent. According to the 1983 National High School Survey on Drug Abuse, 63 percent of high school seniors have tried an illicit drug, and 40 percent have tried a drug other than marijuana. Alcohol abuse is also a serious problem which must be faced.

— For this reason, the Democratic Party believes it is essential to make narcotics control a high priority on the national agenda, and a major consideration in our dealings with producer and transshipment countries, particularly if they are recipients of U.S. assistance.
— At the national level, the effort must begin by introducing a comprehensive management plan to eliminate overlap and friction between the 113 different federal agencies with responsibilities for fighting crime, particularly with respect to the control of drug traffic. We must provide the necessary resources to federal agencies and departments with responsibility for the fight against drugs.
— To spur local law enforcement efforts, establishment of an independent criminal justice corporation should be considered. This corporation could serve as a means of encouraging community-based efforts, such as neighborhood citizen watches, alternative deployment patterns for police, and community service sentencing programs, which have proven effectiveness.
— Violent acts of bigotry, hatred and extremism aimed at women, racial, ethnic and religious minorities, and gay men and lesbians have become an alarmingly common phenomenon. A Democratic

Administration will work vigorously to address, document, and end all such violence.
— We believe that victims of crime deserve a workable program of compensation. We call for sentencing reforms that routinely include monetary or other forms of restitution to victims. The federal government should ensure that victims of violent federal crime receive compensation. We need to establish a federal victim compensation fund, to be financed, in part, by fines and the proceeds from the sale of goods forfeited to the government.
— We support tough restraints on the manufacture, transportation, and sale of snubnosed handguns, which have no legitimate sporting use and are used in a high proportion of violent crimes.
— We will establish a strong federal-state partnership to push for further progress in the nationwide expansion of comprehensive, community-based anti-drunk driving programs. With the support of citizens, private-sector business and government at all levels; we will institutionalize fatality and injury reduction on the nation's highways.
— We support fundamental reform of the sentencing process so that offenders who commit similar crimes receive similar penalties. Reform should begin with the establishment of appropriately drafted sentencing guidelines, and judges deviating from such guidelines should be required to provide written reasons for doing so.
— Finally, we believe that the credibility of our criminal courts must be restored. Our courts should not be attacked for failing to eliminate the major social problem of crime — courts of justice were not designed, and were never intended, to do that. A Democratic Administration will encourage experimentation with alternative dispute-resolution mechanisms, diversion programs for first and nonviolent offenders, and other devices to eliminate the congestion in our courts and restore to them an atmosphere in which they can perform their intended job: doing real individualized justice, in an orderly way.

Chapter III.
Peace, Security, and Freedom

Introduction

Building a safer future for our nation and the world: that is the Democratic agenda for our national security. Every responsibility before our nation, every task that we set, pales beside the most important challenge we face — providing new leadership that enhances our security, promotes our values, and works for peace.

The next American President will preside over a period of historic change in the international system. The relatively stable world order that has prevailed since World War II is bursting at the seams from the powerful forces of change — the proliferation of nuclear and conventional weapons, the relentless Soviet military buildup, the achievement of rough nuclear parity between the Soviet Union and the United States, the increasingly interdependent nature of the international economic order, the recovery and rise of European and Asian powers since the devastation of the Second World War, and the search for a new American political consensus in the wake of Vietnam and Lebanon and in the shadow of a regional crisis in Central America.

The greatest foreign policy imperative of the Democratic Party and of the next President is to learn from past mistakes and adapt to these changes, rather than to resist or ignore them. While not underestimating the Soviet threat, we can no longer afford simplistically to blame all of our troubles on a single "focus of evil," for the sources of international change run even deeper than the sources of superpower competition. We must see change as an opportunity as well as a challenge. In the 1980s and beyond, America must not only make the world safe for diversity; we must learn to thrive on diversity.

The Democratic Party believes that it is time to harness the full range of America's capacity to meet the challenges of a changing world. We reject the notion that America is beset by forces beyond its control. Our commitment to freedom and democracy, our willingness to listen to contrasting viewpoints, and our ingenuity at devising new ideas and arrangements have given us advantages in an increasingly diverse world that no totalitarian system can match.

The Democratic Party has a constructive and confident vision of America's ability to use all of our economic, political, and military resources to pursue our wide-ranging security and economic interests in a diverse and changing world. We believe in a responsible defense policy that will increase our national security. We believe in a foreign policy that respects our allies, builds democracy, and advances the cause of human rights. We believe that our economic future lies in our ability to rise to the challenge of international economic competition by making our own industries more competitive. Above all, we believe that our security requires the direct, personal involvement of the President of the United States to limit the Soviet military threat and to reduce the danger of nuclear war.

We have no illusions about the forces arrayed against the democratic cause in our time. In the year made famous by George Orwell, we can see the realization of many of his grimmest prophecies in the totalitarian Soviet state, which has amassed an arsenal of weapons far beyond its defensive needs. In the communist and non-communist world, we find tyrannical regimes that trample on human rights and repress their

people's cry for economic justice.

The Reagan Administration points to Soviet repression — but has no answer other than to escalate the arms race. It downgrades repression in the noncommunist world, by drawing useless distinctions between "totalitarian" and "authoritarian" regimes.

The Democratic Party understands the challenge posed by the enemies of democracy. Unlike the Reagan Administration, however, we are prepared to work constructively to reduce tensions and make genuine progress toward a safe world.

The Democratic Party is confident that American ideals and American interests reinforce each other in our foreign policy: the promotion of democracy and human rights not only distinguishes us from our adversaries, but it also builds the long-term stability that comes when governments respect their people. We look forward to the 21st Century as a century of democratic solidarity where security, freedom, and peace will flourish.

Peace, freedom and security are the essence of America's dream. They are the future of our children and their children.

This is the test where failure could provide no opportunity to try once more. As President Kennedy once warned: "We have the power to make this the best generation of mankind in the history of the world — or to make it the last."

THE FUTURE IF REAGAN IS REELECTED

"Star Wars is not the path toward a less dangerous world. A direct and safe road exists: equitable and verifiable deep cuts in strategic offensive forces. We must abandon the illusion that ever more sophisticated technology can remove the perils that science and technology have created."

Statement by Dr. Jerome B. Wiesner, Dr. Carl Sagan, Dr. Henry Kendall, and Admiral Noel Gayler (Democratic Platform Committee Hearing, Washington, D.C., June 12, 1984)

"The minister of the apartheid government recently boasted of the fruitful relationship between Pretoria and Washington since the advent of the Reagan regime. Now apartheid South Africa has acquired the military muscle to bomb, to maim, to kill men, women, and children, and to bully these states into negotiating with apartheid through the threat of increased military action. This may be hailed as a victory for apartheid and for the Reagan Administration, but in truth it can only create anger and contempt in the African people."

Professor Dennis Brutus, Northwestern University (former political prisoner in South Africa) (Democratic Platform Committee Hearing, New York, New York, April 9, 1984)

Suppose Mr. Reagan is reelected. How would he deal with the serious threats that

face us and our children?

Under Mr. Reagan, the nuclear arms race would continue to spiral out of control. A new generation of destabilizing missiles will imperil all humanity. We will live in a world where the nuclear arms race has spread from earth into space.

Under Mr. Reagan, we would continue to overemphasize destabilizing and redundant nuclear weapons programs at the expense of our conventional forces. We will spend billions for weapons that do not work. We will continue to ignore proposals to improve defense management, to get a dollar's worth for each dollar spent, and to make our military more combat-effective and our weapons more cost-effective.

Under Mr. Reagan, regional conflicts would continue to be dangerously mismanaged. Young Americans may be sent to fight and die needlessly. The spread of nuclear materials to new nations and the spread of sophisticated conventional weapons to virtually every nation on earth will continue unabated.

Can America afford a President so out of touch with reality that he tells us, "I think the world is safer and further removed from a possible war than it was several years ago"?

Can America afford the recklessness of a President who exposed American Marines to mortal danger and sacrificed 262 of them in a bungled mission in Lebanon against the advice of the Joint Chiefs of Staff, and brought upon us the worst U.S. military disaster since the Vietnam War?

Can America afford the irresponsibility of a President who undermines confidence in our deterrent with misleading allegations of Soviet nuclear "superiority" and whose Administration beguiles the American public with false claims that nuclear war can be survived with enough shovels?

Can America afford the unresponsiveness of a President who thwarts the will of the majority of Americans by waging a secret war against Nicaragua?

In a second Reagan term, will our heavens become a nuclear battleground?

In 1980, candidate Ronald Reagan promised the American people a more secure world. Yet, as President:

— He has raced to deploy new weapons that will be destabilizing and difficult to verify. He has pressed for a multi-billion dollar chemical weapons program. He has launched his trillion dollar "Star Wars" arms race in space.

— He has relaxed controls on nuclear proliferation, thus enhancing the risk that nuclear weapons will be acquired and used by unstable governments and international terrorists.

— He has become the first President since the Cold War to preside over the complete collapse of all nuclear arms negotiations with the Soviets.

— He has rejected SALT II, threatened the ABM Treaty, and abandoned the goal of a complete ban on nuclear weapons tests that has been pursued by every President since Eisenhower. He has refused to seek negotiations to limit anti-satellite weapons that could threaten our vital early-warning and military satellites. Over 250 strategic missiles and bombers that would have been eliminated under SALT II are still in Soviet hands.

Can we afford four more years of a Pentagon spending binge?

In 1980, candidate Ronald Reagan and the Republican Party promised the American people a defense spending increase "to be applied judiciously to critically needed programs." Yet, as President:

— He has initiated the largest peacetime defense build-up in our history with no coherent plan for integrating the increased programs into an effective military posture.

— He has slighted training and readiness of our conventional forces in favor of big ticket nuclear items, "preparing," in the words of General Maxwell Taylor, "for the least possible threats to the neglect of the most probable."

— He has brought us the worst-managed and most wasteful Defense Department in history. Under the Pentagon's wasteful purchasing system, the American taxpayer has paid $435 for a $17 claw hammer, $1100 for a 22-cent plastic steel cap, over $2000 for a 13-cent plain round nut, and $9600 for a $9 Allen wrench.

Can we afford four more years of dangerous foreign policy failures?

In 1980, candidate Ronald Reagan and the Republican Party promised "to put America on a sound, secure footing in the international arena." Yet, as President:

— He has contributed to the decline of U.S.-Soviet relations to a perilous point. Instead of challenges, he has used easy and abusive anti-Soviet rhetoric as a substitute for strength, progress, and careful use of power.

— He has strained vital U.S. alliances through his bungled efforts to stop the Soviet natural gas pipeline, his inflammatory nuclear rhetoric and policies, and his failure to support the efforts of our democratic allies to achieve a negotiated political solution in Central America.

— He has had as many Middle East policies as he has had staff turnovers. First, he offered strategic cooperation to Israel as if it were a gift. Then he took it away to punish Israel as if it were not our ally. Then he pressured Israel to make one-sided concessions to Jordan. Then he demanded that Israel withdraw from Lebanon. Then he pleaded with them to stay. Then he did not accept their offer of medical help for our wounded Marines. He undercut American credibility throughout the Middle East by declaring Lebanon a vital interest of the United States and then withdrawing.

— He has failed to understand the importance for the United States of a solid relationship with the African continent

— not only from the perspective of human decency, but also from enlightened concern for our own self-interest. By his lack of sensitivity and foresight, he has ignored the fate of millions of people who need our help in developing their economies and in dealing with the ravages of drought, and he has jeopardized our relations with countries that are important to U.S. security and well-being.

— He has brought us a strategy in Central America and the Caribbean that has failed. Since he took office, the region has become much more unstable; the hemisphere is much more hostile to us; and the poverty is much deeper. Today in El Salvador, after more than a billion dollars in American aid, the guerrillas are stronger than they were three years ago, and the people are much poorer. In Nicaragua, our support for the *contras* and for the covert war has strengthened the totalitarians at the expense of the moderates. In Honduras, an emerging democracy has been transformed into a staging ground for possible regional war. And in Costa Rica our backing for rebels based there is in danger of dragging that peaceful democracy into a military confrontation with Nicaragua. In Grenada, Mr. Reagan renounced diplomacy for over two years, encouraging extremism, instability, and crisis. By his failure to avoid military intervention, he divided us from our European allies and alienated our friends throughout the Western hemisphere. And by excluding the press, he set a chilling precedent, greatly hampering public scrutiny of his policies. After three and one-half years of Mr. Reagan's tunnel vision, extremism is stronger, our democratic friends are weaker, and we are further than ever from achieving peace and security in the region.

— He is the first President to fail to support publicly the ratification of the Genocide Convention. His Vice President has praised the Philippine dictator for his "love of democracy," his first Secretary of State announced that human rights would be replaced as a foreign policy priority, and his first nominee for Assistant Secretary of State for Human Rights was rejected by the U.S. Senate as unfit for that post. He has closely identified the United States with the apartheid regime in South Africa, and he has time and again failed to confront dictators around the globe.

This is an unprecedented record of failure. But President Reagan is content to make excuses for failure.

President Reagan blames Congress and the Democratic Party. He rebukes Americans deeply and genuinely concerned about the threat of nuclear war. He rails at the Soviet Union — as if words alone, without strategy or effective policy, will make that nation change its course.

It is time for Democrats and Americans to apply a tough standard to Ronald Reagan. Let us paraphrase the question he

asked in 1980: Are we safer today than we were three and a half years ago? Are we further from nuclear war? After more than a thousand days of Mr. Reagan, is the world anywhere less tense, anywhere closer to peace?

Americans throughout this land are answering with a resounding no.

President Reagan himself is responsible — responsible for four years of a failed foreign policy. America elects its President to lead. It does not elect its President to make excuses.

The Democratic Party believes that it is time to harness the full power of America's spirit and capacity to meet the challenges of a changing world.

The Democratic Party has a different and positive vision of America's future. What is at stake may be freedom and survival itself.

THE DEMOCRATIC ALTERNATIVE: A SAFER FUTURE FOR OUR NATION AND THE WORLD

"I do not see why we think of Democracy as so weak and so vulnerable. Let us for heaven's sake have some confidence in America and not tremble, fearing that our society will fall apart at the least rattle of the door. If I were constructing this platform, I would ask that its planks be carved out of self-confidence, and planted in belief in our own system."

Historian Barbara Tuchman (Democratic Platform Committee Hearing, New York, New York, April 9, 1984)

"The Democratic Party requires a foreign policy which approaches the problems that confront us primarily in their national and regional contexts, rather than viewing them, as the Reagan Administration does, almost exclusively as a manifestation of the 'evil empire's' efforts to extend its sway over the entire globe. What we need is a foreign policy which promotes the cause of human rights by opposing tyranny on the part of left as well as right wing governments, rather than a foreign policy, like the one we have now, which supports virtually every reactionary and repressive regime that professes to be anti-communist."

Honorable Stephen J. Solarz, U.S. Representative, New York (Democratic Platform Committee Hearing, New York, New York, April 9, 1984)

There is no higher goal for the Democratic Party than assuring the national security of the United States. This means a strong national defense, vigorous pursuit of nuclear arms control, and a foreign policy dedicated to advancing the interests of America and the forces of freedom and democracy in a period of global transformation. This will require new leadership, strong alliances, skillful diplomacy, effective economic cooperation, and a foreign policy sustained by American strength and ideals. And to hold the support of the

American people, our leaders must also be careful and measured in the use of force.

The Democratic Party is committed to a strong national defense. Democrats know that a relentless Soviet military build-up — well beyond its defensive needs — directly challenges world security, our democratic values, and our free institutions. On the nature of the Soviet threat and on the essential issue of our nation's security, Americans do not divide. On the common interest in human survival, the American and Soviet peoples do not divide.

Maintaining strong and effective military forces is essential to keeping the peace and safeguarding freedom. Our allies and adversaries must never doubt our military power or our will to defend our vital interests. To that end, we pledge a strong defense built in concert with our allies, based on a coherent strategy, and supported by a sound economy.

In an age of about 50,000 nuclear weapons, however, nuclear arms control and reductions are also essential to our security. The most solemn responsibility of a President is to do all that he or she can to prevent a single nuclear weapon from ever being used. Democrats believe that mutual and verifiable controls on nuclear arms can, and must be, a serious integral part of national defense. True national security requires urgent measures to freeze and reverse the arms race, not the pursuit of the phantom of nuclear superiority or futile Star Wars schemes.

The Democratic Party believes that the purpose of nuclear weapons is to deter war, not to fight it. Democrats believe that America has the strength and tenacity to negotiate nuclear arms agreements that will reduce the risk of nuclear war and preserve our military security.

Today we stand at one of the most critical junctures in the arms race since the explosion of the first atomic bomb. Mr. Reagan wants to open the heavens for warfare.

His Star Wars proposal would create a vulnerable and provocative "shield" that would lull our nation into a false sense of security. It would lead our allies to believe that we are retreating from their defense. It would lead to the death of the ABM Treaty — the most successful arms control treaty in history — and this trillion-dollar program would provoke a dangerous offensive and defensive arms race.

If we and our allies could defend our populations effectively against a nuclear war, the Democratic Party would be the first to endorse such a scheme. Unfortunately, our best scientists agree that an effective population defense is probably impossible. Therefore, we must oppose an arms race where the sky is no longer the limit.

Arms Control and Disarmament

Ronald Reagan is the first American President in over twenty years who has not reached any significant arms control agreements with the Soviet Union, and he is the first in over fifty years who has not met face to face with Soviet leaders. The unjustified Soviet walkout from key nuclear talks does not excuse the arms control failures of the Administration.

To reopen the dialogue, a Democratic President will propose an early summit with regular, annual summits to follow, with the Soviet leaders, and meetings between senior civilian and military officials, in order to reduce tensions and explore possible formal agreements. In a Democratic Administration, the superpowers will not communicate through megaphones.

A new Democratic Administration will implement a strategy for peace which makes arms control an integral part of our national security policy. We must move the world back from the brink of nuclear holocaust and set a new direction toward an enduring peace, in which lower levels of military spending will be possible. Our ultimate aim must be to abolish all nuclear weapons in a world safe for peace and freedom.

This strategy calls for immediate steps to stop the nuclear arms race, medium-term measures to reduce the dangers for war, and long-term goals to put the world on a new and peaceful course.

The first practical step is to take the initiative, on January 20, 1985, to challenge the Soviets to halt the arms race quickly. As President Kennedy successfully did in stopping nuclear explosions above ground in 1963, a Democratic President will initiate temporary, verifiable, and mutual moratoria, to be maintained for a fixed period during negotiations so long as the Soviets do the same, on the testing of underground nuclear weapons and anti-satellite weapons; on the testing and deployment of all weapons in space; on the testing and deployment of new strategic ballistic missiles now under development; and on the deployment of nuclear-armed, sea-launched cruise missiles.

These steps should lead promptly to the negotiation of a comprehensive, mutual and verifiable freeze on the testing, production, and deployment of all nuclear weapons.

Building on this initiative, the Democratic President will:

— update and resubmit the SALT II Treaty to the Senate for its advice and consent.

— pursue deep, stabilizing reductions in nuclear arsenals within the framework of SALT II, in the meantime observing the SALT II limits ourselves and insisting that the Soviets do likewise.

— propose the merging of the intermediate-range and strategic arms limitations negotiations, if the President judges that this could advance a comprehensive arms limitation agreement with the Soviet Union.

— immediately resubmit to the Senate for its advice and consent the 1974 Threshold Test Ban Treaty and the 1976 Peaceful Nuclear Explosions Treaty.

— conclude a verifiable and Comprehensive Test Ban Treaty.

— reaffirm our commitment to the ABM Treaty, ensure U.S. compliance, and vigorously demand answers to questions about Soviet compliance through the Standing Consultative Commission and other appropriate channels.

— actively pursue a verifiable, anti-satellite weapons treaty and ban on weapons in space.

— seek a verifiable international ban on the production of nuclear weapons-grade fissile material, such as plutonium and highly enriched uranium.

— undertake all-out efforts to halt nuclear proliferation.

— terminate production of the MX missile and the B-1 bomber.

— prohibit the production of nerve gas and work for a verifiable treaty banning chemical weapons.

— establish U.S.-Soviet nuclear risk reduction centers and other improved communications for a crisis.

— invite the most eminent members of the scientific community to study and report on the worldwide human suffering and the long-term environmental damage which would follow in the days after a nuclear war, and take into account as fully as possible the results of such study in the formulation of our nuclear weapons and arms control policies.

— strengthen broad-based, long-term public support for arms control by working closely with leaders of grass-roots, civic, women's, labor, business, religious and professional groups, including physicians, scientists, lawyers, and educators.

— provide national leadership for economic adjustment for affected communities and industries, and retraining for any defense workers affected by the termination or cutbacks in weapons programs.

— initiate, in close consultation with our NATO allies, a strategy for peace in Europe including:

— achieving a balance of conventional forces in order to reduce reliance on nuclear weapons and to permit the Atlantic Alliance to move toward the adoption of a "no first use" policy;

— mutually pulling back battlefield nuclear weapons from the frontlines of Europe, in order to avoid the necessity of having to make a "use them or lose them" choice should hostilities erupt in Europe.

— negotiating new approaches to intermediate nuclear force limits along the lines of the "walk in the woods" proposal, and then seeking to move closer to zero INF deployments by the U.S. and U.S.S.R.;

— negotiating significant mutual and balanced reductions in conventional forces of both NATO and the Warsaw Pact, and confidence-building measures to reduce the dangers of a surprise attack.

We are under no illusion that these

arms control proposals will be easy to achieve. Most will involve patience and dedication, and above all leadership in the pursuit of peace, freedom, and security. The Soviets are tough negotiators and too often seek to use arms control talks for their propaganda purposes. On this issue — preventing nuclear war — America must lead, and the Democratic Party intends to lead. Without our leadership the nations of the world will be tempted to abandon themselves, perhaps slowly at first, but then relentlessly to the quest for nuclear weapons, and our children will look back with envy upon today's already dangerous nuclear world as a time of relative safety.

Defense Policy

The Reagan Administration measures military might by dollars spent. The Democratic Party seeks prudent defense based on sound planning and a realistic assessment of threats. In the field of defense policy, the Democratic Administration will:
— Work with our NATO and other allies to ensure our collective security, especially by strengthening our conventional defenses so as to reduce our need to rely on nuclear weapons, and to achieve this at increased spending levels, with funding to continue at levels appropriate to our collective security, with the firm hope that successful steps to reduce tensions and to obtain comprehensive and verifiable arms control agreements will guarantee our nation both military security and budgetary relief.
— Cancel destabilizing or duplicative weapons systems, while proceeding in the absence of appropriate arms control agreements with necessary modernization of our strategic forces.
— Scale back the construction of large, expensive and vulnerable nuclear carriers.
— Modernize our conventional forces by balancing new equipment purchases with adequate resources spent on training, fuel, ammunition, maintenance, spare parts, and airlift and sealift to assure combat readiness and mobility, and by providing better equipment for our Reserves and National Guard.
— Reorganize Pentagon management and strengthen the JCS system to reduce interservice rivalries, promote military leadership over bureaucratic skills, assure effective execution of policies and decisions, undertake better multi-year planning based upon realistic projections of available resources, and reduce conflicts of interest.
— Ensure open and fair competitive bidding for procurement of necessary equipment and parts, and establish a system of effective, independent testing of weapons for combat conditions.
— Implement a program of military reform. Our forces must be combat ready; our doctrines should emphasize outthinking and out-maneuvering our adversaries; and our policies should im-

prove military organization and unit cohesion.
— Press our European allies to increase their contributions to NATO defense to levels of effort comparable to our own — an approach that the Administration undercut by abandoning the NATO-wide agreement concluded by its Democratic predecessor — and pursue improved trans-Atlantic economic cooperation and coordination of arms procurement.
— Recognize that the heart of our military strength is people, Americans in uniform who will have the skills and the will to maintain the peace. The men and women of our armed services deserve not only proper pay and benefits, but the nation's recognition, respect and gratitude as well.
— Recognize the importance of the intelligence community and emphasize its mission as being dedicated to the timely collection and analysis of information and data. A Democratic Administration will also recognize the urgent need to depoliticize the intelligence community and to restore professional leadership to it.
— Oppose a peacetime military draft or draft registration.
— Oppose efforts to restrict the opportunities of women in the military based solely on gender. The Reagan Administration has used the combat designation as an arbitrary and inappropriate way to exclude women from work they can legitimately perform. Women nurses and technicians, for example, have long served with distinction on the front lines; women must not be excluded from jobs that they are trained and able to perform.
— Seek ways to expand programs such as VISTA, the Young Adult Conservation Corps, and the Peace Corps.

These and other qualitative improvements will ensure effective American strength at affordable cost. With this strength, we will restore the confidence of our fellow citizens and our allies; we will be able to mount an effective conventional defense; and we will present our adversaries with a credible capability to deter war.

The Democratic Party is committed to reversing the policies of the Reagan Administration in the area of military and defense procurement. Public accounts reveal a four-year record of waste, fraud, conflicts of interest, and indications of wrongdoing. Administration officials have engaged in practices that have cost the taxpayers billions of dollars. Further, the Reagan Administration has ignored legal remedies to stop the abuses, recover the funds, and punish those responsible.

A Democratic President will demand full disclosure of all information, launch a thorough investigation, and seek recovery of any tax funds illegally spent. This will be a major step towards restoring integrity to defense procurements and reducing unnecessary expenditures in the defense budget.

Foreign Policy

The purpose of foreign policy is to attain a strong and secure United States and a world of peace, freedom and justice. On a planet threatened by dictatorships on the left and right, what is at stake may be freedom itself. On a planet shadowed by the threat of a nuclear holocaust, what is at stake may be nothing less than human survival.

A Democratic Administration will comprehend that the gravest political and security dangers in the developing world flow from conditions that open opportunities for the Soviet Union and its surrogates: poverty, repression and despair. Against adversaries such as these, military force is of limited value. Such weapons as economic assistance, economic and political reform, and support for democratic values by, among other steps, funding scholarships to study at U.S. colleges and universities, must be the leading elements of our presence and the primary instruments of American influence in the developing countries.

To this end, a Democratic President will strengthen our Foreign Service, end the present practice of appointing unqualified persons as Ambassadors, strengthen our programs of educational and cultural exchange, and draw upon the best minds in our country in the quest for peace.

A Democratic Administration will initiate and establish a Peace Academy. In the interests of balancing this nation's investment in the study of making war, the Peace Academy will study the disciplines and train experts in the arts of waging peace.

The Democratic Party is committed to ensuring strong representation of women and minorities in military and foreign policy decisionmaking positions in our government.

In addition, a Democratic President will understand that as Commander-in-Chief, he or she directs the forces of peace as well as those of war, and will restore an emphasis on skilled, sensitive, bilateral and multilateral diplomacy as a means to avert and resolve international conflict.

A Democratic President will recognize that the United States, with broad economic, political, and security interests in the world, has an unparalleled stake in the rule of international law. Under a Democratic Administration, there will be no call for clumsy attempts to escape the jurisdiction of the International Court of Justice, such as those put forth by the Reagan Administration in connection with its mining of the harbors of Nicaragua.

A Democratic President will reverse the automatic militarization of foreign policy and look to the causes of conflict to find out whether they are internal or external, whether they are political or primarily social and economic.

In the face of the Reagan Administrations's cavalier approach to the use of the military force around the world, the Democratic Party affirms its commitment to the selective, judicious use of American military power in consonance with Constitutional principles and reinforced by the War Powers Act.

A Democratic President will be prepared to apply military force when vital American interests are threatened, particularly in the event of an attack upon the United States or its immediate allies. But he or she will not hazard American lives or engage in unilateral military involvement:

● Where our objectives are not clear;

● Until all instruments of diplomacy and non-military leverage, as appropriate, have been exhausted;

● Where our objectives threaten unacceptable costs or unreasonable levels of military force;

● Where the local forces supported are not working to resolve the causes of conflict;

● Where multilateral or allied options for the resolution of conflict are available.

Further, a Democratic Administration will take all reasonable domestic action to minimize U.S. vulnerability to international instability, such as reducing Western alliance on Persian Gulf oil and other strategic resources. To this end, a Democratic Administration will implement, with our allies, a multilateral strategy for reduction of allied dependence on critical resources from volatile regions of the world.

U.S. covert operations under a Democratic President will be strictly limited to cases where secrecy is essential to the success of an operation and where there is an unmistakable foreign policy rationale. Secrecy will not be used simply to hide from the American people policies they might be expected to oppose.

Finally, a Democratic President will recognize our democratic process as a source of strength and stability, rather than an unwelcome restraint on the control of foreign policy. He or she will respect the War Powers Resolution as a reflection of wise judgment that the sustained commitment of America's fighting forces must be made with the understanding and support of Congress and the American people. A Democratic President will understand that United States leadership among nations requires a proper respect for law and treaty obligations, and the rights of men and women everywhere.

Europe and the Atlantic Alliance — American leadership is not about standing up to your friends. It is about standing up with them, and for them. In order to have allies, we must act like one.

Maintaining a strong alliance is critically important. We remain absolutely committed to the defense of Europe, and we will work to ensure that our allies carry their fair share of the burden of the common defense. A Democratic Administration in turn will commit itself to increased consultation on security affairs. We must work to sustain and enhance Western unity.

We must persuade the next generation of Europeans that America will use its power responsibly in partnership with them. We Democrats affirm that Western

security is indivisible. We have a vital interest in the security of our allies in Europe. And it must always remain clear that an attack upon them is the same as an attack upon us — by treaty and in reality.

A strong Western alliance requires frank discussions among friends about the issues that from time to time divide us. For example, we must enter into meaningful negotiations with the European Community to reduce their agricultural export subsidies which unfairly impair the competitiveness of American agricultural products in third-country markets.

A Democratic President will encourage our European friends to resolve their long-standing differences over Ireland and Cyprus.

The Democratic Party supports an active role by the United States in safeguarding human rights in Northern Ireland and achieving an enduring peaceful settlement of that conflict. We oppose the use of plastic bullets in Northern Ireland, and we urge all sides to reject the use of violence. The Democratic Party supports a ban on all commercial transactions by the U.S. government with firms in England and Ireland that practice, on an on-going basis, discrimination in Northern Ireland on the basis of race, religion, or sex. We affirm our strong commitment to Irish unity — achieved by consent and based on reconciliation of all the people of Ireland. The Democratic Party is greatly encouraged by the historic and hopeful Report of the New Ireland Forum which holds the promise of a real breakthrough. A Democratic President will promptly appoint a special envoy and urge the British as well as the political leaders in Northern Ireland to review the findings and proposals of the Forum with open hearts and open minds, and will appeal to them to join a new initiative for peace. The Congress and a Democratic President will stand ready to assist this process, and will help promote jobs and investments, on a non-discriminatory basis, that will represent a significant contribution to the cause of peace in Ireland.

In strong contrast to President Reagan's failure to apply effective diplomacy in Cyprus and the Eastern Mediterranean, a Democratic President will act with urgency and determination to make a balanced policy in the area and a peaceful resolution of the Cyprus dispute a key foreign policy priority. A Democratic President will utilize all available U.S. foreign policy instruments and will play an active, instead of a passive, role in the efforts to secure implementation of U.N. Resolutions so as to achieve removal of Turkish troops, the return of refugees, reestablishment of the integrity of the Republic of Cyprus, and respect for all citizens' human rights on Cyprus.

United States — Soviet Relations — U.S. relations with the Soviet Union are a critical element of our security policy. All Americans recognize the threat to world peace posed by the Soviet Union. The U.S.S.R. is the only adversary with the ca-

pability of destroying the United States. Moreover, Americans are more generally concerned about the Soviet leadership's dangerous behavior internationally and the totalitarian nature of their regime. The Brezhnev Doctrine proclaims Soviet willingness to maintain communist regimes against the opposition of their own people. Thus, Soviet troops have invaded and today continue to wage war on the proud people of Afghanistan. In Poland, a military government, acting under Soviet pressure, has sought to crush the indomitable spirit of the Polish people and to destroy Solidarity, a free trade Union movement of ten million members and the first such movement in a communist country. In recent years, the Soviet Union and its allies have played a more aggressive role in countries around the world. At the same time, the Soviet military arsenal, nuclear and conventional, far exceeds that needed for its defense.

Yet we also recognize that the Soviets share a mutual interest in survival. They, too, have no defense against a nuclear war. Our security and their security can only be strengthened by negotiation and cooperation.

To shape a policy that is both firm and wise, we must first stand confident and never fear the outcome of any competition between our systems. We must see the Soviet Union as it is — neither minimizing the threats that Soviet power and policies pose to U.S. interests, nor exaggerating the strength of a Soviet regime beset by economic stagnation and saddled with a bankrupt and sterile ideology. We must join with our allies and friends to maintain an effective deterrent to Soviet power. We must pursue a clear, consistent and firm policy of peaceful competition toward the Soviet Union, a steady and pragmatic approach that neither tolerates Soviet aggression and repression nor fuels Soviet paranoia.

The job of an American President is both to check Soviet challenges to our vital interests, and to meet them on the common ground of survival. The risk of nuclear war cannot be eliminated overnight. But every day it can be either increased or decreased. And one of the surest ways to increase it is to cut off communications.

The Democratic Party condemns continued Soviet persecution of dissidents and refuseniks, which may well have brought Nobel laureate Andrei Sakharov and his wife to the verge of death in internal exile in Gorki. We will not be silent when Soviet actions, such as the imprisonment of Anatoly Shcharansky and Ida Nudel and thousands of others, demonstrate the fundamentally repressive and anti-Semitic nature of the Soviet regime. A Democratic Administration will give priority to securing the freedom to emigrate for these brave men and women of conscience including Jews and other minorities, and to assuring their fair treatment while awaiting permission to leave. These freedoms are guaranteed by the Universal Declaration of Human Rights and by the Helsinki Final Act which the Soviets have signed and with whose provisions they must be required to comply. Jewish emigration, which reached the level of fifty thousand per year during the last Democratic Administration and which has virtually ended under its Republican successor, must be renewed through firm, effective diplomacy. We also recognize that Jewish emigration reached its height at the same time there was an American Administration dedicated to pursuing arms control, expanding mutually beneficial trade, and reducing tensions with the Soviet Union — fully consistent with the interests of the United States and its allies. It is no contradiction to say that while pursuing an end to the arms race and reducing East-West tensions, we can also advance the cause of Soviet Jewish emigration.

Eastern Europe — We must respond to the aspirations and hopes of the peoples of Eastern Europe and encourage, wherever possible, the forces of change and pluralism that will increase these people's freedom from Soviet tyranny and communist dictatorship. We should encourage Western European countries to pursue independent foreign policies and to permit greater liberalization in domestic affairs, and we should seek independent relationships to further these objectives with them.

The Democratic Party condemns the Soviet repression by proxy in Poland and the other countries of Eastern Europe. The emergence of the free trade union Solidarity is one of the most formidable developments in post-war Europe and inspires all who love freedom. The struggle of the Polish people for a democratic society and religious freedom is eloquent testimony to their national spirit and bravery that even a brutal martial law regime cannot stamp out.

Today the Jaruzelski regime claims to have ended the harshest repressive measures. Yet it continues to hold political prisoners, it continues to mistreat them, and it continues to hunt down members of Solidarity.

The Democratic Party agrees with Lech Walesa that the underground Solidarity movement must not be deprived of union freedoms. We call for the release of all political prisoners in Poland and an end to their harassment, the recognition of the free trade union Solidarity, and the resumption of progress toward liberty and human rights in that nation. A Democratic President will continue to press for effective international sanctions against the Polish regime until it makes satisfactory progress toward these objectives.

The Middle East — The Democratic Party believes that the security of Israel and the pursuit of peace in the Middle East are fundamental priorities for American foreign policy. Israel remains more than a trusted friend, a steady ally, and a sister democracy. Israel is strategically important to the United States, and we must enter into meaningful strategic cooperation.

The Democratic Party opposes this Administration's sales of highly advanced weaponry to avowed enemies of Israel, such as AWACS aircraft and Stinger missiles to Saudi Arabia. While helping to meet the legitimate defensive needs of states aligned with our nation, we must ensure Israel's military edge over any combination of Middle East confrontation states. The Democratic Party opposes any consideration of negotiations with the PLO, unless the PLO abandons terrorism, recognizes the state of Israel, and adheres to U.N. Resolutions 242 and 338.

Jerusalem should remain forever undivided with free access to the holy places for people of all faiths. As stated in the 1976 and 1980 platforms, the Democratic Party recognizes and supports the established status of Jerusalem as the capital of Israel. As a symbol of this stand, the U.S. Embassy should be moved from Tel Aviv to Jerusalem.

The Democratic Party condemns this Administration's failure to maintain a high-level Special Negotiator for the Middle East, and believes that the Camp David peace process must be taken up again with urgency. No nation in the Middle East can afford to wait until a new war brings even worse destruction. Once again we applaud and support the example of both Israel and Egypt in taking bold steps for peace. We believe that the United States should press for negotiations among Israel, Jordan, Saudi Arabia, and other Arab states. We re-emphasize the fundamental principle that the prerequisite for a lasting peace in the Middle East remains an Israel with secure and defensible borders, strong beyond a shadow of a doubt; that the basis for peace is the unequivocal recognition of Israel's right to exist by all other states; and that there should be a resolution of the Palestinian issue.

The United States and our allies have vital interests in the Persian Gulf. We must be prepared to work with our allies in defense of those interests. We should stand by our historic support for the principle of freedom of the high seas. At the same time, we and our allies should employ active diplomacy to encourage the earliest possible end to the Iran/Iraq conflict.

The Western Hemisphere — The Western Hemisphere is in trouble. Central America is a region at war. Latin America is experiencing the most serious economic crisis in 50 years. The Inter-American system is on the verge of collapse. Concern about U.S. policies has risen sharply.

It is time to make this Hemisphere a top priority. We need to develop relations based on mutual respect and mutual benefit. Beyond essential security concerns, these relations must emphasize diplomacy, development and respect for human rights. Above all, support for democracy must be pursued. The Reagan Administration is committing the old error of supporting authoritarian military regimes against the wishes of the people they rule, but the United States was not founded, and defended for 200 years with American blood, in order to perpetuate tyranny among our neighbors.

The Hemisphere's nations must strive jointly to find acceptable solutions with judgments and actions based on equally-applied criteria. We must condemn violations of human rights, aggression, and deprivation of basic freedoms wherever they occur. The United States must recognize that the economic and debt crisis of Latin America also directly affects us.

The Reagan Administration has badly misread and mishandled the conflict in Central America. The President has chosen to dwell on the strategic importance of Central America and to cast the struggle in almost exclusively East-West terms. The strategic importance of Central America is not in doubt, nor is the fact that the Soviet Union, Cuba and Nicaragua have all encouraged instability and supported revolution in the region. What the President ignores, however, are the indigenous causes of unrest. Historically, Central America has been burdened by widespread hunger and disease. And the historic pattern of concentrated wealth has done little to produce stable democratic societies.

Sadly, Mr. Reagan has opted for the all too frequent American response to the unrest that has characterized Central America — military assistance. Over the past 100 years, Panama, Nicaragua, and Honduras have all been occupied by U.S. forces in an effort to suppress indigenous revolutionary movements. In 1954, CIA-backed forces successfully toppled the Government of Guatemala.

President Reagan's massive transfusions of military aid to El Salvador are no substitute for the social and economic reforms that are necessary to undermine the appeal the guerrillas hold for many Salvadorans. The changes and upheavals in El Salvador and Nicaragua are home-grown, but they are exacerbated by forces from outside of Central America. The undoubted communist influence on these revolutions cannot be nullified by the dispatch of naval and air armadas to the waters off Nicaragua and thousands of troops to the jungles of Honduras. The solution lies with a new policy that fosters social, economic and political reforms that are compatible with our legitimate vital interests while accommodating the equally legitimate forces of change.

America must find a different approach. All too often, the United States thinks in terms of what it can do *for* the nations of Latin America and the Caribbean region. Rarely does it think in terms of what it can do *with* them. Even with the best of intentions, the difference is more than rhetorical, for paternalism can never be disguised and it is always resented — whether we choose to label it a "special relationship" or to call it a "defensive shield." Acting *for* the nations of the Hemisphere rather than acting in concert *with* them is the surest way of repeating the mistakes of the past and casting a dark shadow over the future.

It need not be. There is an alternative, a good alternative. The great Mexican patriot Benito Juarez pointed the way and said it best: "Between men as between nations, respect for the rights of others is peace." Working *with* our hemispheric neighbors produces understanding and cooperation. Doing someting *for* them produces resentment and conflict.

Democrats know there is a real difference between the two and a Democratic President will seek the advice and counsel of the authentic democratic voices within the region — voices that may be heard north and south, east and west; the voices of President Miguel de la Madrid of Mexico, President Belisario Betancur of Colombia, and President Raul Alfonsin of Argentina; the voices of President Jorge Blanco of the Dominican Republic, Prime Minister Tom Adams of Barbados, and President Alberto Monge of Costa Rica. By consulting with and listening carefully to these leaders and their democratic colleagues elsewhere in the region, the next Democratic President of the United States will fashion a policy toward the region which recognizes that:

— the security and well-being of the Hemisphere are more a function of economic growth and development than of military agreements and arms transfers;

— the mounting debt crisis throughout the region poses a broader threat to democratic institutions and political stability than does any insurgency or armed revolutionary movement;

— there is an urgent and genuine need for far-reaching economic, social and political reforms in much of the region and that such reforms are absolutely essential to the protection of basic human rights;

— the future belongs as much to the people of the region — the politically forgotten and the economically deprived — as it does to the rich and powerful elite;

— preservation and protection of U.S. interests in the Hemisphere requires mutual respect for national sovereignty and demilitarization of the region, prior consultation in accordance with the Rio Treaty and the OAS Charter regarding the application of the Monroe Doctrine, the use of military force, and a multilateral commitment to oppose the establishment of Soviet and Cuban military bases, strategic facilities, or combat presence in Central America or elsewhere in Latin America;

— efforts to isolate Cuba only serve to make it more dependent on the Soviet Union; U.S. diplomatic skills must be employed to reduce that level of dependence and to explore the differences that divide us with a view to stabilizing our relations with Cuba. At the same time we must continue to oppose firmly Cuban intervention in the internal affairs of other nations. Progress in our relationship will depend on Cuba's willingness to end its support for violent revolution, to recognize the sovereignty and independence of other nations by respecting the principle of non-intervention, to demonstrate respect for human rights both inside and outside of Cuba, and to abide by international norms of behavior.

Mindful of these realities and determined to stop widening, militarizing, and Americanizing the conflict, a Democratic President's immediate objective will be to stop the violence and pursue a negotiated political solution in concert with our democratic allies in the Contadora group. He or she will approach Central American policy in the following terms:

— First, there must be unequivocal support for the Contadora process and for the efforts by those countries to achieve political solutions to the conflicts that plague the Central American region.

— Second, there must be a commitment on the part of the United States to reduce tensions in the region. We must terminate our support for the *contras* and other paramilitary groups fighting in Nicaragua. We must halt those U.S. military exercises in the region which are being conducted for no other real purpose than to intimidate or provoke the Nicaraguan government or which may be used as a pretext for deeper U.S. military involvement in the area. And, we must evidence our firm willingness to work for a demilitarized Central America, including the mutual withdrawal of all foreign forces and military advisers from the region. A Democratic President will seek a multilateral framework to protect the security and independence of the region which will include regional agreements to bar new military bases, to restrict the numbers and sophistication of weapons being introduced into Central America, and to permit international inspection of borders. This diplomatic effort can succeed, however, only if all countries in Central America, including Nicaragua, will agree to respect the sovereignty and integrity of their neighbors, to limit their military forces, to reject foreign military bases (other than those provided for in the Panama Canal Treaties), and to deny any external force or power the use of their territories for purposes of subversion in the region. The viability of any security agreement for Central America would be enhanced by the progressive development of pluralism in Nicaragua. To this end, the elections proposed for November are important; how they are conducted will be an indication of Nicaragua's willingness to move in the direction of genuine democracy.

— Third, there must be a clear, concise signal to indicate that we are ready, willing and able to provide substantial economic resources, through the appropriate multilateral channels, to the nations of Central America, as soon as the Contadora process achieves a measure of success in restoring peace and stability in the region. In the meantime, of course, we will continue to provide humanitarian aid and refugee relief assistance. The Democratic Administration will work to help churches and universities which are providing sanctuary and assistance to Guatemalan, Haitian, and Salvadoran refugees, and will give all assistance to such refugees as is consistent with U.S. law.

— Fourth, a Democratic President will support the newly elected President of El Salvador in his efforts to establish civilian democratic control, by channeling U.S. aid through him and by conditioning it on the elimination of government-supported death squads and on progress toward his objectives of land reform, human rights, and serious negotiations with contending forces in El Salvador, in order to achieve a peaceful democratic political settlement of the Salvadoran conflict.

— Fifth, a Democratic President will not use U.S. armed forces in or over El Salvador or Nicaragua for the purpose of engaging in combat unless:

1) Congress has delcared war or otherwise authorized the use of U.S. combat forces, or

2) the use of U.S. combat forces is necessary to meet a clear and present danger of attack upon the U.S., its territories or possessions or upon U.S. embassies or citizens, consistent with the War Powers Act.

These are the key elements that evidence very real differences between the Democrats' approach to Central America and that of the Reagan Administration. And these are the key elements that will offer the American public a choice — a very significant choice — between war and peace in the Central American region.

A Democratic President would seek to work with the countries of the Caribbean to strengthen democratic institutions. He or she would not overlook human rights, by refusing to condemn repression by the regimes of the right or the left in the region. A Democratic President would give high priority to democracy, freedom, and to multilateral development. A Democratic President would encourage regional cooperation and make of that important area a showplace rather than a footstool for economic development. Finally, support for democracy must be pursued in its own right, and not just as a tactic against communism.

Human rights principles were a cornerstone of President Carter's foreign policy and have always been a central concern in the Inter-American system. Regional multilateral action to protect and advance human rights is an international obligation.

A Democratic President must not overlook human rights, refusing to condemn repression by the regimes of the right or the left in the region. Insistence that government respect their obligations to their people is a criterion that must apply equally to all. It is as important in Cuba as in El Salvador, Guatemala as in Nicaragua, in Haiti as in Paraguay and Uruguay.

A Democratic Administration would place protection of human rights in a core position in our relations with Latin America and the Caribbean. It would particularly seek multilateral support for such principles by strengthening and backing the Inter-American Commission on Human Rights, and by encouraging the various private organizations in the hemisphere dedicated to monitoring and protecting human rights.

Africa — The Democratic Party will advocate a set of bold new initiatives for Third World nations in general and Africa in particular. Hunger, drought, and famine have brought untold suffering to millions in Africa. This human misery — and the armies of nationless — requires a policy of substantial increases in humanitarian assistance, a major thrust in agricultural technology transfer, and cessation of the unfortunate tendency to hold such aid hostage to East-West confrontation or other geopolitical aims. The United States also must offer substantially greater economic assistance to these nations, while engaging in a North-South multilateral dialogue that addresses mutual economic development strategies, commodities pricing, and other treaties relevant to international trade. A Democratic President will join with our friends within and outside the continent in support of full respect for the sovereignty and territorial integrity of all African states. Africa is the home of one-eighth of the world's population and a continent of vast resources. Our national interest demands that we give this rich and diverse continent a much higher priority.

A Democratic President will reverse the Reagan Administration's failed policy of "constructive engagement" and strongly and unequivocally oppose the apartheid regime in South Africa. A Democratic Administration will:

— exert maximum pressure on South Africa to hasten the establishment of a democratic, unitary political system within South Africa.

— pursue scrupulous enforcement of the 1977 U.N. arms embargo against South Africa, including enforcement of restrictions on the sale of "dual use" equipment.

— impose a ban on all new loans by U.S. business interests to the South African government and on all new investments and loans to the South African private sector, until there is substantial progress toward the full participation of all the people of South Africa in the social, political, and economic life in that country and toward an end to discrimination based on race or ethnic origin.

— ban the sale or transfer of sophisticated computers and nuclear technology to South Africa and the importation of South African gold coins.

— reimpose export controls in effect during the Carter Administration which were relaxed by the Reagan Administration.

— withdraw landing rights to South African aircraft.

The Democratic Party condemns South Africa for unjustly holding political prisoners. Soviet harassment of the Sakharovs is identical to South African house arrests of political opponents of the South African regime. Specifically, the detention of Nelson Mandela, leader of the African National Congress, and Winnie Mandela must be brought to the world's attention, and we demand their immediate release. In addition, we demand the immediate release of all other political prisoners in South Africa.

A Democratic Administration will work as well toward legitimate rights of self-determination of the peoples of Namibia by:

— demanding compliance with U.N. Security Council Resolution 435 — the six-year-old blueprint for Namibian independence;

— imposing severe fines on U.S. companies that violate the United Nations Decree prohibiting foreign exploitation of Namibian mineral wealth until Namibia attains independence;

— progressively increasing effective sanctions against South Africa unless and until it grants independence to Namibia and abolishes its own abhorrent apartheid system.

Asia — Our relationship with the countries of Asia and the Pacific Basin will continue to be of increasing importance. The political, cultural, economic, and strategic ties which link the United States to this region cannot be ignored.

With our Asian friends and allies, we have a common cause in preserving the security and enhancing democracy in the area.

With our Asian trading partners, we share a common interest in expanding commerce and fair trade between us, as evidenced by the 33 percent of total American trade now conducted with those countries.

And with the growing number of Asian/Pacific-Americans, we welcome the strength and vitality which increased cultural ties bring to this country.

Our relationship with Japan is a key to the maintenance of peace, security, and development in Asia and the Pacific region. Mutual respect, enhanced cooperation, and steady diplomacy must guide our dealings with Japan. At the same time, as allies and friends, we must work to resolve areas of disagreement. A Democratic President, therefore, will press for increased access to Japanese as well as other Asian markets for American firms and their products. Finally, a Democratic President will expect Japan to continue moving toward assuming its fair share of the burden of collective security — in self-defense as well as in foreign assistance and democratic development.

Our security in the Pacific region is also closely tied to the well-being of our long-time allies, Australia and New Zealand. A Democratic President will honor and strengthen our security commitment

to ANZUS as well as to other Southest Asian friends.

Our relationship with the People's Republic of China must also be nurtured and strengthened. The Democratic Party believes that our developing relations with the PRC offer a historic opportunity to bring one quarter of the world's population into the community of nations, to strengthen a counterweight to Soviet expansionism, and to enhance economic relations that offer great potential for mutual advantage. At the same time, we recognize our historic ties to the people on Taiwan and we will continue to honor our commitments to them, consistent with the Taiwan Relations Act.

Our own principles and interests demand that we work with those in Asia, as well as elsewhere, who can encourage democratic institutions and support greater respect for human rights. A Democratic President will work closely with the world's largest democracy, India, and maintain mutually beneficial ties. A Democratic President will press for the restoration of full democracy in the Philippines, further democratization and the elimination of martial law in Taiwan, the return to freedom of speech and press in South Korea, and restoration of human rights for the people of East Timor. Recognizing the strategic importance of Pakistan and the close relationship which has existed between our two countries, a Democratic President would press to restore democracy and terminate its nuclear weapons program. Finally, a Democratic President would press for the fullest possible accounting of Americans still missing in Indochina.

For the past four years, the Soviet Union has been engaged in a brutal effort to crush the resistance of the people of Afghanistan. It denies their right to independence. It is trying to stamp out their culture and to deny them the right to practice their religion, Islam. But despite appalling costs, the people of Afghanistan continue to resist — demonstrating the same qualities of human aspiration and fortitude that made our own nation great. We must continue to oppose Soviet aggression in Afghanistan. We should support the efforts of the Afghanistan freedom fighters with material assistance.

If the Soviet Union is prepared to abide by the principles of international law and human dignity, it should find the U.S. prepared to help produce a peaceful settlement.

Global Debt and Development

The Democratic Party will pursue policies for economic development, for aid and trade that meet the needs of the people of the developing world and that further our own national interest. The next Democratic President will support development policies that meet the basic needs of the poor for food, water, energy, medical care, and shelter rather than "trickle down" policies that never reach those on the bottom.

The next Democratic Administration will give preference in its foreign assistance to countries with democratic institutions and respect for human rights.

A Democratic President will seek to cut back record U.S. budget deficits and interest rates not only for our own economic well-being, but to reduce the economic crisis confronting so many industrialized and developing states alike.

Mr. Reagan has perceived national security in very limited and parochial terms, and thus has failed completely to grasp the significance of the international debt which now has sky-rocketed to some $800 billion. In 1983, some thirty nations accounting for half of this total were forced to seek restructuring of their debts with public and private creditors because they were unable to meet their debt payments.

The U.S. economy is directly linked to the costs of these loans through their variable interest rates (tied to the U.S. prime rate). A rise in the U.S. prime rate by one percent added more than $4 billion to the annual interest costs associated with these external debts. The struggle to meet their external debts has slashed the purchasing power of these developing countries and forced them to curtail imports from the U.S. This accounts for one-third to one-half of the adverse turn in the U.S. trade deficit, which is projected to reach $130 billion this year. The social and political stability of these developing countries is seriously challenged by the debt crisis. In light of the interdependence of the international economy, the crisis also threatens the very foundation of the international financial system. To answer these dangers, the Democratic Administration will:

— Call immediately for discussions on improving the functioning of the international monetary systems and on developing a comprehensive long-term approach to the international debt problem.

— Instruct the Treasury Department to work with the Federal Reserve Board, U.S. bank regulators, key private banks, and the finance ministers and central bankers of Europe and Japan, to develop a short-term program for reducing the debt service obligations of less developed countries, while 1) preserving the safety and soundness of the international banking system and 2) ensuring that the costs of the program are shared equitably among all parties to existing and rescheduled debts.

— Recommend an increase in the lending capacity of the World Bank, as well as an increase in the lending capacity of the Export-Import Bank of the U.S., to ensure that debtor nations obtain adequate capital for investment in export industries.

— Review international trade barriers which limit the ability of these countries to earn foreign exchange.

Security assistance can, in appropriate circumstances, help our friends meet legitimate defense needs. But shifting the balance from economic development toward military sales, as has occurred over the past three and one-half years, sets back the cause of peace and justice, fuels regional arms races, and places sophisticated weapons in the hands of those who could one day turn them back upon us and upon our friends and allies. The Democratic Party seeks now, as in the past, effective international agreements to limit and reduce the transfer of conventional arms.

A Democratic President will seize new opportunities to make major advances at limited cost in the health and survival of the world's poorest people — thus enabling more people to contribute to and share in the world's resources, and promoting stability and popular participation in their societies. Recognizing that unrestrained population growth constitutes a danger for economic progress and political stability, a Democratic President will restore full U.S. support for national and international population programs that are now threatened by the policies of the Reagan Administration.

A Democratic President will work to see the power and prestige of the U.S. fully committed to the reform and strengthening of the United Nations and other international agencies in the pursuit of their original purposes — peace, economic and social welfare, education, and human rights.

Because of the economic instability caused by global debts and by other problems, unprecedented migration into the United States and other parts of the world is occurring in the form of economic refugees. The Democratic Party will support economic development programs so as to aid nations in reducing migration from their countries, and thereby reduce the flow of economic refugees to the U.S. and other parts of the world.

Rather than scuttling the international Law of the Sea negotiations after over a decade of bipartisan U.S. involvement, a Democratic President will actively pursue efforts to achieve an acceptable Treaty and related agreements that protect U.S. interests in all uses of ocean space.

Human Rights and Democratic Solidarity

The Democratic Party believes that we need new approaches to replace the failed Republican policies. We need sustained, personal, presidential leadership in foreign policy and arms control. We need a President who will meet with the Soviets to challenge them to reduce the danger of nuclear war, who will become personally involved in reviving the Camp David peace process, who will give his or her full support to the Contadora negotiations, and who will press the South Africans to repeal their policies of apartheid and destabilization. We need a President who will understand that human rights and national security interests are mutually supportive. We need a President to restore our influence, enhance our security, pursue democracy and freedom, and work unremittingly for peace. With firm purpose, skill, sensitivity, and a recovery of our own pride in what we are — a Democratic President will build an international alliance of free people to promote these great causes.

A Democratic President will pursue a foreign policy that advances basic civil and political rights — freedom of speech, association, thought and religion, the right to leave, freedom of the integrity of the person, and the prohibition of torture, arbitrary detention and cruel, inhuman and degrading treatment — and that seeks as well to attain basic, economic, social, and cultural rights. A Democratic President's concern must extend from the terror of the Russian Gulag to the jails of Latin generals. The banning of South African blacks is no more acceptable than the silencing of Cuban poets. A Democratic President will end U.S. support for dictators throughout the world from Haiti to the Philippines. He or she will support and defend the observance of basic human rights called for in the Universal Declaration of Human Rights and the Helsinki Final Act. He or she will seek, through both quiet diplomacy and public measures, the release of political prisoners and the free immigration of prosecuted individuals and peoples around the world. He or she will seek U.S. ratification of the Genocide Convention, the International Covenants on Human Rights, and the American Convention on Human Rights, as well as the establishment of a U.N. High Commissioner for Human Rights. He or she will fulfill the spirit as well as the letter of our legislation calling for the denial of military and economic assistance to governments and systematically violate human rights.

The Democratic Party believes that whether it is in response to totalitarianism in the Soviet Union or repression in Latin America and East Asia, to apartheid in South Africa or martial law in Poland, to terrorism in Libya or the reign of terror in Iran, or to barbaric aggression in Southeast Asia and Afghanistan, the foreign policy of the United States must be unmistakably on the side of those who love freedom.

As Democrats and as Americans, we will make support for democracy, human rights, and economic and social justice the cornerstone of our policy. These are the most revolutionary ideas on our planet. They are not to be feared. They are the hallmarks of the democratic century that lies before us. ∎

Reagan-Mondale Debate on Domestic Issues

Following is the official record of the nationally televised debate between President Reagan and Walter F. Mondale, sponsored by The League of Women Voters Education Fund, held Oct. 7, in Louisville, Ky.

MRS. DOROTHY S. RIDINGS, Chair, The League of Women Voters Education Fund: Good evening from the Kentucky Center for the Arts in Louisville, Kentucky. I am Dorothy Ridings, President of The League of Women Voters, the sponsor of tonight's first Presidential debate between Republican Ronald Reagan and Democrat Walter Mondale.

Tonight's debate marks the third consecutive Presidential election in which the League is presenting the candidates for the nation's highest office in face-to-face debate. Our panelists are James Wieghart [James G. Wieghart], National Political Correspondent for Scripps-Howard News Service; Diane Sawyer, Correspondent for the CBS program *60 Minutes*; and Fred Barnes, National Political Correspondent for *The Baltimore Sun*. Barbara Walters of ABC News, who is appearing in her fourth Presidential debate, is our moderator. Barbara.

MS. BARBARA WALTERS, Moderator; Correspondent, ABC News: Thank you, Dorothy. A few words as we begin tonight's debate about the format. The position of the candidates — that is, who answers questions first and who gives the last statement — was determined by a toss of the coin between the two candidates. Mr. Mondale won. And that means that he chose to give the final closing statement. It means, too, that the President will answer the first question first. I hope that's clear. If it isn't, it will become clear as the debate goes on.

Further, the candidates will be addressed as they each wanted, and will therefore be called "Mr. President" and "Mr. Mondale." Since there will also be a second debate between the two Presidential candidates, tonight will focus primarily on the economy and other domestic issues. The debate itself is built around questions from the panel. In each of its segments, a reporter will ask the candidate the same general question. Then — and this is important — each candidate will have the chance to rebut what the other has said. In the final segment of the debate will be the closing segment, and the candidates will each have four minutes for their closing statements. And, as I have said, Mr. Mondale will be the last person on the program

to speak.

And now I would like to add a personal note, if I may. As Dorothy Ridings pointed out, I have been involved now in four Presidential debates, either as a moderator or as a panelist. In the past, there was no problem in selecting panelists. Tonight, however, there were to have been four panelists participating in this debate. The candidates were given a list of almost 100 qualified journalists from all the media and could agree on only these three fine journalists. As moderator, and on behalf of my fellow journalists, I very much regret, as does The League of Women Voters, that this situation has occurred.

And now let us begin the debate with the first question from James Wieghart. Mr. Wieghart?

Balanced Budget

MR. JAMES G. WIEGHART, National Political Correspondent, Scripps-Howard News Service: Mr. President, in 1980, you promised the American people, in your campaign, a balanced budget by 1983. We've now had more and bigger deficits in the four years you have been in office. Mr. President, do you have a secret plan to balance the budget sometime in the second turn . . . term? And if so, would you lay out that plan for us tonight?

THE HONORABLE RONALD REAGAN, President of the United States of America: I have a plan, not a secret plan. As a matter of fact, it is the economic recovery program that we presented when I took office in 1981. It is true that earlier, working with some very prominent economists, I had come up, during the campaign, with an economic program that I thought could rectify the great problems confronting us: the double-digit inflation, the high tax rates that I think were hurting the economy, the stagflation that we were undergoing.

Before even the election day, something that none of those economists had even predicted had happened: that the economy was so worsened that I was openly saying that what we had thought, on the basis of our plan, could have brought a balanced budget — no, that was no longer possible. So the plan that we have had and that we are following is a plan that is based on growth in the economy, recovery without inflation, and reducing the share of the . . . of . . . that the Government is taking from the Gross National Product, which has become a drag on the economy.

Already we have a recovery that has been going on for about 21 months, to the point that we can now call it an expansion. Under that, this year we have seen a $21

billion reduction in the deficit from last year, based mainly on the increased revenues the Government is getting without raising tax rates. Our tax cut, we think, was very instrumental in bringing about this economic recovery. We have reduced inflation to about a third of what it was. The interest rates have come down about nine or ten points and, we think, must come down further. In the last 21 months, more than six million people have gotten jobs. We've found. . . . There have been created new jobs for those people, to where there are now 105 million civilians working, where there were only 99 million before, 107 [million] if you count the military.

So we believe that, as we continue to reduce the level of Government spending — the increase, rate of increase in Government spending, which has come down from 17 to 6 percent — and at the same time as the growth in the economy increases the revenues the Government gets without raising taxes, those two lines will meet. And when they meet, that is a balanced budget.

MR. WIEGHART: Mr. President, the Congressional Budget Office has some bad news. The lines aren't about to meet, according to their projections. They project that the budget deficit will continue to climb. In the year 1989, they project a budget deficit of $273 billion. In view of that, and in view of the economic recovery we are now enjoying, would it make sense to propose a tax increase, or take some other fiscal measures to reduce that deficit now, when times are relatively good?

MR. REAGAN: The deficit is a result . . . it is the result of excessive government spending. I do not, very frankly, take seriously the Congressional Budget Office projections, because they have been wrong on virtually all of them, including the fact that our recovery wasn't going to take place to begin with. But it has taken place. But as I said, we have the rate of increase in Government spending down to 6 percent. If the rate of increase in Government spending can be held at 5 percent — we're not far from there — by 1989 that would have reduced budget deficits down to a $30 or $40 billion level. At the same time, if we can have a 4 percent recovery continue through that same period of time, that will mean, without an increase in tax rates, that will mean $400 billion more in Government revenues. And so I think that the lines can meet.

Actually, in constant dollars, in the domestic side of the budget, there has been no spending increase in the four years that we have been here.

MR. WIEGHART: Mr. Mondale, the Carter-Mondale Administration didn't come close to balancing the budget in its four years in office either, despite the fact that President Carter [President Jimmy Carter] did promise a balanced budget during his term. You have proposed a plan, combining tax increases and budgetary cuts and other changes in the administration of the Government, that would reduce the projected budget deficit by two-thirds, to approximately $87 billion in 1989. That still is an enormous deficit that we'll be running for these four years. What other steps do you think should be taken to reduce this deficit and for ... position the country for economic growth?

THE HONORABLE WALTER MONDALE, former Vice President of the United States of America: One of the key tests of leadership is whether one sees clearly the nature of the problems confronted by our nation. And perhaps *the* dominant domestic issue of our times is: What do we do about these enormous deficits? I respect the President. I respect the Presidency, and I think he knows that. But the fact of it is, every estimate by this Administration about the size of the deficit has been off by billions and billions of dollars. As a matter of fact, over four years, they have missed the mark by nearly $600 billion. We were told we would have a balanced budget in 1983. It was a $200 billion deficit instead. And now, we have a major question facing the American people as to whether we'll deal with this deficit and get

it down for the sake of a healthy recovery. Virtually every economic analysis that I've heard of, including that of the distinguished Congressional Budget Office — which is respected by, I think, almost everyone — says that even with historically high levels of economic growth, we will suffer a $263 billion deficit. In other words, it doesn't converge, as the President suggests — it gets larger even with growth.

What that means is that we will continue to have devastating problems with foreign trade: this is the worst trade year in American history, by far. Our rural and farm friends will have continued devastation. Real interest rates, the real cost of interest, will remain very, very high. And many economists are predicting that we're moving into a period of very slow growth because the economy is tapering off, and maybe a recession.

I get it down to a level below 2 percent of Gross National Product with a policy that's fair. I've stood up and told the American people that I think it's a real problem, that it can destroy long-term economic growth, and I've told you what I think should be done. I think this is a test of leadership, and I think the American people know the difference.

MR. WIEGHART: Mr. Mondale, one other way to attack the deficit is further reductions in spending. The President has submitted a number of proposals to Congress to do just that and, in many in-

stances, the House — controlled by the Democrats — has opposed them. Isn't it one aspect of leadership for a prominent Democrat such as yourself to encourage responsible reductions in spending and thereby reduce the deficit?

MR. MONDALE: Absolutely, and I have proposed over $100 billion in cuts in Federal spending over four years. But I am not going to cut it out of Social Security and Medicare and student assistance and things that people need. [Applause] These people depend upon all of us for the little security that they have, and I'm not going to do it that way. The rate of defense spending increase can be slowed. Certainly we can find a coffee pot that costs something less than $7,000. [Laughter] And there are other ways of squeezing this budget without constantly picking on our senior citizens and the most vulnerable in American life. And that's why the Congress, including the Republicans, have not gone along with the President's recommendations.

MS. WALTERS: I would like to ask the audience please to refrain from applauding either side.

It just takes away from the time for your candidates.

And now it is time for the rebuttal. Mr. President, one minute for rebuttal.

MR. REAGAN: Yes. I don't believe that Mr. Mondale has a plan for balancing the budget; he has a plan for raising taxes.

Walter F. Mondale, left, and President Reagan participated Oct. 7 in a debate on domestic issues, in Louisville, Ky. The debate was sponsored by The League of Women Voters Education Fund.

As a matter of fact, the biggest single tax increase in our nation's history took place in 1977. And, for the five years previous to our taking office, taxes doubled in the United States and the budgets increased $318 billion. So, there is no ratio between taxing and balancing a budget. Whether you borrow the money or whether you simply tax it away from the people, you're taking the same amount of money out of the private sector unless and until you bring down government's share of what it is taking.

With regard to Social Security, I hope there will be more time than just this minute to mention that, but I will say this: a President should never say, "Never," but I'm going to violate that rule and say, "Never." I will never stand for a reduction of the Social Security benefits for the people that are now getting them. [Applause]

MS. WALTERS: Mr. Mondale?

MR. MONDALE: Well, that's exactly the commitment that was made to the American people in 1980 — he would never reduce benefits. And of course, what happened right after the election is, they proposed to cut Social Security benefits by 25 percent, reducing the adjustment for inflation, cutting out minimum benefits for the poorest on Social Security, removing educational benefits for dependents whose widows were trying ... with widows trying to get them through college. Everybody remembers that. People know what happened. There is a difference. I have fought for Social Security and Medicare, and for things to help people who are vulnerable, all my life. And I will do it as President of the United States. [Applause]

MS. WALTERS: Thank you very much.

We will now begin with segment number two with my colleague, Diane Sawyer. Ms. Sawyer.

Leadership

MS. DIANE SAWYER, CBS News: Mr. President, Mr. Mondale, the public opinion polls do suggest that the American people are most concerned about the personal leadership characteristics of the two candidates, and each of you has questioned the other's leadership ability. Mr. President, you have said that Mr. Mondale's leadership would take the country down the path of defeatism and despair, and Vice President Bush has called him "whining" and "hoping for bad news." And Mr. Mondale, you have said that President Reagan offers showmanship, not leadership, that he has not mastered what he must know to command his government.

I'd like to ask each of you to substantiate your claims — Mr. Mondale first. Give us specifics to support your claim that President Reagan is a showman, not a leader, has not mastered what he must know to be President after four years. And then second, tell us what personal leadership characteristics you have that he does not.

MR. MONDALE: Well, first of all, I think the first answer this evening suggests exactly what I'm saying. There is no question that we face this massive deficit, and almost everybody agrees unless we get it down the chances for long-term healthy growth are nil. And it's also unfair to dump these tremendous bills on our children. The President says it will disappear overnight because of some reason. No one else believes that's the case. I do, and I'm standing up to the issue with an answer that's fair. I think that's what leadership is all about. There's a difference between being a quarterback and a cheerleader, and when there's a real problem, a President must confront it.

What I was referring to, of course, in the comment that you referred to, was the situation in Lebanon. Now, for three occasions, one after another, our embassies were assaulted in the same way by a truck with demolitions. The first time ... and I did not criticize the President because these things can happen once and sometimes twice. The second time the barracks in Lebanon were assaulted, as we all remember, there were two or three commission reports, recommendations by the CIA, the State Department and the others. And the third time, there was even a warning from the terrorists themselves.

Now, I believe that a President must command that White House and those who work for him. It's the toughest job on earth, and you must master the facts and insist that things that must be done are done. I believe that the way in which I will approach the Presidency is what's needed, because all my life, that has been the way in which I have sought to lead. And that's why, in this campaign, I'm telling you exactly what I want to do. I am answering your questions. I am trying to provide leadership now, before the election, so that the American people can participate in that decision.

MS. SAWYER: You have said, Mr. Mondale, that the polls have given you lower ratings on leadership than President Reagan because your message has failed to get through. Given that you have been in public office for so many years, what accounts for the failure of your message to get through?

MR. MONDALE: Well, I think we're getting better all the time, and I think tonight, as we contrast for the first time our differing approach to government, to values, to the leadership in this country — I think as this debate goes forward, the American people will have, for the first time, a chance to weigh the two of us against each other. And I think, as a process ... as a part of that process, what I am trying to say will come across, and that is that we must lead, we must command, we must direct. And a President must see it like it is. He must stand for the values of decency that the American people stand for, and he must use the power of the White House to try to control these nuclear weapons and lead this world toward a safer world.

MS. SAWYER: Mr. President, the issue is leadership in personal terms. First, do you think, as Vice President Bush said, that Mr. Mondale's campaign is one of whining and hoping for bad news? And, second, what leadership characteristics do you possess that Mr. Mondale does not?

MR. REAGAN: Well, whether he does or not, let me suggest my own idea about the leadership factor — and since you've asked it. And, incidentally, I might say that, with regard to the 25 percent cut to Social Security — before I get to the answer to your question — the only 25 percent cut that I know of was accompanying that huge 1977 tax increase, was a cut of 25 percent in the benefits for every American who was born after 1916.

Now, leadership — first of all, I think you must have some principles you believe in. In mine, I happen to believe in the people, and believe that the people are supposed to be dominant in our society. That they, not government, are to have control of their own affairs to the greatest extent possible with an orderly society. Now, having that, I think also that in leadership.... Well, I believe that you find people, in positions such as I'm in, who have the talent and ability to do the things that are needed in the various departments of government. I don't believe that a leader should be spending his time in the Oval Office deciding who is going to play tennis on the White House court. And you let those people go with the guidelines of overall policy, and not looking over their shoulder and nit-picking the manner in which they go at the job. You are ultimately responsible, however, for that job.

But I also believe something else about that. I believe that.... And when I became Governor of California I started this, and I continue it in this Office — that any issue that comes before me, I have instructed Cabinet members and Staff: they are not to bring up any of the political ramifications that might surround the issue. I don't want to hear them. I want to hear only arguments as to whether it is good or bad for the people. Is it morally right? And on that basis, and that basis alone, we make a decision on every issue.

Now, with regard to my feeling about why I thought that his record bespoke his possible taking us back to the same things that we knew under the previous Administration — his record is that he spoke in praise of deficits several times, said they weren't to be abhorred, that, as a matter of fact, he at one time said he wished the deficit could be doubled because they stimulate the economy and help reduce unemployment.

MS. SAWYER: As a follow-up, let me draw in another specific, if I could, a specific that the Democrats have claimed about your campaign — that it is, essentially, based on imagery. And one specific that they allege is that, for instance, recently you showed up at the opening ceremony of a Buffalo old-age housing project when, in fact, your policy was to cut Federal housing subsidies for the elderly. Yet you were there to have your picture taken with them.

MR. REAGAN: Our policy was not to cut subsidies. We have believed in partnership, and that was an example of a partnership between not only local government and the Federal Government, but also between the private sector that built that particular structure. And this is what we have been trying to do, is involve the Federal Government in such partnerships. We are today subsidizing housing for more than 10 million people. And we're going to continue along that line. We have no thought of throwing people out into the snow, whether because of age or need. We have preserved the safety net for the people with true need in this country. And it has been pure demagoguery that we have in some way shut off all the charitable programs, or many of them, for the people who have real need. The safety net is there, and we are taking care of more people than has ever been taken care of before by any Administration in this country.

MS. WALTERS: Mr. Mondale, the opportunity for you to rebut.

MR. MONDALE: Well, I guess I'm reminded a little bit of what Will Rogers once said about Hoover. He said, "It's not what he doesn't know that bothers me, it's what he knows for sure that just ain't so." [Laughter] The fact of it is ... [Laughter] the fact of it is ... the fact of it is, the President's budget sought to cut Social Security by 25 percent. It's not an opinion — it's a fact. And when the President was asked the other day, "What do you want to cut in the budget?" he said, "Cut those things I asked for but didn't get." That's Social Security and Medicare.

The second fact is that the housing unit for senior citizens that the President dedicated in Buffalo was only made possible through a Federal assistance program for senior citizens that the President's budget sought to terminate. So if he'd had his way, there wouldn't have been any housing project there at all. This Administration has taken a meat cleaver out, in terms of Federal-assisted housing, and the record is there. We have to see the facts before we can draw conclusions.

MS. WALTERS: Mr. President?

MR. REAGAN: Well, let me just respond with regard to Social Security. When we took office, we discovered that the program that the Carter-Mondale Administration had said would solve the fiscal problems of Social Security for the next 50 years, wouldn't solve them for five. Social Security was due to go bankrupt before 1983. Any proposals that I made at that time were at the request of the Chairman — a Democrat — of one of the leading committees, who said we have to do something before the program goes broke and the checks bounce.

And so we made a proposal. And then in 1982 they used that proposal in a demagogic fashion for the 1982 campaign. And three days after the election in 1982 they came to us and said, "Social Security, we know, is broke." Indeed, we had to borrow $17 billion to pay the checks. And then I asked for a bipartisan commission, which I'd asked for from the beginning, to sit down and work out a solution. And so the whole matter of what to do with Social Security has been resolved by bipartisan legislation. And it is on a sound basis now for as far as you can see into the next century.

MS. WALTERS: Mr. President, we begin segment number three with Fred Barnes.

Religion and Politics

MR. FRED BARNES, National Political Correspondent, *The Baltimore Sun*: Mr. President, would you describe your religious beliefs, noting particularly whether you consider yourself a born-again Christian, and explain how these beliefs affect your presidential decisions?

MR. REAGAN: Well, I was raised to have a faith and a belief, and have been a member of a church since I was a small boy. In our particular church we did not use that term, "born again," so I don't know whether I would fit that, that particular term. But I have, thanks to my mother — God rest her soul — the firmest possible belief and faith in God. And I don't believe.... I believe, I should say, as Lincoln once said, that I could not — I would be the most stupid man in the world if I thought I could confront the duties of the office I hold if I could not turn to someone who was stronger and greater than all others. And I do resort to prayer.

At the same time, however, I have not believed that prayer should be introduced into an election, or be a part of a political campaign, or religion a part of that campaign. As a matter of fact, I think religion became a part of this campaign when Mr. Mondale's running mate said I wasn't a good Christian. So it does play a part in my life. I have no hesitancy in saying so. And, as I say, I don't believe that I could carry on unless I had a belief in a higher authority and a belief that prayers are answered.

MR. BARNES: Given those beliefs, Mr. President, why don't you attend services regularly, either by going to church or by inviting a minister to the White House as President Nixon used to do, or someone to Camp David, as President Carter used to do?

MR. REAGAN: The answer to your question is very simple about why I don't go to church. I have gone to church regularly all my life. And I started to here in Washington. And now, in the position I hold, and in the world in which we live, where embassies do get blown up in Beirut.... We're supposed to talk about that on the debate the twenty-first, I understand. But I pose a threat to several hundred people if I go to church. I know the threats that are made against me. We all know the possibilities of terrorism. We have seen the barricades that have had to be built around the White House. And, therefore, I don't feel — and

my minister knows this and supports me in this position — I don't feel that I have a right to go to church knowing that my being there could cause something of the kind that we have seen in other places — in Beirut, for example. I think the Lord understands. [Applause]

MS. WALTERS: May I ask the audience, please to refrain from applause. Fred, your second question.

MR. BARNES: Mr. Mondale, would describe your religious beliefs and mention whether you consider yourself a born-again Christian, and explain how those beliefs would affect your decisions as President?

MR. MONDALE: First of all, I accept President Reagan's affirmation of faith. I am sure that we all accept and admire his commitment to his faith, and we are strengthened, all of us, by that fact. I am a son of a Methodist minister. My wife is the daughter of a Presbyterian minister. I don't know if I've been born again, but I know I was born into a Christian family, and I believe I have sung at more weddings and more funerals than anybody ever to seek the Presidency. Whether that helps or not I don't know. I have a deep religious faith, our family does, it is fundamental, it's probably the reason that I'm in politics. I think our faith tells us ... instructs us about the moral life that we should lead, and I think we are all together on that.

What bothers me is this growing tendency to try to use one's own personal interpretation of faith politically to question others' faith, and to try to use the instrumentalities of government to impose those views on others. All history tells us that that's a mistake. When the Republican platform says that from here on out we're going to have a religious test for judges before they're selected for the Federal Court, and then Jerry Falwell [Dr. Jerry Falwell, President, Moral Majority, Incorporated] announces that that means they get at least two Justices of the Supreme Court, I think that's an abuse of faith in our country.

This nation is the most religious nation on earth. More people go to church and synagogues than any other nation on earth, and it's because we kept the politicians and the state out of the personal exercise of our faith. That's why faith in the United States is pure and unpolluted by the intervention of politicians. And I think if we want to continue, as I do, to have a religious nation let's keep that line and never cross it. [Applause]

MS. WALTERS: Thank you. Mr. Barnes, next question.

We have time for rebuttal now.

MR. BARNES: I think I have a follow-up.

MS. WALTERS: Yes, I asked you if you did. I'm sorry. I thought you waived it.

MR BARNES: Yes, I do. Yes. Mr. Mondale. The ... you've complained, just now, about Jerry Falwell, and you've complained other times about other fundamentalists in politics. Correct me if I'm wrong, but I don't recall you ever complaining about ministers who were involved in the civil rights movement, or in the anti-Vietnam War demonstrations, or about black preachers, who've been so involved in American politics. Is it only conservative ministers that you object to?

MR. MONDALE: No, what I object to [Applause] . . . what I object to . . . what I object to is someone seeking to use his faith to question the faith of another, or to use that faith and seek to use the power of government to impose it on others. A minister who is in civil rights, or in the conservative movement, because he believes his faith instructs him to do that, I admire. The fact that the faith speaks to us, and that we are moral people, hopefully, I accept and rejoice in. It's when you try to use that to undermine the integrity of private political — uh, private religious — faith, and the use of the state is where — for the most personal decisions in American life — that's where I draw the line.

MS. WALTERS: Thank you. Now, Mr. President, rebuttal.

PRESIDENT REAGAN: Yes, it's very difficult to rebut, because I find myself in so much agreement with Mr. Mondale. I, too, want that wall that is in the Constitution of separation of church and state to remain there. The only attacks I have made are on people who have not . . . apparently would break away at that wall from the Government side, using the Government, using the power of the courts and so forth, to hinder that part of the Constitution that says the Government shall not only not establish a religion, it shall not inhibit the practice of religion. And they have been using these things to have government, through court orders, inhibit the practice of religion. A child wants to say grace in its school cafeteria and a court rules that they can't do it, because it's school property. These are the types of things that I think have been happening in a kind of a secular way that have been eroding that separation, and I am opposed to that.

With regard to a platform on the Supreme Court I can only say one thing about that. I don't . . . I have appointed one member of the Supreme Court, Sandra Day O'Connor. I'll stand on my record on that, and if I have the opportunity to appoint any more, I'll do it in the same manner that I did in selecting her.

MS. WALTERS: Mr. Mondale, your rebuttal please.

MR. MONDALE: The platform to which the President refers, in fact, calls for a religious test in the selection of judges. And Jerry Falwell says, "That means we get two or three judges," and it would involve a religious test for the first time in American life. Let's take the example that the President cites; I believe in prayer. My family prays. We've never had any difficulty finding time to pray, but do we want a Constitutional amendment adopted of the kind proposed by the President that gets the local politicians into the business of selecting prayers that our children must either recite in school, or be embarrassed

and asked to excuse themselves? Who would write the prayer? What would it say? How would it be resolved when those disputes occurred?

It seems to me that a moment's reflection tells you why the United States Senate turned that amendment down — because it will undermine the practice of honest faith in our country by politicizing it. We don't want that.

MS. WALTERS: Thank you, Mr. Mondale. Our time is up for this round. We go into the second round of our questioning, begin again with Jim Wieghart. Jim?

Democratic Party

MR. WIEGHART: After that discussion this may be like going from the sublime to the ridiculous, but here it goes: I have a political question for you, Mr. Mondale. [Laughter]

Polls indicate a massive change in the electorate away from the coalition that has long made the Democratic Party a majority. Blue-collar workers, young professionals, their children, and much of the middle class now regard themselvs as independents or Republican, instead of Democrats, and the gap . . . the edge that the Democrats had in party registration seems to be narrowing. I'd like to ask you, Mr. Mondale, what is causing this? Is the Democratic Party out of synch with the majority of Americans, and will it soon be replaced as a majority party by the Republicans? What do you think needs to be done about it as a Democrat?

MR. MONDALE: My answer is that this campaign isn't over yet, and when people vote I think you're going to see a very strong verdict by the American people that they favor the approach that I'm talking about.

The American people want arms control. They don't want this arms race, and they don't want this deadly new effort to bring weapons into the heavens, and they want an American foreign policy that leads toward a safer world. The American people see this debt, and they know it's got to come down, and if it won't come down the economy is gonna slow down, maybe go into a recession. They see this tremendous influx and swamping of cheap foreign imports in this country, that has cost over 3 million jobs, given farmers the worst year in American history, and they know this debt must come down as well, because it's unfair to our children.

The American people want this environment protected. They know that these toxic-waste dumps should have been cleaned up a long time ago, and they know that people's lives and health are being risked because we've had an Administration that has been totally insensitive to the law and the demand for the protection of the environment.

The American people want their children educated, they want to get our edge back in science, and they want a policy headed by the President that helps close this gap that's widening between the

United States and Europe and Japan. The American people want to keep opening doors. They want those civil rights laws enforced, they want the Equal Rights Amendment ratified, they want equal pay for comparable effort for women, and they want it because they've understood from the beginning that when we open doors, we're all stronger, just as we were at the Olympics.

I think as you make the case, the American people will increasingly come to our cause.

MR. WIEGHART: Mr. Mondale, isn't it possible that the American people have heard your message and they are listening, but they are rejecting it?

MR. MONDALE: Well, tonight we had the first debate over the deficit. The President says it will disappear automatically. I have said it is going to take some work. I think the American people will draw their own conclusions. Secondly, I have said that I will not support the cuts in Social Security and Medicare and the rest that the President has proposed. The President answers that it didn't happen, or if it did, it was resolved later in a commission. As the record develops, I think it's going to become increasingly clear that what I am saying and where I want to take this country is exactly where the country wants to go, and the comparison of approaches is such that I think will lead to further strength.

MR. WIEGHART: Mr. President, you and your party are benefiting from what appears to be an erosion of the old Democratic coalition. But you have not laid out a specific agenda to take this shift beyond November 6. What is your program for America for the next decade — with, with some specificity?

MR. REAGAN: Well, again, I am running on the record. I think sometimes Mr. Mondale is running away from his. But I am running on the record of what we have asked for. We will continue to try and get things that we didn't get in the program that has already brought the rate of spending of Government down from 17 percent to 6.1 percent, a program of returning authority and autonomy to the local and state governments that has been unjustly seized by the Federal Government. And you might find those words in a Democratic platform of some years ago. I know because I was a Democrat at that time. And I left the Party eventually because I could no longer follow the turn in the Democratic leadership that they took us down an entirely different path — a path of centralizing authority in the Federal Government, lacking trust in the American people.

I promised when we took office that we would reduce inflation. We have, to one-third of what it was. I promised that we would reduce taxes. We did — 25 percent across the board. That barely held even with, if it did that much, with the gigantic tax increase imposed in 1977. But at least it took that burden away from them. I said that we would create jobs for our people.

And we did — six million in the last 20 or 21 months. I said that we would become respected in the world once again, and that we would refurbish our national defense to the place that we could deal on the world scene, and then seek disarmament, reduction of arms, and, hopefully, an elimination of nuclear weapons. We have done that.

All of the things that I said we would do — from inflation being down, interest rates being down, unemployment falling — all of those things we have done. And I think this is something the American people see.

I think they also know that we have . . . we had a commission that came in a year ago with a recommendation on education, on excellence in education. And today, without the Federal Government being involved other than passing on to them, the school districts, the words from that commission, we find 35 states with task forces now dealing with their educational problems. We find that schools are now extending the curriculum to now have forced teaching of mathematics and science and so forth. All of these things have brought an improvement in the college entrance exams for the first time in some 20 years.

So I think that many Democrats are seeing the same thing this Democrat saw. The leadership isn't taking us where we want to go.

MR. WIEGHART: Mr. President, there is a. . . . Much of what you said affects the quality of life of many Americans — their income, the way they live, and so forth. But there's an aspect to quality of life that lies beyond the private sector, which has to do with our neighborhoods, with our cities, our streets, our parks, our environment. In those areas, I have a difficulty seeing what your program is and what you feel the Federal responsibility is in these areas of the quality of life in the public sector that affects everybody. And even enormous wealth by one individual can't create the kind of environment that he might like.

MR. REAGAN: There are tasks that government legitimately should enforce and tasks that government performs well. And you've named some of them. Crime has come down the last two years for the first time in many, many decades that it has come down — or since we've kept records — two consecutive years. And last year it came down, the biggest drop in crime that we've had. I think that we've had something to do with that, just as we have with the drug problem nationwide.

The environment? Yes, I feel as strongly as anyone about the preservation of the environment. When we took office we found that the national parks were so dirty, and contained so many hazards, lack of safety features, that we stopped buying additional park land until we had rectified this with what was to be a five-year program, but is just about finished already — $1 billion — and now we're going back to budgeting for additional lands for our parks. We have added millions of acres to the wilderness lands, to the game refuges. I think that we are out in front of most. And I see the red light is blinking, so I can't continue, but I've got more.

MS. WALTERS: Well, you'll have a chance when your rebuttal time comes up, perhaps, Mr. President.

MR. REAGAN: All right.

MS. WALTERS: Mr. Mondale, now it's your turn for rebuttal.

MR. MONDALE: The President says that when the Democratic Party made its turn, he left it. The year that he decided we had lost our way was the year that John F. Kennedy was running against Richard Nixon. I was Chairman of Minnesotans for Kennedy. President Reagan was Chairman of a thing called Democrats for Nixon.

Now, maybe we've made a wrong turn with Kennedy, but I'll be proud of supporting him all of our life . . . all of my life, and I'm very happy that John Kennedy was elected. Because John Kennedy looked at the future with courage, saw what needed to be done, and understood his own government. The President just said that his government is shrinking. It's not; it's now the largest peacetime government ever, in terms of the take from the total economy. And instead of retreating where we . . . instead of being strong where we should be strong, he wants to make it strong and intervene in the most private and personal questions in American life. That's where government should not be.

MS. WALTERS: Mr. President?

MR. REAGAN: Before I campaigned as a Democrat for a Republican candidate for President, I had already voted for Dwight Eisenhower to be President of the United States. [Applause] So my change had come earlier than that. I hadn't gotten around to re-registering as yet. I found that was rather difficult to do. But I finally did it.

There are some other things that have been said here, Barb, you said that I might be able to dredge them up. Mr. Mondale referred to the farmers' worst year. The farmers are not the victims of anything this Administration has done. The farmers were the victims of the double-digit inflation and the 21.5 percent interest rates of the Carter-Mondale Administration, and the grain embargo . . . which [Applause] destroyed our reliability nationwide as a supplier. All of these things are presently being rectified, and I think that we are going to salvage the farmers. As a matter of fact, the . . . there has been less than one-quarter of one percent of foreclosures of the 270,000 loans from Government that the farmers have.

MS. WALTERS: Thank you, Mr. President. We will now turn to Diane Sawyer for her round of questions. Diane?

Abortion

MS. SAWYER: I'd like to turn to an area that I think few people enjoy discussing, but that we probably should tonight, because the positions of the two candidates are so clearly different and lead to very different policy consequences — and that is abortion and right to life. I'm exploring for your personal views of abortion, and specifically how you would want them applied as public policy.

First, Mr. President, do you consider abortion murder or a sin? And second, how hard would you work, what kind of priority would you give in your second term legislation to make abortion illegal? And specifically, would you make certain, as your party platform urges, that Federal Justices that you appoint be pro-life?

MR. REAGAN: I believe that in the appointment of judges that all that was specified in the party platform was that they observe . . . have a . . . they respect the sanctity of human life. Now that I would want to see in any judge, and with regard to any issue having to do with human life.

But with regard to abortion — and I have a feeling that this is . . . there's been some reference without naming it here, in remarks of Mr. Mondale, tied to injecting religion into government. With me, abortion is not a problem of religion; it's a problem of the Constitution. I believe that until and unless someone can establish that the unborn child is not a living human being, then that child is already protected by the Constitution which guarantees life, liberty, and the pursuit of happiness to all of us. And I think that this is what we should concentrate on, [Applause] is trying. . . .

I know there was weeks and weeks of testimony before a Senate committee. There were medical authorities, there were religious . . . there were clerics there, everyone talking about this matter of pro-life. And at the end of all of that, not one shred of evidence was introduced that the unborn child was not alive. We have seen premature births that are now grown-up, happy people going around.

Also, there is a strange dichotomy in this whole position about our courts ruling that abortion is not the taking of a human life. In California some time ago, a man beat a woman so savagely that her unborn child was born dead with a fractured skull. And the California state legislature unanimously passed a law that was signed by the then Democratic governor — signed a law that said that any man who so abuses a pregnant woman that he causes the death of her unborn child shall be charged with murder. Now, isn't it strange that that same woman could have taken the life of her unborn child and it was abortion, not murder, but if somebody else does it, that's murder? And it recognizes — it used the term "death of the unborn child."

So this has been my feeling about abortion, that we have a problem now to determine. And all evidence so far comes down on the side of the unborn child being a living human being.

MS. SAWYER: A two-part follow-up — do I take it from what you said about the platform, then, that you don't regard the language, and don't regard in your own appointments, abortion position a test of any kind for justices that it should be? And also, if abortion is made illegal, how would you want it enforced? Who would be the policing units that would investigate, and would you want the women who have abortions to be prosecuted?

MR. REAGAN: The laws regarding that always were state laws. It was only when the Supreme Court handed down a decision that the Federal Government intervened in what had always been a state policy. Our laws against murder are state laws. So, I would think that this would be the — the point of enforcement on this.

I ... as I say, I feel that we have a problem here to resolve, and no one has approached it from that matter. It is ... it does not happen that the church that I belong to had that as part of its dogma. I know that some churches do. Now, it is a sin if you're taking a human life. At the same time, in our Judeo-Christian tradition, we recognize the right of taking human life in self-defense, and therefore I've always believed that a mother — if medically, it is determined that her life is at risk if she goes through with the pregnancy — she has a right then to take the life of even her own unborn child in defense of her own.

MS. SAWYER: Mr. Mondale, to turn to you, do you consider abortion a murder or a sin? And, bridging from what President Reagan said, he has written that if society doesn't know whether life — does human life, in fact, does begin at conception — as long as there is a doubt, that the unborn child should at least be given the benefit of the doubt, and that there should be protection for that unborn child?

MR. MONDALE: This is one of the most emotional and difficult issues that could possibly be debated. I think your questions, however, underscore the fact: there is probably no way that government should or could answer this question in every individual case and in the private lives of the American people.

The Constitutional amendment proposed by President Reagan would make it a crime for a woman to have an abortion if she had been raped or suffered from incest. Is it really the view of the American people, however you feel on the question of abortion, that government ought to be reaching into your living rooms and making choices like this? I think it cannot work, won't work, and will lead to all kinds of cynical evasions of the law. Those who can afford to have them will continue to have them. The disadvantaged will go out in the back alley, as they used to do. I think these questions are inherently personal and moral, and every individual instance is different. Every American should beware ... be aware of the seriousness of the step. But there are some things that government can do, and some things they cannot do.

Now, the example that the President cites has nothing to do with abortion. Somebody went to a woman and nearly killed her. That's always been a serious crime, and always should be a serious

crime. But how does that compare with the problem of a woman who's raped? Do we really want those decisions made by judges who've been picked because they will agree to find the person guilty? I don't think so, and I think it's going in exactly the wrong direction. In America, on basic moral questions, we have always let the people decide in their own personal lives. We haven't felt so insecure that we've reached for the club of state to have our point of view. It's been a good instinct, and we're the most religious people on earth.

One final point. President Reagan, as Governor of California, signed a bill which is perhaps the most liberal pro-abortion bill of any state in the union.

MS. SAWYER: But if I can get you back for a moment on my point, which was the question of when human life begins, a two-part follow-up. First of all, at what point do *you* believe that human life begins in the growth of a fetus, and second of all, you said that government shouldn't be involved in the decisions, yet there are those who would say that government is involved, and the consequence of the involvement was 1.5 million abortions in 1980. And how do you feel about that?

MR. MONDALE: The basic decision of the Supreme Court is that each person has to make this judgment in her own life, and that's the way it's been done. And it's a personal and private moral judgment. I don't know the answer to when life begins, and it's not that simple, either. You've got another life involved. And if it's rape, how do you draw moral judgments on that? If it's incest, how do you draw moral judgments on that? Does every woman in America have to present himself ... herself before some judge picked by Jerry Falwell to clear her personal judgment? It won't work. [Applause]

MS. WALTERS: I'm sorry to do this, but I really must talk to the audience. You're all invited guests. I know I'm wasting time in talking to you, but it really is very unfair of you to applaud, sometimes louder or less loud. And I ask you, as people who were invited here, and polite people, to refrain.

We have our time now, for rebuttal. Mr. President.

MR. REAGAN: Yes. But with regard to this being a personal choice, isn't that what a murderer is insisting on, his or her right to kill someone because of whatever fault they think justifies that?

Now, I'm not capable — and I don't think you are, any of us — to make this determination that must be made with regard to human life. I am simply saying that I believe that that's where the effort should be directed to make that determination. I don't think that any of us should be called upon here to stand and make a decision as to what other things might come under the self-defense tradition. That, too, would have to be worked out then, when you once recognize that we're talking about a life.

But in this great society of ours, wouldn't it make a lot more sense — in this

gentle and kind society — if we had a program that made it possible for when incidents come along in which someone feels they must do away with that unborn child, that instead we make it available for the adoption? There are a million and a half people out there standing in line waiting to adopt children who can't have them any other way.

MS. WALTERS: Mr. Mondale?

MR. MONDALE: I agree with that, and that's why I was the principal sponsor of a liberal adoption law so that more of these children could come to term, so that the young mothers were educated, so that we found an option — an alternative. I'm all for that. But the question is whether this other option, proposed by the President, should be pursued. And I don't agree with it.

Since I've got about 20 seconds, let me just say one thing. The question of agriculture came up a minute ago. Net farm income is off 50 percent in the last three years and every farmer knows it. And the effect of these economic policies is like a massive grain embargo which has caused farm exports to drop 20 percent. It's been a big failure. I opposed the grain embargo in my Administration. I'm opposed to these policies as well.

MS. WALTERS: I'm sitting here like the great schoolteacher letting you both get away with things, because one did it, the other one did it. May I ask in the future that the rebuttals stick to what the rebuttal is. And, also, foreign policy will be the next debate. Stop dragging it in by its ear into this one. [Laughter]

Now, having admonished you, I would like to say to the panel, you are allowed one question and one follow-up. Would you try, as best you could, not to ask two and three. I know it's something we all want to do. Two or three questions is part I, and two and three is part II. Having said that, Fred, it's yours.

Taxes

MR. BARNES: Thank you. Mr. Mondale, let me ask you about middle class Americans and the taxes they pay. I'm talking about, not about the rich or the poor — I know your views on their taxes — but about families earning $25,000 to $45,000 a year. Do you think that those families are overtaxed or undertaxed by the Federal Government?

MR. MONDALE: In my opinion, as we deal with this deficit, people from about $70,000 a year on down have to be dealt with very, very carefully because they are the ones who didn't get any relief the first time around. Under the 1981 tax bill, people making $200,000 a year got $60,000 in tax relief over three years, while people making $30,000 a year, all taxes considered, got no relief at all or their taxes actually went up. That's why my proposal protects everybody from $25,000 a year or less against any tax increases, and treats those $70,000 and under in a way that is more beneficial than the way the President proposes with a sales tax or a flat tax.

What does this mean in real life? Well, the other day Vice President Bush disclosed his tax returns to the American people. He's one of the wealthiest Americans, and he's our Vice President. In 1981, I think he paid about 40 percent in taxes. In 1983, as a result of these tax preferences, he paid a little over 12 percent — 12.8 percent in taxes. That meant that he paid a lower percent in taxes than the janitor who cleaned up his office or the chauffeur who drives him to work.

I believe we need some fairness. And that's why I proposed what I think is a fair and responsible proposal that helps protect these people who have already got no relief or actually got a tax increase.

MR. BARNES: It sounds as if you were saying you think this group of taxpayers making $25,000 to $45,000 a year is already overtaxed. Yet your tax proposal would increase their taxes. I think your aides have said those earning about $25,000 to $35,000, their tax rate ... their tax bill would go up $100, and from $35,000 to $45,000 — more than that, several hundred dollars. Wouldn't that stifle their incentive to work and invest and so on, and also hurt the recovery?

MR. MONDALE: The first thing is, everybody $25,000 and under would have no tax increase. Mr. Reagan, after the election, is going to have to propose a tax increase. And you will have to compare what he proposes. And his Secretary of the Treasury said he is studying a sales tax, or value-added tax. They're the same thing. They hit middle- and moderate-income Americans and leave wealthy Americans largely untouched.

Up until about $70,000, as you go up the ladder, my proposals will be far more beneficial. As soon as we get the economy on a sound ground, as well, I'd like to see the total repeal of indexing. I don't think we can do that for a few years. But at some point we want to do that as well.

MR. BARNES: Mr. President, let me try this on you. Do you think middle-income Americans are overtaxed or undertaxed?

MR. REAGAN: You know, I wasn't going to say this at all, but I can't help it. There you go again. [Laughter.] I don't have a plan to tax or increase taxes. I'm not going to increase taxes. I can understand why you are, Mr. Mondale, because as a Senator you voted 16 times to increase taxes. Now, I believe that our problem has not been that anybody in our country is undertaxed: it's that Government is overfed. And I think that most of our people, this is why we had a 25 percent tax cut across the board, which maintained the same progressivity of our tax structure in the brackets on up. And, as a matter of fact, it just so happens that in the quirks of administering these taxes, those above $50,000 actually did not get quite as big a tax cut, percentage-wise, as did those from $50,000 down. From $50,000 down, those people paid two-thirds of the taxes. And

those people got two-thirds of the tax cut.

Now, the Social Security tax of '77 — this, indeed, was a tax that hit people in the lower brackets the hardest. It had two features. It had several tax increases phased in over a period of time. There are two more yet to come between now and 1989. At the same time every year, it increased the amount of money — virtually every year, there may have been one or two that were skipped in there — that was subject to that tax. Today it is up to about $38,000 of earnings that is subject to the payroll tax for Social Security. And that tax, there are not deductions. So a person making anywhere from ten, fifteen, twenty ... they're paying that tax on the full gross earnings that they have after they have already paid an income tax on that same amount of money.

Now, I don't think that to try and say that we were taxing the rich and not the other way around: it just doesn't work out that way. The system is still where it was with regard to the progressivity, as I've said. And that has not been changed. But if you take it in numbers of dollars instead of percentage, yes, you can say, "Well, that person got ten times as much as this other person." Yes — but he paid ten times as much also. But if you take it in percentages, then you find out that it is fair and equitable across the board.

MR. BARNES: I thought I caught, Mr. President, a glimmer of a stronger statement, there in your answer, than you've made before. I think the operative position you had before was that you would only raise taxes in a second term as a last resort. And I thought you said flatly that, "I'm not going to raise taxes." Is that what you meant to say — that you will flatly not raise taxes in your second term as President?

MR. REAGAN: Yes, I had used.... "Last resort" would always be with me. If you got the Government down to the lowest level that you yourself could say it could not go any lower and still perform the services for the people; and if the recovery was so complete that you knew you were getting the ultimate amount of revenues that you could get through that growth and there was still some slight difference there between those two lines, then I had said once that, "Yes, you would have to then look to see if taxes should not be adjusted." I don't foresee those things happening. So I say with great confidence I'm not going to — I'm not going to go for a tax.

With regard to assailing Mr. Bush about his tax problems, and the difference from the tax he once paid, and then the later tax he paid, I think, if you looked at the deductions, there were great legal expenses in there. It had to do, possibly, with the sale of his home. And they had to do with his setting up of a blind trust. All of those are legally deductions — deductible in computing your tax. And it was a one-year thing with him.

MS. WALTERS: Mr. Mondale, here we go again, this time for rebuttal.

MR. MONDALE: Well, first of all, I gave him the benefit of the doubt on the house deal. I'm just talking about the 12.8 percent that he paid. And that's what's happening all over this country with wealthy Americans. They've got so many loopholes; they don't have to pay much in taxes. Now, Mr. President, you said, "There you go again." Right? Remember the last time you said that?

MR. REAGAN: Um-hummm.

MR. MONDALE: You said it when President Carter said that you were going to cut Medicare. And you said, "Oh no, there you go again, Mr. President." And what did you do right after the election? You went out and tried to cut $20 billion out of Medicare. [Applause.] And so, when you say, "There you go again," people remember this, you know. And people will remember that you signed the biggest tax increase in the history of California, and the biggest tax increase in the history of the United States. And what are you going to do? You've got a $260 billion deficit. You can't wish it away. You won't slow defense spending. You refuse to do that.

MS. WALTERS: Mr. Mondale? I'm afraid your time is up.

MR. MONDALE: Sorry.

MS. WALTERS: Mr. President.

MR. REAGAN: Yes. With regard to Medicare, no. But it's time for us to say that Medicare is in pretty much the same condition that Social Security was. And something is going to have to be done in the next several years to make it fiscally sound. And, no, I never proposed any $20 billion should come out of Medicare. I have proposed that the program we must treat with that particular problem. And maybe part of that problem is because during the four-year period medical costs in this country went up 87 percent.

MS. WALTERS: All right ... fine ... [laughter] ... we can't....

MR. REAGAN: I gave you back some of that time.

MS. WALTERS: We can't keep going back for other rebuttals. There will be time later. We now go to our final round. The way things stand now, we have time for only two sets of questions, and by lot it will be Jim and Diane. And we'll start with Jim Wieghart.

Economic Recovery

MR. WIEGHART: Mr. President, the economic recovery is real but uneven. The Census Bureau, just a month ago, reported that there are more people living under poverty now — a million more people living under it — than when you took office. There have been a number of studies, including studies by the Urban Institute and other nonpolitical organizations, that say that the impact of the tax and budget cuts in your economic policies have impacted severely on certain classes of Americans: working mothers head of households, minority groups, elderly poor. In fact, they're saying the rich are getting richer and the poor are getting poorer under your policies. What relief can you offer to the working poor, to the minorities and the women head of households who have borne the brunt of these economic programs? What can you offer them in the future in your next term?

MR. REAGAN: Well, some of those facts and figures just don't stand up. Yes, there has been an increase in poverty, but it is a lower rate of increase than it was in the preceding years, before we got here. It has begun to decline, but it is still going up. On the other hand, women heads of household — single women heads of household — have for the first time . . . there has been a turn down in the rate of poverty for them. We have found also in our studies that in this increase in poverty it all had to do with their private earnings. It had nothing to do with the transfer payments from Government the . . . by way of many programs. We are spending now 37 percent more on food for the hungry in all the various types of programs that was spent in 1980. We're spending a third more on all of the . . . well, all of the programs of human service. We have more people receiving food stamps than were ever receiving them before — 2,300,000 more are receiving them — even though we took 850,000 off the food-stamp rolls, because they were making an income that was above anything that warranted their fellow citizens having to support them.

We found people making 185 percent of the poverty level were getting Government benefits. We have set a line at 130 percent so that we can direct that aid down to the truly needy. Sometime ago Mr. Mondale said something about education, and college students, and help of that kind. Half — one out of two — of the full-time college students in the United States are receiving some form of federal aid. But there again we've found people that there were . . . under the previous Administration, families that had no limit to income were still eligible for low-interest college loans. We didn't think that was right, and so we have set a standard, but those loans and those grants are directed to the people who otherwise could not go to college, their family incomes were so low. So, there are a host of other figures that reveal that the grant programs are greater than they have ever been, taking care of more people than they ever have. 7.7 million elderly citizens who were living in the lowest 20 percent of earnings . . . 7.7 million have moved up into another bracket since our administration took over, leaving only 5 million of the elderly in that bracket, when there had been more than 13 million.

MR. WIEGHART: Mr. President, in a visit to Texas — in Brownsville, I believe it was in the Rio Grande Valley — you did observe that the economic recovery was uneven in that —

MR. REAGAN: Oh, yes.

MR. WIEGHART: — particular area of Texas, unemployment was over 14 percent, where as state-wide it was the lowest in the country, I believe 5.6 percent. And you made the comment that, however, that man does not live by bread alone. What did you mean by that comment, and, is it . . . if I interpret it correctly, it would be a comment more addressed to the affluent who, obviously, can look beyond just the bread that they need to sustain them with their wherewithal.

MR. REAGAN: That had nothing to do with the other thing of talking about their needs, or anything. I remember distinctly, I was segueing into another subject. I was talking about the things that have been accomplished, and that was referring to the revival of patriotism and optimism, the new spirit that we're finding all over America, and it is a wonderful thing to see when you get out there among the people. So, that was the only place that that was used. I did avoid, I'm afraid, in my previous answer also, the idea of uneven . . . yes, there is no way that the recovery is even across the country, just as in the depths of the recession there was some parts of the country that were worse off, but some that didn't even feel the pain of the recession. We're not going to rest, are not going to be happy until every person in this country who wants a job can have one, until the recovery is complete across the country.

MR. WIEGHART: Mr. Mondale, the . . . as you can gather from the question of the President the celebrated war on poverty obviously didn't end the problem of poverty, although it may have dented it. The poor and the homeless, and the disadvantaged are still with us. What should the Federal Government's role be to turn back the growth in the number of people living below the poverty level, which is now 35 million in the United States, and to help deal with the structural unemployment problems that the President was referring to in an uneven recovery?

MR. MONDALE: Number one, we've got to get the debt down to get the interest rates down so the economy will grow, and people will be employed. Number two, we have to work with cities and others to help generate economic growth in those communities. To the Urban Development Action Grant Program . . . I don't mind those enterprise zones, let's try them, but not as a substitute for the others. Certainly, education and training is crucial. If these young Americans don't have the skills that make them attractive to employees, they're not going to get jobs.

The next thing is to try to get more entrepreneurship in business within the reach of minorities, so that these businesses are located in the communities in which they're found.

The other thing is we need the business community, as well as government, heavily involved in these communities to try to get economic growth. There is no question that the poor are worse off. I think the President genuinely believes that they're better off, but the figures show that about 8 million more people are below the poverty line than 4 years ago. How you can cut school lunches, how you can cut student assistance, how you can cut housing, how you can cut disability benefits, how you can do all of these things, and then the people receiving them — for example, the disabled, who have no alternative. How they're going to do better I don't know. Now, we need a tight budget, but there's no question that this Administration has singled out things that affect the most vulnerable in American life, and they're hurting.

One final point if I might. There's another part of the lopsided economy that we're in today, and that is that these heavy deficits have killed exports, and are swamping the nation with cheap imports. We are now $120 billion of imports, 3 million jobs lost and farmers are having their worst year. That's another reason to get the deficit down.

MR. WIEGHART: Mr. Mondale, is it possible that the vast majority of Americans who appear to be prosperous have lost interest in the kinds of programs you're discussing to help those less privileged than they are?

MR. MONDALE: I think the American people want to make certain that that dollar is wisely spent. I think they stand for civil rights. I know they're all for education and science and training, which I strongly support. They want these young people to have a chance to get jobs, and the rest. I think the business community wants to get involved. I think they're asking for new and creative ways to try to reach it with everyone involved. I think that's part of it.

I think also that the American people want a balanced program that gives us long-term growth, so that they're not having to take money that's desperate to themselves and their families and give it to someone else. I'm opposed to that too.

MS. WALTERS: And now it's time for our rebuttal for this period. Mr. President?

MR. REAGAN: Yes. The connection has been made again between the deficit and the interest rates. There is no connection between them. There is a connection between interest rates and inflation, but I would call to your attention that in 1981, while we were operating still on the Carter-Mondale budget that we inherited, that the interest rates came down from 21.5 [percent] toward the 12 or 13 [percent] figure. And while they were coming down, the deficits had started their great increase. They were going up. Now, if there was a connection, I think that there would be a different parallel between the deficit getting larger and interest rates going down.

The interest rates are based on inflation. And right now, I have to tell you, I don't think there is any excuse for the interest rates being as high as they are because we have brought inflation down so low. I think it can only be that they are anticipating, or hope — or expecting, not hoping, that maybe we don't have a control of inflation, and it's going to go back up again. Well, it isn't going to go back up. We are going to see that it doesn't.

MS. WALTERS: Mr. President —

MR. REAGAN: I haven't got time to

answer with regard to the disabled.

MS. WALTERS: Thank you, Mr. President. Mr. Mondale?

MR. MONDALE: Mr. President, if I heard you correctly, you said that these deficits don't have anything to do with interest rates. I will grant you that interest rates were too high in 1980, and we can have another debate as to why energy prices and so on. There is no way of glossing around that. But when these huge deficits went in place until 1981, what's called the real interest rates — the spread between inflation and what a loan costs you — doubled. And that's still the case today. And the result is interest costs that have never been seen before in terms of real charges. And it's attributable to the deficit.

Everybody — every economist, every businessman — believes that. Your own Council of Economic Advisers — Mr. Feldstein [Martin S. Feldstein, former Chairman, Council of Economic Advisers], in his report, told you that. Every chairman of the [Senate] Finance and [House] Ways and Means Committee[s], Republican leaders in the Senate and House, are telling you that: that deficit is ruining the long-term hopes for this economy. It is causing high interest rates. It is ruining us in trade. It has given us the highest small-business failure in 50 years. The economy is starting downhill, with housing failures —

MS. WALTERS: Thank you, Mr. Mondale.

MR. MONDALE: Go ahead.

MS. WALTERS: They are both very obedient. I have to give you credit for that. [Laughter] We now start our final round of questions. We do want to have time for your rebuttal. And we start with Diane . . . Diane Sawyer.

Campaign Rhetoric

MS. SAWYER: Since we are reaching the end of the question period, and since in every Presidential campaign, the candidates tend to complain that the opposition candidate is not held accountable for what he or she says, let me give you the chance to do that. Mr. Mondale, beginning with you. What do you think the most outrageous thing is your opponent said in this debate tonight? [Laughter]

MR. MONDALE: You want to give me some suggestions? [Laughter] I'm going to use my time a little differently. I'm going to give the President some credit. I think the President has done some things to raise the sense of spirit, morale, good feeling in this country. He is entitled to credit for that. What I think we need, however, is not just that, but to move forward, not just congratulating ourselves, but challenging ourselves to get on with the business of dealing with America's problems.

I think in education, when he lectured the country about the importance of discipline, I didn't like it at first, but I think it helped a little bit. But now we need both that kind of discipline, and the resources, and the consistent leadership that allows

this country to catch up in education and science and training. I like President Reagan. This is not personal. These are deep differences about our future, and that's the basis of my campaign.

MS. SAWYER: To follow up in a similar vein then, what remaining question would you most like to see your opponent forced to answer?

MR. MONDALE: Without any doubt, I have stood up and told the American people that that $263 billion deficit must come down. And I have done what no candidate for President has ever done: I told you before the election what I would do. Mr. Reagan, as you saw tonight . . . President Reagan takes the position that it will disappear by magic. It was once called "voodoo economics." I wish the President would say, "Yes, the CBO is right. Yes, we have a $263 billion deficit. This is how I'm going to get it done." Don't talk about growth, because even though we need growth, that's not helping. It's going to go in the other direction, as they've estimated.

And give us a plan. What will you cut? Whose taxes will you raise? Will you finally touch that defense budget? Are you going to go after Social Security, and Medicare, and student assistance, and the handicapped again, as you did last time? If you'll just tell us what you're going to do, then the American people could compare my plan for the future with your plan. And that's the way it should be. The American people would be in charge.

MS. SAWYER: Mr. President, the most outrageous thing your opponent has said in the debate tonight?

MR. REAGAN: Well now, I have to start with a smile, since his kind words to me. [Laughter] I'll tell you what I think has been the most outrageous thing in political dialogue, both in this campaign and the one in '82. And that is the continued discussion and claim that somehow I am the villain who is going to pull the Social Security checks out from those people who are dependent on them. And why I think it is outrageous — first of all, it isn't true — but why it is outrageous is because, for political advantage, every time they do that, they scare millions of senior citizens who are totally dependent on Social Security, have no place else to turn. And they have to live and go to bed at night thinking, "Is this true? Is someone going to take our check away from us and leave us destitute?" And I don't think that that should be a part of political dialogue.

Now . . . [applause] . . . now to . . . and I still, I just have a minute here?

MS. WALTERS: You have more time.

MR. REAGAN: Oh, I —

MS. WALTERS: You can keep going.

MR. REAGAN: O.K. All right. Now, Social Security, let's lay it to rest once and for all. I told you, never would I do such a thing. But I tell you also now: Social Security has nothing to do with the deficit. Social Security is totally funded by the payroll tax levied on employer and employee. If you reduce the outgo of Social Security,

that money would not go into the General Fund to reduce a deficit. It would go into the Social Security Trust Fund. So Social Security has nothing to do with balancing a budget or erasing or lowering the deficit.

Now, as, again, to get to whether I have . . . I am depending on magic, I think I have talked in straight economic terms about a program of recovery that was . . . I was told wouldn't work. And then after it worked, I was told that lowering taxes would increase inflation. And none of these things happened. It is working, and we are going to continue on that same line.

As to what we might do and find in further savings cuts, no, we're not going to starve the hungry. But we have 2,478 specific recommendations from a commission of more than 2,000 business people in this country, through the Grace Commission, that we're studying right now — and we've already implemented 17 percent of them — that are recommendations as to how to make government more efficient and more economic.

MS. SAWYER: And, to keep it even, what remaining question would you most like to see your opponent forced to answer?

MR. REAGAN: Why the deficits are so much of a problem for him now, but that in 1976, when the deficit was $52 billion and everyone was panicking about that, he said no, that he thought it ought to be bigger, because a bigger deficit would stimulate the economy and would help do away with unemployment. In 1979, he made similar statements . . . the same effect. But . . . but the . . . deficits . . . there was nothing wrong with having deficits. Remember, there was a trillion dollars in debt before we got here. That's got to be paid by our children and grandchildren too, if we don't do it. And I'm hoping we can start some payments on it before we get through here. That's why I want another four years.

MS. WALTERS: Well, we have time now, if you'd like to answer the President's question, or whatever rebuttal.

MR. MONDALE: Well, we just finished almost the whole debate, and the American people don't have the slightest clue about what President Reagan will do about these deficits. And yet that's the most important single issue of our time.

I did support the '76 measure that he told about, because we were in a deep recession and we needed some stimulation. But I will say, as a Democrat, I was a real piker, Mr. President. In 1979, we ran a $29 billion deficit all year. This Administration seems to run that every morning. And the result is exactly what we see. This economy is starting to run downhill. Housing is off. Last report on new purchases, it's the lowest since 1982. Growth is a little over three percent now. Many people are predicting a recession. And the flow of imports into this country is swamping the American people.

We've got to deal with this problem. And those of us who want to be your President should tell you now what we're going to do, so you can make a judgment.

MS. WALTERS: Thank you very

much. We must stop now. I want to give you time for your closing statements. It's indeed time for that. From each of you, we will begin with President Reagan.

I'm sorry. Mr. Reagan, you had your rebuttal, and I just cut you off, because our time is going. You have a chance now for rebuttal before your closing statement. Is that correct?

MR. REAGAN: No. I might as well just go with what I —

MS. WALTERS: Do you want to go with your. . . ?

MR. REAGAN: I don't think so.

MS. WALTERS: Do you want to wait?

MR. REAGAN: I'm all confused now.

MS. WALTERS: Technically, you did. I have little voices that come in my ear. You don't get those same voices. I'm not hearing it from here. I'm hearing it from here.

MR. REAGAN: All right.

MS. WALTERS: You have waived your rebuttal. You can go with your closing statement.

MR. REAGAN: We'll include it in that.

MS. WALTERS: O.K.

Closing Statements

MR. REAGAN: Four years ago, in similar circumstances to this I asked you, the American people, a question. I asked, are you better off than you were four years before. The answer to that, obviously, was no. And as a result I was elected to this office, and promised a new beginning. Now, maybe I'm expected to ask that same question again. I'm not going to because I think that all of you, or almost everyone; those people that have . . . are in the pockets of poverty and haven't caught up. They couldn't answer the way I would want them to. But I think that the most of the people in this country would say yes, they are better off than they were four years ago.

The question, I think, should be enlarged. Is America better off than it was four years ago? And I believe the answer to that has to also be yes.

I'd promised a new beginning. So far it is only a beginning. If the job were finished, I might have thought twice about seeking reelection for this job. But we now have an economy that, for the first time. . . .

Well, let's put it this way. In the first half of 1980, Gross National Product was down, a minus 3.7 percent. First half of '84, it's up eight and a half percent. Productivity in the first half of 1980 was down a minus 2 percent. Today, it is up a plus 4 percent. Personal earnings after taxes, per capita, have gone up almost $3,000 in these four years. In 1980 or 1979, a person with a fixed income of $8,000 would . . . was $500 above the poverty line. And this may explain why there are the numbers still in poverty. By 1980, that same person was $500 below the poverty line.

We have restored much of our economy. With regard to business investment, it is higher than it has been since 1949. So there seems to be no shortage of investment capital. We have, as I said, cut the taxes, but we have reduced inflation, and for two years now it has stayed down there — not at double-digit, but in the range of 4 [percent] or below.

We believe that. . . . We had also promised that we would make our country more secure. Yes, we have an increase in the defense budget. But back then, we had planes that couldn't fly for lack of spare parts or pilots. We had Navy vessels that couldn't leave harbor because of lack of crew, or again, lack of spare parts. Today, we're well on our way to a 600-ship Navy. We have 543 at present. We have. . . . Our military, the morale is high. The . . . I think the people should understand that two-thirds of the defense budget pays for pay and salary, or pay and pension. And then you add to that food and wardrobe and all the other things, and you only have a small portion going for weapons. But I am determined that if ever our men are called on, they should have the best that we can provide in the . . . in the manner of tools and weapons.

There has been reference to expensive spare parts: hammers costing $500. Well, we are the ones who found those.

I think we've given the American people back their spirit. I think there's an optimism in the land and a patriotism. And I think that we're in a position once again to heed the words of Thomas Paine, who said, "We have it in our power to begin the world over again."

MS. WALTERS: Thank you, Mr. Reagan. Mr. Mondale, the closing words are now yours.

MR. MONDALE: I want to thank The League of Women Voters and the City of Louisville for hosting this evening's debate. I want to thank President Reagan for agreeing to debate. He didn't have to, and he did. And we all appreciate it.

The President's favorite question is, "Are you better off?" Well, if you're wealthy, you're better off. If you're middle-income, you're about where you were. And if you're of modest income, you're worse off. That's what the economists tell us. But is that really the question that should be asked? Isn't the real question "Will we be better off? Will our children be better off? Are we building the future that this nation needs?"

I believe that if we ask those questions that bear on our future — not just congratulate ourselves, but challenge us to solve those problems — you'll see that we need new leadership. Are we better off with this arms race? Would we be better off if we start this "Star Wars" escalation into the heavens? Are we better off when we deemphasize our values of human rights? Are we better off when we load our children with this fantastic debt? Would fathers and mothers feel proud of themselves if they loaded their children with debts like this nation is now — over a trillion dollars on the shoulders of our children? Can we be . . . say, really say that we will be better off when we pull away from sort of that basic American instinct of decency and fairness?

I would rather lose a campaign about decency than win a campaign about self-interest. I don't think this nation is composed of people who care only for themselves. And when we sought to assault Social Security and Medicare, as the record shows we did, I think that was mean-spirited. When we terminated 400,000 desperate, hopeless, defenseless Americans who were on disability — confused and unable to defend themselves — and just laid them out on the street, as we did for four years, I don't think that's what America is all about.

America is a fair society, and it is not right that Vice President Bush pays less in taxes than the janitor who helps him. I believe there is fundamental fairness crying out that needs to be achieved in our tax system. I believe that we will be better off if we protect this environment. And contrary to what the President says, I think their record on the environment is inexcusable and often shameful. These laws are not being enforced, have not been enforced, and the public health and the air and the water are paying the price. That's not fair for our future.

I think our future requires a President to lead us in an all-out search to advance our education, our learning, and our science and training, because this world is more complex, and we are being pressed harder all the time.

I believe in opening doors. We won the Olympics in part because we've had civil rights laws and the laws to prohibit discrimination against women. I have been for those efforts all my life. The President's record is quite different.

The question is our future. President Kennedy once said, in response to similar arguments, "We are great, but we can be greater." We can be better if we face our future, rejoice in our strengths, face our problems, and by solving them, build a better society for our children.

Thank you.

[Applause.]

MS. WALTERS: Thank you, Mr. Mondale. Please, we have not finished quite yet. Thank you, Mr. Mondale, and thank you, Mr. President, and our thanks to our panel members as well. And so we bring to a close this first of The League of Women Voters Presidential Debates of 1984. You two can go at each other again in the final League debate on October 21 in Kansas City, Missouri.

And this Thursday night, October 11, at 9 p.m. Eastern Daylight Time, the Vice President, George Bush, will debate Congresswoman Geraldine Ferraro in Philadelphia. And I hope that you will all watch once again.

No matter what the format is, these debates are very important. We all have an extremely vital decision to make. Once more, gentlemen, our thanks. Once more to you our thanks. And now, this is Barbara Walters wishing you a good evening.

[Applause.]

Candidates Debate on Defense, Foreign Policy

Following is the official record of the nationally televised debate between President Reagan and Walter F. Mondale, sponsored by The League of Women Voters Education Fund, held Oct. 21, in Kansas City, Mo.

President Reagan and Walter F. Mondale shake hands at the start of the second 1984 presidential debate, held on Oct. 21 in Kansas City, Mo.

MRS. DOROTHY S. RIDINGS, Chair, The League of Women Voters Education Fund: Good evening. Good evening from the Municipal Auditorium in Kansas City. I'm Dorothy Ridings, the President of the League of Women Voters, the sponsor of this final Presidential debate of the 1984 campaign between Republican Ronald Reagan and Democrat Walter Mondale. Our panelists for tonight's debate on defense and foreign policy issues are Georgie Anne Geyer, syndicated columnist for Universal Press Syndicate, Marvin Kalb, chief diplomatic correspondent for NBC News, Morton Kondracke, executive editor of *The New Republic* magazine, and Henry Trewhitt, diplomatic correspondent for *The Baltimore Sun.* Edwin Newman, formerly of NBC News and now a syndicated columnist for King Features, is our moderator. Ed.

MR. EDWIN NEWMAN, King Features Syndicate: Dorothy Ridings, thank you. A brief word about our procedure tonight. The first question will go to Mr. Mondale. He will have two and a half minutes to reply. Then the panel member who put the question will ask a follow-up. The answer to that will be limited to one minute. After that, the same question will be put to President Reagan. Again, there will be a follow-up, and then each man will have one minute for rebuttal. The second question will go to President Reagan first. After that, the alternating will continue. At the end there will be four-minute summations, with President Reagan going last. We have asked the questioners to be brief. Let's begin. Ms. Geyer, your question to Mr. Mondale.

Central America

MS. GEORGIE ANNE GEYER, Universal Press Syndicate: Mr. Mondale, two related questions on the crucial issue of Central America. You and the Democratic Party have said that the only policy toward the horrendous civil wars in Central America should be on the economic development and negotiations, with perhaps a quarantine of Marxist Nicaragua. Do you believe that these answers would in any way solve the bitter conflicts there? Do you really believe that there is no need to resort to

force at all? Are not these solutions to Central America's gnawing problems simply, again, too weak and too late?

FORMER VICE PRESIDENT MONDALE: I believe that the question oversimplifies the difficulties of what we must do in Central America. Our objectives ought to be to strengthen the democracies, to stop Communist and other extremist influences, and stabilize the community in that area.

To do that, we need a three-pronged attack. One is military assistance to our friends who are being pressured. Secondly, a strong and sophisticated economic aid program and human rights program that offers a better life and a sharper alternative to the alternative offered by the totalitarians who oppose us. And finally, a strong diplomatic effort that pursues the possibilities of peace in the area. That's one of the big disagreements that we have with the President — that they have not pursued the diplomatic opportunities, either within El Salvador or between the countries, and have lost time during which we might have been able to achieve a peace.

This brings up the whole question of what Presidential leadership is all about. I think the lesson in Central America — this

recent embarrassment in Nicaragua, where we are giving instructions for hired assassins, hiring criminals, and the rest — all of this has strengthened our opponents. A President must not only assure that we're tough, but we must also be wise and smart in the exercise of that power.

We saw the same thing in Lebanon, where we spent a good deal of America's assets. But because the leadership of this Government did not pursue wise policies, we have been humiliated and our opponents are stronger. The bottom line of national strength is that the President must be in command. He must lead. And when a President doesn't know that submarine missiles are recallable, says that 70 percent of our strategic forces are conventional, discovers three years into his Administration that our arms control efforts have failed because he didn't know that most Soviet missiles were on land — these are things a President must know to command. A President is called the Commander in Chief. He is called that because he is supposed to be in charge of the facts and run our Government and strengthen our nation.

MS. GEYER: Mr. Mondale, if I could

broaden the question just a little bit. Since World War II, every conflict that we as Americans have been involved with has been in nonconventional or traditional terms — military terms. The Central American wars are very much in the same pattern as China, as Lebanon, as Iran, as Cuba in the early days. Do you see any possibility that we are going to realize the change in warfare in our time or react to it in those terms?

MR. MONDALE: We absolutely must, which is why I responded to your first question the way I did. It's more — it's much more complex. You must understand the region, you must understand the politics of the area, you must provide a strong alternative, and you must show strength — and all at the same time. That's why I object to the covert action in Nicaragua. That's a classic example of a strategy that's embarrassed us, strengthened our opposition, and it undermined the moral authority of our people and our country in the region. Strength requires knowledge, command. We've seen, in the Nicaraguan example, a policy that has actually hurt us, strengthened our opposition, and undermined the moral authority of our country in that region.

MS. GEYER: Mr. President, in the last few months it has seemed more and more that your policies in Central America were beginning to work. Yet, just at this moment, we are confronted with the extraordinary story of a C.I.A. guerrilla manual for the anti-Sandinista Contras whom we are backing which advocates not only assassinations of Sandinistas, but the hiring of criminals to assassinate the guerrillas we are supporting in order to create martyrs. Is this not, in effect, our own state-supported terrorism?

PRESIDENT REAGAN: No, and I'm glad you asked that question, because I know it's on many people's minds. I have ordered an investigation. I know that the C.I.A. is already going forward with one. We have a gentleman down in Nicaragua who is on contract to the C.I.A., advising supposedly on military tactics of the Contras. And he drew up this manual. It was turned over to the Agency head in — of the C.I.A. in Nicaragua to be printed. And a number of pages were excised by that Agency head there — the man in charge — and he sent it on up here to C.I.A., where more pages were excised before it was printed. But some way or other, there were 12 of the original copies that got out down there and were not submitted for this printing process of the C.I.A. Now, those are the details as we have them. And as soon as we have an investigation and find out where any blame lies for the few that did not get excised or changed, we certainly are going to do something about that. We will take the proper action at the proper time.

I was very interested to hear about Central America and our process down there, and I thought for a moment that instead of a debate I was going to find Mr.

Mondale in complete agreement with what we're doing. Because the plan that he has outlined is the one that we have been following for quite some time, including diplomatic processes throughout Central America and working closely with the Contadora Group. So I can only tell you, about the manual, that we're not in the habit of assigning guilt before there has been proper evidence produced and proof of that guilt. But if guilt is established — whoever is guilty — we will treat with that situation then, and they will be removed.

MS. GEYER: Well, Mr. President, you are implying, then, that the C.I.A. in Nicaragua is directing the Contras there? I would also like to ask whether having the C.I.A. investigate its own manual in such a sensitive area is not sort of like sending the fox into the chicken coop a second time?

MR. REAGAN: I'm afraid I misspoke when I said "a C.I.A. head in Nicaragua." There is not someone there directing all of this activity. There are, as you know, C.I.A. men stationed in other countries in the world, and certainly in Central America. And so it was a man down there in that area that this was delivered to, and he recognized that what was in that manual was in direct contravention of my own executive order in December of 1981 that we would have nothing to do with regard to political assassinations.

MR. NEWMAN: Mr. Mondale, your rebuttal.

MR. MONDALE: What is a President charged with doing when he takes his oath of office? He raises his right hand and takes an oath of office to take care to faithfully execute the laws of the land. The President can't know everything, but a President has to know those things that are essential to his leadership and the enforcement of our laws.

This manual, several thousands of which were produced, was distributed, ordering political assassinations, hiring of criminals, and other forms of terrorism. Some of it was excised, but the part dealing with political terrorism was continued. How can this happen? How can something this serious occur in an Administration and have a President of the United States, in a situation like this, say he didn't know? A President must know these things. I don't know which is worse — not knowing or knowing and not stopping it. And what about the mining of the harbors in Nicaragua, which violated international law? This has hurt this country, and a President is supposed to command.

MR. NEWMAN: Mr. President, your rebuttal.

MR. REAGAN: Yes. I have so many things there to respond to, I'm going to pick out something you said earlier. You've been all over the country repeating something that I will admit the press has also been repeating — that I believe that nuclear missiles could be fired and then called back. I never, ever conceived of such a thing. I never said any such thing. In a discussion of our strategic arms negotia-

tions, I said the submarines carrying missiles and airplanes carrying missiles were more conventional type weapons, not as destabilizing as the land-based missiles, and that they were also weapons that . . . or carriers, that if they were sent out and there was a change, you could call them back before they had launched their missiles. But I hope that from here on you will no longer be saying that particular thing, which is absolutely false. How anyone could think that any sane person would believe you could call back a nuclear missile, I think, is as ridiculous as the whole concept has been. So, thank you for giving me a chance to straighten the record. I'm sure that you appreciate that. [Laughter]

MR. NEWMAN: Mr. Kalb . . . Mr. Kalb, your question to President Reagan.

Soviet Union

MR. MARVIN KALB, NBC News: Mr. President, you have often described the Soviet Union as a powerful, evil empire intent on world domination. But this year you have said, and I quote, "If they want to keep their Mickey Mouse system, that's O.K. with me." Which is it, Mr. President? Do you want to contain them within their present borders, and perhaps try to reestablish détente or what goes for détente, or do you really want to roll back their empire?

MR. REAGAN: I have said on a number of occasions exactly what I believe about the Soviet Union. I retract nothing that I have said. I believe that many of the things they have done are evil in any concept of morality that we have. But I also recognize that as the two great superpowers in the world, we have to live with each other. And I told Mr. Gromyko [Andrei Gromyko, Foreign Minister, U.S.S.R.] we don't like their system. They don't like ours. We're not going to change their system, and they sure better not try to change ours. But, between us, we can either destroy the world or we can save it. And I suggested that certainly it was to their common interest, along with ours, to avoid a conflict and to attempt to save the world and remove the nuclear weapons. And I think that, perhaps, we established a little better understanding.

I think that in dealing with the Soviet Union one has to be realistic. I know that Mr. Mondale in the past has made statements as if they were just people like ourselves, and if we were kind and good and did something nice, they would respond accordingly. And the result was unilateral disarmament. We canceled the B-1 under the previous Administration. What did we get for it? Nothing. The Soviet Union has been engaged in the biggest military build-up in the history of man at the same time that we tried the policy of unilateral disarmament — of weakness, if you will. And now we are putting up a defense of our own. And I've made it very plain to them: we seek no superiority. We simply are going to provide a deterrent so that it will be too costly for them if they are nursing any ideas of aggression against us.

Now, they claim they are not. And I made it plain to them, we're not. But this . . . there's been no change in my attitude at all. I just thought, when I came into office, it was time that there was some realistic talk to and about the Soviet Union. And we did get their attention.

MR. KALB: Mr. President, perhaps the other side of the coin — a related question, sir. Since World War II, the vital interests of the United States have always been defined by treaty commitments and by Presidential proclamations. Aside from what is obvious — such as NATO, for example — which countries, which regions in the world do you regard as vital national interests of this country — meaning that you would send American troops to fight there if they were in danger?

MR. REAGAN: Ah, well, now you've added a hypothetical there at the end, Mr. Kalb, about that — where we would send troops in to fight. I am not going to make the decision as to what the tactics could be. But obviously, there are a number of areas in the world that are of importance to us. One is the Middle East. And that is of interest to the whole Western world and the industrialized nations, because of the great supply of energy on which so many depend there. The . . . our neighbors here in America are vital to us. We're working right now and trying to be of help in southern Africa with regard to the independence of Namibia and the removal of the Cuban surrogates — the thousands of them — from Angola. So, I can say there are a great many interests. I believe that we have a great interest in the Pacific Basin. That is where I think the future of the world lies. But I am not going to pick out one and in advance hypothetically say, "Oh yes. We would send troops there." I don't want to send troops any place —

MR. NEWMAN: I'm sorry, Mr. President. Your time was up.

MR. KALB: Mr. Mondale, you have described the Soviet leaders as, and I'm quoting, "cynical, ruthless, and dangerous," suggesting an almost total lack of trust in them. In that case, what makes you think that the annual summit meetings with them that you've proposed will result in agreements that would satisfy the interests of this country?

MR. MONDALE: Because the only type of agreements to reach with the Soviet Union are the types that are specifically defined, so we know exactly what they must do, subject to full verification — which means we know every day whether they're living up to it, and follow-ups wherever we find suggestions that they're violating it, and the strongest possible terms. I have no illusions about the Soviet Union leadership or the nature of that state. They are a tough and a ruthless adversary, and we must be prepared to meet that challenge. And I would.

Where I part with the President is that, despite all of those differences, we must — as past Presidents before this one

have done — meet on the common ground of survival. And that's where the president has opposed practically every arms control agreement by every President of both political parties since the bomb went off. And he now completes this term with no progress toward arms control at all, but with a very dangerous arms race under way instead. There are now over 2,000 more warheads pointed at us today than there were when he was sworn in. And that does not strengthen us. We must be very, very realistic in the nature of that leadership, but we must grind away and talk to find ways to reducing these differences, particularly where arms races are concerned and other dangerous exercises of Soviet power.

There will be no unilateral disarmament under my Administration. I will keep this nation strong. I understand exactly what the Soviets are up to. But that, too, is a part of national strength. To do that, a President must know what is essential to command and to leadership and to strength. And that's where the President's failure to master, in my opinion, the essential elements of arms control has cost us dearly. These four years. . . . Three years into this Administration, he said he just discovered that most Soviet missiles are on land, and that's why his proposal didn't work. I invite the American people tomorrow . . . because I will issue the statement quoting President Reagan. He said exactly what I said he said. He said that these missiles were less dangerous than ballistic missiles because you could fire them and you could recall them if you decide there had been a miscalculation.

MR. NEWMAN: I'm sorry, Mr. —

MR. MONDALE: A President must know those things.

Eastern Europe

MR. KALB: A related question, Mr. Mondale, on Eastern Europe: Do you accept the conventional diplomatic wisdom that Eastern Europe is a Soviet sphere of influence? And, if you do, what could a Mondale Administration realistically do to help the people of Eastern Europe achieve the human rights that were guaranteed to them as a result of the Helsinki Accords?

MR. MONDALE: I think the essential strategy of the United States ought not accept any Soviet control over Eastern Europe. We ought to deal with each of these countries separately. We ought to pursue strategies with each of them, economic and the rest, that help them pull away from their dependence upon the Soviet Union. Where the Soviet Union has acted irresponsibly, as they have in many of those countries — especially, recently, in Poland — I believe we ought to insist that Western credits extended to the Soviet Union bear the market rate. Make the Soviets pay for their irresponsibility. That is a very important objective — to make certain that we continue to look forward to progress toward greater independence by these nations, and work with each of them separately.

MR. NEWMAN: Mr. President, your rebuttal.

MR. REAGAN: Yes. I'm not going to continue trying to respond to these repetitions of the falsehoods that have already been stated here. But with regard to whether Mr. Mondale would be strong, as he said he would be, I know that he has a commercial out where he is appearing on the deck of the [U.S.S.] *Nimitz* and watching the F-14s take off, and that's an image of strength. Except that if he had had his way when the *Nimitz* was being planned, he would have been deep in the water out there, because there wouldn't have been any *Nimitz* to stand on. He was against it. [Laughter] He was against the F-14 fighter; he was against the M-1 tank; he was against the B-1 bomber; he wanted to cut the salary of all of the military; he wanted to bring home half of the American forces in Europe. And he has a record of weakness with regard to our national defense that is second to none. Indeed, he was on that side virtually throughout all his years in the Senate, and he opposed even President Carter when, toward the end of his term, President Carter wanted to increase the defense budget.

MR. NEWMAN: Mr. Mondale, your rebuttal.

MR. MONDALE: Mr. President, I accept your commitment to peace, but I want you to accept my commitment to a strong national defense. [Applause] I have proposed a budget which would increase our nation's strength by . . . in real terms, by double that of the Soviet Union. I'll tell you where we disagree. It is true, over ten years ago, I voted to delay production of the F-14, and I'll tell you why. The plane wasn't flying supposed to . . . the way it was supposed to be. It was a waste of money. Your definition of national strength is to throw money at the Defense Department. My definition of national strength is to make certain that a dollar spent buys us a dollar's worth of defense. There is a big difference between the two of us. A President must manage that budget. I will keep us strong, but you'll not do that unless you command that budget and make certain we get the strength that we need. When you pay out $500 for a $5 hammer, you're not buying strength.

MR. NEWMAN: I would ask the audience not to applaud. All it does is take up time that we would like to devote to the debate. Mr. Kondracke, your question to Mr. Mondale.

Use of Military Force

MR. MORTON M. KONDRACKE, *The New Republic:* Mr. Mondale, in an address earlier this year, you said that before this country resorts to military force, and I'm quoting, "American interests should be sharply defined, publicly supported, Congressionally sanctioned, militarily feasible, internationally defensible, open to independent scrutiny, and alert to regional history." Now, aren't you setting up such a gauntlet of tests here that adversaries could easily suspect that as President you would never use force to protect American interests?

MR. MONDALE: No. As a matter of fact, I believe every one of those standards is essential to the exercise of power by this country. And we can see that in both Lebanon and in Central America. In Lebanon, this President exercised American power all right, but the management of it was such that our Marines were killed; we had to leave in humiliation; the Soviet Union became stronger; terrorists became emboldened. And it was because they did not think through how power should be exercised, did not have the American public with them on a plan that worked, that we ended up the way we did.

Similarly, in Central America, what we're doing in Nicaragua with this covert war — which the Congress, including many Republicans, have tried to stop — is finally end up with the public definition of American power that hurts us, where we get associated with political assassins and the rest. We have to decline, for the first time in modern history, jurisdiction of the World Court, because they will find us guilty of illegal actions.

And our enemies are strengthened from all of this. We need to be strong. We need to be prepared to use that strength. But we must understand that we are a democracy. We are a Government by the people, and when we move, it should be for very severe and extreme reasons that serve our national interest and end up with a stronger country behind us. It is only in that way that we can persevere.

MR. KONDRACKE: You've been quoted as saying that you might quarantine Nicaragua. I'd like to know what that means. Would you stop Soviet ships, as President Kennedy did in 1962, and wouldn't that be more dangerous than President Reagan's covert war?

MR. MONDALE: What I'm referring to there is the mutual self-defense provisions that exist in the Inter-American treaty, the so-called Rio pact, that permits the nations that are friends in that region to combine to take steps, diplomatic and otherwise, to prevent Nicaragua when she acts irresponsibly in asserting power in other parts outside of her border . . . to take those steps, whatever they might be, to stop it.

The Nicaraguans must know that it is the policy of our government that those . . . that that leadership must stay behind the boundaries of their nation, not interfere in other nations. And by working with all of the nations in the region, unlike the policies of this Administration — and unlike the President said, they have *not* supported negotiations in that region — we will be much stronger, because we will have the moral authority that goes with those efforts.

MR. KONDRACKE: President Reagan, you introduced U.S. forces into Lebanon as neutral peacekeepers, but then you made them combatants on the side of the Lebanese Government. Eventually, you were forced to withdraw them under fire, and now Syria, a Soviet ally, is dominant in the country. Doesn't Lebanon represent a major failure on the part of your Administration and raise serious questions about your capacity as a foreign policy strategist and as Commander in Chief?

MR. REAGAN: No, Morton, I don't agree to all of those things. First of all, when we and our allies — the Italians, the French, and the United Kingdom — went into Lebanon, we went in there at the request of what was left of the Lebanese Government, to be a stabilizing force while they tried to establish a government. But the first — pardon me — the first time we went in, we went in at their request, because the war was going on right in Beirut between Israel and the P.L.O. terrorists. Israel could not be blamed for that. Those terrorists had been violating their northern border consistently, and Israel chased them all the way to there. Then, we went in with a multinational force to help remove — and did remove — more than 13,000 of those terrorists from Lebanon. We departed, and then the Government of Lebanon asked us back in as a stabilizing force while they established a government and sought to get the foreign forces all the way out of Lebanon, and that they could then take care of their own borders.

And we were succeeding. We were there for the better part of a year. Our position happened to be at the airport. Oh, there were occasional snipings and sometimes some artillery fire. But we did not engage in conflict that was out of line with our mission. I will never send troops anywhere on a mission of that kind without telling them that if somebody shoots at them, they can darn well shoot back. And this is what we did. We never initiated any kind of action. We defended ourselves there. But we were succeeding to the point that the Lebanese Government had been organized. If you will remember, there were the meetings in Geneva in which they began to meet with the hostile factional forces and try to put together some kind of a peace plan.

We were succeeding, and that was why the terrorist acts began. There are forces there — and that includes Syria, in my mind — who don't want us to succeed, who don't want that kind of a peace with a dominant Lebanon, dominant over its own territory. And so the terrorist acts began, and led to the one great tragedy when they were killed in that suicide bombing of the building. Then the multilateral force withdrew for only one reason: we withdrew because we were no longer able to carry out the mission for which we had been sent in. But we went in in the interest of peace, and to keep Israel and Syria from getting into the sixth war between them. And I have no apologies for our going on a peace mission.

Lebanon and Terrorism

MR. KONDRACKE: Mr. President, four years ago you criticized President Car-

ter for ignoring ample warnings that our diplomats in Iran might be taken hostage. Haven't you done exactly the same thing in Lebanon, not once, but three times, with 300 Americans not hostages but dead. And you vowed swift retaliation against terrorists, but doesn't our lack of response suggest that you're just bluffing?

MR. REAGAN: Morton, no. I think there's a great difference between the Government of Iran threatening our diplomatic personnel — and there is a Government that you can see and can put your hand on. In the terrorist situation, there are terrorist factions all over. . . . In a recent 30-day period, 37 terrorist acts in 20 countries have been committed. The most recent has been the one in Brighton [England]. In dealing with terrorists, yes, we want to retaliate, but only if we can put our finger on the people responsible and not endanger the lives of innocent civilians there in the various communities and in the city of Beirut where these terrorists are operating. I have just signed legislation to add to our ability to deal, along with our allies, with this terrorist problem. And it's going to take all the nations together, just as when we banded together we pretty much resolved the whole problem of skyjackings some time ago. Well, the red light went on. I could have gone on forever.

MR. NEWMAN: Mr. Mondale, your rebuttal.

MR. MONDALE: Groucho Marx said, "Who do you believe — me or your own eyes?" And what we have in Lebanon is something that the American people have seen. The Joint Chiefs urged the President not to put our troops in that barracks because they were undefensible. They urged . . . they went to him five days before they were killed and said, "Please take them out of there." The Secretary of State admitted that this morning. He did not do so. The report following the explosion of the barracks disclosed that we had not taken any of the steps that we should have taken. That was the second time. Then the Embassy was blown up a few weeks ago, and once again, none of the steps that should have been taken were taken. And we were warned five days before that explosives were on their way, and they weren't taken.

The terrorists have won each time. The President told the terrorists he was going to retaliate. He didn't. They called their bluff. And the bottom line is, the United States left in humiliation and our enemies are stronger.

MR. NEWMAN: Mr. President, your rebuttal.

MR. REAGAN: Yes. First of all, Mr. Mondale should know that the President of the United States did not order the Marines into that barracks. That was a command decision made by the commanders on the spot and based with what they thought was best for the men there. That is one.

On the other things that you've just said about the terrorists, I'm tempted to ask you what you would do. These are unidentified people, and, after the bomb goes off, they're blown to bits because they are suicidal individuals who think that they're going to go to paradise if they perpetrate such an act and lose their life in doing it. We are going to ... as I say, we're busy trying to find the centers where these operations stem from, and retaliation will be taken. But we are not going to simply kill some people to say, "Oh, look — we got even." We want to know, when we retaliate, that we're retaliating with those who are responsible for the terrorist acts. And terrorist acts are such that our own United States Capitol in Washington has been bombed twice.

MR. NEWMAN: Mr. Trewhitt, your question to President Reagan.

Age and Missiles

MR. HENRY L. TREWHITT, *The Baltimore Sun:* Mr. President, I want to raise an issue that I think has been lurking out there for two or three weeks, and cast it specifically in national security terms. You already are the oldest President in history, and some of your staff say you were tired after your most recent encounter with Mister ... Mr. Mondale. I recall, yet, that President Kennedy, who had to go for days on end with very little sleep during the Cuba missile crisis.... Is there any doubt in your mind that you would be able to function in such circumstances?

MR. REAGAN: Not at all, Mr. Trewhitt. And I want you to know that also, I will not make age an issue of this campaign. I am not going to exploit, for political purposes, my opponent's youth and inexperience. [Laughter] [Applause]

If I still have time, I might add, Mr. Trewhitt, I might add that it was Seneca or it was Cicero — I don't know which — that said, "If it was not for the elders correcting the mistakes of the young, there would be no state."

MR. TREWHITT: Mr. President, I'd like to head for the fence and try to catch that one before it goes over, but ... but I'll go on to another question. [Laughs]

The ... you and Mr. Mondale have already disagreed about what you had to say about recalling submarine-launched missiles. There's another ... a similar issue out there that relates to your ... it is said, at least, that you were unaware that the Soviet retaliatory power was based on land-based missiles. First, is that correct? Secondly, if it is correct, have you informed yourself in the meantime? And third, is it even necessary for the President to be so intimately involved in strategic details?

MR. REAGAN: Yes. This had to do with our disarmament talks. And the whole controversy about land missiles came up because we thought that the strategic nuclear weapons, the most destabilizing, are the land-based. You put your thumb on a button and somebody blows up twenty minutes later. So, we thought that it would be simpler to negotiate first with those, and then we made it plain, a second phase — take up the submarine-launched ... the air

... the airborne missiles. The Soviet Union — to our surprise, and not just mine — made it plain when we brought this up that they placed, they thought, a greater reliance on the land-based missiles, and therefore they wanted to take up all three. And we agreed; we said, "All right, if that's what you want to do." But it was a surprise to us because they outnumbered us 64 to 36 in submarines and 20 percent more bombers capable of carrying nuclear missiles than we had.

So, why should we believe that they had placed that much more reliance on land-based? But even after we gave in and said, "All right, let's discuss it all," they walked away from the table. We didn't.

MR. TREWHITT: Mr. Mondale, I'm going to hang in there. Should the President's age and stamina be an issue in the political campaign?

MR. MONDALE: No, and I have not made it an issue, nor should it be. What's at issue here is the President's application of his authority to understand what a President must know to lead this nation, secure our defense, and make the decisions and the judgments that are necessary.

A minute ago, the President quoted Cicero, I believe. I want to quote somebody a little closer to home, Harry Truman. He said, "The buck stops here." We just heard the President's answer for the problems at the barracks in Lebanon, where 241 Marines were killed. What happened? First, the Joint Chiefs of Staff went to the President, said, "Don't put those troops there." They did it. And then, five days before the troops were killed, they went back to the President through the Secretary of Defense and said, "Please, Mr. President, take those troops out of there because we can't defend them." They didn't do it. And we know what's ... what happened. After that, once again our Embassy was exploded. This is the fourth time this has happened — an identical attack in the same region, despite warnings, even public warnings from the terrorists. Who's in charge? Who's handling this matter? That's my main point.

Now, on arms control, we're completing four years. This is the first Administration since the bomb went off that made no progress. We have an arms race under way instead. A President has to lead his Government or it won't be done. Different people with different views fight with each other. For three and a half years, this Administration avoided arms control, resisted tabling arms control proposals that had any ... hope of agreeing, rebuked their negotiator in 1981 when he came close to an agreement, at least in principle, on medium-range weapons. And we have this arms race under way.

And a recent book that just came out by the ... perhaps the nation's most respected author in this field, Strobe Talbott, called "The Deadly Gambits," concludes that this President has failed to master the essential details needed to command and lead us, both in terms of security and terms

of arms control. That's why they call the President the Commander in Chief. Good intentions, I grant, but it takes more than that. You must be tough and smart.

MR. TREWHITT: This question of leadership keeps arising in different forms in this discussion already. And the President, Mr. Mondale, has called you "whining and vacillating" — among the more charitable phrases, "weak," I believe. It is ... it is a question of leadership, and he has made the point that you have not repudiated some of the semidiplomatic activity of the Reverend Jackson, particularly in Central America. Do you ... did you approve of his diplomatic activity, and are you prepared to repudiate him now?

MR. MONDALE: I ... I read his statement the other day. I don't admire Fidel Castro at all, and I've said that. Che Guevara was a contemptible figure in civilization's history. I know the Cuban state as a police state, and all my life I've worked in a way that demonstrates that. But Jesse Jackson is an independent person. I don't control him. And let's talk about people we do control. In the last debate, the Vice President of the United States said that I said the Marines had died shamefully and died in shame in Lebanon. I demanded an apology from Vice President Bush because I had instead honored these young men, grieved for their families, and think they were wonderful Americans that honored us all. What does the President have to say about taking responsibility for a Vice President who won't apologize for something like that?

MR. NEWMAN: Mr. President, your rebuttal.

MR. REAGAN: Yes. I know it'll come as a surprise to Mr. Mondale, but I am in charge. And, as a matter of fact, we haven't avoided arms control talks with the Soviet Union. Very early in my Administration I proposed — and I think something that had never been proposed by any previous Administration — I proposed a total elimination of intermediate-range missiles, where the Soviets had better than a ten ... and still have better than a ten-to-one advantage over the Allies in Europe. When they protested that and suggested a smaller number, perhaps, I went along with that. The so-called negotiation that you said I walked out on was the so-called "walk in the wood" between one of our representatives and one of the Soviet Union, and it wasn't me that turned it down; the Soviet Union disavowed it.

MR. NEWMAN: Mr. Mondale, your rebuttal.

MR. MONDALE: Now, there are two distinguished authors in arms control in this country. There are many others, but two that I want to cite tonight. One is Strobe Talbott in his classic book, "The Deadly Gambits." The other is John Newhouse, who's one of the most distinguished arms control specialists in our country. Both said that this Administration turned down the "walk in the woods" agreement first, and that would have been a perfect agreement from the standpoint of the United States and Europe and our security. When Mr. Nitze [Paul Nitze, Chairman, Intermediate Range Nuclear Forces Negotiations], a good negotiator, returned, he was rebuked and his boss was fired.

This is the kind of leadership that we've had in this Administration in the most deadly issue of our times. Now we have a runaway arms race. All they've got to show for four years in U.S.-Soviet relations is one meeting in the last weeks of an Administration and nothing before. They're tough negotiators, but all previous Presidents have made progress. This one has not.

Illegal Immigration

MR. NEWMAN: Miss Geyer, your question to Mr. Mondale.

MS. GEYER: Mr. Mondale, many analysts are now saying that actually our number one foreign policy problem today is one that remains almost totally unrecognized: massive illegal immigration from economically collapsing countries. They are saying that it is the only real territorial threat to the American nation-state. You yourself said in the 1970s that we had a, quote, "hemorrhage on our borders," unquote. Yet today you have backed off any immigration reform, such as the balanced and highly-crafted Simpson-Mazzoli bill. Why? What would you do instead today, if anything?

MR. MONDALE: This is a very serious problem in our country, and it has to be dealt with. I object to that part of the Simpson-Mazzoli bill which I think is very unfair and would prove to be so. That is the part that requires employers to determine the citizenship of an employee before they're hired. I am convinced that the result of this would be that people who are Hispanic, people who have different languages or speak with an accent, would find it difficult to be employed. I think that's wrong. We've never had citizenship tests in our country before, and I don't think we should have a citizenship card today. That is counterproductive.

I do support the other aspects of the Simpson-Mazzoli bill that strengthen enforcement at the border, strengthen other ways of dealing with undocumented workers in this ... in this difficult area, and dealing with the problem of settling people who have lived here for many, many years and do not have an established status. I have further strongly recommended that this Administration do something it has not done, and that is to strengthen enforcement at the border, strengthen the officials in this Government that deal with undocumented workers, and to do so in a way that's responsible and within the Constitution of the United States. We need an answer to this problem, but it must be an American answer that is consistent with justice and due process. Everyone in this room, practically, here tonight, is an immigrant. We came here loving this nation, serving it, and it has served all of our most

bountiful dreams. And one of those dreams is justice. And if we need a measure, and I will support a measure that brings about those objectives but voids that one aspect that I think is very serious.

The second part is to maintain and improve our relations with our friends to the south. We cannot solve this problem all on our own. And that's why the failure of this Administration to deal in effective and good-faith way with Mexico, with Costa Rica, with the other nations, in trying to find a peaceful settlement to the dispute in Central America has undermined our capacity to effectively to deal diplomatic in this ... diplomatically in this area, as well.

MS. GEYER: Sir, people as well-balanced and just as Father Theodore Hesburgh at Notre Dame [University of Notre Dame], who headed the Select Commission on Immigration, have pointed out repeatedly that there will be no immigration reform without employer sanctions, because it would be an unbalanced bill and there would be simply no way to reinforce it.

However, putting that aside for the moment, your critics have also said repeatedly that you have not gone along with the bill, or with any immigration reform, because of the Hispanic groups or Hispanic leadership groups, who actually do not represent what the Hispanic Americans want — because polls show that they overwhelmingly want some kind of immigration reform. Can you say, or ... how can you justify your position on this? And how do you respond to the criticism that this is another, or that this is an example of your flip-flopping and giving in to special interest groups at the expense of the American nation?

MR. MONDALE: I think you're right that the polls show that the majority of Hispanics want that bill. So, I'm not doing it for political reasons. I'm doing it because all my life I've fought for a system of justice in this country, a system in which every American has a chance to achieve the fullness in life without discrimination. This bill imposes upon employers the responsibility of determining whether somebody who applies for a job is an American or not. And, just inevitably, they're going to be reluctant to hire Hispanics or people with a different accent.

If I were dealing with politics here, the polls show the American people want this. I am for reform in this area, for tough enforcement at the border, and for many other aspects of the Simpson-Mazzoli bill. But all my life, I've fought for a fair nation, and despite the politics of it, I stand where I stand and I think I'm right. And before this fight is over, we're going to come up with a better bill, a more effective bill that does not undermine the liberties of our people.

MS. GEYER: Mr. President, you, too, have said that our borders are out of control. Yet, this fall, you allowed the Simpson-Mazzoli bill — which would at least have minimally protected our borders and

the rights of citizenship — because of a relatively unimportant issue of reimbursement to the states for legalized aliens. Given that, may I ask what priority can we expect you to give this forgotten national security element? How sincere are you in your efforts to control, in effect, the nation-state that is the United States?

MR. REAGAN: Georgie Anne, we, believe me, supported the Simpson-Mazzoli bill strongly, and the bill that came out of the Senate. However, there were things added in the House side that we felt made it less of a good bill — as a matter of fact, made it a bad bill. And in conference, we stayed with them in conference all the way to where even Senator Simpson [Alan Kooi Simpson, Republican, Wyoming] did not want the bill in the manner in which it would come out of the conference committee. There were a number of things in there that weakened that bill. I can't go into detail about them here. But it is true, our borders are out of control. It is also true that this has been a situation on our borders back through a number of Administrations. And I supported this bill. I believe in the idea of amnesty for those who have put down roots and who have lived here, even though some time back they ... they may have entered illegally.

With regard to the employer sanctions, this ... we must have that, not only to ensure that we can identify the illegal aliens, but also, while some keep protesting about what it would do to employers, there is another employer that we shouldn't be so concerned about. And these are employers, down through the years, who have encouraged the illegal entry into this country because they then hire these individuals, and hire them at starvation wages, and with none of the benefits that we think are normal and natural for workers in our country. And the individuals can't complain because of their illegal status. We don't think that those people should be allowed to continue operating free. And this was why the provisions that we had in with regard to sanctions and so forth. And I'm going to do everything I can — and all of us in the Administration are — to join in again, when Congress is back at it, to get an immigration bill that will give us, once again, control of our borders.

And with regard to friendship below the border and with the countries down there — yes, no Administration that I know has established the relationship that we have with our Latin friends. But as long as they have an economy that leaves so many people in dire poverty and unemployment, they are going to seek that employment across our borders. And we work with those other countries.

Population Explosion

MS. GEYER: Mr. President, the experts also say that the situation today is terribly different, quantitatively, qualitatively different from what it has been in the past because of the gigantic population growth. For instance, Mexico's population will go from about 60 million today to 120 million at the turn of the century. Many of these people will be coming into the United States not as citizens, but as illegal workers.

You have repeatedly said, recently, that you believe that Armageddon, the destruction of the world, may be imminent in our times. Do you ever feel that we are in for an Armageddon, or a . . . a situation, a time of anarchy regarding the population explosion in the world?

MR. REAGAN: No, as a matter of fact, the population explosion . . . and if you will look at the actual figures, has been vastly exaggerated . . . overexaggerated. As a matter of fact, there are some pretty scientific and solid figures about how much space there still is in the world and how many more people we can have. It's almost like going back to the Malthusian theory, when even then they were saying that everyone would starve, with the limited population they had then. But the problem of population growth is one here with regard to our immigration, and we have been the safety valve, whether we wanted to or not, with the illegal entry here, in Mexico, where their population is increasing and they don't have an economy that can absorb them and provide the jobs. And this is what we're trying to work out, not only to protect our own borders, but have some kind of fairness and recognition of that problem.

MR. NEWMAN: Mr. Mondale, your rebuttal.

MR. MONDALE: One of the biggest problems today is that the countries to our south are so desperately poor that these people, who will almost lose their lives if they don't come north, come north despite all the risks. And if we're going to find a permanent, fundamental answer to this, it goes to American economic and trade policies to permit these nations to have a chance to get on their own two feet and to get prosperity so that they can have jobs for themselves and their people.

And that's why this enormous national debt, engineered by this Administration, is harming these countries and fueling this immigration. These high interest rates, real rates that have doubled under this Administration, have had the same effect on Mexico and so on. And the cost of repaying those debts is so enormous that it results in massive unemployment, hardship, and heartache. And that drives our friends to the north . . . to the south up into our region. And we need to end those deficits, as well.

MR. NEWMAN: Mr. President, your rebuttal.

MR. REAGAN: Well, my rebuttal is, I've heard the national debt blamed for a lot of things, but not for illegal immigration across our border, and it has nothing to do with it. [Laughter] But with regard to these high interest rates too, at least give us the recognition of the fact that when you left office, Mr. Mondale, they were 21.5 [percent], the prime rate. It's now 12.25 [per-

cent], and I predict it will be coming down a little more shortly. So, we're trying to undo some of the things that your Administration did. [Applause]

MR. NEWMAN: Mister . . . no applause, please. Mr. Kalb, your question to President Reagan.

A Nuclear Armageddon?

MR. KALB: Mr. President, I'd like to pick up this Armageddon theme. You've been quoted as saying that you do believe, deep down, that we are heading for some kind of biblical Armageddon. Your Pentagon and your Secretary of Defense have plans for the United States to fight and prevail in a nuclear war. Do you feel that we are now heading, perhaps, for some kind of nuclear Armageddon, and do you feel that this country and the world could survive that kind of calamity?

MR. REAGAN: Mr. Kalb, I think what has been hailed as something I'm supposedly, as President, discussing as principle is the result of just some philosophical discussions with people who are interested in the same things, and that is the prophecies down through the years, the biblical prophecies of what would portend the coming of Armageddon and so forth, and the fact that a number of theologians, for the last decade or more, have believed that this was true, that the prophecies are coming together to portend that. But no one knows whether Armageddon . . . those prophecies mean that Armageddon is a thousand years away or day after tomorrow. So, I have never seriously warned and said, "We must plan according to Armageddon."

Now, with regard to having to say whether we would try to survive in the event of a nuclear war, of course we would. But let me also point out that to several parliaments around the world, in Europe and in Asia, I have made a statement in . . . to each one of them, and I'll repeat it here: A nuclear war cannot be won and must never be fought. And that is why we are maintaining a deterrent and trying to achieve a deterrent capacity to where no one would believe that they could start such a war and escape with limited damage. But the deterrent — and that's what it is for — is also what led me to propose what is now being called the "Star Wars" concept: to propose that we research to see if there isn't a defensive weapon that could defend against incoming missiles. And if such a defense could be found, wouldn't it be far more humanitarian to say that now we can defend against a nuclear war by destroying missiles instead of slaughtering millions of people?

'Star Wars' Technology

MR. KALB: Mr. President, when you made that proposal, the so-called "Star Wars" proposal, you said, if I am not mistaken, that you would share this very supersophisticated technology with the Soviet Union. After all of the distrust over the years, sir, that you have expressed towards the Soviet Union, do you really expect any-

one to take seriously that offer — that you would share the best of America's technology in this weapons area with our principal adversary?

MR. REAGAN: Why not? What if we did? And I hope we can. We're still researching. What if we come up with a weapon that renders those missiles obsolete? There has never been a weapon invented in the history of man that has not led to a defensive, a counterweapon. But suppose we came up with that? Now, some people have said, "Ah, that would make a war imminent, because they would think that we could now launch a first strike, because we could defend against the enemy." But why not do what I have offered to do and ask the Soviet Union to do? Say, "Look, here's what we can do. We'll even give it to you. Now, will you sit down with us and once and for all get rid, all of us, of these nuclear weapons, and free mankind from that threat?" I think that would be the greatest use of a defensive weapon.

MR. KALB: Mr. Mondale, you have been very sharply critical of the President's strategic defense initiative. And yet, what is wrong with a major effort by this country to try to use its best technology to knock out as many incoming nuclear warheads as possible?

MR. MONDALE: First of all, let me sharply disagree with the President on sharing the most advanced, the most dangerous, the most important technology in America with the Soviet Union. We have had for many years, understandably, a system of restraints on high technology, because the Soviets are behind us. And any research or development along the "Star Wars" schemes would inevitably involve our most advanced computers, most advanced engineering, and the thought that we would share this with the Soviet Union is, in my opinion, a total nonstarter. I would not let the Soviet Union get their hands on it at all.

Now what's wrong with "Star Wars?" There's nothing wrong with the theory of it. If we could develop a principle that would say both sides could fire all their missiles and no one would get hurt. I suppose it's a good idea. But the fact of it is, we're so far away from research that even comes close to that, that the director of engineering research in the Defense Department said to get there, we would have to solve eight problems, each of which are more difficult than the atomic bomb and the Manhattan Project. It would cost something like a trillion dollars to test and deploy weapons.

The second thing is, this all assumes that the Soviets wouldn't respond in kind. And they always do. We don't get behind, they won't get behind, and that's been the tragic story of the arms race. We have more at stake in space satellites than they do. If we could stop right now the testing and the deployment of these space weapons — and the President's proposals go clear beyond research — if it was just research, we wouldn't have any argument, because maybe someday somebody will think of something. But to commit this nation to a build-up of antisatellite and space weapons at this time, and their crude state, would bring about an arms race that's very dangerous indeed.

One final point — the most dangerous aspect of this proposal is, for the first time, we would delegate to computers the decision as to whether to start a war. That's dead wrong. There wouldn't be time for a President to decide. It would be decided by these remote computers; it might be an oil fire, it might be a jet exhaust, the computer might decide it's a missile, and off we go. Why don't we stop this madness now and draw a line and keep the heavens free from war? [Applause]

Nuclear Freeze

MR. KALB: Mr. Mondale, in this general area, sir, of arms control, President Carter's National Security Advisor, Zbig Brzezinski [Zbigniew Brzezinski] said, "A nuclear freeze is a hoax." Yet, the basis of your arms proposals, as I understand them, is a mutual and verifiable freeze on existing weapons systems. In your view, which specific weapons systems could be subject to a mutual and verifiable freeze, and which could not?

MR. MONDALE: Every system that is verifiable should be placed on the table for negotiations for an agreement. I would not agree to any negotiations or any agreement that involved conduct on the part of the Soviet Union that we couldn't verify every day. I would not agree to any agreement in which the United States' security interest was not fully recognized and supported. That's ... that's why we say "mutual and verifiable" freezes.

Now, why do I support the freeze? Because this ever-rising arms race madness makes both nations less secure. It's more difficult to defend this nation. It is putting a hair trigger on nuclear war. This Administration, by going into the "Star Wars" system, is going to add a dangerous new escalations. We have to be tough on the Soviet Union. But I think the American people —

MR. NEWMAN: Time is up, Mr. Mondale.

MR. MONDALE: — and the people of the Soviet Union want it to stop.

MR. NEWMAN: President Reagan, your rebuttal.

MR. REAGAN: Yes. My rebuttal, once again, is that this invention that has just been created here of how I would go about the rolling over for the Soviet Union ... no, Mr. Mondale. My idea would be, with that defensive weapon, that we would sit down with them and then say, "Now, are you willing to join us? Here's what we can...." Give them, give them a demonstration. And then say, "Here's what we can do." Now, if you're willing to join us in getting rid of all the nuclear weapons in the world, then we'll give you this one so that we would both know that no one can cheat; that we've both got something that if any-

one tries to cheat.... But when you keep "Star-Warring" it — I never suggested where the weapons should be or what kind. I'm not a scientist. I said, and the Joint Chiefs of Staff agreed with me, that it was time for us to turn our research ability to seeing if we could not find this kind of a defensive weapon. And suddenly somebody says, "Oh, it's got to be up there, and it's 'Star Wars,'" and so forth. I don't know what it would be. But if we can come up with one, I think the world will be better off.

MR. NEWMAN: Mr. Mondale, your rebuttal.

MR. MONDALE: Well, that's what a President's supposed to know — what those weapons are going to be. If they're space weapons, I assume they'll be in space. If they're antisatellite weapons, I assume they're going to be an aid ... armed against antisatellites. [Laughter]

Now, this is the most dangerous technology that we possess. The Soviets try to spy on us, steal this stuff. And to give them technology of this kind, I disagree with. You haven't just accepted research, Mr. President. You've set up a strategic defense initiative, an agency. You're beginning to test. You're talking about deploying. You're asking for a budget of some $30 billion for this purpose. This is an arms escalation, and we will be better off — far better off — if we stop right now, because we have more to lose in space than they do. If someday somebody comes along with an answer, that's something else. But that there would be an answer in our lifetime is unimaginable. Why do we start things that we know the Soviets will match and make us all less secure? That's what the President is for.

MR. NEWMAN: Mr. Kondracke, your question to Mr. Mondale.

MR. KONDRACKE: Mr. Mondale, you say that with respect to the Soviet Union, you want to negotiate a mutual nuclear freeze. Yet you would unilaterally give up the MX missile and the B-1 bomber before the talks have even begun. And you have announced, in advance, that reaching an agreement with the Soviets is the most important thing in the world to you. Aren't you giving away half the store before you even sit down to talk?

MR. MONDALE: No. As a matter of fact, we have a vast range of technology and weaponry right now that provides all the bargaining chips that we need. And I support the air-launched cruise missile, ground-launched cruise missile, the Pershing missile, the Trident submarine, the D-5 submarine, the Stealth technology, the Midgetman — we have a whole range of technology. Why I disagree with the MX is that it's a sitting duck. It'll draw an attack. It puts a hair trigger ... and it is a dangerous, destabilizing weapon. And the B-1 is similarly to be opposed, because for 15 years the Soviet Union has been preparing to meet the B-1. The Secretary of Defense himself said it would be a suicide mission if it were built.

Instead, I want to build the Midgetman, which is mobile and thus less vulnerable, contributing to stability, and a weapon that will give us security and contribute to an incentive for arms control. That's why I'm for Stealth technology: to build the Stealth bomber, which I've supported for years, that can penetrate the Soviet air defense system without any hope that they can perceive where it is because their radar system is frustrated. In other words, a President has to make choices. This makes us stronger.

The final point is, that we can use this money that we save on these weapons to spend on things that we really need. Our conventional strength in Europe is under strength. We need to strengthen that in order to assure our Western allies of our presence there — a strong defense — but also to diminish and reduce the likelihood of a commencement of a war and the use of nuclear weapons. It's in this way, by making wise choices, that we are stronger; we enhance the chances of arms control. Every President till this one has been able to do it. And this nation — the world — is more dangerous as a result.

MR. KONDRACKE: I want to follow up on Mr. Kalb's question. It seems to me on the question of verifiability that you do have some problems with the extent of the freeze. It seems to me, for example, that testing would be very difficult to verify because the Soviets encode their telemetry; research would be impossible to verify; numbers of warheads would be impossible to verify by satellite, except with on-site inspection; and production of any weapon would be impossible to verify. Now, in view of that, what is going to be frozen?

MR. MONDALE: I will not agree to any arms control agreement, including a freeze, that's not verifiable. Let's take your warhead principle. The warhead principle — there've been counting rules for years. Whenever a weapon is tested we count the number of warheads on it, and whenever that warhead is used, we count that number warheads, whether they have that number or less on it or not. These are standard rules. I will not agree to any production restrictions or agreements unless we have the ability to verify those agreements. I don't trust the Russians. I believe that every agreement we reach must be verifiable, and I will not agree to anything that we cannot tell every day. In other words, we've got to be tough. But in order to stop this arms madness we've got to push ahead with tough negotiations that are verifiable, so that we know the Soviets are agreeing and living up to their agreement.

Negotiating with Friends

MR. KONDRACKE: Mr. President, I want to ask you a question about negotiating with friends. You severely criticized President Carter for helping to undermine two friendly dictators who got into trouble with their own people: the Shah of Iran and President Somoza of Nicaragua. Now there are other such leaders heading for trouble,

including President Pincohet [Augusto Pinochet Ugarte] of Chile and President
Marcos [Ferdinand E. Marcos] of the Philippines. What should you do, and what can
you do, to prevent the Philippines from
becoming another Nicaragua?

MR. REAGAN: Morton, I did criticize
the President because of our undercutting
of what was a stalwart ally: the Shah of
Iran. But I am not at all convinced that he
was that far out of line with his people, or
that they wanted that to happen. The Shah
had done our bidding and carried our load
in the Middle East for quite some time,
and I did think that it was a blot on our
record that we let him down. Have things
gotten better? The Shah, whatever he
might have done, was building low-cost
housing, had taken land away from the
mullahs, and was distributing it to the
peasants so they could be landowners —
things of that kind. But we turned it over
to a maniacal fanatic who has slaughtered
thousands and thousands of people, calling
it executions.

The matter of Somoza — no. I never
defended Somoza. As a matter of fact, the
previous Administration stood by him. So
did I. Not that I could have done anything
in my position at that time. But for this
revolution to take place . . . and the promise of the revolution was democracy, human rights, free labor unions, free press.
And then, just as Castro had done in Cuba,
the Sandinistas ousted the other parties to
the revolution. Many of them are now the
Contras. They exiled some, they jailed
some, they murdered some, and they installed a Marxist-Leninist totalitarian government. And what I have to say about this
is: many times — and this has to do with
the Philippines also. . . . I know there are
things there in the Philippines that do not
look good to us from the standpoint, right
now, of democratic rights. But what is the
alternative? It is a large Communist movement to take over the Philippines. They
have been our friend for . . . since their
inception as a nation. And I think that
we've had enough of a record of letting,
under the guise of revolution, someone that
we thought was a little more right than we
would be, letting that person go and then
winding up with totalitarianism, pure and
simple, as the alternative. And I think that
we're better off, for example, with the Philippines, of trying to retain our friendship
and help them right the wrongs we see,
rather than throwing them to the wolves
and then facing a Communist power in the
Pacific.

Philippines

MR. KONDRACKE: Mr. President,
since the United States has two strategically important bases in the Philippines,
would the overthrow of President Marcos
constitute a threat to vital American interests? And, if so, what would you do about
it?

MR. REAGAN: Well, as I say, we have
to look at what an overthrow there would
mean and what the government would be

that would follow. And there is every evidence, every indication, that that government would be hostile to the United States.
And that would be a severe blow to the . . .
to our abilities there in the Pacific.

MR. KONDRACKE: And what would
you do about it?

MR. NEWMAN: Sorry. Sorry, you've
asked the follow-up question. Mr. Mondale, your rebuttal.

MR. MONDALE: Perhaps in no area
do we disagree more than this Administration's policies on human rights. I went to
the Philippines as Vice President, pressed
for human rights, called for the release of
Aquino, *and* made progress that had been
stalled on both the Subic [Bay] and Clark
Airfield bases.

What explains this Administration
cozying up to the Argentine dictators after
they took over? Fortunately, a democracy
took over. But this nation was embarrassed
by this current Administration's adoption
of their policies. What happens in South
Africa where, for example, the Nobel Prize
winner two days ago said this Administration is seen as working with the oppressive
government of that reg . . . of South Africa.
That hurts this nation. We need to stand
for human rights. We need to make it clear
we're for human liberty. National security
and human rights must go together. But
this Administration, time and time again,
has lost its way in this field.

MR. NEWMAN: President Reagan,
your rebuttal.

MR. REAGAN: Well, the invasion of
Afghanistan didn't take place on our
watch. I have described what has happened
in Iran. And we weren't here then, either. I
don't think that our record of human rights
can be assailed. I think that we have observed ourselves and have done our best to
see that human rights are extended
throughout the world. Mr. Mondale has recently announced a plan of his to get the
democracies together and to work with the
whole world to turn to democracy. And I
was glad to hear him say that, because
that's what we've been doing ever since I
announced to the British Parliament that I
thought we should do this.

And human rights are not advanced
when, at the same time, you then stand
back and say, "Whoops, we didn't know the
gun was loaded." And you have another
totalitarian power on your hands.

MR. NEWMAN: In this segment, because of the pressure of time, there will be
no rebuttals and there will be no follow-up
questions. Mr. Trewhitt, your question to
President Reagan.

MR. TREWHITT: One question to
each candidate?

MR. NEWMAN: One question to each
candidate.

Nuclear Strategy

MR. TREWHITT: Mr. President, can
I take you back to something you said earlier? And if I am misquoting you, please
correct me. But I understood you to say
that if the development of space military

technology was successful you might give
the Soviets a demonstration and say, "Here
it is," which sounds to me as if you might
be trying to gain the sort of advantage that
would enable you to dictate terms, and
which, I would then suggest to you, might
mean scrapping a generation of nuclear
strategy called mutual deterrence, in which
we, in effect, hold each other hostage. Is
that your intention?

MR. REAGAN: Well, I can't say that I
have round-tabled that and sat down with
the Chiefs of Staff. But I have said that it
seems to me that this could be a logical
step in what is my ultimate goal, my ultimate dream: and that is the elimination of
nuclear weapons in the world. And it seems
to me that this could be an adjunct, or
certainly a great assisting agent, in getting
that done. I am not going to roll over, as
Mr. Mondale suggests, and give them
something that could turn around and be
used against us. But I think it's a very
interesting proposal — to see if we can
find, first of all, something that renders
those weapons obsolete, incapable of their
mission. But Mr. Mondale seems to approve MAD. MAD is mutual assured destruction, meaning if you use nuclear weapons on us, the only thing we have to keep
you from doing it is that we'll kill as many
people of yours as you'll kill of ours. I think
that to do everything we can to find, as I
say, something that would destroy weapons
and not humans, is a great step forward in
human rights.

MR. TREWHITT: Mr. Mondale,
could I ask you to address the question of
nuclear strategy? Then let's. . . . The formal document is very arcane, but I'm going
to ask you to deal with it anyway. Do you
believe in MAD — mutual assured destruction, mutual deterrence — as it has been
practiced for the last generation.?

MR. MONDALE: I believe in a sensible arms control approach that brings
down these weapons to manageable levels.
I would like to see their elimination. And in
the meantime, we have to be strong enough
to make certain that the Soviet Union
never tempts us. Now, here we have to
decide between generalized objectives and
reality. The President says he wants to
eliminate or reduce the number of nuclear
weapons. But, in fact, these last four years
have seen more weapons built, a wider and
more vigorous arms race than in human
history. He says he wants a system that will
make nuclear arms — wars — safe, so nobody's going to get hurt. Well, maybe
someday somebody can dream of that.
Why threaten our space satellites upon
which we defend? Why pursue a strategy
that would delegate to computers the question of starting a war? A President, to defend this country and to get arms control,
must master what's going on. We all . . . I
accept his objective of . . . and his dreams.
We all do. But the hard reality is that we
must know what we are doing and pursue
those objectives that are possible in our
time. He's opposed every effort of every
President to do so. And the four years of

his Administration he's failed to do so. And if you want a tough President who uses that strength to get arms control and draws the line in the heavens, vote for Walter Mondale. [Applause]

MR. NEWMAN: Please — I must, I must again ask the audience not to applaud, not to cheer, not to demonstrate its feelings in any way.

We've arrived at the point in the debate now where we call for closing statements. You have the full four minutes, each of you. Mr. Mondale, will you go first?

Mondale's Closing Statement

MR. MONDALE: I want to thank The League of Women Voters, the good citizens of Kansas City, and President Reagan for agreeing to debate this evening. This evening we talked about national strength. I believe we need to be strong. And I will keep us strong. By strength ... I think strength must also require wisdom and smarts in its exercise. That's key to the strength of our nation. A President must know the essential facts — essential to command. But a President must also have a vision of where this nation should go. Tonight, as Americans, you have a choice. And you're entitled to know where we would take this country if you decide to elect us.

As President, I would press for long-term, vigorous economic growth. That's why I want to get these debts down and these interest rates down, restore America's exports, help rural America, which is suffering so much, and bring the jobs back here for our children. I want this next generation to be the best educated in American history, to invest in the human mind and science again so we're out front. I want this nation to protect its air, its water, its land, and its public health. America is not temporary. We're forever. And, as Americans, our generation should protect this wonderful land for our children. I want a nation of fairness, where no one is denied the fullness of life or discriminated against, and we deal compassionately with those in our midst who are in trouble. And, above all, I want a nation that's strong. Since we debated two weeks ago, the United States and the Soviet Union have built 100 more warheads, enough to kill millions of Americans and millions of Soviet citizens. This doesn't strengthen us. This weakens the chances of civilization to survive.

I remember the night before I became Vice President. I was given a briefing and told that any time, night or day, I might be called upon to make the most fateful decision on earth: whether to fire these atomic weapons that could destroy the human species. That lesson tells us two things. One,

pick a President that you know will know — if that tragic moment ever comes — what he must know. Because there'd be no time for staffing, committees, or advisors. A President must know right then. But, above all, pick a President who will fight to avoid the day when that god-awful decision ever needs to be made. And that's why this election is so terribly important. America and Americans decide not just what's happening in this country.

We are the strongest and most powerful free society on earth. When you make that judgment, you are deciding not only the future of our nation. In a very profound respect, you're providing the future ... deciding the future of the world. We need to move on. It's time for America to find new leadership. Please join me in this cause to move confidently and with a sense of assurance and command, to build the blessed future of our nation. [Applause]

MR. NEWMAN: President Reagan, your summation please.

Reagan's Closing Statement

MR. REAGAN: Yes. My thanks to The League of Women Voters, to the panelists, the moderator, and to the people of Kansas City for their warm hospitality and greeting.

I think the American people tonight have much to be grateful for: an economic recovery that has become expansion, freedom, and most of all, that we are at peace. I am grateful for the chance to reaffirm my commitment to reduce nuclear weapons and, one day, to eliminate them entirely. The question before you comes down to this: Do you want to see America return to the policies of weakness of the last four years, or do we want to go forward, marching together, as a nation of strength, and that's going to continue to be strong?

The.... [Applause] We shouldn't be dwelling on the past, or even the present. The meaning of this election is the future, and whether we're going to grow and provide the jobs and the opportunities for all Americans, and that they need.

Several years ago, I was given an assignment to write a letter. It was to go into a time capsule and would be read in a hundred years, when that time capsule was opened. I remember driving down the California coast one day. My mind was full of what I was going to put in that letter about the problems and the issues that confront us in our time and what we did about them.

But I couldn't completely neglect the beauty around me: the Pacific out there on one side of the highway, shining in the sunlight, the mountains of the coast range rising on the other side. And I found myself

wondering what it would be like for someone ... wondering if someone, a hundred years from now, would be driving down that highway, and if they would see the same thing.

With that thought, I realized what a job I had with that letter. I would be writing a letter to people who know everything there is to know about us. We know nothing about them. They would know all about our problems. They would know how we solved them and whether our solution was beneficial to them down through the years or whether it hurt them. They would also know that we lived in a world with terrible weapons, nuclear weapons of terrible destructive power aimed at each other, capable of crossing the ocean in a matter of minutes and destroying civilization as we knew it. And then, I thought to myself, "What ... what are they going to say about us? What are those people a hundred years from now going to think?" They will know whether we used those weapons or not.

Well, what they will say about us a hundred years from now depends on how we keep our rendezvous with destiny. Will we do the things that we know must be done, and know that one day, down in history a hundred years, or perhaps before, someone will say, "Thank God for those people back in the 1980s — for preserving our freedom, for saving for us this blessed planet called Earth with all its grandeur and its beauty."

You know, I am grateful to all of you for giving me the opportunity to serve you for these four years, and I seek reelection because I want more than anything else to try to complete the new beginning that we charted four years ago. George Bush — who I think is one of the finest Vice Presidents this country has ever had — George Bush and I have criss-crossed the country, and we've had, in these last few months, a wonderful experience. We have met young America. We have met your sons and daughters.

MR. NEWMAN: Mr. President, I am obliged to cut you off there under the rules of the debate. I'm sorry.

MR. REAGAN: All right. I was just going to.... All right. [Applause]

MR. NEWMAN: Perhaps I ... perhaps I should point out that the rules under which I did that were agreed upon by the two campaigns, with The League, as you know, sir.

MR. REAGAN: I know. I know. Yes.

MR. NEWMAN: Thank you, Mr. President. Thank you, Mr. Mondale. Our thanks also to the panel. Finally, to our audience, we thank you, and The League of Women Voters asks me to say to you: Don't forget to vote on November 6. [Applause] ∎

CQ Vice Presidential Debate

Bush-Ferraro Vice Presidential Debate

Following is the official record of the nationally televised debate between Vice President George Bush and Rep. Geraldine A. Ferraro, sponsored by The League of Women Voters Education Fund, held Oct. 11, in Philadelphia.

MRS. DOROTHY RIDINGS, Chair, League of Women Voters Education Fund: Good evening from the Civic Center in Philadelphia, Pennsylvania. I am Dorothy Ridings, President of The League of Women Voters, the sponsor of tonight's Vice Presidential debate between Republican George Bush and Democrat Geraldine Ferraro.

Our panelists for tonight's debate are John Mashek, National Correspondent for *U.S. News and World Report*, Jack White, Correspondent for *Time* Magazine, Norma Quarles, Correspondent for NBC News, and Robert S. Boyd, Washington Bureau Chief for Knight-Ridder Newspapers. Sander Vanocur, Senior Political Correspondent for ABC News, is our moderator tonight. Sandy.

MR. SANDER VANOCUR, Senior Political Correspondent, ABC News: Thank you, Dorothy. A few words about the order of our format tonight. The order of questioning was determined by a toss of the coin. Congresswoman Ferraro won the toss. She elected to speak last. Therefore, Vice President Bush will get the first question. The debate will be built upon a series of questions from the four reporters on the panel. A reporter will ask a candidate a question, a follow-up question, and then the same to the other candidate. Then each candidate will get to rebut the other. The debate will be divided into two parts. There will be a section, the first one, on domestic affairs, the second on foreign affairs. Now, the manner of address was decided by the candidates. Therefore, it will be "Vice President Bush," "Congresswoman Ferraro."

And we begin our questioning with Mr. Mashek.

Assuming the Presidency

MR. JOHN MASHEK, National Correspondent, *U.S. News & World Report*: John Adams, our nation's first [Vice] President, once said, "Today I am nothing, tomorrow I may be everything." With that in mind, I'd like to ask the following question. Vice President Bush, four years ago you ran against Mr. Reagan for the Republican nomination. You disagreed with him on

such issues as the Equal Rights Amendment, abortion, and you even labeled his economic policies as "voodoo." Now, you apparently agree with him on every issue. If you should be called upon to assume the Presidency, would you follow Mr. Reagan's policies down the line, or would you revert to some of your own ideas?

VICE PRESIDENT GEORGE BUSH: Well, I don't think there's a great difference, Mr. Mashek, between my ideas and President Reagan's. One of the reasons I think we're an effective team is that I believe firmly in his leadership. He has really turned this country around. We agree on the economic program. When we came into office, why, inflation was 12.5 percent. Interest rates, wiping out every single American, were 21.5 percent, if you can believe it. Productivity was down, savings was down; there was despair. In fact, the leadership of the country told the people that there was a "malaise" out there. And this President

has turned it around, and I've been with him every step of the way. And of course, I would continue those kinds of programs, because it's brought America back. America is better off. People are going back to work.

And why Mr. Mondale can't understand that there's a new enthusiasm in this country — that America is back, there is new, strong leadership — I don't know. He has one answer to the problem — raise everybody's taxes. He looked right into that lens and he said out there in San Francisco, he said, "I'm going to raise your taxes." Well, he's had a lot of experience in that, and he's sure going to go ahead and do it. But I remember a statement of Lyndon Johnson's, when he was looking around why his party people weren't supporting him. And he said, "Hey, they painted their tails white and they ran with the antelopes." There's a lot of Democratic whitetails running with the antelopes. Not one single Democrat has introduced the Mondale tax bill into the Congress.

Of course, I support the President's economic program, and I support him in everything else. And I'm not sure, because of my concept of the Vice Presidency, that if I didn't, I'd go doing what Mr. Mondale has done with Jimmy Carter — jump away from it. I couldn't do that to Ronald Reagan — now, next year, or any other time. I have too much trust in him. I have too much friendship for him, and I'd feel very uncomfortable doing that.

MR. MASHEK: Well, some Republicans have criticized Mr. Mondale for now claiming he disagreed privately with Jimmy Carter's decision to impose the grain embargo. Have you ever disagreed with any decision of the Reagan Administration in its inner circles? And, in following that up, where, in your judgment, does loyalty end and principle begin?

MR. BUSH: I owe my President my judgment, and then I owe him loyalty. You can't have the President of the United States out there looking over his shoulder, wondering whether his Vice President is going to be supporting him.

Mrs. Ferraro has quite a few differences with Vice President Mondale, and I understood it when she changed her position on tuition tax credits. They are different on busing. She voted to extend the grain embargo. He now says he was against it. If they win — and I hope they don't — but if they win, she will have to accommodate some views. But she will give him the same kind of loyalty that I am giving President Reagan.

One, we're not far apart on anything. Two, I can walk into that Oval Office any time and give him my judgment, and he might agree or he might not. But he also knows I won't be talking about it to the press, or I won't be knifing in the back by "leaking" to make me look good and complicate the problems of the President of the United States.

Experience

MR. MASHEK: Congresswoman Ferraro, your opponent has served in the House of Representatives, he has been Ambassador to the United Nations, Ambassador to China, Director of the Central Intelligence Agency, and now he has been Vice President for four years. How does your three terms in the House of Representatives stack up against experience like that?

CONGRESSWOMAN GERALDINE FERRARO: Well, let me first say that I wasn't born at the age of 43 when I entered Congress. I did have a life before that as well. I was a prosecutor for almost five years in the District Attorney's Office in Queens County and I was a teacher.

It is not only what is on your paper résumé that makes you qualified to run for or to hold office. It's how you approach problems and what your values are. I think if one has taken a look at my career, they will see that I level with the people, that I

approach problems analytically, that I am able to assess various facts with reference to a problem, and I can make the hard decisions.

I am intrigued when I hear Vice President Bush talk about his support of the President's economic program and how everything is just going so beautifully. I, too, recall when Vice President Bush was running in a primary against President Reagan, and he called the program "voodoo economics," and it was and it is. We are facing absolutely massive deficits. This Administration has chosen to ignore it. The President has failed to put forth a plan to deal with those deficits, and if everything believes that everything is coming up roses, perhaps the Vice President should join me as I travel around the country and speak to people.

People in Johnstown, Pennsylvania, are not terribly thrilled with what's happening in the economy because they are standing in the light of a closed plant, because they've lost their jobs. The people in Youngstown, Ohio, have stores that are boarded up because the economy is not doing well. It's not only the old industries that are failing, but it's also the new ones. In San Jose, California, they are complaining because they can't export their high-tech qualities . . . goods to Japan and other countries. People in the Northwest, in the state of Washington and Oregon, are complaining about what's happening to the timber industry and to the agricultural industry. So things are not as great as the Administration is wanting us to believe in their television commercials. My feeling, quite frankly, is that I have enough experience to see the problems, address them, and make the tough decisions and level with people with reference to those problems.

MR. MASHEK: Despite the historic aspects of your candidacy, how do you account for the fact that the majority of women — at least according to the polls — favor the Reagan-Bush ticket over the Mondale-Ferraro ticket?

MS. FERRARO: I don't. Let me say that I am not a believer in polls. And let me say further that what we are talking about are problems that are facing the entire nation. They're not just problems facing women. The issues in this campaign are the war-peace issues, are the problems of deficits, the problems of trade deficits. We are now facing a $120 billion trade deficit in this country. We are facing problems of the environment. I think what we are going to be doing over the next several weeks, and. . . . I'm absolutely delighted that the League is sponsoring these debates, and that we are able to now speak to the American public and address the issues in a way such as this. I think you are going to see a change in those polls.

MR. VANOCUR: Vice President Bush, you have one minute to rebut.

MR. BUSH: Well, I was glad to get that vote of confidence from Mrs. Ferraro on my economic judgment. So let me make

a statement on the economy. The other day she was in a plant and she said to the workers, "Why are you all voting for," or "Why are so many of you voting for the Reagan-Bush ticket?" And there was a long, deathly silence, and she said, "Come on. We delivered."

That's the problem. I'm not blaming her, except for the liberal voting record in the House. They delivered. They delivered 21.5 percent interest rates. They delivered what they called "malaise." They delivered interest rates that were right off the charts. They delivered pay — take-home pay — checks that were shrinking. And we delivered optimism. People are going back to work — six million of them — and 300,000 jobs a month being created. That's why there was that deathly silence out there in that plant. They delivered the wrong thing. Ronald Reagan is delivering leadership.

MR. VANOCUR: Congresswoman Ferraro, one-minute rebuttal.

MS. FERRARO: I think what I'm going to have to do is I'm going to start correcting the Vice President's statistics. There are six million more people who have jobs, and that's supposed to happen in a growing economy. In fact, in the prior Administration, with all their problems, they created 10 million jobs. The housing interest rates during this Administration — for housing for middle-class Americans — was 14.5 percent. Under the prior Administration, with all their problems, the average rate was 10.6 percent.

If you take a look at the number of people living in poverty as a result of this Administration . . . six million people, 500,000 people knocked off disability rolls, you know, it's. . . . You can walk around saying things are great, and that's what we're going to be hearing. We've been hearing that on those commercials for the past couple of months. I expect they expect the American people to believe that. I'll become a one-woman truth squad, and we'll start tonight.

MR. VANOCUR: Mr. White.

Civil Rights

MR. JACK WHITE, Correspondent, *Time* Magazine: Congresswoman Ferraro, I would like to ask you about civil rights. You have, in the past, been a supporter of tuition tax credits for private and parochial schools, and also of a constitutional amendment to ban busing. Both of these measures were opposed, not only by your running mate, but by just about every educational and civil rights organization in the country. Now that you're Mr. Mondale's running mate, have you changed your position on either of those?

MS. FERRARO: With reference to the busing vote that I cast in 1979, both Fritz Mondale and I agree on the same goal, and that is non-discrimination. I just don't agree on the same direction he does on how to achieve it. But I don't find any problem with that. I think that's been something that's been handled by the courts and is not being handled by Congress and will not be handled by the White House. But we both support non-discrimination and housing and integration of neighborhoods — the goals we both set forth.

With reference to tuition tax credits, I have represented a district in Queens which is 70 percent Catholic. I represented my district. Let me say as well that I have also been a great supporter of public school education. And that is something that Fritz and I feel very, very strongly about for the future of this country.

Now, this Administration, over the past several years, has gutted the educational programs available to our young people. It has attempted to knock out Pell Grants, which are monies to young individuals who are poor and who cannot afford to go to college. It has reduced by 25 percent the amount of monies going into college education, and by a third those going into secondary and primary schools. But Fritz Mondale and I feel very strongly that if you educate your children, that that's an effort, and the way that you build up and make a stronger America.

With reference to civil rights, I think you've got to go beyond that. And if you take a look also at my record in the Congress, and Fritz Mondale's record, both in the Senate and as Vice President, we both have extremely strong civil rights records. This Administration does not. It has come in, in the Bob Jones case, on the side of segregated academies. It came in, in the Grove City case, on the side of discrimination against women, the handicapped, and the elderly. As a matter of fact, in the Congress, we just passed overwhelmingly the Civil Rights Bill of 1984. And this Administration, the Republican-controlled Senate, just killed it in the last week or two in Congress.

So there's a real difference between how the Mondale-Ferraro administration will address the problems of civil rights and the failure of this Administration, specifically in that particular area.

MR. WHITE: In the area of affirmative action, what steps do you think government can take to increase the representation of minorities and women in the work force and in colleges and universities. And, specifically, would you support the use of quotas to achieve those goals?

MS. FERRARO: I do not support the use of quotas. Both Mr. Mondale and I feel very strongly about affirmative action to correct inequities. We believe that steps should be taken both through government and for instance the Small Business Administration. We have supported set-asides for minority and women's businesses. That's a positive thing. We don't feel that you're in any way hurting anybody else by reaching out with affirmative action to help those who have been disenfranchised. On the contrary, if you have a growing economy, if you create the jobs, if you allow for small business the opportunity, with lower interest rates, to reach out and, and grow, there will be more than enough space for everybody — and affirmative action is a

very positive way to deal with the problems of discrimination.

MR. WHITE: Vice President Bush, many critics of your Administration say that it is the most hostile to minorities in recent memory. Have you, inadvertently perhaps, encouraged that view by supporting tuition tax credits, the anti-busing amendment, siding with Bob Jones University in a case before the Supreme Court, the original opposition to the voting Rights Act extension, and so forth?

MR. BUSH: Well, no, Mr. White. I think our record on civil rights is a good record. You mentioned the Voting Rights extension. It was extended for the longest period of time by President Reagan. But we have some problems in attracting the black vote. And I think our record deserves better. We have done more for black colleges than any previous Administration. We favor enterprise zones to give.... And it's been blocked by Tip O'Neill and that House of Representatives. Those liberals in that House blocked a new idea to bring jobs into the black communities across this country. And because it's not an old handout, special Federal spending program, it's blocked there . . . a good idea, and I'd like to see that tried.

We've brought more civil rights cases in the Justice Department than the previous Administration by far. We believe in trying something new to help these black teenage kids. The minimum wage differential — it says, "Look," to an employer, "hire these guys." Yes, they're willing to work for slightly less than the minimum wage. Give them a training job in a private sector. We threw out that old CETA; that didn't train people for jobs that existed, simply rammed them on to the Government payroll. And we put in a thing called the Job Training Partnership Act, wonderful new legislation that's helping blacks more and more.

We think of civil rights as something like crime in your neighborhoods. And, for example, when crime figures are going in the right direction, that's good — that's a civil right. Similarly, we think of it in terms of quality of life. And that means interest rates. You know, it's funny. Mr. Mondale talks about real interest rates. The real interest rate is what you pay when you go down and try to buy a TV set or buy a car or do whatever it is. And the interest rates when we left office were 21.5 percent.

Inflation — is it a civil right to have that going right off the chart so you're busting every American family, those that can afford it the less? We've got a good record. We've got it on civil rights legislation, minority set-asides, more help for black colleges, and we've got it in terms of an economy that's offering people opportunity and hope instead of despair.

MR. WHITE: Along those lines, sir, many recent studies have indicated that the poor and minorities have not really shared in the new prosperity generated by the current economic recovery. Was it right for your Administration to pursue policies

— economic policies — that require those at the bottom of the economic ladder to wait for prosperity to trickle down from people who are much better off than they?

MR. BUSH: Mr. White, it's not trickling down. And I'm not suggesting there's no poverty. But I am suggesting the way to work out of poverty is through real opportunity. And in the meantime, the needy are getting more help. Human resource spending is way, way up. Aid for Dependent Children spending is up. Immunization programs are up. Almost every place you can point, contrary to Mr. Mondale's.... I've got to be careful. Contrary of how he goes around just saying everything bad, if he sees — somebody sees — a silver lining, he finds a big black cloud out there. Whine on, harvest moon. I mean, there's a lot going on, a lot of opportunity.

MR. VANOCUR: Congresswoman Ferraro, your rebuttal.

MS. FERRARO: The Vice President indicates that the President signed the Voting Rights Act. That was after he was . . . he did not support it while it was in the Congress, in the Senate. It was passed despite his opposition, and he did sign it because he was required to do so.

In the civil rights cases that he mentioned, that great number of cases that they have enforced, the reason they enforce them is because under the law they're required to do that — and I'm delighted that the Administration is following the law. [Applause]

With reference — with reference —

MR. VANOCUR: Excuse me. I . . . this'll be out of your . . . my time, not yours.

MS. FERRARO: Thank you.

MR. VANOCUR: Knowing and cherishing the people of this city, and knowing their restraint and diffidence about emotion, especially at athletic contests, of which this is not one, I beseech you: try to hold your applause, please. I'm sorry.

MS. FERRARO: I just have to correct, in my 30 seconds that are left, the comment that the Vice President made with reference specifically to a program like A.F.D.C. If you take A.F.D.C., if you take food stamps, if you take . . . oh, go down the line on poor people's programs, those are the programs that suffered considerably under this Administration's first budget cuts, and those are the ones that, in the second term — second part of their term — we were able to restore some of those terribly, terribly unfair cuts to the poor people of this country.

MR. VANOCUR: Vice President Bush?

MR. BUSH: Well, maybe we have a factual . . . maybe we can ask the experts to go to the books. They'll do it anyway. Spending for food stamps is way, way up under the Reagan Administration. A.F.D.C. is up under the Reagan Administration. And I am not going to be found wrong on that. I am sure of my facts, and we are trying to help, and I think we're doing a reasonable job. But we are not going to rest until every single American that wants a job gets a job, and until this prosperity and this recovery that's benefiting many Americans, benefits *all* Americans.

MR. VANOCUR: Miss Quarles.

Religion and Politics

MS. NORMA QUARLES, Correspondent, NBC News: Vice President Bush, one of the most emotional issues in this campaign has been the question of the separation of church and state. What are your views on the separation of church and state, specifically with regard to abortion, and do you believe it was right for the Archbishop of Philadelphia to have a letter read in 305 churches urging Catholics to fight abortion with their votes?

MR. BUSH: I do believe in pluralism. I do believe in separation of church and state. I don't consider abortion a religious issue. I consider it a moral issue. I believe the Archbishop has every right to do everything he wants in that direction, just as I never faulted Jesse Jackson from taking his message to the black pulpits all across this country, just as I never objected when the nuclear arms . . . the nuclear freeze, or the anti-nuclear people . . . many of those movements were led by priests. Suddenly, because a Catholic bishop or an evangelist feels strongly on a political issue, people are saying it's merging of church and state.

We favor — and I speak confidently for the President — we favor separation of church and state. We favor pluralism. Now, somebody says, "You want to restore prayer in schools. You don't think it's right to prohibit a kid from praying in schools." For years, kids were allowed to pray in schools. We don't think that's a merger of church and state to have a nonmandatory, voluntary, nongovernment-ordered prayer. and yet, some are accusing us of injecting religion into politics. I have no problem with what the Archbishop does. And I have no problem what the evangelists on the right do. And I have no problem what the priests on the left do. And it didn't bother me when, during the Vietnam War, much of the opposition to the government — Democrat *and* Republican governments — was led by priests encouraging people to break the law. And the adage of, you know, the civil disobedience thing.

So our position — separation of church of state, pluralism, so no little kid with a minority religion of some sort is going to feel offended or feel left out or feel uncomfortable. But yes, prayer in schools, on a voluntary basis. It worked for many, many years, until the Supreme Court ruled differently. I am glad we got this question, because I think there has been too much said about religion and politics. We don't believe in denominationally moving in. It wasn't our side that raised the question about our President, whether he was a good Christian or not. [Applause] Please! And so that's our position — separation of church and state, pluralism, respect for all.

MS. QUARLES: Vice President Bush, four years ago, you would have allowed Federal financing of abortions in cases of rape and incest, as well as when the mother's life was threatened. Does your position now agree with that of President Reagan, who in Sunday's debate came very close to saying that abortion is murder?

MR. BUSH: You know, there has been — I have to make a confession — an evolution in my position. There has been 15 million abortions since 1973. And I don't take that lightly. There has been a million and a half this year. The President and I do favor a human rights amendment. I favor one that would have an exception for incest and rape, and he doesn't, but we both . . . only for the life of the mother, and I agree with him on that. So yes, my position has evolved. But I would like to see the American who, faced with 15 million abortions, isn't rethinking his or her position, and. . . . I'll just stand with the answer; I support the President's position — and comfortably, from a moral standpoint.

MS. QUARLES: So you believe it's akin to murder.

MR. BUSH: I support the President's position.

MS. QUARLES: Fine. Congresswoman Ferraro, what are your views on the separation of church and state with regard to abortion, and do you believe it was right for the Archbishop of Philadelphia to have those letters read in the pulpits in this city and urge the voters to fight abortion with their vote?

MS. FERRARO: Let me say, first of all, that I believe very, very sincerely in the separation of church and state. I mean, taking it from the historical viewpoint, if you go back to the 1600s when people came here, the reason they came to this country was to escape religious persecution. And that's the same reason why people are coming here today, and in the 1940s to escape Nazism, and now in the 1980s and 1984 — when they can get out of the country — to escape Communism so they can come here and practice their religion. Our country is founded on the principle that our government should be neutral as far as religion is concerned.

Now what's happened over the past several years — and quite frankly, I'm not going to let you lay on me the intrusion of state and politics into religion, or religion into politics, by my comments with reference to the President's policies. Because it started in 1980, when this Administration was running for office and the Reverend Jerry Falwell became very, very involved in the campaign. What has happened over the past four years has been, I think, a real fudging of that line with the separation of church and state. The actions of the Archbishop's — let me say to you, I feel that they have not only a right, but a responsibility, to speak up. And, even though I've been the person who they have been speaking up about, I feel that they do have the responsibility to do so, and I have no problem with it, no more than I did with the priest who marched in . . . at the time of Vietnam, and no more than I did at the time when Martin Luther King marched at the time of the civil rights marches. I have absolutely no problem with them speaking up. I think they have an obligation as well as a right.

But what I do have a problem with is when the President of the United States gets up in Dallas and addresses a group of individuals and said to them that anybody who doesn't support his Constitutional amendment for prayer in the schools is intolerant of religion. Now, there are numerous groups who don't support that . . . prayer in the school — numerous religious groups. Are they intolerant of religion? Is that what the President is saying? I also object when I am told that the Reverend Falwell has been told that he will pick two of our Supreme Court Justices. That's going a little bit far. In that instance, let me say to you, it is more than a fudging of the line. It is total intrusion, and I think that it's in violation of our Constitution.

MS. QUARLES: Congresswoman Ferraro — [Applause] — as a devout Catholic, does it trouble you that so many of the leaders of your church disagree with you, and do you think that you're being treated unfairly in any way by the Catholic Church?

MS. FERRARO: Let me tell you that I did not come to my position on abortion very lightly. I am a devout Catholic. When I was running for Congress in 1978, I sat and met with a person I felt very close to, a monsignor, currently a bishop. I spoke to him about my personal feelings that I would never have an abortion. But I was not quite sure, if I were ever to become pregnant as a result of a rape, if I would be that self-righteous. I then spoke to him. He said, "Gerry, that's not good enough. You know you can't support that position." And I said, "O.K., that's my religious view. I will accept the teaching of the church, but I cannot impose my religious views on someone else."

I truly take an oath as a public official to represent all the people in my district, not only the Catholics. If there comes a time where I cannot practice my religion and do my job properly, I will resign my job. I said O.K. That's my religious view. I will accept the teaching of the Church. But I cannot impose my religious views on someone else. I truly take an oath as a public official to represent all the people in my district, not only the Catholics. If there comes a time where I cannot practice my religion and do my job properly, I will resign my job.

MR. VANOCUR: Vice President Bush, your rebuttal.

MR. BUSH: I respect that statement. I really . . . I really and truly do. We have a difference on a moral question here, on abortion.

I notice that Mr. Mondale keeps talking in the debate, and now its come up here, about Mr. Falwell. And he keeps . . . I don't know where this canard could have come from about Mr. Falwell picking the Supreme Court Justices. Ronald Reagan has made one superb, outstanding — the only one he's made — appointment to the Supreme Court, and that was Sandra Day O'Connor. Mr. Falwell opposed her nomination. We still have respect for him, but he opposed it. And so, I hope this lays to rest this slander against the President. We want Justices who will ... who will interpret the Constitution, not legislate.

MR. VANOCUR: Congresswoman Ferraro, your rebuttal.

MS. FERRARO: Yes. I still find that very difficult to believe because, in the platform which this ... the Republican Party passed in Dallas, one of the things that they did was, they said that the position on abortion would be a litmus test, not only for Supreme Court Justices, but for other Federal Justices. That, again, seems to me a blurring of the lines of separation between church and state.

MR. VANOCUR: The next questioning, from Mr. Boyd.

Payments in Taxes

MR. ROBERT S. BOYD, Washington Bureau Chief, Knight-Ridder Newspapers: Like many Americans, each of you has recently had an unhappy experience with the Internal Revenue Service. [Laughter] I'm going to prolong your ordeal.

Congresswoman Ferraro, you disagree with the rule that says that a candidate must report the income or assets of his or her spouse if you get any benefit from them. Your husband's tax returns showed that you did benefit, because he paid the mortgage and the property taxes on your homes. Now, the House Ethics Committee is examining this question, but it won't report its findings until after the election. Would you be willing to ask that Committee, which is controlled by Democrats, to hurry up its work and report before the election?

MS. FERRARO: Let me say to you that I already did that. I had wanted them to move ahead. I was.... If you recall, I spent about an hour and 45 minutes speaking to 200 reporters on August 21, which was the day after I was required to file my ... my financial statement. And I sat for as long as they had questions on the issue, and I believe that they were satisfied. I filed more information than any other candidate for a national office in the history of this country. Not only did I agree to file my tax returns, after a little bit of prodding, my husband also agreed to file his with the ... the ... not only the Ethics Committee, but with the F.E.C.

But the action that you're speaking about with the Ethics Committee was started by a right-wing legal organization, a foundation, knowing that I would have to ... that there would be an automatic inquiry. We have filed the necessary papers. I have asked them to move along. Unfortunately, the House, I believe, even went out of session today, so I don't know if they will move. But quite frankly, I would like that to be taken care of anyway, because I just want it cleared up.

MR. BOYD: Since that famous August 21 press conference on your family finances, you filed a new report with the Ethics Committee, and this showed that your previous reports were full of mistakes and omissions. For example, you failed to report about 12 trips that were paid for by special interest groups. In at least 18 cases, your holdings were misstated. Do you think it showed good leadership or attention to duty to blame all this on sloppy work by your accountant?

MS. FERRARO: Well, what it showed was that I ... and it was truly that I hired an accountant who had been with our family for well over 40 years. He was filling out those ethics forms. I did not spend the time with them. I just gave him my tax information and he did it.

I have to tell you what we have done since. I have hired a marvelous accountant. I have spent a lot of money having him go through all those ethics forms, and he will be doing my taxes over the next eight years, while we're in the White House, so that the American public can be sure it's all going to be taken care of. [Applause]

MR. BOYD: Vice President Bush, last year you paid less than 13 percent of your income in Federal taxes. According to the I.R.S., someone in your bracket normally pays about 28 percent of his income. Now, what you did was perfectly legal, but do you think it was fair? And is there something wrong with our tax laws that allows such large deductions for wealthy taxpayers?

MR. BUSH: What that figure, and the way ... I ... I kind of like the way Mrs. Ferraro and Mr. Zaccaro reported, because they reported Federal taxes, state, and local taxes. Gives people a clearer picture. That year, I happened to pay a lot of state and local taxes, which, as you know, are deducted from ... from the other. And so, I looked it up the other day, and we had paid ... I think it's 42 percent of our gross income in taxes.

Now, Mr. Mondale, the other night, took what I ... I'll be honest, I thought it was a cheap shot at me. And we did a little looking around to see about his. We can't find his 91 ... 1981 tax return. It may have been released. Maybe ... maybe my opponent knows whether Mr. Mondale released it. But we did find estimates that his income for those three years is $1,400,000, and I think he paid about the same percentage as I did in ... in total taxes.

He also made a reference that troubled me very much, Mr. Boyd. He started talking about my chauffeur. And you know, I'm driven to work by the Secret Service. So is Mrs. Ferraro. So is Mr. Mondale. They protected his life for ... for ... four years, and now they've done a beautiful job for Barbara and my.... They saved the life of the President of the United States. I thought that was a cheap shot, telling the American people ... to try to divide class, rich and poor.

But the big question is ... isn't whether Mrs. Ferraro's doing well. I think they're doing pretty well. And I know Bar-bara and I are doing well. And it's darn sure that Mr. Mondale's doing well, with $1,400,000 in income. But the question really is, after we get through this disclosure: Is the tax cut fair? Are people getting a fair break? And the answer is: the rich are paying 6 percent more on taxes, and the poor are getting a better break, those lower- and middle-income people that have borne the burden for a long, long time.

So, yes, I favor disclosure, I've always disclosed. This year, I had my taxes and ... and everything I own in a blind trust — so blind, blinder than the President's, where I didn't even sign my tax return. But there seemed to be an interest in it, so we went to the Government Ethics Committee. They agreed to change the trust. The trust has been ... been revealed, and I was sure glad to see that I had paid 42 percent of my gross income in taxes. [Applause]

MR. BOYD: Mister —

MR. BUSH: No, no, no, no, no, no, no, no.

MR. VANOCUR: Please.

MR. BUSH: Please.

MR. BOYD: Mr. Vice President, how can you claim that your home is in Maine for tax purposes, and, at the same time, claim that your home is in Texas for voting purposes?

MR. BUSH: Well —

MR. BOYD: Are you really a Texan or a New Englander? [Applause]

MR. BUSH: I'm really a Texan, but I got one house. And under the law, every taxpayer is allowed, when he sells a house and buys another house, to get the rollover. Everybody, it turns out. And I may ... I may hire.... I notice she said she has a new good accountant. I'd like to get his name and phone number [Laughter] because I think I've paid too much in the way of taxes. And residence, Mr. Boyd, legal residence for voting is very different — the domicile, they call that — very different than the house. But they say, "You're living in the Vice President's house, therefore you don't get what every" — I got problems — "what every other taxpayer gets." I got problems with the I.R.S. But so do a lot of people out there. I think I've paid too much. Nothing ethical. I'd like to get some money back. [Laughter]

MR. VANOCUR: Congresswoman Ferraro, your rebuttal please.

MS. FERRARO: Let ... let me just say that I'd be happy to give the Vice President the name of my accountant, but I warn you, he's expensive. [Laughter] I think the question is whether or not the tax cuts, and the ... the tax system that's currently in our ... that our government uses is fair. I think the tax system is unfair, but it's not something that we can address in the short term. Are the tax cuts that Vice President Bush and I got last time ... last ... three years ago, that this President gave out? No, that's not fair. If you earned $200,000, you got a $25,000 tax cut. If you earned between $20,000 and $40,000, you may have gotten about $1,000, between $10 [thousand] and $20 [thousand], close to

$100. And if you made less than $10,000, with all the budget cuts that came down the line, you suffered a loss of $400. That's not fair. That's basically unfair. And not only is it unfair, but economically it has . . . it has darn near destroyed this country. It was a $750 billion tax cut over a five-year period of time. That's one of the reasons we're facing these enormous deficits that we have today.

MR. VANOCUR: Mr. Vice President.

MR. BUSH: No, I think I've said all I . . . I want to say. I do . . . I didn't fully address myself to Mr. Boyd's question on disclosure. I led the fight, I think in 1968, in the House. I was in the House of Representatives for a couple of terms. [Laughter] And I led the fight for disclosure. I believe in it. Before I went into this job, I disclosed everything we had. We didn't have any private corporations, but I disclosed absolutely everything. Arthur Andersen made out an assets and liabilities statement that I believe went further than any other one. And then, to protect the public interest, we went into this blind trust. I believe in the blind trust, because I believe a public official in this kind of job ought not to know whether he's going to benefit, directly or indirectly, by some holding he might have, or something of that nature. And . . . no, I support full disclosure.

MR. VANOCUR: Thank you. That ends the part of this debate devoted to domestic affairs. We will now turn to foreign affairs. We'll begin the question with Mr. Mashek.

Terrorist Attacks

MR. MASHEK: Vice President Bush, since your Administration came to power, the President has threatened a stern response against terrorism, yet murderous attacks have continued in Lebanon and the Middle East. Who's to blame? And you've been director of the Central Intelligence Agency. What can be done to stop it?

MR. BUSH: Terrorism is very, very difficult to stop. And I think everybody knows that. We had ambassadors killed in Sudan and Lebanon some time ago . . . long time ago. When you see the Israeli building in Lebanon after the death of our Marines, you see that hit by terrorism — the Israelis, with all their experience fighting terrorism, you know it's difficult. When you see Khomeini, with his radical Islam, resorting to government-sponsored terrorists . . . terrorism, it's very difficult.

The intelligence business can do a good job, and I'm always one that defends the Central Intelligence Agency. I believe we ought to strengthen it. And I believe we still have the best foreign intelligence business in the world. But it is very difficult to get the source information that you need to go after something as shadowy as international terror.

There was a difference between Iran and what happened in Lebanon. In Iran, you had a government holding a U.S. Embassy, the government sanctioning the takeover of that Embassy by those . . . by

those students, the government negotiating with the United States Government for their release. In Lebanon, in the terror that happened at the Embassy, you have the Government there, Mr. Gemayel, that wants to help fight against terrorism. But because of the melee in the Middle East that's there today and has been there yesterday and the day before — as everyone that's had experience in that area knows — it is a very different thing.

So, what we've got to do is use absolutely the best security possible. I don't think you can go assigning blame. The President, of course, is the best I've ever seen of accepting that. He's been wonderful about it in absolutely everything that happens. But I think fair-minded people that really understand international terror know that it's very hard to guard against.

And the answer, then, really lies in the Middle East, and terrorism happening all . . . happening all over the world . . . is a solution to the Palestine question. The follow-on to Camp David, under the umbrella of the Reagan September of 1982 initiative — that will reduce terror. It won't eliminate it.

MR. MASHEK: You mentioned Khomeini. Some Republicans charge the previous Administration with being almost helpless against Khomeini and Libya's Khaddafi. Why hasn't your Administration done something to take action against Arab states that foment this kind of terrorism?

MR. BUSH: What we've done is to support Arab states that want to stand up against international terror. Quite different. We believe in supporting, without jeopardizing the security of Israel in any way, because they are our one strategic ally in the area, they are the one democracy in the area, and our relations with them has never been better. . . . But we do believe in reaching out to the . . . what they call the G.C.C., those Gulf Cooperative Council states, those moderate Arab states in that world, and helping them with defensive weapons to guard against international terror or radical Islam perpetuated by Khomeini. And because we've done that, and because the Saudis chopped down a couple of those intruding airplanes a while back, I think we have helped keep the peace in the Persian Gulf.

MR. MASHEK: Congresswoman Ferraro, you and Vice . . . former Vice President Mondale have criticized the President over the bombings in Lebanon. Well, what would you do to prevent such attacks?

MS. FERRARO: Let me first say that terrorism is a . . . a global problem. And let me say secondly that the . . . Mr. Bush has referred to the Embassy that was held in Iran. Well, I was at the White House in January, I guess it was in '81, when those hostages, all 52 of them, came home alive. It was at that time that President Reagan gave a speech welcoming them home — as America did; we were so excited to see them back. But what he said was, "The United States has been embarrassed for the last time. We're going to stand tall, and

if this ever happens again, there is going to be swift and immediate steps taken to address the wrong that our country has founded . . . suffered."

In April of 1983, I was in . . . in Beirut, and visited the Ambassador at the Embassy. Two weeks later, that Embassy was bombed. At that time, you take a look at the crazy activities of terrorists — you can't blame that on anybody. They're going to do crazy things, and you just don't know what's going to happen.

The following October, there was another bombing, and that bombing took place at the Marine barracks, where there were 242 young men who were killed. Right after that bombing occurred, there was a commission set up called the Long Commission, and that commission did a study at the . . . of the security arrangements around where the Marines were sleeping, and found that there was negligence, that they did not have proper gates up, proper precautions to stop those trucks from coming in. And so, the Long Commission issued a report and President Reagan got up and he said "I'm Commander in Chief. I take responsibility." And we all waited for something to be done when he took responsibility.

Well, last month we had our third bombing. The first time, the first Embassy, there was no gate up. The second time with our Marines, the gate was open. The third time, the gate was there but it had not been installed. And what was the President's reaction? Well, the security arrangements were not in. Our people were placed in that Embassy in an unsecure time. And the Marines who were guarding it were left to go away, and there were other people held guarding the Embassy. Again, the President said, "I assume responsibility."

I'd like to know what that means. Are we going to take proper precautions before we put Americans in situations where they're in danger, or are we just going to walk away, throwing our arms up in the air now — quite a reversal from the first time, and from the first time when he said he was going to do something — or is this President going to take some action?

MR. MASHEK: Some Democrats cringe at the words "spying" and "covert activity." Do you believe both of them have a legitimate role in countering terrorist activity around the world?

MS. FERRARO: I think they have a legitimate role in gathering information. And what had happened was, the C.I.A., in the last bombing, had given information to our Administration with reference to the . . . the actual threats that that embassy was going to be bombed, so it wasn't the C.I.A. who was at fault. There's legitimate reason for the . . . the C.I.A. to be in existence, and that's to gather intelligence information for our security. But when I see the C.I.A. doing things like they're doing down in Central America, supporting a covert war, no, I don't support that kind of activity. The C.I.A. is there to . . . meant to protect our Government, not there to subvert other governments. [Applause]

MR. VANOCUR: Vice President Bush.

MR. BUSH: Well, I'm surprised to —

MR. VANOCUR: Please.

MR. BUSH: I think I just heard Mrs. Ferraro say that she would do away with all covert action. And if so, that has very serious ramifications, as the intelligence community knows. This is serious business, and sometimes it's quiet support for a friend. And so, I'll leave that one there.

But let me help you with the difference, Ms. Ferraro, between Iran and the Embassy in Lebanon. In Iran, we were held by a foreign government. In . . . in . . . in . . . Lebanon, you had a wanton terrorist action where the government opposed it. We went to Lebanon to give peace a chance, to stop the bombing of civilians in Beirut, to remove 13,000 terrorists from Lebanon. We did — we saw the formation of a government of reconciliation. And for somebody to suggest, as our two opponents have, that these men died in shame — they better not tell the parents of those young Marines. They gave peace a chance, and our allies were with us: the British, the French, and the Italians.

MR. VANOCUR: Congresswoman Ferraro.

MS. FERRARO: Let me just say, first of all, that I almost resent, Vice President Bush, your patronizing attitude [Applause] that you have to teach me about foreign policy. I've been a member of Congress for six years. I was there when the Embassy was held hostage in Iran, and I have been there, and I have seen what has happened in the past several months — 17 months — with your Administration.

Secondly, please don't categorize my answers either. Leave the interpretation of my answers to the American people who are watching this debate. [Applause] And let me say further that no one has ever said that those young men who were killed — through the negligence of this Administration and others — ever died in shame. No one who has a child who's 19 or 20 years old — a son — would ever say that about the loss of anybody else's child. [Applause]

MR. VANOCUR: Mr. White.

Use of Military Force

MR. WHITE: Congresswomen Ferraro, you've repeatedly said that you would not want your son to die in an undeclared war for an uncertain cause. But recently, your running mate, Mr. Mondale, has suggested that it may become necessary to erect a military quarantine or blockade of Nicaragua. Under what circumstances would you advocate the use of military force, American combat forces, in Central America?

MS. FERRARO: I would advocate the use of force when it was necessary to protect the security of our country, protect our security interests, or protect our people or protect the interest of our friends and neighbors. When President — well, I'm jumping the gun a bit, aren't I? — when

Mr. Mondale [Laughter] . . . when Mr. Mondale referred to the quarantine of Central America, a country in Central America, what he was referring to was a last resort, after all other means of attempting to settle the situation down in that region of the world had been exhausted.

Quite frankly, now what is being done by this Administration is an Americanizing of a regional conflict. They're moving in militarily, instead of promoting the Contadora process — which, as you know is the . . . the process that is in place with the support of Mexico and Colombia and Panama and Venezuela. Instead of supporting the process, our Administration has, in Nicaragua, been supporting covert activities to keep that revolution going in order to overthrow the Sandinista government. In El Salvador . . . was not pushing the head of the Government to move toward correction of the civil rights . . . human rights problems that existed there. And now, this Administration seems almost befuddled by the fact that Nicaragua is moving to participate in the Contadora process. And El Salvador, through its President Duarte [José Napoleón Duarte, President of El Salvador], is reaching out to the guerrillas in order to negotiate a peace.

What Fritz Mondale and I feel about the situation down there is that what you do is, you deal first through negotiation. That force is not a first resort, but certainly a last resort in any instance.

MR. WHITE: A follow-up, please. Many times in its history, the United States has gone to war in order to defend freedom in other lands. Does your answer mean that you would be willing to forego the use of military force even if it meant the establishment of a Soviet-backed dictatorship so close to our own borders?

MS. FERRARO: No. I think what we have to do is work with the government — and I assume you are speaking about the government of Nicaragua — work with that government to achieve a pluralistic society. I mean, they do have elections that are coming up on November 4. I think we have to work with them to achieve a peaceful solution to bring about a pluralistic country. No, I'm not willing to . . . to live with a . . . a force that could be a danger to our country. Certainly, I would see that our country would be there, putting all kinds of pressure on the neighboring countries of Honduras, of Costa Rica, of El Salvador, to promote the kind of society that we can all live with in security in this country.

MR. WHITE: Vice President Bush, both Cuba and Nicaragua are reported to be making extensive preparations to defend themselves against an American invasion, which they claim could come this fall. And even some of your Democratic opponents in Congress have suggested that the Administration may be planning a December surprise invasion. Can you tell us under what circumstances a re-elected Reagan Administration would consider use of force in Central America or the Caribbean?

MR. BUSH: I don't think we're . . . to

be required to use force. Let me point out that there are 2,000 Cuban military and 7,500 so-called Cuban advisers in Nicaragua. There are 55 American military in El Salvador. I went down, on the instructions of the President, to speak to the commandantes in El Salvador, and told them that they had to move with Mr. Magaña [Alvaro Alfredo Magaña Borjo], then the President of El Salvador, to respect human rights. They have done that. They're moving well. I'm not saying it's perfect, but the difference between El Salvador and Nicaragua is like the difference between night and day. El Salvador went to the polls. Mr. Duarte was elected by 70 percent of the people . . . in a . . . in 70 percent voting . . . in a certifiably free election. In Nicaragua you have something very different. You have a Marxist-Leninist group, the Sandinistas, that came into power talking democracy. They have aborted their democracy. They have humiliated the Holy Father. They have cracked down on the only press organ there, *La Prensa*, censoring the press, something that should concern every American. They have not had any human rights at all. They will not permit free elections. Mr. Cruz, who was to be the only viable challenger to Nicaragua . . . to the Sandinistas, to the junta, to Mr. Ortega [Daniel Ortega Saavedra, coordinator, Nicaraguan government], went down there and found that the ground rules were so unfair that he couldn't even wage a campaign.

One country is devoid of human rights. The other is struggling to perfect their democracy. We don't like it, frankly, when Nicaragua exports its revolution or serves as a conduit for supplies coming in from such democracies as North Korea, Bulgaria, the Soviet Union, and Cuba, to try to destabilize El Salvador. Yes, we're concerned about that, because we want to see this trend towards democracy that's . . . continue. There have been something like 13 countries since we've come in move towards the democratic route.

And let me say that Grenada is not unrelated. And now I have a big difference with Ms. Ferraro on that one. We gave those four tiny Caribbean countries a chance. We saved the lives . . . and most of those, the thousand students, said that they were in jeopardy. Grenada was a proud moment, because we did stand up for democracy. But in terms of threat of these countries . . . nuclear . . . I mean [Laughs] . . . weapons, no, there's not that kind of a threat. It's Mr. Mondale that proposed the quarantine, not Ronald Reagan. [Applause] Please.

MR. WHITE: Considering this country's long respect for the rule of international law, was it right for the United States to be involved in mining the harbors of Nicaragua, a country we're not at war with, and to subsequently refuse to allow the World Court to adjudicate that dispute and the complaint from Nicaragua?

MR. BUSH: I support what we're doing. It was reported to the Congress under the law. I support it. My only regret is that the aid for the ... for the contras, those people that are fighting — we call them freedom fighters. They want to see the democracy perfected in Nicaragua. Am I to understand from this assault on covert action that nowhere in the world would we do something that was considered just off-base by ... when Mrs. Ferraro said she'd never support it? Would she never support it if the violation of human rights was so great and quiet support was necessary for freedom fighters? Yes, we're for the contras.

And let me tell you another fact about the contras. Everyone that's not for this, everyone who wants to let that Sandinista government prevail, just like that Castro did, all of that — the contras are not Somocistas. Less than 5 percent of the contras supported Somoza [Anastasio Somoza Debayle, late President of Nicaragua]. These were people that wanted a revolution. These are people that felt the revolution was betrayed. These are people that support human rights. Yes, we should support them.

MR. VANOCUR: Congresswoman Ferraro.

MS. FERRARO: I spent a good deal of time in Central America in January and had an opportunity to speak to the contras after being in ... in Nicaragua and in ... El Salvador. And let me just say that the situation as it exists now, because of this Administration's policies — we're not getting better. We're not moving toward a more secure area of the world. As a matter of fact, the number of troops that the Sandinistas have accumulated since the Administration has started its covert activities has risen from 12 [thousand] to 50,000. And of course, the number of Soviet and Cuban advisers has also increased.

I did not support the mining of the harbors in Nicaragua. It is a violation of international law. Congress did not support it, and, as a matter of fact, just this week the Congress voted to cut off covert aid to Nicaragua unless and until a request is made and there is evidence of need for it and the Congress approves it again in March. So the Congress doesn't get laid on. The covert activities which I oppose in Nicaragua, those C.I.A. covert activities in that specific country, are not supported by the Congress. And, believe it or not, not supported by the majority of people throughout this country. [Applause]

MR. VANOCUR: Vice President Bush.

MR. BUSH: Well, I would simply like to make the distinction again between those countries that are searching for democracy and the handful of countries that have totally violated human rights and are going the Marxist route. Ortega, the commandante who is head of the Nicaraguan Sandinistas, is an avowed Marxist. They don't believe in the church. They don't believe in the free elections. They don't believe in all the values that we believe in. So it is our policy to support the

democracies there, and when you have freedom fighters that want to perfect that revolution and go the democratic route, we believe in giving them support. We are for democracy in the hemisphere. We are for negotiation. Three dollars out of every four that we've sent down there has been for economic aid, to support the people's chance to eat and live and be happy and enjoy life. And one-fourth only was military. You wouldn't get that from listening to Mr. Mondale.

MR. VANOCUR: Ms. Quarles.

Meeting With Soviet Leaders

MS. QUARLES: Vice President Bush, the last three Republican administrations — Eisenhower, Nixon, and Ford, none of them soft on Communism — met with the Soviets and got agreements on arms control. The Soviets haven't changed that much. Can you tell us why President Reagan has not met with the Soviet ministers at all, and only met with Foreign Minister Gromyko [Andrei Gromyko, Foreign Minister, U.S.S.R.] less than a month ago?

MR. BUSH: Yes, I can. The ... you mentioned the Gromyko meeting. Those were broken off under the Carter-Mondale days. There have been three separate Soviet leaders — Mr. Brezhnev [Leonid Brezhnev, late President of the U.S.S.R.], Mr. Andropov [Yuri Andropov, late President of the U.S.S.R.], and now Chernenko [Konstantin Chernenko, President of the U.S.S.R.] — during their ... that's three and a half ... in three and a half years, three separate leaders. The Soviets have not been willing to talk. We are the ones that went to the table in I.N.F. [Intermediate-Range Nuclear Force Negotiations]. We had a good proposal, a moral proposal — ban an entire generation of intermediate nuclear-force weapons. And if you won't do that, don't leave your allies in Europe in a monopoly position — the Soviets with 1,200 of these things and the Alliance with none. We didn't think that is the way you deter aggression and keep the peace.

The President went ... the first thing he did when he came into office was make a proposal in the most destabilizing weapons of all, START, and when the ... the strategic weapons. ... And when the Soviets said, "Well, we don't like that proposal," we said, "All right. We'll be more flexible." I, at the urging of the President, went to Geneva and laid on the table a treaty to ban all chemical weapons. We don't want them to have a monopoly. But we said, "Look, let's come together. You come over here and see what we're doing. We'll go over there and see what you're doing. But let's save the kids of this world from chemical weapons" — a brilliant proposal to get rid of all of them. And the Soviets — "Nyet, nyet, nyet."

And the mutual balance force reduction to reduce conventional force — they're not even willing to tell us the base — Mrs. Ferraro knows that — of how many troops they have. There's four sessions. We have had an agreement with them on the hot

line. But the Carter-Mondale made an agreement, the SALT II agreement, but the Democratic Senate — they were a Democratic Administration — the Democratic Senate wouldn't even ratify that agreement. It was flawed, it was unverifiable, and it was not good.

Our President wants to reduce — not just to stop — he wants to reduce, dramatically, nuclear weapons. And when the Soviets know they're going to have this strong President to deal with, and when this new Administration, Mr. Chernenko's, given more than a few months in office, can solidify its position, then they'll talk. But if they think the opposition, before they sit down, are going to give up the MX, give up the B-1, go for a freeze that locks in inferiority in Europe — all of these things, unilaterally, before they're willing to talk — they may just sweat it out for four more weeks. Who knows?

MS. QUARLES: You were once quoted as saying that a nuclear war is winnable. Is that still your belief? And, if not, under what circumstances would you use nuclear weapons if you were President?

MR. BUSH: No. I don't think it's winnable. I was quoted wrong, obviously, because I never thought that. The Soviet planning — I did learn that when I was director of Central Intelligence, and I don't ... I don't think there'd be any disagreement — is based on that ugly concept. But I agree with the President. It should never be fought. Nuclear weapons should never be fought with. And that's our approach.

So, therefore, let's encourage the Soviets to come to the table, as we did at the Gromyko meeting. I wish everybody could have seen that one. The President, giving the facts to Gromyko in all of these nuclear ... nuclear meetings — excellent. Right on top of that subject matter. And I'll bet you that Gromyko went back to the Soviet Union saying, "Hey, listen. This President is calling the shots. We'd better move."

But you know why I think we'll get an agreement? Because I think it is in the interests of the Soviet Union to make it, just as it is in the interests of the United States. They're not deterred by rhetoric. I listened to the rhetoric for two years at the United Nations. I've lived in a Communist country. It's not rhetoric that decides agreements; it's self interest of those countries.

MS. QUARLES: Congresswoman Ferraro, you and Mr. Mondale are for a verifiable nuclear freeze. Some Democrats had said that verification may not be possible. How would you verify such an agreement and make sure that the Soviets are not cheating?

MS. FERRARO: Let me say, first of all, that I don't think that there is an issue that is more important in this campaign, in this election, than the issue of war and peace. And since today is Eleanor Roosevelt's 100th birthday, let me quote her. She said, "It is not enough to want peace; you must believe in it. And it's not enough to believe in it; you must work for it."

This Administration's policies have indicated quite the opposite. The last time I heard Vice President Bush blame the fact that they didn't meet with a Soviet leader — and this is the first president in 40 years not to meet with a Soviet counterpart — he said the reason was because there were three Soviet leaders in the past three and a half years. I went and got a computer printout. It's five pages of the leaders, world leaders, that the Soviet leaders have met with. And they are not little people. They are people like Mitterrand of France, and Kohl of Germany, and President Spyros Kyprianou of Cyprus. And you go down the line — five pages of people that the Soviet leaders have managed to meet with — and, somehow, they couldn't meet with the President of the United States.

In addition to not meeting with its Soviet counterpart, this is the first President — and you're right — since the start of negotiating arms control agreements, who has not negotiated an arms control agreement. But not only has he not negotiated one, he's been opposed to every single one that every other President has negotiated — including Eisenhower, including Ford, and including Nixon. Now, let me just say that, with reference to the Vice President's comments about the intent and the desire of the United States in this Administration — the Soviet Union did walk out of the talks. I agree. But it seems to me that in 1982, when the Administration presented its START proposal, that it wasn't a realistic proposal. And that is the comment that was made by Secretary Haig after he left office. Because what it dealt with was, it dealt just with land-based nuclear missiles, which is where the Soviets had the bulk of their missiles.

But that aside, in 1982, I believe it was, their own negotiator, Nitze, came out with a proposal called "the walk in the woods proposal," which would have limited the number of nuclear arms in Europe. That proposal was turned down by the Administration — a proposal presented by its own Administrator. Now, I'm delighted that they met with Mr. Gromyko. But they could have had that opportunity to meet with him in 1981, when he came to the UN — which he had done with every other President before — and in 1982 as well. I guess my —

MR. VANOCUR: Congresswoman? I'm sorry. Speaking of limits, I have to impose a limit on you.

MS. FERRARO: O.K.

MR. VANOCUR: Vice President Bush.

MR. BUSH: Well, I think there's quite a difference between Mr. Kyprianou in Cyprus and the leader of the free world, Ronald Reagan, in terms of meeting. [Applause] And the Soviet Union ... the Soviet Union ... the Soviet Union will meet with a lot of different people. We've been in very close touch with Mr. Mitterrand, Mr. Kohl, and others that have met with the leaders of the Soviet Union. But that's quite different than meeting with the President of the United States. The Soviets say, "We'll have a meeting when we think there can be progress." And, yet, they left those talks. I'd like to correct my opponent on "the walk in the woods." It was the Soviet Union that was unwilling to discuss "the walk in the woods." They were the ones that gunned it down first, and the record is very, very clear on that. Miss Ferraro mentioned the inflexibility of our position on strategic arms. Yes, we offered first to get rid of all those ... you try to reduce the SS-18s in those weapons. But then we said, "If that's not good enough, there is flexibility. Let's talk about the bombers and the planes." So, that's a very important point in terms of negotiation.

MR. VANOCUR: Congresswoman, he that taketh away has to give back. I robbed you of your rebuttal. Therefore, you will have two minutes to rebut. Forgive me.

MS. FERRARO: You robbed me of my follow-up. That's what you robbed me. So why I don't let her give me the follow-up —

MR. VANOCUR: All right. And then give your rebuttal.

MS. FERRARO: O.K.

MS. QUARLES: Congresswoman Ferraro, most polls show that the American ... Americans feel that the Republicans, more than the Democrats, are better able to keep the U.S. out of war. We've had four years of relative peace under President Reagan. How can you convince the American public that the world would be a safer place under Carter-Mondale?

MS. FERRARO: I think, first of all, you have to take a look at the current situation. We now have 50,000 nuclear warheads. We have ... we are building at the rate of five or six a day between us, and we have been doing that since this Administration came into office. I think that what you can do is look at what they've done and recognize that they're not going to do very much in the future. And so, since they've done nothing, do we continue to build? Because an arms race doesn't lead to anything; it leads to another arms race, and that's it.

Vice President Mondale has indicated that what he would do, first of all, as soon as he gets into office, is contact his Soviet counterpart and set up an annual summit meeting. That's number one. I don't think you can start negotiating until you start talking.

Secondly, he would issue a challenge. And the challenge would be — in the nature of temporary, mutual, verifiable moratoria to halt testing in the air, in the atmosphere — that would ... respond with a challenge from the Soviet Union, we hope, to sit down and negotiate a treaty. That was done in 1960. I don't know what your lights are doing, Sandy.

MR. VANOCUR: You have another minute.

MS. FERRARO: O.K. I'm watching them blinking, so I have another minute. What that would do is, it would give us the opportunity to sit down and negotiate a treaty. That was done in 1960 by President Kennedy — in 1963. What he did was, he issued a challenge to the Soviet Union. He said, "We will not test in space ... in the atmosphere, if you will not." They did not. In two months, they sat down and they negotiated a treaty. We do not now have to worry about that ... about that type of testing. It can be done. It will be done, if only you have the will to do it. Again, remember — it's mutual, it is verifiable. And is a challenge — that once that challenge is not met, if testing were to resume, then we would continue testing as well.

MR. VANOCUR: Our last series of questions on foreign affairs from Mr. Boyd.

National Security

MR. BOYD: Congresswoman Ferraro, you have little or no experience in military matters, and yet you might someday find yourself Commander in Chief of the Armed Forces. How can you convince the American people, and a potential enemy, that you would know what to do to protect this nation's security? And do you think, in any way, that the Soviets might be tempted to try to take advantage of you simply because you are a woman?

MS. FERRARO: Are you saying that I would have to have fought in a war in order to love peace?

MR. BOYD: I'm not saying that. I'm asking you ... you know what I asked. [Applause]

MS. FERRARO: All right. I think what happens is, when you try to equate whether or not I've had military experience, that's the natural conclusion. It's about as valid as saying that you would have to be black in order to despise racism, that you'd have to be female in order to be terribly offended by sexism. That's just not so.

I think if you take a look at where I've been, both in the Congress and where I intend to go — the type of person I am — I think that the people of this country can rely upon the fact that I will be a leader. I don't think that the Soviet Union for one minute can sit down and make a determination on what I will do if I'm ever in a position to have to do something with reference to the Soviet Union. Quite frankly, I'm prepared to do whatever is necessary in order to secure this country and make sure that that security is maintained.

Secondly, if the Soviet Union were to ever believe that they could challenge the United States with any sort of nuclear forces or otherwise — if I were in a position of leadership in this country, they would be assured that they would be met with swift, concise, and certain retaliation.

MR. BOYD: I —

MS. FERRARO: Let me just say one other thing now.

MR. BOYD: O.K.

MS. FERRARO: The most important thing, though, I think, as a leader, that what one has to do, is get to the point where you're not put into that position. And the way you get to that position of moving away from having to make a decision on force or anything else, is by moving toward arms control. And that's not what's been done over the past four years. I think that if you were to take a look at the failures of this Administration, that would have to be number one. I will not put myself in that position as a leader in this country. I will move immediately toward arms control negotiations.

MR. BOYD: For my follow [up] I'm going to borrow a leaf from the Sunday night debate between your principals, and ask you what is the single question you would most like to ask your opponent here on foreign policy?

MS. FERRARO: Oh, I don't . . . I don't have a single-most question. I guess the concern that I have is a concern not only as the Vice Presidential candidate, but as a citizen in this country. My concern is that we are not doing anything to stop the arms race. And it seems to me that if we keep talking about military inferiority, which we do not have. . . . We are at a comparable level with the Soviet Union. Our Joint Chiefs of Staff have said they'd never exchange our military power for theirs. I guess the thing that I'd want is a commitment that, you know, pretty soon they're going to do something about making this a safer world, you know, for all of us.

MR. BOYD: Vice President Bush, four years ago President Reagan insisted that military buildup would bring the Soviets to negotiate seriously. Since then, we have spent almost a trillion dollars on defense, but the Soviets are still building their military forces as rapidly as we are, and there are no negotiations. Was the President's original premise, his whole strategy, wrong?

MR. BUSH: No. I think his strategy not only was correct, but is correct. You have to go back where we were. Clearly, when we came into office, the American people recognized that we had slipped into positions of inferiority on various things. Some of our planes, as the President points out, were older than the . . . older than the pilots . . . ships that couldn't . . . couldn't go out to sea. And you had a . . . you had a major problem with the military. Actually, the morale wasn't very good either. So, we have had to strengthen the military, and we're well on the way to getting that job done. America is back in terms of military strength, in terms of our ability to deter aggression and keep the peace.

At the same time, however, we have made proposals and proposals and proposals — sound proposals — on reducing nuclear weapons. The Strategic Arms Reduction Talks were good proposals. And it's the Soviets that left the table. The Intermediate Nuclear Force Talks were sound talks. And I wish the Soviet Union had continued them. The chemical weapon treaty to ban all chemical weapons — it was our initiative, not the Soviets'. And we wish they would think anew, and move forward to verification, so that everybody would know whether the other side was keeping its word. But, much more impor-

tant, you'd reduce the level of terror. Similarly, we're reducing, trying to talk to them, and are talking to them in Vienna, about conventional force reductions. We've talked to them about human rights. I've met with Mr. Andropov and Mr. Chernenko, and we mention, and we try to do something about the human rights question. This oppression of Soviet Jews is absolutely intolerable. And so we have to keep pushing forward on the moral grounds, as well as on the arms reduction grounds.

But it is my view that, because this President has been strong, and because we've redressed the imbalances — and I think we're very close to having . . . getting that job done — the Soviets are more likely to make a deal. The Soviets made an ABM treaty when they thought we were going to deploy an ABM system. So I am optimistic for the future, once they realize that they will have this strong, principled President to negotiate with — strong leadership — and yet with demonstrable flexibility on arms control.

MR. BOYD: And now I'll give you a chance, Mr. Vice President, to ask the question you'd most like to ask of your opponent.

MR. BUSH: I have . . . I have none I'd like to ask of her. But I'd sure like to use the time — talk about the World Series, or something of that nature.

Let me put it this way. I don't have any questions. We are so different from the. . . . The Reagan-Bush Administration is so different from the Carter-Mondale Administration, that the American people are going to have the clearest choice. It's the question of going back to the failed ideas of the past, where we came in: 21.5 percent on those interest rates, inflation, despair, malaise, no leadership, blaming the American people for failed leadership. Or another option — keep this recovery going till it benefits absolutely everybody. Peace at home, peace abroad, prosperity, opportunity — I'd like to hear her talk on those things, but I think the yellow light is flashing, and so we'll leave it there.

MR. VANOCUR: Nothing on the World Series?

MR. BUSH: Well . . . I'll go. . . .

MR. VANOCUR: Congresswoman Ferraro?

MS. FERRARO: I think the Vice President's comment about the Carter-Mondale Administration is an indication of just . . . it really typifies this Administration. It's an Administration that looks backwards, not forwards and into the future. I must say that I'm also tickled by their comments on human rights. [Applause] The Soviet Union, in 1979, allowed 51,000 people to emigrate. Because, in the large measure of this Administration's policies over the past four years, 1,313 people got out of the Soviet Union in 1983 and 1984. That's not a great record on human rights. It's certainly not a record on human rights achievements. This Administration spent a trillion dollars on defense, but it hasn't

gotten a trillion dollars of national security.

MR. VANOCUR: Vice President Bush, your rebuttal.

MR. BUSH: No rebuttal.

Closing Statements

MR. VANOCUR: Well, we then can go to the closing statements. Each statement will be four minutes in length, and we'll begin with the Vice President.

MR. BUSH: Well, in a couple of weeks, you, the American people will be faced — three weeks — with a choice. It's the clearest choice in some 50 years. And the choice is, do we move forward with strength and with prosperity, or do we go back to weakness, despair, disrespect? Ronald Reagan and I have put our trust in the American people. We've moved some of the power away from Washington, D.C., and put it back with the people. We're pulling together. The neighborhoods are safer because crime is going down. Your sons and daughters are doing better in school. Test scores are going up. There's a new opportunity lying out there in the future: science, technology, and space offering opportunity to everybody — all the young ones coming up. And abroad, there's new leadership and respect. And Ronald Reagan is clearly the strong leader of the free world. And I'll be honest with you: it's a joy to serve with a President who does not apologize for the United States of America.

Mr. Mondale, on the other hand, has one idea — go out and tax the American people. And then he wants to repeal indexing, to wipe out the one protection that those at the lowest end of the economic scale have — protecting them against being rammed into higher and higher tax brackets. We just owe our country too much to go back to that kind of an approach.

I'd like to say something to the young people. I started a business. I know what it is to have a dream and have a job and work hard to employ others and really to participate in the American dream. And some of you out there are finishing high school or college, and some of you are starting out in the working place. And we want for you America's greatest gift. And that is opportunity. And then on peace — yes, I did serve in combat. I was shot down when I was a young kid, scared to death. And all that did . . . saw friends die. But that heightened my convictions about peace. It is absolutely essential that we guarantee the young people that they will not know the agony of war. America's gift — opportunity and peace.

And now, we do have some unfinished business. We must continue to go ahead. The world is too complex to go back to vacillation and weakness. There's too much going on to go back to the failed policies of the past. The future is too bright not to give it our best shot. Together, we can go forward and lift America up to meet her greatest dreams. Thank you very much. [Applause]

MR. VANOCUR: Thank you very

much. I must say now, in matters of equity, you will be allowed applause at the end of your closing statement, so if you'd begin it now, please.

MS. FERRARO: I hope somebody wants to applaud. [Scattered laughter]

Being the candidate for Vice President of my party is the greatest honor I have ever had. But it's not only a personal achievement for Geraldine Ferraro, and certainly not only the bond that I feel as I go across this country with women throughout the country. I wouldn't be standing here if Fritz Mondale didn't have the courage and my party didn't stand for the values that it does: the values of fairness and equal opportunity. Those values make our country strong. And the future of this country, and how strong it will be, is what this election is all about.

Over the last two months, I've been traveling all over the country talking to the people about the future. I was in Kentucky and I spoke to the Deihaus family. He works as a ... for a car dealer, and he's worried about the deficits and how high interest rates are going to affect his job. Every place I go, I see young parents with their children, and they say to me, "What are we going to do to stop this nuclear arms race?" I was in Dayton, Ohio, a week and a half ago, and I sat with the Allen family, who live next door to a toxic dump, and they're very, very concerned about the fact

that those toxics are seeping into the water that they and their neighbors drink.

Those people love this country and they're patriotic. It's not the patriotism that you're seeing in the commercials as you watch television these days. Their patriotism is not only a pride in the country as it is, but pride in this country that is strong enough to meet the challenges of the future.

Do you know, when we find jobs for the eight and a half million people who are unemployed in this country, we will make our economy stronger, and that will be a patriotic act. When we reduce the deficits, we cut interest rates. And I know the President doesn't believe that, but it's so. We cut those interest rates — young people can buy houses. That's pro-family. And that will be a patriotic act. When we educate our children — oh, good Lord, they're going to be able to compete in a world economy, and that makes us stronger, and that's a patriotic act. When we stop the arms race, make this a safer, saner world, and that's a patriotic act. And when we keep the peace, young men don't die, and that's a patriotic act.

Those are the key to the future. And who can be the leader for the future? When Walter Mondale was Attorney General of Minnesota, he led the fight for a man who could not afford to get justice because he couldn't afford a lawyer. When he was in

the Senate, he fought for child nutrition programs. He wrote the House ... the Fair Housing Act. He even ... he even investigated the concerns and the abuses of migrant workers. And why did he do that? Those weren't popular causes. You know, no one had ever heard of ... Clarence Gideon, the man without a lawyer. Children don't vote and migrant workers aren't exactly a powerful lobby in this country. But he did it because it was right. Fritz Mondale has said that he'd rather lose a battle over decency than win one over self-interest and I agree with him.

This campaign is not over. For our country, for our future, for the principles we believe in, Walter Mondale and I have just begun to fight. [Applause]

MR. VANOCUR: Thank you very much. I'd like to thank Vice President Bush, Congresswoman Ferraro, the members of our panel, for joining us in this League of Women Voters debate. I'd like to join you in thanking them, the City of Philadelphia, and The League of Women Voters.

The League of Women Voters' next debate, the Presidential debate, will take place in Kansas City on October 21st. The subject will be foreign affairs, and it will begin at 8:00 p.m., Eastern time.

Again, our thanks. We hope you'll join us on the 21st.

Thank you.

VOTING STUDIES

CQ

Congress Seeks to Increase Role in Election Year

In the fourth year of President Reagan's administration, Congress sought to increase its role in shaping his domestic and foreign policy.

The main thrust of the president's programs remained intact. But through pivotal votes in the House and Senate, members were able to make the White House accept conditions on some programs to meet congressional objections — particularly on defense spending and Central America.

Members did not forget that 1984 was an election year, and concerns about the November balloting seemed most apparent in their votes on issues related to religion, crime and the "right to life."

The Senate dealt Reagan a clear defeat by rejecting a proposed constitutional amendment on school prayer. But four months later, under pressure from fundamentalist Christian religious groups, Congress cleared legislation that would allow student religious organizations to meet in high schools on the same terms and conditions as other student groups.

The final legislation was less sweeping than Reagan and his conservative allies had wanted, but it nevertheless was a vote that enabled members, concerned about the prayer issue, to cast what constituents might see as a "pro-religion" vote.

Consideration of the prayer amendment made 1984 the third year in a row that the Republican-controlled Senate had given Reagan a vote on a proposed constitutional amendment.

In 1982, the Senate passed a proposal to require a balanced federal budget, but the House rejected a similar amendment. And in 1983, the Senate rejected an anti-abortion amendment backed by Reagan.

Although there was no vote in 1984 on legislation to outlaw abortions, Congress addressed one aspect of the so-called right-to-life issue. Anti-abortion groups and those representing the disabled pushed successfully for legislation designed to protect severely handicapped infants from medical neglect.

Congress cleared major anti-crime legislation, after House Republicans forced a Senate-passed crime package (S 1762) onto the fiscal 1985 continuing appropriations resolution (H J Res 648). The president played a large role on this issue, hammering away at the Democratic-controlled House all year for stalling, even though the Judiciary Committee had been working steadily on individual anti-crime bills.

On balance, the administration pronounced the second session of the 98th Congress a success. Said M. B. Oglesby Jr., chief White House lobbyist: "We won more than we lost."

On some issues, such as crime, Oglesby said, "We had to keep the pressure on and it paid off." Among the biggest disappointments, he said, were failure to resolve proposed funding for Nicaraguan "contras," guerrillas who are fighting that country's leftist Sandinista government, and the school prayer vote.

"We put a lot of time into that," he said of the prayer issue. "Any time you lose, it's a disappointment."

One administration official conceded privately that because 1984 was an election year, the administration "played as much offense as defense. We had to try to stop some things, keep things under control," the official said.

Scraps Over MX, 'Contras'

Members' desire to play a larger role in 1984 was most apparent in foreign policy and defense, two areas where the president traditionally has wide discretion.

The administration had made production of the MX missile its highest priority among a number of controversial nuclear arms issues. While congressional opponents failed to kill the MX, they succeeded in putting limits on funding for production of the missile. If the president decided to pursue MX production in 1985, the House and Senate each must approve resolutions allowing the production money to be spent.

Similarly, Congress carved out a continuing role for itself in funding for the Nicaraguan contras. Members voted to bar any further aid to the contras until March 1985. Thus, if assistance to the Nicaraguan rebels was to continue, it would have to be approved by Congress.

Congress was even able to show some strength on economic policy, an area that Reagan had dominated early in his administration. The Republican-controlled Senate, hung up for a month on deficit reduction plans, finally reached a compromise agreement that was crafted with the White House at the insistence of Senate Republican leaders.

The final plan was agreed to only after other alternatives were rejected — one of them a Democratic plan that lost on a 49-49 tie and had drawn support from Republican moderates.

How Votes Were Selected

Congressional Quarterly each year selects a series of key votes on major issues.

Selection of Issues. An issue is judged by the extent it represents one or more of the following:

● A matter of major controversy.

● A matter of presidential or political power.

● A decision of potentially great impact on the nation and lives of Americans.

Selection of Votes. For each group of related votes on an issue, one key vote usually is chosen. This is the vote, in the opinion of Congressional Quarterly editors, that was important in determining the outcome.

In the description of the key votes, the designation "ND" denotes Northern Democrats and "SD" denotes Southern Democrats.

Senate Key Votes

1. School Prayer

The Senate March 20 rejected a proposed constitutional amendment to permit organized, recited prayer in public schools and other public places. It was the first time since 1970 that the Senate had voted on a constitutional amendment on school prayer; then, a similar though not identical proposal was rejected. The House did not consider any constitutional amendment on prayer in 1984.

The vote on the Senate proposal (S J Res 73) was 56-44, 11 shy of the two-thirds majority required. Republicans voted for the amendment 37-18, while Democrats opposed it, 19-26 (ND 6-25, SD 13-1).

The vote was a setback for President Reagan, who had lobbied for the amendment, and for fundamentalist Christian groups, which had pressed for a constitutional amendment to overturn a series of Supreme Court decisions since 1962 that barred prayers and Bible readings in the public schools.

Before voting on S J Res 73, the Senate defeated, 81-15, an alternative proposal that would have allowed group silent prayer in public schools.

The defeat of the prayer amendment resulted in a strategy shift by proponents of school prayer. Within weeks, they turned their attention to enacting a law to allow student religious groups to meet in public schools on the same terms as other student groups. *(House key vote 6)*

2. Farm Bill

The administration won a qualified victory after trying for more than a year to halt scheduled increases in a major type of crop price support, target prices. What began as a thrift measure became, for many members, an election-year cornucopia of concessions to farmers by the time it cleared the House April 3.

Still, the target price freeze (HR 4072 — PL 98-258) was an achievement for the administration because it meant that bidding on future levels for the important price support program would start at lower levels in 1985, when Congress was scheduled to reauthorize farm programs in an omnibus farm bill.

The target price program provided cash to farmers when market prices for major crops dropped below statutory "targets." In its 1981 farm bill the administration had sought, without success, to end the program. By 1983, administration officials were urging Congress to halt the expensive annual boosts in the targets, arguing that they encouraged farmers to overproduce for surplus-glutted markets.

Farm lobbyists told the administration they would give up the scheduled support increases if they got something in return. The basic bill was negotiated in private sessions with the administration and farm-state senators; progress occasionally stalled as commodity groups voiced new requests. As the Senate was winding up debate on the bill, a final adjustment for rice producers was being completed off the floor. The freeze bill passed the Senate March 22 on a 78-10 vote, with Republicans voting 50-2, Democrats 28-8 (ND 20-4, SD 8-4). By that time, it had acquired paid acreage reductions for crops in 1985 (with early payments to participants in 1984), liberalized loan terms for Farmers Home Administration borrowers, and administration commitments to boost farm exports and food donations abroad.

The final version of the farm measure emerged from the House-Senate conference little changed from the Senate-passed bill.

3. El Salvador Aid

Nearly three years after the Reagan administration began providing substantial amounts of military aid to help the government of El Salvador fight leftist guerrillas, the Senate in March and April held its first major debate on U.S. policy in the region.

Pending before the Senate, as it acted on an "urgent" fiscal 1984 supplemental appropriations bill (H J Res 492 — PL 98-332) was a Reagan request for $92.7 million in military aid to the Salvadoran regime, on top of $64.8 million that Congress had approved previously for the year. Early during Senate consideration of the issue, the administration settled for a compromise figure of $61.75 million, negotiated by Daniel K. Inouye, D-Hawaii. But other Democrats, among them leading critics of Reagan's policies in Central America, pressed for a much lower figure of $21 million, which they said was enough to keep the Salvadoran army supplied through that country's presidential election in May.

On April 2, the Senate rejected an amendment by Edward M. Kennedy, D-Mass., that would have allowed only $21 million in additional Salvador aid. The vote was 25-63: R 2-48; D 23-15 (ND 21-5, SD 2-10).

Coupled with House approval on May 10 of a foreign aid authorizations bill (HR 5119) containing all of Reagan's requests for El Salvador, the Senate's April 2 vote helped end a longstanding debate in Congress about the wisdom of U.S. involvement in the civil war in that country.

Congress eventually approved the $61.75 million included in the urgent supplemental, plus another $70 million for El Salvador in a later supplemental (HR 6040 — PL 98-396), bringing the total for fiscal 1984 to $196.55 million. *(House key vote 5)*

4. Troops in El Salvador

During Senate debate on the "urgent" supplemental appropriations bill for fiscal 1984 (H J Res 492 — PL 98-332), a majority of Democrats decided to put that chamber on record on the question of limiting the president's discretion to send combat troops to Central America. Reagan long had insisted that he had no intention of involving U.S. forces directly in Central America's civil wars. But some Democrats expressed a belief that Reagan would send troops to the region to avert the spread of communism, and they wanted Congress to play a direct role in any such decision.

The Senate on March 29 rejected, by wide margins, two proposals by Edward M. Kennedy, D-Mass., requiring congressional authorization for the introduction of combat troops in Central America.

Early in April, most Senate Democrats reached agreement on another proposal that would have required the president to seek congressional authorization before sending combat troops into or over El Salvador. An exception would be made if introduction of troops was needed immediately to evacuate U.S. citizens. On April 4, Patrick J. Leahy, D-Vt., offered that proposal as an amendment to H J Res 492, and it was tabled on a 59-36 vote: R 49-5; D 10-31 (ND 2-25, SD 8-6). Because the amendment had support from a broad range of Democrats, it was the clearest test in 1984 of congressional sentiment on the issue of direct U.S. involvement in Central America's wars.

5. Tax Indexing

Ever since Congress agreed in 1981 to index federal income taxes to offset the effects of inflation, Democrats and some moderate Republicans had been trying to repeal or delay the law, set to go into effect in 1985. They had argued that a country with annual budget deficits approaching $200 billion could ill afford to reduce taxes approximately $51 billion over the next three years.

But they had been defeated every time — in part because of Reagan's strong support of indexing. He repeatedly threatened to veto any change in indexing or the across-the-board income tax cuts in the Economic Recovery Tax Act of 1981.

In a last attempt to change indexing before it went into effect, Sen. John H. Chafee, R-R.I., proposed an amendment to the Deficit Reduction Act of 1984 (HR 2163) to delay the Jan. 1, 1985, effective date for three years. Critics argued that the delay would hit middle-income taxpayers the hardest. But Chafee replied that the best way to help "the taxpayers of this country is to reduce the deficit."

His arguments failed to convince most of his GOP colleagues and even some Democrats, whose standard-bearer Walter F. Mondale had made an indexing delay part of his economic program. A motion by Finance Committee Chairman Robert Dole, R-Kan., to table (kill) Chafee's amendment was agreed to April 10, 57-38: R 46-7; D 11-31 (ND 8-22, SD 3-9).

6. Real Estate Taxes

Congress tried again, as it had done for the past three years, to help reduce the federal deficit by raising revenues through a hodgepodge of tax measures, including some to close loopholes and improve taxpayer compliance. As before, legislators faced strong lobbying pressure from interest groups to back away from proposed tax hikes.

A key challenge to 1984 efforts came from the real estate industry, which objected to a Finance Committee proposal to increase from 15 to 20 years the minimum time period over which a building could be depreciated, or written off against taxes. Proponents of the change argued that the shorter time period was overly generous and had spurred the growth of abusive real estate tax shelters. Opponents argued that a 20-year depreciation requirement would inhibit investment in real estate.

But the influence of the real estate industry was evident during the Senate floor debate on the Deficit Reduction Act of 1984 (HR 2163), which included provisions to raise $47.7 billion in taxes through fiscal 1987. An amendment by Rudy Boschwitz, R-Minn., to set the real estate depreciation period at 20 years in 1984, 19 years in 1985 and 18 years thereafter was adopted early April 13, 62-19: R 37-8; D 25-11 (ND 17-10, SD 8-1). To help offset revenue losses, the Boschwitz amendment included a provision to reduce tax credits for the rehabilitation of old buildings.

Finance Committee Chairman Robert Dole, R-Kan., who had fought to keep the committee package intact, said: "You do around here what you have the votes to do. The point is [the real estate interests] have the votes."

In conference, the rehabilitation tax credit change was dropped and the real estate depreciation period was set at 18 years (PL 98-369).

7. Deficit-Reduction Plan

In the culmination of four weeks of bitter debate, the Senate on May 17 accepted a modified deficit-reduction package backed by Reagan and the Senate GOP leadership.

The plan was adopted 65-32: R 53-0; D 12-32 (ND 6-24, SD 6-8). But the margin of approval belied the intensity of the chamber's struggle over budget-cutting proposals.

Acceptance of the "Rose Garden" plan, so called because Reagan endorsed it in the White House Rose Garden March 15, was guaranteed once Senate Majority Leader Howard H. Baker Jr., R-Tenn., and White House officials struck a deal with GOP dissidents who had been pressing for higher domestic spending.

Proposals aimed at trimming federal deficits were debated at length in both the House and Senate. The House approved a measure to slash deficits by $182 billion through 1987. The Rose Garden plan called for $140 billion in deficit cuts through the same period. *(House key vote 3)*

Key components of the Senate plan were three-year spending caps on defense and domestic spending. Under the caps, military spending authority would rise by 7 percent annually; the budget for other discretionary spending would be $139.8 billion in fiscal 1985, $144.3 billion in fiscal 1986 and $151.5 billion in fiscal 1987. Taxes would increase by $47.7 billion under the Senate plan, about the same as in the House budget. The House budget called for annual defense spending to rise at a 3.5 percent rate, adjusted for inflation.

Passage of the Rose Garden plan was preceded by close votes on several alternative spending cut/tax increase measures. In one plan, Senate Democrats sought to cut deficits by $204 billion; among the provisions were limiting defense growth to 4 percent and delaying tax indexing for two years. That plan failed May 8 on a 49-49 tie. On May 10 the Senate, 48-46, shelved a plan supported by GOP moderates that would have combined the defense and domestic spending caps and given appropriating committees some leeway in shifting money from defense to social programs.

The GOP leadership broke the logjam May 16 when it convinced five moderate Republicans to support a proposal adding $2 billion to the non-defense appropriations cap. The Senate accepted the plan, 62-37.

The Rose Garden plan vote came the next day on an amendment to HR 2163, a miscellaneous trade bill. The tax provisions were added to HR 4170 (PL 98-369); the spending targets were incorporated in S Con Res 106.

House-Senate agreement on defense spending hung up resolution of spending questions until the closing days of the session.

8. Anti-Missile Defense

By a margin of two votes, the Senate on June 13 killed an amendment that would have trimmed $100 million from Reagan's proposal to develop a space-based defense against Soviet ballistic missiles. This was the first vote taken in either house on Reagan's "strategic defense initiative" — which critics had labeled "Star Wars."

The vote came on an amendment to the fiscal 1985 defense authorization bill (S 2723). Reagan requested $1.78 billion for development of the anti-missile project and the Senate Armed Services Committee had trimmed the amount to $1.63 billion. An amendment by Charles H. Percy, R-Ill., that would have further reduced the amount was tabled, and thus killed, 47-45: R 40-10; D 7-35 (ND 3-26, SD 4-9).

When Reagan called for the initiative in a televised address on March 23, 1983, he set the sweeping goal of making nuclear weapons "impotent and obsolete." Many observers took this statement to mean that the new program would substitute a "leak-proof" defense for the long-standing U.S. policy of deterring Soviet attack by threat of nuclear retaliation.

Critics of Reagan's Star Wars plan argued almost unanimously that a perfect defense would be impossible. At best, they warned, a U.S. effort to develop such weapons would extend the arms race to outer space and shatter the 1972 U.S.-Soviet treaty limiting anti-missile defenses.

There was no corresponding floor vote in the House, where opponents of Reagan's plans for new weapons in space concentrated on trying to block tests of the anti-satellite (ASAT) missile. The House version of the fiscal 1985 defense appropriations bill slashed funding for the anti-missile plan to $1.1 billion. The final appropriations compromise was $1.4 billion.

9. MX Missile

The Senate June 14 approved continued production of MX intercontinental missiles, but only by the vote of Vice President George Bush. Bush broke a 48-48 tie, to table, and thus kill, an amendment to the fiscal 1985 defense authorization bill (S 2723) that would have barred production of additional MXs in fiscal 1985.

In 1983, Congress had narrowly approved production of the first 21 MXs.

Though barring production of more missiles in fiscal 1985, the June 14 amendment would have approved several hundred million dollars in MX-related procurement funds so that the missile production line would be kept available to resume production if the missile were approved in fiscal 1986. The precise mechanics of the amendment were obscure, but its intent was clear: it gave senators a chance to register their unhappiness with Reagan's MX plan without taking political responsibility for voting to kill the program.

MX, which would be the first U.S. long-range ballistic missile with enough power and accuracy to attack armored Soviet missile launchers and command posts, had been the centerpiece of the administration's nuclear arms program. The administration argued that the rapidity with which they could hit their targets gave ICBMs much more symbolic "clout" than other nuclear weapons and that the current Soviet advantage in such weapons was intolerable.

Most MX opponents rejected the administration's focus on land-based missiles such as the MX, arguing that Soviet advantages in such weapons could be offset by U.S. advantages in other kinds of nuclear arms. Moreover, they said, since MX would be deployed in existing missile silos, which were vulnerable to Soviet attack, the new and more powerful missile would simply increase Moscow's incentive to launch a first strike in case of a severe superpower crisis.

The GOP-led Senate clearly was not prepared to vote to kill MX: Shortly before the key vote, it voted 55-41 to kill an amendment that would have denied MX production funds in fiscal 1985. But by abandoning in early 1983 the long search for an invulnerable way to deploy MX, Reagan paved the way for a weakening of support for the program reflected in the June 14 vote to table the anti-production amendment: R 43-10; D 5-38 (ND 2-28, SD 3-10) with Bush casting a "yea" vote to break the 48-48 tie.

The House had voted to block additional MX production unless Congress voted in 1985 to allow it. *(House key vote 9)*

The final compromise allowed production of a second batch of 21 MXs if Congress passed two resolutions approving that move in the spring of 1985.

10. Aid to Nicaraguan 'Contras'

For Congress and the Reagan administration, the most contentious foreign policy issue was the so-called "secret" war in Nicaragua. Since early 1982, thousands of U.S.-paid and equipped guerrillas, called "contras," were battling the leftist government of Nicaragua. The House Democratic leadership in 1983 staked out a clear position in opposition to the war. But until early 1984, the administration had backing for the war from key Democrats in the Senate, especially from members of the Intelligence Committee.

In April, Senate Intelligence Committee Chairman Barry Goldwater, R-Ariz., disclosed on the Senate floor that the CIA had helped the contras mine three Nicaraguan harbors. Goldwater and other committee members were outraged, not so much by the mining as by the fact that the CIA had not notified them in advance.

The immediate product of that outrage was the Senate's adoption on April 10 of a non-binding statement opposing the mining. Also as a result of the mining, several Democrats on the Senate Intelligence Committee — among them committee Vice Chairman Daniel Patrick Moynihan, N.Y., and former Chairman Daniel K. Inouye, Hawaii — decided to drop their support for the Nicaraguan war.

On June 18, as the Senate was debating the fiscal 1985 defense authorizations bill (S 2723), Edward M. Kennedy, D-Mass., offered an amendment stating that the bill did not authorize U.S. aid to the contras. To that amendment, Inouye offered a substitute authorizing $2 million to move the contras out of Nicaragua and $4 million for their "humanitarian support" once they left.

The Senate tabled the underlying Kennedy amendment, taking with it Inouye's substitute proposal, by a vote of 58-38: R 48-6; D 10-32 (ND 2-26, SD 8-6). Nevertheless, the vote showed that support for the Nicaraguan war was fading in the Senate. Among the 38 who opposed the war were five Intelligence Committee members who previously had backed it: Moynihan; Inouye; Lloyd Bentsen, D-Texas; Walter D. Huddleston, D-Ky., and William S. Cohen, R-Maine.

A week later, on June 25, the Senate voted 88-1 to delete Reagan's pending request for $21 million to continue aid to the contras through fiscal 1984. In October, conferees on a fiscal 1985 continuing appropriations resolution (H J Res 648 — PL 98-473) decided to bar any aid to the contras until March 1985. *(House key vote 8)*

11. Drunken Driving

Faced with an intense lobbying effort by relatives of victims of drunken driving, Congress acted to pressure states into raising their minimum drinking age to 21. The law (HR 4616 — PL 98-363) would withhold a portion of federal highway funds if a state did not set its minimum drinking age at 21 by 1987.

When the proposal surfaced in a House committee early in 1984, it was opposed by the administration as an infringement on states' rights. The administration argued that establishing the legal drinking age had been a state prerogative, and 27 states allowed people younger than 21 to purchase or possess alcohol.

Nevertheless, in June the House by voice vote added to a highway funding bill an amendment that would withhold certain funds from states that did not have a 21-year limit. As Congress raced toward the July 4 recess, prospects for enactment were clouded because floor action on the Senate's highway bill had been blocked by various disputes.

A group called Mothers Against Drunk Drivers (MADD) and a number of other organizations continued their crusade backing a national drinking age limit, maintaining that the varying laws created a patchwork quilt of "blood borders" that let young people drive across state lines to drink in states with low minimum ages, causing accidents on their way home.

The mothers buttonholed legislators like veteran campaigners, creating an atmosphere that Sen. Gordon J. Humphrey, R-N.H., called "a public relations effort over the last 10 days which has panicked half the town." The president switched position and supported the legislation.

The path for the legislation was cleared June 21 when senators reached a compromise that combined the withholding of funds if the 21-year limit was not established and providing incentive grants for states to establish other safety programs. When the compromise came up on the Senate floor June 26 in the form of an amendment offered by Frank R. Lautenberg, D-N.J., it was opposed by a handful of members who opposed the coercive approach of withholding funds, and by some who thought it unfairly discriminated against an age group.

But after rejecting an attempt to substitute a financial incentive program for the punitive approach, the Senate whisked the Lautenberg amendment through by a vote of 81-16: R 45-10; D 36-6 (ND 25-3, SD 11-3). Two days later the House agreed to the Senate amendment, clearing the measure for the president.

12. Appropriations Holdup

Upset with Senate unwillingness to resolve defense spending issues and angered at the chamber's virtual dismissal of the congressional budget process, Democrats led by Lawton Chiles, D-Fla., stopped the chamber's work for a week in early August. The first attempt to limit the Democratic filibuster failed, 54-31: R 46-3; D 8-28 (ND 4-20, SD 4-8). Although a second motion to cut off debate succeeded, the Democrats' ploy eventually forced the GOP leadership to agree to negotiations with the House leaders on Pentagon spending.

The Democratic filibuster began Aug. 1, when Chiles objected to a motion to waive provisions of the 1974 Congressional Budget and Impoundment Control Act (PL 93-344) and take up the fiscal 1985 agriculture appropriations bill (HR 5743). The act required Congress to adopt a budget resolution before considering appropriations bills. The Senate had previously agreed to waive the Budget Act to debate fiscal 1985 funding bills; the House May 22 approved a blanket waiver for all 1985 appropriations bills.

A House-Senate conference on the budget resolution (H Con Res 280) had stalled over setting a fiscal 1985 spending level for defense. The Senate plan envisioned a 7 percent increase; the House plan, 3.5 percent.

Chiles' crusade struck a chord among his colleagues, and Majority Leader Howard H. Baker Jr., R-Tenn., Aug. 6 fell six votes short of the necessary 60 to cut off the Chiles-led filibuster. Cloture was invoked Aug. 8, 68-30, but Chiles immediately threatened to object to a Budget Act waiver when the GOP leadership put the District of Columbia appropriations bill on the schedule.

Chiles Aug. 9 suggested that the defense spending impasse could be broken at a "summit" meeting of the Republican and Democratic leadership and the chairmen of the Budget and defense authorizing committees and the Defense appropriations subcommittees. Baker, faced with Chiles' vow to continue objecting to budget waiver, endorsed the summit meeting proposal, and Chiles withdrew his filibuster threat.

13. Civil Rights

Civil rights advocates were stymied in an effort to pass legislation ensuring that no part of an institution receiving federal funds could discriminate on the basis of race, sex, age or handicap.

The bill (HR 5490, S 2568) would have overturned the Supreme Court's Feb. 28 ruling in *Grove City College v. Bell*, which narrowed the reach of Title IX of the 1972 Education Amendments. The court ruled that the law's ban on sex bias in any education "program or activity" receiving federal funds applied only to the program getting aid and not to the entire institution. Three other laws barring discrimination on race, age or handicap had similar wording, and civil rights lawyers warned that the court's ruling could restrict their enforcement as well. The *Grove City* bill would have amended all four laws to make clear that any "recipient" of aid, not just the program or activity involved, would have to conform to the anti-bias laws.

The House passed HR 5490 by a 375-32 margin June 26. But in the Senate, opponents led by Orrin G. Hatch, R-Utah, kept S 2568 bottled up in the Labor and Human Resources Committee. Majority Leader Howard H. Baker Jr., R-Tenn., refused to call up the House version for floor debate, so supporters of the measure sought to attach the measure to the fiscal 1985 continuing appropriations resolution (H J Res 648).

The key vote came Sept. 27 when Minority Leader Robert C. Byrd, D-W.Va., offered the civil rights measure as an amendment to H J Res 648 and asked the Senate to determine whether the amendment, a legislative proposal, was "germane" to the funding bill. The Senate decided that it was germane, and therefore eligible for further action, by a vote of 51-48: R 12-42; D 39-6 (ND 30-1, SD 9-5).

However, Hatch had offered amendments to the funding bill on school busing, gun control and tuition tax credits. The Senate became tied in a procedural knot, with these issues obstructing movement on the funding bill. After four days, Sen. Bob Packwood, R-Ore., a chief sponsor of the civil rights bill, moved to table, and thus kill, the *Grove City* amendment. His motion was agreed to 53-45, ending the civil rights fight for the 98th Congress. The other amendments then fell.

House Key Votes

1. Handicapped Infants

Entering a touchy area of medical and ethical controversy, the House Feb. 2 approved legislation (HR 1904 — PL 98-457) designed to protect severely handicapped infants from medical neglect.

Backed by the administration, right-to-life groups and advocates for the disabled, the legislation was drafted in response to widely publicized "Baby Doe" cases, in which doctors and families had withheld medical treatment and care that handicapped infants needed to stay alive.

HR 1904 required states, as a condition of receiving federal aid for child abuse prevention programs, to have procedures for reporting cases in which handicapped infants were denied treatment for life-threatening conditions. The American Medical Association (AMA) and other critics saw the bill as an unwarranted government intrusion in the decisions of families and physicians.

The key House vote came on an amendment by Rod Chandler, R-Wash., to strike the "Baby Doe" language and instead require the Department of Health and Human Services to issue guidelines for hospitals that wanted to set up advisory panels on the treatment of handicapped babies.

The Chandler amendment, supported by the AMA and other medical organizations, was rejected by the House 182-231: R 31-131; D 151-100 (ND 97-69, SD 54-31).

The opposition of many medical groups to the bill was later blunted, when the Senate adopted a revised version that made clear that doctors would not have to take heroic steps to save the life of an infant if treatment would be futile. But even the compromise language, which was largely incorporated by a conference committee into the final version of the bill, did not go far enough to win the support of the AMA.

2. Water Project Cost-Sharing

The administration and Western states triumphed March 20 when the House voted against asking local beneficiaries of federal dams in the West to help pay for safety repairs. The vote, which pitted region against region, came on an amendment that substituted a mostly federal payment formula for a beneficiary-pays formula sought by environmentalists and taxpayer groups.

The amendment was adopted 194-192: R 75-73; D 119-119 (ND 61-91, SD 58-28).

This was a crucial vote on the cost-sharing issue, which had split Congress for at least eight years and stopped the authorization of most new water projects. The bill in question (HR 1652) authorized $650 million in work to repair and rebuild unsafe, aging dams located largely in the West.

The vote represented a turnaround from April 29, 1982, when the House by 212-140 adopted a user-pays amendment to a similar dam repair bill. But the House was following the lead of Reagan, who had done his own about-face on cost-sharing for dam safety projects. The president's switch, outlined in a Jan. 24 policy statement, seemed a direct response to the pleas of Republicans from the West, a bastion of Reagan support in the 1980 election. Fifteen Western GOP senators had warned Reagan in 1983 that his re-election hopes, and their own, could be damaged by policies that appeared "anti-West" and "anti-water."

The House's vote was partly offset by the Senate, which approved a version with some cost-sharing requirements after filibuster threats by Howard M. Metzenbaum, D-Ohio. That version was enacted (PL 98-404).

3. Adoption of the Budget Resolution

House approval of a fiscal 1985 budget resolution capped an effort by House Democratic leaders to devise a deficit-cutting strategy that would be easy to explain to constituents and exhibit the party's commitment to fiscal discipline. The vote was 250-168: R 21-139; D 229-29 (ND 159-13, SD 70-16).

The resolution (H Con Res 280) did nothing to reduce federal deficits; rather, it set fiscal targets. Once adopted April 5, however, it led the way to House approval of a measure (HR 4170 — PL 98-369) raising $49.2 billion in taxes through fiscal 1987, and other deficit-cutting measures. H Con Res 280 envisioned deficit reductions totaling $182 billion through 1987. The Senate's "Rose Garden" plan called for cuts of $140 billion through the same period. *(Senate key vote 7)*

The plan's key feature was the "pay-as-you-go" concept, which barred spending boosts above inflation, except for defense and a small number of programs for the poor, for which there would have to be offsetting tax hikes. Republicans attacked pay-as-you-go as a "simple sham," but the scheme's apparent appeal as prudent budgeting and the Democratic leaders' backing ensured its approval.

The plan called for defense spending to grow at 3.5 percent a year, adjusted for inflation. Differences with the GOP-led Senate, whose package would have raised Pentagon spending 7 percent a year, blocked consideration of the budget resolution until the end of the session.

4. Physician Fee Freeze

Having previously clamped new Medicare spending limits on hospitals and raised beneficiaries' out-of-pocket costs, Congress in 1984 turned to doctors to cut costs of the financially troubled program.

The basic plan — a freeze on increases in Medicare payments to doctors — was backed by congressional leaders, the administration and the American Medical Association (AMA).

But the AMA objected vehemently to a related "mandatory assignment" plan that would force doctors to accept the "frozen" Medicare fees as full payment for their services. (Assignment, optional under existing law, meant that a doctor would bill Medicare directly and accept program payment as full reimbursement for his services. The law also permitted doctors to bill Medicare beneficiaries directly, charging more than Medicare would pay and requiring the beneficiary to pay the difference.)

The House in April rejected freeze plans, both with mandatory assignment provisions and without. Yet by June, Congress had approved a Medicare fee freeze along with a "voluntary" assignment plan that levied substantial financial penalties on doctors who did not accept assignment. Both were included in a larger "deficit reduction" tax and spending-cut bill (HR 4170 — PL 98-369), cleared by the Senate June 27.

When the House debated an earlier version of the bill (HR 5394) on April 12, Rep. Andrew Jacobs Jr., D-Ind., proposed a yearlong freeze on Medicare physician fees for inpatient hospital care, with provisions that would have effectively deprived doctors of hospital admitting privileges if they refused assignment. Jacobs offered the amendment on the floor after failing to get majority support for it in the Ways and Means Committee.

Opponents argued that assignment would harm elderly Medicare beneficiaries by discouraging doctors from treating them. And, they said, assignment would not in itself save the government any money. (Government savings from the freeze had been estimated at nearly a billion dollars.)

Supporters said mandatory assignment was essential to keep doctors from raising their fees despite the freeze and passing along the extra cost to Medicare patients.

But the House rejected Jacobs' plan by voice vote. It then rejected by 172-242 a Republican motion to recommit the bill to committee with instructions to add a freeze on both inpatient and outpatient fees for Medicare, without mandatory assignment. The vote on recommittal reflected mixed motives. Some members were unwilling to freeze the doctor fees without an assignment plan to protect Medicare patients against higher costs.

The recommittal motion also forced a rare choice between competing health priorities because it also would have struck from the bill a new Medicaid child health initiative that was backed by the Democratic leadership.

And finally, a vote to recommit is generally viewed by the majority as an undesirable surrender to the minority. The 172-242 vote against the recommittal motion split along party lines: R 157-2; D 15-240 (ND 3-170, SD 12-70).

The Senate subsequently included in its deficit reduction plan a one-year Medicare fee freeze, with a new voluntary assignment program and a modified second-year freeze for doctors not participating in assignment.

That plan also disturbed the AMA, but the final bill coupled a "voluntary" plan with a 15-month Medicare freeze on both inpatient and outpatient services. Doctors staying out of the assignment plan were still subject to the freeze and faced penalties in future calculations of Medicare fees at the end of the freeze. The AMA subsequently filed a lawsuit challenging the constitutionality of the assignment provisions.

5. El Salvador Aid

On May 6, voters in El Salvador went to the polls and made José Napoleón Duarte, leader of the center-left Christian Democratic Party, their first freely elected president in some 50 years.

Four days later, members of the U.S. House of Representatives cast their first votes in three years on the issue of U.S. military aid to El Salvador. The result was a close, but decisive, victory for Reagan's program of increasing financial backing of the Salvadoran regime.

The key vote came as the House was considering a bill (HR 5119) authorizing foreign aid programs in fiscal 1984-85. The House adopted an amendment by William S. Broomfield, R-Mich., approving all the aid Reagan sought for El Salvador and other Central American countries. The vote was 212-208: R 156-8; D 56-200 (ND 7-167, SD 49-33).

The immediate effect of the vote was to break a political logjam on another piece of legislation — an "urgent" supplemental spending bill (H J Res 492) including $61.75 million for El Salvador. Over the longer term, the vote demonstrated that members of Congress were willing to give Duarte enough aid to keep his government afloat in its battle against leftist guerrillas. *(Senate key vote 3)*

6. Religious Groups in Schools

In the wake of the Senate's rejection of a constitutional amendment to allow prayer in public schools, controversy over religion in the schools shifted to another legislative battleground. *(Senate key vote 1)*

An administration-backed bill (HR 5345) to allow student religious groups to meet in public high schools was narrowly defeated by the House May 15. Another version of the so-called "equal access" proposal later cleared Congress (HR 1310 — PL 98-377), but only after supporters agreed to several key changes to address criticisms made during House debate on HR 5345.

HR 5345 would have cut off federal funds to high schools that refused to allow religious groups to meet on school premises if other student organizations were granted such access. Critics saw it as a "back door" effort to bring prayer into the schools. But supporters of HR 5345 included some members who opposed the prayer amendment; many in Congress saw the access bill as a way to show constituents that they were not hostile to religion.

HR 5345 garnered a majority of votes, but it fell short of the two-thirds margin needed to pass because it had been brought up under special procedures that barred amendments. The House vote was 270-151: R 147-17; D 123-134 (ND 47-122, SD 76-12).

In later Senate action, a companion school access proposal was redrawn to extend the bill's protections to political and other student groups — not just religious ones. That and other changes blunted the opposition of some critics who objected to singling out religious groups for special protection. The revised Senate proposal was cleared by Congress as an amendment to a popular education bill.

7. Anti-Satellite Test Ban

By a hefty margin, the House voted for a moratorium on tests of the anti-satellite (ASAT) missile against a target in space, so long as Moscow observed a similar restriction.

Pointing out that the Soviet Union had tested ASAT weapons about 20 times since the late 1960s, the administration argued that a similar U.S. weapon was needed to give the Russians an incentive to negotiate the mutual abolition of ASATs. But that argument was clouded by the administration's insistence that the U.S. ASAT was needed to neutralize some Soviet satellites that could guide Soviet weapons against U.S. units in case of war.

ASAT opponents argued that the current Soviet version was primitive and could not be used in any realistic military scenario to blind U.S. satellites. However, they warned, U.S. deployment of its superior weapon would move Moscow to develop an equally capable ASAT. This would threaten communications satellites, on which the United States was more dependent than was Moscow. Accordingly, the critics argued, it would be worth allowing the Russians a symbolic monopoly on ASATs in hopes of averting development of effective anti-satellite arms.

The key House vote came May 23 on an amendment to the fiscal 1985 defense authorization bill that was adopted 238-181: R 39-122; D 199-59 (ND 162-10, SD 37-49).

The Senate voted to bar ASAT target tests unless the president certified his willingness to negotiate "the strictest possible limits" on the weapons. The final version of the defense authorization bill (HR 5167) allowed only two "successful" ASAT target tests in fiscal 1985. The final defense appropriations measure, included in an omnibus continuing resolution (H J Res 648 — PL 98-473) barred any target tests until March 1, 1985, and allowed only three tests in the remainder of the fiscal year.

8. Aid to Nicaraguan 'Contras'

Reaffirming its opposition to the U.S.-backed war in Nicaragua, the House on May 24 rejected Reagan's request for $21 million to continue aiding Nicaraguan rebels in fiscal 1984. The vote was 241-177: R 24-132; D 217-45 (ND 169-6, SD 48-39). The Democratic-controlled House had voted twice in 1983 against CIA aid to several thousand guerrillas, called "contras," who were battling to overthrow the leftist government of Nicaragua. Coupled with diminishing support in the Senate for aiding the rebels, the May 24 vote on a 1984 supplemental funding bill (H J Res 492) forced Reagan to back down on his request. The vote also gave House leaders a strong hand in negotiations later on aid to the contras for fiscal 1985. With House leaders refusing to back down, the administration was forced to accept a prohibition on further aid until February 1985. *(Senate key vote 10)*

9. MX Missile

A yearlong campaign against the MX missile finally eked out a two-vote margin of victory on the night of May 31. The House adopted an amendment to the defense authorization bill (HR 5167) barring production of additional MX missiles in fiscal 1985 unless Congress adopted a joint resolution after April 1, 1985, approving the move.

MX production had been the administration's highest political priority among many controversial nuclear arms issues. According to the administration, it was imperative to break the Soviets' monopoly on large, accurate, land-based missiles to persuade them to negotiate sharp reductions in their arsenal of more than 600 such weapons.

Opponents warned that since MX could attack Soviet missiles but would itself be vulnerable to Soviet attack, the nuclear balance would be much less stable if MX were deployed. In a series of votes in 1983, an intense, grass-roots lobbying campaign closed in on the MX.

On May 15, 1984, an effort to kill outright MX procurement failed by six votes. But two weeks later, after the House Democratic leadership lent new horsepower to the anti-MX campaign, the amendment blocking MX production until after a vote in the spring of 1985 was adopted 199-197: R 17-141; D 182-56 (ND 149-15, SD 33-41).

The Senate had narrowly agreed to production of 21 of the 40 MXs Reagan had requested. In the end, Congress approved 21 missiles, but barred use of the funds unless it passed two joint resolutions of approval next March.

10. Immigration

In a dramatic June 20 roll call, the House passed a comprehensive immigration reform bill by a five-vote margin. The controversial measure (HR 1510) had been working its way through the legislative process since 1981, and had twice passed the Senate, but this was the first time the House had voted on the legislation.

The legislation was designed to stem the flood of illegal immigration into the United States, primarily by penalizing employers who knowingly hire illegal aliens. At the same time, it would have permitted millions of individuals already in the United States illegally to obtain legal status.

The vote was a cliffhanger, seesawing for most of the 15-minute roll call. Only in the final seconds did proponents edge ahead, 216-211: R 91-73; D 125-138 (ND 76-98, SD 49-40).

The vote produced an unusual coalition, with some liberal Democrats joining conservatives of both parties in opposing the bill. The liberal Democrats sided with Hispanic members, who charged that employer sanctions would make businesses reluctant to hire any worker who appeared foreign or spoke with an accent. Conservatives opposing the measure disliked its amnesty provisions.

The closeness of the vote on final passage was a surprise, because amendments considered during the debate had been adopted or rejected, as sponsors had wished, by comfortable margins. However, the narrow victory reflected the deep divisions among members of Congress over how to rewrite immigration laws. Despite a monthlong House-Senate conference in September, members of the two chambers could not reach an accord on a final compromise version. The measure died in the conference committee as the 98th Congress drew to a close.

11. Synfuels Corporation Cutback

In an unexpected defeat for House Majority Leader Jim Wright, D-Texas, and a victory for the Reagan administration, the House July 25 demanded a say on the fate of the trouble-plagued U.S. Synthetic Fuels Corporation (SFC). The House defeated a rule for consideration of the Interior appropriations bill (HR 5973) that would have barred any amendments to rescind SFC funds.

The vote was 148-261: R 21-135; D 127-126 (ND 66-101, SD 61-25).

The White House May 14 had asked Congress to rescind $9.5 billion in SFC funds, roughly two-thirds of its available money. A rash of resignations that came amid charges of mismanagement and conflict-of-interest had left the SFC without a quorum and virtually paralyzed.

Set up in 1980 after a decade of oil supply disruptions, the SFC was meant to encourage commercialization of fuels made from coal, shale, and tar sands by giving loans and price supports to private companies. But the corporation was slow to spend the $20 billion Congress gave it, and firms began withdrawing project proposals as oil prices dropped.

Wright, an SFC backer, made a speech supporting the rule and buttonholed members at the door during the vote. David A. Stockman, director of the Office of Management and Budget, called some members before the vote, asking them to oppose the rule.

Defeat of a rule having House leadership backing was relatively uncommon. It was only the second time in the 98th Congress that such a rule had been rejected.

Congress stripped $2 billion from the corporation as part of its deficit-reduction package (HR 4170 — PL 98-369) and another $5.375 billion as part of the fiscal 1984 continuing resolution, H J Res 648 (PL 98-473).

12. Education Spending

House Republicans challenged Democrats to live up to their campaign promises of fiscal restraint when a five-year omnibus education bill (HR 11) came to the House floor July 26.

But with support for education looming as another election-year issue, the House rejected an amendment by Bill Goodling, R-Pa., to cut the amount authorized by the bill from about $1.7 billion to $974 million in fiscal 1985.

Republicans reminded Democrats of the "new realism" about federal spending that Walter F. Mondale had promised just one week earlier, when he accepted the Democratic presidential nomination.

Goodling said his proposal would have authorized $33.6 million more than was appropriated in 1984 for the 10 education programs included in the bill, but his amendment was rejected 169-233: R 133-20; D 36-213 (ND 13-154, SD 23-59).

After turning down that proposal, Democrats introduced their own amendment to scale back spending levels — although not as far as Goodling had proposed. As amended and approved by the House, the bill authorized $1.32 billion in fiscal 1985. Before clearing Congress and being signed by the president, however, the bill's 1985 price tag was further trimmed in conference with the Senate to about $1.2 billion (PL 98-511).

13. Superfund Right to Sue

The House voted Aug. 9 against giving citizens the right to sue in federal court for damages caused by hazardous-waste dumping, yielding to opposition from the Reagan administration and chemical and insurance companies.

The issue came up during floor consideration of a bill (HR 5640) to renew the "superfund" hazardous-waste cleanup law. The citizen's right to sue had been included in the version of the bill reported by the House Energy Committee, but the House adopted an amendment by Harold S. Sawyer, R-Mich., to strike that provision, 208-200: R 135-

22; D 73-178 (ND 23-146, SD 50-32).

The vote went to the heart of one of the most controversial aspects of the superfund renewal — whether and how to compensate victims of incidents such as the one at Love Canal in New York, where residents were faced with medical problems and houses they could not live in.

The Energy Committee language would have allowed citizens to sue dumpers in federal court for compensation in such cases. Currently, citizens could sue under liability laws in most states, but standards of proof and other legal obstacles made such suits very hard to win.

The House vote was uncluttered by the issue of whether the federal government could afford to compensate victims. The superfund renewal bill was eventually passed by the House but died in the Senate.

14. Crime

In a move that capped a yearlong GOP drive to force a House vote on a comprehensive anti-crime package, the House Sept. 25 voted to send the fiscal 1985 continuing appropriations resolution (H J Res 648 — PL 98-473) back to committee with instructions to attach the crime legislation to it. The vote was 243-166: R 154-3; D 89-163 (ND 35-134, SD 54-29).

That vote effectively ensured that the crime legislation, which Reagan backed, would clear the 98th Congress. The Senate had passed the crime package by a 91-1 vote on Feb. 2. But advocates of the Senate measure had been frustrated by the House Judiciary Committee's bill-by-bill approach to crime, and by its failure to act on key elements of the package until late in the session. They decided the procedural move was the best way to guarantee action.

The Senate kept the crime provisions in its version of H J Res 648, and a compromise that actually expanded the package was cleared Oct. 11 as part of the final funding bill.

The crime package included provisions that overhauled federal sentencing procedures, requiring judges to stay within guidelines to be drawn up by a special commission; authorized pretrial detention of suspects deemed dangerous to the community; tightened the definition of insanity; stiffened penalties for drug trafficking; prohibited trafficking in goods bearing counterfeit trademarks; reestablished a program of anti-crime grants for the states; authorized federal aid to victims of crime and set stiff new penalties for terrorist activities.

15. Duty-Free Exports

The House flirted with handing the Reagan administration a major trade defeat, before rejecting a proposal that would have dropped Taiwan, Hong Kong and South Korea from a program that gave special treatment to exports from developing nations. The Oct. 3 vote was 174-233: R 14-142; D 160-91 (ND 128-38, SD 32-53).

The amendment, offered by Richard A. Gephardt, D-Mo., to an omnibus trade package (HR 3398), would have made the three nations ineligible for the generalized system of preferences (GSP), which permitted some exports from Third World nations to enter the United States duty-free. The trio received more than half the GSP benefits offered by Washington.

Administration officials argued that the carrot of duty-free status was needed to entice beneficiaries to open their markets to U.S. goods, stop counterfeiting U.S. products and meet U.S. standards of worker rights. They also stressed GSP's importance to developing nations and industrialized countries with similar programs as a symbol of the U.S. commitment to free trade.

However, many lawmakers objected to "giving away" benefits to the three countries, which competed vigorously with the United States.

In the final version of HR 3398 benefits to the comparatively wealthier developing nations were phased out. The program was renewed for eight and one-half years, instead of the 10 years requested by the administration. And, for the first time, benefits were tied to recipients' steps to comply with U.S. requirements to lower trade barriers.

16. Export Administration Act/South Africa

Defying the Senate and White House, the House Oct. 11 insisted upon a ban on new commercial bank loans to the South African government to protest the racial policy of apartheid. The vote was 269-62: R 96-50; D 173-12 (ND 121-2, SD 52-10). It effectively killed plans to renew the Export Administration Act.

The ban had been agreed to in a House-Senate conference on the original version of a bill (S 979). However, after the conference deadlocked, the Senate Oct. 10 approved a last-ditch compromise bill (HR 4230) that gave up one provision the Senate wanted — greater Pentagon review of export licenses — and one proposal the House insisted on — the ban on bank loans.

However, the House members voted to restore the ban, knowing that it probably would kill the bill in the Senate.

The administration strongly opposed the ban, preferring inducements, rather than sanctions, to prod South Africa to overturn its policy of separating the races.

Seventeen members of the Black Caucus voted present to protest the ban as too mild. ∎

	1	2	3	4	5	6	7
ALABAMA							
Denton	Y	Y	N	Y	Y	+	Y
Heflin	Y	Y	N	Y	Y	Y	Y
ALASKA							
Murkowski	Y	Y	N	Y	Y	Y	Y
Stevens	Y	Y	N	Y	Y	?	Y
ARIZONA							
Goldwater	N	N	N	Y	Y	?	Y
DeConcini	N	?	?	?	Y	?	N
ARKANSAS							
Bumpers	N	N	?	N	N	Y	N
Pryor	Y	N	N	N	Y	Y	Y
CALIFORNIA							
Wilson	Y	Y	N	Y	Y	Y	Y
Cranston	N	?	Y	N	N	?	N
COLORADO							
Armstrong	Y	Y	N	Y	Y	Y	Y
Hart	N	?	?	?	?	?	?
CONNECTICUT							
Weicker	N	?	Y	N	-	?	Y
Dodd	N	?	Y	N	N	Y	Y
DELAWARE							
Roth	Y	N	N	Y	Y	Y	Y
Biden	N	Y	Y	N	N	Y	Y
FLORIDA							
Hawkins	Y	Y	N	Y	Y	Y	Y
Chiles	Y	Y	N	Y	N	Y	N
GEORGIA							
Mattingly	Y	Y	N	Y	Y	Y	Y
Nunn	Y	Y	N	Y	N	Y	Y
HAWAII							
Inouye	N	Y	N	N	N	Y	N
Matsunaga	N	Y	Y	N	N	Y	N
IDAHO							
McClure	Y	Y	N	Y	Y	?	Y
Symms	Y	Y	N	Y	Y	?	Y
ILLINOIS							
Percy	Y	?	N	Y	Y	Y	Y
Dixon	N	+	N	N	N	Y	N
INDIANA							
Lugar	Y	Y	N	Y	N	Y	Y
Quayle	Y	Y	-	Y	Y	Y	Y

	1	2	3	4	5	6	7
IOWA							
Grassley	Y	Y	N	Y	Y	Y	Y
Jepsen	Y	Y	N	Y	Y	Y	?
KANSAS							
Dole	Y	Y	N	Y	Y	Y	Y
Kassebaum	N	+	N	Y	Y	N	Y
KENTUCKY							
Ford	Y	Y	Y	N	N	Y	N
Huddleston	Y	?	?	Y	N	?	Y
LOUISIANA							
Johnston	Y	N	N	Y	N	?	N
Long	Y	X	N	Y	N	N	Y
MAINE							
Cohen	N	Y	N	Y	N	Y	N
Mitchell	N	Y	Y	N	N	N	N
MARYLAND							
Mathias	N	Y	N	Y	?	N	?
Sarbanes	N	Y	Y	N	N	N	N
MASSACHUSETTS							
Kennedy	N	Y	N	Y	N	N	N
Tsongas	N	Y	Y	?	N	Y	N
MICHIGAN							
Levin	N	Y	Y	N	Y	Y	N
Riegle	N	Y	Y	N	N	Y	N
MINNESOTA							
Boschwitz	N	Y	N	Y	Y	Y	Y
Durenberger	N	Y	N	Y	Y	?	Y
MISSISSIPPI							
Cochran	Y	Y	N	Y	Y	Y	Y
Stennis	Y	Y	N	Y	?	?	N
MISSOURI							
Danforth	N	Y	N	Y	Y	N	Y
Eagleton	N	Y	Y	N	N	?	N
MONTANA							
Baucus	N	Y	Y	N	Y	Y	Y
Melcher	Y	Y	Y	N	Y	Y	N
NEBRASKA							
Exon	Y	N	Y	N	Y	Y	Y
Zorinsky	Y	N	Y	Y	Y	Y	Y
NEVADA							
Hecht	Y	Y	N	Y	Y	Y	Y
Laxalt	Y	Y	N	Y	Y	Y	Y

	1	2	3	4	5	6	7
NEW HAMPSHIRE							
Humphrey	Y	Y	N	Y	Y	N	Y
Rudman	N	Y	N	Y	Y	Y	Y
NEW JERSEY							
Bradley	N	Y	N	N	Y	N	N
Lautenberg	N	Y	Y	N	N	N	N
NEW MEXICO							
Domenici	Y	Y	N	Y	Y	Y	Y
Bingaman	N	Y	Y	N	N	Y	N
NEW YORK							
D'Amato	Y	Y	?	Y	Y	Y	Y
Moynihan	N	#	?	N	N	N	N
NORTH CAROLINA							
East	Y	Y	N	Y	Y	Y	Y
Helms	Y	Y	N	Y	Y	Y	Y
NORTH DAKOTA							
Andrews	N	Y	N	N	N	Y	Y
Burdick	N	Y	?	?	N	Y	N
OHIO							
Glenn	N	Y	N	Y	N	Y	N
Metzenbaum	N	N	?	N	N	N	N
OKLAHOMA							
Nickles	Y	Y	?	Y	Y	Y	Y
Boren	Y	Y	N	Y	Y	Y	Y
OREGON							
Hatfield	N	Y	Y	N	Y	Y	Y
Packwood	N	Y	?	Y	Y	?	Y
PENNSYLVANIA							
Heinz	N	Y	N	N	Y	N	Y
Specter	N	Y	N	N	Y	Y	Y
RHODE ISLAND							
Chafee	N	Y	N	N	N	Y	Y
Pell	N	N	Y	N	N	N	N
SOUTH CAROLINA							
Thurmond	Y	Y	N	Y	Y	Y	Y
Hollings	Y	N	N	N	N	?	N
SOUTH DAKOTA							
Abdnor	Y	Y	N	Y	Y	Y	Y
Pressler	Y	Y	N	N	N	?	Y
TENNESSEE							
Baker	Y	Y	N	Y	Y	Y	Y
Sasser	Y	Y	Y	N	N	Y	N

	1	2	3	4	5	6	7
TEXAS							
Tower	Y	Y	N	Y	Y	Y	Y
Bentsen	Y	Y	N	N	?	?	N
UTAH							
Garn	Y	Y	N	Y	Y	Y	Y
Hatch	Y	Y	N	Y	Y	Y	Y
VERMONT							
Stafford	N	Y	?	?	N	?	Y
Leahy	N	Y	Y	N	N	N	N
VIRGINIA							
Trible	Y	Y	N	Y	Y	Y	Y
Warner	Y	Y	N	Y	Y	Y	Y
WASHINGTON							
Evans	N	Y	N	Y	N	N	Y
Gorton	N	Y	N	Y	Y	Y	Y
WEST VIRGINIA							
Byrd	Y	Y	N	Y	N	Y	N
Randolph	Y	+	Y	N	N	Y	N
WISCONSIN							
Kasten	Y	Y	N	Y	Y	Y	Y
Proxmire	Y	Y	N	Y	N	N	Y
WYOMING							
Simpson	Y	Y	N	Y	Y	Y	Y
Wallop	Y	Y	N	Y	Y	Y	Y

KEY

Y   Voted for (yea).
\#   Paired for.
\+   Announced for.
N   Voted against (nay).
X   Paired against.
-   Announced against.
P   Voted "present".
C   Voted "present" to avoid possible conflict of interest.
?   Did not vote or otherwise make a position known.

Democrats   *Republicans*

ND - Northern Democrats   SD - Southern Democrats (Southern states - Ala., Ark., Fla., Ga., Ky., La., Miss., N.C., Okla., S.C., Tenn., Texas, Va.)

1. S J Res 73. Constitutional Amendment on School Prayer. Passage of the joint resolution to propose an amendment to the Constitution to permit organized, recited prayer in public schools and other public places. Rejected 56-44: R 37-18; D 19-26 (ND 6-25, SD 13-1), March 20, 1984. A two-thirds majority of those present and voting (67 in this case) of both houses is required for passage of a joint resolution proposing an amendment to the Constitution. A "yea" was a vote supporting the president's position.

2. HR 4072. Agricultural Programs Adjustment Act. Passage of the bill to cut target prices for wheat in 1984 and 1985 and to freeze 1985 target prices for corn, cotton and rice at 1984 levels. It also set terms for a wheat acreage reduction program in 1984 and 1985, required acreage reduction programs in 1985 for corn, cotton and rice if certain levels of surpluses were reached, enlarged farm credit programs, authorized changes in disaster loan programs and expanded farm export programs. Passed 78-10: R 50-2; D 28-8 (ND 20-4, SD 8-4), March 22, 1984. A "yea" was a vote supporting the president's position.

3. H J Res 492. Department of Agriculture, Fiscal 1984 Urgent Supplemental Appropriations. Kennedy, D-Mass., amendment to cut funding for military assistance to El Salvador from $61.75 million to $21 million. Rejected 25-63: R 2-48; D 23-15 (ND 21-5, SD 2-10), April 2, 1984. A "nay" was a vote supporting the president's position.

4. H J Res 492. Department of Agriculture, Fiscal 1984 Urgent Supplemental Appropriations. Baker, R-Tenn., motion to table (kill) the Leahy, D-Vt., amendment to require congressional authorization for the introduction of combat troops in or over El Salvador. Motion agreed to 59-36: R 49-5; D 10-31 (ND 2-25, SD 8-6), April 4, 1984. A "yea" was a vote supporting the president's position.

5. HR 2163. Deficit Reduction. Dole, R-Kan., motion to table (kill) the Chafee, R-R.I., amendment to the Dole, R-Kan., amendment, to delay until Jan. 1, 1988, the effective date for indexing tax brackets to offset inflation. Motion agreed to 57-38: R 46-7; D 11-31 (ND 8-22, SD 3-9), April 10, 1984. A "yea" was a vote supporting the president's position. (The Dole amendment, to raise $48 billion in new tax revenues through fiscal 1987, subsequently was adopted 76-5.)

6. HR 2163. Deficit Reduction. Boschwitz, R-Minn., amendment to the Dole, R-Kan., amendment, to change the current 15-year depreciation life for real property to 20 years in 1984, 19 years in 1985 and 18 years thereafter, and to reduce the investment tax credits available for rehabilitation of old buildings. Adopted 62-19: R 37-8; D 25-11 (ND 17-10, SD 8-1), in the session that began April 12, 1984. (The Dole amendment, to raise $48 billion in new tax revenues through fiscal 1987, subsequently was adopted 76-5.)

7. HR 2163. Deficit Reduction. Baker, R-Tenn., amendment to reduce federal deficits by $140 billion through fiscal 1987 by increasing taxes, limiting the increases in military spending, cutting federal benefit and other non-defense programs. Adopted 65-32: R 53-0; D 12-32 (ND 6-24, SD 6-8), May 17, 1984. A "yea" was a vote supporting the president's position.

	8	9	10	11	12	13
ALABAMA						
Denton	Y	Y	Y	Y	Y	N
Heflin	Y	Y	Y	Y	Y	N
ALASKA						
Murkowski	Y	Y	Y	Y	Y	N
Stevens	Y	Y	Y	Y	Y	N
ARIZONA						
Goldwater	Y	Y	Y	N	Y	N
DeConcini	Y	#	Y	Y	#	Y
ARKANSAS						
Bumpers	?	N	N	Y	N	Y
Pryor	N	N	N	Y	Y	Y
CALIFORNIA						
Wilson	Y	Y	Y	Y	Y	N
Cranston	N	N	N	Y	X	Y
COLORADO						
Armstrong	Y	Y	Y	N	Y	N
Hart	N	N	?	?	N	Y
CONNECTICUT						
Weicker	N	N	N	Y	Y	Y
Dodd	N	N	N	Y	N	Y
DELAWARE						
Roth	?	Y	Y	Y	Y	Y
Biden	N	N	N	Y	N	Y
FLORIDA						
Hawkins	Y	Y	Y	Y	?	N
Chiles	N	N	Y	Y	N	Y
GEORGIA						
Mattingly	Y	Y	Y	Y	Y	N
Nunn	N	Y	Y	Y	N	N
HAWAII						
Inouye	N	N	N	Y	N	Y
Matsunaga	N	N	N	Y	N	Y
IDAHO						
McClure	Y	Y	Y	N	?	N
Symms	Y	Y	Y	N	Y	N
ILLINOIS						
Percy	N	?	?	Y	?	?
Dixon	N	N	Y	+	N	Y
INDIANA						
Lugar	Y	Y	Y	Y	Y	N
Quayle	Y	Y	Y	Y	Y	N

	8	9	10	11	12	13
IOWA						
Grassley	Y	N	Y	N	?	N
Jepsen	Y	Y	Y	Y	Y	N
KANSAS						
Dole	Y	Y	Y	Y	Y	N
Kassebaum	Y	Y	N	Y	Y	N
KENTUCKY						
Ford	N	N	N	Y	Y	Y
Huddleston	N	N	N	Y	Y	Y
LOUISIANA						
Johnston	N	N	Y	N	N	Y
Long	Y	N	Y	N	N	N
MAINE						
Cohen	N	Y	N	Y	?	Y
Mitchell	N	N	N	Y	N	Y
MARYLAND						
Mathias	N	N	Y	Y	Y	Y
Sarbanes	N	N	N	Y	N	Y
MASSACHUSETTS						
Kennedy	-	N	N	Y	N	Y
Tsongas	?	N	N	Y	X	Y
MICHIGAN						
Levin	N	N	N	Y	N	Y
Riegle	N	N	N	Y	N	Y
MINNESOTA						
Boschwitz	N	Y	Y	Y	Y	Y
Durenberger	N	N	Y	Y	?	Y
MISSISSIPPI						
Cochran	Y	Y	Y	Y	Y	N
Stennis	N	Y	Y	N	N	N
MISSOURI						
Danforth	Y	Y	Y	Y	Y	N
Eagleton	N	N	N	Y	N	Y
MONTANA						
Baucus	N	N	N	N	-	Y
Melcher	N	N	N	N	N	Y
NEBRASKA						
Exon	N	N	?	Y	Y	Y
Zorinsky	Y	Y	N	Y	Y	N
NEVADA						
Hecht	Y	Y	Y	Y	Y	N
Laxalt	Y	Y	Y	Y	Y	N

	8	9	10	11	12	13
NEW HAMPSHIRE						
Humphrey	Y	N	Y	N	N	N
Rudman	Y	Y	Y	Y	Y	N
NEW JERSEY						
Bradley	N	N	N	Y	X	Y
Lautenberg	N	N	N	Y	N	Y
NEW MEXICO						
Domenici	Y	Y	Y	Y	Y	N
Bingaman	N	N	N	Y	N	Y
NEW YORK						
D'Amato	Y	Y	Y	Y	Y	Y
Moynihan	N	N	N	Y	N	Y
NORTH CAROLINA						
East	Y	Y	Y	Y	Y	N
Helms	Y	Y	Y	Y	Y	N
NORTH DAKOTA						
Andrews	?	?	Y	Y	Y	Y
Burdick	N	N	N	+	#	Y
OHIO						
Glenn	Y	N	N	Y	N	Y
Metzenbaum	N	N	N	Y	N	Y
OKLAHOMA						
Nickles	Y	Y	Y	Y	Y	N
Boren	Y	N	Y	Y	#	N
OREGON						
Hatfield	N	N	N	Y	N	Y
Packwood	Y	N	Y	Y	Y	Y
PENNSYLVANIA						
Heinz	N	Y	N	Y	Y	Y
Specter	Y	N	Y	Y	Y	Y
RHODE ISLAND						
Chafee	N	Y	N	Y	Y	Y
Pell	N	N	-	Y	Y	Y
SOUTH CAROLINA						
Thurmond	Y	Y	Y	N	Y	N
Hollings	Y	N	Y	N	Y	N
SOUTH DAKOTA						
Abdnor	Y	Y	Y	Y	Y	N
Pressler	N	N	N	Y	Y	N
TENNESSEE						
Baker	#	Y	Y	Y	Y	N
Sasser	N	N	N	Y	N	Y

KEY

Y Voted for (yea).
Paired for.
+ Announced for.
N Voted against (nay).
X Paired against.
- Announced against.
P Voted "present".
C Voted "present" to avoid possible conflict of interest.
? Did not vote or otherwise make a position known.

Democrats   *Republicans*

	8	9	10	11	12	13
TEXAS						
Tower	Y	Y	Y	Y	Y	N
Bentsen	N	X	N	Y	?	Y
UTAH						
Garn	Y	Y	Y	Y	Y	N
Hatch	Y	Y	Y	Y	Y	N
VERMONT						
Stafford	X	N	N	Y	Y	Y
Leahy	N	N	N	N	?	Y
VIRGINIA						
Trible	Y	Y	Y	Y	Y	N
Warner	Y	Y	Y	Y	Y	N
WASHINGTON						
Evans	Y	Y	Y	N	N	N
Gorton	Y	Y	Y	N	N	N
WEST VIRGINIA						
Byrd	N	Y	N	Y	N	Y
Randolph	N	N	N	Y	Y	Y
WISCONSIN						
Kasten	+	Y	Y	Y	Y	N
Proxmire	N	N	N	Y	N	Y
WYOMING						
Simpson	Y	Y	Y	N	Y	N
Wallop	Y	Y	Y	N	Y	N

ND - Northern Democrats   SD - Southern Democrats (Southern states - Ala., Ark., Fla., Ga., Ky., La., Miss., N.C., Okla., S.C., Tenn., Texas, Va.)

8. S 2723. Omnibus Defense Authorization. Tower, R-Texas, motion to table (kill) the Percy, R-Ill., amendment to reduce by $100 million the amount authorized for the strategic defense initiative. Motion agreed to 47-45: R 40-10; D 7-35 (ND 3-26, SD 4-9), June 13, 1984. A "yea" was a vote supporting the president's position.

9. S 2723. Omnibus Defense Authorization. Tower, R-Texas, motion to table (kill) the Moynihan, D-N.Y., amendment to produce no additional MX missiles in fiscal 1985 but to keep the MX production line ready for production pending completion of a new study of the mobile, single-warhead "Midgetman" missile. Motion agreed to 49-48: R 43-10; D 5-38 (ND 2-28, SD 3-10), June 14, 1984, with Vice President Bush casting a "yea" vote to break the 48-48 tie. A "yea" was a vote supporting the president's position.

10. S 2723. Omnibus Defense Authorization. Tower, R-Texas, motion to table (kill) the Kennedy, D-Mass., amendment to provide that nothing in the bill shall be construed as authorization for funds to assist insurgent military forces in Nicaragua (the so-called "contras"). Motion agreed to 58-38: R 48-6; D 10-32 (ND 2-26, SD 8-6), June 18, 1984. A "yea" was a vote supporting the president's position.

11. HR 4616. Motor Vehicle Safety/Minimum Drinking Age. Lautenberg, D-N.J., amendment to withhold a percentage of highway funds from states whose minimum drinking ages are under 21 and to provide incentives for other actions aimed at reducing drunken driving. Adopted 81-16: R 45-10; D 36-6 (ND 25-3, SD 11-3), June 26, 1984. A "yea" was a vote supporting the president's position.

12. HR 5743. Agriculture Appropriations, Fiscal 1985. Baker, R-Tenn., motion to invoke cloture (thus limiting debate) on the Baker motion to waive provisions of the Congressional Budget Act that would bar consideration of an appropriations bill prior to adoption of the conference report on the first budget resolution. Motion rejected 54-31: R 46-3; D 8-28 (ND 4-20, SD 4-8), Aug. 6, 1984. A three-fifths majority vote (60) of the total Senate is required to invoke cloture.

13. H J Res 648. Continuing Appropriations, Fiscal 1985. Judgment of the Senate whether the Byrd, D-W.Va., amendment to attach S 2568, civil rights legislation overturning the Supreme Court's ruling in *Grove City College v. Bell*, to the continuing appropriations resolution was germane. Ruled germane 51-48: R 12-42; D 39-6 (ND 30-1, SD 9-5), Sept. 27, 1984.

1. HR 1904. Child Abuse Amendments. Chandler, R-Wash., substitute to the Murphy, D-Pa., amendment, to strike language requiring states that receive federal child-protection grants to ensure that severely handicapped infants receive adequate medical treatment and nutrition, and instead to establish a study commission and require the Department of Health and Human Services to issue guidelines for hospitals that want to establish advisory panels on the treatment of the handicapped infants. Rejected 182-231: R 31-131; D 151-100 (ND 97-69, SD 54-31), Feb. 2, 1984. (The Murphy amendment, clarifying the intent of the infant-protection provisions, subsequently was adopted by voice vote.) A "nay" was a vote supporting the president's position.

2. HR 1652. Reclamation Dam Safety. Kazen, D-Texas, substitute to the Solomon, R-N.Y., amendment, to require reimbursement only for new project benefits by local users and beneficiaries of projects in the bill, which authorized an additional $650 million for safety-related repair of dams administered by the Bureau of Reclamation. Adopted 194-192: R 75-73; D 119-119 (ND 61-91, SD 58-28), March 20, 1984. A "yea" was a vote supporting the president's position.

3. H Con Res 280. First Budget Resolution, Fiscal 1985. Adoption of the first concurrent budget resolution for fiscal 1985 to set targets for the fiscal year ending Sept. 30, 1985, as follows: budget authority, $1,002.1 billion; outlays, $918.2 billion; revenues, $742.7 billion; and deficit, $174.5 billion. The resolution also set preliminary goals for fiscal 1986-87, revised budget levels for fiscal 1984 and included reconciliation instructions requiring House and Senate committees to recommend legislative savings to meet the budget targets. Adopted 250-168: R 21-139; D 229-29 (ND 159-13, SD 70-16), April 5, 1984.

4. HR 5394. Omnibus Budget Reconciliation Act. Moore, R-La., motion to recommit the bill to the House Ways and Means Committee with instructions to include provisions imposing a one-year physician fee freeze for Medicare services and to strike provisions in the measure that increased spending. Motion rejected 172-242: R 157-2; D 15-240 (ND 3-170, SD 12-70), April 12, 1984.

5. HR 5119. Foreign Assistance Authorization. Broomfield, R-Mich., amendment to authorize President Reagan's requests for military, economic and development aid for Central American countries in fiscal 1984-85, and to allow military aid for El Salvador in fiscal 1985 if the president certified to Congress that the government had made "demonstrated progress" on human rights and other issues. Adopted 212-208: R 156-8; D 56-200 (ND 7-167, SD 49-33), May 10, 1984. A "yea" was a vote supporting the president's position.

6. HR 5345. Equal Access Act. Perkins, D-Ky., motion to suspend the rules and pass the bill to allow student religious groups to meet in public secondary schools during non-class hours if other groups do so. Motion rejected 270-151: R 147-17; D 123-134 (ND 47-122, SD 76-12), May 15, 1984. A two-thirds majority of those present and voting (281 in this case) is required for passage under suspension of the rules. A "yea" was a vote supporting the president's position.

7. HR 5167. Department of Defense Authorization. Gore, D-Tenn., amendment to the Brown, D-Calif., amendment, to provide that no funds may be used to test the anti-satellite missile (ASAT) against a target in space unless the Soviet Union conducts a test of its ASAT after enactment of the bill. Adopted 238-181: R 39-122; D 199-59 (ND 162-10, SD 37-49), May 23, 1984. A "nay" was a vote supporting the president's position.

8. H J Res 492. Department of Agriculture, Fiscal 1984 Urgent Supplemental Appropriations. Boland, D-Mass., motion that the House recede from its disagreement to the Senate amendment providing $21 million in covert aid to Nicaraguan rebels, with an amendment providing no funds for Nicaraguan rebels. Motion agreed to 241-177: R 24-132; D 217-45 (ND 169-6, SD 48-39), May 24, 1984. A "nay" was a vote supporting the president's position.

KEY

- Y Voted for (yea).
- # Paired for.
- + Announced for.
- N Voted against (nay).
- X Paired against.
- - Announced against.
- P Voted "present".
- C Voted "present" to avoid possible conflict of interest.
- ? Did not vote or otherwise make a position known.

Democrats   *Republicans*

	1	2	3	4	5	6	7	8
ALABAMA								
1 *Edwards*	N	Y	N	Y	Y	Y	N	N
2 *Dickinson*	N	Y	N	#	Y	Y	N	N
3 Nichols	?	Y	Y	?	Y	Y	N	N
4 Bevill	N	Y	Y	N	?	Y	N	N
5 Flippo	Y	Y	Y	N	N	Y	N	N
6 Erdreich	N	Y	N	Y	N	Y	N	N
7 Shelby	N	Y	N	Y	Y	Y	N	N
ALASKA								
AL *Young*	N	Y	N	Y	Y	Y	N	N
ARIZONA								
1 *McCain*	N	Y	N	Y	Y	Y	N	N
2 Udall	Y	Y	Y	N	N	N	Y	Y
3 *Stump*	N	Y	N	Y	Y	Y	N	N
4 *Rudd*	N	Y	N	#	Y	Y	N	N
5 McNulty	N	Y	Y	N	N	N	Y	Y
ARKANSAS								
1 Alexander	Y	Y	Y	N	N	Y	Y	Y
2 *Bethune*	N	Y	N	Y	Y	Y	N	N
3 *Hammerschmidt*	N	Y	N	Y	Y	Y	N	N
4 Anthony	Y	N	Y	N	N	Y	N	Y
CALIFORNIA								
1 Bosco	Y	?	Y	N	N	N	Y	Y
2 *Chappie*	N	Y	N	Y	Y	Y	N	N
3 Matsui	Y	Y	Y	N	N	N	Y	Y
4 Fazio	Y	Y	Y	N	N	?	Y	Y
5 Burton	Y	Y	Y	N	N	N	Y	Y
6 Boxer	Y	?	Y	N	N	N	Y	Y
7 Miller	Y	Y	Y	N	N	N	Y	Y
8 Dellums	Y	N	Y	N	N	N	Y	Y
9 Stark	Y	N	Y	N	N	N	Y	Y
10 Edwards	Y	N	Y	N	N	N	Y	Y
11 Lantos	Y	Y	Y	X	N	N	Y	Y
12 *Zschau*	Y	N	N	Y	N	Y	N	Y
13 Mineta	Y	Y	Y	N	N	N	Y	Y
14 *Shumway*	N	Y	N	Y	Y	Y	N	N
15 Coelho	Y	Y	Y	N	N	N	Y	Y
16 Panetta	Y	Y	Y	N	N	N	Y	Y
17 *Pashayan*	N	Y	N	Y	Y	Y	N	N
18 Lehman	Y	Y	Y	N	N	N	Y	Y
19 *Lagomarsino*	N	Y	N	Y	Y	Y	N	N
20 *Thomas*	Y	?	N	Y	Y	Y	N	N
21 *Fiedler*	Y	Y	Y	N	Y	Y	N	N
22 *Moorhead*	N	Y	N	Y	Y	Y	N	N
23 Beilenson	Y	N	N	N	N	N	Y	Y
24 Waxman	Y	Y	Y	N	N	N	Y	Y
25 Roybal	Y	Y	Y	N	N	N	Y	Y
26 Berman	Y	N	Y	N	N	N	Y	Y
27 Levine	Y	N	Y	N	N	N	Y	Y
28 Dixon	Y	Y	Y	N	N	N	Y	Y
29 Hawkins	Y	Y	#	N	N	N	Y	Y
30 Martinez	Y	Y	Y	N	N	N	Y	Y
31 Dymally	Y	N	Y	N	N	N	Y	Y
32 Anderson	Y	Y	Y	N	N	N	Y	Y
33 *Dreier*	N	?	N	Y	Y	Y	N	N
34 Torres	Y	Y	Y	N	N	N	Y	Y
35 *Lewis*	N	Y	N	Y	Y	Y	N	?
36 Brown	Y	Y	Y	N	N	N	Y	Y
37 *McCandless*	Y	Y	N	Y	Y	Y	N	N
38 *Patterson*	Y	Y	Y.	N	N	Y	?	Y
39 *Dannemeyer*	N	Y	N	Y	Y	Y	N	N
40 *Badham*	N	Y	N	Y	Y	Y	N	N
41 *Lowery*	N	Y	N	Y	Y	Y	N	N
42 *Lungren*	N	Y	N	Y	Y	Y	N	N

	1	2	3	4	5	6	7	8
43 *Packard*	N	Y	N	Y	Y	Y	N	N
44 Bates	Y	Y	Y	N	N	?	Y	Y
45 *Hunter*	N	Y	N	Y	Y	Y	N	N
COLORADO								
1 Schroeder	Y	Y	Y	N	N	N	Y	Y
2 Wirth	Y	Y	Y	N	N	N	Y	Y
3 Kogovsek	Y	Y	Y	N	N	N	Y	Y
4 *Brown*	Y	Y	N	Y	Y	Y	Y	N
5 *Kramer*	N	Y	N	Y	Y	Y	N	N
6 *Schaefer*	N	Y	N	Y	Y	Y	N	N
CONNECTICUT								
1 Kennelly	Y	?	Y	N	N	N	Y	Y
2 Gejdenson	Y	Y	Y	N	N	N	Y	Y
3 Morrison	Y	N	Y	N	N	N	Y	Y
4 *McKinney*	Y	Y	Y	N	N	N	Y	Y
5 Ratchford	Y	Y	Y	N	N	N	Y	Y
6 *Johnson*	Y	N	Y	Y	Y	N	Y	N
DELAWARE								
AL Carper	Y	N	Y	N	N	N	Y	Y
FLORIDA								
1 Hutto	N	Y	Y	Y	Y	Y	N	N
2 Fuqua	N	Y	Y	N	Y	Y	N	N
3 Bennett	N	Y	Y	Y	Y	Y	N	N
4 Chappell	Y	Y	Y	N	Y	Y	N	N
5 *McCollum*	N	N	N	Y	Y	Y	N	N
6 MacKay	Y	N	N	N	Y	Y	Y	Y
7 Gibbons	Y	N	N	N	N	N	N	N
8 *Young*	N	N	Y	Y	Y	Y	N	N
9 *Bilirakis*	N	N	N	Y	Y	Y	N	N
10 *Ireland*	N	?	N	Y	Y	Y	N	N
11 Nelson	N	N	N	Y	Y	Y	N	N
12 *Lewis*	N	N	N	Y	Y	Y	N	N
13 *Mack*	N	N	N	Y	Y	Y	N	N
14 Mica	N	Y	N	Y	Y	Y	N	N
15 *Shaw*	N	N	N	Y	Y	Y	N	N
16 Smith	Y	N	N	N	N	N	Y	Y
17 Lehman	Y	N	Y	N	N	N	Y	Y
18 Pepper	#	Y	Y	N	N	N	Y	Y
19 Fascell	Y	N	Y	N	N	N	Y	N
GEORGIA								
1 Thomas	Y	N	Y	N	Y	Y	N	N
2 Hatcher	Y	N	Y	N	Y	Y	N	?
3 Ray	N	N	?	N	Y	Y	N	N
4 Levitas	Y	N	Y	N	Y	Y	Y	N
5 Fowler	Y	Y	Y	N	N	Y	N	Y
6 *Gingrich*	N	N	N	Y	Y	Y	N	N
7 Darden	Y	N	N	Y	Y	Y	N	N
8 Rowland	Y	N	Y	N	Y	Y	N	N
9 Jenkins	Y	N	Y	N	Y	Y	N	N
10 Barnard	Y	N	N	N	Y	Y	?	N
HAWAII								
1 Heftel	?	?	?	?	N	Y	Y	Y
2 Akaka	Y	Y	Y	N	N	N	N	Y
IDAHO								
1 *Craig*	N	Y	N	#	Y	Y	N	N
2 *Hansen*	N	?	?	?	?	?	?	?
ILLINOIS								
1 Hayes	Y	?	Y	N	N	N	Y	Y
2 Savage	#	?	Y	N	N	N	Y	Y
3 Russo	N	N	Y	N	N	N	Y	Y
4 *O'Brien*	N	?	N	Y	Y	Y	N	N
5 Lipinski	N	?	N	Y	Y	N	N	N
6 *Hyde*	N	?	X	Y	Y	Y	N	N
7 Collins	Y	?	Y	N	N	N	Y	Y
8 Rostenkowski	N	?	Y	N	?	?	Y	Y
9 Yates	Y	N	Y	N	N	N	Y	Y
10 *Porter*	Y	Y	Y	N	Y	N	Y	N
11 Annunzio	N	?	Y	N	N	N	Y	Y
12 *Crane, P.*	N	N	N	Y	Y	Y	N	N
13 *Erlenborn*	N	?	?	Y	Y	Y	N	N
14 *Corcoran*	X	?	N	Y	Y	Y	N	N
15 *Madigan*	N	N	N	Y	Y	Y	N	N
16 *Martin*	Y	?	N	Y	Y	Y	N	N
17 Evans	N	?	Y	N	N	N	Y	Y
18 *Michel*	N	?	Y	N	Y	Y	N	N
19 *Crane, D.*	N	?	N	Y	Y	Y	N	N
20 Durbin	N	?	Y	N	N	N	Y	Y
21 Price	N	?	Y	N	N	N	Y	Y
22 Simon	?	?	Y	X	N	N	Y	Y
INDIANA								
1 Hall	Y	?	Y	N	?	?	Y	Y
2 Sharp	N	N	Y	N	N	Y	-	Y
3 *Hiler*	N	N	N	Y	Y	Y	N	N
4 *Coats*	N	N	N	Y	Y	Y	N	N
5 Hillis	N	N	N	Y	Y	Y	N	N

ND - Northern Democrats   SD - Southern Democrats

	1	2	3	4	5	6	7	8
6 ***Burton***	N	N	N	Y	Y	Y	N	N
7 ***Myers***	N	Y	N	Y	Y	Y	N	N
8 McCloskey	N	?	Y	N	N	Y	Y	Y
9 Hamilton	N	N	Y	N	N	Y	Y	Y
10 Jacobs	Y	N	Y	N	N	Y	Y	Y
IOWA								
1 ***Leach***	N	N	N	Y	N	N	Y	Y
2 ***Tauke***	N	N	N	Y	Y	Y	Y	Y
3 ***Evans***	N	N	N	Y	Y	Y	Y	Y
4 Smith	?	Y	N	N	N	N	Y	Y
5 Harkin	N	?	N	N	N	Y	Y	Y
6 Bedell	N	N	Y	N	N	Y	Y	Y
KANSAS								
1 ***Roberts***	N	Y	N	Y	Y	Y	N	N
2 Slattery	N	N	N	N	N	N	Y	Y
3 ***Winn***	N	Y	N	Y	Y	Y	N	N
4 Glickman	N	N	Y	N	N	N	Y	Y
5 ***Whittaker***	Y	Y	N	Y	Y	Y	N	N
KENTUCKY								
1 Hubbard	Y	Y	?	Y	Y	Y	N	N
2 Natcher	N	Y	Y	N	N	Y	N	Y
3 Mazzoli	N	N	Y	N	N	Y	Y	Y
4 ***Snyder***	N	Y	N	Y	Y	Y	N	N
5 ***Rogers***	Y	Y	N	Y	Y	Y	N	?
6 ***Hopkins***	Y	Y	N	Y	Y	Y	Y	N
7 Perkins [1]	N	Y	Y	N	N	Y	N	Y
LOUISIANA								
1 ***Livingston***	N	Y	N	Y	Y	Y	N	N
2 Boggs	N	Y	Y	N	?	Y	Y	Y
3 Tauzin	X	Y	N	X	Y	Y	N	N
4 Roemer	N	N	N	N	Y	Y	Y	N
5 Huckaby	N	Y	Y	N	Y	Y	Y	N
6 ***Moore***	N	Y	N	Y	Y	Y	Y	N
7 Breaux	Y	Y	N	N	Y	Y	N	N
8 Long	N	Y	Y	N	N	Y	Y	Y
MAINE								
1 ***McKernan***	Y	N	Y	Y	Y	Y	Y	Y
2 ***Snowe***	Y	N	Y	Y	Y	Y	Y	Y
MARYLAND								
1 Dyson	N	N	Y	Y	Y	Y	N	N
2 Long	Y	N	Y	N	N	N	Y	Y
3 Mikulski	Y	N	Y	N	N	N	?	Y
4 ***Holt***	N	?	N	Y	Y	Y	N	N
5 Hoyer	N	Y	Y	N	N	N	Y	Y
6 Byron	N	N	N	N	Y	Y	N	N
7 Mitchell	Y	?	Y	N	N	N	Y	Y
8 Barnes	N	Y	Y	N	N	N	Y	Y
MASSACHUSETTS								
1 ***Conte***	N	N	Y	Y	N	N	Y	Y
2 Boland	X	N	Y	N	N	N	Y	Y
3 Early	?	N	Y	N	N	N	Y	Y
4 Frank	Y	N	Y	N	N	N	Y	Y
5 Shannon	?	?	Y	N	N	N	Y	Y
6 Mavroules	N	N	Y	N	N	N	Y	Y
7 Markey	Y	?	Y	N	N	N	+	Y
8 O'Neill								
9 Moakley	N	N	Y	N	N	N	Y	Y
10 Studds	Y	N	Y	N	N	N	Y	Y
11 Donnelly	X	Y	Y	N	N	N	Y	Y
MICHIGAN								
1 Conyers	Y	N	Y	N	N	N	Y	Y
2 ***Pursell***	Y	?	N	Y	Y	Y	Y	Y
3 Wolpe	Y	N	Y	N	N	N	Y	Y
4 ***Siljander***	N	?	N	Y	Y	Y	N	N
5 ***Sawyer***	N	Y	N	Y	Y	Y	N	?
6 Carr	N	N	N	N	N	Y	Y	Y
7 Kildee	N	N	Y	N	N	N	Y	Y
8 Traxler	N	N	Y	N	N	Y	Y	?
9 ***Vander Jagt***	N	N	N	#	Y	Y	N	N
10 Albosta	N	N	Y	N	N	Y	Y	Y
11 ***Davis***	N	?	Y	Y	Y	Y	N	N
12 Bonior	N	N	Y	N	N	N	Y	Y
13 Crockett	Y	Y	N	N	N	N	Y	Y
14 Hertel	N	N	Y	N	N	N	Y	Y
15 Ford	#	Y	Y	N	N	N	Y	Y
16 Dingell	Y	N	Y	N	N	Y	Y	Y
17 Levin	Y	N	Y	N	N	N	Y	Y
18 ***Broomfield***	N	N	Y	Y	Y	Y	Y	N
MINNESOTA								
1 Penny	N	N	Y	N	N	Y	Y	Y
2 ***Weber***	N	N	N	Y	Y	Y	N	N
3 ***Frenzel***	Y	?	N	Y	Y	Y	Y	N
4 Vento	N	N	Y	N	N	N	Y	Y
5 Sabo	Y	Y	Y	N	N	N	Y	Y
6 Sikorski	N	N	Y	N	N	Y	Y	Y
7 ***Stangeland***	N	Y	N	Y	Y	Y	N	N
8 Oberstar	N	N	Y	N	N	N	Y	Y
MISSISSIPPI								
1 Whitten	N	Y	Y	N	N	Y	N	Y
2 ***Franklin***	Y	Y	N	Y	Y	Y	N	N
3 Montgomery	N	Y	Y	Y	Y	Y	N	N
4 Dowdy	Y	Y	Y	N	Y	Y	N	N
5 ***Lott***	N	Y	N	Y	Y	Y	N	N
MISSOURI								
1 Clay	Y	?	Y	N	N	N	Y	Y
2 Young	N	Y	Y	N	N	N	N	Y
3 Gephardt	N	N	Y	N	N	N	Y	Y
4 Skelton	N	Y	Y	N	Y	Y	N	N
5 Wheat	Y	N	Y	N	N	N	Y	Y
6 ***Coleman***	N	N	N	Y	Y	N	N	N
7 ***Taylor***	N	Y	N	Y	Y	Y	N	N
8 ***Emerson***	N	?	N	Y	Y	Y	N	N
9 Volkmer	N	N	Y	N	N	Y	Y	Y
MONTANA								
1 Williams	Y	N	Y	N	N	N	Y	Y
2 ***Marlenee***	N	Y	N	Y	Y	Y	N	N
NEBRASKA								
1 ***Bereuter***	N	Y	Y	Y	Y	Y	Y	N
2 ***Daub***	N	Y	N	Y	Y	Y	N	N
3 ***Smith***	N	Y	N	Y	Y	Y	N	N
NEVADA								
1 Reid	N	Y	Y	N	N	N	Y	Y
2 ***Vucanovich***	N	Y	N	Y	Y	Y	N	N
NEW HAMPSHIRE								
1 D'Amours	N	N	Y	N	N	Y	Y	Y
2 ***Gregg***	N	N	N	Y	Y	Y	N	N
NEW JERSEY								
1 Florio	N	N	Y	N	N	N	Y	Y
2 Hughes	Y	N	Y	N	N	Y	Y	Y
3 Howard	Y	Y	Y	N	N	N	Y	Y
4 ***Smith***	N	N	N	Y	Y	Y	Y	N
5 ***Roukema***	N	N	N	Y	N	Y	Y	?
6 Dwyer	Y	N	Y	N	N	N	Y	Y
7 ***Rinaldo***	N	N	N	N	Y	Y	Y	N
8 Roe	N	Y	Y	N	N	N	Y	Y
9 Torricelli	Y	N	Y	N	N	N	N	Y
10 Rodino	Y	N	Y	N	N	N	Y	Y
11 Minish	N	N	Y	N	Y	N	Y	Y
12 ***Courter***	N	Y	N	Y	Y	Y	?	N
13 ***Forsythe*** [2]	?	?						
14 Guarini	Y	N	Y	N	N	N	Y	Y
NEW MEXICO								
1 ***Lujan***	N	Y	N	Y	Y	Y	N	N
2 ***Skeen***	N	Y	N	Y	Y	Y	N	N
3 Richardson	Y	Y	Y	N	N	Y	Y	Y
NEW YORK								
1 ***Carney***	N	Y	N	Y	Y	Y	N	N
2 Downey	Y	N	Y	N	N	N	Y	Y
3 Mrazek	Y	N	Y	N	N	N	Y	Y
4 ***Lent***	N	N	X	Y	Y	N	N	N
5 ***McGrath***	N	N	N	Y	Y	N	N	N
6 Addabbo	N	N	Y	N	N	N	Y	Y
7 Ackerman	Y	N	Y	N	N	N	Y	Y
8 Scheuer	Y	N	Y	N	N	N	Y	Y
9 Ferraro	Y	N	Y	N	N	?	Y	Y
10 Schumer	Y	N	Y	N	N	N	Y	Y
11 Towns	Y	N	Y	N	N	N	Y	Y
12 Owens	Y	N	Y	N	N	N	Y	Y
13 Solarz	Y	N	Y	N	N	X	Y	Y
14 ***Molinari***	N	N	N	Y	Y	Y	N	N
15 ***Green***	Y	N	N	N	N	N	Y	Y
16 Rangel	Y	N	Y	N	N	N	Y	Y
17 Weiss	Y	N	Y	N	N	N	Y	Y
18 Garcia	Y	Y	Y	N	N	N	Y	Y
19 Biaggi	N	Y	Y	N	N	Y	Y	Y
20 Ottinger	Y	N	Y	N	N	N	Y	Y
21 ***Fish***	N	N	N	Y	Y	N	Y	Y
22 ***Gilman***	Y	N	N	Y	Y	N	Y	N
23 Stratton	N	N	Y	N	Y	Y	N	N
24 ***Solomon***	N	N	N	Y	Y	Y	N	N
25 ***Boehlert***	N	N	#	Y	Y	Y	Y	Y
26 ***Martin***	N	N	N	Y	Y	Y	N	N
27 ***Wortley***	N	N	N	Y	Y	Y	N	N
28 McHugh	N	N	Y	N	N	N	Y	Y
29 ***Horton***	Y	N	Y	Y	Y	Y	Y	Y
30 ***Conable***	Y	N	N	Y	Y	Y	N	N
31 ***Kemp***	N	N	N	Y	Y	Y	N	N
32 LaFalce	N	N	Y	N	N	Y	Y	#
33 Nowak	N	N	Y	N	N	Y	Y	Y
34 Lundine	N	N	Y	N	N	Y	?	Y
NORTH CAROLINA								
1 Jones	Y	Y	Y	?	N	Y	Y	Y
2 Valentine	Y	Y	Y	N	Y	Y	N	Y
3 Whitley	Y	Y	Y	N	Y	Y	N	Y
4 Andrews	Y	N	Y	N	?	Y	?	Y
5 Neal	Y	N	Y	N	N	Y	Y	Y
6 Britt	Y	N	Y	N	N	Y	Y	Y
7 Rose	Y	Y	Y	N	N	Y	Y	Y
8 Hefner	N	Y	Y	N	N	Y	Y	Y
9 ***Martin***	N	Y	N	Y	Y	Y	?	?
10 ***Broyhill***	N	N	Y	Y	Y	Y	N	N
11 Clarke	Y	Y	Y	N	N	Y	Y	Y
NORTH DAKOTA								
AL Dorgan	N	Y	N	N	N	N	Y	Y
OHIO								
1 Luken	N	Y	Y	N	N	Y	Y	Y
2 ***Gradison***	N	N	N	Y	Y	N	Y	Y
3 Hall	N	N	?	N	N	Y	Y	Y
4 ***Oxley***	N	N	N	Y	Y	Y	Y	N
5 ***Latta***	N	N	N	Y	Y	Y	N	N
6 ***McEwen***	N	Y	N	Y	Y	Y	N	N
7 ***DeWine***	N	N	N	Y	Y	Y	N	N
8 ***Kindness***	N	N	N	Y	Y	Y	N	N
9 Kaptur	Y	N	Y	N	N	Y	Y	Y
10 ***Miller***	N	N	N	Y	Y	Y	N	N
11 Eckart	Y	N	N	N	N	Y	Y	Y
12 ***Kasich***	N	N	N	Y	Y	Y	N	N
13 Pease	N	N	Y	N	N	Y	Y	Y
14 Seiberling	Y	Y	Y	N	N	N	Y	Y
15 ***Wylie***	N	Y	Y	Y	Y	Y	N	N
16 ***Regula***	N	Y	N	Y	Y	Y	Y	Y
17 ***Williams***	N	Y	Y	Y	Y	Y	Y	?
18 Applegate	N	N	N	N	N	Y	N	Y
19 Feighan	Y	N	N	N	N	N	Y	Y
20 Oakar	N	N	Y	N	N	N	Y	Y
21 Stokes	#	N	Y	N	N	N	Y	Y
OKLAHOMA								
1 Jones	N	Y	Y	N	N	Y	N	Y
2 Synar	Y	Y	Y	N	N	N	Y	Y
3 Watkins	Y	Y	Y	N	?	Y	N	?
4 McCurdy	Y	Y	Y	N	Y	Y	N	Y
5 ***Edwards***	N	Y	N	Y	Y	Y	N	N
6 English	N	Y	N	N	Y	Y	N	N
OREGON								
1 AuCoin	Y	Y	N	Y	N	N	Y	Y
2 ***Smith, R.***	N	Y	N	Y	Y	Y	N	N
3 Wyden	Y	Y	Y	N	N	N	Y	Y
4 Weaver	Y	?	Y	N	N	Y	Y	Y
5 ***Smith, D.***	N	Y	N	Y	Y	#	N	N
PENNSYLVANIA								
1 Foglietta	Y	?	#	N	N	N	Y	Y
2 Gray	Y	N	Y	N	N	N	Y	Y
3 Borski	N	N	Y	N	N	N	Y	Y
4 Kolter	N	Y	Y	N	N	Y	Y	Y
5 ***Schulze***	N	N	N	Y	Y	Y	N	N
6 Yatron	N	N	Y	N	N	Y	Y	Y
7 Edgar	Y	N	Y	N	N	N	Y	Y
8 Kostmayer	Y	N	Y	N	N	N	Y	Y
9 ***Shuster***	Y	N	N	Y	Y	Y	N	N
10 ***McDade***	N	N	N	Y	Y	Y	N	N
11 Harrison	N	?	Y	?	N	Y	Y	Y
12 Murtha	N	Y	Y	N	Y	?	Y	N
13 ***Coughlin***	N	N	N	Y	Y	N	Y	N
14 Coyne	N	N	Y	N	N	N	Y	Y
15 ***Ritter***	N	N	N	Y	Y	Y	Y	N
16 ***Walker***	N	N	N	Y	Y	Y	N	N
17 ***Gekas***	Y	N	N	Y	Y	Y	N	N
18 Walgren	Y	N	Y	N	N	N	Y	Y
19 ***Goodling***	X	Y	Y	Y	Y	Y	Y	Y
20 Gaydos	N	Y	N	N	N	Y	Y	N
21 ***Ridge***	N	N	Y	Y	Y	Y	Y	Y
22 Murphy	N	Y	N	Y	N	Y	Y	Y
23 ***Clinger***	N	N	Y	Y	Y	Y	Y	N
RHODE ISLAND								
1 St Germain	N	Y	Y	N	N	Y	Y	Y
2 ***Schneider***	Y	N	Y	Y	N	N	N	Y
SOUTH CAROLINA								
1 ***Hartnett***	N	N	N	Y	Y	Y	N	N
2 ***Spence***	N	N	N	Y	Y	Y	N	N
3 Derrick	Y	Y	Y	N	N	Y	Y	Y
4 ***Campbell***	N	N	N	Y	Y	Y	N	N
5 Spratt	Y	N	Y	N	N	Y	Y	Y
6 Tallon	Y	N	Y	N	Y	Y	Y	N
SOUTH DAKOTA								
AL Daschle	Y	Y	Y	N	N	Y	Y	Y
TENNESSEE								
1 ***Quillen***	Y	Y	N	Y	Y	Y	N	N
2 ***Duncan***	Y	Y	N	Y	Y	Y	N	N
3 Lloyd	N	Y	N	N	Y	Y	N	N
4 Cooper	Y	N	Y	N	N	N	Y	Y
5 Boner	Y	Y	Y	X	Y	Y	Y	Y
6 Gore	N	Y	Y	N	N	Y	Y	Y
7 ***Sundquist***	N	Y	N	Y	Y	Y	N	N
8 Jones	Y	Y	Y	N	?	Y	Y	Y
9 Ford	Y	Y	Y	N	?	N	Y	Y
TEXAS								
1 Hall, S.	N	Y	Y	Y	Y	Y	N	N
2 Wilson	N	Y	Y	?	Y	Y	N	Y
3 ***Bartlett***	N	Y	N	Y	Y	Y	N	N
4 Hall, R.	N	Y	N	Y	Y	Y	N	N
5 Bryant	Y	?	Y	N	N	N	Y	Y
6 ***Gramm***	N	Y	N	Y	Y	Y	?	?
7 ***Archer***	N	N	N	Y	Y	Y	N	N
8 ***Fields***	N	N	N	Y	Y	Y	N	N
9 Brooks	Y	Y	Y	N	N	Y	?	Y
10 Pickle	Y	Y	Y	N	Y	Y	Y	Y
11 Leath	Y	Y	N	Y	Y	Y	N	N
12 Wright	Y	Y	Y	N	Y	Y	N	Y
13 Hightower	Y	Y	Y	Y	Y	Y	N	N
14 Patman	Y	Y	N	N	Y	Y	N	N
15 de la Garza	N	?	Y	N	Y	Y	N	Y
16 Coleman	Y	Y	Y	N	Y	Y	N	Y
17 Stenholm	N	Y	Y	Y	Y	Y	N	N
18 Leland	#	N	Y	N	N	N	Y	Y
19 Hance	?	?	X	X	?	#	?	X
20 Gonzalez	Y	Y	N	N	N	N	N	Y
21 ***Loeffler***	Y	Y	N	Y	Y	Y	N	N
22 ***Paul***	?	?	?	?	N	Y	N	Y
23 Kazen	Y	Y	?	?	?	Y	N	N
24 Frost	Y	Y	Y	?	N	N	N	Y
25 Andrews	Y	Y	Y	N	Y	Y	N	Y
26 Vandergriff	Y	Y	N	N	Y	P	N	N
27 Ortiz	N	Y	Y	N	Y	Y	N	Y
UTAH								
1 ***Hansen***	N	Y	N	Y	?	Y	N	N
2 ***Marriott***	N	Y	N	#	Y	Y	N	?
3 ***Nielson***	N	Y	N	Y	Y	Y	N	N
VERMONT								
AL ***Jeffords***	?	N	Y	Y	N	Y	Y	Y
VIRGINIA								
1 ***Bateman***	N	Y	N	Y	Y	Y	N	N
2 ***Whitehurst***	Y	Y	N	Y	Y	Y	N	N
3 ***Bliley***	N	N	N	Y	Y	Y	N	N
4 Sisisky	Y	N	Y	N	Y	Y	N	N
5 Daniel	N	N	N	Y	Y	Y	N	N
6 Olin	Y	N	Y	N	N	Y	Y	Y
7 ***Robinson***	N	N	N	Y	Y	Y	N	N
8 ***Parris***	N	N	N	Y	Y	Y	N	N
9 Boucher	Y	N	Y	N	N	Y	Y	Y
10 ***Wolf***	N	N	N	Y	Y	Y	N	N
WASHINGTON								
1 ***Pritchard***	Y	Y	Y	Y	Y	Y	Y	Y
2 Swift	Y	Y	Y	N	N	N	Y	Y
3 Bonker	N	Y	Y	N	N	Y	Y	Y
4 ***Morrison***	Y	Y	N	Y	Y	Y	N	N
5 Foley	Y	Y	Y	N	N	N	Y	Y
6 Dicks	Y	Y	Y	N	N	N	Y	Y
7 Lowry	Y	Y	Y	N	N	N	Y	Y
8 ***Chandler***	Y	Y	Y	Y	Y	Y	Y	Y
WEST VIRGINIA								
1 Mollohan	N	Y	Y	N	Y	Y	Y	Y
2 Staggers	N	N	Y	N	N	Y	Y	Y
3 Wise	N	Y	Y	N	N	Y	Y	Y
4 Rahall	N	Y	Y	N	N	?	Y	Y
WISCONSIN								
1 Aspin	N	N	Y	N	N	N	Y	Y
2 Kastenmeier	Y	N	Y	N	N	N	Y	Y
3 ***Gunderson***	N	N	N	Y	Y	Y	Y	Y
4 Kleczka [3]				N	N	N	Y	Y
5 Moody	Y	N	Y	N	?	N	Y	Y
6 ***Petri***	N	N	Y	Y	Y	Y	N	N
7 Obey	N	N	Y	N	N	N	Y	Y
8 ***Roth***	N	?	N	Y	Y	Y	N	N
9 ***Sensenbrenner***	N	N	N	Y	Y	Y	?	?
WYOMING								
AL ***Cheney***	N	Y	N	Y	Y	Y	N	N

[1] *Died Aug. 3, 1984.*
[2] *Died March 29, 1984.*
[3] *Sworn in April 10, 1984.*

Southern states - Ala., Ark., Fla., Ga., Ky., La., Miss., N.C., Okla., S.C., Tenn., Texas, Va.

9. HR 5167. Department of Defense Authorization. Bennett, D-Fla., amendment to the Dickinson, R-Ala., amendment, to prohibit the obligation of funds appropriated for production of MX missiles unless Congress had given its approval by passing a joint resolution after April 1, 1985. Adopted 199-197: R 17-141; D 182-56 (ND 149-15, SD 33-41), May 31, 1984. (The Dickinson amendment, as amended, subsequently was adopted 198-197.) A "nay" was a vote supporting the president's position.

10. HR 1510. Immigration Reform and Control Act. Passage of the bill to revise immigration laws to impose sanctions on employers who knowingly hire illegal aliens, provide legal status for many illegal aliens already in the United States, expand an existing temporary foreign worker program, create a new guest-worker program and overhaul procedures for handling asylum, deportation and exclusion cases. Passed 216-211: R 91-73; D 125-138 (ND 76-98, SD 49-40), June 20, 1984. A "yea" was a vote supporting the president's position.

11. HR 5973. Interior Appropriations, Fiscal 1985. Adoption of the rule (H Res 551) providing for House floor consideration of the bill to make fiscal 1985 appropriations for the Interior Department and related agencies. H Res 551 would not have waived points of order against amendments to rescind appropriated funds from the U.S. Synthetic Fuels Corporation. Rejected 148-261: R 21-135; D 127-126 (ND 66-101, SD 61-25), July 25, 1984. A "nay" was a vote supporting the president's position.

12. HR 11. Education Amendments/School Prayer. Goodling, R-Pa., perfecting amendment to the Ford, D-Mich., substitute for the Goodling amendment to reduce fiscal 1985 authorizations for education programs in the bill from $1.7 billion to $974 million. The perfecting amendment was identical to the original Goodling proposal that the Ford substitute would have blocked from coming to a vote. Rejected 169-233: R 133-20; D 36-213 (ND 13-154, SD 23-59), July 26, 1984.

13. HR 5640. Superfund Expansion. Sawyer, R-Mich., amendment to delete from the bill a section giving citizens the right to sue in federal court for damages caused by hazardous-waste dumping. Adopted 208-200: R 135-22; D 73-178 (ND 23-146, SD 50-32), Aug. 9, 1984.

14. H J Res 648. Continuing Appropriations, Fiscal 1985. Lungren, R-Calif., motion to recommit the joint resolution to the Committee on Appropriations with instructions to attach the provisions of HR 5963, the Comprehensive Crime Control Act of 1984. Motion agreed to 243-166: R 154-3; D 89-163 (ND 35-134, SD 54-29), Sept. 25, 1984. A "yea" was a vote supporting the president's position.

15. HR 6023. Generalized System of Preferences Renewal Act. Gephardt, D-Mo., amendment to remove Taiwan, Hong Kong and South Korea from the list of countries eligible for duty-free treatment under the generalized system of preferences. Rejected 174-233: R 14-142; D 160-91 (ND 128-38, SD 32-53), Oct. 3, 1984. (The bill subsequently was passed by voice vote.) A "nay" was a vote supporting the president's position.

16. HR 4230. Export Administration Act. Fascell, D-Fla., motion to concur in the Senate amendment with an amendment to ban U.S. commercial bank loans to the government of South Africa. Motion agreed to 269-62: R 96-50; D 173-12 (ND 121-2, SD 52-10), Oct. 11, 1984.

KEY

Y	Voted for (yea).
#	Paired for.
+	Announced for.
N	Voted against (nay).
X	Paired against.
-	Announced against.
P	Voted "present".
C	Voted "present" to avoid possible conflict of interest.
?	Did not vote or otherwise make a position known.

Democrats   *Republicans*

	9	10	11	12	13	14	15	16
ALABAMA								
1 *Edwards*	N	Y	?	Y	Y	Y	N	Y
2 *Dickinson*	N	N	N	Y	Y	Y	N	?
3 Nichols	N	N	Y	N	Y	N	N	Y
4 Bevill	N	N	Y	N	Y	N	N	Y
5 Flippo	N	N	Y	?	Y	Y	Y	Y
6 Erdreich	-	N	N	N	Y	Y	Y	Y
7 Shelby	N	N	N	?	Y	Y	Y	Y
ALASKA								
AL *Young*	N	N	N	Y	Y	Y	?	Y
ARIZONA								
1 *McCain*	N	N	N	Y	Y	Y	N	Y
2 Udall	Y	N	N	N	N	N	?	?
3 *Stump*	N	N	?	?	Y	Y	N	N
4 *Rudd*	N	N	Y	?	Y	Y	?	?
5 McNulty	Y	N	N	N	Y	N	?	?
ARKANSAS								
1 Alexander	?	Y	Y	?	N	X	Y	?
2 *Bethune*	N	N	N	Y	?	?	N	?
3 *Hammerschmidt*	N	Y	N	Y	Y	Y	N	?
4 Anthony	?	Y	#	Y	?	N	N	Y
CALIFORNIA								
1 Bosco	Y	N	N	N	Y	N	Y	Y
2 *Chappie*	N	N	N	?	Y	Y	N	N
3 Matsui	Y	N	Y	N	N	N	Y	Y
4 Fazio	N	N	Y	N	N	N	Y	Y
5 Burton	Y	N	N	N	?	?	Y	Y
6 Boxer	Y	N	N	?	N	Y	Y	Y
7 Miller	Y	N	N	N	N	N	Y	Y
8 Dellums	Y	N	N	N	N	N	N	P
9 Stark	Y	Y	N	N	N	N	Y	Y
10 Edwards	Y	N	N	N	N	N	Y	Y
11 Lantos	Y	N	Y	N	N	N	Y	Y
12 *Zschau*	Y	N	Y	Y	Y	Y	N	Y
13 Mineta	Y	N	N	N	N	N	Y	Y
14 *Shumway*	N	N	N	Y	Y	Y	N	N
15 Coelho	Y	N	N	N	N	N	Y	?
16 *Panetta*	Y	Y	N	N	Y	N	Y	Y
17 *Pashayan*	N	N	N	Y	Y	Y	N	Y
18 Lehman	Y	N	N	N	N	N	Y	Y
19 *Lagomarsino*	N	N	N	Y	Y	Y	N	Y
20 *Thomas*	N	Y	N	?	Y	Y	N	Y
21 *Fiedler*	N	N	N	Y	Y	N	N	Y
22 *Moorhead*	N	N	Y	Y	Y	Y	N	N
23 Beilenson	Y	Y	Y	N	Y	N	Y	Y
24 Waxman	Y	N	?	N	N	N	Y	?
25 Roybal	Y	N	N	N	N	N	Y	?
26 Berman	Y	N	N	N	N	N	Y	Y
27 Levine	Y	N	N	N	N	N	Y	Y
28 Dixon	#	N	Y	N	N	N	N	P
29 Hawkins	?	N	Y	N	N	N	N	Y
30 Martinez	Y	N	N	N	N	N	N	Y
31 Dymally	?	N	N	N	N	N	N	Y
32 Anderson	N	N	N	N	N	N	Y	Y
33 *Dreier*	N	N	N	Y	Y	Y	N	N
34 Torres	Y	N	N	N	N	N	Y	Y
35 *Lewis*	N	N	N	Y	Y	Y	N	Y
36 Brown	Y	N	N	N	N	N	?	?
37 *McCandless*	N	Y	N	Y	Y	Y	N	N
38 Patterson	N	N	Y	N	Y	N	N	Y
39 *Dannemeyer*	N	Y	Y	+	Y	Y	N	N
40 *Badham*	N	N	N	Y	Y	Y	N	N
41 *Lowery*	N	Y	N	Y	Y	Y	N	Y
42 *Lungren*	N	Y	N	Y	Y	Y	N	Y

	9	10	11	12	13	14	15	16
43 *Packard*	N	Y	N	Y	Y	Y	N	?
44 *Bates*	Y	Y	N	N	N	N	Y	Y
45 *Hunter*	N	N	N	Y	Y	Y	N	N
COLORADO								
1 Schroeder	Y	N	N	N	N	N	N	?
2 Wirth	Y	N	N	N	N	N	N	Y
3 Kogovsek	Y	N	Y	?	N	N	N	Y
4 *Brown*	N	N	N	Y	Y	Y	N	Y
5 *Kramer*	N	N	Y	Y	Y	Y	N	Y
6 *Schaefer*	N	Y	N	Y	Y	Y	N	N
CONNECTICUT								
1 Kennelly	Y	N	N	Y	N	Y	N	Y
2 Gejdenson	Y	N	N	N	N	N	Y	Y
3 Morrison	Y	N	N	N	Y	N	Y	?
4 *McKinney*	#	Y	Y	N	N	Y	N	Y
5 Ratchford	Y	N	N	N	N	N	Y	?
6 *Johnson*	Y	Y	N	N	Y	Y	N	Y
DELAWARE								
AL Carper	Y	Y	Y	N	N	Y	N	Y
FLORIDA								
1 Hutto	N	Y	Y	N	Y	Y	N	N
2 Fuqua	N	Y	Y	Y	Y	Y	N	?
3 Bennett	Y	Y	Y	N	Y	Y	N	N
4 Chappell	N	Y	N	Y	N	Y	N	N
5 *McCollum*	N	N	Y	Y	Y	N	N	N
6 MacKay	Y	Y	N	N	Y	N	Y	?
7 Gibbons	?	Y	Y	N	Y	N	Y	Y
8 *Young*	N	Y	N	Y	Y	Y	N	N
9 *Bilirakis*	N	N	N	Y	Y	Y	N	N
10 *Ireland*	N	Y	N	Y	Y	Y	N	N
11 Nelson	N	Y	Y	Y	Y	Y	N	Y
12 *Lewis*	N	Y	N	Y	Y	Y	N	N
13 *Mack*	N	N	N	Y	Y	Y	N	N
14 Mica	Y	Y	N	Y	N	Y	N	Y
15 *Shaw*	N	Y	N	?	Y	Y	N	?
16 Smith	Y	Y	N	N	N	N	Y	Y
17 Lehman	Y	Y	N	N	N	N	Y	Y
18 Pepper	N	Y	N	N	?	?	Y	Y
19 Fascell	Y	Y	Y	N	N	N	Y	Y
GEORGIA								
1 Thomas	N	N	N	N	N	N	N	Y
2 Hatcher	?	N	Y	?	?	?	Y	Y
3 Ray	N	N	Y	Y	Y	Y	N	Y
4 Levitas	N	Y	N	N	Y	N	Y	Y
5 Fowler	Y	Y	N	N	Y	N	N	Y
6 *Gingrich*	N	Y	?	Y	Y	Y	N	N
7 Darden	N	N	Y	N	N	Y	N	Y
8 Rowland	N	N	Y	N	Y	N	N	Y
9 Jenkins	?	N	Y	N	Y	Y	Y	?
10 Barnard	?	N	N	N	N	Y	?	N
HAWAII								
1 Heftel	Y	Y	?	N	Y	N	N	?
2 Akaka	Y	N	N	N	N	N	Y	Y
IDAHO								
1 *Craig*	N	N	N	Y	Y	Y	N	Y
2 *Hansen*	?	?	?	?	?	Y	?	?
ILLINOIS								
1 Hayes	Y	N	N	N	N	N	Y	P
2 Savage	Y	N	N	N	N	N	Y	P
3 Russo	Y	Y	N	N	N	N	N	Y
4 *O'Brien*	N	Y	X	Y	Y	Y	N	Y
5 Lipinski	N	Y	N	N	N	N	Y	Y
6 *Hyde*	N	Y	Y	Y	Y	Y	N	N
7 Collins	Y	N	N	N	N	N	Y	P
8 Rostenkowski	Y	Y	?	?	N	N	Y	Y
9 Yates	Y	N	N	N	N	N	Y	Y
10 *Porter*	N	Y	N	N	N	N	N	Y
11 Annunzio	Y	Y	Y	N	N	N	Y	Y
12 *Crane, P.*	N	N	N	Y	Y	Y	N	N
13 *Erlenborn*	N	Y	N	Y	Y	?	?	Y
14 *Corcoran*	N	Y	N	Y	Y	+	N	Y
15 *Madigan*	N	Y	N	Y	N	Y	N	Y
16 *Martin*	N	N	N	Y	Y	Y	N	Y
17 Evans	N	N	N	N	N	N	Y	Y
18 *Michel*	N	Y	N	Y	Y	Y	N	Y
19 *Crane, D.*	N	N	N	Y	Y	Y	N	N
20 Durbin	Y	Y	N	N	N	Y	Y	Y
21 Price	N	Y	N	N	N	N	Y	Y
22 Simon	?	N	?	?	?	?	?	?
INDIANA								
1 Hall	Y	N	N	N	N	N	Y	P
2 Sharp	Y	Y	N	N	N	Y	N	Y
3 *Hiler*	N	Y	N	Y	Y	Y	N	?
4 *Coats*	N	Y	N	Y	Y	Y	N	?
5 Hillis	N	N	N	Y	Y	Y	N	?

ND - Northern Democrats   SD - Southern Democrats

	9	10	11	12	13	14	15	16
6 ***Burton***	N	Y	N	Y	Y	Y	N	N
7 ***Myers***	N	Y	Y	Y	Y	N	N	Y
8 McCloskey	Y	Y	N	N	N	Y	Y	Y
9 Hamilton	Y	Y	N	N	N	Y	N	Y
10 Jacobs	Y	N	N	N	N	N	Y	Y
IOWA								
1 ***Leach***	Y	Y	N	N	Y	Y	N	Y
2 ***Tauke***	Y	Y	N	Y	Y	Y	?	Y
3 ***Evans***	Y	Y	N	Y	Y	Y	N	Y
4 Smith	Y	Y	Y	N	N	Y	Y	Y
5 Harkin	Y	Y	N	N	N	Y	N	?
6 Bedell	Y	Y	N	N	N	Y	P	Y
KANSAS								
1 ***Roberts***	N	N	N	Y	Y	Y	N	Y
2 Slattery	Y	Y	N	Y	Y	Y	Y	Y
3 ***Winn***	N	Y	Y	Y	Y	Y	N	Y
4 Glickman	Y	Y	N	N	Y	N	Y	Y
5 ***Whittaker***	N	Y	N	Y	Y	Y	N	Y
KENTUCKY								
1 Hubbard	Y	N	Y	?	Y	Y	N	N
2 Natcher	Y	Y	Y	N	Y	N	Y	Y
3 Mazzoli	Y	Y	Y	N	Y	Y	N	Y
4 ***Snyder***	N	N	N	Y	Y	Y	N	N
5 ***Rogers***	N	N	Y	Y	Y	Y	N	N
6 ***Hopkins***	N	N	N	Y	Y	Y	N	N
7 Perkins[1]	Y	N	Y	N				
LOUISIANA								
1 ***Livingston***	N	Y	N	Y	Y	Y	N	N
2 Boggs	Y	Y	Y	N	N	?	N	P
3 Tauzin	N	N	N	Y	Y	Y	Y	Y
4 Roemer	N	N	N	Y	Y	Y	N	Y
5 Huckaby	N	N	Y	Y	Y	Y	N	Y
6 ***Moore***	N	N	N	Y	Y	Y	N	Y
7 Breaux	N	Y	Y	Y	Y	Y	N	?
8 Long	Y	Y	Y	N	Y	N	Y	?
MAINE								
1 ***McKernan***	N	Y	N	Y	N	Y	Y	Y
2 ***Snowe***	N	Y	Y	Y	N	Y	Y	Y
MARYLAND								
1 Dyson	Y	N	N	N	Y	Y	Y	?
2 Long	Y	Y	Y	N	N	Y	N	Y
3 Mikulski	Y	?	N	N	N	N	Y	?
4 ***Holt***	N	Y	N	Y	Y	Y	N	Y
5 Hoyer	Y	Y	N	N	?	X	Y	Y
6 Byron	N	Y	Y	Y	Y	Y	N	Y
7 Mitchell	Y	N	N	N	N	N	Y	P
8 Barnes	Y	Y	N	N	N	N	Y	Y
MASSACHUSETTS								
1 ***Conte***	Y	Y	N	N	N	Y	Y	Y
2 Boland	Y	Y	Y	?	N	N	Y	Y
3 Early	Y	Y	Y	?	N	N	Y	?
4 Frank	Y	Y	N	N	N	N	Y	Y
5 Shannon	Y	?	?	N	N	N	?	?
6 Mavroules	Y	Y	Y	N	N	N	Y	Y
7 Markey	Y	N	N	N	N	N	Y	Y
8 O'Neill	Y							
9 Moakley	Y	Y	Y	N	N	N	Y	Y
10 Studds	Y	Y	N	?	N	N	Y	Y
11 Donnelly	Y	Y	Y	N	N	N	Y	Y
MICHIGAN								
1 Conyers	Y	N	N	N	N	N	Y	P
2 ***Pursell***	N	N	N	Y	?	Y	?	?
3 Wolpe	Y	N	N	N	N	N	Y	Y
4 ***Siljander***	N	N	N	Y	Y	Y	N	?
5 ***Sawyer***	X	Y	N	Y	Y	Y	N	?
6 Carr	Y	N	Y	N	N	Y	Y	Y
7 Kildee	Y	N	N	N	N	N	Y	Y
8 Traxler	Y	Y	Y	N	N	N	Y	Y
9 ***Vander Jagt***	X	N	N	Y	Y	Y	N	?
10 Albosta	Y	N	Y	Y	N	Y	Y	?
11 ***Davis***	N	Y	N	N	N	Y	N	Y
12 Bonior	Y	Y	Y	N	?	N	Y	?
13 Crockett	?	N	Y	N	N	N	Y	?
14 Hertel	Y	N	N	N	N	Y	Y	Y
15 Ford	Y	N	N	N	N	N	Y	Y
16 Dingell	Y	Y	Y	N	N	N	Y	Y
17 Levin	Y	Y	N	N	N	N	Y	Y
18 ***Broomfield***	N	N	N	Y	Y	Y	N	Y
MINNESOTA								
1 Penny	Y	Y	N	Y	N	N	N	Y
2 ***Weber***	N	Y	N	Y	N	Y	N	Y
3 ***Frenzel***	N	Y	N	Y	Y	Y	N	Y
4 Vento	Y	N	N	?	N	N	Y	Y
5 Sabo	#	Y	Y	N	N	N	N	Y
6 Sikorski	Y	N	N	N	N	N	Y	Y

	9	10	11	12	13	14	15	16
7 ***Stangeland***	N	Y	N	Y	Y	Y	N	Y
8 Oberstar	Y	N	Y	N	N	N	Y	Y
MISSISSIPPI								
1 Whitten	Y	N	Y	N	Y	N	Y	Y
2 ***Franklin***	N	Y	N	Y	Y	#	N	Y
3 Montgomery	N	Y	Y	Y	Y	Y	Y	?
4 Dowdy	?	Y	N	N	N	Y	Y	?
5 ***Lott***	N	Y	N	Y	Y	Y	N	N
MISSOURI								
1 Clay	Y	N	?	N	N	N	Y	P
2 Young	Y	N	#	N	X	Y	Y	Y
3 Gephardt	Y	N	N	N	N	N	Y	?
4 Skelton	N	N	Y	N	N	N	Y	?
5 Wheat	Y	N	Y	N	N	N	Y	P
6 ***Coleman***	N	N	N	Y	Y	Y	N	Y
7 ***Taylor***	N	Y	N	?	Y	Y	N	N
8 ***Emerson***	N	N	N	Y	Y	Y	N	Y
9 Volkmer	Y	N	Y	N	N	Y	Y	Y
MONTANA								
1 Williams	Y	-	N	N	N	N	?	Y
2 ***Marlenee***	N	N	N	Y	Y	?	N	Y
NEBRASKA								
1 ***Bereuter***	Y	Y	N	Y	Y	Y	N	Y
2 ***Daub***	N	N	N	Y	Y	Y	N	Y
3 ***Smith***	Y	Y	N	Y	Y	Y	N	Y
NEVADA								
1 Reid	N	N	Y	N	N	N	Y	?
2 ***Vucanovich***	N	Y	N	Y	Y	Y	N	Y
NEW HAMPSHIRE								
1 D'Amours	Y	Y	N	Y	N	#	Y	?
2 ***Gregg***	N	Y	N	Y	N	Y	N	Y
NEW JERSEY								
1 Florio	Y	N	N	N	N	N	Y	Y
2 Hughes	N	N	N	Y	Y	N	N	Y
3 Howard	?	Y	N	N	N	N	Y	?
4 ***Smith***	N	Y	N	N	N	Y	Y	Y
5 ***Roukema***	Y	N	N	Y	Y	Y	N	Y
6 Dwyer	Y	Y	Y	N	N	Y	Y	Y
7 ***Rinaldo***	N	N	N	?	N	Y	Y	Y
8 Roe	?	Y	N	N	Y	N	Y	Y
9 Torricelli	Y	Y	N	N	N	N	Y	Y
10 Rodino	#	Y	Y	N	N	N	Y	Y
11 Minish	Y	Y	N	N	N	Y	?	Y
12 ***Courter***	N	N	N	?	Y	Y	N	N
13 ***Forsythe***[2]								
14 Guarini	?	N	Y	N	N	X	Y	Y
NEW MEXICO								
1 ***Lujan***	N	N	N	Y	Y	Y	N	N
2 ***Skeen***	N	N	N	Y	Y	Y	N	N
3 Richardson	Y	N	N	N	N	N	Y	Y
NEW YORK								
1 ***Carney***	N	N	N	Y	Y	Y	N	Y
2 Downey	Y	Y	N	N	N	N	N	Y
3 Mrazek	Y	Y	N	N	N	Y	Y	Y
4 ***Lent***	N	N	N	Y	N	Y	N	N
5 ***McGrath***	N	N	N	Y	N	#	?	Y
6 Addabbo	Y	N	Y	N	N	N	Y	Y
7 Ackerman	#	N	N	N	N	N	N	Y
8 Scheuer	Y	Y	N	N	N	N	N	Y
9 Ferraro	Y	N	?	?	N	?	?	?
10 Schumer	Y	Y	N	N	?	N	Y	Y
11 Towns	Y	N	N	N	N	N	Y	P
12 Owens	Y	N	N	N	N	N	Y	P
13 Solarz	Y	Y	N	N	N	N	N	Y
14 ***Molinari***	N	Y	N	Y	N	Y	N	Y
15 ***Green***	Y	Y	N	N	N	N	Y	Y
16 Rangel	Y	N	N	N	N	N	Y	P
17 Weiss	Y	N	N	N	N	N	N	Y
18 Garcia	Y	N	N	N	N	N	Y	Y
19 Biaggi	Y	N	?	N	N	N	N	Y
20 Ottinger	Y	Y	N	N	N	N	Y	?
21 ***Fish***	N	Y	N	Y	Y	Y	?	Y
22 ***Gilman***	N	Y	N	N	N	Y	Y	Y
23 Stratton	N	N	?	N	Y	Y	N	N
24 ***Solomon***	N	N	N	Y	Y	Y	Y	N
25 ***Boehlert***	N	Y	N	N	N	Y	N	Y
26 ***Martin***	N	N	N	Y	Y	Y	N	Y
27 ***Wortley***	N	Y	N	Y	Y	Y	N	N
28 McHugh	Y	Y	N	N	N	N	Y	Y
29 ***Horton***	N	N	X	N	N	Y	N	?
30 ***Conable***	N	Y	N	?	Y	Y	N	N
31 ***Kemp***	N	N	N	Y	Y	Y	N	Y
32 LaFalce	Y	Y	Y	N	N	N	?	Y
33 Nowak	Y	Y	Y	N	N	N	Y	Y
34 Lundine	?	Y	Y	Y	N	Y	Y	?

	9	10	11	12	13	14	15	16
NORTH CAROLINA								
1 Jones	Y	N	Y	N	Y	N	?	Y
2 Valentine	N	Y	Y	N	Y	Y	Y	Y
3 Whitley	N	Y	Y	N	Y	Y	N	?
4 Andrews	Y	Y	N	N	Y	Y	N	Y
5 Neal	Y	Y	N	?	N	Y	N	Y
6 Britt	N	Y	Y	N	Y	Y	Y	Y
7 Rose	Y	Y	Y	N	Y	Y	Y	Y
8 Hefner	N	Y	Y	N	Y	Y	N	?
9 ***Martin***	N	Y	N	Y	?	?	?	?
10 ***Broyhill***	N	Y	N	Y	Y	Y	Y	Y
11 Clarke	Y	Y	N	N	?	N	Y	?
NORTH DAKOTA								
AL Dorgan	Y	Y	Y	N	N	N	Y	Y
OHIO								
1 Luken	Y	Y	N	N	Y	Y	Y	Y
2 ***Gradison***	Y	Y	N	Y	Y	Y	N	Y
3 Hall	Y	N	N	N	N	N	Y	Y
4 ***Oxley***	N	Y	N	+	Y	Y	N	Y
5 ***Latta***	N	N	N	Y	Y	Y	N	Y
6 ***McEwen***	N	Y	N	Y	#	Y	N	?
7 ***DeWine***	N	Y	N	Y	Y	Y	N	N
8 ***Kindness***	N	N	N	Y	Y	Y	N	N
9 Kaptur	Y	N	N	N	N	Y	N	?
10 ***Miller***	N	Y	N	Y	Y	Y	N	N
11 Eckart	Y	Y	N	N	N	Y	Y	Y
12 ***Kasich***	N	Y	N	Y	Y	Y	Y	N
13 Pease	Y	Y	N	N	Y	N	N	Y
14 Seiberling	Y	Y	N	N	N	N	Y	Y
15 ***Wylie***	N	Y	N	Y	Y	Y	N	Y
16 ***Regula***	N	N	Y	Y	Y	Y	Y	Y
17 ***Williams***	N	N	N	N	?	?	Y	?
18 Applegate	Y	N	Y	Y	Y	Y	Y	N
19 Feighan	Y	Y	N	N	N	N	Y	Y
20 Oakar	Y	N	N	N	N	N	Y	?
21 Stokes	Y	N	N	N	N	N	Y	P
OKLAHOMA								
1 Jones	Y	Y	N	N	Y	Y	N	Y
2 Synar	Y	Y	N	N	Y	N	N	Y
3 Watkins	N	N	N	Y	Y	Y	N	?
4 McCurdy	?	Y	N	N	Y	Y	N	?
5 ***Edwards***	X	N	Y	Y	Y	Y	N	N
6 English	?	N	N	Y	Y	Y	N	Y
OREGON								
1 AuCoin	Y	N	Y	N	N	Y	N	Y
2 ***Smith, R.***	N	N	N	Y	Y	Y	N	Y
3 Wyden	Y	N	Y	N	N	N	N	Y
4 Weaver	Y	Y	N	N	N	N	Y	?
5 ***Smith, D.***	N	Y	N	Y	Y	Y	N	N
PENNSYLVANIA								
1 Foglietta	Y	N	N	N	N	N	Y	?
2 Gray	Y	N	Y	N	N	N	Y	?
3 Borski	Y	N	N	N	N	N	Y	Y
4 Kolter	?	N	Y	Y	N	N	Y	Y
5 ***Schulze***	N	Y	Y	Y	Y	Y	N	?
6 Yatron	N	N	Y	N	N	Y	?	Y
7 Edgar	Y	N	N	N	N	N	Y	Y
8 Kostmayer	Y	Y	N	N	N	Y	Y	Y
9 ***Shuster***	N	N	Y	Y	Y	Y	N	N
10 ***McDade***	N	Y	Y	Y	N	Y	N	Y
11 Harrison	Y	Y	Y	N	?	?	Y	Y
12 Murtha	N	Y	Y	N	Y	N	Y	Y
13 ***Coughlin***	Y	Y	N	N	N	Y	N	Y
14 Coyne	Y	Y	Y	N	N	N	Y	Y
15 ***Ritter***	N	Y	N	Y	N	Y	Y	Y
16 ***Walker***	N	Y	N	Y	Y	Y	N	Y
17 ***Gekas***	N	N	Y	N	Y	Y	N	N
18 Walgren	Y	Y	N	Y	N	N	Y	?
19 ***Goodling***	Y	N	N	Y	Y	Y	N	Y
20 Gaydos	Y	N	Y	N	N	N	Y	Y
21 ***Ridge***	Y	Y	N	Y	Y	Y	Y	Y
22 Murphy	Y	N	Y	N	Y	N	Y	?
23 ***Clinger***	N	Y	Y	Y	Y	Y	N	Y
RHODE ISLAND								
1 St Germain	Y	Y	N	?	N	N	Y	Y
2 ***Schneider***	Y	Y	N	N	N	Y	Y	Y
SOUTH CAROLINA								
1 ***Hartnett***	N	N	N	Y	Y	Y	N	N
2 ***Spence***	N	N	N	Y	Y	Y	N	N
3 Derrick	Y	Y	Y	Y	Y	Y	N	?
4 ***Campbell***	N	Y	?	Y	Y	Y	N	Y
5 Spratt	Y	Y	N	N	Y	N	N	Y
6 Tallon	Y	Y	N	N	Y	Y	N	?
SOUTH DAKOTA								
AL Daschle	Y	Y	Y	Y	Y	N	N	Y

	9	10	11	12	13	14	15	16
TENNESSEE								
1 ***Quillen***	N	Y	Y	N	Y	N	N	N
2 ***Duncan***	N	N	N	Y	Y	Y	N	Y
3 Lloyd	N	Y	Y	N	Y	Y	N	N
4 Cooper	N	Y	Y	N	N	N	N	?
5 Boner	N	Y	Y	N	N	N	Y	?
6 Gore	N	Y	N	N	N	N	Y	Y
7 ***Sundquist***	N	N	N	N	Y	Y	N	Y
8 Jones	N	Y	?	?	N	N	Y	Y
9 Ford	Y	Y	N	N	N	N	Y	P
TEXAS								
1 Hall, S.	N	N	Y	Y	?	Y	N	N
2 Wilson	X	Y	?	N	Y	Y	?	Y
3 ***Bartlett***	N	N	N	Y	Y	Y	N	Y
4 Hall, R.	N	N	Y	Y	N	Y	N	N
5 Bryant	#	N	Y	N	N	N	Y	Y
6 ***Gramm***	N	N	?	?	Y	?	?	?
7 ***Archer***	N	N	N	Y	Y	Y	N	Y
8 ***Fields***	N	N	N	Y	Y	Y	N	Y
9 Brooks	Y	N	Y	N	Y	N	Y	Y
10 Pickle	Y	Y	Y	N	Y	Y	N	?
11 Leath	X	N	Y	N	Y	Y	N	?
12 Wright	Y	Y	Y	N	N	N	N	Y
13 Hightower	N	N	Y	Y	Y	Y	N	Y
14 Patman	N	N	Y	Y	Y	Y	Y	N
15 de la Garza	N	N	Y	N	N	N	N	?
16 Coleman	Y	N	Y	N	Y	Y	N	?
17 Stenholm	N	N	N	Y	Y	Y	N	?
18 Leland	#	?	Y	N	N	X	Y	P
19 Hance	X	N	Y	Y	N	Y	N	?
20 Gonzalez	Y	N	Y	N	N	N	Y	N
21 ***Loeffler***	N	N	Y	Y	Y	Y	N	Y
22 ***Paul***	Y	N	N	Y	Y	N	N	?
23 Kazen	N	N	Y	N	Y	N	N	Y
24 Frost	X	N	Y	?	N	N	Y	Y
25 Andrews	N	N	Y	N	Y	Y	N	Y
26 Vandergriff	N	N	Y	N	Y	N	Y	Y
27 Ortiz	N	N	N	N	N	N	N	Y
UTAH								
1 ***Hansen***	N	Y	N	Y	Y	Y	N	N
2 ***Marriott***	X	N	?	?	?	Y	N	?
3 ***Nielson***	N	Y	Y	Y	Y	Y	N	N
VERMONT								
AL ***Jeffords***	#	Y	N	Y	N	Y	N	Y
VIRGINIA								
1 ***Bateman***	N	Y	N	Y	?	Y	N	N
2 ***Whitehurst***	N	Y	N	Y	Y	Y	N	Y
3 ***Bliley***	N	N	N	Y	Y	Y	N	Y
4 Sisisky	Y	Y	N	N	Y	Y	N	N
5 Daniel	N	N	Y	Y	Y	Y	N	N
6 Olin	Y	N	N	Y	?	Y	Y	Y
7 ***Robinson***	N	N	-	Y	Y	Y	N	N
8 ***Parris***	N	N	Y	Y	Y	Y	N	Y
9 Boucher	Y	Y	Y	N	N	N	N	Y
10 ***Wolf***	N	Y	N	Y	Y	Y	N	Y
WASHINGTON								
1 ***Pritchard***	N	Y	?	?	?	Y	N	Y
2 Swift	Y	N	N	N	N	N	N	Y
3 Bonker	?	Y	N	N	N	N	N	Y
4 ***Morrison***	N	Y	N	N	Y	N	Y	Y
5 Foley	Y	Y	Y	N	Y	N	N	Y
6 Dicks	N	Y	N	N	N	N	N	Y
7 Lowry	Y	N	N	N	N	N	N	Y
8 ***Chandler***	N	Y	N	N	Y	Y	N	Y
WEST VIRGINIA								
1 Mollohan	N	N	Y	N	Y	N	Y	Y
2 Staggers	Y	N	Y	N	N	N	Y	Y
3 Wise	Y	N	Y	N	N	Y	Y	Y
4 Rahall	Y	Y	Y	N	?	Y	Y	Y
WISCONSIN								
1 Aspin	N	Y	Y	N	N	N	Y	?
2 Kastenmeier	Y	Y	N	N	N	N	Y	Y
3 ***Gunderson***	N	Y	N	Y	Y	Y	N	Y
4 Kleczka[3]	Y	Y	N	N	Y	N	Y	Y
5 Moody	Y	Y	N	Y	N	?	Y	Y
6 ***Petri***	Y	Y	N	Y	Y	Y	N	Y
7 Obey	Y	Y	N	N	N	N	N	Y
8 ***Roth***	N	N	Y	Y	Y	Y	N	Y
9 ***Sensenbrenner***	?	?	N	Y	Y	Y	N	Y
WYOMING								
AL ***Cheney***	N	Y	N	Y	Y	#	?	N

[1] *Died Aug. 3, 1984.*
[2] *Died March 29, 1984.*
[3] *Sworn in April 10, 1984.*

Southern states - Ala., Ark., Fla., Ga., Ky., La., Miss., N.C., Okla., S.C., Tenn., Texas, Va.

1984 Partisanship More Rhetoric Than Voting

An analysis of congressional voting in 1984 showed that President Reagan's Capitol Hill support stayed at roughly the same level as it was the year before, while partisan voting in the House and Senate tapered off.

In addition, Southern Democrats and Republicans infrequently forged a conservative coalition against Northern Democrats, reflecting a general decline in the appearance of this traditional alliance.

These and other findings were based on four statistical vote studies conducted by Congressional Quarterly.

The annual studies measured presidential support, party unity, voting participation and the strength of the conservative coalition in Congress.

While it was difficult to draw conclusions based on the statistics for Congress as a whole, the vote scores of individual lawmakers could be revealing. They showed, for example, how election-year pressures influenced a member's votes and how other factors, such as regional interests, could color a member's choices more than the party's position on certain votes.

Because of the criteria used to select votes in CQ's studies, the results were more useful in charting changes in individual members' voting patterns than they were in measuring levels of presidential power or party loyalty.

In comparing 1984 voting trends with those in 1983, it also was risky to make generalizations because the nature of the votes changed.

While lawmakers were voting on Lebanon in 1983, this year they were preoccupied with El Salvador and Nicaragua. And some issues in 1984 were fresh topics, and there was no basis for comparison with earlier years. (1983 Vote Studies, 1983 Almanac p. 18-C)

One of the interesting trends this year was the low number of roll calls taken in the House and Senate.

Reflecting a decline over the past few years, there were 683 recorded congressional votes in 1984, 408 of them in the House and 275 in the Senate. This was the lowest number since 1969.

"Congress is just doing less," observed Norman Ornstein, a congressional scholar at the American Enterprise Institute. "Members just don't feel any incentive to go to the floor to offer amendments. People want to avoid conflicts, and much of the conflict is channeled into the budget resolution and appropriations bills."

The shrinking number of roll calls also affected the 1984 voting participation scores of members of Congress. On the average, members recorded a position on 91 percent of the votes taken, a high level for an election year. But because there were fewer roll calls, there was less demand on members' time and it was easier to show up for the votes that were held.

Presidential Support

Although Congressional Quarterly's presidential support study showed a minimal change in overall support for Reagan's positions, the study revealed significant changes among certain groups.

For example, there was an increase in support for Reagan's position among House Democrats from the East, Midwest and West, while Southern Democrats in the House backed him about as often in 1984 as they did the year before.

This trend, Ornstein said, suggests that "some Northern Democrats are a little worried about their competition and President Reagan's popularity, and they decided they had to hedge their bets a little bit" by moving closer to the president's positions.

While Southern Democrats continued to rank higher in presidential support than House Democrats from other regions, in the past three years their scores have not reached their 1981 high, when they joined forces with House Republicans to give Reagan his victories on economic legislation.

Because Southern Democrats did not feel compelled to line up with Reagan this year as they did in 1981, "it could mean that Ronald Reagan isn't able to put together the Boll Weevil coalition again next year," Ornstein suggested.

Another interesting trend in the 1984 presidential support study showed a 10 percentage point decline in support for Reagan's policies among House Republicans.

This drop reflected two things: an effort by some Republicans to demonstrate their political independence from the president and a decision by House Republican leaders to focus on Reagan's top priorities while allowing members to vote as they wished on less critical matters.

A House Republican leadership aide said Minority Leader Robert H. Michel, R-Ill., told the White House to "pick your best shots . . . try to isolate your issues as much as possible."

As a result, Republican leaders whipped members into line on key votes, such as an anti-crime bill the president wanted. But they did not ask members to toe the party line on minor bills or measures on which there was overwhelming opposition to Reagan's position, such as Social Security disability legislation.

"You can only go to the well so often," the aide said.

Republicans also seemed to split most often on "pork-barrel" votes, where benefits to their districts outweighed the party's demand for fiscal conservatism.

The 1984 party unity study showed a decline in partisan voting on the House and Senate floors, which could be attributed to a number of factors.

In the House, at least, Democratic leaders did not flex their political muscle to the extent that they did in 1983, when their 26-seat gain allowed them to take steps to reverse some of Reagan's earlier victories.

Also, while partisan rhetoric was often heated on Capitol Hill, many divisive issues were worked out before they reached the floor, or they never came to a vote at all. Therefore, some of the bitter partisanship was not reflected in the vote study.

"For some of these incumbents up for re-election," Ornstein said, "it is better to channel [partisanship] through rhetoric than votes that your opponent could use against you." In some situations, he said, "talk is better than action."

Scores Up in House:

Congress' Backing for Reagan Declines Only Slightly in 1984

Congressional backing for Ronald Reagan's positions waned only slightly in 1984, almost stopping the decline that has occurred since 1981.

Congressional Quarterly's annual presidential support study showed that Congress agreed with the president on 66 percent of the roll-call votes on which his stance was well-known.

That was about 1 percentage point less than in 1983, and a fraction of the 5 percentage point erosion between 1982 and 1983, and the 10 percentage point drop between 1981 and 1982. *(Box, below)*

The study showed the dip even though support for Reagan's positions increased in the House and stayed the same in the Senate. This resulted because far more of the votes on which Reagan had a clear stand took place in the Democratic-controlled House, where he was less likely to win, than in the Republican Senate.

Overall, his support in Congress has slipped nearly 17 percentage points from the level in 1981, his first year in office, a year in which Congress reacted to the mandate of his landslide victory by enacting much of Reagan's program.

Reagan's slippage from his 1981 success rate of 82 percent was the third largest decline of the last seven

presidents. President Eisenhower suffered a 19 point drop in his first term and President Johnson had an 18 point loss over his term that began in 1965.

In 1984, on recorded Senate votes on which he took a stand, Reagan won 86 percent of the time, the same success rate he enjoyed in 1983. In the House, Reagan's support increased slightly more than 4 percentage points from 1983, to just over 52 percent.

While the volume of partisan, election-year rhetoric increased in the Democratic-controlled House in 1984, the presidential support scores took a curious turn. Democrats' scores went up, while those of Republicans went down.

Study's Limitations

For its analysis, CQ considered 190 recorded votes on which Reagan had a known position. Of those, 77 votes were in the Senate; 113 were in the House. Had there been a more equal division of votes between the chambers, Reagan's overall score of 66 percent likely would have been higher, benefiting from his broader Senate support. Last year's study was almost an even split — 85 Senate votes and 82 House votes.

Although the study illustrated the political differences between Reagan and Congress, it did not measure how much of his program actually was enacted. And as an indicator of a member's loyalty to the president, the study should be used with care, caution and caveats.

First, the study counted only issues that reached a roll-call vote on the House or Senate floor. It did not consider items on the White House agenda that were scuttled or defeated before they reached the floor, privately compromised or passed on a voice vote.

Second, the analysis counted only votes where Reagan's public support or opposition was clear.

Third, all votes received equal weight. No distinction was made between major and minor votes, narrow and overwhelming outcomes, administration initiatives and congressional proposals. *(Ground rules, box, p. 21-C)*

For example, a close, largely party-line Senate vote to reject conditions on military aid to El Salvador, which was a major foreign policy victory for Reagan, counted the same in CQ's analysis of Senate support as the unanimous vote on a popular bill aimed at collecting money from parents who fail to make child-support payments.

Finally, issues that took many roll calls to resolve may have influenced the study more than matters settled by a single vote. The classic recent example was in 1978, when President Carter's Senate support score was dramatically enhanced by 55 winning roll-call votes — mostly procedural — on ratification of the Panama Canal treaties.

In 1984, some controversial issues required several roll calls, giving them added importance in assessing Reagan's support rating. To illustrate, 17 roll-call votes were taken when the Senate debated a supplemental appropriations bill that included Reagan's request for aid to El Salvador and to Nicaraguan rebels, and 11 of those votes were considered in the CQ study.

In contrast, the Senate had one roll call on its first budget resolution to set spending and revenue targets for fiscal 1985. The vote, a clear party split, was a key indicator of support for the president's economic policy.

Although some issues were important to the president, he did not take an evident position on various aspects of legislation. In such cases, CQ's study did not reflect Reagan's stance, or whether Congress supported it.

A reporter or researcher interested in how an individ-

Success Rate

Following are the annual percentages of presidential victories since 1953 on congressional votes where the presidents took a clear-cut position:

Eisenhower		Nixon	
1953	89.0%	1969	74.0%
1954	82.8	1970	77.0
1955	75.0	1971	75.0
1956	70.0	1972	66.0
1957	68.0	1973	50.6
1958	76.0	1974	59.6
1959	52.0	**Ford**	
1960	65.0	1974	58.2%
		1975	61.0
Kennedy		1976	53.8
1961	81.0%	**Carter**	
1962	85.4	1977	75.4%
1963	87.1	1978	78.3
		1979	76.8
		1980	75.1
Johnson			
1964	88.0%	**Reagan**	
1965	93.0	1981	82.4%
1966	79.0	1982	72.4
1967	79.0	1983	67.1
1968	75.0	1984	65.8

ual member of Congress voted on aspects of the president's program is advised to look at the specifics of the member's legislative actions, including his or her record on CQ's selected key votes. *(Key votes, p. 3-C)*

Still, the presidential support score was a rough gauge of the relationship between the president and Congress. Over time, the score reflected numerically the rises and dips in those relations, and the individual's ratings showed how particular members fit the trends.

The study was begun in 1953, Eisenhower's first year in office, and long was considered a yardstick of presidential success on Capitol Hill. A careful reading of the study's ground rules shows its drawbacks as a measure of executive clout, but not all readers have used the figures with discrimination.

During the 1980 presidential campaign, President Carter's supporters cited his 77 percent presidential support score for 1979 as evidence that Congress had passed four-fifths of the president's program. A Carter aide later acknowledged that CQ's statistics had been "mistranslated or misused."

Party, Regional Differences

As would be expected, Republicans agreed with Reagan more often than did Democrats. In the Senate, the Republican majority supported his positions on 76 percent of the votes, for a 3 point increase. But the president lost 10 points among House Republicans, falling from a 70 percent to a 60 percent support score.

Among Senate Democrats, Reagan's support barely changed, slipping a single point, from 42 percent to 41 percent. House Democrats backed the president on 34 percent of the roll calls, up six points from 1983.

A breakdown by party and region (East, West, South, Midwest) shows that, in the Senate, Reagan had greatest support in 1984 among Southern Republicans (84 percent, up 10 points) and the least backing from Western Democrats (32 percent, down 6 points). In the House, agreeing with Reagan most often were Western Republicans (65 percent, down 10 points), and least often were Democrats from the same area (28 percent, up 8 points).

In both chambers, Democrats from every region gave Reagan low support scores; only Southern senators backed him more than half the time (52 percent, a 10 point rise).

But House Democrats from all four regions voted more often with the president in 1984 than 1983, while his support declined among House Republicans from every region.

Senate

The president's biggest supporters in the Senate, with tie scores of 92 percent, were Republicans Richard G. Lugar, Ind., also the top scorer of 1983 and 1981, and Majority Leader Howard H. Baker Jr., Tenn., the top scorer of 1982.

Next were two influential Republicans who were absent from the 1983 list of Reagan's top supporters: Robert Dole, Kan., with 90 percent, and Pete V. Domenici, N.M., with 88 percent. Both men parted with Reagan on key economic questions in 1983. Domenici, whose score increased by 14 points in 1984, was up for re-election, but his rival was not viewed as a serious threat. Thad Cochran, R-Miss., who faced a re-election challenge, joined the field of Reagan's top Senate supporters for the first time. His score of 87 percent was 16 points higher than 1983.

Among Senate Republicans, only Lowell P. Weicker Jr., Conn., voted contrary to the president's position more than half the time — 55 percent. Others who disagreed most often with Reagan generally included Weicker's moderate-to-liberal cohorts, except for conservative Gordon J. Humphrey, N.H., who was facing a tough re-election fight.

Reagan's top eight Democratic supporters in the Senate included two Southerners who more often opposed him in 1983. Howell Heflin, Ala., who was up for re-election, led Democrats in support for the president with a score of 75 percent — 33 percentage points higher than 1983.

David L. Boren, Okla., also running for re-election, tied for third at 62 percent — 21 points higher than 1983.

Eleven Democrats agreed with Reagan more than half the time, including Minority Leader Robert C. Byrd,

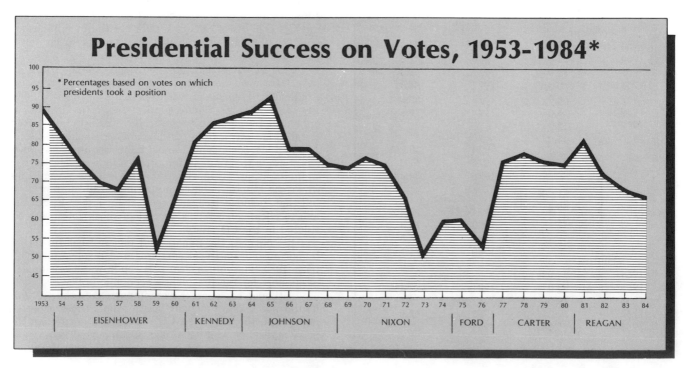

Presidential Success on Votes, 1953-1984*

* Percentages based on votes on which presidents took a position

EISENHOWER   KENNEDY   JOHNSON   NIXON   FORD   CARTER   REAGAN

Ground Rules for CQ Presidential Support-Opposition

Presidential Issues — CQ tries to determine what the president personally, as distinct from other administration officials, does and does not want in the way of legislative action by analyzing his messages to Congress, press conference remarks and other public statements and documents. Members must be aware of the position when the vote is taken.

Borderline Cases — By the time an issue reaches a vote, it may differ from the original form in which the president expressed himself. In such cases, CQ analyzes the measure to determine whether, on balance, the features favored by the president outweigh those he opposed or vice versa. Only then is the vote classified.

Some Votes Excluded — Occasionally, important measures are so extensively amended on the floor that it is impossible to characterize final passage as a victory or defeat for the president.

Procedural Votes — Votes on motions to recommit, to reconsider or to table often are key tests that govern the legislative outcome. Such votes are necessarily included in the presidential support tabulations.

Appropriations — Generally, votes on passage of appropriations bills are not included in the tabulations, since it is rarely possible to determine the president's position on the revisions Congress almost invariably makes in the sums allowed. However, votes on amendments to cut or increase specific amounts requested in the president's budget are included.

Failure to Vote — In tabulating the support or opposition scores of members on the selected presidential-issue votes, CQ counts only "yea" and "nay" votes on the ground that only these affect the outcome. Most failures to vote reflect absences because of illness or official business. Failures to vote lower both support and opposition scores equally.

Weighting — All presidential-issue votes have equal statistical weight in the analysis.

Changed Positions — Presidential support is determined by the position of the president at the time of a vote, even though that position may be different from an earlier position, or may have been reversed after the vote was taken.

W.Va., who scored 53 percent.

Democrats voting against the Reagan position most often were Howard M. Metzenbaum, Ohio, and John Melcher, Mont., both of whom opposed the president 69 percent of the time, and Donald W. Riegle Jr., Mich., whose opposition score was 68 percent. Metzenbaum and Riegle made the list of top Reagan foes in every year of the president's term.

Two names from the 1983 list of chief opponents were notably missing in 1984. David Pryor, Ark., who opposed Reagan more than any other Senate Democrat in 1983, had an opposition score of 47 percent — down 24 points from 1983. And Walter D. Huddleston, Ky., who disagreed with Reagan on 59 percent of 1983 roll calls, opposed the president 40 percent of the time in 1984. Both men were facing re-election fights against conservative opponents.

House

In the House, Steve Bartlett, R-Texas, backed Reagan's position more frequently than any other member — 81 percent of the time. Others heading the ranks of supporters included some of the House's most conservative members, and Minority Leader Robert H. Michel, Ill., who had a 75 percent score.

Liberal-to-moderate "Gypsy Moth" Republicans from the North and East once again composed the GOP group most often voting against Reagan's stance. They were led, as in 1983, by Claudine Schneider, R.I., who opposed the White House position 57 percent of the time. Schneider was on the list of House Republicans frequently at odds with Reagan in every year of his term.

So was Jim Leach, Iowa, whose 1984 opposition score was 53 percent. Prior to the 1984 Republican National Convention, Leach was the organizer, and Schneider an early supporter, of a moderate group trying to fight the party's rightward drift.

Among House Democrats, the group most supportive of the president was led, as twice before, by Dan Daniel,

Va., with 64 percent. G. V. "Sonny" Montgomery, Miss., and Charles W. Stenholm, Texas, were next with support scores of 59 percent and 58 percent, respectively. With Daniel, they were the only House Democrats who had appeared every year on CQ's list of Reagan's top backers.

Other top Democratic supporters were mostly "Boll Weevils" and two other conservatives — Ike Skelton, Mo., at 54 percent and Samuel S. Stratton, N.Y., at 53 percent.

Not surprisingly, Reagan's most consistent opponents in the House included its most liberal Democrats. Charles A. Hayes, Ill., topped their ranks, with an opposition score of 80 percent.

Average Scores

Following are composites of Democratic and Republican scores for 1984 and 1983:

	1984		**1983**	
	Dem.	**Rep.**	**Dem.**	**Rep.**
SUPPORT				
Senate	41%	76%	42%	73%
House	34	60	28	70
OPPOSITION				
Senate	49%	18%	51%	22%
House	58	33	66	25

Regional Averages

SUPPORT

Regional presidential support scores for 1984; scores for 1983 are in parentheses:

	East		West		South		Midwest	
DEMOCRATS								
Senate	35%	(42)	32%	(38)	52%	(42)	40%	(45)
House	31	(22)	28	(20)	43	(42)	30	(21)
REPUBLICANS								
Senate	63	(68)	79	(73)	84	(74)	76	(77)
House	54	(60)	65	(75)	62	(74)	60	(71)

OPPOSITION

Regional presidential opposition scores for 1984; scores for 1983 are in parentheses:

	East		West		South		Midwest	
DEMOCRATS								
Senate	57%	(54)	52%	(49)	37%	(49)	53%	(51)
House	61	(73)	64	(73)	48	(52)	63	(75)
REPUBLICANS								
Senate	30	(27)	14	(20)	10	(23)	19	(20)
House	40	(35)	28	(19)	30	(22)	33	(25)

*(CQ defines regions of the United States as follows: **East:** Conn., Del., Maine, Md., Mass., N.H., N.J., N.Y., Pa., R.I., Vt., W.Va. **West:** Alaska, Ariz., Calif., Colo., Hawaii, Idaho, Mont., Nev., N.M., Ore., Utah, Wash., Wyo. **South:** Ala., Ark., Fla., Ga., Ky., La., Miss., N.C., Okla., S.C., Tenn., Texas, Va. **Midwest:** Ill., Ind., Iowa, Kan., Mich., Minn., Mo., Neb., N.D., Ohio, S.D., Wis.)*

Highest Scorers — Support

Highest individual scorers in presidential support — those who voted most often for Reagan's position in 1984:

SENATE

Democrats		Republicans	
Heflin, Ala.	75%	Lugar, Ind.	92%
Nunn, Ga.	69	Baker, Tenn.	92
Long, La.	62	Dole, Kan.	90
Boren, Okla.	62	Domenici, N.M.	88
Stennis, Miss.	61	Abdnor, S.D.	88
Zorinsky, Neb.	61	Denton, Ala.	87
Johnston, La.	61	Thurmond, S.C.	87
Exon, Neb.	58	Cochran, Miss.	87

HOUSE

Democrats		Republicans	
Daniel, Va.	64%	Bartlett, Texas	81%
Montgomery, Miss.	59	Nielson, Utah	80
Stenholm, Texas	58	Lungren, Calif.	78
Hutto, Fla.	57	Badham, Calif.	77
Thomas, Ga.	54	Dannemeyer, Calif.	77
Sam B. Hall Jr., Texas	54	Mack, Fla.	76
Sisisky, Va.	54	Livingston, La.	75
Skelton, Mo.	54	Michel, Ill.	75
Whitley, N.C.	53	Conable, N.Y.	74
Stratton, N.Y.	53	Hansen, Utah	74
Bevill, Ala.	53	Shumway, Calif.	74
		Robinson, Va.	74
		Bliley, Va.	74

1984 Presidential Position Votes

Following is a list of all Senate and House recorded votes in 1984 on which President Reagan took a position. The votes, listed by CQ vote number, appear in the vote charts beginning on pages 1-S and 1-H.

Senate Votes (77)

Presidential Victories (66) — 1, 5, 6, 7, 8, 9, 11, 12, 14, 17, 19, 31, 39, 41, 42, 46, 47, 48, 49, 50, 51, 52, 54, 55, 61, 77, 79, 93, 96, 100, 101, 103, 107, 109, 110, 115, 125, 127, 130, 131, 132, 140, 141, 149, 158, 159, 160, 161, 184, 185, 192, 205, 209, 221, 222, 225, 226, 227, 245, 254, 257, 261, 262, 266, 272, 275.

Presidential Defeats (11) — 18, 34, 35, 123, 146, 148, 162, 176, 177, 268, 273.

House Votes (113)

Presidential Victories (59) — 13, 42, 54, 71, 75, 89, 90, 95, 99, 106, 107, 114, 115, 116, 120, 122, 124, 125, 126, 127, 133, 134, 136, 137, 138, 140, 144, 147, 148, 149, 159, 161, 171, 182, 196, 205, 206, 209, 210, 212, 213, 224, 225, 226, 245, 270, 282, 285, 319, 352, 355, 358, 370, 377, 379, 380, 385, 388, 399.

Presidential Defeats (54) — 9, 12, 19, 31, 33, 37, 38, 44, 45, 47, 53, 64, 79, 82, 94, 98, 102, 129, 135, 141, 142, 152, 162, 178, 179, 183, 198, 201, 202, 211, 220, 228, 238, 243, 256, 257, 269, 275, 276, 279, 294, 296, 305, 317, 333, 353, 361, 365, 375, 387, 394, 395, 397, 400.

High Scorers — Opposition

Highest individual scorers in presidential opposition — those who voted most often against Reagan's position in 1984:

SENATE

Democrats		Republicans	
Metzenbaum, Ohio	69%	Weicker, Conn.	55%
Melcher, Mont.	69	Hatfield, Ore.	45
Riegle, Mich.	68	Mathias, Md.	42
Pell, R.I.	66	Pressler, S.D.	39
Biden, Del.	65	Specter, Pa.	35
Sarbanes, Md.	64	Humphrey, N.H.	32
Leahy, Vt.	62	Boschwitz, Minn.	31

HOUSE

Democrats		Republicans	
Hayes, Ill.	80%	Schneider, R.I.	57%
Owens, N.Y.	78	Conte, Mass.	56
Dellums, Calif.	78	Green, N.Y.	56
Wheat, Mo.	77	Gilman, N.Y.	55
Wolpe, Mich.	76	Leach, Iowa	53
Edwards, Calif.	75	Snowe, Maine	51
Wyden, Ore.	75	McKernan, Maine	50
Mineta, Calif.	74	Ridge, Pa.	50
Weiss, N.Y.	74	Evans, Iowa	49
Kildee, Mich.	74	Rinaldo, N.J.	49
Lowry, Wash.	74	Petri, Wis.	46

	1	2
ALABAMA		
Denton	87	6
Heflin	75	21
ALASKA		
Murkowski	84	12
Stevens	84	12
ARIZONA		
Goldwater	81	6
DeConcini	42	39
ARKANSAS		
Bumpers	36	53
Pryor	45	47
CALIFORNIA		
Wilson	84	14
Cranston	19	61
COLORADO		
Armstrong	68	14
Hart	12	22
CONNECTICUT		
Weicker	36	55
Dodd	32	61
DELAWARE		
Roth	74	18
Biden	35	65
FLORIDA		
Hawkins	73	19
Chiles	57	35
GEORGIA		
Mattingly	81	14
Nunn	69	29
HAWAII		
Inouye	39	52
Matsunaga	32	60
IDAHO		
McClure	83	10
Symms	81	12
ILLINOIS		
Percy	57	12
Dixon	42	45
INDIANA		
Lugar	92	8
Quayle	86	12

	1	2
IOWA		
Grassley	74	25
Jepsen	74	18
KANSAS		
Dole	90	9
Kassebaum	79	19
KENTUCKY		
Ford	45	51
Huddleston	38	40
LOUISIANA		
Johnston	61	30
Long	62	19
MAINE		
Cohen	62	30
Mitchell	36	61
MARYLAND		
Mathias	51	42
Sarbanes	30	64
MASSACHUSETTS		
Kennedy	30	58
Tsongas	25	52
MICHIGAN		
Levin	34	61
Riegle	31	68
MINNESOTA		
Boschwitz	69	31
Durenberger	71	23
MISSISSIPPI		
Cochran	87	8
Stennis	61	26
MISSOURI		
Danforth	86	13
Eagleton	29	56
MONTANA		
Baucus	40	58
Melcher	30	69
NEBRASKA		
Exon	58	36
Zorinsky	61	38
NEVADA		
Hecht	84	9
Laxalt	82	5

	1	2
NEW HAMPSHIRE		
Humphrey	68	32
Rudman	81	17
NEW JERSEY		
Bradley	42	45
Lautenberg	35	61
NEW MEXICO		
Domenici	88	8
Bingaman	40	56
NEW YORK		
D'Amato	68	25
Moynihan	36	53
NORTH CAROLINA		
East	83	10
Helms	86	10
NORTH DAKOTA		
Andrews	61	27
Burdick	31	56
OHIO		
Glenn	39	43
Metzenbaum	26	69
OKLAHOMA		
Nickles	83	14
Boren	62	29
OREGON		
Hatfield	43	45
Packwood	65	27
PENNSYLVANIA		
Heinz	64†	30†
Specter	65	35
RHODE ISLAND		
Chafee	71	26
Pell	31	66
SOUTH CAROLINA		
Thurmond	87	10
Hollings	32	44
SOUTH DAKOTA		
Abdnor	88	10
Pressler	61	39
TENNESSEE		
Baker	92	3
Sasser	34	58

KEY

† Not eligible for all recorded votes in 1984 (sworn in after Jan. 23, died or resigned during session, or voted "present" to avoid possible conflict of interest).

Democrats   *Republicans*

	1	2
TEXAS		
Tower	86	0
Bentsen	52	34
UTAH		
Garn	83	14
Hatch	78	19
VERMONT		
Stafford	57	25
Leahy	30	62
VIRGINIA		
Trible	82	17
Warner	86	13
WASHINGTON		
Evans	78	19
Gorton	83	17
WEST VIRGINIA		
Byrd	53	45
Randolph	44	51
WISCONSIN		
Kasten	74	21
Proxmire	45	55
WYOMING		
Simpson	86	9
Wallop	86	4

Presidential Support and Opposition: Senate

1. Reagan Support Score, 1984. Percentage of 77 Reagan-issue recorded votes in 1984 on which senator voted "yea" or "nay" *in agreement* with the president's position. Failures to vote lower both Support and Opposition scores.

2. Reagan Opposition Score, 1984. Percentage of 77 Reagan-issue recorded votes in 1984 on which senator voted "yea" or "nay" *in disagreement* with the president's position. Failures to vote lower both Support and Opposition scores.

Presidential Support and Opposition: House

1. Reagan Support Score, 1984. Percentage of 113 Reagan-issue recorded votes in 1984 on which representative voted "yea" or "nay" *in agreement* with the president's position. Failures to vote lower both Support and Opposition scores.

2. Reagan Opposition Score, 1984. Percentage of 113 Reagan-issue recorded votes in 1984 on which representative voted "yea" or "nay" *in disagreement* with the president's position. Failures to vote lower both Support and Opposition scores.

1. Rep. Carl D. Perkins, D-Ky., died Aug. 3, 1984.
2. Rep. Thomas P. O'Neill Jr., D-Mass., as Speaker, votes at his own discretion.
3. Rep. Edwin B. Forsythe, R-N.J., died March 29, 1984.
4. Rep. Gerald D. Kleczka, D-Wis., sworn in April 10, 1984, to succeed Clement J. Zablocki, D, who died Dec. 3, 1983.

KEY

† Not eligible for all recorded votes in 1984 (sworn in after Jan. 23, died or resigned during session, or voted "present" to avoid possible conflict of interest).

Democrats   *Republicans*

	1	2
ALABAMA		
1 *Edwards*	61	28
2 *Dickinson*	64	26
3 Nichols	50	40
4 Bevill	53	35
5 Flippo	50	42
6 Erdreich	50	45
7 Shelby	43	45
ALASKA		
AL *Young*	55	43
ARIZONA		
1 *McCain*	64	27
2 Udall	31	59
3 *Stump*	67	27
4 *Rudd*	66	19
5 McNulty	35	60
ARKANSAS		
1 Alexander	34	44
2 *Bethune*	53	24
3 *Hammerschmidt*	58	32
4 Anthony	37	47
CALIFORNIA		
1 Bosco	26	63
2 *Chappie*	55	36
3 Matsui	32	65
4 Fazio	31	64
5 Burton	24	70
6 Boxer	20	68
7 Miller	22	69
8 Dellums	21	78
9 Stark	25	56
10 Edwards	24	75
11 Lantos	27	69
12 *Zschau*	57	43
13 Mineta	26	74
14 *Shumway*	74	25
15 Coelho	23	64
16 Panetta	31	66
17 *Pashayan*	57	36
18 Lehman	23	64
19 *Lagomarsino*	68	32
20 *Thomas*	64	28
21 *Fiedler*	58	36
22 *Moorhead*	67	28
23 Beilenson	34	65
24 Waxman	25	66
25 Roybal	24	67
26 Berman	29	62
27 Levine	28	68
28 Dixon	25	61
29 Hawkins	19	58
30 Martinez	27	71
31 Dymally	24	55
32 Anderson	36	61
33 *Dreier*	73	25
34 Torres	26	73
35 *Lewis*	71	22
36 Brown	27	69
37 *McCandless*	71	27
38 Patterson	38	53
39 *Dannemeyer*	77	21
40 *Badham*	77	15
41 *Lowery*	69	28
42 *Lungren*	78	19

	1	2
43 *Packard*	69	28
44 Bates	26	68
45 *Hunter*	73	24
COLORADO		
1 Schroeder	28	68
2 Wirth	27	65
3 Kogovsek	21	61
4 *Brown*	65	35
5 *Kramer*	61	33
6 *Schaefer*	70	30
CONNECTICUT		
1 Kennelly	31	65
2 Gejdenson	27	69
3 Morrison	25	66
4 *McKinney*	42	45
5 Ratchford	35	65
6 *Johnson*	52	44
DELAWARE		
AL Carper	41	58
FLORIDA		
1 Hutto	57	40
2 Fuqua	49	39
3 Bennett	51	49
4 Chappell	49	46
5 *McCollum*	66	33
6 MacKay	38	56
7 Gibbons	45	47
8 *Young*	54	38
9 *Bilirakis*	63	34
10 *Ireland*	56	35
11 Nelson	52	44
12 *Lewis*	58	40
13 *Mack*	76	21
14 Mica	49	47
15 *Shaw*	61	37
16 Smith	34	59
17 Lehman	30	59
18 Pepper	39	50
19 Fascell	40	54
GEORGIA		
1 Thomas	54	46
2 Hatcher	43	41
3 Ray	52	44
4 Levitas	48	50
5 Fowler	40	45
6 *Gingrich*	60	29
7 Darden	48	51
8 Rowland	50	48
9 Jenkins	42	46
10 Barnard	44	39
HAWAII		
1 Heftel	31†	34†
2 Akaka	31	63
IDAHO		
1 *Craig*	73	22
2 *Hansen*	19	2
ILLINOIS		
1 Hayes	19	80
2 Savage	15	70
3 Russo	27	63
4 *O'Brien*	65	29
5 Lipinski	45	46
6 *Hyde*	71	25
7 Collins	21	65
8 Rostenkowski	39	42
9 Yates	28	71
10 *Porter*	58	40
11 Annunzio	42	57
12 *Crane, P.*	73	21
13 *Erlenborn*	62	17
14 *Corcoran*	69	15
15 *Madigan*	63	33
16 *Martin*	53	43
17 Evans	24	73
18 *Michel*	75	20
19 *Crane, D.*	68	23
20 Durbin	32	66
21 Price	47	51
22 Simon	12	31
INDIANA		
1 Hall	13	51
2 Sharp	38	50
3 *Hiler*	66	31
4 *Coats*	67	30
5 Hillis	63	30

	1	2
6 *Burton*	73	20
7 *Myers*	59	40
8 McCloskey	37	59
9 Hamilton	49	51
10 Jacobs	27	68
IOWA		
1 *Leach*	42	53
2 *Tauke*	54	42
3 *Evans*	47	49
4 Smith	38	55
5 Harkin	29	66
6 Bedell	33	61
KANSAS		
1 *Roberts*	63	35
2 Slattery	39	61
3 *Winn*	70	26
4 Glickman	40	59
5 *Whittaker*	67	31
KENTUCKY		
1 Hubbard	46	43
2 Natcher	34	66
3 Mazzoli	40	57
4 *Snyder*	58	41
5 *Rogers*	54	41
6 *Hopkins*	60	39
7 Perkins[1]	40†	59†
LOUISIANA		
1 *Livingston*	75	24
2 Boggs	40	47
3 Tauzin	44	53
4 Roemer	50	50
5 Huckaby	49	46
6 *Moore*	58	42
7 Breaux	50	38
8 Long	45	52
MAINE		
1 *McKernan*	50	50
2 *Snowe*	49	51
MARYLAND		
1 Dyson	45	54
2 Long	29	66
3 Mikulski	24	65
4 *Holt*	67	27
5 Hoyer	42	57
6 Byron	50	48
7 Mitchell	19	73
8 Barnes	40	59
MASSACHUSETTS		
1 *Conte*	38	56
2 Boland	37	53
3 Early	23	62
4 Frank	30	66
5 Shannon	15	46
6 Mavroules	33	62
7 Markey	17	58
8 O'Neill[2]		
9 Moakley	29	63
10 Studds	23	66
11 Donnelly	35	56
MICHIGAN		
1 Conyers	21	73
2 *Pursell*	50	40
3 Wolpe	23	76
4 *Siljander*	56	34
5 *Sawyer*	55	32
6 Carr	26	72
7 Kildee	26	74
8 Traxler	28	59
9 *Vander Jagt*	56	30
10 Albosta	27	66
11 Davis	52	38
12 Bonior	25	69
13 Crockett	17	66
14 Hertel	27	71
15 Ford	23	65
16 Dingell	30	59
17 Levin	30	70
18 *Broomfield*	61	31
MINNESOTA		
1 Penny	35	65
2 *Weber*	60	37
3 *Frenzel*	73	23
4 Vento	28	67
5 Sabo	26	70
6 Sikorski	33	67

	1	2
7 *Stangeland*	63	36
8 Oberstar	19	71
MISSISSIPPI		
1 Whitten	39	58
2 *Franklin*	56	34
3 Montgomery	59	41
4 Dowdy	44	47
5 *Lott*	73	25
MISSOURI		
1 Clay	19	65
2 Young	38	52
3 Gephardt	33	60
4 Skelton	54	38
5 Wheat	23	77
6 *Coleman*	55	43
7 *Taylor*	64	32
8 *Emerson*	57	42
9 Volkmer	42	56
MONTANA		
1 Williams	30	65
2 *Marlenee*	54	34
NEBRASKA		
1 *Bereuter*	54	43
2 *Daub*	65	34
3 *Smith*	64	36
NEVADA		
1 Reid	42	58
2 *Vucanovich*	64	31
NEW HAMPSHIRE		
1 D'Amours	34	50
2 *Gregg*	67	28
NEW JERSEY		
1 Florio	26	70
2 Hughes	41	58
3 Howard	28	58
4 *Smith*	56	44
5 *Roukema*	51	45
6 Dwyer	37	60
7 *Rinaldo*	50	49
8 Roe	34	59
9 Torricelli	31	61
10 Rodino	27	59
11 Minish	35	56
12 *Courter*	51	40
13 *Forsythe[3]*	0†	0†
14 Guarini	27	60
NEW MEXICO		
1 *Lujan*	59	39
2 *Skeen*	62	38
3 Richardson	31	66
NEW YORK		
1 *Carney*	59	37
2 Downey	29	67
3 Mrazek	28	68
4 *Lent*	55	35
5 *McGrath*	49	34
6 Addabbo	26	65
7 Ackerman	22	66
8 Scheuer	32	64
9 Ferraro	15	52
10 Schumer	29	68
11 Towns	18	69
12 Owens	18	78
13 Solarz	35	59
14 Molinari	60	40
15 *Green*	42	56
16 Rangel	23	67
17 Weiss	21	74
18 Garcia	30	62
19 Biaggi	35	50
20 Ottinger	21	67
21 *Fish*	50	43
22 *Gilman*	45	55
23 Stratton	53	45
24 *Solomon*	64	34
25 *Boehlert*	58	39
26 *Martin*	54	38
27 *Wortley*	65	33
28 McHugh	35	62
29 *Horton*	48	45
30 *Conable*	74	20
31 *Kemp*	65	28
32 LaFalce	35	56
33 Nowak	32	64
34 Lundine	31	58

	1	2
NORTH CAROLINA		
1 Jones	30	50
2 Valentine	43	44
3 Whitley	53	41
4 Andrews	34	38
5 Neal	39	51
6 Britt	42	52
7 Rose	35	50
8 Hefner	48	45
9 *Martin*	44	23
10 *Broyhill*	70	30
11 Clarke	38	57
NORTH DAKOTA		
AL Dorgan	33	61
OHIO		
1 Luken	35	58
2 *Gradison*	65	32
3 Hall	27	63
4 *Oxley*	67	26
5 *Latta*	64	28
6 *McEwen*	60	29
7 *DeWine*	69	28
8 *Kindness*	62	33
9 Kaptur	26	63
10 *Miller*	60	38
11 Eckart	31	67
12 *Kasich*	61	38
13 Pease	40	59
14 Seiberling	28	70
15 *Wylie*	53	42
16 *Regula*	58	41
17 *Williams*	39	38
18 Applegate	39	60
19 Feighan	26	71
20 Oakar	25	73
21 Stokes	22	68
OKLAHOMA		
1 Jones	52	45
2 Synar	44	51
3 Watkins	45	48
4 McCurdy	46	45
5 *Edwards*	58	36
6 English	52	44
OREGON		
1 AuCoin	29	68
2 *Smith, B.*	53	38
3 Wyden	25	75
4 Weaver	19	72
5 *Smith D.*	73	21
PENNSYLVANIA		
1 Foglietta	22	57
2 Gray	19	73
3 Borski	30	68
4 Kolter	29	65
5 *Schulze*	62	27
6 Yatron	41	53
7 Edgar	25	71
8 Kostmayer	35	63
9 *Shuster*	63	37
10 *McDade*	57	35
11 Harrison	27	55
12 Murtha	52	43
13 *Coughlin*	50	44
14 Coyne	30	68
15 *Ritter*	56	42
16 *Walker*	66	30
17 *Gekas*	62	35
18 Walgren	27	72
19 *Goodling*	50	44
20 Gaydos	37	60
21 *Ridge*	42	50
22 Murphy	35	63
23 *Clinger*	56	42
RHODE ISLAND		
1 St Germain	39	49
2 *Schneider*	37	57
SOUTH CAROLINA		
1 *Hartnett*	65	22
2 *Spence*	59	36
3 Derrick	39	54
4 *Campbell*	60	28
5 Spratt	41	58
6 Tallon	40	54
SOUTH DAKOTA		
AL Daschle	32	60

	1	2
TENNESSEE		
1 *Quillen*	69	20
2 *Duncan*	63	35
3 Lloyd	52	42
4 Cooper	42	52
5 Boner	39	40
6 Gore	46	45
7 *Sundquist*	73	26
8 Jones	40	46
9 Ford	29	57
TEXAS		
1 Hall, S.	54	44
2 Wilson	36	32
3 *Bartlett*	81	18
4 Hall, R.	49	50
5 Bryant	22	62
6 *Gramm*	37	27
7 *Archer*	70	30
8 *Fields*	58	37
9 Brooks	30	58
10 Pickle	47	47
11 Leath	50	38
12 Wright	42	47
13 Hightower	50	46
14 Patman	42	54
15 de la Garza	44	46
16 Coleman	42	55
17 Stenholm	58	37
18 Leland	19	65
19 Hance	15	33
20 Gonzalez	26	72
21 *Loeffler*	72	26
22 *Paul*	29	32
23 Kazen	32	44
24 Frost	33	48
25 Andrews	48	50
26 Vandergriff	47	50
27 Ortiz	41	51
UTAH		
1 *Hansen*	74	16
2 *Marriott*	54	20
3 *Nielson*	80	19
VERMONT		
AL *Jeffords*	47	42
VIRGINIA		
1 *Bateman*	71	27
2 *Whitehurst*	65	26
3 *Bliley*	74	25
4 Sisisky	54	42
5 Daniel	64	34
6 Olin	43	55
7 *Robinson*	74	21
8 *Parris*	61	37
9 Boucher	35	56
10 *Wolf*	64	33
WASHINGTON		
1 *Pritchard*	61	26
2 Swift	33	65
3 Bonker	38	57
4 *Morrison*	60	38
5 Foley	38	57
6 Dicks	43	49
7 Lowry	25	74
8 *Chandler*	62	36
WEST VIRGINIA		
1 Mollohan	49	50
2 Staggers	30	70
3 Wise	33	61
4 Rahall	32	58
WISCONSIN		
1 Aspin	40	51
2 Kastenmeier	25	73
3 *Gunderson*	61	39
4 Kleczka[4]	42†	56†
5 Moody	23	68
6 *Petri*	54	46
7 Obey	31	68
8 *Roth*	51	44
9 *Sensenbrenner*	45	20
WYOMING		
AL *Cheney*	72	11

Party Unity:

Congress' Partisanship Drops Despite Hot Electoral Rhetoric

Despite election-year jousting between Republicans and Democrats, partisan voting on the House floor decreased in the second session of the 98th Congress, according to a Congressional Quarterly vote analysis.

Significantly fewer recorded votes in the House split along party lines this year than in 1983, when partisan voting reached a high-water mark.

In Congress as a whole, the CQ annual study of party unity found that a majority of Republicans voted against a majority of Democrats in 44 percent of the recorded votes taken in 1984 — down from 51 percent in 1983.

The proportion of partisan votes also dropped in the Senate. But on those votes that did split along party lines, Senate Republicans showed more solidarity than in 1983 — despite continued tension between GOP moderates and conservatives.

The average Senate Republican toed the party line and voted with the GOP majority in 78 percent of the partisan votes in 1984 — up from a 74 percent party unity rating in 1983.

Party-Line Votes

In the House, the proportion of votes that pitted a majority of Democrats against a majority of Republicans declined from 56 percent in 1983 to 47 percent in 1984.

In 1983, partisan voting in the House reached the highest level since CQ began its party unity studies in 1954. House leaders were buoyed by Democratic gains in the 1982 congressional elections and actively pushed the party's agenda, including such issues as the Equal Rights Amendment and job-creation measures, during the first session of the 98th Congress.

Much of the partisan cast of the second session arose not from the issues brought to the floor by Democratic leaders, but from the issues they neglected.

The leadership was regularly lambasted by a group of junior Republicans for failing to bring to a vote key items

---

Definitions

Party Unity Votes. Recorded votes in the Senate and House that split the parties, a majority of voting Democrats opposing a majority of voting Republicans.

Party Unity Scores. Percentage of Party Unity votes on which a member votes "yea" or "nay" *in agreement* with a majority of his party. Failure to vote, even if a member announced his stand, lowers his score.

Opposition-to-Party Scores. Percentage of Party Unity votes on which a member votes "yea" or "nay" *in disagreement* with a majority of his party. A member's Party Unity and Opposition-to-Party scores add up to 100 percent only if he voted on all Party Unity votes.

---

on the conservative agenda, including constitutional amendments to require a balanced federal budget and to ban abortion.

Although the 1984 party-line voting in the House dropped from the 1983 peak, the 1984 partisanship rating of 47 percent was still significantly higher than in the first two years of the Reagan administration. In 1982, 36 percent of House votes were identified as partisan; in 1981 the figure was 37 percent.

Recorded votes in the Senate in 1984 split along partisan lines 40 percent of the time — down from 44 percent in 1983 and the lowest level since 1976.

But in racking up an average 78 percent party unity score on partisan votes in 1984, Senate Republicans showed more solidarity than did the Democrats. The party unity score represented the percentage of partisan roll calls on which members, on average, voted with the majority of their party.

The average Senate Democrat voted with the majority of the party on 68 percent of partisan votes — down from a party unity rating of 71 percent in 1983.

In the House, there was not such a wide difference in the degree of party unity displayed by Republicans and Democrats. The average House Democrat voted with the majority of his party 74 percent of the time, while Republicans averaged a unity score of 71 percent. Both parties saw a decline in unity compared with 1983, when the Democrats' score was 76 percent and the Republicans' was 74 percent.

The composite party unity score, which took account of votes in both the House and Senate, was 74 percent for Democrats as a whole and 72 percent for Republicans. Both parties saw a drop of 2 percentage points from their composite ratings in 1983.

In both chambers, Democrats were more likely to be on the losing side of partisan votes in 1984 than in the previous year. Of the 192 House votes identified as partisan in 1984, Democrats won and Republicans lost 141, or 73 percent of the total. In 1983, House Democrats prevailed on 77 percent of the 277 party-line votes.

Democrats in the Senate won only 20 of the 110 partisan votes in 1984, or 18 percent. Last year, Senate Democrats were victorious in 35 percent of the 162 party-line tallies.

Party Dissenters

Southern Democrats voted with their party less frequently in 1984 in both the House and Senate. On partisan Senate roll calls, Southern Democrats voted with the party majority 55 percent of the time — down 10 percentage points from 1983. In the House, the score for Southern Democrats dropped slightly, from 62 percent to 61 percent.

Not surprisingly, then, Southerners were well represented in the ranks of the Democrats who voted most consistently in opposition to the majority of their party.

In the House, Charles W. Stenholm of Texas, was the Democrat who strayed most frequently from the party line, with an opposition score of 70 percent. However, that was lower than the 77 percent opposition score he racked up in 1983.

Including Stenholm, five Texans were among the nine Democrats with the highest records of opposition to the party majority.

At the top of the list of Senate Democrats in their opposition-to-party ratings was Howell Heflin of Alabama, who voted against the Democratic majority on 59 percent of partisan votes. His opposition score jumped significantly from 1983, when he voted against the Democratic majority only 41 percent of the time.

Another Senate Democrat with a high opposition score that marked a notable increase over 1983 was David L. Boren of Oklahoma, who opposed the Democratic majority on 53 percent of party-line roll calls — up from 35 percent in 1983.

Both Boren and Heflin were running for re-election from states that were expected to back Reagan in 1984.

Among House Republicans, representatives from the Northeast dominated the top ranks of those who were most likely to oppose their party. Leading the pack was Silvio O. Conte, R-Mass., ranking minority member of the House Appropriations Committee, who voted against the GOP majority in 70 percent of the partisan votes.

In the Senate, another Northeastern Republican was most likely to oppose the majority GOP sentiment. William S. Cohen, R-Maine, scored 53 percent in opposition-to-party voting — up sharply from his 36 percent opposition score in 1983.

Mark O. Hatfield, R-Ore., chairman of the Senate Appropriations Committee, increased his opposition voting to 48 percent, making him the Republican who was third most likely to vote against the GOP majority on partisan votes this year. In 1983, Hatfield disagreed with the GOP position on 33 percent of partisan votes.

Party Loyalists

The Senate Republican who most consistently supported his party majority was Judiciary Committee Chairman Strom Thurmond, R-S.C., who had a 95 percent party unity score.

In a particularly sharp change in GOP support, Thad Cochran, R-Miss., neared the top of the list of party loyalists with a unity score of 93 percent — up from 69 percent in 1983. Cochran was facing a tough re-election contest in 1984.

Senate Democrats could count most consistently on the support of Paul S. Sarbanes, D-Md., who voted with the party majority on 94 percent of partisan votes. Last year, Sarbanes had a party unity score of 88 percent.

Norman Y. Mineta, D-Calif., was the House Democrat who voted most consistently with the party majority. Supporting the Democrats on 97 percent of partisan votes, Mineta racked up the highest party unity rating in Congress in 1984.

The House Republican who was most likely to vote with his party was David Dreier of California, whose party unity score was 95 percent.

Party Unity Scoreboard

The following table shows the proportion of Party Unity recorded votes in recent years:

	Total Recorded Votes	Party Unity Recorded Votes	Percentage of Total
1984			
Both Chambers	683	302	44%
Senate	275	110	40
House	408	192	47
1983			
Both Chambers	869	439	51
Senate	371	162	44
House	498	277	56
1982			
Both Chambers	924	369	40
Senate	465	202	43
House	459	167	36
1981			
Both Chambers	836	363	43
Senate	483	231	48
House	353	132	37
1980			
Both Chambers	1,135	470	41
Senate	531	243	46
House	604	227	38
1979			
Both Chambers	1,169	550	47
Senate	497	232	47
House	672	318	47
1978			
Both Chambers	1,350	510	38
Senate	516	233	45
House	834	277	33
1977			
Both Chambers	1,341	567	42
Senate	635	269	42
House	706	298	42
1976			
Both Chambers	1,349	493	37
Senate	688	256	37
House	661	237	36
1975			
Both Chambers	1,214	584	48
Senate	602	288	48
House	612	296	48
1974			
Both Chambers	1,081	399	37
Senate	544	241	44
House	537	158	29
1973			
Both Chambers	1,135	463	41
Senate	594	237	40
House	541	226	42
1972			
Both Chambers	861	283	33
Senate	532	194	36
House	329	89	27
1971			
Both Chambers	743	297	40
Senate	423	176	42
House	320	121	38
1970			
Both Chambers	684	219	32
Senate	418	147	35
House	266	72	27
1969			
Both Chambers	422	144	34
Senate	245	89	36
House	177	55	31

Victories, Defeats

	Senate	House	Total
Democrats won, Republicans lost	20	141	161
Republicans won, Democrats lost	90	51	141
Democrats voted unanimously	4	3	7
Republicans voted unanimously	8	8	16

Party Scores

Party Unity and Opposition-to-Party scores below are composites of individual scores and show the percentage of time the average Democrat and Republican voted with his party majority in disagreement with the other party's majority. Failures to vote lower both Party Unity and Opposition-to-Party scores. Averages are closer to House figures because the House has more members.

	1984		1983	
	Dem.	Rep.	Dem.	Rep.
Party Unity	74%	72%	76%	74%
Senate	68	78	71	74
House	74	71	76	74
Opposition	17%	21%	17%	20%
Senate	23	16	22	20
House	17	21	17	19

Sectional Support, Opposition

SENATE	Support	Opposition
Northern Democrats	74%	18%
Southern Democrats	55	35
Northern Republicans	76	19
Southern Republicans	87	8

HOUSE	Support	Opposition
Northern Democrats	81%	11%
Southern Democrats	61	29
Northern Republicans	69	23
Southern Republcians	75	17

Party Unity History

Composite Party Unity scores showing the percentage of time the average Democrat and Republican voted with his party majority in partisan votes in recent years:

Year	Democrats	Republicans
1984	74%	72%
1983	76	74
1982	72	71
1981	69	76
1980	68	70
1979	69	72
1978	64	67
1977	67	70
1976	65	66
1975	69	70

Individual Scores

Highest Party Unity Scores. Those who in 1984 most consistently voted with their party majority against the majority of the other party:

SENATE

Democrats		Republicans	
Sarbanes, Md.	94%	Thurmond, S.C.	95%
Riegle, Mich.	92	Hecht, Nev.	95
Levin, Mich.	89	Garn, Utah	95
Melcher, Mont.	88	Lugar, Ind.	94
Sasser, Tenn.	88	Cochran, Miss.	93
Matsunaga, Hawaii	87	Wilson, Calif.	93

HOUSE

Democrats		Republicans	
Mineta, Calif.	97%	Dreier, Calif.	95%
Wheat, Mo.	96	Archer, Texas	94
Lowry, Wash.	95	Mack, Fla.	94
Kildee, Mich.	94	Shumway, Calif.	94
Edwards, Calif.	94	Bartlett, Texas	93
Torres, Calif.	94	Burton, Ind.	93
Evans, Ill.	94	Schaefer, Colo.	93
Matsui, Calif.	94	Walker, Pa.	92
Oakar, Ohio	94	Coats, Ind.	92

Highest Opposition-to-Party Scores. Those who in 1984 most consistently voted against their party majority:

SENATE

Democrats		Republicans	
Heflin, Ala.	59%	Cohen, Maine	53%
Nunn, Ga.	55	Weicker, Conn.	49
Zorinsky, Neb.	55	Hatfield, Ore.	48
Boren, Okla.	53	Pressler, S.D.	44
Long, La.	52	Andrews, N.D.	41

HOUSE

Democrats		Republicans	
Stenholm, Texas	70%		
Daniel, Va.	68	Conte, Mass.	70%
Roemer, La.	68	Green, N.Y.	69
Ireland, Fla.[1]	62	Schneider, R.I.	67
Montgomery, Miss.	59	McKinney, Conn.	61
Sam B. Hall Jr., Texas	59	Boehlert, N.Y.	59
Vandergriff, Texas	56	Horton, N.Y.	59
Ralph M. Hall, Texas	54	Gilman, N.Y.	57
Patman, Texas	53	Rinaldo, N.J.	54
Ray, Ga.	53	McKernan, Maine	54

[1] *Switched from Democratic to Republican Party on July 5, 1984.*

	1	2		1	2		1	2	KEY
ALABAMA			**IOWA**			**NEW HAMPSHIRE**			† Not eligible for all recorded votes in 1984 (sworn in after Jan. 23, died or resigned during session, or voted "present" to avoid possible conflict of interest).
Denton	91	5	*Grassley*	79	18	*Humphrey*	76	23	
Heflin	36	59	*Jepsen*	77	14	*Rudman*	79	19	
ALASKA			**KANSAS**			**NEW JERSEY**			
Murkowski	90	5	*Dole*	90	8	Bradley	66	25	
Stevens	85	8	*Kassebaum*	75	24	Lautenberg	85	12	
ARIZONA			**KENTUCKY**			**NEW MEXICO**			
Goldwater	84	4	Ford	76†	22†	*Domenici*	86	14	
DeConcini	50†	24†	Huddleston	55	25	Bingaman	79	19	Democrats *Republicans*
ARKANSAS			**LOUISIANA**			**NEW YORK**			
Bumpers	76	14	Johnston	51	44	*D'Amato*	67	25	
Pryor	60	25	Long	35	52	Moynihan	68	25	
CALIFORNIA			**MAINE**			**NORTH CAROLINA**			
Wilson	93	5	*Cohen*	42	53	*East*	85	5	
Cranston	74	7	Mitchell	84	15	*Helms*	90	8	
COLORADO			**MARYLAND**			**NORTH DAKOTA**			
Armstrong	84	9	*Mathias*	52	39	*Andrews*	48	41	
Hart	44	4	Sarbanes	94	2	Burdick	78	11	

	1	2		1	2		1	2		1	2
CONNECTICUT			**MASSACHUSETTS**			**OHIO**			**TEXAS**		
Weicker	37	49	Kennedy	84	7	Glenn	55	25	*Tower*	88	4
Dodd	85	8	Tsongas	69	15	Metzenbaum	79	16	Bentsen	46	28
DELAWARE			**MICHIGAN**			**OKLAHOMA**			**UTAH**		
Roth	85	10	Levin	89	8	*Nickles*	85	13	*Garn*	95	5
Biden	79	21	Riegle	92	6	Boren	41	53	*Hatch*	91	9
FLORIDA			**MINNESOTA**			**OREGON**			**VERMONT**		
Hawkins	69	19	*Boschwitz*	73	26	*Hatfield*	48	48	*Stafford*	54	26
Chiles	61	37	*Durenberger*	68	25	*Packwood*	58	36	Leahy	85	11
GEORGIA			**MISSISSIPPI**			**PENNSYLVANIA**			**VIRGINIA**		
Mattingly	90	7	*Cochran*	93	5	*Heinz*	68	29	*Trible*	87	9
Nunn	44	55	Stennis	41	45	*Specter*	67	32	*Warner*	87	12
HAWAII			**MISSOURI**			**RHODE ISLAND**			**WASHINGTON**		
Inouye	78	14	*Danforth*	85	15	*Chafee*	66	28	*Evans*	76	20
Matsunaga	87	7	Eagleton	81	14	Pell	82	14	*Gorton*	83	16
IDAHO			**MONTANA**			**SOUTH CAROLINA**			**WEST VIRGINIA**		
McClure	80	6	Baucus	76	21	*Thurmond*	95	5	Byrd	77	22
Symms	89	3	Melcher	88	9	Hollings	59	22	Randolph	71	27
ILLINOIS			**NEBRASKA**			**SOUTH DAKOTA**			**WISCONSIN**		
Percy	57	15	Exon	51	45	*Abdnor*	92	7	*Kasten*	83	13
Dixon	56	35	Zorinsky	45	55	*Pressler*	50	44	Proxmire	65	35
INDIANA			**NEVADA**			**TENNESSEE**			**WYOMING**		
Lugar	94	6	*Hecht*	95	2	*Baker*	87	6	*Simpson*	90	8
Quayle	90	8	*Laxalt*	85	4	Sasser	88	8	*Wallop*	91	1

Party Unity and Party Opposition: Senate

1. Party Unity, 1984. Percentage of 110 Senate Party Unity votes in 1984, on which senator voted "yea" or "nay" *in agreement* with a majority of his party. (Party Unity roll calls are those on which a majority of voting Democrats opposed a majority of voting Republicans. Failures to vote lower both Party Unity and Party Opposition score.)

2. Party Opposition, 1984. Percentage of 110 Senate Party Unity votes in 1984, on which senator voted "yea" or "nay" *in disagreement* with a majority of his party.

Party Unity and Party Opposition: House

1. Party Unity, 1984. Percentage of 192 House Party Unity recorded votes in 1984 on which representative voted "yea" or "nay" *in agreement* with a majority of his party. (Party unity roll calls are those on which a majority of voting Demócrats opposed a majority of voting Republicans. Failures to vote lower both Party Unity and Party Opposition scores.)

2. Party Opposition, 1984. Percentage of 192 House Party Unity recorded votes in 1984 on which representative voted "yea" or "nay" *in disagreement* with a majority of his party.

1. *Rep. Andy Ireland, Fla., switched from the Democratic to Republican Party on July 5, 1984. His scores as a Democrat were 24 percent party support and 62 percent opposition.*

2. *Rep. Carl D. Perkins, D-Ky., died Aug. 3, 1984.*

3. *Rep. Thomas P. O'Neill Jr., D-Mass., as Speaker, votes at his own discretion.*

4. *Rep. Edwin B. Forsythe, R-N.J., died March 29, 1984.*

5. *Rep. Gerald D. Kleczka, D-Wis., sworn in April 10, 1984, to succeed Clement J. Zablocki, D, who died Dec. 3, 1983.*

KEY

† Not eligible for all recorded votes in 1984 (sworn in after Jan. 23, died or resigned during session, or voted "present" to avoid possible conflict of interest).

———

Democrats   *Republicans*

	1	2
ALABAMA		
1 *Edwards*	50	32
2 *Dickinson*	72	18
3 Nichols	43	39
4 Bevill	55	29
5 Flippo	61	29
6 Erdreich	52	41
7 Shelby	44	45
ALASKA		
AL *Young*	60	39
ARIZONA		
1 *McCain*	74†	13†
2 Udall	85	7
3 *Stump*	84	7
4 *Rudd*	71	13
5 McNulty	82	10
ARKANSAS		
1 Alexander	57	11
2 *Bethune*	66	10
3 *Hammerschmidt*	67	22
4 Anthony	58	18
CALIFORNIA		
1 Bosco	71	14
2 *Chappie*	76	14
3 Matsui	94	3
4 Fazio	88	8
5 Burton	89	2
6 Boxer	86	3
7 Miller	85	6
8 Dellums	89	6
9 Stark	78	4
10 Edwards	94	5
11 Lantos	83	4
12 *Zschau*	70	30
13 Mineta	97	1
14 *Shumway*	94	6
15 Coelho	85	3
16 Panetta	86	14
17 *Pashayan*	80	12
18 Lehman	81	7
19 *Lagomarsino*	89	11
20 *Thomas*	71	17
21 *Fiedler*	78	18
22 *Moorhead*	91	7
23 Beilenson	87	10
24 Waxman	80	5
25 Roybal	85	4
26 Berman	84	6
27 Levine	88	5
28 Dixon	79	4
29 Hawkins	76	4
30 Martinez	93	5
31 Dymally	65	5
32 Anderson	74	24
33 *Dreier*	95	4
34 Torres	94	2
35 *Lewis*	72	18
36 Brown	91	5
37 *McCandless*	90	8
38 Patterson	74	15
39 *Dannemeyer*	90	6
40 *Badham*	78	8
41 *Lowery*	76	16
42 Lungren	91	6

	1	2
43 *Packard*	89	8
44 Bates	84	9
45 *Hunter*	80	15
COLORADO		
1 Schroeder	73	23
2 Wirth	89	7
3 Kogovsek	78	4
4 *Brown*	85	15
5 *Kramer*	80	10
6 *Schaefer*	93	6
CONNECTICUT		
1 Kennelly	88	7
2 Gejdenson	91	7
3 Morrison	85	8
4 *McKinney*	24	61
5 Ratchford	93	7
6 *Johnson*	48	47
DELAWARE		
AL Carper	76	24
FLORIDA		
1 Hutto	51	46
2 Fuqua	62	27
3 Bennett	59	41
4 Chappell	61	29
5 *McCollum*	85	11
6 MacKay	63	26
7 Gibbons	59	24
8 *Young*	68	24
9 *Bilirakis*	86	14
10 *Ireland* [1]	66	32
11 Nelson	48	48
12 *Lewis*	81	16
13 *Mack*	94	4
14 Mica	65	30
15 *Shaw*	82	14
16 Smith	83	7
17 Lehman	86	4
18 Pepper	78	10
19 Fascell	84	10
GEORGIA		
1 Thomas	70	29
2 Hatcher	58	20
3 Ray	44	53
4 Levitas	57	42
5 Fowler	66	21
6 *Gingrich*	83	9
7 Darden	58	39
8 Rowland	71	27
9 Jenkins	57	33
10 Barnard	48	34
HAWAII		
1 Heftel	49	15†
2 Akaka	85	8
IDAHO		
1 *Craig*	86	4
2 *Hansen*	27	0
ILLINOIS		
1 Hayes	93	4
2 Savage	76	5
3 Russo	74	18
4 *O'Brien*	60	32
5 Lipinski	71	14
6 *Hyde*	79	15
7 Collins	82	5
8 Rostenkowski	68	11
9 Yates	91	8
10 *Porter*	65	31
11 Annunzio	86	12
12 *Crane, P.*	86	7
13 *Erlenborn*	64	13
14 *Corcoran*	69	9
15 *Madigan*	69	24
16 *Martin*	73	23
17 Evans	94	6
18 *Michel*	80	11
19 *Crane, D.*	88	7
20 Durbin	82	18
21 Price	84	14
22 Simon	42	3
INDIANA		
1 Hall	74	4
2 Sharp	63	31
3 *Hiler*	91	5
4 *Coats*	92	8
5 Hillis	69	18

	1	2
6 Burton	93	3
7 Myers	69	26
8 McCloskey	84	9
9 Hamilton	71	29
10 Jacobs	65	29
IOWA		
1 Leach	51	42
2 Tauke	65	31
3 Evans	65	30
4 Smith	71	17
5 Harkin	79	14
6 Bedell	74	16
KANSAS		
1 Roberts	84	8
2 Slattery	60	39
3 Winn	79	13
4 Glickman	69	29
5 Whittaker	83	14
KENTUCKY		
1 Hubbard	37	52
2 Natcher	85	15
3 Mazzoli	79	20
4 Snyder	66	32
5 Rogers	66	28
6 Hopkins	77	22
7 Perkins[2]	85†	13†
LOUISIANA		
1 Livingston	86	12
2 Boggs	71	11
3 Tauzin	46	47
4 Roemer	32	68
5 Huckaby	48	42
6 Moore	74	26
7 Breaux	49	36
8 Long	82	13
MAINE		
1 McKernan	46	54
2 Snowe	47	53
MARYLAND		
1 Dyson	65	33
2 Long	83	11
3 Mikulski	84	6
4 Holt	73	19
5 Hoyer	89	9
6 Byron	47	45
7 Mitchell	88	5
8 Barnes	90	8
MASSACHUSETTS		
1 Conte	25	70
2 Boland	78	7
3 Early	72	11
4 Frank	87	7
5 Shannon	52	2
6 Mavroules	87	8
7 Markey	76	3
8 O'Neill[3]		
9 Moakley	86	5
10 Studds	85	5
11 Donnelly	83	7
MICHIGAN		
1 Conyers	88	6
2 Pursell	53	32
3 Wolpe	93	6
4 Siljander	77	10
5 Sawyer	54	34
6 Carr	87	11
7 Kildee	94	6
8 Traxler	80	8
9 Vander Jagt	62	19
10 Albosta	81	14
11 Davis	48	44
12 Bonior	84	4
13 Crockett	76	6
14 Hertel	84	13
15 Ford	82	5
16 Dingell	84	7
17 Levin	93†	7†
18 Broomfield	78	17
MINNESOTA		
1 Penny	69	31
2 Weber	85	11
3 Frenzel	77	17
4 Vento	90	6
5 Sabo	92	4
6 Sikorski	85	15

	1	2
7 Stangeland	74	21
8 Oberstar	88	4
MISSISSIPPI		
1 Whitten	76	18
2 Franklin	72	15
3 Montgomery	34	59
4 Dowdy	66	26
5 Lott	86	8
MISSOURI		
1 Clay	83	3
2 Young	74	13
3 Gephardt	87	7
4 Skelton	63	27
5 Wheat	96	4
6 Coleman	66	27
7 Taylor	75	19
8 Emerson	78	19
9 Volkmer	72	27
MONTANA		
1 Williams	72	14
2 Marlenee	72	15
NEBRASKA		
1 Bereuter	64	35
2 Daub	85	14
3 Smith	73	27
NEVADA		
1 Reid	84	16
2 Vucanovich	83	11
NEW HAMPSHIRE		
1 D'Amours	58	24
2 Gregg	82	15
NEW JERSEY		
1 Florio	87	7
2 Hughes	71	24
3 Howard	82	4
4 Smith	45	48
5 Roukema	57	38
6 Dwyer	91	7
7 Rinaldo	42	54
8 Roe	86	8
9 Torricelli	76	17
10 Rodino	79	3
11 Minish	73	17
12 Courter	66	21
13 Forsythe[4]	0†	0†
14 Guarini	80	5
NEW MEXICO		
1 Lujan	77	19
2 Skeen	84	15
3 Richardson	89	9
NEW YORK		
1 Carney	75	22
2 Downey	92	4
3 Mrazek	88	7
4 Lent	65	24
5 McGrath	60	26
6 Addabbo	85	4
7 Ackerman	85	5
8 Scheuer	84	8
9 Ferraro	56	3
10 Schumer	87	6
11 Towns	78	4
12 Owens	90	4
13 Solarz	85	6
14 Molinari	73	27
15 Green	29	69
16 Rangel	84	4
17 Weiss	88	7
18 Garcia	81	4
19 Biaggi	74	9
20 Ottinger	83	7
21 Fish	38	51
22 Gilman	43	57
23 Stratton	64	30
24 Solomon	85	10
25 Boehlert	38	59
26 Martin	58	28
27 Wortley	71	28
28 McHugh	89	9
29 Horton	35	59
30 Conable	78	16
31 Kemp	73	14
32 LaFalce	78	13
33 Nowak	88	7
34 Lundine	78	9

	1	2
NORTH CAROLINA		
1 Jones	70	12
2 Valentine	51	38
3 Whitley	63	33
4 Andrews	52	22
5 Neal	65	22
6 Britt	76	21
7 Rose	77	13
8 Hefner	64	25
9 Martin	53	11
10 Broyhill	79	19
11 Clarke	79	14
NORTH DAKOTA		
AL Dorgan	75	22
OHIO		
1 Luken	74	21
2 Gradison	68	30
3 Hall	72	15
4 Oxley	86	8
5 Latta	83	5
6 McEwen	81	9
7 DeWine	86	13
8 Kindness	86	9
9 Kaptur	79	12
10 Miller	84	16
11 Eckart	81	16
12 Kasich	82	17
13 Pease	85	15
14 Seiberling	88	8
15 Wylie	65	24
16 Regula	63	35
17 Williams	33	41
18 Applegate	65	32
19 Feighan	81	17
20 Oakar	94	5
21 Stokes	88	3
OKLAHOMA		
1 Jones	59	40
2 Synar	80	13
3 Watkins	63	31
4 McCurdy	56	29
5 Edwards	78	15
6 English	43	50
OREGON		
1 AuCoin	72	18
2 Smith, B.	70	20
3 Wyden	88	12
4 Weaver	75	17
5 Smith D.	85	5
PENNSYLVANIA		
1 Foglietta	80	2
2 Gray	90	3
3 Borski	93	6
4 Kolter	80	14
5 Schulze	68	21
6 Yatron	70	25
7 Edgar	89	7
8 Kostmayer	83	13
9 Shuster	83	15
10 McDade	41	48
11 Harrison	65	7
12 Murtha	77	18
13 Coughlin	49	44
14 Coyne	91	6
15 Ritter	74	21
16 Walker	92	6
17 Gekas	81	17
18 Walgren	81	15
19 Goodling	66	28
20 Gaydos	77	18
21 Ridge	45	49
22 Murphy	65	28
23 Clinger	54	42
RHODE ISLAND		
1 St Germain	72	9
2 Schneider	29	67
SOUTH CAROLINA		
1 Hartnett	84	7
2 Spence	84	13
3 Derrick	73	25
4 Campbell	83	8
5 Spratt	77	22
6 Tallon	65	31
SOUTH DAKOTA		
AL Daschle	67	17

	1	2
TENNESSEE		
1 Quillen	60	27
2 Duncan	69	30
3 Lloyd	48	47
4 Cooper	74	20
5 Boner	65	19
6 Gore	69	22
7 Sundquist	76	20
8 Jones	68	19
9 Ford	81	4
TEXAS		
1 Hall, S.	31	59
2 Wilson	44	21
3 Bartlett	93	6
4 Hall, R.	44	54
5 Bryant	74	6
6 Gramm	58	5
7 Archer	94	6
8 Fields	84	12
9 Brooks	77	14
10 Pickle	70	22
11 Leath	36	50
12 Wright	73	16
13 Hightower	55	40
14 Patman	43	53
15 de la Garza	66	21
16 Coleman	76	21
17 Stenholm	23	70
18 Leland	74	4
19 Hance	34	20
20 Gonzalez	89	10
21 Loeffler	86	12
22 Paul	50	16
23 Kazen	51	28
24 Frost	63	14
25 Andrews	64	33
26 Vandergriff	41	56
27 Ortiz	77	17
UTAH		
1 Hansen	88	5
2 Marriott	53	7
3 Nielson	90	9
VERMONT		
AL Jeffords	31	52
VIRGINIA		
1 Bateman	71	26
2 Whitehurst	66	25
3 Bliley	82	14
4 Sisisky	66	32
5 Daniel	28	68
6 Olin	65	31
7 Robinson	79	16
8 Parris	72	23
9 Boucher	78	12
10 Wolf	71	27
WASHINGTON		
1 Pritchard	45	32
2 Swift	91†	7†
3 Bonker	78	11
4 Morrison	63	35
5 Foley	81	12
6 Dicks	79	15
7 Lowry	95	5
8 Chandler	63	32
WEST VIRGINIA		
1 Mollohan	76	22
2 Staggers	88	10
3 Wise	76	17
4 Rahall	83	9
WISCONSIN		
1 Aspin	73	16
2 Kastenmeier	90	6
3 Gunderson	74	26
4 Kleczka[5]	84†	15†
5 Moody	82	16
6 Petri	76	24
7 Obey	89	9
8 Roth	61	28
9 Sensenbrenner	56	9
WYOMING		
AL Cheney	78	4

9 of 10 Votes:

Voting Participation Stays High Despite Election Campaigning

Although hometown voters were on their minds for much of the year, members of Congress showed a remarkably high voting participation record in 1984, missing less than one in 10 recorded votes taken.

Congressional Quarterly's study of 1984 voting participation showed that members on average recorded a position on 91 percent of the votes taken, just 1 percentage point below the 1983 score, which tied the highest percentage in 30 years.

Voting participation levels are generally lower in election years, when members must campaign for re-election. As in prior years, the leadership of both chambers tried to accommodate members who were home campaigning, by scheduling most votes for Tuesday, Wednesday or Thursday.

Generally, in 1984, those with the lowest scores had the toughest election contests. Among the lowest voting participation records were those tallied by four senators who ran for the Democratic presidential nomination. Partly because two of them are from the West, Democratic senators from the West were statistically the most likely to miss a vote.

The voting participation study is the closest approach to an attendance record in Congress, but it is only an approximation. *(Definition, box, p. 33-C)*

In 1984, as in most years, Republicans voted more often than Democrats. Senate Democrats have outscored their Republican counterparts in only four of the last 33 years; House Democrats only twice.

Two senators and eight representatives had perfect voting participation scores in 1984, five more representatives than in 1983. Two senators and 14 representatives had scores below 70 percent.

Chamber, Party Scores

Total 1984 recorded votes in Congress numbered 683, far fewer than the 869 votes in 1983. The record was 1,350 votes in 1978.

There were 275 Senate votes, 96 fewer than in 1983, and 413 fewer than the record 688 in 1976.

House members answered 408 roll calls, 90 fewer than in 1983 and 426 fewer than the record 834 in 1978.

Senators' and representatives' voting participation scores were the same in 1984, 91 percent. In 1983, both chambers scored 92 percent.

Senate Republicans on average voted 93 percent of the time in 1984, compared with 94 percent the year before. In 1982, Senate Republicans scored 95 percent. Senate Democrats had an average voting participation score of 90 percent in 1984, compared with a 91 percent score in 1983 and a 94 percent score in 1982.

House Republicans had a 92 percent voting participation score in 1984. In 1983, their average score was 93 percent. In 1982, it was 90 percent.

House Democrats, like their Senate counterparts, scored an average 90 percent in 1984, compared with 92 percent in 1983. In 1982, House Democrats averaged 88 percent.

For the two chambers combined, the 1984 scores were 92 percent for Republicans and 90 percent for Democrats. In 1983, Republicans edged Democrats 93 percent to 92 percent. In 1982, Republicans averaged 91 percent; Democrats, 89 percent.

Individual Highs and Lows

Two senators, Democrat William Proxmire of Wisconsin and Republican Richard G. Lugar of Indiana answered every roll call in 1984, as they had done in 1983. Proxmire last missed a vote in 1966 and extended his record of consecutive votes to 8,618. Six other senators — four Republicans and two Democrats — scored 99 percent.

Eight House members, four from each party, had perfect voting participation scores in 1984. William H. Natcher, D-Ky., had not missed a vote since his election to Congress in 1954 and extended his record to 9,919 consecutive votes. Charles E. Bennett, D-Fla., had answered every roll call since 1979; Dale E. Kildee, D-Mich., had had perfect scores since 1981.

The lowest scoring senator was Gary Hart, of Colorado, 37 percent. Hart was a candidate for the Democratic nomination for president. On the Democratic side, Hart was followed by Walter D. Huddleston of Kentucky, 77 percent, who was up for re-election, and three of Hart's rivals for the Democratic nomination: Alan Cranston of California, 78 percent; Ernest F. Hollings of South Carolina, 79 percent; and John Glenn of Ohio, 80 percent. Paul E. Tsongas of Massachusetts scored 79 percent.

The lowest scoring Senate Republican was Charles H. Percy of Illinois, who was running for re-election.

In the House, the lowest scoring member was George Hansen, R-Idaho, 25 percent. Hansen was convicted April 2 of filing false financial disclosure statements, and had had tough primary and general election campaigns. The lowest scoring Democrat at 40 percent was Paul Simon of Illinois, who was running for the Senate against Percy. Simon was followed by two unsuccessful Senate candidates: Democrats James M. Shannon of Massachusetts, 51 percent, and Kent Hance of Texas, 53 percent.

Absences

Among members of Congress absent for a day or more in 1984 because they were sick or because of illness or death in their families were:

Senate Democrats: Kennedy, Mass.; Leahy, Vt.; Matsunaga, Hawaii; Mitchell, Maine.

House Democrats: Collins, Ill.; Gray, Pa.; Hall, Ind.; Hefner, N.C.; Kastenmeier, Wis.; Leland, Texas; Moody, Wis.; Neal, N.C.; Rodino, N.J.; Russo, Ill.; Weiss, N.Y.

House Republicans: Badham, Calif.; Bateman, Va.; Campbell, S.C.; Cheney, Wyo.; McGrath, N.Y.; Pashayan, Calif.; Pritchard, Wash.; Ritter, Pa.; Sensenbrenner, Wis.; Stangeland, Minn.; Tauke, Iowa; Williams, Ohio

Failure to vote often is due to conflicting duties. Members frequently have to be away from Washington on official business. Leaves of absence, not listed here, are granted members for these purposes.

Party Scores

Composites of Democratic and Republican voting participation scores for 1984 and 1983:

	1984		1983	
	Dem.	Rep.	Dem.	Rep.
Senate	90%	93%	91%	94%
House	90	92	92	93

Regional Scores

Regional voting participation breakdowns for 1984 with 1983 scores in parentheses:

	East		West		South		Midwest	
DEMOCRATS								
Senate	92%	(94)	84%	(85)	88%	(90)	93%	(93)
House	90	(92)	90	(90)	90	(92)	92	(93)
REPUBLICANS								
Senate	93%	(94)	92%	(91)	93%	(95)	93%	(95)
House	93	(93)	91	(91)	91	(94)	92	(94)

(CQ defines regions of the United States as follows: **East:** *Conn., Del., Maine, Md., Mass., N.H., N.J., N.Y., Pa., R.I., Vt., W.Va.* **West:** *Alaska, Ariz., Calif., Colo., Hawaii, Idaho, Mont., Nev., N.M., Ore., Utah, Wash., Wyo.* **South:** *Ala., Ark., Fla., Ga., Ky., La., Miss., N.C., Okla., S.C., Tenn., Texas, Va.* **Midwest:** *Ill., Ind., Iowa, Kan., Mich., Minn., Mo., Neb., N.D., Ohio, S.D., Wis.)*

Definition

Voting Participation. Percentage of recorded votes on which a member voted "yea" or "nay." Failures to vote "yea" or "nay" lower scores — even if the member votes "present," enters a live pair or announces his stand in the *Congressional Record.* Only votes of "yea" or "nay" directly affect the outcome of a vote. Voting participation is the closest approach to an attendance record, but it is only an approximation. A member may be present and nevertheless decline to vote "yea" or "nay" — usually because he has entered a live pair with an absent member.

Pease, Ohio	99	Archer, Texas	99
Panetta, Calif.	99	Gunderson, Wis.	99
Carper, Del.	99	Molinari, N.Y.	99
Slattery, Kan.	99	Nielson, Utah	99
Yates, Ill.	99	Coats, Ind.	99
Sikorski, Minn.	99	Snowe, Maine	99
Wheat, Mo.	99	Gilman, N.Y.	99
Staggers, W.Va.	99	DeWine, Ohio	99
Roemer, La.	99	Shuster, Pa.	99
Wolpe, Mich.	99	Miller, Ohio	99
Reid, Nev.	99	Zschau, Calif.	99
Levitas, Ga.	99	Kasich, Ohio	99
Mineta, Calif.	99		
Lowry, Wash.	99		
Ratchford, Conn.	99		
Wyden, Ore.	99		

Highest Scorers

SENATE

Democrats		Republicans	
Proxmire, Wis.	100%	Lugar, Ind.	100%
Zorinsky, Neb.	99	Specter, Pa.	99
Biden, Del.	99	Garn, Utah	99
Mitchell, Maine	98[2]	Danforth, Mo.	99
Baucus, Mont.	98	Gorton, Wash.	99
Bingaman, N.M.	98	Rudman, N.H.	98
Byrd, W.Va.	98	Wilson, Calif.	98
Randolph, W.Va.	97	Warner, Va.	98
Melcher, Mont.	97	Nickles, Okla.	98
Riegle, Mich.	97	Helms, N.C.	98
		Hatch, Utah	98

HOUSE

Democrats		Republicans	
Natcher, Ky.	100%	Lagomarsino, Calif.	100%
Bennett, Fla.	100	Petri, Wis.	100
Kildee, Mich.	100	Brown, Colo.	100
Penny, Minn.	100	Smith, Neb.	100
Thomas, Ga.	99	Moore, La.	99
Hamilton, Ind.	99	Shumway, Calif.	99
Levin, Mich.	99[1]	McKernan, Maine	99

Lowest Scorers

SENATE

Democrats		Republicans	
Hart, Colo.	37%	Percy, Ill.	69%
Huddleston, Ky.	77	Goldwater, Ariz.	82
Cranston, Calif.	78	Weicker, Conn.	84
Tsongas, Mass.	79	Tower, Texas	85
Hollings, S.C.	79	Stafford, Vt.	85
Glenn, Ohio	80	McClure, Idaho	85
Bentsen, Texas	80	Armstrong, Colo.	85

HOUSE

Democrats		Republicans [3]	
Simon, Ill.	40%	Hansen, Idaho	25%
Shannon, Mass.	51	Gramm, Texas	58
Hance, Texas	53	Paul, Texas	61
Heftel, Hawaii	58[1]	Martin, N.C.	62
Ferraro, N.Y.	59	Marriott, Utah	64
Wilson, Texas	64	Sensenbrenner, Wis.	66[2]
Dymally, Calif.	67	Bethune, Ark.	72
Alexander, Ark.	67	Williams, Ohio	73[2]

[1] *Not eligible for all votes in 1984.*
[2] *Members absent a day or more in 1984 because they were sick or because of illness or death in family.*
[3] *Edwin B. Forsythe, R-N.J., who died March 29, 1984, scored zero.*

Voting Participation Scores: House

Voting Participation, 1984. Percentage of 408 recorded votes in 1984 on which representative voted "yea" or "nay."

KEY

† Not eligible for all recorded votes in 1984 (sworn in after Jan. 23, died or resigned during session, or voted "present" to avoid possible conflict of interest).

\# Member absent a day or more in 1984 due to illness or illness or death in family.

———

Democrats   *Republicans*

ALABAMA

1	*Edwards*	85
2	*Dickinson*	90
3	Nichols	88
4	Bevill	87
5	Flippo	91
6	Erdreich	95
7	Shelby	86

ALASKA

AL	*Young*	98

ARIZONA

1	*McCain*	89†
2	Udall	89
3	*Stump*	90
4	*Rudd*	83
5	McNulty	92

ARKANSAS

1	Alexander	67
2	*Bethune*	72
3	*Hammerschmidt*	90
4	Anthony	78

CALIFORNIA

1	Bosco	85
2	*Chappie*	91
3	Matsui	95
4	Fazio	95
5	Burton	92
6	Boxer	89
7	Miller	90
8	Dellums	95
9	Stark	79
10	Edwards	98
11	Lantos	91
12	*Zschau*	99
13	Mineta	99
14	*Shumway*	99
15	Coelho	88
16	Panetta	99
17	*Pashayan*	91#
18	Lehman	88
19	*Lagomarsino*	100
20	*Thomas*	88
21	*Fiedler*	95
22	*Moorhead*	97
23	Beilenson	96
24	Waxman	84
25	Roybal	90
26	Berman	91
27	Levine	93
28	Dixon	84
29	Hawkins	76
30	Martinez	96
31	Dymally	67
32	Anderson	98
33	*Dreier*	98
34	Torres	94
35	*Lewis*	89
36	Brown	94
37	*McCandless*	98
38	Patterson	88
39	*Dannemeyer*	96
40	*Badham*	88#
41	*Lowery*	91
42	*Lungren*	97
43	*Packard*	96
44	Bates	94
45	*Hunter*	95

COLORADO

1	Schroeder	95
2	Wirth	93
3	Kogovsek	83
4	*Brown*	100
5	*Kramer*	90
6	*Schaefer*	98

CONNECTICUT

1	Kennelly	95
2	Gejdenson	96
3	Morrison	91
4	*McKinney*	86
5	Ratchford	99
6	*Johnson*	96

DELAWARE

AL	Carper	99

FLORIDA

1	Hutto	97
2	Fuqua	87
3	Bennett	100
4	Chappell	90
5	*McCollum*	97
6	MacKay	89
7	Gibbons	85
8	*Young*	91
9	*Bilirakis*	98
10	*Ireland*	88
11	Nelson	95
12	*Lewis*	96
13	*Mack*	97
14	Mica	95
15	*Shaw*	96
16	Smith	90
17	Lehman	90
18	Pepper	86
19	Fascell	91

GEORGIA

1	Thomas	99
2	Hatcher	80
3	Ray	96
4	Levitas	99
5	Fowler	85
6	*Gingrich*	90
7	Darden	97
8	Rowland	98
9	Jenkins	90
10	Barnard	83

HAWAII

1	Heftel	58†
2	Akaka	91

IDAHO

1	*Craig*	91†
2	*Hansen*	25

ILLINOIS

1	Hayes	97
2	Savage	77
3	Russo	91#
4	*O'Brien*	93
5	Lipinski	86
6	*Hyde*	92
7	Collins	87#
8	Rostenkowski	80
9	Yates	99
10	*Porter*	95
11	Annunzio	98
12	*Crane, P.*	92
13	*Erlenborn*	77
14	*Corcoran*	79
15	*Madigan*	93
16	*Martin*	95
17	Evans	98
18	*Michel*	92
19	*Crane, D.*	93
20	Durbin	98
21	Price	98
22	Simon	40

INDIANA

1	Hall	73#
2	Sharp	92
3	*Hiler*	95
4	*Coats*	99
5	*Hillis*	90

1. Rep. Carl D. Perkins, D-Ky., died Aug. 3, 1984.

2. Rep. Thomas P. O'Neill Jr., D-Mass., as Speaker, votes at his own discretion.

3. Rep. Edwin B. Forsythe, R-N.J., died March 29, 1984.

4. Rep. Gerald D. Kleczka, D-Wis., sworn in April 10, 1984, to succeed Clement J. Zablocki, D, who died Dec. 3, 1983.

6 Burton	95	
7 Myers	97	
8 McCloskey	94	
9 Hamilton	99	
10 Jacobs	93	
IOWA		
1 Leach	91	
2 Tauke	95#	
3 Evans	95	
4 Smith	91	
5 Harkin	92	
6 Bedell	92	
KANSAS		
1 Roberts	94	
2 Slattery	99	
3 Winn	91	
4 Glickman	98	
5 Whittaker	96	
KENTUCKY		
1 Hubbard	87	
2 Natcher	100	
3 Mazzoli	98	
4 Snyder	97	
5 Rogers	95	
6 Hopkins	98	
7 Perkins[1]	97†	
LOUISIANA		
1 Livingston	97	
2 Boggs	81	
3 Tauzin	94	
4 Roemer	99	
5 Huckaby	93	
6 Moore	99	
7 Breaux	83	
8 Long	94	
MAINE		
1 McKernan	99	
2 Snowe	99	
MARYLAND		
1 Dyson	96	
2 Long	91	
3 Mikulski	89	
4 Holt	92	
5 Hoyer	97	
6 Byron	93	
7 Mitchell	91	
8 Barnes	98	
MASSACHUSETTS		
1 Conte	95†	
2 Boland	88	
3 Early	82	
4 Frank	93	
5 Shannon	51	
6 Mavroules	93	
7 Markey	73	
8 O'Neill[2]		
9 Moakley	93	
10 Studds	88	
11 Donnelly	90	
MICHIGAN		
1 Conyers	93	
2 Pursell	85	
3 Wolpe	99	
4 Siljander	87	
5 Sawyer	89	
6 Carr	97	
7 Kildee	100	
8 Traxler	88	
9 Vander Jagt	82	
10 Albosta	93	
11 Davis	91	
12 Bonior	88	
13 Crockett	77	
14 Hertel	98	
15 Ford	81	
16 Dingell	91	
17 Levin	99†	
18 Broomfield	94	
MINNESOTA		
1 Penny	100	
2 Weber	96	
3 Frenzel	94	
4 Vento	95	
5 Sabo	97	
6 Sikorski	99	

7 Stangeland	95#
8 Oberstar	87
MISSISSIPPI	
1 Whitten	95
2 Franklin	85
3 Montgomery	95
4 Dowdy	88
5 Lott	96
MISSOURI	
1 Clay	84
2 Young	90
3 Gephardt	92
4 Skelton	90
5 Wheat	99
6 Coleman	94
7 Taylor	94
8 Emerson	98
9 Volkmer	98
MONTANA	
1 Williams	88
2 Marlenee	87
NEBRASKA	
1 Bereuter	98
2 Daub	98
3 Smith	100
NEVADA	
1 Reid	99
2 Vucanovich	93
NEW HAMPSHIRE	
1 D'Amours	81
2 Gregg	95
NEW JERSEY	
1 Florio	90
2 Hughes	97
3 Howard	86
4 Smith	95
5 Roukema	96
6 Dwyer	98
7 Rinaldo	96
8 Roe	96
9 Torricelli	92
10 Rodino	85#
11 Minish	90
12 Courter	89
13 Forsythe[3]	0†
14 Guarini	87
NEW MEXICO	
1 Lujan	97
2 Skeen	98
3 Richardson	97
NEW YORK	
1 Carney	94
2 Downey	95
3 Mrazek	96
4 Lent	88
5 McGrath	85#
6 Addabbo	88
7 Ackerman	90
8 Scheuer	92†
9 Ferraro	59
10 Schumer	93
11 Towns	76
12 Owens	92
13 Solarz	92
14 Molinari	99
15 Green	98
16 Rangel	88
17 Weiss	95#
18 Garcia	86
19 Biaggi	84
20 Ottinger	84
21 Fish	91
22 Gilman	99
23 Stratton	96
24 Solomon	96
25 Boehlert	95
26 Martin	89
27 Wortley	98
28 McHugh	97
29 Horton	92
30 Conable	93
31 Kemp	86
32 LaFalce	91
33 Nowak	95
34 Lundine	85

NORTH CAROLINA	
1 Jones	80
2 Valentine	89
3 Whitley	94
4 Andrews	76
5 Neal	87#
6 Britt	97
7 Rose	87
8 Hefner	89#
9 Martin	62
10 Broyhill	97
11 Clarke	91
NORTH DAKOTA	
AL Dorgan	96
OHIO	
1 Luken	96
2 Gradison	96
3 Hall	86
4 Oxley	92
5 Latta	90
6 McEwen	89
7 DeWine	99
8 Kindness	95
9 Kaptur	88
10 Miller	99
11 Eckart	98
12 Kasich	99
13 Pease	99
14 Seiberling	96
15 Wylie	92
16 Regula	97
17 Williams	73#
18 Applegate	92
19 Feighan	96
20 Oakar	96
21 Stokes	90
OKLAHOMA	
1 Jones	96
2 Synar	92
3 Watkins	94
4 McCurdy	85
5 Edwards	93
6 English	95
OREGON	
1 AuCoin	91
2 Smith, B.	87
3 Wyden	99
4 Weaver	88
5 Smith D.	90
PENNSYLVANIA	
1 Foglietta	79
2 Gray	90#
3 Borski	98
4 Kolter	95
5 Schulze	88
6 Yatron	95
7 Edgar	94
8 Kostmayer	97
9 Shuster	99
10 McDade	89
11 Harrison	71
12 Murtha	95
13 Coughlin	95
14 Coyne	95
15 Ritter	95#
16 Walker	97
17 Gekas	98
18 Walgren	93
19 Goodling	93
20 Gaydos	93
21 Ridge	93
22 Murphy	95
23 Clinger	96
RHODE ISLAND	
1 St Germain	79
2 Schneider	94
SOUTH CAROLINA	
1 Hartnett	90
2 Spence	96
3 Derrick	94
4 Campbell	90#
5 Spratt	98
6 Tallon	93
SOUTH DAKOTA	
AL Daschle	87

TENNESSEE	
1 Quillen	89
2 Duncan	98
3 Lloyd	93
4 Cooper	91
5 Boner	81
6 Gore	90
7 Sundquist	96
8 Jones	87
9 Ford	86
TEXAS	
1 Hall, S.	92
2 Wilson	64
3 Bartlett	97
4 Hall, R.	98
5 Bryant	80
6 Gramm	58
7 Archer	99
8 Fields	96
9 Brooks	87
10 Pickle	94
11 Leath	86
12 Wright	86
13 Hightower	96
14 Patman	96
15 de la Garza	86
16 Coleman	95
17 Stenholm	92
18 Leland	78#
19 Hance	53
20 Gonzalez	98
21 Loeffler	98
22 Paul	61
23 Kazen	77
24 Frost	77
25 Andrews	98
26 Vandergriff	96
27 Ortiz	93
UTAH	
1 Hansen	92
2 Marriott	64
3 Nielson	99
VERMONT	
AL Jeffords	83
VIRGINIA	
1 Bateman	97#
2 Whitehurst	91
3 Bliley	95
4 Sisisky	98
5 Daniel	95
6 Olin	97
7 Robinson	96
8 Parris	97
9 Boucher	89
10 Wolf	98
WASHINGTON	
1 Pritchard	75#
2 Swift	96†
3 Bonker	89
4 Morrison	98
5 Foley	92
6 Dicks	93
7 Lowry	99
8 Chandler	96
WEST VIRGINIA	
1 Mollohan	97
2 Staggers	99
3 Wise	94
4 Rahall	92
WISCONSIN	
1 Aspin	89
2 Kastenmeier	97#
3 Gunderson	99
4 Kleczka[4]	97†
5 Moody	91#
6 Petri	100
7 Obey	98
8 Roth	89
9 Sensenbrenner	66#
WYOMING	
AL Cheney	80#

ALABAMA			IOWA			NEW HAMPSHIRE		
Denton	93		*Grassley*	97		*Humphrey*	97	
Heflin	93		*Jepsen*	87		*Rudman*	98	
ALASKA			**KANSAS**			**NEW JERSEY**		
Murkowski	92		*Dole*	97		Bradley	86	
Stevens	92		*Kassebaum*	94		Lautenberg	94	
ARIZONA			**KENTUCKY**			**NEW MEXICO**		
Goldwater	82		Ford	94†		*Domenici*	96	
DeConcini	82†		Huddleston	77		Bingaman	98	
ARKANSAS			**LOUISIANA**			**NEW YORK**		
Bumpers	90†		Johnston	91		*D'Amato*	93	
Pryor	87		Long	88		Moynihan	90†	
CALIFORNIA			**MAINE**			**NORTH CAROLINA**		
Wilson	98		*Cohen*	93		*East*	91	
Cranston	78		Mitchell	98#		*Helms*	98	
COLORADO			**MARYLAND**			**NORTH DAKOTA**		
Armstrong	85		*Mathias*	91		*Andrews*	90	
Hart	37		Sarbanes	91		Burdick	93	
CONNECTICUT			**MASSACHUSETTS**			**OHIO**		
Weicker	84		Kennedy	83#		Glenn	80	
Dodd	91		Tsongas	79		Metzenbaum	95	
DELAWARE			**MICHIGAN**			**OKLAHOMA**		
Roth	96		Levin	92		*Nickles*	98	
Biden	99		Riegle	97		Boren	90	
FLORIDA			**MINNESOTA**			**OREGON**		
Hawkins	88†		*Boschwitz*	97		*Hatfield*	88	
Chiles	96		*Durenberger*	89		*Packwood*	95	
GEORGIA			**MISSISSIPPI**			**PENNSYLVANIA**		
Mattingly	96		*Cochran*	91		*Heinz*	94†	
Nunn	95		Stennis	84		*Specter*	99	
HAWAII			**MISSOURI**			**RHODE ISLAND**		
Inouye	87		*Danforth*	99		*Chafee*	95	
Matsunaga	93#		Eagleton	87		Pell	93	
IDAHO			**MONTANA**			**SOUTH CAROLINA**		
McClure	85		Baucus	98		*Thurmond*	97	
Symms	91		Melcher	97		Hollings	79	
ILLINOIS			**NEBRASKA**			**SOUTH DAKOTA**		
Percy	69		Exon	94		*Abdnor*	97	
Dixon	90		Zorinsky	99		*Pressler*	94	
INDIANA			**NEVADA**			**TENNESSEE**		
Lugar	100		*Hecht*	96		*Baker*	90	
Quayle	97		*Laxalt*	87†		Sasser	95	

			TEXAS		
			Tower	85	
			Bentsen	80	
			UTAH		
			Garn	99	
			Hatch	98	
			VERMONT		
			Stafford	85	
			Leahy	93#	
			VIRGINIA		
			Trible	95	
			Warner	98	
			WASHINGTON		
			Evans	96	
			Gorton	99	
			WEST VIRGINIA		
			Byrd	98	
			Randolph	97	
			WISCONSIN		
			Kasten	95	
			Proxmire	100	
			WYOMING		
			Simpson	92	
			Wallop	91	

KEY

† Not eligible for all recorded votes in 1984 (sworn in after Jan. 23, died or resigned during session, or voted "present" to avoid possible conflict of interest).

\# Member absent a day or more in 1984 due to illness or illness or death in family.

Democrats   *Republicans*

Voting Participation Scores: Senate

Voting Participation, 1984. Percentage of 275 roll calls in 1984 on which senator voted "yea" or "nay."

Coalition Vote Study:

Conservative Strength Still High for Fourth Reagan Year

The voting strength of Republicans and Southern Democrats, when they joined forces in opposition to Northern Democrats, remained high in 1984, as it has throughout Ronald Reagan's presidency.

The so-called "conservative coalition" won 83 percent of the votes in which it appeared in 1984, up from a 77 percent success score in 1983, according to a Congressional Quarterly vote analysis.

At the same time, the conservative coalition appeared in only 16 percent of recorded votes in 1984. This was only one point above last year's rate, which marked a 19-year low.

The conservative coalition, as defined for the Congressional Quarterly study, does not refer to any organized group or to an ideological definition of conservatism. It refers, rather, to the voting alliance that occurs when a majority of Republicans and Southern Democrats vote against a majority of Northern Democrats. *(See definitions box, this page)*

Congressional Quarterly has been studying the voting patterns of this conservative coalition since 1957. In recent years, Republicans and Southern Democrats have been joined in opposition to Northern Democrats' forces less often — perhaps reflecting greater support for Reagan's programs among Democrats generally — but the coalition has shown greater effectiveness.

In the Senate, the coalition saw its strength almost unchallenged, winning 94 percent of the votes. This was five percentage points above 1983 and only one point below the success rate of 1981, when Republicans took control of the Senate.

The conservative coalition in 1981 was more successful than in any year since 1957, when it scored a perfect 100 percent.

In the House, the coalition was successful 75 percent of the time in 1984, up from 71 percent the previous year. This was still well below the 1981 post-election high of 88 percent.

The number of votes on which the study was based was relatively small, because the 1984 session's 683 recorded votes were the fewest since 1969. Some sessions in the mid-1970s provided almost twice as many votes.

The coalition appeared in just 59 House votes, only two-thirds as many as last year and less than half as often as in the late 1970s.

The 47 Senate votes in which the coalition surfaced was a slight increase from 44 last year, but only a third as often as in the mid-1970s.

In the Senate, Southerners — Democrats and Republicans alike — were more likely to stick with the coalition than they were in 1983.

Also, Senate Republicans from regions other than the South were more likely to support the coalition than in the previous year. But Senate Democrats from regions other than the South supported the coalition less often, with Midwestern support dipping from 38 percent in 1983 to 31 percent.

In the House, support from both parties and from all regions was close to the levels of the previous year.

Definitions

Conservative Coalition. As used in this study, the term "conservative coalition" means a voting alliance of Republicans and Southern Democrats against the Northern Democrats in Congress. This meaning, rather than any philosophic definition of the "conservative coalition" position, provides the basis for CQ's selection of coalition votes.

Conservative Coalition Vote. Any vote in the Senate or the House on which a majority of voting Southern Democrats and a majority of voting Republicans opposed the stand taken by a majority of voting Northern Democrats. Votes on which there is an even division within the ranks of voting Northern Democrats, Southern Democrats or Republicans are not included.

Southern States. The Southern states are Alabama, Arkansas, Florida, Georgia, Kentucky, Louisiana, Mississippi, North Carolina, Oklahoma, South Carolina, Tennessee, Texas and Virginia. The other 37 are grouped as the North in this study.

Conservative Coalition Support Score. Percentage of conservative coalition votes on which member votes "yea" or "nay" *in agreement* with the position of the conservative coalition. Failures to vote, even if a member announces a stand, lower the score.

Conservative Coalition Opposition Score. Percentage of conservative coalition votes on which a member votes "yea" or "nay" *in disagreement* with the position of the conservative coalition.

By region, the group with the highest level of opposition to the coalition was House Democrats from the West, who were recorded in opposition 77 percent of the time. Members from the East were only slightly less likely to oppose the coalition, with Senate Democrats voting in opposition 75 percent of the time and House Democrats voting in opposition 71 percent of the time.

Eastern Republicans voted in opposition to the coalition 34 percent of the time in the Senate and 30 percent of the time in the House. Both figures were down slightly from the previous year.

Individual Scores

Three members of Congress had perfect scores in votes where the conservative coalition appeared:

Sens. Jesse Helms, R-N.C. and James Abdnor, R-S.D., voted with the coalition 100 percent of the time, while Rep. Ronald V. Dellums, D-Calif., voted against it every time.

In the Senate, four other Republicans closely followed Helms and Abdnor in their support of the coalition with 98 percent scores: Paul S. Trible Jr., Va.; Orrin G. Hatch, Utah; Jake Garn, Utah; and Strom Thurmond, S.C.

The Southern Democrats with the highest support scores were two senators up for re-election: David L. Boren, Okla., with 91 percent, and Howell Heflin, Ala., with 89 percent. For the fourth year in a row, Edward Zorinsky, D-Neb., received the highest score in support of the coalition among Northern Democrats.

The leaders in opposing the conservative coalition in the Senate were Paul S. Sarbanes, D-Md., and Donald W. Riegle Jr., D-Mich. Their 98 percent scores were the highest registered in opposition to the coalition since 1959. For the second consecutive year, Lowell P. Weicker Jr., Conn., led Senate Republican opposition to the coalition. Jim Sasser, Tenn., was the leading Southern Democrat in the Senate to oppose the coalition.

In the House, John J. Duncan, R-Tenn., joined two Mississippians, Democrat G. V. "Sonny" Montgomery and Republican Whip Trent Lott, in voting most often with the conservative coalition (97 percent). Beverly B. Byron, Md., led supportive House Northern Democrats with 81 percent.

Several House Democrats almost matched Dellums' perfect score in opposition: Don Edwards, Calif., at 98 percent, and at 97 percent: Norman Y. Mineta, Calif.; Alan Wheat, Mo.; Bob Edgar, Pa.; and Charles A. Hayes, Ill.

Among House Republicans, Silvio O. Conte, Mass., voted against the coalition most often — 76 percent. Texan Mickey Leland led Southern Democrats in voting against the coalition — 86 percent — for the third year in a row.

In the Senate, a large proportion of the conservative coalition's victories (14 of 44) came on Central America policy. Central America issues provided six victories for the conservative coalition in the House. But the coalition did not surface at the end of the session, when Congress voted to halt aid to Nicaraguan "contras" as part of the continuing appropriations resolution.

Defense issues triggered the coalition in the House on 17 of the 59 votes, with results almost evenly split. The president won nine defense votes with the help of the coalition, most on major weapons systems such as Trident II and Pershing II missiles, the B-1 bomber and anti-aircraft guns. But the coalition was defeated on eight issues — losing votes on binary chemical weapons, anti-satellite missile testing and three key MX votes.

In the House, immigration reform provided a series of nine victories for the conservative coalition, on matters such as setting up a guest worker program for growers. But the coalition was defeated on a major vote on granting amnesty to millions of illegal aliens already in the country.

Coalition Appearances

Following is the percentage of the recorded votes for both houses of Congress on which the coalition appeared:

Year	%	Year	%
1965	24%	1975	28
1966	25	1976	24
1967	20	1977	26
1968	24	1978	21
1969	27	1979	20
1970	22	1980	18
1971	30	1981	21
1972	27	1982	18
1973	23	1983	15
1974	24	1984	16

Coalition Victories

Year	Total	Senate	House
1965	33%	39%	25%
1966	45	51	32
1967	63	54	73
1968	73	80	63
1969	68	67	71
1970	66	64	70
1971	83	86	79
1972	69	63	79
1973	61	54	67
1974	59	54	67
1975	50	48	52
1976	58	58	59
1977	68	74	60
1978	52	46	57
1979	70	65	73
1980	72	75	67
1981	92	95	88
1982	85	90	78
1983	77	89	71
1984	83	94	75

Average Scores

Following are the composite conservative coalition support and opposition scores for 1984 (scores for 1983 are in parentheses):

	Southern Democrats	Republicans	Northern Democrats
Coalition Support			
Senate	67% (62)	80% (75)	25% (28)
House	63 (65)	79 (78)	21 (21)
Coalition Opposition			
Senate	23% (28)	14% (18)	67% (64)
House	29 (30)	15 (18)	72 (74)

Regional Scores

Following are the parties' coalition support and opposition scores by region for 1984 (scores for 1983 are in parentheses):

SUPPORT

	East	West	South	Midwest
DEMOCRATS				
Senate	20% (21)	23% (28)	67% (62)	31% (38)
House	22 (21)	17 (18)	63 (65)	24 (24)
REPUBLICANS				
Senate	60% (58)	84% (77)	92% (88)	81% (75)
House	66 (63)	83 (86)	86 (88)	80 (77)

OPPOSITION

	East	West	South	Midwest
DEMOCRATS				
Senate	75% (74)	60% (57)	23% (28)	61% (56)
House	71 (74)	77 (75)	29 (30)	70 (72)
REPUBLICANS				
Senate	34% (37)	9% (13)	3% (8)	15% (20)
House	30 (33)	9 (9)	8 (9)	14 (19)

*(CQ defines regions of the United States as follows: **East:** Conn., Del., Maine, Md., Mass., N.H., N.J., N.Y., Pa., R.I., Vt., W.Va. **West:** Alaska, Ariz., Calif., Colo., Hawaii, Idaho, Mont., Nev., N.M., Ore., Utah, Wash., Wyo. **South:** Ala., Ark., Fla., Ga., Ky., La., Miss., N.C., Okla., S.C., Tenn., Texas, Va. **Midwest:** Ill., Ind., Iowa, Kan., Mich., Minn., Mo., Neb., N.D., Ohio, S.D., Wis.)*

Individual Scores

SUPPORT

Highest Coalition Support Scores. Those who voted with the conservative coalition most consistently in 1984:

SENATE

Southern Democrats		Republicans	
Boren, Okla.	91%	Helms, N.C.	100%
Heflin, Ala.	89	Abdnor, S.D.	100
Nunn, Ga.	83	Trible, Va.	98
Johnston, La.	83	Hatch, Utah	98
Stennis, Miss.	81	Garn, Utah	98
Chiles, Fla.	77	Thurmond, S.C.	98

Northern Democrats

Zorinsky, Neb.	77%
Exon, Neb.	68
Randolph, W.Va.	60
Dixon, Ill.	49
DeConcini, Ariz.	45
Byrd, W.Va.	45

HOUSE

Southern Democrats		Republicans	
Montgomery, Miss.	97%	Lott, Miss.	97%
Hutto, Fla.	95	Duncan, Tenn.	97
Daniel, Va.	92	Livingston, La.	95
Lloyd, Tenn.	90	Packard, Calif.	95
Sam B. Hall Jr., Texas	88	Holt, Md.	95
Whitley, N.C.	88	Bartlett, Texas	95
Hightower, Texas	88	Schaefer, Colo.	95

Northern Democrats

Byron, Md.	81%
Skelton, Mo.	76
Stratton, N.Y.	76
Dyson, Md.	71
Mollohan, W.Va.	63
Murtha, Pa.	63
Yatron, Pa.	58
Volkmer, Mo.	56
Applegate, Ohio	54
Hamilton, Ind.	54
Dicks, Wash.	54
Price, Ill.	53

OPPOSITION

Highest Coalition Opposition Scores. Those who voted against the conservative coalition most consistently in 1984:

SENATE

Southern Democrats		Republicans	
Sasser, Tenn.	62%	Weicker, Conn.	64%
Bumpers, Ark.	51	Hatfield, Ore.	51
Ford, Ky.	38	Mathias, Md.	49
Hollings, S.C.	26	Cohen, Maine	47

1984 Coalition Votes

Following is a list of all 1984 Senate and House votes on which the conservative coalition appeared. The votes are listed by CQ vote number and may be found in the vote charts beginning on pages 1-S and 1-H.

SENATE VOTES (47)

Coalition Victories (44) — 8, 10, 12, 13, 14, 29, 41, 42, 46, 47, 48, 49, 50, 51, 52, 56, 58, 62, 65, 70, 71, 72, 75, 101, 140, 141, 183, 187, 192, 198, 199, 200, 201, 202, 204, 227, 240, 241, 242, 247, 252, 255, 261, 266.

Coalition Defeats (3) — 34, 69, 239.

HOUSE VOTES (59)

Coalition Victories (44) — 5, 42, 44, 62, 89, 90, 120, 124, 125, 126, 127, 133, 134, 136, 137, 144, 147, 148, 149, 161, 177, 182, 205, 208, 209, 212, 215, 216, 222, 225, 226, 247, 261, 270, 324, 329, 331, 343, 350, 354, 359, 367, 370, 388.

Coalition Defeats (15) — 3, 6, 67, 129, 135, 152, 154, 155, 178, 179, 183, 224, 254, 287, 313.

Pryor, Ark.	23	Specter, Pa.	45
Huddleston, Ky.	23		

Northern Democrats

Sarbanes, Md.	98%
Riegle, Mich.	98
Metzenbaum, Ohio	91
Lautenberg, N.J.	91
Kennedy, Mass.	91

HOUSE

Southern Democrats		Republicans	
Leland, Texas	86%	Conte, Mass.	76%
Lehman, Fla.	81	Schneider, R.I.	71
Ford, Tenn.	76	Green, N.Y.	69
Gonzalez, Texas	75	Leach, Iowa	58
Smith, Fla.	69	Jeffords, Vt.	49
Fascell, Fla.	66	McKinney, Conn.	47
Bryant, Texas	64	Coughlin, Pa.	46
Natcher, Ky.	54	Rinaldo, N.J.	44
Long, La.	53	Ridge, Pa.	44
Synar, Okla.	53	Johnson, Conn.	42
Mazzoli, Ky.	53	Roukema, N.J.	42
		Gilman, N.Y.	42

Northern Democrats

Dellums, Calif.	100%
Edwards, Calif.	98
Hayes, Ill.	97
Mineta, Calif.	97
Wheat, Mo.	97
Edgar, Pa.	97
Gejdenson, Conn.	95
Torres, Calif.	95
Vento, Minn.	95
Wolpe, Mich.	95

Conservative Coalition Support and Opposition: House

1. Conservative Coalition Support, 1984. Percentage of 59 conservative coalition recorded votes in 1984 on which representative voted "yea" or "nay" *in agreement* with the position of the conservative coalition. Failures to vote lower both support and opposition scores.

2. Conservative Coalition Opposition, 1984. Percentage of 59 conservative coalition recorded votes in 1984 on which representative voted "yea" or "nay" *in disagreement* with the position of the conservative coalition. Failures to vote lower both support and opposition scores.

1. Rep. Carl D. Perkins, D-Ky., died Aug. 3, 1984.
2. Rep. Thomas P. O'Neill Jr., D-Mass., as Speaker, votes at his own discretion.
3. Rep. Edwin B. Forsythe, R-N.J., died March 29, 1984.
4. Rep. Gerald D. Kleczka, D-Wis., sworn in April 10, 1984, to succeed Clement J. Zablocki, D, who died Dec. 3, 1983.

KEY

† Not eligible for all recorded votes in 1984 (sworn in after Jan. 23, died or resigned during session, or voted "present" to avoid possible conflict of interest).

Democrats   *Republicans*

	1	2
ALABAMA		
1 *Edwards*	83	7
2 *Dickinson*	90	5
3 Nichols	80	10
4 Bevill	83	7
5 Flippo	86	10
6 Erdreich	81	10
7 Shelby	78	12
ALASKA		
AL *Young*	88	10
ARIZONA		
1 *McCain*	83	8
2 Udall	22	69
3 *Stump*	86	7
4 *Rudd*	88	3
5 McNulty	29	64
ARKANSAS		
1 Alexander	42	24
2 *Bethune*	71	8
3 *Hammerschmidt*	92	3
4 Anthony	51	32
CALIFORNIA		
1 Bosco	25	63
2 *Chappie*	81	12
3 Matsui	12	88
4 Fazio	25	68
5 Burton	5	86
6 Boxer	2	92
7 Miller	7	86
8 Dellums	0	100
9 Stark	3	83
10 Edwards	2	98
11 Lantos	14	81
12 *Zschau*	63	37
13 Mineta	3	97
14 *Shumway*	90	10
15 Coelho	20	71
16 Panetta	25	75
17 *Pashayan*	88	10
18 Lehman	20	71
19 *Lagomarsino*	93	7
20 *Thomas*	78	12
21 *Fiedler*	88	8
22 *Moorhead*	90	7
23 Beilenson	12	88
24 Waxman	5	93
25 Roybal	5	90
26 Berman	7	88
27 Levine	5	88
28 Dixon	12	75
29 Hawkins	3	64
30 Martinez	10	85
31 Dymally	10	66
32 Anderson	42	58
33 *Dreier*	88	8
34 Torres	5	95
35 *Lewis*	83	10
36 Brown	12	81
37 *McCandless*	92	8
38 Patterson	32	59
39 *Dannemeyer*	88	8
40 *Badham*	81	5
41 *Lowery*	86	7
42 *Lungren*	90	10

	1	2
43 *Packard*	95	5
44 Bates	14	78
45 *Hunter*	90	8
COLORADO		
1 Schroeder	17	81
2 Wirth	10	83
3 Kogovsek	12	80
4 *Brown*	83	17
5 *Kramer*	86	7
6 *Schaefer*	95	5
CONNECTICUT		
1 Kennelly	15	78
2 Gejdenson	5	95
3 Morrison	5	93
4 *McKinney*	39	47
5 Ratchford	24	76
6 *Johnson*	51	42
DELAWARE		
AL Carper	46	54
FLORIDA		
1 Hutto	95	3
2 Fuqua	81	12
3 Bennett	75	25
4 Chappell	86	7
5 *McCollum*	93	7
6 MacKay	47	46
7 Gibbons	51	36
8 *Young*	85	8
9 *Bilirakis*	90	10
10 *Ireland*	88	7
11 Nelson	83	17
12 *Lewis*	93	7
13 *Mack*	92	8
14 Mica	58	39
15 *Shaw*	90	5
16 Smith	25	69
17 Lehman	10	81
18 Pepper	41	49
19 Fascell	32	66
GEORGIA		
1 Thomas	86	14
2 Hatcher	66	10
3 Ray	81	15
4 Levitas	73	24
5 Fowler	51	42
6 *Gingrich*	86	8
7 Darden	86	12
8 Rowland	78	19
9 Jenkins	66	19
10 Barnard	69	8
HAWAII		
1 Heftel	46	37
2 Akaka	22	75
IDAHO		
1 *Craig*	93	5
2 *Hansen*	15	0
ILLINOIS		
1 Hayes	2	97
2 Savage	0	85
3 Russo	22	69
4 *O'Brien*	88	8
5 Lipinski	46	41
6 *Hyde*	88	7
7 Collins	5	83
8 Rostenkowski	34	46
9 Yates	5	93
10 *Porter*	80	19
11 Annunzio	39	58
12 *Crane, P.*	85	10
13 *Erlenborn*	78	3
14 *Corcoran*	83	3
15 *Madigan*	88	10
16 *Martin*	73	22
17 Evans	7	92
18 *Michel*	90	3
19 *Crane, D.*	86	8
20 Durbin	29	69
21 Price	53	46
22 Simon	7	44
INDIANA		
1 Hall	5	66
2 Sharp	47	36
3 *Hiler*	88	8
4 *Coats*	90	10
5 Hillis	86	3

	1	2
6 *Burton*	90	5
7 *Myers*	93	7
8 McCloskey	25	69
9 Hamilton	54	46
10 Jacobs	15	80
IOWA		
1 *Leach*	36	58
2 *Tauke*	56	39
3 *Evans*	56	37
4 Smith	42	47
5 Harkin	17	80
6 Bedell	24	68
KANSAS		
1 *Roberts*	85	10
2 Slattery	49	51
3 *Winn*	88	5
4 Glickman	44	53
5 *Whittaker*	85	10
KENTUCKY		
1 Hubbard	73	20
2 Natcher	46	54
3 Mazzoli	47	53
4 *Snyder*	85	12
5 *Rogers*	92	7
6 *Hopkins*	80	20
7 Perkins[1]	46†	52†
LOUISIANA		
1 *Livingston*	95	5
2 Boggs	32	44
3 Tauzin	83	17
4 Roemer	78	22
5 Huckaby	80	14
6 *Moore*	86	12
7 Breaux	80	8
8 Long	44	53
MAINE		
1 *McKernan*	59	41
2 *Snowe*	64	36
MARYLAND		
1 Dyson	71	29
2 Long	32	66
3 Mikulski	12	75
4 *Holt*	95	2
5 Hoyer	32	63
6 Byron	81	17
7 Mitchell	5	83
8 Barnes	19	81
MASSACHUSETTS		
1 *Conte*	20	76
2 Boland	25	68
3 Early	12	71
4 Frank	8	88
5 Shannon	0	68
6 Mavroules	20	75
7 Markey	0	85
8 O'Neill[2]		
9 Moakley	12	76
10 Studds	5	83
11 Donnelly	24	71
MICHIGAN		
1 Conyers	5	92
2 *Pursell*	63	20
3 Wolpe	5	95
4 *Siljander*	83	7
5 *Sawyer*	73	10
6 Carr	34	66
7 Kildee	7	93
8 Traxler	22	66
9 *Vander Jagt*	80	3
10 Albosta	34	63
11 *Davis*	78	17
12 Bonior	10	83
13 Crockett	10	69
14 Hertel	20	75
15 Ford	17	75
16 Dingell	31	63
17 Levin	15	85
18 *Broomfield*	90	10
MINNESOTA		
1 Penny	36	64
2 *Weber*	80	17
3 *Frenzel*	71	20
4 Vento	3	95
5 Sabo	12	80
6 Sikorski	22	78

	1	2
7 *Stangeland*	90	7
8 Oberstar	5	83
MISSISSIPPI		
1 Whitten	56	39
2 *Franklin*	86	3
3 Montgomery	97	3
4 Dowdy	64	22
5 *Lott*	97	2
MISSOURI		
1 Clay	2	92
2 Young	42	47
3 Gephardt	27	69
4 Skelton	76	15
5 Wheat	3	97
6 *Coleman*	80	14
7 *Taylor*	90	5
8 *Emerson*	93	5
9 Volkmer	56	44
MONTANA		
1 *Williams*	17	75
2 *Marlenee*	81	8
NEBRASKA		
1 *Bereuter*	71	29
2 *Daub*	90	10
3 *Smith*	80	20
NEVADA		
1 Reid	42	58
2 *Vucanovich*	90	5
NEW HAMPSHIRE		
1 D'Amours	34	56
2 *Gregg*	83	15
NEW JERSEY		
1 Florio	19	76
2 Hughes	46	47
3 Howard	12	71
4 *Smith*	63	37
5 *Roukema*	56	42
6 Dwyer	24	75
7 *Rinaldo*	54	44
8 Roe	29	61
9 Torricelli	31	66
10 Rodino	8	78
11 Minish	36	59
12 *Courter*	71	12
13 *Forsythe*[3]	0†	0†
14 Guarini	15	64
NEW MEXICO		
1 *Lujan*	86	12
2 *Skeen*	93	7
3 Richardson	19	80
NEW YORK		
1 *Carney*	88	10
2 Downey	5	93
3 Mrazek	17	83
4 *Lent*	80	14
5 *McGrath*	73	17
6 Addabbo	5	90
7 Ackerman	5	86
8 Scheuer	15	80
9 Ferraro	7	66
10 Schumer	3	93
11 Towns	3	86
12 Owens	3	93
13 Solarz	15	78
14 *Molinari*	81	19
15 *Green*	29	69
16 Rangel	8	85
17 Weiss	2	93
18 Garcia	7	86
19 Biaggi	34	61
20 Ottinger	7	88
21 *Fish*	53	37
22 *Gilman*	58	42
23 Stratton	76	22
24 *Solomon*	83	14
25 *Boehlert*	61	37
26 *Martin*	81	10
27 *Wortley*	85	15
28 McHugh	24	75
29 *Horton*	68	32
30 *Conable*	86	14
31 *Kemp*	85	12
32 LaFalce	25	68
33 Nowak	19	76
34 Lundine	20	56

	1	2
NORTH CAROLINA		
1 Jones	49	41
2 Valentine	86	7
3 Whitley	88	8
4 Andrews	56	17
5 Neal	51	36
6 Britt	61	39
7 Rose	47	39
8 Hefner	80	17
9 *Martin*	73	3
10 *Broyhill*	93	7
11 Clarke	47	42
NORTH DAKOTA		
AL Dorgan	31	68
OHIO		
1 Luken	37	58
2 *Gradison*	69	31
3 Hall	25	63
4 *Oxley*	93	5
5 *Latta*	83	8
6 *McEwen*	88	5
7 *DeWine*	88	12
8 *Kindness*	86	10
9 Kaptur	20	73
10 *Miller*	83	17
11 Eckart	27	71
12 *Kasich*	92	8
13 Pease	22	78
14 Seiberling	10	83
15 *Wylie*	92	5
16 *Regula*	78	19
17 *Williams*	58	17
18 Applegate	54	44
19 Feighan	17	81
20 Oakar	8	90
21 Stokes	0	93
OKLAHOMA		
1 Jones	69	31
2 Synar	36	53
3 Watkins	78	12
4 McCurdy	71	12
5 *Edwards*	80	12
6 English	75	12
OREGON		
1 AuCoin	22	71
2 *Smith, B.*	83	14
3 Wyden	20	80
4 Weaver	17	76
5 *Smith D.*	88	7
PENNSYLVANIA		
1 Foglietta	7	83
2 Gray	7	86
3 Borski	17	81
4 Kolter	27	64
5 *Schulze*	85	10
6 Yatron	58	37
7 Edgar	2	97
8 Kostmayer	20	80
9 *Shuster*	90	8
10 *McDade*	63	25
11 Harrison	20	63
12 Murtha	63	34
13 *Coughlin*	53	46
14 Coyne	17	78
15 Ritter	73	20
16 *Walker*	88	12
17 *Gekas*	88	12
18 Walgren	19	80
19 *Goodling*	71	29
20 Gaydos	47	53
21 *Ridge*	53	44
22 Murphy	46	51
23 *Clinger*	64	34
RHODE ISLAND		
1 St Germain	29	61
2 *Schneider*	27	71
SOUTH CAROLINA		
1 *Hartnett*	83	5
2 *Spence*	88	8
3 Derrick	61	39
4 *Campbell*	90	3
5 Spratt	56	44
6 Tallon	63	32
SOUTH DAKOTA		
AL Daschle	41	53

	1	2
TENNESSEE		
1 *Quillen*	81	12
2 *Duncan*	97	3
3 Lloyd	90	10
4 Cooper	49	51
5 Boner	66	22
6 Gore	56	34
7 *Sundquist*	90	7
8 Jones	64	25
9 Ford	15	76
TEXAS		
1 Hall, S.	88	7
2 Wilson	59	15
3 *Bartlett*	95	5
4 Hall, R.	81	17
5 Bryant	17	64
6 *Gramm*	69	8
7 *Archer*	88	12
8 *Fields*	80	15
9 Brooks	46	46
10 Pickle	69	27
11 Leath	83	3
12 Wright	58	37
13 Hightower	88	8
14 Patman	83	14
15 de la Garza	59	25
16 Coleman	61	37
17 Stenholm	85	8
18 Leland	2	86
19 Hance	29	15
20 Gonzalez	20	75
21 *Loeffler*	93	5
22 *Paul*	41	36
23 Kazen	66	19
24 Frost	42	47
25 Andrews	81	17
26 Vandergriff	78	20
27 Ortiz	53	41
UTAH		
1 *Hansen*	85	5
2 *Marriott*	68	3
3 *Nielson*	90	10
VERMONT		
AL *Jeffords*	32	49
VIRGINIA		
1 *Bateman*	90	3
2 *Whitehurst*	90	7
3 *Bliley*	88	8
4 *Sisisky*	73	24
5 Daniel	92	8
6 Olin	53	42
7 *Robinson*	88	8
8 *Parris*	88	10
9 Boucher	44	47
10 *Wolf*	86	12
WASHINGTON		
1 *Pritchard*	61	24
2 Swift	22	78
3 Bonker	27	63
4 *Morrison*	85	14
5 Foley	32	56
6 Dicks	54	42
7 Lowry	7	93
8 *Chandler*	80	17
WEST VIRGINIA		
1 Mollohan	63	36
2 Staggers	29	71
3 Wise	37	61
4 Rahall	22	64
WISCONSIN		
1 Aspin	42	54
2 Kastenmeier	8	92
3 *Gunderson*	75	25
4 Kleczka[4]	28†	72†
5 Moody	12	75
6 *Petri*	75	25
7 Obey	17	81
8 *Roth*	83	14
9 *Sensenbrenner*	44	12
WYOMING		
AL *Cheney*	81	2

	1	2		1	2		1	2	KEY
ALABAMA			**IOWA**			**NEW HAMPSHIRE**			
Denton	89	2	*Grassley*	89	11	*Humphrey*	79	17	Democrats *Republicans*
Heflin	89	11	*Jepsen*	87	6	*Rudman*	74	26	
ALASKA			**KANSAS**			**NEW JERSEY**			
Murkowski	94	2	*Dole*	96	2	Bradley	28	60	
Stevens	94	4	*Kassebaum*	81	17	Lautenberg	6	91	
ARIZONA			**KENTUCKY**			**NEW MEXICO**			
Goldwater	77	4	Ford	55	38	*Domenici*	91	9	
DeConcini	45	21	Huddleston	51	23	Bingaman	28	72	

	1	2		1	2		1	2		1	2
ARKANSAS			**LOUISIANA**			**NEW YORK**			**TEXAS**		
Bumpers	45	51	Johnston	83	11	*D'Amato*	72	19	*Tower*	85	2
Pryor	72	23	Long	72	15	Moynihan	21	66	Bentsen	53	17
CALIFORNIA			**MAINE**			**NORTH CAROLINA**			**UTAH**		
Wilson	89	6	*Cohen*	53	47	*East*	91	0	*Garn*	98	2
Cranston	13	72	Mitchell	15	85	*Helms*	100	0	*Hatch*	98	2
COLORADO			**MARYLAND**			**NORTH DAKOTA**			**VERMONT**		
Armstrong	81	4	*Mathias*	49	49	*Andrews*	77	23	*Stafford*	43	34
Hart	2	34	Sarbanes	0	98	Burdick	26	57	Leahy	15	77
CONNECTICUT			**MASSACHUSETTS**			**OHIO**			**VIRGINIA**		
Weicker	23	64	Kennedy	6	91	Glenn	28	51	*Trible*	98	2
Dodd	6	89	Tsongas	13	68	Metzenbaum	4	91	*Warner*	91	6
DELAWARE			**MICHIGAN**			**OKLAHOMA**			**WASHINGTON**		
Roth	83	15	Levin	9	85	*Nickles*	96	2	*Evans*	77	23
Biden	28	72	Riegle	2	98	Boren	91	0	*Gorton*	81	19
FLORIDA			**MINNESOTA**			**OREGON**			**WEST VIRGINIA**		
Hawkins	77	11	*Boschwitz*	66	34	*Hatfield*	45	51	Byrd	45	55
Chiles	77	21	*Durenberger*	70	21	*Packwood*	62	32	Randolph	60	40
GEORGIA			**MISSISSIPPI**			**PENNSYLVANIA**			**WISCONSIN**		
Mattingly	96	4	*Cochran*	96	2	*Heinz*	70	23	*Kasten*	87	11
Nunn	83	17	Stennis	81	13	*Specter*	55	45	Proxmire	28	72
HAWAII			**MISSOURI**			**RHODE ISLAND**			**WYOMING**		
Inouye	30	62	*Danforth*	83	17	*Chafee*	60	36	*Simpson*	89	2
Matsunaga	17	79	Eagleton	26	68	Pell	15	81	*Wallop*	94	0
IDAHO			**MONTANA**			**SOUTH CAROLINA**					
McClure	83	2	Baucus	34	66	*Thurmond*	98	0			
Symms	89	0	Melcher	19	77	Hollings	49	26			
ILLINOIS			**NEBRASKA**			**SOUTH DAKOTA**					
Percy	57	19	Exon	68	28	*Abdnor*	100	0			
Dixon	49	38	Zorinsky	77	21	*Pressler*	72	23			
INDIANA			**NEVADA**			**TENNESSEE**					
Lugar	87	13	*Hecht*	91	2	*Baker*	83	2			
Quayle	81	15	*Laxalt*	85	2	Sasser	30	62			

Conservative Coalition
Support and Opposition: Senate

1. Conservative Coalition Support, 1984. Percentage of 47 conservative coalition votes in 1984 on which senator voted "yea" or "nay" *in agreement* with the position of the conservative coalition. Failures to vote lower both support and opposition scores.

2. Conservative Coalition Opposition 1984. Percentage of 47 conservative coalition votes in 1984 on which senator voted "yea" or "nay" *in disagreement* with the position of the conservative coalition. Failures to vote lower both support and opposition scores.

LOBBY REGISTRATIONS

CQ

November 1983 Registrations

Corporations and Businesses

AMERISERV INC., 3471 N. Federal Highway, Fort Lauderdale, Fla. 33306. Filed for self 11/30/83. Legislative interest — "HR 1955, S 1108, HR 2355, S 1228, S 1323, S 1050." Lobbyist — Marti Forman.

BABCOCK & BROWN, San Francisco, Calif. Lobbyist — Patton, Boggs & Blow, 2550 M St. N.W., Washington, D.C. 20037. Filed 11/16/83. Legislative interest — "Legislation relating to the Tax Exempt Entity Leasing Act of 1983 and the Governmental Lease Financing Reform Act of 1983. . . ."

BANKAMERICA CORP., BankAmerica Center, San Francisco, Calif. Filed for self 11/28/83. Legislative interest — Not specified. Lobbyist — Nancy Camm, 1800 K St. N.W., Washington, D.C. 20006.

BECKER, GURMAN & LUCAS, MEYERS & O'BRIEN, 2501 M St. N.W., Washington, D.C. 20037. Filed for self 11/16/83. Legislative interest — "All legislation involving the conduct of lotteries for the selection of cellular telephone licenses by the FCC . . . opposition to FCC plans to switch from established comparative hearing procedure to lotteries." Lobbyist — Christopher L. Davis.

BELLSOUTH CORP., Washington, D.C. Lobbyist — King & Spalding, 1915 I St. N.W., Washington, D.C. 20006. Filed 11/20/83. Legislative interest — ". . . telecommunications industry."

BEVERLY ENTERPRISES INC., 1901 N. Fort Meyer Drive, Rosslyn, Va. 22209. Filed for self 11/8/83. Legislative interest — "Health, Tax, Social Security and Housing Legislation; HR 4170 - 'Tax Exempt Bond Limitation Act of 1983'. . . ." Lobbyists — Jack A. MacDonald, Barbara Stinson.

BKK CORP., Torrance, Calif. Lobbyist — Bill Hecht, 499 South Capitol St., Washington, D.C. 20003. Filed 11/28/83. Legislative interest — "General legislative interests in hazardous waste management . . . Resource Conservation and Recovery Act Reauthorization . . . HR 2867, [HR] 5757. . . ."

BLUE CROSS AND BLUE SHIELD ASSOCIATION, 676 N. St. Clair, Chicago, Ill. 60611. Filed for self 11/10/83. Legislative interest — "Legislation impacting the financing of Title XVIII, Title XIX, and CHAMPUS. HR 4071 - Tax Reform Act of 1983; HR 4136 - Medicare/Medicaid Budget Reconciliation Amendments of 1983; HR 4185 — FY 84 Defense Appropriations." Lobbyists — Susan E. Phillips, Alan P. Spielman, 1709 New York Ave. N.W., Washington, D.C. 20006.

BURNS AND ROE INC., Washington, D.C. Lobbyist — Luman & Schoor, 1050 17th St. N.W., Washington, D.C. 20036. Filed 11/23/83. Legislative interest — "General interest in matters affecting engineering and design. Specific interest in matters affecting the continuation of the Clinch River Breeder Reactor project. . . ."

CENERGY EXPLORATION CO., Dallas, Texas. Lobbyist — Foreman & Dyess, 1920 N St. N.W., Washington, D.C. 20036. Filed 11/17/83. Legislative interest — "Natural gas legislation including S 1715 and HR 4277." Lobbyist — Daniel A. Dutko, 412 First St. S.E., Washington, D.C. 20003. Filed 11/21/83. Legislative interest — ". . . oil and gas matters."

CENTRAL SERVICES ORGANIZATION, Washington, D.C. Lobbyist — Arnold & Porter, 1200 New Hampshire Ave. N.W., Washington, D.C. 20036. Filed 11/1/83. Legislative interest — ". . . involves antitrust matters contained in HR 4102 and S 1660."

JERRY CHAMBERS EXPLORATION CO., Chicago, Ill. Lobbyist — Holme, Roberts & Owen, 1700 Broadway, Denver, Colo. 80290. Filed 11/28/83. Legislative interest — "Seeking amendment and passage of S 1661 . . . relating to availability of percentage depletion allowance for oil produced using secondary and tertiary recovery methods."

CITIBANK N.A., New York, N.Y. Lobbyist — Webster & Sheffield, 1200 New Hampshire Ave. N.W., Washington, D.C. 20036. Filed 11/16/83. Legislative interest — "Pending Tax Reform Act of 1983 . . . HR 4170. . . ."

THE CLEVELAND ELECTRIC ILLUMINATING CO., P.O. Box 5000, Cleveland, Ohio 44101. Filed for self 11/15/83. Legislative interest — "Legislative activities affecting electric utilities in nuclear, clean air, finance and other related areas." Lobbyist — Michael E. Smith.

COMMERZBANK AG, Dusseldorf, Federal Republic of Germany. Lobbyist — Caplin & Drysdale, 1101 17th St. N.W., Washington, D.C. 20036. Filed 11/11/83. Legislative interest — "None this session."

COMMUNICATIONS COUNSEL, Washington, D.C. Lobbyist — O'Connor & Hannan, 1919 Pennsylvania Ave. N.W., Washington, D.C. 20006. Filed 11/15/83. Legislative interest — "Follow communications legislation."

COMMUNICATIONS SATELLITE CORP., Washington, D.C. Lobbyist — Crowell & Moring, 1100 Connecticut Ave. N.W., Washington, D.C. 20036. Filed 11/10/83. Legislative interest — ". . . leasing provisions of HR 4170 and similar legislation."

CONGER LIFE INSURANCE CO., Miami, Fla. Lobbyist — Bill Hecht, 499 South Capitol St., Washington, D.C. 20003. Filed 11/28/83. Legislative interest — "General legislative interests in life insurance taxation, other legislation affecting the life insurance industry, including HR 1001 and HR 4170."

CONTINENTAL AIRLINES, Houston, Texas. Lobbyist — Akin, Gump, Strauss, Hauer & Feld, 1333 New Hampshire Ave. N.W., Washington, D.C. 20036. Filed 11/1/83. Legislative interest — Not specified.

DAILY EXPRESS INC., Carlisle, Pa. Lobbyist — Jones & Winburn, 1101 15th St. N.W., Washington, D.C. 20005. Filed 11/16/83. Legislative interest — "The Surface Transportation Assistance Act of 1982 and The Technical Corrections Act of 1982."

EASTDIL EQUITY, San Francisco, Calif. Lobbyist — Morrison & Foerster, 1920 N St. N.W., Washington, D.C. 20036. Filed 11/10/83. Legislative interest — ". . . Tax Reform Act of 1983 (HR 4170) and all related tax legislation."

THE ESTES CO., Tucson, Ariz. Lobbyist — Bracy, Williams & Co., 1000 Connecticut Ave. N.W., Washington, D.C. 20036. Filed 11/17/83. Legislative interest — "General legislation affecting business, particularly home building, disaster relief, improvement of city infrastructure. For S 752."

FOREMOST INSURANCE CO., Grand Rapids, Mich. Lobbyist — Witkowski, Weiner, McCaffrey & Brodsky, 1575 I St. N.W., Washington, D.C. 20005. Filed 11/11/83. Legislative interest — ". . . Banking, housing, and insurance legislation . . . Banking Deregulation Bill."

SAMUEL GARY OIL PRODUCER INC., Englewood, Colo. Lobbyist — Holme, Roberts & Owen, 1700 Broadway, Denver, Colo. 80290. Filed 11/28/83. Legislative interest — "Seeking amendment and passage of S 1661 . . . relating to availability of percentage depletion allowance for oil produced using secondary and tertiary recovery methods."

GTE SERVICE CORP., Washington, D.C. Lobbyist — Garvey, Schubert, Adams & Barber, 1000 Potomac St. N.W., Washington, D.C. 20007. Filed 11/10/83. (Former U.S. Rep. Brock Adams, D-Wash., 1965-77, was listed as agent for this client.) Legislative interest — "HR 3621, HR 4102, S 253, S 1660 and any legislation related thereto."

GTE SPRINT COMMUNICATIONS CORP., 1828 L St. N.W., Washington, D.C. 20036. Filed for self 11/29/83. Legislative interest — "... HR 4102, Universal Telephone Service Act - for. S 1660, Universal Telephone Service Act - for." Lobbyist — Marybeth Griswold.

HUGHES HELICOPTERS INC., Culver City, Calif. Lobbyist — Andrews & Kurth, 1747 Pennsylvania Ave. N.W., Washington, D.C. 20006. Filed 11/18/83. Legislative interest — "Tax legislation."

HULES MEXICANOS, S.A., Mexico City, Mexico. Lobbyist — O'Connor & Hannan, 1919 Pennsylvania Ave. N.W., Washington, D.C. 20006. Filed 11/23/83. Legislative interest — "To oppose certain trade remedies legislation; specifically, the Trade Remedies Act of 1983."

INDUSTRIAS NEGROMEX S.A. de C.V., Mexico City, Mexico. Lobbyist — O'Connor & Hannan, 1919 Pennsylvania Ave. N.W., Washington, D.C. 20006. Filed 11/23/83. Legislative interest — "To oppose certain trade remedies legislation; specifically, the Trade Remedies Act of 1983."

KAUFMAN AND BROAD INC., Los Angeles, Calif. Lobbyist — Manatt, Phelps, Rothenberg & Tunney, 1200 New Hampshire Ave. N.W., Washington, D.C. 20036. Filed 11/11/83. Legislative interest — "Tax Legislation relating to life insurance companies."

LOCKHEED AIR TERMINALS INC., Burbank, Calif. Lobbyist — Morrison & Foerster, 1920 N St. N.W., Washington, D.C. 20036. Filed 11/10/83. Legislative interest — "... Tax Reform Act of 1983 and related tax legislation."

LUKENS INC., 50 S. First Ave., Coatesville, Pa. 19320. Lobbyist — Collier, Shannon, Rill & Scott, 1055 Thomas Jefferson St. N.W., Washington, D.C. 20007. Filed 11/23/83. Legislative interest — "... including, but not limited to, international trade issues, energy, taxes, environmental concerns." Filed for self 11/22/83. Legislative interest — "... including, but not limited to, international trade issues, energy, taxes, environmental concerns." Lobbyist — Charles L. Huston III.

LYKES BROTHERS STEAMSHIP CO., Washington, D.C. Lobbyist — R. Duffy Wall & Associates Inc., 11 Dupont Circle N.W., Washington, D.C. 20036. Filed 11/11/83. Legislative interest — "Issues relating to ship-building."

MAGNAVOX GOVERNMENT AND INDUSTRIAL ELECTRONICS CO., Fort Wayne, Ind. Lobbyist — Finley, Kumble, Wagner, Heine, Underberg, Manley & Casey, 1120 Connecticut Ave. N.W., Washington, D.C. 20036. Filed 11/14/83. Legislative interest — "General in the nature of legislative proposals affecting international communications common carriers; S 999...."

McDERMOTT INTERNATIONAL, New Orleans, La. Lobbyist — David F. Stang, 1629 K St. N.W., Washington, D.C. 20006. Filed 11/21/83. Legislative interest — "S 38, Longshoremen's and Harbor Workers' Compensation Act."

JACK McDONALD ASSOCIATES INC., 1120 20th St. N.W., Washington, D.C. 20036. Filed for self 11/23/83. Legislative interest — "Life Insurance Taxation."

MEDTRONIC INC., P.O. Box 1453, 3055 Old Highway 8, Minneapolis, Minn. 55440. Filed for self 11/8/83. Legislative interest — "... legislation affecting health care, prospective payment, Medicare/Medicaid changes, Social Security Act, product liability, trade, hazardous waste, Caribbean Trade Plan, research, tax measures, etc." Lobbyist — Luise Forseth.

MERRILL LYNCH & CO. INC., 1828 L St. N.W., Washington, D.C. 20036. Filed for self 11/10/83. Legislative interest — "Financial, banking, securities, taxation, real estate and related legislation." Lobbyist — John F. Kelly.

MESA PETROLEUM CO., Amarillo, Texas. Lobbyist — Beveridge & Diamond, 1333 New Hampshire Ave. N.W., Washington, D.C. 20036. Filed 11/22/83. Legislative interest — "Tax legislation."

METROPOLITAN INSURANCE COS., One Madison Ave., New York, N.Y. 10010. Lobbyist — D L Associates, 1730 Rhode Island Ave. N.W., Washington, D.C. 20036. Filed 11/21/83. Legislative interest — Not specified. Filed for self 11/15/83. Legislative interest — "The enactment of legislation which supports the well-being and objectives of the life and health insurance industry, related pension matters and casualty insurance business,

such as prospective amendments to the Employee Retirement Income Security Act and the National Labor Relations Act, among others, as well as matters involving the tax and administrative operations of our business. Pending bills of interest are HR 4065 ... HR 100/S 372...." Lobbyists — Miriam A. MacDonald, Vincent P. Reusing, 1025 Connecticut Ave. N.W., Washington, D.C. 20036.

MITCHELL ENERGY & DEVELOPMENT CORP., Washington, D.C., and Woodlands, Texas. Lobbyist — Foreman & Dyess, 1920 N St. N.W., Washington, D.C. 20036. Filed 11/17/83. Legislative interest — "Natural gas including S 1715 and HR 4722." Lobbyist — Daniel A. Dutko, 412 First St. S.E., Washington, D.C. 20003. Filed 11/21/83. Legislative interest — "... oil and gas matters."

MONTANA POWER CO., Butte, Mont. Lobbyist — James A. Rock, 1730 M St. N.W., Washington, D.C. 20036. Filed 11/11/83. Legislative interest — "... includes but is not limited to ... Internal Revenue Code, Atomic Energy Act, Federal Power Act, Rural Electrification Act, Reclamation Acts, Flood Control Act, Appropriations Acts, Rivers and Harbors and Flood Control Authorization Acts, Federal Water Pollution Control Act, Clean Air Act, Occupational Health and Safety, Equal Employment Opportunity Act, Employee Retirement Income Security Act, Wild and Scenic Rivers Act, National Energy Act."

D. MOODY & CO. INC., Tulsa, Okla. Lobbyist — Bowman, Conner, Touhey & Petrillo, 2828 Pennsylvania Ave. N.W., Washington, D.C. 20007. Filed 11/18/83. Legislative interest — "Legislation to amend the Walsh-Healey Act."

MORGAN GUARANTY TRUST COMPANY OF NEW YORK, New York, N.Y. Lobbyist — Davis, Polk & Wardwell, 1575 I Street N.W., Washington, D.C. 20005. Filed 11/16/83. Legislative interests — "Bankruptcy legislation."

MUTUAL BENEFIT LIFE INSURANCE CO., Newark, N.J. Lobbyist — Jack McDonald Associates Inc., 1120 20th St. N.W., Washington, D.C. 20036. Filed 11/23/83. Legislative interest — "Life insurance taxation."

NATIONAL BROADCASTING CO., 1825 K St. N.W., Washington, D.C. 20006. Lobbyist — Vorys, Sater, Seymour & Pease, 1828 L St. N.W., Washington, D.C. 20036. Filed 11/11/83. Legislative interest — "Financial Interests and Network Syndication Rules of the Federal Communications Commission and legislative (authorization and appropriation) activities in respect to them." Filed for self 11/11/83. Legislative interest — "... principally broadcasting including S 1707, HR 2250, S 55 and HR 2382." Lobbyist — Thomas C. Sawyer.

OGLETHORPE POWER CORP., Atlanta, Ga. Lobbyist — Paul, Hastings, Janofsky & Walker, 1050 Thomas Jefferson St. N.W., Washington, D.C. 20007. Filed 11/29/83. Legislative interest — "Legislation affecting rural electric cooperatives, generally and client specifically, particularly tax and financing issues."

PITTS ENERGY GROUP, Dallas, Texas. Lobbyist — Foreman & Dyess, 1920 N St. N.W., Washington, D.C. 20036. Filed 11/17/83. Legislative interest — "Natural gas legislation including S 1715 and HR 4277." Lobbyist — Daniel A. Dutko, 412 First St. S.E., Washington, D.C. 20003. Filed 11/21/83. Legislative interest — "... oil and gas matters."

RAUSCHER, PIERCE REFSNES INC., Dallas, Texas. Lobbyist — Akin, Gump, Strauss, Hauer & Feld, 1333 New Hampshire Ave. N.W., Washington, D.C. 20036. Filed 11/10/83. Legislative interest — "Hearings and any legislation relating to restrictions on the use of industrial development bonds including HR 4170, the 'Tax Reform Act of 1983.'"

ROLLINS ENVIRONMENTAL SERVICES, Wilmington, Del. Lobbyist — O'Connor & Hannan, 1919 Pennsylvania Ave. N.W., Washington, D.C. 20006. Filed 11/14/83. Legislative interest — Not specified.

SANCHEZ-O'BRIEN OIL AND GAS CORP., Laredo, Texas. Lobbyist — Akin, Gump, Strauss, Hauer & Feld, 1333 New Hampshire Ave. N.W., Washington, D.C. 20036. Filed 11/9/83. Legislative interest — "Hearings and any legislation relating to changes in federal taxation of corporations including HR 4170, the 'Tax Reform Act of 1983.'"

LEVI STRAUSS & CO., San Francisco, Calif. Lobbyist —

Akin, Gump, Strauss, Hauer & Feld, 1333 New Hampshire Ave. N.W., Washington, D.C. 20036. Filed 11/9/83. Legislative interest — "Hearings and any legislation relating to foreign tax deferral and foreign tax credits; and proposals relating to the factoring of receivables in S 1804 and HR 3810, the 'Foreign Sales Corporation Act of 1983.'"

TELLABS, Lisle, Ill. Lobbyist — Finley, Kumble, Wagner, Heine, Wagner, Underberg & Manley, 1120 Connecticut Ave. N.W., Washington, D.C. 20036. Filed 11/10/83. Legislative interest — "General in the nature of legislative proposals affecting international communications common carriers; S 999...."

TEXAS INSTRUMENTS INC., 13500 North Central Expressway, Dallas, Texas 75243. Filed for self 11/29/83. Legislative interest — "Matters affecting conduct of business, including but not limited to: Taxation, telecommunications, Defense, Trade, energy, and government relations." Lobbyist — Gary Howell, 1745 Jefferson Davis Highway, Arlington, Va. 22202.

TEXAS OIL & GAS CORP., Dallas, Texas. Lobbyist — Foreman & Dyess, 1920 N St. N.W., Washington, D.C. 20036. Filed 11/17/83. Legislative interest — "Natural gas legislation including S 1715 and HR 4277." Lobbyist — Daniel A. Dutko, 412 First St. S.E., Washington, D.C. 20003. Filed 11/21/83. Legislative interest — "... oil and gas matters."

TRANSCO ENERGY CO., Houston, Texas. Lobbyist — Andrews & Kurth, 1747 Pennsylvania Ave. N.W., Washington, D.C. 20006. Filed 11/11/83. Legislative interest — "Tax Legislation."

TRANSCO EXPLORATION PARTNERS LTD., Houston, Texas. Lobbyist — Andrews & Kurth, 1747 Pennsylvania Ave. N.W., Washington, D.C. 20006. Filed 11/11/83. Legislative interest — "Tax Legislation."

TURNER BROADCASTING SYSTEM INC., 1050 Techwood Drive N.W., Atlanta, Ga. 30318. Lobbyist — Linda Freeman, 1140 Connecticut Ave. N.W., Washington, D.C. 20036. Filed 11/22/83. Legislative interest — "Copyright legislation, financial interest syndication rules, and legislation affecting the telecommunications industry."

U.S. TELEPHONE INC., Washington, D.C. Lobbyist — Foreman & Dyess, 1920 N St. N.W., Washington, D.C. 20036. Filed 11/17/83. Legislative interest — "Telecommunications legislation including Universal Telephone Service Preservation Act (HR 4102)."

U.S. TOBACCO CO., 100 W. Putnam Ave., Greenwich, Conn. 06830. Filed for self 11/23/83. Legislative interest — "All legislation that could affect our industry; HR 4114 and S 2162, Employees Stock Ownership Assistance Acts." Lobbyist — Keith Rogers.

WASHINGTON WATER POWER CO., Spokane, Wash. Lobbyist — James A. Rock, 1730 M St. N.W., Washington, D.C. 20036. Filed 11/11/83. Legislative interest — "... includes but is not limited to ... Internal Revenue Code, Atomic Energy Act, Federal Power Act, Rural Electrification Act, Reclamation Acts, Flood Control Act, Appropriations Acts, Rivers and Harbors and Flood Control Authorization Acts, Federal Water Pollution Control Act, Clean Air Act, Occupational Health and Safety, Equal Employment Opportunity Act, Employee Retirement Income Security Act, Wild and Scenic Rivers Act, National Energy Act."

WESSELY ENERGY CORP., Dallas, Texas. Lobbyist — Foreman & Dyess, 1920 N St. N.W., Washington, D.C. 20036. Filed 11/17/83. Legislative interest — "Natural gas legislation including S 1715 and HR 4277." Lobbyist — Daniel A. Dutko, 412 First St. S.E., Washington, D.C. 20003. Filed 11/21/83. Legislative interest — "... oil and gas matters."

International Relations

REPUBLIC OF HAITI, Port-au-Prince, Haiti. Lobbyist — Gray & Co., 3255 Grace St. N.W., Washington, D.C. 20007. Filed 11/18/83. Legislative interest — "To encourage a more positive U.S. attitude toward the Republic of Haiti through dialogue with Members of Congress, U.S. Government officials and the Media, resulting in increased foreign investment, foreign aid and tourism."

Labor Groups

AIR LINE PILOTS ASSOCIATION, Washington, D.C. Lobbyist — Bracy, Williams & Co., 1000 Connecticut Ave. N.W., Washington, D.C. 20036. Filed 11/17/83. Legislative interest — "Legislation affecting Chapter 11 of the U.S. Bankruptcy Code and other matters affecting labor unions. Also, a sense of the Senate Resolution dealing with Continental Airlines."

INDUSTRIAL UNION DEPARTMENT, AFL-CIO, 815 16th St. N.W., Washington, D.C. 20006. Filed for self 11/17/83. Legislative interest — "... generally and specifically bills affecting workers such as: trade, OSHA pension and employment legislation." Lobbyist — David Mallino.

INTERNATIONAL UNION OF ELECTRICAL, RADIO AND MACHINE WORKERS - AFL-CIO, 1126 16th St. N.W., Washington, D.C. 20036. Filed for self 11/23/83. Legislative interest — Not specified.

Trade Associations

AMERICAN CHAMBER OF COMMERCE IN GERMANY, Frankfurt, Federal Republic of Germany. Lobbyist — Squire, Sanders & Dempsey, 1201 Pennsylvania Ave. N.W., Washington, D.C. 20004. Filed 11/16/83. Legislative interest — "... HR 1234, S 144, S 414...."

AMERICAN COLLEGE OF NEUROPSYCHO-PHARMACOLOGY, Nashville, Tenn. Lobbyist — Perito, Duerk, Carlson & Pinco, 1140 Connecticut Ave. N.W., Washington, D.C. 20036. Filed 11/7/83. Legislative interest — "Legislation supporting biomedical research."

AMERICAN INDEPENDENT REFINERS ASSOCIATION, Washington, D.C. Lobbyist — Sisk, Foley, Hultin & Driver, 2501 M St. N.W., Washington, D.C. 20037. Filed 11/17/83. Legislative interest — "Legislation with impact upon independent refiners, including any legislation with impact upon the distribution of the Strategic Petroleum Reserve."

AMERICAN IRON AND STEEL INSTITUTE, 1000 16th St. N.W., Washington, D.C. 20036. Filed for self 11/28/83. Legislative interest — Not specified.

AMERICAN MEDICAL ASSOCIATION, 535 N. Dearborn St., Chicago, Ill. 60610. Filed for self 11/16/83. Legislative interest — Not specified. Lobbyist — W. Scott Wilber, 1101 Vermont Ave. N.W., Washington, D.C. 20005.

CAROLINAS COTTON GROWERS ASSOCIATION, Raleigh, N.C. Lobbyist — Neal A. Jackson, 1156 15th St. N.W., Washington, D.C. 20005. Filed 11/18/83. Legislative interest — "Supporting legislation to permit employer to file judicial claim against USDA for cotton misgrading (S 2067)."

CONSORTIUM OF SOCIAL SCIENCE ASSOCIATIONS, 1755 Massachusetts Ave. N.W., Washington, D.C. 20036. Filed for self 11/29/83. Legislative interest — Not specified. Lobbyist — Howard J. Silver.

DAIRYMEN INC., Washington, D.C. Lobbyist — Barnett & Alagia, 1000 Thomas Jefferson St. N.W., Washington, D.C. 20007. Filed 11/21/83. Legislative interest — "... Dairy/Tobacco Adjustment Act ... HR 3385...."

DISTILLED SPIRITS COUNCIL OF THE U.S. INC., Washington, D.C. Lobbyist — Palumbo & Cerrell Inc., 11 Dupont Circle N.W., Washington, D.C. 20036. Filed 11/21/83. Legislative interest — "HR 3870."

LEAF TOBACCO EXPORTERS ASSOCIATION, Raleigh, N.C. Lobbyist — Barnett & Alagia, 1000 Thomas Jefferson St. N.W., Washington, D.C. 20007. Filed 11/21/83. Legislative interest — "... Dairy/Tobacco Adjustment Act ... HR 3385...."

MEXICAN CEMENT CHAMBER, Mexico City, Mexico. Lobbyist — O'Connor & Hannan, 1919 Pennsylvania Ave. N.W., Washington, D.C. 20006. Filed 11/21/83. Legislative interest —

"To oppose certain trade remedies legislation; specifically, the Trade Remedies Act of 1983."

MOTION PICTURE ASSOCIATION OF AMERICA, 522 Fifth Ave., New York, N.Y. 10036. Filed for self 11/10/83. Legislative interest — "Legislation dealing with: amendments to the Copyright Act of 1976, HR 1027, HR 1029, HR 1030, S 31, S 32, S 33; and financial interest and syndication rule, HR 2250, S 1707, and amendments to appropriations bills pertaining to the rule; cable copyright rates, HR 2902, HR 3419, and S 1270; antitrust, censorship of motion pictures and audiovisual works; miscellaneous copyright bills affecting films and television programs." Lobbyist — Michael R. Klipper.

NATIONAL ASSOCIATION OF CHILDREN'S HOSPITALS AND RELATED INSTITUTIONS INC., Alexandria, Va. Lobbyist — King & Spalding, 1915 I St. N.W., Washington, D.C. 20006. Filed 11/16/83. (Former U.S. Sen. Charles E. Goodell, R-N.Y., 1968-71; House 1959-68, was listed as agent for this client.) Legislative interest — "General interest is on HR 1904, Child Abuse Prevention, Treatment and Adoption Reform Amendments Act of 1983 and any other similar legislation."

NATIONAL ASSOCIATION OF PERSONNEL CONSULTANTS, Alexandria, Va. Lobbyist — Luman & Schoor, 1050 17th St. N.W., Washington, D.C. 20036. Filed 11/23/83. Legislative interest — "... General interest in all matters affecting national employment laws and their impact on the personnel consulting industry.... Specific interest in the immigration reform legislation (HR 1510 and S 529) - Support."

NATIONAL CABLE TELEVISION ASSOCIATION, Washington, D.C. Lobbyist — Akin, Gump, Strauss, Hauer & Feld, 1333 New Hampshire Ave. N.W., Washington, D.C. 20036. Filed 11/18/83. Legislative interest — "Hearings and any legislation relating to regulation of cable television systems including but not limited to HR 4103, the 'Cable Telecommunications Act of 1983' and HR 4299, the 'Cable Consumer Protection Act of 1983.' "

NATIONAL FEDERATION OF INDEPENDENT BUSINESS, 600 Maryland Ave. S.W., Washington, D.C. 20024 and 150 W. 20th Ave., San Mateo, Calif. 94403. Filed for self 11/12/83. Legislative interest — Not specified. Lobbyist — John E. Sloan Jr.

NATIONAL GUARD ASSOCIATION OF THE UNITED STATES, Washington, D.C. Lobbyist — Webster, Chamberlain & Bean, 1747 Pennsylvania Ave. N.W., Washington, D.C. 20036. Filed 11/8/83. Legislative interest — "National Defense appropriations and expenditures as well as other legislation affecting the National Guard of the United States, its members and former members ... amendment to the Internal Revenue Code ... S 2017...."

NATIONAL ROOFING CONTRACTORS ASSOCIATION, 8600 Bryn Mawr Ave., Chicago, Ill. 60631. Filed for self 11/10/83. Legislative interest — Not specified. Lobbyist — Kenneth E. Nyquist.

OKLAHOMA INDEPENDENT COMMUNICATIONS ASSOCIATION, Oklahoma City, Okla. Lobbyist — Hartz/Meek International, 806 15th St. N.W., Washington, D.C. 20005. Filed 11/28/83. Legislative interest — "Legislation related to rural telephones."

SHIPBUILDERS COUNCIL OF AMERICA, 1110 Vermont Ave. N.W., Washington, D.C. 20005. Filed for self 11/11/83. Legislative interest — "Maritime legislation, tax law related thereto, naval shipbuilding, government procurement regulations, maritime related labor, health and environmental." Lobbyist — W. Patrick Morris.

THE SOCIETY OF THE PLASTICS INDUSTRY INC., 355 Lexington Ave., New York, N.Y. 10017. Filed for self 11/9/83. Legislative interest — "Product Liability Tort Reform, Natural Gas Deregulation, Food Safety, Energy Taxes, Hazardous Air Pollutants, Clean Water Act Effluent Guidelines, Hazardous Materials Transportation, Hazardous Waste Small Generator Exemption, Toxic Victims Compensation Fund, Export-Import Bank Rechartering, Federal Spending, Social Security, Chlorofluorocarbons...." Lobbyist — James M. Bennett, 642 Dakota Trail, Franklin Lakes, N.J. 07417.

TOBACCO MARKETING BOARD OF ZIMBABWE, Harare, Zimbabwe. Lobbyist — Dow, Lohnes & Albertson, 1225 Connecticut Ave. N.W., Washington, D.C. 20036. Filed 11/15/83. Legislative interest — "Dairy and Tobacco Act of 1983 and other international trade legislation affecting tobacco imports from Zimbabwe ... S 1529; HR 3385 ... in opposition to provisions within such legislation which restricts tobacco imports from Zimbabwe."

UNITED STATES PHOTOVOLTAICS MANUFACTURERS' AD HOC COMMITTEE, Washington, D.C. Lobbyist — Adkinson & Lebow, 11 Dupont Circle N.W., Washington, D.C. 20036. Filed 11/23/83. Legislative interest — "... renewable energy tax credits legislation."

Miscellaneous

CITIZENS POLITICAL ACTION COMMITTEE, P.O. Box 645, 228 South A St., Oxnard, Calif. 93032-0645. Filed for self 11/23/83. Legislative interest — "... Export and Import ... Foreign Trade Zone ... Veterans' affairs ... Senior Citizens ... Housing ... Economic assistance ... Citizen Economic Independence programs ... Nutrition based health programs, alternative therapies ... Affordable and real justice in the courts ... Voters rights and civil liberties ... Human rights programs ... Political equality of citizens rights as to corporate or government agency authority." Lobbyist — Gilbert G. Beezley.

COMMITTEE FOR PRIVATE EDUCATION, Washington, D.C. Lobbyist — Shaw, Pittman, Potts & Trowbridge, 1800 M St. N.W., Washington, D.C. 20036. Filed 11/9/83. Legislative interest — "Support tuition tax credit legislation including S 528."

F. S. FALLON JR., P.O. Box 888-F-9, Ashland, Ky. 41101. Filed for self 11/18/83. Legislative interest — "Lobby House and Senate for fair and equal enforcement and administration of the laws of the United States of America. And for better protection of the rights and liberties of our citizens in the Courts. And/or any other matter that may be in the public interest."

ESTATE OF HELEN W. HALBACH, Gladstone, N.J. Lobbyist — Cummings & Lockwood, 1090 Vermont Ave. N.W., Washington, D.C. 20005. Filed 11/15/83. Legislative interest — "The estate favors passage of S 1180 and HR 2813 seeking to amend section 2518(c) of IRS Code of 1954."

GREATER HOUSTON HOSPITAL COUNCIL, 2925 Richmond Ave., Houston, Texas 77098. Filed for self 11/10/83. Legislative interest — "Ongoing and intermittent interest in legislation dealing with hospitals, health care provisions and health care financing." Lobbyist — Daniel Joseph Cassidy.

LUMMI INDIAN TRIBE, Washington, D.C. Lobbyist — SENSE Inc., 1010 Vermont Ave. N.W., Washington, D.C. 20005. Filed 11/28/83. Legislative interest — "... HR 3363...."

MENOMINEE INDIAN TRIBE, Keshena, Wis. Lobbyist — Hobbs, Straus, Dean & Wilder, 1735 New York Ave. N.W., Washington, D.C. 20006. Filed 11/15/83. Legislative interest — Not specified.

CHRISTOPHER L. MEYER, P.O. Box 888, Ashland, Ky. 41101. Filed for self 11/28/83. Legislative interest — "To support all matters before Congress whether Bills, Resolutions, or Amendments to the betterment of mankind. Oppose all matters before Congress that are not in the best interests of mankind."

MORALITY IN MEDIA INC., 475 Riverside Drive, New York, N.Y. 10115. Filed for self 11/28/83. Legislative interest — "Effective and constitutional Federal Obscenity legislation ... S 2136 ... S 2172 ... S 2572 ... S 66 ... S 57 ... HR 2106 ... S 1469 ... HR 3635...." Lobbyists — Morton A. Hill, Paul J. McGeade, Evelyn Dukovic, Christopher M. Beermann.

MUCKLESHOOT INDIAN TRIBE, Washington, D.C. Lobbyist — SENSE Inc., 1010 Vermont Ave. N.W., Washington, D.C. 20005. Filed 11/28/83. Legislative interest — " ... HR 3363...."

THE NATIONAL ORGANIZATION FOR WOMEN, Washington, D.C. Lobbyist — Eleanor Smeal and Associates, 2600 Virginia Ave. N.W., Washington, D.C. 20037. Filed 11/10/83. Legislative interest — "For the Equal Rights Amendment, H J Res 1 and S J Res 10."

NATIONAL TRUST FOR HISTORIC PRESERVATION, 1785 Massachusetts Ave. N.W., Washington, D.C. 20036. Filed for self 11/17/83. Legislative interest — "All legislation affecting historic preservation including appropriations; tax legislation; community development and housing authorizations and appropriations; public lands legislation; environmental review requirements; postal rates; legislation relating to maritime and archaeological resources; and any amendments to the National Historic Preservation Act (16 U.S.C. 470)." Lobbyists — Ruth M. Goltzer, Ian D. Spatz.

NEBRASKA HIGHER EDUCATION LOAN PROGRAM INC., Lincoln, Neb. Lobbyist — O'Connor & Hannan, 1919 Pennsylvania Ave. N.W., Washington, D.C. 20006. Filed 11/11/83. Legislative interest — "Student loan provisions of Tax Reform Act of 1983 (HR 4170)."

THE SOCIETY FOR AMERICAN ARCHAEOLOGY, Laramie, Wyo. Lobbyist — Foresight Inc., 2000 P St. N.W., Washington, D.C. 20036. Filed 11/15/83. Legislative interest — "Convention on Cultural Properties Implementation Act; Interior Appropriations; Historic Shipwreck Preservation Act ... S 1723; HR 3194...."

SUQUAMISH INDIAN TRIBE, Washington, D.C. Lobbyist — SENSE Inc., 1010 Vermont Ave. N.W., Washington, D.C. 20005. Filed 11/28/83. Legislative interest — "... HR 3363...."

THE WASIE FOUNDATION, 909 Foshay Tower, Minneapolis, Minn. 55402. Lobbyist — Moss & Bennett, 1200 Pillsbury Center, Minneapolis, Minn. 55402. Filed 11/10/83. Legislative interest — "HR 4170...." Filed for self 11/10/83. Legislative interest — "Opposed to HR 4170...." Lobbyist — David A. Odahouski.

WESTERN FARMERS ELECTRIC COOPERATIVE, Anadarko, Okla. Lobbyist — Paul, Hastings, Janofsky, & Walker, 1050 Thomas Jefferson St. N.W., Washington, D.C. 20007. Filed 11/27/83. Legislative interest — "Legislation affecting rural electric cooperatives, generally and client specifically, particularly tax financing issues."

December 1983 Registrations

Corporations and Businesses

APACHE CORP., Minneapolis, Minn. Lobbyist — Wilmer, Cutler & Pickering, 1666 K St. N.W., Washington, D.C. 20006. Filed 12/2/83. Legislative interest — "... including proposed amendments to HR 4170, to tax tradable limited partnerships as corporations and related tax matters affecting partnerships." Lobbyist — Jon G. Massey, 610 Poydras St., New Orleans, La. 70130. Filed 12/2/83. Legislative interest — "... including proposed amendments to HR 4170, to tax tradable limited partnerships as corporations and related tax matters affecting partnerships."

BENDIX AEROSPACE SECTOR, 1000 Wilson Blvd., Arlington, Va. 22209. Filed for self 12/22/83. Legislative interest — "Defense authorization and appropriations legislation, NASA and FAA legislation...." Lobbyists — John M. Chapman, David S. Osterhout.

CARR-GOTTSTEIN PROPERTIES INC., 1341 Fairbanks St., Anchorage, Alaska 99501. Filed 12/12/83. Legislative interest — "Any legislation dealing with College Housing loans."

COMMUNICATIONS SATELLITE CORP., 950 L'Enfant Plaza S.W., Washington, D.C. 20024. Filed for self 12/19/83. Legislative interest — "... matters pertaining to communications especially the Communications Act of 1934 and the Communications Satellite Act of 1962. Issues pertaining to S 999 and HR 4464." Lobbyist — G. Stephen Perry.

DELAWARE NORTH COS. INC., Buffalo, N.Y. Lobbyist — Ragan & Mason, 900 17th St. N.W., Washington, D.C. 20036. Filed 12/1/83. Legislative interest — "Amendments to Title 46, U.S. Code, pertaining to Fishing and fish processing vessels."

ELBE PRODUCTS INC., Melville, N.Y. Lobbyist — Morris J. Amitay, 400 North Capitol St. N.W., Washington, D.C. 20001. Filed 12/7/83. Legislative interest — "Legislation pertaining to modification of tariff regulations (S 702)."

EXECUTIVE AFFILIATES, Big Rock, Ill. Lobbyist — Daley and George, 111 W. Washington St., Chicago, Ill. 60602. Filed 12/9/83. Legislative interest — "Consideration of certain tax treatments under the Tax Reform Act of 1983 — HR 4170."

FAMARCO LTD. INC., Virginia Beach, Va. Lobbyist — Baker & McKenzie, 815 Connecticut Ave. N.W., Washington, D.C. 20006. Filed 12/8/83. Legislative interest — "Promote enactment of HR 4321 to repeal law suspending duty on carob hulls."

FLORIDA POWER CORP., P.O. Box 14042, St. Petersburg, Fla. 33733. Filed for self 12/14/83. Legislative interest — "... concerning electric utilities, energy and the environment. Specifically: Nuclear Decommissioning Bill (HR 2820) Support. Acid Rain Legislation." Lobbyist — T. Gary Connett.

GEORESEARCH INC., 2001 Wisconsin Ave. N.W., Washington, D.C. 20007. Filed for self 12/1/83. Legislative interest — "Legislation dealing with the research and control of acid rain; specifically ... National Acid Deposition Control Act of 1983 ... Clean Air Act Amendments of 1983 ... HR 3400, S 769, S 768, HR 2794, HR 3251...."

HOUDAILLE INDUSTRIES INC., 1 Financial Plaza, Fort Lauderdale, Fla. 33394. Filed for self 12/27/83. Legislative interest — "Amendments to various sections of the Trade Act." Lobbyist — John Latona.

INDEPENDENT LIFE & ACCIDENT INSURANCE CO., Jacksonville, Fla. Lobbyist — Deloitte, Haskins & Sells, 655 15th St. N.W., Washington, D.C. 20005. Filed 12/6/83. Legislative interest — "... tax legislation which might have an impact on the business of employer."

McDONNELL DOUGLAS CORP., 1225 Jefferson Davis Highway, Arlington, Va. 22202. Filed for self 12/1/83. Legislative interest — Not specified.

MEDTRONIC INC., P.O. Box 1453, 3055 Old Highway 8, Minneapolis, Minn. 55440. Filed for self 12/8/83. Legislative interest — "... legislation affecting health care, prospective payment, Medicare/Medicaid changes, Social Security Act, product liability, trade, hazardous waste, Caribbean Trade Plan, research, tax measures, etc." Lobbyists — Luise Forseth, B. Kristine Johnson.

THE MOUNTAIN STATES TELEPHONE CO., Denver, Colo. Lobbyist — Wilkinson, Barker, Knauer & Quinn, 1735 New York Ave. N.W., Washington, D.C. 20036. Filed 12/12/83. Legislative interest — "Following HR 3621 to amend the Communications Act of 1934 to assure universal telephone service within the U.S. and for other purposes; S 1660 relating to the preservation of universal telephone service and S 66, the Cable Telecommunications Act of 1983."

THE MUTUAL LIFE INSURANCE COMPANY OF NEW YORK, New York, N.Y. Lobbyist — Hogan & Hartson, 815 Connecticut Ave. N.W., Washington, D.C. 20006. Filed 12/20/83. Legislative interest — "... legislation amending the Internal Revenue Code, including HR 4170 and S 1992."

NORTHWESTERN BELL TELEPHONE CO., Omaha, Neb. Lobbyist — Wilkinson, Barker, Knauer & Quinn, 1735 New York Ave. N.W., Washington, D.C. 20036. Filed 12/12/83. Legislative interest — "Following HR 3621 to amend the Communications Act of 1934 to assure universal telephone service within the U.S. and for other purposes; S 1660 relating to the preservation of universal telephone service and S 66, the Cable Telecommunications Act of 1983."

PACIFIC AGRICULTURAL SERVICES INC., Fresno, Calif. Lobbyist — Santarelli & Bond, 2033 M St. N.W., Washington, D.C. 20036. Filed 12/5/83. Legislative interest — "The consideration and enactment of legislation dealing with jojoba cultivation."

PACIFIC NORTHWEST BELL TELEPHONE CO., Portland, Ore. Lobbyist — Wilkinson, Barker, Knauer & Quinn, 1735 New York Ave. N.W., Washington, D.C. 20036. Filed 12/12/83. Legislative interest — "Following HR 3621 to amend the Communications Act of 1934 to assure universal telephone service within the U.S. and for other purposes; S 1660 relating to the preservation of universal telephone service and S 66, the Cable Telecommunications Act of 1983."

PEPSICO INC., 700 Anderson Hill Road, Purchase, N.Y. 10577. Filed for self 12/5/83. Legislative interest — Not specified. Lobbyist — Max L. Friedersdorf.

THOMPSON & CO., 1924 S. Utica St., Tulsa, Okla. 74104. Lobbyist — Susan Bingham-Neal, 3255 Grace St., Washington, D.C. 20007. Filed 12/8/83. Legislative interest — ". . . Industrial Development Bonds, HR 4170 - 1983 Tax Reform Act. HR 2163 Dingell-Johnson Excise Tax, Proposed 1983 Senate Tax Bill. Proposed Trade Restrictions. Restrictions on Insurance Policyholders . . . House conferees on HR 4170 And Proposed Senate Tax Bill. NSC/Commerce/State Department to Develop Panama/Utility Project. Immigration Information. . . ." Filed for self 12/5/83. Legislative interest — ". . . Industrial Development Bonds, HR 4170 - 1983 Tax Reform Act. HR 2163 Dingell-Johnson Excise Tax, Proposed 1983 Senate Tax Bill. Proposed Trade Restrictions. Restrictions on Insurance Policyholders . . . House conferees on HR 4170 And Proposed Senate Tax Bill. NSC/Commerce/State Department to Develop Panama/Utility Project. Immigration Information. . . ." Lobbyist — Robert J. Thompson.

THOMPSON MEDICAL, New York, N.Y. Lobbyist — Morris J. Amitay, 400 North Capitol St. N.W., Washington, D.C. 20001. Filed 12/7/83. Legislative interest — "Legislation pertaining to drug abuse and FDA regulation of the drug industry (S 503)."

UNITED PARCEL SERVICE, Greenwich, Conn. Lobbyist — James A. Rogers, James F. Fort, 316 Pennsylvania Ave. S.E., Washington, D.C. 20003. Filed 12/1/83. Legislative interest — ". . . transportation, postal laws, taxation and energy."

HANK WILSON & ASSOCIATES, 3 Washington Circle N.W., Washington, D.C. 20037. Filed for self 12/7/83. Legislative interest — Not specified. Lobbyist — H. Hank Wilson.

ZALE CORP., P.O. Box 152777 5B-7, Irving, Texas 75015-2777. Filed for self 12/20/83. Legislative interest — Not specified. Lobbyist — Mary A. Garza.

State and Local Governments

CITY OF MIAMI, Miami, Fla. Lobbyist — Arnold & Porter, 1200 New Hampshire Ave. N.W., Washington, D.C. 20036. Filed 12/29/83. Legislative interest — ". . . involves cable television and related matters contained in S 66 and HR 4103."

CITY OF NEW YORK, New York, N.Y. Lobbyist — Arnold & Porter, 1200 New Hampshire Ave. N.W., Washington, D.C. 20036. Filed 12/29/83. Legislative interest — ". . . involves cable television and related matters contained in S 66 and HR 4103."

COMMISSIONER OF PUBLIC LANDS FOR STATE OF NEW MEXICO, Santa Fe, N.M. Lobbyist — Eric M. Rubin, 1730 M St. N.W., Washington, D.C. 20036. Filed 12/1/83. Legislative interest — ". . . compensation for lands within White Sands Test Range."

Trade Associations

ALABAMA FARM BUREAU FEDERATION, P.O. Box 11000, Montgomery, Ala. 36198. Filed for self 12/22/83. Legislative interest — "All agricultural legislation, foreign trade and fiscal legislation related to agriculture." Lobbyist — Richard G. Fifield.

ALABAMA RAILROAD ASSOCIATION, P.O. Box 21, Montgomery, Ala. 36101. Filed for self 12/7/83. Legislative interest — Not specified. Lobbyist — Margie A. Taylor.

AMERICAN IRON AND STEEL INSTITUTE, Washington, D.C. Lobbyist — Wexler, Reynolds, Harrison & Schule Inc., 1317 F St. N.W., Washington, D.C. 20004. Filed 12/12/83. Legislative interest — ". . . passage of HR 4352 - the Fair Trade in Steel Act of 1983."

AMERICAN WIND ENERGY ASSOCIATION, Alexandria, Va. Lobbyist — Samuel E. Enfield, 2300 40th St. N.W.,

Washington, D.C. 20007. Filed 12/8/83. Legislative interest — "Various bills relating to energy tax credits: S 1305, S 1396, S 1939, S 1564, HR 3072, HR 4078, HR 3358, HR 3110."

CANADIAN ASBESTOS INFORMATION CENTRE, Montreal, Quebec, Canada. Lobbyist — Gray & Co., 3255 Grace St. N.W., Washington, D.C. 20007. Filed 12/23/83. Legislative interest — "Including but not limited to legislation affecting the asbestos industry."

COALITION TO PRESERVE THE INTEGRITY OF AMERICAN TRADEMARKS, Washington, D.C. Lobbyist — Covington & Burling, 1201 Pennsylvania Ave. N.W., Washington, D.C. 20044. Filed 12/2/83. Legislative interest — ". . . may concern issues relating to the importation of items bearing U.S. trademarks."

FEDERAL LAW ENFORCEMENT OFFICERS ASSOCIATION, Carle Place, N.Y. Lobbyist — Brand, Lowell, Nickerson & Dole, 923 15th St. N.W., Washington, D.C. 20005. Filed 12/14/83. Legislative interest — "All legislation concerning the financing, operation and regulation for law enforcement agencies, including HR 1900, HR 622 and HR 624."

INTERNATIONAL ASSOCIATION OF PSYCHO-SOCIAL REHABILITATION SERVICES, McLean, Va. Lobbyist — Washington Alternatives Inc., 1702 Woodman Drive, McLean, Va. 22101. Filed 12/5/83. Legislative interest — "Mental health legislation impacting on chronically mentally ill adults. Disability legislation, HR 4170/S 467. Appropriations for National Institute of Mental Health. Fair Housing Act."

NATIONAL ASSOCIATION OF BLACK OWNED BROADCASTERS, Washington, D.C. Lobbyist — James L. Winston, 1730 M St. N.W., Washington, D.C. 20036. Filed 12/1/83. Legislative interest — "Amendments to the Communications Act and related legislation."

NATIONAL ASSOCIATION OF ENERGY SERVICE COS., 1800 M St. N.W., Washington, D.C. 20036. Lobbyist — Lane & Edson, 1800 M St. N.W., Washington, D.C. 20036. Filed 12/20/83. Legislative interest — "Energy Legislation and legislation relative to third party financing of energy equipment - S 2062, HR 4170." Filed for self 12/20/83. Legislative interest — "Energy Legislation, legislation relating to third party financing. S 2062, HR 4170."

NATIONAL COTTON COUNCIL OF AMERICA, P.O. Box 12285, Memphis, Tenn. 38112. Filed for self 12/12/83. Legislative interest — Not specified. Lobbyist — K. Adrian Hunnings, 1030 15th St. N.W., Washington, D.C. 20005.

NATIONAL GRAIN AND FEED ASSOCIATION, 725 15th St. N.W., Washington, D.C. 20005. Filed for self 12/12/83. Legislative interest — Not specified. Lobbyist — Kenneth W. Dorsch.

NATIONAL MULTIFAMILY HOUSING FINANCE ASSOCIATION, Washington, D.C. Lobbyist — Austin & Lewis, P.O. Box 11208, 1529 Laurel St., Columbia, S.C. 29211. Filed 12/7/83. Legislative interest — "HR 4170 - For Bill as amended."

NATIONAL WATER WELL ASSOCIATION, 500 W. Wilson Bridge Road, Worthington, Ohio 43085. Lobbyist — Brock R. Landry, 1333 New Hampshire Ave. N.W., Washington, D.C. 20036. Filed 12/27/83. Legislative interest — "Enactment of legislation permitting tax credits for ground water heat pumps. HR 2927, S 1939, S 1303, S 1305, S 1237." Filed for self 12/27/83. Legislative interest — "Enactment of legislation permitting tax credits for ground water heat pumps. HR 2927, S 1939, S 1303, S 1305, S 1237."

TELECOMMUNICATIONS USERS COALITION, Washington, D.C. Lobbyist — Gray & Co., 3255 Grace St. N.W., Washington, D.C. 20007. Filed 12/22/83. Legislative interest — "Including but not limited to the legislation limitation of the 'access' telephone charges preliminarily fixed by the FCC (S 1660 and HR 4102)."

UNITED FEDERATION OF POLICE, Hawthorne, N.Y. Lobbyist — Robert D. Gordon, 117 C St. S.E., Washington, D.C. 20003. Filed 12/5/83. Legislative interest — ". . . affecting law enforcement."

WATER SYSTEMS COUNCIL, 221 N. Lasalle St., Chicago, Ill. 60601. Lobbyist — Brock R. Landry, 1333 New Hampshire Ave. N.W., Washington, D.C. 20036. Filed 12/27/83. Legislative interest — "Enactment of legislation permitting energy tax credits for ground water heat pumps (HR 2927, S 1939, S 1303, S 1305, S 1237) and uniform product liability (S 44 and HR 2729)." Filed for self 12/27/83. Legislative interest — "Enactment of legislation permitting energy tax credits for ground water heat pumps (HR 2927, S 1939, S 1303, S 1305, S 1237) and uniform product liability (S 44 and HR 2729)."

Miscellaneous

CERTAIN TRUSTEES OF THE FRENCH AND POLYCLINIC MEDICAL SCHOOL AND HEALTH CENTER INC., Washington, D.C. Lobbyist — Jones, Day, Reavis & Pogue, 1735 I St. N.W., Washington, D.C. 20006. Filed 12/17/83. Legislative interest — "Lobbying activities in connection with HR 4494, 'A Bill to Amend the Internal Revenue Code of 1954 to clarify that volunteer trustees, directors, and officers of public charities shall not be penalized under the tax laws as a result of such public service.'"

INSTITUTE FOR PUBLIC REPRESENTATION, 600 New Jersey Ave. N.W., Washington, D.C. 20001. Filed for self 12/22/83. Legislative interest — "...The Voting Rights of the Handicapped and the Elderly Act; The Equal Access to Voting Rights Act ... S 1676/S 444 and HR 1250...." Lobbyist — Deborah M. Chalfie.

CHARLES C. PIXLEY, 15809 Anamosa Drive, Derwood, Md. 20855. Filed for self 12/5/83. Legislative interest — "Congressional liaison for Health and Human Services."

PUBLIC BROADCASTING SERVICE, Washington, D.C. Lobbyist — Arnold & Porter, 1200 New Hampshire Ave. N.W., Washington, D.C. 20036. Filed 12/27/83. Legislative interest — "Tax exempt leasing legislation."

TULANE UNIVERSITY, New Orleans, La. Lobbyist — Arnold & Porter, 1200 New Hampshire Ave. N.W., Washington, D.C. 20036. Filed 12/27/83. Legislative interest — "Tax exempt leasing legislation."

FRANCISCA WEI, Albany, Calif. Lobbyist — Baker & McKenzie, 815 Connecticut Ave. N.W., Washington, D.C. 20006. Filed 12/8/83. Legislative interest — "Support enactment of Private Immigration legislation (HR 4401)."

January 1984 Registrations

Corporations and Businesses

AMEV HOLDINGS INC., New York, N.Y. Lobbyist — Hansell & Post, 1915 I St. N.W., Washington, D.C. 20006. Filed 1/27/84. Legislative interest — "Legislative action relating to the taxation of the U.S. insurance industry."

THE ANDERSONS, P.O. Box 119, Maumee, Ohio 43537. Filed for self 1/31/84. Legislative interest — "All legislative matters directly or indirectly affecting The Andersons ... will also be involved in promoting agricultural research and cooperative extension before Congress." Lobbyist — Thomas L. Irmen.

ARROW TRANSPORTATION CO., Sheffield, Ala. Lobbyist — Don Wallace Associates Inc., 232 E. Capitol St., Washington, D.C. 20003. Filed 1/23/84. Legislative interest — "Legislation related to agricultural commodities; user fees; and inland waterway transportation systems."

BHC INC., New York, N.Y. Lobbyist — O'Neill and Haase, 1333 New Hampshire Ave. N.W., Washington, D.C. 20036. Filed 1/26/84. Legislative interest — "Communications legislation."

FREDERICK M. BUSH & ASSOCIATES, 2000 L St. N.W., Washington, D.C. 20036. Filed for self 1/31/84. Legislative interest — Not specified. Lobbyist — Frances Patricia Wade.

CELANESE CORP., New York, N.Y. Lobbyist — Akin, Gump, Strauss, Hauer & Feld, 1333 New Hampshire Ave. N.W., Washington, D.C. 20036. Filed 1/5/84. Legislative interest — "Hearings and any legislation relating to the use of methanol as a fuel."

COLUMBUS AND SOUTHERN OHIO ELECTRIC CO., 215 N. Front St., Columbus, Ohio 43215. Filed for self 1/26/84. Legislative interest — Not specified. Lobbyist — William J. Lhota.

FOLEY, LARDNER, HOLLABAUGH & JACOBS, 1775 Pennsylvania Ave. N.W., Washington, D.C. 20006. Filed for self 1/30/84. Legislative interest — "Legislation relating to payment of claims under the crude oil entitlements program." Lobbyists — Dennis A. Henigan, Jack L. Lahr.

GREAT AMERICAN RESERVE INSURANCE CO., 2020 Live Oak, Dallas, Texas 75221. Filed for self 1/27/84. Legislative interest — "The general legislative interest involves Federal Tax Legislation regarding HR 4170 and S 1992. The general position of the Company at this time is that it supports these proposals with certain modifications." Lobbyist — John Howard Stecker.

HEUBLEIN INC., Munson Road, Farmington, Conn. 06032. Filed for self 1/30/84. Legislative interest — Not specified. Lobbyist — Joseph M. McGarry.

INTERNATIONAL BUSINESS MACHINES CORP., Washington, D.C. Lobbyist — Charls E. Walker Associates Inc., 1730 Pennsylvania Ave. N.W., Washington, D.C. 20006. Filed 1/20/84. Legislative interest — "...may concern proposals which alter, amend, or otherwise affect the Internal Revenue Code as it relates to the activities of corporations."

MOTOROLA INC., 1776 K St. N.W., Washington, D.C. 20006. Filed for self 1/30/84. Legislative interest — "Monitor and follow the progress of legislation pertaining to communications, taxation, defense and other legislation affecting the electronics industry. Specifically HR 1887, to end the current moratorium of Treasury regulations by permanently repealing Section 861-8. S 764 - Air Travelers Security Act of 1983." Lobbyist — Joan Piccolo.

PACIFIC STOCK EXCHANGE INC., Los Angeles, Calif. Lobbyist — Covington & Burling, P.O. Box 7566, Washington, D.C. 20044. Filed 1/31/84. Legislative interest — "Taxation of stock options; S 2062."

SCHENLEY INDUSTRIES INC., New York, N.Y. Lobbyist — Fried, Frank, Harris, Shriver & Kampelman, 600 New Hampshire Ave. N.W., Washington, D.C. 20037. Filed 1/5/84. Legislative interest — "... Opposing changes to General Headnote 3(a), TSUS (19 U.S.C. 1202) as proposed by S 2194 and HR 4560. ... Seeking expanded import injury remedies for manufacturers in the U.S. insular possessions."

SCHLENKER & LEBECK, P.O. Box 925, Albuquerque, N.M. 87103. Filed for self 1/3/84. Legislative interest — "S 1864, Declaratory Judgment Act Relating to Section 6166 of the Internal Revenue Code. HR 4018, Declaratory Judgment Act Relating to Section 6166 of the Internal Revenue Code." Lobbyists — A. Michael Lebeck, Kurt A. Sommer.

SERVICE CORPORATION INTERNATIONAL, Houston, Texas. Lobbyist — Don Wallace Associates Inc., 232 E. Capitol St., Washington, D.C. 20003. Filed 1/23/84. Legislative interest — "Legislation affecting the funeral industry."

STARSTRUCK INC., 837 Second Ave., Redwood City, Calif. 94063. Filed for self 1/23/84. Legislative interest — "Matters affecting space commercialization...." Lobbyist — Courtney A. Stadd, 199 S. Capitol St. S.W., Washington, D.C. 20003.

STELCO INC., Royal Trust Tower, Toronto Dominion Center, Toronto, Ontario, Canada M5K 1J4. Filed for self 1/27/84. Legislative interest — "(1) Fair Trade in Steel Act; (b) HR 4352; (c) in opposition to any legislation which restricts U.S. imports of steel mill products from Canada." Lobbyist — Donald K. Belch.

SUNMAR SHIPPING INC., Seattle, Wash. Lobbyist — Preston, Thorgrimson, Ellis & Holman, 1735 New York Ave. N.W., Washington, D.C. 20006. Filed 1/19/84. Legislative interest — "Legislation affecting vessel inspection requirements, HR 4579; S 1102."

TEXAS AIR CORP., Houston, Texas. Lobbyist — Williams & Jensen, 1101 Connecticut Ave. N.W., Washington, D.C. 20036. Filed 1/30/84. Legislative interest — "Develop and implement strategy to prevent legislation that would (a) re-regulate the airline industry, (b) modify the bankruptcy law and voluntary reorganization provisions in a manner adverse to TAC or (c) make any other changes in laws or regulations adversely affecting TAC."

TURNER BROADCASTING SYSTEM INC., 1050 Techwood Drive N.W., Atlanta, Ga. 30318. Filed for self 1/24/84. Legislative interest — "Copyright legislation, financial interest and syndication rules, and legislation affecting the telecommunications industry." Lobbyist — Linda Freeman, 1140 Connecticut Ave. N.W., Washington, D.C. 20036.

UNIDYNAMICS/ST. LOUIS INC., St. Louis, Mo. Lobbyist — Seymour Halpern Inc., 425 E. 58th St., New York, N.Y. 10022. (Former U.S. rep., R-N.Y., 1959-73.) Filed 1/31/84. Legislative interest — "Monitor matters pertaining to appropriations for military procurement, specifically in regard to cruise missiles launching systems."

UNITED TELEVISION INC., Minneapolis, Minn. Lobbyist — Kaye, Scholer, Fierman, Hays & Handler, 1575 I St. N.W., Washington, D.C. 20005. Filed 1/26/84. Legislative interest — Not specified.

Labor Groups

NATIONAL EDUCATION ASSOCIATION, 1201 16th St. N.W., Washington, D.C. 20036. Filed for self 1/30/84. Legislative interest — ". . . Collective Bargaining, Mobile Teacher Retirement (HR 2504), Continuing Appropriations Resolution (H J Res 325), Labor-HHS Appropriations Bill, Tuition Tax Credits (HR 1323), Constitutional Rights Issues such as (Prayer in Schools (HR 72), Discrimination based on Sexual Orientation (HR 1454), Assignment of Public School Students (H J Res 86), Busing (H J Res 91), Right to Life (HR 92)), Funding Education Proposal (HR 394), Child Care Act (HR 573), Tax Exempt Status Private Schools (HR 802), Youth Employment Act (HR 924), Terminating Federal Involvement in Education (HR 985), Extending Head Start (S 181), Tax Legislation, Veterans Education Benefits (HR 815), New G. I. Education Bill (S 25), Martin Luther King Holiday (HR 1522), Voting Rights Act Extension, Social Security issues, Comprehensive Elementary School Guidance programs, Department of Education proposals, Budget Resolutions, Truth in Testing proposals, Federal Assistance Programs, Consolidation, School Lunch issues, Overseas Schools, Impact Aid, Education Consolidation and Improvement Act, AWACs, El Salvador Aid, Family Protection Act." Lobbyist — Joel Packer.

State and Local Governments

GUAM ECONOMIC DEVELOPMENT AUTHORITY, Agana, Guam. Lobbyist — Dickstein, Shapiro & Morin, 2101 L St. N.W., Washington, D.C. 20037. Filed 1/30/84. Legislative interest — ". . . tax legislation."

Trade Associations

AIR LINE PILOTS ASSOCIATION, 1625 Massachusetts Ave. N.W., Washington, D.C. 20036. Filed for self 1/25/84. Legislative interest — Not specified. Lobbyists — Gerald E. Baker, Paul L. Hallisay, Frederick P. Somers.

AMERICAN ASSOCIATION OF MINORITY ENTERPRISE SMALL BUSINESS INVESTMENT COS., Washington, D.C. Lobbyist — Diane Kay Thomas, 6962 Hanover Parkway, Greenbelt, Md. 20770. Filed 1/31/84. Legislative interest — "In support of bills assisting minority entrepreneurs and investments in small business."

AMERICAN BANKERS ASSOCIATION, 1120 Connecticut Ave. N.W., Washington, D.C. 20036. Filed for self 1/5/84. Legislative interest — "HR 4170 (Tax Reform Act of 1983), HR 2918, HR 3001, S 1225 (Multistate Taxation of Financial Depositories), HR 973, S 1509 (Loan Loss Reserve for banks), HR 3025, S 1557 (30 percent tax on nonresident alien portfolio investments), S 1564, HR 3110 (lease financing reform)." Lobbyist — Charles M. Wheeler.

AMERICAN DENTAL ASSOCIATION, 1101 17th St. N.W., Washington, D.C. 20036. Filed for self 1/30/84. Legislative interest — ". . . Specific legislative interests include S 640 and HR 2754. . . ." Lobbyist — Stuart M. Ginsberg.

AMERICAN GAS ASSOCIATION, 1515 Wilson Blvd., Arlington, Va. 22209. Filed for self 1/30/84. Legislative interest — "Clean Air Act Amendments, Land Use Policy, OCS, Pipeline Safety/NTSB, Public Utilities Holding Company Act, Safe Drinking Water Act, Underground Storage." Lobbyist — Diane R. Brown.

ASSOCIATION FOR ADVANCEMENT OF PSYCHOLOGY, 1200 17th St. N.W., Washington, D.C. 20036. Filed for self 1/25/84. Legislative interest — Not specified. Lobbyists — Clarence J. Martin, Lisa Shuger.

ASSOCIATION OF THE FOOD INDUSTRIES, New York, N.Y. Lobbyist — Kent & O'Connor Inc., 1919 Pennsylvania Ave. N.W., Washington, D.C. 20006. Filed 1/19/84. Legislative interest — "FDA regulation (no specific bill)."

BUSINESS EXECUTIVES FOR NATIONAL SECURITY, 21 Dupont Circle N.W., Washington, D.C. 20036. Filed for self 1/20/84. Legislative interest — "National security; arms control; military spending issues; U.S.-Soviet relations." Lobbyist — Michael Burns.

CANADIAN ASBESTOS INFORMATION CENTRE, Montreal, Quebec, Canada. Lobbyist — Gray & Co., 3255 Grace St. N.W., Washington, D.C. 20007. Filed 1/26/84. Legislative interest — "Including but not limited to regulation on and legislation affecting the asbestos industry."

THE ERISA INDUSTRY COMMITTEE, 1726 M St. N.W., Washington, D.C. 20036. Filed for self 1/31/84. Legislative interest — "Legislation relating to the Employee Retirement Income Security Act and other matters regarding employee benefits." Lobbyists — Janice M. Gregory, Mark J. Ugoretz.

GROCERY MANUFACTURERS OF AMERICA INC., Washington, D.C. Lobbyist — Taft, Stettinius & Hollister, First National Bank Center, Cincinnati, Ohio 45202 and 21 Dupont Circle N.W., Washington, D.C. 20036. (Former U.S. Sen. Robert Taft Jr., R-Ohio, 1971-76; House 1963-65, 1967-71, was listed as agent for this client.) Filed 1/20/84. Legislative interest — "Advice regarding legislation dealing with corporate income surtax."

IDAHO FOREST GROUP, Washington, D.C. Lobbyist — F. H. Hutchison & Co., 1744 R St. N.W., Washington, D.C. 20009. Filed 1/20/84. Legislative interest — "S 916 and other timber contract termination proposals; legislation affecting the Small Business Timber Set Aside Program; legislation to designate additional national forest wilderness in Idaho; legislation affecting the timber appraisal system used by the U.S. Forest Service."

IDAHO FOREST INDUSTRY COUNCIL, Coeur d'Alene, Idaho. Lobbyist — F. H. Hutchison & Co., 1744 R St. N.W., Washington, D.C. 20009. Filed 1/20/84. Legislative interest — ". . . to the termination of federal timber sale contracts, legislation to make all purchaser road credits 'effective.' "

IDAHO WILDERNESS GROUP, Washington, D.C. Lobbyist — F. H. Hutchison & Co., 1744 R St. N.W., Washington, D.C. 20009. Filed 1/20/84. Legislative interest — "Proposed legislation to designate additional national forest wilderness areas in Idaho (preparation of testimony for hearings conducted by the Senate Energy and Natural Resources Committee in Boise, Coeur d'Alene, and Lewiston, Idaho)."

JAPAN ECONOMIC INSTITUTE OF AMERICA, 1000 Connecticut Ave. N.W., Washington, D.C. 20036. Filed for self 1/27/84. Legislative interest — ". . . monitors developments affecting U.S. tariff and trade policy, foreign investment and banking activity in the U.S., American exports and export financing, and U.S.-Japan economic relations." Lobbyist — Michael W. Chinworth.

LATIN AMERICAN MANUFACTURERS ASSOCIATION, Washington, D.C. Lobbyist — Neece, Cator & Associates Inc., 1050 17th St. N.W., Washington, D.C. 20036. Filed 1/27/84. Legislative interest — "HR 3020 - Small Business Administration Authorizations."

LEAGUE OF AMERICAN INVESTORS, 32123 Lindero Canyon Road, Westlake Village, Calif. 91361. Filed for self 1/30/84. Legislative interest — "None at present."

LIFE INSURANCE COALITION OF AMERICA, 1800 K St. N.W., Washington, D.C. 20006. Filed for self 1/27/84. Legislative interest — "Life Insurance Act of 1983 - HR 4170/S 1992." Lobbyist — William C. Chasey.

MAN-MADE FIBER PRODUCERS ASSOCIATION INC., 1150 17th St. N.W., Washington, D.C. 20036. Filed for self 1/27/84. Legislative interest — "HR 4124, S 2139, trade reform legislation; HR 3398 omnibus tariff bill. All bills supported." Lobbyist — Charles R. Carlisle.

NATIONAL ASSOCIATION OF FEDERAL CREDIT UNIONS, 1111 N. 19th St., Arlington, Va. 22209. Filed for self 1/31/84. Legislative interest — ". . . HR 3 - Bankruptcy Judgeship, HR 1800 - Consumer Debtor Bankruptcy Amendments, S 1714 - FTC Act Amendments of '83, HR 2000 - Savings Incentive Act, HR 3535 - Demand Deposit Equity Act, S 730 - Credit Deregulation Availability Act, HR 3879 - Payroll Allotments Facilities Act, HR 3868 - Class D Directors Act, S 573 - Fair Deposit Availability Act, S 445 - Consumer Bankruptcy Reform Bill, S 2181 - Financial Services Competitive Equity Act, S 2120, 2121, 2122 - Legislation to amend the Federal Credit Union Act." Lobbyist — Kenneth L. Robinson.

NATIONAL BANKERS ASSOCIATION, Washington, D.C. Lobbyist — MMB Associates Inc., 122 C St. N.W., Washington, D.C. 20001. Filed 1/27/84. Legislative interest — "The Small Business Act, The Depository Instruments Act."

NATIONAL COUNCIL OF SAVINGS INSTITUTIONS, 1101 15th St. N.W., Washington, D.C. 20005. Filed for self 1/5/84. Legislative interest — "Support of bills to improve facilities of savings institutions for encouragement of thrift and home financing. Oppose legislation adverse to thrift and home financing." Lobbyist — Peter E. Knight.

NATIONAL FEDERATION OF INDEPENDENT BUSINESS, Capital Gallery East, 600 Maryland Ave. S.W., Washington, D.C. 20024. Filed for self 1/5/84. Legislative interest — "All legislation affecting small business and the economic well-being of the country, including tax bills, spending cuts, regulation bills, balancing budget bills and paperwork reduction bills." Lobbyist — Margaret Renken Hudson.

NATIONAL MULTIFAMILY HOUSING FINANCE ASSOCIATION, Washington, D.C. Lobbyist — Anderson, Hibey, Nauheim & Blair, 1708 New Hampshire Ave. N.W., Washington, D.C. 20009. Filed 1/30/84. Legislative interest — "HR 4170 and Related Legislation."

SOLAR ENERGY INDUSTRIES ASSOCIATION, Washington, D.C. Lobbyist — Blum & Nash, 1015 18th St. N.W., Washington, D.C. 20036. Filed 1/26/84. Legislative interest — "Tax credits for solar energy equipment purchases."

Miscellaneous

AMERICANS FOR DEMOCRATIC ACTION, 1411 K St. N.W., Washington, D.C. 20005. Filed for self 1/30/84. Legislative interest — "Domestic Policy: . . . Increases in Human needs area of the Federal Budget . . . Fair and Equitable tax code . . . Full Employment Legislation . . . Passage of Equal Rights amendment to the Constitution . . . Death Penalty Legislation (Against) . . . Oppose legislation to restrict a woman's right to choose abortion . . . Civil Rights Legislation (For)." Lobbyist — Mitchell H. Edelstein.

ELEANOR CLARK, Portland, Ore. Lobbyist — Lane & Mittendorf, 1750 K St. N.W., Washington, D.C. 20006. Filed 1/31/84. Legislative interest — ". . . HR 2813 & S 1180."

NATIONAL COMMUNITY ACTION FOUNDATION, Washington, D.C. Lobbyist — MMB Associates Inc., 122 C St. N.W., Washington, D.C. 20001. Filed 1/27/84. Legislative interest — "Community Services Block Grant Act, Labor/HHS Appropriations Act."

NATIONAL CONSUMERS LEAGUE INC., 1522 K St. N.W., Washington, D.C. 20005. Filed for self 1/20/84. Legislative interest — "FTC reauthorization, health care cost containment legislation, product liability legislation." Lobbyist — Barbara F. Warden.

NATIONAL PARKS & CONSERVATION ASSOCIATION, 1701 18th St. N.W., Washington, D.C. 20009. Filed for self 1/4/84. Legislative interest — "General legislative interests relating to natural resource conservation and National Park System management and development. . . . The introduction of legislation pertaining to the National Park System, House and Senate numbers undetermined at this time (to be introduced this session)." Lobbyist — Robert R. Pierce, 5719 Beach Ave., Bethesda, Md. 20817.

NATIONAL RURAL DEVELOPMENT & FINANCE CORP., Washington, D.C. Lobbyist — MMB Associates Inc., 122 C St. N.W., Washington, D.C. 20001. Filed 1/27/84. Legislative interest — "Community Services Block Grant Act, Labor/HHS Appropriations Act, Community Economic Development Act."

ROBERT O. REDDING, 3519 S.W. 147th Ln. Road, Ocala, Fla. 32673. Filed for self 1/24/84. Legislative interest — "All legislation connected with the citrus industry."

GEORGE ROWE JR., New York, N.Y. Lobbyist — Covington & Burling, P.O. Box 7566, Washington, D.C. 20044. Filed 1/5/84. Legislative interest — "To urge that Congress make Section 2503(e) of the Internal Revenue Code of 1954, as amended, retroactive for transfers made before December 31, 1981."

LELAND MICHAEL ROYAN, 9 Inwood Road, Staten Island, N.Y. 10301. Filed for self 1/20/84. Legislative interest — Not specified.

MacKENZIE TURNIPSEED, Tacoma, Wash. Lobbyist — Sonosky, Chambers, Sachse & Guido, 1050 31st St. N.W., Washington, D.C. 20007. Filed 1/23/84. Legislative interest — ". . . HR 4566."

UNIVERSITY OF MICHIGAN HOSPITALS, Ann Arbor, Mich. Lobbyist — Williams & Jensen, 1101 Connecticut Ave. N.W., Washington, D.C. 20036. Filed 1/27/84. Legislative interest — Not specified.

February Registrations

Corporations and Businesses

THE ALLIED CORP., Washington, D.C. Lobbyist — Wexler, Reynolds, Harrison & Schule Inc., 1317 F St. N.W., Washington, D.C. 20004. Filed 2/14/84. Legislative interest — "Registrant seeks to obtain Congressional support for S 44, Product Liability Act; and other matters of interest to The Allied Corporation."

B. ALTMAN & CO., New York, N.Y. Lobbyist — Rogers & Wells, 1737 H St. N.W., Washington, D.C. 20006. Filed 2/24/84. Legislative interest — "Amendments to Section 4946 of the Internal Revenue Code of 1954."

AMERICAN EXPRESS CO., Washington, D.C. Lobbyist — Rogers & Wells, 1737 H St. N.W., Washington, D.C. 20006. Filed 2/24/84. Legislative interest — "Amendment to sections 301-308 of Public Law 97-248, (9/3/82), HR 4170 and S 2062."

AMERISERV INC., Fort Lauderdale, Fla. Lobbyist — Paul Suplizio Associates, 2948 University Terrace N.W., Washington, D.C. 20016. Filed 2/23/84. Legislative interest — "Support tax credit for hiring structurally unemployed, summer youth, and disadvantaged workers. Support retention of provisions of 26 U.S. Code 44B and 51-53 pertaining to targeted jobs tax credit. Support S 2185 which extends targeted jobs tax credit until December 31, 1989."

ARKANSAS ELECTRIC COOPERATIVE CORP., Little Rock, Ark. Lobbyist — Deloitte, Haskins & Sells, 655 15th St. N.W., Washington, D.C. 20005. Filed 2/14/84. Legislative interest — "... tax legislation...."

ASHLAND OIL INC., P.O. Box 391, Ashland, Ky. 41114. Filed for self 2/2/84. Legislative interest — "All legislation concerning the petroleum industry, including but not limited to bills relating to energy, taxes, coal mining, marine transportation, synthetic fuels, and environment." Lobbyist — Patricia T. Clarey, 1025 Connecticut Ave. N.W., Washington, D.C. 20036.

ATCOR INC., 16100 South Lathrop Ave., Harvey, Ill. 60426. Filed for self 2/10/84. Legislative interest — "Budget of legislative items affecting fire safety research or building standards: for. Trade legislation, particularly as to steel tariffs, S 114, S 144, HR 1319: for."

AMERICAN TELEPHONE & TELEGRAPH, New York, N.Y. Lobbyist — Nick J. Volcheff, 2509 E. San Miguel, Phoenix, Ariz. 95016. Filed 2/29/84. Legislative interest — "Hearings and any related legislation affecting the communications industry (*e.g.*, S 1660)."

BAILARD, BIEHL & KAISER INC., San Mateo, Calif. Lobbyists — George W. Beatty & James C. Warner, 1200 18th St. N.W., Washington, D.C. 20036. Filed 2/7/84. Legislative interest — "HR 3529 (to amend IRC re: tax treatment of regulated investment companies). S 1809 (to amend IRC re: attribution between limited partners of stock of publicly owned company for IRC section 542 and section 851 purposes). For both bills."

BHC INC., New York, N.Y. Lobbyist — The Hannaford Co. Inc., 655 15th St. N.W., Washington, D.C. 20005. Filed 2/21/84. Legislative interest — "Legislation affecting television and communications."

BLOUNT INC., Montgomery, Ala. Lobbyist — Philip D. Morrison, 1700 Pennsylvania Ave. N.W., Washington, D.C. 20006. Filed 2/3/84. Legislative interest — "... all legislation relating to federal income taxation of corporations. Specifically, lobbying relating to section 103."

THE BOEING CO., Rosslyn, Va. Lobbyist — Denny Miller Associates, 203 Maryland Ave. N.E., Washington, D.C. 20002. Filed 2/1/84. Legislative interest — "Military Construction and DOD Authorization Acts." Lobbyist — Manatt, Phelps, Rothenberg & Tunney, 1200 New Hampshire Ave. N.W., Washington, D.C. 20036. Filed 2/23/84. Legislative interest — "Tax related issues during the second session of the 98th Congress."

BROWNING & KALECZYC, Box 162, Helena, Mont. 59624. Filed for self 2/29/84. Legislative interest — "General legislative matters dealing with federal contracting, taxes, rural electric and telephone cooperatives, non-profit nursing homes, federal irrigation projects, outdoor advertising and related federal issues coming before congressional review." Lobbyist — R. Stephen Browning.

CALIFORNIA MICROWAVE INC., Sunnyvale, Calif. Lobbyist — Peter Kyros, 1120 Connecticut Ave. N.W., Washington, D.C. 20036. (Former U.S. rep., D-Maine, 1967-75.) Filed 2/7/84. Legislative interest — "International telecommunications issues, HR 4464."

CALVERT GROUP LTD., Bethesda, Md. Lobbyist — Kirkpatrick, Lockhart, Hill, Christopher & Phillips, 1900 M St. N.W., Washington, D.C. 20036. Filed 2/29/84. Legislative interest — "Legislation and legislative activities relative to brokering of deposits in financial institutions; such activity is supported."

CATERPILLAR TRACTOR CO., 1850 K St. N.W., Washington, D.C. 20006. Filed for self 2/27/84. Legislative interest — "Federal budget and tax policy, energy, environmental protection, product liability, health care, OSHA, pension and social security, unemployment insurance, workers compensation, transportation." Lobbyist — William F. Canis.

CENTRAL AND SOUTH WEST CORP., 2121 San Jacinto St., Dallas, Texas 75266-0164. Filed for self 2/16/84. Legislative interest — "The Resource Conservation and Recovery Act (RCRA), Toxic Substances Control Act (TSCA), Safe Drinking Water Act (SDWA) and amendments thereto...." Lobbyist — H. P. (Trey) Harbert III.

CHRIS-CRAFT INDUSTRIES INC., New York, N.Y.

Lobbyist — Hogan & Hartson, 815 Connecticut Ave. N.W., Washington, D.C. 20006. Filed 2/14/84. Legislative interest — "Represents employer's interest with respect to legislation amending the Communications Act of 1934."

THE COCA-COLA CO., P.O. Drawer 1734, Atlanta, Ga. 30301. Filed for self 2/3/84. Legislative interest — Not specified. Lobbyist — Connell Stafford.

COFFEE, SUGAR & COCOA EXCHANGE INC., 4 World Trade Center, New York, N.Y. 10048. Filed for self 2/7/84. Legislative interest — "Legislation which affects commodity futures trading or the commodities related thereto, in particular that which relates to coffee, sugar, cocoa, the Commodity Futures Trading Commission, taxation and bankruptcy." Lobbyists — James J. Bowe, Peter A. Nalewaik.

CONNELL FINANCE CO. INC., Westfield, N.J. Lobbyist — James C. Corman, 1420 16th St. N.W., Washington, D.C. 20036. (Former U.S. rep., D-Calif., 1961-81.) Filed 2/13/84. Legislative interest — "To monitor proposed legislation and treasury regulations and all pending matters affecting the Leasing Industry."

CONSOLIDATED FOODS CORP., Chicago, Ill. Lobbyist — Donald C. Evans Jr., 214 Massachusetts Ave. N.W., Washington, D.C. 20002. Filed 2/3/84. Legislative interest — "Tax matters of interest to the Company and its subsidiaries."

COUNSELORS FOR MANAGEMENT INC., 900 17th St. N.W., Washington, D.C. 20006. Filed 2/16/84. Legislative interest — "HR 2882, S 1711, Legislation to extend patent numbered 3,376,198; for passage." Lobbyist — Janice C. Lipsen.

CTI-CONTAINER TRANSPORT INTERNATIONAL INC., White Plains, N.Y. Lobbyist — Dickey, Knorr & Moore, 1825 I St. N.W., Washington, D.C. 20006. Filed 2/28/84. Legislative interest — "... proposals which alter, amend, or otherwise affect the internal revenue code as it relates to the activities of corporations and businesses in using capital cost recovery allowances for investments in productive equipment."

DENELCOR INC., Aurora, Colo. Lobbyist — Hoog and Associates, 1877 Broadway, Boulder, Colo. 80302. Filed 2/2/84. Legislative interest — "Analysis of future high technology legislation."

DESTILERIA SERRALLES INC., Mercedita, Puerto Rico. Lobbyist — O'Connor & Hannan, 1919 Pennsylvania Ave. N.W., Washington, D.C. 20006. Filed 2/29/84. Legislative interest — "Legislation affecting taxes on cane neutral and other distilled spirits."

DIRECT BROADCAST SATELLITE CORP., Washington, D.C. Lobbyist — Peter Kyros, 1120 Connecticut Ave. N.W., Washington, D.C. 20036. (Former U.S. rep., D-Maine, 1967-75.) Filed 2/7/84. Legislative interest — "International telecommunications issues, HR 4464."

DOFASCO INC., 1330 Burlington St. East, Box 460, Hamilton, Ontario, Canada L8N 3J5. Filed for self 2/8/84. Legislative interest — "... Fair Trade in Steel Act ... HR 4352 ... in opposition to any legislation which restricts U.S. imports of steel mill products from Canada." Lobbyists — Robert Clarke Varah, H. Graham Wilson.

DONREY INC., Fort Smith, Ark. Lobbyist — Cohen and Uretz, 1775 K St. N.W., Washington, D.C. 20006. Filed 2/6/84. Legislative interest — "Introduction and enactment of amendment to Internal Revenue Code to coordinate the excess business holdings rules applicable to private foundations (section 4943) with partial ownership of corporate stock by an employee stock ownership plan."

DOW CHEMICAL U.S.A., Midland, Mich. 48640. Filed for self 2/27/84. Legislative interest — "Energy Legislation - in favor of good national policy. Clean Air Legislation - in favor of good national policy." Lobbyist — Patrick H. McNamara, 1800 M St. N.W., Washington, D.C. 20036.

E. I. DU PONT DE NEMOURS CO., 1007 Market St., Wilmington, Del. 19898. Filed for self 2/6/84. Legislative interest — "All legislation directly related to employer's business, including especially bills related to energy, the environment, taxation, economic policy, governmental regulations, and programs supported by employer contributions." Lobbyist — David T. Modi, 1701 Pennsylvania Ave. N.W., Washington, D.C. 20006.

EMPIRE DISTRICT ELECTRIC CO., Joplin, Mo. Lobbyist — Dana W. Haas, 1112 Stafford St., Arlington, Va. 22201. Filed 2/6/84. Legislative interest — "Legislation including but not limited to the following statutes and amendments thereto: Internal Revenue Code, TVA Act, Atomic Energy Act, Federal Power Act, Rural Electrification Act, Bonneville Power Act, Reclamation acts, Flood Control acts, Appropriations acts, Rivers Harbors Flood Control authorizations, Water Pollution Control Act, Clean Air Act, OSHA, Equal Employment Opportunity Act, Employee Retirement Income Security Act, Wild and Scenic Rivers Act, National Energy Act."

ENERGY RECOVERY SYSTEMS INC., Great Neck, N.Y. Lobbyist — Wisner & Schwarz, 1762 Church St. N.W., Washington, D.C. 20036. Filed 2/6/84. Legislative interest — "Resource Conservation and Recovery Act Reauthorization."

FINLEY, KUMBLE, WAGNER, HEINE, UNDERBERG, MANLEY & CASEY, Washington, D.C. Lobbyist — Peter Kyros, 1120 Connecticut Ave. N.W., Washington, D.C. 20036. (Former U.S. rep., D-Maine, 1967-75.) Filed 2/7/84. Legislative interest — "International telecommunications issues, HR 4464."

FLEXI-VAN LEASING INC., New York, N.Y. Lobbyist — Dickey, Knorr & Moore, 1825 I St. N.W., Washington, D.C. 20006. Filed 2/28/84. Legislative interest — "Legislation of interest concerns proposals which alter, amend, or otherwise affect the internal revenue code as it relates to the activities of corporations and businesses in using capital cost recovery allowances for investments in productive equipment."

GCA CORP., 209 Burlington Road, Bedford, Mass. 01730. Filed for self 2/2/84. Legislative interest — "Legislation affecting and concerning the domestic and international development, manufacturing or production, taxation, and research and development of microelectronic production equipment, robotics, factory automation, and general laboratory instrumentation." Lobbyist — Robert Wayne Sayer, 4545 42nd St. N.W., Washington, D.C. 20016.

GLOBAL IDENTIFICATION CORP., Arlington, Va. Lobbyist — Roxton Inc., 2000 S. Eads St., Arlington, Va. 22202. Filed 2/29/84. Legislative interest — "Our legislative interests involve support of legislation in the health field. . . ."

GPU NUCLEAR CORP., 100 Interpace Parkway, Parsippany, N.J. 07054. Filed for self 2/17/84. Legislative interest — "Legislative matters of interest to GPU Nuclear Corporation including but not limited to the operation of Three Mile Island Nuclear Generating Station." Lobbyist — William L. Gifford, 600 Maryland Ave. S.W., Washington, D.C. 20024.

HANSEN ENGINE CORP., 14920 Minnetonka Industrial Road, Minnetonka, Minn. Filed for self 2/7/84. Legislative interest — ". . . relates to Department of Defense research and development program, HR 4185." Lobbyist — Robert D. Hansen.

HAYT, HAYT AND LANDAU, Great Neck, N.Y. Lobbyist — Patton, Boggs & Blow, 2550 M St. N.W., Washington, D.C. 20037. Filed 2/29/84. Legislative interest — "For legislation to allow referral of federal debt collection litigation to private counsel. Such as a) Debt Collection Act of 1982 and b) S 1668."

IMPRO, 900 17th St. N.W., Washington, D.C. 20006. Filed for self 2/16/84. Legislative interest — "HR 2882, S 1711, Legislation to extend patent numbered 3,376,198; for passage." Lobbyist — Janice C. Lipsen.

INTEL CORP., 3065 Bowers Ave., Santa Clara, Calif. 95051. Filed for self 2/13/84. Legislative interest — "Trade, tax, copyright and antitrust legislation. . . ." Lobbyist — Michael C. Maibach.

THE IRVINE CO., Newport Beach, Calif. Lobbyist — William Ferguson Jr., 2555 M St. N.W., Washington, D.C. 20037. Filed 2/23/84. Legislative interest — "Legislative interests include: a) for technical amendments to the Surface Transportation Assistance Act; b) for reauthorization with amendments of the Clean Water Act; c) for Secondary Mortgage Market Enhancement legislation; d) for Omnibus Water legislation."

KANALKU TIMBER MANAGEMENT CO., Angoon, Alaska. Lobbyist — Thomas J. Barlow III, 4717 Drummond Ave., Chevy Chase, Md. 20815. Filed 2/28/84. Legislative interest — "Forest Service appropriations legislation — current year — seeking changes in amounts of funding for certain Forest Service activities in southeast Alaska."

KANSAS CITY POWER & LIGHT CO., Kansas City, Mo. Lobbyist — Dana W. Haas, 1112 Stafford St., Arlington, Va. 22201. Filed 2/6/84. Legislative interest — "Legislation including but not limited to the following statutes and amendments thereto: Internal Revenue Code, TVA Act, Atomic Energy Act, Federal Power Act, Rural Electrification Act, Bonneville Power Act, Reclamation acts, Flood Control acts, Appropriations acts, Rivers Harbors Flood Control authorizations, Water Pollution Control Act, Clean Air Act, OSHA, Equal Employment Opportunity Act, Employee Retirement Income Security Act, Wild and Scenic Rivers Act, National Energy Act."

KANSAS GAS & ELECTRIC CO., Wichita, Kan. Lobbyist — Dana W. Haas, 1112 Stafford St., Arlington, Va. 22201. Filed 2/6/84. Legislative interest — "Legislation including but not limited to the following statutes and amendments thereto: Internal Revenue Code, TVA Act, Atomic Energy Act, Federal Power Act, Rural Electrification Act, Bonneville Power Act, Reclamation acts, Flood Control Act, Appropriations acts, Rivers Harbors Flood Control authorizations, Water Pollution Control Act, Clean Air Act, OSHA, Equal Employment Opportunity Act, Employee Retirement Income Security Act, Wild and Scenic Rivers Act, National Energy Act."

KIMBERLY-CLARK CORP., 401 N. Lake St., Neenah, Wis. 54956. Filed for self 2/27/84. Legislative interest — "Generally interested in tax, trade, environmental, energy, transportation, antitrust, health, benefits, labor, consumer and other legislative proposals which directly affect the Corporation, its employees or its stockholders." Lobbyist — Bonnie B. Wan, 1201 Pennsylvania Ave. N.W., Washington, D.C. 20004.

K-MART CORP., Troy, Mich. Lobbyist — Howrey & Simon, 1730 Pennsylvania Ave. N.W., Washington, D.C. 20006. Filed 2/13/84. Legislative interest — "Pending intellectual property legislation including S 875 and HR 2447."

LTV AEROSPACE AND DEFENSE CO., P.O. Box 225907, Dallas, Texas 75265. Filed for self 2/29/84. Legislative interest — "Annual Department of Defense and NASA authorization and appropriations and other defense related legislation." Lobbyists — Grant Miller, Jack L. Stempler, 1725 Jefferson Davis Highway, Arlington, Va. 22202.

M/A-COM DEVELOPMENT CORP., Rockville, Md. Lobbyist — Peter Kyros, 1120 Connecticut Ave. N.W., Washington, D.C. 20036. (Former U.S. rep., D-Maine, 1967-75.) Filed 2/7/84. Legislative interest — "International telecommunications issues, HR 4464."

MAGNAVOX GOVERNMENT & INDUSTRIAL ELECTRONICS CO., Fort Wayne, Ind. Lobbyist — Peter Kyros, 1120 Connecticut Ave. N.W., Washington, D.C. 20036. (Former U.S. rep., D-Maine, 1967-75.) Filed 2/7/84. Legislative interest — "International telecommunications issues, HR 4464."

MANAGEMENT INSIGHTS INC., Dallas, Texas. Lobbyist — Paul Suplizio Associates, 2948 University Terrace N.W., Washington, D.C. 20016. Filed 2/23/84. Legislative interest — "Support tax credit for hiring structurally unemployed, summer youth, and disadvantaged workers. Support retention of provisions of 26 U.S. Code 44B and 51-53 pertaining to targeted jobs tax credit. Support S 2185 which extends targeted jobs tax credit to December 31, 1989."

MANVILLE CORP., Washington, D.C. Lobbyist — Steven F. Stockmeyer, 1120 20th St. N.W., Washington, D.C. 20036. Filed 2/9/84. Legislative interest — "Asbestos health related legislation supported by Manville Corporation not yet introduced."

MARK AIR INC., Anchorage, Alaska. Lobbyist — Cliff Madison Government Relations Inc., P.O. Box 3482, Granada Hills, Calif. 91344. Filed 2/17/84. Legislative interest — "CAB Sunset legislation - for. Defense appropriations - for."

McDONNELL DOUGLAS CORP., St. Louis, Mo. Lobbyist — J. C. Steen, 412 First St. S.E., Washington, D.C. 20003. Filed 2/26/84. Legislative interest — "Defense authorization and appropriation bills."

MERCEDES-BENZ OF NORTH AMERICA, Montvale, N.J. Lobbyist — Mudge, Rose, Guthrie, Alexander & Ferdon, 2121

K St. N.W., Washington, D.C. 20037. Filed 2/9/84. Legislative interest — "Bills to amend the Internal Revenue Code of 1954 to limit the amount of depreciation, Investment Tax Credit, and Deductions Allowable for Luxury Automobiles (S 2231, S 2232, HR 4135)."

MILES LABORATORIES INC., Elkhart, Ind. 46515. Filed for self 2/7/84. Legislative interest — "Health care, energy, environmental and tax-related legislation including HR 3502 and S 1306, patent term restoration; S 503, imitation controlled substances act; HR 3818, Federal Insecticide, Fungicide and Rodenticide Reform Act; H J Res 271, National Investors' Day." Lobbyist — Lester L. Rosen, 1025 Vermont Ave. N.W., Washington, D.C. 20005. Filed for self 2/7/84. Legislative interest — "HR 3502, HR 3605 and other legislation pertaining to the health-care system and the pharmaceutical industry in particular." Lobbyist — David M. Jenkins II, Kathleen M. Henderson, 1025 Vermont Ave. N.W., Washington, D.C. 20005.

TERRENCE W. MODGLIN & ASSOCIATES, 2001 S St. N.W., Washington, D.C. 20009. Filed for self 2/28/84. Legislative interest — "HR 4900, Panama Canal Authorization - Canal Commission Employee (U.S. citizen) cost of living adjustment for loss of APO, PX and commissary privileges." Lobbyist — Jean F. O'Neil, 884 College Parkway, Rockville, Md. 20850.

MOLLER STEAMSHIP CO. INC., New York, N.Y. Lobbyist — John E. Bouchard, 1667 K St. N.W., Washington, D.C. 20036. Filed 2/24/84. Legislative interest — "Any legislative matter of concern to Moller Steamship Co. Inc. . . ."

MURPHY MOTOR FREIGHT LINES INC., St. Paul, Minn. Lobbyist — Maun, Green, Hayes, Simon, Johanneson and Brehl, 332 Hamm Building, St. Paul, Minn. 55102. Filed 2/17/84. Legislative interest — "Tax Reform bill of 1983 . . . HR 4170 . . . section 313 of HR 4170 . . . in favor of passage. . . ."

NATIONAL MULTI-FAMILY HOUSING FINANCE ASSOCIATION, Washington, D.C. Lobbyist — Patton, Boggs & Blow, 2550 M St. N.W., Washington, D.C. 20037. Filed 2/10/84. Legislative interest — "Legislation to amend the Tax Bill, HR 4170."

NATIONAL MULTI HOUSING COUNCIL, Washington, D.C. Lobbyist — Gray & Co., 3255 Grace St. N.W., Washington, D.C. 20007. Filed 2/1/84. Legislative interest — "Including but not limited to tax legislation."

NEW YORK MERCANTILE EXCHANGE, New York, N.Y. Lobbyist — Barrett, Smith, Schapiro, Simon & Armstrong, 26 Broadway, New York, N.Y. 10004. Filed 2/15/84. Legislative interest — "Positions for and against various proposed amendments to the Internal Revenue Code, to the Commodity Exchange Act and various other legislation."

NORTHERN NATURAL GAS CO., 2223 Dodge St., Omaha, Neb. 68102. Filed for self 2/27/84. Legislative interest — "Natural gas legislation, tax legislation, environmental legislation." Lobbyist — Thomas C. Jetton.

NORTHROP CORP., Los Angeles, Calif. Lobbyist — J. C. Steen, 412 First St. S.E., Washington, D.C. 20003. Filed 2/28/84. Legislative interest — "Defense authorization and appropriation bills."

OLYMPIA & YORK DEVELOPMENT LTD., Toronto, Ontario, Canada. Lobbyist — Donald C. Evans Jr., 214 Massachusetts Ave. N.E., Washington, D.C. 20002. Filed 2/3/84. Legislative interest — "Tax legislative matters of interest to the Company, its subsidiaries and shareholders."

OLYMPIA & YORK EQUITY CORP., New York, N.Y. Lobbyist — Donald C. Evans Jr., 214 Massachusetts Ave. N.E., Washington, D.C. 20002. Filed 2/3/84. Legislative interest — "Tax legislation of interest to the Company."

ORION SATELLITE CORP., 2000 L St. N.W., Washington, D.C. 20036. Filed for self 2/6/84. Legislative interest — "Any and all legislation concerning domestic and international telecommunications. Amendments and/or interpretation of the Communications Satellite Act of 1962."

PAINE, WEBBER, JACKSON & CURTIS INC., New York, N.Y. Lobbyist — Kirkpatrick, Lockhart, Hill, Christopher & Phillips, 1900 M St. N.W., Washington, D.C. 20036. Filed 2/29/84. Legislative interest — "Legislation and legislative activities rela-

tive to brokering of deposits in financial institutions; such activity is supported."

PLANNING RESEARCH CORP., 1500 Planning Research Drive, McLean, Va. 22102. Filed for self 2/14/84. Legislative interest — "Legislation affecting the professional service industry and impacting the Planning Research Corporation." Lobbyist — JoAnn Spevacek.

POLAROID CORP., 549 Technology Square, Cambridge, Mass. 02139. Lobbyist — Goodwin, Proctor & Hoar, 28 State St., Boston, Mass. 02109. Filed 2/10/84. Legislative interest — ". . . Toxic Substances Control Act ('TSCA') Reauthorization Legislation and Amendments . . . HR 4304 . . . For amendments increasing protection of trade secrets and confidential business information obtained by the federal government under TSCA." Filed for self 2/10/84. Legislative interest — ". . . Toxic Substances Control Act ('TSCA') Reauthorization Legislation and Amendments . . . HR 4304 . . . For amendments increasing protection of trade secrets and confidential business information obtained by the federal government under TSCA." Lobbyist — Richard F. de Lima.

PSC ASSOCIATES, 1609 Barnstead Drive, Reston, Va. 22094. Filed for self 2/16/84. Legislative interest — "On going interest in shipping, fishing export/import." Lobbyist — Pamela A. Chaiet.

RCA CORP., Moorestown, N.J. Lobbyist — Finley, Kumble, Wagner, Heine, Underberg, Manley & Casey, 1120 Connecticut Ave. N.W., Washington, D.C. 20036. Filed 2/24/84. Legislative interest — "In favor of increased funding of Advanced Communication Technology Satellite programs (NASA sponsored project)."

ROCKCOR INC., Redmond, Wash. Lobbyist — Denny Miller Associates, 203 Maryland Ave. N.E., Washington, D.C. 20002. Filed 2/1/84. Legislative interest — "Military Construction and DOD Authorization Acts."

SATELLITE BUSINESS SYSTEMS, 8283 Greensboro Drive, McLean, Va. 22102. Filed for self 2/23/84. Legislative interest — "Telecommunications legislation, including S 1660, HR 4102 and successors. (Support competition, equitable access charges, oppose large subsidies). Also, cable and international legislation affecting telecommunications. . . ." Lobbyist — Michael C. Cushing.

SATELLITE SYSTEMS ENGINEERING, Washington, D.C. Lobbyist — Peter Kyros, 1120 Connecticut Ave. N.W., Washington, D.C. 20036. (Former U.S. rep., D-Maine, 1967-75.) Filed 2/7/84. Legislative interest — "International telecommunications issues, HR 4464."

SIMPLEX TIME RECORDER CO., Gardner, Mass. Lobbyist — Vorys, Sater, Seymour & Pease, 1828 L St. N.W., Washington, D.C. 20036. Filed 2/2/84. Legislative interest — "Advance client's interest in international trade matters, specifically legislation dealing with the Generalized System of Preferences."

TELLABS, Lisle, Ill. Lobbyist — Peter Kyros, 1120 Connecticut Ave. N.W., Washington, D.C. 20036. (Former U.S. rep., D-Maine, 1967-75.) Filed 2/7/84. Legislative interest — "International telecommunications issues, HR 4464."

TEXAS AIR CORP., 333 Clay St., Houston, Texas 77002. Filed for self 2/6/84. Legislative interest — "Opposition to any legislation that would (a) reregulate the airline industry, (b) modify the bankruptcy laws that affect any voluntary reorganization under Chapter 11, that was filed prior to September 25, 1983, or (c) modify the present Federal law concerning labor protective provisions." Lobbyist — Clark H. Onstad, 1201 Pennsylvania Ave. N.W., Washington, D.C. 20004.

TEXAS EASTERN TRANSMISSION CORP., P.O. Box 2521, Houston, Texas 77252. Filed for self 2/8/84. Legislative interest — "General legislative interests affecting energy, especially matters relating to the natural gas and pipeline industries, such as coal slurry legislation, S 276 and HR 1010; Natural Gas Policy Act Amendments; Oil Pipeline Deregulation; Clean Air Act Amendments." Lobbyist — Frances M. Turk, 1090 Vermont Ave. N.W., Washington, D.C. 20005.

TEXAS GAS TRANSMISSION CORP., 3800 Frederica

St., Owensboro, Ky. 42301. Filed for self 2/17/84. Legislative interest — "All matters relating to the natural gas industry." Lobbyists — John P. Dring, Cheryl L. Jones, Ray H. Lancaster, 1875 I St. N.W., Washington, D.C. 20006.

TEXTRON INC., 1090 Vermont Ave. N.W., Washington, D.C. 20005. Filed for self 2/15/84. Legislative interest — "Tax and budget issues, uniform federal product liability legislation (S 44); Contractor Liability and Indemnification Act (S 1839); Sales Representatives Contractual Relations Act (HR 3591); foreign trade issues." Lobbyist — Steven A. Wein.

THORNTON AND EARLY, Boston, Mass. Lobbyist — Martin J. Curry, 52 Hilma St., North Quincy, Mass. 02171. Filed 2/9/84. Legislative interest — "To promote the preservation of common law rights and remedies afforded persons adversely affected by toxic materials and to oppose efforts to establish Federal legislation limiting or abrogating such rights. . . ."

TITAN OCEAN SYSTEMS INC., Oakdale, Pa. Lobbyist — Ballard, Spahr, Andrews & Ingersoll, 1850 K St. N.W., Washington, D.C. 20006. Filed 2/17/84. Legislative interest — "Historic Shipwreck legislation."

TORCHMARK CORP., 2001 3rd Ave. South, Birmingham, Ala. 35233. Filed for self 2/6/84. Legislative interest — "Any legislation, proposed or contemplated, considered to affect Torchmark Corporation . . . including HR 4170, S 1992." Lobbyist — Robert I. Stewart.

THE TRANE CO., 3600 Pammel Creek Road, La Crosse, Wis. 54601. Filed for self 2/21/84. Legislative interest — "Legislation affecting the air conditioning and heat transfer industry . . . Clean Air Act Amendments of 1983, S 768 and HR 3087 - Favor . . . Appliance Standards Program, HR 3244 - Oppose." Lobbyist — David F. Martin, 2020 14th St. North, Arlington, Va. 22201.

TRANSAMERICA-ICS INC., New York, N.Y. Lobbyist — Dickey, Knorr & Moore, 1825 I St. N.W., Washington, D.C. 20006. Filed 2/28/84. Legislative interest — "Legislation of interest concerns proposals which alter, amend, or otherwise affect the internal revenue code as it relates to the activities of corporations and businesses in using capital cost recovery allowances for investments in productive equipment."

TRAVENOL LABORATORIES INC., 1050 17th St. N.W., Washington, D.C. 20036. Filed for self 2/7/84. Legislative interest — Not specified. Lobbyist — Julie L. Arnold.

TRITON CONTAINER INTERNATIONAL INC., San Francisco, Calif. Lobbyist — Dickey, Knorr & Moore, 1825 I St. N.W., Washington, D.C. 20006. Filed 2/28/84. Legislative interest — "Legislation of interest concerns proposals which alter, amend, or otherwise affect the internal revenue code as it relates to the activities of corporations and businesses in using capital cost recovery allowances for investments in productive equipment."

UNITED SERVICES LIFE COMPANIES, Washington, D.C. Lobbyist — R. Duffy Wall & Associates Inc., 1317 F St. N.W., Washington, D.C. 20004. Filed 2/1/84. Legislative interest — "Issues relating to life insurance taxation."

WARNER COMMUNICATIONS INC., New York, N.Y., and Washington, D.C. Lobbyist — Wexler, Reynolds, Harrison & Schule Inc., 1317 F St. N.W., Washington, D.C. 20004. Filed 2/14/84. Legislative interest — "To encourage support for legislation limiting alien ownership of certain broadcast licenses and media distribution facilities." Lobbyist — Akin, Gump, Strauss, Hauer & Feld, 1333 New Hampshire Ave. N.W., Washington, D.C. 20036. Filed 2/24/84. Legislative interest — "Hearings and any legislation relating to amendments to the Securities Exchange Act of 1934 to provide uniform margin requirements in transactions involving the acquisition of the securities of U.S. corporations, including but not limited to HR 2371 and amendments to section 310 of the Federal Communications Act regarding alien ownership including but not limited to S 2282 and HR 4840."

WESTERN AIRLINES, Los Angeles, Calif. Lobbyist — Cliff Madison Government Relations Inc., P.O. Box 3482, Granada Hills, Calif. 91344. Filed 2/17/84. Legislative interest — "CAB Sunset legislation - For. Customs appropriations - For."

WESTERN PIONEER, Buffalo, N.Y. Lobbyist — Ragan & Mason, 900 17th St. N.W., Washington, D.C. 20006. Filed 2/2/84. Legislative interest — "Amendments to Title 46, U.S. Code, pertaining to fishing and fish processing vessels."

XTRA INC., Boston, Mass. Lobbyist — Dickey, Knorr & Moore, 1825 I St. N.W., Washington, D.C. 20006. Filed 2/28/84. Legislative interest — "Legislation of interest concerns proposals which alter, amend, or otherwise affect the internal revenue code as it relates to the activities of corporations and businesses in using capital cost recovery allowances for investments in productive equipment."

International Relations

GOVERNMENT OF CANADA, Ottawa, Ontario, Canada. Lobbyist — Gray & Co., 3255 Grace St. N.W., Washington, D.C. 20007. Filed 2/13/84. Legislative interest — "Including but not limited to issues concerning acid rain, economic, trade and tourism matters."

GOVERNMENT OF CYPRUS, Nicosia, Cyprus. Lobbyist — O'Connor & Hannan, 1919 Pennsylvania Ave. N.W., Washington, D.C. 20008. Filed 2/6/84. Legislative interest — Not specified.

GOVERNMENT OF HAITI, Port-au-Prince, Haiti. Lobbyist — Gray & Co., 3255 Grace St. N.W., Washington, D.C. 20007. Filed 2/13/84. Legislative interest — "Including but not limited to economic, tourism and trade matters."

REPUBLIC OF KOREA, Seoul, Korea. Lobbyist — Gray & Co., 3255 Grace St. N.W., Washington D.C. 20007. Filed 2/13/84. Legislative interest — "Including but not limited to economic and trade matters."

REPUBLIC OF TURKEY, Ankara, Turkey. Lobbyist — Gray & Co., 3255 Grace St. N.W., Washington, D.C. 20007. Filed 2/13/84. Legislative interest — "Including but not limited to economic and security issues."

Labor Groups

COLUMBIA TYPOGRAPHICAL UNION NO. 101 (AFL-CIO), 4626 Wisconsin Ave. N.W., Washington, D.C. 20016. Filed for self 2/7/84. Legislative interest — "Legislative appropriations and Title 44 of the U.S. Code." Lobbyist — William J. Boarman.

INDUSTRIAL UNION DEPARTMENT (AFL-CIO), 815 16th St. N.W., Washington, D.C. 20006. Filed for self 2/14/84. Legislative interest — "All bills affecting the welfare of the country generally and specifically bills affecting workers such as trade, OSHA, pension and employment legislation." Lobbyist — William Briggs.

INTERNATIONAL ASSOCIATION OF FIRE FIGHTERS, 1750 New York Ave. N.W., Washington, D.C. 20006. Filed for self 2/3/84. Legislative interest — "HR 622 (Fed.) law officers and firefighters death benefits. HR 1066 Social Security, benefits, minimum. HR 1175 Government pension plans, exemption from rules. S 1163 Death benefits for federal firefighters. S 809 Fire prevention and control, authorizations. S 640 Income tax exclusions, employer health plan contributions. HR 624 Public Safety officers death benefits. HR 77 Retirement income tax exemption. S 1164 Death benefits for medical conditions. S 135 Income tax, fringe benefits reg. prohibition." Lobbyist — Gilman Udell.

INTERNATIONAL UNION OF OPERATING ENGINEERS, 1125 17th St. N.W., Washington, D.C. 20036. Filed for self 2/21/84. Legislative interest — Not specified. Lobbyist — James H. Thomas.

MARINE ENGINEERS' BENEFICIAL ASSOCIATION (MEBA), Washington, D.C. Lobbyist — Denny Miller Associates, 203 Maryland Ave. N.E., Washington, D.C. 20002. Filed 2/1/84. Legislative interest — "Jones Act Waiver ('Cunard Bill'), HR 4333, S 1197. Export Administration Act of 1978."

NATIONAL RURAL LETTER CARRIERS ASSOCIATION, 1448 Duke St., Alexandria, Va. 22314. Filed for self 2/15/84. Legislative interest — Not specified. Lobbyist — Ken Parmelee.

RADIO OFFICERS UNION, 30 Montgomery St., Jersey City, N.J. 07302. Filed for self 2/9/84. Legislative interest — "General maritime affairs. Marine communications and navigation." Lobbyists — Charles D. Calhoun, Samuel D. Blunt.

UNITED TRANSPORTATION UNION, 400 First St. N.W., Washington, D.C. 20001. Filed for self 2/21/84. Legislative interest — Not specified. Lobbyist — Don R. Beavers.

State and Local Governments

COMMONWEALTH OF PUERTO RICO, San Juan, Puerto Rico. Lobbyist — Hamel & Park, 888 16th St. N.W., Washington, D.C. 20006. Filed 2/21/84. Legislative interest — "Puerto Rico opposes passage of HR 4702 and S 2246."

PORT OF TACOMA, Tacoma, Wash. Lobbyist — Denny Miller Associates, 203 Maryland Ave. N.E., Washington, D.C. 20002. Filed 2/1/84. Legislative interest — "Water Resources Act of 1983 (S 947, HR 367); Third Proviso Legislation (HR 1076)."

SOUTHERN CALIFORNIA RAPID TRANSIT DISTRICT, Los Angeles, Calif. Lobbyist — Cliff Madison Government Relations Inc., P.O. Box 3482, Granada Hills, Calif. 91344. Filed 2/17/84. Legislative interest — "DOT appropriations - for. Surface Transportation Assistance Act - for."

Trade Associations

AMERICAN ASSOCIATION OF BLOOD BANKS, 1117 N. 19th St., Arlington, Va. 22209. Filed for self 2/13/84. Legislative interest — "Health care legislation in general."

AMERICAN ASSOCIATION OF MEAT PROCESSORS, P.O. Box 269, Elizabethtown, Pa. 17022. Filed for self 2/22/84. Legislative interest — "Meat Inspection Amendments of 1983 and Federal Meat and Poultry Products Inspection Act of 1983. HR 1795 and S 593...." Lobbyist — John J. Auciello.

AMERICAN DENTAL ASSOCIATION, 1101 17th St. N.W., Washington, D.C. 20036. Filed for self 2/13/84. Legislative interest — "Legislation affecting: dental education, federal dental programs and the organization, financing and delivery of dental services." Lobbyist — Leonard P. Wheat.

AMERICAN DIETETIC ASSOCIATION, Chicago, Ill. Lobbyist — Latham, Watkins & Hills, 1333 New Hampshire Ave. N.W., Washington, D.C. 20036. Filed 2/17/84. Legislative interest — "Reauthorization of the Older Americans Act of 1965."

AMERICAN IRON AND STEEL INSTITUTE, Washington, D.C. Lobbyist — O'Neill and Haase, 1333 New Hampshire Ave. N.W., Washington, D.C. 20036. Filed 2/28/84. Legislative interest — "HR 4352 - Fair Trade in Steel Act of 1983."

AMERICAN PETROLEUM INSTITUTE, 1220 L St. N.W., Washington, D.C. 20005. Filed for self 2/10/84. Legislative interest — Not specified. Lobbyists — Thomas H. Fitzpatrick, 410 Asylum St., Hartford, Conn. 06103; H. Kim Anderson, 1809 Staples Mill Road, Richmond, Va. 23230.

AMERICAN POLYGRAPH ASSOCIATION, Severna Park, Md. Lobbyist — John Fochtman, 801 S. Pitt St., Alexandria, Va. 22314. Filed 2/28/84. Legislative interest — "Concerned with HR 4681, Polygraph Regulatory Act of 1984. Against bill."

AMERICAN SOCIETY OF COMPOSERS, AUTHORS, AND PUBLISHERS (ASCAP), New York, N.Y. Lobbyist — Wilmer, Cutler & Pickering, 1666 K St. N.W., Washington, D.C. 20006. Filed 2/16/84. Legislative interest — "Legislation affecting copyright royalties and fees paid to composers, authors, and publishers; specifically (a) Coin-Operated Phonorecord Player Copyright Act of 1983, (b) HR 3858, S 1734, (c) 17 U.S. Code, section 116, (d) against bills, for statute."

ASSOCIATION OF BANK HOLDING COMPANIES, 730 15th St. N.W., Washington, D.C. 20005. Filed for self 2/21/84. Legislative interest — "All legislation affecting the association's member companies. In support of the proposed Financial Institutions Deregulation Act, S 1609, and the proposed Competitive Banking Act. In opposition to 'moratorium' legislation such as S 1532 and HR 3499." Lobbyist — Richard M. Whiting.

CONSEJO NACIONAL DE COMERCIO EXTERIOR DEL NORESTE A.C., Apartado 2674, Monterrey, Mexico. Filed for self 2/17/84. Legislative interest — "Support of extension of Generalized System of Preferences. Submission of testimony to House Ways and Means Trade Subcommittee on proposed 'Generalized System of Preferences Renewal Act of 1983.'"

THE CONSORTIUM OF PUBLIC TV STATIONS, Chicago, Ill. Lobbyist — Wexler, Reynolds, Harrison & Schule Inc., 1317 F St. N.W., Washington, D.C. 20004. Filed 2/14/84. Legislative interest — "Registrant seeks to obtain Congressional support for the concept of limited advertising on a voluntary basis by public television stations; Public Broadcasting Act Amendments of 1984."

GREATER PROVIDENCE CHAMBER OF COMMERCE, 10 Dorrance St., Providence, R.I. 02903. Filed for self 2/21/84. Legislative interest — Not specified. Lobbyist — William D. Moore.

INSTITUTE OF MAKERS OF EXPLOSIVES, 1575 I St. N.W., Washington, D.C. 20005. Filed for self 2/23/84. Legislative interest — "Opposition to legislation requiring taggants in explosives materials ... section 9, HR 380...." Lobbyists — Frederick P. Smith Jr., Theresa A. Schneider.

JOINT MARITIME CONGRESS, 444 N. Capitol St. N.W., Washington, D.C. 20001. Filed for self 2/17/84. Legislative interest — Not specified. Lobbyists — Thomas W. Scoville, Benjamin L. Webster, Anthony V. Dresden.

LABOR MANAGEMENT MARITIME COMMITTEE INC., 100 Indiana Ave. N.W., Washington, D.C. 20001. Filed for self 2/29/84. Legislative interest — "None." Lobbyists — Talmage E. Simpkins, Robert S. Agman.

NATIONAL AGRICULTURAL CHEMICALS ASSOCIATION, 1155 15th St. N.W., Washington, D.C. 20005. Filed for self 2/3/84. Legislative interest — "All legislation affecting pesticides."

NATIONAL ASSOCIATION OF BEVERAGE IMPORTERS INC., Washington, D.C. Lobbyist — Malmgren Inc., 1120 20th St. N.W., Washington, D.C. 20036. Filed 2/10/84. Legislative interest — "Wine Equity Act, HR 3795, S 2182, Against."

NATIONAL ASSOCIATION OF MANUFACTURERS, 1776 F St. N.W., Washington, D.C. 20006. Filed for self 2/6/84. Legislative interest — "General energy legislation, including but not limited to natural gas decontrol, synthetic fuels, energy taxes, coal conversion, energy conservation and commercialization of energy technologies." Lobbyist — Ann A. Michel. Filed for self 2/16/84. Legislative interest — "Legislation affecting employee/labor relations ... HR 2847 National Employment Priorities Act; Davis-Bacon Reform - HR 3846/S 1172; Hobbs Act amendments - S 462/HR 49; Labor-Management Racketeering legislation - S 336; Office Machine and Equipment Dealers' Act - HR 1159/S 286; and Sales Representatives Contractual Relations Act - HR 3591." Lobbyist — Francis M. Lunnie Jr.

NATIONAL ASSOCIATION OF REALTORS, 777 14th St. N.W., Washington, D.C. 20005. Filed for self 2/10/84. Legislative interest — "Any legislation that affects the real estate industry, including subsidized housing issues and housing authorization and appropriations legislations; condominium legislation; public buildings legislation; Farmers Home Administration legislation and enterprise zone legislation." Lobbyist — Lisa Lausier. Filed for self 2/10/84. Legislative interest — "Tax legislation." Lobbyist — Gerald M. Howard.

NATIONAL CABLE TELEVISION ASSOCIATION INC., 1724 Massachusetts Ave. N.W., Washington, D.C. 20036. Filed for self 2/9/84. Legislative interest — "Amendments to the Communications Act of 1934 and other legislation affecting cable television generally." Lobbyist — Valerie F. Pinson.

NATIONAL COALITION FOR EMERGENCY MEDICAL SERVICES, Washington, D.C. Lobbyist — Michael J. Dyer, 1331 Pennsylvania Ave. N.W., Washington, D.C. 20004. Filed 2/21/84. Legislative interest — "General legislative interest - (a) Emergency Medical Services Legislation, Department of Health and Human Services Appropriations Bills, Department of Transportation Appropriations Bills, Preventive Health Block

Grant, Surface Transportation Assistance Act; (b) HR 4616; (c) Section 402 of title 23 U.S. Code; (d) for these bills."

NATIONAL FOREST PRODUCTS ASSOCIATION, 1619 Massachusetts Ave. N.W., Washington, D.C. 20036. Filed for self 2/10/84. Legislative interest — "Legislation directly or indirectly affecting the interest of the forest products industry including Forest Service appropriations, federal land management policies, Wilderness proposals, housing and mortgage finance, public financing, lobby law reform, RARE II, Regulatory and Taxation and Federal Timber Contracts legislation." Lobbyist — David E. Stahl.

NATIONAL HEALTH CARE FINANCING ASSOCIATION, P.O. Box 946, Holly Hill, Fla. 32017. Filed for self 2/22/84. Legislative interest — Not specified. Lobbyist — H. Radford Bishop II.

NATIONAL INHOLDERS ASSOCIATION, Sonoma, Calif. Lobbyist — Rosemarie J. Craven, 1919 Pennsylvania Ave. N.W., Washington, D.C. 20006. Filed 2/8/84. Legislative interest — "Public lands issues."

NATIONAL OIL JOBBERS COUNCIL, 1707 H St. N.W., Washington, D.C. 20006. Filed for self 2/22/84. Legislative interest — Not specified. Lobbyist — Robert Lauterberg.

NATIONAL SOCIETY OF PROFESSIONAL ENGINEERS, 2029 K St. N.W., Washington, D.C. 20006. Filed for self 2/9/84. Legislative interest — "All legislation affecting interests of professional engineers." Lobbyist — Kathy S. Prager.

PUBLIC SECURITIES ASSOCIATION, 1110 Vermont Ave. N.W., Washington, D.C. 20005. Filed for self 2/28/84. Legislative interest — "(a) Tax bills (generally) and particularly those affecting municipal finance, mortgage-backed securities, and securities of the federal government and its agencies. (b) HR 4170 and S 2062...." Lobbyist — Jon R. Tumler.

RICE MILLERS' ASSOCIATION, Arlington, Va. Lobbyist — Patton, Boggs & Blow, 2550 M St. N.W., Washington, D.C. 20037. Filed 2/10/84. Legislative interest — "Legislation affecting the export of rice from the United States and the Importation from third countries affecting U.S. markets.... To amend the Trade Act of 1974, S 2191 with respect to beneficiary developing countries which engage in unfair trade practices ... to amend titles III and V of the Trade Act of 1974, HR 4489."

SATELLITE TV VIEWING RIGHTS SUPERFUND INC., Washington, D.C. Lobbyist — Brown & Finn, 1920 N St. N.W., Washington, D.C. 20036. Filed 2/21/84. Legislative interest — "Legislation dealing with a rewrite of the Communications Act and with satellites."

SENIOR EXECUTIVES ASSOCIATION, P.O. Box 7610, Ben Franklin Station, Washington, D.C. 20044. Filed for self 2/9/84. Legislative interest — "Legislation affecting pay, benefits and job security of federal government SES and supergrade employee; affecting improvements in government and management, efficiency and effectiveness; affecting the liability of government employees to suit ... support bills to amend the Federal Tort Claims Act to substitute the government as defendant for the employee when 'Constitutional Torts' are committed within scope of employment ... HR 2097 - support bill to establish 'Little Hoover' commission to study future of civil service ... HR3852/S 1879 - support bills to improve relocation reimbursements for federal employees ... S 958, support the measure to amend the CSRA ... Support legislation to improve the Federal Health Benefits Program." Lobbyist — David S. Burckman.

TOBACCO-CIGARETTE LOBBY, P.O. Box 24891, Richmond, Va. 23224. Filed for self 2/24/84. Legislative interest — Not specified. Lobbyist — C. L. Clay Jr.

WESTERN FUELS ASSOCIATION INC., 1225 19th St. N.W., Washington, D.C. 20036. Filed for self 2/2/84. Legislative interest — "Supporting changes in laws relating to transportation of coal such as slurry legislation (HR 1010 and S 267), the Rahall Bill (HR 2584) and Ford Bills (S 1081 and S 1082), the Seiberling Bill (HR 4559) and others which would limit railroads' monopoly pricing powers. We also are interested in federal coal leasing matters, re-authorization of Clean Air Act (supporting a moderate acid rain control amendment). Clean Water Act, etc." Lobbyist — Ken Holum.

Miscellaneous

AMERICAN ASSOCIATION OF RETIRED PERSONS, 1909 K St. N.W., Washington, D.C. 20049. Filed for self 2/10/84. Legislative interest — "Support of ... Improved Social Security and Medicare/Medicaid Laws ... Improved Tax Treatment of Older Americans ... Improved Nursing Home Standards ... Consumer Protection Legislation ... Employment of Older Workers ... National Health Insurance ... Transportation of the Elderly ... Housing for the Elderly." Lobbyists — David Certner, Meredith Cote.

THE ATLANTIC ALLIANCE FOR MARITIME HERITAGE CONSERVATION, Washington, D.C. Lobbyist — Ballard, Spahr, Andrews & Ingersoll, 1850 K St. N.W., Washington, D.C. 20005. Filed 2/17/84. Legislative interest — "Historic shipwreck legislation."

AVIATION CONSUMER ACTION PROJECT, Box 19029, Washington, D.C. Filed for self 2/23/84. Legislative interest — "... Air Travelers Security Act ... S 764 and HR 2053 ... 49 U.S. Code 1301 *et seq.* ... Against. CAB sunset legislation ... 49 U.S. Code 1301 *et seq.* ... for." Lobbyist — Cornish F. Hitchcock.

ARCHIE BENNETT JR., Houston, Texas. Lobbyist — Thomas P. Marinis Jr., 3418 First City Tower, Houston, Texas 77002. Filed 2/10/84. Legislative interest — "Tax legislation."

BLANCHARD VALLEY HOSPITAL, Findlay, Ohio. Lobbyist — Sutherland, Asbill & Brennan, 1666 K St. N.W., Washington, D.C. 20006. Filed 2/17/84. Legislative interest — Not specified.

NICHOLAS G. CAVAROCCHI, 2010 Massachusetts Ave. N.W., Washington, D.C. 20036. Filed for self 2/7/84. Legislative interest — "General interest in legislation pertaining to authorizations and appropriations for health and education programs."

CITIZENS AGAINST PACs, Washington, D.C. Lobbyist — Sklare, Idelson, 800 18th St. N.W., Washington, D.C. 20006. Filed 2/7/84. Legislative interest — "Generally to support reform of the existing federal campaign finance system which permits political action committee contributions."

JAMES F. DONOVAN, 1835 K St. N.W., Washington, D.C. 20006. Filed for self 2/16/84. Legislative interest — "Health and Trade Legislation."

THE ENVIRONMENTAL FUND, 1302 18th St. N.W., Washington, D.C. 20036. Filed for self 2/23/84. Legislative interest — "HR 1510/S 529, The Immigration Reform and Control Act (for); S 2140, The Immigration Ceiling Act (for); HR 3070, the Critical Trends Assessment Act; HR 907/S 1771, the Global Resources, Environment and Population Act (undecided); unnumbered, the annual appropriations bill for State, Justice, Commerce, the Judiciary, and Related Agencies." Lobbyists — Charles Vern Dinges IV, M. Rupert Cutler.

ENVIRONMENTAL POLICY INSTITUTE, 218 D St. N.E., Washington, D.C. 20003. Filed for self 2/13/84. Legislative interest — "Legislation relating to energy and environmental policy; communications policy, especially information access; and science and technology policy." Lobbyist — Tom Lewis.

FELIPE M. FLORESCA, 67 Wall St., New York, N.Y. 10005. Filed for self 2/8/84. Legislative interest — "... (a) Technological Assessment; (b) Immigration - Foreign Matters relating to Nationals and Corporations; (c) Immigration - Political Refugees; (d) Corporate/Banking Ethics and Practices."

FRED T. FRANZIA, JOHN C. FRANZIA & JOSEPH S. FRANZIA, Ceres, Calif. Lobbyist — Rogers & Wells, 1737 H St. N.W., Washington, D.C. 20006. Filed 2/24/84. Legislative interest — "Amendment to PL 97-34 ..."

CAROL DIANE HENDRICKS, 2601 Park Center Drive, Alexandria, Va. 22302. Filed for self 2/15/84. Legislative interest — "For passage of S 1197, HR 2883, HR 4333."

JAPANESE AMERICAN CITIZENS LEAGUE, San Francisco, Calif. Lobbyist — Colleen A. Darling, 1730 Rhode Island Ave. N.W., Washington, D.C. 20036. Filed 2/9/84. Legislative interest — Not specified.

KAMEHAMEHA SCHOOLS/BERNICE P. BISHOP ESTATE, Honolulu, Hawaii. Lobbyist — Rogers & Wells, 1737 H

St. N.W., Washington, D.C. 20006. Filed 2/24/84. Legislative interest — "Amendment to Section 514 of the Internal Revenue Code of 1954."

NATIONAL ASSOCIATION OF ARAB AMERICANS, 2033 M St. N.W., Washington, D.C. 20036. Filed for self 2/29/84. Legislative interest — "Middle East related legislation: a) FY '84 Foreign Assistance; b) S 637, HR 1850 . . . against." Lobbyists — Aline Kalbian, Annette Najjar, Karen Sasahara, Patrick J. Tyrrell, Robert A. Clark, John Keller.

NATIONAL INTERRELIGIOUS SERVICE BOARD FOR CONSCIENTIOUS OBJECTORS, 15th St. & New York Ave. N.W., Washington, D.C. 20005. Filed for self 2/23/84. Legislative interest — "Conscientious Objection to Military Conscription . . . HUD-Independent Agencies Appropriations Act, 1985 . . . S 1697 . . . HR 1500 . . . HR 1611. . . ." Lobbyist — Irwin E. Bomberger.

NATIONAL RIGHT TO WORK COMMITTEE, 8001 Braddock Road, Springfield, Va. 22160. Filed for self 2/1/84. Legislative interest — "Legislative proposals related to compulsory unionism in private industry, farm labor, public sector employees. . . . Hobbs Act Amendments . . . S 462 and HR 287 . . . Compulsory dues for politics . . . S 1881 and HR 3024 . . . National Right to Work bills . . . S 1200 and HR 511 . . . Contract Debarment . . . S 1079 and HR 1743 . . . ERISA . . . HR 3989 and S 2152 . . . Right to work protection on federal enclaves . . . S 1748 and HR 3344 . . . Right to work protection for construction industry . . . HR 4183. . . ." Lobbyist — Laura Marie Green.

NATIONAL TRUST FOR HISTORIC PRESERVATION, 1785 Massachusetts Ave. N.W., Washington, D.C. 20036. Filed for self 2/6/84. Legislative interest — "All legislation affecting historic preservation including appropriations; tax legislation; community development and housing authorization and appropriations; public lands legislation; environmental review requirements; postal rates; legislation related to maritime and archaeological resources; and any amendments to the National Historic Preservation Act (16 U.S. Code 470)." Lobbyists — Kate M. Perry, Andrea J. Yank.

CHARLES ALBERT O'CONNOR JR., 2300 S. 24th Road, Arlington, Va. 22206. Filed for self 2/16/84. Legislative interest — "Environment issues, veterans affairs, urban renewal. . . ."

DOMENIC R. RUSCIO, 2010 Massachusetts Ave. N.W., Washington, D.C. 20036. Filed for self 2/7/84. Legislative interest — "General interest in legislation pertaining to authorizations and appropriations for health and education programs."

SAVE OUR SECURITY, 1201 16th St. N.W., Washington, D.C. 20036. Filed for self 2/27/84. Legislative interest — "Support legislation preserving all aspects of Social Security (Old Age and Survivors' Insurance, Disability Insurance, Medicare, Medicaid, Supplemental Security Income) and oppose cuts in benefits, changes in qualifications or increased contributions; secure fair treatment for Federal and Postal employees being brought under Social Security." Lobbyist — Keith Tarr-Whelan.

70001 LTD., 600 Maryland Ave. S.W., Washington, D.C. 20024. Filed for self 2/29/84. Legislative interest — ". . . employment, education, and training for disadvantaged youth and families." Lobbyist — Mary Elise DeGonia.

THE WILDERNESS SOCIETY, 1901 Pennsylvania Ave. N.W., Washington, D.C. 20006. Filed for self 2/23/84. Legislative interest — "Wetlands Conservation Act HR 3082; '85 Appropriations; Alaska Hunting Bill S 49." Lobbyists — Bill Reffalt, Lawrence Laundry. Filed for self 2/23/84. Legislative interest — "Interior Appropriations; National Parks Budget; Columbia Gorge National Scenic Area Legislation (for); National Parks Protection Act; Land and Water Fund; Wilderness Legislation strategy." Lobbyist — Eric Olson. Filed for self 2/23/84. Legislative interest — "Florida Wilderness Bill (for); Oregon Wilderness Bill (for); Pennsylvania Wilderness Bill; Wisconsin Wilderness bill; California Wilderness Bill; Wyoming Wilderness Bill; RARE II." Lobbyist — Carla Kish.

BARNABY W. ZALL, 1424 16th St. N.W., Washington, D.C. 20036. Filed for self 2/14/84. Legislative interest — "HR 1510, Immigration Reform and Control Act, for. Appropriations acts for Department of Justice and Immigration and Naturalization Service, for. Generally, immigration-related legislation."

March Registrations

Corporations and Businesses

ALLEGHANY CORP., New York, N.Y. Lobbyist — White & Case, 1747 Pennsylvania Ave. N.W., Washington, D.C. 20006. Filed 3/30/84. Legislative interest — ". . . interested in legislation relating to the disposition of the interest of the United States in Consolidated Railroad, specifically the AMTRAK Improvement Act of 1983, HR 3648."

AMCOR GROUP LTD., Canoga Park, Calif. Lobbyist — Morris J. Amitay, 400 North Capitol St. N.W., Washington, D.C. 20001. Filed 3/26/84. Legislative interest — "Legislation pertaining to extension of residential renewable energy tax credits, Senate tax bill (no bill assigned yet); HR 4170, support extension of credit."

AMERICAN ACTUARIES INC., Grand Rapids, Mich. Lobbyist — Wagner & Baroody Inc., 1100 17th St. N.W., Washington, D.C. 20036. Filed 3/26/84. Legislative interest — "In support of continuation of the Voluntary Employee Benefit Association (VEBA)."

AMERICAN EXPRESS CO., New York, N.Y. Lobbyist — Akin, Gump, Strauss, Hauer & Feld, 1333 New Hampshire Ave. N.W., Washington, D.C. 20036. Filed 3/30/84. Legislative interest — "Hearings and any legislation relating to surcharges for credit card purchases including but not limited to HR 5026 and S 2336."

AMERICAN FAMILY LIFE ASSURANCE CO., Columbus, Ga. Lobbyist — Parry and Romani Associates Inc., 1140 Connecticut Ave. N.W., Washington, D.C. 20036. Filed 3/5/84. Legislative interest — "General insurance related issues."

AMERICUS SHAREOWNER SERVICE CORP., New York, N.Y. Lobbyist — Charls E. Walker Associates Inc., 1730 Pennsylvania Ave. N.W., Washington, D.C. 20036. Filed 3/5/84. Legislative interest — "Legislative interest may concern issues relating to possible changes in the tax treatment of various grantor trusts or the holders of units (or components) thereof."

AMERITRUST CO., 900 Euclid Ave., Cleveland, Ohio 44101. Filed for self 3/2/84. Legislative interest — "Banking legislation: e.g., S 2181, S 2134, HR 3537 — banking deregulation." Lobbyist — Peter E. Brereton.

ARMCO, 1747 Pennsylvania Ave. N.W., Washington, D.C. 20006. Filed for self 3/22/84. Legislative interest — "Energy Legislation; Capital Formation; Steel Industry Trade Legislation." Lobbyist — John L. Bauer Jr.

A.R.M. INC., Dallas, Texas. Lobbyist — Daniel A. Dutko, 412 First St. S.E., Washington, D.C. 20003. Filed 3/12/84. Legislative interest — Not specified.

ARTERY ORGANIZATION INC., Chevy Chase, Md. Lobbyist — Mark B. Sandground, 1025 Connecticut Ave. N.W., Washington, D.C. 20036. Filed 3/30/84. Legislative interest — "Lobby for amendments to section 73(a) of the Tax Reform Act of 1984. Applicable bills are HR 4170 and S 2062."

ATLANTIC RICHFIELD CO., Washington, D.C. Lobbyist — Wexler, Reynolds, Harrison & Schule Inc., 1317 F St. N.W., Washington, D.C. 20004. Filed 3/14/84. Legislative interest — "The registrant seeks to help employer with regards to merger legislation."

BALCOR/AMERICAN EXPRESS INC., Skokie, Ill. Lobbyist — R. Duffy Wall & Associates Inc., 1317 F St. N.W., Washington, D.C. 20004. Filed 3/8/84. Legislative interest — "Issues relating to real estate taxation."

BEAR STEARNS & CO., New York, N.Y. Lobbyist — Powell, Goldstein, Frazer & Murphy, 1110 Vermont Ave. N.W., Washington, D.C. 20005. Filed 3/29/84. Legislative interest — "Any tax or other legislation affecting securities or investment banking industry."

BECHTEL POWER CORP., 50 Beale St., San Francisco, Calif. 94119. Filed for self 3/28/84. Legislative interest — Not specified. Lobbyists — Dennis A. Bitz, 999 Meredith Court, Sonoma, Calif. 95476; Frank M. Staszesky Jr., 1535 Seneca Lane, San Mateo, Calif. 94402.

BIOGEN, Cambridge, Mass. Lobbyist — Patton, Boggs &

Blow, 2550 M St. N.W., Washington, D.C. 20037. Filed 3/8/84. Legislative interest — "Assistance on various pending revenue and tax bills which potentially affect Biogen...."

BORG-WARNER CORP., Chicago, Ill. Lobbyist — Philip D. Morrison, 1700 Pennsylvania Ave. N.W., Washington, D.C. 20006. Filed 3/26/84. Legislative interest — "Generally, all legislation relating to federal income taxation of corporations. Specifically, lobbying relating to section 401(k)."

THE BUDD CO., Troy, Mich. Lobbyist — Gray and Co., 3255 Grace St. N.W., Washington, D.C. 20007. Filed 3/22/84. Legislative interest — "Including but not limited to transportation and trade legislation."

CALIFORNIA VISION SERVICE PLAN, Sacramento, Calif. Lobbyist — James C. Corman, 1420 16th St. N.W., Washington, D.C. 20036. (Former U.S. rep., D-Calif., 1961-81.) Filed 3/13/84. Legislative interest — "To oppose the proposed cap on employer contributions to health insurance premiums."

CAN-AM CORP., Tucson, Ariz. Lobbyist — Squire, Sanders & Dempsey, 1201 Pennsylvania Ave. N.W., Washington, D.C. 20004. Filed 3/22/84. Legislative interest — "Tariff and trade matters of interest to the company."

CARE ENTERPRISES, Orange, Calif. Lobbyist — Parry and Romani Associates Inc., 1140 Connecticut Ave. N.W., Washington, D.C. 20036. Filed 3/5/84. Legislative interest — "General health care issues."

CATHEDRAL CORP., Arlington, Va. Lobbyist — Skadden, Arps, Slate, Meagher & Flom, 919 18th St. N.W., Washington, D.C. 20006. Filed 3/26/84. Legislative interest — "Real Estate provisions in Senate Tax Bill."

CHEVRON USA INC., Washington, D.C. Lobbyist — Anderson, Hibey, Nauheim & Blair, 1708 New Hampshire Ave. N.W., Washington, D.C. 20009. Filed 3/23/84. Legislative interest — "Legislation affecting proposed merger of Socal/Gulf including S 2362, S 2277, HR 5042, HR 3561, and HR 5137; opposition to such legislation." Lobbyist — Charls E. Walker Associates Inc., 1730 Pennsylvania Ave. N.W., Washington, D.C. 20006. Filed 3/16/84. Legislative interest — "... may concern issues relating to merger acquisitions activities." Lobbyist — Morris J. Amitay, 400 North Capitol St. N.W., Washington, D.C. 20001. Filed 3/21/84. Legislative interest — "... legislation placing moratoriums on mergers within oil industry. Opposing reintroduction of Johnston and Metzenbaum amendments."

COASTAL TRADING CO., Seattle, Wash. Lobbyist — Preston, Thorgrimson, Ellis & Holman, 1735 New York Ave. N.W., Washington, D.C. 20006. Filed 3/12/84. Legislative interest — "Legislation affecting vessel inspection requirements, HR 1579; S 1102."

COLONIAL LIFE & ACCIDENT INSURANCE CO., Columbia, S.C. Lobbyist — Paul M. Hawkins, 25 Audubon Place, Hilton Head Island, S.C. 29928. Filed 3/8/84. Legislative interest — "HR 4170 (Stark/Moore Insurance Tax Provision)."

CONSOLIDATED BANK, Miami, Fla. Lobbyist — Baker & Botts, 1701 Pennsylvania Ave. N.W., Washington, D.C. 20006. Filed 3/19/84. Legislative interest — "Legislation to amend the Export/Import Bank Act affecting small exports, and related matters."

CONSOLIDATED FOODS CORP., Chicago, Ill. Lobbyist — Akin, Gump, Strauss, Hauer & Feld, 1333 New Hampshire Ave. N.W., Washington, D.C. 20036. Filed 3/30/84. Legislative interest — "Hearings and any legislation relating to amendments to the Securities Exchange Act of 1934 to provide uniform margin requirements for the acquisition of securities of U.S. corporations including but not limited to HR 2371." Lobbyist — Donald C. Evans Jr., 214 Massachusetts Ave. N.E., Washington, D.C. 20002. Filed 3/22/84. Legislative interest — "Tax matters of interest to the Company and its subsidiaries."

CONSOLIDATED FREIGHTWAYS, Palo Alto, Calif. Lobbyist — Morrison & Foerster, 1920 N St. N.W., Washington, D.C. 20036. Filed 3/8/84. Legislative interest — "... related to tax legislation, and include specifically the Tax Reform Act of 1983-1984, S 2062 and HR 4170, and related provisions. The Employer is in favor of some provisions of the legislation and opposed to other provisions."

CONTINENTAL AMERICAN LIFE INSURANCE CO., Wilmington, Del. Lobbyist — Scriber, Hall & Thompson, 1875 I St. N.W., Washington, D.C. 20006. Filed 3/8/84. Legislative interest — "Proposed legislation with respect to the taxation of life insurance companies."

DAMSON OIL CORP., New York, N.Y. Lobbyist — King & Spalding, 1915 I St. N.W., Washington, D.C. 20006. Filed 3/21/84. Legislative interest — "... is in the Tax Reform Act of 1984 (HR 4170) or similar subsequent legislation."

DEPOSIT GUARANTEE NATIONAL BANK, Jackson, Miss. Lobbyist — Baker & Botts, 1701 Pennsylvania Ave. N.W., Washington, D.C. 20006. Filed 3/19/84. Legislative interest — "Legislation to amend the Export/Import Bank Act affecting small exports, and related matters."

DIAMOND SHAMROCK CORP., 717 N. Harwood St., Dallas, Texas 75201. Filed for self 3/14/84. Legislative interest — Not specified. Lobbyist — Robert S. Long, 919 18th St. N.W., Washington, D.C. 20006.

DIGITAL EQUIPMENT CORP., Maynard, Mass. Lobbyist — Ropes & Gray, 1001 22nd St. N.W., Washington, D.C. 20037. Filed 3/23/84. Legislative interest — "Semiconductor Chip Copyright Protection, S 1201, HR 1028, for enactment."

DORSEY & WHITNEY, 2200 First Bank Place East, Minneapolis, Minn. 55402. Filed for self 3/12/84. Legislative interest — "Tax and Deficit Reduction Bills: HR 4170, S 7062; Interest is to obtain amendments limiting retroactive effect of *Dickman v. Commissioner of Internal Revenue* ... legislative proposals that would make interest-free or low interest loans gifts by the lender and would impute income on the amount loaned to the lender." Lobbyist — David R. Brink, 1800 M St. N.W., Washington, D.C. 20036.

DREYFUS DOLLAR FUND, New York, N.Y. Lobbyist — Stroock & Stroock & Lavan, 1150 17th St. N.W., Washington, D.C. 20036. Filed 3/29/84. Legislative interest — "... proposed tax legislation concerning foreign investment income."

E. F. HUTTON & CO. INC., New York, N.Y. Lobbyist — The Keefe Co., 444 North Capitol St., Washington, D.C. 20001. Filed 3/13/84. Legislative interest — "Legislative interest lobbying to amend House Ways & Means and Senate Finance Committees' deficit reduction legislation, HR 4170."

47TH STREET PHOTO, New York, N.Y. Lobbyist — Miller, Cassidy, Larroca & Lewin, 2555 M St. N.W., Washington, D.C. 20037. Filed 3/5/84. Legislative interest — "Trademark Counterfeiting Act of 1983 — S 875."

FREEPORT-McMORAN INC., New York, N.Y. Lobbyist — R. Duffy Wall & Associates Inc., 1317 F St. N.W., Washington, D.C. 20004. Filed 3/8/84. Legislative interest — "Issues relating to legislation affecting natural gas pricing. Against legislation to violate the sanctity of contracts for the purchase or sale of domestic natural gas...."

GENERAL DYNAMICS CORP., St. Louis, Mo. Lobbyist — Finley, Kumble, Wagner, Heine, Underberg, Manley & Casey, 1120 Connecticut Ave. N.W., Washington, D.C. 20036. Filed 3/23/84. Legislative interest — "The Universal Telephone Service Preservation Act of 1983, S 1660. We are opposed to this legislation."

GREAT WESTERN FINANCIAL CORP., Beverly Hills, Calif. Lobbyist — Leff & Mason, 1700 Pennsylvania Ave. N.W., Washington, D.C. 20006. Filed 3/1/84. Legislative interest — Not specified.

HERON CORP., Tucson, Ariz. Lobbyist — Leff & Mason, 1700 Pennsylvania Ave. N.W., Washington, D.C. 20006. Filed 3/1/84. Legislative interest — Not specified.

HOECHST-ROUSSEL PHARMACEUTICALS INC., Sommerville, N.J. Lobbyist — Wexler, Reynolds, Harrison & Schule Inc., 1317 F St. N.W., Washington, D.C. 20004. Filed 3/14/84. Legislative interest — "The registrant seeks passage of patent term extension legislation directly related to oral diabetic drugs."

HUSKY OIL LTD., Calgary, Alberta, Canada. Lobbyist — McHenry & Staffier, 1300 19th St. N.W., Washington, D.C. 20036. Filed 3/21/84. Legislative interest — "... HR 5042, S 2362, S 2277, HR 3561, HR 5137, and HR 5153."

INTEL CORP., Santa Clara, Calif. Lobbyist — Ropes & Gray, 1001 22nd St. N.W., Washington, D.C. 20037. Filed 3/23/84. Legislative interest — "Semiconductor Chip Copyright Protection, S 1201, HR 1028, for enactment."

INTERCONTINENTAL BANK, Miami, Fla. Lobbyist — Baker & Botts, 1701 Pennsylvania Ave. N.W., Washington, D.C. 20006. Filed 3/19/84. Legislative interest — "Legislation to amend the Export/Import Bank Act affecting small exports, and related matters."

INTERFIRST BANK FT. WORTH, Ft. Worth, Texas. Lobbyist — Baker & Botts, 1701 Pennsylvania Ave. N.W., Washington, D.C. 20006. Filed 3/19/84. Legislative interest — "Legislation to amend the Export/Import Bank Act affecting small exports, and related matters."

INTERNATIONAL AFFAIRS INC., 7374 Eldorado St., McLean, Va. 22102. Filed for self 3/8/84. Legislative interest — "Issues dealing with international relations & trade." Lobbyist — Donnie E. Wilson.

JMB REALTY CORP., Chicago, Ill. Lobbyist — R. Duffy Wall & Associates Inc., 1317 F St. N.W., Washington, D.C. 20004. Filed 3/8/84. Legislative interest — "Issues relating to real estate taxation."

KYOCERA CORP., Kyoto, Japan. Lobbyist — Global USA Inc., 1823 Jefferson Place N.W., Washington, D.C. 20036. Filed 3/28/84. Legislative interest — ". . . general trade related issues. . . ."

LIBERTY NATIONAL, Birmingham, Ala. Lobbyist — R. Duffy Wall & Associates Inc., 1317 F St. N.W., Washington, D.C. 20004. Filed 3/8/84. Legislative interest — "Issues relating to life insurance taxation."

LIFE OF GEORGIA, Atlanta, Ga. Lobbyist — King & Spalding, 1915 I St. N.W., Washington, D.C. 20006. Filed 3/21/84. Legislative interest — ". . . Tax Reform Act of 1984 (HR 4170) or similar subsequent legislation."

LIFE OF VIRGINIA, Richmond, Va. Lobbyist — R. Duffy Wall & Associates Inc., 1317 F St. N.W., Washington, D.C. 20004. Filed 3/8/84. Legislative interest — "Issues relating to life insurance taxation."

LINCOLN PROPERTY CO., Foster City, Calif. Lobbyist — King & Spalding, 1915 I St. N.W., Washington, D.C. 20006. Filed 3/21/84. Legislative interest — ". . . Tax Reform Act of 1984 (HR 4170) or similar subsequent legislation."

LONGNECKER & ASSOCIATES, P.O. Box 24209, Washington, D.C. 20024. Filed for self 3/2/84. Legislative interest — "General interests will be in the field of Cable Television and Telecommunications . . . specific interest will be affirming: HR 4103 & S 66 . . . specific interest will be against: HR 4229 & HR 4299 . . . or any additional Resolutions or Bills that may be introduced during this session of Congress affecting this issue." Lobbyist — Kenneth T. Longnecker.

LOYAL AMERICAN LIFE INSURANCE CO., Mobile, Ala. Lobbyist — Parry and Romani Associates Inc., 1140 Connecticut Ave. N.W., Washington, D.C. 20036. Filed 3/16/84. Legislative interest — "General insurance related issues."

MANSFIELD & PONTICELLI, 2100 M St. N.W., Washington, D.C. 20037. Filed for self 3/1/84. Legislative interest — "Legislation affecting the construction industry, including infrastructure, capital budgeting, highway programs & gasoline taxes, ERISA, FEC reform, federal procurement, Clean Water Act, Clean Air Act, Federal Election Campaign Act, Surface Transportation Assistance Act." Lobbyist — Anthony M. Ponticelli.

LOUIS T. MARCH ASSOCIATES INC., 1400 I St. N.W., Washington, D.C. 20005. Filed for self 3/21/84. Legislative interest — "The general legislative interests to be pursued are those affecting small businesses and government contractors." Lobbyist — Louis T. March.

MECHANICAL TECHNOLOGY INC., Latham, N.Y. Lobbyist — Ginn & Edington Inc., 121 S. Columbus St., Alexandria, Va. 22314. Filed 3/12/84. Legislative interest — "Dept. of Defense and Dept. of Energy Authorization and Appropriations Bills."

MERCEDES-BENZ OF NORTH AMERICA INC., Montvale, N.J. Lobbyist — O'Connor & Hannan, 1919 Pennsylvania Ave. N.W., Washington, D.C. 20006. Filed 3/22/84. Legislative interest — "To resist efforts in House Ways and Means and Senate Finance Committees to impose arbitrary limitations to tax aspects of ownership of certain automobiles."

MERRILL LYNCH CAPITAL INVESTMENTS, Washington, D.C. Lobbyist — Gray and Co., 3255 Grace St. N.W., Washington, D.C. 20007. Filed 3/22/84. Legislative interest — Not specified.

MESA PETROLEUM CO., Amarillo, Texas. Lobbyist — McNair, Glenn, Konduros, Corley, Singletary, Porter & Dibble, 1155 15th St. N.W., Washington, D.C. 20005. Filed 3/14/84. Legislative interest — "Legislation affecting corporate mergers."

MID-AMERICA ASSOCIATES, Philadelphia, Pa. Lobbyist — Powell, Goldstein, Frazer & Murphy, 1110 Vermont Ave. N.W., Washington, D.C. 20005. Filed 3/12/84. Legislative interest — "Tax legislation dealing with the taxation of insurance company policyholders."

MILLER BREWING CO., Milwaukee, Wis. Lobbyist — King & Spalding, 1730 Pennsylvania Ave. N.W., Washington, D.C. 20006. Filed 3/21/84. Legislative interest — "General legislative interest is in the Malt Beverage Interbrand Competition Act of 1984 (S 1680, HR 2262) and similar legislation."

MOBIL CORP., New York, N.Y. Lobbyist — Wagner & Baroody Inc., 1100 17th St. N.W., Washington, D.C. 20036. Filed 3/26/84. Legislative interest — "Issues affecting the oil and gas industry; oil merger legislation."

MONARCH RESOURCES INC., New York, N.Y. Lobbyist — R. Duffy Wall & Associates Inc., 1317 F St. N.W., Washington, D.C. 20004. Filed 3/8/84. Legislative interest — "Issues relating to life insurance taxation."

D. MOODY & CO. INC., P.O. Box 55389, Tulsa, Okla. 74155. Filed for self 3/14/84. Legislative interest — "Legislation to amend the Walsh-Healey Act." Lobbyist — Dale M. Moody.

MORGAN STANLEY & CO., New York, N.Y. Lobbyist — Covington & Burling, 1201 Pennsylvania Ave. N.W., Washington, D.C. 20044. Filed 3/19/84. Legislative interest — "Legislation affecting mergers and acquisitions, including but not limited to those involving the oil industry such as HR 5042 ('Domestic Petroleum Company Acquisition Act of 1984'); S 2277 ('Domestic Petroleum Company Acquisition Act of 1984'); S 2362 (Mineral Lands Leasing Act of 1920 amendments)." Lobbyist — The Laxalt Corp., 813 Maryland Ave. N.E., Washington, D.C. 20002. Filed 3/23/84. Legislative interest — "Legislation affecting mergers and acquisitions, including but not limited to those involving the oil industry such as HR 5042 ('Domestic Petroleum Company Acquisition Act of 1984'); S 2277 ('Domestic Petroleum Company Act Acquisition of 1984'); S 2362 (Mineral Lands Leasing Act of 1920 amendments)."

MURPHY MOTOR FREIGHT LINES INC., P.O. Box 43640, St. Paul, Minn. 55164. Filed for self 3/7/84. Legislative interest — ". . . Tax Reform Bill of 1983 . . . HR 4170 . . . Section 313 of HR 4170 . . . In favor of passage." Lobbyist — E. L. Murphy Jr.

MUTUAL OF OMAHA INSURANCE CO., Omaha, Neb. Lobbyist — Gray and Co., 3255 Grace St. N.W., Washington, D.C. 20007. Filed 3/22/84. Legislative interest — "Including but not limited to tax legislation."

NATIONAL INVESTMENT DEVELOPMENT CORP., Los Angeles, Calif. Lobbyist — Powell, Goldstein, Frazer & Murphy, 1110 Vermont Ave. N.W., Washington, D.C. 20005. Filed 3/7/84. Legislative interest — "Various Bills Dealing with Amendments to the Internal Revenue Code."

NATIONAL REVENUE CORP., Columbus, Ohio. Lobbyist — The Keefe Co., 444 North Capitol St. N.W., Washington, D.C. 20001. Filed 3/13/84. Legislative interest — "Legislative interest lobbying for House introduction of legislation S 1668 — To authorize contracts retaining private counsel to furnish collection services in the case of indebtedness owed to the U.S."

NEW ENGLAND ELECTRIC SYSTEM, Westborough, Mass. Lobbyist — Wexler, Reynolds, Harrison & Schule Inc., 1317 F St. N.W., Washington, D.C. 20004. Filed 3/29/84. Legislative interest — ". . . to stop legislation overturning a F.E.R.C. decision on Construction Work in Progress."

NEW JERSEY NATURAL GAS CO., 1415 Wyckoff Road, Wall, N.J. 07719. Filed for self 3/29/84. Legislative interest — "... energy, business, regulation and consumer issues, and other issues which may affect the employer's activities." Lobbyist — Daniel M. Klucsik.

NEW YORK STOCK EXCHANGE INC., 11 Wall St., New York, N.Y. 10005. Filed for self 3/1/84. Legislative interest — Not specified. Lobbyists — John L. McConnell, Stephen J. Paradise, David P. Lambert, Henry F. Day, Stephen Storch, 1800 K St. N.W., Washington, D.C. 20006.

NORFOLK SOUTHERN CORP., Washington, D.C. Lobbyist — McNair, Glenn, Konduros, Corley, Singletary, Porter & Dibble, 1155 15th St. N.W., Washington, D.C. 20005. Filed 3/14/84. Legislative interest — "Railroad issues."

NORTH AMERICAN VAN LINES, Fort Wayne, Ind. Lobbyist — Patton, Boggs & Blow, 2550 M St. N.W., Washington, D.C. 20037. Filed 3/22/84. Legislative interest — "To amend HR 4170 so that there is a retention of one year delay in increase of highway use tax for small owner-operators."

OCCIDENTAL CHEMICAL CORP., 1747 Pennsylvania Ave. N.W., Washington, D.C. 20001. Filed for self 3/14/84. Legislative interest — "Federal Issues: International Trade, Environment, Energy." Lobbyist — Harris C. Miller.

OHIO DEPOSIT GUARANTY FUND, Cincinnati, Ohio. Lobbyist — Vorys, Sater, Seymour & Pease, 1828 L St. N.W., Washington, D.C. 20036. Legislative interest — "Financial institutions — regulatory reform."

OVERSEAS MILITARY SALES GROUP, Woodbury, N.Y. Lobbyist — Patton, Boggs & Blow, 2550 M St. N.W., Washington, D.C. 20037. Filed 3/26/84. Legislative interest — "For amendment to end Department of Defense program that authorizes shipment of Japanese autos through Guam at government expense, and substitute a new compensation program that benefits all service members stationed in Japan who incur extra auto-related expenses due to embargo on U.S. cars in Japan. (No specific bills are at this time known.)"

PENNZOIL CO., Washington, D.C. Lobbyist — Patton, Boggs & Blow, 2550 M St. N.W., Washington, D.C. 20037. Filed 3/8/84. Legislative interest — "To extend the expiration of Section 252 of the Energy Policy and Conservation Act, such as HR 4194 and S 1982."

PERFORMANCE ENGINEERING INC., P.O. Box 872, Smithtown, N.Y. 11787. Filed for self 3/30/84. Legislative interest — "U.S. and Foreign Military Sales." Lobbyist — Albert M. Sims.

THE PERMANENTE MEDICAL GROUP INC., Oakland, Calif. Lobbyist — McCutchen, Doyle, Brown & Emerson, 3 Embarcadero Center, San Francisco, Calif. 94111. Filed 3/28/84. Legislative interest — "... employee benefit plans ... sections 404 and 415 of the Internal Revenue Code."

PLANNING RESEARCH CORP., 1500 Planning Research Drive, McLean, Va. 22102. Filed 3/2/84. Legislative interest — "Legislation affecting the professional service industry and impacting the Planning Research Corporation." Lobbyist — Bert M. Concklin.

PORTALS INC., Washington, D.C. Lobbyist — Gray and Co., 3255 Grace St. N.W., Washington, D.C. 20007. Filed 3/22/84. Legislative interest — "Including but not limited to legislation relating to government and private sector sales of security paper."

PPG INDUSTRIES INC., Pittsburgh, Pa. Lobbyist — Cleary, Gottlieb, Steen & Hamilton, 1752 N St. N.W., Washington, D.C. 20036. Filed 3/30/84. Legislative interest — "Proposed and draft amendments to the Natural Gas Policy Act (15 U.S.C. section 3301 *et seq.*), including S 1715 and HR 4277."

QUIXOTE CORP., Washington, D.C. Lobbyist — Gray and Co., 3255 Grace St. N.W., Washington, D.C. 20007. Filed 3/22/84. Legislative interest — "Including but not limited to legislation concerning electronic recording of courtroom proceedings."

RALSTON PURINA CO., Washington, D.C. Lobbyist — Bracewell & Patterson, 1825 I St. N.W., Washington, D.C. 20036. Filed 3/8/84. Legislative interest — "Matters relating to taxes on partnership."

REPUBLICBANK HOUSTON, Houston, Texas. Lobbyist — Baker & Botts, 1701 Pennsylvania Ave. N.W., Washington, D.C.

20006. Filed 3/19/84. Legislative interest — "Legislation to amend the Export/Import Bank Act affecting small exports, and related matters."

RIGGS NATIONAL CORP., Washington, D.C. Lobbyist — Fulbright & Jaworski, 1150 Connecticut Ave. N.W., Washington, D.C. 20036. Filed 3/19/84. Legislative interest — "HR 4170."

RKO, Rockville, Md. Lobbyist — McNair, Glenn, Konduros, Corley, Singletary, Porter and Dibble, 1155 15th St. N.W., Washington, D.C. 20005. Filed 3/14/84. Legislative interest — "Broadcasting matters."

SALOMON BROTHERS INC., Washington, D.C. Lobbyist — Gray and Co., 3255 Grace St. N.W., Washington, D.C. 20007. Filed 3/22/84. Legislative interest — "Including but not limited to legislation affecting corporate mergers."

SANTA FE INTERNATIONAL CORP., Alhambra, Calif. Lobbyist — Gray and Co., 3255 Grace St. N.W., Washington, D.C. 20007. Filed 3/22/84. Legislative interest — "Including but not limited to legislation dealing with Mineral Lands Leasing Act."

SCHULMAN MANAGEMENT CO., Hollywood, Calif. Lobbyist — R. Duffy Wall & Associates Inc., 1317 F St. N.W., Washington, D.C. 20004. Filed 3/8/84. Legislative interest — "Issues relating to real estate taxation."

SCIENCE APPLICATIONS INC., La Jolla, Calif. Lobbyist — D L Associates Inc., 1730 Rhode Island Ave. N.W., Washington, D.C. 20036. Filed 3/26/84. Legislative interest — "S 1730 and HR 2133."

SEAGATE COMMUNITY DEVELOPMENT CORP., Toledo, Ohio. Lobbyist — Vorys, Sater, Seymour & Pease, 1828 L St., Washington, D.C. 20036. Filed 3/1/84. Legislative interest — "Community assistance programs."

SEARS, ROEBUCK AND CO., Chicago, Ill. Lobbyist — Mayer, Brown & Platt, 888 17th St. N.W., Washington, D.C. 20006. Filed 3/1/84. Legislative interest — "Registrant's interest is limited to the Internal Revenue Code and/or the Employee Retirement Income Security Act of 1974."

SHAKLEE CORP., San Francisco, Calif. Lobbyist — Gray and Co., 3255 Grace St. N.W., Washington, D.C. 20007. Filed 3/22/84. Legislative interest — "Including but not limited to tax legislation."

SOLID-TEK SYSTEMS INC., Buffalo, N.Y. Lobbyist — Heron, Burchette, Ruckert & Rothwell, 1200 New Hampshire Ave. N.W., Washington, D.C. 20036. Filed 3/5/84. Legislative interest — "All legislation affecting hazardous waste disposal HR 2867, HR 1813, HR 4915, S 757."

SONY CORP., New York, N.Y. Lobbyist — Parry and Romani Associates Inc., 1140 Connecticut Ave. N.W., Washington, D.C. 20036. Filed 3/5/84. Legislative interest — "Unitary Tax and Greymarket."

SOUTHWESTERN LIFE INSURANCE CO., Dallas, Texas. Lobbyist — R. Duffy Wall & Associates Inc., 1317 F St. N.W., Washington, D.C. 20004. Filed 3/8/84. Legislative interest — "Issues relating to life insurance taxation."

SPARX CORP., New York, N.Y. Lobbyist — Dennis J. Burnett, 6014 Waterbury Court, Springfield, Va. Filed 3/2/84. Legislative interest — "General: Remote Sensing Legislation. Specific: Land Remote Sensing Commercialization Act of 1984 ... HR 4836, S 2292...."

STANDARD OIL COMPANY OF CALIFORNIA, 225 Bush St., San Francisco, Calif. 94105 and 1700 K St. N.W., Washington, D.C. 20006. Lobbyist — Bliss, Craft & Richards, 1050 Thomas Jefferson St. N.W., Washington, D.C. 20007. Filed 3/19/84. Legislative interest — "All legislation in the House and the Senate relating to antimerger." Lobbyist — Corcoran, Hardesty, Whyte, Hemphill & Ligon, 1575 I St. N.W., Washington, D.C. 20005. Filed 3/23/84. Legislative interest —"Monitoring legislation relating to divestiture, divorcement and mergers and the tax treatment thereof." Lobbyist — Latham, Watkins & Hills, 1333 New Hampshire Ave. N.W., Washington, D.C. 20036. Filed 3/20/84. Legislative interest — "... Legislation imposing a moratorium on oil industry acquisitions. ... Against such bills." Lobbyist — Van Ness, Feldman, Sutcliffe, Curtis & Levenberg, 1050 Thomas Jefferson St. N.W., Washington, D.C. 20007. Filed 3/14/84. Legislative interest — "Monitoring Legislation relating to divestiture, divorcement and mergers and the tax treatment thereof." Filed for self 3/14/84. Legislative interest — Not specified. Lobbyist — David T. Van Camp.

STANDARD OIL OF INDIANA, Washington, D.C. Lobbyist — David P. Stang, 1629 K St. N.W., Washington, D.C. 20006. Filed 3/5/84. Legislative interest — "Issues related to the 'Hazardous Substance Response Revenue Act of 1980.'"

TECHLAW, 12011 Lee-Jackson Highway, Fairfax, Va. 22033. Filed for self 3/26/84. Legislative interest — "Environmental & safety laws affecting autos, Clean Air Act, National Traffic and Motor Vehicle Safety Act. . . ."

TEXACO INC., White Plains, N.Y., and Washington, D.C. Lobbyist — Williams & Jensen, 1101 Connecticut Ave. N.W., Washington, D.C. 20036. Filed 3/13/84. Legislative interest — "Various legislative proposals relating to mergers, energy and taxation of interest to the clients and its subsidiaries." Lobbyist — Akin, Gump, Strauss, Hauer & Feld, 1333 New Hampshire Ave. N.W., Washington, D.C. 20036. Filed 3/6/84. Legislative interest — "Hearings and any legislation affecting oil company mergers and acquisitions, including, but not limited to S 2277."

TEXAS INDUSTRIES INC., Dallas, Texas. Lobbyist — Morgan, Lewis & Bockius, 1800 M St. N.W., Washington, D.C. 20036. Filed 3/29/84. Legislative interest — "Finance Leasing Provisions — Tax Reform Act of 1984."

TEXAS INSTRUMENTS INC., Dallas, Texas. Lobbyist — Ginn & Edington Inc., 121 S. Columbus St., Alexandria, Va. 22314. Filed 3/12/84. Legislative interest — "Dept. of Defense Authorization and Appropriations Bills."

UNITED BRANDS CO., New York, N.Y. Lobbyist — Patton, Boggs & Blow, 2550 M St. N.W., Washington, D.C. 20037. Filed 3/22/84. Legislative interest — "In support of a technical amendment concerning foreign lessees of equipment. To amend . . . HR 4170 and . . . S 2062."

UNITED GAS PIPE LINE CO., P.O. Box 1478, Houston, Texas 77001. Filed for self 3/19/84. Legislative interest — ". . . legislation affecting the natural gas industry, including but not limited to: S 615, Natural Gas Consumer Relief Act; HR 1441, Natural Gas Import Policy Act of 1983; S 531, Uniform Relocation Act Amendments of 1983." Lobbyist — Dennis R. McCoy, 1101 17th St. N.W., Washington, D.C. 20036.

UNITED SERVICES LIFE COS., Washington, D.C. Lobbyist — R. Duffy Wall & Associates Inc., 1317 F St. N.W., Washington, D.C. 20004. Filed 3/8/84. Legislative interest — "Issues relating to life insurance taxation."

WARNER COMMUNICATIONS INC., Washington, D.C. Lobbyist — Gray and Co., 3255 Grace St. N.W., Washington, D.C. 20007. Filed 3/22/84. Legislative interest — "Including but not limited to communications legislation."

WESTINGHOUSE ELECTRIC CORP., Pittsburgh, Pa. Lobbyist — Surrey & Morse, 1250 I St. N.W., Washington, D.C. 20005. Filed 3/14/84. Legislative interest — "General interest in legislation dealing with Export Control matters (Export Administration Act) and nuclear export matters."

THE WICKLIFE PARTNERSHIP, Russell, Ohio. Lobbyist — Jones, Day, Reavis & Pogue, 1735 I St. N.W., Washington, D.C. 20006. Filed 3/22/84. Legislative interest — "Desire equitable transition rules for partnership contribution tax changes; changes now contained in HR 4170."

WILLIAMS-KUEBELBECK & ASSOCIATES, Redwood City, Calif. Lobbyist — Robert P. Will, 955 L'Enfant Plaza S.W., Washington, D.C. 20024. Filed 3/13/84. Legislative interest — "Federal public works cost recovery."

International Relations

PROVINCE OF NOVA SCOTIA, Halifax, Nova Scotia, Canada. Lobbyist — Corcoran, Hardesty, Whyte, Hemphill & Ligon, 1575 I St. N.W., Washington, D.C. 20005. Filed 3/7/84. Legislative interest — "Natural gas importation under the Natural Gas Act, Natural Gas Policy Act of 1978, and future legislation."

REPUBLIC OF SOUTH AFRICA, Washington, D.C. Lobbyist — Bill Hecht and Associates Inc., 499 South Capitol St. S.E., Washington, D.C. 20003. Filed 3/12/84. Legislative interest — "All matters of interest to the Republic of South Africa and the territory of Namibia/Southwest Africa, including but not limited to HR 3231 and S 979."

REPUBLIC OF TOGO, Washington, D.C. Lobbyist — David Apter & Associates, 1625 K St. N.W., Washington, D.C. 20006. Filed 2/22/84. Legislative interest — Not specified.

REPUBLIC OF TURKEY, Washington, D.C. Lobbyist — Gray & Co., 3255 Grace St. N.W., Washington, D.C. 20007. Filed 3/22/84. Legislative interest — "Including but not limited to economic and security assistance issues."

Labor Groups

INTERNATIONAL UNION, UNITED AUTOMOBILE, AEROSPACE & AGRICULTURAL IMPLEMENT WORKERS OF AMERICA, 8000 E. Jefferson Ave., Detroit, Mich. 48214. Filed for self 3/1/84. Legislative interest — "International trade and investment legislation, e.g., HR 1234/S 707 - Fair Practices in Automotive Products Act; Export Administration Act; International Trade & Investment Act." Lobbyist — Lee Price, 1757 N St. N.W., Washington, D.C. 20036. Filed for self 3/5/84. Legislative interest — "International Affairs issues such as Central America, South Africa, Export-Import Administration Act and Foreign Aid. Trade issues such as domestic content and reorganization." Lobbyist — Don Stillman, 1757 N St. N.W., Washington, D.C. 20036.

NATIONAL ASSOCIATION OF GOVERNMENT EMPLOYEES, 2139 Wisconsin Ave. N.W., Washington, D.C. 20007. Filed for self 3/19/84. Legislative interest — "All legislation concerning the pay, benefits and working conditions of federal employees." Lobbyist — Edward L. Murphy.

NATIONAL RURAL LETTER CARRIERS' ASSOCIATION, 1448 Duke St., Alexandria, Va. 22314. Filed for self 3/26/84. Legislative interest — Not specified. Lobbyist — Tom W. Griffith.

State and Local Governments

CHELAN (NO. 1) PUBLIC UTILITY DISTRICT, Wenatchee, Wash. Lobbyist — Van Ness, Feldman, Sutcliffe, Curtis & Levenberg, 1050 Thomas Jefferson St. N.W., Washington, D.C. 20007. Filed 3/14/84. Legislative interest — "Monitor all legislation impacting financing of hydroelectric project for fisheries enhancement, fish passage, recreational facilities and other purposes mandated by Federal laws or regulations."

DOUGLAS (NO. 1) PUBLIC UTILITY DISTRICT, Wenatchee, Wash. Lobbyist — Van Ness, Feldman, Sutcliffe, Curtis & Levenberg, 1050 Thomas Jefferson St. N.W., Washington, D.C. 20007. Filed 3/14/84. Legislative interest — "Monitor all legislation impacting financing of hydroelectric project for fisheries enhancement, fish passage, recreational facilities and other purposes mandated by Federal laws or regulations."

EAST BAY REGIONAL PARK DISTRICT, Oakland, Calif. Lobbyist — Philip Chabot, 1317 F St. N.W., Washington, D.C. 20004. Filed 3/1/84. Legislative interest — "Legislative interests are those related generally to park and recreation matters."

GRANT (NO. 2) PUBLIC UTILITY DISTRICT, Wenatchee, Wash. Lobbyist — Van Ness, Feldman, Sutcliffe, Curtis & Levenberg, 1050 Thomas Jefferson St. N.W., Washington, D.C. 20007. Filed 3/14/84. Legislative interest — "Monitor all legislation impacting financing of hydroelectric project for fisheries enhancement, fish passage, recreational facilities and other purposes mandated by Federal laws or regulations."

PEOPLE OF ENEWETAK, Enewetak, Marshall Islands, Trust Territory of the Pacific. Lobbyist — Wilmer, Cutler & Pickering, 1666 K St. N.W., Washington, D.C. 20006. Filed 3/27/84. Legislative interest — "Legislation affecting the U.S. Administration of Enewetak, including legislation dealing with ratification of the Compact of Free Association."

Trade Associations

AMERICAN COUNCIL ON EDUCATION, Washington, D.C. Lobbyist — Bracewell & Patterson, 1825 I St. N.W., Washington, D.C. 20006. Filed 3/8/84. Legislative interest — "Matters relating to the taxation of charitable gifts."

AMERICAN ELECTRONICS ASSOCIATION, 1612 K St. N.W., Washington, D.C. 20006. Filed for self 3/27/84. Legislative interest — "Any legislation affecting business, international trade, or Federal procurement issues pertaining to electronic companies." Lobbyists — Geoffrey A. Feiss, Jean E. Hungiville.

AMERICAN INSTITUTE OF MERCHANT SHIPPING, 1625 K St. N.W., Washington, D.C. 20006. Filed for self 3/28/84. Legislative interest — "Legislation affecting the maritime industry.... HR 1197 ... HR 1307 ... S 768 ... S 822 ... S 865 ... HR 1512 ... HR 1566 ... HR 2114 ... HR 2115, 2222, and 2368 ... S 970 ... S 976 ... S 979 ... S 1037 ... S 1038 ... S 1159 ... S 1197 ... S 1238 ... S 1441 ... HR 2321, 2322 ... HR 2381 ... HR 2406 ... HR 2689 ... HR 2692 ... HR 2853 ... HR 2883...." Lobbyist — Thomas J. Lengyel.

AMERICAN PSYCHOLOGICAL ASSOCIATION, 1200 17th St. N.W., Washington, D.C. 20036. Filed for self 3/19/84. Legislative interest — Not specified. Lobbyists — Michael S. Pallak, Alan G. Kraut, Larry D. Rickards, Joan A. Heffernan, Ruby Takanishi, Deborah J. Marquis, Sarah W. Duffy, Mary Uyeda, Walter Batchelor.

AMERICAN PUBLIC POWER ASSOCIATION, Washington, D.C. Lobbyist — Ely, Ritts, Pietrowski & Brickfield, Watergate 600 Building, Washington, D.C. 20037. Filed 3/20/84. Legislative interest — "S 1069, 'The Construction Work in Progress Policy Act' ... HR 555, 'Construction Work in Progress Policy Act of 1983.' For enactment."

AMERICAN SUGARBEET GROWERS ASSOCIATION, 1156 15th St. N.W., Washington, D.C. 20005. Filed for self 3/19/84. Legislative interest — "Interests include general agricultural policy (Farm Bill, etc.) and specifically the domestic sugar industry." Lobbyist — Ruthann Geib.

ASSOCIATED BUILDERS & CONTRACTORS INC., 729 15th St. N.W., Washington, D.C. 20005. Filed for self 3/5/84. Legislative interest — Not specified. Lobbyists — Charles E. Hawkins III, Debi Hall, Daniel Bennet, Richard F. Ali.

COALITION FOR REGIONAL BANKING AND ECONOMIC DEVELOPMENT, Washington, D.C. Lobbyist — Reynolds, Allen & Cook, 1667 K St. N.W., Washington, D.C. 20006. Filed 3/28/84. Legislative interest — "... will seek to prevent the undermining of each state's rights under federal banking laws to determine its own future with respect to bank expansion across state borders. Bills which may be followed include: S 2113, 'Interstate Banking Act of 1983' and S 2181, 'Financial Services Competitive Equity Act.' "

COALITION OF PUBLICLY TRADED LIMITED PARTNERSHIPS, Washington, D.C. Lobbyist — Chambers Associates Inc., 1411 K St. N.W., Washington, D.C. 20005. Filed 3/27/84. Legislative interest — "Tax Reform Act of 1984 ... HR 4170, HR 821, S 1549 ... Corporate Tax Reform."

CREDIT UNION NATIONAL ASSOCIATION, Washington, D.C. Lobbyist — Sutherland, Asbill & Brennan, 1666 K St. N.W., Washington, D.C. 20006. Filed 3/14/84. Legislative interest — "Oppose legislation to revoke tax-exempt status of credit unions."

FEDERAL JUDGES ASSOCIATION, 1355 Market St., San Francisco, Calif. 94103. Lobbyist — Pierson, Ball & Dowd, 1200 18th St. N.W., Washington, D.C. 20036. (Former U.S. Rep. Charles E. Wiggins, R-Calif., 1967-79, was listed as agent for this client.) Filed 3/1/84. Legislative interest — "All legislation affecting the judiciary." Filed for self 3/1/84. Legislative interest — "All legislation affecting the judiciary." Lobbyist — Spencer Williams.

THE FERTILIZER INSTITUTE, Washington, D.C. Lobbyist — McKenna, Conner & Cuneo, 1575 I St. N.W., Washington, D.C. 20005. Filed 3/6/84. Legislative interest is in the reauthorization of CERCLA ... HR 4813 and HR 4915...."

FOOD MARKETING INSTITUTE, Washington, D.C. Lobbyist — McNair, Glenn, Konduros, Corley, Singletary, Porter

& Dibble, 1155 15th St. N.W., Washington, D.C. 20005. Filed 3/14/84. Legislative interest — "Antitrust ... Malt Beverage Interbrand Competition Act ... S 1680...."

MARITIME INSTITUTE FOR RESEARCH AND INDUSTRIAL DEVELOPMENT, Washington, D.C. Lobbyist — Terrence W. Modglin & Associates, 2001 S St. N.W., Washington, D.C. 20009. Filed 3/9/84. Legislative interest — "HR 4900 and related bills. Panama Canal Authorization Act, Fiscal Year 1985, Provisions on cost of living allowance and retention of military services."

MASSACHUSETTS MEDICAL SOCIETY, 1440 Main St., Waltham, Mass. 02254. Filed for self 3/13/84. Legislative interest — Not specified. Lobbyist — Cornelius J. Foley Jr.

MINING AND RECLAMATION COUNCIL OF AMERICA, 1575 I St. N.W., Washington, D.C. 20005. Filed for self 3/1/84. Legislative interest — Not specified. Lobbyists — Thomas H. Altmeyer, Daniel R. Gerkin.

MOTION PICTURE ASSOCIATION OF AMERICA INC., Washington, D.C. Lobbyist — Parry and Romani Associates Inc., 1140 Connecticut Ave. N.W., Washington, D.C. 20036. Filed 3/5/84. Legislative interest — "Matters affecting the motion picture industry, including S 33 in favor."

THE NATIONAL ASSOCIATION OF LIFE UNDERWRITERS, 1922 F St. N.W., Washington, D.C. 20006. Filed for self 3/15/84. Legislative interest — "Legislation affecting life and health insurance, currently S 1992, HR 4170, S 2181, S 2134." Lobbyists — Danea K. Martin, Michael L. Kerkey, David A. Winston.

NATIONAL ASSOCIATION OF PRIVATE PSYCHIATRIC HOSPITALS, 1319 F St. N.W., Washington, D.C. 20004. Filed for self 3/19/84. Legislative interest — "Issues affecting mental health, hospitals, manpower, and patients." Lobbyists — Lana Buck, Mary Peters.

NATIONAL ASSOCIATION OF REALTORS, 777 14th St. N.W., Washington, D.C. 20005. Filed for self 3/2/84. Legislative interest — "Any and all legislation affecting the real estate industry including specifically tax relief; independent contractor; restructuring of financial institutions; emergency tax proposals to spur housing; rent control; FY '84 budget; spending reductions; and mortgage revenue bonds." Lobbyist — David W. Joyner.

NATIONAL ASSOCIATION OF STATE DIRECTORS OF COMMUNITY & JUNIOR COLLEGES, Olympia, Wash. Lobbyist — Preston, Thorgrimson, Ellis & Holman, 1735 New York Ave. N.W., Washington, D.C. 20006. (Former U.S. Rep. Lloyd Meeds, D-Wash., 1965-79, was listed as agent for this client.) Filed 3/5/84. Legislative interest — "Following legislation: HR 4164, HR 4475, HR 2568, S 249, S 2165, S 108, S 1285, S 801 and other legislation affecting Post Secondary Education."

NATIONAL ASSOCIATION OF TRUCK STOP OPERATORS, 1199 N. Fairfax St., Alexandria, Va. 22314. Filed for self 3/22/84. Legislative interest — "The interests are those that affect the truck stop industry, including but not limited to, fuel and energy issues, trucking and highway regulation, agricultural and food services issues, labor issues, and regulatory reform." Lobbyist — Alan J. Thiemann.

NATIONAL BEER WHOLESALERS ASSOCIATION, Falls Church, Va. Lobbyist — Parry and Romani Associates Inc., 1140 Connecticut Ave. N.W., Washington, D.C. 20036. Filed 3/5/84. Legislative interest — "Matters affecting the alcoholic beverage industry, including S 1680 and HR 2262 in favor."

NATIONAL CUSTOMS BROKERS & FORWARDERS ASSOCIATION OF AMERICA, New York, N.Y. Lobbyist — Kent & O'Connor Inc., 1919 Pennsylvania Ave. N.W., Washington, D.C. 20006. Filed 3/5/84. Legislative interest — "Trade, customs and maritime legislation (no bills designated)."

NATIONAL KNITWEAR & SPORTSWEAR ASSOCIATION, 386 Park Ave. South, New York, N.Y. 10016. Filed for self 3/21/84. Legislative interest — "Registrant's general interest is in legislation affecting United States apparel manufacturing, with particular interest in international trade legislation. Specific bills of interest — HR 3398 (Tariff Schedules Amendment) ... HR 4643 and S 1816 (Textile Fibers and Wool Products Identification Improvement Act)." Lobbyist — Seth M. Bodner.

NATIONAL MULTI-HOUSING COUNCIL, Washington, D.C. Lobbyist — Gray and Co., 3255 Grace St. N.W., Washington, D.C. 20007. Filed 3/22/84. Legislative interest — "Including but not limited to tax legislation."

NATIONAL RESTAURANT ASSOCIATION, 311 First St. N.W., Washington, D.C. 20001. Filed for self 3/12/84. Legislative interest — "Any legislation affecting the restaurant and foodservice industries is of interest to the Association. Generally, this is legislation involving small business, labor laws, wages and hours, taxation, consumer protection, food marketing and economic stabilization." Lobbyist — William P. Fisher.

PRIVATE TRUCK COUNCIL OF AMERICA INC., 2022 P St. N.W., Washington, D.C. 20036. Filed for self 3/8/84. Legislative interest — "The Private Truck Council of America Inc. maintains an interest in Congressional Oversight of the Motor Carrier Act of 1980, and pending legislation in truck safety, sizes and weights, and highway funding matters." Lobbyist — Richard P. Schweitzer.

PROFESSIONAL SERVICES COUNCIL, McLean, Va. Lobbyist — Patton, Boggs & Blow, 2550 M St. N.W., Washington, D.C. 20037. Filed 3/22/84. Legislative interest — "In favor of legislation amending the Small Business Act. . . . Such as HR 2133."

SCIENTIFIC APPARATUS MAKERS ASSOCIATION, Washington, D.C. Lobbyist — Leva, Hawes, Symington & Martin, 815 Connecticut Ave. N.W., Washington, D.C. 20006. Filed 3/26/84. Legislative interest — "Legislation relating to customs and trade matters (HR 3398), seeking modification of one aspect of the bill." Lobbyist — Hogan and Hartson, 815 Connecticut Ave. N.W., Washington, D.C. 20006. Filed 3/29/84. Legislative interest — "Legislation generally to provide tax incentives for high technology companies and in particular HR 4475 and S 2165 to increase research activities, to foster university research and scientific training and to encourage contributions of scientific equipment."

SEMICONDUCTOR INDUSTRY ASSOCIATION, San Jose, Calif. Lobbyist — Hogan & Hartson, 815 Connecticut Ave. N.W., Washington, D.C. 20006. Filed 3/29/84. Legislative interest — "Legislation generally to provide tax incentives for high technology companies and in particular HR 4475 and S 2165 to increase research activities, to foster university research and scientific training and to encourage contributions of scientific equipment."

STEEL TANK INSTITUTE, Northbrook, Ill. Lobbyist — Kent & O'Connor, 1919 Pennsylvania Ave. N.W., Washington, D.C. 20006. Filed 3/6/84. Legislative interest — "Environmental legislation (no bill)."

THE TOBACCO INSTITUTE, Washington, D.C. Lobbyist — Gray and Co., 3255 Grace St. N.W., Washington, D.C. 20007. Filed 3/22/84. Legislative interest — "Including but not limited to legislation and amendments relating to taxation and other issues affecting the tobacco industry."

UNITED SATELLITE ACTION, Washington, D.C. Lobbyist — Finley, Kumble, Wagner, Heine, Underberg, Manley & Casey, 1120 Connecticut Ave. N.W., Washington, D.C. 20036. Filed 3/23/84. Legislative interest — "HR 4464 - 'The International Telecommunications Act of 1983'; we are in support of this legislation."

UNITED STATES LEAGUE OF SAVINGS INSTITUTIONS, Chicago, Ill. Lobbyist — Leff & Mason, 1700 Pennsylvania Ave. N.W., Washington, D.C. 20006. Filed 3/1/84. Legislative interest — Not specified.

U.S. PHOTOVOLTAICS MANUFACTURERS' AD HOC COMMITTEE, Washington, D.C. Lobbyist — Bliss, Craft & Richards, 1050 Thomas Jefferson St. N.W., Washington, D.C. 20007. Filed 3/26/84. Legislative interest — "All legislation in the House and the Senate relating to tax legislation providing tax credits for solar voltaic equipment."

VOLUME FOOTWEAR RETAILERS OF AMERICA, Washington, D.C. Lobbyist — R. Duffy Wall & Associates Inc., 1317 F St. N.W., Washington, D.C. 20004. Filed for self 3/8/84. Legislative interest — "Issues relating to the restrictions on the importation of new rubber footwear."

WASHINGTON PUBLIC UTILITY DISTRICTS' ASSOCIATION INC., Seattle, Wash. Lobbyist — Thomas P. Graves, 410 11th St. S.E., Washington, D.C. 20003. Filed 3/5/84. Legislative interest — Not specified.

WESTERN INDEPENDENT BANKERS, 167 S. San Antonio Road, Los Altos, Calif. 94022. Filed for self 3/12/84. Legislative interest — "Banking." Lobbyist — Jon C. Bednerik.

Miscellaneous

PETER ALLSTROM, 400 Seward Square S.E., Washington, D.C. 20003. Filed for self 3/27/84. Legislative interest — "General interest in Immigration Policy; specific interests in the immigration reform and control legislation now pending; supporting amendments and passage of balanced legislation."

BARTHOLOMEW COUNTY HOSPITAL, Columbus, Ind. Lobbyist — Ice, Miller, Donadio & Ryan, One American Square, Indianapolis, Ind. 46282. Filed 3/13/84. Legislative interest — ". . . proposed amendments to Title 18 of the Social Security Act, including Senate Bill S 2352 '[t]o provide equitable treatment for certain hospitals in high wage areas.' We are in favor of such proposed amendments."

EDWARD M. BURNS, 14 Beacon St., Boston, Mass. 02108. Filed for self 3/12/84. Legislative interest — Not specified.

CHILI-USA, 1919 Pennsylvania Ave. N.W., Washington, D.C. 20006. Filed for self 3/6/84. Legislative interest — "For H J Res 465, a Joint Resolution to provide for the designation of chili as the official food of the United States of America." Lobbyist — R. N. Dunagan III.

COMMON CAUSE, 2030 M St. N.W., Washington, D.C. 20036. Filed for self 3/21/84. Legislative interest — ". . . are in such areas as open government, campaign finance reform, Federal Election Commission, Lobby disclosure, government ethics, Senate confirmation process, extension of the Clean Air Act, court jurisdiction issues, congressional budget process, congressional reform, freedom of information, energy policy, waste in government, merit selection of Federal Judges and U.S. Attorneys, regulatory reform, public participation in federal agency proceedings, Legal Services Corporation, the Equal Rights Amendment, and nuclear arms control and military spending. . . ."

COMPETITIVE ENTERPRISE INSTITUTE, 2039 New Hampshire Ave. N.W., Washington, D.C. 20009. Filed for self 3/16/84. Legislative interest — Not specified. Lobbyists — Fred L. Smith, Cesar V. Conda.

CONSERVATIVE ALLIANCE, 1001 Prince St., Alexandria, Va. 22314. Filed for self 3/28/84. Legislative interest — "Human Rights and National Survival Act of 1984 — Legislation as of date of filing has not been introduced." Lobbyist — R. D. Patrick Mahoney.

CONSUMER FEDERATION OF AMERICA, 1314 14th St. N.W., Washington, D.C. 20005. Filed for self 3/14/84. Legislative interest — "Specifically: HR 2668, Consumer Product Safety Commission Reauthorization: For. S 44, Product Liability Act: Against. Natural Gas Decontrol: Against. S 730, Usury Ceiling Preemption: Against. HR 1742, Credit Control Act: For. HR 555, Construction Work in Progress Act: For . . . Generally support legislation which we believe benefits consumers' overall health, safety and pocketbook. Oppose legislation which harms same." Lobbyist — Glenn Nishimura.

THE ENVIRONMENTAL FUND, 1302 18th St. N.W., Washington, D.C. 20036. Filed for self 3/22/84. Legislative interest — "HR 1510/S 529, The Immigration Reform and Control Act (for). S 2140, The Immigration Ceilings Act (for). HR 3070, The Critical Trends Assessment Act. HR 907/S 1771, The Global Resources, Environment and Population Act (undecided). Unnumbered, The annual appropriations bill for State, Justice, Commerce, The Judiciary, and Related Agencies." Lobbyist — Charles Vern Dinges IV.

JOHN R. EVANS, 9208 Seven Locks Road, Bethesda, Md. 20817. Filed for self 3/23/84. Legislative interest — ". . . will be primarily issues in connection with securities, banking, and housing laws and other economic and financial matters. Present activity is in opposition to legislation to prohibit oil company mergers temporarily or permanently and in support of legislation to broaden the authority of the National Corporation of Housing Partnerships."

FOND DU LAC RESERVATION, Cloquet, Minn. Lobbyist — Manny D. Fierro, 1555 Wilson Blvd., Rosslyn, Va. 22209. Filed 3/5/84. Legislative interest — "Legislative issue related to American Indians."

DAVID TROY SAXTON GETTY, P.O. Box 7000-A, Texarkana, Texas 75501. Filed for self 3/26/84. Legislative interest — "U.S. Constitutional Amendments, Bill of Rights, FOI & Privacy Acts, Criminal Justice Act, Immigration & Nationality Acts, United States Postal Service, Bureau of Land Management, Equal Opportunity Employment Act, Social Security Act, U.S. Bureau of Prisons, United States Parole Commission, Fair Credit Reporting Act, Federal Communications Commission, House and Senate proposals, bills, and statutes numbers of same."

GREAT LAKES INDIAN FISH AND WILDLIFE COMMISSION, Odanah, Wis. Lobbyist — Manny D. Fierro, 1555 Wilson Blvd., Rosslyn, Va. 22209. Filed 3/5/84. Legislative interest — "Legislative issues related to Great Lakes Fish & Wildlife Management."

JAMES L. KANE JR., 1315 Vincent Place, McLean, Va. 22101. Filed for self 3/6/84. Legislative interest — "Housing, Banking, Federal Construction, Small Business."

ELROY J. KULAS TRUST NO. 1, 900 Euclid Ave., Cleveland, Ohio. 44101. Lobbyist — Jones, Day, Reavis & Pogue, 1735 I St. N.W., Washington, D.C. 20006. Filed 3/5/84. Legislative interest — "Legislation of interest to charitable foundations, e.g., HR 3043."

LaPORTE HOSPITAL INC., Laporte, Ind. Lobbyist — Ice, Miller, Donadio & Ryan, One American Square, Indianapolis, Ind. 46282. Filed 3/13/84. Legislative interest — "... proposed amendments to Title 18 of the Social Security Act, including Senate Bill S 2352 '[t]o provide equitable treatment for certain hospitals in high wage areas.' We are in favor of such proposed amendments."

JAMES D. & LOIS M. LaROSA AND JAMES J. LaROSA, Clarksville, W.Va., and Bridgeport, W.Va. Lobbyist — Cole & Corette, 1110 Vermont Ave. N.W., Washington, D.C. 20005. Filed 3/22/84. Legislative interest — "Representation of client concerning pending tax reform legislation in the House and Senate of Congress as it affects intra-family Interest-Free Loans."

MARION GENERAL HOSPITAL, Marion, Ind. Lobbyist — Ice, Miller, Donadio & Ryan, One American Square, Indianapolis, Ind. 46282. Filed 3/13/84. Legislative interest — "... proposed amendments to Title 18 of the Social Security Act, including Senate Bill S 2352 '[t]o provide equitable treatment for certain hospitals in high wage areas.' We are in favor of such proposed amendments."

NATIONAL ASSOCIATION OF ARAB AMERICANS, 2033 M St. N.W., Washington, D.C. 20036. Filed for self 3/7/84. Legislative interest — "Middle East related legislation ... FY '84 Foreign Assistance ... S 637, HR 1850. ..." Lobbyists — Claire Pettengill, Nizar Jwaideh.

NATIONAL CLEAN AIR COALITION, 530 7th St. S.E., Washington, D.C. 20003. Filed for self 3/14/84. Legislative interest — "These are to provide legislation to preserve, restore, and insure the rational use of the ecosphere, particularly legislation dealing with clean air issues: HR 145; HR 3400; HR 4404; S 132; S 768; S 769; and S 2159." Lobbyist — Samuel E. Collier.

NATIONAL COMMITTEE TO PRESERVE SOCIAL SECURITY, Washington, D.C. Lobbyist — James C. Corman, 1420 16th St. N.W., Washington, D.C. 20036. (Former U.S. rep., D-Calif., 1961-81.) Filed 3/13/84. Legislative interest — "To advocate federal legislation and regulations affecting Social Security and Medicare programs."

NEIGHBORHOOD HOUSING SERVICES OF AMERICA, 1951 Webster St., Oakland, Calif. 94612. Filed for self 3/20/84. Legislative interest — "Legislation directly affecting the efforts of Neighborhood Housing Services programs such as a joint Congressional Resolution authorizing the President to proclaim a

national NHS Week; the Housing and Community Development Amendments and/or legislation making appropriations for HUD & Independent Agencies." Lobbyist — Mary Lynn Reilly.

ORGANIZATION OF CHINESE AMERICANS, 2025 I St. N.W., Washington, D.C. 20006. Filed for self 3/28/84. Legislative interest — "Advance the interests of Chinese Americans, including immigration bills HR 1510, S 529 (against); HR 4909 (for); HR 2131 (for); amend Communications Act HR 3105 (for)." Lobbyist — Laura Chin.

REVIVAL WAY HOUSE OF PRAYER OF JESUS CHRIST INC., Memphis, Tenn. Filed for self 3/2/84. Legislative interest — "Education (Theology & Religious Education)." Lobbyist — Bishop Willie J. Morris Sr.

SMITH RIVER ALLIANCE, Crescent City, Calif. Lobbyist — David M. Weiman, 517 Albany Ave., Tacoma Park, Md. 20912. Filed 3/21/84. Legislative interest — "Defense Production Act, S 1852."

April Registrations

Corporations and Businesses

AGRI-ENERGY INC., Crookston, Minn. Lobbyist — Heron, Burchette, Ruckert & Rothwell, 1200 New Hampshire Ave. N.W., Washington, D.C. 20036. Filed 4/12/84. Legislative interest — "Support legislation to extend energy investment tax credits for renewable fuel projects. Support increased excise tax exemption for alcohol enhanced fuels."

ALLAN RONSON CO., La Jolla, Calif. Lobbyist — The William Chasey Organization, 1800 K St. N.W., Washington, D.C. 20006. Filed 4/13/84. Legislative interest — "Admit Certain Passenger Vessels to the Coastal Trade. HR 2883; HR 4333; S 1197."

ALLEGHENY INTERNATIONAL, Pittsburgh, Pa. Lobbyist — Morgan, Lewis & Bockius, 1800 M St. N.W., Washington, D.C. 20036. Filed 4/9/84. Legislative interest — "Tax Reform Act of 1984."

ALLIANCE FOR CLEAN ENERGY UNION PACIFIC RAILROAD, New York, N.Y. Lobbyist — Cummings & Lockwood, 1090 Vermont Ave. N.W., Washington, D.C. 20005. Filed 4/2/84. Legislative interest — "Elimination of acid rain."

ALLSTATE INSURANCE GROUP, Northbrook, Ill. Lobbyist — Carl M. Parks, 633 Pennsylvania Ave. N.W., Washington, D.C. 20004. Filed 4/16/84. Legislative interest — "Legislation generally affecting companies of the Allstate Insurance Group, including the property and casualty lines, life, health and commercial insurance, and financial institutions. Also, a general interest in legislation on antitrust, arson and fire safety, automobile (including damageability, safety and theft), bankruptcy, consumer issues, drunk driving, financial institutions, investments and securities, labor relations, pensions, privacy, product liability, taxation, telecommunications, and trade."

AMERICAN EXPRESS CORP., New York, N.Y. Lobbyist — Gray and Co., 3255 Grace St. N.W., Washington, D.C. 20007. Filed 4/10/84. Legislative interest — "Including but not limited to the credit card surcharge legislation."

AMERICAN HOECHST CORP., Somerville, N.J. Lobbyist — Swidler, Berlin & Strelow, 1000 Thomas Jefferson St. N.W., Washington, D.C. 20007. Filed 4/2/84. Legislative interest — "Passage of patent restoration legislation."

AMERICAN SOUTHWEST FINANCIAL CO., Tucson, Ariz. Lobbyist — Bracy Williams & Co., 1000 Connecticut Ave. N.W., Washington, D.C. 20036. Filed 4/20/84. Legislative interest — "Issues concerning the building industry, specifically tax legislation. S Con Res 91 (for); H Con Res 253 (for)."

ARIZONA PUBLIC SERVICE CO., P.O. Box 21666, Phoenix, Ariz. 85036. Filed for self 4/24/84. Legislative interest — "Bills that impact the operation of an electric and gas utility; clean air, DOE budget, clean water, hazardous waste, endangered species, nuclear waste." Lobbyist — Terry D. Hudgins.

BANK OF BOSTON CORP., 100 Federal St., Boston,

Mass. 02110. Filed for self 4/9/84. Legislative interest — Not specified. Lobbyist — Deirdre B. Phillips.

BANK AMERILEASE GROUP, San Francisco, Calif. Lobbyist — James C. Corman, 1420 16th St. N.W., Washington, D.C. 20036. (Former U.S. rep., D-Calif., 1961-81.) Filed 4/16/84. Legislative interest — "To monitor proposed legislation and treasury regulations and all pending matters affecting the Leasing Industry."

BANKERS TRUST CO., New York, N.Y. Lobbyist — Manatt, Phelps, Rothenberg & Tunney, 1200 New Hampshire Ave. N.W., Washington, D.C. 20036. Filed 4/13/84. Legislative interest — "Legislation relating to the banking industry."

BAUMANN INC., Barrington, Ill. Lobbyist — Gnau, Carter, Jacobsen and Associates Inc., 1250 I St. N.W., Washington, D.C. 20005. Filed 4/16/84. Legislative interest — "Legislation affecting the importation of foreign goods and the solicitation of goods to the government."

BEAR STEARNS & CO., New York, N.Y. Lobbyist — Reid & Priest, 1111 19th St. N.W., Washington, D.C. 20036. Filed 4/17/84. Legislative interest — "Revisions of the Internal Revenue Code Relating to discount obligations and taxation of securities under HR 4170 and HR 2163."

BECHTEL GROUP INC., 50 Beale St., San Francisco, Calif. 94119. Filed for self 4/5/84. Legislative interest — ". . . all matters which may be of special interest to an international engineering and construction enterprise." Lobbyist — W. Kenneth Davis, 209 Fairhills Drive, San Rafael, Calif. 94901.

BERMANS, THE LEATHER EXPERTS, Brooklyn Park, Minn. Lobbyist — Paul H. DeLaney Jr., 1120 20th St. N.W., Washington, D.C. 20036. Filed 4/27/84. Legislative interest — "International trade considerations."

BINGHAM, DANA & GOULD, Boston, Mass. Lobbyist — Miller & Chevalier, 655 15th St. N.W., Washington, D.C. 20005. Filed 4/16/84. Legislative interest — "Legislation affecting Title 26 of the U.S. Code."

BLAIR & BLAIR LTD., 1120 19th St. N.W., Washington, D.C. 20036. Filed for self 4/13/84. Legislative interest — ". . . Clean Air Act; Acidic Deposition Study and Ecosystem Mitigation Act; National Acidic Deposition Control Act of 1983 . . . HR 3400 and HR 1405. . . . Will lobby against HR 3400 and for HR 1405." Lobbyist — Steven R. Blair.

BURGESS & LEITH INC., Boston, Mass. Lobbyist Sullivan & Worcester, 1025 Connecticut Ave. N.W., Washington, D.C. 20036. Filed 4/24/84. Legislative interest — "To oppose enactment of new Sections 1276 and 1277 and related sections to the Internal Revenue Code of 1954, as amended."

BURLINGTON NORTHERN, Billings, Mont. Lobbyist — Crowell & Moring, 1100 Connecticut Ave. N.W., Washington, D.C. 20036. Filed 4/20/84. Legislative interest — "Supporting enactment of legislation to repeal a section of the Mineral Leasing Act of 1920 concerning Federal coal lease ownership."

THE BURNELLI CO. INC., Accomac, Va. Lobbyist — Aker Associates Inc., 1341 G St. N.W., Washington, D.C. 20005. Filed 4/17/84. Legislative interest — "Any legislative interest relating to aviation."

CATERPILLAR TRACTOR CO., 100 N.E. Adams St., Peoria, Ill. 61629. Lobbyist — McDermott, Will and Emery, 1850 K St. N.W., Washington, D.C. 20006. Filed 4/13/84. Legislative interest — "Issues regarding the taxation of related party transactions and foreign sales corporation legislation." Filed for self 4/12/84. Legislative interest — ". . . Employee Relations issues. Have followed developments of deficit downpayment bills in House and Senate as they pertain to Employee Relations issues (HR 4170, S 2062)." Lobbyist — Douglas P. Crew. Filed for self 4/12/84. Legislative interest — ". . . primarily corporate taxation and economic policy, with involvement in environment, employee relations, trade, and other domestic and international issues which may affect Caterpillar Tractor Co. Example of a specific interest is HR 4170." Lobbyist — David A. Henson.

CENERGY EXPLORATION CO., Dallas, Texas. Lobbyist — D'Amico, Luedtke, Demarest & Golden, 1920 N St. N.W., Washington, D.C. 20036. Filed 4/10/84. Legislative interest — "Natural gas legislation."

CENTRAL TRANSPORT, Sterling Heights, Mich. Lobbyist — Linton, Mields, Reisler & Cottone, 1015 18th St. N.W., Washington, D.C. 20036. Filed 4/19/84. Legislative interest — "We will monitor congressional consideration of the collective bargaining agreements in bankruptcy reorganization."

CHADBOURNE, PARKE, WHITESIDE & WOLFF, 1101 Vermont Ave. N.W., Washington, D.C. 20005. Filed for self 4/19/84. Legislative interest — "HR 2163, HR 4170 and other tax legislation." Lobbyist — Leslie J. Schreyer.

CHEVRON U.S.A. INC., Washington, D.C. Lobbyist — Pillsbury, Madison & Sutro, 1050 17th St. N.W., Washington, D.C. 20036. Filed 4/2/84. Legislative interest — "Monitoring legislation relating to divestiture, divorcement & mergers, and tax treatment thereof." Lobbyist — Pierson, Ball & Dowd, 1200 18th St. N.W., Washington, D.C. 20036. (Former U.S. Rep. Charles E. Wiggins, R-Calif., 1967-79, was listed as agent for this client.) Filed 4/5/84. Legislative interest — "Any legislation affecting corporate mergers."

CHRONAR CORP., Princeton, N.J. Lobbyist — O'Connor & Hannan, 1919 Pennsylvania Ave. N.W., Washington, D.C. 20006. (Former U.S. Rep. Thomas B. Evans Jr., R-Del., 1977-83, was listed as agent for this client.) Filed 4/26/84. Legislative interest — "Represent generally matters of interest to the client including, but not limited to, providing tax credits for photovoltaic energy."

CH2M HILL, Corvallis, Ore. Lobbyist — Elaine J. Jones, 1201 Pennsylvania Ave. N.W., Washington, D.C. 20004. Filed 4/16/84. Legislative interest — ". . . the environment; public health and safety; public works, transportation, water, energy, military construction; and governmental procurement."

THE CLEVELAND ELECTRIC ILLUMINATING CO., Cleveland, Ohio. Filed for self 4/30/84. Legislative interest — "Legislative activities affecting electric utilities in nuclear, clean air, finance and other related areas." Lobbyist — Linda Carol Haslett, 10 N. Center Road, Perry, Ohio 44081.

COLUMBIA INC., Fairfield, N.J. Lobbyist — Patton, Boggs & Blow, 2550 M St. N.W., Washington, D.C. 20037. Filed 4/27/84. Legislative interest — "Legislation amending the Copyright Act that affects the home recording of television and radio broadcasts and the 'first sale' doctrine such as HR 175, S 175, S 3131, S 3132, and S 3133."

COMMUNITY CARE SYSTEMS INC., Boston, Mass. Lobbyist — Schlossberg-Cassidy & Associates Inc., 955 L'Enfant Plaza S.W., Washington, D.C. 20024. Filed 4/10/84. Legislative interest — "Legislation relating to health care, financing and administration."

CONSOLIDATED NATURAL GAS CO., New York, N.Y. Lobbyist — Philip D. Morrison, 1700 Pennsylvania Ave. N.W., Washington, D.C. 20006. Filed 4/23/84. Legislative interest — "Generally, all legislation relating to federal income taxation of corporations. Specifically, lobbying relating to Tax Act of 1984."

CONTROL DATA CORP., 1201 Pennsylvania Ave. N.W., Washington, D.C. 20004. Filed for self 4/11/84. Legislative interest — "Assist Control Data Corporation in furnishing technical and legal services in connection with Congressional consideration of amendments to or replacement of the Communications Act of 1934, and other legislation affecting communications, information and computers." Lobbyist — William H. Warner.

CORPORACION NACIONAL DEL COBRE, Santiago, Chile. Lobbyist — Anderson & Pendleton, 1000 Connecticut Ave. N.W., Washington, D.C. 20036. Filed 4/20/84. Legislative interest — "Legislation affecting copper."

CRUISE AMERICA LINES INC., Fort Lauderdale, Fla. Lobbyist — George H. Denison, 4801 Massachusetts Ave. N.W., Washington, D.C. 20016. Filed 4/27/84. Legislative interest — "General interest in legislation affecting the domestic cruise industry. Specific interest in S 1197 and HR 2883, bills 'to admit certain passenger vessels to the coastwise trade,' legislation which Cruise America favors."

DAFASCO INC., 1330 Burlington St. East, Hamilton, Ontario, Canada L8N 3J5. Filed for self 4/24/84. Legislative interest — ". . . Fair Trade in Steel Act . . . S 2380/HR 5081. . . . In opposition to any legislation which restricts imports of steel mill products from Canada." Lobbyist — John A. Armstrong.

DAIN BOSWORTH INC., Minneapolis, Minn. Lobbyist — Foley & Lardner, 1775 Pennsylvania Ave. N.W., Washington, D.C. 20006. Legislative interest — ". . . those provisions of HR 4170 and HR 2163 relating to student loan bonds."

DAKOTA LAY'D EGG CO., Cando, N.D. Lobbyist — Hagedorn-Cando Inc., 1201 S. Jefferson-Davis Highway, Arlington, Va. 22202. (Former U.S. Rep. Tom Hagedorn, R-Minn., 1975-83, was listed as agent for this client.) Filed 4/9/84. Legislative interest — "HR 4647 - a bill to reduce tariffs on dried egg yolks."

D'ANCONA & PFLAUM, Chicago, Ill. Lobbyist — Williams & Jensen, 1101 Connecticut Ave. N.W., Washington, D.C. 20036. Filed 4/19/84. Legislative interest — "Federal income, estate, and gift tax legislation of interest to the law firm and its clients."

DEAN WITTER REALTY INC., New York, N.Y. Lobbyist — R. Duffy Wall & Associates Inc., 1317 F St. N.W., Washington, D.C. 20004. Filed 4/2/84. Legislative interest — "Issues relating to real estate taxation."

DEERE & CO., Moline, Ill. Lobbyist — Dickey, Knorr & Moore, 1825 I St. N.W., Washington, D.C. 20006. Filed 4/10/84. Legislative interest — "Legislation of interest will concern proposals which alter, amend or otherwise affect the internal revenue code as it relates to the activities of corporations and businesses."

DRUMMOND CO., Jasper, Ala. Lobbyist — Kaye, Scholer, Fierman, Hays & Handler, 1575 I St. N.W., Washington, D.C. 20005. Filed 4/10/84. Legislative interest — "General legislation affecting the coal industry."

EDSI, Ann Arbor, Mich. Lobbyist — Gnau, Carter, Jacobsen and Associates Inc., 1250 I St. N.W., Washington, D.C. 20005. Filed 4/16/84. Legislative interest — "Research and development funding and continuing funding from various agencies within the Federal government for energy cost savings programs."

ENDOWMENT MANAGEMENT & RESEARCH CORP., Boston, Mass. Lobbyist — Sullivan & Worcester, 1025 Connecticut Ave. N.W., Washington, D.C. 20036. Filed 4/24/84. Legislative interest — "To oppose enactment of new Sections 1276 and 1277 and related sections to the Internal Revenue Code of 1954, as amended."

ENHANCED ENERGY RESOURCES INC., Sugarland, Texas. Lobbyist — D'Amico, Luedtke, Demarest & Golden, 1920 N St. N.W., Washington, D.C. 20036. Filed 4/10/84. Legislative interest — "Natural gas legislation."

THE EQUITABLE LIFE ASSURANCE SOCIETY OF THE UNITED STATES, 1285 Avenue of the Americas, New York, N.Y. 10019. Filed for self 4/5/84. Legislative interest — "Life Insurance Taxation." Lobbyist — Harry D. Garber.

FIRST CHICAGO LEASING CORP., Chicago, Ill. Lobbyist — James C. Corman, 1420 16th St. N.W., Washington, D.C. 20036. (Former U.S. rep., D-Calif., 1961-81.) Filed 4/16/84. Legislative interest — "To monitor proposed legislation and treasury regulations and all pending matters affecting the Leasing Industry."

THE FIRST NATIONAL BANK OF BOSTON, 100 Federal St., Boston, Mass. 02110. Lobbyist — James C. Corman, 1420 16th St. N.W., Washington, D.C. 20036. (Former U.S. rep., D-Calif., 1961-81.) Filed 4/16/84. Legislative interest — "To monitor proposed legislation and treasury regulations and all pending matters affecting the Leasing Industry." Filed for self 4/9/84. Legislative interest — Not specified. Lobbyist — Deirdre B. Phillips.

FIRST NATIONAL BANK OF MINNEAPOLIS, Minneapolis, Minn. Lobbyist — James C. Corman, 1420 16th St. N.W., Washington, D.C. 20036. (Former U.S. rep., D-Calif., 1961-81.) Filed 4/16/84. Legislative interest — "To monitor proposed legislation and treasury regulations and all pending matters affecting the Leasing Industry."

GATX LEASING CORP., San Francisco, Calif. Lobbyist — James C. Corman, 1420 16th St. N.W., Washington, D.C. 20036. (Former U.S. rep., D-Calif., 1961-81.) Filed 4/16/84. Legislative interest — "To monitor proposed legislation and treasury regulations and all pending matters affecting the Leasing Industry."

GENERAL ELECTRIC CREDIT CORP., Stamford, Conn. Lobbyist — James C. Corman, 1420 16th St. N.W., Wash-

ington, D.C. 20036. (Former U.S. rep., D-Calif., 1961-81.) Filed 4/16/84. Legislative interest — "To monitor proposed legislation and treasury regulations and all pending matters affecting the Leasing Industry."

GENERAL PUBLIC UTILITIES CORP., Parsippany, N.J. Lobbyist — Miller & Chevalier, 655 15th St. N.W., Washington, D.C. 20005. Filed 4/16/84. Legislative interest — "Revisions to federal laws and regulations in regard to emergency evacuation plans in areas adjacent to nuclear power plants."

GEORGE PALMITER RIVER MANAGEMENT CONSULTANT CO., Risingsun, Ohio. Lobbyist — Thomas J. Barlow III, 4717 Drummond Ave., Chevy Chase, Md. 20815. Filed 4/11/84. Legislative interest — Not specified.

GEORGIA-PACIFIC CORP., 133 Peachtree St. N.E., Atlanta, Ga. 30303. Filed for self 4/17/84. Legislative interest — "Future legislation that will be covered is legislation directly or indirectly affecting interests of the forest products industry as well as matters relating to gypsum, coal, gas and chemicals. Specific future legislative interests will include environment (Clean Water Act, Clean Air Act, Superfund) and health and chemical safety laws through FFDCA, OSHA, CPSC AND FHSA." Lobbyist — C. T. Howlett Jr., 1875 I St. N.W., Washington, D.C. 20006.

GODFREY ASSOCIATES INC., 918 16th St. N.W., Washington, D.C. 20006. Filed for self 4/27/84. Legislative interest — "Primary area of interest in agricultural legislation - the farm bill as it pertains to sugar. Also follow closely labor, tax and environmental issues as related to agriculture." Lobbyist — Michael L. Morton.

GOLDEN NUGGET INC., Las Vegas, Nev. Lobbyist — James E. Ritchie, 499 S. Capitol St. S.W., Washington, D.C. 20003. Filed 4/12/84. Legislative interest — "Monitor Legislation: S 1876 - A bill to allow Advertising of any State-sponsored lottery, gift enterprise, or similar scheme. HR 5097 - A bill to allow Advertising of any State sponsored lottery, gift enterprise, or similar scheme."

GTE SPRINT COMMUNICATIONS, Washington, D.C. Lobbyist — McNair, Glenn, Konduros, Corley, Singletary, Porter & Dibble, 1155 15th St. N.W., Washington, D.C. 20005. Filed 4/11/84. Legislative interest — "Legislation affecting the communications industry." Lobbyist — Patton, Boggs & Blow, 2550 M St. N.W., Washington, D.C. 20037. Filed 4/27/84. Legislative interest — "Interested in incorporating the International Trade Commission's amendment regarding tax exempt definition into the Boat Safety Bill, HR 2163."

GULF COAST WASTE DISPOSAL AUTHORITY, Houston, Texas. Lobbyist — John D. Raffaelli, 1317 F St. N.W., Washington, D.C. 20004. Filed 4/2/84. Legislative interest — "Issues relating to tax-exempt finance."

HALLMARK CARDS INC., 1201 Pennsylvania Ave. N.W., Washington, D.C. 20004. Lobbyist — Miller & Chevalier, 655 15th St. N.W., Washington, D.C. 20005. Filed 4/10/84. Legislative interest — "Interest is in tax legislation which might have an impact on the business of employer." Filed for self 4/13/84. Legislative interest — "Interest is in tax legislation which might have an impact on the business of employer." Lobbyist — Rae F. Evans.

HARRIS CORP., 2600 Virginia Ave. N.W., Washington, D.C. 20037. Filed for self 4/10/84. Legislative interest — "Defense Authorization - For. Defense Appropriations - For." Lobbyists — William A. Doyle, Thomas H. O'Brien.

HARTFORD FIRE INSURANCE CO., Hartford, Conn. Lobbyist — Kaye, Scholer, Fierman, Hays & Handler, 1575 I St. N.W., Washington, D.C. 20005. Filed 4/12/84. Legislative interest — "General and tax legislation affecting insurance companies."

HAWAIIAN ELECTRIC CO. INC., Honolulu, Hawaii. Lobbyist — Cades, Schutte, Fleming & Wright, 1001 22nd St. N.W., Washington, D.C. 20037. Filed 4/17/84. Legislative interest — ". . . Tax legislation."

HAZOX INC., Wilmington, Del. Lobbyist — Joseph Browder, 1317 F St. N.W., Washington, D.C. 20004. Filed 4/17/84. Legislative interest — "HR 3129, other hazardous waste legislation."

THE HIGH FRONTIER GROUP, P.O. Box 5768, Charlottesville, Va. 22905-0768. Filed for self 4/30/84. Legislative interest — "Defense policy, space policy freeze: against. Quick freeze: against. MX funding: for. Sale of earth sensing satellites to private concerns: against. Funding for civilian space station: for." Lobbyist — Thomas W. J. C. McCrystal.

HOLLAND ASSOCIATES, Hampton, Va. Lobbyist — Holtzman & Associates, 214 Massachusetts Ave. N.E., Washington, D.C. 20002. Filed 4/14/84. Legislative interest — "General legislative interests: passage of private legislation allowing fishing vessel to fish and engage in coastal trading. Specific legislative interests: Fishery Conservation and Management Act of 1975, oppose."

HOLLYWOOD MARINE SERVICES INC., Houston, Texas. Lobbyist — Camp, Carmouche, Barsh, Hunter, Gray & Hoffman, 2550 M St. N.W., Washington, D.C. 20037. Filed 4/13/84. Legislative interest — "S 1739."

HOSPITAL CORPORATION OF AMERICA, 2000 L St. N.W., Washington, D.C. 20036. Filed for self 4/9/84. Legislative interest — "Tax and Health related legislation." Lobbyist — James P. Smith.

HUSKY OIL LTD., Calgary, Alberta, Canada. Lobbyist — Wexler, Reynolds, Harrison & Schule Inc., 1317 F St. N.W., Washington, D.C. 20004. Filed 4/9/84. Legislative interest — "Bills HR 5042, S 2362, S 2277, HR 3561, HR 5137, HR 5153."

INTERNATIONAL AGRICULTURAL DEVELOPMENT SERVICE, Arlington, Va. Lobbyist — Vorys, Sater, Seymour & Pease, 1828 L St. N.W., Washington, D.C. 20036. Filed 4/20/84. Legislative interest — "Advance client's interest re taxation of US citizens employed in foreign countries, specifically re House & Senate '84 tax legislation to amend IRC sec 911-913."

JOHNSON & JOHNSON, 1667 K St. N.W., Washington, D.C. 20006. Filed for self 4/11/84. Legislative interest — "... Health Care Related Issues. S 44 Product Liability. HR 3502 Patent Term Restoration Act. HR 3851 Federal Food & Drug Act. HR 3250 Animal Testing." Lobbyists — Bertram J. Levine, Nicholas L. Ruggieri, Patricia Q. Sheehan.

LIFE CARE SERVICES CORP., Washington, D.C. Lobbyist — Gray and Co., 3255 Grace St. N.W., Washington, D.C. 20007. Filed 4/23/84. Legislative interest — "Including but not limited to tax legislation affecting continuing care retirement communities."

LUCASFILM LTD., San Rafael, Calif. Lobbyist — Lud Ashley, 1735 New York Ave. N.W., Washington, D.C. 20006. (Former U.S. rep., D-Ohio, 1955-81.) Filed 4/28/84. Legislative interest — "For HR 3490, to amend the Internal Revenue Code of 1954 re the definition of produced film rents for purposes of the personal holding company."

LYKES BROTHERS STEAMSHIP CO. INC., New Orleans, La. Lobbyist — Hill, Betts & Nash, 1220 19th St. N.W., Washington, D.C. 20036. Filed 4/11/84. Legislative interest — "... in connection with efforts to obtain an amendment to House Joint Resolution 413; to allow them to acquire four foreign-built vessels."

MANUFACTURERS HANOVER LEASING CORP., New York, N.Y. Lobbyist — James C. Corman, 1420 16th St. N.W., Washington, D.C. 20036. (Former U.S. rep., D-Calif., 1961-81.) Filed 4/16/84. Legislative interest — "To monitor proposed legislation and treasury regulations and all pending matters affecting the Leasing Industry."

MARINE MART INC., Port Isabel, Texas. Lobbyist — Ely, Ritts, Pietrowski & Brickfield, Watergate 600 Building, Washington, D.C. 20037. Filed 4/20/84. Legislative interest — "HR 5051 - The bill to give permanent effect to the provision of the FPA of 1967 relating to the reimbursement of U.S. commercial fishermen for certain losses incurred incident to the seizure of their vessels by foreign nations."

MASCO INC., Taylor, Mich. Lobbyist — Patton, Boggs & Blow, 2550 M St. N.W., Washington, D.C. 20037. Filed 4/27/84. Legislative interest — "Legislation amending the Tax Reform Act of 1984 and the Deficit Reduction Act of 1984 so that a transition rule for certain distributions of appreciated property is included in the above acts. Such as HR 4170."

MERCEDES-BENZ OF NORTH AMERICA INC., Montvale, N.J. Lobbyist — Hogan & Hartson, 815 Connecticut Ave. N.W., Washington, D.C. 20006. Filed 4/9/84. Legislative interest — "Represents employer's interest with respect to legislation amending the Internal Revenue Code including HR 4135, HR 4170, S 2231 and S 2232."

MERRILL LYNCH CAPITAL INVESTMENTS, New York, N.Y. Lobbyist — Gray and Co., 3255 Grace St. N.W., Washington, D.C. 20007. Filed 4/10/84. Legislative interest — "Including but not limited to possible legislation on brokered deposits."

MIDLAND CAPITAL CORP., New York, N.Y. Lobbyist — Jack Ferguson Associates Inc., 203 Maryland Ave. N.E., Washington, D.C. 20002. Filed 4/9/84. Legislative interest — "HR 4170 - House Tax Reform bill; Senate Deficit Reduction Package."

MITCHELL ENERGY & DEVELOPMENT CORP., The Woodlands, Texas. Lobbyist — D'Amico, Luedtke, Demarest & Golden, 1920 N St. N.W., Washington, D.C. 20036. Filed 4/10/84. Legislative interest — "Natural Gas legislation."

MOBIL OIL CORP., 150 East 42nd St., New York, N.Y. 10017. Filed for self 4/10/84. Legislative interest — Not specified. Lobbyist — Peter A. Spina. Filed for self 4/10/84. Legislative interest — "... S 757 Solid Waste Disposal Act ... HR 2867 Hazardous Waste Control ... HR 2891 Antitrust Laws ... HR 3361 Clayton Act Amendment ... HR 3688 Clayton Act Amendment. S 1578 Local Government...." Lobbyist — Robert B. Andrews, 1100 Connecticut Ave. N.W., Washington, D.C. 20036.

MORGAN STANLEY & CO., New York, N.Y. Lobbyist — The Laxalt Corp., 813 Maryland Ave. N.E., Washington, D.C. 20002. Filed 4/23/84. Legislative interest — "Legislation affecting mergers and acquisitions, including but not limited to those involving the oil industry such as HR 5042 ('Domestic Petroleum Company Acquisition Act of 1984'); S 2277 ('Domestic Petroleum Company Acquisition Act of 1984'); S 2362 (Mineral Lands Leasing Act of 1920 amendments)."

N & F DEVELOPMENT CORP. INC., Arlington, Va. Lobbyist — Powell, Goldstein, Frazer & Murphy, 1110 Vermont Ave. N.W., Washington, D.C. 20005. Filed 4/18/84. Legislative interest — "Transition rule for new tax legislation (Tax Reform Act of 1984)."

NORTHVILLE INDUSTRIES, Melville, N.Y. Lobbyist — Vinson & Elkins, 1101 Connecticut Ave. N.W., Washington, D.C. 20036. Filed 4/16/84. Legislative interest — "In support of HR 1997 (Wolpe-McKinney Bill)."

NORWEST MORTGAGE INC., Minneapolis, Minn. Lobbyist — Brownstein, Zeidman & Schomer, 1025 Connecticut Ave. N.W., Washington, D.C. 20036. Filed 4/26/84. Legislative interest — "All legislation and regulatory matters relating to the secondary mortgage market, finance, real estate and security issues and related tax issues."

ONKYO U.S.A. CORP., Ramsey, N.J. Lobbyist — Patton, Boggs & Blow, 2550 M St. N.W., Washington, D.C. 20037. Filed 4/27/84. Legislative interest — "Legislation amending the Copyright Act that affects the home recording of television and radio broadcasts and the 'first sale' doctrine such as HR 175, S 175, S 3131, S 3132, and S 3133."

ORRICK, HERRINGTON & SUTCLIFFE, 520 Capitol Mall, Sacramento, Calif. 95814. Filed for self 4/18/84. Legislative interest — "Liaison for governmental relations & public affairs for law firm clients." Lobbyist — James W. Bruner Jr.

PACIFIC BELL, 140 New Montgomery St., San Francisco, Calif. 94105. Filed for self 4/2/84. Legislative interest — Not specified. Lobbyists — Harold Boel, Colleen Crossland, Brian D. Kidney, 444 N. Capitol St. N.W., Washington, D.C. 20001.

PACIFIC LUMBER SALES CO., Packwood, Wash. Lobbyist — Ullman Consultants Inc., 1000 Potomac St. N.W., Washington, D.C. 20007. (Former U.S. Rep. Al Ullman, D-Ore., 1957-81, was listed as agent for this client.) Filed 4/18/84. Legislative interest — "Tax issues affecting the timber industry."

PARSONS CORP., Washington, D.C. Lobbyist — Taft, Stettinius & Hollister, 21 Dupont Circle N.W., Washington, D.C. 20036. (Former U.S. Sen. Robert Taft Jr., R-Ohio, 1971-76; House 1963-65, 1967-71, was listed as agent for this client.) Filed 4/12/84. Legislative interest — "To advise on tax legislation relating to water treatment and wastewater projects."

PAULUCCI ENTERPRISES, Sanford, Fla. Lobbyist — Dickstein, Shapiro & Morin, 2101 L St. N.W., Washington, D.C. 20037. Filed 4/30/84. Legislative interest — "Amendment to S 2527 for I-4 'design and build' interchange."

J. C. PENNEY CO. INC., Washington, D.C. Lobbyist — Lud Ashley, 1735 New York Ave. N.W., Washington, D.C. (Former U.S. rep., D-Ohio, 1955-81.) Filed 4/23/84. Legislative interest — "Nonbank bank legislation."

PITTS ENERGY GROUP, Dallas, Texas. Lobbyist — D'Amico, Luedtke, Demarest & Golden, 1920 N St. N.W., Washington, D.C. 20036. Filed 4/10/84. Legislative interest — "Natural Gas Legislation."

POTOMAC ELECTRIC POWER CO., 1900 Pennsylvania Ave. N.W., Washington, D.C. 20068. Filed for self 4/6/84. Legislative interest — "All legislative matters directly or indirectly affecting public utilities, specifically but not exclusively including the Clean Air and Water Act amendments, all energy related legislation, railroad deregulation proposals, and tax proposals relating to capital formation." Lobbyist — Edward F. Mitchell.

PRECISION MAGNETICS AND CERAMICS, Rochester, N.H. Lobbyist — Gnau, Carter, Jacobsen and Associates Inc., 1250 I St. N.W., Washington, D.C. 20005. Filed 4/16/84. Legislative interest — "Government business loan guarantees."

PROGRESS TRADING CO., New York, N.Y. Lobbyist — Olwine, Connelly, Chase, O'Donnell & Weyher, 1850 K St. N.W., Washington, D.C. 20006. Filed 4/30/84. Legislative interest — "To support free trade in the importation of genuine trademarked products and legislation which may be introduced in support of such free trade and to oppose legislation designed to restrict such free trade, including legislation directed against parallel importers or any so-called 'gray market' and legislation relating to Sec. 526 of the Tariff Act (19 U.S.C. section 1526) or to Customs Regulations 19 C.F.R. section 133.21."

PURPLE CROSS INSURANCE CO., Seattle, Wash. Lobbyist — Reid & Priest, 1111 19th St. N.W., Washington, D.C. 20036. Legislative interest — "Effective date provisions relating to definition of life insurance under HR 4170 and HR 2163."

RAYMARK CORP., Trumbull, Conn. Lobbyist — Kaye, Scholer, Fierman, Hays & Handler, 1575 I St. N.W., Washington, D.C. 20005. Filed 4/10/84. Legislative interest — "General legislation affecting asbestos manufacturers and the asbestos industry."

REAL PROPERTY SERVICES CORP., Los Angeles, Calif. Lobbyist — The William Chasey Organization, 1800 K St. N.W., Washington, D.C. 20006. Filed 4/13/84. Legislative interest — "Deficit Reduction Act of 1984, S 2062/HR 4170, Equity Refinancing - Low Income Rental Housing."

RECON/OPTICAL INC., 550 W. Northwest Highway, Barrington, Ill. 60010. Lobbyist — Quinn, Racusin, Young & Delaney, 1730 K St. N.W., Washington, D.C. 20006. Legislative interest — "Interest in Department of Defense authorization and appropriation legislation." Lobbyist — Zuckert, Scoutt, Rasenberger & Johnson, 888 17th St. N.W., Washington, D.C. 20006. Filed 4/23/84. Legislative interest — "Interest in Department of Defense authorization and appropriation legislation." Filed for self 4/20/84. Legislative interest — "Interest in Department of Defense authorization and appropriation legislation." Lobbyist — O. O. Johnson.

SALEN DRY CARGO INC., Washington, D.C. Lobbyist — Gray and Co., 3255 Grace St. N.W., Washington, D.C. 20007. Filed 4/10/84. Legislative interest — "Including but not limited to maritime legislation."

SALOMON BROTHERS INC., New York, N.Y. Lobbyist — Black, Manafort & Stone, 324 N. Fairfax St., Alexandria, Va. 22314. Filed 4/12/84. Legislative interest — "Tax, banking, investment and international financial legislation ... Deficit Reduction Act of 1984, banking regulations legislation ... HR 4170, others. ..."

SAMARITAN HEALTH SERVICE, Phoenix, Ariz. Lobbyist — Casson, Calligaro & Mutryn, 2600 Virginia Ave. N.W., Washington, D.C. 20037. Filed 4/20/84. Legislative interest — "Legislation related to the Public Health Service Act, Social Security Act, Medicare and Medicaid."

SAMCOR INC., Phoenix, Ariz. Lobbyist — Perito, Duerk & Pinco, 1140 Connecticut Ave. N.W., Washington, D.C. 20036. Filed

4/23/84. Legislative interest — "Health policy issues, including Medicare prospective payment system and hospital capital financing."

SEA-LAND INDUSTRIES INC., P.O. Box 800, Iselin, N.J. 08830. Filed for self 4/17/84. Legislative interest — "All maritime and maritime related issues, including rail and motor legislation, international trade legislation, tax legislation." Lobbyist — Rebecca Jane Berg, 1140 Connecticut Ave. N.W., Washington, D.C. 20036.

SEARS, ROEBUCK AND CO., Sears Tower, Chicago, Ill. 60684. Filed for self 4/16/84. Legislative interest — "Legislation affecting the operation of Sears, Roebuck and Co. as part of the retail industry, its employees and customers, including, but not limited to the areas of competition, Regulatory Reform, PAC's and Trade Regulations." Lobbyist — Talis Dzenitis, 633 Pennsylvania Ave. N.W., Washington, D.C. 20004.

SECURITY INVESTMENT CO., Baltimore, Md. Lobbyist — Wexler, Reynolds, Harrison & Schule Inc., 1317 F St. N.W., Washington, D.C. 20004. Filed 4/9/84. Legislative interest — "The registrant seeks to represent the employer with respect to legislation concerning Federal Real Property cost savings specifically regarding property leased for the benefit of the Department of Health and Human Services in Maryland, and other interests concerning real property."

SECURITY PACIFIC NATIONAL BANK, 333 S. Hope St., Los Angeles, Calif. 90071. Filed for self 4/20/84. Legislative interest — "All legislation affecting financial institutions, including specific banking legislation, housing, agricultural and other financial matters." Lobbyist — Tessa Morris, 1819 L St. N.W., Washington, D.C. 20036.

SHELL OIL CO., P.O. Box 2463, Houston, Texas 77001. Lobbyist — Edward D. Heffernan, 1875 I St. N.W., Washington, D.C. 20006. Filed 4/17/84. Legislative interest — "HR 4784 - Trade Remedies Reform Act of 1984 (Gibbons) - oppose." Filed for self 4/9/84. Legislative interest — "... oil and gas production, chemicals, health, safety and the environment, taxation concerns, and employee/employer relations." Lobbyist — Janie L. Lawson, 1025 Connecticut Ave. N.W., Washington, D.C. 20036.

SHINY ROCK MINING CORP., Lyons, Ore. Lobbyist — Morris J. Levin, 1050 17th St. N.W., Washington, D.C. 20036. Filed 4/14/84. Legislative interest — "Interested in the Oregon Wilderness Legislation, HR 1149, and like legislation."

SIEMENS-ALLIS INC., 223 Perimeter Center Parkway, Atlanta, Ga. 30338. Filed for self 4/2/84. Legislative interest — "... Trade Remedies Reform Act ... HR 4784 ... For ... Patent Term Restoration Act ... S 1306 ... For." Lobbyists — Frederick W. Powers III, James V. Sheahan.

SMITH BARNEY, HARRIS UPHAM & CO. INC., New York, N.Y. Lobbyist — Foley & Lardner, 1775 Pennsylvania Ave. N.W., Washington, D.C. 20006. Filed 4/26/84. Legislative interest "... provisions of HR 4170 and HR 2163 relating to student loan bonds."

SMITHKLINE CORP., Washington, D.C. Lobbyist — Birch, Horton, Bittner, Pestinger and Anderson, 1140 Connecticut Ave. N.W., Washington, D.C. 20036. Filed 4/10/84. Legislative interest — "Legislative tax work concerning Sections 936 and 861 of the Internal Revenue Code."

SONATRACH, Algiers, Algeria. Lobbyist — Garvey, Schubert, Adams & Barer, The Bank of California Center, Seattle, Wash. 98164. Filed 4/11/84. Legislative interest — "Natural gas deregulation legislation."

SOUTH DAKOTA STUDENT LOAN ASSISTANCE CORP., Aberdeen, S.D. Lobbyist — Foley & Lardner, 1775 Pennsylvania Ave. N.W., Washington, D.C. 20006. Filed 4/26/84. Legislative interest — "... provisions of HR 4170 and HR 2163 relating to student loan bonds."

SPACE AMERICA INC., 600 Water St. S.W., Washington, D.C. 20024. Lobbyist — Ely, Ritts, Pietrowski & Brickfield, Watergate 600 Building, Washington, D.C. 20037. Filed 4/20/84. Legislative interest — "S 2292 and HR 5155 - The Land Remote Sensing Commercialization Act 1982." Filed for self 4/10/84. Legislative interest — "Interested in all bills concerning transfer of ownership of remote sensing satellites from the Government to the private sector. Generally, in support of commercializing land remote sensing satellites. Also interested in bills concerning regulation of expendable launch vehicle payloads." Lobbyist — Kathleen B. Kronmiller.

SPARX CORP., New York, N.Y. Lobbyist — O'Connor & Hannan, 1919 Pennsylvania Ave. N.W., Washington, D.C. 20006. Filed 4/13/84. Legislative interest — "S 2292, to provide for continued access by the Federal Government to land remote sensing data from satellites, and for other purposes. HR 5155, to establish a system to promote the use of land remote-sensing satellite data, and for other purposes."

SQUIBB CORP., 1700 K St. N.W., Washington, D.C. 20006. Filed for self 4/6/84. Legislative interest — "Legislation affecting Corporation and operating companies. Drug Regulation Reform Legislation. Tax Legislation." Lobbyist — Richard L. Thompson.

STANDARD OIL OF SOUTHERN CALIFORNIA, Washington, D.C. Lobbyist — Parry and Romani Associates Inc., 1140 Connecticut Ave. N.W., Washington, D.C. 20036. Filed 4/4/84. Legislative interest — "Pending bills and amendments offering mergers and acquisitions among domestic companies in general and oil companies in particular."

SYSCON CORP., Washington, D.C. Lobbyist — Patton, Boggs & Blow, 2550 M St. N.W., Washington, D.C. 20037. Filed 4/27/84. Legislative interest — "For legislation amending Section IV of the Small Business Competition for Federal Procurements Act such as HR 2133."

TASTY BAKING CO., Philadelphia, Pa. Lobbyist — Philip D. Morrison, 1700 Pennsylvania Ave. N.W., Washington, D.C. 20006. Filed 4/23/84. Legislative interest — "Generally, all legislation relating to federal income taxation of corporations. Specifically, lobbying relating to Tax Act of 1984."

TAYLOR & MIZELL, Dallas, Texas. Lobbyist — R. Duffy Wall & Associates, 1317 F St. N.W., Washington, D.C. 20004. Filed 4/17/84. Legislative interest — "Title 26 of the U.S. Revenue Code."

TEKTRONIX CORP., Beavertown, Ore. Lobbyist — Deloitte, Haskins & Sells, 655 15th St. N.W., Washington, D.C. 20005. Filed 4/17/84. Legislative interest — "Interest is in tax legislation which might have an impact on the business of the employer."

TESORO PETROLEUM CORP., 8700 Tesoro Drive, San Antonio, Texas 78286. Filed for self 4/10/84. Legislative interest — "Tax Legislation, Natural Gas Legislation, Export Administration Act, Resource Conservation and Recovery Act." Lobbyist — Jean A. Becherer, 1800 K St. N.W., Washington, D.C. 20006.

TEXAS OIL & GAS CORP., Dallas, Texas. Lobbyist — D'Amico, Luedtke, Demarest & Golden, 1920 N St. N.W., Washington, D.C. 20036. Filed 4/10/84. Legislative interest — "Natural gas legislation."

TICOR, Los Angeles, Calif. Lobbyist — Piper & Marbury, 888 16th St. N.W., Washington, D.C. 20006. Filed 4/25/84. Legislative interest — "For a technical amendment to pending tax legislation regarding non-taxable exchanges (such as in section 61 to HR 2163) deleting advance property designation requirements."

TIMES MIRROR CO., 1875 I St. N.W., Washington, D.C. 20006. Filed for self 4/16/84. Legislative interest — "All legislation affecting communications industry."

TRIANGLE INDUSTRIES INC., New Brunswick, N.J. Lobbyist — Deloitte, Haskins & Sells, 655 15th St. N.W., Washington, D.C. 20005. Filed 4/17/84. Legislative interest — "Interest in tax legislation which might have an impact on the business of the employer."

TRW INC., 1000 Wilson Blvd., Arlington, Va. 22209. Filed for self 4/17/84. Legislative interest — "General legislation of interest to TRW Inc., including aerospace, electronics, transportation, energy, foreign trade, etc." Lobbyist — Henry J. Steenstra Jr.

UNION PACIFIC CORP., 345 Park Ave., New York, N.Y. 10154. Filed for self 4/10/84. Legislative interest — "Pending and prospective legislation affecting the petroleum and natural gas industries." Lobbyist — Mary Margaret Collins, 1120 20th St. N.W., Washington, D.C. 20036.

UNITED AIRLINES, Chicago, Ill. Lobbyist — Wilmer, Cutler & Pickering, 1666 K St. N.W., Washington, D.C. 20006. Filed 4/11/84. Legislative interest — "Effective date clarification ... Tax Reform Act of 1984; Deficit Reduction Act of 1984 ... HR 4170; Senate Finance Committee Deficit Reduction Act of 1984 ... Effective date clarification/deferred rent."

UNITED STATES CRUISES INC., Seattle, Wash. Lobbyist — Robertson, Monagle, Eastaugh & Bradley, 210 Ferry Way, Juneau, Alaska 99801. Filed 4/17/84. Legislative interest — "Any and all matters relating to shipping and maritime."

UNITED STATES TELEPHONE INC., Dallas, Texas. Lobbyist — D'Amico, Luedtke, Demarest & Golden, 1920 N St. N.W., Washington, D.C. 20036. Filed 4/10/84. Legislative interest — "Telecommunications legislation."

UNITED STATES TRUST CO., New York, N.Y. Lobbyist — Curtis, Mallet-Prevost, Colt & Mosle, 101 Park Ave., New York, N.Y. 10178. Filed 4/20/84. Legislative interest — Not specified.

U.S. WEST, Washington, D.C. Lobbyist — Chambers Associates Inc., 1411 K St. N.W., Washington, D.C. 20005. Filed 4/10/84. Legislative interest — "... general legislation related to taxation, pensions, and employee benefits, and labor issues."

WASTE MANAGEMENT INC., 600 Maryland Ave. S.W., Washington, D.C. 20024. Filed for self 4/16/84. Legislative interest — "Legislation relating to the solid waste, hazardous waste industry. Resource Recovery and Conservation Act amendments, Superfund amendments." Lobbyist — James D. Range.

WESSELY ENERGY CORP., Dallas, Texas. Lobbyist — D'Amico, Luedtke, Demarest & Golden, 1920 N St. N.W., Washington, D.C. 20036. Filed 4/10/84. Legislative interest — "Natural gas legislation."

International Relations

GOVERNMENT OF THE REPUBLIC OF TOGO, Lome, Togo. Lobbyist — David Apter & Associates, 1625 K St. N.W., Washington, D.C. 20006. Filed 4/22/84. Legislative interest — Not specified.

REPUBLIC OF NICARAGUA, Managua, Nicaragua. Lobbyist — Reichler & Appelbaum, 1776 K St. N.W., Washington, D.C. 20006. Filed 4/27/84. Legislative interest — "Appropriations and other legislation affecting Nicaragua." Lobbyist — Agendas International, 820 Second Ave., New York, N.Y. 10017. Filed 4/26/84. Legislative interest — "Appropriations and other measures affecting Nicaragua."

Labor Groups

ALASKA TEAMSTERS-EMPLOYER PENSION TRUST, Anchorage, Alaska. Lobbyist — Birch, Horton, Bittner, Pestinger and Anderson, 1140 Connecticut Ave. N.W., Washington, D.C. 20036. Filed 4/10/84. Legislative interest — "Pension law developments."

INDUSTRIAL UNION DEPARTMENT, AFL-CIO, 815 16th St. N.W., Washington, D.C. 20006. Filed for self 4/18/84. Legislative interest — "All bills affecting the welfare of the country, generally and specifically bills affecting workers such as trade, OSHA, pension and employment legislation." Lobbyist — Nancy Rodgers.

INTERNATIONAL BROTHERHOOD OF TEAMSTERS, Washington, D.C. Lobbyist — Parry and Romani Associates Inc., 1140 Connecticut Ave. N.W., Washington, D.C. 20036. Filed 4/14/84. Legislative interest — "Legislation affecting the rights of current and retired American working men and women."

INTERNATIONAL FEDERATION OF PROFESSIONAL & TECHNICAL ENGINEERS, AFL-CIO, 818 Roeder Road, Silver Spring, Md. 20910. Filed for self 4/17/84. Legislative interest — Not specified. Lobbyist — Lois Rowan.

State and Local Governments

CITY OF ROCHESTER, MINN., Rochester, Minn. Lobbyist — LeFevere, Lefler, Kennedy, O'Brien & Drawz, 120 S. 6th

St., Minneapolis, Minn. 55402. Filed 4/20/84. Legislative interest — "... an action on appropriation or reprogramming of funds for acquisition of property for a federal corrections facility in Rochester, Minn."

CITY OF ST. GEORGE, St. George, Alaska. Lobbyist — Birch, Horton, Bittner, Pestinger and Anderson, 1140 Connecticut Ave. N.W., Washington, D.C. 20036. Filed 4/10/84. Legislative interest — "Economic development and social issues."

CITY OF ST. LOUIS, St. Louis, Mo. Lobbyist — Brown & Associates, 301 Sovereign Court, St. Louis, Mo. 63011. Filed 4/4/84. Legislative interest — "Aviation Legislation. Mass Transit Legislation."

CITY OF STARKE, Starke, Fla. Lobbyist — Spiegel & McDiarmid, 2600 Virginia Ave. N.W., Washington, D.C. 20037. Filed 4/17/84. Legislative interest — "Energy, power supply and environmental matters."

THE GOVERNMENT OF THE FEDERATED STATES OF MICRONESIA, Ponape, Trust Territory of the Pacific. Lobbyist — Development Associates Inc., 2924 Columbia Pike, Arlington, Va. 22204. Filed 4/2/84. Legislative interest — "To help attain the passage by Congress of legislation implementing the Compact of Free Association and related agreements between the Federated States of Micronesia and the United States of America, signed Oct. 1, 1982."

GOVERNMENT OF PUERTO RICO, San Juan, Puerto Rico. Lobbyist — Edward L. Merrigan, 6000 Connecticut Ave. N.W., Washington, D.C. 20815. Filed 4/24/84. Legislative interest — "Pending tax legislation involving Puerto Rico."

GUAM ECONOMIC DEVELOPMENT AUTHORITY, Agana, Guam. Lobbyist — Jones and Winburn, 1101 15th St. N.W., Washington, D.C. 20005. Filed 4/14/84. Legislative interest — "Legislation relating to provisions of the Internal Revenue Code."

NEW YORK CITY TEACHERS RETIREMENT SYSTEM, New York, N.Y. Lobbyist — Groom and Nordberg, 1775 Pennsylvania Ave. N.W., Washington, D.C. 20006. Filed 4/10/84. Legislative interest — "Federal legislation affecting Title 26 of U.S.C. and Title 29 of the U.S.C."

STATE OF MICHIGAN, Washington, D.C. Lobbyist — James C. Corman, 1420 16th St. N.W., Washington, D.C. 20036. (Former U.S. rep., D-Calif., 1961-81.) Filed 4/10/84. Legislative interest — "Legislative and regulatory proposals affecting the following programs: Federal unemployment compensation programs, AFDC, SSI, Title XX Social Services, IV-D Child Support Enforcement, IV-E Adoption Assistance and Foster Care, IV-B Child Welfare Services and Medicaid."

Trade Associations

AIRLINE PILOTS ASSOCIATION, Washington, D.C. Lobbyist — McNair, Glenn, Konduros, Corley, Singletary, Porter & Dibble, 1155 15th St. N.W., Washington, D.C. 20005. Filed 4/24/84. Legislative interest — "Bankruptcy legislation."

AMERICAN BAR ASSOCIATION, 1155 E. 60th St., Chicago, Ill. 60637. Filed for self 4/12/84. Legislative interest — "Matters of general interest to the legal profession including: Bankruptcy Court Reform (HR 3, S 443, S 792 - oppose; HR 1401 - support); Removal of Mandatory Jurisdiction of U.S. Supreme Court (S 385, Title I of S 645 - support); Creation of a State Justice Institute (S 584, Title IV of S 645 - support); Criminal Code Reform (HR 2013 - favor with amendments); Abolition of the Exclusionary Rule (S 101, S 283, HR 2239 - oppose); Gun Control (S 511, HR 1543 - favor with amendments; S 914 - oppose); Restrictions of Habeas Corpus (S 217 - oppose); Equal Rights Amendment (H J Res 1, S J Res 10 - support); Federal Court Subject Matter Limitations (HR 46, S 26, et al. - oppose); Improved Judicial Survivors Annuities (Title III, S 645 - favor); Reauthorization of the Legal Services Corporation (no bill - favor); Regulatory Reform (HR 220, HR 2327 - favor with amendments)." Lobbyist — Maurice A. Barboza, 1800 M St. N.W., Washington, D.C. 20036.

AMERICAN BUSINESS CONFERENCE, 1025 Connecticut Ave. N.W., Washington, D.C. 20036. Filed for self 4/11/84. Legislative interest — "The general legislative interest is tax and regulatory reform legislation for high-growth, mid-range business organizations. The specific legislative interest is the Reagan tax program." Lobbyists — Rhonda Lee Halverson, Leslie H. Smith.

AMERICAN HOSPITAL ASSOCIATION, 444 N. Capitol St. N.W., Washington, D.C. 20001. Lobbyist — Chambers Associates Inc., 1411 K St. N.W., Washington, D.C. 20005. Filed 4/10/84. Legislative interest — "General legislation related to health care." Filed for self 4/13/84. Legislative interest — "... all legislation which may affect the ability of hospitals to render good care or which may affect the health of the American people." Lobbyist — Patricia R. Goldman.

THE AMERICAN INSTITUTE OF ARCHITECTS, 1735 New York Ave. N.W., Washington, D.C. 20006. Filed for self 4/14/84. Legislative interest — "In general all legislation relating to the practice of architecture, specifically, HR 5172, National Bureau of Standards authorization; HR 4170 Tax Reform Act of 1984; HR 1735 to establish revitalization areas; HR 2889 to fund National Building Museum; S J Res 173 HABS." Lobbyist — Herschel Lipow.

AMERICAN MALTING BARLEY ASSOCIATION INC., 735 N. Water St., Milwaukee, Wis. 53202. Filed for self 4/11/84. Legislative interest — "General Farm Legislation, Energy, Environmental, Taxation, Occupational Health and Safety, Research, Food Safety and Transportation Legislation and Regulation." Lobbyist — W. Kirk Miller.

AMERICAN PEANUT PRODUCT MANUFACTURERS INC., 412 First St. S.E., Washington, D.C. 20003. Filed for self 4/13/84. Legislative interest — "Legislation pertaining to peanuts." Lobbyist — William C. Wampler (Former U.S. rep., R-Va., 1953-55; 1967-83.)

THE AMERICAN PUBLIC TRANSIT ASSOCIATION, 1225 Connecticut Ave. N.W., Washington, D.C. 20036. Filed for self 4/10/84. Legislative interest — "Interested in all legislation affecting Association members including all budget resolutions, appropriations acts, and authorizing legislation. H J Res 282. 49 U.S.C. 1601." Lobbyist — Ralph de la Cruz.

AMERICAN SOCIETY FOR PHARMACOLOGY AND EXPERIMENTAL THERAPEUTICS, Bethesda, Md. Lobbyist — Perito, Duerk & Pinco, 1140 Connecticut Ave. N.W., Washington, D.C. 20036. Filed 4/19/84. Legislative interest — "Legislation supporting biomedical research and responsible use of animals and research subjects in furtherance of biomedical research."

AMERICAN TRUCKING ASSOCIATION, Washington, D.C. Lobbyist — John Daniel Reaves and Barbara S. Blaine, 910 16th St. N.W., Washington, D.C. 20006. Filed 4/10/84. Legislative interest — "Passage of diesel fuel tax (HR 2124) in lieu of heavy vehicle use tax enacted in Surface Transportation Assistance Act of 1982."

ASSOCIATED GENERAL CONTRACTORS OF AMERICA, 1957 E St. N.W., Washington, D.C. 20006. Filed 4/4/84. Legislative interest — "Unemployment Compensation." Lobbyist — E. Richard Soper.

ASSOCIATED LOCKSMITHS OF AMERICA, Dallas, Texas. Lobbyist — Chwat/Weigend Associates, 400 First St. N.W., Washington, D.C. 20001. Filed 4/11/84. Legislative interest — "General legislative interests affecting the locksmith industry such as tax credits for installation of locks; and federal regulations such as U.S. Postal Service procurement practices."

ASSOCIATION FOR ADVANCEMENT OF PSYCHOLOGY, 1200 17th St. N.W., Washington, D.C. 20036. Filed for self 4/25/84. Legislative interest — Not specified. Lobbyists — Clarence J. Martin, Charlotte Voorde, Lisa Shuger.

EDISON ELECTRIC INSTITUTE, 1111 19th St. N.W., Washington, D.C. 20036. Lobbyist — Blair & Blair Ltd., 1120 19th St. N.W., Washington, D.C. 20036. Filed 4/13/84. Legislative interest — "... Clean Air Act; Acidic Deposition Study and Ecosystem Mitigation Act; National Acidic Deposition Control Act of 1983 ... HR 3400 and HR 1405 ... Clean Air Act...." Filed for self 4/17/84. Legislative interest — "...HR 555, HR 1914, HR 2510, HR 2511, HR 2512, HR 3277, HR 3132, HR 1943, HR 2483, HR 2582, S 211, S 388, S 893, S 894, S 917, S 1800, S 921, S 11, S 946." Lobbyist — William A. Edwards.

FAMILY-BACKED MORTGAGE ASSOCIATION INC., Oakland, Calif. Lobbyist — Leighton, Lemov, Jacobs & Buckley, 2033 M St. N.W., Washington, D.C. 20036. Filed 4/14/84. Legislative interest — "Specific legislative interest is S 1914, the Home Equity Conversion Act."

FARM CREDIT COUNCIL, 1800 Massachusetts Ave. N.W., Washington, D.C. 20036. Filed for self 4/26/84. Legislative interest — Not specified. Lobbyist — John A. Waits.

THE FARMERS' EDUCATIONAL AND CO-OPERATIVE UNION OF AMERICA (NATIONAL FARMERS UNION), 600 Maryland Ave. S.W., Washington, D.C. 20024. Filed for self 4/11/84. Legislative interest — "... authorities of and the appropriations for the Department of Agriculture, bills relating to labor, health and medical care, welfare, taxation, revenue, tariffs, farm price supports, crop insurance, farm credit, REA, public power, natural resources, marketing and distribution of farm commodities, exportation and importation of agricultural products, foreign aid, defense, reclamation, education, marketing and consumer cooperatives, social security, reciprocal trade agreements, transportation, and antitrust legislation." Lobbyist — Cy Carpenter.

FEDERATION OF AMERICAN HOSPITALS, 1111 19th St. N.W., Washington, D.C. 20036. Filed for self 4/10/84. Legislative interest — "Specifically Medicare, National Health Insurance and Hospital Cost Containment Legislation." Lobbyist — Mary R. Grealy.

FOOD MARKETING INSTITUTE, 1750 K St. N.W., Washington, D.C. 20006. Filed for self 4/6/84. Legislative interest — "Generally, interest in communications legislation, postal legislation, and small business legislation." Lobbyist — Karen E. Theibert. Filed for self 4/13/84. Legislative interest — "Generally, legislation of interest to the Food Distribution Industry, such as: Tax Legislation, the Farm bill, amendments to ERISA, Labor related Legislation, Transportation legislation, lobby laws ... small business legislation, consumer legislation, energy legislation, Food Safety legislation, item pricing, beverage container Legislation, regulatory reforms and postal legislation...." Lobbyist — Robert O. Aders.

GETTY NORTHEAST JOBBERS & DISTRIBUTORS ASSOCIATION, Washington, D.C. Lobbyist — Blum, Nash & Railsback, 1015 18th St. N.W., Washington, D.C. 20036. Filed 4/6/84. Legislative interest — "Legislation relating to petroleum mergers, all antitrust legislation and the FTC authorization act."

HOME HEALTH SERVICES & STAFFING ASSOCIATION, Washington, D.C. Lobbyist — Hogan & Hartson, 815 Connecticut Ave. N.W., Washington, D.C. 20006. Filed 4/11/84. Legislative interest — Not specified.

INTERSTATE NATURAL GAS ASSOCIATION OF AMERICA, 1660 L St. N.W., Washington, D.C. 20036. Filed for self 4/12/84. Legislative interest — "Any legislation pertaining to natural gas: Natural gas legislation (S 1715) and legislation concerning utility relocations (S 531, S 1739 & HR 3678)." Lobbyist — Glenn Jackson.

INVESTMENT COMPANY INSTITUTE, 1775 K St. N.W., Washington, D.C. 20006. Lobbyist — Scott Hodes, 180 North La Salle St., Chicago, Ill. 60610. Filed 4/19/84. Legislative interest — "Legislative interest in banking - securities industry legislation, S 2181, S 2134 'opposed in part.'" Lobbyist — Irving M. Pollack, 13010 Carney St., Wheaton, Md. 20906. Filed 4/18/84. Legislative interest — "Legislative interest in banking - securities industry legislation, S 2181, S 2134 'opposed in part.'" Filed for self 4/10/84. Legislative interest — "S 1532, HR 3413, HR 3499, S 2071, HR 4506 ... S 1609, HR 3537, S 2181, S 2134, S 2107 ... HR 3529, HR 3805, HR 3592 ... S 1080, HR 2327 ... S 645 ... HR 2852, HR 3418 ... HR 4574 ... S 2040, S 1822 ... HR 5342...." Lobbyist — Mary K. Bellamy.

MORTGAGE INSURANCE COMPANIES OF AMERICA, 1725 K St. N.W., Washington, D.C. 20006. Filed for self 4/9/84. Legislative interest — "Any legislation before Congress this session dealing with housing, financial institutions, or insurance." Lobbyist — John E. Gunther.

MUNICIPAL CASTINGS FAIR TRADE COUNCIL, Denham Springs, La. Lobbyist — Adduci, Dinan & Mastriani, 1140 Connecticut Ave. N.W., Washington, D.C. 20036. Filed 4/5/84. Legislative interest — "... include HR 3398, S 50 and S 1672. In support of this legislation."

NATIONAL-AMERICAN WHOLESALE GROCERS' ASSOCIATION, 201 Park Washington Court, Falls Church, Va. 22046. Filed for self 4/12/84. Legislative interest — "Matters affecting the U.S. wholesale grocery and food distribution industries including, HR 7233 (Multiemployer pension withdrawal liability); S 44 (Product liability); S 529 (Immigration Reform); HR 4961 (Tax Equity Fiscal Responsibility Act)." Lobbyist — Elaine Zarafonetis.

NATIONAL ASSOCIATION OF BROADCASTERS, 1771 N St. N.W., Washington, D.C. 20036. Filed for self 4/4/84. Legislative interest — "General legislative interest: Those relating directly or indirectly to the radio and television broadcasting industry, especially amendments relating to Communications Act of 1934, 47 U.S.C. 151, Copyright Law of 1909, 17 U.S.C. 1, Communications Satellite Act of 1962, 47 U.S.C. 701, Regulation of advertising, taxation, appropriations, public broadcasting, newsmen's privilege and consumer protection." Lobbyists — John B. Summers, Stephen Jacobs, Sharon Goldener, Theresa Gibson, Howard E. Woolley, Andrew Vitali Jr., Kevin Burke, Dennis McIntosh.

NATIONAL ASSOCIATION OF COMPANION SITTER AGENCIES AND REFERRAL SERVICES, Birmingham, Ala. Lobbyist — Chwat/Weigend Associates, 400 First St. N.W., Washington, D.C. 20001. Filed 4/11/84. Legislative interest — "General legislative interests affecting the home health industry, nurse's aides, baby sitter agencies, and sitters for the elderly; including Title III of Public Law 89-73 (long-term care), HR 5135, HR 5141, S 233, S 2301, and Public Law 95-171; and regulations in general relating to the Health Care Financing Administration, Social Security Administration and subjects such as hospice."

NATIONAL ASSOCIATION OF FEDERAL CREDIT UNIONS, 1111 N. 19th St., Arlington, Va. 22209. Filed for self 4/10/84. Legislative interest — "Legislative interests are: HR 5174, S 2507 ... S 1714 ... HR 3535 ... S 2522 ... S 2181 ... HR 2371 ... S 573, HR 4187, HR 5301 ... HR 5026 ... HR 5278 ... HR 5038 ... HR 5232...." Lobbyist — Thomas J. Delaney.

NATIONAL ASSOCIATION OF MANUFACTURERS, 1776 F St. N.W., Washington, D.C. 20006. Filed for self 4/8/84. Legislative interest — "Legislation affecting employee/labor relations including but not limited to HR 2847 National Employment Priorities Act; Davis-Bacon Reform - HR 3846/S 1172; Office Machine & Equipment Dealers' Act - HR 1159/S 286 and Sales Representatives Contractual Relations Act - HR 3591." Lobbyist — Renee R. Krause.

NATIONAL ASSOCIATION OF TEMPORARY SERVICES INC., Alexandria, Va. Lobbyist — Miller & Chevalier, 655 15th St. N.W., Washington, D.C. 20005. Filed 4/11/84. Legislative interest — "Obtaining an exemption from Section 414(n) of 1954 Internal Revenue Code for temporary assignments made by temporary help service companies." Filed for self 4/18/84. Legislative interest — "Obtaining an exemption from Section 414(n) of 1954 Internal Revenue Code for temporary assignments made by temporary help service companies." Lobbyist — Samuel R. Sacco.

NATIONAL FEDERATION OF INDEPENDENT BUSINESS, 600 Maryland Ave. S.W., Washington, D.C. 20024. Filed for self 4/14/84. Legislative interest — "All legislation affecting small business and the economic well-being of the country, including Social Security, spending cuts, balanced budget and taxes." Lobbyist — Mary Jane Norville.

NATIONAL FISHERIES INSTITUTE, Washington, D.C. Lobbyist — Jones and Wilburn, 1101 15th St. N.W., Washington, D.C. 20005. Filed 4/14/84. Legislative interest — "General legislative development of Tax Issues and Capital Construction Fund."

NATIONAL MULTI HOUSING COUNCIL, 1150 17th St. N.W., Washington, D.C. 20036. Filed for self 4/17/84. Legislative interest — Not specified. Lobbyists — Stephen D. Driesler, Susan Riley.

NATIONAL RURAL ELECTRIC COOPERATIVE ASSOCIATION, 1800 Massachusetts Ave. N.W., Washington, D.C. 20036. Filed for self 4/17/84. Legislative interest — "All legislative interests affecting the Rural Electrification Act of 1936, as amended." Lobbyist — Michael D. Oldak. Filed for self 4/17/84. Legislative interest — "All legislation affecting the rural electrification program provided for under the REA Act of 1936, as amended." Lobbyist — Bob Bergland (Former U.S. rep., D-Minn., 1971-77; secretary of agriculture, 1977-81.)

NATIONAL SOCIETY OF PROFESSIONAL ENGINEERS, 2029 K St. N.W., Washington, D.C. 20006. Filed for self 4/11/84. Legislative interest — "... S 1714, HR 2970 ... HR 1010, S 267 ... HR 2057 ... HR 1310, S 1285 ... HR 2066 ... S 431, S 1031, HR 3282 ... HR 6114 ... S 532 ... HR 1244, S 23, S 1432 ... HR 2293 ... S 338 ... S 632, HR 428, HR 3443 ... HR 2782 ... HR 2867, S 757 ... S 1001, S 338, HR 2293 ... HR 3286 ... HR 3846...." Lobbyist — Jeffrey T. Cox.

OHIO OIL AND GAS ASSOCIATION, Granville, Ohio. Lobbyist — Vorys, Sater, Seymour and Pease, 1828 L St. N.W., Washington, D.C. 20036. Filed 4/10/84. Legislative interest — "To advance client's interests with respect to HR 4170 and Senate Amendments to HR 2163, the Tax Reform Acts of 1984. Client is for the Senate version and against the House version."

ORGANIZATION OF PROFESSIONAL EMPLOYEES OF THE U.S. DEPARTMENT OF AGRICULTURE, South Building, USDA, Washington, D.C. 20250. Filed for self 4/19/84. Legislative interest — "... are in large part, but not exclusively exemplified in the bills which are listed in the Digest of Public Bills issued by the Library of Congress and indexed under the caption 'Public Officers and Employees, Retirement, and Income Tax Exemption, etc.'" Lobbyist — John H. Miner.

PHARMACEUTICAL MANUFACTURERS ASSOCIATION, 1100 15th St. N.W., Washington, D.C. 20005. Lobbyist — Blair & Blair Ltd., 1120 19th St. N.W., Washington, D.C. 20036. Filed 4/19/84. Legislative interest — "... Food, Drug and Cosmetic Act, any and all legislation pending before the Energy and Commerce Committee relating to the Pharmaceutical industry." Filed for self 4/16/84. Legislative interest — "All matters relating to health care and, particularly, prescription medicines." Lobbyist — David E. Johnson.

PRINTING INDUSTRIES OF AMERICA INC., Arlington, Va. Lobbyist — Blair & Blair Ltd., 1120 19th St. N.W., Washington, D.C. 20036. Filed 4/19/84. Legislative interest — "... Clean Air Act; Hazardous Air Pollutants Amendments Act of 1984 ... Will lobby against HR 5084."

PROCOMPETITIVE RAIL STEERING COMMITTEE, 1090 Vermont Ave. N.W., Washington, D.C. 20005. Lobbyist — Donelan, Cleary, Wood & Maser, 914 Washington Building, Washington, D.C. 20005. Filed 4/16/84. Legislative interest — "Legislation relating to rail transportation issues." Filed for self 4/17/84. Legislative interest — "Legislation relating to rail transportation issues." Lobbyists — James E. Bartley, John F. Donelan.

RISK AND INSURANCE MANAGEMENT SOCIETY INC., New York, N.Y. Lobbyist — Hansell & Post, 1915 I St. N.W., Washington, D.C. 20006. Filed 4/10/84. Legislative interest — "Legislative action relating to the treatment and taxation of property and casualty insurance."

SECURITIES INDUSTRY ASSOCIATION, Washington, D.C. Lobbyist — Lud Ashley, 1735 New York Ave. N.W., Washington, D.C. 20036. (Former U.S. rep., D-Ohio, 1955-81.) Filed 4/23/84. Legislative interest — "Brokered accounts."

SOLAR ENERGY INDUSTRY ASSOCIATION, Alexandria, Va. Lobbyist — Black, Manafort & Stone, 324 N. Fairfax St., Alexandria, Va. 22314. Filed 4/12/84. Legislative interest — "Deficit Reduction Act of 1984; HR 4170 as amended."

TRUCK TRAILER MANUFACTURERS ASSOCIATION, 1020 Princess St., Alexandria, Va. 22314. Filed for self 4/17/84. Legislative interest — "Transportation, tax, general government regulation; S 44; HR 4170." Lobbyist — Richard P. Bowling.

UNITED FRESH FRUIT AND VEGETABLE ASSOCIATION, 727 N. Washington St., Alexandria, Va. 22314. Filed for self 4/19/84. Legislative interest — "... HR 3867 & S 2052, amending the Perishable Agricultural Commodities Act; HR 1510 & S 529, Immigration Reform and Control Act; and various other pieces of legislation affecting the fresh fruit and vegetable industry." Lobbyist — Milan P. Yager.

U.S. LEAGUE OF SAVINGS INSTITUTIONS, Chicago, Ill. Lobbyist — Nicholas J. Spiezio, 1709 New York Ave. N.W., Washington, D.C. 20006. Filed 4/16/84. Legislative interest — "... HR 1179 ... HR 3025 ... HR 4029 ... HR 4243 ... HR 4557 ... S 831 ... S 1557 ... S 1914 ... S 2040 ... S 2096 ... HR 4861 ... HR 4871 ... H Res 442 ... HR 4919 ... H Con Res 262 ... HR 4950 ... HR 5026 ... HR 5038 ... HR 5112 ... HR 4581 ... HR 4614 ... HR 4618 ... HR 4632 ... H J Res 448 ... HR 4685 ... H J Res 464 ... HR 4724 ... H Con Res 250 ... H Con Res 253 ... HR 4774 ... HR 4776 ... HR 4794 ... HR 4795 ... H J Res 474 ... HR 4823 ... S 2226 ... S 2229 ... S 2243 ... S 2249 ... S Con Res 91 ... S 2264 ... S 2265 ... S 2270 ... S 2283 ... S 2294 ... S Res 349 ... S 2322 ... S 2326 ... S Con Res 96 ... S 2335 ... S 2336 ... S 2343 ... S 2345 ... S 2375 ... S 2390 ... S 2391 ... S 2400 ... S 2415...."

WASHINGTON INDEPENDENT WRITERS, Washington, D.C. Lobbyist — Goldfarb, Singer & Austern, 918 16th St. N.W., Washington, D.C. 20006. Filed 4/17/84. Legislative interest — "... include issues of importance to freelance writers. Specifically ... amendments to the work-for-hire provisions of the Copyright Act, 17 U.S.C. 101 *et seq.*"

Miscellaneous

ALL INDIAN PUEBLO COUNCIL, Albuquerque, N.M. Lobbyist — Ella Mae Horse, 1234 Massachusetts Ave. N.W., Washington, D.C. 20005. Filed 4/23/84. Legislative interest — Not specified.

ALLIANCE TO SAVE ENERGY, 1925 K St. N.W., Washington, D.C. 20006. Filed for self 4/11/84. Legislative interest — "Promotion of energy efficiency. Authorizations, appropriations, tax credits, depreciation provisions, and other financial incentives promoting energy efficiency (e.g., appropriations for Department of Energy energy efficiency programs; legislation involving utility participation in energy efficiency initiatives; weatherization legislation (e.g., S 1953); low income energy assistance, particularly as it authorizes expenditures for weatherizing buildings (e.g., S 1165); and deregulation of natural gas and other energy supplies). We favor deregulation and measures promoting energy efficiency."

AMERICAN AUTOMOBILE ASSOCIATION, 8111 Gatehouse Road, Falls Church, Va. 22047. Filed 4/11/84. Legislative interest — "Legislation relating to American motorists and travel generally. Repeal of 55 mph National Speed Limit - AAA Opposes. Motor Vehicle Theft Prevention Act - AAA Supports. Amendments to the Clean Air Act to eliminate or modify the requirement for mandatory auto emission inspection/maintenance programs for states and for other related purposes - AAA Supports. Any legislation promoting the Strategic Petroleum Reserve - AAA Generally Supports. Air Travelers Security Act (HR 2053/S 764) - legislation overturning the CAB decision in the competitive marketing case - AAA Supports. Legislation promoting alternative fuels - AAA Generally Supports. Legislation promoting highway development - AAA Generally Supports. Legislation or administrative action imposing a crude oil tax or fee - AAA Opposes. Substitution of diesel fuel tax for highway use tax - AAA Generally Opposes. Substitution of weight-distance tax for highway use tax - AAA Generally Supports. Age 21 - support grants to promote minimum age 21 drinking laws, oppose sanctions." Lobbyists — Thomas A. Kube, Cynthia Elliot Skiff.

AMERICANS FOR DEMOCRATIC ACTION, 1411 K St. N.W., Washington, D.C. 20005. Filed for self 4/20/84. Legislative interest — "Central America ... Promote regional peace settlement ... No military aid to Guatemala ... No covert military operations against Nicaragua ... Limit aid to El Salvador/promote negotiated settlement." Lobbyist — Bruce Cameron. Filed for self 4/30/84. Legislative interest — "Foreign Policy/Defense Policy ... Arms control legislation (for) ... United States international relations, treaties, agreements and military relations ... Authorization and appropriation bills." Lobbyist — Martin F. Stone.

ANATOLIA COLLEGE, BOARD OF TRUSTEES, Boston, Mass. Lobbyist — Schlossberg-Cassidy & Associates Inc., 955 L'Enfant Plaza S.W., Washington, D.C. 20024. Filed 4/10/84. Legislative interest — "Legislation relating to federal research, education and development programs."

BALTIMORE FOOTBALL ASSOCIATES INC., Baltimore, Md. Lobbyist — Piper & Marbury, 888 16th St. N.W., Washington, D.C. 20006. Filed 4/24/84. Legislative interest — "To seek clarifying amendments to interest free loan provisions of Tax Reform Act of 1984 and Deficit Reduction Act of 1984."

CALIFORNIA URBAN INDIAN HEALTH COUNCIL, Oakland, Calif. Lobbyist — Ella Mae Horse, 1234 Massachusetts Ave. N.W., Washington, D.C. 20005. Filed 4/23/84. Legislative interest — Not specified.

CAMPUS CRUSADE FOR CHRIST INC., San Bernardino, Calif. Lobbyist — The William Chasey Organization, 1800 K St. N.W., Washington, D.C. 20006. Filed 4/13/84. Legislative interest — "Deficit Reduction Act of 1984 - S 2062/HR 4170. Church Audits. Social Security Coverage for Church Employees."

CLEAN COAL COALITION INC., Washington, D.C. Lobbyist — Energy Conversion Alternatives Ltd., 2101 Connecticut Ave. N.W., Washington, D.C. 20005. Filed 4/22/84. Legislative interest — "... relate to legislation regarding regulation of acid rain." Lobbyist — Wickwire, Gavin & Gibbs, 1828 L St. N.W., Washington, D.C. 20036. Filed 4/22/84. Legislative interest — "... relate to legislation regarding regulation of acid rain."

CLEAN WATER ACTION PROJECT, Washington, D.C. Lobbyist — Vance Hughes, 8216 Maple Ridge Road, Bethesda, Md. Filed 4/23/84. Legislative interest — "Superfund Reauthorization, HR 4813 - Support. Safe Drinking Water Act Reauthorization, HR 3200 - Support."

COALITION FOR LOW INCOME & MODERATE INCOME HOUSING, Washington, D.C. Lobbyist — Patton, Boggs & Blow, 2550 M St. N.W., Washington, D.C. 20037. Filed 4/27/84. Legislative interest — "Legislation amending the Tax Reform Act of 1984 and the Deficit Reduction Tax Act of 1984 so that resyndications of low income housing can be exempt from tax accounting provisions of pending tax bills. Such as HR 4170."

COLUMBIA GORGE UNITED, P.O. Box 328, Stevenson, Wash. 98648. Filed for self 4/2/84. Legislative interest — "... opposed to enactment of S 627 (House version, HR 1747) and HR 3853 (introduced in the Senate as an amendment to S 627). Both measures are entitled 'Columbia River Gorge Act of 1983.'" Lobbyists — John Fisher, Joseph T. Wrabek.

COMMITTEE FOR THE STUDY OF THE AMERICAN ELECTORATE, 421 New Jersey Ave. S.E., Washington, D.C. 20003. Filed for self 4/5/84. Legislative interest — "Efforts directed at having legislation concerning truth in TV political campaign advertising introduced. Interests include voter registration and participation, campaign finance, campaign advertising." Lobbyist — Curtis B. Gans.

CONSERVATIVE ALLIANCE, 1001 Prince St., Alexandria, Va. 22314. Filed for self 4/17/84. Legislative interest — "Foreign affairs, national security, defense, human rights and all other legislative issues pertaining to the well-being and the preservation of freedom in the U.S. and around the world." Lobbyist — Lori A. Antolock.

COOK INLET REGION INC., Anchorage, Alaska. Lobbyist — Crowell & Moring, 1100 Connecticut Ave. N.W., Washington, D.C. 20036. Legislative interest — "... include public lands matters affecting Alaska, including the Alaska Native Claims Settlement Act (43 U.S.C. sections 1601 *et seq.*), S 1232 and the Alaska National Interests Lands Conservation Act (16 U.S.C. sections 3101 *et seq.*)."

DETROIT DOCTOR'S HOSPITAL, Detroit, Mich. Lobbyist — Gnau, Carter, Jacobsen and Associates Inc., 1250 I St. N.W., Washington, D.C. 20005. Filed 4/16/84. Legislative interest — "Health Care Legislation and possible location of government financing."

ESTATE OF VIRGINIA S. DU PONT, Wilmington, Del. Lobbyists — H. Stewart Dunn Jr. and Philip D. Morrison, 1700 Pennsylvania Ave. N.W., Washington, D.C. 20006. Filed 4/11/84. Legislative interest — "Lobbying with respect to changes to the estate and gift tax maximum rate. Specifically, against proposed raise in HR 4170 (section 21)."

ENVIRONMENTAL POLICY INSTITUTE, 218 D St. S.E., Washington, D.C. 20003. Filed for self 4/25/84. Legislative interest — "Legislation relating to nuclear energy and health effects of radiation." Lobbyist — Caroline Petti. Filed for self 4/25/84. Legislative interest — "Legislation relating to the Chesapeake Bay, Clean Water Act, related agriculture and Soil Conservation Service legislation." Lobbyist — Chuck Fox.

FRIENDS COMMITTEE ON NATIONAL LEGISLATION, 245 Second St. N.E., Washington, D.C. 20002. Filed for self 4/27/84. Legislative interest — Not specified. Lobbyist — Nancy L. Alexander.

FRIENDS OF THE EARTH, 530 7th St. S.E., Washington, D.C. 20003. Filed for self 4/2/84. Legislative interest — "... are to provide legislation to preserve, restore and insure rational use of the ecosphere, specifically: ... all legislative efforts to promote arms control, especially involving nuclear and chemical weapons, and to oppose wasteful military spending ... DOD and Military Construction Authorization and Appropriation bills; Energy and Water Authorization and Appropriation bills; arms control treaties as introduced...." Lobbyist — David A. Lewis.

GRAY PANTHERS, Philadelphia, Pa. Lobbyist — Brown & Seymour, 100 Park Ave., New York, N.Y. 10017. Filed 4/5/84. Legislative interest — "... Medicare Program ... 42 USC Sec. 1395j et al. ... For improvements in existing procedures."

HALT: AMERICANS FOR LEGAL REFORM, 201 Massachusetts Ave. N.E., Washington, D.C. 20002. Filed for self 4/2/84. Legislative interest — "... FTC Re-Authorization (S 1714, HR 2970) in favor ... Tort Reform (S 44 Uniform Product Liability Act) opposed ... HR 3175 Occupational Disease Compensation Act, in favor ... Crime Victim Compensation Act (HR 3498) in favor." Filed for self 4/2/84. Legislative interest — "HR 4325 Child Support Enforcement Amendments of 1983 ... S Con Res 40, Grandparents Visitation Rights Resolution; and custody legislation." Lobbyist — Karen Leichtman.

LAC COURTE OREILLES OJIBWA TRIBE, Hayward, Wis. Lobbyist — Ella Mae Horse, 1234 Massachusetts Ave. N.W., Washington, D.C. 20005. Filed 4/23/84. Legislative interest — Not specified.

JAMES D. LaROSA, Clarksburg, W.Va. Lobbyist — R. Duffy Wall & Associates Inc., 1317 F St. N.W., Washington, D.C. 20004. Filed 4/17/84. Legislative interest — "Issues relating to interest free loan tax legislation."

LEAGUE OF WOMEN VOTERS OF THE UNITED STATES, 1730 M St. N.W., Washington, D.C. 20036. Filed for self 4/20/84. Legislative interest — Not specified. Lobbyist — David Baker.

MASSACHUSETTS COLLEGE STUDENT LOAN AUTHORITY, Boston, Mass. Lobbyist — Larry S. Snowhite, 1875 I St. N.W., Washington, D.C. 20006. Filed 4/16/84. Legislative interest — "Legislation affecting student loan bonds."

McDERMOTT, WILL & EMERY, 1850 K St. N.W., Washington, D.C. 20006. Filed 4/13/84. Legislative interest — "Registrant's lobbying activities are in connection with their duties as *guardians ad litem*. On February 22, 1979, Judge Louis F. Oberdorfer of the United States District Court for the District of Columbia appointed registrant as *guardians ad litem* to represent the interests of the surviving infants of an airplane crash. *In Re Air Crash Disaster Near Saigon, South Vietnam on April 4, 1975*, Misc. No. 75-0205 (D.D.C., February 22, 1979)."

NATIONAL CLEAN AIR COALITION, 530 7th St. S.E., Washington, D.C. 20003. Filed for self 4/23/84. Legislative interest — "These are to provide legislation to preserve, restore, and insure the rational use of the ecosphere, particularly legislation dealing with clean air issues: HR 3400 (House Acid Rain bill); HR 4404 (New England Caucus Acid Rain bill); HR 5084 (Toxic Air Pollutants bill); S 768 (Senate Committee bill); and S 2159 (Hazardous Air Pollutants)." Lobbyist — Pamela Brodie.

NATIONAL CORPORATION FOR HOUSING PARTNERSHIPS, Washington, D.C. Lobbyist — John R. Evans, 9208

Seven Locks Road, Bethesda, Md. 20817. Filed 4/17/84. Legislative interest — ". . . broaden the authority of the National Corporation for Housing Partnerships."

NATIONAL HEALTH CARE FINANCING ASSOCIATION, P.O. Box 946, Holly Hill, Fla. 32017. Filed for self 4/19/84. Legislative interest — Not specified. Lobbyist — H. Radford Bishop.

NATIONAL UNIVERSITY, San Diego, Calif. Lobbyist — The William Chasey Organization, 1800 K St. N.W., Washington, D.C. 20006. Filed 4/13/84. Legislative interest — "Caribbean Basin Initiative/Kissinger Report. Support."

PEACE POLITICAL ACTION COMMITTEE, 100 Maryland Ave. N.E., Washington, D.C. 20002. Filed for self 4/20/84. Legislative interest — "Legislation on arms control and disarmament, FY 1985 authorization & appropriation bills for DOD, State, AEC, ACDA, etc., in U.S. House of Representatives." Lobbyist — Julie Tang.

JAMES RUSSELL, Brownsville, Texas. Lobbyist — Ely, Ritts, Pietrowski & Brickfield, Watergate 600 Building, Washington, D.C. 20037. Filed 4/20/84. Legislative interest — "HR 5051 - The bill to give permanent effect to the provision of the FPA of 1967 relating to the reimbursement of U.S. commercial fishermen for certain losses incurred incident to the seizure of their vessels by foreign nations."

SOCIAL SECURITY LOBBY, 529 14th St. N.W., Washington, D.C. 20045. Filed for self 4/23/84. Legislative interest — "Interest in persuading Congress to maintain Social Security benefits to all qualified workers both disabled and retired." Lobbyist — Dan Darling.

THE TRUST FOR PUBLIC LANDS, San Francisco, Calif. Lobbyist — Crowell & Moring, 1100 Connecticut Ave. N.W., Washington, D.C. 20036. Filed 4/20/84. Legislative interest — "Seek appropriations for purchase of park, wildlife habitat and other lands."

May Registrations

Corporations and Businesses

ALASKA AIRLINES INC., Washington, D.C. Lobbyist — The McNair Law Firm, 1155 15th St. N.W., Washington, D.C. 20005. Filed 5/17/84. Legislative interest — "Tax issues."

ALLEGHANY CORP., New York, N.Y. Lobbyist — Preston, Thorgrimson, Ellis & Holman, 1735 New York Ave. N.W., Washington, D.C. 20006. Filed 5/8/84. Legislative interest — "All legislation with respect to the transfer of the Consolidated Rail Corporation to private interests, including specifically Alleghany."

AMAX INC., New York, N.Y. Lobbyist — Dewey, Ballantine, Bushby, Palmer & Wood, 1775 Pennsylvania Ave. N.W., Washington, D.C. 20006. Filed 5/29/84. Legislative interest — Not specified.

AMERICAN EXPRESS CO., New York, N.Y. Lobbyist — Gray and Co. Public Communications International Inc., 3255 Grace St. N.W., Washington, D.C. 20007. Filed 5/7/84. Legislative interest — "Including but not limited to legislation to imposition credit card surcharges."

AMERICAN SECURITY CORP., Washington, D.C. Lobbyist — Covington & Burling, 1201 Pennsylvania Ave. N.W., Washington, D.C. 20044. Filed 5/17/84. Legislative interest — "Legislation affecting bank holding companies, banks and/or trust companies, including but not limited to S 2071, S 2134, S 2181, and HR 3499."

AMERICAN TRADING AND PRODUCTION CORP., Baltimore, Md. Lobbyist — Arnold & Porter, 1200 New Hampshire Ave. N.W., Washington, D.C. 20036. Filed 5/1/84. Legislative interest — "Bills to amend the Internal Revenue Code of 1954 with respect to treatment of closely-held active businesses, including revision of limitations on depreciation and investment tax credits on HR 4170."

APCOA INC., Atlanta, Ga. Lobbyist — Dorsey & Whitney, 1800 M St. N.W., Washington, D.C. 20036. Filed 5/3/84. Legislative interest — "HR 5409 and related bills regarding Kennedy Center debt repayment. No position taken at present time."

THE ARBUTUS CORP., Newport Beach, Calif. Lobbyist — Finley, Kumble, Wagner, Heine, Underberg, Manley & Casey, 1120 Connecticut Ave. N.W., Washington, D.C. 20036. Filed 5/21/84. Legislative interest — "Tax Reform Act, HR 4170."

AUTOMOTIVE RENTALS INC., Maple Shade, N.J. Lobbyist — Cohen and Uretz, 1775 K St. N.W., Washington, D.C. 20006. Filed 5/10/84. Legislative interest — ". . . HR 4170, sec. 166(b) and HR 2163, sec. 179. . . ."

AUTO RENTAL CORP., Worcester, Mass. Lobbyist — Cohen and Uretz, 1775 K St. N.W., Washington, D.C. 20006. Filed 5/10/84. Legislative interest — ". . . HR 4170, sec. 166(b) and HR 2163, sec. 179. . . ."

BALFOUR BEATTY LTD., Thorton Heath, Surrey, England. Lobbyist — O'Connor & Hannan, 1919 Pennsylvania Ave. N.W., Washington, D.C. 20006. Legislative interest — ". . . including, but not limited to, matters of construction and transportation."

BANCTEXAS GROUP INC., Dallas, Texas. Lobbyist — Vester T. Hughes Jr., 1000 Mercantile Dallas Building, Dallas, Texas 75201. Filed 5/23/84. Legislative interest — "In favor of the extension of time to make Internal Revenue Code Section 338 elections set forth in HR 4170, the Tax Reform Act of 1984, and HR 2163, the Deficit Reduction Tax Bill of 1984 (if modified to be identical to HR 4170)."

BANKERS LEASING CORP., San Mateo, Calif. Lobbyist — Cohen and Uretz, 1775 K St. N.W., Washington, D.C. 20006. Filed 5/10/84. Legislative interest — ". . . HR 4170, sec. 166(b) and HR 2163, sec. 179. . . ."

BECHTEL INTERNATIONAL INC., 1620 I St. N.W., Washington, D.C. 20006. Filed for self 5/21/84. Legislative interest — Not specified. Lobbyist — Richard R. Buta, 6535 Old Chesterbrook Road, McLean, Va. 22101.

BENEFICIAL LIFE INSURANCE CO., Salt Lake City, Utah. Lobbyist — David P. Stang, 1629 K St. N.W., Washington, D.C. 20006. Filed 5/7/84. Legislative interest — "HR 4170, certain provisions affecting taxation of life insurance companies."

BERKELEY BIO-MEDICAL INC., Scarsdale, N.Y. Lobbyist — Philip D. Morrison, 1700 Pennsylvania Ave. N.W., Washington, D.C. 20006. Filed 5/29/84. Legislative interest — "Generally, lobbying relating to the Tax Act of 1984. Specifically, lobbying relating to the revaluation of assets for Medicare reimbursement purposes (Deficit Reduction Act section 907)."

BEVERIDGE & DIAMOND, Washington, D.C. Lobbyist — Goldberg, Cottingham, Easterling & Napier, Drawer 655, Bennettsville, S.C. 29512. Filed 5/22/84. (Former U.S. Rep. John L. Napier, R-S.C., 1981-83, was listed as agent for this client.) Legislative interest — "Natural Gas Legislation."

BEVERLY ENTERPRISES, 1901 N. Fort Myer Drive, Rosslyn, Va. 22209. Filed for self 5/8/84. Legislative interest — "Health, Tax, Social Security and Housing Legislation and Statutes; HR 4170; S 2062, 'Omnibus Reconciliation Act of 1983' (In Support of Provisions); S 2053, 'Community and Family Living Amendments Act of 1983' (In Opposition to Provisions)." Lobbyist — Barbara A. Rudolph.

BHC INC., New York, N.Y. Lobbyist — Charles E. Walker Associates Inc., 1730 Pennsylvania Ave. N.W., Washington, D.C. 20006. Legislative interest — "Legislative interests may concern issues concerning the effective date of proposed legislation relating to the allowable dividends received deduction for dividends with respect to debt-financed portfolio stock."

BIG RIVERS ELECTRIC CORP., Henderson, Ky. Lobbyist — Mudge, Rose, Guthrie, Alexander & Ferdon, 2121 K St. N.W., Washington, D.C. 20037. Filed 5/14/84. Legislative interest — "Tax legislation affecting Rural Electric Administration Cooperatives; HR 4170, S 2163."

BOSTON & MAINE CORP., Iron Horse Park, North Billerica, Mass. 01862-1692. Filed for self 5/22/84. Legislative interest — "Any legislation relating to sale of Consolidated Rail Corporation ('Conrail'); other legislation relating to transportation." Lobbyist — F. Colin Pease.

BP NORTH AMERICA INC., New York, N.Y. Lobbyist — Sullivan & Cromwell, 125 Broad St., New York, N.Y. 10004. Filed 5/22/84. Legislative interest — "Provisions of HR 4170 and HR 2163 relating to proposed changes to tax accounting principles, foreign tax credit limitation, the taxation of corporations and shareholders, and other tax matters affecting the Employer, supporting or opposing as Employer's interests dictate."

BRISTOL BAY AREA HEALTH CORP., Dillingham, Ala. Lobbyist — Hobbs, Straus, Dean & Wilder, 1735 New York Ave. N.W., Washington, D.C. 20006. Filed 5/29/84. Legislative interest — "Federal legislation concerning health care matters."

BROADHURST, BROOK, MANGHAM, HARDY & REED, 1730 Pennsylvania Ave. N.W., Washington, D.C. 20006. Filed for self 5/3/84. Legislative interest — ". . . Any legislation dealing with energy price, supply, distribution or regulation. . . . Any legislation dealing with banking deregulation, i.e., interest deposits, non-bank banks, expanded powers, etc. . . . Any legislation dealing with environmental and trade issues."

CAMBRIDGE RESEARCH AND DEVELOPMENT GROUP, Westport, Conn. Lobbyist — Baker & McKenzie, 815 Connecticut Ave. N.W., Washington, D.C. 20006. Filed 5/17/84. Legislative interest — "Modification of Section 91(a) of HR 4170."

A. F. CAMPBELL & CO. INC., Dallas, Texas. Lobbyist — R. Duffy Wall & Associates Inc., 1317 F St. N.W., Washington, D.C. 20004. Filed 5/7/84. Legislative interest — "Issues relating to general tax legislation."

CANNON FINANCIAL GROUP, San Diego, Calif. Lobbyist — Finley, Kumble, Wagner, Heine, Underberg, Manley & Casey, 1120 Connecticut Ave. N.W., Washington, D.C. 20036. Filed 5/21/84. Legislative interest — "Tax Reform Act, HR 4170."

CAPITAL HOLDING CORP., Louisville, Ky. Lobbyist — Sutherland, Asbill & Brennan, 1666 K St. N.W., Washington, D.C. 20006. Filed 5/7/84. Legislative interest — "Legislation regarding life insurance company taxation especially with regard to S 1990 and HR 4170."

CARGILL LEASING CORP., Wayzata, Minn. Lobbyist — James C. Corman, 1420 16th St. N.W., Washington, D.C. 20036. (Former U.S. rep., D-Calif., 1961-81.) Filed 5/29/84. Legislative interest — "To monitor proposed legislation and treasury regulations and all pending matters affecting the Leasing Industry."

CAROLINA POWER AND LIGHT CO., Raleigh, N.C. Lobbyist — Charles L. Fishman, 1717 K St. N.W., Washington, D.C. 20036. Filed 5/2/84. Legislative interest — "To oppose passage of S 817, S 1069 or other efforts to alter existing Construction Work in Progress (CWIP) formulas."

CENTURIAN LIFE INSURANCE CO., Des Moines, Iowa. Lobbyist — Riddell, Fox, Holroyd & Jackson, 723 Washington Building, Washington, D.C. 20005. Filed 5/25/84. Legislative interest — "HR 4170, Tax Reform Act of 1984, and Senate tax legislation."

CHEMCRETE INTERNATIONAL CORP., Belmont, Calif. Lobbyist — Camp, Carmouche, Barsh, Hunter, Gray, Hoffman & Gill, 2550 M St. N.W., Washington, D.C. 20037. Filed 5/21/84. Legislative interest — "Matters pertaining to corporate taxation."

CHEVRON U.S.A. INC., 1700 K St. N.W., Washington, D.C. 20006. Filed for self 5/10/84. Legislative interest — Not specified. Lobbyist — Thomas M. Bresnahan III.

CHRIS-CRAFT INDUSTRIES INC., New York, N.Y. Lobbyist — Charls E. Walker Associates Inc., 1730 Pennsylvania Ave. N.W., Washington, D.C. 20006. Filed 5/9/84. Legislative interest — "Legislative interests may concern issues concerning the effective date of proposed legislation relating to the allowable dividends received deduction for dividends with respect to debt-financed portfolio stock."

COM DISCO INC., Rosemont, Ill. Lobbyist — Williams & Jensen, 1101 Connecticut Ave. N.W., Washington, D.C. 20036. Filed 5/14/84. Legislative interest — "Tax matters of interest to the company."

COMPREHENSIVE HEALTH CARE SERVICES OF DETROIT INC., Detroit, Mich. Lobbyist — Miller, Canfield, Paddock & Stone, 2555 M St. N.W., Washington, D.C. 20037. Filed

5/15/84. Legislative interest — "HR 5394 (Section 363 only)."

COMPUTERVISION, 8921 Burdette Road, Bethesda, Md. 20817. Filed for self 5/3/84. Legislative interest — ". . . Armed Services appropriations. . . ." Lobbyist — John H. Forehand III, 95 East Wayne Ave., Silver Spring, Md. 20901.

CONSOLIDATED NATURAL GAS CO., Pittsburgh, Pa. Lobbyist — Wickwire, Gavin & Gibbs, 1819 L St. N.W., Washington, D.C. 20036. Filed 5/7/84 and 5/16/84. Legislative interest — "In support of legislation to facilitate cogeneration activities, including HR 4467."

COOPERATIVE OF AMERICAN PHYSICIANS INC., Los Angeles, Calif. Lobbyist — Ullman Consultants Inc., 1000 Potomac St. N.W., Washington, D.C. 20007. Filed 5/18/84. Legislative interest — "Legislation involving medical malpractice protection."

COVE MARITIME COS., New York, N.Y. Lobbyist — Bogle & Gates, One Thomas Circle N.W., Washington, D.C. 20005. Filed 5/8/84. Legislative interest — "Registrant opposes administration efforts to allow existing foreign built ships to engage in carriage of U.S. preference cargoes without waiting three (3) years from date of U.S. registry as now required."

CPT CORP., 8100 Mitchell Road, Minneapolis, Minn. 55440. Filed for self 5/25/84. Legislative interest — "Opposition to bills S 286 and HR 1159 or any comparable bills to regulate contractual arrangements between suppliers and retailers in the office machine and equipment industry." Lobbyist — David C. Priebe.

CROWLEY MARITIME CORP., San Francisco, Calif. Lobbyist — Kominers, Fort, Schlefer & Boyer, 1776 F St. N.W., Washington, D.C. 20006. Filed 5/2/84. Legislative interest — ". . . HR 5220."

CUSATI/HEISE PARTNERSHIP, Rolling Meadows, Ill. Lobbyist — Williams & Jensen, 1101 Connecticut Ave. N.W., Washington, D.C. 20036. Filed 5/11/84. Legislative interest — "Legislative developments affecting the taxation of partnerships and their partners."

DART & KRAFT, Northbrook, Ill. Lobbyist — Baker & McKenzie, 815 Connecticut Ave. N.W., Washington, D.C. 20006. Filed 5/16/84. Legislative interest — "Modification of section 612(1) of HR 4170."

CECIL B. DAY COS., Atlanta, Ga. Lobbyist — Sutherland, Asbill & Brennan, 1666 K St. N.W., Washington, D.C. 20006. Filed 5/7/84. Legislative interest — "Tax legislation affecting gifts of appreciated properties to private foundations."

DEXTER DEVELOPMENT CO., Aberdeen, Wash. Lobbyist — Murphy & Davenport, 711 Capitol Way, Olympia, Wash. 98501. Filed 5/2/84. Legislative interest — "Indian land claims, S 1735."

DIGITAL EQUIPMENT CORP., Acton, Mass. Lobbyist — Philip D. Morrison, 1700 Pennsylvania Ave. N.W., Washington, D.C. 20006. Filed 5/29/84. Legislative interest — "Generally, all legislation relating to federal income taxation of corporations. Specifically, lobbying relating to technical changes to section 44F legislation."

WALT DISNEY PRODUCTIONS, Burbank, Calif. Lobbyist — Blum, Nash & Railsback, 1015 18th St. N.W., Washington, D.C. 20036. (Former U.S. Rep. Thomas Railsback, R-Ill., 1967-83, was listed among agents for this client.) Filed 5/14/84. Legislative interest — "Legislation relating to amendments to Copyright Act of 1976, HR 1027, interest & syndication rules, HR 4260, S 1707: cable copyright rates, S 1270, HR 3419 & HR 2902; 'works made for hire,' S 2138; export trade & misc. copyright bills affecting films and television programs."

DONREY INC., Fort Smith, Ark. Lobbyist — Steven L. Engelberg, 2033 M St. N.W., Washington, D.C. 20036. Filed 5/14/84. Legislative interest — "Provisions of law relating to private foundations and ESOPs now found in Section 314(D) of the Deficit Reduction Tax Bill of 1984."

DRESSER LEASING CORP., Pittsburgh, Pa. Lobbyist — Cohen and Uretz, 1775 K St. N.W., Washington, D.C. 20006. Filed 5/10/84. Legislative interest — ". . . HR 4170, sec. 166(b) and HR 2163, sec. 179. . . ."

THE DREYFUS CORP., New York, N.Y. Lobbyist — Charls E. Walker Associates Inc., 1730 Pennsylvania Ave. N.W.,

Washington, D.C. 20006. Filed 5/7/84. Legislative interest — "... may concern issues relating to taxes on interest and dividends from foreign sources and permissible activities of subsidiary banks."

DUKE POWER CO., Charlotte, N.C. Lobbyist — Charles L. Fishman, 1717 K St. N.W., Washington, D.C. 20036. Filed 5/2/84. Legislative interest — "To oppose passage of S 817, S 1069 or other efforts to alter existing Construction Work in Progress (CWIP) formulas."

EAST LAKE COMMUNICATIONS, Chicago, Ill. Lobbyist — MMB Associates Inc., 122 C St. N.W., Washington, D.C. 20001. Filed 5/8/84. Legislative interest — "Broadcast Regulation Legislation."

EASTMAN KODAK CO., Rochester, N.Y. Lobbyist — Philip D. Morrison, 1700 Pennsylvania Ave. N.W., Washington, D.C. 20006. Filed 5/29/84. Legislative interest — "Generally, lobbying relating to the Tax Act of 1984. Specifically, lobbying relating to the deductibility of year end bonus pay and (S 195) start-up expenses."

EATON VANCE CORP., Boston, Mass. Lobbyist — Covington & Burling, 1201 Pennsylvania Ave. N.W., Washington, D.C. 20044. Filed 5/17/84. Legislative interest — "Legislation affecting bank holding companies, banks and/or trust companies, including but not limited to S 2071, S 2134, S 2181, and HR 3499."

EMPACADORA DEL NORTE, San Juan, Puerto Rico. Lobbyist — Wald, Harkrader & Ross, 1300 19th St. N.W., Washington, D.C. 20036. Filed 5/18/84. Legislative interest — "... seeking legislation involving the corporation's property interests in Honduras."

ENERGY RESEARCH CORP., Danbury, Conn. Lobbyist — Donald R. Glenn, 1627 K St. N.W., Washington, D.C. 20006. Filed 5/8/84. Legislative interest — "All matters affecting energy R&D, electrochemical systems R&D, and manufacturing/sales, fuel supplies and utilization."

THE EQUITABLE LIFE ASSURANCE SOCIETY OF THE UNITED STATES, 1285 Avenue of the Americas, New York, N.Y. 10019. Filed for self 5/7/84. Legislative interest — "Life insurance taxation." Lobbyist — Robert F. Froehlke. Filed for self 5/4/84. Legislative interest — "Banking deregulation legislation." Lobbyist — Edward S. Cabot.

EQUITY CARRIERS I INC., Houston, Texas. Lobbyist — Bogle & Gates, One Thomas Circle N.W., Washington, D.C. 20005. Filed 5/8/84. Legislative interest — "Registrant is in favor of amendments to Section 614 of the Merchants Marine Act of 1936 (46 U.S.C. section 1184; the 'Snyder Amendment'). Registrant opposes administration efforts to allow existing foreign built ships to engage in carriage of U.S. preference cargoes without waiting three (3) years from date of U.S. registry as now required."

EQUITY CARRIERS III INC., Houston, Texas. Lobbyist — Bogle & Gates, One Thomas Circle N.W., Washington, D.C. 20005. Filed 5/8/84. Legislative interest — "Registrant is in favor of amendments to Section 614 of the Merchant Marine Act of 1936 (46 U.S.C. section 1184; the 'Snyder Amendment'). Registrant opposes administration efforts to allow existing foreign built ships to engage in carriage of U.S. preference cargoes without waiting three (3) years from date of U.S. registry as now required."

EXECUTIVE LIFE INSURANCE CO., Beverly Hills, Calif. Lobbyist — Cohen and Uretz, 1775 K St. N.W., Washington, D.C. 20006. Filed 5/31/84. Legislative interest — "Taxation of insurance companies and products. HR 4170; Deficit Reduction Act of 1984."

FAIRCHILD INDUSTRIES, Washington, D.C. Lobbyist — PM Consulting Corp., 333 Perry Brooks Building, Austin, Texas 78701. Filed 5/25/84. Legislative interest — Not specified.

FALCON TANKERS INC., Houston, Texas. Lobbyist — Bogle & Gates, One Thomas Circle N.W., Washington, D.C. 20005. Filed 5/8/84. Legislative interest — "... HR 5071 ... in favor of this bill."

FAMILY LIFE INSURANCE CO., Seattle, Wash. Lobbyist — Morgan, Lewis & Bockius, 1800 M St. N.W., Washington, D.C. 20036. Filed 5/7/84. Legislative interest — "Legislation affecting the tax treatment of insurance and annuity products."

FIDELITY BANKERS LIFE INSURANCE CO., Richmond, Va. Lobbyist — Sutherland, Asbill & Brennan, 1666 K St. N.W., Washington, D.C. 20006. Filed 5/30/84. Legislative interest — "Interest in the treatment of retired lives reserves under the 'funded welfare benefit plan provisions' of the Senate version of the 1984 tax bill."

47th STREET PHOTO, New York, N.Y. Lobbyist — Hughes, Hubbard & Reed, 1201 Pennsylvania Ave. N.W., Washington, D.C. 20004. Filed 5/24/84. Legislative interest — "To bring to the attention of relevant committees, members and staff of the House and Senate positions on importation of trademarked products."

GELCO CORP., Eden Prairie, Minn. Lobbyist — Cohen and Uretz, 1775 K St. N.W., Washington, D.C. 20006. Filed 5/10/84. Legislative interest — "... HR 4170, sec. 166(b) and HR 2163, sec. 179...."

GENERAL SHALE PRODUCTS CORP., Johnson City, Tenn. Lobbyist — Philip D. Morrison, 1700 Pennsylvania Ave. N.W., Washington, D.C. 20006. Filed 5/29/84. Legislative interest — "Generally, all legislation relating to federal income taxation of corporation. Specifically, lobbying relating to the Tax Act of 1984."

GILMORE STEEL CORP., Portland, Ore. Lobbyist — Government Relations Associates Inc., 655 15th St. N.W., Washington, D.C. 20005. Filed 5/11/84. Legislative interest — "International trade, steel quota legislation, other legislative matters as they arise."

SUSAN HOWLAND-KELLY & ASSOCIATES, 20 Black Oak Mews, Newtown, Pa. 18940. Filed for self 5/16/84. Legislative interest — "Any interest or action affecting the Maritime or Electrical Industry." Lobbyists — Shelley Ann Gardner, Susan Howland-Kelly.

HUGHES AIRCRAFT CO., Arlington, Va. Lobbyist — Dickstein, Shapiro & Morin, 2101 L St. N.W., Washington, D.C. 20037. Filed 5/8/84. Legislative interest — "Authorization bills and appropriations bill affecting industry."

INTERMOUNTAIN HEALTH CARE, Salt Lake City, Utah. Lobbyist — Bonneville Associates Inc., 444 North Capitol St. N.W., Washington, D.C. 20001. Filed 5/21/84. Legislative interest — "Health care legislation, including Titles XVIII and XIX of the Social Security Act and Title XV of the Public Health Service Act...."

J. L. INTERNATIONAL LTD., Westmount, Quebec, Canada. Lobbyist — Finley, Kumble, Wagner, Heine, Underberg, Manley & Casey, 1120 Connecticut Ave. N.W., Washington, D.C. 20036. Filed 5/21/84. Legislative interest — "HR 4170, Tax Reform Act."

ITEL RAILROAD CORP., San Francisco, Calif. Lobbyist — Hanson, Bridgett, Marcus, Vlahos & Stromberg, 333 Market St., San Francisco, Calif. 94105. Filed 5/7/84. Legislative interest — "... pertain to an amendment to the Staggers Act (49 U.S.C. Section 1122), regarding deregulation of rates for commodities shipped in boxcars. The specific legislative interests involve an amendment to Senate Resolution 2257 that would extend to July 1, 1985, the action of the Interstate Commerce Commission in *Ex Parte* 346, Subdivision 8. The legislative interests are for this amendment."

K-MART, Washington, D.C. Lobbyist — Parry & Romani Associates Inc., 1140 Connecticut Ave. N.W., Washington, D.C. 20036. Filed 5/30/84. Legislative interest — "Anti-Counterfeiting Bill."

LAUREL STEEL PRODUCTS LTD., Burlington, Ontario, Canada. Lobbyist — Barry Alexander Herring, 66 Valecrest Ave., Hamilton, Ontario, Canada L7L 5N5. Filed 5/9/84. Legislative interest — "... Fair Trade in Steel Act and other trade related bills.... HR 4352, HR 5081, HR 4124, HR 4784, S 2380.... Opposition to any legislation which restricts U.S. imports of steel mill products from Canada."

LAWRENCE KUDLOW ASSOCIATES, Washington, D.C. Lobbyist — J. L. Associates, One Thomas Circle N.W., Washington, D.C. 20005. Filed 5/1/84. Legislative interest — Not specified.

LEAD MARKETING INTERNATIONAL, 2000 L St. N.W., Washington, D.C. 20036. Filed for self 5/1/84. Legislative interest — "High Technology Legislation."

LEASEWAY TRANSPORTATION CORP., Cleveland, Ohio. Lobbyist — Cohen and Uretz, 1775 K St. N.W., Washington, D.C. 20006. Filed 5/10/84. Legislative interest — "... HR 4170, sec. 166(b) and HR 2163, sec. 179...."

LINCOLN NATIONAL LIFE INSURANCE CO., Fort Wayne, Ind. Lobbyist — Sutherland, Asbill & Brennan, 1666 K St. N.W., Washington, D.C. 20006. Filed 5/7/84. Legislative interest — "Legislation regarding life insurance company taxation and deregulation of financial services industry and other matters affecting the insurance industry."

LOMAS & NETTLETON FINANCIAL CORP., Dallas, Texas. Lobbyist — Vester T. Hughes Jr., 1000 Mercantile Dallas Building, Dallas, Texas 75201. Filed 5/23/84. Legislative interest — "In favor of the real estate depreciation and employee benefit provisions of HR 4170, the Tax Reform Act of 1984, and HR 2163, the Deficit Reduction Tax Bill of 1984 (if modified to be identical to HR 4170)."

LTV AEROSPACE AND DEFENSE CO., Arlington, Va. Lobbyist — Dickstein, Shapiro & Morin, 2101 L St. N.W., Washington, D.C. 20037. Filed 5/8/84. Legislative interest — "Authorization bills and appropriations bill affecting industry."

McDONNELL DOUGLAS CORP., Arlington, Va. Lobbyist — Dickstein, Shapiro & Morin, 2101 L St. N.W., Washington, D.C. 20037. Filed 5/8/84. Legislative interest — "Authorization bills and appropriation bills affecting industry."

DAVY McKEE CORP., Lakeland, Fla. Lobbyist — Hagedorn-Cando Inc., 1704 23rd St. South, Arlington, Va. 22202. Filed 5/11/84. Legislative interest — "1985 FY Authorization of the Dept. of Energy. All issues relating to the Methanol Fuel industry and in particular, funding for the study of methane to methanol plants using remote gas fields or low quality natural gas as feedstock for relocatable methanol plants."

MERCANTILE STORES INC., New York, N.Y. Lobbyist — Philip D. Morrison, 1700 Pennsylvania Ave. N.W., Washington, D.C. 20006. Filed 5/29/84. Legislative interest — "Generally, lobbying relating to the Tax Act of 1984. Specifically, lobbying relating to the deductibility of year end bonus pay."

MERCHANTS TERMINAL CORP., Baltimore, Md. Lobbyist — Covington & Burling, P.O. Box 7566, Washington, D.C. 20044. Filed 5/14/84. Legislative interest — "Multiemployer pension plan withdrawal liability.... Bankruptcy Amendments ... HR 5174 ... For."

MERRILL LYNCH HUBBARD, New York, N.Y. Lobbyist — Rodgers & Wells, 1737 H St. N.W., Washington, D.C. 20006. Filed 5/14/84. Legislative interest — "Tax legislation generally; HR 4170 and HR 2163 (as amended) specifically."

MILLIKEN MILLS, Spartanburg, S.C. Lobbyist — McNair, Glenn, Konduros, Corley, Singletary, Porter & Dibble, 1155 15th St. N.W., Washington, D.C. 20005. Filed 5/29/84. Legislative interest — "All bankruptcy legislation."

MOLLER STEAMSHIP CO. INC., New York, N.Y. Lobbyist — Mark R. Johnson, 1667 K St. N.W., Washington, D.C. 20036. Filed 5/17/84. Legislative interest — Not specified.

MORGAN GUARANTY TRUST CO., New York, N.Y. Lobbyist — R. Duffy Wall & Associates Inc., 1317 F St. N.W., Washington, D.C. 20004. Filed 5/31/84. Legislative interest — "Issues relating to general tax legislation."

MORGAN STANLEY & CO. INC., New York, N.Y. Lobbyist — Akin, Gump, Strauss, Hauer & Feld, 1333 New Hampshire Ave. N.W., Washington, D.C. 20036. Filed 5/25/84. Legislative interest — "Legislation affecting regulation of banking and securities industries."

NEW ENGLAND ELECTRIC SYSTEM, Westborough, Mass. Lobbyist — Charles L. Fishman, 1717 K St. N.W., Washington, D.C. 20036. Filed 5/7/84. Legislative interest — "To oppose passage of S 817, S 1069 or other efforts to alter existing Construction Work in Progress (CWIP) formulas."

NEW ENGLAND MUTUAL LIFE INSURANCE CO., Boston, Mass. Lobbyist — Fried, Frank, Harris, Shriver & Kampelman, 600 New Hampshire Ave. N.W., Washington, D.C. 20037. Filed 5/1/84. Legislative interest — "Propose changes to HR 2163 and HR 4170."

OMNI-TECH OF AMERICA INC., Portland, Texas. Lobbyist — John H. Forehand III, 95 East Wayne Ave., Silver Spring, Md. 20901. Filed 5/3/84. Legislative interest — "... Housing, Armed Services...."

PENNSYLVANIA ENGINEERING CORP., Pittsburgh, Pa. Lobbyist — Cramer, Haber & Lukis, 818 Connecticut Ave. N.W., Washington, D.C. 20006. (Former U.S. Rep. William C. Cramer, R-Fla., 1955-71, was listed among agents for this client.) Filed 5/4/84. Legislative interest — "Tax legislation limiting authority to issue Industrial Development Bonds for the construction of a solid waste disposal facility."

PHH GROUP INC., Hunt Valley, Md. Lobbyist — Cohen and Uretz, 1775 K St. N.W., Washington, D.C. 20006. Filed 5/10/84. Legislative interest — "... HR 4170, sec. 166(b) and HR 2163, sec. 179...."

PHOENIX BULKSHIP I INC., Houston, Texas. Lobbyist — Bogle & Gates, One Thomas Circle N.W., Washington, D.C. 20005. Filed 5/8/84. Legislative interest — "Registrant opposes administration efforts to allow existing foreign built ships to engage in carriage of U.S. preference cargoes without waiting three (3) years from date of U.S. registry as now required."

PHOENIX BULKSHIP II INC., Houston, Texas. Lobbyist — Bogle & Gates, One Thomas Circle N.W., Washington, D.C. 20005. Filed 5/8/84. Legislative interest — "Registrant opposes administration efforts to allow existing foreign built ships to engage in carriage of U.S. preference cargoes without waiting three (3) years from date of U.S. registry as now required."

PLAINS ELECTRIC GENERATION AND TRANSMISSION COOPERATIVE INC., Albuquerque, N.M. Lobbyist — Mudge, Rose, Guthrie, Alexander & Ferdon, 2121 K St. N.W., Washington, D.C. 20037. Filed 5/14/84. Legislative interest — "Tax legislation affecting Rural Electric Administration Cooperatives; HR 4170, S 2163."

PPG INDUSTRIES INC., 1730 Rhode Island Ave. N.W., Washington, D.C. 20036. Filed for self 5/11/84. Legislative interest — "Issues affecting the company's business concerned with energy and environmental issues ... S 1715, HR 4277, S 431, HR 3282, S 768...." Lobbyist — Edward L. Jaffee. Filed for self 5/15/84. Legislative interest — "Taxation, international trade, general business issues. S 1804 - in favor of Patent Term Restoration, S 44 — in favor of Product Liability Reform." Lobbyist — Michal W. Mainwaring. Filed for self 5/21/84. Legislative interest — "... taxes, environmental statutes, energy, transportation and general commerce. S 1715 ... HR 3818, S 757, HR 2867...." Lobbyist — Robert Gary Wilson.

RADAR DEVICES INC., San Leandro, Calif. Lobbyist — Foresight Science & Technology Inc., 2000 P St. N.W., Washington, D.C. 20036. Filed 5/7/84. Legislative interest — "Issues relating to marine navigation and communications ... DOT Appropriations ... for."

REPUBLIC INDUSTRIES INC., Washington, D.C. Lobbyist — Reed, Smith, Shaw & McClay, 1150 Connecticut Ave. N.W., Washington, D.C. 20036. Filed 5/17/84. Legislative interest — "Deficit Reduction Act of 1984; HR 2162."

RHINECHEM CORP., Pittsburgh, Pa. Lobbyist — Philip D. Morrison, 1700 Pennsylvania Ave. N.W., Washington, D.C. 20006. Filed 5/29/84. Legislative interest — "... Tax Act of 1984...."

SALEN DRY CARGO INC., Washington, D.C. Lobbyist — Gray and Co., 3255 Grace St. N.W., Washington, D.C. 20007. Filed 5/7/84. Legislative interest — "Including but not limited to maritime legislation."

SAND LIVESTOCK SYSTEMS INC., Columbus, Neb. Lobbyist — Erickson & Sederstrom, 400 Corn Husker Plaza, Lincoln, Neb. 68508. (Former U.S. Rep. Charles Thone, R-Neb., 1971-79; gov., 1979-83, was listed as agent for this client.) Filed 5/17/84. Legislative interest — "Against Senate amendment No. 2994 to HR 2163."

SANLANDO UTILITIES CORP., Orlando, Fla. Lobbyist — Sutherland, Asbill & Brennan, 1666 K St. N.W., Washington, D.C. 20006. Legislative interest — "Legislation revising rules for collapsible corporations."

SATELLITE SYNDICATED SYSTEMS INC., Tulsa,

Okla. Lobbyist — Pepper & Corazzini, 1776 K St. N.W., Washington, D.C. 20006. Filed 5/18/84. Legislative interest — "Copyright Act of 1976, PL 94-553, 90 Stat. 17 U.S.C. sec. 101, *et seq.*"

SCHULMAN MANAGEMENT, Hollywood, Calif. Lobbyist — Theodore Waller, 2501 M St. N.W., Washington, D.C. 20037. Filed 5/24/84. Legislative interest — "Tax Legislation Generally."

SCOTT PAPER CO., Philadelphia, Pa. Lobbyist — Morgan, Lewis & Bockius, 1800 M St. N.W., Washington, D.C. 20036. Filed 5/23/84. Legislative interest — "Federal Income Tax Issues - HR 4170 and HR 2163."

JOSEPH E. SEAGRAM & SONS INC., 1201 Pennsylvania Ave. N.W., Washington, D.C. 20004. Filed for self 5/23/84. Legislative interest — "Any legislation affecting the distilled spirits and wine industry, specifically tax and trade legislation. Any legislation affecting, directly or indirectly, the existing legal right of any U.S. subsidiary of a Canadian parent company to hold leases on federal lands or to make any investment in the United States."

SECURITY-CONNECTICUT LIFE INSURANCE CO., Avon, Conn. Lobbyist — Sutherland, Asbill & Brennan, 1666 K St. N.W., Washington, D.C. 20006. Filed 5/30/84. Legislative interest — "Interest in the treatment of retired lives reserves under the 'funded welfare benefit plan provisions' of the Senate version of the 1984 tax bill."

SEMINOLE ELECTRIC COOPERATIVE INC., Tampa, Fla. Lobbyist — Mudge, Rose, Gutherie, Alexander & Ferdon, 2121 K St. N.W., Washington, D.C. 20037. Filed 5/14/84. Legislative interest — "Tax legislation affecting Rural Electric Administration Cooperatives; HR 4170, S 2163."

SENTRY LIFE INSURANCE CO., Stevens Point, Wis. Lobbyist — Sutherland, Asbill & Brennan, 1666 K St. N.W., Washington, D.C. 20006. Filed 5/30/84. Legislative interest — "Interest in the treatment of retired lives reserves under the 'funded welfare benefit plan provisions' of the Senate version of the 1984 tax bill."

SMC INTERNATIONAL, Washington, D.C. Lobbyist — John L. Zorack, 1140 19th St. N.W., Washington, D.C. 20036. Filed 5/4/84. Legislative interest — "Long distance directory charges. No specific legislation pending. For reduction of proposed long distance directory services charges."

SNYDER OIL CO., Denver, Colo. Lobbyist — Davis, Graham & Stubbs, 1001 22nd St. N.W., Washington, D.C. 20037. Filed 5/14/84. Legislative interest — "Amendments to California Wilderness Bill, HR 1437, S 5, S 1515."

SOUTHERN CALIFORNIA EDISON, Rosemead, Calif. Lobbyist — Nossaman, Guthner, Knox & Elliot, 1140 19th St. N.W., Washington, D.C. 20036. Filed 5/21/84. Legislative interest — "Concerning legislation related to relicensing of hydro-power projects."

SOUTHERN COMPANY SERVICES INC., Birmingham, Ala. Lobbyist — Balch, Bingham, Baker, Ward, Smith, Bowman & Thagard, P.O. Box 306, Birmingham, Ala. 35201. Filed 5/29/84. Legislative interest — ". . . proposed legislation dealing with relicensing of hydroelectric plants. Specifically: Federal Power Act, 16 U.S.C. Section 791a *et seq.* - favor amendment thereof; Electric Consumers Protection Act of 1983, HR 4402 - for passage; Public Interest Hydroelectric Facility Relicensing Reform Act of 1984, HR 5299 - oppose; Electric Utility Compensation Act of 1984, HR 5416 - oppose."

THE SOUTHLAND CORP., Dallas, Texas. Lobbyist — Simon, Twombly & Terry, 17130 Dallas Parkway, Dallas, Texas 75248. Filed 5/21/84. Legislative interest — "HR 4170 and HR 2163, generally for with modifications." Lobbyist — D'Amico, Luedtke, Demarest & Golden, 1920 N St. N.W., Washington, D.C. 20036. Filed 5/25/84. Legislative interest — "Petroleum marketing legislation, HR 5023; energy legislation - legislation re: imported petroleum products: HR 5455, HR 4232, HR 2479, S 1718."

THE STANDARD OIL CO. (OHIO), Cleveland, Ohio. Filed for self 5/7/84. Legislative interest — "General legislative matters pertaining to the interests of the company respecting petroleum products, refining and distribution, petro-chemical and coal, and metal/non-metal minerals." Lobbyist — Ross J. Heide, 1001 22nd St. N.W., Washington, D.C. 20037.

STELCO INC., Toronto Dominion Center, Toronto, Ontario, Canada M5K 1J4. Filed for self 5/9/84. Legislative interest — ". . . Fair Trade in Steel Act . . . HR 4352 . . . in opposition to any legislation which restricts U.S. imports of steel mill products in Canada." Lobbyist — John D. Allan.

STEPHENS & KREBS, 1800 Old Meadow Road, McLean, Va. 22101. Filed for self 5/25/84. Legislative interest — "General legislative matters dealing with taxes, labor relations, small business and other federal issues coming under federal congressional review."

STEPTOE & JOHNSON, Washington, D.C. Lobbyist — Ullman Consultants Inc., 1000 Potomac St. N.W., Washington, D.C. 20007. (Former U.S. Rep. Al Ullman, D-Ore., 1957-81, was listed as agent for this client.) Filed 5/18/84. Legislative interest — "Trade legislation."

TACOMA CITY LIGHT, Tacoma, Wash. Lobbyist — Denny Miller Associates, 203 Maryland Ave. N.E., Washington, D.C. 20002. Filed 5/3/84. Legislative interest — "Rare II; S 837."

TALLEY CORP., Phoenix, Ariz. Lobbyist — PM Consulting Corp., 333 Perry Brooks Building, Austin, Texas 78701. Filed 5/25/84. Legislative interest — Not specified.

O. C. TANNER CO., Salt Lake City, Utah. Lobbyist — Caplin & Drysdale, 1101 17th St. N.W., Washington, D.C. 20036. Filed 5/16/84. Legislative interest — "General legislative interest in changes to the employee awards provisions of Internal Revenue Code Section 274(b). Specific legislative interest in: (a) the Deficit Reduction Act of 1984, offered as an amendment to the Federal Boat Safety Act (S 2163); (b) the Tax Reform Act of 1984 (HR 4170)."

TOSCO CORP., Santa Monica, Calif. Lobbyist — Marcus W. Sisk Jr., 2828 Pennsylvania Ave. N.W., Washington, D.C. 20007. Filed 5/24/84. Legislative interest — "In opposition to provisions in HR 4170 or similar legislation which would retroactively tax recapitalization or the restructuring of debt by corporations. In support of legislation to provide relief for small and independent re-refiners with remaining claims under the petroleum control and allocation program administered by the Department of Energy."

TUBBS CORDAGE CO., San Francisco, Calif. Lobbyist — Pillsbury, Madison & Sutro, 1050 17th St. N.W., Washington, D.C. 20036. Filed 5/21/84. Legislative interest — "Monitoring legislation relating to the importation of cordage products."

UNITED AIRLINES, Washington, D.C. Lobbyist — Thomas A. Davis, 499 South Capitol St. S.W., Washington, D.C. 20003. Filed 5/21/84. Legislative interest — "Legislation concerning the tax treatment of deferred rent payments ... Deficit Reduction Act of 1984 ... S 2163, HR 4170 ... Proposed IRC Section 467 ... Seek modification." Lobbyist — Corporation Consulting Services Inc., P.O. Box 2768, Key Largo, Fla. 33037. (Former U.S. Rep. L. A. "Skip" Bafalis, R-Fla., 1973-83, was listed as agent for this client.) Filed 5/30/84. Legislative interest — "Legislation concerning the tax treatment of deferred rent payments ... Deficit Reduction Act of 1984 ... S 2163, HR 4170 ... Proposed IRC Section 467 ... Seek modification."

UNITED BRANDS CO., New York, N.Y. Lobbyist — Dickstein, Shapiro & Morin, 2101 L St. N.W., Washington, D.C. 20037. Filed 5/8/84. Legislative interest — "Provisions of tax bill relating to foreign tax exempt leasing."

UNITED COAL CO., Bristol, Va. Lobbyist — McGuire, Woods & Battle, 1400 Ross Building, Richmond, Va. 23219. Filed 5/2/84. Legislative interest — "Interests include all legislation dealing with the production and sale of coal, acid rain legislation and bills affecting PL 96-294, including S 145, S 768, S 769, S 2001, S 454, S 766, HR 132, HR 3400, HR 1405, HR 1404. Will generally support a 'least cost' alternative type of acid rain legislation."

U.S. CAPITAL CORP., Columbia, S.C. Lobbyist — Adams, Quackenbush, Herring & Stuart, P.O. Box 394, Columbia, S.C. 29202. Filed 5/18/84. Legislative interest — "Intend to lobby the Alabama Beach Mouse becoming an endangered species under Endangered Species Act; intend to lobby for exemption of part of Gulf Shores, Alabama from Barrier Islands Act; and intend to secure exemption of 'Mills-Babcock Complex' from new Federal Tax Package."

UNITED STATES FIDELITY AND GUARANTY CO., Baltimore, Md. Lobbyist — Charls E. Walker Associates Inc., 1730 Pennsylvania Ave. N.W., Washington, D.C. 20006. Filed 5/18/84. Legislative interest — "... may concern issues relating to the treatment of income earned by a regulated investment company."

U.S. SUGAR, Clewiston, Fla. Lobbyist — Thomas A. Davis, 499 South Capitol St. S.W., Washington, D.C. 20003. Filed 5/21/84. Legislative interest — "Tax legislation concerning employee stock option plans ... Deficit Reduction Act of 1984 ... S 2163 and HR 4170 ... 26 U.S.C. Section 422 A (Internal Revenue Code) ... Seek Modification."

VIRGINIA ELECTRIC AND POWER CO., Richmond, Va. Lobbyist — Charles L. Fishman, 1717 K St. N.W., Washington, D.C. 20036. Filed 5/2/84. Legislative interest — "To oppose passage of S 817, S 1069 or other efforts to alter existing Construction Work in Progress (CWIP) formulas."

WESTERN SOUTHERN, Cincinnati, Ohio. Lobbyist — The Hoving Group, 2550 M St. N.W., Washington, D.C. 20037. Filed 5/15/84. Legislative interest — "Matters relating to tax policy."

WESTINGHOUSE, Washington, D.C. Lobbyist — O'Connor & Hannan, 1919 Pennsylvania Ave. N.W., Washington, D.C. 20006. Filed 5/17/84. Legislative interest — Not specified.

WHEELS INC., Chicago, Ill. Lobbyist — Cohen and Uretz, 1775 K St. N.W., Washington, D.C. 20006. Filed 5/10/84. Legislative interest — "... HR 4170, sec. 166(b) and HR 2163, sec. 179...."

WILKIE, FARR & GALLAGHER, New York, N.Y. Lobbyist — Williams & Jensen, 1101 Connecticut Ave. N.W., Washington, D.C. 20036. Filed 5/12/84. Legislative interest — "Legislative developments affecting the taxation of real estate."

WINN ENTERPRISES, Los Angeles, Calif. Lobbyist — Parry and Romani Associates Inc., 1140 Connecticut Ave. N.W. Washington, D.C. 20036. Filed 5/29/84. Legislative interest — "Legislation affecting the dairy and food industries."

XEROX CORP., Stamford, Conn. Lobbyist — Philip D. Morrison, 1700 Pennsylvania Ave. N.W., Washington, D.C. 20006. Filed 5/29/84. Legislative interest — "Generally, lobbying relating to the Tax Act of 1984. Specifically, lobbying relating to the characterization of a transaction as a lease or service contract for tax purposes."

International Relations

REPUBLIC OF KOREA, Seoul, South Korea. Lobbyist — Gray and Co., 3255 Grace St. N.W., Washington, D.C. 20007. Filed 5/3/84. Legislative interest — "Including but not limited to economic and trade matters."

State and Local Governments

BROWARD COUNTY, Ft. Lauderdale, Fla. Lobbyist — Cramer, Haber & Lukis, 818 Connecticut Ave. N.W., Washington, D.C. 20006. (Former U.S. Rep. William C. Cramer, R-Fla., 1955-71, was listed among agents for this client.) Filed 5/4/84. Legislative interest — "Tax legislation limiting Broward County's authority to issue Industrial Development Bonds for the construction of a solid waste disposal facility."

DELAWARE ECONOMIC DEVELOPMENT AUTHORITY, Dover, Del. Lobbyist — Ballard, Spahr, Andrews & Ingersoll, 1850 K St. N.W., Washington, D.C. 20006. Filed 5/1/84. Legislative interest — "General interest: HR 4170/HR 2163. Specific Interest: Claymont Delaware Project."

JACKSONVILLE TRANSPORTATION AUTHORITY, Jacksonville, Fla. Lobbyist — Florida Business Associates, 2000 L St. N.W., Washington, D.C. 20036. Filed 5/15/84. Legislative interest — "Seeking UMPTA Funding For Transportation projects. House and Senate Transportation appropriations."

METROPOLITAN TRANSPORTATION AUTHORITY, New York, N.Y. Lobbyist — Brand, Lowell & Dole, 923 15th St. N.W., Washington, D.C. 20005. Filed 5/16/84. Legislative interest — "Representation of the client before committees and the House with respect to Grumman Flexible buses."

THE REDEVELOPMENT AGENCY OF THE CITY OF BURBANK, Burbank, Calif. Lobbyist — Dickey, Knorr & Moore, 1825 I St. N.W., Washington, D.C. 20006. Filed 5/15/84. Legislative interest — "... concern tax and financing issues affecting the City of Burbank and its redevelopment efforts, and include bills such as HR 4170 and any tax amendments to HR 2163."

STATE OF NEVADA, NUCLEAR WASTE PROJECT OFFICE, Carson City, Nev. Lobbyist — Murphy & Davenport, 711 Capitol Way, Olympia, Wash. 98501. Filed 5/2/84. Legislative interest — "All matters pertaining to or affecting the Nuclear Waste Policy Act of 1982."

STATE OF SOUTH CAROLINA BUDGET & CONTROL BOARD, Columbia, S.C. Lobbyist — Adams, Quackenbush, Herring & Stuart, P.O. Box 394, Columbia, S.C. 29202. Filed 5/18/84. Legislative interest — "Intend to lobby regarding the Alabama Beach Mouse becoming an endangered species under Endangered Species Act; intend to lobby for exemption of part of Gulf Shores, Alabama from Barrier Islands Act; and intend to secure exemption of 'Mills-Babcock Complex' from new Federal Tax Package."

TURLOCK IRRIGATION DISTRICT, Turlock, Calif. Lobbyist — Herrick & Smith, 1800 Massachusetts Ave. N.W., Washington, D.C. 20036. Filed 5/27/84. Legislative interest — "The Tuolumne River ... Wild and Scenic Rivers Act ... HR 2474, HR 5083, HR 5291, S 1515, S 5, and any other bill concerning the Tuolumne River ... For: HR 5291; Against HR 2474, HR 5083, S 1515, S 5."

Trade Associations

AD HOC ALTERNATIVE ENERGY LEASING TASK FORCE, Washington, D.C. Lobbyist — Wickwire, Gavin & Gibbs, 1819 L St. N.W., Washington, D.C. 20036. Filed 5/7/84. Legislative interest — "Equitable tax treatment of alternative energy projects. Support for the Wallop Service Contract Amendment, section 22 of HR 2163."

AGRICULTURISTS FOR RESPONSIBLE LEGISLATION, Amarillo, Texas. Lobbyist — Cramer, Haber & Lukis, 818 Connecticut Ave. N.W., Washington, D.C. 20006. (Former U.S. Rep. William C. Cramer, R-Fla., 1955-71, was listed among agents for this client.) Filed 5/3/84. Legislative interest — "To protect the interests of cattle feeders by having the Conference Committee and the Congress sustain the Senate position regarding Limitation on Certain Prepaid Farming Expenses under Section 464 of the Code; or strike limitation."

ALIGNPAC, Portland, Ore. Lobbyist — Morgan, Lewis & Bockius, 1800 M St. N.W., Washington, D.C. 20036. Filed 5/7/84. Legislative interest — "Legislation affecting the tax treatment of insurance and annuity products."

AMERICAN AMBULANCE ASSOCIATION, Sacramento, Calif. Lobbyist — The David Epstein Group, 1000 Potomac St. N.W., Washington, D.C. 20007. Filed 5/17/84. Legislative interest — "... S 1578, Local Government Antitrust Act of 1983 ... HR 2981, To exempt local governments from antitrust laws, Against ... HR 3361, To amend Clayton Act to limit antitrust liability of local governments, Against ... HR 3688, To amend Clayton Act to limit antitrust liability of local governments, Against...."

AMERICAN ASSOCIATION OF DENTAL SCHOOLS, Washington, D.C. Lobbyist — Bracewell & Patterson, 1825 I St. N.W., Washington, D.C. 20006. Filed 5/15/84. Legislative interest — "Matters relating to student loan bonds in tax bill."

AMERICAN ASSOCIATION OF HOMES FOR THE AGING, 1050 17th St. N.W., Washington, D.C. 20036. Filed for self 5/18/84. Legislative interest — "Federal health and housing programs serving the elderly and other issues of concern to the aging (for example, Social Security, Medicare and Medicaid legislation and the Older Americans Act)." Lobbyist — Mary Beth Curry.

AMERICAN COUNCIL OF LIFE INSURANCE INC., 1850 K St. N.W., Washington, D.C. 20006. Filed for self 5/8/84. Legislative interest — "Proposed legislation which affects the life insurance industry; specifically HR 100, S 372." Lobbyist — John K. Booth.

AMERICAN FINANCIAL SERVICES ASSOCIATION, 1101 14th St. N.W., Washington, D.C. 20005. Filed for self 5/15/84. Legislative interest — "Any and all legislation affecting the consumer credit industry including but not limited to the following: Consumer bankruptcy reform, S 5174; financial institutions deregulation, S 2181, S 1609, S 2134; telecommunications legislation, S 1660, HR 4102." Lobbyist — E. Geoffrey Littlehale.

AMERICAN NURSES' ASSOCIATION, 2420 Pershing Road, Kansas City, Mo. 64108. Filed for self 5/14/84. Legislative interest — "Legislation relating to nurses, nursing and health including but not limited to Nurses Training Act, Nurse Research, Community Health Grants, Medicare, Medicaid, Mental Health, Block Grants, Pro-Competition Proposals, Appropriations and Budget." Lobbyist — Donna Richardson, 1101 14th St. N.W., Washington, D.C. 20005.

AMERICAN PSYCHOLOGICAL ASSOCIATION, 1200 17th St. N.W., Washington, D.C. 20036. Filed for self 5/18/84. Legislative interest — Not specified. Lobbyist — Ellen F. Greenberg.

AMERICAN RETREADERS ASSOCIATION, P.O. Box 17203, Louisville, Ky. 40217. Filed for self 5/15/84. Legislative interest — "Taxes: HR 4170. Government Procurement: S 757, HR 2867. Clean Air: HR 3476. Product Liability: S 44. Fair Labor Standards Act: S 2009." Lobbyist — Roy Littlefield, 15900 Pinecroft Lane, Bowie, Md. 20716.

AMERICAN SOCIETY OF ASSOCIATION EXECUTIVES, 1575 I St. N.W., Washington, D.C. 20005. Filed for self 5/11/84. Legislative interest — "Interests include all legislative matter of unique concern to associations, specific areas of concern include taxation of association income, postal rates for non-profit mailers, and association liability for voluntary standards." Lobbyist — James J. Albertine.

AMERICAN TEXTILE MANUFACTURERS INSTITUTE INC., Washington, D.C. Lobbyist — Philip D. Morrison, 1700 Pennsylvania Ave. N.W., Washington, D.C. 20006. Filed 5/29/84. Legislative interest — "Generally, all legislation relating to federal income taxation of corporations. Specifically, lobbying relating to the Tax Act of 1984."

ASSOCIATION OF AMERICAN RAILROADS, Washington, D.C. Lobbyist — James C. Corman, 1420 16th St. N.W., Washington, D.C. 20036. (Former U.S. rep., D-Calif., 1961-81.) Filed 5/29/84. Legislative interest — "Legislative activities affecting the Railroad Unemployment Insurance (RUI) and related programs."

ASSOCIATION OF MAXIMUM SERVICE TELECASTERS INC., 1735 DeSales St. N.W., Washington, D.C. 20036. Filed for self 5/25/84. Legislative interest — "General legislative interests are the Communications Act of 1934, as amended, and legislation related to television." Lobbyist — Gregory L. DePriest.

BUSINESS EXECUTIVES FOR NATIONAL SECURITY, 21 Dupont Circle N.W., Washington, D.C. 20036. Filed for self 5/2/84. Legislative interest — "National security; arms control; military spending issues; U.S.-Soviet relations." Lobbyist — James Morrison.

CHOCOLATE MANUFACTURERS ASSOCIATION OF THE USA, 7900 Westpark Drive, McLean, Va. 22102. Filed for self 5/7/84. Legislative interest — "Food Safety legislation and other legislation relative to the food industry." Lobbyist — Susan Snyder Smith.

EMPLOYEE RELOCATION COUNCIL, Washington, D.C. Lobbyist — Philip D. Morrison, 1700 Pennsylvania Ave. N.W., Washington, D.C. 20006. Filed 5/21/84. Legislative interest — "Generally, lobbying relating to the Tax of Act of 1984. Specifically, lobbying relating to any legislation relating to the relocation of employees."

FEDERATION OF AMERICAN HOSPITALS, 1111 19th St. N.W., Washington, D.C. 20036. Filed for self 5/7/84. Legislative interest — "... Medicare, National Health Insurance and Hospital Cost Containment Legislation." Lobbyist — Mary R. Grealy.

GENERIC PHARMACEUTICAL INDUSTRY ASSOCIATION INC., New York, N.Y. Lobbyist — Parry and Romani Associates Inc., 1140 Connecticut Ave. N.W., Washington, D.C. 20036. Filed 5/29/84. Legislative interest — Not specified.

HORSEMEN'S BENEVOLENT & PROTECTIVE ASSOCIATION, Rockville, Md. Lobbyist — David Vienna & Associates, 510 C St. N.E., Washington, D.C. 20002. Filed 5/8/84. Legislative interest — "Opposition to HR 1694 and S 1233, the Corrupt Racing Practices Act."

HOSPITAL SERVICE ASSOCIATION OF NORTHEAST PENNSYLVANIA, 70 N. Main St., Wilkes-Barre, Pa. 18711. Filed for self 5/31/84. Legislative interest — "Deficit Reduction Act of 1984. (For some provisions, but against others.) Medicare Solvency & Health Care Financing Reform Act of 1984 (Kennedy-Gephardt Bill) HR 4870 (Against)." Lobbyist — Gilbert D. Tough, P.O. Box 33, Lehman, Pa. 18627.

INDEPENDENT PETROLEUM ASSOCIATION OF AMERICA, 1101 16th St. N.W., Washington, D.C. 20036. Filed for self 5/2/84. Legislative interest — "... legislation that might affect the petroleum industry ... all tax bills dealing with taxation of natural resources, land use legislation, particularly if related to public lands, pricing and allocation of crude oil and natural gas, and legislation dealing with activities of the Environmental Protection Agency and Occupational Safety and Health Administration, if pertaining to activities of petroleum producer."

JOB TRAINING ASSOCIATION, Boston, Mass. Lobbyist — MMB Associates Inc., 122 C St. N.W., Washington, D.C. 20001. Filed 5/18/84. Legislative interest — "The Job Training Partnership Act and Related Legislation, The Labor/HHS/Education Appropriations Bill."

JOINT MARITIME CONGRESS, Washington, D.C. Lobbyist — Gray and Co., 3255 Grace St. N.W., Washington, D.C. 20007. Filed 5/31/84. Legislative interest — "Including but not limited to maritime legislation."

MUTUAL PROTECTION TRUST COOPERATIVE OF AMERICAN PHYSICIANS INC., Los Angeles, Calif. Lobbyist — Finley, Kumble, Wagner, Heine, Underberg, Manley & Casey, 1120 Connecticut Ave. N.W., Washington, D.C. 20036. Filed 5/21/84. Legislative interest — "Tax Reform Act of 1984 (HR 4170) and Deficit Reduction Act of 1984."

NATIONAL AGRICULTURAL CHEMICAL ASSOCIATION, Washington, D.C. Lobbyist — Blum, Nash & Railsback, 1015 18th St. N.W., Washington, D.C. 20005. (Former U.S. Rep. Tom Railsback, R-Ill., 1967-83, was listed as agent for this client.) Filed 5/14/84. Legislative interest — "Legislation relating to Patent Term Restoration (S 1306; HR 3502)."

NATIONAL ASSOCIATION OF BROADCASTERS, Washington, D.C. Lobbyist — Blum, Nash & Railsback, 1015 18th St. N.W., Washington, D.C. 20005. (Former U.S. Rep. Tom Railsback, R-Ill., 1967-83, was listed as agent for this client.) Filed 5/14/84. Legislative interest — Not specified.

NATIONAL ASSOCIATION OF CONVENIENCE STORES, 5201 Leesburg Pike, Falls Church, Va. 22041. Filed for self 5/7/84. Legislative interest — "Legislation in the general areas of agriculture, labor and energy with specific regard to farm and food stamp legislation, clean air and water acts and Fair Labor Standards Act." Lobbyist — Teri Richman.

NATIONAL ASSOCIATION OF IMMIGRATION JUDGES, Washington, D.C. Lobbyist — Gray and Co., 3255 Grace St. N.W., Washington, D.C. 20007. Filed 5/11/84. Legislative interest — "Including but not limited to immigration legislation."

NATIONAL ASSOCIATION OF PUBLIC TELEVISION STATIONS, 21 Dupont Circle N.W., Washington, D.C. 20036. Filed for self 5/31/84. Legislative interest — "Specific interests include appropriations for the Corporation for Public Broadcasting (Labor-HHS Appropriation Bill), and for the Public Telecommunications Facilities Program (State, Justice, Commerce Appropriation Bill) and legislative amendments to the Communications Act of 1934 which affect public broadcasting." Lobbyist — Peter M. Fannon.

NATIONAL ASSOCIATION OF STATE SAVINGS INSURERS, Baltimore, Md. Lobbyist — Vorys, Sater, Seymour & Pease, 1828 L St. N.W., Washington, D.C. 20036. Filed 5/16/84. Legislative interest — "Advance client's interest in regard to financial institutions regulatory reform."

NATIONAL CABLE TELEVISION ASSOCIATION, Washington, D.C. Lobbyist — McNair, Glenn, Konduros, Corley, Singletary, Porter & Dibble, 1155 15th St. N.W., Washington, D.C. 20005. Filed 5/29/84. Legislative interest — "Antitrust issues. Copyright issues."

NATIONAL RAILWAY LABOR CONFERENCE, Washington, D.C. Lobbyist — James C. Corman, 1420 16th St. N.W., Washington, D.C. 20036. (Former U.S. rep., D-Calif., 1961-81.) Filed 5/29/84. Legislative interest — ". . . Railroad Unemployment Insurance (RUI) and related programs."

PHARMACEUTICAL MANUFACTURERS OF AMERICA, Washington, D.C. Lobbyist — Blum, Nash & Railsback, 1015 18th St. N.W., Washington, D.C. 20036. (Former U.S. Rep. Tom Railsback, R-Ill., 1967-83, was listed as agent for this client.) Filed 5/14/84. Legislative interest — Not specified.

SOCIETY OF AMERICAN FLORISTS, 901 N. Washington St., Alexandria, Va. 22314. Filed for self 5/18/84. Legislative interest — "Natural Gas Deregulation (S 1715). Minimum Wage (HR 3652). Immigration Reform (HR 1510). Federal Workers Compensation (HR 3175). National Employment Priorities Act (HR 2867). Small Business and Agricultural Trade Remedies Act of 1983 (S 50). Unfair Trade Remedies Simplification Act (S 1672). Accounting Cost Recovery Simplification Act of 1983 (S 1758)." Lobbyist — Dwayne E. Mann.

SOUTHERN FOREST PRODUCTS ASSOCIATION, P.O. Box 52468, New Orleans, La. 70152. Filed for self 5/8/84. Legislative interest — ". . . support of retention of estate tax reduction approved by Congress in 1981 and for a balance approach to wilderness legislation." Lobbyist — Dudley Digges Morgan III.

U.S. TUNA FOUNDATION, Washington, D.C. Lobbyist — Bracewell & Patterson, 1825 I St. N.W., Washington, D.C. 20006. Filed 5/15/84. Legislative interest — "To get a tariff bill passed on behalf of the U.S. Tuna Foundation."

WINE & SPIRITS WHOLESALERS OF AMERICA INC., Washington, D.C. Lobbyist — R. Duffy Wall & Associates Inc., 1317 F St. N.W., Washington, D.C. 20004. Filed 5/7/84. Legislative interest — "Issues relating to general tax legislation."

Miscellaneous

AMERICAN ASSOCIATION OF RETIRED PERSONS, 1909 K St. N.W., Washington, D.C. 20049. Filed for self 5/29/84. Legislative interest — "Support of: . . . Improved Tax Treatment of Older Americans . . . Improved Social Security and Medicare/Medicaid Laws . . . Improved Nursing Home Standards . . . Consumer Protection Legislation . . . Employment of Older Workers . . . National Health Insurance . . . Transportation of the Elderly . . . Housing for the Elderly." Lobbyist — Christine W. McEntee.

AMERICAN HERITAGE CENTRE, 13924 Braddock Road, Centerville, Va. 22020. Filed for self 5/21/84. Legislative interest — ". . . to seek the limitation of federal regulation of newsletters and media commentaries . . . ." Lobbyist — Neal B. Blair.

BANKRUPTCY COURTS BILL COALITION, Washington, D.C. Lobbyist — David Vienna & Associates, 510 C St. N.E., Washington, D.C. 20002. Filed 5/8/84. Legislative interest — "Enactment of legislation to resolve bankruptcy courts constitutional crisis."

ARCHIE BENNETT, Houston, Texas. Lobbyist — Vinson & Elkins, 1101 Connecticut Ave. N.W., Washington, D.C. 20036. Filed 5/10/84. Legislative interest — "1984 Tax Legislation."

JESSE B. BROWN, 605 10th St. N.E., Washington, D.C. 20002. Filed for self 5/11/84. Legislative interest — "All legislative matters directly or indirectly affecting public utilities, specifically,

but not exclusively relating to the Sharp-Madigan Bill; *all* energy-related legislation, railroad deregulation proposals and tax proposals relating to capital information."

BURING ESTATE, Washington, D.C. Lobbyist — Steven L. Engelberg, 2033 M St. N.W., Washington, D.C. 20036. Filed 5/16/84. Legislative interest — "Amendment to Internal Revenue Code relating to estate tax alternate valuation date election."

CALIFORNIA STATE UNIVERSITY, Long Beach, Calif. Lobbyist — Patton, Boggs & Blow, 2550 M St. N.W., Washington, D.C. 20037. Filed 5/26/84. Legislative interest — "To amend the Higher Education Act of 1965 such as . . . HR 5240."

COMMON CAUSE, 2030 M St. N.W., Washington, D.C. 20036. Filed for self 5/10/84. Legislative interest — ". . . are in such areas as open government, campaign finance reform, Federal Election Commission, lobby disclosure, government ethics, Senate confirmation process, extension of the Clean Air Act, court jurisdiction issues, congressional budget process, congressional reform, freedom of information, energy policy, waste in government, merit selection of Federal judges and U.S. Attorneys, regulatory reform, public participation in federal agency proceedings, Legal Services Corporation, the Equal Rights Amendment, nuclear arms control, and military spending . . . ." Lobbyist — Philip Simon.

CONCERNED WOMEN FOR AMERICA, 499 S. Capitol St., Washington, D.C. 20003. Filed for self 5/17/84. Legislative interest — "Issues affecting the family and moral values including for school prayer (S J Res 73); equal access (HR 4996); ERA (against) (H J Res 1); abortion (HR 618) (for the bill)." Lobbyists — Michael P. Farris, Diane White, Michael Jameson.

CONFEDERATED SALISH AND KOOTENAI TRIBES OF THE FLATHEAD RESERVATION, Flathead Reservation, Mont. Lobbyist — Wilkinson, Barker, Knauer & Quinn, 1735 New York Ave. N.W., Washington, D.C. 20006. Filed 5/21/84. Legislative interest — "Our lobbying representation relates to all legislation activities directly or indirectly affecting Indian affairs, including but not limited to tribal lands and natural resources, jurisdiction, taxation, health, education and welfare."

CONSUMERS UNION OF U.S. INC., 256 Washington St., Mt. Vernon, N.Y. 10553. Filed for self 5/7/84. Legislative interest — "Issues affecting consumer . . . Federal Trade Commission . . . federal regulation of broadcasting or common carrier services . . . telecommunications policy planning . . . legislative veto, sunset of statutory authority, public participation or other federal government organization and administration process issues . . . Consumer Product Safety Commission . . . Consumer Class Action and Standing to Sue legislation and any other legislation relating to citizen access to justice. Drug Reform legislation, amendments to the Delaney Clause, food safety clause, drug safety and efficiency requirements, food labeling legislation and any other legislation affecting food, drug, cosmetics or hair dye safety, quality or information disclosure . . . National Highway Traffic Safety Administration . . . vehicle safety issues or highway or vehicle safety . . . consumer redress for product-related injury . . . Hospital Cost Containment and National Health Insurance legislation, and any other legislation affecting medical or health care . . . international trade . . . Amendments to the Freedom of Information Act . . . federal feeding programs, including but not limited to food stamps, school lunches and WIC . . . Legal Services Corporation . . . the price or supply of agricultural commodities . . . Value-added tax . . . Legislation to control wages, prices or profits and any other legislation relating to inflation or to regulation of the national economy . . . Pensions, Individual Retirement Accounts or any other income security issues . . . Electronic Funds Transfer Act Amendments . . . Privacy of Electronic Fund Transfers Act, Fair Financial Information Practices Act . . . Truth in Lending Act Amendments . . . Environmental legislation, including the Clean Air Act." Lobbyists — Linda A. Lipsen, Michelle Meier, 2001 S St. N.W., Washington, D.C. 20009.

EL POMAR, Colorado Springs, Colo. Lobbyist — Pierson, Ball & Dowd, 1200 18th St. N.W., Washington, D.C. 20036. Filed 5/7/84. Legislative interest — "S 2062, Deficit Reduction Act of 1984; support provisions relating to private foundations."

THE ENVIRONMENTAL FUND, 1302 18th St. N.W., Washington, D.C. 20036. Filed for self 5/15/84. Legislative interest

— "HR 1510, The Immigration Reform and Control Act (for). S 2140, The Immigration Ceiling Act (for). S 1025/HR 2491, The Global Resources, Environment and Population Act (undecided). . . . the annual appropriation bill for the Immigration & Naturalization Service (for)." Lobbyists — M. Rupert Cutler, Charles Dinges.

FEDERATION FOR AMERICAN IMMIGRATION REFORM (FAIR), 1424 16th St. N.W., Washington, D.C. 20036. Filed for self 5/14/84. Legislative interest — "In general, immigration-related legislation. In specific, HR 1510/S 529, Immigration Reform & Control Act - For. Unnumbered Immigration Service appropriation bill - For." Lobbyist — Curtis C. Deane.

MANUEL GARCIA JR., LOUISE GARCIA MEYER, CHARLES A. GARCIA AND JOSEPHINE GARCIA PERRY, Tampa, Fla. Lobbyist — Covington & Burling, P.O. Box 7566, Washington, D.C. 20044. Filed 5/10/84. Legislative interest — "Retroactive multiemployer pension plan withdrawal liability. . . . Deficit Reduction Act of 1984 . . . HR 2163, S 111. . . . For."

LEECH LAKE RESERVATION BUSINESS COMMITTEE, Case Lake, Minn. Lobbyist — Gerard, Byler & Associates, 1100 17th St. N.W., Washington, D.C. 20036. Filed 5/18/84. Legislative interest — "Monitoring legislation affecting Indian tribes; general work on authorizing legislation and appropriations matters."

NANA REGIONAL CORP., Kotzebue, Alaska. Lobbyist — Wilkinson, Barker, Knauer & Quinn, 1735 New York Ave. N.W., Washington, D.C. 20006. Filed 5/21/84. Legislative interest — ". . . including but not limited to all matters relating generally to Alaska, its lands and natural resources, the Alaska Native Claims Settlement Act, matters relating to Indians, Eskimos and Aleuts, generally."

NATIONAL ASSOCIATION FOR UNIFORM SERVICES, 5535 Hempstead Way, Springfield, Va. 22151. Filed for self 5/16/84. Legislative interest — Not specified. Lobbyist — Charles C. Partridge.

NATIONAL AUDUBON SOCIETY, New York, N.Y. Lobbyist — Elvis J. Stahr Jr., 1815 H St. N.W., Washington, D.C. 20006. Legislative interest — "Natural Resources: . . . Garrison Diversion Project of Bureau of Reclamation . . . Energy & Water Bill . . . Against Appropriation for Garrison Diversion."

NATIONAL COMMITTEE TO PRESERVE SOCIAL SECURITY, 1300 19th St. N.W., Washington, D.C. 20036. Filed for self 5/4/84. Legislative interest — ". . . legislation of concern to senior citizens." Lobbyist — William Wewer.

NATIONAL CORPORATION FOR HOUSING PARTNERSHIPS, Washington, D.C. Lobbyist — Finley, Kumble, Wagner, Heine, Underberg, Manley & Casey, 1120 Connecticut Ave. N.W., Washington, D.C. 20036. Filed 5/31/84. Legislative interest — "Seeking an amendment to the Housing and Urban Development Act of 1968."

SHEE ATIKA INC., Sitka, Alaska. Lobbyist — Wilkinson, Barker, Knauer & Quinn, 1735 New York Ave. N.W., Washington, D.C. 20006. Filed 5/21/84. Legislative interest — ". . . including but not limited to all matters relating generally to Alaska, its lands and natural resources, the Alaska Native Claims Settlement Act, matters relating to Indians, Eskimos, and Aleuts, generally."

TANANA CHIEFS CONFERENCE INC., Fairbanks, Alaska. Lobbyist — Hobbs, Strauss, Dean & Wilder, 1735 New York Ave. N.W., Washington, D.C. 20006. Filed 5/29/84. Legislative interest — "Federal legislation concerning health care matters."

TEMPLE UNIVERSITY, Philadelphia, Pa. Lobbyist — Ballard, Spahr, Andrews & Ingersoll, 1850 K St. N.W., Washington, D.C. 20006. Filed 5/11/84. Legislative interest — "General interest: Legislation affecting universities. Specific interest: HR 4170."

THE UTE MOUNTAIN UTE TRIBE, Towaoc, Colo. Lobbyist — Hobbs, Straus, Dean & Wilder, 1735 New York Ave. N.W., Washington, D.C. 20006. Filed 5/29/84. Legislative interest — ". . . involve authorizing appropriations legislation relevant to Indian tribes, in particular, the FY 1984 and 1985 Department of the Interior Appropriations Acts for the Ute Mt. Ute Tribe of Colorado."

WHITE EARTH RESERVATION BUSINESS COMMITTEE, White Earth, Minn. Lobbyist — Gerard, Byler & Associates, 1100 17th St. N.W., Washington, D.C. 20036. Filed 5/18/84. Legislative interest — "Monitoring legislation affecting Indian tribes; general work on authorizing legislation and appropriations matters."

June Registrations

Corporations and Businesses

THE ALGOMA STEEL CORP. LTD., 503 Queen St. East, Sault Ste. Marie, Ontario, Canada P6A 5P2. Filed for self 6/21/84. Legislative interest — ". . . Fair Trade in Steel Act . . . S 2380; HR 5081 . . . in opposition to any legislation which restricts U.S. imports of steel mill products from Canada." Lobbyist — Peter Nixon.

AMERICAN CAN CO., Greenwich, Conn. Lobbyist — Covington & Burling, 1201 Pennsylvania Ave. N.W., Washington, D.C. 20044. Filed 6/14/84. Legislative interest — "Retroactive multiemployer pension plan withdrawal liability . . . Deficit Reduction Act of 1984 . . . HR 4170. . . ."

AMERICAN HOME PRODUCTS CORP., New York, N.Y., and Washington, D.C. Lobbyist — Clifford & Warnke, 815 Connecticut Ave. N.W., Washington, D.C. 20006. Filed 6/31/84. Legislative interest — "In connection with matters regarding abbreviated new drug applications and patent term restoration; specifically, the Drug Price Competition Act of 1983, HR 3605, and the Drug Price Competition and Patent Term Restoration Act of 1984, S 2748." Lobbyist — Williams & Jensen, 1101 Connecticut Ave. N.W., Washington, D.C. 20036. Filed 6/15/84. Legislative interest — "Patent legislation of interest to the company, in particular HR 3605 and S 2748." Lobbyist — Patton, Boggs & Blow, 2550 M St. N.W., Washington, D.C. 20037. Filed 6/13/84. Legislative interest — "Efforts to restore patent term and provide for abbreviated new drug applications. Such as . . . Federal Food, Drug and Cosmetic Act and . . . HR 3605."

ASSOCIATES CORPORATION OF AMERICA, Dallas, Texas. Lobbyist — Dutko & Associates, 412 First St. S.E., Washington, D.C. 20003. Filed 6/28/84. Legislative interest — "To influence banking legislation; HR 5734 and S 2181."

BATEMAN, EICHLER, HILL, RICHARDS INC., Los Angeles, Calif. Lobbyist — Gibson, Dunn & Crutcher, 1050 Connecticut Ave. N.W., Washington, D.C. 20036. Legislative interest — ". . . encouraging the passage of legislation that would exempt from the provisions of section 91 of HR 4170 (prepayment of expenses), R&D limited partnership transactions already in progress. The passage of the Senate version of this provision (section 71 of HR 2163) will be encouraged."

THE BOEING CO., Seattle, Wash. Lobbyist — Wilmer, Cutler & Pickering, 1666 K St. N.W., Washington, D.C. 20006. Filed 6/14/84. Legislative interest — "For Foreign Sales Corporation provisions of the [Deficit Reduction] Act."

BRISTOL-MYERS INC., Washington, D.C. Lobbyist — Williams & Jensen, 1101 Connecticut Ave. N.W., Washington, D.C. 20036. Filed 6/15/84. Legislative interest — "Patent legislation of interest to the company, in particular HR 3605 and S 2748." Lobbyist — Patton, Boggs & Blow, 2550 M St. N.W., Washington, D.C. 20037. Filed 6/13/84. Legislative interest — "Efforts to restore patent term and provide for abbreviated new drug applications. Such as . . . Federal Food, Drug and Cosmetic Act and . . . HR 3605."

CARBONTEK TRADING CO. LTD., 1201 Jefferson Davis Highway, Arlington, Va. 22202. Filed for self 6/26/84. Legislative interest — "National energy utilization policy and planning." Lobbyist — W. Wayne Beall.

CIC ENTERPRISES, Indianapolis, Ind. Lobbyist — Bill Hecht and Associates Inc., 499 South Capitol St. S.E., Washington, D.C. 20003. Filed 6/28/84. Legislative interest — ". . . to include but not limited to certain modifications in HR 4170."

COMMUNICATIONS SATELLITE CORP., 950 L'Enfant Plaza S.W., Washington, D.C. 20024. Filed for self 6/7/84. Legislative interest — "... Matters pertaining to telecommunications and related fields ... The International Telecommunications Act of 1983 (HR 4464); The Satellite Communications Act of 1984 (HR 5724); The International Telecommunications Act of 1983 (S 999)." Lobbyist — Robert F. Allnutt.

COMWORLD PRODUCTIONS, Sherman Oaks, Calif. Lobbyist — Manatt, Phelps, Rothenburg & Tunney, 1200 New Hampshire Ave. N.W., Washington, D.C. 20036. Filed 6/5/84. Legislative interest — "Legislative tax issues affecting the movie/video/sound recording industry."

DIMENSION FINANCIAL CORP., Denver, Colo. Lobbyist — Nelson & Yudin, 1707 H St. N.W., Washington, D.C. 20006. Filed 6/25/84. Legislative interest — "Legislation affecting the chartering and operation of banks, including HR 5734, HR 5916 and other bills to amend the Bank Holding Company Act."

EDS FINANCIAL CORP., Dallas, Texas. Lobbyist — James C. Corman, 1420 16th St. N.W., Washington, D.C. 20036. Filed 6/27/84. (Former U.S. rep., D-Calif., 1961-81.) Legislative interest — "To monitor proposed legislation and treasury regulations and all pending matters affecting the Leasing Industry."

ELLMARK ASSOCIATES, San Francisco, Calif. Lobbyist — Lillick, McHose & Charles, 21 Dupont Circle N.W., Washington, D.C. 20037. Filed 6/19/84. Legislative interest — "... Financial Services Competitive Equity Act/Home Owners Loan Act of 1933 ... S 2181 ... 12 U.S.C. Section 1461 et seq. ... Seeking amendments to 12 U.S.C. Section 1464(c)(1)(Q) or (c)(1)(R)."

EL PASO NATURAL GAS CO., 1050 Connecticut Ave. N.W., Washington, D.C. 20036. Filed for self 6/1/84. Legislative interest — "... any legislation affecting the natural gas industry, particularly legislation affecting energy, environment, natural resources, taxes, natural gas production and pricing, and operation of natural gas pipelines. S 1715, HR 4277, HR 5313, S 2688, HR 5640, S 757." Lobbyists — Robert N. Harbor, Randall I. Cole.

EMHART CORP., Farmington, Conn. Lobbyist — Holland & Knight, 600 Maryland Ave. S.W., Washington, D.C. 20024. Filed 6/12/84. Legislative interest — "... Environmental legislation including bills regulating underground storage tanks ... Including HR 5640, S 757 ... In favor of certain provisions."

FEDERATION EMPLOYMENT & GUIDANCE SERVICE, New York, N.Y. Lobbyist — R. William Barton, 1000 Potomac St. N.W., Washington, D.C. 20007. Filed 6/12/84. Legislative interest — "HR 2557 & S 899 (private relief bills on behalf of employer)."

FRAZIER LANIER CO., Montgomery, Ala. Lobbyist — King & Spalding, 1730 Pennsylvania Ave. N.W., Washington, D.C. 20006-4706. Filed 6/19/84. Legislative interest — "... is in opposing the proposed repeal of section 103(b)(7) of the Internal Revenue Code by section 725(i) of HR 4170."

FREDERICK CO., Chicago, Ill. Lobbyist — Skadden, Arps, Slate, Meagher & Flom, 919 18th St. N.W., Washington, D.C. 20006. Filed 6/11/84. Legislative interest — "Partnership provisions in pending tax bills (HR 4170)."

GOLDEN NUGGET INC., Las Vegas, Nev. Lobbyist — Finley, Kumble, Wagner, Heine, Underberg, Manley & Casey, 1120 Connecticut Ave. N.W., Washington, D.C. 20036. Filed 6/22/84. Legislative interest — "HR 5097, 'State-sponsored Lottery Advertising' and S 1876, 'Crimes and Criminal Procedure, Title 18 U.S.C., Amendment'; in favor of passage."

GRAND MET USA INC., Montvale, N.J. Lobbyist — Sullivan & Cromwell, 125 Broad St., New York, N.Y. 10004 and 1775 Pennsylvania Ave. N.W., Washington, D.C. 20006. Filed 6/1/84. Legislative interest — "Provisions of HR 4170 and HR 2163 relating to the use of the last-in first-out method of inventory accounting."

GROUP HOSPITALIZATION INC., Washington, D.C. Lobbyist — Finley, Kumble, Wagner, Heine, Underberg, Manley & Casey, 1120 Connecticut Ave. N.W., Washington, D.C. 20036. Filed 6/29/84. Legislative interest — "HR 5853, in favor of passage."

HEYL & PATTERSON INC., Pittsburgh, Pa. Lobbyist — Covington & Burling, 1201 Pennsylvania Ave. N.W., Washington,

D.C. 20044. Filed 6/1/84. Legislative interest — "Retroactive multiemployer pension plan withdrawal liability ... Deficit Reduction Act of 1984 ... HR 4170, section 111 ... For."

HOFFMAN-LA ROCHE, Washington, D.C. Lobbyist — Williams & Jensen, 1101 Connecticut Ave. N.W., Washington, D.C. 20036. Filed 6/15/84. Legislative interest — "Patent legislation of interest to the company, in particular HR 3605 and S 2748." Lobbyist — Arnold & Porter, 1200 New Hampshire Ave. N.W., Washington, D.C. 20036. Filed 6/20/84. Legislative interest — "Person filing is advocating certain amendments to the New Drug Application and Patent Term Restoration Act (HR 3605 and companion Senate legislation)." Lobbyist — Patton, Boggs & Blow, 2550 M St. N.W., Washington, D.C. 20037. Filed 6/13/84. Legislative interest — "Efforts to restore patent term and provide for abbreviated new drug applications. Such as ... Federal Food, Drug and Cosmetic Act and ... HR 3605."

J. L. ASSOCIATES, 1300 Army Navy Drive, Arlington, Va. 22202. Filed for self 6/19/84. Legislative interest — "... investment/banking interests ... tax interests ... tourism ... defense...." Lobbyist — Jonna Lynne Cullen.

JOHNSON & JOHNSON, New Brunswick, N.J., and Washington, D.C. Lobbyist — Williams & Jensen, 1101 Connecticut Ave. N.W., Washington, D.C. 20036. Filed 6/15/84. Legislative interest — "Patent legislation of interest to the company, in particular HR 3605 and S 2748." Lobbyist — Patton, Boggs & Blow, 2550 M St. N.W., Washington, D.C. 20037. Filed 6/13/84. Legislative interest — "Efforts to restore patent term and provide for abbreviated new drug applications. Such as ... Federal Food, Drug and Cosmetic Act and ... HR 3605."

KINGS ENTERTAINMENT CO., Kings Island, Ohio. Lobbyist — Taft, Stettinius & Hollister, First National Bank Center, Cincinnati, Ohio 45202. Filed 6/13/84. (Former U.S. Sen. Robert Taft Jr., R-Ohio, 1971-76; House 1963-65, 1967-71, was listed among agents for this client.) Legislative interest — "Representation relating to regulation of amusement parks by the CPSC or other Federal agencies. Of particular interest at this time are HR 5790, HR 5788, HR 5630, and S 2650."

LAUREL STEEL PRODUCTS LTD., Burlington, Ontario, Canada. Lobbyist — Dow, Lohnes & Albertson, 1225 Connecticut Ave. N.W., Washington, D.C. 20036. Filed 6/6/84. Legislative interest — "... Fair Trade in Steel Act ... HR 5081/S 2380 ... Opposition to any legislation which restricts U.S. imports of steel mill products from Canada."

LIFE CARE SERVICE CORP., Washington, D.C. Lobbyist — Gray and Co., 3255 Grace St. N.W., Washington, D.C. 20007. Filed 6/14/84. Legislative interest — "Including but not limited to tax legislation affecting continuing care retirement communities."

LUCASFILM LTD., San Rafael, Calif. Lobbyist — Swidler, Berlin & Strelow, 1000 Thomas Jefferson St. N.W., Washington, D.C. 20007. Filed 6/7/84. Legislative interest — "Tax legislation."

R. H. MACY & CO. INC., New York, N.Y. Lobbyist — Skadden, Arps, Slate, Meagher & Flom, 919 18th St. N.W., Washington, D.C. 20006. Filed 6/11/84. Legislative interest — "Corporate Provisions in Pending Tax Bills (HR 4170)."

MAIN HURDMAN, CPAs, 1050 17th St. N.W., Washington, D.C. 20036. Filed for self 6/15/84. Legislative interest — "From time to time clients of Main Hurdman may have interests in various types and subject matter of legislation where my assistance will be requested. I expect early interest in HR 2163 and HR 4170, the 1984 major tax bill." Lobbyist — Robert B. Carleson.

McDONNELL DOUGLAS CORP., Arlington, Va. Lobbyist — Jones & Winburn, 1101 15th St. N.W., Washington, D.C. 20005. Filed 6/12/84. Legislative interest — "Tax Reform Act of 1984."

MCI COMMUNICATIONS CORP., Washington, D.C. Lobbyist — Morgan, Lewis & Bockius, 1800 M St. N.W., Washington, D.C. 20036. Filed 6/6/84. Legislative interest — "HR 4280 - Technical changes."

MERCHANTS TERMINAL CORP., Baltimore, Md. Lobbyist — Gordon, Feinblatt, Rothman, Hoffberger & Hollander, 233 E. Redwood St., Baltimore, Md. 21202. Filed 6/18/84. Legislative interest — "Multiemployer pension plan withdrawal liability ... Bankruptcy Amendments ... HR 5174 ... For."

MERCK & CO. INC., P.O. Box 2000, Rahway, N.J. 07065. Lobbyist — Williams & Jensen, 1101 Connecticut Ave. N.W., Washington, D.C. 20036. Filed 6/15/84. Legislative interest — "Patent legislation of interest to the company, in particular HR 3605 and S 2748." Lobbyist — Patton, Boggs & Blow, 2550 M St. N.W., Washington, D.C. 20037. Filed 6/13/84. Legislative interest — "Efforts to restore patent term and provide for abbreviated new drug applications. Such as . . . Federal Food, Drug and Cosmetic Act and . . . HR 3605." Filed for self 6/21/84. Legislative interest — "Patent Term Restoration - favor . . . Product Liability - favor. . . ." Lobbyist — R. Teel Oliver, 1050 17th St. N.W., Washington, D.C.

METROPOLITAN ANALYSIS AND RETRIEVAL SYSTEMS INC., Missoula, Mont. Lobbyist — Bill Hecht & Associates Inc., 499 South Capitol St. S.E., Washington, D.C. 20003. Filed 6/28/84. Legislative interest — ". . . to include but not limited to certain modifications in HR 4170."

MORGAN GUARANTY TRUST CO., New York, N.Y. Lobbyist — Pillsbury, Madison & Sutro, 1050 17th St. N.W., Washington, D.C. 20036. Filed 6/8/84. Legislative interest — "Monitoring legislation regarding the removal of the 30 percent withholding tax on interest paid to foreign investors. Specifically items 77 & 87 of the House-Senate Conference Report on HR 4170, and any other legislation dealing with this subject."

NATURAL GAS SUPPLY, Washington, D.C. Lobbyist — Kenneth L. Holland, P.O. Drawer 940, Gaffney, S.C. 29342. Filed 6/28/84. (Former U.S. rep., D-S.C., 1975-83.) Legislative interest — "HR 4277."

OMAHA NATIONAL BANK, TRUSTEES OF KIEWIT ROYALTY TRUST, Omaha, Neb. Lobbyist — Sutherland, Ashill & Brennan, 1666 K St. N.W., Washington, D.C. 20006. Filed 6/6/84. Legislative interest — "Legislation altering rules under section 631(c) for coal royalty interests."

J. C. PENNEY CO. INC., Washington, D.C. Lobbyist — Wilkinson, Barker, Knauer & Quinn, 1735 New York Ave. N.W., Washington, D.C. 20006. Filed 6/7/84. Legislative interest — "Nonbank bank legislation."

PENNZOIL CO., Pennzoil Place, Houston, Texas 77001. Filed for self 6/27/84. Legislative interest — "Refinery policy; deregulation of natural gas; end use controls; environmental matters; tax matters; international matters; public lands; and related matters." Lobbyist — Paul R. Kruse, 1155 15th St. N.W., Washington, D.C. 20005.

PROCTER & GAMBLE, Washington, D.C. Lobbyist — Williams & Jensen, 1101 Connecticut Ave. N.W., Washington, D.C. 20036. Filed 6/15/84. Legislative interest — "Patent legislation of interest to the company, in particular HR 3605 and S 2748." Lobbyist — Patton, Boggs & Blow, 2550 M St. N.W., Washington, D.C. 20037. Filed 6/12/84. Legislative interest — "Efforts to restore patent term and provide for abbreviated new drug applications. Such as . . . Federal Food, Drug and Cosmetic Act and . . . HR 3605."

SCHERING-PLOUGH CO., Washington, D.C. Lobbyist — Williams & Jensen, 1101 Connecticut Ave. N.W., Washington, D.C. 20036. Filed 6/15/84. Legislative interest — "Patent legislation of interest to the company, in particular HR 3605 and S 2748." Lobbyist — Patton, Boggs & Blow, 2550 M St. N.W., Washington, D.C. 20037. Filed 6/13/84. Legislative interest — "Efforts to restore patent term and provide for abbreviated new drug applications. Such as . . . Federal Food, Drug and Cosmetic Act and . . . HR 3605."

SCHWINN BICYCLE CO., Chicago, Ill. Lobbyist — Keck, Mahin & Cate, 1333 New Hampshire Ave. N.W., Washington, D.C. 20036. Filed 6/25/84. Legislative interest — "Schwinn has a general interest in legislative matters affecting tariffs on bicycles and bicycle parts. Schwinn is particularly interested in HR 5754, a bill to increase the tariffs on bicycles and bicycle parts. Schwinn opposes that legislation."

SEARS, ROEBUCK AND CO., Chicago, Ill. Lobbyist — Latham, Watkins & Hills, 1333 New Hampshire Ave. N.W., Washington, D.C. 20036. Filed 6/28/84. Legislative interest — ". . . banking and securities matters; HR 5734, HR 5342, HR 5881." Lobbyist — Camp, Carmouche, Barsh, Hunter, Gray, Hoffman &

Gill, 2550 M St. N.W., Washington, D.C. 20037. Filed 6/21/84. Legislative interest — "Legislation affecting the regulation and ownership of financial institutions, security firms, real estate companies, insurance companies, holding companies possessing an interest in these and other businesses, including HR 5734 and HR 5851."

SEGAL, GOLDMAN & MACNOW, Beverly Hills, Calif. Lobbyist — Manatt, Phelps, Rothenburg & Tunney, 1200 New Hampshire Ave. N.W., Washington, D.C. 20036. Filed 6/5/84. Legislative interest — "Legislative tax issues affecting the movie/video/sound recording industry."

SPECTRA-PHYSICS INC., San Jose, Calif. Lobbyist — Shaw, Pittman, Potts & Trowbridge, 1800 M St. N.W., Washington, D.C. 20036. Filed 6/11/84. Legislative interest — "HR 4170 (Omnibus Deficit Reduction Act of 1984) - favor amendment re changing effective date on a provision affecting incentive stock option plans."

SQUIBB CORP., Washington, D.C. Lobbyist — Williams & Jensen, 1101 Connecticut Ave. N.W., Washington, D.C. 20036. Filed 6/15/84. Legislative interest — "Patent legislation of interest to the company, in particular HR 3605 and S 2748." Lobbyist — Patton, Boggs & Blow, 2550 M St. N.W., Washington, D.C. 20037. Filed 6/13/84. Legislative interest — "Efforts to restore patent term and provide for abbreviated new drug applications. Such as . . . Food, Drug and Cosmetic Act and . . . HR 3605."

STAUFFER CHEMICAL CO., Nyala Farm Road, Westport, Conn. 06881. Filed for self 6/8/84. Legislative interest — "Environmental, tax, international trade, and miscellaneous legislation . . . S 768, HR 3400 . . . HR 3200 . . . S 431 . . . S 757, HR 2867 . . . HR 4813." Lobbyists — A. Allan Noe, John P. Murphy, 1828 L St. N.W., Washington, D.C. 20036.

STUART PHARMACEUTICALS, Wilmington, Del. Lobbyist — Patton, Boggs & Blow, 2550 M St. N.W., Washington, D.C. 20037. Filed 6/26/84. Legislative interest — "Efforts to restore patent term and provide for abbreviated new drug applications. Such as . . . Federal Food, Drug and Cosmetic Act and . . . HR 3605."

SUBURBAN PROPANE GAS CORP., Morristown, N.J. Lobbyist — Black, Manafort & Stone Inc., 324 N. Fairfax St., Alexandria, Va. 22314. Filed 6/14/84. Legislative interest — "Monitor S 2370 and related legislation."

UNITED SATELLITE COMMUNICATIONS INC., New York, N.Y. Lobbyist — Pierson, Ball & Dowd, 1200 18th St. N.W., Washington, D.C. 20036. Filed 6/26/84. Legislative interest — "Legislation affecting satellite-to-home television programming business . . . Satellite Viewing Rights Act of 1984 . . . S 2437, HR 5176 . . . Communications Act of 1934 . . . opposes S 2437 and HR 5176."

VIRATEK, Covina, Calif. Lobbyist — Bayh, Tabbert & Capehart, 1575 I St. N.W., Washington, D.C. 20005. Filed 6/21/84. Legislative interest — "Appropriations for Food & Drug Administration & related matters."

WICKES COS. INC., Santa Monica, Calif. Lobbyist — Stroock, Stroock & Lavan, 1150 17th St. N.W., Washington, D.C. 20036. Filed 6/20/84. Legislative interest — "Generally concerned with bankruptcy legislation and certain provisions of HR 5174, the Bankruptcy Amendments of 1984."

ZENITH RADIO CORP., Glenview, Ill. Lobbyist — Brand, Lowell & Dole, 923 15th St. N.W., Washington, D.C. 20005. Filed 6/20/84. Legislative interest — "Representation of the client in matters concerning . . . Japanese Electronic Products Antitrust Litigation, Zenith Radio Corporation and National Union Electric Corporation."

State and Local Governments

STATE OF UTAH, Salt Lake City, Utah. Lobbyist — Hobbs, Straus, Dean & Wilder, 1735 New York Ave. N.W., Washington, D.C. 20006. Filed 6/14/84. Legislative interest — "HR 4103 - Amendments to Communications Act of 1934 to provide national policy regarding cable television."

Trade Associations

AMERICAN APPAREL MANUFACTURERS ASSOCIATION INC., 1611 N. Kent St., Arlington, Va. 22209. Filed for self 6/5/84. Legislative interest — "Legislation affecting the apparel industry ... bills to repeal sections 806.33 and 807 of Tariff Act (oppose) ... the President's Economic Program (support) ... Preventing Traden.ark Counterfeiting (support) ... salesmen protection act (oppose) ... bills to amend the Buy American Act (surveillance) ... state taxation of interstate commerce (support) ... lobby reform (oppose provisions relating to dues disclosure, drafting) ... capital formation (support) ... regulatory reform (surveillance) ... export promotion (support) ... small business legislation (surveillance) ... bills to restructure U.S. trade activities and affecting U.S. apparel trade policy (surveillance) ... multiemployer pension plan act amendments (surveillance) and Pension Equity Tax Act, HR 6410 (oppose) ... immigration legislation (support parts) ... amendments to Fair Labor Standards Act to prevent sweatshops in apparel industry (support) ... uniform product liability law (support) ... anti-counterfeiting law (support) ... trade reciprocity (surveillance) ... Enterprise Zone (surveillance) ... Caribbean Basin initiative (support)...." Lobbyist — Larry K. Martin.

AMERICAN AUTOMOTIVE LEASING ASSOCIATION, Milwaukee, Wis. Lobbyist — Jones and Winburn, 1101 15th St. N.W., Washington, D.C. 20005. Filed 6/12/84. Legislative interest — "The Tax Reform Act of 1984."

AMERICAN PAPER INSTITUTE INC., New York, N.Y. Lobbyist — Marilyn Beth Haugen, 1619 Massachusetts Ave. N.W., Washington, D.C. 20036. Filed 6/20/84. Legislative interest — "Legislative interests are those affecting the pulp, paper and paperboard industry, its operation, practices and properties; tax legislation and environmental legislation, air, water and energy."

AMERICAN PETROLEUM INSTITUTE, Washington, D.C. Lobbyist — Pillsbury, Madison & Sutro, 1050 17th St. N.W., Washington, D.C. 20036. Filed 6/18/84. Legislative interest — "Monitoring legislation affecting the industry; specifically, environmental legislation, HR 5640."

THE AMERICAN PUBLIC TRANSIT ASSOCIATION, 1225 Connecticut Ave. N.W., Washington, D.C. 20036. Filed for self 6/27/84. Legislative interest — "Interested in all legislation affecting Association members including all budget resolutions, transportation appropriations acts, transit authorizing legislation, and tax laws. 49 U.S.C. 1601, HR 5813, HR 5504, S 2554, S 1578, HR 4170." Lobbyist — Charles O. Bishop Jr.

AMERICAN SCHOOL FOOD SERVICE ASSOCIATION, Denver, Colo. Lobbyist — Scott, Harrison & McLeod, 2501 M St. N.W., Washington, D.C. 20037. Filed 6/22/84. Legislative interest — "All issues dealing with child nutrition, commodity distribution and food assistance."

AMERICAN SOCIETY OF COMPOSERS, AUTHORS AND PUBLISHERS, New York, N.Y. Lobbyist — Van Cott, Bagley, Cornwall & McCarthy, 50 S. Main St., Salt Lake City, Utah 84110-3400. Filed 6/11/84. Legislative interest — "... oppose Senate Bill 1734."

ASSOCIATION OF MAXIMUM SERVICE TELECASTERS INC., 1735 DeSales St. N.W., Washington, D.C. 20036. Filed for self 6/5/84. Legislative interest — "General legislative interests are the Communications Act of 1934, as amended, and legislation related to television." Lobbyist — Ann Hagemann.

BUS TRANSIT CAUCUS, Washington, D.C. Lobbyist — Nelson & Yudin, 1707 H St. N.W., Washington, D.C. 20006. Filed 6/26/84. Legislative interest — "All authorizing and appropriating bills dealing with mass transportation, particularly HR 5504; any and all amendments to the Urban Mass Transportation Act of 1964."

CHICAGO ASSOCIATION OF COMMERCE AND INDUSTRY, Chicago, Ill. Lobbyist — Thomas J. Scanlon, 3248 Prospect St. N.W., Washington, D.C. 20007. Filed 6/14/84. Legislative interest — "Have worked to obtain legislative support for the Center for Economic Development Initiatives at the Chicago Association of Commerce and Industry for the FY 84 general supplemental appropriations bill."

COMMITTEE ON PIPE AND TUBE IMPORTS, Washington, D.C. Lobbyist — Roger B. Schagrin, 923 15th St. N.W., Washington, D.C. 20005. Filed 6/11/84. Legislative interest — "Proposals to reform trade remedy laws and general industrial policy issues."

CONSUMERS UNITED FOR RAIL EQUITY, 1050 Thomas Jefferson St. N.W., Washington, D.C. 20007. Lobbyist — Van Ness, Feldman, Sutcliffe, Curtis & Levenberg, 1050 Thomas Jefferson St. N.W., Washington, D.C. 20007. Filed 6/19/84. Legislative interest — "Legislation designed to achieve rail rate and service equity for producers and purchasers of bulk commodities." Filed for self 6/19/84. Legislative interest — "Legislation designed to achieve rail rate and service equity for producers and purchasers of bulk commodities." Lobbyist — Robert G. Szabo.

FEDERAL JUDGES ASSOCIATION, San Francisco, Calif. Lobbyist — Pillsbury, Madison & Sutro, 1050 17th St. N.W., Washington, D.C. 20036. Filed 6/18/84. Legislative interest — "Monitoring legislation affecting the judiciary."

FLORIDA FRUIT & VEGETABLE ASSOCIATION, Orlando, Fla. Lobbyist — Scott, Harrison & McLeod, 2501 M St. N.W., Washington, D.C. 20037. Filed 6/13/84. Legislative interest — Not specified.

FLORIDA TOMATO EXCHANGE, Orlando, Fla. Lobbyist — Scott, Harrison & McLeod, 2501 M St. N.W., Washington, D.C. 20037. Filed 6/12/84. Legislative interest — Not specified.

FLUE CURED TOBACCO COOPERATIVE, Raleigh, N.C. Lobbyist — Patton, Boggs & Blow, 2550 M St. N.W., Washington, D.C. 20037. Filed 6/20/84. Legislative interest — "To establish a national program to increase the availability of information on the health consequences of smoking, to amend the Federal Cigarette Labeling and Advertising Act; to change the label requirements for cigarettes, and for other purposes. Such as ... HR 1824, Federal Cigarette Labeling and Advertising Act."

GROCERY MANUFACTURERS OF AMERICA INC., Washington, D.C. Lobbyist — Baker & McKenzie, 815 Connecticut Ave. N.W., Washington, D.C. 20006. Filed 6/18/84. (Former U.S. Rep. Robert McClory, R-Ill., 1963-83, was listed as agent for this client.) Legislative interest — "Support S 1910 (International Organizations Public Procedures Act of 1983)."

INDEPENDENT TANKER OWNERS COMMITTEE, New York, N.Y. Lobbyist — Hansell & Post, 1915 I St. N.W., Washington, D.C. 20006. Filed 6/18/84. Legislative interest — "Legislative action relating to the transfer of merchant vessels built with federal subsidy from the foreign trade of the U.S. to the domestic trade. Specifically, amendment to the DOD authorization bills."

INDIANA FARM BUREAU INC., 130 E. Washington St., Indianapolis, Ind. 46204. Filed for self 6/14/84. Legislative interest — "Agricultural and insurance legislation. (All general legislation affecting the above.)"

MAN-MADE FIBER PRODUCERS ASSOCIATION INC., 1150 17th St. N.W., Washington, D.C. 20036. Filed for self 6/7/84. Legislative interest — "HR 4124, S 2139, trade reform legislation; HR 3398 omnibus tariff bill. All bills supported." Lobbyist — Robert D. Umphrey Jr.

NATIONAL FOREIGN TRADE COUNCIL INC., 100 E. 42nd St., New York, N.Y. 10017. Filed for self 6/29/84. Legislative interest — "The NFTC generally is interested in legislation affecting international trade and investment." Lobbyists — Paul T. Murphy, Richard W. Roberts, Howard M. Haug.

NATIONAL TIRE DEALERS AND RETREADERS ASSOCIATION INC., 1250 I St. N.W., Washington, D.C. 20005. Filed for self 4/19/84. Legislative interest — "... status of bills and other matters before the Congress which affect the interests of independent tire dealers and retreaders ... particular interest in bills to amend regulations concerning tire identification and recordkeeping, the Internal Revenue Code provisions dealing with the excise tax on tires and tread rubber, the Motor Vehicle Safety Act, regulations promulgated under the Occupational Safety and Health Act, exemptions under the Fair Labor Standards Act, the Clean Air Act, and the issue of allowing post exchanges to retail and service new tires." Lobbyist — Don T. Wilson.

PROFESSIONAL MANAGERS' ASSOCIATION, P.O. Box 7762, Ben Franklin Station, Washington, D.C. 20044. Lobbyist — Riselli & Pressler, 2033 M St. N.W., Washington, D.C. 20036. Filed 6/15/84. Legislative interest — "PMA is concerned with all general and specific legislative interests concerning GS/GM-13, 14 & 15 employees in the Federal Civil Service, including, but not limited to, issues and concerns arising under the Civil Service Reform Act of 1978, PL 95-454, 92 Stat. 1111 (Oct. 13, 1978)." Filed for self 6/15/84. Legislative interest — "PMA is concerned with all general and specific legislative interests concerning GS/GM-13, 14 & 15 employees in the Federal Civil Service, including, but not limited to, issues and concerns arising under the Civil Service Reform Act of 1978, PL 95-454, 92 Stat. 1111 (Oct. 13, 1978)." Lobbyist — Lisa Carlson, 3735 Kanawha St. N.W., Washington, D.C. 20015.

SEMICONDUCTOR INDUSTRY ASSOCIATION, San Jose, Calif. Lobbyist — Richard H. Stern, 2101 L St. N.W., Washington, D.C. 20037. Filed 6/15/85. Legislative interest — "Promoting passage of copyright legislation to protect interests of proprietors of graphic works relating to semiconductor chip products, against the unauthorized duplication thereof. Specifically, S 1201, 'The Semiconductor Chip Protection Act of 1983' and HR 1028, 'The Semiconductor Chip Protection Act.'"

SOUTHERN FOREST PRODUCTS ASSOCIATION, P.O. Box 52468, New Orleans, La. 70152. Filed for self 6/21/84. Legislative interest — "...support of retention of estate tax reduction approved by Congress in 1981 and for a balanced approach to wilderness legislation." Lobbyist — Dudley Digges Morgan III.

UNITED STATES BUSINESS AND INDUSTRIAL COUNCIL, 7000 Executive Center Drive, Brentwood, Tenn. 37027. Filed for self 6/18/84. Legislative interest — "... Duration of matters related to business and industry particularly in areas related to reduced taxes, lower federal spending, less federal regulation ... For passage of uniform product liability laws, S 44; For abolition of Synfuels Corp., HR 4098; For elimination of capital gains tax; Against S 1300 - REA bailout bill; Against comparable worth legislation; Against HR 5174; For repeal of Davis-Bacon Act; For amending Hobbs Act, S 62; For budget reductions based on recommendations of President's Private Sector Survey on Cost Control." Lobbyist — John P. Cregan, 1000 Connecticut Ave. N.W., Washington, D.C. 20036.

Miscellaneous

CHILD DEFENSE LEAGUE, 12686 Westport Circle, West Palm Beach, Fla. 33414. Filed for self 6/18/84. Legislative interest — "Repeal of Lindbergh Act of 1932; and Parental Kidnapping Prevention Act 1980." Lobbyist — Cathy Plotkin.

CONFEDERATED SALISH & KOOTENAI TRIBES OF THE FLATHEAD RESERVATION, Pablo, Mont. Lobbyist — Heron, Burchette, Ruckert & Rothwell, 1200 New Hampshire Ave. N.W., Washington, D.C. 20036. Filed 6/18/84. Legislative interest — "HR 4402, 'The Electric Consumers Protection Act of 1983' - Against. HR 5299, 'Public Interest Hydroelectric Facility Reform Act of 1984' - Against. HR 5416, 'Electric Utility Competition Act of 1984' - Neutral."

CONSERVATIVE ALLIANCE, 1001 Prince St., Alexandria, Va. 22314. Filed for self 6/18/84. Legislative interest — "Human Rights and National Survival Program of 1984 - Legislation as of date of filing has not been introduced." Lobbyist — John T. Dolan.

FINANCIAL ACCOUNTING FOUNDATION, P.O. Box 3821, Stamford, Conn. 06905-0821. Filed for self 6/20/84. Legislative interest — "The Financial Accounting Foundation ... has a general interest in legislation affecting or otherwise relating to the establishment or improvement of standards of financial accounting and reporting." Lobbyist — Patricia Pride, 1129 20th St. N.W., Washington, D.C. 20036.

SIR JAMES GOLDSMITH, Richmond, Surrey, England. Lobbyists — H. Stewart Dunn Jr. and Philip D. Morrison, 1700 Pennsylvania Ave. N.W., Washington, D.C. 20006. Filed 6/8/84 and 6/28/84. Legislative interest — "Lobbying in support of Section 451 of the Tax Reform Act of 1984 (HR 4170)."

HUNTINGTON MEMORIAL HOSPITAL, Pasadena, Calif. Lobbyist — Gibson, Dunne & Crutcher, 1050 Connecticut Ave. N.W., Washington, D.C. 20036. Filed 6/1/84. Legislative interest — "... encouraging the passage of legislation that would allow the scheduled reduction in gift and estate tax rates to go into effect. The Senate's rejection of section 21 of HR 4170 would be encouraged."

MARCH OF DIMES BIRTH DEFECTS FOUNDATION, 1275 Mamaroneck Ave., White Plains, N.Y. 10605. Filed for self 6/27/84. Legislative interest — "Maternal & Child Health Block Grant, Child Health Assurance Program (HR 4136). Reauthorization of WIC program (HR 7). Postal subsidy for Third Class Nonprofit Mailers. Adolescent Pregnancy & Parenthood Act of 1984 (HR 5534). Safe Food Amendments (HR 5495)...." Lobbyist — Nancy Jo Merrill, 1707 H St. N.W., Washington, D.C. 20006.

MAYOR'S COMMITTEE (BALTIMORE) TO RESTORE NFL FOOTBALL, Baltimore, Md. Lobbyist — Hartz/Meek International, 806 15th St. N.W., Washington, D.C. 20005. Filed 6/12/84. Legislative interest — "Legislation related to the movement of professional sports teams from one community to another."

McINTOSH FOUNDATION, New York, N.Y. Lobbyist — Patton, Boggs & Blow, 2550 M St. N.W., Washington, D.C. 20037. Filed 6/26/84. Legislative interest — "Legislation amending the Coast Guard Authorization bill, HR 4841 and S 2526. In support of an amendment to designate a vessel for inspection purposes."

LARRY A. MIZEL, Denver, Colo. Lobbyist — Akin, Gump, Strauss, Hauer & Feld, 1333 New Hampshire Ave. N.W., Washington, D.C. 20036. Filed 6/7/84. Legislative interest — "Tax Reform Act of 1983, HR 4170."

NATIONAL AUDUBON SOCIETY, Washington, D.C. Lobbyist — Perkins, Coie, Stone, Olsen & Williams, 1110 Vermont Ave. N.W., Washington, D.C. 20005. Filed 6/4/84. Legislative interest — "FY 1985 appropriations legislation." Lobbyist — Chambers Associates Inc., 1411 K St. N.W., Washington, D.C. 20005. Filed 6/4/84. Legislative interest — "Water Development Act ... appropriations bill for fiscal year 1985."

JACK JOHN OLIVERO, 255 East Shore Trail, Lake Mohawk, N.J. 07871. Filed for self 6/4/84. Legislative interest — "... including, but not limited to ... Technological assessment ... Immigration - foreign matters relating to nationals and corporations ... Immigration - political refugees ... Corporate/Banking Ethics and Practices."

WESTERN GOVERNORS' ASSOCIATION, 333 Quebec St., Denver, Colo. 80207. Filed for self 6/28/84. Legislative interest — "Hearings and any legislation affecting Western States interests, including, but not limited to, grant programs, resource development and environmental legislation." Lobbyist — R. Philip Shimer, 444 North Capitol St. N.W., Washington, D.C. 20001.

July Registrations

Corporations and Businesses

THE ACACIA GROUP, Washington, D.C. Lobbyist — Sutherland, Asbill & Brennan, 1666 K St. N.W., Washington, D.C. 20006. Filed 7/24/84. Legislative interest — "Amendment to HR 5916 and S 2851 to grandfather acquisition of a savings and loan association."

THE ALGOMA STEEL CORP. LTD., 503 Queen St. East, Sault Ste. Marie, Ontario, Canada P6A 5P2. Filed for self 7/16/84. Legislative interest — "... Fair Trade in Steel Act ... S 2380, HR 5081 ... in opposition to any legislation which restricts U.S. imports of steel mill products from Canada." Lobbyists — James

T. Melville, John Macnamara; Allen Scott Pack, 1250 One Valley Square, Charleston, W.Va. 25301.

ALLIS-CHALMERS ENERGY AND MINERALS SYSTEMS CO., Milwaukee, Wis. Lobbyist — Bliss, Craft & Richards, 1050 Thomas Jefferson St. N.W., Washington, D.C. 20007. Filed 7/27/84. Legislative interest — "All legislation in the House and Senate relating to appropriation for KILnGAS project continuation."

ALTMAN REALTY CO. INC., Glenside, Pa. Lobbyist — S. R. Wojdak and Associates Inc., 8 Penn Center Plaza, Philadelphia, Pa. 19103. Filed 7/11/84. Legislative interest — "Real estate and housing issues."

ALUMINUM COMPANY OF AMERICA, Pittsburgh, Pa. Lobbyist — Groom and Nordberg, 1775 Pennsylvania Ave. N.W., Washington, D.C. 20006. Filed 7/11/84. Legislative interest — "Federal legislation affecting Title 26 of the U.S.C."

AMERADA HESS, New York, N.Y. Lobbyist — Birch, Horton, Bittner, Pestinger and Anderson, 1140 Connecticut Ave. N.W., Washington, D.C. 20036. Filed 7/11/84. Legislative interest — "Oil and gas tax related matters."

AMERICAN GENERAL, Houston, Texas. Lobbyist — Corporation Consulting Services Inc., P.O. Box 2768, Key Largo, Fla. 33037. Filed 7/2/84. (Former U.S. Rep. L. A. "Skip" Bafalis, R-Fla., 1973-83, was listed as agent for this client.) Legislative interest — "...HR 3881 ... HR 5734 ... S 2181 ... Seek modification."

AMERICAN HOSPITAL SUPPLY CORP., 1090 Vermont Ave. N.W., Washington, D.C. 20005. Filed for self 7/19/84. Legislative interest — "...tax, trade, transportation, antitrust, health, benefits, product liability, and other legislative proposals which affect the corporation, its employees, shareholders or customers." Lobbyists — David J. Aho, Sarah Massengale Billock.

AMERICAN SAVINGS BANK, New York, N.Y. Lobbyist — Thacher, Proffitt & Wood, 1140 Connecticut Ave. N.W., Washington, D.C. 20036. Filed 7/12/84. Legislative interest — "HR 5916/S 2181, financial reform legislation (proposed) affecting Federal savings banks and thrift institutions."

ANHEUSER-BUSCH COS., St. Louis, Mo. Lobbyist — David W. Wilmot, 1029 Vermont Ave. N.W., Washington, D.C. 20005. Filed 7/17/84. Legislative interest — Not specified.

ATLANTIC RICHFIELD CO., 515 S. Flower St., Los Angeles, Calif. 90071. Filed for self 7/12/84. Legislative interest — Not specified. Lobbyist — Janet S. Fisher, 1333 New Hampshire Ave. N.W., Washington, D.C. 20036.

B. D. I. INVESTMENT CORP., San Diego, Calif. Lobbyist — Caplin & Drysdale, 1101 17th St. N.W., Washington, D.C. 20036. Filed 7/5/84. Legislative interest — "...changes to the regulated investment company provisions of the Deficit Reduction Act of 1984 (HR 4170)."

BLUE CROSS AND BLUE SHIELD ASSOCIATION, 1709 New York Ave. N.W., Washington, D.C. 20006. Filed for self 7/13/84. Legislative interest — "Legislation impacting the financing and delivery of health care." Lobbyist — Linda L. Lanam.

BREEDER REACTOR CORP., Chicago, Ill. Lobbyist — Swidler, Berlin & Strelow, 1000 Thomas Jefferson St. N.W., Washington, D.C. 20007. Filed 7/23/84. Legislative interest — "...appropriations for Clinch River Breeder Reactor."

BRIGGS & STRATTON, Milwaukee, Wis. Lobbyist — D L Associates Inc., 1730 Rhode Island Ave. N.W., Washington, D.C. 20036. Filed 7/3/84. Legislative interest — Not specified.

BRISTOL-MYERS CO., Washington, D.C. Lobbyist — D L Associates Inc., 1730 Rhode Island Ave. N.W., Washington, D.C. 20036. Filed 7/3/84. Legislative interest — "S 2748 and HR 3605."

BROWN-FORMAN CORP., Louisville, Ky. Lobbyist — Barnes, Richardson & Colburn, 1819 H St. N.W., Washington, D.C. 20006. Filed 7/25/84. Legislative interest — "...The 'Wine Equity Act' of 1983 ... S 2182, HR 3795 ... Oppose passage of these bills."

CABLEVISION SYSTEMS DEVELOPMENT CO., Woodbury, N.Y. Lobbyist — Mintz, Levin, Cohn, Ferris, Glovsky & Popeo, 1825 I St. N.W., Washington, D.C. 20006. Filed 7/12/84. Legislative interest — "...communications and tax."

CHEVRON USA, Washington, D.C. Lobbyist — Charles E. Wiggins, 1050 17th St. N.W., Washington, D.C. 20036. Filed 7/10/84. (Former U.S. rep., R-Calif., 1967-79.) Legislative interest — "Legislation affecting mergers in the oil industry."

CHRONAR CORP., Princeton, N.J. Lobbyist — Schwabe, Williamson, Wyatt, Moore & Roberts, 1000 Potomac St. N.W., Washington, D.C. 20007. Filed 7/12/84. Legislative interest — "Energy tax credits for photovoltaics in HR 4170, tax legislation."

CITICORP CAPITAL INVESTORS LTD., New York, N.Y. Lobbyist — Brown, Roady, Bonvillian & Gold, 1300 19th St. N.W., Washington, D.C. 20035. Filed 7/30/84. Legislative interest — "Enactment of Conrail disposition legislation, and selection of transferee."

DEERE & CO., John Deere Road, Moline, Ill. 61265. Filed for self 7/10/84. Legislative interest — Not specified. Lobbyist — Terrie M. Carter, 910 17th St. N.W., Washington, D.C. 20006.

THE DENVER AND RIO GRANDE WESTERN RAILROAD CO., Denver, Colo. Lobbyist — Fred B. Rooney, 1050 Thomas Jefferson St. N.W., Washington, D.C. 20007. Filed 7/10/84. (Former U.S. rep., D-Pa., 1963-79.) Legislative interest — "Tax legislation."

DOLLAR SAVINGS BANK, Pittsburgh, Pa. Lobbyist — Donald H. Brazier, P.O. Box 12266, Seattle, Wash. 98102. Filed 7/13/84. Legislative interest — "Tax incentives to encourage savings; additional powers for savings banks; conversion from mutual to stock form etc."

EBASCO SERVICES INC., 2 World Trade Center, New York, N.Y. 10048. Filed for self 7/5/84. Legislative interest — "...include tax, energy regulation, international trade, appropriations, authorizations, government operations, environmental & safety legislative matters...." Lobbyist — Robert Michael Hartman, 1025 Connecticut Ave. N.W., Washington, D.C. 20036.

EMS DEVELOPMENT CORP., Farmingdale, N.Y. Lobbyist — Gnau, Carter, Jacobsen & Associates Inc., 1250 I St. N.W., Washington, D.C. 20005. Filed 7/10/84. Legislative interest — "Providing Federal government liaison on marketing and contracting endeavors."

ENSERCH CORP., Dallas, Texas. Lobbyist — Bishop, Liberman, Cook, Purcell & Reynolds, 1200 17th St. N.W., Washington, D.C. 20036. Filed 7/12/84. (Former U.S. Rep. Graham B. Purcell, D-Texas, 1962-73, was listed as agent for this client.) Legislative interest — "...all natural gas legislation...."

ETA SYSTEMS INC., Washington, D.C. Lobbyist — Florida Business Associates Inc., 2000 L St. N.W., Washington, D.C. 20036. Filed 7/12/84. Legislative interest — "Policies involving the use of large scale computational equipment."

FINNIGAN CORP., San Jose, Calif. Lobbyist — Swidler, Berlin & Strelow, 1000 Thomas Jefferson St. N.W., Washington, D.C. 20007. Filed 7/19/84. Legislative interest — "...legislative reform to the Clean Water Act, HR 3282."

FISCAL ASSOCIATES INC., Canton, Ohio. Lobbyist — Stanley A. Cmich & Associates Inc., 1700 Gateway Blvd. S.E., Canton, Ohio 44707. Filed 7/12/84. Legislative interest — "Business, environmental and general legislation...."

FLOATING POINT SYSTEMS INC., Portland, Ore. Lobbyist — Blum, Nash & Railsback, 1015 18th St. N.W., Washington, D.C. 20036. Filed 7/19/84. Legislative interest — "Export Administration legislation, S 979."

FLOW WIND CORP., Lake Oswego, Ore. Lobbyist — Schwabe, Williamson, Wyatt, Moore & Roberts, 1000 Potomac St. N.W., Washington, D.C. 20007. Filed 7/12/84. (Former U.S. Rep. Robert Duncan, D-Ore., 1963-67, 1975-81, was listed as agent for this client.) Legislative interest — "Solar energy tax credits; tax legislation (HR 4170)."

GENERAL MOTORS CORP., Washington, D.C. Lobbyist — Wexler, Reynolds, Harrison & Schule Inc., 1317 F St. N.W., Washington, D.C. 20004. Filed 7/10/84. Legislative interest — "...HR 4175, to encourage the enactment of mandatory safety belt laws by the states."

THE GIBBONS-GRABLE CO., Canton, Ohio. Lobbyist — Stanley A. Cmich & Associates Inc., 1700 Gateway Blvd. S.E., Canton, Ohio 44707. Filed 7/12/84. Legislative interest — "Business, environmental and general legislation...."

GTE/SPRINT COMMUNICATIONS, Washington, D.C. Lobbyist — J. T. Rutherford & Associates Inc., 1301 North Courthouse Road, Arlington, Va. 22201. Filed 7/11/84. Legislative interest — "HR 4170."

GUARDIAN SAVINGS & LOAN, Washington, D.C. Lobbyist — Vinson & Elkins, 1101 Connecticut Ave. N.W., Washington, D.C. 20036. Filed 7/12/84. Legislative interest — "Banking legislation affecting savings and loans."

HARTFORD FIRE INSURANCE CO., Hartford Plaza, Hartford, Conn. 06115. Filed for self 7/13/84. Legislative interest — "... Financial Services Deregulation, Longshore Act Amendments, Pollution and Superfund Legislation, Taxation, Non-Discrimination in Insurance Act, Minimum Financial Responsibility Requirements, Occupational Disease Legislation, Casualty Loss Reporting, Product Liability Tort Reform." Lobbyist — Joel Freedman, 1600 M St. N.W., Washington, D.C. 20036.

HEUBLEIN INC., Farmington, Conn. Lobbyist — Barnes, Richardson & Colburn, 1819 H St. N.W., Washington, D.C. 20006. Filed 7/25/84. Legislative interest — "... The 'Wine Equity Act' of 1983 ... S 2182, HR 3795 ... Oppose passage of these bills."

HIRAM WALKER & SONS INC., Detroit, Mich. Lobbyist — Barnes, Richardson & Colburn, 1819 H St. N.W., Washington, D.C. 20006. Filed 7/25/84. Legislative interest — "... The 'Wine Equity Act' of 1983 ... S 2182, HR 3795 ... Oppose passage of these bills."

HOUSEHOLD INTERNATIONAL, Prospect Heights, Ill. Lobbyist — McNair, Glenn, Konduros, Corley, Singletary, Porter & Dibble, 1155 15th St. N.W., Washington, D.C. 20005. Filed 7/2/84. Legislative interest — "Tax matters."

HYDRIL CO., Los Angeles, Calif. Lobbyist — Deloitte, Haskins & Sells, 655 15th St. N.W., Washington, D.C. 20005. Filed 7/27/84. Legislative interest — "Interest is in tax legislation which might have impact on business of employer."

INVESTORS FIDUCIARY TRUST CO., Kansas City, Mo. Lobbyist — Kirkpatrick, Lockhart, Hill, Christopher & Phillips, 1900 M St. N.W., Washington, D.C. 20036. Filed 7/9/84. Legislative interest — "HR 5342, HR 5916, S 2181 and similar banking legislation; support in part, oppose in part."

ITT CORP., New York, N.Y. Lobbyist — Zuckert, Scoutt, Rasenberger & Johnson, 888 17th St. N.W., Washington, D.C. 20006. Filed 7/6/84. Legislative interest — "Proponent of clarification of the provisions extending the Glass-Steagall Act which are contained in HR 5881, HR 5916 and S 2181."

JAFFE, SNIDER, RAITT & HEUER, 1800 First National Building, Detroit, Mich. 48226. Filed for self 7/30/84. Legislative interest — "Legislation regarding tax matters, specifically the Deficit Reduction Tax Bill of 1984, and the Tax Reform Act of 1984, HR 4170. More specifically, the provisions regarding regulated investment companies were a matter of concern." Lobbyist — Gary R. Glenn. Filed for self 7/30/84. Legislative interest — "Legislation regarding general business matters, including but not limited to federal taxation and municipal finance issues." Lobbyists — F. Thomas Lewand, Clunet R. Lewis, David H. Raitt, Stephen G. Schafer, Arthur A. Weiss.

J. L. ASSOCIATES, 1300 Army-Navy Drive, Arlington, Va. 22202. Filed for self 7/10/84. Legislative interest — "U.S. Tuna Foundation - Tariff on Oil and Water products." Lobbyist — Joanna Lynne Cullen.

K MART CORP., Troy, Mich. Lobbyist — Steele, Simmons & Fornaciari, 2020 K St. N.W., Washington, D.C. 20006. Filed 7/9/84. Legislative interest — "Pending intellectual property legislation including S 875 and HR 2447."

NEAL KNOX ASSOCIATES, P.O. Box 6537, Silver Spring, Md. 20906. Filed for self 7/23/84. Legislative interest — "... all legislation affecting the ownership, acquisition or use of firearms and ammunition, such as S 914, the Firearms Owners Protection Act, and S 2766/HR 5845/HR 5835, the armor-piercing bullet bill." Lobbyist — Neal Knox.

LLOYD'S OF LONDON, London, England. Lobbyist — LeBoeuf, Lamb, Leiby & MacRae, 1333 New Hampshire Ave. N.W., Washington, D.C. 20036 and 520 Madison Ave., New York, N.Y. 10022. Filed 7/17/84. Legislative interest — "HR 4170 (Deficit Reduction Act of 1984; amendment of federal excise tax on insurance (section 4371 of Internal Revenue Code).)"

M/A-COM INC., Rockville, Md. Lobbyist — George R. Moses, 1341 G St. N.W., Washington, D.C. 20005. Filed 7/16/84. Legislative interest — "Legislative and oversight activities affecting high technology manufacturing and government contracting."

MANUFACTURERS HANOVER BANK, New York, N.Y. Lobbyist — Bishop, Liberman, Cook, Purcell & Reynolds, 1200 17th St. N.W., Washington, D.C. 20036. Filed 7/12/84. Legislative interest — "... Promote favorable tax amendments to HR 4170."

MASSACHUSETTS MUTUAL LIFE INSURANCE CO., Springfield, Mass. Lobbyist — Steptoe & Johnson, 1250 Connecticut Ave. N.W., Washington, D.C. 20036. Filed 7/13/84. Legislative interest — "Congressional monitoring of financial services legislation."

MERCHANTS SAVINGS BANK, Manchester, N.H. Lobbyist — Donald H. Brazier, P.O. Box 12266, Seattle, Wash. 98102. Filed 7/13/84. Legislative interest — "Tax incentives to encourage savings; additional powers for savings banks; conversion from mutual to stock form etc."

MERRILL LYNCH & CO. INC., Lobbyist — O'Connor & Hannan, 1919 Pennsylvania Ave. N.W., Washington, D.C. 20006. Filed 7/13/84. Legislative interest — "... including, but not limited to, S 2181."

MIDWEST TELEVISION, Champaign, Ill. Lobbyist — Covington & Burling, 1201 Pennsylvania Ave. N.W., Washington, D.C. 20044. Filed 7/6/84. Legislative interest — "... supports a proposal that would authorize a power increase for its AM radio station in San Diego, California ... opposes legislative efforts to repeal Section 325(b) of the Communications Act."

MINNESOTA MINING & MANUFACTURING CO., 3M Center, St. Paul, Minn. 55144. Filed for self 7/6/84. Legislative interest — "... include product liability, energy and transportation, and government regulatory agencies." Lobbyist — Andrew J. Donelson, 1101 15th St. N.W., Washington, D.C. 20005. Filed for self 7/9/84. Legislative interest — "... include copyright and patent issues, office machines or other products, trade and government regulatory agencies." Lobbyist — Helena C. Hutton, 1101 15th St. N.W., Washington, D.C. 20005. Filed for self 7/9/84. Legislative interest — "... include the environment and government regulatory agencies." Lobbyist — Mary K. Killorin, 1101 15th St. N.W., Washington, D.C. 20005.

MISSISSIPPI POWER & LIGHT, Jackson, Miss. Lobbyist — Bishop, Liberman, Cook, Purcell & Reynolds, 1200 17th St. N.W., Washington, D.C. 20036. Filed 7/12/84. (Former U.S. Rep. Graham B. Purcell, D-Texas, 1962-73, was listed as agent for this client.) Legislative interest — "... all legislation affecting nuclear plant licensing...."

MORTGAGE INSURANCE COMPANIES OF AMERICA, 1725 K St. N.W., Washington, D.C. 20006. Filed for self 7/6/84. Legislative interest — "Any legislation ... dealing with housing, financial institutions, or insurance." Lobbyist — T. I. Wilder.

NABISCO INC., Parsippany, N.J. Lobbyist — Shea & Gould, 330 Madison Ave., New York, N.Y. 10017. Filed 7/11/84. Legislative interest — "Legislation regarding factoring of overseas receivables."

NATIONAL STEEL & SHIPBUILDING CO., 1725 K St. N.W., Washington, D.C. 20006. Filed for self 7/18/84. Legislative interest — Not specified. Lobbyist — Edwin M. Hood.

NOVA, Calgary, Alberta, Canada. Lobbyist — McHenry & Staffier, 1300 19th St. N.W., Washington, D.C. 20036. Filed 7/26/84. Legislative interest — "... opposed to the provisions of HR 4784 which would result in the imposition of countervailing duties upon imported petrochemicals."

NOVACOR CHEMICALS LTD., Calgary, Alberta, Canada. Lobbyist — McHenry & Staffier, 1300 19th St. N.W., Washington, D.C. 20036. Filed 7/26/84. Legislative interest — "... opposed to the provisions of HR 4784 which would result in the imposition of countervailing duties upon imported petrochemicals."

NUCLEAR FUEL SERVICES INC., Rockville, Md. Lobbyist — Miller & Chevalier, 655 15th St. N.W., Washington, D.C.

20005. Filed 7/13/84. Legislative interest — "Revision to federal laws relating to transportation of nuclear materials."

PFIZER INC., New York, N.Y. Lobbyist — Barnes, Richardson & Colburn, 1819 H St. N.W., Washington, D.C. 20006. Filed 7/13/84. Legislative interest — ". . . A bill to extend the tariff suspension for tartaric acid and certain tartaric chemicals . . . HR 4513, S 2493 . . . 19 USC section 1202 . . . support passage. . . ."

PHILLIPS PETROLEUM CO., Bartlesville, Okla. 74004. Filed for self 7/9/84. Legislative interest — "Trade Reciprocity Bill, S 144 & HR 3398 - for. Trade Remedies Bill, HR 4784 - against. Export Administration Act, S 979 & HR 3231 - for modifications. Domestic Content Bill, S 707 - against." Lobbyist — Ernest Johnston, 1825 K St. N.W., Washington, D.C. 20006.

THE PITTSBURGH & LAKE ERIE RAILROAD CO., Pittsburgh, Pa. Lobbyist — Vorys, Sater, Seymour & Pease, 1828 L St. N.W., Washington, D.C. 20036. Filed 7/10/84. Legislative interest — "Legislation re disposition by U.S. Government of Consolidated Rail Corporation (CONRAIL)."

PRIDE AIR INC., 6151 W. Century Blvd., Los Angeles, Calif. 90045. Filed for self 7/23/84. Legislative interest — ". . . legislation affecting business, particularly ADAP authorizing legislation and appropriations." Lobbyist — Donna S. Shaffer, P.O. Box 17309, Washington, D.C. 20041.

RIO GRANDE INDUSTRIES, Denver, Colo. Lobbyist — Bishop, Liberman, Cook, Purcell & Reynolds, 1200 17th St. N.W., Washington, D.C. 20036. Filed 7/12/84. Legislative interest — ". . . railroad taxation . . . Support legislation to provide deduction for railroad construction and rehabilitation expenditures."

ROOSEVELT RACEWAY ASSOCIATES LTD., New York, N.Y. Lobbyist — Seward & Kissel, 919 18th St. N.W., Washington, D.C. 20006. Filed 7/10/84. Legislative interest — "Legislation regarding Tax Reform Act of 1984, lobbied for Section 723 of the Senate version of HR 4170." Lobbyist — Brownstein, Zeidman and Schomer, 1025 Connecticut Ave. N.W., Washington, D.C. 20036. Filed 7/12/84. Legislative interest — "All tax legislation, specifically HR 4170."

RUBIN & ASSOCIATES, Studio City, Calif. Lobbyist — Grove, Engelberg & Gross, 2033 M St. N.W., Washington, D.C. 20036. Filed 7/9/84. Legislative interest — "Omnibus Bankruptcy Improvements Act of 1984 - HR 5174."

SALOMON BROTHERS INC., New York, N.Y. Lobbyist — Bishop, Liberman, Cook, Purcell & Reynolds, 1200 17th St. N.W., Washington, D.C. 20036. Filed 7/12/84. (Former U.S. Rep. Graham B. Purcell, D-Texas, 1962-73, was listed as agent for this client.) Legislative interest — "HR 4170 Deficit Reduction Act of 1984 - for."

SANLANDO UTILITIES CORP., Orlando, Fla. Lobbyist — Sutherland, Asbill & Brennan, 1666 K St. N.W., Washington, D.C. 20006. Filed 7/9/84. Legislative interest — "To obtain appropriate transition rule in connection with amendment of IRC Section 341 (See Section 164 of HR 4170)."

SCHIEFFELIN & CO., New York, N.Y. Lobbyist — Barnes, Richardson & Colburn, 1819 H St. N.W., Washington, D.C. 20006. Filed 7/25/84. Legislative interest — ". . . The 'Wine Equity Act' of 1983 . . . S 2182, HR 3795 . . . Oppose passage of these bills."

JOSEPH E. SEAGRAM & SONS INC., New York, N.Y. Lobbyist — Barnes, Richardson & Colburn, 1819 H St. N.W., Washington, D.C. 20006. Filed 7/25/84. Legislative interest — ". . . The 'Wine Equity Act' of 1983 . . . S 2182, HR 3795 . . . Oppose passage of these bills."

SOUTH CENTRAL BELL, Birmingham, Ala. Lobbyist — Camp, Carmouche, Barsh, Hunter, Gray, Hoffman & Gill, 2550 M St. N.W., Washington, D.C. 20037. Filed 7/17/84. Legislative interest — "Income tax provision of HR 4170 applicable to corporations."

SOUTHWESTERN PUBLIC SERVICE CO., P.O. Box 1261, Amarillo, Texas 79170. Filed for self 7/9/84. Legislative interest — "Legislation affecting the electric utility industry including energy, environment and regulatory issues." Lobbyist — Thomas F. Williams, 6812 Old Kent Road, Amarillo, Texas 79109.

SUPERIOR ENGINEERING & ELECTRONICS, Alexandria, Va. Lobbyist — James C. Corman, 1420 16th St. N.W.,

Washington, D.C. 20036. Filed 7/9/84. (Former U.S. rep., D-Calif., 1961-81.) Legislative interest — "To support legislation favorable to small business engaged in contracting with the Federal Government."

TARTARIC CHEMICALS CORP., New York, N.Y. Lobbyist — Barnes, Richardson & Colburn, 1819 H St. N.W., Washington, D.C. 20006. Filed 7/13/84. Legislative interest — ". . . A bill to extend the tariff suspension for tartaric acid and certain tartaric chemicals . . . HR 4513, S 2493 . . . 19 USC section 1202 . . . Support passage of the bills."

TERWILLIGER, WAKEEN, PIEHLER, CONWAY & KLINGBERG, Wausau, Wis. Lobbyist — D L Associates Inc., 1730 Rhode Island Ave. N.W., Washington, D.C. 20036. Filed 7/3/84. Legislative interest — "HR 4170."

TEXAS-NEW MEXICO POWER CO., 501 W. 6th St., Fort Worth, Texas 76102. Filed for self 7/2/84. Legislative interest — "Legislation affecting the electric utility industry including energy, environment and regulatory issues. Bills of interest include HR 3050, HR 4170, HR 4550, HR 4813, HR 4965, HR 5002 and HR 4032; S J Res 5; and S 768, S 764, S 2390 and S 2356."

THOMSON-CSF DIVISION SYSTEMS ELECTRONIQUE, Bagneux, France. Lobbyist — DGA International Inc., 1225 19th St. N.W., Washington, D.C. 20036. Filed 7/13/84. Legislative interest — "Department of Defense Authorization and Appropriations Bills."

THORNTON & EARLY, Boston, Mass. Lobbyist — MJC Associates Inc., 52 Hilma St., North Quincy, Mass. 02171. Filed 7/20/84. Legislative interest — ". . . Occupational Health Hazards Compensation Act . . . HR 3175/Position: Against."

THE TIMKEN CO., Canton, Ohio. Lobbyist — Stanley A. Cmich & Associates Inc., 1700 Gateway Blvd., Canton, Ohio 44707. Filed 7/12/84. Legislative interest — "Business, environmental and general legislation. . . ."

TOLLAND BANK, Tolland, Conn. Lobbyist — Thacher, Profitt & Wood, 1140 Connecticut Ave. N.W., Washington, D.C. 20036. Filed 7/12/84. Legislative interest — "HR 5916/S 2181, financial reform legislation (proposed) affecting Federal savings banks and thrift institutions."

UNICOVER CORP., Cheyenne, Wyo. Lobbyist — Bingham, Dana & Gould, 1724 Massachusetts Ave. N.W., Washington, D.C. 20036. Filed 7/10/84. Legislative interest — "Supporting passage of the Deficit Reduction Act of 1984 as amended by Committee of Conference."

UNION PACIFIC CORP., 345 Park Ave., New York, N.Y. 10154. Filed for self 7/3/84. Legislative interest — ". . . legislation affecting the transportation and energy industries, particularly so-called 'acid rain' legislation." Lobbyist — W. Dan Boone.

U.S. WINDPOWER INC., San Francisco, Calif. Lobbyist — Cades, Schutte, Fleming & Wright, 1001 22nd St. N.W., Washington, D.C. 20037. Filed 7/10/84. Legislative interest — ". . . tax legislation."

UNR INDUSTRIES INC., Chicago, Ill. Lobbyist — Spriggs, Bode & Hollingsworth, 1015 15th St. N.W., Washington, D.C. 20005. Filed 7/13/84. Legislative interest — "Legislation which involves bankruptcy (HR 5174) and toxic management, including HR 3175, HR 5966 and S 2708."

USAA FINANCIAL SERVICE CO., San Antonio, Texas. Lobbyist — Williams & Jensen, 1101 Connecticut Ave. N.W., Washington, D.C. 20036. Filed 7/30/84. Legislative interest — "Seeking a technical amendment to the effective date section of the Financial Institutions Equity Act (HR 5916/S 2131)."

VALLEY VIEW HOLDINGS INC., Dallas, Texas. Lobbyist — Bishop, Liberman, Cook, Purcell & Reynolds, 1200 17th St. N.W., Washington, D.C. 20036. Filed 7/12/84. (Former U.S. Rep. Graham B. Purcell, D-Texas, 1962-73, was listed as agent for this client.) Legislative interest — ". . . concern futures industry and livestock and meat packing industry. HR 4170 Deficit Reduction Act of 1984 - for passage."

WASHINGTON MUTUAL SAVINGS BANK, Seattle, Wash. Lobbyist — Donald H. Brazier, P.O. Box 12266, Seattle, Wash. 98102. Filed 7/13/84. Legislative interest — "Tax incentives to encourage savings; additional powers for savings banks; conversion from mutual to stock form etc."

WASTE MANAGEMENT INC., Oak Brook, Ill. Lobbyist — McNair, Glenn, Konduros, Corley, Singletary, Porter & Dibble, 1155 15th St. N.W., Washington, D.C. 20005. Filed 7/2/84. Legislative interest — "All matters pertaining to antitrust."

WEDTECH CORP., New York, N.Y. Lobbyist — Gnau, Carter, Jacobsen & Associates Inc., 1250 I St. N.W., Washington, D.C. 20005. Filed 7/10/84. Legislative interest — Not specified.

WESCLAG, Los Angeles, Calif. Lobbyist — Stuart A. Lewis, 1919 Pennsylvania Ave. N.W., Washington, D.C. 20006. Filed 7/23/84. Legislative interest — "HR 4170."

WHITE ENGINES INC., Canton, Ohio. Lobbyist — Stanley A. Cmich & Associates Inc., 1700 Gateway Blvd. S.E., Canton, Ohio 44707. Filed 7/12/84. Legislative interest — "Business, environmental and general legislation...."

THE WILLIAMS COS., P.O. Box 2400, Tulsa, Okla. 74102. Filed for self 7/11/84. Legislative interest — "Any legislation regarding fertilizer, energy, metals ... promotion of U.S. exports; deregulation of natural gas; importation of anhydrous ammonia from U.S.S.R.; petroleum pipeline regulatory reform; corporate taxation matters; and extension of the Export Administration Act." Lobbyist — Judy M. Sullivan, 1120 20th St. N.W., Washington, D.C. 20036.

XEROX CORP., Stamford, Conn. Lobbyist — H. Stewart Dunn Jr., 1700 Pennsylvania Ave. N.W., Washington, D.C. 20006. Filed 7/12/84. Legislative interest — "... federal income taxation of corporations ... lobbying relating to the characterization of a transaction as a lease or service contract for tax purposes."

Labor Groups

AMERICAN FEDERATION OF LABOR AND CONGRESS OF INDUSTRIAL ORGANIZATIONS, 815 16th St. N.W., Washington, D.C. 20006. Filed for self 7/16/84. Legislative interest — Not specified. Lobbyist — Ernest DuBester.

UNITED BROTHERHOOD OF CARPENTERS AND JOINERS OF AMERICA, 101 Constitution Ave. N.W., Washington, D.C. 20001. Filed for self 7/12/84. Legislative interest — Not specified. Lobbyist — Wayne Pierce.

State and Local Governments

BAY AREA RAPID TRANSIT DISTRICT, Oakland, Calif. Lobbyist — Heron, Burchette, Ruckert & Rothwell, 4200 New Hampshire Ave. N.W., Washington, D.C. 20036. Filed 7/12/84. Legislative interest — "Surface Transportation Bill - monitoring. DOT Appropriations bill - support funds for mass transit."

CITY OF ANAHEIM, Anaheim, Calif. Lobbyist — Spiegel & McDiarmid, 2600 Virginia Ave. N.W., Washington, D.C. 20037. Filed 7/5/84. Legislative interest — "Maintain present legislation in Part I of the Federal Power Act; promote competition in hydro relicensing cases, and encourage transmission ... HR 4402 (against); HR 5299 (against); HR 5416 (for) ... HR 5608 (for)."

CITY OF AZUSA, Azusa, Calif. Lobbyist — Spiegel & McDiarmid, 2600 Virginia Ave. N.W., Washington, D.C. 20037. Filed 7/5/84. Legislative interest — "Maintain present legislation in Part I of the Federal Power Act; promote competition in hydro relicensing cases, and encourage transmission ... HR 4402 (against); HR 5299 (against); HR 5416 (for) ... HR 5608 (for)."

CITY OF BANNING, Banning, Calif. Lobbyist — Spiegel & McDiarmid, 2600 Virginia Ave. N.W., Washington, D.C. 20037. Filed 7/5/84. Legislative interest — "Maintain present legislation in Part I of the Federal Power Act; promote competition in hydro relicensing cases, and encourage transmission ... HR 4402 (against); HR 5299 (against); HR 5416 (for) ... HR 5608 (for)."

CITY OF COLTON, Colton, Calif. Lobbyist — Spiegel & McDiarmid, 2600 Virginia Ave. N.W., Washington, D.C. 20037. Filed 7/5/84. Legislative interest — "Maintain present legislation in Part I of the Federal Power Act; promote competition in hydro relicensing cases, and encourage transmission ... HR 4402 (against); HR 5299 (against); HR 5416 (for) ... HR 5608 (for)."

CITY OF NEW BRIGHTON, New Brighton, Minn. Lobbyist — LeFevere, Lefler, Kennedy, O'Brien & Drawz, 120 South 6th St., Minneapolis, Minn. 55402. Filed 7/18/84. Legislative interest — "... to recover costs incurred by the City of New Brighton, Minn., for contamination of its groundwater supply pursuant to CERCLA, 42 U.S.C. section 9601, RCRA, 42 U.S.C. 6901, and Federal Torts Claims Act."

CITY OF RIVERSIDE, Riverside, Calif. Lobbyist — Spiegel & McDiarmid, 2600 Virginia Ave. N.W., Washington, D.C. 20037. Filed 7/5/84. Legislative interest — "Maintain present legislation in Part I of the Federal Power Act; promote competition in hydro relicensing cases, and encourage transmission ... HR 4402 (against); HR 5299 (against); HR 5416 (for) ... HR 5608 (for)."

CITY OF SANTA CLARA, Santa Clara, Calif. Lobbyist — Spiegel & McDiarmid, 2600 Virginia Ave. N.W., Washington, D.C. 20037. Filed 7/5/84. Legislative interest — "Maintain present legislation in Part I of the Federal Power Act; promote competition in hydro relicensing cases, and encourage transmission ... HR 4402 (against); HR 5299 (against); HR 5416 (for) ... HR 5608 (for)."

NORTHERN CALIFORNIA POWER AGENCY, Citrus Heights, Calif. Lobbyist — Spiegel & McDiarmid, 2600 Virginia Ave. N.W., Washington, D.C. 20037. Filed 7/5/84. Legislative interest — "Maintain present legislation in Part I of the Federal Power Act; promote competition in hydro relicensing cases, and encourage transmission ... HR 4402 (against); HR 5299 (against); HR 5416 (for) ... HR 5608 (for)."

ORANGE COUNTY WATER DISTRICT, Fountain Valley, Calif. Lobbyist — McDonough, Holland & Allen, 1875 I St. N.W., Washington, D.C. 20006. Filed 7/9/84. Legislative interest — "S 1739 - for; HR 3678 - for; other issues of concern to a local water district."

PUERTO RICO FEDERAL AFFAIRS ADMINISTRATION, Washington, D.C. Lobbyist — Verner, Liipfert, Bernhard & McPherson, 1660 L St. N.W., Washington, D.C. 20036. Filed 7/11/84. Legislative interest — "Legislation concerning excise tax cover-overs."

Trade Associations

ALLIANCE FOR CLEAN ENERGY, Rosslyn, Va. Lobbyist — W. Dan Boone, 345 Park Ave., New York, N.Y. 10154. Filed 7/3/84. Legislative interest — "Pending and prospective legislation affecting the transportation and energy industries, particularly so-called 'acid rain' legislation."

AMERICAN BAKERS ASSOCIATION, 1111 14th St. N.W., Washington, D.C. 20005. Filed for self 7/9/84. Legislative interest — Not specified. Lobbyist — Michael B. Howland.

AMERICAN BANKERS ASSOCIATION, 1120 Connecticut Ave. N.W., Washington, D.C. 20036. Filed for self 7/19/84. Legislative interest — "Legislation affecting the banking industry." Lobbyist — Clifford R. Northup.

AMERICAN BUSINESS CONFERENCE, 1025 Connecticut Ave. N.W., Washington, D.C. 20036. Filed for self 7/10/84. Legislative interest — "... tax and regulatory reform legislation for high-growth, mid-range business organizations. The specific legislative interest is the Reagan tax program." Lobbyist — Joseph M. Smith.

AMERICAN COUNCIL OF LIFE INSURANCE INC., 1850 K St. N.W., Washington, D.C. 20006. Lobbyist — Kirkpatrick, Lockhart, Hill, Christopher & Phillips, 1900 M St. N.W., Washington, D.C. 20036. Filed 7/9/84. Legislative interest — "HR 5342, HR 5916, S 2181 and similar banking legislation; support in part, oppose in part." Filed for self 7/10/84. Legislative interest — "Proposed legislation that affects the life insurance industry; specifically amendments to the Federal Election Campaign Law." Lobbyist — Jeanne M. Ritchie.

AMERICAN ELECTRONICS ASSOCIATION, Palo Alto, Calif. Lobbyist — Swidler, Berlin & Strelow, 1000 Thomas Jefferson St. N.W., Washington, D.C. 20007. Filed 7/19/84. Legislative interest — "The interests of AEA are in securing legislative reforms to the Clean Water Act, HR 3282 and the Clean Air Act, HR 5084, HR 5314, S 768 and S 2159."

AMERICAN FLAGSHIPS, Washington, D.C. Lobbyist — Gray & Co., 3255 Grace St. N.W., Washington, D.C. 20007. Filed 7/11/84. Legislative interest — "Including but not limited to assistance with U.S. flagships."

AMERICAN INSURANCE ASSOCIATION, 1025 Connecticut Ave. N.W., Washington, D.C. 20036. Filed for self 7/19/84. Legislative interest — "All legislative matters relating to property/casualty insurance and suretyship, together with all matters that will indirectly impact on the markets, costs, regulation, etc., of such business." Lobbyist — Jeanne H. McGowen.

AMERICAN IRON AND STEEL INSTITUTE, Washington, D.C. Lobbyist — Tucker & Vaught, 718 17th St., Denver, Colo. 80202. Filed 7/9/84. Legislative interest — "Steel quota legislation - HR 5081, S 2380." Lobbyist — Wellford, Wegman, Krulwich, Gold & Hoff, 1775 Pennsylvania Ave. N.W., Washington, D.C. 20036. Filed 7/10/84. Legislative interest — "Developing legislative support for S 2380 and HR 5081, the Fair Trade in Steel Act." Lobbyist — Gray & Co., 3255 Grace St. N.W., Washington, D.C. 20007. Filed 7/11/84. Legislative interest — "Including but not limited to clean air and clean water legislation."

AMERICAN LICENSED PRACTICAL NURSES ASSOCIATION, Washington, D.C. Lobbyist — Paul Tendler Associates Inc., 1110 Vermont Ave. N.W., Washington, D.C. 20005. Filed 7/5/84. Legislative interest — "Legislation regarding nursing care, health care in general, labor issues, nursing homes, hospices, hospitals and Medicare/Medicaid."

AMERICAN PUBLIC POWER ASSOCIATION, 2301 M St. N.W., Washington, D.C. 20037. Filed for self 7/6/84. Legislative interest — "Legislation pertaining to energy and municipally-owned utilities, including HR 4170 (the Deficit Reduction Act); HR 5946 (extending the Residential Conservation Service); HR 4277 (natural gas legislation); HR 5640 (hazardous waste Superfund); HR 2867 and S 757 (Resource Conservation and Recovery Act); S 2631 (appliance efficiency standards); S 2630 (reauthorizing the Solar Energy and Energy Conservation Bank); HR 2584 and S 1082 (providing greater protections for captive shippers)." Lobbyist — Randall Swisher.

AMERICAN SOCIETY OF CLINICAL ONCOLOGY, Chicago, Ill. Lobbyist — John T. Grupenhoff, 10000 Falls Road, Potomac, Md. 20854. Filed 7/24/84. Legislative interest — "All legislation dealing with appropriations for biomedical clinical research, authorization legislation regarding biomedical research, animals used in research, Medicare and Medicaid programs relating to biomedical research."

AMERICAN UROLOGICAL ASSOCIATION/AMERICAN ASSOCIATION OF CLINICAL UROLOGISTS, Baltimore, Md. Lobbyist — John T. Grupenhoff, 10000 Falls Road, Potomac, Md. 20854. Filed 7/24/84. Legislative interest — "All legislation dealing with urology practice and research, especially authorization legislation relating to biomedical research, Medicare/Medicaid reimbursement for care; and appropriations for NIH."

ANIMAL HEALTH INSTITUTE, Alexandria, Va. Lobbyist — Taggart & Associates, 1015 15th St. N.W., Washington, D.C. 20005. Filed 7/13/84. Legislative interest — ". . . Animal health drugs."

ASSOCIATED GENERAL CONTRACTORS OF AMERICA, 1957 E St. N.W., Washington, D.C. 20006. Filed for self 7/12/84. Legislative interest — "Federal tax legislation." Lobbyist — Mary Jo Peterson.

THE BANKING ISSUES GROUP, Washington, D.C. Lobbyist — Sutherland, Asbill & Brennan, 1666 K St. N.W., Washington, D.C. 20006. Filed 7/24/84. Legislative interest — "Financial Services legislation including, but not limited to, HR 5916 and S 2851."

BERING SEA FISHERMEN'S ASSOCIATION, Anchorage, Alaska. Lobbyist — C. Deming Cowles, 1050 Thomas Jefferson St. N.W., Washington, D.C. 20007. Filed 7/11/84. Legislative interest — "Monitor and communicate interest in OCS lease sale legislation. OCS revenue sharing legislation and OCS consistency legislation."

BRITISH INSURANCE ASSOCIATION, London, England. Lobbyist — LeBoeuf, Lamb, Leiby & MacRae, 1333 New Hampshire Ave. N.W., Washington, D.C. 20036 and 520 Madison Ave., New York, N.Y. 10022. Filed 7/17/84. Legislative interest — "HR 4170 (Deficit Reduction Act of 1984); amendment of federal excise tax on insurance (section 4371 of Internal Revenue Code)."

CHAMBER OF COMMERCE OF THE U.S., 1615 H St. N.W., Washington, D.C. 20062. Filed for self 7/13/84. Legislative interest — Not specified. Lobbyist — Albert D. Bourland.

COMMITTEE OF ANNUITY INSURERS, Washington, D.C. Lobbyist — Sutherland, Asbill & Brennan, 1666 K St. N.W., Washington, D.C. 20006. Filed 7/18/84. Legislative interest — "Tax and security proposals affecting the Annuity Insurers."

COOPERATIVE LEAGUE OF THE USA, 1828 L St. N.W., Washington, D.C. 20036. Filed for self 7/12/84. Legislative interest — "Housing cooperative taxation issues." Lobbyist — Barbara Thompson, Mary K. Donny.

DISTILLED SPIRITS COUNCIL OF THE U.S., 1250 I St. N.W., Washington, D.C. 20004. Filed for self 7/10/84. Legislative interest — "Legislation dealing with taxes, warning labels, alcohol abuse and any other legislation affecting the distilled spirits industry." Lobbyist — Sydney Probst.

ELECTRONIC INDUSTRIES ASSOCIATION CONSUMER ELECTRONICS GROUP, 2001 I St. N.W., Washington, D.C. 20006. Filed for self 7/10/84. Legislative interest — ". . . S 175 & HR 175 (Support); S 31 & HR 1030 (Oppose); S 33, HR 1029, S 32, HR 1027 & HR 5938 (Oppose); S 286 & HR 1059." Lobbyists — M. K. Blevins, Gary J. Shapiro.

THE FARM CREDIT COUNCIL, 1800 Massachusetts Ave. N.W., Washington, D.C. 20036. Filed for self 7/11/84. Legislative interest — Not specified. Lobbyist — Teresa D. Hay.

FEDERAL JUDGES ASSOCIATION, San Francisco, Calif. Lobbyist — Charles E. Wiggins, 1050 17th St. N.W., Washington, D.C. 20036. Filed 7/10/84. (Former U.S. rep., R-Calif., 1967-79.) Legislative interest — "Bills relating to Federal Court jurisdiction, judicial compensation, and allowances."

GETTY NORTHEAST JOBBERS & DISTRIBUTORS ASSOCIATION, Washington, D.C. Lobbyist — Blum, Nash & Railsback, 1015 18th St. N.W., Washington, D.C. 20036. Filed 7/23/84. Legislative interest — "Legislation relating to petroleum mergers, all antitrust legislation and the FTC authorization act."

HEALTH INDUSTRY MANUFACTURERS ASSOCIATION, 1030 15th St. N.W., Washington, D.C. 20005. Filed for self 7/13/84. Legislative interest — ". . . health and business issues. Specific interest in reimbursement of health care costs . . . changes in medical device legislation." Lobbyist — Bette Anne Starkey.

THE INCENTIVE FEDERATION INC., New York, N.Y. Lobbyist — Zuckert, Scoutt, Rasenberger & Johnson, 888 17th St. N.W., Washington, D.C. 20006. Filed 7/12/84. Legislative interest — "Interest in HR 4170, HR 5261, S 2639."

INDEPENDENT BANKERS ASSOCIATION OF AMERICA, 1168 S. Main St., Sauk Center, Minn. 56378. Filed for self 7/20/84. Legislative interest — "S 1609 . . . Financial Institutions Deregulation Act . . . For. S 2181 . . . Financial Services Competitive Equity Act . . . Against." Lobbyist — Stephen J. Verdier, 1625 Massachusetts Ave. N.W., Washington, D.C. 20036.

INDUSTRY COUNCIL FOR TANGIBLE ASSETS, 214 Massachusetts Ave. N.E., Washington, D.C. 20002. Filed for self 7/27/84. Legislative interest — "Matters affecting the bullion or numismatic industries." Lobbyist — Donald C. Evans Jr.

INSURANCE ASSOCIATION OF CONNECTICUT, Hartford, Conn. Lobbyist — Blum, Nash & Railsback, 1015 18th St. N.W., Washington, D.C. 20036. Filed 7/10/84. (Former U.S. Rep. Tom Railsback, R-Ill., 1967-83, was listed as agent for this client.) Legislative interest — ". . . banking deregulation . . . HR 5734 & S 2181."

INTERNATIONAL ANTICOUNTERFEITING COALITION, San Francisco, Calif. Lobbyist — Verner, Liipfert, Bernhard & McPherson, 1660 L St. N.W., Washington, D.C. 20036. Filed 7/11/84. Legislative interest — "Legislation imposing civil and criminal penalties for trademark counterfeiting."

INVESTMENT COMPANY INSTITUTE, Washington, D.C. Lobbyist — Daniel J. Piliero II, 1750 Pennsylvania Ave.

N.W., Washington, D.C. 20006. Filed 7/10/84. Legislative interest — "... legislation affecting the use of mutual funds as funding vehicles for variable life and annuities. ICI supports the use of mutual funds for these purposes."

MILK INDUSTRY FOUNDATION/INTERNATIONAL ASSOCIATION OF ICE CREAM MANUFACTURERS, 888 16th St. N.W., Washington, D.C. 20006. Filed for self 7/9/84. Legislative interest — "Any legislation affecting the dairy industry." Lobbyist — William C. Tinklepaugh.

MORTGAGE BANKERS ASSOCIATION OF AMERICA, 1125 15th St. N.W., Washington, D.C. 20005. Filed for self 7/17/84. Legislative interest — "... all legislation affecting the mortgage lending, banking and construction industries ... HR 3420, Mortgage Credit - FNMA/FHLMC Limits; HR 3768, Non-Bank Moratorium; HR 4170, 1984 Taxation; HR 4243, Mortgage Credit - ERISA; HR 4557, Secondary Mortgage Market Enhancement Act; HR 4629, Budget - Federal Financing Bank; HR 4709, Taxation - Mortgage Credit Certificate; HR 4774, Appropriations - Line-Item Veto; HR 5174, Consumer - Bankruptcy; HR 5247, Budget - Budget Process; HR 5270, Consumer - Bankruptcy; HR 5288, Budget - FFB; HR 5342, Banking - Moratorium; HR 5367, VA - Home Loan Guaranty; HR 5617, VA - Loan Guaranty Amount; HR 5713, Appropriations - FY 85; H Con Res 280, Budget - FY 1985; H Res 476, Budget - FY 1984; H J Res 517, Appropriations - FY 1984; S 792, Consumer - Bankruptcy; S 1013, Bankruptcy; S 1679, Banking - Federal Financing Bank; S 1822, Taxation - TIMs; S 2040, Secondary Mortgage Market Enhancement Act; S 2062, Omnibus Budget Reconciliation; S 2130, Secondary Mortgage Market Equity Act; S 2181, Banking - Financial Institution Deregulation; S 2213, Budget - Federal Financing Bank; S 2265, VA - Guaranty Amount; S 2391, VA - Funding Fee; S 2500, Budget - FFB; S 2699, Banking - FDIC; S 2700, Banking - FSLIC." Lobbyist — J. Ballard Everett.

NATIONAL ASSOCIATION OF GROWERS AND PRODUCERS FOR FREE TRADE, Stockton, Calif. Lobbyist — Heron, Burchette, Ruckert & Rothwell, 1200 New Hampshire Ave. N.W., Washington, D.C. 20036. Filed 7/12/84. Legislative interest — "HR 5377 - support amendments exempting certain products from Free Trade Area."

NATIONAL ASSOCIATION OF REALTORS, 430 N. Michigan Ave., Chicago, Ill. 60611. Filed for self 7/11/84. Legislative interest — "Legislation affecting real estate generally and mortgage finance; bank holding companies legislation, financial institutions legislation, finance reform legislation." Lobbyist Marlisa Senchak, 777 14th St. N.W., Washington, D.C. 20005.

NATIONAL ASSOCIATION OF SMALL BUSINESS INVESTMENT COMPANIES, Washington, D.C. Lobbyist — Neece, Cator & Associates Inc., 1050 17th St. N.W., Washington, D.C. 20036. Filed 7/13/84. Legislative interest — "S 2686, HR 5687."

NATIONAL ASSOCIATION OF STATE SAVINGS AND LOAN SUPERVISORS, 1001 Connecticut Ave. N.W., Washington, D.C. 20036. Filed for self 7/9/84. Legislative interest — "HR 5916 - Financial Institutions Act of 1984/S 2181. Against certain provisions of the bills." Lobbyist — Robbi-Lynn Watnik.

NATIONAL COUNCIL OF FARMER COOPERATIVES, 1800 Massachusetts Ave. N.W., Washington, D.C. 20036. Filed for self 7/11/84. Legislative interest — Not specified. Lobbyist — Ronald J. Wilson.

NATIONAL COUNCIL SOCIAL SECURITY MANAGEMENT ASSOCIATIONS INC., Grand Rapids, Mich. Lobbyist — Neill, Mullenholz, Shaw & Seeger, 900 17th St. N.W., Washington, D.C. 20006. Filed 7/10/84. Legislative interest — "Legislation affecting the pay, benefits and job security of federal government employees; legislation affecting improvements in government management, efficiency and effectiveness; and legislation affecting the liability of government employees to suit."

NATIONAL FEDERATION OF FEDERAL EMPLOYEES, 1016 16th St. N.W., Washington, D.C. 20036. Filed for self 7/12/84. Legislative interest — "Legislation affecting Federal Employees - General legislative interest include First and Second Concurrent Budget Resolutions, Agency Appropriations and Authorizations, Budget Reconciliation, Social Security Benefits,

Mandatory Social Security coverage, contracting out (OMB circular A-76) Federal Employees Compensation Act, Civil Service Reform Act (U.S.C. Title V), overall compensation and working conditions for Federal employees and retirees. Specific legislative interests include: Fiscal Year 1985 appropriations (support or oppose); HR 5680, to eliminate wage discrimination in the Federal workforce (support); HR 3466, provided Secretary of Army and Air Force authority to establish regulations governing the performance of National Guard civilian technicians (oppose); HR 3511, to eliminate 30 day notice of termination for civilian technicians who cease to be members of the National Guard (oppose); HR 5799, to restrict the contracting out of certain Veterans' position (support); HR 656, to restructure Federal Employees Health Benefit Program; HR 622, to provide death benefits for Federal Law Enforcement Officers and Firefighters (support); Private Sector Survey on Cost Control recommendation cutting Federal pay/benefit/workforce (oppose); Office of Personnel Management's revised personnel regulations (oppose); Supplemental Federal Retirement System." Lobbyist — Michael F. Crim.

NATIONAL FEDERATION OF LICENSED PRACTICAL NURSES, Durham, N.C. Lobbyist — Bruce D. Thevenot, 1155 15th St. N.W., Washington, D.C. 20005. Filed 7/10/84. Legislative interest — "Amendments to Nurse Training Act. Amendments to Titles XVIII and XIX of Social Security Act. Amendments to Veterans Administration medical programs."

NATIONAL GROCERS ASSOCIATION, 1910 K St. N.W., Washington, D.C. 20005. Filed for self 7/15/84. Legislative interest — "General legislation affecting the retail grocer and wholesale food distribution industry as well as legislation affecting small business, in general." Lobbyists — Rose Kuiumgian, J. Patrick Boyle.

NATIONAL NEWSPAPER ASSOCIATION, 1627 K St. N.W., Washington, D.C. 20006. Filed for self 7/11/84. Legislative interest — Not specified. Lobbyist — Matthew J. Gichtin.

NATIONAL PORK PRODUCERS COUNCIL, 1015 15th St. N.W., Washington, D.C. 20005. Filed for self 7/13/84. Legislative interest — "... agricultural issues." Lobbyist — Doyle Talkington.

NATIONAL RURAL ELECTRIC COOPERATIVE ASSOCIATION, 1800 Massachusetts Ave. N.W., Washington, D.C. 20036. Filed for self 7/12/84. Legislative interest — "All legislative interests affecting the RE Act of 1936, as amended." Lobbyists — Thomas P. Graves, Robert W. Lively.

NATIONAL SOFT DRINK ASSOCIATION, 1101 16th St. N.W., Washington, D.C. 20036. Filed for self 7/5/84. Legislative interest — "... Sugar Act Legislation ... legislation affecting the soft drunk industry in the United States ... Solid Waste Recovery and similar measures ... Saccharin legislation ... Food Safety legislation...." Lobbyist — Frederick L. Webber.

PIPE LINE EQUITY ACT COALITION, Owensboro, Ky. Lobbyist — Bishop, Liberman, Cook, Purcell & Reynolds, 1200 17th St. N.W., Washington, D.C. 20036. Filed 7/12/84. Legislative interest — "... General interest - Participate in legislative process involving bills or amendments affecting gas pipeline taxation ... Specific interest - Support legislation to prohibit discrimination by state authorities on property taxation of interstate natural gas pipeline companies."

PUBLIC SECURITIES ASSOCIATION, New York, N.Y. Lobbyist — Bishop, Liberman, Cook, Purcell & Reynolds, 1200 17th St. N.W., Washington, D.C. 20036. Filed 7/12/84. (Former U.S. Rep. Graham B. Purcell, D-Texas, 1962-73, was listed as agent for this client.) Legislative interest — "HR 5174 Bankruptcy Act amendments - for passage."

SECONDARY LEAD SMELTERS ASSOCIATION, Washington, D.C. Lobbyist — Brown, Roady, Bonvillian & Gold, 1300 19th St. N.W., Washington, D.C. 20036. Filed 7/30/84. Legislative interest — "The SLSA is concerned with legislation falling under the jurisdiction of the EPA and OSHA; in particular, CERCLA, 42 USC section 9601; RCRA, 212 USC section 6901; and the OSH Act, 29 USC section 651. Legislation currently being considered by Congress includes HR 5640 and S 757. SLSA favors the legislation, subject to certain amendments."

TEXTILE AND APPAREL GROUP OF THE AMERICAN ASSOCIATION OF EXPORTERS & IMPORTERS, New York, N.Y. Lobbyist — Daniels, Houlihan & Palmeter, 1331 Pennsylvania Ave. N.W., Washington, D.C. 20004. Legislative interest — "... to oppose any legislation which further restricts or affects the imports of textile and apparel products into the United States."

THAI FOOD PROCESSORS ASSOCIATION, Washington, D.C. Lobbyist — Scott, Harrison & McLeod, 2501 M St. N.W., Washington, D.C. 20037. Filed 7/30/84. Legislative interest — "... HR 3398 - Tariff and Trade; HR 5188 - ITC Authorization ... HR 3398 and HR 5188 ... Against various expected amendments to HR 3398 and HR 5188."

THIRD CLASS MAIL ASSOCIATION, 1133 15th St. N.W., Washington, D.C. 20005. Filed for self 7/3/84. Legislative interest — "All legislation pertaining to postal laws and regulations (HR 5798 in support of)." Lobbyist — Gene A. Del Polito.

VOLUNTEER TRUSTEES OF NOT-FOR-PROFIT HOSPITALS, 1825 I St. N.W., Washington, D.C. 20006. Filed for self 7/24/84. Legislative interest — "Selective review of existing and proposed health and hospital legislation and regulations including titles 18 and 19 of the Social Security Act, health planning laws and other provisions which affect the organization and operations of hospitals and related health care entities." Lobbyist — Linda B. Miller.

Miscellaneous

AD HOC COALITION FOR LOW AND MODERATE INCOME HOUSING, Washington, D.C. Lobbyist — Latham, Watkins & Hills, 1333 New Hampshire Ave. N.W., Washington, D.C. 20036. Filed 7/11/84. Legislative interest — "... Deficit Reduction Act of 1984 ... HR 4170 ... Against certain provisions that would adversely affect low-income housing."

THE AMERICAN RIVERS CONSERVATION COUNCIL, 323 Pennsylvania Ave. S.E., Washington, D.C. 20003. Filed for self 7/26/84. Legislative interest — "Preservation of free-flowing rivers: generally in favor of additions to the National Wild and Scenic Rivers System and other proposals which protect rivers; opposed to those water resource projects which unwisely or unnecessarily destroy rivers...." Lobbyist — David Dickson.

AMHERST COLLEGE, Amherst, Mass. Lobbyist — Covington & Burling, P.O. Box 7566, Washington, D.C. 20044. Filed 7/25/84. Legislative interest — "Federal tax treatment of faculty housing; HR 677 and S 777 (for)."

STEVEN MICHAEL CLEMENT, 533 4th St. S.E., Washington, D.C. 20003. Filed for self 7/12/84. Legislative interest — "... HR 2624 - S 430 Amendment to 1964 & 1968 Civil Rights Act - For. HR 5796 - For the Relief of Richard Longstaff - For."

CONCERNED WOMEN FOR AMERICA, P.O. Box 5100, San Diego, Calif. 92105. Filed for self 7/30/84. Legislative interest — "Issues affecting the family and moral values including: Voluntary School Prayer Amendment; Equal Access (HR 4996); ERA (H J Res 1); Abortion (HR 618)." Lobbyist — Michael Jameson.

COUNCIL OF CALIFORNIA TRIBAL GOVERNMENTS, Central Valley, Calif. Lobbyist — Anne Howard & Associates, 888 17th St. N.W., Washington, D.C. 20006. Filed 7/12/84. Legislative interest — "Monitoring status of HR 4566, Indian Gambling Control Act of 1984...."

ENVIRONMENTAL POLICY INSTITUTE, 218 D St. S.E., Washington, D.C. 20003. Filed for self 7/27/84. Legislative interest — "Legislation relating to energy and environmental policy; communications policy, especially information access; and science and technology policy." Lobbyist — Juanita Alvarez. Filed for self 7/27/84. Legislative interest — "Legislation relating to coal development and federal coal leasing." Lobbyist — Suellen Keiner. Filed 7/27/84. Legislative interest — "Legislation relating to synthetic fuels development and subsidization." Lobbyist — Jennifer March.

THE FLORIDA STATE UNIVERSITY GRADUATE STUDIES AND RESEARCH, Tallahassee, Fla. Lobbyist — Florida Business Associates, 2000 L St. N.W., Washington, D.C. 20036. Filed 7/11/84. Legislative interest — "Seeking funding for DOE R&D projects."

JOBS WITH PEACE INC., 129 E St. N.W., Washington, D.C. 20001. Filed for self 7/13/84. Legislative interest — "Disarmament/Arms Control legislation and Domestic Social Programs." Lobbyist — Edward Guinan.

JOHN F. KENNEDY CENTER FOR THE PERFORMING ARTS, Washington, D.C. Lobbyist — Verner, Liipfert, Bernhard & McPherson, 1660 L St. N.W., Washington, D.C. 20036. Filed 7/11/84. Legislative interest — "Legislation affecting the Kennedy Center's obligation to the Treasury."

LEAGUE TO SAVE LAKE TAHOE, P.O. Box 10110, South Lake Tahoe, Calif. 95731. Filed for self 7/9/84. Legislative interest — "PL 96-586 - land acquisition bill (for). HR 1437 (for)." Lobbyist — Thomas A. Martens.

MARITIME INSTITUTE FOR RESEARCH AND INDUSTRIAL DEVELOPMENT, Washington, D.C. Lobbyist — Terrence W. Modglin & Associates, 2001 S St. N.W., Washington, D.C. 20009. Filed 7/12/84. Legislative interest — "HR 4900. Panama Canal Authorization for FY 1985 ... HR 5813 and HR 5921...."

MIAMI TRIBE OF OKLAHOMA, Miami, Okla. Lobbyist — Anne Howard & Associates, 888 M St. N.W., Washington, D.C. 20006. Filed 7/11/84. Legislative interest — "... HR 4566 - The Indian Gambling Control Act of 1984 ... in support..."

NATIONAL COALITION OF INDEPENDENT COLLEGE AND UNIVERSITY STUDENTS, Washington, D.C. Lobbyist — Roy Littlefield, 15900 Pinecroft Lane, Bowie, Md. 20716. Filed 7/3/84. Legislative interest — "Student aid, loans, and grants."

NATIONAL COMMITTEE TO PRESERVE SOCIAL SECURITY AND MEDICARE, 1300 19th St. N.W., Washington, D.C. 20036. Filed for self 7/12/84. Legislative interest — "... legislation of concern to senior citizens." Lobbyist — William Wewer.

NATIONAL HEAD INJURY FOUNDATION INC., Framingham, Mass. Lobbyist — Brand, Lowell & Dole, 923 15th St. N.W., Washington, D.C. 20005. Filed 7/12/84. Legislative interest — "All legislation concerning traumatic head injury."

NATIONAL HEMOPHILIA FOUNDATION, New York, N.Y. Lobbyist — John T. Grupenhoff, 10000 Falls Road, Potomac, Md. 20854. Filed 7/24/84. Legislative interest — "... issues of hemophilia (research and care for patients), in appropriations, authorization, and Medicare/Medicaid legislation."

NATIONAL TAXPAYERS UNION, 325 Pennsylvania Ave. S.E., Washington, D.C. 20003. Filed for self 7/26/84. Legislative interest — "... lower taxes, reduction of government waste and spending, fiscal reforms, tax structure ... S J Res 5 - for Balanced Budget Constitutional Amendment, Omnibus Water Resources Bills, Defense, Transportation, Energy and Water Authorization, Foreign Aid Authorization, and Appropriations Bills. Also the FY 1985 Tax and Budget Resolutions ... in all cases for provisions to control or cut spending." Lobbyist — Jeffrey Stant.

NATURAL RESOURCES DEFENSE COUNCIL INC., 1350 New York Ave. N.W., Washington, D.C. 20005. Filed for self 7/26/84. Legislative interest — "Legislation concerning agricultural conservation and national forest management." Lobbyist — Justin R. Ward.

NORTHEASTERN UNIVERSITY, Boston, Mass. Lobbyist — Swidler, Berlin & Strelow, 1000 Thomas Jefferson St. N.W., Washington, D.C. 20007. Filed 7/20/84. Legislative interest — "Legislation affecting higher education."

THE OCEANIC INSTITUTE, Waimanalo, Hawaii. Lobbyist — Schlossberg-Cassidy & Associates Inc., 955 L'Enfant Plaza S.W., Washington, D.C. 20024. Filed 7/8/84. Legislative interest — "Legislation relating to federal research, education and development programs relating to aquaculture."

W. A. REYNOLDS, Oklahoma City, Okla. Lobbyist — Ted Risenhoover, 505 Plaza Drive, Tahlequah, Okla. 74464. (Former U.S. rep., D-Okla., 1975-79.) Filed 7/27/84. Legislative interest — "... 26 U.S.C. 5723(c)."

SMITH COLLEGE, Northampton, Mass. Lobbyist — Covington & Burling, P.O. Box 7566, Washington, D.C. 20044. Filed

7/25/84. Legislative interest — "Federal tax treatment of faculty housing; HR 677 and S 777 (for)."

U.S.O.C.A., P.O. Box 42404, Washington, D.C. 20015-0404. Filed for self 7/11/84. Legislative interest — "... U.S. foreign policy and aid to Central America ... S 2131 - a bill to suspend deportations of Salvadorans (against) ... HR 5119 - House Foreign Aid Authorization bill and any supplements to it (with respect to aid for Central America) (against military aid to Central America) ... S 2582 - Senate Foreign Aid Bill (with respect to aid to Central America) (against military aid to Central America) ... Foley amendment - bill passed in the House which prohibits introduction of U.S. troops into Central America without prior Congressional approval. We would support any equivalent legislation that was introduced in the Senate." Lobbyist — Sara Theiss.

WELLESLEY COLLEGE, Wellesley, Mass. Lobbyist — Covington & Burling, P.O. Box 7566, Washington, D.C. 20044. Filed 7/25/84. Legislative interest — "Federal tax treatment of faculty housing; HR 677 and S 777 (for)."

WESLEYAN UNIVERSITY, Middletown, Conn. Lobbyist — Covington & Burling, P.O. Box 7566, Washington, D.C. 20044. Filed 7/25/84. Legislative interest — "Federal tax treatment of faculty housing; HR 677 and S 777 (for)." ∎

August Registrations

Corporations and Businesses

AMERICAN ELECTRIC POWER SERVICE CORP., 1 Riverside Plaza, Columbus, Ohio 43215. Filed for self 8/13/84. Legislative interest — Not specified. Lobbyist — Thomas J. Dennis.

AMERICAN PETROFINA INC., P.O. Box 2159, Dallas, Texas 75221. Lobbyist — O'Connor & Hannan, 1919 Pennsylvania Ave. N.W., Washington, D.C. 20006. Filed 8/8/84. Legislative interest — "... including, but not limited to, amendments to HR 5712." Filed for self 8/15/84. Legislative interest — "... including but not limited to, HR 5712, the House Appropriations bill for Commerce, State, and the Judiciary, and any and all amendments which relate to construction differential subsidies for ships." Lobbyists — Joe A. Moss, Gary W. Bruner.

ARMCO INC., 1747 Pennsylvania Ave. N.W., Washington, D.C. 20006. Lobbyist — O'Connor & Hannan, 1919 Pennsylvania Ave. N.W., Washington, D.C. 20006. Filed 8/10/84. Legislative interest — "Monitor any and all legislation affecting the steel industry...." Filed for self 8/8/84. Legislative interest — "... International Trade Legislation ... Foreign Corrupt Practices Act Amendments - S 414 - Support; Reciprocity in Trade - S 144 - Support; Domestic Content - S 707, HR 1234 - Oppose; Revenue Act of 1916 Amendments - S 418 and S 127 - Support; Export Administration Act Reauthorization - S 397 - Support; Foreign Tax Credit Conformity Act - HR 3140 - Support; Fair Trade in Steel Act - HR 5081 - Support."

BEAR STEARNS & CO., New York, N.Y. Lobbyist — Don L. Ricketts, 2550 M St. N.W., Washington, D.C. 20037. Filed 8/5/84. Legislative interest — "Proposals with respect to the Internal Revenue Service."

CADENCE CHEMICAL RESOURCES INC., Michigan City, Ind. Lobbyist — Collier, Shannon, Rill & Scott, 1055 Thomas Jefferson St. N.W., Washington, D.C. 20007. Filed 8/17/84. Legislative interest — "... include but are not limited to Superfund reauthorization and the Resource Conservation and Recovery Act."

CAPITAL MARKETS GROUP, New York, N.Y. Lobbyist — Akin, Gump, Strauss, Hauer & Feld, 1333 New Hampshire Ave. N.W., Washington, D.C. 20036. Filed 8/10/84. Legislative interest — "Hearings and legislation related to capital formation, including but not limited to, HR 5693; Tender Offer Reform Act of 1984." Lobbyist — Timmons & Co. Inc., 1850 K St. N.W., Washington, D.C. 20006. Filed 8/3/84. Legislative interest — "Hearings and legislation related to capital formation, including but not limited to, HR 5693; Tender Offer Reform Act of 1984."

CAROLINA POWER AND LIGHT CO., Raleigh, N.C. Lobbyist — Charlie McBride Associates Inc., 1717 K St. N.W., Washington, D.C. 20036. Filed 8/9/84. Legislative interest — "To oppose passage of S 817, S 1069 or other efforts to alter existing Construction Work in Progress (CWIP) formulas."

CBS INC., New York, N.Y. Lobbyist — Wiley & Rein, 1776 K St. N.W., Washington, D.C. 20006. Filed 8/2/84. Legislative interest — "... opposition to efforts to impose moratorium on FCC broadcast station ownership rules."

COSMETICS CENTER INC., Beltsville, Md. Lobbyist — Dutko and Associates, 412 First St. S.E., Washington, D.C. 20003. Filed 8/9/84. Legislative interest — "Legislation affecting trademark infringements; S 875, HR 5929, HR 5532."

D & B WHOLESALE COSMETIC INC., Fairfield, N.J. Lobbyist — Dutko and Associates, 412 First St. S.E., Washington, D.C. 20003. Filed 8/9/84. Legislative interest — "Legislation affecting trademark infringements; S 875, HR 5929, HR 5532."

DIGITAL EQUIPMENT CORP., Marlboro, Mass. Lobbyist — Powell, Goldstein, Frazer & Murphy, 1110 Vermont Ave. N.W., Washington, D.C. 20005. Filed 8/1/84. Legislative interest — "HR 3398."

DOFASCO INC., 1330 Burlington St. East, Hamilton, Ontario, Canada L8N 3J5. Filed for self 8/1/84. Legislative interest — "... Fair Trade in Steel Act ... S 2380/HR 5081 ... In opposition to any legislation which restricts imports of steel mill products from Canada." Lobbyist — Paul J. Phoenix.

DUKE POWER CO., Charlotte, N.C. Lobbyist — Charlie McBride Associates Inc., 1717 K St. N.W., Washington, D.C. 20036. Filed 8/9/84. Legislative interest — "To oppose passage of S 817, S 1069 or other efforts to alter existing Construction Work in Progress (CWIP) formulas."

ETHYL CORP., 1155 15th St. N.W., Washington, D.C. 20005. Filed for self 8/8/84. Legislative interest — "... Clean Air Act Amendments, HR 5084, HR 5314 ... Superfund Reauthorization, HR 5640 ... Export Administration Act, HR 3231, S 979 ... Toxic Substances Control Act, S 1281 ... Resource Conservation and Recovery Act, S 757, HR 2867 ... Life Insurance Taxation ... HR 3398, Section 130 and S 144 ... S 2746 and HR 5377 - U.S.-Israel Free Trade Agreement ... HR 4170 - Foreign Sales Corporation and Applicable Treasury Regulations ... S 1718 and HR 5136 - Generalized System of Preferences ... HR 4784 - Trade Remedies Reform Act ... HR 5952 - Congressional Approval of President's Remedies on import injuries." Lobbyist — Max Turnipseed.

FOREMOST DAIRIES-HAWAII, Honolulu, Hawaii. Lobbyist — Johnson & Associates, 3240 N. Albemarle St., Arlington, Va. 22207. Filed 8/6/84. Legislative interest — "Laws and regulations pertaining to the dairy industry, farmer cooperatives and taxation."

FRUPAC INTERNATIONAL CORP., Philadelphia, Pa. Lobbyist — Akin, Gump, Strauss, Hauer & Feld, 1333 New Hampshire Ave. N.W., Washington, D.C. 20036. Filed 8/10/84. Legislative interest — "Hearings and any legislation related to import duties on imported fruits and vegetables."

GENERAL AMERICAN LIFE INSURANCE CO., St. Louis, Mo. Lobbyist — Don L. Ricketts, 2550 M St. N.W., Washington, D.C. 20037. Filed 8/15/84. Legislative interest — "Proposals relating to life insurance company taxation under subchapter of the Internal Revenue Code."

THE GOODYEAR TIRE AND RUBBER CO., 1144 E. Market St., Akron, Ohio 44316. Filed for self 8/6/84. Legislative interest — "... legislation affecting business in general and the tire industry in particular." Lobbyist — Frederick W. Rhodes, 1800 K St. N.W., Washington, D.C. 20006.

INMONT CORP., Clifton, N.J. Lobbyist — Taft, Stettinius & Hollister, First National Bank Center, Cincinnati, Ohio 45202 and 21 Dupont Circle N.W., Washington, D.C. 20036. Filed 8/3/84. Legislative interest — "To advise in regard to legislation relating to water pollution and related matters."

INTERNATIONAL PETCHEMCO INC., New York, N.Y. Lobbyist — Rogers & Wells, 1737 H St. N.W., Washington, D.C. 20006. Filed 8/6/84. Legislative interest — "Tax legislation - Deficit Reduction Act of 1984 - opposition to the provisions increasing the tariff rate for ethyl alcohol imports."

LTV CORP., Pittsburgh, Pa. Lobbyist — Collier, Shannon, Rill & Scott, 1055 Thomas Jefferson St. N.W., Washington, D.C. 20007. Filed 8/17/84. Legislative interest — "... include but are not limited to Superfund reauthorization and the Resource Conservation and Recovery Act."

MARATHON MANUFACTURING CO., Houston, Texas. Lobbyist — O'Neill and Haase, 1333 New Hampshire Ave. N.W., Washington, D.C. 20036. Filed 8/3/84. Legislative interest — "Amendments to Coastal Zone Management Act of 1972 and legislation related to Outer Continental Shelf Leasing."

MAREMONT CORP., Saco, Maine. Lobbyist — Dickstein, Shapiro & Morin, 2101 L St. N.W., Washington, D.C. 20037. Filed 8/3/84. Legislative interest — "Department of Defense authorizations and appropriations."

MASSACHUSETTS MUTUAL LIFE INSURANCE CO., Springfield, Mass. Lobbyist — Don L. Ricketts, 2550 M St. N.W., Washington, D.C. 20037. Filed 8/15/84. Legislative interest — "Proposals relating to life insurance company taxation under subchapter of the Internal Revenue Service."

MEADOWGOLD DAIRIES-HAWAII, Honolulu, Hawaii. Lobbyist — Johnson & Associates, 3240 N. Albemarle St., Arlington, Va. 22207. Filed 8/6/84. Legislative interest — "Laws and regulations pertaining to the dairy industry, farmer co-operatives and taxation."

NEW ENGLAND ELECTRIC SYSTEM, Westborough, Mass. Lobbyist — Charlie McBride Associates Inc., 1717 K St. N.W., Washington, D.C. 20036. Filed 8/9/84. Legislative interest — "To oppose passage of S 817, S 1069 or other efforts to alter existing Construction Work in Progress (CWIP) formulas."

NORTHWESTERN MUTUAL LIFE, Milwaukee, Wis. Lobbyist — Don L. Ricketts, 2550 M St. N.W., Washington, D.C. 20037. Filed 8/15/84. Legislative interest — "Proposals relating to life insurance company taxation under subchapter of the Internal Revenue Code."

NOVA, AN ALBERTA CORP., Calgary, Alberta, Canada. Lobbyist — Wexler, Reynolds, Harrison & Schule Inc., 1317 F St. N.W., Washington, D.C. 20004. Filed 8/15/84. Legislative interest — "... opposed to the provisions of HR 4784 which would result in the imposition of countervailing duties upon imported petrochemicals."

NOVACOR CHEMICALS LTD., Calgary, Alberta, Canada. Lobbyist — Wexler, Reynolds, Harrison & Schule, 1317 F St. N.W., Washington, D.C. 20004. Filed 8/15/84. Legislative interest — "... opposed to the provisions of HR 4784 which would result in the imposition of countervailing duties upon imported petrochemicals."

PACIFIC GAS AND ELECTRIC CO., San Francisco, Calif. Lobbyist — Charlie McBride Associates Inc., 1717 K St. N.W., Washington, D.C. 20036. Filed 8/9/84. Legislative interest — "To work for passage of HR 4402 or similar legislation pertaining to relicensing of hydroelectric power facilities."

PENNZOIL CO., Washington, D.C. Lobbyist — Wexler, Reynolds, Harrison & Schule, 1317 F St. N.W., Washington, D.C. 20004. Filed 8/15/84. Legislative interest — "... legislative activity relating to international copper trade."

POTOMAC ELECTRIC POWER CO., 1900 Pennsylvania Ave. N.W., Washington, D.C. 20068. Filed for self 8/17/84. Legislative interest — "All legislative matters directly or indirectly affecting public utilities, specifically but not exclusively including the Clean Air and Water Act amendments, all energy related legislation, railroad deregulation proposals and tax proposals relating to capital formation." Lobbyist — Harold E. Brazil.

SATELLITE SYNDICATED SYSTEMS INC., Tulsa, Okla. Lobbyist — Pepper & Corazzini, 1776 K St. N.W., Washington, D.C. 20006. Filed 8/2/84. Legislative interest — "Copyright Act of 1976, PL 94-553, 90 STAT 17 U.S. Code sec. 101, *et seq.*"

SEARS, ROEBUCK AND CO., Chicago, Ill. Lobbyist — O'Neill and Haase, 1333 New Hampshire Ave. N.W., Washington, D.C. 20036. Filed 8/17/84. Legislative interest — "... HR 5916, Financial Institutions Equity Act of 1984 ... S 2851, Financial Services Competitive Equity Act."

SOUTHERN CALIFORNIA EDISON CO., Rosemead, Calif. Lobbyist — Charlie McBride Associates Inc., 1717 K St.

N.W., Washington, D.C. 20036. Filed 8/9/84. Legislative interest — "To work for the passage of HR 4402 or similar legislation pertaining to relicensing of hydroelectric power facilities."

THE STANDARD CORP., Ogden, Utah. Lobbyist — Philip D. Morrison, 1700 Pennsylvania Ave. N.W., Washington, D.C. 20006. Filed 8/1/84. Legislative interest — "Generally all legislation relating to federal income taxation of corporations. Specifically lobbying relating to the Tax Act of 1984."

TAFT BROADCASTING CO., Cincinnati, Ohio. Lobbyist — Koteen & Naftalin, 1150 Connecticut Ave. N.W., Washington, D.C. 20036. Filed 8/3/84. Legislative interest — "... legislative matters relating to the multiple ownership rules of the Federal Communications Commission."

THERMAL ENERGY CO., Seattle, Wash. Filed for self 8/6/84. Legislative interest — "National Energy Act, Wild and Scenic Rivers Act, Reclamation Acts, Internal Revenue Code, Clean Air Act, Clean Water Act, Equal Employment Opportunity Act, Flood Control Acts, Federal Power Acts, Rivers and Harbors and Flood Control Authorization Act." Lobbyist — Patricia M. Wilson, 2910 3rd Ave. North, Billings, Mont. 59103.

THOMPSON, GOLD & LIEBENGOOD, 1050 Connecticut Ave. N.W., Washington, D.C. 20036. Filed for self 8/13/84. Legislative interest — "... 1985 Tax Reform, any technical corrections bill to the 1984 Tax Act, Banking deregulation, Antitrust laws.... Small Business Administration size standards and federal procurement legislation.... Legislation concerning transportation, public works, waterways, user fees. ... Legislation concerning sports franchise locations.... Legislation concerning bank powers, Market Mutual Funds. ... Legislation concerning steel quotas, trade laws.... Legislation to deregulate natural gas.... Appropriations bills for Justice, Health and Human Services, Housing and Urban Development and Transportation; Office of Management and Budget regulations of agency block grant programs.... Medicare reform...." Lobbyists — Robert J. Thompson, Martin B. Gold, Howard S. Liebengood, Susan B. Neal.

TIMEX CORP., Waterbury, Conn. Lobbyist — Busby, Rehm & Leonard, 1629 K St. N.W., Washington, D.C. 20006. Filed 8/13/84. Legislative interest — "Legislation affecting importation of watches, including HR 3398 (for)."

TRW INC., 23555 Euclid Ave., Cleveland, Ohio 44117. Filed for self 7/24/84. Legislative interest — "General legislation of broad interest to TRW Inc., including that related to antitrust, securities, automotive safety, trade, intellectual properties, regulatory reform, etc." Lobbyist — Ivan E. Sinclair, 1000 Wilson Blvd., Arlington, Va. 22209.

TUBULAR CORPORATION OF AMERICA INC., Muskogee, Okla. Lobbyist — Arent, Fox, Kintner, Plotkin & Kahn, 1050 Connecticut Ave. N.W., Washington, D.C. 20036. Filed 8/13/84. Legislative interest — "Opposed to imposition of trade restrictions on imports of green tubes (HR 3398, and related bills)."

VIRGINIA ELECTRIC AND POWER CO., Richmond, Va. Lobbyist — Charlie McBride Associates Inc., 1717 K St. N.W., Washington, D.C. 20036. Filed 8/9/84. Legislative interest — "To oppose passage of S 817, S 1069 or other efforts to alter existing Construction Work in Progress (CWIP) formulas."

WESTINGHOUSE ELECTRIC CORP., Washington, D.C. Lobbyist — Vierra Associates Inc., 923 15th St. N.W., Washington, D.C. 20005. Filed 8/1/84. Legislative interest — "All legislation concerning the financing, operation and regulation of public mass transportation."

International Relations

EMBASSY OF THE PEOPLE'S REPUBLIC OF CHINA, Washington, D.C. Lobbyist — Akin, Gump, Strauss, Hauer & Feld, 1333 New Hampshire Ave. N.W., Washington, D.C. 20036. Filed 8/8/84. Legislative interest — "Export Administration Act Amendments, HR 3231, S 979, Sense of the Senate re: future of Taiwan, S Res 74."

UNITED NATIONS EDUCATIONAL, SCIENTIFIC AND CULTURAL ORGANIZATION, New York, N.Y. Lobbyist — Wagner & Baroody Inc., 1100 17th St. N.W., Washington, D.C. 20036. Filed 8/20/84. Legislative interest — "To inform the Congress and the public about the purpose of UNESCO and of any current activities by said organization. . . ."

State and Local Governments

ARIZONA POWER AUTHORITY, Phoenix, Ariz. Lobbyist — McCarty, Noone & Williams, 490 L'Enfant Plaza East S.W., Washington, D.C. 20024. Filed 8/1/84. Legislative interest — "Legislation with respect to federal hydroelectric power such as S 268."

MODESTO IRRIGATION DISTRICT, Modesto, Calif. Lobbyist — Charlie McBride Associates Inc., 1717 K St. N.W., Washington, D.C. 20036. Filed 8/8/84. Legislative interest — "To oppose any legislation in the Congress that would designate the Tuolumne River in California wild and scenic under the Wild and Scenic Rivers Act, which action would foreclose for the clients the opportunity to continue to study the feasibility of constructing a hydroelectric facility on the Tuolumne."

CITY OF NORFOLK, Norfolk, Va. Lobbyist — Arnold & Porter, 1200 New Hampshire Ave. N.W., Washington, D.C. 20036. Filed 8/20/84. Legislative interest — "Supporting passage of HR 5993, 'The Local Government Antitrust Act of 1984.' Supporting passage of S 1578, 'The Local Government Antitrust Act of 1983.' "

SPOKANE COUNTY, Spokane, Wash. Lobbyist — Preston, Thorgrimson, Ellis & Holman, 1735 New York Ave. N.W., Washington, D.C. 20006. Filed 8/15/84. Legislative interest — ". . . possible amendments to legislation for protection of municipal water supply (sole source aquifer) and related activities. HR 5959, S 2649, S 2006."

TURLOCK IRRIGATION DISTRICT, Turlock, Calif. Lobbyist — Charlie McBride Associates Inc., 1717 K St. N.W., Washington, D.C. 20036. Filed 8/8/84. Legislative interest — "To oppose any legislation in the Congress that would designate the Tuolumne River in California wild and scenic under the Wild and Scenic Rivers Act, which action would foreclose for the clients the opportunity to continue to study the feasibility of constructing a hydroelectric facility on the Tuolumne."

Trade Associations

AMERICAN ACADEMY OF OTOLARYNGOLOGY, Washington, D.C. Lobbyist — John T. Grupenhoff, 10000 Falls Road, Potomac, Md. 20854. Filed 8/13/84. Legislative interest — ". . . Federal programs for research and care in the field of otolaryngology/head and neck surgery including legislation, appropriations, Medicare/Medicaid and other legislation affecting otolaryngology."

AMERICAN ASSOCIATION OF EXPORTERS AND IMPORTERS, New York, N.Y. Lobbyist — Arnold & Porter, 1200 New Hampshire Ave. N.W., Washington, D.C. 20036. Filed 8/15/84. Legislative interest — "Legislation related to international trade."

AMERICAN INSURANCE ASSOCIATION, Washington, D.C. Lobbyist — O'Connor & Hannan, 1919 Pennsylvania Ave. N.W., Washington, D.C. 20006. Filed 8/16/84. Legislative interest — ". . . including, but not limited to, amendments to Superfund legislation."

ASSOCIATED BUILDERS AND CONTRACTORS INC., 729 15th St. N.W., Washington, D.C. 20005. Filed for self 8/10/84. Legislative interest — "Coal slurry - S 267, HR 1010 - Support; Compressed Workweek - HR 2766, HR 143, HR 277, S 870 - Support; Contracting Out - S 1746 - Support; Davis-Bacon Repeal/Reform - HR 3846, HR 87, HR 141, HR 148, HR 178, HR 284, HR 635, HR 692, HR 1174, S 1803 - Support; ERISA-Single Employer - S 1227 - No formal position; Health Insurance for the Unemployed - HR 3021, S 242, S 291 - Oppose; Immigration Reform - S 529, HR 1510 - No formal position; Jobs Creation-Training - HR 1036, HR 2544 - Oppose; Labor Violence/Corruption - S 336, HR 2635 - Support; Labor Violence/Hobbs Act - S 462, HR 287 - Support; Minority Business Enterprise - S 273 -

Oppose; MSHA/OSHA - HR 112, HR 144, HR 2073, HR 3338, S 980, S 1173 - Support; Retainage - HR 835, S 1181 - Support; Regulatory Reform - HR 220 - Support." Lobbyist — Barbara F. Beatty.

ASSOCIATION OF FOOD INDUSTRIES INC. (TUNA GROUP), New York, N.Y. Lobbyist — Barnett & Alagia, 1000 Thomas Jefferson St. N.W., Washington, D.C. 20007. Filed 8/1/84. Legislative interest — "Opposition to any legislative bill (HR 3398, for example) which attempts to impose tariffs against imported canned tuna."

THE BANKING ISSUES GROUP, Washington, D.C. Lobbyist — Sutherland, Asbill & Brennan, 1666 K St. N.W., Washington, D.C. 20006. Filed 7/24/84. Legislative interest — "Financial Service Legislation including, but not limited to, HR 5916 and S 2851."

BICYCLE MANUFACTURERS ASSOCIATION OF AMERICA, Washington, D.C. Lobbyist — Collier, Shannon, Rill & Scott, 1055 Thomas Jefferson St. N.W., Washington, D.C. 20007. Filed 8/17/84. Legislative interest — "All legislation affecting bicycle manufacturers."

BUSINESS ROUNDTABLE, Washington, D.C. Lobbyist — Charles E. Bangert, 1825 I St. N.W., Washington, D.C. 20006. Filed 8/2/84. Legislative interest — ". . . antitrust matters."

CHAMBER OF COMMERCE OF THE UNITED STATES, 1615 H St. N.W., Washington, D.C. 20062. Filed for self 8/15/84. Legislative interest — Not specified. Lobbyist — Deborah L. Aiken.

CHEMICAL MANUFACTURERS ASSOCIATION, Washington, D.C. Lobbyist — Bracewell & Patterson, 1825 I St. N.W., Washington, D.C. 20006. Filed 8/9/84. Legislative interest — "Legislation relating to Superfund tax, HR 5640 and S 2892."

COALITION TO PROMOTE AMERICA'S TRADE, 1875 I St. N.W., Washington, D.C. 20006. Filed for self 8/1/84. Legislative interest — "Trade and Remedies Reform Act of 1984 . . . HR 4784. . . ." Lobbyist — Jeremiah J. Kenney Jr.

EDISON ELECTRIC INSTITUTE, Washington, D.C. Lobbyist — Vierra Associates Inc., 923 15th St. N.W., Washington, D.C. 20005. Filed 8/1/84. Legislative interest — "Appropriations for the Railroad Accounting Principles Board."

FRIENDS OF THE HOP MARKETING ORDER, Los Angeles, Calif. Lobbyist — Seyfarth, Shaw, Fairweather & Geraldson, 1111 19th St. N.W., Washington, D.C. 20036. Filed 8/15/84. Legislative interest — ". . . legislation affecting the hop industry, such as matters relating to agricultural marketing orders."

GETTY NORTHEAST JOBBERS & DISTRIBUTORS ASSOCIATION, Washington, D.C. Lobbyist — Blum, Nash & Railsback, 1015 18th St. N.W., Washington, D.C. 20036. Filed 7/23/84. Legislative interest — "Legislation relating to petroleum mergers, all antitrust legislation and the FTC authorization act."

INCENTIVE FEDERATION INC., P.O. Box 774, Madison Square Station, New York, N.Y. 10159. Filed for self 8/6/84. Legislative interest — ". . . Incentive and Business Gifts Legislation, S 2639, HR 5261, HR 4170."

INDEPENDENT REFINERS COALITION, Washington, D.C. Lobbyist — Charls E. Walker Associates, 1730 Pennsylvania Ave. N.W., Washington, D.C. 20006. Filed 8/6/84. Legislative interest — ". . . interests may concern issues which could affect the competitive position of independent refiners such as, for example, HR 5455."

INTERNATIONAL ASSOCIATION OF AMUSEMENT PARKS & ATTRACTIONS, Washington, D.C. Lobbyist — David Vienna & Associates, 510 C St. N.E., Washington, D.C. 20002. Filed 8/21/84. Legislative interest — ". . . developing appropriate legislation regarding the amusement park industry."

MID-CONTINENT OIL & GAS ASSOCIATION, Tulsa, Okla. Filed for self 8/9/84. Legislative interest — "Legislation of interest to the petroleum industry." Lobbyist — Stephen E. Ward, 1919 Pennsylvania Ave. N.W., Washington, D.C. 20006.

NATIONAL EDUCATION ASSOCIATION, 1201 16th St. N.W., Washington, D.C. 20036. Filed for self 8/1/84. Legislative interest — "Bills pending before Congress relating to public education." Lobbyist — Gary G. Timmons.

ROCHESTER TAX COUNCIL, Rochester, N.Y. Lobbyist — H. Stewart Dunn Jr., 1700 Pennsylvania Ave. N.W., Washington, D.C. 20006. Filed 8/13/84. Legislative interest — "Generally, all legislation relating to federal income taxation of corporations. Specifically, lobbying in favor of the 'High Technology Research and Scientific Education Act of 1983' (S 2165 and HR 4475), the 'Foreign Sales Corporation Act of 1983' (S 1804), and the 'Foreign Tax Credit Act' (S 1584 and HR 3140)."

THAI FOOD PROCESSORS ASSOCIATION, Bangkok, Thailand. Lobbyist — Barnett & Alagia, 1000 Thomas Jefferson St. N.W., Washington, D.C. 20007. Filed 8/1/84. Legislative interest — "Opposition to any legislative bill (HR 3398, for example) which attempts to impose tariffs against imported canned tuna."

Miscellaneous

THE CONSERVATIVE ALLIANCE, 1001 Prince St., Alexandria, Va. 22314. Filed for self 8/8/84. Legislative interest — "Foreign affairs, national security, defense, human rights, and all other legislative issues pertaining to the well-being and the preservation of freedom in the U.S. and around the world." Lobbyist — Jay L. Young.

CONSUMER ENERGY COUNCIL OF AMERICA, 2000 L St. N.W., Washington, D.C. 20036. Filed for self 8/2/84. Legislative interest — "Energy related issues." Lobbyist — Stephen O. Andersen.

HOOPA VALLEY TRIBE, Hoopa, Calif. Lobbyist — Ziontz, Pirtle, Morisset, Ernstoff & Chestnut, 1100 Olive Way, Seattle, Wash. 98101. Filed 8/6/84. Legislative interest — "All bills relating to Native American interests, land use planning, environmental protection, mining, water rights and welfare."

JUSTICE FELLOWSHIP, P.O. Box 17181, Washington, D.C. 20041. Filed for self 8/6/84. Legislative interest — "Criminal justice reforms generally (principally Title 18, U.S. Code)." Lobbyist — Daniel W. Van Ness.

MILLE LACS BAND OF CHIPPEWA INDIANS, Vineland, Minn. Lobbyist — Ziontz, Pirtle, Morisset, Ernstoff & Chestnut, 1100 Olive Way, Seattle, Wash. 98101. Filed 8/6/84. Legislative interest — "All bills relating to Native American interests, land use planning, environmental protection, mining, water rights and welfare."

RICHARD H. MITMAN, 6520 Goodland Ave., North Hollywood, Calif. 91606. Filed for self 8/13/84. Legislative interest — Not specified.

NATIONAL DEBT REPAYMENT FOUNDATION, Washington, D.C. Lobbyist — Wagner & Baroody Inc., 1100 17th St. N.W., Washington, D.C. 20036. Filed 8/20/84. Legislative interest — "To promote an overall legislative measure to retire the national debt in a fashion similar to the National Highway Trust Fund."

NATURAL RESOURCES DEFENSE COUNCIL INC., New York, N.Y. Lobbyist — W. J. Chandler Associates, 1511 K St. N.W., Washington, D.C. 20005. Filed 8/6/84. Legislative interest — "Highway beautification and sign control on transportation systems: Highway Beautification Act; highway and mass transit authorizing and appropriations legislation (e.g., HR 5504). For beautification and sign control."

RICHARD H. SCHECK, 167 Pelham Road, New Rochelle, N.Y. 10805. Filed for self 8/20/84. Legislative interest — "All legislation pertaining to the U.S. space program."

VILLIERS ADVOCACY ASSOCIATES, Concord, Mass. Lobbyists — Edward F. Howard, Ah Quon McElrath, 1334 G St. N.W., Washington, D.C. 20005. Filed 8/1/84. Legislative interest — ". . . improvement in treatment of low-income older persons, especially in the areas of health and income security. . . ."

September Registrations

Corporations and Businesses

THE ALTER GROUP, Wilmette, Ill. Lobbyist — Davis, Polk & Wardwell, 1575 I St. N.W., Washington, D.C. 20005. Filed 9/7/84. Legislative interest — "Antitrust legislation affecting municipalities."

AM INTERNATIONAL INC., Chicago, Ill. Lobbyist — Wilmer, Cutler & Pickering, 1666 K St. N.W., Washington, D.C. 20006. Filed 9/13/84. Legislative interest — "Bankruptcy Amendments and Federal Judgeship Act of 1984."

BLYTHE EASTMAN/PAINE WEBBER, San Francisco, Calif. Lobbyist — Liz Robbins Associates, 132 D St. S.E., Washington, D.C. 20003. Filed 9/7/84. Legislative interest — "Tax exempt bond projects - HR 4170."

BREED CORP., Lincoln Park, N.J. Lobbyist — Arent, Fox, Kintner, Plotkin & Kahn, 1050 Connecticut Ave. N.W., Washington, D.C. 20036. Filed 9/24/84. (Former U.S. Sen. John C. Culver, D-Iowa, 1975-81; House 1965-75, was listed as agent for this client.) Legislative interest — "Appropriations and other legislation respecting research, demonstration, development, usage of automobile air bag systems and defense programs."

CARTER-WALLACE CO., New York, N.Y. Lobbyist — Patton, Boggs & Blow, 2550 M St. N.W., Washington, D.C. 20037. Filed 9/7/84. Legislative interest — "Efforts to restore patent term and provide abbreviated new drug applications. Such as a) the Federal Food, Drug and Cosmetic Act and b) HR 3605."

CHASE MANHATTAN CORP., Washington, D.C. Lobbyist — Dewey, Ballantine, Bushby, Palmer & Wood, 1775 Pennsylvania Ave. N.W., Washington, D.C. 20006. Filed 9/12/84. Legislative interest — "Bank legislation, S 2851; HR 2431; HR 5446."

CHATTEM INC., 1715 W. 38th St., Chattanooga, Tenn. 37409. Filed for self 9/11/84. Legislative interest — "Amendments to the Federal Food, Drug and Cosmetic Act seeking to limit the ability of the Secretary of Health and Human Services to approve Abbreviated New Drug Applications for over-the-counter drugs."

CHROMALLOY AMERICAN CORP., 120 South Central Ave., St. Louis, Mo. 63105. Filed for self 9/27/84. Legislative interest — Not specified. Lobbyist — Peter H. Hahn, 1100 17th St. N.W., Washington, D.C. 20036.

COLT INDUSTRIES INC., New York, N.Y. Lobbyist — Webster, Chamberlain & Bean, 1747 Pennsylvania Ave. N.W., Washington, D.C. 20006. Filed 9/24/84. Legislative interest — "HR 3475 in favor of."

CONTINENTAL GRAIN CO., New York, N.Y. Lobbyist — Paul H. DeLaney Jr., 1120 20th St. N.W., Washington, D.C. 20036. Filed 9/4/84. Legislative interest — "International tax and trade considerations including possible amendments of United States Domestic International Sales Corporation in the context of United States commitments and understandings in General Agreement of Tariffs and Trade proceedings including possible changes to the United States Internal Revenue Code pursuant to legislative consideration of the Tax Reform Act of 1984 (HR 4170)."

COTTAGE INDUSTRIES, P.O. Box 12148, Arlington, Va. 22209. Filed for self 9/25/84. Legislative interest — ". . . HR 2133 to amend the Small Business Act - Support; S 2489 to amend the Small Business Act to enhance competition in Government Procurement - Support." Lobbyists — Deborah A. Lawrence, Gary V. King.

DESIGN PROFESSIONALS, Washington, D.C. Lobbyist — Thompson, Gold & Liebengood, 1050 Connecticut Ave. N.W., Washington, D.C. 20036. Filed 9/5/84. Legislative interest — "Small Business Administration size standards and federal procurement legislation."

DIGITAL EQUIPMENT CORP., Maynard, Mass. Lobbyist — Verner, Liipfert, Bernhard and McPherson, 1660 L St. N.W., Washington, D.C. 20036. Filed 9/6/84. Legislative interest — "Tax and trade legislation (HR 3398)."

E. I. DU PONT DE NEMOURS CO., 1007 Market St., Wilmington, Del. 19898. Filed for self 9/12/84. Legislative interest — "All legislation directly related to employer's business, including especially bills related to energy, the environment, taxation, economic policy, government regulation, and programs supported by employer contributions." Lobbyist — Ellan K. Wharton.

FIRST BANK SYSTEMS INC., Minneapolis, Minn. Lobbyist — Williams & Jensen, 1101 Connecticut Ave. N.W., Washington, D.C. 20036. Filed 9/20/84. Legislative interest — "Interstate banking legislation . . . specifically S 2851."

GC SERVICES CORP., Houston, Texas. Lobbyist — SMC International, 1825 I St. N.W., Washington, D.C. 20006. Filed 9/28/84. Legislative interest — "Debt collection. HR 3069, S 376, S 1356, S 1668."

GLOBAL ASSOCIATES, Oakland, Calif. Lobbyist — Marcus G. Faust, 2121 K St. N.W., Washington, D.C. 20037. Filed 9/21/84. Legislative interest — "Compact of Free Association for Marshall Islands and Micronesia."

H & W DRILLING INC., Los Angeles, Calif. Lobbyist — Schramm & Raddue, 15 W. Carrillo St., Santa Barbara, Calif. 93101. Filed 9/27/84. Legislative interest — ". . . income tax matters . . . PL 95-618 . . . IRC Sections 38, 48, 612, 613."

HEAVY OIL PROCESS INC., Denver, Colo. Lobbyist — Marcus W. Sisk Jr., 2828 Pennsylvania Ave. N.W., Washington, D.C. 20007. Filed 9/25/84. Legislative interest — "In support of reasonable funding for synthetic fuels development."

IC INDUSTRIES, Chicago, Ill. Lobbyist — Patton, Boggs & Blow, 2550 M St. N.W., Washington, D.C. 20037. Filed 9/7/84. Legislative interest — "Matters related to withholding rates on interest paid foreign lenders such as the Deficit Reduction Act of 1984."

ISFA CORP., Tampa, Fla. Lobbyist — Cadwalader, Wickersham & Taft, One Wall St., New York, N.Y. 10005. Filed 9/26/84. Legislative interest — "General legislative interests relate to legislation regarding the securities activities of financial institutions. Specific legislative interests include S 2851, the Financial Institutions Competitive Equity Act, HR 5916, the Financial Institutions Equity Act, and HR 5881, the Financial Institutions Act of 1984."

JOHNSON & JOHNSON, New Brunswick, N.J. Lobbyist — Parry & Romani Associates Inc., 1140 Connecticut Ave. N.W., Washington, D.C. 20036. Filed 9/10/84. Legislative interest — "Legislation affecting marketing of certain drugs."

KAISER STEEL CORP., Fontana, Calif. Lobbyist — Thompson, Gold & Liebengood, 1050 Connecticut Ave. N.W., Washington, D.C. 20036. Filed 9/5/84. Legislative interest — "Legislation concerning steel quotas, trade laws."

KOENIG & CO., New York, N.Y. Lobbyist — Liz Robbins Associates, 132 D St. S.E., Washington, D.C. 20003. Filed 9/7/84. Legislative interest — "Monitoring tax legislation - HR 5170."

LINCOLN SAVINGS & LOAN ASSOCIATION, P.O. Box 19614, Irvine, Calif. 92714. Lobbyist — Miller & Chevalier, 655 15th St. N.W., Washington, D.C. 20005. Filed 9/5/84. Legislative interest — "Revisions to federal laws governing state-chartered savings and loan association investment activities." Filed for self 9/18/84. Legislative interest — "Revisions to federal laws governing state-chartered savings and loan association investment activities." Lobbyist — James J. Grogan.

LISA ENTERPRISES INC., P.O. Box 1160, Deerfield Beach, Fla. 33441. Filed for self 9/10/84. Legislative interest — "Domestic Content, Against HR 1234." Lobbyist — George B. Herbert Sr.

LOWRANCE ELECTRONICS, Tulsa, Okla. Lobbyist — Thompson, Gold & Liebengood, 1050 Connecticut Ave. N.W., Washington, D.C. 20036. Filed 9/5/84. Legislative interest — "1985 Tax Reform, any technical corrections bill to the 1984 Tax Act."

HERMAN MILLER INC., 8500 Byron Road, Zeeland, Mich. 49464. Filed for self 9/13/84. Legislative interest — "HR 5693. Tender offer legislation in the House & Senate. For legislation that curbs and prohibits hostile takeovers." Lobbyist — Michele Hunt.

THE NATIONAL FOOTBALL LEAGUE, New York, N.Y. Lobbyist — Thompson, Gold & Liebengood, 1050 Connecticut Ave. N.W., Washington, D.C. 20036. Filed 9/5/84. Legislative interest — "Legislation concerning sports franchise locations."

PEPSICO, Purchase, N.Y. 10577. Filed for self 9/18/84. Legislative interest — Not specified. Lobbyist — David L. Wright.

PIEDMONT AIRLINES INC., Winston-Salem, N.C. Lobbyist — SMC International, 1825 I St. N.W., Washington, D.C. 20006. Filed 9/28/84. Legislative interest — ". . . aviation issues."

RES-CARE INC., 1300 Embassy Square Office Park, Louisville, Ky. 40299. Lobbyist — N. Clark Rechtin, 6100 Longview Lane, Louisville, Ky. 40222. Filed 9/13/84. Legislative interest —

"Seeking F.Y. 1984 supplemental appropriations for the Job Corps program . . . HR 6040 . . . support added funds in HR 6040 to meet capital and equipment needs of Job Corps, and subsequent enactment of HR 6040." Filed for self 9/13/84. Legislative interest — "Seeking F.Y. supplemental appropriations for the Job Corps program . . . HR 6040 . . . support added funds in HR 6040 to meet capital and equipment needs of Job Corps, and subsequent enactment of HR 6040." Lobbyist — Edwin T. Paris.

RORER GROUP INC., Fort Washington, Pa. Lobbyist — Patton, Boggs & Blow, 2550 M St. N.W., Washington, D.C. 20037. Filed 9/7/84. Legislative interest — "Efforts to restore patent term and provide for abbreviated new drug applications. Such as a) Federal Food, Drug and Cosmetic Act and b) HR 3605."

SAFECARD SERVICES INC., Fort Lauderdale, Fla. Lobbyist — SMC International, 1825 I St. N.W., Washington, D.C. 20006. Filed 9/28/84. Legislative interest — "Credit card legislation. S 1555, S 1870, HR 3181."

SCHWINN BICYCLE CO., 1856 N. Kostner Ave., Chicago, Ill. 60639. Lobbyist — J. C. Steen, 412 First St. S.E., Washington, D.C. 20003. Filed 9/25/84. Legislative interest — "Opposition to HR 5754 and similar legislation designed to increase tariffs on bicycles and bicycle parts." Lobbyist — Keck, Mahin & Cate, 1333 New Hampshire Ave. N.W., Washington, D.C. 20036. Filed 9/13/84. Legislative interest — "Schwinn has a general interest in legislative matters affecting tariffs on bicycles and bicycle parts. Schwinn is particularly interested in HR 5754, a bill to increase the tariffs on bicycles and bicycle parts. Schwinn opposes that legislation." Filed for self 9/13/84. Legislative interest — "Schwinn has a general interest in legislative matters affecting tariffs on bicycles and bicycle parts. Schwinn is particularly interested in HR 5754, a bill to increase the tariffs on bicycles and bicycle parts. Schwinn opposes that legislation." Lobbyist — John R. F. Baer.

THE STANDARD OIL CO. (OHIO), Midland Building, Cleveland, Ohio 44115. Lobbyist — Marcus G. Faust, 2121 K St. N.W., Washington, D.C. 20037. Filed 9/21/84. Legislative interest — "Clean Air Act." Filed for self 9/19/84. Legislative interest — "General legislative matters pertaining to the interests of the company respecting petroleum products, refining and distribution, petro-chemicals and coal, metal/non-metal minerals and taxes." Lobbyist — David E. Franasiak, 1001 22nd St. N.W., Washington, D.C. 20037.

TRACOR INC., Austin, Texas. Lobbyist — Charls E. Walker Associates Inc., 1730 Pennsylvania Ave. N.W., Washington, D.C. 20006. Filed 9/27/84. Legislative interest — "Legislation which would provide exemptions to the January 1, 1989, deadline for compliance with provisions of PL 96-193 for international operations at Miami International Airport."

TRAWEEK INVESTMENT CO. INC., Marina del Rey, Calif. Lobbyist — Bill Hecht and Associates Inc., 499 South Capitol St. S.E., Washington, D.C. 20003. Filed 9/14/84. Legislative interest — "General legislative interests, to include but not limited to HR 6027 and S 1578."

THE TUPMAN THURLOW CO. INC., New York, N.Y. Lobbyist — Morgan, Lewis & Bockius, 1800 M St. N.W., Washington, D.C. 20036. Filed 9/13/84. Legislative interest — "HR 3398."

UNITED TELECOM COMMUNICATIONS INC., Kansas City, Kan. 66205. Lobbyist — Dutko & Associates, 412 First St. S.E., Washington, D.C. 20003. Filed 9/10/84. Legislative interest — "Legislation affecting telecommunications matters - HR 4102 and S 1665."

WEBER, HALL, SALE & ASSOCIATES INC., Dallas, Texas. Lobbyist — Akin, Gump, Strauss, Hauer & Feld, 1333 New Hampshire Ave. N.W., Washington, D.C. 20036. Filed 9/20/84. Legislative interest — "Hearings and any legislation relating to banking, savings and loan, and financial institution matters."

THE WELK MUSIC GROUP, Santa Monica, Calif. Lobbyist — Liz Robbins Associates, 132 D St. S.E., Washington, D.C. 20003. Filed 9/7/84. Legislative interest — "Commemorative Day in honor of a Broadway Composer - Jerome Kern."

WHYTE & HIRSCHBOECK, Milwaukee, Wis. Lobbyist — Franklin R. Silbey Associates, 1919 Pennsylvania Ave. N.W., Washington, D.C. 20006. Legislative interest — "(For) S 2723 (Authorization)."

International Relations

GOVERNMENT OF BOLIVIA, La Paz, Bolivia. Lobbyist — Martin Associates International, 1711 Connecticut Ave. N.W., Washington, D.C. 20009. Filed 9/27/84. Legislative interest — "Foreign Assistance Legislation; Monitoring legislation of a general nature affecting the Government of Bolivia...."

GOVERNMENT OF PERU, Lima, Peru. Lobbyist — Martin Associates International, 1711 Connecticut Ave. N.W., Washington, D.C. 20009. Filed 9/27/84. Legislative interest — "Foreign Assistance legislation; Monitoring legislation of a general nature affecting the Government of Peru...."

Labor Groups

INTERNATIONAL LADIES' GARMENT WORKERS' UNION, 1710 Broadway, New York, N.Y. 10019. Filed for self 9/17/84. Legislative interest — "Civil rights legislation, educational opportunities, Labor and social welfare legislation, housing, trade, health care, full employment and consumer protective legislation and the Budget." Lobbyist — Iris Sunshine.

State and Local Governments

ASSOCIATION OF LOCAL HOUSING FINANCE AGENCIES, 1101 Connecticut Ave. N.W., Washington, D.C. 20036. Lobbyist — Liz Robbins Associates, 132 D St. S.E., Washington, D.C. 20003. Filed 9/7/84. Legislative interest — "To advocate local housing agencies positions on legislation regarding tax-exempt financing."

TURLOCK IRRIGATION DISTRICT, Turlock, Calif. Lobbyist — Damrell, Damrell & Nelson, 911 13th St., Modesto, Calif. 95353. Filed 9/14/84. Legislative interest — "Any legislation affecting hydroelectric power."

WAYNE COUNTY ROAD COMMISSION, Detroit, Mich. Lobbyist — Thompson, Gold & Liebengood, 1050 Connecticut Ave. N.W., Washington, D.C. 20036. Filed 9/5/84. Legislative interest — "Appropriations bills for Justice, Health and Human Services, Housing and Urban Development and Transportation, and Office of Management and Budget regulations of agency block grant programs."

Trade Associations

AMERICAN ASSOCIATION OF EXPORTERS AND IMPORTERS, 11 W. 42nd St., New York, N.Y. 10036. Filed for self 9/28/84. Legislative interest — "... international trade." Lobbyist — Eugene Milosh.

AMERICAN ASSOCIATION OF HOMES FOR THE AGING, 1050 17th St. N.W., Washington, D.C. 20036. Filed for self 9/18/84. Legislative interest — "Federal health and housing programs serving the elderly and other issues of concern to the aging (for example, Social Security, Medicare and Medicaid legislation and the Older Americans Act)." Lobbyists — Howard Bedlin, Dean Sagar.

AMERICAN ASSOCIATION OF MESBICS, Washington, D.C. Lobbyist — Brown, Wood, Ivey, Mitchell & Petty, One Farragut Square South, Washington, D.C. 20006. Filed 9/20/84. Legislative interest — "... Corporation for Small Business Investment Act ... S 2686 ... HR 4773...."

AMERICAN FINANCIAL SERVICES ASSOCIATION, 1101 14th St. N.W., Washington, D.C. 20005. Filed for self 9/12/84. Legislative interest — "Any and all legislation affecting the consumer credit industry including but not limited to the following: financial institutions deregulation, S 2181, S 1609, S 2134; telecommunications legislation, S 1660, HR 4102." Lobbyist — Carol A. Higgins.

AMERICAN SOCIETY OF ASSOCIATION EXECUTIVES, Washington, D.C. Lobbyist — Sanders, Schnabel & Brandenburg, 1110 Vermont Ave N.W., Washington, D.C. 20005. Filed 9/14/84. Legislative interest — "Legislation relating to employee benefits, i.e., Deficit Reduction Act of 1984 (generally in favor of several provisions)."

ASSOCIATION OF TRIAL LAWYERS, Washington, D.C. Lobbyist — Alan A. Parker, 1050 31st St. N.W., Washington, D.C. 20007. Filed 9/24/84. Legislative interest — "Legislation relative to admiralty, automobile reparation, aviation, consumer protection, criminal law, the environment, health, the administration of justice, legal services, and workers' compensation."

THE CHLORINE INSTITUTE INC., 70 W. 40th St., New York, N.Y. 10018. Lobbyist — LaRoe, Winn & Moerman, 1120 G St. N.W., Washington, D.C. 20005. Filed 9/6/84. Legislative interest — "General legislative interest: Legislation affecting chemical manufacturing generally and chlorine and its derivatives in particular. Chemical transportation, marketing and use. Environmental regulation and taxation of production and use. Specific legislative interest: The Superfund Expansion and Protection Act of 1984, HR 5640; and related Superfund legislation. Seeking modification of the tax on sodium hydroxide and potassium hydroxide. Seeking addition of waste end tax to Superfund legislation." Filed for self 9/19/84. Legislative interest — "General legislative interest: Legislation affecting chemical manufacturing generally and chlorine and its derivatives in particular. Chemical transportation, marketing and use. Environmental regulation and taxation of production and use. Specific legislative interest: The Superfund Expansion and Protection Act of 1984, HR 5640; and related Superfund legislation. Seeking modification of the tax on sodium hydroxide and potassium hydroxide. Seeking addition of waste end tax to Superfund legislation." Lobbyist — Robert L. Mitchell.

COALITION FOR NATIONAL AIRPORT, Arlington, Va. Lobbyist — Patton, Boggs & Blow, 2550 M St. N.W., Washington, D.C. 20037. Filed 9/9/84. Legislative interest — "Monitoring legislation affecting Washington National Airport such as a) DOT Appropriations Bill (FY 1985) Act to rename Dulles Airport and b) S 2483."

COALITION TO PROMOTE AMERICA'S TRADE, Washington, D.C. Lobbyist — Steptoe & Johnson, 1250 Connecticut Ave. N.W., Washington, D.C. 20036. Filed 9/18/84. Legislative interest — "... Trade Remedies Reform Act of 1984 ... HR 4784 ... Against."

COLD FINISHED STEEL BAR INSTITUTE, Washington, D.C. Lobbyist — Thompson & Mitchell, 1120 Vermont Ave. N.W., Washington, D.C. 20005. Filed 9/13/84. Legislative interest — "International trade; U.S. steel imports."

COLLEGE OF AMERICAN PATHOLOGISTS, Washington, D.C. Lobbyist — Thompson, Gold & Liebengood, 1050 Connecticut Ave. N.W., Washington, D.C. 20036. Filed 9/5/84. Legislative interest — "Medicare reform."

COMMITTEE AGAINST NETWORK DOMINANCE, Washington, D.C. Lobbyist — Akin, Gump, Strauss, Hauer & Feld, 1333 New Hampshire Ave. N.W., Washington, D.C. 20036. Filed 9/25/84. Legislative interest — "Hearings and legislation (HR 6134 and S 2962) related to Congressional consideration of recent FCC decision to modify television station ownership rules."

COMMITTEE OF RAILROAD SHIPPERS, Washington, D.C. Lobbyist — Patton, Boggs & Blow, 2550 M St. N.W., Washington, D.C. 20037. Filed 9/7/84. Legislative interest — "Legislation to implement sale of Conrail such as Northeast Rail Services Act of 1981."

CONSORTIUM OF SOCIAL SCIENCE ASSOCIATIONS, 1200 17th St. N.W., Washington, D.C. 20036. Filed for self 9/5/84. Legislative interest — Not specified. Lobbyist — David Jenness.

FEDERATION DES EXPORTATEURS DE VINS & SPIRITUEUX DE FRANCE, Paris, France. Lobbyist — Max N. Berry, 3213 O St. N.W., Washington, D.C. 20007. Filed 9/25/84. Legislative interest — "Inform client of legislation affecting imported wine. 'Wine Equity Act' - a bill, HR 3795. Against HR 3795."

FEDERATION OF APPAREL MANUFACTURERS, New York, N.Y. Lobbyist — Buchanan Ingersoll, 1667 K St. N.W. Washington, D.C. 20006. Filed 9/27/84. Legislative interest — "Sales Representatives Contractual Relations Act ... HR 3591 ... opposed...."

INVESTMENT COMPANY INSTITUTE, 1775 K St. N.W., Washington, D.C. 20006. Lobbyist — Thompson, Gold & Liebengood, 1050 Connecticut Ave. N.W., Washington, D.C. 20036. Filed 9/5/84. Legislative interest — "Legislation concerning bank powers, Market Mutual Funds." Filed for self 9/10/84. Legislative interest — "General tax legislation before the Ways and Means & Finance Committees." Lobbyist — David B. Rosenauer, 1600 M St. N.W., Washington, D.C. 20036.

JOINT COMMITTEE OF KNITWEAR ASSOCIATIONS, Kowloon, Hong Kong. Lobbyist — O'Connor & Hannan, 1919 Pennsylvania Ave. N.W., Washington, D.C. 20006. Filed 9/12/84. Legislative interest — ". . . proposed apparel import restrictions."

NATIONAL ASSOCIATION OF HOME BUILDERS OF THE UNITED STATES, 15th & M Sts. N.W., Washington, D.C. 20005. Filed for self 9/19/84. Legislative interest — Not specified. Lobbyist — Kent W. Colton.

NATIONAL ASSOCIATION OF SMALL BUSINESS INVESTMENT COMPANIES, Washington, D.C. Lobbyist — Brown, Wood, Ivey, Mitchell & Petty, One Farragut Square South, Washington, D.C. 20006. Filed 9/20/84. Legislative interest — ". . . Corporation for Small Business Investment Act . . . S 2686 . . . HR 4773. . . ."

NATIONAL PORK PRODUCERS COUNCIL, 1015 15th St. N.W., Washington, D.C. 20005. Filed for self 9/16/84. Legislative interest — Not specified. Lobbyist — Peter J. Hapworth.

NATIONAL RURAL TELECOM ASSOCIATION, Blair, Neb. Lobbyist — John F. O'Neal, 600 New Hampshire Ave. N.W., Washington, D.C. 20037. Filed 9/4/84. Legislative interest — ". . . legislation affecting REA telephone program, including S 508, HR 3027, HR 2211 and related legislation. Supporting S 1300 and HR 3050, legislation amending the REA of 1936, as amended. Supporting REA telephone loan program provisions of Agriculture Appropriations legislation for FY 1984."

NATURAL GAS SUPPLY ASSOCIATION, Washington, D.C. Lobbyist — Thompson, Gold & Liebengood, 1050 Connecticut Ave. N.W., Washington, D.C. 20036. Filed 9/5/84. Legislative interest — "Legislation to de-regulate natural gas." Lobbyist — Miller & Chevalier, 655 15th St. N.W., Washington, D.C. 20005. Filed 9/24/84. Legislative interest — "Registrant's general interest is in oversight of the Natural Gas Policy Act of 1978, and amending same with a view toward consumer and national defense."

SHEET METAL AND AIR CONDITIONING CONTRACTORS' NATIONAL ASSOCIATION, 8224 Old Courthouse Road, Tysons Corner, Va. 22180. Filed for self 9/5/84. Legislative interest — "Legislative interests include issues of concern to construction industry; i.e., infrastructure, business taxes, ERISA, small business programs." Lobbyists — Margaret P. Thaxton, Stanley E. Kolbe Jr., 418 South Capitol St. S.E., Washington, D.C. 20003.

THE SOUTHERN BAPTIST PRESS ASSOCIATION, Dallas, Texas. Lobbyist — Liz Robbins Associates, 132 D St. S.E., Washington, D.C. 20003. Filed 9/7/84. Legislative interest — "Postal Rate legislation."

THE TOBACCO INSTITUTE, Washington, D.C. Lobbyist — Ronald A. White, 1500 Chestnut St., Philadelphia, Pa. 19102. Filed 9/24/84. Legislative interest — Not specified. Lobbyist — Thompson, Gold & Liebengood, 1050 Connecticut Ave. N.W., Washington, D.C. 20036. Filed 9/5/84. Legislative interest — "1985 Tax Reform, any technical corrections bill to the 1984 Tax Act."

UNITED FRESH FRUIT AND VEGETABLE ASSOCIATION, 727 N. Washington St., Alexandria, Va. 22314. Filed for self 9/20/84. Legislative interest — ". . . HR 5605, the Federal Food Irradiation Development Control Act of 1984; HR 5529, Agriculture Patent Restoration Act; HR 5495, Pesticide Tolerance Emergency Authority Act; HR 1510, S 529, Immigration Reform and Control Act; S 1718, HR 3581, Extension of the Generalized System of Preferences; HR 5377, S 2746, U.S./Israel Free Trade Agreement and other issues affecting the fresh fruit and vegetable industry." Lobbyist — Sharon E. Bomer.

Miscellaneous

AMERICAN ASSOCIATION OF RETIRED PERSONS, Washington, D.C. Lobbyist — Daniel Saphire, 1909 K St. N.W., Washington, D.C. 20036. Filed 9/12/84. Legislative interest — "Medicare; improved tax treatment of older Americans; consumer protection legislation; pharmaceuticals; health care."

AMERICAN CANCER SOCIETY, 777 Third Ave., New York, N.Y. 10017. Filed for self 9/20/84. Legislative interest — "The Comprehensive Smoking Education Act (HR 3979, S 772); cigarette excise tax legislation; appropriations for the National Cancer Institute (HR 6028, S 2836); Charitable Contributions legislation (S 337, HR 1315); The Civil Aeronautics Board Sunset Act of 1984 (HR 5297); elimination of the five-month waiting period for disability insurance benefits for the terminally ill (HR 507, S 1785); a bill to reauthorize the National Cancer Institute; Revenue Foregone and Third Class Nonprofit Postal Rate Subsidies (HR 5798, S 2853); and, the Comprehensive Environmental Response, Compensation Act of 1980 ('Superfund' or 'CERCLA') (HR 5640, S 2892)." Lobbyist — John H. Madigan Jr., 1575 I St. N.W., Washington, D.C. 20005.

THE BIPARTISAN BUDGET COALITION, P.O. Box 5203, F.D.R. Station, New York, N.Y. 10150. Filed for self 9/10/84. Legislative interest — Not specified.

COUNCIL FOR A LIVABLE WORLD, 11 Beacon St., Boston, Mass. 02108. Filed for self 9/28/84. Legislative interest — "Legislation on arms control and disarmament, FY 1985 authorization and appropriation bill for DOD, State, AEC, ACDA, etc., in the U.S. Senate." Lobbyist — Linda Staheli, 100 Maryland Ave. N.W., Washington, D.C. 20002.

METROPOLITAN HOSPITAL OF PHILADELPHIA, Philadelphia, Pa. Lobbyist — Ronald A. White, 1500 Chestnut St., Philadelphia, Pa. 19102. Filed 9/24/84. Legislative interest — Not specified.

NATIONAL COALITION FOR PORT PROGRESS, Washington, D.C. Lobbyist — Thompson, Gold & Liebengood, 1050 Connecticut Ave. N.W., Washington, D.C. 20036. Filed 9/5/84. Legislative interest — ". . . transportation, public works, waterways, user fees."

NATURAL RESOURCES DEFENSE COUNCIL INC., 1350 New York Ave. N.W., Washington, D.C. 20005. Filed for self 9/19/84. Legislative interest — ". . . the environmental and biological consequences of nuclear weapons and nuclear war; legislation concerning the study of such issues by agencies of the federal government." Lobbyist — Estelle H. Rogers.

ORGANIZATION OF CHINESE AMERICANS, 2025 I St. N.W., Washington, D.C. 20006. Filed for self 9/26/84. Legislative interest — "Advance the interests of Chinese Americans including: immigration bills (HR 1510 (against); HR 2909 (for); S 529 (against); HR 2131 (for)); amend Communications Act, HR 3105 (for)." Lobbyist — Henry K. Mui.

RELIGIOUS COALITION FOR ABORTION RIGHTS INC., 100 Maryland Ave. N.E., Washington, D.C. 20002. Filed for self 9/18/84. Legislative interest — Not specified. Lobbyist — Judith Logan-White.

SIERRA CLUB, 530 Bush St., San Francisco, Calif. 94108. Filed for self 9/24/84. Legislative interest — "Environmental protection . . . Wyoming Wilderness Bill/against . . . Clean Water Act/for . . . Superfund/for . . . Interior Appropriations." Lobbyist — Larry Mehlhaff, 23 N. Scott, Sheridan, Wyo. 82801.

TEMIS RAMIRES DE ARELLANO, Washington, D.C. Lobbyist — Pillsbury, Madison & Sutro, 1050 17th St. N.W., Washington, D.C. 20036. Filed 9/21/84. Legislative interest — "Assist Mr. Ramires in his effort to obtain legislative relief for usurpation of his property in Honduras by the U.S. military."

ZERO POPULATION GROWTH INC., 1346 Connecticut Ave. N.W., Washington, D.C. 20036. Filed for self 9/13/84. Legislative interest — "Support legislation to establish a national population policy and foresight capability: 'The Global Resources, Environment and Population Act of 1983,' S 1025, and HR 2491. Support legislation to reform U.S. immigration policy: 'Immigration Reform and Control Act of 1983,' HR 1510. . . ." Lobbyists — Mark Esherick, Susan Weber.

October Registrations

Corporations and Businesses

ABBOTT LABORATORIES, Abbott Park, North Chicago, Ill. 60064. Filed for self 10/13/84. Legislative interest — "...legislation affecting the health care industry ... general nutrition issues, patent restoration, and tax legislation." Lobbyist — David W. Landsidle, 1710 Rhode Island Ave. N.W., Washington, D.C. 20036.

AEROJET-GENERAL INC., Sacramento, Calif. Lobbyist — Breed, Abbott & Morgan, 1875 I St. N.W., Washington, D.C. 20006. Filed 10/5/84. Legislative interest — "...proposed amendments to the 'Superfund' Law; specifically: (a) Superfund Expansion and Protection Act of 1984, and Superfund Amendments of 1984; (b) HR 5640, S 2892; (c) 42 U.S.C. Sec. 9601 *et seq.*; (d) modification."

AFFILIATED CAPITAL CORP., Houston, Texas. Lobbyist — Parry and Romani Associates, 1140 Connecticut Ave. N.W., Washington, D.C. 20036. Filed 10/19/84. Legislative interest — "Municipal Liability Bill."

ALLIED CORP., P.O. Box 3000-R, Morristown, N.J. 07960. Filed for self 10/13/84. Legislative interest — "Health and safety, environmental, technology and other matters affecting Allied Corporation." Lobbyist — Thomas M. Hellman, 1150 Connecticut Ave. N.W., Washington, D.C. 20036.

ALMET INC., Bernardsville, N.J. Lobbyist — Harris, Berg & Creskoff, 1100 15th St. N.W., Washington, D.C. 20005. Filed 10/12/84. (Former U.S. Rep. Herbert E. Harris II, D-Va., 1975-81, was listed as agent for this client.) Legislative interest — "To oppose the ferroalloys amendment (Section 126) added to the omnibus tariff and trade bill (HR 3398) in the 98th Congress, 2nd Session."

THE ALTER GROUP, Wilmette, Ill. Lobbyist — Powell, Goldstein, Frazer & Murphy, 1110 Vermont Ave. N.W., Washington, D.C. 20005. Filed 10/26/84. Legislative interest — "...to oppose the retroactive application of the City of Boulder bill (antitrust immunity for cities)."

AMERICAN EXPRESS CO., Washington, D.C. Lobbyist — Communication Counsel Inc., 1045 31st St. N.W., Washington, D.C. 20007. Filed 10/12/84. Legislative interest — "Credit Card Surcharge - against surcharge." Lobbyist — Jack McDonald Associates Inc., 1120 20th St. N.W., Washington, D.C. 20036. Filed 10/1/84. Legislative interest — "Surcharge ban."

AMERICAN INDIAN NATIONAL BANK, Washington, D.C. Lobbyist — Fried, Frank, Harris, Shriver & Kampelman, 600 New Hampshire Ave. N.W., Washington, D.C. 20037. Filed 10/12/84. Legislative interest — "...American Indian legislation and programs and banking; specific interests: in favor of amendments to Indian Financing Act of 1974, S 2614."

AMOSKEAG SAVINGS BANK, Manchester, N.H. Lobbyist — Thacher, Proffitt & Wood, 1140 Connecticut Ave. N.W., Washington, D.C. 20036. Filed 10/15/84. Legislative interest — "HR 5916/S 2181, financial reform legislation (proposed), affecting Federal savings banks and thrift institutions."

ASARCO INC., New York, N.Y. Lobbyist — Breed, Abbott & Morgan, 1875 I St. N.W., Washington, D.C. 20006. Filed 10/5/84. Legislative interest — "...proposed amendments to the 'Superfund' Law; specifically: (a) Superfund Expansion and Protection Act of 1984, and Superfund Amendments of 1984; (b) HR 5640, S 2892; (c) 42 U.S.C. Sec. 9601 *et seq.*; (d) modification."

ATLAS CORP., Princeton, N.J. Lobbyist — A. Ray Tyrrell, 700 Madison Building, Washington, D.C. 20005. Filed 10/10/84. Legislative interest — "Legislation affecting operations of mining and manufacturing industries."

BAUSCH & LOMB, Rochester, N.Y. Lobbyist — Nixon, Hargrave, Devans & Doyle, 1090 Vermont Ave. N.W., Washington, D.C. 20005. Filed 10/15/84. Legislative interest — "Trade legislation."

BAYBANKS INC., Boston, Mass. Lobbyist — Timothy D. Naegele & Associates, 1850 K St. N.W., Washington, D.C. 20006. Filed 10/11/84. Legislative interest — "Legislation relating to banks and financial institutions, including S 2851, the Financial Services Competitive Equity Act and HR 5916, the Financial Institutions Equity Act of 1984."

PETER L. BERMONT, Miami, Fla. Lobbyist — Wilmer, Cutler & Pickering, 1666 K St. N.W., Washington, D.C. 20006. Filed 10/1/84. Legislative interest — "...legislation to preclude Federal Home Loan Bank Board (FHLBB) from promulgating regulations that insulate incumbent managers of thrift institutions in stock form from shareholder accumulations otherwise consistent with FHLBB supervision of charges in control."

BROADCAST MUSIC INC., New York, N.Y. Lobbyist — Endicott Peabody, 71 Spit Brook Road, Nashua, N.H. 03060. Filed 10/28/84. Legislative interest — "Opposing S 1734 and HR 3858 - The Coin Operated Phono-Record Player Copyright Act."

CAPITOL AIR INC., Smyrna, Tenn. Lobbyist — SMC International, 1825 I St. N.W., Washington, D.C. 20006. Filed 10/16/84. Legislative interest — "Exemption from airport noise standards: H J Res 648, Miami Noise exemption."

CASSIDY & ASSOCIATES INC., Washington, D.C. Lobbyist — Elvis J. Stahr Jr., 1815 H St. N.W., Washington, D.C. 20006. Filed 10/28/84. Legislative interest — "...higher education...."

CASTLE & COOKE, San Francisco, Calif. Lobbyist — Heron, Burchette, Ruckert & Rothwell, 1200 New Hampshire Ave. N.W., Washington, D.C. 20036. Filed 10/31/84. Legislative interest — "Provisions of CERCLA concerning exemption for pesticide application - support."

CEMENTOS ANAHUAC DEL GOLFO S.A., Mexico City, Mexico. Lobbyist — Rogers & Wells, 1737 H St. N.W., Washington, D.C. 20006. Filed 10/11/84. Legislative interest — "Legislation dealing with international trade, particularly imports."

CENTEX COMMUNICATIONS INC., Austin, Texas. Lobbyist — Schlossberg-Cassidy & Associates Inc., 955 L'Enfant Plaza S.W., Washington, D.C. 20024. Filed 10/10/84. Legislative interest — "All legislative matters affecting radio common carriers, including Congressional oversight of FCC licensing for cellular telephone systems."

CF INDUSTRIES INC., Long Grove, Ill. Lobbyist — Brigid A. Holleran, 2550 M St. N.W., Washington, D.C. 20037. Filed 10/3/84. Legislative interest — "Fertilizer, transportation, farm cooperative and related agricultural issues."

COMMAND CONTROL AND COMMUNICATIONS CORP., Torrance, Calif. Lobbyist — Schlossberg-Cassidy & Associates Inc., 955 L'Enfant Plaza S.W., Washington, D.C. 20024. Filed 10/10/84. Legislative interest — "All legislative matters dealing with military funding."

COMMUNICATIONS SATELLITE CORP., Washington, D.C. Lobbyist — Wexler, Reynolds, Harrison & Schule Inc., 1317 F St. N.W., Washington, D.C. 20004. Filed 10/11/84. Legislative interest — "...to obtain passage of as yet unspecified legislation related to international communications satellite systems."

CONNOR FOREST INDUSTRIES INC., Wausau, Wis. Lobbyist — Ronald D. Waterman, 4802 Tabard Place, Annandale, Va. 22003. Filed 10/3/84. Legislative interest — "Renewal of GSP; HR 6023 and S 1718 (now HR 3398); Title 6 of the Trade Act of 1974; For passage of HR 6023 and HR 3398."

THE CONSOLIDATED CAPITAL COS., Emeryville, Calif. Lobbyist — James C. Corman, 1420 16th St. N.W., Washington, D.C. 20036. Filed 10/9/84. (Former U.S. rep., D-Calif., 1961-81.) Legislative interest — "To support legislation matters relating to changes in Section 483 of the Internal Revenue Code."

CORPORACION NACIONAL DEL COBRE DE CHILE (CODELCO), Santiago, Chile. Lobbyist — Manchester Associates Ltd., 1155 15th St. N.W., Washington, D.C. 20005. Filed 10/5/84. Legislative interest — "To oppose import restrictions on copper or similar proposals; Omnibus Trade Act of 1984; HR 3398. Opposed to the two provisions concerning copper. No position on the bill generally."

CPC INTERNATIONAL INC., Englewood Cliffs, N.J. Lobbyist — Breed, Abbott & Morgan, 1875 I St. N.W., Washington, D.C. 20006. Filed 10/5/84. Legislative interest — "...proposed amendments to the 'Superfund' Law; specifically: (a) Superfund Expansion and Protection Act of 1984, and Superfund Amendments of 1984; (b) HR 5640, S 2892; (c) 42 U.S.C. Sec. 9601 *et seq.*; (d) modification."

THE DOW CHEMICAL CO., Midland, Mich. Lobbyist — Groom & Nordberg, 1775 Pennsylvania Ave. N.W., Washington, D.C. 20006. Filed 10/11/84. Legislative interest — "Federal legislation affecting Title 26 of U.S.C."

ELECTRONIC DATA SYSTEMS, Washington, D.C. Lobbyist — Scott, Harrison & McLeod, 2501 M St. N.W., Washington, D.C. 20037. Filed 10/12/84. Legislative interest — ". . . food stamp eligibility verification procedures."

THE EMPIRE DISTRICT ELECTRIC CO., Joplin, Mo. Lobbyist — Thomas L. Holloway, 1920 N St. N.W., Washington, D.C. 20036. Filed 10/17/84. Legislative interest — ". . . Internal Revenue Code; TVA Act; Atomic Energy Act; Federal Power Act; Rural Electrification Act; Bonneville Power Act; Reclamation Acts; Flood Control Acts; Appropriation Acts; National Energy Acts; Clean Air Act; Water Pollution Control Act; OSHA; Natural Gas Policy Act."

FIRST ARKANSAS BANKSTOCK CORP., Worthen Bank Building, 200 West Capitol Ave., Little Rock, Ark. 72201. Filed for self 10/11/84. Legislative interest — "Banking, regulatory and taxation issues."

FORT HOWARD PAPER CO., Green Bay, Wis. Lobbyist — McDermott, Will & Emery, 1850 K St. N.W., Washington, D.C. 20006. Filed 10/12/84. Legislative interest — "Issues regarding Superfund Legislation."

GENERAL ELECTRIC CREDIT CORP., Stamford, Conn. Lobbyist — King & Spalding, 1730 Pennsylvania Ave. N.W., Washington, D.C. 20006. Filed 10/5/84. Legislative interest — ". . . S 2851, the banking bill, or other similar subsequent legislation."

GEORGIA POWER CO., P.O. Box 4545, Atlanta, Ga. 30302. Filed for self 10/11/84. Legislative interest — ". . . interests affecting the electric utility industry, including energy, regulatory, environmental, taxation, and transportation issues." Lobbyist — Doug B. Bowles, 205 Spring Hill Terrace, Roswell, Ga. 30075.

GRUMMAN DATA SYSTEMS CORP., Bethpage, N.Y. Lobbyist — Leo C. Zeferetti, 9912 Fort Hamilton Parkway, Brooklyn, N.Y. 11209. Filed 10/31/84. (Former U.S. rep., D-N.Y., 1975-83.) Legislative interest — Not specified.

HALLMARK CARDS INC., 1201 Pennsylvania Ave. N.W., Washington, D.C. 20004. Filed for self 10/10/84. Legislative interest — Not specified. Lobbyist — Barbara G. Burchett.

HEMET VALLEY FLYING SERVICE, Sacramento, Calif. Lobbyist — A-K Associates, 1225 8th St., Sacramento, Calif. 95814. Filed 10/15/84. Legislative interest — "Fiscal bills relating to five management programs and aircraft development."

INTEGRATED RESOURCES INC., 666 3rd Ave., New York, N.Y. 10017. Filed for self 10/10/84. Legislative interest — ". . . tax legislation affecting investment and capital formation. Specifically . . . the possible effects of the various flat tax and modified flat tax proposals pending before Congress." Lobbyist — Richard Rosenbaum.

INTERNATIONAL FIVE MANAGEMENT, Sacramento, Calif. Lobbyist — A-K Associates, 1225 8th St., Sacramento, Calif. 95814. Filed 10/15/84. Legislative interest — "Fiscal bills relating to five management programs and aircraft development."

INTERNATIONAL MEDICAL CENTERS, Miami, Fla. Lobbyist — Black, Manafort & Stone, 324 North Fairfax St., Alexandria, Va. 22314. Filed 10/10/84. Legislative interest — ". . . legislation affecting HMO's such as TEFRA regulations and tax legislation."

ITEL CONTAINER CORP., 55 Francisco St., San Francisco, Calif. 94133. Filed for self 10/28/84. Legislative interest — ". . . container leasing generally and specifically in connection with support of bill to accelerate, eliminate tariff on containers."

KANSAS CITY POWER AND LIGHT CO., Kansas City, Mo. Lobbyist — Thomas L. Holloway, 1920 N St. N.W., Washington, D.C. 20036. Filed 10/17/84. Legislative interest — ". . . Internal Revenue Code; TVA Act; Atomic Energy Act; Federal Power

Act; Rural Electrification Act; Bonneville Power Act; Reclamation Acts; Flood Control Acts; Appropriation Acts; National Energy Acts; Clean Air Act; Water Pollution Control Act; OSHA; Natural Gas Policy Act."

KEMPER FINANCIAL SERVICES INC., 120 S. LaSalle St., Chicago, Ill. 60603. Filed for self 10/15/84. Legislative interest — ". . . including but not limited to financial services institutions legislation." Lobbyist — Michael F. Dineen, 600 Pennsylvania Ave. S.E., Washington, D.C. 20003.

LINCOLN SAVINGS & LOAN ASSOCIATION, Irvine, Calif. Lobbyist — Miller & Chevalier, 655 15th St. N.W., Washington, D.C. 20005. Filed 10/3/84. Legislative interest — "Revisions to federal laws governing state-chartered savings and loan association investment activities."

MAINE SAVINGS BANK, Portland, Maine. Lobbyist — Thacher, Proffitt & Wood, 1140 Connecticut Ave. N.W., Washington, D.C. 20036. Filed 10/15/84. Legislative interest — "HR 5916/S 2181, financial reform legislation (proposed), affecting federal savings banks and thrift institutions."

MANCHESTER ASSOCIATES LTD., 1155 15th St. N.W., Washington, D.C. 20005. Filed for self 10/5/84. Legislative interest — "To oppose import restrictions on copper or similar proposals. Omnibus Trade Act of 1984; HR 3398. Opposed to the two provisions concerning copper. No position on the bill generally." Lobbyist — John V. Moller.

THE MAY DEPARTMENT STORES CO., St. Louis, Mo. Lobbyist — Hogan & Hartson, 815 Connecticut Ave. N.W., Washington, D.C. 20006. Filed 10/10/84. Legislative interest — "Legislation affecting imports of apparel, textile, footwear or other merchandise."

MISSOURI PUBLIC SERVICE CO., Kansas City, Mo. Lobbyist — Thomas L. Holloway, 1920 N St. N.W., Washington, D.C. 20036. Filed 10/17/84. Legislative interest — ". . . Internal Revenue Code; TVA Act; Atomic Energy Act; Federal Power Act; Rural Electrification Act; Bonneville Power Act; Reclamation Acts; Flood Control Acts; Appropriation Acts; National Energy Acts; Clean Air Act; Water Pollution Control Act; OSHA; Natural Gas Policy Act."

MUTUAL SAVINGS CENTRAL FUND INC., Boston, Mass. Lobbyist — Thacher, Proffitt & Wood, 1140 Connecticut Ave. N.W., Washington, D.C. 20036. Filed 10/15/84. Legislative interest — ". . . legislative proposals affecting deposit insurance."

NABISCO BRANDS INC., 7 Campus Drive, Parsippany, N.J. 07054. Filed for self 10/8/84. Legislative interest — Not specified. Lobbyist — Lynette Lenard, 1050 Connecticut Ave. N.W., Washington, D.C. 20036.

NCR CORP., Dayton, Ohio 45479. Filed for self 10/19/84. Legislative interest — "Legislation affecting the computer industry." Lobbyist — James H. Skidmore, 1140 19th St. N.W., Washington, D.C. 20036.

NEW HAMPSHIRE SAVINGS BANK, Concord, N.H. Lobbyist — Thacher, Proffitt & Wood, 1140 Connecticut Ave. N.W., Washington, D.C. 20036. Filed 10/15/84. Legislative interest — "HR 5916/S 2181, financial reform legislation (proposed), affecting federal savings banks and thrift institutions."

NIKE INC., Beaverton, Ore. Lobbyist — Garvey, Schubert, Adams & Barer, 1011 Western Ave., Seattle, Wash. 98104. Filed 10/10/84. Legislative interest — "Trade legislation involving footwear."

NORTHERN NATURAL GAS CO., 2223 Dodge St., Omaha, Neb. 68102. Filed for self 10/10/84. Legislative interest — "Deregulation of Natural Gas (HR 4277 and S 1715); budget and tax issues as they affect the Natural Gas industry; pipeline safety legislation (HR 5313 and S 2688); Synthetic Fuels Corporation; any legislation relating to restructuring of DOE/FERC (Administrative Law Judge Corps Act, S 1275 and HR 3539)." Lobbyist — H. Spofford Canfield, 1015 15th St. N.W., Washington, D.C. 20005.

NORWEST MORTGAGE INC., 330 2nd Ave. South, Minneapolis, Minn. 55401. Filed for self 10/18/84. Legislative interest — "Housing and banking issues." Lobbyists — Iris S. Kandel, 1981 Greenberry Road, Baltimore, Md. 21209; Jessica Maitzen, 5755 Thunder Hill Road, Columbia, Md. 21045.

PAN AMERICAN WORLD SERVICES, New York, N.Y. Lobbyist — Rogers & Wells, 200 Park Ave., New York, N.Y. 10016. Filed 10/10/84. Legislative interest — "Amendment to Section 531 of the Tax Reform Act of 1984 (PL 98-369, 7/18/84)."

PETER FENN & ASSOCIATES INC., Washington, D.C. Lobbyist — Randall K. Hulme, 618 A St. S.E., Washington, D.C. 20003. Filed 10/12/84. Legislative interest — Not specified.

PFIZER INC., Washington, D.C. Lobbyist — Rogers & Wells, 200 Park Ave., New York, N.Y. 10016. Filed 10/10/84. Legislative interest — "Extension of 26 U.S.C. Sec. 127. . . ."

PHILLIPS PETROLEUM CO., Bartlesville, Okla. 74004. Filed for self 10/3/84. Legislative interest — "S 2892/HR 5640 - 'Superfund Expansion and Protection Act of 1984': generally against; HR 5959/S 2649 - 'Safe Drinking Water Act': generally for; HR 5314/S 768 - 'Clean Air Act Amendments': generally against." Lobbyist — James W. Godlove, 1825 K St. N.W., Washington, D.C. 20006.

PIONEER SYSTEMS INC., New York, N.Y. Lobbyist — Kaye, Scholer, Fierman, Hays & Handler, 1575 I St. N.W., Washington, D.C. 20005. Filed 10/22/84. Legislative interest — ". . . Congressional activities affecting: government procurement policy and aircraft safety regulation."

PORTALS, Washington, D.C. Lobbyist — Gray & Co., 3255 Grace St. N.W., Washington, D.C. 20007. Filed 10/10/84. Legislative interest — "Including but not limited to odometer fraud legislation."

PRATT & WHITNEY, Washington, D.C. Lobbyist — Leo C. Zeferetti, 9912 Fort Hamilton Parkway, Brooklyn, N.Y. 11209. Filed 10/31/84. (Former U.S. rep., D-N.Y., 1975-83.) Legislative interest — "Legislation affecting the client including but not limited to their aircraft engines."

PRIMARK CORP., 1050 17th St. N.W., Washington, D.C. 20036. Filed for self 10/9/84. Legislative interest — "Legislation affecting the banking industry, health care, natural gas and environmental issues." Lobbyist — Julie S. Jones.

R. J. REYNOLDS INDUSTRIES INC., Winston-Salem, N.C. Lobbyist — Burleigh C. W. Leonard, 2550 M St. N.W., Washington, D.C. 20037. Filed 10/11/84. Legislative interest — "Any legislation affecting the general business community, especially the tobacco and consumer products industries: (a) Multinational Corporations; (b) Tax Legislation (and Tax Reform); (c) Agriculture Programs and Services; (d) National Health Program; (e) Consumer Protection; (f) Product Liability; (g) Antitrust; (h) Campaign Financing; (i) Trade Reform; (j) Land Use; (k) Environmental: Air and Water Pollution, Toxic Substances; (l) Smoking Regulation."

SCHWINN BICYCLE CO., 1856 North Kostner Ave., Chicago, Ill. 60639. Lobbyist — Keck, Mahin, & Cate, 1333 New Hampshire Ave. N.W., Washington, D.C. 20036. Filed 10/22/84. Legislative interest — ". . . legislative matters affecting tariffs on bicycles and bicycle parts . . . particularly interested in HR 5754, a bill to increase the tariffs on bicycles and bicycle parts . . . opposes that legislation." Filed for self 10/22/84. Legislative interest — ". . . legislative matters affecting tariffs on bicycles and bicycle parts . . . particularly interested in HR 5754, a bill to increase the tariffs on bicycles and bicycle parts . . . opposes that legislation." Lobbyist — Jay C. Townley.

SINGAPORE AIRLINES LTD., Washington, D.C. Lobbyist — Bracy Williams & Co., 1000 Connecticut Ave. N.W., Washington, D.C. 20036. Filed 10/4/84. Legislative interest — "Legislation affecting the aviation industry in general and international transportation."

RICHARD SINNOT & CO., Washington, D.C. Lobbyist — Thompson, Gold & Liebengood, 1050 Connecticut Ave. N.W., Washington, D.C. 20036. Filed 10/11/84. Legislative interest — "Legislation concerning appropriations for the vessel *Potomac*."

SOUTHWEST MARINE INC., Arlington, Va. Lobbyist — Schlossberg-Cassidy & Associates, 955 L'Enfant Plaza S.W., Washington, D.C. 20024. Filed 10/10/84. Legislative interest — ". . . matters affecting naval overhaul and ship repair contracts."

SPACE SERVICES INC. OF AMERICA, 7015 Gulf Freeway, Houston, Texas 77087. Filed for self 10/24/84. Legislative interest — ". . . all bills concerning commercialization of space, including S 2931, the Commercial Space Launch Act; HR 3942, the Commercial Space Launch Act; and PL 98-365, the Land Remote Sensing Commercialization Act of 1984 . . . any commercial space tax incentives that may develop into legislative initiatives." Lobbyist — Kathleen Bonner Kronmiller, 600 Water St. S.W., Washington, D.C. 20024.

SQUIBB CORP., Washington, D.C. Lobbyist — Black, Manafort & Stone Inc., 324 North Fairfax St., Alexandria, Va. 22314. Filed 10/10/84. Legislative interest — "Patent reform legislation. General tax legislation."

STANDARD MANUFACTURING CO., Dallas, Texas. Lobbyist — Dickstein, Shapiro & Morin, 2101 L St. N.W., Washington, D.C. 20037. Filed 10/10/84. Legislative interest — Not specified.

STEPHENS INC., 114 East Capitol Ave., Little Rock, Ark. 72201. Filed for self 10/11/84. Legislative interest — "Investment banking, small business, banking, corporate and regulatory issues." Lobbyist — A. Vernon Weaver.

STEPHENS OVERSEAS SERVICES INC., 2121 K St. N.W., Washington, D.C. 20037. Filed for self 10/11/84. Legislative interest — "Banking, small business, international and corporate regulatory issues." Lobbyist — Sharon D. Prinz.

STRATOS TANKER INC., Sacramento, Calif. Lobbyist — A-K Associates, 1225 8th St., Sacramento, Calif. 95814. Filed 10/15/84. Legislative interest — "Fiscal bills relating to five management programs and aircraft development."

SYSTEMATICS INC., 4001 Rodney Parham Road, Little Rock, Ark. 72212. Filed for self 10/11/84. Legislative interest — "Small business and taxation and regulatory issues." Lobbyist — A. Vernon Weaver.

3M INC., St. Paul, Minn. Lobbyist — Breed, Abbott & Morgan, 1875 I St. N.W., Washington, D.C. 20006. Filed 10/5/84. Legislative interest — ". . . proposed amendments to the 'Superfund' Law; specifically: (a) Superfund Expansion and Protection Act of 1984, and Superfund Amendments of 1984; (b) HR 5640, S 2892; (c) 42 U.S.C. Sec. 9601 *et seq.*; (d) modification."

TOYOTA MOTOR SALES U.S.A. INC., 19001 S. Western Ave., Torrance, Calif. 90509. Filed for self 10/4/84. Legislative interest — "Japan-U.S. trade and auto related legislation." Lobbyist — Kenji Ueno, 919 18th St. N.W., Washington, D.C. 20006.

UNION ELECTRIC CO., St. Louis, Mo. Lobbyist — Thomas L. Holloway, 1920 N St. N.W., Washington, D.C. 20036. Filed 10/17/84. Legislative interest — ". . . Internal Revenue Code; TVA Act; Atomic Energy Act; Federal Power Act; Rural Electrification Act; Bonneville Power Act; Reclamation Acts; Flood Control Acts; Appropriation Acts; National Energy Acts; Clean Air Act; Water Pollution Control Act; OSHA; Natural Gas Policy Act."

VOLVO CAR B.V., Helmond, The Netherlands. Lobbyist — Bishop, Liberman, Cook, Purcell & Reynolds, 1200 17th St. N.W., Washington, D.C. 20036. Filed 10/12/84. Legislative interest — ". . . legislation affecting the auto industry. 'For' Domestic Content Legislation, S 707."

WESTINGHOUSE ELECTRIC CORP., Washington, D.C. Lobbyist — The Keefe Co., 444 North Capitol St., Washington, D.C. 20001. Filed 10/11/84. Legislative interest — "Support of appropriation funding levels for FAA/Department of Transportation, UMTA."

WESTVACO, New York, N.Y. Lobbyist — John J. Adams, 2000 Pennsylvania Ave. N.W., Washington, D.C. 20036. Filed 10/10/84. Legislative interest — ". . . Virginia Wilderness Bills (HR 5121 and S 2805)."

International Relations

BANCO CENTRAL DE LA REPUBLICA DOMINICANA, Santo Domingo, Dominican Republic. Lobbyist — Black, Manafort & Stone, 324 North Fairfax St., Alexandria, Va. 22314. Filed 10/10/84. Legislative interest — "Monitor Continuing Resolution, 1984 Supplemental Funding food aid, 1985 authorization and appropriations, International Development Security Act, congressional hearings on foreign economic assistance. 'For' bills."

GOVERNMENT OF BARBADOS, Bridgetown, Barbados. Lobbyist — Black, Manafort & Stone, 324 North Fairfax St., Alexandria, Va. 22314. Filed 10/10/84. Legislative interest — "Foreign appropriations bills; U.S./Barbados tax treaty issues."

GOVERNMENT OF HAITI, Port au Prince, Haiti. Lobbyist — Gray & Co. Public Communications International Inc., 3255 Grace St. N.W., Washington, D.C. 20007. Filed 10/22/84. Legislative interest — "Including, but not limited to economic, tourism and trade matters."

REPUBLIC OF KOREA, Seoul, South Korea. Lobbyist — Gray & Co. Public Communications International Inc., 3255 Grace St. N.W., Washington, D.C. 20007. Filed 10/22/84. Legislative interest — "Including, but not limited to economic and trade matters."

GOVERNMENT OF ST. LUCIA, Castries, St. Lucia, West Indies. Lobbyist — Black, Manafort & Stone, 324 North Fairfax St., Alexandria, Va. 22314. Filed 10/10/84. Legislative interest — "Monitor Continuing Resolution, 1984 Supplemental Funding food aid, 1985 authorization and appropriations, International Development Security Act, congressional hearings on foreign economic assistance. 'For' bills."

REPUBLIC OF TURKEY, Ankara, Turkey. Lobbyist — Gray & Co. Public Communications International Inc., 3255 Grace St. N.W., Washington, D.C. 20007. Filed 10/22/84. Legislative interest — "Including, but not limited to economic and security matters; in particular, foreign military matters."

Labor Organizations

NATIONAL FEDERATION OF FEDERAL EMPLOY-EES, 1016 16th St. N.W., Washington, D.C. 20036. Filed for self 10/5/84. Legislative interest — "Legislation affecting Federal Employees . . . First and Second Concurrent Budget Resolutions, Agency Appropriations and Authorizations, Budget Reconciliation, Social Security Benefits, Mandatory Social Security coverage, contracting out (OMB circular A-76), Federal Employees Compensation Act, Civil Service Reform Act (U.S.C. Title V), overall compensation and working conditions for Federal employees and retirees. Specific legislative interests include: Fiscal Year 1985 appropriations (support or oppose); HR 5680, to eliminate wage discrimination in the Federal workforce (support); HR 3466, provided Secretary of Army and Air Force authority to establish regulations governing the performance of National Guard civilian technicians (oppose); HR 3511, to eliminate 30-day notice of termination for civilian technicians who cease to be members of the National Guard (oppose); HR 5799, to restrict the contracting out of certain Veterans' position (support); HR 656, to restructure Federal Employees Health Benefit Program; HR 622, to provide death benefits for Federal Law Enforcement Officers and Firefighters (support); Private Sector Survey on Cost Control recommendation cutting Federal pay/benefit/workforce (oppose); Office of Personnel Management's revised personnel regulations (oppose); Supplemental Federal Retirement System." Lobbyist — Stephan H. Gordon.

NATIONAL WEATHER SERVICE EMPLOYEES ORGANIZATION, Washington, D.C. Lobbyist — Chwat/Weigend Associates, 400 First St. N.W., Washington, D.C. 20001. Filed 10/11/84. Legislative interest — ". . . NOAA authorizations, appropriations and other legislation affecting NOAA."

State and Local Governments

MASSACHUSETTS BAY TRANSPORTATION AU-THORITY, Boston, Mass. Lobbyist — John D. Cahill, 444 North Capitol St. N.W., Washington, D.C. 20001. Filed 10/19/84. Legislative interest — "Transportation issues related to transit; i.e., Transportation Appropriations, Highway/Mass Transit (Legislation HR 5504)."

MILWAUKEE COUNTY INTERGOVERNMENTAL RELATIONS, Milwaukee, Wis. Lobbyist — Ronald D. Waterman, 4802 Tabard Place, Annandale, Va. 22003. Filed 10/9/84. Legislative interest — Not specified.

MODESTO IRRIGATION DISTRICT, Modesto, Calif. Lobbyist — White, Fine and Verville, 1156 15th St. N.W., Washington, D.C. 20005. Filed 10/11/84. Legislative interest — "Title II of the California Wilderness Act."

SOUTH CAROLINA PUBLIC SERVICE AUTHOR-ITY, Monks Corner, S.C. Lobbyist — Bishop, Liberman, Cook, Purcell & Reynolds, 1200 17th St. N.W., Washington, D.C. 20036. Filed 10/11/84. Legislative interest — ". . . Support enactment of S 648, to facilitate land exchange in South Carolina."

SOUTHERN CALIFORNIA RAPID TRANSIT DIS-TRICT, Los Angeles, Calif. Lobbyist — Palumbo & Cerrell, 11 Dupont Circle N.W., Washington, D.C. 20036. Filed 10/10/84. Legislative interest — "Mass transit appropriations bills, for (with amendment to increase)."

STATE OF IDAHO, DEPARTMENT OF EMPLOY-MENT, Boise, Idaho. Lobbyist — Chambers Associates Inc., 1411 K St. N.W., Washington, D.C. 20005. Filed 10/10/84. Legislative interest — "Senate and House Appropriations Bills, HR 6028."

TURLOCK IRRIGATION DISTRICT, Turlock, Calif. Lobbyist — Birch, Horton, Bittner, Pestinger & Anderson, 1140 Connecticut Ave. N.W., Washington, D.C. 20036. Filed 10/11/84. Legislative interest — "Continuing Resolution issues."

WASHINGTON METROPOLITAN AREA TRANSIT AUTHORITY, Washington, D.C. Lobbyist — Hogan & Hartson, 815 Connecticut Ave. N.W., Washington, D.C. 20006. Filed 10/12/84. Legislative interest — ". . . legislation amending The Longshoremen's and Harbor Workers' [Compensation] Act Amendments of 1984, Public Law No. 98-426."

WISCONSIN COUNTIES ASSOCIATION, Madison, Wis. Lobbyist — Ronald D. Waterman, 4802 Tabard Place, Annandale, Va. 22003. Filed 10/9/84. Legislative interest — Not specified.

Trade Associations

ALLIANCE OF AMERICAN INSURERS, Schaumburg, Ill. Lobbyist — David M. Farmer, Stephen W. Broadie, 1629 K St. N.W., Washington, D.C. 20006. Filed 10/10/84. Legislative interest — "All legislation affecting property and casualty insurance; Educational Assistance Tax Exemption (HR 2568); Legal Services Tax Exemption (HR 5361)."

AMERICAN ASSOCIATION OF PRESIDENTS OF INDEPENDENT COLLEGES AND UNIVERSITIES, Rexburg, Idaho. Lobbyist — Wilkinson, Barker, Knauer & Quinn, 1735 New York Ave. N.W., Washington, D.C. 20006. Filed 10/15/84. Legislative interest — ". . . S 2568/HR 5490, 'The Civil Rights Act of 1984'; undertake efforts to defeat passage. . . ."

AMERICAN COLLEGE OF NURSE-MIDWIVES, 1522 K St. N.W., Washington, D.C. 20005. Filed for self 10/16/84. Legislative interest — ". . . maternal and child health legislation, funding for nursing education, health care financing, social welfare and nutrition programs, and bills affecting the ability of professionals to practice . . . bill to amend title XVIII of the Social Security Act to provide reimbursement to nurse-midwives under Medicare and the Nurse Training Act." Lobbyist — Karen Ehrnman.

AMERCIAN DENTAL TRADE ASSOCIATION, Washington, D.C. Lobbyist — Jenner & Block, 21 Dupont Circle N.W., Washington, D.C. 20036. Filed 10/11/84. Legislative interest — Not specified.

AMERICAN FILM MARKETING ASSOCIATION, Los Angeles, Calif. Lobbyist — Jenner & Block, 21 Dupont Circle N.W., Washington, D.C. 20036. Filed 10/11/84. Legislative interest — Not specified.

AMERICAN FINANCIAL SERVICES ASSOCIA-TION, 1101 14th St. N.W., Washington, D.C. 20005. Filed for self 10/1/84. Legislative interest — ". . . legislation affecting the consumer credit industry including but not limited to the following:

financial institutions deregulation, S 2181, S 2134, S 1609; telecommunications legislation, S 1660, HR 4102." Lobbyist — Nancy A. Miller.

AMERICAN FREE TRADE ASSOCIATION INC., Miami, Fla. Lobbyist — Nixon, Hargrave, Devans & Doyle, 1090 Vermont Ave. N.W., Washington, D.C. 20005. Filed 10/9/84. Legislative interest — "Legislation affecting or potentially affecting parallel imports."

AMERICAN GRAPE GROWERS ALLIANCE FOR FAIR TRADE, Fresno, Calif. Lobbyist — Heron, Burchette, Ruckert & Rothwell, 1200 New Hampshire Ave. N.W., Washington, D.C. 20036. Filed 10/31/84. Legislative interest — "Amendments to Tariff Act of 1930 regarding standing of grape growers in ITC proceedings in HR 3398 - supported."

AMERICAN HEALTH CARE ASSOCIATION, 1200 15th St. N.W., Washington, D.C. 20005. Filed for self 10/9/84. Legislative interest — ". . . legislation related to long term care and the nursing home industry." Lobbyists — Paul R. Willging, William Hermelin, Gary Capistrant, Cheryl Beversdorf, Donna R. Barnako, Thomas Truax.

THE AMERICAN INSTITUTE OF ARCHITECTS, 1735 New York Ave. N.W., Washington, D.C. 20006. Filed for self 10/18/84. Legislative interest — Not specified. Lobbyists — James V. Siena, Mark A. Casso.

AMERICAN INTRA-OCULAR IMPLANT SOCIETY, Brentwood, Calif. Lobbyist — Jenner & Block, 21 Dupont Circle N.W., Washington, D.C. 20036. Filed 10/11/84. Legislative interest — Not specified.

AMERICAN NURSES' ASSOCIATION, 2420 Pershing Road, Kansas City, Mo. 64108. Filed for self 10/16/84. Legislative interest — "Legislation relating to nurses, nursing and health including but not limited to Nurse Training Act, Nurse Research, Community Health Grants, Medicare, Medicaid, Mental Health, Block Grants, Pro-Competitive Proposals, Appropriations and Budget." Lobbyist — Kathleen Michels, 1101 14th St. N.W., Washington, D.C. 20005.

AMERICAN PORTRAIT SOCIETY, Beverly Hills, Calif. Lobbyist — Jenner & Block, 21 Dupont Circle N.W., Washington, D.C. 20036. Filed 10/11/84. Legislative interest — Not specified.

AMERICAN SOCIETY OF ASSOCIATION EXECUTIVES, Washington, D.C. Lobbyist — Birch, Horton, Bittner, Pestinger and Anderson, 1140 Connecticut Ave. N.W., Washington, D.C. 20036. Filed 10/11/84. Legislative interest — "General tax legislation issues." Lobbyist — Jenner & Block, 21 Dupont Circle N.W., Washington, D.C. 20036. Legislative interest — ". . . legislative proposals affecting self-regulation in associations."

AMERICAL SOCIETY OF COMPOSERS, AUTHORS AND PUBLISHERS, New York, N.Y. Lobbyist — Palumbo & Cerrell, 11 Dupont Circle N.W., Washington, D.C. 20036. Filed 10/10/84. Legislative interest — "HR 3858, S 1734, legislation affecting music copyrights - against."

AMERICAN SUBCONTRACTORS ASSOCIATION, 1004 Duke St., Alexandria, Va. 22314. Filed for self 10/11/84. Legislative interest — ". . . HR 876, Small Business Contract Payment Procedures Act, support; S 1181, Construction Contracts Payment Procedures Act, support; S 1746, Freedom from Government Competition Act, support; HR 4759, Miller Act Amendments, support; HR 4843, S 2329, No-Fault Multiemployer Plan Termination Insurance Reform Act, support; Legislation to require bid listing on Federal construction contracts, support; Legislation to establish trust funds for payment on Federal construction projects, support." Lobbyist — Dorothy E. Stucke.

ARKANSAS ASSOCIATION OF BANK HOLDING COS., Boyle Building, Little Rock, Ark. 72201. Filed for self 10/11/84. Legislative interest — Not specified.

ASSOCIATED BUILDERS AND CONTRACTORS INC., 729 15th St. N.W., Washington, D.C. 20005. Filed for self 10/12/84. Legislative interest — ". . . Compressed Workweek, HR 277, S 267. . . Davis-Bacon Repeal/Reform, HR 87, HR 141, HR 148, HR 178, HR 284, HR 635, HR 692, HR 1174 . . . Jobs Bill, HR 1036 . . . Labor Extortion, S 462 . . . Minority Set-Asides, S 273 . . . MSHA Reform, HR 112, HR 144, HR 2073, S 980 . . . Regulatory

Reform, HR 220. . . ." Lobbyist — Steven W. Unglesbee.

ASSOCIATED GENERAL CONTRACTORS OF AMERICA, 1957 E St. N.W., Washington, D.C. 20006. Filed for self 10/2/84. Legislative interest — "Occupational Safety and Health issues affecting the construction industry." Lobbyist — Michael J. Pennington.

ASSOCIATION OF OPERATING ROOM NURSES, Denver, Colo. Lobbyist — Jenner & Block, 21 Dupont Circle N.W., Washington, D.C. 20036. Filed 10/11/84. Legislative interest — Not specified.

AUTO GLASS INDUSTRY COMMITTEE, Dallas, Texas. Lobbyist — Jenner & Block, 21 Dupont Circle N.W., Washington, D.C. 20036. Filed 10/11/84. Legislative interest — Not specified.

CHAMBER OF COMMERCE OF THE UNITED STATES, 1615 H St. N.W., Washington, D.C. 20062. Filed for self 10/18/84. Legislative interest — Not specified. Lobbyist — James A. Klein.

COMPUTER AND BUSINESS EQUIPMENT MANUFACTURERS ASSOCIATION, 311 First St. N.W., Washington, D.C. 20001. Filed for self 10/9/84. Legislative interest — Not specified. Lobbyists — Ted A. Heydinger, Gregory Kilgore, William A. Maxwell.

CONSUMERS UNITED FOR RAIL EQUITY, Washington, D.C. Lobbyist — Craft & Richards, 1050 Thomas Jefferson St. N.W., Washington, D.C. 20007. Filed 10/13/84. Legislative interest — "All legislation . . . relating to Staggers Rail Act Amendments."

DENTAL GOLD INSTITUTE, Boston, Mass. Lobbyist — Jenner & Block, 21 Dupont Circle N.W., Washington, D.C. 20036. Filed 10/11/84. Legislative interest — Not specified.

FAMILY-BACKED MORTGAGE ASSOCIATION INC., Oakland, Calif. Lobbyist — Thacher, Proffitt & Wood, 1140 Connecticut Ave. N.W., Washington, D.C. 20036. Filed 10/15/84. Legislative interest — ". . . S 1914, the Home Equity Conversion Act."

FIVE STATE RICE PRODUCERS LEGISLATIVE GROUP, Houston, Texas. Lobbyist — Bishop, Liberman, Cook, Purcell & Reynolds, 1200 17th St. N.W., Washington, D.C. 20036. Filed 10/12/84. (Former U.S. Rep. Graham B. Purcell, D-Texas, 1962-73, was listed as agent for this client.) Legislative interest — ". . . monitoring of drafting of 1984 Agriculture legislation. . . ."

FOOTWEAR INDUSTRIES OF AMERICA, Arlington, Va. Lobbyist — Collier, Shannon, Rill & Scott, 1055 Thomas Jefferson St. N.W., Washington, D.C. 20007. Filed 10/12/84. Legislative interest — ". . . international trade bills and all other legislation affecting general corporate organizations."

HAWAII CONSUMER FINANCE ASSOCIATION INC., Honolulu, Hawaii. Lobbyist — Cades, Schutte, Fleming & Wright, 1001 22nd St. N.W., Washington, D.C. 20037. Filed 10/11/84. Legislative interest — "Financial institution legislation."

INTERNATIONAL ASSOCIATION OF FIRE FIGHTERS, 1750 New York Ave. N.W., Washington, D.C. 20006. Filed for self 10/4/84. Legislative interest — "HR 622, (Fed) law officers & fire fighters death benefits; HR 1066, Social Security benefits minimum; HR 1175, Government pension plans, exemption from rules; HR 624, Public Safety Officers Death Benefits; HR 77, Retirement Income Tax Exemption; S 1163, Death Benefits for Fed. Fire Fighters; S 809, Fire prevention & control authorizations; S 1164, Death Benefits for medical conditions; S 640, Income Tax Exclusion, Employer Health Plan Contributions; S 135, Income Tax, Fringe Benefits Reg. Prohibition." Lobbyist — Thomas K. Reilly.

INTERNATIONAL FRANCHISE ASSOCIATION, 1025 Connecticut Ave. N.W., Washington, D.C. 20036. Filed for self 10/17/84. Legislative interest — Not specified. Lobbyist — Neil A. Simon.

JAPAN AUTOMOBILE TIRE MANUFACTURERS ASSOCIATION, Tokyo, Japan. Lobbyist — Tanaka, Walders & Ritger, 1919 Pennsylvania Ave. N.W., Washington, D.C. 20006. Filed 10/16/84. Legislative interest — ". . . proposals which may affect the importation and marketing of tires in the U.S."

NATIONAL CABLE TELEVISION ASSOCIATION, 1724 Massachusetts Ave. N.W., Washington, D.C. 20036. Filed for self 10/16/84. Legislative interest — "Amendments to the Communications Act of 1934 and other legislation affecting cable television generally." Lobbyist — Bertram W. Carp.

NATIONAL COTTON COUNCIL OF AMERICA, P.O. Box 12285, Memphis, Tenn. 38112. Filed for self 10/9/84. Legislative interest — ". . . favors such action on any legislation affecting the raw cotton industry as will promote the purposes for which the Council is organized." Lobbyist — A. John Maguire, 1030 15th St. N.W., Washington, D.C. 20005.

NATIONAL COUNCIL OF FARMER COOPERATIVES, 1800 Massachusetts Ave. N.W., Washington, D.C. 20036. Filed for self 10/26/84. Legislative interest — "None." Lobbyist — Leslie S. Mead.

NATIONAL FROZEN FOOD ASSOCIATION, Hershey, Pa. Lobbyist — John R. Purcell, 204 E St. N.E., Washington, D.C. 20002. Filed 10/15/84. Legislative interest — "National School Lunch and Child Nutrition Acts and Amendatory Legislation, Emergency Standby Petroleum Allocation Legislation, Highway Trust Fund, Social Security and Multiemployer Pension Plan Legislation."

NATIONAL PEST CONTROL ASSOCIATION, 8100 Oak St., Dunn Loring, Va. 22027. Filed for self 10/11/84. Legislative interest — "Federal Pesticide Legislation - Structural." Lobbyist — Harvey S. Gold.

NATIONAL SCHOOL TRANSPORTATION ASSOCIATION, Springfield, Va. Lobbyist — Palumbo & Cerrell, 11 Dupont Circle N.W., Washington, D.C. 20036. Filed 10/18/84. Legislative interest — "HR 4170, Tax Reform Act of 1984, for, with amendment; HR 5511 requiring seat belts on school buses, against."

NATIONAL TIRE DEALERS AND RETREADERS ASSOCIATION INC., 1250 I St. N.W., Washington, D.C. 20005. Filed for self 10/17/84. Legislative interest — ". . . particular interest in bills to amend regulations concerning tire identification and recordkeeping, the Internal Revenue Code provisions dealing with the excise tax on tires and tread rubber, the Motor Vehicle Safety Act, regulations promulgated under the Occupational Safety and Health Act, exemptions under the Fair Labor Standards Act, the Clean Air Act, the Resource Conservation and Recovery Act and the Hazardous Waste Control Act." Lobbyist — K. Wayne Malbon.

OUTDOOR ADVERTISING ASSOCIATION OF AMERICA, Washington, D.C. Lobbyist — Thompson, Gold & Liebengood, 1050 Connecticut Ave. N.W., Washington, D.C. 20036. Filed 10/11/84. Legislative interest — "Legislation concerning the highway bill."

PROCOMPETITIVE RAIL STEERING COMMITTEE, 1090 Vermont Ave. N.W., Washington, D.C. 20005. Filed for self 10/10/84. Legislative interest — "Legislation affecting railroad transportation." Lobbyist — James E. Bartley.

RETAIL TRADE ACTION COALITION, Washington, D.C. Lobbyist — Akin, Gump, Strauss, Hauer & Feld, 1333 New Hampshire Ave. N.W., Washington, D.C. 20036. Filed 10/10/84. Legislative interest — "Legislation affecting U.S. Trade, particularly with respect to textiles, apparel, and footwear, including HR 3398, the Tariff and Trade Act of 1984; HR 5823, H Res 172 and S Res 122, textile and apparel quotas; HR 5791 and S 2701, footwear quotas; S 2845, amendments to Section 201; HR 6023, GSP renewal; HR 5377, Israel free trade zone; and HR 5929, textile and apparel labeling."

SAVINGS BANKS ASSOCIATION OF MASSACHUSETTS, Boston, Mass. Lobbyist — Thacher, Proffitt & Wood, 1140 Connecticut Ave. N.W., Washington, D.C. 20036. Filed 10/15/84. Legislative interest — ". . . powers of federally-chartered savings banks . . . tax incentives for savings."

SCIENTIFIC APPARATUS MAKERS ASSOCIATION, 1101 16th St. N.W., Washington, D.C. 20036. Filed for self 10/11/84. Legislative interest — "Issues affecting makers of scientific apparatus, including tax policy, product liability, international trade, national health care policy. . . ." Lobbyist — James A. Kaitz.

TOBACCO INSTITUTE, Washington, D.C. Lobbyist — SMC International, 1825 I St. N.W., Washington, D.C. 20006.

Filed 10/16/84. Legislative interest — "Continuation of smoking rules after CAB Sunset: HR 5297, S 2796."

WATERBED MANUFACTURERS ASSOCIATION, Los Angeles, Calif. Lobbyist — Webster, Chamberlain & Bean, 1747 Pennsylvania Ave. N.W., Washington, D.C. 20006. Filed 10/9/84. Legislative interest — "Legislation affecting the waterbed industry, including HR 5469, concerning tariff on imported water mattresses and liners (in favor of increased tariff)."

Miscellaneous

AMERICAN SYMPHONY ORCHESTRA LEAGUE, 633 E St. N.W., Washington, D.C. 20004. Filed for self 10/9/84. Legislative interest — "Any legislation affecting America's symphony orchestra." Lobbyist — Donald E. Fraher.

BAYLOR UNIVERSITY MEDICAL CENTER, Dallas, Texas. Lobbyist — Winstead, McGuire, Sechrest & Minick, 1700 Mercantile Dallas Building, Dallas, Texas 75201. Filed 10/9/84. Legislative interest — "S 2910 - Grove City Reversal Act - Support; S 2568 - Civil Rights Act of 1984 - Support, if language is clarified to limit impact of bill to only overturn Grove City College case."

CALIFORNIA SPACE INSTITUTE, La Jolla, Calif. Lobbyist — Dutko and Associates, 412 First St. S.E., Washington, D.C. 20003. Filed 10/18/84. Legislative interest — "NASA authorization and appropriation bills."

COMMON CAUSE, 2030 M St. N.W., Washington, D.C. 20036. Filed for self 10/15/84. Legislative interest — ". . . open government, campaign finance reform, Federal Election Commission, lobby disclosure, government ethics, Senate confirmation process, extension of the Clean Air Act, court jurisdiction issues, congressional budget process, congressional reform, freedom of information, waste in government, merit selection of Federal judges and U.S. attorneys, regulatory reform, public participation in federal agency proceedings, Legal Services Corporation, civil rights, the Equal Rights Amendment, nuclear arms control, and military spending . . . supported legislation to reform congressional campaign financing, including creating a new 100 percent tax credit, PAC limits and response time on independent expenditures (HR 4428) . . . opposed production funds for the MX missile and supported a proposal by Senator Nunn to establish nuclear risk reduction centers in Washington and Moscow (S Res 239 and HR 408) . . . supported a moratorium on the testing of anti-satellite weapons against objects in space, a $407 million cut in the President's Strategic Defense Initiative program and two amendments to the FY 85 DoD Authorization bill offered in the Senate. One of the amendments called for the U.S. to continue its current policy of not undercutting the terms of existing arms control agreements and the other directed the President to seek immediate resumption of the U.S.-Soviet negotiations for a comprehensive test ban treaty . . . favored investigation by the House Foreign Affairs Committee of the President's possible violation of the War Powers Resolution of 1973 and opposed covert aid in Nicaragua . . . supported legislation intended to limit prepublication review requirements and polygraph examinations imposed on Federal employees (HR 4681) . . . worked for stronger lobby disclosure laws, opposed the nomination of Edwin Meese III as Attorney General and urged the Senate Ethics Committee to investigate possible conflict of interest violations by Senator Mark Hatfield . . . urged the House Energy and Commerce Committee and Senate Labor Committee to investigate the process by which the FDA approved aspartame . . . supported legislation that would limit the value of tax treatment for luxury cars and maintain a one-year hold period on capital gains . . . favored legislation (S 2468) to broaden interpretation of the Civil Rights Act in response to a Supreme Court decision regarding Grove City College and the 1985 appropriations bill for the Legal Services Corporation." Lobbyist — Carole Sonnenfeld.

CONCERNED WOMEN FOR AMERICA, 122 C St. N.W., Washington, D.C. 20001. Filed for self 10/23/84. Legislative interest — "Issues affecting the family and moral values including for school prayer and equal access and against ERA and abortion." Lobbyist — Shannon O'Chester.

THE CONSERVATIVE ALLIANCE, 1001 Prince St., Alexandria, Va. 22314. Filed for self 10/17/84. Legislative interest — "Foreign affairs, national security, defense, human rights, and all other legislative issues pertaining to the well-being and the preservation of freedom in the U.S. and around the world." Lobbyist — Tamara S. Davis.

DAYLIGHT SAVING TIME COALITION, Washington, D.C. Lobbyist — Bracy Williams & Co., 1000 Connecticut Ave. N.W., Washington, D.C. 20036. Filed 10/17/84. Legislative interest — "Advocate the extension of daylight saving time. HR 1398 (for)."

FEDERATION FOR AMERICAN AFGHAN ACTION, 236 Massachusetts Ave. N.E., Washington, D.C. 20002. Lobbyist — Donald C. Evans Jr., 214 Massachusetts Ave. N.E., Washington, D.C. 20002. Filed 10/12/84. Legislative interest — "S Con Res 74/H Con Res 237."

JAPANESE AMERICAN CITIZENS LEAGUE, 1765 Sutter St., San Francisco, Calif. 94115. Filed for self 10/31/84. Legislative interest — "... S 2116 (To Accept and Implement the Recommendations of the CWRIC) and HR 4110 (The Civil Liberties Act of 1983)." Lobbyist — George Timothy Gojio, 1730 Rhode Island Ave. N.W., Washington, D.C. 20036.

ALBERT AND DIANE KANEB, Weston, Mass. Lobbyist — Capitol Associates Inc., 1156 15th St. N.W., Washington, D.C. 20005. Filed 10/16/84. Legislative interest — "For legislation affecting health research."

NATIONAL ASSOCIATION OF ARAB AMERICANS, 2033 M St. N.W., Washington, D.C. 20036. Filed for self 10/12/84. Legislative interest — "Middle East related legislation; FY 1985 Foreign Aid Authorization (S 2582, HR 5119) - against; FY 1985 Foreign Aid Appropriations ... against; Strategic Development Aid (HR 5424) - against; Free Trade Area Legislation (S 2746, HR 5377) - against; U.S. Embassy in Jerusalem (S 2031, HR 4788) - against; Export Administration Act (S 979, HR 3231) - against." Lobbyists — Omar Sbitani, Tanya A. Rahall, George J. Karam, C. Sargent Carleton.

NATIONAL COMMITTEE TO PRESERVE SOCIAL SECURITY AND MEDICARE, 1300 19th St. N.W., Washington, D.C. 20036. Filed for self 10/13/84. Legislative interest — "... changes in the Social Security Act; Medicare amendment to HR 4170." Lobbyist — William J. Lessard Jr.

SIERRA CLUB, 530 Bush St., San Francisco, Calif. 94108. Filed for self 10/15/84. Legislative interest — "Environmental protection; Wyoming Wilderness Bill/against; Clean Water Act/for; Superfund/for; Interior Appropriation." Lobbyist — Larry Mehlhaff, 23 N. Scott, Sheriden, Wyo. 82801. ∎

PRESIDENTIAL MESSAGES

CQ

Reagan Message on Soviet Treaty Violations

Following is the White House text of the Jan. 23 message to Congress transmitting President Reagan's report on Soviet noncompliance with arms control agreements.

TO THE CONGRESS OF
THE UNITED STATES:

If the concept of arms control is to have meaning and credibility as a contribution to global or regional stability, it is essential that all parties to agreements comply with them. Because I seek genuine arms control, I am committed to ensuring that existing agreements are observed. In 1982 increasing concerns about Soviet noncompliance with arms control agreements led me to establish a senior group within the Administration to examine verification and compliance issues. For its part the Congress, in the FY 1984 Arms Control and Disarmament Act, asked me to report to it on compliance. I am herewith enclosing a Report to the Congress on Soviet Noncompliance with Arms Control Agreements.

After a careful review of many months, and numerous diplomatic exchanges with the Soviet Union, the Administration has determined that with regard to seven initial issues analyzed, violations and probable violations have occurred with respect to a number of Soviet legal obligations and political commitments in the arms control field.

The United States Government has determined that the Soviet Union is violating the Geneva Protocol on Chemical Weapons, the Biological Weapons Convention, the Helsinki Final Act, and two provisions of SALT II: telemetry encryption and a rule concerning ICBM modernization. In addition, we have determined that the Soviet Union has almost certainly violated the ABM Treaty, probably violated the SALT II limit on new types, probably violated the SS-16 deployment prohibition of SALT II, and is likely to have violated the nuclear testing yield limit of the Threshold Test Ban Treaty.

Soviet noncompliance is a serious matter. It calls into question important security benefits from arms control, and could create new security risks. It undermines the confidence essential to an effective arms control process in the future. It increases doubts about the reliability of the U.S.S.R. as a negotiating partner, and thus damages the chances for establishing a more constructive U.S.-Soviet relationship.

The United States will continue to press its compliance concerns with the Soviet Union through diplomatic channels, and insist upon explanations, clarifications, and corrective actions. At the same time, the United States is continuing to carry out its own obligations and commitments under relevant agreements. For the future, the United States is seeking to negotiate new arms control agreements that reduce the risk of war, enhance the security of the

United States and its Allies, and contain effective verification and compliance provisions.

We should recognize, however, that ensuring compliance with arms control agreements remains a serious problem. Better verification and compliance provisions and better treaty drafting will help, and we are working toward this in ongoing negotiations. It is fundamentally important, however, that the Soviets take a constructive attitude toward compliance.

The Executive and Legislative branches of our government have long had a shared interest in supporting the arms control process.

Finding effective ways to ensure compliance is central to that process. I look forward to continued close cooperation with the Congress as we seek to move forward in negotiating genuine and enduring arms control agreements.

Sincerely,
/s/ Ronald Reagan

The Fact Sheet provided to the Congress with the classified report is quoted below:

Fact Sheet

The President's Report to the Congress on Soviet Noncompliance with Arms Control Agreements

Commitment to genuine arms control requires that all parties comply with agreements. Over the last several years the U.S.S.R. has taken a number of actions that have prompted renewed concern about an expanding pattern of Soviet violations or possible violations of arms control agreements. Because of the critical importance of compliance with arms control agreements, about one year ago the President established an interagency Arms Control Verification Committee, chaired by his Assistant for National Security Affairs, to address verification and compliance issues. In addition, many members of Congress expressed their serious concerns, and the Congress mandated in the FY 84 Arms Control and Disarmament Act Authorization that "The President shall prepare and transmit to the Congress a report of the compliance or noncompliance of the Soviet Union with existing arms control agreements to which the Soviet Union is a Party."

The President's Report to Congress covers seven different matters of serious concern regarding Soviet compliance: chemical, biological, and toxin weapons, the notification of military exercises, a large new Soviet radar being deployed in the Soviet interior, encryption of data needed to verify arms control provisions,

the testing of a second new intercontinental ballistic missile (ICBM), the deployment status of an existing Soviet ICBM, and the yields of underground nuclear tests. Additional issues of concern are under active study.

Soviet violations of arms control agreements could create new security risks. Such violations deprive us of the security benefits of arms control directly because of the military consequences of known violations, and indirectly by inducing suspicion about the existence of undetected violations that might have additional military consequences.

We have discussed with the Soviets all of the activities covered in the report, but the Soviets have not been willing to meet our basic concerns which we raised in the Standing Consultative Commission in Geneva and in several diplomatic demarches. Nor have they met our requests to cease these activities. We will continue to pursue these issues.

The Findings

The Report examines the evidence concerning Soviet compliance with: the 1972 Biological Weapons Convention (BWC) and the 1925 Geneva Protocol and customary international law, the 1975 Helsinki Final Act, the 1972 ABM Treaty, the unratified SALT II Treaty, and the unratified Threshold Test Ban Treaty (TTBT) signed in 1974. Preparation of the Report entailed a comprehensive review of the legal obligations, political commitments under existing arms control agreements, and documented interpretations of specific obligations, analyses of all the evidence available on applicable Soviet actions, and a review of the diplomatic exchanges on compliance issues between the U.S. and the Soviet Union.

The findings for the seven issues covered in the Report, as reviewed in terms of the agreements involved, are as follows:

1. Chemical, Biological, and Toxin Weapons

● **Treaty Status:** The 1972 Biological and Toxin Weapons Convention (the BWC) and the 1925 Geneva Protocol are multilateral treaties to which both the U.S. and U.S.S.R. are parties. Soviet actions not in accord with these treaties and customary international law relating to the 1925 Geneva Protocol are violations of the legal obligations.

● **Obligations:** The BWC bans the development, production, stockpiling or possession, and transfer of: microbial or other biological agents or toxins except for a small quantity for prophylactic, protective or other peaceful purposes. It also bans weapons, equipment and means of delivery of agents or toxins. The 1925 Geneva Protocol and related rules of customary international law prohibit the first use in war of asphyxiating, poisonous or other gases and of all analogous liquids, materials or devices; and prohibits use of bacteriological methods of warfare.

● **Issues:** The study addressed whether the Soviets are in violation of provisions that ban the development, production, transfer, possession and use of biological and toxin weapons.

● **Finding:** The Soviets, by maintaining an offensive biological warfare program and capabilities and through their involvement in the production, transfer and use of toxins and other lethal chemical warfare agents that have been used in Laos, Kampuchea and Afghanistan, have repeatedly violated their legal obligations under the BWC and customary international law as codified in the 1925 Geneva Protocol.

2. Helsinki Final Act - Notification of Military Exercises

● **Legal Status:** The Final Act of the Conference on Security and Cooperation in Europe was signed in Helsinki in 1975. This document represents a political commitment and was signed by the United States and the Soviet Union, along with many other states. Soviet actions not in accord with that document are violations of their political commitment.

● **Obligation:** All signatory states of the Helsinki Final Act are committed to give prior notification of, and other details concerning, major military maneuvers, defined as those involving more than 25,000 ground troops.

● **Issues:** The study examined whether notification of the Soviet military exercise Zapad-81, which occurred on September 4-12, 1981, was inadequate and therefore a violation of their political commitment.

● **Finding:** With respect to the Helsinki Final Act, the U.S.S.R. by its inadequate notification of the Zapad-81 military exercise, violated its political commitment under this Act to observe the Confidence-Building Measure requiring appropriate prior notification of certain military exercises.

3. ABM Treaty - Krasnoyarsk Radar

● **Treaty Status:** The 1972 ABM Treaty and its subsequent Protocol ban deployment of ABM systems except that each party can deploy one ABM system around the national capital or at a single ICBM deployment area. The ABM Treaty is in force and is of indefinite duration. Soviet actions not in accord with the ABM Treaty are therefore a violation of a legal obligation.

● **Obligation:** In an effort to preclude a territorial ABM defense, the Treaty limited the deployment of ballistic missile early warning radars, including large phased-array radars used for that purpose, to locations along the national periphery of each party and required that they be oriented outward. The Treaty permits deployment (without regard to location or orientation) of large phased-array radars for purposes of tracking objects in outer space or for use as national technical means of

verification of compliance with arms control agreements.

● **Issue:** The study examined the evidence on whether the Soviet deployment of a large phased-array radar near Krasnoyarsk in central Siberia is in violation of the legal obligation to limit the location and orientation of such radars.

● **Finding:** The new radar under construction at Krasnoyarsk almost certainly constitutes a violation of legal obligations under the Anti-Ballistic Missile Treaty of 1972 in that in its associated siting, orientation, and capability, it is prohibited by this Treaty.

SALT II

● **Treaty Status:** SALT II was signed in June 1979. It has not been ratified. In 1981 the United States made clear its intention not to ratify the Treaty. Prior to 1981 both nations were obligated under international law not to take actions which would "defeat the object and purpose" of the signed but unratified Treaty; such Soviet actions before 1981 are violations of legal obligations. Since 1981 the U.S. has observed a political commitment to refrain from actions that undercut SALT II as long as the Soviet Union does likewise. The Soviets have told us they would abide by these provisions also. Soviet actions contrary to SALT II after 1981 are therefore violations of their political commitment.

Three SALT II concerns are addressed: encryption, SS-X-25, and SS-16.

4. Encryption - Impeding Verification

● **Obligation:** The provisions of SALT II ban deliberate concealment measures that impede verification by national technical means. The agreement permits each party to use various methods of transmitting telemetric information during testing, including encryption, but bans deliberate denial of telemetry, such as through encryption, whenever such denial impedes verification.

● **Issue:** The study examined the evidence whether the Soviets have engaged in encryption of missile test telemetry (radio signals) so as to impede verification.

● **Finding:** Soviet encryption practices constitute a violation of a legal obligation prior to 1981 and a violation of their political commitment subsequent to 1981. The nature and extent of encryption of telemetry on new ballistic missiles is an example of deliberate impeding of verification of compliance in violation of this Soviet political commitment.

5. SS-X-25 - 2nd New Type, RV Weight to Throw-weight Ratio, Encryption

● **Obligation:** In an attempt to constrain the modernization and the proliferation of new, more capable types of ICBMs, the provisions of SALT II permit each side to "flight test and deploy" just one new type of "light" ICBM. A new type is defined as one that differs from an existing type by more than 5 percent in length, largest diameter, launch-weight and throw-weight or

differs in number of stages or propellant type. In addition, it was agreed that no single reentry vehicle ICBM of an existing type with a post-boost vehicle would be flight-tested or deployed whose reentry vehicle weight is less than 50 percent of the throw-weight of that ICBM. This latter provision was intended to prohibit the possibility that single warhead ICBMs could quickly be converted to MIRVed systems.

● **Issue:** The study examined the evidence: whether the Soviets have tested a second new type of ICBM (the SS-X-25) which is prohibited (the Soviets have declared the SS-X-24 to be their allowed one new type ICBM); whether the reentry vehicle (RV) on that missile, if it is not a new type, is in compliance with the provision that for existing types of single RV missiles, the weight of the RV be equal to at least 50 percent of total throw-weight; and whether encryption of its tests impedes verification.

● **Finding:** While the evidence is somewhat ambiguous, the SS-X-25 is a probable violation of the Soviets' political commitment to observe the SALT II provision limiting each party to one new type of ICBM. Furthermore, even if we were to accept the Soviet argument that the SS-X-25 is not a prohibited new type of ICBM, based on the one test for which data are available, it would be a violation of their political commitment to observe the SALT II provision which prohibits (for existing types of single reentry vehicle ICBMs) the testing of such an ICBM with a reentry vehicle whose weight is less than 50 percent of the throw-weight of that ICBM. Encryption on this missile is illustrative of the impeding of verification problem cited earlier.

6. SS-16 ICBM - Banned Deployment

● **Obligation:** The Soviet Union agreed in SALT II not to produce, test or deploy ICBMs of the SS-16 type and, in particular, not to produce the SS-16 third stage, the reentry vehicle of that missile.

● **Issue:** The study examined the evidence whether the Soviets have deployed the SS-16 ICBM in spite of the ban on its deployment.

● **Finding:** While the evidence is somewhat ambiguous and we cannot reach a definitive conclusion, the available evidence indicates that the activities at Plesetsk are a probable violation of their legal obligation not to defeat the object and purpose of SALT II prior to 1981 during the period when the Treaty was pending ratification, and a probable violation of a political commitment subsequent to 1981.

7. TTBT - 150 kt Test Limit

● **Treaty Status:** The Threshold Test Ban Treaty was signed in 1974. The Treaty has not been ratified but neither Party has indicated an intention not to ratify. Therefore, both Parties are subject to the obligation under international law to refrain from acts which would "defeat the object and purpose" of the TTBT. Soviet actions that would defeat the object and purpose of the TTBT are therefore violations of their obligation. The U.S. is seeking to negotiate improved verification measures for the Treaty. Both Parties have each separately stated they would observe the 150 kt threshold of the TTBT.

● **Obligation:** The Treaty prohibits any underground nuclear weapon test having a yield exceeding 150 kilotons at any place under the jurisdiction or control of the Parties, beginning March 31, 1976. In view of the technical uncertainties associated with predicting the precise yield of nuclear weapons tests, the sides agreed that one or two slight unintended breaches per year would not be considered a violation.

● **Issue:** The study examined whether the Soviets have conducted nuclear tests in excess of 150 kilotons.

● **Finding:** While the available evidence is ambiguous, in view of ambiguities in the pattern of Soviet testing and in view of verification uncertainties, and we have been unable to reach a definitive conclusion, this evidence indicates that Soviet nu-

clear testing activities for a number of tests constitute a likely violation of legal obligations under the TTBT.

Conclusions

The President has said that the U.S. will continue to press compliance issues with the Soviets through confidential diplomatic channels, and to insist upon explanations, clarifications, and corrective actions. At the same time we are continuing to carry out our obligations and commitments under relevant agreements. We should recognize, however, that ensuring compliance with arms control agreements remains a serious problem. Improved verification and compliance provisions and better treaty drafting will help, and we are working toward this in ongoing negotiations. It is fundamentally important, however, that the Soviets take a constructive attitude toward compliance. ∎

State of the Union Address

Following is the Congressional Record *text of President Reagan's State of the Union address to a joint session of Congress Jan. 25.*

The PRESIDENT. Mr. Speaker, Mr. President, distinguished Members of the Congress, honored guests and fellow citizens. Once again, in keeping with time-honored tradition, I have come to report to you on the state of the Union. I am pleased to report that America is much improved, and there is good reason to believe that improvement will continue through the days to come.

You and I have had some honest and open differences in the year past. But they did not keep us from joining hands in bipartisan cooperation to stop a long decline that has drained this Nation's spirit and eroded its health. There is renewed energy and optimism throughout the land. America is back — standing tall, looking to the eighties with courage, confidence, and hope.

The problems we are overcoming are not the heritage of one person, party, or even one generation. It is just the tendency of government to grow, for practices and programs to become the nearest thing to eternal life we will ever see on this Earth. And there is always that well-intentioned chorus of voices saying, "with a little more power and a little more money, we could do so much for the people." For a time we forgot the American dream is not one of making Government bigger; it is keeping faith with the mighty spirit of free people under God.

The Decade of the '80s

As we came to the decade of the eighties we faced the worst crisis in our postwar

history. The seventies were years of rising problems and falling confidence. There was a feeling Government had grown beyond the consent of the governed. Families felt helpless in the face of mounting inflation and the indignity of taxes that reduced reward for hard work, thrift, and risk-taking. All this was overlaid by an ever-growing web of rules and regulations.

On the international scene, we had an uncomfortable feeling that we had lost the respect of friend and foe. Some questioned whether we had the will to defend peace and freedom.

But America is too great for small dreams. There was a hunger in the land for a spiritual revival, if you will, a crusade for renewal. The American people said: Let us look to the future with confidence, both at home and abroad. Let us give freedom a chance.

Americans were ready to make a new beginning, and together we have done it. We are confronting our problems one by one. Hope is alive tonight for millions of young families and senior citizens set free from unfair tax increases and crushing inflation. Inflation has been beaten down from 12.4 to 3.2 percent, and that is a great victory for all the people. The prime rate has been cut almost in half and we must work together to bring it down even more.

Together, we passed the first across-the-board tax reduction for everyone since the Kennedy tax cuts. Next year, tax rates will be indexed so inflation cannot push people into higher brackets when they get cost-of-living pay raises. Government must never again use inflation to profit at the people's expense.

Today, a working family earning $25,000, has $1,100 more in purchasing power than if tax and inflation rates were still at the 1980 levels. Real after-tax in-

come increased 5 percent last year. And economic deregulation of key industries like transportation has offered more choices to consumers and new chances for entrepreneurs, and protecting the safety. Tonight, we can report and be proud of one of the best recoveries in decades. Send away the handwringers and the doubting Thomases. Hope is reborn for couples dreaming of owning homes, for risk-takers with vision to create tomorrow's opportunities.

The spirit of enterprise is sparked by the sunrise industries of high-tech, and by small business people with big ideas, people like Barbara Proctor, who rose from a ghetto to build a multimillion-dollar advertising agency in Chicago; and Carlos Perez, a Cuban refugee, who turned $27 and a dream into a successful importing business in Coral Gables, Fla.

People like these are heroes for the eighties. They helped 4 million Americans find jobs in 1983. More people are drawing paychecks tonight than ever before. And Congress helps — or progress helps everyone. Well, Congress does, too. In 1983, women filled 73 percent of all the new jobs in managerial, professional, and technical fields.

But we know that many of our fellow countrymen are still out of work, wondering what will come of their hopes and dreams. Can we love America and not reach out to tell them: You are not forgotten; we will not rest until each of you can reach as high as your God-given talents will take you.

The heart of America is strong; it is good and true. The cynics were wrong — America never was a sick society. We are seeing rededication to bedrock values of faith, family, work, neighborhood, peace and freedom — values that help bring us together as one people, from the youngest child to the most senior citizen.

The Congress deserves America's thanks for helping us restore pride and credibility to our military. And I hope that you are as proud as I am of the young men and women in uniform who have volunteered to man the ramparts in defense of freedom and whose dedication, valor, and skill increases so much our chance of living in a world at peace.

People everywhere hunger for peace and a better life. The tide of the future is a freedom tide, and our struggle for democracy cannot and will not be denied. This Nation champions peace that enshrines liberty, democratic rights, and dignity for every individual. America's new strength, confidence, and purpose are carrying hope and opportunity far from our shores. A world economic recovery is underway. It began here.

Four Goals to Keep America Free

We have journeyed far. But we have much farther to go. Franklin Roosevelt told us 50 years ago this month: "Civilization cannot go back; civilization must not stand still. We have undertaken new methods. It is our task to perfect, to improve, to alter when necessary, but in all cases to go forward."

It is time to move forward again, time for America to take freedom's next step. Let us unite tonight behind four great goals to keep America free, secure, and at peace in the eighties. Together:

We can ensure steady economic growth.

We can develop America's next frontier.

We can strengthen our traditional values.

And we can build a meaningful peace to protect our loved ones and this shining star of faith that has guided millions from tyranny to the safe harbor of freedom, progress, and hope.

Federal Deficits

Doing these things will open wider the gates of opportunity and provide greater security for all, with no barriers of bigotry or discrimination. The key to a dynamic decade is vigorous economic growth, our first great goal. We might well begin with common sense in Federal budgeting: Government spending no more than Government takes in.

We must bring Federal deficits down, but how we do that makes all the difference. We can begin by limiting the size and scope of Government. Under the leadership of Vice President Bush, we have reduced the growth of Federal regulations by more than 25 percent, and cut well over 300 million hours of Government-required paperwork each year. This will save the public more than $150 billion over the next 10 years.

The Grace Commission has given us some 2,500 recommendations for reducing wasteful spending, and they are being examined throughout the administration. Federal spending growth has been cut from 17.4 percent in 1980 to less than half of that today. And we have already achieved over $300 billion in budget savings for the period of 1982 to 1986. But that is only a little more than half of what we sought. Government is still spending too large a percentage of the total economy.

Now, some insist that any further budget savings must be obtained by reducing the portion spent on defense. This ignores the fact that national defense is solely the responsibility of the Federal Government. Indeed, it is its prime responsibility. And yet defense spending is less than a third of the total budget. During the years of President Kennedy, and in the years before that, defense was almost half the total budget. Then came several years in which our military capability was allowed to deteriorate to a very dangerous degree. We are just now restoring, through the essential modernization of our conventional and strategic forces, our capability to meet our present and future security needs. We dare not shirk our responsibility to keep America free, secure, and at peace.

The last decade saw domestic spending surge literally out of control. But the basis for such spending had been laid in previous years. A pattern of overspending has been in place for half a century. As the national debt grew, we were told not to worry, that we owed it to ourselves.

Now we know the deficits are a cause for worry. But there is a difference of opinion as to whether taxes should be increased, spending cut, or some of both. Fear is expressed that Government borrowing to fund the deficit could inhibit the economic recovery by taking capital needed for business and industrial expansion. I think that debate is missing an important point. Whether government borrows or increases taxes, it will be taking the same amount of money from the private sector and, either way, that is too much. Simple fairness dictates that Government must not raise taxes on families struggling to pay their bills. The root of the problem is that Government's share is more than we can afford if we are to have a sound economy.

We must bring down the deficits to ensure continued economic growth. In the budget that I will submit on February 1, I will recommend measures that will reduce the deficit over the next 5 years. Many of these will be unfinished business from last year's budget. Some could be enacted quickly if we could join in a serious effort to address this problem. I spoke today with Speaker of the House O'Neill, Senate Majority Leader Baker, Senate Minority Leader Byrd and House Minority Leader Michel. I asked them if they would designate congressional representatives to meet with representatives of the administration to try to reach prompt agreement on a bipartisan deficit reduction plan. I know it will take a long hard struggle to agree on a full-scale plan. So what I have proposed is that we first see if we can agree on a downpayment.

Now, I believe there is basis for such an agreement, one that could reduce the deficits by about $100 billion over the next 3 years. We could focus on some of the less contentious spending cuts that are still pending before the Congress. These could be combined with measures to close certain tax loopholes, measures that the Treasury Department has previously said to be worthy of support. In addition, we could examine the possibility of achieving further outlay savings based on the work of the Grace Commission.

If the congressional leadership is willing, my representatives will be prepared to meet with theirs at the earliest possible time. I would hope the leadership might agree on an expedited timetable in which to develop and enact that downpayment.

But a downpayment alone is not enough to break us out of the deficit problem. It could help us start on the right path. Yet we must do more. So I propose that we begin exploring how together we can make structural reforms to curb the built-in growth of spending.

Budgeting Process

I also propose improvements in the budgeting process. Some 43 of our 50 states grant their Governors the right to veto individual items in appropriation bills without having to veto the entire bill. California is one of those 43 states. As Governor, I found this "line-item veto" was a powerful tool against wasteful or extravagant spending. It works in 43 states. Let us put it to work in Washington for all the people.

It would be most effective if done by constitutional amendment. The majority of Americans approve of such an amendment, just as they and I approve of an amendment mandating a balanced federal budget. Many states also have this protection in their constitutions.

To talk of meeting the present situation by increasing taxes is a Band-Aid solution which does nothing to cure an illness that has been coming on for half a century, to say nothing of the fact that it poses a real threat to economic recovery. Let us remember that a substantial amount of income tax is presently owed and not paid by people in the underground economy. It would be immoral to make those who are paying taxes pay more to compensate for those who are not paying their share.

Simplifying the Tax Code

There is a better way: Let us go forward with an historic reform for fairness, simplicity and incentives for growth. I am asking Secretary Don Regan for a plan for action to simplify the entire tax code so all taxpayers, big and small, are treated more fairly. And I believe such a plan could result in that "underground economy" being brought into the sunlight of honest tax compliance; and it could make the tax base broader so personal tax rates could come down, not go up. I have asked that specific recommendations, consistent with those objectives, be presented to me by December 1984. [Laughter.]

Space: The Next Frontier

Our second great goal is to build on America's pioneer spirit — I said something funny? I said this is America's next frontier, and that is to develop that frontier. A sparkling economy spurs initiative and ingenuity to create sunrise industries and make older ones more competitive.

Nowhere is this more important than our next frontier: Space. Nowhere do we so effectively demonstrate our technological leadership and ability to make life better on Earth. The Space Age is barely a quarter of a century old, but already we have pushed civilization forward with our advances in science and technology. Opportunities and jobs will multiply as we cross new thresholds of knowledge and reach deeper into the unknown.

Our progress in space, taking giant steps for all mankind, is a tribute to American teamwork and excellence. Our finest minds in government, industry, and academia have all pulled together, and we can be proud to say: We are first, we are the best, and we are so because we are free.

America has always been greatest when we dared to be great. We can reach for greatness again. We can follow our dreams to distant stars, living and working in space for peaceful, economic, and scientific gain. Tonight, I am directing NASA to develop a permanently manned space station and to do it within a decade.

A space station will permit quantum leaps in our research in science, communications, in metals and in lifesaving medicines which can be manufactured only in space. We want our friends to help us meet these challenges and share in their benefits. NASA will invite other countries to participate so we can strengthen peace, build prosperity, and expand freedom for all who share our goals.

Just as the oceans opened up a new world for clipper ships and Yankee traders, space holds enormous potential for commerce today. The market for space transportation could surpass our capacity to develop it. Companies interested in putting payloads into space must have ready access to private-sector launch services. The Department of Transportation will help an expendable launch services industry to get off the ground. We will soon implement a number of executive initiatives, develop proposals to ease regulatory constraints, and, with NASA's help, promote private-sector investment in space.

The Environment

As we develop the frontier of space, let us remember our responsibility to preserve our older resources here on Earth. Preservation of our environment is not a liberal or conservative challenge. It is commonsense.

Though this is a time of budget constraints, I have requested for EPA one of the largest percentage budget increases of any agency. We will begin the long, necessary effort to clean up a productive, recreational area and a special national resource — the Chesapeake Bay.

To reduce the threat posed by abandoned hazardous waste dumps, EPA will spend $410 million, and I will request a supplemental increase of $50 million; and because the Superfund law expires in 1985, I have asked Bill Ruckelshaus to develop a proposal for its extension so there will be additional time to complete this important task.

On the question of acid rain, which concerns people in many areas of the United States and Canada, I am proposing a research program that doubles our current funding. And we will take additional action to restore our lakes and develop new technology to reduce pollution that causes acid rain.

We have greatly improved the conditions of our national resources. We will ask the Congress for $157 million beginning in 1985 to acquire new park and conservation lands. The Department of the Interior will encourage careful, selective exploration and production of our vital resources in an Exclusive Economic Zone within the 200-mile limit off our coasts — but with strict adherence to environmental laws and with fuller state and public participation.

Traditional Values

But our most precious resources, our greatest hope for the future, are the minds and hearts of our people, especially our children. We can help them build tomorrow by strengthening our community of shared values. This must be our third great goal. For us, faith, work, family, neighborhood, freedom and peace are not just words. They are expressions of what America means, definitions of what makes us a good and loving people.

Education

Families stand at the center of our society. And every family has a personal stake in promoting excellence in education. Excellence does not begin in Washington. A 600-percent increase in Federal spending on education between 1960 and 1980 was accompanied by a steady decline in Scholastic Aptitude Test scores. Excellence must begin in our homes and neighborhood schools, where it is the responsibility of every parent and teacher and the right of every child.

Our children come first. And that is why I established a bipartisan National Commission on Excellence in Education, to help us chart a commonsense course for better education. Already, communities are implementing the Commission's recommendations. Schools are reporting progress in math and reading skills. But we must do more to restore discipline to schools; and we must encourage the teaching of new basics, reward teachers of merit, enforce tougher standards, and put our parents back in charge.

I will continue to press for tuition tax credits to expand opportunities for families, and to soften the double payment for those paying public school taxes and private school tuition. Our proposal would target assistance to low- and middle-income families. Just as more incentives are needed within our schools, greater competition is needed among our schools. Without standards and competition there can be no champions, no records broken, no excellence — in education or any other walk of life.

Prayer in School

And while I am on this subject, each day, your Members observe a 200-year-old tradition meant to signify America is one Nation under God. I must ask: If you can begin your day with a member of the clergy standing right here leading you in prayer, then why cannot freedom to acknowledge God be enjoyed again by children in every schoolroom across this land?

America was founded by people who believed that God was their rock of safety. He is ours. I recognize we must be cautious in claiming that God is on our side. But I think it is all right to keep asking if we are on His side.

Abortion

During our first 3 years, we have joined bipartisan efforts to restore protection of the law to unborn children. Now, I know this issue is very controversial. But unless and until it can be proven that an unborn child is not a living human being, can we justify assuming without proof that it is not? No one has yet offered such proof. Indeed, all the evidence is to the contrary. We should rise above bitterness and reproach. And if Americans could come together in a spirit of understanding and helping, then we could find positive solutions to the tragedy of abortion.

Crime

Economic recovery, better education, rededication to values all show the spirit or renewal gaining the upper hand. And all will improve family life in the 80's. But families need more. They need assurance that they and their loved ones can walk the streets of America without being afraid. Parents need to know their children will not be victims of child pornography and abduction. This year we will intensify our drive against these and other horrible crimes like sexual abuse and family violence. Already, our efforts to crack down on career criminals, organized crime, drug pushers, and to enforce tougher sentences and paroles are having effect. In 1982, the crime rate dropped by 4.3 percent, the biggest decline since 1972. Protecting victims is just as important as safeguarding the rights of defendants.

Creating Opportunities

Opportunities for all Americans will increase if we move forward on fair housing, and work to ensure women's rights, provide for equitable treatment in pension benefits and Individual Retirement Accounts, facilitate child care, and enforce delinquent parent support payments.

It is not just the home but the workplace and community that sustain our values and shape our future. So I ask your help in assisting more communities to break the bondage of dependency. Help us to free enterprise by permitting debate and voting "yes" on our proposal for enterprise zones in America. This has been before you for 2 years. Its passage can help high-unemployment areas by creating jobs and restoring neighborhoods.

A society bursting with opportunities, reaching for its future with confidence, sustained by faith, fair play, and a conviction that good and courageous people will flourish when they are free — these are the secrets of a strong and prosperous America, at peace with itself and the world.

Lasting and Meaningful Peace

A lasting and meaningful peace is our fourth great goal. It is our highest aspiration. And our record is clear: Americans resort to force only when we must. We have never been aggressors. We have always struggled to defend freedom and democracy.

We have no territorial ambitions. We occupy no countries. We build no walls to lock people in. Americans build the future. And our vision of a better life for farmers, merchants, and working people, from the Americas to Asia, begins with a simple premise: The future is best decided by ballots, not bullets.

Governments which rest upon the consent of the governed do not wage war on their neighbors. Only when people are given a personal stake in deciding their own destiny and benefitting from their own risks do they create societies that are prosperous, progressive, and free. Tonight, it is democracies that offer hope by feeding the hungry, prolonging life, and eliminating drudgery.

When it comes to keeping America strong, free and at peace, there should be no Republicans or Democrats, just patriotic Americans. We can decide the tough issues not by who is right, but by what is right.

Together, we can continue to advance our agenda for peace. We can:

Establish a more stable basis for peaceful relations with the Soviet Union;

Strengthen allied relationships across the board;

Achieve real and equitable reductions in the levels of nuclear arms;

Reinforce our peacemaking efforts in the Middle East, Central America, and Southern Africa;

Assist developing countries, particularly our neighbors in the Western Hemisphere; and

Assist in the development of democratic institutions throughout the world.

The wisdom of our bipartisan cooperation was seen in the work of the Scowcroft Commission, which strengthened our ability to deter war and protect peace. In that same spirit, I urge you to move forward with the Henry Jackson plan to implement the recommendations of the Bipartisan Commission on Central America.

Your joint resolution on the multinational peacekeeping force in Lebanon is also serving the cause of peace. We are making progress in Lebanon. For nearly 10 years the Lebanese have lived from tragedy to tragedy, with no hope for their future. Now the multinational peacekeeping force and our Marines are helping them to break their cycle of despair. There is hope for a free, independent, and sovereign Lebanon. We must have the courage to give peace a chance. And we must not be driven from our objectives for peace in Lebanon by state-sponsored terrorism. We have seen this ugly spectre in Beirut, Kuwait, and Rangoon. It demands international attention. I will forward shortly legislative proposals to help combat terrorism, and I will be seeking support from our allies for concerted action.

Our NATO Alliance is strong; 1983 was a banner year for political courage. And we have strengthened our partnerships and our friendships in the Far East. We are committed to dialogue, deterrence, and promoting prosperity. We will work with our trading partners for a new round of negotiations in support of freer world

trade, greater competition, and more open markets.

A rebirth of bipartisan cooperation, of economic growth and military deterrence, and a growing spirit of unity among our people at home and our allies abroad underline a fundamental and far-reaching change. The United States is safer, stronger, and more secure in 1984 than before. We can now move with confidence to seize the opportunities for peace — and we will.

Addressing the Soviet Union

Tonight I want to speak to the people of the Soviet Union to tell them: It is true that our governments have had serious differences. But our sons and daughters have never fought each other in war. And if we Americans have our way, they never will.

People of the Soviet Union, there is only one sane policy, for your country and mine, to preserve our civilization in this modern age: A nuclear war cannot be won and must never be fought. The only value in our two nations possessing nuclear weapons is to make sure they will never be used. But then would it not be better to do away with them entirely?

People of the Soviet: President Dwight Eisenhower, who fought by your side in World War II, said the essential struggle "is not merely man against man or nation against nation. It is man against war."

Americans are people of peace. If your government wants peace, there will be peace. We can come together in faith and friendship to build a safer and far better world for our children and our children's children. And the whole world will rejoice. That is my message to you.

American Heroes

Some days when life seems hard and we reach out for values to sustain us, or a friend to help us, we find a person who reminds us what it means to be Americans.

Sgt. Stephen Trujillo, a medic in the 2d Ranger Battalion, 75th Infantry, was in the first helicopter to land at the compound held by Cuban forces in Grenada. He saw three other helicopters crash. Despite the imminent explosion of the burning aircraft, he never hesitated. He ran across 25 yards of open terrain through enemy fire to rescue wounded soldiers. He directed two other medics, administered first aid, and returned again and again to the crash site to carry his wounded friends to safety.

Sergeant Trujillo, you and your fellow servicemen and women not only saved innocent lives, you set a nation free. You

inspire us as a force for freedom, not for despotism, and yes, for peace, not conquest. God bless you.

And then there are unsung heroes. Single parents, couples, church and civic volunteers, their hearts carry without complaint the pains of family and community problems. They soothe our sorrow, heal our wounds, calm our fears, and share our joy.

A person like Father Ritter is always there. His Covenant House programs in New York and Houston provide shelter and help to thousands of frightened and abused children each year. The same is true of Dr. Charles Carson. Paralyzed in a plane crash, he still believed nothing is impossible. Today, in Minnesota, he works 80 hours a week without pay, helping pioneer the field of computer-controlled walking. He has given hope to 500,000 paralyzed Americans that someday they may walk again.

The Greatness of America

How can we not believe in the greatness of America? How can we not do what is right and needed to preserve this last best hope of man on Earth?

After all our struggles to restore America, to revive confidence in our country and hope for our future, after all our hard-won victories earned through the patience and courage of every citizen, we cannot, must not and will not turn back. We will finish our job. How could we do less? We are Americans.

Carl Sandburg said: I see America, not in the setting sun of a black night of despair * * *. I see America in the crimson light of a rising sun fresh from the burning, creative hand of God * * *. I see great days ahead for men and women of will and vision.

I have never felt more strongly that America's best days and democracy's best days lie ahead. We are a powerful force for good. With faith and courage, we can perform great deeds and take freedom's next step. And we will. We will carry on the traditions of a good and worthy people who have brought light where there was darkness, warmth where there was cold, medicine where there was disease, food where there was hunger, and peace where there was only bloodshed.

Let us be sure that those who come after will say of us in our time that in our time we did everything that could be done: We finished the race, we kept them free, we kept the faith.

Thank you very much, God bless you, and God bless America.

[Applause, the Members rising.] ∎

President's Budget Message

Following is the text of President Reagan's Feb. 1 budget message to Congress.

TO THE CONGRESS OF
THE UNITED STATES:

In the past year, the Nation's prospects have brightened considerably. The economy has grown strongly — beyond expectation. Inflation has been reduced to its lowest rate in 16 years. Unemployment has declined faster than at any other time in 30 years. We are well on our way to sustained long-term prosperity without runaway inflation.

Our national security is being restored. Our domestic programs are being streamlined to reflect more accurately the proper scope of Government responsibility and intervention in our lives. Government operations are being made more effective and efficient, as steps are taken to reduce costs.

These developments are the result of the program I proposed 3 years ago to correct the severe economic and political problems caused by previous short-sighted and misguided policies and priorities. That program focused on long-range real growth. My tax proposals were designed to provide badly needed incentives for saving and productive investment. I supported the Federal Reserve in its pursuit of sound monetary policy. I worked with the Congress to reverse the growth of Government programs that had become too large or had outlived their usefulness, and as a result, domestic programs, which had been growing rapidly for 3 decades, have finally been contained. I worked to eliminate or simplify unnecessary or burdensome regulations.

To the Nation's great good fortune, the preceding Congress appreciated the fundamental soundness of this program and joined with my administration in helping to make it a reality. Frequently, because of entrenched constituency special interests, the political risks involved in doing so were great. I thanked Members then, and continue to be grateful, for the crucial support my program received. The Nation is now beginning to reap the solid fruits of our joint perseverance and foresight.

The economy's response has fully vindicated my economic program. During the past 2 years the percentage rise in consumer price index has been no more than it was during the first 6 months of 1980. Economic recovery has been vigorous during the past year, with real GNP rising over 6% and industrial production by 16%. Unemployment, though still unacceptably high, has declined by a record 2½ percentage points in a single year. Capacity utilization in American plants has risen dramatically. Business investment in new plant and equipment has risen 11½% in the past year, in real terms. American productivity, stagnant from 1977 to 1981, climbed 3.7% between the third quarter of 1982 and the third quarter of 1983. Interest rates declined substantially in mid-1982, followed by a major, sustained rally of the stock market that added half a trillion dollars to the net financial worth of American households. Real disposable personal income rose 5.1% in 1983. After a substantial decline, the U.S. dollar has rallied powerfully to its highest level in more than a decade.

We are not, however, out of the woods yet. Despite our success in reducing the rate of growth of nondefense spending in the last three budgets, spending in 1985 will exceed 1981 levels by 41%, reflecting continued increases in basic entitlement programs, essential increases in defense

spending, and rapid growth of interest costs. Clearly, much remains to be done. The task of rebuilding our military forces to adequate levels must be carried to completion, and our commitment to provide economic and military support to small, poor nations that are struggling to preserve democracy must be honored. At the same time, further action is required to curb the size and growth of many programs and to achieve managerial efficiencies throughout Government, wherever the opportunity is present.

Three Years of Accomplishment

Last year, I reviewed the dramatic improvements during the preceding 2 years in Government operations, and in the way they affect the economy. I am happy to report that these improvements continued through a third year.

● Where the growth rate of spending was almost out of control at 17.4% a year in 1980, it will decline to 7.3% this year.

● Where spending grew 64% over the 4 years from 1977 to 1981, it will rise by only 41% over the 4-year period from 1981 to 1985, despite legislated cost-of-living adjustments and the needed defense buildup.

● The Federal tax system has been significantly restructured. Marginal income tax rates have been substantially reduced, greatly improving the climate for saving and investment. Depreciation reform has been enacted, restoring the value of depreciation allowances eroded by inflation. Tax loopholes have been closed, making the tax structure more equitable. Efforts have been made to shift to financing Government programs through user fees commensurate with benefits and services provided.

● Our military strength is being restored to more adequate levels.

● Domestic spending, which grew nearly 3-fold in real terms in a little more than 2 decades, will actually be lower this year than it was in 1981.

● The rapid growth of means-tested entitlement programs has been curbed. Eligibility criteria have been tightened to target benefits more to the truly needy, and significant steps have been taken to improve the efficiency and effectiveness of these programs. Unnecessarily frequent cost-of-living adjustments were pared back.

● The social security system has been rescued from the threat of insolvency raised by rampant inflation, excessive liberalizations, and lagging growth of its tax base.

● Unnecessary or excessive Federal credit activities have been eliminated or cut back. Improvements in the management and control of Federal credit activities are being pursued. The administration has supported the basic intent of proposed legislation that would move off-budget lending onto

the unified budget, in order to provide better budgetary control over Federal lending.

● Proliferation of regulations and red tape has been stopped. The number of new Federal rules has fallen by over a quarter during the past three years, and hundreds of unnecessary old rules have been eliminated. For the first time, the *Federal Register* of new regulatory actions has grown shorter for three consecutive years; it is now one-third shorter than in 1980. Federal paperwork requirements have been cut by well over 300 million hours annually, and will be reduced even further in 1984. This has saved the American public over 150,000 work-years that had been spent every year filling out unnecessary Federal forms and reports. Our regulatory reform efforts to date will save individual citizens, businesses, and State and local governments over $150 billion over the next decade.

● Major management improvement initiatives are underway that will fundamentally change the way the Federal Government operates. The President's Council on Integrity and Efficiency has reported $31 billion in cost reductions or funds put to better use.

● The Federal nondefense work force has been reduced by 71,000 employees since I took office.

These are impressive accomplishments — accomplishments to be proud of and to build on. And together we can build on them. With this budget I call on all Members of the Congress once again for additional steps to ensure the firmness of our foundations and overcome the Nation's budget problem.

Maintaining Economic Recovery

Before us stands the prospect of an extended era of peace, prosperity, growth, and a rising standard of living for all Americans. What must we do to ensure that that promise shall be realized and enjoyed in the years to come? What must we do to ensure that the high price of adjustment to this new era paid by the Nation in recent years shall not have been paid in vain?

All signs point to continued strong economic growth, vigorous investment, and rising productivity, without renewed inflation — all but one. Only the threat of indefinitely prolonged high budget deficits threatens the continuation of sustained noninflationary growth and prosperity. It raises the specter of sharply higher interest rates, choked-off investment, renewed recession, and rising unemployment.

This specter must be laid to rest: just as fears of rampant inflation and its attendant evils are being laid to rest; just as fears of helplessness before growth in Soviet military might and all it threatens are being laid to rest; just as fears that the Nation's social security system would "go under" have been laid to rest. A number of actions will be required to lay it to rest. This budget requests these actions of Congress; it calls for measures to continue to curb the upward momentum of Federal spending and to increase Federal receipts. Other actions involve such fundamental reform of our fiscal procedures that they will require that the Constitution be amended.

Congress has each year enacted a portion of my budget proposals, while ignoring others for the time being. It is moving slowly, year by year, toward the full needed set of budget adjustments. I urge the Congress to enact this year not only the proposals contained in this budget, but also constitutional amendments providing for a line-item veto and for a balanced budget — rather than the fitful policy of enacting a half-hearted reform this year, another one next year, and so on.

Where Congress lacks the will to enforce upon itself the strict fiscal diet that is now necessary, it needs the help of the Executive Branch. We need a constitutional amendment granting the President power to veto individual items in appropriations bills. Forty-three of the fifty States give this authority to their governors. Congress has approved a line item veto for the District of Columbia, Puerto Rico, and the trust territories. It is now time for Congress to grant this same authority to the President. As Governor of California, I was able to use the line-item veto as a powerful tool against wasteful government spending. It works, and works well, in State government. Every number in this document bears testimony to the urgent need for the Federal Government to adopt this fundamental fiscal reform.

Let us also heed the people and finally support a constitutional amendment mandating balanced Federal budgets and spending limits. I encourage our citizens to keep working for this at the grassroots. If you want to make it happen, it will happen.

We must seek a bipartisan basis for fundamental reforms of Government spending programs. We need to reexamine just what, how, and how much the Federal Government should be doing — given our need for security and well-being and our desire to leave power and resources with the people. The President's Private Sector Survey on Cost Control (Grace Commission) has already come up with some interesting suggestions in this regard that, with the help of the Congress, will be adopted wherever possible.

To those who say we must raise taxes, I say wait. Tax increases pile unfair burdens on the people, hurt capital formation, and destroy incentives for growth. Tax cuts helped sustain the recovery, leading to faster growth and more jobs. Rather than risk sabotaging our future, let us go forward with an historic reform for fairness, simplicity, and growth. It is time to simplify the entire tax code so everyone is on equal footing.

The tax system must be made simpler and fairer; honest people should not pay for cheaters; the underground economy should come back into the sunlight; and everyone's tax rates should be reduced to spark more savings, investment, and incentives for work and economic growth. This is the blueprint for a brighter future and a fairer tax system. Therefore, I am directing the Department of the Treasury to complete a study with recommendations by the end of the year.

With these changes completed and the necessary fiscal tools in place, I am confident that we can devise a sweeping set of fiscal policy changes designed to reduce substantially the persistent Federal deficits that cloud our otherwise bright economic future. The plan must be based on these cardinal principles:

● It must be bipartisan. Overcoming the deficits and putting the Government's house in order will require everyone's best efforts.

● It must be fair. Just as all Americans will share in the benefits that are coming from recovery, all should share fairly in the burden of transition to a more limited role of Government in our society.

● It must be prudent. The strength of our national defense must be restored so that we can pursue prosperity in peace and freedom, while maintaining our commitment to the truly needy.

● Finally, it must be realistic. Government spending will not be curbed by wishful thinking.

In the meantime, the proposals in this budget provide important additional steps toward reducing the deficit.

Meeting Federal Responsibilities

My administration seeks to limit the size, intrusiveness, and cost of Federal activities as much as possible and to achieve the needed increase in our defense capabilities in the most cost-effective manner possible. This does not mean that appropriate Federal responsibilities are being abandoned, neglected, or inadequately supported. Instead, ways are being found to streamline Federal activity, to limit it to those areas and responsibilities that are truly Federal in nature; to ensure that these appropriate Federal responsibilities are performed in the most cost-effective and efficient manner; and to aid State and local governments in carrying out their appropriate public responsibilities in a similarly cost-effective manner. The Nation must ask for no more publicly-provided services and benefits than the taxpayers can reasonably be asked to finance.

Education. I have devoted considerable time this year to the problems of our schools. The record of the last two decades is not good, though relieved in places by the efforts of many dedicated teachers, administrators, parents, and students. It has been extremely gratifying to observe the response all across the country to my call for a renewed commitment to educational excellence. Excellence in education will only happen when the States and school districts, parents and teachers, and our children devote themselves to the hard work necessary to achieve it. Federal money cannot buy educational excellence. It has not in the past and will not in the future. What we will do in this budget is seek resources to help the States plan and carry out education reforms. My budget includes $729 million, about 50% more than Congress appropriated for 1984, for the education block grant and discretionary fund. States and localities will receive this increase in resources and be able to use the funds for education reform without Federal prescription and interference.

The budget also provides for stabilizing funding for almost all major education State grant programs at the 1984 level and in the future allows room for modest growth for most of these programs.

Finally, the budget reflects continued support of several more important initiatives that will strengthen American education:

● Enactment of tuition tax credits for parents who send their children to qualified private or religiously-affiliated schools.

● Establishment of education savings accounts to give middle- and lower-income families an incentive to save for their children's college education and, at the same time, to encourage a real increase in saving for economic growth.

● Reorientation of student aid programs to ensure that students and families meet their responsibilities for financing higher education.

● Permission for States or localities, if they so choose, to use their compensatory education funds to establish voucher programs to broaden family choice of effective schooling methods for educationally disadvantaged children.

● Assistance to States to train more mathematics and science teachers.

Training and employment. While the economic forecast predicts continuing improvement in the economy and further steady declines in the unemployment rate, I recognize that there are those who lack the skills to find and hold steady jobs. This is particularly true for some of our youth. In the past, Federal training and employment programs have not always helped these people gain the skills needed for success in the job market. Instead the Government spent precious tax dollars funding temporary, dead-end, make-work jobs that did little, if anything, to prepare these people for holding real jobs in the private sector. My administration worked with the Congress to change that. The Job Training Partnership Act, which I signed into law in 1982, involves private industry in the design and delivery of job training programs. Each year it will train 1.5 million disadvantaged adults and youths, dislocated workers, and welfare recipients in skills needed for private sector jobs. Additional work experience for over 700,000 disadvantaged youths will be provided during the summer months. What is needed now is not more Government programs, but removal of Government-created barriers that make it difficult for youths who want to work to find jobs. It has long been acknowledged that the minimum wage is a barrier to job finding for youths, especially minority youths, who lack skills. Therefore, I am again asking the Congress to authorize a wage of 75% of the minimum wage for youths newly hired for jobs during the summer months. This will let employers lower their costs to levels more in line with the skills youths possess, and it will help many young people find jobs and gain valuable work experience. The legislation I have proposed includes protections for adult workers.

Research. Recognizing the Federal responsibility to maintain and strengthen U.S. leadership in science and technology, the budget proposes further increases of more than 10% in Government-wide funding for basic research. The $8 billion planned for support of such research represents a relatively small share of the budget, but it is a critical investment in the Nation's future. Basic research lays the foundation for a strong defense in the years to come and for new technologies and industries that will maintain U.S. industrial leadership, create new jobs, and improve our quality of life.

Space. Our civilian space program has made remarkable progress in the past year. The space shuttle, the world's most advanced space transportation system, has made eight pathbreaking trips into space and is progressing rapidly towards achieving routine operational status.

We can now look forward confidently to the next major challenge in space — a space station. The space station, to be placed in permanent Earth orbit in the early 1990's, is intended to enhance the Nation's science and application programs, to help develop advanced technologies potentially useful to the economy, and to encourage greater commercial use of space. The budget provides planning money to initiate this program.

National defense. During the past 3 years, we have also taken decisive measures to increase our military strength to levels necessary to protect our Nation and our friends and allies around the world. At the same time, we have vigorously pursued diplomatic approaches, such as arms reduction talks, in an effort to ensure the principles of security and freedom for all.

The improvement in our defense posture has been across the board. Long-overdue modernization of our strategic forces is proceeding, while our conventional forces are also being modernized and strengthened. Successful recruiting and retention over the past 3 years have resulted in all of our armed services being more fully manned with capable, high-caliber men and women.

Energy. My administration has significantly reoriented the country's approach to energy matters toward reliance on market forces — instead of Government regulation and massive, indiscriminate Federal spending. This has resulted in greater energy production, more efficient use of energy, and more favorable energy prices. For example:

• The U.S. economy currently is using 30% less oil and gas per dollar's worth of output than it did 10 years ago when energy prices began to rise.

• Heating oil prices have been lower this past year than they were in January 1981, when I removed oil price controls. Gasoline prices have fallen to levels which, after adjustments for general inflation and sales taxes, are within 5% of those that prevailed in the U.S. in the 1950's.

Energy programs proposed in the budget are designed to complement market forces by focusing resources on limited but appropriate responsibilities of the Federal Government and by managing these programs well. Thus, for example, the budget proposes increased spending for basic and other long-term energy research. In addition, the administration continues its commitment to filling the strategic petroleum reserve. The reserve has more than tripled in size in the last three years.

Health care. Progress has been made in slowing the explosive growth of health costs. As part of the Social Security Amendments of 1983, Congress enacted the Administration's proposed fixed price prospective payment system for hospital care. This replaced the previous Medicare hospital reimbursement system under which hospitals were reimbursed for their costs. The new prospective payment system has altered incentives and should lessen the rate of increase in hospital costs.

Under the proposals in this budget, physicians will be asked to maintain present fee levels for medicare through the next fiscal year. Tax incentives prompting overly-costly employee health insurance benefits would be revised to make users and providers more sensitive to costs. Finally, resources for biomedical research will increase.

Transportation. My administration has sought to shift much of the costs of transportation from the general taxpayer to those who use transportation services and facilities. I signed into law several administration-backed proposals to increase excise taxes on aviation and highway users and thereby provide funding needed to revitalize and modernize these important segments of the Nation's transportation system. The proportion of the Department of Transportation's budget financed by user fees has risen from 49% in 1982 to 72% in 1985. The budget reflects the administration's continued commitment to the "users pay" principle by including receipts proposals for nautical and aviation aids, the inland waterway system, and construction and maintenance of deep-draft ports.

Recognizing the importance of safety in our transportation systems, the budget provides for significant improvements in this area. In addition, my administration secured passage of legislation designed to rebuild the Nation's highway and public transportation facilities. This legislation substantially increased funds available to the States and local communities to complete and repair the aging interstate highway system, to rehabilitate principal rural and urban highways and bridges, and to improve mass transit systems. The budget also provides for improvements in the safety of our transportation systems.

Improved ports and channels will help to make U.S. coal exports competitive in world markets. My administration will work with the Congress to provide for timely and efficient port construction. A system that recovers a significant portion of the cost of existing port maintenance and new port construction must be enacted prior to any new construction. In the last 3 years, my administration has sent several reasonable proposals to the Congress, and progress is being made. It is time for action on this important issue.

Reducing the Federal presence in commercial transportation, currently regulated by the Interstate Commerce Commission, the Civil Aeronautics Board, and the Federal Maritime Commission, will improve the efficiency of the industry. Authority for the Civil Aeronautics Board will expire next year, and its residual functions will be assumed by other agencies. The administration will continue to seek legislation to deregulate ocean shipping, and will propose legislation to deregulate oil pipelines and natural gas. Experience since the adoption of initial transportation deregulation legislation has shown clearly that both consumers and industry benefit from reduced Federal involvement in these activities.

Criminal justice. My administration has continued to strengthen the Federal criminal justice system by seeking major legislative changes in immigration policy, sentencing, and bail procedures, and by seeking increased funding for law enforcement activities. An additional organized crime drug enforcement task force will be established in Florida, bringing the total number of task forces to 13. The budget proposes to bolster immigration control by strengthening border enforcement and improving the effectiveness of border inspection programs. Additional attorneys will be sought for the Internal Revenue Service and the Justice Department, underscoring my administration's determination to tackle the serious problem of tax protesters and evaders. The administration will enhance its efforts to identify, neutralize, and defeat foreign agents who pose a threat to the Nation.

International affairs. Our foreign policy is oriented toward maintaining peace through military strength and diplomatic negotiation; promoting market-oriented solutions to international economic problems; telling the story abroad of America's democratic, free-enterprise way of life; and reducing barriers to free trade both here and abroad.

● The security assistance portion of the international affairs program has been increased to assist friendly governments facing threats from the Soviet Union, its surrogates, and from other radical regimes.

● Development aid emphasizes encouraging the private sectors of developing nations and increasing U.S. private sector involvement in foreign assistance.

● The budget provides for continuing the major expansion of international broadcasting activities started last year. Television, exchanges of people, and other programs to improve communications with foreign countries are included.

● My administration will continue to work with the Congress to strengthen the management and coordination of the Government's international trade functions by consolidating them in a Department of International Trade and Industry.

The United States faces threats to its interests in many parts of the world. The Middle East, with its vital energy resources, is still in turmoil. In Central America, Marxist forces continue to threaten democratic governments, exploiting temporary economic dislocations and the continuing poverty of less developed countries. In Africa, the poorest nations of the world are facing the prospect of great privation, accentuated by drought. This budget addresses each of these concerns:

● It continues military and economic support for Israel and Egypt, with improved financial terms.

● It provides for a significant increase in assistance to Central America, the specific nature of which will be defined after our review of the recommendations of the National Bipartisan Commission on Central America.

● It provides special humanitarian aid to counter the immediate effects of African drought and proposes a longer-term program aimed at the root causes of Africa's economic problem.

Although now less than 2% of the budget, international programs are critical to American world leadership and to the success of our foreign policy.

Civil service retirement. There is growing recognition that civil service retirement has far more generous benefits and is much more costly than retirement programs in the private sector or in State and local governments. Accordingly, the administration continues its strong support of the civil service reform proposals advanced in last year's budget. In 1985, the administration will focus its legislative effort on three of those proposals, in modified form: cost-of-living adjustment (COLA) reform, a high 5-year salary average for the benefit formula, and increased employee and agency retirement contributions.

GI bill rate increase. The budget proposes legislation to provide a 15% increase in the rates of educational assistance and special training allowances to GI bill trainees and disabled veterans receiving vocational rehabilitation assistance, effective January 1985. The increase will offset increased costs since GI bill benefits were last raised in 1981. It will provide an increase in monthly education benefit checks to 544,000 veterans and their dependents and survivors.

Continuing Reform of Our Federal System

The overall efficiency of Government in the United States can also be improved by a more rational sorting out of governmental responsibilities among the various levels of government in our Federal system — Federal, State, and local — and by eliminating or limiting overlap and duplication.

In 1981, the Congress responded to my proposals by consolidating 57 categorical programs into nine block grants. In 1982, a block grant was created for job training in the Jobs Training Partnership Act.

The administration is improving the management of intergovernmental assistance by providing State and local elected officials with greater opportunity to express their views on proposed Federal development and assistance actions before final decisions are made. Under Executive Order 12372, Intergovernmental Review of Federal Programs, which I signed in July 1982, Federal agencies must consult with State and local elected officials early in the assistance decision process and make every effort to accommodate their views. The Order also encourages the simplification of State planning requirements imposed by Federal law, and allows for the substitution of State-developed plans for federally required State plans where statutes and regulations allow.

Controlling Federal Credit Programs

Federal credit in all its forms imposes costs on the U.S. economy that must be weighed against its benefits. Federal intervention through guarantees and direct loans may misdirect investment and preempt capital that could be used more efficiently by unsubsidized, private borrowers. Because federally assisted borrowers are frequently less productive than private borrowers, large Federal credit demands, and the degree of subsidy involved in Federal credit activity, must be reduced if we are to improve prospects for economic growth.

The administration continues its strong commitment to control Federal direct loans and loan guarantees. It has supported the basic intent of proposed legislation to move off-budget Federal lending into the unified budget. It seeks other basic reforms in the way in which direct loans and loan guarantees are presented and controlled.

In the coming year, my administration will issue a directive establishing Government-wide policies on credit. This directive will be both an explicit statement of the administration's goal in providing credit assistance and a means of controlling the manner in which that assistance is provided.

Regulatory Reform

Federal regulation grew explosively throughout the 1970's. Whether well or poorly designed, whether aimed at worthy or dubious objectives, these rules have one thing in common: they "tax" and "spend" billions of dollars entirely within the private sector of the economy, unconstrained by public budget or appropriations controls.

My administration has taken steps to correct this problem. Under Executive Order 12291, all Federal regulations must be reviewed by the Office of Management and Budget before being issued to determine whether their social benefits will exceed their social costs. As a result of this review process, we have reversed the rate of growth of Federal regulations. Hundreds of ill-conceived proposals have been screened out, and hundreds of existing rules have been stricken from the books because they were unnecessary or ineffective. Equally important, numerous existing regulations have been improved, and new rules have been made as cost-effective as possible within statutory limits. We are steadily winding down economic controls that regulate prices, form barriers to entry for new firms, and other anti-competitive regulations. At the same time we are increasing the effectiveness of our programs promoting health, safety, and environmental quality.

Our regulatory reform program has been open and public. New rules and changes to existing rules now require public notice and comment. My Executive Order requires regulatory agencies to consider the interests of the general public as well as special interest groups in rulemaking proceedings. The Task Force on Regulatory Relief and the Office of Management and Budget have issued regular reports detailing the progress of regulatory reform efforts. *The Unified Agenda of Federal Regulations*, issued twice each year, describes all planned and pending regulatory changes in virtually all Federal agencies. The administration's *Regulatory Policy Guidelines*, published in August 1983, is the first comprehensive statement of regulatory policy ever to be issued.

I believe it is time the policies and procedures of Executive Order 12291 were enacted into law. Individual regulatory decisions will always be contentious and controversial, but surely we can all agree on the general need for regulatory reform. Making each Government rule as cost-effective as possible benefits everyone and strengthens the individual regulatory statutes. Regulation has become such an important role of the Federal Government that strong and balanced central oversight is becoming a necessity and a bi-partisan objective. The Laxalt-Leahy Regulatory

Reform Act, which passed the Senate unanimously in 1982, would have accomplished this reform. I strongly urge the Congress to take up and pass similar legislation this year. In addition, my administration continues to support measures to deregulate financial institutions.

Improving the Efficiency of Government

It is important to continue to reduce the size of Government. It is equally important to use the remaining resources as efficiently and effectively as possible. My administration has begun to make great strides in doing exactly that.

During the past 3 years, we have initiated several Government-wide management improvement efforts under the guidance of the Cabinet Council on Management and Administration. They are:

—Reform 88;
—Personnel management reform;
—Federal field structure reform; and
—The President's Private Sector Survey on Cost Control.

These management improvement and cost reduction programs focus on 4 objectives:

—Reducing fraud, waste, and mismanagement;
—Improving agency operations;
—Developing streamlined Federal Government management systems; and
—Improving the delivery of services.

Reducing fraud, waste, and mismanagement. This objective seeks better use of appropriated dollars. The President's Council on Integrity and Efficiency (PCIE) was formed in early 1981 and is made up of 18 department and agency Inspectors General. They recently reported $8.4 billion in cost reductions or funds put to better use in the last 6 months of 1983 and a total of $31 billion since they were appointed. The PCIE is beginning to direct its efforts toward preventing problems before they occur, through improved technology and better audit processes, as described in their latest report.

The PCIE also found that enormous waste was occurring because the Federal Government had never established an effective cash management system — despite the fact that it handles almost a trillion dollars in cash annually. This is currently being corrected by installing sophisticated, up-to-date systems that the Department of the Treasury estimates could save as much as $3½ billion a year.

When my administration came to office we found delinquent debt owed the Government rising at a rate of over 40% per year — with a total debt outstanding of over $240 billion. After only 2 years' efforts, this annual growth rate has been reduced to 2%. A credit pre-screening system is now being put in place, and automated collection centers are being installed.

Federal procurement involves annual expenditures of $170 billion. Procurement was an overly complex process with only 50% of our contract dollars awarded under competitive bid. My administration has replaced three sets of regulations with one, and we are now setting up a new pro-competitive policy to cut costs.

We have extended our fight to reduce waste and mismanagement to a direct attack on that nemesis that has always characterized the Federal Government: red tape and paperwork. We have already reduced the paperwork burden placed on the private sector by the Federal Government by well over 300 million hours. In this current fiscal year we intend to reduce the burden by another 130 million hours.

Further savings and improvements are possible. The President's Private Sector Survey on Cost Control (Grace Commission) developed numerous recommendations for savings and cost avoidance. These recommendations range from reducing costs of Federal employee retirement programs to upgrading the Government's seriously outdated and inefficient management and administrative systems. I have already included many of these ideas in this budget and will include more in future budgets. My administration will develop a tracking system to make sure they are carried out.

These are but a few of the efforts underway to make sure that appropriated funds go further and are used for the purposes for which they were intended.

Improving agency operations. I am directing Federal agencies to coordinate their administrative activities so that they reduce their current operating costs immediately, rather than wait for future improvements in systems and technologies. Savings resulting from these efforts are reflected in this budget. These efforts include: (1) consolidating headquarters and regional administrative services; (2) requiring service centers to meet minimum productivity standards for processing documents; (3) using private sector contractors to provide support services where appropriate and economical; (4) reducing Federal civilian employment by 75,000 by the beginning of 1985, reducing higher graded staff, and improving personnel planning; (5) reducing office space by 10%; (6) reducing printing plants by 25% and publications by 25%; and (7) eliminating the processing of documents altogether for most small agencies, by requiring them to obtain services from larger agencies that have efficient centers.

Developing streamlined Federal Government management systems. As we are reducing the size of Government and reducing fraud, waste, and abuse, we also need to change fundamentally the way the Federal Government is managed. When I came into office, we found that the Federal Government lacked a well-planned compatible management process, so we set about developing one. This effort involves five major projects: (1) planning and budgeting, (2) financial management and accounting, (3) personnel management and payroll, (4) personal and real property, and (5) automatic data processing and telecommunications management. Responsibilities and resources for the development of each of these management systems have been assigned to those agencies that have or are capable of developing the most advanced management system in each category. Without this effort, the Federal Government would continue to operate in an inefficient manner that does not serve our citizens well.

Improving the delivery of services. My administration is looking seriously at the way the delivery of Federal services is handled across the country. The objective of this effort is to achieve improved service at lower cost, through improved technology and management techniques such as prescreening, computer matching, adjusted payment schedules, contractor and grantee performance incentives, and a streamlined field structure. All of these efforts are being planned and coordinated centrally as part of the budget process. The results of these efforts will be reported to the Congress together with resulting savings and proposals to upgrade management of the Federal Government.

Conclusion

Vigorous, noninflationary economic recovery is well underway. The long winter of transition from the misguided policies of the past, with their inflationary and growth-deadening side-effects, is now yielding to a new springtime of hope for America. The hope of continued recovery to long-term noninflationary prosperity can be realized if we are able to work together on further deficit reduction measures. Bold, vigorous fiscal policy action to break the momentum of entrenched spending programs, together with responsible and restrained monetary policy, is essential to keep the recovery on track; essential to the Nation's future economic health and vitality. Limited measures to increase receipts will also be necessary to make our tax system fairer and more efficient. But it is important — more than important, *crucial* — to get the mix of spending restraint and receipts increases right. There must be substantial reductions in spending and strictly limited increases in receipts.

I call urgently upon the Congress, therefore, to take the actions proposed in this budget. Far too much is at stake to permit casual dismissal of these essential belt-tightening measures. The Nation has paid a high price for the prospect of a secure, prosperous, noninflationary future; that prospect must not be sacrificed to a sense of complacency, to an expedient ducking of the issues.

With confidence in the ultimate beneficial effects of our actions, let us seize the high ground and secure, for ourselves and our posterity, a bright and prosperous future — a future in which the glory that was America is again restored.

RONALD W. REAGAN
February 1, 1984

Reagan's Economic Report

Following is the text of President Reagan's Economic Report sent to Congress Feb. 2.

TO THE CONGRESS OF
THE UNITED STATES:

I have long believed that the vitality of the American economy and the prosperity of the American people have been diminished by inappropriate policies of the Federal Government: unnecessary government regulations that discouraged initiative and wasted scarce capital and labor; an inefficient and unfair tax system that penalized effort, saving, and investment; excessive government spending that wasted taxpayers' money, misused our Nation's resources, and created budget deficits that reduced capital formation and added to the burden of the national debt; and monetary policies that produced frequent business cycles and a path of increasing inflation.

I came to Washington to change these policies. The needed reforms are far from complete, but substantial progress can already be seen: the burden of regulation has been reduced, tax rates have been lowered and the tax structure improved, government spending on a wide range of domestic programs has been curtailed, and a sound monetary policy has been established.

Although the full favorable effect of those reforms on our Nation's rate of economic growth will take time to develop, some of the benefit of our economic policies is already visible in the current recovery. The economy's performance in 1983 was very gratifying to me. The 3.2 percent rise in consumer prices between 1982 and 1983 was the lowest rate of inflation since 1967. The recovery produced a sharp drop in unemployment and a substantial increase in the income of American families. The number of people at work increased by more than 4 million and the unemployment rate fell from a high of 10.7 percent in December 1982 to 8.2 percent in December 1983. The 6.1 percent rise in real gross national product (GNP) last year means that real annual income per person in the United States rose $700.

Reducing Unemployment

Despite the substantial reduction in unemployment, the number of unemployed workers remains unacceptably high. Continued economic recovery will mean millions of additional jobs in the years ahead and further declines in the rate of unemployment. In 1984 alone, the American economy is expected to add more than 3 million additional jobs. By the end of the decade, we will need 16 million new jobs to absorb a growing labor force. Only a strong and expanding economy can provide those jobs while achieving a progressively lower level of unemployment over the next 6 years.

Although economic growth is by far the most important way to reduce unemployment, special policies to help the structurally unemployed and particularly disadvantaged groups can also be helpful. To assist these individuals in developing job-related skills that will lead to productive careers in the private sector, I proposed the Job Training Partnership Act that I signed into law in 1982. Last year I proposed additional measures to increase opportunities for training and retraining. Although the Congress has enacted some of my employment proposals, I am still waiting for congressional action on others.

Of particular concern to me is the unemployment among teenagers. Such unemployment is not only a problem in itself, but is also indicative of lost opportunities to acquire on-the-job training and job-related skills. It is widely recognized that the minimum wage law is a substantial barrier to the employment of teenagers, especially minority teenagers. I have proposed that during the summer months the minimum wage for teenagers be reduced to 75 percent of the regular minimum wage. This reform would give many teenagers the opportunity to get a first job and acquire the skills needed to help them with subsequent employment and would not hurt adult employment. With an unemployment rate of nearly 50 percent among black teenagers and with only about 20 percent of black teenagers employed, we must act. The Federal Government must not be the source of barriers to employment.

Inflation and Monetary Policy

Reducing the rate of inflation was my most immediate economic goal when I arrived in Washington. In the preceding 24 months, the consumer price level had increased more than 27 percent. Many people feared the U.S. Government had lost its ability to control inflation. Until inflation was brought under control, a healthy recovery could not get under way.

The inflation rate has declined dramatically over the past 3 years. Between 1982 and 1983, the consumer price index rose only 3.2 percent. Americans can again have confidence in the value of the dollar, and they can save for the future without fearing that the purchasing power of these savings will be destroyed by inflation. I am firmly committed to keeping inflation on a downward path. We must never relax in our pursuit of price stability.

The basic requirement for a continued moderation of inflation is a sound monetary policy. I continue to support the Federal Reserve in its pursuit of price stability through sound monetary policy. Last year was a particularly difficult time for monetary policy because of the substantial changes in financial regulations. I am pleased that, in spite of these difficulties, the monetary aggregates at the end of the year were within their target ranges. I expect that in 1984 the Federal Reserve will expand the money stock at a moderate rate that is consistent with both a sustained recovery and continuing progress against inflation.

There are those who advocate a fast rate of money growth in an attempt to depress interest rates. Experience shows, however, that rapid money growth inevitably leads to an increased rate of inflation and higher interest rates. The only monetary policy that can bring interest rates down, and keep them down, is one that promotes confidence that inflation will continue to decline in the years ahead.

The Dollar and the Trade Deficit

The high interest rates in the United States and our low rate of inflation continue to make dollar securities an appealing investment for individuals and businesses around the world. In addition, the United States has been an attractive place for stock market investment and for direct business investment. The result has been a continued rise in the dollar's exchange value relative to other currencies of the world.

The sharp rise in the value of the dollar since 1980 has made it cheaper for Americans to purchase products from overseas, thereby helping us fight inflation. But the dollar's sharp rise has made it difficult for American businesses and farmers to compete in world markets. The decline in U.S. exports and the substantial rise in our imports has resulted in record trade deficits in 1982 and 1983. The trade deficit has been temporarily exacerbated by the international debt problems and by the more advanced stage of recovery in the United States than in the world at large.

Despite these problems, I remain committed to the principle of free trade as the best way to bring the benefits of competition to American consumers and businesses. It would be totally inappropriate to respond by erecting trade barriers or by using taxpayers' dollars to subsidize exports. Instead, we must work with the other nations of the world to reduce the export subsidies and import barriers that currently hurt U.S. farmers, businesses, and workers.

I am also firmly opposed to any attempt to depress the dollar's exchange value by intervention in international currency markets. Pure exchange market intervention cannot offset the fundamental factors that determine the dollar's value. Intervention in the foreign exchange market would be an exercise in futility that would probably enrich currency speculators at the expense of American taxpayers. A combination of exchange market intervention and expansionary monetary policy could reduce the dollar's exchange value, but only by causing an unacceptable increase in the rate of inflation. The dollar must therefore be allowed to seek its natural value without exchange market intervention.

Regulation

One of the four key elements of my program for economic recovery is a far-reaching program of regulatory relief. Substantial progress has been made during the last 3 years. The growth of new regulations has been reduced by more than a third. The demands on the private sector of government paperwork have been reduced by several hundred million hours a year. The Congress approved legislation that has led to substantial deregulation of financial markets and intercity bus transportation. The Federal Communications Commission, with our support, has reduced the regulation of broadcasting and of new communications technology, and the Interstate Commerce Commission and the Civil Aeronautics Board have gone far down the path of deregulation of competitive transportation markets. The benefits of these and other deregulation measures are now increasingly apparent to American consumers and businesses.

It is also apparent that substantial further deregulation and regulatory reform will require changes in the basic regulatory legislation. I urge the Congress to act on the several measures that I proposed last year on natural gas decontrol, financial deregulation, and reform of private pension regulation. I remain confident that there is a basis for agreement on measures that would reduce the burden of Federal regulations, while protecting our shared values and not jeopardizing safety.

Tax Reforms

The final installment of the 3-year personal tax cut took effect in July, giving a helpful boost to the economic recovery. The income tax rate at each income level has been reduced by about 25 percent since 1980. In 1984 a median income four-person family will pay about $1,100 less than it would have without these tax reductions. And, beginning in 1985, the tax brackets will be adjusted automatically so that inflation will no longer push taxpayers into higher brackets and increase the share of their income taken in taxes.

The Economic Recovery Tax Act of 1981 went beyond reducing tax rates to establish important reforms in the structure of the tax system. For businesses, the Accelerated Cost Recovery System increased the after-tax profitability of investments in plant and equipment. The sharp fall in inflation has also increased after-tax profitability. As a result, investment in business equipment has recently been quite strong despite the high real interest rates.

For individuals, the Economic Recovery Tax Act reduced the marriage tax penalty, the estate tax burden, and tax discrimination against saving. The response to the universal eligibility of Individual Retirement Accounts (IRAs) has been far greater than was originally expected. It is estimated that more than 15 million individuals now use IRAs to save for their retirement. Last year, I proposed to expand the opportunity for all married couples to use IRAs fully by allowing them to contribute up to $2,000 each per year to an IRA even if only one has wage income.

Further improvement and simplification of our tax system are sorely needed. The burden of taxation depends not only on the quantity of tax revenue that is collected but also on the quality of the tax system. I have asked the Secretary of the Treasury to develop a plan of action with specific recommendations to make our tax system fairer, simpler, and less of a burden on our Nation's economy. By broadening the tax base, personal tax rates could come down, not go up. Our tax system would stimulate greater economic growth and provide more revenue.

Government Spending

One of my principal goals when I came to Washington was to reverse the dramatic growth of Federal spending on domestic programs and to shift more resources to our Nation's defense. Although many doubted this could be done, both goals are being achieved. We must do everything that we can to avoid waste in defense as in other areas of government. But we must also be willing to pay the cost of providing the military capability to defend our country and to meet our responsibilities as the leading Nation of the free world. Outlays for defense had declined to only 5.2 percent of GNP in 1980, less than one-fourth of total government outlays. By the current fiscal year, defense outlays have increased to 6.7 percent of GNP and 28 percent of total outlays. Real defense outlays have grown 39 percent since 1980. Our spending on defense, however, remains a far smaller percentage of our national income than it was in 1960, when defense outlays took 9.7 percent of GNP.

Real spending has been cut on a wide range of domestic programs and activities. Many wasteful bureaucratic activities have been eliminated and the number of nondefense employees on the Federal payroll has been reduced by 71,000. We have examined every area of Federal Government spending, and sought to eliminate unnecessary and wasteful spending while protecting the benefits needed by the poor and the aged. As a result, total nondefense spending now takes a smaller share of our GNP than it did in 1980. Moreover, under present law, nondefense spending will continue to take a declining share of our GNP in the years ahead.

This reduction has been accomplished without any decrease in existing social security benefits or any change in the medicare benefits for the elderly. Spending on all other nondefense activities and programs has actually declined over 12 percent in real terms since 1980. Even with no further reductions in these activities and programs, their share of GNP in 1986 will be nearly back to the level of 1965.

I am committed to continuing the search for ways to reduce government spending. The budget that I am submitting to the Congress identifies significant savings in entitlement programs and reductions in outlays for other programs that are excessive or that are not the proper responsibility of the Federal Government. The

Grace Commission has given us some 2500 ways to reduce wasteful spending that could save billions of dollars in the years ahead.

Budget Deficits

I have long believed that our Nation's budget must be balanced. A pattern of overspending by the Federal Government has produced a deficit in 22 of the last 23 years. My most serious economic disappointment in 1983 was therefore the failure of the Congress to enact the deficit reduction proposals that I submitted last January in my budget for fiscal 1984. We would be much closer to a balanced budget today if the Congress had enacted all of the spending cuts that I have requested since assuming office, and if the long recession and the sharp decline in inflation had not substantially reduced real tax revenue. In last year's budget I proposed changes in outlays and revenues that could put the deficit on a sharply declining path that, by 1988, would have been less than 2 percent of GNP and on its way to a balance of revenues and outlays.

The unwillingness of the Congress to accept the proposals that I offered has made it clear to me that we must wait until after this year's election to enact spending reductions coupled with tax simplification that will eventually eliminate our budget deficit. But we cannot delay until 1985 to start reducing the deficits that are threatening to prevent a sustained and healthy recovery. I have therefore called on the Democratic and Republican leaders in the Congress to designate representatives to work with the Administration on the development of a "downpayment" deficit reduction program.

I believe that this bipartisan group could develop a package that could be enacted this spring which would reduce the deficit by about $100 billion over the next 3 fiscal years. The package could include a number of the less contentious spending cuts that are pending before the Congress plus additional outlay savings based on the proposals of the Grace Commission. Additional revenue could be provided by measures to close certain tax loopholes — measures that the Department of the Treasury has previously said are worthy of support.

These deficit reductions can increase the public's confidence in our economic future and their faith in the ability of the political system to deal satisfactorily with the deficit. The downpayment package can be a first step toward full elimination of the remaining deficits. Even with a 3-year $100 billion package, the deficits projected for fiscal 1986 and beyond are totally unacceptable to me. They would be a serious threat to our Nation's economic health and a heavy burden to future generations. I am committed to finding ways to reduce further the growth of spending and to put the budget on a path that will lead to a balance between outlays and receipts. In 1985 I will submit a budget that can achieve this goal. But we must go further and make basic structural reforms in the budgetary process

— including the line-item veto and the balanced budget amendment — that will keep spending under control and prevent deficits in the future.

Looking Ahead

As I look ahead, I am very optimistic about the prospects for the American economy. Substantial progress has been made in reforming the economic policies that will shape our economic future. If we continue to develop and pursue sound policies, our Nation can achieve a long period of strong economic growth with low inflation, and the American people can enjoy unprecedented prosperity and economic security.

Ronald Reagan

February 2, 1984

Statement on Redeployment of Marines

Following is the United Press International text of the Feb. 7 statement by President Reagan on the redeployment of United States Marines in Lebanon.

The bloodshed we have witnessed in Lebanon over the last several days only demonstrates once again the length to which the forces of violence and intimidation are prepared to go to prevent a peaceful reconciliation process from taking place. If a moderate government is overthrown because it had the courage to turn in the direction of peace, what hope can there be that other moderates in the region will risk committing themselves to a similar course?

Yielding to violence and terrorism today may seem to provide temporary relief, but such a course is sure to lead to a more dangerous and less manageable future crisis. Even before the last outbreak of violence, we had been considering ways of reconcentrating our forces and the nature of our support in order to take the initiative away from the terrorists.

Far from deterring us from this course, recent events only confirm the importance of the decisive new steps I want to outline for you now.

Thus, after consultation with our M.N.F. partners and President Gemayel and at his request, we are prepared to do the following:

● First, to enhance the safety of American and other M.N.F. personnel in Lebanon, I have authorized U.S. naval forces, under the existing mandate of the M.N.F., to provide naval gunfire and air support against any units firing into greater Beirut from parts of Lebanon controlled by Syria as well as against any units directly attacking American or M.N.F. personnel and facilities. Those who conduct these attacks will no longer have sanctuary from which to bombard Beirut at will. We will stand firm to deter those who seek to influence Lebanon's future by intimidation.

● Second, when the Government of Lebanon is able to reconstitute itself into a broadly based representative government, we will vigorously accelerate the training, equipping and support of the Lebanese armed forces on whom the primary responsibility rests for maintaining stability in Lebanon. We will speed up delivery of equipment, we will improve the flow of information to help counter hostile bombardments and we will intensify training in counterterrorism to help the Lebanese confront the terrorist threat that poses such danger to Lebanon, to Americans in Lebanon and, indeed, to peace in the Middle East.

● Third, in conjunction with these steps, I have asked Secretary of Defense Weinberger to present to me a plan for redeployment of the Marines from Beirut airport to their ships offshore. This redeployment will begin shortly and proceed in stages. U.S. military personnel will remain on the ground in Lebanon for training and equipping the Lebanese Army and protecting the remaining personnel. These are traditional functions that U.S. personnel perform in many friendly countries. Our naval and Marine forces offshore will stand ready, as before, to provide support for the protection of American and other M.N.F. personnel in Lebanon and thereby help assure security in the Beirut area as I have described.

These measures, I believe, will strengthen our ability to do the job we set out to do and to sustain our efforts over the long term. They are consistent with the compromise joint resolution worked out last October with the Congress with respect to our participation in the multinational force.

Report on Lebanon Situation

Following is the White House text of President Reagan's Feb. 13 report to Congress on the situation in Lebanon.

U.S. Foreign Policy Interests Served by U.S. Participation in the MNF

U.S. foreign policy interests remain as stated in the report of December 12, 1983. The Government of Lebanon (GOL) requested the return of the Multinational Force (MNF) to the Beirut area following the tragedy of Sabra/Shatilla. The presence of the MNF was requested specifically to facilitate the restoration of Lebanese Government sovereignty and authority over the Beirut area and thereby to further efforts of the Lebanese Government to assure the safety of persons in the area and to bring an end to the violence. The MNF remains in Lebanon to help provide the Lebanese Government and Lebanese communities an opportunity to reach agreement on broadening the government and to negotiate the withdrawal of foreign forces. The presence of U.S. forces is a critical part of a shared effort with our Western allies — the British, French and Italians — in the Multinational Force. They are as committed as we to assisting the Lebanese to restore peace and stability to their country. The presence of this Multinational Force further symbolizes Western support for Lebanon's efforts not only to withstand external pressure but to enter serious negotiations with Syria on troop withdrawals.

In order to use U.S. assets in Lebanon most effectively, on February 7 the President announced several changes in the orientation of our political and military resources, all of which are consistent with the existing mandate of the MNF. First, in order to enhance the safety of MNF personnel, authority has been given to U.S. naval forces offshore to provide naval gunfire and air support against any units in Syrian-controlled parts of Lebanon firing into the greater Beirut area, as well as against any units directly attacking MNF or U.S. personnel and facilities. Second is more intensified support and training for the Lebanese Armed Forces (LAF), including counter-terrorism training and an increase in our exchange of intelligence information. Third, we have decided that the large contingent of Marines dug in at the Beirut Airport is no longer the most effective way of maintaining an MNF presence. They have become a target in an area that is no longer under government control. Their redeployment to ships offshore will take place in phases based on an assessment of the situation, but with a tentative goal of completion within 30 days, as discussed later in this report. Military personnel will remain on the ground for the purpose of protecting our remaining personnel including those engaged in training and equipping the LAF.

The intention is to redeploy our military resources in a way that can best help the Lebanese, without signalling a lessening in our resolve. The United States will remain fully engaged. We will continue our intensive efforts to bring all sides to the bargaining table. We will continue to press the Lebanese government and the opposition alike to move toward political accommodation.

Until stability is at hand, Lebanon will be a flashpoint for conflict between Israel and Syria and therefore potentially between the United States and the USSR. Instability in Lebanon affects Israel's security directly. Indirectly, the ability of the Government of Lebanon to deal with its security problems, aided by the U.S. and other responsible members of the international community, will affect the confidence of the moderate Arab governments. Our relationship with those governments will be strongly affected by our record in Lebanon, as will the prospects for a wider peace in the area.

Situation in Lebanon: Level of Fighting and Status of Ceasefire

There was an extensive breakdown in the security situation at the end of this reporting period which resulted in the LAF's losing control of West Beirut. Fighting intensified throughout the greater Beirut area involving both heavy exchanges of fire between the LAF and opposing forces on the ground and extensive barrages of artillery and rocket fire. Two Navy A-6 aircraft conducted strikes against artillery positions in response to firing endangering the U.S. MNF or diplomatic facilities. During the course of this fighting the LAF lost effective control of West Beirut, and was experiencing difficulty in maintaining discipline and morale. The LAF re-established its lines along the "Green Line" dividing East and West Beirut. Indications are that although some units suffered significant personnel losses through surrender, desertion, or refusal to fight, the bulk of the force remains intact and loyal to the Government of Lebanon.

February 8 was marked by extensive use of naval gunfire. USS *New Jersey* and USS *Caron* conducted naval gunfire throughout the day against artillery and rocket positions in Syrian controlled portions of Lebanon which were firing on Beirut. A large number of hostile shells fell in the vicinity of the Ambassador's residence at Yarze. The two ships fired a total of 790 rounds (340 16-inch and 450 5-inch).

On February 9 naval gunfire was again employed to respond to hostile fire received from Syrian-controlled portions of Lebanon. The area around Yarze, which contains U.S. diplomatic and MNF personnel, was deliberately fired upon. Recurring artillery and small arms duels continue to spill over into U.S. MNF areas. Occasionally the U.S. MNF is directly targeted. The threat and incidence of terrorist attack on individuals and units of the MNF continues.

In addition to the substantial use of naval gunfire in early February, there were three other instances — on December 13, 14 and 18 — of Syrian or Syrian-backed firing on U.S. reconnaissance planes; in each instance U.S. naval gunfire was used to respond to the sources of fire. The USS *New Jersey's* 16-inch guns were used for the first time on December 14. We were forced to use naval gunfire to silence batteries used to shell Marine positions in an outbreak of fighting in mid-January. On

January 8, one Marine assigned to chancery protection duties was killed by small arms fire at a helicopter pad not far from the Embassy. Two Marines were killed on January 30 in fighting at the airport. The U.S. airman captured on December 4 was released by Syria on January 2 at the request of the USG and the Reverend Jackson.

Two important security problems were resolved during this reporting period. The first of these was the lifting of the siege of Dayr al-Qamar pursuant to an agreement that provided for the safe exodus of thousands of refugees, the withdrawal of a 2,000-man militia and the insertion of government forces into the town to maintain order and keep the peace. The operation was completed in mid-December; all sides have respected the agreement, and the Christian population of Dayr al-Qamar is living in peace. That agreement was an encouraging development; Lebanese government and militia leaders negotiated in good faith and both Syria and Israel were also involved in various ways in ensuring that the agreement could be implemented. It is this kind of political compromise that is being worked on for other areas of Lebanon.

In addition, Saudi Arabia mediated an agreement between Palestinian Liberation Organization Chairman Arafat and Syria that halted the fighting in the Tripoli area between pro- and anti-Arafat factions and permitted the evacuation from Lebanon of Arafat and 4,000 of his troops. The United States supported on humanitarian grounds the consensus in the UN Security Council for the use of UN flags on the evacuation ships, and we urged both publicly and privately the safe departure from the port of Tripoli, which began on December 20. The issue from our perspective was not to support any particular party involved, but the brutality of the shelling of Palestinian camps and the city of Tripoli by Syrian and Syrian-supported Palestinian forces needed to be stopped as a humanitarian matter.

On December 24, a French MNF unit withdrew from a position it had been occupying at an United Nations Relief and Works Agency school adjacent to the Sabra/Shatilla camp area. As the Lebanese Armed Forces moved in to take over this position, it met some resistance from the camps, sparking fighting which drew in the Shi'a Amal the next day. This Christmas fighting ended in the LAF succeeding in sealing off the camp area as a terrorist infiltration route from the southern suburbs into downtown Beirut.

Responsibilities, Activities and Composition of the MNF

Under its mandate, which remains unchanged, the MNF provides a multinational presence requested by the Lebanese government to assist it and the LAF in the Beirut area. The MNF is not authorized to engage in combat, but may exercise the right of self-defense. The U.S. MNF fol-

lows a policy of active self-defense in response to attacks and to improve its security. In order to enhance the safety of MNF personnel, authority has been given to U.S. naval forces offshore to provide naval gunfire and air support against any units in Syrian-controlled parts of Lebanon firing into greater Beirut, as well as against any units directly attacking MNF or U.S. personnel and facilities.

The MNF is currently composed of the following units which perform the functions indicated at the request of the Lebanese government. Their precise functions within the MNF mission have varied over time and continue to be subject to adjustment in light of changing circumstances.

● One U.S. Marine Amphibious Unit (MAU) is ashore at Beirut International Airport as a 1,400-man force which also provides external security troops at U.S. diplomatic facilities in the greater Beirut area. Additional elements of the MAU in reserve, mainly combat support and combat service support elements, are aboard amphibious ships offshore Beirut. Pending the conclusion of consultations with the GOL and our MNF allies, this force will be redeployed as soon as conditions warrant, with a tentative goal of completion within 30 days. As noted above, U.S. military personnel currently with the MNF will remain on the ground for the protection of our remaining personnel.

● Two Italian battalions are in a 1,400-man force in southwest Beirut and also help protect the Sabra and Shatilla refugee camps. The Italian government has nearly completed the four-month process of returning the size of its force to that level from a high of 2,200 men. The Italians announced on February 8 their intention to withdraw further forces, but to leave a portion of their MNF contingent to protect the camp areas.

● The French battalions serve as a force in and near the port of Beirut. The French have returned approximately 460 personnel from the MNF to the United Nations Interim Force in Lebanon (UNIFIL) in southern Lebanon, which leaves them at a level of 1,600 men, well above their original troop commitment.

● One British motorized reconnaissance company of 100 men withdrew from their position east of Beirut International Airport on February 8 and embarked in a Royal Navy ship offshore until the situation clarifies.

In addition, each contingent of the MNF has naval and/or air support forces in the region.

Estimated Cost of U.S. Participation in the MNF*

MNF Deployment:

U.S. Marine Corps (FY 1984 estimated costs)

Operations and Maintenance	$12.1 million
Military Personnel	5.5 million
TOTAL	$17.6 million

*This estimate encompasses all of Fiscal Year 1984 to the present.

Support for the MNF:

U.S. Navy (FY 1984 estimated costs)

Ship Operations in the Eastern	
Mediterranean	$36.1 million
Augmentation Resupply	3.9 million
Cargo Handling	.7 million
Medical Support	2.1 million
Other Support	2.0 million
TOTAL	$44.8 million

MNF Military Casualties

The following military casualties have occurred since the MNF deployed to Beirut in September 1982 and since the last report to Congress:

	Killed In Action		Wounded In Action		Captured	
	Total	Since 12/12/83	Total	Since 12/12/83	Total	Since 12/12/83
U.S.	264	14	134	4	1*	0
Italy	2	0	26	8		
France	77	2	60	4		
UK	0	0	1	0		

* 1 (Released)

Efforts to Reduce the MNF

The Marines are in Lebanon as part of a broadly based international peacekeeping effort to help keep the peace. Together with our MNF partners and the troop contributors to UNIFIL in southern Lebanon, the U.S. is one of a dozen nations that provide forces for this purpose.

Despite the changing situation on the ground, our basic strategy to reduce and eventually eliminate the need for the MNF remains unchanged and continues to center on our diplomatic efforts to encourage reconciliation among Lebanese factions, help expand the control of the Lebanese government over the territory of Lebanon, and create circumstances that will lead to removal of all foreign troops from Lebanon. At the President's direction, the number of men ashore will be reduced in phases and redeployed to ships offshore, with a tentative goal of completion within 30 days, as discussed herein. *It is not possible at this time to predict the exact duration of the need for the MNF.* We will continue to assess this question in the light of progress toward the objectives of national reconciliation and establishment of Lebanese government control.

Meanwhile, the possibility of supplementing or replacing the MNF with a UN peacekeeping operation is also being kept open, although this can be accomplished only if the Lebanese situation calms sufficiently to permit progress in the political dialogue among the parties concerned. We have carried out consultations with the UN Security Council members, the UN Secretariat and our MNF partners to assess prospects for an expanded UN peacekeeping role in various parts of Lebanon. France has informally raised in the Security Council the idea of replacing the MNF with a UN presence. The outlook for a UN role in Beirut remains uncertain; deployments anywhere in the country would depend on agreement of the UN Security Council, the parties on the ground, and potential contributing states.

Our long-term goal in Lebanon remains the same, but should not be confused with the mission of the MNF. The MNF is not a permanent or long-term force. It is not intended that it remain until the U.S. achieves its long-term goals in Lebanon.

Contributions to Lebanon By MNF Members

In addition to their contributions of troops to the MNF, members of the MNF are providing military and economic assistance to Lebanon.

The U.S. is providing $150 million (no year funds) in economic assistance, which it plans to have fully obligated by the end of FY 84. France has reportedly offered $256.6 million in 1983/84, mostly in commercial credits, while Italy is providing $142 million, largely in soft loans, over the next 3-4 years. The UK has provided $3 million, but it and the others are channeling additional contributions to Lebanon through the European Economic Community.

The Administration is considering a substantial supplemental funding request in 1984 in grants or credits for military equipment and training as part of our concerted effort to reconstitute the LAF and make it a strong arm of the central government's authority. The difficulties the Lebanese Army is now experiencing will be closely watched in this context. We plan to expend $46.8 million in FY 84 funds ($15 million appropriated for Lebanon and $31 million in reprogrammed FMS funds). Italy is supplying armored personnel carriers to Lebanon. France has provided 30 AMX tanks, 40 APCs and 10 light helicopters. In addition, the French are training units of the LAF and the Internal Security Force (ISF).

Progress in Training The Lebanese Armed Forces

Our training efforts have focused on four general areas: logistics, maintenance and supply; operational deployment of U.S.-supplied equipment; and, management and operations planning, all conducted by mobile training teams. We have sent 37 training teams — ranging in size from one person to 26 members — to Lebanon since January 1, 1983; 25 have completed their missions and have departed.

There are now 118 trainers in Lebanon, near our average of 100 trainers in Lebanon at any one time. Ten more teams may be scheduled for deployment over the next few months. All of this training has been provided under Foreign Military sales (FMS) procedures and paid for by the Lebanese. We are also conducting some training within the U.S. funded partly through International Military Education and Training funds and partly through FMS. Since the security situation in Lebanon precludes the sending of many LAF officers to the U.S., for 1984, the GOL has chosen to focus its training in the U.S. on individual programs like helicopter and fighter pilot training. The French have provided some training in logistics and operations for the LAF brigade equipped with French-origin heavy equipment.

Given recent events, reflected above, it is not possible to gauge when the LAF will be capable of maintaining internal security in Lebanon. As reflected in the President's announcement of February 7, a vigorous acceleration of training, equipping and support of the LAF is planned to enhance LAF effectiveness.

Progress Toward National Reconciliation

Progress toward national reconciliation was set back by the serious deterioration in the security situation in Beirut in early February. We are working with the Lebanese, Syrians, Israelis and Saudis to try to find a formula for a negotiated solution, and the Saudis have recently sent a senior emissary to Damascus to follow up these efforts.

Progress in Negotiations Toward Political Settlement

Negotiations on a security plan had been underway for some time when the attacks on West Beirut brought them to a halt. Political level contacts continue behind the scenes. The United States continues to press for a political dialogue between the government and leaders of Lebanon's communities. This in turn would pave the way for an expanded, broadly representative government able to deal with fundamental questions of political, social and economic reform and the withdrawal of foreign forces. If Syria and others are convinced of the resolve of the MNF partners to remain in Lebanon until progress is made, it would have a positive effect on reconciliation. ∎

Reagan Proposes Legislation Regarding Central America

Following is the White House text of President Reagan's Feb. 17 message to Congress proposing legislation based on the recommendations of the National Bipartisan Commission on Central America.

TO THE CONGRESS OF
THE UNITED STATES:

I herewith transmit proposed legislation that embodies the consensus arrived at by the National Bipartisan Commission on Central America. Its unifying thread is the spirit of the late Senator Henry M. Jackson — to advance the twin purposes of national security and human development.

Peace and individual betterment are universal purposes. They are at the heart of the American dream. Yet, today in Central America these goals are not realized. Poverty and violence are widespread. As a consequence, democratic forces are not able to flourish, and those who seek to disrupt freedom and opportunity threaten the heart of those nations.

Throughout our history, our leaders have put country before party on issues in foreign affairs important to the national interest. The Commission identifies the situation in Central America as this kind of issue. The 12 Commissioners — Democrats and Republicans alike — conclude "that Central America is both vital and vulnerable, and that whatever other crises may arise to claim the nation's attention, the United States cannot afford to turn away from that threatened region."

We face an inescapable reality: we must come to the support of our neighbors. The democratic elements in Central America need our help. For them to overcome the problems of accumulated historical inequities and immediate armed threats will take time, effort, and resources. We must support those efforts.

As the Commission recommends, our policy must be based on the principles of democratic self-determination, economic and social improvement that fairly benefits all, and cooperation in meeting threats to the security of the region.

Accordingly, I propose the "Central America Democracy, Peace and Development Initiative Act of 1984." This Act calls for an increased commitment of resources beginning immediately and extending regularly over the next five years. This assistance is necessary to support the balance of economic, political, diplomatic, and security measures that will be pursued simultaneously.

I propose authorization for an $8 billion, five-year reconstruction and development program for Central America, composed of $6 billion in direct appropriations and $2 billion in insurance and guarantee authority. For fiscal year 1985 the figures are $1.1 billion and $600 million, respectively. In addition, the plan calls for $400 million in supplemental appropriations for an emergency economic stabilization program for fiscal year 1984.

These resources will support agricultural development, education, health services, export promotion, land reform, housing, humanitarian relief, trade credit insurance, aid for small businesses, and other activities. Because democracy is essential to effective development, special attention will be given to increasing scholarships, leadership training, educational exchanges, and support for the growth of democratic institutions.

Regional institutions such as the Central American Common Market (CACM) and the Central American Bank for Economic Integration (CABEI) made a major contribution to the region's economic growth in the 1960's and early 70's. I am proposing a substantial assistance program to revitalize these institutions and thereby stimulate intra-regional trade and economic activity.

To enable the countries of Central America to participate directly in the planning of these efforts, I shall explore the creation of a Central American Development Organization (CADO). This would enable political and private leaders from both the United States and Central America to review objectives and progress, and make recommendations on the nature and levels of our assistance efforts. The organization would, in effect, help to oversee and coordinate the major efforts that must be made. The legislation I am proposing sets out a series of principles to guide the negotiations for the establishment of this new regional institution. I intend to respect those principles in these negotiations and in our subsequent participation in CADO. As the Commission recognized, the ultimate control of aid funds will always rest with the donors. Consistent with the Constitution and this precept, final disposition of funds appropriated under this legislation will be subject to the ultimate control of the Congress and the President.

The National Bipartisan Commission specifically recommends significantly increased levels of military aid to the region, especially in El Salvador. In the words of the Report, "the worst possible policy for El Salvador is to provide just enough aid to keep the war going, but too little to wage it successfully." I propose authorization for a $259 million supplemental appropriation for the region for fiscal year 1984 and a $256 million program for fiscal year 1985.

U.S. military assistance is vital to shield progress on human rights and democratization against violence from extremes of both left and right. I shall ensure that this assistance is provided under conditions necessary to foster human rights and political and economic development, and our Administration will consult with the Members of the Congress to make certain that our assistance is used fairly and effectively.

No new laws are needed to carry out many of the commission's recommendations. There is, for example, a consensus on an integral part of our strategy in Central America: support for actions implementing the 21 Contadora objectives to help bring about peace. The Contadora objectives are in Central America's interest and in ours. Similarly, we are urging other nations to increase their assistance to the area.

I believe it is no accident that the Commission reached many of the same conclusions about comprehensive solutions to Central America's problems as have the participants in the Contadora process. As Dr. Kissinger noted in his January 10 letter to me, "the best route to consensus on U.S. policy toward Central America is by exposure to the realities of Central America."

The National Bipartisan Commission on Central America has done its work. Now it is our turn. Unless we act — quickly, humanely, and firmly — we shall face a crisis that is much worse for everyone concerned. We owe it to our children to make sure that our neighbors have a chance to live decent lives in freedom.

I, therefore, ask that the enclosed legislation be given your urgent attention and early and favorable action.

RONALD REAGAN

The White House,
February 17, 1984 ∎

President's Veto Message On Water Resources Research

Following is the White House text of President Reagan's Feb. 21 message accompanying his veto of S 684, to authorize an ongoing program of water resources research. It was President Reagan's eighth veto of a public bill during the 98th Congress.

TO THE SENATE OF
THE UNITED STATES:

I am returning herewith without my approval S. 684, an act "To authorize an ongoing program of water resources research, and for other purposes."

Title I would authorize appropriations totalling $36 million annually for the fiscal years 1985-1989 for a variety of water resources research activities throughout the nation, including a new, separate authorization of grants for the development of water technology, which is not an appropriate Federal activity.

Title II would convey desalting test facilities that are no longer in Federal use to Wrightsville Beach, North Carolina, and Roswell, New Mexico. The administration has supported these conveyances. I would be pleased to sign a bill that provides only for them.

For some twenty years, the Federal government has provided "seed money" for the type of water research that would be authorized by Title I. This Federal support has produced a number of successful State water research institutes. I believe that these State institutes are now at a point where further Federal involvement in their research activities is not necessary. They can stand and continue to succeed on their own.

Moreover, the water research that S. 684 would promote can be characterized as mostly local or in some cases regional in nature. The focus of such research will of course vary from State to State because water problems and needs often differ by region. The States and private industry should be fully responsible for financing research necessary to deal with their own particular problems and needs.

If we are to truly succeed in reducing Federal spending we must sort out those responsibilities which are appropriately Federal from those which can be more effectively and fairly implemented at the State and local level. Accordingly, I feel constrained to disapprove S. 684.

RONALD REAGAN

The White House,
February 21, 1984   ∎

Report to Congress on ASAT Arms Control

Following are excerpts from the White House text of President Reagan's March 31 report to Congress regarding U.S. policy on anti-satellite arms control.

Preface

The Congressional conference report for the Department of Defense Appropriations Act for the Fiscal Year ending September 30, 1984 states:

The conferees agree to provide $19,409,000 for advance procurement for the Antisatellite (ASAT) program as proposed by the Senate, instead of no funds as proposed by the House. However, the conferees direct that these funds not be obligated or expended until 45 days following submission to the Congress of a comprehensive report on U.S. policy on arms control plans and objectives in the field of ASAT systems. In no event shall such report be submitted later than March 31, 1984. Such report should include specific steps the Administration contemplates undertaking, within the context of U.S.-Soviet negotiations, to seek a verifiable agreement with the Soviet Union to ban or strictly limit existing and future ASAT systems. The report should be unclassified, with classified addenda as required, and suitable for general release.

This report to Congress fulfills that requirement. It summarizes U.S. national security requirements pertaining to ASAT weaponry, and the problems and possibilities for ASAT arms control. The Report is in two versions, one is unclassified and the other, containing additional detail, is classified.

U.S. Policy on ASAT Arms Control

Overview

U.S. arms control policy must serve our fundamental national security objectives. In particular, arms control arrangements should reduce the risk of war (through measures which strengthen deterrence, increase confidence, and enhance strategic stability) or reduce the destructiveness of warfare. Arms control arrangements for space are desirable if they contribute to our overall deterrence posture and reduce the risk of conflict, not as ends in themselves. Similarly, possible limits or bans on anti-satellite (ASAT) arms must be judged not only in their ability to limit damage to space objects, but also in their contribution to achieving the basic objectives of arms control with respect to terrestrial conventional and nuclear conflict.

The U.S. National Space Policy, announced by the President July 4, 1982, is consistent with the long-standing U.S. approach to space arms control in previous agreements. It states:

"The United States will continue to study space arms control options. The United States will consider verifiable and equitable arms control measures that would ban or otherwise limit testing and deployment of specific weapons systems, should those measures be compatible with United States national security."

Guided by these criteria, the United States has been studying a range of possible options for space arms control with a view to possible negotiations with the Soviet Union and other nations, if such negotiations would serve U.S. interests. The United States is also prepared to examine space arms control issues in the Conference on Disarmament (CD). However, no arrangements or agreements beyond those already governing military activities in outer space have been found to date that are judged to be in the overall interest of the United States and its Allies. The factors which impede the identification of effective ASAT arms control measures include significant difficulties of verification, diverse sources of threats to U.S. and Allied satellites and threats posed by Soviet targeting and reconnaissance satellites which undermine conventional and nuclear deterrence.

Notwithstanding these difficulties, the United States is continuing to study space arms control, in search of selected limits on specific types of space systems or activities in space which could satisfactorily deal with problems such as those described above. Until we have determined whether there are, in fact, practical solutions to these problems, we do not believe it would be productive to engage in formal international negotiations. The United States remains ready, however, to examine the problems and potential of space arms control at the Conference on Disarmament. . . .

Potential Benefits of Space Arms Control

. . . The spectrum of possible space arms control measures includes bans on specialized ASAT weapons and much less ambitious undertakings. To be acceptable any measure must be equitable, effectively verifiable and compatible with our national security. If any space arms control measures met these criteria, and were complied with, then they would have a number of potential benefits. For example, depending on the scope and effectiveness of an agreement, it might:

1. Limit specialized threats to satellites and constrain future threats to such key satellites as those for early warning. Such limitations on specialized threats to satellites, together with satellite survivability measures, could help preserve and enhance stability.

2. Raise the political threshold for attacks against satellites. Restricting threatening activity and/or prohibiting attacks on satellites would add to existing international law aimed at lowering the likelihood of conflict in space.

3. Meet some international concerns regarding the use of space for military purposes.

Problems Facing ASAT Arms Control

In addition to the potential benefits of space arms control, a balanced study of this topic must take into account a number of problems. . . .

Verification. Effective verification is fundamental to arms control. . . . The Congressional language mandating ASAT arms control efforts has been uniformly specific on the matter of verification: any ban on ASAT systems is to be verifiable.

. . . The open U.S. society makes the Soviet task of monitoring U.S. activities regarding arms control compliance a relatively easy matter. In contrast, the closed Soviet society and the general Soviet tendency toward secrecy make U.S. monitoring and verification of compliance much more difficult. This problem is aggravated for ASAT systems because the satellites which serve U.S. and Allied security are few in number. Cheating on anti-satellite limitations, even on a small scale, could pose a disproportionate risk to the United States.

In this regard, the Soviets would have a far easier problem of verifying compliance with limitations on the U.S. ASAT system than we would have on the Soviet system. For example, a ban on all ASAT systems would require that the Soviet ASAT interceptor system be eliminated. The Soviet interceptor is relatively small and is launched by a type of space booster that the Soviets use for other space launch missions. It is not clear how many interceptors or boosters have been manufactured. The USSR could maintain a covert supply of interceptors which could be readied quickly for operational use, probably without risk of U.S. detection. Launch vehicles could be diverted from other missions to launch ASAT interceptors.

Verification problems apply to other aspects of space arms control as well. For instance, tests of a ground-based laser ASAT weapon could be concealed. In addition, determining with confidence whether an object hundreds of kilometers above the earth has been damaged could, in practice, be extremely difficult, and from what source it had been damaged could be extremely difficult or impossible. It may be difficult to determine whether a satellite has been damaged by electronic countermeasures. It is also difficult, or in some cases could be impossible, to determine whether an orbiting satellite contains a weapon.

Additional verification problems arise if ASAT testing is banned or limited. The wide variety of ASAT systems listed below in the discussion of problems of definition, and the fact that ASAT capabilities can be a by-product of systems developed for other missions, create problems of identifying what would be prohibited under testing limitations. The fact that ASAT capabilities are inherent in some systems developed for other missions or are amenable to undetected or surreptitious development makes it impossible to verify compliance with a truly comprehensive testing limitation that would eliminate tests of all methods of countering satellites. Test bans for a more limited class of ASAT systems may be verifiable, and these are being studied to determine if they are in our national interest. The breakout potential of that limited class of ASAT systems is very troublesome and creates doubt that limited test bans could be effective.

The difficult verification problems could, in some cases, be mitigated by future technological developments, or by cooperative measures contained in future arms control agreements. Such possibilities are under study.

Breakout. Among the criteria which must be used in evaluating the implications for national security of any potential arms control measure is that of "breakout." This is the risk that a nation could gain a unilateral advantage if the agreement ceased to remain in force for any reason, for example through sudden abrogation, and obtain a head start in building or deploying a type of weapon which has been banned or severely limited. The importance of certain critical U.S. satellites, which are limited in numbers, could create an incentive for the Soviets to maintain a breakout capability.

Breakout potential could exist even if the Soviets, upon agreeing to a ban on ASAT systems, were to destroy all of their existing systems. The Soviets could retain the capability to redeploy quickly a system in which they would have confidence. If prior to the ban the United States had not tested its MV ASAT system, the Soviets alone would possess such proven technology." The Soviets a year or less to deploy their system again.

Under a strict ASAT arms control regime, it is conceivable that the Soviets could change the basic character of their ASAT program. The USSR could have additional ASAT capability in equipment amenable to undetected or surreptitious development, which could be brought to operational status, or to a status that would permit rapid breakout. For example, any nation routinely conducting space rendezvous and docking operations, as the USSR does, could, under the guise of that activity, develop spacecraft equipped to maneuver into the path of, or detonate next to, another nation's spacecraft. Other types of systems amenable to such development include ballistic missiles with modified guidance software such as ICBMs, SLBMs and MRBMs, as well as space boosters with nuclear payloads. There is little reason to believe that the USSR would use any of these non-optimum capabilities in lieu of the system with known ASAT capabilities. However, a ban on the more readily identifiable ASAT systems could increase the likelihood that other systems would be covertly developed to have ASAT capability.

Disclosure of Information. While the difficult verification problems associated with ASAT arms control might be decreased with the establishment of cooperative measures, in some instances these measures could cause other problems. Information regarding certain U.S. space systems that are associated with national security is among the most sensitive information within the government. Cooperative measures with the objective of enhancing verification of an ASAT arms control agreement might require access to U.S. space systems that were alleged by the Soviets to have ASAT capabilities, and hence could create an unacceptable risk of compromising the protection of that information. Such measures could also have adverse effects on civil uses of space.

Definition. It is difficult to define what constitutes a space weapon for arms control purposes. There are technologies and systems designed for purposes other than ASAT, even some with little or no ASAT capabilities, which may be difficult to exclude from an ASAT definition. Likewise, there are technologies and systems which could have an ASAT application that might not be included in an ASAT definition.

The U.S. Congress has shown concern over space system survivability problems, especially in legislation which each chamber has passed relating the U.S. ASAT program to arms control. The Senate passed a measure to establish criteria governing the testing of ASAT warheads; in the deliberations over that provision, it was argued that "unless (ASAT) development is stopped, our most important and sensitive military satellites will be in jeopardy." The House of Representatives passed a measure deleting advanced procurement funds for the U.S. ASAT program; in those deliberations, it was argued "that the survival of current and projected U.S. space systems is vital to the national security of the United States." In keeping with those broadly-based satellite survivability concerns we need to recognize that "ASAT capability" relates to all systems capable of damaging, destroying or otherwise interrupting the functioning of satellites. Such systems include:

- maneuvering spacecraft (equipped to maneuver into the path of, or to detonate next to, another nation's spacecraft) such as the coorbital interceptor operationally deployed by the USSR.
- Direct ascent interceptors such as exo-atmospheric ABM missiles, ballistic missiles with modified guidance logic, space boosters carrying nuclear payloads, and homing vehicles such as the miniature vehicle system undergoing development by the United States.
- Directed energy weapons such as lasers and particle beams, (either ground-based or space-based, having sufficient power to damage satellites or their sensors).
- Electronic countermeasures of sufficient power output to damage or interrupt satellite functions.
- Weapons which could be carried by manned space planes or orbital complexes.

Furthermore, problems of weapon definition are compounded because some non-weapon space systems, including civil and commercial systems, could have characteristics which would make it difficult to frame a definition to distinguish them from weapon systems. An effective space arms control measure should take into account weapon capabilities beyond those of specialized ASAT systems, and at the same time it must not unduly constrain the legitimate functions of non-weapon space systems.

In seeking ways to verify an ASAT weapon ban, the Administration has been confronted with critical definitional problems: (1) there are many different types of systems which could be used to destroy satellites; (2) in general, many activities related to space give rise to capabilities inherently useful for ASAT purposes, for example, the rendezvous and docking operations routinely conducted by the Soviets could be used to attempt to conceal development of one or more types of ASAT techniques, and (3) restricting the definition of what is an ASAT weapon could make an agreement easier to verify, but ineffective in achieving its purpose of protecting satellites. These definition problems interact with and compound the verification problems described above.

Vulnerability of Satellite Support Systems. ASAT arms control would not provide for survivability of all components of space systems. For example, attacks on other elements of a space system (e.g., ground stations, launch facilities, or communications links) may in some cases be easier and more effective than attacks on satellites themselves. Attacks on ground-based support systems can be carried out with strikes by conventional weapons, such as by cruise missiles with conventional warheads launched from ships or aircraft.

The Soviet Non-Weapon Military Space Threat. Examination of space arms control needs to include a discussion of the growing threat posed by present and projected Soviet space systems which, while not weapons themselves, are designed to support directly the USSR's terrestrial forces in the event of a conflict. These include ocean reconnaissance satellites which use radar and electronic intelligence in efforts to provide targeting data to Soviet weapon platforms which can quickly attack U.S. and Allied surface fleets. In view of the fundamental importance of U.S. and Allied access to the seas in wartime, including for Allied reinforcement by sea, the protection of U.S. and Allied navies against such targeting is critical. Furthermore, as Soviet military space technology improves, the capabilities of Soviet satellites that can be used for targeting are likely to be enhanced and represent a greater threat to U.S. and Allied security. This point is explained at greater length below.

National Security Considerations Regarding Space

Beyond the significant limitations inherent in space arms control discussed above, other national security interests must be taken into account. These would pertain even if verification were not so significant a concern.

Strengthening Deterrence

A fundamental purpose of defense and arms control policies is to maintain and strengthen deterrence, both conventional and nuclear deterrence. ASAT limitations could, unfortunately, undermine deterrence in some instances.

Since the Soviet Union has an operational capability to destroy satellites while the United States does not, the current situation is destabilizing. If, for example, during a crisis or conflict, the Soviet Union were to destroy a U.S. satellite, the United States would lack the capability to respond in kind to avoid escalating the conflict. Thus, in present circumstances a U.S. capability to destroy satellites clearly responds to the need to deter such Soviet

attacks on U.S. satellites in a crisis or conflict.

A comprehensive ASAT ban would afford a sanctuary to existing Soviet satellites designed to target U.S. naval and land conventional forces. The absence of a U.S. ASAT capability to prevent Soviet targeting aided by satellites could be seen by the Soviets as a substantial factor in their ability to attack U.S. and Allied forces and might offset Soviet concerns about the effectiveness of U.S. and Allied naval warfare capabilities. Uncertainty over their ability to employ satellites to target naval forces would decrease the Soviet perception of their chance for success, thereby adding to deterrence and stability. A U.S. ASAT capability would contribute to deterrence of conventional conflict.

For U.S. and Allied security, the United States must continue its efforts to protect against threatening satellites. ASAT capabilities complement the other measures that must be used throughout a conflict. To do otherwise would undermine both conventional and nuclear deterrence. (Further discussion of the above factors is provided in the classified version of this report.) . . .

Soviet Threats to U.S. Satellites

The current Soviet ASAT capabilities include an operational orbital interceptor system, ground-based test lasers with probable ASAT capabilities, and possibly, the nuclear-armed GALOSH ABM interceptors, and the technological capability to conduct electronic warfare against space systems.

The orbital interceptor must go into approximately the same orbit as its target and close at a specific velocity. There have been more than a dozen tests of the interceptor system, which we consider operational, including testing during a Soviet strategic forces exercise in 1982.

A Soviet high-altitude orbital interceptor capability is a possible threat, but we have no direct evidence of such a program by the Soviets, and we may not obtain such evidence before testing. Other techniques for accomplishing this objective may appear preferable to the Soviets. For example, they could also use their developing electronic warfare capabilities against high-altitude satellites. We cannot now say which, if any, such high-altitude capabilities may be developed by the USSR.

Continuing, or possible future, Soviet efforts that could produce ASAT systems include developments in directed energy weapons. We have indications that the Soviets are continuing development of ground-based lasers for ASAT applications. In addition, we believe the Soviets are conducting research and development in the area of space-based laser ASAT systems. We have, as yet, no evidence of Soviet programs to develop ASAT weapons based on particle beam technology.

(Additional data concerning Soviet threats to U.S. satellites are contained in the classified version of this report.) . . .

Utility of a U.S. ASAT Capability

The U.S. ASAT program is focused explicitly on those Soviet satellites which threaten U.S. and Allied terrestrial interests in time of war. All of these threatening Soviet satellites operate at low altitude. Without low altitude satellites to confirm detections of terrestrial targets, Soviet space-based targeting data would be significantly degraded. While the U.S. MV ASAT will be able to attack only a portion of the Soviet satellites, in doing so it would be able seriously to degrade the Soviet reconnaissance capability and thus serves U.S. deterrence objectives. It cannot and need not attack Soviet early warning satellites at high altitudes.

Because of their high launch rates and payload capacity, the Soviet space force has the inherent resiliency to make replacement of satellites a viable alternative (as long as ground facilities are intact). On-orbit spares, surge of launches in a crisis or prior to a hostility, and satellite replacement following ASAT attack are possible methods of replenishment. The U.S. program is structured to provide a number of readily available ASAT systems sufficient to counter expected Soviet surge and replenishment. . . .

Alternatives to Offset the Threat Posed by Soviet Satellites

U.S. force structure plans include a balanced package of complementary defensive measures. The capability to counter Soviet satellites is an important element of those plans. To the extent that we limit our capabilities to counter Soviet satellites, we tend to increase our need to augment our conventional forces to perform their terrestrial missions in the face of the Soviet threat from space, with attending costs.

To counter Soviet satellites by attacking their ground facilities would be an uncertain alternative to an ASAT capability and one which risked escalation of a conflict. A U.S. ASAT capability is a less risky and more effective and flexible way to deal militarily with the Soviet space-based threat.

The ASAT MV complements other protective measures which must be used throughout a conflict. These measures include communications and emissions security, evasive maneuvers and electronic countermeasures. These countermeasures are, however, reactive and cannot provide permanent protection. Moreover, they can impose sharp constraints on the operational effectiveness of U.S. forces in a conflict.

Arms Control Prospects in Light of Policy and National Security Considerations

The balance between the benefits and risks of ASAT arms control is quite sensitive. For example, there is a dilemma as to whether arms control restrictions that would constrain our ability to deal with Soviet targeting satellites, are in our national security interest. Our need to counter such Soviet satellites so as to support our terrestrial forces must be balanced against our interest in limiting threats to critical U.S. satellites. Our studies of possible ASAT arms control regimes are considering these concerns.

Soviet ASAT Arms Control Activities

Although the Soviets have periodically tested their operational ASAT interceptor, they regularly advance space arms control measures in international fora, without acknowledging their own ASAT capability. In their latest initiative last August, the Soviet Union submitted to the 38th United Nations General Assembly a draft treaty, the stated objectives of which are to prohibit testing and deployment of space-based weapons. It calls for elimination of existing ASAT systems, for a ban on the development of new ASAT weapons, and for a ban on attacks on satellites. The USSR also announced a "unilateral moratorium" on the launching of any type of ASAT weapon, to remain in effect as long as other countries refrain from putting into space ASAT weapons of any type.

U.S. Evaluation of Soviet Initiatives

The wording of these proposals had certain ambiguities and loopholes. For example, it would appear that the moratorium did not cover tests of ground-based systems, such as lasers. In any case, the Soviet moratorium appeared to be designed to block tests of the U.S. miniature vehicle ASAT interceptor, while allowing the USSR to maintain the world's only operational ASAT system. This is inconsistent with the USSR's profession "not to be the first to put into outer space any type of ASAT weapon."

The Soviet initiatives have fundamental shortcomings. Lack of effective verification is one of the major weaknesses of the draft treaty. It provides for national technical means of verification, but nothing beyond that. Indeed, the draft does not even prohibit actions that would impede verification. In addition to the problem of verifying the elimination of the Soviet ASAT system, the draft treaty's proposal for a ban on destruction, damaging, and disruption of other states' space objects could also pose verification problems. The Soviet draft treaty is unclear with regard to Soviet targeting and reconnaissance satellites. The draft also does not deal with residual ASAT capabilities. For example, dismantling of the Soviet co-orbital ASAT system would still leave the USSR the option of using some of its Galosh ABM interceptor missiles in an antisatellite role. In addition, the draft treaty proposes that "piloted" spacecraft not be used for "military purposes." We strongly suspect that this provision is intended to constrain the

use of the U.S. Space Transportation System (the Space Shuttle), which in the years ahead will serve as the primary U.S. launch system for national security as well as civil space missions. At the same time, the treaty would apparently not constrain the Soviet unpiloted space station.

Similarly, the possible motives behind the Soviet offer of a "moratorium" are suspect. In addition to their operational ASAT system the Soviets currently have other systems with ASAT capability. The Soviet moratorium deals only with their operational system, allowing the others to continue. For example, the Soviets could test ground-based lasers in an ASAT mode without violating their moratorium. Moreover, the Soviet offer came on the eve of the commencement of flight testing of the U.S. MV system. Thus, the timing suggests that the Soviet offer is designed to curtail the U.S. MV program and thereby leave the Soviet Union with a unilateral advantage in ASAT capability. Furthermore, a test moratorium would not necessarily cause their operational system to atrophy: after a hiatus of several years in ASAT testing, the Soviets were able to resume testing of their ASAT system without any apparent degradation in its performance. Programs in research and development pay a much higher price for a test moratorium. Even a short delay in the test program would delay the time that the U.S. ASAT could be operational. This would decrease the Soviet incentive to negotiate in good faith. (A full analysis of the Soviet draft treaty is provided in the classified version of this report.)

It appears that the Soviet objectives in their initiatives are to limit disproportionately the U.S. ASAT capability and to enhance the Soviet international image.

In sum, it appears that Soviet initiatives on ASAT arms control pose profound verification problems, as in the case of the Soviet treaty, or would leave the USSR with a destabilizing advantage, as in the case of both the treaty and the moratorium.

Multilateral Space Arms Control Activities

The United States has supported discussion of a broad range of questions on space arms control at the Conference on Disarmament (CD). The United States supported in 1983 the establishment of a CD Working Group on Outer Space. The United States does not favor having a working group undertake negotiations. Rather, we believe that a working group should address a broad range of space arms control issues, beginning with a thorough examination of the existing legal regime for space, before any conclusions can be drawn about negotiations which might be pursued in the CD. In 1983, the Soviets insisted that a working group on outer space in the CD be commissioned to begin negotiations. While the United States, our Allies, and the neutral and non-aligned nations of the CD all were ready to establish a working

group without authority to negotiate, the Soviets blocked such action. The U.S. position this year in the CD is unchanged: the United States remains ready to proceed with a serious and responsible examination in the CD of space arms control.

Future Directions of ASAT Arms Control

U.S. space arms control policy seeks to reduce the risk of conflict and enhance strategic stability. Consistent with this purpose, the Administration has been evaluating a number of possible ASAT arms control options in light of whether they support our overall deterrence posture and are effectively verifiable. Despite efforts by this and the previous administration, no way has yet been found to design a comprehensive ASAT ban that meets these criteria.

The major problems for ASAT arms control discussed in detail in this report have hindered our efforts to develop effective arms control measures. In fact, it appears that the problems of verification tend to be greater the more comprehensive the limitation. Some less sweeping options under study would seek to limit or ban specific types of weapons systems. Since we must in any event be able to protect our satellites against threats that could be developed without our knowledge, there is a premium on finding ways to limit in arms control those ASAT systems that create the most difficult survivability problems. We are searching for limits on such systems which are effectively verifiable and which allow us to protect U.S. and Allied forces from threatening Soviet satellites, such as targeting satellites. Other options under examination would regulate certain threatening activities related to space.

The future of space arms control must also be considered in the broader context of U.S.-Soviet arms control relations. Soviet actions in other negotiating fora and Soviet actions with respect to compliance with existing arms control agreements must also be taken into account to determine the most appropriate course of action for the United States concerning arms control for outer space. In the meantime, the U.S. evaluation of possible future courses for ASAT arms control will be judged not simply in light of their ability to limit damage to space objects, but also in light of their contributions to the basic objectives of U.S. arms control policy with respect to terrestrial conventional and nuclear conflict.

The door is not closed to effective ASAT arms control measures. As noted earlier, the President has said that the United States will consider verifiable and equitable arms control measures that would ban or otherwise limit testing and deployment of specific weapons systems, should those measures be compatible with U.S. national security.

This remains the policy of the Administration. The active search for viable arms control opportunities in the ASAT area is continuing. ∎

Public Broadcasting Veto

Following is the White House text of President Reagan's Aug. 29 message accompanying his veto of S 2436, to authorize funding for the Corporation for Public Broadcasting. It was Reagan's ninth veto of a public bill during the 98th Congress.

TO THE SENATE OF
THE UNITED STATES:

Since the adjournment of the Congress has prevented my return of S 2436 within the meaning of Article I, section 7, clause 2 of the Constitution, my withholding of approval from the bill precludes its becoming a law. Notwithstanding what I believe to be my constitutional power regarding the use of the "pocket veto" during an adjournment of Congress, however, I am sending S 2436 to the Senate with my objections, consistent with the Court of Appeals decision in *Kennedy v. Sampson*, 511 F.2d 430 (D.C. Cir. 1974).

Public broadcasting constitutes an important national resource and contributes to the diversity of news, information, and entertainment choices available to the American public. Under S 2436, however, Federal funding for public broadcasting would be increased by too much too fast. The Fiscal Year 1987 authorization of $238 million for the Corporation for Public Broadcasting represents a 49 percent increase over the already enacted funding level for 1986. Likewise, next year's spending on new public broadcasting facilities grants would be authorized at $50 million or four times this year's appropriation.

When all of the demands on the Federal budget are taken into account, increases in spending on public broadcasting of the magnitude contemplated by this legislation cannot be justified. They are incompatible with the clear and urgent need to reduce Federal spending. Moreover, this view is clearly shared by a large portion of the House of Representatives as indicated by the 176 votes in favor of the Oxley amendment to reduce the three-year authorizations by 25 percent.

In disapproving this bill, therefore, I urge the Congress to consider a revised bill providing more reasonable and moderate increases for the Board for Public Broadcasting along the lines of the Oxley amendment. I also reiterate my strong opposition to the huge increases for public facilities grants contained in S 2436 and the unjustified expansion of this program to include repair and replacement of existing equipment.

I must also stress that my firm insistence on scaling this bill back to more fiscally responsible levels in no way jeopardizes the continued operations of public broadcasting stations across the Nation. Under the established funding mechanism, ample appropriations have already been enacted into law for all of Fiscal Years 1985 and 1986. Funding for another 25 months is already guaranteed.

Thus, the issue regarding S 2436 is really one of long-range fiscal prudence. Given the magnitude of the deficit cuts that will be needed in the years ahead, I do not believe we can justify locking-in public broadcasting funding levels for 1987-1989 that are so obviously excessive. To do so would be wholly inconsistent with our pledge to slow the growth of spending and reduce the size of the deficit.

Accordingly, I am disapproving S 2436.

RONALD REAGAN

The White House,
August 29, 1984 ∎

Indian Compensation Veto

Following is the White House text of President Reagan's Oct. 17 memorandum of disapproval (pocket veto) on S 1967, to compensate the Gros Ventre and Assiniboine Tribes for irrigation construction expenses. It was Reagan's 10th veto of a public bill during the 98th Congress.

I am withholding my approval from S. 1967, a bill "To compensate the Gros Ventre and Assiniboine Tribes of the Fort Belknap Indian Community for irrigation construction expenditures."

S. 1967 would reimburse the Gros Ventre and Assiniboine Tribes of the Fort Belknap Indian Community for $107,759.58 in tribal funds expended under applicable law for the construction of irrigation projects on the Fort Belknap Indian Reservation from 1895 to 1913. In addition, interest would be paid at 4 percent from the date of expenditure of the tribal funds until the date of payment of the principal pursuant to the bill.

On November 20, 1962, the Indian Claims Commission, after due deliberation, issued a detailed opinion carefully considering and dismissing (among other claims) a claim for the same reimbursement that would be provided by the bill. Fort Belknap Indian Community v. United States, 11 Ind. Cl. Comm. 479, 510-518, 543-549 (1962). The Commission found that construction of the irrigation system was "requested by the members of the Fort Belknap Community," that it has been of great and continuing benefit to the tribes, and "that its construction and maintenance have been consonant with the fair and honorable dealings clause within the meaning of the Indian Claims Commission Act." 11 Ind. Cl. Comm. 518-519. The tribes took no appeal from that decision.

The fair and impartial administration of justice and the protection of public resources from meritless special appropriations both require that those who have availed themselves of judicial remedies in asserting claims against the United States, and have had their claims fully and fairly adjudicated under our Constitution and laws, receive no more or less than that to which they have been adjudged to be entitled. Twenty-two years after the claims of these two tribes were dismissed by an impartial tribunal established by the Congress specifically to adjudicate such claims, this bill would authorize and appropriate to them all that they were previously found not to be entitled to.

Under the circumstances, the enactment of the bill would set aside established principles of justice and thereby encourage other and future efforts to obtain by legislation that which has been denied by a just adjudication.

For these reasons, I find the bill unacceptable.

RONALD REAGAN

The White House,
October 17, 1984 ∎

NOAA Veto

Following is the White House text of President Reagan's Oct. 19 memorandum of disapproval (pocket veto) on S 1097, the National Oceanic and Atmospheric Administration's Atmospheric and Oceanic Research and Services Act. It was Reagan's 11th veto of a public bill during the 98th Congress.

I have withheld my approval from S. 1097, the "National Oceanic and Atmospheric Administration's Atmospheric and Oceanic Research and Services Act of 1984." S. 1097 would, among other things, authorize appropriations for various National Oceanic and Atmospheric Administration (NOAA) programs for fiscal year 1985, for which appropriations have already been enacted.

S. 1097 also contains, however, a number of undesirable provisions that would unduly effect the ability of the Department of Commerce to manage its programs responsibly and effectively. The provisions in Title VI concerning the closings and consolidations of National Weather Service offices are particularly generous and would have the effect of virtually precluding the consolidation of closing of such offices, even when such closings or consolidations are fully justified.

In addition, S. 1097 contains other highly objectionable provisions concerning the Department's activities. Section 205 of S. 1097 would result in excessive and unjustifiable delays in Department contracting-out activities, even when such contracting would be in the clear interest of the Nation's taxpayers. And, Section 202(b), which concerns the weather satellite program, is objectionable because it would lessen the Secretary of Commerce's discretion in managing that program, as well as require the inefficient use of a government asset.

This Act represents an unwarranted intrusion by Congress into matters normally and properly within the management discretion of the Executive branch. In the interest of efficient and economical conduct of government activities, therefore, I am constrained to withhold my approval of S. 1097.

RONALD REAGAN

The White House,
October 19, 1984 ∎

Broadcasting Funds Veto

Following is the White House text of President Reagan's Oct. 19 memorandum of disapproval (pocket veto) on S 607, to authorize appropriations for the Corporation for Public Broadcasting and the Public Telecommunications Facilities Program. It was Reagan's 12th veto of a public bill during the 98th Congress.

I have withheld my approval from S. 607, the "Public Broadcasting Amendments Act of 1984."

This bill would authorize appropriations of $200 million, $225 million, and $250 million, respectively, for fiscal years 1987, 1988, and 1989 for the Corporation for Public Broadcasting. It would also authorize appropriations of $25 million, $35 million, and $40 million for the Public Telecommunications Facilities Program administered by the Department of Commerce for fiscal years 1985, 1986, and 1987.

Public broadcasting has an important role to play in assuring that a wise variety of information and entertainment choices are made available to American viewers and listeners. Under S. 607, however, the authorizations for Federal subsidies to public broadcasting would increase dramatically. When all of the demands on the Federal budget are taken into account, I cannot endorse the levels of spending contemplated by this legislation. They are incompatible with the clear and urgent need to reduce Federal spending.

It is important to note that current-year funding for these two programs totals only $174 million. The Oxley amendment would have resulted in a generous and barely affordable increase of 15 percent, to $200 million. S. 607 goes much further and raises first-year funding by 29 percent to $225 million for the two programs. By the third year under S. 607, combined funding would be $290 million, a 67 percent increase from the current budget year. Under present fiscal conditions, unrestrained increases of this magnitude — no matter how worthy the programs — are unacceptable.

Legislation that provides for Federal support of public broadcasting at realistic and reasonable levels and that provides public broadcasters with the means and incentives to explore alternative revenue sources would be both appropriate and welcome. If, however, we are to succeed in reducing Federal spending — as we must — the levels of spending contemplated by S. 607 cannot be justified.

In withholding my approval of S. 607, I want to emphasize that the continued operations of the Corporation for Public Broadcasting are not at risk. Funds for the Corporation have already been appropriated for 1985 and 1986, and funds for 1987 are contained in H.R. 6028, the Labor-Health and Human Services-Education 1985 appropriations bill, which recently passed both Houses of Congress.

I vetoed an earlier version of this legislation on August 29, 1984, for precisely the same reasons that I am withholding my approval of S. 607. I will continue to oppose and reject bills of this nature until and unless Congress presents me with a bill that is consistent with sound budget policy. This one is certainly not, and I decline to approve it.

RONALD REAGAN

The White House,
October 19, 1984 ∎

Indian Health Care Veto

Following is the White House text of President Reagan's Oct. 19 memorandum of disapproval (pocket veto) on S 2166, to extend and amend the Indian Health Care Improvement Act. It was Reagan's 13th veto of a public bill during the 98th Congress.

I am withholding my approval of S. 2166, the "Indian Health Care Amendments of 1984," which would extend and amend the Indian Health Care Improvement Act.

Although I fully support the intent and objectives of the Indian Health Care Improvement Act, I believe this bill is seriously deficient in fulfilling those goals. My disapproval of the bill will in no way affect the continued delivery of health care services to our country's Indian population. Earlier this month I signed the Continuing Resolution Appropriations Act for fiscal year 1985, which includes $855 million for the Indian Health Service, an increase of $30 million over the prior year.

A number of serious flaws in S. 2166 compel my disapproval of this bill. Two provisions are especially troublesome.

First, a provision that I find totally unacceptable would actually reduce access to health services for Indians. That provision would have the effect of making Indians residing in Montana ineligible for certain benefits of State and locally supported health programs until and unless the availability of such benefits from the Indian Health Service has been exhausted. In my view, this provision for Indian citizens of Montana would set a precedent for potentially changing the fundamental relationship of the Indian Health Service to State and local entities, as well as depriving eligible Indians of benefits that should be due them by virtue of their citizenship in the State. As a matter of both principle and precedent, I cannot accept this provision.

Second, the mechanism established in section 602(d) of the bill for effecting the removal of the Indian Health Service from the Health Resources and Services Administration (HRSA) is unconstitutional and can have no legal effect. The Department of Justice has advised me that the Congress may not constitutionally delegate to a congressionally appointed body, such as the Commission on the Organizational Placement of the Indian Health Service established by this bill, the legislative authority to determine when legislation will take effect. Because section 602(d) does not comply with the clear requirements of the Constitution, I cannot give my approval to this bill.

Other serious flaws in S. 2166 that compel my disapproval would:
— duplicate existing authorities in most of its provisions;
— unnecessarily and wastefully change the organization of the Indian Health Service; and
— place increased emphasis on services that are not oriented toward the primary mission of the Indian Health Service.

The bill would allocate a significant portion of funding for various peripheral projects, such as unnecessary reports, interagency agreements, and regulations development. This would lead either to an unacceptable increase in total funding or to underfunding of the most critical area — provision of clinical health services to reservation Indians. The Administration has, on the other hand, proposed using most

Indian health funds for this purpose, so that resources can be most effectively spent where the need is the greatest.

For all these reasons, I find S. 2166 unacceptable.

As I indicated earlier, the action I am taking will have no adverse impact on the delivery of health services to Indians living on or near a reservation because the existing provisions of the Snyder Act provide all necessary authority for such services. Since 1955, utilizing the Snyder Act authorities:

— 30 hospitals have been constructed;

— 30 clinics and 58 field health stations have been constructed;

— Annual admissions to Indian Health Service and contract hospitals have more than doubled; out-patient visits have multiplied by approximately eight times; and the number of dental services provided has increased ten-fold.

Even more important are the achievements in terms of improved health status, which is, after all, the goal of the Indian Health Service:

— The infant mortality rate has decreased by 77 percent and the maternal death rate by 86 percent;

— The death rate resulting from pneumonia and influenza has decreased by 73 percent; and

— Death from tuberculosis has been reduced by 94 percent and the incidence of new active tuberculosis has been reduced by 84 percent.

Over the last decade, the Federal Government has supported the Indian Health Service with over $5 billion. The last budget that I submitted to the Congress projected spending an additional $4 billion through 1989.

My Administration's commitment to ensuring the continuing improvement of health services delivery to Indian people and Alaska natives is strong and clear.

RONALD REAGAN

The White House,
October 19, 1984 ∎

The new role for the Federal government contemplated by Title III could also serve as the basis for a Federal industrial policy to influence our Nation's technological development. This Administration has steadfastly opposed such a role for the Federal government.

My Administration has fostered the development of a robust and improving economy, which will do more than anything to improve the growth and productivity of the industrial sector. We will continue our efforts to improve the general economy, the regulatory environment, and tax policies that are essential if U.S. industry is to remain competitive. I cannot, however, approve legislation that would result in significant Federal expenditures with litle or no assurance that there are any benefits to be gained.

I am, therefore, constrained to withhold my approval from H.R. 5172.

RONALD REAGAN

The White House,
October 30, 1984 ∎

Armed Career Criminals Veto

Following is the White House text of President Reagan's Oct. 19 memorandum of disapproval (pocket veto) on HR 6248, the Armed Career Criminal Act of 1984. It was Reagan's 14th veto of a public bill during the 98th Congress.

I am withholding my approval from H.R. 6248, the "Armed Career Criminal Act of 1984."

This legislation would generally enhance the penalties under existing law applicable to a felon who has been convicted three times in a United States or State court of robbery or burglary and who receives, possesses, or transports firearms.

Although I certainly support the aims

of H.R. 6248, I note that identical provisions were contained in the Administration's "Comprehensive Crime Control Act," which I approved on October 12, 1984, as part of P.L. 98-473. That legislation — marking the culmination of much hard work and effort on the part of members of my Administration and the Congress — is the most comprehensive revision of Federal criminal statutes to be enacted in many years.

Inasmuch as H.R. 6248 merely duplicates existing law, it is unnecessary. Accordingly, I decline to approve it.

RONALD REAGAN

The White House,
October 19, 1984 ∎

Bureau of Standards Veto

Following is the White House text of President Reagan's Oct. 30 memorandum of disapproval (pocket veto) on HR 5172, the National Bureau of Standards Authorization Act for fiscal 1985. It was Reagan's 15th veto of a public bill during the 98th Congress.

I am withholding my approval of H.R. 5172, which includes the "National Bureau of Standards Authorization Act for Fiscal Year 1985" (Title I), clarifications of the role of the National Science Foundation in engineering research and education (Title II), and the "Manufacturing Sciences and Robotics Research and Development Act of 1984" (Title III). Title I would, among other things, authorize appropriations for

certain Department of Commerce programs for fiscal year 1985, for which appropriations have already been enacted.

Title III of H.R. 5172 would establish a new program providing Federal financial support for a variety of research, development, education, and training activities, whose purported purpose would be to improve manufacturing technologies, including robotics and automation. These activities would total $250 million during fiscal years 1985-1988, and represent an unwarranted role for the Federal government. The decisions on how to allocate investments for research on manufacturing technologies are best left to American industry. It is highly doubtful that this Act and resulting Federal expenditures would improve the competitiveness of U.S. manufacturing.

Health Research Veto Message

Following is the White House text of President Reagan's Oct. 30 memorandum of disapproval (pocket veto) on S 540, to extend and amend the biomedical research authorities of the National Institutes of Health. It was Reagan's 16th veto of a public bill during the 98th Congress.

I am withholding my approval of S. 540, the "Health Research Extension Act of 1984," which would extend and amend the biomedical research authorities of the National Institutes of Health (NIH).

I have been assured by the Department of Health and Human Services that the Continuing Resolution gives adequate authority for current NIH activities in fiscal year 1985.

This Administration has a record of strong commitment to the support and conduct of biomedical research by the NIH. Each year since taking office, I have requested increases for biomedical research. In 1985, the NIH will receive its largest increase in appropriated funds in history. This increase will ensure the continued operation of the NIH for the coming year and will continue to assist in improving medical practice and the health of the American people.

Rather than improve our research efforts, however, the unfortunate result of S. 540 would be to impede the progress of this important health activity by:

● Creating unnecessary, expensive new organizational entities;

— two institutes would be created, an

arthritis and a nursing institute. This reorganization of the NIH is premature in light of a study of the NIH organizational structure to be released in a few weeks by the Institute of Medicine/National Academy of Sciences.

— numerous bodies, such as a National Commission on Orphan Diseases, an Interagency Committee on Learning Disabilities, and a Lupus Erythematosus Coordinating Committee, would be created for which there are existing mechanisms that could or already perform such functions.

● Mandating overly specific requirements for the management of research that place undue constraints on Executive branch authorities and functions;

— new positions would be created and numerous reports required that would divert scarce resources away from the NIH central mission of basic biomedical research.

— the various NIH peer review groups would be exempted from the provisions of the Federal Advisory Committee Act and Office of Management and Budget oversight. This represents an unwarranted interference with internal Executive branch management over the largest number of advisory groups for any Federal agency.

● Going beyond the Administration's request to extend only expiring authorities by rewriting all the relevant statutes of the NIH;

— current law contains sufficient authority and flexibility to carry out the important research and training activities of NIH, to respond to public concerns, and to meet scientific needs and opportunities. Imposing a uniform set of authorities for each research institution disregards the more extensive mission of some institutes and overburdens smaller institutes which do not need these additional programmatic and advisory responsibilities.

— this attempt to recodify existing statutory language has resulted in some so-called technical revisions that will result in undesired operational changes in some of the institute programs.

I want to underscore my commitment to biomedical research and the National Institutes of Health. The NIH has stood as an example of excellence for 40 years. I do not believe that it is either necessary or wise to revise completely the laws under which it has so successfully operated.

I therefore find no reasonable justification for the extensive changes to the NIH mandated by S. 540. In order to better serve the promise and the future of our national biomedical research enterprise, I am withholding my approval of this bill.

RONALD REAGAN
The White House,
October 30, 1984   ▪

Public Health Service Veto

Following is the White House text of President Reagan's Oct. 30 memorandum of disapproval (pocket veto) on S 2574, the Public Health Service Amendments of 1984. It was Reagan's 17th veto of a public bill during the 98th Congress.

I am withholding my approval of S. 2574, the "Public Health Service Act Amendments of 1984," which would extend and amend various health professions and services authorities. I have been assured by the Department of Health and Human Services that the Continuing Resolution provides adequate authority for these programs for fiscal year 1985. S. 2574 is a seriously flawed piece of legislation. The most serious of its many objectionable provisions include the following:

First, this bill contains authorization levels substantially in excess of my 1985 Budget. Full funding of all the programs in the bill through 1987 would total $2.4 billion, 41 percent more than the $1.7 billion contained in the Budget.

Moreover, S. 2574 would continue to increase obsolete Federal subsidies to health professions students and would maintain the static and rigid categorical framework to deliver such aid. The ability of medical schools to supply our society with health professionals has changed dramatically in the last 20 years. Today, our medical schools are producing nearly 16,000 new doctors each year. Although there may be some shortages of physicians and nurses in particular areas of the country, the Nation as a whole is facing a future surplus — not shortage — of physicians and nurses. Under these circumstances, S. 2574, a bill which continues excessive taxpayer subsidies to health professionals and maintains a rigid unworkable categorical framework, cannot be justified.

S. 2574 takes the wrong approach to health professions training. In contrast to the Administration's proposal for a single, omnibus reauthorization of all health pro-

fessions authorities, which would permit maximum program flexibility to address current needs, the bill not only reauthorizes the existing plethora of narrow, categorical authorities, but also creates new programs. This approach to health professions training is outdated and fails to respond to the rapidly changing health care environment.

A more appropriate approach would recognize that the surplus of physicians has reduced the need for Federal financial assistance and would improve incentives for health professionals to locate in areas of the country where shortages exist. The Administration's health professions proposals would help meet these objectives.

S. 2574 would also repeal the Primary Care Block Grant authority — a key reform proposed by the Administration and enacted by the Congress in 1981 designed to restore State control, strengthen administrative efficiencies, and improve the delivery of health services. Thus, this bill would reverse a successful trend of increased State acceptance of health care responsibility that the Administration initiated. The block grant programs for preventive health and health services and alcohol and drug abuse have been successful. The primary care block grant was made optional by the Congress, and States have been hesitant to accept it. However, to close out the option at a time when States should be willing to consider another step toward greater autonomy is counterproductive and unacceptable.

This bill contains numerous other provisions that are either unnecessary or unacceptable, including authorization for new Federal National Health Service Corps scholarships that are not needed, since the number of scholarship recipients already bound to subsidized medical practice in rural areas is adequate.

For all these reasons, I find S. 2574 unacceptable.

RONALD REAGAN
The White House,
October 30, 1984   ▪

Conservation Corps Veto

Following is the White House text of President Reagan's Oct. 30 memorandum of disapproval (pocket veto) on HR 999, the American Conservation Corps Act of 1984. It was Reagan's 18th veto of a public bill during the 98th Congress.

I am withholding my approval from H.R. 999, the "American Conservation Corps Act of 1984." This legislation would establish, within the Departments of Agriculture and the Interior, conservation-re-

lated employment programs for youths.

The programs that H.R. 999 would in effect reestablish — the Youth Conservation Corps (YCC) and the Young Adult Conservation Corps (YACC) — were terminated by Congress at my recommendation because they had been proven to be costly and unnecessary. The American Conservation Corps (ACC) would duplicate other efforts for youth financed by the Job Training Partnership Act (JTPA), such as the Job Corps, JTPA State Block Grants, and the Summer Youth program. In fiscal year 1985, the Federal Government will spend nearly $2.2 billion on these programs, which will train about 1.5 million people. This training is done at a much lower per-capita cost than would be the case under the ACC, and is much more likely to result in permanent private sector jobs for their graduates because they involve the private sector in job training.

The ACC, however, would be based on the discredited approach to youth unemployment that relies on artificial public sector employment, just as did the Public Service Employment program operated under the Comprehensive Employment and Training Act until it was terminated by Congress in 1981.

Moreover, the ACC is not a necessary or effective way of managing Federal lands. The Federal Government currently spends over $4 billion annually on land management. This amount is adequate to fund all activities needed to ensure the preservation of these precious resources for this and future generations of Americans. Any conservation project that could be performed by the ACC could be done better and for less money under existing programs, because of less overhead for residential centers and the greater productivity of existing workers who are already well trained. In addition, I have recently signed S. 864, which would expand the National Park Service's volunteer program, and allow such a program to be established in the Bureau of Land Management. Under these worthwhile programs, including those administered by the Forest Service and the Fish and Wildlife Service, citizens offer valuable volunteer services to assist the Departments of Agriculture and the Interior in the management of Federal lands.

Finally, while the three year, $225 million ACC authorization is itself unwarranted, it would almost certainly grow. The Youth Conservation Corps began in 1971 as a $1 million pilot program, and was subsequently given a permanent authorization of $60 million annually, notwithstanding its inability to provide enduring, meaningful benefits for the trainees or the public. Moreover, the proponents of the ACC have already served notice that they intend to attempt in the next Congress to increase the ACC authorization to $300 million annually. I believe that America's unemployed youth would be better served by reducing Federal spending so that more resources are available to the private sector of our economy to fuel a continuation of the current economic expansion that has added 6 million new jobs to the workforce over the last two years. If given the opportunity, the private sector is much more likely to offer young people promising career opportunities than temporary make-work Federal job programs such as the American Conservation Corps.

RONALD REAGAN

The White House,
October 30, 1984 ∎

Indian Land Claims Veto

Following is the White House text of President Reagan's Oct. 30 memorandum of disapproval (pocket veto) on HR 5760, to declare that the United States holds certain lands in trust for the Cocopah Indian Tribe of Arizona. It was Reagan's 19th veto of a public bill during the 98th Congress.

I am withholding my approval of H.R. 5760, a bill "To declare that the United States holds certain lands in trust for the Cocopah Indian Tribe of Arizona, and for other purposes."

Title I of H.R. 5760 would declare that almost 4,000 acres of Federal land in Yuma County, Arizona, be held in trust by the United States for the benefit of the Cocopah Indian Tribe. I do not object to this provision.

Title II of H.R. 5760 would allow the Navajo Tribe to reassert against the United States, vague and uncertain claims originally brought in July 1950, but voluntarily and legally withdrawn by their counsel in October 1969. The propriety and finality of counsel's action were subsequently given exhaustive consideration. *Navajo Tribe v. United States*, 220 Ct. Cl. 350, 601 F.2d 536 (1979), *cert. denied*, 444 U.S. 1072 (1980). In the meantime, some claims which might be affected by H.R. 5760 have been settled or litigated, and others have been placed on a detailed trial schedule. Enactment of H.R. 5760 could compel protracted renegotiation, retrial or delay in the trial of these claims, based upon vague and speculative allegations.

Absent a compelling showing that a substantial injustice would result from adherence to procedural norms, the limitations of the Indian Claims Act and the procedures adopted for the adjudication of claims under the Act should not be frustrated by special legislation, such as that contained in title II of H.R. 5760. No such showing has been made here.

Title II would interfere with the fair and orderly adjudication of the claims of the Navajo Tribe and would constitute an affront to established rules, procedures, and principles for the resolution of Indian claims. It could serve to encourage other and future efforts to obtain by legislation that which has been unattainable through adjudication.

For these reasons, I find the bill unacceptable. If Title I were presented as a separate bill, I would have no objection to its enactment.

RONALD REAGAN

The White House,
October 30, 1984 ∎

Equal Access Veto

Following is the White House text of President Reagan's Nov. 8 memorandum of disapproval (pocket veto) on HR 5479, to permanently reauthorize and amend the Equal Access to Justice Act. It was Reagan's 20th veto of a public bill during the 98th Congress.

I am withholding my approval of H.R. 5479, a bill "to amend section 504 of title 5, United States Code, and section 2412 of title 28, United States Code, with respect to awards of expenses of certain agency and court proceedings, and for other purposes."

H.R. 5479 would permanently reauthorize and make a number of significant changes to the Equal Access to Justice Act. The Act allows the award of attorneys' fees to certain parties who successfully litigate against the government unless the government demonstrates that its position is substantially justified or that special circumstances exist that make a fee award unjust. Because the Equal Access to Justice Act expired on September 30, 1984, legislation is needed to reauthorize the Act.

I am firmly committed to the policies underlying the Equal Access to Justice Act and will make the permanent and retroactive reauthorization of the Act a high legislative priority of the Administration in the next Congress. Where the Federal government has taken a position in litigation that is not substantially justified, and thereby has caused a small business or individual to incur unnecessary attorneys' fees and legal costs, I believe it proper for the government to reimburse that small business or individual for those expenses. The Equal Access to Justice Act thus serves an important salutary purpose that should become a permanent part of our government. Unfortunately, H.R. 5479 makes certain changes to the Equal Access to Justice Act that do not further the Act's basic purposes and that are inconsistent with fundamental principles of good government. The most objectionable of these provisions is the change the bill would make in the definition of "position of the United States." Under this changed definition, the Act would no longer apply only to the government's position taken in the administrative or court litigation, but would extend to the underlying agency action. This would result in needless and wasteful litigation over what is supposed to be a subsidiary issue, the award of attorneys' fees, and would further burden the courts, which would have to hear the claims in each case not once, but twice. In addition, this change could also undermine the free exchange of ideas and positions within each agency that is essential for good government.

For example, this change would require courts in making fee determinations to examine the conduct of agency even where that conduct is not at issue in the court's review of the merits of the case before it. This would mean that a fee proceeding could result in an entirely new and subsidiary inquiry in the circumstances that gave rise to the original lawsuit. This inquiry only could lead to far lengthier proceedings than required if the court is merely to examine arguments made in court, but also could lead to extensive discovery of how the underlying agency position was formulated, and who advocated what position and for what reasons at what time. In effect, every step of the agency decision-making process, at whatever level, could become the subject of litigation discovery. Such extensive discovery could inhibit free discussion within an agency prior to any final agency policy decision or action for fear that any internal disagreements or reservations would be the subject of discovery and judicial inquiry.

In addition, H.R. 5479 contains a provision that would require the United States to pay interest on any awarded attorneys' fees not paid within 60 days after the date of the award. As noted by the Comptroller General of the United States, this provision would give lawyers who have received awards under the Act more favorable treatment than any other group entitled to interest payments from the United States. I agree with the Comptroller General that to the extent any interest should be paid under the Act, it should be paid on the same basis as other interest payments made by the government on court judgments.

The Department of Justice, the Office of Management and Budget, and other concerned agencies have repeatedly expressed to the Congress their serious reservations about these and other provisions of H.R. 5479. I wholly support the prompt reauthorization of the Equal Access to Justice Act and believe that the reauthorization should be retroactively effective to October 1, 1984. In light of the permanent nature of a reauthorization, such a reauthorization should include modifications and improvements in the Act, which the Administration is willing to explore with the Congress.

Concurrently with this memorandum, I am issuing a memorandum to all agency heads concerning the Equal Access to Justice Act. This memorandum reaffirms my strong commitment to the policies underlying the Act and instructs agency heads to review the procedures of their agencies to ensure that agency positions continue to be substantially justified. Special attention is to be given to those agency positions that affect small businesses. In addition, each agency is to accept and assist in the preparation of fee applications which can be considered once the Act is reauthorized.

I look forward to approving an acceptable reauthorization of the Equal Access to Justice Act early next year. For the reasons indicated, however, I am compelled to withhold my approval of H.R. 5479.

RONALD REAGAN

The White House,
November 8, 1984

PUBLIC LAWS

Public Laws, 98th Congress, 2nd Session

PL 98-216 (HR 2727) Amend title 31 and title 49 of the U.S. Code to reflect changes in those titles by laws that did not specifically amend such titles. Introduced by RODINO, D-N.J., April 25, 1983. House passed, under suspension of the rules, Aug. 1. Senate Judiciary discharged. Senate passed Jan. 31, 1984. President signed Feb. 14, 1984.

PL 98-217 (HR 3969) Authorize the secretary of defense to act by proxy for any member of the Board of the Panama Canal Commission. Introduced by JONES, D-N.C., Sept. 22, 1983. House Merchant Marine and Fisheries reported Nov. 9 (H Rept 98-515). House passed, under suspension of the rules, Nov. 15. Senate Armed Services reported Nov. 17. Senate passed Jan. 31, 1984. President signed Feb. 14, 1984.

PL 98-218 (H J Res 290) Permit free entry into the United States of the personal effects, equipment and other related articles of foreign participants, officials and other accredited members of delegations involved in the games of the XXIII Olympiad, to be held in the United States in 1984. Introduced by ROSTENKOWSKI, D-Ill., June 6, 1983. House Ways and Means reported June 24 (H Rept 98-268). House passed, under suspension of the rules, June 28. Senate Finance reported Nov. 10. Senate passed, amended, Nov. 18. House agreed to Senate amendment with an amendment Feb. 2, 1984. Senate agreed to House amendment Feb. 6. President signed Feb. 17, 1984.

PL 98-219 (HR 2898) Declare certain lands to be held in trust for the benefit of certain Indian tribes. Introduced by MARRIOTT, R-Utah, May 4, 1983. House Interior and Insular Affairs reported Oct. 18 (H Rept 98-414). House passed, under suspension of the rules, Oct. 21. Senate Indian Affairs discharged. Senate passed, amended, Nov. 18. House agreed to Senate amendments Feb. 7, 1984. President signed Feb. 17, 1984.

PL 98-220 (S J Res 146) Designate March 23, 1984, as "National Energy Education Day." Introduced by HEINZ, R-Pa., Aug. 3, 1983. Senate Judiciary reported Sept. 15. Senate passed Sept. 20. House Post Office and Civil Service discharged. House passed Feb. 8, 1984. President signed Feb. 21, 1984.

PL 98-221 (S 1340) Authorize funds for fiscal years 1984-86 for the Rehabilitation Act. Introduced by HATCH, R-Utah, May 23, 1983. Senate Labor and Human Resources reported May 23 (S Rept 98-168). Senate passed July 26. House passed, amended, Sept. 13. House agreed to conference report Feb. 9, 1984 (H Rept 98-595). Senate agreed to conference report Feb. 9. President signed Feb. 22, 1984.

PL 98-222 (HR 4956) Extend the authorities under the Export Administration Act of 1979 until March 30, 1984. Introduced by BONKER, D-Wash., Feb. 28, 1984. House passed, under suspension of the rules, Feb. 28. Senate passed Feb. 29. President signed Feb. 29, 1984.

PL 98-223 (S 1388) Increase the rates of disability compensation for disabled veterans and increase the rate of dependency and indemnity compensation for surviving spouses and children of veterans. Introduced by SIMPSON, R-Wyo., May 26, 1983. Senate Veterans' Affairs reported Sept. 28 (S Rept 98-249). Senate passed Nov. 18. House passed, amended, Feb. 8, 1984. Senate agreed to House amendments Feb. 9. President signed March 2, 1984.

PL 98-224 (HR 4336) Make certain miscellaneous changes in laws relating to the civil service. Introduced by SCHROEDER, D-Colo., Nov. 9, 1983. House passed, under suspension of the rules, Nov. 16. Senate passed, amended, Feb. 9, 1984. House agreed to Senate amendments Feb. 21. President signed March 2, 1984.

PL 98-225 (S J Res 184) Designate the week of March 4-10, 1984, as "National Beta Club Week." Introduced by HOLLINGS, D-S.C., Oct. 24, 1983. Senate Judiciary reported Feb. 23, 1984. Senate passed Feb. 27. House Post Office and Civil Service discharged. House passed Feb. 29. President signed March 2, 1984.

PL 98-226 (S J Res 193) Designate March 6, 1984, as "Frozen Food Day." Introduced by HAWKINS, R-Fla., Nov. 4, 1983. Senate Judiciary reported Feb. 23, 1984. Senate passed Feb. 27. House Post Office and Civil Service discharged. House passed Feb. 29. President signed March 5, 1984.

PL 98-227 (H J Res 422) Designate the week beginning March 4, 1984, as "Women's History Week." Introduced by BOXER, D-Calif., Nov. 16, 1983. House Post Office and Civil Service discharged. House passed Feb. 29, 1984. Senate passed March 1. President signed March 5, 1984.

PL 98-228 (H J Res 292) Designate the week of June 3-9, 1984, as "National Theatre Week." Introduced by GREEN, R-N.Y., June 8, 1983. House Post Office and Civil Service discharged. House passed Oct. 26. Senate Judiciary reported Feb. 23, 1984. Senate passed Feb. 27. President signed March 7, 1984.

PL 98-229 (HR 4957) Appropriate certain funds for construction of the National System of Interstate and Defense Highways for fiscal year 1985, and increase the amount authorized to be expended for emergency relief under title 23, U.S. Code. Introduced by HOWARD, D-N.J., Feb. 28, 1984. House Public Works and Transportation discharged. House passed Feb. 29. Senate passed March 2. President signed March 9, 1984.

PL 98-230 (S J Res 161) Designate the month of April 1984 as "National Child Abuse Prevention Month." Introduced by CHAFEE, R-R.I., Sept. 15, 1983. Senate Judiciary reported Nov. 8. Senate passed Nov. 10. House Post Office and Civil Service discharged. House passed Feb. 29, 1984. President signed March 12, 1984.

PL 98-231 (S 2354) Rename the "River of No Return Wilderness," in the state of Idaho, as the "Frank Church River of No Return Wilderness." Introduced by McCLURE, R-Idaho, Feb. 27, 1984. Senate Energy and Natural Resources reported Feb. 29. Senate passed March 1. House passed March 8. President signed March 14, 1984.

PL 98-232 (S J Res 112) Proclaim the month of March 1984 as "National Social Work Month." Introduced by INOUYE, D-Hawaii, June 7, 1983. Senate Judiciary reported Feb. 23, 1984. Senate passed Feb. 27. House Post Office and Civil Service discharged. House passed March 8. President signed March 14, 1984.

PL 98-233 (S J Res 225) Designate the month of March 1984 as "National Eye Donor Month." Introduced by MOYNIHAN, D-N.Y., Feb. 2, 1984. Senate Judiciary reported Feb. 23. Senate passed Feb. 27. House Post Office and Civil Service discharged. House passed March 8. President signed March 14, 1984.

PL 98-234 (S J Res 205) Authorize and request the president to designate the second full week in March of each year as "National Employ the Older Worker Week." Introduced by HEINZ, R-Pa., Nov. 18, 1983. Senate Judiciary reported Feb. 23, 1984. Senate passed Feb. 27. House Post Office and Civil Service discharged. House passed March 14. President signed March 16, 1984.

PL 98-235 (HR 3655) Raise the retirement age for judges of the Superior Court of the District of Columbia Court of Appeals, and increase the number of Superior Court judges in the District of Columbia. Introduced by FAUNTROY, D-D.C., July 26, 1983. House District of Columbia reported Sept. 28 (H Rept 98-394). House passed Oct. 4. Senate Governmental Affairs reported Nov. 17. Senate passed, amended, Feb. 9, 1984. House agreed to Senate amendment with an amendment Feb. 22. Senate agreed to House amendment March 2. President signed March 19, 1984.

PL 98-236 (HR 2173) Authorize additional funds to carry out the provisions of the Contract Services for Drug Dependent Federal Offenders Act of 1978. Introduced by HUGHES, D-N.J., March 17, 1983. House Judiciary reported May 4 (H Rept 98-87). House passed, under suspension of the rules, May 9. Senate Judiciary reported Sept. 30. Senate passed March 8, 1984. President signed March 20, 1984.

PL 98-237 (S 47) Improve the international ocean commerce transportation system of the United States. Introduced by GORTON, R-Wash., Jan. 26, 1983. Senate Commerce, Science and Transportation reported Feb. 17. Senate passed March 1. House passed, amended, Oct. 17. Senate agreed to conference report Feb. 23, 1984 (H Rept 98-600). House agreed to conference report March 6. President signed March 20, 1984.

PL 98-238 (S J Res 132) Designate the week beginning May 6, 1984, as "National Correctional Officers Week." Introduced by RIEGLE, D-Mich., July 15, 1983. Senate Judiciary reported Nov. 10. Senate passed Nov. 15. House passed March 8, 1984. President signed March 20, 1984.

PL 98-239 (HR 4194) Extend the expiration date of section 252 of the Energy Policy and Conservation Act. Introduced by SHARP, D-Ind., Oct. 21, 1983. House Energy and Commerce reported Nov. 2 (H Rept 98-472). House passed, under suspension of the rules, Nov. 7. Senate passed, amended, Nov. 17. House disagreed to Senate amendment Nov. 18. House agreed to conference report March 15, 1984 (H Rept 98-620). Senate agreed to conference report March 15. President signed March 20, 1984.

PL 98-240 (H J Res 200) Designate March 11, 1984, as "National Single Parent Day." Introduced by TORRICELLI, D-N.J., March 15, 1983. House Post Office and Civil Service discharged. House passed March 14. Senate passed March 20. President signed March 21, 1984.

PL 98-241 (S 820) Amend section 7 of the Earthquake Hazards Reduction Act of 1977 (42 U.S. Code 7706) to extend authorizations for appropriations. Introduced by GORTON, R-Wash., March 16, 1983. Senate Commerce, Science and Transportation reported March 31 (S Rept 98-42). Senate passed April 7. House Interior and Insular Affairs and House Science and Technology discharged. House passed, amended, Feb. 1, 1984. Senate agreed to House amendments March 8. President signed March 22, 1984.

PL 98-242 (S 684) Authorize an ongoing program of water resources research. Introduced by ABDNOR, R-S.D., March 3, 1983. Senate

Environment and Public Works reported May 16 (S Rept 98-91). Senate passed May 25. House Interior and Insular Affairs discharged. House passed, amended, Oct. 31. Senate agreed to House amendments with an amendment Nov. 18. House agreed to Senate amendment Feb. 7, 1984. President vetoed Feb. 21. Senate passed over presidential veto March 21. House passed over presidential veto March 22. Became public law without presidential approval March 22, 1984.

PL 98-243 (S 912) Modify the authority for the Richard B. Russell Dam and Lake project. Introduced by STAFFORD, R-Vt., March 23, 1983. Senate Environment and Public Works reported Nov. 10 (S Rept 98-306). Senate passed Nov. 16. House Public Works and Transportation discharged. House passed March 13, 1984. President signed March 26, 1984.

PL 98-244 (HR 2809) Establish a National Fish and Wildlife Foundation. Introduced by BREAUX, D-La., April 28, 1983. House Merchant Marine and Fisheries reported May 16 (H Rept 98-134, Part I). House Ways and Means reported July 1 (H Rept 98-134, Part II). House passed, under suspension of the rules, July 12. Senate Environment and Public Works reported Oct. 19 (S Rept 98-272). Senate passed, amended, Nov. 2. House agreed to Senate amendments with an amendment Feb. 6, 1984. Senate agreed to House amendment March 8. President signed March 26, 1984.

PL 98-245 (H J Res 454) Honor the contribution of blacks to American independence. Introduced by JOHNSON, R-Conn., Jan. 26, 1984. House Post Office and Civil Service discharged. House passed Feb. 29. Senate Judiciary reported March 8. Senate passed March 12. President signed March 27, 1984.

PL 98-246 (S J Res 250) Designate the week of May 7-13, 1984, as "National Photo Week." Introduced by BAKER, R-Tenn., Feb. 29, 1984. Senate passed March 22. House Post Office and Civil Service discharged. House passed March 22. President signed March 27, 1984.

PL 98-247 (S J Res 241) Authorize and request the president to issue a proclamation designating May 6-13, 1984, as "Jewish Heritage Week." Introduced by D'AMATO, R-N.Y., Feb. 22, 1984. Senate Judiciary reported March 8. Senate passed March 12. House Post Office and Civil Service discharged. House passed March 14. President signed March 28, 1984.

PL 98-248 (H J Res 493) Appropriate urgent supplemental funds for the Department of Health and Human Services for the fiscal year ending Sept. 30, 1984. Introduced by WHITTEN, D-Miss., Feb. 28, 1984. House Appropriations reported Feb. 29 (H Rept 98-605). House passed March 6. Senate Appropriations reported March 8. Senate passed, amended, March 15. House agreed to conference report March 27 (H Rept 98-632). Senate agreed to conference report March 27. President signed March 30, 1984.

PL 98-249 (S 2507) Continue the transition provisions of the Bankruptcy Act until May 1, 1984. Introduced by BAKER, R-Tenn., March 30, 1984. Senate passed March 30. House passed, amended, March 30. Senate agreed to House amendment March 30. President signed March 31, 1984.

PL 98-250 (S 1530) Make technical amendments to the Indian Self-Determination and Education Assistance Act and other acts. Introduced by ANDREWS, R-N.D., June 23, 1983. Senate Indian Affairs reported Sept. 28. Senate passed Sept. 30. House Interior and Insular Affairs reported March 1, 1984 (H Rept 98-611). House passed March 20. President signed April 3, 1984.

PL 98-251 (H J Res 271) Designate Feb. 11, 1984, as "National Inventors' Day." Introduced by KASTENMEIER, D-Wis., May 17, 1983. House Post Office and Civil Service discharged. House passed Feb. 8, 1984. Senate Judiciary discharged. Senate passed March 26. President signed April 6, 1984.

PL 98-252 (H J Res 443) Designate the month of June 1984 as "Student Awareness of Drunk Driving Month." Introduced by McGRATH, R-N.Y., Jan. 23, 1984. House Post Office and Civil Service discharged. House passed Feb. 29. Senate Judiciary reported March 15. Senate passed March 26. President signed April 6, 1984.

PL 98-253 (S 1365) Designate the air traffic control tower at the Chattanooga Municipal Airport (Lovell Field), Chattanooga, Tenn., as the "Harry Porter Control Tower." Introduced by BAKER, R-Tenn., May 25, 1983. Senate Commerce, Science and Transportation reported Aug. 4. Senate passed Aug. 4. House Public Works and Transportation discharged. House passed April 2, 1984. President signed April 6, 1984.

PL 98-254 (S J Res 203) Designate the week beginning April 8, 1984, as "National Mental Health Counselors Week." Introduced by HUDDLESTON, D-Ky., Nov. 17, 1983. Senate Judiciary reported March 8, 1984. Senate passed March 12. House Post Office and Civil Service discharged. House passed April 3. President signed April 9, 1984.

PL 98-255 (H J Res 432) Designate the week of April 8-14, 1984, as "Parkinson's Disease Awareness Week." Introduced by WAXMAN, D-Calif., Nov. 16, 1983. House Post Office and Civil Service discharged. House passed March 22, 1984. Senate passed March 27. President signed April 9, 1984.

PL 98-256 (S 2392) Authorize the president to appoint Donald D. Engen

to the Office of Administrator of the Federal Aviation Administration. Introduced by KASSEBAUM, R-Kan., March 6, 1984. Senate Commerce, Science and Transportation reported March 29 (S Rept 98-371). Senate passed April 2. House passed April 4. President signed April 10, 1984.

PL 98-257 (HR 3249) Charter the National Academy of Public Administration. Introduced by BROOKS, D-Texas, June 8, 1983. House Judiciary reported Nov. 7 (H Rept 98-491). House passed, under suspension of the rules, Nov. 14. Senate Judiciary discharged. Senate passed March 27, 1984. President signed April 10, 1984.

PL 98-258 (HR 4072) Reduce 1984 and 1985 wheat target prices and set forth a combined 1984 acreage reduction and land division program. Introduced by FOLEY, D-Wash., Oct. 4, 1983. House passed, under suspension of the rules, Nov. 16. Senate Agriculture, Nutrition and Forestry reported March 12, 1984. Senate passed, amended, March 22. Senate agreed to conference report April 2 (H Rept 98-646). House agreed to conference report April 3. President signed April 10, 1984.

PL 98-259 (HR 4206) Amend the Internal Revenue Code of 1954 to exempt from federal income taxes certain military and civilian employees of the United States dying as a result of injuries sustained overseas. Introduced by ARCHER, R-Texas, Oct. 25, 1983. House Ways and Means discharged. House passed Feb. 22, 1984. Senate Finance reported March 12 (S Rept 98-364). Senate passed April 5. President signed April 10, 1984.

PL 98-260 (HR 4202) Designate the air traffic control tower at Midway Airport, Chicago, as the "John G. Fary Tower." Introduced by STANGELAND, R-Minn., Oct. 24, 1983. House Public Works and Transportation reported March 20, 1984 (H Rept 98-623). House passed April 2. Senate passed April 5. President signed April 13, 1984.

PL 98-261 (S J Res 148) Designate the week of May 6-13, 1984, as "National Tuberous Sclerosis Week." Introduced by KENNEDY, D-Mass., Aug. 3, 1983. Senate Judiciary reported Feb. 23, 1984. Senate passed Feb. 27. House Post Office and Civil Service discharged. House passed April 3. President signed April 13, 1984.

PL 98-262 (S J Res 171) Provide for the designation of July 20, 1984, as "National P.O.W./M.I.A. Recognition Day." Introduced by STENNIS, D-Miss., Sept. 28, 1983. Senate Judiciary reported Feb. 23, 1984. Senate passed Feb. 27. House Post Office and Civil Service discharged. House passed April 3. President signed April 13, 1984.

PL 98-263 (H J Res 407) Designate the week beginning April 8, 1984, as "National Hearing Impaired Awareness Week." Introduced by GUARINI, D-N.J., Oct. 31, 1983. House Post Office and Civil Service discharged. House passed April 3, 1984. Senate Judiciary discharged. Senate passed April 11. President signed April 13, 1984.

PL 98-264 (H J Res 520) Designate April 13, 1984, as "Education Day, U.S.A." Introduced by WRIGHT, D-Texas, March 19, 1984. House Post Office and Civil Service discharged. House passed April 3. Senate passed April 5. President signed April 13, 1984.

PL 98-265 (S 1852) Extend the expiration date of the Defense Production Act of 1950. Introduced by TRIBLE, R-Va., Sept. 19, 1983. Senate Banking, Housing and Urban Affairs reported Sept. 29. Senate passed Sept. 30. House passed, amended, Oct. 6. Senate agreed to House amendment with an amendment Oct. 7. House disagreed to Senate amendment March 20, 1984. Senate agreed to conference report April 5 (H Rept 98-651). House agreed to conference report April 10. President signed April 17, 1984.

PL 98-266 (HR 4835) Authorize funds for the Clement J. Zablocki Memorial Outpatient Facility at the American Children's Hospital in Krakow, Poland. Introduced by FASCELL, D-Fla., Feb. 9, 1984. House passed, under suspension of the rules, March 6. Senate Foreign Relations reported March 14. Senate passed April 5. President signed April 17, 1984.

PL 98-267 (H J Res 466) Designate May 1984 as "Older Americans Month." Introduced by McCOLLUM, R-Fla., Feb. 2, 1984. House Post Office and Civil Service discharged. House passed Feb. 8. Senate Judiciary reported April 5. Senate passed April 11. President signed April 17, 1984.

PL 98-268 (S J Res 173) Commend the Historic American Buildings Survey, a program of the National Park Service, Department of the Interior. Introduced by JOHNSTON, D-La., Sept. 28, 1983. Senate Energy and Natural Resources reported Nov. 14 (S Rept 98-311). Senate passed Nov. 18. House Interior and Insular Affairs reported April 9, 1984 (H Rept 98-662). House passed, amended, April 9. Senate agreed to House amendments April 11. President signed April 17, 1984.

PL 98-269 (HR 596) Transfer responsibility for furnishing certified copies of Miller Act payment bonds from the comptroller general to the officer that awarded the contract for which the bond was given. Introduced by SAM B. HALL JR., D-Texas, Jan. 6, 1983. House Judiciary reported April 14 (H Rept 98-63). House passed May 3. Senate Judiciary reported Dec. 14 (S Rept 98-344). Senate passed April 11, 1984. President signed April 18, 1984.

PL 98-270 (HR 4169) Provide for reconciliation pursuant to section 3 of the first concurrent resolution on the budget for fiscal year 1984. Introduced by JONES, D-Okla., Oct. 20, 1983. House Budget reported Oct. 20 (H Rept 98-425). House passed Oct. 25. Senate passed April 5, 1984. President signed April 18, 1984.

PL 98-271 (S 2570) Continue the transition provisions of the Bankruptcy Act until May 26, 1984. Introduced by BAKER, R-Tenn., April 12, 1984. Senate passed April 12. House passed April 26. President signed April 30, 1984.

PL 98-272 (S J Res 210) Designate the period commencing Jan. 1, 1984, and ending Dec. 31, 1984, as the "Year of Excellence in Education." Introduced by TRIBLE, R-Va., Jan. 23, 1984. Senate Judiciary reported March 8. Senate passed March 12. House Post Office and Civil Service discharged. House passed, amended, April 11. Senate agreed to House amendments April 12. President signed May 3, 1984.

PL 98-273 (HR 3867) Amend the Perishable Agricultural Commodities Act of 1930 by impressing a trust on the commodities and sales proceeds of perishable agricultural commodities for the benefit of the unpaid seller. Introduced by DE LA GARZA, D-Texas, Sept. 13, 1983. House Agriculture reported Nov. 12 (H Rept 98-543). House passed, under suspension of the rules, Nov. 15. Senate passed April 12, 1984. President signed May 7, 1984.

PL 98-274 (H J Res 478) Designate the week of April 29-May 5, 1984, as "National Week of the Ocean." Introduced by SHAW, R-Fla., Feb. 8, 1984. House Post Office and Civil Service discharged. House passed Feb. 29. Senate Judiciary reported April 26. Senate passed May 1. President signed May 7, 1984.

PL 98-275 (S J Res 136) Recognize "Volunteer Firefighters Recognition Day" as a tribute to the bravery and self-sacrifice of volunteer firefighters. Introduced by GLENN, D-Ohio, July 27, 1983. Senate passed Aug. 4. House Post Office and Civil Service discharged. House passed, amended, March 22, 1984. Senate agreed to House amendments April 26. President signed May 8, 1984.

PL 98-276 (HR 5298) Provide for a White House Conference on Small Business. Introduced by MITCHELL, D-Md., March 29, 1984. House Small Business reported April 5 (H Rept 98-652). House passed, under suspension of the rules, April 9. Senate passed April 11. President signed May 8, 1984.

PL 98-277 (S 2460) Designate a federal building in Augusta, Maine, as the "Edmund S. Muskie Federal Building." Introduced by MITCHELL, D-Maine, March 22, 1984. Senate Environment and Public Works reported April 6 (S Rept 98-384). Senate passed April 11. House Public Works and Transportation discharged. House passed April 26. President signed May 8, 1984.

PL 98-278 (S 2597) Authorize the awarding of special congressional gold medals to the daughter of Harry S Truman, to Lady Bird Johnson, and to Elie Wiesel. Introduced by GARN, R-Utah, April 25, 1984. Senate Banking, Housing and Urban Affairs reported April 25. Senate passed April 26. House passed April 26. President signed May 8, 1984.

PL 98-279 (S 2461) Designate a federal building in Bangor, Maine, as the "Margaret Chase Smith Federal Building." Introduced by MITCHELL, D-Maine, March 22, 1984. Senate Environment and Public Works reported April 6 (S Rept 98-385). Senate passed April 11. House Public Works and Transportation discharged. House passed April 26. President signed May 8, 1984.

PL 98-280 (HR 3555) Declare certain lands held by the Seneca Nation of Indians to be part of the Allegany Reservation in the state of New York. Introduced by LUNDINE, D-N.Y., July 13, 1983. House Interior and Insular Affairs reported Oct. 19 (H Rept 98-420). House passed Nov. 7. Senate Indian Affairs discharged. Senate passed April 26, 1984. President signed May 9, 1984.

PL 98-281 (S J Res 244) Designate the week beginning May 6, 1984, as "National Asthma and Allergy Awareness Week." Introduced by DOLE, R-Kan., Feb. 23, 1984. Senate Judiciary reported April 12. Senate passed April 25. House Post Office and Civil Service discharged. House passed May 3. President signed May 11, 1984.

PL 98-282 (HR 3376) Declare that the United States holds certain lands in trust for the Makah Indian Tribe, Washington. Introduced by SWIFT, D-Wash., June 21, 1983. House Interior and Insular Affairs reported Nov. 2 (H Rept 98-462). House passed Nov. 18. Senate Indian Affairs discharged. Senate passed April 24, 1984. President signed May 14, 1984.

PL 98-283 (S J Res 232) Authorize and request the president to designate the month of May 1984 as "National Physical Fitness and Sports Month." Introduced by THURMOND, R-S.C., Feb. 9, 1984. Senate Judiciary reported Feb. 23. Senate passed Feb. 27. House Post Office and Civil Service discharged. House passed May 1. President signed May 15, 1984.

PL 98-284 (HR 2733) Extend and improve the existing program of research, development and demonstration in the production and manufacture of guayule rubber, and broaden such program to include other critical agricultural materials. Introduced by BROWN, D-Calif., April 26, 1983. House Agriculture reported May 12 (H Rept 98-109,

Part I). House Science and Technology reported May 16 (H Rept 98-109, Part II). House passed, under suspension of the rules, May 17. Senate Agriculture, Nutrition and Forestry reported June 23 (S Rept 98-164). Senate passed May 1, 1984. President signed May 16, 1984.

PL 98-285 (HR 3240) Authorize the president to present on behalf of Congress a specially struck medal to the widow of Roy Wilkins. Introduced by RANGEL, D N.Y., June 7, 1983. House passed, under suspension of the rules, March 13, 1984. Senate passed May 8. President signed May 17, 1984.

PL 98-286 (S J Res 220) Designate the week of May 20-26, 1984, as "National Arts With the Handicapped Week." Introduced by KENNEDY, D-Mass., Jan. 31, 1984. Senate Judiciary reported Feb. 23. Senate passed Feb. 27. House Post Office and Civil Service discharged. House passed May 3. President signed May 17, 1984.

PL 98-287 (S 597) Convey certain lands to Show Low, Ariz. Introduced by DeCONCINI, D-Ariz., Feb. 24, 1983. Senate Energy and Natural Resources discharged. Senate passed April 13. House Interior and Insular Affairs reported March 1, 1984 (H Rept 98-609). House passed, amended, under suspension of the rules, March 5. Senate agreed to House amendments with an amendment April 11. House agreed to Senate amendment May 2. President signed May 21, 1984.

PL 98-288 (S 1129) Authorize funds through fiscal year 1986 for programs under the Domestic Volunteer Service Act, and allow volunteers to be locally recruited and assigned to projects in order to alleviate poverty and poverty-related human problems. Introduced by HATCH, R-Utah, April 21, 1983. Senate Labor and Human Resources reported July 14 (S Rept 98-182). Senate passed Sept. 14. House passed, amended, Oct. 28. Senate agreed to conference report April 11, 1984 (H Rept 98-679). House agreed to conference report May 8. President signed May 21, 1984.

PL 98-289 (S 64) Establish the Irish Wilderness in Mark Twain National Forest, Missouri. Introduced by DANFORTH, R-Mo., Jan. 26, 1983. Senate Energy and Natural Resources reported March 31 (S Rept 98-45). Senate passed April 13. House Interior and Insular Affairs reported Aug. 1 (H Rept 98-337, Part I). House Agriculture discharged. House passed, amended, under suspension of the rules, Aug. 2. House agreed to conference report May 2, 1984 (H Rept 98-663). Senate agreed to conference report May 3. President signed May 21, 1984.

PL 98-290 (HR 4176) Confirm the boundaries of the Southern Ute Indian Reservation in the state of Colorado, and define jurisdiction within such reservation. Introduced by KOGOVSEK, D-Colo., Oct. 20, 1983. House Interior and Insular Affairs reported April 26, 1984 (H Rept 98-716). House passed, under suspension of the rules, April 30. Senate passed May 3. President signed May 21, 1984.

PL 98-291 (S 1188) Relieve the General Accounting Office of duplicative audit requirements with respect to the Disabled American Veterans. Introduced by THURMOND, R-S.C., May 2, 1983. Senate Judiciary reported Nov. 17. Senate passed Nov. 18. House passed May 7, 1984. President signed May 21, 1984.

PL 98-292 (HR 3635) Amend chapter 110 of title 18, U.S. Code, relating to sexual exploitation of children. Introduced by SAWYER, R-Mich., July 21, 1983. House Judiciary reported Nov. 10 (H Rept 98-536). House passed, under suspension of the rules, Nov. 14. Senate passed, amended, March 30, 1984. House agreed to Senate amendment May 8. President signed May 21, 1984.

PL 98-293 (H J Res 537) Designate the Brigantine and Barnegat units of the National Wildlife Refuge System as the Edwin B. Forsythe National Wildlife Refuge. Introduced by BREAUX, D-La., April 3, 1984. House Merchant Marine and Fisheries reported April 25 (H Rept 98-706). House passed, under suspension of the rules, May 1. Senate passed May 3. President signed May 22, 1984.

PL 98-294 (S J Res 198) Designate April 26, 1985, as "National Nursing Home Residents Day." Introduced by PRYOR, D-Ark., Nov. 15, 1983. Senate Judiciary reported April 12, 1984. Senate passed April 25. House Post Office and Civil Service discharged. House passed, amended, May 1. Senate agreed to House amendments May 10. President signed May 22, 1984.

PL 98-295 (S J Res 228) Designate the week of May 20-26, 1984, as "National Digestive Diseases Awareness Week." Introduced by RANDOLPH, D-W.Va., Feb. 8, 1984. Senate Judiciary reported Feb. 23. Senate passed Feb. 27. House Post Office and Civil Service discharged. House passed May 17. President signed May 22, 1984.

PL 98-296 (HR 4107) Designate the federal building in Salisbury, Md., as the "Maude R. Toulson Federal Building." Introduced by DYSON, D-Md., Oct. 6, 1983. House Public Works and Transportation discharged. House passed Nov. 18. Senate Environment and Public Works reported May 10, 1984. Senate passed May 16. President signed May 24, 1984.

PL 98-297 (HR 5576) Designate certain land and improvements of the National Institutes of Health as the "Mary Woodard Lasker Center for Health Research and Education." Introduced by WAXMAN, D-Calif., May 3, 1984. House passed May 3. Senate passed May 9.

President signed May 24, 1984.

PL 98-298 (S J Res 252) Designate May 25, 1984, as "Missing Children Day." Introduced by HAWKINS, R-Fla., March 1, 1984. Senate Judiciary reported March 8. Senate passed March 12. House Post Office and Civil Service discharged. House passed May 17. President signed May 24, 1984.

PL 98-299 (HR 2174) Continue the transition provisions of the Bankruptcy Act until June 20, 1984. Introduced by HUGHES, D-N.J., March 17, 1983. House Judiciary reported May 9 (H Rept 98-93). House passed, under suspension of the rules, May 9. Senate passed, amended, May 24, 1984. House agreed to Senate amendments May 24. President signed May 25, 1984.

PL 98-300 (HR 2211) Exempt electric and telephone facilities assisted under the Rural Electrification Act from certain right-of-way rental payments under the Federal Land Policy and Management Act of 1976. Introduced by MARLENEE, R-Mont., March 21, 1983. House Interior and Insular Affairs reported Nov. 3 (H Rept 98-475). House passed, under suspension of the rules, Nov. 8. Senate Energy and Natural Resources reported April 11, 1984 (S Rept 98-388). Senate passed May 10. President signed May 25, 1984.

PL 98-301 (HR 5515) Authorize the president to award the Medal of Honor to the unknown American who lost his life while serving in the Armed Forces of the United States in Southeast Asia during the Vietnam era and who has been selected to be buried in the Memorial Amphitheater at Arlington National Cemetery. Introduced by PRICE, D-Ill., April 25, 1984. House Armed Services discharged. House passed May 3. Senate passed May 16. President signed May 25, 1984.

PL 98-302 (HR 5692) Provide for an increase in the public debt limit. Introduced by ROSTENKOWSKI, D-Ill., May 22, 1984. House Ways and Means discharged. House passed May 24. Senate passed, amended, May 24. House agreed to Senate amendment May 24. President signed May 25, 1984.

PL 98-303 (H J Res 526) Designate the week of May 27-June 2, 1984, as "National Animal Health Week." Introduced by TAYLOR, R-Mo., March 21, 1984. House Post Office and Civil Service discharged. House passed May 17. Senate passed May 22. President signed May 25, 1984.

PL 98-304 (S 2079) Amend the charter of AMVETS by extending eligibility for membership to individuals who qualify on or after May 8, 1983. Introduced by THURMOND, R-S.C., Nov. 10, 1983. Senate Judiciary reported Nov. 17. Senate passed Nov. 18. House passed, amended, May 7, 1984. Senate agreed to House amendments May 16. President signed May 31, 1984.

PL 98-305 (S 422) Provide a criminal penalty for robbery of a controlled substance. Introduced by JEPSEN, R-Iowa, Feb. 3, 1983. Senate Judiciary reported Feb. 8, 1984 (S Rept 98-353). Senate passed Feb. 23. House Judiciary discharged. House passed, amended, May 8. Senate agreed to House amendment May 17. President signed May 31, 1984.

PL 98-306 (HR 2751) Increase the authorization of funds for the National Endowment for the Humanities, the National Endowment for the Arts, and for the Institute of Museum Services. Introduced by SIMON, D-Ill., April 26, 1983. House Education and Labor reported May 16 (H Rept 98-163). Supplemental report filed Oct. 26 (H Rept 98-163, Part II). House passed Feb. 21, 1984. Senate passed, amended, April 5. House agreed to Senate amendment May 17. President signed May 31, 1984.

PL 98-307 (S J Res 94) Designate May 13-June 17, 1984, as "Family Reunion Month." Introduced by MATTINGLY, R-Ga., May 5, 1983. Senate passed May 6. House Post Office and Civil Service discharged. House passed, amended, May 17, 1984. Senate agreed to House amendments May 22. President signed May 31, 1984.

PL 98-308 (S J Res 211) Designate the week of Nov. 18-24, 1984, as "National Family Week." Introduced by BURDICK, D-N.D., Jan. 24, 1984. Senate Judiciary reported March 8. Senate passed March 12. House Post Office and Civil Service discharged. House passed May 17. President signed May 31, 1984.

PL 98-309 (S J Res 239) Designate the week of Oct. 21-27, 1984, as "Lupus Awareness Week." Introduced by CHILES, D-Fla., Feb. 21, 1984. Senate Judiciary reported March 8. Senate passed March 12. House Post Office and Civil Service discharged. House passed May 17. President signed May 31, 1984.

PL 98-310 (H J Res 451) Designate the month of November 1984 as "National Alzheimer's Disease Month." Introduced by LOWERY, R-Calif., Jan. 25, 1984. House Post Office and Civil Service discharged. House passed May 1. Senate Judiciary reported May 17. Senate passed May 22. President signed May 31, 1984.

PL 98-311 (H J Res 487) Designate June 6, 1984, as "D-Day National Remembrance." Introduced by LANTOS, D-Calif., Feb. 21, 1984. House Post Office and Civil Service discharged. House passed April 11. Senate Judiciary discharged. Senate passed May 24. President signed May 31, 1984.

PL 98-312 (HR 5287) Amend title III of the Higher Education Act of 1965, permitting additional funds to be used to continue awards under certain multi-year grants. Introduced by SIMON, D-Ill., March 29, 1984. House passed, under suspension of the rules, May 1. Senate passed, amended, May 16. House agreed to Senate amendments May 23. President signed June 12, 1984.

PL 98-313 (S 518) Authorize funds through fiscal year 1986 to assist federal, state and local environmental agencies in carrying out projects of pollution prevention, abatement and control. Introduced by CHAFEE, R-R.I., Feb. 17, 1983. Senate Environment and Public Works reported Nov. 16. Senate passed March 26, 1984. House passed, amended, May 23. Senate agreed to House amendment May 24. President signed June 12, 1984.

PL 98-314 (S 2413) Recognize the organization known as the American Gold Star Mothers Inc. Introduced by DENTON, R-Ala., March 12, 1984. Senate Judiciary reported April 5 (S Rept 98-379). Senate passed April 25. House passed, amended, May 10. Senate agreed to House amendment May 22. President signed June 12, 1984.

PL 98-315 (HR 3547) Amend the District of Columbia Self-Government and Governmental Reorganization Act, extend the authority of the mayor to accept certain interim loans from the United States and extend the authority of the secretary of the Treasury to make such loans. Introduced by DELLUMS, D-Calif., July 13, 1983. House District of Columbia reported July 20 (H Rept 98-302). House passed July 25. Senate Governmental Affairs reported May 15, 1984 (S Rept 98-447). Senate passed May 24. President signed June 12, 1984.

PL 98-316 (HR 5308) Amend the District of Columbia Self-Government and Governmental Reorganization Act, and increase the amount authorized to be appropriated as the annual federal payment to the District of Columbia. Introduced by FAUNTROY, D-D.C., March 30, 1984. House District of Columbia reported May 8 (H Rept 98-736). House passed May 14. Senate passed May 24. President signed June 12, 1984.

PL 98-317 (S J Res 285) Designate June 13, 1984, as "Harmon Killebrew Day." Introduced by McCLURE, R-Idaho, April 30, 1984. Senate Judiciary reported May 10. Senate passed May 16. House Post Office and Civil Service discharged. House passed June 12. President signed June 15, 1984.

PL 98-318 (S J Res 296) Designate June 14, 1984, as "Baltic Freedom Day." Introduced by D'AMATO, R-N.Y., May 15, 1984. Senate Judiciary reported June 7. Senate passed June 8. House passed June 11. President signed June 15, 1984.

PL 98-319 (S J Res 289) Designate June 18, 1984, as "National Child Passenger Safety Awareness Day." Introduced by HAWKINS, R-Fla., May 8, 1984. Senate Judiciary reported May 17. Senate passed May 22. House Post Office and Civil Service discharged. House passed June 6. President signed June 18, 1984.

PL 98-320 (S J Res 261) Provide for the designation of the last week of June 1984 as "Helen Keller Deaf-Blind Awareness Week." Introduced by LEAHY, D-Vt., March 20, 1984. Senate Judiciary reported April 26. Senate passed May 1. House Post Office and Civil Service discharged. House passed June 6. President signed June 18, 1984.

PL 98-321 (HR 3578) Establish certain specified lands in Wisconsin as wilderness. Introduced by OBEY, D-Wis., July 14, 1983. House Interior and Insular Affairs reported Nov. 10 (H Rept 98-531, Part I). House passed, under suspension of the rules, Nov. 16. Senate Agriculture, Nutrition and Forestry reported April 26, 1984 (S Rept 98-413). Senate passed, amended, May 24. House agreed to Senate amendments June 4. President signed June 19, 1984.

PL 98-322 (HR 4198) Designate certain national forest system lands in the state of Vermont for inclusion in the National Wilderness Preservation System, and designate a national recreation area. Introduced by JEFFORDS, R-Vt., Oct. 24, 1983. House Interior and Insular Affairs reported Nov. 10 (H Rept 98-533). House passed, under suspension of the rules, Nov. 15. Senate Agriculture, Nutrition and Forestry reported April 26, 1984 (S Rept 98-416). Senate passed, amended, May 24. House agreed to Senate amendments June 4. President signed June 19, 1984.

PL 98-323 (HR 3921) Establish certain specified lands in New Hampshire as wilderness. Introduced by GREGG, R-N.H., Sept. 19, 1983. House Interior and Insular Affairs reported Nov. 14 (H Rept 98-545, Part I). House passed, under suspension of the rules, Nov. 15. Senate Agriculture, Nutrition and Forestry reported April 26, 1984 (S Rept 98-414). Senate passed, amended, May 24. House agreed to Senate amendments June 6. President signed June 19, 1984.

PL 98-324 (HR 3960) Designate certain public lands in North Carolina as additions to the National Wilderness Preservation System. Introduced by CLARKE, D-N.C., Sept. 22, 1983. House Interior and Insular Affairs reported Nov. 10 (H Rept 98-532, Part I). House passed, under suspension of the rules, Nov. 16. Senate Agriculture, Nutrition and Forestry reported April 26, 1984 (S Rept 98-415). Senate passed, amended, May 24. House agreed to Senate amendment June 4. President signed June 19, 1984.

PL 98-325 (S 2776) Continue the transition provisions of the Bankruptcy Act until June 27, 1984. Introduced by BAKER, R-Tenn., June 19, 1984. Senate passed June 19. House passed June 20. President signed June 20, 1984.

PL 98-326 (HR 5517) Provide for certain additional experts and consultants for the General Accounting Office, and provide for certain additional positions within the General Accounting Office Senior Executive Service. Introduced by SCHROEDER, D-Colo., April 25, 1984. House passed, under suspension of the rules, May 21. Senate passed June 8. President signed June 22, 1984.

PL 98-327 (HR 1723) Authorize funds through fiscal 1986 for the Great Dismal Swamp, Minnesota Valley, and San Francisco Bay National Wildlife Refuges. Introduced by BREAUX, D-La., March 1, 1983. House Merchant Marine and Fisheries reported April 18 (H Rept 98-66). House passed, under suspension of the rules, April 19. Senate Environment and Public Works reported May 16 (S Rept 98-93). Senate passed, amended, Nov. 17. House agreed to Senate amendments with an amendment Feb. 6, 1984. Senate agreed to House amendment to Senate amendment June 8. President signed June 25, 1984.

PL 98-328 (HR 1149) Designate certain lands in Oregon as wilderness. Introduced by WEAVER, D-Ore., Feb. 1, 1983. House Interior and Insular Affairs reported March 2 (H Rept 98-13, Part I). House passed March 21. Senate Energy and Natural Resources reported May 18, 1984 (S Rept 98-465). Senate passed, amended, May 24. House agreed to Senate amendment, under suspension of the rules, June 6. President signed June 26, 1984.

PL 98-329 (HR 4201) Transfer methaqualone from Schedule II (abuse potential, but with accepted U.S. medical use) to Schedule I (abuse potential, with no accepted U.S. medical use) of the Controlled Substances Act. Introduced by ROWLAND, D-Ga., Oct. 24, 1983. House Energy and Commerce reported Nov. 10 (H Rept 98-534). House passed, under suspension of the rules, Nov. 16. Senate Judiciary reported April 5, 1984. Senate passed June 15. President signed June 29, 1984.

PL 98-330 (S J Res 297) Designate the month of June 1984 as "Veterans Preference Month." Introduced by THURMOND, R-S.C., May 16, 1984. Senate Judiciary reported June 14. Senate passed June 15. House Post Office and Civil Service discharged. House passed June 26. President signed June 30, 1984.

PL 98-331 (S J Res 257) Designate the period July 1, 1984, through July 1, 1985, as the "Year of the Ocean." Introduced by STEVENS, R-Alaska, March 8, 1984. Senate Judiciary reported June 7. Senate passed June 8. House Post Office and Civil Service discharged. House passed June 26. President signed July 2, 1984.

PL 98-332 (H J Res 492) Appropriate urgent supplemental funds for the fiscal year ending Sept. 30, 1984. Introduced by WHITTEN, D-Miss., Feb. 28, 1984. House Appropriations reported Feb. 29 (H Rept 98-604). House passed March 6. Senate Appropriations reported March 14 (S Rept 98-365). Senate passed, amended, April 5. House agreed to conference report May 24 (H Rept 98-792). Senate agreed to conference report June 25. President signed July 2, 1984.

PL 98-333 (S J Res 298) Proclaim the month of July 1984 as "National Ice Cream Month," and July 15, 1984, as "National Ice Cream Day." Introduced by HUDDLESTON, D-Ky., May 17, 1984. Senate Judiciary reported June 7. Senate passed June 8. House Post Office and Civil Service discharged. House passed June 26. President signed July 2, 1984.

PL 98-334 (S 1135) Consent to the Goose Lake Basin Compact between the states of California and Oregon. Introduced by HATFIELD, R-Ore., April 21, 1983. Senate Judiciary reported April 12, 1984 (S Rept 98-397). Senate passed May 1. House Interior and Insular Affairs reported June 14 (H Rept 98-841). House passed June 18. President signed July 2, 1984.

PL 98-335 (S J Res 59) Authorize and request the president to designate Feb. 27, 1986, as "Hugo LaFayette Black Day." Introduced by HEFLIN, D-Ala., March 10, 1983. Senate Judiciary reported Feb. 23, 1984. Senate passed Feb. 27. House Post Office and Civil Service discharged. House passed June 26. President signed July 3, 1984.

PL 98-336 (S J Res 150) Designate Aug. 4, 1984, as "Coast Guard Day." Introduced by PACKWOOD, R-Ore., Aug. 4, 1983. Senate Judiciary reported Sept. 15. Senate passed Sept. 20. House Post Office and Civil Service discharged. House passed June 26, 1984. President signed July 3, 1984.

PL 98-337 (S J Res 230) Designate the week of Oct. 7-13, 1984, as "National Birds of Prey Conservation Week." Introduced by SPECTER, R-Pa., Feb. 9, 1984. Senate Judiciary reported June 7. Senate passed June 8. House Post Office and Civil Service discharged. House passed June 26. President signed July 3, 1984.

PL 98-338 (S J Res 303) Designate the week of Dec. 9-15, 1984, as "National Drunk and Drugged Driving Awareness Week." Introduced by HUMPHREY, R-N.H., May 24, 1984. Senate Judiciary reported June 7. Senate passed June 8. House Post Office and Civil Service

discharged. House passed June 26. President signed July 3, 1984.

PL 98-339 (S 837) Designate certain national forest system lands in the state of Washington for inclusion in the National Wilderness Preservation System. Introduced by GORTON, R-Wash., March 17, 1983. Senate Energy and Natural Resources reported May 18, 1984 (S Rept 98-461). Senate passed May 24. House passed, under suspension of the rules, June 18. President signed July 3, 1984.

PL 98-340 (HR 5565) Direct the architect of the Capitol and the District of Columbia to enter into an agreement for the conveyance of certain real property, direct the secretary of the interior to permit the District of Columbia and the Washington Metropolitan Area Transit Authority to construct, maintain and operate certain transportation improvements on federal property, and direct the architect of the Capitol to provide the Washington Metropolitan Area Transit Authority access to certain real property. Introduced by FAUNTROY, D-D.C., May 2, 1984. House District of Columbia reported May 31 (H Rept 98-810, Part I). House passed June 11. Senate passed June 21. President signed July 3, 1984.

PL 98-341 (S J Res 270) Designate the week of July 1-8, 1984, as "National Duck Stamp Week," and 1984 as the "Golden Anniversary Year of the Duck Stamp." Introduced by COCHRAN, R-Miss., April 3, 1984. Senate Judiciary reported June 14. Senate passed June 15. House Post Office and Civil Service discharged. House passed June 26. President signed July 3, 1984.

PL 98-342 (HR 5953) Increase the statutory limit on the public debt. Introduced by ROSTENKOWSKI, D-Ill., June 28, 1984. House Ways and Means reported June 28 (H Rept 98-878). House passed June 29. Senate passed June 29. President signed July 6, 1984.

PL 98-343 (S J Res 238) Designate the week beginning Nov. 19, 1984, as "National Adoption Week." Introduced by HATCH, R-Utah, Feb. 9, 1984. Senate Judiciary reported Feb. 23. Senate passed Feb. 27. House Post Office and Civil Service discharged. House passed June 26. President signed July 9, 1984.

PL 98-344 (S 2403) Declare that the United States holds certain lands in trust for the Pueblo de Cochiti. Introduced by DOMENICI, R-N.M., March 8, 1984. Senate Indian Affairs reported April 18 (S Rept 98-409). Senate passed May 10. House passed June 21. President signed July 9, 1984.

PL 98-345 (H J Res 555) Designate July 20, 1984, as "Space Exploration Day." Introduced by FUQUA, D-Fla., April 25, 1984. House Post Office and Civil Service discharged. House passed June 26. Senate passed June 29. President signed July 9, 1984.

PL 98-346 (H J Res 544) Designate the week beginning Sept. 2, 1984, as "National Schoolage Child Care Awareness Week." Introduced by McKERNAN, R-Maine, April 11, 1984. House Post Office and Civil Service discharged. House passed June 26. Senate passed June 29. President signed July 9, 1984.

PL 98-347 (HR 4921) Provide for the selection of additional lands for inclusion within the Bon Secour National Wildlife Refuge. Introduced by EDWARDS, R-Ala., Feb. 23, 1984. House Merchant Marine and Fisheries reported April 25 (H Rept 98-703). House passed, under suspension of the rules, April 30. Senate Environment and Public Works reported June 19. Senate passed June 21. President signed July 9, 1984.

PL 98-348 (S J Res 278) Commemorate the one hundredth anniversary of the Bureau of Labor Statistics. Introduced by QUAYLE, R-Ind., April 24, 1984. Senate Judiciary reported June 7. Senate passed June 21. House Post Office and Civil Service discharged. House passed June 26. President signed July 9, 1984.

PL 98-349 (S J Res 306) Proclaim July 10, 1984, as "Food for Peace Day." Introduced by DOLE, R-Kan., June 6, 1984. Senate Judiciary reported June 14. Senate passed June 15. House Post Office and Civil Service discharged. House passed June 29. President signed July 9, 1984.

PL 98-350 (H J Res 566) Designate the week beginning Oct. 7, 1984, as "National Neighborhood Housing Services Week." Introduced by MINETA, D-Calif., May 10, 1984. House Post Office and Civil Service discharged. House passed June 26. Senate passed June 29. President signed July 9, 1984.

PL 98-351 (H J Res 604) Designate July 9, 1984, as "African Refugees Day." Introduced by DIXON, D-Calif., June 25, 1984. House Post Office and Civil Service discharged. House passed June 26. Senate Judiciary discharged. Senate passed June 29. President signed July 9, 1984.

PL 98-352 (S 2375) Amend the Small Business Act to improve the operation of the secondary market for loans guaranteed by the Small Business Administration. Introduced by WEICKER, R-Conn., Feb. 29, 1984. Senate Small Business reported June 20 (S Rept 98-542). Senate passed June 21. House passed, under suspension of the rules, June 25. President signed July 10, 1984.

PL 98-353 (HR 5174) Provide for the appointment of United States bankruptcy judges under article III of the Constitution, amend title II of the U.S. Code for the purpose of making certain changes in the personal bankruptcy law, and make certain changes regarding grain storage facilities. Introduced by RODINO, D-N.J., March 19, 1984. House passed March 21. Senate passed, amended, June 19. House agreed to conference report June 29 (H Rept 98-882). Senate agreed to conference report June 29. President signed July 10, 1984.

PL 98-354 (HR 5404) Allow William R. Giannelli to continue to serve as a member of the Board of the Panama Canal Commission after his retirement as an officer of the Department of Defense. Introduced by CARNEY, R-N.Y., April 10, 1984. House Merchant Marine and Fisheries reported May 3 (H Rept 98-732). House passed, under suspension of the rules, May 14. Senate Armed Services discharged. Senate passed June 28. President signed July 10, 1984.

PL 98-355 (HR 5950) Increase the federal contribution for the quadrennial political party presidential national nominating conventions. Introduced by ROSTENKOWSKI, D-Ill., June 28, 1984. House Ways and Means reported June 28 (H Rept 98-877, Part I). House passed June 29. Senate passed June 29. President signed July 11, 1984.

PL 98-356 (H J Res 567) Designate 1984 as the "Year of the St. Lawrence Seaway," and June 27, 1984, as "St. Lawrence Seaway Day." Introduced by PURSELL, R-Mich., May 10, 1984. House Post Office and Civil Service discharged. House passed June 6. Senate Judiciary discharged. Senate passed June 28. President signed July 11, 1984.

PL 98-357 (HR 3825) Establish a boundary for the Black Canyon of the Gunnison National Monument. Introduced by KOGOVSEK, D-Colo., Aug. 4, 1983. House Interior and Insular Affairs reported March 1, 1984 (H Rept 98-608). House passed, under suspension of the rules, March 5. Senate Energy and Natural Resources reported June 27 (S Rept 98-549). Senate passed, amended, June 28. House agreed to Senate amendment June 29. President signed July 13, 1984.

PL 98-358 (HR 4308) Grant the consent of the Congress to an interstate compact for the preparation of a feasibility study for the development of a system of high-speed intercity rail passenger service. Introduced by KOLTER, D-Pa., Nov. 3, 1983. House Judiciary reported June 6 (H Rept 98-823). House passed, under suspension of the rules, June 19. Senate passed June 28. President signed July 13, 1984.

PL 98-359 (HR 3922) Establish a one-year limitation on the filing of claims for unpaid accounts formerly maintained in the Postal Savings System. Introduced by SAM B. HALL JR., D-Texas, Sept. 19, 1983. House Judiciary reported Nov. 8 (H Rept 98-502, Part I). House passed, under suspension of the rules, Nov. 16. Senate Judiciary reported June 26, 1984 (S Rept 98-533). Senate passed June 28. President signed July 13, 1984.

PL 98-360 (HR 5653) Appropriate funds for fiscal year 1985 for energy and water development programs. Introduced by BEVILL, D-Ala., May 18, 1984. House Appropriations reported May 15 (H Rept 98-755). House passed May 22. Senate Appropriations reported June 5 (S Rept 98-502). Senate passed, amended, June 21. House agreed to conference report June 27 (H Rept 98-866). Senate agreed to conference report June 27. President signed July 16, 1984.

PL 98-361 (HR 5154) Authorize funds to the National Aeronautics and Space Administration for research and development, space flight, control and data communications, construction of facilities, and research and program management. Introduced by FUQUA, D-Fla., March 15, 1984. House Science and Technology reported March 21 (H Rept 98-629). House passed March 28. Senate Commerce, Science and Transportation reported May 17 (S Rept 98-455). Senate passed, amended, June 21. Senate agreed to conference report June 27 (H Rept 98-873). House agreed to conference report June 28. President signed July 16, 1984.

PL 98-362 (HR 3075) Amend the Small Business Act to establish a small business computer security and education program. Introduced by WYDEN, D-Ore., May 19, 1983. House Small Business reported Oct. 20 (H Rept 98-423, Part I). House passed, under suspension of the rules, Oct. 24. Senate Small Business reported May 10, 1984 (S Rept 98-438). Senate passed, amended, May 24. House agreed to Senate amendments with amendments June 27. Senate agreed to House amendments June 27. President signed July 16, 1984.

PL 98-363 (HR 4616) Amend the Surface Transportation Assistance Act of 1982, increase the authorization of funds for highway safety programs for fiscal year 1985 and 1986, and require each state to expend a specified amount of such funds for programs concerning child restraint systems. Introduced by ANDERSON, D-Calif., Jan. 24, 1984. House Public Works and Transportation reported March 28 (H Rept 98-641). House passed, under suspension of the rules, April 30. Senate passed, amended, June 26. House agreed to Senate amendments June 28. President signed July 17, 1984.

PL 98-364 (HR 4997) Authorize funds to carry out the Marine Mammal Protection Act of 1972, for fiscal years 1985-88. Introduced by BREAUX, D-La., March 1, 1984. House Merchant Marine and Fisheries reported May 15 (H Rept 98-758). House passed, under suspension of the rules, June 5. Senate Commerce, Science and Transportation discharged. Senate passed, amended, June 27. House agreed to Senate

amendment June 28. President signed July 17, 1984.

PL 98-365 (HR 5155) Establish a system to promote the use of land remote-sensing satellite data. Introduced by FUQUA, D-Fla., March 15, 1984. House Science and Technology reported April 3 (H Rept 98-647). House passed, under suspension of the rules, April 9. Senate Commerce, Science and Transportation reported May 17 (S Rept 98-458). Senate passed, amended, June 8. House agreed to Senate amendment with an amendment June 28. Senate agreed to House amendment June 29. President signed July 17, 1984.

PL 98-366 (HR 5740) Enact the "Barrow Gas Field Transfer Act of 1984." Introduced by YOUNG, R-Alaska, May 24, 1984. House Interior and Insular Affairs reported June 14 (H Rept 98-843). House passed, under suspension of the rules, June 18. Senate Energy and Natural Resources discharged. Senate passed June 28. President signed July 17, 1984.

PL 98-367 (HR 5753) Appropriate funds for fiscal year 1985 for the legislative branch of the federal government. Introduced by FAZIO, D-Calif., May 31, 1984. House Appropriations reported May 31 (H Rept 98-811). House passed June 6. Senate Appropriations reported June 14 (S Rept 98-515). Senate passed, amended, June 21. House agreed to conference report June 28 (H Rept 98-870). Senate agreed to conference report June 28. President signed July 17, 1984.

PL 98-368 (H J Res 548) Authorize the President's Commission on Organized Crime to compel the attendance and testimony of witnesses and the production of information. Introduced by HUGHES, D-N.J., April 12, 1984. House Judiciary reported May 7 (H Rept 98-734). House passed, under suspension of the rules, May 7. Senate passed, amended, June 15. House agreed to Senate amendment June 26. President signed July 17, 1984.

PL 98-369 (HR 4170) Provide for certain spending reductions and revenue increases, and reduce deficits by including reconciliations and appropriations caps for the defense and non-defense discretionary spending for fiscal years 1985-87. Introduced by ROSTENKOWSKI, D-Ill., Oct. 20, 1983. House Ways and Means reported Oct. 21 (H Rept 98-432). Supplemental report filed March 5, 1984 (H Rept 98-432, Part II). House passed April 11. Senate passed, amended, May 17. House agreed to conference report June 27 (H Rept 98-861). Senate agreed to conference report June 27. President signed July 18, 1984.

PL 98-370 (HR 3169) Amend the Energy Policy and Conservation Act to facilitate commerce by the domestic renewable energy industry and related service industries. Introduced by WYDEN, D-Ore., May 26, 1983. House Energy and Commerce reported Nov. 11 (H Rept 98-537). House passed, under suspension of the rules, Nov. 16. Senate Energy and Natural Resources reported June 8, 1984 (S Rept 98-508). Senate passed, amended, June 28. House agreed to Senate amendment June 29. President signed July 18, 1984.

PL 98-371 (HR 5713) Appropriate funds for fiscal year 1985 for the Department of Housing and Urban Development and certain independent agencies. Introduced by BOLAND, D-Mass., May 23, 1984. House Appropriations reported May 23 (H Rept 98-803). House passed May 30. Senate Appropriations reported June 7 (S Rept 98-506). Senate passed, amended, June 21. House agreed to conference report June 27 (H Rept 98-867). Senate agreed to conference report June 27. President signed July 18, 1984.

PL 98-372 (HR 29) Recognize the organization known as the Polish Legion of American Veterans, USA. Introduced by ANNUNZIO, D-Ill., Jan. 3, 1983. House Judiciary reported Nov. 7 (H Rept 98-489). House passed, under suspension of the rules, Nov. 14. Senate Judiciary reported June 19, 1984 (S Rept 98-525). Senate passed June 27. President signed July 23, 1984.

PL 98-373 (S 373) Establish the Arctic Research Council to coordinate a comprehensive Arctic research policy. Introduced by MURKOWSKI, R-Alaska, Feb. 1, 1983. Senate Governmental Affairs reported June 21 (S Rept 98-159). Senate passed June 27. House Science and Technology reported Jan. 31, 1984 (H Rept 98-593, Part I). House Armed Services discharged March 16. House Merchant Marine and Fisheries reported March 16 (H Rept 98-593, Part II). House passed, amended, April 24. Senate agreed to House amendments with amendments June 21. House agreed to Senate amendments June 26. President signed July 31, 1984.

PL 98-374 (H J Res 577) Designate August 1984 as "Polish American Heritage Month." Introduced by BORSKI, D-Pa., May 24, 1984. House Post Office and Civil Service discharged. House passed June 26. Senate Judiciary discharged. Senate passed July 31. President signed Aug. 7, 1984.

PL 98-375 (HR 1492) Establish the Christopher Columbus Quincentenary Jubilee Commission. Introduced by RODINO, D-N.J., Feb. 15, 1983. House Post Office and Civil Service reported May 16 (H Rept 98-150). House passed, under suspension of the rules, June 21. Senate passed, amended, Feb. 1, 1984. Senate agreed to conference report June 27 (H Rept 98-876). House agreed to conference report July 25. President signed Aug. 7, 1984.

PL 98-376 (HR 559) Amend the Securities Exchange Act of 1934 to permit the Securities and Exchange Commission to assess civil penalties for trade in securities while in possession of material non-public information. Introduced by DINGELL, D-Mich., Jan. 6, 1983. House Energy and Commerce reported Sept. 15 (H Rept 98-355). House passed, under suspension of the rules, Sept. 19. Senate Banking, Housing and Urban Affairs discharged. Senate passed, amended, June 29, 1984. House agreed to Senate amendment July 25. President signed Aug. 10, 1984.

PL 98-377 (HR 1310) Authorize funds for fiscal years 1984 and 1985 to upgrade instruction in mathematics, science, computer technology and foreign languages in the nation's educational institutions, and to provide assistance for employment-based vocational training programs. Introduced by PERKINS, D-Ky., Feb. 8, 1983. House Education and Labor reported Feb. 17 (H Rept 98-6, Part I). House Science and Technology reported Feb. 25 (H Rept 98-6, Part II). House passed March 2. Senate passed, amended, June 27, 1984. House concurred in Senate amendment, under suspension of the rules, July 25. President signed Aug. 11, 1984.

PL 98-378 (HR 4325) Amend Part D of Title IV of the Social Security Act, to assure improvement in the child support enforcement program. Introduced by KENNELLY, D-Conn., Nov. 8, 1983. House Ways and Means reported Nov. 10 (H Rept 98-527). House passed, under suspension of the rules, Nov. 16. Senate Finance reported April 9, 1984 (S Rept 98-387). Senate passed, amended, April 25. Senate agreed to conference report Aug. 1 (H Rept 98-925). House agreed to conference report Aug. 8. President signed Aug. 16, 1984.

PL 98-379 (HR 4952) Authorize the secretary of defense to provide assistance to certain Indian tribes for expenses incurred for community impact planning activities relating to the planned deployment of the MX missile system in Nevada and Utah in the same manner that state and local governments were provided assistance for such expenses. Introduced by NICHOLS, D-Ala., Feb. 27, 1984. House Armed Services reported April 9 (H Rept 98-661). House passed, under suspension of the rules, May 1. Senate Armed Services discharged. Senate passed Aug. 1. President signed Aug. 16, 1984.

PL 98-380 (S J Res 302) Designate the month of September 1984 as "National Sewing Month." Introduced by EAST, R-N.C., May 24, 1984. Senate Judiciary reported June 7. Senate passed June 8. House Post Office and Civil Service discharged. House passed Aug. 8. President signed Aug. 17, 1984.

PL 98-381 (S 268) Authorize the secretary of the interior to construct, operate and maintain hydroelectric power plants at various existing water projects. Introduced by McCLURE, R-Idaho, Jan. 27, 1983. Senate Energy and Natural Resources reported May 20 (S Rept 98-137). Senate passed Aug. 4. House Interior and Insular Affairs discharged. House passed, amended, May 3, 1984. Senate agreed to House amendments July 31. President signed Aug. 17, 1984.

PL 98-382 (S 1145) Recognize the organization known as the Catholic War Veterans of the United States of America Inc. Introduced by DENTON, R-Ala., April 26, 1983. Senate Judiciary reported Nov. 17 (S Rept 98-315). Senate passed Nov. 18. House Judiciary discharged. House passed Aug. 6, 1984. President signed Aug. 17, 1984.

PL 98-383 (S J Res 248) Designate Aug. 21, 1984, as "Hawaii Statehood Silver Jubilee Day." Introduced by INOUYE, D-Hawaii, Feb. 28, 1984. Senate Judiciary reported April 5. Senate passed April 11. House Post Office and Civil Service discharged. House passed Aug. 8. President signed Aug. 17, 1984.

PL 98-384 (S J Res 272) Recognize the anniversaries of the Warsaw Uprising and the Polish resistance to invasion of Poland during World War II. Introduced by MURKOWSKI, R-Alaska, April 10, 1984. Senate Judiciary discharged. Senate passed July 27. House passed Aug. 1. President signed Aug. 17, 1984.

PL 98-385 (H J Res 529) Designate the week of Sept. 23-29, 1984, as "National Drug Abuse Education and Prevention Week." Introduced by BENNETT, D-Fla., March 27, 1984. House Post Office and Civil Service discharged. House passed Aug. 8. Senate passed Aug. 10. President signed Aug. 21, 1984.

PL 98-386 (H J Res 574) Designate the week beginning Sept. 9, 1984, as "National Community Leadership Week." Introduced by FRENZEL, R-Minn., May 23, 1984. House Post Office and Civil Service discharged. House passed Aug. 8. Senate passed Aug. 10. President signed Aug. 21, 1984.

PL 98-387 (H J Res 583) Designate Jan. 27, 1985, as "National Jerome Kern Day." Introduced by LEVINE, D-Calif., June 5, 1984. House Post Office and Civil Service discharged. House passed Aug. 8. Senate passed Aug. 10. President signed Aug. 21, 1984.

PL 98-388 (H J Res 587) Designate the month of August 1984 as "Ostomy Awareness Week." Introduced by HOYER, D-Md., June 6, 1984. House Post Office and Civil Service discharged. House passed Aug. 8. Senate passed Aug. 10. President signed Aug. 21, 1984.

PL 98-389 (H J Res 597) Designate the week beginning Sept. 2, 1984, as "Youth America Week." Introduced by KEMP, R-N.Y., June 19, 1984.

PL 98-390 (S 1224) Provide for the disposition of certain undistributed judgment funds awarded the Creek Nation. Introduced by NICKLES, R-Okla., May 5, 1983. Senate Indian Affairs reported May 1, 1984 (S Rept 98-421). Senate passed May 10. House Interior and Insular Affairs reported June 27 (H Rept 98-869). House passed Aug. 6. President signed Aug. 21, 1984.

PL 98-391 (S 1806) Recognize the organization known as the Jewish War Veterans of the United States of America. Introduced by BRADLEY, D-N.J., Aug. 4, 1983. Senate Judiciary reported April 9, 1984 (S Rept 98-386). Senate passed April 26. House Judiciary discharged. House passed, amended, Aug. 6. Senate agreed to House amendment Aug. 10. President signed Aug. 21, 1984.

PL 98-392 (S 2556) Authorize funds for the American Folklife Center for fiscal years 1985-89. Introduced by MATHIAS, R-Md., April 11, 1984. Senate Rules and Administration reported May 8 (S Rept 98-433). Senate passed May 22. House passed, amended, Aug. 8. Senate agreed to House amendments Aug. 9. President signed Aug. 21, 1984.

PL 98-393 (S 2820) Name the federal building in McAlester, Okla., the "Carl Albert Federal Building." Introduced by BOREN, D-Okla., June 28, 1984. Senate Environment and Public Works reported Aug. 2. Senate passed Aug. 8. House passed Aug. 9. President signed Aug. 21, 1984.

PL 98-394 (S J Res 338) Congratulate the athletes of the United States Olympic Team for their performance and achievements in the 1984 Winter Olympic Games in Sarajevo, Yugoslavia, and the 1984 Summer Olympic Games in Los Angeles. Introduced by BAKER, R-Tenn., Aug. 2, 1984. Senate passed Aug. 3. House Post Office and Civil Service discharged. House passed Aug. 8. President signed Aug. 21, 1984.

PL 98-395 (S 1429) Amend the Small Business Act to extend and strengthen the Small Business Development Center Program. Introduced by WEICKER, R-Conn., June 8, 1983. Senate Small Business reported Nov. 11 (S Rept 98-309). Senate passed Nov. 17. House passed, amended, May 14, 1984. Senate agreed to conference report Aug. 6 (H Rept 98-955). House agreed to conference report Aug. 8. President signed Aug. 21, 1984.

PL 98-396 (HR 6040) Make further supplemental appropriations for the fiscal year ending Sept. 30, 1984. Introduced by WHITTEN, D-Miss., July 27, 1984. House Appropriations reported July 27 (H Rept 98-916). House passed Aug. 1. Senate Appropriations reported Aug. 2 (S Rept 98-570). Senate passed, amended, Aug. 8. House agreed to conference report Aug. 10 (H Rept 98-977). Senate agreed to conference report Aug. 10. President signed Aug. 22, 1984.

PL 98-397 (HR 4280) Improve the delivery of retirement benefits and provide for greater equity under private pension plans for workers and their spouses and dependents. Introduced by CLAY, D-Mo., Nov. 2, 1983. House Education and Labor reported April 5, 1984 (H Rept 98-655, Part I). House Ways and Means reported May 17 (H Rept 98-655, Part II). House passed, under suspension of the rules, May 22. Senate Finance reported Aug. 2 (S Rept 98-575). Senate passed, amended, Aug. 6. House agreed to Senate amendment Aug. 9. President signed Aug. 23, 1984.

PL 98-398 (S 746) Establish the Illinois and Michigan Canal National Heritage Corridor in the state of Illinois. Introduced by PERCY, R-Ill., March 9, 1983. Senate Energy and Natural Resources reported Feb. 21, 1984 (S Rept 98-355). Senate passed Feb. 27. House passed, amended, Feb. 28. Senate agreed to House amendment with an amendment June 28. House agreed to Senate amendment June 29. President signed Aug. 24, 1984.

PL 98-399 (HR 5890) Establish a commission to assist in the first observance of the federal legal holiday honoring Martin Luther King Jr. Introduced by HALL, D-Ind., June 19, 1984. House Post Office and Civil Service reported July 23 (H Rept 98-893). House passed, under suspension of the rules, July 24. Senate passed, amended, Aug. 1. House agreed to Senate amendment Aug. 8. President signed Aug. 27, 1984.

PL 98-400 (S 1547) Amend the conditions of a grant of certain lands to the town of Olathe, Colo. Introduced by ARMSTRONG, R-Colo., June 27, 1983. Senate Energy and Natural Resources reported May 10, 1984 (S Rept 98-436). Senate passed Aug. 9. House passed Aug. 10. President signed Aug. 27, 1984.

PL 98-401 (S 2036) Require the secretary of the interior to convey to the city of Brigham City, Utah, certain land and improvements in Box Elder County, Utah. Introduced by GARN, R-Utah, Nov. 1, 1983. Senate Energy and Natural Resources reported July 17, 1984 (S Rept 98-554). Senate passed Aug. 9. House passed Aug. 10. President signed Aug. 27, 1984.

PL 98-402 (HR 4596) Amend section 1601(d) of PL 96-607, to permit the secretary of the interior to acquire title in fee simple to McClintock House at 16 East Williams St., Waterloo, N.Y. Introduced by HORTON, R-N.Y., Jan. 23, 1984. House Interior and Insular Affairs reported April 26 (H Rept 98-722). House passed, under suspension of the rules, May 1. Senate Energy and Natural Resources reported July 17 (S Rept 98-558). Senate passed Aug. 9. President signed Aug. 28, 1984.

PL 98-403 (S 2085) Amend section 3a of the Cotton Statistics and Estimates Act to provide continuing authority to the secretary of agriculture for recovering costs associated with cotton classing services to producers. Introduced by COCHRAN, R-Miss., Nov. 11, 1983. Senate Agriculture, Nutrition and Forestry reported April 12, 1984 (S Rept 98-395). Senate passed May 2. House passed, amended, May 21. Senate agreed to House amendment Aug. 10. President signed Aug. 28, 1984.

PL 98-404 (HR 1652) Amend the Reclamation Safety of Dams Act of 1978, to authorize additional funds for fiscal year 1984 to preserve the structural safety of federal dams. Introduced by KAZEN, D-Texas, Feb. 24, 1983. House Interior and Insular Affairs reported May 16 (H Rept 98-168). House passed March 20, 1984. Senate passed, amended, Aug. 9. House agreed to Senate amendments Aug. 10. President signed Aug. 28, 1984.

PL 98-405 (HR 3787) Amend the National Trails System Act by adding the California Trail to the study list. Introduced by BROWN, D-Calif., Aug. 4, 1983. House Interior and Insular Affairs reported April 26, 1984 (H Rept 98-719). House passed, under suspension of the rules, May 1. Senate Energy and Natural Resources reported July 17 (S Rept 98-557). Senate passed Aug. 9. President signed Aug. 28, 1984.

PL 98-406 (HR 4707) Designate certain national forest lands in the state of Arizona as wilderness. Introduced by UDALL, D-Ariz., Feb. 1, 1984. House Interior and Insular Affairs reported March 30 (H Rept 98-643, Part I). House passed, under suspension of the rules, April 3. Senate passed, amended, Aug. 9. House agreed to Senate amendment Aug. 10. President signed Aug. 28, 1984.

PL 98-407 (HR 5604) Authorize funds for fiscal year 1985 for military construction programs of the Department of Defense. Introduced by PRICE, D-Ill., May 7, 1984. House Armed Services reported May 15 (H Rept 98-765). House passed June 22. Senate passed, amended, June 26. House agreed to conference report Aug. 8 (H Rept 98-962). Senate agreed to conference report Aug. 9. President signed Aug. 28, 1984.

PL 98-408 (S 2201) Convey certain lands to the Zuni Indian Tribe for religious purposes. Introduced by GOLDWATER, R-Ariz., Jan. 23, 1984. Senate Indian Affairs reported May 14 (S Rept 98-441). Senate passed July 31. House passed, amended, Aug. 8. Senate agreed to House amendment Aug. 10. President signed Aug. 28, 1984.

PL 98-409 (HR 4214) Establish a State Mining and Mineral Resources Research Institute program. Introduced by McNULTY, D-Ariz., Oct. 25, 1983. House Interior and Insular Affairs reported April 5, 1984 (H Rept 98-653). House passed, under suspension of the rules, April 9. Senate Energy and Natural Resources reported May 10 (S Rept 98-437). Senate passed, amended, Aug. 9. House agreed to Senate amendment Aug. 10. President signed Aug. 29, 1984.

PL 98-410 (H J Res 452) Recognize the important contributions of the arts to a complete education. Introduced by DOWNEY, D-N.Y., Jan. 26, 1984. House Education and Labor reported June 18 (H Rept 98-844). House passed, under suspension of the rules, June 18. Senate Labor and Human Resources reported Aug. 9. Senate passed Aug. 10. President signed Aug. 29, 1984.

PL 98-411 (HR 5712) Appropriate funds for fiscal year 1985 for the Departments of Commerce, Justice, and State, the Judiciary and certain related agencies. Introduced by SMITH, D-Iowa, May 23, 1984. House Appropriations reported May 23 (H Rept 98-802). House passed May 31. Senate Appropriations reported June 13 (H Rept 98-514). Senate passed, amended, June 28. House agreed to conference report Aug. 8 (H Rept 98-952). Senate agreed to conference report Aug. 9. President signed Aug. 30, 1984.

PL 98-412 (H J Res 600) Amend the Agriculture and Food Act of 1981, to provide for the establishment of a commission to study and make recommendations concerning agriculture-related trade and export policies, programs and practices of the United States. Introduced by DE LA GARZA, D-Texas, June 21, 1984. House Agriculture reported Aug. 6 (H Rept 98-956, Part I). House passed, under suspension of the rules, Aug. 6. Senate passed Aug. 10. President signed Aug. 30, 1984.

PL 98-413 (H J Res 505) Designate the week beginning Sept. 23, 1984, as "National Adult Day Care Center Week." Introduced by HERTEL, D-Mich., March 6, 1984. House Post Office and Civil Service discharged. House passed Aug. 8. Senate Judiciary reported Sept. 13. Senate passed Sept. 17. President signed Sept. 21, 1984.

PL 98-414 (H J Res 545) Designate the week of Sept. 16-22, 1984, as "Emergency Medicine Week." Introduced by VANDERGRIFF, D-Texas, April 11, 1984. House Post Office and Civil Service discharged. House passed Sept. 12. Senate passed Sept. 20. President signed Sept. 24, 1984.

PL 98-415 (S J Res 333) Designate Sept. 21, 1984, as "World War I Aces and Aviators Day." Introduced by HELMS, R-N.C., June 29, 1984. Senate Judiciary reported Aug. 9. Senate passed Aug. 10. House Post

Office and Civil Service discharged. House passed Sept. 20. President signed Sept. 24, 1984.

PL 98-416 (S J Res 340) Designate the week of Sept. 23, 1984, as "National Historically Black Colleges Week." Introduced by THURMOND, R-S.C., Aug. 6, 1984. Senate Judiciary reported Aug. 9. Senate passed Aug. 10. House Post Office and Civil Service discharged. House passed Sept. 20. President signed Sept. 24, 1984.

PL 98-417 (S 1538) Amend the Federal Food, Drug and Cosmetic Act, to revise the procedures of new drug applications and amend Title 35, U.S. Code, to authorize the extension of patents for certain regulated products. Introduced by MATHIAS, R-Md., June 23, 1983. Senate Judiciary reported June 26, 1984 (S Rept 98-547). Senate passed June 29. House passed, amended, Sept. 6. Senate agreed to House amendments Sept. 12. President signed Sept. 24, 1984.

PL 98-418 (S J Res 275) Designate the month of October 1984 as "National Spina Bifida Month." Introduced by DIXON, D-Ill., April 12, 1984. Senate Judiciary reported Aug. 9. Senate passed Aug. 10. House Post Office and Civil Service discharged. House passed Sept. 12. President signed Sept. 25, 1984.

PL 98-419 (S 1546) Provide for a partial deregulation of deepwater port facilities. Introduced by JOHNSTON, D-La., June 27, 1983. Senate Commerce, Science and Transportation reported Nov. 16 (S Rept 98-314). Senate Environment and Public Works reported Feb. 29, 1984. Senate passed March 30. House passed Aug. 9. President signed Sept. 25, 1984.

PL 98-420 (HR 5177) Grant the consent of Congress to an amendment to the Wheeling Creek Watershed Protection and Flood Prevention District Compact entered into by the states of West Virginia and Pennsylvania. Introduced by MOLLOHAN, D-W.Va., March 19, 1984. House Judiciary reported June 6 (H Rept 98-821). House passed, under suspension of the rules, June 18. Senate Judiciary discharged. Senate passed Sept. 10. President signed Sept. 25, 1984.

PL 98-421 (S 806) Provide for a plan to reimburse the Okefenokee Rural Electric Membership Corporation for the costs incurred in installing electrical service to the Cumberland Island National Seashore. Introduced by NUNN, D-Ga., March 15, 1983. Senate Energy and Natural Resources reported July 17, 1984 (S Rept 98-556). Senate passed Aug. 9. House passed Sept. 6. President signed Sept. 25, 1984.

PL 98-422 (S J Res 25) Redesignate the Saint Croix Island National Monument in the state of Maine as the "Saint Croix Island International Historic Site." Introduced by COHEN, R-Maine, Jan. 27, 1983. Senate Energy and Natural Resources reported Feb. 23 (S Rept 98-8). Senate passed March 2. House Interior and Insular Affairs reported April 26, 1984 (H Rept 98-720). House passed, amended, under suspension of the rules, April 30. Senate agreed to House amendment with an amendment Aug. 9. House agreed to Senate amendment Sept. 6. President signed Sept. 25, 1984.

PL 98-423 (S J Res 98-334) Provide for the designation of the month of November 1984 as "National Hospice Month." Introduced by DOLE, R-Kan., July 24, 1984. Senate Judiciary reported Aug. 9. Senate passed Aug. 10. House Post Office and Civil Service discharged. House passed Sept. 12. President signed Sept. 25, 1984.

PL 98-424 (S J Res 335) Designate the week beginning May 19, 1985, as "National Tourism Week." Introduced by WARNER, R-Va., July 25, 1984. Senate Judiciary reported Aug. 9. Senate passed Aug. 10. House Post Office and Civil Service discharged. House passed Sept. 12. President signed Sept. 25, 1984.

PL 98-425 (HR 1437) Designate certain lands in California as wilderness. Introduced by BURTON, D-Calif., Feb. 15, 1983. House Interior and Insular Affairs reported March 18 (H Rept 98-40). House passed April 12. Senate Energy and Natural Resources reported Aug. 7, 1984 (S Rept 98-582). Senate passed, amended, Aug. 9. House agreed to Senate amendment Sept. 12. President signed Sept. 28, 1984.

PL 98-426 (S 38) Revise provisions relating to coverage, benefits, medical treatment and claims procedures under the Longshoremen's and Harbor Workers' Compensation Act. Introduced by NICKLES, R-Okla., Jan. 26, 1983. Senate Labor and Human Resources reported May 10 (S Rept 98-81). Senate passed June 16. House Education and Labor reported Nov. 18 (H Rept 98-570). Supplemental report filed Feb. 7, 1984 (H Rept 98-570, Part II). House passed, amended, under suspension of the rules, April 10. House agreed to conference report Sept. 18 (H Rept 98-1027). Senate agreed to conference report Sept. 20. President signed Sept. 28, 1984.

PL 98-427 (S 2418) Authorize and direct the librarian of Congress, subject to the supervision and authority of a federal civilian or military agency, to proceed with construction of the Library of Congress Mass Book Deacidification Facility. Introduced by MATHIAS, R-Md., March 13, 1984. Senate Rules and Administration reported May 8 (S Rept 98-429). Senate passed May 18. House Public Works and Transportation discharged. House passed, amended, Sept. 11. Senate agreed to House amendment Sept. 17. President signed Sept. 28, 1984.

PL 98-428 (S 2155) Designate certain national forest system lands in the state of Utah for inclusion in the National Wilderness Preservation

System and release other forest lands for multiple use management. Introduced by GARN, R-Utah, Nov. 18, 1983. Senate Energy and Natural Resources reported Aug. 6, 1984 (S Rept 98-581). Senate passed Aug. 9. House Interior and Insular Affairs reported Sept. 13 (H Rept 98-1019, Part I). House passed, under suspension of the rules, Sept. 17. President signed Sept. 28, 1984.

PL 98-429 (S J Res 336) Proclaim Oct. 23, 1984, as "A Time of Remembrance" for all victims of terrorism throughout the world. Introduced by DENTON, R-Ala., July 26, 1984. Senate Judiciary reported Aug. 9. Senate passed Aug. 10. House Post Office and Civil Service discharged. House passed Sept. 12. President signed Sept. 28, 1984.

PL 98-430 (HR 9) Designate components of the National Wilderness Preservation System in the state of Florida. Introduced by FUQUA, D-Fla., Jan. 3, 1983. House Interior and Insular Affairs reported May 11 (H Rept 98-102, Part I). House Agriculture reported June 1 (H Rept 98-102, Part II). House passed, under suspension of the rules, June 6. Senate Energy and Natural Resoures reported Aug. 6, 1984 (S Rept 98-580). Senate passed, amended, Aug. 9. House agreed to Senate amendments Sept. 12. President signed Sept. 28, 1984.

PL 98-431 (H J Res 453) Designate the week of Sept. 30-Oct. 6, 1984, as "National High-Tech Week." Introduced by DYMALLY, D-Calif., Jan. 26, 1984. House Post Office and Civil Service discharged. House passed Aug. 1. Senate passed Sept. 17. President signed Sept. 28, 1984.

PL 98-432 (S 1735) Authorize the secretary of the interior to pay a specified amount to the Shoalwater Bay Indian Tribe of Washington to settle claims regarding a previous transfer by the United States of certain land with the Shoalwater Bay Reservation. Introduced by GORTON, R-Wash., Aug. 3, 1983. Senate Indian Affairs reported May 14, 1984 (S Rept 98-439). Senate passed May 24. House Interior and Insular Affairs discharged. House passed Sept. 11. President signed Sept. 28, 1984.

PL 98-433 (H J Res 153) Designate the week beginning Oct. 7, 1984, as "National Children's Week." Introduced by FOWLER, D-Ga., Feb. 22, 1983. House Post Office and Civil Service discharged. House passed June 6, 1984. Senate Judiciary reported Sept. 13. Senate passed Sept. 17. President signed Sept. 28, 1984.

PL 98-434 (HR 71) Authorize and direct the secretary of the interior to engage in a special study of the potential for groundwater recharge in the High Plains States. Introduced by BEREUTER, R-Neb., Jan. 3, 1983. House Interior and Insular Affairs reported May 16 (H Rept 98-167). House passed, under suspension of the rules, June 20. Senate Energy and Natural Resources reported March 29, 1984 (S Rept 98-372). Senate passed, amended, Aug. 10. House agreed to Senate amendments Sept. 14. President signed Sept. 28, 1984.

PL 98-435 (HR 1250) Provide that registration and polling places for federal elections be accessible to handicapped and elderly individuals. Introduced by FISH, R-N.Y., Feb. 3, 1983. House Administration reported June 21, 1984 (H Rept 98-852). House passed, under suspension of the rules, June 25. Senate Rules and Administration reported Aug. 9 (S Rept 98-590). Senate passed, amended, Aug. 10. House agreed to Senate amendments Sept. 12. President signed Sept. 28, 1984.

PL 98-436 (S J Res 304) Designate the month of October 1984 as "National Quality Month." Introduced by HELMS, R-N.C., June 6, 1984. Senate Judiciary reported Sept. 13. Senate passed Sept. 17. House Post Office and Civil Service discharged. House passed Sept. 20. President signed Sept. 28, 1984.

PL 98-437 (S J Res 254) Designate the month of October 1984 as "National Down's Syndrome Month." Introduced by LUGAR, R-Ind., March 5, 1984. Senate Judiciary reported May 17. Senate passed May 22. House Post Office and Civil Service discharged. House passed Sept. 12. President signed Sept. 28, 1984.

PL 98-438 (S J Res 227) Designate the week beginning Nov. 11, 1984, as "National Women Veterans Recognition Week." Introduced by CRANSTON, D-Calif., Feb. 7, 1984. Senate Judiciary reported April 12. Senate passed April 25. House Post Office and Civil Service discharged. House passed Sept. 12. President signed Sept. 28, 1984.

PL 98-439 (S 598) Authorize the conveyance of land from the Department of Agriculture to Payson, Ariz. Introduced by DeCONCINI, D-Ariz., Feb. 24, 1983. Senate Energy and Natural Resources reported July 17, 1984 (S Rept 98-555). Senate passed Aug. 9. House passed Sept. 17. President signed Sept. 28, 1984.

PL 98-440 (S 2040) Amend the Securities Act of 1933 and the Securities Exchange Act of 1934 with respect to the treatment of mortgage backed securities and increase the authority of the Federal Home Loan Mortgage Corporation. Introduced by GARN, R-Utah, Nov. 2, 1983. Senate Banking, Housing and Urban Affairs reported Nov. 2 (S Rept 98-293). Senate passed Nov. 17. Senate vacated passage Feb. 9, 1984. Senate passed Feb. 9. House passed, amended, Sept. 11. Senate agreed to House amendments Sept. 26. President signed Oct. 3, 1984.

PL 98-441 (H J Res 653) Make continuing appropriations for the fiscal year 1985 through Wednesday, Oct. 3, 1984. Introduced by WHIT-TEN, D-Miss., Oct. 1, 1984. House Appropriations discharged. House passed Oct. 1. Senate passed Oct. 1. President signed Oct. 3, 1984.

PL 98-442 (H J Res 392) Designate Dec. 7, 1984, as "National Pearl Harbor Remembrance Day," on the occasion of the anniversary of the attack on Pearl Harbor. Introduced by SISISKY, D-Va., Oct. 20, 1983. House Post Office and Civil Service discharged. House passed Sept. 12, 1984. Senate passed Sept. 21. President signed Oct. 3, 1984.

PL 98-443 (HR 5297) Amend the Federal Aviation Act of 1958 to terminate certain functions of the Civil Aeronautics Board and to transfer certain functions of the board to the secretary of transportation. Introduced by MINETA, D-Calif., March 29, 1984. House Public Works and Transportation reported May 21 (H Rept 98-793). House passed, under suspension of the rules, June 5. Senate Commerce, Science and Transportation discharged. Senate passed, amended, Aug. 8. House agreed to conference report Sept. 19 (H Rept 98-1025). Senate agreed to conference report Sept. 20. President signed Oct. 4, 1984.

PL 98-444 (S 2732) Amend the Wild and Scenic Rivers Act to permit the control of the lamprey eel in the Pere Marquette River and to designate a portion of the Au Sable River, Mich., as a component of the National Wild and Scenic Rivers System. Introduced by LEVIN, D-Mich., June 6, 1984. Senate Energy and Natural Resources reported Aug. 3 (S Rept 98-574). Senate passed Aug. 9. House passed Sept. 24. President signed Oct. 4, 1984.

PL 98-445 (HR 5147) Implement the Eastern Pacific Ocean Tuna Fishing Agreement signed in San Jose, Costa Rica, March 15, 1983. Introduced by BREAUX, D-La., March 15, 1984. House Merchant Marine and Fisheries reported April 26 (H Rept 98-721). House passed, under suspension of the rules, May 1. Senate Commerce, Science and Transportation reported July 17 (S Rept 98-559). Senate passed Sept. 21. President signed Oct. 4, 1984.

PL 98-446 (H J Res 554) Designate the week of Nov. 11-17, 1984, as "Women in Agriculture Week." Introduced by FOLEY, D-Wash., April 25, 1984. House Post Office and Civil Service discharged. House passed Aug. 8. Senate Judiciary reported Sept. 20. Senate passed Sept. 21. President signed Oct. 4, 1984.

PL 98-447 (H J Res 605) Reaffirm that it is the continuing policy of the United States government to be in opposition to the practice of torture by any foreign government. Introduced by FASCELL, D-Fla., June 26, 1984. House passed, under suspension of the rules, Sept. 11. Senate passed Sept. 21. President signed Oct. 4, 1984.

PL 98-448 (H J Res 606) Designate the week of Oct. 14-21, 1984, as "National Housing Week." Introduced by AuCOIN, D-Ore., June 26, 1984. House Post Office and Civil Service discharged. House passed Aug. 8. Senate Judiciary discharged. Senate passed Sept. 28. President signed Oct. 4, 1984.

PL 98-449 (S 2614) Amend the Indian Financing Act of 1974. Introduced by ANDREWS, R-N.D., May 1, 1984. Senate Indian Affairs reported May 18 (S Rept 98-459). Senate passed June 8. House Interior and Insular Affairs discharged. House passed, amended, Sept. 11. Senate agreed to House amendments with an amendment Sept. 21. House agreed to Senate amendment Sept. 24. President signed Oct. 4, 1984.

PL 98-450 (S 32) Prohibit the owner of certain audio material from renting, leasing or lending for commercial advantage without the authorization of the copyright owner. Introduced by MATHIAS, R-Md., Jan. 26, 1983. Senate Judiciary reported June 23 (S Rept 98-162). Senate passed June 28. House Judiciary discharged. House passed, amended, Sept. 11, 1984. Senate agreed to House amendment Sept. 21. President signed Oct. 4, 1984.

PL 98-451 (S 2000) Allow variable interest rates for Indian funds held in trust by the United States. Introduced by ANDREWS, R-N.D., Oct. 25, 1983. Senate Indian Affairs reported April 24, 1984 (S Rept 98-410). Senate passed May 23. House Interior and Insular Affairs reported Sept. 5 (H Rept 98-988). House passed, amended, Sept. 17. Senate agreed to House amendment Sept. 21. President signed Oct. 4, 1984.

PL 98-452 (S 1770) Extend the lease terms of federal oil and gas lease numbered U-39711. Introduced by GARN, R-Utah, Aug. 4, 1983. Senate Energy and Natural Resources reported June 28, 1984 (S Rept 98-540). Senate passed Aug. 9. House passed Sept. 24. President signed Oct. 4, 1984.

PL 98-453 (H J Res 656) Make continuing appropriations for fiscal 1985 through 6:00 p.m. EDT, Friday, Oct. 5, 1984. Introduced by WHIT-TEN, D-Miss., Oct. 4, 1984. House Appropriations discharged. House passed Oct. 4. Senate passed Oct. 4. President signed Oct. 5, 1984.

PL 98-454 (HR 5561) Enhance the economic development of Guam, the Virgin Islands, American Samoa, the Northern Mariana Islands. Introduced by WON PAT, D-Guam, May 1, 1984. House Interior and Insular Affairs reported May 15 (H Rept 98-784). House passed June 28. Senate Energy and Natural Resources discharged. Senate passed, amended, Aug. 10. House agreed to Senate amendments with amendments Sept. 14. Senate agreed to House amendments Sept. 21. President signed Oct. 5, 1984.

PL 98-455 (H J Res 659) Make further continuing appropriations for fiscal year 1985. Introduced by WHITTEN, D-Miss., Oct. 5, 1984. House passed Oct. 5. Senate passed Oct. 5. President signed Oct. 6, 1984.

PL 98-456 (H J Res 649) Change the date for the counting of the electoral votes in 1985 to Jan. 7. Introduced by WRIGHT, D-Texas, Sept. 19, 1984. House passed Sept. 19. Senate passed Sept. 25. President signed Oct. 9, 1984.

PL 98-457 (HR 1904) Extend and improve the provisions of the Child Abuse Prevention and Treatment Act and the Child Abuse Prevention and Treatment and Adoption Reform Act of 1978. Introduced by MURPHY, D-Pa., March 3, 1983. House Education and Labor reported May 16 (H Rept 98-159). House passed Feb. 2, 1984. Senate passed, amended, July 26. House agreed to conference report Sept. 26 (H Rept 98-1038). Senate agreed to conference report Sept. 28. President signed Oct. 9, 1984.

PL 98-458 (S J Res 322) Designate the week beginning Oct. 7, 1984, as "Mental Illness Awareness Week." Introduced by QUAYLE, R-Ind., June 26, 1984. Senate Judiciary reported Aug. 9. Senate passed Aug. 10. House Post Office and Civil Service discharged. House passed Oct. 2. President signed Oct. 9, 1984.

PL 98-459 (S 2603) Extend the authorization of appropriations for and revise the Older Americans Act of 1965. Introduced by GRASSLEY, R-Iowa, April 26, 1984. Senate Labor and Human Resources reported May 18 (S Rept 98-467). Senate passed May 24. House passed, amended, Aug. 8. Senate agreed to conference report Sept. 26 (H Rept 98-1037). House agreed to conference report Sept. 26. President signed Oct. 9, 1984.

PL 98-460 (HR 3755) Revise the old age, survivors and disability insurance provisions of the Social Security Act. Introduced by PICKLE, D-Texas, Aug. 3, 1983. House Ways and Means reported March 14, 1984 (H Rept 98-618). House passed March 27. Senate passed, amended, May 22. Senate agreed to conference report Sept. 19 (H Rept 98-1039). House agreed to conference report Sept. 19. President signed Oct. 9, 1984.

PL 98-461 (H J Res 663) Make further continuing appropriations for fiscal year 1985. Introduced by WHITTEN, D-Miss., Oct. 9, 1984. House Appropriations discharged. House passed, under suspension of the rules, Oct. 9. Senate passed Oct. 9. President signed Oct. 10, 1984.

PL 98-462 (S 1841) Modify the federal antitrust and intellectual property laws, to stimulate U.S. productivity and enhance the competitiveness of U.S. industries in international markets. Introduced by THURMOND, R-S.C., Sept. 14, 1983. Senate Judiciary reported May 3, 1984 (S Rept 98-427). Senate passed July 31. House passed, amended, Aug. 9. Senate agreed to conference report Sept. 26 (H Rept 98-1044). House agreed to conference report Oct. 1. President signed Oct. 11, 1984.

PL 98-463 (S J Res 201) Designate the week of Nov. 25-Dec. 1, 1984, as "National Epidermolysis Bullosa Awareness Week." Introduced by HATFIELD, R-Ore., Nov. 17, 1983. Senate Judiciary reported Feb. 23, 1984. Senate passed Sept. 17. House Post Office and Civil Service discharged. House passed Oct. 2. President signed Oct. 11, 1984.

PL 98-464 (S 2688) Amend the Natural Gas Pipeline Safety Act of 1968 and the Hazardous Liquid Pipeline Safety Act of 1979 to authorize appropriations for fiscal years 1985-86. Introduced by PACKWOOD, R-Ore., May 17, 1984. Senate Commerce, Science and Transportation reported May 17 (S Rept 98-456). Senate passed June 21. House passed, amended, June 25. Senate agreed to House amendments with an amendment Sept. 21. House agreed to Senate amendment Sept. 26. President signed Oct. 11, 1984.

PL 98-465 (S J Res 237) Designate the week of Nov. 25-Dec. 1, 1984, as "National Home Care Week." Introduced by HATCH, R-Utah, Feb. 9, 1984. Senate Judiciary reported March 8. Senate passed March 12. House Post Office and Civil Service discharged. House passed Oct. 2. President signed Oct. 11, 1984.

PL 98-466 (S 197) Direct the secretary of transportation to conduct an independent study to determine the adequacy of certain industry practices and Federal Aviation Administration rules and regulations. Introduced by INOUYE, D-Hawaii, Feb. 26, 1983. Senate Commerce, Science and Transportation reported May 21, 1984 (S Rept 98-468). Senate passed June 15. House Public Works and Transportation discharged. House passed Oct. 1. President signed Oct. 11, 1984.

PL 98-467 (S J Res 273) Designate the week of Aug. 5-11, 1984, as "Smokey Bear Week." Introduced by HEFLIN, D-Ala., April 12, 1984. Senate Judiciary reported May 3. Senate passed May 8. House Post Office and Civil Service discharged. House passed, amended, Oct 2. Senate agreed to House amendments Oct. 4. President signed Oct. 11, 1984.

PL 98-468 (S J Res 324) Designate November 1984 as "National Christmas Seal Month." Introduced by HATCH, R-Utah, June 27, 1984. Senate Judiciary reported Aug. 2. Senate passed Aug. 3. House Post Office and Civil Service discharged. House passed Oct. 2. President signed Oct. 11, 1984.

PL 98-469 (HR 5221) Extend through Sept. 30, 1988, the period during which amendments to the U.S. Grain Standards Act contained in section 155 of the Omnibus Budget Reconciliation Act of 1981 remain effective. Introduced by FOLEY, D-Wash., March 22, 1984. House Agriculture reported May 15 (H Rept 98-756). House passed, under suspension of the rules, May 21. Senate Agriculture, Nutrition and Forestry reported Sept. 18 (S Rept 98-617). Senate passed Sept. 28. President signed Oct. 11, 1984.

PL 98-470 (HR 3130) Authorize amendments to certain repayment and water service contracts for the Frenchman unit of the Pick-Sloan Missouri River Basin Program. Introduced by SMITH, R-Neb., May 24, 1983. House Interior and Insular Affairs reported June 14, 1984 (H Rept 98-840). House passed, under suspension of the rules, June 18. Senate Energy and Natural Resources reported Sept. 19 (S Rept 98-624). Senate passed Sept. 28. President signed Oct. 11, 1984.

PL 98-471 (S J Res 260) Designate the week beginning Nov. 11, 1984, as "National Blood Pressure Awareness Week." Introduced by QUAYLE, R-Ind., March 15, 1984. Senate Judiciary reported May 3. Senate passed May 8. House Post Office and Civil Service discharged. House passed Oct. 2. President signed Oct. 11, 1984.

PL 98-472 (S J Res 295) Designate the week of Oct. 14-20, 1984, as "Myasthenia Gravis Awareness Week." Introduced by METZENBAUM, D-Ohio, May 15, 1984. Senate Judiciary reported Aug. 9. Senate passed Aug. 10. House Post Office and Civil Service discharged. House passed Oct. 2. President signed Oct. 11, 1984.

PL 98-473 (H J Res 648) Make continuing appropriations for the fiscal year 1985. Introduced by WHITTEN, D-Miss., Sept. 17, 1984. House Appropriations reported Sept. 17 (H Rept 98-1030). House passed Sept. 25. Senate passed, amended, Oct. 4. House agreed to conference report Oct. 10 (H Rept 98-1159). Senate agreed to conference report Oct. 11. President signed Oct. 12, 1984.

PL 98-474 (HR 3979) Establish a national program to increase the availability of information on the health consequences of smoking and amend the Federal Cigarette Labeling and Advertising Act to change the label requirements. Introduced by WAXMAN, D-Calif., Sept. 22, 1983. House Energy and Commerce reported May 23, 1984 (H Rept 98-805). House passed, under suspension of the rules, Sept. 10. Senate passed, amended, Sept. 26. House agreed to Senate amendments Sept. 26. President signed Oct. 12, 1984.

PL 98-475 (H J Res 654) Increase the statutory limit on the public debt. Introduced by MURTHA, D-Pa., Oct. 1, 1984. House passed Oct. 1. Senate passed Oct. 12. President signed Oct. 13, 1984.

PL 98-476 (S J Res 332) Proclaim Oct. 16, 1984, as "World Food Day." Introduced by DOLE, R-Kan., June 29, 1984. Senate Judiciary reported Aug. 9. Senate passed Aug. 10. House Post Office and Civil Service discharged. House passed Oct. 2. President signed Oct. 15, 1984.

PL 98-477 (HR 5164) Amend the National Security Act of 1947 to regulate public disclosure of information held by the Central Intelligence Agency. Introduced by MAZZOLI, D-Ky., March 15, 1984. House Intelligence reported May 1 (H Rept 98-726, Part I). House Government Operations reported Sept. 10 (H Rept 98-726, Part II). House passed, under suspension of the rules, Sept. 19. Senate passed Sept. 28. President signed Oct. 15, 1984.

PL 98-478 (HR 2838) Authorize the secretaries of the interior and agriculture to provide assistance to groups and organizations volunteering to plant tree seedlings on public lands. Introduced by WEAVER, D-Ore., April 28, 1983. House Interior and Insular Affairs reported June 22 (H Rept 98-255, Part I). House Agriculture reported Nov. 11 (H Rept 98-255, Part II). House passed, under suspension of the rules, Nov. 16. Senate Energy and Natural Resources reported Aug. 27, 1984 (S Rept 98-596). Senate passed, amended, Sept. 26. House agreed to Senate amendments, under suspension of the rules, Oct. 1. President signed Oct. 16, 1984.

PL 98-479 (S 2819) Make essential technical corrections to the Housing and Urban-Rural Recovery Act of 1983. Introduced by GARN, R-Utah, June 28, 1984. Senate Banking, Finance and Urban Affairs reported June 28. Senate passed June 29. House passed, amended, under suspension of the rules, Sept. 11. House agreed to conference report Oct. 2 (H Rept 98-1103). Senate agreed to conference report Oct. 3. President signed Oct. 17, 1984.

PL 98-480 (HR 2878) Amend and extend the Library Services and Construction Act. Introduced by SIMON, D-Ill., May 3, 1983. House Education and Labor reported May 16 (H Rept 98-165). House passed Jan. 31, 1984. Senate Labor and Human Resources discharged. Senate passed, amended, June 21. House agreed to conference report Oct. 2 (H Rept 98-1075). Senate agreed to conference report Oct. 3. President signed Oct. 17, 1984.

PL 98-481 (HR 5540) Provide for the restoration of federal recognition to the Confederated Tribes of Coos, Lower Umpqua and Siuslaw Indians, to institute for such tribes those federal services provided to Indians who are recognized by the federal government and who receive such services because of federal trust responsibility. Introduced by

WEAVER, D-Ore., April 26, 1984. House Interior and Insular Affairs reported July 25 (H Rept 98-904). House passed, under suspension of the rules, Aug. 6. Senate Indian Affairs discharged. Senate passed, amended, Sept. 28. House agreed to Senate amendment Oct. 2. President signed Oct. 17, 1984.

PL 98-482 (HR 3697) Modify federal land acquisition and disposal policies carried out with respect to Fire Island National Seashore. Introduced by DOWNEY, D-N.Y., July 28, 1983. House Interior and Insular Affairs reported Sept. 24, 1984 (H Rept 98-1065). House passed, under suspension of the rules, Sept. 24. Senate passed Oct. 3. President signed Oct. 17, 1984.

PL 98-483 (HR 2889) Amend section 306 of the National Historic Preservation Act. Introduced by CLINGER, R-Pa., May 4, 1983. House Interior and Insular Affairs reported May 15, 1984 (H Rept 98-761). House passed, under suspension of the rules, June 4. Senate Energy and Natural Resources reported Sept. 19 (S Rept 98-623). Senate passed, amended, Oct. 3. House agreed to Senate amendment Oct. 4. President signed Oct. 17, 1984.

PL 98-484 (HR 3601) Modify the boundary of the Pike National Forest in the state of Colorado. Introduced by KRAMER, R-Colo., July 19, 1983. House Interior and Insular Affairs reported Sept. 24, 1984 (H Rept 98-1066). House passed, under suspension of the rules, Sept. 24. Senate Energy and Natural Resources discharged. Senate passed Oct. 3. President signed Oct. 17, 1984.

PL 98-485 (HR 4932) Withdraw and reserve for the Department of the Air Force certain public lands within the Nellis Air Force Range, within Clark, Nye and Lincoln counties, Nev., for use as a training and weapons testing area. Introduced by PRICE, D-Ill., Feb. 23, 1984. House Interior and Insular Affairs reported Sept. 24 (H Rept 98-1046, Part I). House passed, under suspension of the rules, Sept. 24. Senate passed Oct. 2. President signed Oct. 17, 1984.

PL 98-486 (HR 4994) Exempt from taxation by the District of Columbia certain property of the Jewish War Veterans, U.S.A. National Memorial Inc. Introduced by SMITH, D-Fla., Feb. 29, 1984. House District of Columbia reported Sept. 13 (H Rept 98-1023). Supplemental report filed Sept. 14 (H Rept 98-1023, Part II). House passed Sept. 17. Senate Governmental Affairs discharged. Senate passed Oct. 3. President signed Oct. 17, 1984.

PL 98-487 (HR 5223) Exempt restaurant central kitchens from federal inspection requirements. Introduced by DE LA GARZA, D-Texas, March 22, 1984. House Agriculture reported June 29 (H Rept 98-885). House passed, under suspension of the rules, July 24. Senate Agriculture, Nutrition and Forestry discharged. Senate passed, amended, Oct. 2. House agreed to Senate amendments Oct. 3. President signed Oct. 17, 1984.

PL 98-488 (HR 5513) Designate the Delta States Research Center in Stoneville, Miss., as the "Jamie Whitten Delta States Research Center." Introduced by MONTGOMERY, D-Miss., April 25, 1984. House Agriculture reported Sept. 24 (H Rept 98-1064). House passed, under suspension of the rules, Sept. 24. Senate Agriculture, Nutrition and Forestry discharged. Senate passed Oct. 3. President signed Oct. 17, 1984.

PL 98-489 (HR 5631) Authorize the acquisition of land for a visitor contact and administrative site for the Big Thicket National Preserve in Texas. Introduced by WILSON, D-Texas, May 9, 1984. House Interior and Insular Affairs reported Aug. 6 (H Rept 98-957). House passed, under suspension of the rules, Aug. 6. Senate Energy and Natural Resources discharged. Senate passed Oct. 3. President signed Oct. 17, 1984.

PL 98-490 (HR 5782) Grant the consent of Congress to an amendment to the Delaware River Basin Compact. Introduced by HUGHES, D-N.J., June 6, 1984. House Judiciary reported Sept. 24 (H Rept 98-1055). House passed, under suspension of the rules, Sept. 24. Senate Judiciary reported Sept. 28. Senate passed Oct. 3. President signed Oct. 17, 1984.

PL 98-491 (HR 5818) Amend the Federal Hazardous Substances Act to apply the notice and repair, replacement, and refund provisions of that act to defective toys and other articles intended for use by children. Introduced by WAXMAN, D-Calif., June 11, 1984. House Energy and Commerce reported July 24 (H Rept 98-895). House passed, under suspension of the rules, Aug. 6. Senate Commerce, Science and Transportation discharged. Senate passed, amended, Oct. 3. House agreed to Senate amendments Oct. 3. President signed Oct. 17, 1984.

PL 98-492 (HR 5997) Designate the U.S. post office and courthouse in Pendleton, Ore., as the "John F. Kilkenny U.S. Post Office and Courthouse." Introduced by ROBERT F. SMITH, R-Ore., June 29, 1984. House Public Works and Transportation reported Aug. 1 (H Rept 98-928). House passed Aug. 9. Senate Environment and Public Works discharged. Senate passed Oct. 3. President signed Oct. 17, 1984.

PL 98-493 (HR 6223) Amend the act providing for the incorporation of certain persons as Group Hospitalization Inc. Introduced by FAUNT-ROY, D-D.C., Sept. 12, 1984. House District of Columbia reported Sept. 13 (H Rept 98-1022). Supplemental report filed Sept. 14 (H Rept 98-1022, Part II). House passed Sept. 17. Senate Governmental Affairs discharged. Senate passed Oct. 3. President signed Oct. 17, 1984.

PL 98-494 (S 416) Designate a segment of the Illinois and Owyhee Rivers in Oregon as components of the National Wild and Scenic River System. Introduced by HATFIELD, R-Ore., Feb. 3, 1983. Senate Energy and Natural Resources reported May 18, 1984 (S Rept 98-460). Senate passed May 24. House Interior and Insular Affairs reported Sept. 24 (H Rept 98-1068). House passed, amended, under suspension of the rules, Sept. 24. Senate agreed to House amendments Oct. 3. President signed Oct. 17, 1984.

PL 98-495 (S 566) Direct the secretary of agriculture to release on behalf of the United States a reversionary interest in certain land conveyed to the South Carolina State Commission of Forestry, and direct the secretary of the interior to convey certain mineral interests of the United States in such land to such commission. Introduced by HOLLINGS, D-S.C., Feb. 23, 1983. Senate Agriculture, Nutrition and Forestry reported Oct. 31 (S Rept 98-286). Senate passed Nov. 18. House passed, under suspension of the rules, Oct. 2, 1984. President signed Oct. 19, 1984.

PL 98-496 (S 648) Facilitate the exchange of certain lands in South Carolina. Introduced by THURMOND, R-S.C., March 2, 1983. Senate Energy and Natural Resources reported Aug. 3, 1984 (S Rept 98-573). Senate passed Aug. 9. House passed, amended, under suspension of the rules, Oct. 2. Senate agreed to House amendment Oct. 4. President signed Oct. 19, 1984.

PL 98-497 (S 905) Establish the National Archives and Records Administration as an independent agency. Introduced by EAGLETON, D-Mo., March 23, 1983. Senate Governmental Affairs reported April 3, 1984 (S Rept 98-373). Senate passed June 21, 1984. House passed, amended, Aug. 2. Senate agreed to conference report Oct. 3 (H Rept 98-1124). House agreed to conference report Oct. 4. President signed Oct. 19, 1984.

PL 98-498 (S 1102) Authorize funds for certain programs of the Marine Protection, Research and Sanctuaries Act of 1972. Introduced by PACKWOOD, R-Ore., April 19, 1983. Senate Commerce, Science and Transportation reported Oct. 26 (S Rept 98-280). Senate passed Nov. 18. House passed, amended, Sept. 14, 1984. Senate agreed to House amendment Oct. 2. President signed Oct. 19, 1984.

PL 98-499 (S 1146) Combat the use of aircraft in illegal drug trafficking. Introduced by BENTSEN, D-Texas, April 26, 1983. Senate Commerce, Science and Transportation reported Sept. 15 (S Rept 98-228). Senate passed Sept. 27. House Public Works and Transportation discharged. House passed, amended, July 24, 1984. Senate agreed to conference report Oct. 2 (H Rept 98-1085). House agreed to conference report Oct. 4. President signed Oct. 19, 1984.

PL 98-500 (S 1151) Compensate heirs of deceased Indians for improper payments from trust estates to states or political subdivisions thereof as reimbursements for old age assistance received by decendents during their lifetime. Introduced by ANDREWS, R-N.D., April 27, 1983. Senate Indian Affairs reported Sept. 18, 1984 (S Rept 98-605). Senate passed Sept. 28. House Interior and Insular Affairs discharged. House Public Works and Transportation discharged. House passed Oct. 4. President signed Oct. 19, 1984.

PL 98-501 (S 1330) Authorize the U.S. Army Corps of Engineers to provide grants to the several states to encourage and foster the construction of necessary public capital investment projects. Introduced by STAFFORD, R-Vt., May 19, 1983. Senate Environment and Public Works reported Nov. 18 (S Rept 98-341). Senate passed Feb. 9, 1984. House Government Operations discharged. House Public Works and Transportation discharged. House passed, amended, May 15. House agreed to conference report Oct. 4 (H Rept 98-1134). Senate agreed to conference report Oct. 5. President signed Oct. 19, 1984.

PL 98-502 (S 1510) Establish uniform single financial audit requirements for state and local governments and other recipients of federal assistance. Introduced by DURNBERGER, R-Minn., June 21, 1983. Senate Governmental Affairs reported Aug. 3 (H Rept 98-234). Senate passed Nov. 2. House Government Operations discharged. House passed, amended, May 15, 1984. Senate agreed to House amendments with amendments Oct. 4. House agreed to Senate amendments Oct. 4. President signed Oct. 19, 1984.

PL 98-503 (S 1688) Amend the Act of Oct. 18, 1972, to modify the authorization of appropriations for the Sitka National Park, Alaska. Introduced by MURKOWSKI, R-Alaska, July 27, 1983. Senate Energy and Natural Resources reported July 17, 1984 (S Rept 98-550). Senate passed Oct. 3. House Interior and Insular Affairs discharged. House passed Oct. 5. President signed Oct. 19, 1984.

PL 98-504 (S 1790) Provide assistance in the preservation of the Art Barn and Pierce Mill located in Rock Creek Park within the District of Columbia. Introduced by THURMOND, R-S.C., Aug. 4, 1983. Senate Energy and Natural Resources reported July 17, 1984 (S Rept 98-551). Senate passed Aug. 9. House Interior and Insular Affairs reported Sept. 18 (H Rept 98-1031). House passed, amended, under suspension of the rules, Oct. 2. Senate agreed to House amendment Oct. 4. President signed Oct. 19, 1984.

PL 98-505 (S 1868) Provide for new acquisitions at Sleeping Bear Dunes National Lakeshore. Introduced by RIEGLE, D-Mich., Sept. 21, 1983. Senate Energy and Natural Resources reported May 1, 1984 (S Rept 98-419). Senate passed Aug. 9. House Interior and Insular Affairs reported Sept. 18 (H Rept 98-1032). House passed, under suspension of the rules, Oct. 2. President signed Oct. 19, 1984.

PL 98-506 (S 1889) Provide that at such time as the principal visitor center of the Congaree Swamp National Monument is established, such center shall be designated as the "Harry R. E. Hampton Visitor Center." Introduced by THURMOND, R-S.C., Sept. 27, 1983. Senate Energy and Natural Resources reported July 17, 1984 (S Rept 98-553). Senate passed Aug. 9. House Interior and Insular Affairs reported Sept. 24 (H Rept 98-1069). House passed, amended, under suspension of the rules, Sept. 24. Senate agreed to House amendments Oct. 5. President signed Oct. 19, 1984.

PL 98-507 (S 2048) Provide for the establishment of a Task Force in Organ Procurement and Transplantation and an Organ Procurement and Transplantation Registry. Introduced by HATCH, R-Utah, Nov. 3, 1983. Senate Labor and Human Resources reported April 6, 1984 (S Rept 98-382). Senate passed April 11. House passed, amended, June 21. House agreed to conference report Oct. 3 (H Rept 98-1127). Senate agreed to conference report Oct. 4. President signed Oct. 19, 1984.

PL 98-508 (S 2125) Designate certain lands in Arkansas as wilderness. Introduced by BUMPERS, D-Ark., Nov. 17, 1983. Senate Energy and Natural Resources reported May 18, 1984 (S Rept 98-462). Senate passed Aug. 9. House Interior and Insular Affairs reported Sept. 28 (H Rept 98-1097, Part I). House passed, amended, under suspension of the rules, Oct. 2. Senate agreed to House amendment Oct. 4. President signed Oct. 19, 1984.

PL 98-509 (S 2303) Authorize funds for fiscal years 1985-87 for alcohol, drug abuse and mental health services block grants. Introduced by HATCH, R-Utah, Feb. 9, 1984. Senate Labor and Human Resources reported April 6 (S Rept 98-381). Senate passed April 26. House Energy and Commerce discharged. House passed, amended, June 28. House agreed to conference report Oct. 4 (H Rept 98-1123). Senate agreed to conference report Oct. 4. President signed Oct. 19, 1984.

PL 98-510 (S 2483) Rename Dulles International Airport in Virginia as the "Washington Dulles International Airport." Introduced by TRIBLE, R-Va., March 27, 1984. Senate Commerce, Science and Transportation reported May 17 (S Rept 98-453). Senate passed June 15. House passed Oct. 4. President signed Oct. 19, 1984.

PL 98-511 (S 2496) Authorize funds through fiscal 1987 for vocational education assistance programs. Introduced by QUAYLE, R-Ind., March 29, 1984. Senate Labor and Human Resources reported May 23 (S Rept 98-503). Senate passed June 28. House Education and Labor discharged. House passed, amended, July 26. Senate agreed to conference report Oct. 3 (H Rept 98-1128). House agreed to conference report Oct. 4. President signed Oct. 19, 1984.

PL 98-512 (S 2616) Authorize funds for fiscal years 1985-87 for the adolescent family life demonstration program. Introduced by DENTON, R-Ala., May 1, 1984. Senate Labor and Human Resources reported May 25 (S Rept 98-496). Senate passed June 29. House passed, amended, Aug. 10. House agreed to conference report, under suspension of the rules, Oct. 9 (H Rept 98-1154). Senate agreed to conference report Oct. 9. President signed Oct. 19, 1984.

PL 98-513 (S 2663) Inheritance of trust or restricted land on the Lake Traverse Indian Reservation, in North Dakota and South Dakota. Introduced by ABDNOR, R-S.D., May 10, 1984. Senate Indian Affairs reported Sept. 18 (S Rept 98-607). Senate passed Oct. 3. House Interior and Insular Affairs discharged. House passed Oct. 4. President signed Oct. 19, 1984.

PL 98-514 (S 2773) Designate certain national forest system lands in the state of Georgia to the National Wilderness Preservation System. Introduced by NUNN, D-Ga., June 19, 1984. Senate Agriculture, Nutrition and Forestry reported Sept. 18 (S Rept 98-611). Senate passed Oct. 2. House passed Oct. 4. President signed Oct. 19, 1984.

PL 98-515 (S 2808) Designate certain national forest system lands in the state of Mississippi as wilderness. Introduced by COCHRAN, R-Miss., June 28, 1984. Senate Agriculture, Nutrition and Forestry reported Sept. 18 (S Rept 98-613). Senate passed Oct. 2. House passed Oct. 4. President signed Oct. 19, 1984.

PL 98-516 (S J Res 80) Grant posthumously full rights of citizenship to William Penn and to Hannah Callowhill Penn. Introduced by HEINZ, R-Pa., April 12, 1983. Senate Judiciary reported Nov. 17. Senate passed Nov. 18. House Judiciary discharged. House passed Oct. 4, 1984. President signed Oct. 19, 1984.

PL 98-517 (S J Res 259) Designate the week of Nov. 12-18, 1984, as "National Reye's Syndrome Week." Introduced by KENNEDY, D-Mass., March 15, 1984. Senate Judiciary reported March 22. Senate passed March 26. House Post Office and Civil Service discharged. House passed Oct. 5. President signed Oct. 19, 1984.

PL 98-518 (S J Res 299) Designate November 1984 as "National Diabetes Month." Introduced by ABDNOR, R-S.D., May 21, 1984. Senate Judiciary reported Aug. 9. Senate passed Aug. 10. House Post Office and Civil Service discharged. House passed Oct. 2. President signed Oct. 19, 1984.

PL 98-519 (S J Res 309) Authorize and request the president to designate January 1985 as "National Cerebral Palsy Month." Introduced by BENTSEN, D-Texas, June 7, 1984. Senate Judiciary reported Aug. 9. Senate passed Aug. 10. House Post Office and Civil Service discharged. House passed Oct. 2. President signed Oct. 19, 1984.

PL 98-520 (HR 2372) Recognize the organization known as the "Navy Wives Clubs of America." Introduced by FORD, D-Tenn., March 24, 1983. House Judiciary discharged. House passed Oct. 4. Senate passed Oct. 5. President signed Oct. 19, 1984.

PL 98-521 (HR 3401) Designate the U.S. post office and courthouse at 245 East Capital St. in Jackson, Miss., as the "James O. Eastland Federal United States Courthouse." Introduced by DOWDY, D-Miss., June 23, 1983. House Public Works and Transportation reported May 30, 1984 (H Rept 98-807). House passed June 18. Senate Environment and Public Works reported Sept. 26. Senate passed Oct. 5. President signed Oct. 19, 1984.

PL 98-522 (HR 3402) Designate that hereafter the federal building at 100 West Capital St. in Jackson, Miss., will be known as the "Dr. A. H. McCoy Federal Building." Introduced by DOWDY, D-Miss., June 23, 1983. House Public Works and Transportation reported May 30, 1984 (H Rept 98-808). House passed June 18. Senate Environment and Public Works reported Sept. 26. Senate passed Oct. 5. President signed Oct. 19, 1984.

PL 98-523 (HR 4025) Authorize the administrator of general services to transfer to the Smithsonian Institution without reimbursement the General Post Office Building and the site thereof located in the District of Columbia. Introduced by YOUNG, D-Mo., Sept. 28, 1983. House Public Works and Transportation reported May 15, 1984 (H Rept 98-778, Part I). House passed, under suspension of the rules, Sept 18. Senate Environment and Public Works and Senate Rules and Administration jointly reported Sept. 29 (S Rept 98-651). Senate passed Oct. 5. President signed Oct. 19, 1984.

PL 98-524 (HR 4164) Authorize funds for vocational education assistance programs. Introduced by PERKINS, D-Ky., Oct. 19, 1983. House Education and Labor reported March 5, 1984 (H Rept 98-612). House passed March 8. Senate Labor and Human Resources discharged. Senate passed, amended, Aug. 8. Senate agreed to conference report Oct. 3 (H Rept 98-1129). House agreed to conference report Oct. 4. President signed Oct. 19, 1984.

PL 98-525 (HR 5167) Authorize appropriations for fiscal year 1985 for the Department of Defense. Introduced by PRICE, D-Ill., March 15, 1984. House Armed Services reported April 19 (H Rept 98-691). House passed June 1. Senate passed, amended, June 21. House agreed to conference report Sept. 26 (H Rept 98-1080). Senate agreed to conference report Sept. 27. President signed Oct. 19, 1984.

PL 98-526 (HR 5183) Direct the secretary of agriculture to convey certain national forest system lands to Craig County, Va. Introduced by BOUCHER, D-Va., March 20, 1984. House Agriculture reported June 22 (H Rept 98-860). House passed, under suspension of the rules, June 25. Senate Agriculture, Nutrition and Forestry reported Sept. 20 (S Rept 98-630). Senate passed Oct. 4. President signed Oct. 19, 1984.

PL 98-527 (HR 5603) Revise and extend programs for persons with developmental disabilities. Introduced by WAXMAN, D-Calif., May 3, 1984. House Energy and Commerce reported June 6 (H Rept 98-826). House passed, under suspension of the rules, June 11. Senate Labor and Human Resources discharged. Senate passed, amended, June 28. House agreed to conference report Oct. 3 (H Rept 98-1074). Senate agreed to conference report Oct. 4. President signed Oct. 19, 1984.

PL 98-528 (HR 5618) Require the Veterans Administration to develop guidance for the provisions of care to veterans suffering from alcohol or drug dependence. Introduced by MONTGOMERY, D-Miss., May 8, 1984. House Veterans' Affairs reported May 15 (H Rept 98-779). House passed, under suspension of the rules, May 21. Senate Veterans' Affairs discharged. Senate passed, amended, Aug. 9. House agreed to Senate amendments with amendments Oct. 2. Senate agreed to House amendments Oct. 3. President signed Oct. 19, 1984.

PL 98-529 (HR 5787) Remove an impediment to oil and gas leasing of certain federal lands in Corpus Christi, Texas, and Port Hueneme, Calif. Introduced by ORTIZ, D-Texas, June 6, 1984. House Interior and Insular Affairs reported Sept. 24 (H Rept 98-1047, Part I). House passed, under suspension of the rules, Sept. 24. Senate Energy and Natural Resources discharged. Senate passed Oct. 5. President signed Oct. 19, 1984.

PL 98-530 (HR 6206) Amend PL 95-238 relating to the water rights of the Ak-Chin Indian Community. Introduced by UDALL, D-Ariz., Sept. 10, 1984. House Interior and Insular Affairs reported Sept. 14 (H Rept 98-1026). House passed, under suspension of the rules, Sept. 17.

Senate passed, amended, Sept. 25. House agreed to Senate amendments Oct. 2. President signed Oct. 19, 1984.

PL 98-531 (HR 6216) Amend the Bankruptcy Amendments and Federal Judgeships Act of 1984 to make technical corrections with respect to the retirement of certain bankruptcy judges. Introduced by EDWARDS, D-Calif., Sept. 11, 1984. House passed, under suspension of the rules, Oct. 1. Senate passed Oct. 4. President signed Oct. 19, 1984.

PL 98-532 (HR 6225) Prevent disruption of the structure and functioning of the government by ratifying all reorganization plans as a matter of law. Introduced by BROOKS, D-Texas, Sept. 12, 1984. House Government Operations reported Sept. 28 (H Rept 98-1104). House passed, under suspension of the rules, Oct. 1. Senate passed Oct. 4. President signed Oct. 19, 1984.

PL 98-533 (HR 6311) Combat international terrorism. Introduced by FASCELL, D-Fla., Sept. 26, 1984. House passed, under suspension of the rules, Oct. 1. Senate passed Oct. 5. President signed Oct. 19, 1984.

PL 98-534 (H J Res 482) Authorize the Law Enforcement Officers Memorial Fund Inc. to establish a National Law Enforcement Heroes Memorial. Introduced by BIAGGI, D-N.Y., Feb. 9, 1984. House Administration reported Sept. 26 (H Rept 98-1084). House passed, under suspension of the rules, Oct. 1. Senate passed Oct. 5. President signed Oct. 19, 1984.

PL 98-535 (H J Res 551) Provide for the reappointment of Anne Legendre Armstrong as a citizen regent of the Smithsonian Institution. Introduced by BOLAND, D-Mass., April 24, 1984. House Administration reported Sept. 13 (H Rept 98-1014). House passed, under suspension of the rules, Sept. 17. Senate Rules and Administration reported Sept. 29 (S Rept 98-644). Senate passed Oct. 4. President signed Oct. 19, 1984.

PL 98-536 (H J Res 552) Provide for the reappointment of A. Leon Higginbotham Jr. as a citizen regent of the Smithsonian Institution. Introduced by BOLAND, D-Mass., April 24, 1984. House Administration reported Sept. 13 (H Rept 98-1013). House passed, under suspension of the rules, Sept. 17. Senate Rules and Administration reported Sept. 29 (S Rept 98-645). Senate passed Oct. 4. President signed Oct. 19, 1984.

PL 98-537 (H J Res 580) Authorize the Kahlil Gibran Centennial Foundation of Washington, D.C., to erect a memorial in the District of Columbia. Introduced by KAZEN, D-Texas, May 30, 1984. House Administration reported Sept. 24 (H Rept 98-1051). House passed, under suspension of the rules, Sept. 24. Senate Rules and Administration reported Sept. 27 (S Rept 98-640). Senate passed Oct. 4. President signed Oct. 19, 1984.

PL 98-538 (H J Res 638) Designate October 1984 as "National Head Injury Awareness Month." Introduced by DICKS, D-Wash., Aug. 9, 1984. House Post Office and Civil Service discharged. House passed Oct. 2. Senate passed Oct. 5. President signed Oct. 19, 1984.

PL 98-539 (H J Res 655) Designate Feb. 16, 1985, as "Lithuanian Independence Day." Introduced by HALL, D-Ind., Oct. 3, 1984. House Post Office and Civil Service discharged. House passed Oct. 5. Senate passed Oct. 5. President signed Oct. 19, 1984.

PL 98-540 (S 864) Eliminate the ceiling on the authorization for the volunteers in parks programs for any one year. Introduced by McCLURE, R-Idaho, March 18, 1983. Senate Energy and Natural Resources reported Aug. 4 (S Rept 98-208). Senate passed Sept. 15. House Interior and Insular Affairs reported Aug. 6, 1984 (H Rept 98-960). House passed, amended, under suspension of the rules, Aug. 6. Senate agreed to House amendment with an amendment Oct. 4. House agreed to Senate amendment Oct. 4. President signed Oct. 24, 1984.

PL 98-541 (HR 1438) Provide for the restoration of the fish and wildlife in the Trinity River Basin, Calif. Introduced by CHAPPIE, R-Calif., Feb. 15, 1983. House Merchant Marine and Fisheries reported Sept. 18, 1984 (H Rept 98-1035, Part I). House passed, under suspension of the rules, Sept. 24. Senate Environment and Public Works reported Sept. 29 (S Rept 98-647). Senate passed Oct. 4. President signed Oct. 24, 1984.

PL 98-542 (HR 1961) Amend title 38, U.S. Code, to provide a presumption of service connection for the occurrence of certain diseases related to exposure to herbicides or other environmental hazards or conditions in veterans who served in Southeast Asia during the Vietnam era. Introduced by DASCHLE, D-S.D., March 8, 1983. House Veterans' Affairs reported Jan. 25, 1984 (H Rept 98-592). House passed, under suspension of the rules, Jan. 30. Senate passed, amended, May 22. House agreed to Senate amendments with amendments Oct. 3. Senate agreed to House amendments Oct. 4. President signed Oct. 24, 1984.

PL 98-543 (HR 5688) Amend title 38, U.S. Code, to provide a cost-of-living increase for fiscal year 1985 in the rates of compensation paid to veterans with service-connected disabilities and the rates of dependency and indemnity compensation paid to survivors of such veterans. Introduced by MONTGOMERY, D-Miss., May 21, 1984. House Veterans' Affairs reported June 7 (H Rept 98-828). House passed, under suspension of the rules, June 18. Senate passed, amended, Oct. 2.

House agreed to Senate amendments with amendments Oct. 5. Senate agreed to House amendments Oct. 9. President signed Oct. 24, 1984.

PL 98-544 (HR 6027) Clarify the application of the Clayton Act to the official conduct of local governments. Introduced by RODINO, D-N.J., July 26, 1984. House Judiciary reported Aug. 8 (H Rept 98-965). House passed, under suspension of the rules, Aug. 8. Senate passed, amended, Oct. 4. House agreed to conference report Oct. 11 (H Rept 98-1158). Senate agreed to conference report Oct. 11. President signed Oct. 24, 1984.

PL 98-545 (S 2583) Authorize United States participation in the Office International de la Vigne et du Vin (the International Office of the Vine and Wine). Introduced by PERCY, R-Ill., April 24, 1984. Senate Foreign Relations reported Sept. 17 (S Rept 98-602). Senate passed Sept. 26. House Foreign Affairs discharged. House passed Oct. 10. President signed Oct. 25, 1984.

PL 98-546 (S 2947) Designate the lock and dam on the Warrior River in Hale County, Ala., as the "Armistead I. Selden Lock and Dam." Introduced by DENTON, R-Ala., Aug. 10, 1984. Senate Environment and Public Works reported Sept. 29 (S Rept 98-649). Senate passed Oct. 4. House passed Oct. 10. President signed Oct. 25, 1984.

PL 98-547 (HR 6257) Amend the Motor Vehicle and Information Cost Savings Act to impede those motor vehicle thefts that occur for purposes of dismantling the vehicles and reselling the major parts by requiring passenger motor vehicles and major replacement parts to have identifying numbers or symbols. Introduced by WIRTH, D-Colo., Sept. 17, 1984. House Energy and Commerce reported Sept. 26 (H Rept 98-1087, Part I). House passed, under suspension of the rules, Oct. 1. Senate passed Oct. 4. President signed Oct. 25, 1984.

PL 98-548 (HR 5271) Extend the Wetlands Loan Act. Introduced by BREAUX, D-La., March 28, 1984. House Merchant Marine and Fisheries reported April 25 (H Rept 98-705). House passed, under suspension of the rules, Sept. 24. Senate passed, amended, Oct. 4. House agreed to Senate amendments Oct. 4. President signed Oct. 26, 1984.

PL 98-549 (S 66) Create a jurisdictional framework to apportion the authority regulating cable systems between federal and state governments, and provide for a competitive marketplace for cable systems in the telecommunications industry. Introduced by GOLDWATER, R-Ariz., Jan. 26, 1983. Senate Commerce, Science and Transportation reported April 27 (S Rept 98-67). Senate passed June 14. House Energy and Commerce discharged. House passed, amended, Oct. 1, 1984. Senate agreed to House amendments with amendments Oct. 11. House agreed to Senate amendments Oct. 11. President signed Oct. 30, 1984.

PL 98-550 (S 543) Designate certain national forest system lands in the state of Wyoming for inclusion in the National Wilderness Preservation System, release other forest lands for multiple use management, and withdraw designated wilderness areas in Wyoming from minerals activity. Introduced by WALLOP, R-Wyo., Feb. 22, 1983. Senate Energy and Natural Resources reported April 5 (S Rept 98-54). Senate passed April 13. House Interior and Insular Affairs discharged. House Agriculture discharged. House passed, amended, Oct. 2, 1984. Senate agreed to House amendment Oct. 4. President signed Oct. 30, 1984.

PL 98-551 (S 771) Authorize funds through fiscal 1986 for health promotion and disease prevention programs of the Department of Health and Human Services. Introduced by HATCH, R-Utah, March 11, 1983. Senate Labor and Human Resources reported June 21 (S Rept 98-158). Senate passed Sept. 21. House passed, amended, under suspension of the rules, Oct. 9, 1984. Senate agreed to House amendment Oct. 11. President signed Oct. 30, 1984.

PL 98-552 (S 1160) Authorize Douglas County, Nev., to transfer certain land to a private owner. Introduced by LAXALT, R-Nev., April 27, 1983. Senate Energy and Natural Resources reported Sept. 19, 1984 (S Rept 98-620). Senate passed Sept. 26. House Interior and Insular Affairs discharged. House passed, amended, Oct. 4. Senate agreed to House amendment Oct. 10. President signed Oct. 30, 1984.

PL 98-553 (S 1291) Authorize appropriations to the Nuclear Regulatory Commission, in accordance with section 261 of the Atomic Energy Act of 1954 and section 305 of the Energy Reorganization Act of 1974. Introduced by SIMPSON, R-Wyo., May 16, 1983. Senate Environment and Public Works reported May 16 (S Rept 98-118). Senate passed Oct. 10, 1984. House passed Oct. 11. President signed Oct. 30, 1984.

PL 98-554 (S 2217) Provide for exemptions, based on safety concerns, from certain length and width limitations for commercial motor vehicles. Introduced by MOYNIHAN, D-N.Y., Jan. 26, 1984. Senate Commerce, Science and Transportation reported June 6 (S Rept 98-505). Senate passed Oct. 2. House passed, amended, Oct. 11. Senate agreed to House amendment Oct. 11. President signed Oct. 30, 1984.

PL 98-555 (S 2301) Authorize funds through fiscal 1987 for the health-care training program and the tuberculosis, venereal disease and immunization programs, and authorize funds through fiscal 1988 for the preventive health and human services block grant programs. Introduced by HATCH, R-Utah, Feb. 9, 1984. Senate Labor and Human

Resources reported April 12 (S Rept 98-393). Senate passed Sept. 28. House passed, amended, Oct. 1. Senate agreed to House amendment with an amendment Oct. 9. House agreed to Senate amendment, under suspension of the rules, Oct. 9. President signed Oct. 30, 1984.

PL 98-556 (S 2499) Authorize funds for certain maritime programs for fiscal year 1985. Introduced by STEVENS, R-Alaska, March 29, 1984. Senate Commerce, Science and Transportation reported May 14 (S Rept 98-445). Senate passed Oct. 11. House passed Oct. 11. President signed Oct. 30, 1984.

PL 98-557 (S 2526) Authorize appropriations for the Coast Guard for fiscal years 1985-86. Introduced by PACKWOOD, R-Ore., April 3, 1984. Senate Commerce, Science and Transportation reported May 17 (S Rept 98-454). Senate passed Oct. 5. House passed Oct. 9. President signed Oct. 30, 1984.

PL 98-558 (S 2565) Extend programs under the Head Start Act. Introduced by DENTON, R-Ala., April 12, 1984. Senate Labor and Human Resources reported May 24 (S Rept 98-484). Senate passed Oct. 4. House passed Oct. 9. President signed Oct. 30, 1984.

PL 98-559 (S 2706) Amend the Hazardous Materials Transportation Act to authorize appropriations for fiscal years 1985-86. Introduced by PACKWOOD, R-Ore., May 23, 1984. Senate Commerce, Science and Transportation reported May 23 (S Rept 98-479). Senate passed June 15. House passed, amended, Oct. 11. Senate agreed to House amendment Oct. 11. President signed Oct. 30, 1984.

PL 98-560 (S 3021) Name the federal building in Elkins, W.Va., as the "Jennings Randolph Federal Center." Introduced by STAFFORD, R-Vt., Sept. 25, 1984. Senate Environment and Public Works reported Sept. 29 (S Rept 98-650). Senate passed Oct. 4. House passed Oct. 11. President signed Oct. 30, 1984.

PL 98-561 (S 3034) Grant a federal charter to the National Society, Daughters of the American Colonists. Introduced by KASSEBAUM, R-Kan., Sept. 28, 1984. Senate Judiciary discharged. Senate passed Oct. 10. House passed Oct. 10. President signed Oct. 30, 1984.

PL 98-562 (S J Res 236) Relating to cooperative East-West ventures in space as an alternative to a space arms race. Introduced by MATSUNAGA, D-Hawaii, Feb. 9, 1984. Senate Foreign Relations reported Oct. 2. Senate passed Oct. 10. House Foreign Affairs discharged. House passed, amended, Oct. 11. Senate agreed to House amendment Oct. 11. President signed Oct. 30, 1984.

PL 98-563 (HR 89) Permit the transportation of passengers between Puerto Rico and other U.S. ports on foreign flag vessels when U.S. flag service or such transportation is not available. Introduced by CO-RRADA, New Prog.-Puerto Rico, Jan. 3, 1983. House Merchant Marine and Fisheries reported May 3, 1984 (H Rept 98-733). House passed, under suspension of the rules, May 15. Senate Commerce, Science and Transportation reported Oct. 4 (S Rept 98-658). Senate passed, amended, Oct. 11. House agreed to Senate amendment Oct. 11. President signed Oct. 30, 1984.

PL 98-564 (HR 597) Amend sections 2733, 2734 and 2736 of title 10, U.S. Code, and section 715 of title 32, U.S. Code, to increase the maximum amount of a claim against the United States that may be paid administratively under those sections and to allow increased delegation of authority to settle and pay certain of those claims. Introduced by SAM B. HALL JR., D-Texas, Jan. 6, 1983. House Judiciary reported Oct. 6 (H Rept 98-407). House passed, under suspension of the rules, Oct. 24. Senate Judiciary reported Oct. 3, 1984. Senate passed Oct. 11. President signed Oct. 30, 1984.

PL 98-565 (HR 1095) Grant a federal charter to the 369th Veterans' Association. Introduced by RANGEL, D-N.Y., Jan. 31, 1983. House Judiciary reported Nov. 7 (H Rept 98-490). House passed, under suspension of the rules, Nov. 14. Senate Judiciary discharged. Senate passed, amended, Oct. 10, 1984. House agreed to Senate amendment Oct. 10. President signed Oct. 30, 1984.

PL 98-566 (HR 1870) Require the secretary of the Treasury to coin and sell a national medal in honor of the members and former members of the armed forces of the United States who served in the Vietnam conflict. Introduced by ANNUNZIO, D-Ill., March 3, 1983. House Banking, Finance and Urban Affairs discharged. House passed, under suspension of the rules, Oct. 18. Senate Banking, Housing and Urban Affairs reported Nov. 2. Senate passed Oct. 9, 1984. President signed Oct. 30, 1984.

PL 98-567 (HR 1880) Establish an interagency committee and a technical study group on cigarette safety. Introduced by MOAKLEY, D-Mass., March 3, 1983. House Energy and Commerce reported July 30, 1984 (H Rept 98-917). House passed, under suspension of the rules, Aug. 6. Senate passed, amended, Sept. 21. House agreed to Senate amendment with an amendment Oct. 1. Senate agreed to House amendment Oct. 4. President signed Oct. 30, 1984.

PL 98-568 (HR 2645) Amend the act of Aug. 15, 1978, revising the boundaries of the Chattahoochee River National Recreation Area in Georgia, setting forth requirements with respect to land acquisition. Introduced by LEVITAS, D-Ga., April 20, 1983. House Interior and Insular Affairs reported March 1, 1984 (H Rept 98-607). House passed,

under suspension of the rules, March 5. Senate Energy and Natural Resources reported Sept. 25 (S Rept 98-633). Senate passed, amended, Oct. 3. House agreed to Senate amendments Oct. 4. President signed Oct. 30, 1984.

PL 98-569 (HR 2790) Amend the Colorado River Basin Salinity Control Act to authorize certain additional measures to assure accomplishment of the objectives of title II of such act. Introduced by KOGOVSEK, D-Colo., April 27, 1983. House Interior and Insular Affairs reported Sept. 13, 1984 (H Rept 98-1018). House passed, under suspension of the rules, Oct. 2. Senate passed, amended, Oct. 5. House agreed to Senate amendments Oct. 9. President signed Oct. 30, 1984.

PL 98-570 (HR 2823) Amend title I of the Reclamation Project Authorization Act of 1972 to provide for the establishment of the Russell Lakes Waterfowl Management Area as a replacement for the authorized Mishak National Wildlife Refuge. Introduced by KOGOVSEK, D-Colo., April 28, 1983. House Interior and Insular Affairs reported Sept. 13, 1984 (H Rept 98-1020, Part I). House Merchant Marine and Fisheries discharged. House passed Oct. 1. Senate Environment and Public Works discharged. Senate passed Oct. 10. President signed Oct. 30, 1984.

PL 98-571 (HR 3150) Direct the secretary of agriculture to convey, for certain specified consideration, to the Sabine River Authority of Texas approximately 31,000 acres of land within the Sabine National Forest to be used for the purposes of the Toledo Bend Project, Louisiana and Texas. Introduced by WILSON, D-Texas, May 25, 1983. House passed, under suspension of the rules, Oct. 2. Senate passed Oct. 10. President signed Oct. 30, 1984.

PL 98-572 (HR 3331) Authorize the exchange of certain lands between the Bureau of Land Management and the city of Los Angeles for purposes of the Santa Monica Mountains National Recreation Area. Introduced by BERMAN, D-Calif., June 16, 1983. House Interior and Insular Affairs reported June 29, 1984 (H Rept 98-884). House passed Aug. 2. Senate Energy and Natural Resources discharged. Senate passed, amended, Oct. 5. House agreed to Senate amendments Oct. 9. President signed Oct. 30, 1984.

PL 98-573 (HR 3398) Make certain changes in the tariff treatment of specified articles and grant duty-free treatment to specified articles. Introduced by GIBBONS, D-Fla., June 23, 1983. House Ways and Means reported June 24 (H Rept 98-267). House passed, under suspension of the rules, June 28. Senate Finance reported Nov. 10 (S Rept 98-308). Senate passed, amended, Sept. 20, 1984. House agreed to conference report Oct. 9 (H Rept 98-1156). Senate agreed to conference report Oct. 9. President signed Oct. 30, 1984.

PL 98-574 (HR 3788) Designate various areas as components of National Wilderness Preservation System in the national forests in the state of Texas. Introduced by BRYANT, D-Texas, Aug. 4, 1983. House Interior and Insular Affairs reported May 2, 1984 (H Rept 98-730, Part I). House Agriculture discharged. House passed, under suspension of the rules, May 8. Senate Agriculture, Nutrition and Forestry reported Sept. 18 (S Rept 98-614). Senate passed, amended, Oct. 2. House agreed to Senate amendment Oct. 4. President signed Oct. 30, 1984.

PL 98-575 (HR 3942) Prohibit persons from launching a space object from the territory of the United States unless they are properly licensed, and direct the secretary of commerce to issue such licenses. Introduced by AKAKA, D-Hawaii, Sept. 21, 1983. House Science and Technology reported May 31, 1984 (H Rept 98-816). House passed, under suspension of the rules, June 5. Senate Commerce, Science and Transportation reported Oct. 3 (S Rept 98-656). Senate passed, amended, Oct. 9. House agreed to Senate amendment Oct. 9. President signed Oct. 30, 1984.

PL 98-576 (HR 3971) Provide that any Osage headright or restricted real estate or funds that are part of the estate of a deceased Osage Indian who did not possess a certificate of competency at the time of death shall be exempt from any estate or inheritence tax imposed by the state of Oklahoma. Introduced by JONES, D-Okla., Sept. 22, 1983. House Interior and Insular Affairs reported Oct. 1, 1984 (H Rept 98-1114). House passed, under suspension of the rules, Oct. 2. Senate passed Oct. 9. President signed Oct. 30, 1984.

PL 98-577 (HR 4209) Amend the Small Business and Federal Procurement Competition Enhancement Act. Introduced by BOXER, D-Calif., Oct. 25, 1983. House Small Business reported Nov. 10 (H Rept 98-528). House passed, under suspension of the rules, May 21, 1984. Senate passed, amended Aug. 7. House agreed to Senate amendments with amendments Oct. 2. Senate agreed to House amendments Oct. 4. President signed Oct. 30, 1984.

PL 98-578 (HR 4263) Designate certain lands in the Cherokee National Forest, Tenn., as wilderness areas, and allow management of certain lands for uses other than wilderness. Introduced by DUNCAN, R-Tenn., Nov. 1, 1983. House Interior and Insular Affairs reported April 26, 1984 (H Rept 98-714, Part I). House passed, under suspension of the rules, May 1. Senate Agriculture, Nutrition and Forestry reported Sept. 18 (S Rept 98-615). Senate passed, amended, Oct. 2. House agreed to Senate amendment Oct. 4. President signed Oct. 30, 1984.

PL 98-579 (HR 4354) Designate the federal building and U.S. courthouse in Ocala, Fla., as the "Golden-Collum Memorial Federal Building and United States Courthouse." Introduced by MacKAY, D-Fla., Nov. 10, 1983. House Public Works and Transportation reported Aug. 1, 1984 (H Rept 98-933). House passed Aug. 9. Senate Environment and Public Works reported Sept. 26. Senate passed Oct. 11. President signed Oct. 30, 1984.

PL 98-580 (HR 4473) Designate the Federal Archives and Records Center in San Bruno, Calif., as the "Leo J. Ryan Memorial Federal Archives and Records Center." Introduced by LANTOS, D-Calif., Nov. 18, 1983. House Public Works and Transportation discharged. House passed Nov. 18. Senate Governmental Affairs discharged. Senate passed Oct. 10, 1984. President signed Oct. 30, 1984.

PL 98-581 (HR 4585) Authorize appropriations for the Office of Environmental Quality and the Council on Environmental Quality for fiscal years 1985-86. Introduced by BREAUX, D-La., Jan. 23, 1984. House Merchant Marine and Fisheries reported April 25 (H Rept 98-702). House passed, under suspension of the rules, May 1. Senate Environment and Public Works discharged. Senate passed, amended, June 21. House agreed to Senate amendment with amendments Aug. 9. Senate agreed to House amendments Oct. 10. President signed Oct. 30, 1984.

PL 98-582 (HR 4700) Designate the federal building and U.S. courthouse at 1961 Stout St., Denver, Colo., as the "Byron G. Rogers Federal Building and United States Courthouse." Introduced by STANGELAND, R-Minn., Jan. 31, 1984. House Public Works and Transportation reported March 20 (H Rept 98-625). House passed April 2. Senate Environment and Public Works reported Sept. 26. Senate passed, amended, Oct. 11. House agreed to Senate amendments Oct. 11. President signed Oct. 30, 1984.

PL 98-583 (HR 4717) Designate the federal building and U.S. courthouse in Las Vegas, Nev., as the "Foley Federal Building and United States Courthouse." Introduced by REID, D-Nev., Feb. 1, 1984. House Public Works and Transportation reported Aug. 1 (H Rept 98-932). House passed Aug. 9. Senate Environment and Public Works reported Sept. 26. Senate passed Oct. 11. President signed Oct. 30, 1984.

PL 98-584 (HR 4966) Recognize the organization known as the Women's Army Corps Veterans' Association. Introduced by WHITEHURST, R-Va., Feb. 28, 1984. House Judiciary discharged. House passed Sept. 26. Senate passed, amended, Oct. 4. House agreed to Senate amendments Oct. 5. President signed Oct. 30, 1984.

PL 98-585 (HR 5076) Designate certain areas in the Allegheny National Forest as wilderness and recreation areas. Introduced by CLINGER, R-Pa., March 8, 1984. House Interior and Insular Affairs reported April 26 (H Rept 98-713, Part I). House passed, under suspension of the rules, May 1. Senate Agriculture, Nutrition and Forestry reported Sept. 18 (S Rept 98-616). Senate passed, amended, Oct. 2. House agreed to Senate amendment Oct. 4. President signed Oct. 30, 1984.

PL 98-586 (HR 5121) Designate certain national forest system lands in the state of Virginia as wilderness. Introduced by BOUCHER, D-Va., March 14, 1984. House Interior and Insular Affairs reported April 25 (H Rept 98-712, Part I). House passed, under suspension of the rules, May 8. Senate Agriculture, Nutrition and Forestry discharged. Senate passed, amended, Oct. 4. House agreed to Senate amendment Oct. 9. President signed Oct. 30, 1984.

PL 98-587 (HR 5189) Amend section 3056 of title 18, U.S. Code, to update the authorities of the U.S. Secret Service. Introduced by SAM B. HALL JR., D-Texas, March 20, 1984. House Judiciary reported Sept. 10 (H Rept 98-1001). House passed, under suspension of the rules, Sept. 17. Senate Finance discharged. Senate passed Oct. 11. President signed Oct. 30, 1984.

PL 98-588 (HR 5252) Redesignate the Veterans Administration Medical Center located in Poplar Bluff, Mo., as the "John J. Pershing Regional Veterans Administration Medical Center." Introduced by EMERSON, R-Mo., March 27, 1984. House Veterans' Affairs discharged. House passed Oct. 3. Senate Veterans' Affairs discharged. Senate passed Oct. 10. President signed Oct. 30, 1984.

PL 98-589 (HR 5323) Designate the U.S. courthouse building in Hato Rey, Puerto Rico, as the "Clemente Ruiz Nazario United States Courthouse." Introduced by CORRADA, New Prog.-Puerto Rico, April 3, 1984. House Public Works and Transportation reported Aug. 1 (H Rept 98-931). House passed Aug. 9. Senate Environment and Public Works reported Sept. 26. Senate passed Oct. 11. President signed Oct. 30, 1984.

PL 98-590 (HR 5358) Enable honey producers and handlers to finance a nationally coordinated research, promotion and consumer information program designed to expand their markets for honey. Introduced by DE LA GARZA, D-Texas, April 4, 1984. House Agriculture reported July 23 (H Rept 98-892). House passed, under suspension of the rules, July 24. Senate Agriculture, Nutrition and Forestry discharged. Senate passed Oct. 4. President signed Oct. 30, 1984.

PL 98-591 (HR 5402) Designate the U.S. post office and courthouse in Utica, N.Y., as the "Alexander Pirnie Federal Building." Introduced by BOEHLERT, R-N.Y., April 10, 1984. House Public Works and Transportation reported Sept. 12 (H Rept 98-1012). House passed Sept. 18. Senate Environment and Public Works reported Sept. 26. Senate passed Oct. 11. President signed Oct. 30, 1984.

PL 98-592 (HR 5716) Provide for the conveyance of public lands, Seneca County, Ohio. Introduced by LATTA, R-Ohio, May 23, 1984. House Interior and Insular Affairs discharged. House passed Oct. 9. Senate passed Oct. 11. President signed Oct. 30, 1984.

PL 98-593 (HR 5747) Designate the federal building in Oak Ridge, Tenn., as the "Joe L. Evins Federal Building." Introduced by LLOYD, D-Tenn., May 30, 1984. House Public Works and Transportation reported Aug. 1 (H Rept 98-930). House passed Aug. 9. Senate Environment and Public Works reported Sept. 26. Senate passed Oct. 11. President signed Oct. 30, 1984.

PL 98-594 (HR 5832) Authorize two additional assistant secretaries for the department of the Treasury. Introduced by HOYER, D-Md., June 12, 1984. House passed, under suspension of the rules, Oct. 2. Senate passed Oct. 11. President signed Oct. 30, 1984.

PL 98-595 (HR 5833) Improve certain maritime programs of the Department of Transportation and the Department of Commerce. Introduced by BIAGGI, D-N.Y., June 12, 1984. House Merchant Marine and Fisheries reported July 10 (H Rept 98-888). House passed, under suspension of the rules, July 24. Senate Commerce, Science and Transportation reported Oct. 2 (S Rept 98-652). Senate passed, amended, Oct. 10. House agreed to Senate amendments Oct. 11. President signed Oct. 30, 1984.

PL 98-596 (HR 5846) Amend title 18, U.S. Code, to improve collection and administration of criminal fines. Introduced by BOUCHER, D-Va., June 14, 1984. House Judiciary reported July 25 (H Rept 98-906). House passed, under suspension of the rules, July 30. Senate passed, amended, Oct. 11. House agreed to Senate amendments Oct. 11. President signed Oct. 30, 1984.

PL 98-597 (HR 6000) Designate the Table Rock Lake Visitors Center building in the vicinity of Branson, Mo., as the "Dewey J. Short Table Rock Lake Visitors Center." Introduced by TAYLOR, R-Mo., June 29, 1984. House Public Works and Transportation reported Aug. 1 (H Rept 98-929). House passed Aug. 9. Senate Environment and Public Works reported Sept. 26. Senate passed Oct. 11. President signed Oct. 30, 1984.

PL 98-598 (HR 6007) Establish certain procedures regarding the judicial service of retired judges of District of Columbia courts. Introduced by DYMALLY, D-Calif., July 24, 1984. House District of Columbia reported July 25 (H Rept 98-910). House passed July 30. Senate Governmental Affairs reported Sept. 27. Senate passed, amended, Sept. 28. House agreed to Senate amendments Oct. 9. President signed Oct. 30, 1984.

PL 98-599 (HR 6100) Clarify the intent of Congress with respect to the families eligible for a commemorative medal authorized for the families of Americans missing or otherwise unaccounted for in Southeast Asia. Introduced by MAVROULES, D-Mass., Aug. 8, 1984. House Armed Services discharged. House passed Oct. 1. Senate Armed Services discharged. Senate passed Oct. 10. President signed Oct. 30, 1984.

PL 98-600 (HR 6101) Amend the Panama Canal Act of 1979 to authorize quarters allowances for certain employees of the Department of Defense serving in the area formerly known as the Canal Zone. Introduced by OAKAR, D-Ohio, Aug. 8, 1984. House Merchant Marine and Fisheries reported Sept. 25 (H Rept 98-1077, Part I). House passed, under suspension of the rules, Oct. 1. Senate passed Oct. 5. President signed Oct. 30, 1984.

PL 98-601 (HR 6112) Amend the Tax Equity and Fiscal Responsibility Act of 1982 with respect to the effect of the 1985 increase in the federal unemployment tax rate on certain small business provisions contained in state unemployment compensation laws. Introduced by ROSTENKOWSKI, D-Ill., Aug. 9, 1984. House Ways and Means reported Sept. 20 (H Rept 98-1043). House passed, under suspension of the rules, Oct. 1. Senate passed Oct. 11. President signed Oct. 30, 1984.

PL 98-602 (HR 6221) Provide for the use and distribution of certain funds awarded to the Wyandotte Tribe of Oklahoma and restore certain mineral rights to the Three Affiliated Tribes of the Fort Berthold Reservation. Introduced by SYNAR, D-Okla., Sept. 11, 1984. House Interior and Insular Affairs reported Sept. 24 (H Rept 98-1067). House passed, under suspension of the rules, Sept. 24. Senate passed, amended, Oct. 2. House agreed to Senate amendments Oct. 4. President signed Oct. 30, 1984.

PL 98-603 (HR 6296) Enact the San Juan Basin Wilderness Protection Act of 1984. Introduced by RICHARDSON, D-N.M., Sept. 24, 1984. House Interior and Insular Affairs discharged. House passed Oct 3. Senate passed, amended, Oct. 5. House agreed to Senate amendment Oct. 5. President signed Oct. 30, 1984.

PL 98-604 (HR 6299) Ensure the payment in 1985 of cost-of-living increases under the OASDI program in title II of the Social Security

Act, and provide for a study of certain changes that might be made in the provisions authorizing cost-of-living adjustments under that program. Introduced by ROSTENKOWSKI, D-Ill., Sept. 25, 1984. House Ways and Means reported Sept. 28 (H Rept 98-1099). House passed, under suspension of the rules, Oct. 2. Senate passed Oct. 11. President signed Oct. 30, 1984.

PL 98-605 (HR 6303) Make certain technical corrections in various acts relating to the Osage Tribe of Indians of Oklahoma. Introduced by JONES, D-Okla., Sept. 25, 1984. House Interior and Insular Affairs reported Oct. 1 (H Rept 98-1115). House passed, under suspension of the rules, Oct. 2. Senate passed Oct. 9. President signed Oct. 30, 1984.

PL 98-606 (HR 6430) Amend the River and Harbor Act of 1946. Introduced by BATEMAN, R-Va., Oct. 10, 1984. House passed Oct. 11. Senate passed Oct. 11. President signed Oct. 30, 1984.

PL 98-607 (HR 6441) Eliminate restrictions with respect to the imposition and collection of tolls on the Richmond-Petersburg Turnpike upon repayment by the Commonwealth of Virginia of certain federal-aid highway funds used on such turnpike. Introduced by BLILEY, R-Va., Oct. 11, 1984. House passed Oct. 11. Senate passed Oct. 11. President signed Oct. 30, 1984.

PL 98-608 (H J Res 158) Make technical corrections in the act of Jan. 25, 1983 (PL 97-459). Introduced by UDALL, D-Ariz., Feb. 23, 1983. House Interior and Insular Affairs reported April 7 (H Rept 98-49). House passed April 19. Senate Indian Affairs reported Sept. 24, 1984 (S Rept 98-632). Senate passed, amended, Oct. 3. House agreed to Senate amendment Oct. 4. President signed Oct. 30, 1984.

PL 98-609 (H J Res 332) Designate the week beginning May 21, 1985, as "National Medical Transcriptionist Week." Introduced by HUNTER, R-Calif., July 27, 1983. House Post Office and Civil Service discharged. House passed Oct. 2, 1984. Senate Judiciary discharged. Senate passed Oct. 10. President signed Oct. 30, 1984.

PL 98-610 (H J Res 594) Designate the week beginning Feb. 17, 1985, as a time to recognize volunteers who give their time to become Big Brothers and Big Sisters to youths in need of adult companionship. Introduced by LLOYD, D-Tenn., June 18, 1984. House Post Office and Civil Service discharged. House passed Aug. 8. Senate Judiciary discharged. Senate passed Oct. 10. President signed Oct. 30, 1984.

PL 98-611 (HR 2568) Amend the Internal Revenue Code of 1954 to extend for 2 years the exclusion from gross income with respect to educational assistance programs. Introduced by SHANNON, D-Mass., April 14, 1983. House Ways and Means reported Sept. 24, 1984 (H Rept 98-1049). House passed, under suspension of the rules, Oct. 1. Senate passed Oct. 11. President signed Oct. 31, 1984.

PL 98-612 (HR 5361) Amend the Internal Revenue Code of 1954 to extend for one year the exclusion from gross income with respect to group legal services plans. Introduced by STARK, D-Calif., April 4, 1984. House Ways and Means reported Sept. 24 (H Rept 98-1050). House passed, under suspension of the rules, Oct. 1. Senate passed, amended, Oct. 11. House agreed to Senate amendment with an amendment Oct. 11. Senate agreed to House amendment with an amendment Oct. 11. House agreed to Senate amendment Oct. 11. President signed Oct. 31, 1984.

PL 98-613 (HR 5492) Provide for the conservation and management of Atlantic striped bass. Introduced by STUDDS, D-Mass., April 12, 1984. House Merchant Marine and Fisheries reported Sept. 17 (H Rept 98-1029). Supplemental report filed Sept. 25 (H Rept 98-1029, Part II). House passed Oct. 4. Senate passed, amended, Oct. 11. House agreed to Senate amendment Oct. 11. President signed Oct. 31, 1984.

PL 98-614 (HR 1314) Extend and revise the authority of the president under chapter 9 of title 5, U.S. Code, to transmit to the Congress plans for the reorganization of the agencies of the executive branch of the government. Introduced by BROOKS, D-Texas, Feb. 8, 1983. House Government Operations reported May 16 (H Rept 98-128, Part I). House Rules reported March 30, 1984 (H Rept 98-128, Part II). House passed, under suspension of the rules, April 10. Senate passed Oct. 11. President signed Nov. 8, 1984.

PL 98-615 (HR 2300) Provide that a former spouse of a federal employee who is married to such employee for 10 years or more shall be entitled to a portion of the annuity of any surviving spouse of such employee. Introduced by SCHROEDER, D-Colo., March 23, 1983. House Post Office and Civil Service reported Sept. 24, 1984 (H Rept 98-1054). House passed, under suspension of the rules, Sept. 24. Senate passed, amended, Oct. 10. House agreed to Senate amendments Oct. 10. President signed Nov. 8, 1984.

PL 98-616 (HR 2867) Authorize funds and revise certain provisions for hazardous waste control and enforcement under the Solid Waste Disposal Act. Introduced by FLORIO, D-N.J., May 3, 1983. House Energy and Commerce reported May 17 (H Rept 98-198, Part I). Supplemental report filed June 9 (H Rept 98-198, Part II). House Judiciary reported June 17 (H Rept 98-198, Part III). House passed Nov. 3. Senate Environment and Public Works discharged. Senate passed, amended, July 25, 1984. House agreed to conference report Oct. 3 (H Rept 98-1133). Senate agreed to conference report Oct. 5. President signed Nov. 8, 1984.

PL 98-617 (HR 5386) Amend part A of title XVIII of the Social Security Act with respect to the payment rates for routine home health care and other services included in hospice care. Introduced by PANETTA, D-Calif., April 5, 1984. House Ways and Means reported Sept. 28 (H Rept 98-1100). House passed, under suspension of the rules, Oct. 1. Senate passed, amended, Oct. 11. House agreed to Senate amendments Oct. 11. President signed Nov. 8, 1984.

PL 98-618 (HR 5399) Authorize appropriations for fiscal year 1985 for intelligence and intelligence-related activities of the U.S. government, the intelligence community staff, and the Central Intelligence Agency Retirement and Disability System. Introduced by BOLAND, D-Mass., April 10, 1984. House Intelligence reported May 10 (H Rept 98-743, Part I). House Armed Services reported May 23 (H Rept 98-743, Part II). House passed Aug. 2. Senate passed, amended, Oct. 11. House agreed to Senate amendment Oct. 11. President signed Nov. 8, 1984.

PL 98-619 (HR 6028) Appropriate funds for fiscal year 1985 for the Departments of Labor, Health and Human Services, and Education, and related agencies. Introduced by NATCHER, D-Ky., July 26, 1984. House Appropriations reported July 26 (H Rept 98-911). House passed Aug. 1. Senate Appropriations discharged. Senate passed, amended, Sept. 25. House agreed to conference report Oct. 10 (H Rept 98-1132). Senate agreed to conference report Oct. 10. President signed Nov. 8, 1984.

PL 98-620 (HR 6163) Amend title 28, U.S. Code, with respect to the places where court shall be held in certain judicial districts. Introduced by KASTENMEIER, D-Wis., Aug. 10, 1984. House Judiciary reported Sept. 24 (H Rept 98-1062). House passed, under suspension of the rules, Sept. 24. Senate Judiciary reported Sept. 28. Senate passed, amended, Oct. 3. House agreed to Senate amendments Oct. 9. President signed Nov. 8, 1984.

PL 98-621 (HR 6224) Provide for the assumption of selected functions, programs and resources of Saint Elizabeths Hospital by the District of Columbia, and provide for the establishment of a comprehensive mental health care system in the District of Columbia. Introduced by DELLUMS, D-Calif., Sept. 12, 1984. House District of Columbia reported Sept. 13 (H Rept 98-1024, Part I). Supplemental report filed Sept. 14 (H Rept 98-1024, Part II). House passed, under suspension of the rules, Oct. 2. Senate passed, amended, Oct. 5. House agreed to Senate amendments Oct. 9. President signed Nov. 8, 1984.

PL 98-622 (HR 6286) Amend title 35, U.S. Code, to increase the effectiveness of the patent laws. Introduced by KASTENMEIER, D-Wis., Sept. 20, 1984. House passed, under suspension of the rules, Oct. 1. Senate Judiciary discharged. Senate passed, amended, Oct. 11. House agreed to Senate amendments with an amendment Oct. 11. Senate agreed to House amendment Oct. 11. President signed Nov. 8, 1984.

PL 98-623 (HR 6342) Approve the governing international fishery agreements with Iceland and the European Economic Community. Introduced by JONES, D-N.C., Oct. 1, 1984. House Merchant Marine and Fisheries discharged. House passed Oct. 4. Senate passed Oct. 10. President signed Nov. 8, 1984. ∎

SENATE ROLL-CALL VOTES

	1	2		1	2		1	2		1	2
ALABAMA			**IOWA**			**NEW HAMPSHIRE**					
Denton	Y	Y	Grassley	N	Y	Humphrey	Y	Y			
Heflin	Y	Y	Jepsen	N	Y	Rudman	Y	N			
ALASKA			**KANSAS**			**NEW JERSEY**					
Murkowski	N	N	Dole	Y	Y	Bradley	Y	Y			
Stevens	X	N	Kassebaum	N	Y	Lautenberg	Y	Y			
ARIZONA			**KENTUCKY**			**NEW MEXICO**					
Goldwater	Y	N	Ford	Y	Y	Domenici	N	Y			
DeConcini	#	Y	Huddleston	N	Y	Bingaman	N	Y			
ARKANSAS			**LOUISIANA**			**NEW YORK**					
Bumpers	N	Y	Johnston	?	?	D'Amato	Y	N			
Pryor	N	Y	Long	Y	Y	Moynihan	Y	Y			
CALIFORNIA			**MAINE**			**NORTH CAROLINA**					
Wilson	Y	Y	Cohen	N	Y	East	Y	Y			
Cranston	?	?	Mitchell	Y	Y	Helms	Y	Y			
COLORADO			**MARYLAND**			**NORTH DAKOTA**					
Armstrong	+	+	Mathias	N	N	Andrews	N	Y			
Hart	?	?	Sarbanes	N	N	Burdick	N	Y			
CONNECTICUT			**MASSACHUSETTS**			**OHIO**					
Weicker	Y	N	Kennedy	N	?	Glenn	N	N			
Dodd	Y	Y	Tsongas	N	N	Metzenbaum	N	N			
DELAWARE			**MICHIGAN**			**OKLAHOMA**					
Roth	?	?	Levin	N	Y	Nickles	Y	Y			
Biden	Y	Y	Riegle	N	Y	Boren	Y	Y			
FLORIDA			**MINNESOTA**			**OREGON**					
Hawkins	Y	Y	Boschwitz	N	Y	Hatfield	?	+			
Chiles	N	Y	Durenberger	Y	N	Packwood	N	N			
GEORGIA			**MISSISSIPPI**			**PENNSYLVANIA**					
Mattingly	#	?	Cochran	Y	Y	Heinz	N	Y			
Nunn	Y	Y	Stennis	?	?	Specter	Y	Y			
HAWAII			**MISSOURI**			**RHODE ISLAND**					
Inouye	?	?	Danforth	N	Y	Chafee	Y	N			
Matsunaga	?	?	Eagleton	N	Y	Pell	N	Y			
IDAHO			**MONTANA**			**SOUTH CAROLINA**					
McClure	N	Y	Baucus	N	Y	Thurmond	N	Y			
Symms	?	?	Melcher	N	Y	Hollings	?	?			
ILLINOIS			**NEBRASKA**			**SOUTH DAKOTA**					
Percy	Y	Y	Exon	Y	Y	Abdnor	N	Y			
Dixon	Y	Y	Zorinsky	N	Y	Pressler	N	Y			
INDIANA			**NEVADA**			**TENNESSEE**					
Lugar	Y	N	Hecht	Y	Y	Baker	Y	Y			
Quayle	Y	Y	Laxalt	Y	Y	Sasser	N	Y			

KEY

- Y Voted for (yea).
- # Paired for.
- + Announced for.
- N Voted against (nay).
- X Paired against.
- − Announced against.
- P Voted "present".
- C Voted "present" to avoid possible conflict of interest.
- ? Did not vote or otherwise make a position known.

Democrats   *Republicans*

	1	2
TEXAS		
Tower	Y	N
Bentsen	?	?
UTAH		
Garn	Y	Y
Hatch	N	Y
VERMONT		
Stafford	Y	N
Leahy	X	?
VIRGINIA		
Trible	Y	Y
Warner	Y	Y
WASHINGTON		
Evans*	Y	N
Gorton	Y	N
WEST VIRGINIA		
Byrd	N	Y
Randolph	N	Y
WISCONSIN		
Kasten	N	Y
Proxmire	N	Y
WYOMING		
Simpson	Y	Y
Wallop	Y	Y

ND - Northern Democrats   SD - Southern Democrats (Southern states - Ala., Ark., Fla., Ga., Ky., La., Miss., N.C., Okla., S.C., Tenn., Texas, Va.)

* Sen. Daniel J. Evans, R-Wash., was sworn in Jan. 23, 1984, to fill the seat left vacant by Sen. Henry M. Jackson, D-Wash., who died Sept. 1, 1983. He was appointed to the Senate on an interim basis after Jackson's death, serving until the end of the first session of the 98th Congress. Having won the Nov. 8, 1983, special election, Evans now will serve the five years remaining in Jackson's term.

1. S 1660. Universal Telephone Service Preservation Act. Goldwater, R-Ariz., motion to table (kill) the Baker, R-Tenn., motion to proceed to the consideration of the bill to delay the imposition of an access charge on residential telephone users, and establish a Universal Service Fund to subsidize low-income and rural users. Motion agreed to 44-40: R 31-18; D 13-22 (ND 8-17, SD 5-5), Jan. 26, 1984. A "yea" was a vote supporting the president's position.

2. S 2211. Congressional Pay Reduction. Passage of the bill to rescind the 3.5 percent pay increase for members of Congress that took effect Jan. 1, 1984. Passed 66-19: R 35-15; D 31-4 (ND 21-4, SD 10-0), Jan. 26, 1984.

	3	4	5	6	7			3	4	5	6	7			3	4	5	6	7
ALABAMA							**IOWA**							**NEW HAMPSHIRE**					
Denton	Y	-	N	Y	Y		*Grassley*	Y	Y	N	Y	Y		*Humphrey*	Y	Y	Y	Y	Y
Heflin	Y	Y	N	Y	N		*Jepsen*	?	Y	Y	Y	Y		*Rudman*	Y	N	Y	Y	Y
ALASKA							**KANSAS**							**NEW JERSEY**					
Murkowski	Y	N	N	Y	Y		*Dole*	Y	Y	N	Y	Y		Bradley	?	Y	Y	Y	Y
Stevens	Y	Y	N	Y	Y		*Kassebaum*	?	?	N	Y	Y		Lautenberg	Y	Y	Y	Y	Y
ARIZONA							**KENTUCKY**							**NEW MEXICO**					
Goldwater	?	N	N	Y	?		Ford	?	Y	Y	Y	Y		*Domenici*	Y	Y	N	Y	Y
DeConcini	?	Y	N	Y	Y		Huddleston	?	Y	Y	Y	Y		Bingaman	Y	Y	Y	Y	Y
ARKANSAS							**LOUISIANA**							**NEW YORK**					
Bumpers	?	Y	Y	Y	Y		Johnston	Y	Y	N	Y	Y		*D'Amato*	Y	Y	N	Y	Y
Pryor	Y	Y	Y	Y	Y		Long	?	Y	?	+	?		Moynihan	Y	Y	Y	Y	Y
CALIFORNIA							**MAINE**							**NORTH CAROLINA**					
Wilson	Y	N	N	Y	Y		*Cohen*	Y	N	Y	Y	Y		*East*	Y	N	N	Y	Y
Cranston	?	?	?	?	?		Mitchell	Y	Y	Y	Y	Y		*Helms*	Y	N	N	Y	Y
COLORADO							**MARYLAND**							**NORTH DAKOTA**					
Armstrong	Y	?	?	?	?		*Mathias*	N	Y	Y	N	N		*Andrews*	Y	N	Y	Y	Y
Hart	?	?	?	?	?		Sarbanes	?	Y	Y	Y	Y		Burdick	Y	N	Y	Y	Y
CONNECTICUT							**MASSACHUSETTS**							**OHIO**					
Weicker	Y	Y	Y	Y	Y		Kennedy	?	Y	N	Y	Y		Glenn	Y	?	?	?	?
Dodd	Y	Y	Y	Y	Y		Tsongas	Y	Y	Y	Y	Y		Metzenbaum	Y	Y	Y	Y	Y
DELAWARE							**MICHIGAN**							**OKLAHOMA**					
Roth	Y	Y	N	Y	Y		Levin	Y	Y	Y	Y	Y		*Nickles*	?	N	N	Y	Y
Biden	Y	Y	N	Y	Y		Riegle	Y	Y	Y	Y	Y		Boren	Y	N	Y	Y	Y
FLORIDA							**MINNESOTA**							**OREGON**					
Hawkins	Y	Y	N	Y	Y		*Boschwitz*	?	Y	Y	Y	Y		*Hatfield*	?	Y	Y	Y	N
Chiles	Y	Y	Y	Y	?		*Durenberger*	?	Y	N	Y	Y		*Packwood*	Y	Y	Y	Y	Y
GEORGIA							**MISSISSIPPI**							**PENNSYLVANIA**					
Mattingly	Y	N	N	Y	Y		*Cochran*	Y	Y	N	Y	Y		*Heinz*	Y	Y	N	Y	?
Nunn	Y	Y	N	Y	Y		Stennis	?	Y	N	Y	Y		*Specter*	Y	Y	N	Y	Y
HAWAII							**MISSOURI**							**RHODE ISLAND**					
Inouye	?	Y	Y	Y	Y		*Danforth*	Y	Y	N	Y	Y		*Chafee*	Y	Y	N	Y	Y
Matsunaga	Y	Y	Y	Y	Y		Eagleton	?	?	?	+	?		Pell	Y	Y	Y	Y	Y
IDAHO							**MONTANA**							**SOUTH CAROLINA**					
McClure	Y	?	N	Y	Y		Baucus	Y	Y	Y	Y	Y		*Thurmond*	Y	Y	N	Y	Y
Symms	Y	N	N	Y	Y		Melcher	Y	Y	Y	Y	Y		Hollings	Y	?	?	+	?
ILLINOIS							**NEBRASKA**							**SOUTH DAKOTA**					
Percy	?	Y	N	Y	Y		Exon	Y	N	Y	Y	Y		*Abdnor*	Y	Y	N	Y	Y
Dixon	Y	Y	Y	Y	Y		Zorinsky	Y	N	N	Y	Y		*Pressler*	Y	N	Y	Y	Y
INDIANA							**NEVADA**							**TENNESSEE**					
Lugar	Y	Y	N	Y	Y		*Hecht*	Y	Y	N	Y	Y		*Baker*	Y	Y	N	Y	Y
Quayle	Y	Y	N	Y	Y		*Laxalt*	Y	Y	N	Y	+		Sasser	Y	Y	Y	Y	Y

KEY

- Y   Voted for (yea).
- \#   Paired for.
- +   Announced for.
- N   Voted against (nay).
- X   Paired against.
- -   Announced against.
- P   Voted "present".
- C   Voted "present" to avoid possible conflict of interest.
- ?   Did not vote or otherwise make a position known.

Democrats   *Republicans*

	3	4	5	6	7
TEXAS					
Tower	Y	Y	?	?	?
Bentsen	Y	?	Y	Y	Y
UTAH					
Garn	Y	N	N	Y	Y
Hatch	Y	Y	N	Y	Y
VERMONT					
Stafford	Y	Y	N	Y	Y
Leahy	Y	Y	Y	Y	Y
VIRGINIA					
Trible	?	N	N	Y	Y
Warner	Y	Y	N	Y	Y
WASHINGTON					
Evans	Y	Y	N	Y	Y
Gorton	Y	Y	N	Y	Y
WEST VIRGINIA					
Byrd	Y	Y	Y	Y	Y
Randolph	Y	N	Y	Y	Y
WISCONSIN					
Kasten	+	N	N	Y	Y
Proxmire	Y	N	Y	Y	Y
WYOMING					
Simpson	Y	N	N	Y	Y
Wallop	Y	N	N	Y	Y

ND - Northern Democrats   SD - Southern Democrats (Southern states - Ala., Ark., Fla., Ga., Ky., La., Miss., N.C., Okla., S.C., Tenn., Texas, Va.)

3. S 1762. Comprehensive Crime Control Act. Thurmond, R-S.C., motion to table (kill) the Mathias, R-Md., amendment to direct a proposed federal sentencing commission to ensure that new sentencing guidelines not result in an increase in the aggregate length of federal prison terms, the average prison term served or the inmate population of federal prisons. Motion agreed to 76-1: R 44-1; D 32-0 (ND 23-0, SD 9-0), Jan. 30, 1984.

4. HR 1492. Christopher Columbus Quincentenary Jubilee Act. Passage of the bill to create a Christopher Columbus Quincentenary Commission, to plan and conduct the 500th anniversary commemoration of Columbus' voyage, and to authorize $200,000 a year in fiscal 1984-92 for the commission. Passed 67-23: R 34-17; D 33-6 (ND 22-5, SD 11-1), Feb. 1, 1984.

5. S 1762. Comprehensive Crime Control Act. Metzenbaum, D-Ohio, amendment to prohibit government officials from tape recording their telephone conversations without consent of the other party, with exceptions permitted for law enforcement and intelligence officers. Rejected 41-51: R 10-43; D 31-8 (ND 23-4, SD 8-4), Feb. 2, 1984. A "nay" was a vote supporting the president's position.

6. S 1762. Comprehensive Crime Control Act. Passage of the bill to revise federal sentencing procedures, expand use of pretrial detention, stiffen drug laws, overhaul the insanity defense, expand the government's authority to require forfeiture of proceeds from organized crime and narcotics trafficking, create a program of anti-crime grants to states and make other changes in the federal criminal code. Passed 91-1: R 52-1; D 39-0 (ND 27-0, SD 12-0), Feb. 2, 1984. A "yea" was a vote supporting the president's position.

7. S 668. Sentencing Reform Act. Passage of the bill to create a commission to write sentencing guidelines for use by federal judges; authorize sentences imposing prison terms, fines or probation; require judges to state reasons for sentences imposed; prohibit parole and abolish the U.S. Parole Commission; and permit either the defendant or the prosecution to appeal a sentence. Passed 85-3: R 48-2; D 37-1 (ND 27-0, SD 10-1), Feb. 2, 1984. A "yea" was a vote supporting the president's position.

	8	9	10	11	12	13
ALABAMA						
Denton	N	Y	Y	Y	Y	Y
Heflin	Y	Y	Y	Y	Y	Y
ALASKA						
Murkowski	N	Y	Y	Y	Y	Y
Stevens	N	Y	Y	Y	Y	Y
ARIZONA						
Goldwater	N	Y	Y	Y	Y	Y
DeConcini	-	Y	Y	Y	Y	Y
ARKANSAS						
Bumpers	N	Y	Y	Y	N	Y
Pryor	N	Y	?	?	Y	Y
CALIFORNIA						
Wilson	N	Y	Y	Y	Y	Y
Cranston	?	?	N	N	?	?
COLORADO						
Armstrong	?	?	?	?	?	+
Hart	?	?	?	?	?	?
CONNECTICUT						
Weicker	Y	Y	N	N	N	N
Dodd	Y	Y	?	?	N	N
DELAWARE						
Roth	N	Y	Y	Y	Y	Y
Biden	Y	Y	N	N	N	Y
FLORIDA						
Hawkins	N	Y	Y	Y	+	Y
Chiles	N	Y	Y	Y	Y	Y
GEORGIA						
Mattingly	N	Y	Y	Y	Y	Y
Nunn	N	Y	Y	Y	Y	Y
HAWAII						
Inouye	Y	Y	#	Y	N	N
Matsunaga	Y	Y	N	#	N	N
IDAHO						
McClure	Y	Y	Y	Y	Y	Y
Symms	N	Y	Y	Y	Y	Y
ILLINOIS						
Percy	N	Y	?	?	+	Y
Dixon	-	+	Y	Y	Y	Y
INDIANA						
Lugar	N	Y	Y	Y	Y	Y
Quayle	N	Y	Y	Y	Y	Y
IOWA						
Grassley	N	Y	Y	Y	Y	Y
Jepsen	N	Y	?	?	Y	Y
KANSAS						
Dole	N	Y	Y	Y	Y	Y
Kassebaum	N	Y	Y	Y	Y	Y
KENTUCKY						
Ford	N	Y	Y	Y	Y	Y
Huddleston	N	?	Y	Y	Y	Y
LOUISIANA						
Johnston	N	Y	Y	Y	Y	Y
Long	?	?	?	+	Y	Y
MAINE						
Cohen	N	Y	Y	Y	Y	N
Mitchell	Y	Y	N	Y	N	N
MARYLAND						
Mathias	Y	Y	N	N	N	N
Sarbanes	Y	Y	?	?	N	N
MASSACHUSETTS						
Kennedy	Y	Y	-	X	N	N
Tsongas	Y	Y	Y	Y	?	N
MICHIGAN						
Levin	Y	Y	N	N	Y	N
Riegle	Y	Y	N	Y	N	N
MINNESOTA						
Boschwitz	Y	Y	N	N	N	N
Durenberger	Y	Y	N	N	Y	Y
MISSISSIPPI						
Cochran	N	Y	Y	Y	Y	Y
Stennis	Y	Y	Y	Y	Y	Y
MISSOURI						
Danforth	N	Y	Y	Y	Y	N
Eagleton	?	?	?	?	N	N
MONTANA						
Baucus	Y	Y	N	Y	N	Y
Melcher	Y	Y	N	N	N	N
NEBRASKA						
Exon	N	Y	Y	Y	Y	Y
Zorinsky	N	Y	Y	Y	Y	Y
NEVADA						
Hecht	?	?	?	?	?	Y
Laxalt	-	+	+	+	+	?
NEW HAMPSHIRE						
Humphrey	N	Y	Y	Y	Y	Y
Rudman	N	Y	Y	Y	Y	Y
NEW JERSEY						
Bradley	?	?	?	?	Y	Y
Lautenberg	Y	Y	?	?	N	N
NEW MEXICO						
Domenici	N	Y	Y	Y	Y	Y
Bingaman	Y	Y	Y	Y	Y	N
NEW YORK						
D'Amato	N	Y	Y	Y	Y	Y
Moynihan	Y	Y	X	?	N	N
NORTH CAROLINA						
East	N	Y	Y	Y	Y	Y
Helms	N	Y	Y	Y	Y	Y
NORTH DAKOTA						
Andrews	N	Y	Y	Y	Y	Y
Burdick	Y	Y	Y	Y	N	N
OHIO						
Glenn	?	?	?	?	?	?
Metzenbaum	Y	Y	N	N	N	N
OKLAHOMA						
Nickles	N	Y	Y	Y	Y	Y
Boren	N	Y	Y	Y	Y	Y
OREGON						
Hatfield	Y	Y	-	-	+	N
Packwood	Y	Y	N	Y	N	Y
PENNSYLVANIA						
Heinz	N	Y	Y	Y	Y	Y
Specter	Y	Y	Y	Y	N	Y
RHODE ISLAND						
Chafee	Y	Y	N	Y	N	N
Pell	N	Y	N	Y	N	Y
SOUTH CAROLINA						
Thurmond	N	Y	Y	Y	Y	Y
Hollings	?	?	?	?	?	?
SOUTH DAKOTA						
Abdnor	N	Y	Y	Y	Y	Y
Pressler	N	Y	Y	Y	Y	Y
TENNESSEE						
Baker	N	Y	Y	Y	Y	Y
Sasser	?	+	?	?	Y	N
TEXAS						
Tower	?	?	?	?	Y	?
Bentsen	N	Y	?	?	Y	Y
UTAH						
Garn	N	Y	Y	Y	Y	Y
Hatch	N	Y	Y	Y	Y	Y
VERMONT						
Stafford	N	Y	Y	Y	Y	Y
Leahy	?	?	?	?	?	-
VIRGINIA						
Trible	N	Y	Y	Y	Y	Y
Warner	N	Y	Y	Y	+	Y
WASHINGTON						
Evans	Y	Y	Y	Y	Y	N
Gorton	Y	Y	Y	Y	Y	Y
WEST VIRGINIA						
Byrd	N	Y	Y	Y	Y	Y
Randolph	N	Y	Y	Y	Y	Y
WISCONSIN						
Kasten	N	Y	+	+	Y	Y
Proxmire	N	Y	N	Y	N	N
WYOMING						
Simpson	N	Y	Y	Y	Y	?
Wallop	?	?	Y	Y	Y	Y

KEY

Y	Voted for (yea).
#	Paired for.
+	Announced for.
N	Voted against (nay).
X	Paired against.
-	Announced against.
P	Voted "present".
C	Voted "present" to avoid possible conflict of interest.
?	Did not vote or otherwise make a position known.

Democrats   *Republicans*

ND - Northern Democrats   SD - Southern Democrats (Southern states - Ala., Ark., Fla., Ga., Ky., La., Miss., N.C., Okla., S.C., Tenn., Texas, Va.)

---

8. S 215. Bail Reform Act. Mitchell, D-Maine, amendment to require that defendants detained before trial be tried within 60 days of their incarceration. Current law requires trial within 90 days. Rejected 30-54: R 11-39; D 19-15 (ND 17-6, SD 2-9), Feb. 3, 1984. A "nay" was a vote supporting the president's position.

9. S 215. Bail Reform Act. Passage of the bill to revise federal bail law to permit judges to order pretrial detention of defendants deemed dangerous to the community; to tighten criteria for post-conviction release; provide increased penalties for crimes committed while on bail, coupled with bail revocation; and stiffen penalties for bail-jumping. Passed 84-0: R 50-0; D 34-0 (ND 24-0, SD 10-0), Feb. 3, 1984. A "yea" was a vote supporting the president's position.

10. S 1763. Reform of Federal Intervention in State Proceedings Act. Baker, R-Tenn., motion to table (kill) the Baucus, D-Mont., amendment to delete from the bill a provision requiring federal courts to defer to state court decisions on prisoner claims given a "full and fair" adjudication in state courts. Motion agreed to 59-17: R 41-6; D 18-11 (ND 9-11, SD 9-0), Feb. 6, 1984.

11. S 1763. Reform of Federal Intervention in State Proceedings Act. Passage of the bill to make it more difficult for state prisoners to challenge their state convictions by *habeas corpus* proceedings in federal court. Passed 67-9: R 43-4; D 24-5 (ND 15-5, SD 9-0), Feb. 6, 1984. A "yea" was a vote supporting the president's position.

12. S 1764. Exclusionary Rule Limitation Act. Passage of the bill to modify the "exclusionary rule," which forbids use in trials of illegally obtained evidence, by permitting use in federal criminal trials of evidence obtained by law enforcement officers acting in a "good-faith" belief that they were proceeding legally. Passed 63-24: R 42-6; D 21-18 (ND 9-17, SD 12-1), Feb. 7, 1984. A "yea" was a vote supporting the president's position.

13. S 1765. Capital Punishment. Baker, R-Tenn., motion to invoke cloture (thus limiting debate) on the bill to re-establish a federal death penalty, provide for a separate hearing on the issue of punishment following conviction and require the sentencing body to consider aggravating and mitigating factors. Motion agreed to 65-26: R 43-8; D 22-18 (ND 10-17, SD 12-1), Feb. 9, 1984. A three-fifths majority vote (60) of the total Senate is required to invoke cloture.

	14	15	16	17		14	15	16	17		14	15	16	17
ALABAMA					**IOWA**					**NEW HAMPSHIRE**				
Denton	Y	Y	Y	Y	*Grassley*	Y	Y	Y	Y	*Humphrey*	Y	Y	Y	N
Heflin	Y	Y	Y	Y	*Jepsen*	Y	Y	Y	Y	*Rudman*	Y	Y	Y	Y
ALASKA					**KANSAS**					**NEW JERSEY**				
Murkowski	?	?	?	?	*Dole*	Y	?	Y	Y	Bradley	Y	Y	Y	Y
Stevens	Y	Y	Y	Y	*Kassebaum*	Y	Y	Y	Y	Lautenberg	N	Y	Y	Y
ARIZONA					**KENTUCKY**					**NEW MEXICO**				
Goldwater	Y	Y	Y	Y	Ford	Y	Y	Y	Y	*Domenici*	Y	?	Y	Y
DeConcini	Y	Y	Y	Y	Huddleston	Y	Y	Y	Y	Bingaman	N	Y	Y	N
ARKANSAS					**LOUISIANA**					**NEW YORK**				
Bumpers	Y	Y	Y	Y	Johnston	Y	Y	Y	?	D'Amato	Y	N	Y	Y
Pryor	Y	Y	Y	Y	Long	Y	Y	Y	Y	Moynihan	Y	Y	Y	Y
CALIFORNIA					**MAINE**					**NORTH CAROLINA**				
Wilson	Y	Y	Y	Y	*Cohen*	N	Y	Y	Y	*East*	Y	Y	Y	Y
Cranston	?	?	?	?	Mitchell	N	Y	Y	Y	*Helms*	Y	Y	Y	Y
COLORADO					**MARYLAND**					**NORTH DAKOTA**				
Armstrong	Y	Y	+	?	*Mathias*	N	Y	Y	Y	*Andrews*	N	Y	Y	?
Hart	N	?	?	?	Sarbanes	N	Y	Y	Y	Burdick	N	Y	Y	Y
CONNECTICUT					**MASSACHUSETTS**					**OHIO**				
Weicker	N	Y	Y	Y	Kennedy	N	Y	Y	Y	Glenn	-	?	?	?
Dodd	N	Y	Y	Y	Tsongas	?	?	?	?	Metzenbaum	N	Y	Y	N
DELAWARE					**MICHIGAN**					**OKLAHOMA**				
Roth	Y	Y	Y	N	Levin	N	N	Y	N	*Nickles*	Y	Y	Y	N
Biden	N	Y	Y	N	Riegle	N	Y	Y	Y	Boren	Y	Y	Y	N
FLORIDA					**MINNESOTA**					**OREGON**				
Hawkins	Y	N	Y	N	*Boschwitz*	N	N	Y	Y	*Hatfield*	N	+	+	?
Chiles	Y	Y	Y	?	*Durenberger*	N	Y	Y	N	Packwood	Y	N	Y	Y
GEORGIA					**MISSISSIPPI**					**PENNSYLVANIA**				
Mattingly	Y	Y	Y	Y	*Cochran*	Y	Y	Y	Y	Heinz	Y	N	Y	Y
Nunn	Y	Y	Y	Y	Stennis	Y	Y	Y	Y	Specter	Y	N	Y	Y
HAWAII					**MISSOURI**					**RHODE ISLAND**				
Inouye	N	?	Y	Y	*Danforth*	N	Y	Y	Y	*Chafee*	N	Y	Y	Y
Matsunaga	N	N	Y	Y	Eagleton	N	Y	Y	Y	Pell	N	Y	Y	Y
IDAHO					**MONTANA**					**SOUTH CAROLINA**				
McClure	Y	Y	Y	Y	Baucus	Y	Y	Y	Y	*Thurmond*	Y	Y	Y	Y
Symms	Y	Y	Y	Y	Melcher	N	Y	Y	?	Hollings	?	?	?	?
ILLINOIS					**NEBRASKA**					**SOUTH DAKOTA**				
Percy	N	Y	Y	?	Exon	Y	Y	Y	Y	*Abdnor*	Y	Y	Y	Y
Dixon	Y	N	Y	N	Zorinsky	Y	Y	Y	Y	*Pressler*	Y	Y	Y	Y
INDIANA					**NEVADA**					**TENNESSEE**				
Lugar	Y	N	Y	Y	*Hecht*	Y	Y	Y	Y	*Baker*	Y	Y	Y	Y
Quayle	Y	Y	Y	Y	*Laxalt*	Y	?	Y	Y	Sasser	N	Y	Y	Y

KEY

Y	Voted for (yea).
#	Paired for.
+	Announced for.
N	Voted against (nay).
X	Paired against.
-	Announced against.
P	Voted "present".
C	Voted "present" to avoid possible conflict of interest.
?	Did not vote or otherwise make a position known.

Democrats   Republicans

	14	15	16	17
TEXAS				
Tower	Y	Y	Y	Y
Bentsen	N	Y	Y	Y
UTAH				
Garn	Y	Y	Y	Y
Hatch	Y	Y	Y	Y
VERMONT				
Stafford	Y	Y	Y	Y
Leahy	N	Y	Y	Y
VIRGINIA				
Trible	Y	Y	Y	Y
Warner	Y	Y	Y	Y
WASHINGTON				
Evans	N	Y	Y	?
Gorton	Y	Y	Y	Y
WEST VIRGINIA				
Byrd	Y	Y	Y	Y
Randolph	Y	Y	Y	Y
WISCONSIN				
Kasten	Y	N	Y	Y
Proxmire	N	Y	Y	N
WYOMING				
Simpson	Y	Y	Y	Y
Wallop	Y	N	Y	Y

ND - Northern Democrats   SD - Southern Democrats (Southern states - Ala., Ark., Fla., Ga., Ky., La., Miss., N.C., Okla., S.C., Tenn., Texas, Va.)

14. S 1765. Capital Punishment. Passage of the bill to reinstitute the death penalty for certain federal crimes, including assassination or attempted assassination of a president, treason, espionage and specified other federal crimes resulting in the death of another person. The bill requires a separate hearing on the issue of punishment after the defendant is convicted of an offense carrying the death penalty. Passed 63-32: R 43-11; D 20-21 (ND 9-19, SD 11-2), Feb. 22, 1984. A "yea" was a vote supporting the president's position.

15. S 52. Armed Career Criminal Act. Kennedy, D-Mass., amendment specifying that the federal government may prosecute a defendant with at least two prior state burglary or robbery convictions only if the third offense charged is a federal crime involving use of a firearm. Adopted 77-12: R 41-9; D 36-3 (ND 23-3, SD 13-0), Feb. 23, 1984.

16. S 52. Armed Career Criminal Act. Passage of the bill to allow federal prosecutions of defendants with at least two prior state burglary or robbery convictions if the defendant is charged with a third offense that is a federal crime involving use of a firearm. The bill mandates a 15-year prison term with no probation or parole upon conviction. Passed 92-0: R 52-0; D 40-0 (ND 27-0, SD 13-0), Feb. 23, 1984.

17. S 47. Shipping Antitrust Act. Adoption of the conference report on the bill to broaden exemptions from antitrust prosecution for international shipping conferences, and expediting Federal Maritime Commission approval of conference agreements. Adopted 74-12: R 44-5; D 30-7 (ND 20-6, SD 10-1), Feb. 23, 1984. A "yea" was a vote supporting the president's position.

KEY

Y	Voted for (yea).
#	Paired for.
+	Announced for.
N	Voted against (nay).
X	Paired against.
-	Announced against.
P	Voted "present".
C	Voted "present" to avoid possible conflict of interest.
?	Did not vote or otherwise make a position known.

Democrats   **Republicans**

State / Senator	18	19	20	21	22	23	24	25
ALABAMA								
Denton	Y	Y	Y	N	N	Y	Y	Y
Heflin	N	N	Y	Y	N	Y	Y	Y
ALASKA								
Murkowski	Y	Y	Y	Y	Y	Y	Y	Y
Stevens	Y	Y	Y	Y	Y	Y	Y	N
ARIZONA								
Goldwater	Y	?	?	N	Y	Y	Y	Y
DeConcini	Y	N	Y	Y	N	C	C	Y
ARKANSAS								
Bumpers	N	N	Y	Y	N	N	N	Y
Pryor	N	N	Y	Y	N	Y	N	Y
CALIFORNIA								
Wilson	Y	Y	Y	N	N	Y	Y	Y
Cranston	?	?	?	?	?	?	?	?
COLORADO								
Armstrong	N	N	Y	Y	N	Y	Y	Y
Hart	-	?	?	?	?	?	?	?
CONNECTICUT								
Weicker	N	Y	Y	Y	Y	N	Y	Y
Dodd	N	N	Y	?	?	?	?	Y
DELAWARE								
Roth	N	N	Y	Y	N	Y	Y	Y
Biden	N	N	Y	Y	N	N	N	Y
FLORIDA								
Hawkins	N	Y	Y	N	N	N	N	Y
Chiles	Y	N	Y	N	N	N	N	Y
GEORGIA								
Mattingly	N	N	Y	Y	N	Y	Y	Y
Nunn	N	N	Y	Y	N	Y	N	Y
HAWAII								
Inouye	N	N	Y	Y	N	Y	N	Y
Matsunaga	N	N	Y	Y	N	N	N	Y
IDAHO								
McClure	Y	?	?	N	N	Y	Y	Y
Symms	Y	N	Y	N	N	Y	Y	Y
ILLINOIS								
Percy	Y	N	Y	N	Y	N	Y	?
Dixon	N	Y	Y	Y	N	Y	Y	Y
INDIANA								
Lugar	Y	N	Y	N	N	Y	Y	Y
Quayle	Y	N	Y	Y	N	Y	Y	Y

State / Senator	18	19	20	21	22	23	24	25
IOWA								
Grassley	N	N	Y	Y	N	Y	Y	Y
Jepsen	N	Y	Y	Y	N	Y	Y	Y
KANSAS								
Dole	Y	N	Y	N	Y	N	Y	Y
Kassebaum	N	N	Y	?	N	Y	Y	Y
KENTUCKY								
Ford	N	N	Y	Y	N	N	N	Y
Huddleston	?	?	?	Y	N	Y	Y	Y
LOUISIANA								
Johnston	Y	N	Y	N	N	N	N	Y
Long	Y	N	?	N	N	Y	Y	Y
MAINE								
Cohen	?	?	?	Y	N	N	N	Y
Mitchell	N	Y	Y	Y	N	Y	N	Y
MARYLAND								
Mathias	N	N	Y	Y	Y	Y	Y	N
Sarbanes	N	N	Y	Y	N	N	N	Y
MASSACHUSETTS								
Kennedy	N	?	?	Y	N	N	N	Y
Tsongas	N	N	Y	?	?	Y	N	Y
MICHIGAN								
Levin	N	N	Y	Y	N	N	N	Y
Riegle	N	Y	Y	Y	N	N	N	Y
MINNESOTA								
Boschwitz	N	N	Y	Y	N	N	N	Y
Durenberger	N	N	Y	?	?	Y	Y	Y
MISSISSIPPI								
Cochran	Y	N	Y	Y	N	Y	Y	Y
Stennis	N	?	?	Y	N	N	N	Y
MISSOURI								
Danforth	N	N	Y	Y	N	Y	Y	Y
Eagleton	N	Y	Y	Y	N	Y	Y	Y
MONTANA								
Baucus	N	N	Y	N	N	Y	N	Y
Melcher	N	N	Y	Y	N	N	N	Y
NEBRASKA								
Exon	N	N	Y	Y	N	N	N	Y
Zorinsky	Y	N	Y	Y	N	N	N	Y

State / Senator	18	19	20	21	22	23	24	25
NEW HAMPSHIRE								
Humphrey	N	N	Y	Y	Y	N	N	Y
Rudman	?	?	?	?	Y	Y	N	Y
NEW JERSEY								
Bradley	N	N	Y	Y	Y	Y	N	Y
Lautenberg	N	N	Y	Y	N	N	N	Y
NEW MEXICO								
Domenici	Y	N	Y	Y	N	Y	Y	Y
Bingaman	N	N	Y	Y	N	Y	N	Y
NEW YORK								
D'Amato	N	Y	Y	Y	Y	N	N	Y
Moynihan	N	Y	Y	Y	Y	Y	N	Y
NORTH CAROLINA								
East	Y	N	Y	N	N	Y	Y	Y
Helms	Y	N	Y	N	Y	N	Y	Y
NORTH DAKOTA								
Andrews	N	Y	Y	Y	N	Y	Y	Y
Burdick	N	Y	Y	Y	N	Y	Y	Y
OHIO								
Glenn	?	?	?	?	?	?	?	?
Metzenbaum	N	?	?	Y	N	N	N	Y
OKLAHOMA								
Nickles	N	N	Y	Y	N	Y	Y	Y
Boren	N	N	Y	Y	N	Y	Y	Y
OREGON								
Hatfield	N	Y	?	Y	N	N	N	Y
Packwood	N	N	Y	Y	N	N	N	Y
PENNSYLVANIA								
Heinz	Y	N	Y	Y	Y	Y	Y	Y
Specter	Y	Y	Y	Y	Y	N	N	Y
RHODE ISLAND								
Chafee	Y	N	Y	Y	N	Y	Y	Y
Pell	N	N	Y	Y	N	Y	N	Y
SOUTH CAROLINA								
Thurmond	Y	Y	Y	N	N	Y	Y	Y
Hollings	?	?	?	?	N	N	N	Y
SOUTH DAKOTA								
Abdnor	Y	Y	?	N	N	Y	Y	Y
Pressler	N	Y	Y	Y	N	N	?	Y
TENNESSEE								
Baker	Y	N	Y	N	N	Y	Y	Y
Sasser	Y	N	Y	N	N	N	N	Y

State / Senator	18	19	20	21	22	23	24	25
TEXAS								
Tower	Y	N	Y	?	Y	Y	Y	Y
Bentsen	N	N	Y	Y	N	Y	Y	Y
UTAH								
Garn	Y	N	Y	N	Y	Y	Y	Y
Hatch	Y	N	Y	Y	Y	Y	Y	Y
VERMONT								
Stafford	N	N	Y	Y	N	N	N	Y
Leahy	N	N	Y	Y	N	Y	N	Y
VIRGINIA								
Trible	Y	N	Y	Y	N	Y	Y	Y
Warner	N	N	Y	Y	N	Y	N	Y
WASHINGTON								
Evans	Y	N	Y	Y	N	Y	Y	Y
Gorton	Y	N	Y	Y	N	N	N	Y
WEST VIRGINIA								
Byrd	N	N	Y	N	N	Y	N	Y
Randolph	N	N	Y	Y	N	Y	Y	Y
WISCONSIN								
Kasten	Y	Y	Y	Y	N	Y	N	Y
Proxmire	N	N	Y	Y	N	Y	N	Y
WYOMING								
Simpson	Y	N	Y	N	Y	N	Y	Y
Wallop	Y	N	Y	N	N	Y	Y	Y

ND - Northern Democrats   SD - Southern Democrats (Southern states - Ala., Ark., Fla., Ga., Ky., La., Miss., N.C., Okla., S.C., Tenn., Texas, Va.)

18. S 979. Export Administration Act Amendments. Mc-Clure, R-Idaho, substitute for the Humphrey, R-N.H.-Roth, R-Del., amendment, to allow the president discretion to continue exports of nuclear materials and technology to countries not submitting to international inspection of their nuclear facilities. Rejected 38-55: R 32-21; D 6-34 (ND 2-26, SD 4-8), Feb. 28, 1984. A "yea" was a vote supporting the president's position. (The Humphrey-Roth amendment to ban exports of nuclear materials and technology to the countries in question subsequently was adopted by voice vote.)

19. S 2336. Credit Card Surcharge. D'Amato, R-N.Y., amendment to strike language allowing merchants to impose credit card surcharges and instead make permanent the ban on such surcharges. Rejected 22-66: R 16-35; D 6-31 (ND 6-20, SD 0-11), Feb. 28, 1984. A "nay" was a vote supporting the president's position.

20. S 2335. Credit Card Surcharge. Passage of the bill to extend the ban on credit-card surcharges from Feb. 27, 1984, until May 15, 1984. Passed 84-0: R 48-0; D 36-0 (ND 26-0, SD 10-0), Feb. 28, 1984.

21. S 979. Export Administration Act Amendments. Proxmire, D-Wis., amendment to the Atomic Energy Act of 1954 to replace congressional veto procedures with a requirement of a joint resolution or a bill to approve international nuclear cooperation agreements. Adopted 74-16: R 37-14; D 37-2 (ND 26-0, SD 11-2), Feb. 29, 1984.

22. S 979. Export Administration Act Amendments. Heinz, R-Pa., amendment to the Dixon, D-Ill., amendment, to allow the president to renew control on agricultural exports for successive, 60-day periods if he certifies to Congress that controls are necessary, effective and not harmful to farmers. Rejected 20-74: R 16-38; D 4-36 (ND 4-22, SD 0-14), Feb. 29, 1984. (The Dixon amendment to end agricultural export embargoes after 60 days unless approved by Congress subsequently was adopted by voice vote.)

23. S 979. Export Administration Act Amendments. Heinz, R-Pa., motion to table (kill) the Metzenbaum, D-Ohio, amendment to halt major oil company mergers for five years unless it can be demonstrated that the merger is necessary for development of new energy sources. Motion agreed to 61-34: R 42-13; D 19-21 (ND 12-14, SD 7-7), Feb. 29, 1984.

24. S 979. Export Administration Act Amendments/Oil Company Mergers. Heinz, R-Pa., motion to table (kill) the Johnston, D-La., amendment to the Mineral Lands Leasing Act to deny benefits of federal leases or federal rights of way to major oil companies involved in a merger occurring in the period beginning Feb. 27 and ending six months after enactment of S 979. Motion agreed to 52-42: R 43-11; D 9-31 (ND 4-22, SD 5-9), Feb. 29, 1984.

25. S 979. Export Administration Act Amendments. Heinz, R-Pa., motion to table (kill) the Murkowski, R-Alaska, amendment to allow the secretary of commerce five working days to notify Congress after receipt of an export license application for a petroleum product. The amendment was an unsuccessful tactical move to force a second vote that would have put senators on record on the question of oil exports before debating a subsequent amendment to lift a ban on Alaskan oil exports. Motion agreed to 94-2: R 52-2; D 42-0 (ND 28-0, SD 14-0), March 1, 1984.

	26	27	28	29	30	31		26	27	28	29	30	31		26	27	28	29	30	31
ALABAMA							**IOWA**							**NEW HAMPSHIRE**						
Denton	Y	Y	N	N	Y	Y	*Grassley*	Y	Y	N	Y	Y	Y	*Humphrey*	Y	Y	Y	Y	N	Y
Heflin	N	Y	N	Y	Y	Y	*Jepsen*	Y	N	N	Y	Y	N	*Rudman*	Y	Y	Y	Y	N	Y
ALASKA							**KANSAS**							**NEW JERSEY**						
Murkowski	Y	N	Y	Y	Y	Y	*Dole*	Y	Y	Y	Y	Y	Y	Bradley	Y	Y	?	?	?	Y
Stevens	Y	N	Y	Y	N	Y	*Kassebaum*	N	N	Y	Y	Y	Y	Lautenberg	Y	Y	Y	N	N	Y
ARIZONA							**KENTUCKY**							**NEW MEXICO**						
Goldwater	Y	Y	Y	?	?	Y	Ford	N	Y	N	?	?	N	*Domenici*	Y	Y	Y	Y	Y	Y
DeConcini	N	Y	N	N	Y	Y	Huddleston	N	+	?	?	?	Y	Bingaman	N	Y	N	Y	Y	N
ARKANSAS							**LOUISIANA**							**NEW YORK**						
Bumpers	N	Y	N	Y	Y	N	Johnston	N	Y	N	Y	Y	Y	*D'Amato*	Y	Y	Y	Y	N	Y
Pryor	N	Y	N	Y	Y	N	Long	Y	Y	N	Y	Y	Y	Moynihan	Y	Y	?	?	?	Y
CALIFORNIA							**MAINE**							**NORTH CAROLINA**						
Wilson	Y	Y	Y	Y	Y	Y	*Cohen*	Y	Y	Y	N	Y	Y	*East*	Y	Y	N	Y	Y	N
Cranston	?	?	?	?	?	N	Mitchell	N	Y	N	N	Y	Y	*Helms*	Y	Y	N	Y	Y	N
COLORADO							**MARYLAND**							**NORTH DAKOTA**						
Armstrong	Y	N	N	N	Y	Y	*Mathias*	Y	Y	Y	Y	N	Y	*Andrews*	N	Y	N	Y	Y	Y
Hart	?	?	?	?	?	?	Sarbanes	N	Y	N	N	Y	Y	Burdick	N	Y	N	Y	Y	N
CONNECTICUT							**MASSACHUSETTS**							**OHIO**						
Weicker	?	?	?	?	?	N	Kennedy	N	Y	N	N	Y	Y	Glenn	?	?	?	?	?	?
Dodd	N	Y	N	N	N	Y	Tsongas	Y	Y	N	N	Y	Y	Metzenbaum	Y	Y	?	N	N	N
DELAWARE							**MICHIGAN**							**OKLAHOMA**						
Roth	Y	N	Y	Y	N	Y	Levin	N	Y	N	N	Y	Y	*Nickles*	N	N	N	Y	Y	Y
Biden	Y	Y	N	Y	Y	Y	Riegle	N	Y	N	N	Y	Y	Boren	N	Y	N	Y	Y	Y
FLORIDA							**MINNESOTA**							**OREGON**						
Hawkins	Y	Y	Y	Y	N	Y	*Boschwitz*	N	N	Y	Y	Y	Y	*Hatfield*	N	Y	Y	Y	Y	N
Chiles	N	Y	N	N	Y	Y	*Durenberger*	N	Y	N	Y	Y	Y	*Packwood*	Y	Y	N	Y	Y	Y
GEORGIA							**MISSISSIPPI**							**PENNSYLVANIA**						
Mattingly	Y	Y	N	Y	N	Y	*Cochran*	Y	Y	Y	Y	N	Y	*Heinz*	Y	Y	Y	Y	Y	Y
Nunn	N	Y	N	Y	Y	Y	Stennis	N	Y	N	?	?	Y	*Specter*	Y	N	Y	Y	Y	Y
HAWAII							**MISSOURI**							**RHODE ISLAND**						
Inouye	N	Y	N	N	Y	Y	*Danforth*	Y	Y	Y	Y	Y	Y	*Chafee*	Y	?	?	?	?	Y
Matsunaga	N	Y	N	N	Y	Y	Eagleton	N	Y	N	Y	Y	+	Pell	N	Y	N	N	?	Y
IDAHO							**MONTANA**							**SOUTH CAROLINA**						
McClure	?	?	?	Y	Y	N	Baucus	N	Y	N	Y	Y	+	*Thurmond*	Y	N	N	Y	Y	Y
Symms	Y	N	Y	Y	N	Y	Melcher	N	Y	N	N	Y	Y	Hollings	N	?	?	?	?	?
ILLINOIS							**NEBRASKA**							**SOUTH DAKOTA**						
Percy	?	+	?	?	?	+	Exon	N	Y	N	Y	N	Y	*Abdnor*	N	Y	N	Y	Y	Y
Dixon	N	Y	N	Y	Y	Y	Zorinsky	N	Y	N	Y	N	Y	*Pressler*	N	Y	N	Y	Y	Y
INDIANA							**NEVADA**							**TENNESSEE**						
Lugar	Y	N	Y	Y	N	Y	*Hecht*	Y	Y	Y	Y	Y	Y	*Baker*	Y	Y	Y	?	?	Y
Quayle	Y	Y	Y	Y	N	Y	*Laxalt*	Y	N	Y	Y	Y	Y	Sasser	N	Y	N	N	Y	Y

KEY

Y Voted for (yea).
\# Paired for.
+ Announced for.
N Voted against (nay).
X Paired against.
- Announced against.
P Voted "present".
C Voted "present" to avoid possible conflict of interest.
? Did not vote or otherwise make a position known.

Democrats *Republicans*

	26	27	28	29	30	31
TEXAS						
Tower	Y	N	Y	Y	Y	Y
Bentsen	N	Y	N	Y	Y	Y
UTAH						
Garn	Y	Y	Y	Y	N	Y
Hatch	Y	N	Y	Y	N	Y
VERMONT						
Stafford	Y	Y	Y	Y	?	Y
Leahy	N	Y	N	Y	Y	Y
VIRGINIA						
Trible	Y	?	?	Y	N	Y
Warner	Y	Y	N	Y	N	Y
WASHINGTON						
Evans	Y	N	Y	Y	Y	Y
Gorton	Y	N	Y	Y	Y	Y
WEST VIRGINIA						
Byrd	N	Y	N	Y	Y	Y
Randolph	N	Y	N	Y	Y	Y
WISCONSIN						
Kasten	Y	Y	Y	N	Y	Y
Proxmire	Y	Y	Y	N	Y	Y
WYOMING						
Simpson	Y	N	Y	Y	Y	Y
Wallop	Y	N	Y	Y	Y	Y

ND - Northern Democrats   SD - Southern Democrats (Southern states - Ala., Ark., Fla., Ga., Ky., La., Miss., N.C., Okla., S.C., Tenn., Texas, Va.)

26. S 979. Export Administration Act Amendments. Baker, R-Tenn., motion to table (kill) the Melcher, D-Mont., amendment to reduce target prices — a major price support — for wheat and also reduce the amount of unplanted acreage required to participate in the Department of Agriculture's wheat program. Motion agreed to 52-42: R 44-8; D 8-34 (ND 7-21, SD 1-13), March 1, 1984.

27. S 979. Export Administration Act Amendments. Heinz, R-Pa., motion to table (kill) the Murkowski, R-Alaska, amendment to allow Alaskan oil exports of up to 200,000 barrels per day provided the cargo is carried on U.S. ships, which would be repaired in U.S. shipyards. Motion agreed to 70-20: R 31-19; D 39-1 (ND 27-1, SD 12-0), March 1, 1984.

28. S 979. Export Administration Act Amendments. Heinz, R-Pa., motion to table (kill) the Pryor, D-Ark., amendment to urge the president to nominate a person with experience in agriculture or small business for the next vacancy on the Federal Reserve Board. Motion rejected 37-50: R 35-15; D 2-35 (ND 2-23, SD 0-12), March 1, 1984.

29. S 979. Export Administration Act Amendments. Heinz, R-Pa., motion to table (kill) the Dodd, D-Conn., amendment to allow the president to apply export controls even if they would have the effect of breaking existing export contracts provided the controls are related to actual or impending acts of aggression and terrorism, violations of human rights, or nuclear weapons tests. Motion agreed to 65-21: R 46-4; D 19-17 (ND 11-15, SD 8-2), March 1, 1984.

30. S 979. Export Administration Act Amendments. Boren, D-Okla., amendment to express the sense of the Senate in favor of reducing target prices — a major price support — for wheat and also reducing the amount of unplanted acreage required to qualify for the Department of Agriculture's wheat program. Adopted 62-22: R 32-17; D 30-5 (ND 20-5, SD 10-0), March 1, 1984.

31. Wilson Nomination. Confirmation of President Reagan's nomination of William A. Wilson of California to be U.S. ambassador to the Holy See. Confirmed 81-13: R 48-6; D 33-7 (ND 23-4, SD 10-3), March 7, 1984. A "yea" was a vote supporting the president's position.

	32	33		32	33		32	33
ALABAMA			**IOWA**			**NEW HAMPSHIRE**		
Denton	Y	Y	*Grassley*	Y	Y	*Humphrey*	Y	Y
Heflin	Y	Y	*Jepsen*	Y	Y	*Rudman*	Y	N
ALASKA			**KANSAS**			**NEW JERSEY**		
Murkowski	Y	Y	*Dole*	Y	Y	Bradley	Y	Y
Stevens	Y	Y	*Kassebaum*	Y	Y	Lautenberg	Y	Y
ARIZONA			**KENTUCKY**			**NEW MEXICO**		
Goldwater	Y	Y	Ford	Y	Y	*Domenici*	Y	Y
DeConcini	Y	N	Huddleston	Y	Y	Bingaman	Y	Y
ARKANSAS			**LOUISIANA**			**NEW YORK**		
Bumpers	Y	Y	Johnston	Y	Y	*D'Amato*	Y	N
Pryor	Y	Y	Long	Y	N	Moynihan	Y	Y
CALIFORNIA			**MAINE**			**NORTH CAROLINA**		
Wilson	Y	Y	*Cohen*	Y	Y	*East*	Y	Y
Cranston	Y	Y	Mitchell	Y	N	*Helms*	Y	Y
COLORADO			**MARYLAND**			**NORTH DAKOTA**		
Armstrong	Y	Y	*Mathias*	?	Y	*Andrews*	Y	N
Hart	?	?	Sarbanes	Y	Y	Burdick	Y	Y
CONNECTICUT			**MASSACHUSETTS**			**OHIO**		
Weicker	Y	Y	Kennedy	Y	Y	Glenn	?	N
Dodd	Y	N	Tsongas	Y	Y	Metzenbaum	Y	Y
DELAWARE			**MICHIGAN**			**OKLAHOMA**		
Roth	Y	Y	Levin	Y	Y	*Nickles*	Y	Y
Biden	Y	N	Riegle	Y	Y	Boren	Y	Y
FLORIDA			**MINNESOTA**			**OREGON**		
Hawkins	Y	Y	*Boschwitz*	Y	Y	*Hatfield*	Y	#
Chiles	Y	Y	*Durenberger*	Y	Y	*Packwood*	Y	Y
GEORGIA			**MISSISSIPPI**			**PENNSYLVANIA**		
Mattingly	Y	Y	*Cochran*	Y	Y	*Heinz*	Y	N
Nunn	Y	N	Stennis	Y	Y	*Specter*	Y	Y
HAWAII			**MISSOURI**			**RHODE ISLAND**		
Inouye	Y	Y	*Danforth*	Y	Y	*Chafee*	Y	Y
Matsunaga	Y	Y	Eagleton	Y	Y	Pell	Y	N
IDAHO			**MONTANA**			**SOUTH CAROLINA**		
McClure	Y	Y	Baucus	Y	Y	*Thurmond*	Y	Y
Symms	Y	Y	Melcher	Y	N	Hollings	Y	Y
ILLINOIS			**NEBRASKA**			**SOUTH DAKOTA**		
Percy	+	X	Exon	Y	Y	*Abdnor*	Y	Y
Dixon	Y	N	Zorinsky	Y	Y	*Pressler*	Y	Y
INDIANA			**NEVADA**			**TENNESSEE**		
Lugar	Y	Y	*Hecht*	Y	Y	*Baker*	Y	Y
Quayle	Y	Y	*Laxalt*	Y	Y	Sasser	Y	N

	32	33
TEXAS		
Tower	Y	Y
Bentsen	Y	Y
UTAH		
Garn	Y	?
Hatch	Y	Y
VERMONT		
Stafford	Y	Y
Leahy	Y	Y
VIRGINIA		
Trible	Y	Y
Warner	Y	Y
WASHINGTON		
Evans	Y	Y
Gorton	Y	Y
WEST VIRGINIA		
Byrd	Y	Y
Randolph	Y	Y
WISCONSIN		
Kasten	Y	Y
Proxmire	Y	Y
WYOMING		
Simpson	Y	Y
Wallop	Y	Y

KEY

Y Voted for (yea).
\# Paired for.
\+ Announced for.
N Voted against (nay).
X Paired against.
\- Announced against.
P Voted "present".
C Voted "present" to avoid possible conflict of interest.
? Did not vote or otherwise make a position known.

Democrats   *Republicans*

ND - Northern Democrats   SD - Southern Democrats (Southern states - Ala., Ark., Fla., Ga., Ky., La., Miss., N.C., Okla., S.C., Tenn., Texas, Va.)

32. S J Res 73. Constitutional Amendment on School Prayer. Judiciary Committee amendment to provide that neither the federal government nor any state government shall compose the words to any school prayer. S J Res 73 would allow organized, vocal prayer in public schools. Adopted 96-0: R 53-0; D 43-0 (ND 29-0, SD 14-0), March 14, 1984.

33. S J Res 73. Constitutional Amendment on School Prayer. Baker, R-Tenn., motion to table (kill) the Dixon, D-Ill., amendment to allow individual group or silent prayer or reflection in public schools. A second section provided that it would not be an establishment of a state religion to allow "voluntary student religious groups" to meet in public facilities. Motion agreed to 81-15: R 48-4; D 33-11 (ND 22-8, SD 11-3), March 15, 1984.

	34	35	36	37	38	39
ALABAMA						
Denton	Y	Y	Y	Y	Y	Y
Heflin	Y	Y	Y	Y	N	Y
ALASKA						
Murkowski	Y	Y	Y	Y	Y	Y
Stevens	Y	Y	Y	Y	Y	Y
ARIZONA						
Goldwater	N	Y	Y	Y	Y	N
DeConcini	N	Y	?	?	?	?
ARKANSAS						
Bumpers	N	Y	N	N	N	N
Pryor	Y	Y	N	N	N	N
CALIFORNIA						
Wilson	Y	Y	Y	Y	Y	Y
Cranston	N	Y	?	?	?	?
COLORADO						
Armstrong	Y	N	Y	Y	Y	Y
Hart	N	Y	?	?	?	?
CONNECTICUT						
Weicker	N	Y	Y	Y	?	?
Dodd	N	Y	N	?	?	?
DELAWARE						
Roth	Y	Y	Y	Y	Y	N
Biden	N	Y	N	Y	Y	Y
FLORIDA						
Hawkins	Y	Y	Y	Y	Y	Y
Chiles	Y	Y	N	Y	Y	Y
GEORGIA						
Mattingly	Y	Y	Y	Y	Y	Y
Nunn	Y	Y	Y	N	Y	Y
HAWAII						
Inouye	N	Y	N	N	N	Y
Matsunaga	N	Y	N	N	N	Y
IDAHO						
McClure	Y	Y	Y	Y	Y	Y
Symms	Y	Y	Y	Y	Y	Y
ILLINOIS						
Percy	Y	?	?	?	?	?
Dixon	N	Y	N	N	Y	+
INDIANA						
Lugar	Y	N	Y	Y	Y	Y
Quayle	Y	Y	Y	Y	Y	Y

	34	35	36	37	38	39
IOWA						
Grassley	Y	Y	Y	N	Y	Y
Jepsen	Y	Y	Y	N	Y	Y
KANSAS						
Dole	Y	N	Y	Y	Y	Y
Kassebaum	N	Y	Y	Y	Y	+
KENTUCKY						
Ford	Y	Y	N	N	N	Y
Huddleston	Y	Y	?	?	?	?
LOUISIANA						
Johnston	Y	Y	N	N	N	N
Long	Y	Y	N	Y	Y	X
MAINE						
Cohen	N	Y	Y	Y	Y	Y
Mitchell	N	Y	Y	Y	Y	Y
MARYLAND						
Mathias	N	?	Y	Y	Y	Y
Sarbanes	N	Y	N	N	N	Y
MASSACHUSETTS						
Kennedy	N	Y	N	N	N	Y
Tsongas	N	Y	N	Y	Y	Y
MICHIGAN						
Levin	N	Y	N	N	Y	Y
Riegle	N	Y	N	N	N	Y
MINNESOTA						
Boschwitz	N	Y	Y	Y	Y	Y
Durenberger	N	Y	Y	Y	Y	Y
MISSISSIPPI						
Cochran	Y	N	Y	Y	Y	Y
Stennis	Y	Y	N	N	N	Y
MISSOURI						
Danforth	N	N	Y	Y	Y	Y
Eagleton	N	Y	N	N	N	Y
MONTANA						
Baucus	N	Y	N	N	N	Y
Melcher	Y	Y	N	N	N	Y
NEBRASKA						
Exon	Y	Y	N	N	N	N
Zorinsky	Y	Y	N	N	N	N
NEVADA						
Hecht	Y	Y	Y	Y	Y	Y
Laxalt	Y	Y	Y	Y	Y	Y

	34	35	36	37	38	39
NEW HAMPSHIRE						
Humphrey	Y	Y	Y	Y	Y	Y
Rudman	N	Y	Y	Y	Y	Y
NEW JERSEY						
Bradley	N	Y	N	Y	Y	Y
Lautenberg	N	Y	N	N	Y	Y
NEW MEXICO						
Domenici	Y	N	Y	Y	Y	Y
Bingaman	N	Y	N	N	Y	Y
NEW YORK						
D'Amato	Y	Y	Y	Y	Y	Y
Moynihan	N	Y	Y	Y	Y	#
NORTH CAROLINA						
East	Y	Y	Y	Y	Y	Y
Helms	Y	Y	Y	Y	Y	Y
NORTH DAKOTA						
Andrews	N	Y	Y	Y	N	Y
Burdick	N	Y	N	N	N	Y
OHIO						
Glenn	N	Y	N	N	Y	Y
Metzenbaum	N	Y	N	N	Y	N
OKLAHOMA						
Nickles	Y	N	Y	Y	Y	Y
Boren	Y	Y	N	N	N	Y
OREGON						
Hatfield	N	Y	N	Y	Y	Y
Packwood	N	Y	N	Y	N	Y
PENNSYLVANIA						
Heinz	N	Y	Y	Y	Y	Y
Specter	N	N	Y	Y	Y	Y
RHODE ISLAND						
Chafee	N	Y	Y	Y	Y	Y
Pell	N	Y	Y	N	Y	N
SOUTH CAROLINA						
Thurmond	Y	Y	Y	Y	Y	Y
Hollings	Y	Y	N	N	N	N
SOUTH DAKOTA						
Abdnor	Y	Y	Y	Y	Y	Y
Pressler	Y	Y	Y	Y	Y	Y
TENNESSEE						
Baker	Y	N	Y	Y	Y	Y
Sasser	Y	Y	N	N	N	Y

KEY

Y	Voted for (yea).
#	Paired for.
+	Announced for.
N	Voted against (nay).
X	Paired against.
-	Announced against.
P	Voted "present".
C	Voted "present" to avoid possible conflict of interest.
?	Did not vote or otherwise make a position known.

Democrats   *Republicans*

	34	35	36	37	38	39
TEXAS						
Tower	Y	N	Y	Y	Y	Y
Bentsen	Y	Y	N	N	N	Y
UTAH						
Garn	Y	Y	Y	Y	Y	Y
Hatch	Y	Y	Y	Y	Y	Y
VERMONT						
Stafford	N	Y	Y	Y	Y	Y
Leahy	N	Y	N	N	N	Y
VIRGINIA						
Trible	Y	Y	Y	Y	Y	Y
Warner	Y	Y	Y	Y	Y	Y
WASHINGTON						
Evans	N	N	Y	Y	Y	Y
Gorton	N	Y	Y	Y	Y	Y
WEST VIRGINIA						
Byrd	Y	Y	N	N	N	Y
Randolph	Y	Y	N	N	N	+
WISCONSIN						
Kasten	Y	Y	Y	Y	Y	Y
Proxmire	Y	N	Y	Y	Y	Y
WYOMING						
Simpson	Y	Y	Y	Y	Y	Y
Wallop	Y	Y	Y	Y	Y	Y

ND - Northern Democrats   SD - Southern Democrats (Southern states - Ala., Ark., Fla., Ga., Ky., La., Miss., N.C., Okla., S.C., Tenn., Texas, Va.)

34. S J Res 73. Constitutional Amendment on School Prayer. Passage of the joint resolution to propose an amendment to the Constitution to permit organized, recited prayer in public schools and other public places. Rejected 56-44: R 37-18; D 19-26 (ND 6-25, SD 13-1), March 20, 1984. A two-thirds majority of those present and voting (67 in this case) of both houses is required for passage of a joint resolution proposing an amendment to the Constitution. A "yea" was a vote supporting the president's position.

35. S 684. Water Research Veto. Passage, over President Reagan's Feb. 21 veto, of the bill to authorize $36 million annually for fiscal years 1985 through 1989 for water resources research programs to be administered by the Interior Department, including matching grants for state water research institutes. Passed 86-12: R 42-11; D 44-1 (ND 30-1, SD 14-0), March 21, 1984. A two-thirds majority of those present and voting (66 in this case) of both houses is required to override a veto. A "nay" was a vote supporting the president's position.

36. HR 4072. Agricultural Programs Adjustment Act. Baker, R-Tenn., motion to table (kill) the Pryor, D-Ark., amendment to compensate farmers who suffered losses due to grain elevator failures. Motion agreed to 61-34: R 54-0; D 7-34 (ND 5-23, SD 2-11), March 22, 1984.

37. HR 4072. Agricultural Programs Adjustment Act. Baker, R-Tenn., motion to table (kill) the Bumpers, D-Ark., amendment to require that land left unplanted because a farmer was participating in a crop reduction program would not be included in evaluations of disaster loan applications. Motion agreed to 58-36: R 50-4; D 8-32 (ND 6-21, SD 2-11), March 22, 1984.

38. HR 4072. Agricultural Programs Adjustment Act. Baker, R-Tenn., motion to table (kill) the Melcher, D-Mont., amendment to raise the wheat target price support in 1985 from $4.38 per bushel to $4.45 per bushel. Motion agreed to 68-25: R 52-1; D 16-24 (ND 13-14, SD 3-10), March 22, 1984.

39. HR 4072. Agricultural Programs Adjustment Act. Passage of the bill to cut target prices for wheat in 1984 and 1985 and to freeze 1985 target prices for corn, cotton and rice at 1984 levels. It also set terms for a wheat acreage reduction program in 1984 and 1985, required acreage reduction programs in 1985 for corn, cotton and rice if certain levels of surpluses were reached, enlarged farm credit programs, authorized changes in disaster loan programs and expanded farm export programs. Passed 78-10: R 50-2; D 28-8 (ND 20-4, SD 8-4), March 22, 1984. A "yea" was a vote supporting the president's position.

	40 41 42		40 41 42		40 41 42	KEY
ALABAMA		**IOWA**		**NEW HAMPSHIRE**		Y Voted for (yea).
Denton	? + N	*Grassley*	N N N	*Humphrey*	Y Y N	# Paired for.
Heflin	N Y N	*Jepsen*	N Y N	*Rudman*	Y Y N	+ Announced for.
ALASKA		**KANSAS**		**NEW JERSEY**		N Voted against (nay).
Murkowski	N Y N	*Dole*	N Y N	Bradley	Y Y N	X Paired against.
Stevens	N Y N	*Kassebaum*	Y Y N	Lautenberg	Y N Y	- Announced against.
ARIZONA		**KENTUCKY**		**NEW MEXICO**		P Voted "present".
Goldwater	N Y N	Ford	Y ? ?	*Domenici*	N Y N	C Voted "present" to avoid possible conflict of interest.
DeConcini	N Y N	Huddleston	Y ? ?	Bingaman	N N Y	
ARKANSAS		**LOUISIANA**		**NEW YORK**		? Did not vote or otherwise make a position known.
Bumpers	Y Y N	Johnston	Y Y N	*D'Amato*	N Y N	
Pryor	N Y N	Long	N Y N	Moynihan	Y ? N	Democrats *Republicans*
CALIFORNIA		**MAINE**		**NORTH CAROLINA**		
Wilson	N Y N	*Cohen*	Y Y N	*East*	N Y N	
Cranston	Y N Y	Mitchell	Y Y Y	*Helms*	N Y N	
COLORADO		**MARYLAND**		**NORTH DAKOTA**		40 41 42
Armstrong	N + -	*Mathias*	N Y Y	*Andrews*	Y Y N	
Hart	? ? +	Sarbanes	Y N Y	Burdick	N N Y	
CONNECTICUT		**MASSACHUSETTS**		**OHIO**		**TEXAS**	
Weicker	Y N Y	Kennedy	N N Y	Glenn	Y Y N	*Tower*	N Y N
Dodd	Y N Y	Tsongas	N N Y	Metzenbaum	Y N Y	Bentsen	N Y N
DELAWARE		**MICHIGAN**		**OKLAHOMA**		**UTAH**	
Roth	N Y N	Levin	Y N Y	*Nickles*	N Y N	*Garn*	N Y N
Biden	N Y N	Riegle	Y N Y	Boren	N Y N	*Hatch*	N Y N
FLORIDA		**MINNESOTA**		**OREGON**		**VERMONT**	
Hawkins	? ? N	*Boschwitz*	Y Y N	*Hatfield*	Y N Y	*Stafford*	N Y N
Chiles	Y Y N	*Durenberger*	N Y N	*Packwood*	Y Y N	Leahy	Y N Y
GEORGIA		**MISSISSIPPI**		**PENNSYLVANIA**		**VIRGINIA**	
Mattingly	N Y N	*Cochran*	N Y N	*Heinz*	Y ? N	*Trible*	N Y N
Nunn	Y Y N	Stennis	Y Y N	*Specter*	N N Y	*Warner*	N Y N
HAWAII		**MISSOURI**		**RHODE ISLAND**		**WASHINGTON**	
Inouye	Y Y N	*Danforth*	Y Y N	*Chafee*	N Y N	*Evans*	N Y N
Matsunaga	Y ? Y	Eagleton	Y Y N	Pell	Y N Y	*Gorton*	Y Y N
IDAHO		**MONTANA**		**SOUTH CAROLINA**		**WEST VIRGINIA**	
McClure	N Y N	Baucus	N Y N	*Thurmond*	N Y -	Byrd	N Y N
Symms	N Y N	Melcher	Y N Y	Hollings	? Y N	Randolph	N Y Y
ILLINOIS		**NEBRASKA**		**SOUTH DAKOTA**		**WISCONSIN**	
Percy	N Y N	Exon	N Y N	*Abdnor*	Y Y N	*Kasten*	N Y N
Dixon	N Y N	Zorinsky	N Y N	*Pressler*	Y Y N	Proxmire	Y N Y
INDIANA		**NEVADA**		**TENNESSEE**		**WYOMING**	
Lugar	N Y N	*Hecht*	N Y N	*Baker*	N Y N	*Simpson*	N Y N
Quayle	N Y N	*Laxalt*	N Y N	Sasser	N N Y	*Wallop*	N Y N

ND - Northern Democrats   SD - Southern Democrats (Southern states - Ala., Ark., Fla., Ga., Ky., La., Miss., N.C., Okla., S.C., Tenn., Texas, Va.)

40. H J Res 492. Department of Agriculture, Fiscal 1984 Urgent Supplemental Appropriations. Rudman, R-N.H., motion to table (kill) the Baker, R-Tenn., substitute to the Johnston, D-La., amendment, to strike an 11-month moratorium on oil mergers, requiring instead that Senate committees study the issue. Motion rejected 39-57: R 14-39; D 25-18 (ND 18-12, SD 7-6), March 28, 1984. (The Baker amendment and the Johnston amendment, as amended, subsequently were adopted by voice vote.)

41. H J Res 492. Department of Agriculture, Fiscal 1984 Urgent Supplemental Appropriations. Baker, R-Tenn., motion to table (kill) the Kennedy, D-Mass., amendment to require congressional authorization for the introduction of combat forces in or over El Salvador, Honduras or Nicaragua. Motion agreed to 71-20: R 47-4; D 24-16 (ND 13-15, SD 11-1), March 29, 1984. A "yea" was a vote supporting the president's position.

42. H J Res 492. Department of Agriculture, Fiscal 1984 Urgent Supplemental Appropriations. Kennedy, D-Mass., amendment to require congressional authorization for the introduction of combat forces in or over El Salvador or Nicaragua. Rejected 23-72: R 4-49; D 19-23 (ND 18-12, SD 1-11), March 29, 1984. A "nay" was a vote supporting the president's position.

	43	44	45	46	47	48	49	50
ALABAMA								
Denton	?	+	+	N	N	Y	Y	Y
Heflin	Y	Y	Y	N	N	Y	Y	Y
ALASKA								
Murkowski	Y	Y	Y	N	N	Y	Y	Y
Stevens	Y	Y	Y	N	N	Y	Y	Y
ARIZONA								
Goldwater	Y	N	Y	N	N	Y	Y	Y
DeConcini	?	?	?	?	?	?	?	?
ARKANSAS								
Bumpers	Y	Y	Y	?	?	Y	N	N
Pryor	Y	Y	Y	N	Y	Y	N	Y
CALIFORNIA								
Wilson	Y	?	Y	N	N	Y	Y	?
Cranston	?	?	?	Y	Y	N	N	N
COLORADO								
Armstrong	?	?	?	N	N	Y	Y	Y
Hart	?	?	?	?	?	?	?	?
CONNECTICUT								
Weicker	Y	Y	Y	Y	N	N	N	N
Dodd	?	?	?	Y	Y	N	N	N
DELAWARE								
Roth	Y	N	Y	N	N	Y	Y	Y
Biden	Y	Y	Y	Y	Y	N	N	N
FLORIDA								
Hawkins	?	?	?	N	N	Y	Y	Y
Chiles	Y	Y	Y	N	N	Y	Y	Y
GEORGIA								
Mattingly	Y	N	Y	N	N	Y	Y	Y
Nunn	?	?	?	N	N	Y	Y	Y
HAWAII								
Inouye	Y	Y	Y	N	N	Y	Y	Y
Matsunaga	?	Y	Y	Y	Y	N	N	N
IDAHO								
McClure	Y	Y	Y	N	N	Y	Y	Y
Symms	?	?	?	N	N	Y	Y	Y
ILLINOIS								
Percy	Y	Y	Y	N	N	Y	Y	Y
Dixon	Y	Y	Y	N	N	?	?	?
INDIANA								
Lugar	Y	N	Y	N	N	Y	Y	Y
Quayle	?	?	?	-	-	Y	Y	Y
IOWA								
Grassley	Y	N	Y	N	N	Y	Y	Y
Jepsen	?	?	?	N	N	Y	Y	Y
KANSAS								
Dole	Y	N	Y	N	N	Y	Y	?
Kassebaum	Y	N	Y	N	N	Y	Y	Y
KENTUCKY								
Ford	?	?	?	Y	N	N	N	Y
Huddleston	?	?	?	?	?	N	N	N
LOUISIANA								
Johnston	Y	Y	Y	N	Y	Y	Y	Y
Long	Y	Y	Y	N	N	Y	Y	Y
MAINE								
Cohen	Y	Y	Y	N	N	Y	N	Y
Mitchell	Y	Y	Y	N	N	N	N	N
MARYLAND								
Mathias	Y	Y	Y	N	N	Y	N	Y
Sarbanes	Y	Y	Y	Y	N	N	N	N
MASSACHUSETTS								
Kennedy	?	?	?	Y	N	N	N	N
Tsongas	?	?	?	Y	Y	N	?	?
MICHIGAN								
Levin	Y	Y	Y	Y	N	N	Y	Y
Riegle	Y	Y	Y	Y	N	N	N	N
MINNESOTA								
Boschwitz	Y	Y	Y	N	N	Y	Y	Y
Durenberger	Y	?	Y	N	N	Y	Y	Y
MISSISSIPPI								
Cochran	Y	?	?	N	Y	Y	Y	Y
Stennis	Y	Y	Y	N	N	Y	Y	Y
MISSOURI								
Danforth	Y	Y	Y	N	N	Y	Y	Y
Eagleton	Y	Y	Y	Y	N	N	N	N
MONTANA								
Baucus	Y	Y	Y	Y	N	N	Y	Y
Melcher	Y	Y	Y	Y	N	N	N	N
NEBRASKA								
Exon	?	Y	Y	Y	Y	N	Y	N
Zorinsky	Y	Y	Y	Y	Y	N	Y	N
NEVADA								
Hecht	Y	N	Y	N	N	Y	Y	Y
Laxalt	?	Y	Y	N	?	Y	Y	Y
NEW HAMPSHIRE								
Humphrey	N	N	Y	N	N	Y	Y	Y
Rudman	Y	Y	Y	N	N	Y	Y	Y
NEW JERSEY								
Bradley	?	?	?	N	N	N	N	N
Lautenberg	?	?	?	Y	N	N	N	N
NEW MEXICO								
Domenici	Y	N	Y	N	N	Y	Y	Y
Bingaman	Y	N	Y	N	Y	N	N	N
NEW YORK								
D'Amato	Y	Y	Y	?	?	Y	N	Y
Moynihan	?	Y	Y	?	?	Y	N	Y
NORTH CAROLINA								
East	Y	Y	Y	N	N	Y	Y	Y
Helms	Y	Y	Y	N	N	Y	Y	Y
NORTH DAKOTA								
Andrews	Y	Y	Y	N	Y	Y	Y	Y
Burdick	?	?	?	?	?	?	?	?
OHIO								
Glenn	Y	Y	Y	N	N	N	N	Y
Metzenbaum	Y	Y	Y	?	?	Y	N	N
OKLAHOMA								
Nickles	Y	N	Y	?	N	Y	Y	Y
Boren	Y	N	Y	N	N	Y	Y	?
OREGON								
Hatfield	+	?	+	Y	Y	N	N	N
Packwood	Y	Y	Y	?	?	Y	N	N
PENNSYLVANIA								
Heinz	Y	Y	Y	N	N	Y	N	Y
Specter	Y	Y	Y	N	N	Y	N	Y
RHODE ISLAND								
Chafee	Y	N	Y	N	N	Y	Y	Y
Pell	Y	Y	Y	Y	N	N	N	N
SOUTH CAROLINA								
Thurmond	Y	N	Y	N	N	Y	Y	Y
Hollings	Y	Y	Y	N	N	Y	Y	?
SOUTH DAKOTA								
Abdnor	Y	Y	Y	N	N	Y	Y	Y
Pressler	Y	Y	Y	N	Y	N	N	Y
TENNESSEE								
Baker	Y	Y	Y	N	N	?	?	?
Sasser	Y	Y	Y	Y	Y	?	N	N
TEXAS								
Tower	?	?	?	N	N	Y	Y	Y
Bentsen	Y	Y	Y	N	N	Y	Y	Y
UTAH								
Garn	Y	Y	Y	N	N	Y	Y	Y
Hatch	Y	Y	Y	N	N	Y	Y	Y
VERMONT								
Stafford	?	?	?	?	?	?	?	?
Leahy	Y	Y	Y	Y	N	N	N	N
VIRGINIA								
Trible	?	Y	Y	N	N	Y	Y	Y
Warner	Y	N	Y	N	N	Y	Y	Y
WASHINGTON								
Evans	Y	N	Y	N	N	Y	Y	Y
Gorton	Y	N	Y	N	N	Y	Y	Y
WEST VIRGINIA								
Byrd	Y	Y	Y	N	N	Y	N	Y
Randolph	Y	Y	Y	Y	Y	Y	N	Y
WISCONSIN								
Kasten	Y	Y	Y	N	N	Y	Y	Y
Proxmire	N	N	Y	Y	N	N	N	N
WYOMING								
Simpson	?	Y	Y	N	N	Y	Y	Y
Wallop	Y	Y	Y	N	?	Y	Y	Y

ND - Northern Democrats   SD - Southern Democrats (Southern states - Ala., Ark., Fla., Ga., Ky., La., Miss., N.C., Okla., S.C., Tenn., Texas, Va.)

43. H J Res 492. Department of Agriculture, Fiscal 1984 Urgent Supplemental Appropriations. Cochran, R-Miss., amendment to provide $175 million for credits under the "Food for Peace" program, and reduce emergency food aid to Africa from $150 million to $60 million. Adopted 71-2: R 42-1; D 29-1 (ND 18-1, SD 11-0), March 30, 1984.

44. H J Res 492. Department of Agriculture, Fiscal 1984 Urgent Supplemental Appropriations. Melcher, D-Mont., amendment to provide $5 million in emergency food aid to the Philippines. Adopted 57-19: R 27-16; D 30-3 (ND 20-2, SD 10-1), March 30, 1984.

45. S 2507. Bankruptcy Act Extension. Passage of the bill to extend a transitional period of 1978 bankruptcy reform legislation (PL 95-598) for 30 days, from March 31, 1984, to April 30, 1984. Passed 78-0: R 45-0; D 33-0 (ND 22-0, SD 11-0), March 30, 1984.

46. H J Res 492. Department of Agriculture, Fiscal 1984 Urgent Supplemental Appropriations. Kennedy, D-Mass., amendment to cut funding for military assistance to El Salvador from $61.75 million to $21 million. Rejected 25-63: R 2-48; D 23-15 (ND 21-5, SD 2-10), April 2, 1984. A "nay" was a vote supporting the president's position.

47. H J Res 492. Department of Agriculture, Fiscal 1984 Urgent Supplemental Appropriations. Melcher, D-Mont., amendment to cut funding for El Salvador from $61.75 million to $35.4 million. Rejected 24-63: R 4-45; D 20-18 (ND 18-8, SD 2-10), April 2, 1984. A "nay" was a vote supporting the president's position.

48. H J Res 492. Department of Agriculture, Fiscal 1984 Urgent Supplemental Appropriations. Kasten, R-Wis., motion to table (kill) the Kennedy, D-Mass., amendment to withhold 15 percent of the military aid contained in the bill until the Salvadoran government has obtained a verdict with respect to the murder of two U.S. labor advisers in January 1981 in El Salvador. Motion agreed to 69-24: R 50-3; D 19-21 (ND 8-19, SD 11-2), April 3, 1984. A "yea" was a vote supporting the president's position.

49. H J Res 492. Department of Agriculture, Fiscal 1984 Urgent Supplemental Appropriations. Kasten, R-Wis., motion to table (kill) the Specter, R-Pa., amendment to withhold 30 percent of the aid in the bill or subsequently appropriated until the Salvadoran government has obtained a verdict in the murder of four U.S. churchwomen in El Salvador. Motion agreed to 54-39: R 44-9; D 10-30 (ND 1-25, SD 9-5), April 3, 1984. A "yea" was a vote supporting the president's position.

50. H J Res 492. Department of Agriculture, Fiscal 1984 Urgent Supplemental Appropriations. Kasten, R-Wis., motion to table (kill) the Kennedy, D-Mass., amendment to withhold military aid to El Salvador until the government agrees to participate in unconditional negotiations with major parties to the conflict in that country. Motion agreed to 63-26: R 47-4; D 16-22 (ND 7-19, SD 9-3), April 3, 1984. A "yea" was a vote supporting the president's position.

KEY

- Y Voted for (yea).
- # Paired for.
- + Announced for.
- N Voted against (nay).
- X Paired against.
- - Announced against.
- P Voted "present".
- C Voted "present" to avoid possible conflict of interest.
- ? Did not vote or otherwise make a position known.

Democrats   *Republicans*

ND - Northern Democrats   SD - Southern Democrats (Southern states - Ala., Ark., Fla., Ga., Ky., La., Miss., N.C., Okla., S.C., Tenn., Texas, Va.)

	51	52	53	54	55	56	57
ALABAMA							
Denton	Y	N	Y	Y	Y	Y	Y
Heflin	Y	N	Y	Y	Y	Y	N
ALASKA							
Murkowski	Y	N	Y	Y	Y	Y	Y
Stevens	Y	N	Y	Y	Y	Y	Y
ARIZONA							
Goldwater	Y	N	Y	Y	Y	Y	?
DeConcini	?	?	?	?	?	?	?
ARKANSAS							
Bumpers	N	Y	N	N	N	Y	N
Pryor	N	Y	N	N	N	Y	N
CALIFORNIA							
Wilson	Y	N	Y	Y	Y	Y	Y
Cranston	N	Y	N	N	N	N	N
COLORADO							
Armstrong	Y	N	Y	Y	Y	Y	Y
Hart	?	#	?	?	X	?	?
CONNECTICUT							
Weicker	N	?	?	N	N	N	N
Dodd	N	Y	N	N	N	N	Y
DELAWARE							
Roth	Y	N	Y	Y	Y	Y	Y
Biden	N	Y	N	N	N	N	N
FLORIDA							
Hawkins	Y	-	?	Y	Y	Y	Y
Chiles	Y	N	N	Y	N	Y	Y
GEORGIA							
Mattingly	Y	N	Y	Y	Y	Y	Y
Nunn	Y	N	N	?	N	Y	Y
HAWAII							
Inouye	N	?	N	N	N	Y	N
Matsunaga	N	Y	N	N	N	N	N
IDAHO							
McClure	Y	N	Y	Y	Y	Y	Y
Symms	Y	N	Y	Y	Y	Y	Y
ILLINOIS							
Percy	Y	N	Y	Y	Y	Y	Y
Dixon	N	N	N	N	N	Y	Y
INDIANA							
Lugar	Y	N	Y	Y	Y	Y	Y
Quayle	Y	N	Y	Y	Y	Y	Y
IOWA							
Grassley	Y	N	N	N	Y	Y	Y
Jepsen	Y	N	Y	Y	Y	Y	Y
KANSAS							
Dole	Y	N	Y	Y	Y	Y	Y
Kassebaum	Y	Y	Y	Y	Y	Y	Y
KENTUCKY							
Ford	N	N	N	N	N	Y	N
Huddleston	Y	N	N	N	N	Y	?
LOUISIANA							
Johnston	Y	N	N	Y	N	Y	N
Long	Y	X	Y	Y	#	Y	N
MAINE							
Cohen	Y	N	N	N	Y	N	Y
Mitchell	N	Y	N	N	N	N	N
MARYLAND							
Mathias	Y	N	?	N	N	Y	Y
Sarbanes	N	Y	N	N	N	N	N
MASSACHUSETTS							
Kennedy	N	Y	N	N	N	N	N
Tsongas	?	Y	N	N	?	N	Y
MICHIGAN							
Levin	N	Y	N	N	N	N	N
Riegle	N	Y	N	N	N	N	N
MINNESOTA							
Boschwitz	Y	N	N	Y	Y	Y	Y
Durenberger	Y	N	Y	Y	Y	Y	Y
MISSISSIPPI							
Cochran	Y	N	Y	Y	Y	Y	Y
Stennis	Y	N	?	N	N	Y	Y
MISSOURI							
Danforth	Y	N	Y	Y	Y	Y	Y
Eagleton	N	Y	N	N	N	Y	N
MONTANA							
Baucus	N	Y	N	N	N	N	N
Melcher	N	Y	N	N	N	N	N
NEBRASKA							
Exon	N	Y	N	N	N	N	N
Zorinsky	Y	Y	N	N	N	Y	N
NEW HAMPSHIRE							
Humphrey	Y	N	Y	Y	Y	Y	Y
Rudman	Y	N	Y	Y	Y	Y	Y
NEW JERSEY							
Bradley	N	Y	N	N	N	Y	N
Lautenberg	N	Y	N	N	N	Y	N
NEW MEXICO							
Domenici	Y	N	Y	Y	Y	Y	Y
Bingaman	N	Y	N	N	N	N	Y
NEW YORK							
D'Amato	Y	N	Y	Y	Y	Y	Y
Moynihan	N	N	N	N	N	N	Y
NORTH CAROLINA							
East	Y	N	Y	Y	Y	Y	Y
Helms	Y	N	Y	Y	Y	Y	Y
NORTH DAKOTA							
Andrews	N	N	N	N	Y	Y	?
Burdick	?	?	?	?	?	?	?
OHIO							
Glenn	Y	Y	?	N	N	N	Y
Metzenbaum	N	Y	N	N	N	N	Y
OKLAHOMA							
Nickles	Y	N	Y	Y	Y	Y	Y
Boren	Y	N	N	Y	N	Y	N
OREGON							
Hatfield	N	Y	N	N	N	N	N
Packwood	Y	N	Y	Y	Y	Y	Y
PENNSYLVANIA							
Heinz	Y	N	Y	Y	Y	Y	Y
Specter	N	Y	Y	Y	Y	Y	Y
RHODE ISLAND							
Chafee	Y	N	Y	Y	Y	Y	Y
Pell	N	Y	N	N	N	N	N
SOUTH CAROLINA							
Thurmond	Y	N	Y	Y	Y	Y	Y
Hollings	N	N	Y	N	N	Y	N
SOUTH DAKOTA							
Abdnor	Y	N	Y	Y	Y	Y	Y
Pressler	N	Y	Y	N	N	Y	Y
TENNESSEE							
Baker	Y	N	Y	Y	Y	Y	Y
Sasser	N	Y	N	N	N	Y	N

	51	52	53	54	55	56	57
TEXAS							
Tower	Y	N	Y	Y	Y	Y	Y
Bentsen	N	N	?	N	N	Y	Y
UTAH							
Garn	Y	N	Y	Y	Y	Y	Y
Hatch	Y	N	Y	Y	Y	Y	Y
VERMONT							
Stafford	?	?	?	?	?	?	?
Leahy	N	Y	N	N	N	N	Y
VIRGINIA							
Trible	Y	N	Y	Y	Y	Y	Y
Warner	Y	N	Y	Y	Y	Y	Y
WASHINGTON							
Evans	Y	N	Y	Y	+	Y	Y
Gorton	Y	N	Y	Y	Y	Y	Y
WEST VIRGINIA							
Byrd	N	N	N	N	N	Y	N
Randolph	N	N	N	N	N	Y	N
WISCONSIN							
Kasten	Y	N	Y	Y	Y	Y	Y
Proxmire	N	Y	N	N	N	N	Y
WYOMING							
Simpson	Y	N	Y	Y	Y	Y	Y
Wallop	Y	N	Y	Y	Y	Y	Y

51. H J Res 492. Department of Agriculture, Fiscal 1984 Urgent Supplemental Appropriations. Baker, R-Tenn., motion to table (kill) the Leahy, D-Vt., amendment to require congressional authorization for the introduction of combat troops in or over El Salvador. Motion agreed to 59-36: R 49-5; D 10-31 (ND 2-25, SD 8-6), April 4, 1984. A "yea" was a vote supporting the president's position.

52. H J Res 492. Department of Agriculture, Fiscal 1984 Urgent Supplemental Appropriations. Kennedy, D-Mass., amendment to delete $21 million in the bill for covert aid to Nicaraguan rebels. Rejected 30-61: R 4-47; D 26-14 (ND 23-4, SD 3-10), April 4, 1984. A "nay" was a vote supporting the president's position.

53. H J Res 492. Department of Agriculture, Fiscal 1984 Urgent Supplemental Appropriations. Rudman, R-N.H., motion to table (kill) the Dodd, D-Conn., amendment to bar the use of covert funds for sabotage or terrorism in Nicaragua. Motion agreed to 47-43: R 44-7; D 3-36 (ND 0-27, SD 3-9), April 4, 1984.

54. H J Res 492. Department of Agriculture, Fiscal 1984 Urgent Supplemental Appropriations. Stevens, R-Alaska, motion to table (kill) the Levin, D-Mich., amendment to bar the use of covert funds to overthrow a government of a country with which the U.S. has full diplomatic relations. Motion agreed to 51-44: R 46-8; D 5-36 (ND 0-28, SD 5-8), April 5, 1984. A "yea" was a vote supporting the president's position.

55. H J Res 492. Department of Agriculture, Fiscal 1984 Urgent Supplemental Appropriations. Stevens, R-Alaska, motion to table (kill) the Sasser, D-Tenn., amendment to bar the use of Department of Defense operations and maintenance funds to convert temporary facilities in Honduras used for military exercises to permanent facilities. Motion agreed to 50-44: R 49-4; D 1-40 (ND 0-28, SD 1-12), April 5, 1984. A "yea" was a vote supporting the president's position.

56. H J Res 492. Department of Agriculture, Fiscal 1984 Urgent Supplemental Appropriations. Passage of the joint resolution to provide $1,145,105,000 in fiscal 1984 emergency appropriations for food assistance programs of the Department of Agriculture, for assistance to El Salvador, covert aid to Nicaraguan rebels and for other purposes. Passed 76-19: R 53-1; D 23-18 (ND 9-18, SD 14-0), April 5, 1984. The president had requested $90 million in food aid for 18 African nations, $92,750,000 in military assistance to El Salvador and $21 million in covert aid to Nicaraguan rebels.

57. HR 4169. Omnibus Reconciliation Act. Passage of the bill to reduce federal spending by $8.2 billion from fiscal 1984-87 by delaying cost-of-living adjustments for federal retirees' benefits and veterans' compensation, and limiting and delaying federal civilian pay raises. Passed (thus cleared for the president) 67-26: R 50-2; D 17-24 (ND 13-15, SD 4-9), April 5, 1984.

	58	59	60	61	62	63	64	65
ALABAMA								
Denton	N	N	N	Y	N	N	N	Y
Heflin	Y	Y	N	Y	N	Y	N	Y
ALASKA								
Murkowski	N	Y	N	Y	N	N	N	Y
Stevens	N	Y	N	Y	N	N	N	Y
ARIZONA								
Goldwater	N	N	N	Y	?	?	?	?
DeConcini	N	Y	N	Y	?	?	?	?
ARKANSAS								
Bumpers	N	Y	C	N	N	N	Y	N
Pryor	N	Y	N	Y	N	N	N	Y
CALIFORNIA								
Wilson	?	Y	N	Y	N	N	N	N
Cranston	N	Y	N	N	Y	N	N	N
COLORADO								
Armstrong	N	Y	N	Y	N	N	N	Y
Hart	?	?	?	?	?	?	?	?
CONNECTICUT								
Weicker	N	Y	-	-	Y	?	N	Y
Dodd	N	Y	N	N	Y	N	N	N
DELAWARE								
Roth	?	Y	N	Y	N	N	N	N
Biden	N	Y	N	N	Y	N	N	N
FLORIDA								
Hawkins	?	Y	N	Y	Y	N	N	Y
Chiles	Y	Y	Y	N	N	N	N	N
GEORGIA								
Mattingly	N	Y	N	Y	N	N	N	Y
Nunn	Y	Y	N	N	N	N	N	N
HAWAII								
Inouye	Y	Y	N	Y	N	Y	N	N
Matsunaga	?	Y	N	Y	N	Y	N	Y
IDAHO								
McClure	N	Y	N	Y	N	N	Y	Y
Symms	N	N	N	Y	N	N	N	Y
ILLINOIS								
Percy	N	Y	N	Y	Y	N	N	Y
Dixon	N	Y	N	Y	?	N	Y	
INDIANA								
Lugar	N	Y	N	N	N	N	N	N
Quayle	N	Y	N	Y	Y	N	N	N

	58	59	60	61	62	63	64	65
IOWA								
Grassley	N	Y	N	Y	N	Y	N	N
Jepsen	?	Y	N	Y	Y	Y	N	N
KANSAS								
Dole	N	N	N	Y	N	N	N	Y
Kassebaum	?	Y	N	Y	N	N	N	N
KENTUCKY								
Ford	N	Y	C	N	Y	N	N	Y
Huddleston	?	Y	N	N	Y	Y	?	?
LOUISIANA								
Johnston	N	Y	N	N	N	N	N	Y
Long	N	N	N	N	N	N	N	Y
MAINE								
Cohen	Y	Y	N	Y	Y	N	Y	N
Mitchell	Y	Y	N	N	N	N	Y	N
MARYLAND								
Mathias	N	+	?	?	Y	N	N	Y
Sarbanes	Y	Y	N	Y	N	N	N	N
MASSACHUSETTS								
Kennedy	Y	Y	N	N	Y	N	Y	N
Tsongas	N	Y	N	N	Y	N	N	N
MICHIGAN								
Levin	Y	Y	N	Y	N	Y	N	Y
Riegle	N	Y	N	N	Y	N	N	N
MINNESOTA								
Boschwitz	N	Y	N	Y	Y	N	Y	N
Durenberger	N	Y	N	Y	N	Y	N	N
MISSISSIPPI								
Cochran	N	?	N	Y	Y	N	N	Y
Stennis	N	Y	N	?	N	N	N	Y
MISSOURI								
Danforth	N	Y	N	N	N	N	N	Y
Eagleton	N	Y	N	N	Y	N	Y	N
MONTANA								
Baucus	Y	Y	N	Y	N	Y	N	N
Melcher	Y	Y	N	Y	Y	Y	Y	N
NEBRASKA								
Exon	Y	Y	N	N	N	N	N	N
Zorinsky	Y	Y	N	Y	N	Y	N	Y
NEVADA								
Hecht	N	N	N	Y	N	N	N	Y
Laxalt	N	Y	N	Y	N	N	N	Y

	58	59	60	61	62	63	64	65
NEW HAMPSHIRE								
Humphrey	?	Y	N	Y	N	N	N	N
Rudman	N	Y	N	Y	N	N	N	Y
NEW JERSEY								
Bradley	?	Y	N	Y	N	N	N	N
Lautenberg	N	Y	N	N	Y	N	N	N
NEW MEXICO								
Domenici	N	Y	N	Y	N	N	N	Y
Bingaman	Y	Y	N	N	Y	N	Y	Y
NEW YORK								
D'Amato	N	Y	N	Y	Y	N	N	N
Moynihan	?	Y	N	N	Y	N	N	N
NORTH CAROLINA								
East	N	N	N	Y	N	Y	N	Y
Helms	N	N	N	Y	N	Y	N	Y
NORTH DAKOTA								
Andrews	N	Y	N	N	N	N	N	Y
Burdick	Y	Y	N	Y	N	N	N	Y
OHIO								
Glenn	?	Y	N	Y	N	N	N	N
Metzenbaum	Y	Y	Y	N	Y	N	Y	N
OKLAHOMA								
Nickles	N	Y	N	Y	N	N	N	Y
Boren	N	Y	N	Y	N	N	N	Y
OREGON								
Hatfield	N	Y	N	N	N	N	N	Y
Packwood	N	Y	N	Y	N	N	N	Y
PENNSYLVANIA								
Heinz	N	Y	N	Y	N	N	N	Y
Specter	N	Y	N	Y	Y	N	N	Y
RHODE ISLAND								
Chafee	N	Y	N	N	N	N	N	Y
Pell	N	Y	N	N	Y	N	Y	Y
SOUTH CAROLINA								
Thurmond	N	N	N	Y	N	N	N	Y
Hollings	?	Y	?	N	N	N	Y	N
SOUTH DAKOTA								
Abdnor	N	Y	N	Y	N	Y	N	Y
Pressler	N	Y	N	N	N	Y	N	N
TENNESSEE								
Baker	?	Y	N	Y	N	N	N	Y
Sasser	N	Y	N	N	Y	N	N	N

	58	59	60	61	62	63	64	65
TEXAS								
Tower	?	N	?	Y	N	N	N	Y
Bentsen	?	?	?	?	?	N	N	?
UTAH								
Garn	N	Y	N	Y	N	N	N	Y
Hatch	N	N	N	Y	N	N	N	Y
VERMONT								
Stafford	?	Y	N	N	N	N	N	N
Leahy	Y	Y	N	Y	N	N	N	N
VIRGINIA								
Trible	N	Y	N	Y	N	N	N	Y
Warner	N	Y	N	Y	N	N	N	Y
WASHINGTON								
Evans	N	Y	N	Y	Y	N	N	Y
Gorton	N	Y	N	Y	N	N	N	Y
WEST VIRGINIA								
Byrd	N	Y	N	Y	Y	N	N	Y
Randolph	N	Y	N	N	Y	N	N	Y
WISCONSIN								
Kasten	N	Y	N	Y	Y	N	N	N
Proxmire	Y	Y	Y	N	Y	N	Y	N
WYOMING								
Simpson	?	Y	N	Y	N	N	N	Y
Wallop	N	N	N	Y	N	N	N	Y

KEY

Y   Voted for (yea).
\#   Paired for.
\+   Announced for.
N   Voted against (nay).
X   Paired against.
-   Announced against.
P   Voted "present".
C   Voted "present" to avoid possible conflict of interest.
?   Did not vote or otherwise make a position known.

Democrats   *Republicans*

ND - Northern Democrats   SD - Southern Democrats (Southern states - Ala., Ark., Fla., Ga., Ky., La., Miss., N.C., Okla., S.C., Tenn., Texas, Va.)

58. HR 2163. Deficit Reduction. Metzenbaum, D-Ohio, amendment to the Dole, R-Kan., amendment, to delete a provision allowing a tax exclusion for employee service awards. Rejected 18-64: R 1-44; D 17-20 (ND 14-12, SD 3-8), April 9, 1984. (The Dole amendment, to raise $48 billion in new tax revenues through fiscal 1987, subsequently was adopted *(see vote 77, p. 15-S)*.)

59. HR 2163. Deficit Reduction. Kennedy, D-Mass., amendment to the Dole, R-Kan., amendment, to express the sense of Congress that no U.S. funds shall be used for the mining of ports or territorial waters of Nicaragua. Adopted 84-12: R 42-11; D 42-1 (ND 30-0, SD 12-1), April 10, 1984. (The Dole amendment, to raise $48 billion in new tax revenues through fiscal 1987, subsequently was adopted *(see vote 77, p. 15-S)*.)

60. HR 2163. Deficit Reduction. Metzenbaum, D-Ohio, amendment to the Dole, R-Kan., amendment, to delete or phase out a number of tax breaks for the life insurance industry, for a savings of over $1 billion through fiscal 1987. Rejected 3-89: R 0-52; D 3-37 (ND 2-28, SD 1-9), April 10, 1984. (The Dole amendment, to raise $48 billion in new tax revenues through fiscal 1987, subsequently was adopted *(see vote 77, p. 15-S)*.)

61. HR 2163. Deficit Reduction. Dole, R-Kan., motion to table (kill) the Chafee, R-R.I., amendment to the Dole, R-Kan., amendment, to delay until Jan. 1, 1988, the effective date for indexing tax brackets to offset inflation. Motion agreed to 57-38: R 46-7; D 11-31 (ND 8-22, SD 3-9), April 10, 1984. (The Dole amendment, to raise $48 billion in new tax revenues through fiscal 1987, subsequently was adopted *(see vote 77, p. 15-S)*.) A "yea" was a vote supporting the president's position.

62. HR 2163. Deficit Reduction. Heinz, R-Pa., amendment to the Dole, R-Kan., amendment, to make $700 million in federal grants to states to provide health benefits to the long-term unemployed. Rejected 39-57: R 11-43; D 28-14 (ND 25-4, SD 3-10), April 11, 1984. (The Dole amendment, to raise $48 billion in new tax revenues through fiscal 1987, subsequently was adopted *(see vote 77, p. 15-S)*.)

63. HR 2163. Deficit Reduction. Pressler, R-S.D., amendment to the Dole, R-Kan., amendment, to eliminate an increase in highway user fees for trucks set to go into effect July 1. Rejected 14-81: R 9-44; D 5-37 (ND 3-25, SD 2-12), April 11, 1984. (The Dole amendment, to raise $48 billion in new tax revenues through fiscal 1987, subsequently was adopted *(see vote 77, p. 15-S)*.)

64. HR 2163. Deficit Reduction. Bumpers, D-Ark., amendment to the Dole, R-Kan., amendment, to strike a provision reducing from one year to six months the length of time an asset must be held before the proceeds from its sale can receive preferential capital gains tax treatment. Rejected 14-82: R 3-51; D 11-31 (ND 9-20, SD 2-11), April 11, 1984. (The Dole amendment, to raise $48 billion in new tax revenues through fiscal 1987, subsequently was adopted *(see vote 77, p. 15-S)*.)

65. HR 2163. Deficit Reduction. Wallop, R-Wyo., motion to table (kill) the Bradley, D-N.J., amendment to the Dole, R-Kan., amendment, to forbid synthetic fuels projects from receiving energy tax credits and financing from the Synthetic Fuels Corp. at the same time. Motion agreed to 52-43: R 36-18; D 16-25 (ND 9-20, SD 7-5), April 11, 1984. (The Dole amendment, to raise $48 billion in new tax revenues through fiscal 1987, subsequently was adopted *(see vote 77, p. 15-S)*.)

	66	67	68	69	70	71	72
ALABAMA							
Denton	N	N	Y	Y	Y	Y	?
Heflin	N	N	N	Y	Y	Y	Y
ALASKA							
Murkowski	N	N	Y	Y	Y	Y	Y
Stevens	N	?	N	Y	Y	Y	Y
ARIZONA							
Goldwater	?	?	?	?	?	?	#
DeConcini	?	?	?	?	?	?	?
ARKANSAS							
Bumpers	N	N	Y	N	Y	Y	N
Pryor	N	N	Y	N	Y	Y	N
CALIFORNIA							
Wilson	N	N	Y	N	Y	Y	Y
Cranston	N	Y	Y	N	N	N	N
COLORADO							
Armstrong	N	N	Y	Y	Y	Y	Y
Hart	?	?	?	?	?	?	?
CONNECTICUT							
Weicker	N	?	-	?	N	?	?
Dodd	N	Y	N	N	N	N	Y
DELAWARE							
Roth	Y	N	Y	Y	Y	N	Y
Biden	N	N	N	N	N	N	N
FLORIDA							
Hawkins	N	N	Y	N	Y	Y	Y
Chiles	Y	N	N	Y	N	Y	Y
GEORGIA							
Mattingly	N	N	Y	N	Y	Y	Y
Nunn	Y	N	Y	Y	Y	Y	N
HAWAII							
Inouye	N	N	N	Y	N	Y	N
Matsunaga	N	N	N	N	Y	N	N
IDAHO							
McClure	?	?	?	?	?	?	?
Symms	?	?	?	?	?	?	?
ILLINOIS							
Percy	N	N	Y	N	Y	N	Y
Dixon	N	N	Y	N	Y	N	Y
INDIANA							
Lugar	Y	N	N	Y	N	Y	N
Quayle	Y	N	N	Y	Y	Y	Y
IOWA							
Grassley	N	N	Y	N	Y	Y	Y
Jepsen	N	N	Y	N	Y	Y	Y
KANSAS							
Dole	Y	N	Y	Y	Y	Y	Y
Kassebaum	Y	N	Y	Y	Y	N	Y
KENTUCKY							
Ford	N	Y	N	N	Y	Y	N
Huddleston	N	Y	N	?	?	?	?
LOUISIANA							
Johnston	N	Y	N	Y	Y	Y	Y
Long	N	Y	N	Y	Y	Y	X
MAINE							
Cohen	Y	N	Y	N	N	Y	N
Mitchell	Y	N	N	N	N	Y	N
MARYLAND							
Mathias	Y	?	N	N	Y	N	Y
Sarbanes	N	N	N	N	N	N	N
MASSACHUSETTS							
Kennedy	N	Y	N	N	N	N	N
Tsongas	N	N	Y	N	N	N	N
MICHIGAN							
Levin	N	N	Y	N	N	Y	N
Riegle	N	N	N	N	N	N	N
MINNESOTA							
Boschwitz	N	N	N	N	Y	N	Y
Durenberger	Y	Y	Y	Y	?	?	?
MISSISSIPPI							
Cochran	N	N	Y	Y	Y	Y	Y
Stennis	N	Y	N	Y	Y	Y	Y
MISSOURI							
Danforth	Y	N	N	Y	Y	N	Y
Eagleton	Y	N	Y	N	N	Y	Y
MONTANA							
Baucus	N	Y	N	Y	Y	Y	Y
Melcher	N	Y	N	N	N	Y	N
NEBRASKA							
Exon	N	N	N	Y	Y	Y	Y
Zorinsky	N	N	Y	Y	Y	Y	Y
NEVADA							
Hecht	N	N	Y	Y	Y	Y	Y
Laxalt	N	N	Y	Y	Y	Y	Y
NEW HAMPSHIRE							
Humphrey	Y	N	N	N	Y	?	Y
Rudman	Y	N	Y	N	Y	N	Y
NEW JERSEY							
Bradley	Y	N	Y	N	N	N	N
Lautenberg	Y	N	N	N	N	N	N
NEW MEXICO							
Domenici	N	N	Y	N	N	Y	Y
Bingaman	N	Y	Y	N	N	N	N
NEW YORK							
D'Amato	N	N	Y	N	Y	Y	Y
Moynihan	N	N	Y	N	Y	N	N
NORTH CAROLINA							
East	N	N	Y	Y	Y	?	Y
Helms	N	N	Y	Y	Y	Y	Y
NORTH DAKOTA							
Andrews	N	N	N	N	N	N	N
Burdick	N	N	Y	N	N	Y	N
OHIO							
Glenn	Y	?	Y	N	Y	Y	Y
Metzenbaum	Y	N	Y	N	N	Y	N
OKLAHOMA							
Nickles	Y	N	Y	Y	Y	Y	Y
Boren	N	N	Y	Y	Y	Y	Y
OREGON							
Hatfield	Y	N	Y	N	N	N	Y
Packwood	Y	N	Y	Y	Y	N	Y
PENNSYLVANIA							
Heinz	Y	N	Y	N	N	Y	Y
Specter	N	N	Y	N	Y	N	Y
RHODE ISLAND							
Chafee	Y	N	N	N	Y	N	Y
Pell	N	N	N	N	N	N	Y
SOUTH CAROLINA							
Thurmond	N	N	Y	N	Y	Y	Y
Hollings	N	Y	N	N	N	Y	Y
SOUTH DAKOTA							
Abdnor	N	N	Y	N	Y	Y	Y
Pressler	N	N	Y	N	Y	Y	Y
TENNESSEE							
Baker	Y	N	Y	Y	?	Y	Y
Sasser	N	Y	N	N	Y	Y	N
TEXAS							
Tower	Y	N	Y	Y	Y	Y	Y
Bentsen	N	N	N	Y	Y	?	?
UTAH							
Garn	Y	N	Y	Y	Y	Y	Y
Hatch	N	N	Y	Y	Y	Y	Y
VERMONT							
Stafford	Y	N	Y	N	N	N	Y
Leahy	N	N	Y	N	N	N	N
VIRGINIA							
Trible	N	N	Y	Y	Y	Y	Y
Warner	N	N	N	N	Y	Y	Y
WASHINGTON							
Evans	Y	N	Y	N	Y	N	Y
Gorton	Y	N	Y	Y	Y	N	Y
WEST VIRGINIA							
Byrd	N	N	N	Y	N	Y	N
Randolph	N	Y	Y	N	Y	Y	Y
WISCONSIN							
Kasten	N	N	Y	N	Y	N	N
Proxmire	N	N	Y	N	N	N	Y
WYOMING							
Simpson	Y	N	Y	Y	Y	Y	Y
Wallop	Y	N	Y	Y	Y	Y	Y

KEY

Y Voted for (yea).
Paired for.
+ Announced for.
N Voted against (nay).
X Paired against.
- Announced against.
P Voted "present".
C Voted "present" to avoid possible conflict of interest.
? Did not vote or otherwise make a position known.

Democrats   *Republicans*

ND - Northern Democrats   SD - Southern Democrats (Southern states - Ala., Ark., Fla., Ga., Ky., La., Miss., N.C., Okla., S.C., Tenn., Texas, Va.)

66. HR 2163. Deficit Reduction. Chafee, R-R.I., motion to table (kill) the D'Amato, R-N.Y., amendment to the Dole, R-Kan., amendment, to delete tax-exempt income from a calculation used to determine if a retiree must pay income taxes on Social Security benefits. Motion rejected 32-63: R 24-28; D 8-35 (ND 6-23, SD 2-12), April 12, 1984. (The D'Amato amendment subsequently was adopted by voice vote. The Dole amendment, to raise $48 billion in new tax revenues through fiscal 1987, subsequently was adopted (*see vote 77, p. 15-S*).)

67. HR 2163. Deficit Reduction. Ford, D-Ky., amendment to the Dole, R-Kan., amendment, to delete a provision increasing excise taxes on distilled liquor $2 a gallon and provisions allowing special tax advantages in economically distressed areas designated as "enterprise zones." Rejected 15-76: R 1-48; D 14-28 (ND 7-21, SD 7-7), April 12, 1984. (The Dole amendment, to raise $48 billion in new tax revenues through fiscal 1987, subsequently was adopted (*see vote 77, p. 15-S*).)

68. HR 2163. Deficit Reduction. Wilson, R-Calif., motion to table (kill) the Ford, D-Ky., amendment to the Dole, R-Kan., amendment, to increase excise taxes on distilled liquor by only $1 a gallon, instead of $2, and to raise taxes on wine by approximately 20 cents a gallon. Motion agreed to 62-32: R 41-10; D 21-22 (ND 16-13, SD 5-9), April 12, 1984. (The Dole amendment, to raise $48 billion in new tax revenues through fiscal 1987, subsequently was adopted (*see vote 77, p. 15-S*).)

69. HR 2163. Deficit Reduction. Packwood, R-Ore., motion to table (kill) the Cohen, R-Maine, amendment to the Dole, R-Kan., amendment, to delete provisions eliminating existing resi-

dential energy tax credits on the date of enactment. Motion rejected 38-55: R 28-23; D 10-32 (ND 3-26, SD 7-6), April 12, 1984. (The Cohen amendment subsequently was adopted by voice vote. The Dole amendment, to raise $48 billion in new tax revenues through fiscal 1987, subsequently was adopted (*see vote 77, p. 15-S*).)

70. HR 2163. Deficit Reduction. Dole, R-Kan., motion to table (kill) the Metzenbaum, D-Ohio, amendment to the Dole amendment, to impose a 15 percent tax on corporate profits over $50,000. Motion agreed to 62-30: R 43-7; D 19-23 (ND 8-21, SD 11-2), April 12, 1984. (The Dole amendment, to raise $48 billion in new tax revenues through fiscal 1987, subsequently was adopted (*see vote 77, p. 15-S*).)

71. HR 2163. Deficit Reduction. Dole, R-Kan., motion to table (kill) the Bradley, D-N.J., amendment to the Dole amendment, to impose a tax on the lead content of gasoline to raise funds for the federal "Superfund" to clean up toxic wastes. Motion agreed to 61-28: R 36-12; D 25-16 (ND 13-16, SD 12-0), April 12, 1984. (The Dole amendment, to raise $48 billion in new tax revenues through fiscal 1987, subsequently was adopted (*see vote 77, p. 15-S*).)

72. HR 2163. Deficit Reduction. Dole, R-Kan., motion to table (kill) the Bradley, D-N.J., amendment to the Dole amendment, to provide a cost-of-living adjustment in the earned income tax credit available to low-income wage earners with dependent children. Motion agreed to 64-25: R 47-2; D 17-23 (ND 11-18, SD 6-5), April 12, 1984. (The Dole amendment, to raise $48 billion in new tax revenue through fiscal 1987, subsequently was adopted (*see vote 77, p. 15-S*).)

	73 74 75 76 77		73 74 75 76 77		73 74 75 76 77	KEY
ALABAMA		**IOWA**		**NEW HAMPSHIRE**		Y Voted for (yea).
Denton	+ + + + +	*Grassley*	Y Y Y Y Y	*Humphrey*	Y N Y Y N	# Paired for.
Heflin	Y Y Y N Y	*Jepsen*	Y Y Y N Y	*Rudman*	Y Y Y Y Y	+ Announced for.
ALASKA		**KANSAS**		**NEW JERSEY**		N Voted against (nay).
Murkowski	Y Y Y Y Y	*Dole*	Y Y Y Y Y	Bradley	Y N N Y Y	X Paired against.
Stevens	? ? ? ? ?	*Kassebaum*	Y N Y Y Y	Lautenberg	N N N N Y	- Announced against.
ARIZONA		**KENTUCKY**		**NEW MEXICO**		P Voted ''present''.
Goldwater	? ? ? ? ?	Ford	N Y N N Y	*Domenici*	Y Y Y N Y	C Voted ''present'' to avoid possi-
DeConcini	? ? ? ? ?	Huddleston	? ? ? ? ?	Bingaman	Y Y Y N Y	ble conflict of interest.
ARKANSAS		**LOUISIANA**		**NEW YORK**		? Did not vote or otherwise make a
Bumpers	Y Y N Y Y	Johnston	? ? ? ? ?	*D'Amato*	Y Y Y N Y	position known.
Pryor	Y Y Y N Y	Long	Y N Y Y Y	Moynihan	? N Y N Y	
CALIFORNIA		**MAINE**		**NORTH CAROLINA**		Democrats *Republicans*
Wilson	Y Y Y Y Y	*Cohen*	Y N Y Y Y	*East*	Y Y Y Y Y	
Cranston	N ? ? ? ?	Mitchell	N N N N Y	*Helms*	Y Y Y Y Y	
COLORADO		**MARYLAND**		**NORTH DAKOTA**		
Armstrong	Y Y Y Y Y	*Mathias*	Y N N Y Y	*Andrews*	Y Y Y N Y	73 74 75 76 77
Hart	? ? ? ? ?	Sarbanes	N N N N Y	Burdick	N Y N N Y	
CONNECTICUT		**MASSACHUSETTS**		**OHIO**		**TEXAS**	
Weicker	? ? ? ? ?	Kennedy	N N N N Y	Glenn	Y Y Y Y Y	*Tower*	N Y Y Y Y
Dodd	N Y N N Y	Tsongas	Y Y Y Y Y	Metzenbaum	Y N N N N	Bentsen	? ? ? ? ?
DELAWARE		**MICHIGAN**		**OKLAHOMA**		**UTAH**	
Roth	Y Y Y Y Y	Levin	N Y N N Y	*Nickles*	Y Y Y Y Y	*Garn*	N Y Y Y N
Biden	Y Y Y Y N	Riegle	N Y N N Y	Boren	Y Y ? ? ?	*Hatch*	Y Y Y Y N
FLORIDA		**MINNESOTA**		**OREGON**		**VERMONT**	
Hawkins	Y Y Y Y Y	*Boschwitz*	Y Y Y Y Y	*Hatfield*	Y Y Y Y Y	*Stafford*	? ? ? ? ?
Chiles	Y Y Y Y Y	*Durenberger*	? ? ? ? ?	*Packwood*	Y ? ? ? ?	Leahy	N N Y Y Y
GEORGIA		**MISSISSIPPI**		**PENNSYLVANIA**		**VIRGINIA**	
Mattingly	Y Y Y Y Y	*Cochran*	Y Y Y Y Y	*Heinz*	Y N Y Y Y	*Trible*	Y Y Y Y Y
Nunn	Y Y Y N Y	Stennis	Y ? ? ? ?	*Specter*	Y Y Y Y Y	*Warner*	Y Y Y Y Y
HAWAII		**MISSOURI**		**RHODE ISLAND**		**WASHINGTON**	
Inouye	Y Y N N Y	*Danforth*	Y N Y Y Y	*Chafee*	Y N Y Y Y	*Evans*	Y N Y Y Y
Matsunaga	Y Y Y N Y	Eagleton	? ? ? ? ?	Pell	Y N N Y Y	*Gorton*	Y Y Y Y Y
IDAHO		**MONTANA**		**SOUTH CAROLINA**		**WEST VIRGINIA**	
McClure	? ? ? ? ?	Baucus	Y Y Y N Y	*Thurmond*	Y Y Y Y Y	Byrd	N Y N N Y
Symms	? ? ? ? ?	Melcher	N Y Y N Y	Hollings	? ? ? ? ?	Randolph	N Y N N Y
ILLINOIS		**NEBRASKA**		**SOUTH DAKOTA**		**WISCONSIN**	
Percy	Y Y N Y Y	Exon	Y Y Y N Y	*Abdnor*	Y Y Y Y Y	*Kasten*	Y Y Y N Y
Dixon	Y Y N N Y	Zorinsky	Y Y Y N Y	*Pressler*	? ? Y Y Y	Proxmire	Y N Y Y Y
INDIANA		**NEVADA**		**TENNESSEE**		**WYOMING**	
Lugar	Y Y Y Y Y	*Hecht*	Y Y Y Y Y	*Baker*	Y Y Y Y Y	*Simpson*	Y Y Y Y Y
Quayle	Y Y Y Y Y	*Laxalt*	Y Y Y Y Y	Sasser	N Y Y N Y	*Wallop*	Y Y Y Y Y

ND - Northern Democrats   SD - Southern Democrats (Southern states - Ala., Ark., Fla., Ga., Ky., La., Miss., N.C., Okla., S.C., Tenn., Texas, Va.)

73. HR 2163. Deficit Reduction. Dole, R-Kan., motion to table (kill) the Cranston, D-Calif., amendment to the Dole amendment *(see vote 77, below)*, to exempt for one year low- and moderate-income housing from provisions to eliminate certain real estate tax shelters involving deferred interest payments. Motion agreed to 66-17: R 44-2; D 22-15 (ND 14-13, SD 8-2), in the session that began April 12, 1984.

74. HR 2163. Deficit Reduction. Boschwitz, R-Minn., amendment to the Dole, R-Kan., amendment *(see vote 77, below)*, to change the current 15-year depreciation life for real property to 20 years in 1984, 19 years in 1985 and 18 years thereafter, and to reduce the investment tax credits available for rehabilitation of old buildings. Adopted 62-19: R 37-8; D 25-11 (ND 17-10, SD 8-1), in the session that began April 12, 1984.

75. HR 2163. Deficit Reduction. Dole, R-Kan., motion to table (kill) the Levin, D-Mich., amendment to the Dole amendment *(see vote 77, below)*, to increase the tax deduction for two-income couples from 10 percent to 10.5 percent and to pay for the change by retaining the maximum estate tax at 60 percent. Motion agreed to 62-19: R 44-2; D 18-17 (ND 12-15, SD 6-2), in the session that began April 12, 1984.

76. HR 2163. Deficit Reduction. Dole, R-Kan., motion to table (kill) the Melcher, D-Mont., amendment to the Dole amendment *(see vote 77, below)*, to liberalize travel and transportation deductions for construction workers who work at sites more than 40 miles away from home. Motion agreed to 50-31: R 41-5; D 9-26 (ND 6-21, SD 3-5), in the session that began April 12, 1984.

77. HR 2163. Deficit Reduction. Dole, R-Kan., amendment, as amended, to raise $47 billion in new tax revenues through fiscal 1987 by closing a wide range of tax loopholes, revamping taxation of the life insurance industry, raising liquor taxes by $2 a gallon and making a number of other changes. Floor amendments had cut $1 billion from the original Dole proposal. Adopted 76-5: R 43-3; D 33-2 (ND 25-2, SD 8-0), in the session that began April 12, 1984. A "yea" was a vote supporting the president's position.

	78	79	80	81
ALABAMA				
Denton	Y	Y	N	N
Heflin	Y	Y	N	N
ALASKA				
Murkowski	Y	Y	N	Y
Stevens	N	Y	N	Y
ARIZONA				
Goldwater	Y	Y	Y	N
DeConcini	N	Y	N	N
ARKANSAS				
Bumpers	N	Y	N	N
Pryor	N	Y	N	N
CALIFORNIA				
Wilson	Y	Y	N	N
Cranston	N	Y	N	N
COLORADO				
Armstrong	N	Y	Y	N
Hart	?	?	?	?
CONNECTICUT				
Weicker	N	Y	N	Y
Dodd	N	?	N	N
DELAWARE				
Roth	N	Y	N	N
Biden	N	Y	N	N
FLORIDA				
Hawkins	N	Y	N	?
Chiles	N	Y	N	N
GEORGIA				
Mattingly	Y	Y	N	N
Nunn	Y	Y	N	N
HAWAII				
Inouye	N	Y	N	N
Matsunaga	N	Y	N	N
IDAHO				
McClure	Y	Y	Y	Y
Symms	Y	Y	Y	N
ILLINOIS				
Percy	N	Y	N	N
Dixon	N	Y	N	N
INDIANA				
Lugar	N	Y	N	Y
Quayle	N	Y	N	N

	78	79	80	81
IOWA				
Grassley	N	Y	N	N
Jepsen	N	Y	N	N
KANSAS				
Dole	N	Y	N	Y
Kassebaum	N	Y	N	N
KENTUCKY				
Ford	N	Y	N	N
Huddleston	?	+	N	N
LOUISIANA				
Johnston	N	Y	N	N
Long	Y	Y	N	N
MAINE				
Cohen	?	+	N	N
Mitchell	N	Y	N	N
MARYLAND				
Mathias	N	Y	N	Y
Sarbanes	N	Y	N	N
MASSACHUSETTS				
Kennedy	?	?	?	?
Tsongas	N	Y	N	N
MICHIGAN				
Levin	N	Y	N	N
Riegle	N	Y	N	N
MINNESOTA				
Boschwitz	N	Y	N	N
Durenberger	N	Y	N	Y
MISSISSIPPI				
Cochran	N	Y	N	Y
Stennis	N	Y	N	N
MISSOURI				
Danforth	N	Y	N	Y
Eagleton	N	Y	N	N
MONTANA				
Baucus	N	Y	N	N
Melcher	N	Y	?	N
NEBRASKA				
Exon	Y	Y	N	N
Zorinsky	Y	Y	N	N
NEVADA				
Hecht	Y	Y	N	N
Laxalt	Y	Y	N	N

	78	79	80	81
NEW HAMPSHIRE				
Humphrey	Y	Y	Y	N
Rudman	Y	Y	Y	N
NEW JERSEY				
Bradley	N	Y	N	N
Lautenberg	N	Y	N	N
NEW MEXICO				
Domenici	N	Y	N	Y
Bingaman	N	Y	N	N
NEW YORK				
D'Amato	Y	Y	N	N
Moynihan	N	Y	N	Y
NORTH CAROLINA				
East	?	?	?	?
Helms	Y	Y	Y	N
NORTH DAKOTA				
Andrews	Y	Y	N	N
Burdick	N	Y	N	N
OHIO				
Glenn	N	Y	N	Y
Metzenbaum	N	Y	N	N
OKLAHOMA				
Nickles	Y	Y	Y	N
Boren	Y	Y	N	N
OREGON				
Hatfield	N	Y	N	Y
Packwood	N	Y	N	N
PENNSYLVANIA				
Heinz	N	Y	N	N
Specter	N	Y	N	N
RHODE ISLAND				
Chafee	N	Y	N	Y
Pell	N	Y	N	N
SOUTH CAROLINA				
Thurmond	Y	Y	Y	N
Hollings	N	Y	N	N
SOUTH DAKOTA				
Abdnor	N	Y	N	N
Pressler	N	Y	N	N
TENNESSEE				
Baker	N	Y	N	Y
Sasser	N	Y	N	N

KEY

Y	Voted for (yea).
#	Paired for.
+	Announced for.
N	Voted against (nay).
X	Paired against.
-	Announced against.
P	Voted "present".
C	Voted "present" to avoid possible conflict of interest.
?	Did not vote or otherwise make a position known.

Democrats   *Republicans*

	78	79	80	81
TEXAS				
Tower	N	Y	?	?
Bentsen	N	Y	N	N
UTAH				
Garn	Y	Y	Y	N
Hatch	Y	Y	Y	N
VERMONT				
Stafford	N	Y	N	N
Leahy	N	Y	N	N
VIRGINIA				
Trible	Y	Y	N	N
Warner	Y	Y	N	N
WASHINGTON				
Evans	N	Y	N	?
Gorton	N	Y	N	N
WEST VIRGINIA				
Byrd	N	Y	N	N
Randolph	N	Y	N	N
WISCONSIN				
Kasten	Y	Y	N	N
Proxmire	N	Y	N	N
WYOMING				
Simpson	N	Y	N	?
Wallop	N	Y	N	N

ND - Northern Democrats   SD - Southern Democrats (Southern states - Ala., Ark., Fla., Ga., Ky., La., Miss., N.C., Okla., S.C., Tenn., Texas, Va.)

78. HR 2163. Deficit Reduction. Helms, R-N.C., amendment to cut spending by 10 percent in all federal programs, except Social Security, Medicare and defense, saving $200 billion through 1987. Rejected 27-68: R 21-32; D 6-36 (ND 2-27, SD 4-9), April 25, 1984.

79. HR 4325. Child Support Enforcement. Passage of the bill to amend the Social Security Act to require states to establish procedures for mandatory withholding from the wages of parents in arrears on child support and to make other changes in the federal-state child support enforcement program. Passed 94-0: R 53-0; D 41-0 (ND 28-0, SD 13-0), April 25, 1984. A "yea" was a vote supporting the president's position.

80. HR 2163. Deficit Reduction. Symms, R-Idaho, amendment to reduce federal outlays by $285.9 billion over fiscal years 1985-87 by reducing non-defense discretionary spending 10 percent from fiscal 1984 levels; reducing defense spending $70.5 billion from fiscal 1985-87; and freezing cost-of-living adjustments for federal benefit programs, except those for the poor or aged. Rejected 11-84: R 11-42; D 0-42 (ND 0-28, SD 0-14), April 26, 1984.

81. HR 2163. Deficit Reduction. Hatfield, R-Ore., motion to table (kill) the DeConcini, D-Ariz., amendment to save $4.4 billion in fiscal 1985 by implementing cost savings in areas such as travel expenses, consultant fees, and public affairs. Motion rejected 15-78: R 13-37; D 2-41 (ND 2-27, SD 0-14), April 26, 1984. (The DeConcini amendment subsequently was adopted by voice vote.)

	82	83	84	85	86	87
ALABAMA						
Denton	+	Y	N	N	Y	Y
Heflin	?	Y	N	N	N	Y
ALASKA						
Murkowski	?	?	?	+	?	?
Stevens	N	Y	N	N	Y	N
ARIZONA						
Goldwater	Y	N	N	N	Y	N
DeConcini	?	Y	N	N	N	Y
ARKANSAS						
Bumpers	N	N	Y	Y	N	Y
Pryor	N	N	Y	Y	?	?
CALIFORNIA						
Wilson	Y	Y	N	N	Y	N
Cranston	N	Y	N	N	N	Y
COLORADO						
Armstrong	?	N	N	Y	Y	N
Hart	?	?	?	?	?	?
CONNECTICUT						
Weicker	N	Y	Y	N	Y	
Dodd	N	Y	Y	Y	N	Y
DELAWARE						
Roth	N	Y	N	N	Y	N
Biden	?	Y	Y	Y	Y	Y
FLORIDA						
Hawkins	?	Y	N	N	?	?
Chiles	N	Y	Y	N	Y	
GEORGIA						
Mattingly	Y	N	N	Y	Y	N
Nunn	Y	Y	Y	N	Y	Y
HAWAII						
Inouye	N	Y	Y	Y	N	Y
Matsunaga	N	Y	Y	N	Y	
IDAHO						
McClure	Y	N	Y	N	Y	N
Symms	Y	N	N	N	Y	N
ILLINOIS						
Percy	N	Y	N	N	Y	Y
Dixon	N	?	+	Y	Y	N
INDIANA						
Lugar	N	Y	N	N	Y	N
Quayle	?	Y	Y	N	Y	N
IOWA						
Grassley	N	N	Y	Y	Y	N
Jepsen	N	N	N	Y	Y	N
KANSAS						
Dole	?	Y	N	N	Y	N
Kassebaum	N	N	Y	Y	Y	Y
KENTUCKY						
Ford	N	Y	N	N	N	Y
Huddleston	?	Y	N	N	N	Y
LOUISIANA						
Johnston	N	Y	Y	N	N	Y
Long	Y	Y	Y	N	N	Y
MAINE						
Cohen	N	Y	N	Y	N	Y
Mitchell	N	Y	Y	Y	N	Y
MARYLAND						
Mathias	?	Y	Y	N	N	Y
Sarbanes	N	Y	N	N	N	Y
MASSACHUSETTS						
Kennedy	?	Y	?	N	N	Y
Tsongas	?	Y	Y	Y	?	?
MICHIGAN						
Levin	-	Y	Y	N	N	Y
Riegle	?	Y	N	N	N	Y
MINNESOTA						
Boschwitz	N	Y	N	N	Y	N
Durenberger	N	Y	-	N	N	Y
MISSISSIPPI						
Cochran	N	Y	N	N	Y	N
Stennis	N	Y	Y	N	N	Y
MISSOURI						
Danforth	N	Y	N	N	N	Y
Eagleton	N	Y	Y	N	N	Y
MONTANA						
Baucus	N	N	N	Y	N	Y
Melcher	N	Y	Y	Y	N	Y
NEBRASKA						
Exon	?	N	Y	Y	Y	N
Zorinsky	?	N	Y	Y	Y	N
NEVADA						
Hecht	Y	Y	N	N	Y	N
Laxalt	N	Y	N	N	Y	?
NEW HAMPSHIRE						
Humphrey	Y	N	N	Y	Y	N
Rudman	Y	Y	N	N	N	Y
NEW JERSEY						
Bradley	?	Y	N	N	N	Y
Lautenberg	?	Y	N	N	N	Y
NEW MEXICO						
Domenici	N	N	N	N	N	Y
Bingaman	N	Y	Y	Y	N	Y
NEW YORK						
D'Amato	?	Y	N	N	Y	N
Moynihan	N	Y	N	N	N	Y
NORTH CAROLINA						
East	?	?	N	N	Y	N
Helms	Y	N	N	N	Y	N
NORTH DAKOTA						
Andrews	?	N	Y	Y	N	Y
Burdick	N	N	Y	Y	N	Y
OHIO						
Glenn	N	Y	N	N	?	?
Metzenbaum	?	N	N	N	N	Y
OKLAHOMA						
Nickles	Y	N	Y	Y	Y	Y
Boren	Y	N	Y	Y	Y	Y
OREGON						
Hatfield	N	N	N	Y	N	Y
Packwood	N	N	N	N	N	Y
PENNSYLVANIA						
Heinz	?	Y	N	N	Y	N
Specter	N	Y	Y	Y	Y	N
RHODE ISLAND						
Chafee	N	Y	N	N	Y	Y
Pell	?	Y	N	N	N	Y
SOUTH CAROLINA						
Thurmond	Y	Y	N	N	Y	N
Hollings	N	Y	Y	Y	?	?
SOUTH DAKOTA						
Abdnor	N	?	N	N	Y	N
Pressler	?	N	Y	Y	Y	N
TENNESSEE						
Baker	N	Y	N	N	N	Y
Sasser	N	Y	Y	Y	N	Y
TEXAS						
Tower	N	Y	N	N	N	Y
Bentsen	N	Y	Y	N	?	?
UTAH						
Garn	Y	N	N	N	Y	N
Hatch	Y	Y	N	N	N	Y
VERMONT						
Stafford	N	Y	Y	N	N	Y
Leahy	?	Y	Y	N	Y	Y
VIRGINIA						
Trible	?	Y	N	N	Y	N
Warner	Y	Y	N	N	Y	N
WASHINGTON						
Evans	N	Y	N	Y	N	Y
Gorton	?	Y	N	N	N	Y
WEST VIRGINIA						
Byrd	N	N	N	N	N	Y
Randolph	N	N	N	Y	N	Y
WISCONSIN						
Kasten	+	N	N	Y	Y	N
Proxmire	Y	N	Y	Y	Y	N
WYOMING						
Simpson	?	Y	N	Y	Y	Y
Wallop	N	N	N	N	?	?

KEY

Y Voted for (yea).
\# Paired for.
+ Announced for.
N Voted against (nay).
- Announced against.
P Voted "present".
C Voted "present" to avoid possible conflict of interest.
? Did not vote or otherwise make a position known.

Democrats *Republicans*

ND - Northern Democrats   SD - Southern Democrats (Southern states - Ala., Ark., Fla., Ga., Ky., La., Miss., N.C., Okla., S.C., Tenn., Texas, Va.)

82. HR 2163. Deficit Reduction. Symms, R-Idaho, amendment to make a 7.5 percent across-the-board cut in fiscal 1985-87 spending for all federal programs except Social Security, Medicare and defense. Rejected 18-50: R 14-25; D 4-25 (ND 1-16, SD 3-9), April 30, 1984.

83. HR 2163. Deficit Reduction. Mitchell, D-Maine, amendment to authorize a 3.5 percent pay raise for federal judges retroactive to January 1984, costing $1.7 million over one year. Adopted 67-28: R 35-17; D 32-11 (ND 21-8, SD 11-3), May 1, 1984.

84. HR 2163. Deficit Reduction. Hollings, D-S.C., amendment to cut the federal budget deficit $316 billion over three years by raising $137 billion in new revenues; providing a 4 percent inflation-adjusted growth rate for defense in fiscal 1985 and 1986, and 3 percent in fiscal 1987; freezing cost-of-living adjustments for entitlements in fiscal 1985, then allowing a 3 percent increase in fiscal 1986 and 1987. Rejected 38-57: R 12-41; D 26-16 (ND 15-13, SD 11-3), May 1, 1984.

85. HR 2163. Deficit Reduction. Grassley, R-Iowa, amendment to freeze all fiscal 1985 military and domestic spending except to cover new recipients in social programs such as food stamps and Medicare. The freeze would reduce the deficit approximately $260 billion over three years, including the $48 billion tax increase already approved by the Senate. Rejected 33-65: R 14-40; D 19-25 (ND 14-16, SD 5-9), May 2, 1984.

86. HR 2163. Deficit Reduction. Mattingly, R-Ga., motion to table (kill) the Chiles, D-Fla., point of order (see vote 87, below) that the Mattingly amendment to give the president authority to veto line items in appropriations bills is unconstitutional. Motion rejected 45-46: R 37-15; D 8-31 (ND 6-22, SD 2-9), May 3, 1984.

87. HR 2163. Deficit Reduction. Chiles, D-Fla., point of order that the Mattingly, R-Ga., amendment to give the president authority to veto line items in appropriations bills is unconstitutional. Point of order upheld 56-34: R 21-30; D 35-4 (ND 24-4, SD 11-0), May 3, 1984.

	88	89	90	91	92	93			88	89	90	91	92	93			88	89	90	91	92	93
ALABAMA								**IOWA**								**NEW HAMPSHIRE**						
Denton	N	Y	Y	Y	N	Y		*Grassley*	N	Y	Y	Y	N	N		*Humphrey*	N	Y	Y	Y	N	Y
Heflin	Y	N	N	N	N	Y		*Jepsen*	N	Y	Y	Y	N	Y		*Rudman*	N	Y	Y	Y	Y	Y
ALASKA								**KANSAS**								**NEW JERSEY**						
Murkowski	N	Y	Y	Y	N	Y		*Dole*	N	Y	Y	Y	N	Y		Bradley	Y	N	N	N	N	N
Stevens	N	?	?	?	?	Y		*Kassebaum*	N	Y	Y	Y	N	Y		Lautenberg	Y	N	N	N	N	N
ARIZONA								**KENTUCKY**								**NEW MEXICO**						
Goldwater	N	Y	Y	Y	N	Y		Ford	Y	N	N	N	N	N		*Domenici*	N	Y	Y	Y	N	Y
DeConcini	Y	N	N	N	Y	N		Huddleston	Y	N	N	N	N	N		Bingaman	Y	N	N	N	N	N
ARKANSAS								**LOUISIANA**								**NEW YORK**						
Bumpers	Y	N	?	?	?	N		Johnston	Y	N	Y	Y	Y	N		*D'Amato*	N	Y	Y	Y	N	Y
Pryor	Y	N	N	N	N	N		Long	Y	Y	Y	Y	Y	N		Moynihan	Y	N	N	N	N	N
CALIFORNIA								**MAINE**								**NORTH CAROLINA**						
Wilson	N	Y	Y	Y	N	Y		*Cohen*	N	N	N	N	N	N		*East*	N	Y	Y	Y	N	Y
Cranston	Y	N	N	N	N	N		Mitchell	Y	N	N	N	N	N		*Helms*	N	Y	Y	Y	N	Y
COLORADO								**MARYLAND**								**NORTH DAKOTA**						
Armstrong	N	Y	Y	Y	N	Y		*Mathias*	Y	Y	?	?	+	-		*Andrews*	Y	Y	Y	Y	N	Y
Hart	Y	N	N	N	N	?		Sarbanes	Y	N	N	N	N	N		Burdick	Y	N	N	N	N	N
CONNECTICUT								**MASSACHUSETTS**								**OHIO**						
Weicker	Y	N	Y	Y	Y	N		Kennedy	Y	N	N	N	N	N		Glenn	?	?	?	?	?	?
Dodd	Y	N	N	N	Y	N		Tsongas	Y	N	N	N	N	?		Metzenbaum	Y	N	N	N	N	N
DELAWARE								**MICHIGAN**								**OKLAHOMA**						
Roth	N	Y	Y	Y	N	Y		Levin	Y	N	N	N	N	N		*Nickles*	N	Y	Y	Y	Y	Y
Biden	Y	N	N	N	N	N		Riegle	Y	N	N	N	N	N		Boren	Y	N	Y	Y	Y	N
FLORIDA								**MINNESOTA**								**OREGON**						
Hawkins	N	?	?	?	?	Y		*Boschwitz*	N	Y	Y	Y	N	Y		*Hatfield*	N	Y	Y	N	N	Y
Chiles	Y	N	N	N	N	N		*Durenberger*	N	Y	Y	Y	N	Y		*Packwood*	N	Y	Y	N	N	Y
GEORGIA								**MISSISSIPPI**								**PENNSYLVANIA**						
Mattingly	N	Y	Y	Y	N	Y		*Cochran*	N	Y	Y	Y	N	Y		*Heinz*	Y	Y	Y	Y	N	N
Nunn	Y	Y	Y	Y	Y	Y		Stennis	Y	Y	Y	Y	N	N		*Specter*	N	N	N	Y	N	Y
HAWAII								**MISSOURI**								**RHODE ISLAND**						
Inouye	Y	N	N	N	N	?		*Danforth*	N	Y	Y	Y	Y	Y		*Chafee*	Y	Y	Y	N	N	N
Matsunaga	Y	N	N	N	N	N		Eagleton	Y	N	N	N	Y	N		Pell	Y	N	N	N	N	N
IDAHO								**MONTANA**								**SOUTH CAROLINA**						
McClure	N	Y	Y	Y	Y	Y		Baucus	Y	N	Y	Y	N	N		*Thurmond*	N	Y	Y	Y	N	Y
Symms	N	Y	Y	Y	Y	Y		Melcher	Y	N	N	Y	N	N		Hollings	?	?	N	N	N	N
ILLINOIS								**NEBRASKA**								**SOUTH DAKOTA**						
Percy	N	N	Y	Y	N	Y		Exon	Y	N	Y	N	Y	N		*Abdnor*	N	Y	Y	Y	N	Y
Dixon	Y	Y	N	Y	Y	N		Zorinsky	Y	Y	Y	N	Y	Y		*Pressler*	Y	N	Y	Y	N	Y
INDIANA								**NEVADA**								**TENNESSEE**						
Lugar	N	Y	Y	Y	N	Y		*Hecht*	N	Y	Y	Y	N	?		*Baker*	N	Y	?	Y	N	Y
Quayle	N	Y	Y	Y	Y	Y		*Laxalt*	N	+	Y	Y	N	Y		Sasser	Y	N	N	N	N	N

KEY

Y	Voted for (yea).
#	Paired for.
+	Announced for.
N	Voted against (nay).
X	Paired against.
-	Announced against.
P	Voted "present".
C	Voted "present" to avoid possible conflict of interest.
?	Did not vote or otherwise make a position known.

Democrats   *Republicans*

	88	89	90	91	92	93
TEXAS						
Tower	N	Y	Y	Y	N	Y
Bentsen	Y	N	Y	Y	N	N
UTAH						
Garn	N	Y	Y	Y	N	Y
Hatch	N	Y	Y	Y	N	Y
VERMONT						
Stafford	N	Y	Y	Y	N	N
Leahy	Y	N	N	N	N	N
VIRGINIA						
Trible	N	Y	Y	Y	N	Y
Warner	N	+	Y	Y	N	Y
WASHINGTON						
Evans	N	Y	Y	Y	Y	Y
Gorton	N	Y	Y	Y	Y	Y
WEST VIRGINIA						
Byrd	Y	N	N	N	N	N
Randolph	Y	N	N	N	N	N
WISCONSIN						
Kasten	N	Y	Y	Y	N	Y
Proxmire	Y	N	Y	Y	N	N
WYOMING						
Simpson	N	Y	Y	Y	Y	Y
Wallop	N	Y	Y	Y	N	Y

ND - Northern Democrats   SD - Southern Democrats (Southern states - Ala., Ark., Fla., Ga., Ky., La., Miss., N.C., Okla., S.C., Tenn., Texas, Va.)

88. HR 2163. Deficit Reduction. Chiles, D-Fla., amendment to reduce federal deficits by $204 billion over fiscal 1984-87 by limiting inflation-adjusted growth in defense to 4 percent, increasing taxes by $81.3 billion and reducing domestic discretionary spending by $17.4 billion. Rejected 49-49: R 6-49; D 43-0 (ND 30-0, SD 13-0), May 8, 1984.

89. HR 2163. Deficit Reduction. Domenici, R-N.M., motion to table (kill) the Bradley, D-N.J., amendment to modify the GOP-leadership deficit-reduction package by limiting inflation-adjusted growth for defense to 5 percent, increase non-defense discretionary programs from fiscal 1985-87 by $8.2 billion, and restore 7 percent of the savings in Medicare. Motion agreed to 51-43: R 46-5; D 5-38 (ND 2-28, SD 3-10), May 8, 1984.

90. HR 2163. Deficit Reduction. Dole, R-Kan., motion to table (kill) the Kennedy, D-Mass., amendment to the GOP-leadership deficit plan eliminating the increases in Part B, covering out-of-pocket patient costs, in Medicare premiums and deductible. Motion agreed to 58-36: R 48-3; D 10-33 (ND 4-26, SD 6-7), May 9, 1984.

91. HR 2163. Deficit Reduction. Dole, R-Kan., motion to table (kill) the Kennedy, D-Mass., amendment to the GOP-leader-

ship plan eliminating the delay in the eligibility for Medicare recipients from the first day of the month in which they turn 65 to the first day of the month after turning 65. Motion agreed to 59-36: R 48-4; D 11-32 (ND 5-25, SD 6-7), May 9, 1984.

92. HR 2163. Deficit Reduction. Gorton, R-Wash., substitute deficit-reduction plan reducing deficits by $234.3 billion from fiscal 1984-87 by capping the cost-of-living adjustment in non-means tested federal benefit programs at the Consumer Price Index (CPI) minus 3 percent; capping personal income tax indexing at the CPI minus 3 percent; reducing defense spending authority by about $2 billion in 1985; and increasing the level of non-defense discretionary spending by $2.7 billion in 1985. Rejected 23-72: R 12-40; D 11-32 (ND 7-23, SD 4-9), May 9, 1984.

93. HR 2163. Deficit Reduction. Baker, R-Tenn., motion to table (kill) the Chafee, R-R.I., amendment to merge the three-year defense and domestic statutory spending caps in the GOP-leadership deficit-reduction package and set the cap at $434.5 billion in fiscal 1985; $472.3 billion in 1986, and $514.6 billion in 1987. The amendment also would have reduced the defense spending level in the leadership plan by $37 billion over the three years and increased domestic spending by $20.3 billion. Motion agreed to 48-46: R 45-8; D 3-38 (ND 1-26, SD 2-12), May 10, 1984. A "yea" was a vote supporting the president's position.

KEY

- Y Voted for (yea).
- # Paired for.
- + Announced for.
- N Voted against (nay).
- X Paired against.
- - Announced against.
- P Voted "present".
- C Voted "present" to avoid possible conflict of interest.
- ? Did not vote or otherwise make a position known.

Democrats *Republicans*

	94	95	96	97	98	99	100	101
ALABAMA								
Denton	Y	N	Y	N	Y	N	Y	Y
Heflin	Y	Y	N	Y	Y	Y	Y	N
ALASKA								
Murkowski	Y	Y	Y	N	Y	Y	Y	Y
Stevens	Y	Y	Y	N	Y	Y	Y	Y
ARIZONA								
Goldwater	Y	Y	Y	N	Y	N	Y	Y
DeConcini	Y	Y	N	Y	Y	Y	Y	N
ARKANSAS								
Bumpers	Y	N	N	Y	N	Y	N	N
Pryor	Y	Y	N	?	?	Y	Y	Y
CALIFORNIA								
Wilson	?	Y	Y	Y	N	Y	Y	Y
Cranston	Y	N	N	Y	N	Y	N	N
COLORADO								
Armstrong	Y	Y	N	Y	N	Y	Y	Y
Hart	?	?	Y	?	?	?	?	?
CONNECTICUT								
Weicker	N	N	N	Y	N	Y	N	Y
Dodd	Y	N	N	Y	N	N	N	Y
DELAWARE								
Roth	Y	Y	Y	N	Y	N	Y	Y
Biden	Y	Y	Y	N	Y	N	Y	Y
FLORIDA								
Hawkins	Y	Y	Y	N	Y	N	Y	Y
Chiles	Y	Y	N	Y	Y	N	N	Y
GEORGIA								
Mattingly	Y	Y	Y	N	Y	N	Y	Y
Nunn	Y	N	N	Y	N	Y	N	Y
HAWAII								
Inouye	?	?	N	Y	N	?	N	Y
Matsunaga	?	?	N	?	N	Y	N	N
IDAHO								
McClure	Y	Y	Y	N	Y	N	Y	Y
Symms	Y	Y	Y	N	Y	N	Y	Y
ILLINOIS								
Percy	Y	Y	Y	N	Y	Y	Y	Y
Dixon	Y	Y	N	Y	Y	Y	N	N
INDIANA								
Lugar	Y	Y	Y	N	Y	N	Y	Y
Quayle	Y	Y	Y	N	Y	N	Y	Y

	94	95	96	97	98	99	100	101
IOWA								
Grassley	Y	Y	Y	N	Y	N	Y	Y
Jepsen	Y	Y	Y	?	?	?	?	?
KANSAS								
Dole	Y	Y	Y	N	Y	Y	Y	Y
Kassebaum	Y	Y	Y	Y	N	Y	N	Y
KENTUCKY								
Ford	Y	Y	N	Y	N	Y	N	Y
Huddleston	Y	Y	N	Y	N	Y	Y	Y
LOUISIANA								
Johnston	Y	N	N	N	Y	N	Y	Y
Long	Y	N	N	N	N	Y	Y	Y
MAINE								
Cohen	Y	Y	Y	N	N	Y	Y	Y
Mitchell	Y	Y	N	Y	Y	N	N	N
MARYLAND								
Mathias	Y	N	Y	N	?	?	?	?
Sarbanes	Y	Y	?	Y	N	Y	N	N
MASSACHUSETTS								
Kennedy	Y	?	Y	Y	N	Y	N	N
Tsongas	Y	Y	Y	Y	N	Y	N	N
MICHIGAN								
Levin	Y	Y	N	Y	N	Y	N	Y
Riegle	Y	N	Y	?	N	N	N	N
MINNESOTA								
Boschwitz	Y	Y	Y	N	Y	N	Y	Y
Durenberger	Y	Y	Y	N	Y	N	Y	Y
MISSISSIPPI								
Cochran	Y	Y	Y	N	Y	N	Y	Y
Stennis	Y	Y	N	Y	N	Y	Y	Y
MISSOURI								
Danforth	Y	Y	Y	N	Y	N	Y	Y
Eagleton	Y	Y	N	Y	N	Y	N	N
MONTANA								
Baucus	Y	Y	N	Y	N	Y	N	Y
Melcher	Y	Y	N	Y	N	N	N	N
NEBRASKA								
Exon	?	?	N	N	Y	N	Y	Y
Zorinsky	Y	N	N	Y	Y	N	Y	Y
NEVADA								
Hecht	Y	Y	Y	N	Y	N	Y	Y
Laxalt	Y	Y	Y	N	Y	N	Y	Y

	94	95	96	97	98	99	100	101
NEW HAMPSHIRE								
Humphrey	Y	Y	N	N	Y	N	Y	N
Rudman	Y	Y	Y	N	Y	N	Y	Y
NEW JERSEY								
Bradley	Y	N	Y	Y	N	N	N	N
Lautenberg	Y	Y	Y	Y	N	N	N	N
NEW MEXICO								
Domenici	Y	Y	Y	N	Y	N	Y	Y
Bingaman	Y	Y	N	Y	N	N	N	Y
NEW YORK								
D'Amato	Y	Y	Y	N	Y	Y	Y	Y
Moynihan	Y	Y	Y	N	Y	N	N	N
NORTH CAROLINA								
East	Y	Y	Y	N	Y	N	Y	Y
Helms	Y	Y	Y	N	Y	N	Y	Y
NORTH DAKOTA								
Andrews	Y	Y	Y	N	Y	N	Y	Y
Burdick	Y	Y	N	Y	N	N	N	Y
OHIO								
Glenn	Y	N	N	N	N	N	N	N
Metzenbaum	Y	N	Y	N	N	N	N	N
OKLAHOMA								
Nickles	Y	Y	Y	N	Y	N	Y	Y
Boren	Y	Y	N	Y	N	Y	Y	Y
OREGON								
Hatfield	Y	N	Y	N	Y	N	Y	Y
Packwood	Y	Y	Y	N	Y	Y	Y	Y
PENNSYLVANIA								
Heinz	Y	Y	Y	N	Y	N	Y	Y
Specter	Y	Y	Y	Y	Y	Y	Y	Y
RHODE ISLAND								
Chafee	Y	Y	Y	N	Y	N	Y	Y
Pell	Y	Y	Y	Y	N	Y	N	N
SOUTH CAROLINA								
Thurmond	Y	Y	Y	N	Y	N	Y	Y
Hollings	Y	N	N	Y	N	N	N	N
SOUTH DAKOTA								
Abdnor	Y	Y	Y	N	Y	N	Y	Y
Pressler	Y	Y	Y	Y	Y	Y	Y	Y
TENNESSEE								
Baker	Y	Y	Y	N	Y	N	Y	Y
Sasser	Y	Y	N	Y	N	Y	N	N

	94	95	96	97	98	99	100	101
TEXAS								
Tower	Y	Y	Y	N	Y	N	Y	Y
Bentsen	Y	N	N	Y	Y	N	N	Y
UTAH								
Garn	Y	Y	Y	N	Y	N	Y	Y
Hatch	?	?	Y	N	Y	N	Y	Y
VERMONT								
Stafford	Y	Y	Y	?	?	N	Y	Y
Leahy	Y	Y	N	Y	N	Y	N	N
VIRGINIA								
Trible	Y	Y	Y	N	Y	N	Y	Y
Warner	Y	Y	Y	N	Y	Y	Y	Y
WASHINGTON								
Evans	Y	Y	Y	N	Y	N	Y	Y
Gorton	Y	Y	Y	N	Y	N	Y	Y
WEST VIRGINIA								
Byrd	Y	N	N	Y	N	N	N	N
Randolph	Y	N	N	Y	N	N	N	Y
WISCONSIN								
Kasten	Y	Y	Y	N	Y	N	Y	Y
Proxmire	Y	Y	N	Y	N	Y	N	Y
WYOMING								
Simpson	Y	Y	Y	N	Y	N	Y	Y
Wallop	Y	N	Y	N	Y	N	Y	Y

ND - Northern Democrats   SD - Southern Democrats (Southern states - Ala., Ark., Fla., Ga., Ky., La., Miss., N.C., Okla., S.C., Tenn., Texas, Va.)

94. HR 2163. Deficit Reduction. Kasten, R-Wis., amendment to require congressional authorizing committees to recommend, no later than Sept. 30, 1984, ways to reduce the deficit over three years by $20 billion through cost-control measures such as those called for by the Grace commission, a businessmen's group that in January recommended ways to cut waste in the federal government. The administration also would be called on to adopt such recommendations to achieve $20 billion in cost savings. Adopted 93-1: R 52-1; D 41-0 (ND 27-0, SD 14-0), May 15, 1984.

95. HR 2163. Deficit Reduction. Boschwitz, R-Minn., amendment to direct the Congressional Budget Office and the Office of Management and Budget to study the feasibility of a "fair-play" approach to the budget process. This would allow an increase by the same percentage in every major part of the budget. Adopted 74-20: R 49-5; D 25-15 (ND 17-9, SD 8-6), May 15, 1984.

96. HR 2163. Deficit Reduction. Baker, R-Tenn., amendment to increase by $2 billion the spending authority levels for non-defense discretionary programs contained in the GOP-leadership plan to: $139.8 billion in fiscal 1985; $144.3 billion in fiscal 1986; and $151.5 billion in fiscal 1987. Adopted 62-37: R 53-2; D 9-35 (ND 9-21, SD 0-14), May 16, 1984. A "yea" was a vote supporting the president's position.

97. HR 2163. Deficit Reduction. Baucus, D-Mont., amendment to restore $588 million of the $9 billion in Medicare savings

that were included in the GOP-leadership plan. Rejected 44-50: R 7-46; D 37-4 (ND 26-2, SD 11-2), May 17, 1984.

98. HR 2163. Deficit Reduction. Weicker, R-Conn., motion to table (kill) the Kennedy, D-Mass., amendment to provide an additional $326.4 million over the next three years for child abuse services and five health programs, including childhood immunization and migrant health centers. Motion agreed to 63-32: R 50-2; D 13-30 (ND 7-23, SD 6-7), May 17, 1984.

99. HR 2163. Deficit Reduction. Specter, R-Pa., amendment to earmark $200 million to alleviate prison and jail overcrowding in federal, state and local facilities. Rejected 36-60: R 14-39; D 22-21 (ND 13-16, SD 9-5), May 17, 1984.

100. HR 2163. Deficit Reduction. Baker, R-Tenn., amendment to reduce federal deficits by $140 billion through fiscal 1987 by increasing taxes, limiting the increases in military spending, cutting federal benefit and other non-defense programs. Adopted 65-32: R 53-0; D 12-32 (ND 6-24, SD 6-8), May 17, 1984. A "yea" was a vote supporting the president's position.

101. HR 4170. Deficit Reduction. Passage of the bill to increase taxes $47.7 billion; reduce costs in benefit programs by $18.4 billion; and place three-year spending caps on military and non-defense spending, which combined would reduce federal deficits $140 billion through fiscal 1987. Passed 74-23: R 52-1; D 22-22 (ND 12-18, SD 10-4), May 17, 1984. A "yea" was a vote supporting the president's position.

KEY

Y	Voted for (yea).
#	Paired for.
+	Announced for.
N	Voted against (nay).
X	Paired against.
-	Announced against.
P	Voted "present".
C	Voted "present" to avoid possible conflict of interest.
?	Did not vote or otherwise make a position known.

Democrats *Republicans*

Senator	102	103	104	105	106	107	108	109
ALABAMA								
Denton	Y	Y	Y	?	+	Y	N	Y
Heflin	?	?	?	Y	Y	Y	Y	Y
ALASKA								
Murkowski	Y	Y	Y	Y	Y	Y	N	Y
Stevens	?	?	?	Y	?	Y	Y	Y
ARIZONA								
Goldwater	N	Y	Y	N	Y	N	Y	N
DeConcini	Y	N	Y	Y	Y	Y	Y	Y
ARKANSAS								
Bumpers	?	?	?	?	?	?	Y	Y
Pryor	?	?	Y	Y	Y	Y	Y	Y
CALIFORNIA								
Wilson	Y	Y	Y	Y	Y	Y	N	Y
Cranston	Y	N	Y	Y	Y	Y	Y	Y
COLORADO								
Armstrong	Y	N	Y	Y	Y	Y	N	Y
Hart	?	?	?	?	?	?	?	?
CONNECTICUT								
Weicker	?	?	?	?	?	Y	Y	Y
Dodd	?	N	Y	?	?	Y	Y	Y
DELAWARE								
Roth	Y	Y	Y	Y	Y	Y	N	Y
Biden	Y	N	Y	Y	Y	Y	Y	Y
FLORIDA								
Hawkins	Y	Y	Y	Y	Y	Y	N	Y
Chiles	Y	N	+	Y	Y	Y	Y	Y
GEORGIA								
Mattingly	?	?	?	Y	Y	Y	Y	Y
Nunn	Y	N	Y	?	+	Y	Y	Y
HAWAII								
Inouye	?	?	?	?	?	Y	Y	Y
Matsunaga	?	?	Y	Y	Y	?	Y	Y
IDAHO								
McClure	Y	Y	Y	Y	Y	Y	N	Y
Symms	Y	Y	Y	Y	Y	Y	N	Y
ILLINOIS								
Percy	?	+	+	?	?	Y	Y	Y
Dixon	Y	N	Y	?	?	Y	Y	Y
INDIANA								
Lugar	Y	Y	Y	Y	Y	Y	N	Y
Quayle	N	Y	N	Y	Y	Y	Y	Y
IOWA								
Grassley	Y	Y	Y	Y	Y	Y	N	Y
Jepsen	?	?	?	Y	Y	Y	N	Y
KANSAS								
Dole	Y	Y	Y	?	?	Y	N	Y
Kassebaum	Y	Y	Y	Y	Y	Y	Y	Y
KENTUCKY								
Ford	?	?	?	Y	Y	Y	Y	Y
Huddleston	Y	N	Y	?	?	?	?	Y
LOUISIANA								
Johnston	?	?	?	N	Y	Y	Y	Y
Long	Y	N	Y	Y	Y	Y	Y	Y
MAINE								
Cohen	Y	?	?	Y	Y	Y	Y	Y
Mitchell	Y	N	Y	Y	Y	Y	Y	Y
MARYLAND								
Mathias	?	?	?	?	?	Y	Y	Y
Sarbanes	?	?	Y	Y	Y	Y	Y	Y
MASSACHUSETTS								
Kennedy	Y	N	Y	?	?	Y	Y	Y
Tsongas	Y	N	Y	?	?	Y	Y	Y
MICHIGAN								
Levin	Y	N	Y	?	+	Y	Y	Y
Riegle	?	?	+	Y	Y	Y	Y	Y
MINNESOTA								
Boschwitz	Y	Y	Y	Y	Y	Y	Y	Y
Durenberger	?	?	Y	Y	Y	Y	Y	Y
MISSISSIPPI								
Cochran	?	?	?	?	?	Y	N	Y
Stennis	Y	N	Y	Y	Y	Y	Y	Y
MISSOURI								
Danforth	Y	Y	Y	Y	Y	Y	Y	Y
Eagleton	Y	N	Y	Y	Y	Y	Y	Y
MONTANA								
Baucus	Y	N	Y	Y	Y	Y	?	Y
Melcher	Y	N	Y	Y	Y	Y	Y	Y
NEBRASKA								
Exon	Y	-	+	?	Y	Y	Y	Y
Zorinsky	Y	N	Y	Y	Y	Y	N	Y
NEVADA								
Hecht	Y	Y	Y	Y	Y	Y	N	Y
Laxalt	?	?	?	?	?	Y	N	Y
NEW HAMPSHIRE								
Humphrey	Y	N	Y	Y	Y	Y	N	Y
Rudman	Y	Y	Y	Y	Y	Y	N	Y
NEW JERSEY								
Bradley	?	?	?	?	?	Y	Y	Y
Lautenberg	Y	N	Y	Y	Y	Y	Y	Y
NEW MEXICO								
Domenici	Y	Y	Y	Y	Y	Y	Y	Y
Bingaman	Y	N	Y	Y	Y	Y	Y	Y
NEW YORK								
D'Amato	Y	Y	Y	?	?	Y	Y	?
Moynihan	Y	N	Y	?	?	?	Y	Y
NORTH CAROLINA								
East	Y	Y	Y	Y	Y	Y	N	Y
Helms	Y	Y	Y	Y	Y	Y	N	Y
NORTH DAKOTA								
Andrews	Y	Y	Y	Y	Y	Y	Y	Y
Burdick	Y	N	Y	Y	Y	Y	Y	Y
OHIO								
Glenn	Y	N	Y	?	?	Y	Y	Y
Metzenbaum	Y	N	Y	?	Y	Y	Y	Y
OKLAHOMA								
Nickles	Y	N	Y	Y	Y	Y	N	Y
Boren	?	?	?	Y	Y	Y	Y	Y
OREGON								
Hatfield	Y	Y	Y	Y	Y	Y	Y	Y
Packwood	Y	Y	Y	Y	Y	Y	Y	Y
PENNSYLVANIA								
Heinz	Y	Y	Y	Y	Y	Y	Y	Y
Specter	Y	Y	Y	?	Y	Y	Y	Y
RHODE ISLAND								
Chafee	Y	Y	Y	?	Y	Y	Y	Y
Pell	Y	N	Y	?	+	Y	Y	Y
SOUTH CAROLINA								
Thurmond	?	+	+	Y	Y	Y	N	Y
Hollings	Y	N	Y	?	?	Y	Y	Y
SOUTH DAKOTA								
Abdnor	Y	Y	Y	Y	Y	Y	N	Y
Pressler	Y	Y	Y	?	?	Y	Y	Y
TENNESSEE								
Baker	Y	Y	Y	Y	Y	Y	Y	Y
Sasser	Y	N	Y	Y	?	Y	Y	Y
TEXAS								
Tower	Y	Y	Y	Y	Y	Y	N	?
Bentsen	Y	N	Y	Y	Y	Y	Y	Y
UTAH								
Garn	Y	Y	Y	Y	Y	Y	N	Y
Hatch	Y	Y	Y	Y	Y	Y	N	Y
VERMONT								
Stafford	Y	Y	Y	Y	Y	Y	Y	Y
Leahy	Y	N	Y	?	+	Y	Y	Y
VIRGINIA								
Trible	Y	Y	Y	Y	Y	Y	N	Y
Warner	Y	Y	Y	Y	Y	Y	N	Y
WASHINGTON								
Evans	Y	Y	Y	?	Y	Y	Y	Y
Gorton	Y	Y	Y	Y	Y	Y	Y	Y
WEST VIRGINIA								
Byrd	Y	N	Y	Y	Y	Y	Y	Y
Randolph	Y	N	Y	Y	Y	Y	Y	Y
WISCONSIN								
Kasten	Y	Y	Y	Y	Y	Y	N	Y
Proxmire	N	Y	Y	N	Y	Y	Y	Y
WYOMING								
Simpson	?	?	?	Y	Y	Y	N	Y
Wallop	Y	Y	Y	?	?	Y	N	+

ND - Northern Democrats   SD - Southern Democrats (Southern states - Ala., Ark., Fla., Ga., Ky., La., Miss., N.C., Okla., S.C., Tenn., Texas, Va.)

102. Procedural Motion. Baker, R-Tenn., motion to instruct the sergeant-at-arms to request the attendance of absent senators. Motion agreed to 73-3: R 42-2; D 31-1 (ND 23-1, SD 8-0), May 18, 1984.

103. H Con Res 280. First Budget Resolution, Fiscal 1985. Adoption of the concurrent resolution to set spending and revenue targets for fiscal 1985 as follows: budget authority, $1,012.7 billion; outlays, $925.5 billion; revenues, $743.8 billion; and deficit, $181.7 billion. Adopted 41-34: R 40-3; D 1-31 (ND 1-23, SD 0-8), May 18, 1984. A "yea" was a vote supporting the president's position.

104. H Con Res 304. Andrei Sakharov and Yelena Bonner. Adoption of the concurrent resolution to express the sense of Congress in protest against the Soviet Union's continued violation of the human rights of dissident Andrei Sakharov and his wife Yelena Bonner, and state that Yelena Bonner should be allowed to emigrate from the Soviet Union to seek medical treatment. Adopted 76-0: R 43-0; D 33-0 (ND 25-0, SD 8-0), May 18, 1984.

105. Procedural Motion. Baker, R-Tenn., motion to instruct the sergeant-at-arms to request the attendance of absent senators. Motion agreed to 65-4: R 40-2; D 25-2 (ND 16-1, SD 9-1), May 21, 1984.

106. HR 5174. Bankruptcy Court Act. Exon, D-Neb., amendment to prevent the parents of children born out of wedlock from escaping child support payments by filing for bankruptcy. Adopted 70-0: R 42-0; D 28-0 (ND 19-0, SD 9-0), May 21, 1984.

107. S 1651. Veterans' Dioxin and Radiation Exposure Compensation Standards. Simpson, R-Wyo.-Cranston, D-Calif., amendment to require the Veterans Administration to decide whether to grant compensation for Vietnam-era veterans exposed to Agent Orange, and for veterans exposed to radiation during atomic testing or the occupation of Nagasaki and Hiroshima. Adopted 95-0: R 55-0; D 40-0 (ND 28-0, SD 12-0), May 22, 1984. A "yea" was a vote supporting the president's position.

108. HR 5174. Bankruptcy Court Act. Mathias, R-Md., motion to table (kill) the Helms, R-N.C., amendment to amend the Federal Election Campaign Act to bar the use of compulsory union dues for political purposes. Motion agreed to 65-32: R 24-31; D 41-1 (ND 28-1, SD 13-0), May 22, 1984.

109. HR 3755. Social Security Disability Reform Act. Passage of the bill to revamp the Social Security disability review process and to provide payment of benefits to individuals whose cases are under appeal. Passed 96-0: R 52-0; D 44-0 (ND 30-0, SD 14-0), May 22, 1984. A "yea" was a vote supporting the president's position.

	110		110		110
ALABAMA		**IOWA**		**NEW HAMPSHIRE**	
Denton	N	*Grassley*	N	*Humphrey*	N
Heflin	N	*Jepsen*	N	*Rudman*	Y
ALASKA		**KANSAS**		**NEW JERSEY**	
Murkowski	N	*Dole*	N	Bradley	?
Stevens	N	*Kassebaum*	N	Lautenberg	Y
ARIZONA		**KENTUCKY**		**NEW MEXICO**	
Goldwater	?	Ford	Y	*Domenici*	N
DeConcini	X	Huddleston	Y	Bingaman	?
ARKANSAS		**LOUISIANA**		**NEW YORK**	
Bumpers	Y	Johnston	N	*D'Amato*	N
Pryor	Y	Long	Y	Moynihan	#
CALIFORNIA		**MAINE**		**NORTH CAROLINA**	
Wilson	N	*Cohen*	N	*East*	N
Cranston	Y	Mitchell	Y	*Helms*	N
COLORADO		**MARYLAND**		**NORTH DAKOTA**	
Armstrong	N	*Mathias*	Y	*Andrews*	N
Hart	?	Sarbanes	Y	Burdick	Y
CONNECTICUT		**MASSACHUSETTS**		**OHIO**	
Weicker	N	Kennedy	Y	Glenn	Y
Dodd	Y	Tsongas	Y	Metzenbaum	Y
DELAWARE		**MICHIGAN**		**OKLAHOMA**	
Roth	N	Levin	Y	*Nickles*	N
Biden	Y	Riegle	Y	Boren	N
FLORIDA		**MINNESOTA**		**OREGON**	
Hawkins	?	*Boschwitz*	N	*Hatfield*	Y
Chiles	Y	*Durenberger*	N	*Packwood*	?
GEORGIA		**MISSISSIPPI**		**PENNSYLVANIA**	
Mattingly	N	*Cochran*	N	*Heinz*	Y
Nunn	N	Stennis	Y	*Specter*	Y
HAWAII		**MISSOURI**		**RHODE ISLAND**	
Inouye	Y	*Danforth*	N	*Chafee*	N
Matsunaga	?	Eagleton	Y	Pell	Y
IDAHO		**MONTANA**		**SOUTH CAROLINA**	
McClure	N	Baucus	N	*Thurmond*	N
Symms	N	Melcher	Y	Hollings	Y
ILLINOIS		**NEBRASKA**		**SOUTH DAKOTA**	
Percy	N	Exon	N	*Abdnor*	N
Dixon	N	Zorinsky	N	*Pressler*	N
INDIANA		**NEVADA**		**TENNESSEE**	
Lugar	N	*Hecht*	N	*Baker*	N
Quayle	N	*Laxalt*	N	Sasser	Y

KEY

Y Voted for (yea).
Paired for.
+ Announced for.
N Voted against (nay).
X Paired against.
- Announced against.
P Voted "present".
C Voted "present" to avoid possible conflict of interest.
? Did not vote or otherwise make a position known.

Democrats   *Republicans*

	110
TEXAS	
Tower	N
Bentsen	Y
UTAH	
Garn	N
Hatch	N
VERMONT	
Stafford	N
Leahy	Y
VIRGINIA	
Trible	N
Warner	N
WASHINGTON	
Evans	N
Gorton	N
WEST VIRGINIA	
Byrd	Y
Randolph	Y
WISCONSIN	
Kasten	N
Proxmire	Y
WYOMING	
Simpson	N
Wallop	?

ND - Northern Democrats   SD - Southern Democrats (Southern states - Ala., Ark., Fla., Ga., Ky., La., Miss., N.C., Okla., S.C., Tenn., Texas, Va.)

110. Wilkinson Nomination. Kennedy, D-Mass., motion to recommit the nomination of J. Harvie Wilkinson III of Virginia to be a federal appeals court judge to the Judiciary Committee to allow for an additional day of hearings. Motion rejected 36-54: R 5-46; D 31-8 (ND 21-4, SD 10-4), May 24, 1984. A "nay" was a vote supporting the president's position.

	111	112	113	114	115	116
ALABAMA						
Denton	Y	Y	Y	Y	Y	Y
Heflin	?	Y	Y	Y	Y	Y
ALASKA						
Murkowski	Y	Y	Y	Y	Y	Y
Stevens	?	Y	Y	Y	N	Y
ARIZONA						
Goldwater	N	?	Y	N	Y	Y
DeConcini	?	Y	Y	Y	Y	Y
ARKANSAS						
Bumpers	?	Y	Y	Y	Y	Y
Pryor	?	Y	Y	Y	Y	Y
CALIFORNIA						
Wilson	Y	Y	Y	Y	Y	Y
Cranston	Y	Y	Y	Y	Y	Y
COLORADO						
Armstrong	?	Y	Y	Y	Y	Y
Hart	?	?	Y	?	Y	?
CONNECTICUT						
Weicker	?	?	Y	Y	Y	Y
Dodd	Y	Y	?	?	Y	Y
DELAWARE						
Roth	Y	Y	Y	Y	Y	Y
Biden	?	Y	Y	Y	Y	Y
FLORIDA						
Hawkins	Y	Y	Y	Y	Y	Y
Chiles	Y	Y	Y	Y	Y	Y
GEORGIA						
Mattingly	Y	Y	Y	Y	Y	Y
Nunn	?	Y	Y	Y	Y	Y
HAWAII						
Inouye	Y	Y	Y	Y	Y	Y
Matsunaga	Y	Y	Y	Y	Y	Y
IDAHO						
McClure	Y	Y	Y	Y	Y	Y
Symms	Y	N	N	Y	Y	Y
ILLINOIS						
Percy	Y	Y	Y	Y	?	?
Dixon	Y	Y	Y	Y	Y	Y
INDIANA						
Lugar	Y	Y	Y	Y	Y	Y
Quayle	?	Y	Y	Y	Y	Y

	111	112	113	114	115	116
IOWA						
Grassley	Y	Y	Y	Y	Y	Y
Jepsen	?	Y	?	?	?	?
KANSAS						
Dole	?	Y	Y	Y	Y	Y
Kassebaum	?	?	Y	Y	Y	Y
KENTUCKY						
Ford	Y	Y	Y	Y	Y	Y
Huddleston	?	Y	Y	Y	N	Y
LOUISIANA						
Johnston	Y	Y	Y	Y	Y	Y
Long	?	Y	Y	Y	N	Y
MAINE						
Cohen	?	Y	Y	Y	Y	Y
Mitchell	Y	Y	Y	Y	?	?
MARYLAND						
Mathias	Y	Y	Y	N	Y	Y
Sarbanes	?	Y	Y	Y	Y	Y
MASSACHUSETTS						
Kennedy	?	+	Y	Y	Y	Y
Tsongas	Y	?	Y	Y	N	Y
MICHIGAN						
Levin	Y	Y	Y	Y	Y	Y
Riegle	Y	Y	Y	Y	N	Y
MINNESOTA						
Boschwitz	Y	Y	Y	Y	N	Y
Durenberger	Y	Y	Y	N	Y	Y
MISSISSIPPI						
Cochran	?	Y	Y	Y	Y	Y
Stennis	Y	Y	Y	Y	Y	Y
MISSOURI						
Danforth	Y	Y	Y	Y	Y	Y
Eagleton	Y	Y	Y	?	?	?
MONTANA						
Baucus	?	Y	Y	Y	N	Y
Melcher	Y	Y	Y	Y	N	Y
NEBRASKA						
Exon	?	Y	Y	Y	Y	Y
Zorinsky	Y	Y	Y	Y	N	Y
NEVADA						
Hecht	Y	Y	Y	Y	Y	Y
Laxalt	Y	Y	Y	Y	Y	Y

	111	112	113	114	115	116
NEW HAMPSHIRE						
Humphrey	?	Y	Y	Y	N	Y
Rudman	Y	Y	Y	Y	Y	Y
NEW JERSEY						
Bradley	?	?	Y	Y	?	?
Lautenberg	?	Y	Y	Y	Y	Y
NEW MEXICO						
Domenici	Y	Y	Y	Y	Y	Y
Bingaman	?	Y	Y	Y	Y	Y
NEW YORK						
D'Amato	?	Y	Y	Y	N	Y
Moynihan	?	Y	Y	Y	Y	Y
NORTH CAROLINA						
East	?	N	Y	Y	Y	Y
Helms	Y	N	Y	Y	Y	Y
NORTH DAKOTA						
Andrews	Y	Y	Y	Y	Y	?
Burdick	Y	Y	Y	Y	Y	Y
OHIO						
Glenn	Y	Y	Y	Y	Y	Y
Metzenbaum	Y	Y	Y	Y	N	Y
OKLAHOMA						
Nickles	Y	Y	Y	Y	N	Y
Boren	Y	Y	Y	Y	Y	Y
OREGON						
Hatfield	Y	Y	+	+	+	+
Packwood	Y	Y	Y	Y	Y	Y
PENNSYLVANIA						
Heinz	Y	Y	Y	Y	Y	Y
Specter	Y	Y	Y	Y	Y	Y
RHODE ISLAND						
Chafee	Y	Y	Y	Y	Y	Y
Pell	?	Y	Y	Y	N	Y
SOUTH CAROLINA						
Thurmond	?	+	Y	Y	Y	Y
Hollings	Y	?	Y	Y	Y	Y
SOUTH DAKOTA						
Abdnor	Y	Y	Y	Y	N	Y
Pressler	Y	Y	Y	Y	N	Y
TENNESSEE						
Baker	Y	Y	Y	Y	Y	Y
Sasser	Y	Y	Y	Y	Y	Y

	111	112	113	114	115	116
TEXAS						
Tower	Y	Y	Y	Y	Y	Y
Bentsen	Y	Y	Y	Y	Y	Y
UTAH						
Garn	Y	Y	Y	Y	Y	Y
Hatch	Y	Y	Y	Y	Y	Y
VERMONT						
Stafford	Y	Y	Y	Y	Y	Y
Leahy	?	Y	Y	Y	Y	Y
VIRGINIA						
Trible	Y	Y	Y	Y	?	?
Warner	?	?	Y	Y	Y	Y
WASHINGTON						
Evans	?	Y	Y	Y	Y	Y
Gorton	Y	Y	Y	Y	Y	Y
WEST VIRGINIA						
Byrd	Y	Y	Y	Y	Y	Y
Randolph	?	Y	Y	Y	Y	Y
WISCONSIN						
Kasten	?	Y	Y	Y	Y	Y
Proxmire	N	Y	Y	Y	Y	Y
WYOMING						
Simpson	Y	?	?	?	?	?
Wallop	?	Y	Y	Y	Y	Y

ND - Northern Democrats   SD - Southern Democrats (Southern states - Ala., Ark., Fla., Ga., Ky., La., Miss., N.C., Okla., S.C., Tenn., Texas, Va.)

111. Procedural Motion. Baker, R-Tenn., motion to instruct the sergeant-at-arms to request the attendance of absent senators. Motion agreed to 61-2: R 37-1; D 24-1 (ND 16-1, SD 8-0), June 4, 1984.

112. S 1285. Emergency Mathematics and Science Education Act. Baker, R-Tenn., amendment (offered on behalf of Hatch, R-Utah) to authorize $75 million annually in aid in fiscal 1984-86 to magnet schools in school districts carrying out a desegregation plan. Adopted 86-3: R 46-3; D 40-0 (ND 27-0, SD 13-0), June 6, 1984.

113. S 2723. Omnibus Defense Authorization. Hollings, D-S.C., amendment expressing the sense of Congress that the current limitation on cost-of-living adjustments for federal retirees who are under 62 years of age should not be continued beyond fiscal 1985. Adopted 95-1: R 51-1; D 44-0 (ND 30-0, SD 14-0), June 7, 1984.

114. S 2723. Omnibus Defense Authorization. Proxmire, D-Wis., amendment expressing the sense of Congress that the president should insist that members of the NATO alliance increase their defense budgets by at least 3 percent, in addition to the cost of inflation in 1984 and 1985, and that Japan increase its planned defense spending in those years. Adopted 91-3: R 49-3; D 42-0 (ND 28-0, SD 14-0), June 7, 1984.

115. S 2723. Omnibus Defense Authorization. Tower, R-Texas, motion to table (kill) the Pressler, R-S.D., amendment to limit the rate of annual increase in U.S. defense expenditures in Europe to the average rate of annual increase in defense spending by the members of the NATO alliance. Motion agreed to 76-16: R 43-7; D 33-9 (ND 21-7, SD 12-2), June 7, 1984. A "yea" was a vote supporting the president's position.

116. S 2723. Omnibus Defense Authorization. Byrd, D-W.Va., amendment to prohibit diversion to other purposes of any of the secret amount of money authorized for the so-called "stealth" bomber and an improved air-launched cruise missile. Adopted 90-0: R 49-0; D 41-0 (ND 27-0, SD 14-0), June 7, 1984.

KEY

- Y Voted for (yea).
- # Paired for.
- + Announced for.
- N Voted against (nay).
- X Paired against.
- - Announced against.
- P Voted "present".
- C Voted "present" to avoid possible conflict of interest.
- ? Did not vote or otherwise make a position known.

Democrats *Republicans*

	117	118	119	120	121	122	123	124
ALABAMA								
Denton	N	Y	Y	Y	N	Y	Y	N
Heflin	Y	Y	Y	Y	N	Y	N	Y
ALASKA								
Murkowski	Y	N	Y	Y	Y	Y	Y	Y
Stevens	Y	+	Y	N	?	Y	Y	Y
ARIZONA								
Goldwater	Y	N	Y	Y	N	Y	Y	Y
DeConcini	Y	Y	N	N	Y	Y	N	Y
ARKANSAS								
Bumpers	Y	Y	N	N	Y	Y	Y	?
Pryor	Y	Y	Y	N	Y	Y	N	Y
CALIFORNIA								
Wilson	Y	Y	Y	Y	N	Y	Y	N
Cranston	Y	Y	N	N	Y	Y	N	Y
COLORADO								
Armstrong	?	Y	Y	N	Y	Y	N	Y
Hart	?	Y	N	N	?	?	N	Y
CONNECTICUT								
Weicker	Y	N	N	N	Y	Y	N	Y
Dodd	Y	?	N	N	Y	Y	N	Y
DELAWARE								
Roth	Y	Y	Y	N	Y	Y	?	?
Biden	Y	Y	N	N	Y	Y	N	Y
FLORIDA								
Hawkins	Y	?	Y	N	Y	?	N	Y
Chiles	Y	Y	N	N	Y	Y	Y	N
GEORGIA								
Mattingly	Y	Y	Y	Y	N	Y	Y	N
Nunn	?	Y	N	N	Y	Y	Y	N
HAWAII								
Inouye	Y	?	?	?	?	Y	N	Y
Matsunaga	Y	Y	N	N	Y	Y	N	Y
IDAHO								
McClure	N	?	Y	Y	N	Y	Y	N
Symms	N	Y	Y	Y	N	Y	Y	N
ILLINOIS								
Percy	?	Y	N	N	Y	Y	Y	N
Dixon	?	Y	N	N	Y	Y	Y	N
INDIANA								
Lugar	Y	Y	Y	Y	N	Y	Y	N
Quayle	Y	N	Y	Y	N	Y	Y	N
IOWA								
Grassley	Y	Y	Y	N	Y	Y	Y	N
Jepsen	?	Y	?	N	Y	Y	Y	N
KANSAS								
Dole	Y	Y	Y	Y	N	Y	N	N
Kassebaum	Y	?	Y	N	Y	Y	N	Y
KENTUCKY								
Ford	Y	Y	N	N	Y	Y	N	Y
Huddleston	Y	Y	N	N	Y	Y	N	Y
LOUISIANA								
Johnston	Y	Y	N	N	Y	Y	N	N
Long	Y	Y	Y	N	N	Y	Y	N
MAINE								
Cohen	?	Y	N	N	Y	Y	N	Y
Mitchell	+	Y	N	N	Y	Y	N	Y
MARYLAND								
Mathias	Y	Y	N	N	Y	Y	Y	N
Sarbanes	Y	Y	N	N	Y	Y	Y	N
MASSACHUSETTS								
Kennedy	Y	Y	-	-	+	Y	N	?
Tsongas	Y	Y	N	N	Y	Y	N	?
MICHIGAN								
Levin	Y	Y	N	N	Y	Y	N	Y
Riegle	Y	Y	N	N	Y	Y	N	Y
MINNESOTA								
Boschwitz	Y	?	Y	N	Y	Y	N	Y
Durenberger	Y	?	N	N	Y	Y	N	Y
MISSISSIPPI								
Cochran	?	Y	N	Y	Y	Y	N	Y
Stennis	Y	Y	N	Y	?	Y	Y	N
MISSOURI								
Danforth	Y	Y	Y	Y	N	Y	Y	N
Eagleton	?	?	?	?	?	Y	Y	N
MONTANA								
Baucus	Y	Y	Y	N	Y	Y	N	Y
Melcher	Y	Y	N	N	Y	Y	N	Y
NEBRASKA								
Exon	Y	Y	N	N	Y	Y	N	Y
Zorinsky	Y	Y	Y	N	Y	Y	N	N
NEVADA								
Hecht	Y	?	?	?	?	Y	Y	N
Laxalt	Y	Y	Y	Y	N	Y	Y	N
NEW HAMPSHIRE								
Humphrey	Y	Y	Y	N	Y	Y	Y	N
Rudman	Y	Y	Y	Y	N	Y	Y	N
NEW JERSEY								
Bradley	?	Y	N	N	Y	Y	N	Y
Lautenberg	?	Y	N	N	Y	Y	N	Y
NEW MEXICO								
Domenici	Y	Y	Y	N	Y	Y	Y	N
Bingaman	Y	Y	N	N	Y	Y	Y	N
NEW YORK								
D'Amato	Y	Y	Y	N	Y	Y	N	Y
Moynihan	Y	Y	N	N	Y	Y	N	Y
NORTH CAROLINA								
East	Y	Y	Y	Y	N	Y	Y	N
Helms	Y	Y	Y	Y	N	Y	N	N
NORTH DAKOTA								
Andrews	?	Y	+	-	+	?	?	?
Burdick	Y	Y	N	N	Y	Y	N	Y
OHIO								
Glenn	?	Y	N	N	Y	Y	Y	N
Metzenbaum	Y	Y	N	N	Y	Y	Y	N
OKLAHOMA								
Nickles	Y	Y	Y	Y	N	Y	Y	N
Boren	Y	Y	Y	Y	N	Y	N	Y
OREGON								
Hatfield	+	Y	N	N	Y	Y	Y	N
Packwood	Y	Y	N	N	?	Y	Y	N
PENNSYLVANIA								
Heinz	Y	Y	N	N	Y	Y	N	Y
Specter	Y	Y	Y	N	Y	Y	Y	N
RHODE ISLAND								
Chafee	Y	Y	N	N	Y	Y	Y	N
Pell	Y	Y	N	N	Y	N	N	Y
SOUTH CAROLINA								
Thurmond	Y	Y	Y	N	Y	Y	Y	N
Hollings	Y	?	Y	Y	?	Y	N	Y
SOUTH DAKOTA								
Abdnor	Y	Y	Y	Y	N	Y	Y	N
Pressler	Y	Y	N	N	Y	Y	N	?
TENNESSEE								
Baker	Y	Y	Y	Y	N	Y	Y	N
Sasser	Y	Y	N	N	Y	Y	N	Y
TEXAS								
Tower	Y	Y	Y	N	Y	Y	Y	N
Bentsen	Y	Y	N	N	Y	Y	Y	N
UTAH								
Garn	Y	Y	Y	Y	N	Y	N	Y
Hatch	Y	Y	Y	N	Y	N	Y	N
VERMONT								
Stafford	Y	?	N	N	Y	Y	N	Y
Leahy	Y	Y	N	N	Y	Y	N	Y
VIRGINIA								
Trible	Y	?	?	?	?	Y	N	Y
Warner	Y	Y	N	N	Y	Y	Y	N
WASHINGTON								
Evans	Y	Y	N	N	Y	Y	N	Y
Gorton	Y	Y	Y	N	Y	Y	N	Y
WEST VIRGINIA								
Byrd	Y	Y	N	N	N	Y	N	Y
Randolph	Y	Y	N	N	Y	Y	N	Y
WISCONSIN								
Kasten	Y	Y	Y	Y	N	Y	-	+
Proxmire	Y	N	N	N	Y	Y	Y	N
WYOMING								
Simpson	?	Y	Y	Y	Y	Y	Y	N
Wallop	N	Y	Y	Y	N	Y	Y	?

ND - Northern Democrats   SD - Southern Democrats (Southern states - Ala., Ark., Fla., Ga., Ky., La., Miss., N.C., Okla., S.C., Tenn., Texas, Va.)

117. S 2723. Omnibus Defense Authorization. Byrd, D-W.Va., amendment to provide that the Competition Advocate General, established for each of the armed services, would be a general or admiral appointed to the position for a two-year term. Adopted 80-4: R 43-4; D 37-0 (ND 24-0, SD 13-0), June 8, 1984.

118. Procedural Motion. Baker, R-Tenn., motion to instruct the sergeant-at-arms to request the attendance of absent senators. Motion agreed to 82-5: R 42-4; D 40-1 (ND 27-1, SD 13-0), June 12, 1984.

119. S 2723. Omnibus Defense Authorization. Wallop, R-Wyo., amendment to the Warner, R-Va., amendment *(see vote 121, below)*, to provide that nothing in the Warner amendment would prevent the president from acting in the national security interests of the United States. Rejected 45-48: R 38-13; D 7-35 (ND 2-26, SD 5-9), June 12, 1984.

120. S 2723. Omnibus Defense Authorization. Goldwater, R-Ariz., motion to table (kill) the Warner, R-Va., amendment *(see vote 121, below)*. Motion rejected 29-65: R 25-27; D 4-38 (ND 0-28, SD 4-10), June 12, 1984.

121. S 2723. Omnibus Defense Authorization. Warner, R-Va., amendment to bar tests of an anti-satellite missile (ASAT) against a target in space unless the president certifies his willingness to seek ASAT arms control limitations with the Soviet Union. Adopted 61-28: R 26-24; D 35-4 (ND 26-1, SD 9-3), June 12, 1984.

122. S 2723. Omnibus Defense Authorization. Tower, R-Texas, amendment to the Glenn, D-Ohio, amendment, to call for a "Citizen-Soldier GI Bill," to limit an educational benefit program for military personnel to a test period of Sept. 30, 1984, to Sept. 30, 1988, and restrict participation to 12,500 persons. Adopted 96-1: R 53-0; D 43-1 (ND 29-1, SD 14-0), June 13, 1984.

123. S 2723. Omnibus Defense Authorization. Tower, R-Texas, motion to table (kill) the Armstrong, R-Colo., amendment to establish a GI Bill program of educational benefits for veterans who complete their service or for active-duty personnel who complete 10 years of service and to scrap the Veterans Educational Assistance Program. Motion rejected 46-51: R 33-19; D 13-32 (ND 7-24, SD 6-8), June 13, 1984. A "yea" was a vote supporting the president's position. (The Senate subsequently tabled the Armstrong amendment *(see vote 125, p. 24-S).*)

124. S 2723. Omnibus Defense Authorization. Armstrong, R-Colo., motion to waive relevant portions of the Budget Act preventing floor consideration of a floor amendment creating an entitlement program unless the Senate has first adopted a budget resolution incorporating the program for the year that the entitlement would take effect. Motion rejected 44-48: R 16-34; D 28-14 (ND 21-8, SD 7-6), June 13, 1984.

KEY

- Y Voted for (yea).
- # Paired for.
- + Announced for.
- N Voted against (nay).
- X Paired against.
- - Announced against.
- P Voted "present".
- C Voted "present" to avoid possible conflict of interest.
- ? Did not vote or otherwise make a position known.

Democrats *Republicans*

	125	126	127	128	129	130	131	132
ALABAMA								
Denton	Y	Y	Y	Y	Y	Y	Y	Y
Heflin	N	Y	Y	Y	Y	Y	Y	Y
ALASKA								
Murkowski	Y	Y	Y	Y	Y	Y	Y	Y
Stevens	Y	Y	Y	Y	Y	Y	Y	Y
ARIZONA								
Goldwater	Y	Y	Y	Y	Y	Y	Y	Y
DeConcini	N	N	Y	Y	Y	Y	N	#
ARKANSAS								
Bumpers	?	?	?	?	?	?	N	N
Pryor	N	Y	N	Y	Y	N	N	N
CALIFORNIA								
Wilson	Y	Y	Y	Y	Y	Y	Y	Y
Cranston	N	N	N	Y	Y	N	N	N
COLORADO								
Armstrong	N	N	Y	Y	Y	Y	Y	Y
Hart	N	Y	N	Y	Y	N	N	N
CONNECTICUT								
Weicker	?	Y	N	Y	?	N	N	N
Dodd	N	Y	N	Y	Y	N	N	N
DELAWARE								
Roth	?	?	?	?	?	Y	Y	Y
Biden	N	Y	N	Y	Y	N	N	N
FLORIDA								
Hawkins	N	Y	Y	Y	Y	Y	Y	Y
Chiles	Y	N	N	Y	Y	N	N	N
GEORGIA								
Mattingly	Y	Y	Y	Y	Y	Y	Y	Y
Nunn	Y	Y	N	Y	Y	Y	Y	Y
HAWAII								
Inouye	N	Y	N	Y	Y	Y	N	N
Matsunaga	N	N	N	Y	Y	N	N	N
IDAHO								
McClure	Y	Y	Y	Y	Y	Y	Y	Y
Symms	Y	Y	Y	Y	Y	Y	Y	Y
ILLINOIS								
Percy	Y	Y	N	Y	Y	?	?	?
Dixon	Y	Y	N	Y	Y	N	N	N
INDIANA								
Lugar	Y	N	Y	Y	Y	Y	Y	Y
Quayle	Y	Y	Y	Y	Y	Y	Y	Y

	125	126	127	128	129	130	131	132
IOWA								
Grassley	Y	N	Y	Y	Y	N	Y	N
Jepsen	Y	Y	Y	Y	Y	Y	Y	Y
KANSAS								
Dole	N	N	Y	Y	Y	Y	Y	Y
Kassebaum	Y	Y	Y	Y	Y	Y	Y	Y
KENTUCKY								
Ford	N	N	N	Y	Y	N	N	N
Huddleston	N	Y	N	Y	Y	N	N	N
LOUISIANA								
Johnston	Y	Y	N	Y	Y	Y	Y	N
Long	Y	Y	Y	Y	?	Y	Y	N
MAINE								
Cohen	N	N	N	Y	Y	Y	Y	Y
Mitchell	N	N	N	Y	Y	N	N	N
MARYLAND								
Mathias	Y	Y	N	Y	Y	N	N	N
Sarbanes	N	Y	N	Y	Y	N	N	N
MASSACHUSETTS								
Kennedy	?	?	-	?	?	N	N	N
Tsongas	?	?	?	?	?	N	N	N
MICHIGAN								
Levin	N	N	N	Y	N	N	N	N
Riegle	N	N	N	Y	Y	N	N	N
MINNESOTA								
Boschwitz	N	Y	N	Y	Y	Y	Y	Y
Durenberger	N	Y	N	Y	?	Y	N	N
MISSISSIPPI								
Cochran	N	Y	N	Y	Y	Y	Y	Y
Stennis	Y	Y	N	Y	?	Y	Y	Y
MISSOURI								
Danforth	Y	Y	Y	Y	Y	Y	Y	Y
Eagleton	Y	Y	N	Y	Y	N	N	N
MONTANA								
Baucus	N	Y	N	Y	Y	N	N	N
Melcher	N	Y	N	Y	Y	N	N	N
NEBRASKA								
Exon	Y	Y	N	Y	Y	Y	N	N
Zorinsky	N	N	Y	Y	Y	Y	Y	Y
NEVADA								
Hecht	Y	Y	Y	Y	Y	Y	Y	Y
Laxalt	Y	Y	Y	Y	Y	Y	Y	Y

	125	126	127	128	129	130	131	132
NEW HAMPSHIRE								
Humphrey	Y	Y	Y	Y	Y	Y	N	N
Rudman	Y	Y	Y	Y	Y	Y	Y	Y
NEW JERSEY								
Bradley	N	Y	N	Y	N	N	N	N
Lautenberg	N	Y	N	Y	Y	N	N	N
NEW MEXICO								
Domenici	Y	Y	Y	Y	Y	Y	Y	Y
Bingaman	Y	Y	N	Y	Y	N	N	N
NEW YORK								
D'Amato	N	Y	Y	Y	Y	Y	Y	Y
Moynihan	N	Y	N	Y	Y	N	N	N
NORTH CAROLINA								
East	Y	Y	Y	Y	Y	Y	Y	Y
Helms	Y	Y	Y	Y	Y	Y	Y	Y
NORTH DAKOTA								
Andrews	?	?	?	?	?	?	?	?
Burdick	N	N	N	Y	Y	N	N	N
OHIO								
Glenn	Y	Y	Y	Y	Y	Y	N	N
Metzenbaum	Y	Y	N	Y	Y	N	N	N
OKLAHOMA								
Nickles	Y	Y	Y	Y	Y	Y	Y	Y
Boren	N	Y	Y	Y	Y	N	N	N
OREGON								
Hatfield	Y	Y	N	Y	Y	N	N	N
Packwood	Y	Y	Y	Y	Y	Y	N	N
PENNSYLVANIA								
Heinz	N	Y	N	Y	?	Y	Y	Y
Specter	N	Y	Y	Y	Y	Y	Y	N
RHODE ISLAND								
Chafee	Y	Y	N	Y	Y	N	?	Y
Pell	N	Y	N	Y	Y	N	N	N
SOUTH CAROLINA								
Thurmond	Y	Y	Y	Y	Y	Y	Y	Y
Hollings	N	N	Y	Y	Y	N	N	N
SOUTH DAKOTA								
Abdnor	Y	Y	Y	Y	Y	Y	Y	Y
Pressler	N	N	Y	Y	Y	N	N	N
TENNESSEE								
Baker	Y	?	#	?	?	Y	Y	Y
Sasser	N	Y	N	Y	Y	N	N	N

	125	126	127	128	129	130	131	132
TEXAS								
Tower	Y	Y	Y	Y	Y	Y	Y	Y
Bentsen	Y	Y	N	Y	Y	N	?	X
UTAH								
Garn	N	Y	Y	Y	Y	Y	Y	Y
Hatch	N	Y	Y	Y	Y	Y	Y	Y
VERMONT								
Stafford	?	?	X	Y	Y	N	N	N
Leahy	N	Y	N	Y	Y	N	N	N
VIRGINIA								
Trible	N	Y	N	Y	Y	Y	Y	Y
Warner	Y	Y	Y	Y	Y	Y	Y	Y
WASHINGTON								
Evans	N	N	Y	Y	Y	N	N	N
Gorton	Y	Y	Y	Y	Y	Y	Y	Y
WEST VIRGINIA								
Byrd	N	N	N	Y	Y	N	Y	N
Randolph	N	N	N	Y	Y	N	Y	N
WISCONSIN								
Kasten	-	?	+	+	+	Y	Y	Y
Proxmire	Y	Y	N	Y	Y	N	N	N
WYOMING								
Simpson	Y	Y	Y	Y	Y	N	Y	Y
Wallop	Y	Y	Y	Y	Y	Y	Y	Y

ND - Northern Democrats   SD - Southern Democrats (Southern states - Ala., Ark., Fla., Ga., Ky., La., Miss., N.C., Okla., S.C., Tenn., Texas, Va.)

125. S 2723. Omnibus Defense Authorization. Tower, R-Texas, motion to table (kill) the Armstrong, R-Colo., amendment to establish a GI Bill program of educational benefits for veterans who complete their service or for active-duty personnel who complete 10 years of service and to scrap the Veterans Educational Assistance Program. This version of Armstrong's amendment had revised language saying that no payment would be made except from annual appropriations. Motion agreed to 47-45: R 34-16; D 13-29 (ND 7-22, SD 6-7), June 13, 1984. A "yea" was a vote supporting the president's position.

126. S 2723. Omnibus Defense Authorization. Glenn, D-Ohio, amendment to establish a "Citizen-Soldier GI Bill" program open to recruits in certain job specialties who could contribute $250 of their pay a month and, upon completion of two years of service, be eligible for educational benefits of $500 a month for three years. Adopted 72-20: R 43-7; D 29-13 (ND 19-10, SD 10-3), June 13, 1984.

127. S 2723. Omnibus Defense Authorization. Tower, R-Texas, motion to table (kill) the Percy, R-Ill., amendment to reduce by $100 million the amount authorized for the strategic defense initiative. Motion agreed to 47-45: R 40-10; D 7-35 (ND 3-26, SD 4-9), June 13, 1984. A "yea" was a vote supporting the president's position.

128. S 2723. Omnibus Defense Authorization. Exon, D-Neb., amendment to urge the president to press for a resolution of the issue of Americans missing in Indochina and to seek the immediate release of Americans still held captive there and of the remains not yet returned of those who died there. Adopted 93-0: R 51-0; D 42-0 (ND 29-0, SD 13-0), June 13, 1984.

129. S 2723. Omnibus Defense Authorization. Goldwater, R-Ariz., amendment to reduce by $7.9 million the authorization for purchase of the Army's UH-60 Blackhawk helicopter, without affecting the number of helicopters to be acquired. Adopted 88-0: R 48-0; D 40-0 (ND 29-0, SD 11-0), June 13, 1984.

130. S 2723. Omnibus Defense Authorization. Baker, R-Tenn., motion to table (kill) the Dixon, D-Ill., motion to recommit the bill to the Armed Services Committee for five days with instructions to report back to the Senate with a $293.7 billion defense authorization bill so as to have 5 percent inflation-adjusted defense growth in fiscal 1985 compared to the previous year. Motion agreed to 55-43: R 46-7; D 9-36 (ND 3-28, SD 6-8), June 14, 1984. A "yea" was a vote supporting the president's position.

131. S 2723. Omnibus Defense Authorization. Tower, R-Texas, motion to table (kill) the Leahy, D-Vt., amendment to delete $2.622 billion for production of the MX missile in fiscal 1985 and transfer $1.4 billion of the savings into a variety of nonnuclear equipment and improvements in defense readiness. Motion agreed to 55-41: R 45-7; D 10-34 (ND 4-27, SD 6-7), June 14, 1984. A "yea" was a vote supporting the president's position.

132. S 2723. Omnibus Defense Authorization. Tower, R-Texas, motion to table (kill) the Moynihan, D-N.Y., amendment to produce no additional MX missiles in fiscal 1985 but to keep the MX production line ready for production pending completion of a new study of the mobile, single-warhead "Midgetman" missile. Motion agreed to 49-48: R 43-10; D 5-38 (ND 2-28, SD 3-10), June 14, 1984, with Vice President Bush casting a "yea" vote to break the 48-48 tie. A "yea" was a vote supporting the president's position.

KEY

- Y Voted for (yea).
- # Paired for.
- + Announced for.
- N Voted against (nay).
- X Paired against.
- - Announced against.
- P Voted "present".
- C Voted "present" to avoid possible conflict of interest.
- ? Did not vote or otherwise make a position known.

Democrats *Republicans*

	133	134	135	136	137	138	139	140
ALABAMA								
Denton	N	Y	Y	Y	N	Y	N	Y
Heflin	Y	Y	Y	Y	N	Y	Y	Y
ALASKA								
Murkowski	Y	Y	Y	Y	Y	Y	N	Y
Stevens	Y	Y	Y	Y	N	Y	N	Y
ARIZONA								
Goldwater	Y	Y	?	?	Y	?	N	Y
DeConcini	N	N	Y	Y	Y	Y	Y	N
ARKANSAS								
Bumpers	N	Y	Y	Y	?	?	?	Y
Pryor	N	Y	Y	Y	?	?	?	N
CALIFORNIA								
Wilson	Y	Y	Y	Y	N	Y	Y	Y
Cranston	N	Y	Y	Y	?	?	?	?
COLORADO								
Armstrong	N	Y	Y	N	Y	N	Y	Y
Hart	?	?	?	?	?	?	?	?
CONNECTICUT								
Weicker	Y	Y	Y	Y	Y	N	Y	N
Dodd	N	Y	Y	Y	?	Y	?	N
DELAWARE								
Roth	Y	Y	Y	Y	N	Y	N	Y
Biden	N	Y	Y	Y	Y	Y	Y	N
FLORIDA								
Hawkins	N	Y	Y	Y	?	+	N	Y
Chiles	Y	Y	Y	Y	Y	Y	Y	Y
GEORGIA								
Mattingly	Y	Y	Y	Y	?	?	N	Y
Nunn	Y	Y	Y	Y	Y	Y	Y	Y
HAWAII								
Inouye	N	?	+	+	Y	Y	Y	Y
Matsunaga	N	Y	Y	Y	Y	Y	Y	N
IDAHO								
McClure	Y	Y	Y	N	Y	N	Y	Y
Symms	Y	Y	N	Y	Y	Y	N	Y
ILLINOIS								
Percy	?	?	?	?	?	?	?	?
Dixon	Y	Y	Y	Y	Y	Y	Y	Y
INDIANA								
Lugar	Y	Y	Y	Y	Y	N	Y	Y
Quayle	Y	Y	N	Y	N	Y	Y	Y
IOWA								
Grassley	Y	Y	Y	Y	N	Y	N	Y
Jepsen	Y	Y	?	?	?	?	?	Y
KANSAS								
Dole	N	Y	Y	Y	N	Y	N	Y
Kassebaum	Y	Y	Y	Y	Y	Y	N	Y
KENTUCKY								
Ford	N	Y	?	?	Y	Y	Y	N
Huddleston	N	Y	Y	Y	?	?	?	Y
LOUISIANA								
Johnston	Y	Y	Y	Y	Y	Y	Y	Y
Long	N	Y	Y	Y	Y	Y	Y	Y
MAINE								
Cohen	N	Y	Y	Y	Y	Y	Y	Y
Mitchell	N	Y	Y	Y	Y	Y	Y	N
MARYLAND								
Mathias	Y	Y	?	?	Y	Y	Y	Y
Sarbanes	N	Y	Y	Y	?	?	Y	N
MASSACHUSETTS								
Kennedy	N	Y	Y	Y	?	Y	Y	N
Tsongas	N	Y	Y	Y	?	N	Y	N
MICHIGAN								
Levin	N	Y	Y	Y	Y	Y	Y	N
Riegle	N	Y	?	?	Y	Y	Y	N
MINNESOTA								
Boschwitz	Y	Y	?	+	N	Y	N	Y
Durenberger	Y	Y	Y	?	N	N	Y	Y
MISSISSIPPI								
Cochran	Y	Y	Y	Y	?	?	?	Y
Stennis	?	?	Y	?	Y	Y	Y	Y
MISSOURI								
Danforth	Y	Y	?	?	Y	Y	Y	Y
Eagleton	?	Y	Y	Y	Y	Y	Y	N
MONTANA								
Baucus	N	Y	Y	Y	Y	Y	Y	N
Melcher	N	Y	Y	Y	Y	Y	Y	N
NEBRASKA								
Exon	Y	Y	Y	?	?	?	?	?
Zorinsky	Y	Y	Y	Y	P	Y	Y	?
NEVADA								
Hecht	Y	Y	Y	Y	N	Y	Y	Y
Laxalt	Y	?	?	?	Y	Y	Y	Y
NEW HAMPSHIRE								
Humphrey	Y	Y	N	Y	?	?	Y	Y
Rudman	Y	Y	N	Y	Y	Y	Y	Y
NEW JERSEY								
Bradley	N	N	Y	Y	Y	Y	N	Y
Lautenberg	N	N	Y	Y	+	Y	Y	N
NEW MEXICO								
Domenici	N	Y	?	?	Y	Y	Y	Y
Bingaman	N	Y	Y	Y	Y	Y	Y	N
NEW YORK								
D'Amato	N	Y	Y	Y	?	?	?	Y
Moynihan	N	?	Y	Y	Y	Y	?	Y
NORTH CAROLINA								
East	Y	Y	Y	Y	N	Y	N	Y
Helms	Y	Y	Y	Y	Y	Y	N	Y
NORTH DAKOTA								
Andrews	?	?	?	?	?	Y	Y	N
Burdick	Y	Y	Y	Y	+	Y	Y	N
OHIO								
Glenn	N	Y	Y	Y	Y	Y	Y	Y
Metzenbaum	N	Y	?	?	?	?	?	N
OKLAHOMA								
Nickles	Y	Y	Y	Y	N	Y	N	Y
Boren	Y	Y	Y	Y	Y	Y	Y	Y
OREGON								
Hatfield	N	Y	Y	Y	Y	Y	Y	N
Packwood	Y	?	Y	Y	Y	Y	Y	Y
PENNSYLVANIA								
Heinz	Y	Y	?	?	N	Y	N	Y
Specter	Y	Y	Y	Y	Y	Y	Y	N
RHODE ISLAND								
Chafee	Y	Y	Y	Y	Y	Y	Y	Y
Pell	N	Y	Y	Y	+	?	?	-
SOUTH CAROLINA								
Thurmond	N	Y	Y	Y	N	Y	N	Y
Hollings	N	Y	Y	Y	N	Y	Y	Y
SOUTH DAKOTA								
Abdnor	Y	Y	Y	Y	?	Y	N	Y
Pressler	N	Y	Y	Y	?	?	?	Y
TENNESSEE								
Baker	N	Y	Y	Y	Y	Y	?	Y
Sasser	N	Y	Y	Y	Y	Y	Y	N
TEXAS								
Tower	Y	Y	Y	?	Y	Y	N	Y
Bentsen	?	?	Y	Y	Y	Y	Y	N
UTAH								
Garn	Y	Y	Y	Y	Y	Y	N	Y
Hatch	N	Y	Y	Y	N	Y	N	Y
VERMONT								
Stafford	Y	Y	Y	Y	?	?	?	N
Leahy	N	Y	Y	Y	?	?	Y	N
VIRGINIA								
Trible	Y	Y	Y	Y	?	Y	Y	Y
Warner	Y	Y	Y	Y	?	Y	Y	Y
WASHINGTON								
Evans	Y	Y	Y	N	Y	N	Y	Y
Gorton	Y	Y	Y	N	Y	N	Y	Y
WEST VIRGINIA								
Byrd	N	Y	Y	Y	Y	Y	Y	N
Randolph	N	Y	Y	Y	Y	Y	Y	N
WISCONSIN								
Kasten	N	N	Y	Y	Y	Y	Y	N
Proxmire	N	N	N	Y	Y	Y	Y	N
WYOMING								
Simpson	Y	N	Y	Y	Y	N	Y	N
Wallop	Y	Y	Y	Y	N	Y	N	Y

ND - Northern Democrats   SD - Southern Democrats (Southern states - Ala., Ark., Fla., Ga., Ky., La., Miss., N.C., Okla., S.C., Tenn., Texas, Va.)

133. S 2723. Omnibus Defense Authorization. Tower, R-Texas, motion to table (kill) the Cohen, R-Maine, amendment to institute a 5.5 percent pay raise for all military personnel, effective Jan. 1, 1985. Motion agreed to 49-45: R 40-13; D 9-32 (ND 4-25, SD 5-7), June 14, 1984.

134. S 2723. Omnibus Defense Authorization. Tower, R-Texas, motion to table (kill) the Proxmire, D-Wis., amendment to delete a provision allowing chauffeur-driven transportation between home and work for certain senior Pentagon officials. Motion agreed to 85-6: R 49-2; D 36-4 (ND 24-4, SD 12-0), in the session that began June 14, 1984.

135. S 2723. Omnibus Defense Authorization. Byrd, D-W.Va., amendment to create a commission on the Merchant Marine and defense. Adopted 80-5: R 41-4; D 39-1 (ND 26-1, SD 13-0), June 15, 1984.

136. S 2723. Omnibus Defense Authorization. Nunn, D-Ga., amendment to support establishment of nuclear risk reduction centers in the United States and the Soviet Union. Adopted 82-0: R 43-0; D 39-0 (ND 26-0, SD 13-0), June 15, 1984.

137. S 2723. Omnibus Defense Authorization. Bradley, D N.J., amendment expressing the sense of Congress that a permanent site for the Olympic Games should be established that would insulate the games from international politics. Adopted 48-22: R 22-20; D 26-2 (ND 18-0, SD 8-2), June 18, 1984.

138. S 2723. Omnibus Defense Authorization. Symms, R-Idaho, amendment expressing the sense of the Senate that the United States prevent the extension of Cuban aggressive activities in the Western Hemisphere. Adopted 77-3: R 43-2; D 34-1 (ND 23-1, SD 11-0), June 18, 1984.

139. S 2723. Omnibus Defense Authorization. Hatfield, R-Ore., motion to table (kill) the Murkowski, R-Alaska, amendment to require a study of the export of U.S.-produced crude oil. Motion agreed to 54-29: R 20-28; D 34-1 (ND 23-1, SD 11-0), June 18, 1984.

140. S 2723. Omnibus Defense Authorization. Tower, R-Texas, motion to table (kill) the Kennedy, D-Mass., amendment to require prior congressional approval for the introduction of U.S. combat troops into El Salvador or Nicaragua. Motion agreed to 63-31: R 49-5; D 14-26 (ND 5-21, SD 9-5), June 18, 1984. A "yea" was a vote supporting the president's position.

CQ Senate Votes 141 - 148

Corresponding to Congressional Record Votes 141, 142, 143, 144, 145, 146, 147, 148

	141	142	143	144	145	146	147	148
ALABAMA								
Denton	Y	Y	Y	N	N	Y	Y	N
Heflin	Y	Y	Y	N	Y	Y	Y	N
ALASKA								
Murkowski	Y	Y	Y	Y	Y	Y	Y	Y
Stevens	Y	Y	Y	Y	Y	Y	Y	N
ARIZONA								
Goldwater	Y	Y	Y	N	N	Y	Y	N
DeConcini	Y	Y	Y	Y	Y	N	Y	Y
ARKANSAS								
Bumpers	N	Y	Y	Y	Y	N	Y	Y
Pryor	N	Y	Y	Y	Y	N	Y	Y
CALIFORNIA								
Wilson	Y	Y	Y	N	Y	Y	Y	N
Cranston	N	Y	Y	Y	Y	N	Y	Y
COLORADO								
Armstrong	Y	Y	Y	Y	Y	Y	Y	N
Hart	?	?	?	?	?	?	?	?
CONNECTICUT								
Weicker	N	Y	Y	Y	Y	N	Y	Y
Dodd	N	Y	Y	Y	Y	N	Y	Y
DELAWARE								
Roth	Y	Y	Y	Y	N	Y	Y	Y
Biden	N	Y	Y	Y	Y	N	Y	Y
FLORIDA								
Hawkins	Y	Y	Y	Y	Y	Y	Y	Y
Chiles	Y	Y	Y	Y	Y	N	Y	Y
GEORGIA								
Mattingly	Y	Y	Y	N	Y	N	Y	N
Nunn	Y	Y	Y	Y	N	N	Y	Y
HAWAII								
Inouye	N	Y	Y	Y	Y	N	Y	Y
Matsunaga	N	Y	Y	Y	Y	N	Y	Y
IDAHO								
McClure	Y	Y	Y	Y	N	Y	Y	N
Symms	Y	Y	Y	N	N	Y	Y	N
ILLINOIS								
Percy	?	Y	Y	Y	Y	N	Y	Y
Dixon	Y	Y	Y	Y	N	N	Y	Y
INDIANA								
Lugar	Y	Y	Y	N	N	Y	Y	N
Quayle	Y	Y	Y	N	N	Y	Y	N
IOWA								
Grassley	Y	Y	Y	Y	N	Y	Y	Y
Jepsen	Y	Y	Y	Y	N	Y	Y	Y
KANSAS								
Dole	Y	Y	Y	Y	N	Y	Y	Y
Kassebaum	N	Y	Y	Y	Y	N	Y	Y
KENTUCKY								
Ford	N	Y	Y	Y	Y	N	Y	Y
Huddleston	N	Y	Y	Y	Y	N	Y	Y
LOUISIANA								
Johnston	Y	Y	Y	Y	N	N	Y	Y
Long	Y	Y	Y	N	N	Y	Y	N
MAINE								
Cohen	N	Y	Y	Y	Y	N	Y	Y
Mitchell	N	Y	Y	Y	Y	N	Y	Y
MARYLAND								
Mathias	Y	Y	Y	Y	Y	N	Y	Y
Sarbanes	N	Y	Y	Y	Y	N	Y	Y
MASSACHUSETTS								
Kennedy	N	Y	Y	Y	Y	N	Y	Y
Tsongas	N	Y	Y	Y	Y	N	Y	Y
MICHIGAN								
Levin	N	Y	Y	Y	Y	N	Y	Y
Riegle	N	Y	Y	Y	Y	N	Y	Y
MINNESOTA								
Boschwitz	Y	Y	Y	Y	Y	Y	Y	Y
Durenberger	Y	Y	Y	Y	Y	N	Y	Y
MISSISSIPPI								
Cochran	Y	Y	Y	Y	N	Y	Y	Y
Stennis	Y	Y	Y	Y	N	N	Y	Y
MISSOURI								
Danforth	Y	Y	Y	Y	Y	N	Y	Y
Eagleton	N	Y	Y	Y	Y	N	Y	Y
MONTANA								
Baucus	N	Y	Y	Y	N	N	Y	Y
Melcher	N	Y	Y	Y	N	N	Y	Y
NEBRASKA								
Exon	?	Y	Y	Y	Y	N	Y	Y
Zorinsky	N	Y	Y	Y	Y	Y	Y	N
NEVADA								
Hecht	Y	Y	Y	N	Y	Y	Y	N
Laxalt	Y	Y	Y	N	Y	Y	Y	N
NEW HAMPSHIRE								
Humphrey	Y	Y	Y	Y	Y	N	Y	Y
Rudman	Y	Y	Y	Y	Y	N	Y	Y
NEW JERSEY								
Bradley	N	Y	Y	Y	Y	N	Y	Y
Lautenberg	N	Y	Y	Y	Y	N	Y	Y
NEW MEXICO								
Domenici	Y	Y	Y	Y	Y	Y	Y	Y
Bingaman	N	Y	Y	Y	Y	N	Y	Y
NEW YORK								
D'Amato	Y	Y	Y	Y	Y	N	Y	Y
Moynihan	N	Y	Y	Y	Y	N	Y	Y
NORTH CAROLINA								
East	Y	Y	Y	N	N	Y	Y	N
Helms	Y	Y	Y	N	Y	Y	Y	N
NORTH DAKOTA								
Andrews	Y	Y	Y	Y	Y	N	Y	Y
Burdick	N	Y	Y	Y	Y	N	Y	Y
OHIO								
Glenn	N	?	?	Y	Y	N	Y	Y
Metzenbaum	N	Y	Y	Y	Y	N	Y	Y
OKLAHOMA								
Nickles	Y	Y	Y	N	Y	Y	Y	N
Boren	Y	Y	Y	Y	Y	N	Y	Y
OREGON								
Hatfield	N	Y	Y	Y	Y	N	Y	Y
Packwood	Y	Y	Y	Y	Y	N	Y	Y
PENNSYLVANIA								
Heinz	Y	Y	Y	Y	Y	N	Y	Y
Specter	Y	Y	Y	Y	Y	N	Y	Y
RHODE ISLAND								
Chafee	Y	Y	Y	Y	Y	N	Y	Y
Pell	-	Y	Y	Y	Y	N	Y	Y
SOUTH CAROLINA								
Thurmond	Y	Y	Y	Y	N	Y	Y	N
Hollings	Y	Y	Y	Y	Y	N	Y	Y
SOUTH DAKOTA								
Abdnor	Y	Y	Y	Y	N	Y	Y	N
Pressler	N	Y	Y	Y	N	N	Y	Y
TENNESSEE								
Baker	Y	Y	?	Y	N	Y	Y	N
Sasser	N	Y	Y	Y	Y	N	Y	Y
TEXAS								
Tower	Y	Y	Y	Y	N	Y	Y	N
Bentsen	N	Y	Y	Y	N	N	Y	Y
UTAH								
Garn	Y	Y	Y	N	Y	Y	Y	Y
Hatch	Y	Y	Y	N	Y	Y	Y	Y
VERMONT								
Stafford	N	Y	Y	Y	N	N	Y	Y
Leahy	N	Y	Y	Y	Y	N	Y	Y
VIRGINIA								
Trible	Y	Y	Y	Y	Y	N	Y	Y
Warner	Y	Y	Y	Y	Y	Y	Y	Y
WASHINGTON								
Evans	Y	Y	Y	Y	Y	N	Y	Y
Gorton	Y	Y	Y	Y	Y	N	Y	Y
WEST VIRGINIA								
Byrd	N	Y	Y	Y	Y	N	Y	Y
Randolph	N	Y	Y	Y	Y	N	Y	Y
WISCONSIN								
Kasten	Y	Y	Y	Y	N	Y	Y	Y
Proxmire	N	Y	Y	N	N	Y	Y	Y
WYOMING								
Simpson	Y	Y	Y	Y	N	N	Y	Y
Wallop	Y	Y	Y	N	N	Y	Y	N

ND - Northern Democrats   SD - Southern Democrats (Southern states - Ala., Ark., Fla., Ga., Ky., La., Miss., N.C., Okla., S.C., Tenn., Texas, Va.)

141. S 2723. Omnibus Defense Authorization. Tower, R-Texas, motion to table (kill) the Kennedy, D-Mass., amendment to provide that nothing in the bill shall be construed as authorization for funds to assist insurgent military forces in Nicaragua (the so-called "contras"). Motion agreed to 58-38: R 48-6; D 10-32 (ND 2-26, SD 8-6), June 18, 1984. A "yea" was a vote supporting the president's position.

142. S 2723. Omnibus Defense Authorization. Byrd, D-W.Va., amendment expressing the sense of Congress that the free world should take steps to ensure that the people of Afghanistan have food and medical supplies. Adopted 98-0: R 55-0; D 43-0 (ND 29-0, SD 14-0), June 19, 1984.

143. S 2723. Omnibus Defense Authorization. Cohen, R-Maine, amendment to the Mathias, R-Md., amendment, expressing the sense of Congress that the president should try to discuss with the Soviet Union ways of verifying limitations on nuclear-armed, sea-launched cruise missiles. Adopted 97-0: R 54-0; D 43-0 (ND 29-0, SD 14-0), June 19, 1984. (The Mathias amendment, as amended, subsequently was adopted by voice vote.)

144. S 2723. Omnibus Defense Authorization. Bumpers, D-Ark., amendment expressing the sense of Congress that the United States should continue to abide by certain limits contained in the U.S.-Soviet strategic arms limitation treaty (SALT II) signed in 1979 but never ratified, so long as the Soviet Union observes those limits. Adopted 82-17: R 40-15; D 42-2 (ND 30-0, SD 12-2), June 19, 1984.

145. S 2723. Omnibus Defense Authorization. Trible, R-Va., motion to table (kill) the Jepsen, R-Iowa, amendment to the Trible amendment, to limit certain benefits to the divorced spouses of military personnel whose marriages continued during at least 20 years of the former spouse's military service. Motion agreed to 70-29: R 35-20; D 35-9 (ND 26-4, SD 9-5), June 19, 1984. (The Trible amendment, subsequently adopted by voice vote, would extend the benefits to former spouses who were married to a military member during at least 15 years of military service.)

146. S 2723. Omnibus Defense Authorization. Tower, R-Texas, motion to table (kill) the Kennedy, D-Mass., amendment *(see vote 148, below)*. Motion rejected 34-65: R 31-24; D 3-41 (ND 1-29, SD 2-12), June 20, 1984. A "yea" was a vote supporting the president's position.

147. S 2723. Omnibus Defense Authorization. Symms, R-Idaho, amendment to the Kennedy, D-Mass., amendment *(see vote 148, below)*, declaring that, in accordance with international law, the United States had no obligation to continue abiding by any arms control treaty the Soviet Union had violated. Adopted 99-0: R 55-0; D 44-0 (ND 30-0, SD 14-0), June 20, 1984.

148. S 2723. Omnibus Defense Authorization. Kennedy, D-Mass., amendment expressing the sense of Congress that the president should seek Senate approval of two treaties banning underground nuclear explosions larger than 150 kilotons, and should resume negotiations with the Soviet Union seeking a comprehensive nuclear test ban treaty. Adopted 77-22: R 36-19; D 41-3 (ND 29-1, SD 12-2), June 20, 1984. A "nay" was a vote supporting the president's position.

KEY

Y Voted for (yea).
\# Paired for.
+ Announced for.
N Voted against (nay).
X Paired against.
- Announced against.
P Voted "present".
C Voted "present" to avoid possible conflict of interest.
? Did not vote or otherwise make a position known.

Democrats   Republicans

	149	150	151	152	153
ALABAMA					
Denton	Y	Y	Y	Y	?
Heflin	Y	Y	Y	Y	N
ALASKA					
Murkowski	Y	Y	Y	Y	Y
Stevens	Y	Y	Y	Y	Y
ARIZONA					
Goldwater	Y	Y	Y	Y	Y
DeConcini	N	Y	N	Y	N
ARKANSAS					
Bumpers	N	Y	N	Y	Y
Pryor	N	Y	N	Y	N
CALIFORNIA					
Wilson	Y	Y	Y	Y	Y
Cranston	N	Y	N	Y	N
COLORADO					
Armstrong	Y	Y	Y	Y	Y
Hart	Y	Y	?	?	?
CONNECTICUT					
Weicker	Y	Y	Y	Y	Y
Dodd	Y	Y	N	Y	N
DELAWARE					
Roth	N	Y	N	Y	Y
Biden	N	Y	N	Y	N
FLORIDA					
Hawkins	Y	Y	Y	Y	N
Chiles	N	Y	N	Y	N
GEORGIA					
Mattingly	Y	Y	Y	Y	Y
Nunn	N	Y	N	Y	N
HAWAII					
Inouye	N	Y	N	Y	N
Matsunaga	N	Y	N	Y	?
IDAHO					
McClure	Y	Y	N	Y	Y
Symms	?	Y	Y	Y	Y
ILLINOIS					
Percy	Y	Y	Y	Y	Y
Dixon	N	Y	Y	Y	N
INDIANA					
Lugar	Y	Y	Y	Y	Y
Quayle	Y	Y	Y	Y	Y

	149	150	151	152	153
IOWA					
Grassley	N	Y	Y	?	Y
Jepsen	Y	Y	Y	Y	Y
KANSAS					
Dole	Y	Y	Y	Y	?
Kassebaum	Y	Y	?	?	Y
KENTUCKY					
Ford	N	Y	Y	Y	N
Huddleston	?	?	?	?	Y
LOUISIANA					
Johnston	N	Y	N	Y	Y
Long	?	?	?	?	?
MAINE					
Cohen	Y	Y	Y	Y	Y
Mitchell	Y	Y	N	Y	N
MARYLAND					
Mathias	Y	N	N	Y	N
Sarbanes	N	Y	N	Y	N
MASSACHUSETTS					
Kennedy	N	Y	Y	N	N
Tsongas	Y	Y	N	N	?
MICHIGAN					
Levin	N	Y	Y	Y	Y
Riegle	N	Y	Y	Y	N
MINNESOTA					
Boschwitz	Y	Y	Y	Y	Y
Durenberger	Y	Y	?	?	Y
MISSISSIPPI					
Cochran	Y	Y	Y	Y	Y
Stennis	N	Y	?	?	N
MISSOURI					
Danforth	Y	Y	Y	Y	Y
Eagleton	N	Y	N	Y	Y
MONTANA					
Baucus	N	Y	N	Y	Y
Melcher	N	Y	N	Y	N
NEBRASKA					
Exon	N	Y	Y	Y	Y
Zorinsky	N	Y	N	Y	Y
NEVADA					
Hecht	Y	Y	Y	Y	Y
Laxalt	Y	Y	Y	Y	Y

	149	150	151	152	153
NEW HAMPSHIRE					
Humphrey	N	Y	Y	Y	Y
Rudman	Y	Y	Y	Y	Y
NEW JERSEY					
Bradley	N	Y	N	Y	N
Lautenberg	N	Y	N	Y	N
NEW MEXICO					
Domenici	Y	Y	Y	Y	Y
Bingaman	N	Y	N	Y	Y
NEW YORK					
D'Amato	Y	Y	Y	Y	N
Moynihan	Y	Y	N	Y	N
NORTH CAROLINA					
East	Y	Y	Y	Y	Y
Helms	Y	Y	Y	Y	Y
NORTH DAKOTA					
Andrews	Y	Y	N	Y	Y
Burdick	N	N	N	Y	N
OHIO					
Glenn	N	Y	Y	Y	N
Metzenbaum	N	Y	N	N	N
OKLAHOMA					
Nickles	Y	Y	Y	Y	Y
Boren	N	Y	Y	Y	N
OREGON					
Hatfield	Y	N	N	N	Y
Packwood	Y	Y	?	?	Y
PENNSYLVANIA					
Heinz	Y	Y	Y	Y	N
Specter	Y	Y	Y	Y	Y
RHODE ISLAND					
Chafee	?	?	?	?	?
Pell	N	Y	N	N	Y
SOUTH CAROLINA					
Thurmond	Y	Y	Y	Y	Y
Hollings	N	Y	?	?	Y
SOUTH DAKOTA					
Abdnor	Y	Y	Y	Y	Y
Pressler	N	Y	?	?	Y
TENNESSEE					
Baker	Y	Y	Y	Y	Y
Sasser	N	Y	N	Y	N

	149	150	151	152	153
TEXAS					
Tower	Y	Y	Y	Y	Y
Bentsen	N	Y	N	Y	N
UTAH					
Garn	Y	Y	Y	Y	Y
Hatch	Y	Y	Y	Y	Y
VERMONT					
Stafford	Y	Y	?	?	Y
Leahy	N	Y	N	Y	N
VIRGINIA					
Trible	Y	Y	Y	Y	Y
Warner	Y	Y	Y	Y	Y
WASHINGTON					
Evans	Y	Y	N	Y	N
Gorton	Y	Y	Y	Y	Y
WEST VIRGINIA					
Byrd	N	Y	N	Y	N
Randolph	N	Y	N	Y	N
WISCONSIN					
Kasten	Y	Y	Y	Y	Y
Proxmire	N	Y	N	N	N
WYOMING					
Simpson	Y	Y	N	Y	N
Wallop	Y	Y	Y	Y	Y

ND - Northern Democrats   SD - Southern Democrats (Southern states - Ala., Ark., Fla., Ga., Ky., La., Miss., N.C., Okla., S.C., Tenn., Texas, Va.)

149. S 2723. Omnibus Defense Authorization. Tower, R-Texas, motion to table (kill) the Nunn, D-Ga., amendment to reduce the number of U.S. military personnel stationed in Europe by 30,000 per year for three years, beginning at the end of 1987, unless other NATO member nations had increased their defense spending by certain amounts. Motion agreed to 55-41: R 49-4; D 6-37 (ND 5-26, SD 1-11), June 20, 1984. A "yea" was a vote supporting the president's position.

150. S 2723. Omnibus Defense Authorization. Cohen, R-Maine, amendment to set a limit of 326,414 on the number of U.S. military personnel stationed in Europe after Sept. 30, 1985, and to encourage the president to seek increased defense spending by other NATO member nations. Adopted 94-3: R 52-2; D 42-1 (ND 30-1, SD 12-0), June 20, 1984. (For parliamentary reasons, the Cohen amendment was offered as an amendment to an earlier version of the Nunn, D-Ga., amendment, which was tabled *(see vote 149, above)*.)

151. S 2723. Omnibus Defense Authorization. Tower, R-Texas, motion to table (kill) the Roth, R-Del., amendment to bar the purchase of HMMWV trucks until certain tests had been completed. Motion agreed to 51-38: R 42-7; D 9-31 (ND 6-24, SD 3-7), in the session that began June 20, 1984.

152. HR 5167. Defense Authorization. Passage of the bill to authorize $213.5 billion for weapons procurement, military research and operations, and maintenance programs of the Department of Defense in fiscal 1985. Passed 82-6: R 47-1; D 35-5 (ND 25-5, SD 10-0), in the session that began June 20, 1984.

153. HR 5653. Energy and Water Development Appropriations, Fiscal 1985. Hatfield, R-Ore., motion to table (kill) the DeConcini, D-Ariz., amendment to increase by $5 million the funding available for solar-thermal research in the Department of Energy. Motion agreed to 60-33: R 48-4; D 12-29 (ND 8-20, SD 4-9), June 21, 1984.

	154	155	156	157	158	159	160	161
ALABAMA								
Denton	N	Y	Y	Y	Y	Y	N	Y
Heflin	N	?	?	Y	Y	Y	N	Y
ALASKA								
Murkowski	Y	Y	Y	Y	Y	Y	N	Y
Stevens	?	?	Y	N	Y	Y	N	Y
ARIZONA								
Goldwater	?	Y	Y	Y	N	Y	?	?
DeConcini	N	Y	Y	N	Y	Y	Y	N
ARKANSAS								
Bumpers	Y	Y	Y	N	Y	Y	N	Y
Pryor	?	?	?	N	Y	Y	N	Y
CALIFORNIA								
Wilson	?	Y	Y	N	Y	Y	N	Y
Cranston	Y	Y	Y	N	Y	N	N	Y
COLORADO								
Armstrong	?	Y	?	Y	N	Y	N	Y
Hart	?	?	?	?	?	?	?	?
CONNECTICUT								
Weicker	?	?	Y	N	Y	N	N	Y
Dodd	?	Y	Y	N	Y	Y	N	Y
DELAWARE								
Roth	Y	Y	Y	N	Y	Y	Y	N
Biden	N	Y	Y	N	Y	Y	Y	N
FLORIDA								
Hawkins	Y	?	N	N	Y	Y	N	Y
Chiles	Y	Y	Y	N	Y	Y	N	Y
GEORGIA								
Mattingly	N	Y	Y	Y	Y	Y	N	Y
Nunn	N	Y	Y	Y	Y	Y	Y	Y
HAWAII								
Inouye	Y	Y	Y	N	Y	N	N	Y
Matsunaga	Y	Y	Y	N	Y	Y	N	Y
IDAHO								
McClure	?	Y	Y	Y	N	Y	N	Y
Symms	N	Y	Y	Y	N	Y	N	Y
ILLINOIS								
Percy	Y	?	Y	N	Y	N	N	Y
Dixon	N	Y	Y	?	+	Y	N	Y
INDIANA								
Lugar	Y	Y	Y	N	Y	N	N	Y
Quayle	Y	Y	Y	N	Y	Y	Y	Y

	154	155	156	157	158	159	160	161
IOWA								
Grassley	N	Y	Y	N	N	Y	N	Y
Jepsen	N	?	Y	N	Y	Y	N	Y
KANSAS								
Dole	N	Y	Y	N	Y	Y	N	Y
Kassebaum	N	Y	Y	N	Y	Y	N	Y
KENTUCKY								
Ford	Y	Y	Y	Y	Y	Y	N	Y
Huddleston	?	Y	Y	Y	Y	Y	N	Y
LOUISIANA								
Johnston	Y	Y	?	Y	N	Y	N	Y
Long	?	Y	Y	Y	N	Y	N	Y
MAINE								
Cohen	N	Y	Y	N	Y	Y	N	Y
Mitchell	?	Y	Y	N	Y	Y	N	Y
MARYLAND								
Mathias	Y	Y	Y	Y	Y	N	N	Y
Sarbanes	?	Y	?	N	Y	Y	N	Y
MASSACHUSETTS								
Kennedy	?	?	Y	N	Y	Y	N	Y
Tsongas	?	?	?	N	Y	Y	N	Y
MICHIGAN								
Levin	N	Y	+	N	Y	Y	N	Y
Riegle	Y	Y	Y	N	Y	Y	N	Y
MINNESOTA								
Boschwitz	Y	Y	Y	N	Y	N	N	Y
Durenberger	Y	Y	Y	N	Y	Y	N	Y
MISSISSIPPI								
Cochran	Y	?	Y	N	Y	Y	N	Y
Stennis	N	Y	Y	N	N	Y	N	Y
MISSOURI								
Danforth	N	Y	Y	N	Y	N	N	Y
Eagleton	Y	?	?	N	Y	Y	N	Y
MONTANA								
Baucus	N	N	Y	Y	N	Y	N	Y
Melcher	Y	Y	Y	N	Y	N	Y	Y
NEBRASKA								
Exon	N	Y	Y	N	Y	Y	Y	Y
Zorinsky	N	Y	Y	N	Y	Y	Y	Y
NEVADA								
Hecht	Y	Y	Y	N	Y	Y	N	Y
Laxalt	?	?	Y	Y	Y	Y	N	Y

	154	155	156	157	158	159	160	161
NEW HAMPSHIRE								
Humphrey	N	?	Y	Y	N	Y	Y	N
Rudman	N	Y	Y	Y	Y	Y	N	Y
NEW JERSEY								
Bradley	N	Y	Y	N	Y	N	N	Y
Lautenberg	Y	Y	Y	N	Y	Y	N	Y
NEW MEXICO								
Domenici	Y	Y	Y	N	Y	Y	N	Y
Bingaman	Y	Y	Y	N	Y	Y	N	Y
NEW YORK								
D'Amato	?	Y	Y	Y	Y	Y	N	Y
Moynihan	Y	Y	Y	Y	Y	Y	N	Y
NORTH CAROLINA								
East	N	Y	Y	Y	Y	Y	Y	N
Helms	?	Y	Y	N	Y	Y	N	Y
NORTH DAKOTA								
Andrews	Y	Y	Y	Y	Y	Y	N	Y
Burdick	N	Y	Y	?	+	N	N	Y
OHIO								
Glenn	?	Y	Y	N	Y	Y	Y	N
Metzenbaum	N	Y	N	Y	N	Y	N	Y
OKLAHOMA								
Nickles	N	Y	Y	Y	Y	Y	Y	Y
Boren	N	Y	Y	N	Y	Y	N	Y
OREGON								
Hatfield	Y	Y	Y	N	Y	Y	N	Y
Packwood	Y	Y	Y	N	Y	Y	N	Y
PENNSYLVANIA								
Heinz	Y	+	Y	N	Y	Y	N	Y
Specter	Y	Y	Y	N	Y	Y	Y	Y
RHODE ISLAND								
Chafee	?	Y	Y	N	Y	N	N	Y
Pell	N	+	+	N	Y	Y	N	Y
SOUTH CAROLINA								
Thurmond	N	Y	Y	N	Y	Y	N	Y
Hollings	Y	Y	Y	N	Y	Y	Y	N
SOUTH DAKOTA								
Abdnor	Y	?	?	Y	Y	Y	N	Y
Pressler	N	?	Y	Y	Y	Y	N	Y
TENNESSEE								
Baker	Y	Y	Y	N	Y	Y	N	Y
Sasser	N	Y	Y	N	Y	Y	N	Y

KEY

- **Y** Voted for (yea).
- **#** Paired for.
- **+** Announced for.
- **N** Voted against (nay).
- **X** Paired against.
- **-** Announced against.
- **P** Voted "present".
- **C** Voted "present" to avoid possible conflict of interest.
- **?** Did not vote or otherwise make a position known.

Democrats   *Republicans*

	154	155	156	157	158	159	160	161
TEXAS								
Tower	?	Y	Y	N	Y	Y	N	Y
Bentsen	?	Y	Y	N	Y	Y	N	Y
UTAH								
Garn	Y	Y	Y	Y	Y	Y	N	N
Hatch	Y	Y	Y	Y	Y	Y	Y	N
VERMONT								
Stafford	?	Y	Y	N	Y	Y	N	Y
Leahy	Y	?	Y	Y	N	Y	N	Y
VIRGINIA								
Trible	?	Y	Y	N	Y	Y	N	Y
Warner	N	Y	Y	N	Y	Y	N	Y
WASHINGTON								
Evans	N	Y	Y	N	Y	N	N	Y
Gorton	Y	Y	Y	N	Y	N	N	Y
WEST VIRGINIA								
Byrd	Y	Y	Y	N	Y	Y	N	Y
Randolph	+	Y	Y	N	Y	Y	N	Y
WISCONSIN								
Kasten	N	Y	Y	Y	Y	Y	Y	N
Proxmire	N	N	Y	N	Y	Y	N	Y
WYOMING								
Simpson	N	Y	Y	N	Y	Y	N	Y
Wallop	Y	Y	Y	N	Y	Y	N	Y

ND - Northern Democrats   SD - Southern Democrats (Southern states - Ala., Ark., Fla., Ga., Ky., La., Miss., N.C., Okla., S.C., Tenn., Texas, Va.)

154. HR 5753. Legislative Branch Appropriations, Fiscal 1985. Appropriations Committee amendment to restore a 2 percent across-the-board cut in fiscal 1985 legislative branch appropriations. Adopted 39-36: R 23-19; D 16-17 (ND 11-12, SD 5-5), June 21, 1984.

155. H J Res 492. Department of Agriculture, Fiscal 1984 Urgent Supplemental Appropriations. Adoption of the conference report on the bill to appropriate $1,123,705,000 in fiscal 1984 for the Department of Agriculture and several other programs. Adopted 79-2: R 44-0; D 35-2 (ND 23-2, SD 12-0), June 25, 1984. The president had requested $916,280,000.

156. H J Res 492. Department of Agriculture, Fiscal 1984 Urgent Supplemental Appropriations. Hatfield, R-Ore., motion to table (kill) the Senate amendment to provide $21 million in covert aid to Nicaraguan rebels. Motion agreed to 88-1: R 52-1; D 36-0 (ND 25-0, SD 11-0), June 25, 1984.

157. HR 4616. Motor Vehicle Safety/Minimum Drinking Age. Humphrey, R-N.H., amendment to provide financial incentives to encourage, but not require, states to raise their legal drinking age to 21. Rejected 35-62: R 25-30; D 10-32 (ND 4-24, SD 6-8), June 26, 1984.

158. HR 4616. Motor Vehicle Safety/Minimum Drinking Age. Lautenberg, D-N.J., amendment to withhold a percentage of highway funds from states whose minimum drinking ages are under 21 and to provide incentives for other actions aimed at reducing drunk driving. Adopted 81-16: R 45-10; D 36-6 (ND 25-3, SD 11-3), June 26, 1984. A "yea" was a vote supporting the president's position.

159. S 1285. Emergency Mathematics and Science Education Act. Hatfield, R-Ore., amendment to make it unlawful for high schools receiving federal funds to deny use of their buildings to religious, political and other student groups if such access is granted to other extracurricular groups before and after school. Adopted 88-11: R 49-6; D 39-5 (ND 25-5, SD 14-0), June 27, 1984. A "yea" was a vote supporting the president's position.

160. HR 4170. Deficit Reduction. D'Amato, R-N.Y., motion to table (kill) the conference report on the bill to raise $50 billion in new taxes and to cut Medicare and other spending by about $13 billion through fiscal year 1987. Motion rejected 22-76: R 13-41; D 9-35 (ND 7-23, SD 2-12), June 27, 1984. A "nay" was a vote supporting the president's position.

161. HR 4170. Deficit Reduction. Adoption of the conference report on the bill to raise $50 billion in new taxes and to cut Medicare and other spending by about $13 billion through fiscal year 1987. Adopted 83-15: R 45-9; D 38-6 (ND 25-5, SD 13-1), June 27, 1984. A "yea" was a vote supporting the president's position.

CQ Senate Votes 162 - 168

Corresponding to Congressional Record Votes 162, 163, 164, 165, 166, 167, 168, 169, 170, 171, 172, 173, 174, 175, 176, 177, 178, 179, 180, 181, 182, 183

	162	163	164	165	166	167	168
ALABAMA							
Denton	Y	Y	Y	N	N	N	N
Heflin	Y	Y	N	Y	Y	Y	Y
ALASKA							
Murkowski	Y	Y	N	Y	N	N	Y
Stevens	Y	Y	N	Y	N	N	Y
ARIZONA							
Goldwater	?	Y	Y	N	N	?	?
DeConcini	N	Y	N	Y	Y	Y	N
ARKANSAS							
Bumpers	N	Y	N	Y	Y	Y	Y
Pryor	N	Y	N	Y	Y	Y	Y
CALIFORNIA							
Wilson	Y	Y	Y	Y	N	N	Y
Cranston	N	Y	N	Y	N	?	?
COLORADO							
Armstrong	Y	Y	Y	N	N	Y	Y
Hart	?	Y	N	Y	Y	?	?
CONNECTICUT							
Weicker	Y	Y	N	Y	N	Y	Y
Dodd	N	Y	N	Y	Y	Y	N
DELAWARE							
Roth	Y	Y	N	Y	N	N	N
Biden	N	Y	N	Y	N	N	N
FLORIDA							
Hawkins	N	Y	Y	Y	N	N	C
Chiles	N	Y	N	Y	Y	N	Y
GEORGIA							
Mattingly	Y	Y	Y	N	N	Y	Y
Nunn	Y	Y	N	Y	Y	Y	Y
HAWAII							
Inouye	?	Y	N	Y	Y	N	N
Matsunaga	N	Y	N	Y	Y	N	Y
IDAHO							
McClure	Y	Y	Y	N	?	?	?
Symms	Y	Y	Y	N	N	Y	Y
ILLINOIS							
Percy	Y	Y	N	Y	N	N	N
Dixon	Y	Y	N	Y	Y	N	Y
INDIANA							
Lugar	Y	Y	N	Y	N	N	N
Quayle	Y	Y	Y	Y	N	Y	Y
IOWA							
Grassley	Y	Y	Y	N	N	Y	Y
Jepsen	Y	Y	Y	N	N	Y	Y
KANSAS							
Dole	Y	Y	N	Y	N	Y	Y
Kassebaum	N	Y	N	Y	N	Y	Y
KENTUCKY							
Ford	N	Y	N	Y	Y	N	N
Huddleston	Y	Y	N	Y	Y	N	N
LOUISIANA							
Johnston	N	Y	N	Y	Y	N	N
Long	N	Y	Y	Y	Y	N	Y
MAINE							
Cohen	N	Y	N	Y	N	N	Y
Mitchell	N	Y	N	Y	N	N	N
MARYLAND							
Mathias	Y	Y	N	Y	N	Y	N
Sarbanes	N	Y	N	Y	Y	N	N
MASSACHUSETTS							
Kennedy	N	Y	N	Y	N	N	N
Tsongas	N	Y	N	Y	N	N	Y
MICHIGAN							
Levin	N	Y	N	Y	Y	N	Y
Riegle	N	Y	N	Y	N	N	N
MINNESOTA							
Boschwitz	Y	Y	N	Y	Y	N	N
Durenberger	?	Y	N	Y	N	N	N
MISSISSIPPI							
Cochran	Y	Y	Y	N	N	Y	Y
Stennis	?	Y	N	Y	Y	Y	?
MISSOURI							
Danforth	Y	Y	N	Y	N	N	N
Eagleton	N	Y	N	Y	N	N	Y
MONTANA							
Baucus	N	Y	N	Y	N	Y	Y
Melcher	N	Y	N	Y	Y	Y	Y
NEBRASKA							
Exon	N	Y	N	Y	Y	Y	Y
Zorinsky	Y	Y	Y	N	Y	Y	Y
NEVADA							
Hecht	Y	Y	Y	N	N	N	Y
Laxalt	Y	Y	N	Y	Y	C	C
NEW HAMPSHIRE							
Humphrey	Y	Y	Y	N	N	Y	Y
Rudman	Y	Y	N	Y	N	Y	Y
NEW JERSEY							
Bradley	N	Y	N	Y	N	Y	Y
Lautenberg	N	Y	N	Y	N	+	N
NEW MEXICO							
Domenici	Y	Y	N	Y	N	N	Y
Bingaman	N	Y	N	Y	N	N	Y
NEW YORK							
D'Amato	N	Y	N	Y	Y	N	Y
Moynihan	N	Y	N	Y	Y	N	C
NORTH CAROLINA							
East	Y	Y	?	N	N	+	Y
Helms	Y	Y	Y	N	N	Y	Y
NORTH DAKOTA							
Andrews	N	Y	N	Y	N	Y	Y
Burdick	N	Y	N	Y	Y	Y	Y
OHIO							
Glenn	N	Y	N	Y	N	Y	Y
Metzenbaum	N	Y	N	Y	N	Y	Y
OKLAHOMA							
Nickles	Y	Y	Y	N	N	Y	Y
Boren	Y	Y	N	Y	Y	Y	Y
OREGON							
Hatfield	N	Y	N	Y	N	Y	Y
Packwood	N	Y	N	Y	N	N	N
PENNSYLVANIA							
Heinz	Y	Y	N	Y	N	N	N
Specter	Y	Y	N	Y	N	N	Y
RHODE ISLAND							
Chafee	Y	Y	N	Y	N	Y	Y
Pell	N	Y	N	Y	Y	N	N
SOUTH CAROLINA							
Thurmond	Y	Y	Y	N	N	Y	Y
Hollings	N	Y	N	Y	Y	Y	N
SOUTH DAKOTA							
Abdnor	Y	Y	N	Y	Y	Y	Y
Pressler	N	Y	N	Y	N	Y	Y
TENNESSEE							
Baker	Y	Y	N	Y	N	N	N
Sasser	N	Y	N	Y	Y	N	N
TEXAS							
Tower	?	Y	Y	N	N	N	N
Bentsen	?	Y	N	Y	Y	N	N
UTAH							
Garn	Y	Y	Y	N	N	N	Y
Hatch	Y	Y	Y	N	N	N	Y
VERMONT							
Stafford	Y	Y	N	Y	N	N	Y
Leahy	N	Y	N	Y	N	Y	N
VIRGINIA							
Trible	Y	Y	Y	Y	N	N	Y
Warner	Y	Y	Y	Y	N	Y	Y
WASHINGTON							
Evans	Y	Y	N	Y	N	N	N
Gorton	Y	Y	N	Y	N	N	N
WEST VIRGINIA							
Byrd	N	Y	N	N	Y	Y	Y
Randolph	N	Y	N	N	Y	Y	Y
WISCONSIN							
Kasten	Y	Y	N	Y	N	N	Y
Proxmire	Y	Y	Y	N	N	N	Y
WYOMING							
Simpson	Y	Y	Y	N	N	N	Y
Wallop	Y	Y	Y	N	N	Y	Y

KEY

- Y Voted for (yea).
- \# Paired for.
- + Announced for.
- N Voted against (nay).
- X Paired against.
- - Announced against.
- P Voted "present".
- C Voted "present" to avoid possible conflict of interest.
- ? Did not vote or otherwise make a position known.

Democrats *Republicans*

ND - Northern Democrats SD - Southern Democrats (Southern states - Ala., Ark., Fla., Ga., Ky., La., Miss., N.C., Okla., S.C., Tenn., Texas, Va.)

162. S 1285. Emergency Mathematics and Science Education Act. Baker, R-Tenn., motion to table (kill) the Riegle, D-Mich., amendment to authorize $15 million annually over three years for establishing after-school child care programs in school facilities. Motion agreed to 51-42: R 44-8; D 7-34 (ND 3-26, SD 4-8), June 27, 1984. A "nay" was a vote supporting the president's position. (HR 1310, which authorized almost $1 billion over two years for mathematics and science education, subsequently was passed by voice vote.)

163. Treaties. Adoption of the resolutions of ratification for **Exec T, 96th Cong, 2nd Sess,** Convention with Canada with respect to Taxes on Income and Capital; **Treaty Doc. No. 98-7,** Protocol Amending the Tax Convention with Canada; **Treaty Doc. No. 98-22,** Second Protocol Amending the 1980 Tax Convention with Canada; **Treaty Doc. No. 98-21,** Protocol to the Tax Convention with the French Republic; **Treaty Doc. No. 98-11,** Estate and Gift Tax Convention with the Government of Sweden; **Treaty Doc. No. 98-4,** Supplementary Convention on Extradition with Sweden; **Treaty Doc. No. 98-15,** Convention with France on the Transfer of Sentenced Persons; **Treaty Doc. No. 98-16,** Extradition Treaty with Thailand; **Treaty Doc. No. 98-17,** Extradition Treaty with Costa Rica; **Treaty Doc. No. 98-18,** Extradition Treaty with Jamaica; **Treaty Doc. No. 98-19,** Extradition Treaty with Ireland; **Treaty Doc. No. 98-20,** Extradition Treaty with Italy; **Treaty Doc. No. 98-23,** Convention on the Transfer of Sentenced Persons; **Treaty Doc. No. 98-24,** Convention on Mutual Legal Assistance with the Kingdom of Morocco; **Treaty Doc. No. 98-25,** Mutual Legal Assistance Treaty with Italy; **Treaty Doc. No. 98-26,** Treaty with Canada relating to the Skagit River and Ross Lake in the state of Washington and the Seven Mile Reservoir on the Pend D'Oreille River in the Province of British Columbia. Adopted en bloc 100-0: R 55-0; D 45-0 (ND 31-0, SD 14-0), June 28, 1984. A two-thirds majority of those present and voting (67 in this case) is required for adoption of resolutions of ratification.

164. HR 5712. Commerce, Justice, State and the Judiciary Appropriations, Fiscal 1985. Judgment of the Senate affirming the chair's ruling that the Appropriations Committee amendment (see vote 165, below) was out of order because it constituted legislation on an appropriations bill. Ruling of the chair rejected 27-72: R 24-30; D 3-42 (ND 2-29, SD 1-13), June 28, 1984.

165. HR 5712. Commerce, Justice, State and the Judiciary Appropriations, Fiscal 1985. Appropriations Committee amendment to provide $297.55 million for the Legal Services Corporation and to specify that none of the funds could be used to promulgate or enforce regulations without 15 days' advance notice to the Appropriations committees of both houses. Adopted 78-22: R 37-18; D 41-4 (ND 27-4, SD 14-0), June 28, 1984.

166. HR 5712. Commerce, Justice, State and the Judiciary Appropriations, Fiscal 1985. Hollings, D-S.C., amendment to prohibit use by the Federal Trade Commission of any funds in the bill to commence or enforce antitrust actions against local governments. Rejected 36-63: R 6-48; D 30-15 (ND 16-15, SD 14-0), June 28, 1984.

167. HR 5712. Commerce, Justice, State and the Judiciary Appropriations, Fiscal 1985. Weicker, R-Conn., amendment to delete from the bill the $31.3 million provided for the National Endowment for Democracy. Rejected 42-51: R 22-29; D 20-22 (ND 13-15, SD 7-7), June 28, 1984.

168. HR 5712. Commerce, Justice, State and the Judiciary Appropriations, Fiscal 1985. Rudman, R-N.H., amendment to reduce to $21.3 million, from $31.3 million, the funds provided in the bill for the National Endowment for Democracy, and to bar use of any of those funds for institutes connected with any political party operating in the United States. Adopted 62-30: R 37-14; D 25-16 (ND 18-10, SD 7-6), June 28, 1984.

	169	170	171	172	173	174
ALABAMA						
Denton	N	N	N	Y	Y	Y
Heflin	Y	N	N	Y	N	N
ALASKA						
Murkowski	?	?	?	Y	Y	?
Stevens	N	N	Y	Y	Y	?
ARIZONA						
Goldwater	?	?	?	?	?	?
DeConcini	N	N	Y	Y	Y	?
ARKANSAS						
Bumpers	Y	N	N	Y	Y	?
Pryor	Y	N	N	Y	Y	?
CALIFORNIA						
Wilson	N	N	N	Y	Y	Y
Cranston	?	?	?	?	?	?
COLORADO						
Armstrong	Y	N	N	Y	N	?
Hart	?	?	?	?	?	N
CONNECTICUT						
Weicker	Y	N	Y	Y	Y	?
Dodd	N	N	Y	Y	Y	N
DELAWARE						
Roth	N	N	N	Y	N	Y
Biden	Y	N	N	Y	Y	N
FLORIDA						
Hawkins	N	N	Y	Y	Y	N
Chiles	Y	N	Y	Y	Y	N
GEORGIA						
Mattingly	Y	N	N	Y	Y	Y
Nunn	Y	N	N	Y	N	N
HAWAII						
Inouye	N	N	Y	Y	Y	Y
Matsunaga	N	Y	Y	Y	Y	Y
IDAHO						
McClure	?	?	?	?	?	?
Symms	Y	N	N	Y	N	?
ILLINOIS						
Percy	N	N	Y	Y	Y	?
Dixon	N	N	N	Y	Y	?
INDIANA						
Lugar	N	N	N	Y	Y	Y
Quayle	Y	N	N	Y	Y	Y
IOWA						
Grassley	Y	N	N	Y	Y	Y
Jepsen	Y	N	N	Y	Y	?
KANSAS						
Dole	Y	N	N	Y	Y	Y
Kassebaum	Y	N	N	Y	Y	?
KENTUCKY						
Ford	N	N	Y	Y	Y	Y
Huddleston	N	N	Y	Y	Y	?
LOUISIANA						
Johnston	N	N	Y	Y	Y	?
Long	N	N	Y	Y	Y	Y
MAINE						
Cohen	N	N	Y	Y	Y	?
Mitchell	N	N	Y	Y	Y	?
MARYLAND						
Mathias	Y	Y	Y	Y	Y	?
Sarbanes	N	N	Y	Y	Y	N
MASSACHUSETTS						
Kennedy	N	N	Y	Y	Y	?
Tsongas	Y	Y	Y	Y	Y	?
MICHIGAN						
Levin	N	N	Y	Y	Y	N
Riegle	N	N	N	Y	Y	N
MINNESOTA						
Boschwitz	N	Y	Y	Y	Y	N
Durenberger	N	Y	Y	Y	Y	Y
MISSISSIPPI						
Cochran	Y	N	Y	Y	Y	?
Stennis	?	?	?	?	?	?
MISSOURI						
Danforth	N	Y	N	Y	Y	Y
Eagleton	N	N	N	Y	Y	N
MONTANA						
Baucus	Y	N	N	Y	N	N
Melcher	Y	N	N	Y	N	N
NEBRASKA						
Exon	Y	N	N	Y	N	?
Zorinsky	Y	N	N	Y	N	N
NEVADA						
Hecht	N	N	N	Y	Y	?
Laxalt	P	N	Y	Y	Y	?
NEW HAMPSHIRE						
Humphrey	Y	N	N	Y	N	?
Rudman	Y	N	Y	Y	Y	Y
NEW JERSEY						
Bradley	Y	N	Y	Y	Y	?
Lautenberg	N	N	Y	Y	Y	?
NEW MEXICO						
Domenici	N	N	Y	Y	Y	N
Bingaman	N	N	N	Y	Y	N
NEW YORK						
D'Amato	N	N	Y	Y	Y	Y
Moynihan	N	Y	Y	Y	Y	?
NORTH CAROLINA						
East	Y	N	N	Y	Y	Y
Helms	Y	N	N	Y	N	N
NORTH DAKOTA						
Andrews	Y	N	Y	Y	Y	?
Burdick	Y	N	Y	Y	Y	N
OHIO						
Glenn	Y	N	Y	Y	Y	N
Metzenbaum	Y	Y	Y	Y	Y	Y
OKLAHOMA						
Nickles	Y	N	N	Y	N	?
Boren	Y	N	N	Y	N	N
OREGON						
Hatfield	Y	N	Y	Y	Y	?
Packwood	N	Y	Y	Y	Y	?
PENNSYLVANIA						
Heinz	N	N	Y	Y	Y	?
Specter	N	N	Y	Y	Y	?
RHODE ISLAND						
Chafee	Y	Y	N	Y	Y	?
Pell	N	Y	Y	Y	Y	?
SOUTH CAROLINA						
Thurmond	N	N	N	Y	Y	Y
Hollings	Y	Y	Y	Y	Y	?
SOUTH DAKOTA						
Abdnor	N	N	N	Y	Y	?
Pressler	Y	N	N	Y	Y	?
TENNESSEE						
Baker	Y	N	Y	Y	?	Y
Sasser	N	N	N	Y	Y	?
TEXAS						
Tower	N	N	Y	Y	Y	?
Bentsen	N	?	?	Y	Y	Y
UTAH						
Garn	N	N	Y	Y	Y	Y
Hatch	N	N	N	Y	Y	Y
VERMONT						
Stafford	N	Y	Y	Y	Y	?
Leahy	Y	N	N	Y	Y	?
VIRGINIA						
Trible	Y	N	N	Y	Y	?
Warner	Y	N	N	Y	Y	?
WASHINGTON						
Evans	N	Y	Y	Y	Y	?
Gorton	N	N	N	Y	Y	Y
WEST VIRGINIA						
Byrd	Y	N	N	Y	Y	?
Randolph	Y	N	Y	Y	Y	N
WISCONSIN						
Kasten	N	N	N	Y	Y	N
Proxmire	Y	N	N	Y	N	Y
WYOMING						
Simpson	N	N	Y	Y	Y	Y
Wallop	N	N	N	Y	N	Y

KEY

Y   Voted for (yea).
\#   Paired for.
+   Announced for.
N   Voted against (nay).
X   Paired against.
-   Announced against.
P   Voted "present".
C   Voted "present" to avoid possible conflict of interest.
?   Did not vote or otherwise make a position known.

Democrats   *Republicans*

ND - Northern Democrats   SD - Southern Democrats (Southern states - Ala., Ark., Fla., Ga., Ky., La., Miss., N.C., Okla., S.C., Tenn., Texas, Va.)

169. HR 5712. Commerce, Justice, State and the Judiciary Appropriations, Fiscal 1985. Hollings, D-S.C., amendment to delete funding for the National Endowment for Democracy and increase the amount for educational and cultural exchanges abroad by $11.86 million. Rejected 44-49: R 23-28; D 21-21 (ND 14-15, SD 7-6), June 28, 1984.

170. HR 5712. Commerce, Justice, State and the Judiciary Appropriations, Fiscal 1985. Chafee, R-R.I., motion to table (kill) the Helms, R-N.C., amendment to bar the Commerce and State departments from spending any funds in the bill to promote trade with Bulgaria and to state the sense of Congress that Bulgaria be declared to be engaged in state-sponsored terrorism. Motion rejected 14-79: R 8-44; D 6-35 (ND 5-24, SD 1-11), June 28, 1984.

171. HR 5712. Commerce, Justice, State and the Judiciary Appropriations, Fiscal 1985. Rudman, R-N.H., motion to table (kill) the Nickles, R-Okla., amendment to trim 4 percent across-the-board from appropriations in the bill. Motion agreed to 49-44: R 26-26; D 23-18 (ND 17-12, SD 6-6), June 28, 1984.

172. HR 5712. Commerce, Justice, State and the Judiciary Appropriations, Fiscal 1985. Nickles, R-Okla., amend-

ment expressing the sense of the Senate condemning Black Muslim leader Louis Farrakhan, a prominent supporter of Democratic presidential candidate Jesse Jackson, for "anti-Jewish and racist" statements and urging the Democratic and Republican national chairmen to repudiate in writing the sentiments reportedly expressed by Farrakhan. Adopted 95-0: R 53-0; D 42-0 (ND 29-0, SD 13-0), June 28, 1984.

173. HR 5712. Commerce, Justice, State and the Judiciary Appropriations, Fiscal 1985. Passage of the bill to provide $11,441,835,000 for the Commerce, Justice and State departments, several related agencies, and the federal judiciary in fiscal 1985. Passed 79-15: R 45-7; D 34-8 (ND 24-5, SD 10-3), June 28, 1984. The president had requested $11,175,884,000 in new budget authority.

174. HR 4170. Deficit Reduction. Dole, R-Kan., motion to table (kill) the Melcher, D-Mont., amendment to the concurrent resolution (H Con Res 328) making corrections in the enrollment of HR 4170 — the tax increase/spending cut legislation — to exempt farms, residences costing up to $250,000 and small businesses costing up to $500,000 from a provision penalizing those who finance sale of property with a below-market interest rate loan. Motion agreed to 30-23: R 22-5; D 8-18 (ND 5-14, SD 3-4), June 29, 1984.

KEY

Y	Voted for (yea).
#	Paired for.
+	Announced for.
N	Voted against (nay).
X	Paired against.
-	Announced against.
P	Voted "present".
C	Voted "present" to avoid possible conflict of interest.
?	Did not vote or otherwise make a position known.

Democrats *Republicans*

	175	176	177	178	179	180	181
ALABAMA							
Denton	Y	Y	N	Y	Y	Y	Y
Heflin	Y	N	Y	Y	N	Y	Y
ALASKA							
Murkowski	Y	N	Y	Y	Y	Y	Y
Stevens	Y	Y	N	Y	Y	Y	Y
ARIZONA							
Goldwater	Y	N	N	N	Y	Y	Y
DeConcini	Y	N	Y	Y	Y	Y	Y
ARKANSAS							
Bumpers	Y	N	Y	Y	Y	Y	Y
Pryor	Y	N	Y	Y	Y	Y	Y
CALIFORNIA							
Wilson	Y	N	Y	Y	Y	N	Y
Cranston	Y	N	Y	Y	Y	Y	Y
COLORADO							
Armstrong	Y	Y	N	Y	Y	Y	Y
Hart	?	?	?	?	?	?	?
CONNECTICUT							
Weicker	Y	N	Y	Y	Y	Y	?
Dodd	?	?	Y	Y	Y	Y	Y
DELAWARE							
Roth	Y	N	Y	Y	Y	N	Y
Biden	Y	N	Y	Y	Y	Y	Y
FLORIDA							
Hawkins	Y	N	Y	Y	Y	?	?
Chiles	Y	N	Y	Y	Y	Y	Y
GEORGIA							
Mattingly	Y	N	Y	Y	Y	?	?
Nunn	Y	N	Y	Y	Y	Y	Y
HAWAII							
Inouye	Y	N	Y	Y	Y	Y	Y
Matsunaga	Y	N	Y	Y	Y	Y	Y
IDAHO							
McClure	Y	Y	N	Y	Y	Y	Y
Symms	Y	Y	N	Y	Y	N	Y
ILLINOIS							
Percy	Y	N	Y	Y	Y	Y	Y
Dixon	Y	N	Y	Y	Y	Y	Y
INDIANA							
Lugar	Y	N	Y	Y	Y	Y	Y
Quayle	Y	N	Y	Y	Y	Y	Y
IOWA							
Grassley	Y	N	Y	Y	Y	N	Y
Jepsen	Y	N	Y	Y	Y	Y	Y
KANSAS							
Dole	Y	N	N	Y	Y	Y	Y
Kassebaum	Y	Y	Y	Y	Y	Y	Y
KENTUCKY							
Ford	Y	N	Y	Y	Y	Y	Y
Huddleston	?	?	?	Y	Y	Y	Y
LOUISIANA							
Johnston	Y	N	Y	Y	Y	Y	Y
Long	'Y	N	Y	Y	Y	Y	Y
MAINE							
Cohen	Y	N	Y	Y	Y	Y	Y
Mitchell	Y	N	Y	Y	Y	Y	Y
MARYLAND							
Mathias	Y	N	Y	Y	Y	Y	Y
Sarbanes	Y	N	Y	Y	Y	Y	Y
MASSACHUSETTS							
Kennedy	Y	N	Y	Y	Y	Y	Y
Tsongas	?	?	?	?	Y	Y	Y
MICHIGAN							
Levin	Y	N	Y	Y	Y	Y	Y
Riegle	Y	N	Y	Y	Y	Y	Y
MINNESOTA							
Boschwitz	Y	N	Y	Y	Y	Y	+
Durenberger	Y	Y	N	Y	Y	Y	Y
MISSISSIPPI							
Cochran	Y	N	Y	Y	Y	Y	Y
Stennis	Y	N	Y	Y	Y	Y	Y
MISSOURI							
Danforth	Y	N	Y	Y	Y	Y	Y
Eagleton	Y	N	Y	Y	Y	Y	Y
MONTANA							
Baucus	Y	N	Y	Y	Y	N	Y
Melcher	Y	N	Y	Y	Y	Y	Y
NEBRASKA							
Exon	Y	N	Y	Y	Y	Y	Y
Zorinsky	Y	N	Y	Y	Y	N	Y
NEVADA							
Hecht	Y	Y	N	Y	Y	Y	Y
Laxalt	Y	Y	N	Y	Y	Y	Y
NEW HAMPSHIRE							
Humphrey	Y	N	Y	Y	Y	N	Y
Rudman	Y	N	Y	Y	Y	Y	Y
NEW JERSEY							
Bradley	Y	N	Y	Y	Y	Y	Y
Lautenberg	Y	N	Y	Y	Y	Y	Y
NEW MEXICO							
Domenici	?	?	?	Y	Y	Y	Y
Bingaman	Y	N	Y	Y	Y	Y	Y
NEW YORK							
D'Amato	Y	N	Y	Y	Y	Y	Y
Moynihan	Y	N	Y	Y	Y	Y	Y
NORTH CAROLINA							
East	Y	Y	N	Y	Y	N	Y
Helms	Y	Y	N	Y	Y	N	Y
NORTH DAKOTA							
Andrews	Y	N	Y	Y	Y	Y	Y
Burdick	Y	N	Y	Y	Y	Y	Y
OHIO							
Glenn	Y	N	Y	Y	Y	Y	Y
Metzenbaum	Y	N	Y	Y	Y	Y	Y
OKLAHOMA							
Nickles	Y	Y	N	Y	Y	N	Y
Boren	Y	N	Y	Y	Y	N	Y
OREGON							
Hatfield	Y	N	Y	Y	Y	Y	Y
Packwood	Y	N	Y	Y	Y	Y	Y
PENNSYLVANIA							
Heinz	Y	N	Y	Y	Y	Y	Y
Specter	Y	N	Y	Y	Y	Y	Y
RHODE ISLAND							
Chafee	Y	N	Y	Y	Y	Y	Y
Pell	Y	N	Y	Y	Y	Y	Y
SOUTH CAROLINA							
Thurmond	Y	Y	N	Y	Y	-	+
Hollings	Y	N	Y	Y	Y	Y	Y
SOUTH DAKOTA							
Abdnor	Y	Y	N	Y	Y	Y	Y
Pressler	Y	N	Y	Y	Y	Y	Y
TENNESSEE							
Baker	Y	Y	N.	Y	Y	?	?
Sasser	Y	N	Y	Y	Y	Y	Y
TEXAS							
Tower	Y	Y	N	?	?	?	?
Bentsen	Y	N	Y	Y	Y	Y	Y
UTAH							
Garn	?	?	?	Y	Y	Y	Y
Hatch	?	?	?	Y	Y	N	Y
VERMONT							
Stafford	Y	N	Y	Y	Y	Y	Y
Leahy	Y	N	Y	Y	Y	Y	Y
VIRGINIA							
Trible	Y	N	Y	Y	Y	Y	Y
Warner	Y	N	Y	Y	Y	Y	Y
WASHINGTON							
Evans	Y	N	Y	Y	Y	Y	Y
Gorton	Y	N	Y	Y	Y	Y	Y
WEST VIRGINIA							
Byrd	Y	N	?	?	?	?	Y
Randolph	Y	N	Y	Y	Y	Y	Y
WISCONSIN							
Kasten	Y	N	Y	Y	Y	Y	Y
Proxmire	Y	N	Y	Y	Y	N	Y
WYOMING							
Simpson	Y	Y	N	Y	Y	Y	Y
Wallop	Y	Y	N	Y	Y	N	Y

ND - Northern Democrats   SD - Southern Democrats (Southern states - Ala., Ark., Fla., Ga., Ky., La., Miss., N.C., Okla., S.C., Tenn., Texas, Va.)

175. H Con Res 332. Andrei Sakharov and Yelena Bonner. Adoption of the concurrent resolution to call on the Soviet Union to provide information to signatories of the Helsinki Final Act about the whereabouts, health and legal status of Nobel Prize laureate physicist Andrei Sakharov and his wife, Yelena Bonner. Adopted 93-0: R 52-0; D 41-0 (ND 28-0, SD 13-0), July 24, 1984.

176. HR 5798. Treasury, Postal Service and General Government Appropriations, Fiscal 1985. Abdnor, R-S.D., motion to table (kill) the Kennedy, D-Mass., amendment to urge President Reagan to withdraw his appointment of Anne M. Burford, former administrator of the Environmental Protection Agency, to head the National Advisory Committee on Oceans and Atmosphere. Motion rejected 18-75: R 18-34; D 0-41 (ND 0-28, SD 0-13), July 24, 1984. A "yea" was a vote supporting the president's position.

177. HR 5798. Treasury, Postal Service and General Government Appropriations, Fiscal 1985. Kennedy, D-Mass., amendment to urge President Reagan to withdraw his appointment of Anne M. Burford, former administrator of the Environmental Protection Agency, to head the National Advisory Committee on Oceans and Atmosphere. Adopted 74-19: R 33-19; D 41-0 (ND 28-0, SD 13-0), July 24, 1984. A "nay" was a vote supporting the president's position.

178. S 1668. Federal Debt Collection. Metzenbaum, D-Ohio, amendments to require the attorney general to seek competitive bids in awarding contracts for debt collection, to require limits on contingency fees based on successful litigation, and to require the General Accounting Office to conduct annual audits of contracts and fees awarded by the attorney general. Adopted 95-1: R 53-1; D 42-0 (ND 28-0, SD 14-0), July 25, 1984.

179. S 1668. Federal Debt Collection. Passage of the bill to allow the Justice Department to contract with private attorneys to litigate federal debt collection cases. Passed 96-1: R 54-0; D 42-1 (ND 29-0, SD 13-1), July 25, 1984.

180. HR 5798. Treasury, Postal Service and General Government Appropriations, Fiscal 1985. Passage of the bill to provide $12,738,652,000 in fiscal 1985 funding for the Treasury Department, the Postal Service, the Executive Office of the President and other independent agencies. Passed 78-15: R 40-10; D 38-5 (ND 25-4, SD 13-1), July 25, 1984. The president had requested $12,349,688,000 in new budget authority.

181. HR 2867. Hazardous Waste Disposal. Passage of the bill to amend the Resource Conservation and Recovery Act of 1976 and reauthorize funding for programs under the act for fiscal years 1985 through 1989. Passed 93-0: R 49-0; D 44-0 (ND 30-0, SD 14-0), July 25, 1984.

	182 183 184 185		182 183 184 185		182 183 184 185
ALABAMA		**IOWA**		**NEW HAMPSHIRE**	
Denton	Y Y Y Y	Grassley	Y Y Y Y	Humphrey	Y N Y Y
Heflin	Y Y Y Y	Jepsen	Y Y Y Y	Rudman	Y N Y Y
ALASKA		**KANSAS**		**NEW JERSEY**	
Murkowski	Y Y Y Y	Dole	Y Y Y Y	Bradley	Y N Y Y
Stevens	Y Y Y Y	Kassebaum	Y Y Y Y	Lautenberg	Y N Y Y
ARIZONA		**KENTUCKY**		**NEW MEXICO**	
Goldwater	Y Y Y Y	Ford	Y Y Y Y	Domenici	Y Y Y Y
DeConcini	Y Y Y Y	Huddleston	Y N Y Y	Bingaman	Y Y Y Y
ARKANSAS		**LOUISIANA**		**NEW YORK**	
Bumpers	Y N Y Y	Johnston	Y N ? N	D'Amato	Y N Y Y
Pryor	Y Y Y Y	Long	Y N Y Y	Moynihan	Y N Y Y
CALIFORNIA		**MAINE**		**NORTH CAROLINA**	
Wilson	Y Y Y Y	Cohen	Y N Y Y	East	Y Y Y Y
Cranston	Y Y Y Y	Mitchell	Y N Y Y	Helms	Y Y Y Y
COLORADO		**MARYLAND**		**NORTH DAKOTA**	
Armstrong	? ? ? ?	Mathias	Y N Y Y	Andrews	Y Y Y Y
Hart	? ? ? ?	Sarbanes	Y N Y Y	Burdick	Y Y Y Y
CONNECTICUT		**MASSACHUSETTS**		**OHIO**	
Weicker	Y Y Y Y	Kennedy	Y Y Y Y	Glenn	Y N Y Y
Dodd	Y N Y Y	Tsongas	? ? ? ?	Metzenbaum	Y N Y Y
DELAWARE		**MICHIGAN**		**OKLAHOMA**	
Roth	Y N Y Y	Levin	Y N Y Y	Nickles	Y Y Y Y
Biden	Y N Y Y	Riegle	Y N Y Y	Boren	Y Y Y Y
FLORIDA		**MINNESOTA**		**OREGON**	
Hawkins	Y N Y Y	Boschwitz	Y N Y Y	Hatfield	Y Y Y Y
Chiles	? ? ? ?	Durenberger	Y N Y Y	Packwood	Y Y ? ?
GEORGIA		**MISSISSIPPI**		**PENNSYLVANIA**	
Mattingly	Y N Y Y	Cochran	Y Y Y Y	Heinz	Y N + Y
Nunn	Y N Y Y	Stennis	Y Y Y N	Specter	Y N Y Y
HAWAII		**MISSOURI**		**RHODE ISLAND**	
Inouye	? ? ? ?	Danforth	Y N Y Y	Chafee	Y N Y Y
Matsunaga	Y Y Y Y	Eagleton	Y N Y Y	Pell	Y N Y Y
IDAHO		**MONTANA**		**SOUTH CAROLINA**	
McClure	Y Y Y Y	Baucus	Y Y Y Y	Thurmond	Y Y Y Y
Symms	Y Y ? ?	Melcher	Y Y Y Y	Hollings	Y Y Y N
ILLINOIS		**NEBRASKA**		**SOUTH DAKOTA**	
Percy	Y Y ? Y	Exon	Y Y Y Y	Abdnor	Y Y Y Y
Dixon	? ? Y Y	Zorinsky	Y Y Y Y	Pressler	Y Y Y Y
INDIANA		**NEVADA**		**TENNESSEE**	
Lugar	Y N Y Y	Hecht	Y Y Y Y	Baker	Y Y Y Y
Quayle	N N Y Y	Laxalt	Y Y Y Y	Sasser	Y Y Y Y

KEY

Y Voted for (yea).
Paired for.
+ Announced for.
N Voted against (nay).
X Paired against.
- Announced against.
P Voted "present".
C Voted "present" to avoid possible conflict of interest.
? Did not vote or otherwise make a position known.

Democrats *Republicans*

	182 183 184 185
TEXAS	
Tower	Y Y Y Y
Bentsen	Y N Y Y
UTAH	
Garn	Y Y Y Y
Hatch	Y Y Y Y
VERMONT	
Stafford	Y Y ? ?
Leahy	Y N Y Y
VIRGINIA	
Trible	Y Y Y Y
Warner	Y Y Y Y
WASHINGTON	
Evans	Y Y Y Y
Gorton	Y Y Y Y
WEST VIRGINIA	
Byrd	Y N Y Y
Randolph	Y Y Y Y
WISCONSIN	
Kasten	Y Y Y Y
Proxmire	N N Y Y
WYOMING	
Simpson	Y Y Y ?
Wallop	Y Y Y Y

ND - Northern Democrats   SD - Southern Democrats (Southern states - Ala., Ark., Fla., Ga., Ky., La., Miss., N.C., Okla., S.C., Tenn., Texas, Va.)

182. Procedural Motion. Baker, R-Tenn., motion to instruct the sergeant-at-arms to request the attendance of absent senators. Motion agreed to 92-2: R 53-1; D 39-1 (ND 26-1, SD 13-0), July 26, 1984.

183. S 268. Hydroelectric Power Plants. Cranston, D-Calif., motion to table (kill) the Metzenbaum, D-Ohio, amendment to extend contracts for inexpensive electrical power from Hoover Dam for 18 months after their current expiration date of May 31, 1987, rather than for 30 years as provided by the bill. Motion agreed to 56-38: R 38-16; D 18-22 (ND 11-16, SD 7-6), July 26, 1984.

184. HR 1904. Child Abuse Amendments. Passage of the bill to authorize $174 million in fiscal 1984-87 for child protection and adoption assistance programs and $35 million in fiscal 1985-87 to aid victims of family violence. The bill included language requiring states receiving federal child-protection aid to establish procedures for protecting severely handicapped infants from medical neglect. Passed 89-0: R 49-0; D 40-0 (ND 28-0, SD 12-0), July 26, 1984. A "yea" was a vote supporting the president's position.

185. HR 1428. Social Security Cost-of-Living Adjustment. Moynihan, D-N.Y., amendment to provide a cost-of-living adjustment equal to the rate of inflation in January 1985 to Social Security, disability and Supplemental Security Income beneficiaries. The measure also increases the wage base for paying Social Security payroll taxes, and the amount retirees can earn from wages without having to forfeit Social Security benefits. Adopted 87-3: R 50-0; D 37-3 (ND 27-0, SD 10-3), July 26, 1984. A "yea" was a vote supporting the president's position.

	186	187	188	189	190	191	192	193
ALABAMA								
Denton	Y	Y	Y	N	Y	Y	Y	Y
Heflin	Y	Y	Y	N	Y	Y	Y	Y
ALASKA								
Murkowski	?	?	?	?	?	Y	Y	Y
Stevens	Y	Y	Y	N	Y	Y	Y	Y
ARIZONA								
Goldwater	Y	Y	N	N	Y	N	Y	Y
DeConcini	Y	Y	Y	N	Y	Y	Y	Y
ARKANSAS								
Bumpers	Y	N	Y	N	Y	Y	Y	N
Pryor	Y	Y	?	?	?	Y	Y	N
CALIFORNIA								
Wilson	Y	Y	Y	N	Y	Y	Y	Y
Cranston	Y	Y	Y	N	Y	Y	Y	N
COLORADO								
Armstrong	Y	Y	?	?	?	Y	Y	Y
Hart	?	?	?	?	?	?	?	?
CONNECTICUT								
Weicker	N	Y	?	?	?	N	Y	Y
Dodd	Y	N	Y	N	N	Y	N	N
DELAWARE								
Roth	Y	N	Y	N	Y	Y	N	Y
Biden	Y	N	Y	N	Y	Y	N	N
FLORIDA								
Hawkins	Y	Y	Y	N	Y	N	Y	Y
Chiles	Y	N	Y	N	N	Y	N	N
GEORGIA								
Mattingly	Y	Y	Y	N	Y	Y	Y	Y
Nunn	Y	N	?	?	?	Y	N	N
HAWAII								
Inouye	?	?	?	?	?	Y	Y	N
Matsunaga	Y	Y	Y	N	Y	Y	Y	N
IDAHO								
McClure	Y	Y	Y	N	Y	Y	Y	Y
Symms	Y	Y	Y	N	Y	Y	Y	Y
ILLINOIS								
Percy	?	-	?	?	?	Y	N	Y
Dixon	?	-	?	?	-	Y	N	N
INDIANA								
Lugar	Y	Y	Y	N	Y	N	Y	Y
Quayle	N	N	N	N	Y	N	N	Y

	186	187	188	189	190	191	192	193
IOWA								
Grassley	Y	Y	Y	N	Y	Y	Y	Y
Jepsen	Y	Y	Y	N	Y	Y	Y	Y
KANSAS								
Dole	Y	Y	Y	N	Y	Y	Y	Y
Kassebaum	Y	Y	?	?	?	Y	Y	Y
KENTUCKY								
Ford	Y	Y	Y	N	Y	Y	Y	N
Huddleston	Y	Y	?	?	?	Y	Y	N
LOUISIANA								
Johnston	Y	Y	Y	N	Y	Y	Y	N
Long	Y	N	Y	Y	N	Y	Y	Y
MAINE								
Cohen	Y	N	Y	Y	N	Y	N	Y
Mitchell	Y	N	Y	N	N	Y	N	N
MARYLAND								
Mathias	Y	N	Y	N	Y	Y	N	N
Sarbanes	Y	N	?	?	?	Y	N	N
MASSACHUSETTS								
Kennedy	Y	Y	Y	N	Y	Y	Y	X
Tsongas	?	?	?	?	?	Y	N	N
MICHIGAN								
Levin	Y	N	Y	N	Y	Y	N	N
Riegle	Y	N	Y	N	Y	Y	N	N
MINNESOTA								
Boschwitz	Y	Y	Y	N	Y	Y	N	Y
Durenberger	Y	Y	?	?	?	?	N	Y
MISSISSIPPI								
Cochran	?	?	?	?	?	Y	Y	Y
Stennis	Y	Y	?	?	?	Y	Y	Y
MISSOURI								
Danforth	Y	Y	Y	N	Y	Y	N	Y
Eagleton	Y	N	Y	N	Y	Y	Y	N
MONTANA								
Baucus	Y	Y	Y	N	Y	Y	Y	N
Melcher	Y	Y	Y	N	Y	Y	Y	N
NEBRASKA								
Exon	Y	Y	Y	Y	Y	Y	Y	Y
Zorinsky	Y	Y	Y	Y	Y	Y	Y	Y
NEVADA								
Hecht	Y	Y	Y	N	Y	Y	Y	Y
Laxalt	Y	Y	Y	N	Y	Y	Y	Y

	186	187	188	189	190	191	192	193
NEW HAMPSHIRE								
Humphrey	Y	Y	Y	N	Y	Y	N	Y
Rudman	Y	Y	Y	N	Y	Y	N	Y
NEW JERSEY								
Bradley	Y	N	Y	N	Y	N	N	N
Lautenberg	Y	N	Y	N	Y	N	N	N
NEW MEXICO								
Domenici	Y	Y	Y	N	Y	Y	Y	Y
Bingaman	Y	Y	Y	N	Y	Y	Y	N
NEW YORK								
D'Amato	Y	N	Y	N	N	Y	N	Y
Moynihan	Y	N	Y	Y	N	?	N	N
NORTH CAROLINA								
East	Y	Y	Y	N	Y	Y	Y	Y
Helms	Y	Y	Y	N	Y	Y	Y	Y
NORTH DAKOTA								
Andrews	Y	Y	Y	N	Y	Y	Y	Y
Burdick	Y	Y	Y	N	Y	Y	Y	N
OHIO								
Glenn	Y	N	Y	N	Y	N	N	N
Metzenbaum	Y	N	Y	N	Y	N	N	N
OKLAHOMA								
Nickles	Y	Y	Y	N	Y	Y	Y	Y
Boren	?	?	?	?	?	?	Y	Y
OREGON								
Hatfield	Y	Y	Y	N	Y	Y	Y	Y
Packwood	Y	Y	Y	N	Y	Y	Y	N
PENNSYLVANIA								
Heinz	Y	N	Y	N	Y	Y	N	Y
Specter	Y	N	Y	N	Y	Y	N	Y
RHODE ISLAND								
Chafee	?	?	Y	N	Y	Y	N	Y
Pell	Y	Y	Y	Y	N	Y	N	#
SOUTH CAROLINA								
Thurmond	Y	Y	Y	N	Y	Y	Y	Y
Hollings	Y	Y	Y	Y	Y	Y	Y	N
SOUTH DAKOTA								
Abdnor	Y	Y	Y	N	Y	Y	Y	Y
Pressler	Y	Y	Y	N	Y	Y	Y	Y
TENNESSEE								
Baker	?	?	?	?	?	Y	Y	Y
Sasser	Y	Y	?	Y	Y	?	?	?

	186	187	188	189	190	191	192	193
TEXAS								
Tower	Y	Y	Y	N	Y	?	Y	Y
Bentsen	?	?	?	?	?	?	Y	N
UTAH								
Garn	Y	Y	Y	N	Y	Y	Y	Y
Hatch	Y	Y	Y	N	Y	Y	Y	Y
VERMONT								
Stafford	Y	N	Y	N	Y	N	Y	Y
Leahy	Y	N	Y	N	N	Y	N	N
VIRGINIA								
Trible	Y	Y	Y	N	Y	Y	Y	Y
Warner	Y	N	Y	N	Y	Y	Y	Y
WASHINGTON								
Evans	Y	Y	Y	N	Y	Y	Y	Y
Gorton	Y	Y	Y	N	Y	Y	Y	Y
WEST VIRGINIA								
Byrd	Y	N	Y	N	N	Y	N	N
Randolph	Y	Y	Y	Y	Y	Y	Y	N
WISCONSIN								
Kasten	Y	Y	Y	N	Y	Y	Y	Y
Proxmire	N	N	N	Y	N	N	N	N
WYOMING								
Simpson	?	?	?	?	?	Y	Y	Y
Wallop	Y	Y	Y	N	Y	Y	Y	Y

KEY

- **Y** Voted for (yea).
- **#** Paired for.
- **+** Announced for.
- **N** Voted against (nay).
- **X** Paired against.
- **-** Announced against.
- **P** Voted "present".
- **C** Voted "present" to avoid possible conflict of interest.
- **?** Did not vote or otherwise make a position known.

Democrats   *Republicans*

ND - Northern Democrats   SD - Southern Democrats (Southern states - Ala., Ark., Fla., Ga., Ky., La., Miss., N.C., Okla., S.C., Tenn., Texas, Va.)

186. S 268. Hydroelectric Power Plants. Stevens, R-Alaska, motion to instruct the sergeant-at-arms to request the attendance of absent senators. Motion agreed to 85-3: R 47-2; D 38-1 (ND 26-1, SD 12-0), July 30, 1984.

187. S 268. Hydroelectric Power Plants. Baker, R-Tenn., motion to invoke cloture (thus limiting debate) on the Baker motion to concur in the House amendments to the bill to extend contracts for power from the Hoover Dam. Motion agreed to 60-28: R 40-9; D 20-19 (ND 12-15, SD 8-4), July 30, 1984. A three-fifths majority vote (60) of the total Senate is required to invoke cloture.

188. S 268. Hydroelectric Power Plants. Stevens, R-Alaska, motion to instruct the sergeant-at-arms to request the attendance of absent senators. Motion agreed to 76-3: R 44-2; D 32-1 (ND 25-1, SD 7-0), July 30, 1984.

189. S 268. Hydroelectric Power Plants. Metzenbaum, D-Ohio, motion to recess until 11:00 a.m. July 31, 1984. Rejected 16-64: R 1-45; D 15-19 (ND 12-14, SD 3-5), July 30, 1984.

190. S 268. Hydroelectric Power Plants. Stevens, R-Alaska, motion to table (kill) the Metzenbaum, D-Ohio, amendment to change from one year to five years the period during which legal claims for Hoover Dam power could be filed. Motion agreed to 62-18: R 43-3; D 19-15 (ND 13-13, SD 6-2), July 30, 1984.

191. Procedural Motion. Stevens, R-Alaska, motion to instruct the sergeant-at-arms to request the attendance of absent senators. Motion agreed to 89-4: R 49-3; D 40-1 (ND 28-1, SD 12-0), July 31, 1984.

192. S 268. Hydroelectric Power Plants. Baker, R-Tenn., motion to concur in the House amendment to the bill to authorize 30-year extensions of contracts for electric power from the Hoover Dam that were scheduled to expire May 31, 1987. Motion agreed to 64-34: R 40-15; D 24-19 (ND 13-17, SD 11-2), July 31, 1984. A "yea" was a vote supporting the president's position.

193. Wilkinson Nomination. Baker, R-Tenn., motion to invoke cloture (thus limiting debate) on the nomination of James Harvie Wilkinson III of Virginia to be a judge on the 4th U.S. Circuit Court of Appeals. Motion rejected 57-39: R 51-4, D 6-35 (ND 2-26, SD 4-9), July 31, 1984. A three-fifths majority vote (60) of the total Senate is required to invoke cloture.

	194 195			194 195			194 195		KEY
ALABAMA			**IOWA**			**NEW HAMPSHIRE**			Y Voted for (yea).
Denton	Y Y		*Grassley*	Y Y		*Humphrey*	Y Y		# Paired for.
Heflin	Y Y		*Jepsen*	Y Y		*Rudman*	Y Y		+ Announced for.
ALASKA			**KANSAS**			**NEW JERSEY**			N Voted against (nay).
Murkowski	Y Y		*Dole*	Y Y		Bradley	Y Y		X Paired against.
Stevens	Y Y		*Kassebaum*	Y Y		Lautenberg	Y Y		- Announced against.
ARIZONA			**KENTUCKY**			**NEW MEXICO**			P Voted "present".
Goldwater	Y Y		Ford	Y Y		*Domenici*	Y Y		C Voted "present" to avoid possi-
DeConcini	Y Y		Huddleston	Y Y		Bingaman	Y Y		ble conflict of interest.
ARKANSAS			**LOUISIANA**			**NEW YORK**			? Did not vote or otherwise make a
Bumpers	Y Y		Johnston	Y Y		*D'Amato*	Y Y		position known.
Pryor	Y Y		Long	Y Y		Moynihan	Y Y		
CALIFORNIA			**MAINE**			**NORTH CAROLINA**			Democrats *Republicans*
Wilson	Y Y		*Cohen*	Y Y		*East*	Y Y		
Cranston	Y Y		Mitchell	Y Y		*Helms*	Y Y		
COLORADO			**MARYLAND**			**NORTH DAKOTA**			
Armstrong	Y Y		*Mathias*	Y Y		*Andrews*	Y Y		194 195
Hart	? ?		Sarbanes	Y Y		Burdick	Y Y		
CONNECTICUT			**MASSACHUSETTS**			**OHIO**			**TEXAS**
Weicker	? Y		Kennedy	Y Y		Glenn	Y Y		*Tower* Y Y
Dodd	Y Y		Tsongas	Y Y		Metzenbaum	Y Y		Bentsen Y Y
DELAWARE			**MICHIGAN**			**OKLAHOMA**			**UTAH**
Roth	Y Y		Levin	? Y		*Nickles*	Y Y		*Garn* Y Y
Biden	Y Y		Riegle	Y Y		Boren	Y Y		*Hatch* Y Y
FLORIDA			**MINNESOTA**			**OREGON**			**VERMONT**
Hawkins	Y Y		*Boschwitz*	Y Y		*Hatfield*	Y Y		*Stafford* Y Y
Chiles	Y Y		*Durenberger*	Y Y		*Packwood*	Y Y		Leahy Y Y
GEORGIA			**MISSISSIPPI**			**PENNSYLVANIA**			**VIRGINIA**
Mattingly	Y Y		*Cochran*	Y Y		*Heinz*	Y Y		*Trible* Y Y
Nunn	Y Y		Stennis	Y Y		*Specter*	Y Y		*Warner* Y Y
HAWAII			**MISSOURI**			**RHODE ISLAND**			**WASHINGTON**
Inouye	Y Y		*Danforth*	Y Y		*Chafee*	Y Y		*Evans* Y Y
Matsunaga	Y Y		Eagleton	Y Y		Pell	Y Y		*Gorton* Y Y
IDAHO			**MONTANA**			**SOUTH CAROLINA**			**WEST VIRGINIA**
McClure	Y Y		Baucus	Y Y		*Thurmond*	Y Y		Byrd Y Y
Symms	Y Y		Melcher	Y Y		Hollings	Y Y		Randolph Y Y
ILLINOIS			**NEBRASKA**			**SOUTH DAKOTA**			**WISCONSIN**
Percy	Y Y		Exon	Y Y		*Abdnor*	Y Y		*Kasten* Y Y
Dixon	Y Y		Zorinsky	Y Y		*Pressler*	Y Y		Proxmire Y Y
INDIANA			**NEVADA**			**TENNESSEE**			**WYOMING**
Lugar	Y Y		*Hecht*	Y Y		*Baker*	Y Y		*Simpson* Y Y
Quayle	Y Y		*Laxalt*	Y Y		Sasser	Y Y		*Wallop* Y Y

ND - Northern Democrats   SD - Southern Democrats (Southern states - Ala., Ark., Fla., Ga., Ky., La., Miss., N.C., Okla., S.C., Tenn., Texas, Va.)

194. S 1841. National Productivity and Innovation Act. Passage of the bill to ease antitrust obstacles for companies that undertake joint ventures in research and development. Passed 97-0: R 54-0; D 43-0 (ND 29-0, SD 14-0), July 31, 1984.

195. HR 4325. Child Support Enforcement. Adoption of the conference report on the bill to assure, through incentive payments to states, mandatory withholding of wages and other methods, that parents meet child support obligations. Adopted 99-0: R 55-0; D 44-0 (ND 30-0, SD 14-0), Aug. 1, 1984.

	196 197 198 199 200 201 202 203		196 197 198 199 200 201 202 203		196 197 198 199 200 201 202 203	KEY

KEY
- Y Voted for (yea).
- # Paired for.
- + Announced for.
- N Voted against (nay).
- X Paired against.
- - Announced against.
- P Voted "present".
- C Voted "present" to avoid possible conflict of interest.
- ? Did not vote or otherwise make a position known.

Democrats   *Republicans*

	196 197 198 199 200 201 202 203

State / Senator	196 197 198 199 200 201 202 203
ALABAMA	
Denton	Y Y Y Y N N N N
Heflin	Y Y Y Y N N N Y
ALASKA	
Murkowski	Y Y Y Y N N N N
Stevens	Y Y Y Y N N N Y
ARIZONA	
Goldwater	Y Y Y ? N N N Y
DeConcini	# Y Y Y Y N N Y
ARKANSAS	
Bumpers	N Y Y Y Y N Y Y
Pryor	Y Y Y Y Y N N Y
CALIFORNIA	
Wilson	Y Y Y Y N N N Y
Cranston	X Y N N Y Y Y Y
COLORADO	
Armstrong	Y Y Y Y N N N N
Hart	N Y N N Y Y Y Y
CONNECTICUT	
Weicker	Y Y Y N Y Y Y Y
Dodd	N Y N N Y Y Y Y
DELAWARE	
Roth	Y Y Y Y N N Y N
Biden	N Y N N Y N N Y
FLORIDA	
Hawkins	? Y Y Y N N N Y
Chiles	N Y N N N N N Y
GEORGIA	
Mattingly	Y Y Y Y N N N N
Nunn	N Y N N N N N Y
HAWAII	
Inouye	N Y N N Y Y Y Y
Matsunaga	N Y N N Y Y Y Y
IDAHO	
McClure	? ? ? ? N N N N
Symms	Y Y Y Y N N N N
ILLINOIS	
Percy	? + Y Y N N ? Y
Dixon	N Y N Y N N Y Y
INDIANA	
Lugar	Y Y Y Y N N N N
Quayle	Y Y Y Y N N N N
IOWA	
Grassley	? Y Y N N N N N
Jepsen	Y Y Y Y N N N N
KANSAS	
Dole	Y Y Y Y N N N N
Kassebaum	Y ? Y Y N N Y Y
KENTUCKY	
Ford	Y Y Y Y Y Y N Y
Huddleston	Y Y Y Y N N N Y
LOUISIANA	
Johnston	N Y N N N N N Y
Long	N Y N N N N N Y
MAINE	
Cohen	? Y Y Y N N Y Y
Mitchell	N Y N N Y Y Y Y
MARYLAND	
Mathias	Y Y Y Y N N Y Y
Sarbanes	N Y N N Y Y Y Y
MASSACHUSETTS	
Kennedy	N Y N N Y Y Y Y
Tsongas	X ? N Y N Y N Y
MICHIGAN	
Levin	N Y N N Y Y ? Y
Riegle	N Y N N Y Y Y Y
MINNESOTA	
Boschwitz	Y Y Y Y N N N Y
Durenberger	? Y Y Y N N N N
MISSISSIPPI	
Cochran	Y Y Y Y N N N N
Stennis	N Y Y Y Y N Y Y
MISSOURI	
Danforth	Y Y Y Y N N N N
Eagleton	N Y N N Y Y N Y
MONTANA	
Baucus	- Y N N Y Y Y Y
Melcher	N Y N N Y Y N Y
NEBRASKA	
Exon	Y Y Y Y Y Y N N
Zorinsky	Y Y Y Y Y Y N N
NEVADA	
Hecht	Y Y Y Y N N N N
Laxalt	Y Y Y Y N N N N
NEW HAMPSHIRE	
Humphrey	N Y Y Y N N N N
Rudman	Y Y Y Y N N Y N
NEW JERSEY	
Bradley	X Y N N N N Y Y
Lautenberg	N Y N N Y Y Y Y
NEW MEXICO	
Domenici	Y Y Y Y N N N N
Bingaman	N Y N N Y Y Y Y
NEW YORK	
D'Amato	Y Y Y Y N N ? ?
Moynihan	N Y N N Y N Y Y
NORTH CAROLINA	
East	Y Y Y Y N N N N
Helms	Y Y Y Y N N N N
NORTH DAKOTA	
Andrews	Y Y Y Y N N N N
Burdick	# Y Y Y Y Y Y Y
OHIO	
Glenn	N Y N N Y Y Y N
Metzenbaum	N Y N N Y Y Y Y
OKLAHOMA	
Nickles	Y Y Y Y N N N N
Boren	# Y Y Y N N N Y
OREGON	
Hatfield	Y Y Y Y N N N N
Packwood	Y Y Y Y N N Y Y
PENNSYLVANIA	
Heinz	Y Y Y Y N N Y Y
Specter	Y Y Y Y N N Y N
RHODE ISLAND	
Chafee	Y Y Y Y N N Y Y
Pell	Y Y Y N Y Y Y Y
SOUTH CAROLINA	
Thurmond	Y Y Y Y N N N N
Hollings	N Y N N N ? ? ?
SOUTH DAKOTA	
Abdnor	Y Y Y Y N N N N
Pressler	Y Y Y Y N N N Y
TENNESSEE	
Baker	Y Y Y Y N N N Y
Sasser	N Y N N Y Y Y Y
TEXAS	
Tower	Y Y Y Y N N Y N
Bentsen	? ? ? ? ? ? ? ?
UTAH	
Garn	Y Y Y Y N N N N
Hatch	Y Y Y Y N N N N
VERMONT	
Stafford	Y Y Y Y N N Y N
Leahy	? Y Y N Y Y Y Y
VIRGINIA	
Trible	Y Y Y Y N N N N
Warner	Y Y Y Y N N N N
WASHINGTON	
Evans	N Y Y Y N N Y Y
Gorton	N Y N N N N N Y
WEST VIRGINIA	
Byrd	N Y N N Y Y Y Y
Randolph	Y Y Y N Y Y N Y
WISCONSIN	
Kasten	Y Y Y Y N N N N
Proxmire	N Y N N Y N N Y
WYOMING	
Simpson	Y Y Y Y N N N N
Wallop	Y ? Y Y N N N N

ND - Northern Democrats   SD - Southern Democrats (Southern states - Ala., Ark., Fla., Ga., Ky., La., Miss., N.C., Okla., S.C., Tenn., Texas, Va.)

196. HR 5743. Agriculture Appropriations, Fiscal 1985. Baker, R-Tenn., motion to invoke cloture (thus limiting debate) on the Baker motion to waive provisions of the Congressional Budget Act that would bar consideration of an appropriations bill prior to adoption of the conference report on the first budget resolution. Motion rejected 54-31: R 46-3; D 8-28 (ND 4-20, SD 4-8), Aug. 6, 1984. A three-fifths majority vote (60) of the total Senate is required to invoke cloture.

197. HR 4209. Small Business and Federal Procurement Competition Enhancement Act. Passage of the bill to promote competition and small business participation in federal procurement. Passed 94-0: R 51-0; D 43-0 (ND 30-0, SD 13-0), Aug. 7, 1984.

198. HR 5743. Agriculture Appropriations, Fiscal 1985. Baker, R-Tenn., motion to invoke cloture (thus limiting debate) on the Baker motion to waive provisions of the Congressional Budget Act that would bar consideration of an appropriations bill prior to adoption of the conference report on the first budget resolution. Motion agreed to 68-30: R 54-0; D 14-30 (ND 7-24, SD 7-6), Aug. 8, 1984. A three-fifths majority vote (60) of the total Senate is required to invoke cloture.

199. HR 5743. Agriculture Appropriations, Fiscal 1985. Baker, R-Tenn., motion to waive provisions of the Congressional Budget Act that would bar consideration of an appropriations bill prior to adoption of the conference report on the first budget resolution. Motion agreed to 63-34: R 50-3; D 13-31 (ND 6-25, SD 7-6), Aug. 8, 1984.

200. HR 6040. Supplemental Appropriations, Fiscal 1984. Dodd, D-Conn., amendment to reduce overall foreign aid spending levels from $1 billion to $643.9 million to reflect current authorized expenditures. Rejected 37-62: R 3-52; D 34-10 (ND 29-2, SD 5-8), Aug. 8, 1984.

201. HR 6040. Supplemental Appropriations, Fiscal 1984. Inouye, D-Hawaii, amendment to delete $116.9 million in military aid to El Salvador from the supplemental bill. Rejected 29-69: R 2-53; D 27-16 (ND 25-6, SD 2-10), Aug. 8, 1984.

202. HR 6040. Supplemental Appropriations, Fiscal 1984. Packwood, R-Ore., motion to table (kill) the Helms, R-N.C., amendment to commend President Reagan on his anti-abortion stance. Motion rejected 43-52: R 18-35; D 25-17 (ND 22-8, SD 3-9), Aug. 8, 1984. (The Helms amendment did not become part of the bill because it was written as an amendment to an amendment by Packwood supporting international family planning assistance. Packwood withdrew his amendment when the Senate failed to kill the Helms amendment.)

203. HR 6040. Supplemental Appropriations, Fiscal 1984. Dixon, D-Ill., amendment to appropriate an additional $60 million for the Emergency Food and Shelter Program. Adopted 57-40: R 18-36; D 39-4 (ND 27-4, SD 12-0), Aug. 8, 1984.

	204 205 206 207		204 205 206 207		204 205 206 207
ALABAMA		**IOWA**		**NEW HAMPSHIRE**	
Denton	N Y Y Y	*Grassley*	N N Y Y	Humphrey	N Y N Y
Heflin	N N Y ?	*Jepsen*	N N Y Y	*Rudman*	N Y Y Y
ALASKA		**KANSAS**		**NEW JERSEY**	
Murkowski	N Y Y Y	*Dole*	N Y N Y	Bradley	N Y Y Y
Stevens	N Y Y Y	*Kassebaum*	N Y N Y	Lautenberg	Y N Y Y
ARIZONA		**KENTUCKY**		**NEW MEXICO**	
Goldwater	N Y Y Y	Ford	Y N Y Y	*Domenici*	N Y Y Y
DeConcini	N N Y Y	Huddleston	Y N Y Y	Bingaman	Y N Y Y
ARKANSAS		**LOUISIANA**		**NEW YORK**	
Bumpers	N N Y Y	Johnston	Y N Y Y	*D'Amato*	? ? Y Y
Pryor	N N Y ?	Long	? N ? Y	Moynihan	Y N Y Y
CALIFORNIA		**MAINE**		**NORTH CAROLINA**	
Wilson	N Y N Y	*Cohen*	N Y Y Y	*East*	? Y Y Y
Cranston	Y N ? Y	Mitchell	Y N N Y	*Helms*	N Y N Y
COLORADO		**MARYLAND**		**NORTH DAKOTA**	
Armstrong	N Y N Y	*Mathias*	N Y Y Y	*Andrews*	N Y N Y
Hart	? ? Y Y	Sarbanes	Y N Y Y	Burdick	Y N Y Y
CONNECTICUT		**MASSACHUSETTS**		**OHIO**	
Weicker	N Y Y Y	Kennedy	Y N N Y	Glenn	Y Y ? Y
Dodd	? N N Y	Tsongas	Y N Y Y	Metzenbaum	Y N Y Y
DELAWARE		**MICHIGAN**		**OKLAHOMA**	
Roth	N Y N Y	Levin	Y N Y Y	*Nickles*	N Y N Y
Biden	N N N Y	Riegle	Y N Y Y	Boren	N N Y Y
FLORIDA		**MINNESOTA**		**OREGON**	
Hawkins	N Y Y Y	*Boschwitz*	N Y Y Y	*Hatfield*	N Y N Y
Chiles	N N N Y	*Durenberger*	N Y Y Y	*Packwood*	N Y Y Y
GEORGIA		**MISSISSIPPI**		**PENNSYLVANIA**	
Mattingly	N Y N Y	*Cochran*	N Y Y Y	*Heinz*	N Y N Y
Nunn	N N N Y	Stennis	Y N ? Y	*Specter*	N Y Y Y
HAWAII		**MISSOURI**		**RHODE ISLAND**	
Inouye	N N N Y	*Danforth*	N Y Y Y	*Chafee*	N Y Y Y
Matsunaga	Y N Y Y	Eagleton	Y N Y Y	Pell	Y N Y Y
IDAHO		**MONTANA**		**SOUTH CAROLINA**	
McClure	N Y N Y	Baucus	Y N N Y	*Thurmond*	N Y Y Y
Symms	N Y N Y	Melcher	Y N Y Y	Hollings	? ? Y Y
ILLINOIS		**NEBRASKA**		**SOUTH DAKOTA**	
Percy	N Y Y Y	Exon	N N N Y	*Abdnor*	N Y Y Y
Dixon	N N Y Y	Zorinsky	N N N Y	*Pressler*	N N Y Y
INDIANA		**NEVADA**		**TENNESSEE**	
Lugar	N Y Y Y	*Hecht*	N Y N Y	*Baker*	N Y Y Y
Quayle	N Y Y Y	*Laxalt*	N Y Y Y	Sasser	N N N Y

KEY

Y Voted for (yea).
\# Paired for.
+ Announced for.
N Voted against (nay).
X Paired against.
- Announced against.
P Voted "present".
C Voted "present" to avoid possible conflict of interest.
? Did not vote or otherwise make a position known.

Democrats   *Republicans*

	204 205 206 207
TEXAS	
Tower	N Y ? Y
Bentsen	? ? ? ?
UTAH	
Garn	N Y N Y
Hatch	N Y N Y
VERMONT	
Stafford	? Y Y Y
Leahy	N N N Y
VIRGINIA	
Trible	N Y N Y
Warner	N Y N Y
WASHINGTON	
Evans	N Y Y Y
Gorton	N Y Y Y
WEST VIRGINIA	
Byrd	N N N Y
Randolph	N N Y Y
WISCONSIN	
Kasten	N Y Y Y
Proxmire	Y N N Y
WYOMING	
Simpson	N Y Y Y
Wallop	N Y N Y

ND - Northern Democrats   SD - Southern Democrats (Southern states - Ala., Ark., Fla., Ga., Ky., La., Miss., N.C., Okla., S.C., Tenn., Texas, Va.)

204. HR 6040. Supplemental Appropriations, Fiscal 1984. Judgment of the Senate whether the Pell, D-R.I., amendment dealing with the U.S. policy regarding Taiwan was germane. Ruled non-germane 23-69: R 0-52; D 23-17 (ND 19-10, SD 4-7), Aug. 8, 1984.

205. HR 6040. Supplemental Appropriations, Fiscal 1984. Hatfield, R-Ore., motion to table (kill) the Baucus, D-Mont., amendment to urge that President Reagan withdraw the appointment of Martha Seger to the Federal Reserve Board. Motion agreed to 53-43: R 51-3; D 2-40 (ND 2-28, SD 0-12), Aug. 8, 1984. A "yea" was a vote supporting the president's position.

206. HR 6040. Supplemental Appropriations, Fiscal 1984. Passage of the bill to provide $6,983,228,070 in supplemental appropriations for fiscal 1984. Passed 62-32: R 36-18; D 26-14 (ND 18-11, SD 8-3), in the session that began Aug. 8, 1984. The president had requested $5,953,340,170.

207. Treaties. Adoption of the resolutions of ratification for **Treaty Doc. 98-6,** Estate and Gift Tax Convention with the Kingdom of Denmark; **Treaty Doc. 98-8,** Treaty with the Kingdom of Thailand on Cooperation in the Execution of Penal Sentences; **Treaty Doc. 98-13,** Cartagena Convention for the Protection and Development of the Marine Environment of the Wider Caribbean Region. Adopted en bloc 97-0: R 55-0; D 42-0 (ND 31-0, SD 11-0), Aug. 9, 1984. A two-thirds majority of those present and voting (65 in this case) is required for adoption of resolutions of ratification.

	208 209 210 211 212 213 214		208 209 210 211 212 213 214		208 209 210 211 212 213 214
ALABAMA		**IOWA**		**NEW HAMPSHIRE**	
Denton	Y Y N Y N Y Y	*Grassley*	Y Y Y Y Y Y Y	*Humphrey*	Y Y Y Y Y Y N
Heflin	? ? Y Y Y N ?	*Jepsen*	Y Y Y Y Y Y Y	*Rudman*	Y N N ? Y Y N
ALASKA		**KANSAS**		**NEW JERSEY**	
Murkowski	Y Y N Y Y Y Y	*Dole*	Y Y N Y Y Y Y	Bradley	N N Y Y Y N Y
Stevens	Y N Y Y Y Y Y	*Kassebaum*	Y Y N Y ? Y Y	Lautenberg	N N Y Y Y ? ?
ARIZONA		**KENTUCKY**		**NEW MEXICO**	
Goldwater	Y Y N Y N Y Y	Ford	N N Y N ? ? ?	*Domenici*	Y Y N Y Y Y Y
DeConcini	Y Y N Y Y Y N	Huddleston	N N Y N Y N Y	Bingaman	N N Y Y Y N Y
ARKANSAS		**LOUISIANA**		**NEW YORK**	
Bumpers	N N Y N Y N Y	Johnston	N N Y N Y ? ?	*D'Amato*	Y Y Y Y Y Y Y
Pryor	? ? ? ? ? ? ?	Long	Y Y Y N Y N Y	Moynihan	N N Y ? + - +
CALIFORNIA		**MAINE**		**NORTH CAROLINA**	
Wilson	Y Y N Y Y Y N	*Cohen*	Y Y Y Y Y ? ?	*East*	Y Y Y Y Y Y Y
Cranston	N N ? ? ? ? ?	Mitchell	N N Y Y Y N N	*Helms*	Y Y Y Y Y Y Y
COLORADO		**MARYLAND**		**NORTH DAKOTA**	
Armstrong	Y Y N Y ? ? ?	*Mathias*	Y N Y Y Y Y N	*Andrews*	Y Y Y N Y Y Y
Hart	N N Y N ? ? Y	Sarbanes	N N Y N Y N Y	Burdick	N N Y N Y N Y
CONNECTICUT		**MASSACHUSETTS**		**OHIO**	
Weicker	Y Y N Y Y ? ?	Kennedy	N N Y N Y ? ?	Glenn	N N Y Y Y N Y
Dodd	N N Y Y Y N N	Tsongas	N N Y Y Y N Y	Metzenbaum	N N Y Y Y N Y
DELAWARE		**MICHIGAN**		**OKLAHOMA**	
Roth	Y Y Y Y Y Y N	Levin	N N Y Y Y N Y	*Nickles*	Y Y Y Y N Y Y
Biden	N N N Y Y N N	Riegle	N N Y N Y N Y	Boren	Y Y Y N Y N Y
FLORIDA		**MINNESOTA**		**OREGON**	
Hawkins	Y Y N Y Y Y Y	*Boschwitz*	Y Y Y Y Y Y Y	*Hatfield*	Y N N Y Y Y Y
Chiles	Y N Y Y Y N Y	*Durenberger*	Y Y Y Y Y Y Y	*Packwood*	N N N Y Y Y Y
GEORGIA		**MISSISSIPPI**		**PENNSYLVANIA**	
Mattingly	Y Y N Y Y Y Y	*Cochran*	Y Y N Y Y Y Y	*Heinz*	Y Y Y Y + + Y
Nunn	N N Y Y Y N Y	Stennis	Y Y Y N Y ? Y	*Specter*	Y Y N Y Y Y Y
HAWAII		**MISSOURI**		**RHODE ISLAND**	
Inouye	N N Y N Y N Y	*Danforth*	Y Y Y Y Y Y Y	*Chafee*	Y Y Y Y Y Y N
Matsunaga	N N Y N Y N Y	Eagleton	N N Y N Y N Y	Pell	Y N Y Y Y N N
IDAHO		**MONTANA**		**SOUTH CAROLINA**	
McClure	Y Y N ? Y Y Y	Baucus	Y Y Y N Y N Y	*Thurmond*	Y Y N Y Y Y Y
Symms	Y Y N Y Y Y Y	Melcher	N N Y N + - +	Hollings	N N Y N Y N Y
ILLINOIS		**NEBRASKA**		**SOUTH DAKOTA**	
Percy	Y Y Y Y Y Y Y	Exon	Y Y Y N Y N Y	*Abdnor*	Y Y N Y Y Y Y
Dixon	Y Y Y Y Y Y N	Zorinsky	Y Y Y N Y N Y	*Pressler*	Y Y N Y Y Y Y
INDIANA		**NEVADA**		**TENNESSEE**	
Lugar	Y Y N Y Y Y Y	*Hecht*	Y Y N Y Y Y Y	*Baker*	Y Y N Y Y Y Y
Quayle	Y Y N Y Y Y Y	*Laxalt*	Y Y ? ? ? ? ?	Sasser	N N Y N Y N Y

	208 209 210 211 212 213 214
TEXAS	
Tower	Y Y N ? ? ? ?
Bentsen	? ? ? ? ? ? ?
UTAH	
Garn	Y Y N Y Y Y Y
Hatch	Y Y N Y Y Y Y
VERMONT	
Stafford	Y Y Y Y ? ? ?
Leahy	N N Y Y Y N Y
VIRGINIA	
Trible	Y Y N Y Y Y Y
Warner	Y Y N Y Y Y Y
WASHINGTON	
Evans	Y Y N Y Y Y Y
Gorton	Y Y N Y Y Y Y
WEST VIRGINIA	
Byrd	N N Y Y Y N Y
Randolph	Y N Y N Y N Y
WISCONSIN	
Kasten	Y Y N ? Y Y Y
Proxmire	N N Y Y N N N
WYOMING	
Simpson	Y Y Y Y Y ? ?
Wallop	Y Y N Y Y ? ?

KEY

Y Voted for (yea).
\# Paired for.
\+ Announced for.
N Voted against (nay).
X Paired against.
- Announced against.
P Voted "present".
C Voted "present" to avoid possible conflict of interest.
? Did not vote or otherwise make a position known.

Democrats *Republicans*

ND - Northern Democrats   SD - Southern Democrats (Southern states - Ala., Ark., Fla., Ga., Ky., La., Miss., N.C., Okla., S.C., Tenn., Texas, Va.)

208. Wilkinson Nomination. Baker, R-Tenn., motion to invoke cloture (thus limiting debate) on the nomination of James Harvie Wilkinson III of Virginia to be a judge on the 4th U.S. Circuit Court of Appeals. Motion agreed to 65-32: R 54-1; D 11-31 (ND 7-24, SD 4-7), Aug. 9, 1984. A three-fifths majority (60) of the total Senate is required to invoke cloture.

209. Wilkinson Nomination. Confirmation of President Reagan's nomination of James Harvie Wilkinson III of Virginia to be a judge on the 4th U.S. Circuit Court of Appeals. Confirmed 58-39: R 50-5; D 8-34 (ND 5-26, SD 3-8), Aug. 9, 1984. A "yea" was a vote supporting the president's position.

210. HR 5743. Agriculture Appropriations, Fiscal 1985. Melcher, D-Mont., substitute for the Armstrong, R-Colo., amendment, to bar federal price supports and other farm program benefits for a crop if part of the crop was produced on easily erodible land. Adopted 62-34: R 22-32; D 40-2 (ND 28-2, SD 12-0), Aug. 9, 1984.

211. HR 5743. Agriculture Appropriations, Fiscal 1985. Cochran, R-Miss., motion to table (kill) the Exon, D-Neb., amendment to raise 1984 and 1985 wheat target prices and 1985 corn target prices. Motion agreed to 66-25: R 47-3; D 19-22 (ND 16-13, SD 3-9), Aug. 9, 1984.

212. HR 5743. Agriculture Appropriations, Fiscal 1985. Kennedy, D-Mass., amendment to increase by $29 million the appropriation for the supplemental nutrition program for women, infants and children (WIC). Adopted 83-4: R 46-3; D 37-1 (ND 26-1, SD 11-0), Aug. 10, 1984.

213. HR 5743. Agriculture Appropriations, Fiscal 1985. Cochran, R-Miss., motion to table (kill) the Bumpers, D-Ark., amendment to require the executive branch to report to Congress on its plans to increase farm income, expand farm exports, lower interest rates and otherwise ameliorate farmers' economic problems, and on changes contemplated in farm commodity and credit programs. Motion agreed to 46-34: R 46-0; D 0-34 (ND 0-25, SD 0-9), Aug. 10, 1984.

214. HR 5743. Agriculture Appropriations, Fiscal 1985. Passage of the bill to appropriate $35,781,315,710 in fiscal 1985 for the Agriculture Department, the Food and Drug Administration and the Commodity Futures Trading Commission. Passed 71-11: R 41-6; D 30-5 (ND 21-5, SD 9-0), Aug. 10, 1984. The president had requested $34,521,717,000 in new budget authority.

	215	216	217	218	219	220	221
ALABAMA							
Denton	Y	Y	Y	Y	Y	Y	Y
Heflin	?	Y	Y	Y	Y	N	Y
ALASKA							
Murkowski	Y	Y	N	Y	Y	Y	Y
Stevens	Y	Y	Y	Y	Y	N	Y
ARIZONA							
Goldwater	Y	Y	Y	N	Y	Y	Y
DeConcini	Y	Y	Y	Y	Y	N	Y
ARKANSAS							
Bumpers	Y	Y	N	Y	Y	N	N
Pryor	Y	Y	N	Y	Y	N	N
CALIFORNIA							
Wilson	Y	Y	Y	Y	Y	Y	Y
Cranston	Y	Y	Y	Y	Y	N	Y
COLORADO							
Armstrong	Y	Y	Y	N	Y	Y	Y
Hart	Y	Y	Y	Y	Y	Y	N
CONNECTICUT							
Weicker	Y	Y	N	N	Y	N	Y
Dodd	Y	Y	Y	Y	Y	N	Y
DELAWARE							
Roth	Y	Y	Y	Y	Y	Y	Y
Biden	Y	Y	N	Y	Y	Y	Y
FLORIDA							
Hawkins	Y	Y	Y	Y	Y	N	Y
Chiles	Y	Y	Y	Y	Y	?	?
GEORGIA							
Mattingly	Y	Y	N	Y	Y	Y	Y
Nunn	Y	Y	Y	Y	Y	Y	Y
HAWAII							
Inouye	Y	Y	N	Y	Y	N	Y
Matsunaga	Y	Y	Y	Y	Y	N	Y
IDAHO							
McClure	Y	Y	Y	Y	Y	N	Y
Symms	Y	Y	Y	Y	Y	Y	Y
ILLINOIS							
Percy	Y	Y	Y	Y	Y	?	?
Dixon	Y	Y	Y	Y	Y	N	Y
INDIANA							
Lugar	Y	Y	Y	Y	Y	Y	Y
Quayle	Y	Y	Y	N	Y	N	Y

	215	216	217	218	219	220	221
IOWA							
Grassley	Y	Y	Y	Y	Y	N	Y
Jepsen	Y	Y	Y	Y	Y	Y	Y
KANSAS							
Dole	Y	Y	Y	Y	Y	N	Y
Kassebaum	Y	Y	Y	Y	Y	N	Y
KENTUCKY							
Ford	Y	Y	Y	Y	Y	C	Y
Huddleston	Y	Y	Y	Y	Y	N	Y
LOUISIANA							
Johnston	Y	Y	Y	Y	Y	N	Y
Long	Y	Y	Y	Y	Y	N	Y
MAINE							
Cohen	Y	Y	Y	Y	Y	N	Y
Mitchell	Y	Y	Y	Y	Y	N	Y
MARYLAND							
Mathias	Y	Y	Y	Y	N	Y	Y
Sarbanes	Y	Y	Y	Y	Y	N	Y
MASSACHUSETTS							
Kennedy	?	Y	Y	Y	Y	N	Y
Tsongas	Y	Y	Y	Y	Y	?	?
MICHIGAN							
Levin	?	?	Y	Y	Y	N	Y
Riegle	Y	Y	N	Y	Y	N	Y
MINNESOTA							
Boschwitz	Y	Y	Y	Y	Y	Y	Y
Durenberger	?	Y	Y	Y	Y	Y	Y
MISSISSIPPI							
Cochran	?	Y	Y	Y	Y	N	Y
Stennis	Y	Y	Y	Y	Y	Y	Y
MISSOURI							
Danforth	Y	Y	N	Y	Y	N	Y
Eagleton	Y	Y	Y	Y	Y	N	Y
MONTANA							
Baucus	Y	Y	N	Y	Y	N	Y
Melcher	Y	Y	Y	?	Y	N	Y
NEBRASKA							
Exon	Y	Y	Y	Y	Y	N	Y
Zorinsky	Y	Y	Y	Y	Y	N	Y
NEVADA							
Hecht	Y	Y	Y	Y	Y	Y	Y
Laxalt	Y	Y	Y	Y	Y	Y	Y

	215	216	217	218	219	220	221
NEW HAMPSHIRE							
Humphrey	Y	Y	Y	Y	Y	Y	Y
Rudman	Y	Y	Y	Y	Y	Y	Y
NEW JERSEY							
Bradley	?	Y	?	Y	Y	Y	Y
Lautenberg	Y	Y	Y	Y	Y	N	Y
NEW MEXICO							
Domenici	?	?	Y	Y	Y	N	Y
Bingaman	Y	Y	Y	Y	Y	N	Y
NEW YORK							
D'Amato	N	N	?	Y	N	N	N
Moynihan	N	Y	N	Y	N	N	N
NORTH CAROLINA							
East	Y	Y	Y	Y	Y	Y	Y
Helms	Y	Y	Y	Y	Y	Y	Y
NORTH DAKOTA							
Andrews	Y	Y	N	Y	Y	N	Y
Burdick	Y	Y	Y	Y	Y	N	Y
OHIO							
Glenn	Y	Y	Y	Y	Y	N	Y
Metzenbaum	?	Y	Y	Y	Y	N	Y
OKLAHOMA							
Nickles	Y	Y	N	Y	Y	Y	Y
Boren	Y	Y	N	Y	Y	Y	Y
OREGON							
Hatfield	Y	Y	+	?	+	+	+
Packwood	Y	Y	Y	Y	Y	Y	Y
PENNSYLVANIA							
Heinz	Y	Y	N	Y	N	N	Y
Specter	Y	Y	Y	Y	Y	N	Y
RHODE ISLAND							
Chafee	Y	Y	Y	Y	Y	N	Y
Pell	Y	Y	Y	Y	Y	N	Y
SOUTH CAROLINA							
Thurmond	Y	+	N	Y	Y	Y	Y
Hollings	Y	Y	Y	Y	Y	N	Y
SOUTH DAKOTA							
Abdnor	N	N	Y	N	Y	N	N
Pressler	Y	Y	Y	Y	N	N	Y
TENNESSEE							
Baker	Y	Y	?	?	?	Y	Y
Sasser	Y	Y	N	Y	N	Y	N

	215	216	217	218	219	220	221
TEXAS							
Tower	Y	Y	Y	Y	Y	Y	?
Bentsen	Y	Y	Y	Y	Y	N	Y
UTAH							
Garn	Y	Y	Y	Y	Y	Y	Y
Hatch	Y	Y	Y	Y	Y	Y	Y
VERMONT							
Stafford	Y	Y	Y	Y	Y	N	Y
Leahy	Y	Y	Y	Y	Y	N	Y
VIRGINIA							
Trible	Y	Y	N	Y	Y	N	Y
Warner	Y	Y	Y	?	Y	N	Y
WASHINGTON							
Evans	Y	Y	Y	Y	Y	N	Y
Gorton	Y	Y	Y	Y	Y	Y	Y
WEST VIRGINIA							
Byrd	Y	Y	Y	Y	Y	N	Y
Randolph	Y	Y	Y	Y	Y	-	+
WISCONSIN							
Kasten	Y	Y	Y	Y	Y	Y	Y
Proxmire	Y	Y	Y	N	Y	N	Y
WYOMING							
Simpson	Y	Y	Y	Y	Y	Y	Y
Wallop	Y	Y	N	Y	Y	Y	Y

KEY

Y   Voted for (yea).
Paired for.
+   Announced for.
N   Voted against (nay).
X   Paired against.
-   Announced against.
P   Voted "present".
C   Voted "present" to avoid possible conflict of interest.
?   Did not vote or otherwise make a position known.

Democrats   *Republicans*

ND - Northern Democrats   SD - Southern Democrats (Southern states - Ala., Ark., Fla., Ga., Ky., La., Miss., N.C., Okla., S.C., Tenn., Texas, Va.)

215. S 2851. Financial Services Competitive Equity Act. Baker, R-Tenn., motion to invoke cloture (thus limiting debate) on the Baker motion to proceed to the consideration of the bill to close several loopholes in banking law, authorize regional interstate banking and permit banks to underwrite some securities. Motion agreed to 89-3: R 50-2; D 39-1 (ND 26-1, SD 13-0), Sept. 10, 1984. A three-fifths majority (60) of the total Senate is required to invoke cloture.

216. S 2851. Financial Services Competitive Equity Act. Baker, R-Tenn., motion to proceed to the consideration of the bill to close several loopholes in banking law, authorize regional interstate banking and permit banks to underwrite some securities. Motion agreed to 95-2: R 51-2; D 44-0 (ND 30-0, SD 14-0), Sept. 11, 1984.

217. S 2851. Financial Services Competitive Equity Act. Proxmire, D-Wis., amendment to strike a section of the bill requiring the Federal Reserve to pay banks interest on certain reserves they maintain with the Fed. Adopted 76-20: R 41-11; D 35-9 (ND 25-5, SD 10-4), Sept. 12, 1984.

218. S 2851. Financial Services Competitive Equity Act. Stevens, R-Alaska, motion to instruct the sergeant-at-arms to compel the attendance of absent senators. Motion agreed to 92-4: R 49-3; D 43-1 (ND 29-1, SD 14-0), Sept. 13, 1984.

219. S 2851. Financial Services Competitive Equity Act. Baker, R-Tenn., motion to invoke cloture (thus limiting debate) on the bill to permit bank affiliates to underwrite certain securities, close loopholes in federal banking law and allow regional interstate banking. Motion agreed to 92-6: R 48-5; D 44-1 (ND 30-1, SD 14-0), Sept. 13, 1984. A three-fifths majority (60) of the total Senate is required to invoke cloture.

220. S 2851. Financial Services Competitive Equity Act. Gorton, R-Wash., amendment to permit state-chartered subsidiaries of bank holding companies to market certain kinds of insurance within their home states. Rejected 38-56: R 32-21; D 6-35 (ND 3-26, SD 3-9), Sept. 13, 1984.

221. S 2851. Financial Services Competitive Equity Act. Passage of the bill to permit bank affiliates to underwrite certain securities, close loopholes in federal banking law and allow regional interstate banking. Passed 89-5: R 50-2; D 39-3 (ND 28-1, SD 11-2), Sept. 13, 1984. A "yea" was a vote supporting the president's position.

	222	223	224	225	226	227
ALABAMA						
Denton	?	Y	Y	N	Y	?
Heflin	N	Y	Y	Y	Y	N
ALASKA						
Murkowski	Y	Y	N	Y	Y	Y
Stevens	Y	Y	Y	Y	Y	Y
ARIZONA						
Goldwater	N	N	N	Y	Y	Y
DeConcini	Y	Y	Y	N	Y	N
ARKANSAS						
Bumpers	N	Y	Y	N	Y	Y
Pryor	N	Y	Y	Y	Y	Y
CALIFORNIA						
Wilson	Y	Y	Y	Y	Y	Y
Cranston	Y	Y	Y	N	Y	N
COLORADO						
Armstrong	N	Y	Y	Y	Y	N
Hart	N	Y	Y	N	Y	Y
CONNECTICUT						
Weicker	N	Y	Y	Y	Y	Y
Dodd	N	N	N	?	Y	N
DELAWARE						
Roth	N	Y	Y	Y	Y	Y
Biden	N	Y	Y	Y	Y	N
FLORIDA						
Hawkins	N	Y	Y	N	Y	Y
Chiles	N	Y	Y	N	Y	Y
GEORGIA						
Mattingly	N	N	N	N	Y	Y
Nunn	N	N	N	N	Y	Y
HAWAII						
Inouye	Y	N	N	N	Y	N
Matsunaga	Y	Y	Y	Y	Y	Y
IDAHO						
McClure	Y	Y	Y	Y	Y	Y
Symms	Y	Y	Y	Y	Y	Y
ILLINOIS						
Percy	N	Y	Y	Y	Y	Y
Dixon	N	Y	Y	N	Y	N
INDIANA						
Lugar	N	Y	Y	Y	Y	Y
Quayle	N	Y	Y	Y	Y	Y

	222	223	224	225	226	227
IOWA						
Grassley	N	N	N	Y	Y	Y
Jepsen	N	Y	Y	Y	Y	Y
KANSAS						
Dole	Y	Y	Y	Y	Y	Y
Kassebaum	N	Y	Y	Y	Y	Y
KENTUCKY						
Ford	N	N	N	N	Y	N
Huddleston	N	N	N	Y	Y	N
LOUISIANA						
Johnston	Y	N	N	N	Y	Y
Long	Y	N	N	N	Y	Y
MAINE						
Cohen	Y	Y	Y	Y	Y	N
Mitchell	Y	Y	Y	N	Y	Y
MARYLAND						
Mathias	N	Y	Y	Y	Y	N
Sarbanes	N	Y	Y	N	Y	N
MASSACHUSETTS						
Kennedy	N	Y	Y	N	Y	N
Tsongas	?	?	?	?	?	?
MICHIGAN						
Levin	N	Y	Y	Y	Y	N
Riegle	N	Y	Y	N	Y	N
MINNESOTA						
Boschwitz	N	N	N	Y	Y	N
Durenberger	N	Y	N	Y	Y	Y
MISSISSIPPI						
Cochran	N	Y	Y	Y	Y	Y
Stennis	N	N	N	N	Y	Y
MISSOURI						
Danforth	P	Y	Y	Y	Y	Y
Eagleton	N	N	N	N	Y	N
MONTANA						
Baucus	N	Y	Y	Y	Y	N
Melcher	N	Y	Y	N	Y	N
NEBRASKA						
Exon	N	Y	Y	Y	Y	Y
Zorinsky	N	Y	Y	N	Y	Y
NEVADA						
Hecht	N	N	N	Y	Y	N
Laxalt	Y	N	N	Y	Y	N

	222	223	224	225	226	227
NEW HAMPSHIRE						
Humphrey	N	Y	Y	Y	Y	Y
Rudman	N	Y	Y	Y	Y	N
NEW JERSEY						
Bradley	N	Y	Y	N	Y	Y
Lautenberg	N	Y	Y	N	Y	Y
NEW MEXICO						
Domenici	Y	Y	Y	Y	Y	N
Bingaman	N	Y	Y	N	Y	Y
NEW YORK						
D'Amato	N	N	N	N	Y	N
Moynihan	N	Y	Y	N	Y	N
NORTH CAROLINA						
East	N	N	N	N	Y	Y
Helms	N	N	N	N	Y	Y
NORTH DAKOTA						
Andrews	N	Y	Y	Y	Y	N
Burdick	N	N	N	N	Y	Y
OHIO						
Glenn	N	Y	N	Y	Y	Y
Metzenbaum	N	Y	Y	Y	Y	N
OKLAHOMA						
Nickles	N	Y	Y	N	Y	Y
Boren	N	N	N	N	Y	Y
OREGON						
Hatfield	N	N	N	Y	Y	Y
Packwood	N	Y	Y	Y	Y	Y
PENNSYLVANIA						
Heinz	C	Y	Y	Y	Y	N
Specter	N	Y	Y	Y	Y	N
RHODE ISLAND						
Chafee	N	Y	Y	Y	Y	Y
Pell	N	Y	N	N	Y	N
SOUTH CAROLINA						
Thurmond	Y	Y	Y	Y	Y	Y
Hollings	Y	N	Y	N	Y	N
SOUTH DAKOTA						
Abdnor	N	Y	Y	Y	Y	Y
Pressler	N	Y	Y	Y	Y	Y
TENNESSEE						
Baker	N	Y	Y	Y	Y	Y
Sasser	N	Y	Y	N	Y	N

	222	223	224	225	226	227
TEXAS						
Tower	N	N	N	Y	Y	Y
Bentsen	N	N	N	N	Y	Y
UTAH						
Garn	Y	Y	Y	Y	Y	N
Hatch	Y	Y	Y	N	Y	N
VERMONT						
Stafford	N	Y	N	Y	Y	Y
Leahy	N	Y	Y	Y	Y	Y
VIRGINIA						
Trible	N	Y	Y	N	Y	Y
Warner	N	Y	Y	N	Y	Y
WASHINGTON						
Evans	N	Y	Y	N	Y	Y
Gorton	Y	Y	Y	Y	Y	Y
WEST VIRGINIA						
Byrd	N	Y	Y	N	Y	N
Randolph	-	N	N	N	Y	N
WISCONSIN						
Kasten	Y	Y	Y	Y	Y	N
Proxmire	N	N	N	Y	Y	Y
WYOMING						
Simpson	N	Y	N	Y	Y	?
Wallop	N	Y	N	Y	Y	Y

ND - Northern Democrats   SD - Southern Democrats (Southern states - Ala., Ark., Fla., Ga., Ky., La., Miss., N.C., Okla., S.C., Tenn., Texas, Va.)

---

222. HR 3398. Miscellaneous Tariff, Trade and Customs Matters. Wilson, R-Calif., amendment to establish the same duty for imported water-packed tuna and imported oil-packed tuna. Currently, there is a 6 percent duty on imported water-packed canned tuna and a 35 percent duty on imported tuna canned in oil. Rejected 22-73: R 14-38; D 8-35 (ND 5-24, SD 3-11), Sept. 18, 1984. A "nay" was a vote supporting the president's position.

223. S Res 66. Senate Television. Baker, R-Tenn., motion to invoke cloture (thus limiting debate) on the Baker motion to proceed to the consideration of the bill to authorize television and radio coverage of Senate proceedings. Motion agreed to 73-26: R 44-11; D 29-15 (ND 24-6, SD 5-9), Sept. 18, 1984. A three-fifths majority (60) of the total Senate is required to invoke cloture.

224. S Res 66. Senate Television. Baker, R-Tenn., motion to proceed to consideration of the bill to authorize television and radio coverage of Senate proceedings. Motion agreed to 67-32: R 39-16; D 28-16 (ND 22-8, SD 6-8), Sept. 19, 1984.

225. Beaudin Nomination. Confirmation of President Reagan's nomination of Bruce D. Beaudin of the District of Columbia to be an associate judge of the Superior Court of the District of Columbia. Confirmed 57-41: R 45-10; D 12-31 (ND 9-20, SD 3-11), Sept. 19, 1984. A "yea" was a vote supporting the president's position.

226. HR 3755. Social Security Disability Amendments. Adoption of the conference report on the bill to overhaul the Social Security disability review process and to provide for the continuation of benefits for individuals thrown off the rolls who decide to appeal. Adopted 99-0: R 55-0; D 44-0 (ND 30-0, SD 14-0), Sept. 19, 1984. A "yea" was a vote supporting the president's position.

227. HR 3398. Miscellaneous Tariff, Trade and Customs Matters. Danforth, R-Mo., motion to table (kill) the Specter, R-Pa., amendment to allow the district court of the District of Columbia to hear cases alleging that foreign nations are engaging in unfair trade practices. Motion agreed to 61-36: R 39-14; D 22-22 (ND 13-17, SD 9-5), Sept. 19, 1984. A "yea" was a vote supporting the president's position.

	228		228		228		228
ALABAMA		**IOWA**		**NEW HAMPSHIRE**			
Denton	+	Grassley	+	Humphrey	Y		
Heflin	Y	Jepsen	?	Rudman	Y		
ALASKA		**KANSAS**		**NEW JERSEY**			
Murkowski	Y	Dole	Y	Bradley	Y		
Stevens	Y	Kassebaum	Y	Lautenberg	Y		
ARIZONA		**KENTUCKY**		**NEW MEXICO**			
Goldwater	Y	Ford	Y	Domenici	Y		
DeConcini	Y	Huddleston	Y	Bingaman	Y		
ARKANSAS		**LOUISIANA**		**NEW YORK**			
Bumpers	Y	Johnston	Y	D'Amato	Y		
Pryor	Y	Long	Y	Moynihan	Y		
CALIFORNIA		**MAINE**		**NORTH CAROLINA**			
Wilson	Y	Cohen	Y	East	Y		
Cranston	Y	Mitchell	Y	Helms	Y		
COLORADO		**MARYLAND**		**NORTH DAKOTA**			
Armstrong	Y	Mathias	Y	Andrews	Y		
Hart		Sarbanes	Y	Burdick	Y		
CONNECTICUT		**MASSACHUSETTS**		**OHIO**		**TEXAS**	
Weicker	Y	Kennedy	Y	Glenn	Y	Tower	Y
Dodd	Y	Tsongas	Y	Metzenbaum	Y	Bentsen	Y
DELAWARE		**MICHIGAN**		**OKLAHOMA**		**UTAH**	
Roth	Y	Levin	Y	Nickles	Y	Garn	Y
Biden	Y	Riegle	Y	Boren	Y	Hatch	Y
FLORIDA		**MINNESOTA**		**OREGON**		**VERMONT**	
Hawkins	Y	Boschwitz	Y	Hatfield	Y	Stafford	Y
Chiles	Y	Durenberger	Y	Packwood	Y	Leahy	Y
GEORGIA		**MISSISSIPPI**		**PENNSYLVANIA**		**VIRGINIA**	
Mattingly	Y	Cochran	Y	Heinz	Y	Trible	Y
Nunn	Y	Stennis	Y	Specter	Y	Warner	Y
HAWAII		**MISSOURI**		**RHODE ISLAND**		**WASHINGTON**	
Inouye	?	Danforth	Y	Chafee	Y	Evans	Y
Matsunaga	Y	Eagleton	Y	Pell	Y	Gorton	Y
IDAHO		**MONTANA**		**SOUTH CAROLINA**		**WEST VIRGINIA**	
McClure	Y	Baucus	Y	Thurmond	Y	Byrd	Y
Symms	Y	Melcher	Y	Hollings	Y	Randolph	Y
ILLINOIS		**NEBRASKA**		**SOUTH DAKOTA**		**WISCONSIN**	
Percy	Y	Exon	Y	Abdnor	Y	Kasten	Y
Dixon	Y	Zorinsky	Y	Pressler	Y	Proxmire	Y
INDIANA		**NEVADA**		**TENNESSEE**		**WYOMING**	
Lugar	Y	Hecht	Y	Baker	Y	Simpson	Y
Quayle	Y	Laxalt	Y	Sasser	Y	Wallop	Y

KEY

Y   Voted for (yea).
\#   Paired for.
\+   Announced for.
N   Voted against (nay).
X   Paired against.
\-   Announced against.
P   Voted "present".
C   Voted "present" to avoid possible conflict of interest.
?   Did not vote or otherwise make a position known.

Democrats   *Republicans*

ND - Northern Democrats   SD - Southern Democrats (Southern states - Ala., Ark., Fla., Ga., Ky., La., Miss., N.C., Okla., S.C., Tenn., Texas, Va.)

228. HR 3398. Miscellaneous Tariff, Trade and Customs Matters. Passage of the bill to alter tariffs and customs on more than 70 items, broaden the president's authority to respond to a wide range of unfair trade practices by foreign competitors, renew for 10 years duty-free treatment of developing nations' exports, authorize negotiations for a free trade area with Israel and Canada and aid the domestic shoe, steel and copper industries. Passed 96-0: R 52-0; D 44-0 (ND 30-0, SD 14-0), Sept. 20, 1984.

	229	230	231	232	233	234	235
ALABAMA							
Denton	Y	Y	Y	Y	Y	N	Y
Heflin	?	?	?	?	?	Y	Y
ALASKA							
Murkowski	Y	N	Y	Y	Y	Y	Y
Stevens	Y	Y	Y	Y	Y	Y	Y
ARIZONA							
Goldwater	N	N	N	Y	N	Y	Y
DeConcini	?	?	?	?	?	N	Y
ARKANSAS							
Bumpers	Y	N	Y	Y	Y	Y	Y
Pryor	?	?	?	?	?	Y	Y
CALIFORNIA							
Wilson	Y	Y	Y	N	Y	Y	Y
Cranston	Y	N	Y	Y	Y	Y	Y
COLORADO							
Armstrong	Y	Y	?	?	?	N	Y
Hart	?	?	Y	Y	Y	Y	Y
CONNECTICUT							
Weicker	N	Y	?	?	?	Y	Y
Dodd	Y	N	Y	Y	Y	Y	Y
DELAWARE							
Roth	Y	Y	Y	Y	Y	N	Y
Biden	Y	N	Y	Y	Y	N	Y
FLORIDA							
Hawkins	Y	?	Y	Y	Y	Y	Y
Chiles	Y	N	Y	Y	Y	Y	Y
GEORGIA							
Mattingly	Y	N	Y	Y	Y	N	Y
Nunn	Y	N	Y	Y	Y	N	Y
HAWAII							
Inouye	?	?	Y	Y	Y	Y	Y
Matsunaga	Y	N	?	?	?	Y	Y
IDAHO							
McClure	Y	Y	Y	N	Y	Y	Y
Symms	Y	Y	Y	Y	Y	N	Y
ILLINOIS							
Percy	?	?	?	-	?	+	?
Dixon	?	?	N	N	N	Y	Y
INDIANA							
Lugar	Y	Y	Y	Y	Y	Y	Y
Quayle	N	Y	N	Y	N	Y	Y

	229	230	231	232	233	234	235
IOWA							
Grassley	?	?	Y	N	Y	N	Y
Jepsen	?	?	?	?	N	Y	Y
KANSAS							
Dole	Y	N	Y	Y	?	?	Y
Kassebaum	Y	Y	Y	Y	Y	Y	Y
KENTUCKY							
Ford	Y	N	Y	Y	Y	Y	Y
Huddleston	?	?	Y	Y	Y	Y	Y
LOUISIANA							
Johnston	Y	N	Y	Y	Y	Y	Y
Long	Y	N	Y	Y	Y	?	Y
MAINE							
Cohen	?	?	Y	Y	Y	Y	Y
Mitchell	Y	Y	Y	Y	Y	Y	Y
MARYLAND							
Mathias	Y	Y	Y	Y	Y	Y	Y
Sarbanes	?	?	?	?	?	?	Y
MASSACHUSETTS							
Kennedy	Y	N	Y	Y	Y	?	?
Tsongas	?	N	Y	Y	Y	Y	Y
MICHIGAN							
Levin	Y	N	?	?	?	Y	Y
Riegle	Y	N	Y	Y	Y	Y	Y
MINNESOTA							
Boschwitz	?	?	Y	Y	?	Y	Y
Durenberger	Y	N	Y	Y	Y	Y	Y
MISSISSIPPI							
Cochran	Y	Y	Y	N	Y	Y	Y
Stennis	Y	N	Y	Y	Y	Y	Y
MISSOURI							
Danforth	Y	N	Y	Y	Y	Y	Y
Eagleton	Y	N	?	?	?	Y	Y
MONTANA							
Baucus	?	?	Y	Y	Y	N	Y
Melcher	Y	N	Y	Y	Y	Y	Y
NEBRASKA							
Exon	Y	Y	Y	Y	Y	N	Y
Zorinsky	Y	Y	Y	Y	Y	N	Y
NEVADA							
Hecht	Y	N	Y	N	Y	Y	Y
Laxalt	Y	N	Y	N	?	Y	Y

	229	230	231	232	233	234	235
NEW HAMPSHIRE							
Humphrey	Y	Y	Y	Y	Y	?	N
Rudman	Y	Y	Y	Y	Y	Y	Y
NEW JERSEY							
Bradley	Y	N	?	Y	Y	Y	Y
Lautenberg	Y	N	Y	Y	Y	Y	Y
NEW MEXICO							
Domenici	Y	N	?	?	?	Y	Y
Bingaman	Y	N	Y	Y	Y	Y	Y
NEW YORK							
D'Amato	Y	N	Y	Y	Y	Y	Y
Moynihan	Y	Y	Y	Y	Y	Y	Y
NORTH CAROLINA							
East	Y	N	Y	N	Y	?	Y
Helms	Y	N	Y	N	Y	Y	Y
NORTH DAKOTA							
Andrews	Y	Y	Y	Y	Y	Y	Y
Burdick	Y	N	Y	Y	Y	Y	Y
OHIO							
Glenn	Y	N	Y	Y	?	Y	Y
Metzenbaum	Y	Y	Y	Y	Y	Y	Y
OKLAHOMA							
Nickles	?	?	Y	Y	Y	N	Y
Boren	?	?	?	?	N	Y	Y
OREGON							
Hatfield	Y	N	Y	Y	Y	Y	Y
Packwood	Y	Y	Y	Y	Y	Y	Y
PENNSYLVANIA							
Heinz	Y	Y	Y	Y	Y	Y	Y
Specter	Y	Y	Y	Y	Y	Y	Y
RHODE ISLAND							
Chafee	Y	Y	Y	Y	Y	Y	Y
Pell	Y	Y	?	+	?	+	Y
SOUTH CAROLINA							
Thurmond	Y	Y	Y	N	Y	Y	Y
Hollings	Y	N	?	?	?	Y	Y
SOUTH DAKOTA							
Abdnor	Y	Y	Y	Y	Y	Y	Y
Pressler	Y	Y	Y	Y	Y	Y	Y
TENNESSEE							
Baker	Y	Y	?	?	Y	Y	?
Sasser	Y	N	?	Y	Y	Y	Y

KEY

Y	Voted for (yea).
#	Paired for.
+	Announced for.
N	Voted against (nay).
X	Paired against.
-	Announced against.
P	Voted "present".
C	Voted "present" to avoid possible conflict of interest.
?	Did not vote or otherwise make a position known.

Democrats *Republicans*

	229	230	231	232	233	234	235
TEXAS							
Tower	?	?	Y	N	Y	Y	Y
Bentsen	Y	N	Y	Y	Y	Y	Y
UTAH							
Garn	Y	Y	Y	Y	Y	N	Y
Hatch	Y	Y	Y	N	N	N	Y
VERMONT							
Stafford	Y	N	Y	Y	Y	Y	Y
Leahy	Y	N	Y	Y	Y	Y	Y
VIRGINIA							
Trible	Y	Y	Y	Y	Y	N	Y
Warner	Y	Y	Y	Y	Y	Y	Y
WASHINGTON							
Evans	?	?	?	?	?	?	Y
Gorton	Y	Y	Y	Y	Y	Y	Y
WEST VIRGINIA							
Byrd	Y	N	Y	Y	Y	Y	Y
Randolph	Y	N	Y	Y	Y	Y	Y
WISCONSIN							
Kasten	Y	Y	Y	Y	Y	Y	+
Proxmire	N	N	N	Y	N	N	N
WYOMING							
Simpson	Y	N	Y	Y	Y	Y	Y
Wallop	Y	Y	?	?	?	?	Y

ND - Northern Democrats   SD - Southern Democrats (Southern states - Ala., Ark., Fla., Ga., Ky., La., Miss., N.C., Okla., S.C., Tenn., Texas, Va.)

229. Procedural Motion. Baker, R-Tenn., motion to instruct the sergeant-at-arms to request the attendance of absent senators. Motion agreed to 77-4: R 44-3; D 33-1 (ND 23-1, SD 10-0), Sept. 21, 1984.

230. S Res 66. Senate Television. Baker, R-Tenn., motion to invoke cloture (thus limiting debate) on the bill to authorize television and radio coverage of Senate proceedings. Motion rejected 37-44: R 31-15; D 6-29 (ND 6-19, SD 0-10), Sept. 21, 1984. A three-fifths majority (60) of the total Senate is required to invoke cloture.

231. Procedural Motion. Stevens, R-Alaska, motion to instruct the sergeant-at-arms to request the attendance of absent senators. Motion agreed to 76-4: R 45-2; D 31-2 (ND 22-2, SD 9-0), Sept. 24, 1984.

232. S 2527. Surface Transportation and Uniform Relocation Assistance Act. Baker, R-Tenn., motion to invoke cloture (thus limiting debate) on the Baker motion to proceed to the consideration of the bill to approve cost estimates for construction and repairs to the Interstate Highway System. Motion agreed to 70-12: R 36-11; D 34-1 (ND 24-1, SD 10-0), Sept. 24, 1984. A three-fifths majority (60) of the total Senate is required to invoke cloture.

233. Procedural Motion. Baker, R-Tenn., motion to instruct the sergeant-at-arms to require the attendance of absent senators. Motion agreed to 74-5: R 42-3; D 32-2 (ND 22-2, SD 10-0), Sept. 24, 1984.

234. HR 6028. Labor, Health and Human Services, Education Appropriations, Fiscal 1985. Passage of the bill to appropriate $105,903,623,000 in fiscal 1985 for the Labor Department, the Department of Health and Human Services, the Education Department and related agencies. The total included $11.1 billion in advance funding for fiscal 1986-87 for certain programs. The bill allows Medicaid funding to be used for abortions in cases of rape or incest, as well as when the mother's life is endangered. Passed 71-20: R 38-12; D 33-8 (ND 22-6, SD 11-2), Sept. 25, 1984. The president had requested $99,685,346,000 in new budget authority, but the Senate did not consider $373,047,000 for programs that had not been authorized.

235. HR 2838. Timber Contract Relief. Passage of the bill to allow contract purchasers of federal timber to be relieved of the obligation to purchase up to 55 percent of the volume of timber for which they contracted before Jan. 1, 1982, upon payment of certain buy-out charges. Passed 94-2: R 51-1; D 43-1 (ND 29-1, SD 14-0), Sept. 26, 1984.

CQ Senate Vote 236

Corresponding to Congressional Record Vote 253

	236
ALABAMA	
Denton	N
Heflin	N
ALASKA	
Murkowski	N
Stevens	N
ARIZONA	
Goldwater	N
DeConcini	Y
ARKANSAS	
Bumpers	Y
Pryor	Y
CALIFORNIA	
Wilson	N
Cranston	Y
COLORADO	
Armstrong	N
Hart	Y
CONNECTICUT	
Weicker	Y
Dodd	Y
DELAWARE	
Roth	N
Biden	Y
FLORIDA	
Hawkins	N
Chiles	Y
GEORGIA	
Mattingly	N
Nunn	N
HAWAII	
Inouye	Y
Matsunaga	Y
IDAHO	
McClure	N
Symms	N
ILLINOIS	
Percy	?
Dixon	Y
INDIANA	
Lugar	N
Quayle	N

	236
IOWA	
Grassley	N
Jepsen	N
KANSAS	
Dole	N
Kassebaum	N
KENTUCKY	
Ford	Y
Huddleston	Y
LOUISIANA	
Johnston	Y
Long	N
MAINE	
Cohen	Y
Mitchell	Y
MARYLAND	
Mathias	Y
Sarbanes	Y
MASSACHUSETTS	
Kennedy	Y
Tsongas	Y
MICHIGAN	
Levin	Y
Riegle	Y
MINNESOTA	
Boschwitz	Y
Durenberger	Y
MISSISSIPPI	
Cochran	N
Stennis	N
MISSOURI	
Danforth	N
Eagleton	Y
MONTANA	
Baucus	Y
Melcher	Y
NEBRASKA	
Exon	Y
Zorinsky	N
NEVADA	
Hecht	N
Laxalt	N

	236
NEW HAMPSHIRE	
Humphrey	N
Rudman	N
NEW JERSEY	
Bradley	Y
Lautenberg	Y
NEW MEXICO	
Domenici	N
Bingaman	Y
NEW YORK	
D'Amato	Y
Moynihan	Y
NORTH CAROLINA	
East	N
Helms	N
NORTH DAKOTA	
Andrews	Y
Burdick	Y
OHIO	
Glenn	Y
Metzenbaum	Y
OKLAHOMA	
Nickles	N
Boren	N
OREGON	
Hatfield	N
Packwood	Y
PENNSYLVANIA	
Heinz	Y
Specter	Y
RHODE ISLAND	
Chafee	Y
Pell	Y
SOUTH CAROLINA	
Thurmond	N
Hollings	Y
SOUTH DAKOTA	
Abdnor	N
Pressler	N
TENNESSEE	
Baker	N
Sasser	Y

KEY

- Y Voted for (yea).
- # Paired for.
- + Announced for.
- N Voted against (nay).
- X Paired against.
- \- Announced against.
- P Voted "present".
- C Voted "present" to avoid possible conflict of interest.
- ? Did not vote or otherwise make a position known.

Democrats ***Republicans***

	236
TEXAS	
Tower	N
Bentsen	Y
UTAH	
Garn	N
Hatch	N
VERMONT	
Stafford	Y
Leahy	Y
VIRGINIA	
Trible	N
Warner	N
WASHINGTON	
Evans	N
Gorton	N
WEST VIRGINIA	
Byrd	Y
Randolph	Y
WISCONSIN	
Kasten	N
Proxmire	Y
WYOMING	
Simpson	N
Wallop	N

ND - Northern Democrats SD - Southern Democrats (Southern states - Ala., Ark., Fla., Ga., Ky., La., Miss., N.C., Okla., S.C., Tenn., Texas, Va.)

236. H J Res 648. Continuing Appropriations, Fiscal 1985. Judgment of the Senate whether the Byrd, D-W.Va., amendment to attach S 2568, civil rights legislation overturning the Supreme Court's ruling in *Grove City v. Bell*, to the continuing appropriations resolution was germane. Ruled germane 51-48: R 12-42; D 39-6 (ND 30-1, SD 9-5), Sept. 27, 1984.

	237	238	239	240	241	242	243	244
ALABAMA								
Denton	Y	Y	N	N	Y	N	N	Y
Heflin	Y	Y	N	N	Y	N	N	Y
ALASKA								
Murkowski	N	Y	Y	N	Y	N	N	Y
Stevens	Y	Y	Y	N	Y	N	N	Y
ARIZONA								
Goldwater	N	Y	N	N	Y	N	N	?
DeConcini	Y	Y	N	N	Y	N	N	Y
ARKANSAS								
Bumpers	Y	Y	Y	N	N	N	N	Y
Pryor	Y	Y	N	N	Y	N	N	Y
CALIFORNIA								
Wilson	Y	Y	N	N	Y	N	N	Y
Cranston	Y	Y	Y	N	N	Y	N	Y
COLORADO								
Armstrong	Y	Y	N	N	Y	N	N	Y
Hart	Y	Y	Y	Y	N	Y	Y	Y
CONNECTICUT								
Weicker	N	Y	Y	Y	N	Y	N	N
Dodd	Y	Y	Y	Y	N	Y	Y	Y
DELAWARE								
Roth	Y	Y	N	N	Y	N	N	Y
Biden	?	Y	N	Y	Y	N	N	Y
FLORIDA								
Hawkins	Y	?	?	?	Y	Y	N	Y
Chiles	Y	Y	N	N	Y	N	N	Y
GEORGIA								
Mattingly	Y	Y	N	N	Y	N	N	Y
Nunn	Y	Y	N	N	Y	N	N	Y
HAWAII								
Inouye	Y	Y	Y	Y	N	Y	Y	Y
Matsunaga	Y	Y	Y	Y	N	Y	Y	Y
IDAHO								
McClure	Y	Y	N	N	Y	N	N	Y
Symms	Y	Y	N	N	Y	N	N	Y
ILLINOIS								
Percy	?	Y	Y	N	?	Y	N	Y
Dixon	Y	Y	Y	Y	N	Y	N	Y
INDIANA								
Lugar	Y	N	Y	Y	Y	N	N	Y
Quayle	N	N	Y	Y	Y	N	N	N
IOWA								
Grassley	Y	Y	N	N	Y	N	N	Y
Jepsen	Y	Y	N	N	Y	N	N	Y
KANSAS								
Dole	Y	Y	Y	N	Y	N	N	Y
Kassebaum	Y	Y	N	N	Y	N	N	Y
KENTUCKY								
Ford	Y	Y	N	N	Y	N	N	Y
Huddleston	Y	Y	N	N	Y	N	N	Y
LOUISIANA								
Johnston	?	?	?	?	Y	N	N	Y
Long	Y	Y	Y	Y	Y	Y	N	Y
MAINE								
Cohen	Y	Y	Y	N	N	Y	N	Y
Mitchell	Y	Y	Y	N	N	Y	N	Y
MARYLAND								
Mathias	Y	Y	Y	Y	N	Y	Y	Y
Sarbanes	Y	Y	Y	Y	N	Y	Y	Y
MASSACHUSETTS								
Kennedy	Y	Y	Y	Y	N	Y	Y	Y
Tsongas	Y	Y	Y	Y	N	Y	Y	Y
MICHIGAN								
Levin	Y	Y	Y	?	N	?	?	Y
Riegle	Y	Y	Y	Y	N	Y	N	Y
MINNESOTA								
Boschwitz	Y	Y	Y	N	N	Y	N	Y
Durenberger	Y	Y	Y	N	N	Y	N	Y
MISSISSIPPI								
Cochran	Y	Y	N	N	Y	N	N	Y
Stennis	Y	Y	Y	Y	Y	N	N	Y
MISSOURI								
Danforth	Y	Y	Y	Y	N	Y	N	Y
Eagleton	Y	Y	N	N	Y	N	N	Y
MONTANA								
Baucus	Y	Y	Y	N	N	Y	N	Y
Melcher	Y	Y	Y	N	-	+	-	Y
NEBRASKA								
Exon	Y	Y	N	N	Y	N	N	Y
Zorinsky	Y	Y	N	N	Y	N	N	Y
NEVADA								
Hecht	Y	Y	N	N	Y	N	N	Y
Laxalt	Y	Y	N	N	Y	N	N	Y
NEW HAMPSHIRE								
Humphrey	Y	Y	N	Y	N	Y	N	N
Rudman	Y	Y	Y	Y	N	Y	Y	Y
NEW JERSEY								
Bradley	Y	Y	Y	Y	N	Y	Y	Y
Lautenberg	Y	Y	Y	Y	N	Y	Y	Y
NEW MEXICO								
Domenici	Y	Y	N	Y	N	Y	N	Y
Bingaman	Y	Y	Y	N	N	Y	N	Y
NEW YORK								
D'Amato	Y	Y	N	Y	N	Y	N	Y
Moynihan	Y	Y	Y	Y	N	Y	N	Y
NORTH CAROLINA								
East	Y	N	N	N	Y	N	N	Y
Helms	Y	N	N	N	N	N	N	Y
NORTH DAKOTA								
Andrews	Y	Y	Y	N	Y	N	N	Y
Burdick	Y	Y	Y	N	N	Y	N	Y
OHIO								
Glenn	Y	?	?	?	N	Y	Y	Y
Metzenbaum	Y	Y	Y	Y	N	Y	Y	Y
OKLAHOMA								
Nickles	Y	Y	N	N	Y	N	N	Y
Boren	Y	Y	N	N	Y	N	N	Y
OREGON								
Hatfield	Y	Y	Y	Y	Y	Y	N	Y
Packwood	Y	Y	Y	N	Y	N	N	Y
PENNSYLVANIA								
Heinz	Y	Y	?	?	N	Y	N	Y
Specter	Y	Y	Y	N	Y	Y	N	Y
RHODE ISLAND								
Chafee	Y	Y	Y	Y	N	Y	Y	Y
Pell	?	Y	Y	Y	N	Y	Y	Y
SOUTH CAROLINA								
Thurmond	Y	Y	N	N	Y	N	N	Y
Hollings	Y	Y	N	N	Y	N	N	Y
SOUTH DAKOTA								
Abdnor	Y	Y	N	N	Y	N	N	Y
Pressler	Y	Y	N	N	?	?	?	Y
TENNESSEE								
Baker	Y	Y	Y	N	Y	N	N	Y
Sasser	Y*	Y	Y	N	Y	N	N	Y
TEXAS								
Tower	Y	?	?	?	Y	N	N	Y
Bentsen	Y	Y	Y	Y	Y	Y	Y	Y
UTAH								
Garn	Y	Y	N	N	Y	N	N	Y
Hatch	Y	Y	N	N	Y	N	N	Y
VERMONT								
Stafford	Y	Y	Y	Y	N	Y	N	Y
Leahy	Y	Y	Y	N	N	Y	N	Y
VIRGINIA								
Trible	Y	Y	N	N	Y	N	N	Y
Warner	Y	Y	N	N	Y	N	N	Y
WASHINGTON								
Evans	Y	Y	Y	Y	N	Y	N	Y
Gorton	Y	Y	Y	N	Y	N	Y	Y
WEST VIRGINIA								
Byrd	Y	Y	Y	Y	N	Y	Y	Y
Randolph	Y	Y	Y	N	Y	N	Y	Y
WISCONSIN								
Kasten	Y	Y	N	N	Y	N	N	Y
Proxmire	N	Y	N	N	Y	N	N	N
WYOMING								
Simpson	Y	Y	N	N	Y	N	N	Y
Wallop	Y	Y	-	N	Y	N	N	Y

KEY

Y Voted for (yea).
Paired for.
+ Announced for.
N Voted against (nay).
X Paired against.
- Announced against.
P Voted "present".
C Voted "present" to avoid possible conflict of interest.
? Did not vote or otherwise make a position known.

Democrats **Republicans**

ND - Northern Democrats   SD - Southern Democrats (Southern states - Ala., Ark., Fla., Ga., Ky., La., Miss., N.C., Okla., S.C., Tenn., Texas, Va.)

237. Procedural Motion. Baker, R-Tenn., motion to instruct the sergeant-at-arms to request the attendance of absent senators. Motion agreed to 91-5: R 50-4; D 41-1 (ND 28-1, SD 13-0), Sept. 28, 1984.

238. H J Res 648. Continuing Appropriations, Fiscal 1985. Byrd, D-W.Va. (for Riegle, D-Mich.), motion to invoke cloture (thus limiting debate) on the Byrd amendment to overturn the Feb. 28, 1984, Supreme Court decision in *Grove City College v. Bell* narrowing the reach of Title IX of the 1972 Education Amendments, a law designed to bar sex discrimination in educational institutions receiving federal aid. Motion agreed to 92-4: R 49-4; D 43-0 (ND 30-0, SD 13-0), Sept. 29, 1984. A three-fifths majority vote (60) of the total Senate is required to invoke cloture.

239. H J Res 648. Continuing Appropriations, Fiscal 1985. Baker, R-Tenn., motion to table (kill) the Hatch, R-Utah, appeal of the chair's ruling that the Baker (for Hatch) amendment, to restrict the right of federal courts to order busing of schoolchildren to achieve desegregation, was non-germane. Motion agreed to 55-39: R 25-26; D 30-13 (ND 25-5, SD 5-8), Sept. 29, 1984. (Upon reconsideration, the Baker motion subsequently was rejected (see vote 242, below).)

240. H J Res 648. Continuing Appropriations, Fiscal 1985. Baker, R-Tenn., motion to table (kill) the McClure, R-Idaho, appeal of the chair's ruling that the Baker (for Hatch, R-Utah) amendment to ease restrictions on the sale of shotguns, rifles and some handguns was non-germane. Motion rejected 31-63: R 12-40; D 19-23 (ND 16-13, SD 3-10), Sept. 29, 1984.

241. H J Res 648. Continuing Appropriations, Fiscal 1985. Baker, R-Tenn., motion to reconsider the vote by which the Baker motion to table (kill) the Hatch, R-Utah, appeal of the chair's ruling on the Baker (for Hatch) amendment was agreed to (see vote 239, above). Motion agreed to 60-37: R 41-12; D 19-25 (ND 6-24, SD 13-1), Oct. 1, 1984.

242. H J Res 648. Continuing Appropriations, Fiscal 1985. Baker, R-Tenn., motion to table (kill) the Hatch, R-Utah, appeal of the chair's ruling that the Baker (for Hatch) amendment was non-germane (see vote 239, above). Motion rejected 41-56: R 15-39; D 26-17 (ND 24-5, SD 2-12), Oct. 1, 1984. (The Baker motion to reconsider the vote by which the Baker motion to table was agreed to (see vote 239, above) previously had been agreed to (see vote 241, above).)

243. H J Res 648. Continuing Appropriations, Fiscal 1985. Baker, R-Tenn., motion to reconsider the vote by which the Baker motion to table (kill) the McClure, R-Idaho, appeal of the chair's ruling on the Baker (for Hatch, R-Utah) amendment was rejected (see vote 240, above). Motion rejected 20-77: R 5-49; D 15-28 (ND 14-15, SD 1-13), Oct. 1, 1984.

244. Procedural Motion. Baker, R-Tenn., motion to instruct the sergeant-at-arms to request the attendance of absent senators. Motion agreed to 96-3: R 52-2; D 44-1 (ND 30-1, SD 14-0), Oct. 2, 1984.

KEY

- Y Voted for (yea).
- # Paired for.
- + Announced for.
- N Voted against (nay).
- X Paired against.
- - Announced against.
- P Voted "present".
- C Voted "present" to avoid possible conflict of interest.
- ? Did not vote or otherwise make a position known.

Democrats *Republicans*

	245	246	247	248	249	250	251	252
ALABAMA								
Denton	Y	N	N	N	Y	N	N	N
Heflin	N	Y	N	Y	N	N	N	N
ALASKA								
Murkowski	Y	N	N	N	Y	N	Y	N
Stevens	Y	N	N	N	Y	Y	N	N
ARIZONA								
Goldwater	Y	N	N	N	Y	N	N	N
DeConcini	N	Y	N	Y	N	N	Y	Y
ARKANSAS								
Bumpers	N	Y	Y	Y	N	N	Y	Y
Pryor	N	Y	N	Y	N	N	Y	Y
CALIFORNIA								
Wilson	Y	N	N	N	Y	Y	N	N
Cranston	N	Y	Y	N	N	Y	N	Y
COLORADO								
Armstrong	Y	N	N	N	Y	N	Y	N
Hart	N	N	Y	N	N	N	Y	Y
CONNECTICUT								
Weicker	N	N	N	N	Y	Y	Y	Y
Dodd	N	N	Y	N	N	N	N	Y
DELAWARE								
Roth	Y	N	N	N	Y	N	N	N
Biden	N	Y	Y	Y	N	N	Y	Y
FLORIDA								
Hawkins	Y	N	Y	N	Y	Y	N	N
Chiles	N	Y	Y	Y	N	N	N	N
GEORGIA								
Mattingly	Y	N	N	N	Y	N	N	N
Nunn	N	N	N	N	N	N	N	N
HAWAII								
Inouye	N	N	Y	Y	N	Y	N	Y
Matsunaga	N	N	N	?	N	N	N	Y
IDAHO								
McClure	Y	N	N	N	Y	Y	N	N
Symms	Y	N	N	N	Y	Y	N	N
ILLINOIS								
Percy	N	N	Y	N	Y	?	N	N
Dixon	N	Y	Y	Y	N	N	Y	N
INDIANA								
Lugar	Y	N	N	N	Y	Y	N	N
Quayle	Y	N	N	N	Y	Y	N	N
IOWA								
Grassley	Y	N	N	N	Y	Y	Y	N
Jepsen	Y	N	N	N	Y	Y	Y	N
KANSAS								
Dole	Y	N	N	N	Y	Y	N	N
Kassebaum	Y	N	N	N	Y	Y	Y	Y
KENTUCKY								
Ford	N	Y	Y	Y	N	N	Y	Y
Huddleston	N	N	Y	Y	N	N	N	Y
LOUISIANA								
Johnston	N	N	N	N	N	N	N	N
Long	N	N	N	N	?	N	N	N
MAINE								
Cohen	N	Y	Y	Y	N	N	Y	Y
Mitchell	N	Y	Y	Y	N	N	Y	Y
MARYLAND								
Mathias	Y	N	N	N	Y	Y	Y	N
Sarbanes	N	Y	Y	Y	N	N	Y	Y
MASSACHUSETTS								
Kennedy	N	N	Y	N	N	N	Y	Y
Tsongas	N	N	Y	N	N	N	Y	Y
MICHIGAN								
Levin	N	Y	Y	Y	N	N	Y	?
Riegle	N	Y	Y	Y	N	N	Y	Y
MINNESOTA								
Boschwitz	Y	N	Y	N	Y	Y	N	N
Durenberger	Y	N	N	Y	Y	Y	N	N
MISSISSIPPI								
Cochran	Y	N	N	N	Y	Y	N	N
Stennis	?	?	?	?	?	Y	N	N
MISSOURI								
Danforth	Y	N	N	N	Y	Y	N	N
Eagleton	N	Y	Y	Y	N	N	Y	Y
MONTANA								
Baucus	N	Y	Y	N	N	N	Y	Y
Melcher	N	Y	Y	N	N	N	Y	Y
NEBRASKA								
Exon	Y	N	N	N	N	N	Y	N
Zorinsky	Y	Y	N	N	N	N	Y	Y
NEVADA								
Hecht	Y	N	N	N	Y	Y	N	N
Laxalt	Y	?	N	N	Y	Y	N	N
NEW HAMPSHIRE								
Humphrey	Y	N	Y	Y	Y	Y	Y	N
Rudman	Y	N	Y	N	Y	Y	N	N
NEW JERSEY								
Bradley	N	N	Y	Y	N	N	Y	?
Lautenberg	N	N	Y	Y	N	N	Y	Y
NEW MEXICO								
Domenici	Y	N	N	N	Y	N	N	N
Bingaman	N	N	Y	N	N	N	N	Y
NEW YORK								
D'Amato	Y	Y	N	N	Y	Y	N	N
Moynihan	N	N	Y	N	Y	N	Y	Y
NORTH CAROLINA								
East	Y	N	?	?	?	N	N	N
Helms	Y	N	N	N	Y	N	N	N
NORTH DAKOTA								
Andrews	Y	N	N	N	N	Y	Y	Y
Burdick	N	Y	Y	N	N	N	Y	Y
OHIO								
Glenn	?	?	?	?	N	N	Y	Y
Metzenbaum	N	N	Y	N	N	Y	Y	Y
OKLAHOMA								
Nickles	Y	N	N	N	Y	N	Y	N
Boren	N	Y	N	N	N	N	N	N
OREGON								
Hatfield	Y	N	N	N	Y	Y	Y	Y
Packwood	Y	N	N	Y	Y	N	Y	Y
PENNSYLVANIA								
Heinz	Y	N	N	N	Y	N	N	N
Specter	N	N	N	N	Y	Y	N	N
RHODE ISLAND								
Chafee	Y	N	Y	Y	Y	Y	N	N
Pell	N	N	Y	Y	N	N	Y	Y
SOUTH CAROLINA								
Thurmond	Y	N	N	N	Y	N	N	N
Hollings	N	Y	Y	Y	N	N	Y	Y
SOUTH DAKOTA								
Abdnor	Y	N	N	N	Y	N	N	N
Pressler	Y	Y	N	N	N	N	Y	Y
TENNESSEE								
Baker	Y	N	N	N	Y	N	N	N
Sasser	N	Y	Y	Y	N	N	Y	Y
TEXAS								
Tower	Y	N	N	N	Y	Y	N	N
Bentsen	N	N	N	N	N	N	Y	N
UTAH								
Garn	Y	N	N	N	Y	Y	N	N
Hatch	Y	N	N	N	Y	N	N	N
VERMONT								
Stafford	Y	N	N	N	Y	Y	N	Y
Leahy	N	Y	Y	Y	N	N	Y	Y
VIRGINIA								
Trible	Y	N	N	N	Y	Y	N	N
Warner	Y	N	N	N	Y	Y	N	N
WASHINGTON								
Evans	Y	-	N	N	Y	Y	N	N
Gorton	Y	-	N	N	Y	Y	N	N
WEST VIRGINIA								
Byrd	N	Y	Y	Y	N	N	Y	Y
Randolph	N	Y	N	N	N	N	Y	Y
WISCONSIN								
Kasten	Y	N	N	N	Y	Y	N	N
Proxmire	N	Y	N	Y	N	N	Y	Y
WYOMING								
Simpson	Y	N	N	N	Y	Y	N	N
Wallop	Y	N	N	N	Y	Y	N	N

ND - Northern Democrats   SD - Southern Democrats (Southern states - Ala., Ark., Fla., Ga., Ky., La., Miss., N.C., Okla., S.C., Tenn., Texas, Va.)

245. H J Res 648. Continuing Appropriations, Fiscal 1985. Packwood, R-Ore., motion to table (kill) the Byrd, D-W.Va., amendment to overturn the Feb. 28, 1984, Supreme Court decision in *Grove City College v. Bell* narrowing the reach of Title IX of the 1972 Education Amendments, a law designed to bar sex discrimination in educational institutions receiving federal aid. Motion agreed to 53-45: R 51-4; D 2-41 (ND 2-28, SD 0-13), Oct. 2, 1984. A "yea" was a vote supporting the president's position.

246. H J Res 648. Continuing Appropriations, Fiscal 1985. Judgment of the Senate whether the DeConcini, D-Ariz., amendment, to provide antitrust exemptions to arrangements between breweries and beer distributors allowing distributors exclusive distribution rights in particular territories, was germane. Ruled non-germane 28-67: R 3-49; D 25-18 (ND 17-13, SD 8-5), Oct. 2, 1984.

247. H J Res 648. Continuing Appropriations, Fiscal 1985. Judgment of the Senate whether the Bradley, D-N.J., amendment, to establish a $6 billion "superfund" toxic waste cleanup program for fiscal years 1986-90, was germane. The existing $1.6 billion superfund program is due to expire at the end of fiscal 1985. Ruled non-germane 38-59: R 8-46; D 30-13 (ND 24-6, SD 6-7), Oct. 2, 1984.

248. H J Res 648. Continuing Appropriations, Fiscal 1985. Judgment of the Senate whether the Bumpers, D-Ark., amendment, to require the government to use competitive bidding practices for leasing onshore land for oil and gas development, was

germane. Ruled non-germane 33-63: R 5-49; D 28-14 (ND 20-9, SD 8-5), in the session that began Oct. 2, 1984.

249. H J Res 648. Continuing Appropriations, Fiscal 1985. Kasten, R-Wis., motion to table (kill) the Melcher, D-Mont., amendment to earmark 5 percent (about $144 million) of the funds in the foreign aid appropriation bill's Economic Support Fund for health programs abroad. Motion agreed to 51-46: R 51-3; D 0-43 (ND 0-31, SD 0-12), in the session that began Oct. 2, 1984.

250. H J Res 648. Continuing Appropriations, Fiscal 1985. Kasten, R-Wis., motion to table (kill) the Zorinsky, D-Neb., amendment to prohibit U.S. participation in the Inter-American Investment Corporation. Motion agreed to 50-49: R 46-8; D 4-41 (ND 2-29, SD 2-12), Oct. 3, 1984.

251. H J Res 648. Continuing Appropriations, Fiscal 1985. Pryor, D-Ark., amendment to reduce the funds appropriated in the bill for military grants to foreign nations under the Military Assistance Program from $917 million to $705.5 million. Rejected 46-54: R 11-44; D 35-10 (ND 28-3, SD 7-7), Oct. 3, 1984.

252. H J Res 648. Continuing Appropriations, Fiscal 1985. Inouye, D-Hawaii, amendment to prohibit the expenditure of government intelligence agencies' funds on activities directed against the government of Nicaragua and to provide $6 million for the withdrawal and resettlement of guerrillas opposing the Nicaraguan government. Rejected 42-57: R 8-47; D 34-10 (ND 29-1, SD 5-9), Oct. 3, 1984.

	253	254	255	256	257	258	259	260
ALABAMA								
Denton	Y	N	N	N	Y	Y	Y	Y
Heflin	Y	N	N	N	Y	N	N	N
ALASKA								
Murkowski	Y	N	N	N	Y	Y	Y	N
Stevens	Y	N	N	N	N	Y	Y	Y
ARIZONA								
Goldwater	Y	N	N	N	Y	N	Y	N
DeConcini	Y	Y	Y	Y	N	N	N	N
ARKANSAS								
Bumpers	Y	Y	Y	Y	N	N	N	N
Pryor	Y	Y	Y	N	N	N	N	N
CALIFORNIA								
Wilson	Y	N	N	N	Y	N	Y	Y
Cranston	Y	Y	Y	Y	N	N	Y	Y
COLORADO								
Armstrong	Y	N	N	N	Y	Y	Y	N
Hart	Y	Y	Y	Y	N	N	N	N
CONNECTICUT								
Weicker	Y	Y	N	N	N	Y	N	Y
Dodd	Y	Y	Y	Y	N	N	Y	Y
DELAWARE								
Roth	Y	N	N	N	Y	Y	N	Y
Biden	Y	Y	Y	Y	Y	N	Y	Y
FLORIDA								
Hawkins	Y	N	N	N	Y	Y	Y	N
Chiles	Y	Y	Y	Y	N	N	N	N
GEORGIA								
Mattingly	Y	N	N	N	Y	Y	Y	Y
Nunn	Y	N	N	N	N	N	Y	N
HAWAII								
Inouye	Y	Y	Y	Y	N	N	N	N
Matsunaga	Y	Y	Y	Y	N	N	N	N
IDAHO								
McClure	Y	N	N	N	Y	Y	N	N
Symms	Y	N	N	N	Y	Y	N	N
ILLINOIS								
Percy	Y	?	?	?	?	?	?	?
Dixon	Y	Y	N	Y	N	Y	N	Y
INDIANA								
Lugar	Y	N	N	N	Y	Y	Y	N
Quayle	Y	N	N	N	Y	Y	Y	Y

	253	254	255	256	257	258	259	260
IOWA								
Grassley	Y	N	N	N	Y	Y	Y	Y
Jepsen	Y	N	N	N	Y	Y	N	N
KANSAS								
Dole	Y	N	N	N	Y	Y	Y	N
Kassebaum	Y	N	N	N	N	Y	Y	Y
KENTUCKY								
Ford	Y	Y	N	Y	Y	N	N	Y
Huddleston	Y	Y	Y	N	Y	Y	N	N
LOUISIANA								
Johnston	Y	N	N	N	Y	N	N	N
Long	Y	N	N	N	Y	N	N	?
MAINE								
Cohen	Y	Y	N	Y	N	Y	Y	N
Mitchell	Y	Y	Y	Y	Y	N	Y	N
MARYLAND								
Mathias	Y	N	N	N	N	Y	N	Y
Sarbanes	Y	Y	Y	Y	N	N	N	N
MASSACHUSETTS								
Kennedy	Y	Y	Y	Y	N	N	Y	N
Tsongas	Y	Y	Y	Y	N	N	N	Y
MICHIGAN								
Levin	Y	Y	Y	Y	N	N	N	N
Riegle	Y	Y	Y	Y	N	N	Y	N
MINNESOTA								
Boschwitz	Y	Y	N	N	Y	Y	Y	Y
Durenberger	Y	N	N	N	Y	Y	Y	Y
MISSISSIPPI								
Cochran	Y	N	N	N	Y	Y	Y	Y
Stennis	Y	N	N	N	Y	Y	N	N
MISSOURI								
Danforth	Y	N	N	N	Y	Y	Y	Y
Eagleton	Y	Y	N	Y	Y	N	Y	N
MONTANA								
Baucus	Y	Y	N	Y	N	N	Y	N
Melcher	Y	Y	Y	Y	N	N	N	N
NEBRASKA								
Exon	Y	Y	N	Y	Y	Y	N	Y
Zorinsky	Y	Y	N	N	Y	Y	N	Y
NEVADA								
Hecht	Y	N	N	N	Y	Y	Y	Y
Laxalt	Y	N	N	N	Y	Y	Y	N

	253	254	255	256	257	258	259	260
NEW HAMPSHIRE								
Humphrey	Y	N	N	N	Y	Y	Y	Y
Rudman	Y	N	N	N	N	Y	Y	N
NEW JERSEY								
Bradley	?	?	?	Y	N	Y	N	Y
Lautenberg	Y	Y	Y	Y	N	N	Y	Y
NEW MEXICO								
Domenici	Y	N	N	N	Y	Y	Y	N
Bingaman	Y	Y	Y	Y	N	Y	Y	N
NEW YORK								
D'Amato	Y	N	N	N	Y	Y	Y	N
Moynihan	Y	Y	Y	Y	N	Y	Y	Y
NORTH CAROLINA								
East	Y	N	N	?	?	?	?	?
Helms	Y	N	N	N	Y	Y	Y	N
NORTH DAKOTA								
Andrews	Y	Y	N	Y	Y	Y	N	N
Burdick	Y	Y	Y	Y	N	N	N	Y
OHIO								
Glenn	Y	Y	N	Y	N	N	Y	N
Metzenbaum	Y	Y	Y	Y	N	N	Y	N
OKLAHOMA								
Nickles	Y	N	N	N	Y	Y	N	Y
Boren	?	N	N	N	Y	N	N	Y
OREGON								
Hatfield	?	Y	N	N	Y	N	N	Y
Packwood	Y	Y	N	Y	N	Y	Y	Y
PENNSYLVANIA								
Heinz	Y	Y	N	N	N	Y	Y	Y
Specter	Y	N	N	N	N	Y	Y	Y
RHODE ISLAND								
Chafee	Y	Y	N	N	N	Y	Y	N
Pell	Y	Y	Y	Y	N	N	N	N
SOUTH CAROLINA								
Thurmond	Y	N	N	N	Y	Y	Y	N
Hollings	Y	N	Y	N	N	N	N	N
SOUTH DAKOTA								
Abdnor	Y	N	N	N	Y	Y	N	Y
Pressler	Y	Y	N	Y	Y	Y	Y	Y
TENNESSEE								
Baker	Y	N	N	N	Y	Y	Y	N
Sasser	Y	Y	N	Y	N	N	N	N

	253	254	255	256	257	258	259	260
TEXAS								
Tower	Y	N	N	N	Y	Y	Y	N
Bentsen	Y	Y	N	Y	N	N	N	N
UTAH								
Garn	Y	N	N	N	Y	Y	N	N
Hatch	Y	N	N	N	Y	Y	Y	N
VERMONT								
Stafford	Y	Y	N	Y	Y	Y	Y	Y
Leahy	Y	Y	N	Y	N	N	Y	N
VIRGINIA								
Trible	Y	N	N	N	Y	Y	Y	Y
Warner	Y	N	N	N	Y	Y	Y	N
WASHINGTON								
Evans	Y	N	N	N	Y	Y	Y	N
Gorton	Y	N	N	N	N	Y	Y	Y
WEST VIRGINIA								
Byrd	Y	N	Y	N	Y	N	N	N
Randolph	Y	N	N	Y	N	N	N	Y
WISCONSIN								
Kasten	Y	N	N	N	Y	Y	N	N
Proxmire	Y	Y	Y	Y	Y	N	Y	N
WYOMING								
Simpson	Y	N	N	N	N	Y	Y	Y
Wallop	Y	N	N	N	Y	Y	Y	N

ND - Northern Democrats   SD - Southern Democrats (Southern states - Ala., Ark., Fla., Ga., Ky., La., Miss., N.C., Okla., S.C., Tenn., Texas, Va.)

253. S Con Res 74. Supporting People of Afghanistan. Adoption of the concurrent resolution to call on the United States "to effectively support" the people of Afghanistan in their resistance of the occupation by the Soviet Union. Adopted 97-0: R 54-0; D 43-0 (ND 30-0, SD 13-0), Oct. 3, 1984.

254. H J Res 648. Continuing Appropriations, Fiscal 1985. Dodd, D-Conn., amendment to bar the use of U.S. aid to rebels fighting the Nicaraguan government for "terrorist" activities. Rejected 45-53: R 10-44; D 35-9 (ND 28-2, SD 7-7), Oct. 3, 1984. A "nay" was a vote supporting the president's position.

255. H J Res 648. Continuing Appropriations, Fiscal 1985. Judgment of the Senate whether the Moynihan, D-N.Y., amendment to regulate the sale of armor-piercing ammunition, so-called "cop-killer" bullets, was germane. Ruled non-germane 24-74: R 0-54; D 24-20 (ND 21-9, SD 3-11), Oct. 3, 1984.

256. H J Res 648. Continuing Appropriations, Fiscal 1985. Judgment of the Senate whether the Cranston, D-Calif., amendment to require the federal government to study its pay and classification system to determine if wage differences are caused by sex discrimination was germane. Ruled non-germane 41-57: R 4-49; D 37-8 (ND 30-1, SD 7-7), Oct. 3, 1984.

257. H J Res 648. Continuing Appropriations, Fiscal 1985. Baker, R-Tenn., motion to table (kill) the Weicker, R-Conn., amendment to allow for Medicaid payments for abortion in cases of rape or incest. Motion agreed to 54-44: R 39-14; D 15-30 (ND 9-22, SD 6-8), Oct. 3, 1984. A "yea" was a vote supporting the president's position.

258. H J Res 648. Continuing Appropriations, Fiscal 1985. Rudman, R-N.H., motion to table (kill) the Biden, D-Del., amendment to require that the president certify that funds provided were sufficient to secure U.S. embassies abroad. Motion agreed to 61-37: R 53-0; D 8-37 (ND 6-25, SD 2-12), Oct. 3, 1984.

259. H J Res 648. Continuing Appropriations, Fiscal 1985. Rudman, D-N.H., amendment to restore the Federal Trade Commission's authority to bring injunctive antitrust actions against municipalities. Adopted 56-42: R 40-13; D 16-29 (ND 15-16, SD 1-13), Oct. 3, 1984.

260. H J Res 648. Continuing Appropriations, Fiscal 1985. Packwood, R-Ore., motion to table (kill) the Chiles, D-Fla., amendment to provide an extension for compliance with noise standards for foreign carriers that operate international services at Miami International Airport and Bangor, Maine, airport. Motion rejected 47-50: R 30-23; D 17-27 (ND 13-18, SD 4-9), Oct. 3, 1984. (The Chiles amendment subsequently was adopted by voice vote.)

KEY

- Y Voted for (yea).
- # Paired for.
- + Announced for.
- N Voted against (nay).
- X Paired against.
- - Announced against.
- P Voted "present".
- C Voted "present" to avoid possible conflict of interest.
- ? Did not vote or otherwise make a position known.

Democrats   *Republicans*

	261	262	263	264	265	266	267	268
ALABAMA								
Denton	Y	N	N	Y	Y	Y	Y	Y
Heflin	N	N	N	Y	Y	Y	N	Y
ALASKA								
Murkowski	Y	N	N	Y	Y	Y	?	N
Stevens	Y	N	N	Y	Y	Y	Y	N
ARIZONA								
Goldwater	Y	N	N	Y	?	Y	Y	Y
DeConcini	N	N	Y	Y	Y	N	N	N
ARKANSAS								
Bumpers	N	N	Y	Y	N	N	N	?
Pryor	N	N	Y	Y	N	?	?	N
CALIFORNIA								
Wilson	Y	Y	N	Y	Y	Y	Y	N
Cranston	N	Y	Y	Y	Y	N	Y	N
COLORADO								
Armstrong	Y	N	N	Y	Y	Y	N	N
Hart	N	N	N	Y	Y	Y	N	N
CONNECTICUT								
Weicker	N	Y	N	Y	N	N	Y	N
Dodd	N	Y	Y	Y	N	N	N	N
DELAWARE								
Roth	N	Y	N	Y	Y	Y	Y	Y
Biden	N	Y	N	Y	N	N	N	N
FLORIDA								
Hawkins	Y	N	N	Y	N	Y	?	N
Chiles	Y	N	N	Y	Y	Y	N	?
GEORGIA								
Mattingly	Y	Y	N	Y	Y	Y	N	N
Nunn	Y	N	N	Y	Y	Y	N	?
HAWAII								
Inouye	N	N	N	Y	N	N	N	N
Matsunaga	N	N	N	Y	Y	N	N	N
IDAHO								
McClure	Y	N	N	Y	Y	Y	N	N
Symms	Y	N	?	Y	Y	Y	N	N
ILLINOIS								
Percy	?	?	?	?	?	?	?	?
Dixon	N	N	Y	Y	Y	N	N	N
INDIANA								
Lugar	Y	Y	N	Y	N	Y	Y	Y
Quayle	Y	Y	N	Y	Y	Y	Y	N

	261	262	263	264	265	266	267	268
IOWA								
Grassley	N	Y	Y	Y	Y	Y	N	N
Jepsen	Y	Y	Y	Y	Y	Y	N	N
KANSAS								
Dole	Y	Y	Y	Y	Y	Y	Y	Y
Kassebaum	Y	Y	Y	Y	Y	Y	N	N
KENTUCKY								
Ford	N	N	N	Y	N	N	N	N
Huddleston	Y	N	Y	Y	N	N	N	N
LOUISIANA								
Johnston	Y	N	N	Y	Y	Y	?	?
Long	?	?	?	?	Y	Y	N	?
MAINE								
Cohen	Y	N	N	Y	N	Y	N	N
Mitchell	N	N	Y	Y	N	N	N	?
MARYLAND								
Mathias	Y	N	N	Y	Y	N	Y	Y
Sarbanes	N	Y	N	Y	Y	N	Y	N
MASSACHUSETTS								
Kennedy	N	Y	Y	Y	N	N	Y	?
Tsongas	N	Y	Y	Y	N	N	N	N
MICHIGAN								
Levin	N	N	N	Y	Y	N	N	-
Riegle	N	N	N	Y	Y	N	N	N
MINNESOTA								
Boschwitz	Y	Y	N	Y	Y	Y	Y	N
Durenberger	Y	Y	Y	Y	Y	Y	Y	N
MISSISSIPPI								
Cochran	Y	N	N	Y	Y	Y	Y	?
Stennis	Y	N	N	Y	Y	Y	N	?
MISSOURI								
Danforth	Y	N	N	Y	Y	Y	Y	Y
Eagleton	N	Y	N	Y	Y	N	N	N
MONTANA								
Baucus	N	N	Y	Y	Y	N	N	N
Melcher	N	N	Y	Y	Y	N	N	N
NEBRASKA								
Exon	N	N	N	Y	Y	Y	N	N
Zorinsky	N	Y	N	Y	Y	Y	N	N
NEVADA								
Hecht	Y	N	N	Y	Y	Y	N	N
Laxalt	Y	N	N	Y	?	Y	Y	Y

	261	262	263	264	265	266	267	268
NEW HAMPSHIRE								
Humphrey	N	Y	Y	Y	Y	Y	N	Y
Rudman	Y	N	N	Y	Y	Y	N	Y
NEW JERSEY								
Bradley	N	Y	Y	Y	N	N	Y	?
Lautenberg	N	Y	Y	N	N	?	?	Y
NEW MEXICO								
Domenici	Y	N	N	Y	Y	Y	Y	N
Bingaman	N	N	N	Y	Y	N	N	N
NEW YORK								
D'Amato	N	N	N	Y	N	Y	N	N
Moynihan	N	Y	Y	N	N	N	N	?
NORTH CAROLINA								
East	?	?	?	?	N	Y	Y	N
Helms	Y	Y	N	Y	N	Y	N	N
NORTH DAKOTA								
Andrews	Y	N	Y	Y	Y	N	N	N
Burdick	N	N	Y	Y	Y	N	N	N
OHIO								
Glenn	N	N	N	Y	N	N	N	N
Metzenbaum	N	N	N	Y	N	N	N	N
OKLAHOMA								
Nickles	Y	Y	Y	Y	Y	Y	N	N
Boren	Y	N	Y	Y	?	?	-	N
OREGON								
Hatfield	Y	N	N	Y	Y	N	?	N
Packwood	N	Y	N	Y	Y	N	Y	Y
PENNSYLVANIA								
Heinz	N	N	N	Y	N	Y	?	N
Specter	N	N	Y	N	N	N	N	N
RHODE ISLAND								
Chafee	Y	Y	Y	Y	Y	N	Y	Y
Pell	N	Y	N	Y	Y	N	N	N
SOUTH CAROLINA								
Thurmond	Y	N	N	Y	Y	Y	Y	Y
Hollings	N	N	N	Y	Y	N	N	?
SOUTH DAKOTA								
Abdnor	Y	N	Y	Y	Y	Y	N	N
Pressler	N	Y	Y	Y	Y	Y	N	N
TENNESSEE								
Baker	Y	N	N	Y	Y	Y	Y	Y
Sasser	N	N	Y	Y	N	N	N	?

	261	262	263	264	265	266	267	268
TEXAS								
Tower	Y	N	N	Y	Y	Y	Y	Y
Bentsen	Y	N	Y	Y	Y	Y	N	?
UTAH								
Garn	Y	N	N	Y	Y	Y	N	N
Hatch	Y	N	Y	Y	Y	Y	N	N
VERMONT								
Stafford	Y	Y	Y	Y	Y	N	Y	Y
Leahy	N	Y	N	Y	Y	N	N	?
VIRGINIA								
Trible	N	Y	N	Y	Y	Y	N	Y
Warner	N	N	N	Y	Y	Y	N	N
WASHINGTON								
Evans	Y	Y	Y	Y	Y	N	Y	Y
Gorton	Y	N	Y	Y	Y	Y	Y	N
WEST VIRGINIA								
Byrd	Y	N	N	Y	N	N	Y	N
Randolph	N	N	Y	Y	N	N	N	N
WISCONSIN								
Kasten	Y	Y	N	Y	Y	Y	N	N
Proxmire	Y	Y	N	Y	N	N	N	Y
WYOMING								
Simpson	Y	N	Y	Y	Y	Y	N	Y
Wallop	Y	N	N	Y	Y	Y	Y	Y

ND - Northern Democrats   SD - Southern Democrats (Southern states - Ala., Ark., Fla., Ga., Ky., La., Miss., N.C., Okla., S.C., Tenn., Texas, Va.)

261. H J Res 648. Continuing Appropriations, Fiscal 1985. Baker, R-Tenn., motion to table (kill) the Pressler, R-S.D., amendment to bar military aid to Turkey until Turkey relinquished control of the town of Varosha on Cyprus. Motion agreed to 51-46: R 42-11; D 9-35 (ND 2-29, SD 7-6), in the session that began Oct. 3, 1984. A "yea" was a vote supporting the president's position.

262. H J Res 648. Continuing Appropriations, Fiscal 1985. Bradley, D-N.J., amendment to rescind funding for the Synthetic Fuels Corporation by $9 billion. Rejected 37-60: R 23-30; D 14-30 (ND 14-17, SD 0-13), in the session that began Oct. 3, 1984. A "nay" was a vote supporting the president's position.

263. H J Res 648. Continuing Appropriations, Fiscal 1985. Judgment of the Senate whether the Abdnor, R-S.D., amendment to authorize about $11 billion in water projects was germane. Ruled non-germane 36-60: R 16-36; D 20-24 (ND 14-17, SD 6-7), in the session that began Oct. 3, 1984.

264. H J Res 648. Continuing Appropriations, Fiscal 1985. Thurmond, R-S.C., motion to table (kill) the first division of the committee amendment. The effect of the motion was to retain in H J Res 648 the text of the crime bill attached to the measure during House consideration. Motion agreed to 97-0: R 53-0; D 44-0 (ND 31-0, SD 13-0), in the session that began Oct. 3, 1984.

265. S 3024. Surface Transportation and Uniform Relocation Assistance Act. Baker, R-Tenn., motion to table (kill) the Specter, R-Pa., amendment to change the Department of Transportation's formula for allocating money to the states for repair and maintenance of the Interstate Highway System. Motion agreed to 75-21: R 43-9; D 32-12 (ND 22-9, SD 10-3), Oct. 4, 1984.

266. H J Res 654. Debt Limit Increase. Baker, R-Tenn., motion to table (kill) the Kennedy, D-Mass., amendment to call for a mutual and verifiable freeze on the production, testing and deployment of nuclear weapons and a reduction in nuclear weapons stockpiles worldwide. Motion agreed to 55-42: R 46-8; D 9-34 (ND 2-29, SD 7-5), Oct. 5, 1984. A "yea" was a vote supporting the president's position.

267. H J Res 654. Debt Limit Increase. Baker, R-Tenn., motion to table (kill) the Tsongas, D-Mass., amendment to require Congress to vote on a proposal to freeze government appropriations at fiscal 1985 levels for fiscal 1986 before it votes again to raise the debt limit and to increase the debt limit to $1.73 trillion. (The House-passed measure would increase the debt limit to $1.824 trillion.) Motion rejected 30-61: R 25-25; D 5-36 (ND 5-25, SD 0-11), Oct. 5, 1984.

268. H J Res 654. Debt Limit Increase. Baker, R-Tenn., motion to table (kill) the Melcher, D-Mont., amendment to extend limits on imputed interest charges by the Internal Revenue Service on seller-financed sales of property. (The Internal Revenue Service computes taxes on imputed interest when a seller in a sale of self-financed property charges interest rates lower than those set by the Treasury.) Motion rejected 23-59: R 20-32; D 3-27 (ND 2-23, SD 1-4), Oct. 9, 1984. A "yea" was a vote supporting the president's position.

	269	270	271	272		269	270	271	272		269	270	271	272
ALABAMA					**IOWA**					**NEW HAMPSHIRE**				
Denton	Y	N	Y	N	*Grassley*	Y	Y	Y	Y	*Humphrey*	Y	N	Y	Y
Heflin	Y	Y	Y	Y	*Jepsen*	Y	Y	Y	Y	*Rudman*	Y	Y	Y	Y
ALASKA					**KANSAS**					**NEW JERSEY**				
Murkowski	Y	Y	Y	Y	*Dole*	Y	Y	Y	Y	Bradley	?	Y	Y	Y
Stevens	Y	Y	Y	Y	*Kassebaum*	Y	Y	Y	Y	Lautenberg	Y	Y	Y	Y
ARIZONA					**KENTUCKY**					**NEW MEXICO**				
Goldwater	Y	?	?	?	Ford	Y	Y	Y	Y	*Domenici*	Y	Y	Y	Y
DeConcini	Y	Y	Y	N	Huddleston	Y	?	?	?	Bingaman	Y	Y	Y	Y
ARKANSAS					**LOUISIANA**					**NEW YORK**				
Bumpers	?	Y	Y	N	Johnston	?	Y	Y	Y	*D'Amato*	Y	Y	Y	Y
Pryor	Y	Y	Y	N	Long	?	Y	Y	Y	Moynihan	?	Y	Y	Y
CALIFORNIA					**MAINE**					**NORTH CAROLINA**				
Wilson	Y	Y	Y	N	*Cohen*	Y	?	?	?	*East*	Y	N	N	N
Cranston	Y	Y	Y	Y	Mitchell	?	Y	Y	Y	*Helms*	Y	N	Y	-
COLORADO					**MARYLAND**					**NORTH DAKOTA**				
Armstrong	Y	Y	Y	N	*Mathias*	Y	Y	Y	Y	*Andrews*	Y	Y	Y	Y
Hart	?	Y	Y	Y	Sarbanes	Y	Y	Y	Y	Burdick	Y	Y	Y	Y
CONNECTICUT					**MASSACHUSETTS**					**OHIO**				
Weicker	Y	Y	Y	N	Kennedy	?	?	?	?	Glenn	Y	Y	Y	Y
Dodd	Y	Y	Y	Y	Tsongas	Y	Y	Y	Y	Metzenbaum	Y	Y	Y	Y
DELAWARE					**MICHIGAN**					**OKLAHOMA**				
Roth	Y	Y	Y	Y	Levin	+	+	+	+	*Nickles*	Y	Y	Y	N
Biden	Y	Y	Y	Y	Riegle	Y	Y	Y	Y	Boren	?	N	Y	?
FLORIDA					**MINNESOTA**					**OREGON**				
Hawkins	Y	Y	Y	N	*Boschwitz*	Y	Y	Y	N	*Hatfield*	Y	-	+	-
Chiles	?	Y	Y	Y	*Durenberger*	Y	Y	Y	N	*Packwood*	Y	Y	Y	Y
GEORGIA					**MISSISSIPPI**					**PENNSYLVANIA**				
Mattingly	Y	Y	Y	N	*Cochran*	?	Y	Y	?	*Heinz*	Y	Y	Y	N
Nunn	?	Y	Y	Y	Stennis	?	Y	Y	?	*Specter*	Y	Y	Y	Y
HAWAII					**MISSOURI**					**RHODE ISLAND**				
Inouye	Y	Y	Y	Y	*Danforth*	Y	Y	Y	Y	*Chafee*	Y	Y	Y	Y
Matsunaga	Y	Y	Y	Y	Eagleton	Y	?	?	?	Pell	Y	N	Y	Y
IDAHO					**MONTANA**					**SOUTH CAROLINA**				
McClure	Y	?	?	?	Baucus	Y	N	Y	N	*Thurmond*	Y	Y	Y	N
Symms	Y	N	N	N	Melcher	Y	Y	Y	N	Hollings	?	Y	Y	Y
ILLINOIS					**NEBRASKA**					**SOUTH DAKOTA**				
Percy	?	?	?	?	Exon	Y	N	Y	N	*Abdnor*	Y	Y	Y	Y
Dixon	Y	Y	Y	?	Zorinsky	Y	N	Y	N	*Pressler*	Y	Y	Y	Y
INDIANA					**NEVADA**					**TENNESSEE**				
Lugar	Y	Y	Y	Y	*Hecht*	Y	Y	Y	N	*Baker*	Y	Y	Y	Y
Quayle	Y	Y	Y	N	*Laxalt*	Y	Y	Y	?	Sasser	?	Y	Y	Y

KEY

- Y Voted for (yea).
- # Paired for.
- + Announced for.
- N Voted against (nay).
- X Paired against.
- - Announced against.
- P Voted "present".
- C Voted "present" to avoid possible conflict of interest.
- ? Did not vote or otherwise make a position known.

Democrats   Republicans

	269	270	271	272
TEXAS				
Tower	Y	?	?	?
Bentsen	?	Y	Y	Y
UTAH				
Garn	Y	Y	Y	N
Hatch	Y	Y	Y	N
VERMONT				
Stafford	Y	Y	Y	Y
Leahy	?	Y	Y	Y
VIRGINIA				
Trible	Y	Y	Y	N
Warner	Y	Y	Y	Y
WASHINGTON				
Evans	Y	Y	Y	Y
Gorton	Y	Y	Y	Y
WEST VIRGINIA				
Byrd	Y	Y	Y	Y
Randolph	Y	Y	Y	Y
WISCONSIN				
Kasten	Y	Y	Y	N
Proxmire	Y	N	Y	Y
WYOMING				
Simpson	Y	Y	Y	Y
Wallop	Y	-	?	?

ND - Northern Democrats   SD - Southern Democrats (Southern states - Ala., Ark., Fla., Ga., Ky., La., Miss., N.C., Okla., S.C., Tenn., Texas, Va.)

269. H J Res 654. Debt Limit Increase. Jepsen, R-Iowa, amendment to exempt sales of primary residences and vacation homes for $250,000 or less, farms or ranches for $2 million or less and small businesses for $1 million or less from a law, to go into effect Jan. 1, 1985, that would impose a tax penalty on certain seller-financed real estate transactions in which below-market interest rates are charged. Adopted 81-0: R 53-0; D 28-0 (ND 24-0, SD 4-0), Oct. 9, 1984.

270. H J Res 648. Continuing Appropriations, Fiscal 1985. Adoption of the conference report on the fiscal 1985 continuing appropriations resolution providing funds for programs and agencies contained in the nine appropriations measures that had not been signed into law by the Oct. 1 start of the fiscal year. Adopted 78-11: R 43-5; D 35-6 (ND 23-5, SD 12-1), Oct. 11, 1984.

271. S Res 478. Support for the Genocide Treaty. Adoption of the resolution expressing support for the principles contained in the International Convention on the Prevention and Punishment of the Crime of Genocide, and stating that the Senate would act on it "expeditiously" in the 99th Congress. Adopted 87-2: R 46-2; D 41-0 (ND 28-0, SD 13-0), Oct. 11, 1984.

272. H J Res 654. Debt Limit Increase. Dole, R-Kan., motion to table (kill) the Symms, R-Idaho, amendment to repeal a law, set to go into effect Jan. 1, 1985, that would impose a tax penalty on certain seller-financed real estate transactions in which below-market interest rates are charged. Motion agreed to 57-26: R 26-19; D 31-7 (ND 22-5, SD 9-2), Oct. 11, 1984. A "yea" was a vote supporting the president's position.

	273	274	275		273	274	275		273	274	275
ALABAMA				**IOWA**				**NEW HAMPSHIRE**			
Denton	?	Y	Y	*Grassley*	N	?	X	*Humphrey*	N	Y	N
Heflin	N	?	?	*Jepsen*	N	?	?	*Rudman*	Y	Y	Y
ALASKA				**KANSAS**				**NEW JERSEY**			
Murkowski	?	Y	Y	*Dole*	Y	Y	Y	Bradley	?	?	#
Stevens	N	Y	Y	*Kassebaum*	N	Y	N	Lautenberg	?	?	?
ARIZONA				**KENTUCKY**				**NEW MEXICO**			
Goldwater	?	?	?	Ford	N	Y	N	*Domenici*	?	Y	Y
DeConcini	N	Y	N	Huddleston	?	?	?	Bingaman	?	?	X
ARKANSAS				**LOUISIANA**				**NEW YORK**			
Bumpers	N	?	?	Johnston	?	Y	N	*D'Amato*	?	?	?
Pryor	-	?	-	Long	Y	?	?	Moynihan	N	Y	N
CALIFORNIA				**MAINE**				**NORTH CAROLINA**			
Wilson	N	Y	Y	*Cohen*	?	Y	Y	*East*	?	Y	Y
Cranston	N	?	?	Mitchell	N	Y	N	*Helms*	?	?	X
COLORADO				**MARYLAND**				**NORTH DAKOTA**			
Armstrong	N	?	?	*Mathias*	N	Y	Y	*Andrews*	?	?	?
Hart	?	?	?	Sarbanes	?	?	?	Burdick	N	Y	N
CONNECTICUT				**MASSACHUSETTS**				**OHIO**			
Weicker	?	N	Y	Kennedy	?	?	?	Glenn	N	Y	N
Dodd	N	Y	N	Tsongas	N	Y	N	Metzenbaum	N	?	?
DELAWARE				**MICHIGAN**				**OKLAHOMA**			
Roth	?	Y	Y	Levin	?	?	?	*Nickles*	?	Y	N
Biden	N	Y	N	Riegle	N	Y	N	Boren	-	?	-
FLORIDA				**MINNESOTA**				**OREGON**			
Hawkins	?	?	?	*Boschwitz*	Y	Y	Y	*Hatfield*	?	?	#
Chiles	N	?	N	*Durenberger*	?	Y	Y	*Packwood*	Y	Y	Y
GEORGIA				**MISSISSIPPI**				**PENNSYLVANIA**			
Mattingly	-	?	-	*Cochran*	?	Y	Y	*Heinz*	?	Y	Y
Nunn	N	N	N	Stennis	?	?	?	*Specter*	N	Y	Y
HAWAII				**MISSOURI**				**RHODE ISLAND**			
Inouye	N	Y	N	*Danforth*	Y	Y	Y	*Chafee*	Y	Y	Y
Matsunaga	N	Y	N	Eagleton	?	?	?	Pell	N	Y	N
IDAHO				**MONTANA**				**SOUTH CAROLINA**			
McClure	?	?	?	Baucus	N	Y	N	*Thurmond*	N	Y	Y
Symms	N	?	?	Melcher	N	Y	N	Hollings	N	?	?
ILLINOIS				**NEBRASKA**				**SOUTH DAKOTA**			
Percy	?	?	?	Exon	?	Y	N	*Abdnor*	?	Y	Y
Dixon	?	?	?	Zorinsky	N	Y	N	*Pressler*	N	Y	Y
INDIANA				**NEVADA**				**TENNESSEE**			
Lugar	Y	Y	Y	*Hecht*	N	Y	Y	*Baker*	N	Y	Y
Quayle	Y	N	Y	*Laxalt*	?	Y	Y	Sasser	N	Y	N

KEY

Y   Voted for (yea).
\#   Paired for.
\+   Announced for.
N   Voted against (nay).
X   Paired against.
\-   Announced against.
P   Voted "present".
C   Voted "present" to avoid possible conflict of interest.
?   Did not vote or otherwise make a position known.

Democrats   *Republicans*

	273	274	275
TEXAS			
Tower	?	Y	Y
Bentsen	?	Y	N
UTAH			
Garn	Y	Y	Y
Hatch	N	Y	Y
VERMONT			
Stafford	Y	Y	Y
Leahy	N	Y	N
VIRGINIA			
Trible	N	Y	Y
Warner	N	Y	Y
WASHINGTON			
Evans	Y	Y	Y
Gorton	Y	Y	Y
WEST VIRGINIA			
Byrd	N	Y	N
Randolph	N	Y	N
WISCONSIN			
Kasten	N	Y	N
Proxmire	N	N	N
WYOMING			
Simpson	Y	Y	Y
Wallop	?	?	#

ND - Northern Democrats   SD - Southern Democrats (Southern states - Ala., Ark., Fla., Ga., Ky., La., Miss., N.C., Okla., S.C., Tenn., Texas, Va.)

273. H J Res 654. Debt Limit Increase. Passage of the joint resolution to increase the public debt limit from $1,573,000,000,000 to $1,824,000,000,000. Rejected 14-46: R 13-18; D 1-28 (ND 0-21, SD 1-7), in the session that began Oct. 11, 1984. A "yea" was a vote supporting the president's position. (This resolution subsequently was passed upon reconsideration of the vote *(see vote 275, below)*.)

274. Procedural Motion. Baker, R-Tenn., motion to instruct the sergeant-at-arms to request the presence of absent senators. Motion agreed to 62-4: R 39-2; D 23-2 (ND 19-1, SD 4-1), Oct. 12, 1984.

275. H J Res 654. Debt Limit Increase. Passage of the joint resolution to increase the public debt limit from $1,573,000,000,000 to $1,824,000,000,000. Passed 37-30: R 37-4; D 0-26 (ND 0-20, SD 0-6), Oct. 12, 1984. A "yea" was a vote supporting the president's position.

HOUSE ROLL-CALL VOTES

CQ

1. Procedural Motion. Walker, R-Pa., motion to approve the House *Journal* of Monday, Jan. 23. Motion agreed to 322-28: R 122-14; D 200-14 (ND 128-13, SD 72-1), Jan. 24, 1984.

2. H Res 393. *Congressional Record* **Investigation.** Frost, D-Texas, motion to table (kill) the resolution to call for a Rules Committee investigation of instances where House documents, including the *Congressional Record*, have been altered, and report back to the House in 45 days with recommendations for changes necessary to ensure the accuracy of the *Congressional Record*. Motion agreed to 213-144: R 0-136; D 213-8 (ND 145-3, SD 68-5), Jan. 24, 1984.

3. HR 2615. Weatherization and Employment Act. Gekas, R-Pa., amendment to prohibit use of funds authorized under the bill in any fiscal year unless the secretary of the Treasury certified to Congress that such expenditures would not increase the national debt. Rejected 168-205: R 118-24; D 50-181 (ND 9-147, SD 41-34), Jan. 24, 1984.

4. HR 2615. Weatherization and Employment Act. Gramm, R-Texas, amendment to authorize the president to eliminate or reduce, by executive order, any authorization or appropriation made under the bill upon a declaration such action would aid in balancing the budget or reducing the national debt, to become effective after 60 days unless Congress voted to override the executive order. Rejected 131-245: R 118-25; D 13-220 (ND 2-155, SD 11-65), Jan. 24, 1984.

5. HR 2615. Weatherization and Employment Act. Carper, D-Del., amendment to reduce the fiscal 1985 authorization from $500 million to $200 million, authorize such sums as may be necessary for fiscal 1986-89 and reduce the authorization from 10 years to five years. Adopted 233-142: R 125-18; D 108-124 (ND 44-112, SD 64-12), Jan. 24, 1984.

6. HR 2615. Weatherization and Employment Act. Passage of the bill to authorize $200 million in fiscal 1985 and such sums as may be necessary in fiscal 1986-89 for weatherization of the homes of low-income people. Passed 222-157: R 30-114; D 192-43 (ND 156-3, SD 36-40), Jan. 24, 1984.

7. Procedural Motion. Wright, D-Texas, motion to dispense with Calendar Wednesday business on Jan. 25. Motion rejected 222-140: R 2-139; D 220-1 (ND 148-0, SD 72-1), Jan. 24, 1984. A two-thirds majority of those present and voting (242 in this case) is required to dispense with Calendar Wednesday business. (Calendar Wednesday is a procedure developed in the early 20th Century to bypass the Rules Committee. Under the complicated procedure, the committees, in alphabetical order, may call up legislation for House floor consideration. In this case, the Agriculture Committee Jan. 25 called up HR 2714 for debate.)

* Rep. Clement J. Zablocki, D-Wis., died Dec. 3, 1983. The last vote for which he was eligible was CQ vote 498, the last vote of the first session of the 98th Congress.

KEY

Y Voted for (yea).
Paired for.
+ Announced for.
N Voted against (nay).
X Paired against.
- Announced against.
P Voted "present".
C Voted "present" to avoid possible conflict of interest.
? Did not vote or otherwise make a position known.

Democrats   *Republicans*

	1	2	3	4	5	6	7
ALABAMA							
1 *Edwards*	Y	N	Y	N	Y	N	N
2 *Dickinson*	N	N	Y	Y	Y	N	N
3 Nichols	?	?	?	?	?	?	?
4 Bevill	Y	Y	N	Y	N	Y	Y
5 Flippo	Y	Y	Y	N	Y	N	Y
6 Erdreich	Y	Y	Y	N	Y	N	Y
7 Shelby	Y	Y	N	N	Y	N	Y
ALASKA							
AL *Young*	N	N	Y	Y	Y	Y	N
ARIZONA							
1 *McCain*	?	?	#	#	?	X	?
2 Udall	Y	N	N	N	Y	Y	?
3 *Stump*	Y	N	Y	Y	Y	N	N
4 *Rudd*	Y	N	Y	Y	N	N	N
5 McNulty	Y	Y	N	N	Y	Y	Y
ARKANSAS							
1 Alexander	?	?	?	?	?	?	?
2 *Bethune*	Y	N	Y	Y	Y	N	N
3 *Hammerschmidt*	Y	N	Y	Y	Y	N	N
4 Anthony	Y	Y	N	N	Y	Y	Y
CALIFORNIA							
1 Bosco	Y	Y	N	N	Y	Y	Y
2 *Chappie*	P	N	N	Y	N	Y	N
3 Matsui	?	Y	N	N	Y	Y	Y
4 Fazio	Y	Y	N	N	Y	Y	Y
5 Burton	Y	?	N	N	Y	Y	?
6 Boxer	Y	Y	N	N	Y	Y	Y
7 Miller	?	Y	N	N	Y	Y	Y
8 Dellums	?	Y	N	N	N	Y	Y
9 Stark	Y	Y	N	N	Y	Y	?
10 Edwards	Y	Y	N	N	Y	Y	Y
11 Lantos	?	?	X	?	?	#	?
12 *Zschau*	Y	N	Y	N	N	Y	N
13 Mineta	Y	Y	N	N	Y	Y	Y
14 *Shumway*	Y	N	Y	Y	Y	N	N
15 Coelho	Y	?	N	N	Y	Y	Y
16 Panetta	Y	Y	N	N	Y	Y	Y
17 *Pashayan*	Y	?	Y	Y	Y	N	N
18 Lehman	Y	Y	N	N	Y	Y	Y
19 *Lagomarsino*	Y	N	Y	Y	N	N	N
20 *Thomas*	?	?	#	#	?	X	N
21 *Fiedler*	Y	N	Y	Y	Y	N	N
22 *Moorhead*	Y	N	Y	Y	Y	N	N
23 Beilenson	Y	Y	N	N	Y	Y	Y
24 Waxman	Y	Y	N	N	Y	Y	Y
25 Roybal	Y	Y	N	N	Y	Y	Y
26 Berman	P	Y	N	?	?	#	?
27 Levine	Y	Y	N	N	Y	Y	Y
28 Dixon	Y	?	N	N	Y	Y	Y
29 Hawkins	Y	Y	N	N	Y	Y	?
30 Martinez	Y	Y	N	N	Y	Y	Y
31 Dymally	?	?	X	?	?	Y	Y
32 Anderson	Y	Y	N	N	Y	Y	Y
33 *Dreier*	Y	N	Y	Y	Y	N	N
34 Torres	Y	Y	N	N	Y	Y	Y
35 *Lewis*	Y	N	Y	Y	Y	N	Y
36 Brown	Y	Y	N	N	Y	Y	Y
37 *McCandless*	Y	N	Y	Y	Y	N	N
38 Patterson	Y	Y	N	N	Y	Y	Y
39 *Dannemeyer*	N	N	Y	Y	Y	N	N
40 *Badham*	?	?	#	#	?	X	?
41 *Lowery*	?	?	?	?	?	?	?
42 *Lungren*	Y	N	Y	Y	Y	N	N

	1	2	3	4	5	6	7
43 *Packard*	Y	N	Y	Y	Y	N	?
44 Bates	Y	Y	N	N	Y	Y	Y
45 *Hunter*	Y	N	Y	Y	N	N	N
COLORADO							
1 Schroeder	N	N	N	N	N	Y	Y
2 Wirth	Y	Y	N	N	N	Y	Y
3 Kogovsek	Y	Y	N	N	N	Y	Y
4 *Brown*	N	N	Y	Y	N	N	N
5 *Kramer*	?	?	?	?	?	?	?
6 *Schaefer*	Y	N	Y	Y	N	N	N
CONNECTICUT							
1 Kennelly	Y	Y	N	N	N	Y	Y
2 Gejdenson	N	Y	N	N	N	Y	Y
3 Morrison	Y	Y	N	N	N	Y	Y
4 *McKinney*	?	?	?	X	?	#	?
5 Ratchford	Y	Y	N	N	N	Y	Y
6 *Johnson*	?	?	?	?	?	?	?
DELAWARE							
AL Carper	Y	Y	Y	N	Y	Y	Y
FLORIDA							
1 Hutto	Y	N	Y	N	Y	N	Y
2 Fuqua	Y	Y	N	N	Y	N	Y
3 Bennett	Y	N	N	Y	Y	Y	Y
4 Chappell	?	?	?	?	?	?	?
5 *McCollum*	Y	N	Y	Y	Y	N	N
6 MacKay	Y	Y	N	N	Y	Y	Y
7 Gibbons	Y	N	N	N	N	Y	Y
8 *Young*	Y	N	Y	Y	Y	N	N
9 *Bilirakis*	Y	N	Y	Y	Y	N	N
10 Ireland	Y	N	Y	N	Y	Y	N
11 Nelson	Y	N	Y	N	Y	N	N
12 *Lewis*	N	N	Y	Y	N	N	N
13 *Mack*	N	N	Y	Y	N	N	N
14 Mica	Y	N	N	N	Y	Y	Y
15 *Shaw*	Y	N	Y	Y	Y	N	N
16 Smith	Y	N	N	Y	Y	Y	Y
17 Lehman	Y	N	N	N	Y	Y	Y
18 Pepper	Y	N	N	N	Y	Y	Y
19 Fascell	Y	Y	N	N	Y	Y	Y
GEORGIA							
1 Thomas	Y	Y	Y	N	Y	N	Y
2 Hatcher	Y	Y	N	N	Y	N	Y
3 Ray	Y	Y	N	N	Y	N	Y
4 Levitas	Y	Y	N	N	Y	N	Y
5 Fowler	Y	Y	N	N	Y	Y	Y
6 *Gingrich*	Y	N	Y	Y	Y	N	N
7 Darden	Y	Y	Y	N	Y	N	Y
8 Rowland	Y	Y	N	N	Y	N	Y
9 Jenkins	Y	Y	N	N	Y	N	Y
10 Barnard	Y	Y	N	Y	N	Y	Y
HAWAII							
1 Heftel	?	?	?	?	?	?	?
2 Akaka	Y	Y	N	N	N	Y	Y
IDAHO							
1 *Craig*	Y	N	Y	Y	Y	N	N
2 *Hansen*	Y	N	?	#	?	X	N
ILLINOIS							
1 Hayes	Y	Y	N	N	N	Y	Y
2 Savage	?	?	X	X	?	#	?
3 Russo	Y	Y	N	N	Y	Y	Y
4 *O'Brien*	Y	N	Y	Y	N	N	N
5 Lipinski	?	?	?	?	?	?	?
6 *Hyde*	· Y	N	Y	Y	Y	N	N
7 Collins	?	?	X	X	?	#	?
8 Rostenkowski	?	?	?	?	?	?	?
9 Yates	N	Y	N	N	N	Y	Y
10 *Porter*	Y	N	Y	Y	N	N	N
11 Annunzio	Y	Y	N	N	Y	Y	Y
12 *Crane, P.*	?	?	#	#	?	X	?
13 *Erlenborn*	?	?	Y	Y	N	N	N
14 *Corcoran*	+	-	#	#	+	X	-
15 *Madigan*	Y	N	Y	Y	N	N	N
16 *Martin*	Y	N	Y	Y	Y	N	N
17 Evans	Y	N	N	N	Y	Y	Y
18 *Michel*	Y	N	Y	Y	Y	N	N
19 *Crane, D.*	Y	N	Y	Y	Y	N	N
20 Durbin	N	Y	N	N	Y	Y	Y
21 Price	Y	Y	N	N	Y	Y	Y
22 Simon	?	N	N	?	?	Y	Y
INDIANA							
1 Hall	Y	Y	N	N	N	Y	Y
2 Sharp	Y	Y	N	N	N	Y	Y
3 *Hiler*	Y	N	Y	Y	Y	N	N
4 *Coats*	Y	N	Y	Y	Y	N	N
5 *Hillis*	?	?	?	?	?	?	?

ND - Northern Democrats   SD - Southern Democrats

	1	2	3	4	5	6	7
6 ***Burton***	Y	N	Y	Y	Y	N	N
7 ***Myers***	Y	N	Y	N	Y	N	N
8 McCloskey	Y	Y	N	N	N	Y	Y
9 Hamilton	Y	Y	N	N	N	Y	Y
10 Jacobs	N	Y	N	N	N	Y	Y
IOWA							
1 ***Leach***	?	?	?	?	?	?	?
2 ***Tauke***	Y	N	Y	N	Y	Y	N
3 ***Evans***	N	N	Y	N	Y	Y	N
4 Smith	?	?	?	?	?	?	?
5 Harkin	N	Y	N	N	N	Y	Y
6 Bedell	?	?	?	?	?	?	?
KANSAS							
1 ***Roberts***	?	?	?	?	?	?	?
2 Slattery	Y	Y	Y	N	Y	Y	Y
3 ***Winn***	?	?	?	?	?	?	?
4 Glickman	Y	Y	Y	N	Y	Y	Y
5 ***Whittaker***	Y	N	Y	Y	Y	N	N
KENTUCKY							
1 Hubbard	Y	Y	Y	N	Y	N	?
2 Natcher	Y	Y	N	N	N	Y	Y
3 Mazzoli	Y	Y	N	N	Y	Y	Y
4 ***Snyder***	Y	N	Y	N	Y	N	N
5 ***Rogers***	Y	N	Y	Y	Y	Y	N
6 ***Hopkins***	Y	N	Y	Y	Y	N	N
7 Perkins	Y	Y	N	N	N	Y	Y
LOUISIANA							
1 ***Livingston***	Y	N	Y	Y	Y	N	N
2 Boggs	Y	?	N	N	N	Y	Y
3 Tauzin	Y	Y	Y	Y	Y	Y	Y
4 Roemer	N	Y	Y	Y	Y	N	Y
5 Huckaby	?	?	?	?	?	?	?
6 ***Moore***	Y	N	Y	Y	Y	N	N
7 Breaux	Y	Y	?	?	?	?	?
8 Long	?	?	N	N	N	Y	Y
MAINE							
1 ***McKernan***	Y	N	N	N	N	Y	N
2 ***Snowe***	Y	N	N	N	N	Y	N
MARYLAND							
1 Dyson	Y	Y	N	N	Y	N	Y
2 Long	?	Y	N	N	N	Y	?
3 Mikulski	Y	Y	N	N	N	Y	Y
4 ***Holt***	Y	N	Y	Y	Y	N	N
5 Hoyer	Y	Y	N	N	N	Y	Y
6 Byron	?	?	N	N	Y	Y	Y
7 Mitchell	N	Y	N	N	N	Y	Y
8 Barnes	Y	Y	N	N	N	Y	Y
MASSACHUSETTS							
1 ***Conte***	Y	N	N	N	N	Y	N
2 Boland	Y	Y	N	N	N	Y	Y
3 Early	Y	Y	N	N	N	Y	Y
4 Frank	Y	Y	N	N	N	Y	Y
5 Shannon	Y	Y	N	N	N	Y	Y
6 Mavroules	Y	Y	N	N	N	Y	Y
7 Markey	Y	Y	N	N	N	Y	Y
8 O'Neill							
9 Moakley	?	?	X	X	?	#	?
10 Studds	Y	Y	N	N	N	?	?
11 Donnelly	Y	Y	N	N	N	Y	Y
MICHIGAN							
1 Conyers	Y	Y	N	N	N	Y	Y
2 ***Pursell***	?	?	?	?	?	?	?
3 Wolpe	Y	Y	N	N	N	Y	Y
4 ***Siljander***	?	?	?	?	?	?	N
5 ***Sawyer***	Y	N	Y	Y	Y	Y	N
6 Carr	Y	Y	N	N	Y	Y	Y
7 Kildee	Y	Y	N	N	N	Y	Y
8 Traxler	N	Y	N	N	N	Y	Y
9 ***Vander Jagt***	?	?	?	?	?	?	?
10 Albosta	Y	Y	Y	N	N	Y	Y
11 ***Davis***	Y	N	N	N	N	Y	N
12 Bonior	Y	Y	N	N	N	Y	?
13 Crockett	?	Y	N	N	N	Y	Y
14 Hertel	Y	Y	N	N	N	Y	Y
15 Ford	Y	Y	N	N	N	Y	?
16 Dingell	Y	Y	?	N	N	Y	Y
17 Levin	Y	Y	N	N	Y	Y	Y
18 ***Broomfield***	Y	N	Y	Y	Y	N	N
MINNESOTA							
1 Penny	N	Y	N	N	Y	Y	Y
2 ***Weber***	N	N	Y	Y	Y	N	N
3 ***Frenzel***	?	?	?	#	?	?	?
4 Vento	Y	Y	N	N	N	Y	Y
5 Sabo	N	Y	N	N	Y	Y	Y
6 Sikorski	N	?	N	N	N	Y	Y
7 ***Stangeland***	Y	N	Y	Y	Y	Y	N
8 Oberstar	Y	Y	N	N	N	Y	Y
MISSISSIPPI							
1 Whitten	Y	?	?	N	N	Y	Y
2 ***Franklin***	Y	N	Y	Y	Y	N	N
3 Montgomery	Y	Y	Y	Y	Y	N	Y
4 Dowdy	Y	Y	N	N	Y	Y	Y
5 ***Lott***	Y	?	Y	Y	Y	N	N
MISSOURI							
1 Clay	N	Y	N	N	N	Y	Y
2 Young	Y	Y	N	N	Y	Y	Y
3 Gephardt	?	Y	N	N	Y	Y	Y
4 Skelton	Y	Y	N	N	Y	Y	Y
5 Wheat	Y	Y	N	N	N	Y	Y
6 ***Coleman***	?	?	?	?	?	?	?
7 ***Taylor***	Y	N	Y	Y	Y	N	N
8 ***Emerson***	N	N	Y	Y	Y	N	N
9 Volkmer	Y	Y	N	Y	Y	Y	Y
MONTANA							
1 Williams	?	Y	N	N	N	Y	Y
2 ***Marlenee***	Y	N	Y	Y	Y	Y	N
NEBRASKA							
1 ***Bereuter***	Y	N	N	Y	Y	N	N
2 ***Daub***	Y	N	Y	Y	Y	N	N
3 ***Smith***	Y	N	Y	Y	Y	N	N
NEVADA							
1 Reid	Y	Y	N	N	N	Y	Y
2 ***Vucanovich***	Y	N	Y	Y	Y	N	N
NEW HAMPSHIRE							
1 D'Amours	Y	N	N	N	N	Y	Y
2 ***Gregg***	Y	N	Y	Y	Y	N	N
NEW JERSEY							
1 Florio	?	Y	N	N	N	Y	Y
2 Hughes	?	?	?	?	?	N	Y
3 Howard	Y	Y	N	N	N	Y	Y
4 ***Smith***	Y	N	N	Y	N	Y	N
5 ***Roukema***	Y	N	N	N	Y	N	Y
6 Dwyer	Y	Y	N	N	Y	Y	Y
7 ***Rinaldo***	Y	N	N	N	N	Y	N
8 Roe	Y	Y	N	N	N	Y	Y
9 Torricelli	Y	Y	N	N	N	Y	Y
10 Rodino	?	Y	N	N	N	Y	Y
11 Minish	Y	Y	N	N	N	Y	Y
12 ***Courter***	Y	N	Y	Y	Y	N	N
13 ***Forsythe***	?	?	?	?	?	?	?
14 Guarini	Y	Y	N	N	Y	Y	Y
NEW MEXICO							
1 ***Lujan***	Y	N	Y	Y	Y	N	?
2 ***Skeen***	?	?	Y	Y	Y	N	N
3 Richardson	Y	Y	N	N	N	Y	Y
NEW YORK							
1 ***Carney***	Y	N	N	N	Y	Y	N
2 Downey	Y	Y	N	N	N	Y	Y
3 Mrazek	Y	Y	N	N	N	Y	Y
4 ***Lent***	?	?	Y	Y	Y	Y	N
5 ***McGrath***	Y	N	Y	Y	Y	Y	N
6 Addabbo	Y	Y	N	N	N	Y	Y
7 Ackerman	Y	Y	N	N	N	Y	Y
8 Scheuer	?	Y	?	N	N	?	Y
9 Ferraro	Y	Y	N	N	N	Y	Y
10 Schumer	Y	Y	N	N	N	Y	Y
11 Towns	Y	Y	N	N	N	Y	Y
12 Owens	Y	Y	N	N	N	Y	Y
13 Solarz	?	?	X	X	?	#	?
14 ***Molinari***	Y	N	N	Y	Y	N	N
15 ***Green***	Y	N	N	N	N	Y	N
16 Rangel	Y	Y	N	N	N	Y	Y
17 Weiss	Y	Y	N	N	N	Y	Y
18 Garcia	Y	Y	N	N	N	Y	Y
19 Biaggi	Y	Y	N	N	N	Y	Y
20 Ottinger	?	Y	N	X	N	Y	Y
21 ***Fish***	Y	N	N	N	N	Y	N
22 ***Gilman***	Y	N	N	N	N	Y	N
23 Stratton	Y	Y	Y	N	N	Y	Y
24 ***Solomon***	?	?	?	Y	Y	N	N
25 ***Boehlert***	Y	N	N	N	N	Y	N
26 ***Martin***	Y	N	N	Y	Y	Y	N
27 ***Wortley***	Y	N	N	Y	Y	Y	N
28 McHugh	Y	Y	N	N	N	Y	Y
29 ***Horton***	Y	N	N	N	N	Y	N
30 ***Conable***	Y	N	Y	Y	Y	N	N
31 ***Kemp***	?	N	Y	Y	Y	N	N
32 LaFalce	Y	Y	N	N	Y	Y	Y
33 Nowak	Y	Y	N	N	N	Y	Y
34 Lundine	Y	Y	N	N	Y	Y	?
NORTH CAROLINA							
1 Jones	Y	Y	N	N	Y	N	Y
2 Valentine	Y	Y	Y	N	Y	N	Y
3 Whitley	Y	Y	Y	N	Y	N	Y
4 Andrews	?	?	?	?	?	?	?
5 Neal	Y	Y	Y	N	Y	N	Y
6 Britt	Y	Y	Y	N	Y	Y	Y
7 Rose	Y	Y	N	N	Y	Y	Y
8 Hefner	Y	Y	Y	N	Y	N	Y
9 ***Martin***	?	N	Y	Y	Y	N	N
10 ***Broyhill***	Y	N	Y	Y	Y	N	N
11 Clarke	P	Y	N	N	Y	Y	?
NORTH DAKOTA							
AL Dorgan	Y	Y	N	N	Y	Y	Y
OHIO							
1 Luken	Y	Y	N	N	N	Y	Y
2 ***Gradison***	Y	N	Y	N	Y	N	N
3 Hall	?	?	?	N	Y	Y	Y
4 ***Oxley***	Y	N	Y	Y	Y	N	N
5 ***Latta***	Y	N	Y	Y	Y	N	N
6 ***McEwen***	Y	N	Y	Y	Y	N	N
7 ***DeWine***	Y	N	Y	Y	Y	N	N
8 ***Kindness***	Y	N	Y	Y	Y	N	N
9 Kaptur	Y	Y	N	N	Y	Y	?
10 ***Miller***	N	N	Y	Y	Y	N	N
11 Eckart	Y	?	N	N	Y	Y	Y
12 ***Kasich***	Y	N	Y	Y	Y	N	N
13 Pease	Y	Y	N	N	Y	Y	Y
14 Seiberling	?	?	?	?	?	?	?
15 ***Wylie***	Y	N	Y	Y	Y	N	N
16 ***Regula***	Y	N	Y	Y	Y	N	N
17 ***Williams***	?	?	?	X	?	#	?
18 Applegate	?	Y	?	N	Y	Y	Y
19 Feighan	Y	Y	N	N	Y	Y	Y
20 Oakar	Y	Y	N	N	N	Y	Y
21 Stokes	Y	Y	N	N	N	Y	Y
OKLAHOMA							
1 Jones	Y	Y	N	N	Y	Y	Y
2 Synar	+	+	-	-	+	Y	Y
3 Watkins	Y	Y	N	N	Y	Y	Y
4 McCurdy	?	?	?	?	?	?	?
5 ***Edwards***	Y	N	Y	N	Y	N	N
6 English	?	?	?	?	?	?	?
OREGON							
1 AuCoin	?	?	?	?	?	?	?
2 ***Smith, R.***	Y	N	Y	N	Y	N	N
3 Wyden	Y	Y	N	N	N	Y	Y
4 Weaver	?	?	N	N	?	Y	Y
5 ***Smith, D.***	Y	N	Y	Y	Y	N	N
PENNSYLVANIA							
1 Foglietta	Y	Y	N	N	N	Y	Y
2 Gray	Y	?	N	N	N	Y	Y
3 Borski	Y	Y	N	N	Y	Y	Y
4 Kolter	Y	?	Y	N	Y	Y	Y
5 ***Schulze***	N	N	Y	Y	Y	N	?
6 Yatron	Y	Y	Y	N	Y	Y	Y
7 Edgar	Y	Y	N	N	N	Y	?
8 Kostmayer	Y	Y	N	N	N	Y	Y
9 ***Shuster***	Y	N	Y	Y	Y	N	N
10 ***McDade***	Y	N	N	N	N	Y	N
11 Harrison	Y	Y	N	N	N	Y	Y
12 Murtha	Y	Y	N	N	Y	Y	Y
13 ***Coughlin***	N	N	N	N	N	Y	?
14 Coyne	P	Y	N	N	N	Y	Y
15 ***Ritter***	?	?	?	?	?	?	?
16 ***Walker***	N	N	Y	Y	Y	N	N
17 ***Gekas***	Y	N	Y	Y	Y	N	N
18 Walgren	Y	Y	N	N	N	Y	?
19 ***Goodling***	N	N	Y	Y	Y	N	N
20 Gaydos	Y	Y	Y	N	Y	Y	Y
21 ***Ridge***	Y	?	N	Y	Y	Y	?
22 Murphy	N	Y	Y	N	Y	Y	Y
23 ***Clinger***	Y	N	N	Y	N	Y	N
RHODE ISLAND							
1 St Germain	?	?	?	?	?	?	?
2 ***Schneider***	Y	N	N	N	N	Y	N
SOUTH CAROLINA							
1 ***Hartnett***	?	?	?	?	?	N	N
2 ***Spence***	Y	N	Y	Y	Y	N	N
3 Derrick	?	Y	Y	N	Y	N	Y
4 ***Campbell***	Y	N	Y	Y	Y	N	N
5 Spratt	Y	Y	Y	N	Y	Y	Y
6 Tallon	Y	Y	N	N	Y	Y	Y
SOUTH DAKOTA							
AL Daschle	Y	Y	N	N	Y	Y	Y
TENNESSEE							
1 ***Quillen***	Y	N	Y	Y	Y	N	N
2 ***Duncan***	Y	N	Y	Y	Y	N	N
3 Lloyd	Y	Y	Y	N	Y	N	Y
4 Cooper	Y	Y	Y	N	Y	N	Y
5 Boner	Y	Y	Y	N	Y	Y	Y
6 Gore	?	?	?	?	?	?	?
7 ***Sundquist***	Y	N	Y	Y	Y	N	N
8 Jones	Y	Y	N	N	Y	Y	Y
9 Ford	Y	Y	N	N	N	Y	Y
TEXAS							
1 Hall, S.	Y	Y	Y	Y	Y	N	Y
2 Wilson	?	?	?	?	?	?	?
3 ***Bartlett***	Y	N	Y	Y	Y	N	N
4 Hall, R.	Y	Y	Y	Y	Y	N	Y
5 Bryant	Y	Y	N	N	Y	?	?
6 ***Gramm***	Y	N	Y	Y	Y	N	N
7 ***Archer***	Y	N	Y	Y	Y	N	N
8 ***Fields***	Y	N	Y	Y	Y	N	N
9 Brooks	Y	Y	N	N	Y	Y	Y
10 Pickle	Y	Y	N	N	Y	N	Y
11 Leath	Y	Y	Y	N	Y	N	Y
12 Wright	?	?	N	N	Y	Y	Y
13 Hightower	Y	Y	Y	N	Y	N	Y
14 Patman	Y	Y	Y	Y	Y	N	Y
15 de la Garza	?	?	?	?	?	?	?
16 Coleman	Y	Y	Y	N	Y	N	Y
17 Stenholm	?	?	?	?	?	?	?
18 Leland	Y	Y	N	N	N	Y	Y
19 Hance	?	?	?	X	?	X	?
20 Gonzalez	Y	Y	N	N	N	Y	Y
21 ***Loeffler***	Y	N	Y	Y	Y	N	N
22 ***Paul***	Y	N	Y	Y	Y	N	?
23 Kazen	Y	Y	Y	N	Y	Y	Y
24 Frost	Y	Y	N	N	Y	Y	?
25 Andrews	Y	Y	Y	N	Y	N	Y
26 Vandergriff	Y	Y	Y	Y	Y	N	Y
27 Ortiz	Y	Y	N	N	N	Y	Y
UTAH							
1 ***Hansen***	Y	N	Y	Y	Y	N	N
2 ***Marriott***	?	?	#	#	?	X	?
3 ***Nielson***	Y	N	Y	Y	Y	N	N
VERMONT							
AL ***Jeffords***	Y	N	N	N	N	Y	N
VIRGINIA							
1 ***Bateman***	Y	N	Y	Y	Y	N	N
2 ***Whitehurst***	Y	N	Y	Y	Y	N	N
3 ***Bliley***	?	?	Y	Y	Y	N	N
4 Sisisky	Y	Y	Y	N	Y	N	Y
5 Daniel	Y	Y	Y	Y	Y	N	N
6 Olin	Y	Y	Y	N	Y	N	Y
7 ***Robinson***	Y	N	Y	N	Y	N	N
8 ***Parris***	Y	N	Y	Y	Y	N	N
9 Boucher	Y	Y	N	N	N	Y	Y
10 ***Wolf***	Y	N	Y	Y	Y	N	N
WASHINGTON							
1 ***Pritchard***	Y	N	Y	Y	Y	N	Y
2 Swift	Y	Y	N	N	N	Y	Y
3 Bonker	Y	Y	N	N	N	Y	?
4 ***Morrison***	Y	N	Y	Y	Y	N	N
5 Foley	?	?	?	?	?	?	?
6 Dicks	Y	Y	N	N	Y	Y	Y
7 Lowry	Y	Y	N	N	N	Y	Y
8 ***Chandler***	Y	N	Y	Y	Y	N	N
WEST VIRGINIA							
1 Mollohan	Y	Y	N	N	N	Y	Y
2 Staggers	Y	?	N	N	N	Y	Y
3 Wise	Y	+	N	N	N	Y	Y
4 Rahall	?	Y	N	N	N	Y	Y
WISCONSIN							
1 Aspin	Y	Y	N	N	Y	Y	Y
2 Kastenmeier	Y	Y	N	N	N	Y	Y
3 ***Gunderson***	Y	N	Y	Y	Y	N	N
4 Vacancy*							
5 Moody	Y	Y	N	N	?	Y	Y
6 ***Petri***	Y	N	Y	Y	Y	N	N
7 Obey	Y	Y	N	N	N	Y	Y
8 ***Roth***	Y	N	Y	Y	Y	N	N
9 ***Sensenbrenner***	Y	N	Y	Y	Y	N	N
WYOMING							
AL ***Cheney***	Y	N	Y	Y	Y	N	N

Southern states - Ala., Ark., Fla., Ga., Ky., La., Miss., N.C., Okla., S.C., Tenn., Texas, Va.

KEY

Y Voted for (yea).
Paired for.
+ Announced for.
N Voted against (nay).
X Paired against.
- Announced against.
P Voted "present".
C Voted "present" to avoid possible conflict of interest.
? Did not vote or otherwise make a position known.

Democrats *Republicans*

8. H Res 403. Proxy Voting Investigation. Frost, D-Texas, motion to table (kill) the resolution to demand an investigation of proxy voting in committees. Motion agreed to 236-155: R 0-152; D 236-3 (ND 156-0, SD 80-3), Jan. 26, 1984.

9. HR 2714. Agricultural Productivity Act. Passage of the bill to authorize $10.5 million for fiscal years 1985-89 for pilot research projects and other research and information activities on organic farming; also to authorize cost-sharing federal conservation payments for "intercropping," a planting practice that conserves and improves soil. Passed 206-184: R 15-138; D 191-46 (ND 143-14, SD 48-32), Jan. 26, 1984. A "nay" was a vote supporting the president's position.

10. HR 2900. National Oceanic and Atmospheric Administration Authorization. Andrews, D-Texas, amendment to prohibit the agency from contracting out any services to the private sector until Congress has been notified and has had 45 legislative days to review the proposal. Adopted 257-124: R 28-118; D 229-6 (ND 158-1, SD 71-5), Jan. 26, 1984.

	8	9	10
ALABAMA			
1 *Edwards*	?	?	?
2 *Dickinson*	N	N	N
3 Nichols	?	?	?
4 Bevill	Y	N	Y
5 Flippo	Y	Y	?
6 Erdreich	Y	Y	#
7 Shelby	Y	Y	Y
ALASKA			
AL *Young*	N	N	Y
ARIZONA			
1 *McCain*	N	N	N
2 Udall	Y	Y	Y
3 *Stump*	N	N	N
4 *Rudd*	N	N	N
5 McNulty	Y	Y	Y
ARKANSAS			
1 Alexander	Y	Y	Y
2 *Bethune*	?	N	?
3 *Hammerschmidt*	N	N	N
4 Anthony	Y	Y	Y
CALIFORNIA			
1 Bosco	Y	Y	Y
2 *Chappie*	N	N	N
3 Matsui	Y	Y	Y
4 Fazio	Y	Y	Y
5 Burton	Y	Y	Y
6 Boxer	Y	Y	Y
7 Miller	Y	Y	Y
8 Dellums	Y	Y	Y
9 Stark	Y	Y	Y
10 Edwards	Y	Y	Y
11 Lantos	Y	Y	Y
12 *Zschau*	N	N	N
13 Mineta	Y	Y	Y
14 *Shumway*	N	N	N
15 Coelho	Y	Y	?
16 Panetta	Y	Y	Y
17 *Pashayan*	N	N	N
18 Lehman	Y	Y	Y
19 *Lagomarsino*	N	N	N
20 *Thomas*	N	N	X
21 *Fiedler*	N	X	N
22 *Moorhead*	N	N	N
23 Beilenson	Y	Y	Y
24 Waxman	Y	Y	?
25 Roybal	Y	Y	Y
26 Berman	Y	Y	Y
27 Levine	Y	Y	Y
28 Dixon	?	#	#
29 Hawkins	Y	Y	Y
30 Martinez	Y	Y	Y
31 Dymally	Y	Y	Y
32 Anderson	Y	N	Y
33 *Dreier*	N	N	N
34 Torres	Y	Y	Y
35 *Lewis*	N	N	Y
36 Brown	Y	Y	Y
37 *McCandless*	N	N	N
38 Patterson	Y	Y	Y
39 *Dannemeyer*	N	N	N
40 *Badham*	N	N	N
41 *Lowery*	N	N	N
42 *Lungren*	N	N	N

	8	9	10
43 *Packard*	N	N	N
44 Bates	Y	Y	Y
45 *Hunter*	N	N	N
COLORADO			
1 Schroeder	Y	Y	Y
2 Wirth	Y	Y	Y
3 Kogovsek	Y	Y	Y
4 *Brown*	N	N	N
5 *Kramer*	N	N	N
6 *Schaefer*	N	N	N
CONNECTICUT			
1 Kennelly	Y	Y	Y
2 Gejdenson	Y	Y	Y
3 Morrison	Y	Y	Y
4 *McKinney*	?	X	X
5 Ratchford	Y	N	Y
6 *Johnson*	N	N	N
DELAWARE			
AL Carper	Y	?	Y
FLORIDA			
1 Hutto	Y	N	Y
2 Fuqua	?	?	?
3 Bennett	N	N	Y
4 Chappell	Y	N	Y
5 *McCollum*	N	N	N
6 MacKay	Y	N	Y
7 Gibbons	Y	N	Y
8 *Young*	?	X	?
9 *Bilirakis*	N	N	N
10 Ireland	Y	N	N
11 Nelson	Y	N	Y
12 *Lewis*	N	N	N
13 *Mack*	N	N	N
14 Mica	Y	Y	Y
15 *Shaw*	N	N	N
16 Smith	Y	Y	Y
17 Lehman	Y	Y	Y
18 Pepper	Y	Y	Y
19 Fascell	Y	Y	Y
GEORGIA			
1 Thomas	Y	Y	Y
2 Hatcher	Y	N	Y
3 Ray	Y	N	Y
4 Levitas	Y	N	?
5 Fowler	Y	N	Y
6 *Gingrich*	N	N	?
7 Darden	Y	N	Y
8 Rowland	Y	Y	Y
9 Jenkins	Y	N	N
10 Barnard	Y	N	Y
HAWAII			
1 Heftel	?	?	?
2 Akaka	Y	Y	Y
IDAHO			
1 *Craig*	N	N	N
2 *Hansen*	N	N	N
ILLINOIS			
1 Hayes	Y	Y	Y
2 Savage	Y	Y	Y
3 Russo	Y	Y	Y
4 *O'Brien*	?	?	?
5 Lipinski	Y	Y	Y
6 *Hyde*	N	N	N
7 Collins	?	#	#
8 Rostenkowski	?	?	?
9 Yates	Y	Y	Y
10 *Porter*	N	N	N
11 Annunzio	Y	Y	Y
12 *Crane, P.*	N	N	N
13 *Erlenborn*	N	N	N
14 *Corcoran*	-	X	X
15 *Madigan*	?	X	X
16 *Martin*	N	N	N
17 Evans	Y	Y	Y
18 *Michel*	N	N	N
19 *Crane, D.*	N	N	N
20 Durbin	Y	Y	Y
21 Price	Y	Y	Y
22 Simon	?	?	Y
INDIANA			
1 Hall	Y	Y	?
2 Sharp	Y	Y	Y
3 *Hiler*	N	N	N
4 *Coats*	N	N	N
5 *Hillis*	N	N	N

ND - Northern Democrats   SD - Southern Democrats

	8	9	10
6 Burton	N	N	N
7 Myers	N	N	Y
8 McCloskey	Y	Y	Y
9 Hamilton	Y	Y	Y
10 Jacobs	Y	N	Y
IOWA			
1 Leach	N	Y	?
2 Tauke	N	Y	N
3 Evans	?	Y	N
4 Smith	?	?	?
5 Harkin	Y	Y	?
6 Bedell	Y	Y	Y
KANSAS			
1 Roberts	?	?	?
2 Slattery	Y	N	Y
3 Winn	N	N	N
4 Glickman	Y	Y	Y
5 Whittaker	N	N	N
KENTUCKY			
1 Hubbard	Y	N	Y
2 Natcher	Y	Y	Y
3 Mazzoli	Y	Y	Y
4 Snyder	N	N	Y
5 Rogers	N	N	N
6 Hopkins	N	N	N
7 Perkins	Y	Y	Y
LOUISIANA			
1 Livingston	N	N	N
2 Boggs	Y	Y	Y
3 Tauzin	Y	N	Y
4 Roemer	Y	N	N
5 Huckaby	?	?	?
6 Moore	N	N	N
7 Breaux	Y	Y	Y
8 Long	Y	Y	Y
MAINE			
1 McKernan	N	Y	Y
2 Snowe	N	N	Y
MARYLAND			
1 Dyson	Y	N	Y
2 Long	Y	Y	Y
3 Mikulski	Y	Y	Y
4 Holt	N	N	N
5 Hoyer	Y	Y	Y
6 Byron	Y	N	Y
7 Mitchell	Y	Y	Y
8 Barnes	Y	Y	Y
MASSACHUSETTS			
1 Conte	N	N	Y
2 Boland	?	N	?
3 Early	Y	N	Y
4 Frank	Y	Y	Y
5 Shannon	Y	Y	Y
6 Mavroules	Y	Y	Y
7 Markey	Y	Y	Y
8 O'Neill			
9 Moakley	?	?	?
10 Studds	Y	Y	Y
11 Donnelly	?	?	?
MICHIGAN			
1 Conyers	Y	Y	Y
2 Pursell	N	N	N
3 Wolpe	Y	Y	Y
4 Siljander	N	N	N
5 Sawyer	N	N	N
6 Carr	Y	Y	Y
7 Kildee	Y	Y	Y
8 Traxler	Y	Y	Y
9 Vander Jagt	N	N	N
10 Albosta	Y	Y	Y
11 Davis	N	Y	?
12 Bonior	Y	Y	Y
13 Crockett	Y	Y	Y
14 Hertel	Y	Y	Y
15 Ford	Y	Y	Y
16 Dingell	?	?	Y
17 Levin	Y	Y	Y
18 Broomfield	N	N	N
MINNESOTA			
1 Penny	Y	Y	Y
2 Weber	N	N	N
3 Frenzel	N	N	N
4 Vento	Y	Y	Y
5 Sabo	Y	Y	Y
6 Sikorski	Y	Y	Y

	8	9	10
7 Stangeland	N	N	N
8 Oberstar	Y	Y	Y
MISSISSIPPI			
1 Whitten	Y	N	?
2 Franklin	N	Y	N
3 Montgomery	Y	N	N
4 Dowdy	Y	Y	Y
5 Lott	N	N	N
MISSOURI			
1 Clay	Y	Y	Y
2 Young	Y	Y	Y
3 Gephardt	Y	Y	Y
4 Skelton	?	?	Y
5 Wheat	Y	Y	Y
6 Coleman	N	N	N
7 Taylor	N	N	N
8 Emerson	N	N	N
9 Volkmer	Y	Y	Y
MONTANA			
1 Williams	Y	Y	Y
2 Marlenee	N	N	N
NEBRASKA			
1 Bereuter	N	Y	Y
2 Daub	N	N	N
3 Smith	N	N	Y
NEVADA			
1 Reid	Y	Y	Y
2 Vucanovich	N	N	N
NEW HAMPSHIRE			
1 D'Amours	Y	N	Y
2 Gregg	N	N	N
NEW JERSEY			
1 Florio	Y	Y	Y
2 Hughes	?	?	?
3 Howard	Y	Y	Y
4 Smith	N	N	Y
5 Roukema	N	N	N
6 Dwyer	Y	N	Y
7 Rinaldo	N	N	Y
8 Roe	Y	Y	Y
9 Torricelli	Y	Y	Y
10 Rodino	?	#	Y
11 Minish	Y	N	Y
12 Courter	N	N	N
13 Forsythe	?	X	?
14 Guarini	Y	Y	Y
NEW MEXICO			
1 Lujan	N	N	N
2 Skeen	N	N	N
3 Richardson	Y	Y	Y
NEW YORK			
1 Carney	N	N	Y
2 Downey	Y	Y	Y
3 Mrazek	+	#	+
4 Lent	N	N	N
5 McGrath	N	N	N
6 Addabbo	Y	Y	Y
7 Ackerman	Y	Y	Y
8 Scheuer	Y	Y	Y
9 Ferraro	Y	Y	Y
10 Schumer	Y	Y	Y
11 Towns	Y	Y	Y
12 Owens	Y	Y	Y
13 Solarz	?	#	?
14 Molinari	N	N	Y
15 Green	N	N	N
16 Rangel	?	Y	Y
17 Weiss	Y	Y	Y
18 Garcia	?	#	#
19 Biaggi	Y	Y	Y
20 Ottinger	Y	Y	Y
21 Fish	N	Y	Y
22 Gilman	N	Y	Y
23 Stratton	Y	Y	Y
24 Solomon	N	N	N
25 Boehlert	N	N	Y
26 Martin	N	N	N
27 Wortley	N	N	N
28 McHugh	Y	Y	Y
29 Horton	N	Y	Y
30 Conable	N	N	N
31 Kemp	N	N	?
32 LaFalce	?	Y	N
33 Nowak	Y	Y	Y
34 Lundine	Y	Y	Y

	8	9	10
NORTH CAROLINA			
1 Jones	Y	Y	Y
2 Valentine	Y	?	Y
3 Whitley	Y	N	Y
4 Andrews	?	?	?
5 Neal	Y	Y	Y
6 Britt	Y	N	Y
7 Rose	?	?	?
8 Hefner	Y	N	Y
9 Martin	N	N	N
10 Broyhill	N	N	N
11 Clarke	Y	Y	Y
NORTH DAKOTA			
AL Dorgan	Y	Y	Y
OHIO			
1 Luken	Y	N	Y
2 Gradison	N	N	N
3 Hall	Y	Y	Y
4 Oxley	N	N	N
5 Latta	N	N	N
6 McEwen	N	N	N
7 DeWine	N	N	N
8 Kindness	N	N	N
9 Kaptur	Y	Y	Y
10 Miller	N	N	N
11 Eckart	Y	Y	Y
12 Kasich	N	N	N
13 Pease	Y	Y	Y
14 Seiberling	Y	Y	Y
15 Wylie	?	X	?
16 Regula	N	N	N
17 Williams	N	N	N
18 Applegate	Y	N	Y
19 Feighan	Y	Y	Y
20 Oakar	Y	Y	Y
21 Stokes	Y	Y	Y
OKLAHOMA			
1 Jones	Y	N	Y
2 Synar	Y	Y	Y
3 Watkins	Y	N	Y
4 McCurdy	Y	N	Y
5 Edwards	N	N	N
6 English	Y	Y	Y
OREGON			
1 AuCoin	?	#	Y
2 Smith, R.	N	N	N
3 Wyden	Y	Y	Y
4 Weaver	Y	Y	Y
5 Smith, D.	N	N	N
PENNSYLVANIA			
1 Foglietta	Y	Y	Y
2 Gray	Y	Y	Y
3 Borski	Y	Y	Y
4 Kolter	Y	Y	Y
5 Schulze	N	N	N
6 Yatron	Y	Y	Y
7 Edgar	Y	Y	Y
8 Kostmayer	Y	Y	Y
9 Shuster	N	N	N
10 McDade	N	Y	N
11 Harrison	Y	Y	Y
12 Murtha	Y	Y	Y
13 Coughlin	?	?	?
14 Coyne	Y	Y	Y
15 Ritter	N	Y	N
16 Walker	N	N	N
17 Gekas	N	N	N
18 Walgren	Y	Y	Y
19 Goodling	N	Y	N
20 Gaydos	Y	Y	Y
21 Ridge	N	N	N
22 Murphy	Y	N	Y
23 Clinger	-	-	-
RHODE ISLAND			
1 St Germain	?	?	?
2 Schneider	N	Y	Y
SOUTH CAROLINA			
1 Hartnett	N	N	Y
2 Spence	N	N	Y
3 Derrick	Y	Y	N
4 Campbell	N	N	N
5 Spratt	Y	Y	Y
6 Tallon	Y	Y	Y
SOUTH DAKOTA			
AL Daschle	Y	Y	Y

	8	9	10
TENNESSEE			
1 Quillen	N	N	?
2 Duncan	N	N	N
3 Lloyd	Y	N	Y
4 Cooper	Y	Y	Y
5 Boner	Y	Y	Y
6 Gore	Y	Y	Y
7 Sundquist	N	N	N
8 Jones	Y	Y	Y
9 Ford	Y	Y	?
TEXAS			
1 Hall, S.	N	Y	Y
2 Wilson	?	?	?
3 Bartlett	N	N	N
4 Hall, R.	N	Y	Y
5 Bryant	?	#	?
6 Gramm	N	N	?
7 Archer	N	N	N
8 Fields	N	N	N
9 Brooks	Y	Y	Y
10 Pickle	Y	?	?
11 Leath	Y	Y	Y
12 Wright	Y	Y	Y
13 Hightower	Y	N	Y
14 Patman	Y	N	Y
15 de la Garza	Y	Y	Y
16 Coleman	Y	Y	Y
17 Stenholm	Y	N	Y
18 Leland	Y	Y	Y
19 Hance	Y	Y	Y
20 Gonzalez	Y	Y	Y
21 Loeffler	N	N	N
22 Paul	?	X	X
23 Kazen	Y	Y	Y
24 Frost	Y	Y	Y
25 Andrews	Y	N	Y
26 Vandergriff	Y	?	Y
27 Ortiz	Y	Y	Y
UTAH			
1 Hansen	N	N	N
2 Marriott	N	N	N
3 Nielson	N	N	N
VERMONT			
AL Jeffords	?	?	?
VIRGINIA			
1 Bateman	N	N	Y
2 Whitehurst	N	N	Y
3 Bliley	N	N	N
4 Sisisky	Y	N	?
5 Daniel	Y	N	Y
6 Olin	Y	Y	Y
7 Robinson	N	N	N
8 Parris	N	N	N
9 Boucher	Y	Y	Y
10 Wolf	N	N	N
WASHINGTON			
1 Pritchard	N	N	Y
2 Swift	Y	Y	Y
3 Bonker	Y	Y	Y
4 Morrison	N	N	Y
5 Foley	Y	Y	Y
6 Dicks	Y	?	Y
7 Lowry	Y	Y	Y
8 Chandler	N	N	N
WEST VIRGINIA			
1 Mollohan	Y	Y	Y
2 Staggers	Y	Y	Y
3 Wise	Y	Y	Y
4 Rahall	Y	Y	Y
WISCONSIN			
1 Aspin	Y	Y	Y
2 Kastenmeier	Y	Y	Y
3 Gunderson	N	N	N
4 Vacancy			
5 Moody	Y	Y	Y
6 Petri	N	Y	Y
7 Obey	Y	Y	Y
8 Roth	N	N	N
9 Sensenbrenner	N	N	N
WYOMING			
AL Cheney	N	N	N

Southern states - Ala., Ark., Fla., Ga., Ky., La., Miss., N.C., Okla., S.C., Tenn., Texas, Va.

KEY

Y Voted for (yea).
\# Paired for.
\+ Announced for.
N Voted against (nay).
X Paired against.
- Announced against.
P Voted "present".
C Voted "present" to avoid possible conflict of interest.
? Did not vote or otherwise make a position known.

Democrats   *Republicans*

11. HR 2878. Library Services and Construction Act. Gingrich, R-Ga., amendment to authorize the president to eliminate or reduce, by executive order, any authorization made under the bill if he declared that the action would help balance the budget or reduce the national debt, to become effective after 60 days unless Congress voted to override the executive order. Rejected 144-248; R 132-20; D 12-228 (ND 2-162, SD 10-66), Jan. 31, 1984.

12. HR 2878. Library Services and Construction Act. Passage of the bill to authorize $156 million in fiscal 1985, rising to $186 million in fiscal 1988, for the improvement and construction of public libraries. Passed 357-39: R 120-36; D 237-3 (ND 160-1, SD 77-2), Jan. 31, 1984. A "nay" was a vote supporting the president's position.

13. HR 1904. Child Abuse Amendments. Chandler, R-Wash., substitute to the Murphy, D-Pa., amendment, to strike language requiring states that receive federal child-protection grants to ensure that severely handicapped infants receive adequate medical treatment and nutrition, and instead to establish a study commission and require the Department of Health and Services to issue guidelines for hospitals that want to establish advisory panels on the treatment of the handicapped infants. Rejected 182-231: R 31-131; D 151-100 (ND 97-69, SD 54-31), Feb. 2, 1984. (The Murphy amendment, clarifying the intent of the infant protection provisions, subsequently was adopted by voice vote.) A "nay" was a vote supporting the president's position.

14. HR 1904. Child Abuse Amendments. Miller, D-Calif., amendment to authorize $65 million for fiscal 1984-86 for programs to prevent family violence and to provide shelter to victims of family violence. Adopted 367-31: R 129-28; D 238-3 (ND 157-0, SD 81-3), Feb. 2, 1984.

15. HR 1904. Child Abuse Amendments. Passage of the bill to authorize $196 million over four years for child-protection programs, adoption assistance, and projects to prevent family violence, and to require states receiving funds under the bill to ensure that severely handicapped infants receive adequate medical treatment and nutrition. Passed 396-4: R 155-4; D 241-0 (ND 158-0, SD 83-0), Feb. 2, 1984.

	11	12	13	14	15
ALABAMA					
1 *Edwards*	N	Y	N	Y	Y
2 *Dickinson*	Y	Y	N	Y	Y
3 Nichols	N	Y	?	Y	Y
4 Bevill	N	Y	N	Y	Y
5 Flippo	?	?	Y	Y	Y
6 Erdreich	N	Y	N	Y	Y
7 Shelby	N	Y	N	Y	Y
ALASKA					
AL *Young*	N	Y	N	Y	Y
ARIZONA					
1 *McCain*	Y	Y	N	Y	Y
2 Udall	N	Y	Y	Y	Y
3 *Stump*	Y	N	N	N	Y
4 *Rudd*	Y	N	N	?	?
5 McNulty	N	Y	N	Y	Y
ARKANSAS					
1 Alexander	N	Y	Y	Y	Y
2 *Bethune*	Y	Y	N	?	?
3 *Hammerschmidt*	N	Y	N	Y	Y
4 Anthony	N	Y	Y	Y	Y
CALIFORNIA					
1 Bosco	N	Y	Y	Y	?
2 *Chappie*	Y	Y	N	Y	Y
3 Matsui	N	Y	Y	Y	Y
4 Fazio	N	Y	Y	Y	Y
5 Burton	N	Y	Y	Y	?
6 Boxer	N	Y	Y	Y	Y
7 Miller	?	?	Y	Y	Y
8 Dellums	N	Y	Y	Y	Y
9 Stark	N	Y	Y	Y	Y
10 Edwards	N	Y	Y	Y	Y
11 Lantos	N	Y	Y	Y	Y
12 *Zschau*	Y	N	Y	N	Y
13 Mineta	N	Y	Y	Y	Y
14 *Shumway*	Y	N	N	N	Y
15 Coelho	N	Y	Y	?	Y
16 Panetta	N	Y	Y	Y	Y
17 *Pashayan*	Y	Y	N	Y	Y
18 Lehman	N	Y	Y	+	Y
19 *Lagomarsino*	Y	Y	N	Y	Y
20 *Thomas*	Y	Y	Y	Y	Y
21 *Fiedler*	Y	Y	Y	Y	Y
22 *Moorhead*	Y	Y	Y	Y	Y
23 Beilenson	N	Y	Y	Y	Y
24 Waxman	N	Y·	Y	Y	Y
25 Roybal	N	Y	Y	Y	Y
26 Berman	N	Y	Y	Y	Y
27 Levine	N	Y	Y	Y	Y
28 Dixon	?	?	Y	Y	Y
29 Hawkins	N	Y	Y	Y	Y
30 Martinez	N	Y	Y	Y	Y
31 Dymally	N	Y	Y	Y	Y
32 Anderson	N	Y	Y	Y	Y
33 *Dreier*	Y	N	N	N	Y
34 Torres	N	Y	Y	Y	Y
35 *Lewis*	Y	N	Y	Y	Y
36 Brown	N	Y	Y	Y	?
37 *McCandless*	Y	N	Y	Y	Y
38 Patterson	Y	Y	Y	Y	Y
39 *Dannemeyer*	Y	N	N	N	N
40 *Badham*	Y	N	N	N	N
41 *Lowery*	Y	Y	Y	Y	Y
42 *Lungren*	Y	N	N	N	Y

	11	12	13	14	15
43 *Packard*	Y	Y	N	Y	Y
44 Bates	?	Y	Y	Y	Y
45 *Hunter*	Y	N	N	N	Y
COLORADO					
1 Schroeder	N	Y	Y	Y	Y
2 Wirth	N	Y	Y	?	?
3 Kogovsek	?	?	Y	Y	Y
4 *Brown*	Y	N	Y	Y	Y
5 *Kramer*	Y	Y	N	Y	Y
6 *Schaefer*	Y	Y	N	Y	Y
CONNECTICUT					
1 Kennelly	N	Y	Y	Y	Y
2 Gejdenson	N	Y	Y	Y	Y
3 Morrison	N	Y	Y	Y	Y
4 *McKinney*	?	Y	Y	Y	Y
5 Ratchford	N	Y	Y	Y	Y
6 *Johnson*	Y	Y	Y	Y	Y
DELAWARE					
AL Carper	N	Y	Y	Y	Y
FLORIDA					
1 Hutto	N	Y	N	Y	Y
2 Fuqua	N	Y	N	Y	Y
3 Bennett	Y	Y	N	Y	Y
4 Chappell	?	Y	Y	Y	Y
5 *McCollum*	Y	N	N	Y	Y
6 MacKay	N	Y	Y	Y	+
7 Gibbons	N	Y	Y	Y	Y
8 *Young*	Y	Y	N	Y	Y
9 *Bilirakis*	Y	N	N	Y	Y
10 Ireland	Y	Y	Y	Y	Y
11 Nelson	N	Y	N	Y	Y
12 *Lewis*	Y	Y	N	Y	Y
13 *Mack*	Y	N	N	N	Y
14 Mica	N	Y	Y	Y	Y
15 *Shaw*	Y	Y	N	Y	Y
16 Smith	N	Y	Y	Y	Y
17 Lehman	N	Y	Y	Y	Y
18 Pepper	?	Y	\#	?	?
19 Fascell	N	Y	Y	Y	Y
GEORGIA					
1 Thomas	N	Y	Y	Y	Y
2 Hatcher	?	?	Y	Y	Y
3 Ray	N	Y	N	Y	Y
4 Levitas	N	Y	Y	Y	Y
5 Fowler	?	?	Y	Y	Y
6 *Gingrich*	Y	Y	N	Y	Y
7 Darden	N	Y	Y	Y	Y
8 Rowland	N	Y	Y	Y	Y
9 Jenkins	N	Y	Y	Y	Y
10 Barnard	N	Y	Y	Y	Y
HAWAII					
1 Heftel	?	?	?	?	?
2 Akaka	N	Y	Y	Y	Y
IDAHO					
1 *Craig*	Y	N	N	N	Y
2 *Hansen*	?	N	N	N	Y
ILLINOIS					
1 Hayes	N	Y	Y	Y	Y
2 Savage	?	?	\#	?	Y
3 Russo	N	Y	N	Y	Y
4 *O'Brien*	?	?	N	Y	Y
5 Lipinski	N	Y	N	Y	Y
6 *Hyde*	Y	N	Y	N	Y
7 Collins	N	Y	Y	Y	Y
8 Rostenkowski	N	Y	N	Y	Y
9 Yates	N	Y	Y	Y	Y
10 *Porter*	+	+	Y	Y	Y
11 Annunzio	N	Y	N	Y	Y
12 *Crane, P.*	?	?	N	N	N
13 *Erlenborn*	Y	N	N	N	Y
14 *Corcoran*	+	+	X	+	+
15 *Madigan*	Y	Y	N	Y	Y
16 *Martin*	Y	Y	Y	Y	Y
17 Evans	N	Y	N	Y	Y
18 *Michel*	Y	Y	N	Y	Y
19 *Crane, D.*	Y	N	N	N	N
20 Durbin	N	Y	N	Y	Y
21 Price	N	Y	N	Y	Y
22 Simon	N	Y	?	Y	Y
INDIANA					
1 Hall	?	?	Y	Y	Y
2 Sharp	N	Y	N	Y	Y
3 *Hiler*	Y	Y	N	Y	Y
4 *Coats*	Y	Y	N	Y	Y
5 Hillis	Y	Y	N	Y	Y

ND · Northern Democrats   SD · Southern Democrats

	11	12	13	14	15
6 Burton	Y	N	N	Y	Y
7 Myers	N	Y	N	Y	Y
8 McCloskey	N	Y	N	Y	Y
9 Hamilton	N	Y	N	Y	Y
10 Jacobs	N	?	Y	Y	Y
IOWA					
1 Leach	Y	Y	N	Y	Y
2 Tauke	?	?	N	Y	Y
3 Evans	Y	Y	N	Y	Y
4 Smith	?	?	?	?	?
5 Harkin	N	Y	N	Y	Y
6 Bedell	N	Y	N	Y	Y
KANSAS					
1 Roberts	Y	Y	N	Y	Y
2 Slattery	N	N	N	Y	Y
3 Winn	Y	Y	N	Y	Y
4 Glickman	N	Y	N	Y	Y
5 Whittaker	Y	Y	Y	Y	Y
KENTUCKY					
1 Hubbard	N	Y	Y	Y	Y
2 Natcher	N	Y	N	Y	Y
3 Mazzoli	N	Y	N	Y	Y
4 Snyder	N	Y	N	Y	Y
5 Rogers	Y	Y	Y	Y	Y
6 Hopkins	Y	Y	Y	?	Y
7 Perkins	N	Y	N	Y	Y
LOUISIANA					
1 Livingston	Y	Y	N	Y	Y
2 Boggs	N	Y	N	Y	Y
3 Tauzin	Y	Y	X	?	?
4 Roemer	Y	Y	N	Y	Y
5 Huckaby	?	?	N	Y	Y
6 Moore	Y	Y	N	Y	Y
7 Breaux	Y	Y	Y	Y	Y
8 Long	N	Y	N	Y	Y
MAINE					
1 McKernan	N	Y	Y	Y	Y
2 Snowe	N	Y	Y	Y	Y
MARYLAND					
1 Dyson	N	Y	N	Y	Y
2 Long	N	Y	Y	Y	Y
3 Mikulski	N	Y	Y	Y	Y
4 Holt	Y	N	N	N	Y
5 Hoyer	N	Y	N	Y	Y
6 Byron	N	Y	N	Y	Y
7 Mitchell	N	Y	Y	Y	Y
8 Barnes	N	Y	N	Y	Y
MASSACHUSETTS					
1 Conte	N	Y	N	Y	Y
2 Boland	N	Y	X	?	?
3 Early	N	Y	?	?	?
4 Frank	N	Y	?	?	?
5 Shannon	N	Y	?	?	?
6 Mavroules	N	Y	N	Y	Y
7 Markey	N	Y	Y	Y	Y
8 O'Neill					
9 Moakley	N	Y	N	Y	Y
10 Studds	N	Y	Y	Y	Y
11 Donnelly	?	?	X	?	?
MICHIGAN					
1 Conyers	N	Y	N	Y	Y
2 Pursell	N	Y	Y	?	?
3 Wolpe	N	Y	Y	Y	Y
4 Siljander	Y	Y	N	Y	Y
5 Sawyer	Y	Y	N	Y	Y
6 Carr	N	Y	N	Y	Y
7 Kildee	N	Y	N	Y	Y
8 Traxler	N	Y	N	Y	Y
9 Vander Jagt	?	?	N	Y	Y
10 Albosta	N	Y	N	?	?
11 Davis	Y	Y	N	Y	Y
12 Bonior	N	Y	N	Y	Y
13 Crockett	N	Y	Y	Y	Y
14 Hertel	N	Y	N	Y	Y
15 Ford	?	?	#	?	?
16 Dingell	N	Y	Y	Y	Y
17 Levin	N	Y	N	Y	Y
18 Broomfield	Y	Y	N	Y	Y
MINNESOTA					
1 Penny	N	Y	N	Y	Y
2 Weber	Y	Y	N	Y	Y
3 Frenzel	Y	Y	Y	Y	Y
4 Vento	N	P	N	Y	Y
5 Sabo	N	Y	Y	Y	Y
6 Sikorski	N	Y	N	+	Y

	11	12	13	14	15
7 Stangeland	Y	Y	N	Y	Y
8 Oberstar	N	Y	N	Y	Y
MISSISSIPPI					
1 Whitten	N	Y	N	Y	Y
2 Franklin	Y	Y	Y	Y	Y
3 Montgomery	Y	Y	Y	N	Y
4 Dowdy	N	Y	Y	Y	Y
5 Lott	Y	Y	N	Y	Y
MISSOURI					
1 Clay	N	Y	Y	Y	Y
2 Young	N	Y	N	Y	Y
3 Gephardt	N	Y	N	Y	Y
4 Skelton	N	Y	N	?	?
5 Wheat	N	Y	N	Y	Y
6 Coleman	Y	Y	N	Y	Y
7 Taylor	Y	Y	N	Y	Y
8 Emerson	Y	Y	N	Y	Y
9 Volkmer	Y	Y	N	Y	Y
MONTANA					
1 Williams	N	Y	Y	Y	Y
2 Marlenee	Y	Y	N	Y	Y
NEBRASKA					
1 Bereuter	Y	Y	N	Y	Y
2 Daub	Y	N	N	N	Y
3 Smith	Y	Y	N	Y	Y
NEVADA					
1 Reid	N	Y	N	Y	Y
2 Vucanovich	Y	Y	N	Y	Y
NEW HAMPSHIRE					
1 D'Amours	N	?	N	Y	Y
2 Gregg	Y	Y	N	N	Y
NEW JERSEY					
1 Florio	N	Y	N	Y	Y
2 Hughes	N	Y	Y	Y	Y
3 Howard	N	Y	Y	?	?
4 Smith	Y	Y	N	Y	Y
5 Roukema	Y	Y	N	Y	Y
6 Dwyer	N	Y	Y	Y	Y
7 Rinaldo	Y	Y	N	Y	Y
8 Roe	N	Y	Y	Y	Y
9 Torricelli	N	Y	Y	Y	Y
10 Rodino	N	Y	Y	Y	Y
11 Minish	N	Y	N	Y	Y
12 Courter	Y	Y	N	Y	Y
13 Forsythe	?	?	?	?	?
14 Guarini	N	Y	Y	Y	Y
NEW MEXICO					
1 Lujan	Y	Y	N	Y	Y
2 Skeen	Y	Y	N	Y	Y
3 Richardson	N	Y	Y	Y	Y
NEW YORK					
1 Carney	N	Y	N	Y	Y
2 Downey	N	Y	Y	Y	Y
3 Mrazek	N	Y	Y	Y	Y
4 Lent	Y	Y	N	Y	Y
5 McGrath	Y	Y	N	Y	Y
6 Addabbo	N	Y	N	Y	Y
7 Ackerman	N	Y	Y	Y	Y
8 Scheuer	N	Y	Y	Y	Y
9 Ferraro	N	Y	?	?	?
10 Schumer	N	Y	Y	Y	Y
11 Towns	N	Y	Y	Y	Y
12 Owens	N	Y	Y	Y	Y
13 Solarz	N	Y	Y	Y	Y
14 Molinari	N	Y	N	Y	Y
15 Green	N	Y	Y	Y	Y
16 Rangel	N	Y	Y	Y	Y
17 Weiss	N	Y	Y	Y	Y
18 Garcia	N	Y	Y	Y	Y
19 Biaggi	N	Y	Y	Y	Y
20 Ottinger	N	Y	Y	Y	Y
21 Fish	N	Y	N	Y	Y
22 Gilman	N	Y	N	Y	Y
23 Stratton	Y	Y	N	Y	Y
24 Solomon	Y	Y	N	Y	Y
25 Boehlert	N	Y	N	Y	Y
26 Martin	Y	Y	N	?	Y
27 Wortley	Y	Y	N	Y	Y
28 McHugh	N	Y	Y	Y	Y
29 Horton	?	Y	Y	Y	Y
30 Conable	?	Y	Y	Y	Y
31 Kemp	Y	Y	N	Y	Y
32 LaFalce	N	Y	N	Y	Y
33 Nowak	N	Y	N	Y	Y
34 Lundine	N	Y	N	Y	Y

	11	12	13	14	15
NORTH CAROLINA					
1 Jones	?	Y	Y	?	?
2 Valentine	N	Y	Y	?	?
3 Whitley	N	Y	Y	Y	Y
4 Andrews	?	?	Y	Y	Y
5 Neal	N	Y	Y	Y	Y
6 Britt	N	Y	Y	Y	Y
7 Rose	N	?	Y	Y	Y
8 Hefner	N	Y	N	Y	Y
9 Martin	Y	Y	N	Y	Y
10 Broyhill	Y	Y	N	Y	Y
11 Clarke	N	Y	Y	Y	Y
NORTH DAKOTA					
AL Dorgan	N	?	N	Y	Y
OHIO					
1 Luken	N	Y	N	Y	Y
2 Gradison	N	N	N	Y	Y
3 Hall	N	Y	N	Y	Y
4 Oxley	Y	N	Y	Y	Y
5 Latta	Y	N	N	Y	Y
6 McEwen	Y	Y	N	Y	Y
7 DeWine	Y	N	Y	Y	Y
8 Kindness	N	Y	N	Y	Y
9 Kaptur	N	Y	Y	Y	Y
10 Miller	Y	Y	N	Y	Y
11 Eckart	N	Y	N	Y	Y
12 Kasich	Y	Y	N	Y	Y
13 Pease	N	Y	Y	Y	Y
14 Seiberling	N	Y	Y	Y	Y
15 Wylie	Y	Y	N	Y	Y
16 Regula	Y	Y	N	Y	Y
17 Williams	?	?	N	Y	Y
18 Applegate	N	Y	N	Y	Y
19 Feighan	N	Y	Y	Y	Y
20 Oakar	N	Y	N	Y	Y
21 Stokes	N	Y	#	?	?
OKLAHOMA					
1 Jones	N	Y	N	Y	Y
2 Synar	N	N	Y	Y	Y
3 Watkins	N	Y	Y	Y	Y
4 McCurdy	?	?	Y	Y	Y
5 Edwards	N	Y	N	Y	Y
6 English	N	Y	N	Y	Y
OREGON					
1 AuCoin	N	Y	Y	Y	Y
2 Smith, R.	N	Y	Y	Y	Y
3 Wyden	N	Y	Y	?	?
4 Weaver	N	Y	Y	Y	Y
5 Smith, D.	Y	N	N	N	Y
PENNSYLVANIA					
1 Foglietta	?	?	Y	Y	Y
2 Gray	N	Y	Y	Y	Y
3 Borski	N	Y	N	Y	Y
4 Kolter	N	Y	N	Y	Y
5 Schulze	Y	Y	N	Y	Y
6 Yatron	N	Y	N	Y	Y
7 Edgar	N	Y	Y	Y	Y
8 Kostmayer	N	Y	Y	Y	Y
9 Shuster	Y	Y	N	Y	N
10 McDade	Y	Y	N	Y	Y
11 Harrison	N	Y	N	Y	Y
12 Murtha	N	Y	N	Y	Y
13 Coughlin	Y	Y	N	Y	Y
14 Coyne	N	Y	N	Y	Y
15 Ritter	Y	Y	N	Y	Y
16 Walker	Y	Y	N	Y	Y
17 Gekas	Y	Y	Y	N	Y
18 Walgren	N	Y	Y	Y	Y
19 Goodling	?	?	X	Y	Y
20 Gaydos	N	Y	N	Y	Y
21 Ridge	Y	Y	N	Y	Y
22 Murphy	N	Y	N	Y	Y
23 Clinger	Y	Y	N	Y	Y
RHODE ISLAND					
1 St Germain	N	Y	N	Y	Y
2 Schneider	Y	Y	Y	Y	Y
SOUTH CAROLINA					
1 Hartnett	Y	N	N	N	Y
2 Spence	Y	Y	N	Y	Y
3 Derrick	N	Y	Y	Y	Y
4 Campbell	Y	Y	N	Y	Y
5 Spratt	N	Y	Y	Y	Y
6 Tallon	N	Y	Y	Y	Y
SOUTH DAKOTA					
AL Daschle	?	?	Y	Y	Y

	11	12	13	14	15
TENNESSEE					
1 Quillen	Y	Y	Y	Y	Y
2 Duncan	Y	Y	Y	Y	Y
3 Lloyd	N	Y	N	Y	Y
4 Cooper	N	Y	Y	Y	Y
5 Boner	N	Y	Y	Y	Y
6 Gore	N	Y	N	Y	Y
7 Sundquist	Y	Y	Y	Y	Y
8 Jones	N	Y	Y	Y	Y
9 Ford	N	Y	Y	Y	Y
TEXAS					
1 Hall, S.	Y	Y	N	Y	Y
2 Wilson	?	?	N	Y	Y
3 Bartlett	Y	Y	N	N	Y
4 Hall, R.	?	Y	N	Y	Y
5 Bryant	N	Y	Y	Y	Y
6 Gramm	Y	N	N	N	Y
7 Archer	Y	Y	N	?	?
8 Fields	Y	Y	N	Y	Y
9 Brooks	N	Y	N	Y	Y
10 Pickle	?	?	Y	Y	Y
11 Leath	N	Y	N	Y	Y
12 Wright	N	Y	N	Y	Y
13 Hightower	N	Y	Y	Y	Y
14 Patman	N	Y	Y	Y	Y
15 de la Garza	N	Y	N	Y	Y
16 Coleman	N	Y	N	Y	Y
17 Stenholm	N	Y	N	Y	Y
18 Leland	N	Y	#	?	+
19 Hance	?	?	?	?	?
20 Gonzalez	N	Y	Y	Y	Y
21 Loeffler	Y	N	Y	N	Y
22 Paul	?	?	?	?	?
23 Kazen	?	?	Y	Y	Y
24 Frost	N	Y	Y	Y	Y
25 Andrews	N	Y	N	Y	Y
26 Vandergriff	Y	Y	Y	Y	Y
27 Ortiz	N	Y	N	Y	Y
UTAH					
1 Hansen	Y	N	N	Y	Y
2 Marriott	Y	Y	N	Y	Y
3 Nielson	Y	N	N	N	Y
VERMONT					
AL Jeffords	?	?	?	?	?
VIRGINIA					
1 Bateman	Y	N	N	N	Y
2 Whitehurst	Y	Y	N	N	Y
3 Bliley	Y	N	N	Y	Y
4 Sisisky	N	Y	Y	Y	Y
5 Daniel	Y	Y	N	Y	Y
6 Olin	N	Y	N	Y	Y
7 Robinson	N	N	N	Y	Y
8 Parris	Y	Y	N	Y	Y
9 Boucher	N	Y	N	Y	Y
10 Wolf	Y	Y	N	Y	Y
WASHINGTON					
1 Pritchard	Y	Y	Y	Y	Y
2 Swift	N	Y	Y	Y	Y
3 Bonker	N	Y	N	Y	Y
4 Morrison	Y	Y	Y	Y	Y
5 Foley	N	Y	N	Y	Y
6 Dicks	N	Y	Y	Y	Y
7 Lowry	N	Y	Y	Y	Y
8 Chandler	Y	Y	Y	Y	Y
WEST VIRGINIA					
1 Mollohan	N	Y	N	Y	Y
2 Staggers	N	Y	N	Y	Y
3 Wise	N	Y	N	Y	Y
4 Rahall	N	Y	N	Y	Y
WISCONSIN					
1 Aspin	N	Y	N	?	?
2 Kastenmeier	N	Y	Y	Y	Y
3 Gunderson	Y	Y	N	Y	Y
4 Vacancy					
5 Moody	N	Y	N	Y	Y
6 Petri	Y	Y	N	Y	Y
7 Obey	N	Y	N	Y	Y
8 Roth	Y	Y	N	Y	Y
9 Sensenbrenner	Y	Y	N	Y	Y
WYOMING					
AL Cheney	Y	N	N	N	Y

Southern states - Ala., Ark., Fla., Ga., Ky., La., Miss., N.C., Okla., S.C., Tenn., Texas, Va.

16. Procedural Motion. Walker, R-Pa., motion to approve the House *Journal* of Tuesday, Feb. 7. Motion agreed to 365-23: R 144-12; D 221-11 (ND 136-11, SD 85-0), Feb. 8, 1984.

17. H Con Res 255. Congressional Recess. Adoption of the concurrent resolution to adjourn the House from Feb. 9 to Feb. 21, and the Senate from Feb. 9 or 10 to Feb. 20 for the Lincoln's Birthday recess. Adopted 268-137: R 51-108; D 217-29 (ND 150-11, SD 67-18), Feb. 8, 1984.

18. HR 555. Construction Work in Progress. Moorhead, R-Calif., substitute to codify a ruling of the Federal Energy Regulatory Commission that permits public utilities to include in their rate base up to 50 percent of the interest costs incurred during the construction of a power plant. Rejected 135-266: R 101-52; D 34-214 (ND 3-160, SD 31-54), Feb. 8, 1984.

19. HR 555. Construction Work in Progress. Passage of the bill to allow public utilities subject to Federal Energy Regulatory Commission jurisdiction to recover the interest costs of construction work in progress through rate increases only upon showing financial need and demonstrating the need for the new construction. Passed 288-113: R 66-87; D 222-26 (ND 165-1, SD 57-25), Feb. 8, 1984. A "nay" was a vote supporting the president's position.

20. H Res 436. Committee Elections. Dannemeyer, R-Calif., motion to recommit to the Committee on Rules the resolution making committee appointments, with instructions to constitute committees in actual proportion to the House's political party memberships. Motion rejected 153-237: R 153-1; D 0-236 (ND 0-160, SD 0-76), Feb. 9, 1984.

21. S 1340. Rehabilitation Act Amendments. Adoption of the conference report on the bill to reauthorize the Rehabilitation Act of 1973 through fiscal 1986, including $1.038 billion in 1984 and additional sums in subsequent years for state grants for vocational rehabilitation of the handicapped. Adopted 384-3: R 145-3; D 239-0 (ND 162-0, SD 77-0), Feb. 9, 1984.

22. HR 2899. Environmental Research. Adoption of the rule (H Res 429) providing for House floor consideration of the bill to authorize $283,510,000 in fiscal 1984 and $297,686,000 in fiscal 1985 for Environmental Protection Agency research and development programs. Adopted 378-0: R 146-0; D 232-0 (ND 158-0, SD 74-0), Feb. 9, 1984.

23. HR 2899. Environmental Research. Passage of the bill to authorize $283,510,000 in fiscal 1984 and $297,686,000 in fiscal 1985 for Environmental Protection Agency research and development programs. Passed 362-9: R 136-9; D 226-0 (ND 157-0, SD 69-0), Feb. 9, 1984.

KEY

Y	Voted for (yea).
#	Paired for.
+	Announced for.
N	Voted against (nay).
X	Paired against.
-	Announced against.
P	Voted "present".
C	Voted "present" to avoid possible conflict of interest.
?	Did not vote or otherwise make a position known.

Democrats   *Republicans*

	16	17	18	19	20	21	22	23
ALABAMA								
1 *Edwards*	Y	Y	Y	N	Y	Y	?	Y
2 *Dickinson*	N	Y	Y	Y	Y	Y	?	Y
3 Nichols	Y	Y	Y	N	N	Y	?	?
4 Bevill	Y	Y	Y	N	N	Y	Y	?
5 Flippo	Y	Y	Y	N	N	Y	Y	Y
6 Erdreich	Y	Y	Y	N	N	Y	Y	Y
7 Shelby	Y	Y	Y	N	N	Y	Y	Y
ALASKA								
AL *Young*	N	N	Y	Y	Y	Y	Y	Y
ARIZONA								
1 *McCain*	?	?	#	X	Y	Y	Y	Y
2 Udall	Y	Y	N	Y	N	Y	Y	Y
3 *Stump*	Y	N	Y	N	Y	Y	Y	N
4 *Rudd*	Y	Y	Y	N	Y	Y	Y	Y
5 McNulty	Y	Y	N	Y	N	Y	Y	Y
ARKANSAS								
1 Alexander	Y	Y	N	Y	N	Y	Y	Y
2 *Bethune*	Y	N	?	Y	?	?	Y	Y
3 *Hammerschmidt*	Y	Y	Y	N	Y	Y	Y	Y
4 Anthony	Y	Y	N	Y	?	?	?	?
CALIFORNIA								
1 Bosco	Y	?	N	Y	N	Y	Y	Y
2 *Chappie*	N	N	Y	N	Y	Y	Y	Y
3 Matsui	Y	Y	N	Y	N	Y	Y	Y
4 Fazio	Y	Y	N	Y	N	Y	Y	Y
5 Burton	Y	Y	N	Y	N	Y	Y	Y
6 Boxer	Y	Y	N	Y	N	Y	Y	Y
7 Miller	?	Y	N	Y	N	Y	Y	Y
8 Dellums	Y	Y	N	Y	N	Y	Y	Y
9 Stark	?	?	?	?	?	?	?	?
10 Edwards	Y	Y	N	Y	N	Y	Y	Y
11 Lantos	Y	Y	N	Y	N	Y	Y	Y
12 *Zschau*	Y	Y	N	Y	Y	Y	Y	Y
13 Mineta	Y	Y	N	Y	N	Y	Y	Y
14 *Shumway*	Y	N	Y	N	Y	Y	Y	Y
15 Coelho	Y	Y	N	Y	N	Y	Y	Y
16 Panetta	Y	Y	N	Y	N	Y	Y	Y
17 *Pashayan*	Y	N	Y	N	Y	Y	Y	Y
18 Lehman	?	?	?	?	N	Y	Y	Y
19 *Lagomarsino*	Y	N	Y	N	Y	Y	Y	Y
20 *Thomas*	?	Y	Y	N	Y	Y	Y	Y
21 *Fiedler*	Y	Y	N	Y	Y	Y	Y	Y
22 *Moorhead*	Y	N	Y	N	Y	Y	Y	Y
23 Beilenson	Y	Y	N	Y	N	Y	Y	Y
24 Waxman	?	Y	N	Y	N	Y	Y	Y
25 Roybal	Y	Y	N	Y	N	Y	Y	Y
26 Berman	?	?	?	?	N	Y	Y	Y
27 Levine	Y	Y	N	Y	N	Y	Y	Y
28 Dixon	Y	Y	N	Y	N	Y	Y	Y
29 Hawkins	N	Y	N	Y	X	?	?	?
30 Martinez	P	N	N	Y	N	Y	Y	Y
31 Dymally	P	Y	N	Y	N	Y	Y	Y
32 Anderson	Y	N	Y	N	N	Y	Y	Y
33 *Dreier*	Y	N	Y	N	Y	Y	Y	Y
34 Torres	Y	Y	N	Y	N	Y	?	Y
35 *Lewis*	Y	N	Y	N	Y	Y	Y	Y
36 Brown	Y	Y	N	Y	N	Y	Y	Y
37 *McCandless*	P	N	Y	N	Y	Y	Y	Y
38 Patterson	Y	Y	N	Y	N	Y	Y	Y
39 *Dannemeyer*	Y	N	Y	N	Y	Y	Y	N
40 *Badham*	Y	N	Y	N	Y	Y	Y	Y
41 *Lowery*	Y	Y	Y	N	Y	Y	Y	Y
42 *Lungren*	Y	N	?	?	Y	Y	Y	Y

	16	17	18	19	20	21	22	23
43 *Packard*	Y	Y	Y	N	Y	Y	Y	Y
44 Bates	Y	Y	N	Y	N	Y	Y	Y
45 *Hunter*	Y	N	Y	N	Y	Y	Y	Y
COLORADO								
1 Schroeder	N	N	N	Y	N	Y	N	Y
2 Wirth	Y	Y	N	Y	N	Y	Y	Y
3 Kogovsek	Y	Y	N	Y	N	Y	Y	Y
4 *Brown*	Y	N	N	Y	N	Y	Y	Y
5 *Kramer*	Y	N	Y	N	Y	Y	Y	Y
6 *Schaefer*	P	N	Y	N	#	?	?	?
CONNECTICUT								
1 Kennelly	Y	Y	N	Y	N	Y	Y	Y
2 Gejdenson	N	Y	N	Y	N	Y	Y	Y
3 Morrison	Y	Y	N	Y	N	Y	Y	Y
4 *McKinney*	Y	N	?	Y	#	?	?	?
5 Ratchford	Y	Y	N	Y	N	Y	Y	Y
6 *Johnson*	Y	N	Y	N	Y	Y	Y	Y
DELAWARE								
AL Carper	Y	N	N	Y	N	Y	Y	Y
FLORIDA								
1 Hutto	Y	Y	Y	N	Y	Y	Y	Y
2 Fuqua	Y	Y	Y	N	Y	Y	Y	Y
3 Bennett	Y	N	N	N	N	Y	Y	Y
4 Chappell	Y	Y	Y	N	Y	Y	Y	Y
5 *McCollum*	Y	N	Y	N	Y	Y	Y	?
6 MacKay	Y	Y	N	Y	N	Y	Y	?
7 Gibbons	Y	Y	Y	N	Y	Y	Y	Y
8 *Young*	Y	N	N	Y	Y	Y	Y	Y
9 *Bilirakis*	Y	N	Y	N	Y	Y	Y	Y
10 *Ireland*	Y	N	Y	N	?	Y	Y	Y
11 Nelson	Y	-	Y	N	Y	Y	Y	Y
12 *Lewis*	N	N	Y	N	Y	Y	Y	Y
13 *Mack*	Y	N	Y	N	Y	Y	Y	Y
14 Mica	Y	Y	Y	N	N	Y	Y	?
15 *Shaw*	Y	N	Y	N	Y	Y	Y	Y
16 Smith	Y	N	N	Y	?	Y	Y	Y
17 Lehman	Y	Y	N	Y	N	Y	Y	Y
18 Pepper	Y	Y	N	Y	N	Y	Y	Y
19 Fascell	Y	Y	Y	N	?	?	?	?
GEORGIA								
1 Thomas	Y	Y	N	Y	N	Y	Y	Y
2 Hatcher	Y	Y	Y	N	N	Y	Y	Y
3 Ray	Y	N	N	Y	N	Y	Y	Y
4 Levitas	Y	N	N	Y	N	Y	Y	Y
5 Fowler	Y	Y	N	?	N	Y	Y	Y
6 *Gingrich*	Y	N	Y	N	Y	Y	Y	Y
7 Darden	Y	Y	N	Y	N	Y	Y	Y
8 Rowland	Y	N	Y	N	Y	Y	Y	Y
9 Jenkins	Y	Y	N	Y	N	Y	Y	Y
10 Barnard	Y	Y	N	Y	N	Y	Y	Y
HAWAII								
1 Heftel	?	?	?	?	?	?	?	?
2 Akaka	Y	N	N	Y	N	Y	Y	Y
IDAHO								
1 *Craig*	Y	N	Y	N	Y	Y	Y	?
2 *Hansen*	?	N	Y	N	?	?	?	?
ILLINOIS								
1 Hayes	Y	Y	N	Y	N	Y	Y	Y
2 Savage	?	?	?	Y	X	?	?	?
3 Russo	Y	Y	N	Y	N	Y	Y	Y
4 *O'Brien*	Y	Y	Y	Y	Y	Y	Y	Y
5 Lipinski	P	Y	N	Y	N	Y	Y	Y
6 *Hyde*	Y	Y	Y	N	Y	Y	Y	Y
7 Collins	Y	N	Y	N	Y	Y	?	Y
8 Rostenkowski	Y	Y	N	Y	N	Y	Y	Y
9 Yates	N	Y	N	Y	N	Y	Y	Y
10 *Porter*	Y	N	Y	N	Y	Y	Y	Y
11 Annunzio	Y	?	?	Y	N	Y	Y	Y
12 *Crane, P.*	Y	N	Y	N	Y	N	Y	N
13 *Erlenborn*	Y	Y	Y	N	Y	Y	Y	Y
14 *Corcoran*	+	-	#	X	#	+	+	+
15 *Madigan*	Y	N	Y	N	Y	Y	Y	Y
16 *Martin*	Y	N	N	Y	Y	Y	Y	Y
17 Evans	Y	Y	N	Y	N	Y	Y	Y
18 *Michel*	Y	Y	Y	N	Y	Y	Y	Y
19 *Crane, D.*	Y	N	Y	N	Y	N	Y	N
20 Durbin	N	N	Y	N	Y	Y	Y	Y
21 Price	Y	Y	N	Y	N	Y	Y	Y
22 Simon	P	Y	N	Y	N	Y	Y	Y
INDIANA								
1 Hall	Y	Y	N	Y	?	Y	Y	Y
2 Sharp	Y	Y	N	Y	N	Y	Y	Y
3 *Hiler*	Y	N	Y	N	Y	Y	Y	Y
4 *Coats*	Y	N	Y	N	Y	Y	Y	Y
5 Hillis	?	?	?	?	?	?	?	?

ND - Northern Democrats   SD - Southern Democrats

	16	17	18	19	20	21	22	23
6 ***Burton***	Y	N	Y	N	Y	Y	Y	N
7 ***Myers***	Y	N	Y	N	Y	Y	Y	Y
8 McCloskey	Y	N	N	Y	N	Y	Y	Y
9 Hamilton	Y	Y	N	Y	N	Y	Y	Y
10 Jacobs	N	Y	N	Y	N	Y	Y	Y
IOWA								
1 ***Leach***	Y	N	N	Y	Y	Y	Y	Y
2 ***Tauke***	Y	N	N	Y	Y	?	?	Y
3 ***Evans***	N	?	N	Y	Y	?	Y	Y
4 Smith	Y	Y	N	Y	N	Y	Y	Y
5 Harkin	N	Y	N	Y	N	Y	Y	Y
6 Bedell	Y	Y	N	Y	N	?	Y	Y
KANSAS								
1 ***Roberts***	N	N	?	?	Y	Y	Y	Y
2 Slattery	Y	Y	N	Y	N	Y	Y	Y
3 ***Winn***	Y	Y	Y	N	Y	Y	Y	Y
4 Glickman	Y	Y	N	Y	N	Y	Y	Y
5 ***Whittaker***	Y	N	Y	Y	Y	Y	Y	Y
KENTUCKY								
1 Hubbard	Y	N	N	Y	N	Y	Y	Y
2 Natcher	Y	Y	N	Y	N	Y	Y	Y
3 Mazzoli	Y	Y	N	Y	N	Y	Y	Y
4 ***Snyder***	Y	Y	N	Y	Y	Y	Y	Y
5 ***Rogers***	Y	N	Y	Y	Y	Y	Y	Y
6 ***Hopkins***	Y	N	N	Y	Y	Y	?	Y
7 Perkins	Y	Y	N	Y	N	Y	Y	Y
LOUISIANA								
1 ***Livingston***	Y	N	Y	N	Y	Y	Y	Y
2 Boggs	Y	Y	Y	N	N	Y	Y	?
3 Tauzin	Y	Y	Y	N	N	Y	Y	Y
4 Roemer	Y	N	N	Y	N	Y	Y	Y
5 Huckaby	Y	N	Y	N	N	Y	Y	Y
6 ***Moore***	Y	Y	Y	N	Y	Y	Y	Y
7 Breaux	Y	Y	Y	N	N	Y	Y	Y
8 Long	?	?	?	?	?	?	?	?
MAINE								
1 ***McKernan***	Y	N	N	Y	Y	Y	Y	Y
2 ***Snowe***	Y	N	N	Y	Y	Y	Y	Y
MARYLAND								
1 Dyson	Y	Y	Y	Y	N	Y	Y	Y
2 Long	Y	Y	N	Y	N	Y	Y	Y
3 Mikulski	Y	N	N	Y	N	Y	Y	Y
4 ***Holt***	Y	N	Y	N	#	Y	Y	Y
5 Hoyer	Y	Y	N	Y	N	Y	Y	?
6 Byron	Y	Y	Y	Y	N	Y	Y	Y
7 Mitchell	N	Y	N	Y	N	Y	Y	Y
8 Barnes	Y	Y	N	Y	N	Y	Y	Y
MASSACHUSETTS								
1 ***Conte***	Y	Y	N	Y	Y	Y	Y	Y
2 Boland	Y	Y	N	Y	N	Y	Y	Y
3 Early	?	?	?	?	?	?	?	?
4 Frank	Y	Y	N	Y	N	Y	Y	Y
5 Shannon	Y	Y	N	Y	?	?	?	?
6 Mavroules	Y	Y	N	Y	N	Y	Y	Y
7 Markey	?	?	?	?	X	+	+	+
8 O'Neill								
9 Moakley	Y	Y	N	Y	N	Y	Y	Y
10 Studds	Y	Y	N	Y	N	Y	Y	Y
11 Donnelly	Y	Y	N	Y	N	Y	Y	Y
MICHIGAN								
1 Conyers	Y	Y	N	Y	N	Y	Y	Y
2 ***Pursell***	Y	N	N	Y	Y	Y	Y	Y
3 Wolpe	Y	Y	N	Y	N	Y	Y	Y
4 ***Siljander***	Y	N	Y	Y	Y	Y	Y	Y
5 ***Sawyer***	Y	Y	N	Y	N	Y	Y	Y
6 Carr	P	Y	N	Y	N	Y	?	Y
7 Kildee	Y	Y	N	Y	N	Y	Y	Y
8 Traxler	Y	Y	N	Y	N	Y	Y	Y
9 ***Vander Jagt***	?	?	?	?	#	?	?	?
10 Albosta	Y	Y	N	Y	N	Y	Y	Y
11 ***Davis***	Y	N	?	+	Y	Y	Y	Y
12 Bonior	Y	Y	N	Y	N	Y	Y	Y
13 Crockett	?	Y	N	Y	N	Y	?	Y
14 Hertel	Y	Y	N	Y	N	Y	Y	Y
15 Ford	?	Y	N	Y	N	Y	Y	?
16 Dingell	Y	Y	N	Y	N	Y	Y	Y
17 Levin	Y	Y	N	Y	N	Y	Y	Y
18 ***Broomfield***	Y	N	Y	?	Y	Y	Y	Y
MINNESOTA								
1 Penny	N	Y	N	Y	N	Y	Y	Y
2 ***Weber***	Y	N	N	Y	Y	Y	Y	Y
3 ***Frenzel***	Y	Y	Y	N	Y	Y	Y	?
4 Vento	Y	Y	N	Y	N	Y	Y	Y
5 Sabo	N	Y	N	Y	N	Y	Y	?
6 Sikorski	P	Y	N	Y	N	Y	Y	Y

	16	17	18	19	20	21	22	23
7 ***Stangeland***	Y	Y	Y	N	Y	Y	Y	Y
8 Oberstar	P	Y	N	Y	N	Y	Y	Y
MISSISSIPPI								
1 Whitten	Y	Y	N	Y	N	Y	Y	Y
2 ***Franklin***	Y	Y	N	Y	Y	Y	Y	Y
3 Montgomery	Y	Y	Y	N	N	Y	Y	Y
4 Dowdy	Y	Y	N	Y	N	Y	Y	Y
5 ***Lott***	Y	N	Y	N	Y	Y	Y	Y
MISSOURI								
1 Clay	N	Y	N	Y	N	Y	Y	Y
2 Young	Y	Y	N	Y	N	Y	Y	Y
3 Gephardt	Y	Y	N	Y	N	Y	Y	?
4 Skelton	Y	Y	N	Y	N	Y	Y	Y
5 Wheat	Y	Y	N	Y	N	Y	Y	Y
6 ***Coleman***	Y	N	N	Y	Y	Y	Y	Y
7 ***Taylor***	Y	Y	N	Y	Y	Y	Y	Y
8 ***Emerson***	N	N	N	Y	Y	Y	Y	Y
9 Volkmer	P	Y	N	Y	N	Y	Y	Y
MONTANA								
1 Williams	?	?	N	Y	X	Y	Y	Y
2 ***Marlenee***	Y	Y	N	Y	Y	?	?	?
NEBRASKA								
1 ***Bereuter***	Y	N	N	Y	Y	Y	Y	Y
2 ***Daub***	Y	N	Y	N	Y	Y	Y	Y
3 ***Smith***	Y	N	N	Y	Y	Y	Y	Y
NEVADA								
1 Reid	Y	Y	N	Y	N	Y	Y	Y
2 ***Vucanovich***	Y	N	Y	N	Y	Y	Y	Y
NEW HAMPSHIRE								
1 D'Amours	Y	N	N	Y	N	Y	Y	Y
2 ***Gregg***	Y	N	N	Y	Y	Y	Y	Y
NEW JERSEY								
1 Florio	?	Y	N	Y	N	Y	Y	Y
2 Hughes	Y	Y	N	Y	N	Y	Y	Y
3 Howard	Y	Y	N	Y	N	Y	Y	Y
4 ***Smith***	Y	N	N	Y	Y	Y	Y	Y
5 ***Roukema***	Y	Y	N	Y	Y	Y	Y	Y
6 Dwyer	Y	Y	N	Y	N	Y	Y	Y
7 ***Rinaldo***	Y	N	N	Y	Y	Y	Y	Y
8 Roe	Y	Y	N	Y	N	Y	Y	Y
9 Torricelli	Y	Y	N	Y	N	Y	Y	Y
10 Rodino	Y	Y	N	Y	N	Y	Y	Y
11 Minish	?	?	X	#	X	?	?	?
12 ***Courter***	Y	N	Y	N	Y	Y	Y	Y
13 ***Forsythe***	?	?	?	?	?	?	?	?
14 Guarini	Y	Y	N	Y	N	Y	Y	Y
NEW MEXICO								
1 ***Lujan***	Y	N	Y	N	#	?	?	?
2 ***Skeen***	Y	N	Y	N	Y	Y	Y	Y
3 Richardson	Y	N	N	Y	N	Y	Y	Y
NEW YORK								
1 ***Carney***	Y	Y	N	Y	Y	Y	Y	Y
2 Downey	Y	Y	N	Y	?	Y	Y	Y
3 Mrazek	Y	Y	N	Y	X	Y	Y	Y
4 ***Lent***	Y	Y	N	Y	Y	Y	Y	Y
5 ***McGrath***	Y	Y	N	Y	Y	Y	Y	Y
6 Addabbo	Y	Y	N	Y	N	Y	Y	Y
7 Ackerman	Y	Y	N	Y	N	Y	Y	Y
8 Scheuer	Y	Y	N	Y	?	?	?	?
9 Ferraro	Y	Y	N	Y	N	Y	Y	Y
10 Schumer	Y	Y	N	Y	N	Y	Y	Y
11 Towns	?	?	?	?	?	?	?	?
12 Owens	Y	Y	N	Y	N	Y	Y	Y
13 Solarz	Y	Y	N	Y	N	Y	Y	Y
14 ***Molinari***	Y	N	N	Y	Y	Y	Y	Y
15 ***Green***	Y	N	?	?	Y	Y	Y	Y
16 Rangel	Y	Y	N	Y	N	Y	Y	Y
17 Weiss	Y	Y	N	Y	N	Y	Y	Y
18 Garcia	Y	Y	N	Y	N	Y	Y	Y
19 Biaggi	Y	Y	N	Y	N	Y	Y	Y
20 Ottinger	Y	Y	N	Y	N	Y	Y	Y
21 ***Fish***	Y	Y	N	Y	Y	Y	Y	Y
22 ***Gilman***	Y	N	N	Y	Y	Y	Y	Y
23 Stratton	Y	Y	N	Y	N	Y	Y	Y
24 ***Solomon***	N	N	Y	N	Y	Y	Y	Y
25 ***Boehlert***	Y	Y	N	Y	Y	Y	Y	Y
26 ***Martin***	Y	Y	Y	Y	Y	Y	Y	Y
27 ***Wortley***	Y	Y	Y	N	Y	Y	Y	Y
28 McHugh	Y	Y	N	Y	N	Y	Y	Y
29 ***Horton***	Y	Y	N	Y	?	?	?	?
30 ***Conable***	?	?	?	?	Y	Y	Y	Y
31 ***Kemp***	Y	N	N	Y	#	?	?	?
32 LaFalce	Y	Y	N	Y	N	Y	Y	Y
33 Nowak	Y	Y	N	Y	N	Y	Y	Y
34 Lundine	Y	Y	N	Y	N	Y	?	Y

	16	17	18	19	20	21	22	23
NORTH CAROLINA								
1 Jones	Y	Y	?	?	X	?	?	?
2 Valentine	Y	Y	N	Y	N	Y	Y	Y
3 Whitley	Y	Y	N	Y	N	Y	Y	Y
4 Andrews	Y	N	N	Y	?	?	?	?
5 Neal	Y	N	N	Y	N	Y	Y	Y
6 Britt	Y	Y	N	Y	N	Y	Y	Y
7 Rose	Y	Y	N	Y	N	?	?	Y
8 Hefner	Y	Y	N	Y	N	Y	Y	Y
9 ***Martin***	Y	N	Y	N	Y	Y	Y	Y
10 ***Broyhill***	Y	Y	Y	N	Y	Y	Y	Y
11 Clarke	Y	Y	Y	Y	N	Y	Y	Y
NORTH DAKOTA								
AL Dorgan	Y	Y	N	Y	N	Y	Y	Y
OHIO								
1 Luken	Y	Y	N	Y	N	Y	Y	Y
2 ***Gradison***	Y	N	N	Y	Y	?	?	?
3 Hall	Y	Y	N	Y	N	Y	Y	Y
4 ***Oxley***	Y	N	Y	N	Y	Y	Y	Y
5 ***Latta***	Y	N	Y	N	Y	?	Y	Y
6 ***McEwen***	Y	N	Y	N	Y	Y	Y	?
7 ***DeWine***	Y	N	Y	N	Y	Y	Y	Y
8 ***Kindness***	Y	N	Y	N	Y	Y	Y	Y
9 Kaptur	Y	Y	N	Y	N	Y	Y	Y
10 ***Miller***	N	N	Y	N	Y	Y	Y	Y
11 Eckart	Y	Y	N	Y	N	Y	Y	Y
12 ***Kasich***	Y	Y	N	Y	Y	Y	Y	Y
13 Pease	Y	Y	N	Y	N	Y	Y	Y
14 Seiberling	Y	Y	N	Y	N	Y	Y	Y
15 ***Wylie***	Y	Y	?	?	#	?	?	?
16 ***Regula***	Y	N	N	Y	Y	Y	Y	Y
17 ***Williams***	Y	N	Y	Y	Y	Y	Y	Y
18 Applegate	?	Y	N	Y	N	Y	Y	Y
19 Feighan	Y	Y	N	Y	N	Y	Y	Y
20 Oakar	Y	Y	N	Y	N	Y	Y	Y
21 Stokes	Y	Y	N	Y	N	Y	Y	Y
OKLAHOMA								
1 Jones	Y	Y	N	Y	N	Y	Y	Y
2 Synar	Y	N	N	Y	N	+	+	+
3 Watkins	Y	Y	N	Y	N	Y	Y	?
4 McCurdy	Y	Y	N	Y	?	?	?	?
5 ***Edwards***	Y	N	N	Y	Y	Y	Y	Y
6 English	Y	N	N	Y	N	Y	Y	Y
OREGON								
1 AuCoin	Y	Y	N	Y	N	Y	Y	Y
2 ***Smith, R.***	Y	N	Y	N	Y	Y	Y	Y
3 Wyden	Y	Y	N	Y	N	Y	Y	Y
4 Weaver	Y	Y	N	Y	N	Y	Y	Y
5 ***Smith, D.***	Y	N	Y	N	Y	Y	Y	Y
PENNSYLVANIA								
1 Foglietta	Y	Y	N	Y	N	Y	Y	?
2 Gray	Y	?	N	Y	N	Y	Y	?
3 Borski	Y	Y	N	Y	N	Y	Y	Y
4 Kolter	Y	Y	N	Y	N	Y	Y	Y
5 ***Schulze***	Y	N	Y	N	Y	Y	Y	Y
6 Yatron	Y	Y	N	Y	N	Y	Y	Y
7 Edgar	P	Y	N	Y	N	Y	Y	Y
8 Kostmayer	?	?	N	Y	N	Y	Y	Y
9 ***Shuster***	Y	N	Y	N	Y	Y	Y	Y
10 ***McDade***	Y	Y	N	Y	Y	Y	Y	Y
11 Harrison	Y	Y	N	Y	N	Y	Y	Y
12 Murtha	Y	Y	N	Y	N	Y	Y	Y
13 ***Coughlin***	N	N	X	#	Y	Y	Y	Y
14 Coyne	Y	Y	N	Y	N	Y	Y	Y
15 ***Ritter***	Y	N	Y	N	Y	?	Y	Y
16 ***Walker***	N	N	N	Y	Y	Y	Y	Y
17 ***Gekas***	Y	N	N	?	Y	Y	Y	Y
18 Walgren	Y	Y	N	Y	N	Y	Y	Y
19 ***Goodling***	N	?	N	Y	Y	Y	Y	?
20 Gaydos	Y	Y	N	Y	N	Y	Y	Y
21 ***Ridge***	?	N	N	Y	Y	Y	Y	Y
22 Murphy	Y	Y	?	Y	N	Y	Y	Y
23 ***Clinger***	Y	N	N	Y	Y	Y	Y	Y
RHODE ISLAND								
1 St Germain	?	?	?	?	?	?	?	?
2 ***Schneider***	Y	Y	N	Y	Y	?	?	Y
SOUTH CAROLINA								
1 ***Hartnett***	Y	N	Y	N	Y	Y	?	?
2 ***Spence***	Y	N	Y	Y	Y	Y	Y	Y
3 Derrick	Y	Y	N	Y	N	Y	Y	Y
4 ***Campbell***	Y	N	N	Y	Y	Y	Y	Y
5 Spratt	Y	Y	N	Y	N	Y	Y	Y
6 Tallon	Y	Y	N	Y	N	Y	Y	Y
SOUTH DAKOTA								
AL Daschle	?	?	?	?	N	Y	Y	Y

	16	17	18	19	20	21	22	23
TENNESSEE								
1 ***Quillen***	Y	Y	Y	N	Y	Y	Y	?
2 ***Duncan***	Y	Y	Y	N	Y	Y	Y	Y
3 Lloyd	Y	N	N	N	N	Y	Y	Y
4 Cooper	Y	Y	N	Y	N	Y	Y	Y
5 Boner	Y	Y	N	Y	?	?	?	?
6 Gore	Y	Y	N	Y	N	Y	Y	Y
7 ***Sundquist***	Y	N	Y	N	Y	Y	Y	Y
8 Jones	Y	Y	N	Y	N	Y	Y	Y
9 Ford	Y	Y	N	Y	N	Y	Y	Y
TEXAS								
1 Hall, S.	Y	N	Y	N	N	Y	Y	Y
2 Wilson	Y	Y	N	Y	?	Y	Y	Y
3 ***Bartlett***	Y	N	Y	N	Y	Y	Y	N
4 Hall, R.	Y	N	Y	N	N	Y	Y	Y
5 Bryant	?	Y	N	Y	N	Y	Y	?
6 ***Gramm***	Y	N	Y	N	Y	Y	Y	Y
7 ***Archer***	Y	N	Y	N	Y	Y	Y	Y
8 ***Fields***	Y	N	Y	N	Y	Y	Y	Y
9 Brooks	Y	Y	Y	N	N	Y	Y	Y
10 Pickle	Y	Y	Y	Y	N	Y	Y	Y
11 Leath	Y	Y	Y	N	N	Y	Y	Y
12 Wright	Y	Y	?	?	N	Y	Y	?
13 Hightower	Y	Y	Y	N	N	Y	Y	Y
14 Patman	Y	N	Y	N	N	Y	Y	Y
15 de la Garza	Y	?	N	Y	?	?	?	?
16 Coleman	Y	Y	N	Y	N	Y	?	Y
17 Stenholm	Y	N	Y	N	N	Y	Y	?
18 Leland	Y	Y	N	Y	N	Y	Y	Y
19 Hance	?	?	?	?	X	?	?	?
20 Gonzalez	Y	Y	N	Y	N	Y	Y	Y
21 ***Loeffler***	Y	N	Y	N	Y	Y	Y	Y
22 ***Paul***	Y	Y	N	Y	Y	N	Y	N
23 Kazen	?	?	?	?	?	?	?	?
24 Frost	Y	Y	Y	?	?	?	?	?
25 Andrews	Y	Y	N	?	N	Y	Y	Y
26 Vandergriff	Y	Y	Y	Y	N	Y	Y	Y
27 Ortiz	Y	N	N	N	N	Y	Y	Y
UTAH								
1 ***Hansen***	Y	N	Y	N	Y	Y	Y	N
2 ***Marriott***	Y	Y	Y	N	Y	Y	Y	Y
3 ***Nielson***	Y	N	Y	N	Y	Y	Y	Y
VERMONT								
AL ***Jeffords***	Y	N	N	Y	Y	Y	?	?
VIRGINIA								
1 ***Bateman***	Y	Y	N	N	Y	Y	Y	Y
2 ***Whitehurst***	Y	Y	Y	N	Y	Y	Y	Y
3 ***Bliley***	Y	Y	Y	N	Y	Y	Y	Y
4 Sisisky	Y	Y	N	Y	N	Y	Y	Y
5 Daniel	P	Y	N	Y	N	Y	Y	Y
6 Olin	Y	Y	N	Y	N	Y	Y	Y
7 ***Robinson***	Y	Y	Y	N	Y	Y	Y	Y
8 ***Parris***	Y	N	Y	N	Y	Y	Y	Y
9 Boucher	Y	Y	N	Y	N	Y	Y	Y
10 ***Wolf***	Y	N	Y	N	Y	Y	Y	Y
WASHINGTON								
1 ***Pritchard***	Y	Y	Y	N	Y	Y	?	?
2 Swift	Y	Y	N	Y	N	Y	Y	Y
3 Bonker	?	Y	N	Y	?	?	?	?
4 ***Morrison***	Y	Y	Y	N	Y	Y	Y	Y
5 Foley	Y	Y	N	Y	N	Y	Y	Y
6 Dicks	Y	Y	N	Y	N	Y	Y	Y
7 Lowry	Y	Y	N	Y	N	Y	Y	Y
8 ***Chandler***	Y	Y	Y	N	Y	Y	Y	Y
WEST VIRGINIA								
1 Mollohan	Y	N	N	Y	N	Y	Y	Y
2 Staggers	Y	Y	N	Y	N	Y	Y	Y
3 Wise	Y	N	N	Y	N	Y	Y	Y
4 Rahall	Y	N	N	Y	N	Y	Y	Y
WISCONSIN								
1 Aspin	Y	Y	N	Y	N	Y	Y	?
2 Kastenmeier	Y	Y	N	Y	N	Y	Y	Y
3 ***Gunderson***	Y	Y	Y	N	Y	Y	Y	Y
4 Vacancy								
5 Moody	Y	Y	N	Y	N	Y	Y	Y
6 ***Petri***	Y	N	Y	Y	Y	Y	Y	Y
7 Obey	Y	Y	N	Y	N	Y	Y	Y
8 ***Roth***	Y	N	N	Y	Y	Y	Y	Y
9 ***Sensenbrenner***	Y	N	Y	N	Y	Y	Y	Y
WYOMING								
AL ***Cheney***	Y	Y	Y	N	Y	Y	Y	N

Southern states - Ala., Ark., Fla., Ga., Ky., La., Miss., N.C., Okla., S.C., Tenn., Texas, Va.

24. H Res 15. Select Committee on Hunger. Hall, D-Ohio, motion to order the previous question (thus ending debate and the possibility of amendment) on the Rules Committee substitute to establish a Select Committee on Hunger. Motion agreed to 263-122: R 34-117; D 229-5 (ND 155-0, SD 74-5), Feb. 22, 1984.

25. H Res 15. Select Committee on Hunger. Adoption of the resolution to establish a Select Committee on Hunger. Adopted 309-78: R 85-66; D 224-12 (ND 154-4, SD 70-8), Feb. 22, 1984.

26. HR 2708. Foreign Language Assistance. Gekas, R-Pa., amendment to prohibit appropriation of funds to carry out the bill unless the money were provided in a measure containing no other appropriations. Rejected 145-243: R 129-22; D 16-221 (ND 2-159, SD 14-62), Feb. 23, 1984.

27. HR 2708. Foreign Language Assistance. Passage of the bill to authorize a total of $150 million in fiscal 1984-86 for aid to schools and colleges to improve instruction in foreign languages. Passed 265-120: R 63-87; D 202-33 (ND 154-9, SD 48-24), Feb. 23, 1984.

KEY

Y Voted for (yea).
\# Paired for.
+ Announced for.
N Voted against (nay).
X Paired against.
- Announced against.
P Voted "present".
C Voted "present" to avoid possible conflict of interest.
? Did not vote or otherwise make a position known.

Democrats *Republicans*

	24	25	26	27
ALABAMA				
1 *Edwards*	N	N	Y	Y
2 *Dickinson*	N	N	Y	N
3 Nichols	Y	Y	Y	N
4 Bevill	Y	Y	N	N
5 Flippo	Y	Y	N	?
6 Erdreich	Y	Y	?	?
7 Shelby	Y	Y	Y	N
ALASKA				
AL *Young*	N	Y	Y	Y
ARIZONA				
1 *McCain*	N	Y	Y	N
2 Udall	Y	Y	N	Y
3 *Stump*	?	?	Y	N
4 *Rudd*	?	?	Y	N
5 McNulty	Y	Y	N	Y
ARKANSAS				
1 Alexander	Y	Y	N	Y
2 *Bethune*	N	N	Y	N
3 *Hammerschmidt*	?	?	Y	Y
4 Anthony	Y	Y	X	?
CALIFORNIA				
1 Bosco	?	Y	N	Y
2 *Chappie*	N	N	Y	N
3 Matsui	Y	Y	N	Y
4 Fazio	Y	Y	N	Y
5 Burton	Y	Y	N	Y
6 Boxer	Y	Y	N	Y
7 Miller	?	Y	N	Y
8 Dellums	Y	Y	N	Y
9 Stark	Y	Y	N.	Y
10 Edwards	Y	Y	N	Y
11 Lantos	Y	Y	N	Y
12 *Zschau*	N	N	Y	N
13 Mineta	Y	Y	N	Y
14 *Shumway*	N	N	Y	N
15 Coelho	Y	X	X	Y
16 Panetta	Y	Y	N	Y
17 *Pashayan*	N	Y	N	Y
18 Lehman	Y	Y	N	Y
19 *Lagomarsino*	N	Y	Y	N
20 *Thomas*	N	N	Y	N
21 *Fiedler*	N	Y	Y	N
22 *Moorhead*	N	Y	Y	N
23 Beilenson	Y	Y	N	Y
24 Waxman	Y	Y	N	?
25 Roybal	Y	Y	N	Y
26 Berman	Y	Y	N	Y
27 Levine	Y	Y	N	Y
28 Dixon	Y	Y	N	Y
29 Hawkins	Y	Y	N	Y
30 Martinez	Y	Y	N	Y
31 Dymally	Y	Y	N	Y
32 Anderson	Y	Y	N	Y
33 *Dreier*	N	N	Y	N
34 Torres	Y	Y	N	Y
35 *Lewis*	N	Y	N	N
36 Brown	Y	Y	N	Y
37 *McCandless*	N	N	Y	N
38 Patterson	Y	Y	?	?
39 *Dannemeyer*	N	N	Y	N
40 *Badham*	N	N	Y	N
41 *Lowery*	Y	Y	N	Y
42 *Lungren*	N	N	Y	N
43 *Packard*	N	N	Y	Y
44 Bates	Y	Y	N	Y
45 *Hunter*	N	Y	Y	N
COLORADO				
1 Schroeder	Y	Y	N	Y
2 Wirth	Y	Y	N	Y
3 Kogovsek	?	?	N	Y
4 *Brown*	N	N	Y	N
5 *Kramer*	N	N	N	N
6 *Schaefer*	N	Y	Y	N
CONNECTICUT				
1 Kennelly	Y	Y	N	Y
2 Gejdenson	Y	Y	N	Y
3 Morrison	Y	Y	N	Y
4 *McKinney*	Y	Y	N	Y
5 Ratchford	Y	Y	N	Y
6 *Johnson*	N	N	Y	N
DELAWARE				
AL Carper	Y	Y	N	N
FLORIDA				
1 Hutto	Y	Y	N	N
2 Fuqua	Y	Y	?	?
3 Bennett	Y	Y	Y	N
4 Chappell	?	?	N	Y
5 *McCollum*	N	N	Y	Y
6 MacKay	Y	?	N	N
7 Gibbons	N	N	N	Y
8 *Young*	N	Y	Y	Y
9 *Bilirakis*	N	N	Y	Y
10 Ireland	Y	Y	N	N
11 Nelson	Y	Y	N	N
12 *Lewis*	N	Y	Y	N
13 *Mack*	N	N	Y	N
14 Mica	Y	Y	N	Y
15 *Shaw*	N	Y	Y	N
16 Smith	Y	Y	N	Y
17 Lehman	Y	Y	N	Y
18 Pepper	Y	Y	N	Y
19 Fascell	Y	Y	N	Y
GEORGIA				
1 Thomas	Y	Y	N	Y
2 Hatcher	?	?	?	?
3 Ray	Y	Y	N	Y
4 Levitas	Y	Y	N	Y
5 Fowler	Y	Y	N	Y
6 *Gingrich*	N	Y	Y	Y
7 Darden	Y	Y	N	Y
8 Rowland	Y	Y	N	Y
9 Jenkins	N	N	N	Y
10 Barnard	Y	Y	?	?
HAWAII				
1 Heftel	?	?	?	?
2 Akaka	Y	Y	N	Y
IDAHO				
1 *Craig*	N	N	Y	N
2 *Hansen*	?	N	Y	N
ILLINOIS				
1 Hayes	Y	Y	N	Y
2 Savage	?	Y	N	Y
3 Russo	Y	Y	N	Y
4 *O'Brien*	Y	Y	Y	Y
5 Lipinski	Y	Y	N	Y
6 *Hyde*	N	N	Y	N
7 Collins	?	?	X	Y
8 Rostenkowski	Y	Y	N	Y
9 Yates	Y	Y	N	Y
10 *Porter*	+	+	\#	\#
11 Annunzio	Y	Y	N	Y
12 *Crane, P.*	N	N	Y	N
13 *Erlenborn*	?	?	\#	?
14 *Corcoran*	-	+	+	+
15 *Madigan*	N	Y	\#	?
16 *Martin*	N	N	Y	Y
17 Evans	Y	Y	N	Y
18 *Michel*	?	?	Y	N
19 *Crane, D.*	N	N	Y	N
20 Durbin	Y	Y	N	Y
21 Price	Y	Y	N	Y
22 Simon	?	?	N	Y
INDIANA				
1 Hall	Y	Y	N	Y
2 Sharp	Y	Y	N	Y
3 *Hiler*	N	N	Y	N
4 *Coats*	N	N	Y	N
5 Hillis	N	Y	Y	Y

ND - Northern Democrats SD - Southern Democrats

	24	25	26	27
6 Burton	N	N	Y	N
7 Myers	N	Y	N	N
8 McCloskey	Y	Y	N	Y
9 Hamilton	Y	Y	N	Y
10 Jacobs	Y-	Y	N	N
IOWA				
1 *Leach*	N	Y	Y	Y
2 *Tauke*	N	N	N	N
3 *Evans*	N	Y	N	N
4 Smith	Y	Y	N	Y
5 Harkin	Y	Y	N	Y
6 Bedell	Y	Y	N	Y
KANSAS				
1 *Roberts*	N	N	Y	N
2 Slattery	Y	Y	N	N
3 *Winn*	Y	Y	Y	N
4 Glickman	Y	N	N	N
5 *Whittaker*	N	Y	Y	N
KENTUCKY				
1 Hubbard	N	N	Y	N
2 Natcher	Y	Y	N	Y
3 Mazzoli	Y	Y	N	Y
4 *Snyder*	N	Y	Y	N
5 *Rogers*	N	Y	Y	N
6 *Hopkins*	N	N	Y	Y
7 Perkins	Y	Y	N	Y
LOUISIANA				
1 *Livingston*	N	N	Y	N
2 Boggs	Y	Y	N	Y
3 Tauzin	?	?	?	?
4 Roemer	Y	Y	Y	N
5 Huckaby	Y	Y	Y	N
6 *Moore*	Y	Y	Y	N
7 Breaux	N	Y	N	Y
8 Long	Y	?	N	Y
MAINE				
1 *McKernan*	N	Y	Y	Y
2 *Snowe*	Y	Y	Y	Y
MARYLAND				
1 Dyson	Y	Y	N	N
2 Long	?	?	N	Y
3 Mikulski	Y	Y	N	Y
4 *Holt*	?	?	Y	N
5 Hoyer	Y	Y	N	Y
6 Byron	Y	N	Y	N
7 Mitchell	Y	Y	N	Y
8 Barnes	Y	Y	N	Y
MASSACHUSETTS				
1 *Conte*	Y	Y	N	Y
2 Boland	Y	Y	N	Y
3 Early	Y	Y	N	Y
4 Frank	Y	Y	N	Y
5 Shannon	?	Y	?	?
6 Mavroules	Y	Y	N	Y
7 Markey	?	?	N	Y
8 O'Neill				
9 Moakley	Y	Y	N	Y
10 Studds	Y	Y	N	Y
11 Donnelly	Y	Y	N	Y
MICHIGAN				
1 Conyers	Y	Y	N	Y
2 *Pursell*	Y	Y	Y	Y
3 Wolpe	Y	Y	N	N
4 *Siljander*	Y	Y	Y	Y
5 *Sawyer*	Y	Y	N	Y
6 Carr	Y	Y	N	Y
7 Kildee	Y	Y	N	Y
8 Traxler	Y	Y	N	Y
9 *Vander Jagt*	N	Y	Y	N
10 Albosta	Y	Y	N	Y
11 *Davis*	N	Y	Y	Y
12 Bonior	Y	Y	?	Y
13 Crockett	Y	Y	N	Y
14 Hertel	Y	Y	N	Y
15 Ford	Y	Y	N	Y
16 Dingell	Y	Y	N	Y
17 Levin	Y	Y	N	Y
18 *Broomfield*	Y	Y	Y	Y
MINNESOTA				
1 Penny	Y	Y	N	Y
2 *Weber*	N	N	Y	Y
3 *Frenzel*	N	N	Y	N
4 Vento	Y	Y	N	Y
5 Sabo	Y	Y	N	Y
6 Sikorski	Y	Y	N	Y

	24	25	26	27
7 *Stangeland*	Y	Y	Y	Y
8 Oberstar	Y	Y	N	Y
MISSISSIPPI				
1 Whitten	Y	Y	N	Y
2 *Franklin*	N	Y	Y	Y
3 Montgomery	?	?	Y	N
4 Dowdy	Y	Y	N	Y
5 *Lott*	N	N	Y	?
MISSOURI				
1 Clay	Y	Y	N	Y
2 Young	Y	Y	N	Y
3 Gephardt	Y	Y	N	Y
4 Skelton	Y	Y	Y	N
5 Wheat	Y	Y	N	Y
6 *Coleman*	N	Y	N	Y
7 *Taylor*	N	Y	Y	N
8 *Emerson*	N	N	Y	N
9 Volkmer	Y	Y	N	N
MONTANA				
1 Williams	Y	Y	N	Y
2 *Marlenee*	?	?	?	?
NEBRASKA				
1 *Bereuter*	N	Y	Y	Y
2 *Daub*	N	N	Y	Y
3 *Smith*	N	N	Y	Y
NEVADA				
1 Reid	Y	Y	N	Y
2 *Vucanovich*	N	N	Y	N
NEW HAMPSHIRE				
1 D'Amours	Y	Y	?	Y
2 *Gregg*	N	?	Y	N
NEW JERSEY				
1 Florio	Y	Y	N	Y
2 Hughes	Y	N	N	Y
3 Howard	Y	Y	N	Y
4 *Smith*	Y	Y	Y	Y
5 *Roukema*	N	N	N	N
6 Dwyer	Y	Y	N	Y
7 *Rinaldo*	Y	Y	N	Y
8 Roe	Y	Y	N	Y
9 Torricelli	Y	Y	N	Y
10 Rodino	Y	Y	N	Y
11 Minish	Y	Y	N	Y
12 *Courter*	?	?	Y	Y
13 *Forsythe*	?	?	?	?
14 Guarini	Y	+	N	Y
NEW MEXICO				
1 *Lujan*	N	Y	Y	Y
2 *Skeen*	N	N	Y	Y
3 Richardson	Y	Y	N	Y
NEW YORK				
1 *Carney*	N	Y	Y	N
2 Downey	Y	Y	N	Y
3 Mrazek	Y	Y	N	Y
4 *Lent*	Y	Y	Y	Y
5 *McGrath*	Y	Y	Y	Y
6 Addabbo	?	?	X	#
7 Ackerman	Y	Y	N	Y
8 Scheuer	?	?	?	?
9 Ferraro	Y	Y	N	Y
10 Schumer	Y	Y	N	Y
11 Towns	Y	Y	X	?
12 Owens	Y	Y	N	Y
13 Solarz	Y	Y	N	Y
14 *Molinari*	Y	Y	N	N
15 *Green*	N	N	N	Y
16 Rangel	Y	Y	N	Y
17 Weiss	Y	Y	N	Y
18 Garcia	Y	Y	N	Y
19 Biaggi	Y	Y	N	Y
20 Ottinger	Y	Y	N	Y
21 *Fish*	Y	Y	Y	Y
22 *Gilman*	Y	Y	N	Y
23 Stratton	Y	Y	N	Y
24 *Solomon*	N	Y	Y	N
25 *Boehlert*	Y	Y	N	Y
26 *Martin*	Y	Y	?	?
27 *Wortley*	Y	Y	N	Y
28 McHugh	?	?	?	?
29 *Horton*	Y	Y	N	Y
30 *Conable*	N	N	?	?
31 *Kemp*	N	N	Y	N
32 LaFalce	Y	Y	N	Y
33 Nowak	Y	Y	N	Y
34 Lundine	Y	Y	N	Y

	24	25	26	27
NORTH CAROLINA				
1 Jones	Y	Y	N	Y
2 Valentine	Y	Y	N	Y
3 Whitley	Y	Y	N	Y
4 Andrews	?	Y	N	Y
5 Neal	?	?	N	Y
6 Britt	Y	Y	N	Y
7 Rose	Y	Y	N	Y
8 Hefner	Y	Y	N	Y
9 *Martin*	N	Y	Y	N
10 *Broyhill*	N	N	?	?
11 Clarke	Y	Y	N	Y
NORTH DAKOTA				
AL Dorgan	Y	Y	N	Y
OHIO				
1 Luken	Y	Y	N	Y
2 *Gradison*	N	N	Y	N
3 Hall	Y	Y	N	Y
4 *Oxley*	N	N	Y	N
5 *Latta*	N	Y	#	X
6 *McEwen*	N	Y	?	?
7 *DeWine*	Y	Y	Y	Y
8 *Kindness*	N	N	Y	N
9 Kaptur	Y	Y	N	Y
10 *Miller*	N	Y	N	Y
11 Eckart	?	?	?	?
12 *Kasich*	Y	Y	N	N
13 Pease	Y	Y	N	Y
14 Seiberling	Y	Y	N	Y
15 *Wylie*	N	Y	Y	N
16 *Regula*	N	Y	N	Y
17 Williams	Y	Y	Y	Y
18 Applegate	Y	Y	N	Y
19 Feighan	Y	Y	N	Y
20 Oakar	Y	Y	N	Y
21 Stokes	?	?	N	Y
OKLAHOMA				
1 Jones	Y	N	N	N
2 Synar	Y	Y	N	Y
3 Watkins	Y	Y	?	?
4 McCurdy	Y	Y	N	?
5 *Edwards*	N	Y	N	N
6 English	Y	Y	N	N
OREGON				
1 AuCoin	Y	Y	N	Y
2 *Smith, R.*	?	?	?	?
3 Wyden	Y	Y	N	Y
4 Weaver	?	?	N	Y
5 *Smith, D.*	N	N	Y	N
PENNSYLVANIA				
1 Foglietta	?	?	?	?
2 Gray	Y	Y	N	Y
3 Borski	Y	Y	N	Y
4 Kolter	Y	Y	N	Y
5 *Schulze*	N	N	Y	N
6 Yatron	Y	Y	N	Y
7 Edgar	Y	Y	N	Y
8 Kostmayer	Y	Y	N	Y
9 *Shuster*	N	N	Y	N
10 *McDade*	Y	Y	Y	Y
11 Harrison	?	?	N	Y
12 Murtha	Y	Y	N	Y
13 *Coughlin*	N	N	N	Y
14 Coyne	Y	Y	N	Y
15 *Ritter*	N	Y	Y	Y
16 *Walker*	N	N	Y	N
17 *Gekas*	Y	Y	N	Y
18 Walgren	Y	Y	N	Y
19 *Goodling*	N	Y	Y	N
20 Gaydos	Y	Y	N	Y
21 *Ridge*	Y	Y	Y	Y
22 Murphy	Y	N	Y	N
23 *Clinger*	N	Y	Y	Y
RHODE ISLAND				
1 St Germain	?	?	?	?
2 *Schneider*	Y	Y	N	Y
SOUTH CAROLINA				
1 *Hartnett*	N	N	Y	N
2 *Spence*	?	?	N	Y
3 Derrick	Y	Y	N	Y
4 *Campbell*	N	N	Y	#
5 Spratt	Y	Y	N	Y
6 Tallon	Y	Y	N	Y
SOUTH DAKOTA				
AL Daschle	Y	Y	N	Y

	24	25	26	27
TENNESSEE				
1 *Quillen*	Y	Y	#	?
2 *Duncan*	Y	Y	Y	N
3 Lloyd	Y	Y	?	?
4 Cooper	Y	Y	N	N
5 Boner	Y	Y	?	?
6 Gore	Y	Y	N	N
7 *Sundquist*	N	N	Y	N
8 Jones	Y	Y	N	Y
9 Ford	Y	Y	N	?
TEXAS				
1 Hall, S.	?	?	?	?
2 Wilson	?	?	?	?
3 *Bartlett*	N	N	Y	N
4 Hall, R.	Y	Y	N	Y
5 Bryant	Y	Y	N	Y
6 *Gramm*	N	N	Y	N
7 *Archer*	N	N	Y	N
8 *Fields*	N	N	Y	N
9 Brooks	Y	Y	N	Y
10 Pickle	Y	N	N	N
11 Leath	?	?	?	?
12 Wright	Y	Y	?	?
13 Hightower	Y	Y	N	Y
14 Patman	Y	Y	N	Y
15 de la Garza	Y	Y	N	Y
16 Coleman	Y	Y	Y	Y
17 Stenholm	Y	N	Y	N
18 Leland	Y	Y	N	Y
19 Hance	?	?	?	?
20 Gonzalez	Y	Y	N	Y
21 *Loeffler*	N	N	Y	N
22 *Paul*	?	?	?	X
23 Kazen	Y	Y	N	?
24 Frost	Y	Y	N	Y
25 Andrews	Y	Y	N	N
26 Vandergriff	Y	Y	Y	Y
27 Ortiz	?	?	N	Y
UTAH				
1 *Hansen*	N	N	Y	N
2 *Marriott*	N	N	Y	N
3 *Nielson*	N	N	Y	N
VERMONT				
AL *Jeffords*	?	?	?	?
VIRGINIA				
1 *Bateman*	N	Y	Y	N
2 *Whitehurst*	N	Y	Y	Y
3 *Bliley*	N	Y	N	N
4 Sisisky	Y	Y	N	N
5 Daniel	N	N	Y	N
6 Olin	Y	N	Y	N
7 *Robinson*	N	N	N	Y
8 *Parris*	Y	Y	Y	Y
9 Boucher	Y	Y	N	Y
10 *Wolf*	Y	Y	Y	Y
WASHINGTON				
1 *Pritchard*	N	Y	N	Y
2 Swift	Y	Y	N	Y
3 Bonker	?	?	?	?
4 *Morrison*	N	Y	Y	Y
5 Foley	Y	Y	N	Y
6 Dicks	Y	Y	N	Y
7 Lowry	Y	Y	N	Y
8 *Chandler*	N	Y	Y	Y
WEST VIRGINIA				
1 Mollohan	?	+	N	Y
2 Staggers	Y	Y	N	Y
3 Wise	Y	Y	N	Y
4 Rahall	Y	Y	N	Y
WISCONSIN				
1 Aspin	Y	Y	N	Y
2 Kastenmeier	Y	Y	N	Y
3 *Gunderson*	N	Y	N	N
4 Vacancy				
5 Moody	Y	Y	N	Y
6 *Petri*	N	N	Y	Y
7 Obey	Y	Y	N	Y
8 *Roth*	N	Y	?	?
9 *Sensenbrenner*	N	Y	N	Y
WYOMING				
AL *Cheney*	N	N	Y	N

Southern states - Ala., Ark., Fla., Ga., Ky., La., Miss., N.C., Okla., S.C., Tenn., Texas, Va.

28. H Res 446. Committee Funds. Adoption of the resolution to authorize House committees to spend a total of $45.4 million in 1984. Adopted 252-141: R 35-120; D 217-21 (ND 145-12, SD 72-9), March 1, 1984.

29. HR 3050. Rural Electrification Administration Financing. Bethune, R-Ark., substitute to raise interest rates to Rural Electrification Administration (REA) borrowers by a variable rate formula that differed from that contained in HR 3050, require REA repayment of outstanding notes to the U.S. Treasury and make other revisions in terms of REA loans. Rejected 107-289: R 76-80; D 31-209 (ND 24-136, SD 7-73), March 1, 1984.

30. HR 3050. Rural Electrification Administration Financing. Bethune, R-Ark., motion to recommit the bill to the Agriculture Committee with instructions to consider amendments to assure the financial integrity of the Rural Electrification Administration (REA) revolving loan fund without restricting the availability of credit or increasing cost of credit to borrowers other than those using REA. Motion rejected 127-268: R 96-61; D 31-207 (ND 27-131, SD 4-76), March 1, 1984.

31. HR 3050. Rural Electrification Administration Financing. Passage of the bill to raise interest rates to Rural Electrification Administration (REA) borrowers by a variable rate formula, to relieve REA of required repayment of long-term notes to the U.S. Treasury and make other revisions in terms of REA loans. Passed 283-111: R 84-71; D 199-40 (ND 122-38, SD 77-2), March 1, 1984. A "nay" was a vote supporting the president's position.

32. H J Res 492. Department of Agriculture, Fiscal 1984 Urgent Supplemental Appropriations. Passage of the joint resolution to appropriate $150 million in fiscal 1984 for emergency food aid to 18 African nations and to authorize the sale of up to $90 million in Commodity Credit Corporation stocks to those nations or to countries helping them meet their emergency food needs. Passed 374-29: R 130-29; D 244-0 (ND 163-0, SD 81-0), March 6, 1984. The president had requested $90 million in food aid.

33. HR 3648. Amtrak Improvement Act. Broyhill, R-N.C., amendment to permit the Department of Transportation to sell Conrail unless Congress passes a law disapproving the sale. The bill would require Congress to approve any sale for it to take effect. Rejected 147-254: R 129-26; D 18-228 (ND 3-158, SD 15-70), March 6, 1984. A "yea" was a vote supporting the president's position.

34. Procedural Motion. Gekas, R-Pa., motion to approve the House *Journal* of Wednesday, March 7. Motion agreed to 350-25: R 134-13; D 216-12 (ND 138-11, SD 78-1), March 8, 1984.

35. HR 4164. Vocational Technical Education Amendments. Roukema, R-N.J., amendment to prohibit the use of funds under the bill to buy equipment, if the purchase results in financial benefit to an organization representing the interests of the purchaser or its employees. Adopted 205-173: R 140-9; D 65-164 (ND 32-121, SD 33-43), March 8, 1984.

KEY

Y	Voted for (yea).
#	Paired for.
+	Announced for.
N	Voted against (nay).
X	Paired against.
-	Announced against.
P	Voted "present".
C	Voted "present" to avoid possible conflict of interest.
?	Did not vote or otherwise make a position known.

Democrats *Republicans*

	28	29	30	31	32	33	34	35
ALABAMA								
1 Edwards	Y	N	N	Y	Y	Y	Y	Y
2 *Dickinson*	Y	N	N	Y	Y	N	N	Y
3 Nichols	Y	N	N	Y	Y	?	Y	Y
4 Bevill	Y	X	?	?	Y	N	Y	Y
5 Flippo	Y	N	N	Y	Y	N	Y	?
6 Erdreich	Y	N	N	Y	Y	N	Y	?
7 Shelby	Y	N	N	Y	Y	Y	Y	Y
ALASKA								
AL *Young*	Y	N	N	Y	Y	N	N	Y
ARIZONA								
1 *McCain*	N	N	Y	N	Y	Y	Y	Y
2 Udall	Y	N	N	Y	Y	N	Y	?
3 *Stump*	N	N	N	N	N	Y	N	Y
4 *Rudd*	Y	N	Y	N	?	?	?	#
5 McNulty	Y	N	N	Y	?	N	Y	Y
ARKANSAS								
1 Alexander	Y	N	N	Y	Y	N	Y	N
2 *Bethune*	N	Y	Y	N	Y	Y	?	Y
3 *Hammerschmidt*	Y	N	N	Y	Y	Y	Y	Y
4 Anthony	Y	N	N	Y	Y	N	Y	N
CALIFORNIA								
1 Bosco	Y	N	N	Y	Y	N	Y	?
2 *Chappie*	N	Y	Y	N	Y	Y	N	Y
3 Matsui	Y	N	N	Y	Y	N	Y	N
4 Fazio	Y	N	N	Y	Y	N	Y	N
5 Burton	Y	N	N	Y	Y	N	Y	N
6 Boxer	?	?	?	?	Y	N	Y	N
7 Miller	Y	N	N	Y	Y	N	Y	N
8 Dellums	Y	N	N	N	Y	N	Y	N
9 Stark	Y	Y	N	?	?	?	?	?
10 Edwards	Y	N	N	N	Y	N	Y	N
11 Lantos	Y	N	N	Y	Y	N	Y	N
12 *Zschau*	Y	Y	Y	N	Y	Y	Y	Y
13 Mineta	Y	N	N	Y	Y	N	Y	X
14 *Shumway*	N	Y	N	N	Y	Y	N	Y
15 Coelho	Y	N	N	Y	Y	N	Y	?
16 Panetta	Y	Y	N	Y	N	Y	Y	Y
17 *Pashayan*	N	N	Y	N	Y	Y	Y	Y
18 Lehman	Y	N	N	Y	Y	N	Y	N
19 *Lagomarsino*	N	Y	Y	N	Y	Y	Y	Y
20 *Thomas*	Y	Y	Y	N	Y	Y	N	Y
21 *Fiedler*	N	Y	N	Y	Y	Y	Y	Y
22 *Moorhead*	N	Y	Y	N	Y	Y	Y	Y
23 Beilenson	Y	Y	N	Y	Y	N	Y	?
24 Waxman	Y	N	N	Y	Y	N	Y	N
25 Roybal	Y	N	N	Y	Y	?	Y	N
26 Berman	Y	N	N	Y	?	Y	N	N
27 Levine	Y	N	N	Y	N	P	N	?
28 Dixon	Y	N	N	Y	Y	?	P	N
29 Hawkins	Y	N	N	Y	N	N	N	N
30 Martinez	Y	N	N	Y	Y	N	Y	N
31 Dymally	Y	N	N	Y	N	P	N	?
32 Anderson	Y	Y	N	Y	N	P	Y	Y
33 *Dreier*	N	Y	Y	N	N	Y	Y	Y
34 Torres	Y	N	N	Y	Y	N	Y	N
35 *Lewis*	N	Y	Y	N	Y	Y	Y	Y
36 Brown	Y	N	N	Y	Y	N	Y	N
37 *McCandless*	N	Y	N	N	Y	Y	Y	Y
38 Patterson	Y	N	N	Y	Y	N	Y	?
39 *Dannemeyer*	N	Y	Y	N	N	Y	Y	#
40 *Badham*	Y	Y	Y	N	N	Y	Y	Y
41 *Lowery*	?	?	?	?	Y	Y	Y	Y
42 *Lungren*	N	Y	Y	N	N	Y	Y	Y

	28	29	30	31	32	33	34	35
43 *Packard*	N	Y	Y	N	N	Y	Y	Y
44 Bates	Y	Y	Y	N	Y	N	Y	N
45 *Hunter*	N	Y	Y	N	Y	Y	Y	Y
COLORADO								
1 Schroeder	N	Y	N	Y	N	N	N	Y
2 Wirth	Y	N	N	Y	Y	N	Y	N
3 Kogovsek	Y	N	N	Y	Y	?	Y	N
4 *Brown*	N	N	N	Y	N	Y	Y	Y
5 *Kramer*	N	Y	Y	N	Y	Y	Y	Y
6 *Schaefer*	N	Y	Y	N	Y	Y	Y	Y
CONNECTICUT								
1 Kennelly	Y	N	N	N	Y	N	Y	N
2 Gejdenson	Y	Y	Y	N	Y	N	N	N
3 Morrison	Y	N	N	Y	Y	N	Y	Y
4 *McKinney*	Y	N	Y	N	Y	N	?	X
5 Ratchford	Y	N	N	Y	Y	N	Y	N
6 *Johnson*	N	Y	Y	N	Y	Y	Y	Y
DELAWARE								
AL Carper	N	Y	N	Y	N	Y	N	Y
FLORIDA								
1 Hutto	N	N	N	Y	N	Y	N	Y
2 Fuqua	Y	N	N	?	?	N	Y	N
3 Bennett	Y	N	N	Y	N	Y	Y	Y
4 Chappell	Y	N	N	Y	Y	N	?	?
5 *McCollum*	N	Y	Y	N	Y	Y	Y	Y
6 MacKay	Y	Y	N	Y	Y	N	Y	N
7 Gibbons	Y	N	N	Y	N	Y	N	?
8 *Young*	N	N	Y	Y	Y	N	Y	Y
9 *Bilirakis*	N	N	Y	N	Y	N	?	?
10 Ireland	N	N	Y	Y	Y	Y	Y	Y
11 Nelson	Y	Y	Y	+	N	Y	Y
12 *Lewis*	N	Y	N	Y	Y	Y	Y	Y
13 *Mack*	?	Y	Y	N	N	Y	Y	Y
14 Mica	Y	Y	N	Y	Y	N	Y	N
15 *Shaw*	N	Y	Y	N	Y	Y	Y	Y
16 Smith	?	?	?	?	Y	N	Y	N
17 Lehman	?	?	?	?	Y	N	Y	N
18 Pepper	Y	N	N	Y	Y	N	?	X
19 Fascell	Y	N	N	Y	N	Y	?	?
GEORGIA								
1 Thomas	Y	N	N	Y	N	Y	Y	Y
2 Hatcher	Y	N	N	Y	N	Y	Y	?
3 Ray	Y	N	N	Y	N	Y	N	Y
4 Levitas	Y	N	N	Y	N	Y	Y	Y
5 Fowler	Y	N	N	Y	N	Y	Y	N
6 *Gingrich*	N	N	Y	Y	Y	Y	Y	Y
7 Darden	Y	N	N	Y	N	Y	Y	Y
8 Rowland	Y	N	N	Y	N	Y	Y	Y
9 Jenkins	Y	N	N	Y	N	Y	Y	N
10 Barnard	Y	N	N	Y	N	Y	N	Y
HAWAII								
1 Heftel	?	?	?	?	?	?	?	?
2 Akaka	Y	N	N	Y	Y	N	Y	?
IDAHO								
1 *Craig*	N	Y	Y	N	N	Y	Y	Y
2 *Hansen*	N	Y	Y	N	N	Y	Y	Y
ILLINOIS								
1 Hayes	Y	N	N	Y	N	Y	N	N
2 Savage	?	?	?	?	Y	N	?	?
3 Russo	Y	N	N	Y	N	Y	N	N
4 *O'Brien*	N	N	N	Y	Y	Y	Y	Y
5 Lipinski	Y	N	N	Y	N	N	N	N
6 *Hyde*	?	Y	Y	N	Y	Y	Y	Y
7 Collins	?	?	?	?	?	?	?	X
8 Rostenkowski	Y	Y	Y	N	Y	N	Y	N
9 Yates	Y	Y	Y	N	Y	N	Y	N
10 *Porter*	N	N	Y	N	Y	Y	?	Y
11 Annunzio	Y	N	N	Y	Y	N	Y	N
12 *Crane, P.*	N	Y	Y	N	N	Y	?	#
13 *Erlenborn*	Y	Y	N	Y	N	Y	Y	Y
14 *Corcoran*	-	+	+	+	+	+	+	#
15 *Madigan*	Y	N	N	Y	N	Y	N	Y
16 *Martin*	N	Y	N	Y	N	Y	?	Y
17 Evans	Y	N	N	Y	N	N	Y	N
18 *Michel*	N	Y	Y	N	Y	Y	Y	Y
19 *Crane, D.*	N	Y	Y	N	N	Y	Y	Y
20 Durbin	N	N	N	Y	N	N	Y	N
21 Price	Y	N	N	Y	N	Y	Y	N
22 Simon	?	?	?	?	Y	N	?	?
INDIANA								
1 Hall	Y	N	N	Y	Y	N	Y	N
2 Sharp	Y	N	N	Y	N	Y	Y	Y
3 *Hiler*	N	Y	N	Y	Y	Y	Y	Y
4 *Coats*	N	Y	N	Y	Y	N	Y	N
5 *Hillis*	N	N	N	Y	Y	Y	Y	Y

ND - Northern Democrats   SD - Southern Democrats

	28	29	30	31	32	33	34	35
6 ***Burton***	N	Y	Y	N	N	Y	Y	Y
7 ***Myers***	Y	N	N	Y	Y	Y	Y	Y
8 McCloskey	Y	N	N	Y	?	N	Y	N
9 Hamilton	Y	N	N	Y	Y	N	Y	Y
10 Jacobs	N	Y	Y	N	Y	N	N	N
IOWA								
1 ***Leach***	N	Y	Y	Y	Y	Y	Y	Y
2 ***Tauke***	N	N	N	Y	Y	Y	Y	N
3 ***Evans***	N	Y	Y	Y	Y	Y	N	N
4 Smith	Y	N	N	Y	Y	N	Y	N
5 Harkin	Y	N	N	Y	Y	N	N	N
6 Bedell	Y	N	N	Y	Y	N	Y	N
KANSAS								
1 ***Roberts***	N	N	N	Y	Y	Y	N	Y
2 Slattery	N	N	N	Y	Y	N	Y	N
3 ***Winn***	Y	Y	Y	N	Y	Y	Y	#
4 Glickman	N	N	N	Y	Y	Y	Y	Y
5 ***Whittaker***	N	N	N	Y	Y	Y	Y	Y
KENTUCKY								
1 Hubbard	?	?	?	?	Y	N	Y	N
2 Natcher	Y	N	N	Y	Y	N	Y	N
3 Mazzoli	Y	Y	Y	N	+	+	Y	Y
4 ***Snyder***	Y	N	Y	Y	Y	Y	Y	Y
5 ***Rogers***	N	N	N	Y	Y	Y	Y	Y
6 ***Hopkins***	N	N	N	Y	Y	Y	Y	Y
7 Perkins	Y	N	N	Y	Y	N	Y	N
LOUISIANA								
1 ***Livingston***	N	Y	Y	N	?	?	Y	Y
2 Boggs	Y	N	N	Y	Y	N	Y	N
3 Tauzin	Y	Y	N	Y	Y	Y	Y	Y
4 Roemer	N	Y	Y	Y	Y	N	N	Y
5 Huckaby	Y	?	?	?	Y	N	Y	Y
6 ***Moore***	N	Y	Y	Y	Y	Y	Y	Y
7 Breaux	Y	N	N	Y	Y	Y	Y	Y
8 Long	Y	N	N	Y	Y	N	Y	N
MAINE								
1 ***McKernan***	N	N	Y	Y	Y	Y	Y	Y
2 ***Snowe***	N	N	Y	Y	Y	Y	Y	Y
MARYLAND								
1 Dyson	Y	N	N	Y	Y	N	Y	N
2 Long	Y	?	N	Y	Y	N	Y	?
3 Mikulski	Y	N	N	Y	Y	?	Y	N
4 ***Holt***	N	N	Y	Y	Y	Y	Y	Y
5 Hoyer	Y	N	N	Y	Y	N	Y	N
6 Byron	Y	N	N	Y	Y	N	Y	Y
7 Mitchell	?	N	N	Y	Y	N	N	N
8 Barnes	Y	N	N	Y	Y	N	Y	N
MASSACHUSETTS								
1 ***Conte***	N	Y	Y	N	Y	N	Y	N
2 Boland	?	?	?	?	Y	N	?	?
3 Early	N	Y	Y	N	Y	N	Y	N
4 Frank	Y	Y	Y	N	Y	N	Y	Y
5 Shannon	N	Y	Y	N	?	?	?	?
6 Mavroules	Y	Y	Y	N	Y	N	Y	N
7 Markey	?	?	?	?	?	?	?	?
8 O'Neill								
9 Moakley	Y	N	N	Y	Y	N	Y	N
10 Studds	Y	N	N	Y	Y	N	Y	Y
11 Donnelly	Y	N	N	Y	Y	N	Y	Y
MICHIGAN								
1 Conyers	?	?	?	?	Y	N	Y	N
2 ***Pursell***	N	N	Y	Y	Y	Y	Y	Y
3 Wolpe	Y	N	N	Y	Y	N	Y	N
4 ***Siljander***	?	Y	Y	N	Y	?	Y	#
5 ***Sawyer***	N	Y	N	?	Y	N	Y	Y
6 Carr	Y	N	N	Y	Y	N	Y	N
7 Kildee	Y	N	N	Y	Y	N	Y	N
8 Traxler	Y	N	N	Y	?	N	Y	N
9 ***Vander Jagt***	N	N	N	Y	Y	Y	?	Y
10 Albosta	Y	N	N	Y	Y	N	?	N
11 ***Davis***	N	N	N	Y	Y	Y	Y	N
12 Bonior	Y	N	N	Y	Y	N	Y	N
13 Crockett	?	N	N	Y	Y	N	Y	N
14 Hertel	Y	Y	N	N	Y	?	Y	N
15 Ford	Y	N	N	Y	Y	N	?	N
16 Dingell	Y	Y	N	Y	Y	N	Y	N
17 Levin	Y	N	Y	N	Y	N	Y	N
18 ***Broomfield***	Y	?	?	?	Y	Y	Y	?
MINNESOTA								
1 Penny	Y	N	N	Y	Y	N	N	N
2 ***Weber***	N	N	N	Y	Y	Y	Y	?
3 ***Frenzel***	Y	Y	Y	N	Y	Y	N	+
4 Vento	Y	N	N	Y	?	N	Y	N
5 Sabo	Y	N	N	Y	Y	N	N	N
6 Sikorski	Y	N	N	Y	Y	N	N	N
7 ***Stangeland***	Y	N	N	Y	Y	Y	Y	Y
8 Oberstar	Y	N	N	Y	Y	N	Y	N
MISSISSIPPI								
1 Whitten	Y	N	N	Y	Y	N	Y	N
2 ***Franklin***	Y	N	N	Y	Y	Y	?	Y
3 Montgomery	Y	N	N	Y	Y	Y	Y	Y
4 Dowdy	?	?	?	?	Y	N	?	N
5 ***Lott***	N	N	Y	Y	Y	Y	Y	Y
MISSOURI								
1 Clay	Y	N	N	Y	?	N	?	N
2 Young	Y	N	?	?	Y	N	Y	N
3 Gephardt	Y	N	N	Y	Y	N	Y	N
4 Skelton	Y	N	N	Y	Y	N	Y	Y
5 Wheat	Y	N	N	Y	Y	N	Y	N
6 ***Coleman***	N	N	N	Y	Y	Y	Y	Y
7 ***Taylor***	Y	N	N	Y	Y	Y	Y	Y
8 ***Emerson***	N	N	N	Y	Y	Y	N	Y
9 Volkmer	Y	N	N	Y	Y	N	Y	Y
MONTANA								
1 Williams	N	N	N	Y	Y	N	Y	Y
2 ***Marlenee***	Y	N	N	Y	Y	N	Y	Y
NEBRASKA								
1 ***Bereuter***	N	N	N	Y	Y	Y	?	Y
2 ***Daub***	N	Y	Y	Y	Y	Y	Y	Y
3 ***Smith***	N	N	N	Y	Y	Y	Y	N
NEVADA								
1 Reid	Y	N	N	Y	Y	N	Y	N
2 ***Vucanovich***	Y	N	N	Y	N	Y	Y	Y
NEW HAMPSHIRE								
1 D'Amours	N	N	?	N	Y	N	Y	N
2 ***Gregg***	N	N	N	Y	Y	Y	Y	Y
NEW JERSEY								
1 Florio	Y	N	N	Y	Y	N	Y	Y
2 Hughes	N	N	Y	N	Y	N	Y	Y
3 Howard	?	?	?	?	Y	N	Y	N
4 ***Smith***	N	Y	Y	N	Y	Y	Y	Y
5 ***Roukema***	N	Y	Y	N	Y	Y	Y	Y
6 Dwyer	Y	Y	Y	N	Y	N	Y	N
7 ***Rinaldo***	Y	Y	Y	N	Y	N	Y	Y
8 Roe	Y	N	N	Y	Y	N	Y	N
9 Torricelli	Y	N	Y	Y	Y	N	Y	N
10 Rodino	Y	N	N	Y	Y	N	Y	N
11 Minish	Y	N	N	Y	Y	N	Y	Y
12 ***Courter***	N	N	Y	N	Y	N	Y	Y
13 ***Forsythe***	?	?	?	?	?	?	?	?
14 Guarini	Y	N	N	Y	Y	N	Y	N
NEW MEXICO								
1 ***Lujan***	N	N	N	Y	Y	Y	Y	Y
2 ***Skeen***	N	N	N	Y	Y	Y	Y	Y
3 Richardson	Y	N	N	Y	Y	N	Y	N
NEW YORK								
1 ***Carney***	Y	Y	Y	N	Y	?	Y	Y
2 Downey	Y	N	N	N	Y	N	?	?
3 Mrazek	Y	N	Y	N	Y	N	?	?
4 ***Lent***	Y	Y	Y	?	Y	Y	Y	Y
5 ***McGrath***	Y	Y	Y	N	?	?	Y	Y
6 Addabbo	Y	N	N	Y	Y	N	Y	N
7 Ackerman	Y	N	Y	N	Y	-	+	?
8 Scheuer	?	?	?	?	Y	N	Y	N
9 Ferraro	Y	N	N	Y	Y	N	Y	N
10 Schumer	Y	N	Y	N	Y	N	Y	N
11 Towns	?	N	N	Y	Y	N	Y	N
12 Owens	Y	N	Y	N	Y	N	Y	N
13 Solarz	Y	N	N	Y	?	N	Y	N
14 ***Molinari***	N	Y	Y	N	Y	Y	Y	Y
15 ***Green***	N	Y	Y	N	Y	Y	Y	Y
16 Rangel	Y	N	N	Y	Y	N	Y	N
17 Weiss	Y	Y	Y	N	Y	N	Y	N
18 Garcia	Y	N	N	N	Y	N	Y	N
19 Biaggi	?	?	?	?	Y	?	Y	N
20 Ottinger	Y	Y	Y	N	Y	N	?	N
21 ***Fish***	Y	N	N	Y	Y	N	Y	Y
22 ***Gilman***	Y	N	N	Y	Y	N	Y	N
23 Stratton	Y	N	N	Y	Y	N	Y	Y
24 ***Solomon***	?	Y	Y	N	?	Y	N	Y
25 ***Boehlert***	N	N	N	Y	Y	Y	Y	N
26 ***Martin***	?	N	Y	N	Y	Y	Y	Y
27 ***Wortley***	N	Y	Y	N	Y	Y	Y	Y
28 McHugh	Y	N	N	Y	Y	N	Y	Y
29 ***Horton***	Y	N	Y	N	Y	N	P	X
30 ***Conable***	Y	Y	Y	N	Y	Y	Y	Y
31 ***Kemp***	?	Y	Y	N	Y	Y	?	Y
32 LaFalce	Y	Y	Y	N	Y	N	Y	?
33 Nowak	Y	Y	Y	N	Y	N	Y	N
34 Lundine	Y	N	N	Y	Y	N	Y	N
NORTH CAROLINA								
1 Jones	Y	N	N	Y	Y	N	?	N
2 Valentine	N	N	N	Y	Y	N	Y	Y
3 Whitley	Y	N	N	Y	Y	N	Y	N
4 Andrews	Y	N	N	Y	Y	N	Y	N
5 Neal	Y	N	N	Y	Y	N	Y	Y
6 Britt	Y	N	N	+	Y	N	Y	N
7 Rose	Y	N	N	Y	Y	N	?	N
8 Hefner	?	X	?	?	?	N	Y	N
9 ***Martin***	N	Y	Y	Y	Y	Y	Y	Y
10 ***Broyhill***	N	N	N	Y	Y	Y	Y	Y
11 Clarke	Y	N	N	Y	Y	N	Y	N
NORTH DAKOTA								
AL Dorgan	Y	N	N	Y	Y	N	Y	N
OHIO								
1 Luken	Y	N	N	Y	Y	N	Y	N
2 ***Gradison***	N	Y	Y	N	Y	Y	Y	Y
3 Hall	Y	N	N	Y	Y	N	?	?
4 ***Oxley***	N	N	N	Y	Y	Y	Y	Y
5 ***Latta***	N	Y	Y	N	Y	Y	Y	Y
6 ***McEwen***	N	N	?	?	Y	Y	Y	Y
7 ***DeWine***	N	Y	Y	N	?	?	Y	Y
8 ***Kindness***	N	Y	Y	Y	Y	?	?	?
9 Kaptur	Y	N	N	Y	Y	N	Y	Y
10 ***Miller***	N	Y	Y	Y	Y	Y	N	Y
11 Eckart	Y	N	N	Y	Y	N	Y	Y
12 ***Kasich***	N	Y	Y	N	Y	Y	Y	Y
13 Pease	Y	N	N	Y	Y	Y	Y	N
14 Seiberling	Y	N	N	Y	Y	N	P	N
15 ***Wylie***	N	N	N	Y	?	?	Y	Y
16 ***Regula***	Y	N	Y	Y	Y	N	Y	Y
17 ***Williams***	N	N	N	Y	Y	N	Y	N
18 Applegate	Y	N	N	Y	Y	N	?	N
19 Feighan	Y	N	N	Y	Y	N	Y	Y
20 Oakar	Y	N	N	Y	Y	N	Y	N
21 Stokes	Y	?	?	Y	Y	N	?	N
OKLAHOMA								
1 Jones	Y	N	Y	Y	Y	N	Y	Y
2 Synar	Y	N	N	Y	Y	N	Y	-
3 Watkins	Y	N	N	Y	Y	N	Y	Y
4 McCurdy	Y	N	N	Y	Y	N	?	?
5 ***Edwards***	N	N	Y	Y	Y	N	N	?
6 English	Y	N	N	Y	Y	N	Y	Y
OREGON								
1 AuCoin	Y	N	Y	N	Y	N	Y	N
2 ***Smith, R.***	N	N	Y	Y	Y	Y	Y	Y
3 Wyden	Y	N	N	Y	Y	N	Y	N
4 Weaver	Y	N	N	Y	?	?	Y	N
5 ***Smith, D.***	N	Y	Y	N	N	Y	Y	Y
PENNSYLVANIA								
1 Foglietta	?	?	?	?	?	?	?	?
2 Gray	Y	N	N	Y	Y	N	Y	N
3 Borski	Y	N	N	Y	Y	N	Y	N
4 Kolter	Y	N	N	Y	Y	N	Y	N
5 ***Schulze***	N	Y	Y	N	Y	Y	Y	Y
6 Yatron	Y	N	N	Y	Y	N	Y	N
7 Edgar	Y	N	N	Y	Y	N	Y	N
8 Kostmayer	Y	N	N	Y	Y	N	Y	N
9 ***Shuster***	N	N	N	Y	N	N	Y	Y
10 ***McDade***	Y	N	N	Y	Y	N	Y	Y
11 Harrison	Y	N	N	Y	Y	N	Y	N
12 Murtha	?	N	N	Y	Y	N	Y	N
13 ***Coughlin***	N	#	?	?	Y	Y	N	N
14 Coyne	Y	N	N	Y	Y	N	Y	N
15 ***Ritter***	N	Y	Y	N	Y	N	?	Y
16 ***Walker***	N	?	?	?	N	Y	N	Y
17 ***Gekas***	N	N	N	Y	Y	N	Y	Y
18 Walgren	Y	Y	Y	Y	Y	N	Y	N
19 ***Goodling***	N	N	N	Y	Y	N	?	Y
20 Gaydos	Y	N	N	Y	Y	N	Y	N
21 ***Ridge***	N	?	N	Y	Y	N	Y	Y
22 Murphy	?	?	?	?	Y	N	Y	N
23 ***Clinger***	N	N	N	Y	Y	N	Y	Y
RHODE ISLAND								
1 St Germain	?	?	?	?	Y	N	P	N
2 ***Schneider***	N	Y	Y	N	Y	N	Y	Y
SOUTH CAROLINA								
1 ***Hartnett***	N	N	N	Y	Y	Y	Y	Y
2 ***Spence***	N	N	N	Y	Y	Y	Y	Y
3 Derrick	Y	N	N	Y	Y	N	Y	?
4 ***Campbell***	N	N	N	Y	Y	Y	Y	Y
5 Spratt	Y	N	N	Y	Y	N	Y	N
6 Tallon	Y	N	N	Y	Y	N	Y	Y
SOUTH DAKOTA								
AL Daschle	Y	N	N	Y	Y	N	Y	N
TENNESSEE								
1 ***Quillen***	Y	N	N	Y	Y	Y	Y	Y
2 ***Duncan***	Y	N	N	Y	Y	Y	Y	Y
3 Lloyd	?	N	N	Y	Y	N	Y	N
4 Cooper	Y	N	N	Y	?	N	Y	N
5 Boner	Y	N	N	Y	Y	N	Y	N
6 Gore	Y	N	N	Y	Y	N	Y	N
7 ***Sundquist***	N	N	N	Y	Y	Y	Y	Y
8 Jones	Y	N	N	Y	Y	N	?	X
9 Ford	Y	N	N	Y	Y	N	Y	N
TEXAS								
1 Hall, S.	N	Y	N	Y	Y	Y	Y	Y
2 Wilson	Y	N	N	Y	?	N	?	?
3 ***Bartlett***	N	?	Y	N	Y	Y	Y	Y
4 Hall, R.	Y	N	N	Y	Y	Y	Y	N
5 Bryant	?	N	N	Y	Y	N	Y	N
6 ***Gramm***	?	?	?	?	N	Y	Y	Y
7 ***Archer***	N	Y	Y	N	N	Y	Y	Y
8 ***Fields***	N	Y	Y	N	N	Y	Y	Y
9 Brooks	Y	N	N	Y	Y	N	Y	N
10 Pickle	Y	N	N	Y	?	?	Y	N
11 Leath	N	N	N	Y	Y	Y	Y	Y
12 Wright	Y	?	?	?	Y	N	?	N
13 Hightower	N	N	N	Y	Y	N	Y	Y
14 Patman	Y	N	N	Y	Y	Y	Y	N
15 de la Garza	Y	N	N	Y	Y	N	Y	N
16 Coleman	Y	N	N	Y	Y	N	Y	N
17 Stenholm	N	N	N	Y	Y	Y	Y	Y
18 Leland	?	?	?	?	Y	N	Y	N
19 Hance	?	?	?	?	?	?	?	X
20 Gonzalez	Y	N	N	Y	Y	N	Y	N
21 ***Loeffler***	N	N	Y	Y	Y	Y	Y	Y
22 ***Paul***	?	#	?	?	?	?	?	#
23 Kazen	Y	N	N	Y	Y	Y	Y	N
24 Frost	Y	N	N	Y	?	N	Y	N
25 Andrews	Y	N	N	Y	Y	Y	Y	Y
26 Vandergriff	N	N	N	Y	Y	Y	Y	N
27 Ortiz	Y	N	N	Y	Y	N	Y	Y
UTAH								
1 ***Hansen***	N	Y	Y	N	N	Y	Y	Y
2 ***Marriott***	N	N	N	Y	Y	Y	?	#
3 ***Nielson***	N	Y	Y	N	N	Y	Y	Y
VERMONT								
AL ***Jeffords***	Y	N	N	Y	Y	N	Y	Y
VIRGINIA								
1 ***Bateman***	N	N	N	Y	Y	Y	Y	Y
2 ***Whitehurst***	?	?	?	?	Y	Y	Y	Y
3 ***Bliley***	N	Y	Y	N	Y	Y	Y	Y
4 Sisisky	Y	N	N	Y	Y	?	?	?
5 Daniel	Y	N	N	Y	Y	Y	Y	Y
6 Olin	Y	N	N	Y	Y	N	Y	N
7 ***Robinson***	N	N	N	Y	Y	Y	Y	Y
8 ***Parris***	N	N	N	Y	Y	Y	Y	Y
9 Boucher	Y	N	N	Y	Y	N	Y	N
10 ***Wolf***	N	N	N	Y	Y	Y	Y	Y
WASHINGTON								
1 ***Pritchard***	N	Y	Y	N	Y	Y	Y	Y
2 Swift	Y	N	N	Y	Y	N	Y	N
3 Bonker	Y	N	N	Y	Y	N	Y	N
4 ***Morrison***	N	N	N	Y	Y	Y	Y	Y
5 Foley	Y	N	N	Y	Y	N	Y	Y
6 Dicks	Y	N	?	?	Y	N	Y	Y
7 Lowry	Y	Y	N	N	Y	N	Y	Y
8 ***Chandler***	Y	Y	Y	N	Y	Y	Y	Y
WEST VIRGINIA								
1 Mollohan	Y	N	N	Y	Y	N	Y	N
2 Staggers	?	N	N	Y	Y	N	Y	N
3 Wise	N	N	N	Y	Y	N	Y	N
4 Rahall	Y	N	N	Y	Y	N	?	N
WISCONSIN								
1 Aspin	Y	N	N	Y	Y	N	Y	Y
2 Kastenmeier	Y	N	N	Y	Y	N	Y	N
3 ***Gunderson***	N	N	N	Y	Y	Y	Y	Y
4 Vacancy								
5 Moody	Y	N	N	Y	Y	N	?	?
6 ***Petri***	N	N	Y	Y	Y	Y	Y	Y
7 Obey	Y	N	N	Y	Y	N	Y	N
8 ***Roth***	N	N	N	Y	Y	Y	?	Y
9 ***Sensenbrenner***	N	N	Y	N	Y	?	Y	Y
WYOMING								
AL ***Cheney***	N	N	Y	Y	N	Y	Y	Y

Southern states - Ala., Ark., Fla., Ga., Ky., La., Miss., N.C., Okla., S.C., Tenn., Texas, Va.

36. HR 4164. Vocational Technical Education Amendments. Bartlett, R-Texas, amendment to prohibit the use of funds under the bill for maintaining existing vocational education programs and to provide aid, in general, only for the improvement and expansion of training programs. Rejected 60-313: R 60-85; D 0-228 (ND 0-150, SD 0-78), March 8, 1984.

37. HR 4164. Vocational Technical Education Amendments. Passage of the bill to extend aid to vocational education through fiscal 1989, authorizing "such sums" as Congress considers necessary. Passed 373-4: R 143-4; D 230-0 (ND 154-0, SD 76-0), March 8, 1984. A "nay" was a vote supporting the president's position.

38. HR 3020. Small Business Authorization. Bliley, R-Va., amendment to eliminate Small Business Administration direct loans, except loans to the handicapped and to minority businesses. Rejected 72-331: R 70-89; D 2-242 (ND 0-161, SD 2-81), March 14, 1984. A "yea" was a vote supporting the president's position.

39. HR 3020. Small Business Authorization. Passage of the bill to authorize $986 million in fiscal 1984, $1.08 billion in fiscal 1985 and $1.12 billion in fiscal 1986 for Small Business Administration programs. Passed 386-11: R 148-8; D 238-3 (ND 162-1, SD 76-2), March 15, 1984.

KEY

Y Voted for (yea).
\# Paired for.
\+ Announced for.
N Voted against (nay).
X Paired against.
- Announced against.
P Voted "present".
C Voted "present" to avoid possible conflict of interest.
? Did not vote or otherwise make a position known.

Democrats *Republicans*

	36	37	38	39
ALABAMA				
1 *Edwards*	Y	Y	N	Y
2 *Dickinson*	Y	Y	Y	Y
3 Nichols	N	Y	?	?
4 Bevill	N	Y	N	Y
5 Flippo	N	Y	N	Y
6 Erdreich	?	+	N	Y
7 Shelby	N	Y	N	Y
ALASKA				
AL *Young*	N	Y	N	Y
ARIZONA				
1 *McCain*	Y	Y	N	Y
2 Udall	N	Y	N	Y
3 *Stump*	Y	Y	Y	Y
4 *Rudd*	?	?	Y	Y
5 McNulty	N	Y	N	Y
ARKANSAS				
1 Alexander	N	Y	N	?
2 *Bethune*	N	Y	N	Y
3 *Hammerschmidt*	N	Y	N	Y
4 Anthony	N	Y	N	Y
CALIFORNIA				
1 Bosco	N	Y	N	Y
2 *Chappie*	Y	Y	N	Y
3 Matsui	N	Y	N	Y
4 Fazio	N	Y	N	Y
5 Burton	N	Y	N	Y
6 Boxer	N	Y	N	?
7 Miller	N	Y	N	Y
8 Dellums	N	Y	N	Y
9 Stark	?	?	?	?
10 Edwards	N	Y	N	Y
11 Lantos	N	Y	N	Y
12 *Zschau*	Y	Y	Y	N
13 Mineta	N	Y	N	Y
14 Shumway	N	N	N	N
15 Coelho	?	?	N	Y
16 Panetta	N	Y	N	Y
17 *Pashayan*	N	Y	N	Y
18 Lehman	N	Y	N	Y
19 *Lagomarsino*	N	Y	N	Y
20 *Thomas*	N	Y	Y	Y
21 *Fiedler*	N	Y	N	Y
22 *Moorhead*	Y	Y	Y	Y
23 Beilenson	N	Y	N	Y
24 Waxman	?	Y	N	Y
25 Roybal	N	Y	?	Y
26 Berman	?	Y	Y	Y
27 Levine	?	Y	N	Y
28 Dixon	N	Y	N	Y
29 Hawkins	N	Y	?	?
30 Martinez	N	Y	N	Y
31 Dymally	N	Y	N	Y
32 Anderson	N	Y	N	Y
33 *Dreier*	Y	Y	Y	Y
34 Torres	N	Y	N	Y
35 *Lewis*	?	Y	Y	Y
36 Brown	N	Y	N	Y
37 *McCandless*	Y	Y	Y	Y
38 Patterson	N	Y	N	Y
39 *Dannemeyer*	Y	Y	Y	Y
40 *Badham*	Y	N	?	Y
41 *Lowery*	Y	Y	N	Y
42 *Lungren*	Y	Y	Y	Y

	36	37	38	39
43 *Packard*	Y	Y	Y	Y
44 Bates	N	Y	N	Y
45 *Hunter*	Y	Y	Y	Y
COLORADO				
1 Schroeder	N	Y	N	Y
2 Wirth	?	?	N	Y
3 Kogovsek	N	Y	N	Y
4 *Brown*	N	Y	Y	Y
5 *Kramer*	Y	Y	Y	Y
6 *Schaefer*	N	Y	N	Y
CONNECTICUT				
1 Kennelly	N	Y	N	Y
2 Gejdenson	N	Y	N	Y
3 Morrison	N	Y	N	Y
4 *McKinney*	?	?	N	Y
5 Ratchford	N	Y	N	Y
6 *Johnson*	N	Y	N	Y
DELAWARE				
AL Carper	N	Y	N	Y
FLORIDA				
1 Hutto	N	Y	N	Y
2 Fuqua	N	?	N	Y
3 Bennett	N	Y	N	Y
4 Chappell	N	Y	N	Y
5 *McCollum*	Y	Y	N	Y
6 MacKay	?	?	N	Y
7 Gibbons	?	?	N	Y
8 *Young*	Y	Y	N	Y
9 *Bilirakis*	?	?	N	Y
10 Ireland	N	Y	N	?
11 Nelson	N	Y	N	Y
12 *Lewis*	N	Y	N	Y
13 *Mack*	Y	Y	Y	Y
14 Mica	N	Y	N	Y
15 *Shaw*	Y	Y	N	Y
16 Smith	N	Y	N	Y
17 Lehman	N	Y	N	Y
18 Pepper	?	?	N	Y
19 Fascell	?	?	N	Y
GEORGIA				
1 Thomas	N	Y	N	Y
2 Hatcher	N	Y	N	Y
3 Ray	N	Y	Y	Y
4 Levitas	N	Y	N	Y
5 Fowler	N	Y	?	?
6 *Gingrich*	Y	Y	Y	Y
7 Darden	N	Y	N	Y
8 Rowland	N	Y	N	Y
9 Jenkins	N	Y	N	Y
10 Barnard	N	Y	N	?
HAWAII				
1 Heftel	?	?	?	?
2 Akaka	N	Y	?	Y
IDAHO				
1 *Craig*	N	Y	Y	Y
2 *Hansen*	N	Y	Y	Y
ILLINOIS				
1 Hayes	N	Y	N	Y
2 Savage	?	Y	?	?
3 Russo	N	Y	N	Y
4 *O'Brien*	Y	Y	N	Y
5 Lipinski	N	Y	N	Y
6 *Hyde*	N	Y	N	Y
7 Collins	?	?	?	?
8 Rostenkowski	N	Y	N	Y
9 Yates	N	Y	N	Y
10 *Porter*	Y	Y	N	Y
11 Annunzio	N	Y	N	Y
12 *Crane, P.*	?	?	Y	N
13 *Erlenborn*	Y	Y	Y	N
14 *Corcoran*	-	+	-	+
15 *Madigan*	Y	Y	N	Y
16 *Martin*	Y	Y	Y	Y
17 Evans	N	Y	N	Y
18 *Michel*	N	Y	N	Y
19 *Crane, D.*	Y	N	Y	?
20 Durbin	N	Y	N	Y
21 Price	N	Y	N	Y
22 Simon	?	?	?	?
INDIANA				
1 Hall	N	Y	N	Y
2 Sharp	N	Y	N	Y
3 *Hiler*	N	Y	Y	?
4 *Coats*	N	Y	N	Y
5 Hillis	Y	Y	Y	Y

ND - Northern Democrats SD - Southern Democrats

	36	37	38	39
6 Burton	Y	Y	Y	N
7 Myers	N	Y	N	Y
8 McCloskey	N	Y	N	Y
9 Hamilton	N	Y	N	Y
10 Jacobs	N	Y	N	Y
IOWA				
1 Leach	?	?	Y	Y
2 Tauke	N	Y	Y	?
3 Evans	N	Y	N	Y
4 Smith	N	Y	N	Y
5 Harkin	N	Y	N	Y
6 Bedell	N	Y	N	Y
KANSAS				
1 Roberts	N	Y	N	Y
2 Slattery	N	Y	N	N
3 Winn	?	?	N	Y
4 Glickman	N	Y	N	Y
5 Whittaker	Y	Y	Y	Y
KENTUCKY				
1 Hubbard	N	Y	N	Y
2 Natcher	N	Y	N	Y
3 Mazzoli	N	Y	N	Y
4 Snyder	N	Y	N	Y
5 Rogers	N	Y	N	Y
6 Hopkins	N	Y	Y	Y
7 Perkins	N	Y	N	Y
LOUISIANA				
1 Livingston	N	Y	Y	Y
2 Boggs	N	Y	N	Y
3 Tauzin	N	Y	N	?
4 Roemer	N	Y	N	Y
5 Huckaby	N	Y	N	Y
6 Moore	N	Y	N	Y
7 Breaux	N	Y	N	Y
8 Long	N	Y	N	Y
MAINE				
1 McKernan	N	Y	N	Y
2 Snowe	N	Y	N	Y
MARYLAND				
1 Dyson	N	Y	N	Y
2 Long	N	Y	N	Y
3 Mikulski	N	Y	N	Y
4 Holt	Y	Y	N	Y
5 Hoyer	N	Y	N	Y
6 Byron	N	Y	N	Y
7 Mitchell	N	Y	N	Y
8 Barnes	N	Y	N	Y
MASSACHUSETTS				
1 Conte	N	Y	N	Y
2 Boland	?	?	N	Y
3 Early	N	Y	?	Y
4 Frank	N	Y	N	Y
5 Shannon	?	?	N	Y
6 Mavroules	N	Y	N	Y
7 Markey	?	?	?	?
8 O'Neill				
9 Moakley	N	Y	N	Y
10 Studds	N	Y	N	Y
11 Donnelly	N	Y	N	Y
MICHIGAN				
1 Conyers	N	Y	N	Y
2 Pursell	N	Y	N	Y
3 Wolpe	N	Y	N	Y
4 Siljander	N	Y	Y	Y
5 Sawyer	N	Y	N	Y
6 Carr	N	Y	N	Y
7 Kildee	N	Y	N	Y
8 Traxler	N	Y	N	Y
9 Vander Jagt	Y	Y	Y	Y
10 Albosta	+	+	N	Y
11 Davis	N	Y	N	Y
12 Bonior	N	Y	N	Y
13 Crockett	N	Y	N	Y
14 Hertel	N	Y	N	Y
15 Ford	N	Y	N	Y
16 Dingell	N	Y	N	Y
17 Levin	N	Y	N	Y
18 Broomfield	?	?	Y	Y
MINNESOTA				
1 Penny	N	Y	N	Y
2 Weber	N	Y	Y	Y
3 Frenzel	+	+	Y	Y
4 Vento	N	Y	N	Y
5 Sabo	N	Y	N	Y
6 Sikorski	N	Y	N	Y

	36	37	38	39
7 Stangeland	N	Y	Y	Y
8 Oberstar	N	Y	N	+
MISSISSIPPI				
1 Whitten	N	Y	N	Y
2 Franklin	N	Y	Y	Y
3 Montgomery	N	Y	N	Y
4 Dowdy	N	Y	N	Y
5 Lott	Y	Y	N	Y
MISSOURI				
1 Clay	?	?	N	Y
2 Young	N	Y	?	Y
3 Gephardt	N	Y	N	Y
4 Skelton	N	Y	N	Y
5 Wheat	N	Y	N	Y
6 Coleman	N	Y	N	Y
7 Taylor	N	Y	Y	Y
8 Emerson	N	Y	N	Y
9 Volkmer	N	Y	N	Y
MONTANA				
1 Williams	N	Y	N	Y
2 Marlenee	N	?	N	Y
NEBRASKA				
1 Bereuter	Y	Y	N	Y
2 Daub	N	Y	N	Y
3 Smith	N	Y	N	Y
NEVADA				
1 Reid	N	Y	N	Y
2 Vucanovich	Y	Y	Y	Y
NEW HAMPSHIRE				
1 D'Amours	?	?	N	Y
2 Gregg	N	Y	Y	Y
NEW JERSEY				
1 Florio	N	Y	N	Y
2 Hughes	N	Y	N	Y
3 Howard	N	Y	N	Y
4 Smith	N	Y	N	Y
5 Roukema	Y	Y	N	Y
6 Dwyer	N	Y	N	Y
7 Rinaldo	N	Y	N	Y
8 Roe	N	Y	N	Y
9 Torricelli	N	Y	N	Y
10 Rodino	N	Y	N	Y
11 Minish	N	Y	N	Y
12 Courter	N	Y	N	Y
13 Forsythe	?	?	?	?
14 Guarini	N	Y	N	Y
NEW MEXICO				
1 Lujan	Y	Y	N	Y
2 Skeen	Y	Y	Y	Y
3 Richardson	N	Y	N	Y
NEW YORK				
1 Carney	?	?	N	Y
2 Downey	?	?	N	Y
3 Mrazek	N	Y	N	Y
4 Lent	N	Y	N	Y
5 McGrath	N	Y	N	Y
6 Addabbo	N	Y	N	Y
7 Ackerman	-	-	N	Y
8 Scheuer	N	Y	N	Y
9 Ferraro	N	Y	N	Y
10 Schumer	N	Y	N	Y
11 Towns	N	Y	?	Y
12 Owens	N	Y	N	Y
13 Solarz	N	Y	N	Y
14 Molinari	N	Y	N	Y
15 Green	N	Y	N	?
16 Rangel	N	Y	N	Y
17 Weiss	N	Y	N	Y
18 Garcia	N	Y	N	Y
19 Biaggi	N	Y	N	Y
20 Ottinger	?	?	N	Y
21 Fish	N	Y	N	Y
22 Gilman	N	Y	N	Y
23 Stratton	N	Y	N	Y
24 Solomon	Y	Y	?	?
25 Boehlert	N	Y	N	Y
26 Martin	Y	Y	N	Y
27 Wortley	Y	Y	N	Y
28 McHugh	?	Y	N	Y
29 Horton	?	?	N	Y
30 Conable	?	Y	Y	Y
31 Kemp	?	Y	Y	Y
32 LaFalce	?	?	N	Y
33 Nowak	N	Y	N	Y
34 Lundine	?	?	N	Y

	36	37	38	39
NORTH CAROLINA				
1 Jones	N	Y	N	Y
2 Valentine	N	Y	N	?
3 Whitley	N	Y	N	Y
4 Andrews	N	?	N	Y
5 Neal	N	Y	N	Y
6 Britt	N	Y	N	Y
7 Rose	N	Y	N	Y
8 Hefner	N	Y	N	Y
9 Martin	N	Y	?	Y
10 Broyhill	N	Y	N	Y
11 Clarke	N	Y	N	Y
NORTH DAKOTA				
AL Dorgan	N	Y	N	Y
OHIO				
1 Luken	N	?	N	Y
2 Gradison	N	Y	?	Y
3 Hall	?	?	N	Y
4 Oxley	N	Y	Y	Y
5 Latta	Y	Y	N	Y
6 McEwen	Y	Y	N	Y
7 DeWine	Y	Y	Y	Y
8 Kindness	?	?	N	Y
9 Kaptur	N	Y	N	Y
10 Miller	N	Y	N	Y
11 Eckart	N	Y	N	Y
12 Kasich	N	Y	N	Y
13 Pease	N	+	N	Y
14 Seiberling	N	+	N	Y
15 Wylie	Y	Y	N	Y
16 Regula	N	Y	N	Y
17 Williams	?	?	N	?
18 Applegate	N	Y	N	Y
19 Feighan	N	Y	N	?
20 Oakar	N	Y	N	Y
21 Stokes	?	?	N	Y
OKLAHOMA				
1 Jones	N	Y	N	Y
2 Synar	+	+	N	N
3 Watkins	N	Y	?	Y
4 McCurdy	?	?	N	Y
5 Edwards	N	Y	N	Y
6 English	N	Y	N	Y
OREGON				
1 AuCoin	N	Y	N	Y
2 Smith, R.	Y	Y	N	Y
3 Wyden	N	Y	N	Y
4 Weaver	N	Y	N	Y
5 Smith, D.	Y	Y	Y	Y
PENNSYLVANIA				
1 Foglietta	?	?	?	?
2 Gray	N	Y	N	Y
3 Borski	N	Y	N	Y
4 Kolter	N	Y	N	Y
5 Schulze	Y	Y	N	Y
6 Yatron	N	Y	N	Y
7 Edgar	N	Y	?	Y
8 Kostmayer	N	Y	?	Y
9 Shuster	Y	Y	Y	Y
10 McDade	N	Y	N	Y
11 Harrison	N	Y	N	Y
12 Murtha	N	Y	N	Y
13 Coughlin	N	Y	N	Y
14 Coyne	N	Y	N	Y
15 Ritter	N	Y	?	Y
16 Walker	Y	Y	Y	Y
17 Gekas	?	?	Y	Y
18 Walgren	N	Y	N	Y
19 Goodling	N	Y	Y	Y
20 Gaydos	N	Y	N	Y
21 Ridge	Y	Y	N	Y
22 Murphy	N	Y	N	Y
23 Clinger	N	Y	N	Y
RHODE ISLAND				
1 St Germain	N	Y	N	?
2 Schneider	N	Y	N	Y
SOUTH CAROLINA				
1 Hartnett	?	?	Y	Y
2 Spence	Y	Y	N	Y
3 Derrick	?	?	N	Y
4 Campbell	N	Y	N	Y
5 Spratt	N	Y	N	Y
6 Tallon	N	Y	N	Y
SOUTH DAKOTA				
AL Daschle	N	Y	N	Y

	36	37	38	39
TENNESSEE				
1 Quillen	N	?	Y	Y
2 Duncan	N	Y	N	Y
3 Lloyd	N	Y	N	Y
4 Cooper	N	Y	N	Y
5 Boner	N	Y	N	Y
6 Gore	N	Y	N	Y
7 Sundquist	N	Y	Y	+
8 Jones	?	+	N	Y
9 Ford	N	Y	N	N
TEXAS				
1 Hall, S.	N	Y	N	Y
2 Wilson	?	?	?	?
3 Bartlett	Y	N	Y	N
4 Hall, R.	N	Y	N	Y
5 Bryant	N	Y	N	?
6 Gramm	Y	Y	Y	N
7 Archer	Y	Y	Y	Y
8 Fields	Y	Y	Y	Y
9 Brooks	N	Y	N	Y
10 Pickle	N	Y	N	Y
11 Leath	N	Y	?	?
12 Wright	N	Y	N	Y
13 Hightower	N	Y	N	Y
14 Patman	N	Y	N	Y
15 de la Garza	N	Y	N	Y
16 Coleman	N	Y	N	Y
17 Stenholm	N	Y	N	Y
18 Leland	N	Y	?	?
19 Hance	?	?	?	?
20 Gonzalez	N	Y	N	Y
21 Loeffler	N	Y	Y	Y
22 Paul	?	?	?	?
23 Kazen	N	Y	N	Y
24 Frost	N	Y	N	Y
25 Andrews	N	Y	N	Y
26 Vandergriff	N	Y	N	Y
27 Ortiz	?	?	N	Y
UTAH				
1 Hansen	?	Y	Y	Y
2 Marriott	?	?	Y	Y
3 Nielson	Y	Y	Y	N
VERMONT				
AL Jeffords	N	Y	N	Y
VIRGINIA				
1 Bateman	Y	Y	Y	Y
2 Whitehurst	N	Y	N	Y
3 Bliley	Y	Y	Y	?
4 Sisisky	N	Y	N	Y
5 Daniel	N	Y	N	Y
6 Olin	N	Y	N	Y
7 Robinson	Y	Y	Y	Y
8 Parris	Y	Y	N	Y
9 Boucher	N	Y	N	Y
10 Wolf	Y	Y	N	Y
WASHINGTON				
1 Pritchard	N	Y	N	Y
2 Swift	N	Y	N	Y
3 Bonker	N	Y	N	Y
4 Morrison	N	Y	N	Y
5 Foley	N	Y	?	Y
6 Dicks	N	Y	N	Y
7 Lowry	N	Y	N	Y
8 Chandler	N	Y	N	Y
WEST VIRGINIA				
1 Mollohan	N	Y	N	?
2 Staggers	N	Y	N	Y
3 Wise	N	Y	N	Y
4 Rahall	N	Y	N	Y
WISCONSIN				
1 Aspin	?	Y	N	Y
2 Kastenmeier	N	Y	N	Y
3 Gunderson	N	Y	N	Y
4 Vacancy				
5 Moody	N	Y	N	Y
6 Petri	N	Y	N	Y
7 Obey	N	Y	N	Y
8 Roth	N	Y	N	Y
9 Sensenbrenner	N	Y	Y	Y
WYOMING				
AL Cheney	Y	Y	Y	Y

Southern states - Ala., Ark., Fla., Ga., Ky., La., Miss., N.C., Okla., S.C., Tenn., Texas, Va.

KEY

Y	Voted for (yea).
#	Paired for.
+	Announced for.
N	Voted against (nay).
X	Paired against.
-	Announced against.
P	Voted "present".
C	Voted "present" to avoid possible conflict of interest.
?	Did not vote or otherwise make a position known.

Democrats   *Republicans*

40. Procedural Motion. Gingrich, R-Ga., motion to approve the House *Journal* of Monday, March 19. Motion agreed to 327-22: R 121-13; D 206-9 (ND 130-8, SD 76-1), March 20, 1984.

41. HR 1652. Reclamation Dam Safety. Edgar, D-Pa., amendment to the Solomon, R-N.Y., amendment, to strike the word "substantially." Both the first- and second-degree amendments required reimbursement by local users and beneficiaries of projects in the bill, which authorized an additional $650 million for safety-related repair of dams administered by the Interior Department's Bureau of Reclamation. Adopted 382-0: R 147-0; D 235-0 (ND 150-0, SD 85-0), March 20, 1984.

42. HR 1652. Reclamation Dam Safety. Kazen, D-Texas, substitute to the Solomon, R-N.Y., amendment, to require reimbursement only for new project benefits by local users and beneficiaries of projects in the bill, which authorized an additional $650 million for safety-related repair of dams administered by the Bureau of Reclamation. Adopted 194-192: R 75-73; D 119-119 (ND 61-91, SD 58-28), March 20, 1984. A "yea" was a vote supporting the president's position.

43. HR 5174. Bankruptcy Court Act. Adoption of the rule (H Res 465) providing for House floor consideration of the bill to provide lifetime appointments for bankruptcy court judges, tighten standards for consumer bankruptcy, make changes affecting grain elevator bankruptcies and limit the circumstances under which union contracts can be rejected by companies that file for bankruptcy. The rule allowed only the Kastenmeier, D-Wis., amendment *(see vote 44, below)* to be offered. Adopted 242-166: R 14-145; D 228-21 (ND 162-4, SD 66-17), March 21, 1984.

44. HR 5174. Bankruptcy Court Act. Kastenmeier, D-Wis., amendment to provide for the appointment of bankruptcy judges as adjuncts to federal district courts, striking the bill's language providing for the appointment of life-tenured bankruptcy judges. Adopted 250-161: R 122-36; D 128-125 (ND 74-96, SD 54-29), March 21, 1984. A "nay" was a vote supporting the president's position. (The bill subsequently was passed by voice vote.)

45. S 684. Water Research Veto. Passage, over President Reagan's Feb. 21 veto, of the bill to authorize $36 million annually for fiscal years 1985 through 1989 for water resources research programs to be administered by the Interior Department, including matching grants for state water research institutes. Passed (thus enacted into law) 309-81: R 69-80; D 240-1 (ND 161-1, SD 79-0), March 22, 1984. A two-thirds majority of those present and voting (260 in this case) of both houses is required to override a veto. A "nay" was a vote supporting the president's position.

46. HR 3755. Social Security Disability Reform Act. Adoption of the rule (H Res 466) providing for House floor consideration of the bill to revamp the Social Security disability review process and to provide payment of benefits to individuals whose cases are under appeal. Adopted 340-40: R 111-37; D 229-3 (ND 157-1, SD 72-2), March 22, 1984.

	40	41	42	43	44	45	46
ALABAMA							
1 *Edwards*	Y	Y	Y	N	Y	Y	Y
2 *Dickinson*	N	Y	Y	N	Y	N	N
3 Nichols	Y	Y	Y	N	Y	Y	Y
4 Bevill	Y	Y	Y	?	Y	Y	Y
5 Flippo	Y	Y	Y	Y	Y	Y	Y
6 Erdreich	Y	Y	Y	Y	N	Y	Y
7 Shelby	Y	Y	Y	N	Y	Y	Y
ALASKA							
AL *Young*	?	Y	Y	N	Y	Y	Y
ARIZONA							
1 *McCain*	Y	Y	Y	N	Y	Y	N
2 Udall	Y	Y	Y	Y	Y	Y	Y
3 *Stump*	Y	Y	Y	N	Y	N	N
4 *Rudd*	Y	Y	Y	N	#	?	?
5 McNulty	Y	Y	Y	Y	Y	Y	Y
ARKANSAS							
1 Alexander	Y	Y	Y	?	?	?	?
2 *Bethune*	Y	Y	Y	N	?	?	?
3 *Hammerschmidt*	Y	Y	Y	N	Y	Y	Y
4 Anthony	Y	Y	N	Y	?	Y	Y
CALIFORNIA							
1 Bosco	?	?	?	Y	N	?	?
2 *Chappie*	N	Y	Y	N	Y	N	Y
3 Matsui	Y	Y	Y	Y	N	Y	Y
4 Fazio	Y	Y	Y	Y	N	Y	Y
5 Burton	Y	Y	Y	Y	Y	Y	Y
6 Boxer	?	?	?	Y	N	Y	Y
7 Miller	Y	Y	Y	Y	Y	Y	Y
8 Dellums	Y	Y	N	Y	N	Y	Y
9 Stark	Y	Y	N	Y	N	Y	Y
10 Edwards	Y	Y	N	Y	N	Y	Y
11 Lantos	Y	Y	Y	Y	N	Y	Y
12 *Zschau*	Y	Y	N	N	Y	N	Y
13 Mineta	Y	Y	Y	Y	N	Y	Y
14 *Shumway*	Y	Y	Y	N	Y	N	N
15 Coelho	Y	Y	Y	Y	Y	Y	Y
16 Panetta	Y	Y	Y	Y	Y	Y	Y
17 *Pashayan*	Y	Y	Y	N	Y	Y	Y
18 Lehman	Y	Y	Y	Y	N	Y	Y
19 *Lagomarsino*	Y	Y	Y	N	Y	N	Y
20 *Thomas*	?	?	?	N	Y	N	N
21 *Fiedler*	Y	Y	Y	N	Y	N	Y
22 *Moorhead*	Y	Y	Y	N	Y	N	N
23 Beilenson	Y	Y	N	Y	N	Y	Y
24 Waxman	?	Y	Y	Y	N	Y	Y
25 Roybal	Y	Y	Y	Y	N	Y	Y
26 Berman	Y	Y	N	Y	N	Y	Y
27 Levine	Y	Y	N	Y	N	Y	Y
28 Dixon	Y	Y	Y	Y	Y	Y	Y
29 Hawkins	N	Y	Y	Y	N	Y	Y
30 Martinez	Y	Y	Y	Y	N	Y	Y
31 Dymally	P	Y	N	Y	N	Y	?
32 Anderson	Y	Y	Y	Y	N	Y	N
33 *Dreier*	?	?	?	X	N	?	?
34 Torres	Y	Y	Y	Y	N	Y	Y
35 *Lewis*	Y	Y	Y	N	Y	N	N
36 Brown	Y	Y	Y	Y	N	Y	Y
37 *McCandless*	Y	Y	Y	-	Y	N	N
38 Patterson	Y	Y	Y	Y	N	Y	Y
39 *Dannemeyer*	Y	Y	Y	N	Y	N	N
40 *Badham*	Y	Y	Y	N	Y	N	N
41 *Lowery*	?	?	Y	N	N	N	Y
42 *Lungren*	Y	Y	Y	N	Y	N	N

	40	41	42	43	44	45	46
43 *Packard*	Y	Y	Y	N	Y	?	?
44 Bates	Y	Y	Y	Y	Y	Y	Y
45 *Hunter*	Y	Y	Y	N	Y	N	N
COLORADO							
1 Schroeder	N	Y	Y	Y	Y	+	+
2 Wirth	Y	Y	Y	Y	N	Y	Y
3 Kogovsek	Y	Y	Y	?	Y	Y	Y
4 *Brown*	Y	Y	Y	N	Y	N	N
5 *Kramer*	Y	Y	Y	N	Y	N	N
6 *Schaefer*	Y	Y	Y	N	Y	N	N
CONNECTICUT							
1 Kennelly	?	?	?	Y	N	Y	Y
2 Gejdenson	N	Y	Y	Y	N	Y	Y
3 Morrison	Y	Y	N	Y	N	Y	Y
4 *McKinney*	?	Y	Y	N	N	Y	Y
5 Ratchford	Y	Y	Y	Y	N	Y	Y
6 *Johnson*	Y	Y	N	Y	N	Y	Y
DELAWARE							
AL Carper	Y	Y	N	Y	N	Y	Y
FLORIDA							
1 Hutto	Y	Y	Y	N	Y	Y	Y
2 Fuqua	Y	Y	Y	Y	Y	Y	Y
3 Bennett	Y	Y	Y	Y	Y	Y	Y
4 Chappell	Y	Y	Y	Y	Y	Y	Y
5 *McCollum*	Y	Y	N	Y	N	Y	N
6 MacKay	Y	N	Y	Y	Y	Y	Y
7 Gibbons	P	Y	N	N	Y	Y	Y
8 *Young*	Y	Y	N	N	Y	N	Y
9 *Bilirakis*	N	Y	N	N	Y	N	N
10 Ireland	?	?	?	?	?	?	?
11 Nelson	+	Y	N	Y	N	Y	Y
12 *Lewis*	Y	Y	N	N	Y	Y	Y
13 *Mack*	Y	Y	N	N	Y	N	N
14 Mica	Y	Y	Y	N	#	?	?
15 *Shaw*	?	Y	N	N	Y	N	N
16 Smith	Y	Y	N	Y	N	Y	Y
17 Lehman	Y	Y	Y	Y	N	Y	Y
18 Pepper	Y	Y	Y	N	Y	?	?
19 Fascell	Y	Y	N	Y	N	Y	Y
GEORGIA							
1 Thomas	Y	Y	N	Y	Y	Y	Y
2 Hatcher	Y	Y	N	?	Y	Y	Y
3 Ray	Y	Y	N	Y	Y	Y	Y
4 Levitas	Y	Y	N	Y	Y	Y	Y
5 Fowler	Y	Y	Y	N	Y	Y	?
6 *Gingrich*	N	Y	N	N	Y	N	Y
7 Darden	Y	Y	N	Y	Y	Y	Y
8 Rowland	Y	Y	N	Y	Y	Y	Y
9 Jenkins	Y	Y	N	Y	Y	Y	Y
10 Barnard	Y	Y	N	Y	Y	?	?
HAWAII							
1 Heftel	?	?	?	?	?	?	?
2 Akaka	Y	Y	Y	Y	N	Y	Y
IDAHO							
1 *Craig*	Y	Y	Y	N	Y	Y	N
2 *Hansen*	Y	?	?	X	?	?	?
ILLINOIS							
1 Hayes	?	?	?	Y	N	Y	Y
2 Savage	?	?	?	?	?	?	?
3 Russo	Y	Y	N	Y	Y	Y	Y
4 *O'Brien*	?	?	?	N	Y	?	?
5 Lipinski	?	?	Y	N	Y	Y	Y
6 *Hyde*	?	?	N	N	Y	N	Y
7 Collins	?	?	?	#	?	?	?
8 Rostenkowski	?	?	?	Y	Y	?	?
9 Yates	N	Y	N	Y	Y	Y	Y
10 *Porter*	?	Y	Y	N	N	Y	Y
11 Annunzio	?	?	?	#	N	Y	Y
12 *Crane, P.*	P	Y	N	N	Y	N	N
13 *Erlenborn*	?	?	?	N	Y	N	Y
14 *Corcoran*	?	?	?	X	?	?	Y
15 *Madigan*	Y	Y	N	N	Y	?	?
16 *Martin*	?	?	?	N	Y	N	Y
17 Evans	?	?	?	Y	N	Y	Y
18 *Michel*	?	?	?	N	Y	N	N
19 *Crane, D.*	?	?	?	N	Y	N	N
20 Durbin	?	?	?	Y	N	Y	Y
21 Price	?	?	?	Y	N	Y	Y
22 Simon	?	?	Y	?	?	?	?
INDIANA							
1 Hall	?	?	?	Y	N	Y	Y
2 Sharp	Y	Y	N	Y	N	Y	Y
3 *Hiler*	Y	Y	N	N	Y	N	N
4 *Coats*	Y	Y	N	N	Y	N	N
5 Hillis	Y	Y	N	N	Y	N	Y

ND - Northern Democrats   SD - Southern Democrats

Corresponding to Congressional Record Votes 47, 48, 49, 51, 52, 53, 54

	40	41	42	43	44	45	46
6 ***Burton***	Y	Y	N	N	Y	N	N
7 ***Myers***	Y	Y	Y	N	Y	Y	Y
8 McCloskey	Y	Y	?	Y	N	Y	Y
9 Hamilton	Y	Y	N	N	Y	Y	Y
10 Jacobs	N	Y	N	N	Y	Y	Y
IOWA							
1 ***Leach***	Y	Y	N	N	N	N	Y
2 ***Tauke***	Y	Y	N	N	N	N	Y
3 ***Evans***	N	Y	N	N	Y	N	?
4 Smith	Y	Y	Y	Y	Y	Y	Y
5 Harkin	?	?	?	Y	N	Y	Y
6 Bedell	Y	Y	N	Y	N	Y	Y
KANSAS							
1 ***Roberts***	N	Y	Y	N	Y	Y	Y
2 Slattery	Y	Y	N	Y	Y	Y	Y
3 ***Winn***	Y	Y	Y	N	Y	N	?
4 Glickman	Y	Y	N	Y	N	Y	Y
5 ***Whittaker***	?	Y	Y	N	Y	Y	Y
KENTUCKY							
1 Hubbard	Y	Y	Y	Y	N	Y	Y
2 Natcher	Y	Y	Y	Y	Y	Y	Y
3 Mazzoli	Y	Y	N	Y	Y	Y	Y
4 ***Snyder***	?	Y	Y	N	Y	N	Y
5 ***Rogers***	Y	Y	Y	N	Y	N	Y
6 ***Hopkins***	Y	Y	Y	N	Y	Y	N
7 Perkins	Y	Y	Y	Y	Y	Y	N
LOUISIANA							
1 ***Livingston***	N	Y	Y	N	Y	Y	Y
2 Boggs	Y	Y	Y	Y	N	Y	Y
3 Tauzin	Y	Y	Y	N	Y	Y	Y
4 Roemer	N	Y	N	N	Y	Y	Y
5 Huckaby	Y	Y	Y	N	Y	Y	Y
6 ***Moore***	Y	Y	Y	N	Y	Y	N
7 Breaux	?	Y	Y	N	Y	Y	?
8 Long	Y	Y	Y	Y	N	Y	Y
MAINE							
1 ***McKernan***	Y	Y	N	N	N	Y	Y
2 ***Snowe***	Y	Y	N	N	N	Y	Y
MARYLAND							
1 Dyson	Y	Y	N	Y	N	Y	Y
2 Long	?	Y	N	Y	Y	Y	Y
3 Mikulski	Y	Y	N	Y	N	Y	Y
4 ***Holt***	Y	?	?	N	Y	N	Y
5 Hoyer	Y	Y	Y	Y	N	Y	Y
6 Byron	Y	Y	N	Y	N	Y	Y
7 Mitchell	?	?	?	#	?	#	?
8 Barnes	Y	Y	Y	Y	N	Y	?
MASSACHUSETTS							
1 ***Conte***	Y	Y	N	Y	N	Y	Y
2 Boland	Y	?	N	#	N	?	?
3 Early	Y	Y	N	Y	N	Y	Y
4 Frank	Y	Y	N	Y	N	Y	Y
5 Shannon	?	?	?	Y	N	Y	Y
6 Mavroules	Y	Y	N	Y	N	Y	Y
7 Markey	?	?	?	Y	N	Y	?
8 O'Neill							
9 Moakley	Y	Y	N	Y	N	Y	Y
10 Studds	Y	Y	N	Y	N	Y	Y
11 Donnelly	Y	Y	Y	Y	N	Y	Y
MICHIGAN							
1 Conyers	Y	Y	N	Y	Y	Y	?
2 ***Pursell***	?	?	?	N	Y	Y	Y
3 Wolpe	Y	Y	N	Y	Y	Y	Y
4 ***Siljander***	?	?	?	N	Y	?	?
5 ***Sawyer***	Y	Y	Y	N	N	Y	Y
6 Carr	Y	Y	N	Y	Y	Y	Y
7 Kildee	Y	Y	N	Y	Y	Y	Y
8 Traxler	Y	Y	N	Y	Y	Y	Y
9 ***Vander Jagt***	Y	Y	N	N	Y	N	Y
10 Albosta	Y	Y	N	Y	Y	+	?
11 ***Davis***	P	?	?	N	Y	Y	Y
12 Bonior	Y	Y	N	Y	Y	Y	Y
13 Crockett	Y	Y	Y	Y	Y	Y	?
14 Hertel	Y	Y	N	Y	Y	Y	Y
15 Ford	?	Y	Y	Y	Y	Y	Y
16 Dingell	?	Y	N	Y	Y	Y	Y
17 Levin	Y	Y	N	Y	Y	Y	Y
18 ***Broomfield***	Y	Y	N	N	Y	N	?
MINNESOTA							
1 Penny	N	Y	N	Y	Y	Y	Y
2 ***Weber***	Y	Y	N	N	Y	N	Y
3 ***Frenzel***	?	?	?	N	Y	N	N
4 Vento	?	Y	N	Y	N	Y	Y
5 Sabo	N	Y	Y	Y	Y	Y	Y
6 Sikorski	P	Y	N	Y	Y	Y	Y
7 ***Stangeland***	Y	Y	Y	N	Y	Y	N
8 Oberstar	?	Y	N	?	Y	Y	Y
MISSISSIPPI							
1 Whitten	Y	Y	Y	Y	Y	Y	Y
2 ***Franklin***	?	Y	Y	N	Y	Y	Y
3 Montgomery	Y	Y	Y	N	Y	Y	Y
4 Dowdy	?	Y	Y	?	N	Y	Y
5 ***Lott***	Y	Y	Y	N	Y	N	Y
MISSOURI							
1 Clay	?	?	?	Y	N	Y	Y
2 Young	Y	Y	Y	Y	Y	Y	Y
3 Gephardt	Y	Y	N	Y	N	Y	Y
4 Skelton	Y	Y	Y	Y	Y	Y	Y
5 Wheat	Y	Y	N	Y	Y	Y	Y
6 ***Coleman***	Y	Y	N	N	Y	Y	Y
7 ***Taylor***	Y	Y	Y	N	Y	N	Y
8 ***Emerson***	N	?	?	N	Y	Y	Y
9 Volkmer	Y	?	N	Y	Y	Y	Y
MONTANA							
1 Williams	Y	Y	N	Y	Y	Y	Y
2 ***Marlenee***	Y	Y	Y	N	N	Y	Y
NEBRASKA							
1 ***Bereuter***	Y	Y	Y	N	Y	Y	Y
2 ***Daub***	Y	Y	Y	N	Y	Y	N
3 ***Smith***	Y	Y	Y	N	N	Y	Y
NEVADA							
1 Reid	Y	Y	Y	Y	N	Y	Y
2 ***Vucanovich***	Y	Y	Y	N	N	Y	Y
NEW HAMPSHIRE							
1 D'Amours	Y	Y	N	Y	N	Y	Y
2 ***Gregg***	Y	Y	N	N	Y	N	N
NEW JERSEY							
1 Florio	Y	Y	N	Y	N	Y	Y
2 Hughes	Y	Y	N	N	N	Y	Y
3 Howard	Y	Y	Y	Y	N	Y	Y
4 ***Smith***	Y	Y	N	Y	N	N	Y
5 ***Roukema***	Y	Y	N	N	N	N	Y
6 Dwyer	Y	Y	N	Y	N	Y	Y
7 ***Rinaldo***	?	Y	N	Y	N	Y	Y
8 Roe	Y	Y	Y	Y	N	Y	Y
9 Torricelli	Y	Y	N	Y	N	Y	Y
10 Rodino	Y	Y	N	Y	N	Y	Y
11 Minish	Y	Y	N	Y	N	#	?
12 ***Courter***	Y	Y	Y	?	Y	N	Y
13 ***Forsythe***	?	?	?	?	?	?	?
14 Guarini	Y	Y	N	Y	N	Y	Y
NEW MEXICO							
1 ***Lujan***	Y	Y	Y	N	Y	Y	Y
2 ***Skeen***	Y	Y	Y	N	Y	Y	Y
3 Richardson	Y	Y	Y	Y	Y	Y	Y
NEW YORK							
1 ***Carney***	Y	Y	Y	N	Y	Y	Y
2 Downey	Y	Y	N	Y	N	Y	Y
3 Mrazek	Y	Y	N	Y	N	Y	Y
4 ***Lent***	Y	Y	N	N	Y	Y	Y
5 ***McGrath***	Y	Y	N	Y	N	Y	Y
6 Addabbo	Y	Y	N	Y	N	Y	Y
7 Ackerman	Y	Y	N	Y	N	Y	Y
8 Scheuer	Y	Y	N	Y	N	?	?
9 Ferraro	Y	Y	N	Y	N	Y	Y
10 Schumer	Y	Y	N	Y	N	Y	Y
11 Towns	?	Y	N	#	N	Y	Y
12 Owens	Y	Y	N	Y	Y	Y	Y
13 Solarz	Y	Y	N	Y	N	Y	Y
14 ***Molinari***	Y	Y	N	N	Y	Y	Y
15 ***Green***	Y	Y	N	Y	N	Y	Y
16 Rangel	Y	Y	N	Y	N	Y	Y
17 Weiss	Y	Y	N	Y	N	Y	Y
18 Garcia	Y	Y	Y	Y	N	Y	Y
19 Biaggi	?	Y	Y	Y	N	Y	Y
20 Ottinger	P	Y	N	Y	Y	Y	Y
21 ***Fish***	Y	Y	N	N	N	Y	?
22 ***Gilman***	Y	Y	N	Y	N	Y	Y
23 Stratton	Y	Y	N	Y	N	Y	Y
24 ***Solomon***	N	Y	N	N	Y	N	Y
25 ***Boehlert***	Y	Y	N	Y	N	Y	Y
26 ***Martin***	Y	Y	N	N	Y	Y	Y
27 ***Wortley***	Y	Y	N	Y	N	?	Y
28 McHugh	Y	Y	N	Y	N	Y	Y
29 ***Horton***	Y	Y	N	Y	N	Y	?
30 ***Conable***	?	Y	N	N	Y	N	Y
31 ***Kemp***	Y	Y	N	N	Y	N	Y
32 LaFalce	Y	Y	N	Y	Y	Y	Y
33 Nowak	Y	Y	N	Y	Y	Y	Y
34 Lundine	Y	?	N	Y	Y	Y	Y
NORTH CAROLINA							
1 Jones	?	Y	Y	Y	Y	Y	Y
2 Valentine	Y	Y	Y	Y	?	?	?
3 Whitley	Y	Y	Y	Y	?	?	?
4 Andrews	Y	Y	N	Y	N	Y	Y
5 Neal	Y	Y	N	Y	N	Y	Y
6 Britt	Y	Y	N	N	Y	Y	Y
7 Rose	Y	Y	Y	Y	Y	Y	Y
8 Hefner	Y	Y	Y	Y	Y	Y	Y
9 ***Martin***	Y	Y	N	Y	Y	Y	Y
10 ***Broyhill***	Y	Y	N	N	Y	Y	Y
11 Clarke	P	Y	Y	Y	Y	Y	Y
NORTH DAKOTA							
AL Dorgan	N	Y	Y	Y	Y	?	Y
OHIO							
1 Luken	Y	Y	Y	Y	N	Y	Y
2 ***Gradison***	Y	Y	N	N	N	N	Y
3 Hall	Y	Y	N	Y	Y	Y	Y
4 ***Oxley***	Y	Y	N	N	Y	N	Y
5 ***Latta***	Y	Y	N	N	Y	N	Y
6 ***McEwen***	Y	Y	Y	N	Y	N	Y
7 ***DeWine***	Y	Y	N	N	N	N	Y
8 ***Kindness***	Y	Y	N	N	Y	N	Y
9 Kaptur	?	Y	N	Y	N	Y	Y
10 ***Miller***	N	Y	N	N	Y	N	Y
11 Eckart	Y	Y	N	Y	Y	Y	Y
12 ***Kasich***	Y	Y	N	N	Y	N	Y
13 Pease	Y	Y	N	Y	N	Y	Y
14 Seiberling	Y	Y	Y	Y	N	N	Y
15 ***Wylie***	Y	Y	Y	N	Y	N	Y
16 ***Regula***	Y	Y	Y	N	N	N	Y
17 ***Williams***	Y	Y	Y	Y	N	N	Y
18 Applegate	Y	Y	N	Y	Y	Y	Y
19 Feighan	?	Y	N	Y	N	Y	Y
20 Oakar	Y	Y	N	Y	N	Y	Y
21 Stokes	Y	Y	N	Y	?	Y	Y
OKLAHOMA							
1 Jones	Y	Y	Y	Y	N	?	?
2 Synar	Y	Y	Y	Y	N	Y	Y
3 Watkins	?	Y	Y	Y	Y	Y	Y
4 McCurdy	Y	Y	Y	Y	Y	Y	Y
5 ***Edwards***	Y	Y	Y	N	Y	Y	Y
6 English	Y	Y	Y	Y	Y	Y	Y
OREGON							
1 AuCoin	Y	Y	Y	Y	Y	Y	Y
2 ***Smith, R.***	Y	Y	Y	N	Y	Y	Y
3 Wyden	Y	Y	Y	Y	Y	Y	Y
4 Weaver	?	?	?	Y	Y	Y	Y
5 ***Smith, D.***	Y	Y	Y	N	Y	Y	N
PENNSYLVANIA							
1 Foglietta	?	?	?	Y	N	?	?
2 Gray	Y	Y	N	Y	Y	Y	Y
3 Borski	Y	Y	N	Y	N	Y	Y
4 Kolter	Y	Y	Y	Y	Y	Y	Y
5 ***Schulze***	Y	Y	N	N	N	Y	Y
6 Yatron	Y	Y	N	Y	Y	Y	Y
7 Edgar	Y	Y	N	+	N	Y	Y
8 Kostmayer	Y	Y	N	Y	Y	Y	Y
9 ***Shuster***	Y	Y	N	N	Y	N	Y
10 ***McDade***	?	Y	N	Y	N	N	Y
11 Harrison	?	?	?	Y	Y	Y	Y
12 Murtha	Y	Y	Y	N	Y	Y	Y
13 ***Coughlin***	N	Y	N	N	Y	Y	Y
14 Coyne	Y	Y	N	Y	Y	Y	Y
15 ***Ritter***	Y	Y	N	Y	N	N	Y
16 ***Walker***	N	Y	N	N	Y	N	N
17 ***Gekas***	Y	Y	N	N	Y	?	Y
18 Walgren	Y	Y	N	Y	N	Y	Y
19 ***Goodling***	N	Y	Y	N	Y	N	Y
20 Gaydos	Y	Y	Y	Y	Y	Y	Y
21 ***Ridge***	Y	Y	N	N	N	Y	Y
22 Murphy	Y	Y	Y	Y	Y	Y	Y
23 ***Clinger***	Y	Y	N	N	N	Y	Y
RHODE ISLAND							
1 St Germain	P	Y	Y	Y	Y	Y	Y
2 ***Schneider***	Y	Y	N	Y	X	X	?
SOUTH CAROLINA							
1 ***Hartnett***	?	Y	N	X	?	?	?
2 ***Spence***	Y	Y	N	N	Y	Y	Y
3 Derrick	Y	Y	Y	Y	Y	Y	Y
4 ***Campbell***	?	Y	N	N	Y	Y	Y
5 Spratt	Y	Y	N	Y	N	Y	Y
6 Tallon	Y	Y	N	Y	Y	Y	Y
SOUTH DAKOTA							
AL Daschle	Y	Y	Y	Y	Y	Y	Y
TENNESSEE							
1 ***Quillen***	Y	Y	Y	N	N	N	Y
2 ***Duncan***	Y	Y	Y	N	Y	Y	Y
3 Lloyd	Y	Y	Y	Y	N	Y	Y
4 Cooper	Y	Y	N	Y	N	Y	Y
5 Boner	Y	Y	Y	Y	N	?	?
6 Gore	Y	Y	Y	Y	N	Y	Y
7 ***Sundquist***	Y	Y	Y	N	Y	N	Y
8 Jones	Y	Y	Y	Y	N	Y	Y
9 Ford	Y	Y	Y	Y	N	Y	Y
TEXAS							
1 Hall, S.	Y	Y	Y	N	Y	Y	Y
2 Wilson	?	?	Y	?	?	?	?
3 ***Bartlett***	Y	Y	Y	N	Y	N	N
4 Hall, R.	Y	Y	Y	N	Y	Y	Y
5 Bryant	?	?	?	Y	Y	Y	Y
6 ***Gramm***	Y	Y	Y	N	Y	N	N
7 ***Archer***	Y	Y	N	N	Y	N	Y
8 ***Fields***	?	Y	N	N	Y	N	Y
9 Brooks	Y	Y	Y	Y	Y	Y	Y
10 Pickle	Y	Y	Y	Y	Y	Y	Y
11 Leath	Y	Y	Y	N	Y	Y	Y
12 Wright	Y	Y	Y	Y	Y	Y	?
13 Hightower	Y	Y	Y	N	Y	Y	Y
14 Patman	Y	Y	Y	N	Y	Y	Y
15 de la Garza	?	?	?	Y	Y	Y	?
16 Coleman	Y	Y	Y	Y	Y	Y	Y
17 Stenholm	Y	Y	Y	N	Y	Y	Y
18 Leland	?	Y	N	Y	N	Y	Y
19 Hance	?	?	?	?	?	?	?
20 Gonzalez	Y	Y	Y	Y	Y	Y	Y
21 ***Loeffler***	Y	Y	Y	N	Y	N	Y
22 ***Paul***	?	?	?	X	?	X	?
23 Kazen	Y	Y	Y	N	Y	Y	Y
24 Frost	Y	Y	Y	Y	Y	Y	Y
25 Andrews	Y	Y	Y	Y	Y	Y	Y
26 Vandergriff	Y	Y	Y	N	Y	Y	Y
27 Ortiz	Y	Y	Y	Y	Y	#	?
UTAH							
1 ***Hansen***	Y	Y	Y	N	Y	?	?
2 ***Marriott***	Y	Y	Y	N	Y	?	?
3 ***Nielson***	Y	Y	Y	N	Y	?	N
VERMONT							
AL ***Jeffords***	Y	Y	N	N	N	Y	Y
VIRGINIA							
1 ***Bateman***	Y	Y	Y	N	Y	Y	Y
2 ***Whitehurst***	Y	Y	Y	N	N	Y	Y
3 ***Bliley***	Y	Y	N	N	N	N	N
4 Sisisky	Y	Y	N	Y	N	Y	Y
5 Daniel	Y	Y	N	Y	N	Y	N
6 Olin	Y	Y	N	Y	N	Y	Y
7 ***Robinson***	Y	Y	N	N	Y	N	Y
8 ***Parris***	Y	Y	N	N	Y	Y	Y
9 Boucher	Y	Y	N	Y	N	Y	Y
10 ***Wolf***	Y	Y	N	N	Y	N	Y
WASHINGTON							
1 ***Pritchard***	?	Y	Y	N	Y	N	Y
2 Swift	Y	Y	Y	Y	Y	Y	Y
3 Bonker	Y	Y	Y	Y	Y	Y	Y
4 ***Morrison***	Y	Y	Y	N	Y	Y	Y
5 Foley	Y	Y	Y	Y	N	Y	Y
6 Dicks	Y	Y	Y	Y	Y	Y	Y
7 Lowry	Y	Y	Y	Y	Y	Y	Y
8 ***Chandler***	Y	Y	Y	N	Y	Y	Y
WEST VIRGINIA							
1 Mollohan	?	Y	Y	Y	Y	Y	Y
2 Staggers	Y	Y	N	Y	Y	Y	Y
3 Wise	Y	Y	Y	Y	Y	Y	Y
4 Rahall	Y	Y	Y	Y	N	Y	Y
WISCONSIN							
1 Aspin	Y	Y	N	Y	Y	Y	Y
2 Kastenmeier	Y	Y	N	Y	Y	Y	Y
3 ***Gunderson***	P	Y	N	N	N	N	Y
4 Vacancy							
5 Moody	Y	Y	N	Y	Y	Y	Y
6 ***Petri***	Y	Y	N	N	Y	N	Y
7 Obey	Y	Y	N	Y	Y	Y	Y
8 ***Roth***	?	?	?	N	Y	Y	Y
9 ***Sensenbrenner***	Y	Y	N	N	Y	N	Y
WYOMING							
AL ***Cheney***	Y	Y	Y	N	Y	N	?

Southern states - Ala., Ark., Fla., Ga., Ky., La., Miss., N.C., Okla., S.C., Tenn., Texas, Va.

KEY

Y Voted for (yea).
\# Paired for.
\+ Announced for.
N Voted against (nay).
X Paired against.
- Announced against.
P Voted "present".
C Voted "present" to avoid possible conflict of interest.
? Did not vote or otherwise make a position known.

———

Democrats *Republicans*

47. HR 3755. Social Security Disability Reform Act. Passage of the bill to revamp the Social Security disability review process and to provide payment of benefits to individuals whose cases were under appeal. Passed 410-1: R 160-1; D 250-0 (ND 164-0, SD 86-0), March 27, 1984. A "nay" was a vote supporting the president's position.

48. Procedural Motion. Weber, R-Minn., motion to approve the House *Journal* of Tuesday, March 27. Motion agreed to 363-27: R 143-14; D 220-13 (ND 138-12, SD 82-1), March 28, 1984.

49. HR 5154. National Aeronautics and Space Administration Authorization. Passage of the bill to authorize $7.5 billion in fiscal 1985 for programs of the National Aeronautics and Space Administration and to establish a National Commission on Space. Passed 389-11: R 158-3; D 231-8 (ND 148-8, SD 83-0), March 28, 1984.

50. H J Res 517. Department of Housing and Urban Development, Fiscal 1984 Urgent Supplemental Appropriations. Passage of the joint resolution to allocate $2.5 billion of reserved and unused budget authority for subsidized housing. Passed 340-55: R 113-43; D 227-12 (ND 156-6, SD 71-6), March 29, 1984.

51. H Res 443. Hunger Committee Funds. Adoption of the resolution to provide $449,250 between March 1, 1984, and Jan. 3, 1985, for investigations and other expenses of the House Select Committee on Hunger. Adopted 288-109: R 64-92; D 224-17 (ND 157-5, SD 67-12), March 29, 1984.

52. HR 4841. Coast Guard Authorization. Adoption of the rule (H Res 472) providing for House floor consideration of the bill to authorize appropriations of $2.4 billion in fiscal 1985 and $2.6 billion in fiscal 1986 for the Coast Guard. Adopted 394-0: R 156-0; D 238-0 (ND 160-0, SD 78-0), March 29, 1984.

53. HR 4841. Coast Guard Authorization. Passage of the bill to authorize appropriations of $2.4 billion in fiscal 1985 and $2.6 billion in fiscal 1986 for the Coast Guard. Passed 348-38: R 122-34; D 226-4 (ND 151-4, SD 75-0), March 29, 1984. A "nay" was a vote supporting the president's position.

	47	48	49	50	51	52	53
ALABAMA							
1 Edwards	Y	Y	Y	Y	N	Y	Y
2 *Dickinson*	Y	N	Y	Y	N	Y	N
3 Nichols	Y	Y	Y	Y	Y	Y	Y
4 Bevill	Y	Y	Y	Y	Y	Y	Y
5 Flippo	Y	Y	Y	Y	Y	Y	Y
6 Erdreich	Y	Y	Y	Y	Y	Y	Y
7 Shelby	Y	Y	Y	Y	Y	Y	Y
ALASKA							
AL *Young*	Y	N	Y	?	N	Y	Y
ARIZONA							
1 *McCain*	Y	Y	Y	Y	Y	Y	Y
2 Udall	Y	Y	Y	Y	Y	Y	Y
3 *Stump*	Y	Y	Y	N	N	Y	N
4 *Rudd*	Y	Y	Y	?	?	?	?
5 McNulty	Y	Y	Y	Y	Y	Y	Y
ARKANSAS							
1 Alexander	Y	Y	?	?	?	Y	Y
2 *Bethune*	Y	Y	Y	Y	N	Y	Y
3 *Hammerschmidt*	Y	Y	Y	Y	Y	Y	Y
4 Anthony	Y	Y	?	?	Y	Y	Y
CALIFORNIA							
1 Bosco	Y	Y	Y	Y	Y	Y	Y
2 *Chappie*	Y	N	Y	N	Y	Y	Y
3 Matsui	Y	Y	Y	Y	Y	Y	Y
4 Fazio	+	Y	Y	Y	Y	Y	Y
5 Burton	Y	Y	Y	Y	Y	Y	Y
6 Boxer	Y	Y	Y	Y	Y	Y	Y
7 Miller	Y	P	Y	Y	Y	Y	Y
8 Dellums	Y	Y	Y	Y	Y	Y	Y
9 Stark	Y	Y	?	?	Y	Y	Y
10 Edwards	Y	Y	Y	Y	Y	Y	Y
11 Lantos	Y	Y	Y	Y	Y	Y	Y
12 Zschau	Y	Y	Y	Y	N	Y	Y
13 Mineta	Y	Y	Y	Y	Y	Y	Y
14 *Shumway*	Y	Y	Y	N	N	Y	N
15 Coelho	Y	Y	Y	Y	Y	Y	Y
16 Panetta	Y	Y	Y	Y	Y	Y	Y
17 *Pashayan*	Y	Y	Y	Y	?	?	?
18 Lehman	Y	Y	Y	Y	Y	Y	Y
19 *Lagomarsino*	Y	Y	Y	Y	N	Y	Y
20 *Thomas*	Y	Y	Y	Y	N	Y	Y
21 *Fiedler*	Y	Y	Y	Y	Y	?	Y
22 *Moorhead*	Y	Y	Y	N	N	Y	Y
23 Beilenson	Y	Y	Y	Y	Y	Y	Y
24 Waxman	?	?	?	Y	Y	?	Y
25 Roybal	Y	Y	Y	Y	Y	Y	Y
26 Berman	Y	Y	Y	Y	Y	Y	Y
27 Levine	Y	Y	Y	Y	Y	Y	Y
28 Dixon	Y	Y	Y	?	Y	Y	Y
29 Hawkins	Y	N	?	Y	Y	?	Y
30 Martinez	Y	?	Y	Y	Y	Y	Y
31 Dymally	Y	P	Y	Y	Y	?	?
32 Anderson	Y	Y	Y	Y	Y	Y	Y
33 *Dreier*	Y	Y	Y	N	N	Y	N
34 Torres	Y	Y	Y	Y	Y	Y	Y
35 *Lewis*	Y	Y	Y	Y	N	Y	Y
36 Brown	Y	Y	Y	Y	Y	Y	Y
37 *McCandless*	Y	Y	Y	N	N	Y	Y
38 Patterson	Y	Y	Y	Y	Y	Y	Y
39 *Dannemeyer*	Y	Y	Y	N	N	Y	N
40 *Badham*	Y	Y	Y	Y	N	Y	Y
41 *Lowery*	Y	Y	Y	Y	N	Y	Y
42 *Lungren*	Y	Y	Y	N	N	Y	N
43 *Packard*	Y	Y	Y	Y	N	Y	Y
44 Bates	Y	Y	Y	Y	Y	Y	Y
45 *Hunter*	Y	Y	Y	N	Y	Y	Y
COLORADO							
1 Schroeder	Y	N	Y	Y	Y	Y	Y
2 Wirth	Y	Y	?	Y	Y	Y	Y
3 Kogovsek	Y	Y	Y	Y	Y	Y	Y
4 *Brown*	Y	Y	Y	N	N	Y	N
5 *Kramer*	Y	Y	Y	N	Y	Y	Y
6 *Schaefer*	Y	Y	Y	N	Y	Y	N
CONNECTICUT							
1 Kennelly	Y	Y	Y	Y	Y	Y	Y
2 Gejdenson	Y	N	Y	Y	Y	Y	Y
3 Morrison	?	Y	Y	Y	Y	Y	Y
4 *McKinney*	Y	Y	Y	Y	Y	Y	Y
5 Ratchford	Y	Y	Y	Y	Y	Y	Y
6 *Johnson*	Y	?	Y	Y	N	Y	Y
DELAWARE							
AL Carper	Y	Y	Y	Y	Y	Y	Y
FLORIDA							
1 Hutto	Y	Y	Y	Y	N	Y	Y
2 Fuqua	Y	Y	Y	Y	Y	Y	?
3 Bennett	Y	Y	Y	Y	Y	Y	Y
4 Chappell	Y	Y	Y	Y	Y	Y	Y
5 *McCollum*	Y	Y	Y	N	N	Y	Y
6 MacKay	Y	Y	Y	N	Y	Y	Y
7 Gibbons	Y	Y	Y	N	N	Y	Y
8 *Young*	Y	Y	Y	Y	N	Y	Y
9 *Bilirakis*	Y	Y	Y	N	N	Y	Y
10 Ireland	?	?	?	?	?	?	?
11 Nelson	Y	Y	Y	Y	Y	+	Y
12 *Lewis*	Y	Y	Y	Y	Y	Y	Y
13 *Mack*	Y	Y	Y	N	N	Y	Y
14 Mica	Y	Y	Y	Y	Y	Y	Y
15 *Shaw*	Y	Y	Y	Y	Y	Y	Y
16 Smith	Y	Y	Y	Y	Y	Y	Y
17 Lehman	Y	Y	Y	Y	Y	Y	Y
18 Pepper	Y	Y	Y	Y	Y	Y	Y
19 Fascell	Y	Y	Y	Y	Y	Y	Y
GEORGIA							
1 Thomas	Y	Y	Y	Y	Y	Y	Y
2 Hatcher	Y	Y	Y	Y	Y	Y	Y
3 Ray	Y	Y	Y	Y	Y	Y	Y
4 Levitas	Y	Y	Y	Y	Y	Y	Y
5 Fowler	Y	Y	Y	Y	Y	Y	Y
6 *Gingrich*	Y	Y	Y	Y	Y	Y	Y
7 Darden	Y	Y	Y	Y	Y	Y	Y
8 Rowland	Y	Y	Y	Y	Y	Y	Y
9 Jenkins	Y	Y	Y	Y	N	Y	Y
10 Barnard	Y	Y	Y	Y	Y	Y	?
HAWAII							
1 Heftel	?	?	?	?	?	?	?
2 Akaka	Y	Y	Y	Y	Y	?	Y
IDAHO							
1 *Craig*	Y	Y	Y	?	?	?	?
2 *Hansen*	?	?	?	?	?	?	?
ILLINOIS							
1 Hayes	Y	Y	Y	Y	Y	Y	Y
2 Savage	Y	?	?	?	?	?	?
3 Russo	Y	Y	N	N	Y	Y	Y
4 *O'Brien*	Y	Y	Y	Y	Y	Y	Y
5 Lipinski	Y	N	Y	Y	Y	Y	Y
6 *Hyde*	Y	Y	Y	Y	N	Y	Y
7 Collins	Y	Y	Y	Y	Y	Y	Y
8 Rostenkowski	Y	Y	Y	Y	Y	Y	Y
9 Yates	Y	N	Y	Y	Y	Y	Y
10 *Porter*	Y	P	Y	Y	Y	Y	Y
11 Annunzio	Y	Y	Y	Y	Y	Y	Y
12 *Crane, P.*	N	Y	Y	N	N	Y	N
13 *Erlenborn*	?	Y	Y	Y	N	Y	Y
14 *Corcoran*	Y	+	+	+	+	+	+
15 *Madigan*	Y	Y	Y	N	N	Y	N
16 *Martin*	Y	Y	Y	N	N	Y	N
17 Evans	Y	Y	Y	Y	Y	Y	Y
18 *Michel*	Y	Y	Y	Y	N	Y	Y
19 *Crane, D.*	Y	N	Y	N	N	Y	N
20 Durbin	Y	N	Y	Y	Y	Y	Y
21 Price	Y	Y	Y	Y	Y	Y	Y
22 Simon	Y	Y	Y	Y	Y	Y	Y
INDIANA							
1 Hall	?	Y	Y	Y	Y	Y	Y
2 Sharp	Y	Y	Y	Y	Y	Y	Y
3 *Hiler*	Y	Y	Y	Y	N	Y	N
4 *Coats*	Y	Y	Y	Y	N	Y	Y
5 Hillis	Y	Y	Y	N	N	Y	Y

Corresponding to Congressional Record Votes 55, 56, 57, 58, 59, 60, 61

	47	48	49	50	51	52	53
6 *Burton*	Y	N	Y	N	N	Y	N
7 *Myers*	Y	Y	Y	Y	Y	Y	Y
8 McCloskey	Y	Y	Y	Y	Y	Y	Y
9 Hamilton	Y	Y	Y	Y	Y	Y	Y
10 Jacobs	Y	N	N	Y	N	Y	Y
IOWA							
1 *Leach*	Y	Y	Y	Y	Y	Y	Y
2 *Tauke*	Y	Y	Y	N	N	Y	N
3 *Evans*	Y	N	Y	N	N	Y	Y
4 Smith	Y	Y	Y	Y	Y	Y	Y
5 Harkin	Y	N	Y	Y	?	Y	Y
6 Bedell	Y	Y	Y	Y	Y	Y	Y
KANSAS							
1 *Roberts*	Y	N	Y	N	N	Y	N
2 Slattery	Y	Y	N	N	Y	Y	N
3 *Winn*	Y	Y	Y	N	N	Y	N
4 Glickman	Y	Y	Y	N	N	Y	N
5 *Whittaker*	Y	Y	Y	Y	N	Y	N
KENTUCKY							
1 Hubbard	Y	Y	Y	N	N	Y	Y
2 Natcher	Y	Y	Y	Y	Y	Y	Y
3 Mazzoli	Y	Y	Y	Y	Y	Y	Y
4 *Snyder*	Y	Y	Y	N	N	Y	Y
5 *Rogers*	Y	Y	Y	Y	Y	Y	Y
6 *Hopkins*	Y	Y	Y	Y	N	Y	Y
7 Perkins	Y	Y	Y	?	?	?	?
LOUISIANA							
1 *Livingston*	Y	Y	Y	Y	N	Y	Y
2 Boggs	Y	Y	Y	Y	Y	Y	Y
3 Tauzin	Y	Y	Y	Y	Y	Y	Y
4 Roemer	Y	N	Y	Y	N	Y	Y
5 Huckaby	Y	Y	Y	Y	Y	Y	Y
6 *Moore*	Y	Y	Y	Y	Y	Y	Y
7 Breaux	?	Y	Y	Y	Y	Y	Y
8 Long	Y	Y	Y	Y	Y	Y	Y
MAINE							
1 *McKernan*	Y	Y	Y	Y	Y	Y	Y
2 *Snowe*	Y	Y	Y	Y	Y	Y	Y
MARYLAND							
1 Dyson	Y	Y	Y	Y	Y	Y	Y
2 Long	Y	Y	Y	Y	Y	Y	Y
3 Mikulski	Y	Y	Y	Y	Y	Y	Y
4 *Holt*	Y	Y	Y	Y	N	Y	Y
5 Hoyer	Y	Y	Y	Y	Y	Y	Y
6 Byron	Y	Y	Y	Y	N	Y	Y
7 Mitchell	Y	N	Y	Y	Y	Y	Y
8 Barnes	Y	Y	Y	Y	Y	Y	Y
MASSACHUSETTS							
1 *Conte*	Y	Y	Y	Y	Y	Y	Y
2 Boland	Y	Y	Y	Y	Y	Y	Y
3 Early	Y	Y	Y	Y	Y	Y	?
4 Frank	Y	Y	Y	Y	Y	Y	Y
5 Shannon	Y	?	Y	Y	Y	Y	Y
6 Mavroules	Y	Y	?	Y	Y	Y	Y
7 Markey	Y	?	?	?	?	?	?
8 O'Neill							
9 Moakley	Y	Y	Y	Y	Y	Y	Y
10 Studds	Y	Y	Y	Y	Y	Y	Y
11 Donnelly	Y	Y	?	?	?	?	?
MICHIGAN							
1 Conyers	Y	Y	N	Y	Y	Y	Y
2 *Pursell*	Y	Y	Y	N	N	Y	Y
3 Wolpe	Y	Y	Y	Y	Y	Y	Y
4 *Siljander*	Y	Y	Y	Y	?	Y	Y
5 *Sawyer*	Y	Y	Y	Y	Y	Y	Y
6 Carr	Y	Y	Y	Y	Y	Y	Y
7 Kildee	Y	Y	Y	Y	Y	Y	Y
8 Traxler	Y	Y	Y	Y	Y	Y	?
9 *Vander Jagt*	Y	Y	Y	Y	Y	Y	Y
10 Albosta	Y	Y	Y	Y	Y	Y	Y
11 *Davis*	Y	Y	Y	Y	Y	Y	Y
12 Bonior	Y	Y	?	Y	Y	Y	Y
13 Crockett	Y	?	Y	Y	Y	?	Y
14 Hertel	Y	Y	Y	Y	Y	Y	Y
15 Ford	Y	Y	Y	Y	Y	Y	Y
16 Dingell	Y	Y	Y	Y	Y	Y	?
17 Levin	Y	Y	Y	Y	Y	Y	Y
18 *Broomfield*	Y	Y	Y	Y	Y	Y	Y
MINNESOTA							
1 Penny	Y	N	N	Y	Y	Y	Y
2 *Weber*	Y	Y	Y	N	N	Y	Y
3 *Frenzel*	Y	?	N	N	N	Y	N
4 Vento	Y	Y	Y	Y	Y	Y	Y
5 Sabo	Y	N	Y	Y	Y	Y	Y
6 Sikorski	Y	P	Y	Y	Y	Y	Y

	47	48	49	50	51	52	53
7 *Stangeland*	Y	Y	Y	Y	Y	Y	Y
8 Oberstar	Y	Y	N	Y	Y	Y	Y
MISSISSIPPI							
1 Whitten	Y	?	Y	Y	Y	Y	?
2 *Franklin*	Y	Y	Y	Y	Y	Y	Y
3 Montgomery	Y	Y	Y	N	N	Y	Y
4 Dowdy	Y	Y	Y	Y	Y	Y	Y
5 *Lott*	Y	Y	Y	N	N	Y	Y
MISSOURI							
1 Clay	Y	N	Y	Y	Y	Y	Y
2 Young	Y	Y	Y	?	?	?	?
3 Gephardt	+	Y	Y	Y	Y	Y	Y
4 Skelton	Y	Y	Y	Y	Y	Y	Y
5 Wheat	Y	Y	Y	Y	Y	Y	Y
6 *Coleman*	Y	Y	Y	Y	Y	Y	Y
7 *Taylor*	Y	Y	Y	N	N	Y	Y
8 *Emerson*	Y	N	Y	Y	N	Y	Y
9 Volkmer	Y	Y	Y	Y	N	Y	Y
MONTANA							
1 Williams	Y	Y	Y	Y	Y	Y	Y
2 *Marlenee*	?	Y	Y	Y	N	Y	Y
NEBRASKA							
1 *Bereuter*	Y	Y	Y	Y	Y	Y	Y
2 *Daub*	Y	Y	Y	Y	N	Y	Y
3 *Smith*	Y	Y	Y	Y	N	Y	Y
NEVADA							
1 Reid	Y	Y	Y	Y	Y	Y	Y
2 *Vucanovich*	Y	Y	Y	Y	N	Y	N
NEW HAMPSHIRE							
1 D'Amours	Y	Y	Y	Y	Y	Y	Y
2 *Gregg*	Y	Y	Y	Y	N	Y	?
NEW JERSEY							
1 Florio	Y	Y	Y	Y	Y	Y	Y
2 Hughes	Y	Y	Y	N	Y	Y	Y
3 Howard	Y	Y	Y	Y	Y	Y	Y
4 *Smith*	Y	Y	Y	Y	Y	Y	Y
5 *Roukema*	Y	Y	Y	Y	Y	Y	Y
6 Dwyer	Y	Y	Y	Y	Y	Y	Y
7 *Rinaldo*	Y	Y	Y	Y	Y	Y	Y
8 Roe	Y	Y	Y	Y	Y	Y	Y
9 Torricelli	Y	Y	Y	Y	Y	Y	Y
10 Rodino	Y	Y	Y	Y	Y	Y	Y
11 Minish	Y	Y	?	Y	Y	Y	Y
12 *Courter*	Y	Y	Y	Y	Y	Y	Y
13 *Forsythe* *	?	?	?				
14 Guarini	Y	Y	Y	Y	Y	Y	Y
NEW MEXICO							
1 *Lujan*	Y	Y	Y	Y	Y	Y	N
2 *Skeen*	Y	Y	Y	Y	N	Y	N
3 Richardson	Y	Y	Y	Y	Y	Y	Y
NEW YORK							
1 *Carney*	Y	?	Y	Y	Y	Y	Y
2 Downey	Y	Y	Y	Y	Y	Y	Y
3 Mrazek	Y	Y	Y	Y	?	Y	Y
4 *Lent*	Y	Y	Y	Y	N	Y	Y
5 *McGrath*	Y	Y	Y	Y	Y	Y	Y
6 Addabbo	Y	Y	Y	Y	Y	Y	Y
7 Ackerman	Y	Y	Y	Y	Y	Y	Y
8 Scheuer	Y	Y	Y	Y	Y	Y	Y
9 Ferraro	?	Y	Y	Y	Y	Y	Y
10 Schumer	Y	Y	Y	Y	Y	Y	Y
11 Towns	Y	Y	Y	?	Y	Y	Y
12 Owens	Y	Y	Y	?	Y	Y	Y
13 Solarz	Y	Y	Y	Y	Y	Y	Y
14 *Molinari*	Y	Y	Y	Y	Y	Y	Y
15 *Green*	Y	Y	Y	Y	N	Y	Y
16 Rangel	Y	Y	Y	Y	?	?	?
17 Weiss	Y	Y	Y	Y	Y	Y	Y
18 Garcia	Y	Y	Y	Y	Y	Y	Y
19 Biaggi	?	?	?	?	?	?	?
20 Ottinger	Y	?	?	Y	Y	Y	Y
21 *Fish*	Y	?	Y	Y	Y	Y	Y
22 *Gilman*	Y	Y	Y	Y	Y	Y	Y
23 Stratton	Y	P	Y	Y	?	?	?
24 *Solomon*	Y	N	Y	N	?	Y	Y
25 *Boehlert*	Y	Y	Y	Y	Y	Y	Y
26 *Martin*	Y	Y	Y	Y	Y	Y	Y
27 *Wortley*	Y	Y	Y	Y	Y	Y	Y
28 McHugh	Y	?	Y	Y	Y	Y	Y
29 *Horton*	Y	Y	Y	Y	Y	Y	Y
30 *Conable*	Y	Y	N	Y	N	Y	N
31 *Kemp*	Y	Y	Y	Y	N	?	Y
32 LaFalce	Y	Y	Y	Y	Y	Y	Y
33 Nowak	Y	Y	Y	Y	Y	Y	Y
34 Lundine	Y	?	Y	Y	Y	Y	Y

	47	48	49	50	51	52	53
NORTH CAROLINA							
1 Jones	Y	Y	Y	Y	Y	Y	Y
2 Valentine	Y	Y	Y	Y	Y	Y	Y
3 Whitley	Y	Y	Y	?	?	?	?
4 Andrews	Y	Y	?	?	?	?	?
5 Neal	Y	Y	Y	Y	Y	Y	Y
6 Britt	Y	Y	Y	Y	Y	Y	Y
7 Rose	Y	Y	?	?	?	?	?
8 Hefner	Y	Y	Y	Y	Y	Y	Y
9 *Martin*	Y	Y	Y	?	N	Y	Y
10 *Broyhill*	Y	Y	Y	N	N	Y	Y
11 Clarke	Y	P	Y	Y	Y	Y	Y
NORTH DAKOTA							
AL Dorgan	Y	Y	Y	N	Y	Y	N
OHIO							
1 Luken	Y	Y	Y	Y	Y	Y	Y
2 *Gradison*	Y	Y	Y	Y	N	Y	Y
3 Hall	Y	Y	Y	?	?	?	?
4 *Oxley*	Y	Y	Y	Y	N	Y	Y
5 *Latta*	Y	Y	Y	N	N	Y	Y
6 *McEwen*	Y	Y	Y	Y	Y	Y	Y
7 *DeWine*	Y	Y	Y	Y	N	Y	N
8 *Kindness*	Y	Y	Y	N	N	Y	Y
9 Kaptur	Y	?	Y	Y	Y	Y	?
10 *Miller*	Y	N	Y	Y	Y	Y	Y
11 Eckart	Y	Y	Y	Y	Y	Y	Y
12 *Kasich*	Y	Y	Y	Y	Y	Y	Y
13 Pease	Y	Y	Y	Y	Y	Y	Y
14 Seiberling	Y	Y	Y	Y	Y	Y	Y
15 *Wylie*	Y	Y	Y	Y	Y	Y	Y
16 *Regula*	Y	Y	Y	Y	Y	Y	Y
17 *Williams*	Y	Y	Y	Y	Y	Y	Y
18 Applegate	Y	Y	Y	Y	Y	Y	Y
19 Feighan	Y	Y	Y	Y	Y	Y	?
20 Oakar	Y	Y	Y	Y	Y	Y	?
21 Stokes	Y	?	Y	Y	Y	Y	+
OKLAHOMA							
1 Jones	Y	Y	Y	Y	N	Y	Y
2 Synar	Y	Y	Y	Y	Y	Y	Y
3 Watkins	Y	Y	Y	Y	Y	Y	Y
4 McCurdy	Y	Y	Y	?	?	?	?
5 *Edwards*	Y	N	Y	Y	N	Y	Y
6 English	Y	Y	Y	Y	Y	Y	Y
OREGON							
1 AuCoin	Y	Y	Y	Y	Y	Y	Y
2 *Smith, R.*	Y	Y	Y	Y	N	Y	Y
3 Wyden	Y	Y	Y	Y	Y	Y	Y
4 Weaver	Y	Y	N	Y	Y	Y	Y
5 *Smith, D.*	Y	?	Y	N	N	Y	N
PENNSYLVANIA							
1 Foglietta	?	?	?	?	?	?	?
2 Gray	Y	?	?	Y	Y	Y	Y
3 Borski	Y	Y	Y	Y	Y	Y	Y
4 Kolter	Y	Y	Y	Y	Y	Y	Y
5 *Schulze*	Y	Y	?	Y	Y	Y	N
6 Yatron	Y	Y	Y	Y	Y	Y	Y
7 Edgar	Y	?	Y	Y	Y	Y	Y
8 Kostmayer	Y	Y	Y	Y	Y	Y	Y
9 *Shuster*	Y	Y	Y	N	N	Y	N
10 *McDade*	Y	Y	Y	Y	Y	Y	Y
11 Harrison	Y	?	?	Y	Y	Y	?
12 Murtha	Y	Y	Y	Y	Y	Y	Y
13 *Coughlin*	?	N	Y	Y	Y	Y	Y
14 Coyne	Y	Y	Y	Y	Y	Y	Y
15 *Ritter*	Y	Y	Y	Y	Y	Y	Y
16 *Walker*	Y	N	Y	N	N	Y	N
17 *Gekas*	Y	Y	Y	Y	Y	Y	Y
18 Walgren	Y	Y	Y	Y	Y	Y	Y
19 *Goodling*	Y	N	Y	?	?	?	?
20 Gaydos	?	?	?	?	?	?	?
21 *Ridge*	Y	Y	Y	Y	Y	Y	Y
22 Murphy	Y	Y	Y	Y	N	Y	Y
23 *Clinger*	Y	Y	Y	Y	Y	Y	Y
RHODE ISLAND							
1 St Germain	Y	P	Y	Y	Y	Y	?
2 *Schneider*	Y	Y	Y	Y	Y	Y	Y
SOUTH CAROLINA							
1 *Hartnett*	Y	Y	N	N	N	Y	Y
2 *Spence*	Y	Y	Y	Y	N	Y	Y
3 Derrick	Y	Y	Y	Y	Y	Y	Y
4 *Campbell*	Y	Y	?	Y	N	Y	Y
5 Spratt	Y	Y	Y	Y	Y	Y	Y
6 Tallon	Y	Y	Y	#	?	?	?
SOUTH DAKOTA							
AL Daschle	?	Y	?	Y	Y	Y	Y

	47	48	49	50	51	52	53
TENNESSEE							
1 *Quillen*	Y	Y	Y	Y	Y	Y	?
2 *Duncan*	Y	Y	Y	Y	Y	Y	Y
3 Lloyd	Y	Y	Y	Y	Y	Y	Y
4 Cooper	Y	Y	Y	Y	Y	Y	Y
5 Boner	Y	Y	Y	Y	Y	Y	Y
6 Gore	Y	Y	Y	Y	Y	Y	Y
7 *Sundquist*	Y	Y	Y	Y	N	Y	Y
8 Jones	Y	Y	Y	Y	Y	Y	Y
9 Ford	Y	Y	Y	Y	Y	Y	?
TEXAS							
1 Hall, S.	Y	Y	Y	Y	Y	Y	Y
2 Wilson	?	Y	Y	Y	Y	?	?
3 *Bartlett*	Y	Y	Y	Y	N	Y	N
4 Hall, R.	Y	Y	Y	Y	N	Y	Y
5 Bryant	Y	Y	Y	Y	Y	Y	Y
6 *Gramm*	Y	Y	Y	N	N	Y	N
7 *Archer*	Y	Y	Y	N	N	Y	Y
8 *Fields*	Y	Y	Y	N	N	Y	Y
9 Brooks	Y	Y	Y	Y	Y	Y	Y
10 Pickle	Y	Y	Y	Y	Y	Y	Y
11 Leath	Y	Y	Y	N	N	Y	Y
12 Wright	Y	Y	Y	?	Y	Y	Y
13 Hightower	Y	Y	Y	Y	Y	Y	Y
14 Patman	Y	Y	Y	Y	Y	Y	Y
15 de la Garza	Y	Y	Y	Y	Y	Y	Y
16 Coleman	Y	Y	Y	Y	Y	Y	Y
17 Stenholm	Y	Y	Y	N	N	Y	Y
18 Leland	Y	?	Y	Y	Y	Y	Y
19 Hance	?	?	?	X	?	?	?
20 Gonzalez	Y	Y	Y	Y	Y	Y	Y
21 *Loeffler*	Y	Y	Y	N	N	Y	N
22 *Paul*	?	?	?	?	?	?	?
23 Kazen	Y	?	?	?	?	?	?
24 Frost	Y	Y	Y	Y	Y	Y	Y
25 Andrews	Y	Y	Y	Y	Y	Y	Y
26 Vandergriff	Y	Y	Y	Y	Y	Y	Y
27 Ortiz	Y	?	Y	Y	Y	Y	Y
UTAH							
1 *Hansen*	Y	Y	Y	N	N	Y	Y
2 *Marriott*	Y	Y	Y	Y	N	Y	Y
3 *Nielson*	Y	Y	Y	N	N	Y	N
VERMONT							
AL *Jeffords*	Y	Y	Y	Y	Y	Y	N
VIRGINIA							
1 *Bateman*	Y	Y	Y	Y	N	Y	Y
2 *Whitehurst*	Y	Y	Y	Y	Y	Y	Y
3 *Bliley*	Y	Y	Y	Y	Y	Y	Y
4 Sisisky	Y	Y	Y	Y	Y	Y	Y
5 Daniel	Y	Y	Y	Y	N	Y	Y
6 Olin	Y	Y	Y	Y	N	Y	Y
7 *Robinson*	Y	Y	Y	?	N	Y	Y
8 *Parris*	Y	Y	Y	N	Y	Y	Y
9 Boucher	Y	Y	Y	?	?	?	?
10 *Wolf*	Y	Y	Y	Y	Y	Y	Y
WASHINGTON							
1 *Pritchard*	Y	Y	Y	Y	Y	Y	Y
2 Swift	Y	Y	Y	Y	Y	Y	Y
3 Bonker	Y	?	?	?	?	Y	Y
4 *Morrison*	Y	Y	Y	Y	Y	Y	Y
5 Foley	+	Y	Y	Y	Y	Y	Y
6 Dicks	Y	?	Y	Y	Y	Y	Y
7 Lowry	Y	Y	Y	Y	Y	Y	Y
8 *Chandler*	Y	Y	Y	Y	N	Y	Y
WEST VIRGINIA							
1 Mollohan	Y	Y	Y	Y	Y	Y	Y
2 Staggers	Y	Y	Y	Y	Y	Y	Y
3 Wise	Y	Y	?	Y	Y	Y	Y
4 Rahall	Y	Y	Y	Y	Y	Y	Y
WISCONSIN							
1 Aspin	Y	Y	Y	Y	Y	Y	Y
2 Kastenmeier	Y	Y	Y	Y	Y	Y	Y
3 *Gunderson*	Y	Y	Y	Y	Y	Y	N
4 Vacancy							
5 Moody	Y	Y	Y	N	Y	Y	N
6 *Petri*	Y	Y	Y	N	N	Y	Y
7 Obey	Y	?	N	Y	Y	Y	Y
8 *Roth*	Y	Y	Y	Y	N	Y	Y
9 *Sensenbrenner*	Y	Y	Y	N	N	Y	N
WYOMING							
AL *Cheney*	Y	Y	Y	?	?	?	?

** Rep. Edwin B. Forsythe, R-N.J., died March 29, 1984. The last vote for which he was eligible was CQ vote 49.*

Southern states - Ala., Ark., Fla., Ga., Ky., La., Miss., N.C., Okla., S.C., Tenn., Texas, Va.

54. HR 4072. Agricultural Programs Adjustment. Adoption of the conference report on the bill to cut 1984 and 1985 target prices for wheat and freeze 1985 target prices for corn, cotton and rice at 1984 levels, to provide for 1985 acreage reduction programs for these crops and to revise certain conditions for Farmers Home Administration loans. Adopted 379-11: R 152-2; D 227-9 (ND 151-8, SD 76-1), April 3, 1984. A "yea" was a vote supporting the president's position.

55. HR 4707. Arizona Wilderness. McNulty, D-Ariz., motion to suspend the rules and pass the bill to designate approximately 1.2 million acres of national forest and Bureau of Land Management land in Arizona as federally protected wilderness. Motion agreed to 335-56: R 113-42; D 222-14 (ND 157-3, SD 65-11), April 3, 1984. A two-thirds majority of those present and voting (261 in this case) is required for passage under suspension of the rules.

56. HR 5026. Credit Card Surcharge Ban. Annunzio, D-Ill., motion to suspend the rules and pass the bill to extend until May 31, 1985, the ban on merchants' adding a surcharge for purchases made with credit cards. Motion agreed to 355-34: R 135-19; D 220-15 (ND 150-9, SD 70-6), April 3, 1984. A two-thirds majority of those present and voting (260 in this case) is required for passage under suspension of the rules.

57. H Con Res 280. First Budget Resolution, Fiscal 1985. Adoption of the rule (H Res 476) providing for House floor consideration of the concurrent resolution to set budget targets for the fiscal year ending Sept. 30, 1985. Under the rule, the budget committee's "pay-as-you-go" budget plan plus seven substitute budgets were made in order. Adopted 302-89: R 72-83; D 230-6 (ND 150-5, SD 80-1), April 4, 1984.

58. H Con Res 280. First Budget Resolution, Fiscal 1985. Wirth, D-Colo., substitute to provide spending and revenue levels for fiscal 1985 as submitted by President Reagan on Feb. 1, 1984. Rejected 1-401: R 1-155; D 0-246 (ND 0-165, SD 0-81), April 4, 1984.

59. H Con Res 280. First Budget Resolution, Fiscal 1985. Dannemeyer, R-Calif., substitute to reduce federal deficits $206 billion over three years by cutting spending $136 billion and raising taxes $7 billion. Rejected 51-354: R 50-107; D 1-247 (ND 0-168, SD 1-79), April 4, 1984.

60. H Con Res 280. First Budget Resolution, Fiscal 1985. Roemer, D-La., substitute proposed by the Conservative Democratic Forum to reduce deficits $225 billion over three years by cutting spending $53 billion and raising revenues $70 billion. Rejected 59-338: R 33-123; D 26-215 (ND 4-158, SD 22-57), April 4, 1984.

KEY

- **Y** Voted for (yea).
- **#** Paired for.
- **+** Announced for.
- **N** Voted against (nay).
- **X** Paired against.
- **-** Announced against.
- **P** Voted "present".
- **C** Voted "present" to avoid possible conflict of interest.
- **?** Did not vote or otherwise make a position known.

Democrats *Republicans*

	54	55	56	57	58	59	60
43 *Packard*	Y	N	Y	N	N	Y	Y
44 Bates	Y	Y	Y	Y	N	N	N
45 *Hunter*	Y	N	Y	Y	N	Y	N
COLORADO							
1 Schroeder	Y	Y	Y	Y	N	N	N
2 Wirth	Y	Y	N	Y	N	N	N
3 Kogovsek	Y	Y	Y	Y	N	N	N
4 *Brown*	Y	Y	N	N	Y	N	Y
5 *Kramer*	Y	Y	Y	N	N	N	N
6 *Schaefer*	Y	N	N	N	N	Y	N
CONNECTICUT							
1 Kennelly	Y	Y	Y	Y	N	N	N
2 Gejdenson	Y	Y	Y	Y	N	N	N
3 Morrison	Y	Y	Y	Y	N	N	N
4 *McKinney*	?	?	?	Y	N	N	N
5 Ratchford	Y	Y	Y	Y	N	N	N
6 *Johnson*	?	Y	Y	N	N	N	N
DELAWARE							
AL Carper	Y	Y	Y	Y	N	N	N
FLORIDA							
1 Hutto	Y	Y	Y	Y	N	N	Y
2 Fuqua	Y	Y	Y	Y	N	N	Y
3 Bennett	Y	Y	Y	Y	N	N	N
4 Chappell	Y	Y	Y	Y	N	N	Y
5 *McCollum*	Y	Y	Y	N	N	Y	N
6 MacKay	Y	Y	Y	Y	N	N	N
7 Gibbons	Y	Y	N	Y	N	N	N
8 *Young*	Y	Y	Y	N	N	N	N
9 *Bilirakis*	Y	Y	Y	N	N	Y	N
10 Ireland	Y	N	Y	N	N	Y	Y
11 Nelson	N	Y	Y	Y	N	N	N
12 *Lewis*	Y	Y	Y	N	N	N	N
13 *Mack*	Y	Y	Y	N	N	Y	N
14 Mica	Y	Y	Y	Y	N	N	N
15 *Shaw*	Y	Y	Y	N	N	N	N
16 Smith	Y	Y	Y	N	N	N	N
17 Lehman	Y	Y	Y	Y	?	?	?
18 Pepper	Y	Y	Y	Y	N	N	N
19 Fascell	?	?	?	Y	?	?	?
GEORGIA							
1 Thomas	Y	Y	Y	Y	N	N	N
2 Hatcher	Y	Y	Y	Y	N	N	N
3 Ray	Y	N	Y	#	?	?	#
4 Levitas	Y	Y	Y	N	N	N	Y
5 Fowler	Y	Y	Y	N	N	N	N
6 *Gingrich*	Y	Y	Y	N	N	Y	N
7 Darden	Y	Y	Y	?	N	N	Y
8 Rowland	Y	Y	Y	N	N	N	N
9 Jenkins	Y	Y	Y	N	N	N	N
10 Barnard	Y	N	Y	N	N	N	Y
HAWAII							
1 Heftel	?	?	?	?	?	?	?
2 Akaka	Y	Y	Y	Y	N	N	N
IDAHO							
1 *Craig*	Y	Y	Y	N	N	Y	N
2 *Hansen*	?	?	?	?	?	?	?
ILLINOIS							
1 Hayes	Y	Y	Y	?	N	N	N
2 Savage	?	?	?	?	?	?	?
3 Russo	N	Y	Y	N	N	N	N
4 *O'Brien*	Y	Y	Y	N	N	N	N
5 Lipinski	Y	Y	Y	Y	N	N	N
6 *Hyde*	?	?	?	?	?	?	?
7 Collins	Y	Y	Y	?	N	N	N
8 Rostenkowski	Y	Y	Y	?	N	N	N
9 Yates	N	Y	Y	Y	N	N	N
10 *Porter*	Y	Y	Y	N	N	N	Y
11 Annunzio	Y	Y	Y	Y	N	N	N
12 *Crane, P.*	?	?	?	N	N	Y	N
13 *Erlenborn*	N	N	N	Y	?	?	?
14 *Corcoran*	Y	Y	Y	N	N	N	N
15 *Madigan*	Y	Y	Y	N	N	N	N
16 *Martin*	Y	Y	Y	N	N	N	N
17 Evans	Y	Y	Y	N	N	N	N
18 *Michel*	Y	Y	Y	N	N	N	N
19 *Crane, D.*	Y	N	N	X	N	Y	N
20 Durbin	Y	Y	Y	Y	N	N	N
21 Price	Y	Y	Y	Y	N	N	N
22 Simon	?	?	?	Y	N	N	N
INDIANA							
1 Hall	?	?	?	Y	N	N	N
2 Sharp	Y	Y	Y	Y	N	N	N
3 *Hiler*	Y	Y	Y	N	N	N	N
4 *Coats*	Y	Y	Y	N	N	N	N
5 *Hillis*	Y	Y	Y	Y	N	Y	Y

	54	55	56	57	58	59	60
ALABAMA							
1 *Edwards*	Y	Y	Y	Y	N	Y	N
2 *Dickinson*	Y	N	Y	Y	N	?	?
3 Nichols	Y	Y	Y	Y	N	N	N
4 Bevill	Y	Y	Y	Y	N	N	N
5 Flippo	Y	Y	Y	Y	N	N	N
6 Erdreich	Y	Y	Y	Y	N	N	N
7 Shelby	Y	Y	Y	Y	N	N	N
ALASKA							
AL *Young*	Y	N	N	N	N	N	N
ARIZONA							
1 *McCain*	Y	Y	Y	N	N	Y	N
2 Udall	?	Y	Y	Y	N	N	N
3 *Stump*	Y	N	N	N	N	N	N
4 *Rudd*	Y	N	?	Y	N	Y	N
5 McNulty	Y	Y	Y	Y	N	N	N
ARKANSAS							
1 Alexander	Y	Y	Y	Y	N	?	N
2 *Bethune*	Y	Y	Y	N	N	N	N
3 *Hammerschmidt*	Y	N	Y	Y	N	N	Y
4 Anthony	Y	Y	Y	?	N	N	Y
CALIFORNIA							
1 Bosco	Y	Y	Y	Y	?	N	N
2 *Chappie*	Y	Y	Y	N	N	N	N
3 Matsui	Y	Y	Y	?	N	N	N
4 Fazio	Y	Y	Y	?	N	N	N
5 Burton	Y	Y	Y	N	N	N	N
6 Boxer	Y	Y	Y	N	N	N	N
7 Miller	Y	Y	N	N	N	N	N
8 Dellums	Y	Y	Y	N	N	N	N
9 Stark	Y	Y	N	Y	N	N	?
10 Edwards	Y	Y	Y	N	N	N	N
11 Lantos	?	?	?	Y	N	N	N
12 *Zschau*	Y	Y	Y	N	N	N	Y
13 Mineta	Y	Y	Y	N	N	N	N
14 *Shumway*	Y	N	N	N	N	N	N
15 Coelho	?	?	?	Y	N	N	N
16 Panetta	Y	Y	Y	Y	N	N	N
17 *Pashayan*	Y	Y	Y	N	N	N	N
18 Lehman	Y	Y	Y	?	N	N	N
19 *Lagomarsino*	Y	Y	Y	N	N	N	N
20 *Thomas*	Y	N	N	Y	N	N	N
21 *Fiedler*	Y	Y	Y	N	N	N	N
22 *Moorhead*	Y	Y	Y	N	Y	N	N
23 Beilenson	Y	Y	N	?	N	N	N
24 Waxman	Y	Y	Y	N	N	N	N
25 Roybal	Y	Y	Y	Y	N	N	N
26 Berman	Y	Y	?	Y	?	N	N
27 Levine	Y	Y	N	N	N	N	N
28 Dixon	Y	Y	Y	Y	N	N	N
29 Hawkins	?	?	?	#	?	?	?
30 Martinez	Y	Y	Y	Y	N	N	N
31 Dymally	Y	Y	Y	N	N	N	N
32 Anderson	N	Y	Y	N	N	N	N
33 *Dreier*	Y	N	N	N	Y	N	N
34 Torres	Y	Y	Y	Y	N	N	N
35 *Lewis*	Y	N	Y	N	N	N	N
36 Brown	Y	Y	Y	N	N	N	N
37 *McCandless*	Y	N	Y	N	N	Y	N
38 Patterson	Y	Y	Y	N	N	N	Y
39 *Dannemeyer*	Y	N	N	N	N	N	N
40 *Badham*	Y	N	N	N	Y	N	N
41 *Lowery*	Y	Y	Y	N	N	N	Y
42 *Lungren*	?	?	?	X	N	Y	N

ND - Northern Democrats   SD - Southern Democrats

Corresponding to Congressional Record Votes 62, 63, 64, 65, 66, 67, 68

	54	55	56	57	58	59	60
6 ***Burton***	Y	N	Y	N	N	Y	N
7 ***Myers***	Y	N	Y	N	N	N	N
8 McCloskey	Y	Y	Y	Y	N	N	N
9 Hamilton	Y	Y	Y	Y	N	N	N
10 Jacobs	N	Y	Y	N	N	N	N
IOWA							
1 ***Leach***	Y	Y	Y	Y	?	N	N
2 ***Tauke***	Y	Y	Y	Y	N	N	Y
3 ***Evans***	Y	Y	Y	?	N	N	N
4 Smith	Y	Y	Y	Y	N	N	N
5 Harkin	Y	Y	Y	?	N	N	N
6 Bedell	Y	Y	Y	Y	N	N	N
KANSAS							
1 ***Roberts***	Y	N	Y	N	N	N	Y
2 Slattery	Y	Y	Y	Y	N	N	Y
3 ***Winn***	Y	Y	Y	Y	N	N	N
4 Glickman	Y	Y	Y	Y	N	N	N
5 ***Whittaker***	Y	N	Y	Y	N	N	Y
KENTUCKY							
1 Hubbard	?	?	?	?	?	?	?
2 Natcher	Y	Y	Y	Y	N	N	N
3 Mazzoli	Y	Y	Y	Y	N	N	N
4 ***Snyder***	Y	Y	Y	N	N	N	N
5 ***Rogers***	Y	N	Y	Y	N	N	N
6 ***Hopkins***	Y	N	N	N	N	N	N
7 Perkins	Y	Y	N	Y	N	N	N
LOUISIANA							
1 ***Livingston***	Y	N	?	N	N	Y	Y
2 Boggs	Y	Y	Y	Y	N	N	N
3 Tauzin	Y	Y	Y	Y	N	N	Y
4 Roemer	Y	Y	N	Y	N	N	Y
5 Huckaby	Y	Y	Y	Y	N	N	Y
6 ***Moore***	Y	Y	Y	N	N	N	Y
7 Breaux	Y	Y	Y	Y	N	N	Y
8 Long	Y	Y	Y	Y	N	N	N
MAINE							
1 ***McKernan***	Y	Y	Y	Y	N	N	N
2 ***Snowe***	Y	Y	Y	Y	N	N	N
MARYLAND							
1 Dyson	Y	Y	Y	Y	N	N	N
2 Long	Y	Y	Y	Y	N	N	Y
3 Mikulski	Y	Y	Y	Y	N	N	N
4 ***Holt***	Y	N	Y	Y	N	N	Y
5 Hoyer	Y	Y	?	Y	N	N	N
6 Byron	Y	N	Y	Y	N	N	Y
7 Mitchell	Y	Y	Y	Y	N	N	X
8 Barnes	Y	Y	Y	Y	N	N	N
MASSACHUSETTS							
1 ***Conte***	Y	Y	Y	N	N	N	N
2 Boland	Y	Y	Y	Y	N	N	N
3 Early	Y	Y	Y	Y	N	N	N
4 Frank	N	Y	N	Y	?	?	?
5 Shannon	?	?	?	?	N	N	N
6 Mavroules	Y	Y	Y	Y	N	N	N
7 Markey	?	?	?	?	-	-	-
8 O'Neill							
9 Moakley	Y	Y	Y	Y	N	N	N
10 Studds	Y	Y	Y	Y	N	N	N
11 Donnelly	Y	Y	Y	Y	N	N	N
MICHIGAN							
1 Conyers	Y	Y	Y	Y	N	N	N
2 ***Pursell***	Y	Y	Y	N	N	N	N
3 Wolpe	Y	Y	Y	Y	N	N	N
4 ***Siljander***	Y	Y	Y	N	N	Y	N
5 ***Sawyer***	Y	Y	Y	N	N	N	N
6 Carr	Y	Y	Y	Y	N	N	?
7 Kildee	Y	Y	Y	Y	N	N	N
8 Traxler	Y	Y	Y	Y	N	N	N
9 ***Vander Jagt***	Y	Y	Y	?	?	?	?
10 Albosta	Y	Y	Y	Y	N	N	N
11 ***Davis***	Y	Y	Y	Y	N	N	N
12 Bonior	Y	Y	Y	Y	N	N	N
13 Crockett	Y	Y	Y	Y	N	N	N
14 Hertel	Y	Y	Y	Y	N	N	N
15 Ford	Y	Y	Y	Y	N	N	N
16 Dingell	Y	Y	Y	Y	N	N	N
17 Levin	Y	Y	Y	Y	N	N	N
18 ***Broomfield***	Y	Y	Y	N	N	Y	N
MINNESOTA							
1 Penny	Y	Y	Y	Y	N	N	N
2 ***Weber***	Y	Y	Y	N	N	Y	N
3 ***Frenzel***	Y	Y	Y	N	N	N	N
4 Vento	Y	Y	Y	Y	N	N	N
5 Sabo	Y	Y	Y	Y	N	N	N
6 Sikorski	Y	Y	Y	Y	N	N	N

	54	55	56	57	58	59	60
7 ***Stangeland***	Y	?	Y	Y	?	N	N
8 Oberstar	Y	Y	Y	Y	N	N	N
MISSISSIPPI							
1 Whitten	Y	Y	Y	Y	N	N	N
2 ***Franklin***	Y	Y	Y	N	N	N	Y
3 Montgomery	Y	N	N	Y	N	N	Y
4 Dowdy	?	?	?	Y	N	N	N
5 ***Lott***	Y	Y	Y	Y	N	N	N
MISSOURI							
1 Clay	Y	Y	Y	Y	N	N	N
2 Young	Y	Y	Y	Y	N	N	N
3 Gephardt	Y	Y	Y	Y	N	N	N
4 Skelton	Y	N	Y	Y	N	N	N
5 Wheat	Y	Y	Y	Y	N	N	N
6 ***Coleman***	Y	Y	Y	Y	N	N	N
7 ***Taylor***	Y	N	Y	Y	N	N	N
8 ***Emerson***	Y	N	Y	?	N	N	N
9 Volkmer	Y	Y	Y	Y	N	N	N
MONTANA							
1 Williams	Y	Y	Y	Y	N	N	?
2 ***Marlenee***	Y	Y	Y	Y	N	N	N
NEBRASKA							
1 ***Bereuter***	Y	Y	Y	Y	N	N	Y
2 ***Daub***	Y	Y	Y	N	N	Y	N
3 ***Smith***	Y	Y	Y	Y	N	N	N
NEVADA							
1 Reid	Y	Y	Y	Y	N	N	N
2 ***Vucanovich***	Y	N	N	N	N	Y	N
NEW HAMPSHIRE							
1 D'Amours	N	Y	Y	Y	N	N	N
2 ***Gregg***	Y	Y	Y	N	N	N	N
NEW JERSEY							
1 Florio	Y	Y	Y	Y	N	N	N
2 Hughes	N	Y	Y	N	N	N	N
3 Howard	Y	Y	Y	Y	N	N	N
4 ***Smith***	Y	Y	Y	Y	N	N	N
5 ***Roukema***	Y	Y	Y	N	N	N	Y
6 Dwyer	Y	Y	Y	Y	N	N	N
7 ***Rinaldo***	Y	Y	Y	Y	N	N	N
8 Roe	Y	Y	Y	?	N	N	N
9 Torricelli	Y	Y	Y	Y	N	N	N
10 Rodino	Y	Y	Y	Y	N	N	N
11 Minish	?	?	?	Y	N	N	N
12 ***Courter***	Y	Y	N	Y	N	N	N
13 Vacancy							
14 Guarini	Y	Y	Y	Y	N	N	N
NEW MEXICO							
1 ***Lujan***	Y	Y	Y	N	N	Y	Y
2 ***Skeen***	Y	N	Y	Y	N	N	N
3 Richardson	Y	Y	Y	Y	N	N	N
NEW YORK							
1 ***Carney***	Y	Y	Y	N	N	N	N
2 Downey	Y	Y	Y	Y	N	N	N
3 Mrazek	Y	Y	Y	Y	N	N	N
4 ***Lent***	?	?	?	N	N	N	?
5 ***McGrath***	Y	Y	Y	N	N	N	N
6 Addabbo	Y	Y	Y	Y	N	N	?
7 Ackerman	Y	Y	Y	Y	N	N	N
8 Scheuer	Y	Y	Y	Y	N	N	N
9 Ferraro	Y	Y	Y	Y	N	N	N
10 Schumer	Y	Y	Y	Y	N	N	N
11 Towns	?	?	?	?	?	N	N
12 Owens	+	+	+	Y	N	N	N
13 Solarz	Y	Y	Y	Y	N	N	N
14 ***Molinari***	Y	Y	Y	N	N	N	N
15 ***Green***	Y	Y	Y	Y	N	N	N
16 Rangel	Y	Y	Y	#	N	N	N
17 Weiss	Y	Y	Y	Y	N	N	N
18 Garcia	Y	Y	Y	Y	N	N	N
19 Biaggi	Y	Y	Y	Y	N	N	N
20 Ottinger	Y	Y	N	Y	?	?	?
21 ***Fish***	Y	Y	Y	N	N	N	N
22 ***Gilman***	Y	Y	Y	N	N	N	N
23 Stratton	Y	N	Y	Y	N	N	N
24 ***Solomon***	Y	Y	Y	N	N	Y	N
25 ***Boehlert***	?	?	?	X	?	X	?
26 ***Martin***	Y	N	Y	Y	N	N	N
27 ***Wortley***	Y	N	Y	Y	N	N	Y
28 McHugh	Y	Y	Y	Y	N	N	N
29 ***Horton***	Y	Y	Y	N	N	N	N
30 ***Conable***	N	Y	Y	Y	N	Y	N
31 ***Kemp***	Y	Y	Y	X	Y	Y	N
32 LaFalce	Y	Y	N	N	N	N	N
33 Nowak	Y	Y	Y	Y	N	N	N
34 Lundine	Y	Y	Y	Y	N	N	N

	54	55	56	57	58	59	60
NORTH CAROLINA							
1 Jones	Y	Y	Y	Y	N	N	N
2 Valentine	?	?	?	Y	N	N	N
3 Whitley	Y	Y	Y	Y	N	N	N
4 Andrews	Y	Y	Y	Y	N	N	N
5 Neal	Y	Y	Y	Y	N	N	Y
6 Britt	Y	Y	Y	Y	N	N	N
7 Rose	Y	Y	Y	Y	N	N	N
8 Hefner	Y	Y	Y	Y	N	N	N
9 ***Martin***	Y	Y	Y	Y	N	N	Y
10 ***Broyhill***	Y	Y	Y	Y	N	N	N
11 Clarke	Y	Y	Y	Y	N	N	N
NORTH DAKOTA							
AL Dorgan	Y	Y	Y	Y	N	N	N
OHIO							
1 Luken	Y	Y	Y	Y	N	N	N
2 ***Gradison***	Y	Y	N	Y	N	N	N
3 Hall	?	?	?	?	?	?	?
4 ***Oxley***	Y	Y	Y	Y	N	Y	Y
5 ***Latta***	Y	N	Y	Y	N	N	N
6 ***McEwen***	Y	Y	Y	Y	N	N	N
7 ***DeWine***	Y	Y	Y	N	N	N	N
8 ***Kindness***	Y	Y	Y	Y	N	Y	Y
9 Kaptur	Y	Y	Y	#	N	N	N
10 ***Miller***	Y	Y	Y	N	N	N	Y
11 Eckart	Y	Y	Y	Y	N	N	N
12 ***Kasich***	Y	Y	Y	Y	N	N	N
13 Pease	Y	Y	N	Y	N	N	N
14 Seiberling	Y	Y	Y	Y	N	N	N
15 ***Wylie***	Y	Y	Y	Y	N	N	N
16 ***Regula***	Y	Y	Y	N	N	N	N
17 ***Williams***	Y	Y	Y	Y	N	N	N
18 Applegate	Y	Y	Y	Y	N	N	N
19 Feighan	Y	Y	Y	Y	N	N	N
20 Oakar	Y	Y	Y	Y	N	N	N
21 Stokes	Y	Y	Y	Y	N	N	N
OKLAHOMA							
1 Jones	Y	Y	Y	Y	N	N	Y
2 Synar	Y	Y	N	Y	N	N	N
3 Watkins	Y	Y	Y	Y	N	N	N
4 McCurdy	Y	Y	Y	Y	N	N	Y
5 ***Edwards***	Y	Y	Y	Y	N	N	N
6 English	Y	N	Y	Y	N	N	N
OREGON							
1 AuCoin	Y	Y	Y	N	N	N	N
2 ***Smith, R.***	Y	N	Y	Y	N	N	N
3 Wyden	Y	Y	Y	Y	N	N	N
4 Weaver	Y	Y	Y	Y	N	N	N
5 ***Smith, D.***	Y	N	N	N	N	Y	N
PENNSYLVANIA							
1 Foglietta	?	?	?	Y	?	?	?
2 Gray	Y	Y	Y	Y	N	N	N
3 Borski	Y	Y	Y	Y	N	N	N
4 Kolter	Y	Y	Y	Y	N	N	N
5 ***Schulze***	Y	Y	N	Y	?	N	Y
6 Yatron	Y	Y	Y	Y	N	N	N
7 Edgar	Y	Y	Y	?	N	N	N
8 Kostmayer	Y	Y	Y	Y	N	N	N
9 ***Shuster***	Y	Y	Y	N	N	N	N
10 ***McDade***	Y	Y	Y	N	N	N	N
11 Harrison	?	?	?	?	N	N	N
12 Murtha	Y	Y	Y	Y	N	N	N
13 ***Coughlin***	Y	Y	Y	N	N	N	N
14 Coyne	Y	Y	Y	Y	N	N	N
15 ***Ritter***	Y	Y	Y	N	N	N	N
16 ***Walker***	Y	Y	N	N	N	Y	N
17 ***Gekas***	Y	Y	Y	N	N	Y	N
18 Walgren	N	Y	Y	Y	N	N	N
19 ***Goodling***	Y	Y	Y	N	N	N	N
20 Gaydos	Y	Y	Y	Y	N	N	N
21 ***Ridge***	Y	Y	Y	Y	N	N	N
22 Murphy	Y	Y	Y	Y	N	N	N
23 ***Clinger***	Y	Y	Y	N	N	N	Y
RHODE ISLAND							
1 St Germain	?	?	?	Y	N	N	N
2 ***Schneider***	Y	Y	Y	Y	N	N	N
SOUTH CAROLINA							
1 ***Hartnett***	Y	N	Y	N	N	N	N
2 ***Spence***	?	N	Y	N	N	N	N
3 Derrick	Y	Y	?	Y	N	N	N
4 ***Campbell***	Y	Y	Y	Y	N	N	Y
5 Spratt	Y	Y	Y	Y	N	N	N
6 Tallon	Y	Y	Y	Y	N	N	N
SOUTH DAKOTA							
AL Daschle	Y	Y	Y	Y	N	N	N

	54	55	56	57	58	59	60
TENNESSEE							
1 ***Quillen***	Y	N	Y	Y	N	N	N
2 ***Duncan***	Y	N	Y	Y	N	N	N
3 Lloyd	Y	N	Y	Y	N	N	Y
4 Cooper	?	?	?	Y	N	Y	Y
5 Boner	?	?	?	Y	N	N	N
6 Gore	?	?	?	Y	N	N	N
7 ***Sundquist***	Y	Y	Y	Y	N	Y	Y
8 Jones	Y	Y	Y	Y	N	N	N
9 Ford	Y	Y	Y	Y	N	N	?
TEXAS							
1 Hall, S.	+	+	+	?	N	N	Y
2 Wilson	?	?	?	?	?	?	?
3 ***Bartlett***	Y	Y	N	N	N	Y	Y
4 Hall, R.	Y	N	Y	Y	N	N	?
5 Bryant	Y	Y	Y	Y	N	N	N
6 ***Gramm***	?	?	?	?	?	#	?
7 ***Archer***	Y	Y	N	N	N	Y	Y
8 ***Fields***	Y	N	Y	N	N	N	N
9 Brooks	Y	Y	Y	Y	N	N	N
10 Pickle	Y	Y	Y	Y	N	N	N
11 Leath	Y	N	Y	Y	N	N	Y
12 Wright	Y	?	Y	Y	N	N	N
13 Hightower	Y	N	Y	Y	N	N	Y
14 Patman	Y	N	Y	Y	N	N	N
15 de la Garza	Y	Y	Y	Y	N	N	N
16 Coleman	Y	Y	Y	Y	N	N	N
17 Stenholm	Y	N	N	Y	N	N	Y
18 Leland	Y	Y	Y	Y	N	N	N
19 Hance	?	?	?	#	?	?	?
20 Gonzalez	Y	Y	Y	Y	?	N	N
21 ***Loeffler***	Y	N	Y	Y	N	N	N
22 ***Paul***	?	?	?	X	?	?	?
23 Kazen	?	?	?	?	?	?	?
24 Frost	Y	Y	Y	Y	N	N	N
25 Andrews	Y	Y	Y	Y	N	N	N
26 Vandergriff	Y	Y	Y	Y	N	N	N
27 Ortiz	Y	Y	Y	Y	N	N	N
UTAH							
1 ***Hansen***	Y	Y	Y	Y	N	Y	?
2 ***Marriott***	Y	Y	Y	N	N	N	N
3 ***Nielson***	Y	Y	Y	N	N	Y	Y
VERMONT							
AL ***Jeffords***	?	?	?	N	N	N	N
VIRGINIA							
1 ***Bateman***	Y	Y	Y	Y	N	N	N
2 ***Whitehurst***	Y	Y	Y	Y	N	Y	Y
3 ***Bliley***	Y	N	Y	Y	N	Y	Y
4 Sisisky	Y	Y	Y	Y	N	N	N
5 Daniel	?	?	?	?	?	?	?
6 Olin	Y	Y	Y	Y	N	N	N
7 ***Robinson***	Y	N	Y	Y	N	Y	N
8 ***Parris***	Y	Y	Y	N	N	N	N
9 Boucher	?	?	?	Y	N	N	N
10 ***Wolf***	Y	Y	Y	N	N	N	N
WASHINGTON							
1 ***Pritchard***	Y	Y	Y	Y	N	?	Y
2 Swift	Y	Y	Y	Y	N	N	?
3 Bonker	Y	Y	Y	Y	N	N	N
4 ***Morrison***	Y	Y	Y	Y	N	N	Y
5 Foley	Y	Y	Y	Y	N	N	N
6 Dicks	Y	Y	Y	Y	N	N	N
7 Lowry	Y	Y	Y	Y	N	N	N
8 ***Chandler***	Y	Y	Y	Y	N	N	N
WEST VIRGINIA							
1 Mollohan	Y	Y	Y	Y	N	N	N
2 Staggers	Y	Y	Y	Y	N	N	N
3 Wise	Y	Y	Y	Y	N	N	N
4 Rahall	Y	Y	Y	Y	N	N	N
WISCONSIN							
1 Aspin	Y	Y	Y	?	N	N	N
2 Kastenmeier	Y	Y	Y	Y	N	N	N
3 ***Gunderson***	Y	Y	Y	N	N	N	N
4 Vacancy							
5 Moody	Y	Y	Y	?	N	N	N
6 ***Petri***	Y	Y	N	N	N	N	N
7 Obey	Y	Y	Y	Y	N	N	N
8 ***Roth***	Y	Y	Y	Y	N	Y	N
9 ***Sensenbrenner***	Y	Y	Y	N	N	Y	N
WYOMING							
AL ***Cheney***	Y	Y	Y	Y	N	Y	N

Southern states - Ala., Ark., Fla., Ga., Ky., La., Miss., N.C., Okla., S.C., Tenn., Texas, Va.

61. H Con Res 280. First Budget Resolution, Fiscal 1985. Dixon, D-Calif., substitute offered by the Congressional Black Caucus to reduce deficits by $324 billion over three years by cutting military spending by $203 billion and increasing taxes by $181 billion. Domestic spending would increase $99 billion. Rejected 76-333: R 0-160; D 76-173 (ND 70-99, SD 6-74), April 5, 1984.

62. H Con Res 280. First Budget Resolution, Fiscal 1985. McHugh, D-N.Y., substitute offered by the Democratic Study Group to reduce deficits by $261 billion over three years by limiting domestic spending, holding defense increases to the rate of inflation and increasing taxes by $76.2 billion. Rejected 132-284: R 5-156; D 127-128 (ND 117-53, SD 10-75), April 5, 1984.

63. H Con Res 280. First Budget Resolution, Fiscal 1985. MacKay, D-Fla., substitute to impose a modified spending freeze, providing for inflation adjustments only in defense spending and most entitlement programs. Taxes would be increased by $47.2 billion. Rejected 108-310: R 28-132; D 80-178 (ND 50-122, SD 30-56), April 5, 1984.

64. H Con Res 280. First Budget Resolution, Fiscal 1985. Latta, R-Ohio, substitute offered by House Republicans calling for $205 billion in three-year deficit reductions by cutting defense spending by $40.2 billion, domestic spending by $26.3 billion, entitlements by $23.2 billion, raising taxes by $47.2 billion and finding other savings totaling $61.6 billion. The plan would have resulted in a $174.6 billion fiscal 1985 deficit. Rejected 107-311: R 105-55; D 2-256 (ND 0-172, SD 2-84), April 5, 1984. A "yea" was a vote supporting the president's position.

65. H Con Res 280. First Budget Resolution, Fiscal 1985. Adoption of the first concurrent budget resolution for fiscal 1985 to set targets for the fiscal year ending Sept. 30, 1985, as follows: budget authority, $1,002.1 billion; outlays, $918.2 billion; revenues, $742.7 billion; and deficit, $174.5 billion. The resolution also set preliminary goals for fiscal 1986-87, revised budget levels for fiscal 1984 and included reconciliation instructions requiring House and Senate committees to recommend legislative savings to meet the budget targets. Adopted 250-168: R 21-139; D 229-29 (ND 159-13, SD 70-16), April 5, 1984.

KEY

- Y Voted for (yea).
- # Paired for.
- + Announced for.
- N Voted against (nay).
- X Paired against.
- - Announced against.
- P Voted "present".
- C Voted "present" to avoid possible conflict of interest.
- ? Did not vote or otherwise make a position known.

Democrats **Republicans**

	61	62	63	64	65
ALABAMA					
1 Edwards	N	N	N	Y	N
2 Dickinson	N	N	N	Y	N
3 Nichols	N	N	N	N	Y
4 Bevill	N	N	N	N	Y
5 Flippo	N	N	N	N	Y
6 Erdreich	N	N	Y	N	Y
7 Shelby	X	N	N	N	N
ALASKA					
AL Young	N	N	Y	Y	N
ARIZONA					
1 McCain	N	N	N	Y	N
2 Udall	N	Y	N	N	Y
3 Stump	N	N	N	N	N
4 Rudd	N	N	N	N	N
5 McNulty	N	Y	Y	N	Y
ARKANSAS					
1 Alexander	?	N	N	N	Y
2 Bethune	N	N	N	Y	N
3 Hammerschmidt	N	N	N	Y	N
4 Anthony	N	N	N	N	Y
CALIFORNIA					
1 Bosco	N	Y	Y	N	Y
2 Chappie	N	N	N	Y	N
3 Matsui	N	Y	N	N	Y
4 Fazio	N	Y	N	N	Y
5 Burton	Y	Y	N	N	Y
6 Boxer	Y	Y	Y	N	Y
7 Miller	Y	Y	N	N	Y
8 Dellums	Y	Y	N	N	Y
9 Stark	Y	Y	N	N	Y
10 Edwards	Y	Y	N	N	Y
11 Lantos	N	N	N	N	Y
12 Zschau	N	N	N	N	N
13 Mineta	N	Y	N	N	Y
14 Shumway	N	N	N	N	N
15 Coelho	N	Y	N	N	Y
16 Panetta	N	N	N	Y	Y
17 Pashayan	N	N	N	Y	N
18 Lehman	N	Y	N	N	Y
19 Lagomarsino	N	N	N	Y	N
20 Thomas	N	N	N	Y	N
21 Fiedler	N	N	N	Y	N
22 Moorhead	N	N	N	Y	N
23 Beilenson	Y	Y	N	N	Y
24 Waxman	Y	Y	N	N	Y
25 Roybal	Y	Y	N	N	Y
26 Berman	Y	Y	N	N	Y
27 Levine	N	Y	Y	N	Y
28 Dixon	Y	Y	N	N	Y
29 Hawkins	#	#	?	X	#
30 Martinez	Y	Y	N	N	Y
31 Dymally	Y	Y	N	N	Y
32 Anderson	Y	N	N	N	Y
33 Dreier	N	N	N	Y	N
34 Torres	N	Y	N	N	Y
35 Lewis	N	N	N	Y	N
36 Brown	Y	Y	Y	N	Y
37 McCandless	N	N	N	?	N
38 Patterson	N	N	N	N	Y
39 Dannemeyer	N	N	N	N	N
40 Badham	N	N	N	Y	N
41 Lowery	N	N	N	Y	N
42 Lungren	N	N	N	Y	N
43 Packard	N	N	N	Y	N
44 Bates	Y	Y	Y	N	Y
45 Hunter	N	N	N	Y	N
COLORADO					
1 Schroeder	Y	Y	Y	N	Y
2 Wirth	Y	N	N	N	Y
3 Kogovsek	N	Y	N	N	Y
4 Brown	N	N	Y	N	N
5 Kramer	N	N	N	N	N
6 Schaefer	N	N	N	Y	N
CONNECTICUT					
1 Kennelly	N	N	N	N	Y
2 Gejdenson	N	Y	N	N	Y
3 Morrison	N	Y	Y	N	Y
4 McKinney	N	Y	Y	N	Y
5 Ratchford	N	N	N	N	Y
6 Johnson	N	N	N	N	Y
DELAWARE					
AL Carper	N	N	Y	N	Y
FLORIDA					
1 Hutto	N	N	N	N	Y
2 Fuqua	N	N	N	N	Y
3 Bennett	N	N	N	N	Y
4 Chappell	N	N	N	N	Y
5 McCollum	N	N	N	Y	N
6 MacKay	N	N	Y	N	Y
7 Gibbons	N	N	Y	N	Y
8 Young	N	N	N	Y	N
9 Bilirakis	N	N	N	N	N
10 Ireland	N	N	Y	N	Y
11 Nelson	N	N	Y	N	Y
12 Lewis	N	N	N	Y	N
13 Mack	N	N	N	Y	N
14 Mica	N	N	N	N	Y
15 Shaw	N	N	N	Y	N
16 Smith	N	N	Y	N	Y
17 Lehman	?	Y	N	N	Y
18 Pepper	N	N	N	N	Y
19 Fascell	N	N	Y	N	Y
GEORGIA					
1 Thomas	N	N	Y	N	Y
2 Hatcher	?	N	Y	N	Y
3 Ray	X	X	?	?	?
4 Levitas	N	N	Y	N	N
5 Fowler	Y	N	Y	N	Y
6 Gingrich	N	N	N	Y	N
7 Darden	N	N	N	N	N
8 Rowland	N	N	Y	N	Y
9 Jenkins	N	N	Y	N	Y
10 Barnard	N	N	N	N	N
HAWAII					
1 Heftel	?	?	?	?	?
2 Akaka	Y	Y	N	N	Y
IDAHO					
1 Craig	N	N	Y	N	N
2 Hansen	?	?	?	?	?
ILLINOIS					
1 Hayes	Y	Y	N	N	Y
2 Savage	Y	Y	N	N	Y
3 Russo	N	Y	Y	N	Y
4 O'Brien	N	N	N	N	Y
5 Lipinski	N	N	Y	N	Y
6 Hyde	?	?	?	#	X
7 Collins	Y	Y	N	N	Y
8 Rostenkowski	N	N	N	N	Y
9 Yates	Y	Y	N	N	Y
10 Porter	N	N	N	Y	Y
11 Annunzio	N	Y	N	N	Y
12 Crane, P.	N	N	N	N	N
13 Erlenborn	?	N	N	Y	?
14 Corcoran	N	N	N	Y	N
15 Madigan	N	N	N	Y	N
16 Martin	N	N	Y	N	N
17 Evans	N	N	N	Y	Y
18 Michel	N	N	N	N	N
19 Crane, D.	N	N	N	N	N
20 Durbin	N	N	Y	N	Y
21 Price	N	Y	N	N	Y
22 Simon	N	Y	N	N	Y
INDIANA					
1 Hall	Y	Y	N	N	Y
2 Sharp	N	N	Y	N	Y
3 Hiler	N	N	N	N	N
4 Coats	N	N	N	Y	N
5 Hillis	N	N	N	Y	N

ND - Northern Democrats   SD - Southern Democrats

Member	61	62	63	64	65
6 Burton	N	N	N	Y	N
7 Myers	N	N	N	N	N
8 McCloskey	?	Y	Y	N	Y
9 Hamilton	N	N	Y	N	Y
10 Jacobs	Y	Y	N	N	Y
IOWA					
1 Leach	N	N	Y	N	N
2 Tauke	N	N	Y	N	N
3 Evans	N	Y	Y	N	N
4 Smith	N	Y	Y	N	N
5 Harkin	N	Y	Y	N	N
6 Bedell	N	Y	Y	N	Y
KANSAS					
1 Roberts	N	N	Y	N	N
2 Slattery	N	N	Y	N	Y
3 Winn	N	N	N	Y	N
4 Glickman	N	N	Y	N	Y
5 Whittaker	N	N	N	Y	N
KENTUCKY					
1 Hubbard	?	?	?	?	?
2 Natcher	N	N	N	N	N
3 Mazzoli	N	N	N	N	Y
4 Snyder	N	N	N	N	N
5 Rogers	N	N	N	Y	N
6 Hopkins	N	N	N	N	N
7 Perkins	N	N	N	N	Y
LOUISIANA					
1 Livingston	N	N	N	Y	N
2 Boggs	Y	N	N	N	Y
3 Tauzin	N	N	N	N	N
4 Roemer	N	N	N	N	N
5 Huckaby	N	N	N	N	Y
6 Moore	N	N	N	N	N
7 Breaux	N	N	N	N	N
8 Long	N	Y	N	N	Y
MAINE					
1 McKernan	N	N	N	N	Y
2 Snowe	N	N	N	N	Y
MARYLAND					
1 Dyson	N	N	N	Y	N
2 Long	N	?	N	N	Y
3 Mikulski	N	Y	N	N	Y
4 Holt	N	N	N	N	N
5 Hoyer	N	Y	N	N	Y
6 Byron	N	N	N	N	N
7 Mitchell	Y	N	N	N	Y
8 Barnes	N	Y	N	N	Y
MASSACHUSETTS					
1 Conte	N	N	N	N	Y
2 Boland	N	Y	N	N	Y
3 Early	Y	Y	N	N	Y
4 Frank	Y	Y	N	N	Y
5 Shannon	Y	Y	N	N	Y
6 Mavroules	N	N	N	N	Y
7 Markey	Y	Y	N	N	Y
8 O'Neill					
9 Moakley	Y	Y	N	N	Y
10 Studds	Y	Y	N	N	Y
11 Donnelly	N	N	N	N	Y
MICHIGAN					
1 Conyers	Y	N	N	N	Y
2 Pursell	N	N	N	N	N
3 Wolpe	N	Y	Y	N	Y
4 Siljander	N	N	N	N	N
5 Sawyer	N	N	N	N	N
6 Carr	N	N	N	N	N
7 Kildee	Y	Y	N	N	Y
8 Traxler	N	Y	N	N	Y
9 Vander Jagt	N	N	N	Y	N
10 Albosta	N	Y	Y	N	Y
11 Davis	N	N	N	Y	Y
12 Bonior	Y	Y	N	N	Y
13 Crockett	Y	Y	N	N	N
14 Hertel	N	N	N	N	Y
15 Ford	?	?	N	N	Y
16 Dingell	N	N	N	N	Y
17 Levin	N	N	N	N	Y
18 Broomfield	N	N	N	Y	Y
MINNESOTA					
1 Penny	N	N	Y	N	Y
2 Weber	N	N	Y	N	N
3 Frenzel	N	N	Y	N	Y
4 Vento	Y	Y	N	N	Y
5 Sabo	Y	Y	N	N	Y
6 Sikorski	N	N	Y	N	Y

Member	61	62	63	64	65
7 Stangeland	N	N	N	Y	N
8 Oberstar	Y	Y	N	N	Y
MISSISSIPPI					
1 Whitten	N	N	N	N	Y
2 Franklin	N	N	N	N	N
3 Montgomery	N	N	N	N	N
4 Dowdy	N	N	N	N	Y
5 Lott	N	N	N	Y	N
MISSOURI					
1 Clay	Y	N	N	N	Y
2 Young	N	N	N	N	Y
3 Gephardt	N	N	N	N	Y
4 Skelton	N	N	N	N	Y
5 Wheat	Y	Y	N	N	Y
6 Coleman	N	N	N	Y	N
7 Taylor	N	N	N	Y	N
8 Emerson	N	N	Y	N	N
9 Volkmer	N	N	N	N	Y
MONTANA					
1 Williams	N	Y	N	N	Y
2 Marlenee	N	N	N	Y	N
NEBRASKA					
1 Bereuter	N	N	N	N	Y
2 Daub	N	N	Y	Y	N
3 Smith	N	N	Y	Y	N
NEVADA					
1 Reid	N	N	Y	N	Y
2 Vucanovich	N	N	N	N	N
NEW HAMPSHIRE					
1 D'Amours	N	Y	N	N	Y
2 Gregg	N	N	Y	Y	N
NEW JERSEY					
1 Florio	Y	N	N	N	Y
2 Hughes	N	N	Y	N	Y
3 Howard	Y	Y	N	N	Y
4 Smith	N	N	N	N	Y
5 Roukema	N	N	N	N	Y
6 Dwyer	N	Y	N	N	Y
7 Rinaldo	N	N	N	N	Y
8 Roe	N	Y	N	N	Y
9 Torricelli	N	N	N	N	Y
10 Rodino	Y	Y	N	N	Y
11 Minish	Y	Y	N	N	Y
12 Courter	N	N	N	N	N
13 Vacancy					
14 Guarini	N	Y	N	N	Y
NEW MEXICO					
1 Lujan	N	N	Y	Y	N
2 Skeen	N	N	N	Y	N
3 Richardson	N	Y	Y	N	Y
NEW YORK					
1 Carney	N	N	N	N	N
2 Downey	Y	Y	N	N	Y
3 Mrazek	N	N	Y	N	Y
4 Lent	?	?	?	?	X
5 McGrath	N	N	N	N	N
6 Addabbo	Y	Y	N	N	Y
7 Ackerman	Y	Y	N	N	Y
8 Scheuer	Y	Y	N	N	Y
9 Ferraro	Y	Y	N	N	Y
10 Schumer	Y	Y	N	N	Y
11 Towns	Y	Y	N	N	Y
12 Owens	N	N	N	N	Y
13 Solarz	N	N	N	N	Y
14 Molinari	N	N	N	N	N
15 Green	N	N	N	N	N
16 Rangel	#	N	N	N	Y
17 Weiss	Y	Y	N	N	Y
18 Garcia	Y	Y	N	N	Y
19 Biaggi	Y	N	N	N	Y
20 Ottinger	Y	Y	N	N	Y
21 Fish	N	N	N	N	Y
22 Gilman	N	N	-	N	N
23 Stratton	N	N	N	N	Y
24 Solomon	N	N	N	N	N
25 Boehlert	?	?	?	X	#
26 Martin	N	N	N	N	N
27 Wortley	N	N	N	Y	N
28 McHugh	N	Y	N	N	Y
29 Horton	N	N	N	N	Y
30 Conable	N	N	N	N	N
31 Kemp	N	N	N	N	N
32 LaFalce	N	Y	Y	N	Y
33 Nowak	N	Y	Y	N	Y
34 Lundine	N	Y	Y	N	Y

Member	61	62	63	64	65
NORTH CAROLINA					
1 Jones	N	N	N	N	Y
2 Valentine	N	N	N	N	Y
3 Whitley	N	N	N	N	Y
4 Andrews	N	N	N	N	Y
5 Neal	N	Y	Y	N	Y
6 Britt	N	N	N	N	Y
7 Rose	N	Y	N	N	Y
8 Hefner	N	N	N	N	Y
9 Martin	N	N	N	Y	N
10 Broyhill	N	N	Y	Y	Y
11 Clarke	N	N	N	N	Y
NORTH DAKOTA					
AL Dorgan	N	Y	Y	N	N
OHIO					
1 Luken	N	Y	Y	N	Y
2 Gradison	N	N	Y	Y	N
3 Hall	?	?	?	?	?
4 Oxley	N	N	Y	N	Y
5 Latta	N	N	N	N	N
6 McEwen	N	N	N	Y	N
7 DeWine	N	N	N	N	N
8 Kindness	N	N	N	N	N
9 Kaptur	N	Y	N	N	Y
10 Miller	N	N	N	Y	N
11 Eckart	N	N	Y	N	N
12 Kasich	N	N	N	Y	N
13 Pease	N	Y	Y	N	Y
14 Seiberling	Y	Y	N	N	Y
15 Wylie	N	N	N	Y	Y
16 Regula	N	N	N	N	Y
17 Williams	N	N	N	N	Y
18 Applegate	N	N	Y	N	N
19 Feighan	N	N	Y	N	Y
20 Oakar	Y	Y	N	N	Y
21 Stokes	Y	Y	N	N	Y
OKLAHOMA					
1 Jones	N	N	Y	N	Y
2 Synar	-	Y	Y	N	Y
3 Watkins	N	N	Y	N	Y
4 McCurdy	N	N	Y	N	Y
5 Edwards	N	N	N	Y	N
6 English	N	N	Y	N	N
OREGON					
1 AuCoin	N	Y	N	N	Y
2 Smith, R.	N	N	N	N	N
3 Wyden	N	Y	N	N	Y
4 Weaver	Y	Y	N	N	Y
5 Smith, D.	N	N	N	N	N
PENNSYLVANIA					
1 Foglietta	Y	Y	N	?	#
2 Gray	Y	Y	N	N	Y
3 Borski	N	Y	N	N	Y
4 Kolter	N	Y	N	N	Y
5 Schulze	N	N	N	N	Y
6 Yatron	N	N	N	N	Y
7 Edgar	Y	Y	N	N	Y
8 Kostmayer	Y	Y	N	N	Y
9 Shuster	N	N	N	N	N
10 McDade	N	N	Y	N	Y
11 Harrison	?	?	N	N	Y
12 Murtha	N	N	N	N	Y
13 Coughlin	N	N	Y	N	N
14 Coyne	Y	Y	N	N	Y
15 Ritter	N	N	Y	N	N
16 Walker	N	N	N	N	N
17 Gekas	N	N	N	Y	N
18 Walgren	N	Y	N	N	Y
19 Goodling	N	Y	Y	Y	Y
20 Gaydos	N	N	N	N	Y
21 Ridge	N	N	N	Y	N
22 Murphy	N	Y	Y	N	N
23 Clinger	N	N	Y	Y	N
RHODE ISLAND					
1 St Germain	N	Y	N	N	Y
2 Schneider	N	Y	N	Y	N
SOUTH CAROLINA					
1 Hartnett	N	N	N	N	N
2 Spence	N	N	N	Y	N
3 Derrick	N	N	N	Y	Y
4 Campbell	N	N	N	Y	N
5 Spratt	N	N	N	N	Y
6 Tallon	N	N	N	Y	N
SOUTH DAKOTA					
AL Daschle	N	N	Y	N	Y

Member	61	62	63	64	65
TENNESSEE					
1 Quillen	N	N	N	Y	N
2 Duncan	N	N	N	Y	N
3 Lloyd	N	N	N	N	N
4 Cooper	Y	Y	Y	Y	Y
5 Boner	N	N	Y	N	Y
6 Gore	N	N	Y	N	Y
7 Sundquist	N	N	N	Y	N
8 Jones	N	N	Y	N	Y
9 Ford	Y	N	N	N	Y
TEXAS					
1 Hall, S.	N	N	N	N	Y
2 Wilson	N	?	Y	N	Y
3 Bartlett	N	N	N	Y	N
4 Hall, R.	N	N	N	N	N
5 Bryant	N	Y	N	N	Y
6 Gramm	N	N	N	Y	N
7 Archer	N	N	N	Y	N
8 Fields	N	N	N	Y	N
9 Brooks	N	N	N	N	Y
10 Pickle	N	N	Y	N	Y
11 Leath	N	N	N	N	N
12 Wright	N	N	N	N	Y
13 Hightower	N	N	N	N	Y
14 Patman	N	N	N	Y	N
15 de la Garza	N	N	N	N	Y
16 Coleman	N	N	N	N	Y
17 Stenholm	N	N	N	N	Y
18 Leland	Y	Y	N	N	Y
19 Hance	?	?	?	?	X
20 Gonzalez	Y	Y	N	N	N
21 Loeffler	N	N	N	Y	N
22 Paul	?	?	?	#	?
23 Kazen	?	?	?	?	?
24 Frost	N	Y	N	N	Y
25 Andrews	N	N	Y	N	Y
26 Vandergriff	N	N	N	N	Y
27 Ortiz	N	N	N	N	Y
UTAH					
1 Hansen	N	N	Y	Y	N
2 Marriott	N	N	N	Y	N
3 Nielson	N	N	N	Y	N
VERMONT					
AL Jeffords	N	N	N	N	Y
VIRGINIA					
1 Bateman	N	N	N	Y	N
2 Whitehurst	N	N	N	Y	N
3 Bliley	N	N	N	Y	N
4 Sisisky	N	N	N	N	Y
5 Daniel	N	N	N	N	N
6 Olin	-	N	N	N	Y
7 Robinson	N	N	N	Y	N
8 Parris	N	N	N	N	N
9 Boucher	N	N	N	N	Y
10 Wolf	N	N	N	N	N
WASHINGTON					
1 Pritchard	N	Y	Y	Y	Y
2 Swift	N	Y	N	N	Y
3 Bonker	N	Y	N	N	Y
4 Morrison	N	N	N	Y	N
5 Foley	N	Y	N	N	Y
6 Dicks	N	Y	N	N	Y
7 Lowry	Y	Y	N	N	Y
8 Chandler	N	N	N	Y	Y
WEST VIRGINIA					
1 Mollohan	N	N	N	N	Y
2 Staggers	N	N	N	N	Y
3 Wise	N	N	N	N	Y
4 Rahall	Y	Y	?	N	Y
WISCONSIN					
1 Aspin	N	Y	N	N	Y
2 Kastenmeier	Y	Y	Y	N	Y
3 Gunderson	N	N	Y	N	N
4 Vacancy					
5 Moody	N	Y	N	N	Y
6 Petri	N	N	Y	N	Y
7 Obey	Y	Y	Y	N	Y
8 Roth	N	N	N	N	Y
9 Sensenbrenner	N	N	Y	N	N
WYOMING					
AL Cheney	N	N	N	Y	N

Southern states - Ala., Ark., Fla., Ga., Ky., La., Miss., N.C., Okla., S.C., Tenn., Texas, Va.

66. HR 7. Child Nutrition. Adoption of the rule (H Res 478) providing for House floor consideration of the bill to reauthorize child nutrition programs through 1988, to liberalize eligibility and benefits in certain programs, and make other changes. Adopted 275-125: R 36-122; D 239-3 (ND 158-0, SD 81-3), April 10, 1984.

67. HR 4900. Panama Canal Authorization. Carney, R-N.Y., amendment to reduce funding for the operation and maintenance of the Panama Canal in fiscal 1985 from $443,946,000 to $435,653,000. Rejected 188-214: R 109-50; D 79-164 (ND 37-124, SD 42-40), April 10, 1984.

68. HR 4900. Panama Canal Authorization. Passage of the bill to authorize fiscal 1985 spending of $443,946,000 by the Panama Canal Commission for the operation and maintenance of the Panama Canal. Passed 307-89: R 87-68; D 220-21 (ND 155-5, SD 65-16), April 10, 1984.

69. Procedural Motion. Bliley, R-Va., motion to approve the House *Journal* of Tuesday, April 10. Motion agreed to 366-21: R 148-8; D 218-13 (ND 139-11, SD 79-2), April 11, 1984.

70. HR 7. Child Nutrition. Erlenborn, R-Ill., amendment to strike authorization for "tiering" in the federal child-care food program. Under this system, if certain percentages of children in a home child-care program were poor enough to qualify for free or reduced-price meals, all children in the program may receive such meals. Rejected 140-262: R 130-24; D 10-238 (ND 0-165, SD 10-73), April 11, 1984.

71. HR 4170. Deficit Reduction. Passage of the bill to raise $49.2 billion in new taxes through fiscal 1987 by closing a wide range of tax loopholes; increasing taxes on distilled liquor, cigarettes and telephones; revamping taxation of the life insurance industry; and making other changes. Passed 318-97: R 95-66; D 223-31 (ND 155-14, SD 68-17), April 11, 1984. A "yea" was a vote supporting the president's position.

KEY

Y	Voted for (yea).
#	Paired for.
+	Announced for.
N	Voted against (nay).
X	Paired against.
-	Announced against.
P	Voted "present".
C	Voted "present" to avoid possible conflict of interest.
?	Did not vote or otherwise make a position known.

Democrats   *Republicans*

	66	67	68	69	70	71
ALABAMA						
1 *Edwards*	N	N	Y	?	Y	Y
2 *Dickinson*	N	N	N	N	Y	N
3 Nichols	Y	Y	N	?	N	Y
4 Bevill	Y	Y	Y	Y	N	Y
5 Flippo	Y	N	Y	Y	N	Y
6 Erdreich	Y	Y	N	Y	N	Y
7 Shelby	Y	Y	N	Y	N	N
ALASKA						
AL *Young*	Y	Y	Y	N	N	N
ARIZONA						
1 *McCain*	N	Y	Y	Y	Y	N
2 Udall	Y	N	Y	N	?	N
3 *Stump*	N	Y	N	Y	N	Y
4 *Rudd*	N	Y	N	Y	N	Y
5 McNulty	Y	Y	Y	Y	N	N
ARKANSAS						
1 Alexander	Y	?	?	Y	?	Y
2 *Bethune*	N	Y	Y	Y	Y	N
3 *Hammerschmidt*	Y	Y	Y	Y	N	N
4 Anthony	Y	N	Y	Y	N	Y
CALIFORNIA						
1 Bosco	Y	N	Y	Y	N	Y
2 *Chappie*	N	N	N	Y	Y	Y
3 Matsui	Y	N	Y	N	Y	Y
4 Fazio	Y	N	Y	Y	N	Y
5 Burton	?	?	#	Y	N	Y
6 Boxer	Y	N	Y	N	Y	Y
7 Miller	Y	N	Y	Y	N	Y
8 Dellums	Y	N	Y	Y	N	Y
9 Stark	Y	N	Y	N	Y	Y
10 Edwards	Y	N	Y	Y	N	Y
11 Lantos	Y	N	Y	?	?	Y
12 *Zschau*	N	Y	Y	Y	Y	Y
13 Mineta	Y	N	Y	Y	N	Y
14 *Shumway*	N	N	Y	Y	Y	N
15 Coelho	?	N	Y	Y	N	Y
16 Panetta	Y	N	Y	Y	N	Y
17 *Pashayan*	N	Y	N	Y	Y	N
18 Lehman	Y	N	Y	Y	N	Y
19 *Lagomarsino*	N	N	Y	Y	Y	N
20 *Thomas*	N	N	Y	Y	Y	Y
21 *Fiedler*	N	Y	Y	Y	Y	N
22 *Moorhead*	N	N	Y	Y	Y	Y
23 Beilenson	Y	N	Y	Y	N	Y
24 Waxman	Y	N	Y	?	Y	Y
25 Roybal	Y	N	Y	Y	N	Y
26 Berman	Y	N	Y	Y	N	Y
27 Levine	Y	N	Y	Y	N	Y
28 Dixon	Y	N	Y	Y	N	Y
29 Hawkins	?	N	Y	N	N	Y
30 Martinez	Y	N	Y	Y	N	N
31 Dymally	Y	N	Y	P	N	Y
32 Anderson	Y	N	Y	Y	N	N
33 *Dreier*	N	Y	N	Y	N	N
34 Torres	Y	N	Y	Y	N	Y
35 *Lewis*	N	N	Y	Y	Y	N
36 Brown	Y	?	?	Y	?	Y
37 *McCandless*	N	Y	N	Y	N	N
38 Patterson	Y	N	Y	Y	N	Y
39 *Dannemeyer*	N	Y	N	Y	Y	N
40 *Badham*	N	N	Y	Y	Y	Y
41 *Lowery*	N	Y	Y	P	Y	N
42 *Lungren*	N	N	Y	Y	Y	N

	66	67	68	69	70	71
43 *Packard*	N	N	Y	Y	Y	Y
44 Bates	Y	N	Y	Y	N	Y
45 *Hunter*	N	Y	N	Y	Y	N
COLORADO						
1 Schroeder	Y	Y	Y	N	N	N
2 Wirth	Y	N	Y	Y	N	Y
3 Kogovsek	Y	N	Y	Y	N	Y
4 *Brown*	N	Y	N	Y	Y	N
5 *Kramer*	N	Y	N	Y	Y	N
6 *Schaefer*	N	Y	N	Y	Y	N
CONNECTICUT						
1 Kennelly	Y	Y	Y	Y	N	Y
2 Gejdenson	Y	N	Y	N	N	Y
3 Morrison	Y	N	Y	Y	N	Y
4 *McKinney*	Y	N	Y	Y	Y	Y
5 Ratchford	Y	Y	Y	Y	N	Y
6 *Johnson*	Y	Y	Y	Y	N	Y
DELAWARE						
AL Carper	Y	N	Y	?	N	Y
FLORIDA						
1 Hutto	Y	Y	Y	Y	Y	Y
2 Fuqua	Y	N	Y	Y	N	Y
3 Bennett	Y	Y	Y	Y	Y	Y
4 Chappell	Y	Y	N	Y	N	Y
5 *McCollum*	N	Y	N	Y	Y	N
6 MacKay	Y	Y	Y	Y	N	Y
7 Gibbons	?	N	Y	Y	Y	Y
8 *Young*	N	Y	Y	Y	N	N
9 *Bilirakis*	N	N	N	Y	Y	N
10 Ireland	Y	Y	N	Y	N	Y
11 Nelson	Y	Y	Y	+	Y	Y
12 *Lewis*	N	Y	N	Y	Y	N
13 *Mack*	N	Y	N	Y	Y	N
14 Mica	Y	N	Y	Y	N	Y
15 *Shaw*	N	Y	N	Y	Y	N
16 Smith	Y	N	Y	Y	N	Y
17 Lehman	Y	N	Y	Y	N	Y
18 Pepper	Y	N	Y	Y	N	Y
19 Fascell	Y	N	Y	Y	N	Y
GEORGIA						
1 Thomas	Y	N	Y	Y	N	Y
2 Hatcher	Y	N	Y	Y	N	Y
3 Ray	Y	N	Y	Y	N	Y
4 Levitas	Y	Y	Y	Y	N	Y
5 Fowler	Y	N	Y	Y	N	Y
6 *Gingrich*	N	Y	Y	Y	Y	Y
7 Darden	Y	Y	Y	Y	N	Y
8 Rowland	Y	N	Y	Y	N	Y
9 Jenkins	Y	N	Y	?	N	Y
10 Barnard	Y	N	Y	Y	N	Y
HAWAII						
1 Heftel	?	?	?	?	?	?
2 Akaka	Y	N	Y	Y	N	Y
IDAHO						
1 *Craig*	N	Y	N	Y	Y	N
2 *Hansen*	?	?	?	?	?	?
ILLINOIS						
1 Hayes	Y	N	Y	Y	N	Y
2 Savage	?	?	?	?	?	Y
3 Russo	Y	N	Y	Y	N	Y
4 *O'Brien*	Y	N	Y	Y	Y	Y
5 Lipinski	Y	N	Y	N	N	Y
6 *Hyde*	N	N	Y	N	Y	N
7 Collins	Y	N	Y	Y	N	Y
8 Rostenkowski	Y	N	Y	Y	N	Y
9 Yates	Y	N	Y	Y	N	Y
10 *Porter*	N	Y	Y	Y	Y	?
11 Annunzio	Y	N	Y	Y	N	Y
12 *Crane, P.*	N	Y	N	Y	Y	N
13 *Erlenborn*	N	Y	Y	Y	Y	Y
14 *Corcoran*	N	Y	Y	Y	Y	N
15 *Madigan*	N	N	Y	Y	Y	N
16 *Martin*	N	Y	N	Y	#	N
17 Evans	Y	N	Y	Y	N	Y
18 *Michel*	N	Y	Y	Y	Y	Y
19 *Crane, D.*	N	Y	N	Y	Y	N
20 Durbin	Y	Y	Y	N	N	Y
21 Price	Y	N	Y	Y	N	Y
22 Simon	Y	N	Y	Y	N	?
INDIANA						
1 Hall	?	?	?	?	?	Y
2 Sharp	Y	Y	Y	Y	N	Y
3 *Hiler*	N	Y	N	Y	Y	N
4 *Coats*	N	Y	N	Y	Y	N
5 Hillis	N	Y	N	Y	?	Y

ND - Northern Democrats   SD - Southern Democrats

	66	67	68	69	70	71
6 ***Burton***	?	Y	N	Y	Y	Y
7 ***Myers***	Y	Y	N	Y	Y	N
8 McCloskey	Y	N	Y	Y	N	Y
9 Hamilton	Y	N	Y	Y	N	Y
10 Jacobs	Y	Y	Y	N	N	Y
IOWA						
1 ***Leach***	Y	Y	Y	Y	Y	Y
2 ***Tauke***	Y	N	Y	Y	Y	Y
3 ***Evans***	Y	N	N	N	Y	Y
4 Smith	Y	N	Y	Y	N	Y
5 Harkin	Y	N	Y	N	N	Y
6 Bedell	Y	N	Y	Y	N	Y
KANSAS						
1 ***Roberts***	N	Y	?	Y	Y	N
2 Slattery	Y	Y	Y	Y	N	Y
3 ***Winn***	N	Y	N	Y	Y	Y
4 Glickman	Y	Y	Y	Y	N	Y
5 ***Whittaker***	N	Y	N	Y	Y	Y
KENTUCKY						
1 Hubbard	Y	N	Y	Y	N	N
2 Natcher	Y	N	Y	Y	N	N
3 Mazzoli	Y	N	Y	Y	N	N
4 ***Snyder***	N	N	N	Y	Y	Y
5 ***Rogers***	N	?	?	Y	Y	N
6 ***Hopkins***	N	N	N	Y	?	N
7 Perkins	Y	N	Y	Y	N	Y
LOUISIANA						
1 ***Livingston***	N	Y	Y	Y	Y	N
2 Boggs	Y	N	Y	Y	N	Y
3 Tauzin	Y	N	Y	Y	N	N
4 Roemer	Y	Y	N	N	N	N
5 Huckaby	Y	Y	Y	Y	N	Y
6 ***Moore***	Y	Y	Y	Y	Y	Y
7 Breaux	Y	N	Y	P	N	Y
8 Long	Y	N	Y	Y	N	Y
MAINE						
1 ***McKernan***	N	N	Y	Y	N	Y
2 ***Snowe***	Y	Y	Y	Y	N	Y
MARYLAND						
1 Dyson	Y	Y	N	Y	N	N
2 Long	Y	N	Y	Y	N	Y
3 Mikulski	Y	?	?	Y	N	#
4 ***Holt***	Y	Y	Y	Y	Y	Y
5 Hoyer	Y	N	Y	Y	N	Y
6 Byron	Y	Y	Y	Y	N	N
7 Mitchell	Y	N	Y	?	N	Y
8 Barnes	Y	N	Y	Y	N	Y
MASSACHUSETTS						
1 ***Conte***	Y	N	Y	Y	Y	C
2 Boland	Y	N	Y	Y	N	Y
3 Early	Y	Y	?	Y	N	N
4 Frank	Y	N	Y	Y	N	Y
5 Shannon	?	?	?	?	N	Y
6 Mavroules	?	N	Y	Y	N	Y
7 Markey	Y	N	Y	Y	N	Y
8 O'Neill						
9 Moakley	Y	N	Y	Y	X	Y
10 Studds	Y	N	Y	Y	N	Y
11 Donnelly	Y	Y	Y	Y	N	Y
MICHIGAN						
1 Conyers	Y	N	Y	?	N	Y
2 ***Pursell***	Y	Y	Y	Y	N	N
3 Wolpe	Y	N	Y	Y	X	Y
4 ***Siljander***	N	Y	Y	Y	Y	N
5 ***Sawyer***	Y	N	Y	Y	Y	Y
6 Carr	Y	N	Y	P	N	N
7 Kildee	Y	N	Y	Y	N	Y
8 Traxler	Y	N	Y	Y	N	N
9 ***Vander Jagt***	N	Y	Y	Y	#	Y
10 Albosta	Y	N	Y	Y	N	N
11 ***Davis***	Y	N	Y	Y	N	Y
12 Bonior	Y	N	Y	Y	N	Y
13 Crockett	Y	N	Y	Y	N	Y
14 Hertel	Y	N	Y	Y	N	N
15 Ford	Y	N	Y	Y	N	Y
16 Dingell	Y	N	Y	Y	N	Y
17 Levin	Y	N	Y	Y	N	C
18 ***Broomfield***	N	N	Y	Y	Y	Y
MINNESOTA						
1 Penny	Y	Y	Y	N	N	Y
2 ***Weber***	N	Y	Y	Y	Y	N
3 ***Frenzel***	N	Y	Y	Y	Y	Y
4 Vento	Y	N	Y	Y	N	Y
5 Sabo	Y	N	Y	N	N	Y
6 Sikorski	Y	Y	Y	N	N	Y
7 ***Stangeland***	N	Y	?	Y	Y	N
8 Oberstar	Y	N	Y	Y	N	Y
MISSISSIPPI						
1 Whitten	Y	Y	Y	Y	N	N
2 ***Franklin***	N	Y	Y	Y	N	Y
3 Montgomery	N	Y	?	Y	Y	Y
4 Dowdy	Y	Y	Y	Y	N	Y
5 ***Lott***	N	Y	N	Y	Y	Y
MISSOURI						
1 Clay	Y	N	Y	N	N	Y
2 Young	Y	N	Y	Y	N	Y
3 Gephardt	Y	N	Y	?	N	Y
4 Skelton	Y	N	Y	Y	N	Y
5 Wheat	Y	N	Y	Y	N	Y
6 ***Coleman***	N	N	Y	?	?	?
7 ***Taylor***	N	N	Y	Y	Y	Y
8 ***Emerson***	N	Y	Y	N	Y	N
9 Volkmer	Y	Y	Y	Y	N	Y
MONTANA						
1 Williams	?	Y	N	?	N	Y
2 ***Marlenee***	N	N	?	Y	Y	N
NEBRASKA						
1 ***Bereuter***	N	Y	Y	Y	Y	Y
2 ***Daub***	N	Y	N	Y	Y	Y
3 ***Smith***	Y	Y	N	Y	Y	Y
NEVADA						
1 Reid	Y	Y	Y	Y	N	Y
2 ***Vucanovich***	N	Y	N	Y	Y	N
NEW HAMPSHIRE						
1 D'Amours	Y	N	Y	Y	N	Y
2 ***Gregg***	N	Y	N	Y	Y	N
NEW JERSEY						
1 Florio	Y	Y	Y	?	N	N
2 Hughes	Y	N	Y	Y	N	Y
3 Howard	Y	N	Y	Y	N	Y
4 ***Smith***	Y	Y	Y	Y	N	Y
5 ***Roukema***	Y	Y	Y	Y	Y	Y
6 Dwyer	Y	N	Y	Y	N	Y
7 ***Rinaldo***	Y	Y	Y	Y	N	Y
8 Roe	Y	N	Y	Y	N	Y
9 Torricelli	Y	N	Y	Y	N	Y
10 Rodino	Y	N	Y	Y	N	Y
11 Minish	Y	Y	Y	Y	N	Y
12 ***Courter***	N	Y	N	Y	Y	N
13 Vacancy						
14 Guarini	Y	X	Y	Y	N	Y
NEW MEXICO						
1 ***Lujan***	Y	Y	?	Y	Y	Y
2 ***Skeen***	Y	N	Y	Y	Y	N
3 Richardson	Y	Y	Y	Y	N	Y
NEW YORK						
1 ***Carney***	N	Y	N	Y	Y	N
2 Downey	Y	N	Y	?	N	Y
3 Mrazek	Y	Y	Y	Y	N	Y
4 ***Lent***	?	?	?	?	?	Y
5 ***McGrath***	N	Y	N	Y	Y	Y
6 Addabbo	Y	N	Y	Y	N	Y
7 Ackerman	Y	N	Y	Y	N	Y
8 Scheuer	Y	N	Y	Y	N	Y
9 Ferraro	?	?	?	?	?	Y
10 Schumer	Y	N	Y	Y	N	Y
11 Towns	Y	N	Y	?	?	Y
12 Owens	Y	N	Y	Y	N	Y
13 Solarz	Y	N	Y	Y	N	Y
14 ***Molinari***	Y	N	Y	Y	Y	N
15 ***Green***	Y	Y	Y	Y	N	Y
16 Rangel	Y	N	Y	Y	N	Y
17 Weiss	Y	N	Y	Y	N	Y
18 Garcia	Y	N	Y	Y	N	Y
19 Biaggi	Y	N	Y	Y	N	Y
20 Ottinger	Y	N	Y	P	N	Y
21 ***Fish***	N	N	Y	Y	N	Y
22 ***Gilman***	Y	Y	Y	Y	N	Y
23 Stratton	Y	N	Y	Y	N	Y
24 ***Solomon***	N	Y	N	N	Y	N
25 ***Boehlert***	Y	N	Y	Y	N	Y
26 ***Martin***	Y	N	Y	Y	Y	Y
27 ***Wortley***	N	N	N	Y	Y	Y
28 McHugh	Y	N	Y	Y	N	Y
29 ***Horton***	?	N	Y	Y	N	Y
30 ***Conable***	N	Y	Y	Y	Y	Y
31 ***Kemp***	N	N	Y	Y	Y	N
32 LaFalce	Y	N	Y	Y	N	Y
33 Nowak	Y	N	Y	Y	N	Y
34 ***Lundine***	Y	N	Y	?	N	Y
NORTH CAROLINA						
1 Jones	?	?	?	?	X	?
2 Valentine	Y	Y	Y	Y	N	Y
3 Whitley	Y	Y	N	Y	N	Y
4 Andrews	Y	Y	Y	Y	N	Y
5 Neal	Y	Y	Y	Y	N	Y
6 Britt	Y	Y	N	Y	N	Y
7 Rose	Y	N	N	Y	N	Y
8 Hefner	Y	Y	Y	Y	N	Y
9 ***Martin***	N	Y	N	?	Y	Y
10 ***Broyhill***	N	Y	N	Y	Y	Y
11 Clarke	Y	Y	Y	Y	N	Y
NORTH DAKOTA						
AL Dorgan	Y	Y	N	Y	N	Y
OHIO						
1 Luken	Y	N	Y	Y	N	Y
2 ***Gradison***	N	Y	Y	Y	Y	Y
3 Hall	Y	?	?	?	N	Y
4 ***Oxley***	N	Y	N	Y	Y	Y
5 ***Latta***	N	Y	N	Y	Y	Y
6 ***McEwen***	N	Y	N	Y	Y	N
7 ***DeWine***	N	Y	Y	Y	Y	Y
8 ***Kindness***	N	N	Y	Y	Y	Y
9 Kaptur	Y	N	Y	Y	N	Y
10 ***Miller***	N	Y	N	N	Y	Y
11 Eckart	Y	Y	Y	?	N	Y
12 ***Kasich***	N	Y	Y	Y	Y	Y
13 Pease	Y	N	Y	Y	N	Y
14 Seiberling	Y	N	Y	Y	N	Y
15 ***Wylie***	N	Y	Y	Y	Y	Y
16 ***Regula***	N	Y	N	Y	Y	Y
17 ***Williams***	Y	Y	N	Y	Y	Y
18 Applegate	Y	Y	N	?	N	Y
19 Feighan	Y	Y	Y	Y	N	Y
20 Oakar	Y	N	?	Y	N	Y
21 Stokes	Y	N	Y	Y	N	Y
OKLAHOMA						
1 Jones	Y	Y	Y	Y	N	Y
2 Synar	Y	-	+	Y	N	Y
3 Watkins	Y	Y	Y	Y	N	Y
4 McCurdy	Y	N	Y	Y	N	Y
5 ***Edwards***	N	N	Y	Y	Y	N
6 English	Y	N	Y	Y	N	N
OREGON						
1 AuCoin	?	N	Y	Y	N	Y
2 ***Smith, R.***	N	Y	Y	Y	Y	N
3 Wyden	Y	Y	Y	Y	N	Y
4 Weaver	Y	Y	Y	Y	N	Y
5 ***Smith, D.***	N	Y	N	Y	Y	N
PENNSYLVANIA						
1 Foglietta	?	?	?	?	?	?
2 Gray	?	?	?	Y	N	Y
3 Borski	Y	N	Y	Y	N	Y
4 Kolter	Y	Y	Y	Y	N	Y
5 ***Schulze***	?	?	?	Y	N	Y
6 Yatron	?	?	?	Y	N	Y
7 Edgar	?	?	?	Y	N	Y
8 Kostmayer	Y	Y	Y	Y	N	Y
9 ***Shuster***	N	N	Y	Y	Y	N
10 ***McDade***	?	?	?	Y	N	Y
11 Harrison	?	?	?	?	?	?
12 Murtha	Y	N	Y	Y	N	Y
13 ***Coughlin***	N	Y	Y	N	N	Y
14 Coyne	?	?	?	?	?	Y
15 ***Ritter***	N	Y	Y	Y	Y	Y
16 ***Walker***	N	Y	N	?	?	?
17 ***Gekas***	Y	N	Y	Y	N	Y
18 Walgren	Y	Y	Y	Y	N	Y
19 ***Goodling***	Y	Y	N	N	Y	Y
20 Gaydos	Y	Y	Y	P	N	Y
21 ***Ridge***	Y	N	Y	Y	N	Y
22 Murphy	?	Y	Y	Y	N	N
23 ***Clinger***	N	N	N	-	Y	Y
RHODE ISLAND						
1 St Germain	Y	N	Y	P	N	Y
2 ***Schneider***	Y	N	Y	Y	N	Y
SOUTH CAROLINA						
1 ***Hartnett***	N	Y	N	Y	Y	N
2 ***Spence***	N	Y	N	Y	Y	Y
3 Derrick	Y	Y	Y	Y	N	Y
4 ***Campbell***	N	Y	N	Y	Y	Y
5 Spratt	Y	Y	Y	Y	N	Y
6 Tallon	Y	N	Y	Y	N	Y
SOUTH DAKOTA						
AL Daschle	Y	Y	Y	Y	N	N
TENNESSEE						
1 ***Quillen***	N	Y	N	Y	Y	Y
2 ***Duncan***	Y	Y	N	Y	#	Y
3 Lloyd	Y	Y	N	Y	N	Y
4 Cooper	Y	Y	Y	Y	N	Y
5 Boner	Y	Y	Y	Y	N	Y
6 Gore	Y	N	Y	Y	N	Y
7 ***Sundquist***	N	Y	N	Y	Y	Y
8 Jones	Y	Y	N	Y	N	Y
9 Ford	Y	N	Y	Y	N	Y
TEXAS						
1 Hall, S.	Y	Y	N	Y	Y	N
2 Wilson	?	N	Y	?	?	?
3 ***Bartlett***	N	Y	Y	Y	Y	Y
4 Hall, R.	Y	Y	N	Y	N	N
5 Bryant	Y	N	Y	Y	N	Y
6 ***Gramm***	N	Y	N	Y	Y	N
7 ***Archer***	N	Y	N	Y	Y	N
8 ***Fields***	N	N	Y	Y	Y	N
9 Brooks	Y	N	Y	Y	N	Y
10 Pickle	Y	N	Y	Y	N	Y
11 Leath	Y	Y	N	Y	N	N
12 Wright	Y	N	Y	Y	N	Y
13 Hightower	Y	Y	Y	Y	N	Y
14 Patman	Y	Y	N	Y	N	N
15 de la Garza	Y	?	?	Y	N	Y
16 Coleman	Y	N	Y	Y	N	N
17 Stenholm	N	?	?	N	Y	Y
18 Leland	Y	N	Y	?	X	#
19 Hance	?	#	X	?	?	?
20 Gonzalez	Y	N	Y	Y	N	N
21 ***Loeffler***	N	Y	N	Y	Y	N
22 ***Paul***	?	?	?	?	#	X
23 Kazen	?	?	?	?	?	X
24 Frost	?	N	Y	Y	N	N
25 Andrews	Y	Y	Y	Y	N	Y
26 Vandergriff	Y	Y	N	P	Y	N
27 Ortiz	Y	N	Y	Y	N	Y
UTAH						
1 ***Hansen***	N	N	N	Y	Y	Y
2 ***Marriott***	N	Y	Y	Y	Y	Y
3 ***Nielson***	N	Y	N	Y	Y	N
VERMONT						
AL ***Jeffords***	Y	Y	Y	Y	Y	Y
VIRGINIA						
1 ***Bateman***	N	Y	Y	Y	Y	Y
2 ***Whitehurst***	N	Y	Y	Y	Y	Y
3 ***Bliley***	N	N	Y	Y	Y	Y
4 Sisisky	Y	Y	Y	Y	N	Y
5 Daniel	N	Y	Y	Y	Y	N
6 Olin	Y	-	+	Y	N	Y
7 ***Robinson***	N	Y	Y	Y	Y	Y
8 ***Parris***	N	Y	N	Y	Y	N
9 Boucher	Y	Y	Y	Y	N	Y
10 ***Wolf***	N	Y	Y	Y	Y	Y
WASHINGTON						
1 ***Pritchard***	Y	N	Y	Y	Y	Y
2 Swift	Y	N	Y	Y	N	Y
3 Bonker	Y	N	Y	Y	N	Y
4 ***Morrison***	N	N	Y	Y	Y	Y
5 Foley	?	N	Y	Y	N	Y
6 Dicks	Y	N	Y	Y	N	Y
7 Lowry	Y	N	Y	Y	N	Y
8 ***Chandler***	N	N	Y	Y	Y	Y
WEST VIRGINIA						
1 Mollohan	Y	N	Y	Y	N	Y
2 Staggers	Y	Y	N	Y	N	Y
3 Wise	Y	N	Y	Y	N	Y
4 Rahall	Y	Y	Y	Y	N	Y
WISCONSIN						
1 Aspin	Y	N	Y	Y	N	Y
2 Kastenmeier	Y	N	Y	Y	N	Y
3 ***Gunderson***	Y	N	Y	Y	Y	Y
4 Kleczka *	Y	N	Y	Y	N	Y
5 Moody	Y	Y	Y	Y	N	Y
6 ***Petri***	N	N	Y	Y	Y	Y
7 Obey	Y	N	Y	Y	N	Y
8 ***Roth***	?	?	?	?	?	Y
9 ***Sensenbrenner***	N	Y	N	Y	Y	N
WYOMING						
AL ***Cheney***	N	Y	N	Y	Y	N

** Rep. Gerald D. Kleczka, D-Wis., was sworn in April 10, 1984. The first vote for which he was eligible was CQ vote 66.*

Southern states - Ala., Ark., Fla., Ga., Ky., La., Miss., N.C., Okla., S.C., Tenn., Texas, Va.

72. HR 5394. Omnibus Budget Reconciliation Act. Derrick, D-S.C., motion to order the previous question (thus ending debate and the possibility of amendment) on the rule (H Res 483) providing for House floor consideration of the bill to cut spending during fiscal 1985-87 in a variety of federal benefit programs. Motion agreed to 241-173: R 0-161; D 241-12 (ND 166-5, SD 75-7), April 12, 1984.

73. HR 5394. Omnibus Budget Reconciliation Act. Adoption of the rule (H Res 483) providing for House floor consideration of the bill to cut spending during fiscal 1985-87 in a variety of federal benefit programs. Adopted 217-196: R 0-160; D 217-36 (ND 162-9, SD 55-27), April 12, 1984.

74. HR 5394. Omnibus Budget Reconciliation Act. Moore, R-La., motion to recommit the bill to the House Ways and Means Committee with instructions to include provisions imposing a one-year physician fee freeze for Medicare services and to strike provisions in the measure that increased spending. Motion rejected 172-242: R 157-2; D 15-240 (ND 3-170, SD 12-70), April 12, 1984.

75. HR 5394. Omnibus Budget Reconciliation Act. Passage of the bill to reduce federal spending $3.9 billion during fiscal 1985-87 by reducing costs in Medicare, welfare, veterans', and other benefit programs. Passed 261-152: R 26-132; D 235-20 (ND 165-8, SD 70-12), April 12, 1984. A "yea" was a vote supporting the president's position.

76. H Con Res 290. Mining of Nicaraguan Waters. Adoption of the rule (H Res 485) providing for House floor consideration of the concurrent resolution stating the sense of Congress that no appropriated funds should be used for planning, directing, executing or supporting the mining of ports or territorial waters of Nicaragua. Adopted 230-153: R 8-144; D 222-9 (ND 156-1, SD 66-8), April 12, 1984.

KEY

Y Voted for (yea).
Paired for.
+ Announced for.
N Voted against (nay).
X Paired against.
- Announced against.
P Voted "present".
C Voted "present" to avoid possible conflict of interest.
? Did not vote or otherwise make a position known.

Democrats *Republicans*

	72	73	74	75	76
ALABAMA					
1 *Edwards*	N	N	Y	N	N
2 *Dickinson*	X	?	#	X	X
3 Nichols	Y	N	?	X	?
4 Bevill	Y	Y	N	Y	?
5 Flippo	Y	Y	N	Y	?
6 Erdreich	Y	Y	N	Y	Y
7 Shelby	N	N	Y	N	?
ALASKA					
AL *Young*	N	N	Y	Y	N
ARIZONA					
1 *McCain*	N	N	Y	N	N
2 Udall	Y	Y	N	Y	Y
3 *Stump*	N	N	Y	N	N
4 *Rudd*	X	?	#	X	X
5 McNulty	Y	Y	N	Y	+
ARKANSAS					
1 Alexander	Y	Y	N	Y	Y
2 *Bethune*	N	N	Y	N	N
3 *Hammerschmidt*	N	N	Y	N	N
4 Anthony	Y	Y	N	Y	Y
CALIFORNIA					
1 Bosco	Y	Y	N	Y	?
2 *Chappie*	N	N	Y	N	N
3 Matsui	Y	Y	N	Y	Y
4 Fazio	Y	Y	N	Y	Y
5 Burton	Y	Y	N	Y	Y
6 Boxer	Y	Y	N	Y	Y
7 Miller	Y	Y	N	Y	Y
8 Dellums	Y	Y	N	Y	Y
9 Stark	Y	Y	N	Y	Y
10 Edwards	Y	Y	N	Y	Y
11 Lantos	#	#	X	#	?
12 *Zschau*	N	N	Y	N	N
13 Mineta	Y	Y	N	Y	Y
14 *Shumway*	N	N	Y	N	N
15 Coelho	Y	Y	N	Y	Y
16 Panetta	Y	Y	N	Y	Y
17 *Pashayan*	N	N	Y	X	N
18 Lehman	Y	Y	N	Y	Y
19 *Lagomarsino*	N	N	Y	N	N
20 *Thomas*	N	N	Y	N	X
21 *Fiedler*	N	N	Y	N	N
22 *Moorhead*	N	N	Y	N	N
23 Beilenson	Y	Y	N	Y	Y
24 Waxman	Y	Y	N	Y	Y
25 Roybal	Y	Y	N	Y	Y
26 Berman	Y	Y	N	Y	Y
27 Levine	Y	Y	N	Y	Y
28 Dixon	Y	Y	N	Y	Y
29 Hawkins	Y	Y	N	Y	Y
30 Martinez	Y	Y	N	Y	Y
31 Dymally	Y	Y	N	Y	#
32 Anderson	N	N	N	Y	Y
33 *Dreier*	N	N	Y	N	N
34 Torres	Y	Y	N	Y	?
35 *Lewis*	N	N	Y	N	N
36 Brown	Y	Y	N	Y	Y
37 *McCandless*	N	N	Y	N	N
38 Patterson	Y	Y	N	Y	Y
39 *Dannemeyer*	N	N	Y	N	N
40 *Badham*	N	N	Y	N	N
41 *Lowery*	N	N	Y	N	N
42 *Lungren*	N	N	Y	N	N

	72	73	74	75	76
43 *Packard*	N	N	Y	N	N
44 Bates	Y	Y	N	Y	Y
45 *Hunter*	N	N	Y	N	N
COLORADO					
1 Schroeder	Y	Y	N	Y	Y
2 Wirth	Y	Y	N	Y	Y
3 Kogovsek	Y	Y	N	Y	Y
4 *Brown*	N	N	Y	N	N
5 *Kramer*	N	N	Y	N	N
6 *Schaefer*	N	N	Y	N	N
CONNECTICUT					
1 Kennelly	Y	Y	N	Y	Y
2 Gejdenson	Y	Y	N	Y	Y
3 Morrison	Y	Y	N	Y	Y
4 *McKinney*	N	N	Y	N	Y
5 Ratchford	Y	Y	N	Y	Y
6 *Johnson*	N	N	Y	N	Y
DELAWARE					
AL Carper	Y	Y	N	Y	Y
FLORIDA					
1 Hutto	Y	N	Y	N	N
2 Fuqua	Y	Y	N	Y	Y
3 Bennett	Y	Y	Y	Y	Y
4 Chappell	Y	Y	N	Y	Y
5 *McCollum*	N	N	Y	N	N
6 MacKay	Y	Y	N	Y	Y
7 Gibbons	Y	Y	N	Y	Y
8 *Young*	N	N	Y	N	N
9 *Bilirakis*	N	N	Y	N	N
10 Ireland	?	Y	Y	N	?
11 Nelson	Y	Y	N	Y	Y
12 *Lewis*	N	N	Y	N	N
13 *Mack*	N	N	Y	N	N
14 Mica	Y	Y	N	Y	Y
15 *Shaw*	N	N	Y	N	N
16 Smith	Y	Y	N	Y	Y
17 Lehman	Y	Y	N	Y	Y
18 Pepper	Y	Y	N	Y	Y
19 Fascell	Y	Y	N	Y	Y
GEORGIA					
1 Thomas	Y	Y	N	Y	Y
2 Hatcher	Y	Y	N	Y	Y
3 Ray	Y	N	Y	N	Y
4 Levitas	Y	Y	N	Y	Y
5 Fowler	Y	Y	N	Y	Y
6 *Gingrich*	N	N	Y	N	N
7 Darden	Y	Y	N	Y	Y
8 Rowland	Y	Y	N	Y	Y
9 Jenkins	Y	N	N	Y	Y
10 Barnard	Y	N	N	Y	?
HAWAII					
1 Heftel	?	?	?	?	?
2 Akaka	Y	Y	N	Y	?
IDAHO					
1 *Craig*	X	?	#	?	X
2 *Hansen*	?	?	?	?	?
ILLINOIS					
1 Hayes	Y	Y	N	Y	Y
2 Savage	?	?	N	Y	Y
3 Russo	Y	Y	N	Y	#
4 *O'Brien*	N	N	Y	N	N
5 Lipinski	Y	Y	N	Y	?
6 *Hyde*	N	N	Y	N	N
7 Collins	Y	Y	N	Y	Y
8 Rostenkowski	Y	Y	N	Y	Y
9 Yates	Y	Y	N	Y	Y
10 *Porter*	N	N	Y	N	N
11 Annunzio	Y	Y	N	Y	Y
12 *Crane, P.*	N	N	Y	N	N
13 *Erlenborn*	N	N	Y	N	N
14 *Corcoran*	N	N	Y	N	N
15 *Madigan*	N	N	Y	N	N
16 *Martin*	N	N	Y	N	N
17 Evans	Y	Y	N	Y	Y
18 *Michel*	N	N	Y	N	N
19 *Crane, D.*	N	N	Y	N	N
20 Durbin	Y	Y	N	Y	Y
21 Price	Y	Y	N	Y	Y
22 Simon	#	#	X	#	?
INDIANA					
1 Hall	Y	Y	N	Y	Y
2 Sharp	Y	Y	N	Y	Y
3 *Hiler*	N	N	Y	N	N
4 *Coats*	N	N	Y	N	N
5 Hillis	N	N	Y	N	N

ND - Northern Democrats   SD - Southern Democrats

	72	73	74	75	76
6 Burton	N	N	Y	N	N
7 Myers	N	N	Y	N	N
8 McCloskey	N	N	N	Y	Y
9 Hamilton	N	N	N	Y	Y
10 Jacobs	Y	Y	N	Y	?
IOWA					
1 *Leach*	N	N	Y	N	Y
2 *Tauke*	N	N	Y	N	N
3 *Evans*	N	N	Y	N	N
4 Smith	N	N	N	N	Y
5 Harkin	Y	Y	N	Y	Y
6 Bedell	Y	Y	N	Y	?
KANSAS					
1 *Roberts*	N	N	Y	N	N
2 Slattery	Y	Y	N	Y	Y
3 *Winn*	N	N	Y	N	N
4 Glickman	Y	Y	N	Y	Y
5 *Whittaker*	N	N	Y	N	N
KENTUCKY					
1 Hubbard	Y	N	Y	N	N
2 Natcher	N	N	N	Y	Y
3 Mazzoli	Y	Y	N	Y	Y
4 *Snyder*	N	N	Y	N	Y
5 *Rogers*	N	N	Y	N	N
6 *Hopkins*	N	N	Y	N	N
7 Perkins	Y	Y	N	N	Y
LOUISIANA					
1 *Livingston*	N	N	Y	N	N
2 Boggs	Y	N	N	Y	N
3 Tauzin	?	X	X	#	#
4 Roemer	Y	N	N	Y	Y
5 Huckaby	Y	N	N	Y	Y
6 *Moore*	N	N	Y	N	N
7 Breaux	Y	N	N	Y	Y
8 Long	Y	Y	N	Y	Y
MAINE					
1 *McKernan*	N	N	Y	Y	N
2 *Snowe*	N	N	Y	Y	N
MARYLAND					
1 Dyson	Y	N	Y	N	Y
2 Long	Y	Y	N	Y	Y
3 Mikulski	Y	Y	N	Y	Y
4 *Holt*	N	N	Y	N	N
5 Hoyer	Y	Y	N	Y	Y
6 Byron	Y	N	Y	N	?
7 Mitchell	Y	Y	N	Y	Y
8 Barnes	Y	Y	N	Y	Y
MASSACHUSETTS					
1 *Conte*	N	N	Y	Y	Y
2 Boland	Y	Y	N	Y	Y
3 Early	Y	Y	N	Y	Y
4 Frank	Y	Y	N	Y	Y
5 Shannon	Y	Y	N	Y	Y
6 Mavroules	Y	Y	N	Y	Y
7 Markey	Y	Y	N	Y	Y
8 O'Neill					
9 Moakley	Y	Y	N	Y	Y
10 Studds	Y	Y	N	Y	Y
11 Donnelly	Y	Y	N	Y	Y
MICHIGAN					
1 Conyers	Y	Y	N	Y	Y
2 *Pursell*	N	N	Y	N	Y
3 Wolpe	Y	Y	N	Y	Y
4 *Siljander*	N	N	Y	N	N
5 *Sawyer*	N	N	Y	N	N
6 Carr	Y	Y	N	Y	Y
7 Kildee	Y	Y	N	Y	Y
8 Traxler	Y	Y	N	Y	Y
9 *Vander Jagt*	N	X	#	X	X
10 Albosta	N	N	Y	N	N
11 *Davis*	N	N	Y	N	N
12 Bonior	Y	Y	N	Y	Y
13 Crockett	Y	Y	N	Y	Y
14 Hertel	Y	Y	N	Y	Y
15 Ford	Y	Y	N	Y	Y
16 Dingell	Y	Y	N	Y	?
17 Levin	Y	Y	N	Y	Y
18 *Broomfield*	N	N	Y	N	N
MINNESOTA					
1 Penny	Y	Y	N	Y	Y
2 *Weber*	N	N	Y	N	N
3 *Frenzel*	N	N	Y	N	N
4 Vento	Y	Y	N	Y	Y
5 Sabo	Y	Y	N	Y	Y
6 Sikorski	Y	Y	N	Y	Y

	72	73	74	75	76
7 *Stangeland*	N	N	Y	N	#
8 Oberstar	Y	Y	N	Y	Y
MISSISSIPPI					
1 Whitten	N	N	N	Y	Y
2 *Franklin*	N	N	Y	N	N
3 Montgomery	Y	N	Y	N	N
4 Dowdy	N	N	N	Y	Y
5 *Lott*	N	N	Y	N	N
MISSOURI					
1 Clay	Y	Y	N	Y	Y
2 Young	Y	Y	N	Y	Y
3 Gephardt	Y	Y	N	Y	Y
4 Skelton	Y	Y	N	Y	Y
5 Wheat	Y	Y	N	Y	Y
6 *Coleman*	N	N	Y	N	N
7 *Taylor*	N	N	Y	N	N
8 *Emerson*	N	N	Y	N	N
9 Volkmer	Y	N	N	Y	Y
MONTANA					
1 Williams	Y	Y	N	Y	Y
2 *Marlenee*	N	N	Y	N	N
NEBRASKA					
1 *Bereuter*	N	N	Y	Y	N
2 *Daub*	N	N	Y	N	N
3 *Smith*	N	N	Y	N	N
NEVADA					
1 Reid	Y	Y	N	Y	Y
2 *Vucanovich*	N	N	Y	N	N
NEW HAMPSHIRE					
1 D'Amours	Y	Y	N	Y	Y
2 *Gregg*	N	N	Y	N	N
NEW JERSEY					
1 Florio	Y	Y	N	Y	Y
2 Hughes	Y	N	Y	N	Y
3 Howard	Y	Y	N	Y	Y
4 *Smith*	N	N	Y	N	N
5 *Roukema*	N	N	Y	N	Y
6 Dwyer	Y	Y	N	Y	Y
7 *Rinaldo*	N	N	N	Y	N
8 Roe	Y	Y	N	Y	?
9 Torricelli	Y	Y	N	Y	Y
10 Rodino	Y	Y	N	Y	Y
11 Minish	Y	Y	N	Y	Y
12 *Courter*	N	N	Y	N	N
13 Vacancy					
14 Guarini	Y	Y	N	Y	Y
NEW MEXICO					
1 *Lujan*	N	N	Y	N	N
2 *Skeen*	N	N	Y	N	N
3 Richardson	Y	Y	N	Y	Y
NEW YORK					
1 *Carney*	N	N	Y	N	N
2 Downey	Y	Y	N	Y	Y
3 Mrazek	Y	Y	N	Y	Y
4 *Lent*	N	N	Y	N	N
5 *McGrath*	N	N	Y	N	N
6 Addabbo	Y	Y	N	Y	Y
7 Ackerman	Y	Y	N	Y	Y
8 Scheuer	Y	Y	N	Y	Y
9 Ferraro	Y	Y	N	Y	Y
10 Schumer	Y	Y	N	Y	Y
11 Towns	Y	Y	N	Y	Y
12 Owens	Y	Y	N	Y	Y
13 Solarz	Y	Y	N	Y	Y
14 *Molinari*	N	N	Y	N	N
15 *Green*	N	N	N	Y	Y
16 Rangel	Y	Y	N	Y	Y
17 Weiss	Y	Y	N	N	Y
18 Garcia	Y	Y	N	Y	Y
19 Biaggi	N	Y	N	Y	#
20 Ottinger	Y	Y	N	Y	N
21 *Fish*	N	N	Y	N	N
22 *Gilman*	N	N	Y	N	N
23 Stratton	Y	Y	N	Y	N
24 *Solomon*	N	N	Y	N	N
25 *Boehlert*	N	N	Y	N	N
26 *Martin*	N	N	Y	N	N
27 *Wortley*	N	N	Y	N	N
28 McHugh	Y	Y	N	Y	Y
29 *Horton*	N	N	Y	Y	?
30 *Conable*	N	N	Y	N	N
31 *Kemp*	N	N	Y	N	N
32 LaFalce	Y	Y	N	Y	Y
33 Nowak	Y	Y	N	Y	Y
34 Lundine	Y	Y	N	Y	?

	72	73	74	75	76
NORTH CAROLINA					
1 Jones	?	?	?	?	?
2 Valentine	Y	Y	N	Y	?
3 Whitley	Y	N	Y	N	N
4 Andrews	Y	Y	N	Y	Y
5 Neal	Y	Y	N	Y	Y
6 *Britt*	Y	Y	N	Y	Y
7 Rose	Y	Y	N	Y	Y
8 Hefner	Y	?	N	Y	Y
9 *Martin*	N	N	Y	N	N
10 *Broyhill*	N	N	Y	N	N
11 Clarke	Y	Y	N	Y	Y
NORTH DAKOTA					
AL Dorgan	Y	Y	N	Y	Y
OHIO					
1 Luken	Y	Y	N	Y	Y
2 *Gradison*	N	N	Y	N	Y
3 Hall	Y	Y	N	Y	Y
4 *Oxley*	N	N	Y	N	N
5 *Latta*	N	N	Y	N	?
6 *McEwen*	N	N	Y	N	N
7 *DeWine*	N	N	Y	N	N
8 *Kindness*	N	N	Y	N	X
9 *Kaptur*	Y	Y	N	Y	Y
10 *Miller*	N	N	Y	N	N
11 Eckart	Y	Y	N	Y	Y
12 *Kasich*	N	N	Y	N	N
13 Pease	Y	Y	N	Y	Y
14 Seiberling	Y	Y	N	Y	Y
15 *Wylie*	N	N	Y	N	N
16 *Regula*	N	N	Y	N	N
17 *Williams*	N	N	Y	N	N
18 Applegate	Y	Y	N	Y	N
19 Feighan	Y	Y	N	Y	Y
20 Oakar	Y	Y	N	Y	Y
21 Stokes	Y	Y	N	Y	Y
OKLAHOMA					
1 Jones	Y	Y	N	Y	Y
2 Synar	Y	Y	N	Y	Y
3 Watkins	Y	Y	N	Y	Y
4 *McCurdy*	Y	Y	N	Y	Y
5 *Edwards*	N	N	Y	N	N
6 English	Y	N	N	Y	Y
OREGON					
1 AuCoin	Y	N	Y	Y	Y
2 *Smith, R.*	N	N	Y	N	N
3 Wyden	Y	Y	N	Y	Y
4 Weaver	Y	Y	N	Y	Y
5 *Smith, D.*	N	N	Y	N	N
PENNSYLVANIA					
1 Foglietta	Y	Y	N	Y	Y
2 Gray	Y	Y	N	Y	Y
3 Borski	Y	Y	N	Y	Y
4 Kolter	Y	Y	N	Y	Y
5 *Schulze*	N	N	Y	N	N
6 Yatron	Y	Y	N	Y	Y
7 Edgar	Y	Y	N	Y	Y
8 Kostmayer	Y	Y	N	Y	Y
9 *Shuster*	N	N	Y	N	N
10 *McDade*	N	N	Y	Y	N
11 Harrison	?	?	?	?	?
12 Murtha	Y	Y	N	Y	Y
13 *Coughlin*	N	N	Y	Y	N
14 Coyne	Y	Y	N	Y	Y
15 *Ritter*	N	N	Y	N	N
16 *Walker*	N	N	Y	N	N
17 *Gekas*	N	N	Y	N	N
18 Walgren	Y	Y	N	Y	Y
19 *Goodling*	N	N	Y	N	Y
20 Gaydos	Y	Y	N	Y	Y
21 *Ridge*	N	N	Y	N	N
22 Murphy	Y	Y	Y	N	?
23 *Clinger*	N	N	Y	N	N
RHODE ISLAND					
1 St Germain	Y	Y	N	Y	Y
2 *Schneider*	N	N	Y	Y	Y
SOUTH CAROLINA					
1 *Hartnett*	N	N	Y	N	N
2 *Spence*	N	N	Y	N	N
3 Derrick	Y	Y	N	Y	Y
4 *Campbell*	N	N	Y	N	N
5 Spratt	Y	Y	N	Y	Y
6 Tallon	Y	Y	N	Y	Y
SOUTH DAKOTA					
AL Daschle	Y	Y	N	Y	?

	72	73	74	75	76
TENNESSEE					
1 *Quillen*	N	N	Y	Y	X
2 *Duncan*	N	N	Y	N	N
3 Lloyd	Y	N	N	N	Y
4 Cooper	Y	Y	N	Y	Y
5 Boner	#	#	X	#	#
6 Gore	Y	Y	N	Y	Y
7 *Sundquist*	N	N	Y	N	N
8 Jones	Y	Y	N	Y	Y
9 Ford	Y	Y	N	Y	Y
TEXAS					
1 Hall, S.	Y	N	Y	Y	Y
2 Wilson	?	?	?	?	?
3 *Bartlett*	N	N	Y	N	N
4 Hall, R.	Y	N	Y	N	N
5 Bryant	Y	Y	N	Y	Y
6 *Gramm*	N	N	Y	N	N
7 *Archer*	N	N	Y	N	N
8 *Fields*	N	N	Y	N	N
9 Brooks	Y	Y	N	Y	Y
10 Pickle	Y	N	Y	N	N
11 Leath	Y	N	Y	N	N
12 Wright	Y	Y	N	Y	Y
13 Hightower	Y	Y	N	Y	Y
14 Patman	N	N	N	Y	Y
15 de la Garza	Y	Y	N	Y	Y
16 Coleman	Y	Y	N	Y	Y
17 Stenholm	Y	N	Y	N	N
18 Leland	Y	Y	N	Y	Y
19 Hance	#	X	X	#	?
20 Gonzalez	Y	Y	N	Y	Y
21 *Loeffler*	N	N	Y	N	N
22 *Paul*	X	?	?	?	#
23 Kazen	?	?	?	?	?
24 Frost	?	?	?	?	?
25 Andrews	Y	Y	N	Y	?
26 Vandergriff	N	N	N	Y	N
27 Ortiz	Y	Y	N	Y	Y
UTAH					
1 *Hansen*	N	N	Y	N	N
2 *Marriott*	N	N	#	?	X
3 *Nielson*	N	N	Y	N	N
VERMONT					
AL *Jeffords*	N	N	Y	Y	#
VIRGINIA					
1 *Bateman*	N	N	Y	N	N
2 *Whitehurst*	N	N	Y	N	N
3 *Bliley*	N	N	Y	N	N
4 Sisisky	Y	Y	N	Y	Y
5 Daniel	N	N	Y	N	N
6 Olin	Y	Y	N	Y	Y
7 *Robinson*	N	N	Y	N	N
8 *Parris*	N	N	Y	N	N
9 Boucher	Y	Y	N	Y	?
10 *Wolf*	N	N	Y	N	N
WASHINGTON					
1 *Pritchard*	N	N	Y	N	N
2 Swift	?	?	N	Y	Y
3 Bonker	Y	Y	N	Y	Y
4 *Morrison*	N	N	Y	N	N
5 Foley	Y	Y	N	Y	Y
6 Dicks	Y	Y	N	Y	Y
7 Lowry	Y	Y	N	Y	Y
8 *Chandler*	N	N	Y	N	N
WEST VIRGINIA					
1 Mollohan	Y	Y	N	Y	Y
2 Staggers	Y	Y	N	Y	Y
3 Wise	Y	Y	N	Y	Y
4 Rahall	Y	Y	N	Y	Y
WISCONSIN					
1 Aspin	Y	Y	N	Y	Y
2 Kastenmeier	Y	Y	N	Y	Y
3 *Gunderson*	N	N	Y	N	N
4 Kleczka	Y	Y	N	Y	Y
5 Moody	Y	Y	N	Y	Y
6 *Petri*	N	N	Y	N	N
7 Obey	Y	Y	N	Y	Y
8 *Roth*	N	N	Y	N	N
9 *Sensenbrenner*	N	N	Y	N	N
WYOMING					
AL *Cheney*	N	N	Y	N	N

Southern states - Ala., Ark., Fla., Ga., Ky., La., Miss., N.C., Okla., S.C., Tenn., Texas, Va.

KEY

Y Voted for (yea).
Paired for.
+ Announced for.
N Voted against (nay).
X Paired against.
- Announced against.
P Voted "present".
C Voted "present" to avoid possible conflict of interest.
? Did not vote or otherwise make a position known.

Democrats *Republicans*

77. H Con Res 290. Mining of Nicaraguan Waters. Hyde, R-Ill., motion to recommit the concurrent resolution to the House Foreign Affairs Committee with instructions to substitute for it new language stating the sense of Congress that no appropriated funds should be used for planning, directing, executing or supporting the mining of ports or territorial waters of Nicaragua if Congress certified that the Nicaraguan government had ceased its support of forces aimed at the subversion of neighboring nations. Motion rejected 144-249: R 132-21; D 12-228 (ND 2-160, SD 10-68), April 12, 1984.

78. H Con Res 290. Mining of Nicaraguan Waters. Adoption of the concurrent resolution stating the sense of Congress that no appropriated funds should be used for planning, directing, executing or supporting the mining of ports or territorial waters of Nicaragua. Adopted 281-111: R 57-96; D 224-15 (ND 158-3, SD 66-12), April 12, 1984.

	77	78
ALABAMA		
1 *Edwards*	Y	N
2 *Dickinson*	#	X
3 Nichols	X	#
4 Bevill	N	Y
5 Flippo	N	Y
6 Erdreich	N	Y
7 Shelby	?	?
ALASKA		
AL *Young*	Y	Y
ARIZONA		
1 *McCain*	Y	N
2 Udall	N	Y
3 *Stump*	Y	N
4 *Rudd*	#	X
5 McNulty	?	+
ARKANSAS		
1 Alexander	N	Y
2 *Bethune*	Y	N
3 *Hammerschmidt*	Y	N
4 Anthony	N	Y
CALIFORNIA		
1 Bosco	N	Y
2 *Chappie*	?	?
3 Matsui	N	Y
4 Fazio	N	Y
5 Burton	N	Y
6 Boxer	N	Y
7 Miller	N	Y
8 Dellums	N	Y
9 Stark	N	Y
10 Edwards	N	Y
11 Lantos	?	?
12 *Zschau*	N	Y
13 Mineta	N	Y
14 *Shumway*	Y	N
15 Coelho	N	Y
16 Panetta	N	Y
17 *Pashayan*	Y	N
18 Lehman	N	Y
19 *Lagomarsino*	Y	Y
20 *Thomas*	Y	Y
21 *Fiedler*	Y	Y
22 *Moorhead*	Y	N
23 Beilenson	N	Y
24 Waxman	N	Y
25 Roybal	N	Y
26 Berman	N	Y
27 Levine	N	Y
28 Dixon	N	Y
29 Hawkins	N	Y
30 Martinez	N	Y
31 Dymally	X	?
32 Anderson	N	Y
33 *Dreier*	Y	N
34 Torres	N	Y
35 *Lewis*	Y	N
36 Brown	N	Y
37 *McCandless*	Y	Y
38 Patterson	N	Y
39 *Dannemeyer*	Y	N
40 *Badham*	Y	N
41 *Lowery*	Y	N
42 *Lungren*	Y	N

	77	78
43 *Packard*	Y	N
44 Bates	N	Y
45 *Hunter*	Y	N
COLORADO		
1 Schroeder	N	Y
2 Wirth	N	Y
3 Kogovsek	N	Y
4 *Brown*	N	Y
5 *Kramer*	Y	Y
6 *Schaefer*	Y	N
CONNECTICUT		
1 Kennelly	N	Y
2 Gejdenson	N	Y
3 Morrison	N	Y
4 *McKinney*	N	Y
5 Ratchford	N	Y
6 *Johnson*	Y	Y
DELAWARE		
AL Carper	N	Y
FLORIDA		
1 Hutto	Y	N
2 Fuqua	N	Y
3 Bennett	N	Y
4 Chappell	N	Y
5 *McCollum*	Y	N
6 MacKay	N	Y
7 Gibbons	N	Y
8 *Young*	Y	N
9 *Bilirakis*	Y	N
10 Ireland	?	?
11 Nelson	N	Y
12 *Lewis*	Y	N
13 *Mack*	Y	N
14 Mica	N	Y
15 *Shaw*	Y	N
16 Smith	N	Y
17 Lehman	N	Y
18 Pepper	N	Y
19 Fascell	N	Y
GEORGIA		
1 Thomas	N	Y
2 Hatcher	N	Y
3 Ray	Y	N
4 Levitas	N	Y
5 Fowler	N	Y
6 *Gingrich*	Y	N
7 Darden	N	N
8 Rowland	N	Y
9 Jenkins	N	Y
10 Barnard	?	?
HAWAII		
1 Heftel	?	?
2 Akaka	?	?
IDAHO		
1 *Craig*	#	X
2 *Hansen*	?	?
ILLINOIS		
1 Hayes	?	?
2 Savage	N	Y
3 Russo	X	#
4 *O'Brien*	Y	N
5 Lipinski	?	?
6 *Hyde*	Y	N
7 Collins	N	Y
8 Rostenkowski	N	Y
9 Yates	N	Y
10 *Porter*	Y	N
11 Annunzio	N	Y
12 *Crane, P.*	Y	N
13 *Erlenborn*	Y	N
14 *Corcoran*	Y	N
15 *Madigan*	Y	Y
16 *Martin*	Y	Y
17 Evans	N	Y
18 *Michel*	Y	N
19 *Crane, D.*	Y	N
20 Durbin	N	Y
21 Price	?	?
22 Simon	?	?
INDIANA		
1 Hall	N	Y
2 Sharp	N	Y
3 *Hiler*	Y	N
4 *Coats*	Y	N
5 *Hillis*	Y	N

ND - Northern Democrats   SD - Southern Democrats

	77	78		77	78		77	78		77	78
6 Burton	Y	N	7 Stangeland	X	#	NORTH CAROLINA			TENNESSEE		
7 Myers	Y	N	8 Oberstar	N	Y	1 Jones	?	?	1 Quillen	#	X
8 McCloskey	N	Y	MISSISSIPPI			2 Valentine	N	Y	2 Duncan	Y	N
9 Hamilton	N	Y	1 Whitten	N	Y	3 Whitley	N	Y	3 Lloyd	N	N
10 Jacobs	N	Y	2 Franklin	Y	N	4 Andrews	N	Y	4 Cooper	N	Y
IOWA			3 Montgomery	Y	N	5 Neal	N	Y	5 Boner	X	?
1 Leach	N	Y	4 Dowdy	N	Y	6 Britt	N	Y	6 Gore	N	Y
2 Tauke	N	Y	5 Lott	Y	N	7 Rose	N	Y	7 Sundquist	Y	N
3 Evans	N	Y	MISSOURI			8 Hefner	N	Y	8 Jones	N	Y
4 Smith	N	Y	1 Clay	N	Y	9 Martin	Y	Y	9 Ford	N	Y
5 Harkin	N	Y	2 Young	N	Y	10 Broyhill	Y	Y	TEXAS		
6 Bedell	?	?	3 Gephardt	N	Y	11 Clarke	N	Y	1 Hall, S.	Y	N
KANSAS			4 Skelton	N	Y	NORTH DAKOTA			2 Wilson	?	?
1 Roberts	Y	N	5 Wheat	N	Y	AL Dorgan	N	Y	3 Bartlett	Y	N
2 Slattery	N	Y	6 Coleman	Y	N	OHIO			4 Hall, R.	Y	N
3 Winn	Y	N	7 Taylor	Y	N	1 Luken	N	Y	5 Bryant	N	Y
4 Glickman	N	Y	8 Emerson	Y	N	2 Gradison	N	Y	6 Gramm	Y	N
5 Whittaker	Y	Y	9 Volkmer	N	Y	3 Hall	N	Y	7 Archer	Y	N
KENTUCKY			MONTANA			4 Oxley	Y	N	8 Fields	Y	N
1 Hubbard	Y	N	1 Williams	N	Y	5 Latta	?	?	9 Brooks	N	Y
2 Natcher	N	Y	2 Marlenee	Y	N	6 McEwen	Y	N	10 Pickle	N	Y
3 Mazzoli	N	Y	NEBRASKA			7 DeWine	Y	N	11 Leath	Y	N
4 Snyder	Y	N	1 Bereuter	Y	Y	8 Kindness	#	X	12 Wright	N	Y
5 Rogers	Y	N	2 Daub	Y	Y	9 Kaptur	Y	Y	13 Hightower	N	Y
6 Hopkins	Y	N	3 Smith	Y	Y	10 Miller	Y	Y	14 Patman	N	Y
7 Perkins	N	Y	NEVADA			11 Eckart	N	Y	15 de la Garza	N	Y
LOUISIANA			1 Reid	N	Y	12 Kasich	Y	N	16 Coleman	N	Y
1 Livingston	Y	N	2 Vucanovich	Y	N	13 Pease	N	Y	17 Stenholm	Y	N
2 Boggs	N	Y	NEW HAMPSHIRE			14 Seiberling	N	Y	18 Leland	N	Y
3 Tauzin	?	?	1 D'Amours	N	Y	15 Wylie	Y	N	19 Hance	?	?
4 Roemer	Y	N	2 Gregg	Y	Y	16 Regula	Y	Y	20 Gonzalez	N	Y
5 Huckaby	Y	N	NEW JERSEY			17 Williams	Y	Y	21 Loeffler	Y	N
6 Moore	Y	N	1 Florio	N	Y	18 Applegate	N	Y	22 Paul	?	#
7 Breaux	N	Y	2 Hughes	N	Y	19 Feighan	N	Y	23 Kazen	?	?
8 Long	N	Y	3 Howard	N	Y	20 Oakar	N	Y	24 Frost	?	?
MAINE			4 Smith	N	Y	21 Stokes	N	Y	25 Andrews	N	Y
1 McKernan	N	Y	5 Roukema	N	Y	OKLAHOMA			26 Vandergriff	N	Y
2 Snowe	N	Y	6 Dwyer	N	Y	1 Jones	N	Y	27 Ortiz	N	Y
MARYLAND			7 Rinaldo	N	Y	2 Synar	N	Y	UTAH		
1 Dyson	N	N	8 Roe	N	Y	3 Watkins	N	Y	1 Hansen	Y	N
2 Long	N	Y	9 Torricelli	N	Y	4 McCurdy	N	Y	2 Marriott	?	?
3 Mikulski	N	Y	10 Rodino	N	Y	5 Edwards	Y	N	3 Nielson	Y	N
4 Holt	Y	N	11 Minish	N	Y	6 English	N	Y	VERMONT		
5 Hoyer	N	Y	12 Courter	Y	N	OREGON			AL Jeffords	X	#
6 Byron	Y	N	13 Vacancy			1 AuCoin	N	Y	VIRGINIA		
7 Mitchell	N	Y	14 Guarini	N	Y	2 Smith, R.	Y	Y	1 Bateman	Y	N
8 Barnes	N	Y	NEW MEXICO			3 Wyden	N	Y	2 Whitehurst	Y	N
MASSACHUSETTS			1 Lujan	Y	N	4 Weaver	N	Y	3 Bliley	Y	N
1 Conte	N	Y	2 Skeen	Y	N	5 Smith, D.	Y	Y	4 Sisisky	N	Y
2 Boland	N	Y	3 Richardson	N	Y	PENNSYLVANIA			5 Daniel	Y	N
3 Early	N	Y	NEW YORK			1 Foglietta	N	Y	6 Olin	N	Y
4 Frank	N	Y	1 Carney	Y	N	2 Gray	N	Y	7 Robinson	Y	N
5 Shannon	N	Y	2 Downey	N	Y	3 Borski	N	Y	8 Parris	Y	N
6 Mavroules	N	Y	3 Mrazek	N	Y	4 Kolter	N	Y	9 Boucher	?	?
7 Markey	N	Y	4 Lent	Y	Y	5 Schulze	Y	Y	10 Wolf	Y	N
8 O'Neill			5 McGrath	Y	Y	6 Yatron	N	Y	WASHINGTON		
9 Moakley	N	Y	6 Addabbo	N	Y	7 Edgar	N	Y	1 Pritchard	Y	Y
10 Studds	N	Y	7 Ackerman	N	Y	8 Kostmayer	N	Y	2 Swift	N	Y
11 Donnelly	N	Y	8 Scheuer	N	Y	9 Shuster	Y	N	3 Bonker	N	Y
MICHIGAN			9 Ferraro	N	Y	10 McDade	Y	Y	4 Morrison	Y	Y
1 Conyers	N	Y	10 Schumer	N	Y	11 Harrison	?	?	5 Foley	N	Y
2 Pursell	Y	Y	11 Towns	N	Y	12 Murtha	N	Y	6 Dicks	N	Y
3 Wolpe	N	Y	12 Owens	N	Y	13 Coughlin	N	Y	7 Lowry	N	Y
4 Siljander	Y	N	13 Solarz	N	?	14 Coyne	N	Y	8 Chandler	Y	Y
5 Sawyer	Y	N	14 Molinari	Y	N	15 Ritter	Y	N	WEST VIRGINIA		
6 Carr	N	Y	15 Green	Y	N	16 Walker	Y	N	1 Mollohan	N	Y
7 Kildee	N	Y	16 Rangel	N	Y	17 Gekas	Y	N	2 Staggers	N	Y
8 Traxler	N	Y	17 Weiss	N	Y	18 Walgren	N	Y	3 Wise	N	Y
9 Vander Jagt	#	X	18 Garcia	N	Y	19 Goodling	Y	Y	4 Rahall	N	Y
10 Albosta	N	Y	19 Biaggi	?	#	20 Gaydos	N	Y	WISCONSIN		
11 Davis	Y	N	20 Ottinger	N	Y	21 Ridge	N	Y	1 Aspin	N	Y
12 Bonior	N	Y	21 Fish	N	N	22 Murphy	?	?	2 Kastenmeier	N	Y
13 Crockett	N	Y	22 Gilman	N	Y	23 Clinger	Y	Y	3 Gunderson	Y	Y
14 Hertel	N	Y	23 Stratton	Y	N	RHODE ISLAND			4 Kleczka	N	Y
15 Ford	N	Y	24 Solomon	Y	N	1 St Germain	N	Y	5 Moody	Y	Y
16 Dingell	N	Y	25 Boehlert	N	Y	2 Schneider	N	Y	6 Petri	Y	Y
17 Levin	N	Y	26 Martin	Y	N	SOUTH CAROLINA			7 Obey	N	Y
18 Broomfield	Y	Y	27 Wortley	Y	N	1 Hartnett	Y	N	8 Roth	Y	Y
MINNESOTA			28 McHugh	N	Y	2 Spence	Y	N	9 Sensenbrenner	Y	Y
1 Penny	N	Y	29 Horton	N	Y	3 Derrick	N	Y	WYOMING		
2 Weber	Y	N	30 Conable	Y	N	4 Campbell	Y	N	AL Cheney	Y	N
3 Frenzel	Y	Y	31 Kemp	Y	N	5 Spratt	N	Y			
4 Vento	N	Y	32 LaFalce	N	Y	6 Tallon	N	Y			
5 Sabo	N	Y	33 Nowak	N	Y	SOUTH DAKOTA					
6 Sikorski	N	Y	34 Lundine	?	?	AL Daschle	N	Y			

Southern states - Ala., Ark., Fla., Ga., Ky., La., Miss., N.C., Okla., S.C., Tenn., Texas, Va.

KEY

Y Voted for (yea).
Paired for.
+ Announced for.
N Voted against (nay).
X Paired against.
- Announced against.
P Voted "present".
C Voted "present" to avoid possible conflict of interest.
? Did not vote or otherwise make a position known.

———

Democrats *Republicans*

79. S 373. Arctic Research and Critical Materials Policy. Passage of the bill to establish an Arctic Research Commission and an Interagency Arctic Research Policy Committee to coordinate federal Arctic research and to establish a National Critical Materials Council to coordinate federal policies on materials critical to the national economy and security. Passed 253-1: R 115-1; D 138-0 (ND 89-0, SD 49-0), April 24, 1984. A "nay" was a vote supporting the president's position.

80. HR 4974. National Science Foundation Authorization. Gregg, R-N.H., amendment to reduce by $58.5 million certain fiscal 1985 funding authorizations for the National Science Foundation. Rejected 175-180: R 140-10; D 35-170 (ND 16-115, SD 19-55), April 25, 1984.

81. HR 4974. National Science Foundation Authorization. Walker, R-Pa., amendment to reduce fiscal 1985 funding for the National Science Foundation by 3.9 percent. Rejected 170-183: R 134-14; D 36-169 (ND 16-115, SD 20-54), April 25, 1984.

82. HR 4974. National Science Foundation Authorization. Passage of the bill to authorize $1.56 billion for the fiscal 1985 activities of the National Science Foundation. Passed 252-99: R 57-93; D 195-6 (ND 128-1, SD 67-5), April 25, 1984. A "nay" was a vote supporting the president's position.

83. Procedural Motion. Weber, R-Minn., motion to approve the House *Journal* of Wednesday, April 25. Motion agreed to 319-22: R 137-12; D 182-10 (ND 115-9, SD 67-1), April 26, 1984.

84. S 2570. Bankruptcy Court Transition Extension. Adoption of the rule (H Res 490) providing for House floor consideration of the bill to extend from April 30, 1984, to May 26, 1984, a period of transition to a new bankruptcy court system established under a 1978 law (PL 95-598). Adopted 295-47: R 99-46; D 196-1 (ND 129-1, SD 67-0), April 26, 1984.

85. S 2570. Bankruptcy Court Transition Extension. Sensenbrenner, R-Wis., motion to recommit the bill to the Judiciary Committee with instructions to change the end of a transition period to a new bankruptcy court system established under a 1978 law (PL 98-598) from May 26, 1984, to midnight May 23, 1984. Motion rejected 33-304: R 32-114; D 1-190 (ND 0-128, SD 1-62), April 26, 1984.

86. S 2570. Bankruptcy Court Transition Extension. Passage of the bill to extend from April 30, 1984, to May 26, 1984, a period of transition to a new bankruptcy court system established under a 1978 law (PL 95-598). Passed 322-13: R 133-10; D 189-3 (ND 130-0, SD 59-3), April 26, 1984.

	79	80	81	82	83	84	85	86
ALABAMA								
1 *Edwards*	?	#	?	?	?	?	?	?
2 *Dickinson*	Y	Y	Y	N	N	N	Y	Y
3 Nichols	Y	N	N	Y	Y	Y	N	Y
4 Bevill	?	?	?	?	?	?	?	?
5 Flippo	?	N	N	Y	Y	Y	N	Y
6 Erdreich	Y	N	Y	Y	Y	Y	N	Y
7 Shelby	Y	N	N	Y	Y	Y	N	Y
ALASKA								
AL *Young*	Y	Y	Y	Y	N	Y	N	Y
ARIZONA								
1 *McCain*	?	Y	Y	N	Y	?	?	?
2 Udall	Y	N	N	Y	Y	Y	N	Y
3 *Stump*	?	Y	Y	N	Y	N	Y	N
4 *Rudd*	Y	Y	Y	N	Y	Y	N	Y
5 McNulty	?	?	?	?	?	?	?	?
ARKANSAS								
1 Alexander	Y	?	?	?	?	?	?	?
2 *Bethune*	Y	Y	Y	N	?	N	N	Y
3 *Hammerschmidt*	Y	Y	Y	N	Y	N	N	Y
4 Anthony	?	N	N	Y	Y	Y	N	Y
CALIFORNIA								
1 Bosco	?	?	?	?	?	?	?	?
2 *Chappie*	Y	#	#	X	?	?	?	?
3 Matsui	Y	N	N	Y	Y	Y	N	Y
4 Fazio	Y	N	N	Y	Y	Y	N	Y
5 Burton	?	?	?	?	?	?	?	?
6 Boxer	?	?	?	?	?	?	?	?
7 Miller	?	X	?	#	?	?	?	?
8 Dellums	?	N	N	Y	?	Y	N	Y
9 Stark	?	N	N	?	Y	Y	N	Y
10 Edwards	Y	N	N	Y	Y	Y	N	Y
11 Lantos	?	N	N	Y	Y	Y	N	Y
12 *Zschau*	Y	Y	Y	N	Y	Y	N	Y
13 Mineta	Y	N	N	Y	Y	Y	N	Y
14 *Shumway*	Y	Y	Y	N	Y	N	N	N
15 Coelho	?	?	?	?	?	?	?	?
16 Panetta	?	N	N	Y	Y	Y	N	Y
17 *Pashayan*	Y	Y	Y	N	Y	?	?	?
18 Lehman	?	X	X	?	?	?	?	?
19 *Lagomarsino*	Y	Y	Y	N	Y	Y	N	Y
20 *Thomas*	Y	Y	Y	N	Y	N	N	Y
21 *Fiedler*	Y	Y	Y	N	Y	N	Y	Y
22 *Moorhead*	Y	Y	Y	N	Y	N	N	Y
23 Beilenson	Y	N	N	Y	Y	Y	N	Y
24 Waxman	Y	N	N	Y	Y	Y	N	Y
25 Roybal	?	?	?	?	?	?	?	?
26 Berman	Y	N	N	Y	Y	Y	N	Y
27 Levine	Y	X	?	?	?	?	?	?
28 Dixon	?	N	N	Y	Y	Y	N	Y
29 Hawkins	Y	N	N	Y	Y	?	N	Y
30 Martinez	Y	N	N	Y	Y	Y	N	Y
31 Dymally	?	?	?	?	?	?	?	?
32 Anderson	Y	Y	N	Y	N	N	Y	Y
33 *Dreier*	Y	Y	Y	N	Y	N	N	Y
34 Torres	Y	N	N	Y	Y	Y	N	Y
35 *Lewis*	Y	Y	N	N	Y	Y	?	?
36 Brown	Y	N	N	Y	Y	Y	N	Y
37 *McCandless*	?	Y	Y	N	Y	N	N	N
38 Patterson	?	?	?	?	?	?	?	?
39 *Dannemeyer*	Y	Y	Y	N	Y	N	Y	Y
40 *Badham*	Y	Y	Y	N	Y	N	Y	N
41 *Lowery*	Y	Y	Y	Y	?	Y	Y	N
42 *Lungren*	Y	Y	Y	N	Y	N	Y	Y

	79	80	81	82	83	84	85	86
43 *Packard*	Y	Y	Y	N	Y	Y	N	Y
44 Bates	Y	Y	N	Y	Y	Y	N	Y
45 *Hunter*	Y	Y	Y	N	Y	?	Y	Y
COLORADO								
1 Schroeder	+	Y	N	Y	N	Y	N	Y
2 Wirth	Y	N	N	Y	Y	Y	N	Y
3 Kogovsek	?	?	?	?	?	?	?	?
4 *Brown*	Y	Y	Y	N	Y	N	Y	N
5 *Kramer*	Y	Y	Y	N	Y	N	Y	N
6 *Schaefer*	Y	Y	Y	N	N	N	Y	Y
CONNECTICUT								
1 Kennelly	?	?	?	?	?	?	?	?
2 Gejdenson	?	N	N	Y	N	Y	N	Y
3 Morrison	?	N	N	Y	Y	Y	N	Y
4 *McKinney*	?	N	N	Y	Y	Y	N	Y
5 Ratchford	Y	N	N	Y	Y	Y	N	Y
6 *Johnson*	?	Y	Y	Y	Y	Y	N	Y
DELAWARE								
AL Carper	Y	Y	Y	Y	Y	Y	N	Y
FLORIDA								
1 Hutto	Y	N	N	Y	Y	Y	N	Y
2 Fuqua	?	N	N	Y	Y	Y	N	Y
3 Bennett	Y	N	N	Y	Y	Y	N	Y
4 Chappell	?	N	N	Y	Y	Y	N	Y
5 *McCollum*	Y	Y	Y	N	Y	N	Y	N
6 MacKay	Y	N	N	Y	Y	Y	N	Y
7 Gibbons	Y	N	N	Y	Y	Y	?	?
8 *Young*	Y	Y	Y	Y	N	Y	N	Y
9 *Bilirakis*	?	Y	Y	N	Y	N	N	Y
10 Ireland	?	N	N	Y	Y	Y	N	Y
11 Nelson	+	N	Y	Y	Y	Y	N	Y
12 *Lewis*	+	Y	N	N	N	N	N	Y
13 *Mack*	Y	Y	Y	N	Y	N	Y	N
14 Mica	Y	N	N	Y	Y	Y	N	Y
15 *Shaw*	Y	Y	Y	N	Y	Y	N	Y
16 Smith	Y	N	N	Y	Y	Y	N	Y
17 Lehman	?	N	N	Y	Y	Y	N	Y
18 Pepper	Y	N	N	Y	?	?	?	?
19 Fascell	Y	N	N	Y	Y	Y	N	Y
GEORGIA								
1 Thomas	Y	N	N	Y	Y	Y	N	Y
2 Hatcher	?	N	N	Y	Y	Y	N	Y
3 Ray	Y	Y	Y	Y	Y	Y	N	Y
4 Levitas	Y	N	N	Y	Y	Y	N	Y
5 Fowler	?	?	?	?	Y	Y	?	?
6 *Gingrich*	Y	Y	Y	Y	Y	?	N	Y
7 Darden	?	N	N	Y	Y	Y	N	Y
8 Rowland	?	N	N	Y	Y	Y	N	?
9 Jenkins	?	N	N	Y	Y	?	?	?
10 Barnard	?	N	N	Y	Y	N	N	Y
HAWAII								
1 Heftel	?	?	?	?	?	?	?	?
2 Akaka	Y	N	N	Y	Y	Y	N	Y
IDAHO								
1 *Craig*	Y	Y	Y	N	Y	N	Y	Y
2 *Hansen*	?	?	?	?	?	?	?	?
ILLINOIS								
1 Hayes	Y	N	N	Y	Y	Y	N	Y
2 Savage	Y	N	N	Y	Y	Y	N	Y
3 Russo	?	?	?	?	?	?	?	?
4 *O'Brien*	Y	Y	Y	Y	Y	Y	N	Y
5 Lipinski	?	?	?	?	?	?	?	?
6 *Hyde*	Y	Y	Y	N	Y	N	N	Y
7 Collins	?	X	X	?	Y	Y	N	Y
8 Rostenkowski	?	?	?	?	?	?	?	?
9 Yates	Y	N	N	Y	Y	Y	N	Y
10 *Porter*	Y	Y	Y	Y	N	Y	N	Y
11 Annunzio	?	N	N	Y	Y	Y	N	Y
12 *Crane, P.*	N	Y	Y	N	Y	N	Y	N
13 *Erlenborn*	Y	Y	Y	Y	Y	Y	N	Y
14 *Corcoran*	Y	Y	Y	N	Y	N	N	Y
15 *Madigan*	Y	Y	N	Y	Y	Y	N	Y
16 *Martin*	?	Y	Y	N	N	N	N	Y
17 Evans	Y	N	N	Y	Y	Y	N	Y
18 *Michel*	Y	Y	Y	N	Y	?	?	?
19 *Crane, D.*	?	Y	Y	N	N	N	Y	N
20 Durbin	?	N	N	Y	N	Y	N	Y
21 Price	Y	N	N	Y	Y	Y	N	Y
22 Simon	Y	N	N	Y	Y	?	Y	Y
INDIANA								
1 Hall	?	?	?	?	?	?	?	?
2 Sharp	Y	N	Y	Y	Y	Y	N	Y
3 *Hiler*	Y	Y	Y	N	Y	N	Y	Y
4 *Coats*	?	Y	Y	N	Y	N	Y	N
5 *Hillis*	Y	Y	Y	Y	Y	Y	Y	Y

ND - Northern Democrats   SD - Southern Democrats

Corresponding to Congressional Record Votes 91, 93, 94, 95, 96, 97, 98, 99

	79	80	81	82	83	84	85	86
6 ***Burton***	?	Y	Y	N	Y	N	N	Y
7 ***Myers***	?	N	Y	Y	Y	Y	Y	Y
8 McCloskey	?	N	N	Y	?	?	?	?
9 Hamilton	Y	N	Y	Y	Y	Y	N	Y
10 Jacobs	Y	?	?	?	?	?	?	?
IOWA								
1 ***Leach***	?	Y	N	Y	Y	?	N	Y
2 ***Tauke***	Y	Y	Y	Y	Y	Y	N	Y
3 ***Evans***	Y	Y	Y	Y	N	Y	N	Y
4 Smith	?	?	?	?	?	?	?	?
5 Harkin	Y	N	N	Y	N	Y	N	Y
6 Bedell	?	N	N	Y	Y	Y	N	Y
KANSAS								
1 ***Roberts***	Y	Y	Y	N	N	N	N	Y
2 Slattery	Y	Y	Y	N	Y	Y	N	Y
3 ***Winn***	Y	Y	Y	N	Y	N	N	Y
4 Glickman	?	N	N	Y	Y	Y	N	Y
5 ***Whittaker***	Y	Y	Y	N	Y	N	N	Y
KENTUCKY								
1 Hubbard	Y	Y	Y	N	Y	Y	N	Y
2 Natcher	Y	N	N	Y	Y	Y	N	Y
3 Mazzoli	Y	N	N	Y	Y	Y	N	Y
4 ***Snyder***	?	Y	Y	N	Y	Y	Y	Y
5 ***Rogers***	?	Y	Y	N	Y	Y	N	Y
6 ***Hopkins***	Y	Y	Y	N	Y	Y	N	Y
7 Perkins	Y	N	N	Y	Y	Y	N	Y
LOUISIANA								
1 ***Livingston***	Y	Y	Y	N	Y	Y	N	Y
2 Boggs	?	N	N	Y	?	?	?	?
3 Tauzin	?	Y	Y	Y	Y	Y	N	Y
4 Roemer	Y	Y	Y	N	N	Y	N	N
5 Huckaby	Y	Y	N	Y	Y	Y	N	Y
6 ***Moore***	Y	Y	Y	Y	Y	Y	N	Y
7 Breaux	?	N	Y	Y	P	Y	N	Y
8 Long	?	N	N	Y	Y	Y	N	Y
MAINE								
1 ***McKernan***	Y	Y	N	Y	Y	Y	N	Y
2 ***Snowe***	Y	Y	N	Y	Y	Y	N	Y
MARYLAND								
1 Dyson	?	Y	N	Y	Y	Y	N	Y
2 Long	?	N	N	Y	Y	?	N	Y
3 Mikulski	?	N	N	Y	Y	Y	N	Y
4 ***Holt***	Y	Y	Y	Y	Y	N	N	Y
5 Hoyer	Y	N	N	Y	Y	Y	N	Y
6 Byron	Y	Y	Y	Y	Y	Y	N	Y
7 Mitchell	Y	N	N	Y	N	Y	N	Y
8 Barnes	Y	N	N	Y	Y	Y	N	Y
MASSACHUSETTS								
1 ***Conte***	?	?	?	#	?	?	?	?
2 Boland	Y	N	N	Y	Y	Y	N	Y
3 Early	Y	N	N	Y	Y	Y	N	Y
4 Frank	Y	N	N	Y	Y	Y	N	Y
5 Shannon	?	?	?	?	?	Y	?	?
6 Mavroules	?	N	N	Y	Y	Y	N	Y
7 Markey	?	?	?	?	?	?	?	?
8 O'Neill								
9 Moakley	Y	N	N	Y	Y	Y	N	Y
10 Studds	?	N	N	Y	Y	Y	?	?
11 Donnelly	?	?	?	?	?	?	?	?
MICHIGAN								
1 Conyers	Y	N	N	Y	Y	Y	N	Y
2 ***Pursell***	?	?	?	#	?	?	?	?
3 Wolpe	Y	N	N	Y	Y	Y	N	Y
4 ***Siljander***	?	Y	Y	N	Y	Y	Y	Y
5 ***Sawyer***	?	?	?	?	?	?	?	?
6 Carr	Y	N	N	Y	Y	Y	N	Y
7 Kildee	Y	N	N	Y	Y	Y	N	Y
8 Traxler	Y	N	N	?	Y	Y	N	Y
9 ***Vander Jagt***	Y	Y	Y	Y	Y	Y	N	Y
10 Albosta	?	N	N	Y	Y	Y	N	Y
11 ***Davis***	?	N	Y	Y	Y	Y	N	Y
12 Bonior	Y	N	N	Y	Y	Y	N	Y
13 Crockett	Y	N	N	Y	?	?	?	?
14 Hertel	Y	N	N	Y	Y	Y	N	Y
15 Ford	Y	N	N	Y	?	Y	N	Y
16 Dingell	?	N	N	Y	Y	Y	N	Y
17 Levin	Y	N	N	Y	Y	Y	N	Y
18 ***Broomfield***	?	Y	Y	N	Y	Y	Y	N
MINNESOTA								
1 Penny	Y	Y	Y	Y	N	Y	N	Y
2 ***Weber***	?	Y	Y	N	Y	N	N	Y
3 ***Frenzel***	Y	Y	Y	N	N	Y	N	Y
4 Vento	Y	N	N	Y	Y	Y	N	Y
5 Sabo	Y	N	N	Y	N	Y	N	Y
6 Sikorski	Y	N	Y	Y	N	Y	N	Y
7 ***Stangeland***	Y	Y	?	N	?	Y	N	Y
8 Oberstar	Y	N	N	Y	Y	Y	N	Y
MISSISSIPPI								
1 Whitten	Y	Y	N	Y	Y	Y	Y	Y
2 ***Franklin***	?	Y	Y	N	Y	Y	N	Y
3 Montgomery	Y	Y	Y	Y	Y	Y	N	Y
4 Dowdy	?	N	N	Y	Y	Y	N	Y
5 ***Lott***	Y	Y	Y	N	Y	Y	N	Y
MISSOURI								
1 Clay	Y	N	N	Y	N	Y	N	Y
2 Young	Y	N	N	Y	Y	Y	N	Y
3 Gephardt	?	?	?	?	Y	Y	N	Y
4 Skelton	?	?	?	?	?	?	?	?
5 Wheat	Y	N	N	Y	Y	Y	N	Y
6 ***Coleman***	Y	Y	Y	Y	Y	N	Y	Y
7 ***Taylor***	Y	Y	Y	N	Y	Y	N	Y
8 ***Emerson***	Y	#	#	?	N	Y	N	Y
9 Volkmer	Y	N	N	Y	Y	Y	N	Y
MONTANA								
1 Williams	Y	N	N	Y	Y	Y	N	Y
2 ***Marlenee***	?	?	?	?	?	?	?	?
NEBRASKA								
1 ***Bereuter***	?	?	?	?	Y	Y	N	Y
2 ***Daub***	?	Y	Y	N	Y	Y	Y	Y
3 ***Smith***	Y	Y	Y	N	Y	Y	N	Y
NEVADA								
1 Reid	?	N	N	Y	Y	Y	N	Y
2 ***Vucanovich***	?	?	#	X	?	?	?	?
NEW HAMPSHIRE								
1 D'Amours	Y	?	?	?	?	?	?	?
2 ***Gregg***	Y	Y	Y	N	Y	Y	N	Y
NEW JERSEY								
1 Florio	Y	N	N	Y	?	?	?	?
2 Hughes	Y	Y	Y	Y	Y	Y	N	Y
3 Howard	Y	N	N	Y	Y	Y	N	Y
4 ***Smith***	Y	N	Y	Y	Y	Y	N	Y
5 ***Roukema***	Y	Y	Y	N	Y	Y	N	Y
6 Dwyer	?	N	N	Y	Y	Y	N	Y
7 ***Rinaldo***	Y	Y	Y	Y	Y	Y	N	Y
8 Roe	?	N	N	Y	Y	Y	N	Y
9 Torricelli	Y	N	N	Y	Y	Y	?	?
10 Rodino	?	?	?	?	?	?	?	?
11 Minish	?	?	?	?	?	?	?	?
12 ***Courter***	Y	Y	Y	N	?	?	?	?
13 Vacancy								
14 Guarini	?	X	X	?	?	?	?	?
NEW MEXICO								
1 ***Lujan***	Y	Y	Y	Y	Y	Y	Y	Y
2 ***Skeen***	Y	Y	Y	Y	Y	Y	N	Y
3 Richardson	P	N	N	Y	Y	Y	N	Y
NEW YORK								
1 ***Carney***	Y	Y	Y	Y	Y	Y	N	Y
2 Downey	Y	N	N	Y	Y	Y	N	Y
3 Mrazek	Y	N	N	Y	Y	Y	N	Y
4 ***Lent***	Y	Y	Y	Y	Y	Y	N	?
5 ***McGrath***	?	Y	Y	Y	Y	N	N	Y
6 Addabbo	?	X	X	#	?	?	?	?
7 Ackerman	?	?	?	?	?	?	?	?
8 Scheuer	?	N	N	Y	Y	Y	N	Y
9 Ferraro	?	?	?	?	?	?	?	?
10 Schumer	?	N	N	Y	Y	Y	N	Y
11 Towns	?	N	N	Y	Y	Y	N	Y
12 Owens	Y	N	N	Y	Y	Y	N	Y
13 Solarz	Y	N	N	Y	Y	Y	N	Y
14 ***Molinari***	Y	Y	Y	Y	Y	Y	N	Y
15 ***Green***	Y	N	N	Y	Y	Y	N	Y
16 Rangel	?	?	?	?	?	?	?	?
17 Weiss	+	-	-	+	+	+	-	+
18 Garcia	?	N	N	Y	Y	Y	N	Y
19 Biaggi	Y	N	N	Y	Y	Y	N	Y
20 Ottinger	?	N	N	Y	P	Y	N	Y
21 ***Fish***	Y	Y	Y	Y	Y	Y	N	Y
22 ***Gilman***	Y	N	N	Y	Y	Y	N	Y
23 Stratton	Y	N	N	Y	Y	Y	N	Y
24 ***Solomon***	Y	Y	Y	N	N	N	Y	N
25 ***Boehlert***	Y	N	N	Y	Y	Y	N	Y
26 ***Martin***	Y	Y	Y	Y	Y	Y	N	?
27 ***Wortley***	Y	Y	Y	Y	Y	Y	N	Y
28 McHugh	?	N	N	Y	Y	Y	N	Y
29 ***Horton***	?	N	N	Y	Y	Y	N	Y
30 ***Conable***	Y	Y	Y	N	Y	N	Y	Y
31 ***Kemp***	Y	Y	Y	N	Y	Y	N	Y
32 LaFalce	?	?	?	?	?	?	?	?
33 Nowak	?	?	?	?	?	?	?	?
34 Lundine	Y	N	N	Y	?	Y	N	Y
NORTH CAROLINA								
1 Jones	?	N	N	?	Y	Y	N	Y
2 Valentine	?	?	?	?	?	?	?	?
3 Whitley	Y	N	Y	Y	Y	Y	N	Y
4 Andrews	?	N	Y	Y	Y	Y	N	?
5 Neal	Y	N	Y	Y	Y	Y	N	Y
6 Britt	?	N	Y	Y	Y	Y	N	Y
7 Rose	Y	N	N	Y	Y	Y	N	Y
8 Hefner	Y	N	Y	Y	?	?	?	?
9 ***Martin***	?	Y	Y	Y	Y	Y	Y	Y
10 ***Broyhill***	Y	Y	Y	N	Y	Y	N	Y
11 Clarke	Y	N	N	?	Y	Y	N	Y
NORTH DAKOTA								
AL Dorgan	?	N	N	Y	Y	Y	N	Y
OHIO								
1 Luken	?	N	Y	Y	Y	Y	N	Y
2 ***Gradison***	Y	Y	Y	Y	Y	Y	Y	Y
3 Hall	Y	Y	Y	Y	?	Y	N	Y
4 ***Oxley***	Y	Y	Y	N	Y	Y	N	Y
5 ***Latta***	?	Y	Y	N	Y	Y	N	Y
6 ***McEwen***	Y	Y	Y	N	Y	N	Y	Y
7 ***DeWine***	?	Y	Y	N	Y	N	Y	Y
8 ***Kindness***	?	Y	Y	N	Y	Y	N	Y
9 Kaptur	?	?	X	?	?	?	?	?
10 ***Miller***	?	Y	Y	N	N	Y	N	Y
11 Eckart	Y	N	N	Y	Y	Y	N	Y
12 ***Kasich***	Y	Y	Y	N	Y	Y	N	Y
13 Pease	Y	N	N	Y	Y	Y	N	Y
14 Seiberling	?	N	N	Y	Y	Y	N	Y
15 ***Wylie***	Y	Y	Y	Y	Y	Y	N	Y
16 ***Regula***	Y	Y	Y	Y	Y	Y	?	?
17 ***Williams***	Y	N	Y	Y	Y	N	N	Y
18 Applegate	Y	Y	Y	Y	?	Y	N	Y
19 Feighan	Y	N	N	Y	Y	Y	N	Y
20 Oakar	?	N	N	Y	Y	Y	N	Y
21 Stokes	?	?	?	?	?	?	?	?
OKLAHOMA								
1 Jones	?	Y	N	Y	?	?	?	?
2 Synar	Y	N	N	Y	Y	Y	?	+
3 Watkins	Y	N	Y	Y	Y	Y	N	Y
4 McCurdy	Y	N	N	Y	Y	Y	N	Y
5 ***Edwards***	Y	Y	?	N	Y	N	N	Y
6 English	Y	Y	Y	Y	Y	Y	N	Y
OREGON								
1 AuCoin	?	Y	N	Y	Y	Y	?	Y
2 ***Smith, R.***	Y	Y	Y	Y	Y	N	N	Y
3 Wyden	Y	N	N	Y	Y	Y	N	Y
4 Weaver	?	N	N	Y	Y	Y	N	Y
5 ***Smith, D.***	Y	Y	Y	N	?	?	?	?
PENNSYLVANIA								
1 Foglietta	?	?	?	?	?	?	?	?
2 Gray	Y	N	N	Y	?	Y	N	Y
3 Borski	Y	N	N	Y	Y	Y	N	Y
4 Kolter	Y	Y	Y	Y	Y	Y	N	Y
5 ***Schulze***	?	Y	Y	Y	Y	Y	N	Y
6 Yatron	?	Y	Y	Y	Y	Y	N	Y
7 Edgar	Y	N	N	Y	Y	Y	N	Y
8 Kostmayer	?	N	Y	Y	Y	Y	N	Y
9 ***Shuster***	Y	Y	Y	N	Y	N	N	Y
10 ***McDade***	?	?	?	?	?	?	?	?
11 Harrison	Y	?	?	?	Y	Y	N	Y
12 Murtha	Y	N	N	Y	Y	Y	N	Y
13 ***Coughlin***	Y	Y	Y	Y	N	Y	N	Y
14 Coyne	?	N	N	Y	Y	Y	N	Y
15 ***Ritter***	?	Y	Y	N	Y	Y	N	Y
16 ***Walker***	Y	Y	Y	N	N	N	Y	N
17 ***Gekas***	Y	Y	Y	N	Y	N	Y	Y
18 Walgren	Y	N	N	Y	Y	Y	N	Y
19 ***Goodling***	Y	Y	Y	N	N	N	N	Y
20 Gaydos	?	Y	Y	Y	?	Y	N	Y
21 ***Ridge***	?	Y	N	Y	Y	Y	N	?
22 Murphy	?	Y	Y	Y	Y	Y	N	Y
23 ***Clinger***	?	Y	Y	Y	Y	Y	Y	Y
RHODE ISLAND								
1 St Germain	?	?	?	?	?	?	?	?
2 ***Schneider***	?	Y	N	N	Y	Y	N	Y
SOUTH CAROLINA								
1 ***Hartnett***	Y	Y	Y	N	Y	N	N	Y
2 ***Spence***	Y	Y	Y	N	Y	Y	N	Y
3 Derrick	?	N	N	Y	Y	Y	N	Y
4 ***Campbell***	?	?	?	?	Y	Y	N	Y
5 Spratt	Y	N	N	Y	Y	Y	N	Y
6 Tallon	?	Y	Y	Y	Y	Y	N	Y
SOUTH DAKOTA								
AL Daschle	?	?	?	?	?	?	?	?
TENNESSEE								
1 ***Quillen***	?	Y	Y	Y	Y	Y	N	Y
2 ***Duncan***	Y	Y	Y	Y	Y	Y	N	Y
3 Lloyd	?	N	N	Y	Y	Y	N	Y
4 Cooper	Y	Y	N	Y	Y	Y	N	Y
5 Boner	?	N	N	Y	?	?	N	Y
6 Gore	?	N	N	Y	Y	Y	?	?
7 ***Sundquist***	Y	Y	Y	N	Y	?	?	?
8 Jones	?	?	?	?	?	?	?	?
9 Ford	Y	?	?	?	?	?	?	?
TEXAS								
1 Hall, S.	Y	Y	Y	N	Y	?	?	Y
2 Wilson	?	?	?	?	?	?	?	?
3 ***Bartlett***	Y	Y	Y	N	Y	Y	N	Y
4 Hall, R.	Y	N	N	Y	Y	Y	N	Y
5 Bryant	Y	?	?	?	?	?	?	?
6 ***Gramm***	Y	Y	Y	N	Y	N	Y	Y
7 ***Archer***	Y	Y	Y	N	Y	Y	N	Y
8 ***Fields***	Y	Y	Y	N	Y	N	N	Y
9 Brooks	Y	N	N	Y	Y	Y	N	Y
10 Pickle	?	?	?	?	?	?	?	?
11 Leath	Y	N	N	Y	Y	Y	N	Y
12 Wright	Y	?	?	?	?	?	?	?
13 Hightower	?	?	?	?	?	?	?	?
14 Patman	?	?	?	?	?	?	?	?
15 de la Garza	Y	Y	N	Y	Y	Y	N	Y
16 Coleman	Y	N	N	Y	Y	Y	N	Y
17 Stenholm	?	Y	Y	N	Y	Y	N	N
18 Leland	?	N	N	Y	Y	Y	N	Y
19 Hance	?	?	?	?	?	?	?	?
20 Gonzalez	Y	N	N	Y	Y	Y	N	Y
21 ***Loeffler***	Y	Y	Y	N	Y	Y	N	Y
22 ***Paul***	?	#	#	X	?	?	?	?
23 Kazen	?	?	?	?	?	?	?	?
24 Frost	?	?	?	?	?	?	?	?
25 Andrews	Y	Y	N	Y	Y	Y	N	Y
26 Vandergriff	?	Y	Y	Y	Y	?	N	Y
27 Ortiz	?	?	?	?	?	?	?	+
UTAH								
1 ***Hansen***	Y	Y	Y	N	Y	Y	N	Y
2 ***Marriott***	?	#	#	X	?	?	?	?
3 ***Nielson***	Y	Y	Y	N	Y	Y	N	Y
VERMONT								
AL ***Jeffords***	Y	N	N	Y	Y	Y	N	Y
VIRGINIA								
1 ***Bateman***	?	Y	Y	Y	Y	Y	N	Y
2 ***Whitehurst***	Y	Y	Y	Y	Y	Y	N	Y
3 ***Bliley***	?	Y	Y	N	Y	Y	N	Y
4 Sisisky	Y	Y	Y	Y	Y	Y	N	Y
5 Daniel	Y	Y	Y	N	Y	Y	N	N
6 Olin	Y	Y	N	Y	Y	Y	N	Y
7 ***Robinson***	?	#	?	?	?	?	?	?
8 ***Parris***	Y	Y	Y	N	Y	Y	N	Y
9 Boucher	Y	N	N	Y	Y	Y	?	?
10 ***Wolf***	Y	Y	Y	Y	Y	Y	N	Y
WASHINGTON								
1 ***Pritchard***	Y	Y	Y	Y	Y	Y	N	Y
2 Swift	?	N	N	Y	Y	Y	N	Y
3 Bonker	?	?	?	?	?	?	?	?
4 ***Morrison***	Y	Y	Y	N	Y	Y	N	Y
5 Foley	?	N	N	Y	Y	Y	N	Y
6 Dicks	?	?	?	?	?	?	?	?
7 Lowry	Y	N	N	Y	Y	Y	N	Y
8 ***Chandler***	Y	Y	Y	Y	Y	Y	N	Y
WEST VIRGINIA								
1 Mollohan	?	N	N	Y	Y	Y	N	Y
2 Staggers	Y	N	N	Y	Y	Y	N	Y
3 Wise	Y	N	N	Y	Y	Y	N	Y
4 Rahall	Y	N	N	Y	Y	Y	N	Y
WISCONSIN								
1 Aspin	?	?	?	?	Y	Y	N	Y
2 Kastenmeier	Y	N	N	Y	Y	Y	N	Y
3 ***Gunderson***	Y	Y	Y	N	Y	Y	N	Y
4 Kleczka	?	N	N	Y	Y	Y	N	Y
5 Moody	?	N	N	Y	Y	Y	N	Y
6 ***Petri***	Y	Y	Y	N	Y	N	N	Y
7 Obey	Y	N	N	Y	Y	Y	N	Y
8 ***Roth***	Y	?	?	?	Y	Y	Y	Y
9 ***Sensenbrenner***	Y	Y	Y	N	Y	N	Y	N
WYOMING								
AL ***Cheney***	?	Y	Y	N	Y	Y	N	Y

Southern states - Ala., Ark., Fla., Ga., Ky., La., Miss., N.C., Okla., S.C., Tenn., Texas, Va.

KEY

Y Voted for (yea).
Paired for.
+ Announced for.
N Voted against (nay).
X Paired against.
- Announced against.
P Voted "present".
C Voted "present" to avoid possible conflict of interest.
? Did not vote or otherwise make a position known.

———

Democrats *Republicans*

---

87. HR 5172. National Bureau of Standards Authorization. Adoption of the rule (H Res 481) providing for House floor consideration of the bill to authorize appropriations for the National Bureau of Standards and related agencies for fiscal 1984 and fiscal 1985. Adopted 282-47: R 96-47; D 186-0 (ND 126-0, SD 60-0), April 26, 1984.

88. HR 5172. National Bureau of Standards Authorization. Fuqua, D-Fla., amendment to the Gregg, R-N.H., substitute to the Walker, R-Pa., amendment, to cut the fiscal 1985 authorization by approximately $2.5 million. Adopted 164-151: R 9-131; D 155-20 (ND 111-6, SD 44-14), April 26, 1984. (The Gregg substitute subsequently was rejected *(see vote 90, below)*.)

89. HR 5172. National Bureau of Standards Authorization. Gregg, R-N.H., amendment to the Walker, R-Pa., amendment, to cut the fiscal 1985 authorization by $6 million. Adopted 185-126: R 135-1; D 50-125 (ND 20-98, SD 30-27), April 26, 1984. A "yea" was a vote supporting the president's position.

90. HR 5172. National Bureau of Standards Authorization. Gregg, R-N.H., substitute to the Walker, R-Pa., amendment, as amended by the Fuqua, D-Fla., amendment *(see vote 88, above)*, to cut the fiscal 1985 authorization by $2.5 million. Rejected 123-172: R 1-129; D 122-43 (ND 97-13, SD 25-30), April 26, 1984. A "nay" was a vote supporting the president's position.

91. HR 5172. National Bureau of Standards Authorization. Rudd, R-Ariz., amendment to eliminate a $500,000 authorization for a study on conversion to the metric system. Adopted 146-143: R 101-25; D 45-118 (ND 20-89, SD 25-29), April 26, 1984.

92. HR 5172. National Bureau of Standards Authorization. Fuqua, D-Fla., motion that the Committee of the Whole rise without coming to a resolution on the bill. Motion agreed to 159-129: R 3-122; D 156-7 (ND 108-0, SD 48-7), April 26, 1984.

93. HR 7. Child Nutrition. Bartlett, R-Texas, substitute to cut the authorizations in the bill for child nutrition programs from four to three years, through fiscal 1987, providing a total of $4.6 billion in budget authority for the programs. Rejected 136-270: R 116-45; D 20-225 (ND 1-167, SD 19-58), May 1, 1984.

94. HR 7. Child Nutrition. Passage of the bill to reauthorize child nutrition programs through fiscal 1988, providing a four-year total of $9 billion in budget authority for the programs. Passed 343-72: R 95-67; D 248-5 (ND 171-0, SD 77-5), May 1, 1984. A "nay" was a vote supporting the president's position.

	87	88	89	90	91	92	93	94
ALABAMA								
1 *Edwards*	?	?	?	?	?	?	Y	Y
2 *Dickinson*	N	N	Y	N	N	N	Y	Y
3 Nichols	?	?	?	?	?	?	Y	Y
4 Bevill	?	?	?	?	?	?	N	Y
5 Flippo	Y	Y	N	Y	N	Y	N	Y
6 Erdreich	Y	Y	Y	N	Y	Y	N	Y
7 Shelby	Y	?	?	?	?	?	?	?
ALASKA								
AL *Young*	Y	Y	Y	N	Y	Y	Y	Y
ARIZONA								
1 *McCain*	?	X	?	?	?	?	Y	N
2 Udall	Y	Y	N	Y	N	Y	N	Y
3 *Stump*	N	N	Y	N	Y	N	Y	N
4 *Rudd*	Y	N	Y	N	Y	N	Y	N
5 McNulty	?	?	?	?	?	?	N	Y
ARKANSAS								
1 Alexander	?	?	?	?	?	?	N	Y
2 *Bethune*	N	N	Y	N	?	?	Y	N
3 *Hammerschmidt*	Y	N	Y	N	Y	N	Y	Y
4 Anthony	Y	Y	N	Y	N	Y	N	Y
CALIFORNIA								
1 Bosco	?	?	?	?	?	?	N	Y
2 *Chappie*	?	X	?	?	?	?	Y	Y
3 Matsui	Y	Y	N	Y	N	Y	?	Y
4 Fazio	Y	Y	N	?	?	?	N	Y
5 Burton	?	#	?	?	?	?	N	Y
6 Boxer	?	?	?	?	?	?	N	Y
7 Miller	?	#	?	?	?	?	N	Y
8 Dellums	Y	Y	N	Y	N	Y	N	Y
9 Stark	Y	Y	N	?	Y	Y	N	Y
10 Edwards	Y	Y	N	Y	N	Y	N	Y
11 Lantos	Y	Y	N	Y	N	Y	N	Y
12 *Zschau*	Y	N	Y	N	Y	N	Y	Y
13 Mineta	Y	Y	N	Y	N	Y	N	Y
14 *Shumway*	N	N	Y	N	Y	N	Y	N
15 Coelho	?	?	?	?	?	?	N	Y
16 Panetta	Y	Y	Y	N	Y	Y	N	Y
17 *Pashayan*	Y	N	Y	?	?	?	Y	Y
18 Lehman	?	#	?	?	?	?	N	Y
19 *Lagomarsino*	Y	N	Y	N	Y	N	Y	N
20 *Thomas*	Y	N	Y	N	N	N	Y	N
21 *Fiedler*	Y	N	Y	N	Y	N	Y	N
22 *Moorhead*	N	N	Y	N	Y	N	Y	N
23 Beilenson	Y	Y	N	Y	N	Y	N	Y
24 Waxman	Y	Y	N	Y	N	Y	N	Y
25 Roybal	?	?	?	?	?	?	N	Y
26 Berman	Y	Y	N	?	N	Y	?	Y
27 Levine	?	?	?	?	?	?	N	Y
28 Dixon	Y	?	N	Y	N	Y	N	Y
29 Hawkins	Y	Y	?	Y	N	Y	N	Y
30 Martinez	Y	Y	N	Y	N	Y	N	Y
31 Dymally	?	?	?	?	?	?	N	Y
32 Anderson	Y	?	N	N	N	Y	N	Y
33 *Dreier*	N	N	Y	N	Y	N	Y	N
34 Torres	Y	?	N	Y	N	?	N	Y
35 *Lewis*	?	?	?	?	?	?	Y	N
36 Brown	Y	Y	N	Y	N	Y	N	Y
37 *McCandless*	N	N	Y	N	Y	N	Y	N
38 Patterson	?	?	?	?	?	?	N	Y
39 *Dannemeyer*	N	N	Y	?	Y	N	Y	N
40 *Badham*	N	N	?	?	?	?	Y	N
41 Lowery	Y	N	Y	N	Y	N	Y	Y
42 Lungren	N	N	Y	N	Y	N	Y	N
43 *Packard*	Y	N	Y	N	Y	N	Y	Y
44 Bates	Y	Y	Y	?	?	?	N	Y
45 *Hunter*	N	N	Y	?	?	?	Y	N
COLORADO								
1 Schroeder	Y	Y	Y	N	Y	N	N	Y
2 Wirth	Y	Y	N	Y	N	Y	?	?
3 Kogovsek	?	?	?	?	?	?	N	Y
4 *Brown*	N	N	N	N	N	N	Y	N
5 *Kramer*	Y	N	Y	N	Y	N	Y	N
6 *Schaefer*	N	Y	Y	N	Y	N	Y	N
CONNECTICUT								
1 Kennelly	?	?	?	?	?	?	N	Y
2 Gejdenson	Y	Y	N	Y	N	Y	N	Y
3 Morrison	Y	Y	N	Y	?	Y	N	Y
4 *McKinney*	Y	Y	Y	N	N	N	N	Y
5 Ratchford	Y	Y	Y	Y	Y	Y	N	Y
6 *Johnson*	Y	N	Y	N	Y	N	Y	N
DELAWARE								
AL Carper	Y	Y	Y	N	N	Y	N	Y
FLORIDA								
1 Hutto	Y	Y	Y	N	Y	N	Y	N
2 Fuqua	Y	Y	N	Y	N	Y	?	Y
3 Bennett	Y	Y	N	Y	Y	Y	Y	Y
4 Chappell	?	Y	N	Y	N	Y	N	Y
5 *McCollum*	N	N	Y	N	N	N	Y	N
6 MacKay	Y	Y	?	?	?	?	N	Y
7 Gibbons	?	?	?	?	?	?	N	Y
8 *Young*	N	N	Y	N	N	N	Y	N
9 *Bilirakis*	N	N	Y	N	N	Y	N	N
10 Ireland	Y	Y	N	Y	N	Y	N	Y
11 Nelson	Y	Y	N	Y	N	Y	N	Y
12 *Lewis*	Y	N	Y	N	N	N	Y	N
13 *Mack*	N	N	Y	N	Y	N	Y	N
14 Mica	Y	Y	N	Y	N	Y	N	Y
15 *Shaw*	N	N	Y	N	N	N	Y	N
16 Smith	Y	Y	N	Y	N	Y	N	Y
17 Lehman	Y	Y	N	?	N	Y	N	Y
18 Pepper	?	#	?	?	?	?	N	Y
19 Fascell	Y	Y	N	Y	N	Y	X	Y
GEORGIA								
1 Thomas	Y	Y	Y	N	N	Y	N	Y
2 Hatcher	Y	?	?	?	?	?	N	Y
3 Ray	Y	N	Y	N	Y	Y	Y	Y
4 Levitas	Y	N	Y	N	Y	N	Y	Y
5 Fowler	?	?	?	?	?	?	N	Y
6 *Gingrich*	N	N	Y	N	Y	N	Y	N
7 Darden	Y	Y	N	N	N	Y	N	Y
8 Rowland	Y	?	?	?	?	?	N	Y
9 Jenkins	?	?	?	?	?	?	N	Y
10 Barnard	Y	Y	Y	N	N	Y	N	Y
HAWAII								
1 Heftel	?	?	?	?	?	?	?	?
2 Akaka	Y	Y	N	Y	N	Y	N	Y
IDAHO								
1 *Craig*	N	N	Y	N	Y	N	Y	N
2 *Hansen*	?	?	?	?	?	?	?	?
ILLINOIS								
1 Hayes	Y	Y	N	Y	N	Y	N	Y
2 Savage	Y	Y	N	Y	N	Y	N	Y
3 Russo	?	?	?	?	?	?	N	Y
4 *O'Brien*	Y	N	Y	N	N	N	N	Y
5 Lipinski	?	?	?	?	?	?	N	Y
6 *Hyde*	Y	N	Y	N	Y	N	Y	N
7 Collins	Y	Y	N	Y	N	Y	N	Y
8 Rostenkowski	?	?	?	?	?	?	N	Y
9 Yates	Y	Y	N	Y	N	Y	N	Y
10 *Porter*	Y	N	Y	N	Y	N	Y	N
11 Annunzio	Y	Y	N	Y	N	Y	N	Y
12 *Crane, P.*	N	N	Y	N	Y	N	Y	N
13 *Erlenborn*	Y	N	?	?	?	?	Y	N
14 *Corcoran*	Y	N	Y	N	Y	N	Y	N
15 *Madigan*	Y	N	Y	N	Y	N	Y	N
16 *Martin*	N	N	N	N	N	N	Y	N
17 Evans	Y	N	Y	N	Y	N	Y	N
18 *Michel*	?	X	?	?	?	?	Y	N
19 *Crane, D.*	N	N	Y	?	?	?	Y	N
20 Durbin	Y	Y	Y	N	Y	N	N	Y
21 Price	Y	Y	N	Y	N	Y	N	Y
22 Simon	Y	Y	?	?	?	?	?	?
INDIANA								
1 Hall	?	?	?	?	?	?	?	?
2 Sharp	Y	Y	Y	N	Y	N	Y	Y
3 *Hiler*	N	N	Y	N	Y	N	Y	N
4 *Coats*	Y	N	Y	N	Y	N	Y	Y
5 Hillis	Y	?	?	?	?	?	Y	Y

ND - Northern Democrats   SD - Southern Democrats

Corresponding to Congressional Record Votes 100, 102, 103, 104, 105, 106, 108, 109

	87	88	89	90	91	92	93	94
6 ***Burton***	N	N	Y	N	Y	N	Y	N
7 ***Myers***	Y	N	Y	N	Y	N	Y	Y
8 McCloskey	?	?	?	?	?	?	N	Y
9 Hamilton	Y	Y	Y	N	Y	Y	N	Y
10 Jacobs	?	?	?	?	?	?	N	Y
IOWA								
1 ***Leach***	Y	N	Y	N	N	Y	Y	Y
2 ***Tauke***	Y	N	Y	N	N	N	Y	Y
3 ***Evans***	Y	N	?	?	?	?	Y	Y
4 Smith	?	?	?	?	?	?	N	Y
5 Harkin	Y	Y	N	Y	N	Y	N	Y
6 Bedell	Y	Y	N	Y	N	Y	N	Y
KANSAS								
1 ***Roberts***	N	N	Y	N	Y	N	Y	N
2 Slattery	Y	N	Y	N	Y	Y	N	Y
3 ***Winn***	Y	N	Y	N	Y	N	Y	N
4 Glickman	Y	N	Y	N	Y	Y	N	Y
5 ***Whittaker***	Y	N	Y	?	?	?	Y	N
KENTUCKY								
1 Hubbard	Y	N	Y	N	Y	N	N	Y
2 Natcher	Y	Y	N	Y	N	Y	N	Y
3 Mazzoli	Y	Y	Y	N	Y	Y	N	Y
4 ***Snyder***	Y	N	Y	N	Y	N	N	Y
5 ***Rogers***	Y	N	Y	N	Y	N	N	Y
6 ***Hopkins***	Y	N	Y	N	Y	N	Y	N
7 Perkins	Y	Y	N	Y	N	Y	N	Y
LOUISIANA								
1 ***Livingston***	N	N	Y	N	Y	N	Y	N
2 Boggs	?	?	?	?	?	?	N	Y
3 Tauzin	Y	N	Y	N	N	Y	Y	Y
4 Roemer	Y	N	Y	N	Y	N	Y	Y
5 Huckaby	Y	N	Y	?	?	?	N	Y
6 ***Moore***	Y	N	Y	N	Y	N	Y	Y
7 Breaux	Y	Y	Y	N	Y	Y	Y	Y
8 Long	Y	Y	N	Y	N	Y	N	Y
MAINE								
1 ***McKernan***	Y	N	Y	N	N	N	N	Y
2 ***Snowe***	Y	N	Y	N	N	N	N	Y
MARYLAND								
1 Dyson	Y	Y	N	N	Y	Y	N	Y
2 Long	Y	Y	N	Y	N	Y	N	Y
3 Mikulski	Y	Y	N	Y	Y	Y	N	Y
4 ***Holt***	N	N	Y	N	Y	N	Y	Y
5 Hoyer	Y	Y	N	Y	N	Y	N	Y
6 Byron	Y	Y	N	Y	Y	Y	Y	Y
7 Mitchell	Y	Y	N	Y	N	Y	N	Y
8 Barnes	?	Y	N	Y	N	Y	N	Y
MASSACHUSETTS								
1 ***Conte***	?	?	?	?	?	?	N	Y
2 Boland	Y	Y	N	Y	?	?	N	Y
3 Early	Y	Y	N	?	?	?	?	Y
4 Frank	Y	Y	N	?	?	?	N	Y
5 Shannon	Y	?	?	?	?	?	N	Y
6 Mavroules	Y	?	?	?	?	?	N	Y
7 Markey	?	?	?	?	?	?	?	?
8 O'Neill								
9 Moakley	Y	Y	N	Y	N	Y	N	Y
10 Studds	?	?	?	?	?	?	N	Y
11 Donnelly	?	?	?	?	?	?	N	Y
MICHIGAN								
1 Conyers	?	?	?	?	?	?	N	Y
2 ***Pursell***	?	?	?	?	?	?	N	Y
3 Wolpe	Y	Y	N	Y	N	Y	N	Y
4 ***Siljander***	N	N	Y	N	Y	N	Y	N
5 ***Sawyer***	?	?	?	?	?	?	N	Y
6 Carr	Y	Y	N	Y	N	Y	N	Y
7 Kildee	Y	Y	N	Y	N	Y	N	Y
8 Traxler	Y	?	?	?	?	?	N	Y
9 ***Vander Jagt***	Y	N	Y	N	Y	N	Y	Y
10 Albosta	Y	?	?	?	?	?	N	Y
11 ***Davis***	Y	N	Y	N	N	N	Y	Y
12 Bonior	Y	?	N	Y	N	Y	N	Y
13 Crockett	?	?	?	?	?	?	N	Y
14 Hertel	Y	Y	N	Y	N	Y	N	Y
15 Ford	Y	?	?	?	?	?	N	Y
16 Dingell	Y	Y	N	Y	N	Y	N	Y
17 Levin	Y	Y	Y	Y	N	?	N	Y
18 ***Broomfield***	Y	N	Y	N	Y	N	Y	Y
MINNESOTA								
1 Penny	Y	N	Y	N	Y	Y	N	Y
2 ***Weber***	Y	N	Y	N	Y	N	Y	N
3 ***Frenzel***	Y	N	Y	N	N	N	Y	Y
4 Vento	Y	N	N	Y	N	Y	N	Y
5 Sabo	Y	Y	N	Y	N	Y	N	Y
6 Sikorski	Y	N	Y	N	Y	Y	N	Y
7 ***Stangeland***	Y	N	Y	N	Y	N	Y	Y
8 Oberstar	Y	Y	N	Y	N	Y	N	Y
MISSISSIPPI								
1 Whitten	?	Y	N	Y	N	Y	?	Y
2 ***Franklin***	Y	N	Y	N	Y	N	Y	Y
3 Montgomery	Y	Y	Y	N	Y	Y	Y	N
4 Dowdy	Y	Y	N	Y	N	Y	N	Y
5 ***Lott***	Y	N	Y	N	Y	N	Y	N
MISSOURI								
1 Clay	Y	Y	?	?	?	?	N	Y
2 Young	Y	?	?	?	?	?	N	Y
3 Gephardt	Y	Y	N	Y	N	Y	N	Y
4 Skelton	?	?	?	?	?	?	N	Y
5 Wheat	Y	Y	N	Y	N	Y	N	Y
6 ***Coleman***	N	N	Y	N	N	N	Y	Y
7 ***Taylor***	Y	N	?	?	?	?	Y	Y
8 ***Emerson***	Y	N	Y	N	Y	N	Y	Y
9 Volkmer	Y	Y	N	Y	Y	Y	N	Y
MONTANA								
1 Williams	Y	Y	N	Y	Y	Y	N	Y
2 ***Marlenee***	?	?	?	?	?	?	Y	Y
NEBRASKA								
1 ***Bereuter***	N	N	Y	N	Y	N	N	Y
2 ***Daub***	N	N	Y	N	Y	N	Y	N
3 ***Smith***	Y	N	Y	N	Y	N	Y	N
NEVADA								
1 Reid	Y	Y	N	Y	N	Y	N	Y
2 ***Vucanovich***	?	X	?	?	?	?	Y	N
NEW HAMPSHIRE								
1 D'Amours	?	?	?	?	?	?	N	Y
2 ***Gregg***	N	N	Y	N	Y	N	Y	Y
NEW JERSEY								
1 Florio	?	?	?	?	?	?	N	Y
2 Hughes	Y	Y	N	N	N	Y	N	Y
3 Howard	Y	Y	N	Y	N	Y	N	Y
4 ***Smith***	Y	Y	Y	N	Y	?	N	Y
5 ***Roukema***	Y	N	Y	N	Y	N	N	Y
6 Dwyer	Y	Y	N	Y	N	Y	N	Y
7 ***Rinaldo***	Y	Y	Y	N	Y	N	N	Y
8 Roe	Y	Y	N	Y	Y	Y	N	Y
9 Torricelli	?	#	?	?	?	?	N	Y
10 Rodino	?	#	?	?	?	?	N	Y
11 Minish	?	?	?	?	?	?	N	Y
12 ***Courter***	?	?	?	?	?	?	N	Y
13 Vacancy								
14 Guarini	?	#	?	?	?	?	N	Y
NEW MEXICO								
1 ***Lujan***	Y	N	Y	N	Y	N	Y	N
2 ***Skeen***	Y	N	Y	N	Y	N	Y	N
3 Richardson	Y	Y	N	Y	N	Y	N	Y
NEW YORK								
1 ***Carney***	Y	N	Y	N	N	N	Y	Y
2 Downey	Y	Y	N	Y	N	Y	N	Y
3 Mrazek	Y	Y	N	Y	Y	Y	N	Y
4 ***Lent***	Y	?	?	?	?	?	N	Y
5 ***McGrath***	Y	Y	Y	N	N	N	N	Y
6 Addabbo	?	#	?	?	?	?	N	Y
7 Ackerman	?	?	?	?	?	?	N	Y
8 Scheuer	Y	Y	N	Y	N	Y	N	Y
9 Ferraro	?	?	?	?	?	?	N	Y
10 Schumer	Y	Y	N	Y	N	Y	N	Y
11 Towns	Y	Y	N	Y	N	Y	N	Y
12 Owens	Y	Y	N	Y	N	Y	N	Y
13 Solarz	Y	Y	N	Y	N	Y	N	Y
14 ***Molinari***	Y	N	Y	N	Y	N	Y	Y
15 ***Green***	Y	Y	N	Y	Y	N	Y	Y
16 Rangel	?	#	?	?	?	?	N	Y
17 Weiss	+	#	-	+	-	+	N	Y
18 Garcia	Y	Y	N	Y	N	Y	N	Y
19 Biaggi	Y	Y	N	Y	N	Y	N	Y
20 Ottinger	Y	?	?	?	?	?	N	Y
21 ***Fish***	?	?	?	?	?	?	N	Y
22 ***Gilman***	Y	N	Y	N	Y	N	N	Y
23 Stratton	Y	Y	N	Y	N	Y	N	Y
24 ***Solomon***	N	N	Y	N	Y	N	Y	N
25 ***Boehlert***	Y	N	Y	N	Y	N	N	Y
26 ***Martin***	?	?	?	?	?	?	N	Y
27 ***Wortley***	Y	N	Y	N	Y	N	N	Y
28 McHugh	Y	Y	N	Y	N	Y	N	Y
29 ***Horton***	Y	Y	Y	N	Y	N	N	Y
30 ***Conable***	Y	N	Y	N	N	N	Y	N
31 ***Kemp***	?	N	Y	N	Y	N	?	Y
32 LaFalce	?	?	?	?	N	Y	N	Y
33 Nowak	?	?	?	?	?	?	N	Y
34 Lundine	Y	Y	N	Y	N	Y	N	Y
NORTH CAROLINA								
1 Jones	Y	Y	N	Y	N	Y	?	#
2 Valentine	?	?	?	?	?	?	Y	Y
3 Whitley	Y	Y	N	?	?	?	N	Y
4 Andrews	Y	?	?	?	?	?	?	?
5 Neal	Y	?	?	?	?	?	N	Y
6 Britt	Y	N	Y	N	N	Y	N	Y
7 Rose	Y	Y	N	Y	N	Y	N	Y
8 Hefner	?	?	?	?	?	?	N	Y
9 ***Martin***	Y	N	Y	?	?	?	Y	Y
10 ***Broyhill***	Y	N	Y	N	Y	N	Y	N
11 Clarke	?	?	?	?	?	?	N	Y
NORTH DAKOTA								
AL Dorgan	Y	Y	N	Y	Y	Y	N	Y
OHIO								
1 Luken	Y	?	?	?	?	?	N	Y
2 ***Gradison***	Y	N	Y	N	Y	N	Y	Y
3 Hall	Y	?	?	?	?	?	N	Y
4 ***Oxley***	Y	N	Y	N	Y	N	Y	Y
5 ***Latta***	Y	X	?	?	?	?	Y	Y
6 ***McEwen***	Y	N	Y	N	?	?	Y	Y
7 ***DeWine***	N	N	Y	N	Y	N	Y	N
8 ***Kindness***	Y	N	Y	N	Y	N	Y	Y
9 Kaptur	?	#	?	?	?	?	N	Y
10 ***Miller***	Y	N	Y	N	Y	N	Y	Y
11 Eckart	Y	Y	Y	?	N	Y	N	Y
12 ***Kasich***	N	N	Y	N	Y	N	Y	Y
13 Pease	Y	Y	N	Y	N	Y	N	Y
14 Seiberling	Y	Y	N	Y	N	Y	N	Y
15 ***Wylie***	Y	N	Y	N	?	?	N	Y
16 ***Regula***	?	?	?	?	?	?	N	Y
17 ***Williams***	Y	N	Y	N	Y	N	N	Y
18 Applegate	?	Y	Y	N	?	?	N	Y
19 Feighan	Y	Y	Y	Y	Y	Y	N	Y
20 Oakar	Y	Y	N	Y	N	Y	N	Y
21 Stokes	?	?	?	?	?	?	N	Y
OKLAHOMA								
1 Jones	Y	N	Y	N	N	Y	N	Y
2 Synar	+	+	-	-	+	+	N	Y
3 Watkins	Y	Y	N	Y	Y	Y	N	Y
4 McCurdy	Y	Y	N	Y	N	Y	N	Y
5 ***Edwards***	Y	N	Y	N	Y	N	Y	Y
6 English	Y	Y	Y	N	Y	Y	N	Y
OREGON								
1 AuCoin	Y	Y	N	Y	N	Y	N	Y
2 ***Smith, R.***	Y	N	Y	N	Y	N	?	?
3 Wyden	Y	Y	N	Y	N	Y	N	Y
4 Weaver	Y	Y	N	Y	Y	Y	N	Y
5 ***Smith, D.***	?	X	?	?	?	?	Y	N
PENNSYLVANIA								
1 Foglietta	?	?	?	?	?	?	N	Y
2 Gray	Y	Y	N	Y	N	Y	N	Y
3 Borski	Y	Y	N	Y	N	Y	N	Y
4 Kolter	Y	Y	N	Y	N	Y	N	Y
5 ***Schulze***	Y	N	Y	N	Y	N	N	Y
6 Yatron	Y	Y	N	Y	Y	Y	N	Y
7 Edgar	Y	Y	N	Y	N	Y	N	Y
8 Kostmayer	Y	N	Y	N	N	Y	N	Y
9 ***Shuster***	N	N	Y	N	Y	N	Y	N
10 ***McDade***	?	?	?	?	?	?	N	Y
11 Harrison	?	Y	N	Y	Y	Y	N	Y
12 Murtha	Y	Y	N	Y	N	Y	N	Y
13 ***Coughlin***	Y	N	Y	?	?	?	N	Y
14 Coyne	Y	Y	N	Y	N	Y	N	Y
15 ***Ritter***	Y	N	Y	N	N	N	Y	N
16 ***Walker***	N	N	Y	N	Y	N	Y	N
17 ***Gekas***	Y	N	Y	N	Y	N	N	Y
18 Walgren	Y	Y	Y	Y	N	Y	N	Y
19 ***Goodling***	?	N	Y	N	Y	N	N	Y
20 Gaydos	Y	Y	N	Y	N	Y	N	Y
21 ***Ridge***	Y	N	Y	N	N	N	N	Y
22 Murphy	Y	Y	N	?	?	?	N	Y
23 ***Clinger***	Y	N	Y	N	Y	N	N	Y
RHODE ISLAND								
1 St Germain	?	?	?	?	?	?	N	Y
2 ***Schneider***	Y	N	Y	N	Y	N	N	Y
SOUTH CAROLINA								
1 ***Hartnett***	N	N	Y	N	Y	N	Y	N
2 ***Spence***	Y	N	Y	N	Y	N	Y	Y
3 Derrick	Y	Y	N	Y	Y	Y	N	Y
4 ***Campbell***	Y	N	Y	N	Y	N	Y	Y
5 Spratt	Y	Y	N	N	N	Y	N	Y
6 Tallon	Y	Y	Y	N	Y	Y	N	Y
SOUTH DAKOTA								
AL Daschle	?	?	?	?	?	?	N	Y
TENNESSEE								
1 ***Quillen***	Y	N	Y	N	N	Y	N	Y
2 ***Duncan***	Y	N	Y	N	Y	N	N	Y
3 Lloyd	Y	Y	Y	N	N	Y	N	Y
4 Cooper	Y	Y	Y	N	N	Y	N	Y
5 Boner	Y	?	?	?	?	?	N	Y
6 Gore	?	?	?	?	?	?	N	Y
7 ***Sundquist***	?	?	?	?	?	?	Y	N
8 Jones	?	?	?	?	?	?	N	Y
9 Ford	?	?	?	?	?	?	N	Y
TEXAS								
1 Hall, S.	Y	Y	Y	N	Y	N	Y	Y
2 Wilson	?	?	?	?	?	?	?	?
3 ***Bartlett***	N	N	Y	N	Y	N	Y	N
4 Hall, R.	Y	Y	N	N	N	Y	Y	Y
5 Bryant	?	?	?	?	?	?	?	Y
6 ***Gramm***	N	N	Y	N	Y	N	?	?
7 ***Archer***	N	N	Y	N	Y	N	Y	N
8 ***Fields***	Y	X	?	?	?	?	Y	N
9 Brooks	Y	Y	N	Y	Y	Y	?	?
10 Pickle	?	?	?	?	?	?	N	Y
11 Leath	Y	N	Y	N	Y	Y	Y	N
12 Wright	?	?	?	?	?	Y	N	Y
13 Hightower	?	?	?	?	?	?	Y	Y
14 Patman	?	?	?	?	?	?	N	Y
15 de la Garza	?	Y	Y	Y	N	?	?	Y
16 Coleman	Y	Y	N	Y	Y	Y	N	Y
17 Stenholm	Y	N	Y	N	Y	N	Y	N
18 Leland	Y	Y	N	Y	N	Y	N	Y
19 Hance	?	?	?	?	?	?	?	?
20 Gonzalez	?	Y	N	Y	N	Y	N	Y
21 ***Loeffler***	Y	N	Y	N	Y	N	Y	N
22 ***Paul***	?	X	?	?	?	?	#	X
23 Kazen	?	?	?	?	?	?	?	?
24 Frost	?	?	?	?	?	?	?	?
25 Andrews	Y	N	Y	N	Y	Y	Y	Y
26 Vandergriff	Y	N	Y	N	Y	N	Y	Y
27 Ortiz	?	?	?	?	?	?	N	Y
UTAH								
1 ***Hansen***	N	N	Y	N	?	?	Y	N
2 ***Marriott***	?	X	?	?	?	?	Y	Y
3 ***Nielson***	N	N	Y	N	Y	N	Y	N
VERMONT								
AL ***Jeffords***	Y	Y	Y	N	N	N	N	Y
VIRGINIA								
1 ***Bateman***	N	N	Y	N	Y	N	Y	N
2 ***Whitehurst***	Y	N	Y	N	N	N	Y	N
3 ***Bliley***	Y	N	Y	N	Y	N	Y	N
4 Sisisky	Y	N	Y	N	Y	Y	N	Y
5 Daniel	Y	N	Y	N	Y	N	Y	N
6 Olin	Y	Y	Y	N	N	Y	N	Y
7 ***Robinson***	?	X	?	?	?	?	Y	N
8 ***Parris***	Y	N	Y	N	Y	N	Y	Y
9 Boucher	?	?	?	?	?	?	N	Y
10 ***Wolf***	Y	N	Y	N	Y	N	Y	Y
WASHINGTON								
1 ***Pritchard***	Y	N	Y	N	N	N	N	Y
2 Swift	Y	Y	Y	Y	N	Y	?	Y
3 Bonker	?	?	?	?	?	?	N	Y
4 ***Morrison***	N	N	Y	N	N	N	N	Y
5 Foley	?	Y	N	Y	N	Y	N	Y
6 Dicks	?	?	?	?	?	?	N	Y
7 Lowry	Y	Y	N	Y	N	Y	N	Y
8 ***Chandler***	Y	N	Y	N	N	N	N	Y
WEST VIRGINIA								
1 Mollohan	Y	Y	N	Y	Y	Y	N	Y
2 Staggers	Y	Y	N	Y	N	Y	N	Y
3 Wise	Y	Y	N	-	-	+	N	Y
4 Rahall	Y	Y	N	?	?	?	N	Y
WISCONSIN								
1 Aspin	Y	Y	N	Y	N	Y	N	Y
2 Kastenmeier	Y	Y	N	Y	N	Y	N	+
3 ***Gunderson***	Y	N	Y	N	Y	N	Y	Y
4 Kleczka	Y	Y	N	Y	N	Y	N	Y
5 Moody	Y	Y	Y	Y	N	Y	N	Y
6 ***Petri***	Y	N	Y	N	Y	N	N	Y
7 Obey	Y	Y	N	Y	N	Y	N	Y
8 ***Roth***	Y	N	Y	N	Y	N	Y	Y
9 ***Sensenbrenner***	N	N	Y	N	Y	N	Y	N
WYOMING								
AL ***Cheney***	N	X	?	?	?	?	Y	N

Southern states - Ala., Ark., Fla., Ga., Ky., La., Miss., N.C., Okla., S.C., Tenn., Texas, Va.

95. HR 5041. Joint Research and Development Antitrust Act. Edwards, D-Calif., motion to suspend the rules and pass the bill to protect companies, under certain circumstances, from treble antitrust damages when they engage in joint research and development ventures. Motion agreed to 417-0: R 162-0; D 255-0 (ND 173-0, SD 82-0), May 1, 1984. A two-thirds majority of those present and voting (278 in this case) is required for passage under suspension of the rules. A "yea" was a vote supporting the president's position.

96. H Con Res 275. Colombian Drug Eradication. Fascell, D-Fla., motion to suspend the rules and adopt the concurrent resolution to congratulate the government of Colombia on its recent decision to conduct experimental testing of herbicidal methods for the eradication of plants used to produce narcotic drugs. Motion agreed to 416-0: R 162-0; D 254-0 (ND 172-0, SD 82-0), May 1, 1984. A two-thirds majority of those present and voting (278 in this case) is required for adoption under suspension of the rules.

97. H Con Res 261. Contadora Group Initiative. Barnes, D-Md., motion to suspend the rules and adopt the concurrent resolution to support the efforts of the so-called "Contadora group" of Colombia, Mexico, Panama and Venezuela to negotiate a peace agreement in Central America and calling on the U.S. government to support those efforts. Motion agreed to 416-0: R 162-0; D 254-0 (ND 172-0, SD 82-0), May 1, 1984. A two-thirds majority of those present and voting (278 in this case) is required for adoption under suspension of the rules.

98. HR 5188. Customs Service Authorization. Gibbons, D-Fla., motion to suspend the rules and pass the bill to authorize $686.4 million for the U.S. Customs Service, $28.4 million for the U.S. International Trade Commission and $14.2 million for the Office of the U.S. Trade Representative in fiscal 1985. Motion agreed to 289-127: R 47-114; D 242-13 (ND 166-7, SD 76-6), May 1, 1984. A two-thirds majority of those present and voting (278 in this case) is required for passage under suspension of the rules. A "nay" was a vote supporting the president's position.

99. HR 5147. Tuna Fishing Agreement. Breaux, D-La., motion to suspend the rules and pass the bill to implement the Eastern Pacific Ocean Tuna Fishing Agreement, signed in San Jose, Costa Rica, on March 15, 1983. Motion agreed to 416-0: R 161-0; D 255-0 (ND 173-0, SD 82-0), May 1, 1984. A two-thirds majority of those present and voting (278 in this case) is required for passage under suspension of the rules. A "yea" was a vote supporting the president's position.

100. HR 4585. Environmental Quality Authorizations. Breaux, D-La., motion to suspend the rules and pass the bill to authorize $480,000 for the Office of Environmental Quality in each of fiscal years 1985-87, and to establish a fund to finance joint studies and projects involving the Council on Environmental Quality and other entities. Motion agreed to 412-4: R 159-3; D 253-1 (ND 171-1, SD 82-0), May 1, 1984. A two-thirds majority of those present and voting (278 in this case) is required for passage under suspension of the rules.

101. H J Res 537. Edwin B. Forsythe Refuge. Breaux, D-La., motion to suspend the rules and pass the joint resolution to designate the Brigantine and Barnegat units of the National Wildlife Refuge System, located in New Jersey, as the Edwin B. Forsythe National Wildlife Refuge, in honor of the late Rep. Forsythe, R-N.J. (1970-84), who died March 29. Motion agreed to 416-0: R 162-0; D 254-0 (ND 172-0, SD 82-0), May 1, 1984. A two-thirds majority of those present and voting (278 in this case) is required for passage under suspension of the rules.

102. HR 5050. Fisheries Loan Fund. Breaux, D-La., motion to suspend the rules and pass the bill to extend for two more years, until Oct. 1, 1986, the authorization for a fisheries loan fund established under the Fish and Wildlife Act of 1956. Motion agreed to 309-104: R 69-93; D 240-11 (ND 164-6, SD 76-5), May 1, 1984. A two-thirds majority of those present and voting (276 in this case) is required for passage under suspension of the rules. A "nay" was a vote supporting the president's position.

KEY

Y	Voted for (yea).
#	Paired for.
+	Announced for.
N	Voted against (nay).
X	Paired against.
-	Announced against.
P	Voted "present".
C	Voted "present" to avoid possible conflict of interest.
?	Did not vote or otherwise make a position known.

Democrats   *Republicans*

	95	96	97	98	99	100	101	102
ALABAMA								
1 *Edwards*	Y	Y	Y	Y	Y	Y	Y	Y
2 *Dickinson*	Y	Y	Y	N	Y	Y	Y	N
3 Nichols	Y	Y	Y	N	Y	Y	Y	Y
4 Bevill	Y	Y	Y	Y	Y	Y	Y	Y
5 Flippo	Y	Y	Y	Y	Y	Y	Y	Y
6 Erdreich	Y	Y	Y	Y	Y	Y	Y	Y
7 Shelby	?	?	?	?	?	?	?	?
ALASKA								
AL *Young*	Y	Y	Y	N	Y	Y	Y	Y
ARIZONA								
1 *McCain*	Y	Y	Y	N	Y	Y	Y	N
2 Udall	Y	Y	Y	Y	Y	Y	Y	Y
3 *Stump*	Y	Y	Y	N	Y	N	Y	N
4 *Rudd*	Y	Y	Y	N	Y	Y	Y	N
5 McNulty	Y	Y	Y	Y	Y	Y	Y	Y
ARKANSAS								
1 Alexander	Y	Y	Y	Y	Y	Y	Y	Y
2 *Bethune*	Y	Y	Y	N	Y	Y	Y	N
3 *Hammerschmidt*	Y	Y	Y	Y	Y	Y	Y	Y
4 Anthony	Y	Y	Y	Y	Y	Y	Y	Y
CALIFORNIA								
1 Bosco	Y	Y	Y	Y	Y	Y	Y	Y
2 *Chappie*	Y	Y	Y	N	Y	Y	Y	N
3 Matsui	Y	Y	Y	Y	Y	Y	Y	Y
4 Fazio	Y	Y	Y	Y	Y	Y	Y	Y
5 Burton	Y	Y	Y	Y	Y	Y	Y	Y
6 Boxer	Y	Y	Y	Y	Y	Y	Y	Y
7 Miller	Y	Y	Y	Y	Y	Y	Y	Y
8 Dellums	Y	Y	Y	Y	Y	Y	Y	Y
9 Stark	Y	Y	Y	Y	Y	Y	Y	Y
10 Edwards	Y	Y	Y	Y	Y	Y	Y	Y
11 Lantos	Y	Y	Y	Y	Y	Y	Y	Y
12 *Zschau*	Y	Y	Y	N	Y	Y	Y	N
13 Mineta	Y	Y	Y	Y	Y	Y	Y	Y
14 *Shumway*	Y	Y	Y	N	Y	Y	Y	N
15 Coelho	Y	Y	Y	Y	Y	Y	Y	Y
16 Panetta	Y	Y	Y	Y	Y	Y	Y	Y
17 *Pashayan*	Y	Y	Y	N	Y	Y	Y	Y
18 Lehman	Y	Y	Y	Y	Y	Y	Y	Y
19 *Lagomarsino*	Y	Y	Y	N	Y	Y	Y	N
20 *Thomas*	Y	Y	Y	N	Y	Y	Y	N
21 *Fiedler*	Y	Y	Y	N	Y	Y	Y	N
22 *Moorhead*	Y	Y	Y	N	Y	Y	Y	Y
23 Beilenson	Y	Y	Y	Y	Y	Y	Y	Y
24 Waxman	Y	Y	Y	Y	Y	Y	Y	Y
25 Roybal	Y	Y	Y	Y	Y	Y	Y	Y
26 Berman	Y	Y	Y	Y	Y	Y	Y	?
27 Levine	Y	Y	Y	Y	Y	Y	Y	Y
28 Dixon	Y	Y	Y	Y	Y	Y	Y	Y
29 Hawkins	Y	Y	Y	Y	Y	Y	?	Y
30 Martinez	Y	Y	Y	Y	Y	Y	?	Y
31 Dymally	Y	Y	Y	Y	Y	Y	Y	Y
32 Anderson	Y	?	Y	Y	Y	Y	Y	Y
33 *Dreier*	Y	Y	Y	N	Y	Y	Y	N
34 Torres	Y	Y	Y	Y	Y	Y	Y	Y
35 *Lewis*	Y	Y	Y	N	Y	Y	Y	Y
36 Brown	Y	Y	Y	Y	Y	Y	Y	Y
37 *McCandless*	Y	Y	Y	N	Y	Y	Y	N
38 Patterson	Y	Y	Y	Y	Y	Y	Y	Y
39 *Dannemeyer*	Y	Y	Y	N	Y	N	Y	N
40 *Badham*	Y	Y	Y	N	Y	Y	Y	N
41 *Lowery*	Y	Y	Y	N	Y	Y	Y	Y
42 *Lungren*	Y	Y	Y	N	Y	Y	Y	N
43 *Packard*	Y	Y	Y	Y	Y	Y	Y	N
44 Bates	Y	Y	Y	Y	Y	Y	Y	Y
45 *Hunter*	Y	Y	Y	?	Y	Y	Y	Y
COLORADO								
1 Schroeder	Y	Y	Y	Y	Y	Y	Y	N
2 Wirth	Y	Y	Y	Y	Y	Y	Y	Y
3 Kogovsek	Y	Y	Y	Y	Y	Y	Y	Y
4 *Brown*	Y	Y	Y	N	Y	Y	Y	N
5 *Kramer*	Y	Y	Y	N	Y	Y	Y	N
6 *Schaefer*	Y	Y	Y	N	Y	Y	Y	N
CONNECTICUT								
1 Kennelly	Y	Y	Y	Y	Y	Y	Y	Y
2 Gejdenson	Y	Y	Y	Y	Y	Y	Y	Y
3 Morrison	Y	Y	Y	Y	Y	Y	Y	Y
4 *McKinney*	Y	Y	Y	Y	Y	Y	Y	Y
5 Ratchford	Y	Y	Y	Y	Y	Y	Y	Y
6 *Johnson*	Y	Y	Y	Y	Y	Y	Y	Y
DELAWARE								
AL Carper	Y	Y	Y	Y	Y	Y	Y	Y
FLORIDA								
1 Hutto	Y	Y	Y	Y	Y	Y	Y	Y
2 Fuqua	Y	Y	Y	Y	Y	Y	Y	Y
3 Bennett	Y	Y	Y	Y	Y	Y	Y	Y
4 Chappell	Y	Y	Y	Y	Y	Y	Y	Y
5 *McCollum*	Y	Y	Y	N	Y	Y	Y	N
6 MacKay	Y	Y	Y	Y	Y	Y	Y	Y
7 Gibbons	Y	Y	Y	Y	Y	Y	Y	N
8 *Young*	Y	Y	Y	Y	Y	Y	Y	N
9 *Bilirakis*	Y	Y	Y	N	Y	Y	Y	Y
10 Ireland	Y	Y	Y	Y	Y	Y	Y	Y
11 Nelson	Y	Y	Y	Y	Y	Y	Y	Y
12 *Lewis*	Y	Y	Y	N	Y	Y	Y	Y
13 *Mack*	Y	Y	Y	N	Y	Y	Y	N
14 Mica	Y	Y	Y	Y	Y	Y	Y	Y
15 *Shaw*	Y	Y	Y	N	Y	Y	Y	Y
16 Smith	Y	Y	Y	Y	Y	Y	Y	Y
17 Lehman	Y	Y	Y	Y	Y	Y	Y	?
18 Pepper	Y	Y	Y	Y	Y	Y	Y	Y
19 Fascell	Y	Y	Y	Y	Y	Y	Y	Y
GEORGIA								
1 Thomas	Y	Y	Y	Y	Y	Y	Y	Y
2 Hatcher	Y	Y	Y	Y	Y	Y	Y	Y
3 Ray	Y	Y	Y	N	Y	Y	Y	Y
4 Levitas	Y	Y	Y	Y	Y	Y	Y	Y
5 Fowler	Y	Y	Y	Y	Y	Y	Y	Y
6 *Gingrich*	Y	Y	Y	N	?	Y	Y	N
7 Darden	Y	Y	Y	Y	Y	Y	Y	Y
8 Rowland	Y	Y	Y	Y	Y	Y	Y	Y
9 Jenkins	Y	Y	Y	Y	Y	Y	Y	Y
10 Barnard	Y	Y	Y	Y	Y	Y	Y	Y
HAWAII								
1 Heftel	?	?	?	?	?	?	?	?
2 Akaka	Y	Y	Y	Y	Y	Y	Y	Y
IDAHO								
1 *Craig*	Y	Y	Y	N	Y	Y	Y	N
2 *Hansen*	?	?	?	?	?	?	?	?
ILLINOIS								
1 Hayes	Y	Y	Y	Y	Y	Y	Y	N
2 Savage	Y	Y	?	Y	Y	Y	Y	Y
3 Russo	Y	Y	Y	Y	Y	Y	Y	Y
4 *O'Brien*	Y	Y	Y	N	Y	Y	Y	Y
5 Lipinski	Y	Y	Y	Y	Y	Y	Y	Y
6 *Hyde*	Y	Y	Y	N	Y	Y	Y	N
7 Collins	Y	Y	Y	Y	Y	Y	Y	Y
8 Rostenkowski	Y	Y	Y	Y	Y	Y	Y	Y
9 Yates	Y	Y	Y	Y	Y	Y	Y	Y
10 *Porter*	Y	Y	Y	Y	Y	Y	Y	N
11 Annunzio	Y	Y	Y	Y	Y	Y	Y	Y
12 *Crane, P.*	Y	Y	Y	N	Y	N	Y	N
13 *Erlenborn*	Y	Y	Y	N	Y	Y	Y	N
14 *Corcoran*	Y	Y	Y	N	Y	Y	Y	N
15 *Madigan*	Y	Y	Y	N	Y	Y	Y	N
16 *Martin*	Y	Y	Y	N	Y	Y	Y	N
17 Evans	Y	Y	Y	Y	Y	Y	Y	Y
18 *Michel*	Y	Y	Y	N	Y	Y	Y	N
19 *Crane, D.*	Y	Y	Y	N	Y	N	Y	N
20 Durbin	Y	Y	Y	Y	Y	Y	Y	Y
21 Price	Y	Y	Y	Y	Y	Y	Y	Y
22 Simon	?	?	?	?	?	?	?	?
INDIANA								
1 Hall	?	?	?	?	?	?	?	?
2 Sharp	Y	Y	Y	Y	Y	Y	Y	Y
3 *Hiler*	Y	Y	Y	N	Y	Y	Y	N
4 *Coats*	Y	Y	Y	N	Y	Y	Y	N
5 *Hillis*	Y	Y	Y	N	Y	Y	Y	N

ND - Northern Democrats   SD - Southern Democrats

	95	96	97	98	99	100	101	102
6 ***Burton***	Y	Y	Y	N	Y	Y	Y	N
7 ***Myers***	Y	Y	Y	N	Y	Y	Y	Y
8 McCloskey	Y	Y	Y	Y	Y	Y	Y	Y
9 Hamilton	Y	Y	Y	Y	Y	Y	Y	N
10 Jacobs	Y	Y	Y	Y	Y	Y	Y	N
IOWA								
1 ***Leach***	Y	Y	Y	Y	Y	Y	Y	Y
2 ***Tauke***	Y	Y	Y	N	Y	Y	Y	N
3 ***Evans***	Y	Y	Y	N	Y	Y	Y	N
4 Smith	Y	Y	Y	Y	Y	Y	Y	Y
5 Harkin	Y	Y	Y	Y	Y	Y	Y	Y
6 Bedell	Y	Y	Y	Y	Y	Y	Y	Y
KANSAS								
1 ***Roberts***	Y	Y	Y	N	Y	Y	Y	N
2 Slattery	Y	Y	Y	Y	Y	Y	Y	N
3 ***Winn***	Y	Y	Y	N	Y	Y	Y	N
4 Glickman	Y	Y	Y	Y	Y	Y	Y	Y
5 ***Whittaker***	Y	Y	Y	N	Y	Y	Y	N
KENTUCKY								
1 Hubbard	Y	Y	Y	N	Y	Y	Y	Y
2 Natcher	Y	Y	Y	Y	Y	Y	Y	Y
3 Mazzoli	Y	Y	Y	Y	Y	Y	Y	Y
4 ***Snyder***	Y	Y	Y	Y	Y	Y	Y	Y
5 ***Rogers***	Y	Y	Y	N	Y	Y	Y	N
6 ***Hopkins***	Y	Y	Y	Y	Y	Y	Y	N
7 Perkins	Y	Y	Y	Y	Y	Y	Y	Y
LOUISIANA								
1 ***Livingston***	Y	Y	Y	N	Y	Y	Y	Y
2 Boggs	Y	Y	Y	Y	Y	Y	Y	Y
3 Tauzin	Y	Y	Y	Y	Y	Y	Y	Y
4 Roemer	Y	Y	Y	Y	Y	Y	Y	N
5 Huckaby	Y	Y	Y	Y	Y	Y	Y	Y
6 ***Moore***	Y	Y	Y	Y	Y	Y	Y	Y
7 Breaux	Y	Y	Y	Y	Y	Y	Y	Y
8 Long	Y	Y	Y	Y	Y	Y	Y	Y
MAINE								
1 ***McKernan***	Y	Y	Y	N	Y	Y	Y	Y
2 ***Snowe***	Y	Y	Y	N	Y	Y	Y	Y
MARYLAND								
1 Dyson	Y	Y	Y	N	Y	Y	Y	Y
2 Long	Y	Y	Y	Y	Y	?	Y	Y
3 Mikulski	Y	Y	Y	Y	Y	Y	Y	Y
4 ***Holt***	Y	Y	Y	N	Y	Y	Y	Y
5 Hoyer	Y	Y	Y	Y	Y	Y	Y	Y
6 Byron	Y	Y	Y	Y	Y	Y	Y	N
7 Mitchell	Y	Y	Y	Y	Y	Y	Y	Y
8 Barnes	Y	Y	Y	Y	Y	Y	Y	Y
MASSACHUSETTS								
1 ***Conte***	Y	Y	Y	Y	Y	Y	Y	Y
2 Boland	Y	Y	Y	Y	Y	Y	Y	Y
3 Early	Y	Y	Y	N	Y	Y	Y	Y
4 Frank	Y	Y	Y	Y	Y	Y	Y	Y
5 Shannon	Y	Y	Y	Y	Y	Y	Y	Y
6 Mavroules	Y	Y	Y	Y	Y	Y	Y	Y
7 Markey	?	?	?	?	?	?	?	?
8 O'Neill								
9 Moakley	Y	Y	Y	Y	Y	Y	Y	Y
10 Studds	Y	Y	Y	Y	Y	Y	Y	Y
11 Donnelly	Y	Y	Y	Y	Y	Y	Y	Y
MICHIGAN								
1 Conyers	Y	Y	Y	Y	Y	Y	Y	Y
2 ***Pursell***	Y	Y	Y	N	Y	Y	Y	N
3 Wolpe	Y	Y	Y	Y	Y	Y	Y	Y
4 ***Siljander***	Y	Y	Y	N	Y	Y	Y	N
5 ***Sawyer***	Y	Y	Y	Y	Y	Y	Y	Y
6 Carr	Y	Y	Y	Y	Y	Y	Y	Y
7 Kildee	Y	Y	Y	Y	Y	Y	Y	Y
8 Traxler	Y	Y	Y	Y	Y	Y	Y	Y
9 ***Vander Jagt***	Y	Y	Y	N	Y	Y	Y	Y
10 Albosta	Y	Y	Y	Y	Y	Y	Y	Y
11 ***Davis***	Y	Y	Y	Y	Y	Y	Y	Y
12 Bonior	Y	Y	Y	Y	Y	Y	Y	Y
13 Crockett	Y	Y	Y	Y	Y	Y	Y	Y
14 Hertel	Y	Y	Y	Y	Y	Y	Y	Y
15 Ford	Y	Y	Y	Y	Y	Y	Y	Y
16 Dingell	Y	Y	Y	Y	Y	Y	Y	Y
17 Levin	Y	Y	Y	Y	Y	Y	Y	Y
18 ***Broomfield***	Y	Y	Y	N	Y	Y	Y	N
MINNESOTA								
1 Penny	Y	Y	Y	Y	Y	Y	Y	Y
2 ***Weber***	Y	Y	Y	N	Y	Y	Y	Y
3 ***Frenzel***	Y	Y	Y	N	Y	Y	Y	N
4 Vento	Y	Y	Y	Y	Y	Y	Y	Y
5 Sabo	Y	Y	Y	Y	Y	Y	Y	Y
6 Sikorski	Y	Y	Y	Y	Y	Y	Y	Y
7 ***Stangeland***	Y	Y	Y	N	Y	Y	Y	N
8 Oberstar	Y	Y	Y	Y	Y	Y	Y	?
MISSISSIPPI								
1 Whitten	Y	Y	Y	Y	Y	Y	Y	Y
2 ***Franklin***	Y	Y	Y	N	Y	Y	Y	Y
3 Montgomery	Y	Y	Y	Y	Y	Y	Y	Y
4 Dowdy	Y	Y	Y	Y	Y	Y	Y	Y
5 ***Lott***	Y	Y	Y	N	Y	Y	Y	Y
MISSOURI								
1 Clay	Y	Y	Y	Y	Y	Y	Y	Y
2 Young	Y	Y	Y	Y	Y	Y	Y	Y
3 Gephardt	Y	Y	Y	Y	Y	Y	Y	Y
4 Skelton	Y	Y	Y	Y	Y	Y	Y	Y
5 Wheat	Y	Y	Y	Y	Y	Y	Y	Y
6 ***Coleman***	Y	Y	Y	Y	Y	Y	Y	Y
7 ***Taylor***	Y	Y	Y	N	Y	Y	Y	Y
8 ***Emerson***	Y	Y	Y	N	Y	Y	Y	N
9 Volkmer	Y	Y	Y	N	Y	Y	Y	Y
MONTANA								
1 Williams	Y	Y	Y	Y	Y	Y	Y	N
2 ***Marlenee***	Y	Y	Y	Y	Y	Y	Y	Y
NEBRASKA								
1 ***Bereuter***	Y	Y	Y	N	Y	Y	Y	N
2 ***Daub***	Y	Y	Y	N	Y	Y	Y	N
3 ***Smith***	Y	Y	Y	N	Y	Y	Y	N
NEVADA								
1 Reid	Y	Y	Y	Y	Y	Y	Y	Y
2 ***Vucanovich***	Y	Y	Y	N	Y	Y	Y	N
NEW HAMPSHIRE								
1 D'Amours	Y	Y	Y	Y	Y	Y	Y	Y
2 ***Gregg***	Y	Y	Y	N	Y	Y	Y	N
NEW JERSEY								
1 Florio	Y	Y	Y	Y	Y	Y	Y	Y
2 Hughes	Y	Y	Y	Y	Y	Y	Y	Y
3 Howard	Y	Y	Y	Y	Y	Y	Y	Y
4 ***Smith***	Y	Y	Y	N	Y	Y	Y	Y
5 ***Roukema***	Y	Y	Y	N	Y	Y	Y	Y
6 Dwyer	Y	Y	Y	Y	Y	Y	Y	Y
7 ***Rinaldo***	Y	Y	Y	Y	Y	Y	Y	Y
8 Roe	Y	Y	Y	Y	Y	Y	Y	Y
9 Torricelli	Y	Y	Y	Y	Y	Y	Y	Y
10 Rodino	Y	Y	Y	Y	Y	Y	Y	Y
11 Minish	Y	Y	Y	Y	Y	Y	Y	Y
12 ***Courter***	Y	Y	Y	Y	Y	Y	Y	N
13 Vacancy								
14 Guarini	Y	Y	Y	Y	Y	Y	Y	Y
NEW MEXICO								
1 ***Lujan***	Y	Y	Y	Y	Y	Y	Y	N
2 ***Skeen***	Y	Y	Y	Y	Y	Y	Y	N
3 Richardson	Y	Y	Y	Y	Y	Y	Y	Y
NEW YORK								
1 ***Carney***	Y	Y	Y	N	Y	Y	Y	Y
2 Downey	Y	Y	Y	Y	Y	Y	Y	Y
3 Mrazek	Y	Y	Y	Y	Y	Y	Y	Y
4 ***Lent***	Y	Y	Y	N	Y	Y	Y	Y
5 ***McGrath***	Y	Y	Y	N	Y	Y	Y	Y
6 Addabbo	Y	Y	Y	Y	Y	Y	Y	Y
7 Ackerman	Y	Y	Y	Y	Y	Y	Y	Y
8 Scheuer	Y	Y	Y	Y	Y	Y	Y	Y
9 Ferraro	Y	Y	Y	Y	Y	Y	Y	Y
10 Schumer	Y	Y	Y	Y	Y	Y	Y	Y
11 Towns	Y	Y	Y	Y	Y	Y	Y	Y
12 Owens	Y	Y	Y	Y	Y	Y	Y	Y
13 Solarz	Y	Y	Y	Y	Y	Y	Y	Y
14 ***Molinari***	Y	Y	Y	N	Y	Y	Y	Y
15 ***Green***	Y	Y	Y	Y	Y	Y	Y	Y
16 Rangel	Y	Y	Y	Y	Y	Y	Y	Y
17 Weiss	Y	Y	Y	Y	Y	Y	Y	Y
18 Garcia	Y	Y	Y	Y	Y	Y	Y	Y
19 Biaggi	Y	Y	Y	Y	Y	Y	Y	Y
20 Ottinger	Y	Y	Y	Y	Y	Y	Y	Y
21 ***Fish***	Y	Y	Y	Y	Y	Y	Y	Y
22 ***Gilman***	Y	Y	Y	Y	Y	Y	Y	Y
23 Stratton	Y	Y	Y	Y	Y	Y	Y	Y
24 ***Solomon***	Y	Y	Y	N	Y	Y	Y	Y
25 ***Boehlert***	Y	Y	Y	N	Y	Y	Y	Y
26 ***Martin***	Y	Y	Y	N	Y	Y	Y	Y
27 ***Wortley***	Y	Y	Y	N	Y	Y	Y	N
28 McHugh	Y	Y	Y	Y	Y	Y	Y	Y
29 ***Horton***	Y	Y	Y	Y	Y	Y	Y	Y
30 ***Conable***	Y	Y	Y	N	Y	Y	Y	N
31 ***Kemp***	Y	Y	Y	N	Y	Y	Y	Y
32 LaFalce	Y	Y	Y	Y	Y	Y	Y	Y
33 Nowak	Y	Y	Y	Y	Y	Y	Y	Y
34 Lundine	Y	Y	Y	Y	Y	Y	Y	Y
NORTH CAROLINA								
1 Jones	?	?	?	?	?	?	?	?
2 Valentine	Y	Y	Y	Y	Y	Y	Y	Y
3 Whitley	Y	Y	Y	Y	Y	Y	Y	Y
4 Andrews	?	?	?	?	?	?	?	?
5 Neal	Y	Y	Y	Y	Y	Y	Y	Y
6 Britt	Y	Y	Y	Y	Y	Y	Y	Y
7 Rose	Y	Y	Y	Y	Y	Y	Y	Y
8 Hefner	Y	Y	Y	Y	Y	Y	Y	Y
9 ***Martin***	Y	Y	Y	N	Y	Y	Y	N
10 ***Broyhill***	Y	Y	Y	Y	Y	Y	Y	N
11 Clarke	Y	Y	Y	Y	Y	Y	Y	Y
NORTH DAKOTA								
AL Dorgan	Y	Y	Y	Y	Y	Y	Y	Y
OHIO								
1 Luken	Y	Y	Y	Y	Y	Y	Y	Y
2 ***Gradison***	Y	Y	Y	Y	Y	Y	Y	Y
3 Hall	Y	Y	Y	Y	Y	Y	Y	Y
4 ***Oxley***	Y	Y	Y	N	Y	Y	Y	Y
5 ***Latta***	Y	Y	Y	N	Y	Y	Y	N
6 ***McEwen***	Y	Y	Y	N	Y	Y	Y	N
7 ***DeWine***	Y	Y	Y	N	Y	Y	Y	Y
8 ***Kindness***	Y	Y	Y	Y	Y	Y	Y	Y
9 Kaptur	Y	Y	Y	Y	Y	Y	Y	Y
10 ***Miller***	Y	Y	Y	N	Y	Y	Y	N
11 Eckart	Y	Y	Y	Y	Y	Y	Y	Y
12 ***Kasich***	Y	Y	Y	N	Y	Y	Y	Y
13 Pease	Y	Y	Y	Y	Y	Y	Y	Y
14 Seiberling	Y	Y	Y	Y	Y	Y	Y	Y
15 ***Wylie***	Y	Y	Y	N	Y	Y	Y	Y
16 ***Regula***	Y	Y	Y	Y	Y	Y	Y	N
17 ***Williams***	Y	Y	Y	Y	Y	Y	Y	Y
18 Applegate	Y	Y	Y	Y	Y	N	Y	Y
19 Feighan	Y	Y	Y	Y	Y	Y	Y	Y
20 Oakar	Y	Y	Y	Y	Y	Y	Y	Y
21 Stokes	Y	Y	Y	Y	Y	Y	Y	Y
OKLAHOMA								
1 Jones	Y	Y	Y	Y	Y	Y	Y	N
2 Synar	Y	Y	Y	Y	Y	Y	Y	Y
3 Watkins	Y	Y	Y	Y	Y	Y	Y	Y
4 McCurdy	Y	Y	Y	Y	Y	Y	Y	N
5 ***Edwards***	Y	Y	Y	N	Y	Y	Y	N
6 English	Y	Y	Y	Y	Y	Y	Y	Y
OREGON								
1 AuCoin	Y	Y	Y	Y	Y	Y	Y	Y
2 ***Smith, R.***	?	?	?	?	?	?	?	?
3 Wyden	Y	Y	Y	Y	Y	Y	Y	Y
4 Weaver	Y	Y	Y	Y	Y	Y	Y	Y
5 ***Smith, D.***	Y	Y	Y	N	Y	Y	Y	N
PENNSYLVANIA								
1 Foglietta	Y	Y	Y	Y	Y	Y	Y	Y
2 Gray	Y	Y	Y	Y	Y	Y	Y	Y
3 Borski	Y	Y	Y	Y	Y	Y	Y	Y
4 Kolter	Y	Y	Y	N	Y	Y	Y	Y
5 ***Schulze***	Y	Y	Y	N	Y	Y	Y	Y
6 Yatron	Y	Y	Y	Y	Y	Y	Y	Y
7 Edgar	Y	Y	Y	Y	Y	Y	Y	Y
8 Kostmayer	Y	Y	Y	Y	Y	Y	Y	Y
9 ***Shuster***	Y	Y	Y	N	Y	Y	Y	N
10 ***McDade***	Y	Y	Y	N	Y	Y	Y	Y
11 Harrison	Y	Y	Y	Y	Y	Y	Y	Y
12 Murtha	Y	Y	Y	Y	Y	Y	Y	?
13 ***Coughlin***	Y	Y	Y	N	Y	Y	Y	Y
14 Coyne	Y	Y	Y	Y	Y	Y	Y	Y
15 ***Ritter***	Y	Y	Y	N	Y	Y	Y	Y
16 ***Walker***	Y	Y	Y	N	Y	Y	Y	N
17 ***Gekas***	Y	Y	Y	N	Y	Y	Y	N
18 Walgren	Y	Y	Y	Y	Y	Y	Y	Y
19 ***Goodling***	Y	Y	Y	N	Y	Y	Y	N
20 Gaydos	Y	Y	Y	N	Y	Y	Y	Y
21 ***Ridge***	Y	Y	Y	N	Y	Y	Y	Y
22 Murphy	Y	Y	Y	N	Y	Y	Y	Y
23 ***Clinger***	Y	Y	Y	Y	Y	Y	Y	Y
RHODE ISLAND								
1 St Germain	Y	Y	Y	Y	Y	Y	Y	Y
2 ***Schneider***	Y	Y	Y	Y	Y	Y	Y	Y
SOUTH CAROLINA								
1 ***Hartnett***	Y	Y	Y	N	Y	Y	Y	N
2 ***Spence***	Y	Y	Y	N	Y	Y	Y	N
3 Derrick	Y	Y	Y	Y	Y	Y	Y	Y
4 ***Campbell***	Y	Y	Y	Y	Y	Y	Y	N
5 Spratt	Y	Y	Y	Y	Y	Y	Y	Y
6 Tallon	Y	Y	Y	Y	Y	Y	Y	Y
SOUTH DAKOTA								
AL Daschle	Y	Y	Y	Y	Y	Y	Y	Y
TENNESSEE								
1 ***Quillen***	Y	Y	Y	N	Y	Y	Y	Y
2 ***Duncan***	Y	Y	Y	Y	Y	Y	Y	Y
3 Lloyd	Y	Y	Y	Y	Y	Y	Y	N
4 Cooper	Y	Y	Y	Y	Y	Y	Y	Y
5 Boner	Y	Y	Y	Y	Y	Y	Y	Y
6 Gore	Y	Y	Y	Y	Y	Y	Y	Y
7 ***Sundquist***	Y	Y	Y	N	Y	Y	Y	N
8 Jones	Y	Y	Y	Y	Y	Y	Y	Y
9 Ford	Y	Y	Y	Y	Y	Y	Y	Y
TEXAS								
1 Hall, S.	Y	Y	Y	Y	Y	Y	Y	Y
2 Wilson	?	?	?	?	?	?	?	?
3 ***Bartlett***	Y	Y	Y	N	Y	Y	Y	N
4 Hall, R.	Y	Y	Y	N	Y	Y	Y	Y
5 Bryant	Y	Y	Y	Y	Y	Y	Y	Y
6 ***Gramm***	?	?	?	?	?	?	?	?
7 ***Archer***	Y	Y	Y	Y	Y	Y	Y	N
8 ***Fields***	Y	Y	Y	Y	Y	Y	Y	N
9 Brooks	?	?	?	?	?	?	?	?
10 Pickle	Y	Y	Y	Y	Y	Y	Y	Y
11 Leath	Y	Y	Y	Y	Y	Y	Y	Y
12 Wright	Y	Y	Y	Y	Y	Y	Y	Y
13 Hightower	Y	Y	Y	Y	Y	Y	Y	Y
14 Patman	Y	Y	Y	Y	Y	Y	Y	Y
15 de la Garza	Y	Y	Y	Y	Y	Y	Y	Y
16 Coleman	Y	Y	Y	Y	Y	Y	Y	Y
17 Stenholm	Y	Y	Y	Y	Y	Y	Y	Y
18 Leland	Y	Y	Y	Y	Y	Y	Y	Y
19 Hance	?	?	?	?	?	?	?	?
20 Gonzalez	Y	Y	Y	Y	Y	Y	Y	Y
21 ***Loeffler***	Y	Y	Y	Y	Y	Y	Y	N
22 ***Paul***	?	?	?	?	?	?	?	?
23 Kazen	?	?	?	?	?	?	?	?
24 Frost	?	?	?	?	?	?	?	?
25 Andrews	Y	Y	Y	Y	Y	Y	Y	Y
26 Vandergriff	Y	Y	Y	Y	Y	Y	Y	Y
27 Ortiz	Y	Y	Y	Y	Y	Y	Y	Y
UTAH								
1 ***Hansen***	Y	Y	Y	N	Y	Y	Y	N
2 ***Marriott***	Y	Y	Y	N	Y	Y	Y	N
3 ***Nielson***	Y	Y	Y	N	Y	Y	Y	N
VERMONT								
AL ***Jeffords***	Y	Y	Y	Y	Y	Y	Y	Y
VIRGINIA								
1 ***Bateman***	Y	Y	Y	Y	Y	Y	Y	Y
2 ***Whitehurst***	Y	Y	Y	N	Y	Y	Y	N
3 ***Bliley***	Y	Y	Y	N	Y	Y	Y	N
4 Sisisky	Y	Y	Y	N	Y	Y	Y	Y
5 Daniel	Y	Y	Y	N	Y	Y	Y	Y
6 Olin	Y	Y	Y	Y	Y	Y	Y	Y
7 ***Robinson***	Y	Y	Y	N	Y	Y	Y	N
8 ***Parris***	Y	Y	Y	N	Y	Y	Y	Y
9 Boucher	Y	Y	Y	Y	Y	Y	Y	Y
10 ***Wolf***	Y	Y	Y	N	Y	Y	Y	Y
WASHINGTON								
1 ***Pritchard***	Y	Y	Y	Y	Y	Y	Y	Y
2 Swift	Y	Y	Y	Y	Y	Y	Y	Y
3 Bonker	Y	Y	Y	Y	Y	Y	Y	Y
4 ***Morrison***	Y	Y	Y	Y	Y	Y	Y	N
5 Foley	Y	Y	Y	Y	Y	Y	Y	Y
6 Dicks	Y	Y	Y	Y	Y	Y	Y	Y
7 Lowry	Y	Y	Y	Y	Y	Y	Y	Y
8 ***Chandler***	Y	Y	Y	Y	Y	Y	Y	Y
WEST VIRGINIA								
1 Mollohan	Y	Y	Y	Y	Y	Y	Y	Y
2 Staggers	Y	Y	Y	Y	Y	Y	Y	Y
3 Wise	Y	Y	Y	Y	Y	Y	Y	Y
4 Rahall	Y	Y	Y	N	Y	Y	Y	Y
WISCONSIN								
1 Aspin	Y	Y	Y	Y	Y	Y	Y	Y
2 Kastenmeier	Y	Y	Y	Y	Y	Y	Y	Y
3 ***Gunderson***	Y	Y	Y	N	Y	Y	Y	N
4 Kleczka	Y	Y	Y	Y	Y	Y	Y	Y
5 Moody	Y	Y	Y	Y	Y	Y	Y	Y
6 ***Petri***	Y	Y	Y	N	Y	Y	Y	Y
7 Obey	Y	Y	Y	Y	Y	Y	Y	Y
8 ***Roth***	Y	Y	Y	Y	Y	Y	Y	Y
9 ***Sensenbrenner***	Y	Y	Y	Y	Y	Y	Y	N
WYOMING								
AL ***Cheney***	Y	Y	Y	N	Y	Y	Y	N

Southern states - Ala., Ark., Fla., Ga., Ky., La., Miss., N.C., Okla., S.C., Tenn., Texas, Va.

103. HR 5076. Pennsylvania Wilderness Act. Seiberling, D-Ohio, motion to suspend the rules and pass the bill to designate certain areas in the Allegheny National Forest as wilderness and recreation areas. Motion agreed to 387-28: R 137-23; D 250-5 (ND 173-0, SD 77-5), May 1, 1984. A two-thirds majority of those present and voting (277 in this case) is required for passage under suspension of the rules.

104. HR 4263. Tennessee Wilderness Act. Seiberling, D-Ohio, motion to suspend the rules and pass the bill to designate certain lands in the Cherokee National Forest in Tennessee as wilderness areas, and to allow management of certain lands for uses other than wilderness. Motion agreed to 404-12: R 153-8; D 251-4 (ND 173-0, SD 78-4), May 1, 1984. A two-thirds majority of those present and voting (278 in this case) is required for passage under suspension of the rules.

105. HR 4596. Women's Rights Historical Park. Seiberling, D-Ohio, motion to suspend the rules and pass the bill to permit the Interior Department to acquire McClintock House in Waterloo, N.Y., as part of the Women's Rights National Historic Park. Motion agreed to 404-13: R 155-7; D 249-6 (ND 173-0, SD 76-6), May 1, 1984. A two-thirds majority of those present and voting (278 in this case) is required for passage under suspension of the rules.

106. HR 3787. California and Pony Express Trails. Seiberling, D-Ohio, motion to suspend the rules and pass the bill to authorize the Interior Department to study the Pony Express Trail and the California Trail for possible inclusion in the national historic trails system, and to designate the Daniel Boone Heritage Trail. Motion agreed to 401-14: R 156-4; D 245-10 (ND 170-3, SD 75-7), May 1, 1984. A two-thirds majority of those present and voting (277 in this case) is required for passage under suspension of the rules. A "yea" was a vote supporting the president's position.

107. HR 5100. Holocaust Memorial Council Authorization. Seiberling, D-Ohio, motion to suspend the rules and pass the bill to authorize $2,051,000 in fiscal 1985 and $2,151,000 in fiscal 1986 for activities of the U.S. Holocaust Memorial Council. Motion agreed to 410-5: R 159-3; D 251-2 (ND 171-0, SD 80-2), May 1, 1984. A two-thirds majority of those present and voting (277 in this case) is required for passage under suspension of the rules. A "yea" was a vote supporting the president's position.

108. HR 3472. Lamprey Eel Control. Seiberling, D-Ohio, motion to suspend the rules and pass the bill to amend the Wild and Scenic Rivers Act to permit control of the lamprey eel in the Pere Marquette River. Motion agreed to 410-5: R 161-1; D 249-4 (ND 170-1, SD 79-3), May 1, 1984. A two-thirds majority of those present and voting (277 in this case) is required for passage under suspension of the rules.

109. HR 4952. Indian MX Assistance. Nichols, D-Ala., motion to suspend the rules and pass the bill to authorize assistance to certain Indian tribes, similar to that already provided state and local governments, for community planning related to the planned deployment of MX missiles. Motion agreed to 402-11: R 158-2; D 244-9 (ND 171-0, SD 73-9), May 1, 1984. A two-thirds majority of those present and voting (276 in this case) is required for passage under suspension of the rules.

110. Procedural Motion. Weber, R-Minn., motion to approve the House *Journal* of Tuesday, May 1. Motion agreed to 353-27: R 140-13; D 213-14 (ND 143-13, SD 70-1), May 2, 1984.

KEY

Y Voted for (yea).
Paired for.
+ Announced for.
N Voted against (nay).
X Paired against.
- Announced against.
P Voted "present".
C Voted "present" to avoid possible conflict of interest.
? Did not vote or otherwise make a position known.

Democrats *Republicans*

	103	104	105	106	107	108	109	110
ALABAMA								
1 Edwards	Y	Y	Y	Y	Y	Y	Y	Y
2 *Dickinson*	N	Y	Y	Y	Y	Y	Y	N
3 Nichols	Y	Y	Y	Y	Y	Y	Y	Y
4 Bevill	Y	Y	Y	Y	Y	Y	Y	Y
5 Flippo	Y	Y	Y	Y	Y	Y	Y	Y
6 Erdreich	Y	Y	Y	Y	Y	Y	Y	Y
7 Shelby	?	?	?	?	?	?	?	Y
ALASKA								
AL *Young*	Y	Y	Y	Y	Y	Y	Y	N
ARIZONA								
1 *McCain*	Y	Y	Y	Y	Y	Y	Y	Y
2 Udall	Y	Y	Y	Y	Y	Y	Y	Y
3 *Stump*	N	N	N	Y	N	Y	Y	Y
4 *Rudd*	N	Y	Y	Y	Y	Y	Y	Y
5 McNulty	Y	Y	Y	Y	Y	Y	Y	Y
ARKANSAS								
1 Alexander	Y	Y	Y	Y	Y	Y	Y	P
2 *Bethune*	Y	Y	Y	Y	Y	Y	Y	Y
3 *Hammerschmidt*	Y	Y	Y	Y	Y	Y	Y	Y
4 Anthony	Y	Y	Y	Y	Y	Y	Y	Y
CALIFORNIA								
1 Bosco	Y	Y	Y	Y	Y	Y	Y	Y
2 *Chappie*	Y	Y	Y	Y	Y	Y	Y	N
3 Matsui	Y	Y	Y	Y	Y	Y	Y	Y
4 Fazio	Y	Y	Y	Y	Y	Y	Y	Y
5 Burton	Y	Y	Y	Y	Y	Y	Y	Y
6 Boxer	Y	Y	Y	Y	Y	Y	Y	Y
7 Miller	Y	Y	Y	Y	Y	Y	Y	Y
8 Dellums	Y	Y	Y	Y	Y	Y	Y	Y
9 Stark	Y	Y	Y	Y	Y	Y	Y	Y
10 Edwards	Y	Y	Y	Y	Y	Y	Y	Y
11 Lantos	Y	Y	Y	Y	Y	Y	Y	Y
12 *Zschau*	Y	Y	Y	Y	Y	Y	Y	Y
13 Mineta	Y	Y	Y	Y	Y	Y	Y	Y
14 *Shumway*	N	Y	Y	N	Y	N	Y	Y
15 Coelho	Y	Y	Y	Y	?	Y	Y	Y
16 Panetta	Y	Y	Y	Y	Y	Y	Y	Y
17 *Pashayan*	Y	Y	Y	Y	Y	Y	Y	Y
18 Lehman	Y	Y	Y	Y	Y	Y	Y	Y
19 *Lagomarsino*	Y	Y	Y	Y	Y	Y	Y	Y
20 *Thomas*	Y	Y	Y	Y	Y	Y	Y	Y
21 *Fiedler*	Y	Y	Y	Y	Y	Y	Y	Y
22 *Moorhead*	Y	Y	Y	Y	Y	Y	Y	Y
23 Beilenson	Y	Y	Y	Y	Y	Y	Y	Y
24 Waxman	Y	Y	Y	Y	Y	Y	Y	?
25 Roybal	Y	Y	Y	Y	Y	Y	Y	Y
26 Berman	Y	Y	Y	Y	Y	Y	Y	Y
27 Levine	Y	Y	Y	Y	Y	Y	Y	Y
28 Dixon	Y	Y	Y	Y	Y	Y	Y	Y
29 Hawkins	Y	Y	Y	Y	?	?	N	
30 Martinez	Y	Y	Y	?	Y	Y	Y	Y
31 Dymally	Y	Y	Y	Y	Y	Y	Y	P
32 Anderson	Y	Y	Y	Y	Y	Y	Y	Y
33 *Dreier*	Y	Y	Y	Y	Y	Y	Y	Y
34 Torres	Y	Y	Y	Y	Y	Y	Y	Y
35 *Lewis*	Y	Y	Y	Y	Y	Y	Y	Y
36 Brown	Y	Y	Y	Y	Y	Y	Y	
37 *McCandless*	Y	Y	Y	Y	Y	Y	Y	Y
38 Patterson	Y	Y	Y	Y	Y	Y	Y	Y
39 *Dannemeyer*	N	N	N	Y	Y	Y	Y	Y
40 *Badham*	N	N	Y	Y	Y	Y	Y	Y
41 *Lowery*	Y	Y	Y	Y	Y	Y	Y	Y
42 *Lungren*	N	Y	Y	Y	Y	Y	Y	Y

	103	104	105	106	107	108	109	110
43 *Packard*	Y	Y	Y	Y	Y	Y	Y	Y
44 Bates	Y	Y	Y	Y	Y	Y	Y	Y
45 *Hunter*	Y	Y	Y	Y	Y	Y	Y	Y
COLORADO								
1 Schroeder	Y	Y	Y	Y	Y	Y	Y	N
2 Wirth	Y	Y	Y	Y	Y	Y	Y	Y
3 Kogovsek	Y	Y	Y	Y	Y	Y	Y	Y
4 *Brown*	Y	Y	N	Y	Y	Y	Y	Y
5 *Kramer*	Y	Y	Y	Y	Y	Y	Y	Y
6 *Schaefer*	N	Y	Y	Y	Y	Y	Y	Y
CONNECTICUT								
1 Kennelly	Y	Y	Y	Y	Y	Y	Y	Y
2 Gejdenson	Y	Y	Y	Y	Y	Y	Y	N
3 Morrison	Y	Y	Y	Y	Y	Y	Y	Y
4 *McKinney*	Y	Y	Y	Y	Y	Y	Y	Y
5 Ratchford	Y	Y	Y	Y	Y	Y	Y	Y
6 *Johnson*	Y	Y	Y	?	Y	Y	Y	Y
DELAWARE								
AL Carper	Y	Y	Y	Y	Y	Y	Y	Y
FLORIDA								
1 Hutto	Y	Y	Y	Y	Y	Y	Y	Y
2 Fuqua	Y	Y	Y	Y	Y	Y	Y	Y
3 Bennett	Y	Y	Y	Y	Y	Y	Y	Y
4 Chappell	Y	Y	Y	Y	Y	Y	Y	Y
5 *McCollum*	Y	Y	Y	Y	Y	Y	Y	Y
6 MacKay	Y	Y	Y	Y	Y	Y	Y	Y
7 Gibbons	Y	Y	Y	Y	Y	Y	N	?
8 *Young*	Y	Y	Y	Y	Y	Y	Y	Y
9 *Bilirakis*	Y	Y	Y	Y	Y	Y	Y	Y
10 Ireland	Y	Y	Y	Y	Y	Y	Y	Y
11 Nelson	Y	Y	Y	Y	Y	Y	Y	Y
12 *Lewis*	Y	Y	Y	Y	Y	Y	Y	?
13 *Mack*	Y	Y	Y	Y	Y	Y	Y	Y
14 Mica	Y	Y	Y	Y	Y	Y	Y	Y
15 *Shaw*	Y	Y	Y	Y	Y	Y	Y	Y
16 Smith	Y	Y	Y	Y	Y	Y	Y	P
17 Lehman	Y	Y	Y	Y	Y	Y	Y	?
18 Pepper	Y	Y	Y	Y	Y	Y	Y	Y
19 Fascell	Y	Y	Y	Y	Y	Y	Y	?
GEORGIA								
1 Thomas	Y	Y	Y	Y	Y	Y	Y	Y
2 Hatcher	Y	Y	Y	Y	Y	Y	Y	Y
3 Ray	Y	Y	Y	Y	Y	Y	Y	Y
4 Levitas	Y	Y	Y	Y	Y	Y	Y	Y
5 Fowler	Y	Y	Y	Y	Y	Y	Y	Y
6 *Gingrich*	Y	Y	Y	Y	Y	Y	Y	Y
7 *Darden*	Y	Y	Y	Y	Y	Y	Y	Y
8 Rowland	Y	Y	Y	Y	Y	Y	Y	Y
9 Jenkins	Y	Y	Y	Y	Y	Y	Y	Y
10 Barnard	Y	Y	Y	Y	Y	Y	Y	Y
HAWAII								
1 Heftel	?	?	?	?	?	?	?	?
2 Akaka	Y	Y	Y	Y	Y	Y	Y	?
IDAHO								
1 *Craig*	N	Y	Y	Y	Y	Y	Y	Y
2 *Hansen*	?	?	?	?	?	?	?	?
ILLINOIS								
1 Hayes	Y	Y	Y	Y	Y	Y	Y	Y
2 Savage	Y	Y	Y	Y	Y	Y	Y	Y
3 Russo	Y	Y	Y	Y	Y	Y	Y	Y
4 *O'Brien*	?	Y	Y	?	Y	Y	Y	Y
5 Lipinski	Y	Y	Y	Y	Y	Y	Y	Y
6 *Hyde*	Y	Y	Y	Y	Y	Y	Y	Y
7 Collins	Y	Y	Y	Y	Y	Y	Y	Y
8 Rostenkowski	Y	Y	Y	Y	Y	Y	Y	Y
9 Yates	Y	Y	Y	Y	Y	Y	Y	N
10 *Porter*	Y	Y	Y	Y	Y	Y	Y	Y
11 Annunzio	Y	Y	Y	Y	Y	Y	Y	Y
12 *Crane, P.*	N	N	N	N	Y	N	Y	Y
13 *Erlenborn*	Y	Y	Y	Y	Y	Y	Y	Y
14 *Corcoran*	Y	Y	Y	Y	Y	Y	Y	Y
15 *Madigan*	?	Y	Y	Y	Y	Y	Y	Y
16 *Martin*	Y	Y	Y	Y	Y	Y	Y	Y
17 Evans	Y	Y	Y	Y	Y	Y	Y	Y
18 *Michel*	Y	Y	Y	Y	Y	Y	Y	Y
19 *Crane, D.*	N	N	Y	N	N	Y	N	Y
20 Durbin	Y	Y	Y	N	Y	Y	N	Y
21 Price	Y	Y	Y	Y	Y	Y	Y	Y
22 Simon	?	?	?	?	?	?	?	Y
INDIANA								
1 Hall	?	?	?	?	?	?	?	?
2 Sharp	Y	Y	Y	Y	Y	Y	Y	Y
3 *Hiler*	Y	Y	Y	Y	Y	Y	Y	Y
4 *Coats*	Y	Y	Y	Y	Y	Y	Y	Y
5 Hillis	Y	Y	Y	Y	Y	Y	Y	Y

ND - Northern Democrats   SD - Southern Democrats

Corresponding to Congressional Record Votes 118, 119, 120, 121, 122, 123, 124, 125

	103	104	105	106	107	108	109	110
6 ***Burton***	Y	Y	Y	Y	Y	Y	Y	Y
7 ***Myers***	Y	Y	Y	Y	Y	Y	Y	Y
8 McCloskey	Y	Y	Y	Y	Y	Y	Y	Y
9 Hamilton	Y	Y	Y	Y	Y	Y	Y	Y
10 Jacobs	Y	Y	Y	N	Y	N	Y	N
IOWA								
1 ***Leach***	Y	Y	Y	Y	Y	Y	Y	Y
2 ***Tauke***	Y	Y	Y	Y	Y	Y	Y	Y
3 ***Evans***	Y	Y	Y	Y	Y	Y	Y	N
4 Smith	Y	Y	Y	Y	Y	Y	Y	Y
5 Harkin	Y	Y	Y	Y	Y	Y	Y	N
6 Bedell	Y	Y	Y	Y	Y	Y	Y	Y
KANSAS								
1 ***Roberts***	N	Y	Y	Y	Y	Y	Y	N
2 Slattery	Y	Y	Y	N	Y	Y	Y	Y
3 ***Winn***	N	Y	Y	Y	Y	Y	Y	Y
4 Glickman	Y	Y	Y	Y	Y	Y	Y	Y
5 ***Whittaker***	N	Y	Y	Y	Y	Y	Y	Y
KENTUCKY								
1 Hubbard	Y	Y	N	Y	Y	Y	N	Y
2 Natcher	Y	Y	Y	Y	Y	Y	Y	Y
3 Mazzoli	Y	Y	Y	Y	Y	Y	Y	Y
4 ***Snyder***	Y	Y	Y	Y	Y	Y	Y	Y
5 ***Rogers***	Y	Y	Y	Y	Y	Y	Y	Y
6 ***Hopkins***	Y	Y	Y	Y	Y	Y	Y	Y
7 Perkins	Y	Y	Y	Y	Y	Y	Y	Y
LOUISIANA								
1 ***Livingston***	Y	?	Y	Y	Y	Y	Y	?
2 Boggs	Y	Y	Y	Y	Y	Y	Y	Y
3 Tauzin	Y	Y	Y	Y	Y	Y	Y	Y
4 Roemer	Y	Y	N	N	N	N	N	N
5 Huckaby	Y	Y	Y	Y	Y	Y	Y	Y
6 ***Moore***	Y	Y	Y	Y	Y	Y	Y	Y
7 Breaux	Y	Y	Y	Y	Y	Y	Y	Y
8 Long	Y	Y	Y	Y	Y	Y	Y	Y
MAINE								
1 ***McKernan***	Y	Y	Y	Y	Y	Y	Y	Y
2 ***Snowe***	Y	Y	Y	Y	Y	Y	Y	Y
MARYLAND								
1 Dyson	Y	Y	Y	Y	Y	Y	Y	Y
2 Long	Y	Y	Y	Y	Y	Y	Y	Y
3 Mikulski	Y	Y	Y	Y	Y	Y	Y	Y
4 ***Holt***	N	Y	Y	N	Y	Y	Y	Y
5 Hoyer	Y	Y	Y	Y	Y	Y	Y	Y
6 Byron	Y	Y	Y	Y	Y	Y	Y	Y
7 Mitchell	Y	Y	Y	Y	Y	?	?	N
8 Barnes	Y	Y	Y	Y	Y	Y	Y	Y
MASSACHUSETTS								
1 ***Conte***	Y	Y	Y	Y	Y	Y	Y	Y
2 Boland	Y	Y	Y	Y	Y	Y	Y	Y
3 Early	Y	Y	Y	Y	Y	Y	Y	Y
4 Frank	Y	Y	Y	Y	Y	Y	Y	Y
5 Shannon	Y	Y	Y	Y	Y	Y	Y	?
6 Mavroules	Y	Y	Y	Y	Y	Y	Y	Y
7 Markey	?	?	?	?	?	?	?	?
8 O'Neill								
9 Moakley	Y	Y	Y	Y	Y	Y	Y	Y
10 Studds	Y	Y	Y	Y	Y	Y	Y	Y
11 Donnelly	Y	Y	Y	Y	Y	Y	Y	Y
MICHIGAN								
1 Conyers	Y	Y	Y	Y	Y	Y	Y	Y
2 ***Pursell***	Y	Y	Y	Y	Y	Y	Y	Y
3 Wolpe	Y	Y	Y	Y	Y	Y	Y	Y
4 ***Siljander***	Y	Y	Y	Y	Y	Y	Y	Y
5 ***Sawyer***	Y	Y	Y	Y	Y	Y	Y	Y
6 Carr	Y	Y	Y	Y	Y	Y	Y	Y
7 Kildee	Y	Y	Y	Y	Y	Y	Y	Y
8 Traxler	Y	Y	Y	Y	Y	Y	Y	Y
9 ***Vander Jagt***	Y	Y	Y	Y	Y	Y	Y	Y
10 Albosta	Y	Y	Y	Y	Y	Y	Y	Y
11 ***Davis***	Y	Y	Y	Y	Y	Y	Y	Y
12 Bonior	Y	Y	Y	Y	Y	Y	Y	?
13 Crockett	Y	Y	Y	Y	Y	Y	Y	?
14 Hertel	Y	Y	Y	Y	Y	Y	Y	Y
15 Ford	Y	Y	Y	Y	Y	Y	Y	?
16 Dingell	Y	Y	Y	Y	Y	Y	Y	Y
17 Levin	Y	Y	Y	Y	Y	Y	Y	Y
18 ***Broomfield***	Y	Y	Y	Y	Y	Y	Y	Y
MINNESOTA								
1 Penny	Y	Y	Y	Y	Y	Y	Y	N
2 ***Weber***	Y	Y	Y	Y	Y	Y	Y	Y
3 ***Frenzel***	Y	Y	Y	Y	Y	Y	Y	N
4 Vento	Y	Y	Y	Y	Y	Y	Y	Y
5 Sabo	Y	Y	Y	Y	Y	Y	Y	N
6 Sikorski	Y	Y	Y	Y	Y	Y	Y	N

	103	104	105	106	107	108	109	110
7 ***Stangeland***	Y	Y	Y	Y	Y	Y	Y	Y
8 Oberstar	Y	Y	Y	Y	Y	Y	Y	P
MISSISSIPPI								
1 Whitten	Y	Y	Y	Y	Y	Y	Y	Y
2 ***Franklin***	Y	Y	Y	Y	Y	Y	Y	Y
3 Montgomery	Y	Y	Y	N	Y	Y	Y	Y
4 Dowdy	Y	Y	Y	Y	Y	Y	Y	Y
5 ***Lott***	Y	Y	Y	Y	Y	Y	Y	?
MISSOURI								
1 Clay	Y	Y	Y	Y	Y	Y	Y	?
2 Young	Y	Y	Y	Y	Y	Y	Y	Y
3 Gephardt	Y	Y	Y	Y	Y	Y	Y	Y
4 Skelton	Y	Y	Y	Y	Y	Y	Y	Y
5 Wheat	Y	Y	Y	Y	Y	Y	Y	Y
6 ***Coleman***	Y	Y	Y	Y	Y	Y	Y	Y
7 ***Taylor***	Y	Y	Y	Y	Y	Y	Y	Y
8 ***Emerson***	Y	Y	Y	Y	Y	Y	Y	N
9 Volkmer	Y	Y	Y	Y	Y	Y	Y	Y
MONTANA								
1 Williams	Y	Y	Y	Y	Y	Y	Y	?
2 ***Marlenee***	Y	Y	Y	Y	Y	Y	Y	Y
NEBRASKA								
1 ***Bereuter***	Y	Y	Y	Y	Y	Y	Y	Y
2 ***Daub***	N	Y	Y	Y	Y	Y	Y	Y
3 ***Smith***	Y	Y	Y	Y	Y	Y	Y	Y
NEVADA								
1 Reid	Y	Y	Y	Y	Y	Y	Y	Y
2 ***Vucanovich***	N	N	Y	Y	Y	Y	Y	Y
NEW HAMPSHIRE								
1 D'Amours	Y	Y	Y	Y	Y	Y	Y	Y
2 ***Gregg***	Y	Y	Y	Y	Y	Y	Y	Y
NEW JERSEY								
1 Florio	Y	Y	Y	Y	Y	Y	Y	?
2 Hughes	Y	Y	Y	Y	Y	Y	Y	Y
3 Howard	Y	Y	Y	Y	Y	Y	Y	Y
4 ***Smith***	Y	Y	Y	Y	Y	Y	Y	Y
5 ***Roukema***	Y	Y	Y	Y	Y	Y	Y	Y
6 Dwyer	Y	Y	Y	Y	Y	Y	Y	Y
7 ***Rinaldo***	Y	Y	Y	Y	Y	Y	Y	Y
8 Roe	Y	Y	Y	Y	Y	Y	Y	Y
9 Torricelli	Y	Y	Y	Y	Y	Y	Y	Y
10 Rodino	Y	Y	Y	Y	Y	Y	Y	Y
11 Minish	Y	Y	Y	Y	Y	Y	Y	Y
12 ***Courter***	Y	Y	Y	Y	Y	Y	Y	Y
13 Vacancy								
14 Guarini	Y	Y	Y	Y	Y	Y	Y	Y
NEW MEXICO								
1 ***Lujan***	Y	Y	Y	Y	Y	Y	Y	Y
2 ***Skeen***	Y	Y	Y	Y	Y	Y	Y	Y
3 Richardson	Y	Y	Y	Y	Y	Y	Y	?
NEW YORK								
1 ***Carney***	Y	Y	Y	Y	Y	Y	Y	Y
2 Downey	Y	Y	Y	Y	Y	Y	Y	Y
3 Mrazek	Y	Y	Y	Y	Y	Y	Y	Y
4 ***Lent***	Y	Y	Y	Y	Y	Y	Y	Y
5 ***McGrath***	Y	Y	Y	Y	Y	Y	Y	Y
6 Addabbo	Y	Y	Y	Y	Y	Y	Y	Y
7 Ackerman	Y	Y	Y	Y	Y	Y	Y	Y
8 Scheuer	Y	Y	Y	Y	Y	Y	Y	Y
9 Ferraro	Y	Y	Y	Y	Y	Y	Y	Y
10 Schumer	Y	Y	Y	Y	Y	Y	Y	Y
11 Towns	Y	Y	Y	Y	Y	Y	Y	Y
12 Owens	Y	Y	Y	Y	Y	Y	Y	Y
13 Solarz	Y	Y	Y	Y	Y	Y	Y	Y
14 ***Molinari***	Y	Y	Y	Y	Y	Y	Y	Y
15 ***Green***	Y	Y	Y	Y	Y	Y	Y	Y
16 Rangel	Y	Y	Y	Y	Y	Y	Y	Y
17 Weiss	Y	Y	Y	Y	Y	Y	Y	Y
18 Garcia	Y	Y	Y	Y	Y	Y	Y	?
19 Biaggi	Y	Y	Y	Y	Y	Y	Y	Y
20 Ottinger	Y	Y	Y	Y	Y	Y	Y	P
21 ***Fish***	Y	Y	Y	Y	Y	Y	Y	Y
22 ***Gilman***	Y	Y	Y	Y	Y	Y	+	Y
23 Stratton	Y	Y	Y	Y	Y	Y	Y	Y
24 ***Solomon***	Y	Y	Y	Y	Y	Y	Y	N
25 ***Boehlert***	Y	Y	Y	Y	Y	Y	Y	Y
26 ***Martin***	Y	Y	Y	Y	Y	Y	Y	Y
27 ***Wortley***	Y	Y	Y	Y	Y	Y	Y	Y
28 McHugh	Y	Y	Y	Y	Y	Y	Y	Y
29 ***Horton***	Y	Y	Y	Y	Y	Y	Y	Y
30 ***Conable***	Y	Y	Y	Y	Y	Y	Y	Y
31 ***Kemp***	Y	Y	Y	Y	Y	Y	Y	Y
32 LaFalce	Y	Y	Y	Y	Y	Y	Y	Y
33 Nowak	Y	Y	Y	Y	Y	Y	Y	Y
34 Lundine	Y	Y	Y	Y	Y	Y	Y	Y

	103	104	105	106	107	108	109	110
NORTH CAROLINA								
1 Jones	?	?	?	?	?	?	?	?
2 Valentine	Y	Y	Y	Y	Y	Y	Y	?
3 Whitley	Y	Y	Y	Y	Y	Y	Y	Y
4 Andrews	?	?	?	?	?	?	?	?
5 Neal	Y	Y	Y	Y	Y	Y	Y	Y
6 Britt	Y	Y	Y	Y	Y	Y	Y	Y
7 Rose	Y	Y	Y	Y	Y	Y	Y	Y
8 Hefner	Y	Y	Y	Y	Y	Y	Y	Y
9 ***Martin***	Y	Y	Y	Y	Y	Y	Y	Y
10 ***Broyhill***	Y	Y	Y	Y	Y	Y	Y	Y
11 Clarke	Y	Y	Y	Y	Y	Y	Y	Y
NORTH DAKOTA								
AL Dorgan	Y	Y	Y	Y	Y	Y	Y	Y
OHIO								
1 Luken	Y	Y	Y	Y	Y	Y	Y	Y
2 ***Gradison***	Y	Y	Y	Y	Y	Y	Y	Y
3 Hall	Y	Y	Y	Y	Y	Y	Y	Y
4 ***Oxley***	Y	Y	Y	Y	Y	Y	Y	Y
5 ***Latta***	Y	Y	Y	Y	Y	Y	Y	Y
6 ***McEwen***	Y	Y	Y	Y	Y	Y	Y	Y
7 ***DeWine***	Y	Y	Y	Y	Y	Y	Y	Y
8 ***Kindness***	Y	Y	Y	Y	Y	Y	?	?
9 Kaptur	Y	Y	Y	Y	Y	Y	Y	Y
10 ***Miller***	Y	Y	Y	Y	Y	Y	Y	N
11 Eckart	Y	Y	Y	Y	Y	Y	Y	Y
12 ***Kasich***	Y	Y	Y	Y	Y	Y	Y	Y
13 Pease	Y	Y	Y	Y	Y	Y	Y	Y
14 Seiberling	Y	Y	Y	Y	Y	Y	Y	Y
15 ***Wylie***	Y	Y	Y	Y	Y	Y	Y	Y
16 ***Regula***	Y	Y	Y	Y	Y	Y	Y	Y
17 ***Williams***	Y	Y	Y	Y	Y	Y	Y	Y
18 Applegate	Y	Y	Y	Y	Y	Y	Y	?
19 Feighan	Y	Y	Y	Y	Y	Y	Y	Y
20 Oakar	Y	Y	Y	Y	Y	Y	Y	Y
21 Stokes	Y	Y	Y	Y	Y	Y	Y	Y
OKLAHOMA								
1 Jones	Y	Y	Y	Y	Y	Y	Y	Y
2 Synar	Y	Y	Y	Y	Y	Y	Y	Y
3 Watkins	Y	Y	Y	Y	Y	Y	Y	Y
4 McCurdy	Y	Y	Y	Y	Y	Y	Y	Y
5 ***Edwards***	Y	Y	Y	Y	Y	Y	Y	Y
6 English	Y	Y	Y	Y	Y	Y	Y	Y
OREGON								
1 AuCoin	Y	Y	Y	Y	Y	Y	Y	Y
2 ***Smith, R.***	?	?	?	?	?	?	?	?
3 Wyden	Y	Y	Y	Y	Y	Y	Y	Y
4 Weaver	Y	Y	Y	Y	Y	Y	Y	Y
5 ***Smith, D.***	N	N	N	Y	Y	Y	Y	Y
PENNSYLVANIA								
1 Foglietta	Y	Y	Y	Y	Y	Y	Y	Y
2 Gray	Y	Y	Y	Y	Y	Y	Y	Y
3 Borski	Y	Y	Y	Y	Y	Y	Y	Y
4 Kolter	Y	Y	Y	Y	Y	Y	Y	Y
5 ***Schulze***	Y	Y	Y	Y	Y	Y	Y	?
6 Yatron	Y	Y	Y	Y	Y	Y	Y	Y
7 Edgar	Y	Y	Y	Y	Y	Y	Y	Y
8 Kostmayer	Y	Y	Y	Y	Y	Y	Y	Y
9 ***Shuster***	Y	Y	Y	Y	Y	Y	Y	Y
10 ***McDade***	Y	Y	Y	Y	Y	Y	Y	Y
11 Harrison	Y	Y	Y	Y	Y	Y	Y	Y
12 Murtha	Y	Y	Y	Y	Y	Y	Y	Y
13 ***Coughlin***	Y	Y	Y	Y	Y	Y	Y	N
14 Coyne	Y	Y	Y	Y	Y	Y	Y	?
15 ***Ritter***	Y	Y	Y	Y	Y	Y	Y	Y
16 ***Walker***	Y	Y	Y	Y	Y	Y	Y	N
17 ***Gekas***	Y	Y	Y	Y	Y	Y	Y	Y
18 Walgren	Y	Y	Y	Y	Y	Y	Y	?
19 ***Goodling***	Y	Y	Y	Y	Y	Y	Y	?
20 Gaydos	Y	Y	Y	Y	Y	Y	Y	Y
21 ***Ridge***	Y	Y	Y	Y	Y	Y	Y	Y
22 Murphy	Y	Y	Y	Y	Y	Y	Y	N
23 ***Clinger***	Y	Y	Y	Y	Y	Y	Y	Y
RHODE ISLAND								
1 St Germain	Y	Y	Y	Y	Y	Y	Y	P
2 ***Schneider***	Y	Y	Y	Y	Y	Y	Y	P
SOUTH CAROLINA								
1 ***Hartnett***	N	Y	N	Y	Y	Y	Y	N
2 ***Spence***	Y	Y	Y	Y	Y	Y	Y	Y
3 Derrick	Y	Y	Y	Y	Y	Y	Y	Y
4 ***Campbell***	Y	Y	Y	Y	Y	Y	Y	Y
5 Spratt	Y	Y	Y	Y	Y	Y	Y	Y
6 Tallon	Y	Y	Y	Y	Y	Y	Y	Y
SOUTH DAKOTA								
AL Daschle	Y	Y	Y	Y	Y	Y	Y	Y

	103	104	105	106	107	108	109	110
TENNESSEE								
1 ***Quillen***	Y	Y	Y	Y	Y	Y	Y	Y
2 ***Duncan***	Y	Y	Y	Y	Y	Y	Y	Y
3 Lloyd	N	Y	Y	Y	Y	Y	Y	Y
4 Cooper	Y	Y	Y	Y	Y	Y	Y	Y
5 Boner	Y	Y	Y	Y	Y	Y	Y	Y
6 Gore	Y	Y	Y	Y	Y	Y	Y	Y
7 ***Sundquist***	Y	Y	Y	Y	Y	Y	Y	Y
8 Jones	Y	Y	Y	Y	Y	Y	Y	Y
9 Ford	Y	Y	Y	Y	Y	Y	Y	Y
TEXAS								
1 Hall, S.	Y	Y	N	N	Y	Y	N	Y
2 Wilson	?	?	?	?	?	?	?	?
3 ***Bartlett***	Y	Y	Y	Y	Y	Y	Y	Y
4 Hall, R.	Y	Y	N	N	Y	N	N	Y
5 Bryant	Y	Y	Y	Y	Y	Y	Y	?
6 ***Gramm***	?	?	?	?	?	?	?	?
7 ***Archer***	Y	Y	Y	Y	Y	Y	Y	Y
8 ***Fields***	Y	Y	Y	Y	Y	Y	Y	Y
9 Brooks	?	?	?	?	?	?	?	?
10 Pickle	Y	Y	Y	Y	Y	Y	N	Y
11 Leath	N	N	N	N	Y	Y	Y	Y
12 Wright	Y	Y	Y	Y	Y	Y	Y	?
13 Hightower	Y	Y	Y	Y	Y	Y	Y	Y
14 Patman	N	N	Y	Y	N	Y	N	Y
15 de la Garza	Y	Y	Y	Y	Y	Y	Y	?
16 Coleman	Y	Y	Y	Y	Y	Y	Y	Y
17 Stenholm	N	N	N	N	Y	Y	N	Y
18 Leland	Y	Y	Y	Y	Y	Y	Y	?
19 Hance	?	?	?	?	?	?	?	?
20 Gonzalez	Y	Y	Y	Y	Y	Y	Y	Y
21 ***Loeffler***	Y	Y	Y	Y	Y	Y	Y	Y
22 ***Paul***	?	?	?	?	?	?	?	?
23 Kazen	?	?	?	?	?	?	?	?
24 Frost	?	?	?	?	?	?	?	?
25 Andrews	Y	Y	Y	Y	Y	Y	Y	Y
26 Vandergriff	Y	Y	Y	N	Y	Y	N	P
27 Ortiz	Y	Y	Y	Y	Y	Y	Y	Y
UTAH								
1 ***Hansen***	Y	Y	N	Y	Y	Y	Y	Y
2 ***Marriott***	Y	Y	Y	Y	Y	Y	Y	Y
3 ***Nielson***	N	Y	N	Y	Y	Y	Y	Y
VERMONT								
AL ***Jeffords***	Y	Y	Y	Y	Y	Y	Y	Y
VIRGINIA								
1 ***Bateman***	Y	Y	Y	Y	Y	Y	Y	Y
2 ***Whitehurst***	N	Y	Y	Y	Y	Y	Y	Y
3 ***Bliley***	Y	Y	Y	Y	Y	Y	Y	Y
4 Sisisky	Y	Y	Y	Y	Y	Y	Y	Y
5 Daniel	N	N	Y	Y	Y	Y	Y	P
6 Olin	Y	Y	Y	Y	Y	Y	N	Y
7 ***Robinson***	N	N	Y	Y	Y	Y	Y	Y
8 ***Parris***	Y	Y	Y	Y	Y	Y	Y	Y
9 Boucher	Y	Y	Y	Y	Y	Y	Y	Y
10 ***Wolf***	Y	Y	Y	Y	Y	Y	Y	Y
WASHINGTON								
1 ***Pritchard***	Y	Y	Y	Y	Y	Y	Y	?
2 Swift	Y	Y	Y	Y	Y	Y	Y	Y
3 Bonker	Y	Y	Y	Y	Y	Y	Y	Y
4 ***Morrison***	Y	Y	Y	Y	Y	Y	Y	Y
5 Foley	Y	Y	Y	Y	Y	Y	Y	Y
6 Dicks	Y	Y	Y	Y	Y	Y	Y	Y
7 Lowry	Y	Y	Y	Y	Y	Y	Y	N
8 ***Chandler***	Y	Y	Y	Y	Y	Y	Y	Y
WEST VIRGINIA								
1 Mollohan	Y	Y	Y	Y	Y	Y	Y	Y
2 Staggers	Y	Y	Y	Y	Y	Y	Y	Y
3 Wise	Y	Y	Y	Y	Y	Y	Y	Y
4 Rahall	Y	Y	Y	Y	Y	Y	Y	Y
WISCONSIN								
1 Aspin	Y	Y	Y	Y	Y	Y	Y	Y
2 Kastenmeier	Y	Y	Y	Y	Y	Y	Y	Y
3 ***Gunderson***	Y	Y	Y	Y	Y	Y	Y	Y
4 Kleczka	Y	Y	Y	Y	Y	Y	Y	Y
5 Moody	Y	Y	Y	Y	Y	Y	Y	Y
6 ***Petri***	Y	Y	Y	Y	Y	Y	Y	Y
7 Obey	Y	Y	Y	Y	Y	Y	Y	Y
8 ***Roth***	Y	Y	Y	Y	Y	Y	Y	Y
9 ***Sensenbrenner***	Y	Y	Y	Y	Y	Y	Y	Y
WYOMING								
AL ***Cheney***	N	Y	Y	Y	Y	Y	Y	Y

Southern states - Ala., Ark., Fla., Ga., Ky., La., Miss., N.C., Okla., S.C., Tenn., Texas, Va.

111. H J Res 492. Department of Agriculture, Fiscal 1984 Urgent Supplemental Appropriations. Conte, R-Mass., motion to instruct House conferees on the bill to meet with Senate conferees. Motion rejected 159-245: R 158-0; D 1-245 (ND 0-167, SD 1-78), May 2, 1984.

112. S 64. Irish Wilderness Act. Adoption of the conference report on the bill to establish as federal wilderness and protect from development the Irish Wilderness Area of about 16,500 acres in the Mark Twain National Forest, Missouri. Adopted 254-142: R 35-121; D 219-21 (ND 159-3, SD 60-18), May 2, 1984.

113. Procedural Motion. Walker, R-Pa., motion to approve the House *Journal* of Wednesday, May 2. Motion agreed to 344-28: R 136-15; D 208-13 (ND 136-12, SD 72-1), May 3, 1984.

114. HR 4275. Hoover Dam Power Allocation. Boxer, D-Calif., amendment to require the energy secretary to auction hydroelectric power from Hoover Dam and award it to the highest bidder or bidders. Rejected 176-214: R 76-79; D 100-135 (ND 81-82, SD 19-53), May 3, 1984. A "nay" was a vote supporting the president's position.

115. HR 4275. Hoover Dam Power Allocation. Passage of the bill to authorize the interior secretary to increase the generating capacity of existing equipment at the Hoover Dam and Powerplant, and renewing contracts for allocation of hydroelectric power generated from Hoover Dam. Passed 279-95: R 99-49; D 180-46 (ND 117-40, SD 63-6), May 3, 1984. A "yea" was a vote supporting the president's position.

KEY

Y	Voted for (yea).
#	Paired for.
+	Announced for.
N	Voted against (nay).
X	Paired against.
-	Announced against.
P	Voted "present".
C	Voted "present" to avoid possible conflict of interest.
?	Did not vote or otherwise make a position known.

Democrats *Republicans*

	111	112	113	114	115
ALABAMA					
1 *Edwards*	Y	N	Y	N	Y
2 *Dickinson*	Y	N	N	N	Y
3 Nichols	N	Y	Y	N	Y
4 Bevill	N	Y	Y	N	Y
5 Flippo	N	Y	Y	N	Y
6 Erdreich	N	Y	Y	N	Y
7 Shelby	N	Y	Y	N	Y
ALASKA					
AL *Young*	Y	N	N	N	Y
ARIZONA					
1 *McCain*	Y	N	Y	N	Y
2 Udall	N	Y	Y	N	Y
3 *Stump*	Y	N	Y	N	Y
4 *Rudd*	Y	N	Y	N	?
5 McNulty	N	Y	Y	N	Y
ARKANSAS					
1 Alexander	N	Y	Y	Y	Y
2 *Bethune*	Y	Y	Y	Y	?
3 *Hammerschmidt*	Y	N	?	?	?
4 Anthony	N	N	?	?	?
CALIFORNIA					
1 Bosco	N	Y	Y	N	Y
2 *Chappie*	Y	N	N	N	Y
3 Matsui	N	Y	Y	N	Y
4 Fazio	N	Y	Y	N	Y
5 Burton	N	Y	Y	Y	Y
6 Boxer	N	Y	Y	Y	N
7 Miller	N	Y	Y	Y	?
8 Dellums	N	Y	Y	Y	N
9 Stark	?	?	Y	Y	?
10 Edwards	N	Y	?	Y	Y
11 Lantos	N	Y	Y	N	Y
12 *Zschau*	Y	Y	Y	Y	Y
13 Mineta	N	Y	Y	Y	Y
14 *Shumway*	Y	N	Y	N	Y
15 Coelho	N	Y	Y	N	Y
16 Panetta	N	Y	Y	Y	Y
17 *Pashayan*	Y	N	N	N	Y
18 Lehman	N	Y	Y	N	Y
19 *Lagomarsino*	Y	N	Y	N	Y
20 *Thomas*	Y	N	Y	N	Y
21 *Fiedler*	Y	N	?	N	Y
22 *Moorhead*	Y	N	Y	N	Y
23 Beilenson	N	Y	Y	N	Y
24 Waxman	N	Y	Y	N	Y
25 Roybal	N	Y	Y	N	Y
26 Berman	N	Y	Y	N	Y
27 Levine	N	Y	Y	N	Y
28 Dixon	N	Y	Y	N	Y
29 Hawkins	N	Y	?	N	?
30 Martinez	N	Y	Y	N	Y
31 Dymally	N	Y	P	N	Y
32 Anderson	N	Y	Y	N	Y
33 *Dreier*	Y	N	Y	N	Y
34 Torres	N	Y	Y	N	Y
35 *Lewis*	Y	N	Y	N	Y
36 Brown	N	Y	Y	N	Y
37 *McCandless*	Y	N	Y	N	Y
38 Patterson	N	Y	Y	N	Y
39 *Dannemeyer*	Y	N	N	N	Y
40 *Badham*	Y	N	Y	N	Y
41 *Lowery*	Y	N	?	N	Y
42 *Lungren*	Y	N	Y	N	Y

	111	112	113	114	115
43 *Packard*	Y	N	Y	N	Y
44 Bates	N	Y	Y	Y	Y
45 *Hunter*	Y	N	Y	N	Y
COLORADO					
1 Schroeder	N	Y	N	Y	Y
2 Wirth	N	Y	Y	N	?
3 Kogovsek	N	Y	Y	?	?
4 *Brown*	Y	N	Y	N	Y
5 *Kramer*	Y	N	Y	N	Y
6 *Schaefer*	Y	N	Y	N	Y
CONNECTICUT					
1 Kennelly	N	Y	Y	Y	Y
2 Gejdenson	N	Y	N	N	Y
3 Morrison	N	Y	Y	Y	N
4 *McKinney*	Y	Y	Y	?	?
5 Ratchford	N	Y	Y	N	Y
6 *Johnson*	Y	N	Y	Y	Y
DELAWARE					
AL Carper	N	Y	Y	Y	N
FLORIDA					
1 Hutto	N	Y	Y	Y	Y
2 Fuqua	N	Y	Y	?	?
3 Bennett	N	N	Y	Y	Y
4 Chappell	N	N	Y	Y	Y
5 *McCollum*	Y	N	Y	N	Y
6 MacKay	N	Y	Y	Y	Y
7 Gibbons	N	Y	?	Y	Y
8 *Young*	Y	N	Y	N	Y
9 *Bilirakis*	Y	N	Y	Y	Y
10 Ireland	Y	N	Y	N	Y
11 Nelson	N	Y	Y	N	Y
12 *Lewis*	#	-	+	+	-
13 *Mack*	Y	N	?	N	Y
14 Mica	N	Y	Y	Y	Y
15 *Shaw*	Y	Y	Y	N	Y
16 Smith	N	Y	Y	Y	Y
17 Lehman	N	Y	Y	N	Y
18 Pepper	N	Y	Y	?	?
19 Fascell	N	Y	Y	N	Y
GEORGIA					
1 Thomas	N	Y	Y	N	Y
2 Hatcher	N	N	Y	N	Y
3 Ray	N	Y	Y	N	Y
4 Levitas	N	Y	Y	N	Y
5 Fowler	N	N	Y	N	Y
6 *Gingrich*	Y	N	Y	N	Y
7 Darden	N	Y	Y	N	Y
8 Rowland	N	Y	Y	N	Y
9 Jenkins	N	N	Y	N	Y
10 Barnard	N	?	?	N	Y
HAWAII					
1 Heftel	?	?	Y	Y	N
2 Akaka	N	Y	Y	N	Y
IDAHO					
1 *Craig*	Y	N	Y	N	Y
2 *Hansen*	?	?	?	?	?
ILLINOIS					
1 Hayes	X	#	Y	Y	N
2 Savage	N	Y	?	?	?
3 Russo	N	?	?	?	?
4 *O'Brien*	Y	N	Y	Y	N
5 Lipinski	N	Y	N	Y	Y
6 *Hyde*	Y	N	Y	Y	Y
7 Collins	N	Y	Y	Y	Y
8 Rostenkowski	N	Y	Y	Y	Y
9 Yates	N	Y	N	Y	N
10 *Porter*	Y	Y	Y	Y	N
11 Annunzio	N	Y	N	Y	Y
12 *Crane, P.*	Y	N	?	?	?
13 *Erlenborn*	Y	N	Y	Y	Y
14 *Corcoran*	Y	N	Y	Y	Y
15 *Madigan*	Y	N	Y	N	N
16 *Martin*	Y	Y	Y	Y	Y
17 Evans	N	Y	Y	Y	N
18 *Michel*	Y	N	Y	N	N
19 *Crane, D.*	Y	N	Y	Y	N
20 Durbin	N	Y	N	Y	N
21 Price	N	Y	Y	N	Y
22 Simon	N	Y	Y	Y	Y
INDIANA					
1 Hall	?	?	?	?	?
2 Sharp	N	Y	Y	Y	Y
3 *Hiler*	?	?	Y	Y	N
4 *Coats*	Y	N	Y	Y	N
5 Hillis	Y	N	Y	Y	Y

ND - Northern Democrats   SD - Southern Democrats

	111	112	113	114	115
6 Burton	Y	N	Y	Y	N
7 Myers	Y	N	Y	N	Y
8 McCloskey	N	Y	Y	Y	N
9 Hamilton	N	Y	Y	Y	N
10 Jacobs	N	N	N	Y	N
IOWA					
1 *Leach*	Y	Y	Y	Y	N
2 *Tauke*	Y	N	Y	Y	N
3 *Evans*	Y	N	N	Y	Y
4 Smith	N	Y	Y	N	Y
5 Harkin	N	?	N	N	Y
6 Bedell	N	Y	Y	Y	Y
KANSAS					
1 *Roberts*	Y	N	N	N	Y
2 Slattery	N	Y	Y	Y	N
3 *Winn*	Y	N	Y	N	Y
4 Glickman	N	Y	Y	N	Y
5 *Whittaker*	Y	N	Y	N	Y
KENTUCKY					
1 Hubbard	N	N	Y	N	Y
2 Natcher	N	Y	Y	N	Y
3 Mazzoli	N	Y	Y	N	+
4 *Snyder*	Y	N	Y	Y	Y
5 *Rogers*	Y	N	Y	?	?
6 *Hopkins*	Y	N	Y	N	Y
7 Perkins	N	Y	Y	N	Y
LOUISIANA					
1 *Livingston*	?	?	Y	N	N
2 Boggs	N	Y	Y	N	Y
3 Tauzin	N	Y	Y	Y	N
4 Roemer	N	N	N	Y	N
5 Huckaby	N	Y	Y	Y	N
6 *Moore*	Y	Y	Y	N	N
7 Breaux	N	Y	?	#	X
8 Long	N	Y	Y	N	Y
MAINE					
1 *McKernan*	Y	Y	Y	Y	N
2 *Snowe*	Y	N	Y	Y	Y
MARYLAND					
1 Dyson	N	N	Y	N	Y
2 Long	N	Y	Y	Y	N
3 Mikulski	N	Y	Y	Y	Y
4 *Holt*	Y	N	Y	N	?
5 Hoyer	N	Y	Y	Y	Y
6 Byron	N	N	Y	N	Y
7 Mitchell	N	#	N	Y	Y
8 Barnes	N	Y	Y	Y	N
MASSACHUSETTS					
1 *Conte*	Y	Y	Y	Y	N
2 Boland	N	Y	Y	Y	Y
3 Early	N	Y	Y	Y	N
4 Frank	N	Y	Y	Y	N
5 Shannon	?	?	Y	Y	N
6 Mavroules	N	Y	Y	Y	Y
7 Markey	?	?	Y	Y	Y
8 O'Neill					
9 Moakley	N	Y	Y	Y	Y
10 Studds	N	Y	Y	Y	N
11 Donnelly	N	Y	Y	N	Y
MICHIGAN					
1 Conyers	N	Y	Y	Y	Y
2 *Pursell*	Y	Y	Y	Y	Y
3 Wolpe	N	Y	Y	Y	N
4 *Siljander*	Y	N	Y	Y	N
5 *Sawyer*	Y	Y	Y	N	Y
6 Carr	N	Y	Y	Y	N
7 Kildee	N	Y	Y	Y	N
8 Traxler	N	Y	?	?	?
9 *Vander Jagt*	Y	N	Y	Y	Y
10 Albosta	N	Y	Y	Y	Y
11 *Davis*	Y	N	Y	N	Y
12 Bonior	N	Y	Y	N	Y
13 Crockett	N	Y	?	?	?
14 Hertel	N	Y	Y	Y	N
15 Ford	X	Y	?	N	Y
16 Dingell	N	Y	?	?	?
17 Levin	N	Y	Y	N	Y
18 *Broomfield*	Y	N	Y	N	Y
MINNESOTA					
1 Penny	N	Y	N	N	Y
2 *Weber*	Y	N	Y	Y	N
3 *Frenzel*	Y	Y	Y	Y	N
4 Vento	N	Y	Y	N	+
5 Sabo	N	Y	N	N	Y
6 Sikorski	N	Y	N	Y	Y

	111	112	113	114	115
7 *Stangeland*	Y	N	?	N	N
8 Oberstar	N	Y	P	N	?
MISSISSIPPI					
1 Whitten	N	Y	Y	N	Y
2 *Franklin*	Y	N	Y	Y	Y
3 Montgomery	N	N	Y	N	Y
4 Dowdy	N	Y	Y	N	Y
5 *Lott*	Y	N	Y	N	Y
MISSOURI					
1 Clay	N	Y	?	?	?
2 Young	N	Y	Y	N	Y
3 Gephardt	N	Y	?	Y	Y
4 Skelton	N	Y	Y	N	Y
5 Wheat	N	Y	Y	N	Y
6 *Coleman*	Y	Y	Y	N	Y
7 *Taylor*	Y	N	Y	N	Y
8 *Emerson*	Y	N	N	N	Y
9 Volkmer	N	Y	Y	N	Y
MONTANA					
1 Williams	?	?	?	N	Y
2 *Marlenee*	Y	N	Y	N	Y
NEBRASKA					
1 *Bereuter*	Y	Y	Y	N	Y
2 *Daub*	Y	N	N	N	Y
3 *Smith*	Y	N	Y	N	Y
NEVADA					
1 Reid	N	Y	Y	N	Y
2 *Vucanovich*	Y	N	Y	N	Y
NEW HAMPSHIRE					
1 D'Amours	X	Y	Y	Y	N
2 *Gregg*	Y	N	Y	Y	N
NEW JERSEY					
1 Florio	N	Y	Y	N	Y
2 Hughes	N	Y	Y	N	Y
3 Howard	N	Y	Y	N	?
4 *Smith*	Y	Y	Y	Y	Y
5 *Roukema*	Y	N	Y	Y	Y
6 Dwyer	N	Y	Y	Y	Y
7 *Rinaldo*	Y	Y	Y	Y	Y
8 Roe	N	?	Y	N	Y
9 Torricelli	N	Y	Y	Y	Y
10 Rodino	N	Y	Y	Y	Y
11 Minish	N	Y	Y	Y	Y
12 *Courter*	Y	Y	Y	Y	Y
13 Vacancy					
14 Guarini	N	Y	Y	Y	Y
NEW MEXICO					
1 *Lujan*	Y	N	Y	N	Y
2 *Skeen*	Y	N	Y	N	Y
3 Richardson	N	Y	Y	N	Y
NEW YORK					
1 *Carney*	Y	N	Y	Y	N
2 Downey	N	Y	Y	Y	Y
3 Mrazek	N	Y	?	Y	N
4 *Lent*	Y	N	Y	Y	Y
5 *McGrath*	Y	Y	Y	Y	N
6 Addabbo	N	Y	Y	?	?
7 Ackerman	N	Y	Y	Y	N
8 Scheuer	N	Y	?	N	N
9 Ferraro	N	Y	Y	Y	Y
10 Schumer	N	Y	Y	Y	N
11 Towns	N	Y	Y	Y	N
12 Owens	N	Y	Y	Y	Y
13 Solarz	N	Y	Y	Y	Y
14 *Molinari*	Y	N	Y	Y	N
15 *Green*	Y	N	Y	Y	N
16 Rangel	N	Y	Y	N	N
17 Weiss	N	Y	Y	Y	N
18 Garcia	X	?	?	N	Y
19 Biaggi	N	?	?	?	?
20 Ottinger	N	Y	?	N	N
21 *Fish*	Y	Y	Y	Y	Y
22 *Gilman*	Y	Y	Y	Y	Y
23 Stratton	N	Y	Y	N	Y
24 *Solomon*	Y	N	N	Y	N
25 *Boehlert*	Y	Y	Y	Y	Y
26 *Martin*	Y	N	N	N	Y
27 *Wortley*	Y	N	?	N	Y
28 McHugh	N	Y	?	Y	?
29 *Horton*	Y	N	Y	Y	Y
30 *Conable*	Y	Y	Y	Y	Y
31 *Kemp*	Y	N	Y	N	N
32 LaFalce	N	Y	?	N	Y
33 Nowak	N	Y	Y	N	Y
34 Lundine	N	Y	Y	N	Y

	111	112	113	114	115
NORTH CAROLINA					
1 Jones	?	?	?	?	?
2 Valentine	?	?	?	?	?
3 Whitley	N	Y	Y	N	Y
4 Andrews	?	?	?	?	?
5 Neal	N	Y	Y	N	Y
6 Britt	N	Y	Y	N	Y
7 Rose	N	Y	Y	N	Y
8 Hefner	N	Y	Y	N	Y
9 *Martin*	Y	N	Y	N	N
10 *Broyhill*	Y	Y	Y	Y	N
11 Clarke	N	Y	Y	N	Y
NORTH DAKOTA					
AL Dorgan	N	Y	N	N	Y
OHIO					
1 Luken	N	Y	Y	?	?
2 *Gradison*	Y	Y	Y	Y	N
3 Hall	N	Y	Y	N	Y
4 *Oxley*	Y	N	Y	?	?
5 *Latta*	Y	N	?	N	?
6 *McEwen*	Y	N	Y	Y	N
7 *DeWine*	Y	N	Y	N	N
8 *Kindness*	Y	N	Y	N	N
9 Kaptur	N	Y	Y	Y	Y
10 *Miller*	Y	N	N	N	Y
11 Eckart	N	Y	Y	Y	N
12 *Kasich*	Y	N	Y	N	N
13 Pease	N	Y	Y	N	N
14 Seiberling	N	Y	Y	Y	N
15 *Wylie*	Y	N	Y	N	Y
16 *Regula*	Y	Y	Y	N	Y
17 *Williams*	Y	Y	Y	Y	Y
18 Applegate	N	Y	?	N	Y
19 Feighan	N	Y	?	Y	Y
20 Oakar	N	Y	Y	N	Y
21 Stokes	N	Y	Y	N	Y
OKLAHOMA					
1 Jones	N	Y	Y	N	Y
2 Synar	N	Y	Y	N	Y
3 Watkins	N	Y	Y	N	?
4 McCurdy	N	Y	Y	N	Y
5 *Edwards*	Y	N	Y	?	?
6 English	N	Y	Y	N	Y
OREGON					
1 AuCoin	N	Y	Y	N	Y
2 *Smith, R.*	#	?	Y	N	Y
3 Wyden	N	Y	Y	N	Y
4 Weaver	N	Y	Y	Y	N
5 *Smith, D.*	Y	N	Y	N	Y
PENNSYLVANIA					
1 Foglietta	N	Y	Y	Y	N
2 Gray	N	Y	?	?	?
3 Borski	N	Y	?	Y	Y
4 Kolter	N	Y	Y	Y	Y
5 *Schulze*	Y	N	Y	Y	Y
6 Yatron	N	Y	Y	Y	Y
7 Edgar	N	?	Y	Y	N
8 Kostmayer	N	Y	Y	Y	N
9 *Shuster*	Y	N	Y	N	Y
10 *McDade*	Y	Y	Y	Y	Y
11 Harrison	N	Y	?	?	?
12 Murtha	N	Y	Y	Y	Y
13 *Coughlin*	Y	Y	N	Y	?
14 Coyne	N	Y	Y	Y	Y
15 *Ritter*	Y	N	Y	N	Y
16 *Walker*	Y	N	N	Y	N
17 *Gekas*	Y	N	Y	N	Y
18 Walgren	N	?	Y	Y	Y
19 *Goodling*	Y	N	N	Y	N
20 Gaydos	N	Y	Y	N	Y
21 *Ridge*	Y	N	Y	Y	N
22 Murphy	N	Y	Y	Y	N
23 *Clinger*	Y	Y	Y	N	Y
RHODE ISLAND					
1 St Germain	N	Y	P	N	Y
2 *Schneider*	Y	?	Y	Y	Y
SOUTH CAROLINA					
1 *Hartnett*	Y	N	Y	?	?
2 *Spence*	Y	N	Y	N	Y
3 Derrick	N	Y	?	?	?
4 *Campbell*	Y	N	Y	N	Y
5 Spratt	N	Y	Y	N	Y
6 Tallon	N	Y	Y	N	Y
SOUTH DAKOTA					
AL Daschle	N	Y	Y	N	Y

	111	112	113	114	115
TENNESSEE					
1 *Quillen*	Y	N	Y	N	?
2 *Duncan*	Y	N	Y	N	Y
3 Lloyd	N	Y	Y	N	Y
4 Cooper	N	Y	Y	N	Y
5 Boner	N	Y	?	?	?
6 Gore	N	Y	Y	N	Y
7 *Sundquist*	Y	N	Y	N	Y
8 Jones	N	N	Y	?	#
9 Ford	N	Y	Y	N	Y
TEXAS					
1 Hall, S.	N	Y	Y	N	Y
2 Wilson	?	?	?	?	?
3 *Bartlett*	Y	N	?	Y	N
4 Hall, R.	N	N	Y	N	Y
5 Bryant	?	?	?	?	?
6 *Gramm*	#	?	?	?	?
7 *Archer*	Y	N	Y	Y	N
8 *Fields*	Y	N	Y	Y	Y
9 Brooks	?	?	?	?	?
10 Pickle	N	N	Y	N	Y
11 Leath	N	N	Y	N	Y
12 Wright	N	Y	Y	N	Y
13 Hightower	N	N	Y	N	Y
14 Patman	N	N	Y	N	Y
15 de la Garza	?	?	?	?	?
16 Coleman	N	N	Y	N	Y
17 Stenholm	N	N	Y	N	Y
18 Leland	X	?	?	X	?
19 Hance	?	?	?	?	?
20 Gonzalez	N	Y	Y	N	Y
21 *Loeffler*	Y	N	Y	N	Y
22 *Paul*	#	X	?	?	?
23 Kazen	?	?	?	?	?
24 Frost	?	?	?	?	?
25 Andrews	N	Y	Y	Y	Y
26 Vandergriff	N	Y	Y	N	Y
27 Ortiz	N	Y	Y	N	?
UTAH					
1 *Hansen*	Y	N	Y	N	Y
2 *Marriott*	Y	N	Y	N	Y
3 *Nielson*	Y	N	Y	N	Y
VERMONT					
AL *Jeffords*	Y	?	Y	Y	N
VIRGINIA					
1 *Bateman*	Y	N	Y	N	Y
2 *Whitehurst*	Y	N	Y	N	Y
3 *Bliley*	#	X	Y	Y	Y
4 Sisisky	N	Y	Y	Y	Y
5 Daniel	N	N	Y	N	Y
6 Olin	N	Y	Y	N	Y
7 *Robinson*	Y	N	Y	N	Y
8 *Parris*	Y	N	Y	N	Y
9 Boucher	N	Y	Y	N	Y
10 *Wolf*	Y	N	?	Y	N
WASHINGTON					
1 *Pritchard*	Y	Y	Y	Y	N
2 Swift	N	Y	Y	N	Y
3 Bonker	N	Y	?	N	Y
4 *Morrison*	Y	Y	Y	Y	N
5 Foley	N	Y	Y	N	Y
6 Dicks	N	Y	Y	N	Y
7 Lowry	N	Y	Y	Y	N
8 *Chandler*	Y	Y	Y	Y	N
WEST VIRGINIA					
1 Mollohan	N	Y	Y	N	Y
2 Staggers	N	Y	Y	Y	Y
3 Wise	N	Y	Y	Y	Y
4 Rahall	N	Y	Y	N	Y
WISCONSIN					
1 Aspin	N	Y	Y	Y	N
2 Kastenmeier	N	Y	?	Y	Y
3 *Gunderson*	Y	N	Y	N	Y
4 Kleczka	N	Y	Y	Y	N
5 *Moody*	N	Y	Y	Y	Y
6 *Petri*	Y	Y	Y	N	Y
7 Obey	N	Y	Y	Y	Y
8 *Roth*	Y	N	Y	Y	Y
9 *Sensenbrenner*	Y	Y	Y	Y	N
WYOMING					
AL *Cheney*	Y	N	Y	N	Y

Southern states - Ala., Ark., Fla., Ga., Ky., La., Miss., N.C., Okla., S.C., Tenn., Texas, Va.

116. HR 5121. Virginia Wilderness. Seiberling, D-Ohio, motion to suspend the rules and pass the bill to designate as federal wilderness approximately 59,000 acres in the Jefferson and George Washington National Forests, Virginia. Motion agreed to 376-20: R 139-14; D 237-6 (ND 162-0, SD 75-6), May 8, 1984. A two-thirds majority of those present and voting (264 in this case) is required for passage under suspension of the rules. A "yea" was a vote supporting the president's position.

117. S 1129. Domestic Volunteer Service Act. Adoption of the conference report on the bill to authorize $158.4 million in fiscal 1984, $166.1 million in fiscal 1985 and $175.2 million in fiscal 1986 for volunteer programs administered by ACTION. Adopted (thus cleared for the president) 369-25: R 127-25; D 242-0 (ND 161-0, SD 81-0), May 8, 1984.

118. Procedural Motion. Solomon, R-N.Y., motion to approve the House *Journal* of Tuesday, May 8. Motion agreed to 361-23: R 140-10; D 221-13 (ND 143-12, SD 78-1), May 9, 1984.

119. HR 5119. Foreign Assistance Authorization. Feighan, D-Ohio, amendment to set a $670 million limit on military aid to Turkey and authorize $250 million in additional assistance to Cyprus if the president certifies that an agreement has been reached between Greek and Turkish Cypriots that makes substantial progress toward settlement of the Cyprus dispute. Adopted 376-27: R 131-23; D 245-4 (ND 168-1, SD 77-3), May 9, 1984.

120. HR 5119. Foreign Assistance Authorization. Hall, D-Ohio, amendment to eliminate the $25 million in grant military assistance to the Philippines. Rejected 149-259: R 15-139; D 134-120 (ND 106-64, SD 28-56), May 9, 1984. A "nay" was a vote supporting the president's position.

121. HR 5119. Foreign Assistance Authorization. Rahall, D-W.Va., amendment to prohibit the use of foreign military sales funds by foreign countries to develop their own weapons systems outside the United States. Rejected 40-379: R 12-148; D 28-231 (ND 17-158, SD 11-73), May 9, 1984.

122. HR 5119. Foreign Assistance Authorization. Dorgan, D-N.D., amendment to freeze the military assistance program grants to non-Central American countries at the fiscal year 1984 appropriations level of $422.5 million. Rejected 207-208: R 46-110; D 161-98 (ND 112-63, SD 49-35), May 9, 1984. A "nay" was a vote supporting the president's position.

KEY

Y Voted for (yea).
Paired for.
+ Announced for.
N Voted against (nay).
X Paired against.
- Announced against.
P Voted "present".
C Voted "present" to avoid possible conflict of interest.
? Did not vote or otherwise make a position known.

Democrats **Republicans**

	116	117	118	119	120	121	122
ALABAMA							
1 *Edwards*	Y	Y	?	Y	N	N	N
2 *Dickinson*	Y	Y	N	Y	X	N	N
3 Nichols	Y	Y	Y	Y	Y	N	N
4 Bevill	Y	Y	Y	Y	Y	N	N
5 Flippo	Y	Y	Y	Y	N	N	N
6 Erdreich	Y	Y	Y	Y	Y	N	Y
7 Shelby	Y	Y	Y	Y	N	N	N
ALASKA							
AL *Young*	N	Y	N	Y	N	N	N
ARIZONA							
1 *McCain*	Y	Y	Y	Y	N	N	N
2 Udall	Y	Y	?	Y	N	N	Y
3 *Stump*	N	N	Y	N	N	Y	N
4 *Rudd*	N	N	Y	N	N	N	N
5 McNulty	Y	Y	Y	Y	N	N	Y
ARKANSAS							
1 Alexander	Y	Y	?	Y	N	N	N
2 *Bethune*	Y	Y	?	Y	?	N	N
3 *Hammerschmidt*	Y	Y	Y	Y	N	N	N
4 Anthony	Y	Y	Y	?	Y	N	Y
CALIFORNIA							
1 Bosco	Y	Y	Y	Y	?	N	Y
2 *Chappie*	Y	Y	Y	N	N	Y	Y
3 Matsui	Y	Y	Y	Y	Y	N	Y
4 Fazio	Y	Y	Y	Y	Y	N	Y
5 Burton	Y	Y	Y	Y	Y	N	Y
6 Boxer	Y	Y	Y	Y	Y	N	Y
7 Miller	Y	Y	Y	Y	Y	N	Y
8 Dellums	Y	Y	Y	Y	Y	N	Y
9 Stark	Y	Y	Y	Y	Y	N	Y
10 Edwards	Y	Y	Y	Y	Y	N	Y
11 Lantos	Y	Y	Y	Y	N	N	N
12 *Zschau*	Y	N	Y	Y	N	N	N
13 Mineta	Y	Y	Y	Y	Y	N	Y
14 *Shumway*	Y	N	Y	N	Y	Y	Y
15 Coelho	Y	Y	Y	Y	Y	N	N
16 Panetta	Y	Y	Y	Y	Y	N	Y
17 *Pashayan*	Y	Y	Y	Y	N	N	N
18 Lehman	Y	Y	Y	Y	N	N	Y
19 *Lagomarsino*	Y	Y	Y	Y	N	N	N
20 *Thomas*	Y	N	Y	Y	N	N	N
21 *Fiedler*	Y	Y	Y	Y	N	N	Y
22 *Moorhead*	Y	Y	Y	Y	N	N	N
23 Beilenson	Y	Y	Y	Y	Y	N	N
24 Waxman	Y	Y	Y	Y	Y	N	N
25 Roybal	Y	Y	?	?	Y	N	Y
26 Berman	Y	Y	Y	Y	Y	N	N
27 Levine	Y	Y	Y	Y	N	N	N
28 Dixon	Y	Y	Y	Y	Y	N	N
29 Hawkins	?	?	N	?	?	N	N
30 Martinez	Y	Y	Y	Y	N	N	N
31 Dymally	Y	?	P	Y	N	Y	N
32 Anderson	Y	Y	Y	Y	N	N	Y
33 *Dreier*	Y	N	Y	Y	N	N	N
34 Torres	Y	Y	Y	Y	N	N	Y
35 *Lewis*	Y	Y	Y	?	X	N	N
36 Brown	Y	Y	Y	Y	Y	N	Y
37 *McCandless*	Y	Y	Y	+	N	Y	Y
38 Patterson	Y	Y	Y	Y	Y	N	N
39 *Dannemeyer*	Y	N	Y	N	N	N	N
40 *Badham*	Y	N	Y	N	N	Y	N
41 *Lowery*	Y	Y	Y	Y	N	N	N
42 *Lungren*	Y	N	Y	Y	N	N	N

	116	117	118	119	120	121	122
43 *Packard*	Y	Y	Y	Y	N	Y	N
44 Bates	Y	Y	Y	Y	Y	N	Y
45 *Hunter*	Y	Y	?	Y	N	N	N
COLORADO							
1 Schroeder	Y	Y	N	Y	Y	N	Y
2 Wirth	Y	Y	Y	Y	Y	N	Y
3 Kogovsek	Y	Y	Y	Y	Y	N	Y
4 *Brown*	Y	Y	Y	N	N	N	Y
5 *Kramer*	?	?	Y	N	N	N	Y
6 *Schaefer*	Y	Y	Y	N	N	N	Y
CONNECTICUT							
1 Kennelly	Y	Y	Y	Y	Y	N	N
2 Gejdenson	Y	Y	N	Y	Y	N	N
3 Morrison	Y	Y	Y	Y	Y	N	N
4 *McKinney*	Y	Y	Y	Y	N	N	N
5 Ratchford	Y	Y	Y	Y	Y	N	Y
6 Johnson	Y	Y	Y	Y	N	N	Y
DELAWARE							
AL Carper	Y	Y	Y	Y	N	N	Y
FLORIDA							
1 Hutto	Y	Y	Y	Y	N	N	N
2 Fuqua	Y	Y	Y	Y	N	N	N
3 Bennett	Y	Y	Y	Y	N	N	N
4 Chappell	Y	Y	Y	Y	N	N	N
5 *McCollum*	Y	Y	Y	Y	N	N	N
6 MacKay	Y	Y	Y	Y	Y	N	Y
7 Gibbons	Y	Y	Y	Y	N	N	N
8 *Young*	?	?	?	?	?	N	N
9 *Bilirakis*	Y	Y	Y	Y	N	N	N
10 Ireland	Y	Y	?	Y	N	N	N
11 Nelson	Y	Y	Y	Y	N	N	N
12 *Lewis*	Y	Y	Y	Y	N	N	N
13 *Mack*	Y	Y	Y	Y	N	N	N
14 Mica	Y	Y	Y	Y	N	N	N
15 *Shaw*	Y	Y	Y	Y	N	N	N
16 Smith	Y	Y	Y	Y	N	N	N
17 Lehman	Y	Y	Y	Y	Y	N	Y
18 Pepper	Y	Y	Y	Y	N	N	N
19 Fascell	Y	Y	?	Y	N	N	N
GEORGIA							
1 Thomas	Y	Y	Y	Y	N	N	N
2 Hatcher	Y	Y	Y	Y	N	N	Y
3 Ray	Y	Y	N	Y	N	N	N
4 Levitas	Y	Y	Y	Y	N	N	N
5 Fowler	?	?	Y	Y	N	N	N
6 *Gingrich*	Y	Y	Y	Y	N	N	N
7 Darden	Y	Y	Y	Y	Y	Y	Y
8 Rowland	Y	Y	Y	Y	N	N	N
9 Jenkins	?	?	Y	Y	Y	Y	Y
10 Barnard	Y	Y	Y	Y	N	N	Y
HAWAII							
1 Heftel	Y	Y	?	Y	N	N	Y
2 Akaka	Y	Y	Y	?	N	N	Y
IDAHO							
1 *Craig*	Y	N	Y	N	N	N	N
2 *Hansen*	?	?	?	?	?	?	?
ILLINOIS							
1 Hayes	Y	Y	Y	Y	Y	N	Y
2 Savage	?	?	?	?	?	N	Y
3 Russo	Y	Y	Y	Y	N	N	Y
4 *O'Brien*	Y	Y	Y	Y	N	N	N
5 Lipinski	Y	Y	Y	Y	N	N	N
6 *Hyde*	Y	Y	Y	Y	N	N	N
7 Collins	Y	Y	Y	Y	N	N	Y
8 Rostenkowski	Y	Y	Y	Y	N	N	N
9 Yates	Y	Y	Y	Y	Y	N	N
10 *Porter*	Y	Y	Y	Y	-	-	N
11 Annunzio	Y	Y	Y	Y	N	N	N
12 *Crane, P.*	N	N	N	N	N	N	N
13 *Erlenborn*	?	?	?	?	?	?	?
14 *Corcoran*	Y	Y	Y	Y	N	N	N
15 *Madigan*	Y	Y	Y	Y	N	N	N
16 *Martin*	Y	Y	Y	Y	Y	N	Y
17 Evans	Y	Y	Y	Y	Y	N	Y
18 *Michel*	Y	N	Y	Y	N	Y	N
19 *Crane, D.*	N	N	Y	N	N	N	N
20 Durbin	Y	Y	N	Y	N	Y	N
21 Price	Y	Y	Y	Y	N	N	N
22 Simon	Y	Y	Y	Y	Y	N	Y
INDIANA							
1 Hall	?	?	?	?	?	?	?
2 Sharp	Y	Y	Y	Y	N	N	Y
3 *Hiler*	Y	Y	Y	Y	N	N	N
4 *Coats*	Y	Y	Y	Y	N	N	N
5 *Hillis*	Y	Y	Y	?	N	N	N

	116	117	118	119	120	121	122
6 ***Burton***	Y	N	Y	N	N	N	N
7 ***Myers***	Y	Y	Y	Y	N	N	N
8 McCloskey	Y	Y	Y	Y	Y	N	Y
9 Hamilton	Y	Y	Y	Y	N	N	N
10 Jacobs	Y	Y	N	Y	Y	N	Y
IOWA							
1 ***Leach***	Y	Y	Y	Y	Y	N	Y
2 ***Tauke***	Y	Y	Y	Y	N	N	Y
3 ***Evans***	Y	Y	N	N	?	N	Y
4 Smith	Y	Y	Y	Y	N	N	Y
5 Harkin	Y	Y	N	Y	Y	N	Y
6 Bedell	Y	Y	Y	Y	Y	N	Y
KANSAS							
1 ***Roberts***	Y	Y	N	N	N	N	Y
2 Slattery	Y	Y	Y	Y	Y	N	Y
3 ***Winn***	Y	Y	Y	Y	N	N	N
4 Glickman	Y	Y	Y	Y	Y	N	Y
5 ***Whittaker***	Y	Y	Y	Y	N	N	N
KENTUCKY							
1 Hubbard	N	Y	Y	N	Y	Y	Y
2 Natcher	Y	Y	Y	Y	Y	N	Y
3 Mazzoli	Y	Y	Y	Y	N	N	Y
4 ***Snyder***	Y	Y	Y	Y	N	N	Y
5 ***Rogers***	?	?	Y	N	N	N	Y
6 ***Hopkins***	?	?	Y	N	N	N	Y
7 Perkins	Y	Y	Y	Y	Y	Y	Y
LOUISIANA							
1 ***Livingston***	Y	N	Y	Y	N	N	N
2 Boggs	Y	Y	?	Y	N	N	Y
3 Tauzin	Y	Y	Y	Y	Y	N	Y
4 Roemer	Y	Y	N	Y	Y	N	Y
5 Huckaby	Y	Y	Y	Y	N	N	N
6 ***Moore***	Y	Y	Y	Y	N	N	Y
7 Breaux	Y	Y	Y	Y	N	N	N
8 Long	Y	Y	Y	Y	N	N	N
MAINE							
1 ***McKernan***	Y	Y	Y	Y	N	N	Y
2 ***Snowe***	Y	Y	Y	Y	N	N	Y
MARYLAND							
1 Dyson	Y	Y	?	Y	N	N	N
2 Long	Y	Y	Y	Y	N	N	Y
3 Mikulski	?	?	Y	Y	Y	N	Y
4 ***Holt***	Y	Y	Y	N	N	N	N
5 Hoyer	Y	Y	Y	Y	N	N	N
6 Byron	Y	Y	Y	Y	N	Y	Y
7 Mitchell	Y	Y	N	Y	Y	N	Y
8 Barnes	Y	Y	Y	Y	N	N	N
MASSACHUSETTS							
1 ***Conte***	Y	Y	Y	Y	N	N	N
2 Boland	Y	Y	Y	Y	N	N	N
3 Early	Y	Y	Y	Y	Y	Y	N
4 Frank	Y	Y	Y	Y	Y	N	N
5 Shannon	?	?	Y	Y	Y	N	Y
6 Mavroules	Y	Y	Y	Y	N	N	N
7 Markey	Y	Y	Y	#	#	?	?
8 O'Neill							
9 Moakley	Y	Y	?	Y	Y	N	Y
10 Studds	?	?	Y	Y	Y	N	Y
11 Donnelly	Y	Y	Y	Y	Y	N	N
MICHIGAN							
1 Conyers	Y	Y	Y	Y	Y	Y	Y
2 ***Pursell***	Y	Y	Y	Y	N	N	N
3 Wolpe	Y	Y	Y	Y	Y	N	N
4 ***Siljander***	Y	Y	Y	Y	Y	N	N
5 ***Sawyer***	Y	Y	Y	Y	N	N	N
6 Carr	Y	Y	Y	Y	Y	N	Y
7 Kildee	Y	Y	Y	Y	Y	N	Y
8 Traxler	Y	Y	?	Y	Y	N	N
9 ***Vander Jagt***	?	?	?	Y	N	N	N
10 Albosta	Y	Y	Y	Y	Y	Y	N
11 ***Davis***	Y	Y	Y	Y	N	N	N
12 Bonior	Y	Y	?	Y	?	Y	Y
13 Crockett	Y	Y	?	Y	Y	Y	Y
14 Hertel	Y	Y	Y	Y	Y	N	Y
15 Ford	Y	Y	?	Y	N	Y	Y
16 Dingell	Y	Y	Y	Y	Y	Y	N
17 Levin	Y	Y	Y	Y	Y	N	N
18 ***Broomfield***	Y	Y	Y	Y	N	N	N
MINNESOTA							
1 Penny	Y	Y	N	Y	Y	N	Y
2 ***Weber***	Y	Y	Y	Y	N	N	N
3 ***Frenzel***	Y	N	Y	Y	N	N	?
4 Vento	Y	Y	Y	Y	Y	N	Y
5 Sabo	Y	Y	N	Y	Y	N	Y
6 Sikorski	Y	Y	N	Y	Y	N	Y
7 ***Stangeland***	Y	Y	Y	Y	N	Y	Y
8 Oberstar	Y	Y	P	Y	Y	N	Y
MISSISSIPPI							
1 Whitten	Y	Y	Y	Y	Y	N	Y
2 ***Franklin***	Y	Y	Y	Y	N	N	N
3 Montgomery	Y	Y	Y	?	N	Y	N
4 Dowdy	Y	Y	Y	Y	Y	N	N
5 ***Lott***	Y	Y	Y	Y	N	N	N
MISSOURI							
1 Clay	Y	Y	N	Y	Y	N	Y
2 Young	Y	Y	Y	Y	Y	N	N
3 Gephardt	Y	Y	Y	Y	N	N	N
4 Skelton	Y	Y	Y	Y	N	N	N
5 Wheat	Y	Y	Y	Y	Y	N	Y
6 ***Coleman***	Y	Y	Y	Y	N	Y	N
7 ***Taylor***	Y	Y	?	Y	N	N	Y
8 ***Emerson***	N	Y	N	N	N	Y	Y
9 Volkmer	Y	Y	Y	N	Y	N	Y
MONTANA							
1 Williams	Y	Y	?	Y	Y	N	Y
2 ***Marlenee***	Y	Y	Y	Y	N	N	N
NEBRASKA							
1 ***Bereuter***	Y	Y	Y	N	N	Y	N
2 ***Daub***	Y	Y	Y	Y	Y	N	Y
3 ***Smith***	Y	Y	Y	Y	N	N	N
NEVADA							
1 Reid	Y	Y	Y	Y	N	N	N
2 ***Vucanovich***	Y	Y	Y	Y	N	N	N
NEW HAMPSHIRE							
1 D'Amours	?	?	Y	Y	Y	N	Y
2 ***Gregg***	Y	Y	Y	Y	Y	N	N
NEW JERSEY							
1 Florio	Y	Y	Y	Y	N	N	Y
2 Hughes	Y	Y	Y	Y	N	N	Y
3 Howard	Y	Y	Y	Y	N	N	N
4 ***Smith***	Y	Y	Y	Y	N	N	Y
5 ***Roukema***	Y	Y	Y	Y	N	N	Y
6 Dwyer	Y	Y	Y	Y	N	N	N
7 ***Rinaldo***	Y	Y	Y	Y	N	N	N
8 Roe	Y	Y	Y	Y	N	N	Y
9 Torricelli	Y	Y	Y	Y	N	N	N
10 Rodino	Y	Y	Y	Y	Y	N	Y
11 Minish	Y	Y	Y	Y	N	N	N
12 ***Courter***	Y	Y	Y	Y	Y	N	Y
13 Vacancy							
14 Guarini	Y	Y	Y	Y	Y	N	Y
NEW MEXICO							
1 ***Lujan***	Y	?	Y	Y	N	N	?
2 ***Skeen***	Y	Y	Y	Y	N	N	N
3 Richardson	Y	Y	Y	Y	Y	N	N
NEW YORK							
1 ***Carney***	Y	Y	Y	Y	N	N	N
2 Downey	Y	Y	?	Y	Y	N	Y
3 Mrazek	Y	Y	Y	Y	Y	N	Y
4 ***Lent***	Y	Y	Y	Y	N	N	?
5 ***McGrath***	Y	Y	Y	Y	N	N	?
6 Addabbo	Y	Y	Y	Y	N	N	Y
7 Ackerman	Y	Y	Y	Y	N	N	Y
8 Scheuer	Y	Y	Y	Y	N	N	N
9 Ferraro	?	Y	?	?	Y	N	Y
10 Schumer	Y	Y	Y	Y	Y	N	N
11 Towns	Y	Y	Y	Y	Y	N	Y
12 Owens	Y	Y	?	Y	Y	N	Y
13 Solarz	Y	Y	Y	Y	N	N	N
14 ***Molinari***	Y	Y	Y	Y	N	N	N
15 ***Green***	Y	Y	Y	Y	Y	N	N
16 Rangel	Y	Y	Y	Y	N	N	Y
17 Weiss	Y	Y	Y	Y	Y	N	N
18 Garcia	?	?	Y	Y	N	N	N
19 Biaggi	Y	Y	Y	Y	N	N	N
20 Ottinger	?	?	P	Y	Y	N	Y
21 ***Fish***	Y	Y	Y	Y	N	N	Y
22 ***Gilman***	Y	Y	Y	Y	N	N	N
23 Stratton	Y	Y	Y	Y	N	N	N
24 ***Solomon***	Y	Y	N	?	N	N	N
25 ***Boehlert***	Y	Y	Y	Y	N	N	Y
26 ***Martin***	Y	Y	Y	Y	N	N	N
27 ***Wortley***	Y	Y	Y	Y	N	N	N
28 McHugh	Y	Y	Y	Y	?	N	Y
29 ***Horton***	N	Y	Y	Y	N	N	N
30 ***Conable***	Y	Y	Y	Y	N	N	N
31 ***Kemp***	Y	Y	?	Y	N	N	N
32 LaFalce	Y	Y	Y	Y	N	N	Y
33 Nowak	Y	Y	Y	Y	N	N	N
34 Lundine	Y	Y	Y	?	N	N	N
NORTH CAROLINA							
1 Jones	?	?	?	?	?	?	?
2 Valentine	?	?	?	?	?	?	?
3 Whitley	Y	Y	Y	Y	N	N	Y
4 Andrews	?	?	?	?	?	?	?
5 Neal	?	?	?	Y	?	?	N
6 Britt	Y	Y	Y	Y	N	N	N
7 Rose	?	?	Y	Y	N	N	N
8 Hefner	Y	Y	Y	Y	N	N	Y
9 ***Martin***	?	?	?	?	?	?	?
10 ***Broyhill***	Y	Y	Y	Y	N	N	Y
11 Clarke	Y	Y	Y	Y	N	N	Y
NORTH DAKOTA							
AL Dorgan	Y	Y	Y	Y	Y	N	Y
OHIO							
1 Luken	Y	Y	Y	Y	Y	N	Y
2 ***Gradison***	Y	Y	Y	Y	N	N	Y
3 Hall	?	?	Y	Y	Y	N	Y
4 ***Oxley***	?	?	Y	?	N	N	Y
5 ***Latta***	Y	N	Y	N	N	N	N
6 ***McEwen***	Y	Y	Y	Y	N	N	N
7 ***DeWine***	Y	Y	Y	Y	N	N	N
8 ***Kindness***	Y	Y	Y	Y	N	N	N
9 Kaptur	?	?	?	Y	Y	N	Y
10 ***Miller***	Y	Y	N	N	Y	Y	Y
11 Eckart	Y	Y	Y	Y	Y	N	Y
12 ***Kasich***	Y	Y	Y	Y	N	N	N
13 Pease	Y	Y	Y	Y	Y	N	Y
14 Seiberling	Y	Y	Y	Y	Y	N	Y
15 ***Wylie***	Y	Y	Y	Y	N	N	Y
16 ***Regula***	Y	Y	Y	Y	N	N	N
17 ***Williams***	?	?	Y	Y	Y	N	Y
18 Applegate	Y	Y	?	Y	Y	Y	Y
19 Feighan	Y	Y	Y	Y	Y	N	N
20 Oakar	Y	Y	Y	Y	Y	Y	Y
21 Stokes	Y	Y	Y	Y	Y	N	Y
OKLAHOMA							
1 Jones	Y	Y	Y	Y	N	N	Y
2 Synar	Y	Y	Y	Y	N	N	Y
3 Watkins	Y	Y	Y	Y	N	N	Y
4 McCurdy	Y	Y	Y	Y	N	N	Y
5 ***Edwards***	Y	Y	Y	?	N	N	N
6 English	Y	Y	Y	Y	N	N	Y
OREGON							
1 AuCoin	Y	?	Y	Y	Y	N	N
2 ***Smith, R.***	Y	Y	Y	Y	N	N	N
3 Wyden	Y	Y	Y	Y	Y	N	Y
4 Weaver	Y	Y	Y	Y	Y	N	Y
5 ***Smith, D.***	N	N	Y	N	N	N	N
PENNSYLVANIA							
1 Foglietta	Y	Y	Y	Y	Y	N	Y
2 Gray	Y	Y	Y	Y	Y	N	Y
3 Borski	Y	Y	Y	Y	Y	N	Y
4 Kolter	Y	Y	Y	Y	Y	Y	Y
5 ***Schulze***	Y	Y	Y	Y	Y	N	?
6 Yatron	Y	Y	Y	Y	N	N	N
7 Edgar	Y	Y	Y	Y	Y	N	Y
8 Kostmayer	Y	Y	Y	Y	N	N	Y
9 ***Shuster***	N	Y	Y	Y	N	N	N
10 ***McDade***	Y	Y	Y	Y	N	N	N
11 Harrison	?	?	?	Y	Y	N	Y
12 Murtha	Y	Y	Y	Y	N	N	N
13 ***Coughlin***	Y	Y	Y	Y	N	N	N
14 Coyne	Y	Y	Y	Y	Y	N	N
15 ***Ritter***	Y	Y	Y	Y	Y	N	Y
16 ***Walker***	Y	Y	N	Y	Y	N	Y
17 ***Gekas***	Y	Y	Y	Y	N	P	N
18 Walgren	Y	Y	Y	Y	Y	N	Y
19 ***Goodling***	Y	Y	N	Y	Y	N	Y
20 Gaydos	Y	Y	Y	Y	Y	N	Y
21 ***Ridge***	Y	Y	Y	Y	N	N	Y
22 Murphy	Y	Y	Y	Y	Y	Y	Y
23 ***Clinger***	Y	Y	Y	Y	N	N	N
RHODE ISLAND							
1 St Germain	Y	Y	P	Y	Y	N	N
2 ***Schneider***	Y	Y	Y	Y	N	N	Y
SOUTH CAROLINA							
1 ***Hartnett***	N	N	Y	Y	N	N	N
2 ***Spence***	Y	Y	?	?	?	N	N
3 Derrick	Y	Y	Y	Y	Y	N	Y
4 ***Campbell***	Y	Y	Y	Y	N	N	N
5 Spratt	Y	Y	Y	Y	Y	N	Y
6 Tallon	N	Y	Y	Y	Y	N	Y
SOUTH DAKOTA							
AL Daschle	Y	Y	Y	Y	Y	N	Y
TENNESSEE							
1 ***Quillen***	Y	Y	Y	Y	N	N	N
2 ***Duncan***	Y	Y	Y	Y	N	N	N
3 Lloyd	Y	Y	Y	Y	N	N	Y
4 Cooper	Y	Y	Y	Y	Y	N	Y
5 Boner	Y	Y	Y	?	Y	N	Y
6 Gore	Y	Y	Y	Y	N	N	Y
7 ***Sundquist***	Y	Y	Y	Y	N	N	N
8 Jones	Y	Y	Y	Y	Y	Y	Y
9 Ford	Y	Y	Y	Y	Y	N	Y
TEXAS							
1 Hall, S.	Y	Y	Y	Y	N	Y	Y
2 Wilson	Y	Y	Y	Y	N	N	N
3 ***Bartlett***	Y	N	Y	Y	N	N	N
4 Hall, R.	Y	Y	Y	Y	Y	Y	Y
5 Bryant	Y	Y	Y	Y	Y	N	Y
6 ***Gramm***	?	?	?	Y	N	N	N
7 ***Archer***	Y	N	Y	Y	N	N	Y
8 ***Fields***	?	?	?	Y	N	N	?
9 Brooks	Y	Y	Y	Y	Y	N	N
10 Pickle	Y	Y	Y	?	N	N	Y
11 Leath	N	Y	Y	?	Y	Y	N
12 Wright	Y	Y	Y	Y	N	N	N
13 Hightower	Y	Y	Y	Y	N	N	Y
14 Patman	N	Y	Y	N	Y	Y	Y
15 de la Garza	Y	Y	Y	Y	N	N	Y
16 Coleman	Y	Y	Y	Y	N	N	Y
17 Stenholm	N	Y	Y	Y	Y	Y	Y
18 Leland	Y	Y	Y	Y	Y	N	?
19 Hance	?	?	?	X	#	?	?
20 Gonzalez	Y	Y	Y	Y	N	N	Y
21 ***Loeffler***	Y	N	Y	Y	N	N	N
22 ***Paul***	N	N	Y	Y	Y	Y	Y
23 Kazen	?	?	?	?	?	?	?
24 Frost	Y	Y	Y	Y	N	N	N
25 Andrews	Y	Y	Y	Y	N	N	Y
26 Vandergriff	Y	Y	Y	Y	N	N	Y
27 Ortiz	Y	Y	Y	Y	N	N	Y
UTAH							
1 ***Hansen***	?	?	?	?	?	?	?
2 ***Marriott***	Y	Y	Y	Y	N	N	N
3 ***Nielson***	Y	N	Y	N	N	Y	Y
VERMONT							
AL ***Jeffords***	Y	Y	Y	Y	?	N	Y
VIRGINIA							
1 ***Bateman***	Y	Y	?	Y	N	N	N
2 ***Whitehurst***	Y	Y	Y	Y	N	N	N
3 ***Bliley***	N	Y	Y	Y	N	N	N
4 Sisisky	Y	Y	Y	Y	N	N	N
5 Daniel	N	Y	?	Y	N	N	N
6 Olin	Y	Y	Y	Y	N	N	Y
7 ***Robinson***	N	Y	Y	Y	N	N	N
8 ***Parris***	N	Y	Y	Y	N	N	N
9 Boucher	Y	Y	Y	Y	N	N	N
10 ***Wolf***	Y	Y	Y	Y	N	N	N
WASHINGTON							
1 ***Pritchard***	Y	Y	Y	Y	N	N	N
2 Swift	?	?	Y	Y	N	N	N
3 Bonker	Y	Y	Y	Y	Y	N	N
4 ***Morrison***	Y	Y	?	Y	N	N	N
5 Foley	Y	Y	Y	Y	N	N	N
6 Dicks	Y	Y	Y	Y	N	N	N
7 Lowry	Y	Y	N	Y	Y	N	Y
8 ***Chandler***	Y	Y	Y	Y	N	N	N
WEST VIRGINIA							
1 Mollohan	Y	Y	Y	Y	N	N	Y
2 Staggers	Y	Y	Y	Y	Y	Y	Y
3 Wise	Y	Y	Y	Y	N	Y	Y
4 Rahall	?	?	Y	Y	Y	Y	Y
WISCONSIN							
1 Aspin	Y	Y	Y	Y	N	N	N
2 Kastenmeier	Y	Y	Y	Y	Y	Y	Y
3 ***Gunderson***	Y	Y	Y	Y	N	N	Y
4 Kleczka	Y	Y	Y	Y	N	N	N
5 Moody	Y	Y	Y	Y	N	N	N
6 ***Petri***	Y	Y	Y	Y	N	N	N
7 Obey	Y	Y	Y	Y	N	N	Y
8 ***Roth***	Y	Y	Y	N	N	N	N
9 ***Sensenbrenner***	Y	Y	Y	Y	N	N	Y
WYOMING							
AL ***Cheney***	Y	N	Y	Y	N	N	N

Southern states - Ala., Ark., Fla., Ga., Ky., La., Miss., N.C., Okla., S.C., Tenn., Texas, Va.

KEY

Y   Voted for (yea).
Paired for.
+   Announced for.
N   Voted against (nay).
X   Paired against.
-   Announced against.
P   Voted "present".
C   Voted "present" to avoid possible conflict of interest.
?   Did not vote or otherwise make a position known.

Democrats   *Republicans*

123. Procedural Motion. Weber, R-Minn., motion to approve the House *Journal* of Wednesday, May 9. Motion agreed to 233-153: R 7-145; D 226-8 (ND 149-8, SD 77-0), May 10, 1984.

124. HR 5119. Foreign Assistance Authorization. Studds, D-Mass., amendment to prohibit any military aid to El Salvador in fiscal year 1985 unless the president had certified to Congress that the Salvadoran government had achieved three objectives: removing from the security forces individuals responsible for or associated with "death squads" and establishing effective control over the security forces; complying with international agreements on the protection of civilians in civil wars; and participating in good faith negotiations with all parties to the Salvadoran civil war. Rejected 128-287: R 3-156; D 125-131 (ND 119-54, SD 6-77), May 10, 1984. A "nay" was a vote supporting the president's position.

125. HR 5119. Foreign Assistance Authorization. Broomfield, R-Mich., amendment to authorize President Reagan's requests for military, economic and development aid for Central American countries in fiscal 1984-1985, and to allow military aid for El Salvador in fiscal 1985 if the president certified to Congress that the government had made "demonstrated progress" on human rights and other issues. Adopted 212-208: R 156-8; D 56-200 (ND 7-167, SD 49-33), May 10, 1984. A "yea" was a vote supporting the president's position.

126. HR 5119. Foreign Assistance Authorization. Broomfield, R-Mich., amendment to authorize President Reagan's requests for military, economic and development aid for Central American countries in fiscal 1984-1985, and to allow military aid for El Salvador in fiscal 1985 if the president certified to Congress that the government had made "demonstrated progress" on human rights and other issues. Adopted 211-208: R 155-8; D 56-200 (ND 7-167, SD 49-33), May 10, 1984. A "yea" was a vote supporting the president's position. (The amendment previously was adopted in the Committee of the Whole (see vote 125, above).)

127. HR 5119. Foreign Aid Authorization. Passage of the bill to make $361 million in supplemental authorizations for foreign aid programs in fiscal 1984 and $10.95 billion in authorizations for fiscal 1985. Passed 211-206: R 116-46; D 95-160 (ND 44-129, SD 51-31), May 10, 1984. A "yea" was a vote supporting the president's position.

	123	124	125	126	127
ALABAMA					
1 *Edwards*	N	N	Y	#	?
2 *Dickinson*	N	N	Y	Y	Y
3 Nichols	Y	N	Y	Y	N
4 Bevill	Y	N	?	?	?
5 Flippo	Y	N	Y	Y	N
6 Erdreich	Y	N	Y	Y	Y
7 Shelby	Y	N	Y	Y	N
ALASKA					
AL *Young*	N	N	Y	Y	Y
ARIZONA					
1 *McCain*	N	N	Y	Y	Y
2 Udall	?	Y	N	N	Y
3 *Stump*	N	N	Y	Y	Y
4 *Rudd*	N	N	Y	Y	Y
5 McNulty	Y	N	N	N	N
ARKANSAS					
1 Alexander	Y	N	N	N	N
2 *Bethune*	N	?	Y	Y	Y
3 *Hammerschmidt*	N	N	Y	Y	N
4 Anthony	?	N	N	N	N
CALIFORNIA					
1 Bosco	Y	?	N	N	N
2 *Chappie*	N	N	Y	Y	N
3 Matsui	Y	Y	N	N	N
4 Fazio	Y	Y	N	N	N
5 Burton	Y	Y	N	N	N
6 Boxer	Y	Y	N	N	N
7 Miller	Y	Y	N	N	N
8 Dellums	Y	Y	N	N	N
9 Stark	Y	Y	N	N	N
10 Edwards	Y	Y	N	N	N
11 Lantos	Y	Y	N	N	Y
12 *Zschau*	N	N	Y	Y	Y
13 Mineta	?	Y	N	N	N
14 *Shumway*	N	N	Y	Y	N
15 Coelho	Y	Y	N	N	N
16 Panetta	Y	Y	N	N	N
17 *Pashayan*	N	N	Y	Y	N
18 Lehman	Y	Y	N	N	N
19 *Lagomarsino*	N	N	Y	Y	N
20 *Thomas*	N	N	Y	Y	Y
21 *Fiedler*	N	N	Y	Y	Y
22 *Moorhead*	N	N	Y	Y	N
23 Beilenson	Y	Y	N	N	N
24 Waxman	N	Y	N	N	Y
25 Roybal	Y	Y	N	N	N
26 Berman	Y	Y	N	N	N
27 Levine	Y	Y	N	N	Y
28 Dixon	?	Y	N	N	N
29 Hawkins	N	Y	N	N	N
30 Martinez	Y	Y	N	N	Y
31 Dymally	P	Y	N	N	Y
32 Anderson	Y	Y	N	N	N
33 *Dreier*	N	N	Y	Y	Y
34 Torres	Y	Y	N	N	N
35 *Lewis*	Y	N	Y	Y	Y
36 Brown	Y	Y	N	N	N
37 *McCandless*	N	N	Y	Y	Y
38 Patterson	Y	N	N	N	N
39 *Dannemeyer*	N	N	Y	Y	N
40 *Badham*	N	N	Y	Y	Y
41 Lowery	?	N	Y	Y	Y
42 Lungren	N	N	Y	Y	Y

	123	124	125	126	127
43 *Packard*	N	N	Y	Y	Y
44 Bates	Y	Y	N	N	N
45 *Hunter*	?	N	Y	Y	Y
COLORADO					
1 Schroeder	N	Y	N	N	N
2 Wirth	Y	Y	N	N	N
3 Kogovsek	Y	Y	N	N	N
4 *Brown*	N	N	Y	Y	N
5 *Kramer*	N	N	Y	Y	Y
6 *Schaefer*	N	N	Y	Y	Y
CONNECTICUT					
1 Kennelly	Y	Y	N	N	N
2 Gejdenson	Y	Y	N	N	N
3 Morrison	Y	Y	N	N	N
4 *McKinney*	?	N	N	N	Y
5 Ratchford	Y	Y	N	N	N
6 *Johnson*	N	N	Y	Y	N
DELAWARE					
AL Carper	Y	N	N	N	Y
FLORIDA					
1 Hutto	Y	N	Y	Y	Y
2 Fuqua	Y	N	Y	Y	Y
3 Bennett	Y	N	Y	Y	Y
4 Chappell	Y	N	Y	Y	Y
5 *McCollum*	?	N	Y	Y	Y
6 MacKay	Y	N	N	N	Y
7 Gibbons	Y	N	N	N	N
8 *Young*	N	N	Y	Y	Y
9 *Bilirakis*	N	N	Y	Y	Y
10 Ireland	?	N	Y	Y	Y
11 Nelson	Y	N	Y	Y	Y
12 *Lewis*	N	N	Y	Y	Y
13 *Mack*	N	N	Y	Y	Y
14 Mica	Y	N	Y	Y	Y
15 *Shaw*	N	N	Y	Y	Y
16 Smith	Y	N	N	N	Y
17 Lehman	Y	Y	N	N	Y
18 Pepper	Y	N	N	N	Y
19 Fascell	Y	N	N	N	Y
GEORGIA					
1 Thomas	Y	N	Y	Y	Y
2 Hatcher	Y	N	Y	Y	Y
3 Ray	Y	N	Y	Y	Y
4 Levitas	Y	N	Y	Y	Y
5 Fowler	Y	N	N	N	Y
6 *Gingrich*	N	?	Y	Y	Y
7 Darden	Y	N	Y	Y	Y
8 Rowland	Y	N	Y	Y	Y
9 Jenkins	Y	?	Y	Y	N
10 Barnard	Y	Y	Y	Y	Y
HAWAII					
1 Heftel	?	N	N	N	N
2 Akaka	Y	Y	N	N	?
IDAHO					
1 *Craig*	N	N	Y	Y	Y
2 *Hansen*	?	?	?	?	?
ILLINOIS					
1 Hayes	Y	Y	N	N	N
2 Savage	?	Y	N	N	N
3 Russo	Y	Y	N	N	N
4 *O'Brien*	N	N	Y	Y	Y
5 Lipinski	Y	N	N	N	N
6 *Hyde*	N	N	Y	Y	Y
7 Collins	Y	Y	N	N	N
8 Rostenkowski	?	N	?	?	?
9 Yates	Y	Y	N	N	N
10 *Porter*	+	N	Y	Y	Y
11 Annunzio	Y	N	N	N	Y
12 *Crane, P.*	N	N	Y	Y	N
13 *Erlenborn*	N	N	Y	Y	Y
14 *Corcoran*	N	N	Y	Y	Y
15 *Madigan*	?	N	Y	Y	Y
16 *Martin*	N	N	Y	N	Y
17 Evans	Y	Y	N	N	N
18 *Michel*	N	N	Y	Y	Y
19 *Crane, D.*	N	N	Y	Y	Y
20 Durbin	Y	Y	N	N	N
21 Price	Y	N	N	N	Y
22 Simon	Y	Y	N	N	Y
INDIANA					
1 Hall	?	#	?	?	?
2 Sharp	Y	N	N	N	N
3 *Hiler*	N	N	Y	Y	Y
4 *Coats*	N	N	Y	Y	Y
5 *Hillis*	N	N	Y	Y	Y

ND - Northern Democrats   SD - Southern Democrats

	123	124	125	126	127
6 Burton	N	N	Y	Y	Y
7 Myers	N	N	Y	Y	Y
8 McCloskey	Y	N	N	N	N
9 Hamilton	Y	N	N	N	N
10 Jacobs	N	Y	N	N	N
IOWA					
1 Leach	N	Y	N	N	N
2 Tauke	N	N	Y	Y	N
3 Evans	?	N	Y	Y	N
4 Smith	Y	N	N	N	N
5 Harkin	N	Y	N	N	N
6 Bedell	Y	Y	N	N	N
KANSAS					
1 Roberts	N	N	Y	Y	N
2 Slattery	Y	N	N	N	N
3 Winn	N	N	Y	Y	Y
4 Glickman	Y	N	N	N	N
5 Whittaker	N	N	Y	Y	N
KENTUCKY					
1 Hubbard	Y	N	Y	N	N
2 Natcher	Y	N	N	N	N
3 Mazzoli	Y	N	N	N	N
4 Snyder	N	N	Y	Y	N
5 Rogers	N	N	Y	Y	N
6 Hopkins	N	N	Y	Y	N
7 Perkins	Y	N	N	N	N
LOUISIANA					
1 Livingston	N	N	Y	Y	Y
2 Boggs	?	X	?	X	#
3 Tauzin	Y	N	Y	Y	Y
4 Roemer	Y	N	Y	Y	Y
5 Huckaby	Y	N	Y	Y	Y
6 Moore	N	N	Y	Y	Y
7 Breaux	Y	N	Y	Y	Y
8 Long	Y	N	N	N	N
MAINE					
1 McKernan	N	N	Y	Y	Y
2 Snowe	N	N	Y	Y	Y
MARYLAND					
1 Dyson	Y	N	Y	Y	N
2 Long	Y	N	N	N	N
3 Mikulski	Y	Y	N	N	N
4 Holt	N	N	Y	Y	Y
5 Hoyer	Y	N	N	N	Y
6 Byron	Y	N	Y	N	N
7 Mitchell	N	Y	N	N	N
8 Barnes	Y	N	N	N	N
MASSACHUSETTS					
1 Conte	N	Y	N	N	Y
2 Boland	Y	N	N	N	N
3 Early	Y	Y	N	N	N
4 Frank	Y	Y	N	N	N
5 Shannon	Y	Y	N	N	N
6 Mavroules	Y	Y	N	N	N
7 Markey	?	Y	N	N	N
8 O'Neill					
9 Moakley	Y	Y	N	N	N
10 Studds	Y	Y	N	N	N
11 Donnelly	Y	Y	N	N	N
MICHIGAN					
1 Conyers	?	Y	N	N	N
2 Pursell	N	N	Y	Y	Y
3 Wolpe	?	Y	N	N	N
4 Siljander	N	N	Y	Y	Y
5 Sawyer	N	N	Y	Y	Y
6 Carr	Y	N	N	N	N
7 Kildee	Y	Y	N	N	N
8 Traxler	Y	Y	N	N	N
9 Vander Jagt	N	N	Y	Y	Y
10 Albosta	Y	N	N	N	N
11 Davis	N	N	Y	Y	N
12 Bonior	Y	Y	N	N	N
13 Crockett	?	Y	N	N	N
14 Hertel	Y	Y	N	N	N
15 Ford	Y	Y	N	N	N
16 Dingell	Y	N	N	N	N
17 Levin	Y	N	N	N	N
18 Broomfield	N	N	Y	Y	Y
MINNESOTA					
1 Penny	N	N	Y	Y	N
2 Weber	N	N	Y	Y	Y
3 Frenzel	N	N	Y	Y	Y
4 Vento	Y	Y	N	N	N
5 Sabo	Y	Y	N	N	N
6 Sikorski	N	Y	N	N	N

	123	124	125	126	127
7 Stangeland	N	N	Y	Y	N
8 Oberstar	P	Y	N	N	N
MISSISSIPPI					
1 Whitten	?	N	N	N	N
2 Franklin	N	N	Y	Y	Y
3 Montgomery	Y	N	Y	Y	Y
4 Dowdy	Y	N	Y	Y	Y
5 Lott	N	N	Y	Y	Y
MISSOURI					
1 Clay	?	Y	N	N	N
2 Young	Y	N	N	N	N
3 Gephardt	Y	N	N	N	N
4 Skelton	Y	N	Y	Y	Y
5 Wheat	Y	Y	N	N	N
6 Coleman	N	N	Y	Y	N
7 Taylor	N	N	Y	Y	N
8 Emerson	N	N	Y	Y	N
9 Volkmer	Y	N	N	N	N
MONTANA					
1 Williams	?	Y	N	N	N
2 Marlenee	N	N	Y	Y	Y
NEBRASKA					
1 Bereuter	N	N	Y	Y	Y
2 Daub	N	N	Y	Y	N
3 Smith	N	N	Y	Y	N
NEVADA					
1 Reid	Y	N	N	N	Y
2 Vucanovich	?	N	Y	Y	Y
NEW HAMPSHIRE					
1 D'Amours	Y	N	N	N	N
2 Gregg	N	N	Y	Y	Y
NEW JERSEY					
1 Florio	Y	Y	N	N	N
2 Hughes	Y	N	N	N	N
3 Howard	Y	Y	N	N	N
4 Smith	?	N	Y	Y	N
5 Roukema	Y	N	N	N	N
6 Dwyer	Y	Y	N	N	N
7 Rinaldo	?	N	Y	Y	N
8 Roe	Y	N	N	N	N
9 Torricelli	Y	Y	N	N	N
10 Rodino	Y	Y	N	N	N
11 Minish	Y	N	Y	Y	N
12 Courter	?	?	Y	Y	Y
13 Vacancy					
14 Guarini	Y	N	N	N	N
NEW MEXICO					
1 Lujan	N	N	Y	Y	Y
2 Skeen	N	N	Y	Y	Y
3 Richardson	Y	Y	N	N	N
NEW YORK					
1 Carney	N	N	Y	Y	Y
2 Downey	Y	Y	N	N	N
3 Mrazek	Y	Y	N	N	N
4 Lent	N	N	Y	Y	Y
5 McGrath	N	N	Y	Y	Y
6 Addabbo	Y	Y	N	N	N
7 Ackerman	Y	Y	N	N	N
8 Scheuer	Y	Y	N	N	N
9 Ferraro	Y	Y	N	N	N
10 Schumer	Y	Y	N	N	N
11 Towns	Y	Y	N	N	N
12 Owens	Y	Y	N	N	N
13 Solarz	Y	Y	N	N	N
14 Molinari	N	N	Y	Y	Y
15 Green	N	N	N	N	N
16 Rangel	Y	Y	N	N	N
17 Weiss	Y	Y	N	N	N
18 Garcia	?	Y	N	N	N
19 Biaggi	Y	N	N	N	Y
20 Ottinger	Y	Y	N	N	N
21 Fish	?	N	Y	Y	Y
22 Gilman	N	N	Y	Y	N
23 Stratton	Y	N	Y	Y	Y
24 Solomon	N	N	Y	Y	Y
25 Boehlert	N	N	Y	Y	N
26 Martin	N	N	Y	Y	Y
27 Wortley	N	N	Y	Y	Y
28 McHugh	Y	N	N	N	N
29 Horton	N	N	Y	Y	Y
30 Conable	N	N	Y	Y	Y
31 Kemp	N	N	Y	Y	N
32 LaFalce	Y	N	N	N	N
33 Nowak	Y	Y	N	N	N
34 Lundine	Y	Y	N	N	N

	123	124	125	126	127
NORTH CAROLINA					
1 Jones	?	?	N	N	N
2 Valentine	?	N	Y	Y	N
3 Whitley	Y	N	Y	Y	N
4 Andrews	?	?	?	?	?
5 Neal	?	N	N	N	N
6 Britt	Y	N	N	N	N
7 Rose	Y	Y	N	N	N
8 Hefner	Y	N	N	N	N
9 Martin	N	N	Y	Y	N
10 Broyhill	N	N	Y	Y	Y
11 Clarke	Y	N	N	N	N
NORTH DAKOTA					
AL Dorgan	Y	Y	N	N	N
OHIO					
1 Luken	Y	Y	N	N	N
2 Gradison	N	N	Y	Y	Y
3 Hall	Y	Y	N	N	N
4 Oxley	N	N	Y	Y	Y
5 Latta	N	N	Y	Y	N
6 McEwen	Y	N	Y	Y	N
7 DeWine	N	N	Y	Y	Y
8 Kindness	N	N	Y	Y	Y
9 Kaptur	Y	Y	N	N	N
10 Miller	N	N	Y	Y	N
11 Eckart	Y	Y	N	N	N
12 Kasich	Y	N	Y	Y	Y
13 Pease	Y	Y	N	N	N
14 Seiberling	Y	N	N	N	N
15 Wylie	N	N	Y	Y	Y
16 Regula	N	N	Y	Y	N
17 Williams	Y	N	Y	Y	Y
18 Applegate	?	Y	N	N	N
19 Feighan	Y	Y	N	N	N
20 Oakar	Y	Y	N	N	N
21 Stokes	Y	Y	N	N	N
OKLAHOMA					
1 Jones	Y	N	N	N	N
2 Synar	Y	N	N	N	Y
3 Watkins	Y	N	?	?	?
4 McCurdy	Y	N	Y	Y	Y
5 Edwards	N	N	Y	Y	Y
6 English	Y	N	Y	Y	N
OREGON					
1 AuCoin	Y	Y	N	N	N
2 Smith, R.	N	N	Y	Y	N
3 Wyden	Y	Y	N	N	N
4 Weaver	Y	Y	N	N	N
5 Smith, D.	N	N	Y	Y	N
PENNSYLVANIA					
1 Foglietta	Y	N	N	N	Y
2 Gray	Y	Y	N	N	N
3 Borski	Y	N	N	N	Y
4 Kolter	Y	Y	N	N	N
5 Schulze	N	N	Y	Y	Y
6 Yatron	Y	N	N	N	Y
7 Edgar	Y	Y	N	N	N
8 Kostmayer	Y	Y	N	N	N
9 Shuster	N	N	Y	Y	Y
10 McDade	N	N	Y	Y	Y
11 Harrison	?	?	N	N	N
12 Murtha	Y	N	Y	Y	Y
13 Coughlin	N	N	Y	Y	Y
14 Coyne	Y	Y	N	N	N
15 Ritter	N	N	Y	Y	Y
16 Walker	N	N	Y	Y	N
17 Gekas	Y	N	Y	Y	N
18 Walgren	Y	Y	N	N	N
19 Goodling	N	N	Y	Y	N
20 Gaydos	Y	N	N	N	N
21 Ridge	N	N	Y	Y	N
22 Murphy	Y	N	N	N	N
23 Clinger	N	N	Y	Y	Y
RHODE ISLAND					
1 St Germain	P	Y	N	N	N
2 Schneider	N	Y	N	N	Y
SOUTH CAROLINA					
1 Hartnett	N	?	Y	Y	?
2 Spence	N	N	Y	Y	N
3 Derrick	Y	N	N	N	Y
4 Campbell	N	?	Y	Y	Y
5 Spratt	Y	N	N	N	N
6 Tallon	Y	N	Y	Y	N
SOUTH DAKOTA					
AL Daschle	Y	Y	N	N	N

	123	124	125	126	127
TENNESSEE					
1 Quillen	N	N	Y	Y	Y
2 Duncan	N	N	Y	Y	Y
3 Lloyd	Y	N	Y	Y	N
4 Cooper	Y	N	N	N	Y
5 Boner	Y	X	X	Y	Y
6 Gore	Y	N	N	N	Y
7 Sundquist	N	N	Y	Y	Y
8 Jones	Y	N	?	?	X
9 Ford	?	Y	?	#	#
TEXAS					
1 Hall, S.	Y	N	Y	Y	Y
2 Wilson	?	N	Y	Y	Y
3 Bartlett	N	N	Y	Y	Y
4 Hall, R.	Y	N	Y	Y	N
5 Bryant	?	Y	N	N	N
6 Gramm	N	N	Y	Y	N
7 Archer	N	N	Y	Y	N
8 Fields	N	N	Y	Y	N
9 Brooks	Y	N	N	N	N
10 Pickle	Y	N	Y	Y	Y
11 Leath	Y	N	Y	Y	Y
12 Wright	Y	N	Y	Y	Y
13 Hightower	Y	N	Y	Y	N
14 Patman	Y	N	Y	Y	Y
15 de la Garza	Y	N	Y	Y	Y
16 Coleman	Y	N	Y	Y	Y
17 Stenholm	Y	N	Y	Y	Y
18 Leland	Y	Y	N	N	N
19 Hance	?	?	?	?	?
20 Gonzalez	Y	N	N	N	N
21 Loeffler	N	N	Y	Y	Y
22 Paul	Y	N	N	N	N
23 Kazen	?	?	?	?	?
24 Frost	Y	N	N	N	Y
25 Andrews	Y	N	Y	Y	Y
26 Vandergriff	Y	N	Y	Y	Y
27 Ortiz	Y	N	Y	Y	Y
UTAH					
1 Hansen	?	?	?	?	?
2 Marriott	N	N	Y	Y	Y
3 Nielson	N	N	Y	Y	N
VERMONT					
AL Jeffords	N	N	N	N	N
VIRGINIA					
1 Bateman	N	N	Y	Y	Y
2 Whitehurst	N	N	Y	Y	Y
3 Bliley	N	N	Y	Y	Y
4 Sisisky	Y	N	Y	Y	N
5 Daniel	Y	N	Y	Y	Y
6 Olin	Y	N	N	N	N
7 Robinson	N	N	Y	Y	Y
8 Parris	N	N	Y	Y	Y
9 Boucher	Y	N	N	N	N
10 Wolf	N	N	Y	Y	Y
WASHINGTON					
1 Pritchard	Y	N	N	N	N
2 Swift	Y	Y	N	N	N
3 Bonker	Y	Y	N	N	Y
4 Morrison	N	N	Y	Y	Y
5 Foley	Y	N	N	N	N
6 Dicks	Y	N	N	N	N
7 Lowry	Y	Y	N	N	N
8 Chandler	N	N	Y	Y	Y
WEST VIRGINIA					
1 Mollohan	Y	N	Y	N	N
2 Staggers	Y	N	N	N	N
3 Wise	Y	N	N	N	N
4 Rahall	Y	Y	N	N	N
WISCONSIN					
1 Aspin	Y	N	N	N	N
2 Kastenmeier	Y	Y	N	N	N
3 Gunderson	N	N	Y	Y	N
4 Kleczka	N	N	N	N	N
5 Moody	?	#	?	X	X
6 Petri	N	N	Y	Y	N
7 Obey	Y	N	N	N	N
8 Roth	N	N	Y	Y	N
9 Sensenbrenner	N	N	Y	Y	N
WYOMING					
AL Cheney	N	N	Y	Y	Y

Southern states - Ala., Ark., Fla., Ga., Ky., La., Miss., N.C., Okla., S.C., Tenn., Texas, Va.

128. Procedural Motion. Weber, R-Minn., motion to approve the House *Journal* of Monday, May 14. Motion agreed to 348-33: R 126-22; D 222-11 (ND 141-10, SD 81-1), May 15, 1984.

129. HR 5345. Equal Access Act. Perkins, D-Ky., motion to suspend the rules and pass the bill to allow student religious groups to meet in public secondary schools during non-class hours if other groups do so. Motion rejected 270-151: R 147-17; D 123-134 (ND 47-122, SD 76-12), May 15, 1984. A two-thirds majority of those present and voting (281 in this case) is required for passage under suspension of the rules. A "yea" was a vote supporting the president's position.

130. HR 89. Puerto Rico Passenger Service. Biaggi, D-N.Y., motion to suspend the rules and pass the bill to permit foreign-flag vessels to transport passengers between Puerto Rico and other U.S. ports when U.S.-flag ships are not available. Motion agreed to 390-25: R 143-20; D 247-5 (ND 159-4, SD 88-1), May 15, 1984. A two-thirds majority of those present and voting (277 in this case) is required for passage under suspension of the rules.

131. HR 5505. War Risk Insurance. Biaggi, D-N.Y., motion to suspend the rules and pass the bill to extend through fiscal 1989 the authority of the government to provide war risk and certain other insurance to cover U.S. merchant marine vessels, cargoes and crew in an emergency. Motion agreed to 413-0: R 161-0; D 252-0 (ND 163-0, SD 89-0), May 15, 1984. A two-thirds majority of those present and voting (276 in this case) is required for passage under suspension of the rules.

132. Procedural Motion. Weber, R-Minn., motion to approve the House *Journal* of Tuesday, May 15. Motion agreed to 301-91: R 74-77; D 227-14 (ND 147-11, SD 80-3), May 16, 1984.

133. HR 5167. Department of Defense Authorization. Mavroules, D-Mass., amendment to the Bennett, D-Fla., amendment, to bar procurement of MX missiles in fiscal 1985. Rejected 212-218: R 18-146; D 194-72 (ND 161-16, SD 33-56), May 16, 1984. A "nay" was a vote supporting the president's position.

134. HR 5167. Department of Defense Authorization. Dickinson, R-Ala., amendment to the Mavroules, D-Mass., substitute to the Bennett, D-Fla., amendment (*see vote 133, above*), to allow the production of 15 MX missiles subject to certain conditions. Adopted 229-199: R 146-17; D 83-182 (ND 22-154, SD 61-28), May 16, 1984. (The Mavroules substitute, as amended, subsequently was adopted by voice vote.) A "yea" was a vote supporting the president's position.

KEY

Y Voted for (yea).
Paired for.
+ Announced for.
N Voted against (nay).
X Paired against.
- Announced against.
P Voted "present".
C Voted "present" to avoid possible conflict of interest.
? Did not vote or otherwise make a position known.

Democrats *Republicans*

	128	129	130	131	132	133	134
ALABAMA							
1 *Edwards*	Y	Y	Y	Y	Y	N	Y
2 *Dickinson*	N	Y	N	Y	N	N	Y
3 Nichols	Y	Y	Y	Y	N	N	Y
4 Bevill	Y	Y	Y	Y	Y	N	Y
5 Flippo	Y	Y	Y	Y	Y	N	Y
6 Erdreich	Y	Y	Y	Y	Y	N	Y
7 Shelby	?	Y	Y	Y	Y	N	Y
ALASKA							
AL *Young*	N	Y	Y	Y	N	N	Y
ARIZONA							
1 *McCain*	Y	Y	N	Y	N	Y	N
2 Udall	Y	N	Y	Y	Y	Y	N
3 *Stump*	Y	N	Y	Y	N	N	Y
4 *Rudd*	Y	Y	Y	Y	N	N	Y
5 McNulty	Y	N	Y	Y	Y	Y	N
ARKANSAS							
1 Alexander	Y	Y	Y	Y	Y	N	Y
2 *Bethune*	?	Y	Y	Y	Y	N	Y
3 *Hammerschmidt*	Y	Y	N	Y	N	N	Y
4 Anthony	Y	Y	Y	Y	?	Y	N
CALIFORNIA							
1 Bosco	Y	N	Y	Y	Y	Y	N
2 *Chappie*	N	Y	Y	Y	N	N	Y
3 Matsui	Y	N	Y	Y	Y	Y	N
4 Fazio	?	?	?	?	Y	Y	N
5 Burton	Y	N	Y	Y	Y	Y	N
6 Boxer	Y	N	?	?	Y	Y	N
7 Miller	Y	N	Y	Y	Y	Y	N
8 Dellums	Y	N	Y	Y	Y	Y	N
9 Stark	Y	N	Y	Y	Y	Y	N
10 Edwards	Y	N	?	Y	?	Y	N
11 Lantos	Y	N	Y	Y	Y	Y	N
12 *Zschau*	Y	N	Y	N	Y	N	N
13 Mineta	Y	N	Y	Y	Y	Y	N
14 *Shumway*	Y	Y	Y	Y	N	N	Y
15 Coelho	Y	N	Y	Y	Y	Y	N
16 Panetta	Y	N	Y	Y	Y	Y	N
17 *Pashayan*	Y	Y	Y	Y	N	N	Y
18 Lehman	Y	N	Y	Y	Y	Y	N
19 *Lagomarsino*	Y	Y	Y	Y	N	N	Y
20 *Thomas*	Y	Y	Y	Y	Y	N	Y
21 *Fiedler*	Y	Y	Y	?	N	N	Y
22 *Moorhead*	Y	Y	Y	Y	Y	N	Y
23 Beilenson	Y	N	Y	?	Y	Y	N
24 Waxman	Y	N	Y	Y	Y	Y	N
25 Roybal	Y	N	Y	Y	Y	Y	N
26 Berman	Y	N	Y	Y	Y	Y	N
27 Levine	Y	N	Y	Y	Y	Y	N
28 Dixon	P	N	Y	Y	Y	Y	N
29 Hawkins	Y	N	Y	Y	Y	Y	N
30 Martinez	Y	N	Y	Y	Y	Y	N
31 Dymally	P	N	Y	Y	P	Y	N
32 Anderson	Y	N	Y	Y	Y	Y	N
33 *Dreier*	Y	Y	Y	Y	N	N	Y
34 Torres	Y	N	Y	Y	Y	Y	N
35 *Lewis*	Y	Y	Y	Y	N	N	Y
36 Brown	Y	N	Y	Y	Y	Y	N
37 *McCandless*	Y	Y	Y	Y	Y	N	Y
38 Patterson	Y	Y	Y	Y	N	Y	N
39 *Dannemeyer*	N	Y	Y	Y	N	N	Y
40 *Badham*	Y	Y	Y	Y	Y	N	Y
41 *Lowery*	Y	Y	Y	Y	Y	N	Y
42 *Lungren*	N	Y	Y	Y	N	N	Y

	128	129	130	131	132	133	134
43 *Packard*	Y	Y	Y	Y	N	N	Y
44 Bates	?	?	?	?	Y	Y	N
45 *Hunter*	Y	Y	N	Y	N	N	Y
COLORADO							
1 Schroeder	N	N	Y	N	Y	N	Y
2 Wirth	Y	N	Y	Y	Y	Y	N
3 Kogovsek	Y	N	Y	Y	Y	Y	?
4 *Brown*	Y	Y	Y	Y	N	N	Y
5 *Kramer*	Y	Y	Y	Y	Y	N	Y
6 *Schaefer*	Y	Y	N	Y	N	N	Y
CONNECTICUT							
1 Kennelly	Y	N	Y	Y	Y	Y	N
2 Gejdenson	N	N	Y	N	Y	N	Y
3 Morrison	Y	N	Y	Y	Y	Y	N
4 *McKinney*	Y	N	Y	Y	?	Y	N
5 Ratchford	Y	N	Y	Y	Y	Y	N
6 *Johnson*	?	N	Y	Y	Y	?	N
DELAWARE							
AL Carper	Y	Y	Y	Y	Y	Y	N
FLORIDA							
1 Hutto	?	Y	Y	Y	Y	N	Y
2 Fuqua	Y	Y	Y	Y	Y	N	Y
3 Bennett	Y	Y	Y	Y	Y	N	Y
4 Chappell	Y	Y	Y	Y	Y	N	Y
5 *McCollum*	Y	N	Y	Y	N	N	Y
6 MacKay	Y	Y	Y	Y	Y	Y	N
7 Gibbons	Y	N	Y	Y	Y	Y	N
8 *Young*	?	Y	Y	Y	N	N	Y
9 *Bilirakis*	Y	Y	Y	Y	N	N	Y
10 Ireland	Y	Y	Y	Y	N	N	Y
11 Nelson	Y	Y	Y	+	N	Y	N
12 *Lewis*	Y	Y	Y	?	N	N	Y
13 *Mack*	Y	Y	Y	Y	N	N	Y
14 Mica	Y	Y	Y	Y	Y	Y	N
15 *Shaw*	Y	Y	Y	Y	N	N	Y
16 Smith	Y	N	Y	Y	Y	Y	N
17 Lehman	Y	N	Y	Y	Y	Y	N
18 Pepper	Y	N	Y	Y	P	N	Y
19 Fascell	Y	N	Y	Y	Y	Y	N
GEORGIA							
1 Thomas	Y	Y	Y	Y	?	N	Y
2 Hatcher	Y	Y	Y	Y	Y	N	Y
3 Ray	Y	Y	Y	Y	Y	N	Y
4 Levitas	Y	Y	Y	Y	Y	Y	N
5 Fowler	Y	Y	Y	Y	Y	Y	N
6 *Gingrich*	Y	Y	Y	?	N	N	Y
7 Darden	Y	Y	Y	Y	Y	N	Y
8 Rowland	Y	Y	Y	Y	Y	N	Y
9 Jenkins	Y	Y	Y	Y	Y	Y	Y
10 Barnard	Y	Y	Y	Y	Y	N	Y
HAWAII							
1 Heftel	Y	Y	Y	Y	?	Y	N
2 Akaka	Y	N	Y	Y	Y	Y	N
IDAHO							
1 *Craig*	Y	Y	Y	Y	N	N	Y
2 *Hansen*	?	?	?	?	?	?	?
ILLINOIS							
1 Hayes	Y	N	Y	Y	Y	Y	N
2 Savage	Y	N	Y	Y	Y	Y	N
3 Russo	Y	N	Y	Y	Y	Y	N
4 *O'Brien*	Y	Y	Y	Y	Y	Y	N
5 Lipinski	Y	Y	Y	Y	Y	Y	N
6 *Hyde*	Y	Y	Y	Y	N	N	Y
7 Collins	Y	N	Y	Y	Y	Y	N
8 Rostenkowski	?	?	?	?	Y	Y	N
9 Yates	Y	N	Y	Y	Y	Y	N
10 *Porter*	Y	N	Y	Y	Y	N	Y
11 Annunzio	Y	N	Y	Y	Y	Y	N
12 *Crane, P.*	Y	Y	Y	Y	N	N	Y
13 *Erlenborn*	Y	Y	Y	Y	N	N	Y
14 *Corcoran*	Y	Y	Y	Y	N	N	Y
15 *Madigan*	Y	Y	Y	?	N	N	Y
16 *Martin*	Y	Y	Y	Y	N	N	Y
17 Evans	Y	N	Y	Y	Y	Y	N
18 *Michel*	N	Y	Y	Y	?	N	Y
19 *Crane, D.*	Y	Y	Y	Y	N	N	Y
20 Durbin	N	N	Y	N	Y	N	Y
21 Price	Y	Y	Y	Y	Y	Y	N
22 Simon	?	N	?	?	?	Y	N
INDIANA							
1 Hall	?	?	?	?	?	Y	N
2 Sharp	Y	Y	Y	Y	Y	Y	N
3 *Hiler*	N	Y	Y	Y	N	N	Y
4 *Coats*	N	Y	Y	Y	N	N	Y
5 Hillis	Y	Y	Y	Y	N	N	Y

ND - Northern Democrats   SD - Southern Democrats

	128	129	130	131	132	133	134
6 ***Burton***	?	Y	Y	Y	N	N	Y
7 ***Myers***	Y	Y	Y	Y	N	N	Y
8 McCloskey	Y	Y	Y	Y	Y	Y	N
9 Hamilton	Y	Y	Y	Y	Y	Y	N
10 Jacobs	N	Y	Y	Y	N	Y	N
IOWA							
1 ***Leach***	Y	N	Y	?	N	Y	N
2 ***Tauke***	Y	Y	Y	Y	Y	Y	N
3 ***Evans***	N	Y	Y	Y	N	Y	N
4 Smith	Y	N	Y	Y	Y	Y	N
5 Harkin	N	Y	Y	Y	N	Y	N
6 Bedell	Y	Y	Y	Y	Y	Y	N
KANSAS							
1 ***Roberts***	N	Y	Y	Y	N	N	Y
2 Slattery	Y	N	Y	Y	Y	Y	N
3 ***Winn***	Y	Y	Y	Y	Y	N	Y
4 Glickman	Y	N	Y	Y	Y	Y	N
5 ***Whittaker***	?	Y	Y	Y	N	N	Y
KENTUCKY							
1 Hubbard	?	Y	Y	Y	Y	N	Y
2 Natcher	Y	Y	Y	Y	Y	Y	N
3 Mazzoli	Y	Y	Y	Y	Y	Y	N
4 ***Snyder***	?	Y	N	Y	Y	N	Y
5 ***Rogers***	Y	Y	Y	Y	Y	N	Y
6 ***Hopkins***	Y	Y	Y	Y	Y	N	Y
7 Perkins	Y	Y	Y	Y	Y	Y	N
LOUISIANA							
1 ***Livingston***	Y	Y	N	Y	N	N	Y
2 Boggs	Y	Y	Y	Y	Y	Y	N
3 Tauzin	Y	Y	Y	Y	Y	N	Y
4 Roemer	N	Y	Y	Y	N	N	Y
5 Huckaby	Y	Y	Y	Y	Y	N	Y
6 ***Moore***	Y	Y	Y	Y	Y	N	Y
7 Breaux	?	Y	Y	Y	Y	N	Y
8 Long	Y	Y	Y	Y	Y	Y	N
MAINE							
1 ***McKernan***	Y	Y	N	Y	Y	N	Y
2 ***Snowe***	Y	Y	Y	Y	Y	N	Y
MARYLAND							
1 Dyson	Y	Y	Y	Y	Y	Y	N
2 Long	Y	N	Y	?	Y	Y	N
3 Mikulski	Y	N	Y	Y	Y	Y	N
4 ***Holt***	Y	Y	Y	Y	Y	N	Y
5 Hoyer	Y	N	Y	Y	Y	N	Y
6 Byron	Y	Y	Y	Y	Y	N	Y
7 Mitchell	N	N	Y	Y	?	Y	N
8 Barnes	Y	N	Y	Y	Y	Y	N
MASSACHUSETTS							
1 ***Conte***	Y	N	Y	Y	Y	Y	N
2 Boland	Y	N	Y	Y	?	Y	N
3 Early	Y	N	Y	Y	Y	Y	N
4 Frank	Y	N	Y	Y	Y	Y	N
5 Shannon	Y	N	?	?	?	Y	N
6 Mavroules	Y	N	?	?	Y	Y	N
7 Markey	Y	N	Y	Y	Y	Y	N
8 O'Neill							
9 Moakley	Y	N	?	Y	Y	Y	N
10 Studds	Y	N	Y	Y	Y	Y	N
11 Donnelly	?	N	N	Y	Y	Y	N
MICHIGAN							
1 Conyers	Y	N	Y	Y	Y	Y	N
2 ***Pursell***	Y	Y	N	Y	Y	N	Y
3 Wolpe	Y	N	Y	Y	Y	Y	N
4 ***Siljander***	Y	Y	Y	Y	N	N	Y
5 ***Sawyer***	Y	Y	Y	Y	?	N	Y
6 Carr	Y	Y	Y	Y	Y	Y	N
7 Kildee	Y	N	Y	Y	Y	Y	N
8 Traxler	Y	Y	Y	Y	Y	Y	N
9 ***Vander Jagt***	Y	Y	Y	Y	N	N	?
10 Albosta	Y	Y	Y	Y	Y	Y	N
11 ***Davis***	Y	Y	Y	Y	N	N	Y
12 Bonior	Y	N	Y	Y	Y	Y	N
13 Crockett	?	N	Y	Y	Y	Y	N
14 Hertel	Y	N	Y	Y	Y	Y	N
15 Ford	?	N	Y	Y	?	Y	N
16 Dingell	?	Y	N	Y	?	Y	N
17 Levin	Y	N	Y	Y	Y	Y	N
18 ***Broomfield***	Y	Y	Y	Y	N	N	Y
MINNESOTA							
1 Penny	N	Y	Y	Y	N	Y	N
2 ***Weber***	N	Y	Y	Y	N	N	Y
3 ***Frenzel***	?	Y	Y	Y	N	N	Y
4 Vento	Y	N	Y	Y	Y	Y	N
5 Sabo	N	N	Y	Y	N	Y	N
6 Sikorski	N	Y	Y	Y	N	Y	N

	128	129	130	131	132	133	134
7 ***Stangeland***	?	Y	N	Y	N	N	Y
8 Oberstar	P	N	Y	Y	P	Y	N
MISSISSIPPI							
1 Whitten	Y	Y	Y	Y	Y	Y	N
2 ***Franklin***	Y	Y	Y	Y	Y	N	Y
3 Montgomery	Y	Y	Y	Y	Y	N	Y
4 Dowdy	?	Y	Y	Y	Y	Y	N
5 ***Lott***	N	Y	Y	Y	N	N	Y
MISSOURI							
1 Clay	?	N	Y	Y	N	Y	N
2 Young	Y	N	Y	Y	Y	Y	N
3 Gephardt	Y	N	Y	Y	Y	Y	N
4 Skelton	Y	Y	Y	Y	Y	N	Y
5 Wheat	Y	N	Y	Y	Y	Y	N
6 ***Coleman***	?	N	Y	Y	N	N	Y
7 ***Taylor***	?	Y	N	Y	?	N	Y
8 ***Emerson***	N	Y	Y	Y	N	N	Y
9 Volkmer	Y	Y	Y	Y	Y	Y	N
MONTANA							
1 Williams	Y	N	Y	Y	Y	Y	Y
2 ***Marlenee***	Y	Y	Y	Y	Y	N	Y
NEBRASKA							
1 ***Bereuter***	Y	Y	Y	Y	Y	Y	N
2 ***Daub***	Y	Y	Y	Y	N	N	Y
3 ***Smith***	Y	Y	Y	Y	Y	Y	N
NEVADA							
1 Reid	Y	N	Y	Y	Y	N	Y
2 ***Vucanovich***	Y	Y	Y	Y	N	N	Y
NEW HAMPSHIRE							
1 D'Amours	Y	Y	Y	Y	Y	Y	N
2 ***Gregg***	?	Y	Y	Y	Y	N	Y
NEW JERSEY							
1 Florio	Y	N	Y	Y	Y	Y	N
2 Hughes	Y	Y	Y	Y	Y	N	Y
3 Howard	Y	N	Y	Y	Y	Y	N
4 ***Smith***	Y	Y	N	Y	?	N	Y
5 ***Roukema***	Y	Y	Y	Y	Y	Y	N
6 Dwyer	Y	N	Y	Y	Y	Y	N
7 ***Rinaldo***	Y	Y	Y	Y	Y	N	Y
8 Roe	Y	N	Y	Y	Y	Y	N
9 Torricelli	Y	N	N	Y	Y	Y	N
10 Rodino	Y	N	Y	Y	Y	Y	N
11 Minish	Y	N	Y	Y	Y	Y	N
12 ***Courter***	Y	Y	Y	Y	Y	N	Y
13 Vacancy							
14 Guarini	Y	N	Y	Y	Y	Y	N
NEW MEXICO							
1 ***Lujan***	Y	Y	Y	Y	N	N	Y
2 ***Skeen***	Y	Y	Y	Y	N	N	Y
3 Richardson	Y	Y	Y	Y	Y	Y	N
NEW YORK							
1 ***Carney***	Y	Y	Y	Y	N	N	Y
2 Downey	Y	N	Y	Y	Y	Y	N
3 Mrazek	Y	N	Y	Y	Y	Y	N
4 ***Lent***	Y	N	Y	Y	N	N	Y
5 ***McGrath***	Y	N	Y	Y	Y	N	Y
6 Addabbo	Y	N	Y	Y	Y	Y	N
7 Ackerman	Y	N	Y	Y	Y	Y	N
8 Scheuer	Y	N	Y	Y	?	Y	N
9 Ferraro	?	?	?	?	Y	Y	N
10 Schumer	Y	N	Y	Y	Y	Y	N
11 Towns	?	N	Y	Y	Y	Y	N
12 Owens	Y	N	Y	Y	?	Y	N
13 Solarz	?	X	?	?	Y	Y	N
14 ***Molinari***	Y	Y	Y	Y	N	N	Y
15 ***Green***	Y	N	Y	Y	N	Y	?
16 Rangel	Y	N	Y	Y	Y	Y	N
17 Weiss	Y	N	Y	Y	Y	Y	N
18 Garcia	Y	N	Y	Y	Y	Y	N
19 Biaggi	Y	Y	Y	Y	Y	Y	N
20 Ottinger	P	N	Y	Y	?	Y	N
21 ***Fish***	Y	N	Y	Y	N	N	Y
22 ***Gilman***	Y	N	Y	Y	Y	N	Y
23 Stratton	Y	Y	Y	Y	Y	N	Y
24 ***Solomon***	N	Y	Y	Y	N	N	Y
25 ***Boehlert***	Y	Y	Y	Y	Y	N	Y
26 ***Martin***	?	Y	Y	Y	N	N	Y
27 ***Wortley***	Y	Y	Y	Y	N	N	Y
28 McHugh	Y	N	Y	Y	Y	Y	N
29 ***Horton***	Y	Y	Y	Y	Y	N	Y
30 ***Conable***	Y	Y	Y	Y	N	N	Y
31 ***Kemp***	N	Y	Y	Y	?	N	Y
32 LaFalce	Y	Y	Y	Y	P	Y	N
33 Nowak	Y	Y	Y	Y	Y	Y	N
34 Lundine	Y	Y	Y	Y	Y	Y	N

	128	129	130	131	132	133	134
NORTH CAROLINA							
1 Jones	Y	Y	Y	Y	Y	Y	N
2 Valentine	Y	Y	Y	Y	Y	N	Y
3 Whitley	Y	Y	Y	Y	Y	N	Y
4 Andrews	Y	Y	Y	Y	Y	N	Y
5 Neal	Y	Y	Y	Y	Y	Y	Y
6 Britt	Y	Y	Y	Y	Y	N	Y
7 Rose	Y	Y	Y	Y	Y	N	Y
8 Hefner	Y	Y	Y	Y	Y	N	Y
9 ***Martin***	Y	Y	Y	Y	N	N	Y
10 ***Broyhill***	Y	Y	Y	Y	Y	N	Y
11 Clarke	Y	Y	Y	Y	Y	Y	Y
NORTH DAKOTA							
AL Dorgan	N	N	Y	Y	Y	Y	N
OHIO							
1 Luken	Y	Y	Y	Y	Y	Y	Y
2 ***Gradison***	Y	N	Y	Y	Y	Y	N
3 Hall	Y	Y	Y	Y	Y	Y	N
4 ***Oxley***	?	Y	Y	Y	N	N	Y
5 ***Latta***	Y	Y	Y	Y	?	N	Y
6 ***McEwen***	Y	Y	Y	Y	Y	N	Y
7 ***DeWine***	Y	Y	Y	Y	Y	N	Y
8 ***Kindness***	Y	Y	Y	Y	N	N	Y
9 Kaptur	?	Y	Y	Y	Y	Y	N
10 ***Miller***	N	Y	Y	Y	N	N	Y
11 Eckart	Y	Y	Y	Y	Y	Y	N
12 ***Kasich***	Y	Y	Y	Y	Y	N	Y
13 Pease	Y	Y	Y	Y	Y	Y	N
14 Seiberling	Y	N	Y	Y	Y	Y	N
15 ***Wylie***	Y	Y	Y	Y	Y	N	Y
16 ***Regula***	Y	Y	Y	Y	Y	N	Y
17 ***Williams***	?	Y	Y	Y	Y	N	Y
18 Applegate	?	Y	Y	Y	?	Y	Y
19 Feighan	Y	N	Y	Y	Y	Y	N
20 Oakar	Y	N	Y	Y	Y	Y	N
21 Stokes	Y	N	Y	Y	Y	Y	N
OKLAHOMA							
1 Jones	Y	Y	Y	Y	Y	Y	N
2 Synar	Y	N	Y	Y	Y	Y	N
3 Watkins	Y	Y	Y	Y	Y	N	Y
4 McCurdy	Y	Y	Y	Y	Y	N	Y
5 ***Edwards***	Y	Y	Y	Y	N	N	Y
6 English	Y	Y	N	Y	Y	N	Y
OREGON							
1 AuCoin	Y	N	Y	Y	N	Y	N
2 ***Smith, R.***	Y	Y	Y	Y	N	N	Y
3 Wyden	Y	N	Y	Y	Y	Y	N
4 Weaver	Y	Y	Y	Y	Y	Y	N
5 ***Smith, D.***	?	#	?	?	?	N	Y
PENNSYLVANIA							
1 Foglietta	Y	N	Y	Y	Y	Y	N
2 Gray	Y	N	Y	Y	Y	Y	N
3 Borski	Y	N	Y	Y	Y	Y	N
4 Kolter	?	Y	N	Y	Y	Y	N
5 ***Schulze***	Y	Y	Y	Y	Y	N	Y
6 Yatron	Y	Y	Y	Y	Y	N	Y
7 Edgar	Y	N	Y	Y	Y	Y	N
8 Kostmayer	Y	N	Y	Y	Y	Y	N
9 ***Shuster***	Y	Y	N	Y	Y	N	Y
10 ***McDade***	Y	Y	Y	Y	Y	N	Y
11 Harrison	?	Y	Y	Y	?	Y	N
12 Murtha	Y	?	?	?	Y	N	Y
13 ***Coughlin***	N	N	Y	Y	?	Y	N
14 Coyne	?	N	Y	Y	Y	Y	N
15 ***Ritter***	?	Y	Y	Y	N	N	Y
16 ***Walker***	N	Y	Y	Y	N	N	Y
17 ***Gekas***	Y	Y	+	+	N	N	Y
18 Walgren	Y	N	Y	Y	Y	Y	N
19 ***Goodling***	N	Y	Y	Y	N	N	Y
20 Gaydos	Y	Y	Y	Y	Y	Y	N
21 ***Ridge***	Y	Y	Y	Y	Y	Y	N
22 Murphy	?	Y	Y	Y	Y	Y	Y
23 ***Clinger***	Y	Y	Y	Y	N	N	Y
RHODE ISLAND							
1 St Germain	P	Y	Y	Y	P	Y	N
2 ***Schneider***	Y	N	Y	Y	Y	Y	N
SOUTH CAROLINA							
1 ***Hartnett***	N	Y	N	Y	N	N	Y
2 ***Spence***	Y	Y	N	Y	N	N	Y
3 Derrick	Y	Y	Y	Y	Y	Y	N
4 ***Campbell***	Y	Y	Y	Y	N	N	Y
5 Spratt	Y	Y	Y	Y	Y	Y	Y
6 Tallon	?	Y	Y	Y	Y	N	Y
SOUTH DAKOTA							
AL Daschle	Y	Y	Y	Y	N	Y	N

	128	129	130	131	132	133	134
TENNESSEE							
1 ***Quillen***	Y	Y	N	Y	Y	N	Y
2 ***Duncan***	Y	Y	Y	Y	Y	N	Y
3 Lloyd	Y	Y	Y	Y	Y	N	Y
4 Cooper	Y	N	Y	Y	Y	N	Y
5 Boner	Y	Y	Y	Y	Y	N	Y
6 Gore	Y	Y	Y	Y	Y	N	Y
7 ***Sundquist***	Y	Y	Y	Y	Y	N	Y
8 Jones	Y	Y	Y	Y	Y	N	Y
9 Ford	Y	N	Y	Y	Y	Y	N
TEXAS							
1 Hall, S.	Y	Y	Y	Y	Y	N	Y
2 Wilson	Y	Y	Y	Y	?	N	Y
3 ***Bartlett***	Y	Y	Y	Y	Y	N	Y
4 Hall, R.	Y	Y	Y	Y	Y	N	Y
5 Bryant	Y	N	Y	Y	Y	Y	N
6 ***Gramm***	Y	Y	Y	Y	N	N	Y
7 ***Archer***	Y	Y	Y	Y	Y	N	Y
8 ***Fields***	Y	Y	N	Y	N	N	Y
9 Brooks	Y	Y	Y	Y	Y	Y	N
10 Pickle	Y	Y	Y	Y	Y	N	Y
11 Leath	Y	Y	Y	Y	Y	N	Y
12 Wright	Y	Y	Y	Y	Y	Y	N
13 Hightower	Y	Y	Y	Y	Y	N	Y
14 Patman	Y	Y	Y	Y	Y	N	Y
15 de la Garza	Y	Y	Y	Y	Y	N	Y
16 Coleman	Y	Y	Y	Y	Y	N	Y
17 Stenholm	Y	Y	Y	Y	Y	N	Y
18 Leland	?	N	Y	Y	Y	Y	N
19 Hance	?	#	?	?	?	?	?
20 Gonzalez	Y	N	Y	Y	Y	Y	N
21 ***Loeffler***	?	Y	Y	Y	N	N	Y
22 ***Paul***	Y	Y	Y	Y	Y	Y	Y
23 Kazen	Y	Y	Y	Y	Y	N	Y
24 Frost	Y	N	Y	Y	Y	N	Y
25 Andrews	Y	Y	Y	Y	Y	N	Y
26 Vandergriff	Y	P	Y	Y	P	N	Y
27 Ortiz	Y	Y	Y	Y	Y	N	Y
UTAH							
1 ***Hansen***	Y	Y	Y	Y	N	N	Y
2 ***Marriott***	Y	Y	Y	Y	Y	N	Y
3 ***Nielson***	Y	Y	Y	Y	Y	N	Y
VERMONT							
AL ***Jeffords***	Y	Y	Y	Y	Y	Y	N
VIRGINIA							
1 ***Bateman***	Y	Y	N	Y	Y	N	Y
2 ***Whitehurst***	Y	Y	Y	Y	Y	N	Y
3 ***Bliley***	Y	Y	Y	Y	Y	N	Y
4 Sisisky	Y	Y	Y	Y	Y	Y	N
5 Daniel	Y	Y	Y	Y	N	N	Y
6 Olin	Y	Y	Y	Y	Y	Y	Y
7 ***Robinson***	Y	Y	Y	Y	Y	N	Y
8 ***Parris***	Y	Y	Y	Y	Y	N	Y
9 Boucher	Y	Y	Y	Y	Y	Y	N
10 ***Wolf***	Y	Y	Y	Y	N	N	Y
WASHINGTON							
1 ***Pritchard***	Y	Y	Y	Y	Y	N	Y
2 Swift	Y	N	Y	Y	Y	Y	N
3 Bonker	Y	Y	Y	Y	Y	Y	N
4 ***Morrison***	Y	Y	Y	Y	N	N	Y
5 Foley	Y	N	Y	Y	Y	Y	N
6 Dicks	Y	N	Y	Y	Y	N	Y
7 Lowry	Y	N	Y	Y	Y	Y	N
8 ***Chandler***	Y	Y	Y	Y	Y	N	Y
WEST VIRGINIA							
1 Mollohan	Y	Y	Y	Y	Y	N	Y
2 Staggers	Y	Y	Y	Y	Y	Y	Y
3 Wise	Y	Y	Y	Y	Y	Y	Y
4 Rahall	?	?	?	?	Y	Y	N
WISCONSIN							
1 Aspin	Y	N	Y	Y	Y	N	Y
2 Kastenmeier	Y	N	Y	Y	Y	Y	N
3 ***Gunderson***	Y	Y	N	Y	Y	N	Y
4 Kleczka	Y	N	Y	Y	Y	Y	N
5 Moody	?	N	Y	Y	Y	Y	N
6 ***Petri***	N	Y	Y	Y	Y	Y	N
7 Obey	Y	N	Y	Y	P	Y	N
8 ***Roth***	Y	Y	Y	Y	?	N	Y
9 ***Sensenbrenner***	Y	Y	N	Y	N	Y	N
WYOMING							
AL ***Cheney***	N	Y	Y	Y	N	N	Y

Southern states - Ala., Ark., Fla., Ga., Ky., La., Miss., N.C., Okla., S.C., Tenn., Texas, Va.

KEY

Y Voted for (yea).
\# Paired for.
\+ Announced for.
N Voted against (nay).
X Paired against.
- Announced against.
P Voted "present".
C Voted "present" to avoid possible conflict of interest.
? Did not vote or otherwise make a position known.

———

Democrats   *Republicans*

---

135. HR 5167. Department of Defense Authorization. Bethune, R-Ark., amendment to bar the production of binary chemical munitions. Adopted 247-179: R 53-111; D 194-68 (ND 155-18, SD 39-50), May 17, 1984. A "nay" was a vote supporting the president's position.

136. HR 5167. Department of Defense Authorization. Weiss, D-N.Y., amendment to delete funds for production of the Trident II missile. Rejected 93-319: R 3-159; D 90-160 (ND 86-82, SD 4-78), May 17, 1984. A "nay" was a vote supporting the president's position.

137. HR 5167. Department of Defense Authorization. Smith, D-Fla., amendment to bar the use of funds to purchase Sergeant York anti-aircraft guns (also called DIVADs) until certain test results have been reported to Congress. Rejected 157-229: R 32-123; D 125-106 (ND 112-40, SD 13-66), May 17, 1984. A "nay" was a vote supporting the president's position.

	135	136	137
ALABAMA			
1 *Edwards*	N	N	N
2 *Dickinson*	N	N	N
3 Nichols	N	N	N
4 Bevill	N	N	N
5 Flippo	N	N	N
6 Erdreich	N	N	N
7 Shelby	N	N	N
ALASKA			
AL *Young*	N	N	N
ARIZONA			
1 *McCain*	N	N	N
2 Udall	Y	N	N
3 *Stump*	N	N	?
4 *Rudd*	N	N	N
5 McNulty	Y	N	Y
ARKANSAS			
1 Alexander	N	N	N
2 *Bethune*	Y	N	N
3 *Hammerschmidt*	N	N	N
4 Anthony	N	?	?
CALIFORNIA			
1 Bosco	N	Y	?
2 *Chappie*	N	N	N
3 Matsui	Y	N	N
4 Fazio	N	N	Y
5 Burton	Y	Y	Y
6 Boxer	Y	Y	?
7 Miller	Y	Y	Y
8 Dellums	Y	Y	Y
9 Stark	#	?	?
10 Edwards	Y	Y	Y
11 Lantos	Y	N	N
12 *Zschau*	Y	N	Y
13 Mineta	Y	N	Y
14 *Shumway*	N	N	N
15 Coelho	?	?	?
16 Panetta	Y	N	Y
17 *Pashayan*	N	N	N
18 Lehman	Y	N	?
19 *Lagomarsino*	N	N	N
20 *Thomas*	N	N	Y
21 *Fiedler*	N	N	?
22 *Moorhead*	N	N	N
23 Beilenson	Y	Y	Y
24 Waxman	Y	Y	Y
25 Roybal	Y	Y	Y
26 Berman	Y	Y	Y
27 Levine	Y	Y	Y
28 Dixon	Y	Y	Y
29 Hawkins	Y	#	#
30 Martinez	Y	Y	Y
31 Dymally	Y	Y	Y
32 Anderson	Y	N	N
33 *Dreier*	N	N	N
34 Torres	Y	Y	Y
35 *Lewis*	N	N	N
36 Brown	Y	N	N
37 *McCandless*	N	N	N
38 Patterson	Y	N	?
39 *Dannemeyer*	N	N	Y
40 *Badham*	N	N	N
41 *Lowery*	N	N	N
42 *Lungren*	N	N	Y

	135	136	137
43 *Packard*	N	N	N
44 Bates	Y	Y	Y
45 *Hunter*	N	N	N
COLORADO			
1 Schroeder	Y	N	Y
2 Wirth	Y	N	?
3 Kogovsek	Y	Y	Y
4 *Brown*	N	N	Y
5 *Kramer*	N	N	N
6 *Schaefer*	Y	N	Y
CONNECTICUT			
1 Kennelly	Y	Y	N
2 Gejdenson	Y	Y	Y
3 Morrison	Y	Y	N
4 *McKinney*	Y	N	N
5 Ratchford	Y	Y	N
6 *Johnson*	Y	N	N
DELAWARE			
AL Carper	Y	N	N
FLORIDA			
1 Hutto	N	N	?
2 Fuqua	Y	N	N
3 Bennett	N	N	N
4 Chappell	N	N	N
5 *McCollum*	N	N	N
6 MacKay	Y	N	N
7 Gibbons	N	N	N
8 *Young*	N	N	N
9 *Bilirakis*	N	N	Y
10 Ireland	N	N	N
11 Nelson	N	N	Y
12 *Lewis*	Y	N	N
13 *Mack*	N	N	N
14 Mica	Y	?	?
15 *Shaw*	N	N	?
16 Smith	Y	Y	Y
17 Lehman	Y	Y	?
18 Pepper	Y	N	X
19 Fascell	Y	N	Y
GEORGIA			
1 Thomas	N	N	N
2 Hatcher	N	N	N
3 Ray	N	N	N
4 Levitas	N	?	?
5 Fowler	Y	N	N
6 *Gingrich*	N	N	Y
7 Darden	N	N	N
8 Rowland	N	N	N
9 Jenkins	Y	N	N
10 Barnard	N	?	?
HAWAII			
1 Heftel	N	N	Y
2 Akaka	Y	N	Y
IDAHO			
1 *Craig*	N	N	N
2 *Hansen*	?	?	?
ILLINOIS			
1 Hayes	Y	Y	Y
2 Savage	Y	Y	Y
3 Russo	Y	Y	Y
4 *O'Brien*	N	N	N
5 Lipinski	Y	N	Y
6 *Hyde*	N	N	N
7 Collins	Y	Y	Y
8 Rostenkowski	N	Y	N
9 Yates	Y	Y	Y
10 *Porter*	Y	N	Y
11 Annunzio	Y	N	N
12 *Crane, P.*	N	N	N
13 *Erlenborn*	N	N	N
14 *Corcoran*	N	N	N
15 *Madigan*	N	N	N
16 *Martin*	Y	N	?
17 Evans	Y	Y	Y
18 *Michel*	N	N	N
19 *Crane, D.*	N	N	?
20 Durbin	Y	N	Y
21 Price	N	N	N
22 Simon	Y	?	Y
INDIANA			
1 Hall	Y	Y	Y
2 Sharp	+	-	-
3 *Hiler*	Y	N	?
4 *Coats*	Y	N	N
5 *Hillis*	N	N	N

ND - Northern Democrats   SD - Southern Democrats

	135	136	137
6 Burton	N	N	N
7 Myers	N	N	N
8 McCloskey	Y	N	N
9 Hamilton	N	N	N
10 Jacobs	Y	N	Y
IOWA			
1 Leach	Y	Y	N
2 Tauke	Y	N	Y
3 Evans	N	N	Y
4 Smith	Y	N	?
5 Harkin	Y	Y	Y
6 Bedell	Y	Y	Y
KANSAS			
1 Roberts	Y	N	N
2 Slattery	Y	N	N
3 Winn	N	N	N
4 Glickman	Y	N	N
5 Whittaker	Y	N	N
KENTUCKY			
1 Hubbard	N	N	N
2 Natcher	Y	N	N
3 Mazzoli	Y	N	N
4 Snyder	N	N	N
5 Rogers	N	N	N
6 Hopkins	Y	N	Y
7 Perkins	Y	N	N
LOUISIANA			
1 Livingston	N	N	N
2 Boggs	Y	N	N
3 Tauzin	Y	N	Y
4 Roemer	Y	N	Y
5 Huckaby	Y	N	N
6 Moore	N	N	N
7 Breaux	N	N	Y
8 Long	Y	N	N
MAINE			
1 McKernan	Y	N	Y
2 Snowe	Y	N	Y
MARYLAND			
1 Dyson	N	N	N
2 Long	N	N	N
3 Mikulski	Y	N	N
4 Holt	N	N	N
5 Hoyer	Y	N	N
6 Byron	N	N	N
7 Mitchell	Y	Y	?
8 Barnes	Y	N	Y
MASSACHUSETTS			
1 Conte	Y	Y	N
2 Boland	Y	N	?
3 Early	Y	Y	?
4 Frank	Y	Y	Y
5 Shannon	Y	Y	Y
6 Mavroules	Y	Y	N
7 Markey	Y	Y	Y
8 O'Neill			
9 Moakley	Y	?	?
10 Studds	Y	Y	Y
11 Donnelly	Y	N	Y
MICHIGAN			
1 Conyers	Y	Y	Y
2 Pursell	Y	N	N
3 Wolpe	Y	Y	Y
4 Siljander	N	N	N
5 Sawyer	N	N	N
6 Carr	Y	Y	N
7 Kildee	Y	Y	Y
8 Traxler	Y	N	?
9 Vander Jagt	N	N	N
10 Albosta	Y	N	N
11 Davis	Y	N	N
12 Bonior	Y	#	Y
13 Crockett	Y	Y	Y
14 Hertel	Y	N	?
15 Ford	Y	N	Y
16 Dingell	Y	N	Y
17 Levin	Y	Y	Y
18 Broomfield	N	N	N
MINNESOTA			
1 Penny	Y	Y	Y
2 Weber	Y	N	Y
3 Frenzel	Y	N	Y
4 Vento	Y	Y	#
5 Sabo	Y	Y	Y
6 Sikorski	Y	Y	Y

	135	136	137
7 Stangeland	N	N	N
8 Oberstar	Y	Y	Y
MISSISSIPPI			
1 Whitten	Y	N	N
2 Franklin	Y	N	N
3 Montgomery	N	N	N
4 Dowdy	N	N	N
5 Lott	N	N	N
MISSOURI			
1 Clay	Y	Y	Y
2 Young	N	X	?
3 Gephardt	Y	N	N
4 Skelton	N	N	N
5 Wheat	Y	Y	Y
6 Coleman	N	N	?
7 Taylor	N	N	N
8 Emerson	N	N	N
9 Volkmer	Y	N	N
MONTANA			
1 Williams	N	Y	Y
2 Marlenee	N	N	N
NEBRASKA			
1 Bereuter	N	N	N
2 Daub	Y	N	N
3 Smith	N	N	N
NEVADA			
1 Reid	Y	N	Y
2 Vucanovich	N	N	N
NEW HAMPSHIRE			
1 D'Amours	Y	?	N
2 Gregg	Y	N	?
NEW JERSEY			
1 Florio	Y	N	Y
2 Hughes	Y	N	?
3 Howard	Y	Y	?
4 Smith	Y	N	N
5 Roukema	Y	N	Y
6 Dwyer	Y	N	Y
7 Rinaldo	Y	N	N
8 Roe	Y	N	?
9 Torricelli	Y	N	Y
10 Rodino	Y	Y	Y
11 Minish	Y	N	Y
12 Courter	N	N	Y
13 Vacancy			
14 Guarini	Y	N	Y
NEW MEXICO			
1 Lujan	N	N	N
2 Skeen	N	N	N
3 Richardson	Y	N	?
NEW YORK			
1 Carney	N	N	N
2 Downey	Y	Y	Y
3 Mrazek	Y	Y	N
4 Lent	N	N	N
5 McGrath	Y	N	N
6 Addabbo	Y	Y	Y
7 Ackerman	Y	Y	Y
8 Scheuer	Y	Y	Y
9 Ferraro	Y	N	Y
10 Schumer	Y	Y	Y
11 Towns	Y	Y	?
12 Owens	Y	Y	Y
13 Solarz	Y	Y	Y
14 Molinari	Y	N	N
15 Green	Y	N	N
16 Rangel	Y	Y	Y
17 Weiss	Y	Y	Y
18 Garcia	Y	Y	Y
19 Biaggi	Y	N	?
20 Ottinger	Y	Y	Y
21 Fish	Y	N	Y
22 Gilman	N	N	N
23 Stratton	N	N	N
24 Solomon	N	N	N
25 Boehlert	Y	N	N
26 Martin	N	N	N
27 Wortley	Y	N	N
28 McHugh	Y	Y	Y
29 Horton	Y	N	N
30 Conable	N	N	N
31 Kemp	N	N	N
32 LaFalce	Y	Y	Y
33 Nowak	Y	Y	Y
34 Lundine	Y	N	Y

	135	136	137
NORTH CAROLINA			
1 Jones	N	N	N
2 Valentine	N	N	N
3 Whitley	N	N	N
4 Andrews	Y	?	?
5 Neal	Y	N	N
6 Britt	Y	N	N
7 Rose	Y	N	N
8 Hefner	N	N	N
9 Martin	Y	N	N
10 Broyhill	N	N	N
11 Clarke	Y	Y	N
NORTH DAKOTA			
AL Dorgan	Y	Y	Y
OHIO			
1 Luken	Y	N	Y
2 Gradison	Y	N	N
3 Hall	Y	N	N
4 Oxley	N	N	N
5 Latta	N	N	?
6 McEwen	N	N	N
7 DeWine	N	N	N
8 Kindness	N	N	Y
9 Kaptur	Y	N	Y
10 Miller	N	N	Y
11 Eckart	Y	N	Y
12 Kasich	Y	N	Y
13 Pease	Y	N	Y
14 Seiberling	Y	Y	Y
15 Wylie	N	?	N
16 Regula	Y	N	N
17 Williams	Y	?	N
18 Applegate	Y	N	N
19 Feighan	Y	Y	Y
20 Oakar	Y	Y	N
21 Stokes	Y	Y	Y
OKLAHOMA			
1 Jones	N	N	N
2 Synar	Y	N	N
3 Watkins	Y	N	N
4 McCurdy	N	N	N
5 Edwards	N	N	N
6 English	N	N	N
OREGON			
1 AuCoin	Y	Y	Y
2 Smith, R.	Y	N	N
3 Wyden	Y	Y	Y
4 Weaver	Y	Y	Y
5 Smith, D.	N	N	Y
PENNSYLVANIA			
1 Foglietta	Y	N	N
2 Gray	Y	Y	Y
3 Borski	Y	N	Y
4 Kolter	Y	N	Y
5 Schulze	N	N	N
6 Yatron	Y	N	Y
7 Edgar	Y	Y	Y
8 Kostmayer	Y	N	Y
9 Shuster	N	N	N
10 McDade	?	?	N
11 Harrison	Y	N	Y
12 Murtha	N	N	N
13 Coughlin	Y	N	N
14 Coyne	Y	Y	Y
15 Ritter	N	N	Y
16 Walker	Y	N	N
17 Gekas	Y	N	Y
18 Walgren	Y	N	Y
19 Goodling	Y	N	N
20 Gaydos	N	N	N
21 Ridge	N	N	Y
22 Murphy	N	N	N
23 Clinger	Y	N	N
RHODE ISLAND			
1 St Germain	Y	N	N
2 Schneider	Y	Y	Y
SOUTH CAROLINA			
1 Hartnett	N	N	N
2 Spence	N	N	N
3 Derrick	Y	N	N
4 Campbell	N	N	N
5 Spratt	Y	N	N
6 Tallon	Y	N	N
SOUTH DAKOTA			
AL Daschle	Y	N	Y

	135	136	137
TENNESSEE			
1 Quillen	N	N	N
2 Duncan	N	N	N
3 Lloyd	N	N	N
4 Cooper	Y	N	Y
5 Boner	N	N	?
6 Gore	Y	N	Y
7 Sundquist	N	N	N
8 Jones	N	N	N
9 Ford	Y	N	Y
TEXAS			
1 Hall, S.	N	N	N
2 Wilson	N	N	N
3 Bartlett	N	N	N
4 Hall, R.	N	N	N
5 Bryant	Y	N	N
6 Gramm	N	N	N
7 Archer	N	N	N
8 Fields	N	N	N
9 Brooks	N	N	N
10 Pickle	Y	N	N
11 Leath	N	N	N
12 Wright	Y	N	N
13 Hightower	N	N	N
14 Patman	N	N	N
15 de la Garza	N	N	N
16 Coleman	N	N	N
17 Stenholm	N	N	N
18 Leland	Y	Y	Y
19 Hance	X	?	X
20 Gonzalez	Y	P	N
21 Loeffler	N	N	N
22 Paul	Y	N	Y
23 Kazen	N	N	N
24 Frost	Y	N	N
25 Andrews	N	N	N
26 Vandergriff	N	N	N
27 Ortiz	N	X	?
UTAH			
1 Hansen	N	N	N
2 Marriott	N	N	N
3 Nielson	N	N	Y
VERMONT			
AL Jeffords	Y	N	Y
VIRGINIA			
1 Bateman	N	N	N
2 Whitehurst	N	N	N
3 Bliley	N	N	N
4 Sisisky	N	N	N
5 Daniel	N	N	N
6 Olin	Y	N	Y
7 Robinson	N	N	N
8 Parris	Y	N	N
9 Boucher	Y	N	N
10 Wolf	N	N	N
WASHINGTON			
1 Pritchard	Y	N	N
2 Swift	Y	N	Y
3 Bonker	Y	N	N
4 Morrison	N	N	?
5 Foley	Y	N	Y
6 Dicks	Y	N	Y
7 Lowry	Y	Y	Y
8 Chandler	N	N	N
WEST VIRGINIA			
1 Mollohan	N	N	N
2 Staggers	N	N	Y
3 Wise	Y	N	N
4 Rahall	?	Y	?
WISCONSIN			
1 Aspin	Y	N	Y
2 Kastenmeier	Y	Y	Y
3 Gunderson	Y	N	Y
4 Kleczka	Y	N	Y
5 Moody	Y	Y	Y
6 Petri	N	N	N
7 Obey	Y	Y	Y
8 Roth	N	N	Y
9 Sensenbrenner	Y	N	Y
WYOMING			
AL Cheney	N	N	N

Southern states - Ala., Ark., Fla., Ga., Ky., La., Miss., N.C., Okla., S.C., Tenn., Texas, Va.

138. HR 4280. Retirement Equity Act. Rostenkowski, D-Ill., motion to suspend the rules and pass the bill to amend the 1974 Employee Retirement Income Security Act and the Internal Revenue Code to strengthen the pension rights of workers who interrupt their careers to raise a family and of homemakers who depend on the pensions of their working spouses. Motion agreed to 413-0: R 163-0; D 250-0 (ND 164-0, SD 86-0), May 22, 1984. A two-thirds majority of those present and voting (276 in this case) is required for passage under suspension of the rules. A "yea" was a vote supporting the president's position.

139. H Con Res 310. New Ireland Forum. Fascell, D-Fla., motion to suspend the rules and adopt the concurrent resolution to commend the New Ireland Forum and urging the British and Irish governments and all parties in Northern Ireland to consider the forum's recommendations. Composed of Irish political leaders, the forum issued a report on May 2, 1984, suggesting options for resolving the troubles of Northern Ireland. Motion agreed to 417-0: R 163-0; D 254-0 (ND 168-0, SD 86-0), May 22, 1984. A two-thirds majority of those present and voting (278 in this case) is required for adoption under suspension of the rules.

140. HR 4145. State Justice Institute Act. Kastenmeier, D-Wis., motion to suspend the rules and pass the bill to create a state justice institute to make grants to state courts to help them improve their operations. Motion rejected 243-176: R 40-123; D 203-53 (ND 141-28, SD 62-25), May 22, 1984. A two-thirds majority of those present and voting (280 in this case) is required for passage under suspension of the rules. A "nay" was a vote supporting the president's position.

141. HR 4249. U.S. Marshals and Witness Security Reform. Kastenmeier, D-Wis., motion to suspend the rules and pass the bill to tighten controls on a Justice Department program that gives witnesses in federal criminal cases new identities in exchange for their testimony. Motion agreed to 376-41: R 125-37; D 251-4 (ND 165-2, SD 86-2), May 22, 1984. A two-thirds majority of those present and voting (278 in this case) is required for passage under suspension of the rules. A "nay" was a vote supporting the president's position.

142. HR 5665. Public Debt Limit. Passage of the bill to increase the federal debt ceiling by $30 billion from $1.49 trillion to $1.52 trillion to keep the government financed through June 22, 1984. Rejected 150-263: R 46-115; D 104-148 (ND 77-87, SD 27-61), May 22, 1984. A "yea" was a vote supporting the president's position.

143. HR 5653. Energy and Water Development Appropriations, Fiscal 1985. Adoption of the resolution (H Res 501) waiving certain points of order against consideration of the bill to appropriate $15,470,725,000 for energy and water development for fiscal 1985 or any other fiscal 1985 general appropriation bill reported by the Appropriations Committee. Adopted 246-166: R 29-130; D 217-36 (ND 145-20, SD 72-16), May 22, 1984.

144. HR 5653. Energy and Water Development Appropriations, Fiscal 1985. Ottinger, D-N.Y., amendment to delete $43.1 million from breeder reactor research and add $33.1 million to solar energy research, demonstration projects for extended burnup of nuclear fuel and university research reactors. Rejected 171-229: R 31-122; D 140-107 (ND 122-44, SD 18-63), May 22, 1984. A "nay" was a vote supporting the president's position.

145. HR 5653. Energy and Water Development Appropriations, Fiscal 1985. Passage of the bill to appropriate $15,470,725,000 for energy and water development for fiscal 1985. Passed 349-46: R 123-29; D 226-17 (ND 144-17, SD 82-0), May 22, 1984. The president had requested $15,874,791,000 in new budget authority.

KEY

Y	Voted for (yea).
#	Paired for.
+	Announced for.
N	Voted against (nay).
X	Paired against.
-	Announced against.
P	Voted "present".
C	Voted "present" to avoid possible conflict of interest.
?	Did not vote or otherwise make a position known.

Democrats *Republicans*

	138	139	140	141	142	143	144	145
ALABAMA								
1 Edwards	Y	Y	Y	Y	Y	Y	N	Y
2 *Dickinson*	Y	Y	N	N	N	N	N	Y
3 Nichols	Y	Y	Y	Y	N	Y	N	Y
4 Bevill	Y	Y	Y	Y	N	Y	N	Y
5 Flippo	Y	Y	Y	Y	Y	Y	?	Y
6 Erdreich	Y	Y	Y	Y	N	Y	N	Y
7 Shelby	Y	Y	Y	Y	N	Y	N	Y
ALASKA								
AL *Young*	Y	Y	Y	Y	N	N	N	Y
ARIZONA								
1 *McCain*	Y	Y	N	Y	N	Y	N	Y
2 Udall	Y	Y	Y	Y	Y	Y	N	Y
3 *Stump*	Y	Y	N	N	N	N	N	Y
4 *Rudd*	Y	Y	N	N	N	N	N	Y
5 McNulty	Y	Y	Y	Y	Y	Y	N	Y
ARKANSAS								
1 Alexander	Y	Y	Y	Y	N	Y	N	Y
2 *Bethune*	Y	Y	N	Y	N	N	N	Y
3 *Hammerschmidt*	?	?	?	?	?	?	?	?
4 Anthony	Y	Y	N	Y	N	Y	N	Y
CALIFORNIA								
1 Bosco	Y	Y	Y	N	Y	Y	Y	Y
2 *Chappie*	?	?	?	?	?	?	?	?
3 Matsui	Y	Y	Y	Y	Y	Y	Y	Y
4 Fazio	Y	Y	Y	Y	P	Y	N	Y
5 Burton	Y	Y	Y	Y	Y	Y	Y	Y
6 Boxer	Y	Y	Y	N	Y	Y	Y	Y
7 Miller	Y	Y	Y	N	?	?	?	?
8 Dellums	Y	Y	Y	N	Y	Y	Y	Y
9 Stark	Y	Y	Y	Y	Y	Y	Y	Y
10 Edwards	Y	Y	Y	Y	Y	Y	Y	Y
11 Lantos	Y	Y	Y	Y	Y	Y	Y	Y
12 Zschau	Y	Y	N	Y	N	?	Y	Y
13 Mineta	Y	Y	Y	Y	Y	Y	Y	Y
14 *Shumway*	Y	Y	N	N	N	N	N	Y
15 Coelho	Y	Y	Y	Y	N	Y	N	Y
16 Panetta	Y	Y	Y	Y	Y	N	Y	Y
17 *Pashayan*	Y	Y	N	N	N	N	N	Y
18 Lehman	Y	Y	Y	Y	N	Y	N	Y
19 *Lagomarsino*	Y	Y	N	Y	N	N	N	Y
20 *Thomas*	Y	Y	N	Y	N	N	N	Y
21 *Fiedler*	Y	Y	N	Y	N	N	N	Y
22 *Moorhead*	Y	Y	N	N	N	N	N	N
23 Beilenson	Y	Y	Y	Y	Y	Y	Y	Y
24 Waxman	?	?	Y	Y	Y	Y	Y	Y
25 Roybal	Y	Y	Y	Y	Y	Y	Y	Y
26 Berman	Y	Y	Y	Y	?	Y	Y	Y
27 Levine	Y	Y	Y	Y	Y	Y	N	Y
28 Dixon	Y	Y	Y	N	Y	N	Y	Y
29 Hawkins	Y	Y	Y	N	?	?	?	?
30 Martinez	Y	Y	Y	Y	Y	Y	N	Y
31 Dymally	Y	Y	Y	N	Y	N	Y	Y
32 Anderson	Y	Y	Y	Y	N	Y	N	Y
33 *Dreier*	Y	Y	N	Y	N	N	N	N
34 Torres	Y	Y	Y	Y	N	Y	Y	Y
35 *Lewis*	Y	Y	Y	Y	N	N	N	Y
36 Brown	Y	Y	Y	N	Y	Y	N	Y
37 *McCandless*	Y	Y	N	N	N	N	N	Y
38 Patterson	Y	Y	Y	Y	N	Y	N	Y
39 *Dannemeyer*	Y	Y	N	Y	N	N	N	Y
40 *Badham*	Y	Y	N	N	N	N	N	Y
41 *Lowery*	Y	Y	N	Y	N	N	N	Y
42 *Lungren*	Y	Y	N	Y	N	N	N	Y

	138	139	140	141	142	143	144	145
43 *Packard*	Y	Y	N	Y	N	N	N	Y
44 Bates	Y	Y	Y	N	Y	Y	Y	Y
45 *Hunter*	Y	Y	N	Y	Y	N	N	Y
COLORADO								
1 Schroeder	Y	Y	Y	Y	N	N	Y	N
2 Wirth	Y	Y	Y	Y	Y	Y	Y	Y
3 Kogovsek	?	?	?	?	?	?	?	?
4 *Brown*	Y	Y	N	N	N	Y	N	Y
5 *Kramer*	Y	Y	N	Y	N	N	N	Y
6 *Schaefer*	Y	Y	N	Y	N	N	N	Y
CONNECTICUT								
1 Kennelly	Y	Y	Y	N	Y	Y	Y	Y
2 Gejdenson	Y	Y	Y	Y	N	Y	Y	Y
3 Morrison	Y	Y	Y	Y	Y	N	Y	N
4 *McKinney*	Y	Y	Y	Y	N	Y	N	Y
5 Ratchford	Y	Y	Y	Y	Y	Y	Y	Y
6 *Johnson*	Y	Y	Y	Y	N	Y	N	Y
DELAWARE								
AL Carper	Y	Y	N	Y	Y	Y	Y	Y
FLORIDA								
1 Hutto	Y	Y	N	Y	N	Y	N	Y
2 Fuqua	Y	Y	N	Y	N	Y	N	Y
3 Bennett	Y	Y	N	Y	N	Y	N	Y
4 Chappell	Y	Y	N	Y	N	Y	N	Y
5 *McCollum*	Y	Y	N	N	N	N	N	Y
6 MacKay	Y	Y	N	N	N	N	N	Y
7 Gibbons	Y	Y	Y	N	N	N	N	Y
8 *Young*	Y	Y	N	Y	N	N	N	Y
9 *Bilirakis*	Y	Y	N	N	N	N	N	Y
10 Ireland	Y	Y	N	Y	N	N	N	Y
11 Nelson	Y	Y	N	N	N	N	N	Y
12 *Lewis*	Y	Y	N	N	N	N	N	Y
13 *Mack*	Y	Y	N	N	N	N	N	Y
14 Mica	Y	Y	Y	Y	N	Y	N	Y
15 *Shaw*	Y	Y	N	N	N	N	N	Y
16 Smith	Y	Y	N	Y	N	Y	N	Y
17 Lehman	Y	Y	Y	Y	N	Y	N	Y
18 Pepper	Y	Y	Y	Y	Y	Y	Y	Y
19 Fascell	Y	Y	Y	Y	Y	Y	Y	Y
GEORGIA								
1 Thomas	Y	Y	Y	Y	N	Y	N	Y
2 Hatcher	Y	Y	Y	Y	N	Y	N	Y
3 Ray	Y	Y	Y	N	N	Y	N	Y
4 Levitas	Y	Y	Y	N	Y	N	N	Y
5 Fowler	Y	Y	Y	Y	Y	Y	?	?
6 *Gingrich*	Y	Y	N	?	?	?	?	?
7 Darden	Y	Y	Y	N	Y	N	Y	Y
8 Rowland	Y	Y	Y	N	N	Y	N	Y
9 Jenkins	Y	Y	Y	Y	N	Y	N	Y
10 Barnard	Y	Y	Y	Y	N	N	Y	Y
HAWAII								
1 Heftel	Y	Y	Y	N	Y	Y	Y	Y
2 Akaka	Y	Y	Y	N	Y	N	Y	Y
IDAHO								
1 *Craig*	Y	Y	N	N	N	N	N	Y
2 *Hansen*	?	?	?	?	?	?	?	?
ILLINOIS								
1 Hayes	Y	Y	Y	N	Y	Y	Y	Y
2 Savage	Y	Y	Y	N	Y	Y	Y	Y
3 Russo	Y	Y	Y	Y	N	N	N	?
4 *O'Brien*	Y	Y	N	Y	N	Y	N	Y
5 Lipinski	Y	Y	Y	Y	Y	Y	Y	Y
6 *Hyde*	Y	Y	Y	Y	?	?	?	?
7 Collins	Y	Y	Y	N	Y	Y	Y	Y
8 Rostenkowski	Y	Y	Y	Y	N	Y	N	Y
9 Yates	Y	Y	Y	Y	Y	Y	Y	Y
10 *Porter*	Y	Y	Y	Y	N	N	N	Y
11 Annunzio	Y	Y	Y	Y	Y	N	Y	Y
12 *Crane, P.*	Y	Y	N	N	N	N	N	Y
13 *Erlenborn*	Y	Y	N	Y	N	N	N	Y
14 *Corcoran*	Y	Y	N	N	N	N	N	Y
15 *Madigan*	Y	Y	N	Y	N	N	N	Y
16 *Martin*	Y	Y	N	N	N	Y	N	Y
17 Evans	Y	Y	Y	Y	Y	Y	Y	N
18 *Michel*	Y	Y	N	Y	N	Y	N	Y
19 *Crane, D.*	Y	Y	N	N	N	N	N	N
20 Durbin	Y	Y	N	Y	N	Y	N	Y
21 Price	Y	Y	Y	Y	N	Y	N	Y
22 Simon	?	?	?	?	?	?	Y	Y
INDIANA								
1 Hall	?	?	?	?	?	?	?	?
2 Sharp	+	+	-	+	+	+	-	+
3 *Hiler*	Y	Y	N	Y	N	N	N	Y
4 *Coats*	Y	Y	N	N	N	N	N	Y
5 *Hillis*	Y	Y	N	Y	N	N	N	Y

ND - Northern Democrats   SD - Southern Democrats

	138	139	140	141	142	143	144	145
6 ***Burton***	Y	Y	N	N	N	N	N	N
7 ***Myers***	Y	Y	N	Y	N	Y	N	Y
8 McCloskey	Y	Y	N	Y	Y	Y	Y	Y
9 Hamilton	Y	Y	N	Y	Y	N	Y	Y
10 Jacobs	Y	Y	N	Y	N	N	Y	N
IOWA								
1 ***Leach***	Y	Y	N	Y	N	N	Y	N
2 ***Tauke***	Y	Y	N	Y	Y	N	Y	N
3 ***Evans***	Y	Y	N	Y	N	N	Y	N
4 Smith	Y	Y	Y	Y	N	Y	N	Y
5 Harkin	Y	Y	Y	Y	N	Y	Y	Y
6 Bedell	Y	Y	Y	Y	Y	N	Y	Y
KANSAS								
1 ***Roberts***	Y	Y	N	N	N	N	N	Y
2 Slattery	Y	Y	N	Y	N	N	Y	N
3 ***Winn***	Y	Y	N	Y	N	N	N	Y
4 Glickman	Y	Y	Y	Y	N	N	Y	Y
5 ***Whittaker***	Y	Y	N	Y	N	N	N	Y
KENTUCKY								
1 Hubbard	?	?	?	?	?	?	?	?
2 Natcher	Y	Y	Y	Y	N	Y	N	Y
3 Mazzoli	Y	Y	Y	Y	N	N	N	Y
4 ***Snyder***	Y	Y	N	N	N	Y	N	Y
5 ***Rogers***	Y	Y	Y	N	N	Y	N	Y
6 ***Hopkins***	Y	Y	N	N	N	N	Y	N
7 Perkins	Y	Y	Y	Y	Y	Y	N	Y
LOUISIANA								
1 ***Livingston***	Y	Y	N	N	Y	Y	N	Y
2 Boggs	Y	Y	Y	Y	Y	Y	N	?
3 Tauzin	Y	Y	Y	Y	N	Y	N	Y
4 Roemer	Y	Y	Y	Y	N	Y	N	Y
5 Huckaby	Y	Y	Y	Y	N	Y	N	Y
6 ***Moore***	Y	Y	Y	Y	N	Y	N	Y
7 Breaux	Y	Y	Y	Y	N	Y	N	Y
8 Long	Y	Y	Y	Y	Y	Y	N	Y
MAINE								
1 ***McKernan***	Y	Y	Y	Y	Y	N	Y	Y
2 ***Snowe***	Y	Y	Y	Y	Y	N	Y	Y
MARYLAND								
1 Dyson	Y	Y	N	Y	N	Y	N	Y
2 Long	Y	Y	Y	Y	N	Y	N	Y
3 Mikulski	Y	Y	N	Y	Y	Y	Y	Y
4 ***Holt***	Y	Y	N	N	N	N	N	Y
5 Hoyer	Y	Y	Y	Y	Y	Y	N	Y
6 Byron	Y	Y	N	N	N	Y	N	Y
7 Mitchell	Y	Y	Y	Y	N	Y	?	?
8 Barnes	Y	Y	Y	Y	Y	Y	Y	Y
MASSACHUSETTS								
1 ***Conte***	Y	Y	Y	Y	Y	Y	Y	Y
2 Boland	Y	Y	Y	Y	Y	Y	Y	Y
3 Early	Y	Y	Y	Y	N	Y	Y	Y
4 Frank	Y	Y	Y	Y	Y	Y	Y	Y
5 Shannon	Y	Y	Y	Y	Y	Y	Y	Y
6 Mavroules	Y	Y	Y	Y	Y	Y	Y	Y
7 Markey	Y	Y	Y	Y	Y	Y	Y	Y
8 O'Neill								
9 Moakley	Y	Y	Y	Y	Y	Y	Y	Y
10 Studds	Y	Y	Y	Y	Y	N	Y	N
11 Donnelly	Y	Y	Y	Y	Y	N	N	Y
MICHIGAN								
1 Conyers	?	Y	Y	Y	N	Y	Y	Y
2 ***Pursell***	Y	Y	N	Y	N	N	Y	Y
3 Wolpe	Y	Y	Y	Y	N	N	Y	Y
4 ***Siljander***	Y	Y	N	Y	N	N	N	Y
5 ***Sawyer***	Y	Y	Y	Y	N	N	?	?
6 Carr	Y	Y	Y	Y	N	Y	N	Y
7 Kildee	Y	Y	Y	Y	Y	Y	Y	Y
8 Traxler	Y	Y	Y	Y	N	Y	Y	Y
9 ***Vander Jagt***	Y	Y	N	Y	Y	N	?	?
10 Albosta	Y	Y	Y	Y	N	Y	Y	Y
11 ***Davis***	Y	Y	N	Y	N	N	?	?
12 Bonior	Y	Y	Y	Y	Y	Y	Y	N
13 Crockett	Y	Y	Y	Y	N	N	?	?
14 Hertel	Y	Y	Y	Y	N	Y	Y	N
15 Ford	?	Y	Y	Y	Y	Y	Y	?
16 Dingell	?	?	?	?	#	?	?	?
17 Levin	Y	Y	Y	Y	Y	Y	Y	Y
18 ***Broomfield***	Y	Y	N	Y	N	N	N	N
MINNESOTA								
1 Penny	Y	Y	N	Y	N	Y	Y	Y
2 ***Weber***	Y	Y	N	Y	N	N	Y	N
3 ***Frenzel***	Y	Y	N	N	Y	N	N	N
4 Vento	Y	Y	Y	Y	Y	Y	Y	N
5 Sabo	Y	Y	Y	Y	P	Y	N	Y
6 Sikorski	Y	Y	N	Y	N	Y	Y	N
7 ***Stangeland***	Y	Y	N	Y	N	N	N	Y
8 Oberstar	Y	Y	Y	Y	N	Y	Y	Y
MISSISSIPPI								
1 Whitten	Y	Y	N	Y	N	Y	N	Y
2 ***Franklin***	Y	Y	Y	Y	N	Y	N	Y
3 Montgomery	Y	Y	Y	Y	N	Y	N	Y
4 Dowdy	Y	Y	N	Y	N	Y	N	Y
5 ***Lott***	Y	Y	N	Y	Y	N	N	Y
MISSOURI								
1 Clay	Y	Y	Y	Y	Y	Y	Y	Y
2 Young	Y	Y	Y	Y	N	Y	N	Y
3 Gephardt	?	Y	Y	Y	Y	Y	Y	Y
4 Skelton	Y	Y	N	Y	Y	Y	N	Y
5 Wheat	Y	Y	Y	Y	N	Y	Y	Y
6 ***Coleman***	Y	Y	N	Y	N	N	N	Y
7 ***Taylor***	Y	Y	N	N	N	Y	N	Y
8 ***Emerson***	Y	Y	N	N	N	Y	N	Y
9 Volkmer	Y	Y	N	Y	N	Y	N	Y
MONTANA								
1 Williams	Y	Y	Y	N	Y	Y	Y	Y
2 ***Marlenee***	Y	Y	N	Y	N	N	N	Y
NEBRASKA								
1 ***Bereuter***	Y	Y	N	Y	N	N	Y	Y
2 ***Daub***	Y	Y	N	Y	N	N	N	Y
3 ***Smith***	Y	Y	N	Y	N	Y	N	Y
NEVADA								
1 Reid	Y	Y	Y	Y	N	Y	Y	Y
2 ***Vucanovich***	Y	Y	Y	N	N	N	N	Y
NEW HAMPSHIRE								
1 D'Amours	?	Y	N	Y	N	Y	?	?
2 ***Gregg***	Y	Y	Y	Y	Y	N	Y	N
NEW JERSEY								
1 Florio	Y	Y	Y	Y	N	Y	Y	Y
2 Hughes	Y	Y	Y	Y	N	Y	Y	Y
3 Howard	Y	Y	Y	Y	N	Y	Y	Y
4 ***Smith***	Y	Y	Y	Y	N	N	Y	Y
5 ***Roukema***	Y	Y	N	Y	Y	N	N	Y
6 Dwyer	Y	Y	Y	Y	Y	Y	Y	Y
7 ***Rinaldo***	Y	Y	Y	Y	N	Y	Y	Y
8 Roe	Y	Y	Y	?	N	Y	N	Y
9 Torricelli	Y	Y	Y	Y	N	Y	Y	Y
10 Rodino	Y	Y	Y	Y	Y	Y	Y	Y
11 Minish	Y	Y	Y	Y	N	Y	Y	Y
12 ***Courter***	Y	Y	N	Y	N	N	Y	Y
13 Vacancy								
14 Guarini	Y	Y	Y	?	Y	Y	Y	Y
NEW MEXICO								
1 ***Lujan***	Y	Y	N	N	N	N	N	Y
2 ***Skeen***	Y	Y	N	Y	N	N	N	Y
3 Richardson	Y	Y	Y	Y	N	Y	Y	Y
NEW YORK								
1 ***Carney***	Y	Y	N	Y	N	Y	N	Y
2 Downey	Y	Y	Y	Y	Y	Y	Y	Y
3 Mrazek	Y	Y	Y	Y	N	Y	N	Y
4 ***Lent***	Y	Y	N	Y	N	N	N	Y
5 ***McGrath***	Y	Y	Y	Y	N	N	N	Y
6 Addabbo	Y	Y	Y	Y	Y	Y	Y	Y
7 Ackerman	Y	Y	Y	Y	N	Y	Y	N
8 Scheuer	Y	Y	Y	Y	N	Y	Y	Y
9 Ferraro	Y	Y	Y	Y	N	N	Y	Y
10 Schumer	Y	Y	Y	Y	Y	Y	Y	Y
11 Towns	Y	Y	Y	Y	N	Y	Y	Y
12 Owens	Y	Y	Y	Y	N	Y	Y	Y
13 Solarz	Y	Y	Y	Y	Y	Y	Y	Y
14 ***Molinari***	Y	Y	N	Y	N	N	Y	Y
15 ***Green***	Y	Y	Y	Y	Y	Y	Y	Y
16 Rangel	?	?	?	?	Y	Y	Y	Y
17 Weiss	Y	Y	Y	Y	N	Y	Y	N
18 Garcia	Y	Y	Y	Y	Y	Y	Y	Y
19 Biaggi	Y	Y	Y	Y	N	Y	Y	?
20 Ottinger	Y	Y	Y	Y	N	Y	Y	Y
21 ***Fish***	Y	Y	Y	Y	N	N	?	?
22 ***Gilman***	Y	Y	Y	Y	N	Y	Y	Y
23 Stratton	Y	Y	Y	Y	Y	Y	N	Y
24 ***Solomon***	Y	Y	N	Y	N	N	N	N
25 ***Boehlert***	Y	Y	Y	Y	Y	N	Y	Y
26 ***Martin***	Y	Y	Y	Y	N	N	N	Y
27 ***Wortley***	Y	Y	N	Y	N	N	N	Y
28 McHugh	Y	Y	Y	Y	Y	Y	Y	Y
29 ***Horton***	Y	Y	Y	Y	Y	Y	N	Y
30 ***Conable***	Y	Y	N	N	Y	N	N	N
31 ***Kemp***	Y	Y	N	Y	Y	N	N	Y
32 LaFalce	Y	Y	Y	Y	N	Y	Y	?
33 Nowak	Y	Y	Y	Y	Y	Y	Y	Y
34 Lundine	Y	Y	Y	Y	Y	N	Y	Y
NORTH CAROLINA								
1 Jones	Y	Y	N	Y	Y	Y	N	Y
2 Valentine	Y	Y	Y	Y	N	Y	N	Y
3 Whitley	Y	Y	Y	Y	N	Y	N	Y
4 Andrews	Y	Y	Y	Y	N	Y	N	Y
5 Neal	Y	Y	Y	Y	N	Y	Y	Y
6 Britt	?	?	?	Y	N	Y	N	Y
7 Rose	?	?	Y	Y	N	Y	?	Y
8 Hefner	Y	Y	Y	Y	N	Y	N	Y
9 ***Martin***	Y	Y	N	Y	N	N	N	Y
10 ***Broyhill***	Y	Y	N	Y	N	N	N	N
11 Clarke	Y	Y	Y	Y	Y	Y	Y	Y
NORTH DAKOTA								
AL Dorgan	Y	Y	N	Y	N	Y	N	Y
OHIO								
1 Luken	Y	Y	N	Y	N	Y	Y	Y
2 ***Gradison***	Y	Y	N	Y	Y	N	N	Y
3 Hall	Y	Y	N	Y	Y	Y	Y	Y
4 ***Oxley***	Y	Y	Y	Y	N	N	N	Y
5 ***Latta***	Y	Y	N	Y	N	N	N	N
6 ***McEwen***	Y	Y	N	Y	N	N	N	Y
7 ***DeWine***	Y	Y	N	Y	N	N	N	Y
8 ***Kindness***	Y	Y	Y	Y	N	N	N	Y
9 Kaptur	Y	Y	Y	Y	N	Y	Y	Y
10 ***Miller***	Y	Y	N	N	N	Y	N	Y
11 Eckart	Y	Y	N	Y	N	Y	Y	Y
12 ***Kasich***	Y	Y	N	Y	N	N	N	Y
13 Pease	Y	Y	N	Y	Y	N	Y	Y
14 Seiberling	Y	Y	Y	Y	N	Y	Y	Y
15 ***Wylie***	Y	Y	N	N	N	N	N	Y
16 ***Regula***	Y	Y	N	Y	N	N	N	Y
17 ***Williams***	Y	Y	Y	?	N	N	?	?
18 Applegate	Y	Y	N	Y	N	Y	N	Y
19 Feighan	Y	Y	Y	Y	N	Y	Y	N
20 Oakar	Y	Y	Y	Y	N	Y	Y	Y
21 Stokes	Y	Y	Y	Y	Y	Y	Y	Y
OKLAHOMA								
1 Jones	Y	Y	N	Y	Y	Y	N	Y
2 Synar	Y	Y	Y	Y	Y	Y	Y	Y
3 Watkins	Y	Y	N	Y	N	Y	N	Y
4 McCurdy	Y	Y	Y	Y	N	Y	N	Y
5 ***Edwards***	Y	Y	N	Y	N	Y	N	Y
6 English	Y	Y	N	Y	N	Y	N	Y
OREGON								
1 AuCoin	Y	Y	Y	Y	N	Y	Y	Y
2 ***Smith, R.***	Y	Y	N	Y	N	Y	N	Y
3 Wyden	Y	Y	N	Y	N	Y	Y	Y
4 Weaver	Y	Y	Y	Y	N	N	Y	N
5 ***Smith, D.***	Y	Y	N	N	N	N	N	N
PENNSYLVANIA								
1 Foglietta	Y	Y	Y	Y	Y	Y	Y	Y
2 Gray	Y	Y	Y	Y	P	Y	Y	Y
3 Borski	Y	Y	Y	Y	Y	Y	Y	Y
4 Kolter	Y	Y	N	Y	N	Y	N	Y
5 ***Schulze***	Y	Y	N	Y	Y	N	N	N
6 Yatron	Y	Y	Y	Y	N	Y	N	Y
7 Edgar	Y	Y	Y	Y	Y	N	Y	N
8 Kostmayer	Y	Y	N	Y	Y	Y	Y	Y
9 ***Shuster***	Y	Y	N	N	N	N	N	Y
10 ***McDade***	Y	Y	Y	Y	Y	Y	N	?
11 Harrison	Y	Y	Y	Y	Y	Y	N	Y
12 Murtha	Y	Y	Y	Y	Y	Y	N	Y
13 ***Coughlin***	Y	Y	N	Y	N	N	Y	Y
14 Coyne	Y	Y	Y	Y	Y	Y	N	Y
15 ***Ritter***	Y	Y	N	Y	N	N	N	N
16 ***Walker***	Y	Y	N	Y	N	N	N	N
17 ***Gekas***	Y	Y	N	Y	N	N	N	Y
18 Walgren	Y	Y	Y	Y	?	?	?	?
19 ***Goodling***	Y	Y	N	Y	N	N	Y	Y
20 Gaydos	Y	Y	N	Y	N	Y	N	Y
21 ***Ridge***	Y	Y	Y	Y	N	N	Y	Y
22 Murphy	Y	Y	N	Y	N	Y	N	Y
23 ***Clinger***	Y	Y	N	Y	Y	N	N	Y
RHODE ISLAND								
1 St Germain	Y	Y	Y	Y	Y	Y	Y	Y
2 ***Schneider***	Y	Y	Y	Y	Y	N	Y	Y
SOUTH CAROLINA								
1 ***Hartnett***	Y	Y	N	N	N	N	N	Y
2 ***Spence***	Y	Y	N	Y	N	N	N	Y
3 Derrick	Y	Y	N	Y	N	Y	Y	Y
4 ***Campbell***	Y	Y	N	Y	N	N	N	Y
5 Spratt	Y	Y	Y	Y	N	Y	Y	Y
6 Tallon	Y	Y	N	Y	N	Y	Y	Y
SOUTH DAKOTA								
AL Daschle	Y	Y	N	Y	N	Y	N	Y
TENNESSEE								
1 ***Quillen***	Y	Y	N	N	Y	Y	N	Y
2 ***Duncan***	Y	Y	N	Y	Y	N	N	Y
3 Lloyd	Y	Y	Y	Y	N	Y	N	Y
4 Cooper	Y	Y	Y	Y	N	Y	N	Y
5 Boner	Y	Y	Y	Y	N	Y	N	Y
6 Gore	Y	Y	Y	Y	Y	N	?	?
7 ***Sundquist***	Y	Y	N	N	Y	N	N	Y
8 Jones	Y	Y	Y	Y	N	Y	N	Y
9 Ford	Y	Y	Y	Y	Y	Y	N	Y
TEXAS								
1 Hall, S.	Y	Y	Y	Y	N	N	N	Y
2 Wilson	Y	Y	N	Y	N	Y	?	?
3 ***Bartlett***	Y	Y	N	Y	N	N	N	N
4 Hall, R.	Y	Y	Y	Y	N	N	?	?
5 Bryant	Y	Y	Y	Y	N	Y	Y	Y
6 ***Gramm***	Y	Y	N	Y	N	N	N	N
7 ***Archer***	Y	Y	N	Y	N	N	N	N
8 ***Fields***	Y	Y	N	Y	N	N	?	?
9 Brooks	Y	Y	Y	Y	Y	Y	N	Y
10 Pickle	Y	Y	Y	Y	Y	Y	N	Y
11 Leath	Y	Y	N	N	Y	Y	?	?
12 Wright	Y	Y	Y	Y	Y	Y	N	Y
13 Hightower	Y	Y	Y	Y	N	Y	N	Y
14 Patman	Y	Y	Y	Y	N	Y	N	Y
15 de la Garza	Y	Y	Y	Y	N	Y	N	Y
16 Coleman	Y	Y	Y	Y	Y	Y	Y	Y
17 Stenholm	Y	Y	N	Y	N	N	N	Y
18 Leland	Y	Y	Y	Y	N	Y	Y	Y
19 Hance	?	?	?	?	X	?	?	?
20 Gonzalez	Y	Y	Y	Y	N	Y	N	Y
21 ***Loeffler***	Y	Y	N	Y	Y	N	N	Y
22 ***Paul***	Y	Y	N	N	N	N	?	?
23 Kazen	Y	Y	Y	Y	N	Y	N	Y
24 Frost	Y	Y	Y	Y	Y	N	N	Y
25 Andrews	Y	Y	N	Y	Y	Y	N	Y
26 Vandergriff	Y	Y	N	Y	N	N	N	Y
27 Ortiz	Y	Y	Y	Y	N	Y	Y	Y
UTAH								
1 ***Hansen***	Y	Y	N	N	N	N	N	Y
2 ***Marriott***	Y	Y	Y	Y	N	N	N	Y
3 ***Nielson***	Y	Y	N	N	N	N	N	Y
VERMONT								
AL ***Jeffords***	Y	Y	Y	Y	Y	N	Y	Y
VIRGINIA								
1 ***Bateman***	Y	Y	N	N	Y	Y	N	Y
2 ***Whitehurst***	Y	Y	N	Y	Y	N	N	Y
3 ***Bliley***	Y	Y	N	Y	Y	Y	N	Y
4 Sisisky	Y	Y	N	Y	Y	Y	N	Y
5 Daniel	Y	Y	N	Y	N	N	N	Y
6 Olin	Y	Y	N	Y	N	Y	N	Y
7 ***Robinson***	Y	Y	N	N	N	Y	N	Y
8 ***Parris***	Y	Y	N	Y	Y	N	N	Y
9 Boucher	Y	Y	Y	Y	N	Y	N	Y
10 ***Wolf***	Y	Y	Y	Y	Y	N	Y	Y
WASHINGTON								
1 ***Pritchard***	Y	Y	Y	Y	Y	N	?	?
2 Swift	Y	Y	Y	Y	P	Y	N	?
3 Bonker	Y	Y	Y	Y	Y	?	Y	Y
4 ***Morrison***	Y	Y	Y	Y	Y	Y	N	Y
5 Foley	Y	Y	Y	Y	Y	Y	N	Y
6 Dicks	Y	Y	Y	Y	Y	Y	N	Y
7 Lowry	Y	Y	Y	Y	P	N	Y	Y
8 ***Chandler***	Y	Y	N	Y	Y	N	N	Y
WEST VIRGINIA								
1 Mollohan	Y	Y	N	Y	Y	Y	N	Y
2 Staggers	Y	Y	Y	Y	N	Y	Y	Y
3 Wise	+	+	+	+	-	+	Y	Y
4 Rahall	?	?	?	?	?	?	?	?
WISCONSIN								
1 Aspin	Y	Y	Y	Y	Y	Y	Y	Y
2 Kastenmeier	Y	Y	Y	Y	N	Y	Y	Y
3 ***Gunderson***	Y	Y	N	Y	N	N	Y	Y
4 Kleczka	Y	Y	Y	Y	Y	Y	Y	Y
5 Moody	Y	Y	Y	Y	N	Y	Y	N
6 ***Petri***	Y	Y	Y	Y	N	N	N	N
7 Obey	Y	Y	Y	Y	N	Y	Y	N
8 ***Roth***	Y	Y	Y	N	N	?	N	Y
9 ***Sensenbrenner***	Y	Y	N	Y	N	N	N	N
WYOMING								
AL ***Cheney***	Y	Y	N	Y	Y	N	N	Y

Southern states - Ala., Ark., Fla., Ga., Ky., La., Miss., N.C., Okla., S.C., Tenn., Texas, Va.

146. Procedural Motion. Fields, R-Texas, motion to approve the House *Journal* of Tuesday, May 22. Motion agreed to 366-26: R 141-13; D 225-13 (ND 143-10, SD 82-3), May 23, 1984.

147. HR 5167. Department of Defense Authorization. Lowry, D-Wash., amendment to bar the purchase of additional Pershing II missiles until April 1, 1985, allowing such purchases after that date only if the president certified to Congress that the Soviet Union showed no willingness to limit such weapons and if the Congress thereafter approved resumption of Pershing II purchases by joint resolution. Rejected 122-294: R 7-156; D 115-138 (ND 110-57, SD 5-81), May 23, 1984. A "nay" was a vote supporting the president's position.

148. HR 5167. Department of Defense Authorization. Dellums, D-Calif., amendment to delete $7.1 billion for procurement of 34 B-1 bombers. Rejected 163-254: R 19-142; D 144-112 (ND 130-40, SD 14-72), May 23, 1984. A "nay" was a vote supporting the president's position.

149. HR 5167. Department of Defense Authorization. Schroeder, D-Colo., amendment to limit appropriations for procurement in fiscal 1985 to 106.5 percent of the amount appropriated for procurement in fiscal 1984. Rejected 173-250: R 28-136; D 145-114 (ND 130-43, SD 15-71), May 23, 1984. A "nay" was a vote supporting the president's position.

150. HR 4170. Deficit Reduction. Vander Jagt, R-Mich., motion to order the previous question (thus ending debate and the possibility of amendment) on the Vander Jagt motion to instruct House conferees on the deficit-reduction bill not to agree to the Senate amendment to lengthen the depreciation period for real estate and to reduce tax credits available for the rehabilitation of old buildings. Motion agreed to 296-128: R 101-61; D 195-67 (ND 133-41, SD 62-26), May 23, 1984.

151. HR 4170. Deficit Reduction. Vander Jagt, R-Mich., motion to instruct House conferees on the deficit-reduction bill not to agree to the Senate amendment to lengthen the depreciation period for real estate and to reduce tax credits available for the rehabilitation of old buildings. Motion agreed to 397-24: R 162-0; D 235-24 (ND 149-23, SD 86-1), May 23, 1984.

152. HR 5167. Department of Defense Authorization. Gore, D-Tenn., amendment to the Brown, D-Calif., amendment, to provide that no funds may be used to test the anti-satellite missile (ASAT) against a target in space unless the Soviet Union conducts a test of its ASAT after enactment of the bill. Adopted 238-181: R 39-122; D 199-59 (ND 162-10, SD 37-49), May 23, 1984. A "nay" was a vote supporting the president's position.

153. HR 5167. Department of Defense Authorization. Stratton, D-N.Y., amendment to the Brown, D-Calif., amendment, to provide that the anti-satellite missile (ASAT) may be tested against an object in space as many times as the Soviet ASAT has been tested against an object in space. Rejected 178-236: R 124-37; D 54-199 (ND 12-157, SD 42-42), May 23, 1984.

KEY

Y Voted for (yea).
Paired for.
+ Announced for.
N Voted against (nay).
X Paired against.
- Announced against.
P Voted "present".
C Voted "present" to avoid possible conflict of interest.
? Did not vote or otherwise make a position known.

Democrats   *Republicans*

	146	147	148	149	150	151	152	153
ALABAMA								
1 *Edwards*	?	N	N	N	N	Y	N	Y
2 *Dickinson*	N	N	N	N	N	N	Y	N
3 Nichols	Y	N	N	N	N	Y	N	Y
4 Bevill	Y	N	N	N	N	Y	N	Y
5 Flippo	Y	N	N	N	Y	Y	N	Y
6 Erdreich	Y	N	N	N	N	Y	N	Y
7 Shelby	Y	N	N	N	N	Y	N	Y
ALASKA								
AL *Young*	?	N	N	N	N	Y	N	Y
ARIZONA								
1 *McCain*	Y	N	N	N	N	Y	N	Y
2 Udall	Y	Y	Y	Y	N	Y	Y	N
3 *Stump*	Y	N	N	N	N	Y	N	Y
4 *Rudd*	Y	N	N	N	N	Y	N	Y
5 McNulty	Y	Y	Y	N	N	Y	Y	N
ARKANSAS								
1 Alexander	Y	N	N	N	N	Y	N	Y
2 *Bethune*	?	N	N	N	N	Y	N	Y
3 *Hammerschmidt*	Y	N	N	N	N	Y	N	Y
4 Anthony	Y	N	N	Y	N	Y	N	Y
CALIFORNIA								
1 Bosco	Y	Y	Y	N	Y	Y	Y	N
2 *Chappie*	N	N	N	N	Y	Y	N	Y
3 Matsui	Y	Y	Y	N	Y	Y	Y	N
4 Fazio	Y	Y	Y	Y	Y	Y	Y	N
5 Burton	Y	Y	Y	Y	Y	Y	Y	N
6 Boxer	Y	Y	Y	Y	Y	Y	Y	N
7 Miller	?	?	Y	Y	Y	Y	Y	N
8 Dellums	Y	Y	Y	Y	Y	Y	Y	N
9 Stark	Y	Y	Y	Y	Y	N	Y	N
10 Edwards	Y	Y	Y	Y	Y	Y	Y	N
11 Lantos	Y	N	Y	Y	Y	Y	Y	N
12 *Zschau*	Y	N	Y	Y	N	Y	N	Y
13 Mineta	Y	Y	Y	Y	Y	Y	Y	N
14 *Shumway*	Y	N	N	N	N	Y	N	Y
15 Coelho	Y	N	N	Y	Y	Y	Y	N
16 Panetta	Y	Y	Y	Y	Y	Y	Y	N
17 *Pashayan*	Y	N	N	N	N	Y	N	Y
18 Lehman	Y	Y	Y	Y	Y	Y	Y	N
19 *Lagomarsino*	Y	N	N	N	N	Y	N	Y
20 *Thomas*	Y	N	N	N	N	Y	N	Y
21 *Fiedler*	Y	N	N	N	N	Y	N	Y
22 *Moorhead*	Y	N	N	N	N	Y	N	Y
23 Beilenson	Y	Y	Y	Y	Y	N	Y	N
24 Waxman	Y	Y	Y	Y	Y	Y	Y	N
25 Roybal	Y	Y	Y	Y	Y	Y	Y	N
26 Berman	Y	Y	Y	Y	Y	Y	Y	N
27 Levine	Y	Y	Y	N	Y	Y	Y	N
28 Dixon	?	#	N	Y	Y	Y	Y	N
29 Hawkins	Y	Y	Y	Y	Y	Y	Y	?
30 Martinez	Y	Y	Y	Y	Y	Y	Y	N
31 Dymally	P	Y	N	Y	Y	Y	Y	N
32 Anderson	Y	N	N	Y	Y	Y	Y	Y
33 *Dreier*	Y	N	N	N	N	Y	N	Y
34 Torres	Y	Y	N	Y	Y	Y	Y	N
35 *Lewis*	Y	N	N	N	N	Y	N	Y
36 Brown	Y	Y	N	Y	Y	Y	Y	N
37 *McCandless*	Y	N	N	N	N	Y	N	Y
38 Patterson	Y	N	N	N	Y	?	N	Y
39 *Dannemeyer*	Y	N	N	N	N	Y	N	Y
40 *Badham*	Y	N	N	N	N	Y	N	Y
41 *Lowery*	Y	N	N	N	N	Y	N	Y
42 *Lungren*	Y	N	N	N	N	Y	N	Y
43 *Packard*	Y	N	N	N	Y	Y	N	Y
44 Bates	Y	Y	Y	Y	Y	Y	Y	N
45 *Hunter*	Y	N	N	N	Y	Y	N	Y
COLORADO								
1 Schroeder	N	Y	Y	Y	N	Y	Y	N
2 Wirth	Y	Y	Y	Y	N	Y	Y	N
3 Kogovsek	Y	Y	Y	Y	Y	Y	Y	N
4 *Brown*	Y	N	Y	Y	Y	Y	Y	Y
5 *Kramer*	Y	N	N	N	Y	Y	N	Y
6 *Schaefer*	Y	N	N	N	Y	Y	N	Y
CONNECTICUT								
1 Kennelly	Y	Y	Y	Y	N	Y	Y	N
2 Gejdenson	N	Y	Y	Y	N	Y	Y	N
3 Morrison	Y	Y	Y	Y	Y	Y	Y	N
4 *McKinney*	?	Y	Y	Y	Y	Y	Y	N
5 Ratchford	Y	Y	Y	Y	Y	Y	Y	N
6 *Johnson*	Y	N	N	Y	N	Y	Y	N
DELAWARE								
AL Carper	Y	N	Y	N	N	Y	Y	N
FLORIDA								
1 Hutto	Y	N	N	N	Y	Y	N	Y
2 Fuqua	Y	N	N	N	N	Y	N	Y
3 Bennett	Y	N	N	N	Y	Y	N	Y
4 Chappell	Y	N	N	N	Y	Y	N	Y
5 *McCollum*	Y	N	N	N	N	Y	N	Y
6 MacKay	Y	N	Y	Y	Y	Y	Y	N
7 Gibbons	Y	Y	Y	Y	Y	N	Y	N
8 *Young*	?	N	N	N	N	Y	N	Y
9 *Bilirakis*	Y	N	N	N	Y	Y	N	Y
10 Ireland	Y	N	N	?	Y	Y	N	Y
11 Nelson	Y	N	N	N	Y	Y	N	Y
12 *Lewis*	Y	N	N	N	Y	Y	N	Y
13 *Mack*	N	N	N	N	N	Y	N	Y
14 Mica	Y	N	N	N	N	Y	N	Y
15 *Shaw*	Y	N	N	N	N	Y	N	Y
16 Smith	Y	N	Y	N	Y	Y	Y	N
17 Lehman	Y	Y	Y	Y	Y	Y	Y	N
18 Pepper	Y	N	N	N	Y	Y	N	Y
19 Fascell	Y	N	Y	N	Y	Y	Y	N
GEORGIA								
1 Thomas	Y	N	N	N	Y	Y	N	Y
2 Hatcher	Y	N	N	N	Y	Y	N	Y
3 Ray	?	X	N	N	Y	Y	N	Y
4 Levitas	Y	N	N	N	Y	Y	N	Y
5 Fowler	?	?	Y	N	Y	Y	Y	N
6 *Gingrich*	Y	N	N	N	Y	Y	N	Y
7 Darden	Y	N	N	N	N	Y	N	Y
8 Rowland	Y	N	N	Y	Y	Y	N	Y
9 Jenkins	Y	N	?	N	Y	Y	Y	N
10 Barnard	Y	N	?	?	?	?	?	?
HAWAII								
1 Heftel	?	N	N	N	Y	Y	N	Y
2 Akaka	Y	N	N	N	N	Y	N	Y
IDAHO								
1 *Craig*	Y	N	N	N	Y	Y	N	Y
2 *Hansen*	?	?	?	?	?	?	?	?
ILLINOIS								
1 Hayes	Y	Y	Y	Y	Y	Y	Y	N
2 Savage	Y	Y	Y	Y	Y	Y	Y	N
3 Russo	?	?	?	?	Y	Y	Y	N
4 *O'Brien*	Y	N	N	N	Y	Y	N	Y
5 Lipinski	Y	N	N	N	Y	Y	N	Y
6 *Hyde*	Y	N	N	N	N	Y	N	Y
7 Collins	Y	?	Y	Y	Y	Y	Y	N
8 Rostenkowski	Y	N	N	N	Y	Y	N	Y
9 Yates	Y	Y	Y	Y	Y	Y	Y	N
10 *Porter*	Y	N	N	N	-	Y	Y	N
11 Annunzio	Y	N	N	N	Y	Y	N	Y
12 *Crane, P.*	Y	N	N	N	N	Y	N	Y
13 *Erlenborn*	Y	N	N	N	Y	Y	N	Y
14 *Corcoran*	Y	N	N	N	N	Y	N	Y
15 *Madigan*	?	N	N	N	N	Y	N	Y
16 *Martin*	Y	N	N	N	Y	Y	N	Y
17 Evans	Y	Y	Y	Y	N	Y	Y	N
18 *Michel*	Y	N	N	N	Y	Y	N	Y
19 *Crane, D.*	Y	N	N	N	N	Y	N	Y
20 Durbin	N	Y	Y	Y	Y	Y	Y	N
21 Price	Y	N	N	N	Y	Y	N	Y
22 Simon	Y	N	Y	Y	Y	Y	Y	N
INDIANA								
1 Hall	?	?	?	Y	N	Y	Y	N
2 Sharp	+	-	+	-	+	+	-	-
3 *Hiler*	Y	N	N	N	N	Y	N	Y
4 *Coats*	Y	N	N	N	N	Y	N	Y
5 Hillis	Y	N	N	N	Y	Y	N	Y

ND - Northern Democrats   SD - Southern Democrats

	146	147	148	149	150	151	152	153
6 ***Burton***	Y	N	N	N	Y	Y	N	Y
7 ***Myers***	Y	N	N	N	N	Y	N	Y
8 McCloskey	Y	N	Y	Y	Y	Y	Y	N
9 Hamilton	Y	N	Y	N	Y	Y	Y	N
10 Jacobs	N	Y	Y	Y	Y	Y	Y	N
IOWA								
1 ***Leach***	Y	Y	Y	Y	Y	Y	Y	N
2 ***Tauke***	Y	N	Y	Y	Y	Y	Y	N
3 ***Evans***	N	N	N	Y	N	Y	Y	N
4 Smith	Y	N	Y	Y	Y	Y	Y	N
5 Harkin	N	Y	Y	Y	Y	Y	Y	N
6 Bedell	Y	Y	Y	Y	Y	Y	Y	N
KANSAS								
1 ***Roberts***	N	N	N	Y	N	Y	N	Y
2 Slattery	Y	N	N	Y	Y	Y	Y	N
3 ***Winn***	Y	N	N	N	N	Y	N	Y
4 Glickman	Y	N	N	N	Y	Y	Y	?
5 ***Whittaker***	Y	N	N	N	N	Y	N	Y
KENTUCKY								
1 Hubbard	Y	N	N	N	Y	Y	N	Y
2 Natcher	Y	N	N	N	N	Y	N	Y
3 Mazzoli	Y	N	Y	N	Y	Y	Y	N
4 ***Snyder***	Y	N	N	Y	Y	Y	N	Y
5 ***Rogers***	Y	N	N	N	N	Y	N	Y
6 ***Hopkins***	Y	N	N	N	N	Y	Y	N
7 Perkins	Y	N	N	Y	Y	Y	N	N
LOUISIANA								
1 ***Livingston***	Y	N	N	N	N	Y	N	Y
2 Boggs	Y	N	N	N	Y	Y	Y	N
3 Tauzin	Y	N	N	N	Y	Y	N	Y
4 Roemer	N	N	N	Y	Y	Y	Y	N
5 Huckaby	Y	N	N	N	Y	Y	Y	N
6 ***Moore***	Y	N	N	N	Y	Y	Y	N
7 Breaux	Y	N	N	N	Y	?	N	Y
8 Long	Y	N	N	N	Y	Y	Y	N
MAINE								
1 ***McKernan***	Y	N	N	Y	Y	Y	Y	N
2 ***Snowe***	Y	N	N	Y	N	Y	Y	N
MARYLAND								
1 Dyson	Y	N	N	N	Y	Y	N	Y
2 Long	Y	Y	Y	N	Y	Y	Y	N
3 Mikulski	Y	Y	Y	Y	N	?	?	?
4 ***Holt***	?	N	N	N	Y	Y	N	Y
5 Hoyer	Y	N	N	Y	Y	Y	Y	N
6 Byron	Y	N	N	N	Y	Y	N	Y
7 Mitchell	N	#	#	Y	N	N	Y	N
8 Barnes	Y	N	Y	Y	Y	Y	Y	N
MASSACHUSETTS								
1 ***Conte***	Y	Y	Y	Y	N	Y	Y	N
2 Boland	Y	N	Y	?	Y	Y	Y	N
3 Early	Y	Y	Y	Y	Y	N	Y	N
4 Frank	?	Y	Y	Y	N	N	Y	N
5 Shannon	Y	Y	Y	Y	Y	N	Y	N
6 Mavroules	Y	Y	Y	N	N	Y	Y	N
7 Markey	Y	Y	Y	Y	N	Y	+	-
8 O'Neill								
9 Moakley	Y	Y	Y	Y	Y	Y	Y	N
10 Studds	Y	Y	Y	Y	N	Y	Y	N
11 Donnelly	Y	N	Y	Y	Y	N	Y	N
MICHIGAN								
1 Conyers	Y	Y	Y	Y	N	N	Y	N
2 ***Pursell***	Y	N	Y	N	Y	Y	Y	N
3 Wolpe	Y	Y	Y	Y	N	Y	Y	N
4 ***Siljander***	Y	N	N	N	Y	Y	N	Y
5 ***Sawyer***	Y	N	N	N	Y	Y	N	Y
6 Carr	Y	Y	Y	N	Y	Y	Y	N
7 Kildee	Y	Y	Y	Y	N	Y	Y	N
8 Traxler	Y	N	Y	Y	Y	Y	Y	N
9 ***Vander Jagt***	Y	N	N	N	Y	Y	N	Y
10 Albosta	Y	N	Y	Y	N	Y	Y	N
11 ***Davis***	Y	N	N	N	Y	Y	N	Y
12 Bonior	Y	Y	Y	Y	Y	Y	Y	N
13 Crockett	?	Y	Y	Y	N	Y	Y	?
14 Hertel	Y	N	Y	Y	N	Y	Y	N
15 Ford	?	Y	Y	Y	Y	Y	Y	N
16 Dingell	Y	N	Y	N	Y	Y	Y	N
17 Levin	Y	N	Y	Y	Y	N	Y	N
18 ***Broomfield***	Y	N	N	N	Y	Y	Y	Y
MINNESOTA								
1 Penny	N	Y	Y	Y	N	Y	Y	N
2 ***Weber***	Y	N	Y	N	N	Y	N	Y
3 ***Frenzel***	N	N	Y	Y	Y	Y	Y	N
4 Vento	Y	Y	Y	Y	Y	Y	Y	N
5 Sabo	N	Y	Y	Y	Y	N	Y	N
6 Sikorski	N	Y	Y	Y	N	Y	Y	N
7 ***Stangeland***	Y	N	?	N	N	Y	N	Y
8 Oberstar	P	Y	Y	Y	N	Y	Y	N
MISSISSIPPI								
1 Whitten	Y	N	N	Y	N	Y	N	Y
2 ***Franklin***	Y	N	N	N	Y	Y	N	Y
3 Montgomery	Y	N	N	N	N	Y	N	Y
4 Dowdy	Y	N	N	N	Y	Y	N	?
5 ***Lott***	Y	N	N	N	Y	Y	N	Y
MISSOURI								
1 Clay	N	Y	Y	Y	?	?	Y	N
2 Young	Y	N	N	N	N	Y	N	Y
3 Gephardt	Y	N	Y	Y	Y	N	Y	N
4 Skelton	Y	N	N	N	Y	Y	N	Y
5 Wheat	?	Y	Y	Y	Y	Y	Y	N
6 ***Coleman***	Y	N	N	N	Y	Y	N	Y
7 ***Taylor***	Y	N	N	N	N	Y	N	Y
8 ***Emerson***	N	N	N	N	N	Y	N	Y
9 Volkmer	Y	N	N	N	Y	Y	Y	N
MONTANA								
1 Williams	Y	Y	Y	Y	N	Y	Y	N
2 ***Marlenee***	Y	N	N	N	N	Y	N	Y
NEBRASKA								
1 ***Bereuter***	Y	N	N	Y	Y	Y	Y	N
2 ***Daub***	Y	N	N	N	Y	Y	N	Y
3 ***Smith***	Y	N	N	Y	N	Y	N	Y
NEVADA								
1 Reid	Y	N	Y	N	N	Y	Y	N
2 ***Vucanovich***	Y	N	N	N	N	Y	N	Y
NEW HAMPSHIRE								
1 D'Amours	Y	N	Y	N	N	Y	Y	N
2 ***Gregg***	?	N	N	N	N	Y	N	Y
NEW JERSEY								
1 Florio	Y	Y	Y	Y	N	Y	Y	N
2 Hughes	Y	N	Y	N	Y	Y	Y	N
3 Howard	Y	N	Y	Y	Y	Y	Y	N
4 ***Smith***	Y	N	N	N	Y	Y	Y	N
5 ***Roukema***	Y	N	N	Y	Y	Y	Y	N
6 Dwyer	Y	N	Y	Y	Y	Y	Y	N
7 ***Rinaldo***	Y	N	N	N	Y	Y	Y	N
8 Roe	Y	N	Y	N	Y	Y	Y	N
9 Torricelli	Y	Y	Y	Y	Y	Y	N	Y
10 Rodino	Y	Y	Y	Y	Y	Y	Y	N
11 Minish	Y	N	Y	Y	Y	Y	Y	N
12 ***Courter***	Y	N	N	N	Y	?	?	?
13 Vacancy								
14 Guarini	Y	N	Y	Y	Y	N	Y	N
NEW MEXICO								
1 ***Lujan***	Y	N	N	N	N	Y	N	Y
2 ***Skeen***	Y	N	N	N	Y	Y	N	Y
3 Richardson	Y	N	N	Y	N	Y	Y	N
NEW YORK								
1 ***Carney***	Y	N	N	N	N	Y	N	Y
2 Downey	Y	Y	Y	Y	Y	Y	Y	N
3 Mrazek	Y	Y	Y	Y	Y	Y	Y	N
4 ***Lent***	Y	N	N	N	N	Y	N	Y
5 ***McGrath***	N	N	N	N	N	Y	N	Y
6 Addabbo	?	Y	Y	Y	Y	Y	Y	N
7 Ackerman	Y	Y	Y	Y	N	N	Y	N
8 Scheuer	Y	Y	Y	Y	Y	C	Y	N
9 Ferraro	Y	Y	Y	Y	Y	Y	Y	N
10 Schumer	Y	Y	Y	Y	Y	Y	Y	N
11 Towns	Y	Y	Y	Y	Y	Y	Y	N
12 Owens	Y	Y	Y	Y	Y	Y	Y	N
13 Solarz	Y	N	Y	Y	Y	Y	Y	N
14 ***Molinari***	Y	N	N	N	Y	Y	N	Y
15 ***Green***	Y	N	Y	Y	Y	Y	Y	N
16 Rangel	?	Y	Y	Y	Y	N	Y	N
17 Weiss	Y	Y	Y	Y	Y	N	Y	N
18 Garcia	Y	Y	Y	Y	N	Y	Y	N
19 Biaggi	Y	N	Y	N	N	Y	Y	N
20 Ottinger	P	Y	Y	Y	N	Y	Y	N
21 ***Fish***	?	N	Y	N	N	Y	Y	N
22 ***Gilman***	Y	N	N	N	Y	Y	Y	N
23 Stratton	Y	N	N	N	Y	Y	N	Y
24 ***Solomon***	N	N	N	N	Y	Y	N	Y
25 ***Boehlert***	Y	N	N	N	N	Y	Y	N
26 ***Martin***	Y	N	N	N	Y	Y	N	Y
27 ***Wortley***	Y	N	N	N	N	Y	N	Y
28 McHugh	Y	N	Y	N	Y	N	Y	N
29 ***Horton***	Y	N	Y	N	N	Y	Y	N
30 ***Conable***	Y	N	N	N	Y	Y	N	Y
31 ***Kemp***	?	N	?	N	Y	Y	N	Y
32 LaFalce	Y	Y	Y	Y	Y	N	Y	N
33 Nowak	?	Y	Y	Y	Y	Y	Y	N
34 Lundine	?	?	?	?	?	?	?	?
NORTH CAROLINA								
1 Jones	Y	N	N	N	Y	Y	Y	N
2 Valentine	Y	N	N	N	Y	Y	N	Y
3 Whitley	Y	N	N	N	Y	Y	N	Y
4 Andrews	Y	N	N	N	Y	Y	?	?
5 Neal	?	N	N	N	Y	Y	Y	N
6 Britt	Y	N	Y	N	Y	Y	Y	N
7 Rose	Y	N	N	N	Y	Y	Y	N
8 Hefner	Y	N	N	N	Y	Y	Y	N
9 ***Martin***	Y	N	N	N	?	?	?	?
10 ***Broyhill***	Y	N	N	N	Y	Y	N	Y
11 Clarke	Y	Y	N	N	Y	Y	Y	N
NORTH DAKOTA								
AL Dorgan	Y	Y	N	Y	Y	Y	Y	N
OHIO								
1 Luken	Y	N	N	N	Y	Y	Y	N
2 ***Gradison***	Y	N	N	N	Y	Y	Y	N
3 Hall	Y	Y	N	Y	N	Y	Y	N
4 ***Oxley***	Y	N	N	N	Y	Y	Y	Y
5 ***Latta***	Y	N	N	N	Y	Y	N	Y
6 ***McEwen***	Y	?	N	N	Y	Y	N	Y
7 ***DeWine***	Y	N	N	N	Y	Y	N	Y
8 ***Kindness***	Y	N	N	N	N	Y	N	Y
9 Kaptur	Y	Y	Y	Y	Y	Y	Y	N
10 ***Miller***	N	N	N	Y	Y	Y	N	Y
11 Eckart	Y	Y	N	Y	Y	Y	Y	N
12 ***Kasich***	Y	N	N	N	Y	Y	N	Y
13 Pease	Y	N	Y	Y	Y	N	Y	N
14 Seiberling	Y	Y	Y	Y	Y	Y	Y	N
15 ***Wylie***	Y	N	N	Y	Y	Y	N	Y
16 ***Regula***	Y	N	N	N	Y	Y	Y	N
17 ***Williams***	Y	N	N	N	N	Y	Y	Y
18 Applegate	?	N	N	N	Y	Y	N	Y
19 Feighan	Y	Y	Y	Y	Y	Y	Y	N
20 Oakar	Y	Y	N	Y	Y	Y	Y	N
21 Stokes	Y	Y	#	Y	Y	Y	Y	N
OKLAHOMA								
1 Jones	Y	N	N	Y	Y	Y	N	N
2 Synar	Y	N	N	N	Y	Y	Y	N
3 Watkins	Y	N	N	N	Y	Y	N	?
4 McCurdy	Y	N	N	N	Y	Y	N	N
5 ***Edwards***	Y	N	N	N	Y	Y	N	Y
6 English	Y	N	N	N	Y	Y	N	N
OREGON								
1 AuCoin	?	Y	Y	Y	Y	Y	Y	N
2 ***Smith, R.***	Y	N	N	N	Y	Y	N	Y
3 Wyden	Y	Y	Y	Y	Y	Y	Y	N
4 Weaver	Y	Y	Y	Y	Y	N	Y	N
5 ***Smith, D.***	Y	N	N	N	Y	Y	N	Y
PENNSYLVANIA								
1 Foglietta	Y	Y	Y	Y	Y	Y	Y	N
2 Gray	Y	Y	Y	Y	Y	Y	Y	N
3 Borski	Y	N	Y	Y	Y	Y	Y	N
4 Kolter	Y	Y	Y	Y	Y	Y	Y	N
5 ***Schulze***	Y	N	N	Y	Y	Y	N	Y
6 Yatron	Y	N	N	N	N	Y	Y	N
7 Edgar	Y	Y	Y	Y	N	Y	Y	N
8 Kostmayer	Y	Y	Y	Y	N	Y	Y	N
9 ***Shuster***	Y	N	N	N	Y	Y	N	Y
10 ***McDade***	Y	N	X	N	N	Y	N	N
11 Harrison	?	N	Y	Y	N	Y	Y	N
12 Murtha	?	?	N	N	Y	Y	Y	N
13 ***Coughlin***	N	Y	Y	Y	N	Y	Y	N
14 Coyne	Y	Y	Y	Y	Y	Y	Y	N
15 ***Ritter***	Y	N	N	Y	N	Y	Y	N
16 ***Walker***	N	N	N	N	Y	Y	N	Y
17 ***Gekas***	Y	N	N	N	N	Y	N	Y
18 Walgren	?	Y	Y	Y	Y	Y	Y	N
19 ***Goodling***	N	Y	N	Y	Y	Y	Y	N
20 Gaydos	Y	Y	N	N	Y	Y	Y	N
21 ***Ridge***	Y	N	N	N	N	Y	Y	N
22 Murphy	Y	N	N	N	Y	Y	Y	N
23 ***Clinger***	Y	N	Y	N	N	Y	Y	N
RHODE ISLAND								
1 St Germain	P	N	Y	N	Y	Y	Y	N
2 ***Schneider***	Y	Y	Y	Y	N	Y	N	N
SOUTH CAROLINA								
1 ***Hartnett***	Y	N	N	N	Y	Y	N	Y
2 ***Spence***	Y	N	N	N	Y	Y	N	Y
3 Derrick	N	N	Y	Y	N	Y	Y	N
4 ***Campbell***	Y	N	N	N	Y	Y	N	Y
5 Spratt	Y	N	N	N	N	Y	Y	N
6 Tallon	Y	N	N	Y	Y	Y	Y	N
SOUTH DAKOTA								
AL Daschle	Y	Y	N	Y	N	Y	Y	?
TENNESSEE								
1 ***Quillen***	Y	N	N	N	Y	Y	N	Y
2 ***Duncan***	Y	N	N	N	Y	Y	N	Y
3 Lloyd	Y	N	N	N	N	Y	N	Y
4 Cooper	Y	N	Y	N	N	Y	Y	N
5 Boner	Y	N	N	N	Y	Y	Y	N
6 Gore	Y	N	N	N	N	Y	Y	N
7 ***Sundquist***	Y	N	N	N	Y	Y	N	Y
8 Jones	Y	N	N	N	Y	Y	Y	N
9 Ford	Y	Y	Y	Y	Y	Y	Y	N
TEXAS								
1 Hall, S.	Y	N	N	N	Y	Y	N	Y
2 Wilson	?	N	?	N	Y	Y	N	Y
3 ***Bartlett***	Y	N	N	N	Y	Y	N	Y
4 Hall, R.	Y	N	N	N	Y	Y	N	Y
5 Bryant	Y	N	N	Y	Y	Y	Y	N
6 ***Gramm***	Y	N	N	N	N	Y	?	?
7 ***Archer***	Y	N	N	N	Y	Y	N	Y
8 ***Fields***	Y	N	N	N	Y	Y	N	Y
9 Brooks	Y	N	Y	N	N	Y	?	?
10 Pickle	Y	N	N	N	Y	Y	Y	N
11 Leath	Y	N	N	N	Y	Y	N	Y
12 Wright	Y	N	N	N	Y	Y	N	Y
13 Hightower	Y	N	N	N	Y	Y	N	Y
14 Patman	Y	N	N	N	N	Y	N	Y
15 de la Garza	Y	N	N	N	Y	Y	N	Y
16 Coleman	Y	N	N	N	N	Y	N	Y
17 Stenholm	N	N	N	N	Y	Y	N	Y
18 Leland	Y	Y	Y	Y	N	Y	Y	N
19 Hance	?	X	X	?	?	?	?	?
20 Gonzalez	Y	P	N	P	Y	Y	N	N
21 ***Loeffler***	Y	N	N	N	Y	Y	N	Y
22 ***Paul***	Y	Y	Y	Y	Y	Y	N	Y
23 Kazen	Y	N	N	N	N	Y	N	Y
24 Frost	Y	N	N	N	N	Y	N	Y
25 Andrews	Y	N	Y	N	Y	Y	N	Y
26 Vandergriff	Y	N	N	N	N	Y	N	Y
27 Ortiz	Y	N	N	N	N	Y	N	Y
UTAH								
1 ***Hansen***	Y	N	N	N	Y	Y	N	Y
2 ***Marriott***	Y	N	N	N	N	Y	N	Y
3 ***Nielson***	Y	N	N	N	N	Y	N	Y
VERMONT								
AL ***Jeffords***	Y	N	Y	N	N	Y	Y	N
VIRGINIA								
1 ***Bateman***	Y	N	N	N	N	Y	N	Y
2 ***Whitehurst***	Y	N	N	N	N	Y	N	Y
3 ***Bliley***	Y	N	N	N	N	Y	N	Y
4 Sisisky	Y	N	N	N	Y	Y	N	Y
5 Daniel	Y	N	N	N	Y	Y	N	Y
6 Olin	Y	N	N	Y	N	Y	Y	N
7 ***Robinson***	Y	N	N	N	N	Y	N	Y
8 ***Parris***	Y	N	N	N	N	Y	N	Y
9 Boucher	Y	N	N	N	N	Y	Y	N
10 ***Wolf***	Y	N	N	N	N	Y	N	Y
WASHINGTON								
1 ***Pritchard***	Y	N	N	N	Y	Y	Y	N
2 Swift	Y	Y	Y	Y	Y	Y	Y	N
3 Bonker	Y	Y	Y	Y	Y	Y	Y	N
4 ***Morrison***	Y	N	N	N	Y	Y	N	Y
5 Foley	Y	Y	N	N	Y	Y	Y	N
6 Dicks	Y	Y	N	N	Y	Y	Y	N
7 Lowry	Y	Y	Y	Y	Y	Y	Y	N
8 ***Chandler***	Y	N	N	N	Y	Y	Y	N
WEST VIRGINIA								
1 Mollohan	Y	N	N	N	Y	Y	Y	N
2 Staggers	Y	Y	Y	Y	Y	Y	Y	N
3 Wise	Y	N	Y	N	Y	Y	Y	N
4 Rahall	?	?	?	Y	N	Y	Y	N
WISCONSIN								
1 Aspin	Y	N	Y	N	Y	Y	Y	N
2 Kastenmeier	Y	Y	Y	Y	Y	Y	Y	N
3 ***Gunderson***	Y	N	Y	Y	Y	Y	Y	N
4 Kleczka	Y	N	N	N	Y	Y	Y	N
5 Moody	Y	Y	Y	Y	Y	N	Y	N
6 ***Petri***	Y	N	Y	N	Y	Y	N	Y
7 Obey	Y	Y	Y	Y	Y	N	Y	N
8 ***Roth***	Y	N	Y	Y	Y	Y	N	Y
9 ***Sensenbrenner***	?	?	?	?	?	?	?	?
WYOMING								
AL ***Cheney***	Y	N	N	N	Y	Y	N	Y

Southern states - Ala., Ark., Fla., Ga., Ky., La., Miss., N.C., Okla., S.C., Tenn., Texas, Va.

154. HR 5167. Department of Defense Authorization. Byron, D-Md., amendment to the McCurdy, D-Okla., substitute to the Brown, D-Calif., amendment, to provide that the anti-satellite missile (ASAT) may be tested against an object in space as many times as the Soviet ASAT has been tested against an object in space. Rejected 181-229: R 127-33; D 54-196 (ND 9-159, SD 45-37), May 23, 1984.

155. HR 5167. Department of Defense Authorization. McCurdy, D-Okla., substitute to the Brown, D-Calif., amendment, to bar testing of the anti-satellite missile (ASAT) against an object in space through March 31, 1985, and allowing tests thereafter only if the president certifies that he has invited the Soviet Union to resume negotiations to limit ASATs. Rejected 186-228: R 127-33; D 59-195 (ND 12-158, SD 47-37), May 23, 1984. (The Brown amendment, as amended, which provided that no funds may be used to test the anti-satellite missile (ASAT) against a target in space unless the Soviet Union conducts a test of its ASAT after enactment of the bill, subsequently was adopted by voice vote.)

156. HR 5167. Department of Defense Authorization. Foley, D-Wash., amendment to bar the use of authorized funds to introduce combat troops into El Salvador and Nicaragua, except in certain circumstances. Adopted 341-64: R 97-62; D 244-2 (ND 165-0, SD 79-2), May 23, 1984.

157. HR 5167. Department of Defense Authorization. Hartnett, R-S.C., amendment to bar the use of authorized funds to introduce combat troops into Western Europe, the Middle East or Korea, except in certain circumstances. Rejected 27-379: R 7-152; D 20-227 (ND 17-151, SD 3-76), May 23, 1984.

158. Procedural Motion. Fields, R-Texas, motion to approve the House *Journal* of Wednesday, May 23. Motion agreed to 324-51: R 114-36; D 210-15 (ND 139-10, SD 71-5), May 24, 1984.

159. HR 5692. Debt Limit. Passage of the bill to increase temporarily the debt ceiling by $30 billion, from $1.49 trillion to $1.52 trillion, through June 22, 1984. Passed 211-198: R 69-90; D 142-108 (ND 99-66, SD 43-42), May 24, 1984. A "yea" was a vote supporting the president's position.

160. H J Res 492. Department of Agriculture, Fiscal 1984 Urgent Supplemental Appropriations. Adoption of the conference report on the bill to appropriate $1,061,894,000 in fiscal 1984 for the Department of Agriculture and other agencies. Adopted 376-36: R 124-31; D 252-5 (ND 167-4, SD 85-1), May 24, 1984. The president had requested $779,494,000 in new budget authority.

161. H J Res 492. Department of Agriculture, Fiscal 1984 Urgent Supplemental Appropriations. Long, D-Md., motion that the House recede from its disagreement to the Senate amendment providing $61.75 million in military aid to El Salvador. Motion agreed to 267-154: R 152-5; D 115-149 (ND 40-136, SD 75-13), May 24, 1984. A "yea" was a vote supporting the president's position.

KEY

- **Y** Voted for (yea).
- **#** Paired for.
- **+** Announced for.
- **N** Voted against (nay).
- **X** Paired against.
- **-** Announced against.
- **P** Voted "present".
- **C** Voted "present" to avoid possible conflict of interest.
- **?** Did not vote or otherwise make a position known.

Democrats *Republicans*

Member	154	155	156	157	158	159	160	161
ALABAMA								
1 *Edwards*	Y	Y	Y	N	Y	Y	Y	Y
2 *Dickinson*	Y	Y	Y	N	N	N	Y	?
3 Nichols	Y	Y	Y	N	Y	N	Y	Y
4 Bevill	Y	Y	Y	N	Y	Y	Y	Y
5 Flippo	Y	Y	Y	N	Y	Y	Y	Y
6 Erdreich	Y	Y	Y	N	Y	N	Y	Y
7 Shelby	Y	Y	Y	N	?	N	Y	Y
ALASKA								
AL *Young*	Y	Y	Y	N	N	N	Y	Y
ARIZONA								
1 *McCain*	Y	Y	N	N	Y	Y	Y	Y
2 Udall	N	N	Y	N	Y	Y	Y	Y
3 *Stump*	Y	Y	N	N	Y	N	N	Y
4 *Rudd*	Y	Y	N	N	Y	N	N	Y
5 McNulty	N	N	Y	N	Y	Y	Y	N
ARKANSAS								
1 Alexander	?	?	?	?	Y	Y	Y	Y
2 *Bethune*	Y	Y	Y	N	?	N	Y	Y
3 *Hammerschmidt*	Y	Y	Y	N	Y	N	Y	Y
4 Anthony	Y	Y	Y	?	Y	Y	Y	Y
CALIFORNIA								
1 Bosco	N	N	Y	N	Y	N	Y	N
2 *Chappie*	Y	Y	Y	N	Y	N	Y	Y
3 Matsui	N	N	Y	N	Y	Y	Y	N
4 Fazio	N	N	Y	N	Y	Y	Y	N
5 Burton	N	N	Y	N	Y	Y	Y	N
6 Boxer	N	N	Y	N	Y	P	Y	N
7 Miller	N	N	Y	N	Y	N	Y	N
8 Dellums	N	N	Y	Y	?	N	Y	N
9 Stark	N	N	Y	Y	Y	Y	Y	N
10 Edwards	N	N	Y	Y	Y	Y	Y	N
11 Lantos	N	N	Y	N	Y	N	Y	N
12 *Zschau*	N	N	N	N	N	Y	Y	Y
13 Mineta	N	N	Y	N	Y	Y	Y	N
14 *Shumway*	Y	Y	N	N	Y	N	N	Y
15 Coelho	N	N	Y	N	?	?	?	N
16 Panetta	N	N	Y	N	Y	Y	Y	N
17 *Pashayan*	Y	Y	Y	N	Y	N	N	Y
18 Lehman	N	N	Y	N	Y	N	Y	N
19 *Lagomarsino*	Y	Y	Y	N	Y	Y	Y	Y
20 *Thomas*	Y	Y	Y	N	Y	N	Y	Y
21 *Fiedler*	Y	Y	Y	N	N	N	Y	Y
22 *Moorhead*	Y	Y	N	N	Y	N	N	Y
23 Beilenson	N	N	Y	?	Y	Y	Y	N
24 Waxman	N	N	Y	N	?	Y	Y	N
25 Roybal	N	N	Y	N	Y	Y	Y	N
26 Berman	N	N	Y	N	Y	Y	Y	N
27 Levine	N	N	Y	N	Y	Y	Y	N
28 Dixon	N	N	Y	N	Y	Y	Y	N
29 Hawkins	?	N	Y	N	?	N	Y	N
30 Martinez	N	N	Y	N	Y	Y	Y	N
31 Dymally	N	N	Y	N	P	N	Y	N
32 Anderson	Y	N	Y	N	Y	N	Y	N
33 *Dreier*	Y	Y	N	N	Y	N	N	Y
34 Torres	N	N	Y	N	Y	Y	Y	N
35 *Lewis*	Y	Y	Y	N	Y	N	Y	?
36 Brown	N	N	Y	N	Y	Y	Y	N
37 *McCandless*	Y	Y	Y	N	Y	N	N	Y
38 Patterson	N	N	Y	N	?	N	Y	N
39 *Dannemeyer*	Y	Y	N	N	Y	N	N	Y
40 *Badham*	Y	Y	N	N	Y	N	N	Y
41 *Lowery*	Y	Y	N	N	Y	Y	Y	Y
42 *Lungren*	Y	Y	N	N	Y	N	N	Y
43 *Packard*	Y	Y	N	N	N	N	Y	Y
44 Bates	N	N	Y	N	Y	N	Y	N
45 *Hunter*	Y	Y	N	N	?	Y	Y	Y
COLORADO								
1 Schroeder	N	N	Y	N	Y	Y	Y	N
2 Wirth	N	N	Y	N	Y	Y	Y	N
3 Kogovsek	N	N	Y	N	Y	Y	Y	N
4 *Brown*	Y	Y	Y	N	Y	N	N	Y
5 *Kramer*	Y	Y	N	N	N	N	N	Y
6 *Schaefer*	Y	Y	N	N	N	N	N	Y
CONNECTICUT								
1 Kennelly	N	N	Y	N	Y	Y	Y	N
2 Gejdenson	N	N	Y	N	N	N	Y	N
3 Morrison	N	N	Y	N	Y	Y	Y	N
4 *McKinney*	N	N	Y	N	Y	Y	Y	Y
5 Ratchford	N	N	Y	N	Y	Y	Y	N
6 *Johnson*	N	N	Y	N	Y	Y	Y	N
DELAWARE								
AL Carper	N	N	Y	N	Y	Y	Y	Y
FLORIDA								
1 Hutto	Y	Y	Y	N	?	N	Y	Y
2 Fuqua	Y	Y	?	N	Y	Y	Y	Y
3 Bennett	Y	Y	Y	N	Y	Y	Y	Y
4 Chappell	Y	Y	Y	N	Y	N	Y	Y
5 *McCollum*	Y	Y	N	N	?	?	?	Y
6 MacKay	N	N	Y	N	Y	N	Y	N
7 Gibbons	N	N	Y	N	?	Y	Y	Y
8 *Young*	N	N	Y	Y	?	N	N	Y
9 *Bilirakis*	Y	Y	N	N	N	N	N	Y
10 *Ireland*	Y	Y	Y	N	Y	N	Y	Y
11 Nelson	Y	Y	Y	N	Y	N	Y	N
12 *Lewis*	Y	Y	Y	N	Y	N	Y	Y
13 *Mack*	Y	Y	N	N	N	N	N	Y
14 Mica	N	N	Y	N	Y	N	Y	N
15 *Shaw*	Y	Y	N	N	Y	N	N	Y
16 Smith	N	N	Y	N	Y	Y	Y	N
17 Lehman	N	N	Y	N	Y	Y	Y	N
18 Pepper	N	N	Y	N	Y	Y	Y	N
19 Fascell	N	N	Y	N	P	Y	Y	Y
GEORGIA								
1 Thomas	Y	Y	Y	N	Y	Y	Y	Y
2 Hatcher	Y	Y	?	?	Y	Y	Y	Y
3 Ray	Y	Y	Y	N	Y	N	Y	Y
4 Levitas	Y	N	Y	N	Y	Y	Y	Y
5 Fowler	N	N	Y	N	Y	Y	Y	N
6 *Gingrich*	Y	Y	N	N	Y	N	N	Y
7 Darden	Y	Y	Y	N	Y	N	Y	Y
8 Rowland	N	N	Y	N	Y	N	Y	Y
9 Jenkins	N	N	Y	N	N	N	Y	Y
10 Barnard	?	?	?	?	?	Y	Y	Y
HAWAII								
1 Heftel	N	N	Y	N	?	?	?	Y
2 Akaka	N	N	Y	N	Y	Y	Y	N
IDAHO								
1 *Craig*	Y	Y	Y	N	Y	N	N	Y
2 *Hansen*	?	?	?	?	?	?	?	?
ILLINOIS								
1 Hayes	N	N	Y	N	N	N	Y	N
2 Savage	N	N	Y	Y	Y	N	Y	N
3 Russo	N	N	Y	N	Y	N	Y	N
4 *O'Brien*	Y	Y	N	N	Y	Y	Y	Y
5 Lipinski	N	N	Y	N	Y	Y	Y	Y
6 *Hyde*	Y	Y	N	N	Y	N	Y	Y
7 Collins	N	N	Y	N	Y	N	Y	N
8 Rostenkowski	N	N	Y	N	Y	Y	Y	N
9 Yates	N	N	Y	N	Y	Y	Y	N
10 *Porter*	N	N	Y	N	Y	Y	Y	N
11 Annunzio	Y	Y	Y	N	Y	Y	Y	Y
12 *Crane, P.*	Y	Y	N	N	Y	N	N	Y
13 *Erlenborn*	Y	Y	Y	N	Y	Y	Y	Y
14 *Corcoran*	Y	Y	N	N	?	Y	Y	Y
15 *Madigan*	Y	Y	Y	N	Y	Y	Y	Y
16 *Martin*	Y	Y	Y	N	Y	N	?	Y
17 Evans	N	N	Y	Y	Y	Y	Y	N
18 *Michel*	Y	Y	N	N	Y	Y	Y	Y
19 *Crane, D.*	Y	Y	N	N	Y	N	N	Y
20 Durbin	N	N	Y	N	N	N	Y	Y
21 Price	N	Y	Y	N	Y	Y	Y	Y
22 Simon	N	N	Y	N	Y	Y	?	Y
INDIANA								
1 Hall	N	N	Y	N	Y	N	Y	N
2 Sharp	-	+	-	?	?	+	+	?
3 *Hiler*	Y	Y	N	N	Y	N	Y	Y
4 *Coats*	Y	Y	N	N	Y	N	Y	Y
5 *Hillis*	Y	Y	Y	N	Y	Y	Y	Y

ND - Northern Democrats SD - Southern Democrats

Corresponding to Congressional Record Votes 173, 174, 175, 176, 177, 178, 179, 180

	154	155	156	157	158	159	160	161
6 ***Burton***	Y	Y	N	N	N	N	N	Y
7 ***Myers***	Y	Y	Y	N	Y	N	Y	Y
8 McCloskey	N	N	Y	N	Y	Y	Y	N
9 Hamilton	N	N	Y	N	Y	Y	Y	Y
10 Jacobs	N	N	?	N	N	N	N	N
IOWA								
1 ***Leach***	N	N	Y	N	Y	N	Y	N
2 ***Tauke***	N	N	Y	N	Y	Y	Y	Y
3 ***Evans***	N	N	Y	N	?	N	N	Y
4 Smith	N	N	Y	N	Y	N	Y	Y
5 Harkin	N	N	?	?	N	N	Y	N
6 Bedell	N	N	Y	Y	Y	Y	Y	Y
KANSAS								
1 ***Roberts***	Y	Y	Y	N	N	N	Y	Y
2 Slattery	N	Y	Y	N	Y	N	Y	Y
3 ***Winn***	Y	Y	Y	N	Y	N	Y	Y
4 Glickman	?	?	+	N	Y	N	Y	Y
5 ***Whittaker***	Y	Y	Y	N	N	N	Y	Y
KENTUCKY								
1 Hubbard	Y	Y	Y	N	Y	N	Y	Y
2 Natcher	Y	Y	Y	N	Y	N	Y	N
3 Mazzoli	N	N	Y	N	Y	N	Y	N
4 ***Snyder***	Y	Y	Y	Y	Y	N	Y	Y
5 ***Rogers***	Y	Y	N	N	N	Y	Y	Y
6 ***Hopkins***	Y	N	Y	N	Y	N	Y	Y
7 Perkins	Y	Y	Y	N	Y	Y	Y	N
LOUISIANA								
1 ***Livingston***	Y	Y	N	N	Y	Y	Y	Y
2 Boggs	?	N	Y	N	?	Y	Y	Y
3 Tauzin	Y	Y	Y	N	Y	N	Y	Y
4 Roemer	N	N	Y	Y	N	N	Y	Y
5 Huckaby	N	N	Y	N	Y	N	Y	Y
6 ***Moore***	N	N	Y	N	Y	N	Y	Y
7 Breaux	Y	Y	?	?	Y	N	Y	Y
8 Long	N	N	Y	N	Y	Y	Y	Y
MAINE								
1 ***McKernan***	N	N	Y	N	Y	Y	Y	Y
2 ***Snowe***	N	N	Y	N	Y	Y	Y	Y
MARYLAND								
1 Dyson	Y	Y	Y	N	Y	N	Y	Y
2 Long	N	N	Y	N	Y	N	Y	Y
3 Mikulski	?	?	?	?	?	?	Y	N
4 ***Holt***	Y	Y	Y	N	N	Y	Y	Y
5 Hoyer	N	N	Y	N	Y	Y	Y	Y
6 Byron	Y	Y	Y	N	?	N	Y	Y
7 Mitchell	N	N	Y	Y	N	Y	Y	N
8 Barnes	N	N	Y	N	Y	Y	Y	Y
MASSACHUSETTS								
1 ***Conte***	N	N	Y	N	Y	Y	Y	N
2 Boland	N	N	Y	N	Y	Y	Y	Y
3 Early	N	N	Y	N	Y	N	Y	N
4 Frank	N	N	Y	N	Y	Y	Y	N
5 Shannon	N	N	Y	N	Y	Y	Y	N
6 Mavroules	N	N	Y	N	Y	Y	Y	N
7 Markey	-	-	+	-	Y	Y	?	N
8 O'Neill								
9 Moakley	N	N	Y	N	Y	Y	Y	N
10 Studds	N	N	Y	N	Y	Y	Y	N
11 Donnelly	N	N	Y	N	Y	Y	Y	N
MICHIGAN								
1 Conyers	N	N	Y	Y	?	?	Y	N
2 ***Pursell***	N	N	Y	N	Y	N	Y	Y
3 Wolpe	N	N	Y	N	Y	Y	Y	N
4 ***Siljander***	Y	Y	N	N	Y	N	N	Y
5 ***Sawyer***	Y	Y	Y	N	Y	?	?	?
6 Carr	N	N	Y	N	P	N	Y	N
7 Kildee	N	N	Y	N	Y	Y	Y	N
8 Traxler	N	N	Y	N	Y	N	Y	?
9 ***Vander Jagt***	Y	Y	Y	N	?	Y	Y	Y
10 Albosta	N	N	Y	N	Y	N	Y	N
11 ***Davis***	Y	Y	Y	N	Y	Y	Y	Y
12 Bonior	N	N	Y	N	Y	Y	Y	N
13 Crockett	?	?	?	?	?	N	Y	N
14 Hertel	N	N	Y	N	Y	Y	Y	N
15 Ford	N	N	?	?	?	#	?	N
16 Dingell	N	N	Y	N	Y	Y	Y	N
17 Levin	N	N	Y	N	Y	Y	Y	N
18 ***Broomfield***	Y	Y	N	N	N	Y	Y	Y
MINNESOTA								
1 Penny	N	N	Y	N	N	N	Y	N
2 ***Weber***	Y	Y	N	N	Y	N	Y	Y
3 ***Frenzel***	N	N	Y	N	Y	Y	Y	Y
4 Vento	N	N	Y	N	Y	Y	Y	N
5 Sabo	N	N	Y	N	N	Y	Y	N
6 Sikorski	N	N	Y	N	N	Y	Y	N

	154	155	156	157	158	159	160	161
7 ***Stangeland***	Y	Y	?	N	Y	N	Y	Y
8 Oberstar	N	N	Y	N	P	Y	Y	N
MISSISSIPPI								
1 Whitten	Y	Y	Y	N	Y	Y	Y	Y
2 ***Franklin***	Y	Y	N	N	Y	N	Y	Y
3 Montgomery	Y	Y	Y	N	Y	N	Y	Y
4 Dowdy	?	?	?	N	Y	Y	Y	Y
5 ***Lott***	Y	Y	N	N	Y	Y	Y	Y
MISSOURI								
1 Clay	N	N	Y	Y	?	?	Y	N
2 Young	Y	Y	Y	N	Y	Y	Y	Y
3 Gephardt	N	N	Y	N	Y	Y	Y	Y
4 Skelton	Y	Y	Y	N	Y	Y	Y	Y
5 Wheat	N	N	Y	N	?	Y	Y	N
6 ***Coleman***	Y	Y	Y	N	?	Y	Y	Y
7 ***Taylor***	Y	Y	Y	N	Y	N	Y	Y
8 ***Emerson***	Y	Y	Y	N	N	N	Y	Y
9 Volkmer	N	Y	Y	N	Y	Y	Y	N
MONTANA								
1 Williams	N	N	Y	Y	?	Y	Y	N
2 ***Marlenee***	Y	Y	N	N	Y	N	Y	Y
NEBRASKA								
1 ***Bereuter***	N	N	Y	N	Y	N	Y	Y
2 ***Daub***	Y	Y	Y	N	N	N	Y	Y
3 ***Smith***	Y	Y	Y	N	Y	N	Y	Y
NEVADA								
1 Reid	N	N	Y	N	Y	Y	Y	Y
2 ***Vucanovich***	Y	Y	N	N	Y	N	N	Y
NEW HAMPSHIRE								
1 D'Amours	N	N	Y	N	Y	N	Y	Y
2 ***Gregg***	Y	Y	N	N	N	Y	N	Y
NEW JERSEY								
1 Florio	N	N	?	N	Y	N	Y	Y
2 Hughes	N	N	Y	N	Y	N	Y	Y
3 Howard	N	N	Y	N	Y	P	Y	N
4 ***Smith***	N	N	Y	N	Y	N	Y	Y
5 ***Roukema***	N	N	Y	N	?	?	?	?
6 Dwyer	N	N	Y	N	Y	Y	Y	N
7 ***Rinaldo***	N	N	Y	N	Y	N	Y	Y
8 Roe	N	N	Y	N	Y	N	Y	N
9 Torricelli	Y	Y	Y	N	Y	N	Y	N
10 Rodino	N	N	Y	N	Y	Y	Y	N
11 Minish	N	N	Y	N	Y	Y	Y	Y
12 ***Courter***	?	?	?	?	Y	N	Y	Y
13 Vacancy								
14 Guarini	N	N	Y	N	Y	Y	Y	N
NEW MEXICO								
1 ***Lujan***	Y	Y	N	N	Y	N	Y	Y
2 ***Skeen***	Y	Y	N	N	N	N	Y	Y
3 Richardson	N	N	Y	N	Y	N	Y	N
NEW YORK								
1 ***Carney***	Y	Y	Y	Y	Y	N	Y	Y
2 Downey	N	N	Y	N	Y	Y	Y	N
3 Mrazek	N	N	Y	N	Y	N	Y	N
4 ***Lent***	Y	Y	Y	N	?	N	Y	Y
5 ***McGrath***	Y	Y	Y	N	N	N	Y	Y
6 Addabbo	N	N	Y	N	Y	Y	Y	N
7 Ackerman	N	N	Y	N	Y	N	Y	N
8 Scheuer	N	N	Y	N	Y	Y	Y	N
9 Ferraro	N	N	Y	N	Y	N	Y	N
10 Schumer	N	N	Y	N	Y	Y	Y	N
11 Towns	N	N	Y	N	Y	N	Y	N
12 Owens	N	N	Y	N	Y	N	Y	N
13 Solarz	N	N	Y	N	Y	Y	Y	N
14 ***Molinari***	Y	Y	Y	N	Y	N	Y	Y
15 ***Green***	N	N	Y	N	Y	Y	Y	N
16 Rangel	N	N	Y	Y	?	Y	Y	N
17 Weiss	N	N	Y	Y	Y	N	Y	N
18 Garcia	N	N	Y	Y	Y	Y	Y	N
19 Biaggi	N	N	Y	N	Y	Y	Y	Y
20 Ottinger	N	N	Y	N	?	Y	Y	N
21 ***Fish***	N	N	Y	?	Y	Y	Y	Y
22 ***Gilman***	N	Y	Y	N	?	N	Y	Y
23 Stratton	Y	Y	Y	N	Y	Y	Y	Y
24 ***Solomon***	Y	Y	Y	N	N	N	Y	Y
25 ***Boehlert***	N	N	Y	N	Y	Y	Y	Y
26 ***Martin***	Y	Y	N	N	N	Y	Y	Y
27 ***Wortley***	Y	Y	N	N	Y	N	Y	Y
28 McHugh	N	N	Y	N	Y	Y	Y	Y
29 ***Horton***	N	N	Y	N	Y	Y	Y	Y
30 ***Conable***	Y	Y	Y	N	Y	Y	Y	Y
31 ***Kemp***	Y	Y	N	N	Y	Y	Y	Y
32 LaFalce	N	N	Y	N	Y	N	Y	Y
33 Nowak	N	N	Y	N	Y	Y	Y	N
34 Lundine	?	?	?	?	P	Y	Y	N

	154	155	156	157	158	159	160	161
NORTH CAROLINA								
1 Jones	Y	N	Y	?	Y	Y	Y	N
2 Valentine	Y	Y	Y	N	Y	N	Y	Y
3 Whitley	Y	Y	Y	N	Y	Y	Y	Y
4 Andrews	?	Y	Y	?	Y	Y	Y	Y
5 Neal	N	N	Y	N	?	N	Y	Y
6 Britt	N	N	Y	N	Y	N	Y	Y
7 Rose	N	N	Y	N	Y	Y	Y	N
8 Hefner	N	N	Y	N	Y	Y	Y	Y
9 ***Martin***	?	?	?	?	Y	Y	Y	Y
10 ***Broyhill***	Y	Y	Y	N	Y	Y	Y	Y
11 Clarke	N	N	Y	N	Y	Y	Y	Y
NORTH DAKOTA								
AL Dorgan	N	N	Y	N	Y	Y	Y	N
OHIO								
1 Luken	N	N	Y	N	Y	N	Y	N
2 ***Gradison***	N	N	Y	Y	Y	Y	Y	Y
3 Hall	N	N	Y	N	?	Y	Y	N
4 ***Oxley***	Y	Y	N	N	N	Y	Y	Y
5 ***Latta***	Y	Y	Y	N	Y	N	Y	Y
6 ***McEwen***	Y	Y	N	N	Y	N	N	Y
7 ***DeWine***	Y	Y	N	N	Y	N	Y	Y
8 ***Kindness***	?	?	N	N	Y	N	Y	Y
9 Kaptur	N	N	Y	N	?	N	Y	N
10 ***Miller***	Y	Y	Y	N	N	N	Y	Y
11 Eckart	N	N	Y	N	Y	N	Y	N
12 ***Kasich***	Y	Y	Y	N	Y	N	Y	Y
13 Pease	N	N	Y	Y	Y	Y	Y	N
14 Seiberling	N	N	Y	N	Y	N	Y	N
15 ***Wylie***	Y	Y	Y	N	Y	Y	Y	Y
16 ***Regula***	N	N	Y	N	Y	Y	Y	Y
17 ***Williams***	Y	Y	Y	N	Y	Y	Y	?
18 Applegate	Y	Y	Y	Y	?	N	Y	N
19 Feighan	N	N	?	?	Y	N	Y	N
20 Oakar	N	N	Y	Y	Y	N	Y	N
21 Stokes	N	N	Y	N	Y	Y	Y	N
OKLAHOMA								
1 Jones	N	Y	Y	N	N	P	Y	Y
2 Synar	N	N	Y	N	Y	Y	Y	Y
3 Watkins	?	?	?	?	?	?	?	?
4 McCurdy	N	Y	Y	N	Y	N	Y	Y
5 ***Edwards***	Y	Y	Y	N	Y	N	Y	Y
6 English	N	Y	Y	N	Y	N	Y	Y
OREGON								
1 AuCoin	N	N	Y	N	Y	N	Y	N
2 ***Smith, R.***	Y	Y	Y	N	Y	N	Y	Y
3 Wyden	N	N	Y	N	Y	N	Y	N
4 Weaver	N	N	?	Y	Y	N	N	N
5 ***Smith, D.***	Y	Y	N	N	N	N	N	Y
PENNSYLVANIA								
1 Foglietta	N	N	Y	N	Y	Y	Y	N
2 Gray	N	N	Y	N	Y	P	Y	N
3 Borski	N	N	Y	N	Y	Y	Y	N
4 Kolter	N	N	Y	N	Y	N	Y	N
5 ***Schulze***	Y	Y	Y	N	Y	Y	Y	Y
6 Yatron	N	N	Y	N	Y	N	Y	Y
7 Edgar	N	N	Y	N	Y	Y	Y	N
8 Kostmayer	N	N	Y	N	Y	Y	Y	N
9 ***Shuster***	Y	Y	Y	Y	Y	N	N	Y
10 ***McDade***	N	Y	Y	N	Y	Y	Y	Y
11 Harrison	N	N	Y	N	?	Y	Y	N
12 Murtha	N	N	Y	N	Y	Y	Y	Y
13 ***Coughlin***	N	N	Y	N	N	N	Y	Y
14 Coyne	N	N	Y	N	Y	Y	Y	N
15 ***Ritter***	Y	Y	N	N	Y	N	Y	N
16 ***Walker***	Y	Y	N	N	N	N	N	Y
17 ***Gekas***	Y	Y	Y	N	Y	Y	Y	Y
18 Walgren	N	N	Y	N	Y	N	Y	N
19 ***Goodling***	Y	N	Y	Y	N	N	Y	Y
20 Gaydos	N	N	Y	N	?	N	Y	Y
21 ***Ridge***	N	N	Y	N	Y	N	Y	Y
22 Murphy	N	N	Y	N	Y	N	Y	Y
23 ***Clinger***	Y	N	Y	N	N	Y	Y	Y
RHODE ISLAND								
1 St Germain	N	N	Y	N	P	P	Y	N
2 ***Schneider***	N	N	Y	N	Y	Y	Y	N
SOUTH CAROLINA								
1 ***Hartnett***	Y	Y	N	N	Y	N	Y	Y
2 ***Spence***	Y	Y	N	N	Y	N	Y	Y
3 Derrick	N	N	Y	N	?	N	Y	Y
4 ***Campbell***	Y	Y	N	N	Y	Y	Y	Y
5 Spratt	N	N	Y	N	Y	Y	Y	Y
6 Tallon	N	N	Y	N	Y	N	Y	Y
SOUTH DAKOTA								
AL Daschle	?	N	Y	N	Y	N	Y	N

	154	155	156	157	158	159	160	161
TENNESSEE								
1 ***Quillen***	Y	Y	Y	N	Y	Y	Y	Y
2 ***Duncan***	Y	Y	Y	N	Y	Y	Y	Y
3 Lloyd	Y	Y	Y	N	N	N	Y	Y
4 Cooper	N	N	Y	N	Y	Y	Y	Y
5 Boner	N	N	Y	N	Y	N	Y	Y
6 Gore	N	N	Y	N	Y	Y	Y	Y
7 ***Sundquist***	Y	Y	N	N	Y	Y	Y	Y
8 Jones	N	N	Y	N	Y	N	Y	N
9 Ford	N	N	Y	?	?	Y	Y	N
TEXAS								
1 Hall, S.	Y	Y	Y	N	Y	N	N	Y
2 Wilson	Y	Y	N	N	?	?	?	Y
3 ***Bartlett***	Y	Y	Y	N	Y	Y	Y	Y
4 Hall, R.	Y	Y	Y	N	Y	N	Y	Y
5 Bryant	N	N	Y	N	Y	N	Y	N
6 ***Gramm***	?	?	?	?	?	?	?	?
7 ***Archer***	Y	Y	N	N	Y	N	N	Y
8 ***Fields***	Y	Y	Y	N	N	N	N	Y
9 Brooks	?	?	?	N	Y	Y	Y	N
10 Pickle	N	N	Y	N	Y	Y	Y	Y
11 Leath	Y	Y	N	N	?	?	?	Y
12 Wright	Y	Y	Y	N	Y	Y	Y	Y
13 Hightower	Y	Y	Y	N	Y	N	Y	Y
14 Patman	Y	Y	Y	N	Y	N	Y	Y
15 de la Garza	Y	Y	Y	N	?	Y	Y	Y
16 Coleman	Y	Y	Y	N	Y	Y	Y	Y
17 Stenholm	Y	Y	Y	N	N	N	Y	Y
18 Leland	N	N	Y	Y	Y	Y	Y	N
19 Hance	?	?	?	?	?	X	?	?
20 Gonzalez	N	N	Y	N	Y	N	Y	N
21 ***Loeffler***	Y	Y	N	N	Y	Y	Y	Y
22 ***Paul***	Y	Y	?	?	Y	N	N	N
23 Kazen	Y	Y	Y	N	Y	N	Y	Y
24 Frost	Y	Y	Y	?	Y	Y	Y	Y
25 Andrews	Y	Y	Y	N	Y	Y	Y	Y
26 Vandergriff	Y	Y	Y	N	Y	N	Y	Y
27 Ortiz	Y	Y	Y	N	Y	Y	Y	Y
UTAH								
1 ***Hansen***	Y	Y	N	N	N	N	N	Y
2 ***Marriott***	Y	Y	N	N	?	?	?	?
3 ***Nielson***	Y	Y	N	N	N	N	N	Y
VERMONT								
AL ***Jeffords***	N	N	Y	N	Y	Y	Y	Y
VIRGINIA								
1 ***Bateman***	Y	Y	N	N	Y	Y	Y	Y
2 ***Whitehurst***	Y	Y	Y	N	Y	Y	Y	Y
3 ***Bliley***	Y	Y	Y	N	N	Y	Y	Y
4 Sisisky	Y	Y	Y	N	Y	Y	Y	Y
5 Daniel	Y	Y	Y	N	Y	N	Y	Y
6 Olin	N	N	Y	N	Y	Y	Y	Y
7 ***Robinson***	Y	Y	N	N	Y	Y	Y	Y
8 ***Parris***	Y	Y	Y	N	Y	Y	Y	Y
9 Boucher	N	N	Y	N	Y	N	Y	Y
10 ***Wolf***	Y	Y	Y	N	Y	Y	?	Y
WASHINGTON								
1 ***Pritchard***	N	N	Y	N	?	Y	?	Y
2 Swift	N	N	Y	N	Y	Y	Y	N
3 Bonker	N	?	Y	N	Y	Y	Y	Y
4 ***Morrison***	Y	Y	Y	N	Y	Y	Y	Y
5 Foley	?	N	N	Y	N	Y	Y	Y
6 Dicks	N	N	Y	N	Y	Y	Y	Y
7 Lowry	N	N	Y	N	Y	Y	Y	N
8 ***Chandler***	N	N	Y	N	Y	Y	Y	Y
WEST VIRGINIA								
1 Mollohan	N	N	Y	N	Y	Y	Y	Y
2 Staggers	N	N	Y	N	Y	Y	Y	N
3 Wise	N	N	Y	N	+	-	Y	N
4 Rahall	N	N	Y	N	Y	Y	Y	N
WISCONSIN								
1 Aspin	N	N	Y	N	Y	Y	Y	Y
2 Kastenmeier	N	N	Y	Y	Y	N	N	N
3 ***Gunderson***	N	Y	Y	N	Y	N	Y	Y
4 Kleczka	N	N	Y	N	Y	Y	Y	N
5 Moody	N	N	Y	N	Y	N	Y	N
6 ***Petri***	Y	Y	Y	N	Y	N	Y	Y
7 Obey	N	N	Y	N	Y	N	N	N
8 ***Roth***	Y	Y	N	N	Y	N	Y	Y
9 ***Sensenbrenner***	?	?	?	?	?	?	?	?
WYOMING								
AL ***Cheney***	Y	Y	N	N	Y	Y	N	Y

Southern states - Ala., Ark., Fla., Ga., Ky., La., Miss., N.C., Okla., S.C., Tenn., Texas, Va.

162. H J Res 492. Department of Agriculture, Fiscal 1984 Urgent Supplemental Appropriations.
Boland, D-Mass., motion that the House recede from its disagreement to the Senate amendment providing $21 million in covert aid to Nicaraguan rebels, with an amendment providing no funds for Nicaraguan rebels. Motion agreed to 241-177: R 24-132; D 217-45 (ND 169-6, SD 48-39), May 24, 1984. A "nay" was a vote supporting the president's position.

163. HR 5167. Department of Defense Authorization.
Hunter, R-Calif., amendment to bar the use of authorized funds to introduce combat troops into El Salvador or Nicaragua unless the president determines that a communist threat to the region exists. Rejected 99-288: R 93-53; D 6-235 (ND 0-159, SD 6-76), May 24, 1984.

164. HR 2174. Bankruptcy Court Extension.
Rodino, D-N.J., motion to agree with the Senate amendments to the bill to extend from May 25, 1984, until June 20, 1984, a period of transition to a new bankruptcy court system established under the 1978 Bankruptcy Reform Act (PL 95-598). Motion agreed to 349-27: R 117-26; D 232-1 (ND 153-1, SD 79-0), May 24, 1984.

165. Procedural Motion.
Lott, R-Miss., motion to approve the House *Journal* of Thursday, May 24. Motion agreed to 284-25: R 107-15; D 177-10 (ND 118-10, SD 59-0), May 30, 1984.

166. HR 5713. Department of Housing and Urban Development Appropriations, Fiscal 1985.
Adoption of the rule (H Res 511) providing for House floor consideration of the bill to appropriate funds for the Department of Housing and Urban Development and 17 independent agencies for fiscal 1985. Adopted 296-56: R 80-54; D 216-2 (ND 148-0, SD 68-2), May 30, 1984.

167. HR 5713. Department of Housing and Urban Development Appropriations, Fiscal 1985.
Walker, R-Pa., amendment to authorize the president to cut any item in the bill by up to 10 percent. Rejected 133-258: R 114-38; D 19-220 (ND 5-157, SD 14-63), May 30, 1984.

168. HR 5713. Department of Housing and Urban Development Appropriations, Fiscal 1985.
Passage of the bill to appropriate $58,436,496,500 for the Department of Housing and Urban Development and 17 independent agencies in fiscal 1985. Passed 282-110: R 65-87; D 217-23 (ND 155-8, SD 62-15), May 30, 1984. The president had requested $54,668,498,000 in new budget authority.

169. HR 5167. Department of Defense Authorization.
Bedell, D-Iowa, amendment to the Nichols, D-Ala., amendment *(see vote 170, p. 56-H)*, to bar the Pentagon from limiting competitive bidding only to persons on a list of qualified bidders. Adopted 324-75: R 121-34; D 203-41 (ND 147-18, SD 56-23), May 30, 1984.

KEY

Y Voted for (yea).
\# Paired for.
+ Announced for.
N Voted against (nay).
X Paired against.
- Announced against.
P Voted "present".
C Voted "present" to avoid possible conflict of interest.
? Did not vote or otherwise make a position known.

Democrats   *Republicans*

	162	163	164	165	166	167	168	169
ALABAMA								
1 *Edwards*	N	N	Y	Y	Y	N	?	N
2 *Dickinson*	N	Y	Y	N	N	Y	N	N
3 Nichols	N	N	Y	Y	Y	Y	Y	N
4 Bevill	N	N	Y	Y	Y	N	N	Y
5 Flippo	N	N	Y	Y	Y	N	Y	N
6 Erdreich	N	N	Y	Y	Y	N	Y	Y
7 Shelby	N	N	Y	?	Y	N	N	Y
ALASKA								
AL *Young*	N	Y	Y	N	Y	N	Y	Y
ARIZONA								
1 *McCain*	N	Y	Y	Y	Y	Y	N	N
2 Udall	Y	N	Y	?	Y	N	Y	Y
3 *Stump*	N	Y	Y	N	Y	N	Y	N
4 *Rudd*	N	Y	Y	?	?	Y	Y	N
5 McNulty	Y	N	?	?	?	N	Y	Y
ARKANSAS								
1 Alexander	Y	N	Y	Y	Y	N	Y	N
2 *Bethune*	N	Y	Y	?	N	Y	N	Y
3 *Hammerschmidt*	N	Y	Y	Y	Y	Y	N	Y
4 Anthony	Y	N	Y	?	?	?	?	?
CALIFORNIA								
1 Bosco	Y	?	?	Y	Y	N	Y	Y
2 *Chappie*	N	Y	Y	N	Y	Y	N	Y
3 Matsui	Y	N	Y	Y	Y	N	Y	Y
4 Fazio	Y	N	Y	Y	Y	N	Y	Y
5 Burton	Y	?	?	Y	Y	N	Y	Y
6 Boxer	Y	N	Y	Y	Y	N	Y	Y
7 Miller	Y	?	?	Y	Y	N	Y	Y
8 Dellums	Y	N	Y	Y	Y	N	Y	Y
9 Stark	Y	?	?	?	?	?	?	?
10 Edwards	Y	N	Y	Y	Y	N	Y	Y
11 Lantos	Y	N	Y	Y	Y	N	Y	Y
12 *Zschau*	Y	N	Y	Y	Y	Y	N	N
13 Mineta	Y	N	Y	Y	Y	N	Y	Y
14 *Shumway*	N	Y	N	Y	N	Y	N	Y
15 Coelho	Y	N	Y	Y	Y	N	Y	Y
16 Panetta	Y	N	Y	Y	Y	N	Y	Y
17 *Pashayan*	N	N	Y	Y	Y	N	Y	N
18 Lehman	Y	N	Y	?	?	?	?	#
19 *Lagomarsino*	N	N	Y	Y	Y	Y	Y	Y
20 *Thomas*	N	N	?	Y	Y	Y	N	N
21 *Fiedler*	N	Y	N	Y	Y	Y	Y	Y
22 *Moorhead*	N	Y	Y	Y	Y	Y	N	Y
23 Beilenson	Y	N	?	Y	Y	N	Y	Y
24 Waxman	Y	?	Y	Y	Y	N	Y	Y
25 Roybal	Y	N	?	Y	Y	N	Y	Y
26 Berman	Y	N	Y	Y	Y	N	Y	Y
27 Levine	Y	N	Y	Y	Y	N	Y	Y
28 Dixon	Y	N	Y	Y	Y	?	?	?
29 Hawkins	Y	N	Y	Y	Y	N	Y	?
30 Martinez	Y	N	Y	Y	Y	N	Y	Y
31 Dymally	Y	N	Y	?	?	?	?	?
32 Anderson	Y	N	N	Y	Y	N	Y	Y
33 *Dreier*	N	Y	N	Y	N	Y	N	Y
34 Torres	Y	N	Y	Y	Y	N	Y	Y
35 *Lewis*	?	#	?	?	?	?	Y	N
36 Brown	Y	N	Y	Y	Y	N	Y	Y
37 *McCandless*	N	Y	N	Y	N	Y	N	Y
38 Patterson	Y	N	Y	?	?	X	#	Y
39 *Dannemeyer*	N	Y	N	N	N	Y	N	Y
40 *Badham*	N	Y	Y	N	Y	N	Y	Y
41 *Lowery*	N	Y	Y	?	?	Y	N	Y
42 *Lungren*	N	Y	N	Y	N	Y	N	Y
43 *Packard*	N	Y	Y	?	?	?	?	?
44 Bates	Y	N	Y	Y	Y	N	Y	Y
45 *Hunter*	N	Y	Y	Y	Y	Y	Y	N
COLORADO								
1 Schroeder	Y	N	Y	N	Y	Y	Y	Y
2 Wirth	Y	N	Y	?	?	?	?	?
3 Kogovsek	Y	N	Y	Y	Y	N	Y	Y
4 *Brown*	N	N	N	Y	N	Y	N	Y
5 *Kramer*	N	Y	Y	?	?	?	?	Y
6 *Schaefer*	N	Y	N	N	N	Y	N	Y
CONNECTICUT								
1 Kennelly	Y	N	Y	Y	Y	N	Y	N
2 Gejdenson	Y	N	Y	N	Y	N	Y	N
3 Morrison	Y	X	?	?	Y	N	Y	
4 *McKinney*	Y	N	Y	P	Y	N	Y	Y
5 Ratchford	Y	N	Y	Y	Y	N	Y	N
6 *Johnson*	N	N	Y	Y	Y	N	Y	N
DELAWARE								
AL Carper	Y	N	Y	Y	Y	N	Y	Y
FLORIDA								
1 Hutto	N	N	Y	Y	Y	N	Y	N
2 Fuqua	N	N	Y	Y	Y	N	Y	N
3 Bennett	Y	N	Y	Y	Y	N	Y	N
4 Chappell	N	N	Y	Y	?	N	Y	N
5 *McCollum*	N	Y	?	Y	N	Y	N	Y
6 MacKay	Y	N	Y	Y	Y	N	Y	Y
7 Gibbons	Y	?	?	?	?	?	?	?
8 *Young*	N	Y	Y	Y	N	Y	Y	Y
9 *Bilirakis*	N	Y	Y	N	Y	N	Y	Y
10 Ireland	N	Y	Y	?	?	Y	Y	Y
11 Nelson	N	N	Y	Y	Y	N	Y	Y
12 *Lewis*	N	Y	Y	N	Y	N	Y	Y
13 *Mack*	N	Y	N	N	N	Y	N	Y
14 Mica	N	N	Y	Y	Y	N	Y	N
15 *Shaw*	N	Y	Y	N	Y	N	Y	Y
16 Smith	Y	N	Y	?	?	?	Y	Y
17 Lehman	Y	?	?	Y	Y	N	Y	N
18 Pepper	Y	N	Y	?	?	X	?	?
19 Fascell	N	N	Y	Y	Y	N	Y	Y
GEORGIA								
1 Thomas	N	N	Y	Y	Y	N	Y	N
2 Hatcher	?	?	?	Y	Y	N	Y	N
3 Ray	N	N	Y	Y	Y	Y	+	N
4 Levitas	N	N	Y	N	N	N	N	Y
5 Fowler	Y	N	Y	Y	Y	N	Y	Y
6 *Gingrich*	N	Y	N	?	?	Y	N	Y
7 Darden	N	N	Y	Y	N	N	N	N
8 Rowland	N	N	Y	Y	Y	N	Y	N
9 Jenkins	N	N	Y	Y	Y	N	Y	N
10 Barnard	N	N	Y	Y	Y	?	?	?
HAWAII								
1 Heftel	Y	?	?	?	Y	N	Y	Y
2 Akaka	Y	N	Y	?	Y	N	Y	Y
IDAHO								
1 *Craig*	N	N	N	N	N	Y	N	Y
2 *Hansen*	?	?	?	?	?	?	?	?
ILLINOIS								
1 Hayes	Y	N	Y	Y	Y	N	Y	Y
2 Savage	Y	N	Y	?	Y	N	Y	Y
3 Russo	Y	N	Y	?	Y	N	N	Y
4 *O'Brien*	N	#	?	?	?	?	?	Y
5 Lipinski	Y	N	Y	N	Y	N	Y	Y
6 *Hyde*	N	Y	Y	N	Y	N	Y	N
7 Collins	Y	N	Y	Y	Y	N	Y	Y
8 Rostenkowski	Y	N	Y	?	?	N	Y	Y
9 Yates	Y	N	Y	Y	Y	N	Y	Y
10 *Porter*	N	Y	?	+	-	Y	N	Y
11 Annunzio	Y	N	Y	Y	Y	N	Y	N
12 *Crane, P.*	N	Y	Y	N	Y	N	Y	Y
13 *Erlenborn*	N	N	Y	?	?	Y	N	Y
14 *Corcoran*	N	Y	Y	Y	Y	N	Y	Y
15 *Madigan*	N	Y	?	Y	Y	N	Y	Y
16 *Martin*	Y	N	Y	N	Y	N	Y	Y
17 Evans	Y	N	Y	Y	Y	N	Y	Y
18 *Michel*	N	Y	Y	?	?	Y	N	Y
19 *Crane, D.*	N	Y	N	Y	N	Y	N	Y
20 Durbin	Y	N	Y	?	Y	N	Y	Y
21 Price	Y	N	Y	Y	Y	N	Y	N
22 Simon	Y	N	?	?	?	?	?	?
INDIANA								
1 Hall	Y	N	Y	Y	Y	N	Y	Y
2 Sharp	Y	N	Y	Y	Y	Y	N	Y
3 *Hiler*	N	Y	Y	N	Y	N	Y	Y
4 *Coats*	N	Y	Y	N	Y	N	Y	Y
5 Hillis	N	Y	Y	Y	Y	N	Y	N

ND - Northern Democrats   SD - Southern Democrats

Corresponding to Congressional Record Votes 181, 183, 184, 185, 186, 187, 188, 189

	162	163	164	165	166	167	168	169
6 ***Burton***	N	Y	Y	?	?	Y	N	Y
7 ***Myers***	N	Y	?	Y	Y	N	N	N
8 McCloskey	Y	N	Y	Y	Y	N	Y	N
9 Hamilton	Y	N	Y	Y	Y	Y	Y	Y
10 Jacobs	Y	N	Y	N	Y	N	Y	Y
IOWA								
1 ***Leach***	Y	?	Y	Y	Y	Y	Y	Y
2 ***Tauke***	Y	N	Y	Y	N	Y	N	Y
3 ***Evans***	Y	N	N	N	Y	Y	N	Y
4 Smith	Y	N	Y	Y	Y	N	Y	Y
5 Harkin	Y	?	?	N	Y	N	Y	Y
6 Bedell	Y	N	Y	Y	Y	N	Y	Y
KANSAS								
1 ***Roberts***	N	#	?	N	N	Y	N	Y
2 Slattery	Y	N	Y	Y	Y	N	N	Y
3 ***Winn***	N	Y	Y	?	Y	Y	N	Y
4 Glickman	Y	N	Y	?	Y	N	Y	Y
5 ***Whittaker***	N	Y	Y	?	Y	Y	N	Y
KENTUCKY								
1 Hubbard	N	N	Y	Y	Y	Y	N	Y
2 Natcher	Y	N	Y	Y	Y	N	Y	Y
3 Mazzoli	Y	N	Y	Y	Y	N	Y	Y
4 ***Snyder***	N	N	Y	Y	Y	N	Y	Y
5 ***Rogers***	?	?	?	Y	Y	N	Y	Y
6 ***Hopkins***	N	N	Y	Y	Y	Y	Y	N
7 Perkins	Y	N	Y	?	Y	N	Y	Y
LOUISIANA								
1 ***Livingston***	N	Y	?	Y	Y	Y	N	Y
2 Boggs	Y	N	Y	?	Y	N	Y	Y
3 Tauzin	N	N	Y	Y	Y	Y	Y	Y
4 Roemer	N	N	Y	?	?	Y	N	Y
5 Huckaby	N	N	Y	?	?	Y	N	Y
6 ***Moore***	N	N	Y	Y	?	Y	Y	Y
7 Breaux	N	N	Y	?	?	#	?	?
8 Long	Y	N	Y	?	Y	N	Y	N
MAINE								
1 ***McKernan***	Y	N	Y	Y	Y	N	Y	Y
2 ***Snowe***	Y	N	Y	Y	Y	N	Y	Y
MARYLAND								
1 Dyson	N	N	Y	?	?	N	Y	N
2 Long	Y	N	Y	?	Y	N	Y	Y
3 Mikulski	Y	N	Y	Y	Y	N	Y	N
4 ***Holt***	N	N	Y	Y	Y	Y	Y	X
5 Hoyer	Y	N	Y	Y	Y	N	Y	Y
6 Byron	N	N	Y	Y	Y	N	Y	N
7 Mitchell	Y	N	Y	N	Y	N	Y	Y
8 Barnes	Y	N	Y	Y	Y	N	Y	Y
MASSACHUSETTS								
1 ***Conte***	Y	N	Y	Y	Y	N	Y	Y
2 Boland	Y	N	?	?	Y	N	Y	Y
3 Early	Y	N	Y	Y	Y	N	Y	Y
4 Frank	Y	N	Y	Y	Y	N	Y	Y
5 Shannon	Y	?	?	?	?	N	Y	Y
6 Mavroules	Y	N	Y	?	Y	N	Y	N
7 Markey	Y	N	Y	Y	Y	N	Y	Y
8 O'Neill								
9 Moakley	Y	N	Y	Y	Y	N	Y	Y
10 Studds	Y	N	?	Y	Y	N	Y	Y
11 Donnelly	Y	N	Y	Y	Y	N	Y	Y
MICHIGAN								
1 Conyers	Y	N	Y	?	Y	N	Y	Y
2 ***Pursell***	Y	N	Y	Y	N	Y	N	Y
3 Wolpe	Y	N	Y	Y	Y	N	Y	Y
4 ***Siljander***	N	Y	Y	?	N	Y	N	Y
5 ***Sawyer***	?	?	?	Y	Y	Y	Y	Y
6 Carr	Y	N	Y	Y	Y	N	Y	Y
7 Kildee	Y	N	Y	Y	Y	N	Y	Y
8 Traxler	?	?	?	Y	Y	N	Y	Y
9 ***Vander Jagt***	N	?	?	Y	Y	Y	Y	Y
10 Albosta	Y	N	Y	Y	Y	N	Y	Y
11 ***Davis***	N	Y	Y	?	?	Y	Y	Y
12 Bonior	Y	N	Y	Y	?	N	Y	Y
13 Crockett	Y	N	Y	?	?	?	?	#
14 Hertel	Y	N	Y	Y	Y	N	Y	Y
15 Ford	Y	N	Y	?	Y	N	Y	N
16 Dingell	Y	N	Y	Y	Y	N	Y	N
17 Levin	Y	N	Y	Y	Y	N	Y	Y
18 ***Broomfield***	N	Y	Y	Y	Y	Y	N	Y
MINNESOTA								
1 Penny	Y	N	Y	N	Y	N	N	Y
2 ***Weber***	N	Y	N	Y	?	Y	N	Y
3 ***Frenzel***	N	N	Y	Y	N	Y	N	Y
4 Vento	Y	N	Y	Y	Y	N	Y	Y
5 Sabo	Y	N	Y	N	Y	N	Y	Y
6 Sikorski	Y	N	Y	N	Y	N	Y	Y
7 ***Stangeland***	N	Y	Y	Y	N	Y	Y	Y
8 Oberstar	Y	N	Y	P	Y	N	Y	Y
MISSISSIPPI								
1 Whitten	Y	?	Y	Y	Y	N	Y	Y
2 ***Franklin***	N	Y	Y	?	?	?	?	X
3 Montgomery	N	Y	Y	Y	Y	N	Y	N
4 Dowdy	N	N	Y	?	Y	N	Y	Y
5 ***Lott***	N	Y	Y	Y	Y	Y	N	N
MISSOURI								
1 Clay	Y	N	Y	N	Y	N	Y	Y
2 Young	Y	N	Y	Y	Y	N	Y	N
3 Gephardt	Y	N	Y	Y	Y	N	Y	Y
4 Skelton	N	N	Y	?	Y	N	Y	N
5 Wheat	Y	N	Y	Y	Y	N	Y	Y
6 ***Coleman***	N	Y	Y	?	?	?	?	?
7 ***Taylor***	N	N	Y	Y	Y	Y	N	Y
8 ***Emerson***	N	N	Y	N	Y	Y	Y	Y
9 Volkmer	Y	N	Y	Y	Y	Y	Y	Y
MONTANA								
1 Williams	Y	N	Y	?	Y	N	Y	Y
2 ***Marlenee***	N	Y	N	Y	N	Y	N	Y
NEBRASKA								
1 ***Bereuter***	N	N	Y	Y	N	Y	Y	Y
2 ***Daub***	N	N	Y	Y	N	Y	N	Y
3 ***Smith***	N	N	Y	Y	Y	Y	Y	Y
NEVADA								
1 Reid	Y	N	Y	Y	Y	N	Y	Y
2 ***Vucanovich***	N	Y	N	Y	N	Y	N	Y
NEW HAMPSHIRE								
1 D'Amours	Y	?	?	?	?	?	?	?
2 ***Gregg***	N	N	Y	?	?	Y	N	Y
NEW JERSEY								
1 Florio	Y	N	Y	?	?	N	Y	Y
2 Hughes	Y	N	Y	Y	Y	N	Y	Y
3 Howard	Y	N	Y	Y	Y	N	Y	Y
4 ***Smith***	N	Y	Y	?	Y	N	Y	Y
5 ***Roukema***	?	X	?	Y	Y	N	Y	Y
6 Dwyer	Y	N	Y	Y	Y	N	Y	Y
7 ***Rinaldo***	N	Y	Y	Y	Y	N	Y	Y
8 Roe	Y	N	Y	Y	Y	N	Y	Y
9 Torricelli	Y	N	Y	Y	Y	N	Y	Y
10 Rodino	Y	N	Y	Y	Y	N	Y	Y
11 Minish	Y	?	?	Y	Y	N	Y	+
12 ***Courter***	N	Y	Y	Y	N	N	Y	Y
13 Vacancy								
14 Guarini	Y	N	Y	?	?	N	Y	Y
NEW MEXICO								
1 ***Lujan***	N	Y	Y	Y	Y	Y	N	Y
2 ***Skeen***	N	Y	Y	?	?	?	?	Y
3 Richardson	Y	N	Y	?	Y	N	Y	Y
NEW YORK								
1 ***Carney***	N	N	Y	Y	Y	N	Y	Y
2 Downey	Y	N	Y	Y	Y	N	Y	Y
3 Mrazek	Y	N	Y	Y	Y	N	Y	Y
4 ***Lent***	N	Y	Y	Y	Y	N	?	?
5 ***McGrath***	N	N	N	?	?	N	Y	Y
6 Addabbo	Y	X	?	?	?	N	Y	Y
7 Ackerman	Y	N	Y	Y	Y	N	Y	Y
8 Scheuer	Y	N	Y	Y	Y	N	Y	Y
9 Ferraro	Y	N	Y	?	Y	N	Y	Y
10 Schumer	Y	N	Y	?	Y	N	Y	Y
11 Towns	Y	?	Y	?	Y	N	Y	Y
12 Owens	Y	N	Y	?	Y	N	Y	Y
13 Solarz	Y	N	Y	Y	Y	N	Y	Y
14 ***Molinari***	N	N	Y	Y	Y	N	Y	Y
15 ***Green***	Y	N	Y	Y	Y	N	Y	Y
16 Rangel	Y	N	Y	?	?	?	Y	Y
17 Weiss	Y	N	Y	Y	Y	N	Y	Y
18 Garcia	Y	N	?	?	?	?	?	Y
19 Biaggi	Y	N	Y	Y	Y	N	Y	Y
20 Ottinger	Y	N	Y	P	Y	N	Y	Y
21 ***Fish***	Y	N	Y	Y	Y	N	Y	Y
22 ***Gilman***	N	N	Y	Y	Y	N	Y	Y
23 Stratton	N	N	Y	Y	Y	N	Y	N
24 ***Solomon***	N	Y	N	N	N	Y	N	Y
25 ***Boehlert***	Y	N	Y	Y	Y	N	Y	Y
26 ***Martin***	N	Y	Y	Y	Y	N	Y	?
27 ***Wortley***	N	Y	Y	Y	Y	N	Y	Y
28 McHugh	Y	N	Y	?	?	N	Y	Y
29 ***Horton***	Y	N	Y	Y	Y	N	Y	N
30 ***Conable***	N	N	N	?	N	Y	N	Y
31 ***Kemp***	N	Y	Y	Y	?	Y	N	Y
32 LaFalce	#	X	?	Y	Y	N	Y	Y
33 Nowak	Y	N	Y	Y	Y	N	Y	Y
34 Lundine	Y	N	Y	Y	Y	N	Y	Y
NORTH CAROLINA								
1 Jones	Y	N	Y	Y	Y	N	Y	Y
2 Valentine	Y	N	Y	Y	Y	N	Y	Y
3 Whitley	Y	N	Y	Y	Y	N	Y	Y
4 Andrews	Y	N	Y	Y	Y	N	Y	Y
5 Neal	Y	N	Y	Y	Y	N	Y	Y
6 Britt	Y	N	Y	Y	N	N	Y	Y
7 Rose	Y	?	?	Y	Y	N	Y	Y
8 Hefner	Y	N	Y	?	?	?	?	Y
9 ***Martin***	?	?	?	Y	N	Y	N	Y
10 ***Broyhill***	N	Y	?	?	?	Y	N	Y
11 Clarke	Y	N	Y	?	?	N	Y	Y
NORTH DAKOTA								
AL Dorgan	Y	N	Y	Y	Y	N	N	Y
OHIO								
1 Luken	Y	N	Y	Y	Y	N	Y	Y
2 ***Gradison***	Y	N	N	Y	Y	N	N	Y
3 Hall	Y	N	Y	?	?	?	?	?
4 ***Oxley***	N	N	Y	?	?	Y	N	N
5 ***Latta***	N	Y	Y	Y	Y	Y	N	Y
6 ***McEwen***	N	Y	Y	Y	Y	Y	N	N
7 ***DeWine***	N	Y	Y	Y	Y	Y	N	N
8 ***Kindness***	N	Y	N	Y	N	Y	N	Y
9 Kaptur	Y	N	Y	?	?	N	Y	Y
10 ***Miller***	N	Y	Y	N	N	Y	N	Y
11 Eckart	Y	N	Y	Y	Y	N	Y	Y
12 ***Kasich***	N	N	Y	Y	Y	Y	Y	N
13 Pease	Y	N	Y	?	Y	N	Y	Y
14 Seiberling	Y	N	Y	Y	Y	N	Y	Y
15 ***Wylie***	N	N	Y	Y	Y	Y	Y	Y
16 ***Regula***	Y	N	Y	Y	Y	N	Y	Y
17 ***Williams***	?	?	?	Y	Y	N	Y	Y
18 Applegate	Y	N	Y	?	Y	N	Y	Y
19 Feighan	Y	N	Y	Y	?	N	N	Y
20 Oakar	Y	N	?	Y	Y	N	Y	N
21 Stokes	Y	N	Y	Y	Y	N	Y	Y
OKLAHOMA								
1 Jones	Y	N	Y	?	?	N	N	Y
2 Synar	Y	N	Y	?	Y	N	Y	Y
3 Watkins	?	?	?	Y	Y	N	Y	Y
4 McCurdy	Y	N	Y	Y	Y	N	Y	N
5 ***Edwards***	N	Y	Y	?	?	?	?	?
6 English	N	N	Y	Y	Y	N	Y	N
OREGON								
1 AuCoin	Y	N	Y	Y	Y	Y	N	Y
2 ***Smith, R.***	N	N	Y	Y	Y	Y	Y	Y
3 Wyden	Y	N	Y	Y	Y	N	Y	Y
4 Weaver	Y	N	?	?	?	?	?	Y
5 ***Smith, D.***	N	Y	Y	?	?	?	?	N
PENNSYLVANIA								
1 Foglietta	Y	N	Y	Y	Y	N	Y	Y
2 Gray	Y	N	Y	Y	Y	N	Y	Y
3 Borski	Y	N	Y	Y	Y	N	Y	Y
4 Kolter	Y	N	Y	Y	?	N	Y	Y
5 ***Schulze***	N	?	Y	?	?	Y	N	Y
6 Yatron	Y	N	Y	Y	Y	N	Y	Y
7 Edgar	Y	N	Y	Y	Y	N	Y	Y
8 Kostmayer	Y	N	Y	Y	Y	N	Y	Y
9 ***Shuster***	N	N	Y	Y	N	Y	N	N
10 ***McDade***	N	N	Y	?	?	?	Y	Y
11 Harrison	Y	N	Y	Y	Y	N	Y	Y
12 Murtha	N	?	Y	Y	Y	N	Y	Y
13 ***Coughlin***	N	Y	Y	?	Y	Y	Y	Y
14 Coyne	Y	N	Y	Y	Y	N	Y	Y
15 ***Ritter***	N	Y	Y	Y	Y	Y	N	Y
16 ***Walker***	N	Y	N	N	N	Y	N	Y
17 ***Gekas***	N	Y	Y	Y	Y	Y	N	Y
18 Walgren	Y	N	Y	Y	Y	N	Y	Y
19 ***Goodling***	Y	N	Y	P	N	N	N	Y
20 Gaydos	N	N	Y	?	?	?	?	?
21 ***Ridge***	Y	?	N	Y	Y	N	Y	Y
22 Murphy	Y	N	Y	Y	Y	N	Y	Y
23 ***Clinger***	N	N	Y	Y	Y	Y	Y	N
RHODE ISLAND								
1 St Germain	Y	N	Y	?	?	N	Y	Y
2 ***Schneider***	Y	N	Y	?	Y	N	Y	Y
SOUTH CAROLINA								
1 ***Hartnett***	N	Y	?	Y	N	Y	N	N
2 ***Spence***	N	?	Y	?	N	Y	Y	N
3 Derrick	Y	N	Y	Y	Y	N	Y	Y
4 ***Campbell***	N	Y	Y	?	N	Y	N	Y
5 Spratt	Y	N	Y	?	?	N	Y	Y
6 Tallon	N	N	Y	?	?	?	?	?
SOUTH DAKOTA								
AL Daschle	Y	?	Y	?	?	?	?	Y
TENNESSEE								
1 ***Quillen***	N	?	?	Y	Y	Y	Y	N
2 ***Duncan***	N	N	Y	Y	Y	Y	Y	N
3 Lloyd	N	N	Y	Y	Y	N	Y	N
4 Cooper	Y	N	Y	?	Y	N	Y	Y
5 Boner	Y	N	?	Y	Y	N	Y	Y
6 Gore	Y	N	Y	?	?	?	?	?
7 ***Sundquist***	N	Y	Y	N	N	Y	Y	Y
8 Jones	Y	N	Y	?	?	N	Y	Y
9 Ford	Y	N	Y	Y	Y	N	Y	Y
TEXAS								
1 Hall, S.	N	Y	Y	Y	Y	Y	N	Y
2 Wilson	Y	Y	Y	?	?	?	?	?
3 ***Bartlett***	N	Y	Y	?	?	Y	N	Y
4 Hall, R.	N	Y	Y	?	Y	Y	N	Y
5 Bryant	Y	N	Y	?	?	?	?	?
6 ***Gramm***	?	?	?	Y	N	Y	N	Y
7 ***Archer***	N	Y	Y	Y	N	Y	N	Y
8 ***Fields***	N	Y	Y	?	N	Y	Y	Y
9 Brooks	Y	?	?	Y	Y	N	Y	N
10 Pickle	Y	N	Y	Y	Y	N	N	Y
11 Leath	N	N	Y	?	?	?	?	?
12 Wright	Y	N	Y	Y	Y	N	Y	N
13 Hightower	N	N	Y	Y	Y	N	Y	Y
14 Patman	N	N	Y	Y	Y	Y	N	Y
15 de la Garza	Y	N	?	?	Y	N	Y	Y
16 Coleman	Y	N	Y	Y	Y	N	Y	Y
17 Stenholm	N	Y	Y	Y	Y	Y	N	Y
18 Leland	Y	N	Y	?	Y	N	Y	Y
19 Hance	X	?	?	?	?	#	X	?
20 Gonzalez	Y	N	Y	Y	Y	N	Y	Y
21 ***Loeffler***	N	Y	Y	Y	Y	Y	N	Y
22 ***Paul***	Y	N	N	Y	N	Y	N	Y
23 Kazen	N	N	?	Y	Y	N	Y	N
24 Frost	Y	N	Y	?	Y	N	Y	Y
25 Andrews	Y	N	Y	Y	Y	N	Y	Y
26 Vandergriff	N	N	Y	?	Y	Y	N	Y
27 Ortiz	Y	N	Y	Y	Y	N	Y	Y
UTAH								
1 ***Hansen***	N	Y	Y	Y	Y	Y	N	N
2 ***Marriott***	?	?	?	?	?	?	?	?
3 ***Nielson***	N	Y	Y	Y	Y	Y	N	Y
VERMONT								
AL ***Jeffords***	Y	N	Y	?	?	?	?	?
VIRGINIA								
1 ***Bateman***	N	Y	Y	Y	N	Y	Y	N
2 ***Whitehurst***	N	#	?	Y	Y	Y	N	N
3 ***Bliley***	N	Y	Y	Y	Y	Y	N	Y
4 Sisisky	N	N	Y	Y	Y	N	Y	Y
5 Daniel	N	N	Y	Y	Y	Y	N	N
6 Olin	Y	N	Y	Y	Y	N	Y	Y
7 ***Robinson***	N	Y	Y	Y	Y	Y	N	N
8 ***Parris***	N	Y	Y	Y	Y	Y	Y	Y
9 Boucher	Y	N	?	Y	Y	N	Y	Y
10 ***Wolf***	N	Y	Y	?	Y	N	Y	Y
WASHINGTON								
1 ***Pritchard***	Y	N	Y	?	?	N	Y	Y
2 Swift	Y	N	Y	Y	Y	N	Y	Y
3 Bonker	Y	N	Y	Y	Y	N	Y	Y
4 ***Morrison***	N	Y	Y	Y	Y	N	Y	N
5 Foley	Y	N	Y	Y	Y	N	Y	Y
6 Dicks	Y	N	Y	Y	Y	N	Y	Y
7 Lowry	Y	N	Y	Y	Y	N	Y	Y
8 ***Chandler***	Y	?	Y	?	Y	Y	Y	N
WEST VIRGINIA								
1 Mollohan	Y	N	Y	?	?	N	Y	Y
2 Staggers	Y	N	Y	Y	Y	N	Y	Y
3 Wise	Y	N	Y	Y	Y	N	Y	Y
4 Rahall	Y	?	?	Y	Y	N	Y	Y
WISCONSIN								
1 Aspin	Y	N	Y	Y	Y	N	Y	N
2 Kastenmeier	Y	N	Y	Y	Y	N	Y	Y
3 ***Gunderson***	Y	N	Y	Y	N	N	N	Y
4 Kleczka	Y	N	Y	Y	Y	N	Y	Y
5 Moody	Y	N	Y	Y	Y	N	N	Y
6 ***Petri***	N	N	N	Y	Y	N	N	Y
7 Obey	Y	N	Y	Y	Y	N	Y	Y
8 ***Roth***	N	Y	Y	Y	Y	Y	Y	Y
9 ***Sensenbrenner***	?	?	?	?	?	?	?	?
WYOMING								
AL ***Cheney***	N	Y	Y	N	N	Y	N	N

Southern states - Ala., Ark., Fla., Ga., Ky., La., Miss., N.C., Okla., S.C., Tenn., Texas, Va.

170. HR 5167. Department of Defense Authorization. Nichols, D-Ala., amendment to require contractors to identify the manufacturer of parts sold to the Pentagon. Adopted 396-0: R 155-0; D 241-0 (ND 162-0, SD 79-0), May 30, 1984.

171. HR 5167. Department of Defense Authorization. Ottinger, D-N.Y., amendment to bar the use of funds for civil defense intended to prepare for or respond to a nuclear war. Rejected 87-301: R 9-140; D 78-161 (ND 73-91, SD 5-70), May 30, 1984. A "nay" was a vote supporting the president's position.

172. HR 5167. Department of Defense Authorization. Biaggi, D-N.Y., amendment to allow up to two non-U.S.-built cruise ships to be used in trade between U.S. ports. Adopted 237-159: R 60-95; D 177-64 (ND 113-53, SD 64-11), May 30, 1984.

173. Procedural Motion. Gunderson, R-Wis., motion to approve the House *Journal* of Wednesday, May 30. Motion agreed to 344-26: R 131-14; D 213-12 (ND 140-11, SD 73-1), May 31, 1984.

174. HR 5712. Commerce, Justice, State and the Judiciary Appropriations, Fiscal 1985. Ottinger, D-N.Y., amendment to delete $31.3 million for the National Endowment for Democracy, created in 1983 to encourage understanding of U.S.-style democracy in foreign countries through the private sector. Adopted 226-173: R 87-67; D 139-106 (ND 100-67, SD 39-39), May 31, 1984.

175. HR 5712. Commerce, Justice, State and the Judiciary Appropriations, Fiscal 1985. Miller, R-Ohio, motion to recommit the bill to the Appropriations Committee with instructions to trim 4 percent in discretionary funding for fiscal 1985. Motion agreed to 208-194: R 141-13; D 67-181 (ND 28-141, SD 39-40), May 31, 1984.

176. HR 5712. Commerce, Justice, State and the Judiciary Appropriations, Fiscal 1985. Passage of the bill to provide $10,749,649,000 in fiscal 1985 for the Commerce, Justice and State departments, 17 related agencies and the federal judiciary. Passed 303-98: R 76-79; D 227-19 (ND 155-12, SD 72-7), May 31, 1984. The president had requested $11,130,943,000 in new budget authority.

177. HR 5167. Department of Defense Authorization. Price, D-Ill., amendment to the Dickinson, R-Ala., amendment, to authorize the production of 15 MX missiles subject to certain conditions. Adopted 203-182: R 137-15; D 66-167 (ND 16-144, SD 50-23), May 31, 1984. (The Dickinson amendment, as amended by the Price amendment and by the Bennett, D-Fla., amendment *(see vote 178, p. 58-H),* subsequently was adopted *(see vote 179, p. 58-H).)*

KEY

Y	Voted for (yea).
#	Paired for.
+	Announced for.
N	Voted against (nay).
X	Paired against.
-	Announced against.
P	Voted "present".
C	Voted "present" to avoid possible conflict of interest.
?	Did not vote or otherwise make a position known.

Democrats   *Republicans*

	170	171	172	173	174	175	176	177
ALABAMA								
1 *Edwards*	Y	N	Y	Y	Y	N	Y	Y
2 *Dickinson*	Y	N	N	N	Y	Y	Y	Y
3 Nichols	Y	N	Y	Y	N	Y	Y	Y
4 Bevill	Y	N	Y	Y	Y	N	Y	Y
5 Flippo	Y	N	Y	Y	N	Y	Y	Y
6 Erdreich	Y	N	Y	Y	+	-	-	+
7 Shelby	Y	N	Y	N	Y	N	Y	Y
ALASKA								
AL *Young*	Y	N	Y	N	Y	N	Y	Y
ARIZONA								
1 *McCain*	Y	N	N	Y	Y	Y	N	Y
2 Udall	Y	N	N	Y	N	N	Y	N
3 *Stump*	Y	N	N	Y	Y	Y	N	Y
4 *Rudd*	Y	N	N	Y	Y	Y	Y	Y
5 McNulty	Y	N	Y	Y	Y	N	Y	Y
ARKANSAS								
1 Alexander	Y	?	#	Y	N	N	Y	?
2 *Bethune*	Y	N	N	Y	Y	Y	Y	Y
3 *Hammerschmidt*	Y	N	Y	Y	Y	Y	Y	Y
4 Anthony	?	?	?	?	X	?	?	?
CALIFORNIA								
1 Bosco	Y	N	Y	Y	N	Y	Y	N
2 *Chappie*	Y	N	Y	N	Y	Y	Y	Y
3 Matsui	Y	N	Y	N	N	N	Y	N
4 Fazio	Y	N	Y	Y	N	Y	Y	Y
5 Burton	Y	Y	N	N	N	N	Y	N
6 Boxer	Y	Y	N	Y	N	Y	Y	N
7 Miller	Y	N	N	?	Y	N	Y	N
8 Dellums	Y	Y	N	Y	N	Y	Y	N
9 Stark	?	?	?	?	Y	N	Y	N
10 Edwards	Y	Y	N	Y	N	Y	Y	N
11 Lantos	Y	N	Y	Y	N	Y	Y	N
12 *Zschau*	Y	N	Y	Y	Y	Y	Y	Y
13 Mineta	Y	N	Y	Y	N	N	Y	N
14 *Shumway*	Y	N	Y	Y	Y	Y	N	Y
15 *Pashayan*	Y	N	?	N	Y	N	Y	Y
16 Panetta	Y	N	N	Y	N	N	Y	N
17 *Pashayan*	Y	N	N	N	Y	N	Y	Y
18 Lehman	?	?	?	?	Y	N	Y	N
19 *Lagomarsino*	Y	N	N	Y	N	N	Y	Y
20 *Thomas*	Y	?	N	Y	N	Y	Y	Y
21 *Fiedler*	Y	N	N	Y	N	N	Y	Y
22 *Moorhead*	Y	N	N	Y	Y	Y	N	Y
23 Beilenson	Y	N	N	Y	Y	N	Y	N
24 Waxman	Y	Y	Y	N	N	Y	N	N
25 Roybal	Y	Y	N	Y	N	Y	Y	N
26 Berman	Y	Y	Y	N	N	Y	Y	N
27 Levine	Y	Y	Y	Y	N	N	Y	N
28 Dixon	?	?	?	?	?	X	?	X
29 Hawkins	?	Y	Y	?	N	N	Y	?
30 Martinez	Y	N	Y	Y	N	N	Y	N
31 Dymally	?	?	?	?	?	?	?	?
32 Anderson	Y	N	Y	Y	N	Y	Y	Y
33 *Dreier*	Y	N	Y	Y	Y	Y	N	Y
34 Torres	Y	Y	Y	Y	N	N	Y	N
35 *Lewis*	Y	N	Y	Y	N	Y	Y	Y
36 Brown	Y	Y	Y	Y	N	Y	Y	N
37 *McCandless*	Y	N	N	Y	Y	Y	N	Y
38 Patterson	Y	N	N	?	N	N	Y	Y
39 *Dannemeyer*	Y	N	?	?	Y	N	Y	Y
40 *Badham*	Y	N	Y	N	Y	N	Y	#
41 *Lowery*	Y	N	N	Y	N	N	Y	Y
42 Lungren	Y	N	Y	Y	Y	Y	N	Y

	170	171	172	173	174	175	176	177
43 *Packard*	?	?	?	?	Y	Y	N	Y
44 Bates	Y	Y	N	Y	Y	Y	Y	N
45 *Hunter*	Y	N	N	?	N	N	Y	Y
COLORADO								
1 Schroeder	Y	Y	Y	N	Y	Y	Y	N
2 Wirth	?	?	N	Y	Y	N	Y	N
3 Kogovsek	Y	N	N	Y	Y	Y	?	Y	N
4 *Brown*	Y	N	N	Y	Y	Y	Y	N
5 *Kramer*	Y	N	Y	Y	Y	Y	N	Y
6 *Schaefer*	Y	N	N	Y	Y	Y	N	Y
CONNECTICUT								
1 Kennelly	Y	N	Y	Y	N	Y	N	Y
2 Gejdenson	Y	N	Y	N	N	N	Y	N
3 Morrison	Y	N	Y	Y	N	Y	N	Y
4 *McKinney*	Y	N	Y	N	Y	N	?	?	#
5 Ratchford	Y	N	Y	Y	N	Y	N	Y
6 *Johnson*	Y	N	Y	Y	Y	Y	Y	N
DELAWARE								
AL Carper	Y	N	Y	Y	N	Y	N	Y
FLORIDA								
1 Hutto	Y	N	?	Y	Y	Y	Y	Y
2 Fuqua	Y	N	Y	?	N	N	Y	Y
3 Bennett	Y	N	Y	N	Y	N	Y	N
4 *Chappell*	Y	?	Y	N	N	Y	Y	Y
5 *McCollum*	Y	N	Y	Y	Y	Y	N	Y
6 MacKay	Y	N	Y	?	N	Y	N	Y
7 Gibbons	?	?	?	?	?	?	?	?
8 *Young*	Y	N	Y	?	?	#	?	#
9 *Bilirakis*	Y	N	Y	N	Y	N	Y	Y
10 Ireland	Y	N	Y	N	Y	N	Y	Y
11 Nelson	Y	N	Y	Y	Y	Y	Y	Y
12 *Lewis*	Y	N	Y	Y	Y	N	Y	Y
13 *Mack*	Y	N	N	N	N	Y	N	Y
14 Mica	Y	N	Y	N	N	Y	Y	Y
15 *Shaw*	Y	N	Y	Y	Y	Y	Y	#
16 Smith	Y	N	Y	N	N	Y	N	Y
17 Lehman	Y	Y	N	Y	N	Y	N	Y
18 Pepper	?	?	#	Y	N	N	Y	Y
19 Fascell	Y	Y	Y	N	N	Y	N	Y
GEORGIA								
1 Thomas	Y	N	Y	Y	Y	Y	Y	Y
2 Hatcher	Y	N	Y	N	N	Y	Y	?
3 Ray	Y	N	Y	Y	Y	Y	Y	Y
4 Levitas	Y	N	Y	N	Y	Y	Y	Y
5 Fowler	Y	N	Y	N	Y	Y	Y	N
6 *Gingrich*	Y	N	N	Y	N	N	N	Y
7 Darden	Y	N	Y	Y	Y	Y	Y	Y
8 Rowland	Y	N	Y	Y	Y	Y	Y	Y
9 Jenkins	Y	N	Y	?	?	?	?	?
10 Barnard	?	?	?	?	?	?	?	?
HAWAII								
1 Heftel	Y	N	Y	?	N	Y	N	N
2 Akaka	Y	N	N	Y	Y	N	Y	N
IDAHO								
1 *Craig*	Y	N	Y	N	Y	N	Y	Y
2 *Hansen*	?	?	?	?	?	?	?	?
ILLINOIS								
1 Hayes	Y	Y	Y	Y	N	Y	N	N
2 Savage	Y	Y	Y	Y	N	Y	Y	N
3 Russo	Y	N	Y	Y	Y	Y	Y	N
4 *O'Brien*	Y	N	N	N	N	Y	Y	Y
5 Lipinski	Y	Y	Y	N	N	Y	Y	Y
6 *Hyde*	Y	N	N	Y	N	Y	Y	Y
7 Collins	Y	Y	Y	?	N	Y	N	N
8 Rostenkowski	Y	N	N	N	N	N	Y	N
9 Yates	Y	Y	N	N	N	Y	N	N
10 *Porter*	Y	N	Y	N	Y	Y	Y	Y
11 Annunzio	Y	N	Y	N	N	N	Y	Y
12 *Crane, P.*	Y	N	Y	Y	Y	Y	N	Y
13 *Erlenborn*	Y	N	N	N	Y	Y	Y	Y
14 *Corcoran*	Y	N	N	Y	Y	Y	Y	Y
15 *Madigan*	Y	N	N	?	Y	Y	Y	Y
16 *Martin*	Y	N	N	Y	Y	Y	Y	Y
17 Evans	Y	Y	Y	Y	N	Y	Y	N
18 *Michel*	Y	N	N	Y	N	Y	N	Y
19 *Crane, D.*	Y	N	Y	Y	Y	Y	N	Y
20 Durbin	Y	N	Y	N	N	Y	Y	N
21 Price	Y	N	Y	N	N	N	Y	Y
22 Simon	?	?	?	?	?	?	?	?
INDIANA								
1 Hall	Y	N	Y	Y	N	Y	N	N
2 Sharp	Y	N	Y	N	N	Y	N	N
3 *Hiler*	Y	N	N	Y	N	Y	N	Y
4 *Coats*	Y	N	N	Y	Y	Y	N	Y
5 Hillis	Y	N	Y	Y	Y	Y	Y	Y

ND - Northern Democrats   SD - Southern Democrats

	170	171	172	173	174	175	176	177
6 ***Burton***	Y	N	Y	Y	N	Y	N	Y
7 ***Myers***	Y	N	N	Y	N	Y	Y	Y
8 McCloskey	Y	N	N	Y	Y	Y	Y	N
9 Hamilton	Y	N	N	Y	Y	Y	Y	N
10 Jacobs	Y	N	N	N	Y	Y	Y	N
IOWA								
1 ***Leach***	Y	Y	N	Y	Y	Y	Y	N
2 ***Tauke***	Y	Y	N	Y	Y	Y	N	N
3 ***Evans***	Y	Y	Y	N	Y	Y	N	N
4 Smith	Y	Y	N	Y	N	N	Y	N
5 Harkin	Y	Y	Y	N	Y	N	?	N
6 Bedell	Y	Y	Y	Y	Y	N	Y	N
KANSAS								
1 ***Roberts***	Y	N	N	N	Y	Y	N	Y
2 Slattery	Y	N	N	?	Y	Y	N	N
3 ***Winn***	Y	N	N	Y	Y	Y	N	Y
4 Glickman	Y	N	N	Y	Y	Y	N	N
5 ***Whittaker***	Y	N	N	N	Y	Y	N	Y
KENTUCKY								
1 Hubbard	Y	N	N	Y	Y	Y	N	Y
2 Natcher	Y	N	Y	Y	N	N	Y	N
3 Mazzoli	Y	N	Y	Y	Y	N	Y	N
4 ***Snyder***	Y	N	N	Y	Y	Y	Y	Y
5 ***Rogers***	Y	N	Y	Y	Y	Y	Y	Y
6 ***Hopkins***	Y	N	N	Y	Y	Y	Y	Y
7 Perkins	Y	N	Y	Y	N	N	Y	N
LOUISIANA								
1 ***Livingston***	Y	N	Y	Y	N	Y	N	Y
2 Boggs	Y	N	?	Y	N	N	Y	N
3 Tauzin	Y	N	N	Y	N	Y	Y	Y
4 Roemer	Y	N	N	N	Y	Y	N	Y
5 Huckaby	Y	N	Y	Y	Y	Y	Y	Y
6 ***Moore***	Y	N	N	Y	Y	Y	Y	Y
7 Breaux	?	?	?	?	N	N	Y	Y
8 Long	Y	N	Y	Y	N	N	Y	N
MAINE								
1 ***McKernan***	Y	Y	N	Y	Y	Y	Y	Y
2 ***Snowe***	Y	Y	N	Y	Y	Y	Y	Y
MARYLAND								
1 Dyson	Y	N	N	Y	Y	N	Y	N
2 Long	Y	N	N	Y	Y	N	Y	N
3 Mikulski	Y	N	N	Y	Y	N	Y	N
4 ***Holt***	?	?	N	Y	N	N	Y	Y
5 Hoyer	Y	N	N	?	N	N	Y	Y
6 Byron	?	?	Y	Y	?	Y	Y	Y
7 Mitchell	Y	Y	N	N	?	N	Y	N
8 Barnes	Y	N	N	Y	N	N	Y	N
MASSACHUSETTS								
1 ***Conte***	Y	N	N	Y	N	N	Y	N
2 Boland	Y	N	Y	Y	Y	N	Y	N
3 Early	Y	Y	N	Y	N	N	Y	N
4 Frank	Y	Y	Y	Y	Y	N	Y	N
5 Shannon	Y	Y	Y	Y	Y	N	Y	N
6 Mavroules	Y	N	N	Y	Y	N	Y	N
7 Markey	Y	Y	Y	Y	Y	N	Y	N
8 O'Neill								
9 Moakley	Y	N	Y	Y	Y	N	Y	N
10 Studds	Y	Y	Y	Y	Y	N	Y	N
11 Donnelly	Y	N	Y	Y	Y	N	Y	N
MICHIGAN								
1 Conyers	?	Y	N	?	Y	N	Y	N
2 ***Pursell***	Y	N	N	Y	N	N	Y	Y
3 Wolpe	Y	Y	Y	Y	Y	N	Y	N
4 ***Siljander***	Y	N	Y	Y	N	Y	N	Y
5 ***Sawyer***	Y	N	Y	Y	?	?	?	?
6 Carr	Y	N	Y	Y	N	N	Y	N
7 Kildee	Y	N	Y	Y	N	N	Y	N
8 Traxler	Y	N	Y	Y	N	N	Y	N
9 ***Vander Jagt***	Y	?	?	Y	N	#	?	#
10 Albosta	Y	Y	Y	Y	Y	Y	Y	N
11 ***Davis***	Y	N	Y	?	Y	Y	Y	Y
12 Bonior	Y	Y	Y	Y	Y	N	Y	N
13 Crockett	?	#	X	?	?	X	?	X
14 Hertel	Y	N	Y	Y	N	N	N	N
15 Ford	Y	Y	N	?	Y	N	Y	N
16 Dingell	Y	N	Y	Y	Y	N	Y	N
17 Levin	Y	N	Y	Y	N	N	Y	N
18 ***Broomfield***	Y	N	N	Y	N	Y	Y	Y
MINNESOTA								
1 Penny	Y	N	Y	N	Y	N	N	N
2 ***Weber***	Y	N	Y	Y	Y	Y	N	Y
3 ***Frenzel***	Y	N	N	N	Y	Y	N	Y
4 Vento	Y	Y	Y	Y	Y	N	Y	N
5 Sabo	Y	Y	Y	N	N	?	?	X
6 Sikorski	Y	Y	Y	N	Y	N	Y	N
7 ***Stangeland***	Y	N	Y	Y	Y	Y	N	Y
8 Oberstar	Y	Y	Y	?	Y	N	Y	N
MISSISSIPPI								
1 Whitten	Y	N	Y	Y	N	N	Y	N
2 ***Franklin***	?	?	?	?	?	Y	N	Y
3 Montgomery	Y	N	N	Y	Y	Y	N	Y
4 Dowdy	Y	N	N	Y	Y	N	Y	?
5 ***Lott***	Y	N	N	Y	N	Y	N	Y
MISSOURI								
1 Clay	Y	Y	Y	N	Y	N	Y	N
2 Young	Y	N	Y	?	N	Y	Y	N
3 Gephardt	Y	N	Y	Y	N	N	Y	N
4 Skelton	Y	N	Y	Y	N	N	Y	Y
5 Wheat	Y	Y	Y	Y	Y	N	Y	N
6 ***Coleman***	?	N	N	Y	N	Y	Y	Y
7 ***Taylor***	Y	N	Y	Y	Y	Y	Y	Y
8 ***Emerson***	Y	N	N	N	Y	Y	Y	Y
9 Volkmer	Y	N	Y	Y	Y	Y	Y	N
MONTANA								
1 Williams	Y	N	?	Y	Y	N	Y	Y
2 ***Marlenee***	Y	N	N	Y	Y	?	Y	Y
NEBRASKA								
1 ***Bereuter***	Y	N	Y	Y	N	Y	N	N
2 ***Daub***	Y	N	N	Y	Y	Y	N	Y
3 ***Smith***	Y	N	N	Y	Y	Y	Y	N
NEVADA								
1 Reid	Y	Y	Y	Y	N	N	Y	Y
2 ***Vucanovich***	Y	N	N	Y	Y	Y	N	Y
NEW HAMPSHIRE								
1 D'Amours	?	?	?	?	Y	Y	Y	N
2 ***Gregg***	Y	N	N	Y	Y	Y	N	Y
NEW JERSEY								
1 Florio	Y	N	Y	Y	Y	N	Y	N
2 Hughes	Y	N	Y	Y	Y	N	N	?
3 Howard	Y	N	Y	Y	N	N	Y	X
4 ***Smith***	Y	N	N	?	N	Y	Y	Y
5 ***Roukema***	Y	N	N	Y	Y	Y	Y	N
6 Dwyer	Y	N	Y	Y	N	N	Y	?
7 ***Rinaldo***	Y	N	Y	Y	N	N	Y	Y
8 Roe	Y	N	Y	Y	N	N	Y	?
9 Torricelli	Y	N	N	Y	N	N	Y	N
10 Rodino	?	N	Y	Y	N	N	?	X
11 Minish	+	?	#	?	?	N	Y	N
12 ***Courter***	Y	N	Y	Y	N	Y	N	Y
13 Vacancy								
14 Guarini	Y	N	Y	Y	Y	N	Y	?
NEW MEXICO								
1 ***Lujan***	Y	N	N	Y	N	Y	N	Y
2 ***Skeen***	Y	N	N	Y	Y	Y	N	Y
3 Richardson	Y	N	Y	Y	N	N	Y	N
NEW YORK								
1 ***Carney***	Y	N	Y	Y	Y	Y	Y	Y
2 Downey	Y	N	Y	Y	Y	N	Y	N
3 Mrazek	Y	?	Y	Y	Y	N	Y	N
4 ***Lent***	?	?	?	?	N	Y	Y	Y
5 ***McGrath***	Y	N	Y	Y	Y	Y	Y	Y
6 Addabbo	Y	N	Y	Y	N	N	Y	N
7 Ackerman	Y	Y	Y	Y	Y	N	Y	X
8 Scheuer	Y	Y	Y	?	N	N	Y	N
9 Ferraro	Y	N	Y	Y	N	N	Y	N
10 Schumer	Y	N	Y	Y	Y	N	Y	N
11 Towns	Y	Y	Y	Y	Y	N	Y	N
12 Owens	Y	Y	Y	Y	Y	N	Y	N
13 Solarz	Y	Y	Y	Y	N	N	Y	N
14 ***Molinari***	Y	N	Y	Y	N	Y	Y	Y
15 ***Green***	Y	Y	Y	Y	N	N	Y	N
16 Rangel	Y	Y	Y	Y	?	N	Y	N
17 Weiss	Y	Y	Y	Y	Y	N	Y	N
18 Garcia	Y	Y	Y	Y	N	N	Y	N
19 Biaggi	Y	Y	Y	Y	N	N	Y	N
20 Ottinger	Y	Y	Y	P	Y	N	Y	N
21 ***Fish***	Y	N	Y	Y	N	Y	Y	?
22 ***Gilman***	Y	N	Y	Y	N	Y	Y	Y
23 Stratton	Y	N	Y	Y	Y	N	Y	Y
24 ***Solomon***	Y	N	Y	N	N	Y	N	Y
25 ***Boehlert***	Y	N	Y	Y	N	Y	Y	Y
26 ***Martin***	Y	N	Y	?	?	Y	Y	Y
27 ***Wortley***	Y	N	Y	Y	Y	Y	Y	Y
28 McHugh	Y	Y	Y	Y	Y	N	Y	N
29 ***Horton***	Y	?	Y	Y	N	N	Y	Y
30 ***Conable***	Y	N	N	Y	Y	Y	N	Y
31 ***Kemp***	Y	N	N	Y	N	Y	N	Y
32 LaFalce	Y	N	Y	Y	#	N	Y	N
33 Nowak	Y	Y	Y	Y	N	N	Y	N
34 Lundine	Y	Y	Y	Y	?	N	Y	?
NORTH CAROLINA								
1 Jones	Y	N	Y	Y	Y	N	Y	?
2 Valentine	Y	N	Y	Y	Y	Y	Y	Y
3 Whitley	Y	N	Y	Y	Y	Y	Y	Y
4 Andrews	Y	N	?	Y	Y	Y	Y	Y
5 Neal	Y	N	Y	?	Y	Y	Y	P
6 Britt	Y	N	Y	Y	N	Y	Y	Y
7 Rose	Y	N	Y	Y	?	N	Y	N
8 Hefner	Y	N	Y	Y	Y	N	Y	Y
9 ***Martin***	Y	N	N	Y	Y	Y	Y	Y
10 ***Broyhill***	Y	N	N	Y	Y	Y	N	Y
11 Clarke	Y	Y	Y	Y	Y	N	Y	N
NORTH DAKOTA								
AL Dorgan	Y	N	N	Y	Y	N	N	N
OHIO								
1 Luken	Y	N	Y	Y	Y	Y	N	N
2 ***Gradison***	Y	N	Y	Y	Y	Y	Y	N
3 Hall	?	?	?	Y	Y	Y	Y	N
4 ***Oxley***	Y	N	N	Y	Y	Y	N	Y
5 ***Latta***	Y	N	N	Y	N	Y	N	Y
6 ***McEwen***	Y	N	N	Y	N	Y	N	Y
7 ***DeWine***	Y	N	N	Y	N	Y	N	Y
8 ***Kindness***	Y	?	N	Y	Y	Y	N	Y
9 Kaptur	Y	N	Y	Y	Y	Y	Y	N
10 ***Miller***	Y	N	N	N	Y	Y	Y	Y
11 Eckart	Y	N	Y	Y	Y	N	Y	N
12 ***Kasich***	Y	N	N	Y	N	Y	N	Y
13 Pease	Y	N	N	Y	Y	N	Y	N
14 Seiberling	Y	Y	N	Y	Y	N	Y	N
15 ***Wylie***	Y	N	N	Y	N	Y	N	Y
16 ***Regula***	Y	N	N	Y	N	Y	Y	Y
17 ***Williams***	Y	?	Y	Y	Y	Y	Y	Y
18 Applegate	Y	N	N	?	Y	Y	Y	N
19 Feighan	Y	N	Y	Y	Y	N	Y	N
20 Oakar	Y	Y	Y	Y	Y	N	Y	N
21 Stokes	Y	Y	Y	Y	Y	N	Y	N
OKLAHOMA								
1 Jones	Y	N	Y	Y	Y	Y	Y	N
2 Synar	Y	Y	Y	Y	Y	N	Y	N
3 Watkins	Y	N	Y	Y	Y	N	Y	Y
4 McCurdy	Y	?	Y	Y	?	?	?	?
5 ***Edwards***	?	?	?	?	?	?	?	?
6 English	Y	N	Y	Y	Y	?	?	?
OREGON								
1 AuCoin	Y	Y	N	Y	N	N	N	N
2 ***Smith, R.***	Y	N	N	Y	Y	Y	N	Y
3 Wyden	Y	Y	N	Y	Y	N	Y	N
4 Weaver	Y	Y	N	Y	Y	Y	N	N
5 ***Smith, D.***	Y	N	N	Y	Y	Y	N	Y
PENNSYLVANIA								
1 Foglietta	Y	Y	Y	Y	N	N	Y	N
2 Gray	Y	Y	Y	Y	N	N	Y	N
3 Borski	Y	Y	Y	Y	N	N	Y	N
4 Kolter	Y	N	Y	Y	N	?	?	?
5 ***Schulze***	Y	N	Y	Y	N	Y	Y	Y
6 Yatron	Y	N	Y	Y	N	N	Y	Y
7 Edgar	Y	?	N	Y	Y	N	Y	N
8 Kostmayer	Y	N	Y	Y	N	N	Y	N
9 ***Shuster***	Y	N	N	Y	Y	Y	N	#
10 ***McDade***	Y	N	N	Y	N	Y	Y	Y
11 Harrison	Y	N	Y	?	Y	N	Y	N
12 Murtha	Y	N	Y	Y	N	N	Y	Y
13 ***Coughlin***	Y	N	N	N	N	Y	Y	N
14 Coyne	Y	Y	N	Y	N	N	Y	N
15 ***Ritter***	Y	N	N	Y	N	Y	N	Y
16 ***Walker***	Y	N	N	?	Y	Y	N	Y
17 ***Gekas***	Y	N	N	N	Y	Y	N	Y
18 Walgren	Y	Y	Y	Y	Y	Y	Y	N
19 ***Goodling***	Y	N	Y	?	N	Y	Y	Y
20 Gaydos	?	N	Y	Y	N	N	?	N
21 ***Ridge***	Y	N	N	P	N	Y	Y	N
22 Murphy	Y	N	Y	Y	N	Y	Y	X
23 ***Clinger***	Y	N	Y	Y	-	+	+	+
RHODE ISLAND								
1 St Germain	Y	N	Y	P	N	N	Y	N
2 ***Schneider***	Y	N	Y	Y	Y	N	N	N
SOUTH CAROLINA								
1 ***Hartnett***	Y	N	Y	Y	Y	Y	N	Y
2 ***Spence***	Y	N	Y	Y	Y	Y	N	Y
3 Derrick	Y	N	Y	Y	N	Y	Y	N
4 ***Campbell***	Y	N	Y	Y	Y	Y	Y	Y
5 Spratt	Y	N	Y	?	N	N	Y	Y
6 Tallon	?	?	?	Y	Y	Y	Y	Y
SOUTH DAKOTA								
AL Daschle	Y	N	N	Y	Y	Y	Y	N
TENNESSEE								
1 ***Quillen***	Y	N	Y	Y	N	Y	N	Y
2 ***Duncan***	Y	N	Y	Y	Y	Y	Y	Y
3 Lloyd	Y	N	Y	Y	N	N	Y	Y
4 Cooper	Y	N	N	?	N	Y	Y	Y
5 Boner	Y	N	?	Y	Y	Y	Y	Y
6 Gore	?	?	X	Y	Y	Y	Y	Y
7 ***Sundquist***	Y	N	Y	Y	Y	Y	N	Y
8 Jones	Y	N	Y	Y	Y	Y	Y	Y
9 Ford	Y	N	Y	Y	N	N	Y	Y
TEXAS								
1 Hall, S.	Y	N	N	Y	N	Y	Y	Y
2 Wilson	?	?	?	?	?	?	?	#
3 ***Bartlett***	Y	N	N	Y	Y	Y	N	Y
4 Hall, R.	Y	N	Y	Y	Y	Y	Y	Y
5 Bryant	?	?	?	?	?	?	?	?
6 ***Gramm***	Y	?	?	?	?	?	?	Y
7 ***Archer***	Y	N	N	Y	Y	Y	N	Y
8 ***Fields***	Y	N	N	N	Y	Y	N	Y
9 Brooks	Y	N	Y	Y	N	N	Y	N
10 Pickle	Y	N	Y	Y	N	N	Y	Y
11 Leath	?	?	?	?	?	?	?	#
12 Wright	Y	?	Y	Y	N	N	Y	N
13 Hightower	Y	N	N	Y	Y	Y	Y	Y
14 Patman	Y	N	Y	Y	Y	Y	Y	Y
15 de la Garza	Y	N	N	Y	N	N	Y	Y
16 Coleman	Y	N	Y	Y	N	N	Y	Y
17 Stenholm	Y	N	Y	Y	Y	Y	N	Y
18 Leland	Y	Y	N	?	Y	N	Y	X
19 Hance	?	X	X	?	?	?	?	#
20 Gonzalez	Y	N	Y	Y	N	N	Y	N
21 ***Loeffler***	Y	N	N	Y	Y	Y	N	Y
22 ***Paul***	Y	?	?	Y	Y	Y	N	Y
23 Kazen	Y	N	Y	Y	N	N	Y	Y
24 Frost	Y	N	Y	Y	Y	N	Y	Y
25 Andrews	Y	N	Y	Y	Y	Y	Y	Y
26 Vandergriff	Y	N	N	Y	Y	Y	N	Y
27 Ortiz	Y	N	Y	Y	N	N	Y	Y
UTAH								
1 ***Hansen***	Y	N	N	Y	Y	Y	N	Y
2 ***Marriott***	?	?	?	?	?	?	?	?
3 ***Nielson***	Y	N	N	Y	Y	Y	N	Y
VERMONT								
AL ***Jeffords***	?	?	?	?	?	?	?	X
VIRGINIA								
1 ***Bateman***	Y	N	N	Y	Y	Y	Y	Y
2 ***Whitehurst***	Y	N	Y	Y	Y	Y	Y	Y
3 ***Bliley***	Y	N	N	Y	Y	Y	Y	Y
4 Sisisky	Y	N	Y	Y	Y	N	Y	N
5 Daniel	Y	N	Y	Y	Y	Y	Y	Y
6 Olin	Y	N	Y	Y	Y	Y	N	N
7 ***Robinson***	Y	N	N	Y	Y	Y	Y	Y
8 ***Parris***	Y	?	N	Y	Y	Y	Y	Y
9 Boucher	Y	N	Y	Y	N	N	Y	N
10 ***Wolf***	Y	N	N	Y	N	Y	Y	Y
WASHINGTON								
1 ***Pritchard***	?	N	N	?	N	N	Y	Y
2 Swift	Y	N	Y	Y	N	N	Y	N
3 Bonker	Y	Y	N	Y	Y	N	Y	N
4 ***Morrison***	Y	N	N	Y	N	N	Y	Y
5 Foley	Y	Y	N	Y	N	N	Y	N
6 Dicks	Y	N	N	Y	Y	N	Y	Y
7 Lowry	Y	Y	Y	?	Y	N	Y	N
8 ***Chandler***	Y	N	N	?	N	N	Y	Y
WEST VIRGINIA								
1 Mollohan	Y	N	Y	Y	N	?	?	?
2 Staggers	Y	N	N	Y	N	N	Y	N
3 Wise	Y	N	N	Y	Y	N	Y	N
4 Rahall	Y	Y	Y	Y	Y	N	Y	N
WISCONSIN								
1 Aspin	Y	N	N	Y	N	N	Y	Y
2 Kastenmeier	Y	Y	N	Y	Y	N	Y	N
3 ***Gunderson***	Y	N	N	Y	N	Y	N	Y
4 Kleczka	Y	Y	N	?	Y	Y	Y	N
5 Moody	Y	Y	N	?	Y	Y	Y	N
6 ***Petri***	Y	Y	N	Y	N	Y	Y	N
7 Obey	Y	Y	Y	Y	N	N	N	N
8 ***Roth***	Y	N	N	Y	N	Y	Y	Y
9 ***Sensenbrenner***	?	?	?	?	?	?	?	?
WYOMING								
AL ***Cheney***	Y	N	Y	Y	Y	Y	N	Y

Southern states - Ala., Ark., Fla., Ga., Ky., La., Miss., N.C., Okla., S.C., Tenn., Texas, Va.

KEY

Y Voted for (yea).
Paired for.
+ Announced for.
N Voted against (nay).
X Paired against.
- Announced against.
P Voted "present".
C Voted "present" to avoid possible conflict of interest.
? Did not vote or otherwise make a position known.

Democrats   *Republicans*

178. HR 5167. Department of Defense Authorization.
Bennett, D-Fla., amendment to the Dickinson, R-Ala., amendment, to prohibit the obligation of funds appropriated for production of MX missiles unless Congress had given its approval by passing a joint resolution after April 1, 1985. Adopted 199-197: R 17-141; D 182-56 (ND 149-15, SD 33-41), May 31, 1984. (The Dickinson amendment, as amended, subsequently was adopted *(see vote 179, below).)* A "nay" was a vote supporting the president's position.

179. HR 5167. Department of Defense Authorization.
Dickinson, R-Ala., amendment, as amended, to authorize the production of 15 MX missiles but prohibit the obligation of funds appropriated for that purpose unless Congress had given its approval by passing a joint resolution after April 1, 1985. Adopted 198-197: R 17-141; D 181-56 (ND 148-15, SD 33-41), May 31, 1984. A "nay" was a vote supporting the president's position.

180. HR 5167. Department of Defense Authorization.
Price, D-Ill., motion that all debate on the bill and the amendments thereto be completed in one hour (by 10:10 p.m.). Motion agreed to 213-174: R 22-134; D 191-40 (ND 131-27, SD 60-13), May 31, 1984.

181. HR 5167. Department of Defense Authorization.
Hiler, R-Ind., motion that all debate on the Dellums, D-Calif., amendment and all amendments thereto be limited to five minutes. Motion rejected 55-321: R 36-118; D 19-203 (ND 8-141, SD 11-62), May 31, 1984.

182. HR 5167. Department of Defense Authorization.
Dellums, D-Calif., amendment to prohibit, during fiscal 1985, further deployment in Europe of Pershing II or ground-launched cruise missiles unless the North Atlantic Treaty Organization (NATO) notified the United States that there was a NATO consensus that further deployments should be made. Rejected 104-291: R 2-154; D 102-137 (ND 98-66, SD 4-71), May 31, 1984. A "nay" was a vote supporting the president's position.

183. HR 5167. Department of Defense Authorization.
Dickinson, R-Ala., amendment, as amended, to authorize the production of 15 MX missiles but prohibit the obligation of funds appropriated for that purpose unless Congress had given its approval by passing a joint resolution after April 1, 1985. Adopted 199-196: R 17-142; D 182-54 (ND 150-14, SD 32-40), May 31, 1984. A "nay" was a vote supporting the president's position. (This amendment previously had been adopted in the Committee of the Whole *(see vote 179, above).)*

184. HR 5167. Department of Defense Authorization.
Passage of the bill to authorize $207 billion for research and development, weapons procurement, and operations and maintenance in the Department of Defense. Passed 298-98: R 124-35; D 174-63 (ND 104-59, SD 70-4), in the session that began May 31, 1984.

	178	179	180	181	182	183	184
ALABAMA							
1 *Edwards*	N	N	Y	?	N	N	Y
2 *Dickinson*	N	N	Y	Y	N	N	Y
3 Nichols	N	N	Y	Y	N	N	Y
4 Bevill	N	N	Y	N	N	N	Y
5 Flippo	N	N	Y	N	N	N	Y
6 Erdreich	-	-	+	-	-	X	#
7 Shelby	N	N	?	N	N	N	Y
ALASKA							
AL *Young*	N	N	N	N	N	N	Y
ARIZONA							
1 *McCain*	N	N	N	N	N	N	N
2 Udall	Y	?	Y	N	Y	Y	Y
3 *Stump*	N	N	N	Y	N	N	Y
4 *Rudd*	N	N	Y	N	N	N	Y
5 McNulty	Y	Y	Y	Y	N	Y	Y
ARKANSAS							
1 Alexander	?	?	?	?	?	?	?
2 *Bethune*	N	N	N	N	N	N	Y
3 *Hammerschmidt*	N	N	N	N	N	N	Y
4 Anthony	?	?	?	?	X	?	#
CALIFORNIA							
1 Bosco	Y	Y	?	?	N	Y	N
2 *Chappie*	N	N	N	N	N	N	Y
3 Matsui	Y	Y	Y	N	Y	Y	Y
4 Fazio	N	N	Y	N	N	?	?
5 Burton	Y	Y	Y	Y	Y	Y	N
6 Boxer	Y	Y	N	N	Y	Y	N
7 Miller	Y	Y	N	Y	Y	Y	Y
8 Dellums	Y	Y	N	Y	Y	Y	N
9 Stark	Y	Y	Y	?	?	Y	Y
10 Edwards	Y	Y	N	?	Y	Y	N
11 Lantos	Y	Y	Y	N	Y	Y	Y
12 *Zschau*	Y	Y	N	Y	N	Y	Y
13 Mineta	Y	Y	Y	?	Y	Y	Y
14 Shumway	N	N	N	N	N	N	N
15 Coelho	Y	Y	Y	N	Y	Y	Y
16 Panetta	Y	Y	Y	Y	Y	Y	Y
17 *Pashayan*	N	N	N	N	N	N	Y
18 Lehman	Y	Y	Y	N	Y	Y	N
19 *Lagomarsino*	N	N	N	N	N	N	Y
20 *Thomas*	N	N	N	N	N	N	Y
21 *Fiedler*	N	N	N	N	N	N	Y
22 *Moorhead*	N	N	N	N	N	N	Y
23 Beilenson	Y	Y	Y	N	Y	Y	N
24 Waxman	Y	Y	Y	N	Y	Y	N
25 Roybal	Y	Y	N	Y	Y	Y	N
26 Berman	Y	Y	Y	N	Y	Y	N
27 Levine	Y	Y	Y	N	Y	Y	Y
28 Dixon	#	#	?	?	#	#	X
29 Hawkins	?	?	?	?	?	?	?
30 Martinez	Y	Y	Y	N	Y	Y	Y
31 Dymally	?	?	?	?	?	?	?
32 Anderson	N	N	N	N	N	N	N
33 *Dreier*	N	N	N	N	N	N	Y
34 Torres	Y	Y	Y	N	Y	Y	Y
35 *Lewis*	N	N	Y	?	N	N	Y
36 Brown	Y	Y	Y	Y	Y	Y	Y
37 *McCandless*	N	N	N	N	N	N	Y
38 Patterson	N	N	N	N	N	N	Y
39 *Dannemeyer*	N	N	Y	N	N	N	Y
40 *Badham*	N	N	Y	?	N	N	Y
41 *Lowery*	N	N	N	N	N	N	Y
42 *Lungren*	N	N	N	N	N	N	Y

	178	179	180	181	182	183	184
43 *Packard*	N	N	N	N	N	N	N
44 Bates	Y	Y	Y	Y	Y	Y	Y
45 *Hunter*	N	N	N	N	N	N	Y
COLORADO							
1 Schroeder	Y	Y	Y	N	Y	Y	Y
2 Wirth	Y	Y	N	N	Y	Y	Y
3 Kogovsek	Y	Y	Y	N	Y	Y	Y
4 *Brown*	N	N	N	N	N	N	N
5 *Kramer*	N	N	Y	N	N	N	N
6 *Schaefer*	N	N	N	Y	N	N	N
CONNECTICUT							
1 Kennelly	Y	Y	Y	N	Y	Y	Y
2 Gejdenson	Y	Y	Y	N	Y	Y	Y
3 Morrison	Y	Y	Y	N	Y	Y	Y
4 *McKinney*	#	#	?	?	?	#	?
5 Ratchford	Y	Y	Y	N	Y	Y	Y
6 *Johnson*	Y	Y	Y	N	N	Y	Y
DELAWARE							
AL Carper	Y	Y	Y	N	N	Y	Y
FLORIDA							
1 Hutto	N	N	Y	N	N	N	Y
2 Fuqua	N	N	Y	N	N	N	Y
3 Bennett	Y	Y	N	N	Y	Y	Y
4 Chappell	N	N	Y	?	N	N	Y
5 *McCollum*	N	N	N	N	N	N	Y
6 MacKay	Y	Y	N	N	Y	Y	Y
7 Gibbons	?	?	?	?	?	?	?
8 *Young*	N	N	N	N	N	N	Y
9 *Bilirakis*	N	N	N	N	N	N	Y
10 Ireland	N	N	N	N	N	N	Y
11 Nelson	N	N	N	N	N	N	Y
12 *Lewis*	N	N	N	N	N	N	Y
13 *Mack*	N	N	N	N	N	N	N
14 Mica	Y	Y	Y	N	Y	Y	Y
15 *Shaw*	N	N	N	N	N	N	Y
16 Smith	Y	Y	N	N	Y	Y	Y
17 Lehman	Y	Y	Y	Y	Y	Y	N
18 Pepper	N	N	Y	N	N	?	#
19 Fascell	Y	Y	Y	N	Y	Y	Y
GEORGIA							
1 Thomas	N	N	Y	N	N	N	Y
2 Hatcher	?	?	?	?	?	?	?
3 Ray	N	N	Y	N	N	N	Y
4 Levitas	N	N	Y	N	N	N	Y
5 Fowler	Y	Y	N	N	Y	Y	Y
6 *Gingrich*	N	N	N	N	N	N	N
7 Darden	N	N	Y	N	N	N	Y
8 Rowland	N	N	Y	N	N	N	Y
9 Jenkins	?	?	?	?	?	?	?
10 Barnard	?	?	?	?	?	?	?
HAWAII							
1 Heftel	Y	Y	Y	N	N	Y	Y
2 Akaka	Y	Y	Y	N	N	Y	Y
IDAHO							
1 *Craig*	N	N	N	N	N	N	Y
2 *Hansen*	?	?	?	?	?	?	?
ILLINOIS							
1 Hayes	Y	Y	Y	?	Y	Y	N
2 Savage	Y	Y	N	N	Y	Y	N
3 Russo	Y	Y	Y	N	Y	Y	N
4 *O'Brien*	N	N	N	Y	N	N	Y
5 Lipinski	N	N	Y	Y	N	N	Y
6 *Hyde*	N	N	N	N	N	N	N
7 Collins	Y	Y	Y	N	Y	Y	N
8 Rostenkowski	Y	Y	Y	Y	Y	Y	Y
9 Yates	Y	Y	Y	N	Y	Y	Y
10 *Porter*	N	N	N	N	N	N	Y
11 Annunzio	Y	Y	Y	N	Y	Y	Y
12 *Crane, P.*	N	N	N	N	N	N	N
13 *Erlenborn*	N	N	N	N	N	N	Y
14 *Corcoran*	N	N	N	N	N	N	Y
15 *Madigan*	N	N	N	N	N	N	Y
16 *Martin*	N	N	N	N	N	N	Y
17 Evans	Y	Y	Y	N	Y	Y	Y
18 *Michel*	N	N	N	N	N	N	Y
19 *Crane, D.*	N	N	N	N	N	N	N
20 Durbin	Y	Y	Y	N	Y	Y	Y
21 Price	N	N	Y	N	N	N	Y
22 Simon	?	?	?	?	?	?	?
INDIANA							
1 Hall	Y	Y	Y	N	Y	Y	Y
2 Sharp	Y	Y	Y	N	Y	Y	Y
3 *Hiler*	N	N	Y	N	N	N	Y
4 *Coats*	N	N	N	N	N	N	Y
5 Hillis	N	N	Y	Y	N	N	Y

	178	179	180	181	182	183	184
6 ***Burton***	N	N	N	N	N	N	N
7 ***Myers***	N	N	N	N	N	N	Y
8 McCloskey	Y	Y	Y	N	N	Y	Y
9 Hamilton	Y	Y	Y	N	N	Y	Y
10 Jacobs	Y	Y	N	N	Y	Y	Y
IOWA							
1 ***Leach***	Y	Y	N	N	Y	Y	N
2 ***Tauke***	Y	Y	N	Y	N	Y	N
3 ***Evans***	Y	Y	N	N	N	Y	N
4 Smith	Y	Y	Y	Y	N	Y	N
5 Harkin	Y	Y	Y	N	Y	Y	N
6 Bedell	Y	Y	Y	N	Y	Y	N
KANSAS							
1 ***Roberts***	N	N	N	N	N	N	N
2 Slattery	Y	Y	N	N	N	Y	Y
3 ***Winn***	N	N	N	N	N	N	Y
4 Glickman	Y	Y	N	N	N	Y	Y
5 ***Whittaker***	N	N	N	N	N	N	N
KENTUCKY							
1 Hubbard	Y	Y	Y	N	N	Y	Y
2 Natcher	Y	Y	Y	N	N	Y	Y
3 Mazzoli	Y	Y	Y	N	N	Y	Y
4 ***Snyder***	N	N	Y	Y	N	N	Y
5 ***Rogers***	N	N	N	Y	N	N	Y
6 ***Hopkins***	N	N	Y	N	N	N	Y
7 Perkins	Y	Y	Y	N	N	Y	Y
LOUISIANA							
1 ***Livingston***	N	N	N	N	N	N	Y
2 Boggs	Y	Y	Y	N	N	Y	Y
3 Tauzin	N	N	N	N	N	N	Y
4 Roemer	N	N	N	N	N	N	N
5 Huckaby	N	N	N	N	N	N	Y
6 ***Moore***	N	N	N	N	N	N	Y
7 Breaux	N	N	N	N	N	N	Y
8 Long	Y	Y	Y	N	N	Y	Y
MAINE							
1 ***McKernan***	N	N	N	N	N	N	Y
2 ***Snowe***	N	N	N	N	N	N	Y
MARYLAND							
1 Dyson	Y	Y	Y	Y	N	Y	Y
2 Long	Y	Y	Y	Y	N	Y	Y
3 Mikulski	Y	Y	Y	N	Y	Y	Y
4 ***Holt***	N	N	N	Y	N	N	Y
5 Hoyer	Y	Y	Y	N	N	Y	Y
6 Byron	N	N	Y	?	N	N	Y
7 Mitchell	Y	Y	Y	N	Y	Y	N
8 Barnes	Y	Y	Y	N	N	Y	Y
MASSACHUSETTS							
1 ***Conte***	Y	Y	Y	N	Y	Y	Y
2 Boland	Y	Y	Y	N	N	Y	Y
3 Early	Y	Y	Y	N	Y	Y	N
4 Frank	Y	Y	N	N	Y	Y	N
5 Shannon	Y	Y	Y	N	Y	Y	N
6 Mavroules	Y	Y	Y	N	Y	Y	Y
7 Markey	Y	Y	Y	N	Y	Y	N
8 O'Neill	Y	Y					
9 Moakley	Y	Y	Y	N	Y	Y	Y
10 Studds	Y	Y	Y	N	Y	Y	N
11 Donnelly	Y	Y	Y	N	N	Y	N
MICHIGAN							
1 Conyers	Y	Y	N	N	Y	Y	N
2 ***Pursell***	N	N	N	N	N	N	Y
3 Wolpe	Y	Y	Y	N	Y	Y	Y
4 ***Siljander***	N	N	N	N	N	N	Y
5 ***Sawyer***	X	X	?	?	?	X	?
6 Carr	Y	Y	N	N	N	Y	Y
7 Kildee	Y	Y	Y	N	Y	Y	Y
8 Traxler	Y	Y	Y	N	Y	Y	Y
9 ***Vander Jagt***	X	X	?	?	?	N	Y
10 Albosta	Y	Y	Y	N	N	Y	Y
11 ***Davis***	N	N	N	N	N	N	N
12 Bonior	Y	Y	Y	N	Y	Y	N
13 Crockett	?	#	?	?	#	?	X
14 Hertel	Y	Y	Y	N	N	Y	N
15 Ford	Y	Y	Y	?	Y	Y	Y
16 Dingell	Y	Y	Y	N	N	Y	Y
17 Levin	Y	Y	Y	N	N	Y	Y
18 ***Broomfield***	N	N	N	N	N	N	N
MINNESOTA							
1 Penny	Y	Y	Y	N	Y	Y	N
2 ***Weber***	N	N	N	N	N	N	Y
3 ***Frenzel***	N	N	N	N	N	N	N
4 Vento	Y	Y	?	N	Y	Y	N
5 Sabo	#	#	?	?	?	#	X
6 Sikorski	Y	Y	Y	N	Y	Y	N
7 ***Stangeland***	N	N	N	Y	N	N	N
8 Oberstar	Y	Y	N	N	Y	Y	N
MISSISSIPPI							
1 Whitten	Y	Y	Y	N	N	Y	Y
2 ***Franklin***	N	N	N	N	N	N	Y
3 Montgomery	N	N	Y	Y	N	N	Y
4 Dowdy	?	?	?	?	?	?	?
5 ***Lott***	N	N	N	N	N	N	Y
MISSOURI							
1 Clay	Y	Y	?	?	Y	Y	N
2 Young	Y	Y	Y	N	N	Y	Y
3 Gephardt	Y	Y	Y	N	N	Y	Y
4 Skelton	N	N	Y	N	N	N	Y
5 Wheat	Y	Y	Y	N	Y	Y	N
6 ***Coleman***	N	N	N	N	N	N	Y
7 ***Taylor***	N	N	Y	Y	N	N	Y
8 ***Emerson***	N	N	N	N	N	N	Y
9 Volkmer	Y	Y	Y	N	N	Y	Y
MONTANA							
1 Williams	Y	Y	N	N	Y	Y	Y
2 ***Marlenee***	N	N	N	N	N	N	N
NEBRASKA							
1 ***Bereuter***	Y	Y	N	Y	N	Y	N
2 ***Daub***	N	N	N	N	N	N	Y
3 ***Smith***	Y	Y	N	N	N	Y	Y
NEVADA							
1 Reid	N	N	Y	N	N	N	Y
2 ***Vucanovich***	N	N	N	N	N	N	Y
NEW HAMPSHIRE							
1 D'Amours	Y	Y	Y	N	N	Y	Y
2 ***Gregg***	N	N	N	N	N	N	N
NEW JERSEY							
1 Florio	Y	Y	Y	N	N	Y	Y
2 Hughes	N	N	Y	N	N	N	N
3 Howard	?	?	?	?	?	?	?
4 ***Smith***	N	N	N	N	N	N	Y
5 ***Roukema***	Y	Y	N	N	N	Y	Y
6 Dwyer	Y	Y	Y	N	N	Y	Y
7 ***Rinaldo***	N	N	N	N	N	N	Y
8 Roe	?	?	?	?	?	?	?
9 Torricelli	Y	Y	Y	N	Y	Y	Y
10 Rodino	#	#	?	?	?	#	?
11 Minish	Y	Y	Y	N	N	Y	Y
12 ***Courter***	N	N	N	Y	N	N	N
13 Vacancy							
14 Guarini	?	?	?	?	?	?	?
NEW MEXICO							
1 ***Lujan***	N	N	N	N	N	N	N
2 ***Skeen***	N	N	N	N	N	N	Y
3 Richardson	Y	Y	Y	N	N	Y	Y
NEW YORK							
1 ***Carney***	N	N	N	N	N	N	Y
2 Downey	Y	Y	Y	?	Y	Y	Y
3 Mrazek	Y	Y	Y	N	Y	Y	Y
4 ***Lent***	N	N	?	N	N	N	Y
5 ***McGrath***	N	N	N	N	N	N	Y
6 Addabbo	Y	Y	Y	N	Y	Y	Y
7 Ackerman	#	#	Y	N	Y	Y	N
8 Scheuer	Y	Y	N	N	Y	Y	Y
9 Ferraro	Y	Y	Y	N	Y	Y	Y
10 Schumer	Y	Y	Y	N	Y	Y	Y
11 Towns	Y	Y	N	N	Y	Y	N
12 Owens	Y	Y	Y	N	Y	Y	Y
13 Solarz	Y	Y	Y	N	Y	Y	Y
14 ***Molinari***	N	N	N	N	N	N	Y
15 ***Green***	Y	Y	N	N	N	Y	Y
16 Rangel	Y	Y	?	?	Y	Y	N
17 Weiss	Y	Y	Y	N	Y	Y	N
18 Garcia	Y	Y	Y	N	Y	Y	N
19 Biaggi	Y	Y	Y	N	N	Y	Y
20 Ottinger	Y	Y	Y	N	Y	Y	N
21 ***Fish***	N	N	Y	N	N	N	Y
22 ***Gilman***	N	N	N	N	N	N	Y
23 Stratton	N	N	Y	Y	N	N	Y
24 ***Solomon***	N	N	N	N	N	N	Y
25 ***Boehlert***	N	N	N	N	N	N	Y
26 ***Martin***	N	N	N	N	N	N	Y
27 ***Wortley***	N	N	N	?	N	N	Y
28 McHugh	Y	Y	Y	N	N	Y	Y
29 ***Horton***	N	N	N	N	N	N	Y
30 ***Conable***	N	N	N	N	N	N	N
31 ***Kemp***	N	N	N	N	N	N	Y
32 LaFalce	Y	Y	Y	N	Y	Y	N
33 Nowak	Y	Y	Y	N	Y	Y	N
34 Lundine	?	?	?	?	?	?	X
NORTH CAROLINA							
1 Jones	Y	Y	Y	N	N	Y	Y
2 Valentine	N	N	Y	Y	N	N	Y
3 Whitley	N	N	Y	Y	N	N	Y
4 Andrews	Y	Y	Y	N	N	?	Y
5 Neal	Y	Y	Y	N	N	Y	Y
6 Britt	N	N	Y	N	N	N	Y
7 Rose	Y	?	?	?	?	?	?
8 Hefner	N	N	Y	Y	N	N	Y
9 ***Martin***	N	N	N	N	N	N	Y
10 ***Broyhill***	N	N	N	Y	N	N	Y
11 Clarke	Y	Y	Y	N	N	Y	Y
NORTH DAKOTA							
AL Dorgan	Y	Y	Y	N	Y	Y	N
OHIO							
1 Luken	Y	?	?	?	N	Y	Y
2 ***Gradison***	Y	Y	Y	Y	N	Y	Y
3 Hall	Y	Y	Y	N	N	Y	Y
4 ***Oxley***	N	N	N	N	N	N	Y
5 ***Latta***	N	N	N	N	N	N	Y
6 ***McEwen***	N	N	N	Y	N	N	Y
7 ***DeWine***	N	N	N	N	N	N	Y
8 ***Kindness***	N	N	N	Y	N	N	N
9 Kaptur	Y	Y	Y	N	Y	Y	N
10 ***Miller***	N	N	N	N	N	N	Y
11 Eckart	Y	Y	Y	N	Y	Y	Y
12 ***Kasich***	N	N	N	N	N	N	Y
13 Pease	Y	Y	N	N	Y	Y	Y
14 Seiberling	Y	Y	Y	N	Y	Y	Y
15 ***Wylie***	N	N	Y	Y	N	N	N
16 ***Regula***	N	N	N	N	N	N	Y
17 ***Williams***	N	N	N	N	N	N	Y
18 Applegate	Y	Y	Y	?	N	Y	N
19 Feighan	Y	Y	N	N	Y	Y	N
20 Oakar	Y	Y	Y	N	Y	Y	Y
21 Stokes	Y	Y	N	?	Y	Y	N
OKLAHOMA							
1 Jones	Y	Y	Y	N	N	Y	Y
2 Synar	Y	Y	Y	N	N	Y	Y
3 Watkins	N	N	Y	N	N	N	Y
4 McCurdy	?	?	?	?	?	?	?
5 ***Edwards***	X	X	?	?	?	?	?
6 English	?	?	?	?	?	?	?
OREGON							
1 AuCoin	Y	Y	Y	N	Y	Y	N
2 ***Smith, R.***	N	N	Y	N	N	N	Y
3 Wyden	Y	Y	Y	N	Y	Y	N
4 Weaver	Y	Y	Y	N	Y	Y	N
5 ***Smith, D.***	N	N	N	N	N	N	N
PENNSYLVANIA							
1 Foglietta	Y	Y	Y	N	Y	Y	Y
2 Gray	Y	Y	N	N	Y	Y	N
3 Borski	Y	Y	?	?	N	Y	Y
4 Kolter	?	?	?	?	?	?	?
5 ***Schulze***	N	N	Y	N	N	N	Y
6 Yatron	N	N	Y	N	N	N	Y
7 Edgar	Y	Y	N	N	Y	Y	N
8 Kostmayer	Y	Y	Y	N	Y	Y	N
9 ***Shuster***	N	N	N	N	N	N	Y
10 ***McDade***	N	N	Y	Y	N	N	Y
11 Harrison	Y	Y	Y	N	N	Y	Y
12 Murtha	N	N	Y	N	N	N	?
13 ***Coughlin***	Y	Y	N	N	N	Y	Y
14 Coyne	Y	Y	Y	N	Y	Y	Y
15 ***Ritter***	N	N	N	N	N	N	N
16 ***Walker***	N	N	N	N	N	N	Y
17 ***Gekas***	N	N	N	N	N	N	Y
18 Walgren	Y	Y	N	N	N	Y	Y
19 ***Goodling***	Y	Y	Y	N	N	Y	Y
20 Gaydos	Y	Y	Y	N	N	Y	Y
21 ***Ridge***	Y	Y	N	N	?	Y	Y
22 Murphy	Y	Y	?	Y	N	Y	N
23 ***Clinger***	N	N	N	N	N	N	Y
RHODE ISLAND							
1 St Germain	Y	Y	Y	N	N	Y	Y
2 ***Schneider***	Y	Y	N	N	N	Y	N
SOUTH CAROLINA							
1 ***Hartnett***	N	N	N	Y	N	N	Y
2 ***Spence***	N	N	N	N	N	N	Y
3 Derrick	Y	Y	Y	N	N	Y	Y
4 ***Campbell***	N	N	N	N	N	N	Y
5 Spratt	Y	Y	N	N	N	Y	Y
6 Tallon	Y	Y	Y	N	N	Y	Y
SOUTH DAKOTA							
AL Daschle	Y	Y	Y	N	Y	Y	Y
TENNESSEE							
1 ***Quillen***	N	N	Y	Y	N	N	Y
2 ***Duncan***	N	N	N	Y	N	N	Y
3 Lloyd	N	N	Y	Y	N	N	Y
4 Cooper	N	N	Y	N	N	N	Y
5 Boner	N	N	Y	N	N	N	Y
6 Gore	N	N	Y	N	N	N	Y
7 ***Sundquist***	N	N	Y	Y	N	N	Y
8 Jones	N	N	Y	N	N	N	Y
9 Ford	Y	Y	Y	N	Y	Y	Y
TEXAS							
1 Hall, S.	N	N	Y	N	N	N	Y
2 Wilson	X	X	?	?	?	?	?
3 ***Bartlett***	N	N	N	N	N	N	Y
4 Hall, R.	N	N	N	N	N	N	Y
5 Bryant	#	#	?	?	?	#	?
6 ***Gramm***	N	N	N	N	N	N	Y
7 ***Archer***	N	N	N	Y	N	N	Y
8 ***Fields***	N	N	N	Y	N	N	Y
9 Brooks	Y	Y	Y	N	N	Y	Y
10 Pickle	Y	Y	N	N	N	Y	Y
11 Leath	X	X	?	?	?	X	#
12 Wright	Y	Y	Y	?	N	Y	Y
13 Hightower	N	N	Y	Y	N	N	Y
14 Patman	N	N	N	N	N	N	Y
15 de la Garza	N	N	Y	N	N	N	Y
16 Coleman	Y	Y	Y	N	N	Y	Y
17 Stenholm	N	N	N	N	N	N	Y
18 Leland	#	Y	Y	N	Y	Y	N
19 Hance	X	X	?	?	X	X	?
20 Gonzalez	Y	Y	Y	N	Y	Y	Y
21 ***Loeffler***	N	N	N	N	N	N	Y
22 ***Paul***	Y	Y	N	?	?	Y	N
23 Kazen	N	N	Y	N	N	N	Y
24 Frost	X	X	Y	N	N	X	Y
25 Andrews	N	N	Y	N	N	N	Y
26 Vandergriff	N	N	N	N	N	N	N
27 Ortiz	N	N	Y	N	N	N	Y
UTAH							
1 ***Hansen***	N	N	N	Y	N	N	N
2 ***Marriott***	X	X	?	?	?	X	?
3 ***Nielson***	N	N	N	N	N	N	Y
VERMONT							
AL ***Jeffords***	#	#	?	?	?	#	?
VIRGINIA							
1 ***Bateman***	N	N	N	N	N	N	Y
2 ***Whitehurst***	N	N	Y	Y	N	N	Y
3 ***Bliley***	N	N	N	N	N	N	Y
4 Sisisky	Y	Y	?	N	N	Y	Y
5 Daniel	N	N	Y	Y	N	N	Y
6 Olin	Y	Y	Y	N	N	Y	Y
7 ***Robinson***	N	N	Y	N	N	N	Y
8 ***Parris***	N	N	Y	Y	N	N	Y
9 Boucher	Y	Y	Y	N	N	Y	Y
10 ***Wolf***	N	N	N	N	N	N	Y
WASHINGTON							
1 ***Pritchard***	N	N	N	Y	N	N	Y
2 Swift	Y	Y	Y	?	Y	Y	Y
3 Bonker	?	Y	Y	N	Y	Y	N
4 ***Morrison***	N	N	N	N	N	N	Y
5 Foley	Y	Y	Y	N	N	Y	Y
6 Dicks	N	N	N	N	N	N	Y
7 Lowry	Y	Y	Y	?	Y	Y	Y
8 ***Chandler***	N	N	N	N	N	N	Y
WEST VIRGINIA							
1 Mollohan	N	N	Y	N	N	N	Y
2 Staggers	Y	Y	Y	N	Y	Y	Y
3 Wise	Y	Y	Y	N	N	Y	Y
4 Rahall	Y	Y	N	N	Y	Y	Y
WISCONSIN							
1 Aspin	N	N	Y	N	N	N	Y
2 Kastenmeier	Y	Y	N	N	Y	Y	N
3 ***Gunderson***	N	N	N	Y	N	N	N
4 Kleczka	Y	Y	Y	N	N	Y	Y
5 Moody	Y	Y	Y	N	Y	Y	N
6 ***Petri***	Y	Y	N	N	N	Y	Y
7 Obey	Y	Y	Y	N	N	Y	Y
8 ***Roth***	N	N	N	N	N	N	Y
9 ***Sensenbrenner***	?	?	?	?	?	?	?
WYOMING							
AL ***Cheney***	N	N	N	N	N	N	Y

Southern states - Ala., Ark., Fla., Ga., Ky., La., Miss., N.C., Okla., S.C., Tenn., Texas, Va.

185. HR 5743. Agriculture Appropriations, Fiscal 1985. Dannemeyer, R-Calif., amendment to reduce certain programs by $24 million, on the assumption that the Agriculture Department could administratively implement money-saving policy changes recommended by a presidential commission (the Grace commission). Rejected 153-232: R 101-50; D 52-182 (ND 34-120, SD 18-62), June 6, 1984.

186. HR 5743. Agriculture Appropriations, Fiscal 1985. Obey, D-Wis., substitute for the Walker, R-Pa., amendment *(see vote 187, below)*, to reduce appropriations for non-entitlement farm and food programs in fiscal 1985 by 64 percent. Rejected 6-388: R 3-151; D 3-237 (ND 2-157, SD 1-80), June 6, 1984.

187. HR 5743. Agriculture Appropriations, Fiscal 1985. Walker, R-Pa., amendment to reduce appropriations for farm and food programs in fiscal 1985 by 1 percent. Adopted 232-164: R 131-23; D 101-141 (ND 61-100, SD 40-41), June 6, 1984.

188. HR 5753. Legislative Branch Appropriations, Fiscal 1985. Frenzel, R-Minn., amendment to reduce funds for House of Representatives operations by approximately $13 million. Rejected 191-201: R 141-11; D 50-190 (ND 27-133, SD 23-57), June 6, 1984.

189. HR 5753. Legislative Branch Appropriations, Fiscal 1985. Brown, R-Colo., amendment to bar hiring individuals to operate elevators in House office buildings and reduce funds in the bill earmarked for elevator operators' salaries by $88,354. Rejected 176-205: R 121-26; D 55-179 (ND 20-135, SD 35-44), June 6, 1984.

190. HR 5753. Legislative Branch Appropriations, Fiscal 1985. Frenzel, R-Minn., amendment to make a 2 percent across-the-board cut in the bill's funding level. Adopted 201-175: R 133-10; D 68-165 (ND 32-123, SD 36-42), June 6, 1984.

191. HR 5753. Legislative Branch Appropriations, Fiscal 1985. Fazio, D-Calif., motion that the Committee of the Whole rise and report the bill back to the House. Motion agreed to 234-147: R 0-143; D 234-4 (ND 157-2, SD 77-2), June 6, 1984. (By voting to rise, the House refused to consider a pending Lewis, R-Calif., amendment to bar the use of funds for House television coverage unless cameras pan the chamber uniformly from gavel to gavel.)

192. HR 5753. Legislative Branch Appropriations, Fiscal 1985. Frenzel, R-Minn., amendment to make a 2 percent across-the-board cut in the bill's funding level. Adopted 193-190: R 142-5; D 51-185 (ND 24-135, SD 27-50), June 6, 1984. (This amendment previously had been adopted in the Committee of the Whole *(see vote 190, above)*.)

KEY

Y	Voted for (yea).
#	Paired for.
+	Announced for.
N	Voted against (nay).
X	Paired against.
-	Announced against.
P	Voted "present".
C	Voted "present" to avoid possible conflict of interest.
?	Did not vote or otherwise make a position known.

Democrats   *Republicans*

	185	186	187	188	189	190	191	192
ALABAMA								
1 *Edwards*	Y	N	Y	Y	?	?	?	?
2 *Dickinson*	N	N	Y	?	N	Y	N	Y
3 Nichols	?	?	?	?	?	?	?	?
4 Bevill	?	?	?	?	?	?	?	?
5 Flippo	N	N	N	N	Y	N	Y	N
6 Erdreich	Y	N	Y	Y	Y	Y	Y	Y
7 Shelby	N	N	N	N	N	Y	Y	Y
ALASKA								
AL *Young*	N	N	N	N	N	N	N	Y
ARIZONA								
1 *McCain*	Y	N	Y	Y	Y	?	N	Y
2 Udall	N	N	N	N	N	Y	N	N
3 *Stump*	Y	N	Y	Y	Y	Y	N	Y
4 *Rudd*	Y	N	Y	Y	Y	Y	Y	Y
5 McNulty	N	N	N	N	N	N	Y	N
ARKANSAS								
1 Alexander	N	N	N	N	N	N	Y	N
2 *Bethune*	N	N	Y	Y	Y	Y	N	Y
3 *Hammerschmidt*	?	?	?	?	?	?	?	?
4 Anthony	?	?	?	?	?	?	?	?
CALIFORNIA								
1 Bosco	Y	N	Y	N	N	N	Y	N
2 *Chappie*	Y	N	Y	Y	Y	Y	N	Y
3 Matsui	N	N	N	N	N	N	Y	N
4 Fazio	N	N	N	N	N	N	Y	N
5 Burton	?	?	?	N	N	N	Y	N
6 Boxer	N	N	N	N	N	Y	Y	N
7 Miller	N	N	N	N	N	N	Y	N
8 Dellums	?	?	?	?	?	?	?	?
9 Stark	?	?	N	N	N	Y	Y	N
10 Edwards	N	N	N	N	N	N	Y	N
11 Lantos	?	?	?	?	?	?	?	?
12 *Zschau*	Y	N	Y	Y	Y	Y	N	Y
13 Mineta	N	N	N	N	N	N	Y	N
14 *Shumway*	Y	N	Y	Y	Y	Y	N	Y
15 Coelho	N	N	N	N	N	N	Y	N
16 Panetta	Y	N	Y	N	N	N	Y	N
17 *Pashayan*	Y	N	Y	Y	Y	Y	N	Y
18 Lehman	N	N	Y	N	N	Y	Y	N
19 *Lagomarsino*	Y	N	Y	Y	Y	Y	N	Y
20 *Thomas*	Y	N	Y	Y	Y	Y	N	Y
21 *Fiedler*	Y	N	Y	Y	Y	Y	N	Y
22 *Moorhead*	Y	N	Y	Y	Y	Y	N	Y
23 Beilenson	N	N	N	N	N	Y	N	
24 Waxman	?	?	?	?	?	?	?	?
25 Roybal	?	?	?	?	?	?	?	?
26 Berman	N	N	N	N	N	N	Y	N
27 Levine	N	N	N	N	N	N	Y	N
28 Dixon	X	?	?	?	?	?	?	?
29 Hawkins	N	N	N	N	N	N	Y	N
30 Martinez	?	N	N	N	N	N	Y	N
31 Dymally	?	?	?	N	N	N	Y	N
32 Anderson	Y	N	Y	N	Y	N	Y	N
33 *Dreier*	Y	N	Y	Y	Y	Y	N	Y
34 Torres	?	N	N	N	N	N	Y	N
35 *Lewis*	Y	N	Y	N	N	N	N	N
36 Brown	N	N	N	N	N	N	Y	N
37 *McCandless*	Y	N	Y	Y	Y	Y	N	Y
38 Patterson	Y	N	Y	Y	Y	?	Y	Y
39 *Dannemeyer*	Y	N	Y	Y	Y	Y	N	Y
40 *Badham*	#	?	?	?	?	?	?	?
41 *Lowery*	Y	N	Y	Y	?	?	?	Y
42 *Lungren*	Y	N	Y	Y	Y	Y	N	Y

	185	186	187	188	189	190	191	192
43 *Packard*	Y	N	Y	Y	Y	Y	N	Y
44 Bates	N	N	N	N	Y	Y	Y	N
45 *Hunter*	Y	N	Y	Y	Y	Y	N	Y
COLORADO								
1 Schroeder	Y	Y	Y	?	Y	Y	Y	N
2 Wirth	N	N	Y	N	Y	N	Y	N
3 Kogovsek	N	N	N	N	N	N	?	?
4 *Brown*	Y	N	Y	Y	Y	Y	N	Y
5 *Kramer*	N	N	Y	?	Y	Y	?	Y
6 *Schaefer*	Y	N	Y	Y	Y	Y	N	Y
CONNECTICUT								
1 Kennelly	N	N	Y	N	N	N	Y	N
2 Gejdenson	N	N	N	N	N	N	Y	N
3 Morrison	N	N	N	N	N	Y	Y	Y
4 *McKinney*	#	N	Y	N	N	N	Y	N
5 Ratchford	N	N	N	N	N	N	Y	N
6 *Johnson*	Y	N	Y	Y	Y	Y	N	Y
DELAWARE								
AL Carper	N	N	Y	Y	Y	Y	Y	Y
FLORIDA								
1 Hutto	Y	N	Y	N	N	N	Y	N
2 Fuqua	N	N	Y	N	N	N	Y	N
3 Bennett	Y	Y	Y	Y	Y	Y	Y	Y
4 Chappell	?	N	N	N	N	?	Y	N
5 *McCollum*	Y	N	Y	Y	Y	N	Y	Y
6 MacKay	Y	?	#	#	#	?	?	?
7 Gibbons	?	?	?	?	?	?	?	?
8 *Young*	Y	N	Y	Y	Y	Y	N	Y
9 *Bilirakis*	Y	N	Y	Y	Y	Y	N	Y
10 Ireland	Y	N	Y	Y	Y	Y	N	Y
11 Nelson	Y	N	Y	+	Y	Y	Y	Y
12 *Lewis*	Y	N	Y	Y	N	Y	N	Y
13 *Mack*	Y	N	Y	Y	Y	Y	N	Y
14 Mica	N	N	Y	N	Y	N	Y	N
15 *Shaw*	Y	N	Y	Y	Y	Y	N	Y
16 Smith	N	N	N	N	?	N	Y	N
17 Lehman	N	N	N	N	N	N	Y	N
18 Pepper	N	N	N	N	N	N	Y	N
19 Fascell	N	N	N	N	?	?	?	?
GEORGIA								
1 Thomas	N	N	N	N	N	N	Y	N
2 Hatcher	N	N	N	N	N	N	Y	N
3 Ray	Y	N	Y	Y	Y	Y	Y	Y
4 Levitas	Y	N	Y	N	Y	N	Y	N
5 Fowler	N	N	Y	N	Y	Y	Y	N
6 *Gingrich*	Y	N	Y	Y	Y	Y	N	Y
7 Darden	N	N	Y	N	N	N	Y	N
8 Rowland	N	N	N	N	N	N	Y	N
9 Jenkins	Y	N	Y	N	Y	Y	Y	N
10 Barnard	Y	N	Y	N	Y	N	Y	N
HAWAII								
1 Heftel	N	N	Y	Y	Y	Y	Y	N
2 Akaka	N	N	N	N	N	N	Y	N
IDAHO								
1 *Craig*	Y	N	Y	Y	Y	Y	N	Y
2 *Hansen*	?	?	?	?	?	?	?	?
ILLINOIS								
1 Hayes	N	N	N	N	N	N	Y	N
2 Savage	N	N	N	N	N	N	Y	N
3 Russo	Y	N	Y	N	Y	N	Y	N
4 *O'Brien*	N	N	Y	N	N	Y	N	N
5 Lipinski	N	N	N	N	N	N	Y	N
6 *Hyde*	Y	N	Y	Y	?	?	?	?
7 Collins	N	N	N	N	N	N	Y	N
8 Rostenkowski	N	N	Y	N	N	N	N	N
9 Yates	N	N	N	N	N	N	Y	N
10 *Porter*	Y	N	Y	N	N	N	Y	N
11 Annunzio	N	N	N	N	N	N	Y	N
12 *Crane, P.*	Y	Y	Y	Y	Y	Y	N	Y
13 *Erlenborn*	Y	N	Y	Y	Y	?	?	?
14 *Corcoran*	Y	N	Y	Y	Y	Y	?	Y
15 *Madigan*	N	N	Y	N	Y	N	Y	N
16 *Martin*	Y	N	Y	Y	Y	Y	N	Y
17 Evans	N	N	N	N	N	N	Y	N
18 *Michel*	Y	N	Y	Y	Y	Y	N	N
19 *Crane, D.*	Y	N	Y	Y	Y	Y	Y	Y
20 Durbin	N	N	Y	N	Y	N	Y	Y
21 Price	N	N	N	N	N	N	N	N
22 Simon	?	N	N	N	N	N	Y	N
INDIANA								
1 Hall	N	N	N	N	N	N	Y	N
2 Sharp	Y	N	Y	Y	Y	Y	Y	N
3 *Hiler*	Y	N	Y	Y	Y	Y	N	Y
4 *Coats*	Y	N	Y	Y	Y	Y	N	Y
5 Hillis	Y	N	Y	N	Y	N	Y	N

ND - Northern Democrats   SD - Southern Democrats

	185	186	187	188	189	190	191	192
6 **Burton**	Y	N	Y	Y	Y	Y	N	Y
7 **Myers**	?	?	?	?	?	?	?	?
8 McCloskey	N	N	N	?	?	?	?	?
9 Hamilton	Y	N	Y	Y	Y	Y	Y	Y
10 Jacobs	Y	N	Y	Y	N	Y	Y	Y
IOWA								
1 **Leach**	Y	N	Y	Y	Y	Y	N	Y
2 **Tauke**	Y	N	Y	Y	Y	Y	N	Y
3 **Evans**	Y	N	Y	Y	Y	Y	N	Y
4 Smith	N	N	N	N	N	N	Y	N
5 Harkin	N	N	N	N	N	Y	Y	N
6 Bedell	N	N	N	N	N	N	Y	N
KANSAS								
1 **Roberts**	N	N	Y	Y	Y	Y	N	Y
2 Slattery	N	N	Y	Y	Y	Y	Y	Y
3 **Winn**	N	N	Y	N	Y	Y	N	Y
4 Glickman	N	N	Y	Y	Y	Y	Y	N
5 **Whittaker**	N	N	Y	Y	Y	Y	N	Y
KENTUCKY								
1 Hubbard	N	N	N	N	N	Y	Y	Y
2 Natcher	N	N	N	N	N	N	Y	N
3 Mazzoli	N	N	N	N	N	N	Y	N
4 **Snyder**	N	N	Y	Y	N	Y	N	Y
5 **Rogers**	?	?	?	?	?	?	?	?
6 **Hopkins**	N	N	N	Y	Y	Y	N	Y
7 Perkins	N	N	N	N	N	N	Y	?
LOUISIANA								
1 **Livingston**	Y	N	Y	Y	Y	Y	N	Y
2 Boggs	N	N	N	N	N	N	Y	N
3 Tauzin	N	N	Y	Y	Y	Y	Y	N
4 Roemer	Y	N	Y	Y	Y	Y	Y	Y
5 Huckaby	N	N	N	Y	Y	Y	Y	N
6 **Moore**	Y	N	Y	Y	Y	Y	N	Y
7 Breaux	N	N	Y	N	Y	Y	Y	N
8 Long	N	N	N	N	N	N	Y	N
MAINE								
1 **McKernan**	N	N	N	Y	Y	Y	N	Y
2 **Snowe**	N	N	N	Y	Y	Y	N	Y
MARYLAND								
1 Dyson	N	N	N	N	N	N	Y	N
2 Long	N	N	N	N	Y	N	Y	N
3 Mikulski	N	N	N	N	N	N	Y	N
4 **Holt**	?	?	?	?	?	?	?	?
5 Hoyer	N	N	N	N	?	N	Y	N
6 Byron	?	?	?	?	?	?	?	?
7 Mitchell	N	?	N	N	N	N	Y	N
8 Barnes	?	N	Y	N	N	N	Y	N
MASSACHUSETTS								
1 **Conte**	N	N	N	Y	Y	Y	N	Y
2 Boland	N	N	N	N	N	N	Y	N
3 Early	Y	N	N	Y	N	N	Y	N
4 Frank	Y	N	N	N	N	N	Y	N
5 Shannon	?	?	?	?	?	?	?	?
6 Mavroules	N	N	N	N	N	N	Y	N
7 Markey	Y	N	N	N	N	N	Y	N
8 O'Neill								
9 Moakley	N	N	N	N	N	N	Y	N
10 Studds	N	N	N	N	N	N	Y	N
11 Donnelly	Y	N	N	N	N	N	Y	N
MICHIGAN								
1 Conyers	N	N	N	N	N	N	Y	N
2 **Pursell**	#	N	N	Y	N	Y	N	Y
3 Wolpe	N	N	N	N	N	Y	Y	N
4 **Siljander**	Y	N	Y	Y	Y	Y	N	Y
5 **Sawyer**	Y	N	Y	N	N	Y	N	Y
6 Carr	N	N	N	N	N	N	Y	N
7 Kildee	N	N	N	N	N	N	Y	N
8 Traxler	N	N	N	N	N	N	Y	N
9 **Vander Jagt**	Y	N	Y	Y	Y	Y	N	Y
10 Albosta	N	N	N	Y	N	Y	Y	N
11 **Davis**	N	N	Y	Y	N	Y	N	Y
12 Bonior	N	N	N	N	?	?	Y	N
13 Crockett	N	N	N	N	N	N	Y	N
14 Hertel	Y	N	Y	N	N	N	Y	N
15 Ford	N	N	N	N	N	N	Y	N
16 Dingell	N	N	N	N	N	N	Y	N
17 Levin	N	N	N	N	N	N	Y	N
18 **Broomfield**	Y	N	Y	Y	N	Y	N	Y
MINNESOTA								
1 Penny	N	N	Y	Y	N	Y	Y	Y
2 **Weber**	Y	N	Y	Y	Y	Y	N	Y
3 **Frenzel**	Y	N	Y	Y	Y	Y	N	Y
4 Vento	N	N	N	N	N	N	Y	N
5 Sabo	N	N	N	N	N	N	Y	N
6 Sikorski	Y	N	Y	N	N	N	Y	N

	185	186	187	188	189	190	191	192
7 **Stangeland**	N	N	N	Y	N	Y	N	Y
8 Oberstar	?	N	N	N	N	N	Y	N
MISSISSIPPI								
1 Whitten	N	N	N	N	N	N	Y	N
2 **Franklin**	N	N	Y	Y	Y	Y	N	Y
3 Montgomery	?	?	?	?	?	?	?	?
4 Dowdy	N	N	N	Y	N	Y	Y	Y
5 **Lott**	N	N	Y	Y	Y	Y	N	Y
MISSOURI								
1 Clay	?	N	N	N	N	?	Y	N
2 Young	?	?	?	?	?	?	?	?
3 Gephardt	N	N	N	N	N	N	Y	N
4 Skelton	N	N	N	N	N	N	Y	N
5 Wheat	N	N	N	N	N	N	Y	N
6 **Coleman**	N	N	Y	Y	Y	Y	N	Y
7 **Taylor**	N	N	Y	Y	Y	Y	N	Y
8 **Emerson**	N	N	N	Y	?	Y	N	Y
9 Volkmer	N	N	Y	Y	N	Y	Y	Y
MONTANA								
1 Williams	N	N	N	N	N	N	Y	?
2 **Marlenee**	N	N	N	Y	Y	Y	N	Y
NEBRASKA								
1 **Bereuter**	N	N	N	Y	Y	Y	N	Y
2 **Daub**	N	N	N	Y	Y	Y	N	Y
3 **Smith**	N	N	N	Y	Y	Y	N	Y
NEVADA								
1 Reid	Y	N	Y	N	N	N	Y	N
2 **Vucanovich**	Y	N	Y	Y	Y	Y	N	Y
NEW HAMPSHIRE								
1 D'Amours	Y	N	Y	Y	Y	Y	Y	Y
2 **Gregg**	Y	N	Y	Y	Y	Y	N	Y
NEW JERSEY								
1 Florio	N	N	Y	N	N	N	Y	N
2 Hughes	Y	N	Y	N	N	Y	Y	Y
3 Howard	N	N	N	N	N	N	Y	N
4 **Smith**	?	?	?	?	?	?	?	?
5 **Roukema**	Y	N	Y	Y	Y	Y	N	Y
6 Dwyer	N	N	N	N	N	N	Y	N
7 **Rinaldo**	N	N	Y	Y	Y	Y	N	Y
8 Roe	N	N	N	N	N	N	Y	N
9 Torricelli	Y	N	Y	Y	Y	Y	Y	N
10 Rodino	?	?	?	?	?	?	?	?
11 Minish	Y	N	Y	N	N	N	Y	N
12 **Courter**	Y	N	Y	Y	Y	Y	N	Y
13 Vacancy								
14 Guarini	Y	N	Y	N	?	N	Y	N
NEW MEXICO								
1 **Lujan**	Y	N	Y	Y	Y	Y	N	Y
2 **Skeen**	N	N	Y	Y	Y	Y	N	Y
3 Richardson	N	N	N	N	Y	N	Y	N
NEW YORK								
1 **Carney**	N	N	Y	Y	N	Y	N	Y
2 Downey	N	N	N	N	N	N	Y	N
3 Mrazek	N	N	Y	N	N	N	Y	N
4 **Lent**	Y	N	Y	Y	Y	Y	N	Y
5 **McGrath**	Y	N	Y	Y	Y	Y	N	Y
6 Addabbo	N	N	N	N	N	N	Y	N
7 Ackerman	N	N	N	N	N	N	Y	N
8 Scheuer	N	N	N	N	N	N	Y	N
9 Ferraro	N	?	?	?	?	?	?	?
10 Schumer	N	N	N	N	N	N	Y	N
11 Towns	N	N	N	N	N	N	Y	N
12 Owens	N	N	N	N	?	N	Y	N
13 Solarz	N	N	N	N	N	N	Y	N
14 **Molinari**	Y	N	Y	Y	Y	Y	N	Y
15 **Green**	X	?	?	N	N	N	N	Y
16 Rangel	N	N	N	N	N	?	Y	N
17 Weiss	N	N	N	N	N	N	Y	N
18 Garcia	N	N	N	N	?	?	?	N
19 Biaggi	?	N	N	?	?	?	?	?
20 Ottinger	N	N	N	N	N	N	Y	N
21 **Fish**	N	N	Y	Y	Y	?	?	?
22 **Gilman**	N	N	N	Y	Y	Y	N	Y
23 Stratton	?	?	?	?	?	?	?	?
24 **Solomon**	Y	N	Y	Y	Y	Y	N	Y
25 **Boehlert**	N	N	N	Y	Y	N	N	Y
26 **Martin**	N	N	N	?	?	?	?	?
27 **Wortley**	N	N	N	Y	Y	Y	N	Y
28 McHugh	N	N	N	N	N	N	Y	N
29 **Horton**	N	N	N	N	N	N	N	N
30 **Conable**	Y	Y	Y	Y	Y	Y	N	Y
31 **Kemp**	Y	N	Y	?	?	?	?	?
32 LaFalce	Y	N	Y	N	Y	N	Y	N
33 Nowak	Y	N	Y	Y	N	N	Y	N
34 Lundine	N	N	N	N	N	N	Y	N

	185	186	187	188	189	190	191	192
NORTH CAROLINA								
1 Jones	N	N	N	N	N	N	Y	N
2 Valentine	N	N	Y	Y	Y	Y	Y	N
3 Whitley	N	N	Y	Y	Y	Y	Y	Y
4 Andrews	?	?	?	?	?	?	?	?
5 Neal	N	N	Y	Y	N	Y	Y	?
6 Britt	N	N	Y	N	Y	Y	Y	Y
7 Rose	N	N	N	N	N	N	Y	N
8 Hefner	N	N	N	N	N	N	Y	N
9 **Martin**	N	N	Y	Y	Y	Y	N	Y
10 **Broyhill**	Y	N	Y	Y	Y	Y	N	Y
11 Clarke	N	N	Y	N	N	N	Y	N
NORTH DAKOTA								
AL Dorgan	N	N	N	Y	N	Y	Y	Y
OHIO								
1 Luken	Y	N	Y	Y	N	Y	Y	Y
2 **Gradison**	Y	N	Y	Y	Y	Y	N	Y
3 Hall	Y	N	N	N	N	Y	Y	Y
4 **Oxley**	N	N	Y	Y	Y	Y	N	Y
5 **Latta**	?	?	?	?	?	?	?	?
6 **McEwen**	Y	N	Y	Y	Y	Y	N	Y
7 **DeWine**	Y	N	Y	Y	Y	Y	N	Y
8 **Kindness**	Y	N	Y	Y	N	Y	N	Y
9 Kaptur	N	N	Y	Y	N	Y	Y	Y
10 **Miller**	Y	N	Y	Y	Y	Y	N	Y
11 Eckart	N	N	Y	Y	N	Y	Y	Y
12 **Kasich**	Y	N	Y	Y	Y	Y	N	Y
13 Pease	N	N	Y	N	Y	N	Y	N
14 Seiberling	N	N	N	N	Y	N	Y	N
15 **Wylie**	?	?	?	?	?	?	?	?
16 **Regula**	N	N	Y	Y	Y	Y	N	Y
17 **Williams**	N	N	Y	N	N	Y	N	Y
18 Applegate	Y	N	Y	Y	N	Y	Y	Y
19 Feighan	Y	N	Y	Y	N	Y	Y	Y
20 Oakar	N	N	N	N	N	N	Y	N
21 Stokes	N	N	N	N	N	N	Y	N
OKLAHOMA								
1 Jones	Y	N	Y	N	Y	Y	Y	Y
2 Synar	N	N	N	N	N	N	Y	N
3 Watkins	N	N	N	N	Y	N	Y	N
4 McCurdy	N	N	Y	N	N	Y	Y	Y
5 **Edwards**	N	N	Y	Y	Y	Y	N	Y
6 English	N	N	Y	N	Y	Y	Y	Y
OREGON								
1 AuCoin	N	N	Y	N	N	N	Y	N
2 **Smith, R.**	?	N	Y	N	Y	Y	N	Y
3 Wyden	N	N	Y	N	N	N	Y	N
4 Weaver	N	N	Y	N	N	N	Y	N
5 **Smith, D.**	Y	N	Y	Y	Y	Y	N	Y
PENNSYLVANIA								
1 Foglietta	N	N	N	N	N	N	Y	N
2 Gray	N	N	N	N	N	N	Y	N
3 Borski	N	N	Y	N	Y	N	Y	N
4 Kolter	N	N	Y	N	N	N	Y	N
5 **Schulze**	Y	N	Y	Y	Y	Y	N	Y
6 Yatron	Y	N	Y	Y	Y	Y	Y	Y
7 Edgar	N	N	Y	N	N	N	Y	N
8 Kostmayer	?	N	Y	N	N	N	Y	N
9 **Shuster**	Y	N	Y	Y	Y	Y	N	Y
10 **McDade**	N	N	Y	N	Y	N	N	N
11 Harrison	?	?	?	?	?	?	?	?
12 Murtha	N	N	N	N	N	N	Y	N
13 **Coughlin**	Y	N	Y	Y	N	Y	N	Y
14 Coyne	N	N	N	N	N	N	Y	N
15 **Ritter**	Y	N	Y	Y	Y	Y	N	Y
16 **Walker**	Y	N	Y	Y	Y	Y	N	Y
17 **Gekas**	Y	N	Y	Y	Y	Y	N	Y
18 Walgren	Y	N	Y	Y	N	Y	Y	Y
19 **Goodling**	Y	N	Y	Y	Y	Y	N	Y
20 Gaydos	N	N	N	N	N	N	Y	N
21 **Ridge**	N	N	Y	Y	Y	Y	N	Y
22 Murphy	Y	N	Y	N	N	N	Y	N
23 **Clinger**	Y	N	Y	Y	Y	Y	N	Y
RHODE ISLAND								
1 St Germain	N	N	N	N	N	N	Y	N
2 **Schneider**	Y	N	N	Y	Y	Y	N	Y
SOUTH CAROLINA								
1 **Hartnett**	Y	N	Y	Y	Y	Y	N	Y
2 **Spence**	N	N	Y	Y	Y	Y	N	Y
3 Derrick	N	N	N	N	Y	Y	Y	N
4 **Campbell**	Y	N	Y	Y	Y	Y	N	Y
5 Spratt	Y	N	Y	N	Y	Y	Y	Y
6 Tallon	?	N	N	Y	Y	Y	Y	Y
SOUTH DAKOTA								
AL Daschle	Y	N	N	?	?	?	?	?

	185	186	187	188	189	190	191	192
TENNESSEE								
1 **Quillen**	Y	N	Y	Y	?	?	?	?
2 **Duncan**	Y	N	Y	Y	Y	Y	N	Y
3 Lloyd	Y	N	Y	Y	Y	Y	Y	Y
4 Cooper	N	N	Y	N	N	N	Y	N
5 Boner	N	N	N	N	N	N	Y	N
6 Gore	N	N	Y	N	Y	Y	Y	Y
7 **Sundquist**	N	N	Y	Y	Y	Y	N	Y
8 Jones	N	N	N	N	N	N	Y	N
9 Ford	N	N	N	N	N	N	Y	N
TEXAS								
1 Hall, S.	?	?	?	?	?	?	?	?
2 Wilson	N	N	N	N	N	N	Y	N
3 **Bartlett**	Y	N	Y	Y	Y	Y	N	Y
4 Hall, R.	N	N	N	Y	Y	Y	Y	Y
5 Bryant	N	N	Y	N	N	N	Y	N
6 **Gramm**	Y	N	Y	Y	Y	Y	N	Y
7 **Archer**	Y	N	Y	Y	Y	Y	N	Y
8 **Fields**	Y	N	Y	Y	Y	Y	N	Y
9 Brooks	N	N	N	N	Y	N	Y	N
10 Pickle	N	N	Y	N	N	Y	Y	N
11 Leath	N	N	Y	Y	Y	Y	Y	N
12 Wright	N	N	N	N	N	N	Y	N
13 Hightower	N	N	N	N	N	N	Y	N
14 Patman	N	N	Y	N	N	Y	Y	Y
15 de la Garza	N	N	N	N	N	N	Y	N
16 Coleman	Y	N	Y	Y	N	N	Y	N
17 Stenholm	Y	N	Y	Y	Y	Y	Y	Y
18 Leland	X	?	X	X	X	?	?	?
19 Hance	N	N	Y	Y	Y	Y	Y	Y
20 Gonzalez	N	N	N	N	N	N	Y	N
21 **Loeffler**	N	N	Y	Y	Y	Y	N	Y
22 **Paul**	Y	Y	Y	Y	Y	Y	N	Y
23 Kazen	N	N	N	N	N	N	Y	N
24 Frost	N	N	Y	N	N	N	Y	N
25 Andrews	Y	N	Y	Y	Y	Y	Y	Y
26 Vandergriff	Y	N	Y	Y	Y	Y	Y	Y
27 Ortiz	N	N	N	N	N	N	Y	N
UTAH								
1 **Hansen**	Y	N	Y	Y	Y	Y	N	Y
2 **Marriott**	Y	N	Y	Y	N	Y	N	Y
3 **Nielson**	Y	N	Y	Y	Y	?	N	Y
VERMONT								
AL **Jeffords**	N	N	N	Y	N	N	N	Y
VIRGINIA								
1 **Bateman**	Y	N	Y	Y	Y	Y	N	Y
2 **Whitehurst**	Y	N	N	Y	N	Y	N	Y
3 **Bliley**	Y	N	Y	Y	Y	Y	N	Y
4 Sisisky	N	N	N	N	Y	N	Y	N
5 Daniel	N	N	Y	Y	N	?	?	?
6 Olin	N	N	N	Y	Y	Y	Y	Y
7 **Robinson**	N	N	Y	Y	Y	Y	N	Y
8 **Parris**	N	N	Y	Y	N	Y	N	Y
9 Boucher	N	N	Y	N	N	N	Y	N
10 **Wolf**	N	N	Y	Y	Y	Y	N	Y
WASHINGTON								
1 **Pritchard**	Y	N	Y	Y	Y	?	?	?
2 Swift	N	?	N	N	N	N	Y	N
3 Bonker	N	N	Y	N	N	Y	Y	N
4 **Morrison**	N	N	N	Y	Y	Y	N	Y
5 Foley	N	N	N	N	N	N	Y	N
6 Dicks	N	N	N	N	N	N	Y	N
7 Lowry	N	N	N	N	N	N	Y	N
8 **Chandler**	Y	N	Y	Y	Y	?	?	Y
WEST VIRGINIA								
1 Mollohan	N	N	Y	N	N	N	Y	N
2 Staggers	N	N	Y	N	N	N	Y	N
3 Wise	Y	N	Y	Y	Y	Y	Y	Y
4 Rahall	N	N	Y	N	N	N	Y	N
WISCONSIN								
1 Aspin	N	N	Y	N	?	?	?	?
2 Kastenmeier	?	?	?	?	?	?	Y	N
3 **Gunderson**	Y	N	Y	Y	N	Y	N	Y
4 Kleczka	Y	N	N	N	N	N	Y	N
5 Moody	Y	N	Y	N	N	N	Y	N
6 **Petri**	N	N	Y	Y	Y	Y	N	Y
7 Obey	N	Y	N	N	N	N	Y	N
8 **Roth**	?	?	?	?	?	?	?	?
9 **Sensenbrenner**	?	?	?	?	?	?	?	?
WYOMING								
AL **Cheney**	Y	N	Y	Y	Y	Y	N	Y

Southern states - Ala., Ark., Fla., Ga., Ky., La., Miss., N.C., Okla., S.C., Tenn., Texas, Va.

KEY

Y Voted for (yea).
Paired for.
+ Announced for.
N Voted against (nay).
X Paired against.
- Announced against.
P Voted "present".
C Voted "present" to avoid possible conflict of interest.
? Did not vote or otherwise make a position known.

Democrats   *Republicans*

---

193. HR 5753. Legislative Branch Appropriations, Fiscal 1985. Passage of the bill to provide $1,247,450,820 in fiscal 1985 for House of Representatives operations and legislative branch agencies. Passed 247-138: R 36-110; D 211-28 (ND 143-16, SD 68-12), June 6, 1984.

194. HR 1149. Oregon Wilderness. Seiberling, D-Ohio, motion to suspend the rules and concur in the Senate amendment to the bill to designate as federal wilderness and protect from development 945,000 acres in national forests in Oregon. Motion agreed to (thus clearing the bill for the president) 281-99: R 49-95; D 232-4 (ND 157-0, SD 75-4), June 6, 1984. A two-thirds majority of those present and voting (254 in this case) is required under suspension of the rules.

195. Procedural Motion. Mack, R-Fla., motion to approve the House *Journal* of Wednesday, June 6. Motion agreed to 357-38: R 131-23; D 226-15 (ND 142-14, SD 84-1), June 7, 1984.

196. HR 5145. Human Services Amendments. Perkins, D-Ky., motion to suspend the rules and pass the bill to reauthorize Head Start, Community Services Block Grants, and other social services programs through fiscal 1989. Motion rejected 261-156: R 26-133; D 235-23 (ND 167-5, SD 68-18), June 7, 1984. A two-thirds majority of those present and voting (278 in this case) is required for passage under suspension of the rules. A "nay" was a vote supporting the president's position.

197. HR 5504. Surface Transportation Act. McNulty, D-Ariz., amendment to strike the provision in the bill changing the formula for allocating to the states funds for highway resurfacing, restoration, rehabilitation and reconstruction. Rejected 93-315: R 44-113; D 49-202 (ND 39-128, SD 10-74), June 7, 1984.

198. HR 5504. Surface Transportation Act. Passage of the bill to approve Interstate highway and Interstate substitute cost estimates, and to provide relocation assistance. Passed 297-73: R 89-54; D 208-19 (ND 137-17, SD 71-2), June 7, 1984. A "nay" was a vote supporting the president's position.

	193	194	195	196	197	198
ALABAMA						
1 *Edwards*	?	?	Y	N	N	Y
2 *Dickinson*	Y	N	N	N	Y	Y
3 Nichols	?	?	Y	N	Y	Y
4 Bevill	?	?	Y	N	Y	Y
5 Flippo	Y	Y	Y	N	Y	Y
6 Erdreich	N	Y	Y	Y	Y	Y
7 Shelby	N	N	Y	Y	Y	?
ALASKA						
AL *Young*	Y	N	N	Y	Y	Y
ARIZONA						
1 *McCain*	Y	?	?	N	Y	Y
2 Udall	Y	Y	?	Y	Y	Y
3 *Stump*	N	N	Y	N	Y	N
4 *Rudd*	Y	N	Y	N	Y	N
5 McNulty	Y	Y	Y	Y	Y	Y
ARKANSAS						
1 Alexander	Y	Y	Y	Y	N	Y
2 *Bethune*	N	Y	Y	?	?	?
3 *Hammerschmidt*	?	?	Y	?	N	Y
4 Anthony	?	?	Y	N	Y	Y
CALIFORNIA						
1 Bosco	Y	?	Y	Y	N	?
2 *Chappie*	N	N	N	N	N	Y
3 Matsui	Y	Y	Y	Y	?	?
4 Fazio	Y	Y	Y	Y	N	Y
5 Burton	Y	Y	Y	Y	N	Y
6 Boxer	Y	Y	Y	Y	N	Y
7 Miller	Y	Y	Y	Y	N	Y
8 Dellums	#	?	Y	Y	N	Y
9 Stark	Y	Y	Y	Y	N	Y
10 Edwards	Y	Y	Y	Y	N	Y
11 Lantos	#	?	Y	Y	N	Y
12 Zschau	N	Y	Y	N	N	N
13 Mineta	Y	Y	Y	Y	N	Y
14 *Shumway*	N	N	Y	N	N	N
15 Coelho	Y	Y	?	?	?	?
16 Panetta	N	Y	Y	N	N	Y
17 *Pashayan*	N	N	?	?	?	?
18 Lehman	Y	Y	Y	Y	N	Y
19 *Lagomarsino*	N	Y	Y	N	N	N
20 *Thomas*	N	N	Y	N	N	Y
21 *Fiedler*	N	Y	Y	N	N	N
22 *Moorhead*	N	N	Y	N	N	Y
23 Beilenson	Y	Y	Y	Y	N	Y
24 Waxman	?	?	N	Y	N	?
25 Roybal	?	?	Y	Y	N	Y
26 Berman	Y	?	N	Y	N	?
27 Levine	Y	Y	Y	Y	N	Y
28 Dixon	#	?	?	Y	N	Y
29 Hawkins	Y	Y	N	Y	N	?
30 Martinez	Y	Y	Y	Y	N	Y
31 Dymally	Y	Y	P	Y	N	Y
32 Anderson	Y	Y	Y	Y	N	Y
33 *Dreier*	N	N	Y	N	N	N
34 Torres	Y	Y	Y	Y	N	Y
35 *Lewis*	N	N	N	N	N	Y
36 Brown	Y	Y	?	Y	N	Y
37 *McCandless*	N	N	Y	N	N	Y
38 Patterson	Y	Y	Y	Y	?	?
39 *Dannemeyer*	N	N	N	N	N	N
40 *Badham*	X	?	?	N	N	N
41 *Lowery*	N	N	Y	N	N	N
42 *Lungren*	N	N	Y	N	N	N

	193	194	195	196	197	198
43 *Packard*	N	N	Y	N	N	Y
44 Bates	Y	Y	Y	Y	N	Y
45 *Hunter*	N	N	Y	N	N	Y
COLORADO						
1 Schroeder	Y	Y	N	Y	Y	N
2 Wirth	Y	Y	Y	Y	Y	Y
3 Kogovsek	?	Y	Y	Y	Y	?
4 *Brown*	N	N	N	N	Y	N
5 *Kramer*	N	N	Y	N	N	Y
6 *Schaefer*	N	N	Y	N	Y	N
CONNECTICUT						
1 Kennelly	Y	Y	Y	Y	N	Y
2 Gejdenson	N	Y	?	Y	N	Y
3 Morrison	Y	Y	Y	Y	N	Y
4 *McKinney*	Y	Y	Y	Y	N	Y
5 Ratchford	Y	Y	Y	Y	N	Y
6 *Johnson*	N	Y	Y	Y	N	Y
DELAWARE						
AL Carper	Y	Y	Y	Y	Y	Y
FLORIDA						
1 Hutto	Y	Y	Y	N	N	Y
2 Fuqua	Y	Y	Y	Y	N	Y
3 Bennett	Y	Y	Y	Y	N	Y
4 Chappell	Y	Y	Y	Y	N	Y
5 *McCollum*	N	Y	Y	N	N	Y
6 MacKay	X	?	Y	N	N	Y
7 Gibbons	?	?	Y	Y	?	N
8 *Young*	N	N	Y	N	N	Y
9 *Bilirakis*	N	Y	Y	N	N	N
10 Ireland	N	Y	Y	N	Y	Y
11 Nelson	Y	Y	Y	Y	N	Y
12 *Lewis*	N	N	Y	N	N	Y
13 *Mack*	N	Y	N	N	N	Y
14 Mica	Y	Y	Y	Y	N	Y
15 *Shaw*	N	Y	Y	N	N	Y
16 Smith	Y	Y	Y	Y	N	Y
17 Lehman	Y	Y	Y	Y	N	N
18 Pepper	Y	Y	Y	Y	N	Y
19 Fascell	Y	Y	?	Y	N	Y
GEORGIA						
1 Thomas	Y	Y	Y	Y	N	Y
2 Hatcher	Y	Y	Y	Y	?	?
3 Ray	Y	Y	Y	Y	N	Y
4 Levitas	Y	Y	Y	N	N	Y
5 Fowler	Y	Y	Y	Y	N	Y
6 *Gingrich*	N	N	?	N	N	Y
7 Darden	Y	Y	Y	Y	N	Y
8 Rowland	Y	Y	Y	Y	N	Y
9 Jenkins	Y	Y	Y	Y	N	Y
10 Barnard	Y	Y	Y	Y	N	Y
HAWAII						
1 Heftel	Y	Y	?	Y	Y	Y
2 Akaka	Y	Y	Y	Y	Y	N
IDAHO						
1 *Craig*	?	N	Y	N	Y	N
2 *Hansen*	?	?	?	?	?	?
ILLINOIS						
1 Hayes	Y	Y	N	Y	N	Y
2 Savage	Y	Y	?	Y	N	Y
3 Russo	N	Y	Y	Y	N	Y
4 *O'Brien*	Y	Y	Y	Y	N	Y
5 Lipinski	N	Y	Y	Y	N	Y
6 *Hyde*	?	?	Y	Y	N	?
7 Collins	Y	Y	Y	Y	N	Y
8 Rostenkowski	Y	Y	Y	Y	N	Y
9 Yates	Y	Y	Y	Y	N	Y
10 *Porter*	Y	Y	Y	Y	N	Y
11 Annunzio	Y	Y	Y	Y	N	Y
12 *Crane, P.*	N	N	N	Y	N	?
13 *Erlenborn*	X	?	Y	N	N	?
14 *Corcoran*	N	Y	Y	N	N	Y
15 *Madigan*	N	N	Y	N	N	Y
16 *Martin*	N	Y	Y	N	N	Y
17 Evans	Y	Y	Y	Y	?	?
18 *Michel*	X	?	?	N	N	Y
19 *Crane, D.*	N	N	Y	N	?	?
20 Durbin	Y	Y	N	Y	N	Y
21 Price	Y	Y	Y	Y	N	Y
22 Simon	Y	Y	Y	Y	?	?
INDIANA						
1 Hall	Y	Y	Y	Y	N	Y
2 Sharp	Y	Y	Y	Y	N	Y
3 *Hiler*	N	N	Y	N	N	N
4 *Coats*	N	N	N	N	N	N
5 Hillis	N	Y	Y	N	N	Y

ND - Northern Democrats   SD - Southern Democrats

	193	194	195	196	197	198
6 ***Burton***	N	N	Y	N	N	N
7 ***Myers***	?	?	Y	N	N	Y
8 McCloskey	?	?	Y	Y	N	Y
9 Hamilton	Y	Y	Y	Y	N	Y
10 Jacobs	N	Y	N	Y	N	N
IOWA						
1 ***Leach***	N	Y	Y	N	Y	N
2 ***Tauke***	N	N	Y	N	Y	Y
3 ***Evans***	N	N	Y	N	Y	Y
4 Smith	Y	Y	Y	Y	?	N
5 Harkin	Y	Y	N	Y	Y	Y
6 Bedell	Y	Y	Y	Y	Y	?
KANSAS						
1 ***Roberts***	N	N	N	N	Y	N
2 Slattery	Y	Y	Y	N	Y	N
3 ***Winn***	N	N	Y	N	Y	Y
4 Glickman	N	Y	Y	N	Y	Y
5 ***Whittaker***	N	N	N	N	Y	N
KENTUCKY						
1 Hubbard	N	N	Y	Y	?	?
2 Natcher	Y	Y	Y	Y	N	Y
3 Mazzoli	Y	Y	Y	Y	N	?
4 ***Snyder***	N	N	Y	N	N	Y
5 ***Rogers***	?	?	Y	N	N	Y
6 ***Hopkins***	N	N	Y	N	N	Y
7 Perkins	Y	Y	Y	Y	N	Y
LOUISIANA						
1 ***Livingston***	N	N	Y	N	N	N
2 Boggs	Y	Y	Y	Y	N	Y
3 Tauzin	N	Y	Y	Y	N	Y
4 Roemer	N	Y	N	N	N	Y
5 Huckaby	Y	Y	Y	Y	N	Y
6 ***Moore***	N	N	Y	N	N	Y
7 Breaux	Y	?	Y	N	N	Y
8 Long	Y	Y	Y	Y	N	Y
MAINE						
1 ***McKernan***	Y	Y	Y	Y	Y	Y
2 ***Snowe***	Y	Y	Y	N	Y	Y
MARYLAND						
1 Dyson	Y	Y	Y	Y	N	Y
2 Long	Y	Y	Y	Y	N	Y
3 Mikulski	Y	Y	Y	Y	N	Y
4 ***Holt***	?	?	N	N	N	Y
5 Hoyer	Y	Y	Y	Y	N	Y
6 Byron	?	?	Y	Y	N	Y
7 Mitchell	Y	Y	N	Y	N	Y
8 Barnes	Y	Y	Y	Y	N	Y
MASSACHUSETTS						
1 ***Conte***	Y	Y	Y	Y	N	Y
2 Boland	Y	Y	Y	Y	N	Y
3 Early	Y	Y	Y	Y	N	Y
4 Frank	Y	?	Y	Y	N	Y
5 Shannon	?	?	?	?	N	Y
6 Mavroules	Y	Y	?	Y	N	Y
7 Markey	Y	Y	Y	Y	N	Y
8 O'Neill						
9 Moakley	Y	Y	Y	Y	N	Y
10 Studds	Y	Y	?	Y	N	Y
11 Donnelly	N	Y	Y	Y	N	Y
MICHIGAN						
1 Conyers	Y	Y	?	Y	N	Y
2 ***Pursell***	N	Y	Y	Y	N	Y
3 Wolpe	Y	Y	Y	Y	N	Y
4 ***Siljander***	N	N	Y	N	N	?
5 ***Sawyer***	N	Y	Y	N	N	?
6 Carr	Y	Y	Y	Y	N	Y
7 Kildee	Y	Y	Y	Y	N	Y
8 Traxler	Y	Y	Y	Y	N	Y
9 ***Vander Jagt***	N	N	?	N	N	Y
10 Albosta	Y	Y	Y	Y	N	Y
11 ***Davis***	Y	N	Y	Y	N	Y
12 Bonior	Y	Y	Y	Y	?	?
13 Crockett	Y	Y	?	Y	N	?
14 Hertel	N	Y	Y	Y	N	N
15 Ford	Y	Y	?	Y	N	Y
16 Dingell	Y	Y	Y	Y	N	Y
17 Levin	Y	Y	Y	Y	N	Y
18 ***Broomfield***	N	N	Y	N	N	Y
MINNESOTA						
1 Penny	Y	Y	N	Y	Y	Y
2 ***Weber***	N	?	P	N	Y	Y
3 ***Frenzel***	N	Y	Y	N	Y	N
4 Vento	Y	Y	Y	Y	Y	Y
5 Sabo	Y	Y	N	Y	Y	N
6 Sikorski	Y	Y	N	Y	Y	Y
7 ***Stangeland***	Y	N	Y	N	Y	Y
8 Oberstar	Y	Y	P	Y	Y	Y
MISSISSIPPI						
1 Whitten	Y	Y	Y	Y	Y	?
2 ***Franklin***	N	N	Y	Y	Y	Y
3 Montgomery	?	?	Y	N	Y	Y
4 Dowdy	Y	Y	Y	Y	Y	Y
5 ***Lott***	N	N	Y	N	Y	Y
MISSOURI						
1 Clay	Y	Y	N	Y	N	?
2 Young	?	?	Y	Y	N	Y
3 Gephardt	Y	Y	Y	Y	Y	Y
4 Skelton	Y	Y	Y	Y	Y	Y
5 Wheat	N	Y	Y	Y	N	Y
6 ***Coleman***	Y	N	N	N	Y	Y
7 ***Taylor***	N	N	Y	N	Y	Y
8 ***Emerson***	N	N	N	N	N	Y
9 Volkmer	Y	Y	Y	Y	Y	Y
MONTANA						
1 Williams	?	?	Y	?	Y	N
2 ***Marlenee***	Y	N	Y	N	Y	N
NEBRASKA						
1 ***Bereuter***	N	N	Y	Y	Y	N
2 ***Daub***	N	N	Y	N	Y	Y
3 ***Smith***	Y	N	Y	N	Y	N
NEVADA						
1 Reid	Y	Y	Y	Y	Y	N
2 ***Vucanovich***	N	N	Y	N	Y	Y
NEW HAMPSHIRE						
1 D'Amours	Y	Y	Y	Y	Y	Y
2 ***Gregg***	N	N	Y	N	Y	?
NEW JERSEY						
1 Florio	Y	Y	Y	Y	N	Y
2 Hughes	Y	Y	Y	Y	N	Y
3 Howard	Y	Y	Y	Y	N	Y
4 ***Smith***	?	?	?	Y	N	Y
5 ***Roukema***	Y	Y	Y	N	N	Y
6 Dwyer	Y	Y	Y	Y	N	Y
7 ***Rinaldo***	Y	Y	Y	Y	N	Y
8 Roe	Y	Y	Y	Y	N	Y
9 Torricelli	Y	Y	Y	Y	N	Y
10 Rodino	#	?	?	?	?	?
11 Minish	Y	Y	Y	Y	N	Y
12 ***Courter***	N	Y	Y	N	N	Y
13 Vacancy						
14 Guarini	Y	Y	Y	Y	N	Y
NEW MEXICO						
1 ***Lujan***	N	N	Y	Y	Y	N
2 ***Skeen***	N	N	Y	N	Y	N
3 Richardson	N	Y	Y	Y	Y	N
NEW YORK						
1 ***Carney***	Y	N	Y	N	N	Y
2 Downey	Y	Y	Y	Y	N	?
3 Mrazek	Y	Y	Y	Y	N	?
4 ***Lent***	Y	Y	Y	N	N	N
5 ***McGrath***	Y	Y	Y	N	N	N
6 Addabbo	Y	Y	Y	Y	N	Y
7 Ackerman	Y	Y	Y	Y	N	Y
8 Scheuer	Y	Y	Y	Y	N	Y
9 Ferraro	?	?	Y	Y	N	Y
10 Schumer	Y	Y	Y	Y	N	Y
11 Towns	Y	Y	Y	Y	N	Y
12 Owens	Y	Y	Y	Y	N	Y
13 Solarz	Y	Y	Y	Y	N	?
14 ***Molinari***	Y	Y	Y	N	N	N
15 ***Green***	Y	Y	Y	Y	N	Y
16 Rangel	Y	Y	Y	Y	N	Y
17 Weiss	Y	Y	Y	Y	N	Y
18 Garcia	Y	Y	Y	Y	N	Y
19 Biaggi	#	?	Y	Y	N	?
20 Ottinger	Y	Y	?	Y	N	?
21 ***Fish***	?	?	Y	N	N	?
22 ***Gilman***	N	Y	Y	Y	N	Y
23 Stratton	?	?	Y	Y	N	Y
24 ***Solomon***	N	N	N	N	N	N
25 ***Boehlert***	Y	Y	Y	Y	N	?
26 ***Martin***	?	?	?	?	N	?
27 ***Wortley***	Y	N	Y	Y	N	Y
28 McHugh	Y	Y	Y	Y	N	Y
29 ***Horton***	Y	N	Y	Y	N	Y
30 ***Conable***	N	N	Y	N	N	N
31 ***Kemp***	?	?	Y	N	N	?
32 LaFalce	Y	Y	Y	N	N	Y
33 Nowak	Y	Y	Y	Y	N	Y
34 Lundine	Y	Y	Y	Y	N	Y
NORTH CAROLINA						
1 Jones	Y	Y	Y	Y	N	Y
2 Valentine	Y	Y	Y	Y	N	Y
3 Whitley	Y	Y	Y	Y	N	?
4 Andrews	?	?	Y	Y	N	Y
5 Neal	Y	Y	Y	Y	N	Y
6 Britt	Y	Y	Y	Y	N	Y
7 Rose	Y	Y	Y	Y	?	?
8 Hefner	Y	Y	Y	Y	N	Y
9 ***Martin***	N	?	?	?	?	?
10 ***Broyhill***	N	N	Y	N	N	N
11 Clarke	Y	Y	Y	Y	N	Y
NORTH DAKOTA						
AL Dorgan	Y	Y	Y	Y	Y	N
OHIO						
1 Luken	N	Y	Y	Y	N	Y
2 ***Gradison***	N	Y	Y	N	N	N
3 Hall	Y	Y	Y	Y	N	Y
4 ***Oxley***	N	N	Y	N	N	?
5 ***Latta***	X	?	Y	N	N	Y
6 ***McEwen***	N	N	Y	N	N	Y
7 ***DeWine***	N	N	Y	N	N	N
8 ***Kindness***	N	N	Y	N	N	?
9 Kaptur	Y	Y	Y	Y	N	Y
10 ***Miller***	N	Y	N	N	N	Y
11 Eckart	Y	Y	Y	Y	N	Y
12 ***Kasich***	N	Y	Y	N	N	Y
13 Pease	Y	Y	Y	N	N	Y
14 Seiberling	Y	Y	Y	Y	N	Y
15 ***Wylie***	?	?	Y	N	N	Y
16 ***Regula***	N	Y	Y	N	N	Y
17 ***Williams***	Y	Y	Y	Y	?	?
18 Applegate	Y	Y	?	Y	N	Y
19 Feighan	Y	Y	Y	Y	N	Y
20 Oakar	Y	Y	Y	Y	N	Y
21 Stokes	Y	Y	Y	Y	N	?
OKLAHOMA						
1 Jones	Y	Y	Y	N	N	Y
2 Synar	Y	Y	Y	Y	N	Y
3 Watkins	N	Y	Y	Y	N	Y
4 McCurdy	Y	Y	Y	Y	N	Y
5 ***Edwards***	N	N	Y	N	N	N
6 English	Y	Y	Y	N	N	Y
OREGON						
1 AuCoin	N	Y	Y	Y	Y	N
2 ***Smith, R.***	N	N	N	N	Y	Y
3 Wyden	N	Y	Y	Y	Y	N
4 Weaver	N	Y	Y	Y	Y	N
5 ***Smith, D.***	N	N	N	N	Y	N
PENNSYLVANIA						
1 Foglietta	Y	Y	Y	Y	N	Y
2 Gray	Y	Y	Y	Y	N	N
3 Borski	Y	Y	Y	Y	N	Y
4 Kolter	Y	Y	Y	Y	N	Y
5 ***Schulze***	Y	N	Y	Y	N	Y
6 Yatron	Y	Y	Y	Y	N	Y
7 Edgar	Y	Y	Y	Y	N	Y
8 Kostmayer	Y	Y	Y	Y	N	Y
9 ***Shuster***	N	N	Y	N	N	Y
10 ***McDade***	Y	N	Y	N	N	Y
11 Harrison	?	?	?	?	?	?
12 Murtha	Y	Y	Y	Y	?	Y
13 ***Coughlin***	N	Y	N	N	N	N
14 Coyne	Y	Y	Y	Y	N	Y
15 ***Ritter***	N	Y	Y	N	N	Y
16 ***Walker***	N	N	N	N	N	N
17 ***Gekas***	N	Y	N	N	N	Y
18 Walgren	Y	Y	?	Y	N	Y
19 ***Goodling***	N	Y	N	N	N	Y
20 Gaydos	Y	Y	Y	Y	N	Y
21 ***Ridge***	Y	Y	Y	Y	N	Y
22 Murphy	Y	Y	N	Y	N	Y
23 ***Clinger***	Y	N	Y	N	N	Y
RHODE ISLAND						
1 St Germain	Y	Y	P	Y	Y	Y
2 ***Schneider***	Y	Y	Y	Y	Y	Y
SOUTH CAROLINA						
1 ***Hartnett***	N	N	Y	N	Y	?
2 ***Spence***	N	N	Y	N	Y	N
3 Derrick	Y	Y	Y	?	Y	Y
4 ***Campbell***	N	N	Y	N	Y	Y
5 Spratt	Y	Y	Y	Y	Y	Y
6 Tallon	Y	Y	Y	Y	Y	Y
SOUTH DAKOTA						
AL Daschle	?	?	Y	Y	Y	N
TENNESSEE						
1 ***Quillen***	N	N	Y	N	N	Y
2 ***Duncan***	N	N	Y	N	N	Y
3 Lloyd	Y	Y	?	?	N	?
4 Cooper	Y	Y	Y	Y	N	Y
5 Boner	Y	Y	Y	Y	N	?
6 Gore	Y	Y	Y	Y	N	?
7 ***Sundquist***	Y	Y	Y	N	N	Y
8 Jones	Y	Y	Y	Y	N	Y
9 Ford	Y	Y	?	?	?	?
TEXAS						
1 Hall, S.	?	?	Y	N	N	Y
2 Wilson	Y	Y	Y	Y	N	Y
3 ***Bartlett***	N	N	Y	N	N	N
4 Hall, R.	N	Y	Y	Y	N	Y
5 Bryant	Y	Y	Y	Y	N	Y
6 ***Gramm***	N	N	Y	N	N	Y
7 ***Archer***	N	N	Y	N	N	Y
8 ***Fields***	N	N	N	N	N	Y
9 Brooks	Y	Y	?	Y	N	?
10 Pickle	Y	Y	Y	Y	N	Y
11 Leath	Y	Y	Y	Y	N	Y
12 Wright	Y	Y	Y	Y	N	?
13 Hightower	Y	Y	Y	Y	N	?
14 Patman	N	N	Y	Y	N	Y
15 de la Garza	Y	Y	Y	Y	N	?
16 Coleman	Y	Y	Y	Y	N	Y
17 Stenholm	N	N	Y	N	N	Y
18 Leland	#	?	?	?	?	?
19 Hance	N	Y	Y	Y	N	Y
20 Gonzalez	Y	Y	Y	Y	N	Y
21 ***Loeffler***	N	N	Y	N	N	N
22 ***Paul***	N	N	Y	N	N	N
23 Kazen	Y	Y	Y	Y	N	Y
24 Frost	Y	Y	Y	Y	N	Y
25 Andrews	Y	Y	Y	Y	N	Y
26 Vandergriff	N	Y	Y	N	N	Y
27 Ortiz	Y	Y	Y	Y	N	Y
UTAH						
1 ***Hansen***	N	N	N	N	Y	N
2 ***Marriott***	N	N	Y	N	Y	?
3 ***Nielson***	N	N	Y	N	Y	N
VERMONT						
AL ***Jeffords***	Y	Y	Y	Y	Y	N
VIRGINIA						
1 ***Bateman***	N	Y	Y	N	N	Y
2 ***Whitehurst***	N	N	Y	N	N	Y
3 ***Bliley***	N	N	Y	N	N	Y
4 Sisisky	Y	Y	Y	Y	N	Y
5 Daniel	?	?	Y	N	N	Y
6 Olin	Y	Y	Y	Y	N	?
7 ***Robinson***	N	N	Y	N	N	Y
8 ***Parris***	Y	N	Y	N	N	Y
9 Boucher	Y	Y	Y	Y	N	Y
10 ***Wolf***	Y	N	Y	N	Y	Y
WASHINGTON						
1 ***Pritchard***	?	?	Y	N	?	?
2 Swift	Y	Y	Y	Y	Y	Y
3 Bonker	Y	Y	Y	Y	Y	Y
4 ***Morrison***	N	Y	Y	N	N	N
5 Foley	Y	Y	Y	Y	Y	Y
6 Dicks	N	Y	Y	Y	Y	Y
7 Lowry	Y	Y	Y	Y	Y	Y
8 ***Chandler***	N	Y	Y	N	Y	Y
WEST VIRGINIA						
1 Mollohan	Y	Y	Y	Y	Y	Y
2 Staggers	Y	Y	Y	Y	Y	Y
3 Wise	N	Y	Y	Y	Y	+
4 Rahall	Y	Y	Y	Y	Y	Y
WISCONSIN						
1 Aspin	?	?	Y	Y	N	Y
2 Kastenmeier	Y	Y	Y	Y	N	Y
3 ***Gunderson***	N	N	Y	N	N	N
4 Kleczka	Y	Y	Y	Y	N	Y
5 Moody	Y	Y	Y	Y	N	Y
6 ***Petri***	Y	Y	Y	N	N	N
7 Obey	Y	Y	Y	Y	N	Y
8 ***Roth***	X	?	Y	Y	N	Y
9 ***Sensenbrenner***	?	?	?	?	?	?
WYOMING						
AL ***Cheney***	N	N	Y	N	Y	N

Southern states - Ala., Ark., Fla., Ga., Ky., La., Miss., N.C., Okla., S.C., Tenn., Texas, Va.

199. HR 5525. Semiconductor Chip Protection. Kastenmeier, D-Wis., motion to suspend the rules and pass the bill to provide a new form of 10-year copyright protection for semiconductor chips. Motion agreed to 388-0: R 143-0; D 245-0 (ND 162-0, SD 83-0), June 11, 1984. A two-thirds majority of those present and voting (259 in this case) is required for passage under suspension of the rules.

200. HR 4772. Vietnam Veterans of America Charter. Sam B. Hall Jr., D-Texas, motion to suspend the rules and pass the bill to grant a federal charter to the Vietnam Veterans of America. Motion agreed to 295-96: R 54-89; D 241-7 (ND 161-3, SD 80-4), June 11, 1984. A two-thirds majority of those present and voting (261 in this case) is required for passage under suspension of the rules.

201. HR 5600. Preventive Health Services/Family Planning Block Grant Authorization. Waxman, D-Calif., motion to suspend the rules and pass the bill to authorize a total of $906.5 million for fiscal 1985-87 for preventive health services block grants, family planning and the adolescent family life programs. Motion agreed to 290-102: R 66-80; D 224-22 (ND 156-6, SD 68-16), June 11, 1984. A two-thirds majority of those present and voting (262 in this case) is required for passage under suspension of the rules. A "nay" was a vote supporting the president's position.

202. HR 5603. Alcohol, Drug Abuse and Mental Health Services Authorization. Waxman, D-Calif., motion to suspend the rules and pass the bill to authorize $2.3 billion for fiscal 1985-87 for grants for alcohol, drug abuse and mental health programs, and for fiscal 1985-88 for developmental disabilities aid. Motion agreed to 360-33: R 115-30; D 245-3 (ND 163-1, SD 82-2), June 11, 1984. A two-thirds majority of those present and voting (262 in this case) is required for passage under suspension of the rules. A "nay" was a vote supporting the president's position.

203. HR 5496. Medical Technology Assessment. Waxman, D-Calif., motion to suspend the rules and pass the bill to authorize $240 million for the National Center for Health Services and the National Center for Health Services Research and Medical Technology Assessment to provide data on health programs. Motion agreed to 376-16: R 129-16; D 247-0 (ND 165-0, SD 82-0), June 11, 1984. A two-thirds majority of those present and voting (262 in this case) is required for passage under suspension of the rules.

204. HR 1510. Immigration Reform and Control Act. Adoption of the rule (H Res 519) providing for House floor consideration of the bill to revise immigration laws to impose sanctions on employers who hire illegal aliens, provide legal status for many illegal aliens already in the United States, expand an existing temporary foreign worker program, and overhaul procedures for handling asylum, deportation and exclusion cases. Adopted 291-111: R 139-11; D 152-100 (ND 85-80, SD 67-20), June 11, 1984.

205. HR 1510. Immigration Reform and Control Act. Education and Labor Committee amendment (offered by Hawkins, D-Calif.) to restructure provisions penalizing employers who knowingly hire illegal aliens, deleting the criminal sanctions and increasing the fines. The amendment also included a new procedure for handling cases of alleged employment discrimination. Rejected 166-253: R 9-152; D 157-101 (ND 132-38, SD 25-63), June 12, 1984. A "nay" was a vote supporting the president's position.

206. HR 1510. Immigration Reform and Control Act. Lungren, R-Calif., amendment to delete from the bill language that required employers of four or more workers to check documents and keep records on their workers only after federal immigration officials find an illegal alien on the payroll. Adopted 321-97: R 105-55; D 216-42 (ND 151-19, SD 65-23), June 12, 1984. A "yea" was a vote supporting the president's position.

KEY

Y Voted for (yea).
\# Paired for.
+ Announced for.
N Voted against (nay).
X Paired against.
- Announced against.
P Voted "present".
C Voted "present" to avoid possible conflict of interest.
? Did not vote or otherwise make a position known.

Democrats *Republicans*

	199	200	201	202	203	204	205	206
ALABAMA								
1 *Edwards*	Y	Y	Y	Y	Y	Y	N	Y
2 *Dickinson*	?	?	?	?	?	?	X	Y
3 Nichols	Y	N	N	Y	Y	N	N	Y
4 Bevill	?	?	?	?	?	?	N	Y
5 Flippo	Y	Y	Y	Y	Y	Y	N	N
6 Erdreich	Y	Y	Y	Y	Y	Y	N	Y
7 Shelby	Y	Y	Y	Y	Y	N	N	Y
ALASKA								
AL *Young*	Y	Y	Y	Y	Y	Y	N	Y
ARIZONA								
1 *McCain*	Y	C	Y	Y	N	N	N	N
2 Udall	Y	Y	Y	Y	Y	Y	Y	Y
3 *Stump*	Y	N	N	N	N	N	N	N
4 *Rudd*	Y	N	N	N	Y	N	N	N
5 McNulty	Y	Y	Y	Y	Y	Y	Y	N
ARKANSAS								
1 Alexander	Y	Y	Y	Y	Y	Y	Y	Y
2 *Bethune*	?	?	?	?	?	?	N	Y
3 *Hammerschmidt*	Y	N	N	Y	Y	N	N	Y
4 Anthony	Y	Y	Y	Y	Y	Y	N	Y
CALIFORNIA								
1 Bosco	Y	Y	Y	Y	Y	N	N	N
2 *Chappie*	Y	N	Y	Y	Y	N	Y	Y
3 Matsui	Y	Y	Y	Y	Y	N	Y	Y
4 Fazio	Y	Y	Y	Y	Y	N	Y	Y
5 Burton	Y	Y	Y	Y	Y	N	Y	Y
6 Boxer	Y	Y	Y	Y	Y	N	Y	Y
7 Miller	Y	Y	Y	Y	Y	N	Y	Y
8 Dellums	Y	Y	Y	Y	Y	N	Y	Y
9 Stark	Y	Y	Y	Y	Y	N	Y	Y
10 Edwards	Y	Y	Y	Y	Y	N	Y	Y
11 Lantos	Y	Y	Y	Y	Y	N	Y	Y
12 *Zschau*	Y	Y	Y	N	Y	Y	N	Y
13 Mineta	Y	Y	Y	Y	Y	N	Y	Y
14 *Shumway*	Y	N	N	N	N	Y	N	Y
15 Coelho	Y	Y	Y	Y	Y	N	Y	N
16 Panetta	Y	Y	Y	Y	Y	N	Y	Y
17 *Pashayan*	?	?	?	?	?	X	N	Y
18 Lehman	Y	Y	Y	Y	Y	N	N	N
19 *Lagomarsino*	Y	N	Y	Y	Y	Y	N	Y
20 *Thomas*	?	X	?	?	?	\#	N	Y
21 *Fiedler*	Y	N	Y	Y	N	Y	N	Y
22 *Moorhead*	Y	N	N	Y	Y	Y	N	Y
23 Beilenson	Y	Y	Y	Y	Y	N	Y	Y
24 Waxman	Y	Y	Y	Y	Y	N	Y	Y
25 Roybal	Y	Y	Y	Y	Y	N	Y	Y
26 Berman	Y	Y	Y	Y	Y	N	Y	Y
27 Levine	Y	Y	Y	Y	Y	N	Y	Y
28 Dixon	Y	Y	Y	Y	Y	N	Y	Y
29 Hawkins	Y	Y	Y	Y	Y	N	Y	Y
30 Martinez	Y	Y	Y	Y	Y	N	Y	Y
31 Dymally	Y	Y	Y	Y	Y	N	Y	Y
32 Anderson	Y	Y	Y	Y	Y	N	Y	N
33 *Dreier*	Y	N	N	N	Y	Y	N	Y
34 Torres	+	Y	Y	Y	Y	N	Y	Y
35 *Lewis*	Y	N	N	N	Y	Y	N	Y
36 Brown	Y	Y	Y	Y	Y	?	?	?
37 *McCandless*	Y	N	N	N	N	Y	N	Y
38 Patterson	Y	Y	Y	Y	Y	N	Y	Y
39 *Dannemeyer*	Y	N	N	N	N	Y	N	Y
40 *Badham*	Y	N	Y	Y	Y	Y	N	Y
41 *Lowery*	Y	N	Y	Y	Y	N	N	Y
42 *Lungren*	Y	N	N	N	Y	Y	N	N
43 *Packard*	Y	N	N	?	Y	Y	N	Y
44 Bates	Y	Y	Y	?	Y	Y	Y	Y
45 *Hunter*	Y	N	N	N	Y	Y	Y	Y
COLORADO								
1 Schroeder	Y	Y	Y	Y	Y	N	N	Y
2 Wirth	Y	Y	Y	Y	Y	N	Y	Y
3 Kogovsek	Y	Y	Y	Y	Y	N	Y	Y
4 *Brown*	Y	N	N	N	N	N	N	Y
5 *Kramer*	Y	N	N	N	Y	N	Y	?
6 *Schaefer*	Y	N	N	N	N	Y	N	N
CONNECTICUT								
1 Kennelly	Y	Y	Y	Y	Y	N	Y	Y
2 Gejdenson	Y	Y	Y	Y	Y	N	Y	Y
3 Morrison	+	\#	+	+	+	N	Y	Y
4 *McKinney*	Y	Y	Y	Y	Y	N	Y	Y
5 Ratchford	Y	Y	Y	Y	Y	Y	Y	Y
6 *Johnson*	Y	Y	Y	Y	Y	N	Y	Y
DELAWARE								
AL Carper	Y	Y	Y	Y	Y	Y	N	Y
FLORIDA								
1 Hutto	Y	Y	Y	Y	Y	Y	N	Y
2 Fuqua	Y	Y	N	Y	Y	Y	N	N
3 Bennett	Y	Y	Y	Y	Y	N	N	N
4 Chappell	?	?	X	?	?	Y	N	N
5 *McCollum*	Y	N	N	N	Y	N	N	N
6 MacKay	Y	Y	Y	Y	Y	Y	N	Y
7 Gibbons	Y	Y	Y	Y	Y	Y	Y	Y
8 *Young*	?	N	N	Y	N	N	N	N
9 *Bilirakis*	Y	N	N	Y	N	N	N	N
10 Ireland	Y	Y	Y	Y	Y	N	N	N
11 Nelson	Y	N	Y	Y	N	Y	N	N
12 *Lewis*	Y	Y	Y	Y	Y	N	N	N
13 *Mack*	Y	N	N	N	N	Y	N	Y
14 Mica	Y	Y	Y	?	Y	Y	N	Y
15 *Shaw*	Y	Y	Y	Y	Y	N	N	Y
16 Smith	Y	Y	Y	Y	Y	N	Y	Y
17 Lehman	Y	Y	Y	Y	Y	Y	Y	Y
18 Pepper	Y	Y	Y	Y	Y	Y	Y	Y
19 Fascell	Y	Y	Y	Y	Y	Y	N	Y
GEORGIA								
1 Thomas	Y	Y	Y	Y	Y	Y	N	N
2 Hatcher	Y	Y	Y	Y	Y	Y	N	N
3 Ray	Y	Y	Y	Y	N	Y	N	Y
4 Levitas	Y	Y	Y	Y	Y	N	N	Y
5 Fowler	Y	Y	Y	Y	Y	Y	Y	Y
6 *Gingrich*	Y	N	N	N	Y	N	N	Y
7 *Darden*	Y	Y	Y	Y	Y	N	N	Y
8 Rowland	Y	Y	Y	Y	Y	N	N	N
9 Jenkins	Y	Y	Y	Y	Y	Y	N	N
10 Barnard	?	?	?	?	?	?	N	Y
HAWAII								
1 Heftel	Y	Y	Y	Y	Y	Y	N	Y
2 Akaka	?	\#	\#	?	?	X	Y	Y
IDAHO								
1 *Craig*	Y	N	N	Y	Y	?	N	N
2 *Hansen*	?	?	?	?	?	?	?	?
ILLINOIS								
1 Hayes	Y	Y	Y	Y	Y	N	Y	Y
2 Savage	Y	Y	Y	Y	Y	N	Y	Y
3 Russo	Y	Y	Y	Y	Y	N	N	Y
4 *O'Brien*	Y	N	Y	Y	Y	N	Y	Y
5 Lipinski	Y	Y	Y	Y	Y	Y	Y	Y
6 *Hyde*	Y	N	N	Y	Y	N	N	Y
7 Collins	Y	Y	Y	Y	Y	N	Y	Y
8 Rostenkowski	Y	Y	Y	Y	Y	Y	Y	?
9 Yates	Y	Y	Y	Y	Y	N	Y	Y
10 *Porter*	Y	Y	Y	Y	Y	Y	N	Y
11 Annunzio	Y	Y	N	Y	Y	Y	Y	Y
12 *Crane, P.*	Y	N	N	N	N	N	N	N
13 *Erlenborn*	Y	N	Y	Y	Y	Y	Y	Y
14 *Corcoran*	Y	N	Y	Y	Y	Y	Y	Y
15 *Madigan*	Y	N	Y	Y	Y	Y	Y	Y
16 *Martin*	Y	Y	Y	Y	Y	N	N	Y
17 Evans	Y	Y	Y	Y	Y	N	Y	Y
18 *Michel*	?	?	?	?	?	Y	N	Y
19 *Crane, D.*	Y	N	N	N	N	N	N	N
20 Durbin	Y	Y	Y	Y	Y	Y	Y	Y
21 Price	Y	Y	Y	Y	Y	Y	Y	Y
22 Simon	?	?	?	?	?	X	?	?
INDIANA								
1 Hall	Y	Y	Y	Y	Y	N	+	+
2 Sharp	Y	Y	Y	Y	Y	Y	Y	Y
3 *Hiler*	Y	Y	N	Y	N	Y	N	Y
4 *Coats*	Y	Y	N	Y	Y	N	N	Y
5 *Hillis*	Y	Y	Y	Y	Y	Y	N	Y

ND - Northern Democrats   SD - Southern Democrats

Corresponding to Congressional Record Votes 221, 222, 223, 224, 225, 226, 227, 228

	199	200	201	202	203	204	205	206
6 ***Burton***	Y	N	N	Y	N	Y	N	?
7 ***Myers***	Y	Y	Y	Y	Y	Y	N	Y
8 McCloskey	Y	Y	Y	Y	Y	Y	Y	Y
9 Hamilton	Y	Y	Y	Y	Y	Y	N	Y
10 Jacobs	Y	Y	Y	Y	Y	N	Y	Y
IOWA								
1 ***Leach***	?	?	?	?	?	?	N	Y
2 ***Tauke***	Y	Y	Y	Y	Y	Y	N	Y
3 ***Evans***	Y	N	Y	N	Y	Y	N	Y
4 Smith	Y	Y	Y	Y	Y	Y	N	Y
5 Harkin	Y	Y	Y	Y	Y	Y	Y	Y
6 Bedell	?	?	?	Y	Y	Y	N	Y
KANSAS								
1 ***Roberts***	Y	N	N	Y	Y	Y	N	N
2 Slattery	Y	Y	Y	Y	Y	Y	N	N
3 ***Winn***	Y	N	Y	Y	Y	Y	N	Y
4 Glickman	Y	Y	Y	Y	Y	Y	N	Y
5 ***Whittaker***	Y	N	Y	Y	Y	Y	N	Y
KENTUCKY								
1 Hubbard	?	?	?	?	?	?	Y	Y
2 Natcher	Y	Y	Y	Y	Y	Y	N	Y
3 Mazzoli	Y	Y	N	Y	Y	Y	N	Y
4 ***Snyder***	Y	N	N	Y	Y	Y	N	Y
5 ***Rogers***	Y	N	N	Y	Y	Y	N	Y
6 ***Hopkins***	Y	Y	N	Y	Y	Y	N	Y
7 Perkins	Y	Y	Y	Y	Y	Y	Y	Y
LOUISIANA								
1 ***Livingston***	Y	N	N	N	Y	Y	N	Y
2 Boggs	Y	Y	Y	Y	Y	Y	Y	Y
3 Tauzin	Y	Y	Y	Y	Y	Y	N	Y
4 Roemer	Y	Y	N	N	Y	Y	N	Y
5 Huckaby	Y	Y	Y	Y	Y	Y	N	Y
6 ***Moore***	Y	Y	Y	Y	Y	Y	N	N
7 Breaux	Y	Y	Y	Y	Y	Y	N	Y
8 Long	Y	Y	Y	Y	Y	Y	N	Y
MAINE								
1 ***McKernan***	Y	N	Y	Y	Y	Y	N	Y
2 ***Snowe***	Y	N	Y	Y	Y	Y	N	Y
MARYLAND								
1 Dyson	Y	Y	Y	Y	Y	Y	N	Y
2 Long	Y	Y	Y	Y	Y	Y	Y	Y
3 Mikulski	Y	Y	Y	Y	Y	N	Y	Y
4 ***Holt***	Y	N	N	Y	Y	Y	N	N
5 Hoyer	Y	Y	Y	Y	Y	Y	Y	Y
6 Byron	Y	N	N	Y	Y	Y	N	Y
7 Mitchell	Y	Y	Y	Y	Y	N	Y	?
8 Barnes	Y	Y	Y	Y	Y	Y	Y	Y
MASSACHUSETTS								
1 ***Conte***	Y	Y	Y	Y	Y	Y	N	Y
2 Boland	Y	Y	Y	Y	Y	Y	Y	Y
3 Early	Y	Y	Y	Y	Y	Y	Y	Y
4 Frank	Y	Y	Y	Y	Y	Y	N	Y
5 Shannon	?	?	?	?	?	Y	Y	Y
6 Mavroules	Y	Y	Y	Y	Y	Y	Y	Y
7 Markey	Y	Y	?	Y	Y	N	Y	Y
8 O'Neill								
9 Moakley	Y	Y	Y	Y	Y	Y	Y	Y
10 Studds	Y	Y	Y	Y	Y	Y	Y	Y
11 Donnelly	Y	Y	Y	Y	Y	Y	Y	Y
MICHIGAN								
1 Conyers	Y	Y	Y	Y	Y	N	Y	Y
2 ***Pursell***	Y	Y	Y	Y	Y	Y	N	Y
3 Wolpe	Y	Y	Y	Y	Y	N	Y	Y
4 ***Siljander***	Y	N	N	Y	Y	Y	N	N
5 ***Sawyer***	Y	N	Y	Y	Y	Y	N	Y
6 Carr	?	?	?	?	?	?	Y	Y
7 Kildee	Y	Y	Y	Y	Y	N	Y	Y
8 Traxler	Y	Y	Y	Y	Y	Y	N	N
9 ***Vander Jagt***	Y	N	Y	Y	Y	Y	N	N
10 Albosta	Y	Y	Y	Y	Y	N	N	Y
11 ***Davis***	Y	Y	Y	Y	Y	Y	N	Y
12 Bonior	Y	Y	Y	Y	Y	Y	Y	Y
13 Crockett	Y	Y	Y	Y	Y	N	Y	Y
14 Hertel	Y	Y	Y	Y	Y	Y	Y	Y
15 Ford	Y	Y	Y	Y	Y	Y	Y	Y
16 Dingell	Y	Y	Y	Y	Y	Y	Y	Y
17 Levin	Y	Y	Y	Y	Y	Y	Y	Y
18 ***Broomfield***	Y	N	Y	Y	Y	Y	N	Y
MINNESOTA								
1 Penny	Y	Y	Y	Y	Y	Y	N	N
2 ***Weber***	Y	N	N	Y	Y	Y	N	N
3 ***Frenzel***	?	?	Y	Y	Y	Y	N	Y
4 Vento	Y	Y	Y	Y	Y	Y	Y	Y
5 Sabo	Y	Y	Y	Y	Y	N	Y	N
6 Sikorski	Y	Y	Y	Y	Y	Y	Y	Y

	199	200	201	202	203	204	205	206
7 ***Stangeland***	Y	Y	N	Y	Y	Y	N	N
8 Oberstar	?	?	?	?	?	?	?	?
MISSISSIPPI								
1 Whitten	Y	Y	Y	Y	Y	Y	N	Y
2 ***Franklin***	Y	N	N	Y	Y	Y	N	N
3 Montgomery	Y	Y	N	Y	Y	Y	N	N
4 Dowdy	Y	Y	Y	Y	Y	N	N	N
5 ***Lott***	Y	N	N	Y	Y	Y	N	N
MISSOURI								
1 Clay	?	?	?	?	?	?	Y	Y
2 Young	Y	Y	Y	Y	Y	Y	Y	Y
3 Gephardt	Y	Y	Y	Y	Y	N	Y	N
4 Skelton	Y	Y	Y	Y	Y	N	N	Y
5 Wheat	Y	Y	Y	Y	Y	Y	Y	Y
6 ***Coleman***	Y	Y	Y	Y	Y	Y	N	Y
7 ***Taylor***	Y	N	N	Y	Y	Y	N	Y
8 ***Emerson***	Y	N	N	Y	Y	Y	N	N
9 Volkmer	Y	Y	Y	Y	Y	Y	N	Y
MONTANA								
1 Williams	Y	Y	Y	Y	Y	N	Y	Y
2 ***Marlenee***	Y	N	Y	Y	Y	Y	N	N
NEBRASKA								
1 ***Bereuter***	Y	N	N	Y	Y	Y	N	Y
2 ***Daub***	Y	N	N	Y	Y	Y	N	Y
3 ***Smith***	Y	N	N	Y	Y	Y	N	Y
NEVADA								
1 Reid	Y	Y	Y	Y	Y	N	Y	Y
2 ***Vucanovich***	Y	N	N	Y	Y	Y	N	N
NEW HAMPSHIRE								
1 D'Amours	?	?	?	?	?	?	N	Y
2 ***Gregg***	Y	Y	Y	Y	Y	Y	N	Y
NEW JERSEY								
1 Florio	Y	Y	Y	Y	Y	N	Y	Y
2 Hughes	Y	Y	Y	Y	Y	Y	N	Y
3 Howard	Y	Y	Y	Y	Y	Y	Y	Y
4 ***Smith***	Y	Y	N	Y	Y	Y	N	Y
5 ***Roukema***	Y	N	Y	Y	Y	Y	N	Y
6 Dwyer	?	?	#	?	?	#	Y	Y
7 ***Rinaldo***	Y	N	N	Y	Y	Y	Y	Y
8 Roe	Y	Y	Y	Y	Y	Y	Y	Y
9 Torricelli	Y	Y	Y	Y	Y	Y	N	Y
10 Rodino	Y	Y	Y	Y	Y	Y	N	Y
11 Minish	Y	Y	Y	Y	Y	N	Y	Y
12 ***Courter***	Y	N	Y	Y	Y	Y	N	Y
13 Vacancy								
14 Guarini	Y	Y	Y	Y	Y	N	Y	Y
NEW MEXICO								
1 ***Lujan***	Y	Y	Y	Y	Y	N	Y	N
2 ***Skeen***	Y	N	Y	Y	Y	N	N	N
3 Richardson	Y	Y	Y	Y	Y	N	Y	Y
NEW YORK								
1 ***Carney***	?	?	?	?	?	?	N	Y
2 Downey	Y	Y	Y	Y	Y	N	Y	Y
3 Mrazek	Y	Y	Y	Y	Y	N	Y	Y
4 ***Lent***	?	?	N	Y	Y	Y	N	Y
5 ***McGrath***	Y	Y	N	Y	Y	Y	N	Y
6 Addabbo	Y	Y	Y	Y	Y	N	Y	Y
7 Ackerman	Y	Y	Y	Y	Y	N	Y	Y
8 Scheuer	Y	Y	Y	Y	Y	Y	N	Y
9 Ferraro	Y	Y	Y	Y	Y	N	Y	Y
10 Schumer	?	Y	Y	Y	Y	Y	Y	Y
11 Towns	Y	Y	Y	Y	Y	N	Y	Y
12 Owens	Y	Y	Y	Y	Y	N	Y	N
13 Solarz	Y	Y	Y	Y	Y	Y	N	Y
14 ***Molinari***	Y	N	Y	Y	Y	Y	N	Y
15 ***Green***	Y	Y	Y	Y	Y	Y	Y	Y
16 Rangel	Y	Y	Y	Y	Y	N	Y	Y
17 Weiss	Y	Y	Y	Y	Y	N	#	Y
18 Garcia	Y	Y	Y	Y	Y	N	Y	Y
19 Biaggi	Y	Y	Y	Y	Y	Y	Y	Y
20 Ottinger	Y	Y	Y	Y	Y	N	Y	Y
21 ***Fish***	Y	Y	Y	Y	Y	Y	N	Y
22 ***Gilman***	Y	Y	Y	Y	Y	Y	N	Y
23 Stratton	Y	N	Y	Y	Y	N	Y	Y
24 ***Solomon***	Y	N	N	Y	?	Y	N	Y
25 ***Boehlert***	Y	Y	Y	Y	Y	Y	N	Y
26 ***Martin***	Y	N	Y	Y	Y	Y	N	Y
27 ***Wortley***	Y	Y	Y	Y	Y	Y	N	Y
28 McHugh	Y	Y	Y	Y	Y	Y	N	Y
29 ***Horton***	Y	Y	Y	Y	Y	N	Y	N
30 ***Conable***	Y	Y	Y	Y	Y	Y	N	Y
31 ***Kemp***	?	?	?	?	?	?	N	Y
32 LaFalce	Y	Y	N	N	Y	Y	N	Y
33 Nowak	Y	Y	Y	Y	Y	Y	Y	Y
34 Lundine	Y	Y	Y	Y	Y	Y	Y	Y

	199	200	201	202	203	204	205	206
NORTH CAROLINA								
1 Jones	Y	Y	Y	Y	Y	N	Y	Y
2 Valentine	Y	Y	Y	Y	Y	Y	N	Y
3 Whitley	Y	Y	Y	Y	Y	Y	Y	Y
4 Andrews	Y	Y	Y	Y	Y	Y	N	Y
5 Neal	Y	Y	Y	Y	Y	Y	N	Y
6 Britt	Y	Y	Y	Y	Y	Y	Y	Y
7 Rose	Y	Y	Y	Y	Y	Y	?	?
8 Hefner	Y	Y	Y	Y	Y	Y	N	Y
9 ***Martin***	?	?	?	?	?	?	N	?
10 ***Broyhill***	Y	N	Y	Y	Y	Y	N	Y
11 Clarke	?	Y	Y	Y	Y	Y	N	Y
NORTH DAKOTA								
AL Dorgan	Y	Y	Y	Y	Y	Y	N	Y
OHIO								
1 Luken	Y	Y	Y	Y	Y	Y	N	Y
2 ***Gradison***	Y	Y	N	Y	Y	Y	N	Y
3 Hall	Y	Y	Y	Y	Y	Y	Y	Y
4 ***Oxley***	?	?	?	?	?	?	N	Y
5 ***Latta***	Y	N	N	Y	Y	Y	N	N
6 ***McEwen***	Y	Y	N	Y	N	Y	N	Y
7 ***DeWine***	Y	Y	N	Y	Y	Y	N	N
8 ***Kindness***	Y	N	N	N	Y	Y	N	N
9 Kaptur	Y	Y	Y	Y	Y	N	?	Y
10 ***Miller***	Y	Y	N	Y	Y	Y	N	N
11 Eckart	Y	Y	Y	Y	Y	Y	Y	Y
12 ***Kasich***	Y	Y	Y	Y	Y	Y	N	N
13 Pease	Y	Y	Y	Y	Y	Y	Y	Y
14 Seiberling	Y	Y	Y	Y	Y	Y	Y	Y
15 ***Wylie***	Y	Y	Y	Y	Y	Y	N	N
16 ***Regula***	Y	Y	Y	Y	Y	Y	N	N
17 ***Williams***	?	?	?	?	?	?	Y	Y
18 Applegate	Y	Y	Y	Y	Y	Y	N	N
19 Feighan	Y	Y	Y	Y	Y	Y	Y	Y
20 Oakar	Y	Y	Y	Y	Y	N	Y	Y
21 Stokes	Y	Y	Y	Y	Y	N	Y	Y
OKLAHOMA								
1 Jones	Y	Y	N	Y	Y	Y	N	Y
2 Synar	+	+	+	+	+	Y	N	Y
3 Watkins	Y	Y	N	Y	Y	Y	N	Y
4 McCurdy	Y	Y	Y	Y	Y	Y	N	Y
5 ***Edwards***	Y	Y	N	Y	Y	Y	N	N
6 English	Y	Y	N	Y	Y	Y	N	Y
OREGON								
1 AuCoin	Y	Y	Y	Y	Y	N	N	Y
2 ***Smith, R.***	Y	Y	Y	Y	Y	Y	N	N
3 Wyden	Y	Y	Y	Y	Y	Y	N	Y
4 Weaver	Y	Y	Y	Y	Y	N	Y	?
5 ***Smith, D.***	Y	N	N	N	Y	Y	N	N
PENNSYLVANIA								
1 Foglietta	Y	Y	Y	Y	Y	N	Y	Y
2 Gray	Y	Y	Y	Y	Y	N	Y	Y
3 Borski	Y	Y	Y	Y	Y	Y	Y	Y
4 Kolter	?	?	?	?	?	?	Y	Y
5 ***Schulze***	?	?	?	?	?	Y	N	Y
6 Yatron	Y	Y	Y	Y	Y	N	Y	Y
7 Edgar	Y	Y	Y	Y	Y	Y	Y	Y
8 Kostmayer	Y	Y	Y	Y	Y	Y	Y	Y
9 ***Shuster***	Y	N	N	N	Y	Y	N	Y
10 ***McDade***	?	?	?	?	?	Y	Y	Y
11 Harrison	Y	N	Y	Y	Y	Y	Y	N
12 Murtha	Y	Y	Y	Y	Y	Y	N	Y
13 ***Coughlin***	Y	Y	Y	Y	Y	Y	N	Y
14 Coyne	Y	Y	Y	Y	Y	Y	Y	Y
15 ***Ritter***	Y	N	Y	Y	Y	Y	N	N
16 ***Walker***	Y	Y	N	N	N	Y	N	N
17 ***Gekas***	Y	N	Y	N	Y	Y	N	N
18 Walgren	Y	Y	Y	Y	Y	Y	N	Y
19 ***Goodling***	?	?	?	?	?	#	N	Y
20 Gaydos	Y	Y	Y	Y	Y	N	Y	Y
21 ***Ridge***	?	?	?	?	?	Y	N	Y
22 Murphy	Y	Y	Y	Y	Y	Y	Y	N
23 ***Clinger***	Y	N	Y	Y	Y	Y	N	Y
RHODE ISLAND								
1 St Germain	Y	Y	Y	Y	Y	Y	N	Y
2 ***Schneider***	?	?	?	?	?	Y	Y	Y
SOUTH CAROLINA								
1 ***Hartnett***	Y	N	N	N	Y	Y	N	Y
2 ***Spence***	Y	N	N	Y	Y	Y	N	Y
3 Derrick	Y	Y	Y	Y	Y	Y	N	Y
4 ***Campbell***	Y	N	N	Y	Y	Y	N	Y
5 Spratt	Y	Y	Y	Y	Y	Y	N	Y
6 Tallon	Y	Y	Y	Y	Y	Y	?	?
SOUTH DAKOTA								
AL Daschle	Y	Y	Y	Y	Y	Y	N	Y

	199	200	201	202	203	204	205	206
TENNESSEE								
1 ***Quillen***	Y	N	N	Y	Y	Y	?	?
2 ***Duncan***	Y	N	N	Y	Y	Y	N	Y
3 Lloyd	Y	N	N	Y	Y	Y	N	N
4 Cooper	Y	Y	N	Y	Y	Y	N	N
5 Boner	Y	Y	Y	Y	Y	N	N	Y
6 Gore	Y	Y	Y	Y	Y	Y	N	N
7 ***Sundquist***	Y	Y	N	Y	Y	Y	N	Y
8 Jones	Y	Y	Y	Y	Y	N	Y	Y
9 Ford	Y	Y	Y	Y	Y	Y	Y	Y
TEXAS								
1 Hall, S.	Y	Y	N	Y	Y	Y	N	N
2 Wilson	Y	N	Y	Y	Y	Y	N	Y
3 ***Bartlett***	Y	N	N	N	N	Y	N	N
4 Hall, R.	Y	Y	N	Y	Y	N	N	N
5 Bryant	Y	Y	Y	Y	Y	N	Y	Y
6 ***Gramm***	Y	Y	N	Y	Y	N	N	N
7 ***Archer***	Y	N	N	N	Y	Y	N	N
8 ***Fields***	Y	N	N	Y	Y	N	N	N
9 Brooks	Y	Y	Y	Y	Y	N	Y	Y
10 Pickle	Y	Y	Y	Y	Y	Y	N	Y
11 Leath	Y	Y	N	Y	Y	N	N	N
12 Wright	Y	Y	Y	Y	Y	Y	Y	Y
13 Hightower	Y	Y	Y	Y	Y	N	N	Y
14 Patman	Y	N	Y	Y	Y	N	N	N
15 de la Garza	Y	Y	Y	Y	Y	N	Y	Y
16 Coleman	Y	Y	Y	Y	Y	N	Y	Y
17 Stenholm	Y	Y	N	Y	Y	N	N	N
18 Leland	Y	Y	Y	Y	Y	N	Y	Y
19 Hance	Y	Y	Y	Y	Y	N	Y	N
20 Gonzalez	Y	Y	Y	Y	Y	N	Y	Y
21 ***Loeffler***	Y	N	Y	Y	Y	N	N	N
22 ***Paul***	Y	N	N	N	N	N	N	N
23 Kazen	Y	Y	Y	Y	Y	N	Y	N
24 Frost	Y	Y	Y	Y	Y	N	Y	Y
25 Andrews	Y	Y	Y	Y	Y	Y	N	Y
26 Vandergriff	Y	Y	N	N	Y	Y	N	N
27 Ortiz	Y	Y	Y	Y	Y	N	Y	N
UTAH								
1 ***Hansen***	Y	N	N	N	Y	Y	N	Y
2 ***Marriott***	Y	N	N	Y	Y	Y	N	Y
3 ***Nielson***	Y	N	N	N	Y	Y	N	Y
VERMONT								
AL ***Jeffords***	Y	Y	Y	N	Y	Y	N	Y
VIRGINIA								
1 ***Bateman***	Y	N	N	Y	Y	Y	N	Y
2 ***Whitehurst***	?	?	?	?	?	?	?	Y
3 ***Bliley***	Y	N	Y	Y	Y	Y	N	Y
4 Sisisky	Y	Y	Y	Y	Y	Y	N	Y
5 Daniel	?	?	?	?	?	Y	N	Y
6 Olin	Y	Y	Y	Y	Y	Y	Y	Y
7 ***Robinson***	Y	N	N	Y	Y	Y	N	Y
8 ***Parris***	Y	N	N	Y	Y	Y	N	Y
9 Boucher	Y	Y	Y	Y	?	Y	N	Y
10 ***Wolf***	Y	Y	N	Y	Y	Y	N	Y
WASHINGTON								
1 ***Pritchard***	?	?	?	?	?	?	N	Y
2 Swift	Y	Y	Y	Y	Y	Y	Y	Y
3 Bonker	Y	Y	Y	Y	Y	Y	?	Y
4 ***Morrison***	Y	Y	Y	Y	Y	Y	N	N
5 Foley	?	?	?	?	?	?	Y	N
6 Dicks	Y	Y	Y	Y	Y	Y	N	N
7 Lowry	Y	Y	Y	Y	Y	N	Y	Y
8 ***Chandler***	Y	Y	Y	Y	Y	Y	N	N
WEST VIRGINIA								
1 Mollohan	Y	Y	N	Y	Y	Y	N	Y
2 Staggers	Y	Y	N	Y	Y	Y	Y	Y
3 Wise	Y	Y	Y	Y	Y	Y	Y	Y
4 Rahall	Y	Y	Y	Y	Y	?	Y	Y
WISCONSIN								
1 Aspin	Y	Y	Y	Y	Y	N	Y	Y
2 Kastenmeier	Y	Y	Y	Y	Y	Y	Y	Y
3 ***Gunderson***	Y	Y	Y	Y	Y	Y	N	N
4 Kleczka	Y	Y	-	Y	Y	Y	Y	Y
5 Moody	?	?	?	?	?	?	Y	Y
6 ***Petri***	Y	Y	N	Y	Y	Y	N	N
7 Obey	Y	Y	Y	Y	Y	N	Y	N
8 ***Roth***	Y	N	N	Y	Y	Y	N	Y
9 ***Sensenbrenner***	?	?	?	?	?	?	?	?
WYOMING								
AL ***Cheney***	Y	N	N	N	N	Y	N	Y

Southern states - Ala., Ark., Fla., Ga., Ky., La., Miss., N.C., Okla., S.C., Tenn., Texas, Va.

KEY

Y Voted for (yea).
Paired for.
+ Announced for.
N Voted against (nay).
X Paired against.
- Announced against.
P Voted "present".
C Voted "present" to avoid possible conflict of interest.
? Did not vote or otherwise make a position known.

Democrats   *Republicans*

207. HR 1510. Immigration Reform and Control Act. Frank, D-Mass., amendment to establish a new procedure for handling cases of alleged employment discrimination because of national origin or alienage, and to provide remedies for such discrimination. The amendment would create a "special counsel" within a newly created U.S. Immigration Board to handle discrimination cases. Adopted 404-9: R 150-8; D 254-1 (ND 167-1, SD 87-0), June 12, 1984.

208. HR 1510. Immigration Reform and Control Act. Sam B. Hall Jr., D-Texas, amendment to require the federal government to establish a system for employers to validate a prospective employee's Social Security identification number by telephone as a check on the applicant's eligibility to work in the United States. Adopted 242-155: R 122-29; D 120-126 (ND 56-107, SD 64-19), June 12, 1984.

209. HR 1510. Immigration Reform and Control Act. Schroeder, D-Colo., amendment to set a three-year expiration date for provisions that penalize employers who knowingly hire illegal aliens. Rejected 137-274: R 26-130; D 111-144 (ND 89-82, SD 22-62), June 13, 1984. A "nay" was a vote supporting the president's position.

210. HR 1510. Immigration Reform and Control Act. Roybal, D-Calif., amendment to delete the bill's employer sanctions provisions and substitute new funding and requirements for enforcement of existing labor laws on wages, hours and working conditions. Rejected 120-304: R 20-140; D 100-164 (ND 86-89, SD 14-75), June 13, 1984. A "nay" was a vote supporting the president's position.

211. HR 1510. Immigration Reform and Control Act. Fish, R-N.Y., amendment to delete from the bill language requiring federal officials to obtain a warrant before searching "open fields" for illegal aliens. Rejected 133-285: R 63-98; D 70-187 (ND 56-115, SD 14-72), June 13, 1984. A "yea" was a vote supporting the president's position.

212. HR 1510. Immigration Reform and Control Act. McCollum, R-Fla., amendment to streamline procedures for handling asylum deportation or exclusion cases by barring most "class action" lawsuits and by deleting a requirement that aliens be notified of certain procedural rights. Adopted 208-192: R 142-16; D 66-176 (ND 10-149, SD 56-27), June 13, 1984. A "yea" was a vote supporting the president's position.

	207	208	209	210	211	212
ALABAMA						
1 *Edwards*	Y	?	N	N	Y	Y
2 *Dickinson*	Y	Y	N	N	N	Y
3 Nichols	Y	Y	N	N	N	Y
4 Bevill	Y	Y	N	N	N	Y
5 Flippo	Y	Y	N	?	Y	
6 Erdreich	Y	Y	N	N	N	Y
7 Shelby	Y	Y	N	N	N	Y
ALASKA						
AL *Young*	Y	Y	N	N	Y	Y
ARIZONA						
1 *McCain*	Y	Y	Y	Y	N	Y
2 Udall	Y	N	Y	N	Y	N
3 *Stump*	N	Y	N	Y	N	Y
4 *Rudd*	Y	Y	N	N	Y	Y
5 McNulty	Y	N	Y	N	Y	N
ARKANSAS						
1 Alexander	Y	Y	Y	N	Y	N
2 *Bethune*	Y	Y	N	N	Y	Y
3 *Hammerschmidt*	Y	Y	N	Y	N	Y
4 Anthony	Y	Y	N	N	Y	Y
CALIFORNIA						
1 Bosco	Y	N	Y	N	N	N
2 *Chappie*	Y	N	N	Y	N	N
3 Matsui	Y	Y	Y	Y	N	N
4 Fazio	Y	Y	Y	Y	N	N
5 Burton	Y	N	Y	N	N	N
6 Boxer	Y	N	Y	N	N	N
7 Miller	Y	N	Y	N	N	N
8 Dellums	Y	N	Y	N	N	N
9 Stark	Y	?	N	Y	N	?
10 Edwards	Y	N	Y	Y	N	N
11 Lantos	Y	N	Y	N	N	N
12 *Zschau*	Y	Y	N	N	N	Y
13 Mineta	Y	N	Y	N	N	N
14 *Shumway*	N	Y	N	N	Y	Y
15 Coelho	Y	N	Y	N	N	N
16 Panetta	Y	Y	Y	Y	N	N
17 *Pashayan*	Y	Y	Y	Y	N	Y
18 Lehman	N	N	Y	N	N	N
19 *Lagomarsino*	Y	Y	N	N	N	Y
20 *Thomas*	Y	Y	N	N	N	Y
21 *Fiedler*	Y	Y	N	N	N	Y
22 *Moorhead*	Y	Y	N	N	N	Y
23 Beilenson	Y	Y	N	N	N	N
24 Waxman	Y	N	Y	N	N	N
25 Roybal	Y	N	Y	Y	N	?
26 Berman	Y	N	Y	N	N	N
27 Levine	Y	N	Y	N	N	N
28 Dixon	Y	N	Y	Y	N	N
29 Hawkins	Y	?	Y	Y	N	?
30 Martinez	?	Y	Y	Y	N	N
31 Dymally	Y	N	Y	N	N	N
32 Anderson	Y	N	Y	N	N	N
33 *Dreier*	Y	Y	Y	N	N	Y
34 Torres	Y	N	Y	N	Y	N
35 *Lewis*	Y	Y	N	Y	N	Y
36 Brown	?	Y	Y	Y	N	N
37 *McCandless*	Y	N	N	N	N	Y
38 Patterson	Y	N	Y	Y	Y	N
39 *Dannemeyer*	Y	Y	N	N	N	Y
40 *Badham*	N	N	N	N	N	Y
41 *Lowery*	Y	N	N	N	N	Y
42 *Lungren*	Y	N	N	N	N	Y

	207	208	209	210	211	212
43 *Packard*	Y	N	N	N	N	Y
44 Bates	Y	N	Y	N	?	?
45 *Hunter*	Y	Y	N	N	Y	Y
COLORADO						
1 Schroeder	Y	Y	Y	Y	N	N
2 Wirth	Y	Y	Y	Y	N	N
3 Kogovsek	Y	N	Y	Y	N	?
4 *Brown*	Y	N	N	N	N	Y
5 *Kramer*	Y	Y	Y	Y	N	Y
6 *Schaefer*	Y	Y	N	N	N	Y
CONNECTICUT						
1 Kennelly	Y	N	Y	Y	N	N
2 Gejdenson	Y	N	Y	Y	N	N
3 Morrison	Y	N	Y	Y	N	N
4 *McKinney*	Y	N	Y	N	N	Y
5 Ratchford	Y	N	N	N	N	N
6 *Johnson*	Y	Y	N	N	Y	N
DELAWARE						
AL Carper	+	Y	N	N	Y	N
FLORIDA						
1 Hutto	Y	Y	N	N	Y	Y
2 Fuqua	Y	Y	N	N	N	?
3 Bennett	Y	N	N	N	N	Y
4 Chappell	Y	Y	?	N	Y	Y
5 *McCollum*	Y	N	N	Y	N	Y
6 MacKay	Y	Y	N	N	N	N
7 Gibbons	Y	Y	N	Y	N	Y
8 *Young*	Y	N	?	?	?	?
9 *Bilirakis*	Y	Y	N	N	N	Y
10 Ireland	Y	Y	N	N	N	Y
11 Nelson	Y	N	N	Y	N	Y
12 *Lewis*	Y	N	N	N	N	Y
13 *Mack*	Y	Y	Y	N	Y	Y
14 Mica	Y	N	N	Y	N	N
15 *Shaw*	Y	N	N	Y	Y	Y
16 Smith	Y	N	N	N	N	?
17 Lehman	Y	N	N	Y	N	N
18 Pepper	Y	Y	N	N	N	N
19 Fascell	Y	N	N	Y	N	N
GEORGIA						
1 Thomas	Y	Y	N	N	N	Y
2 Hatcher	Y	N	N	N	N	?
3 Ray	Y	Y	N	N	N	Y
4 Levitas	Y	Y	N	N	N	N
5 Fowler	Y	Y	N	N	N	N
6 *Gingrich*	Y	Y	?	N	N	Y
7 Darden	Y	?	N	N	N	Y
8 Rowland	Y	Y	N	N	N	Y
9 Jenkins	Y	Y	N	?	Y	Y
10 Barnard	Y	Y	N	N	N	Y
HAWAII						
1 Heftel	Y	Y	N	N	N	N
2 Akaka	Y	N	Y	Y	N	N
IDAHO						
1 *Craig*	Y	Y	Y	N	N	Y
2 *Hansen*	?	?	?	?	?	?
ILLINOIS						
1 Hayes	Y	N	Y	Y	N	N
2 Savage	Y	N	Y	Y	N	N
3 Russo	Y	Y	N	Y	N	N
4 *O'Brien*	Y	Y	N	N	Y	Y
5 Lipinski	Y	Y	N	N	N	N
6 *Hyde*	?	Y	N	N	Y	Y
7 Collins	Y	N	Y	Y	N	N
8 Rostenkowski	Y	N	N	N	N	N
9 Yates	Y	N	N	Y	N	N
10 *Porter*	Y	Y	N	N	N	N
11 Annunzio	Y	N	N	N	N	N
12 *Crane, P.*	N	Y	N	N	Y	Y
13 *Erlenborn*	N	Y	?	N	Y	Y
14 *Corcoran*	Y	Y	N	N	Y	?
15 *Madigan*	Y	Y	N	N	Y	Y
16 *Martin*	Y	Y	N	N	N	Y
17 Evans	Y	N	Y	N	Y	N
18 *Michel*	Y	?	N	N	Y	Y
19 *Crane, D.*	N	Y	N	N	Y	Y
20 Durbin	Y	N	N	N	N	N
21 Price	Y	N	N	Y	N	N
22 Simon	?	?	?	?	?	?
INDIANA						
1 Hall	+	-	+	Y	N	N
2 Sharp	Y	Y	N	N	Y	N
3 *Hiler*	Y	Y	N	N	N	Y
4 *Coats*	Y	Y	N	N	N	Y
5 *Hillis*	Y	Y	N	N	N	Y

ND - Northern Democrats   SD - Southern Democrats

Corresponding to Congressional Record Votes 229, 230, 231, 232, 234, 236

	207	208	209	210	211	212
6 ***Burton***	?	?	?	?	N	Y
7 ***Myers***	?	Y	N	N	N	Y
8 McCloskey	Y	N	N	N	N	N
9 Hamilton	Y	N	N	N	Y	N
10 Jacobs	Y	N	Y	Y	N	N
IOWA						
1 ***Leach***	Y	Y	N	N	Y	N
2 ***Tauke***	Y	N	N	N	Y	Y
3 ***Evans***	Y	Y	N	N	Y	Y
4 Smith	Y	Y	N	N	Y	Y
5 Harkin	Y	N	N	N	Y	N
6 Bedell	Y	Y	N	N	Y	N
KANSAS						
1 ***Roberts***	Y	Y	N	N	N	Y
2 Slattery	Y	Y	Y	Y	N	N
3 ***Winn***	Y	Y	N	N	N	Y
4 Glickman	Y	N	N	N	N	N
5 ***Whittaker***	Y	Y	N	N	N	Y
KENTUCKY						
1 Hubbard	Y	Y	N	N	N	Y
2 Natcher	Y	N	N	N	N	N
3 Mazzoli	Y	N	N	N	Y	N
4 ***Snyder***	Y	Y	N	N	N	N
5 ***Rogers***	Y	Y	N	N	N	Y
6 ***Hopkins***	Y	Y	N	N	Y	Y
7 Perkins	Y	?	N	N	N	Y
LOUISIANA						
1 ***Livingston***	Y	N	N	N	Y	Y
2 Boggs	Y	?	Y	N	N	Y
3 Tauzin	Y	Y	N	N	N	Y
4 Roemer	Y	Y	Y	N	N	Y
5 Huckaby	Y	Y	N	N	N	Y
6 ***Moore***	Y	?	N	N	Y	Y
7 Breaux	Y	Y	N	N	N	Y
8 Long	Y	Y	N	N	N	N
MAINE						
1 ***McKernan***	Y	Y	N	N	N	Y
2 ***Snowe***	Y	Y	N	N	N	Y
MARYLAND						
1 Dyson	Y	Y	N	N	N	Y
2 Long	Y	Y	Y	Y	N	N
3 Mikulski	Y	Y	Y	Y	N	N
4 ***Holt***	Y	Y	N	N	N	Y
5 Hoyer	Y	N	N	N	N	?
6 Byron	Y	?	N	N	N	Y
7 Mitchell	Y	N	Y	Y	N	N
8 Barnes	Y	N	N	N	N	N
MASSACHUSETTS						
1 ***Conte***	Y	N	N	N	Y	N
2 Boland	+	N	N	N	Y	N
3 Early	Y	N	N	N	?	?
4 Frank	Y	N	N	N	Y	N
5 Shannon	Y	N	Y	Y	?	?
6 Mavroules	Y	N	N	N	N	N
7 Markey	Y	N	Y	Y	N	N
8 O'Neill						
9 Moakley	Y	Y	N	N	Y	?
10 Studds	Y	N	N	N	N	N
11 Donnelly	Y	Y	N	N	Y	N
MICHIGAN						
1 Conyers	Y	N	Y	Y	N	N
2 ***Pursell***	Y	Y	N	N	Y	Y
3 Wolpe	Y	N	Y	Y	N	N
4 ***Siljander***	Y	Y	N	N	N	Y
5 ***Sawyer***	?	Y	N	N	N	Y
6 Carr	Y	Y	Y	Y	N	N
7 Kildee	Y	N	Y	Y	N	N
8 Traxler	Y	?	N	N	Y	N
9 ***Vander Jagt***	Y	Y	N	N	N	Y
10 Albosta	Y	N	Y	Y	N	N
11 ***Davis***	Y	Y	N	N	N	Y
12 Bonior	Y	N	Y	Y	N	N
13 Crockett	Y	N	Y	Y	N	N
14 Hertel	Y	N	Y	Y	Y	N
15 Ford	?	Y	?	Y	N	N
16 Dingell	Y	Y	N	N	Y	?
17 Levin	Y	N	Y	N	N	N
18 ***Broomfield***	Y	Y	N	N	N	Y
MINNESOTA						
1 Penny	Y	N	N	N	N	N
2 ***Weber***	Y	Y	?	N	N	Y
3 ***Frenzel***	Y	N	N	N	Y	Y
4 Vento	Y	N	N	N	Y	N
5 Sabo	Y	N	Y	Y	Y	N
6 Sikorski	Y	N	N	N	Y	N
7 ***Stangeland***	Y	Y	N	N	N	Y
8 Oberstar	?	?	?	?	?	?
MISSISSIPPI						
1 Whitten	Y	?	N	N	N	?
2 ***Franklin***	Y	Y	N	N	Y	Y
3 Montgomery	Y	Y	N	N	N	Y
4 Dowdy	Y	Y	?	N	N	Y
5 ***Lott***	Y	Y	N	N	Y	Y
MISSOURI						
1 Clay	Y	N	Y	Y	N	N
2 Young	Y	Y	N	N	N	N
3 Gephardt	Y	N	N	N	N	N
4 Skelton	Y	Y	N	N	N	?
5 Wheat	Y	N	Y	Y	N	N
6 ***Coleman***	Y	N	N	N	Y	Y
7 ***Taylor***	Y	Y	N	N	N	Y
8 ***Emerson***	Y	Y	N	N	N	Y
9 Volkmer	Y	Y	N	N	Y	Y
MONTANA						
1 Williams	Y	Y	Y	Y	N	N
2 ***Marlenee***	N	Y	N	Y	N	Y
NEBRASKA						
1 ***Bereuter***	Y	N	N	N	Y	Y
2 ***Daub***	Y	Y	N	N	Y	Y
3 ***Smith***	Y	N	N	N	N	Y
NEVADA						
1 Reid	Y	N	Y	Y	N	N
2 ***Vucanovich***	Y	Y	N	N	Y	Y
NEW HAMPSHIRE						
1 D'Amours	Y	Y	N	N	Y	N
2 ***Gregg***	Y	Y	N	N	N	Y
NEW JERSEY						
1 Florio	Y	N	N	N	N	N
2 Hughes	Y	Y	N	N	Y	N
3 Howard	Y	Y	Y	N	Y	?
4 ***Smith***	Y	Y	N	N	Y	N
5 ***Roukema***	Y	N	N	N	N	Y
6 Dwyer	Y	N	N	N	Y	N
7 ***Rinaldo***	Y	Y	N	N	Y	N
8 Roe	Y	Y	N	N	Y	N
9 Torricelli	Y	N	N	N	Y	Y
10 Rodino	Y	N	N	N	Y	N
11 Minish	Y	Y	N	N	Y	N
12 ***Courter***	Y	Y	N	N	N	Y
13 Vacancy						
14 Guarini	Y	N	N	Y	Y	N
NEW MEXICO						
1 ***Lujan***	?	N	Y	Y	Y	Y
2 ***Skeen***	Y	Y	Y	Y	N	Y
3 Richardson	Y	N	Y	Y	N	N
NEW YORK						
1 ***Carney***	Y	Y	N	N	N	Y
2 Downey	Y	N	Y	Y	N	N
3 Mrazek	Y	N	Y	Y	Y	N
4 ***Lent***	Y	Y	N	N	N	Y
5 ***McGrath***	Y	N	N	N	Y	Y
6 Addabbo	Y	N	Y	Y	N	N
7 Ackerman	Y	N	Y	Y	N	N
8 Scheuer	Y	Y	N	N	Y	Y
9 Ferraro	Y	N	Y	Y	?	?
10 Schumer	Y	N	Y	N	N	N
11 Towns	Y	N	Y	Y	N	N
12 Owens	Y	N	Y	Y	N	?
13 Solarz	Y	N	N	N	Y	N
14 ***Molinari***	Y	Y	N	N	Y	Y
15 ***Green***	Y	N	N	N	Y	N
16 Rangel	Y	?	Y	Y	N	N
17 Weiss	Y	N	Y	Y	N	N
18 Garcia	Y	N	Y	Y	N	N
19 Biaggi	Y	?	N	N	N	N
20 Ottinger	Y	Y	Y	Y	N	N
21 ***Fish***	Y	N	N	N	Y	N
22 ***Gilman***	Y	Y	N	N	N	N
23 Stratton	Y	Y	N	Y	Y	Y
24 ***Solomon***	Y	?	N	N	N	Y
25 ***Boehlert***	Y	N	N	N	Y	Y
26 ***Martin***	Y	Y	N	N	?	?
27 ***Wortley***	Y	Y	N	N	Y	Y
28 McHugh	Y	N	N	N	N	N
29 ***Horton***	Y	Y	Y	Y	N	Y
30 ***Conable***	Y	N	N	N	?	Y
31 ***Kemp***	Y	?	Y	Y	N	N
32 LaFalce	Y	Y	N	N	Y	N
33 Nowak	Y	Y	N	N	Y	N
34 Lundine	Y	?	N	N	N	N
NORTH CAROLINA						
1 Jones	?	Y	N	Y	N	Y
2 Valentine	Y	Y	N	N	N	Y
3 Whitley	Y	Y	N	N	N	Y
4 Andrews	Y	Y	N	N	N	Y
5 Neal	Y	Y	N	N	?	?
6 Britt	Y	Y	N	N	N	N
7 Rose	?	?	?	N	N	Y
8 Hefner	Y	Y	N	N	N	Y
9 ***Martin***	Y	Y	N	N	N	Y
10 ***Broyhill***	Y	Y	N	N	N	Y
11 Clarke	Y	Y	N	N	N	N
NORTH DAKOTA						
AL Dorgan	Y	Y	N	N	N	N
OHIO						
1 Luken	Y	N	N	N	N	N
2 ***Gradison***	Y	N	N	N	Y	Y
3 Hall	Y	Y	Y	Y	N	N
4 ***Oxley***	Y	Y	N	N	Y	Y
5 ***Latta***	Y	?	N	Y	N	?
6 ***McEwen***	Y	Y	N	N	N	Y
7 ***DeWine***	Y	Y	N	N	Y	Y
8 ***Kindness***	N	Y	Y	Y	Y	Y
9 Kaptur	Y	N	Y	N	N	N
10 ***Miller***	Y	Y	N	N	Y	Y
11 Eckart	Y	Y	N	N	Y	N
12 ***Kasich***	Y	Y	N	N	Y	Y
13 Pease	Y	Y	N	N	Y	N
14 Seiberling	Y	N	N	N	Y	?
15 ***Wylie***	Y	Y	N	N	N	Y
16 ***Regula***	Y	Y	N	N	Y	Y
17 ***Williams***	Y	?	N	N	N	?
18 Applegate	Y	Y	N	N	Y	Y
19 Feighan	Y	N	N	N	N	N
20 Oakar	Y	N	Y	Y	Y	N
21 Stokes	Y	N	Y	Y	N	N
OKLAHOMA						
1 Jones	Y	Y	N	N	N	Y
2 Synar	Y	N	N	N	N	N
3 Watkins	Y	Y	N	N	N	Y
4 McCurdy	Y	Y	N	N	N	Y
5 ***Edwards***	Y	Y	Y	Y	N	Y
6 English	Y	Y	N	N	N	Y
OREGON						
1 AuCoin	Y	N	Y	Y	N	N
2 ***Smith, R.***	Y	Y	Y	N	N	Y
3 Wyden	Y	N	Y	Y	N	N
4 Weaver	?	?	Y	Y	N	N
5 ***Smith, D.***	Y	Y	N	N	N	Y
PENNSYLVANIA						
1 Foglietta	Y	N	Y	Y	N	N
2 Gray	Y	N	?	Y	N	N
3 Borski	Y	N	Y	N	Y	N
4 Kolter	Y	Y	Y	N	N	N
5 ***Schulze***	Y	Y	?	N	Y	Y
6 Yatron	Y	Y	N	N	Y	Y
7 Edgar	Y	N	Y	Y	N	N
8 Kostmayer	Y	N	N	N	N	N
9 ***Shuster***	Y	Y	N	N	Y	Y
10 ***McDade***	Y	?	N	N	N	Y
11 Harrison	Y	N	N	N	Y	N
12 Murtha	Y	Y	N	N	Y	N
13 ***Coughlin***	Y	N	N	N	Y	Y
14 Coyne	Y	N	N	N	N	N
15 ***Ritter***	Y	Y	N	N	N	Y
16 ***Walker***	Y	Y	N	N	N	Y
17 ***Gekas***	Y	Y	N	?	N	Y
18 Walgren	Y	N	N	N	Y	N
19 ***Goodling***	Y	Y	N	N	N	Y
20 Gaydos	Y	Y	N	N	N	Y
21 ***Ridge***	Y	N	N	N	N	Y
22 Murphy	Y	Y	Y	N	N	N
23 ***Clinger***	Y	N	N	N	Y	N
RHODE ISLAND						
1 St Germain	Y	Y	N	N	Y	N
2 ***Schneider***	Y	N	N	N	N	N
SOUTH CAROLINA						
1 ***Hartnett***	Y	Y	N	N	N	Y
2 ***Spence***	Y	Y	N	N	N	Y
3 Derrick	Y	N	N	N	N	Y
4 ***Campbell***	Y	Y	?	?	N	Y
5 Spratt	Y	Y	N	N	N	N
6 Tallon	?	?	?	N	N	Y
SOUTH DAKOTA						
AL Daschle	Y	Y	N	N	N	N
TENNESSEE						
1 ***Quillen***	?	?	Y	Y	Y	Y
2 ***Duncan***	Y	Y	N	N	Y	Y
3 Lloyd	Y	Y	Y	N	N	Y
4 Cooper	Y	N	N	N	Y	Y
5 Boner	Y	Y	N	N	N	Y
6 Gore	Y	N	N	N	N	Y
7 ***Sundquist***	Y	Y	N	N	Y	Y
8 Jones	Y	Y	N	N	N	Y
9 Ford	Y	N	Y	Y	N	N
TEXAS						
1 Hall, S.	Y	Y	Y	N	N	Y
2 Wilson	Y	N	N	N	Y	Y
3 ***Bartlett***	Y	Y	Y	N	N	Y
4 Hall, R.	Y	Y	Y	N	N	Y
5 Bryant	Y	Y	Y	N	N	N
6 ***Gramm***	Y	Y	Y	Y	N	Y
7 ***Archer***	Y	Y	N	N	Y	Y
8 ***Fields***	Y	Y	Y	Y	Y	Y
9 Brooks	Y	Y	Y	N	N	N
10 Pickle	Y	Y	N	N	N	Y
11 Leath	Y	Y	N	Y	N	Y
12 Wright	Y	Y	Y	N	N	N
13 Hightower	Y	Y	Y	Y	N	Y
14 Patman	Y	Y	Y	Y	N	Y
15 de la Garza	Y	?	Y	Y	N	N
16 Coleman	Y	Y	Y	Y	N	N
17 Stenholm	Y	Y	Y	Y	N	Y
18 Leland	Y	N	Y	Y	N	?
19 Hance	Y	N	Y	Y	N	Y
20 Gonzalez	Y	N	Y	Y	N	N
21 ***Loeffler***	Y	Y	Y	Y	N	Y
22 ***Paul***	N	?	Y	N	N	?
23 Kazen	Y	Y	Y	Y	N	N
24 Frost	Y	Y	Y	N	N	N
25 Andrews	Y	Y	?	N	N	N
26 Vandergriff	Y	Y	Y	Y	N	N
27 Ortiz	Y	N	Y	Y	N	N
UTAH						
1 ***Hansen***	Y	Y	N	N	N	Y
2 ***Marriott***	Y	Y	N	N	N	Y
3 ***Nielson***	Y	Y	Y	N	N	Y
VERMONT						
AL ***Jeffords***	Y	N	N	N	Y	N
VIRGINIA						
1 ***Bateman***	Y	Y	N	N	N	Y
2 ***Whitehurst***	Y	Y	N	N	N	Y
3 ***Bliley***	Y	Y	N	N	N	Y
4 Sisisky	Y	Y	?	?	?	?
5 Daniel	Y	Y	N	N	N	Y
6 Olin	Y	Y	N	N	Y	Y
7 ***Robinson***	Y	Y	N	N	N	Y
8 ***Parris***	Y	Y	N	N	Y	Y
9 Boucher	Y	Y	N	N	Y	N
10 ***Wolf***	Y	Y	N	N	Y	Y
WASHINGTON						
1 ***Pritchard***	Y	N	?	N	Y	Y
2 Swift	Y	Y	N	N	N	N
3 Bonker	Y	?	N	N	N	N
4 ***Morrison***	Y	Y	Y	Y	N	N
5 Foley	Y	?	?	Y	N	N
6 Dicks	Y	Y	N	N	N	N
7 Lowry	Y	N	Y	Y	N	N
8 ***Chandler***	Y	?	N	N	Y	Y
WEST VIRGINIA						
1 Mollohan	Y	Y	Y	Y	Y	N
2 Staggers	Y	N	N	N	Y	N
3 Wise	Y	Y	N	N	Y	N
4 Rahall	Y	Y	N	N	Y	N
WISCONSIN						
1 Aspin	Y	?	N	N	Y	?
2 Kastenmeier	Y	N	N	N	N	N
3 ***Gunderson***	Y	Y	N	N	Y	Y
4 Kleczka	Y	N	N	N	N	N
5 Moody	Y	Y	Y	Y	Y	N
6 ***Petri***	Y	Y	Y	N	N	Y
7 Obey	Y	N	N	N	Y	N
8 ***Roth***	Y	Y	N	N	Y	Y
9 ***Sensenbrenner***	?	?	?	?	?	?
WYOMING						
AL ***Cheney***	Y	?	N	N	N	Y

Southern states - Ala., Ark., Fla., Ga., Ky., La., Miss., N.C., Okla., S.C., Tenn., Texas, Va.

213. HR 1510. Immigration Reform and Control Act. Moorhead, R-Calif., amendment to set a yearly cap of 450,000 on legal immigration into the United States. The cap would not include refugees, defined as those persons fleeing their homeland because of persecution. Rejected 168-231: R 111-46; D 57-185 (ND 17-140, SD 40-45), June 13, 1984. A "nay" was a vote supporting the president's position.

214. HR 1510. Immigration Reform and Control Act. Roybal, D-Calif., amendment to clarify the meaning of "continuous physical presence" in the United States when the issue arises in connection with deportation proceedings. The purpose was to ensure that no alien would be deported because of a brief, emergency absence from the country. Adopted 411-4: R 157-3; D 254-1 (ND 165-1, SD 89-0), June 14, 1984.

215. HR 1510. Immigration Reform and Control Act. Education and Labor Committee amendment (offered by Miller, D-Calif.) to restore most provisions of current law regarding regulation of an existing temporary foreign worker program that would be expanded under the bill, to provide a three-year transition period to that expanded program, and to create a commission to study the subject of a temporary foreign worker program. Rejected 164-256: R 7-153; D 157-103 (ND 135-36, SD 22-67), June 14, 1984.

216. HR 1510. Immigration Reform and Control Act. Agriculture Committee amendment (offered by Panetta, D-Calif.) to create a new, flexible temporary foreign worker program for the agriculture industry permitting growers to apply to the attorney general for workers within 72 hours of need and allowing workers to move from employer to employer within a defined "agricultural region," remaining in the United States for up to 11 months. Adopted 228-172: R 138-15; D 90-157 (ND 36-124, SD 54-33), June 14, 1984.

KEY

Y Voted for (yea).
Paired for.
+ Announced for.
N Voted against (nay).
X Paired against.
- Announced against.
P Voted "present".
C Voted "present" to avoid possible conflict of interest.
? Did not vote or otherwise make a position known.

Democrats *Republicans*

	213	214	215	216
ALABAMA				
1 *Edwards*	N	Y	N	Y
2 *Dickinson*	?	?	N	Y
3 Nichols	N	Y	N	Y
4 Bevill	N	Y	N	N
5 Flippo	Y	Y	N	Y
6 Erdreich	Y	Y	N	N
7 Shelby	Y	Y	N	N
ALASKA				
AL *Young*	Y	Y	N	N
ARIZONA				
1 *McCain*	N	Y	N	Y
2 Udall	?	Y	Y	N
3 *Stump*	Y	Y	N	Y
4 *Rudd*	Y	Y	N	Y
5 McNulty	N	Y	N	N
ARKANSAS				
1 Alexander	N	Y	N	Y
2 *Bethune*	Y	Y	N	Y
3 *Hammerschmidt*	Y	Y	N	Y
4 Anthony	N	Y	N	Y
CALIFORNIA				
1 Bosco	N	Y	N	Y
2 *Chappie*	Y	Y	N	Y
3 Matsui	N	Y	Y	Y
4 Fazio	?	Y	N	Y
5 Burton	N	Y	Y	N
6 Boxer	N	Y	Y	N
7 Miller	N	Y	Y	N
8 Dellums	N	Y	Y	N
9 Stark	?	Y	Y	N
10 Edwards	N	Y	Y	N
11 Lantos	N	Y	Y	N
12 *Zschau*	Y	Y	N	Y
13 Mineta	N	Y	Y	N
14 *Shumway*	Y	Y	N	Y
15 Coelho	?	Y	Y	N
16 Panetta	N	Y	N	Y
17 *Pashayan*	Y	Y	N	Y
18 Lehman	N	Y	N	Y
19 *Lagomarsino*	Y	Y	N	Y
20 *Thomas*	Y	Y	N	Y
21 *Fiedler*	Y	Y	N	Y
22 *Moorhead*	Y	Y	N	Y
23 Beilenson	Y	Y	Y	N
24 Waxman	N	Y	Y	N
25 Roybal	N	Y	Y	N
26 Berman	N	Y	Y	N
27 Levine	N	Y	Y	N
28 Dixon	N	Y	Y	N
29 Hawkins	?	Y	Y	N
30 Martinez	N	Y	Y	N
31 Dymally	N	Y	Y	N
32 Anderson	Y	Y	Y	N
33 *Dreier*	Y	Y	N	Y
34 Torres	N	+	Y	N
35 *Lewis*	N	Y	N	Y
36 Brown	N	Y	Y	N
37 *McCandless*	Y	Y	N	Y
38 Patterson	Y	Y	Y	N
39 *Dannemeyer*	Y	Y	N	Y
40 *Badham*	Y	Y	N	Y
41 *Lowery*	Y	Y	N	Y
42 *Lungren*	Y	Y	N	Y
43 *Packard*	Y	Y	N	Y
44 Bates	?	?	?	?
45 *Hunter*	Y	Y	N	Y
COLORADO				
1 Schroeder	?	Y	Y	N
2 Wirth	N	Y	Y	N
3 Kogovsek	N	Y	Y	N
4 *Brown*	Y	Y	N	Y
5 *Kramer*	Y	Y	N	Y
6 *Schaefer*	Y	Y	N	Y
CONNECTICUT				
1 Kennelly	N	Y	Y	N
2 Gejdenson	N	Y	Y	N
3 Morrison	N	Y	Y	N
4 *McKinney*	N	Y	N	N
5 Ratchford	N	Y	Y	N
6 *Johnson*	N	?	N	N
DELAWARE				
AL Carper	N	Y	Y	N
FLORIDA				
1 Hutto	Y	Y	N	Y
2 Fuqua	?	?	N	Y
3 Bennett	Y	Y	N	N
4 Chappell	Y	Y	N	Y
5 *McCollum*	Y	Y	N	Y
6 MacKay	N	Y	N	Y
7 Gibbons	N	Y	N	Y
8 *Young*	?	Y	N	Y
9 *Bilirakis*	Y	Y	N	Y
10 Ireland	Y	Y	N	Y
11 Nelson	Y	Y	N	Y
12 *Lewis*	Y	Y	N	Y
13 *Mack*	Y	Y	N	Y
14 Mica	Y	Y	N	N
15 *Shaw*	Y	Y	N	Y
16 Smith	N	Y	N	N
17 Lehman	N	Y	N	N
18 Pepper	N	Y	N	N
19 Fascell	N	Y	N	N
GEORGIA				
1 Thomas	Y	Y	N	Y
2 Hatcher	N	Y	N	Y
3 Ray	Y	Y	N	N
4 Levitas	N	Y	N	Y
5 Fowler	?	Y	N	Y
6 *Gingrich*	Y	Y	N	Y
7 Darden	N	Y	N	Y
8 Rowland	N	Y	N	Y
9 Jenkins	Y	Y	N	Y
10 Barnard	N	Y	N	Y
HAWAII				
1 Heftel	N	?	N	Y
2 Akaka	N	Y	Y	N
IDAHO				
1 *Craig*	Y	Y	N	Y
2 *Hansen*	?	?	?	?
ILLINOIS				
1 Hayes	N	Y	Y	N
2 Savage	?	?	Y	N
3 Russo	N	Y	Y	N
4 *O'Brien*	N	Y	N	#
5 Lipinski	N	Y	N	N
6 *Hyde*	Y	Y	N	Y
7 Collins	N	Y	Y	N
8 Rostenkowski	N	Y	N	N
9 Yates	?	Y	Y	N
10 *Porter*	N	Y	N	Y
11 Annunzio	N	Y	N	N
12 *Crane, P.*	N	Y	N	Y
13 *Erlenborn*	Y	Y	N	Y
14 *Corcoran*	N	Y	N	Y
15 *Madigan*	Y	Y	N	Y
16 *Martin*	N	Y	N	Y
17 Evans	N	Y	Y	N
18 *Michel*	Y	Y	N	Y
19 *Crane, D.*	Y	Y	N	Y
20 Durbin	N	Y	N	N
21 Price	N	Y	Y	N
22 Simon	?	?	Y	?
INDIANA				
1 Hall	N	Y	Y	N
2 Sharp	N	Y	N	N
3 *Hiler*	N	Y	N	Y
4 *Coats*	N	Y	N	Y
5 *Hillis*	Y	Y	N	Y

ND - Northern Democrats   SD - Southern Democrats

	213 214 215 216		213 214 215 216		213 214 215 216		213 214 215 216
6 *Burton*	Y Y N Y	7 *Stangeland*	Y Y ? Y	**NORTH CAROLINA**		**TENNESSEE**	
7 *Myers*	Y Y N Y	8 Oberstar	? ? ? ?	1 Jones	N Y N Y	1 *Quillen*	Y Y N Y
8 McCloskey	N Y N Y	**MISSISSIPPI**		2 Valentine	Y Y N Y	2 *Duncan*	Y Y N Y
9 Hamilton	N Y N N	1 *Whitten*	N Y N Y	3 Whitley	N Y N Y	3 Lloyd	Y Y N N
10 Jacobs	N Y Y Y	2 *Franklin*	Y Y N Y	4 Andrews	? Y N Y	4 Cooper	N Y N N
IOWA		3 Montgomery	Y Y N Y	5 Neal	? Y N Y	5 Boner	N Y Y N
1 *Leach*	N Y N Y	4 Dowdy	Y Y N Y	6 Britt	N Y Y N	6 Gore	N Y N Y
2 *Tauke*	N Y N Y	5 *Lott*	? Y N Y	7 Rose	N Y N Y	7 *Sundquist*	Y Y N Y
3 Evans	N Y N Y	**MISSOURI**		8 Hefner	N Y N Y	8 Jones	N Y N Y
4 Smith	N Y N Y	1 Clay	? Y Y N	9 *Martin*	Y Y N Y	9 Ford	? Y Y N
5 Harkin	N Y N Y	2 Young	N Y Y N	10 *Broyhill*	Y Y N Y	**TEXAS**	
6 Bedell	N Y N Y	3 Gephardt	N Y Y N	11 Clarke	N Y N ?	1 Hall, S.	Y Y N Y
KANSAS		4 Skelton	N Y N N	**NORTH DAKOTA**		2 Wilson	Y Y N Y
1 *Roberts*	Y Y N Y	5 Wheat	N Y N Y	AL Dorgan	Y Y N Y	3 *Bartlett*	N Y N Y
2 Slattery	Y Y Y Y	6 *Coleman*	Y Y N Y	**OHIO**		4 Hall, R.	Y Y N Y
3 *Winn*	Y Y N Y	7 *Taylor*	Y N N Y	1 Luken	N Y Y Y	5 Bryant	Y Y Y N
4 Glickman	Y Y Y Y	8 *Emerson*	Y Y N Y	2 *Gradison*	N Y N Y	6 *Gramm*	Y Y N Y
5 *Whittaker*	Y Y N Y	9 Volkmer	N Y N Y	3 Hall	Y Y N Y	7 *Archer*	Y Y N Y
KENTUCKY		**MONTANA**		4 *Oxley*	Y Y N Y	8 *Fields*	Y Y N Y
1 Hubbard	Y Y Y ?	1 Williams	? Y Y N	5 *Latta*	Y N N Y	9 Brooks	Y Y N Y
2 Natcher	N Y N N	2 *Marlenee*	Y Y N ?	6 *McEwen*	Y Y N Y	10 Pickle	N Y N N
3 Mazzoli	N Y N N	**NEBRASKA**		7 *DeWine*	N Y N Y	11 Leath	Y Y N Y
4 *Snyder*	Y Y N Y	1 *Bereuter*	Y Y N Y	8 *Kindness*	Y Y N N	12 Wright	N Y N N
5 *Rogers*	Y Y N Y	2 *Daub*	Y Y Y Y	9 Kaptur	N Y Y N	13 Hightower	Y Y N Y
6 *Hopkins*	Y Y N Y	3 *Smith*	Y Y N Y	10 *Miller*	Y Y N Y	14 Patman	Y Y N Y
7 Perkins	N Y Y N	**NEVADA**		11 Eckart	N Y N Y	15 de la Garza	N Y N Y
LOUISIANA		1 Reid	N Y Y N	12 *Kasich*	Y Y N Y	16 Coleman	N Y Y N
1 *Livingston*	Y Y N Y	2 *Vucanovich*	Y Y N Y	13 Pease	N Y N N	17 Stenholm	Y Y N Y
2 Boggs	N Y Y N	**NEW HAMPSHIRE**		14 Seiberling	Y Y Y N	18 Leland	N Y Y N
3 Tauzin	Y Y N Y	1 D'Amours	N Y Y Y	15 *Wylie*	Y Y N Y	19 Hance	Y Y Y Y
4 Roemer	Y Y N Y	2 *Gregg*	N Y Y Y	16 *Regula*	Y Y N Y	20 Gonzalez	N Y N Y
5 Huckaby	Y Y N Y	**NEW JERSEY**		17 *Williams*	Y Y N N	21 *Loeffler*	Y Y N Y
6 *Moore*	Y Y N Y	1 Florio	N Y N N	18 Applegate	Y N Y N	22 *Paul*	? N N ?
7 Breaux	Y Y ? #	2 Hughes	N Y N N	19 Feighan	N Y N N	23 Kazen	N Y Y N
8 Long	N Y N Y	3 Howard	N Y N N	20 Oakar	N Y ? N	24 Frost	N Y Y N
MAINE		4 *Smith*	N Y N N	21 Stokes	N Y Y N	25 Andrews	Y Y N N
1 *McKernan*	Y Y N Y	5 *Roukema*	Y Y N Y	**OKLAHOMA**		26 Vandergriff	Y Y Y N
2 *Snowe*	Y Y N Y	6 Dwyer	N Y N N	1 Jones	N Y N N	27 Ortiz	N Y Y N
MARYLAND		7 *Rinaldo*	N Y N N	2 Synar	N Y N N	**UTAH**	
1 Dyson	Y Y Y Y	8 Roe	N Y N N	3 Watkins	Y Y N Y	1 *Hansen*	Y Y N #
2 Long	N Y Y N	9 Torricelli	N Y Y Y	4 McCurdy	Y Y N Y	2 *Marriott*	Y Y N ?
3 Mikulski	N Y Y N	10 Rodino	N Y Y N	5 *Edwards*	N Y N Y	3 *Nielson*	Y Y N Y
4 *Holt*	N Y N Y	11 Minish	N Y N N	6 English	Y Y N Y	**VERMONT**	
5 Hoyer	N Y N Y	12 *Courter*	Y Y ? ?	**OREGON**		AL *Jeffords*	N ? ? ?
6 Byron	Y Y N Y	13 Vacancy		1 AuCoin	N Y N N	**VIRGINIA**	
7 Mitchell	? Y Y N	14 Guarini	N Y N X	2 *Smith, R.*	Y Y N Y	1 *Bateman*	Y Y N Y
8 Barnes	N Y Y N	**NEW MEXICO**		3 Wyden	Y Y N N	2 *Whitehurst*	Y Y N Y
MASSACHUSETTS		1 *Lujan*	Y Y N #	4 Weaver	N Y N N	3 *Bliley*	N Y N Y
1 *Conte*	N Y Y N	2 *Skeen*	Y Y N Y	5 *Smith, D.*	Y Y N Y	4 Sisisky	N Y N Y
2 Boland	N Y Y ?	3 Richardson	N Y Y N	**PENNSYLVANIA**		5 Daniel	Y Y N Y
3 Early	? Y Y ?	**NEW YORK**		1 Foglietta	? Y Y N	6 Olin	Y Y N Y
4 Frank	N Y Y N	1 *Carney*	Y Y N Y	2 Gray	N Y Y X	7 *Robinson*	Y Y N Y
5 Shannon	? Y Y ?	2 Downey	N Y Y X	3 Borski	N Y Y ?	8 *Parris*	Y Y ? Y
6 Mavroules	N Y Y ?	3 Mrazek	N Y Y N	4 Kolter	N Y Y N	9 Boucher	Y Y N Y
7 Markey	N Y Y N	4 *Lent*	N Y N Y	5 *Schulze*	N Y N Y	10 *Wolf*	N Y N ?
8 O'Neill		5 *McGrath*	N Y N Y	6 Yatron	Y Y Y Y	**WASHINGTON**	
9 Moakley	N Y Y N	6 Addabbo	N Y Y N	7 Edgar	N Y N N	1 *Pritchard*	N Y N Y
10 Studds	N Y Y X	7 Ackerman	N Y Y N	8 Kostmayer	N Y Y N	2 Swift	N Y Y N
11 Donnelly	N Y Y N	8 Scheuer	Y ? Y ?	9 *Shuster*	Y Y N Y	3 Bonker	N Y N N
MICHIGAN		9 Ferraro	? ? ? ?	10 McDade	N ? Y N	4 *Morrison*	N Y N Y
1 Conyers	N Y Y N	10 Schumer	N Y Y N	11 Harrison	N ? ? N	5 Foley	N Y N Y
2 *Pursell*	Y Y N Y	11 Towns	N Y Y N	12 Murtha	N Y Y Y	6 Dicks	N Y N Y
3 Wolpe	N Y N Y	12 Owens	N Y Y N	13 *Coughlin*	Y Y N Y	7 Lowry	N Y Y Y
4 *Siljander*	Y Y N Y	13 Solarz	N Y Y N	14 Coyne	N ? Y N	8 *Chandler*	Y Y N Y
5 *Sawyer*	Y Y N Y	14 *Molinari*	N Y N Y	15 *Ritter*	Y Y N Y	**WEST VIRGINIA**	
6 Carr	N Y N N	15 *Green*	N Y N N	16 *Walker*	Y Y N Y	1 Mollohan	N Y Y N
7 Kildee	N Y Y N	16 Rangel	N Y Y N	17 *Gekas*	Y Y N Y	2 Staggers	N Y N Y
8 Traxler	N Y N Y	17 Weiss	N Y Y N	18 Walgren	N Y N Y	3 Wise	N Y N Y
9 *Vander Jagt*	Y Y N Y	18 Garcia	N Y Y ?	19 *Goodling*	Y Y N Y	4 Rahall	N Y Y Y
10 Albosta	N Y N Y	19 Biaggi	N ? ? N	20 Gaydos	N Y Y Y	**WISCONSIN**	
11 *Davis*	Y Y N Y	20 Ottinger	N Y N Y	21 *Ridge*	N Y N N	1 Aspin	? Y N N
12 Bonior	? Y Y N	21 *Fish*	? Y N Y	22 Murphy	Y Y Y Y	2 Kastenmeier	N Y Y N
13 Crockett	N Y Y ?	22 *Gilman*	N Y N Y	23 *Clinger*	N Y N N	3 *Gunderson*	N Y N Y
14 Hertel	N Y Y N	23 Stratton	Y Y N N	**RHODE ISLAND**		4 Kleczka	N Y N N
15 Ford	N Y Y N	24 *Solomon*	Y Y N Y	1 St Germain	N Y N Y	5 Moody	N Y N N
16 Dingell	N Y N ?	25 *Boehlert*	N Y N N	2 *Schneider*	N Y Y N	6 *Petri*	Y Y N Y
17 Levin	N Y Y N	26 *Martin*	? Y N Y	**SOUTH CAROLINA**		7 Obey	N Y Y N
18 *Broomfield*	Y Y N Y	27 *Wortley*	N Y N Y	1 *Hartnett*	Y Y N ?	8 Roth	Y Y N N
MINNESOTA		28 McHugh	N Y N Y	2 *Spence*	Y Y N Y	9 *Sensenbrenner*	? ? ? ?
1 Penny	N Y N N	29 *Horton*	N Y N Y	3 Derrick	N Y N Y	**WYOMING**	
2 *Weber*	Y Y N Y	30 *Conable*	N Y N Y	4 *Campbell*	Y Y N Y	AL *Cheney*	? Y N Y
3 *Frenzel*	N Y N ?	31 *Kemp*	N Y N Y	5 Spratt	N Y N Y		
4 Vento	N Y N Y	32 LaFalce	N Y Y N	6 Tallon	Y Y N Y		
5 Sabo	N Y Y N	33 Nowak	N Y Y N	**SOUTH DAKOTA**			
6 Sikorski	N Y Y N	34 Lundine	N Y Y N	AL Daschle	Y Y N Y		

Southern states - Ala., Ark., Fla., Ga., Ky., La., Miss., N.C., Okla., S.C., Tenn., Texas, Va.

217. Procedural Motion. Hartnett, R-S.C., motion to approve the House *Journal* of Thursday, June 14. Motion agreed to 254-24: R 98-9; D 156-15 (ND 96-14, SD 60-1), June 15, 1984.

218. HR 3678. Water Resources Development Authorization. Adoption of the rule (H Res 515) providing for House floor consideration of the bill to authorize appropriations for water resource development and conservation. Adopted 286-7: R 105-7; D 181-0 (ND 119-0, SD 62-0), June 15, 1984.

219. H Con Res 294. Non-delivery of International Mail in the Soviet Union. Clay, D-Mo., motion to suspend the rules and adopt the concurrent resolution stating disapproval of the Soviet Union's systematic non-delivery of mail originating in the United States and calling on the U.S. Postal Service to raise the issue at the Congress of the Universal Postal Union. Motion agreed to 403-0: R 155-0; D 248-0 (ND 163-0, SD 85-0), June 19, 1984. A two-thirds majority of those present and voting (269 in this case) is required for adoption under suspension of the rules.

220. HR 1510. Immigration Reform and Control Act. Lungren, R-Calif., amendment to authorize the attorney general to grant temporary resident status to aliens who could show they arrived in the United States prior to Jan. 1, 1980, and permanent resident status to aliens who could show they had arrived in the United States prior to Jan. 1, 1977. Rejected 181-245: R 133-29; D 48-216 (ND 12-163, SD 36-53), June 19, 1984. A "yea" was a vote supporting the president's position.

221. HR 1510. Immigration Reform and Control Act. Shaw, R-Fla., amendment to authorize the attorney general to grant permanent resident status to aliens who could show they had arrived in the United States before Jan. 1, 1980. Rejected 177-246: R 131-30; D 46-216 (ND 17-157, SD 29-59), June 19, 1984.

222. HR 1510. Immigration Reform and Control Act. Wright, D-Texas, amendment to authorize the attorney general to grant temporary resident status to aliens who could show they had arrived in the United States prior to Jan. 1, 1982. Such aliens could seek permanent resident status after two years, providing they could demonstrate an understanding of English and of U.S. history and government, or were enrolled in a course of study to learn these subjects. Adopted 247-170: R 119-39; D 128-131 (ND 67-102, SD 61-29), June 19, 1984.

223. HR 1510. Immigration Reform and Control Act. Lungren, R-Calif., motion to limit debate on an amendment to strike provisions from the bill providing legal status for illegal aliens already in the United States. Motion agreed to 245-169: R 75-84; D 170-85 (ND 110-57, SD 60-28), June 20, 1984.

224. HR 1510. Immigration Reform and Control Act. McCollum, R-Fla., amendment to strike provisions from the bill providing legal status for illegal aliens already in the country. Rejected 195-233: R 114-50; D 81-183 (ND 26-148, SD 55-35), June 20, 1984. A "nay" was a vote supporting the president's position.

KEY

Y	Voted for (yea).
#	Paired for.
+	Announced for.
N	Voted against (nay).
X	Paired against.
-	Announced against.
P	Voted "present".
C	Voted "present" to avoid possible conflict of interest.
?	Did not vote or otherwise make a position known.

Democrats *Republicans*

	217	218	219	220	221	222	223	224
ALABAMA								
1 *Edwards*	Y	Y	Y	Y	Y	?	Y	N
2 *Dickinson*	N	Y	Y	Y	Y	Y	Y	Y
3 Nichols	Y	Y	Y	N	N	N	N	Y
4 Bevill	?	?	Y	N	N	Y	N	Y
5 Flippo	?	?	Y	N	Y	?	Y	Y
6 Erdreich	Y	Y	Y	N	Y	Y	Y	Y
7 Shelby	Y	Y	Y	Y	Y	Y	N	Y
ALASKA								
AL *Young*	N	Y	Y	Y	Y	Y	N	Y
ARIZONA								
1 *McCain*	?	?	Y	N	N	N	N	N
2 Udall	?	Y	Y	N	N	Y	N	N
3 *Stump*	Y	Y	Y	N	N	?	N	Y
4 *Rudd*	Y	Y	Y	Y	Y	Y	Y	Y
5 McNulty	?	?	Y	N	N	N	N	N
ARKANSAS								
1 Alexander	?	?	Y	N	N	Y	Y	N
2 *Bethune*	?	?	N	N	N	N	Y	Y
3 *Hammerschmidt*	Y	?	Y	N	N	N	N	Y
4 Anthony	?	?	Y	N	N	Y	Y	N
CALIFORNIA								
1 Bosco	?	?	Y	N	N	Y	Y	N
2 *Chappie*	N	Y	Y	Y	Y	Y	Y	Y
3 Matsui	?	?	Y	N	N	N	?	N
4 Fazio	Y	Y	Y	N	N	N	N	N
5 Burton	Y	Y	Y	N	N	N	N	N
6 *Boxer*	?	?	Y	N	N	N	N	N
7 Miller	Y	Y	Y	N	N	N	?	N
8 Dellums	?	?	Y	N	N	N	N	N
9 Stark	Y	Y	Y	N	N	N	N	N
10 Edwards	Y	Y	Y	N	N	N	N	N
11 Lantos	Y	Y	Y	N	N	N	Y	N
12 *Zschau*	Y	Y	Y	Y	Y	Y	Y	N
13 Mineta	?	Y	Y	N	N	N	N	N
14 *Shumway*	Y	N	Y	Y	Y	Y	N	Y
15 Coelho	?	?	Y	N	N	N	Y	N
16 Panetta	Y	?	Y	N	N	N	N	N
17 *Pashayan*	Y	Y	Y	Y	Y	Y	Y	N
18 Lehman	?	?	Y	N	Y	N	N	N
19 *Lagomarsino*	Y	Y	Y	Y	Y	Y	Y	N
20 *Thomas*	Y	Y	Y	Y	Y	Y	Y	N
21 *Fiedler*	?	Y	Y	N	N	N	Y	N
22 *Moorhead*	Y	Y	Y	Y	Y	Y	Y	Y
23 Beilenson	?	Y	Y	N	N	N	Y	N
24 Waxman	?	Y	Y	N	N	Y	N	N
25 Roybal	Y	Y	Y	N	N	N	N	N
26 Berman	Y	Y	Y	N	N	N	Y	N
27 Levine	?	Y	Y	N	N	N	N	N
28 Dixon	?	Y	Y	N	N	N	N	N
29 Hawkins	N	Y	Y	N	N	?	N	N
30 Martinez	Y	Y	Y	N	N	N	N	N
31 Dymally	P	Y	Y	?	X	X	?	N	N
32 Anderson	Y	Y	Y	N	Y	N	N	N
33 *Dreier*	Y	Y	Y	Y	Y	Y	Y	Y
34 Torres	?	Y	Y	N	N	N	N	N
35 *Lewis*	Y	Y	Y	Y	Y	Y	Y	N
36 Brown	Y	Y	Y	N	N	?	N	N
37 *McCandless*	Y	Y	Y	Y	Y	Y	Y	N
38 Patterson	Y	Y	Y	N	N	Y	Y	N
39 *Dannemeyer*	?	?	Y	Y	Y	Y	Y	Y
40 *Badham*	?	?	Y	Y	Y	Y	Y	N
41 *Lowery*	Y	Y	Y	Y	Y	Y	Y	N
42 *Lungren*	Y	Y	Y	Y	Y	Y	Y	N

	217	218	219	220	221	222	223	224
43 *Packard*	Y	Y	Y	Y	Y	Y	Y	Y
44 Bates	Y	Y	?	N	N	N	N	N
45 *Hunter*	?	Y	Y	Y	Y	N	N	Y
COLORADO								
1 Schroeder	?	?	Y	N	N	N	N	N
2 Wirth	Y	Y	Y	N	N	?	N	N
3 Kogovsek	Y	Y	Y	N	N	N	N	N
4 *Brown*	Y	N	Y	Y	Y	Y	N	Y
5 *Kramer*	Y	?	Y	Y	Y	Y	N	Y
6 *Schaefer*	Y	Y	Y	Y	Y	Y	N	Y
CONNECTICUT								
1 Kennelly	Y	Y	Y	N	?	?	?	N
2 Gejdenson	N	?	Y	N	N	N	N	N
3 Morrison	?	?	Y	N	N	N	N	N
4 *McKinney*	Y	Y	Y	N	N	Y	N	N
5 Ratchford	Y	Y	Y	N	N	Y	N	N
6 *Johnson*	Y	Y	Y	N	N	Y	N	N
DELAWARE								
AL Carper	Y	Y	Y	N	Y	Y	Y	N
FLORIDA								
1 Hutto	?	?	Y	Y	Y	Y	Y	Y
2 Fuqua	?	?	Y	N	N	Y	Y	Y
3 Bennett	Y	Y	Y	Y	Y	Y	Y	Y
4 Chappell	Y	Y	Y	N	N	Y	Y	Y
5 *McCollum*	Y	?	Y	Y	Y	Y	Y	Y
6 MacKay	?	?	Y	N	Y	Y	N	N
7 Gibbons	Y	Y	Y	N	Y	N	Y	N
8 *Young*	?	Y	Y	Y	Y	Y	?	Y
9 *Bilirakis*	Y	Y	Y	Y	Y	Y	Y	N
10 Ireland	Y	Y	Y	Y	?	Y	Y	N
11 Nelson	Y	Y	Y	Y	Y	Y	Y	N
12 *Lewis*	Y	Y	Y	Y	Y	Y	Y	N
13 *Mack*	?	Y	Y	Y	Y	Y	Y	Y
14 Mica	Y	Y	Y	Y	Y	Y	Y	Y
15 *Shaw*	Y	Y	Y	Y	Y	Y	Y	Y
16 Smith	Y	Y	Y	N	N	N	N	N
17 Lehman	Y	Y	Y	N	N	N	N	N
18 Pepper	Y	Y	Y	N	N	N	N	N
19 Fascell	Y	Y	Y	N	Y	N	Y	N
GEORGIA								
1 Thomas	Y	Y	Y	Y	Y	Y	Y	Y
2 Hatcher	?	?	Y	Y	Y	Y	Y	Y
3 Ray	Y	Y	Y	Y	Y	Y	Y	Y
4 Levitas	Y	?	Y	Y	Y	Y	N	Y
5 Fowler	?	Y	Y	Y	Y	Y	N	N
6 *Gingrich*	?	?	Y	Y	Y	Y	Y	N
7 Darden	Y	?	Y	Y	Y	Y	Y	N
8 Rowland	?	Y	Y	Y	Y	Y	Y	N
9 Jenkins	Y	Y	Y	Y	Y	Y	Y	N
10 Barnard	?	?	Y	Y	Y	Y	N	Y
HAWAII								
1 Heftel	?	Y	Y	N	N	Y	Y	N
2 Akaka	?	?	Y	N	N	N	N	N
IDAHO								
1 *Craig*	?	Y	Y	Y	Y	Y	N	Y
2 *Hansen*	?	?	?	?	?	?	?	?
ILLINOIS								
1 Hayes	Y	Y	Y	N	N	N	N	N
2 Savage	Y	Y	Y	N	N	N	N	N
3 Russo	?	?	Y	N	Y	Y	Y	Y
4 *O'Brien*	?	?	Y	Y	Y	?	N	Y
5 Lipinski	?	?	N	N	Y	N	N	N
6 *Hyde*	Y	Y	Y	Y	Y	Y	Y	Y
7 Collins	Y	Y	Y	N	N	N	Y	N
8 Rostenkowski	Y	Y	Y	N	N	N	Y	N
9 Yates	Y	Y	Y	N	N	N	N	N
10 *Porter*	?	Y	Y	Y	Y	Y	N	Y
11 Annunzio	Y	Y	Y	N	N	N	N	N
12 *Crane, P.*	Y	N	Y	Y	N	Y	N	Y
13 *Erlenborn*	Y	Y	?	Y	N	N	N	N
14 *Corcoran*	Y	Y	?	#	#	Y	Y	N
15 *Madigan*	?	Y	Y	Y	Y	?	Y	Y
16 *Martin*	Y	Y	Y	Y	N	N	N	N
17 Evans	Y	Y	Y	N	N	N	N	N
18 *Michel*	Y	Y	Y	Y	Y	Y	Y	N
19 *Crane, D.*	?	?	Y	Y	Y	Y	N	N
20 Durbin	N	Y	Y	Y	Y	Y	Y	N
21 Price	Y	Y	Y	N	N	N	N	N
22 Simon	?	?	Y	N	N	Y	Y	N
INDIANA								
1 Hall	Y	Y	?	?	N	N	N	N
2 Sharp	Y	?	Y	N	N	Y	N	N
3 *Hiler*	Y	?	Y	Y	Y	+	Y	Y
4 *Coats*	?	?	Y	Y	Y	Y	Y	N
5 Hillis	Y	Y	?	Y	Y	Y	Y	Y

ND - Northern Democrats   SD - Southern Democrats

Corresponding to Congressional Record Votes 242, 243, 244, 245, 246, 247, 248, 249

	217	218	219	220	221	222	223	224
6 ***Burton***	Y	Y	Y	Y	Y	Y	N	Y
7 ***Myers***	Y	Y	Y	Y	Y	Y	Y	Y
8 McCloskey	Y	Y	Y	N	N	N	Y	N
9 Hamilton	?	?	Y	N	N	N	Y	N
10 Jacobs	N	Y	Y	N	N	N	N	N
IOWA								
1 ***Leach***	Y	?	Y	Y	Y	Y	N	N
2 ***Tauke***	?	?	Y	Y	Y	Y	N	N
3 ***Evans***	?	?	Y	Y	Y	Y	N	Y
4 Smith	?	?	Y	N	Y	Y	Y	N
5 Harkin	N	Y	Y	N	N	N	Y	N
6 Bedell	Y	Y	Y	N	N	Y	Y	N
KANSAS								
1 ***Roberts***	?	?	Y	Y	Y	Y	Y	Y
2 Slattery	?	Y	Y	N	N	Y	Y	N
3 ***Winn***	?	?	Y	Y	Y	Y	Y	N
4 Glickman	Y	Y	Y	N	N	Y	Y	N
5 ***Whittaker***	?	?	Y	Y	Y	Y	Y	Y
KENTUCKY								
1 Hubbard	?	?	Y	N	N	Y	N	Y
2 Natcher	Y	Y	Y	N	N	N	Y	N
3 Mazzoli	Y	Y	Y	N	N	N	Y	N
4 ***Snyder***	Y	Y	Y	Y	Y	Y	Y	Y
5 ***Rogers***	Y	Y	Y	Y	Y	Y	Y	Y
6 ***Hopkins***	Y	Y	Y	Y	N	N	N	Y
7 Perkins	Y	Y	Y	N	N	Y	Y	N
LOUISIANA								
1 ***Livingston***	?	Y	?	Y	Y	Y	Y	Y
2 Boggs	?	Y	?	N	N	Y	N	N
3 Tauzin	?	Y	Y	N	N	Y	N	Y
4 Roemer	N	Y	?	N	N	Y	N	Y
5 Huckaby	Y	Y	Y	N	N	N	N	Y
6 ***Moore***	Y	Y	Y	Y	Y	Y	N	Y
7 Breaux	?	?	Y	Y	N	Y	Y	Y
8 Long	Y	Y	Y	N	N	Y	Y	N
MAINE								
1 ***McKernan***	Y	Y	Y	Y	Y	Y	N	N
2 ***Snowe***	Y	?	Y	Y	Y	Y	N	Y
MARYLAND								
1 Dyson	?	Y	Y	N	N	Y	Y	Y
2 Long	?	Y	Y	N	N	Y	Y	N
3 Mikulski	Y	Y	Y	N	N	N	?	?
4 ***Holt***	Y	?	Y	Y	Y	Y	Y	Y
5 Hoyer	Y	?	Y	N	N	N	Y	N
6 Byron	?	?	Y	Y	Y	Y	Y	Y
7 Mitchell	N	Y	Y	N	N	N	Y	N
8 Barnes	Y	Y	Y	N	N	N	Y	N
MASSACHUSETTS								
1 ***Conte***	?	?	Y	N	N	N	Y	N
2 Boland	?	?	Y	N	N	Y	Y	N
3 Early	?	?	Y	N	N	Y	N	N
4 Frank	Y	Y	Y	N	N	N	Y	N
5 Shannon	?	?	Y	N	N	N	?	?
6 Mavroules	?	?	?	N	N	N	Y	N
7 Markey	Y	Y	+	N	N	N	Y	N
8 O'Neill								
9 Moakley	Y	?	Y	N	N	Y	Y	N
10 Studds	?	?	Y	N	N	N	Y	N
11 Donnelly	Y	?	?	N	Y	Y	Y	N
MICHIGAN								
1 Conyers	?	Y	?	N	N	N	N	N
2 ***Pursell***	?	?	Y	Y	Y	N	Y	Y
3 Wolpe	Y	Y	Y	N	N	N	Y	N
4 ***Siljander***	?	?	Y	N	N	Y	N	Y
5 ***Sawyer***	Y	Y	Y	N	N	Y	N	N
6 Carr	Y	Y	Y	N	N	Y	N	Y
7 Kildee	Y	Y	Y	N	N	N	N	N
8 Traxler	Y	?	Y	N	N	N	Y	N
9 ***Vander Jagt***	Y	Y	?	?	Y	Y	N	Y
10 Albosta	?	?	Y	N	N	Y	Y	Y
11 ***Davis***	?	Y	Y	Y	?	Y	Y	N
12 Bonior	Y	Y	Y	N	N	N	Y	N
13 Crockett	Y	?	Y	N	N	N	Y	N
14 Hertel	?	?	Y	N	N	Y	N	Y
15 Ford	?	?	Y	N	N	N	?	N
16 Dingell	?	Y	Y	N	N	Y	?	N
17 Levin	Y	Y	Y	N	N	N	N	N
18 ***Broomfield***	Y	?	Y	N	N	N	N	Y
MINNESOTA								
1 Penny	N	Y	Y	N	N	Y	Y	N
2 ***Weber***	?	?	Y	Y	Y	Y	Y	N
3 ***Frenzel***	N	N	Y	Y	Y	Y	N	Y
4 Vento	N	?	Y	N	N	N	N	N
5 Sabo	N	?	Y	N	N	N	Y	N
6 Sikorski	N	Y	Y	N	N	Y	Y	N

	217	218	219	220	221	222	223	224
7 ***Stangeland***	Y	Y	Y	Y	Y	N	Y	Y
8 Oberstar	?	?	Y	N	N	N	N	N
MISSISSIPPI								
1 Whitten	Y	Y	Y	N	N	N	Y	Y
2 ***Franklin***	?	?	Y	Y	Y	Y	N	Y
3 Montgomery	Y	Y	Y	N	N	N	Y	Y
4 Dowdy	?	?	?	N	N	N	Y	Y
5 ***Lott***	?	Y	Y	Y	Y	Y	Y	Y
MISSOURI								
1 Clay	N	?	Y	N	N	N	N	N
2 Young	Y	?	Y	N	N	N	Y	N
3 Gephardt	?	?	Y	N	N	N	Y	N
4 Skelton	?	?	Y	Y	N	Y	Y	Y
5 Wheat	Y	Y	Y	N	N	N	N	N
6 ***Coleman***	?	Y	Y	Y	Y	N	N	Y
7 ***Taylor***	Y	?	Y	Y	Y	Y	Y	Y
8 ***Emerson***	N	Y	Y	Y	Y	Y	N	Y
9 Volkmer	Y	Y	Y	Y	N	Y	N	Y
MONTANA								
1 Williams	?	Y	?	N	N	?	?	?
2 ***Marlenee***	?	?	Y	Y	Y	Y	N	Y
NEBRASKA								
1 ***Bereuter***	Y	Y	Y	Y	Y	Y	Y	Y
2 ***Daub***	Y	Y	Y	Y	Y	Y	N	Y
3 ***Smith***	Y	Y	Y	Y	Y	Y	Y	Y
NEVADA								
1 Reid	Y	Y	Y	Y	Y	Y	Y	Y
2 ***Vucanovich***	?	Y	Y	N	N	N	N	Y
NEW HAMPSHIRE								
1 D'Amours	Y	Y	?	Y	Y	Y	Y	Y
2 ***Gregg***	Y	Y	Y	Y	Y	Y	Y	Y
NEW JERSEY								
1 Florio	Y	?	Y	N	N	Y	Y	N
2 Hughes	Y	Y	Y	Y	Y	Y	Y	N
3 Howard	Y	Y	Y	N	N	?	Y	N
4 ***Smith***	?	Y	Y	N	N	N	Y	N
5 ***Roukema***	Y	Y	Y	Y	Y	N	?	Y
6 Dwyer	Y	?	Y	N	N	Y	Y	N
7 ***Rinaldo***	Y	Y	Y	N	N	N	N	Y
8 Roe	Y	Y	Y	N	N	Y	Y	N
9 Torricelli	?	?	Y	Y	Y	Y	Y	Y
10 Rodino	P	Y	Y	N	N	N	Y	N
11 Minish	Y	Y	Y	N	N	Y	Y	N
12 ***Courter***	Y	Y	Y	Y	Y	Y	N	Y
13 Vacancy								
14 Guarini	Y	Y	?	N	N	N	Y	N
NEW MEXICO								
1 ***Lujan***	Y	Y	Y	Y	Y	Y	N	Y
2 ***Skeen***	Y	Y	Y	N	N	N	N	Y
3 Richardson	N	Y	Y	N	N	Y	N	N
NEW YORK								
1 ***Carney***	?	?	Y	Y	Y	Y	N	Y
2 Downey	Y	Y	Y	N	N	N	Y	N
3 Mrazek	Y	Y	Y	N	N	N	Y	N
4 ***Lent***	Y	Y	Y	Y	Y	N	Y	Y
5 ***McGrath***	Y	?	Y	Y	Y	N	N	Y
6 Addabbo	?	?	Y	N	N	N	N	N
7 Ackerman	Y	+	Y	N	N	N	N	N
8 Scheuer	?	?	Y	N	N	Y	Y	N
9 Ferraro	?	?	Y	N	N	N	Y	N
10 Schumer	?	?	Y	N	?	?	Y	N
11 Towns	?	?	?	N	N	N	?	N
12 Owens	Y	Y	Y	N	N	N	N	N
13 Solarz	Y	Y	Y	N	N	N	Y	N
14 ***Molinari***	Y	Y	Y	N	N	Y	N	N
15 ***Green***	Y	Y	Y	N	N	N	Y	N
16 Rangel	?	Y	Y	N	N	N	N	N
17 Weiss	Y	Y	Y	N	N	N	N	N
18 Garcia	?	Y	Y	N	N	N	Y	N
19 Biaggi	Y	Y	?	N	N	Y	Y	N
20 Ottinger	?	Y	Y	N	N	N	N	N
21 ***Fish***	Y	Y	Y	Y	Y	N	Y	N
22 ***Gilman***	Y	Y	Y	N	N	N	N	N
23 Stratton	?	Y	Y	N	N	N	Y	Y
24 ***Solomon***	N	N	Y	Y	Y	N	N	Y
25 ***Boehlert***	Y	Y	Y	Y	Y	Y	?	N
26 ***Martin***	Y	Y	Y	Y	Y	N	N	Y
27 ***Wortley***	Y	Y	Y	Y	Y	Y	N	Y
28 McHugh	Y	Y	Y	N	N	N	Y	N
29 ***Horton***	?	?	Y	Y	Y	Y	Y	Y
30 ***Conable***	Y	N	Y	Y	Y	Y	Y	N
31 ***Kemp***	?	?	Y	N	N	Y	N	N
32 LaFalce	Y	Y	Y	N	N	Y	Y	N
33 Nowak	Y	Y	Y	N	N	N	Y	N
34 Lundine	?	?	Y	N	N	Y	Y	N

	217	218	219	220	221	222	223	224
NORTH CAROLINA								
1 Jones	Y	?	Y	N	N	N	Y	Y
2 Valentine	Y	Y	Y	N	N	N	Y	Y
3 Whitley	?	?	Y	Y	Y	Y	Y	Y
4 Andrews	Y	Y	Y	Y	Y	Y	Y	Y
5 Neal	?	Y	Y	Y	Y	Y	?	Y
6 Britt	Y	Y	Y	N	N	Y	Y	N
7 Rose	Y	Y	Y	N	N	Y	Y	Y
8 Hefner	?	?	Y	Y	N	Y	Y	Y
9 ***Martin***	?	?	Y	Y	Y	Y	Y	Y
10 ***Broyhill***	?	?	Y	Y	Y	Y	Y	Y
11 Clarke	?	?	Y	N	N	Y	Y	N
NORTH DAKOTA								
AL Dorgan	N	Y	Y	N	Y	Y	Y	N
OHIO								
1 Luken	Y	Y	Y	N	N	N	Y	Y
2 ***Gradison***	?	?	Y	Y	Y	Y	Y	Y
3 Hall	Y	Y	Y	N	N	N	Y	N
4 ***Oxley***	Y	Y	Y	Y	Y	Y	Y	N
5 ***Latta***	?	?	Y	Y	Y	Y	Y	Y
6 ***McEwen***	Y	Y	Y	Y	Y	Y	N	Y
7 ***DeWine***	Y	Y	Y	N	N	Y	N	N
8 ***Kindness***	Y	Y	Y	Y	Y	Y	N	Y
9 Kaptur	?	?	Y	N	N	Y	Y	Y
10 ***Miller***	N	Y	Y	Y	Y	Y	N	Y
11 Eckart	Y	Y	Y	N	N	Y	Y	N
12 ***Kasich***	Y	Y	Y	Y	Y	Y	N	Y
13 Pease	Y	Y	Y	N	N	Y	Y	N
14 Seiberling	Y	?	Y	N	N	N	Y	N
15 ***Wylie***	Y	Y	Y	Y	Y	Y	Y	Y
16 ***Regula***	Y	?	Y	Y	Y	Y	N	Y
17 ***Williams***	Y	?	Y	Y	Y	Y	Y	Y
18 Applegate	?	?	Y	N	N	Y	Y	Y
19 Feighan	Y	Y	Y	N	N	Y	N	N
20 Oakar	?	?	Y	N	N	N	N	N
21 Stokes	Y	Y	Y	N	N	N	N	N
OKLAHOMA								
1 Jones	Y	Y	Y	N	Y	Y	Y	N
2 Synar	Y	?	Y	N	N	Y	Y	N
3 Watkins	Y	Y	Y	N	Y	Y	Y	Y
4 McCurdy	?	Y	Y	?	N	N	Y	Y
5 ***Edwards***	Y	Y	Y	Y	N	N	N	Y
6 English	Y	Y	Y	N	N	N	N	Y
OREGON								
1 AuCoin	Y	Y	Y	Y	Y	?	Y	Y
2 ***Smith, R.***	Y	Y	Y	Y	Y	N	N	Y
3 Wyden	Y	Y	Y	N	N	N	Y	Y
4 Weaver	Y	Y	Y	N	N	Y	Y	N
5 ***Smith, D.***	?	?	Y	Y	Y	Y	N	Y
PENNSYLVANIA								
1 Foglietta	?	?	Y	N	N	N	Y	N
2 Gray	?	?	Y	N	N	N	N	N
3 Borski	Y	Y	Y	N	N	Y	Y	N
4 Kolter	Y	Y	Y	N	N	Y	Y	N
5 ***Schulze***	Y	Y	Y	Y	Y	?	Y	Y
6 Yatron	Y	Y	Y	Y	Y	Y	Y	Y
7 Edgar	Y	Y	Y	N	N	N	Y	N
8 Kostmayer	?	Y	Y	N	N	N	Y	N
9 ***Shuster***	Y	Y	Y	Y	Y	Y	Y	Y
10 ***McDade***	N	Y	Y	Y	N	Y	Y	Y
11 Harrison	?	?	Y	Y	Y	Y	?	N
12 Murtha	Y	Y	Y	N	N	Y	Y	N
13 ***Coughlin***	N	Y	?	Y	Y	Y	N	N
14 Coyne	Y	Y	Y	N	N	N	Y	N
15 ***Ritter***	?	?	Y	Y	Y	Y	N	Y
16 ***Walker***	?	Y	Y	Y	Y	Y	N	Y
17 ***Gekas***	Y	Y	Y	Y	Y	Y	N	Y
18 Walgren	?	?	Y	N	N	Y	N	N
19 ***Goodling***	?	?	Y	Y	Y	Y	?	Y
20 Gaydos	Y	Y	Y	N	N	N	Y	Y
21 ***Ridge***	Y	?	Y	Y	Y	Y	N	Y
22 Murphy	Y	Y	Y	Y	Y	Y	Y	Y
23 ***Clinger***	Y	Y	Y	Y	Y	N	Y	N
RHODE ISLAND								
1 St Germain	P	Y	?	N	N	N	Y	N
2 ***Schneider***	Y	Y	Y	N	N	N	N	N
SOUTH CAROLINA								
1 ***Hartnett***	Y	?	Y	Y	Y	Y	Y	Y
2 ***Spence***	Y	Y	Y	Y	Y	Y	N	Y
3 Derrick	?	?	Y	Y	Y	Y	Y	N
4 ***Campbell***	?	Y	Y	Y	Y	Y	N	Y
5 Spratt	Y	Y	Y	Y	Y	Y	Y	N
6 Tallon	Y	?	?	Y	Y	Y	Y	Y
SOUTH DAKOTA								
AL Daschle	Y	?	Y	N	Y	Y	Y	Y

	217	218	219	220	221	222	223	224
TENNESSEE								
1 ***Quillen***	?	Y	Y	Y	Y	N	Y	N
2 ***Duncan***	Y	Y	Y	N	Y	N	Y	Y
3 Lloyd	?	?	Y	N	N	Y	N	Y
4 Cooper	?	?	Y	N	?	N	Y	N
5 Boner	Y	?	Y	Y	N	Y	Y	Y
6 Gore	Y	Y	Y	Y	Y	Y	Y	N
7 ***Sundquist***	Y	Y	Y	Y	Y	N	Y	Y
8 Jones	Y	Y	?	Y	N	Y	Y	Y
9 Ford	Y	Y	Y	N	N	N	N	N
TEXAS								
1 Hall, S.	Y	Y	Y	N	N	Y	N	Y
2 Wilson	?	Y	Y	Y	Y	Y	Y	Y
3 ***Bartlett***	?	?	Y	Y	Y	Y	N	Y
4 Hall, R.	Y	Y	Y	N	N	N	N	N
5 Bryant	?	?	Y	Y	N	N	Y	Y
6 ***Gramm***	?	?	Y	N	N	N	N	Y
7 ***Archer***	Y	Y	Y	N	N	N	N	Y
8 ***Fields***	Y	Y	?	N	N	N	N	Y
9 Brooks	?	?	Y	N	N	Y	Y	Y
10 Pickle	Y	Y	Y	N	N	Y	Y	N
11 Leath	Y	Y	Y	N	N	Y	N	Y
12 Wright	Y	Y	Y	N	N	Y	Y	N
13 Hightower	Y	Y	Y	N	N	N	Y	Y
14 Patman	Y	Y	Y	N	N	N	N	Y
15 de la Garza	Y	Y	Y	N	N	N	N	N
16 Coleman	Y	Y	Y	Y	N	N	N	Y
17 Stenholm	Y	Y	Y	N	N	N	N	Y
18 Leland	?	?	Y	N	N	N	N	N
19 Hance	Y	Y	Y	N	N	N	N	Y
20 Gonzalez	Y	Y	Y	N	N	N	N	N
21 ***Loeffler***	Y	Y	Y	N	N	N	N	Y
22 ***Paul***	?	?	Y	N	N	N	N	Y
23 Kazen	Y	Y	Y	N	Y	Y	N	N
24 Frost	?	?	Y	Y	Y	Y	Y	N
25 Andrews	Y	Y	Y	N	N	N	Y	Y
26 Vandergriff	Y	Y	Y	N	N	N	N	N
27 Ortiz	Y	Y	Y	N	N	N	N	N
UTAH								
1 ***Hansen***	?	?	Y	Y	Y	Y	Y	Y
2 ***Marriott***	?	?	Y	Y	Y	Y	Y	N
3 ***Nielson***	Y	N	Y	Y	Y	Y	Y	N
VERMONT								
AL ***Jeffords***	?	?	Y	Y	Y	Y	Y	N
VIRGINIA								
1 ***Bateman***	Y	Y	Y	Y	Y	+	Y	Y
2 ***Whitehurst***	Y	?	Y	Y	Y	Y	Y	Y
3 ***Bliley***	Y	Y	Y	Y	Y	Y	Y	Y
4 Sisisky	Y	Y	Y	Y	Y	Y	Y	N
5 Daniel	Y	Y	Y	Y	Y	Y	Y	Y
6 Olin	Y	Y	Y	N	N	N	Y	Y
7 ***Robinson***	Y	Y	Y	Y	Y	Y	Y	Y
8 ***Parris***	Y	Y	Y	Y	Y	Y	Y	Y
9 Boucher	Y	Y	Y	N	N	Y	Y	N
10 ***Wolf***	Y	Y	Y	Y	Y	Y	N	Y
WASHINGTON								
1 ***Pritchard***	?	Y	Y	Y	Y	Y	Y	N
2 Swift	Y	Y	Y	N	N	Y	Y	N
3 Bonker	?	Y	Y	N	N	Y	N	N
4 ***Morrison***	?	Y	Y	N	N	Y	N	N
5 Foley	Y	Y	Y	N	N	Y	Y	N
6 Dicks	?	Y	Y	N	N	Y	Y	N
7 Lowry	N	Y	Y	N	N	N	N	N
8 ***Chandler***	?	Y	Y	N	?	Y	N	N
WEST VIRGINIA								
1 Mollohan	Y	Y	Y	N	N	N	Y	Y
2 Staggers	Y	Y	Y	N	N	Y	Y	Y
3 Wise	Y	Y	Y	N	N	N	Y	Y
4 Rahall	Y	Y	Y	N	N	N	Y	N
WISCONSIN								
1 Aspin	?	Y	Y	N	Y	Y	Y	N
2 Kastenmeier	Y	Y	Y	N	N	N	Y	N
3 ***Gunderson***	Y	Y	Y	Y	Y	Y	Y	N
4 Kleczka	Y	Y	Y	N	N	N	N	N
5 Moody	?	?	Y	N	N	Y	Y	N
6 ***Petri***	Y	Y	Y	Y	Y	Y	N	Y
7 Obey	Y	Y	Y	N	N	Y	Y	N
8 ***Roth***	?	?	?	Y	Y	Y	Y	Y
9 ***Sensenbrenner***	?	?	?	?	?	?	?	?
WYOMING								
AL ***Cheney***	?	?	Y	Y	Y	Y	Y	N

Southern states - Ala., Ark., Fla., Ga., Ky., La., Miss., N.C., Okla., S.C., Tenn., Texas, Va.

225. HR 1510. Immigration Reform and Control Act. McCollum, R-Fla., amendment to streamline procedures for handling asylum, deportation and exclusion cases by barring most "class action" lawsuits and by deleting a requirement that aliens seeking to enter the country be notified of certain procedural rights. Adopted 219-208: R 149-15; D 70-193 (ND 10-164, SD 60-29), June 20, 1984. A "yea" was a vote supporting the president's position. (This amendment previously had been adopted in the Committee of the Whole (*see vote 212, p. 66-H*).)

226. HR 1510. Immigration Reform and Control Act. Passage of the bill to revise immigration laws to impose sanctions on employers who knowingly hire illegal aliens, provide legal status for many illegal aliens already in the United States, expand an existing temporary foreign worker program, create a 'new guest-worker program and overhaul procedures for handling asylum, deportation and exclusion cases. Passed 216-211: R 91-73; D 125-138 (ND 76-98, SD 49-40), June 20, 1984. A "yea" was a vote supporting the president's position.

227. HR 5580. Organ Transplant Act. Dannemeyer, R-Calif., substitute to reduce the total authorization to $21 million over three years, dropping funding proposed for certain drugs used by transplant patients. Rejected 25-379: R 23-135; D 2-244 (ND 0-164, SD 2-80), June 21, 1984.

228. HR 5580. Organ Transplant Act. Passage of the bill to facilitate organ transplant surgery by authorizing $78 million over four years for grants to local organ procurement agencies, funding for certain drugs used by transplant patients and a national computerized system for linking organ donors and patients. Passed 396-6: R 149-6; D 247-0 (ND 165-0, SD 82-0), June 21, 1984. A "nay" was a vote supporting the president's position.

229. HR 5798. Treasury, Postal Service and General Government Appropriations, Fiscal 1985. Levitas, D-Ga., amendment to reduce fiscal 1985 spending for the Office of Administration in the Executive Office of the President by $1.5 million. Adopted 326-74: R 115-38; D 211-36 (ND 135-31, SD 76-5), June 21, 1984.

230. HR 5798. Treasury, Postal Service and General Government Appropriations, Fiscal 1985. Lungren, R-Calif., amendment to eliminate $20 million designated for the construction of a federal building in Long Beach, Calif. Rejected 166-226: R 133-19; D 33-207 (ND 14-146, SD 19-61), June 21, 1984.

231. H Res 531. Election of Speaker Pro Tempore. Adoption of the resolution to elect Rep. Jim Wright, D-Texas, Speaker pro tempore during the absence of the Speaker. Adopted 230-148: R 3-147; D 227-1 (ND 150-1, SD 77-0), June 21, 1984. (The resolution was necessary to allow Wright to name extra conferees on the defense authorization bill (HR 5167), in the absence of Speaker Thomas P. O'Neill Jr., D-Mass. The extra conferees were appointed to deal with the MX and anti-satellite missiles`

232. HR 5167. Department of Defense Authorization. Price, D-Ill., motion to allow the conference committee on the bill to hold closed meetings. Motion agreed to 337-28: R 123-26; D 214-2 (ND 143-2, SD 71-0), June 21, 1984.

KEY

- Y Voted for (yea).
- # Paired for.
- + Announced for.
- N Voted against (nay).
- X Paired against.
- - Announced against.
- P Voted "present".
- C Voted "present" to avoid possible conflict of interest.
- ? Did not vote or otherwise make a position known.

Democrats   *Republicans*

	225	226	227	228	229	230	231	232
ALABAMA								
1 *Edwards*	Y	Y	?	?	?	?	?	?
2 *Dickinson*	Y	N	N	Y	Y	N	Y	?
3 Nichols	Y	N	N	Y	Y	Y	Y	Y
4 Bevill	Y	N	N	Y	Y	Y	N	Y
5 Flippo	Y	N	N	Y	Y	N	Y	Y
6 Erdreich	Y	N	N	Y	Y	Y	Y	Y
7 Shelby	Y	N	N	Y	?	?	?	?
ALASKA								
AL *Young*	Y	N	N	Y	N	N	N	Y
ARIZONA								
1 *McCain*	Y	N	N	Y	N	Y	N	N
2 Udall	N	N	N	Y	N	Y	N	?
3 *Stump*	Y	N	Y	N	N	N	N	Y
4 *Rudd*	Y	N	Y	N	Y	N	Y	Y
5 McNulty	N	N	N	Y	Y	N	Y	Y
ARKANSAS								
1 Alexander	N	Y	N	Y	?	N	?	?
2 *Bethune*	Y	N	N	?	Y	Y	N	Y
3 *Hammerschmidt*	Y	Y	N	Y	Y	N	Y	Y
4 Anthony	Y	Y	N	Y	Y	N	Y	Y
CALIFORNIA								
1 Bosco	N	N	N	Y	?	N	Y	Y
2 *Chappie*	Y	N	N	Y	Y	Y	N	Y
3 Matsui	N	N	N	Y	Y	Y	Y	Y
4 Fazio	N	N	N	Y	N	N	Y	Y
5 Burton	N	N	N	Y	Y	N	Y	Y
6 Boxer	N	N	N	Y	Y	N	Y	Y
7 Miller	N	N	N	Y	Y	N	Y	Y
8 Dellums	N	N	N	Y	Y	N	Y	Y
9 Stark	N	Y	N	Y	?	N	Y	Y
10 Edwards	N	N	N	Y	Y	N	Y	Y
11 Lantos	N	N	N	Y	Y	N	Y	Y
12 *Zschau*	Y	N	Y	N	Y	N	Y	Y
13 Mineta	N	N	N	Y	Y	N	Y	Y
14 *Shumway*	Y	N	Y	?	Y	Y	N	Y
15 Coelho	N	N	N	Y	Y	N	Y	Y
16 Panetta	N	Y	N	Y	Y	N	Y	Y
17 *Pashayan*	Y	N	N	Y	Y	N	Y	Y
18 Lehman	N	N	N	Y	Y	N	Y	Y
19 *Lagomarsino*	Y	N	Y	Y	Y	N	Y	Y
20 *Thomas*	Y	Y	N	Y	Y	N	N	N
21 *Fiedler*	Y	N	?	Y	Y	Y	N	Y
22 *Moorhead*	Y	Y	Y	Y	Y	Y	N	Y
23 Beilenson	N	Y	N	Y	N	N	Y	Y
24 Waxman	N	N	N	Y	Y	N	?	?
25 Roybal	N	N	N	Y	Y	N	Y	Y
26 Berman	N	N	N	Y	N	N	Y	Y
27 Levine	N	N	N	Y	Y	N	Y	Y
28 Dixon	N	N	N	Y	Y	N	Y	Y
29 Hawkins	N	N	N	?	N	N	?	Y
30 Martinez	N	N	N	Y	Y	N	Y	Y
31 Dymally	N	N	N	Y	Y	N	Y	Y
32 Anderson	N	N	N	Y	Y	N	N	Y
33 *Dreier*	Y	N	N	Y	Y	Y	Y	N
34 Torres	N	N	N	Y	Y	N	Y	Y
35 *Lewis*	Y	N	N	Y	N	Y	N	Y
36 Brown	N	N	?	?	N	N	Y	Y
37 *McCandless*	Y	Y	Y	Y	Y	Y	N	N
38 Patterson	N	N	N	Y	N	N	Y	Y
39 *Dannemeyer*	Y	Y	Y	Y	Y	N	Y	Y
40 *Badham*	Y	N	N	Y	Y	Y	N	Y
41 *Lowery*	Y	Y	Y	N	Y	N	Y	Y
42 *Lungren*	Y	Y	N	Y	Y	Y	N	Y

	225	226	227	228	229	230	231	232
43 *Packard*	Y	Y	Y	Y	Y	Y	N	Y
44 Bates	N	Y	Y	N	Y	N	Y	Y
45 *Hunter*	Y	N	N	Y	N	Y	?	?
COLORADO								
1 Schroeder	N	N	N	Y	Y	Y	Y	Y
2 Wirth	N	N	N	Y	Y	N	Y	Y
3 Kogovsek	N	N	N	Y	?	?	?	?
4 *Brown*	Y	N	N	Y	N	Y	Y	Y
5 *Kramer*	Y	N	N	Y	N	Y	N	?
6 *Schaefer*	Y	Y	N	Y	Y	Y	N	Y
CONNECTICUT								
1 Kennelly	N	N	N	Y	Y	N	Y	Y
2 Gejdenson	N	N	N	Y	Y	N	Y	Y
3 Morrison	N	N	N	Y	Y	N	Y	Y
4 *McKinney*	N	Y	N	+	Y	Y	N	Y
5 Ratchford	N	N	N	Y	Y	N	Y	Y
6 *Johnson*	N	Y	N	Y	Y	N	N	N
DELAWARE								
AL Carper	N	Y	N	Y	Y	Y	Y	Y
FLORIDA								
1 Hutto	Y	Y	N	Y	Y	N	Y	Y
2 Fuqua	Y	Y	N	Y	Y	N	Y	Y
3 Bennett	Y	Y	N	Y	Y	N	Y	Y
4 Chappell	Y	Y	?	Y	Y	N	?	?
5 *McCollum*	Y	Y	N	Y	Y	Y	N	Y
6 MacKay	Y	Y	N	Y	?	?	?	?
7 Gibbons	Y	Y	N	Y	Y	N	Y	Y
8 *Young*	Y	Y	?	?	?	?	?	?
9 *Bilirakis*	Y	N	N	Y	N	Y	N	Y
10 Ireland	Y	Y	N	Y	Y	Y	?	?
11 Nelson	Y	Y	N	Y	Y	Y	Y	Y
12 *Lewis*	Y	Y	N	Y	Y	N	Y	Y
13 *Mack*	Y	N	N	Y	N	Y	N	Y
14 Mica	Y	Y	N	Y	Y	N	Y	Y
15 *Shaw*	Y	Y	N	Y	N	Y	N	Y
16 Smith	N	Y	N	Y	N	Y	N	?
17 Lehman	N	N	N	Y	Y	N	Y	Y
18 Pepper	N	Y	?	?	Y	N	Y	Y
19 Fascell	N	Y	N	Y	Y	N	Y	Y
GEORGIA								
1 Thomas	Y	N	N	Y	Y	N	Y	Y
2 Hatcher	Y	N	N	Y	Y	?	Y	?
3 Ray	N	N	N	Y	Y	N	Y	Y
4 Levitas	N	N	N	Y	Y	N	Y	Y
5 Fowler	N	Y	?	?	?	?	?	?
6 *Gingrich*	Y	Y	N	Y	?	Y	N	N
7 Darden	Y	N	N	Y	Y	N	Y	Y
8 Rowland	Y	N	N	Y	Y	N	Y	Y
9 Jenkins	Y	N	N	Y	Y	N	Y	Y
10 Barnard	Y	N	N	Y	Y	N	Y	Y
HAWAII								
1 Heftel	Y	Y	N	Y	Y	N	Y	Y
2 Akaka	N	N	N	Y	Y	N	Y	Y
IDAHO								
1 *Craig*	Y	N	N	Y	?	?	?	?
2 *Hansen*	?	?	?	?	?	?	?	?
ILLINOIS								
1 Hayes	N	N	N	Y	Y	N	Y	Y
2 Savage	N	N	N	Y	Y	N	Y	Y
3 Russo	N	Y	N	Y	Y	N	Y	Y
4 *O'Brien*	Y	Y	N	Y	N	N	N	Y
5 Lipinski	N	Y	N	Y	Y	N	Y	Y
6 *Hyde*	Y	Y	N	Y	Y	N	Y	N
7 Collins	N	N	N	Y	Y	N	Y	?
8 Rostenkowski	N	Y	N	Y	Y	N	Y	Y
9 Yates	N	N	N	Y	Y	N	Y	Y
10 *Porter*	N	N	N	Y	N	N	N	Y
11 Annunzio	N	Y	N	Y	Y	N	Y	Y
12 *Crane, P.*	Y	N	Y	N	?	?	?	?
13 *Erlenborn*	Y	Y	N	Y	N	Y	?	?
14 *Corcoran*	Y	Y	Y	Y	Y	N	Y	Y
15 *Madigan*	Y	Y	N	Y	N	Y	N	Y
16 *Martin*	Y	Y	N	Y	?	N	Y	Y
17 Evans	N	N	N	Y	Y	N	Y	Y
18 *Michel*	Y	Y	Y	N	Y	N	Y	Y
19 *Crane, D.*	Y	N	Y	N	Y	Y	?	N
20 Durbin	N	N	N	Y	Y	N	Y	Y
21 Price	N	Y	N	Y	Y	N	Y	Y
22 Simon	N	N	N	Y	?	?	?	?
INDIANA								
1 Hall	N	N	N	Y	Y	N	Y	Y
2 Sharp	N	Y	N	Y	Y	N	Y	Y
3 *Hiler*	Y	Y	N	Y	Y	N	Y	Y
4 *Coats*	Y	Y	N	Y	Y	N	Y	Y
5 Hillis	Y	N	N	Y	Y	Y	N	Y

ND - Northern Democrats   SD - Southern Democrats

Corresponding to Congressional Record Votes 250, 251, 253, 254, 255, 257, 258, 259

	225	226	227	228	229	230	231	232
6 ***Burton***	Y	Y	N	Y	Y	Y	N	N
7 ***Myers***	Y	Y	N	Y	Y	Y	N	N
8 McCloskey	N	Y	N	Y	Y	N	Y	Y
9 Hamilton	N	Y	N	Y	Y	N	Y	Y
10 Jacobs	N	N	N	Y	Y	Y	Y	N
IOWA								
1 ***Leach***	N	Y	N	Y	Y	Y	N	Y
2 ***Tauke***	Y	Y	N	Y	Y	Y	N	Y
3 ***Evans***	Y	Y	N	Y	Y	Y	N	Y
4 Smith	Y	Y	N	Y	N	N	Y	Y
5 Harkin	N	Y	N	Y	Y	N	Y	Y
6 Bedell	N	Y	N	Y	Y	?	?	?
KANSAS								
1 ***Roberts***	Y	N	N	Y	Y	Y	N	N
2 Slattery	N	Y	N	Y	N	Y	Y	Y
3 ***Winn***	Y	Y	N	Y	Y	Y	N	Y
4 Glickman	N	Y	N	Y	Y	N	Y	Y
5 ***Whittaker***	Y	Y	N	Y	Y	Y	N	N
KENTUCKY								
1 Hubbard	Y	N	N	Y	?	?	?	?
2 Natcher	N	Y	N	Y	N	N	Y	Y
3 Mazzoli	N	Y	N	Y	Y	N	Y	Y
4 ***Snyder***	Y	N	N	Y	Y	N	N	Y
5 ***Rogers***	Y	N	N	Y	N	N	N	Y
6 ***Hopkins***	Y	N	N	Y	Y	Y	N	Y
7 Perkins	N	N	N	Y	Y	N	Y	Y
LOUISIANA								
1 ***Livingston***	Y	Y	N	Y	N	Y	N	Y
2 Boggs	N	Y	?	?	?	?	?	?
3 Tauzin	Y	N	N	Y	Y	N	Y	Y
4 Roemer	Y	N	N	Y	Y	Y	Y	Y
5 Huckaby	Y	N	N	Y	Y	Y	Y	Y
6 ***Moore***	Y	N	N	Y	Y	Y	N	Y
7 Breaux	Y	Y	N	Y	Y	N	Y	?
8 Long	N	Y	N	Y	Y	N	Y	Y
MAINE								
1 ***McKernan***	Y	Y	N	Y	Y	Y	N	Y
2 ***Snowe***	Y	Y	N	Y	Y	Y	N	Y
MARYLAND								
1 Dyson	Y	N	N	Y	Y	N	Y	Y
2 Long	N	Y	N	Y	Y	Y	?	?
3 Mikulski	?	?	N	Y	Y	N	Y	Y
4 ***Holt***	Y	Y	N	Y	Y	Y	Y	Y
5 Hoyer	N	Y	N	Y	N	N	Y	Y
6 Byron	Y	Y	N	+	Y	Y	Y	Y
7 Mitchell	N	N	N	Y	Y	N	Y	Y
8 Barnes	N	Y	N	Y	Y	N	Y	Y
MASSACHUSETTS								
1 ***Conte***	N	Y	N	Y	N	Y	N	Y
2 Boland	N	Y	N	Y	N	N	?	?
3 Early	N	Y	N	Y	N	N	Y	Y
4 Frank	N	Y	N	Y	N	N	Y	Y
5 Shannon	?	?	?	?	?	?	?	?
6 Mavroules	N	Y	N	Y	N	N	Y	Y
7 Markey	N	N	N	Y	Y	N	Y	Y
8 O'Neill								
9 Moakley	N	Y	N	Y	N	N	Y	Y
10 Studds	N	Y	N	Y	Y	N	Y	Y
11 Donnelly	N	Y	N	Y	N	N	Y	Y
MICHIGAN								
1 Conyers	N	N	N	Y	Y	N	Y	Y
2 ***Pursell***	Y	N	N	Y	Y	Y	N	Y
3 Wolpe	N	N	N	Y	Y	N	Y	Y
4 ***Siljander***	Y	N	N	Y	Y	Y	N	N
5 ***Sawyer***	Y	Y	N	Y	N	N	N	Y
6 Carr	N	N	?	?	Y	N	Y	Y
7 Kildee	N	N	N	Y	Y	N	Y	Y
8 Traxler	N	Y	N	Y	Y	N	Y	Y
9 ***Vander Jagt***	Y	N	N	?	Y	N	N	Y
10 Albosta	N	N	N	Y	Y	N	Y	Y
11 ***Davis***	Y	Y	N	Y	Y	Y	?	Y
12 Bonior	N	Y	N	Y	Y	N	?	?
13 Crockett	N	N	N	Y	Y	N	Y	Y
14 Hertel	N	N	N	Y	N	N	Y	Y
15 Ford	N	N	?	Y	Y	N	?	?
16 Dingell	N	Y	N	Y	Y	N	Y	Y
17 Levin	N	Y	N	Y	Y	N	Y	Y
18 ***Broomfield***	Y	N	N	Y	Y	Y	N	Y
MINNESOTA								
1 Penny	N	Y	N	Y	Y	N	Y	Y
2 ***Weber***	Y	Y	N	Y	Y	Y	N	N
3 ***Frenzel***	Y	Y	N	Y	Y	Y	N	Y
4 Vento	N	N	N	Y	Y	N	Y	Y
5 Sabo	N	Y	N	Y	N	N	Y	Y
6 Sikorski	N	N	N	Y	Y	N	Y	Y

	225	226	227	228	229	230	231	232
7 ***Stangeland***	Y	Y	N	Y	Y	N	N	Y
8 Oberstar	N	N	N	Y	Y	N	Y	Y
MISSISSIPPI								
1 Whitten	Y	N	N	Y	N	N	Y	Y
2 ***Franklin***	Y	Y	N	Y	Y	Y	N	Y
3 Montgomery	Y	Y	N	Y	Y	N	Y	Y
4 Dowdy	Y	Y	N	Y	Y	N	Y	Y
5 ***Lott***	Y	Y	N	Y	Y	Y	N	Y
MISSOURI								
1 Clay	N	N	N	Y	Y	?	?	?
2 Young	N	N	N	Y	Y	N	Y	Y
3 Gephardt	N	N	N	Y	Y	N	Y	?
4 Skelton	Y	N	N	Y	Y	N	Y	Y
5 Wheat	N	N	N	Y	Y	N	Y	Y
6 ***Coleman***	Y	N	N	Y	Y	Y	N	Y
7 ***Taylor***	Y	Y	N	Y	N	N	N	Y
8 ***Emerson***	Y	N	N	Y	Y	Y	N	N
9 Volkmer	Y	N	N	Y	Y	N	Y	Y
MONTANA								
1 Williams	?	-	?	Y	Y	N	?	?
2 ***Marlenee***	Y	N	N	Y	Y	Y	N	Y
NEBRASKA								
1 ***Bereuter***	Y	Y	N	Y	Y	Y	Y	Y
2 ***Daub***	Y	N	N	Y	?	#	?	?
3 ***Smith***	Y	Y	N	Y	Y	Y	Y	Y
NEVADA								
1 Reid	N	N	N	Y	Y	N	Y	Y
2 ***Vucanovich***	Y	Y	N	Y	N	Y	N	N
NEW HAMPSHIRE								
1 D'Amours	N	Y	N	Y	Y	N	Y	Y
2 ***Gregg***	Y	Y	N	Y	Y	Y	N	N
NEW JERSEY								
1 Florio	N	N	N	Y	Y	N	Y	Y
2 Hughes	N	N	N	Y	Y	N	Y	Y
3 Howard	N	Y	N	Y	Y	N	Y	Y
4 ***Smith***	N	Y	N	Y	Y	Y	N	Y
5 ***Roukema***	Y	N	N	Y	Y	Y	N	Y
6 Dwyer	N	Y	N	Y	Y	N	Y	Y
7 ***Rinaldo***	N	N	N	Y	Y	Y	N	Y
8 Roe	N	Y	N	Y	Y	N	Y	Y
9 Torricelli	Y	Y	N	Y	?	?	?	?
10 Rodino	N	Y	N	Y	Y	N	Y	Y
11 Minish	N	N	N	Y	Y	Y	Y	Y
12 ***Courter***	Y	N	N	Y	N	Y	N	Y
13 Vacancy								
14 Guarini	N	N	N	Y	Y	N	Y	Y
NEW MEXICO								
1 ***Lujan***	Y	N	N	Y	Y	Y	N	Y
2 ***Skeen***	Y	N	N	Y	N	Y	N	Y
3 Richardson	N	N	N	Y	Y	N	Y	Y
NEW YORK								
1 ***Carney***	Y	N	N	Y	Y	Y	N	Y
2 Downey	N	Y	N	?	Y	N	Y	?
3 Mrazek	N	Y	N	Y	Y	N	Y	Y
4 ***Lent***	Y	N	N	Y	Y	Y	N	Y
5 ***McGrath***	Y	N	N	Y	N	Y	N	Y
6 Addabbo	N	N	N	Y	N	N	?	?
7 Ackerman	N	N	N	Y	Y	N	Y	Y
8 Scheuer	N	Y	N	Y	N	N	Y	Y
9 Ferraro	N	N	N	Y	Y	?	?	?
10 Schumer	N	Y	?	?	Y	?	?	?
11 Towns	N	N	?	?	?	?	?	?
12 Owens	N	N	N	Y	Y	?	?	?
13 Solarz	N	Y	N	Y	Y	?	?	?
14 ***Molinari***	Y	Y	N	Y	Y	Y	N	Y
15 ***Green***	N	Y	N	Y	N	Y	N	Y
16 Rangel	N	N	N	Y	Y	N	Y	Y
17 Weiss	N	N	N	Y	Y	N	Y	Y
18 Garcia	N	N	?	?	Y	?	?	?
19 Biaggi	Y	N	N	Y	N	N	Y	Y
20 Ottinger	N	Y	?	Y	Y	N	N	Y
21 ***Fish***	N	Y	N	Y	Y	Y	N	Y
22 ***Gilman***	N	Y	-	Y	Y	Y	N	Y
23 Stratton	Y	N	?	Y	N	N	Y	Y
24 ***Solomon***	Y	N	N	Y	Y	Y	N	Y
25 ***Boehlert***	Y	Y	N	Y	Y	Y	N	Y
26 ***Martin***	Y	N	N	Y	Y	Y	N	Y
27 ***Wortley***	Y	Y	N	Y	Y	Y	N	?
28 McHugh	N	Y	N	Y	Y	N	Y	Y
29 ***Horton***	Y	N	N	Y	N	Y	N	Y
30 ***Conable***	Y	Y	N	Y	N	Y	N	Y
31 ***Kemp***	Y	N	N	Y	Y	Y	N	Y
32 LaFalce	N	Y	N	Y	Y	N	Y	Y
33 Nowak	N	Y	N	Y	Y	N	Y	Y
34 Lundine	N	Y	N	Y	?	?	?	?

	225	226	227	228	229	230	231	232
NORTH CAROLINA								
1 Jones	Y	N	N	Y	Y	N	Y	Y
2 Valentine	Y	Y	N	Y	Y	Y	?	?
3 Whitley	Y	Y	N	Y	Y	N	Y	Y
4 Andrews	Y	Y	N	Y	N	Y	Y	Y
5 Neal	Y	Y	N	Y	Y	N	Y	Y
6 Britt	N	Y	N	Y	Y	N	Y	Y
7 Rose	Y	Y	N	Y	Y	N	Y	Y
8 Hefner	Y	Y	N	Y	Y	N	Y	Y
9 ***Martin***	Y	Y	N	Y	Y	?	?	?
10 ***Broyhill***	Y	Y	Y	N	Y	Y	N	Y
11 Clarke	N	Y	N	Y	Y	N	Y	Y
NORTH DAKOTA								
AL Dorgan	N	Y	N	Y	Y	Y	Y	?
OHIO								
1 Luken	N	Y	N	Y	Y	N	Y	Y
2 ***Gradison***	Y	Y	N	Y	Y	Y	N	Y
3 Hall	N	N	N	Y	Y	N	Y	Y
4 ***Oxley***	Y	Y	N	Y	Y	Y	N	Y
5 ***Latta***	Y	N	N	Y	Y	Y	N	Y
6 ***McEwen***	Y	Y	N	Y	Y	Y	N	N
7 ***DeWine***	Y	Y	N	Y	Y	Y	N	Y
8 ***Kindness***	Y	N	N	Y	Y	Y	N	Y
9 Kaptur	N	N	?	?	Y	N	Y	Y
10 ***Miller***	Y	Y	N	Y	N	Y	N	Y
11 Eckart	N	Y	N	Y	Y	N	Y	Y
12 ***Kasich***	Y	Y	N	Y	Y	Y	N	Y
13 Pease	N	Y	N	Y	Y	Y	Y	Y
14 Seiberling	N	Y	N	Y	Y	N	Y	Y
15 ***Wylie***	Y	Y	N	Y	Y	Y	N	Y
16 ***Regula***	Y	N	N	Y	Y	Y	N	Y
17 ***Williams***	Y	N	N	?	?	#	?	?
18 Applegate	Y	N	N	Y	Y	N	Y	?
19 Feighan	N	Y	N	Y	Y	N	Y	Y
20 Oakar	N	N	N	Y	Y	N	Y	Y
21 Stokes	N	N	N	Y	Y	N	Y	Y
OKLAHOMA								
1 Jones	Y	Y	N	Y	Y	Y	Y	Y
2 Synar	N	Y	N	Y	Y	N	Y	Y
3 Watkins	Y	N	N	Y	Y	N	Y	Y
4 McCurdy	Y	Y	N	Y	Y	Y	Y	Y
5 ***Edwards***	Y	N	N	Y	Y	Y	N	Y
6 English	Y	N	N	Y	Y	Y	Y	Y
OREGON								
1 AuCoin	N	N	N	Y	?	?	?	?
2 ***Smith, R.***	Y	N	N	Y	Y	N	N	Y
3 Wyden	N	N	N	Y	Y	N	Y	Y
4 Weaver	N	Y	N	Y	Y	N	Y	Y
5 ***Smith, D.***	Y	Y	N	Y	Y	Y	N	Y
PENNSYLVANIA								
1 Foglietta	N	N	N	Y	N	N	Y	Y
2 Gray	N	N	N	Y	N	N	Y	Y
3 Borski	N	N	?	?	Y	N	Y	Y
4 Kolter	N	N	N	Y	Y	N	Y	Y
5 ***Schulze***	Y	Y	N	Y	N	Y	N	Y
6 Yatron	N	N	N	Y	Y	N	Y	?
7 Edgar	N	N	N	Y	N	N	Y	Y
8 Kostmayer	N	Y	N	Y	N	N	Y	Y
9 ***Shuster***	Y	N	N	Y	Y	N	N	Y
10 ***McDade***	Y	Y	N	Y	Y	Y	N	Y
11 Harrison	N	Y	?	?	?	?	?	?
12 Murtha	N	Y	N	Y	N	N	Y	Y
13 ***Coughlin***	Y	Y	N	Y	N	N	N	Y
14 Coyne	N	Y	N	Y	Y	N	Y	Y
15 ***Ritter***	Y	Y	N	Y	Y	N	N	N
16 ***Walker***	Y	Y	Y	Y	Y	Y	N	N
17 ***Gekas***	Y	Y	Y	Y	Y	Y	N	N
18 Walgren	N	Y	N	Y	Y	Y	Y	Y
19 ***Goodling***	Y	N	N	Y	Y	Y	N	Y
20 Gaydos	N	N	N	Y	Y	N	Y	Y
21 ***Ridge***	Y	Y	N	Y	Y	Y	N	?
22 Murphy	N	N	N	Y	Y	Y	Y	Y
23 ***Clinger***	N	Y	N	Y	Y	N	N	Y
RHODE ISLAND								
1 St Germain	N	Y	N	Y	Y	N	Y	Y
2 ***Schneider***	N	Y	N	Y	?	?	?	?
SOUTH CAROLINA								
1 ***Hartnett***	Y	N	Y	Y	N	N	N	Y
2 ***Spence***	Y	N	N	Y	Y	Y	N	Y
3 Derrick	Y	Y	N	Y	Y	N	Y	Y
4 ***Campbell***	Y	Y	N	Y	Y	Y	N	Y
5 Spratt	N	Y	N	Y	Y	Y	Y	Y
6 Tallon	Y	Y	N	Y	Y	Y	Y	Y
SOUTH DAKOTA								
AL Daschle	N	Y	N	Y	Y	N	Y	Y

	225	226	227	228	229	230	231	232
TENNESSEE								
1 ***Quillen***	Y	Y	N	Y	N	Y	N	Y
2 ***Duncan***	Y	N	N	Y	Y	Y	N	Y
3 Lloyd	Y	Y	?	?	?	?	?	?
4 Cooper	Y	Y	N	Y	N	Y	Y	Y
5 Boner	Y	Y	?	?	Y	N	Y	Y
6 Gore	Y	Y	N	Y	Y	N	Y	Y
7 ***Sundquist***	Y	N	N	Y	Y	Y	N	Y
8 Jones	Y	Y	N	Y	Y	N	Y	Y
9 Ford	N	Y	N	Y	Y	N	?	?
TEXAS								
1 Hall, S.	Y	N	N	Y	Y	Y	Y	Y
2 Wilson	Y	Y	N	Y	Y	N	Y	Y
3 ***Bartlett***	Y	N	Y	Y	Y	Y	N	Y
4 Hall, R.	Y	N	N	Y	Y	Y	Y	Y
5 Bryant	N	N	?	?	?	?	?	?
6 ***Gramm***	Y	N	?	?	?	?	?	?
7 ***Archer***	Y	N	Y	Y	Y	Y	N	Y
8 ***Fields***	Y	N	Y	Y	Y	Y	N	Y
9 Brooks	Y	N	N	Y	Y	N	Y	Y
10 Pickle	Y	Y	N	Y	Y	N	Y	Y
11 Leath	Y	N	N	Y	Y	N	Y	Y
12 Wright	N	Y	N	Y	Y	N	Y	?
13 Hightower	Y	N	N	Y	Y	N	Y	Y
14 Patman	Y	N	Y	Y	Y	N	Y	Y
15 de la Garza	N	N	N	?	Y	N	Y	Y
16 Coleman	N	N	N	Y	Y	N	Y	Y
17 Stenholm	Y	N	N	Y	Y	Y	Y	Y
18 Leland	?	?	?	?	?	X	?	?
19 Hance	Y	N	N	Y	Y	N	Y	?
20 Gonzalez	N	N	N	Y	Y	N	Y	?
21 ***Loeffler***	Y	N	N	Y	N	Y	N	Y
22 ***Paul***	N	N	Y	N	Y	Y	N	N
23 Kazen	N	N	N	Y	Y	N	Y	Y
24 Frost	N	N	N	Y	Y	N	Y	Y
25 Andrews	N	N	N	Y	Y	Y	Y	Y
26 Vandergriff	N	N	Y	Y	Y	N	Y	Y
27 Ortiz	N	N	N	Y	Y	N	Y	Y
UTAH								
1 ***Hansen***	Y	Y	Y	Y	N	Y	N	?
2 ***Marriott***	Y	N	?	?	?	?	?	?
3 ***Nielson***	Y	Y	Y	Y	Y	Y	N	N
VERMONT								
AL ***Jeffords***	N	Y	N	Y	Y	Y	N	Y
VIRGINIA								
1 ***Bateman***	Y	Y	N	Y	Y	N	N	Y
2 ***Whitehurst***	Y	Y	N	Y	N	Y	N	Y
3 ***Bliley***	Y	N	N	Y	Y	N	N	Y
4 Sisisky	Y	Y	N	Y	Y	N	Y	Y
5 Daniel	Y	N	N	Y	Y	Y	Y	Y
6 Olin	Y	N	N	Y	Y	N	Y	Y
7 ***Robinson***	Y	N	N	Y	N	Y	N	Y
8 ***Parris***	Y	N	N	Y	Y	Y	N	Y
9 Boucher	N	Y	N	Y	Y	N	Y	Y
10 ***Wolf***	Y	Y	N	Y	Y	Y	N	Y
WASHINGTON								
1 ***Pritchard***	Y	Y	N	Y	?	?	N	N
2 Swift	N	N	N	Y	Y	Y	Y	Y
3 Bonker	N	Y	N	Y	Y	N	Y	Y
4 ***Morrison***	N	Y	N	Y	Y	Y	N	Y
5 Foley	N	Y	N	Y	Y	N	Y	Y
6 Dicks	N	Y	N	Y	Y	N	Y	Y
7 Lowry	N	N	N	Y	Y	N	Y	N
8 ***Chandler***	Y	Y	N	Y	Y	Y	N	Y
WEST VIRGINIA								
1 Mollohan	N	N	N	Y	Y	N	Y	Y
2 Staggers	N	N	N	Y	Y	Y	Y	Y
3 Wise	N	N	N	Y	+	+	+	+
4 Rahall	N	Y	N	Y	Y	X	+	-
WISCONSIN								
1 Aspin	N	Y	N	Y	Y	N	Y	?
2 Kastenmeier	N	Y	N	Y	Y	Y	Y	Y
3 ***Gunderson***	Y	Y	N	Y	Y	Y	N	Y
4 Kleczka	N	Y	N	Y	Y	N	Y	Y
5 Moody	N	Y	N	Y	Y	N	Y	Y
6 ***Petri***	Y	Y	N	Y	Y	Y	N	Y
7 Obey	N	Y	N	Y	Y	N	Y	Y
8 ***Roth***	Y	N	N	Y	Y	Y	N	Y
9 ***Sensenbrenner***	?	?	?	?	?	?	?	?
WYOMING								
AL ***Cheney***	Y	Y	Y	Y	Y	Y	N	N

Southern states - Ala., Ark., Fla., Ga., Ky., La., Miss., N.C., Okla., S.C., Tenn., Texas, Va.

233. HR 5490. Civil Rights Act of 1984. Adoption of the rule (H Res 528) providing for House floor consideration of the bill to overturn a Feb. 28 Supreme Court ruling that narrowed the reach of a 1972 law banning sex discrimination by federally aided colleges and universities. The bill seeks to ensure broad application of four major civil rights laws, including the 1972 education law. Adopted 224-136: R 17-125; D 207-11 (ND 143-4, SD 64-7), June 21, 1984.

234. Procedural Motion. Hubbard, D-Ky., motion to approve the House *Journal* of Thursday, June 21. Motion agreed to 286-34: R 109-21; D 177-13 (ND 108-12, SD 69-1), June 22, 1984.

235. HR 5604. Military Construction Authorization. Passage of the bill to authorize $9.2 billion for military construction projects of the Department of Defense in fiscal 1985. Passed 312-49: R 123-16; D 189-33 (ND 114-31, SD 75-2), June 22, 1984.

236. HR 5680. Federal Pay Equity. Adoption of the rule (H Res 526) providing for House floor consideration of the bill to reform the federal merit pay system and require a study of sex-based wage differentials within the federal work force. Adopted 276-58: R 77-57; D 199-1 (ND 135-0, SD 64-1), June 22, 1984.

237. Procedural Motion. Petri, R-Wis., motion to approve the House *Journal* of Monday, June 25. Motion agreed to 360-24: R 139-13; D 221-11 (ND 137-10, SD 84-1), June 26, 1984.

238. HR 5885. Head Start/Human Services Amendments. Andrews, D-N.C., amendment to suspend the rules and pass the bill to reauthorize Head Start and other social services programs through fiscal 1986. Motion agreed to 409-10: R 148-10; D 261-0 (ND 172-0, SD 89-0), June 26, 1984. A two-thirds majority of those present and voting (280 in this case) is required for passage under suspension of the rules. A "nay" was a vote supporting the president's position.

239. H Con Res 321. Early Projections of Election Results. Swift, D-Wash., motion to suspend the rules and adopt the concurrent resolution to ask the news media, particularly broadcasters, to refrain voluntarily from projecting election results until all polls are closed. Motion agreed to 352-65: R 108-50; D 244-15 (ND 159-12, SD 85-3), June 26, 1984. A two-thirds majority of those present and voting (278 in this case) is required for adoption under suspension of the rules.

240. HR 3282. Water Quality Renewal. Passage of the bill to reauthorize and revise programs under the Clean Water Act for fiscal 1985-88. Passed 405-11: R 147-11; D 258-0 (ND 170-0, SD 88-0), June 26, 1984.

KEY

Y	Voted for (yea).
#	Paired for.
+	Announced for.
N	Voted against (nay).
X	Paired against.
-	Announced against.
P	Voted "present".
C	Voted "present" to avoid possible conflict of interest.
?	Did not vote or otherwise make a position known.

Democrats *Republicans*

	233	234	235	236	237	238	239	240
ALABAMA								
1 *Edwards*	?	?	?	?	Y	Y	Y	Y
2 *Dickinson*	N	N	Y	Y	N	+	Y	Y
3 Nichols	Y	Y	Y	Y	Y	Y	Y	Y
4 Bevill	Y	Y	Y	Y	Y	Y	Y	Y
5 Flippo	Y	Y	Y	Y	Y	Y	Y	Y
6 Erdreich	Y	Y	Y	Y	Y	Y	Y	Y
7 Shelby	?	?	#	?	Y	Y	Y	Y
ALASKA								
AL *Young*	N	N	Y	Y	N	Y	Y	Y
ARIZONA								
1 *McCain*	?	?	?	?	Y	Y	Y	Y
2 Udall	Y	?	?	?	Y	Y	Y	Y
3 *Stump*	N	?	?	?	Y	N	N	N
4 *Rudd*	N	Y	Y	Y	Y	Y	Y	Y
5 McNulty	Y	Y	Y	Y	Y	Y	Y	Y
ARKANSAS								
1 Alexander	?	?	?	?	Y	Y	Y	Y
2 *Bethune*	N	?	?	?	?	Y	N	Y
3 *Hammerschmidt*	N	Y	N	Y	N	Y	N	Y
4 Anthony	Y	?	Y	?	Y	Y	Y	Y
CALIFORNIA								
1 Bosco	Y	?	?	?	Y	Y	Y	Y
2 *Chappie*	N	N	Y	N	Y	N	Y	N
3 Matsui	Y	Y	Y	Y	Y	Y	Y	Y
4 Fazio	Y	Y	Y	?	Y	Y	Y	Y
5 Burton	Y	Y	Y	Y	Y	Y	Y	Y
6 Boxer	Y	Y	Y	Y	Y	Y	Y	Y
7 Miller	Y	Y	Y	Y	Y	Y	Y	Y
8 Dellums	Y	Y	N	Y	Y	Y	Y	Y
9 Stark	Y	Y	N	Y	Y	Y	Y	Y
10 Edwards	Y	Y	N	Y	Y	Y	Y	Y
11 Lantos	Y	?	?	?	Y	Y	Y	Y
12 *Zschau*	N	Y	N	Y	Y	Y	N	Y
13 Mineta	Y	Y	Y	Y	Y	Y	Y	Y
14 *Shumway*	N	Y	N	Y	N	Y	N	Y
15 Coelho	Y	Y	Y	Y	Y	Y	Y	Y
16 Panetta	Y	Y	Y	Y	Y	Y	Y	Y
17 *Pashayan*	N	?	?	?	Y	N	Y	Y
18 Lehman	Y	?	Y	Y	Y	Y	Y	Y
19 *Lagomarsino*	N	Y	Y	Y	Y	Y	Y	Y
20 *Thomas*	N	?	?	?	Y	Y	Y	Y
21 *Fiedler*	N	N	Y	N	Y	Y	N	Y
22 *Moorhead*	N	Y	Y	Y	Y	Y	N	Y
23 Beilenson	Y	Y	N	Y	Y	Y	Y	Y
24 Waxman	Y	?	?	?	Y	Y	Y	Y
25 Roybal	Y	Y	N	Y	?	Y	Y	Y
26 Berman	Y	?	?	?	Y	Y	Y	Y
27 Levine	Y	Y	Y	Y	Y	Y	Y	Y
28 Dixon	Y	?	Y	Y	N	?	?	?
29 Hawkins	?	N	Y	N	Y	Y	Y	Y
30 Martinez	Y	Y	Y	Y	Y	Y	Y	Y
31 Dymally	Y	P	Y	Y	?	?	?	?
32 Anderson	Y	Y	Y	Y	Y	Y	Y	Y
33 *Dreier*	N	Y	Y	N	Y	Y	N	Y
34 Torres	Y	Y	Y	Y	Y	Y	Y	Y
35 *Lewis*	N	Y	Y	?	?	?	?	?
36 Brown	Y	Y	Y	Y	Y	Y	Y	Y
37 *McCandless*	N	Y	Y	N	Y	Y	N	Y
38 Patterson	Y	Y	Y	Y	Y	Y	Y	Y
39 *Dannemeyer*	N	Y	Y	N	Y	N	N	N
40 *Badham*	N	?	?	?	Y	N	Y	Y
41 *Lowery*	N	Y	Y	N	Y	N	Y	Y
42 *Lungren*	N	?	Y	N	Y	Y	Y	N

	233	234	235	236	237	238	239	240
43 *Packard*	N	Y	Y	N	Y	Y	Y	Y
44 Bates	N	Y	Y	Y	Y	Y	Y	Y
45 *Hunter*	N	Y	Y	Y	Y	?	Y	Y
COLORADO								
1 Schroeder	Y	N	Y	Y	?	Y	Y	Y
2 Wirth	Y	Y	N	Y	Y	Y	Y	Y
3 Kogovsek	?	?	?	?	?	Y	Y	?
4 *Brown*	N	Y	N	N	N	N	Y	Y
5 *Kramer*	N	Y	Y	Y	Y	Y	N	Y
6 *Schaefer*	N	?	Y	N	Y	N	Y	Y
CONNECTICUT								
1 Kennelly	Y	Y	Y	Y	Y	Y	Y	Y
2 Gejdenson	Y	P	Y	?	N	Y	Y	Y
3 Morrison	Y	Y	Y	Y	Y	Y	Y	Y
4 *McKinney*	N	Y	N	?	?	?	?	?
5 Ratchford	Y	Y	Y	Y	Y	Y	Y	Y
6 *Johnson*	N	Y	N	Y	Y	Y	Y	Y
DELAWARE								
AL Carper	Y	Y	Y	Y	Y	Y	Y	Y
FLORIDA								
1 Hutto	N	Y	Y	Y	Y	Y	Y	Y
2 Fuqua	?	Y	Y	Y	Y	Y	Y	Y
3 Bennett	N	Y	Y	Y	Y	Y	Y	Y
4 Chappell	?	?	Y	?	Y	Y	Y	Y
5 *McCollum*	N	Y	Y	N	Y	N	Y	N
6 MacKay	?	Y	N	Y	Y	Y	Y	Y
7 Gibbons	Y	Y	Y	?	Y	Y	Y	Y
8 *Young*	?	?	Y	N	Y	N	Y	N
9 *Bilirakis*	N	Y	Y	Y	Y	Y	Y	Y
10 Ireland	?	?	?	?	Y	Y	Y	Y
11 Nelson	N	Y	Y	Y	Y	Y	Y	Y
12 *Lewis*	N	Y	Y	Y	Y	Y	Y	Y
13 *Mack*	N	Y	Y	N	Y	Y	Y	Y
14 Mica	Y	Y	Y	Y	Y	Y	Y	Y
15 *Shaw*	N	Y	Y	N	Y	N	Y	N
16 Smith	?	Y	Y	Y	Y	Y	Y	Y
17 Lehman	Y	Y	Y	?	Y	Y	Y	Y
18 Pepper	Y	?	Y	Y	Y	Y	Y	Y
19 Fascell	Y	Y	Y	Y	Y	Y	Y	Y
GEORGIA								
1 Thomas	Y	Y	Y	Y	Y	Y	Y	Y
2 Hatcher	?	Y	Y	?	Y	Y	Y	Y
3 Ray	N	Y	Y	N	Y	Y	Y	Y
4 Levitas	N	Y	Y	Y	Y	Y	N	Y
5 Fowler	?	?	?	?	Y	Y	Y	Y
6 *Gingrich*	N	Y	Y	N	?	?	?	Y
7 Darden	Y	?	#	?	Y	Y	Y	Y
8 Rowland	Y	Y	Y	Y	Y	Y	Y	Y
9 Jenkins	Y	Y	Y	Y	Y	Y	Y	Y
10 Barnard	Y	Y	?	Y	Y	Y	Y	Y
HAWAII								
1 Heftel	Y	?	Y	Y	?	Y	Y	Y
2 Akaka	Y	Y	Y	Y	Y	Y	Y	Y
IDAHO								
1 *Craig*	?	?	?	?	Y	N	Y	Y
2 *Hansen*	?	?	?	?	?	?	?	?
ILLINOIS								
1 Hayes	Y	?	X	?	Y	Y	Y	Y
2 Savage	Y	Y	N	Y	Y	Y	Y	Y
3 Russo	Y	Y	Y	Y	Y	Y	Y	Y
4 *O'Brien*	N	Y	N	Y	N	Y	Y	Y
5 Lipinski	Y	Y	Y	Y	Y	Y	Y	Y
6 *Hyde*	N	Y	Y	Y	Y	Y	Y	N
7 Collins	Y	Y	N	Y	Y	Y	Y	Y
8 Rostenkowski	Y	?	?	Y	Y	Y	Y	Y
9 Yates	Y	Y	N	Y	Y	Y	Y	Y
10 *Porter*	N	?	Y	N	Y	Y	Y	Y
11 Annunzio	?	Y	Y	Y	Y	Y	Y	Y
12 *Crane, P.*	?	Y	Y	N	Y	N	Y	N
13 *Erlenborn*	N	Y	Y	Y	?	?	?	?
14 *Corcoran*	N	?	Y	N	Y	Y	Y	Y
15 *Madigan*	N	Y	?	N	Y	Y	Y	Y
16 *Martin*	N	Y	?	Y	Y	Y	Y	Y
17 Evans	Y	Y	Y	Y	Y	Y	Y	Y
18 *Michel*	?	Y	Y	N	Y	Y	Y	Y
19 *Crane, D.*	N	Y	Y	N	Y	N	Y	N
20 Durbin	Y	N	Y	?	N	Y	Y	Y
21 Price	Y	Y	Y	Y	Y	Y	Y	Y
22 Simon	?	?	?	?	Y	Y	Y	Y
INDIANA								
1 Hall	Y	Y	?	Y	?	?	?	?
2 Sharp	N	?	?	?	Y	Y	Y	Y
3 *Hiler*	N	Y	N	Y	N	Y	N	Y
4 *Coats*	N	N	Y	N	Y	Y	Y	Y
5 *Hillis*	N	Y	Y	Y	Y	Y	Y	Y

ND - Northern Democrats   SD - Southern Democrats

	233	234	235	236	237	238	239	240
6 ***Burton***	N	Y	Y	N	Y	Y	Y	N
7 ***Myers***	N	Y	Y	Y	Y	Y	N	Y
8 McCloskey	Y	Y	Y	Y	Y	Y	Y	Y
9 Hamilton	Y	Y	Y	Y	Y	Y	Y	Y
10 Jacobs	N	N	N	Y	?	Y	N	Y
IOWA								
1 ***Leach***	Y	Y	N	Y	Y	Y	?	Y
2 ***Tauke***	N	Y	N	Y	Y	Y	N	Y
3 ***Evans***	N	N	N	Y	N	Y	Y	Y
4 Smith	Y	?	?	?	Y	Y	Y	Y
5 Harkin	Y	N	Y	Y	N	Y	Y	Y
6 Bedell	?	?	?	?	Y	Y	Y	Y
KANSAS								
1 ***Roberts***	?	N	Y	Y	N	Y	Y	Y
2 Slattery	Y	?	Y	Y	Y	Y	Y	Y
3 ***Winn***	?	Y	Y	Y	?	Y	N	Y
4 Glickman	Y	Y	Y	Y	Y	Y	N	Y
5 ***Whittaker***	N	Y	Y	Y	?	Y	N	Y
KENTUCKY								
1 Hubbard	?	Y	Y	Y	Y	Y	Y	Y
2 Natcher	Y	Y	Y	Y	Y	Y	Y	Y
3 Mazzoli	Y	+	+	+	Y	Y	Y	Y
4 ***Snyder***	N	Y	Y	Y	Y	Y	N	Y
5 ***Rogers***	N	N	Y	Y	Y	Y	Y	Y
6 ***Hopkins***	N	?	?	?	Y	Y	N	Y
7 Perkins	Y	Y	Y	Y	Y	Y	Y	Y
LOUISIANA								
1 ***Livingston***	N	Y	Y	N	Y	Y	N	Y
2 Boggs	?	?	#	?	Y	Y	Y	Y
3 Tauzin	Y	Y	Y	Y	Y	Y	Y	Y
4 Roemer	Y	N	Y	Y	N	Y	N	Y
5 Huckaby	Y	Y	Y	?	Y	Y	Y	Y
6 ***Moore***	Y	Y	Y	Y	Y	Y	Y	Y
7 Breaux	?	Y	Y	Y	Y	Y	Y	Y
8 Long	Y	Y	Y	Y	Y	Y	Y	Y
MAINE								
1 ***McKernan***	N	Y	Y	N	Y	Y	Y	Y
2 ***Snowe***	Y	Y	?	?	Y	Y	Y	Y
MARYLAND								
1 Dyson	Y	Y	Y	Y	Y	Y	Y	Y
2 Long	?	?	Y	Y	?	Y	?	Y
3 Mikulski	N	Y	Y	Y	Y	Y	Y	Y
4 ***Holt***	N	N	Y	N	Y	Y	Y	Y
5 Hoyer	Y	Y	Y	Y	Y	Y	Y	Y
6 Byron	?	Y	Y	Y	Y	Y	Y	Y
7 Mitchell	Y	N	N	Y	?	Y	Y	Y
8 Barnes	Y	Y	Y	Y	Y	Y	Y	Y
MASSACHUSETTS								
1 ***Conte***	Y	Y	Y	Y	Y	Y	Y	Y
2 Boland	?	Y	Y	Y	Y	Y	Y	Y
3 Early	Y	?	Y	Y	Y	Y	Y	Y
4 Frank	?	Y	Y	Y	Y	Y	N	Y
5 Shannon	?	?	?	?	?	?	?	?
6 Mavroules	?	Y	Y	?	Y	Y	Y	Y
7 Markey	Y	N	N	Y	Y	Y	Y	Y
8 O'Neill								
9 Moakley	Y	Y	Y	Y	?	Y	Y	Y
10 Studds	Y	Y	N	?	?	Y	Y	Y
11 Donnelly	Y	Y	Y	Y	?	Y	Y	Y
MICHIGAN								
1 Conyers	Y	?	Y	Y	Y	Y	Y	Y
2 ***Pursell***	Y	Y	N	Y	Y	Y	Y	Y
3 Wolpe	Y	Y	Y	Y	Y	Y	Y	Y
4 ***Siljander***	N	N	Y	Y	Y	Y	Y	Y
5 ***Sawyer***	Y	Y	Y	Y	Y	Y	Y	Y
6 Carr	Y	Y	Y	Y	Y	Y	Y	Y
7 Kildee	Y	Y	Y	Y	Y	Y	Y	Y
8 Traxler	Y	Y	Y	?	Y	Y	Y	Y
9 ***Vander Jagt***	N	?	Y	Y	Y	Y	Y	Y
10 Albosta	Y	Y	?	?	Y	Y	Y	Y
11 ***Davis***	N	?	Y	Y	Y	Y	Y	Y
12 Bonior	?	Y	Y	Y	Y	Y	Y	Y
13 Crockett	Y	?	Y	Y	Y	Y	Y	Y
14 Hertel	Y	Y	Y	Y	Y	Y	N	Y
15 Ford	?	?	#	?	?	Y	Y	Y
16 Dingell	Y	?	Y	Y	Y	Y	Y	Y
17 Levin	Y	Y	Y	Y	Y	Y	Y	Y
18 ***Broomfield***	Y	Y	Y	Y	Y	Y	N	Y
MINNESOTA								
1 Penny	Y	N	N	Y	N	Y	Y	Y
2 ***Weber***	N	N	Y	N	Y	Y	N	Y
3 ***Frenzel***	N	N	N	Y	Y	Y	Y	Y
4 Vento	Y	Y	Y	Y	Y	Y	Y	Y
5 Sabo	Y	N	N	Y	N	Y	Y	Y
6 Sikorski	Y	N	N	Y	N	Y	Y	Y
7 ***Stangeland***	N	Y	N	Y	Y	Y	Y	Y
8 Oberstar	Y	?	N	Y	P	Y	Y	Y
MISSISSIPPI								
1 Whitten	?	Y	Y	Y	Y	Y	Y	Y
2 ***Franklin***	N	Y	Y	Y	Y	Y	Y	Y
3 Montgomery	Y	Y	Y	Y	Y	Y	Y	Y
4 Dowdy	Y	Y	Y	Y	?	Y	Y	Y
5 ***Lott***	N	Y	Y	N	Y	Y	Y	Y
MISSOURI								
1 Clay	Y	N	N	?	?	Y	Y	Y
2 Young	Y	Y	Y	?	Y	Y	Y	Y
3 Gephardt	Y	Y	Y	Y	Y	Y	Y	Y
4 Skelton	Y	Y	Y	Y	Y	Y	Y	Y
5 Wheat	Y	Y	Y	Y	Y	Y	Y	Y
6 ***Coleman***	Y	Y	Y	Y	Y	Y	Y	Y
7 ***Taylor***	N	Y	Y	N	Y	Y	N	Y
8 ***Emerson***	N	N	Y	N	N	Y	Y	?
9 Volkmer	Y	Y	Y	?	Y	Y	Y	Y
MONTANA								
1 Williams	Y	Y	N	Y	?	Y	Y	Y
2 ***Marlenee***	N	Y	?	?	Y	Y	Y	N
NEBRASKA								
1 ***Bereuter***	N	?	N	N	Y	Y	Y	Y
2 ***Daub***	?	N	Y	N	Y	Y	N	Y
3 ***Smith***	N	Y	N	N	Y	Y	Y	Y
NEVADA								
1 Reid	Y	Y	Y	Y	Y	Y	Y	Y
2 ***Vucanovich***	N	Y	Y	N	Y	Y	Y	Y
NEW HAMPSHIRE								
1 D'Amours	Y	?	Y	Y	Y	Y	Y	Y
2 ***Gregg***	N	Y	Y	N	Y	Y	Y	Y
NEW JERSEY								
1 Florio	Y	?	?	?	P	Y	Y	Y
2 Hughes	Y	Y	Y	Y	Y	Y	Y	Y
3 Howard	Y	Y	Y	Y	Y	Y	Y	Y
4 ***Smith***	N	Y	Y	Y	Y	Y	Y	Y
5 ***Roukema***	Y	Y	N	Y	Y	Y	Y	Y
6 Dwyer	Y	Y	Y	Y	Y	Y	Y	Y
7 ***Rinaldo***	N	Y	Y	Y	Y	Y	Y	Y
8 Roe	Y	Y	Y	Y	Y	Y	Y	Y
9 Torricelli	?	?	#	?	Y	Y	Y	Y
10 Rodino	Y	?	Y	Y	Y	Y	Y	Y
11 Minish	Y	Y	Y	Y	Y	Y	Y	Y
12 ***Courter***	N	Y	Y	Y	Y	Y	Y	Y
13 Vacancy								
14 Guarini	Y	Y	Y	Y	Y	Y	Y	Y
NEW MEXICO								
1 ***Lujan***	N	Y	Y	Y	Y	Y	Y	Y
2 ***Skeen***	N	Y	Y	N	Y	Y	Y	Y
3 Richardson	Y	Y	Y	Y	Y	Y	Y	Y
NEW YORK								
1 ***Carney***	N	Y	Y	N	Y	Y	Y	Y
2 Downey	?	Y	N	?	Y	Y	Y	Y
3 Mrazek	Y	Y	N	Y	Y	Y	Y	?
4 ***Lent***	N	?	Y	Y	Y	Y	?	Y
5 ***McGrath***	N	?	?	Y	Y	Y	Y	?
6 Addabbo	?	?	X	?	Y	Y	Y	Y
7 Ackerman	Y	+	-	Y	Y	Y	N	Y
8 Scheuer	Y	Y	N	Y	?	Y	Y	Y
9 Ferraro	?	Y	Y	Y	Y	Y	Y	Y
10 Schumer	?	?	?	?	?	Y	N	Y
11 Towns	?	?	?	?	?	?	?	Y
12 Owens	?	?	X	Y	Y	Y	Y	Y
13 Solarz	?	?	Y	Y	?	Y	Y	Y
14 ***Molinari***	Y	Y	Y	Y	Y	Y	N	Y
15 ***Green***	Y	?	Y	Y	Y	Y	N	Y
16 Rangel	Y	Y	N	Y	Y	Y	Y	Y
17 Weiss	Y	?	N	Y	?	Y	Y	Y
18 Garcia	?	?	X	?	?	Y	Y	Y
19 Biaggi	Y	?	?	Y	?	Y	Y	Y
20 Ottinger	Y	?	N	Y	?	Y	Y	Y
21 ***Fish***	?	Y	Y	Y	Y	Y	Y	Y
22 ***Gilman***	Y	Y	Y	Y	Y	Y	Y	Y
23 Stratton	Y	Y	Y	Y	Y	Y	Y	Y
24 ***Solomon***	N	N	Y	N	N	Y	N	Y
25 ***Boehlert***	N	Y	Y	Y	Y	Y	Y	Y
26 ***Martin***	N	Y	Y	Y	Y	Y	Y	Y
27 ***Wortley***	N	Y	Y	Y	Y	Y	Y	?
28 McHugh	Y	Y	Y	Y	Y	Y	Y	Y
29 ***Horton***	?	Y	Y	Y	Y	Y	Y	Y
30 ***Conable***	N	Y	N	N	Y	Y	Y	Y
31 ***Kemp***	N	?	?	?	Y	Y	N	Y
32 LaFalce	Y	Y	Y	Y	Y	Y	Y	Y
33 Nowak	Y	Y	Y	Y	Y	Y	Y	Y
34 Lundine	Y	?	?	?	Y	Y	Y	Y
NORTH CAROLINA								
1 Jones	Y	Y	Y	Y	Y	Y	Y	Y
2 Valentine	?	Y	Y	Y	Y	Y	Y	Y
3 Whitley	Y	Y	Y	Y	Y	Y	Y	Y
4 Andrews	Y	Y	Y	Y	P	Y	Y	Y
5 Neal	Y	?	Y	Y	Y	Y	Y	Y
6 Britt	Y	Y	Y	Y	Y	Y	Y	Y
7 Rose	Y	?	?	?	Y	Y	Y	?
8 Hefner	Y	Y	Y	?	Y	Y	Y	Y
9 ***Martin***	?	?	?	?	Y	Y	Y	Y
10 ***Broyhill***	N	?	Y	N	Y	Y	N	Y
11 Clarke	Y	Y	?	?	Y	Y	Y	Y
NORTH DAKOTA								
AL Dorgan	Y	?	Y	Y	Y	Y	Y	Y
OHIO								
1 Luken	Y	Y	Y	Y	N	Y	N	Y
2 ***Gradison***	N	Y	Y	N	Y	Y	N	Y
3 Hall	Y	Y	Y	Y	Y	Y	Y	Y
4 ***Oxley***	?	Y	Y	Y	Y	Y	Y	Y
5 ***Latta***	N	?	?	?	Y	Y	N	Y
6 ***McEwen***	N	Y	Y	Y	Y	Y	Y	Y
7 ***DeWine***	N	Y	Y	Y	Y	Y	N	Y
8 ***Kindness***	?	Y	Y	Y	Y	Y	N	Y
9 Kaptur	Y	Y	Y	Y	Y	Y	Y	Y
10 ***Miller***	N	N	Y	Y	N	Y	Y	Y
11 Eckart	Y	Y	Y	Y	Y	Y	Y	Y
12 ***Kasich***	N	Y	Y	Y	Y	Y	Y	Y
13 Pease	Y	Y	Y	Y	Y	Y	Y	Y
14 Seiberling	Y	Y	N	Y	Y	Y	Y	Y
15 ***Wylie***	?	Y	Y	Y	Y	Y	Y	Y
16 ***Regula***	Y	Y	Y	Y	?	Y	Y	Y
17 ***Williams***	?	?	?	?	?	Y	Y	Y
18 Applegate	Y	?	Y	Y	?	Y	Y	Y
19 Feighan	Y	Y	Y	Y	Y	Y	Y	Y
20 Oakar	Y	Y	Y	Y	?	Y	Y	Y
21 Stokes	Y	Y	N	Y	Y	Y	Y	Y
OKLAHOMA								
1 Jones	Y	?	?	?	Y	Y	Y	Y
2 Synar	Y	Y	Y	?	Y	Y	Y	Y
3 Watkins	Y	Y	Y	?	Y	Y	Y	Y
4 McCurdy	Y	Y	Y	Y	Y	Y	Y	Y
5 ***Edwards***	N	Y	Y	Y	Y	Y	Y	Y
6 English	Y	Y	Y	Y	Y	Y	Y	Y
OREGON								
1 AuCoin	?	?	X	?	Y	Y	Y	?
2 ***Smith, R.***	N	?	?	?	Y	Y	Y	Y
3 Wyden	Y	?	?	?	Y	Y	Y	Y
4 Weaver	Y	Y	N	?	Y	Y	Y	Y
5 ***Smith, D.***	N	N	Y	N	N	N	Y	Y
PENNSYLVANIA								
1 Foglietta	Y	Y	Y	Y	Y	Y	Y	Y
2 Gray	Y	?	X	?	Y	Y	Y	Y
3 Borski	Y	Y	Y	Y	Y	Y	Y	Y
4 Kolter	Y	Y	Y	Y	Y	Y	N	Y
5 ***Schulze***	N	Y	Y	Y	Y	Y	Y	Y
6 Yatron	?	Y	Y	Y	Y	Y	N	Y
7 Edgar	Y	?	?	?	Y	Y	Y	Y
8 Kostmayer	Y	Y	Y	Y	Y	Y	N	Y
9 ***Shuster***	N	Y	Y	Y	Y	Y	Y	Y
10 ***McDade***	Y	?	?	?	Y	Y	Y	Y
11 Harrison	?	?	Y	Y	?	Y	Y	Y
12 Murtha	?	?	Y	Y	Y	Y	Y	Y
13 ***Coughlin***	N	N	Y	Y	N	Y	Y	Y
14 Coyne	Y	Y	Y	Y	Y	Y	N	Y
15 ***Ritter***	N	Y	Y	Y	Y	Y	Y	Y
16 ***Walker***	N	N	Y	N	N	Y	N	Y
17 ***Gekas***	N	Y	Y	Y	N	Y	N	Y
18 Walgren	Y	?	?	?	Y	Y	Y	Y
19 ***Goodling***	?	N	Y	Y	N	Y	Y	Y
20 Gaydos	Y	Y	Y	Y	Y	Y	Y	Y
21 ***Ridge***	N	Y	Y	N	Y	Y	Y	Y
22 Murphy	Y	Y	Y	?	Y	Y	N	Y
23 ***Clinger***	N	Y	+	+	Y	Y	Y	Y
RHODE ISLAND								
1 St Germain	Y	P	Y	Y	P	Y	Y	Y
2 ***Schneider***	?	Y	Y	Y	Y	Y	Y	Y
SOUTH CAROLINA								
1 ***Hartnett***	N	Y	?	?	Y	Y	N	Y
2 ***Spence***	N	Y	Y	N	Y	Y	Y	Y
3 Derrick	Y	Y	Y	Y	Y	Y	?	Y
4 ***Campbell***	N	?	Y	Y	Y	Y	Y	Y
5 Spratt	Y	Y	Y	Y	Y	Y	Y	Y
6 Tallon	Y	Y	Y	Y	?	Y	Y	Y
SOUTH DAKOTA								
AL Daschle	Y	?	?	?	Y	Y	Y	Y
TENNESSEE								
1 ***Quillen***	Y	Y	Y	?	Y	Y	Y	Y
2 ***Duncan***	Y	Y	Y	Y	Y	Y	N	Y
3 Lloyd	+	?	#	+	Y	Y	Y	Y
4 Cooper	Y	?	Y	Y	Y	Y	Y	Y
5 Boner	Y	Y	Y	Y	Y	Y	Y	Y
6 Gore	Y	Y	Y	?	Y	Y	Y	Y
7 ***Sundquist***	N	N	Y	N	?	Y	Y	Y
8 Jones	Y	Y	Y	Y	Y	Y	Y	Y
9 Ford	Y	?	Y	Y	Y	Y	Y	Y
TEXAS								
1 Hall, S.	N	Y	Y	Y	Y	Y	Y	Y
2 Wilson	Y	Y	Y	?	Y	Y	Y	Y
3 ***Bartlett***	N	Y	N	?	Y	Y	Y	N
4 Hall, R.	Y	Y	Y	Y	Y	Y	Y	Y
5 Bryant	?	?	?	?	Y	Y	Y	Y
6 ***Gramm***	?	?	?	?	?	Y	N	Y
7 ***Archer***	N	Y	Y	N	Y	Y	N	Y
8 ***Fields***	N	Y	Y	N	Y	Y	N	Y
9 Brooks	Y	?	Y	Y	Y	Y	Y	?
10 Pickle	?	Y	Y	Y	Y	Y	Y	Y
11 Leath	?	Y	Y	Y	Y	Y	Y	Y
12 Wright	Y	Y	Y	Y	Y	Y	Y	Y
13 Hightower	Y	Y	Y	Y	Y	Y	Y	Y
14 Patman	Y	Y	Y	Y	Y	Y	Y	Y
15 de la Garza	Y	Y	Y	Y	Y	Y	Y	Y
16 Coleman	Y	Y	Y	Y	Y	Y	Y	Y
17 Stenholm	Y	Y	Y	Y	Y	Y	Y	Y
18 Leland	?	?	N	Y	Y	Y	Y	Y
19 Hance	Y	Y	Y	Y	Y	Y	Y	Y
20 Gonzalez	Y	Y	Y	Y	Y	Y	N	Y
21 ***Loeffler***	N	Y	Y	N	Y	Y	Y	Y
22 ***Paul***	N	?	?	?	Y	N	N	N
23 Kazen	Y	Y	Y	Y	Y	Y	Y	Y
24 Frost	Y	?	?	?	?	?	?	Y
25 Andrews	Y	Y	Y	Y	Y	Y	Y	Y
26 Vandergriff	N	Y	Y	Y	Y	Y	Y	Y
27 Ortiz	Y	Y	Y	Y	Y	Y	Y	Y
UTAH								
1 ***Hansen***	N	Y	Y	N	Y	Y	Y	Y
2 ***Marriott***	?	?	?	?	Y	Y	Y	Y
3 ***Nielson***	N	Y	Y	N	Y	Y	Y	N
VERMONT								
AL ***Jeffords***	N	Y	Y	Y	?	Y	Y	Y
VIRGINIA								
1 ***Bateman***	N	Y	Y	N	Y	Y	Y	Y
2 ***Whitehurst***	?	Y	Y	?	Y	Y	N	Y
3 ***Bliley***	N	Y	Y	N	Y	Y	N	Y
4 Sisisky	Y	Y	Y	Y	Y	Y	Y	Y
5 Daniel	Y	Y	Y	Y	Y	Y	Y	Y
6 Olin	Y	Y	Y	Y	Y	Y	Y	Y
7 ***Robinson***	N	Y	Y	N	Y	Y	Y	Y
8 ***Parris***	N	Y	Y	Y	Y	Y	Y	Y
9 Boucher	Y	Y	Y	Y	Y	Y	Y	Y
10 ***Wolf***	N	Y	Y	Y	Y	Y	Y	Y
WASHINGTON								
1 ***Pritchard***	?	?	Y	Y	Y	Y	Y	Y
2 Swift	Y	Y	Y	Y	Y	Y	Y	Y
3 Bonker	?	?	Y	Y	Y	Y	Y	Y
4 ***Morrison***	N	Y	Y	Y	Y	Y	Y	Y
5 Foley	Y	?	?	?	?	Y	Y	Y
6 Dicks	Y	Y	Y	Y	Y	Y	Y	Y
7 Lowry	Y	N	Y	Y	N	Y	Y	Y
8 ***Chandler***	N	Y	Y	Y	Y	Y	Y	Y
WEST VIRGINIA								
1 Mollohan	Y	Y	Y	Y	?	Y	Y	Y
2 Staggers	Y	Y	Y	Y	Y	Y	Y	Y
3 Wise	+	Y	Y	Y	Y	Y	Y	Y
4 Rahall	+	Y	Y	Y	Y	Y	Y	Y
WISCONSIN								
1 Aspin	?	?	Y	Y	Y	Y	Y	Y
2 Kastenmeier	Y	Y	N	Y	Y	Y	Y	Y
3 ***Gunderson***	N	Y	Y	Y	Y	Y	Y	Y
4 Kleczka	Y	P	Y	Y	Y	Y	Y	Y
5 Moody	Y	?	N	Y	Y	Y	Y	Y
6 ***Petri***	N	Y	N	Y	Y	Y	N	Y
7 Obey	Y	Y	N	Y	Y	Y	Y	Y
8 ***Roth***	Y	?	Y	Y	Y	Y	Y	Y
9 ***Sensenbrenner***	?	?	?	?	?	?	?	?
WYOMING								
AL ***Cheney***	N	?	?	?	Y	N	Y	N

Southern states - Ala., Ark., Fla., Ga., Ky., La., Miss., N.C., Okla., S.C., Tenn., Texas, Va.

241. HR 5490. Civil Rights Act of 1984. Dannemeyer, R-Calif., appeal of the chair's ruling that the Bartlett, R-Texas, amendment declaring members of Congress to be recipients of federal financial assistance for coverage under the bill was out of order. Ruling of the chair upheld 277-125: R 24-124; D 253-1 (ND 167-1, SD 86-0), June 26, 1984.

242. HR 5490. Civil Rights Act of 1984. Siljander, R-Mich., amendment to define the word "person" under the Age Discrimination Act of 1975 to include unborn children from the moment of conception. Rejected 186-219: R 112-40; D 74-179 (ND 40-127, SD 34-52), June 26, 1984.

243. HR 5490. Civil Rights Act of 1984. Passage of the bill to make clear that the bar to discrimination in Title IX of the 1972 Education Act, Title VI of the Civil Rights Act of 1964, Section 504 of the Rehabilitation Act of 1973 and the Age Discrimination Act of 1975 covers an entire institution if any program or activity within the institution receives federal assistance. Passed 375-32: R 124-29; D 251-3 (ND 168-0, SD 83-3), June 26, 1984. A "nay" was a vote supporting the president's position.

244. Procedural Motion. McKernan, R-Maine, motion to approve the House *Journal* of Tuesday, June 26. Motion agreed to 358-35: R 133-21; D 225-14 (ND 143-12, SD 82-2), June 27, 1984.

245. HR 4170. Deficit Reduction. Adoption of the conference report on the bill to raise $50 billion in new taxes and to cut Medicare and other spending by about $13 billion through fiscal year 1987. Adopted 268-155: R 76-86; D 192-69 (ND 126-46, SD 66-23), June 27, 1984. A "yea" was a vote supporting the president's position.

KEY

Y	Voted for (yea).
#	Paired for.
+	Announced for.
N	Voted against (nay).
X	Paired against.
-	Announced against.
P	Voted "present".
C	Voted "present" to avoid possible conflict of interest.
?	Did not vote or otherwise make a position known.

Democrats   *Republicans*

	241	242	243	244	245
ALABAMA					
1 *Edwards*	Y	N	N	?	Y
2 *Dickinson*	N	N	Y	N	N
3 Nichols	Y	Y	Y	Y	N
4 Bevill	Y	Y	Y	Y	N
5 Flippo	Y	N	Y	Y	Y
6 Erdreich	Y	N	Y	N	Y
7 Shelby	Y	Y	Y	Y	N
ALASKA					
AL *Young*	N	Y	Y	?	Y
ARIZONA					
1 *McCain*	N	Y	N	Y	N
2 Udall	Y	N	Y	Y	Y
3 *Stump*	N	Y	N	Y	N
4 *Rudd*	N	Y	N	Y	N
5 McNulty	Y	N	Y	Y	Y
ARKANSAS					
1 Alexander	Y	N	Y	Y	Y
2 *Bethune*	N	Y	Y	Y	N
3 *Hammerschmidt*	N	?	Y	Y	N
4 Anthony	?	?	Y	Y	Y
CALIFORNIA					
1 Bosco	Y	N	Y	Y	Y
2 *Chappie*	N	Y	Y	N	N
3 Matsui	Y	N	Y	Y	Y
4 Fazio	Y	N	Y	Y	Y
5 Burton	Y	N	Y	Y	Y
6 Boxer	Y	N	Y	Y	Y
7 Miller	Y	N	Y	Y	Y
8 Dellums	Y	N	Y	N	N
9 Stark	Y	N	Y	?	Y
10 Edwards	Y	N	Y	Y	Y
11 Lantos	Y	N	Y	Y	Y
12 *Zschau*	N	N	Y	Y	Y
13 Mineta	Y	N	Y	Y	Y
14 *Shumway*	N	Y	N	Y	N
15 Coelho	Y	N	Y	Y	Y
16 Panetta	Y	N	Y	Y	Y
17 *Pashayan*	N	N	Y	Y	N
18 Lehman	Y	N	Y	Y	Y
19 *Lagomarsino*	N	Y	Y	Y	N
20 *Thomas*	Y	N	Y	Y	Y
21 *Fiedler*	N	N	Y	Y	N
22 *Moorhead*	N	Y	N	Y	N
23 Beilenson	Y	N	Y	Y	Y
24 Waxman	Y	N	Y	Y	Y
25 Roybal	Y	N	Y	Y	Y
26 Berman	Y	N	Y	Y	Y
27 Levine	Y	N	Y	Y	Y
28 Dixon	Y	N	Y	Y	Y
29 Hawkins	Y	N	Y	?	N
30 Martinez	Y	N	Y	Y	Y
31 Dymally	?	?	?	?	X
32 Anderson	Y	N	Y	Y	N
33 *Dreier*	N	Y	Y	Y	N
34 Torres	Y	N	Y	N	Y
35 *Lewis*	?	Y	Y	?	N
36 Brown	Y	N	Y	?	Y
37 *McCandless*	N	N	Y	Y	N
38 Patterson	Y	?	Y	?	Y
39 *Dannemeyer*	N	Y	N	Y	N
40 *Badham*	N	Y	N	Y	N
41 Lowery	N	Y	Y	?	N
42 Lungren	?	?	?	Y	N

	241	242	243	244	245
43 *Packard*	N	Y	N	Y	Y
44 Bates	Y	N	Y	Y	Y
45 *Hunter*	N	Y	?	Y	N
COLORADO					
1 Schroeder	Y	N	Y	N	N
2 Wirth	Y	N	Y	Y	Y
3 Kogovsek	?	?	?	?	?
4 *Brown*	N	N	Y	N	N
5 *Kramer*	N	N	Y	Y	N
6 *Schaefer*	N	Y	Y	Y	Y
CONNECTICUT					
1 Kennelly	Y	N	Y	Y	Y
2 Gejdenson	Y	N	Y	N	Y
3 Morrison	Y	N	Y	Y	Y
4 *McKinney*	?	?	?	?	?
5 Ratchford	Y	N	Y	Y	Y
6 *Johnson*	N	N	Y	Y	Y
DELAWARE					
AL Carper	Y	N	Y	Y	Y
FLORIDA					
1 Hutto	Y	Y	Y	Y	Y
2 Fuqua	Y	Y	Y	Y	Y
3 Bennett	Y	Y	Y	Y	Y
4 Chappell	Y	N	Y	?	Y
5 *McCollum*	N	Y	Y	Y	N
6 MacKay	Y	N	Y	Y	Y
7 Gibbons	Y	Y	Y	Y	Y
8 *Young*	N	Y	Y	N	N
9 *Bilirakis*	N	Y	Y	Y	N
10 Ireland	?	?	?	?	Y
11 Nelson	Y	Y	Y	Y	Y
12 *Lewis*	N	Y	Y	Y	N
13 *Mack*	N	Y	Y	N	N
14 Mica	Y	Y	Y	Y	Y
15 *Shaw*	N	Y	Y	Y	N
16 Smith	Y	N	Y	Y	Y
17 Lehman	Y	N	?	Y	Y
18 Pepper	Y	N	Y	Y	Y
19 Fascell	Y	N	Y	Y	Y
GEORGIA					
1 Thomas	Y	N	Y	Y	Y
2 Hatcher	Y	N	Y	Y	Y
3 Ray	Y	Y	Y	Y	Y
4 Levitas	Y	N	Y	Y	N
5 Fowler	Y	N	Y	Y	Y
6 *Gingrich*	N	Y	Y	?	?
7 Darden	Y	N	Y	Y	N
8 Rowland	Y	N	Y	Y	Y
9 Jenkins	Y	N	Y	Y	Y
10 Barnard	?	?	?	Y	N
HAWAII					
1 Heftel	Y	N	Y	?	Y
2 Akaka	Y	N	?	Y	#
IDAHO					
1 *Craig*	N	Y	Y	Y	N
2 *Hansen*	?	?	?	?	?
ILLINOIS					
1 Hayes	Y	N	Y	N	Y
2 Savage	Y	N	Y	Y	N
3 Russo	Y	Y	Y	Y	Y
4 *O'Brien*	N	Y	Y	Y	Y
5 Lipinski	Y	Y	Y	N	Y
6 *Hyde*	N	Y	Y	Y	N
7 Collins	Y	N	Y	Y	Y
8 Rostenkowski	Y	Y	Y	Y	Y
9 Yates	?	N	Y	Y	Y
10 *Porter*	N	N	Y	Y	Y
11 Annunzio	Y	Y	Y	Y	Y
12 *Crane, P.*	N	Y	N	Y	N
13 *Erlenborn*	?	?	?	?	?
14 *Corcoran*	?	Y	Y	Y	Y
15 *Madigan*	N	Y	Y	Y	Y
16 *Martin*	N	N	Y	Y	N
17 Evans	Y	N	Y	Y	Y
18 *Michel*	Y	Y	Y	Y	Y
19 *Crane, D.*	N	Y	N	Y	N
20 Durbin	Y	Y	Y	N	Y
21 Price	?	?	?	Y	Y
22 Simon	Y	N	Y	Y	Y
INDIANA					
1 Hall	Y	N	Y	Y	N
2 Sharp	Y	N	Y	Y	Y
3 *Hiler*	N	Y	Y	N	N
4 *Coats*	N	Y	N	Y	N
5 *Hillis*	N	Y	Y	Y	Y

	241	242	243	244	245
6 Burton	N	Y	N	Y	N
7 Myers	Y	Y	Y	Y	N
8 McCloskey	Y	N	Y	Y	Y
9 Hamilton	Y	Y	Y	Y	Y
10 Jacobs	N	N	Y	N	Y
IOWA					
1 Leach	Y	N	Y	Y	Y
2 Tauke	N	Y	Y	Y	Y
3 Evans	N	Y	Y	N	Y
4 Smith	Y	N	Y	Y	Y
5 Harkin	Y	N	Y	N	Y
6 Bedell	Y	N	Y	Y	Y
KANSAS					
1 Roberts	N	N	N	N	N
2 Slattery	Y	N	Y	Y	N
3 Winn	N	Y	Y	Y	Y
4 Glickman	Y	N	Y	Y	Y
5 Whittaker	N	N	Y	Y	Y
KENTUCKY					
1 Hubbard	Y	N	Y	Y	N
2 Natcher	Y	Y	Y	Y	N
3 Mazzoli	Y	Y	Y	Y	Y
4 Snyder	Y	Y	Y	Y	Y
5 Rogers	N	Y	Y	Y	N
6 Hopkins	N	Y	Y	Y	N
7 Perkins	Y	Y	Y	Y	Y
LOUISIANA					
1 Livingston	N	Y	N	Y	N
2 Boggs	Y	Y	Y	Y	Y
3 Tauzin	Y	Y	Y	Y	N
4 Roemer	Y	N	Y	N	Y
5 Huckaby	Y	N	Y	Y	Y
6 Moore	N	Y	Y	Y	Y
7 Breaux	Y	Y	Y	Y	Y
8 Long	Y	Y	Y	Y	Y
MAINE					
1 McKernan	N	N	Y	Y	Y
2 Snowe	Y	N	Y	Y	Y
MARYLAND					
1 Dyson	Y	Y	Y	Y	N
2 Long	Y	N	Y	Y	Y
3 Mikulski	Y	N	Y	Y	Y
4 Holt	N	Y	Y	Y	Y
5 Hoyer	Y	N	Y	Y	Y
6 Byron	Y	Y	Y	Y	N
7 Mitchell	Y	N	Y	N	N
8 Barnes	Y	N	Y	Y	Y
MASSACHUSETTS					
1 Conte	Y	Y	Y	Y	Y
2 Boland	Y	Y	Y	Y	Y
3 Early	Y	Y	Y	Y	N
4 Frank	Y	N	Y	?	?
5 Shannon	?	?	?	?	Y
6 Mavroules	Y	Y	Y	Y	Y
7 Markey	Y	N	Y	Y	N
8 O'Neill					
9 Moakley	Y	Y	Y	Y	Y
10 Studds	Y	N	Y	Y	Y
11 Donnelly	Y	Y	Y	Y	Y
MICHIGAN					
1 Conyers	Y	N	Y	N	Y
2 Pursell	N	N	Y	?	N
3 Wolpe	Y	N	Y	Y	Y
4 Siljander	N	Y	N	Y	N
5 Sawyer	N	N	Y	Y	Y
6 Carr	Y	N	Y	Y	N
7 Kildee	Y	Y	Y	Y	Y
8 Traxler	Y	Y	Y	Y	N
9 Vander Jagt	?	?	?	Y	N
10 Albosta	Y	?	+	Y	N
11 Davis	Y	Y	Y	Y	N
12 Bonior	?	?	?	Y	Y
13 Crockett	Y	N	Y	Y	Y
14 Hertel	Y	Y	Y	Y	N
15 Ford	Y	N	Y	?	Y
16 Dingell	Y	N	Y	?	Y
17 Levin	Y	N	Y	Y	C
18 Broomfield	N	Y	Y	Y	N
MINNESOTA					
1 Penny	Y	N	Y	N	Y
2 Weber	N	Y	Y	N	N
3 Frenzel	?	?	Y	N	Y
4 Vento	Y	N	Y	Y	Y
5 Sabo	Y	N	Y	N	Y
6 Sikorski	Y	Y	Y	N	N

	241	242	243	244	245
7 Stangeland	N	Y	Y	Y	N
8 Oberstar	Y	Y	Y	P	Y
MISSISSIPPI					
1 Whitten	Y	Y	Y	?	N
2 Franklin	N	Y	Y	Y	N
3 Montgomery	Y	Y	N	Y	Y
4 Dowdy	Y	Y	Y	Y	Y
5 Lott	N	Y	N	Y	N
MISSOURI					
1 Clay	Y	N	Y	?	N
2 Young	Y	Y	Y	Y	Y
3 Gephardt	Y	?	Y	Y	Y
4 Skelton	Y	Y	Y	Y	Y
5 Wheat	Y	N	Y	Y	Y
6 Coleman	Y	N	Y	Y	N
7 Taylor	N	Y	Y	Y	N
8 Emerson	N	Y	Y	N	N
9 Volkmer	Y	Y	Y	Y	N
MONTANA					
1 Williams	Y	N	Y	?	N
2 Marlenee	N	Y	N	Y	N
NEBRASKA					
1 Bereuter	N	Y	Y	Y	Y
2 Daub	N	Y	Y	Y	Y
3 Smith	N	Y	Y	Y	Y
NEVADA					
1 Reid	Y	Y	Y	Y	Y
2 Vucanovich	N	Y	Y	Y	N
NEW HAMPSHIRE					
1 D'Amours	Y	N	Y	N	Y
2 Gregg	N	Y	Y	Y	Y
NEW JERSEY					
1 Florio	Y	N	Y	Y	Y
2 Hughes	Y	N	Y	Y	Y
3 Howard	Y	N	Y	Y	Y
4 Smith	N	Y	Y	Y	Y
5 Roukema	Y	N	Y	Y	Y
6 Dwyer	Y	N	Y	Y	Y
7 Rinaldo	Y	Y	Y	Y	Y
8 Roe	Y	Y	Y	Y	Y
9 Torricelli	Y	N	Y	Y	N
10 Rodino	Y	N	Y	N	Y
11 Minish	Y	Y	Y	Y	Y
12 Courter	N	Y	Y	Y	N
13 Vacancy					
14 Guarini	Y	N	Y	Y	N
NEW MEXICO					
1 Lujan	N	Y	Y	Y	N
2 Skeen	N	N	Y	Y	N
3 Richardson	Y	N	Y	Y	Y
NEW YORK					
1 Carney	N	Y	Y	Y	N
2 Downey	Y	N	Y	Y	Y
3 Mrazek	?	?	?	Y	Y
4 Lent	?	?	Y	Y	Y
5 McGrath	?	?	Y	Y	Y
6 Addabbo	Y	N	Y	Y	Y
7 Ackerman	Y	N	Y	Y	Y
8 Scheuer	Y	N	Y	Y	Y
9 Ferraro	Y	N	Y	Y	Y
10 Schumer	Y	N	Y	Y	N
11 Towns	?	?	?	?	N
12 Owens	Y	N	Y	Y	N
13 Solarz	Y	N	Y	Y	Y
14 Molinari	N	Y	Y	Y	N
15 Green	Y	N	Y	Y	Y
16 Rangel	Y	N	Y	Y	Y
17 Weiss	Y	N	Y	Y	N
18 Garcia	Y	N	Y	Y	Y
19 Biaggi	Y	N	Y	Y	Y
20 Ottinger	Y	N	Y	?	N
21 Fish	Y	N	Y	Y	Y
22 Gilman	Y	N	Y	Y	Y
23 Stratton	Y	N	Y	Y	Y
24 Solomon	N	Y	Y	N	N
25 Boehlert	Y	N	Y	Y	Y
26 Martin	N	Y	Y	?	Y
27 Wortley	?	?	?	Y	Y
28 McHugh	Y	N	Y	Y	Y
29 Horton	Y	N	Y	Y	Y
30 Conable	Y	N	Y	Y	Y
31 Kemp	?	Y	Y	Y	N
32 LaFalce	Y	N	Y	Y	Y
33 Nowak	Y	N	Y	Y	Y
34 Lundine	Y	N	Y	?	Y

	241	242	243	244	245
NORTH CAROLINA					
1 Jones	Y	N	Y	Y	Y
2 Valentine	Y	N	Y	Y	Y
3 Whitley	Y	N	Y	Y	Y
4 Andrews	Y	N	Y	Y	Y
5 Neal	Y	N	Y	Y	Y
6 Britt	Y	N	Y	Y	Y
7 Rose	?	?	?	Y	Y
8 Hefner	Y	N	Y	Y	Y
9 Martin	N	N	Y	Y	Y
10 Broyhill	Y	N	Y	Y	Y
11 Clarke	Y	N	Y	Y	Y
NORTH DAKOTA					
AL Dorgan	Y	Y	Y	Y	Y
OHIO					
1 Luken	Y	Y	Y	Y	Y
2 Gradison	N	Y	Y	Y	N
3 Hall	Y	N	Y	N	N
4 Oxley	N	N	Y	N	Y
5 Latta	N	Y	Y	Y	N
6 McEwen	N	Y	Y	N	N
7 DeWine	N	Y	Y	Y	Y
8 Kindness	?	Y	N	Y	Y
9 Kaptur	Y	N	Y	N	N
10 Miller	N	Y	N	Y	N
11 Eckart	Y	N	Y	N	Y
12 Kasich	N	Y	Y	N	N
13 Pease	Y	N	Y	Y	N
14 Seiberling	Y	N	Y	Y	Y
15 Wylie	N	Y	Y	N	N
16 Regula	N	Y	Y	Y	Y
17 Williams	N	Y	Y	Y	N
18 Applegate	Y	Y	Y	N	N
19 Feighan	Y	N	Y	Y	Y
20 Oakar	Y	Y	Y	Y	Y
21 Stokes	Y	N	Y	Y	Y
OKLAHOMA					
1 Jones	Y	N	Y	Y	Y
2 Synar	Y	N	Y	Y	Y
3 Watkins	Y	N	Y	Y	Y
4 McCurdy	Y	N	Y	Y	Y
5 Edwards	N	Y	Y	N	N
6 English	Y	Y	Y	Y	N
OREGON					
1 AuCoin	Y	N	Y	?	Y
2 Smith, R.	N	Y	Y	Y	N
3 Wyden	Y	N	Y	Y	Y
4 Weaver	Y	N	Y	?	Y
5 Smith, D.	N	Y	N	N	N
PENNSYLVANIA					
1 Foglietta	Y	N	Y	Y	Y
2 Gray	Y	N	Y	Y	Y
3 Borski	Y	Y	Y	Y	Y
4 Kolter	Y	Y	Y	Y	Y
5 Schulze	?	?	?	Y	Y
6 Yatron	Y	Y	Y	Y	N
7 Edgar	Y	N	Y	Y	Y
8 Kostmayer	Y	N	Y	Y	Y
9 Shuster	N	Y	N	Y	N
10 McDade	?	?	?	Y	Y
11 Harrison	Y	N	Y	?	Y
12 Murtha	Y	Y	Y	Y	Y
13 Coughlin	Y	N	Y	N	Y
14 Coyne	Y	N	Y	Y	Y
15 Ritter	N	Y	Y	Y	N
16 Walker	N	Y	N	N	N
17 Gekas	N	N	Y	N	Y
18 Walgren	Y	N	Y	Y	Y
19 Goodling	N	Y	N	N	N
20 Gaydos	Y	Y	Y	?	N
21 Ridge	N	N	Y	Y	N
22 Murphy	Y	Y	Y	Y	N
23 Clinger	N	Y	Y	Y	N
RHODE ISLAND					
1 St Germain	Y	Y	Y	P	Y
2 Schneider	N	N	Y	Y	Y
SOUTH CAROLINA					
1 Hartnett	N	Y	N	Y	N
2 Spence	N	Y	Y	Y	Y
3 Derrick	Y	N	Y	Y	Y
4 Campbell	?	?	?	Y	Y
5 Spratt	Y	N	Y	Y	Y
6 Tallon	Y	N	Y	Y	Y
SOUTH DAKOTA					
AL Daschle	Y	Y	Y	Y	Y

	241	242	243	244	245
TENNESSEE					
1 Quillen	Y	Y	Y	Y	Y
2 Duncan	N	Y	Y	Y	Y
3 Lloyd	Y	Y	Y	Y	Y
4 Cooper	Y	Y	Y	Y	Y
5 Boner	Y	N	Y	Y	Y
6 Gore	Y	Y	Y	Y	Y
7 Sundquist	N	Y	Y	Y	N
8 Jones	Y	N	Y	Y	Y
9 Ford	Y	N	Y	?	Y
TEXAS					
1 Hall, S.	Y	Y	N	Y	N
2 Wilson	Y	N	Y	?	Y
3 Bartlett	N	Y	Y	Y	Y
4 Hall, R.	Y	Y	Y	Y	N
5 Bryant	Y	N	Y	?	Y
6 Gramm	N	Y	Y	Y	N
7 Archer	N	Y	N	Y	N
8 Fields	N	Y	N	N	N
9 Brooks	Y	N	Y	Y	+
10 Pickle	Y	N	Y	Y	Y
11 Leath	Y	Y	Y	Y	Y
12 Wright	Y	N	Y	Y	Y
13 Hightower	Y	Y	Y	Y	Y
14 Patman	Y	Y	Y	Y	N
15 de la Garza	Y	Y	Y	Y	Y
16 Coleman	Y	N	Y	Y	N
17 Stenholm	Y	Y	Y	N	Y
18 Leland	Y	N	Y	Y	Y
19 Hance	Y	N	Y	Y	Y
20 Gonzalez	Y	N	Y	Y	N
21 Loeffler	N	Y	N	Y	N
22 Paul	N	Y	N	Y	N
23 Kazen	Y	Y	Y	Y	Y
24 Frost	Y	N	Y	Y	Y
25 Andrews	Y	N	Y	Y	Y
26 Vandergriff	Y	N	Y	Y	N
27 Ortiz	Y	Y	Y	Y	Y
UTAH					
1 Hansen	N	Y	N	Y	Y
2 Marriott	N	Y	Y	Y	Y
3 Nielson	N	Y	N	N	N
VERMONT					
AL Jeffords	N	N	Y	Y	Y
VIRGINIA					
1 Bateman	Y	N	N	Y	Y
2 Whitehurst	N	Y	Y	?	Y
3 Bliley	N	Y	Y	Y	Y
4 Sisisky	Y	N	Y	Y	Y
5 Daniel	Y	Y	N	Y	N
6 Olin	Y	N	Y	Y	Y
7 Robinson	N	Y	N	Y	Y
8 Parris	?	Y	Y	N	N
9 Boucher	Y	N	Y	Y	N
10 Wolf	N	Y	Y	Y	Y
WASHINGTON					
1 Pritchard	Y	N	Y	Y	Y
2 Swift	C	N	Y	Y	Y
3 Bonker	Y	N	Y	Y	Y
4 Morrison	N	N	Y	Y	Y
5 Foley	Y	N	Y	Y	Y
6 Dicks	Y	N	Y	Y	Y
7 Lowry	Y	N	Y	Y	Y
8 Chandler	N	N	Y	Y	Y
WEST VIRGINIA					
1 Mollohan	Y	Y	Y	Y	Y
2 Staggers	Y	Y	Y	Y	Y
3 Wise	Y	N	Y	Y	Y
4 Rahall	Y	Y	Y	Y	Y
WISCONSIN					
1 Aspin	Y	N	Y	Y	Y
2 Kastenmeier	Y	N	Y	Y	Y
3 Gunderson	Y	N	Y	Y	Y
4 Kleczka	Y	Y	Y	Y	Y
5 Moody	Y	N	Y	Y	Y
6 Petri	N	Y	Y	Y	N
7 Obey	Y	N	Y	Y	Y
8 Roth	N	Y	Y	Y	Y
9 Sensenbrenner	?	?	?	?	?
WYOMING					
AL Cheney	N	Y	Y	Y	Y

Southern states - Ala., Ark., Fla., Ga., Ky., La., Miss., N.C., Okla., S.C., Tenn., Texas, Va.

246. HR 5653. Energy and Water Development Appropriations, Fiscal 1985. Adoption of the conference report on the bill to appropriate $15,371,359,000 in fiscal 1985 for energy and water development. Adopted 400-23: R 143-17; D 257-6 (ND 167-6, SD 90-0), June 27, 1984. The president had requested $15,874,791,000 in new budget authority.

247. HR 5798. Treasury, Postal Service and General Government Appropriations, Fiscal 1985. Boxer, D-Calif., amendment to strike language from the bill that would prohibit the use of federal employee health insurance to pay for an abortion except when the life of the mother is endangered. Rejected 156-261: R 23-135; D 133-126 (ND 100-70, SD 33-56), June 27, 1984.

248. HR 5798. Treasury, Postal Service and General Government Appropriations, Fiscal 1985. Ratchford, D-Conn., amendment to reduce appropriations in the bill by 1 percent across-the-board except for salaries and expenses for the White House, the Office of Administration and the Office of Management and Budget, all in the Executive Office of the President. Adopted 345-66: R 150-5; D 195-61 (ND 113-53, SD 82-8), June 27, 1984.

249. HR 5798. Treasury, Postal Service and General Government Appropriations, Fiscal 1985. Obey, D-Wis., amendment to reduce by 63 percent all appropriations in the bill not required by previously enacted law. Rejected 10-389: R 4-149; D 6-240 (ND 5-154, SD 1-86), June 27, 1984.

250. HR 5798. Treasury, Postal Service and General Government Appropriations, Fiscal 1985. Jacobs, D-Ind., amendment to reduce by $890,000 the $1.17 million appropriation in the bill for pension, salary and staff of former presidents. Rejected 180-232: R 50-108; D 130-124 (ND 86-82, SD 44-42), June 27, 1984.

251. HR 5798. Treasury, Postal Service and General Government Appropriations, Fiscal 1985. Nelson, D-Fla., amendment to reduce by $147,100 the $1.17 million appropriation in the bill for pension, salary and staff of former presidents. Adopted 347-59: R 128-28; D 219-31 (ND 141-23, SD 78-8), June 27, 1984.

252. HR 5798. Treasury, Postal Service and General Government Appropriations, Fiscal 1985. Passage of the bill to provide fiscal 1985 appropriations of $11,896,587,701 for the Treasury Department, U.S. Postal Service, Executive Office of the President and other agencies. Passed 313-98: R 80-77; D 233-21 (ND 155-10, SD 78-11), June 27, 1984. The president had requested $12,349,687,000 in new budget authority.

253. HR 5898. Military Construction Appropriations, Fiscal 1985. Adoption of the rule (H Res 532) providing for House floor consideration of the bill to appropriate $8,258,471,037 for military construction projects of the Department of Defense in fiscal 1985. Adopted 366-35: R 122-33; D 244-2 (ND 157-2, SD 87-0), June 27, 1984.

KEY

Y Voted for (yea).
\# Paired for.
\+ Announced for.
N Voted against (nay).
X Paired against.
− Announced against.
P Voted "present".
C Voted "present" to avoid possible conflict of interest.
? Did not vote or otherwise make a position known.

Democrats   *Republicans*

	246	247	248	249	250	251	252	253
ALABAMA								
1 *Edwards*	Y	N	Y	N	N	?	?	?
2 *Dickinson*	Y	N	Y	N	Y	Y	N	Y
3 Nichols	Y	N	Y	N	Y	Y	Y	Y
4 Bevill	Y	N	Y	N	Y	Y	Y	Y
5 Flippo	Y	N	Y	N	Y	Y	Y	Y
6 Erdreich	Y	N	Y	N	Y	Y	N	Y
7 Shelby	Y	N	Y	N	Y	Y	N	Y
ALASKA								
AL *Young*	Y	N	Y	N	N	Y	Y	Y
ARIZONA								
1 *McCain*	Y	N	Y	N	Y	N	Y	Y
2 Udall	Y	Y	?	?	N	Y	Y	Y
3 *Stump*	Y	N	Y	N	N	Y	N	Y
4 *Rudd*	Y	N	Y	N	N	Y	Y	Y
5 McNulty	Y	Y	Y	N	Y	Y	Y	Y
ARKANSAS								
1 Alexander	Y	N	N	Y	N	Y	Y	Y
2 *Bethune*	Y	N	Y	N	Y	Y	N	Y
3 *Hammerschmidt*	Y	N	Y	N	Y	Y	Y	Y
4 Anthony	Y	Y	Y	N	Y	Y	Y	Y
CALIFORNIA								
1 Bosco	Y	Y	Y	N	N	?	Y	?
2 *Chappie*	Y	N	Y	N	Y	Y	Y	Y
3 Matsui	Y	Y	Y	N	Y	Y	Y	Y
4 Fazio	Y	N	N	N	Y	Y	Y	Y
5 Burton	Y	Y	Y	N	Y	Y	Y	Y
6 Boxer	Y	Y	Y	N	Y	Y	Y	Y
7 Miller	Y	Y	N	N	Y	Y	Y	Y
8 Dellums	Y	Y	Y	N	Y	Y	Y	Y
9 Stark	Y	Y	Y	N	Y	Y	?	?
10 Edwards	Y	Y	Y	N	Y	Y	Y	Y
11 Lantos	Y	Y	Y	N	Y	Y	Y	Y
12 *Zschau*	Y	Y	Y	N	Y	Y	N	N
13 Mineta	Y	Y	Y	N	Y	Y	Y	Y
14 *Shumway*	Y	N	Y	N	Y	N	Y	N
15 Coelho	Y	Y	Y	N	Y	Y	Y	Y
16 Panetta	Y	Y	Y	N	Y	Y	Y	Y
17 *Pashayan*	Y	N	Y	N	N	Y	N	Y
18 Lehman	Y	Y	Y	N	Y	Y	Y	Y
19 *Lagomarsino*	Y	N	Y	N	N	Y	N	Y
20 *Thomas*	Y	Y	Y	Y	Y	Y	N	N
21 *Fiedler*	Y	Y	Y	N	Y	Y	Y	Y
22 *Moorhead*	Y	N	Y	N	N	Y	N	Y
23 Beilenson	Y	Y	Y	N	N	Y	Y	Y
24 Waxman	?	Y	Y	N	N	Y	?	
25 Roybal	Y	Y	N	N	Y	Y	Y	Y
26 Berman	Y	Y	N	?	N	N	Y	Y
27 Levine	Y	Y	Y	N	Y	Y	Y	Y
28 Dixon	?	Y	N	N	N	Y	Y	Y
29 Hawkins	Y	?	?	?	N	N	Y	?
30 Martinez	Y	?	Y	N	Y	Y	Y	Y
31 Dymally	?	\#	?	?	?	?	?	?
32 Anderson	Y	Y	N	N	Y	Y	Y	Y
33 *Dreier*	N	N	Y	N	Y	N	N	N
34 Torres	Y	Y	Y	?	?	Y	N	?
35 *Lewis*	Y	N	Y	N	N	N	Y	Y
36 Brown	Y	Y	Y	N	N	Y	Y	?
37 *McCandless*	N	N	Y	N	N	Y	N	Y
38 Patterson	Y	Y	Y	?	Y	?	?	Y
39 *Dannemeyer*	N	N	Y	N	Y	N	N	N
40 *Badham*	Y	N	Y	N	N	N	N	?
41 Lowery	Y	N	?	N	N	Y	Y	Y
42 *Lungren*	Y	N	Y	N	N	Y	N	Y

	246	247	248	249	250	251	252	253
43 *Packard*	Y	N	Y	N	N	Y	N	Y
44 Bates	Y	Y	Y	Y	Y	Y	Y	Y
45 *Hunter*	Y	N	Y	N	N	Y	Y	Y
COLORADO								
1 Schroeder	Y	Y	Y	?	?	?	?	?
2 Wirth	Y	Y	Y	N	N	Y	Y	Y
3 Kogovsek	?	Y	Y	N	Y	Y	Y	Y
4 *Brown*	Y	Y	Y	Y	Y	Y	N	N
5 *Kramer*	Y	N	Y	Y	Y	Y	N	Y
6 *Schaefer*	Y	N	Y	N	Y	Y	N	N
CONNECTICUT								
1 Kennelly	Y	Y	N	N	Y	Y	Y	Y
2 Gejdenson	Y	Y	N	N	Y	Y	Y	Y
3 Morrison	N	Y	N	N	Y	Y	Y	Y
4 *McKinney*	Y	Y	N	N	N	N	Y	Y
5 Ratchford	Y	Y	Y	N	Y	Y	Y	Y
6 *Johnson*	Y	Y	Y	N	N	Y	Y	Y
DELAWARE								
AL Carper	Y	Y	Y	N	Y	Y	Y	Y
FLORIDA								
1 Hutto	Y	N	Y	N	Y	Y	Y	Y
2 Fuqua	Y	N	Y	N	N	Y	Y	?
3 Bennett	Y	N	Y	N	Y	Y	Y	Y
4 Chappell	Y	N	Y	N	Y	Y	Y	Y
5 *McCollum*	Y	N	Y	N	N	Y	N	Y
6 MacKay	Y	Y	Y	N	Y	Y	Y	Y
7 Gibbons	Y	N	Y	N	Y	Y	Y	Y
8 *Young*	Y	N	Y	N	N	Y	N	Y
9 *Bilirakis*	Y	N	Y	N	Y	Y	Y	Y
10 Ireland	Y	N	Y	?	?	Y	Y	Y
11 Nelson	Y	N	Y	N	Y	Y	Y	Y
12 *Lewis*	Y	N	Y	N	N	Y	Y	Y
13 *Mack*	Y	N	Y	?	Y	Y	N	N
14 Mica	Y	N	Y	Y	Y	Y	Y	Y
15 *Shaw*	+	N	N	Y	N	N	Y	Y
16 Smith	Y	Y	N	N	?	?	Y	?
17 Lehman	Y	Y	Y	N	N	Y	Y	Y
18 Pepper	Y	N	N	N	?	N	Y	Y
19 Fascell	Y	Y	N	N	N	N	Y	Y
GEORGIA								
1 Thomas	Y	Y	Y	N	N	Y	Y	Y
2 Hatcher	Y	Y	Y	N	N	Y	N	Y
3 Ray	Y	N	Y	N	N	Y	N	Y
4 Levitas	Y	Y	Y	N	Y	Y	Y	Y
5 Fowler	Y	Y	N	N	Y	Y	Y	Y
6 *Gingrich*	Y	N	Y	?	Y	Y	N	Y
7 Darden	Y	Y	N	N	Y	Y	Y	Y
8 Rowland	Y	Y	Y	N	Y	Y	Y	Y
9 Jenkins	Y	N	Y	N	Y	Y	Y	Y
10 Barnard	Y	N	Y	N	N	Y	Y	Y
HAWAII								
1 Heftel	Y	N	Y	N	Y	Y	Y	Y
2 Akaka	Y	Y	N	N	N	Y	Y	Y
IDAHO								
1 *Craig*	Y	N	Y	N	N	Y	N	N
2 *Hansen*	?	?	?	?	?	?	?	?
ILLINOIS								
1 Hayes	Y	Y	N	N	Y	Y	Y	Y
2 Savage	Y	Y	N	?	N	Y	Y	Y
3 Russo	Y	N	N	N	N	Y	N	Y
4 *O'Brien*	Y	N	Y	N	N	Y	Y	Y
5 Lipinski	Y	N	Y	N	N	Y	Y	Y
6 *Hyde*	Y	N	Y	N	Y	Y	Y	Y
7 Collins	Y	Y	N	N	Y	Y	Y	Y
8 Rostenkowski	Y	N	N	N	N	Y	Y	Y
9 Yates	Y	Y	N	N	Y	Y	Y	Y
10 *Porter*	Y	N	Y	N	N	Y	Y	Y
11 Annunzio	Y	N	N	N	Y	Y	Y	Y
12 *Crane, P.*	N	N	Y	N	Y	N	N	N
13 *Erlenborn*	?	?	?	?	?	?	?	?
14 *Corcoran*	Y	N	Y	?	N	Y	Y	Y
15 *Madigan*	Y	N	Y	N	N	Y	Y	Y
16 *Martin*	Y	Y	Y	N	N	Y	N	N
17 Evans	Y	Y	Y	N	Y	Y	Y	Y
18 *Michel*	Y	N	Y	N	N	N	Y	Y
19 *Crane, D.*	N	N	Y	N	Y	N	N	N
20 Durbin	Y	N	Y	N	Y	Y	Y	Y
21 Price	Y	N	Y	N	N	Y	Y	Y
22 Simon	Y	?	?	?	?	?	?	?
INDIANA								
1 Hall	Y	Y	N	N	N	N	Y	Y
2 Sharp	Y	N	Y	N	Y	N	Y	Y
3 *Hiler*	Y	N	Y	N	N	N	Y	Y
4 *Coats*	Y	N	Y	N	N	Y	N	Y
5 Hillis	Y	N	Y	N	N	Y	Y	Y

ND - Northern Democrats   SD - Southern Democrats

Corresponding to Congressional Record Votes 273, 275, 276, 277, 278, 279, 280, 281

	246	247	248	249	250	251	252	253
6 ***Burton***	Y	N	Y	N	Y	Y	N	N
7 ***Myers***	Y	N	Y	N	N	Y	Y	Y
8 McCloskey	Y	N	?	?	?	?	Y	Y
9 Hamilton	Y	N	Y	N	Y	Y	Y	Y
10 Jacobs	N	Y	Y	N	Y	Y	N	Y
IOWA								
1 ***Leach***	N	N	Y	N	N	Y	Y	N
2 ***Tauke***	N	N	Y	N	N	Y	N	N
3 ***Evans***	N	N	Y	N	Y	Y	N	N
4 Smith	Y	N	N	N	N	N	Y	Y
5 Harkin	Y	N	Y	N	Y	Y	Y	Y
6 Bedell	Y	N	Y	N	N	Y	Y	Y
KANSAS								
1 ***Roberts***	Y	N	Y	N	Y	Y	N	Y
2 Slattery	Y	N	Y	N	Y	Y	N	Y
3 ***Winn***	Y	N	Y	N	N	Y	N	Y
4 Glickman	Y	N	Y	N	Y	Y	Y	Y
5 ***Whittaker***	Y	N	Y	N	Y	Y	N	Y
KENTUCKY								
1 Hubbard	Y	N	Y	N	Y	Y	N	Y
2 Natcher	Y	N	Y	N	N	Y	Y	Y
3 Mazzoli	Y	N	Y	N	N	Y	Y	Y
4 ***Snyder***	Y	N	Y	N	N	Y	Y	Y
5 ***Rogers***	Y	N	Y	N	N	Y	Y	Y
6 ***Hopkins***	N	N	Y	N	N	Y	Y	Y
7 Perkins	Y	N	Y	N	N	Y	Y	Y
LOUISIANA								
1 ***Livingston***	Y	N	Y	N	N	N	Y	Y
2 Boggs	Y	N	N	N	?	N	Y	Y
3 Tauzin	Y	N	Y	N	Y	Y	Y	Y
4 Roemer	Y	N	Y	N	Y	Y	N	Y
5 Huckaby	Y	N	Y	N	N	Y	N	Y
6 ***Moore***	Y	N	Y	N	N	Y	Y	Y
7 Breaux	Y	N	Y	?	Y	Y	Y	Y
8 Long	Y	N	Y	N	Y	Y	Y	Y
MAINE								
1 ***McKernan***	Y	Y	Y	N	N	Y	Y	Y
2 ***Snowe***	Y	Y	Y	N	N	Y	Y	Y
MARYLAND								
1 Dyson	Y	N	Y	N	Y	Y	Y	Y
2 Long	Y	N	Y	N	Y	Y	Y	Y
3 Mikulski	Y	Y	?	?	?	?	?	?
4 ***Holt***	Y	N	Y	N	N	N	Y	Y
5 Hoyer	Y	Y	N	N	N	N	Y	Y
6 Byron	Y	N	Y	N	N	Y	Y	Y
7 Mitchell	Y	Y	N	N	N	Y	Y	?
8 Barnes	Y	Y	Y	N	N	Y	Y	Y
MASSACHUSETTS								
1 ***Conte***	Y	N	N	N	N	N	Y	Y
2 Boland	Y	N	N	N	N	Y	Y	Y
3 Early	Y	N	N	N	N	N	Y	?
4 Frank	Y	Y	Y	N	Y	Y	Y	Y
5 Shannon	Y	Y	N	?	?	?	?	?
6 Mavroules	Y	N	Y	N	N	Y	Y	Y
7 Markey	Y	Y	Y	N	Y	Y	Y	Y
8 O'Neill								
9 Moakley	Y	N	N	N	N	Y	Y	Y
10 Studds	Y	Y	Y	N	Y	Y	Y	Y
11 Donnelly	Y	N	N	N	Y	Y	Y	Y
MICHIGAN								
1 Conyers	Y	Y	N	N	Y	Y	Y	Y
2 ***Pursell***	Y	Y	Y	N	N	Y	Y	N
3 Wolpe	Y	Y	Y	N	Y	Y	Y	Y
4 ***Siljander***	Y	N	Y	N	Y	Y	N	N
5 ***Sawyer***	Y	N	Y	N	N	N	Y	Y
6 Carr	Y	Y	Y	N	Y	Y	Y	Y
7 Kildee	Y	N	N	N	Y	Y	Y	Y
8 Traxler	Y	N	Y	N	N	Y	Y	Y
9 ***Vander Jagt***	Y	N	Y	N	?	?	Y	Y
10 Albosta	Y	N	Y	N	Y	Y	Y	Y
11 ***Davis***	Y	N	Y	N	Y	Y	Y	Y
12 Bonior	Y	N	?	?	?	?	?	?
13 Crockett	Y	Y	Y	N	Y	Y	Y	?
14 Hertel	Y	N	Y	N	Y	Y	Y	Y
15 Ford	Y	Y	N	N	N	Y	Y	Y
16 Dingell	Y	Y	N	N	Y	Y	Y	?
17 Levin	Y	Y	Y	N	Y	Y	Y	Y
18 ***Broomfield***	Y	N	Y	N	N	N	N	N
MINNESOTA								
1 Penny	Y	N	Y	N	Y	Y	Y	Y
2 ***Weber***	N	N	Y	N	Y	Y	N	N
3 ***Frenzel***	N	Y	Y	N	N	Y	N	N
4 Vento	Y	Y	Y	N	Y	Y	Y	Y
5 Sabo	Y	Y	N	N	N	Y	Y	Y
6 Sikorski	N	N	Y	N	Y	Y	Y	Y

	246	247	248	249	250	251	252	253
7 ***Stangeland***	Y	N	?	N	Y	Y	N	Y
8 Oberstar	Y	N	N	N	N	Y	Y	Y
MISSISSIPPI								
1 Whitten	Y	N	Y	N	N	Y	Y	Y
2 ***Franklin***	Y	?	?	?	?	?	?	?
3 Montgomery	Y	N	Y	N	Y	Y	Y	Y
4 Dowdy	Y	N	Y	N	Y	Y	Y	Y
5 ***Lott***	Y	N	Y	N	N	N	N	Y
MISSOURI								
1 Clay	Y	Y	N	N	Y	Y	Y	Y
2 Young	Y	N	Y	N	N	N	Y	Y
3 Gephardt	Y	N	Y	N	N	Y	Y	Y
4 Skelton	Y	N	Y	N	Y	Y	Y	Y
5 Wheat	Y	Y	N	N	N	N	Y	Y
6 ***Coleman***	Y	N	Y	N	N	Y	Y	Y
7 ***Taylor***	Y	N	Y	N	N	N	Y	Y
8 ***Emerson***	Y	N	Y	N	Y	Y	Y	Y
9 Volkmer	Y	N	Y	N	Y	Y	Y	Y
MONTANA								
1 Williams	Y	Y	Y	N	N	Y	Y	?
2 ***Marlenee***	Y	N	Y	N	N	Y	N	N
NEBRASKA								
1 ***Bereuter***	Y	N	Y	N	N	Y	N	Y
2 ***Daub***	Y	N	N	N	Y	Y	Y	N
3 ***Smith***	Y	N	Y	N	Y	Y	N	Y
NEVADA								
1 Reid	Y	N	Y	N	Y	Y	Y	Y
2 ***Vucanovich***	Y	N	Y	N	N	N	N	N
NEW HAMPSHIRE								
1 D'Amours	Y	N	Y	N	Y	Y	Y	Y
2 ***Gregg***	Y	N	Y	N	Y	Y	N	N
NEW JERSEY								
1 Florio	Y	N	N	N	N	Y	Y	Y
2 Hughes	Y	Y	Y	N	Y	Y	N	Y
3 Howard	Y	Y	Y	?	N	Y	Y	Y
4 ***Smith***	Y	N	Y	N	Y	Y	Y	Y
5 ***Roukema***	Y	Y	Y	N	N	Y	N	N
6 Dwyer	Y	N	Y	N	N	Y	Y	Y
7 ***Rinaldo***	Y	N	Y	N	Y	Y	Y	Y
8 Roe	Y	N	N	N	N	Y	Y	Y
9 Torricelli	Y	Y	N	N	Y	Y	Y	Y
10 Rodino	Y	N	Y	N	N	Y	Y	Y
11 Minish	Y	N	Y	N	N	Y	Y	Y
12 ***Courter***	Y	N	Y	N	N	Y	Y	Y
13 Vacancy								
14 Guarini	Y	N	Y	N	N	Y	Y	Y
NEW MEXICO								
1 ***Lujan***	Y	N	Y	N	Y	Y	Y	Y
2 ***Skeen***	Y	N	Y	N	N	Y	Y	Y
3 Richardson	Y	N	Y	N	Y	?	?	Y
NEW YORK								
1 ***Carney***	Y	N	Y	N	N	Y	Y	Y
2 Downey	Y	Y	N	?	N	N	Y	Y
3 Mrazek	Y	Y	Y	N	N	Y	Y	Y
4 ***Lent***	Y	N	Y	N	N	Y	Y	Y
5 ***McGrath***	Y	N	Y	N	N	N	Y	Y
6 Addabbo	Y	Y	N	N	N	Y	Y	Y
7 Ackerman	N	Y	N	N	Y	Y	Y	Y
8 Scheuer	Y	Y	N	N	N	Y	Y	Y
9 Ferraro	Y	Y	N	N	N	Y	Y	Y
10 Schumer	Y	Y	N	N	N	Y	Y	Y
11 Towns	Y	Y	Y	N	Y	Y	Y	Y
12 Owens	Y	?	N	N	Y	Y	Y	Y
13 Solarz	Y	Y	N	N	N	Y	Y	Y
14 ***Molinari***	Y	N	?	N	N	N	Y	Y
15 ***Green***	Y	Y	Y	N	N	N	Y	Y
16 Rangel	Y	Y	N	N	N	Y	Y	Y
17 Weiss	N	Y	N	N	N	Y	Y	Y
18 Garcia	Y	?	N	N	N	N	Y	Y
19 Biaggi	Y	Y	Y	N	N	N	Y	Y
20 Ottinger	Y	Y	N	N	Y	Y	Y	N
21 ***Fish***	Y	?	?	?	?	?	?	?
22 ***Gilman***	Y	Y	N	N	N	Y	Y	Y
23 Stratton	Y	N	Y	N	N	N	Y	Y
24 ***Solomon***	Y	N	Y	N	Y	Y	N	Y
25 ***Boehlert***	Y	Y	Y	N	N	Y	Y	Y
26 ***Martin***	Y	N	Y	N	N	Y	Y	Y
27 ***Wortley***	Y	N	Y	N	N	Y	Y	Y
28 McHugh	Y	N	N	N	N	Y	Y	Y
29 ***Horton***	Y	Y	Y	N	N	N	Y	Y
30 ***Conable***	N	Y	Y	N	N	Y	N	Y
31 ***Kemp***	Y	N	Y	N	N	N	N	Y
32 LaFalce	Y	N	Y	N	N	Y	Y	Y
33 Nowak	Y	N	Y	N	Y	Y	Y	Y
34 Lundine	Y	Y	Y	N	N	Y	Y	?

	246	247	248	249	250	251	252	253
NORTH CAROLINA								
1 Jones	Y	N	Y	N	Y	Y	Y	Y
2 Valentine	Y	N	Y	N	Y	Y	Y	Y
3 Whitley	Y	N	Y	N	N	Y	Y	Y
4 Andrews	Y	N	Y	N	N	Y	Y	Y
5 Neal	Y	Y	Y	N	N	Y	Y	Y
6 Britt	Y	Y	Y	N	Y	Y	Y	Y
7 Rose	Y	Y	Y	N	N	Y	Y	Y
8 Hefner	Y	N	Y	N	N	Y	Y	Y
9 ***Martin***	Y	N	Y	N	N	Y	N	Y
10 ***Broyhill***	N	N	Y	N	N	Y	N	N
11 Clarke	Y	N	Y	N	Y	Y	Y	Y
NORTH DAKOTA								
AL Dorgan	Y	N	?	?	Y	Y	N	Y
OHIO								
1 Luken	Y	N	Y	N	Y	Y	N	Y
2 ***Gradison***	Y	N	Y	N	N	Y	N	Y
3 Hall	Y	N	Y	N	N	Y	Y	Y
4 ***Oxley***	Y	N	Y	N	N	Y	N	Y
5 ***Latta***	Y	N	Y	N	N	Y	N	Y
6 ***McEwen***	Y	N	Y	N	Y	Y	N	N
7 ***DeWine***	Y	N	Y	N	N	N	Y	Y
8 ***Kindness***	Y	N	Y	N	N	N	N	Y
9 Kaptur	Y	N	?	N	Y	Y	Y	Y
10 ***Miller***	Y	N	Y	N	N	Y	Y	Y
11 Eckart	Y	Y	Y	N	Y	Y	Y	Y
12 ***Kasich***	Y	N	Y	N	Y	Y	N	Y
13 Pease	Y	Y	Y	N	Y	Y	Y	Y
14 Seiberling	Y	Y	Y	N	Y	Y	Y	Y
15 ***Wylie***	Y	N	Y	N	N	Y	N	Y
16 ***Regula***	Y	N	Y	N	N	N	Y	Y
17 ***Williams***	?	N	?	?	Y	Y	Y	Y
18 Applegate	Y	N	Y	N	N	Y	Y	Y
19 Feighan	Y	Y	Y	N	Y	Y	N	Y
20 Oakar	Y	N	N	N	Y	Y	Y	Y
21 Stokes	Y	Y	N	N	Y	Y	Y	Y
OKLAHOMA								
1 Jones	Y	N	Y	N	N	Y	N	Y
2 Synar	Y	Y	Y	N	N	Y	Y	Y
3 Watkins	Y	N	Y	N	Y	Y	Y	Y
4 McCurdy	Y	Y	Y	N	Y	Y	Y	Y
5 ***Edwards***	Y	N	Y	N	N	Y	Y	Y
6 English	Y	N	Y	N	Y	Y	Y	Y
OREGON								
1 AuCoin	Y	Y	Y	N	Y	Y	N	Y
2 ***Smith, R.***	Y	N	Y	N	Y	Y	N	Y
3 Wyden	Y	Y	Y	N	Y	Y	Y	Y
4 Weaver	N	Y	Y	Y	Y	?	?	N
5 ***Smith, D.***	N	N	Y	N	Y	Y	N	Y
PENNSYLVANIA								
1 Foglietta	Y	Y	Y	N	N	N	Y	Y
2 Gray	Y	?	?	?	N	Y	Y	Y
3 Borski	Y	N	Y	N	Y	Y	Y	Y
4 Kolter	Y	N	Y	N	Y	Y	Y	Y
5 ***Schulze***	Y	N	Y	N	N	N	Y	Y
6 Yatron	Y	N	Y	N	Y	Y	Y	Y
7 Edgar	Y	Y	Y	N	N	Y	Y	Y
8 Kostmayer	Y	Y	Y	N	N	Y	Y	Y
9 ***Shuster***	Y	N	Y	N	N	Y	N	N
10 ***McDade***	Y	N	Y	N	N	Y	Y	Y
11 Harrison	Y	N	N	N	N	N	Y	Y
12 Murtha	Y	N	?	N	N	N	Y	Y
13 ***Coughlin***	Y	N	Y	N	N	N	Y	Y
14 Coyne	Y	N	N	N	N	N	Y	Y
15 ***Ritter***	N	N	Y	N	Y	Y	N	N
16 ***Walker***	Y	N	Y	N	N	Y	N	N
17 ***Gekas***	Y	Y	Y	N	N	Y	Y	N
18 Walgren	Y	Y	Y	N	Y	Y	Y	Y
19 ***Goodling***	Y	N	Y	N	N	Y	Y	Y
20 Gaydos	Y	N	Y	N	?	Y	Y	Y
21 ***Ridge***	Y	N	Y	N	N	Y	Y	Y
22 Murphy	Y	N	Y	Y	Y	Y	N	Y
23 ***Clinger***	Y	N	Y	N	N	Y	Y	Y
RHODE ISLAND								
1 St Germain	Y	N	Y	N	N	Y	Y	Y
2 ***Schneider***	Y	Y	Y	N	Y	Y	Y	Y
SOUTH CAROLINA								
1 ***Hartnett***	Y	N	Y	N	Y	Y	Y	Y
2 ***Spence***	Y	?	Y	N	N	Y	N	Y
3 Derrick	Y	Y	Y	N	Y	Y	Y	Y
4 ***Campbell***	Y	N	Y	N	N	Y	N	Y
5 Spratt	Y	Y	Y	N	N	Y	Y	Y
6 Tallon	Y	N	Y	N	Y	Y	Y	Y
SOUTH DAKOTA								
AL Daschle	Y	Y	Y	N	Y	Y	Y	Y

	246	247	248	249	250	251	252	253
TENNESSEE								
1 ***Quillen***	Y	N	Y	N	N	?	Y	Y
2 ***Duncan***	Y	N	Y	N	N	Y	Y	Y
3 Lloyd	Y	N	Y	N	Y	Y	Y	Y
4 Cooper	Y	Y	Y	N	?	?	?	?
5 Boner	Y	N	Y	N	Y	Y	Y	Y
6 Gore	Y	N	Y	?	Y	Y	Y	Y
7 ***Sundquist***	Y	N	Y	N	N	Y	Y	Y
8 Jones	Y	N	Y	N	Y	Y	Y	Y
9 Ford	Y	Y	Y	N	N	Y	Y	Y
TEXAS								
1 Hall, S.	Y	N	Y	N	Y	Y	Y	Y
2 Wilson	Y	Y	Y	N	N	Y	Y	Y
3 ***Bartlett***	N	N	Y	N	N	Y	N	N
4 Hall, R.	Y	N	Y	N	Y	Y	Y	Y
5 Bryant	Y	Y	Y	N	Y	Y	Y	Y
6 ***Gramm***	?	?	?	?	?	Y	N	Y
7 ***Archer***	Y	N	Y	N	Y	Y	N	Y
8 ***Fields***	Y	N	Y	N	Y	Y	N	Y
9 Brooks	Y	Y	Y	N	N	Y	Y	Y
10 Pickle	Y	Y	Y	N	N	Y	Y	Y
11 Leath	Y	N	Y	N	N	Y	N	Y
12 Wright	Y	N	Y	N	N	Y	Y	Y
13 Hightower	Y	N	Y	N	N	Y	Y	Y
14 Patman	Y	N	Y	N	Y	Y	N	Y
15 de la Garza	Y	N	Y	N	N	Y	Y	Y
16 Coleman	Y	Y	Y	N	Y	Y	Y	Y
17 Stenholm	Y	N	Y	N	Y	Y	N	Y
18 Leland	Y	Y	N	N	N	N	Y	Y
19 Hance	Y	Y	Y	N	Y	Y	Y	Y
20 Gonzalez	Y	Y	N	N	N	N	Y	Y
21 ***Loeffler***	Y	N	Y	N	N	N	Y	Y
22 ***Paul***	N	N	Y	Y	Y	Y	?	?
23 Kazen	Y	N	Y	N	N	Y	Y	Y
24 Frost	Y	Y	Y	N	Y	Y	Y	Y
25 Andrews	Y	Y	Y	N	Y	Y	Y	Y
26 Vandergriff	Y	Y	Y	N	Y	Y	N	Y
27 Ortiz	Y	N	Y	N	N	Y	Y	Y
UTAH								
1 ***Hansen***	Y	N	Y	N	Y	Y	N	Y
2 ***Marriott***	Y	N	Y	N	N	N	Y	Y
3 ***Nielson***	Y	N	Y	N	Y	Y	N	Y
VERMONT								
AL ***Jeffords***	Y	Y	Y	N	N	Y	Y	Y
VIRGINIA								
1 ***Bateman***	Y	N	Y	N	N	Y	Y	Y
2 ***Whitehurst***	Y	N	Y	N	N	Y	Y	Y
3 ***Bliley***	Y	X	?	?	?	?	?	?
4 Sisisky	Y	Y	N	N	Y	Y	Y	Y
5 Daniel	Y	N	Y	N	N	Y	Y	Y
6 Olin	Y	?	Y	N	N	Y	Y	Y
7 ***Robinson***	Y	N	Y	N	N	Y	Y	Y
8 ***Parris***	Y	N	N	N	N	N	Y	Y
9 Boucher	Y	Y	Y	N	Y	Y	Y	Y
10 ***Wolf***	Y	N	N	N	N	Y	Y	Y
WASHINGTON								
1 ***Pritchard***	Y	Y	Y	?	N	N	Y	Y
2 Swift	Y	Y	Y	N	N	Y	Y	?
3 Bonker	Y	N	Y	N	N	Y	Y	Y
4 ***Morrison***	Y	Y	Y	N	N	Y	N	Y
5 Foley	Y	Y	Y	N	N	N	Y	Y
6 Dicks	Y	Y	Y	N	?	Y	Y	Y
7 Lowry	Y	Y	N	Y	N	Y	Y	Y
8 ***Chandler***	Y	Y	Y	N	N	Y	N	Y
WEST VIRGINIA								
1 Mollohan	Y	N	Y	N	Y	Y	Y	Y
2 Staggers	Y	N	Y	N	Y	Y	Y	Y
3 Wise	Y	Y	Y	N	Y	Y	Y	Y
4 Rahall	Y	N	Y	N	N	N	Y	Y
WISCONSIN								
1 Aspin	Y	N	Y	N	Y	Y	Y	Y
2 Kastenmeier	Y	Y	N	N	Y	Y	Y	Y
3 ***Gunderson***	Y	N	Y	N	N	Y	Y	Y
4 Kleczka	Y	N	Y	?	Y	?	?	Y
5 Moody	Y	Y	N	N	Y	Y	Y	Y
6 ***Petri***	Y	N	Y	N	Y	Y	Y	N
7 Obey	Y	N	N	Y	N	Y	Y	Y
8 ***Roth***	Y	N	Y	?	Y	+	+	+
9 ***Sensenbrenner***	?	?	?	?	?	?	?	?
WYOMING								
AL ***Cheney***	Y	N	Y	N	N	N	N	Y

Southern states - Ala., Ark., Fla., Ga., Ky., La., Miss., N.C., Okla., S.C., Tenn., Texas, Va.

254. HR 5898. Military Construction Appropriations, Fiscal 1985. McNulty, D-Ariz., amendment to reduce spending in the bill by $25 million to reflect savings achieved by greater reliance on performance standards in contracting for Pentagon construction projects. Adopted 219-180: R 66-93; D 153-87 (ND 117-36, SD 36-51), in the session that began June 27, 1984.

255. HR 5898. Military Construction Appropriations, Fiscal 1985. Passage of the bill to appropriate $8,258,471,037 for military construction projects of the Department of Defense in fiscal 1985. Passed 347-52: R 139-19; D 208-33 (ND 123-33, SD 85-0), in the session that began June 27, 1984. The president had requested $10,318,200,000 in new budget authority.

256. HR 5927. Debt Limit Increase. Ways and Means Committee amendment to raise the existing public debt limit of $1.52 trillion by $232 billion to $1.753 trillion, an amount estimated to provide sufficient government borrowing authority through June 1985. Rejected 87-332: R 49-112; D 38-220 (ND 30-139, SD 8-81), June 28, 1984. A "yea" was a vote supporting the president's position.

257. HR. 5927. Debt Limit Increase. Passage of the bill to increase the existing public debt limit of $1.52 trillion by $53 billion to $1.573 trillion, an amount estimated to provide sufficient government borrowing through August 1984. Rejected 138-282: R 59-104; D 79-178 (ND 55-114, SD 24-64), June 28, 1984. A "yea" was a vote supporting the president's position.

258. HR 5154. National Aeronautics and Space Administration Authorization. Adoption of the conference report on the bill to authorize $7.5 billion for the National Aeronautics and Space Administration in fiscal 1985. Adopted 298-119: R 71-89; D 227-30 (ND 145-22, SD 82-8), June 28, 1984.

259. HR 5753. Legislative Branch Appropriations, Fiscal 1985. Adoption of the conference report on the bill to appropriate $1,551,015,038 in fiscal 1985 for Congress and related agencies. Adopted 253-157: R 44-116; D 209-41 (ND 144-19, SD 65-22), June 28, 1984.

260. HR 5899. District of Columbia Appropriations, Fiscal 1985. Daschle, D-S.D., amendment to the Walker, R-Pa., amendment (see vote 261, below), to reduce the funding levels in the bill by 1 percent. Rejected 138-286: R 23-140; D 115-146 (ND 71-101, SD 44-45), June 28, 1984. (The Walker amendment subsequently was adopted (see vote 261, below), and then later rejected when the House rose from the Committee of the Whole (see vote 262, p. 82-H).)

261. HR 5899. District of Columbia Appropriations, Fiscal 1985. Walker, R-Pa., amendment to cut the funding levels in the bill by 2 percent. Adopted 239-186: R 137-26; D 102-160 (ND 42-132, SD 60-28), June 28, 1984. (The Walker amendment subsequently was rejected when the House rose from the Committee of the Whole (see vote 262, p. 82-H).)

KEY

Y	Voted for (yea).
#	Paired for.
+	Announced for.
N	Voted against (nay).
X	Paired against.
-	Announced against.
P	Voted "present".
C	Voted "present" to avoid possible conflict of interest.
?	Did not vote or otherwise make a position known.

Democrats   **Republicans**

	254	255	256	257	258	259	260	261
ALABAMA								
1 *Edwards*	N	Y	Y	Y	Y	?	N	Y
2 *Dickinson*	N	Y	N	N	Y	Y	Y	Y
3 Nichols	N	Y	N	N	Y	N	Y	Y
4 Bevill	N	Y	N	Y	Y	Y	N	Y
5 Flippo	N	Y	N	Y	Y	Y	Y	Y
6 Erdreich	Y	Y	N	N	Y	N	Y	Y
7 Shelby	Y	Y	Y	N	Y	N	Y	Y
ALASKA								
AL *Young*	N	Y	N	N	N	Y	N	N
ARIZONA								
1 *McCain*	N	Y	Y	Y	N	N	N	Y
2 Udall	Y	Y	N	N	Y	Y	N	N
3 *Stump*	N	N	N	N	N	N	N	Y
4 *Rudd*	N	Y	N	Y	Y	Y	N	Y
5 McNulty	Y	Y	N	Y	Y	Y	Y	N
ARKANSAS								
1 Alexander	N	Y	N	N	Y	N	Y	N
2 *Bethune*	Y	Y	N	N	?	N	N	Y
3 *Hammerschmidt*	N	Y	Y	Y	N	N	N	Y
4 Anthony	N	Y	N	Y	Y	Y	N	Y
CALIFORNIA								
1 Bosco	Y	Y	N	N	Y	N	Y	Y
2 *Chappie*	Y	Y	N	N	N	N	Y	Y
3 Matsui	Y	Y	Y	Y	Y	Y	N	N
4 Fazio	N	Y	N	N	Y	N	N	N
5 Burton	Y	Y	Y	Y	Y	N	N	N
6 Boxer	Y	Y	N	N	Y	N	N	N
7 Miller	Y	Y	N	N	Y	Y	Y	Y
8 Dellums	Y	N	N	N	Y	N	N	N
9 Stark	Y	N	?	?	?	?	?	?
10 Edwards	Y	N	N	N	Y	N	N	N
11 Lantos	Y	Y	N	N	Y	Y	N	N
12 *Zschau*	Y	N	N	N	N	N	N	Y
13 Mineta	Y	Y	N	N	Y	Y	N	N
14 *Shumway*	N	Y	N	N	N	N	N	Y
15 Coelho	N	Y	N	N	Y	Y	Y	N
16 Panetta	N	Y	N	N	Y	Y	Y	N
17 *Pashayan*	Y	Y	N	N	N	Y	N	Y
18 Lehman	N	Y	N	N	Y	Y	N	N
19 *Lagomarsino*	N	Y	N	N	N	N	N	Y
20 *Thomas*	Y	Y	N	N	N	N	N	Y
21 *Fiedler*	N	?	N	N	Y	N	N	Y
22 *Moorhead*	N	Y	N	N	N	N	N	Y
23 Beilenson	Y	Y	Y	Y	Y	N	N	N
24 Waxman	?	?	N	Y	Y	?	N	N
25 Roybal	Y	Y	N	Y	Y	N	N	N
26 Berman	Y	Y	Y	Y	Y	Y	N	N
27 Levine	Y	Y	N	N	Y	N	N	N
28 Dixon	?	?	N	Y	Y	N	N	N
29 Hawkins	?	?	?	Y	Y	?	N	N
30 Martinez	?	?	N	Y	Y	N	N	N
31 Dymally	?	?	?	?	?	?	?	?
32 Anderson	N	Y	N	N	Y	N	N	N
33 *Dreier*	Y	Y	N	N	N	N	N	Y
34 Torres	Y	Y	N	N	Y	Y	Y	N
35 *Lewis*	N	Y	Y	Y	N	N	N	Y
36 Brown	?	?	N	Y	Y	Y	N	N
37 *McCandless*	Y	Y	N	N	N	N	Y	Y
38 Patterson	Y	Y	N	Y	Y	Y	N	N
39 *Dannemeyer*	Y	Y	N	N	N	N	N	Y
40 *Badham*	N	Y	N	N	N	N	N	Y
41 *Lowery*	N	Y	Y	Y	Y	Y	Y	Y
42 *Lungren*	N	Y	N	N	N	N	N	Y

	254	255	256	257	258	259	260	261
43 *Packard*	N	Y	N	N	N	N	N	Y
44 Bates	Y	Y	N	N	Y	Y	Y	N
45 *Hunter*	N	Y	Y	Y	Y	Y	N	Y
COLORADO								
1 Schroeder	?	?	N	N	N	N	N	Y
2 Wirth	?	?	N	N	Y	Y	N	N
3 Kogovsek	Y	Y	N	Y	Y	Y	Y	N
4 *Brown*	Y	N	N	N	N	N	N	N
5 *Kramer*	N	Y	N	N	N	N	N	Y
6 *Schaefer*	N	Y	N	N	N	N	Y	Y
CONNECTICUT								
1 Kennelly	N	Y	N	Y	Y	Y	N	N
2 Gejdenson	N	Y	N	N	Y	Y	N	N
3 Morrison	Y	N	N	N	Y	N	Y	N
4 *McKinney*	N	N	Y	Y	Y	N	N	N
5 Ratchford	Y	Y	N	N	Y	Y	N	N
6 *Johnson*	Y	N	Y	Y	Y	N	N	N
DELAWARE								
AL Carper	Y	Y	N	N	Y	N	Y	Y
FLORIDA								
1 Hutto	N	Y	N	N	Y	N	N	Y
2 Fuqua	N	Y	N	N	Y	N	N	N
3 Bennett	N	Y	N	N	Y	N	N	Y
4 Chappell	N	Y	N	N	Y	N	N	Y
5 *McCollum*	N	Y	N	N	N	N	N	Y
6 MacKay	Y	Y	N	N	Y	N	N	Y
7 Gibbons	Y	Y	Y	Y	Y	Y	Y	Y
8 *Young*	N	Y	N	N	N	N	N	Y
9 *Bilirakis*	N	Y	N	N	N	N	N	Y
10 Ireland	N	Y	N	N	N	N	N	Y
11 Nelson	N	Y	N	N	Y	N	N	N
12 *Lewis*	N	Y	N	N	N	N	N	Y
13 *Mack*	Y	Y	Y	N	N	N	N	Y
14 Mica	Y	Y	N	N	Y	Y	Y	Y
15 *Shaw*	Y	Y	N	N	N	N	N	Y
16 Smith	Y	Y	?	Y	Y	Y	?	?
17 Lehman	?	?	Y	Y	Y	Y	N	N
18 Pepper	Y	Y	Y	Y	Y	?	N	N
19 Fascell	N	Y	Y	Y	Y	Y	N	N
GEORGIA								
1 Thomas	N	Y	N	N	Y	Y	Y	Y
2 Hatcher	N	Y	Y	Y	Y	Y	N	Y
3 Ray	N	Y	N	N	N	N	N	Y
4 Levitas	Y	Y	N	Y	Y	Y	Y	Y
5 Fowler	N	Y	Y	Y	Y	Y	N	N
6 *Gingrich*	Y	Y	N	N	N	N	N	Y
7 Darden	Y	Y	N	N	Y	Y	Y	Y
8 Rowland	Y	Y	N	N	Y	Y	Y	Y
9 Jenkins	N	Y	N	Y	Y	Y	N	Y
10 Barnard	N	Y	N	Y	?	Y	Y	Y
HAWAII								
1 Heftel	Y	Y	?	Y	Y	Y	Y	Y
2 Akaka	N	Y	N	N	Y	N	N	N
IDAHO								
1 *Craig*	Y	Y	N	N	N	N	N	Y
2 *Hansen*	?	?	?	?	?	?	?	?
ILLINOIS								
1 Hayes	Y	N	N	N	Y	N	N	N
2 Savage	?	Y	N	N	Y	Y	N	N
3 Russo	Y	Y	N	N	N	N	Y	N
4 *O'Brien*	N	Y	Y	Y	Y	N	N	N
5 Lipinski	Y	Y	N	Y	Y	Y	N	N
6 *Hyde*	N	Y	Y	Y	Y	N	N	N
7 Collins	Y	N	N	N	Y	N	N	N
8 Rostenkowski	Y	Y	Y	Y	Y	Y	N	N
9 Yates	?	?	Y	Y	Y	Y	N	N
10 *Porter*	N	Y	Y	Y	Y	N	N	Y
11 Annunzio	?	#	N	Y	Y	Y	N	N
12 *Crane, P.*	N	N	N	N	N	N	N	N
13 *Erlenborn*	?	?	?	?	?	?	?	?
14 *Corcoran*	N	Y	N	N	Y	Y	N	Y
15 *Madigan*	Y	Y	Y	Y	Y	N	N	Y
16 *Martin*	Y	N	N	N	Y	N	N	Y
17 Evans	N	Y	N	N	Y	N	N	N
18 *Michel*	N	Y	Y	Y	Y	N	N	N
19 *Crane, D.*	N	N	N	N	N	N	N	Y
20 Durbin	Y	Y	N	N	Y	N	N	N
21 Price	N	Y	N	Y	Y	N	N	N
22 Simon	?	?	Y	Y	?	Y	N	N
INDIANA								
1 Hall	N	Y	N	N	Y	N	Y	Y
2 Sharp	Y	Y	N	N	Y	N	Y	Y
3 *Hiler*	Y	N	N	N	N	N	N	Y
4 *Coats*	N	Y	N	N	Y	N	N	Y
5 Hillis	N	Y	N	Y	N	N	Y	Y

ND - Northern Democrats   SD - Southern Democrats

Corresponding to Congressional Record Votes 283, 284, 285, 286, 287, 288, 289, 290

	254	255	256	257	258	259	260	261
6 ***Burton***	N	Y	N	N	N	N	N	Y
7 ***Myers***	N	Y	N	N	N	Y	Y	N
8 McCloskey	Y	Y	N	N	Y	Y	N	N
9 Hamilton	Y	Y	Y	Y	Y	Y	Y	Y
10 Jacobs	Y	N	N	N	N	N	Y	Y
IOWA								
1 ***Leach***	Y	N	N	N	Y	N	N	Y
2 ***Tauke***	Y	N	N	Y	N	N	N	Y
3 ***Evans***	Y	N	N	N	N	N	Y	Y
4 Smith	Y	Y	N	N	Y	Y	N	N
5 Harkin	Y	Y	N	N	Y	Y	Y	N
6 Bedell	Y	N	N	N	N	Y	Y	N
KANSAS								
1 ***Roberts***	Y	N	N	N	N	N	N	Y
2 Slattery	Y	N	N	N	Y	N	Y	Y
3 ***Winn***	Y	Y	N	N	N	N	N	Y
4 Glickman	N	Y	N	N	Y	N	Y	Y
5 ***Whittaker***	Y	Y	N	N	N	N	N	Y
KENTUCKY								
1 Hubbard	Y	Y	N	N	N	N	Y	Y
2 Natcher	N	Y	N	N	Y	Y	N	N
3 Mazzoli	N	Y	N	N	Y	Y	N	N
4 ***Snyder***	N	Y	N	N	N	Y	N	Y
5 ***Rogers***	N	Y	N	N	Y	N	Y	Y
6 ***Hopkins***	N	Y	N	N	Y	N	N	Y
7 Perkins	N	Y	N	Y	N	Y	N	Y
LOUISIANA								
1 ***Livingston***	N	Y	N	Y	Y	Y	N	Y
2 Boggs	Y	Y	N	N	Y	Y	N	N
3 Tauzin	Y	Y	N	N	Y	Y	Y	Y
4 Roemer	N	Y	N	N	N	N	N	Y
5 Huckaby	N	Y	N	N	Y	N	N	Y
6 ***Moore***	Y	Y	N	N	N	N	N	Y
7 Breaux	N	?	Y	N	Y	Y	N	N
8 Long	N	Y	Y	Y	Y	Y	Y	N
MAINE								
1 ***McKernan***	Y	Y	?	Y	N	Y	N	N
2 ***Snowe***	N	Y	N	N	N	Y	N	Y
MARYLAND								
1 Dyson	N	Y	N	N	Y	Y	Y	Y
2 Long	N	Y	?	N	Y	Y	Y	Y
3 Mikulski	?	?	N	N	Y	Y	N	Y
4 ***Holt***	N	Y	Y	Y	N	N	N	N
5 Hoyer	N	Y	N	Y	Y	Y	N	N
6 Byron	N	Y	N	N	Y	N	N	Y
7 Mitchell	?	X	N	N	?	Y	N	N
8 Barnes	Y	Y	Y	Y	Y	Y	N	N
MASSACHUSETTS								
1 ***Conte***	N	Y	Y	Y	Y	Y	N	N
2 Boland	N	Y	Y	Y	Y	?	N	N
3 Early	?	?	N	N	Y	?	N	N
4 Frank	Y	Y	Y	Y	Y	Y	N	N
5 Shannon	?	?	?	?	?	?	?	?
6 Mavroules	N	Y	N	Y	Y	Y	N	N
7 Markey	Y	N	N	N	Y	Y	Y	N
8 O'Neill								
9 Moakley	Y	Y	Y	?	Y	Y	N	N
10 Studds	Y	N	N	N	Y	Y	N	N
11 Donnelly	Y	Y	Y	Y	Y	Y	N	N
MICHIGAN								
1 Conyers	Y	N	N	Y	Y	Y	N	N
2 ***Pursell***	Y	N	N	N	Y	N	Y	Y
3 Wolpe	Y	Y	N	N	Y	Y	N	N
4 ***Siljander***	Y	Y	N	N	Y	N	N	Y
5 ***Sawyer***	N	Y	Y	Y	Y	Y	N	Y
6 Carr	N	Y	N	N	Y	Y	N	N
7 Kildee	Y	Y	N	Y	Y	Y	N	N
8 Traxler	Y	Y	N	Y	Y	?	Y	N
9 ***Vander Jagt***	N	Y	Y	Y	Y	Y	N	Y
10 Albosta	Y	Y	N	N	N	Y	N	Y
11 ***Davis***	N	Y	N	Y	Y	Y	N	Y
12 Bonior	?	?	Y	Y	Y	Y	Y	N
13 Crockett	?	?	N	N	N	Y	N	N
14 Hertel	?	Y	N	N	Y	Y	N	N
15 Ford	N	Y	N	N	Y	Y	N	N
16 Dingell	N	N	N	N	?	?	?	N
17 Levin	Y	Y	N	N	Y	Y	N	N
18 ***Broomfield***	Y	Y	N	N	N	N	Y	Y
MINNESOTA								
1 Penny	Y	N	N	N	N	N	Y	Y
2 ***Weber***	?	?	N	N	N	N	N	Y
3 ***Frenzel***	Y	N	Y	Y	N	N	N	Y
4 Vento	Y	Y	N	Y	N	Y	Y	N
5 Sabo	N	N	N	N	Y	Y	N	N
6 Sikorski	Y	N	N	N	Y	Y	Y	Y
7 ***Stangeland***	Y	N	Y	N	N	Y	N	Y
8 Oberstar	Y	N	N	N	N	Y	N	N
MISSISSIPPI								
1 Whitten	N	Y	N	N	Y	Y	N	N
2 ***Franklin***	?	?	N	N	N	N	N	Y
3 Montgomery	N	Y	N	N	N	Y	N	Y
4 Dowdy	N	Y	N	N	Y	Y	Y	Y
5 ***Lott***	N	Y	Y	N	Y	Y	N	Y
MISSOURI								
1 Clay	Y	N	N	N	Y	Y	N	N
2 Young	Y	Y	N	Y	Y	Y	Y	N
3 Gephardt	Y	Y	N	N	Y	Y	Y	N
4 Skelton	N	Y	N	Y	N	Y	Y	N
5 Wheat	Y	Y	N	Y	Y	Y	N	N
6 ***Coleman***	N	Y	N	N	Y	Y	N	Y
7 ***Taylor***	N	Y	N	Y	N	Y	N	Y
8 ***Emerson***	N	Y	N	N	Y	N	N	Y
9 Volkmer	Y	N	N	Y	Y	N	N	Y
MONTANA								
1 Williams	Y	Y	N	Y	Y	Y	N	Y
2 ***Marlenee***	N	Y	N	N	N	?	Y	Y
NEBRASKA								
1 ***Bereuter***	Y	N	N	N	N	N	N	Y
2 ***Daub***	N	Y	N	N	N	N	N	Y
3 ***Smith***	Y	N	N	N	N	N	N	Y
NEVADA								
1 Reid	Y	Y	Y	Y	Y	Y	N	N
2 ***Vucanovich***	N	Y	N	N	N	N	N	Y
NEW HAMPSHIRE								
1 D'Amours	Y	Y	N	N	?	?	Y	Y
2 ***Gregg***	Y	Y	Y	Y	N	N	N	Y
NEW JERSEY								
1 Florio	?	?	N	N	Y	Y	N	N
2 Hughes	Y	Y	N	N	N	?	Y	Y
3 Howard	N	Y	N	N	Y	Y	N	N
4 ***Smith***	N	Y	N	N	Y	N	Y	Y
5 ***Roukema***	Y	N	N	N	N	N	N	Y
6 Dwyer	N	Y	N	Y	Y	?	N	N
7 ***Rinaldo***	Y	Y	N	N	Y	N	N	Y
8 Roe	N	Y	N	N	Y	Y	N	N
9 Torricelli	Y	Y	N	N	Y	N	Y	Y
10 Rodino	Y	N	N	N	Y	Y	N	N
11 Minish	Y	Y	N	N	Y	Y	Y	Y
12 ***Courter***	N	Y	N	N	Y	N	N	Y
13 Vacancy								
14 Guarini	Y	Y	N	N	Y	Y	N	N
NEW MEXICO								
1 ***Lujan***	Y	Y	N	N	Y	N	Y	Y
2 ***Skeen***	N	Y	N	N	Y	N	Y	Y
3 Richardson	Y	Y	N	N	Y	N	Y	N
NEW YORK								
1 ***Carney***	N	Y	N	N	Y	Y	N	N
2 Downey	Y	Y	N	N	Y	Y	Y	N
3 Mrazek	Y	Y	N	N	Y	Y	N	N
4 ***Lent***	N	Y	N	N	Y	N	N	Y
5 ***McGrath***	N	Y	N	N	Y	Y	Y	Y
6 Addabbo	Y	Y	N	N	Y	Y	N	N
7 Ackerman	Y	N	N	N	Y	Y	Y	N
8 Scheuer	Y	Y	N	Y	Y	Y	N	N
9 Ferraro	N	Y	N	N	Y	Y	Y	N
10 Schumer	Y	Y	Y	Y	Y	Y	N	N
11 Towns	?	Y	N	N	Y	Y	N	N
12 Owens	Y	N	N	N	Y	Y	N	N
13 Solarz	Y	Y	Y	Y	Y	Y	Y	N
14 ***Molinari***	N	Y	N	N	N	Y	N	Y
15 ***Green***	N	Y	Y	Y	Y	Y	N	N
16 Rangel	Y	N	N	N	Y	Y	N	N
17 Weiss	Y	N	N	N	Y	Y	N	N
18 Garcia	Y	Y	Y	Y	Y	Y	N	N
19 Biaggi	Y	Y	N	N	Y	Y	Y	N
20 Ottinger	Y	N	Y	Y	Y	Y	N	N
21 ***Fish***	N	Y	Y	Y	Y	Y	N	Y
22 ***Gilman***	Y	Y	N	N	Y	N	N	Y
23 Stratton	N	Y	Y	Y	Y	Y	N	Y
24 ***Solomon***	N	Y	N	N	N	N	N	Y
25 ***Boehlert***	N	Y	Y	Y	Y	Y	N	Y
26 ***Martin***	N	Y	N	N	Y	N	N	Y
27 ***Wortley***	N	Y	N	N	Y	N	N	Y
28 McHugh	Y	Y	N	Y	Y	Y	N	N
29 ***Horton***	N	Y	Y	Y	Y	Y	N	N
30 ***Conable***	Y	N	Y	Y	N	N	N	N
31 ***Kemp***	N	Y	Y	Y	?	Y	N	Y
32 LaFalce	Y	Y	N	N	Y	Y	Y	Y
33 Nowak	Y	Y	N	N	Y	Y	Y	N
34 Lundine	?	?	N	N	Y	Y	Y	N
NORTH CAROLINA								
1 Jones	?	?	N	Y	Y	Y	N	N
2 Valentine	N	Y	N	N	Y	N	Y	Y
3 Whitley	Y	Y	N	Y	Y	Y	Y	N
4 Andrews	?	?	N	N	Y	Y	Y	N
5 Neal	Y	Y	N	N	Y	Y	Y	Y
6 Britt	N	Y	N	N	Y	Y	Y	N
7 Rose	N	Y	N	Y	Y	Y	Y	N
8 Hefner	N	Y	N	N	Y	Y	Y	N
9 ***Martin***	N	Y	N	Y	Y	N	N	Y
10 ***Broyhill***	Y	Y	Y	Y	N	N	Y	Y
11 Clarke	N	Y	N	N	Y	Y	Y	Y
NORTH DAKOTA								
AL Dorgan	Y	Y	N	N	N	N	Y	N
OHIO								
1 Luken	Y	Y	N	N	Y	N	Y	Y
2 ***Gradison***	Y	Y	Y	Y	N	N	N	Y
3 Hall	?	?	N	?	Y	Y	Y	Y
4 ***Oxley***	N	Y	Y	N	N	N	N	Y
5 ***Latta***	N	Y	Y	Y	N	N	N	Y
6 ***McEwen***	Y	Y	N	N	N	N	N	Y
7 ***DeWine***	N	Y	N	N	Y	N	N	Y
8 ***Kindness***	N	Y	N	Y	N	N	N	Y
9 Kaptur	Y	Y	?	?	?	#	Y	N
10 ***Miller***	Y	Y	N	N	N	N	Y	Y
11 Eckart	Y	Y	N	N	Y	N	Y	Y
12 ***Kasich***	Y	Y	N	N	N	N	Y	Y
13 Pease	Y	Y	Y	Y	Y	Y	Y	N
14 Seiberling	Y	N	N	N	Y	Y	Y	N
15 ***Wylie***	Y	Y	N	N	Y	N	N	Y
16 ***Regula***	N	Y	Y	Y	Y	Y	N	Y
17 ***Williams***	Y	Y	N	Y	Y	Y	Y	Y
18 Applegate	Y	Y	N	N	N	Y	N	Y
19 Feighan	Y	Y	N	N	Y	N	Y	Y
20 Oakar	Y	Y	N	N	Y	Y	N	N
21 Stokes	Y	Y	N	N	Y	Y	N	N
OKLAHOMA								
1 Jones	N	Y	N	N	N	N	Y	Y
2 Synar	Y	Y	Y	Y	Y	Y	Y	?
3 Watkins	N	Y	N	N	Y	N	Y	Y
4 McCurdy	N	Y	N	N	Y	N	Y	Y
5 ***Edwards***	N	Y	N	N	Y	N	N	Y
6 English	N	Y	N	N	Y	N	Y	Y
OREGON								
1 AuCoin	Y	N	N	N	?	X	Y	Y
2 ***Smith, R.***	Y	N	N	N	Y	N	Y	Y
3 Wyden	Y	Y	N	N	N	N	Y	Y
4 Weaver	?	?	N	N	N	Y	N	Y
5 ***Smith, D.***	Y	N	N	N	N	N	N	Y
PENNSYLVANIA								
1 Foglietta	Y	Y	N	N	Y	Y	N	N
2 Gray	N	Y	N	N	Y	Y	N	N
3 Borski	Y	Y	N	N	Y	Y	Y	N
4 Kolter	Y	Y	N	N	Y	Y	Y	N
5 ***Schulze***	Y	Y	Y	N	N	N	N	Y
6 Yatron	Y	Y	N	N	Y	Y	Y	Y
7 Edgar	Y	N	N	Y	Y	Y	N	N
8 Kostmayer	Y	Y	Y	Y	Y	Y	Y	Y
9 ***Shuster***	N	Y	N	N	N	N	N	Y
10 ***McDade***	N	Y	N	Y	Y	Y	N	N
11 Harrison	Y	Y	?	?	?	?	N	N
12 Murtha	N	Y	Y	Y	Y	Y	N	N
13 ***Coughlin***	N	Y	N	Y	Y	Y	N	N
14 Coyne	N	Y	Y	Y	Y	Y	N	N
15 ***Ritter***	Y	N	N	N	Y	N	N	Y
16 ***Walker***	Y	Y	Y	N	N	N	N	Y
17 ***Gekas***	Y	Y	N	Y	N	N	N	Y
18 Walgren	Y	N	N	N	Y	Y	N	N
19 ***Goodling***	Y	Y	N	N	N	N	N	Y
20 Gaydos	Y	Y	N	N	Y	Y	Y	N
21 ***Ridge***	Y	Y	N	N	Y	Y	N	N
22 Murphy	Y	Y	N	N	Y	Y	Y	Y
23 ***Clinger***	Y	Y	N	Y	Y	Y	N	N
RHODE ISLAND								
1 St Germain	Y	Y	Y	Y	Y	Y	N	N
2 ***Schneider***	Y	Y	Y	Y	N	N	N	Y
SOUTH CAROLINA								
1 ***Hartnett***	N	Y	N	N	?	N	N	Y
2 ***Spence***	N	Y	N	N	N	N	N	Y
3 Derrick	Y	Y	N	?	Y	Y	N	Y
4 ***Campbell***	Y	Y	N	Y	N	N	N	Y
5 Spratt	Y	Y	N	N	Y	Y	N	Y
6 Tallon	Y	Y	N	N	Y	Y	Y	Y
SOUTH DAKOTA								
AL Daschle	N	Y	N	N	Y	Y	Y	N
TENNESSEE								
1 ***Quillen***	N	Y	Y	Y	N	?	N	N
2 ***Duncan***	N	Y	Y	Y	Y	Y	N	Y
3 Lloyd	N	Y	N	N	Y	N	N	Y
4 Cooper	Y	Y	N	N	Y	Y	Y	Y
5 Boner	Y	Y	N	N	Y	Y	Y	Y
6 Gore	Y	Y	N	Y	Y	Y	Y	Y
7 ***Sundquist***	N	Y	Y	Y	Y	Y	N	Y
8 Jones	N	Y	N	N	Y	Y	Y	Y
9 Ford	Y	Y	N	?	Y	Y	N	N
TEXAS								
1 Hall, S.	Y	Y	N	N	Y	Y	Y	Y
2 Wilson	N	Y	N	N	Y	Y	N	N
3 ***Bartlett***	N	Y	N	N	N	N	N	Y
4 Hall, R.	Y	Y	N	N	Y	N	Y	Y
5 Bryant	Y	Y	N	N	Y	Y	Y	N
6 ***Gramm***	N	Y	N	N	Y	N	N	Y
7 ***Archer***	Y	Y	N	N	N	N	N	Y
8 ***Fields***	Y	Y	N	N	Y	N	N	Y
9 Brooks	N	?	N	N	Y	Y	N	Y
10 Pickle	Y	Y	N	N	Y	Y	Y	Y
11 Leath	N	Y	N	N	Y	Y	N	Y
12 Wright	N	Y	N	Y	Y	Y	Y	N
13 Hightower	N	Y	N	N	Y	Y	N	Y
14 Patman	Y	Y	N	N	Y	N	N	Y
15 de la Garza	Y	Y	N	N	Y	Y	N	N
16 Coleman	N	Y	Y	Y	Y	Y	Y	Y
17 Stenholm	Y	Y	N	N	N	N	N	Y
18 Leland	Y	Y	N	N	Y	Y	N	N
19 Hance	Y	Y	N	Y	Y	?	N	Y
20 Gonzalez	N	Y	N	Y	Y	Y	N	N
21 ***Loeffler***	N	Y	Y	Y	N	N	N	Y
22 ***Paul***	?	?	N	N	N	N	N	Y
23 Kazen	N	Y	N	Y	Y	Y	N	Y
24 Frost	Y	Y	N	N	Y	Y	Y	N
25 Andrews	Y	Y	N	Y	Y	Y	Y	Y
26 Vandergriff	Y	Y	N	N	Y	N	N	Y
27 Ortiz	N	Y	N	N	Y	Y	N	N
UTAH								
1 ***Hansen***	N	Y	N	N	Y	N	N	Y
2 ***Marriott***	N	Y	N	N	N	N	N	Y
3 ***Nielson***	Y	Y	N	N	N	N	N	Y
VERMONT								
AL ***Jeffords***	Y	Y	Y	Y	N	N	Y	N
VIRGINIA								
1 ***Bateman***	N	Y	N	Y	Y	N	N	N
2 ***Whitehurst***	N	Y	N	Y	N	N	N	Y
3 ***Bliley***	?	?	N	Y	N	N	N	N
4 Sisisky	N	Y	N	Y	Y	Y	N	Y
5 Daniel	N	Y	N	N	N	N	N	Y
6 Olin	Y	Y	N	N	Y	Y	N	Y
7 ***Robinson***	N	Y	N	N	N	N	N	N
8 ***Parris***	Y	Y	Y	Y	Y	N	N	N
9 Boucher	N	Y	N	N	Y	Y	N	Y
10 ***Wolf***	Y	Y	Y	Y	Y	N	N	N
WASHINGTON								
1 ***Pritchard***	Y	Y	Y	Y	Y	N	N	N
2 Swift	Y	Y	N	Y	Y	Y	N	N
3 Bonker	Y	Y	Y	Y	Y	N	Y	Y
4 ***Morrison***	N	Y	?	Y	Y	N	Y	Y
5 Foley	N	Y	Y	Y	Y	Y	Y	N
6 Dicks	N	Y	Y	Y	Y	Y	Y	Y
7 Lowry	Y	Y	N	N	Y	Y	Y	N
8 ***Chandler***	Y	Y	N	Y	Y	N	N	Y
WEST VIRGINIA								
1 Mollohan	N	Y	Y	Y	N	Y	N	N
2 Staggers	Y	Y	N	N	N	Y	Y	N
3 Wise	Y	Y	N	N	N	N	Y	Y
4 Rahall	N	N	Y	Y	N	Y	N	N
WISCONSIN								
1 Aspin	Y	Y	N	N	N	Y	Y	N
2 Kastenmeier	Y	N	N	N	N	Y	N	N
3 ***Gunderson***	N	Y	N	N	N	N	N	Y
4 Kleczka	Y	Y	Y	Y	Y	Y	N	N
5 Moody	Y	N	N	N	Y	Y	N	N
6 ***Petri***	Y	N	N	N	N	N	N	Y
7 Obey	Y	N	N	N	N	Y	Y	N
8 ***Roth***	N	Y	N	N	N	N	N	Y
9 ***Sensenbrenner***	?	?	?	?	?	?	?	?
WYOMING								
AL ***Cheney***	N	Y	N	Y	N	N	N	Y

Southern states - Ala., Ark., Fla., Ga., Ky., La., Miss., N.C., Okla., S.C., Tenn., Texas, Va.

262. HR 5899. District of Columbia Appropriations, Fiscal 1985.
Walker, R-Pa., amendment to cut funding in the bill by 2 percent. Rejected 151-273: R 104-59; D 47-214 (ND 20-154, SD 27-60), June 28, 1984. (This amendment previously had been adopted in the Committee of the Whole (*see vote 261, p. 80-H*).)

263. HR 5899. District of Columbia Appropriations, Fiscal 1985.
Passage of the bill to appropriate $639,470,000 in federal funds, and $2,317,875,000 in District funds, for fiscal 1985. Passed 308-116: R 76-87; D 232-29 (ND 165-9, SD 67-20), June 28, 1984. The president had requested $503,470,000 in federal funds and $2,302,962,000 in District funds.

264. HR 5680. Federal Pay Equity.
Daniel B. Crane, R-Ill., amendment to the Oakar, D-Ohio, amendment, to change the definition of discriminatory wage-setting practices to be examined in the study required by the bill from "comparable" duties and working conditions to "substantially equal" duties and working conditions. Rejected 22-395: R 20-141; D 2-254 (ND 0-168, SD 2-86), June 28, 1984.

265. HR 5680. Federal Pay Equity.
Passage of the bill to require a study of possible discriminatory wage-setting practices in the federal government and to establish a federal employee performance management and recognition system. Passed 413-6: R 154-6; D 259-0 (ND 169-0, SD 90-0), June 28, 1984.

266. HR 3678. Water Resources Development Authorization.
Shaw, R-Fla., amendment to deauthorize the Cross-Florida Barge Canal. Rejected 201-204: R 102-54; D 99-150 (ND 80-85, SD 19-65), June 28, 1984.

267. H Con Res 332. Andrei Sakharov and Yelena Bonner.
Adoption of the concurrent resolution expressing the sense of Congress that the Soviet Union should provide signers of the Helsinki Final Act with specific information on the whereabouts, health and legal status of Soviet dissidents Andrei Sakharov and Yelena Bonner (Sakharov's wife). Adopted 399-0: R 153-0; D 246-0 (ND 161-0, SD 85-0), June 29, 1984.

268. HR 5950. Quadrennial Political Party Conventions.
Adoption of the rule (H Res 544) providing for House floor consideration of the bill to increase the federal contribution to the quadrennial political party presidential national nominating conventions. Adopted 267-136: R 33-121; D 234-15 (ND 156-8, SD 78-7), June 29, 1984.

269. HR 5953. Debt Limit Increase.
Ways and Means Committee amendment (offered by Rostenkowski, D-Ill.) to raise the existing public debt limit of $1.52 trillion by $232 billion to $1.753 trillion, an amount estimated to provide sufficient government borrowing authority through June 1985. Rejected 109-300: R 62-94; D 47-206 (ND 33-133, SD 14-73), June 29, 1984. A "yea" was a vote supporting the president's position.

KEY

Y	Voted for (yea).
#	Paired for.
+	Announced for.
N	Voted against (nay).
X	Paired against.
-	Announced against.
P	Voted "present".
C	Voted "present" to avoid possible conflict of interest.
?	Did not vote or otherwise make a position known.

Democrats   *Republicans*

	262	263	264	265	266	267	268	269
ALABAMA								
1 *Edwards*	N	Y	N	Y	N	Y	Y	Y
2 *Dickinson*	N	Y	Y	Y	N	Y	N	Y
3 Nichols	Y	Y	N	Y	N	Y	Y	N
4 Bevill	N	Y	N	Y	N	?	?	Y
5 Flippo	N	Y	N	Y	N	Y	?	Y
6 Erdreich	N	Y	N	Y	N	Y	N	N
7 Shelby	Y	N	N	Y	N	Y	Y	N
ALASKA								
AL *Young*	N	Y	N	Y	N	Y	N	N
ARIZONA								
1 *McCain*	Y	N	N	Y	N	?	N	Y
2 Udall	N	Y	N	Y	Y	?	?	?
3 *Stump*	Y	N	Y	N	N	Y	N	N
4 *Rudd*	Y	N	Y	Y	?	?	?	?
5 McNulty	N	Y	N	Y	N	Y	N	Y
ARKANSAS								
1 Alexander	N	Y	N	Y	?	?	Y	N
2 *Bethune*	Y	N	N	?	Y	?	N	N
3 *Hammerschmidt*	N	Y	N	Y	N	Y	N	Y
4 Anthony	N	Y	N	Y	?	?	Y	N
CALIFORNIA								
1 Bosco	N	N	N	Y	N	Y	Y	N
2 *Chappie*	N	N	N	Y	Y	Y	N	N
3 Matsui	N	Y	N	Y	N	Y	Y	Y
4 Fazio	N	Y	N	Y	N	Y	Y	N
5 Burton	N	Y	N	Y	N	Y	Y	N
6 Boxer	N	Y	N	Y	Y	Y	Y	N
7 Miller	N	Y	N	Y	Y	Y	Y	N
8 Dellums	N	Y	N	Y	Y	Y	Y	N
9 Stark	?	?	?	?	?	?	?	?
10 Edwards	N	Y	N	Y	Y	Y	Y	N
11 Lantos	N	Y	N	Y	N	Y	Y	N
12 *Zschau*	Y	N	N	Y	Y	Y	N	N
13 Mineta	N	Y	N	Y	N	Y	Y	N
14 *Shumway*	Y	N	N	N	Y	N	N	N
15 Coelho	N	Y	N	Y	N	Y	Y	N
16 Panetta	N	Y	N	Y	Y	Y	Y	N
17 *Pashayan*	Y	Y	N	Y	N	Y	N	N
18 Lehman	N	Y	N	Y	N	Y	Y	N
19 *Lagomarsino*	N	N	N	Y	Y	Y	N	N
20 *Thomas*	Y	Y	N	Y	Y	Y	N	N
21 *Fiedler*	Y	N	N	Y	?	?	?	?
22 *Moorhead*	Y	N	N	Y	Y	Y	N	N
23 Beilenson	N	Y	N	Y	Y	Y	Y	Y
24 Waxman	N	Y	N	Y	N	Y	Y	N
25 Roybal	N	Y	?	Y	Y	Y	Y	N
26 Berman	N	Y	N	Y	Y	Y	Y	Y
27 Levine	N	Y	N	Y	Y	Y	Y	N
28 Dixon	N	Y	N	Y	N	Y	Y	N
29 Hawkins	N	Y	N	Y	?	Y	Y	N
30 Martinez	N	Y	N	Y	N	Y	Y	N
31 Dymally	?	?	?	?	?	?	?	?
32 Anderson	N	Y	N	Y	N	Y	N	N
33 *Dreier*	Y	N	N	Y	Y	Y	N	N
34 Torres	N	Y	N	Y	Y	Y	Y	N
35 *Lewis*	Y	N	N	Y	Y	Y	N	Y
36 Brown	N	Y	N	Y	N	Y	Y	Y
37 *McCandless*	Y	N	Y	N	N	Y	N	N
38 Patterson	N	Y	N	Y	N	Y	Y	N
39 *Dannemeyer*	Y	N	Y	Y	Y	N	N	N
40 *Badham*	N	N	N	Y	N	Y	N	Y
41 *Lowery*	N	Y	N	Y	Y	Y	N	Y
42 *Lungren*	Y	Y	Y	Y	Y	Y	N	Y

	262	263	264	265	266	267	268	269
43 *Packard*	Y	N	Y	Y	N	Y	N	N
44 Bates	N	Y	N	Y	Y	Y	Y	N
45 *Hunter*	Y	N	N	N	Y	Y	N	Y
COLORADO								
1 Schroeder	N	Y	N	Y	N	Y	Y	N
2 Wirth	N	Y	N	Y	Y	Y	Y	N
3 Kogovsek	N	Y	N	Y	N	Y	Y	N
4 *Brown*	Y	N	N	Y	N	Y	N	N
5 *Kramer*	Y	N	N	Y	Y	Y	N	N
6 *Schaefer*	Y	N	N	Y	Y	Y	N	N
CONNECTICUT								
1 Kennelly	N	Y	N	Y	N	Y	Y	N
2 Gejdenson	N	Y	Y	Y	Y	Y	Y	N
3 Morrison	N	Y	N	Y	Y	Y	?	N
4 *McKinney*	N	Y	N	Y	Y	Y	Y	Y
5 Ratchford	N	Y	N	Y	N	Y	Y	N
6 *Johnson*	N	Y	N	Y	Y	Y	Y	Y
DELAWARE								
AL Carper	Y	Y	N	Y	Y	Y	Y	N
FLORIDA								
1 Hutto	N	Y	N	Y	N	Y	N	N
2 Fuqua	N	Y	N	Y	N	Y	N	N
3 Bennett	Y	Y	N	Y	Y	Y	Y	Y
4 Chappell	N	Y	?	Y	N	Y	N	N
5 *McCollum*	N	Y	N	Y	Y	Y	N	N
6 MacKay	Y	Y	N	Y	Y	Y	Y	N
7 Gibbons	N	Y	N	Y	N	Y	Y	Y
8 *Young*	Y	Y	N	Y	Y	Y	N	N
9 *Bilirakis*	Y	N	N	Y	Y	N	N	N
10 Ireland	N	N	N	Y	Y	Y	?	N
11 Nelson	N	Y	N	Y	N	Y	Y	N
12 *Lewis*	Y	N	N	Y	Y	N	N	N
13 *Mack*	Y	N	N	Y	N	Y	N	Y
14 Mica	?	?	?	Y	Y	Y	Y	N
15 *Shaw*	N	Y	N	Y	Y	Y	N	N
16 Smith	?	?	N	Y	N	Y	Y	N
17 Lehman	N	Y	N	Y	Y	Y	Y	Y
18 Pepper	N	Y	N	Y	N	Y	Y	N
19 Fascell	N	Y	N	Y	Y	Y	Y	Y
GEORGIA								
1 Thomas	N	Y	N	Y	N	Y	N	N
2 Hatcher	N	Y	N	Y	N	Y	N	N
3 Ray	?	N	N	Y	N	Y	N	N
4 Levitas	Y	Y	N	Y	Y	Y	N	N
5 Fowler	N	Y	N	Y	N	Y	Y	N
6 *Gingrich*	Y	N	N	Y	Y	Y	?	Y
7 Darden	N	Y	N	Y	N	Y	Y	N
8 Rowland	Y	Y	N	Y	N	Y	N	N
9 Jenkins	N	Y	N	Y	N	Y	N	N
10 Barnard	Y	Y	N	Y	N	Y	N	N
HAWAII								
1 Heftel	N	Y	N	Y	N	?	Y	Y
2 Akaka	N	Y	N	Y	N	Y	Y	N
IDAHO								
1 *Craig*	Y	N	N	Y	Y	?	?	?
2 *Hansen*	?	?	?	?	?	?	?	?
ILLINOIS								
1 Hayes	N	Y	N	Y	N	Y	Y	N
2 Savage	N	Y	N	Y	N	Y	Y	N
3 Russo	N	Y	N	Y	Y	Y	Y	N
4 *O'Brien*	N	Y	N	Y	N	Y	Y	Y
5 Lipinski	N	Y	N	Y	N	Y	Y	N
6 *Hyde*	N	Y	N	Y	Y	Y	N	N
7 Collins	N	Y	N	Y	N	Y	Y	N
8 Rostenkowski	N	Y	N	Y	N	Y	Y	N
9 Yates	N	Y	N	Y	Y	Y	Y	N
10 *Porter*	N	Y	N	Y	N	Y	N	Y
11 Annunzio	N	Y	N	Y	N	Y	Y	N
12 *Crane, P.*	Y	N	N	N	N	N	N	N
13 *Erlenborn*	?	?	?	?	?	?	?	?
14 *Corcoran*	Y	N	Y	Y	N	Y	N	Y
15 *Madigan*	Y	N	N	?	Y	Y	Y	Y
16 *Martin*	Y	N	Y	Y	Y	Y	N	Y
17 Evans	N	Y	N	Y	N	Y	Y	N
18 *Michel*	N	Y	N	Y	Y	Y	Y	N
19 *Crane, D.*	Y	N	Y	N	N	Y	N	N
20 Durbin	N	Y	N	Y	Y	Y	Y	N
21 Price	N	Y	N	Y	N	Y	N	N
22 Simon	N	Y	N	Y	?	?	?	?
INDIANA								
1 Hall	N	Y	N	Y	N	Y	Y	N
2 Sharp	N	Y	N	Y	Y	Y	Y	N
3 *Hiler*	Y	N	Y	Y	Y	Y	N	N
4 *Coats*	Y	N	N	Y	Y	Y	N	N
5 Hillis	N	Y	N	Y	Y	Y	N	N

ND - Northern Democrats   SD - Southern Democrats

	262	263	264	265	266	267	268	269
6 ***Burton***	Y	N	N	Y	Y	Y	N	N
7 ***Myers***	N	N	N	Y	N	Y	N	N
8 McCloskey	N	Y	N	Y	N	Y	Y	N
9 Hamilton	Y	Y	N	Y	Y	Y	Y	Y
10 Jacobs	N	Y	N	Y	N	Y	N	N
IOWA								
1 ***Leach***	Y	N	N	Y	Y	Y	N	N
2 ***Tauke***	N	N	N	Y	Y	Y	N	N
3 ***Evans***	Y	N	N	Y	Y	Y	N	N
4 Smith	N	Y	N	Y	N	Y	N	N
5 Harkin	N	Y	N	Y	Y	Y	Y	N
6 Bedell	N	Y	N	Y	Y	Y	Y	N
KANSAS								
1 ***Roberts***	Y	N	N	Y	Y	Y	N	N
2 Slattery	Y	Y	N	Y	Y	Y	Y	N
3 ***Winn***	Y	Y	N	Y	N	Y	N	N
4 Glickman	Y	Y	N	Y	Y	Y	Y	N
5 ***Whittaker***	Y	N	N	Y	N	Y	N	N
KENTUCKY								
1 Hubbard	Y	N	N	Y	N	Y	N	N
2 Natcher	N	Y	N	Y	N	Y	Y	N
3 Mazzoli	N	Y	N	Y	N	Y	Y	N
4 ***Snyder***	N	Y	N	Y	N	Y	N	N
5 ***Rogers***	Y	Y	N	Y	Y	Y	N	N
6 ***Hopkins***	Y	Y	N	Y	Y	Y	N	N
7 Perkins	N	Y	N	Y	N	Y	Y	Y
LOUISIANA								
1 ***Livingston***	Y	N	?	Y	N	Y	N	Y
2 Boggs	N	Y	N	Y	N	Y	Y	N
3 Tauzin	Y	Y	N	Y	N	Y	Y	N
4 Roemer	Y	N	N	Y	N	Y	N	N
5 Huckaby	N	Y	N	Y	N	Y	N	N
6 ***Moore***	Y	Y	N	Y	N	Y	N	N
7 Breaux	N	Y	N	Y	N	?	?	?
8 Long	N	Y	N	Y	N	Y	Y	Y
MAINE								
1 ***McKernan***	N	Y	N	Y	Y	Y	N	Y
2 ***Snowe***	N	Y	N	Y	Y	Y	N	N
MARYLAND								
1 Dyson	Y	Y	N	Y	N	Y	Y	N
2 Long	Y	Y	N	Y	N	?	Y	N
3 Mikulski	N	Y	N	Y	N	Y	Y	N
4 ***Holt***	N	Y	N	Y	N	Y	N	Y
5 Hoyer	N	Y	N	Y	N	?	Y	N
6 Byron	Y	N	N	Y	N	Y	?	N
7 Mitchell	N	Y	N	Y	N	Y	Y	N
8 Barnes	N	Y	N	Y	Y	Y	Y	Y
MASSACHUSETTS								
1 ***Conte***	N	Y	N	Y	Y	Y	N	Y
2 Boland	N	Y	N	Y	Y	Y	Y	Y
3 Early	N	Y	?	?	?	?	?	?
4 Frank	N	Y	N	Y	?	Y	Y	Y
5 Shannon	?	?	?	?	?	?	?	?
6 Mavroules	N	Y	N	Y	N	Y	Y	N
7 Markey	N	Y	N	Y	Y	Y	Y	N
8 O'Neill								
9 Moakley	N	Y	N	Y	N	Y	Y	Y
10 Studds	N	Y	N	Y	Y	Y	Y	N
11 Donnelly	N	Y	N	Y	N	Y	Y	Y
MICHIGAN								
1 Conyers	N	Y	N	Y	Y	Y	Y	Y
2 ***Pursell***	Y	N	N	Y	N	Y	N	N
3 Wolpe	N	Y	N	Y	Y	Y	Y	N
4 ***Siljander***	Y	N	N	Y	Y	Y	N	N
5 ***Sawyer***	Y	Y	N	Y	Y	Y	N	Y
6 Carr	N	Y	N	Y	N	Y	Y	N
7 Kildee	N	Y	N	Y	Y	Y	Y	N
8 Traxler	N	Y	N	Y	N	Y	Y	N
9 ***Vander Jagt***	N	Y	N	?	Y	Y	Y	Y
10 Albosta	N	Y	N	Y	N	Y	Y	N
11 ***Davis***	N	Y	N	Y	N	Y	Y	N
12 Bonior	N	Y	?	Y	N	Y	Y	Y
13 Crockett	N	Y	N	Y	N	?	Y	N
14 Hertel	N	Y	N	Y	Y	Y	Y	N
15 Ford	N	Y	N	Y	N	?	?	?
16 Dingell	N	Y	N	Y	Y	Y	Y	N
17 Levin	N	Y	N	Y	Y	Y	Y	N
18 ***Broomfield***	Y	N	N	Y	N	Y	N	N
MINNESOTA								
1 Penny	Y	N	N	Y	Y	Y	Y	N
2 ***Weber***	Y	N	N	Y	Y	Y	N	N
3 ***Frenzel***	Y	N	N	Y	Y	Y	Y	Y
4 Vento	N	Y	N	Y	Y	Y	Y	N
5 Sabo	N	Y	N	Y	N	Y	Y	N
6 Sikorski	N	Y	N	Y	Y	Y	Y	N
7 ***Stangeland***	Y	N	N	Y	N	Y	N	Y
8 Oberstar	N	Y	N	Y	Y	Y	Y	N
MISSISSIPPI								
1 Whitten	N	Y	N	Y	N	Y	Y	N
2 ***Franklin***	Y	Y	N	Y	N	Y	N	N
3 Montgomery	Y	N	N	Y	N	Y	Y	N
4 Dowdy	N	Y	N	Y	N	Y	Y	N
5 ***Lott***	Y	N	N	Y	?	Y	Y	Y
MISSOURI								
1 Clay	N	Y	N	Y	Y	Y	Y	N
2 Young	N	Y	N	Y	N	Y	Y	N
3 Gephardt	N	Y	N	Y	N	Y	Y	N
4 Skelton	N	Y	N	Y	N	Y	Y	N
5 Wheat	N	Y	N	Y	N	Y	Y	N
6 ***Coleman***	Y	N	N	Y	Y	Y	Y	N
7 ***Taylor***	N	N	N	Y	N	Y	N	N
8 ***Emerson***	N	Y	N	Y	N	Y	N	N
9 Volkmer	N	Y	N	Y	N	Y	Y	N
MONTANA								
1 Williams	Y	N	?	?	?	Y	Y	Y
2 ***Marlenee***	Y	N	N	Y	N	Y	N	N
NEBRASKA								
1 ***Bereuter***	N	N	N	Y	Y	Y	N	N
2 ***Daub***	Y	N	N	Y	N	Y	N	N
3 ***Smith***	Y	N	N	Y	N	Y	N	N
NEVADA								
1 Reid	N	Y	N	Y	Y	Y	Y	Y
2 ***Vucanovich***	Y	N	N	Y	Y	Y	N	N
NEW HAMPSHIRE								
1 D'Amours	Y	Y	N	Y	Y	Y	Y	N
2 ***Gregg***	Y	N	N	Y	Y	Y	Y	Y
NEW JERSEY								
1 Florio	N	Y	N	Y	N	Y	Y	N
2 Hughes	N	Y	N	Y	N	Y	Y	N
3 Howard	N	Y	N	Y	N	Y	Y	N
4 ***Smith***	Y	Y	N	Y	Y	Y	N	N
5 ***Roukema***	N	Y	N	Y	Y	Y	N	N
6 Dwyer	N	Y	N	Y	N	Y	Y	Y
7 ***Rinaldo***	Y	Y	N	Y	Y	Y	N	N
8 Roe	N	Y	N	Y	N	Y	Y	N
9 Torricelli	Y	N	N	Y	N	Y	Y	N
10 Rodino	N	Y	N	Y	N	Y	Y	N
11 Minish	Y	Y	N	Y	Y	Y	Y	N
12 ***Courter***	Y	N	N	Y	Y	Y	N	N
13 Vacancy								
14 Guarini	N	Y	N	Y	N	Y	Y	N
NEW MEXICO								
1 ***Lujan***	Y	N	N	Y	Y	Y	Y	N
2 ***Skeen***	Y	N	N	Y	Y	Y	N	N
3 Richardson	N	Y	N	Y	Y	Y	Y	N
NEW YORK								
1 ***Carney***	N	Y	N	Y	N	Y	N	N
2 Downey	N	Y	N	Y	Y	Y	Y	N
3 Mrazek	N	Y	N	Y	?	Y	Y	N
4 ***Lent***	Y	N	N	Y	N	Y	N	N
5 ***McGrath***	Y	N	N	Y	Y	Y	N	N
6 Addabbo	N	Y	N	Y	N	Y	Y	N
7 Ackerman	N	Y	N	Y	Y	Y	Y	N
8 Scheuer	N	Y	N	Y	Y	Y	Y	N
9 Ferraro	N	Y	?	?	?	Y	Y	N
10 Schumer	N	Y	N	Y	Y	Y	Y	N
11 Towns	N	Y	N	Y	Y	?	?	?
12 Owens	N	Y	N	Y	Y	Y	Y	N
13 Solarz	N	Y	N	Y	Y	Y	Y	Y
14 ***Molinari***	Y	N	N	Y	N	Y	N	N
15 ***Green***	N	Y	N	Y	Y	Y	Y	Y
16 Rangel	N	Y	N	Y	N	Y	Y	N
17 Weiss	N	Y	N	Y	Y	Y	Y	N
18 Garcia	N	Y	N	Y	Y	Y	Y	Y
19 Biaggi	N	Y	N	Y	N	Y	Y	N
20 Ottinger	N	Y	N	Y	Y	Y	Y	N
21 ***Fish***	N	Y	N	Y	Y	Y	Y	Y
22 ***Gilman***	Y	Y	N	Y	Y	Y	N	N
23 Stratton	N	Y	N	Y	N	Y	Y	Y
24 ***Solomon***	Y	N	N	Y	Y	Y	N	N
25 ***Boehlert***	N	Y	N	Y	Y	Y	Y	Y
26 ***Martin***	N	Y	N	Y	Y	Y	N	N
27 ***Wortley***	N	Y	N	Y	Y	Y	N	N
28 McHugh	N	Y	N	Y	N	Y	Y	N
29 ***Horton***	N	Y	N	Y	N	Y	N	Y
30 ***Conable***	N	Y	N	Y	Y	Y	N	Y
31 ***Kemp***	Y	Y	N	Y	Y	Y	N	Y
32 LaFalce	Y	Y	N	Y	N	Y	Y	N
33 Nowak	N	Y	N	Y	N	Y	Y	N
34 Lundine	N	Y	N	Y	Y	Y	Y	N
NORTH CAROLINA								
1 Jones	N	Y	N	Y	N	Y	Y	Y
2 Valentine	Y	Y	N	Y	?	Y	Y	N
3 Whitley	N	Y	N	Y	N	Y	Y	N
4 Andrews	N	Y	N	Y	?	Y	Y	N
5 Neal	N	Y	N	Y	N	Y	Y	N
6 Britt	N	Y	N	Y	N	Y	Y	N
7 Rose	N	Y	N	Y	N	Y	Y	N
8 Hefner	N	Y	N	Y	N	Y	Y	N
9 ***Martin***	N	Y	Y	Y	Y	?	?	?
10 ***Broyhill***	Y	N	N	Y	N	Y	Y	Y
11 Clarke	N	Y	N	Y	?	Y	Y	N
NORTH DAKOTA								
AL Dorgan	N	Y	N	Y	N	Y	Y	N
OHIO								
1 Luken	Y	N	N	Y	N	Y	N	N
2 ***Gradison***	Y	Y	N	Y	Y	Y	N	Y
3 Hall	Y	Y	N	Y	N	Y	Y	N
4 ***Oxley***	Y	N	N	Y	Y	Y	N	N
5 ***Latta***	Y	N	N	Y	Y	Y	N	N
6 ***McEwen***	Y	N	N	Y	N	Y	N	Y
7 ***DeWine***	Y	N	N	Y	Y	Y	Y	N
8 ***Kindness***	Y	Y	N	Y	N	Y	N	Y
9 Kaptur	N	Y	N	Y	N	Y	Y	N
10 ***Miller***	Y	N	N	Y	N	Y	N	N
11 Eckart	Y	Y	N	Y	Y	Y	Y	N
12 ***Kasich***	Y	Y	N	Y	Y	Y	N	N
13 Pease	N	Y	N	Y	Y	Y	Y	Y
14 Seiberling	N	Y	N	Y	Y	?	Y	N
15 ***Wylie***	N	Y	N	Y	Y	Y	N	N
16 ***Regula***	Y	Y	N	Y	Y	Y	N	Y
17 ***Williams***	N	Y	?	Y	?	?	?	?
18 Applegate	N	Y	N	Y	N	Y	Y	N
19 Feighan	Y	Y	N	Y	Y	Y	Y	N
20 Oakar	N	Y	N	Y	N	Y	Y	N
21 Stokes	N	Y	N	Y	N	Y	Y	N
OKLAHOMA								
1 Jones	N	N	N	Y	N	Y	Y	N
2 Synar	N	Y	N	Y	Y	Y	Y	Y
3 Watkins	N	N	N	Y	N	Y	Y	N
4 McCurdy	Y	N	N	Y	Y	Y	N	N
5 ***Edwards***	N	N	N	Y	Y	Y	N	N
6 English	Y	N	N	Y	Y	Y	N	N
OREGON								
1 AuCoin	N	N	N	Y	?	Y	Y	N
2 ***Smith, R.***	Y	N	N	Y	N	Y	Y	N
3 Wyden	N	N	N	Y	Y	Y	Y	N
4 Weaver	Y	N	N	Y	Y	Y	N	N
5 ***Smith, D.***	Y	N	Y	Y	Y	Y	N	N
PENNSYLVANIA								
1 Foglietta	N	Y	N	?	?	?	?	?
2 Gray	N	Y	N	Y	N	Y	Y	N
3 Borski	N	Y	N	Y	Y	Y	Y	N
4 Kolter	N	Y	N	Y	N	Y	Y	N
5 ***Schulze***	Y	N	N	Y	?	Y	N	Y
6 Yatron	N	Y	N	Y	N	?	?	?
7 Edgar	N	Y	N	Y	Y	Y	Y	Y
8 Kostmayer	Y	Y	N	Y	Y	Y	Y	Y
9 ***Shuster***	Y	N	N	Y	N	Y	N	N
10 ***McDade***	N	Y	N	Y	?	Y	N	Y
11 Harrison	N	Y	N	Y	N	?	?	+
12 Murtha	N	Y	N	Y	N	Y	Y	Y
13 ***Coughlin***	N	Y	N	Y	Y	Y	Y	N
14 Coyne	N	Y	N	Y	N	Y	Y	Y
15 ***Ritter***	Y	N	Y	Y	Y	Y	N	N
16 ***Walker***	Y	N	N	Y	Y	Y	N	Y
17 ***Gekas***	N	Y	N	Y	Y	Y	N	Y
18 Walgren	N	Y	N	Y	Y	Y	N	N
19 ***Goodling***	Y	Y	N	Y	Y	Y	N	Y
20 Gaydos	N	Y	N	Y	N	Y	Y	N
21 ***Ridge***	N	Y	N	Y	Y	?	?	?
22 Murphy	N	Y	N	Y	N	Y	Y	N
23 ***Clinger***	N	Y	N	Y	N	Y	Y	Y
RHODE ISLAND								
1 St Germain	N	Y	N	Y	N	Y	N	Y
2 ***Schneider***	N	Y	N	Y	Y	Y	Y	Y
SOUTH CAROLINA								
1 ***Hartnett***	Y	N	N	Y	Y	Y	N	N
2 ***Spence***	Y	N	N	Y	Y	Y	N	N
3 Derrick	N	Y	N	Y	N	Y	Y	N
4 ***Campbell***	Y	N	N	Y	Y	Y	N	N
5 Spratt	N	Y	N	Y	Y	Y	Y	N
6 Tallon	N	Y	N	Y	Y	Y	Y	N
SOUTH DAKOTA								
AL Daschle	N	Y	N	Y	N	Y	Y	N
TENNESSEE								
1 ***Quillen***	N	Y	N	Y	Y	Y	Y	Y
2 ***Duncan***	Y	Y	N	Y	Y	Y	Y	Y
3 Lloyd	Y	N	N	Y	N	Y	Y	N
4 Cooper	N	Y	N	Y	Y	Y	Y	N
5 Boner	N	Y	N	Y	N	Y	Y	N
6 Gore	Y	Y	N	Y	N	Y	Y	N
7 ***Sundquist***	Y	Y	N	Y	N	Y	Y	Y
8 Jones	Y	Y	N	Y	N	Y	Y	N
9 Ford	N	Y	N	Y	N	Y	Y	N
TEXAS								
1 Hall, S.	N	N	N	Y	N	Y	Y	N
2 Wilson	N	Y	N	Y	N	Y	Y	N
3 ***Bartlett***	Y	N	Y	N	Y	Y	Y	Y
4 Hall, R.	Y	N	Y	Y	N	Y	Y	N
5 Bryant	N	Y	N	Y	Y	Y	Y	N
6 ***Gramm***	Y	N	N	Y	Y	Y	N	N
7 ***Archer***	Y	N	N	Y	Y	Y	N	N
8 ***Fields***	Y	N	N	Y	N	Y	N	N
9 Brooks	Y	Y	N	Y	N	Y	Y	Y
10 Pickle	N	Y	N	Y	N	Y	Y	N
11 Leath	Y	?	N	Y	N	Y	Y	Y
12 Wright	N	Y	N	Y	N	Y	Y	N
13 Hightower	Y	N	N	Y	N	Y	N	N
14 Patman	Y	N	N	Y	N	Y	N	N
15 de la Garza	N	Y	N	Y	N	?	?	?
16 Coleman	N	Y	N	Y	Y	Y	Y	Y
17 Stenholm	Y	N	N	Y	N	Y	Y	N
18 Leland	N	Y	N	Y	Y	Y	Y	N
19 Hance	Y	N	N	Y	N	Y	Y	N
20 Gonzalez	N	Y	N	Y	N	Y	Y	N
21 ***Loeffler***	Y	N	Y	Y	?	Y	Y	Y
22 ***Paul***	Y	N	Y	N	Y	?	?	?
23 Kazen	N	N	N	Y	N	Y	Y	N
24 Frost	N	Y	N	Y	N	Y	Y	N
25 Andrews	Y	Y	N	Y	?	Y	Y	N
26 Vandergriff	Y	N	Y	Y	N	Y	Y	N
27 Ortiz	N	Y	N	Y	N	Y	Y	N
UTAH								
1 ***Hansen***	Y	N	Y	Y	Y	Y	N	N
2 ***Marriott***	N	Y	N	Y	Y	Y	N	N
3 ***Nielson***	Y	N	N	Y	Y	Y	N	N
VERMONT								
AL ***Jeffords***	N	Y	N	Y	Y	Y	N	Y
VIRGINIA								
1 ***Bateman***	N	Y	N	Y	N	Y	Y	Y
2 ***Whitehurst***	N	Y	N	Y	N	Y	Y	Y
3 ***Bliley***	N	Y	N	Y	N	Y	N	N
4 Sisisky	N	Y	N	Y	N	Y	Y	N
5 Daniel	N	N	N	Y	N	Y	Y	N
6 Olin	Y	Y	N	Y	Y	Y	Y	N
7 ***Robinson***	N	Y	N	Y	?	Y	N	N
8 ***Parris***	N	Y	N	Y	Y	Y	N	Y
9 Boucher	N	Y	N	Y	N	Y	Y	N
10 ***Wolf***	N	Y	N	Y	Y	Y	N	Y
WASHINGTON								
1 ***Pritchard***	N	Y	N	Y	Y	?	?	Y
2 Swift	N	Y	N	Y	N	Y	Y	N
3 Bonker	N	Y	N	Y	Y	Y	Y	Y
4 ***Morrison***	Y	Y	N	Y	Y	Y	N	N
5 Foley	N	Y	N	Y	N	Y	Y	Y
6 Dicks	N	Y	N	Y	N	Y	Y	Y
7 Lowry	N	Y	N	Y	Y	Y	Y	N
8 ***Chandler***	Y	Y	N	Y	Y	Y	N	N
WEST VIRGINIA								
1 Mollohan	Y	Y	N	Y	N	Y	Y	Y
2 Staggers	N	Y	N	Y	?	Y	Y	N
3 Wise	N	Y	N	Y	Y	Y	Y	N
4 Rahall	N	Y	N	Y	N	Y	Y	Y
WISCONSIN								
1 Aspin	N	Y	N	?	Y	Y	Y	N
2 Kastenmeier	N	Y	N	Y	Y	Y	Y	N
3 ***Gunderson***	N	Y	N	Y	N	Y	N	Y
4 Kleczka	N	Y	N	Y	Y	Y	Y	Y
5 Moody	N	Y	N	Y	Y	Y	Y	N
6 ***Petri***	Y	N	N	Y	Y	Y	N	N
7 Obey	N	Y	?	Y	Y	Y	Y	N
8 ***Roth***	Y	N	Y	Y	N	Y	N	N
9 ***Sensenbrenner***	?	?	?	?	?	?	?	?
WYOMING								
AL ***Cheney***	Y	N	Y	Y	Y	Y	N	Y

Southern states - Ala., Ark., Fla., Ga., Ky., La., Miss., N.C., Okla., S.C., Tenn., Texas, Va.

270. HR 5953. Debt Limit Increase. Passage of the bill to increase the existing public debt limit of $1.52 trillion by $53 billion to $1.573 trillion, an amount estimated to provide sufficient government borrowing authority through August 1984. Passed 208-202: R 84-72; D 124-130 (ND 78-89, SD 46-41), June 29, 1984. A "yea" was a vote supporting the president's position.

271. HR 5950. Quadrennial Political Party Conventions. Passage of the bill to increase the federal contribution to the quadrennial political party presidential national nominating conventions. Passed 226-169: R 27-125; D 199-44 (ND 135-23, SD 64-21), June 29, 1984.

272. HR 5174. Bankruptcy Court Act. Adoption of the conference report on the bill to restructure the bankruptcy courts, bar companies filing for bankruptcy from abrogating their labor contracts without prior court approval, make it more difficult for consumers to declare bankruptcy and cancel their debts, provide expedited procedures for farmers and fishermen to recover their products or proceeds therefrom when grain elevators or processing plants go bankrupt, and bar the discharge in bankruptcy of debts incurred as a result of drunken driving. Adopted 394-0: R 152-0; D 242-0 (ND 159-0, SD 83-0), June 29, 1984.

273. HR 3678. Water Resources Development Authorization. Hopkins, R-Ky., amendment to require state cost-sharing for the construction of the Falmouth Dam in Kentucky. Rejected 148-196: R 66-66; D 82-130 (ND 56-85, SD 26-45), June 29, 1984.

274. H Con Res 334. Adjournment Resolution. Adoption of the concurrent resolution to provide for the adjournment of the House and Senate from June 29 to July 23, 1984. Adopted 319-9: R 122-3; D 197-6 (ND 133-3, SD 64-3), June 29, 1984.

275. HR 3678. Water Resources Development Authorization. Petri, R-Wis., amendment to require non-federal interests to pay certain shares of water project costs during the project's construction, require non-federal interests to pay 30 percent of costs of general cargo ports, and set an annually declining ceiling on obligation of general revenues for inland waterway projects. Rejected 85-213: R 46-68; D 39-145 (ND 34-83, SD 5-62), June 29, 1984. A "yea" was a vote supporting the president's position.

276. HR 3678. Water Resources Development Authorization. Passage of the bill to authorize various water resources development and conservation projects to be constructed by the Army Corps of Engineers. Passed 259-33: R 89-23; D 170-10 (ND 107-9, SD 63-1), June 29, 1984. A "nay" was a vote supporting the president's position.

KEY

Y Voted for (yea).
\# Paired for.
\+ Announced for.
N Voted against (nay).
X Paired against.
- Announced against.
P Voted "present".
C Voted "present" to avoid possible conflict of interest.
? Did not vote or otherwise make a position known.

Democrats *Republicans*

	270	271	272	273	274	275	276
ALABAMA							
1 Edwards	Y	Y	Y	?	?	?	?
2 Dickinson	N	N	Y	Y	Y	N	Y
3 Nichols	N	Y	Y	Y	?	?	?
4 Bevill	?	?	?	?	?	?	?
5 Flippo	Y	Y	Y	N	Y	?	?
6 Erdreich	N	N	Y	N	Y	N	Y
7 Shelby	N	Y	Y	Y	Y	N	Y
ALASKA							
AL Young	N	N	Y	N	Y	N	Y
ARIZONA							
1 McCain	Y	N	Y	Y	Y	?	?
2 Udall	?	?	?	?	?	?	?
3 Stump	N	N	Y	Y	Y	N	Y
4 Rudd	X	?	?	?	?	?	?
5 McNulty	Y	Y	Y	N	Y	N	Y
ARKANSAS							
1 Alexander	Y	Y	Y	?	Y	N	Y
2 Bethune	N	N	Y	?	?	?	?
3 Hammerschmidt	Y	N	Y	?	?	?	?
4 Anthony	Y	Y	Y	Y	Y	N	Y
CALIFORNIA							
1 Bosco	N	Y	Y	N	Y	?	?
2 Chappie	N	N	Y	N	Y	N	Y
3 Matsui	Y	Y	Y	?	?	?	?
4 Fazio	N	Y	Y	Y	Y	N	Y
5 Burton	N	Y	Y	?	?	?	?
6 Boxer	N	Y	Y	?	?	?	?
7 Miller	N	Y	Y	?	?	?	?
8 Dellums	N	Y	Y	N	Y	Y	Y
9 Stark	?	?	?	?	?	?	?
10 Edwards	Y	Y	Y	Y	Y	?	Y
11 Lantos	N	Y	Y	Y	Y	N	Y
12 Zschau	Y	Y	Y	Y	Y	Y	N
13 Mineta	N	Y	Y	N	Y	N	Y
14 Shumway	N	N	Y	N	Y	Y	Y
15 Coelho	N	Y	Y	N	N	N	Y
16 Panetta	N	Y	Y	Y	Y	?	?
17 Pashayan	N	N	Y	N	Y	N	Y
18 Lehman	N	Y	Y	N	?	?	?
19 Lagomarsino	Y	N	Y	Y	Y	Y	Y
20 Thomas	N	Y	Y	?	?	?	?
21 Fiedler	?	?	?	?	?	?	?
22 Moorhead	N	N	Y	?	?	?	?
23 Beilenson	Y	Y	Y	Y	Y	Y	Y
24 Waxman	N	Y	Y	Y	Y	?	?
25 Roybal	Y	Y	Y	?	?	?	?
26 Berman	Y	?	Y	Y	Y	Y	Y
27 Levine	N	Y	Y	Y	Y	Y	Y
28 Dixon	N	Y	Y	N	Y	Y	Y
29 Hawkins	N	Y	Y	?	?	?	?
30 Martinez	N	Y	Y	N	Y	N	Y
31 Dymally	?	?	Y	N	Y	?	?
32 Anderson	N	N	Y	N	Y	?	?
33 Dreier	N	N	Y	Y	Y	Y	N
34 Torres	N	Y	Y	N	Y	N	Y
35 Lewis	Y	Y	Y	N	Y	N	Y
36 Brown	Y	Y	Y	?	Y	N	Y
37 McCandless	N	N	Y	N	Y	N	Y
38 Patterson	N	Y	Y	?	?	?	?
39 Dannemeyer	N	N	Y	Y	Y	Y	Y
40 Badham	N	N	Y	Y	Y	?	?
41 Lowery	Y	Y	Y	Y	Y	Y	Y
42 Lungren	N	N	Y	Y	Y	Y	Y

	270	271	272	273	274	275	276
43 Packard	Y	N	Y	N	Y	N	Y
44 Bates	N	Y	Y	Y	Y	Y	Y
45 Hunter	Y	N	Y	Y	Y	N	Y
COLORADO							
1 Schroeder	N	Y	Y	N	Y	Y	N
2 Wirth	N	Y	?	?	?	?	?
3 Kogovsek	Y	Y	Y	N	Y	N	Y
4 Brown	N	N	Y	Y	N	Y	N
5 Kramer	N	N	Y	?	?	?	?
6 Schaefer	N	N	Y	N	Y	N	Y
CONNECTICUT							
1 Kennelly	Y	Y	Y	Y	Y	Y	Y
2 Gejdenson	N	Y	Y	?	?	?	?
3 Morrison	N	Y	Y	Y	Y	Y	Y
4 McKinney	Y	?	Y	N	Y	Y	Y
5 Ratchford	Y	Y	Y	Y	Y	Y	Y
6 Johnson	Y	N	Y	N	Y	N	N
DELAWARE							
AL Carper	N	N	Y	Y	Y	N	Y
FLORIDA							
1 Hutto	Y	Y	Y	?	?	?	?
2 Fuqua	Y	Y	?	?	?	?	?
3 Bennett	Y	Y	Y	N	Y	N	Y
4 Chappell	Y	Y	Y	N	Y	N	Y
5 McCollum	Y	N	Y	N	Y	Y	Y
6 MacKay	N	Y	Y	Y	Y	Y	Y
7 Gibbons	Y	Y	Y	Y	Y	N	Y
8 Young	N	Y	Y	N	Y	Y	Y
9 Bilirakis	Y	N	Y	N	?	?	?
10 Ireland	N	N	Y	Y	?	?	?
11 Nelson	N	Y	+	X	+	X	+
12 Lewis	N	N	Y	N	Y	N	Y
13 Mack	Y	N	Y	N	Y	N	Y
14 Mica	Y	Y	Y	Y	Y	Y	Y
15 Shaw	N	N	Y	N	Y	N	Y
16 Smith	Y	Y	Y	?	?	?	?
17 Lehman	Y	Y	Y	N	Y	N	Y
18 Pepper	Y	Y	Y	N	Y	N	Y
19 Fascell	Y	Y	Y	?	?	?	?
GEORGIA							
1 Thomas	Y	Y	Y	N	Y	N	Y
2 Hatcher	Y	Y	Y	?	?	?	?
3 Ray	N	N	Y	Y	Y	Y	N
4 Levitas	N	N	Y	N	Y	N	Y
5 Fowler	Y	Y	Y	Y	Y	Y	Y
6 Gingrich	Y	N	Y	N	Y	N	?
7 Darden	N	Y	Y	Y	Y	N	Y
8 Rowland	N	Y	Y	N	Y	N	Y
9 Jenkins	Y	Y	Y	N	Y	N	Y
10 Barnard	Y	Y	Y	N	Y	N	Y
HAWAII							
1 Heftel	Y	N	Y	Y	Y	?	?
2 Akaka	Y	Y	Y	N	Y	N	Y
IDAHO							
1 Craig	?	?	?	?	?	#	?
2 Hansen	?	?	?	?	?	?	?
ILLINOIS							
1 Hayes	N	Y	Y	N	Y	N	Y
2 Savage	N	Y	?	?	?	?	?
3 Russo	N	?	Y	N	?	?	?
4 O'Brien	Y	N	Y	N	Y	Y	Y
5 Lipinski	Y	Y	?	?	?	?	?
6 Hyde	Y	N	Y	N	Y	N	Y
7 Collins	N	Y	Y	Y	Y	Y	Y
8 Rostenkowski	Y	Y	?	?	?	?	?
9 Yates	Y	Y	Y	Y	Y	Y	N
10 Porter	Y	N	Y	N	Y	Y	Y
11 Annunzio	Y	Y	Y	N	Y	N	Y
12 Crane, P.	N	N	Y	Y	Y	Y	N
13 Erlenborn	?	?	?	?	?	?	?
14 Corcoran	Y	Y	Y	N	Y	Y	Y
15 Madigan	Y	Y	Y	N	Y	N	Y
16 Martin	N	N	Y	N	Y	N	Y
17 Evans	Y	N	Y	Y	Y	Y	Y
18 Michel	Y	N	Y	?	?	Y	Y
19 Crane, D.	N	N	Y	N	Y	?	?
20 Durbin	N	Y	Y	Y	Y	N	Y
21 Price	Y	Y	Y	N	Y	N	Y
22 Simon	?	?	?	?	?	?	?
INDIANA							
1 Hall	N	Y	Y	N	Y	N	Y
2 Sharp	Y	N	Y	Y	?	Y	N
3 Hiler	N	N	Y	Y	Y	?	?
4 Coats	N	N	Y	Y	Y	?	?
5 Hillis	Y	N	Y	?	?	?	?

ND - Northern Democrats   SD - Southern Democrats

	270	271	272	273	274	275	276
6 **Burton**	N	?	Y	Y	Y	N	
7 **Myers**	N	N	Y	N	Y	N	Y
8 McCloskey	N	Y	Y	Y	Y	N	Y
9 Hamilton	Y	Y	Y	N	Y	Y	Y
10 Jacobs	N	N	Y	?	?	?	?
IOWA							
1 **Leach**	N	N	Y	Y	Y	Y	N
2 **Tauke**	Y	N	Y	Y	Y	N	Y
3 **Evans**	N	N	Y	Y	Y	N	Y
4 Smith	Y	N	Y	N	Y	N	Y
5 Harkin	N	N	Y	Y	Y	N	Y
6 Bedell	N	N	Y	Y	Y	?	?
KANSAS							
1 **Roberts**	N	N	Y	Y	Y	N	Y
2 Slattery	N	Y	Y	Y	Y	N	Y
3 **Winn**	N	N	Y	N	Y	N	Y
4 Glickman	N	Y	Y	Y	Y	N	Y
5 **Whittaker**	N	N	Y	N	Y	N	Y
KENTUCKY							
1 Hubbard	N	N	Y	Y	Y	N	Y
2 Natcher	N	Y	Y	N	Y	N	Y
3 Mazzoli	N	N	Y	Y	Y	N	Y
4 **Snyder**	N	N	Y	N	Y	N	Y
5 **Rogers**	Y	N	Y	N	Y	N	Y
6 **Hopkins**	N	N	Y	Y	Y	Y	N
7 Perkins	Y	Y	Y	Y	?	N	Y
LOUISIANA							
1 **Livingston**	Y	Y	Y	N	Y	N	Y
2 Boggs	Y	Y	Y	N	Y	N	Y
3 Tauzin	N	Y	Y	N	Y	N	Y
4 Roemer	N	N	Y	Y	Y	N	Y
5 Huckaby	N	Y	Y	N	Y	N	Y
6 **Moore**	N	Y	Y	N	Y	N	Y
7 Breaux	?	?	?	X	?	?	?
8 Long	Y	Y	Y	N	Y	N	Y
MAINE							
1 **McKernan**	Y	N	Y	N	Y	N	Y
2 **Snowe**	Y	N	Y	Y	Y	N	Y
MARYLAND							
1 Dyson	N	N	Y	N	Y	N	Y
2 Long	N	Y	Y	N	Y	N	Y
3 Mikulski	Y	Y	Y	N	Y	N	Y
4 **Holt**	Y	N	Y	Y	Y	N	Y
5 Hoyer	Y	Y	Y	N	Y	N	Y
6 Byron	N	?	Y	N	Y	N	Y
7 Mitchell	Y	Y	Y	Y	Y	N	Y
8 Barnes	Y	Y	Y	Y	Y	Y	Y
MASSACHUSETTS							
1 **Conte**	Y	N	Y	Y	Y	?	?
2 Boland	Y	?	?	?	?	#	?
3 Early	?	?	?	?	?	?	?
4 Frank	Y	?	?	?	?	?	?
5 Shannon	?	?	?	?	?	?	?
6 Mavroules	Y	Y	?	?	?	?	?
7 Markey	N	Y	Y	N	Y	Y	N
8 O'Neill							
9 Moakley	Y	Y	Y	?	?	?	?
10 Studds	Y	Y	?	?	?	?	?
11 Donnelly	Y	Y	Y	N	Y	N	Y
MICHIGAN							
1 Conyers	Y	Y	Y	N	Y	N	Y
2 **Pursell**	Y	N	?	?	?	?	?
3 Wolpe	N	Y	Y	Y	Y	Y	Y
4 **Siljander**	N	N	Y	Y	Y	?	?
5 **Sawyer**	Y	N	Y	Y	Y	N	Y
6 Carr	N	Y	Y	N	Y	N	Y
7 Kildee	Y	Y	Y	Y	Y	Y	Y
8 Traxler	Y	Y	?	?	?	?	?
9 **Vander Jagt**	Y	Y	Y	N	?	?	?
10 Albosta	N	Y	Y	N	Y	N	Y
11 **Davis**	Y	N	Y	N	?	?	?
12 Bonior	Y	?	Y	Y	Y	Y	Y
13 Crockett	N	Y	Y	Y	Y	?	?
14 Hertel	N	Y	Y	Y	Y	Y	N
15 Ford	Y	Y	Y	N	Y	N	Y
16 Dingell	Y	?	Y	N	Y	N	Y
17 Levin	N	Y	Y	Y	Y	N	Y
18 **Broomfield**	Y	N	Y	Y	Y	Y	N
MINNESOTA							
1 Penny	N	Y	Y	N	N	N	Y
2 **Weber**	N	N	Y	Y	N	N	Y
3 **Frenzel**	Y	Y	Y	Y	Y	Y	N
4 Vento	Y	Y	Y	#	?	?	?
5 Sabo	N	Y	Y	Y	Y	N	Y
6 Sikorski	N	Y	Y	Y	Y	Y	N

	270	271	272	273	274	275	276
7 **Stangeland**	Y	N	Y	N	Y	N	Y
8 Oberstar	N	?	Y	N	Y	N	Y
MISSISSIPPI							
1 Whitten	Y	Y	Y	N	Y	N	Y
2 **Franklin**	N	Y	?	?	?	?	?
3 Montgomery	Y	Y	Y	Y	Y	N	Y
4 Dowdy	Y	Y	Y	N	Y	N	Y
5 **Lott**	Y	Y	Y	N	Y	N	Y
MISSOURI							
1 Clay	N	Y	Y	N	Y	Y	Y
2 Young	Y	Y	Y	N	Y	N	Y
3 Gephardt	Y	Y	Y	N	Y	?	?
4 Skelton	Y	Y	Y	Y	Y	?	?
5 Wheat	Y	Y	Y	Y	Y	N	Y
6 **Coleman**	Y	N	Y	N	Y	N	Y
7 **Taylor**	Y	N	Y	N	?	?	?
8 **Emerson**	N	N	Y	N	Y	N	Y
9 Volkmer	Y	N	Y	N	?	?	?
MONTANA							
1 Williams	Y	N	Y	Y	N	N	Y
2 **Marlenee**	N	N	Y	?	?	?	?
NEBRASKA							
1 **Bereuter**	N	N	Y	Y	Y	N	Y
2 **Daub**	N	N	Y	N	N	N	Y
3 **Smith**	N	N	Y	N	Y	N	Y
NEVADA							
1 Reid	Y	Y	Y	N	Y	N	Y
2 **Vucanovich**	N	Y	Y	N	N	N	N
NEW HAMPSHIRE							
1 D'Amours	N	?	Y	Y	Y	N	?
2 **Gregg**	Y	?	Y	?	?	?	?
NEW JERSEY							
1 Florio	N	Y	Y	N	Y	?	?
2 Hughes	N	Y	Y	N	Y	N	Y
3 Howard	N	Y	Y	N	Y	N	Y
4 **Smith**	Y	N	Y	N	Y	N	Y
5 **Roukema**	Y	N	Y	Y	Y	N	Y
6 Dwyer	Y	Y	Y	N	Y	N	Y
7 **Rinaldo**	N	N	Y	N	Y	N	Y
8 Roe	N	Y	Y	N	Y	N	Y
9 Torricelli	N	N	Y	N	?	#	?
10 Rodino	Y	Y	Y	N	Y	N	Y
11 Minish	Y	Y	Y	N	Y	N	Y
12 **Courter**	Y	N	Y	Y	Y	Y	N
13 Vacancy							
14 Guarini	Y	Y	Y	N	Y	N	Y
NEW MEXICO							
1 **Lujan**	N	N	Y	Y	Y	Y	Y
2 **Skeen**	Y	N	Y	Y	Y	Y	Y
3 Richardson	N	Y	Y	Y	Y	Y	Y
NEW YORK							
1 **Carney**	N	N	Y	N	Y	N	Y
2 Downey	N	?	Y	?	?	?	Y
3 Mrazek	N	N	Y	N	Y	N	Y
4 **Lent**	Y	N	Y	?	?	?	?
5 **McGrath**	N	N	Y	Y	Y	N	Y
6 Addabbo	Y	Y	Y	?	?	X	?
7 Ackerman	N	Y	Y	N	Y	?	?
8 Scheuer	Y	Y	Y	N	Y	?	?
9 Ferraro	N	Y	Y	N	?	?	?
10 Schumer	N	Y	Y	Y	Y	N	Y
11 Towns	N	Y	Y	N	Y	N	Y
12 Owens	N	Y	Y	N	Y	?	?
13 Solarz	Y	Y	Y	#	?	?	?
14 **Molinari**	N	N	Y	N	Y	N	Y
15 **Green**	Y	Y	Y	Y	Y	Y	N
16 Rangel	Y	Y	Y	Y	Y	N	Y
17 Weiss	N	Y	Y	Y	Y	Y	Y
18 Garcia	Y	Y	Y	#	?	?	?
19 Biaggi	Y	Y	Y	N	Y	N	Y
20 Ottinger	N	N	Y	Y	Y	Y	Y
21 **Fish**	Y	Y	Y	Y	?	?	?
22 **Gilman**	N	N	Y	Y	Y	N	Y
23 Stratton	Y	Y	Y	Y	Y	N	Y
24 **Solomon**	N	N	Y	?	Y	Y	N
25 **Boehlert**	Y	N	Y	Y	Y	Y	Y
26 **Martin**	Y	Y	Y	Y	Y	N	Y
27 **Wortley**	N	N	Y	Y	?	Y	Y
28 McHugh	Y	Y	Y	N	Y	N	Y
29 **Horton**	Y	N	Y	N	Y	?	?
30 **Conable**	Y	N	Y	Y	Y	Y	N
31 **Kemp**	Y	N	Y	N	Y	Y	Y
32 LaFalce	Y	Y	Y	N	Y	?	?
33 Nowak	Y	Y	Y	N	Y	N	Y
34 Lundine	N	Y	Y	N	Y	N	Y

	270	271	272	273	274	275	276
NORTH CAROLINA							
1 Jones	Y	N	Y	N	Y	N	Y
2 Valentine	N	Y	Y	N	Y	N	Y
3 Whitley	Y	Y	Y	N	?	?	?
4 Andrews	Y	Y	Y	?	?	?	?
5 Neal	N	Y	Y	?	?	?	?
6 Britt	N	Y	Y	N	Y	N	Y
7 Rose	Y	Y	Y	N	Y	N	Y
8 Hefner	N	Y	Y	Y	Y	N	Y
9 **Martin**	?	?	?	?	?	?	?
10 **Broyhill**	Y	Y	Y	N	Y	Y	N
11 Clarke	Y	Y	Y	Y	?	?	?
NORTH DAKOTA							
AL Dorgan	?	Y	?	?	?	?	?
OHIO							
1 Luken	N	?	Y	N	Y	Y	Y
2 **Gradison**	Y	N	Y	?	?	?	?
3 Hall	Y	Y	Y	N	Y	N	Y
4 **Oxley**	Y	N	Y	Y	Y	N	Y
5 **Latta**	Y	N	Y	N	Y	?	?
6 **McEwen**	N	N	Y	N	Y	?	?
7 **DeWine**	N	Y	Y	Y	Y	Y	Y
8 **Kindness**	Y	N	Y	N	Y	N	Y
9 Kaptur	N	N	Y	N	Y	?	?
10 **Miller**	N	N	Y	N	Y	Y	Y
11 Eckart	N	Y	Y	Y	Y	Y	Y
12 **Kasich**	N	N	Y	Y	Y	N	Y
13 Pease	Y	Y	Y	N	Y	N	Y
14 Seiberling	N	N	Y	Y	Y	Y	N
15 **Wylie**	Y	N	Y	N	Y	N	Y
16 **Regula**	N	N	Y	Y	Y	Y	Y
17 **Williams**	#	?	?	?	?	?	?
18 Applegate	N	Y	Y	N	Y	N	Y
19 Feighan	N	Y	Y	Y	Y	Y	?
20 Oakar	N	Y	Y	N	Y	N	Y
21 Stokes	N	Y	Y	N	Y	N	Y
OKLAHOMA							
1 Jones	N	Y	Y	Y	Y	N	Y
2 Synar	Y	Y	Y	N	N	N	Y
3 Watkins	N	N	Y	N	N	N	Y
4 McCurdy	N	?	Y	Y	Y	N	Y
5 **Edwards**	N	N	Y	N	Y	N	Y
6 English	N	Y	Y	Y	Y	N	Y
OREGON							
1 AuCoin	N	Y	Y	N	Y	N	Y
2 **Smith, R.**	N	N	Y	N	Y	N	Y
3 Wyden	N	Y	Y	N	Y	N	Y
4 Weaver	N	N	Y	?	?	?	?
5 **Smith, D.**	N	N	Y	?	?	?	?
PENNSYLVANIA							
1 Foglietta	?	?	?	?	?	?	?
2 Gray	N	Y	Y	N	Y	Y	Y
3 Borski	N	Y	Y	N	Y	N	Y
4 Kolter	Y	Y	Y	N	Y	N	Y
5 **Schulze**	Y	N	Y	?	?	?	?
6 Yatron	?	?	?	?	?	?	?
7 Edgar	Y	N	Y	Y	Y	Y	Y
8 Kostmayer	Y	Y	Y	Y	Y	Y	Y
9 **Shuster**	N	N	Y	N	Y	N	Y
10 **McDade**	Y	N	Y	N	Y	Y	Y
11 Harrison	+	Y	Y	N	Y	N	Y
12 Murtha	Y	Y	Y	N	Y	N	Y
13 **Coughlin**	Y	Y	Y	Y	Y	Y	Y
14 Coyne	Y	Y	Y	N	?	N	Y
15 **Ritter**	N	N	Y	N	Y	Y	N
16 **Walker**	N	N	Y	Y	Y	Y	N
17 **Gekas**	Y	N	Y	N	Y	N	Y
18 Walgren	Y	Y	Y	Y	Y	N	Y
19 **Goodling**	Y	N	Y	Y	Y	Y	N
20 Gaydos	Y	N	Y	N	Y	N	Y
21 **Ridge**	?	?	?	?	?	?	?
22 Murphy	Y	Y	Y	N	Y	N	Y
23 **Clinger**	Y	N	Y	N	Y	N	Y
RHODE ISLAND							
1 St Germain	Y	N	Y	N	Y	?	?
2 **Schneider**	Y	Y	Y	Y	Y	?	?
SOUTH CAROLINA							
1 **Hartnett**	N	N	Y	?	?	?	?
2 **Spence**	N	N	Y	?	?	?	?
3 Derrick	N	N	Y	Y	Y	N	Y
4 **Campbell**	Y	N	Y	Y	?	?	?
5 Spratt	N	Y	Y	Y	Y	Y	Y
6 Tallon	N	N	Y	Y	Y	N	?
SOUTH DAKOTA							
AL Daschle	N	Y	Y	?	?	?	?

	270	271	272	273	274	275	276
TENNESSEE							
1 **Quillen**	Y	Y	Y	?	?	X	?
2 **Duncan**	Y	N	?	?	?	?	?
3 Lloyd	N	N	Y	N	Y	N	?
4 Cooper	N	Y	Y	Y	Y	N	Y
5 Boner	Y	N	Y	N	Y	N	Y
6 Gore	Y	N	Y	N	Y	N	Y
7 **Sundquist**	Y	N	Y	N	Y	N	Y
8 Jones	N	N	Y	?	?	?	?
9 Ford	Y	Y	Y	?	?	?	?
TEXAS							
1 Hall, S.	N	Y	Y	Y	Y	N	Y
2 Wilson	Y	Y	Y	N	Y	N	Y
3 **Bartlett**	Y	Y	Y	Y	Y	Y	?
4 Hall, R.	N	N	Y	N	Y	N	Y
5 Bryant	N	Y	Y	N	Y	N	Y
6 **Gramm**	N	N	Y	Y	Y	N	Y
7 **Archer**	N	N	Y	Y	Y	Y	Y
8 **Fields**	N	N	Y	N	Y	N	Y
9 Brooks	Y	Y	Y	N	Y	N	Y
10 Pickle	Y	Y	Y	N	Y	N	Y
11 Leath	Y	Y	Y	?	?	?	?
12 Wright	Y	Y	Y	?	?	?	?
13 Hightower	Y	N	Y	N	Y	N	Y
14 Patman	N	N	Y	N	Y	N	Y
15 de la Garza	?	?	?	?	?	?	?
16 Coleman	Y	Y	Y	?	?	?	?
17 Stenholm	Y	Y	?	?	?	?	?
18 Leland	N	Y	Y	N	Y	N	Y
19 Hance	Y	Y	Y	N	Y	N	Y
20 Gonzalez	Y	Y	Y	N	Y	N	Y
21 **Loeffler**	Y	Y	Y	Y	?	?	?
22 **Paul**	?	?	?	?	?	?	?
23 Kazen	Y	Y	Y	N	Y	N	Y
24 Frost	N	Y	Y	N	Y	N	Y
25 Andrews	Y	Y	Y	N	Y	N	Y
26 Vandergriff	N	N	Y	N	N	N	Y
27 Ortiz	N	Y	Y	N	Y	N	Y
UTAH							
1 **Hansen**	N	N	Y	Y	Y	?	?
2 **Marriott**	Y	N	Y	Y	Y	N	Y
3 **Nielson**	N	N	Y	Y	Y	Y	N
VERMONT							
AL **Jeffords**	Y	N	Y	Y	Y	Y	N
VIRGINIA							
1 **Bateman**	Y	Y	Y	N	Y	N	Y
2 **Whitehurst**	Y	N	Y	?	?	?	?
3 **Bliley**	Y	N	Y	N	Y	N	Y
4 Sisisky	Y	Y	Y	N	Y	N	Y
5 Daniel	N	N	Y	Y	?	N	N
6 Olin	N	N	Y	N	Y	N	Y
7 **Robinson**	Y	N	Y	Y	Y	Y	N
8 **Parris**	Y	N	Y	N	Y	N	Y
9 Boucher	N	?	?	?	?	?	?
10 **Wolf**	Y	N	Y	N	Y	?	?
WASHINGTON							
1 **Pritchard**	Y	Y	Y	X	?	?	?
2 Swift	Y	Y	Y	N	Y	N	Y
3 Bonker	Y	Y	Y	N	Y	N	Y
4 **Morrison**	Y	N	Y	N	Y	N	Y
5 Foley	Y	Y	Y	N	Y	N	Y
6 Dicks	Y	Y	Y	N	Y	N	?
7 Lowry	N	Y	Y	N	Y	N	Y
8 **Chandler**	Y	N	Y	Y	Y	N	Y
WEST VIRGINIA							
1 Mollohan	Y	Y	Y	N	Y	N	Y
2 Staggers	N	N	Y	Y	Y	N	Y
3 Wise	N	Y	Y	Y	Y	N	Y
4 Rahall	Y	N	Y	N	Y	N	Y
WISCONSIN							
1 Aspin	Y	Y	Y	Y	Y	?	?
2 Kastenmeier	N	Y	Y	?	?	?	?
3 **Gunderson**	N	N	Y	N	Y	N	Y
4 Kleczka	Y	Y	Y	Y	Y	Y	Y
5 Moody	N	Y	Y	Y	Y	N	Y
6 **Petri**	N	N	Y	Y	Y	Y	Y
7 Obey	N	Y	Y	Y	Y	Y	N
8 **Roth**	N	?	?	?	?	?	?
9 **Sensenbrenner**	?	?	?	?	?	?	?
WYOMING							
AL **Cheney**	Y	N	Y	Y	Y	Y	N

Southern states - Ala., Ark., Fla., Ga., Ky., La., Miss., N.C., Okla., S.C., Tenn., Texas, Va.

277. HR 5541. Public Broadcasting Authorization. Dannemeyer, R-Calif., substitute to the Oxley, R-Ohio, amendment *(see vote 278, below),* to limit the authorized funding for the Corporation for Public Broadcasting to $130 million in each of fiscal years 1987-89. Rejected 95-298: R 77-77; D 18-221 (ND 1-158, SD 17-63), July 24, 1984.

278. HR 5541. Public Broadcasting Authorization. Oxley, R-Ohio, amendment to reduce the authorized funding for the Corporation for Public Broadcasting to $186 million in fiscal 1987, $214 million in 1988 and $246 million in 1989; and to reduce the authorized funding for the Public Telecommunications Facilities Program to $14 million in fiscal 1985, $16 million in 1986 and $18 million in 1987. Rejected 176-217: R 125-31; D 51-186 (ND 13-145, SD 38-41), July 24, 1984.

279. HR 5541. Public Broadcasting Authorization. Passage of the bill to authorize funding for the Corporation for Public Broadcasting at $238 million in fiscal 1987, $253 million in 1988 and $270 million in 1989; and for the Public Telecommunications Facilities Program, $50 million in fiscal 1985, $53 million in 1986 and $56 million in 1987. Passed 302-91: R 69-87; D 233-4 (ND 158-0, SD 75-4), July 24, 1984. A "nay" was a vote supporting the president's position.

280. HR 1580. Aviation Drug-Trafficking Control Act. Mineta, D-Calif., motion to suspend the rules and pass the bill to increase penalties for aircraft pilots and owners who knowingly participate in illegal drug trafficking. Motion agreed to 393-1: R 154-1; D 239-0 (ND 158-0, SD 81-0), July 24, 1984. A two-thirds majority of those present and voting (263 in this case) is required for passage under suspension of the rules.

281. HR 5616. Counterfeit Access Device and Computer Fraud and Abuse Act. Hughes, D-N.J., motion to suspend the rules and pass the bill to make it a federal crime to obtain unauthorized access to computers and to set new penalties for trafficking in fraudulent credit cards or bank cards, or cards that are stolen, lost or revoked. Motion agreed to 395-0: R 155-0; D 240-0 (ND 159-0, SD 81-0), July 24, 1984. A two-thirds majority of those present and voting (264 in this case) is required for passage under suspension of the rules.

282. HR 1310. Emergency Mathematics and Science Education Act. Perkins, D-Ky., motion to suspend the rules and discharge the Education and Labor and Judiciary committees from further consideration of the bill and to concur in the Senate amendment to make it unlawful for high schools receiving federal aid to deny use of their building to religious, political and other student groups, if such access is granted to other student groups. Motion agreed to 337-77: R 157-5; D 180-72 (ND 100-66, SD 80-6), July 25, 1984. A two-thirds majority of those present and voting (276 in this case) is required under suspension of the rules. A "yea" was a vote supporting the president's position.

283. HR 1310. Emergency Mathematics and Science Education Act. Perkins, D-Ky., motion to concur in the Senate bill to make it unlawful for high schools receiving federal aid to deny use of their buildings to religious, political and other student groups, if such access is granted to other student groups; and to authorize funds for fiscal 1984-86 for math-science improvement, asbestos abatement, desegregation aid and other programs. Motion agreed to 393-15: R 155-6; D 238-9 (ND 153-9, SD 85-0), July 25, 1984. A two-thirds majority of those present and voting (272 in this case) is required under suspension of the rules.

284. HR 1492. Christopher Columbus Quincentenary Jubilee Act. Adoption of the conference report on the bill to establish a commission to observe the 500th anniversary of Columbus' first voyage to the New World. Adopted 279-130: R 70-88; D 209-42 (ND 153-13, SD 56-29), July 25, 1984.

KEY

Y	Voted for (yea).
#	Paired for.
+	Announced for.
N	Voted against (nay).
X	Paired against.
-	Announced against.
P	Voted "present".
C	Voted "present" to avoid possible conflict of interest.
?	Did not vote or otherwise make a position known.

Democrats *Republicans*

	277	278	279	280	281	282	283	284
ALABAMA								
1 Edwards	N	N	Y	Y	Y	?	?	?
2 Dickinson	Y	Y	N	Y	Y	Y	Y	Y
3 Nichols	?	?	?	Y	Y	Y	Y	Y
4 Bevill	Y	Y	Y	Y	Y	Y	Y	N
5 Flippo	Y	N	Y	Y	Y	Y	Y	Y
6 Erdreich	N	Y	Y	Y	Y	Y	Y	N
7 Shelby	N	N	Y	Y	Y	Y	Y	Y
ALASKA								
AL Young	N	N	Y	Y	Y	Y	Y	Y
ARIZONA								
1 McCain	N	Y	Y	Y	Y	Y	Y	N
2 Udall	N	N	Y	Y	Y	?	?	Y
3 Stump	?	?	?	?	?	?	?	?
4 Rudd	Y	Y	N	Y	Y	Y	Y	N
5 McNulty	N	N	Y	Y	Y	Y	Y	Y
ARKANSAS								
1 Alexander	N	N	Y	Y	Y	Y	Y	Y
2 Bethune	Y	Y	N	Y	Y	Y	Y	N
3 Hammerschmidt	Y	Y	Y	Y	Y	Y	Y	Y
4 Anthony	N	N	Y	Y	Y	Y	Y	?
CALIFORNIA								
1 Bosco	N	Y	Y	?	?	N	Y	Y
2 Chappie	N	Y	Y	Y	Y	Y	Y	N
3 Matsui	N	N	Y	Y	Y	Y	Y	Y
4 Fazio	N	N	Y	Y	Y	Y	Y	Y
5 Burton	N	N	Y	Y	Y	N	Y	Y
6 Boxer	N	N	Y	Y	Y	N	Y	Y
7 Miller	N	N	Y	Y	Y	Y	Y	Y
8 Dellums	N	N	Y	Y	Y	N	N	Y
9 Stark	N	N	Y	Y	Y	Y	Y	Y
10 Edwards	N	N	Y	Y	Y	N	N	Y
11 Lantos	N	N	Y	Y	Y	Y	Y	Y
12 Zschau	N	Y	N	Y	Y	Y	Y	N
13 Mineta	N	N	Y	Y	Y	N	Y	Y
14 Shumway	Y	Y	N	Y	Y	Y	N	N
15 Coelho	N	N	Y	Y	Y	Y	Y	Y
16 Panetta	N	N	Y	Y	Y	Y	Y	Y
17 Pashayan	Y	Y	Y	Y	Y	Y	Y	Y
18 Lehman	N	N	Y	Y	Y	Y	Y	Y
19 Lagomarsino	Y	Y	N	Y	Y	Y	Y	N
20 Thomas	Y	Y	N	Y	Y	Y	Y	N
21 Fiedler	Y	Y	N	Y	Y	Y	Y	N
22 Moorhead	Y	Y	N	Y	Y	Y	Y	N
23 Beilenson	N	N	Y	Y	Y	N	Y	Y
24 Waxman	?	?	?	?	?	X	?	?
25 Roybal	N	N	Y	Y	Y	N	N	Y
26 Berman	N	N	Y	Y	Y	N	Y	Y
27 Levine	N	Y	Y	Y	N	?	?	Y
28 Dixon	N	N	Y	Y	Y	N	Y	Y
29 Hawkins	X	X	#	?	?	N	Y	Y
30 Martinez	N	N	Y	Y	Y	N	Y	Y
31 Dymally	N	N	Y	Y	Y	N	Y	Y
32 Anderson	N	N	Y	Y	Y	Y	Y	Y
33 Dreier	Y	Y	N	Y	Y	Y	Y	N
34 Torres	-	-	+	+	+	Y	Y	Y
35 Lewis	?	?	?	?	?	Y	Y	Y
36 Brown	N	N	Y	?	?	Y	Y	Y
37 McCandless	Y	Y	N	Y	Y	Y	Y	N
38 Patterson	N	N	Y	Y	Y	Y	Y	Y
39 Dannemeyer	Y	Y	N	Y	Y	Y	N	N
40 Badham	Y	Y	N	Y	Y	Y	Y	N
41 Lowery	N	Y	Y	Y	Y	Y	Y	N
42 Lungren	Y	Y	N	Y	Y	Y	Y	N

	277	278	279	280	281	282	283	284
43 Packard	Y	Y	N	Y	Y	Y	Y	N
44 Bates	N	N	Y	Y	Y	N	Y	Y
45 Hunter	Y	Y	Y	Y	Y	Y	Y	N
COLORADO								
1 Schroeder	N	N	Y	Y	Y	N	Y	Y
2 Wirth	N	N	Y	Y	Y	N	Y	Y
3 Kogovsek	?	?	?	?	?	N	Y	Y
4 Brown	Y	Y	N	Y	Y	Y	Y	N
5 Kramer	?	?	?	?	?	Y	Y	N
6 Schaefer	Y	Y	N	Y	Y	Y	Y	N
CONNECTICUT								
1 Kennelly	N	N	Y	Y	Y	N	Y	Y
2 Gejdenson	?	?	?	?	?	N	Y	Y
3 Morrison	N	N	Y	Y	Y	N	Y	Y
4 McKinney	N	N	Y	Y	Y	Y	Y	Y
5 Ratchford	N	N	Y	Y	Y	N	Y	Y
6 Johnson	N	Y	Y	Y	Y	Y	Y	Y
DELAWARE								
AL Carper	N	N	Y	Y	Y	Y	Y	N
FLORIDA								
1 Hutto	Y	Y	Y	Y	Y	Y	Y	Y
2 Fuqua	N	N	Y	Y	Y	Y	Y	Y
3 Bennett	N	Y	Y	Y	Y	Y	Y	Y
4 Chappell	N	N	Y	Y	Y	Y	Y	Y
5 McCollum	Y	Y	N	Y	Y	Y	Y	N
6 MacKay	N	N	Y	Y	Y	Y	Y	Y
7 Gibbons	N	Y	Y	Y	Y	Y	Y	Y
8 Young	Y	Y	N	Y	Y	Y	Y	N
9 Bilirakis	N	Y	N	Y	Y	N	Y	N
10 Ireland *	Y	Y	Y	Y	Y	Y	Y	Y
11 Nelson	N	N	Y	Y	Y	Y	Y	Y
12 Lewis	N	Y	Y	Y	Y	Y	Y	N
13 Mack	Y	Y	N	Y	Y	Y	Y	N
14 Mica	N	N	Y	Y	Y	Y	Y	Y
15 Shaw	N	Y	N	Y	Y	Y	Y	N
16 Smith	N	N	Y	Y	Y	N	Y	Y
17 Lehman	N	N	Y	Y	Y	N	Y	Y
18 Pepper	N	N	Y	Y	Y	Y	Y	Y
19 Fascell	N	N	Y	Y	Y	N	Y	Y
GEORGIA								
1 Thomas	N	N	Y	Y	Y	Y	Y	Y
2 Hatcher	N	N	Y	Y	Y	Y	Y	?
3 Ray	Y	Y	Y	Y	Y	Y	Y	N
4 Levitas	N	Y	Y	Y	Y	Y	Y	Y
5 Fowler	?	?	?	?	?	Y	Y	Y
6 Gingrich	N	Y	N	Y	Y	?	?	?
7 Darden	Y	Y	Y	Y	Y	Y	Y	Y
8 Rowland	N	Y	Y	Y	Y	Y	Y	N
9 Jenkins	Y	Y	Y	Y	Y	Y	Y	Y
10 Barnard	N	Y	Y	Y	Y	Y	Y	Y
HAWAII								
1 Heftel	?	?	?	?	?	?	?	?
2 Akaka	?	N	Y	Y	Y	N	Y	Y
IDAHO								
1 Craig	Y	Y	N	Y	Y	Y	Y	N
2 Hansen	?	?	?	?	?	?	?	?
ILLINOIS								
1 Hayes	N	N	Y	Y	Y	N	Y	Y
2 Savage	N	N	Y	Y	Y	N	Y	Y
3 Russo	N	N	Y	Y	Y	N	Y	Y
4 O'Brien	N	Y	N	Y	Y	Y	Y	Y
5 Lipinski	N	N	Y	Y	Y	Y	Y	Y
6 Hyde	Y	Y	N	Y	Y	Y	Y	Y
7 Collins	N	N	Y	Y	Y	N	Y	Y
8 Rostenkowski	?	?	?	?	?	?	?	?
9 Yates	N	N	Y	Y	Y	N	Y	Y
10 Porter	N	Y	N	Y	Y	Y	Y	Y
11 Annunzio	N	N	Y	Y	Y	N	Y	Y
12 Crane, P.	Y	N	Y	N	Y	Y	N	N
13 Erlenborn	N	Y	N	Y	Y	Y	Y	N
14 Corcoran	N	Y	Y	Y	Y	Y	Y	N
15 Madigan	N	Y	Y	Y	Y	Y	Y	Y
16 Martin	Y	Y	N	Y	Y	Y	Y	Y
17 Evans	N	N	Y	Y	Y	Y	Y	Y
18 Michel	Y	Y	N	Y	Y	Y	Y	Y
19 Crane, D.	Y	Y	N	Y	Y	Y	N	N
20 Durbin	N	N	Y	Y	Y	Y	Y	Y
21 Price	N	N	Y	Y	Y	Y	Y	Y
22 Simon	N	?	?	?	?	?	?	?
INDIANA								
1 Hall	N	N	Y	Y	Y	N	Y	Y
2 Sharp	N	N	Y	Y	Y	Y	Y	N
3 Hiler	Y	Y	N	Y	Y	Y	Y	N
4 Coats	N	Y	N	Y	Y	Y	Y	N
5 Hillis	Y	Y	N	Y	Y	Y	Y	N

ND - Northern Democrats   SD - Southern Democrats

	277	278	279	280	281	282	283	284
6 ***Burton***	Y	Y	N	Y	Y	Y	Y	N
7 ***Myers***	Y	Y	N	Y	Y	Y	Y	Y
8 McCloskey	N	N	Y	Y	Y	Y	Y	Y
9 Hamilton	N	N	Y	Y	Y	Y	Y	Y
10 Jacobs	N	N	Y	Y	Y	Y	Y	N
IOWA								
1 ***Leach***	N	Y	Y	Y	Y	Y	Y	N
2 ***Tauke***	N	N	Y	Y	Y	Y	Y	N
3 ***Evans***	N	Y	Y	Y	Y	Y	Y	N
4 Smith	N	N	Y	Y	Y	Y	Y	Y
5 Harkin	N	N	Y	Y	Y	Y	Y	Y
6 Bedell	N	N	Y	Y	Y	Y	Y	N
KANSAS								
1 ***Roberts***	Y	Y	N	Y	Y	Y	Y	N
2 Slattery	N	Y	Y	Y	Y	Y	Y	N
3 ***Winn***	Y	Y	N	Y	Y	Y	Y	Y
4 Glickman	N	Y	Y	Y	Y	Y	Y	Y
5 ***Whittaker***	Y	Y	N	Y	Y	Y	Y	N
KENTUCKY								
1 Hubbard	N	N	Y	Y	Y	Y	Y	N
2 Natcher	N	N	Y	Y	Y	Y	Y	Y
3 Mazzoli	N	N	Y	Y	Y	Y	Y	Y
4 ***Snyder***	N	Y	Y	Y	Y	Y	Y	N
5 ***Rogers***	N	Y	Y	Y	Y	Y	Y	N
6 ***Hopkins***	N	Y	N	Y	Y	Y	Y	N
7 Perkins	N	N	Y	Y	Y	Y	Y	Y
LOUISIANA								
1 ***Livingston***	Y	Y	N	Y	Y	Y	Y	N
2 Boggs	N	N	Y	Y	Y	Y	Y	Y
3 Tauzin	N	Y	Y	Y	Y	Y	Y	N
4 Roemer	Y	Y	N	Y	Y	Y	Y	N
5 Huckaby	Y	Y	Y	Y	Y	Y	Y	Y
6 ***Moore***	Y	Y	N	Y	Y	Y	Y	N
7 Breaux	N	N	Y	Y	Y	Y	Y	N
8 Long	N	N	Y	Y	Y	Y	Y	Y
MAINE								
1 ***McKernan***	N	Y	Y	Y	Y	Y	Y	Y
2 ***Snowe***	N	N	Y	Y	Y	Y	Y	Y
MARYLAND								
1 Dyson	Y	Y	Y	Y	Y	Y	Y	N
2 Long	N	?	P	Y	Y	N	Y	Y
3 Mikulski	N	N	Y	Y	Y	Y	Y	Y
4 ***Holt***	N	Y	N	Y	Y	Y	Y	N
5 Hoyer	N	N	Y	Y	Y	Y	Y	Y
6 Byron	N	N	Y	Y	Y	Y	Y	N
7 Mitchell	N	N	Y	Y	Y	N	Y	Y
8 Barnes	N	N	Y	Y	Y	N	Y	Y
MASSACHUSETTS								
1 ***Conte***	N	N	Y	Y	Y	Y	Y	Y
2 Boland	N	N	Y	Y	Y	Y	Y	Y
3 Early	N	N	Y	Y	Y	Y	Y	Y
4 Frank	N	N	Y	Y	Y	Y	Y	Y
5 Shannon	?	?	?	?	?	?	?	?
6 Mavroules	N	N	Y	Y	Y	Y	Y	Y
7 Markey	N	N	Y	Y	Y	N	Y	Y
8 O'Neill								
9 Moakley	N	N	Y	Y	Y	Y	Y	Y
10 Studds	N	N	Y	Y	Y	N	Y	Y
11 Donnelly	N	N	Y	Y	Y	Y	Y	Y
MICHIGAN								
1 Conyers	N	N	Y	Y	Y	?	N	Y
2 ***Pursell***	N	Y	Y	Y	Y	Y	Y	N
3 Wolpe	N	N	Y	Y	Y	Y	Y	Y
4 ***Siljander***	Y	Y	N	Y	Y	Y	Y	N
5 ***Sawyer***	Y	N	Y	?	Y	Y	Y	Y
6 Carr	N	N	Y	Y	Y	Y	Y	Y
7 Kildee	N	N	Y	Y	Y	Y	Y	Y
8 Traxler	N	N	Y	Y	Y	Y	Y	Y
9 ***Vander Jagt***	N	Y	Y	Y	Y	Y	Y	N
10 Albosta	N	Y	Y	Y	Y	Y	Y	Y
11 ***Davis***	N	N	Y	Y	Y	Y	Y	Y
12 Bonior	N	N	Y	Y	Y	N	Y	Y
13 Crockett	?	?	?	?	?	N	Y	?
14 Hertel	N	N	Y	Y	Y	Y	Y	Y
15 Ford	N	N	Y	Y	Y	N	N	Y
16 Dingell	N	N	Y	Y	Y	Y	Y	Y
17 Levin	N	N	Y	Y	Y	N	Y	Y
18 ***Broomfield***	N	Y	N	Y	Y	Y	Y	N
MINNESOTA								
1 Penny	N	Y	Y	Y	Y	Y	Y	N
2 ***Weber***	Y	Y	N	Y	Y	Y	Y	N
3 ***Frenzel***	Y	Y	N	Y	Y	Y	Y	N
4 Vento	N	N	Y	Y	Y	N	Y	Y
5 Sabo	N	N	Y	Y	Y	Y	Y	Y
6 Sikorski	N	N	Y	Y	Y	Y	Y	Y

	277	278	279	280	281	282	283	284
7 ***Stangeland***	Y	Y	N	Y	Y	Y	Y	N
8 Oberstar	N	N	Y	Y	Y	N	Y	Y
MISSISSIPPI								
1 Whitten	N	N	Y	Y	Y	Y	Y	Y
2 ***Franklin***	#	#	X	?	?	Y	Y	N
3 Montgomery	Y	Y	Y	Y	Y	Y	Y	N
4 Dowdy	?	?	?	?	?	?	?	Y
5 ***Lott***	Y	Y	N	Y	Y	Y	Y	Y
MISSOURI								
1 Clay	?	?	?	?	?	-	?	?
2 Young	X	X	#	?	?	?	?	?
3 Gephardt	N	N	Y	Y	Y	Y	Y	Y
4 Skelton	N	N	Y	Y	Y	Y	Y	Y
5 Wheat	N	N	Y	Y	Y	N	Y	Y
6 ***Coleman***	N	Y	Y	Y	Y	Y	Y	Y
7 ***Taylor***	Y	Y	Y	Y	Y	Y	Y	Y
8 ***Emerson***	Y	Y	N	Y	Y	Y	Y	N
9 Volkmer	N	N	Y	Y	Y	Y	Y	Y
MONTANA								
1 Williams	N	N	Y	Y	Y	Y	Y	N
2 ***Marlenee***	?	?	?	?	?	Y	Y	N
NEBRASKA								
1 ***Bereuter***	N	Y	Y	Y	Y	Y	Y	N
2 ***Daub***	Y	Y	N	Y	Y	Y	Y	Y
3 ***Smith***	Y	Y	N	Y	Y	Y	Y	N
NEVADA								
1 Reid	N	N	Y	Y	Y	Y	Y	Y
2 ***Vucanovich***	N	N	Y	Y	Y	Y	Y	N
NEW HAMPSHIRE								
1 D'Amours	?	?	?	?	?	Y	Y	Y
2 ***Gregg***	Y	Y	N	Y	Y	Y	Y	?
NEW JERSEY								
1 Florio	N	N	Y	Y	Y	N	?	Y
2 Hughes	N	Y	Y	Y	Y	Y	Y	Y
3 Howard	N	N	Y	Y	Y	Y	Y	Y
4 ***Smith***	N	Y	Y	Y	Y	Y	Y	Y
5 ***Roukema***	N	Y	N	Y	Y	Y	Y	Y
6 Dwyer	N	N	Y	Y	Y	Y	Y	Y
7 ***Rinaldo***	N	N	Y	Y	Y	Y	Y	Y
8 Roe	N	N	Y	Y	Y	Y	Y	Y
9 Torricelli	N	N	Y	Y	Y	N	Y	Y
10 Rodino	?	?	?	?	?	Y	?	Y
11 Minish	N	N	Y	Y	Y	N	Y	Y
12 ***Courter***	N	Y	Y	Y	Y	Y	Y	Y
13 Vacancy								
14 Guarini	N	N	Y	Y	Y	Y	Y	Y
NEW MEXICO								
1 ***Lujan***	N	N	Y	Y	Y	Y	Y	Y
2 ***Skeen***	N	N	Y	Y	Y	Y	Y	N
3 Richardson	N	N	Y	Y	Y	Y	Y	Y
NEW YORK								
1 ***Carney***	Y	Y	N	Y	Y	Y	Y	Y
2 Downey	N	N	Y	Y	Y	Y	Y	Y
3 Mrazek	N	N	Y	Y	Y	Y	Y	Y
4 ***Lent***	N	Y	Y	Y	Y	Y	Y	Y
5 ***McGrath***	Y	Y	N	Y	Y	Y	Y	Y
6 Addabbo	N	N	Y	Y	Y	N	Y	Y
7 Ackerman	N	N	Y	Y	Y	N	N	Y
8 Scheuer	N	N	Y	Y	Y	N	Y	Y
9 Ferraro	N	N	Y	Y	Y	?	?	?
10 Schumer	N	N	Y	Y	Y	N	N	Y
11 Towns	?	?	?	?	Y	?	?	Y
12 Owens	N	N	Y	Y	Y	N	Y	Y
13 Solarz	N	N	Y	Y	Y	N	Y	Y
14 ***Molinari***	N	Y	Y	Y	Y	Y	Y	N
15 ***Green***	N	N	Y	Y	Y	N	Y	Y
16 Rangel	N	N	Y	Y	Y	N	Y	Y
17 Weiss	N	N	Y	Y	Y	N	Y	Y
18 Garcia	N	N	Y	Y	Y	N	Y	Y
19 Biaggi	?	?	?	?	?	#	?	?
20 Ottinger	N	N	Y	Y	Y	N	Y	Y
21 ***Fish***	N	N	Y	Y	Y	N	Y	Y
22 ***Gilman***	Y	Y	Y	Y	Y	N	Y	Y
23 Stratton	N	N	Y	Y	Y	Y	Y	Y
24 ***Solomon***	Y	Y	N	Y	Y	Y	Y	Y
25 ***Boehlert***	N	N	Y	Y	Y	Y	Y	Y
26 ***Martin***	N	N	Y	Y	Y	Y	Y	Y
27 ***Wortley***	N	N	Y	Y	Y	Y	Y	Y
28 McHugh	N	N	Y	Y	Y	N	Y	Y
29 ***Horton***	N	N	Y	Y	Y	Y	Y	Y
30 ***Conable***	N	Y	Y	Y	Y	Y	Y	Y
31 ***Kemp***	Y	Y	N	Y	Y	Y	Y	Y
32 LaFalce	N	N	Y	Y	Y	Y	Y	Y
33 Nowak	N	N	Y	Y	Y	Y	Y	Y
34 Lundine	N	N	Y	Y	Y	Y	Y	Y

	277	278	279	280	281	282	283	284
NORTH CAROLINA								
1 Jones	N	N	Y	Y	Y	Y	Y	Y
2 Valentine	N	Y	Y	Y	Y	Y	Y	Y
3 Whitley	N	N	Y	Y	Y	Y	Y	Y
4 Andrews	?	?	?	?	?	Y	Y	Y
5 Neal	N	N	Y	Y	Y	Y	Y	Y
6 Britt	N	?	?	Y	Y	Y	Y	Y
7 Rose	N	N	Y	Y	Y	Y	Y	Y
8 Hefner	N	N	Y	Y	Y	Y	Y	Y
9 ***Martin***	?	?	?	?	?	Y	Y	Y
10 ***Broyhill***	Y	Y	N	Y	Y	Y	Y	Y
11 Clarke	N	N	Y	Y	Y	Y	Y	Y
NORTH DAKOTA								
AL Dorgan	N	N	Y	Y	Y	Y	Y	N
OHIO								
1 Luken	N	N	Y	Y	Y	Y	Y	Y
2 ***Gradison***	Y	Y	N	Y	Y	Y	Y	N
3 Hall	N	N	Y	Y	Y	Y	Y	N
4 ***Oxley***	N	Y	N	Y	Y	Y	Y	N
5 ***Latta***	Y	Y	N	Y	Y	Y	Y	N
6 ***McEwen***	N	Y	N	Y	Y	Y	Y	Y
7 ***DeWine***	N	Y	N	Y	Y	Y	Y	N
8 ***Kindness***	N	Y	N	Y	Y	Y	Y	Y
9 Kaptur	N	N	Y	Y	Y	Y	Y	Y
10 ***Miller***	N	Y	Y	Y	Y	Y	Y	N
11 Eckart	N	N	Y	Y	Y	Y	Y	Y
12 ***Kasich***	Y	Y	N	Y	Y	Y	Y	N
13 Pease	N	N	Y	Y	Y	Y	Y	Y
14 Seiberling	N	N	Y	Y	Y	Y	N	Y
15 ***Wylie***	N	Y	Y	Y	Y	Y	Y	Y
16 ***Regula***	?	Y	N	Y	Y	Y	Y	Y
17 ***Williams***	N	N	Y	Y	Y	Y	Y	Y
18 Applegate	N	Y	Y	Y	Y	Y	Y	Y
19 Feighan	N	N	Y	Y	Y	N	Y	Y
20 Oakar	N	N	Y	Y	Y	N	Y	Y
21 Stokes	N	N	Y	Y	Y	N	N	Y
OKLAHOMA								
1 Jones	N	Y	Y	Y	Y	Y	Y	N
2 Synar	N	N	Y	Y	Y	Y	Y	N
3 Watkins	N	Y	Y	Y	Y	Y	Y	N
4 McCurdy	N	Y	Y	Y	Y	Y	Y	N
5 ***Edwards***	Y	Y	N	Y	Y	Y	Y	N
6 English	N	Y	Y	Y	Y	Y	Y	N
OREGON								
1 AuCoin	?	?	?	?	?	Y	Y	Y
2 ***Smith, R.***	?	?	?	?	?	Y	Y	Y
3 Wyden	N	N	Y	Y	Y	Y	Y	Y
4 Weaver	N	N	Y	Y	Y	Y	Y	Y
5 ***Smith, D.***	#	#	X	?	?	Y	Y	N
PENNSYLVANIA								
1 Foglietta	N	N	Y	Y	Y	N	Y	Y
2 Gray	N	N	Y	Y	Y	N	Y	Y
3 Borski	N	N	Y	Y	Y	N	Y	Y
4 Kolter	N	Y	Y	Y	Y	Y	Y	Y
5 ***Schulze***	Y	Y	Y	Y	Y	Y	Y	Y
6 Yatron	N	N	Y	Y	Y	Y	Y	Y
7 Edgar	N	N	Y	Y	Y	N	Y	Y
8 Kostmayer	N	N	Y	Y	Y	N	Y	N
9 ***Shuster***	Y	Y	N	Y	Y	Y	Y	Y
10 ***McDade***	N	N	Y	Y	Y	Y	Y	Y
11 Harrison	?	?	?	?	?	Y	Y	Y
12 Murtha	N	N	Y	Y	Y	Y	Y	Y
13 ***Coughlin***	N	Y	Y	Y	Y	N	Y	Y
14 Coyne	N	N	Y	Y	Y	N	Y	Y
15 ***Ritter***	N	Y	N	Y	Y	Y	Y	Y
16 ***Walker***	Y	Y	N	Y	Y	Y	Y	N
17 ***Gekas***	N	Y	Y	Y	Y	Y	Y	N
18 Walgren	N	N	Y	Y	Y	N	Y	Y
19 ***Goodling***	N	Y	Y	Y	Y	Y	Y	N
20 Gaydos	N	N	Y	Y	Y	Y	Y	Y
21 ***Ridge***	N	N	Y	Y	Y	Y	Y	Y
22 Murphy	N	Y	Y	Y	Y	Y	Y	Y
23 ***Clinger***	N	N	Y	Y	Y	Y	Y	Y
RHODE ISLAND								
1 St Germain	N	N	Y	Y	Y	Y	Y	Y
2 ***Schneider***	N	N	Y	Y	Y	Y	Y	Y
SOUTH CAROLINA								
1 ***Hartnett***	Y	Y	N	Y	Y	Y	Y	N
2 ***Spence***	Y	Y	Y	Y	Y	Y	Y	N
3 Derrick	N	Y	Y	Y	Y	Y	Y	?
4 ***Campbell***	Y	Y	N	Y	Y	Y	Y	?
5 Spratt	?	?	?	?	?	Y	Y	Y
6 Tallon	N	Y	Y	Y	Y	Y	?	Y
SOUTH DAKOTA								
AL Daschle	N	N	Y	Y	Y	Y	?	?

	277	278	279	280	281	282	283	284
TENNESSEE								
1 ***Quillen***	Y	Y	N	Y	Y	Y	Y	Y
2 ***Duncan***	N	N	Y	Y	Y	Y	Y	N
3 Lloyd	N	Y	Y	Y	Y	Y	Y	N
4 Cooper	N	N	Y	Y	Y	Y	Y	N
5 Boner	?	?	?	?	?	Y	Y	Y
6 Gore	N	N	Y	Y	Y	Y	Y	N
7 ***Sundquist***	N	Y	Y	Y	Y	Y	Y	N
8 Jones	?	?	?	?	?	?	?	?
9 Ford	?	?	?	?	?	Y	Y	Y
TEXAS								
1 Hall, S.	Y	Y	N	Y	Y	Y	Y	N
2 Wilson	N	N	Y	Y	Y	?	?	N
3 ***Bartlett***	N	Y	N	Y	Y	Y	Y	N
4 Hall, R.	N	Y	Y	Y	Y	Y	Y	N
5 Bryant	N	N	Y	Y	Y	Y	Y	Y
6 ***Gramm***	Y	Y	N	Y	Y	#	?	?
7 ***Archer***	Y	Y	N	Y	Y	Y	Y	N
8 ***Fields***	Y	Y	N	Y	Y	Y	Y	N
9 Brooks	N	N	Y	Y	Y	Y	Y	Y
10 Pickle	Y	Y	Y	Y	Y	Y	Y	Y
11 Leath	Y	Y	Y	Y	Y	Y	Y	N
12 Wright	N	N	Y	Y	Y	Y	Y	Y
13 Hightower	Y	Y	Y	Y	Y	Y	Y	Y
14 Patman	Y	Y	Y	Y	Y	Y	Y	N
15 de la Garza	N	Y	Y	Y	Y	Y	Y	Y
16 Coleman	N	N	Y	Y	Y	Y	Y	Y
17 Stenholm	Y	Y	N	Y	Y	Y	Y	N
18 Leland	N	N	Y	Y	Y	N	Y	Y
19 Hance	Y	Y	Y	Y	Y	Y	Y	N
20 Gonzalez	N	N	Y	Y	Y	N	Y	Y
21 ***Loeffler***	Y	Y	N	Y	Y	Y	Y	N
22 ***Paul***	Y	Y	N	N	Y	Y	N	N
23 Kazen	N	Y	Y	Y	Y	Y	Y	N
24 Frost	?	?	?	?	?	Y	Y	Y
25 Andrews	N	Y	Y	Y	Y	Y	Y	N
26 Vandergriff	N	Y	Y	Y	Y	Y	Y	Y
27 Ortiz	N	N	Y	Y	Y	Y	Y	Y
UTAH								
1 ***Hansen***	?	?	?	?	?	Y	Y	N
2 ***Marriott***	?	?	?	?	?	?	?	?
3 ***Nielson***	N	Y	N	Y	Y	Y	N	N
VERMONT								
AL ***Jeffords***	N	N	Y	Y	Y	Y	Y	Y
VIRGINIA								
1 ***Bateman***	N	Y	N	Y	Y	Y	Y	Y
2 ***Whitehurst***	N	N	Y	Y	Y	Y	Y	N
3 ***Bliley***	Y	Y	N	Y	Y	Y	Y	N
4 Sisisky	N	Y	Y	Y	Y	Y	Y	Y
5 Daniel	Y	Y	N	Y	Y	Y	Y	N
6 Olin	N	Y	Y	Y	Y	Y	Y	N
7 ***Robinson***	Y	Y	N	Y	Y	Y	Y	N
8 ***Parris***	Y	Y	Y	Y	Y	Y	Y	Y
9 Boucher	N	N	Y	Y	Y	Y	Y	Y
10 ***Wolf***	N	Y	Y	Y	Y	Y	Y	Y
WASHINGTON								
1 ***Pritchard***	?	N	Y	Y	?	Y	Y	?
2 Swift	N	N	Y	Y	Y	Y	Y	Y
3 Bonker	N	N	Y	Y	Y	Y	Y	Y
4 ***Morrison***	N	N	Y	Y	Y	Y	Y	Y
5 Foley	N	N	Y	Y	Y	Y	Y	Y
6 Dicks	N	N	Y	Y	Y	Y	Y	Y
7 Lowry	N	N	Y	Y	Y	N	Y	Y
8 ***Chandler***	N	N	Y	Y	Y	Y	Y	Y
WEST VIRGINIA								
1 Mollohan	N	N	Y	Y	Y	Y	Y	Y
2 Staggers	N	N	Y	Y	Y	Y	Y	Y
3 Wise	N	N	Y	Y	Y	Y	Y	Y
4 Rahall	N	N	Y	Y	Y	Y	Y	Y
WISCONSIN								
1 Aspin	N	N	Y	Y	Y	Y	Y	Y
2 Kastenmeier	N	N	Y	Y	Y	N	Y	Y
3 ***Gunderson***	N	Y	N	Y	Y	Y	Y	N
4 Kleczka	N	Y	Y	Y	Y	Y	Y	Y
5 Moody	N	N	Y	Y	Y	N	Y	Y
6 ***Petri***	Y	Y	N	Y	Y	Y	Y	N
7 Obey	N	Y	Y	Y	Y	Y	Y	Y
8 ***Roth***	Y	N	Y	Y	Y	Y	Y	Y
9 ***Sensenbrenner***	N	Y	N	Y	Y	Y	Y	N
WYOMING								
AL ***Cheney***	Y	Y	N	Y	Y	Y	Y	N

** Rep. Andy Ireland switched his party affiliation from Democrat to Republican effective July 5, 1984.*

Southern states - Ala., Ark., Fla., Ga., Ky., La., Miss., N.C., Okla., S.C., Tenn., Texas, Va.

285. HR 5973. Interior Appropriations, Fiscal 1985. Adoption of the rule (H Res 551) providing for House floor consideration of the bill to make fiscal 1985 appropriations for the Interior Department and related agencies. H Res 551 would not have waived points of order against amendments to rescind appropriated funds from the U.S. Synthetic Fuels Corporation. Rejected 148-261: R 21-135; D 127-126 (ND 66-101, SD 61-25), July 25, 1984. A "nay" was a vote supporting the president's position.

286. Procedural Motion. Gregg, R-N.H., motion to approve the House *Journal* of Wednesday, July 25. Motion agreed to 355-28: R 138-10; D 217-18 (ND 139-17, SD 78-1), July 26, 1984.

287. HR 11. Education Amendments/School Prayer. Walker, R-Pa., amendment to the Coats, R-Ind., amendment, to cut off federal education assistance to states and school districts with policies that prohibit silent or vocal prayer in public schools. Rejected 194-215: R 121-33; D 73-182 (ND 18-153, SD 55-29), July 26, 1984.

288. HR 11. Education Amendments/School Prayer. Gunderson, R-Wis., amendment to the Hunter, R-Calif., substitute for the Coats, R-Ind., amendment, to prohibit states and school districts from denying individuals the opportunity to participate in moments of silent prayer in public schools. The Gunderson amendment struck language in the Hunter amendment that would have cut off federal funds to states and schools that prohibit voluntary spoken and silent prayer in schools. Adopted 378-29: R 150-3; D 228-26 (ND 147-24, SD 81-2), July 26, 1984.

289. HR 11. Education Amendments/School Prayer. Coats, R-Ind., amendment as amended by the Hunter, R-Calif., substitute as amended by Gunderson, R-Wis., to prohibit states and school districts from denying individuals the opportunity to participate in moments of silent prayer in public schools; to provide that no person could be required to participate in prayer and to stipulate that federal, state and local officials could not influence the form or content of any prayer. Adopted 356-50: R 150-3; D 206-47 (ND 128-43, SD 78-4), July 26, 1984.

290. HR 11. Education Amendments/School Prayer. Goodling, R-Pa., perfecting amendment to the Ford, D-Mich., substitute for the Goodling amendment to reduce fiscal 1985 authorizations for education programs in the bill from $1.7 billion to $974 million. The perfecting amendment was identical to the original Goodling proposal that the Ford substitute would have blocked from coming to a vote. Rejected 169-233: R 133-20; D 36-213 (ND 13-154, SD 23-59), July 26, 1984.

291. HR 11. Education Amendments/School Prayer. Goodling, R-Pa., amendment as amended by the Ford, D-Mich., substitute, to reduce fiscal 1985 authorizations for education programs in the bill from $1.7 billion to $1.32 billion. Adopted 397-0: R 149-0; D 248-0 (ND 167-0, SD 81-0), July 26, 1984.

292. HR 11. Education Amendments/School Prayer. Passage of the bill to reauthorize through fiscal 1989 11 education programs, including bilingual education, impact aid and grants for the education of adults, immigrants and women, and to prohibit states and school districts from denying individuals the opportunity to participate in moments of silent prayer in public schools. Passed 307-85: R 67-80; D 240-5 (ND 165-0, SD 75-5), July 26, 1984.

KEY

Y	Voted for (yea).
#	Paired for.
+	Announced for.
N	Voted against (nay).
X	Paired against.
-	Announced against.
P	Voted "present".
C	Voted "present" to avoid possible conflict of interest.
?	Did not vote or otherwise make a position known.

Democrats   *Republicans*

	285	286	287	288	289	290	291	292
ALABAMA								
1 *Edwards*	?	Y	Y	Y	Y	Y	Y	Y
2 *Dickinson*	N	P	Y	Y	Y	Y	Y	Y
3 Nichols	Y	Y	Y	Y	Y	N	Y	Y
4 Bevill	Y	Y	Y	Y	Y	N	Y	Y
5 Flippo	Y	Y	Y	Y	Y	?	Y	Y
6 Erdreich	N	Y	Y	Y	Y	N	Y	Y
7 Shelby	N	Y	Y	Y	Y	N	Y	Y
ALASKA								
AL *Young*	N	N	Y	Y	Y	N	Y	Y
ARIZONA								
1 *McCain*	N	Y	Y	Y	Y	Y	Y	N
2 Udall	N	?	N	Y	N	Y	Y	Y
3 *Stump*	?	?	?	?	?	?	?	?
4 *Rudd*	Y	Y	Y	Y	Y	?	Y	X
5 McNulty	N	Y	N	Y	N	Y	N	Y
ARKANSAS								
1 Alexander	Y	?	?	?	?	?	?	?
2 *Bethune*	N	Y	Y	Y	Y	Y	?	?
3 *Hammerschmidt*	N	Y	Y	Y	Y	Y	Y	Y
4 Anthony	#	?	N	Y	Y	Y	Y	Y
CALIFORNIA								
1 Bosco	N	Y	N	Y	Y	N	Y	Y
2 *Chappie*	N	?	?	?	?	?	?	?
3 Matsui	Y	Y	N	Y	Y	N	Y	Y
4 Fazio	Y	Y	N	Y	Y	N	Y	Y
5 Burton	N	Y	N	N	N	N	Y	Y
6 Boxer	N	Y	N	Y	N	?	?	#
7 Miller	N	Y	N	Y	Y	N	Y	Y
8 Dellums	N	Y	N	N	N	N	Y	Y
9 Stark	N	?	N	N	N	N	Y	Y
10 Edwards	Y	Y	N	N	N	N	Y	Y
11 Lantos	Y	Y	N	Y	N	N	Y	Y
12 *Zschau*	N	?	N	Y	Y	Y	Y	N
13 Mineta	Y	Y	N	Y	Y	N	Y	Y
14 *Shumway*	N	Y	Y	Y	Y	Y	Y	N
15 Coelho	Y	Y	N	Y	Y	N	Y	Y
16 Panetta	N	Y	N	Y	Y	N	Y	Y
17 *Pashayan*	N	Y	Y	Y	Y	Y	Y	Y
18 Lehman	N	Y	N	Y	Y	N	Y	Y
19 *Lagomarsino*	N	Y	Y	Y	Y	Y	Y	Y
20 *Thomas*	N	Y	N	Y	Y	Y	?	?
21 *Fiedler*	N	Y	N	Y	Y	Y	Y	Y
22 *Moorhead*	N	Y	Y	Y	Y	Y	Y	N
23 Beilenson	Y	Y	N	N	N	N	Y	Y
24 Waxman	?	Y	N	N	N	N	Y	Y
25 Roybal	N	Y	N	N	N	N	Y	Y
26 Berman	N	Y	N	N	N	N	Y	Y
27 Levine	N	?	X	?	?	N	Y	Y
28 Dixon	Y	Y	N	Y	N	N	Y	Y
29 Hawkins	Y	N	N	N	N	N	Y	Y
30 Martinez	N	Y	N	Y	N	N	Y	Y
31 Dymally	N	P	N	Y	N	N	Y	Y
32 Anderson	N	Y	N	Y	N	N	Y	Y
33 *Dreier*	N	Y	Y	Y	Y	Y	Y	N
34 Torres	Y	?	N	Y	N	Y	N	Y
35 *Lewis*	N	Y	Y	Y	Y	Y	Y	N
36 Brown	N	Y	N	Y	N	Y	N	Y
37 *McCandless*	N	Y	Y	Y	Y	Y	Y	N
38 *Patterson*	Y	Y	N	Y	Y	N	N	Y
39 *Dannemeyer*	Y	+	+	+	+	+	+	?
40 *Badham*	Y	Y	Y	Y	Y	Y	Y	N
41 *Lowery*	N	?	Y	Y	Y	Y	Y	N
42 *Lungren*	N	Y	Y	Y	Y	Y	Y	N
43 *Packard*	N	Y	Y	Y	Y	Y	Y	N
44 Bates	N	Y	N	Y	N	N	Y	Y
45 *Hunter*	N	Y	Y	Y	Y	Y	Y	N
COLORADO								
1 Schroeder	N	N	N	Y	Y	N	Y	Y
2 Wirth	Y	Y	N	Y	Y	Y	Y	Y
3 Kogovsek	Y	Y	N	Y	Y	?	?	?
4 *Brown*	N	Y	Y	Y	Y	Y	Y	N
5 *Kramer*	Y	Y	Y	Y	Y	Y	Y	N
6 *Schaefer*	N	Y	Y	Y	Y	Y	Y	N
CONNECTICUT								
1 Kennelly	N	Y	N	Y	N	Y	N	Y
2 Gejdenson	N	N	N	N	N	N	Y	Y
3 Morrison	N	Y	N	Y	N	N	Y	Y
4 *McKinney*	Y	Y	N	Y	Y	Y	Y	Y
5 Ratchford	Y	Y	N	Y	N	Y	N	Y
6 *Johnson*	N	Y	N	Y	Y	N	Y	Y
DELAWARE								
AL Carper	Y	Y	N	Y	Y	N	Y	Y
FLORIDA								
1 Hutto	Y	Y	Y	Y	Y	N	Y	?
2 Fuqua	Y	Y	Y	Y	Y	Y	Y	Y
3 Bennett	Y	Y	Y	Y	Y	Y	Y	Y
4 Chappell	Y	Y	Y	Y	Y	N	Y	Y
5 *McCollum*	N	Y	Y	Y	Y	Y	Y	Y
6 MacKay	N	Y	Y	Y	Y	Y	Y	Y
7 Gibbons	Y	Y	Y	Y	Y	Y	Y	Y
8 *Young*	N	Y	Y	Y	Y	Y	Y	Y
9 *Bilirakis*	N	Y	Y	Y	Y	Y	Y	Y
10 *Ireland*	N	Y	Y	Y	Y	Y	Y	Y
11 Nelson	Y	Y	Y	Y	Y	Y	Y	Y
12 *Lewis*	N	Y	Y	Y	Y	Y	Y	N
13 *Mack*	N	N	Y	Y	Y	Y	Y	N
14 Mica	Y	Y	N	Y	Y	N	Y	?
15 *Shaw*	N	Y	?	?	?	?	?	?
16 Smith	N	Y	N	Y	N	N	Y	Y
17 Lehman	Y	Y	N	N	N	N	Y	Y
18 Pepper	Y	Y	N	Y	Y	N	Y	Y
19 Fascell	Y	Y	N	Y	N	N	Y	Y
GEORGIA								
1 Thomas	N	Y	Y	Y	Y	N	Y	Y
2 Hatcher	Y	Y	?	?	?	?	?	?
3 Ray	Y	Y	Y	Y	Y	Y	Y	N
4 Levitas	Y	Y	Y	Y	Y	N	Y	Y
5 Fowler	Y	Y	Y	Y	Y	N	Y	Y
6 *Gingrich*	?	Y	Y	Y	Y	Y	Y	N
7 Darden	Y	Y	Y	Y	Y	Y	Y	Y
8 Rowland	Y	Y	Y	Y	N	Y	Y	Y
9 Jenkins	Y	Y	Y	Y	Y	N	Y	Y
10 Barnard	N	Y	Y	Y	N	Y	Y	Y
HAWAII								
1 Heftel	?	Y	N	Y	N	Y	Y	Y
2 Akaka	Y	Y	N	Y	N	Y	N	Y
IDAHO								
1 *Craig*	N	Y	Y	Y	Y	Y	Y	N
2 *Hansen*	?	?	?	?	?	?	?	?
ILLINOIS								
1 Hayes	N	Y	N	Y	N	N	Y	Y
2 Savage	N	Y	N	Y	N	N	Y	Y
3 Russo	N	Y	N	Y	N	Y	Y	Y
4 *O'Brien*	X	Y	Y	Y	Y	Y	Y	Y
5 Lipinski	N	N	Y	Y	Y	Y	Y	Y
6 *Hyde*	N	?	Y	N	Y	Y	N	Y
7 Collins	N	Y	N	N	N	N	Y	Y
8 Rostenkowski	?	?	?	?	?	?	?	?
9 Yates	Y	N	N	N	N	N	Y	Y
10 *Porter*	N	Y	N	Y	Y	Y	Y	Y
11 Annunzio	Y	Y	N	Y	N	Y	N	Y
12 *Crane, P.*	N	Y	Y	Y	Y	Y	Y	N
13 *Erlenborn*	N	Y	Y	Y	Y	Y	Y	Y
14 *Corcoran*	N	Y	Y	Y	Y	Y	?	?
15 *Madigan*	N	Y	Y	Y	Y	Y	Y	Y
16 *Martin*	N	Y	N	Y	Y	Y	Y	Y
17 Evans	N	Y	N	Y	N	Y	N	Y
18 *Michel*	N	Y	Y	Y	Y	Y	Y	Y
19 *Crane, D.*	N	Y	Y	Y	Y	N	Y	N
20 Durbin	Y	N	N	Y	N	Y	N	Y
21 Price	Y	Y	N	Y	Y	Y	Y	Y
22 Simon	?	?	?	?	?	?	?	?
INDIANA								
1 Hall	N	Y	N	Y	N	N	Y	Y
2 Sharp	N	Y	Y	Y	Y	N	Y	Y
3 *Hiler*	N	Y	Y	Y	Y	Y	Y	N
4 *Coats*	N	Y	Y	Y	Y	Y	Y	N
5 Hillis	N	Y	Y	Y	Y	Y	Y	N

ND - Northern Democrats   SD - Southern Democrats

Corresponding to Congressional Record Votes 316, 317, 319, 320, 321, 324, 325, 326

	285	286	287	288	289	290	291	292
6 ***Burton***	N	Y	Y	Y	Y	Y	Y	N
7 ***Myers***	Y	Y	Y	Y	Y	Y	Y	N
8 McCloskey	N	Y	N	Y	Y	N	Y	Y
9 Hamilton	N	Y	Y	Y	Y	N	Y	Y
10 Jacobs	N	N	Y	Y	Y	N	Y	Y
IOWA								
1 ***Leach***	N	?	N	Y	Y	N	Y	?
2 ***Tauke***	N	Y	N	Y	Y	Y	Y	N
3 ***Evans***	N	N	N	Y	Y	Y	Y	Y
4 Smith	Y	Y	N	Y	Y	N	Y	Y
5 Harkin	N	N	N	Y	Y	N	Y	Y
6 Bedell	N	Y	N	Y	Y	N	Y	Y
KANSAS								
1 ***Roberts***	N	N	Y	Y	Y	Y	Y	N
2 Slattery	N	Y	N	Y	Y	Y	Y	Y
3 ***Winn***	Y	Y	Y	Y	Y	Y	Y	N
4 Glickman	N	Y	N	Y	Y	N	Y	Y
5 ***Whittaker***	N	Y	Y	Y	Y	Y	Y	N
KENTUCKY								
1 Hubbard	Y	?	?	?	?	?	?	?
2 Natcher	Y	Y	Y	Y	Y	N	Y	Y
3 Mazzoli	Y	Y	N	Y	Y	N	Y	Y
4 ***Snyder***	N	Y	Y	Y	Y	Y	Y	Y
5 ***Rogers***	Y	Y	Y	Y	Y	Y	Y	Y
6 ***Hopkins***	N	Y	Y	Y	Y	Y	Y	Y
7 Perkins	Y	Y	N	Y	Y	N	Y	Y
LOUISIANA								
1 ***Livingston***	N	?	Y	Y	Y	Y	Y	N
2 Boggs	Y	Y	N	Y	Y	N	Y	?
3 Tauzin	N	Y	Y	Y	Y	Y	Y	Y
4 Roemer	N	N	Y	Y	Y	Y	Y	N
5 Huckaby	Y	P	Y	Y	Y	Y	Y	Y
6 ***Moore***	N	Y	Y	Y	Y	Y	Y	N
7 Breaux	Y	Y	Y	Y	Y	Y	Y	Y
8 Long	Y	Y	N	Y	Y	N	Y	Y
MAINE								
1 ***McKernan***	N	Y	N	Y	Y	Y	Y	Y
2 ***Snowe***	Y	Y	N	Y	Y	Y	Y	Y
MARYLAND								
1 Dyson	N	Y	Y	Y	Y	N	Y	Y
2 Long	Y	Y	N	?	Y	N	Y	Y
3 Mikulski	N	Y	N	Y	Y	N	Y	Y
4 ***Holt***	N	Y	Y	Y	Y	Y	Y	N
5 Hoyer	N	Y	N	Y	Y	N	Y	Y
6 Byron	Y	Y	Y	Y	Y	Y	Y	Y
7 Mitchell	N	N	N	Y	N	N	Y	Y
8 Barnes	N	Y	N	Y	N	N	Y	Y
MASSACHUSETTS								
1 ***Conte***	N	Y	N	Y	Y	N	Y	Y
2 Boland	Y	Y	N	Y	Y	?	?	?
3 Early	Y	Y	?	?	?	?	?	?
4 Frank	N	Y	N	Y	N	N	Y	Y
5 Shannon	?	?	N	Y	N	N	Y	Y
6 Mavroules	Y	Y	N	Y	N	N	Y	Y
7 Markey	N	Y	N	Y	N	N	Y	Y
8 O'Neill								
9 Moakley	Y	Y	N	Y	Y	N	Y	Y
10 Studds	N	Y	N	Y	N	?	?	?
11 Donnelly	Y	Y	N	Y	Y	N	Y	Y
MICHIGAN								
1 Conyers	N	Y	N	N	N	N	Y	Y
2 ***Pursell***	N	Y	N	Y	Y	Y	Y	Y
3 Wolpe	N	Y	N	Y	Y	N	Y	Y
4 ***Siljander***	N	Y	Y	Y	Y	Y	Y	N
5 ***Sawyer***	N	Y	Y	Y	Y	Y	Y	Y
6 Carr	Y	Y	Y	Y	Y	N	Y	Y
7 Kildee	N	Y	N	Y	Y	N	Y	Y
8 Traxler	Y	Y	N	Y	Y	N	Y	Y
9 ***Vander Jagt***	N	Y	Y	Y	Y	Y	Y	Y
10 Albosta	Y	Y	N	Y	Y	Y	Y	Y
11 ***Davis***	N	Y	N	Y	Y	N	Y	Y
12 Bonior	Y	Y	N	Y	Y	N	Y	Y
13 Crockett	Y	Y	N	N	N	N	Y	Y
14 Hertel	N	Y	N	Y	Y	N	Y	Y
15 Ford	N	?	N	Y	Y	N	Y	Y
16 Dingell	Y	Y	N	Y	Y	N	Y	Y
17 Levin	N	Y	N	Y	Y	N	Y	Y
18 ***Broomfield***	N	Y	Y	Y	Y	Y	Y	N
MINNESOTA								
1 Penny	N	N	N	Y	Y	Y	Y	Y
2 ***Weber***	N	Y	Y	Y	Y	Y	Y	Y
3 ***Frenzel***	N	Y	N	Y	Y	Y	Y	N
4 Vento	N	N	N	Y	Y	?	?	?
5 Sabo	Y	N	N	Y	N	N	Y	Y
6 Sikorski	N	N	N	Y	Y	N	Y	Y

	285	286	287	288	289	290	291	292
7 ***Stangeland***	N	Y	Y	Y	Y	Y	Y	Y
8 Oberstar	Y	P	N	Y	Y	N	Y	Y
MISSISSIPPI								
1 Whitten	Y	Y	Y	Y	?	N	Y	Y
2 ***Franklin***	N	Y	Y	Y	Y	Y	Y	N
3 Montgomery	Y	Y	Y	Y	Y	Y	Y	N
4 Dowdy	N	Y	Y	Y	Y	N	Y	Y
5 ***Lott***	N	Y	Y	Y	Y	Y	Y	N
MISSOURI								
1 Clay	?	N	N	N	N	N	Y	Y
2 Young	#	Y	N	Y	Y	N	Y	Y
3 Gephardt	N	Y	N	Y	Y	N	Y	Y
4 Skelton	Y	Y	Y	Y	Y	N	Y	Y
5 Wheat	Y	Y	N	Y	Y	N	Y	Y
6 ***Coleman***	N	?	N	Y	Y	Y	Y	Y
7 ***Taylor***	N	Y	#	?	?	?	?	X
8 ***Emerson***	N	N	Y	Y	Y	Y	Y	Y
9 Volkmer	Y	P	Y	Y	Y	N	Y	Y
MONTANA								
1 Williams	N	?	N	Y	Y	N	Y	Y
2 ***Marlenee***	N	Y	Y	Y	Y	Y	Y	N
NEBRASKA								
1 ***Bereuter***	N	Y	N	Y	Y	Y	Y	Y
2 ***Daub***	N	Y	Y	Y	Y	Y	Y	Y
3 ***Smith***	N	Y	Y	Y	Y	Y	Y	Y
NEVADA								
1 Reid	Y	Y	N	Y	Y	N	Y	Y
2 ***Vucanovich***	N	Y	Y	Y	Y	Y	Y	N
NEW HAMPSHIRE								
1 D'Amours	N	Y	N	Y	Y	Y	Y	Y
2 ***Gregg***	N	Y	Y	Y	Y	Y	Y	N
NEW JERSEY								
1 Florio	N	Y	N	Y	Y	N	Y	Y
2 Hughes	N	Y	N	Y	Y	Y	Y	Y
3 Howard	N	Y	N	Y	Y	N	Y	Y
4 ***Smith***	N	Y	Y	Y	Y	Y	Y	Y
5 ***Roukema***	N	?	N	Y	Y	Y	Y	N
6 Dwyer	Y	Y	N	Y	Y	N	Y	Y
7 ***Rinaldo***	N	?	?	?	?	?	?	?
8 Roe	N	Y	N	Y	Y	N	Y	Y
9 Torricelli	N	Y	N	Y	Y	N	Y	Y
10 Rodino	Y	Y	N	Y	Y	N	Y	Y
11 Minish	N	Y	N	Y	Y	N	Y	Y
12 ***Courter***	N	?	?	?	?	?	?	?
13 Vacancy								
14 Guarini	Y	Y	N	Y	Y	N	Y	Y
NEW MEXICO								
1 ***Lujan***	N	Y	Y	Y	Y	Y	Y	Y
2 ***Skeen***	N	Y	Y	Y	Y	Y	Y	N
3 Richardson	N	Y	N	Y	Y	N	Y	Y
NEW YORK								
1 ***Carney***	N	Y	Y	Y	Y	Y	Y	N
2 Downey	N	Y	N	Y	Y	N	Y	Y
3 Mrazek	N	Y	N	Y	Y	N	Y	Y
4 ***Lent***	N	Y	Y	Y	Y	Y	Y	Y
5 ***McGrath***	N	Y	Y	Y	Y	Y	Y	Y
6 Addabbo	Y	Y	N	Y	N	N	Y	Y
7 Ackerman	N	N	N	N	N	N	Y	Y
8 Scheuer	N	Y	N	N	N	N	Y	Y
9 Ferraro	?	?	N	Y	?	?	?	?
10 Schumer	N	Y	N	N	N	N	Y	Y
11 Towns	N	?	N	Y	Y	N	Y	Y
12 Owens	N	Y	N	Y	Y	N	Y	Y
13 Solarz	N	Y	N	Y	Y	N	Y	Y
14 ***Molinari***	N	Y	Y	Y	Y	Y	Y	N
15 ***Green***	N	Y	N	N	N	N	Y	Y
16 Rangel	N	Y	N	N	N	N	Y	Y
17 Weiss	N	Y	N	N	N	N	Y	Y
18 Garcia	N	Y	N	Y	Y	N	Y	Y
19 Biaggi	?	?	N	Y	Y	N	Y	Y
20 Ottinger	N	P	N	N	N	N	Y	Y
21 ***Fish***	N	?	N	Y	Y	Y	Y	Y
22 ***Gilman***	N	Y	N	Y	Y	N	Y	Y
23 Stratton	?	Y	Y	Y	Y	N	Y	Y
24 ***Solomon***	N	N	Y	Y	Y	Y	Y	N
25 ***Boehlert***	N	Y	N	Y	Y	N	Y	Y
26 ***Martin***	N	Y	Y	Y	Y	Y	Y	?
27 ***Wortley***	N	Y	Y	Y	Y	Y	Y	Y
28 McHugh	N	Y	N	Y	Y	N	Y	Y
29 ***Horton***	X	Y	N	Y	Y	N	Y	Y
30 ***Conable***	N	Y	N	?	?	?	?	?
31 ***Kemp***	N	Y	Y	Y	Y	Y	Y	N
32 LaFalce	Y	Y	N	Y	Y	N	Y	Y
33 Nowak	Y	Y	N	Y	Y	N	Y	Y
34 Lundine	Y	?	N	Y	Y	Y	Y	Y

	285	286	287	288	289	290	291	292
NORTH CAROLINA								
1 Jones	Y	?	N	Y	Y	N	Y	Y
2 Valentine	Y	Y	Y	Y	Y	N	Y	Y
3 Whitley	Y	Y	Y	Y	Y	N	Y	Y
4 Andrews	N	Y	N	Y	Y	N	Y	Y
5 Neal	N	?	?	?	?	?	?	?
6 Britt	Y	Y	N	Y	Y	N	Y	Y
7 Rose	Y	Y	Y	Y	Y	N	Y	Y
8 Hefner	Y	Y	Y	Y	Y	N	Y	Y
9 ***Martin***	N	Y	Y	Y	Y	Y	Y	Y
10 ***Broyhill***	N	Y	Y	Y	Y	Y	Y	N
11 Clarke	N	Y	N	Y	Y	N	Y	Y
NORTH DAKOTA								
AL Dorgan	Y	Y	N	Y	Y	N	Y	Y
OHIO								
1 Luken	N	Y	N	Y	Y	N	Y	Y
2 ***Gradison***	N	Y	N	Y	Y	Y	Y	N
3 Hall	N	Y	Y	N	N	N	Y	Y
4 ***Oxley***	N	Y	+	+	+	+	+	+
5 ***Latta***	N	Y	Y	Y	Y	Y	Y	N
6 ***McEwen***	N	Y	Y	Y	Y	Y	Y	N
7 ***DeWine***	N	Y	Y	Y	Y	Y	Y	N
8 ***Kindness***	N	Y	Y	N	N	Y	Y	N
9 Kaptur	N	Y	N	Y	Y	N	Y	Y
10 ***Miller***	N	N	Y	Y	Y	Y	Y	Y
11 Eckart	N	Y	N	Y	Y	N	Y	Y
12 ***Kasich***	N	Y	Y	Y	Y	Y	Y	Y
13 Pease	N	Y	N	Y	Y	N	Y	Y
14 Seiberling	N	?	N	Y	Y	N	Y	Y
15 ***Wylie***	N	Y	Y	Y	Y	Y	Y	N
16 ***Regula***	Y	Y	Y	Y	Y	Y	Y	Y
17 ***Williams***	N	Y	Y	Y	Y	N	Y	Y
18 Applegate	Y	?	Y	Y	Y	Y	Y	Y
19 Feighan	N	Y	N	Y	Y	N	Y	Y
20 Oakar	N	Y	N	Y	Y	N	Y	Y
21 Stokes	N	Y	N	N	N	N	Y	Y
OKLAHOMA								
1 Jones	N	Y	Y	Y	Y	N	Y	Y
2 Synar	N	Y	N	Y	N	N	Y	Y
3 Watkins	Y	Y	Y	Y	Y	N	Y	Y
4 McCurdy	N	Y	Y	Y	Y	N	Y	Y
5 ***Edwards***	Y	N	Y	Y	Y	Y	Y	N
6 English	N	Y	Y	Y	Y	Y	Y	Y
OREGON								
1 AuCoin	Y	Y	N	Y	Y	N	Y	Y
2 ***Smith, R.***	N	Y	Y	Y	Y	Y	Y	Y
3 Wyden	Y	Y	N	Y	Y	N	Y	Y
4 Weaver	N	Y	N	N	N	N	Y	Y
5 ***Smith, D.***	N	Y	Y	Y	Y	Y	?	?
PENNSYLVANIA								
1 Foglietta	N	Y	N	Y	Y	N	Y	?
2 Gray	Y	Y	N	N	N	N	Y	Y
3 Borski	N	Y	N	Y	Y	N	Y	Y
4 Kolter	Y	Y	Y	Y	Y	Y	Y	Y
5 ***Schulze***	Y	Y	Y	Y	Y	Y	Y	N
6 Yatron	Y	Y	Y	Y	Y	N	Y	Y
7 Edgar	N	N	N	Y	Y	N	Y	Y
8 Kostmayer	N	Y	N	Y	Y	N	Y	Y
9 ***Shuster***	Y	Y	Y	Y	Y	Y	Y	N
10 ***McDade***	Y	Y	Y	Y	Y	Y	Y	Y
11 Harrison	Y	?	N	Y	Y	N	Y	Y
12 Murtha	Y	Y	Y	Y	Y	N	Y	?
13 ***Coughlin***	N	N	N	Y	Y	N	Y	Y
14 Coyne	Y	Y	N	Y	Y	N	Y	Y
15 ***Ritter***	N	Y	Y	Y	Y	Y	Y	N
16 ***Walker***	N	Y	Y	Y	Y	Y	Y	N
17 ***Gekas***	N	Y	Y	Y	Y	Y	Y	N
18 Walgren	N	Y	N	Y	Y	Y	Y	Y
19 ***Goodling***	N	N	Y	Y	Y	Y	Y	N
20 Gaydos	Y	Y	Y	Y	Y	N	Y	Y
21 ***Ridge***	N	Y	N	Y	Y	Y	Y	Y
22 Murphy	Y	Y	Y	Y	Y	N	Y	Y
23 ***Clinger***	Y	Y	Y	Y	Y	Y	Y	Y
RHODE ISLAND								
1 St Germain	N	?	?	?	?	?	?	?
2 ***Schneider***	N	Y	N	Y	Y	N	Y	Y
SOUTH CAROLINA								
1 ***Hartnett***	N	Y	Y	Y	Y	Y	Y	N
2 ***Spence***	N	Y	Y	Y	Y	Y	Y	Y
3 Derrick	Y	Y	Y	Y	Y	Y	Y	Y
4 ***Campbell***	?	?	+	+	Y	Y	Y	Y
5 Spratt	N	Y	N	Y	Y	N	Y	Y
6 Tallon	N	?	Y	Y	Y	N	Y	Y
SOUTH DAKOTA								
AL Daschle	Y	Y	N	Y	Y	Y	Y	Y

	285	286	287	288	289	290	291	292
TENNESSEE								
1 ***Quillen***	Y	Y	Y	Y	Y	N	Y	Y
2 ***Duncan***	Y	Y	Y	Y	Y	N	Y	Y
3 Lloyd	Y	Y	Y	Y	Y	N	Y	Y
4 Cooper	Y	Y	N	Y	Y	N	Y	Y
5 Boner	Y	Y	Y	Y	Y	N	?	Y
6 Gore	N	Y	N	Y	Y	N	Y	Y
7 ***Sundquist***	N	Y	Y	Y	Y	Y	Y	N
8 Jones	?	?	?	?	?	?	?	#
9 Ford	N	?	N	Y	?	N	Y	Y
TEXAS								
1 Hall, S.	Y	Y	Y	Y	Y	Y	Y	Y
2 Wilson	?	?	Y	Y	Y	N	Y	Y
3 ***Bartlett***	N	Y	Y	Y	Y	Y	Y	N
4 Hall, R.	Y	Y	Y	Y	Y	Y	Y	Y
5 Bryant	Y	Y	N	Y	Y	N	Y	Y
6 ***Gramm***	?	?	?	?	?	?	?	?
7 ***Archer***	N	Y	Y	Y	Y	Y	Y	N
8 ***Fields***	N	Y	Y	Y	Y	Y	Y	N
9 Brooks	Y	Y	N	Y	Y	N	Y	Y
10 Pickle	Y	Y	N	Y	Y	N	Y	Y
11 Leath	Y	Y	Y	Y	Y	N	Y	Y
12 Wright	Y	Y	Y	Y	Y	N	Y	Y
13 Hightower	Y	Y	Y	Y	Y	Y	Y	Y
14 Patman	Y	Y	Y	Y	Y	Y	Y	Y
15 de la Garza	Y	Y	Y	Y	Y	N	Y	Y
16 Coleman	Y	Y	N	Y	Y	N	Y	Y
17 Stenholm	N	Y	Y	Y	Y	Y	Y	N
18 Leland	Y	Y	N	?	N	N	Y	Y
19 Hance	Y	Y	Y	Y	Y	Y	Y	Y
20 Gonzalez	Y	Y	N	N	N	N	Y	Y
21 ***Loeffler***	Y	Y	Y	Y	Y	Y	Y	N
22 ***Paul***	N	Y	Y	Y	Y	Y	Y	N
23 Kazen	Y	Y	Y	Y	Y	N	Y	Y
24 Frost	Y	Y	N	Y	Y	?	Y	Y
25 Andrews	Y	Y	Y	Y	Y	N	Y	Y
26 Vandergriff	Y	Y	Y	Y	Y	N	Y	Y
27 Ortiz	N	Y	N	Y	Y	N	Y	Y
UTAH								
1 ***Hansen***	N	Y	Y	Y	Y	Y	Y	N
2 ***Marriott***	?	?	?	?	?	?	?	?
3 ***Nielson***	Y	Y	Y	Y	Y	Y	Y	N
VERMONT								
AL ***Jeffords***	N	Y	N	Y	Y	Y	Y	Y
VIRGINIA								
1 ***Bateman***	N	Y	Y	Y	Y	Y	Y	Y
2 ***Whitehurst***	N	Y	Y	Y	Y	Y	Y	Y
3 ***Bliley***	N	Y	Y	Y	Y	Y	Y	N
4 Sisisky	N	Y	N	Y	Y	N	Y	Y
5 Daniel	Y	Y	Y	Y	Y	Y	Y	N
6 Olin	N	Y	N	Y	Y	Y	?	?
7 ***Robinson***	-	Y	Y	Y	Y	Y	Y	N
8 ***Parris***	Y	Y	Y	Y	Y	Y	Y	Y
9 Boucher	Y	Y	Y	Y	Y	N	Y	Y
10 ***Wolf***	N	Y	Y	Y	Y	Y	Y	Y
WASHINGTON								
1 ***Pritchard***	?	?	?	?	?	?	?	?
2 Swift	N	Y	N	Y	Y	N	Y	Y
3 Bonker	N	Y	N	Y	Y	N	Y	Y
4 ***Morrison***	N	Y	N	Y	Y	Y	Y	Y
5 Foley	Y	Y	N	Y	Y	N	Y	Y
6 Dicks	N	Y	N	Y	Y	N	Y	Y
7 Lowry	N	N	N	Y	Y	N	Y	Y
8 ***Chandler***	N	Y	N	Y	Y	N	Y	Y
WEST VIRGINIA								
1 Mollohan	Y	Y	Y	Y	Y	N	Y	Y
2 Staggers	Y	Y	N	Y	Y	N	Y	Y
3 Wise	Y	Y	N	Y	Y	N	Y	Y
4 Rahall	Y	Y	N	Y	Y	N	Y	Y
WISCONSIN								
1 Aspin	Y	Y	N	Y	Y	N	Y	Y
2 Kastenmeier	N	Y	N	N	N	N	Y	Y
3 ***Gunderson***	N	Y	N	Y	Y	Y	Y	N
4 Kleczka	N	Y	N	Y	Y	N	Y	Y
5 Moody	N	Y	N	Y	Y	Y	Y	Y
6 ***Petri***	N	Y	Y	Y	Y	Y	Y	Y
7 Obey	N	Y	?	Y	Y	N	Y	Y
8 ***Roth***	Y	Y	Y	Y	Y	Y	Y	Y
9 ***Sensenbrenner***	N	Y	Y	Y	Y	Y	Y	N
WYOMING								
AL ***Cheney***	N	Y	Y	Y	Y	Y	Y	N

Southern states - Ala., Ark., Fla., Ga., Ky., La., Miss., N.C., Okla., S.C., Tenn., Texas, Va.

293. HR 4784. Trade Remedies Reform Act. Frenzel, R-Minn., motion to recommit the bill to the Ways and Means Committee with instructions to modify the legislation, including elimination of a provision making the use of unfairly priced parts in manufactured goods imported to the United States an unfair trade practice. Motion rejected 128-231: R 99-40; D 29-191 (ND 15-131, SD 14-60), July 26, 1984.

294. HR 4784. Trade Remedies Reform Act. Passage of the bill to expand the range of unfair trade practices eligible for retaliation by the United States. Passed 259-95: R 66-71; D 193-24 (ND 132-11, SD 61-13), July 26, 1984. A "nay" was a vote supporting the president's position.

295. H Res 558. George Hansen Reprimand. Adoption of the resolution to reprimand Rep. George Hansen, R-Idaho, for failing to disclose his financial dealings as required under the 1978 Ethics in Government Act. Adopted 354-52: R 116-42; D 238-10 (ND 160-5, SD 78-5), July 31, 1984.

296. H Res 555. Anne M. Burford Appointment. D'Amours, D-N.H., motion to suspend the rules and adopt the resolution urging President Reagan to withdraw the appointment of former Environmental Protection Agency Administrator Anne M. Burford to be chairman of the National Advisory Committee on Oceans and Atmosphere. Motion agreed to 363-51: R 110-49; D 253-2 (ND 171-0, SD 82-2), July 31, 1984. A two-thirds majority of those present and voting (276 in this case) is required for adoption under suspension of the rules. A "nay" was a vote supporting the president's position.

297. HR 6028. Labor, Health and Human Services, Education Appropriations, Fiscal 1985. Dannemeyer, R-Calif., amendment to cut spending in the bill by $147.5 million through a variety of cost-saving measures. Rejected 182-226: R 121-35; D 61-191 (ND 27-141, SD 34-50), Aug. 1, 1984.

298. HR 6028. Labor, Health and Human Services, Education Appropriations, Fiscal 1985. Frenzel, R-Minn., amendment to reduce discretionary spending in the bill by 5.9 percent across-the-board, or $1.5 billion. Rejected 144-276: R 116-47; D 28-229 (ND 7-164, SD 21-65), Aug. 1, 1984.

299. HR 6028. Labor, Health and Human Services, Education Appropriations, Fiscal 1985. Passage of the bill to provide $85,579,931,000 in fiscal 1985 appropriations and $10,568,609,000 in advance fiscal 1986 appropriations for the Departments of Labor, Health and Human Services, Education and other related agencies. Passed 329-91: R 78-85; D 251-6 (ND 172-0, SD 79-6), Aug. 1, 1984. The president had requested $92,489,040,000 in new budget authority. The House did not consider an additional $7,196,306,000 in requests for programs that had not been authorized.

300. HR 6040. Supplemental Appropriations, Fiscal 1984. Walker, R-Pa., amendment to reduce the overall spending amount in the bill by 1 percent. Rejected 184-238: R 129-33; D 55-205 (ND 26-148, SD 29-57), Aug. 1, 1984.

KEY

Y	Voted for (yea).
#	Paired for.
+	Announced for.
N	Voted against (nay).
X	Paired against.
-	Announced against.
P	Voted "present".
C	Voted "present" to avoid possible conflict of interest.
?	Did not vote or otherwise make a position known.

Democrats   *Republicans*

	293	294	295	296	297	298	299	300
ALABAMA								
1 Edwards	Y	Y	Y	Y	N	Y	Y	Y
2 *Dickinson*	N	Y	N	?	Y	N	Y	Y
3 Nichols	N	Y	Y	Y	Y	Y	Y	Y
4 Bevill	N	Y	Y	Y	N	N	Y	N
5 Flippo	N	?	Y	Y	Y	N	Y	N
6 Erdreich	N	Y	Y	Y	Y	N	Y	N
7 Shelby	N	Y	Y	Y	N	Y	Y	N
ALASKA								
AL *Young*	N	Y	N	N	N	N	Y	Y
ARIZONA								
1 *McCain*	Y	Y	Y	N	Y	Y	Y	Y
2 Udall	N	Y	Y	Y	N	N	Y	N
3 *Stump*	?	?	N	N	Y	Y	N	Y
4 *Rudd*	?	?	N	N	Y	Y	N	N
5 McNulty	N	Y	Y	Y	Y	N	Y	N
ARKANSAS								
1 Alexander	?	?	?	Y	N	N	Y	N
2 *Bethune*	?	?	?	?	?	Y	Y	Y
3 *Hammerschmidt*	Y	Y	N	N	Y	Y	Y	Y
4 Anthony	N	N	?	?	X	?	?	?
CALIFORNIA								
1 Bosco	?	?	Y	Y	N	Y	Y	N
2 *Chappie*	?	?	Y	N	Y	N	Y	N
3 Matsui	N	Y	Y	Y	N	N	Y	N
4 Fazio	N	Y	Y	Y	N	N	Y	N
5 Burton	N	Y	Y	Y	N	N	Y	N
6 Boxer	X	?	Y	Y	N	N	Y	N
7 Miller	N	Y	Y	Y	N	N	Y	N
8 Dellums	N	Y	?	Y	N	N	Y	N
9 Stark	N	Y	Y	Y	N	N	Y	N
10 Edwards	N	Y	Y	Y	N	N	Y	N
11 Lantos	N	?	Y	Y	N	N	Y	N
12 *Zschau*	Y	N	Y	Y	Y	Y	N	Y
13 Mineta	N	Y	Y	Y	N	N	Y	N
14 *Shumway*	Y	N	N	N	Y	N	Y	Y
15 Coelho	N	Y	Y	Y	N	N	Y	N
16 Panetta	Y	Y	Y	Y	N	N	Y	N
17 *Pashayan*	Y	Y	N	Y	N	Y	N	Y
18 Lehman	?	?	Y	Y	N	N	Y	N
19 *Lagomarsino*	Y	N	Y	Y	Y	Y	Y	Y
20 *Thomas*	#	?	Y	N	Y	N	Y	N
21 *Fiedler*	Y	N	Y	Y	Y	N	Y	Y
22 *Moorhead*	Y	N	N	Y	Y	N	Y	Y
23 Beilenson	Y	Y	Y	Y	N	N	Y	N
24 Waxman	?	?	Y	Y	N	N	Y	?
25 Roybal	N	Y	Y	Y	N	N	Y	N
26 Berman	?	?	Y	Y	N	N	Y	N
27 Levine	Y	Y	Y	Y	N	N	Y	N
28 Dixon	N	Y	Y	Y	N	N	Y	N
29 Hawkins	?	?	Y	Y	X	N	Y	N
30 Martinez	N	Y	Y	Y	N	N	Y	N
31 Dymally	N	Y	P	Y	N	N	Y	N
32 Anderson	N	Y	N	Y	N	N	N	N
33 *Dreier*	Y	N	Y	Y	Y	Y	N	Y
34 Torres	N	Y	N	Y	N	N	Y	N
35 *Lewis*	Y	Y	Y	N	Y	N	Y	Y
36 Brown	N	Y	Y	Y	N	N	Y	N
37 *McCandless*	Y	N	Y	N	Y	N	Y	Y
38 Patterson	N	Y	Y	Y	Y	Y	N	Y
39 *Dannemeyer*	?	?	N	N	Y	Y	N	Y
40 *Badham*	Y	N	N	N	Y	N	Y	Y
41 *Lowery*	Y	N	Y	Y	Y	Y	N	+
42 *Lungren*	Y	N	Y	N	Y	Y	N	Y

	293	294	295	296	297	298	299	300
43 *Packard*	Y	N	Y	Y	Y	Y	N	Y
44 Bates	?	?	Y	Y	N	N	N	N
45 *Hunter*	N	Y	N	N	Y	Y	N	N
COLORADO								
1 Schroeder	Y	N	Y	N	Y	N	Y	N
2 Wirth	N	?	Y	N	Y	N	Y	N
3 Kogovsek	?	?	Y	Y	N	N	Y	N
4 *Brown*	Y	N	N	Y	N	Y	N	Y
5 *Kramer*	Y	N	Y	N	Y	N	Y	Y
6 *Schaefer*	Y	N	Y	N	Y	N	Y	Y
CONNECTICUT								
1 Kennelly	N	Y	Y	Y	N	N	Y	N
2 Gejdenson	N	N	Y	Y	N	N	Y	N
3 Morrison	N	N	Y	Y	Y	N	Y	N
4 *McKinney*	Y	Y	Y	Y	N	N	Y	N
5 Ratchford	N	Y	Y	Y	N	N	Y	N
6 *Johnson*	N	Y	Y	Y	N	N	Y	N
DELAWARE								
AL Carper	N	Y	Y	Y	Y	N	Y	Y
FLORIDA								
1 Hutto	?	?	Y	Y	Y	N	Y	N
2 Fuqua	N	Y	Y	Y	N	N	Y	N
3 Bennett	N	Y	Y	Y	Y	N	Y	N
4 Chappell	N	Y	Y	Y	N	N	Y	N
5 *McCollum*	Y	N	N	Y	Y	Y	N	Y
6 MacKay	N	Y	Y	Y	Y	N	Y	Y
7 Gibbons	N	Y	Y	Y	N	Y	Y	Y
8 *Young*	N	Y	N	Y	N	N	Y	Y
9 *Bilirakis*	Y	N	N	Y	N	Y	N	Y
10 *Ireland*	N	Y	Y	Y	Y	Y	Y	Y
11 Nelson	+	-	Y	Y	Y	Y	Y	N
12 *Lewis*	Y	N	Y	N	Y	N	Y	Y
13 *Mack*	Y	N	Y	N	Y	Y	N	Y
14 Mica	?	?	Y	Y	Y	N	Y	Y
15 *Shaw*	?	?	Y	Y	Y	N	Y	Y
16 Smith	N	Y	Y	Y	N	N	Y	N
17 Lehman	?	?	Y	Y	N	N	Y	N
18 Pepper	N	Y	Y	Y	N	N	Y	N
19 Fascell	N	Y	Y	Y	N	N	Y	N
GEORGIA								
1 Thomas	Y	N	Y	N	Y	N	Y	N
2 Hatcher	?	?	Y	Y	N	N	Y	N
3 Ray	N	Y	Y	Y	Y	Y	Y	Y
4 Levitas	N	Y	Y	Y	Y	Y	Y	Y
5 Fowler	N	Y	Y	Y	N	N	Y	N
6 *Gingrich*	Y	N	Y	Y	Y	Y	Y	Y
7 Darden	N	Y	Y	Y	Y	Y	Y	Y
8 Rowland	Y	N	Y	Y	Y	N	Y	N
9 Jenkins	N	Y	Y	Y	N	N	Y	N
10 Barnard	?	?	Y	Y	Y	Y	Y	N
HAWAII								
1 Heftel	N	Y	P	N	N	N	Y	N
2 Akaka	N	Y	P	Y	?	N	Y	N
IDAHO								
1 *Craig*	Y	N	C	N	#	Y	N	Y
2 *Hansen*	?	?	?	?	Y	Y	N	Y
ILLINOIS								
1 Hayes	N	Y	Y	Y	N	N	Y	N
2 Savage	N	Y	?	Y	?	N	Y	N
3 Russo	N	Y	Y	Y	N	N	Y	N
4 *O'Brien*	?	?	Y	Y	N	N	Y	N
5 Lipinski	N	Y	Y	Y	N	N	Y	N
6 *Hyde*	Y	N	N	Y	Y	Y	Y	Y
7 Collins	N	Y	?	?	N	N	Y	N
8 Rostenkowski	?	?	?	?	N	N	Y	N
9 Yates	N	Y	Y	Y	N	N	Y	N
10 *Porter*	Y	Y	Y	Y	N	N	Y	Y
11 Annunzio	N	Y	Y	Y	N	N	Y	N
12 *Crane, P.*	Y	N	N	N	Y	Y	N	Y
13 *Erlenborn*	Y	N	Y	N	Y	Y	Y	Y
14 *Corcoran*	Y	N	Y	N	Y	Y	N	Y
15 *Madigan*	Y	N	Y	?	N	N	Y	Y
16 *Martin*	N	Y	Y	Y	?	Y	N	Y
17 Evans	N	Y	Y	Y	N	N	Y	N
18 *Michel*	Y	N	Y	N	Y	N	Y	Y
19 *Crane, D.*	?	?	N	N	Y	N	Y	N
20 Durbin	N	Y	Y	Y	N	N	Y	N
21 Price	N	Y	Y	Y	N	N	Y	N
22 Simon	?	?	Y	Y	N	N	Y	N
INDIANA								
1 Hall	N	Y	Y	Y	N	N	Y	N
2 Sharp	N	Y	Y	Y	Y	N	Y	Y
3 *Hiler*	Y	Y	Y	Y	Y	N	Y	Y
4 *Coats*	Y	Y	N	Y	Y	N	Y	Y
5 Hillis	N	Y	N	Y	Y	Y	N	Y

ND - Northern Democrats   SD - Southern Democrats

	293	294	295	296	297	298	299	300
6 ***Burton***	N	N	N	N	Y	Y	N	Y
7 ***Myers***	Y	Y	Y	Y	Y	Y	N	N
8 McCloskey	N	Y	Y	Y	N	N	Y	N
9 Hamilton	Y	Y	Y	Y	Y	N	Y	N
10 Jacobs	N	Y	Y	Y	N	N	Y	Y
IOWA								
1 ***Leach***	Y	N	Y	Y	Y	Y	Y	Y
2 ***Tauke***	Y	N	Y	Y	Y	Y	N	Y
3 ***Evans***	Y	N	Y	Y	Y	Y	N	Y
4 Smith	Y	N	Y	Y	N	N	Y	N
5 Harkin	Y	Y	Y	Y	N	N	Y	Y
6 Bedell	N	Y	Y	Y	N	Y	Y	N
KANSAS								
1 ***Roberts***	Y	N	Y	Y	Y	Y	N	Y
2 Slattery	Y	Y	Y	Y	Y	Y	Y	Y
3 ***Winn***	Y	N	Y	N	Y	Y	N	Y
4 Glickman	N	Y	Y	Y	Y	N	?	Y
5 ***Whittaker***	Y	N	Y	N	Y	Y	N	Y
KENTUCKY								
1 Hubbard	?	?	N	Y	Y	N	Y	Y
2 Natcher	N	Y	Y	Y	N	N	Y	N
3 Mazzoli	N	Y	Y	Y	N	N	Y	N
4 ***Snyder***	Y	N	P	Y	N	N	Y	Y
5 ***Rogers***	Y	Y	N	Y	Y	N	Y	N
6 ***Hopkins***	Y	N	N	Y	Y	N	Y	Y
7 Perkins	N	Y	Y	Y	N	N	Y	N
LOUISIANA								
1 ***Livingston***	Y	N	N	N	Y	N	Y	Y
2 Boggs	?	?	Y	Y	N	N	Y	N
3 Tauzin	Y	Y	Y	Y	Y	Y	Y	Y
4 Roemer	Y	N	Y	Y	Y	Y	N	Y
5 Huckaby	Y	N	Y	Y	?	Y	Y	Y
6 ***Moore***	Y	Y	Y	Y	Y	Y	Y	Y
7 Breaux	Y	Y	Y	Y	Y	Y	Y	Y
8 Long	N	Y	Y	Y	N	N	Y	N
MAINE								
1 ***McKernan***	N	Y	Y	Y	N	N	Y	N
2 ***Snowe***	N	Y	Y	Y	N	N	Y	N
MARYLAND								
1 Dyson	N	Y	N	Y	Y	N	Y	N
2 Long	N	Y	N	Y	N	N	Y	N
3 Mikulski	N	Y	Y	Y	N	N	Y	N
4 ***Holt***	Y	N	Y	Y	Y	N	N	N
5 Hoyer	N	Y	Y	Y	N	N	Y	N
6 Byron	N	Y	Y	Y	Y	N	Y	N
7 Mitchell	N	Y	Y	Y	N	N	Y	N
8 Barnes	N	Y	Y	Y	N	N	Y	N
MASSACHUSETTS								
1 ***Conte***	N	Y	Y	Y	N	N	Y	N
2 Boland	?	?	Y	Y	N	N	Y	N
3 Early	?	?	Y	Y	N	N	Y	N
4 Frank	N	Y	Y	Y	N	N	Y	N
5 Shannon	N	Y	Y	Y	N	N	Y	N
6 Mavroules	N	Y	Y	Y	N	N	Y	N
7 Markey	N	Y	Y	Y	N	N	Y	N
8 O'Neill								
9 Moakley	N	Y	Y	Y	N	N	Y	N
10 Studds	?	?	Y	Y	N	N	Y	N
11 Donnelly	N	Y	Y	Y	N	N	Y	N
MICHIGAN								
1 Conyers	N	Y	Y	Y	N	N	Y	N
2 ***Pursell***	Y	N	Y	Y	N	N	Y	Y
3 Wolpe	N	Y	Y	Y	N	N	Y	N
4 ***Siljander***	Y	?	Y	Y	Y	Y	N	Y
5 ***Sawyer***	Y	Y	N	Y	N	Y	Y	N
6 Carr	N	Y	Y	Y	N	N	Y	N
7 Kildee	N	Y	Y	Y	N	N	Y	N
8 Traxler	?	?	Y	Y	N	N	Y	N
9 ***Vander Jagt***	Y	Y	P	Y	Y	Y	Y	N
10 Albosta	N	Y	Y	Y	Y	Y	Y	N
11 ***Davis***	N	Y	Y	Y	N	N	Y	N
12 Bonior	N	Y	Y	Y	N	N	Y	N
13 Crockett	N	Y	Y	Y	N	N	Y	N
14 Hertel	N	Y	Y	Y	N	N	Y	N
15 Ford	?	?	Y	Y	N	N	Y	N
16 Dingell	N	Y	Y	Y	?	N	Y	N
17 Levin	N	Y	Y	Y	N	N	Y	N
18 ***Broomfield***	Y	Y	Y	Y	Y	Y	N	N
MINNESOTA								
1 Penny	Y	N	Y	Y	Y	Y	Y	Y
2 ***Weber***	Y	N	Y	Y	?	Y	N	Y
3 ***Frenzel***	Y	N	Y	+	Y	Y	N	Y
4 Vento	?	?	Y	Y	N	N	Y	N
5 Sabo	N	Y	Y	Y	N	N	Y	N
6 Sikorski	N	N	Y	Y	N	N	Y	N
7 ***Stangeland***	Y	N	Y	Y	N	Y	Y	N
8 Oberstar	N	Y	Y	Y	N	N	Y	N
MISSISSIPPI								
1 Whitten	N	N	Y	Y	N	N	Y	N
2 ***Franklin***	Y	N	?	?	Y	Y	Y	Y
3 Montgomery	N	Y	Y	Y	Y	Y	N	Y
4 Dowdy	N	Y	Y	Y	N	N	Y	N
5 ***Lott***	Y	Y	Y	N	Y	Y	N	Y
MISSOURI								
1 Clay	?	?	Y	Y	N	N	Y	N
2 Young	X	?	Y	Y	N	N	Y	N
3 Gephardt	?	?	Y	Y	N	N	Y	N
4 Skelton	N	Y	Y	Y	Y	N	Y	N
5 Wheat	N	Y	Y	Y	N	N	Y	N
6 ***Coleman***	Y	Y	N	Y	Y	N	Y	Y
7 ***Taylor***	#	?	N	Y	Y	Y	Y	Y
8 ***Emerson***	Y	N	Y	Y	Y	N	Y	Y
9 Volkmer	N	N	Y	Y	N	N	Y	N
MONTANA								
1 Williams	Y	Y	Y	Y	Y	N	Y	N
2 ***Marlenee***	Y	N	N	N	Y	Y	N	Y
NEBRASKA								
1 ***Bereuter***	Y	N	Y	Y	Y	N	Y	Y
2 ***Daub***	Y	N	Y	Y	Y	Y	Y	Y
3 ***Smith***	Y	N	Y	Y	Y	N	Y	Y
NEVADA								
1 Reid	N	Y	Y	Y	N	N	Y	N
2 ***Vucanovich***	Y	N	Y	N	Y	Y	N	Y
NEW HAMPSHIRE								
1 D'Amours	Y	Y	Y	Y	Y	?	Y	Y
2 ***Gregg***	Y	N	N	Y	Y	Y	N	Y
NEW JERSEY								
1 Florio	N	Y	Y	Y	N	N	Y	N
2 Hughes	N	Y	Y	Y	Y	N	Y	Y
3 Howard	N	Y	Y	Y	N	N	Y	N
4 ***Smith***	N	Y	Y	Y	N	N	Y	N
5 ***Roukema***	N	Y	Y	Y	Y	N	Y	Y
6 Dwyer	N	Y	Y	Y	N	N	Y	N
7 ***Rinaldo***	?	?	Y	Y	N	N	Y	Y
8 Roe	N	Y	Y	Y	N	N	Y	N
9 Torricelli	N	Y	Y	Y	?	N	Y	N
10 Rodino	N	Y	Y	Y	N	N	Y	N
11 Minish	N	Y	Y	Y	N	N	Y	Y
12 ***Courter***	?	?	N	Y	#	Y	Y	Y
13 Vacancy								
14 Guarini	N	Y	Y	Y	N	N	Y	N
NEW MEXICO								
1 ***Lujan***	N	Y	Y	N	Y	Y	N	Y
2 ***Skeen***	N	Y	Y	N	Y	Y	N	Y
3 Richardson	?	+	Y	Y	N	N	Y	N
NEW YORK								
1 ***Carney***	Y	N	N	Y	Y	Y	Y	Y
2 Downey	N	Y	Y	Y	N	N	Y	N
3 Mrazek	N	Y	Y	Y	N	N	Y	N
4 ***Lent***	Y	?	Y	Y	Y	Y	Y	Y
5 ***McGrath***	Y	N	Y	Y	Y	Y	Y	Y
6 Addabbo	X	?	Y	Y	N	N	Y	N
7 Ackerman	?	?	?	?	N	N	Y	N
8 Scheuer	N	Y	Y	Y	N	N	Y	N
9 Ferraro	?	?	?	?	?	?	?	?
10 Schumer	N	Y	Y	Y	N	N	Y	N
11 Towns	N	Y	?	?	N	N	Y	N
12 Owens	N	Y	Y	Y	N	N	Y	N
13 Solarz	N	Y	?	Y	N	N	Y	N
14 ***Molinari***	Y	N	N	N	Y	Y	N	Y
15 ***Green***	Y	N	Y	Y	N	N	Y	N
16 Rangel	N	Y	Y	Y	N	N	Y	N
17 Weiss	N	Y	Y	Y	N	N	Y	N
18 Garcia	?	?	Y	Y	N	N	Y	N
19 Biaggi	?	?	N	Y	N	N	Y	N
20 Ottinger	N	Y	Y	Y	?	N	Y	N
21 ***Fish***	Y	N	N	Y	N	N	Y	N
22 ***Gilman***	N	Y	Y	Y	N	[illegible]	[illegible]	N
23 Stratton	Y	N	Y	Y	N	N	Y	N
24 ***Solomon***	Y	N	Y	Y	Y	Y	N	Y
25 ***Boehlert***	N	Y	Y	Y	N	N	Y	N
26 ***Martin***	?	?	Y	Y	N	N	Y	Y
27 ***Wortley***	Y	N	Y	Y	Y	Y	Y	Y
28 McHugh	N	Y	Y	Y	N	N	Y	N
29 ***Horton***	N	Y	Y	Y	N	N	Y	N
30 ***Conable***	?	?	N	Y	Y	Y	N	Y
31 ***Kemp***	Y	N	Y	N	N	Y	N	Y
32 LaFalce	?	?	Y	Y	N	N	Y	N
33 Nowak	N	Y	Y	Y	N	N	Y	N
34 Lundine	N	?	Y	Y	N	N	Y	Y
NORTH CAROLINA								
1 Jones	N	Y	Y	Y	N	N	Y	N
2 Valentine	N	Y	Y	Y	Y	N	Y	N
3 Whitley	N	N	Y	Y	Y	N	Y	Y
4 Andrews	Y	Y	Y	Y	N	N	Y	Y
5 Neal	?	?	Y	Y	N	N	Y	Y
6 Britt	N	Y	Y	Y	N	N	Y	Y
7 Rose	N	Y	Y	Y	N	N	Y	N
8 Hefner	N	Y	Y	Y	N	N	Y	N
9 ***Martin***	?	?	?	Y	?	?	?	?
10 ***Broyhill***	N	Y	Y	Y	Y	Y	N	Y
11 Clarke	N	Y	Y	Y	N	N	Y	N
NORTH DAKOTA								
AL Dorgan	Y	Y	Y	Y	Y	Y	Y	Y
OHIO								
1 Luken	N	Y	Y	Y	Y	N	Y	Y
2 ***Gradison***	?	?	Y	Y	Y	Y	N	Y
3 Hall	?	?	Y	Y	N	N	Y	Y
4 ***Oxley***	+	-	Y	N	?	Y	N	Y
5 ***Latta***	Y	Y	Y	N	Y	Y	N	Y
6 ***McEwen***	N	N	N	Y	Y	Y	N	Y
7 ***DeWine***	Y	Y	N	Y	Y	Y	N	Y
8 ***Kindness***	Y	Y	N	N	Y	Y	N	Y
9 Kaptur	N	Y	Y	Y	N	N	Y	N
10 ***Miller***	Y	Y	Y	Y	Y	Y	Y	Y
11 Eckart	N	Y	Y	Y	Y	N	Y	N
12 ***Kasich***	N	Y	Y	Y	Y	Y	Y	Y
13 Pease	N	Y	Y	Y	N	N	Y	Y
14 Seiberling	N	Y	Y	Y	N	N	Y	Y
15 ***Wylie***	N	Y	Y	Y	N	Y	Y	Y
16 ***Regula***	N	Y	Y	Y	N	N	Y	Y
17 ***Williams***	?	?	Y	Y	?	?	?	N
18 Applegate	N	Y	Y	Y	N	N	Y	Y
19 Feighan	N	Y	Y	Y	N	Y	Y	Y
20 Oakar	N	Y	?	?	N	N	Y	N
21 Stokes	N	Y	Y	Y	N	X	?	?
OKLAHOMA								
1 Jones	N	Y	Y	Y	N	N	Y	N
2 Synar	N	Y	Y	Y	N	N	Y	N
3 Watkins	Y	Y	Y	Y	N	N	Y	N
4 McCurdy	N	Y	Y	Y	N	N	Y	N
5 ***Edwards***	Y	N	Y	N	Y	Y	N	Y
6 English	Y	N	Y	Y	Y	Y	Y	Y
OREGON								
1 AuCoin	Y	N	Y	Y	N	N	Y	Y
2 ***Smith, R.***	?	?	Y	N	Y	Y	N	Y
3 Wyden	N	Y	Y	Y	N	N	Y	N
4 Weaver	N	Y	Y	Y	Y	N	Y	Y
5 ***Smith, D.***	?	?	N	N	Y	Y	N	Y
PENNSYLVANIA								
1 Foglietta	?	?	Y	Y	N	N	Y	N
2 Gray	N	Y	Y	Y	N	N	Y	N
3 Borski	N	Y	Y	Y	N	N	Y	N
4 Kolter	N	Y	Y	Y	Y	N	Y	N
5 ***Schulze***	N	Y	Y	Y	Y	Y	Y	Y
6 Yatron	N	Y	Y	Y	Y	N	Y	N
7 Edgar	N	Y	Y	Y	N	N	Y	N
8 Kostmayer	N	Y	Y	Y	Y	N	Y	Y
9 ***Shuster***	N	Y	Y	Y	Y	Y	N	Y
10 ***McDade***	N	Y	Y	Y	N	N	Y	N
11 Harrison	N	Y	Y	Y	?	?	?	N
12 Murtha	?	?	Y	Y	N	N	Y	N
13 ***Coughlin***	N	Y	Y	Y	N	N	Y	N
14 Coyne	N	Y	Y	Y	N	N	Y	N
15 ***Ritter***	N	Y	Y	Y	Y	Y	N	Y
16 ***Walker***	N	Y	Y	Y	Y	Y	N	Y
17 ***Gekas***	Y	N	Y	Y	Y	Y	N	Y
18 Walgren	N	Y	Y	Y	?	?	?	Y
19 ***Goodling***	N	Y	Y	Y	Y	Y	Y	Y
20 Gaydos	N	Y	Y	Y	Y	?	N	Y
21 ***Ridge***	N	Y	Y	Y	Y	N	Y	Y
22 Murphy	N	Y	Y	Y	Y	Y	Y	N
23 ***Clinger***	Y	Y	Y	Y	Y	N	Y	Y
RHODE ISLAND								
1 St Germain	?	?	Y	Y	N	N	Y	N
2 ***Schneider***	N	Y	Y	Y	?	N	Y	N
SOUTH CAROLINA								
1 ***Hartnett***	Y	N	N	N	Y	Y	N	Y
2 ***Spence***	Y	Y	Y	Y	Y	Y	N	Y
3 Derrick	N	Y	?	?	N	Y	Y	N
4 ***Campbell***	N	Y	Y	Y	Y	Y	N	Y
5 Spratt	N	Y	Y	Y	N	N	Y	Y
6 Tallon	N	Y	Y	Y	N	N	Y	N
SOUTH DAKOTA								
AL Daschle	N	N	Y	Y	Y	N	Y	N
TENNESSEE								
1 ***Quillen***	#	?	N	N	Y	Y	N	Y
2 ***Duncan***	N	Y	Y	Y	Y	Y	Y	Y
3 Lloyd	N	Y	+	+	N	N	Y	N
4 Cooper	Y	N	Y	Y	N	N	Y	N
5 Boner	N	Y	Y	Y	N	N	Y	N
6 Gore	N	Y	?	?	N	N	Y	Y
7 ***Sundquist***	N	Y	Y	Y	Y	Y	Y	Y
8 Jones	X	?	Y	Y	N	N	Y	N
9 Ford	?	?	Y	Y	N	N	Y	N
TEXAS								
1 Hall, S.	N	Y	Y	Y	Y	Y	N	Y
2 Wilson	N	Y	N	Y	N	N	Y	N
3 ***Bartlett***	?	?	Y	N	Y	Y	N	Y
4 Hall, R.	N	Y	Y	Y	Y	N	Y	Y
5 Bryant	?	?	Y	Y	N	N	Y	N
6 ***Gramm***	?	?	?	?	#	#	?	?
7 ***Archer***	Y	N	Y	Y	Y	Y	N	Y
8 ***Fields***	Y	N	Y	Y	Y	Y	N	Y
9 Brooks	N	Y	Y	Y	N	N	Y	N
10 Pickle	N	Y	Y	Y	Y	N	?	N
11 Leath	N	Y	N	N	N	Y	Y	N
12 Wright	N	Y	Y	Y	N	N	Y	N
13 Hightower	N	Y	Y	Y	N	Y	Y	N
14 Patman	Y	N	N	Y	N	N	Y	Y
15 de la Garza	Y	N	Y	Y	?	N	Y	N
16 Coleman	N	Y	Y	Y	N	N	Y	N
17 Stenholm	Y	N	Y	Y	Y	Y	N	Y
18 Leland	N	Y	?	?	X	?	?	?
19 Hance	N	Y	Y	Y	Y	N	N	Y
20 Gonzalez	N	Y	Y	Y	N	N	Y	N
21 ***Loeffler***	N	Y	N	Y	Y	Y	N	Y
22 ***Paul***	?	?	N	N	Y	Y	N	Y
23 Kazen	N	Y	Y	Y	N	N	Y	N
24 Frost	N	Y	Y	Y	?	?	?	?
25 Andrews	N	Y	Y	Y	Y	N	Y	Y
26 Vandergriff	?	Y	Y	Y	Y	N	Y	Y
27 Ortiz	N	Y	Y	Y	N	N	Y	N
UTAH								
1 ***Hansen***	Y	N	N	N	Y	Y	N	Y
2 ***Marriott***	?	?	?	?	?	?	?	?
3 ***Nielson***	Y	N	Y	N	Y	Y	N	Y
VERMONT								
AL ***Jeffords***	Y	Y	Y	Y	N	N	Y	N
VIRGINIA								
1 ***Bateman***	Y	N	Y	Y	Y	Y	Y	N
2 ***Whitehurst***	#	?	Y	Y	Y	Y	Y	N
3 ***Bliley***	Y	N	Y	Y	Y	Y	N	Y
4 Sisisky	N	Y	Y	Y	Y	N	Y	N
5 Daniel	Y	N	N	N	Y	Y	N	Y
6 Olin	?	?	Y	Y	Y	N	Y	Y
7 ***Robinson***	Y	N	Y	N	Y	Y	N	N
8 ***Parris***	Y	Y	Y	Y	Y	N	Y	N
9 Boucher	N	Y	Y	Y	N	N	Y	N
10 ***Wolf***	Y	Y	N	Y	N	N	Y	N
WASHINGTON								
1 ***Pritchard***	?	?	Y	Y	N	Y	Y	?
2 Swift	N	Y	Y	Y	N	N	Y	N
3 Bonker	N	Y	Y	Y	N	N	Y	N
4 ***Morrison***	Y	N	Y	Y	N	N	Y	Y
5 Foley	Y	N	Y	Y	N	N	Y	N
6 Dicks	N	Y	Y	Y	N	N	Y	N
7 Lowry	N	Y	Y	Y	N	N	Y	N
8 ***Chandler***	Y	N	Y	Y	N	N	Y	Y
WEST VIRGINIA								
1 Mollohan	N	Y	Y	Y	N	N	Y	N
2 Staggers	N	Y	Y	Y	N	N	Y	N
3 Wise	N	Y	Y	Y	N	N	Y	N
4 Rahall	N	Y	Y	Y	N	N	Y	N
WISCONSIN								
1 Aspin	?	?	Y	Y	N	N	Y	N
2 Kastenmeier	N	Y	Y	Y	N	N	Y	N
3 ***Gunderson***	Y	Y	Y	Y	Y	Y	Y	Y
4 Kleczka	N	Y	Y	Y	N	N	Y	N
5 Moody	N	Y	Y	Y	N	N	Y	N
6 ***Petri***	Y	Y	Y	Y	Y	N	Y	Y
7 Obey	N	Y	Y	Y	N	N	Y	N
8 ***Roth***	N	Y	Y	Y	Y	N	Y	N
9 ***Sensenbrenner***	Y	Y	Y	Y	Y	Y	N	Y
WYOMING								
AL ***Cheney***	Y	N	Y	Y	Y	Y	N	Y

Southern states - Ala., Ark., Fla., Ga., Ky., La., Miss., N.C., Okla., S.C., Tenn., Texas, Va.

KEY

Y	Voted for (yea).
#	Paired for.
+	Announced for.
N	Voted against (nay).
X	Paired against.
-	Announced against.
P	Voted "present".
C	Voted "present" to avoid possible conflict of interest.
?	Did not vote or otherwise make a position known.

Democrats   *Republicans*

301. HR 6040. Supplemental Appropriations, Fiscal 1984. Passage of the bill to appropriate $5,384,624,400 in supplemental funds for fiscal 1984. Passed 304-116: R 75-87; D 229-29 (ND 155-18, SD 74-11), Aug. 1, 1984. The president had requested $5,953,340,170.

302. HR 5151. Hunger Relief Act. Emerson, R-Mo., amendment to eliminate language that would allow states to choose whether to require food stamp recipients, as a condition of eligibility, to submit monthly financial reports. Existing law required the reports. Rejected 120-293: R 113-48; D 7-245 (ND 3-165, SD 4-80), Aug. 1, 1984.

303. HR 5151. Hunger Relief Act. Panetta, D-Calif., amendment, to the Coleman, R-Mo., amendment, to authorize increases in the maximum car value used in the food stamp assets test to determine program eligibility. The Panetta amendment retained the existing maximum value of $4,500 for a car, but permitted that maximum to rise over three years at the same rate as the Consumer Price Index, up to $5,500. The Coleman amendment would have maintained the $4,500 maximum in current law; the bill would have raised it to $5,500 upon enactment. Adopted 282-131: R 42-120; D 240-11 (ND 164-5, SD 76-6), Aug. 1, 1984.

304. HR 5151. Hunger Relief Act. Coleman, R-Mo., amendment, as amended by Panetta, D-Calif. *(see vote 303, above)*, to authorize increases in the maximum car value used to determine food stamp eligibility. The amendment retained the existing maximum value of $4,500 for a car, but permitted that maximum to rise over three years at the same rate as the Consumer Price Index, up to $5,500. Adopted 384-25: R 160-1; D 224-24 (ND 146-22, SD 78-2), Aug. 1, 1984.

305. HR 5151. Hunger Relief Act. Passage of the bill to liberalize certain eligibility and benefit levels in the food stamp program, to increase federal penalties against states for program errors and to make other changes. Passed 364-39: R 122-38; D 242-1 (ND 163-0, SD 79-1), Aug. 1, 1984. A "nay" was a vote supporting the president's position.

	301	302	303	304	305
ALABAMA					
1 *Edwards*	Y	Y	Y	Y	Y
2 *Dickinson*	N	Y	N	Y	Y
3 Nichols	Y	N	Y	Y	Y
4 Bevill	Y	N	Y	Y	Y
5 Flippo	Y	N	Y	Y	Y
6 Erdreich	Y	N	Y	Y	Y
7 Shelby	N	N	Y	Y	Y
ALASKA					
AL *Young*	Y	N	Y	Y	Y
ARIZONA					
1 *McCain*	N	N	N	Y	Y
2 Udall	Y	N	Y	Y	Y
3 *Stump*	N	Y	N	Y	N
4 *Rudd*	Y	Y	N	Y	N
5 McNulty	Y	N	Y	Y	Y
ARKANSAS					
1 Alexander	Y	N	?	?	?
2 *Bethune*	Y	Y	N	Y	Y
3 *Hammerschmidt*	Y	Y	N	Y	N
4 Anthony	?	?	?	?	?
CALIFORNIA					
1 Bosco	Y	N	Y	Y	Y
2 *Chappie*	N	N	N	Y	Y
3 Matsui	Y	N	Y	Y	Y
4 Fazio	Y	N	Y	Y	Y
5 Burton	Y	N	Y	N	Y
6 Boxer	Y	N	Y	Y	Y
7 Miller	N	N	N	N	Y
8 Dellums	N	N	N	Y	Y
9 Stark	Y	N	Y	N	Y
10 Edwards	Y	N	Y	Y	Y
11 Lantos	Y	N	Y	Y	Y
12 *Zschau*	N	N	N	Y	Y
13 Mineta	Y	N	Y	Y	Y
14 *Shumway*	N	Y	N	Y	N
15 Coelho	Y	N	Y	Y	Y
16 Panetta	Y	N	Y	Y	Y
17 *Pashayan*	N	+	N	Y	Y
18 Lehman	Y	N	Y	Y	?
19 *Lagomarsino*	N	Y	N	Y	Y
20 *Thomas*	N	Y	N	Y	Y
21 *Fiedler*	N	Y	N	Y	Y
22 *Moorhead*	N	Y	N	Y	N
23 Beilenson	Y	N	Y	Y	Y
24 Waxman	Y	N	Y	Y	Y
25 Roybal	Y	N	Y	Y	Y
26 Berman	Y	N	Y	Y	?
27 Levine	Y	N	Y	Y	Y
28 Dixon	Y	N	?	N	Y
29 Hawkins	Y	N	Y	N	Y
30 Martinez	Y	N	Y	Y	Y
31 Dymally	Y	N	Y	Y	Y
32 Anderson	Y	N	Y	Y	Y
33 *Dreier*	N	Y	N	Y	N
34 Torres	Y	N	Y	Y	Y
35 *Lewis*	N	N	Y	N	Y
36 Brown	Y	N	Y	Y	Y
37 *McCandless*	N	Y	N	Y	Y
38 Patterson	Y	N	Y	Y	Y
39 *Dannemeyer*	N	Y	N	Y	N
40 *Badham*	N	Y	N	Y	N
41 *Lowery*	N	Y	N	Y	N
42 *Lungren*	N	Y	N	Y	N
43 *Packard*	Y	Y	N	Y	Y
44 Bates	Y	N	Y	Y	Y
45 *Hunter*	Y	Y	N	Y	N
COLORADO					
1 Schroeder	N	N	Y	Y	Y
2 Wirth	N	N	Y	Y	Y
3 Kogovsek	Y	N	Y	Y	Y
4 *Brown*	N	N	Y	Y	Y
5 *Kramer*	N	Y	N	Y	N
6 *Schaefer*	N	Y	N	Y	N
CONNECTICUT					
1 Kennelly	Y	N	Y	Y	Y
2 Gejdenson	Y	N	Y	Y	Y
3 Morrison	Y	N	Y	Y	Y
4 *McKinney*	Y	Y	Y	Y	Y
5 Ratchford	Y	N	Y	Y	Y
6 *Johnson*	N	N	Y	Y	Y
DELAWARE					
AL Carper	Y	N	Y	Y	Y
FLORIDA					
1 Hutto	Y	N	Y	Y	Y
2 Fuqua	Y	N	Y	Y	Y
3 Bennett	Y	N	N	N	N
4 Chappell	Y	N	Y	Y	Y
5 *McCollum*	N	Y	Y	Y	N
6 MacKay	N	N	Y	Y	Y
7 Gibbons	Y	N	Y	Y	Y
8 *Young*	Y	Y	Y	Y	Y
9 *Bilirakis*	N	Y	N	Y	Y
10 *Ireland*	N	Y	N	Y	Y
11 Nelson	Y	Y	Y	Y	Y
12 *Lewis*	N	Y	N	Y	Y
13 *Mack*	N	Y	N	Y	N
14 Mica	Y	N	Y	Y	Y
15 *Shaw*	Y	Y	N	Y	Y
16 Smith	Y	N	Y	Y	Y
17 Lehman	Y	N	Y	Y	Y
18 Pepper	Y	N	Y	Y	Y
19 Fascell	Y	N	Y	Y	Y
GEORGIA					
1 Thomas	Y	N	Y	Y	Y
2 Hatcher	Y	N	Y	Y	?
3 Ray	Y	N	Y	Y	Y
4 Levitas	Y	N	Y	Y	Y
5 Fowler	Y	N	Y	Y	Y
6 *Gingrich*	N	Y	N	Y	Y
7 Darden	Y	N	Y	Y	Y
8 Rowland	Y	N	Y	Y	Y
9 Jenkins	Y	N	Y	Y	Y
10 Barnard	Y	N	Y	Y	Y
HAWAII					
1 Heftel	Y	N	Y	Y	Y
2 Akaka	Y	N	Y	Y	Y
IDAHO					
1 *Craig*	N	Y	N	Y	N
2 *Hansen*	N	Y	N	Y	N
ILLINOIS					
1 Hayes	N	N	Y	N	Y
2 Savage	N	N	Y	Y	Y
3 Russo	N	N	Y	Y	Y
4 *O'Brien*	Y	N	Y	Y	Y
5 Lipinski	Y	N	N	Y	Y
6 *Hyde*	Y	N	Y	Y	Y
7 Collins	Y	N	Y	Y	Y
8 Rostenkowski	Y	N	Y	Y	Y
9 Yates	Y	N	Y	N	Y
10 *Porter*	Y	Y	Y	N	Y
11 Annunzio	Y	N	Y	Y	Y
12 *Crane, P.*	N	Y	N	Y	N
13 *Erlenborn*	Y	N	N	Y	Y
14 *Corcoran*	N	Y	N	Y	N
15 *Madigan*	N	N	Y	Y	Y
16 *Martin*	N	Y	N	Y	Y
17 Evans	Y	N	Y	Y	Y
18 *Michel*	N	Y	N	Y	Y
19 *Crane, D.*	N	Y	N	Y	N
20 Durbin	Y	N	Y	Y	Y
21 Price	Y	N	Y	Y	Y
22 Simon	Y	?	?	?	?
INDIANA					
1 Hall	Y	N	Y	Y	Y
2 Sharp	Y	N	Y	Y	Y
3 *Hiler*	N	Y	N	Y	Y
4 *Coats*	N	Y	N	Y	Y
5 Hillis	Y	Y	N	Y	Y

ND - Northern Democrats   SD - Southern Democrats

Corresponding to Congressional Record Votes 337, 339, 340, 341, 342

	301	302	303	304	305
6 Burton	N	Y	N	Y	N
7 Myers	Y	Y	N	Y	Y
8 McCloskey	Y	N	Y	Y	Y
9 Hamilton	Y	N	Y	Y	Y
10 Jacobs	N	N	Y	Y	Y
IOWA					
1 Leach	N	N	Y	Y	Y
2 Tauke	N	N	N	Y	Y
3 Evans	N	N	N	Y	Y
4 Smith	Y	N	Y	Y	Y
5 Harkin	Y	N	Y	Y	Y
6 Bedell	Y	?	Y	Y	Y
KANSAS					
1 Roberts	N	N	N	Y	Y
2 Slattery	N	N	Y	Y	Y
3 Winn	N	Y	N	Y	Y
4 Glickman	Y	N	Y	Y	Y
5 Whittaker	N	N	N	Y	Y
KENTUCKY					
1 Hubbard	N	N	Y	Y	Y
2 Natcher	Y	N	Y	Y	Y
3 Mazzoli	Y	N	Y	?	?
4 Snyder	Y	Y	Y	Y	Y
5 Rogers	Y	Y	N	Y	Y
6 Hopkins	Y	Y	N	Y	Y
7 Perkins	Y	N	Y	Y	Y
LOUISIANA					
1 Livingston	Y	Y	N	Y	Y
2 Boggs	Y	N	Y	Y	Y
3 Tauzin	Y	N	Y	Y	Y
4 Roemer	N	N	Y	Y	Y
5 Huckaby	Y	N	Y	Y	Y
6 Moore	Y	Y	Y	Y	Y
7 Breaux	Y	?	?	?	?
8 Long	Y	N	Y	?	Y
MAINE					
1 McKernan	Y	N	Y	Y	Y
2 Snowe	Y	N	Y	Y	Y
MARYLAND					
1 Dyson	Y	N	Y	Y	Y
2 Long	Y	?	?	?	?
3 Mikulski	?	N	Y	Y	Y
4 Holt	Y	Y	N	Y	N
5 Hoyer	Y	N	Y	Y	Y
6 Byron	Y	N	Y	Y	Y
7 Mitchell	Y	N	Y	Y	Y
8 Barnes	Y	N	Y	Y	Y
MASSACHUSETTS					
1 Conte	Y	N	Y	Y	Y
2 Boland	Y	N	Y	Y	Y
3 Early	Y	N	Y	Y	Y
4 Frank	Y	N	Y	Y	Y
5 Shannon	Y	N	Y	?	?
6 Mavroules	Y	N	Y	Y	Y
7 Markey	Y	?	?	?	?
8 O'Neill					
9 Moakley	Y	N	Y	Y	Y
10 Studds	Y	N	Y	Y	Y
11 Donnelly	Y	N	Y	Y	Y
MICHIGAN					
1 Conyers	N	N	Y	Y	Y
2 Pursell	N	Y	N	Y	Y
3 Wolpe	Y	N	Y	Y	?
4 Siljander	N	Y	N	Y	Y
5 Sawyer	Y	Y	Y	Y	Y
6 Carr	Y	N	Y	Y	Y
7 Kildee	Y	N	Y	N	Y
8 Traxler	Y	N	Y	Y	Y
9 Vander Jagt	Y	Y	N	Y	Y
10 Albosta	Y	N	Y	Y	Y
11 Davis	Y	N	Y	Y	Y
12 Bonior	Y	N	Y	Y	Y
13 Crockett	N	N	Y	N	Y
14 Hertel	N	N	Y	Y	Y
15 Ford	Y	?	?	?	?
16 Dingell	Y	N	Y	?	?
17 Levin	Y	N	Y	Y	Y
18 Broomfield	N	N	N	Y	Y
MINNESOTA					
1 Penny	N	N	N	Y	Y
2 Weber	N	Y	N	Y	Y
3 Frenzel	N	Y	N	Y	Y
4 Vento	Y	N	Y	Y	Y
5 Sabo	Y	N	Y	Y	Y
6 Sikorski	Y	N	Y	Y	Y

	301	302	303	304	305
7 Stangeland	Y	Y	N	N	Y
8 Oberstar	Y	N	Y	Y	Y
MISSISSIPPI					
1 Whitten	Y	N	Y	Y	Y
2 Franklin	Y	N	N	Y	Y
3 Montgomery	Y	N	N	Y	Y
4 Dowdy	Y	N	Y	Y	Y
5 Lott	N	N	N	Y	Y
MISSOURI					
1 Clay	Y	N	Y	Y	Y
2 Young	Y	N	Y	Y	Y
3 Gephardt	Y	N	Y	Y	Y
4 Skelton	Y	Y	Y	Y	Y
5 Wheat	Y	N	Y	Y	Y
6 Coleman	Y	Y	N	Y	Y
7 Taylor	Y	Y	N	Y	Y
8 Emerson	Y	Y	N	Y	Y
9 Volkmer	Y	N	Y	Y	Y
MONTANA					
1 Williams	Y	N	Y	Y	Y
2 Marlenee	Y	Y	Y	Y	Y
NEBRASKA					
1 Bereuter	Y	Y	Y	Y	Y
2 Daub	N	Y	Y	Y	Y
3 Smith	Y	Y	N	Y	Y
NEVADA					
1 Reid	Y	N	Y	Y	Y
2 Vucanovich	N	Y	N	Y	Y
NEW HAMPSHIRE					
1 D'Amours	Y	N	Y	Y	Y
2 Gregg	N	Y	Y	Y	Y
NEW JERSEY					
1 Florio	Y	Y	Y	Y	Y
2 Hughes	Y	N	Y	Y	Y
3 Howard	Y	N	Y	Y	Y
4 Smith	Y	Y	Y	Y	Y
5 Roukema	Y	Y	N	Y	Y
6 Dwyer	Y	N	Y	Y	Y
7 Rinaldo	Y	N	Y	Y	Y
8 Roe	Y	N	Y	Y	Y
9 Torricelli	Y	N	Y	Y	Y
10 Rodino	Y	N	Y	?	?
11 Minish	Y	N	Y	Y	Y
12 Courter	N	N	N	Y	Y
13 Vacancy					
14 Guarini	Y	N	Y	Y	Y
NEW MEXICO					
1 Lujan	N	N	Y	Y	Y
2 Skeen	N	N	Y	Y	Y
3 Richardson	Y	N	Y	Y	Y
NEW YORK					
1 Carney	Y	Y	N	Y	Y
2 Downey	Y	N	Y	N	Y
3 Mrazek	Y	N	Y	Y	Y
4 Lent	N	N	N	Y	Y
5 McGrath	N	N	N	Y	Y
6 Addabbo	Y	N	Y	Y	Y
7 Ackerman	Y	N	Y	N	Y
8 Scheuer	Y	N	Y	Y	Y
9 Ferraro	?	?	?	?	?
10 Schumer	Y	?	?	?	?
11 Towns	N	N	Y	N	Y
12 Owens	Y	N	Y	Y	Y
13 Solarz	Y	N	Y	Y	Y
14 Molinari	Y	Y	Y	Y	Y
15 Green	Y	N	Y	Y	Y
16 Rangel	Y	N	Y	Y	Y
17 Weiss	Y	N	Y	N	Y
18 Garcia	Y	?	Y	N	Y
19 Biaggi	Y	N	Y	Y	?
20 Ottinger	Y	N	Y	N	Y
21 Fish	Y	N	Y	Y	Y
22 Gilman	Y	N	Y	Y	Y
23 Stratton	Y	N	Y	Y	Y
24 Solomon	Y	Y	N	Y	?
25 Boehlert	Y	N	Y	Y	Y
26 Martin	N	N	N	Y	Y
27 Wortley	Y	N	N	Y	Y
28 McHugh	Y	N	Y	Y	Y
29 Horton	Y	N	Y	Y	Y
30 Conable	N	Y	N	Y	Y
31 Kemp	Y	Y	?	?	Y
32 LaFalce	Y	N	Y	Y	Y
33 Nowak	Y	N	Y	Y	Y
34 Lundine	?	N	Y	Y	Y

	301	302	303	304	305
NORTH CAROLINA					
1 Jones	?	N	Y	Y	Y
2 Valentine	Y	N	Y	Y	Y
3 Whitley	Y	N	Y	Y	Y
4 Andrews	Y	N	Y	Y	Y
5 Neal	Y	N	Y	Y	Y
6 Britt	Y	N	Y	Y	Y
7 Rose	Y	N	Y	Y	Y
8 Hefner	Y	N	Y	Y	Y
9 Martin	?	?	?	?	?
10 Broyhill	N	N	Y	N	Y
11 Clarke	Y	N	Y	Y	Y
NORTH DAKOTA					
AL Dorgan	N	N	Y	Y	Y
OHIO					
1 Luken	Y	N	Y	Y	Y
2 Gradison	N	Y	Y	Y	Y
3 Hall	Y	N	Y	Y	Y
4 Oxley	N	Y	N	Y	N
5 Latta	Y	Y	N	Y	Y
6 McEwen	N	Y	Y	Y	N
7 DeWine	N	Y	N	Y	N
8 Kindness	N	Y	N	N	Y
9 Kaptur	Y	N	Y	Y	Y
10 Miller	Y	Y	N	Y	Y
11 Eckart	Y	N	Y	Y	Y
12 Kasich	Y	Y	N	Y	Y
13 Pease	Y	N	Y	Y	Y
14 Seiberling	Y	N	Y	N	Y
15 Wylie	Y	Y	Y	Y	Y
16 Regula	Y	Y	Y	Y	Y
17 Williams	?	?	?	?	?
18 Applegate	Y	N	Y	Y	Y
19 Feighan	Y	N	Y	Y	Y
20 Oakar	Y	N	Y	Y	Y
21 Stokes	?	?	?	?	?
OKLAHOMA					
1 Jones	Y	N	Y	Y	Y
2 Synar	Y	N	Y	Y	Y
3 Watkins	Y	N	Y	Y	Y
4 McCurdy	Y	N	Y	Y	Y
5 Edwards	N	N	N	Y	N
6 English	N	N	Y	Y	Y
OREGON					
1 AuCoin	N	N	Y	Y	Y
2 Smith, R.	Y	Y	N	Y	Y
3 Wyden	N	N	Y	Y	Y
4 Weaver	N	N	Y	Y	Y
5 Smith, D.	N	Y	N	Y	N
PENNSYLVANIA					
1 Foglietta	Y	N	Y	N	Y
2 Gray	Y	N	Y	Y	Y
3 Borski	Y	N	Y	Y	Y
4 Kolter	Y	N	Y	Y	Y
5 Schulze	N	Y	N	Y	Y
6 Yatron	Y	N	Y	Y	Y
7 Edgar	Y	N	Y	Y	Y
8 Kostmayer	Y	N	Y	Y	Y
9 Shuster	N	Y	N	Y	Y
10 McDade	Y	N	Y	Y	Y
11 Harrison	Y	N	Y	Y	Y
12 Murtha	Y	N	Y	Y	Y
13 Coughlin	Y	N	Y	Y	Y
14 Coyne	Y	N	Y	Y	Y
15 Ritter	N	Y	Y	Y	Y
16 Walker	N	Y	N	Y	N
17 Gekas	N	Y	N	Y	Y
18 Walgren	Y	N	Y	Y	Y
19 Goodling	Y	N	Y	Y	Y
20 Gaydos	Y	N	Y	Y	Y
21 Ridge	Y	N	Y	Y	Y
22 Murphy	Y	N	Y	Y	Y
23 Clinger	Y	N	Y	Y	Y
RHODE ISLAND					
1 St Germain	Y	N	Y	Y	Y
2 Schneider	Y	N	Y	Y	Y
SOUTH CAROLINA					
1 Hartnett	N	Y	N	Y	N
2 Spence	N	Y	N	Y	Y
3 Derrick	Y	Y	Y	Y	Y
4 Campbell	N	Y	N	Y	Y
5 Spratt	Y	N	Y	Y	Y
6 Tallon	Y	N	Y	Y	Y
SOUTH DAKOTA					
AL Daschle	Y	N	Y	Y	Y

	301	302	303	304	305
TENNESSEE					
1 Quillen	?	Y	N	Y	Y
2 Duncan	Y	N	N	Y	Y
3 Lloyd	Y	Y	N	Y	Y
4 Cooper	Y	N	Y	Y	Y
5 Boner	Y	N	Y	Y	?
6 Gore	Y	N	Y	Y	Y
7 Sundquist	Y	Y	N	Y	Y
8 Jones	Y	N	N	Y	Y
9 Ford	Y	N	Y	Y	Y
TEXAS					
1 Hall, S.	N	N	Y	Y	Y
2 Wilson	Y	N	?	?	?
3 Bartlett	N	N	N	Y	N
4 Hall, R.	N	?	Y	Y	Y
5 Bryant	Y	N	Y	Y	Y
6 Gramm	?	?	?	?	?
7 Archer	N	Y	N	Y	N
8 Fields	N	N	N	Y	N
9 Brooks	Y	N	Y	Y	Y
10 Pickle	Y	N	Y	Y	Y
11 Leath	Y	Y	N	Y	Y
12 Wright	Y	N	?	?	Y
13 Hightower	Y	N	Y	Y	Y
14 Patman	N	N	Y	Y	Y
15 de la Garza	Y	N	Y	Y	Y
16 Coleman	Y	N	Y	Y	Y
17 Stenholm	N	N	Y	Y	Y
18 Leland	?	?	?	?	?
19 Hance	Y	N	Y	Y	Y
20 Gonzalez	Y	N	Y	N	Y
21 Loeffler	N	N	N	Y	Y
22 Paul	N	Y	N	Y	?
23 Kazen	Y	N	Y	Y	Y
24 Frost	?	?	?	?	?
25 Andrews	Y	N	Y	Y	Y
26 Vandergriff	N	N	Y	Y	Y
27 Ortiz	Y	N	Y	Y	Y
UTAH					
1 Hansen	N	Y	N	Y	N
2 Marriott	?	?	?	?	?
3 Nielson	N	Y	N	Y	N
VERMONT					
AL Jeffords	Y	N	Y	Y	Y
VIRGINIA					
1 Bateman	N	N	N	Y	Y
2 Whitehurst	Y	Y	N	Y	Y
3 Bliley	Y	Y	N	Y	Y
4 Sisisky	Y	N	Y	Y	Y
5 Daniel	Y	N	N	Y	Y
6 Olin	N	N	Y	Y	Y
7 Robinson	Y	Y	N	Y	Y
8 Parris	Y	Y	N	Y	Y
9 Boucher	Y	N	Y	Y	Y
10 Wolf	Y	N	Y	Y	Y
WASHINGTON					
1 Pritchard	Y	Y	Y	?	?
2 Swift	Y	N	Y	Y	Y
3 Bonker	Y	N	Y	Y	Y
4 Morrison	Y	N	Y	Y	Y
5 Foley	Y	N	Y	Y	Y
6 Dicks	Y	N	Y	Y	Y
7 Lowry	Y	N	Y	Y	Y
8 Chandler	Y	N	N	Y	Y
WEST VIRGINIA					
1 Mollohan	Y	N	Y	Y	Y
2 Staggers	Y	N	Y	Y	Y
3 Wise	Y	N	Y	Y	Y
4 Rahall	Y	N	Y	Y	Y
WISCONSIN					
1 Aspin	Y	N	Y	Y	Y
2 Kastenmeier	Y	N	Y	Y	Y
3 Gunderson	N	Y	N	Y	Y
4 Kleczka	Y	N	Y	Y	Y
5 Moody	N	N	Y	Y	Y
6 Petri	Y	Y	N	Y	Y
7 Obey	Y	N	Y	Y	Y
8 Roth	Y	Y	N	Y	Y
9 Sensenbrenner	N	Y	N	Y	Y
WYOMING					
AL Cheney	N	Y	N	Y	N

Southern states - Ala., Ark., Fla., Ga., Ky., La., Miss., N.C., Okla., S.C., Tenn., Texas, Va.

306. HR 5399. Intelligence Agencies Authorizations.
Passage of the bill to make authorizations in fiscal 1985 for the CIA and other intelligence agencies and to prohibit any form of U.S. aid to military or paramilitary groups in Nicaragua. Passed 294-118: R 65-96; D 229-22 (ND 164-3, SD 65-19), Aug. 2, 1984.

307. HR 5973. Interior Appropriations, Fiscal 1985.
Yates, D-Ill., motion to end debate on the Conte, R-Mass., amendment and all amendments thereto except the Ottinger, D-N.Y., amendment. Motion agreed to 285-116: R 69-88; D 216-28 (ND 145-20, SD 71-8), Aug. 2, 1984.

308. HR 5973. Interior Appropriations, Fiscal 1985.
Ratchford, D-Conn., amendment to the Conte, R-Mass., amendment *(see vote 309, below)*, to rescind $5 billion from the U.S. Synthetic Fuels Corporation. The Conte amendment would rescind $10 billion. Adopted 236-177: R 67-94; D 169-83 (ND 94-76, SD 75-7), Aug. 2, 1984.

309. HR 5973. Interior Appropriations, Fiscal 1985.
Conte, R-Mass., amendment, as amended by Ratchford, D-Conn. *(see vote 308, above)*, to rescind $5 billion from the U.S. Synthetic Fuels Corporation. Adopted 410-2: R 161-1; D 249-1 (ND 169-0, SD 80-1), Aug. 2, 1984.

310. HR 5973. Interior Appropriations, Fiscal 1985.
McDade, R-Pa., amendment to reduce by 3 percent across-the-board the budget authority provided in the bill. Adopted 212-181: R 144-8; D 68-173 (ND 29-133, SD 39-40), Aug. 2, 1984.

311. HR 5973. Interior Appropriations, Fiscal 1985.
Passage of the bill to appropriate $3,033,865,000 in fiscal 1985 for the Interior Department and related agencies (includes deduction for $5 billion rescission from U.S. Synthetic Fuels Corporation). Passed 336-57: R 108-46; D 228-11 (ND 159-2, SD 69-9), Aug. 2, 1984. The president had requested $7,679,336,000 in new budget authority. He also had requested a rescission of $9 billion.

KEY

Y Voted for (yea).
Paired for.
+ Announced for.
N Voted against (nay).
X Paired against.
- Announced against.
P Voted "present".
C Voted "present" to avoid possible conflict of interest.
? Did not vote or otherwise make a position known.

Democrats *Republicans*

	306	307	308	309	310	311
ALABAMA						
1 Edwards	Y	Y	N	Y	N	Y
2 *Dickinson*	?	?	Y	Y	Y	Y
3 Nichols	N	Y	Y	Y	Y	Y
4 Bevill	Y	Y	Y	Y	N	Y
5 Flippo	N	?	Y	Y	Y	Y
6 Erdreich	N	Y	Y	Y	Y	Y
7 Shelby	N	Y	Y	Y	N	Y
ALASKA						
AL *Young*	Y	N	Y	Y	Y	Y
ARIZONA						
1 *McCain*	N	N	Y	Y	Y	Y
2 Udall	Y	N	N	Y	N	Y
3 *Stump*	Y	N	Y	Y	Y	N
4 *Rudd*	N	Y	Y	Y	Y	Y
5 McNulty	Y	Y	N	Y	Y	Y
ARKANSAS						
1 Alexander	Y	Y	Y	Y	N	Y
2 *Bethune*	N	N	N	Y	Y	Y
3 *Hammerschmidt*	N	N	Y	Y	Y	Y
4 Anthony	?	?	#	?	X	?
CALIFORNIA						
1 Bosco	Y	Y	Y	Y	?	?
2 *Chappie*	Y	Y	Y	Y	N	Y
3 Matsui	Y	Y	Y	Y	N	Y
4 Fazio	Y	Y	Y	Y	N	Y
5 Burton	Y	Y	Y	Y	N	Y
6 Boxer	Y	Y	N	Y	X	?
7 Miller	Y	N	N	Y	N	Y
8 Dellums	Y	N	N	Y	N	Y
9 Stark	Y	N	N	Y	N	Y
10 Edwards	Y	N	N	Y	N	Y
11 Lantos	Y	Y	Y	Y	N	Y
12 *Zschau*	Y	Y	N	Y	Y	Y
13 Mineta	Y	Y	Y	Y	N	Y
14 *Shumway*	N	N	Y	Y	N	N
15 Coelho	Y	Y	Y	Y	N	Y
16 Panetta	Y	Y	Y	Y	N	Y
17 *Pashayan*	Y	Y	Y	Y	Y	Y
18 Lehman	Y	Y	Y	Y	?	?
19 *Lagomarsino*	N	N	N	Y	Y	Y
20 *Thomas*	N	N	Y	Y	#	?
21 *Fiedler*	N	N	N	Y	Y	Y
22 *Moorhead*	N	Y	Y	Y	Y	N
23 Beilenson	Y	Y	N	Y	N	Y
24 Waxman	Y	?	N	Y	N	Y
25 Roybal	Y	Y	N	Y	N	Y
26 Berman	Y	Y	N	Y	N	Y
27 Levine	Y	Y	Y	Y	N	Y
28 Dixon	Y	Y	N	Y	N	Y
29 Hawkins	Y	Y	Y	Y	N	Y
30 Martinez	Y	Y	Y	Y	N	Y
31 Dymally	P	?	?	?	?	?
32 Anderson	Y	Y	Y	Y	Y	Y
33 *Dreier*	N	N	N	Y	Y	N
34 Torres	Y	Y	Y	Y	N	Y
35 *Lewis*	N	?	?	?	#	?
36 Brown	Y	Y	N	Y	N	Y
37 *McCandless*	N	Y	N	Y	Y	Y
38 Patterson	Y	Y	Y	Y	N	Y
39 *Dannemeyer*	N	Y	Y	Y	Y	N
40 *Badham*	N	N	Y	Y	Y	Y
41 *Lowery*	N	Y	Y	Y	Y	Y
42 *Lungren*	N	Y	N	Y	#	?

	306	307	308	309	310	311
43 *Packard*	N	Y	Y	Y	Y	Y
44 Bates	Y	Y	Y	Y	N	Y
45 *Hunter*	N	Y	Y	Y	Y	Y
COLORADO						
1 Schroeder	Y	N	N	Y	N	N
2 Wirth	Y	Y	Y	Y	Y	Y
3 Kogovsek	Y	N	Y	Y	N	Y
4 *Brown*	N	N	N	N	Y	N
5 *Kramer*	N	N	Y	Y	Y	N
6 *Schaefer*	N	Y	Y	Y	Y	N
CONNECTICUT						
1 Kennelly	Y	Y	N	Y	N	Y
2 Gejdenson	Y	Y	Y	Y	N	Y
3 Morrison	Y	Y	N	Y	N	Y
4 *McKinney*	Y	N	Y	Y	N	Y
5 Ratchford	Y	Y	Y	Y	N	Y
6 *Johnson*	Y	Y	N	Y	N	Y
DELAWARE						
AL Carper	Y	Y	N	Y	Y	Y
FLORIDA						
1 Hutto	Y	Y	Y	Y	N	Y
2 Fuqua	Y	Y	Y	Y	N	Y
3 Bennett	Y	Y	Y	Y	Y	Y
4 Chappell	Y	Y	Y	Y	N	Y
5 *McCollum*	N	N	N	Y	Y	Y
6 MacKay	Y	N	Y	Y	Y	Y
7 Gibbons	Y	Y	Y	Y	N	Y
8 *Young*	Y	Y	Y	Y	N	Y
9 *Bilirakis*	N	N	N	Y	Y	Y
10 *Ireland*	Y	Y	Y	Y	N	Y
11 Nelson	Y	Y	Y	Y	N	Y
12 *Lewis*	N	N	Y	Y	Y	Y
13 *Mack*	N	N	N	Y	Y	Y
14 Mica	Y	Y	Y	Y	N	Y
15 *Shaw*	N	N	N	Y	Y	Y
16 Smith	Y	Y	Y	Y	N	Y
17 Lehman	Y	Y	Y	Y	?	?
18 Pepper	Y	Y	Y	Y	N	Y
19 Fascell	Y	Y	Y	Y	N	Y
GEORGIA						
1 Thomas	Y	Y	Y	Y	N	Y
2 Hatcher	Y	?	Y	Y	N	Y
3 Ray	N	Y	Y	Y	Y	Y
4 Levitas	N	N	Y	Y	Y	Y
5 Fowler	Y	Y	Y	Y	N	Y
6 *Gingrich*	N	N	N	Y	Y	Y
7 Darden	Y	Y	Y	Y	Y	Y
8 Rowland	Y	Y	Y	Y	N	Y
9 Jenkins	Y	N	Y	Y	N	Y
10 Barnard	Y	Y	Y	Y	N	Y
HAWAII						
1 Heftel	Y	Y	Y	Y	N	Y
2 Akaka	Y	N	Y	Y	N	Y
IDAHO						
1 *Craig*	N	N	N	Y	Y	Y
2 *Hansen*	?	?	?	Y	?	Y
ILLINOIS						
1 Hayes	Y	Y	Y	Y	N	Y
2 Savage	Y	P	Y	Y	N	Y
3 Russo	Y	Y	Y	Y	N	Y
4 *O'Brien*	Y	Y	Y	Y	N	Y
5 Lipinski	Y	Y	Y	Y	N	Y
6 *Hyde*	N	N	N	Y	Y	Y
7 Collins	Y	Y	Y	Y	N	Y
8 Rostenkowski	Y	Y	Y	Y	?	?
9 Yates	Y	Y	Y	Y	N	Y
10 *Porter*	Y	N	N	Y	N	Y
11 Annunzio	Y	Y	Y	Y	N	Y
12 *Crane, P.*	N	N	N	Y	Y	N
13 *Erlenborn*	Y	Y	N	Y	N	Y
14 *Corcoran*	N	N	N	Y	Y	Y
15 *Madigan*	Y	Y	N	Y	Y	Y
16 *Martin*	Y	N	N	Y	N	Y
17 Evans	Y	Y	N	Y	N	Y
18 *Michel*	N	Y	N	Y	N	N
19 *Crane, D.*	N	N	Y	Y	N	N
20 Durbin	Y	Y	Y	Y	N	Y
21 Price	Y	Y	Y	Y	N	Y
22 Simon	?	?	?	?	?	?
INDIANA						
1 Hall	Y	Y	Y	Y	N	Y
2 Sharp	?	Y	Y	Y	Y	Y
3 *Hiler*	N	N	N	Y	N	N
4 *Coats*	N	N	N	Y	Y	N
5 Hillis	Y	Y	Y	Y	Y	Y

ND - Northern Democrats   SD - Southern Democrats

Corresponding to Congressional Record Votes 343, 345, 346, 347, 348, 349

	306	307	308	309	310	311
6 ***Burton***	N	N	Y	Y	Y	N
7 ***Myers***	Y	Y	Y	Y	Y	Y
8 McCloskey	Y	Y	Y	Y	N	Y
9 Hamilton	Y	Y	Y	Y	Y	Y
10 Jacobs	N	N	N	Y	?	?
IOWA						
1 ***Leach***	Y	N	N	Y	Y	N
2 ***Tauke***	Y	Y	N	Y	Y	N
3 ***Evans***	N	Y	N	Y	Y	N
4 Smith	Y	?	Y	Y	N	Y
5 Harkin	Y	Y	N	Y	Y	Y
6 Bedell	Y	Y	N	Y	Y	Y
KANSAS						
1 ***Roberts***	N	N	N	Y	Y	N
2 Slattery	Y	Y	Y	Y	Y	Y
3 ***Winn***	N	Y	Y	Y	Y	Y
4 Glickman	Y	Y	Y	Y	Y	Y
5 ***Whittaker***	N	Y	N	Y	Y	N
KENTUCKY						
1 Hubbard	N	Y	Y	N	Y	N
2 Natcher	Y	Y	Y	Y	N	Y
3 Mazzoli	Y	Y	Y	Y	Y	Y
4 ***Snyder***	Y	Y	Y	Y	Y	Y
5 ***Rogers***	Y	Y	Y	Y	Y	Y
6 ***Hopkins***	N	N	Y	Y	Y	N
7 Perkins	Y	Y	Y	Y	N	Y
LOUISIANA						
1 ***Livingston***	N	N	N	Y	Y	Y
2 Boggs	Y	?	Y	Y	N	Y
3 Tauzin	N	N	Y	Y	Y	Y
4 Roemer	N	N	N	Y	Y	N
5 Huckaby	Y	Y	Y	Y	Y	Y
6 ***Moore***	Y	N	N	Y	Y	Y
7 Breaux	Y	Y	Y	Y	N	Y
8 Long	Y	Y	Y	Y	N	Y
MAINE						
1 ***McKernan***	Y	N	N	Y	Y	Y
2 ***Snowe***	Y	Y	Y	Y	Y	Y
MARYLAND						
1 Dyson	Y	?	Y	Y	N	Y
2 Long	Y	Y	Y	Y	N	Y
3 Mikulski	Y	Y	N	Y	N	Y
4 ***Holt***	N	Y	Y	Y	Y	N
5 Hoyer	Y	Y	Y	Y	N	Y
6 Byron	Y	Y	Y	Y	N	Y
7 Mitchell	Y	Y	N	Y	N	Y
8 Barnes	Y	Y	N	Y	N	Y
MASSACHUSETTS						
1 ***Conte***	Y	Y	N	Y	?	Y
2 Boland	Y	Y	Y	Y	N	Y
3 Early	Y	Y	N	?	N	Y
4 Frank	Y	N	N	Y	N	Y
5 Shannon	Y	Y	N	Y	?	?
6 Mavroules	Y	Y	Y	Y	N	Y
7 Markey	Y	Y	N	Y	N	Y
8 O'Neill						
9 Moakley	Y	Y	Y	Y	N	Y
10 Studds	Y	Y	N	Y	N	Y
11 Donnelly	Y	Y	Y	Y	N	Y
MICHIGAN						
1 Conyers	Y	N	N	Y	N	Y
2 ***Pursell***	Y	Y	N	Y	Y	Y
3 Wolpe	Y	Y	N	Y	N	Y
4 ***Siljander***	N	Y	N	Y	Y	N
5 ***Sawyer***	N	Y	Y	Y	Y	Y
6 Carr	Y	Y	N	Y	N	Y
7 Kildee	Y	Y	Y	Y	N	Y
8 Traxler	?	Y	Y	Y	N	Y
9 ***Vander Jagt***	N	N	Y	Y	Y	Y
10 Albosta	Y	Y	Y	Y	Y	Y
11 ***Davis***	?	Y	N	Y	N	Y
12 Bonior	Y	?	Y	Y	N	Y
13 Crockett	Y	Y	N	Y	N	Y
14 Hertel	Y	N	N	Y	N	Y
15 Ford	Y	Y	Y	Y	N	Y
16 Dingell	Y	Y	Y	Y	N	Y
17 Levin	Y	Y	N	Y	N	Y
18 ***Broomfield***	N	Y	N	Y	Y	N
MINNESOTA						
1 Penny	Y	Y	N	Y	Y	Y
2 ***Weber***	N	?	N	Y	Y	N
3 ***Frenzel***	Y	N	N	Y	Y	N
4 Vento	Y	Y	N	?	?	?
5 Sabo	Y	Y	Y	Y	N	Y
6 Sikorski	Y	Y	N	Y	Y	Y
7 ***Stangeland***	Y	Y	Y	Y	Y	Y
8 Oberstar	Y	Y	Y	Y	N	Y
MISSISSIPPI						
1 Whitten	Y	Y	Y	Y	N	Y
2 ***Franklin***	N	N	N	Y	Y	Y
3 Montgomery	N	Y	Y	Y	Y	Y
4 Dowdy	Y	Y	Y	Y	?	?
5 ***Lott***	N	N	N	Y	Y	Y
MISSOURI						
1 Clay	Y	Y	Y	Y	N	Y
2 Young	Y	Y	Y	Y	N	Y
3 Gephardt	Y	Y	N	Y	N	Y
4 Skelton	Y	Y	Y	Y	N	Y
5 Wheat	Y	Y	N	Y	N	Y
6 ***Coleman***	N	N	Y	Y	Y	Y
7 ***Taylor***	N	Y	Y	Y	Y	Y
8 ***Emerson***	N	N	Y	Y	Y	Y
9 Volkmer	Y	Y	Y	Y	N	Y
MONTANA						
1 Williams	Y	N	N	Y	N	Y
2 ***Marlenee***	N	N	N	Y	Y	Y
NEBRASKA						
1 ***Bereuter***	Y	Y	N	Y	Y	Y
2 ***Daub***	Y	N	N	Y	Y	Y
3 ***Smith***	Y	Y	Y	Y	Y	Y
NEVADA						
1 Reid	Y	Y	#	Y	N	Y
2 ***Vucanovich***	N	N	Y	Y	N	Y
NEW HAMPSHIRE						
1 D'Amours	Y	Y	N	Y	Y	Y
2 ***Gregg***	N	N	N	Y	Y	Y
NEW JERSEY						
1 Florio	Y	Y	N	Y	N	Y
2 Hughes	Y	Y	Y	Y	Y	Y
3 Howard	?	?	X	?	?	?
4 ***Smith***	N	N	N	Y	Y	Y
5 ***Roukema***	Y	N	N	Y	Y	Y
6 Dwyer	Y	Y	Y	Y	N	Y
7 ***Rinaldo***	Y	N	N	Y	Y	Y
8 Roe	Y	Y	Y	Y	N	Y
9 Torricelli	Y	Y	N	Y	N	Y
10 Rodino	?	?	X	?	X	?
11 Minish	Y	Y	N	Y	Y	Y
12 ***Courter***	N	N	N	Y	Y	N
13 Vacancy						
14 Guarini	?	Y	N	Y	N	Y
NEW MEXICO						
1 ***Lujan***	N	N	Y	Y	Y	Y
2 ***Skeen***	N	Y	Y	Y	Y	Y
3 Richardson	Y	Y	Y	Y	N	Y
NEW YORK						
1 ***Carney***	N	N	N	Y	Y	Y
2 Downey	Y	Y	N	Y	N	Y
3 Mrazek	Y	Y	Y	Y	N	Y
4 ***Lent***	N	Y	Y	Y	Y	Y
5 ***McGrath***	N	Y	N	Y	#	?
6 Addabbo	Y	Y	N	Y	N	Y
7 Ackerman	Y	Y	Y	Y	N	Y
8 Scheuer	Y	?	Y	Y	N	Y
9 Ferraro	?	?	?	?	?	?
10 Schumer	Y	Y	N	Y	N	Y
11 Towns	Y	Y	Y	Y	N	Y
12 Owens	?	Y	Y	Y	N	Y
13 Solarz	Y	Y	N	Y	N	Y
14 ***Molinari***	N	N	N	Y	Y	N
15 ***Green***	Y	Y	N	Y	N	Y
16 Rangel	Y	Y	N	Y	N	Y
17 Weiss	Y	Y	N	Y	N	Y
18 Garcia	Y	Y	N	Y	N	Y
19 Biaggi	Y	Y	N	Y	N	Y
20 Ottinger	N	Y	N	Y	N	Y
21 ***Fish***	Y	N	Y	Y	Y	Y
22 ***Gilman***	N	N	N	Y	Y	Y
23 Stratton	N	Y	Y	Y	N	Y
24 ***Solomon***	N	N	N	Y	Y	N
25 ***Boehlert***	Y	Y	N	Y	Y	Y
26 ***Martin***	Y	?	N	Y	Y	Y
27 ***Wortley***	Y	N	N	Y	Y	N
28 McHugh	Y	Y	N	Y	N	Y
29 ***Horton***	Y	Y	N	Y	Y	Y
30 ***Conable***	Y	Y	N	Y	Y	N
31 ***Kemp***	N	N	N	Y	Y	N
32 LaFalce	Y	Y	Y	Y	N	Y
33 Nowak	Y	Y	Y	Y	N	Y
34 Lundine	Y	Y	Y	Y	Y	Y
NORTH CAROLINA						
1 Jones	Y	Y	Y	Y	N	Y
2 Valentine	?	Y	Y	Y	Y	Y
3 Whitley	Y	Y	Y	Y	Y	Y
4 Andrews	Y	Y	Y	Y	Y	Y
5 Neal	Y	Y	Y	Y	Y	Y
6 Britt	Y	Y	N	Y	Y	Y
7 Rose	Y	Y	Y	Y	N	Y
8 Hefner	Y	Y	Y	Y	N	Y
9 ***Martin***	N	?	N	Y	?	?
10 ***Broyhill***	Y	Y	N	Y	Y	N
11 Clarke	Y	Y	N	Y	N	Y
NORTH DAKOTA						
AL Dorgan	Y	N	Y	Y	Y	Y
OHIO						
1 Luken	Y	Y	N	Y	Y	Y
2 ***Gradison***	Y	Y	N	Y	Y	Y
3 Hall	Y	Y	Y	Y	Y	Y
4 ***Oxley***	N	N	N	Y	Y	Y
5 ***Latta***	N	Y	N	Y	Y	Y
6 ***McEwen***	N	N	N	Y	Y	Y
7 ***DeWine***	N	N	N	Y	Y	Y
8 ***Kindness***	N	N	N	Y	Y	N
9 Kaptur	Y	Y	Y	Y	Y	Y
10 ***Miller***	N	N	N	Y	Y	N
11 Eckart	Y	Y	N	Y	Y	Y
12 ***Kasich***	N	N	N	Y	Y	Y
13 Pease	Y	Y	N	Y	Y	Y
14 Seiberling	Y	Y	N	Y	N	Y
15 ***Wylie***	Y	N	Y	Y	Y	Y
16 ***Regula***	Y	N	Y	Y	Y	Y
17 ***Williams***	Y	Y	Y	Y	?	?
18 Applegate	Y	Y	Y	Y	N	Y
19 Feighan	Y	N	N	Y	Y	Y
20 Oakar	Y	Y	N	Y	N	Y
21 Stokes	Y	Y	N	Y	N	Y
OKLAHOMA						
1 Jones	Y	N	Y	Y	Y	Y
2 Synar	Y	N	N	Y	N	Y
3 Watkins	Y	Y	Y	Y	N	Y
4 McCurdy	Y	?	?	?	?	?
5 ***Edwards***	N	N	Y	Y	Y	Y
6 English	N	Y	Y	Y	Y	Y
OREGON						
1 AuCoin	Y	Y	Y	Y	N	Y
2 ***Smith, R.***	Y	Y	N	Y	N	Y
3 Wyden	Y	Y	Y	Y	N	Y
4 Weaver	Y	Y	N	Y	Y	N
5 ***Smith, D.***	N	Y	Y	Y	#	?
PENNSYLVANIA						
1 Foglietta	Y	Y	Y	Y	N	Y
2 Gray	Y	Y	N	Y	N	Y
3 Borski	Y	Y	Y	Y	N	?
4 Kolter	Y	Y	Y	Y	N	Y
5 ***Schulze***	Y	N	Y	Y	Y	Y
6 Yatron	Y	Y	Y	Y	N	Y
7 Edgar	Y	N	N	Y	N	Y
8 Kostmayer	Y	N	N	Y	N	Y
9 ***Shuster***	N	Y	Y	Y	Y	N
10 ***McDade***	Y	Y	Y	Y	Y	Y
11 Harrison	Y	Y	N	Y	N	Y
12 Murtha	Y	Y	Y	Y	N	Y
13 ***Coughlin***	Y	N	N	Y	Y	Y
14 Coyne	Y	Y	Y	Y	N	Y
15 ***Ritter***	N	N	Y	Y	Y	N
16 ***Walker***	N	N	N	Y	Y	N
17 ***Gekas***	N	N	Y	Y	Y	N
18 Walgren	Y	N	Y	Y	Y	Y
19 ***Goodling***	Y	Y	Y	Y	Y	Y
20 Gaydos	Y	Y	Y	Y	N	Y
21 ***Ridge***	Y	N	N	Y	Y	Y
22 Murphy	Y	Y	Y	Y	N	Y
23 ***Clinger***	Y	Y	Y	Y	Y	Y
RHODE ISLAND						
1 St Germain	Y	Y	N	Y	N	Y
2 ***Schneider***	Y	Y	N	Y	Y	Y
SOUTH CAROLINA						
1 ***Hartnett***	N	Y	N	Y	Y	N
2 ***Spence***	N	N	N	Y	Y	Y
3 Derrick	Y	Y	N	Y	Y	Y
4 ***Campbell***	N	N	N	Y	Y	Y
5 Spratt	Y	Y	N	Y	Y	Y
6 Tallon	Y	Y	Y	Y	Y	Y
SOUTH DAKOTA						
AL Daschle	Y	N	Y	Y	N	Y
TENNESSEE						
1 ***Quillen***	Y	Y	Y	Y	Y	Y
2 ***Duncan***	Y	Y	N	Y	Y	Y
3 Lloyd	N	?	?	?	?	?
4 Cooper	Y	?	?	?	X	?
5 Boner	Y	Y	Y	Y	N	?
6 Gore	Y	Y	Y	Y	Y	Y
7 ***Sundquist***	N	?	?	#	#	?
8 Jones	Y	Y	Y	Y	N	Y
9 Ford	?	?	?	?	?	?
TEXAS						
1 Hall, S.	N	Y	Y	Y	Y	N
2 Wilson	Y	Y	Y	Y	N	Y
3 ***Bartlett***	N	N	N	Y	Y	Y
4 Hall, R.	N	Y	Y	Y	Y	N
5 Bryant	Y	Y	Y	Y	N	Y
6 ***Gramm***	?	?	?	?	?	?
7 ***Archer***	N	N	Y	Y	Y	N
8 ***Fields***	N	Y	Y	Y	Y	N
9 Brooks	Y	Y	Y	Y	N	Y
10 Pickle	Y	Y	Y	Y	N	Y
11 Leath	Y	Y	Y	Y	Y	N
12 Wright	Y	Y	Y	Y	N	Y
13 Hightower	Y	Y	Y	Y	N	Y
14 Patman	N	Y	Y	Y	Y	Y
15 de la Garza	Y	Y	Y	Y	N	Y
16 Coleman	Y	Y	Y	Y	N	Y
17 Stenholm	N	Y	Y	Y	Y	N
18 Leland	?	?	?	?	X	?
19 Hance	N	Y	Y	Y	Y	N
20 Gonzalez	Y	Y	Y	Y	N	Y
21 ***Loeffler***	N	Y	Y	Y	Y	Y
22 ***Paul***	N	N	N	Y	Y	N
23 Kazen	N	Y	Y	Y	N	Y
24 Frost	?	?	?	?	?	?
25 Andrews	Y	Y	Y	Y	Y	Y
26 Vandergriff	N	N	Y	Y	Y	N
27 Ortiz	Y	Y	Y	?	X	?
UTAH						
1 ***Hansen***	N	Y	Y	Y	?	?
2 ***Marriott***	?	?	?	X	?	?
3 ***Nielson***	N	Y	Y	Y	Y	Y
VERMONT						
AL ***Jeffords***	Y	N	N	Y	N	Y
VIRGINIA						
1 ***Bateman***	Y	N	Y	Y	Y	Y
2 ***Whitehurst***	Y	Y	Y	Y	Y	Y
3 ***Bliley***	N	Y	N	Y	#	?
4 Sisisky	Y	Y	Y	Y	Y	Y
5 Daniel	Y	Y	Y	Y	Y	N
6 Olin	Y	Y	Y	Y	Y	Y
7 ***Robinson***	Y	N	N	Y	Y	N
8 ***Parris***	Y	Y	Y	Y	Y	Y
9 Boucher	Y	Y	Y	Y	N	Y
10 ***Wolf***	Y	N	Y	Y	Y	Y
WASHINGTON						
1 ***Pritchard***	?	?	?	?	?	?
2 Swift	Y	Y	N	Y	X	?
3 Bonker	Y	Y	N	Y	N	Y
4 ***Morrison***	Y	N	Y	Y	Y	Y
5 Foley	Y	Y	Y	Y	N	Y
6 Dicks	Y	Y	Y	Y	N	Y
7 Lowry	Y	N	N	Y	N	Y
8 ***Chandler***	Y	Y	N	Y	Y	Y
WEST VIRGINIA						
1 Mollohan	Y	Y	Y	Y	N	Y
2 Staggers	Y	N	Y	Y	N	Y
3 Wise	+	+	+	+	+	+
4 Rahall	Y	Y	Y	Y	N	Y
WISCONSIN						
1 Aspin	Y	Y	Y	Y	Y	Y
2 Kastenmeier	Y	Y	N	Y	N	Y
3 ***Gunderson***	Y	Y	N	Y	Y	Y
4 Kleczka	Y	Y	N	Y	N	Y
5 Moody	Y	N	Y	Y	N	Y
6 ***Petri***	N	N	N	Y	Y	Y
7 Obey	Y	Y	N	Y	N	Y
8 ***Roth***	Y	Y	Y	Y	Y	Y
9 ***Sensenbrenner***	N	N	N	Y	Y	N
WYOMING						
AL ***Cheney***	N	N	N	Y	Y	N

Southern states - Ala., Ark., Fla., Ga., Ky., La., Miss., N.C., Okla., S.C., Tenn., Texas, Va.

312. HR 5712. Commerce, Justice, State and the Judiciary Appropriations, Fiscal 1985. Adoption of the conference report on the bill to provide $11,520,976,200 for the Commerce, Justice and the State departments, the federal judiciary and related agencies. Adopted 277-135: R 64-94; D 213-41 (ND 150-17, SD 63-24), Aug. 8, 1984. The president had requested $11,145,918,000 in new budget authority.

313. HR 5712. Commerce, Justice, State and the Judiciary Appropriations, Fiscal 1985. Smith, D-Iowa, motion that the House recede from its disagreement to the Senate amendment and concur therein with an amendment to provide $64.31 million for the Federal Trade Commission. Motion agreed to 226-193: R 22-137; D 204-56 (ND 162-11, SD 42-45), Aug. 8, 1984.

314. HR 5712. Commerce, Justice, State and the Judiciary Appropriations, Fiscal 1985. Smith, D-Iowa, motion that the House recede from its disagreement to the Senate amendment and concur therein with an amendment to provide $305 million for the Legal Services Corp. (LSC) and requiring the LSC board of directors to inform the House and Senate Appropriations committees before promulgating or implementing any new regulations. Motion agreed to 278-138: R 46-111; D 232-27 (ND 169-3, SD 63-24), Aug. 8, 1984.

315. HR 5712. Commerce, Justice, State and the Judiciary Appropriations, Fiscal 1985. Smith, D-Iowa, motion that the House recede from its disagreement to the Senate amendment and concur therein with an amendment to provide $18.5 million for the National Endowment for Democracy. Motion agreed to 237-181: R 80-78; D 157-103 (ND 106-67, SD 51-36), Aug. 8, 1984.

316. HR 5886. American Folklife Center. Hawkins, D-Calif., motion to suspend the rules and pass the bill to authorize $839,549 for fiscal 1985 and $867,898 in 1986 for the American Folklife Center of the Library of Congress. Motion agreed to 416-2: R 157-2; D 259-0 (ND 173-0, SD 86-0), Aug. 8, 1984. A two-thirds majority of those present and voting (279 in this case) is required for passage under suspension of the rules.

317. HR 4785. Older Americans. Andrews, D-N.C., motion to suspend the rules and pass the bill to authorize funding for programs of the Older Americans Act of $1.34 billion in fiscal 1985 with increases in 1986-87. Motion agreed to 406-12: R 147-12; D 259-0 (ND 172-0, SD 87-0), Aug. 8, 1984. A two-thirds majority of those present and voting (279 in this case) is required for passage under suspension of the rules. A "nay" was a vote supporting the president's position.

318. HR 6027. Municipal Antitrust Amendments. Seiberling, D-Ohio, motion to suspend the rules and pass the bill to protect municipalities from monetary damage awards in antitrust lawsuits. Motion agreed to 414-5: R 158-1; D 256-4 (ND 172-1, SD 84-3), Aug. 8, 1984. A two-thirds majority of those present and voting (280 in this case) is required for passage under suspension of the rules.

KEY

- Y Voted for (yea).
- # Paired for.
- + Announced for.
- N Voted against (nay).
- X Paired against.
- − Announced against.
- P Voted "present".
- C Voted "present" to avoid possible conflict of interest.
- ? Did not vote or otherwise make a position known.

Democrats   *Republicans*

	312	313	314	315	316	317	318
ALABAMA							
1 *Edwards*	N	N	N	Y	Y	Y	Y
2 *Dickinson*	N	N	N	Y	Y	Y	Y
3 Nichols	Y	Y	Y	Y	Y	Y	Y
4 Bevill	Y	Y	Y	N	Y	Y	Y
5 Flippo	Y	?	?	?	?	?	?
6 Erdreich	N	N	N	Y	Y	Y	Y
7 Shelby	N	N	N	Y	Y	Y	Y
ALASKA							
AL *Young*	Y	N	Y	Y	Y	Y	Y
ARIZONA							
1 *McCain*	Y	N	N	Y	Y	Y	Y
2 Udall	Y	Y	Y	Y	Y	Y	Y
3 *Stump*	N	N	N	N	N	Y	Y
4 *Rudd*	N	N	N	N	Y	Y	Y
5 McNulty	Y	Y	Y	Y	Y	Y	Y
ARKANSAS							
1 Alexander	Y	Y	Y	Y	Y	Y	Y
2 *Bethune*	N	?	N	N	Y	Y	Y
3 *Hammerschmidt*	Y	N	N	Y	Y	Y	Y
4 Anthony	Y	N	Y	N	Y	Y	Y
CALIFORNIA							
1 Bosco	N	Y	?	Y	Y	Y	Y
2 *Chappie*	N	N	N	N	Y	Y	Y
3 Matsui	Y	Y	Y	Y	Y	Y	Y
4 Fazio	Y	Y	Y	Y	Y	Y	Y
5 Burton	Y	Y	Y	Y	Y	Y	Y
6 Boxer	Y	Y	Y	Y	Y	Y	Y
7 Miller	Y	Y	Y	N	Y	Y	Y
8 Dellums	Y	Y	Y	Y	Y	Y	Y
9 Stark	?	Y	Y	N	Y	Y	Y
10 Edwards	Y	Y	Y	N	Y	Y	Y
11 Lantos	Y	Y	Y	Y	Y	Y	Y
12 *Zschau*	Y	N	Y	Y	Y	Y	Y
13 Mineta	Y	Y	Y	Y	Y	Y	Y
14 *Shumway*	N	N	N	N	Y	Y	Y
15 Coelho	Y	Y	Y	Y	Y	Y	Y
16 Panetta	Y	Y	Y	N	Y	Y	Y
17 *Pashayan*	N	N	N	Y	Y	Y	Y
18 Lehman	Y	Y	Y	Y	Y	Y	Y
19 *Lagomarsino*	N	N	N	Y	Y	Y	Y
20 *Thomas*	#	X	X	?	?	?	?
21 *Fiedler*	N	N	N	Y	Y	Y	Y
22 *Moorhead*	N	N	N	Y	Y	Y	Y
23 Beilenson	Y	Y	Y	N	Y	Y	Y
24 Waxman	Y	Y	Y	Y	Y	Y	?
25 Roybal	Y	Y	Y	Y	Y	Y	Y
26 Berman	Y	Y	Y	Y	Y	Y	Y
27 Levine	Y	Y	Y	Y	Y	Y	Y
28 Dixon	Y	Y	Y	?	Y	Y	Y
29 Hawkins	Y	Y	Y	Y	Y	Y	Y
30 Martinez	Y	Y	Y	Y	Y	Y	Y
31 Dymally	Y	Y	Y	Y	Y	Y	Y
32 Anderson	Y	Y	Y	Y	Y	Y	Y
33 *Dreier*	N	N	N	N	Y	Y	Y
34 Torres	Y	Y	Y	Y	Y	Y	Y
35 Lewis	Y	N	N	Y	Y	Y	Y
36 Brown	Y	Y	Y	N	Y	Y	Y
37 *McCandless*	?	N	N	N	Y	Y	Y
38 Patterson	Y	Y	Y	N	Y	Y	Y
39 *Dannemeyer*	N	N	N	N	Y	N	Y
40 *Badham*	N	N	N	Y	Y	Y	Y
41 *Lowery*	N	N	N	Y	Y	Y	Y
42 *Lungren*	N	N	N	Y	Y	Y	Y

	312	313	314	315	316	317	318
43 *Packard*	N	N	N	Y	Y	Y	Y
44 Bates	Y	Y	Y	N	Y	Y	Y
45 *Hunter*	Y	N	Y	Y	Y	Y	Y
COLORADO							
1 Schroeder	N	Y	Y	N	Y	Y	Y
2 Wirth	Y	Y	Y	Y	Y	Y	Y
3 Kogovsek	Y	Y	Y	Y	Y	Y	Y
4 *Brown*	N	N	N	N	Y	Y	Y
5 *Kramer*	?	?	?	?	?	?	?
6 *Schaefer*	N	N	N	N	Y	Y	Y
CONNECTICUT							
1 Kennelly	Y	Y	Y	Y	Y	Y	Y
2 Gejdenson	Y	Y	Y	Y	Y	Y	Y
3 Morrison	Y	Y	Y	N	Y	Y	Y
4 *McKinney*	Y	N	Y	N	Y	Y	Y
5 Ratchford	Y	Y	Y	N	Y	Y	Y
6 *Johnson*	Y	N	N	N	Y	Y	Y
DELAWARE							
AL Carper	Y	Y	Y	Y	Y	Y	Y
FLORIDA							
1 Hutto	Y	Y	N	Y	Y	Y	Y
2 Fuqua	Y	Y	Y	Y	Y	Y	Y
3 Bennett	Y	Y	Y	Y	Y	Y	Y
4 Chappell	Y	Y	Y	Y	Y	Y	Y
5 *McCollum*	N	N	Y	N	Y	Y	Y
6 MacKay	N	Y	Y	N	Y	Y	Y
7 Gibbons	Y	Y	Y	Y	Y	Y	Y
8 *Young*	Y	N	Y	N	Y	Y	Y
9 *Bilirakis*	N	N	N	Y	Y	Y	Y
10 *Ireland*	N	N	N	Y	Y	Y	Y
11 Nelson	N	N	Y	N	Y	Y	Y
12 *Lewis*	N	N	N	Y	Y	Y	Y
13 *Mack*	N	N	N	Y	Y	Y	Y
14 Mica	Y	Y	N	Y	Y	Y	Y
15 *Shaw*	Y	N	N	Y	Y	Y	Y
16 Smith	Y	Y	Y	Y	Y	Y	Y
17 Lehman	Y	Y	Y	Y	Y	Y	Y
18 Pepper	Y	Y	Y	Y	Y	Y	Y
19 Fascell	Y	Y	Y	Y	Y	Y	Y
GEORGIA							
1 Thomas	Y	N	Y	Y	Y	Y	Y
2 Hatcher	Y	N	N	Y	Y	Y	Y
3 Ray	N	N	Y	N	Y	Y	Y
4 Levitas	Y	N	Y	N	Y	Y	Y
5 Fowler	Y	N	Y	Y	Y	Y	Y
6 *Gingrich*	N	N	?	Y	Y	Y	Y
7 Darden	Y	N	Y	N	Y	Y	Y
8 Rowland	Y	N	N	Y	Y	Y	Y
9 Jenkins	Y	N	N	N	Y	Y	Y
10 Barnard	Y	N	N	N	Y	Y	Y
HAWAII							
1 Heftel	Y	Y	Y	Y	Y	Y	Y
2 Akaka	Y	Y	Y	Y	Y	Y	Y
IDAHO							
1 *Craig*	N	N	N	N	N	Y	Y
2 *Hansen*	N	N	N	?	?	?	?
ILLINOIS							
1 Hayes	Y	Y	Y	Y	Y	Y	Y
2 Savage	?	Y	Y	N	Y	Y	Y
3 Russo	N	Y	Y	Y	Y	Y	Y
4 *O'Brien*	Y	Y	Y	Y	Y	Y	Y
5 Lipinski	Y	Y	Y	Y	Y	Y	Y
6 *Hyde*	N	N	Y	Y	Y	Y	Y
7 Collins	Y	Y	Y	N	Y	Y	Y
8 Rostenkowski	Y	Y	Y	N	Y	?	Y
9 Yates	Y	Y	Y	N	Y	Y	Y
10 *Porter*	Y	N	Y	N	Y	Y	Y
11 Annunzio	Y	Y	Y	Y	Y	Y	Y
12 *Crane, P.*	N	N	N	Y	Y	N	N
13 *Erlenborn*	N	N	N	Y	Y	N	N
14 *Corcoran*	N	N	N	Y	Y	Y	Y
15 *Madigan*	Y	N	N	?	Y	Y	Y
16 *Martin*	N	N	Y	N	Y	Y	Y
17 Evans	Y	Y	Y	N	Y	Y	Y
18 *Michel*	N	N	N	Y	Y	Y	Y
19 *Crane, D.*	N	N	N	N	Y	N	Y
20 Durbin	N	Y	Y	Y	Y	Y	Y
21 Price	Y	Y	Y	Y	Y	Y	Y
22 Simon	Y	Y	Y	Y	Y	Y	Y
INDIANA							
1 Hall	N	Y	Y	Y	Y	?	Y
2 Sharp	N	N	Y	N	Y	Y	Y
3 *Hiler*	N	N	N	N	Y	Y	Y
4 *Coats*	N	N	N	Y	Y	Y	Y
5 Hillis	Y	N	N	N	Y	Y	Y

ND - Northern Democrats   SD - Southern Democrats

Corresponding to Congressional Record Votes 350, 351, 352, 353, 354, 355, 356

	312	313	314	315	316	317	318
6 ***Burton***	N	N	N	Y	Y	Y	Y
7 ***Myers***	Y	Y	Y	N	Y	Y	Y
8 McCloskey	Y	Y	Y	N	Y	Y	Y
9 Hamilton	Y	N	Y	N	Y	Y	Y
10 Jacobs	N	Y	Y	N	Y	Y	Y
IOWA							
1 ***Leach***	Y	Y	Y	N	Y	Y	Y
2 ***Tauke***	N	N	Y	N	Y	Y	Y
3 ***Evans***	N	Y	Y	N	Y	Y	Y
4 Smith	Y	Y	Y	Y	Y	Y	Y
5 Harkin	Y	Y	Y	N	Y	Y	Y
6 Bedell	Y	Y	Y	N	Y	Y	Y
KANSAS							
1 ***Roberts***	N	N	N	N	Y	Y	Y
2 Slattery	N	Y	Y	N	Y	Y	Y
3 ***Winn***	?	?	X	?	?	?	?
4 Glickman	N	Y	Y	Y	Y	Y	Y
5 ***Whittaker***	N	N	N	N	Y	Y	Y
KENTUCKY							
1 Hubbard	N	N	Y	Y	Y	Y	Y
2 Natcher	Y	Y	Y	Y	Y	Y	Y
3 Mazzoli	Y	Y	Y	N	Y	Y	Y
4 ***Snyder***	Y	N	N	N	Y	Y	Y
5 ***Rogers***	Y	N	N	N	Y	Y	Y
6 ***Hopkins***	Y	N	N	N	Y	Y	Y
7 Vacancy*							
LOUISIANA							
1 ***Livingston***	N	N	N	Y	Y	Y	Y
2 Boggs	Y	Y	Y	N	Y	Y	Y
3 Tauzin	N	N	N	N	Y	Y	Y
4 Roemer	N	N	N	N	Y	Y	Y
5 Huckaby	N	N	Y	N	Y	Y	Y
6 ***Moore***	Y	N	Y	N	Y	Y	Y
7 Breaux	Y	Y	Y	Y	Y	Y	Y
8 Long	Y	Y	Y	Y	Y	Y	Y
MAINE							
1 ***McKernan***	Y	Y	Y	N	Y	Y	Y
2 ***Snowe***	Y	Y	Y	N	Y	Y	Y
MARYLAND							
1 Dyson	Y	Y	N	N	Y	Y	Y
2 Long	Y	Y	Y	Y	Y	Y	Y
3 Mikulski	Y	Y	Y	N	Y	Y	Y
4 ***Holt***	Y	N	N	Y	Y	Y	Y
5 Hoyer	Y	Y	Y	Y	Y	Y	Y
6 Byron	Y	N	N	Y	Y	Y	Y
7 Mitchell	Y	Y	Y	N	Y	Y	Y
8 Barnes	Y	Y	Y	Y	Y	Y	Y
MASSACHUSETTS							
1 ***Conte***	Y	Y	Y	Y	Y	Y	Y
2 Boland	Y	Y	Y	Y	Y	Y	Y
3 Early	Y	Y	Y	Y	Y	Y	Y
4 Frank	Y	Y	Y	N	Y	Y	Y
5 Shannon	?	?	#	?	?	?	?
6 Mavroules	Y	Y	Y	Y	Y	Y	Y
7 Markey	Y	Y	Y	N	Y	Y	Y
8 O'Neill							
9 Moakley	Y	Y	Y	Y	Y	Y	Y
10 Studds	Y	Y	Y	N	Y	Y	Y
11 Donnelly	?	Y	Y	Y	Y	Y	Y
MICHIGAN							
1 Conyers	Y	Y	Y	N	Y	Y	Y
2 ***Pursell***	Y	N	Y	Y	Y	Y	Y
3 Wolpe	Y	Y	Y	Y	Y	Y	Y
4 ***Siljander***	?	X	?	?	?	?	?
5 ***Sawyer***	Y	N	Y	Y	Y	Y	Y
6 Carr	Y	Y	Y	Y	Y	Y	Y
7 Kildee	Y	Y	Y	Y	Y	Y	Y
8 Traxler	Y	Y	Y	Y	Y	Y	Y
9 ***Vander Jagt***	Y	N	N	Y	Y	Y	Y
10 Albosta	Y	N	Y	N	Y	Y	Y
11 ***Davis***	Y	Y	Y	Y	Y	Y	Y
12 Bonior	Y	Y	Y	Y	Y	Y	Y
13 Crockett	Y	Y	Y	N	Y	Y	Y
14 Hertel	N	Y	Y	Y	Y	Y	Y
15 Ford	Y	Y	Y	Y	Y	Y	Y
16 Dingell	Y	Y	Y	Y	Y	Y	Y
17 Levin	Y	Y	Y	Y	Y	Y	Y
18 ***Broomfield***	N	N	N	Y	Y	Y	Y
MINNESOTA							
1 Penny	N	N	Y	Y	Y	Y	Y
2 ***Weber***	N	N	N	N	Y	Y	Y
3 ***Frenzel***	N	N	Y	N	Y	Y	Y
4 Vento	Y	Y	Y	Y	Y	Y	Y
5 Sabo	Y	Y	Y	Y	Y	Y	Y
6 Sikorski	Y	Y	Y	Y	Y	Y	Y

	312	313	314	315	316	317	318
7 ***Stangeland***	N	N	N	N	Y	Y	Y
8 Oberstar	Y	Y	Y	N	Y	Y	Y
MISSISSIPPI							
1 Whitten	Y	Y	Y	Y	Y	Y	Y
2 ***Franklin***	N	N	N	N	Y	Y	Y
3 Montgomery	N	N	N	Y	Y	Y	Y
4 Dowdy	Y	Y	Y	Y	Y	Y	Y
5 ***Lott***	N	N	N	Y	Y	Y	Y
MISSOURI							
1 Clay	?	?	?	?	?	?	?
2 Young	Y	Y	Y	Y	Y	Y	Y
3 Gephardt	Y	Y	Y	Y	Y	Y	Y
4 Skelton	?	N	N	N	Y	Y	Y
5 Wheat	Y	Y	Y	Y	Y	Y	Y
6 ***Coleman***	?	N	N	Y	Y	Y	Y
7 ***Taylor***	Y	N	N	N	Y	Y	Y
8 ***Emerson***	Y	N	N	N	Y	Y	Y
9 Volkmer	Y	N	Y	N	Y	Y	Y
MONTANA							
1 Williams	Y	Y	Y	N	Y	Y	N
2 ***Marlenee***	N	N	N	N	Y	Y	Y
NEBRASKA							
1 ***Bereuter***	N	N	N	Y	Y	Y	Y
2 ***Daub***	N	N	N	N	Y	Y	Y
3 ***Smith***	N	N	N	N	Y	Y	Y
NEVADA							
1 Reid	Y	N	Y	Y	Y	Y	Y
2 ***Vucanovich***	N	N	N	N	Y	Y	Y
NEW HAMPSHIRE							
1 D'Amours	Y	N	Y	Y	Y	Y	Y
2 ***Gregg***	N	N	N	Y	Y	Y	Y
NEW JERSEY							
1 Florio	Y	Y	Y	Y	Y	Y	Y
2 Hughes	Y	Y	Y	N	Y	Y	Y
3 Howard	Y	Y	Y	Y	Y	Y	Y
4 ***Smith***	Y	Y	Y	Y	Y	Y	Y
5 ***Roukema***	Y	N	N	N	Y	Y	Y
6 Dwyer	Y	Y	Y	Y	Y	Y	Y
7 ***Rinaldo***	Y	Y	Y	Y	Y	Y	Y
8 Roe	Y	Y	Y	Y	Y	Y	Y
9 Torricelli	Y	Y	Y	Y	Y	Y	Y
10 Rodino	Y	Y	Y	Y	Y	Y	Y
11 Minish	Y	Y	Y	N	Y	Y	Y
12 ***Courter***	N	Y	Y	Y	Y	Y	Y
13 Vacancy							
14 Guarini	Y	Y	Y	Y	Y	Y	Y
NEW MEXICO							
1 ***Lujan***	N	N	N	Y	Y	Y	Y
2 ***Skeen***	N	N	N	N	Y	Y	Y
3 Richardson	Y	Y	Y	Y	Y	Y	Y
NEW YORK							
1 ***Carney***	N	N	N	N	Y	Y	Y
2 Downey	Y	Y	Y	Y	Y	Y	Y
3 Mrazek	Y	Y	Y	Y	Y	Y	Y
4 ***Lent***	Y	N	N	Y	Y	Y	Y
5 ***McGrath***	Y	N	N	N	Y	Y	Y
6 Addabbo	Y	Y	Y	Y	Y	Y	Y
7 Ackerman	Y	Y	Y	Y	Y	Y	Y
8 Scheuer	Y	Y	Y	N	Y	Y	Y
9 Ferraro	Y	Y	Y	Y	Y	Y	Y
10 Schumer	?	Y	Y	Y	Y	Y	Y
11 Towns	?	#	#	?	?	?	?
12 Owens	Y	Y	Y	Y	Y	Y	Y
13 Solarz	Y	Y	Y	Y	Y	Y	Y
14 ***Molinari***	Y	N	N	Y	Y	Y	Y
15 ***Green***	Y	Y	Y	Y	Y	Y	Y
16 Rangel	Y	#	Y	Y	Y	Y	Y
17 Weiss	Y	Y	Y	N	Y	Y	Y
18 Garcia	Y	Y	Y	Y	Y	Y	Y
19 Biaggi	Y	Y	Y	Y	Y	Y	Y
20 Ottinger	Y	Y	Y	N	?	Y	Y
21 ***Fish***	Y	N	Y	Y	Y	Y	Y
22 ***Gilman***	Y	Y	Y	Y	Y	Y	Y
23 Stratton	Y	N	Y	Y	Y	Y	Y
24 ***Solomon***	N	N	N	Y	Y	Y	Y
25 ***Boehlert***	Y	Y	Y	Y	Y	Y	Y
26 ***Martin***	Y	N	N	Y	Y	Y	Y
27 ***Wortley***	N	N	N	N	Y	Y	Y
28 McHugh	Y	Y	Y	N	Y	Y	Y
29 ***Horton***	Y	N	#	Y	Y	Y	Y
30 ***Conable***	N	N	Y	N	Y	N	Y
31 ***Kemp***	N	N	N	Y	Y	Y	Y
32 LaFalce	Y	Y	Y	Y	Y	Y	Y
33 Nowak	Y	Y	Y	Y	Y	Y	Y
34 Lundine	Y	Y	Y	Y	Y	Y	Y

	312	313	314	315	316	317	318
NORTH CAROLINA							
1 Jones	Y	Y	Y	Y	Y	Y	Y
2 Valentine	N	N	N	Y	Y	Y	Y
3 Whitley	Y	N	N	Y	Y	Y	Y
4 Andrews	Y	Y	Y	Y	Y	Y	Y
5 Neal	N	N	Y	N	Y	Y	Y
6 Britt	Y	N	Y	Y	Y	Y	Y
7 Rose	Y	Y	Y	Y	Y	Y	Y
8 Hefner	Y	Y	Y	Y	Y	Y	Y
9 ***Martin***	N	N	Y	N	Y	Y	Y
10 ***Broyhill***	N	N	N	N	Y	Y	Y
11 Clarke	Y	Y	Y	Y	Y	Y	Y
NORTH DAKOTA							
AL Dorgan	N	Y	Y	N	Y	Y	Y
OHIO							
1 Luken	N	Y	Y	N	Y	Y	Y
2 ***Gradison***	Y	Y	Y	N	Y	Y	Y
3 Hall	N	Y	Y	N	Y	Y	Y
4 ***Oxley***	N	N	N	N	Y	Y	Y
5 ***Latta***	N	N	N	Y	Y	Y	Y
6 ***McEwen***	N	N	N	Y	Y	Y	Y
7 ***DeWine***	N	N	N	Y	Y	Y	Y
8 ***Kindness***	N	N	Y	N	Y	Y	Y
9 Kaptur	Y	Y	Y	N	Y	Y	Y
10 ***Miller***	Y	Y	N	N	Y	Y	Y
11 Eckart	Y	Y	Y	N	Y	Y	Y
12 ***Kasich***	N	N	N	Y	Y	Y	Y
13 Pease	Y	Y	Y	N	Y	Y	Y
14 Seiberling	Y	Y	Y	N	Y	Y	Y
15 ***Wylie***	N	N	Y	Y	Y	Y	Y
16 ***Regula***	Y	Y	Y	Y	Y	Y	Y
17 ***Williams***	Y	N	Y	Y	Y	Y	Y
18 Applegate	Y	Y	Y	N	Y	Y	Y
19 Feighan	Y	Y	Y	Y	Y	Y	Y
20 Oakar	Y	Y	Y	N	Y	Y	Y
21 Stokes	Y	Y	Y	N	Y	Y	Y
OKLAHOMA							
1 Jones	N	N	N	N	Y	Y	Y
2 Synar	Y	Y	Y	N	Y	Y	Y
3 Watkins	Y	N	Y	N	Y	Y	Y
4 McCurdy	N	N	N	N	Y	Y	Y
5 ***Edwards***	N	N	N	Y	Y	Y	Y
6 English	N	N	N	N	Y	Y	Y
OREGON							
1 AuCoin	N	Y	Y	Y	Y	Y	Y
2 ***Smith, R.***	N	N	N	N	Y	Y	Y
3 Wyden	Y	Y	Y	N	Y	Y	Y
4 Weaver	N	Y	Y	N	Y	Y	Y
5 ***Smith, D.***	N	N	N	N	Y	N	Y
PENNSYLVANIA							
1 Foglietta	Y	Y	Y	Y	Y	Y	Y
2 Gray	Y	Y	Y	Y	Y	Y	Y
3 Borski	Y	Y	Y	Y	Y	Y	Y
4 Kolter	Y	Y	Y	Y	Y	Y	Y
5 ***Schulze***	Y	N	N	Y	Y	Y	Y
6 Yatron	Y	Y	Y	Y	Y	Y	Y
7 Edgar	Y	Y	Y	N	Y	Y	Y
8 Kostmayer	Y	Y	Y	Y	Y	Y	Y
9 ***Shuster***	N	N	N	N	Y	Y	Y
10 ***McDade***	Y	Y	Y	Y	Y	Y	Y
11 Harrison	Y	Y	Y	Y	Y	Y	Y
12 Murtha	Y	Y	Y	Y	Y	Y	Y
13 ***Coughlin***	Y	N	N	Y	Y	Y	Y
14 Coyne	Y	Y	Y	Y	Y	Y	Y
15 ***Ritter***	N	N	N	Y	Y	Y	Y
16 ***Walker***	N	N	N	N	Y	Y	Y
17 ***Gekas***	N	N	?	N	Y	Y	Y
18 Walgren	Y	Y	Y	N	Y	Y	Y
19 ***Goodling***	N	N	N	N	Y	Y	Y
20 Gaydos	Y	Y	Y	Y	Y	Y	Y
21 ***Ridge***	Y	Y	Y	Y	Y	Y	Y
22 Murphy	N	Y	Y	N	Y	Y	Y
23 ***Clinger***	Y	N	Y	Y	Y	Y	Y
RHODE ISLAND							
1 St Germain	?	Y	Y	N	Y	Y	Y
2 ***Schneider***	Y	N	Y	Y	Y	Y	Y
SOUTH CAROLINA							
1 ***Hartnett***	N	N	N	N	Y	Y	Y
2 ***Spence***	N	N	N	N	Y	Y	Y
3 Derrick	Y	N	N	Y	Y	Y	Y
4 ***Campbell***	N	N	N	N	Y	Y	Y
5 Spratt	Y	Y	Y	N	Y	Y	Y
6 Tallon	Y	Y	Y	Y	Y	Y	Y
SOUTH DAKOTA							
AL Daschle	Y	Y	Y	Y	Y	Y	Y

	312	313	314	315	316	317	318
TENNESSEE							
1 ***Quillen***	Y	N	N	Y	Y	Y	Y
2 ***Duncan***	Y	N	N	Y	Y	Y	Y
3 Lloyd	Y	N	Y	Y	Y	Y	Y
4 Cooper	Y	Y	Y	Y	Y	Y	Y
5 Boner	Y	N	Y	Y	Y	Y	Y
6 Gore	Y	Y	Y	N	Y	Y	Y
7 ***Sundquist***	N	N	N	N	Y	Y	Y
8 Jones	Y	N	Y	Y	Y	Y	Y
9 Ford	Y	Y	Y	N	Y	Y	Y
TEXAS							
1 Hall, S.	N	N	N	N	Y	Y	Y
2 Wilson	Y	N	Y	Y	?	Y	Y
3 ***Bartlett***	N	N	N	N	Y	N	Y
4 Hall, R.	N	N	N	N	Y	Y	Y
5 Bryant	Y	Y	Y	N	Y	Y	N
6 ***Gramm***	N	N	N	N	Y	Y	Y
7 ***Archer***	N	N	N	N	Y	N	Y
8 ***Fields***	N	N	N	N	Y	Y	Y
9 Brooks	Y	N	Y	Y	Y	Y	Y
10 Pickle	Y	Y	Y	Y	Y	Y	Y
11 Leath	N	N	N	N	Y	Y	Y
12 Wright	Y	N	Y	Y	Y	Y	Y
13 Hightower	N	Y	N	Y	Y	Y	Y
14 Patman	N	N	N	N	Y	Y	Y
15 de la Garza	Y	Y	Y	Y	Y	Y	Y
16 Coleman	Y	Y	Y	Y	Y	Y	Y
17 Stenholm	N	N	N	N	Y	Y	Y
18 Leland	Y	Y	Y	Y	Y	Y	Y
19 Hance	N	N	N	Y	Y	Y	Y
20 Gonzalez	Y	Y	Y	Y	Y	Y	Y
21 ***Loeffler***	N	N	N	N	Y	Y	Y
22 ***Paul***	X	?	X	?	?	?	?
23 Kazen	Y	N	Y	Y	Y	Y	Y
24 Frost	Y	N	Y	Y	Y	Y	N
25 Andrews	Y	N	Y	N	Y	Y	N
26 Vandergriff	?	N	N	Y	Y	Y	Y
27 Ortiz	Y	Y	Y	Y	Y	Y	Y
UTAH							
1 ***Hansen***	N	N	N	N	N	N	Y
2 ***Marriott***	?	?	?	?	?	?	?
3 ***Nielson***	N	N	N	N	Y	N	Y
VERMONT							
AL ***Jeffords***	Y	N	Y	N	Y	Y	Y
VIRGINIA							
1 ***Bateman***	N	N	N	N	Y	Y	Y
2 ***Whitehurst***	Y	N	Y	Y	Y	Y	Y
3 ***Bliley***	N	N	N	Y	Y	Y	Y
4 Sisisky	Y	N	Y	N	Y	Y	Y
5 Daniel	N	Y	N	N	Y	Y	Y
6 Olin	N	Y	Y	N	Y	Y	Y
7 ***Robinson***	Y	Y	N	Y	Y	Y	Y
8 ***Parris***	Y	N	N	N	Y	Y	Y
9 Boucher	Y	Y	Y	Y	Y	Y	Y
10 ***Wolf***	Y	Y	N	Y	Y	Y	Y
WASHINGTON							
1 ***Pritchard***	?	?	?	?	?	?	?
2 Swift	Y	Y	Y	N	Y	Y	Y
3 Bonker	Y	Y	?	N	Y	Y	Y
4 ***Morrison***	Y	N	Y	Y	Y	Y	Y
5 Foley	?	Y	Y	Y	Y	Y	Y
6 Dicks	Y	Y	Y	Y	Y	Y	Y
7 Lowry	Y	Y	Y	N	Y	Y	Y
8 ***Chandler***	Y	Y	Y	Y	Y	Y	Y
WEST VIRGINIA							
1 Mollohan	Y	N	Y	Y	Y	Y	Y
2 Staggers	Y	Y	Y	Y	Y	Y	Y
3 Wise	Y	Y	Y	N	Y	Y	Y
4 Rahall	Y	Y	Y	Y	Y	Y	Y
WISCONSIN							
1 Aspin	Y	Y	Y	Y	Y	Y	Y
2 Kastenmeier	Y	Y	Y	N	Y	Y	Y
3 ***Gunderson***	N	N	N	Y	Y	Y	Y
4 Kleczka	Y	Y	Y	N	Y	Y	Y
5 Moody	Y	Y	Y	Y	Y	Y	Y
6 ***Petri***	N	N	N	N	Y	Y	Y
7 Obey	Y	Y	Y	N	Y	Y	Y
8 ***Roth***	Y	N	N	N	Y	Y	Y
9 ***Sensenbrenner***	N	N	N	N	Y	Y	Y
WYOMING							
AL ***Cheney***	N	N	N	Y	Y	N	Y

* *Rep. Carl D. Perkins, D-Ky., died Aug. 3, 1984. The last vote for which he was eligible was CQ vote 311.*

Southern states - Ala., Ark., Fla., Ga., Ky., La., Miss., N.C., Okla., S.C., Tenn., Texas, Va.

319. HR 4325. Child Support Enforcement. Adoption of the conference report on the bill to require states to establish certain procedures, including mandatory withholding of wages, to strengthen enforcement of child support payments. Adopted 413-0: R 158-0; D 255-0 (ND 170-0, SD 85-0), Aug. 8, 1984. A "yea" was a vote supporting the president's position.

320. S 2436. Corporation for Public Broadcasting Authorization. Adoption of the rule (H Res 563) providing for House floor consideration of the bill to authorize funding for the Corporation for Public Broadcasting for fiscal 1987-89 and for the Public Telecommunications Facilities Program for fiscal 1985-87. Adopted 324-89: R 78-81; D 246-8 (ND 170-1, SD 76-7), Aug. 8, 1984. (On July 24, a normally routine motion to substitute the text of a House-passed authorization for S 2436 was blocked by opponents. After adopting the rule, the House by voice vote approved the substitution, and the Senate Aug. 9 cleared the measure.)

321. HR 3605. Drug Price Competition/Generic Drug Act. Judgment of the House whether to consider the rule (H Res 569) providing for House floor consideration of the bill to extend patent protection for brand name drugs and authorizing the Food and Drug Administration to use streamlined procedures to approve cheaper generic copies of drugs. Agreed to consider the rule 313-80: R 75-80; D 238-0 (ND 159-0, SD 79-0), Aug. 8, 1984. A two-thirds majority of those present and voting (262 in this case) is required.

322. HR 3605. Drug Price Competition/Generic Drug Act. Adoption of the rule (H Res 569) providing for House floor consideration of the bill to extend patent protection for brand name drugs and authorizing the Food and Drug Administration to use streamlined procedures to approve cheaper generic copies of drugs. Adopted 304-74: R 73-74; D 231-0 (ND 156-0, SD 75-0), Aug. 8, 1984.

323. HR 5640. Superfund Extension. Adoption of the rule (H Res 570) providing for House floor consideration of the bill to renew and expand the "superfund" hazardous waste cleanup program. Adopted 218-199: R 4-154; D 214-45 (ND 151-23, SD 63-22), Aug. 9, 1984.

KEY

Y	Voted for (yea).
#	Paired for.
+	Announced for.
N	Voted against (nay).
X	Paired against.
-	Announced against.
P	Voted "present".
C	Voted "present" to avoid possible conflict of interest.
?	Did not vote or otherwise make a position known.

Democrats *Republicans*

	319	320	321	322	323
ALABAMA					
1 *Edwards*	Y	?	?	?	N
2 *Dickinson*	Y	N	N	N	N
3 Nichols	Y	Y	Y	Y	N
4 Bevill	Y	Y	Y	Y	Y
5 Flippo	?	?	?	?	Y
6 Erdreich	Y	Y	Y	Y	Y
7 Shelby	Y	Y	Y	Y	N
ALASKA					
AL *Young*	Y	Y	Y	Y	N
ARIZONA					
1 *McCain*	Y	N	N	N	N
2 Udall	Y	Y	Y	Y	N
3 *Stump*	Y	N	N	N	N
4 *Rudd*	Y	N	Y	N	N
5 McNulty	Y	Y	Y	Y	N
ARKANSAS					
1 Alexander	Y	Y	Y	?	Y
2 *Bethune*	Y	?	Y	?	?
3 *Hammerschmidt*	Y	N	N	N	N
4 Anthony	Y	Y	Y	Y	Y
CALIFORNIA					
1 Bosco	Y	Y	?	?	Y
2 *Chappie*	Y	N	N	N	N
3 Matsui	Y	Y	Y	Y	Y
4 Fazio	Y	Y	?	?	Y
5 Burton	Y	Y	Y	Y	Y
6 Boxer	Y	Y	Y	Y	Y
7 Miller	Y	Y	Y	Y	Y
8 Dellums	Y	Y	Y	Y	Y
9 Stark	Y	Y	?	Y	Y
10 Edwards	Y	Y	Y	Y	Y
11 Lantos	Y	Y	Y	Y	Y
12 *Zschau*	Y	N	N	N	N
13 Mineta	Y	Y	Y	Y	Y
14 *Shumway*	Y	N	N	N	N
15 Coelho	Y	?	Y	Y	Y
16 Panetta	Y	Y	Y	Y	Y
17 *Pashayan*	Y	N	N	N	N
18 Lehman	Y	Y	Y	Y	Y
19 *Lagomarsino*	Y	N	N	N	N
20 *Thomas*	?	?	?	?	?
21 *Fiedler*	Y	N	N	N	N
22 *Moorhead*	Y	N	Y	N	N
23 Beilenson	Y	Y	Y	Y	Y
24 Waxman	Y	Y	Y	Y	Y
25 Roybal	?	Y	Y	Y	Y
26 Berman	Y	Y	Y	Y	Y
27 Levine	Y	Y	Y	Y	Y
28 Dixon	?	Y	Y	Y	Y
29 Hawkins	Y	Y	Y	?	Y
30 Martinez	Y	Y	Y	Y	Y
31 Dymally	Y	Y	Y	Y	Y
32 Anderson	Y	Y	Y	Y	N
33 *Dreier*	Y	N	N	N	N
34 Torres	Y	Y	Y	Y	Y
35 *Lewis*	Y	Y	N	N	N
36 Brown	Y	Y	Y	?	N
37 *McCandless*	Y	N	N	N	N
38 Patterson	Y	Y	Y	Y	Y
39 *Dannemeyer*	Y	N	N	N	N
40 *Badham*	Y	N	N	N	N
41 *Lowery*	Y	Y	N	N	N
42 *Lungren*	Y	N	Y	N	N

	319	320	321	322	323
43 *Packard*	Y	N	N	N	N
44 Bates	Y	Y	Y	Y	Y
45 *Hunter*	Y	N	N	N	N
COLORADO					
1 Schroeder	Y	Y	Y	Y	Y
2 Wirth	Y	Y	Y	Y	Y
3 Kogovsek	Y	Y	Y	Y	Y
4 *Brown*	Y	N	N	N	N
5 *Kramer*	?	?	?	?	N
6 *Schaefer*	Y	N	N	N	N
CONNECTICUT					
1 Kennelly	Y	Y	Y	Y	Y
2 Gejdenson	Y	Y	Y	Y	Y
3 Morrison	Y	Y	Y	Y	Y
4 *McKinney*	Y	Y	Y	Y	Y
5 Ratchford	Y	Y	Y	Y	Y
6 *Johnson*	Y	N	Y	N	N
DELAWARE					
AL Carper	Y	Y	Y	Y	Y
FLORIDA					
1 Hutto	Y	Y	Y	Y	N
2 Fuqua	Y	Y	Y	Y	Y
3 Bennett	Y	Y	Y	Y	Y
4 Chappell	Y	?	?	?	Y
5 *McCollum*	Y	Y	Y	N	N
6 MacKay	Y	Y	Y	Y	Y
7 Gibbons	Y	Y	Y	Y	Y
8 *Young*	Y	Y	Y	Y	N
9 *Bilirakis*	Y	N	N	N	N
10 *Ireland*	Y	Y	Y	?	N
11 Nelson	Y	Y	Y	Y	Y
12 *Lewis*	Y	Y	Y	N	N
13 *Mack*	Y	N	N	N	N
14 Mica	Y	Y	Y	Y	Y
15 *Shaw*	Y	N	N	N	N
16 Smith	Y	Y	Y	Y	Y
17 Lehman	Y	Y	Y	Y	Y
18 Pepper	Y	Y	Y	Y	Y
19 Fascell	Y	Y	Y	Y	Y
GEORGIA					
1 Thomas	Y	Y	Y	Y	Y
2 Hatcher	Y	Y	?	?	Y
3 Ray	Y	Y	Y	Y	Y
4 Levitas	Y	Y	Y	Y	Y
5 Fowler	Y	Y	Y	Y	?
6 *Gingrich*	Y	N	Y	Y	N
7 Darden	Y	Y	Y	Y	Y
8 Rowland	Y	Y	Y	Y	Y
9 Jenkins	Y	Y	Y	Y	Y
10 Barnard	Y	Y	Y	Y	Y
HAWAII					
1 Heftel	Y	Y	Y	?	Y
2 Akaka	Y	Y	Y	Y	Y
IDAHO					
1 *Craig*	Y	N	N	N	N
2 *Hansen*	Y	N	N	N	N
ILLINOIS					
1 Hayes	Y	Y	Y	Y	Y
2 Savage	Y	Y	Y	Y	Y
3 Russo	Y	Y	Y	Y	Y
4 *O'Brien*	Y	Y	Y	Y	N
5 Lipinski	Y	Y	Y	Y	Y
6 *Hyde*	Y	N	Y	N	N
7 Collins	Y	Y	Y	Y	Y
8 Rostenkowski	Y	Y	Y	Y	Y
9 Yates	Y	Y	Y	Y	Y
10 *Porter*	Y	Y	Y	N	N
11 Annunzio	Y	Y	Y	Y	Y
12 *Crane, P.*	Y	Y	Y	Y	Y
13 *Erlenborn*	Y	N	Y	N	N
14 *Corcoran*	?	N	N	?	N
15 *Madigan*	Y	Y	N	Y	N
16 *Martin*	Y	Y	N	Y	N
17 Evans	Y	Y	Y	Y	Y
18 *Michel*	Y	N	N	N	N
19 *Crane, D.*	Y	N	Y	N	N
20 Durbin	Y	Y	Y	Y	Y
21 Price	Y	Y	Y	Y	Y
22 Simon	Y	Y	?	?	Y
INDIANA					
1 Hall	Y	Y	Y	Y	Y
2 Sharp	Y	Y	Y	Y	Y
3 *Hiler*	Y	N	N	N	N
4 *Coats*	Y	N	N	N	N
5 *Hillis*	Y	Y	?	?	?

ND - Northern Democrats   SD - Southern Democrats

	319	320	321	322	323
6 Burton	Y	N	N	N	N
7 Myers	Y	Y	N	Y	N
8 McCloskey	Y	Y	Y	Y	Y
9 Hamilton	Y	Y	Y	Y	Y
10 Jacobs	Y	Y	Y	Y	N
IOWA					
1 Leach	Y	Y	Y	Y	N
2 Tauke	Y	Y	Y	Y	N
3 Evans	Y	Y	N	Y	N
4 Smith	Y	Y	Y	Y	N
5 Harkin	Y	Y	Y	Y	N
6 Bedell	Y	Y	Y	Y	Y
KANSAS					
1 Roberts	Y	N	N	N	N
2 Slattery	Y	Y	Y	Y	Y
3 Winn	Y	N	N	N	N
4 Glickman	Y	Y	Y	Y	Y
5 Whittaker	Y	N	N	Y	N
KENTUCKY					
1 Hubbard	Y	Y	Y	?	Y
2 Natcher	Y	Y	Y	Y	Y
3 Mazzoli	Y	Y	Y	?	Y
4 Snyder	Y	Y	N	Y	N
5 Rogers	Y	Y	Y	Y	N
6 Hopkins	Y	N	N	N	N
7 Vacancy					
LOUISIANA					
1 Livingston	Y	N	N	N	N
2 Boggs	Y	Y	Y	Y	Y
3 Tauzin	Y	Y	Y	Y	N
4 Roemer	Y	N	Y	Y	N
5 Huckaby	Y	Y	Y	Y	N
6 Moore	Y	Y	Y	Y	N
7 Breaux	Y	Y	Y	Y	Y
8 Long	Y	Y	Y	Y	Y
MAINE					
1 McKernan	Y	Y	Y	Y	N
2 Snowe	Y	Y	Y	Y	N
MARYLAND					
1 Dyson	Y	Y	Y	Y	N
2 Long	Y	Y	Y	Y	Y
3 Mikulski	Y	Y	Y	Y	Y
4 Holt	Y	N	N	?	N
5 Hoyer	Y	Y	Y	Y	Y
6 Byron	Y	Y	Y	Y	N
7 Mitchell	Y	Y	Y	?	Y
8 Barnes	Y	Y	Y	Y	Y
MASSACHUSETTS					
1 Conte	Y	Y	Y	Y	N
2 Boland	Y	Y	Y	Y	Y
3 Early	Y	Y	Y	Y	Y
4 Frank	Y	Y	Y	Y	Y
5 Shannon	?	?	?	?	?
6 Mavroules	?	Y	Y	Y	Y
7 Markey	Y	Y	Y	Y	Y
8 O'Neill					
9 Moakley	Y	Y	Y	Y	Y
10 Studds	Y	Y	Y	Y	Y
11 Donnelly	Y	Y	Y	Y	Y
MICHIGAN					
1 Conyers	Y	Y	Y	Y	Y
2 Pursell	Y	N	N	N	N
3 Wolpe	Y	Y	Y	Y	Y
4 Siljander	?	?	?	?	?
5 Sawyer	Y	Y	Y	N	N
6 Carr	Y	Y	Y	Y	Y
7 Kildee	Y	Y	Y	Y	Y
8 Traxler	Y	Y	Y	Y	Y
9 Vander Jagt	Y	Y	Y	Y	N
10 Albosta	Y	Y	Y	Y	Y
11 Davis	Y	Y	Y	Y	Y
12 Bonior	Y	Y	Y	Y	Y
13 Crockett	Y	?	?	?	Y
14 Hertel	Y	Y	Y	Y	Y
15 Ford	Y	Y	?	?	Y
16 Dingell	Y	Y	Y	Y	Y
17 Levin	Y	Y	Y	Y	Y
18 Broomfield	Y	N	Y	N	N
MINNESOTA					
1 Penny	Y	Y	Y	Y	Y
2 Weber	Y	N	N	N	N
3 Frenzel	?	N	N	N	N
4 Vento	Y	Y	Y	Y	Y
5 Sabo	Y	Y	Y	Y	Y
6 Sikorski	Y	Y	Y	Y	Y

	319	320	321	322	323
7 Stangeland	Y	N	N	N	N
8 Oberstar	Y	Y	Y	Y	Y
MISSISSIPPI					
1 Whitten	Y	Y	Y	?	Y
2 Franklin	Y	N	?	?	N
3 Montgomery	Y	Y	Y	Y	N
4 Dowdy	Y	Y	Y	Y	N
5 Lott	Y	N	Y	N	N
MISSOURI					
1 Clay	?	?	?	?	Y
2 Young	Y	Y	Y	Y	Y
3 Gephardt	?	Y	Y	Y	Y
4 Skelton	Y	Y	Y	?	Y
5 Wheat	Y	Y	Y	Y	Y
6 Coleman	Y	Y	Y	N	N
7 Taylor	Y	N	Y	N	N
8 Emerson	Y	N	N	N	N
9 Volkmer	Y	Y	Y	Y	Y
MONTANA					
1 Williams	Y	?	?	?	N
2 Marlenee	?	Y	Y	N	N
NEBRASKA					
1 Bereuter	Y	Y	Y	N	N
2 Daub	Y	N	N	N	N
3 Smith	Y	N	Y	N	N
NEVADA					
1 Reid	Y	Y	Y	Y	N
2 Vucanovich	Y	Y	N	N	N
NEW HAMPSHIRE					
1 D'Amours	Y	Y	Y	Y	Y
2 Gregg	Y	N	N	N	N
NEW JERSEY					
1 Florio	Y	Y	Y	Y	Y
2 Hughes	Y	Y	Y	Y	Y
3 Howard	Y	Y	Y	Y	Y
4 Smith	Y	Y	Y	Y	Y
5 Roukema	Y	?	?	?	N
6 Dwyer	Y	Y	Y	Y	Y
7 Rinaldo	Y	Y	Y	Y	Y
8 Roe	Y	Y	?	Y	Y
9 Torricelli	Y	Y	Y	Y	Y
10 Rodino	Y	Y	Y	Y	Y
11 Minish	Y	Y	Y	Y	Y
12 Courter	Y	Y	Y	Y	Y
13 Vacancy					
14 Guarini	Y	Y	Y	?	Y
NEW MEXICO					
1 Lujan	Y	Y	Y	Y	N
2 Skeen	Y	N	N	Y	N
3 Richardson	Y	Y	Y	Y	N
NEW YORK					
1 Carney	Y	N	N	Y	N
2 Downey	Y	Y	Y	Y	Y
3 Mrazek	Y	Y	Y	Y	Y
4 Lent	Y	N	N	N	N
5 McGrath	Y	N	N	N	N
6 Addabbo	Y	Y	?	Y	Y
7 Ackerman	Y	Y	Y	Y	Y
8 Scheuer	Y	Y	Y	Y	Y
9 Ferraro	Y	Y	Y	Y	Y
10 Schumer	Y	Y	Y	Y	Y
11 Towns	?	?	?	?	?
12 Owens	Y	Y	Y	Y	Y
13 Solarz	Y	Y	Y	Y	Y
14 Molinari	Y	Y	Y	Y	N
15 Green	Y	Y	Y	Y	N
16 Rangel	Y	Y	Y	Y	Y
17 Weiss	Y	Y	Y	Y	Y
18 Garcia	Y	Y	Y	?	Y
19 Biaggi	Y	Y	Y	Y	Y
20 Ottinger	Y	Y	Y	Y	Y
21 Fish	Y	Y	Y	Y	N
22 Gilman	Y	Y	Y	Y	N
23 Stratton	Y	Y	Y	Y	N
24 Solomon	Y	N	Y	N	N
25 Boehlert	Y	Y	Y	Y	N
26 Martin	Y	Y	Y	Y	N
27 Wortley	Y	Y	Y	Y	N
28 McHugh	Y	Y	Y	Y	Y
29 Horton	Y	Y	Y	?	N
30 Conable	Y	N	N	N	N
31 Kemp	Y	Y	Y	Y	N
32 LaFalce	Y	Y	?	Y	Y
33 Nowak	Y	Y	Y	Y	Y
34 Lundine	Y	Y	Y	Y	Y

	319	320	321	322	323
NORTH CAROLINA					
1 Jones	Y	?	?	?	Y
2 Valentine	Y	Y	Y	Y	N
3 Whitley	Y	Y	Y	Y	Y
4 Andrews	Y	Y	Y	Y	Y
5 Neal	Y	Y	Y	Y	?
6 Britt	Y	Y	Y	Y	Y
7 Rose	Y	Y	Y	Y	Y
8 Hefner	?	?	?	?	Y
9 Martin	Y	Y	Y	Y	?
10 Broyhill	Y	N	Y	N	N
11 Clarke	Y	Y	Y	Y	Y
NORTH DAKOTA					
AL Dorgan	Y	Y	Y	?	Y
OHIO					
1 Luken	Y	Y	Y	N	N
2 Gradison	Y	Y	Y	N	N
3 Hall	Y	Y	?	Y	Y
4 Oxley	Y	N	N	N	N
5 Latta	Y	N	N	N	N
6 McEwen	Y	N	N	N	?
7 DeWine	Y	Y	Y	Y	N
8 Kindness	Y	N	N	N	N
9 Kaptur	Y	Y	Y	Y	Y
10 Miller	Y	Y	Y	Y	N
11 Eckart	Y	Y	Y	Y	Y
12 Kasich	Y	N	N	Y	N
13 Pease	Y	Y	Y	Y	Y
14 Seiberling	Y	Y	Y	?	Y
15 Wylie	Y	Y	Y	Y	Y
16 Regula	Y	N	Y	N	N
17 Williams	?	Y	?	?	N
18 Applegate	Y	N	?	Y	Y
19 Feighan	Y	Y	Y	Y	Y
20 Oakar	Y	Y	Y	Y	Y
21 Stokes	Y	Y	Y	Y	Y
OKLAHOMA					
1 Jones	Y	N	Y	Y	N
2 Synar	Y	Y	Y	?	Y
3 Watkins	Y	Y	Y	Y	Y
4 McCurdy	Y	Y	Y	Y	Y
5 Edwards	Y	N	Y	?	N
6 English	Y	N	Y	Y	Y
OREGON					
1 AuCoin	Y	Y	Y	Y	Y
2 Smith, R.	Y	Y	Y	Y	N
3 Wyden	Y	Y	Y	Y	Y
4 Weaver	Y	Y	?	?	Y
5 Smith, D.	Y	N	N	N	N
PENNSYLVANIA					
1 Foglietta	Y	Y	Y	Y	Y
2 Gray	Y	Y	Y	Y	Y
3 Borski	Y	Y	Y	Y	Y
4 Kolter	Y	Y	Y	Y	N
5 Schulze	Y	Y	Y	Y	N
6 Yatron	Y	Y	Y	Y	Y
7 Edgar	Y	Y	Y	Y	Y
8 Kostmayer	Y	Y	Y	Y	Y
9 Shuster	Y	N	N	Y	N
10 McDade	Y	Y	Y	Y	N
11 Harrison	Y	Y	Y	Y	?
12 Murtha	Y	Y	?	Y	Y
13 Coughlin	Y	Y	Y	Y	Y
14 Coyne	Y	Y	Y	Y	Y
15 Ritter	Y	N	Y	Y	N
16 Walker	Y	N	N	N	N
17 Gekas	Y	N	Y	N	N
18 Walgren	Y	Y	Y	Y	Y
19 Goodling	Y	N	Y	N	N
20 Gaydos	Y	Y	?	Y	Y
21 Ridge	Y	Y	?	?	N
22 Murphy	Y	Y	Y	Y	Y
23 Clinger	Y	Y	Y	Y	N
RHODE ISLAND					
1 St Germain	Y	Y	Y	Y	Y
2 Schneider	Y	Y	Y	Y	N
SOUTH CAROLINA					
1 Hartnett	Y	N	N	Y	N
2 Spence	Y	Y	Y	Y	N
3 Derrick	Y	Y	Y	Y	Y
4 Campbell	Y	N	Y	Y	N
5 Spratt	Y	Y	Y	Y	Y
6 Tallon	Y	Y	Y	Y	Y
SOUTH DAKOTA					
AL Daschle	Y	Y	Y	?	Y

	319	320	322	323
TENNESSEE				
1 Quillen	Y	N	N	Y	N
2 Duncan	Y	Y	Y	Y	N
3 Lloyd	Y	Y	Y	Y	N
4 Cooper	Y	Y	Y	Y	N
5 Boner	?	Y	Y	Y	Y
6 Gore	Y	Y	Y	Y	Y
7 Sundquist	Y	N	Y	Y	N
8 Jones	Y	Y	?	?	Y
9 Ford	Y	Y	Y	Y	Y
TEXAS					
1 Hall, S.	Y	N	Y	Y	N
2 Wilson	Y	Y	Y	?	?
3 Bartlett	Y	N	N	Y	N
4 Hall, R.	Y	Y	Y	Y	N
5 Bryant	Y	Y	Y	Y	Y
6 Gramm	Y	N	N	N	N
7 Archer	Y	N	N	N	N
8 Fields	Y	N	N	N	N
9 Brooks	Y	Y	?	Y	Y
10 Pickle	Y	Y	Y	Y	Y
11 Leath	Y	?	?	?	N
12 Wright	Y	Y	Y	?	Y
13 Hightower	Y	Y	Y	Y	N
14 Patman	Y	Y	Y	Y	N
15 de la Garza	Y	Y	Y	Y	N
16 Coleman	Y	Y	Y	Y	Y
17 Stenholm	Y	N	Y	Y	N
18 Leland	Y	Y	Y	Y	Y
19 Hance	Y	Y	Y	Y	Y
20 Gonzalez	Y	Y	Y	Y	Y
21 Loeffler	Y	N	N	N	N
22 Paul	Y	N	N	N	?
23 Kazen	Y	Y	Y	Y	N
24 Frost	Y	Y	Y	Y	Y
25 Andrews	Y	Y	Y	Y	Y
26 Vandergriff	Y	N	Y	N	N
27 Ortiz	Y	Y	Y	Y	Y
UTAH					
1 Hansen	Y	N	N	N	N
2 Marriott	?	?	?	?	?
3 Nielson	Y	N	Y	N	N
VERMONT					
AL Jeffords	Y	Y	Y	Y	N
VIRGINIA					
1 Bateman	Y	Y	Y	Y	N
2 Whitehurst	Y	Y	Y	?	N
3 Bliley	Y	N	Y	Y	N
4 Sisisky	Y	Y	Y	Y	Y
5 Daniel	Y	N	Y	Y	N
6 Olin	Y	Y	Y	Y	N
7 Robinson	Y	N	N	Y	N
8 Parris	Y	N	?	?	N
9 Boucher	Y	Y	Y	Y	Y
10 Wolf	Y	Y	N	Y	N
WASHINGTON					
1 Pritchard	?	?	?	?	?
2 Swift	Y	Y	Y	Y	Y
3 Bonker	Y	Y	Y	Y	Y
4 Morrison	Y	Y	N	?	N
5 Foley	Y	Y	Y	Y	Y
6 Dicks	Y	Y	Y	Y	Y
7 Lowry	Y	Y	Y	Y	Y
8 Chandler	Y	Y	N	N	N
WEST VIRGINIA					
1 Mollohan	Y	Y	Y	Y	N
2 Staggers	Y	Y	Y	Y	Y
3 Wise	Y	Y	Y	Y	N
4 Rahall	Y	Y	Y	Y	N
WISCONSIN					
1 Aspin	Y	Y	Y	Y	Y
2 Kastenmeier	Y	Y	Y	Y	Y
3 Gunderson	Y	N	Y	N	N
4 Kleczka	Y	Y	Y	Y	Y
5 Moody	Y	Y	Y	Y	Y
6 Petri	Y	N	N	N	N
7 Obey	Y	Y	Y	Y	Y
8 Roth	Y	Y	Y	Y	N
9 Sensenbrenner	Y	N	N	N	N
WYOMING					
AL Cheney	Y	N	N	Y	N

Southern states - Ala., Ark., Fla., Ga., Ky., La., Miss., N.C., Okla., S.C., Tenn., Texas, Va.

324. HR 5640. Superfund Expansion. Sawyer, R-Mich., amendment to delete from the bill a section giving citizens the right to sue in federal court for damages caused by hazardous waste dumping. Adopted 208-200: R 135-22; D 73-178 (ND 23-146, SD 50-32), Aug. 9, 1984.

325. HR 5640. Superfund Expansion. Sawyer, R-Mich., amendment to delete from the bill provisions giving citizens the right to sue in federal court to compel a federal, state or local agency to perform a duty required under the superfund law. Rejected 141-248: R 105-49; D 36-199 (ND 10-151, SD 26-48), Aug. 10, 1984.

326. HR 5640. Superfund Expansion. Florio, D-N.J., amendment to limit to persons with interests adversely affected the right to sue for performance of a duty under the superfund law. Adopted 391-0: R 152-0; D 239-0 (ND 163-0, SD 76-0), Aug. 10, 1984.

327. HR 6040. Supplemental Appropriations, Fiscal 1984. Adoption of the conference report on the bill appropriating supplemental funds for fiscal 1984. Adopted 312-85: R 88-67; D 224-18 (ND 152-13, SD 72-5), Aug. 10, 1984. As cleared, the bill provided $6,176,745,000. The president had requested $5,953,340,170.

328. HR 6040. Supplemental Appropriations, Fiscal 1984. Long, D-Md., motion that the House recede from its disagreement to the Senate amendment appropriating supplemental foreign aid funds with a Long amendment that the House substitute reduced funds for Central America. The Senate included $116.9 million in military funds to El Salvador while the Long amendment would have reduced that to $40 million. Motion rejected 57-340: R 5-149; D 52-191 (ND 38-129, SD 14-62), Aug. 10, 1984.

329. HR 6040. Supplemental Appropriations, Fiscal 1984. Kemp, R-N.Y., motion that the House recede from its disagreement to the Senate amendment appropriating supplemental foreign aid funds with a Kemp amendment that the House adopt revised funds for Central America. The Kemp amendment contained $70 million in military funds to El Salvador. Motion agreed to 234-161: R 146-7; D 88-154 (ND 24-142, SD 64-12), Aug. 10, 1984.

330. HR 6040. Supplemental Appropriations, Fiscal 1984. Whitten, D-Miss., motion that the House insist on its disagreement with the Senate over a provision concerning the U.S. Postal Service. The House position would prohibit the Postal Service from hiring new employees at lower wages than those received by current employees. Motion agreed to 378-1: R 142-1; D 236-0 (ND 161-0, SD 75-0), Aug. 10, 1984.

331. HR 5640. Superfund Expansion. Levitas, D-Ga., amendment to create an administrative mechanism for compensating individuals harmed by exposure to hazardous wastes and to set aside 12 percent of the "superfund" for that purpose. Rejected 159-200: R 21-117; D 138-83 (ND 124-29, SD 14-54), Aug. 10, 1984.

KEY

Y	Voted for (yea).
#	Paired for.
+	Announced for.
N	Voted against (nay).
X	Paired against.
-	Announced against.
P	Voted "present".
C	Voted "present" to avoid possible conflict of interest.
?	Did not vote or otherwise make a position known.

Democrats *Republicans*

	324	325	326	327	328	329	330	331
ALABAMA								
1 *Edwards*	Y	Y	Y	Y	N	Y	Y	N
2 *Dickinson*	Y	Y	Y	Y	N	Y	Y	N
3 Nichols	Y	Y	Y	Y	N	Y	Y	?
4 Bevill	Y	Y	Y	Y	N	Y	Y	N
5 Flippo	Y	Y	Y	Y	N	Y	Y	N
6 Erdreich	Y	Y	Y	Y	N	Y	Y	N
7 Shelby	?	?	?	?	?	?	?	?
ALASKA								
AL *Young*	Y	Y	Y	Y	N	Y	Y	N
ARIZONA								
1 *McCain*	Y	Y	Y	Y	N	Y	Y	N
2 Udall	N	N	Y	Y	Y	Y	Y	?
3 *Stump*	Y	Y	Y	N	Y	Y	Y	N
4 *Rudd*	Y	Y	Y	Y	?	?	?	?
5 McNulty	Y	N	Y	Y	N	N	Y	Y
ARKANSAS								
1 Alexander	N	?	?	?	?	?	?	?
2 Bethune	?	?	?	?	?	?	?	?
3 *Hammerschmidt*	Y	Y	Y	Y	N	Y	Y	N
4 Anthony	?	N	Y	Y	N	N	Y	N
CALIFORNIA								
1 Bosco	Y	Y	Y	Y	N	Y	Y	?
2 *Chappie*	Y	Y	Y	Y	N	Y	Y	N
3 Matsui	N	N	Y	Y	N	N	Y	Y
4 Fazio	N	N	Y	Y	N	N	Y	Y
5 Burton	?	N	Y	Y	N	N	Y	Y
6 Boxer	N	N	Y	Y	N	N	Y	Y
7 Miller	N	N	Y	Y	N	N	Y	Y
8 Dellums	N	N	Y	Y	N	N	Y	Y
9 Stark	N	N	Y	Y	N	N	Y	Y
10 Edwards	N	N	Y	Y	N	N	Y	Y
11 Lantos	N	N	Y	Y	N	N	Y	Y
12 *Zschau*	Y	Y	Y	N	Y	N	Y	N
13 Mineta	N	N	Y	Y	N	N	Y	Y
14 *Shumway*	Y	Y	Y	N	Y	?	N
15 Coelho	N	N	?	Y	N	N	Y	Y
16 Panetta	N	N	Y	Y	N	N	Y	Y
17 *Pashayan*	Y	Y	Y	N	Y	N	Y	N
18 Lehman	N	N	Y	Y	N	N	Y	Y
19 *Lagomarsino*	Y	N	Y	N	Y	N	Y	N
20 *Thomas*	?	Y	Y	N	Y	N	Y	N
21 *Fiedler*	Y	N	Y	N	Y	Y	Y	N
22 *Moorhead*	Y	Y	Y	N	Y	?	?
23 Beilenson	Y	?	?	Y	N	N	Y	Y
24 Waxman	N	?	?	Y	N	N	Y	Y
25 Roybal	N	N	Y	Y	N	N	Y	Y
26 Berman	N	?	Y	Y	N	N	Y	Y
27 Levine	N	N	Y	Y	N	N	Y	+
28 Dixon	N	N	Y	Y	N	N	?	?
29 Hawkins	N	N	Y	Y	N	N	Y	?
30 Martinez	N	N	Y	?	N	N	Y	Y
31 Dymally	N	N	Y	Y	N	N	Y	Y
32 Anderson	N	N	Y	Y	Y	N	Y	Y
33 *Dreier*	Y	Y	Y	N	Y	Y	Y	N
34 Torres	N	N	Y	Y	N	N	Y	Y
35 *Lewis*	Y	#	Y	N	N	Y	Y	N
36 Brown	N	N	Y	Y	N	N	Y	Y
37 *McCandless*	Y	Y	Y	N	Y	Y	Y	N
38 Patterson	N	N	Y	?	N	N	Y	Y
39 *Dannemeyer*	Y	Y	Y	N	Y	Y	Y	N
40 *Badham*	Y	#	?	?	?	?	?	?
41 *Lowery*	Y	?	?	Y	N	Y	Y	N
42 *Lungren*	Y	Y	Y	N	Y	N	Y	N

	324	325	326	327	328	329	330	331
43 *Packard*	Y	Y	Y	N	Y	N	Y	N
44 Bates	N	N	Y	Y	N	N	Y	Y
45 *Hunter*	Y	Y	Y	Y	N	Y	Y	N
COLORADO								
1 Schroeder	N	N	Y	N	N	N	Y	Y
2 Wirth	N	N	Y	Y	N	N	Y	Y
3 Kogovsek	N	N	Y	Y	N	N	Y	Y
4 *Brown*	Y	Y	Y	N	Y	N	Y	N
5 *Kramer*	Y	Y	Y	N	Y	Y	Y	N
6 *Schaefer*	Y	Y	Y	N	Y	N	Y	N
CONNECTICUT								
1 Kennelly	Y	N	Y	Y	N	N	Y	Y
2 Gejdenson	N	N	Y	Y	Y	N	Y	Y
3 Morrison	Y	N	Y	Y	N	N	Y	Y
4 *McKinney*	N	N	Y	Y	N	Y	Y	N
5 Ratchford	N	N	Y	Y	N	Y	Y	Y
6 *Johnson*	Y	N	Y	Y	N	Y	Y	N
DELAWARE								
AL Carper	N	N	Y	Y	N	Y	N	Y
FLORIDA								
1 Hutto	Y	Y	Y	Y	N	Y	Y	N
2 Fuqua	Y	X	?	?	?	#	?	?
3 Bennett	Y	N	Y	Y	N	Y	Y	Y
4 Chappell	Y	Y	Y	Y	N	Y	Y	N
5 *McCollum*	Y	Y	Y	N	Y	Y	Y	N
6 MacKay	N	N	Y	N	Y	Y	Y	?
7 Gibbons	N	N	?	Y	N	Y	Y	N
8 *Young*	Y	N	Y	N	Y	Y	Y	N
9 *Bilirakis*	Y	Y	Y	N	Y	Y	Y	Y
10 *Ireland*	Y	Y	Y	N	Y	Y	Y	N
11 Nelson	Y	Y	Y	Y	N	Y	Y	N
12 *Lewis*	Y	Y	Y	N	Y	Y	Y	N
13 *Mack*	Y	Y	Y	N	Y	Y	Y	N
14 Mica	Y	N	Y	N	Y	Y	Y	Y
15 *Shaw*	Y	Y	Y	N	Y	Y	Y	N
16 Smith	N	N	Y	N	Y	Y	Y	?
17 Lehman	N	N	Y	Y	N	Y	N	?
18 Pepper	N	N	Y	Y	N	Y	Y	?
19 Fascell	N	N	Y	Y	N	Y	Y	?
GEORGIA								
1 Thomas	N	N	Y	N	Y	Y	Y	Y
2 Hatcher	?	?	?	?	?	?	?	?
3 Ray	Y	Y	Y	Y	N	Y	Y	N
4 Levitas	N	N	Y	Y	N	Y	Y	Y
5 Fowler	N	N	Y	Y	N	N	Y	Y
6 *Gingrich*	Y	Y	Y	N	N	Y	Y	N
7 Darden	N	Y	Y	N	Y	N	Y	N
8 Rowland	N	Y	Y	N	Y	Y	Y	N
9 Jenkins	Y	Y	Y	Y	N	Y	Y	Y
10 Barnard	N	Y	Y	N	Y	Y	Y	N
HAWAII								
1 Heftel	Y	?	?	Y	N	N	Y	Y
2 Akaka	N	N	Y	Y	N	N	Y	Y
IDAHO								
1 *Craig*	Y	Y	Y	N	Y	N	?	N
2 *Hansen*	?	?	?	N	N	Y	N	N
ILLINOIS								
1 Hayes	N	N	Y	N	N	N	Y	Y
2 Savage	N	N	Y	N	N	N	Y	Y
3 Russo	N	N	Y	N	N	N	Y	Y
4 *O'Brien*	Y	Y	Y	N	N	Y	Y	N
5 Lipinski	N	?	?	?	?	?	?	?
6 *Hyde*	Y	Y	?	Y	N	Y	Y	N
7 Collins	N	N	Y	N	N	N	Y	Y
8 Rostenkowski	N	N	Y	Y	N	N	Y	Y
9 Yates	N	N	Y	Y	N	N	Y	Y
10 *Porter*	Y	N	Y	N	N	Y	Y	Y
11 Annunzio	N	N	Y	Y	N	Y	Y	Y
12 *Crane, P.*	Y	Y	Y	N	N	Y	?	Y
13 *Erlenborn*	Y	Y	Y	N	Y	Y	?	?
14 *Corcoran*	Y	Y	?	Y	N	Y	Y	N
15 *Madigan*	N	N	Y	N	N	Y	Y	N
16 *Martin*	Y	N	Y	N	Y	Y	Y	N
17 Evans	N	N	Y	N	N	Y	Y	Y
18 *Michel*	Y	Y	Y	N	Y	Y	Y	N
19 *Crane, D.*	Y	Y	Y	N	N	Y	Y	N
20 Durbin	N	N	Y	Y	N	N	Y	Y
21 Price	N	N	Y	Y	N	Y	Y	Y
22 Simon	?	?	?	?	?	?	?	?
INDIANA								
1 Hall	N	N	Y	Y	N	N	Y	Y
2 Sharp	N	N	Y	Y	N	Y	Y	Y
3 *Hiler*	Y	Y	Y	N	Y	#	Y	N
4 *Coats*	Y	Y	Y	N	Y	Y	Y	N
5 *Hillis*	Y	Y	Y	Y	N	Y	Y	?

ND - Northern Democrats   SD - Southern Democrats

Corresponding to Congressional Record Votes 363, 365, 366, 367, 368, 369, 370, 371

	324	325	326	327	328	329	330	331
6 ***Burton***	Y	Y	Y	N	N	Y	Y	?
7 ***Myers***	Y	Y	Y	Y	N	Y	Y	N
8 McCloskey	N	N	Y	Y	N	N	Y	N
9 Hamilton	N	N	Y	Y	Y	Y	Y	N
10 Jacobs	N	N	Y	Y	N	N	Y	Y
IOWA								
1 ***Leach***	Y	N	Y	N	Y	N	Y	Y
2 ***Tauke***	Y	Y	Y	N	Y	Y	Y	?
3 ***Evans***	Y	N	Y	N	Y	Y	Y	Y
4 Smith	N	N	Y	Y	Y	N	Y	Y
5 Harkin	N	N	Y	Y	N	N	Y	Y
6 Bedell	N	N	Y	Y	Y	N	Y	?
KANSAS								
1 ***Roberts***	Y	Y	Y	N	N	Y	Y	N
2 Slattery	Y	N	Y	N	Y	Y	Y	N
3 ***Winn***	Y	Y	Y	Y	N	Y	Y	N
4 Glickman	Y	N	Y	Y	Y	Y	Y	Y
5 ***Whittaker***	Y	Y	Y	N	N	#	?	?
KENTUCKY								
1 Hubbard	Y	N	Y	N	N	Y	Y	N
2 Natcher	Y	N	Y	Y	Y	N	Y	N
3 Mazzoli	Y	Y	Y	Y	Y	N	Y	N
4 ***Snyder***	Y	#	?	?	?	?	?	?
5 ***Rogers***	Y	Y	Y	Y	N	Y	Y	N
6 ***Hopkins***	Y	Y	Y	Y	N	N	Y	N
7 Vacancy								
LOUISIANA								
1 ***Livingston***	Y	Y	Y	Y	N	Y	Y	N
2 Boggs	N	N	Y	Y	N	Y	Y	?
3 Tauzin	Y	N	Y	Y	N	Y	Y	N
4 Roemer	Y	N	Y	Y	N	Y	Y	N
5 Huckaby	Y	Y	Y	Y	N	Y	Y	N
6 ***Moore***	Y	Y	Y	Y	N	Y	Y	N
7 Breaux	Y	N	Y	Y	N	Y	Y	N
8 Long	Y	N	Y	Y	N	Y	Y	N
MAINE								
1 ***McKernan***	N	N	Y	Y	N	Y	Y	Y
2 ***Snowe***	N	N	Y	Y	N	Y	Y	Y
MARYLAND								
1 Dyson	Y	N	Y	Y	N	Y	Y	N
2 Long	N	?	Y	N	Y	N	Y	Y
3 Mikulski	N	N	Y	Y	N	N	Y	Y
4 ***Holt***	Y	N	Y	Y	N	Y	Y	N
5 Hoyer	?	N	Y	Y	Y	N	Y	Y
6 Byron	Y	Y	Y	Y	N	Y	Y	N
7 Mitchell	N	N	Y	Y	N	N	Y	Y
8 Barnes	N	N	Y	Y	Y	N	Y	Y
MASSACHUSETTS								
1 ***Conte***	N	N	Y	Y	N	N	Y	Y
2 Boland	N	N	Y	Y	N	Y	Y	Y
3 Early	N	?	?	?	?	?	?	?
4 Frank	N	N	Y	Y	N	N	Y	Y
5 Shannon	N	?	?	?	N	N	?	?
6 Mavroules	N	N	Y	Y	N	N	Y	Y
7 Markey	N	N	Y	Y	N	N	Y	Y
8 O'Neill								
9 Moakley	N	N	Y	Y	N	N	Y	Y
10 Studds	N	N	Y	Y	N	N	Y	Y
11 Donnelly	N	N	Y	Y	N	N	Y	Y
MICHIGAN								
1 Conyers	N	N	Y	Y	N	N	Y	Y
2 ***Pursell***	?	?	?	?	?	?	?	?
3 Wolpe	N	N	Y	Y	N	N	Y	Y
4 ***Siljander***	Y	Y	Y	N	N	Y	?	N
5 ***Sawyer***	Y	Y	Y	Y	N	Y	Y	N
6 Carr	N	N	Y	Y	N	N	Y	Y
7 Kildee	N	N	Y	Y	N	N	Y	Y
8 Traxler	N	?	?	?	?	X	?	?
9 ***Vander Jagt***	Y	Y	Y	Y	N	Y	Y	N
10 Albosta	N	N	Y	Y	N	N	Y	Y
11 ***Davis***	N	N	Y	Y	N	Y	?	?
12 Bonior	?	N	Y	Y	N	N	Y	N
13 Crockett	N	N	Y	Y	N	N	Y	N
14 Hertel	N	N	Y	N	N	N	Y	Y
15 Ford	N	N	Y	Y	Y	N	Y	N
16 Dingell	N	N	Y	Y	N	N	Y	N
17 Levin	N	N	Y	Y	Y	N	Y	N
18 ***Broomfield***	Y	Y	Y	Y	N	Y	Y	N
MINNESOTA								
1 Penny	N	N	Y	N	N	N	Y	Y
2 ***Weber***	N	N	Y	Y	N	Y	Y	Y
3 ***Frenzel***	Y	Y	Y	N	N	Y	+	N
4 Vento	N	N	Y	Y	N	N	Y	Y
5 Sabo	N	N	Y	Y	N	N	Y	Y
6 Sikorski	N	N	Y	Y	N	N	Y	Y
7 ***Stangeland***	Y	Y	Y	Y	N	Y	Y	N
8 Oberstar	N	N	Y	Y	N	N	Y	Y
MISSISSIPPI								
1 Whitten	Y	N	Y	Y	Y	N	Y	N
2 ***Franklin***	Y	Y	Y	Y	N	Y	Y	?
3 Montgomery	Y	Y	Y	Y	N	Y	Y	N
4 Dowdy	N	N	Y	Y	N	Y	Y	Y
5 ***Lott***	Y	Y	Y	Y	N	Y	?	?
MISSOURI								
1 Clay	N	N	Y	Y	N	N	Y	Y
2 Young	X	Y	Y	Y	N	Y	Y	Y
3 Gephardt	N	N	Y	?	N	?	?	?
4 Skelton	N	N	Y	Y	?	#	?	?
5 Wheat	N	N	Y	Y	N	N	Y	Y
6 ***Coleman***	Y	N	Y	Y	N	Y	Y	N
7 ***Taylor***	Y	Y	Y	Y	N	Y	Y	N
8 ***Emerson***	Y	Y	Y	Y	N	Y	Y	N
9 Volkmer	N	N	Y	Y	Y	N	Y	Y
MONTANA								
1 Williams	N	N	Y	Y	N	N	Y	Y
2 ***Marlenee***	Y	Y	Y	N	N	Y	Y	?
NEBRASKA								
1 ***Bereuter***	Y	Y	Y	Y	N	Y	Y	N
2 ***Daub***	Y	Y	Y	N	N	Y	Y	N
3 ***Smith***	Y	Y	Y	Y	N	Y	Y	N
NEVADA								
1 Reid	N	N	Y	Y	Y	Y	Y	Y
2 ***Vucanovich***	Y	Y	Y	N	N	Y	Y	N
NEW HAMPSHIRE								
1 D'Amours	N	N	Y	Y	Y	N	Y	Y
2 ***Gregg***	N	N	Y	Y	N	Y	Y	Y
NEW JERSEY								
1 Florio	N	N	Y	Y	N	N	Y	Y
2 Hughes	Y	N	Y	Y	Y	N	Y	N
3 Howard	N	X	?	?	?	X	?	?
4 ***Smith***	N	N	Y	Y	N	Y	Y	Y
5 ***Roukema***	Y	N	Y	Y	N	N	Y	N
6 Dwyer	N	N	Y	Y	Y	Y	Y	Y
7 ***Rinaldo***	N	N	Y	Y	N	Y	Y	Y
8 Roe	Y	N	Y	Y	N	N	Y	Y
9 Torricelli	N	N	Y	Y	N	N	Y	Y
10 Rodino	N	N	Y	Y	N	N	?	Y
11 Minish	N	N	Y	Y	N	Y	Y	Y
12 ***Courter***	Y	N	Y	N	N	Y	Y	N
13 Vacancy								
14 Guarini	N	N	Y	Y	Y	Y	Y	Y
NEW MEXICO								
1 ***Lujan***	Y	?	Y	Y	N	Y	Y	N
2 ***Skeen***	Y	Y	Y	N	N	Y	Y	N
3 Richardson	N	N	Y	Y	N	N	Y	Y
NEW YORK								
1 ***Carney***	Y	Y	Y	Y	N	Y	Y	N
2 Downey	N	N	Y	Y	N	N	Y	Y
3 Mrazek	N	N	Y	Y	N	N	Y	Y
4 ***Lent***	N	N	Y	Y	N	Y	Y	N
5 ***McGrath***	N	N	Y	N	N	Y	Y	N
6 Addabbo	N	N	Y	Y	N	N	Y	?
7 Ackerman	N	N	Y	Y	N	N	Y	Y
8 Scheuer	N	N	Y	Y	N	N	Y	Y
9 Ferraro	N	?	?	?	?	?	?	?
10 Schumer	?	N	Y	Y	N	N	Y	Y
11 Towns	N	X	?	?	?	X	?	?
12 Owens	N	N	Y	Y	N	N	Y	Y
13 Solarz	N	N	Y	Y	Y	N	Y	Y
14 ***Molinari***	N	N	Y	Y	N	Y	Y	Y
15 ***Green***	N	N	Y	Y	N	Y	Y	N
16 Rangel	N	N	Y	Y	N	N	Y	Y
17 Weiss	N	N	Y	Y	N	N	Y	Y
18 Garcia	N	X	?	?	?	X	?	?
19 Biaggi	N	Y	Y	Y	N	Y	Y	N
20 Ottinger	N	N	Y	Y	Y	N	Y	N
21 ***Fish***	Y	N	Y	Y	N	Y	Y	Y
22 ***Gilman***	N	N	Y	Y	N	Y	Y	Y
23 Stratton	Y	Y	Y	Y	N	Y	Y	N
24 ***Solomon***	Y	Y	Y	N	N	Y	Y	Y
25 ***Boehlert***	N	N	Y	Y	N	Y	Y	Y
26 ***Martin***	Y	N	Y	Y	N	Y	Y	?
27 ***Wortley***	Y	N	Y	Y	N	Y	Y	N
28 McHugh	N	N	Y	Y	Y	N	Y	Y
29 ***Horton***	N	N	Y	Y	N	Y	Y	N
30 ***Conable***	Y	Y	Y	N	N	Y	Y	N
31 ***Kemp***	Y	Y	Y	Y	N	Y	Y	N
32 LaFalce	N	N	Y	Y	N	Y	Y	Y
33 Nowak	N	N	Y	Y	Y	Y	?	?
34 Lundine	N	N	Y	Y	Y	N	?	?
NORTH CAROLINA								
1 Jones	Y	Y	Y	Y	N	N	Y	N
2 Valentine	Y	Y	Y	Y	N	Y	Y	N
3 Whitley	Y	N	Y	Y	N	Y	Y	N
4 Andrews	Y	N	Y	Y	N	Y	Y	N
5 Neal	N	?	?	?	?	?	?	?
6 Britt	Y	N	Y	Y	N	Y	Y	Y
7 Rose	Y	N	Y	Y	N	Y	Y	?
8 Hefner	Y	Y	Y	Y	N	Y	Y	N
9 ***Martin***	?	?	?	?	?	?	?	?
10 ***Broyhill***	Y	Y	Y	N	N	Y	Y	N
11 Clarke	?	?	?	?	?	?	?	?
NORTH DAKOTA								
AL Dorgan	N	N	Y	N	N	N	Y	N
OHIO								
1 Luken	Y	Y	Y	Y	N	N	Y	N
2 ***Gradison***	Y	Y	Y	N	N	Y	Y	N
3 Hall	N	N	Y	Y	N	N	Y	Y
4 ***Oxley***	Y	Y	Y	N	N	Y	Y	N
5 ***Latta***	Y	Y	Y	N	N	Y	Y	Y
6 ***McEwen***	#	#	?	?	?	#	?	?
7 ***DeWine***	Y	Y	Y	N	N	Y	Y	N
8 ***Kindness***	Y	Y	Y	N	N	Y	Y	N
9 Kaptur	N	N	Y	Y	N	N	Y	?
10 ***Miller***	Y	Y	Y	Y	N	N	Y	N
11 Eckart	N	N	Y	Y	N	N	Y	Y
12 ***Kasich***	Y	N	Y	Y	N	Y	Y	N
13 Pease	Y	N	Y	Y	Y	N	Y	N
14 Seiberling	N	N	Y	Y	N	N	Y	Y
15 ***Wylie***	Y	Y	Y	Y	N	Y	Y	N
16 ***Regula***	Y	N	Y	Y	N	Y	Y	N
17 ***Williams***	?	N	Y	Y	N	Y	Y	?
18 Applegate	Y	Y	Y	Y	N	N	Y	Y
19 Feighan	N	N	Y	Y	N	N	Y	Y
20 Oakar	N	N	Y	Y	N	N	Y	Y
21 Stokes	N	N	Y	Y	N	N	Y	Y
OKLAHOMA								
1 Jones	Y	N	Y	Y	N	Y	Y	N
2 Synar	Y	N	Y	Y	Y	N	Y	N
3 Watkins	Y	N	Y	Y	N	Y	Y	N
4 McCurdy	Y	?	?	?	?	?	?	?
5 ***Edwards***	Y	Y	Y	N	N	Y	Y	N
6 English	Y	N	Y	Y	N	Y	Y	N
OREGON								
1 AuCoin	N	N	Y	N	N	N	Y	Y
2 ***Smith, R.***	Y	Y	Y	?	?	?	?	?
3 Wyden	N	N	Y	N	N	N	Y	Y
4 Weaver	N	N	Y	N	N	N	Y	Y
5 ***Smith, D.***	Y	Y	Y	N	N	Y	Y	N
PENNSYLVANIA								
1 Foglietta	N	N	Y	Y	N	N	Y	Y
2 Gray	N	?	?	Y	N	N	Y	Y
3 Borski	N	N	Y	Y	N	N	Y	N
4 Kolter	N	N	Y	Y	N	N	Y	Y
5 ***Schulze***	Y	Y	Y	N	Y	N	Y	N
6 Yatron	N	N	Y	Y	Y	N	Y	Y
7 Edgar	N	N	Y	N	N	N	Y	Y
8 Kostmayer	N	N	Y	Y	N	N	Y	Y
9 ***Shuster***	Y	Y	Y	N	N	Y	Y	N
10 ***McDade***	N	N	Y	Y	N	Y	Y	Y
11 Harrison	?	N	Y	Y	Y	N	Y	N
12 Murtha	Y	N	Y	Y	N	Y	Y	N
13 ***Coughlin***	N	N	Y	Y	N	Y	Y	N
14 Coyne	N	N	Y	Y	?	?	?	?
15 ***Ritter***	N	N	Y	N	N	Y	Y	N
16 ***Walker***	Y	Y	Y	N	N	Y	?	N
17 ***Gekas***	Y	Y	Y	N	N	Y	Y	N
18 Walgren	N	N	Y	Y	Y	N	Y	N
19 ***Goodling***	Y	N	Y	N	N	Y	Y	N
20 Gaydos	N	?	Y	Y	N	Y	Y	Y
21 ***Ridge***	Y	N	Y	Y	N	Y	Y	N
22 Murphy	Y	Y	Y	Y	N	N	Y	Y
23 ***Clinger***	Y	N	Y	Y	N	Y	Y	N
RHODE ISLAND								
1 St Germain	N	N	Y	Y	N	N	Y	Y
2 ***Schneider***	N	N	Y	Y	Y	Y	Y	Y
SOUTH CAROLINA								
1 ***Hartnett***	Y	Y	Y	N	N	Y	Y	?
2 ***Spence***	Y	Y	Y	N	N	Y	Y	N
3 Derrick	Y	N	Y	Y	Y	Y	Y	N
4 ***Campbell***	Y	Y	Y	Y	N	Y	Y	?
5 Spratt	Y	N	Y	Y	Y	Y	Y	N
6 Tallon	Y	Y	Y	Y	N	Y	Y	N
SOUTH DAKOTA								
AL Daschle	Y	N	Y	N	N	N	Y	?
TENNESSEE								
1 ***Quillen***	Y	Y	Y	?	?	?	?	?
2 ***Duncan***	Y	Y	Y	Y	N	Y	Y	N
3 Lloyd	Y	Y	Y	Y	N	Y	Y	N
4 Cooper	N	N	Y	Y	N	Y	Y	Y
5 Boner	N	N	Y	Y	N	Y	Y	?
6 Gore	N	?	Y	Y	N	Y	Y	N
7 ***Sundquist***	Y	Y	Y	Y	N	Y	Y	Y
8 Jones	N	N	Y	Y	N	N	Y	N
9 Ford	N	N	Y	?	N	N	Y	Y
TEXAS								
1 Hall, S.	?	?	?	?	?	#	?	?
2 Wilson	Y	?	?	Y	N	Y	Y	N
3 ***Bartlett***	Y	Y	Y	N	N	Y	Y	N
4 Hall, R.	N	N	Y	Y	N	Y	Y	N
5 Bryant	N	N	Y	Y	Y	X	Y	N
6 ***Gramm***	Y	N	Y	Y	N	Y	Y	N
7 ***Archer***	Y	Y	Y	N	N	Y	Y	N
8 ***Fields***	Y	N	Y	N	N	Y	Y	N
9 Brooks	Y	?	?	?	?	?	?	?
10 Pickle	Y	N	Y	Y	Y	Y	Y	N
11 Leath	Y	Y	Y	Y	N	Y	?	?
12 Wright	N	?	?	?	?	Y	Y	N
13 Hightower	Y	?	Y	Y	N	Y	Y	N
14 Patman	Y	N	Y	Y	N	Y	Y	N
15 de la Garza	N	N	Y	Y	?	?	?	?
16 Coleman	N	N	Y	Y	Y	N	Y	N
17 Stenholm	Y	Y	Y	Y	N	Y	Y	N
18 Leland	N	N	Y	Y	N	N	Y	Y
19 Hance	N	N	Y	Y	N	Y	Y	N
20 Gonzalez	N	N	Y	N	Y	N	Y	Y
21 ***Loeffler***	Y	Y	Y	N	N	Y	Y	?
22 ***Paul***	Y	Y	?	N	N	N	N	N
23 Kazen	Y	Y	Y	Y	N	Y	Y	N
24 Frost	N	N	Y	Y	Y	Y	Y	Y
25 Andrews	Y	N	Y	Y	N	Y	Y	N
26 Vandergriff	Y	Y	Y	N	N	Y	Y	Y
27 Ortiz	N	N	Y	Y	N	Y	Y	Y
UTAH								
1 ***Hansen***	Y	Y	Y	N	N	Y	Y	N
2 ***Marriott***	?	?	?	?	?	?	?	?
3 ***Nielson***	Y	Y	Y	N	N	Y	Y	N
VERMONT								
AL ***Jeffords***	N	N	?	?	?	?	?	?
VIRGINIA								
1 ***Bateman***	?	?	?	?	?	?	?	?
2 ***Whitehurst***	Y	Y	Y	Y	N	Y	Y	?
3 ***Bliley***	Y	Y	Y	Y	N	Y	Y	N
4 Sisisky	Y	Y	Y	Y	N	Y	Y	N
5 Daniel	Y	Y	Y	Y	N	Y	Y	N
6 Olin	?	Y	Y	N	N	Y	Y	N
7 ***Robinson***	Y	Y	Y	Y	N	Y	Y	N
8 ***Parris***	Y	Y	Y	Y	N	Y	Y	N
9 Boucher	N	?	Y	Y	?	?	?	?
10 ***Wolf***	Y	N	Y	Y	N	Y	Y	N
WASHINGTON								
1 ***Pritchard***	?	?	?	?	?	?	?	?
2 Swift	N	N	Y	Y	N	N	Y	N
3 Bonker	N	N	Y	Y	N	N	Y	Y
4 ***Morrison***	Y	Y	Y	Y	N	Y	Y	N
5 Foley	Y	Y	Y	Y	Y	N	Y	N
6 Dicks	N	N	Y	Y	Y	N	Y	N
7 Lowry	N	N	Y	Y	N	N	Y	Y
8 ***Chandler***	Y	Y	Y	Y	N	Y	Y	N
WEST VIRGINIA								
1 Mollohan	Y	Y	Y	Y	N	Y	Y	N
2 Staggers	N	N	Y	Y	N	N	Y	N
3 Wise	N	N	Y	Y	N	Y	Y	N
4 Rahall	?	N	Y	Y	N	N	Y	Y
WISCONSIN								
1 Aspin	N	N	Y	Y	N	Y	Y	Y
2 Kastenmeier	N	N	Y	Y	Y	N	Y	Y
3 ***Gunderson***	Y	Y	Y	Y	N	Y	Y	N
4 Kleczka	Y	N	Y	Y	Y	N	Y	Y
5 Moody	N	N	Y	Y	N	N	Y	Y
6 ***Petri***	Y	N	Y	Y	N	Y	Y	Y
7 Obey	N	N	Y	N	Y	N	Y	Y
8 ***Roth***	Y	N	Y	Y	N	Y	Y	N
9 ***Sensenbrenner***	Y	N	Y	N	N	Y	Y	Y
WYOMING								
AL ***Cheney***	Y	Y	Y	N	N	Y	Y	N

Southern states - Ala., Ark., Fla., Ga., Ky., La., Miss., N.C., Okla., S.C., Tenn., Texas, Va.

KEY

Y Voted for (yea).
\# Paired for.
\+ Announced for.
N Voted against (nay).
X Paired against.
- Announced against.
P Voted "present".
C Voted "present" to avoid possible conflict of interest.
? Did not vote or otherwise make a position known.

Democrats *Republicans*

332. HR 5640. Superfund Expansion. Conable, R-N.Y., amendment to terminate on Sept. 30, 1986 (instead of Sept. 30, 1990), the taxes imposed under the bill. Rejected 142-205: R 102-32; D 40-173 (ND 13-133, SD 27-40), Aug. 10, 1984.

333. HR 5640. Superfund Expansion. Passage of the bill to renew for fiscal 1986-90 and expand the "superfund" hazardous waste cleanup program. Passed 323-33: R 107-30; D 216-3 (ND 152-0, SD 64-3), Aug. 10, 1984. A "nay" was a vote supporting the president's position.

	332	333
ALABAMA		
1 *Edwards*	Y	Y
2 *Dickinson*	Y	Y
3 Nichols	?	?
4 Bevill	N	Y
5 Flippo	N	Y
6 Erdreich	N	Y
7 Shelby	?	?
ALASKA		
AL *Young*	Y	N
ARIZONA		
1 *McCain*	\#	?
2 Udall	?	?
3 *Stump*	Y	N
4 *Rudd*	\#	?
5 McNulty	N	Y
ARKANSAS		
1 Alexander	?	?
2 *Bethune*	?	?
3 *Hammerschmidt*	Y	N
4 Anthony	N	Y
CALIFORNIA		
1 Bosco	Y	Y
2 *Chappie*	Y	Y
3 Matsui	N	Y
4 Fazio	N	Y
5 Burton	N	Y
6 Boxer	N	Y
7 Miller	N	Y
8 Dellums	N	Y
9 Stark	N	Y
10 Edwards	N	Y
11 Lantos	N	Y
12 *Zschau*	N	Y
13 Mineta	N	Y
14 *Shumway*	Y	N
15 Coelho	N	Y
16 Panetta	N	Y
17 *Pashayan*	Y	Y
18 Lehman	N	Y
19 *Lagomarsino*	N	Y
20 *Thomas*	Y	Y
21 *Fiedler*	N	Y
22 *Moorhead*	?	?
23 Beilenson	N	Y
24 Waxman	N	Y
25 Roybal	N	Y
26 Berman	N	Y
27 Levine	-	+
28 Dixon	X	?
29 Hawkins	?	?
30 Martinez	N	Y
31 Dymally	N	Y
32 Anderson	N	Y
33 *Dreier*	Y	Y
34 Torres	N	Y
35 *Lewis*	Y	N
36 Brown	N	Y
37 *McCandless*	Y	Y
38 Patterson	Y	Y
39 *Dannemeyer*	Y	N
40 *Badham*	\#	?
41 *Lowery*	Y	Y
42 *Lungren*	Y	Y

	332	333
43 *Packard*	Y	Y
44 Bates	N	Y
45 *Hunter*	Y	N
COLORADO		
1 Schroeder	?	?
2 Wirth	N	Y
3 Kogovsek	N	Y
4 *Brown*	Y	Y
5 *Kramer*	Y	Y
6 *Schaefer*	Y	Y
CONNECTICUT		
1 Kennelly	N	Y
2 Gejdenson	N	Y
3 Morrison	N	Y
4 *McKinney*	?	Y
5 Ratchford	N	Y
6 *Johnson*	Y	Y
DELAWARE		
AL Carper	Y	Y
FLORIDA		
1 Hutto	Y	Y
2 Fuqua	X	?
3 Bennett	N	Y
4 Chappell	N	Y
5 *McCollum*	Y	Y
6 MacKay	X	?
7 Gibbons	N	Y
8 *Young*	Y	Y
9 *Bilirakis*	N	Y
10 *Ireland*	Y	Y
11 Nelson	N	Y
12 *Lewis*	N	Y
13 *Mack*	Y	N
14 Mica	N	Y
15 *Shaw*	Y	Y
16 Smith	?	?
17 Lehman	?	?
18 Pepper	N	Y
19 Fascell	?	?
GEORGIA		
1 Thomas	N	Y
2 Hatcher	?	?
3 Ray	Y	Y
4 Levitas	Y	Y
5 Fowler	N	Y
6 *Gingrich*	Y	Y
7 Darden	Y	Y
8 Rowland	N	Y
9 Jenkins	N	Y
10 Barnard	Y	Y
HAWAII		
1 Heftel	N	Y
2 Akaka	N	Y
IDAHO		
1 *Craig*	Y	N
2 *Hansen*	?	N
ILLINOIS		
1 Hayes	N	Y
2 Savage	?	Y
3 Russo	N	Y
4 *O'Brien*	Y	Y
5 Lipinski	?	?
6 *Hyde*	Y	N
7 Collins	N	Y
8 Rostenkowski	?	?
9 Yates	N	Y
10 *Porter*	Y	Y
11 Annunzio	N	Y
12 *Crane, P.*	Y	N
13 *Erlenborn*	?	?
14 *Corcoran*	Y	N
15 *Madigan*	Y	Y
16 *Martin*	Y	Y
17 Evans	N	Y
18 *Michel*	Y	Y
19 *Crane, D.*	\#	?
20 Durbin	N	Y
21 Price	N	Y
22 Simon	?	?
INDIANA		
1 Hall	N	Y
2 Sharp	N	Y
3 *Hiler*	Y	Y
4 *Coats*	Y	Y
5 *Hillis*	?	?

ND - Northern Democrats   SD - Southern Democrats

	332	333
6 Burton	?	?
7 Myers	N	Y
8 McCloskey	N	Y
9 Hamilton	N	Y
10 Jacobs	N	Y
IOWA		
1 Leach	N	Y
2 Tauke	?	?
3 Evans	Y	Y
4 Smith	N	Y
5 Harkin	N	Y
6 Bedell	?	?
KANSAS		
1 Roberts	Y	N
2 Slattery	N	Y
3 Winn	Y	Y
4 Glickman	N	Y
5 Whittaker	#	?
KENTUCKY		
1 Hubbard	Y	Y
2 Natcher	N	Y
3 Mazzoli	N	Y
4 Snyder	?	?
5 Rogers	?	?
6 Hopkins	Y	Y
7 Vacancy		
LOUISIANA		
1 Livingston	Y	Y
2 Boggs	?	?
3 Tauzin	Y	Y
4 Roemer	N	Y
5 Huckaby	Y	Y
6 Moore	N	Y
7 Breaux	Y	Y
8 Long	Y	Y
MAINE		
1 McKernan	N	Y
2 Snowe	N	Y
MARYLAND		
1 Dyson	N	Y
2 Long	N	Y
3 Mikulski	N	Y
4 Holt	Y	Y
5 Hoyer	N	Y
6 Byron	Y	Y
7 Mitchell	N	Y
8 Barnes	N	Y
MASSACHUSETTS		
1 Conte	N	Y
2 Boland	?	Y
3 Early	?	?
4 Frank	N	Y
5 Shannon	X	Y
6 Mavroules	N	Y
7 Markey	N	Y
8 O'Neill		
9 Moakley	?	Y
10 Studds	N	Y
11 Donnelly	N	Y
MICHIGAN		
1 Conyers	N	Y
2 Pursell	?	?
3 Wolpe	N	Y
4 Siljander	Y	Y
5 Sawyer	Y	Y
6 Carr	?	Y
7 Kildee	N	Y
8 Traxler	?	?
9 Vander Jagt	Y	Y
10 Albosta	Y	Y
11 Davis	?	?
12 Bonior	N	Y
13 Crockett	?	?
14 Hertel	N	Y
15 Ford	N	Y
16 Dingell	N	Y
17 Levin	N	Y
18 Broomfield	Y	Y
MINNESOTA		
1 Penny	N	Y
2 Weber	N	Y
3 Frenzel	Y	Y
4 Vento	N	Y
5 Sabo	N	Y
6 Sikorski	N	Y

	332	333
7 Stangeland	Y	Y
8 Oberstar	N	Y
MISSISSIPPI		
1 Whitten	Y	Y
2 Franklin	?	Y
3 Montgomery	Y	Y
4 Dowdy	N	Y
5 Lott	#	?
MISSOURI		
1 Clay	N	Y
2 Young	N	Y
3 Gephardt	?	Y
4 Skelton	X	?
5 Wheat	N	Y
6 Coleman	Y	Y
7 Taylor	Y	N
8 Emerson	Y	Y
9 Volkmer	Y	Y
MONTANA		
1 Williams	N	Y
2 Marlenee	?	?
NEBRASKA		
1 Bereuter	Y	Y
2 Daub	Y	Y
3 Smith	Y	Y
NEVADA		
1 Reid	N	Y
2 Vucanovich	Y	N
NEW HAMPSHIRE		
1 D'Amours	N	Y
2 Gregg	Y	Y
NEW JERSEY		
1 Florio	N	Y
2 Hughes	N	Y
3 Howard	X	?
4 Smith	N	Y
5 Roukema	Y	Y
6 Dwyer	N	Y
7 Rinaldo	N	Y
8 Roe	N	Y
9 Torricelli	N	Y
10 Rodino	N	Y
11 Minish	N	Y
12 Courter	N	Y
13 Vacancy		
14 Guarini	N	Y
NEW MEXICO		
1 Lujan	Y	Y
2 Skeen	Y	Y
3 Richardson	N	Y
NEW YORK		
1 Carney	Y	Y
2 Downey	N	Y
3 Mrazek	N	Y
4 Lent	N	Y
5 McGrath	N	Y
6 Addabbo	X	?
7 Ackerman	N	Y
8 Scheuer	N	Y
9 Ferraro	?	?
10 Schumer	N	Y
11 Towns	X	Y
12 Owens	N	Y
13 Solarz	N	Y
14 Molinari	N	Y
15 Green	N	Y
16 Rangel	N	Y
17 Weiss	N	Y
18 Garcia	X	?
19 Biaggi	N	Y
20 Ottinger	?	?
21 Fish	N	Y
22 Gilman	N	Y
23 Stratton	Y	Y
24 Solomon	Y	Y
25 Boehlert	N	Y
26 Martin	#	?
27 Wortley	Y	Y
28 McHugh	N	Y
29 Horton	Y	Y
30 Conable	Y	N
31 Kemp	Y	N
32 LaFalce	N	Y
33 Nowak	?	?
34 Lundine	?	?

	332	333
NORTH CAROLINA		
1 Jones	Y	Y
2 Valentine	Y	Y
3 Whitley	N	Y
4 Andrews	N	Y
5 Neal	?	?
6 Britt	N	Y
7 Rose	?	?
8 Hefner	N	Y
9 Martin	?	?
10 Broyhill	Y	N
11 Clarke	?	?
NORTH DAKOTA		
AL Dorgan	?	?
OHIO		
1 Luken	Y	Y
2 Gradison	Y	Y
3 Hall	N	Y
4 Oxley	Y	Y
5 Latta	Y	Y
6 McEwen	#	?
7 DeWine	Y	Y
8 Kindness	Y	Y
9 Kaptur	X	?
10 Miller	Y	Y
11 Eckart	N	Y
12 Kasich	Y	Y
13 Pease	N	Y
14 Seiberling	N	Y
15 Wylie	Y	Y
16 Regula	N	Y
17 Williams	N	Y
18 Applegate	Y	Y
19 Feighan	N	Y
20 Oakar	N	Y
21 Stokes	N	Y
OKLAHOMA		
1 Jones	Y	Y
2 Synar	N	Y
3 Watkins	Y	Y
4 McCurdy	?	?
5 Edwards	Y	N
6 English	Y	N
OREGON		
1 AuCoin	N	Y
2 Smith, R.	?	?
3 Wyden	N	Y
4 Weaver	N	Y
5 Smith, D.	Y	N
PENNSYLVANIA		
1 Foglietta	N	Y
2 Gray	N	Y
3 Borski	N	Y
4 Kolter	N	Y
5 Schulze	Y	Y
6 Yatron	Y	Y
7 Edgar	N	Y
8 Kostmayer	N	Y
9 Shuster	Y	Y
10 McDade	N	Y
11 Harrison	N	Y
12 Murtha	N	Y
13 Coughlin	N	Y
14 Coyne	?	?
15 Ritter	N	Y
16 Walker	Y	Y
17 Gekas	Y	Y
18 Walgren	N	Y
19 Goodling	Y	Y
20 Gaydos	Y	Y
21 Ridge	N	Y
22 Murphy	Y	Y
23 Clinger	Y	Y
RHODE ISLAND		
1 St Germain	N	Y
2 Schneider	N	Y
SOUTH CAROLINA		
1 Hartnett	?	?
2 Spence	Y	Y
3 Derrick	X	?
4 Campbell	?	?
5 Spratt	N	Y
6 Tallon	Y	Y
SOUTH DAKOTA		
AL Daschle	?	Y

	332	333
TENNESSEE		
1 Quillen	#	?
2 Duncan	Y	Y
3 Lloyd	Y	Y
4 Cooper	N	Y
5 Boner	?	?
6 Gore	N	Y
7 Sundquist	Y	N
8 Jones	N	Y
9 Ford	N	Y
TEXAS		
1 Hall, S.	?	?
2 Wilson	N	Y
3 Bartlett	Y	N
4 Hall, R.	N	Y
5 Bryant	N	Y
6 Gramm	Y	Y
7 Archer	Y	N
8 Fields	Y	Y
9 Brooks	?	?
10 Pickle	Y	Y
11 Leath	?	?
12 Wright	N	Y
13 Hightower	Y	Y
14 Patman	N	Y
15 de la Garza	?	?
16 Coleman	N	Y
17 Stenholm	Y	Y
18 Leland	N	Y
19 Hance	N	Y
20 Gonzalez	N	Y
21 Loeffler	?	?
22 Paul	Y	N
23 Kazen	N	Y
24 Frost	N	Y
25 Andrews	N	Y
26 Vandergriff	Y	Y
27 Ortiz	N	Y
UTAH		
1 Hansen	Y	N
2 Marriott	?	?
3 Nielson	Y	N
VERMONT		
AL Jeffords	?	?
VIRGINIA		
1 Bateman	#	?
2 Whitehurst	#	?
3 Bliley	Y	N
4 Sisisky	Y	Y
5 Daniel	Y	N
6 Olin	Y	N
7 Robinson	Y	N
8 Parris	Y	Y
9 Boucher	?	?
10 Wolf	Y	Y
WASHINGTON		
1 Pritchard	?	?
2 Swift	N	Y
3 Bonker	N	Y
4 Morrison	Y	Y
5 Foley	N	Y
6 Dicks	N	Y
7 Lowry	N	Y
8 Chandler	Y	Y
WEST VIRGINIA		
1 Mollohan	Y	Y
2 Staggers	N	Y
3 Wise	N	Y
4 Rahall	N	Y
WISCONSIN		
1 Aspin	N	Y
2 Kastenmeier	N	Y
3 Gunderson	N	Y
4 Kleczka	N	Y
5 Moody	N	Y
6 Petri	N	Y
7 Obey	N	Y
8 Roth	Y	Y
9 Sensenbrenner	N	Y
WYOMING		
AL Cheney	Y	N

Southern states - Ala., Ark., Fla., Ga., Ky., La., Miss., N.C., Okla., S.C., Tenn., Texas, Va.

334. HR 3605. Drug Price Competition. Shaw, R-Fla., amendment to the Waxman, D-Calif., amendment, to reduce to 18 months, from 30 months, the period during which the Food and Drug Administration must delay approval of a generic drug that is the subject of patent litigation. Rejected 66-304: R 16-130; D 50-174 (ND 40-113, SD 10-61), Sept. 6, 1984. (The Waxman amendment, to revise federal approval processes for generic drugs, subsequently was adopted by voice vote.)

335. HR 3605. Drug Price Competition. Quillen, R-Tenn., amendment to the Waxman, D-Calif., amendment, to exempt over-the-counter pharmaceuticals from revisions made by the bill in the federal approval process for generic drugs. Rejected 24-347: R 9-135; D 15-212 (ND 9-144, SD 6-68), Sept. 6, 1984. (The Waxman amendment, to revise federal approval processes for generic drugs, subsequently was adopted by voice vote.)

336. HR 3605. Drug Price Competition. Frenzel, R-Minn., amendment to the Derrick, D-S.C., amendment, to extend to 180 days, from 90 days, the period of time for compliance with new requirements that catalogs identify textile merchandise as imported or domestic. Rejected 36-323: R 30-115; D 6-208 (ND 5-143, SD 1-65), Sept. 6, 1984. (The Derrick amendment, to strengthen labeling requirements for textiles and clothing, subsequently was adopted by voice vote.)

337. HR 3605. Drug Price Competition. Passage of the bill to revise federal procedures for approving generic drugs, to authorize extended patents for new drugs, medical devices and food additives, and to revise labeling requirements for textiles and clothing. Passed 362-0: R 147-0; D 215-0 (ND 146-0, SD 69-0), Sept. 6, 1984.

338. HR 5602. Health Professions and Services. Dannemeyer, R-Calif., substitute to authorize about $678 million annually for federal health professions and services programs for fiscal years 1985 through 1988. (The bill provided about $761 million for those programs in fiscal 1985 with increases in following years.) Rejected 78-236: R 68-59; D 10-177 (ND 0-132, SD 10-45), Sept. 6, 1984.

339. HR 5798. Treasury, Postal Service and General Government Appropriations, Fiscal 1985. Adoption of the conference report on the bill to appropriate $12,766,276,000 in fiscal 1985 for the Treasury Department, the Postal Service, the Executive Office of the President and other agencies. Adopted 276-110: R 76-74; D 200-36 (ND 137-17, SD 63-19), Sept. 12, 1984. The president had requested $12,349,678,000 in new budget authority.

340. HR 5798. Treasury, Postal Service and General Government Appropriations, Fiscal 1985. Whitten, D-Miss., motion that the House insist on its disagreement with the Senate amendment to forbid the use of Postal Service funds to implement regulations charging state and local child support enforcement officials a fee for address information. Motion rejected 1-389: R 0-154; D 1-235 (ND 0-157, SD 1-78), Sept. 12, 1984.

341. HR 1437. California Wilderness Act. Adoption of the rule (H Res 573) providing for consideration of the bill to designate as federal wilderness some 1.8 million acres of national forest land in California. Adopted 295-112: R 51-106; D 244-6 (ND 163-1, SD 81-5), Sept. 12, 1984.

KEY

- **Y** Voted for (yea).
- **#** Paired for.
- **+** Announced for.
- **N** Voted against (nay).
- **X** Paired against.
- **-** Announced against.
- **P** Voted "present".
- **C** Voted "present" to avoid possible conflict of interest.
- **?** Did not vote or otherwise make a position known.

Democrats   *Republicans*

Member	334	335	336	337	338	339	340	341
ALABAMA								
1 Edwards	N	N	N	Y	?	Y	N	Y
2 Dickinson	N	N	N	Y	N	Y	N	?
3 Nichols	N	Y	N	Y	N	Y	N	Y
4 Bevill	?	?	N	Y	N	Y	N	Y
5 Flippo	?	?	?	?	?	Y	N	Y
6 Erdreich	N	N	N	Y	N	Y	N	Y
7 Shelby	N	N	?	?	?	N	N	Y
ALASKA								
AL Young	N	N	N	Y	Y	Y	N	N
ARIZONA								
1 McCain	N	N	N	Y	?	Y	N	Y
2 Udall	N	N	N	Y	N	Y	N	Y
3 Stump	?	?	?	?	?	?	?	?
4 Rudd	?	?	?	?	?	Y	N	N
5 McNulty	N	N	N	Y	N	Y	N	Y
ARKANSAS								
1 Alexander	?	?	?	?	?	Y	?	?
2 Bethune	?	?	?	?	?	?	N	Y
3 Hammerschmidt	Y	Y	N	Y	N	Y	N	N
4 Anthony	N	N	N	Y	N	?	?	Y
CALIFORNIA								
1 Bosco	N	N	N	?	?	Y	N	Y
2 Chappie	N	N	N	Y	N	Y	N	N
3 Matsui	?	?	?	?	?	Y	?	Y
4 Fazio	N	N	N	Y	N	Y	N	Y
5 Burton	N	N	N	Y	N	Y	N	Y
6 Boxer	Y	N	N	Y	?	Y	N	Y
7 Miller	N	?	N	Y	?	Y	N	Y
8 Dellums	Y	N	N	Y	N	Y	N	Y
9 Stark	?	?	?	?	?	Y	N	Y
10 Edwards	Y	N	N	Y	N	Y	N	Y
11 Lantos	N	N	N	Y	?	Y	N	Y
12 Zschau	N	N	Y	Y	N	Y	N	Y
13 Mineta	N	N	N	Y	N	Y	?	Y
14 Shumway	N	N	N	Y	N	Y	N	N
15 Coelho	Y	N	N	Y	N	Y	N	Y
16 Panetta	N	N	N	Y	N	Y	N	Y
17 Pashayan	?	?	?	?	?	N	N	N
18 Lehman	N	N	N	Y	N	Y	N	Y
19 Lagomarsino	N	N	N	Y	N	N	N	Y
20 Thomas	N	N	N	Y	?	N	N	N
21 Fiedler	N	N	N	Y	?	N	N	N
22 Moorhead	N	N	N	Y	?	N	N	N
23 Beilenson	?	?	?	?	?	Y	N	Y
24 Waxman	N	N	N	Y	N	Y	?	?
25 Roybal	N	N	N	Y	N	Y	N	Y
26 Berman	N	N	N	Y	N	Y	N	Y
27 Levine	N	N	N	Y	?	Y	N	Y
28 Dixon	N	N	N	Y	N	Y	N	Y
29 Hawkins	?	N	N	Y	N	Y	N	Y
30 Martinez	N	N	N	Y	N	Y	N	Y
31 Dymally	N	N	N	Y	N	Y	N	Y
32 Anderson	N	N	Y	N	Y	N	N	Y
33 Dreier	N	N	N	Y	Y	N	N	N
34 Torres	-	-	-	+	-	?	N	Y
35 Lewis	N	?	Y	Y	Y	N	N	N
36 Brown	N	N	N	Y	N	Y	N	Y
37 McCandless	N	N	Y	Y	N	N	N	N
38 Patterson	N	N	N	Y	N	?	N	Y
39 Dannemeyer	N	N	Y	N	Y	N	N	N
40 Badham	Y	N	N	Y	Y	N	N	N
41 Lowery	N	N	Y	Y	Y	N	N	N
42 Lungren	N	N	Y	Y	Y	N	N	N
43 Packard	N	N	N	Y	N	N	N	N
44 Bates	N	N	N	Y	N	Y	?	Y
45 Hunter	Y	N	N	Y	Y	Y	N	N
COLORADO								
1 Schroeder	Y	N	N	Y	N	N	N	Y
2 Wirth	N	N	N	Y	N	N	N	Y
3 Kogovsek	Y	N	N	Y	N	?	N	Y
4 Brown	Y	N	N	Y	N	N	N	N
5 Kramer	Y	N	Y	Y	N	N	N	N
6 Schaefer	N	N	Y	Y	Y	N	N	N
CONNECTICUT								
1 Kennelly	N	N	N	Y	N	N	N	Y
2 Gejdenson	N	N	N	Y	N	Y	N	Y
3 Morrison	Y	Y	N	Y	N	Y	N	Y
4 McKinney	Y	Y	N	Y	N	Y	?	Y
5 Ratchford	N	N	N	Y	N	Y	N	Y
6 Johnson	N	N	N	Y	N	Y	N	Y
DELAWARE								
AL Carper	N	N	N	Y	N	N	N	Y
FLORIDA								
1 Hutto	N	N	N	Y	N	Y	N	Y
2 Fuqua	?	?	?	?	?	Y	N	Y
3 Bennett	N	N	N	Y	Y	N	N	Y
4 Chappell	?	N	N	Y	?	Y	N	Y
5 McCollum	Y	N	N	Y	N	N	N	N
6 MacKay	Y	N	?	?	?	Y	N	Y
7 Gibbons	N	N	?	Y	N	?	N	Y
8 Young	Y	N	N	Y	N	Y	N	N
9 Bilirakis	Y	N	N	Y	Y	N	N	N
10 Ireland	Y	N	N	Y	Y	Y	N	Y
11 Nelson	#	-	-	+	-	N	N	Y
12 Lewis	+	-	-	+	+	Y	N	N
13 Mack	Y	N	N	Y	N	N	N	N
14 Mica	N	N	?	Y	?	Y	N	Y
15 Shaw	Y	N	N	Y	Y	Y	N	N
16 Smith	Y	N	?	?	?	Y	?	Y
17 Lehman	Y	Y	N	N	Y	N	N	Y
18 Pepper	Y	N	N	Y	?	?	?	Y
19 Fascell	Y	N	?	Y	N	Y	N	Y
GEORGIA								
1 Thomas	N	N	N	Y	N	Y	N	Y
2 Hatcher	N	N	N	Y	N	Y	N	Y
3 Ray	N	N	N	Y	N	Y	N	N
4 Levitas	N	N	N	Y	N	N	N	Y
5 Fowler	?	N	N	Y	N	Y	N	Y
6 Gingrich	N	N	N	Y	Y	?	N	N
7 Darden	N	N	N	Y	N	Y	N	Y
8 Rowland	N	N	N	Y	N	Y	N	Y
9 Jenkins	N	N	N	Y	?	Y	N	Y
10 Barnard	?	?	?	?	?	Y	N	Y
HAWAII								
1 Heftel	?	?	?	?	?	?	N	Y
2 Akaka	?	?	?	?	?	?	?	?
IDAHO								
1 Craig	N	N	N	Y	N	N	N	Y
2 Hansen	?	?	?	?	?	N	N	N
ILLINOIS								
1 Hayes	N	N	N	Y	N	Y	N	Y
2 Savage	N	N	N	Y	N	Y	N	?
3 Russo	Y	N	N	Y	N	Y	N	N
4 O'Brien	N	N	N	Y	?	Y	N	N
5 Lipinski	N	N	N	Y	?	?	?	Y
6 Hyde	N	N	N	Y	N	Y	N	N
7 Collins	N	N	N	Y	N	Y	N	Y
8 Rostenkowski	?	?	?	?	?	Y	N	Y
9 Yates	N	Y	N	Y	N	Y	N	Y
10 Porter	N	N	N	Y	N	N	N	N
11 Annunzio	N	N	N	Y	N	Y	N	Y
12 Crane, P.	N	N	Y	Y	N	N	N	N
13 Erlenborn	N	N	Y	Y	?	Y	N	N
14 Corcoran	?	?	?	?	?	Y	N	Y
15 Madigan	N	N	N	Y	N	Y	?	?
16 Martin	N	N	N	Y	Y	?	N	Y
17 Evans	N	N	N	Y	N	Y	N	Y
18 Michel	N	N	N	Y	?	N	N	N
19 Crane, D.	N	N	Y	Y	N	N	N	N
20 Durbin	Y	N	N	Y	N	N	N	Y
21 Price	N	N	N	Y	N	Y	N	Y
22 Simon	?	?	?	?	?	?	?	?
INDIANA								
1 Hall	?	?	?	?	?	Y	N	Y
2 Sharp	N	N	N	Y	N	Y	N	Y
3 Hiler	N	N	N	Y	N	N	N	N
4 Coats	N	N	N	Y	N	N	N	N
5 Hillis	N	N	N	Y	N	Y	N	N

ND - Northern Democrats   SD - Southern Democrats

	334	335	336	337	338	339	340	341
6 ***Burton***	N	N	Y	Y	?	N	N	N
7 ***Myers***	N	N	N	Y	N	Y	N	N
8 McCloskey	N	N	N	Y	N	Y	N	Y
9 Hamilton	N	N	N	Y	N	Y	N	Y
10 Jacobs	Y	N	N	Y	N	N	N	N
IOWA								
1 ***Leach***	?	?	?	?	?	Y	N	Y
2 ***Tauke***	N	N	Y	Y	Y	N	N	N
3 ***Evans***	N	N	Y	Y	N	N	N	Y
4 Smith	Y	N	Y	Y	N	Y	N	Y
5 Harkin	?	?	?	?	?	Y	N	Y
6 Bedell	N	N	N	Y	N	Y	N	Y
KANSAS								
1 ***Roberts***	?	?	?	?	?	N	N	N
2 Slattery	Y	N	N	Y	N	N	N	Y
3 ***Winn***	?	?	?	?	?	N	N	N
4 Glickman	Y	N	N	Y	N	N	N	Y
5 ***Whittaker***	N	N	N	Y	Y	?	?	N
KENTUCKY								
1 Hubbard	N	N	N	Y	Y	N	N	Y
2 Natcher	N	N	N	Y	N	Y	N	Y
3 Mazzoli	N	N	N	Y	N	Y	N	Y
4 ***Snyder***	Y	N	N	Y	Y	Y	N	N
5 ***Rogers***	N	N	N	Y	Y	Y	N	N
6 ***Hopkins***	N	N	N	Y	Y	N	N	N
7 Vacancy								
LOUISIANA								
1 ***Livingston***	N	N	Y	Y	Y	Y	N	N
2 Boggs	?	N	N	Y	N	?	?	?
3 Tauzin	?	?	?	?	?	Y	N	Y
4 Roemer	Y	N	N	Y	Y	N	N	Y
5 Huckaby	N	N	N	Y	N	N	N	Y
6 ***Moore***	N	N	N	Y	Y	Y	N	N
7 Breaux	N	N	N	Y	N	Y	N	Y
8 Long	N	N	N	Y	?	Y	N	Y
MAINE								
1 ***McKernan***	N	N	N	Y	N	Y	N	Y
2 ***Snowe***	N	N	N	Y	N	Y	N	Y
MARYLAND								
1 Dyson	N	N	N	Y	N	?	?	?
2 Long	Y	N	N	Y	N	Y	N	Y
3 Mikulski	N	N	P	?	N	Y	N	Y
4 ***Holt***	N	N	N	Y	N	Y	N	Y
5 Hoyer	N	N	N	Y	N	Y	N	Y
6 Byron	N	N	N	Y	N	Y	N	Y
7 Mitchell	N	N	N	Y	N	Y	N	Y
8 Barnes	N	N	N	Y	?	Y	N	Y
MASSACHUSETTS								
1 ***Conte***	N	N	N	Y	N	Y	N	Y
2 Boland	N	N	N	Y	?	Y	N	Y
3 Early	?	?	?	?	?	Y	N	Y
4 Frank	Y	N	N	Y	N	Y	N	Y
5 Shannon	?	?	?	?	?	?	?	?
6 Mavroules	N	N	N	Y	N	Y	N	Y
7 Markey	Y	N	N	Y	?	?	?	?
8 O'Neill								
9 Moakley	N	N	N	Y	N	Y	N	Y
10 Studds	N	N	N	Y	?	?	?	?
11 Donnelly	N	N	N	Y	N	Y	N	Y
MICHIGAN								
1 Conyers	Y	N	N	Y	N	Y	N	Y
2 ***Pursell***	N	N	N	Y	N	N	N	Y
3 Wolpe	N	N	N	Y	N	Y	N	Y
4 ***Siljander***	N	N	N	Y	Y	N	N	N
5 ***Sawyer***	N	Y	N	Y	N	Y	N	Y
6 Carr	N	N	N	Y	N	Y	N	Y
7 Kildee	Y	N	N	Y	N	Y	N	Y
8 Traxler	N	N	?	?	?	?	N	Y
9 ***Vander Jagt***	N	Y	N	Y	N	N	N	N
10 Albosta	N	Y	N	Y	N	Y	N	Y
11 ***Davis***	Y	N	N	Y	N	Y	N	N
12 Bonior	Y	N	N	Y	N	?	?	Y
13 Crockett	N	N	N	Y	?	Y	N	Y
14 Hertel	Y	N	N	Y	N	Y	N	Y
15 Ford	N	N	?	?	?	Y	N	Y
16 Dingell	N	N	N	Y	N	Y	N	Y
17 Levin	N	N	N	Y	N	Y	N	Y
18 ***Broomfield***	N	N	N	Y	N	Y	N	N
MINNESOTA								
1 Penny	N	N	N	Y	N	Y	N	Y
2 ***Weber***	N	N	Y	Y	Y	?	N	Y
3 ***Frenzel***	N	N	Y	Y	Y	N	N	N
4 Vento	Y	Y	Y	Y	N	Y	N	Y
5 Sabo	N	N	Y	Y	N	Y	N	Y
6 Sikorski	N	N	N	Y	N	Y	N	Y
7 ***Stangeland***	N	N	Y	Y	Y	N	N	N
8 Oberstar	Y	N	N	Y	N	+	-	+
MISSISSIPPI								
1 Whitten	N	N	N	Y	?	Y	N	Y
2 ***Franklin***	N	N	N	Y	Y	N	N	N
3 Montgomery	N	N	N	Y	Y	N	N	Y
4 Dowdy	?	?	?	?	?	Y	N	Y
5 ***Lott***	N	N	N	Y	Y	N	N	N
MISSOURI								
1 Clay	N	N	N	Y	N	Y	N	Y
2 Young	N	N	N	Y	N	Y	N	Y
3 Gephardt	N	N	N	Y	N	Y	N	Y
4 Skelton	N	Y	N	Y	N	Y	N	Y
5 Wheat	N	N	N	Y	N	Y	N	Y
6 ***Coleman***	N	N	N	Y	N	Y	N	N
7 ***Taylor***	?	?	?	?	?	Y	N	N
8 ***Emerson***	N	N	N	Y	N	Y	N	N
9 Volkmer	Y	N	N	Y	N	Y	N	Y
MONTANA								
1 Williams	N	N	N	Y	?	N	N	Y
2 ***Marlenee***	N	N	N	Y	Y	N	N	N
NEBRASKA								
1 ***Bereuter***	N	N	Y	Y	N	N	N	Y
2 ***Daub***	N	N	Y	Y	Y	Y	N	N
3 ***Smith***	N	N	Y	Y	N	Y	N	Y
NEVADA								
1 Reid	N	N	N	Y	N	Y	?	Y
2 ***Vucanovich***	?	?	?	?	?	N	N	N
NEW HAMPSHIRE								
1 D'Amours	N	N	N	Y	N	?	?	?
2 ***Gregg***	?	?	?	?	?	N	N	Y
NEW JERSEY								
1 Florio	?	?	?	?	?	Y	N	Y
2 Hughes	N	N	N	Y	N	N	N	Y
3 Howard	N	N	N	Y	?	Y	N	Y
4 ***Smith***	N	N	N	Y	N	Y	N	Y
5 ***Roukema***	N	N	N	Y	?	N	N	Y
6 Dwyer	N	N	N	Y	N	Y	N	Y
7 ***Rinaldo***	N	N	N	Y	N	?	N	Y
8 Roe	N	N	N	Y	N	Y	N	Y
9 Torricelli	N	N	N	Y	?	Y	N	Y
10 Rodino	N	N	N	Y	N	Y	N	Y
11 Minish	Y	N	N	Y	N	Y	N	Y
12 ***Courter***	N	N	N	Y	N	Y	N	N
13 Vacancy								
14 Guarini	Y	N	N	Y	N	?	?	?
NEW MEXICO								
1 ***Lujan***	N	N	N	Y	Y	Y	N	Y
2 ***Skeen***	N	N	N	Y	Y	N	N	N
3 Richardson	N	N	N	Y	N	?	?	Y
NEW YORK								
1 ***Carney***	N	N	?	?	?	?	?	?
2 Downey	N	N	N	Y	N	Y	N	Y
3 Mrazek	N	N	N	Y	N	Y	N	Y
4 ***Lent***	N	?	N	Y	N	Y	N	N
5 ***McGrath***	N	N	N	Y	N	Y	N	N
6 Addabbo	?	?	?	?	?	Y	N	Y
7 Ackerman	?	?	?	?	?	?	N	Y
8 Scheuer	N	N	N	Y	N	Y	N	Y
9 Ferraro	?	?	?	?	?	?	?	?
10 Schumer	N	N	N	Y	?	Y	N	Y
11 Towns	?	?	?	?	?	?	?	?
12 Owens	?	?	?	?	?	?	N	Y
13 Solarz	N	N	N	Y	N	Y	N	Y
14 ***Molinari***	N	N	N	Y	N	Y	N	N
15 ***Green***	N	N	Y	Y	N	Y	N	Y
16 Rangel	X	?	?	?	N	Y	N	Y
17 Weiss	Y	N	N	Y	N	?	?	Y
18 Garcia	Y	N	N	Y	N	Y	N	Y
19 Biaggi	N	N	N	Y	N	Y	N	Y
20 Ottinger	N	N	N	?	?	Y	N	Y
21 ***Fish***	N	N	N	Y	?	Y	N	N
22 ***Gilman***	N	N	N	Y	N	Y	N	Y
23 Stratton	Y	N	N	Y	N	Y	N	Y
24 ***Solomon***	N	N	N	Y	Y	N	N	N
25 ***Boehlert***	N	N	N	Y	?	Y	N	Y
26 ***Martin***	N	N	N	Y	?	?	?	?
27 ***Wortley***	N	N	N	Y	N	Y	N	N
28 McHugh	N	N	N	Y	N	Y	N	Y
29 ***Horton***	?	?	?	?	?	Y	N	N
30 ***Conable***	N	?	Y	Y	Y	?	?	N
31 ***Kemp***	N	N	N	Y	N	?	?	?
32 LaFalce	N	N	N	Y	N	Y	N	Y
33 Nowak	N	N	N	Y	N	Y	N	Y
34 Lundine	N	N	N	Y	N	N	N	Y
NORTH CAROLINA								
1 Jones	N	Y	N	Y	N	Y	N	Y
2 Valentine	N	N	N	Y	N	Y	N	Y
3 Whitley	N	N	N	Y	?	Y	N	Y
4 Andrews	N	N	N	Y	N	Y	N	Y
5 Neal	?	?	?	?	?	Y	N	Y
6 Britt	N	N	N	Y	N	Y	N	Y
7 Rose	N	N	N	Y	?	Y	N	Y
8 Hefner	N	N	N	Y	N	Y	?	Y
9 ***Martin***	?	?	?	?	?	?	?	?
10 ***Broyhill***	N	N	N	Y	Y	N	N	N
11 Clarke	N	N	N	Y	N	Y	N	Y
NORTH DAKOTA								
AL Dorgan	N	N	N	Y	N	N	N	Y
OHIO								
1 Luken	N	N	?	?	?	Y	N	Y
2 ***Gradison***	?	?	?	?	?	N	N	Y
3 Hall	N	N	N	Y	N	Y	N	Y
4 ***Oxley***	N	N	N	Y	Y	N	N	N
5 ***Latta***	N	Y	N	Y	Y	?	N	N
6 ***McEwen***	N	N	N	Y	Y	N	N	N
7 ***DeWine***	N	N	N	Y	Y	Y	N	Y
8 ***Kindness***	N	N	N	Y	Y	N	N	N
9 Kaptur	N	N	N	Y	N	Y	N	Y
10 ***Miller***	N	N	Y	Y	Y	Y	N	N
11 Eckart	Y	N	N	Y	N	Y	N	Y
12 ***Kasich***	N	N	N	Y	Y	Y	N	N
13 Pease	N	N	N	Y	N	Y	N	Y
14 Seiberling	Y	Y	N	Y	N	N	N	Y
15 ***Wylie***	N	N	N	Y	N	Y	N	N
16 ***Regula***	N	N	N	Y	N	Y	N	N
17 ***Williams***	N	N	N	Y	N	Y	N	Y
18 Applegate	Y	N	N	Y	N	Y	N	Y
19 Feighan	N	N	N	Y	N	N	N	Y
20 Oakar	N	N	N	Y	N	Y	N	Y
21 Stokes	N	N	N	Y	N	Y	N	Y
OKLAHOMA								
1 Jones	Y	N	N	Y	N	N	N	Y
2 Synar	N	N	N	Y	N	Y	N	Y
3 Watkins	N	N	N	Y	N	Y	N	Y
4 McCurdy	?	?	?	?	?	N	N	Y
5 ***Edwards***	N	N	N	Y	N	N	N	N
6 English	N	N	Y	Y	N	N	N	Y
OREGON								
1 AuCoin	N	N	N	Y	N	N	N	Y
2 ***Smith, R.***	?	?	?	?	?	Y	N	N
3 Wyden	N	N	N	Y	N	Y	N	Y
4 Weaver	Y	N	N	Y	N	?	N	Y
5 ***Smith, D.***	N	N	Y	Y	?	N	N	N
PENNSYLVANIA								
1 Foglietta	Y	N	N	Y	N	Y	N	Y
2 Gray	N	N	N	Y	N	Y	N	Y
3 Borski	N	N	N	Y	N	Y	N	Y
4 Kolter	N	N	N	Y	N	Y	N	Y
5 ***Schulze***	?	?	N	Y	Y	N	N	N
6 Yatron	N	N	N	Y	N	Y	N	Y
7 Edgar	N	N	N	Y	N	Y	N	Y
8 Kostmayer	N	N	N	Y	?	Y	N	Y
9 ***Shuster***	N	N	N	Y	?	N	N	N
10 ***McDade***	?	?	?	?	?	Y	N	Y
11 Harrison	?	?	N	Y	N	Y	N	Y
12 Murtha	N	N	N	Y	N	Y	N	Y
13 ***Coughlin***	N	N	N	Y	N	Y	N	Y
14 Coyne	N	N	N	Y	N	Y	N	Y
15 ***Ritter***	N	N	N	Y	Y	N	N	N
16 ***Walker***	N	N	Y	Y	Y	N	N	N
17 ***Gekas***	N	N	N	Y	N	N	N	N
18 Walgren	N	N	?	?	?	Y	N	Y
19 ***Goodling***	N	N	N	Y	N	Y	N	N
20 Gaydos	N	N	N	Y	N	Y	N	Y
21 ***Ridge***	N	N	N	Y	N	Y	N	Y
22 Murphy	N	N	N	Y	N	N	N	Y
23 ***Clinger***	N	N	Y	Y	N	Y	N	Y
RHODE ISLAND								
1 St Germain	Y	N	N	Y	N	Y	N	Y
2 ***Schneider***	N	N	N	Y	N	Y	N	Y
SOUTH CAROLINA								
1 ***Hartnett***	N	N	N	Y	?	N	N	N
2 ***Spence***	N	N	N	Y	N	Y	N	Y
3 Derrick	N	N	N	Y	N	Y	?	Y
4 ***Campbell***	N	N	N	Y	Y	Y	N	N
5 Spratt	N	N	N	Y	N	Y	N	Y
6 Tallon	N	N	N	Y	?	Y	N	Y
SOUTH DAKOTA								
AL Daschle	N	N	N	Y	?	Y	N	Y
TENNESSEE								
1 ***Quillen***	N	Y	N	Y	?	Y	N	Y
2 ***Duncan***	N	Y	N	Y	N	Y	N	N
3 Lloyd	N	Y	N	Y	N	Y	N	Y
4 Cooper	N	Y	N	Y	N	Y	Y	Y
5 Boner	N	N	N	Y	N	Y	N	Y
6 Gore	Y	Y	N	Y	N	Y	N	Y
7 ***Sundquist***	N	N	N	Y	N	Y	N	N
8 Jones	N	N	N	Y	N	Y	N	Y
9 Ford	N	N	N	Y	?	Y	N	Y
TEXAS								
1 Hall, S.	Y	N	N	Y	Y	N	N	N
2 Wilson	N	N	N	Y	?	?	?	Y
3 ***Bartlett***	N	N	N	Y	Y	N	N	N
4 Hall, R.	N	N	N	Y	N	Y	N	N
5 Bryant	N	N	N	Y	N	Y	N	Y
6 ***Gramm***	N	N	N	Y	?	?	?	?
7 ***Archer***	N	N	N	Y	Y	N	N	N
8 ***Fields***	N	N	N	Y	Y	N	N	N
9 Brooks	N	N	N	Y	N	Y	N	Y
10 Pickle	N	N	N	Y	N	Y	N	Y
11 Leath	N	N	N	Y	Y	N	N	N
12 Wright	?	?	?	?	?	Y	N	Y
13 Hightower	N	N	N	Y	?	Y	N	Y
14 Patman	N	N	N	Y	Y	N	N	N
15 de la Garza	P	N	N	Y	?	Y	N	Y
16 Coleman	N	N	N	Y	N	Y	N	Y
17 Stenholm	N	N	?	?	?	N	N	N
18 Leland	N	N	?	?	?	?	?	Y
19 Hance	N	N	?	?	?	N	N	Y
20 Gonzalez	Y	P	N	Y	N	Y	N	Y
21 ***Loeffler***	N	N	N	Y	Y	N	N	N
22 ***Paul***	N	N	Y	Y	Y	N	N	N
23 Kazen	N	N	?	?	?	Y	N	Y
24 Frost	N	N	N	Y	N	Y	N	Y
25 Andrews	N	N	N	Y	?	Y	N	Y
26 Vandergriff	?	?	?	?	?	Y	N	Y
27 Ortiz	N	N	N	Y	N	Y	N	Y
UTAH								
1 ***Hansen***	N	N	N	Y	?	N	N	N
2 ***Marriott***	N	N	N	Y	N	N	N	N
3 ***Nielson***	N	N	N	Y	Y	N	N	N
VERMONT								
AL ***Jeffords***	N	Y	Y	Y	?	?	?	?
VIRGINIA								
1 ***Bateman***	N	N	N	Y	Y	Y	N	Y
2 ***Whitehurst***	N	N	N	Y	N	Y	N	Y
3 ***Bliley***	?	?	?	?	?	N	N	N
4 Sisisky	N	N	N	Y	N	Y	N	Y
5 Daniel	N	N	N	Y	N	N	N	Y
6 Olin	N	N	N	Y	N	N	N	Y
7 ***Robinson***	N	N	N	Y	N	Y	N	N
8 ***Parris***	N	N	N	Y	N	Y	N	Y
9 Boucher	?	?	?	?	?	Y	N	Y
10 ***Wolf***	N	N	N	Y	N	Y	N	Y
WASHINGTON								
1 ***Pritchard***	N	N	?	Y	?	?	N	?
2 Swift	N	N	N	Y	N	Y	N	Y
3 Bonker	?	?	?	?	?	Y	N	Y
4 ***Morrison***	N	N	Y	Y	N	N	N	N
5 Foley	?	?	?	?	?	Y	N	Y
6 Dicks	N	N	N	?	N	Y	N	Y
7 Lowry	Y	N	N	Y	N	Y	N	Y
8 ***Chandler***	N	N	Y	Y	N	Y	N	N
WEST VIRGINIA								
1 Mollohan	N	N	N	Y	N	Y	N	Y
2 Staggers	N	N	N	Y	N	Y	N	Y
3 Wise	N	N	N	Y	N	Y	N	Y
4 Rahall	Y	N	N	Y	N	Y	N	Y
WISCONSIN								
1 Aspin	?	?	?	Y	N	Y	N	Y
2 Kastenmeier	Y	Y	Y	Y	N	Y	N	Y
3 ***Gunderson***	N	N	N	Y	Y	Y	N	Y
4 Kleczka	Y	N	-	+	-	Y	N	Y
5 Moody	Y	Y	?	?	?	Y	N	Y
6 ***Petri***	Y	Y	Y	Y	N	Y	N	Y
7 Obey	Y	Y	N	Y	N	Y	N	Y
8 ***Roth***	Y	N	N	Y	N	Y	N	Y
9 ***Sensenbrenner***	N	N	N	Y	Y	N	N	Y
WYOMING								
AL ***Cheney***	?	N	N	Y	Y	?	?	?

Southern states - Ala., Ark., Fla., Ga., Ky., La., Miss., N.C., Okla., S.C., Tenn., Texas, Va.

KEY

Y Voted for (yea).
Paired for.
+ Announced for.
N Voted against (nay).
X Paired against.
- Announced against.
P Voted "present".
C Voted "present" to avoid possible conflict of interest.
? Did not vote or otherwise make a position known.

———

Democrats   *Republicans*

342. HR 1437. California Wilderness Act. Udall, D-Ariz., motion to take from the Speaker's table the bill, with a Senate amendment, designating as federal wilderness some 1.8 million acres of national forest land in California, and to agree to the Senate amendment. Motion agreed to (thus clearing the bill for the president) 368-41: R 122-36; D 246-5 (ND 166-0, SD 80-5), Sept. 12, 1984.

343. HR 3347. Extradition Act. Hughes, D-N.J., motion to suspend the rules and pass the bill to revise procedures for extraditing persons to foreign countries seeking them for alleged criminal offenses. Motion rejected 103-307: R 2-157; D 101-150 (ND 89-76, SD 12-74), Sept. 12, 1984. A two-thirds majority of those present and voting (274 in this case) is required for passage under suspension of the rules.

344. HR 6071. Trademark Counterfeiting Act. Hughes, D-N.J., motion to suspend the rules and pass the bill to impose criminal penalties and increase civil remedies against those who produce or sell goods bearing counterfeit trademarks. Motion agreed to 403-0: R 157-0; D 246-0 (ND 162-0, SD 84-0), Sept. 12, 1984. A two-thirds majority of those present and voting (269 in this case) is required for passage under suspension of the rules.

345. Procedural Motion. Fields, R-Texas, motion to approve the House *Journal* of Wednesday, Sept. 12. Motion agreed to 362-30: R 134-19; D 228-11 (ND 146-10, SD 82-1), Sept. 13, 1984.

346. S 2463. Ocean and Coastal Resources. Snyder, D-Ky., motion to recommit to the committee on conference the conference report on the bill to share revenues from drilling leases on federal territory offshore with states and to authorize fisheries programs. Motion rejected 122-282: R 91-64; D 31-218 (ND 13-155, SD 18-63), Sept. 13, 1984.

347. S 2463. Ocean and Coastal Resources. Adoption of the conference report on the bill to share revenues from drilling leases on federal territory offshore with states and to authorize fisheries programs. Adopted 312-94: R 83-71; D 229-23 (ND 158-11, SD 71-12), Sept. 13, 1984.

348. HR 5609. American Defense Education Act. Adoption of the rule (H Res 578) providing for House floor consideration of the bill to authorize an estimated $8.6 billion over fiscal years 1985-87 for school improvement projects. The rule barred amendments that had not been filed and printed in the *Congressional Record* by Sept. 12, the day before floor consideration of the bill. Adopted 311-89: R 63-86; D 248-3 (ND 163-3, SD 85-0), Sept. 13, 1984.

	342	343	344	345	346	347	348
ALABAMA							
1 *Edwards*	Y	N	Y	Y	N	Y	?
2 *Dickinson*	Y	N	Y	N	Y	Y	Y
3 Nichols	Y	N	Y	Y	N	Y	Y
4 Bevill	Y	N	Y	Y	N	Y	Y
5 Flippo	Y	N	Y	Y	N	Y	Y
6 Erdreich	Y	N	Y	Y	N	Y	Y
7 Shelby	Y	N	Y	Y	N	Y	Y
ALASKA							
AL *Young*	N	N	Y	N	N	N	Y
ARIZONA							
1 *McCain*	Y	N	Y	Y	Y	N	N
2 Udall	Y	N	Y	Y	N	Y	Y
3 *Stump*	?	?	?	?	?	?	?
4 *Rudd*	N	N	Y	N	Y	N	N
5 McNulty	Y	N	Y	Y	N	Y	Y
ARKANSAS							
1 Alexander	?	Y	Y	Y	N	Y	Y
2 *Bethune*	Y	N	Y	Y	?	?	?
3 *Hammerschmidt*	N	N	Y	Y	N	Y	Y
4 Anthony	Y	N	Y	Y	N	Y	Y
CALIFORNIA							
1 Bosco	Y	N	Y	Y	N	Y	Y
2 *Chappie*	N	N	Y	N	Y	Y	N
3 Matsui	Y	Y	Y	Y	N	Y	Y
4 Fazio	?	?	?	Y	N	Y	Y
5 Burton	Y	Y	?	Y	N	Y	Y
6 Boxer	Y	Y	Y	Y	N	Y	Y
7 Miller	Y	Y	?	Y	N	Y	Y
8 Dellums	Y	Y	Y	?	N	Y	Y
9 Stark	Y	Y	Y	Y	N	Y	Y
10 Edwards	Y	Y	Y	P	N	Y	Y
11 Lantos	Y	Y	Y	Y	N	Y	Y
12 *Zschau*	Y	N	Y	Y	N	Y	N
13 Mineta	Y	Y	Y	Y	N	Y	Y
14 *Shumway*	N	N	Y	Y	Y	N	N
15 Coelho	Y	N	Y	Y	N	Y	Y
16 Panetta	Y	N	Y	Y	N	Y	Y
17 *Pashayan*	N	N	Y	Y	N	Y	N
18 Lehman	Y	Y	Y	Y	N	Y	Y
19 *Lagomarsino*	Y	N	Y	Y	N	Y	N
20 *Thomas*	Y	N	Y	Y	N	Y	N
21 *Fiedler*	Y	N	Y	Y	N	Y	N
22 *Moorhead*	N	N	Y	Y	N	Y	N
23 Beilenson	Y	Y	Y	Y	N	N	Y
24 Waxman	Y	Y	Y	Y	N	Y	?
25 Roybal	Y	Y	Y	Y	N	Y	Y
26 Berman	Y	Y	Y	Y	N	Y	Y
27 Levine	Y	Y	Y	Y	N	Y	Y
28 Dixon	Y	Y	Y	Y	N	Y	Y
29 Hawkins	Y	Y	Y	Y	N	Y	Y
30 Martinez	Y	Y	Y	Y	N	Y	Y
31 Dymally	Y	Y	Y	P	?	Y	Y
32 Anderson	Y	N	Y	Y	N	Y	Y
33 *Dreier*	N	N	Y	Y	N	N	N
34 Torres	Y	Y	Y	Y	N	Y	Y
35 *Lewis*	N	N	Y	Y	N	Y	N
36 Brown	Y	Y	Y	Y	N	Y	Y
37 *McCandless*	N	N	Y	Y	Y	Y	N
38 Patterson	Y	N	Y	Y	N	Y	Y
39 *Dannemeyer*	N	N	Y	Y	N	N	N
40 *Badham*	N	N	Y	Y	N	Y	N
41 *Lowery*	Y	N	Y	Y	N	Y	N
42 *Lungren*	N	N	Y	Y	N	Y	N

	342	343	344	345	346	347	348
43 *Packard*	N	N	Y	Y	Y	N	Y
44 Bates	Y	N	Y	Y	N	Y	?
45 *Hunter*	Y	N	Y	Y	N	Y	N
COLORADO							
1 Schroeder	Y	N	Y	N	N	N	Y
2 Wirth	Y	Y	Y	Y	N	Y	Y
3 Kogovsek	Y	N	Y	Y	N	Y	Y
4 *Brown*	Y	N	Y	Y	Y	N	Y
5 *Kramer*	Y	N	Y	Y	Y	N	Y
6 *Schaefer*	N	N	N	N	Y	N	Y
CONNECTICUT							
1 Kennelly	Y	N	Y	Y	N	Y	Y
2 Gejdenson	Y	Y	Y	N	N	Y	Y
3 Morrison	Y	Y	Y	Y	N	Y	Y
4 *McKinney*	Y	N	Y	N	N	Y	Y
5 Ratchford	Y	N	Y	Y	N	Y	Y
6 *Johnson*	Y	N	Y	Y	N	Y	Y
DELAWARE							
AL Carper	Y	N	Y	Y	N	Y	Y
FLORIDA							
1 Hutto	Y	N	Y	Y	N	Y	Y
2 Fuqua	Y	N	Y	Y	N	Y	Y
3 Bennett	Y	N	Y	Y	N	Y	Y
4 Chappell	Y	N	Y	Y	N	Y	Y
5 *McCollum*	Y	N	Y	Y	N	Y	N
6 MacKay	Y	N	Y	Y	N	Y	Y
7 Gibbons	Y	N	Y	Y	N	Y	Y
8 *Young*	Y	N	Y	Y	N	Y	N
9 *Bilirakis*	Y	N	Y	Y	N	Y	Y
10 *Ireland*	Y	N	Y	Y	N	Y	Y
11 Nelson	Y	N	Y	Y	N	Y	Y
12 *Lewis*	Y	N	Y	Y	N	Y	N
13 *Mack*	Y	N	Y	Y	N	Y	N
14 Mica	Y	N	Y	Y	N	Y	Y
15 *Shaw*	Y	N	Y	Y	N	Y	N
16 Smith	Y	N	Y	Y	N	Y	Y
17 Lehman	Y	Y	Y	Y	N	Y	Y
18 Pepper	Y	Y	Y	?	N	Y	Y
19 Fascell	Y	Y	Y	Y	N	Y	Y
GEORGIA							
1 Thomas	Y	N	Y	N	N	Y	Y
2 Hatcher	Y	N	Y	?	Y	Y	Y
3 Ray	Y	N	Y	Y	N	Y	Y
4 Levitas	Y	N	Y	Y	N	Y	Y
5 Fowler	Y	N	Y	Y	N	Y	Y
6 *Gingrich*	Y	N	Y	Y	N	Y	N
7 Darden	Y	N	Y	?	Y	?	Y
8 Rowland	Y	N	Y	Y	N	Y	Y
9 Jenkins	Y	N	Y	Y	N	Y	Y
10 Barnard	Y	N	Y	Y	?	?	Y
HAWAII							
1 Heftel	Y	N	Y	?	N	Y	Y
2 Akaka	Y	Y	Y	Y	N	Y	Y
IDAHO							
1 *Craig*	Y	N	Y	Y	Y	N	N
2 *Hansen*	N	N	Y	Y	Y	N	N
ILLINOIS							
1 Hayes	Y	Y	Y	Y	N	Y	Y
2 Savage	Y	Y	Y	Y	N	Y	Y
3 Russo	Y	Y	Y	Y	N	Y	Y
4 *O'Brien*	Y	N	Y	?	Y	Y	Y
5 Lipinski	Y	N	Y	Y	N	Y	Y
6 *Hyde*	Y	N	Y	Y	N	N	N
7 Collins	Y	Y	Y	Y	N	Y	Y
8 Rostenkowski	Y	N	Y	Y	N	Y	Y
9 Yates	Y	Y	Y	Y	Y	N	Y
10 *Porter*	Y	N	Y	Y	Y	N	N
11 Annunzio	Y	N	Y	Y	N	Y	Y
12 *Crane, P.*	N	N	Y	Y	Y	N	N
13 *Erlenborn*	Y	N	Y	Y	Y	N	N
14 *Corcoran*	Y	N	Y	?	?	?	?
15 *Madigan*	Y	N	Y	Y	Y	N	Y
16 *Martin*	Y	N	Y	Y	Y	N	Y
17 Evans	Y	Y	Y	Y	N	Y	Y
18 *Michel*	Y	N	Y	Y	Y	N	?
19 *Crane, D.*	N	N	Y	Y	Y	N	N
20 Durbin	Y	N	N	Y	N	N	Y
21 Price	Y	N	Y	Y	N	Y	Y
22 Simon	?	?	?	?	?	?	?
INDIANA							
1 Hall	Y	N	Y	Y	N	Y	Y
2 Sharp	Y	N	Y	Y	Y	N	Y
3 *Hiler*	Y	N	Y	?	?	?	?
4 *Coats*	Y	N	Y	Y	N	Y	Y
5 Hillis	Y	N	Y	Y	Y	Y	Y

ND - Northern Democrats   SD - Southern Democrats

Corresponding to Congressional Record Votes 385, 386, 387, 388, 389, 390, 391

	342	343	344	345	346	347	348
6 ***Burton***	Y	N	Y	Y	Y	N	N
7 ***Myers***	Y	N	Y	Y	Y	Y	N
8 McCloskey	Y	N	Y	Y	N	Y	Y
9 Hamilton	Y	N	Y	Y	N	Y	Y
10 Jacobs	Y	?	?	N	N	N	Y
IOWA							
1 ***Leach***	Y	N	Y	Y	Y	N	Y
2 ***Tauke***	Y	N	Y	Y	Y	N	Y
3 ***Evans***	Y	N	Y	N	Y	N	Y
4 Smith	Y	N	Y	Y	Y	Y	Y
5 Harkin	Y	N	Y	N	Y	N	Y
6 Bedell	Y	N	Y	Y	Y	N	Y
KANSAS							
1 ***Roberts***	Y	N	Y	N	Y	N	N
2 Slattery	Y	N	Y	Y	Y	N	Y
3 ***Winn***	Y	N	Y	Y	N	N	N
4 Glickman	Y	Y	Y	Y	Y	N	Y
5 ***Whittaker***	Y	N	Y	Y	N	N	N
KENTUCKY							
1 Hubbard	Y	N	Y	Y	N	Y	Y
2 Natcher	Y	Y	Y	Y	N	Y	Y
3 Mazzoli	Y	Y	Y	Y	N	Y	Y
4 ***Snyder***	Y	N	Y	Y	Y	N	Y
5 ***Rogers***	Y	N	Y	Y	Y	N	Y
6 ***Hopkins***	Y	N	Y	Y	Y	N	Y
7 Vacancy							
LOUISIANA							
1 ***Livingston***	N	N	Y	Y	N	Y	N
2 Boggs	?	?	?	?	?	?	?
3 Tauzin	Y	N	Y	Y	N	Y	Y
4 Roemer	Y	N	Y	N	N	Y	Y
5 Huckaby	Y	N	Y	Y	N	Y	Y
6 ***Moore***	Y	N	Y	Y	N	Y	Y
7 Breaux	Y	N	?	Y	N	Y	Y
8 Long	?	?	?	Y	N	Y	Y
MAINE							
1 ***McKernan***	Y	N	Y	Y	N	Y	N
2 ***Snowe***	Y	N	Y	Y	N	Y	N
MARYLAND							
1 Dyson	?	N	Y	Y	N	Y	Y
2 Long	Y	N	Y	?	N	Y	Y
3 Mikulski	Y	Y	Y	Y	N	Y	Y
4 ***Holt***	Y	N	Y	Y	N	Y	Y
5 Hoyer	Y	Y	Y	Y	N	Y	Y
6 Byron	Y	N	Y	Y	N	Y	Y
7 Mitchell	Y	Y	Y	N	N	Y	Y
8 Barnes	Y	Y	Y	Y	N	Y	Y
MASSACHUSETTS							
1 ***Conte***	Y	N	Y	Y	N	Y	Y
2 Boland	Y	N	Y	Y	N	Y	Y
3 Early	Y	N	Y	Y	N	Y	Y
4 Frank	Y	?	?	Y	?	Y	Y
5 Shannon	?	?	?	?	?	?	?
6 Mavroules	Y	N	Y	Y	N	Y	Y
7 Markey	Y	Y	Y	?	N	Y	Y
8 O'Neill							
9 Moakley	Y	Y	Y	Y	N	Y	Y
10 Studds	?	?	?	Y	N	Y	Y
11 Donnelly	Y	Y	Y	Y	N	Y	Y
MICHIGAN							
1 Conyers	Y	Y	Y	Y	N	Y	Y
2 ***Pursell***	Y	N	Y	Y	N	Y	Y
3 Wolpe	Y	Y	Y	Y	N	Y	Y
4 ***Siljander***	Y	N	Y	Y	N	Y	N
5 ***Sawyer***	Y	Y	Y	Y	N	Y	Y
6 Carr	Y	N	Y	Y	N	Y	Y
7 Kildee	Y	Y	Y	Y	N	Y	Y
8 Traxler	Y	Y	Y	Y	N	Y	Y
9 ***Vander Jagt***	Y	N	Y	N	N	Y	Y
10 Albosta	Y	N	Y	Y	N	Y	Y
11 ***Davis***	N	N	Y	P	N	Y	Y
12 Bonior	Y	Y	Y	Y	N	Y	Y
13 Crockett	Y	Y	?	Y	N	Y	Y
14 Hertel	Y	N	Y	Y	N	Y	Y
15 Ford	Y	?	Y	?	?	?	Y
16 Dingell	Y	N	Y	Y	N	N	Y
17 Levin	Y	Y	Y	Y	N	Y	Y
18 ***Broomfield***	Y	N	Y	N	Y	Y	N
MINNESOTA							
1 Penny	Y	N	Y	N	N	Y	Y
2 ***Weber***	Y	N	Y	N	Y	N	Y
3 ***Frenzel***	Y	N	Y	Y	Y	N	Y
4 Vento	Y	Y	Y	Y	N	Y	Y
5 Sabo	Y	Y	Y	N	N	Y	Y
6 Sikorski	Y	N	Y	N	N	Y	Y

	342	343	344	345	346	347	348
7 ***Stangeland***	Y	N	Y	?	?	?	?
8 Oberstar	?	?	?	Y	N	Y	Y
MISSISSIPPI							
1 Whitten	Y	N	Y	Y	N	Y	Y
2 ***Franklin***	Y	N	Y	Y	N	Y	N
3 Montgomery	N	N	Y	Y	N	Y	Y
4 Dowdy	Y	N	Y	Y	N	Y	Y
5 ***Lott***	N	N	Y	Y	N	Y	N
MISSOURI							
1 Clay	Y	Y	Y	N	N	Y	Y
2 Young	?	?	?	Y	Y	Y	Y
3 Gephardt	Y	N	Y	Y	N	Y	Y
4 Skelton	Y	N	Y	Y	N	Y	Y
5 Wheat	Y	Y	Y	Y	N	Y	Y
6 ***Coleman***	Y	N	Y	Y	Y	Y	N
7 ***Taylor***	Y	N	Y	Y	Y	N	?
8 ***Emerson***	Y	N	Y	N	Y	N	N
9 Volkmer	Y	N	Y	Y	Y	N	Y
MONTANA							
1 Williams	Y	N	Y	?	N	Y	Y
2 ***Marlenee***	N	N	Y	Y	Y	N	N
NEBRASKA							
1 ***Bereuter***	Y	N	Y	N	Y	N	Y
2 ***Daub***	Y	N	Y	Y	Y	N	N
3 ***Smith***	Y	N	Y	Y	Y	N	Y
NEVADA							
1 Reid	Y	N	Y	Y	N	Y	Y
2 ***Vucanovich***	N	N	Y	Y	Y	N	N
NEW HAMPSHIRE							
1 D'Amours	?	N	Y	Y	N	Y	Y
2 ***Gregg***	Y	N	Y	Y	N	Y	Y
NEW JERSEY							
1 Florio	Y	N	Y	?	?	?	?
2 Hughes	Y	Y	Y	Y	N	Y	Y
3 Howard	Y	Y	Y	Y	N	Y	Y
4 ***Smith***	Y	N	Y	Y	N	Y	Y
5 ***Roukema***	Y	N	Y	Y	N	Y	N
6 Dwyer	Y	N	Y	Y	N	Y	Y
7 ***Rinaldo***	Y	N	Y	Y	N	Y	Y
8 Roe	Y	Y	?	Y	N	Y	Y
9 Torricelli	Y	Y	Y	Y	N	Y	Y
10 Rodino	Y	Y	Y	Y	N	Y	Y
11 Minish	Y	N	Y	Y	N	Y	Y
12 ***Courter***	Y	N	Y	Y	N	Y	Y
13 Vacancy							
14 Guarini	?	?	?	Y	N	Y	Y
NEW MEXICO							
1 ***Lujan***	Y	N	Y	Y	Y	N	Y
2 ***Skeen***	N	N	Y	Y	Y	N	N
3 Richardson	Y	Y	Y	Y	Y	Y	Y
NEW YORK							
1 ***Carney***	?	?	?	Y	N	Y	N
2 Downey	Y	Y	Y	Y	N	Y	Y
3 Mrazek	Y	N	Y	?	N	Y	Y
4 ***Lent***	Y	N	Y	Y	N	Y	N
5 ***McGrath***	Y	N	Y	Y	N	Y	N
6 Addabbo	Y	Y	Y	Y	N	?	Y
7 Ackerman	Y	Y	Y	Y	N	Y	Y
8 Scheuer	Y	Y	Y	Y	N	Y	?
9 Ferraro	?	?	?	?	?	?	?
10 Schumer	Y	Y	Y	Y	N	Y	Y
11 Towns	?	?	?	?	N	Y	Y
12 Owens	Y	Y	Y	Y	N	Y	Y
13 Solarz	Y	Y	Y	Y	N	Y	Y
14 ***Molinari***	Y	N	Y	Y	N	Y	N
15 ***Green***	Y	N	Y	Y	N	Y	Y
16 Rangel	Y	Y	Y	Y	N	Y	Y
17 Weiss	Y	Y	Y	Y	N	Y	Y
18 Garcia	Y	Y	Y	Y	N	Y	Y
19 Biaggi	Y	N	Y	Y	N	Y	Y
20 Ottinger	Y	Y	Y	?	N	Y	Y
21 ***Fish***	Y	N	Y	Y	Y	Y	Y
22 ***Gilman***	Y	Y	Y	Y	N	Y	Y
23 Stratton	Y	N	Y	Y	N	Y	Y
24 ***Solomon***	N	N	Y	N	N	Y	Y
25 ***Boehlert***	Y	N	Y	Y	N	Y	Y
26 ***Martin***	?	?	?	Y	N	Y	Y
27 ***Wortley***	Y	N	Y	Y	N	Y	N
28 McHugh	Y	Y	Y	Y	N	Y	Y
29 ***Horton***	Y	N	Y	Y	N	?	Y
30 ***Conable***	Y	N	Y	Y	Y	N	N
31 ***Kemp***	?	N	Y	Y	N	Y	Y
32 LaFalce	Y	Y	Y	Y	N	Y	Y
33 Nowak	Y	Y	Y	Y	N	Y	Y
34 Lundine	Y	N	Y	?	N	Y	Y

	342	343	344	345	346	347	348
NORTH CAROLINA							
1 Jones	Y	N	Y	Y	N	Y	Y
2 Valentine	Y	N	Y	Y	N	Y	Y
3 Whitley	Y	N	?	Y	N	Y	Y
4 Andrews	Y	N	Y	Y	N	Y	Y
5 Neal	Y	N	Y	Y	N	Y	Y
6 Britt	Y	N	Y	Y	N	Y	Y
7 Rose	Y	N	Y	Y	?	?	Y
8 Hefner	Y	N	Y	Y	Y	Y	Y
9 ***Martin***	?	?	?	?	?	?	?
10 ***Broyhill***	Y	N	Y	Y	Y	N	N
11 Clarke	Y	N	Y	Y	N	Y	Y
NORTH DAKOTA							
AL Dorgan	Y	N	Y	Y	Y	N	Y
OHIO							
1 Luken	Y	N	Y	Y	N	Y	Y
2 ***Gradison***	Y	N	Y	Y	Y	N	N
3 Hall	Y	Y	Y	Y	N	Y	?
4 ***Oxley***	Y	N	Y	Y	Y	N	N
5 ***Latta***	Y	N	Y	Y	Y	Y	N
6 ***McEwen***	Y	N	Y	Y	Y	Y	N
7 ***DeWine***	Y	N	Y	Y	Y	N	N
8 ***Kindness***	Y	N	Y	N	Y	N	N
9 Kaptur	Y	N	Y	Y	N	Y	Y
10 ***Miller***	Y	N	Y	N	Y	N	N
11 Eckart	Y	N	Y	Y	N	Y	Y
12 ***Kasich***	Y	N	Y	Y	Y	Y	N
13 Pease	Y	Y	Y	Y	N	Y	Y
14 Seiberling	Y	Y	Y	Y	N	Y	Y
15 ***Wylie***	Y	N	Y	Y	Y	N	Y
16 ***Regula***	Y	N	Y	Y	Y	N	N
17 ***Williams***	Y	N	?	?	?	?	?
18 Applegate	Y	N	Y	?	N	Y	Y
19 Feighan	Y	N	Y	Y	N	Y	Y
20 Oakar	Y	Y	Y	Y	N	Y	Y
21 Stokes	Y	Y	Y	Y	N	Y	Y
OKLAHOMA							
1 Jones	Y	N	Y	Y	N	N	Y
2 Synar	Y	Y	Y	Y	N	Y	Y
3 Watkins	Y	N	Y	Y	Y	N	Y
4 McCurdy	Y	N	Y	Y	N	N	Y
5 ***Edwards***	Y	N	Y	Y	Y	N	N
6 English	Y	N	Y	Y	Y	N	Y
OREGON							
1 AuCoin	Y	N	Y	Y	N	Y	N
2 ***Smith, R.***	N	N	Y	?	?	?	?
3 Wyden	Y	N	Y	Y	N	Y	Y
4 Weaver	Y	N	Y	Y	N	Y	Y
5 ***Smith, D.***	N	N	Y	N	Y	N	?
PENNSYLVANIA							
1 Foglietta	Y	Y	Y	Y	N	Y	Y
2 Gray	Y	Y	Y	Y	N	Y	Y
3 Borski	Y	Y	Y	Y	N	Y	Y
4 Kolter	Y	N	Y	Y	N	Y	Y
5 ***Schulze***	Y	N	Y	Y	Y	N	?
6 Yatron	Y	N	Y	Y	N	Y	Y
7 Edgar	Y	Y	Y	Y	N	Y	Y
8 Kostmayer	Y	Y	Y	Y	N	Y	Y
9 ***Shuster***	Y	N	Y	?	Y	Y	N
10 ***McDade***	Y	N	Y	Y	Y	Y	Y
11 Harrison	Y	N	Y	?	?	?	?
12 Murtha	Y	N	Y	Y	N	Y	Y
13 ***Coughlin***	Y	N	Y	N	Y	N	Y
14 Coyne	Y	Y	Y	Y	N	Y	Y
15 ***Ritter***	Y	N	Y	Y	Y	N	Y
16 ***Walker***	Y	N	Y	N	Y	N	N
17 ***Gekas***	N	N	Y	Y	Y	N	N
18 Walgren	Y	Y	Y	Y	N	Y	Y
19 ***Goodling***	Y	N	Y	N	Y	Y	N
20 Gaydos	Y	N	Y	Y	?	?	?
21 ***Ridge***	Y	N	Y	Y	Y	Y	?
22 Murphy	Y	Y	Y	Y	Y	Y	Y
23 ***Clinger***	Y	N	Y	Y	Y	Y	N
RHODE ISLAND							
1 St Germain	Y	N	Y	P	N	Y	Y
2 ***Schneider***	Y	N	?	Y	N	Y	Y
SOUTH CAROLINA							
1 ***Hartnett***	N	N	Y	Y	Y	N	Y
2 ***Spence***	Y	N	Y	Y	N	Y	N
3 Derrick	Y	N	Y	Y	N	Y	Y
4 ***Campbell***	Y	N	Y	Y	N	Y	N
5 Spratt	Y	N	Y	Y	N	Y	Y
6 Tallon	Y	N	Y	Y	N	Y	Y
SOUTH DAKOTA							
AL Daschle	Y	N	Y	Y	N	Y	Y

	342	343	344	345	346	347	348
TENNESSEE							
1 ***Quillen***	Y	N	Y	Y	Y	N	Y
2 ***Duncan***	Y	N	Y	Y	Y	Y	Y
3 Lloyd	Y	N	Y	Y	Y	Y	Y
4 Cooper	Y	Y	Y	Y	N	Y	Y
5 Boner	Y	N	Y	Y	N	Y	Y
6 Gore	Y	N	Y	Y	N	Y	Y
7 ***Sundquist***	Y	N	Y	Y	Y	Y	N
8 Jones	Y	N	Y	?	?	?	?
9 Ford	Y	N	Y	Y	N	Y	Y
TEXAS							
1 Hall, S.	Y	N	Y	Y	Y	Y	Y
2 Wilson	Y	N	Y	Y	Y	Y	Y
3 ***Bartlett***	N	N	Y	Y	Y	N	N
4 Hall, R.	Y	N	Y	Y	Y	N	Y
5 Bryant	Y	N	Y	Y	N	Y	Y
6 ***Gramm***	?	?	?	?	?	?	?
7 ***Archer***	N	N	Y	Y	Y	N	N
8 ***Fields***	N	N	Y	N	Y	N	N
9 Brooks	Y	Y	Y	Y	Y	Y	Y
10 Pickle	Y	N	Y	Y	Y	Y	Y
11 Leath	N	N	Y	Y	Y	Y	Y
12 Wright	Y	N	Y	Y	Y	Y	Y
13 Hightower	Y	N	Y	Y	N	N	Y
14 Patman	N	N	Y	Y	Y	N	Y
15 de la Garza	Y	N	Y	?	N	Y	Y
16 Coleman	Y	N	Y	?	?	?	?
17 Stenholm	N	N	Y	Y	Y	N	Y
18 Leland	Y	Y	Y	Y	N	Y	Y
19 Hance	Y	N	Y	Y	Y	N	Y
20 Gonzalez	Y	Y	Y	Y	N	N	Y
21 ***Loeffler***	N	N	Y	Y	Y	N	N
22 ***Paul***	N	N	Y	Y	Y	N	N
23 Kazen	Y	N	Y	Y	Y	N	Y
24 Frost	Y	N	Y	Y	Y	Y	Y
25 Andrews	Y	N	Y	Y	Y	Y	Y
26 Vandergriff	Y	N	Y	Y	Y	N	Y
27 Ortiz	Y	N	Y	Y	N	Y	Y
UTAH							
1 ***Hansen***	Y	N	Y	Y	Y	N	N
2 ***Marriott***	Y	N	Y	Y	Y	N	N
3 ***Nielson***	N	N	Y	Y	Y	N	Y
VERMONT							
AL ***Jeffords***	?	?	?	?	Y	N	Y
VIRGINIA							
1 ***Bateman***	Y	N	Y	Y	N	Y	Y
2 ***Whitehurst***	Y	N	Y	Y	N	Y	Y
3 ***Bliley***	Y	N	Y	Y	Y	Y	N
4 Sisisky	Y	N	Y	Y	N	Y	Y
5 Daniel	N	N	Y	Y	N	Y	Y
6 Olin	Y	N	Y	Y	N	Y	Y
7 ***Robinson***	N	N	Y	Y	Y	Y	Y
8 ***Parris***	Y	N	Y	?	Y	Y	Y
9 Boucher	Y	Y	Y	Y	N	Y	Y
10 ***Wolf***	Y	N	Y	Y	Y	Y	Y
WASHINGTON							
1 ***Pritchard***	?	?	?	?	?	?	?
2 Swift	Y	Y	Y	Y	N	Y	Y
3 Bonker	Y	N	Y	Y	N	Y	Y
4 ***Morrison***	Y	N	Y	Y	N	Y	Y
5 Foley	Y	Y	Y	Y	N	Y	Y
6 Dicks	Y	N	Y	Y	N	Y	Y
7 Lowry	Y	Y	Y	Y	N	Y	Y
8 ***Chandler***	Y	N	Y	Y	?	?	?
WEST VIRGINIA							
1 Mollohan	Y	N	Y	?	Y	Y	?
2 Staggers	Y	N	Y	Y	N	Y	Y
3 Wise	Y	N	Y	Y	N	Y	Y
4 Rahall	Y	N	Y	Y	N	Y	Y
WISCONSIN							
1 Aspin	Y	N	Y	?	N	Y	Y
2 Kastenmeier	Y	Y	Y	Y	N	Y	Y
3 ***Gunderson***	Y	N	Y	Y	Y	N	Y
4 Kleczka	Y	N	Y	Y	N	Y	Y
5 Moody	Y	Y	Y	Y	N	Y	Y
6 ***Petri***	Y	N	Y	Y	Y	N	Y
7 Obey	Y	Y	Y	Y	N	Y	N
8 ***Roth***	Y	N	Y	Y	N	Y	Y
9 ***Sensenbrenner***	Y	N	Y	Y	N	Y	N
WYOMING							
AL ***Cheney***	?	?	?	?	?	?	?

Southern states - Ala., Ark., Fla., Ga., Ky., La., Miss., N.C., Okla., S.C., Tenn., Texas, Va.

349. Procedural Motion.
Brown, R-Colo., motion to approve the House *Journal* of Thursday, Sept. 13. Motion agreed to 250-16: R 100-9; D 150-7 (ND 94-6, SD 56-1), Sept. 14, 1984.

350. HR 1511. Port-Cargo Diversion.
Biaggi, D-N.Y., motion to suspend the rules and pass the bill to require shippers moving U.S. cargo through ports in Canada and Mexico to file their rates with the Federal Maritime Commission. Motion rejected 188-209: R 42-114; D 146-95 (ND 113-45, SD 33-50), Sept. 18, 1984. A two-thirds majority of those present and voting (265 in this case) is required for passage under suspension of the rules.

351. HR 3336. Insanity Defense Revisions.
Conyers, D-Mich., motion to suspend the rules and pass the bill to revise the insanity defense to make it more restrictive. Motion rejected 225-171: R 33-122; D 192-49 (ND 146-12, SD 46-37), Sept. 18, 1984. A two-thirds majority of those present and voting (264 in this case) is required for passage under suspension of the rules.

352. HR 5656. Dangerous Drug Diversion Control.
Hughes, D-N.J., motion to suspend the rules and pass the bill to curb the diversion of prescription drugs from medical channels to the black market. Motion agreed to 392-1: R 154-1; D 238-0 (ND 155-0, SD 83-0), Sept. 18, 1984. A two-thirds majority of those present and voting (262 in this case) is required for passage under suspension of the rules. A "yea" was a vote supporting the president's position.

353. HR 5959. Safe Drinking Water.
Waxman, D-Calif., motion to suspend the rules and pass the bill to set deadlines for establishing federal standards on contaminants in drinking water, to revise program enforcement and other authorities, to establish new groundwater protection programs, and to authorize $216 million annually for fiscal years 1986-89 for federal safe drinking water programs and the new groundwater programs. Motion agreed to 366-27: R 128-26; D 238-1 (ND 157-0, SD 81-1), Sept. 18, 1984. A two-thirds majority of those present and voting (262 in this case) is required for passage under suspension of the rules. A "nay" was a vote supporting the president's position.

354. HR 5290. Compassionate Pain Relief.
Hughes, D-N.J., amendment to increase penalties for illegal diversion of diacetylmorphine (heroin) authorized for medicinal use, to require physician peer review of decisions to prescribe the drug and to otherwise strengthen protections against illegal diversion of the drug from its intended purpose of relief of intractable pain in dying patients. Rejected 178-232: R 18-141; D 160-91 (ND 134-35, SD 26-56), Sept. 19, 1984.

355. HR 5290. Compassionate Pain Relief.
Passage of the bill to authorize the federal government to provide diacetylmorphine (heroin) to hospital and hospice pharmacies for doctors to prescribe, with certain limits, for treatment of intractable pain in dying patients. Rejected 55-355: R 11-148; D 44-207 (ND 41-129, SD 3-78), Sept. 19, 1984. A "nay" was a vote supporting the president's position.

356. HR 5164. Central Intelligence Agency Information Act.
Boland, D-Mass., motion to suspend the rules and pass the bill to allow the CIA director to close certain operational files from search-and-review provisions of the Freedom of Information Act. Motion agreed to 369-36: R 155-1; D 214-35 (ND 136-33, SD 78-2), Sept. 19, 1984. A two-thirds majority of those present and voting (270 in this case) is required for passage under suspension of the rules.

KEY

Y	Voted for (yea).
#	Paired for.
+	Announced for.
N	Voted against (nay).
X	Paired against.
-	Announced against.
P	Voted "present".
C	Voted "present" to avoid possible conflict of interest.
?	Did not vote or otherwise make a position known.

Democrats   *Republicans*

Member	349	350	351	352	353	354	355	356
ALABAMA								
1 Edwards	Y	Y	Y	Y	Y	N	N	Y
2 Dickinson	N	N	N	Y	Y	N	N	Y
3 Nichols	?	N	Y	Y	Y	N	N	Y
4 Bevill	Y	N	N	Y	Y	N	N	Y
5 Flippo	Y	N	N	Y	Y	N	N	Y
6 Erdreich	Y	N	N	Y	Y	N	N	Y
7 Shelby	Y	N	N	Y	Y	?	?	?
ALASKA								
AL Young	Y	Y	N	Y	Y	N	N	Y
ARIZONA								
1 McCain	?	N	N	Y	N	N	N	Y
2 Udall	Y	N	Y	Y	Y	Y	N	Y
3 Stump	?	N	N	Y	N	N	N	Y
4 Rudd	?	N	N	Y	N	N	N	Y
5 McNulty	?	N	Y	Y	Y	Y	N	Y
ARKANSAS								
1 Alexander	?	?	?	?	?	?	?	?
2 Bethune	?	?	?	?	?	?	?	?
3 Hammerschmidt	Y	N	N	Y	N	N	N	Y
4 Anthony	Y	?	?	?	?	Y	-	Y
CALIFORNIA								
1 Bosco	?	N	N	Y	Y	Y	N	Y
2 Chappie	?	N	N	Y	N	N	N	Y
3 Matsui	Y	Y	Y	Y	Y	Y	N	Y
4 Fazio	Y	Y	Y	Y	Y	Y	N	Y
5 Burton	Y	Y	Y	Y	Y	Y	Y	N
6 Boxer	?	Y	Y	Y	Y	Y	N	N
7 Miller	?	Y	Y	Y	Y	Y	Y	Y
8 Dellums	?	Y	Y	Y	Y	Y	N	N
9 Stark	?	Y	Y	Y	Y	Y	N	N
10 Edwards	Y	Y	Y	Y	Y	Y	N	N
11 Lantos	?	Y	Y	Y	Y	Y	N	Y
12 Zschau	?	N	Y	Y	Y	N	N	Y
13 Mineta	Y	Y	Y	Y	Y	Y	N	Y
14 Shumway	Y	N	N	Y	N	N	N	Y
15 Coelho	?	Y	Y	Y	Y	Y	N	Y
16 Panetta	Y	Y	Y	Y	Y	N	N	Y
17 Pashayan	Y	N	N	Y	Y	N	N	Y
18 Lehman	Y	?	?	?	?	?	?	?
19 Lagomarsino	Y	N	N	Y	Y	N	N	Y
20 Thomas	?	N	N	Y	Y	N	N	Y
21 Fiedler	Y	N	Y	Y	Y	N	N	Y
22 Moorhead	Y	N	N	Y	Y	?	?	?
23 Beilenson	Y	N	Y	Y	Y	N	N	Y
24 Waxman	Y	Y	Y	Y	Y	Y	Y	Y
25 Roybal	Y	Y	Y	Y	Y	Y	N	N
26 Berman	Y	Y	Y	Y	Y	Y	Y	Y
27 Levine	Y	Y	Y	Y	Y	Y	Y	Y
28 Dixon	Y	Y	Y	Y	Y	Y	N	N
29 Hawkins	Y	Y	Y	Y	Y	Y	N	N
30 Martinez	?	Y	Y	Y	Y	Y	N	Y
31 Dymally	P	Y	Y	Y	Y	Y	N	N
32 Anderson	Y	Y	Y	Y	Y	N	N	Y
33 Dreier	Y	N	N	Y	N	N	N	Y
34 Torres	?	Y	Y	Y	Y	Y	N	N
35 Lewis	Y	N	N	Y	Y	N	N	Y
36 Brown	Y	Y	Y	Y	Y	Y	Y	Y
37 McCandless	?	N	N	Y	Y	N	N	Y
38 Patterson	?	Y	Y	Y	Y	Y	N	Y
39 Dannemeyer	?	N	N	N	N	N	N	Y
40 Badham	Y	N	N	Y	Y	N	N	Y
41 Lowery	?	?	?	?	?	N	N	Y
42 Lungren	Y	N	N	Y	N	N	N	Y
43 Packard	Y	N	N	Y	Y	N	N	Y
44 Bates	Y	Y	Y	Y	Y	Y	N	Y
45 Hunter	?	N	N	Y	Y	N	N	Y
COLORADO								
1 Schroeder	?	Y	Y	Y	Y	Y	N	Y
2 Wirth	?	Y	Y	Y	Y	Y	N	Y
3 Kogovsek	Y	N	Y	Y	Y	Y	N	?
4 Brown	Y	N	N	Y	N	N	N	Y
5 Kramer	Y	N	N	Y	Y	N	N	Y
6 Schaefer	Y	N	N	Y	N	N	N	Y
CONNECTICUT								
1 Kennelly	?	Y	Y	Y	Y	Y	N	Y
2 Gejdenson	N	Y	Y	Y	Y	Y	N	Y
3 Morrison	?	Y	Y	Y	Y	+	-	+
4 McKinney	?	Y	N	Y	Y	Y	Y	Y
5 Ratchford	Y	N	Y	Y	Y	Y	N	Y
6 Johnson	Y	N	Y	Y	Y	Y	N	Y
DELAWARE								
AL Carper	?	Y	Y	Y	Y	Y	N	Y
FLORIDA								
1 Hutto	Y	N	N	Y	Y	N	N	Y
2 Fuqua	?	N	N	Y	Y	?	-	N
3 Bennett	Y	Y	Y	Y	Y	N	N	Y
4 Chappell	Y	N	N	Y	Y	N	N	Y
5 McCollum	Y	N	N	Y	N	N	N	Y
6 MacKay	?	-	+	+	Y	N	N	Y
7 Gibbons	?	N	N	Y	Y	N	N	Y
8 Young	Y	N	N	Y	Y	N	N	Y
9 Bilirakis	Y	N	N	Y	Y	N	N	Y
10 Ireland	Y	N	N	Y	Y	N	N	Y
11 Nelson	Y	Y	Y	Y	Y	Y	N	Y
12 Lewis	Y	N	N	Y	Y	N	N	Y
13 Mack	?	N	N	Y	Y	N	N	Y
14 Mica	Y	N	N	Y	Y	N	N	Y
15 Shaw	Y	N	N	Y	Y	N	N	Y
16 Smith	Y	Y	Y	Y	Y	N	N	Y
17 Lehman	Y	?	?	?	?	?	?	?
18 Pepper	?	N	Y	Y	Y	N	N	Y
19 Fascell	?	Y	Y	Y	Y	N	N	Y
GEORGIA								
1 Thomas	Y	Y	Y	Y	Y	N	N	Y
2 Hatcher	Y	N	Y	Y	Y	N	N	Y
3 Ray	Y	N	Y	Y	Y	N	N	Y
4 Levitas	Y	N	Y	Y	Y	N	N	Y
5 Fowler	?	N	N	Y	Y	N	N	Y
6 Gingrich	Y	N	?	?	?	N	N	Y
7 Darden	Y	N	N	Y	Y	N	N	Y
8 Rowland	Y	Y	Y	Y	Y	N	N	Y
9 Jenkins	Y	N	N	Y	Y	N	N	Y
10 Barnard	?	N	N	Y	Y	N	N	Y
HAWAII								
1 Heftel	?	?	?	?	?	Y	Y	Y
2 Akaka	Y	Y	Y	Y	Y	Y	Y	Y
IDAHO								
1 Craig	N	N	N	Y	Y	N	N	Y
2 Hansen	?	N	N	Y	N	N	N	Y
ILLINOIS								
1 Hayes	?	Y	Y	Y	Y	N	N	N
2 Savage	?	Y	Y	Y	Y	Y	N	N
3 Russo	Y	Y	Y	Y	Y	Y	N	Y
4 O'Brien	?	Y	N	Y	Y	N	Y	Y
5 Lipinski	?	Y	Y	Y	Y	Y	N	Y
6 Hyde	Y	N	N	Y	Y	N	N	Y
7 Collins	Y	?	?	?	?	N	N	Y
8 Rostenkowski	?	Y	Y	Y	Y	Y	N	Y
9 Yates	Y	N	Y	Y	Y	Y	N	Y
10 Porter	Y	N	N	Y	Y	N	N	Y
11 Annunzio	Y	Y	Y	Y	Y	Y	N	Y
12 Crane, P.	?	N	N	Y	N	N	N	Y
13 Erlenborn	Y	N	N	Y	Y	N	N	Y
14 Corcoran	Y	N	N	Y	Y	N	N	Y
15 Madigan	Y	N	N	Y	Y	N	N	Y
16 Martin	?	N	N	Y	Y	Y	Y	Y
17 Evans	Y	N	N	Y	Y	Y	N	N
18 Michel	Y	N	N	Y	Y	N	N	Y
19 Crane, D.	?	N	N	Y	N	N	N	Y
20 Durbin	?	N	Y	Y	Y	N	N	Y
21 Price	Y	Y	Y	Y	Y	N	N	Y
22 Simon	?	?	?	?	?	?	?	?
INDIANA								
1 Hall	?	Y	Y	Y	Y	Y	N	Y
2 Sharp	Y	N	N	Y	Y	Y	Y	Y
3 Hiler	?	N	N	Y	N	N	N	Y
4 Coats	Y	N	N	Y	Y	N	N	Y
5 Hillis	Y	N	N	Y	Y	N	N	Y

ND - Northern Democrats   SD - Southern Democrats

Corresponding to Congressional Record Votes 392, 393, 394, 395, 396, 400, 401, 402

	349	350	351	352	353	354	355	356
6 ***Burton***	Y	N	N	Y	Y	N	N	Y
7 ***Myers***	Y	N	Y	Y	N	N	N	Y
8 McCloskey	Y	N	Y	Y	Y	Y	N	Y
9 Hamilton	Y	N	N	Y	Y	Y	Y	Y
10 Jacobs	N	N	N	Y	Y	Y	N	Y
IOWA								
1 ***Leach***	Y	N	Y	Y	Y	N	N	Y
2 ***Tauke***	Y	N	N	Y	Y	N	N	Y
3 ***Evans***	N	N	N	Y	Y	N	N	Y
4 Smith	Y	N	Y	Y	Y	Y	N	Y
5 Harkin	?	?	?	?	?	Y	N	Y
6 Bedell	Y	N	Y	Y	Y	Y	N	N
KANSAS								
1 ***Roberts***	N	N	N	Y	Y	N	N	Y
2 Slattery	Y	N	Y	Y	Y	Y	N	Y
3 ***Winn***	Y	N	N	Y	Y	N	N	Y
4 Glickman	Y	N	Y	Y	Y	N	N	Y
5 ***Whittaker***	Y	N	N	Y	Y	Y	N	Y
KENTUCKY								
1 Hubbard	Y	N	Y	Y	Y	N	N	Y
2 Natcher	Y	N	N	Y	Y	N	N	Y
3 Mazzoli	Y	N	Y	Y	Y	N	N	Y
4 ***Snyder***	?	Y	N	Y	Y	N	N	Y
5 ***Rogers***	Y	Y	N	Y	Y	N	N	Y
6 ***Hopkins***	Y	N	N	Y	Y	N	N	Y
7 Vacancy								
LOUISIANA								
1 ***Livingston***	Y	Y	N	Y	Y	N	N	Y
2 Boggs	?	?	?	?	?	Y	N	Y
3 Tauzin	?	Y	N	Y	Y	N	N	Y
4 Roemer	N	Y	N	Y	Y	N	N	Y
5 Huckaby	Y	N	N	Y	?	N	N	Y
6 ***Moore***	Y	Y	N	Y	Y	N	N	Y
7 Breaux	Y	Y	Y	Y	Y	?	?	?
8 Long	Y	Y	Y	Y	Y	Y	N	Y
MAINE								
1 ***McKernan***	Y	Y	Y	Y	Y	Y	N	Y
2 ***Snowe***	Y	Y	N	Y	Y	Y	N	Y
MARYLAND								
1 Dyson	?	Y	Y	Y	Y	N	N	Y
2 Long	Y	Y	Y	Y	?	Y	Y	Y
3 Mikulski	?	Y	Y	Y	Y	Y	Y	Y
4 ***Holt***	N	?	?	?	?	N	N	Y
5 Hoyer	Y	Y	Y	Y	Y	Y	Y	Y
6 Byron	?	Y	Y	Y	Y	N	N	Y
7 Mitchell	?	Y	Y	Y	Y	N	N	N
8 Barnes	Y	Y	Y	Y	Y	Y	N	Y
MASSACHUSETTS								
1 ***Conte***	Y	Y	Y	Y	Y	Y	N	Y
2 Boland	Y	?	+	+	+	Y	N	Y
3 Early	?	?	?	?	?	N	N	Y
4 Frank	Y	Y	Y	Y	Y	Y	Y	Y
5 Shannon	?	?	?	?	?	?	?	?
6 Mavroules	Y	Y	Y	Y	Y	N	N	Y
7 Markey	?	+	+	+	+	?	?	?
8 O'Neill								
9 Moakley	?	?	?	?	?	Y	Y	Y
10 Studds	?	?	?	?	?	?	?	?
11 Donnelly	?	?	?	?	?	Y	Y	Y
MICHIGAN								
1 Conyers	?	Y	Y	Y	Y	Y	N	N
2 ***Pursell***	Y	N	Y	Y	Y	N	N	Y
3 Wolpe	?	N	Y	Y	Y	Y	N	Y
4 ***Siljander***	?	N	Y	Y	Y	N	N	Y
5 ***Sawyer***	?	N	Y	Y	Y	Y	N	Y
6 Carr	Y	N	Y	Y	Y	Y	N	Y
7 Kildee	Y	N	Y	Y	Y	Y	N	Y
8 Traxler	?	N	Y	?	Y	Y	N	Y
9 ***Vander Jagt***	?	N	N	Y	Y	N	N	Y
10 Albosta	?	N	Y	Y	Y	Y	N	Y
11 ***Davis***	Y	N	Y	Y	Y	N	N	Y
12 Bonior	?	N	Y	Y	Y	Y	Y	Y
13 Crockett	?	N	Y	?	Y	N	N	N
14 Hertel	Y	N	Y	Y	Y	Y	N	Y
15 Ford	?	N	Y	Y	Y	Y	Y	Y
16 Dingell	Y	N	Y	Y	Y	Y	Y	Y
17 Levin	Y	N	Y	Y	Y	Y	N	Y
18 ***Broomfield***	?	N	Y	Y	Y	N	N	Y
MINNESOTA								
1 Penny	N	N	Y	Y	Y	N	N	Y
2 ***Weber***	?	N	N	Y	Y	N	N	?
3 ***Frenzel***	Y	N	N	Y	Y	N	N	Y
4 Vento	Y	Y	Y	Y	Y	Y	Y	Y
5 Sabo	Y	Y	Y	Y	Y	Y	Y	Y
6 Sikorski	N	Y	Y	Y	Y	N	N	Y

	349	350	351	352	353	354	355	356
7 ***Stangeland***	?	N	N	Y	Y	N	N	Y
8 Oberstar	?	Y	Y	Y	Y	Y	N	Y
MISSISSIPPI								
1 Whitten	Y	N	Y	Y	Y	N	N	?
2 ***Franklin***	?	?	?	?	?	N	N	Y
3 Montgomery	Y	N	N	Y	Y	N	N	Y
4 Dowdy	?	N	N	Y	Y	N	N	Y
5 ***Lott***	Y	Y	N	Y	Y	N	N	Y
MISSOURI								
1 Clay	N	N	Y	Y	Y	Y	N	N
2 Young	Y	Y	Y	Y	Y	N	N	Y
3 Gephardt	?	N	Y	Y	Y	Y	N	Y
4 Skelton	?	N	Y	Y	Y	N	N	Y
5 Wheat	Y	Y	Y	Y	Y	Y	N	Y
6 ***Coleman***	Y	N	N	Y	Y	N	N	Y
7 ***Taylor***	Y	Y	N	Y	Y	N	N	Y
8 ***Emerson***	N	N	N	Y	Y	N	N	Y
9 Volkmer	?	N	Y	Y	Y	N	N	Y
MONTANA								
1 Williams	Y	Y	Y	Y	Y	Y	N	Y
2 ***Marlenee***	Y	N	Y	Y	Y	N	N	Y
NEBRASKA								
1 ***Bereuter***	Y	N	N	Y	Y	N	N	Y
2 ***Daub***	?	N	N	Y	Y	N	N	Y
3 ***Smith***	Y	N	N	Y	Y	N	N	Y
NEVADA								
1 Reid	Y	N	N	Y	Y	Y	N	Y
2 ***Vucanovich***	?	?	?	?	?	N	N	Y
NEW HAMPSHIRE								
1 D'Amours	?	N	Y	Y	Y	N	N	Y
2 ***Gregg***	?	N	N	Y	Y	N	N	Y
NEW JERSEY								
1 Florio	?	Y	Y	Y	Y	Y	N	Y
2 Hughes	Y	Y	Y	Y	Y	Y	N	Y
3 Howard	Y	Y	Y	Y	Y	Y	N	Y
4 ***Smith***	?	Y	Y	Y	Y	Y	N	Y
5 ***Roukema***	?	Y	Y	Y	Y	N	N	Y
6 Dwyer	Y	Y	Y	Y	Y	Y	N	Y
7 ***Rinaldo***	Y	Y	Y	Y	Y	Y	N	Y
8 Roe	Y	Y	Y	Y	Y	N	N	Y
9 Torricelli	?	Y	Y	Y	Y	N	N	Y
10 Rodino	Y	?	?	?	?	Y	N	Y
11 Minish	?	Y	Y	Y	Y	N	N	Y
12 ***Courter***	Y	Y	N	Y	Y	?	?	?
13 Vacancy								
14 Guarini	?	?	?	?	?	N	N	Y
NEW MEXICO								
1 ***Lujan***	Y	N	Y	Y	Y	N	N	Y
2 ***Skeen***	?	N	N	Y	Y	N	N	Y
3 Richardson	Y	Y	Y	Y	Y	Y	N	Y
NEW YORK								
1 ***Carney***	?	Y	N	Y	Y	N	N	Y
2 Downey	Y	Y	Y	Y	Y	Y	N	Y
3 Mrazek	Y	Y	Y	Y	Y	Y	N	Y
4 ***Lent***	Y	Y	N	Y	Y	N	N	Y
5 ***McGrath***	Y	?	?	?	?	?	?	?
6 Addabbo	Y	Y	Y	Y	Y	Y	N	Y
7 Ackerman	?	Y	Y	Y	Y	Y	Y	N
8 Scheuer	Y	Y	Y	Y	Y	Y	N	Y
9 Ferraro	?	?	?	?	?	?	?	?
10 Schumer	?	Y	Y	Y	Y	Y	N	Y
11 Towns	?	Y	Y	Y	Y	N	N	N
12 Owens	Y	Y	Y	?	Y	Y	N	N
13 Solarz	Y	Y	Y	Y	Y	Y	Y	Y
14 ***Molinari***	Y	Y	N	Y	Y	N	N	Y
15 ***Green***	Y	Y	Y	Y	Y	Y	Y	Y
16 Rangel	Y	Y	Y	Y	Y	N	N	Y
17 Weiss	Y	Y	Y	Y	Y	Y	Y	N
18 Garcia	?	Y	Y	Y	Y	N	N	N
19 Biaggi	?	Y	Y	Y	Y	Y	N	Y
20 Ottinger	?	Y	Y	Y	Y	Y	Y	N
21 ***Fish***	Y	Y	Y	Y	Y	N	N	Y
22 ***Gilman***	?	Y	Y	Y	Y	N	N	Y
23 Stratton	Y	Y	Y	Y	Y	?	Y	Y
24 ***Solomon***	N	Y	N	Y	Y	N	N	Y
25 ***Boehlert***	?	Y	Y	Y	Y	N	N	Y
26 ***Martin***	Y	N	N	Y	Y	N	N	Y
27 ***Wortley***	Y	N	N	Y	Y	N	N	Y
28 McHugh	Y	Y	Y	Y	Y	Y	N	Y
29 ***Horton***	Y	Y	Y	Y	?	N	N	Y
30 ***Conable***	Y	N	N	Y	Y	N	N	?
31 ***Kemp***	?	N	N	Y	Y	N	N	Y
32 LaFalce	?	?	Y	Y	Y	Y	N	Y
33 Nowak	Y	Y	Y	Y	Y	Y	N	Y
34 Lundine	Y	Y	Y	Y	Y	Y	N	Y

	349	350	351	352	353	354	355	356
NORTH CAROLINA								
1 Jones	Y	Y	Y	Y	Y	Y	N	Y
2 Valentine	Y	N	N	Y	Y	N	N	Y
3 Whitley	?	N	N	Y	Y	N	N	Y
4 Andrews	Y	Y	N	Y	Y	Y	N	Y
5 Neal	?	Y	N	Y	Y	Y	N	Y
6 Britt	?	Y	Y	Y	Y	Y	N	Y
7 Rose	Y	Y	Y	Y	Y	N	N	Y
8 Hefner	Y	Y	Y	Y	Y	N	N	Y
9 ***Martin***	?	?	?	?	?	N	N	Y
10 ***Broyhill***	?	N	N	Y	Y	N	N	Y
11 Clarke	Y	N	Y	Y	Y	Y	N	Y
NORTH DAKOTA								
AL Dorgan	Y	N	Y	Y	Y	Y	N	N
OHIO								
1 Luken	?	N	Y	Y	Y	Y	Y	Y
2 ***Gradison***	Y	N	Y	Y	Y	N	N	Y
3 Hall	Y	Y	Y	Y	Y	Y	N	Y
4 ***Oxley***	?	N	N	Y	Y	N	N	Y
5 ***Latta***	Y	N	N	Y	Y	N	N	Y
6 ***McEwen***	Y	N	Y	Y	Y	N	N	Y
7 ***DeWine***	Y	N	N	Y	Y	Y	Y	Y
8 ***Kindness***	Y	N	N	Y	Y	N	N	Y
9 Kaptur	?	N	Y	Y	Y	N	N	Y
10 ***Miller***	N	N	N	Y	Y	N	N	Y
11 Eckart	Y	Y	Y	Y	Y	Y	N	Y
12 ***Kasich***	Y	N	N	Y	Y	N	N	Y
13 Pease	Y	Y	Y	Y	Y	Y	N	Y
14 Seiberling	?	N	Y	Y	Y	Y	N	N
15 ***Wylie***	Y	N	N	Y	Y	?	?	?
16 ***Regula***	Y	Y	Y	Y	Y	N	N	Y
17 ***Williams***	?	?	?	?	?	?	?	?
18 Applegate	?	Y	N	Y	Y	Y	Y	Y
19 Feighan	?	?	?	?	?	Y	N	Y
20 Oakar	Y	Y	Y	Y	Y	Y	Y	Y
21 Stokes	Y	Y	Y	Y	Y	Y	Y	Y
OKLAHOMA								
1 Jones	Y	N	N	Y	Y	N	N	Y
2 Synar	Y	N	Y	Y	Y	Y	Y	Y
3 Watkins	Y	N	N	Y	Y	N	N	Y
4 McCurdy	Y	N	N	Y	Y	N	N	Y
5 ***Edwards***	Y	N	N	Y	Y	N	N	?
6 English	Y	N	N	Y	Y	N	N	Y
OREGON								
1 AuCoin	?	N	Y	Y	Y	N	N	N
2 ***Smith, R.***	?	Y	N	Y	N	N	N	Y
3 Wyden	Y	N	Y	Y	Y	N	N	Y
4 Weaver	?	N	Y	Y	Y	Y	Y	N
5 ***Smith, D.***	?	N	N	Y	N	N	N	Y
PENNSYLVANIA								
1 Foglietta	Y	?	?	?	?	Y	N	Y
2 Gray	Y	Y	Y	Y	Y	N	N	N
3 Borski	Y	Y	Y	Y	Y	Y	N	Y
4 Kolter	Y	Y	N	Y	Y	Y	N	Y
5 ***Schulze***	?	N	N	Y	Y	N	N	Y
6 Yatron	?	Y	N	Y	Y	N	N	Y
7 Edgar	Y	Y	Y	Y	Y	Y	N	N
8 Kostmayer	Y	Y	?	?	?	Y	N	N
9 ***Shuster***	Y	Y	N	Y	Y	N	N	Y
10 ***McDade***	Y	N	N	Y	Y	N	N	Y
11 Harrison	?	Y	Y	Y	Y	Y	Y	Y
12 Murtha	Y	Y	N	Y	Y	Y	N	Y
13 ***Coughlin***	N	Y	N	Y	Y	N	N	Y
14 Coyne	?	Y	Y	Y	Y	Y	Y	Y
15 ***Ritter***	Y	N	N	Y	Y	Y	N	Y
16 ***Walker***	?	N	N	Y	Y	N	N	Y
17 ***Gekas***	Y	N	N	Y	Y	N	N	Y
18 Walgren	?	Y	N	Y	Y	Y	Y	Y
19 ***Goodling***	Y	Y	Y	Y	Y	N	N	Y
20 Gaydos	?	Y	N	Y	Y	Y	N	Y
21 ***Ridge***	Y	Y	N	Y	Y	N	N	Y
22 Murphy	Y	Y	N	Y	Y	Y	N	N
23 ***Clinger***	Y	Y	N	Y	Y	N	N	Y
RHODE ISLAND								
1 St Germain	?	Y	Y	Y	Y	Y	N	Y
2 ***Schneider***	?	Y	Y	Y	Y	N	Y	Y
SOUTH CAROLINA								
1 ***Hartnett***	?	N	N	Y	N	N	N	Y
2 ***Spence***	Y	N	N	Y	Y	Y	N	Y
3 Derrick	?	N	Y	Y	Y	N	N	Y
4 ***Campbell***	Y	N	N	Y	Y	N	N	Y
5 Spratt	Y	N	Y	Y	Y	N	N	Y
6 Tallon	Y	Y	Y	Y	Y	N	N	Y
SOUTH DAKOTA								
AL Daschle	Y	N	Y	Y	Y	N	N	Y

	349	350	351	352	353	354	355	356
TENNESSEE								
1 ***Quillen***	?	Y	N	Y	N	N	N	Y
2 ***Duncan***	Y	N	N	Y	Y	N	N	Y
3 Lloyd	Y	Y	Y	Y	Y	N	N	Y
4 Cooper	?	Y	Y	Y	Y	Y	Y	Y
5 Boner	Y	Y	Y	Y	Y	?	?	?
6 Gore	Y	Y	Y	Y	Y	Y	N	Y
7 ***Sundquist***	Y	Y	N	Y	Y	N	N	Y
8 Jones	?	N	Y	Y	Y	Y	N	Y
9 Ford	Y	Y	Y	Y	Y	Y	N	Y
TEXAS								
1 Hall, S.	Y	N	Y	Y	Y	N	N	Y
2 Wilson	?	Y	N	Y	Y	Y	N	?
3 ***Bartlett***	?	N	N	Y	N	N	N	Y
4 Hall, R.	Y	N	Y	Y	Y	N	N	Y
5 Bryant	?	Y	Y	Y	Y	Y	N	Y
6 ***Gramm***	?	?	?	?	?	?	?	?
7 ***Archer***	Y	N	N	Y	N	N	N	Y
8 ***Fields***	Y	Y	N	Y	Y	N	N	Y
9 Brooks	?	Y	Y	Y	Y	N	N	Y
10 Pickle	Y	N	Y	Y	Y	Y	N	Y
11 Leath	Y	N	N	Y	Y	N	N	?
12 Wright	?	Y	Y	Y	Y	Y	N	Y
13 Hightower	Y	N	Y	Y	Y	N	N	Y
14 Patman	Y	N	Y	Y	Y	N	N	Y
15 de la Garza	Y	N	N	Y	Y	N	N	Y
16 Coleman	?	Y	Y	Y	Y	Y	N	Y
17 Stenholm	Y	N	N	Y	Y	N	N	Y
18 Leland	?	Y	Y	Y	Y	Y	N	N
19 Hance	Y	N	N	Y	Y	N	N	Y
20 Gonzalez	Y	N	N	Y	Y	N	N	Y
21 ***Loeffler***	Y	N	N	Y	N	N	N	Y
22 ***Paul***	Y	N	N	N	N	N	Y	N
23 Kazen	Y	N	N	Y	Y	N	N	Y
24 Frost	?	Y	Y	Y	Y	Y	N	Y
25 Andrews	Y	N	Y	Y	Y	N	N	Y
26 Vandergriff	?	N	N	Y	Y	N	N	Y
27 Ortiz	?	Y	Y	Y	Y	N	N	Y
UTAH								
1 ***Hansen***	?	N	N	Y	N	N	N	Y
2 ***Marriott***	?	N	N	Y	N	N	N	Y
3 ***Nielson***	?	N	N	Y	N	N	N	Y
VERMONT								
AL ***Jeffords***	Y	N	Y	Y	Y	Y	N	Y
VIRGINIA								
1 ***Bateman***	Y	Y	N	Y	Y	N	N	Y
2 ***Whitehurst***	Y	Y	N	Y	Y	Y	Y	Y
3 ***Bliley***	Y	N	N	Y	Y	N	N	Y
4 Sisisky	?	Y	Y	Y	Y	Y	N	Y
5 Daniel	?	N	N	Y	N	N	N	Y
6 Olin	?	N	N	Y	Y	N	N	Y
7 ***Robinson***	Y	N	N	Y	N	N	N	Y
8 ***Parris***	Y	Y	N	Y	Y	N	N	Y
9 Boucher	Y	N	Y	Y	Y	Y	N	Y
10 ***Wolf***	Y	Y	N	Y	Y	N	Y	Y
WASHINGTON								
1 ***Pritchard***	?	Y	Y	Y	Y	Y	Y	Y
2 Swift	?	Y	Y	Y	Y	Y	N	Y
3 Bonker	Y	Y	Y	Y	Y	Y	N	Y
4 ***Morrison***	Y	N	N	Y	Y	N	N	Y
5 Foley	?	Y	Y	Y	Y	Y	Y	Y
6 Dicks	Y	Y	Y	Y	Y	Y	N	Y
7 Lowry	N	Y	Y	Y	Y	Y	N	N
8 ***Chandler***	?	?	?	?	?	N	N	Y
WEST VIRGINIA								
1 Mollohan	?	Y	Y	Y	Y	Y	N	Y
2 Staggers	Y	Y	Y	Y	Y	Y	N	Y
3 Wise	Y	Y	Y	Y	Y	Y	Y	Y
4 Rahall	Y	Y	Y	Y	Y	Y	N	Y
WISCONSIN								
1 Aspin	?	N	Y	Y	Y	Y	N	Y
2 Kastenmeier	Y	N	Y	Y	Y	Y	N	N
3 ***Gunderson***	Y	N	N	Y	Y	Y	Y	Y
4 Kleczka	Y	Y	N	Y	Y	N	Y	Y
5 Moody	Y	?	?	?	?	Y	N	Y
6 ***Petri***	Y	N	Y	Y	Y	N	N	Y
7 Obey	Y	N	Y	Y	Y	Y	Y	Y
8 ***Roth***	?	N	Y	Y	Y	N	N	Y
9 ***Sensenbrenner***	Y	N	Y	Y	N	N	N	Y
WYOMING								
AL ***Cheney***	?	?	?	?	?	?	?	?

Southern states - Ala., Ark., Fla., Ga., Ky., La., Miss., N.C., Okla., S.C., Tenn., Texas, Va.

357. HR 3082. Wetlands Resources. Adoption of the rule (H Res 579) providing for House floor consideration of the bill to increase revenues for the Migratory Bird Conservation Fund, authorize a new Wetlands Conservation Fund at $75 million annually, accelerate the National Wetlands Inventory, and authorize use of certain federal lands for a jetty construction project at Oregon Inlet, N.C. Adopted 398-0: R 150-0; D 248-0 (ND 166-0, SD 82-0), Sept. 19, 1984.

358. HR 3755. Social Security Disability Amendments. Adoption of the conference report on the bill to overhaul the Social Security disability review process and to provide for the continuation of benefits for individuals thrown off the rolls who decide to appeal. Adopted (thus cleared for the president) 402-0: R 152-0; D 250-0 (ND 168-0, SD 82-0), Sept. 19, 1984. A "yea" was a vote supporting the president's position.

359. HR 3082. Wetlands Resources. Seiberling, D-Ohio, amendment to strike Title IV, authorizing use of lands within the Cape Hatteras National Seashore and the Pea Island National Wildlife Refuge for the Manteo Bay jetty project at Oregon Inlet, N.C. Rejected 194-203: R 76-79; D 118-124 (ND 103-61, SD 15-63), Sept. 20, 1984.

360. HR 3082. Wetlands Resources. Passage of the bill to increase revenues for the Migratory Bird Conservation Fund, authorize a new Wetlands Conservation Fund at $75 million annually, accelerate the National Wetlands Inventory, and authorize use of certain federal lands for a jetty construction project at Oregon Inlet, N.C. Passed 351-45: R 130-21; D 221-24 (ND 149-17, SD 72-7), Sept. 20, 1984.

361. HR 5585. Railroad Safety Improvement Act. Adoption of the rule (H Res 562) providing for House floor consideration of the bill to authorize $55.4 million in fiscal 1985 and $57.7 million in fiscal 1986 for safety programs of the Federal Railroad Administration. Adopted 389-2: R 150-2; D 239-0 (ND 161-0, SD 78-0), Sept. 20, 1984. A "nay" was a vote supporting the president's position.

362. H J Res 648. Continuing Appropriations, Fiscal 1985. Adoption of the rule (H Res 586) providing for House floor consideration of the bill to provide interim funding for agencies and programs included in the nine regular fiscal 1985 appropriations bills that have not been signed into law. Rejected 168-225: 97-54; D 71-171 (ND 44-119, SD 27-52), Sept. 20, 1984.

KEY

Y Voted for (yea).
Paired for.
+ Announced for.
N Voted against (nay).
X Paired against.
- Announced against.
P Voted "present".
C Voted "present" to avoid possible conflict of interest.
? Did not vote or otherwise make a position known.

Democrats   *Republicans*

	357	358	359	360	361	362
ALABAMA						
1 *Edwards*	Y	Y	N	Y	Y	N
2 *Dickinson*	Y	Y	N	Y	Y	N
3 Nichols	Y	Y	N	Y	Y	N
4 Bevill	Y	Y	N	Y	Y	N
5 Flippo	Y	Y	N	Y	Y	N
6 Erdreich	Y	Y	N	Y	Y	N
7 Shelby	?	?	N	Y	Y	N
ALASKA						
AL *Young*	Y	Y	N	Y	Y	N
ARIZONA						
1 *McCain*	Y	Y	Y	Y	Y	Y
2 Udall	Y	Y	?	?	?	?
3 *Stump*	Y	Y	N	N	Y	N
4 *Rudd*	Y	Y	Y	Y	Y	N
5 McNulty	Y	Y	?	?	?	?
ARKANSAS						
1 Alexander	?	?	N	Y	Y	N
2 *Bethune*	?	?	?	?	?	?
3 *Hammerschmidt*	Y	Y	N	Y	Y	N
4 Anthony	Y	Y	N	Y	Y	N
CALIFORNIA						
1 Bosco	Y	Y	N	Y	Y	?
2 *Chappie*	Y	Y	N	Y	Y	N
3 Matsui	Y	Y	N	Y	Y	N
4 Fazio	Y	Y	N	Y	Y	N
5 Burton	Y	Y	Y	Y	Y	N
6 Boxer	Y	Y	Y	Y	Y	N
7 Miller	Y	Y	Y	Y	Y	N
8 Dellums	Y	Y	Y	Y	Y	N
9 Stark	Y	Y	Y	Y	?	Y
10 Edwards	Y	Y	Y	Y	Y	Y
11 Lantos	Y	Y	Y	Y	Y	Y
12 *Zschau*	Y	Y	Y	Y	Y	Y
13 Mineta	Y	Y	Y	Y	Y	N
14 *Shumway*	Y	Y	N	Y	Y	N
15 Coelho	Y	Y	N	Y	Y	N
16 Panetta	Y	Y	Y	Y	Y	Y
17 *Pashayan*	Y	Y	N	Y	Y	N
18 Lehman	?	+	N	Y	Y	N
19 *Lagomarsino*	Y	Y	Y	Y	Y	N
20 *Thomas*	Y	Y	N	Y	Y	N
21 *Fiedler*	Y	Y	Y	Y	Y	N
22 *Moorhead*	?	?	Y	Y	Y	N
23 Beilenson	Y	Y	Y	Y	Y	Y
24 Waxman	Y	Y	Y	Y	?	Y
25 Roybal	Y	Y	N	Y	Y	N
26 Berman	Y	Y	Y	Y	?	N
27 Levine	Y	Y	Y	Y	Y	N
28 Dixon	Y	Y	N	Y	Y	N
29 Hawkins	Y	Y	?	#	?	?
30 Martinez	Y	Y	?	?	?	N
31 Dymally	Y	Y	N	Y	Y	N
32 Anderson	Y	Y	N	Y	Y	N
33 *Dreier*	Y	Y	Y	N	Y	Y
34 Torres	Y	Y	Y	Y	Y	N
35 *Lewis*	Y	Y	N	Y	Y	N
36 Brown	Y	Y	N	Y	Y	N
37 *McCandless*	Y	Y	N	Y	Y	Y
38 Patterson	Y	Y	?	?	?	?
39 *Dannemeyer*	Y	Y	Y	N	Y	N
40 *Badham*	Y	Y	N	Y	Y	N
41 *Lowery*	Y	Y	Y	Y	Y	Y
42 *Lungren*	Y	Y	Y	Y	Y	Y

	357	358	359	360	361	362
43 *Packard*	Y	Y	Y	Y	Y	N
44 Bates	Y	Y	Y	Y	Y	N
45 *Hunter*	Y	Y	Y	Y	Y	Y
COLORADO						
1 Schroeder	Y	Y	Y · Y		Y	N
2 Wirth	Y	Y	?	?	?	N
3 Kogovsek	Y	Y	Y	Y	Y	N
4 *Brown*	Y	Y	N	Y	Y	N
5 *Kramer*	Y	Y	N	Y	Y	N
6 *Schaefer*	Y	Y	N	Y	Y	Y
CONNECTICUT						
1 Kennelly	Y	Y	Y	Y	Y	N
2 Gejdenson	Y	Y	Y	Y	Y	N
3 Morrison	+	+	Y	Y	Y	N
4 *McKinney*	Y	Y	N	Y	?	N
5 Ratchford	Y	Y	Y	Y	Y	N
6 *Johnson*	Y	Y	Y	Y	Y	N
DELAWARE						
AL Carper	Y	Y	N	Y	Y	N
FLORIDA						
1 Hutto	Y	Y	N	Y	Y	N
2 Fuqua	Y	Y	N	Y	Y	Y
3 Bennett	Y	Y	N	Y	Y	N
4 Chappell	Y	Y	N	Y	?	N
5 *McCollum*	Y	Y	Y	Y	Y	Y
6 MacKay	Y	Y	N	Y	Y	N
7 Gibbons	Y	Y	?	Y	Y	Y
8 *Young*	Y	Y	N	Y	Y	N
9 *Bilirakis*	Y	Y	Y	Y	Y	Y
10 *Ireland*	Y	Y	N	Y	Y	N
11 Nelson	Y	Y	Y	X	Y	Y
12 *Lewis*	Y	Y	Y	Y	Y	Y
13 *Mack*	Y	Y	Y	?	Y	Y
14 Mica	Y	Y	Y	Y	Y	Y
15 *Shaw*	Y	Y	N	Y	Y	N
16 Smith	Y	Y	N	Y	Y	N
17 Lehman	Y	Y	Y	Y	Y	N
18 Pepper	Y	Y	Y	Y	Y	N
19 Fascell	Y	Y	N	Y	?	Y
GEORGIA						
1 Thomas	Y	Y	N	Y	Y	N
2 Hatcher	Y	Y	N	Y	Y	N
3 Ray	Y	Y	N	Y	Y	Y
4 Levitas	Y	Y	Y	Y	Y	Y
5 Fowler	Y	Y	N	Y	Y	Y
6 *Gingrich*	?	?	Y	Y	Y	Y
7 Darden	Y	Y	N	Y	Y	Y
8 Rowland	Y	Y	N	Y	Y	Y
9 Jenkins	Y	Y	N	Y	Y	Y
10 Barnard	Y	Y	Y	Y	?	Y
HAWAII						
1 Heftel	Y	Y	N	Y	Y	Y
2 Akaka	Y	Y	?	?	?	?
IDAHO						
1 *Craig*	Y	Y	N	N	Y	N
2 *Hansen*	Y	Y	N	N	Y	?
ILLINOIS						
1 Hayes	Y	Y	Y	Y	Y	N
2 Savage	?	Y	Y	Y	Y	N
3 Russo	Y	Y	N	Y	Y	N
4 *O'Brien*	Y	Y	Y	Y	Y	Y
5 Lipinski	Y	Y	N	Y	Y	N
6 *Hyde*	Y	Y	Y	Y	Y	Y
7 Collins	Y	Y	Y	Y	Y	N
8 Rostenkowski	Y	Y	N	Y	Y	N
9 Yates	Y	Y	Y	N	Y	N
10 *Porter*	Y	Y	Y	Y	Y	Y
11 Annunzio	Y	Y	Y	Y	Y	N
12 *Crane, P.*	?	?	Y	N	N	Y
13 *Erlenborn*	Y	Y	N	Y	Y	Y
14 *Corcoran*	Y	Y	Y	Y	Y	Y
15 *Madigan*	Y	Y	N	Y	Y	Y
16 *Martin*	Y	Y	?	?	Y	Y
17 Evans	Y	Y	Y	Y	Y	N
18 *Michel*	Y	Y	N	Y	Y	Y
19 *Crane, D.*	Y	Y	Y	N	Y	Y
20 Durbin	Y	Y	N	Y	Y	N
21 Price	Y	Y	N	Y	Y	N
22 Simon	?	?	Y	?	Y	?
INDIANA						
1 Hall	Y	Y	N	Y	Y	N
2 Sharp	Y	Y	Y	Y	Y	N
3 *Hiler*	Y	Y	Y	Y	Y	Y
4 *Coats*	Y	Y	Y	Y	Y	Y
5 Hillis	Y	Y	N	Y	Y	Y

ND - Northern Democrats   SD - Southern Democrats

	357	358	359	360	361	362
6 **Burton**	Y	Y	Y	N	Y	Y
7 **Myers**	Y	Y	N	Y	Y	N
8 McCloskey	Y	Y	N	Y	Y	N
9 Hamilton	Y	Y	N	Y	Y	Y
10 Jacobs	Y	Y	Y	Y	Y	Y
IOWA						
1 **Leach**	Y	Y	?	?	?	?
2 **Tauke**	Y	Y	?	?	?	?
3 **Evans**	Y	Y	?	?	?	?
4 Smith	Y	Y	N	Y	Y	N
5 Harkin	?	?	Y	Y	Y	Y
6 Bedell	Y	Y	Y	N	Y	Y
KANSAS						
1 **Roberts**	Y	Y	N	N	Y	Y
2 Slattery	Y	Y	Y	N	Y	Y
3 **Winn**	Y	Y	N	Y	Y	Y
4 Glickman	Y	Y	Y	Y	Y	Y
5 **Whittaker**	Y	Y	Y	Y	Y	Y
KENTUCKY						
1 Hubbard	Y	Y	N	Y	Y	Y
2 Natcher	Y	Y	N	Y	Y	N
3 Mazzoli	Y	Y	N	Y	Y	Y
4 **Snyder**	Y	Y	N	Y	Y	N
5 **Rogers**	Y	Y	N	Y	Y	N
6 **Hopkins**	Y	Y	Y	Y	Y	Y
7 Vacancy						
LOUISIANA						
1 **Livingston**	Y	Y	N	Y	Y	N
2 Boggs	Y	Y	?	?	?	?
3 Tauzin	Y	Y	N	Y	Y	N
4 Roemer	Y	Y	Y	N	Y	Y
5 Huckaby	Y	Y	Y	Y	Y	?
6 **Moore**	Y	Y	N	Y	Y	N
7 Breaux	?	?	N	Y	Y	N
8 Long	Y	Y	?	Y	Y	Y
MAINE						
1 **McKernan**	Y	Y	N	Y	Y	Y
2 **Snowe**	Y	Y	Y	Y	Y	Y
MARYLAND						
1 Dyson	Y	Y	N	Y	Y	N
2 Long	Y	Y	Y	Y	Y	N
3 Mikulski	Y	Y	N	Y	Y	N
4 **Holt**	Y	Y	N	Y	Y	Y
5 Hoyer	Y	Y	N	Y	Y	N
6 Byron	Y	Y	Y	Y	Y	N
7 Mitchell	Y	Y	Y	Y	Y	N
8 Barnes	Y	Y	Y	Y	Y	N
MASSACHUSETTS						
1 **Conte**	Y	Y	Y	N	Y	Y
2 Boland	Y	Y	N	Y	Y	Y
3 Early	Y	Y	Y	Y	Y	Y
4 Frank	Y	Y	N	N	Y	Y
5 Shannon	?	?	?	?	?	?
6 Mavroules	Y	Y	N	Y	Y	Y
7 Markey	?	?	Y	N	Y	N
8 O'Neill						
9 Moakley	Y	Y	N	Y	Y	Y
10 Studds	?	?	Y	Y	Y	Y
11 Donnelly	Y	Y	N	Y	Y	N
MICHIGAN						
1 Conyers	Y	Y	Y	Y	Y	N
2 **Pursell**	Y	Y	Y	Y	Y	Y
3 Wolpe	Y	Y	Y	Y	Y	Y
4 **Siljander**	Y	Y	?	?	?	?
5 **Sawyer**	Y	Y	?	?	?	?
6 Carr	Y	Y	N	Y	Y	N
7 Kildee	Y	Y	Y	Y	Y	Y
8 Traxler	Y	Y	N	Y	Y	N
9 **Vander Jagt**	Y	Y	?	?	?	?
10 Albosta	Y	Y	N	Y	Y	N
11 **Davis**	Y	Y	N	Y	Y	Y
12 Bonior	Y	Y	Y	Y	Y	Y
13 Crockett	?	Y	Y	Y	Y	N
14 Hertel	Y	Y	?	Y	Y	Y
15 Ford	Y	Y	N	Y	Y	N
16 Dingell	Y	Y	N	Y	Y	?
17 Levin	Y	Y	Y	Y	Y	Y
18 **Broomfield**	?	?	N	Y	Y	N
MINNESOTA						
1 Penny	Y	Y	Y	Y	Y	Y
2 **Weber**	Y	Y	Y	Y	Y	Y
3 **Frenzel**	Y	Y	Y	Y	Y	N
4 Vento	Y	Y	Y	Y	Y	Y
5 Sabo	Y	Y	Y	Y	Y	N
6 Sikorski	Y	Y	Y	Y	Y	Y

	357	358	359	360	361	362
7 **Stangeland**	Y	Y	N	Y	Y	N
8 Oberstar	Y	Y	N	Y	Y	N
MISSISSIPPI						
1 Whitten	Y	Y	N	Y	Y	N
2 **Franklin**	Y	Y	N	Y	Y	N
3 Montgomery	Y	Y	N	Y	Y	N
4 Dowdy	Y	Y	N	Y	Y	N
5 **Lott**	Y	Y	N	Y	Y	Y
MISSOURI						
1 Clay	Y	Y	Y	Y	Y	N
2 Young	Y	Y	N	Y	Y	N
3 Gephardt	Y	Y	N	Y	Y	N
4 Skelton	Y	Y	N	Y	Y	N
5 Wheat	Y	Y	Y	Y	Y	Y
6 **Coleman**	Y	Y	N	Y	Y	Y
7 **Taylor**	Y	Y	N	Y	Y	Y
8 **Emerson**	Y	Y	N	Y	Y	Y
9 Volkmer	Y	Y	Y	Y	Y	N
MONTANA						
1 Williams	Y	Y	Y	Y	Y	N
2 **Marlenee**	Y	Y	N	Y	Y	Y
NEBRASKA						
1 **Bereuter**	Y	Y	Y	Y	?	N
2 **Daub**	Y	Y	N	Y	Y	N
3 **Smith**	Y	Y	N	Y	Y	N
NEVADA						
1 Reid	Y	Y	Y	N	Y	Y
2 **Vucanovich**	Y	Y	N	Y	Y	N
NEW HAMPSHIRE						
1 D'Amours	Y	Y	Y	Y	?	?
2 **Gregg**	Y	Y	Y	Y	Y	Y
NEW JERSEY						
1 Florio	Y	Y	N	Y	Y	N
2 Hughes	Y	Y	N	Y	Y	N
3 Howard	Y	Y	N	Y	Y	N
4 **Smith**	Y	Y	Y	Y	Y	Y
5 **Roukema**	Y	Y	N	Y	Y	Y
6 Dwyer	Y	Y	Y	Y	Y	N
7 **Rinaldo**	Y	Y	Y	Y	Y	?
8 Roe	Y	Y	N	Y	Y	N
9 Torricelli	Y	Y	Y	Y	?	N
10 Rodino	Y	Y	Y	Y	Y	N
11 Minish	Y	Y	Y	Y	Y	N
12 **Courter**	?	?	Y	Y	Y	Y
13 Vacancy						
14 Guarini	Y	Y	Y	Y	Y	N
NEW MEXICO						
1 **Lujan**	Y	Y	Y	Y	Y	Y
2 **Skeen**	Y	Y	N	Y	Y	Y
3 Richardson	Y	Y	Y	Y	Y	N
NEW YORK						
1 **Carney**	Y	Y	N	Y	Y	N
2 Downey	Y	Y	Y	Y	Y	N
3 Mrazek	Y	Y	N	Y	Y	N
4 **Lent**	Y	Y	N	Y	Y	Y
5 **McGrath**	?	?	?	?	?	?
6 Addabbo	Y	Y	Y	Y	Y	N
7 Ackerman	Y	Y	Y	Y	Y	?
8 Scheuer	Y	Y	Y	Y	Y	N
9 Ferraro	?	?	?	?	?	?
10 Schumer	Y	Y	Y	Y	Y	N
11 Towns	Y	Y	N	Y	Y	N
12 Owens	Y	Y	Y	Y	Y	N
13 Solarz	Y	Y	Y	Y	Y	N
14 **Molinari**	Y	Y	Y	?	Y	N
15 **Green**	Y	Y	Y	N	Y	N
16 Rangel	Y	Y	N	Y	Y	N
17 Weiss	Y	Y	Y	Y	Y	N
18 Garcia	Y	Y	Y	Y	Y	N
19 Biaggi	?	?	N	Y	Y	N
20 Ottinger	Y	Y	Y	N	Y	N
21 **Fish**	Y	Y	Y	N	Y	N
22 **Gilman**	Y	Y	Y	Y	Y	N
23 Stratton	Y	Y	N	Y	Y	N
24 **Solomon**	Y	Y	Y	Y	Y	Y
25 **Boehlert**	Y	Y	Y	N	Y	Y
26 **Martin**	Y	Y	N	Y	Y	Y
27 **Wortley**	Y	Y	N	Y	Y	Y
28 McHugh	Y	Y	Y	Y	Y	Y
29 **Horton**	Y	Y	N	Y	?	N
30 **Conable**	Y	Y	Y	N	Y	Y
31 **Kemp**	Y	Y	N	Y	Y	Y
32 LaFalce	Y	Y	Y	Y	Y	Y
33 Nowak	Y	Y	N	Y	Y	N
34 Lundine	Y	Y	N	Y	Y	Y

	357	358	359	360	361	362
NORTH CAROLINA						
1 Jones	Y	Y	N	Y	Y	N
2 Valentine	Y	Y	N	Y	Y	N
3 Whitley	Y	Y	N	Y	Y	N
4 Andrews	Y	Y	N	Y	Y	N
5 Neal	Y	Y	N	Y	Y	N
6 Britt	Y	Y	N	Y	Y	N
7 Rose	Y	Y	N	Y	Y	N
8 Hefner	Y	Y	N	Y	Y	N
9 **Martin**	Y	Y	N	Y	Y	?
10 **Broyhill**	Y	Y	N	Y	Y	Y
11 Clarke	Y	Y	N	Y	Y	N
NORTH DAKOTA						
AL Dorgan	Y	Y	Y	N	Y	N
OHIO						
1 Luken	Y	Y	N	Y	Y	N
2 **Gradison**	Y	Y	Y	Y	Y	Y
3 Hall	Y	Y	?	Y	Y	Y
4 **Oxley**	+	+	N	Y	Y	Y
5 **Latta**	?	?	Y	N	Y	Y
6 **McEwen**	?	?	N	Y	Y	N
7 **DeWine**	?	?	Y	Y	Y	?
8 **Kindness**	Y	Y	N	Y	Y	Y
9 Kaptur	Y	Y	Y	Y	Y	N
10 **Miller**	?	?	Y	N	Y	N
11 Eckart	Y	Y	Y	Y	Y	N
12 **Kasich**	Y	Y	Y	Y	Y	N
13 Pease	Y	Y	Y	N	Y	Y
14 Seiberling	Y	Y	Y	N	Y	N
15 **Wylie**	?	?	Y	Y	Y	Y
16 **Regula**	Y	Y	Y	N	Y	Y
17 **Williams**	?	Y	Y	Y	Y	?
18 Applegate	Y	Y	Y	Y	Y	N
19 Feighan	Y	Y	Y	Y	Y	N
20 Oakar	Y	Y	N	Y	Y	N
21 Stokes	Y	Y	Y	Y	Y	N
OKLAHOMA						
1 Jones	Y	Y	Y	Y	Y	?
2 Synar	Y	Y	+	N	Y	N
3 Watkins	Y	Y	N	Y	Y	N
4 McCurdy	Y	Y	N	Y	Y	N
5 **Edwards**	?	Y	Y	Y	Y	Y
6 English	Y	Y	Y	Y	Y	N
OREGON						
1 AuCoin	Y	Y	Y	N	Y	N
2 **Smith, R.**	Y	Y	N	Y	Y	Y
3 Wyden	Y	Y	Y	Y	Y	N
4 Weaver	Y	Y	Y	Y	Y	N
5 **Smith, D.**	Y	Y	N	N	Y	Y
PENNSYLVANIA						
1 Foglietta	Y	Y	Y	N	Y	N
2 Gray	Y	Y	N	Y	Y	N
3 Borski	Y	Y	N	Y	Y	N
4 Kolter	Y	Y	N	Y	Y	N
5 **Schulze**	Y	Y	N	Y	Y	Y
6 Yatron	Y	Y	Y	Y	Y	N
7 Edgar	Y	Y	Y	N	Y	Y
8 Kostmayer	Y	Y	Y	N	Y	Y
9 **Shuster**	Y	Y	N	Y	Y	N
10 **McDade**	Y	Y	Y	Y	Y	Y
11 Harrison	Y	Y	?	?	?	?
12 Murtha	Y	Y	N	Y	Y	N
13 **Coughlin**	Y	Y	Y	Y	Y	Y
14 Coyne	Y	Y	N	Y	Y	N
15 **Ritter**	Y	Y	Y	Y	Y	Y
16 **Walker**	Y	Y	Y	?	?	Y
17 **Gekas**	Y	Y	Y	Y	Y	Y
18 Walgren	Y	Y	Y	Y	Y	N
19 **Goodling**	Y	Y	Y	Y	Y	Y
20 Gaydos	Y	Y	N	Y	Y	N
21 **Ridge**	Y	Y	Y	Y	Y	Y
22 Murphy	Y	Y	Y	Y	Y	N
23 **Clinger**	Y	Y	Y	Y	Y	Y
RHODE ISLAND						
1 St Germain	Y	Y	Y	Y	?	?
2 **Schneider**	Y	Y	Y	Y	Y	N
SOUTH CAROLINA						
1 **Hartnett**	Y	Y	N	Y	Y	Y
2 **Spence**	Y	Y	N	Y	Y	Y
3 Derrick	Y	Y	N	Y	Y	Y
4 **Campbell**	Y	Y	N	?	Y	Y
5 Spratt	?	Y	Y	Y	Y	Y
6 Tallon	Y	Y	N	Y	Y	Y
SOUTH DAKOTA						
AL Daschle	Y	Y	Y	Y	Y	N

	357	358	359	360	361	362
TENNESSEE						
1 **Quillen**	Y	Y	N	Y	Y	N
2 **Duncan**	Y	Y	N	Y	Y	N
3 Lloyd	Y	Y	N	Y	Y	N
4 Cooper	Y	Y	Y	?	Y	Y
5 Boner	?	?	?	?	?	?
6 Gore	Y	Y	Y	Y	Y	N
7 **Sundquist**	Y	Y	N	Y	Y	N
8 Jones	Y	Y	N	N	Y	N
9 Ford	Y	Y	Y	Y	Y	N
TEXAS						
1 Hall, S.	Y	Y	N	Y	Y	N
2 Wilson	Y	Y	N	Y	Y	N
3 **Bartlett**	Y	Y	Y	N	Y	Y
4 Hall, R.	Y	Y	N	N	Y	N
5 Bryant	Y	Y	?	?	?	?
6 **Gramm**	?	?	?	?	?	?
7 **Archer**	Y	Y	Y	Y	Y	Y
8 **Fields**	Y	Y	N	Y	Y	Y
9 Brooks	Y	Y	N	Y	Y	N
10 Pickle	Y	Y	N	Y	Y	N
11 Leath	?	?	?	?	?	?
12 Wright	Y	?	?	?	?	?
13 Hightower	Y	Y	N	Y	Y	N
14 Patman	Y	Y	N	N	Y	N
15 de la Garza	Y	Y	N	Y	Y	N
16 Coleman	Y	Y	?	?	?	?
17 Stenholm	Y	Y	N	N	Y	Y
18 Leland	Y	Y	N	Y	Y	Y
19 Hance	Y	Y	N	N	Y	Y
20 Gonzalez	Y	Y	N	Y	Y	Y
21 **Loeffler**	Y	Y	N	Y	Y	Y
22 **Paul**	Y	Y	Y	N	Y	N
23 Kazen	Y	Y	N	Y	Y	N
24 Frost	Y	Y	?	?	?	?
25 Andrews	Y	Y	N	Y	Y	N
26 Vandergriff	Y	Y	N	Y	Y	N
27 Ortiz	Y	Y	N	Y	Y	N
UTAH						
1 **Hansen**	Y	Y	Y	Y	Y	Y
2 **Marriott**	Y	Y	N	Y	Y	Y
3 **Nielson**	Y	Y	N	N	N	Y
VERMONT						
AL **Jeffords**	Y	Y	Y	Y	?	?
VIRGINIA						
1 **Bateman**	Y	Y	N	Y	Y	N
2 **Whitehurst**	Y	Y	Y	Y	Y	N
3 **Bliley**	Y	Y	N	Y	Y	N
4 Sisisky	Y	Y	N	Y	Y	N
5 Daniel	Y	Y	N	Y	Y	N
6 Olin	Y	Y	Y	Y	Y	Y
7 **Robinson**	Y	Y	N	Y	Y	N
8 **Parris**	Y	Y	N	Y	Y	Y
9 Boucher	Y	Y	N	Y	Y	N
10 **Wolf**	Y	Y	N	Y	Y	Y
WASHINGTON						
1 **Pritchard**	Y	Y	?	?	Y	Y
2 Swift	Y	Y	N	Y	Y	N
3 Bonker	Y	Y	N	Y	Y	N
4 **Morrison**	Y	Y	Y	Y	Y	N
5 Foley	Y	Y	?	Y	Y	N
6 Dicks	Y	Y	Y	Y	Y	N
7 Lowry	Y	Y	Y	Y	Y	N
8 **Chandler**	Y	Y	Y	Y	Y	Y
WEST VIRGINIA						
1 Mollohan	Y	Y	N	Y	Y	N
2 Staggers	Y	Y	Y	Y	Y	N
3 Wise	Y	Y	Y	Y	Y	N
4 Rahall	Y	Y	N	Y	Y	N
WISCONSIN						
1 Aspin	Y	Y	Y	Y	Y	Y
2 Kastenmeier	Y	Y	Y	N	Y	N
3 **Gunderson**	Y	Y	Y	Y	Y	Y
4 Kleczka	Y	Y	Y	Y	Y	Y
5 Moody	Y	Y	Y	N	Y	Y
6 **Petri**	Y	Y	Y	Y	Y	Y
7 Obey	Y	Y	Y	N	Y	Y
8 **Roth**	Y	Y	Y	Y	Y	N
9 **Sensenbrenner**	Y	Y	Y	Y	Y	Y
WYOMING						
AL **Cheney**	?	?	?	?	?	?

Southern states - Ala., Ark., Fla., Ga., Ky., La., Miss., N.C., Okla., S.C., Tenn., Texas, Va.

363. H J Res 648. Continuing Appropriations, Fiscal 1985. Long, D-La., motion to order the previous question (thus ending debate and the possibility of amendment) on the rule (H Res 588) providing for House floor consideration of the joint resolution to provide interim funding for agencies and programs included in the nine regular fiscal 1985 appropriations bills that have not been signed into law. Motion agreed to 218-174: R 3-147; D 215-27 (ND 156-7, SD 59-20), Sept. 25, 1984.

364. H J Res 648. Continuing Appropriations, Fiscal 1985. Adoption of the rule (H Res 588) providing for House floor consideration of the joint resolution to provide interim funding for agencies and programs included in the nine regular fiscal 1985 appropriations bills that have not been signed into law. Adopted 257-135: R 34-114; D 223-21 (ND 159-5, SD 64-16), Sept. 25, 1984.

365. H J Res 648. Continuing Appropriations, Fiscal 1985. Roe, D-N.J., amendment to include provisions of HR 3678, authorizing $18 billion for 300 water resource projects. Adopted 336-64: R 105-46; D 231-18 (ND 156-12, SD 75-6), Sept. 25, 1984. A "nay" was a vote supporting the president's position.

366. H J Res 648. Continuing Appropriations, Fiscal 1985. Williams, D-Mont., amendment to prohibit the federal government from contracting with private companies to administer 30 Job Corps civilian conservation centers that are now administered by the Agriculture and Interior departments. Adopted 242-162: R 23-129; D 219-33 (ND 165-5, SD 54-28), Sept. 25, 1984.

367. H J Res 648. Continuing Appropriations, Fiscal 1985. Brown, R-Colo., amendment to reduce by 2 percent all funding levels for foreign assistance programs, except for funds earmarked for Egypt and Israel. Adopted 273-134: R 133-22; D 140-112 (ND 75-94, SD 65-18), Sept. 25, 1984.

368. H J Res 648. Continuing Appropriations, Fiscal 1985. Frenzel, R-Minn., amendment to reduce by 2 percent all discretionary spending levels in the joint resolution for programs covered by the Labor, Health and Human Services and Education fiscal 1985 appropriations measure. Rejected 122-284: R 93-61; D 29-223 (ND 8-161, SD 21-62), Sept. 25, 1984.

369. H J Res 648. Continuing Appropriations, Fiscal 1985. Miller, D-Calif., amendment to provide $50 million to states to train child-care facility staff and parents of attending children in the prevention of child abuse. Adopted 369-37: R 131-25; D 238-12 (ND 161-6, SD 77-6), Sept. 25, 1984.

370. H J Res 648. Continuing Appropriations, Fiscal 1985. Lungren, R-Calif., motion to recommit the joint resolution to the Committee on Appropriations with instructions to attach the provisions of HR 5963, the Comprehensive Crime Control Act of 1984. Motion agreed to 243-166: R 154-3; D 89-163 (ND 35-134, SD 54-29), Sept. 25, 1984. A "yea" was a vote supporting the president's position.

KEY

- Y Voted for (yea).
- # Paired for.
- + Announced for.
- N Voted against (nay).
- X Paired against.
- - Announced against.
- P Voted "present".
- C Voted "present" to avoid possible conflict of interest.
- ? Did not vote or otherwise make a position known.

Democrats   *Republicans*

	363	364	365	366	367	368	369	370
ALABAMA								
1 *Edwards*	N	Y	Y	N	N	N	Y	Y
2 *Dickinson*	N	N	Y	N	Y	N	Y	Y
3 Nichols	Y	Y	Y	Y	Y	N	Y	Y
4 Bevill	Y	Y	Y	Y	Y	N	Y	N
5 Flippo	Y	Y	Y	Y	Y	N	Y	Y
6 Erdreich	X	#	Y	Y	Y	Y	Y	Y
7 Shelby	N	Y	Y	N	Y	N	Y	Y
ALASKA								
AL *Young*	N	Y	Y	N	Y	N	Y	Y
ARIZONA								
1 *McCain*	N	N	Y	N	Y	Y	Y	Y
2 Udall	Y	Y	Y	Y	Y	N	Y	N
3 *Stump*	N	N	Y	N	Y	N	Y	Y
4 *Rudd*	N	Y	Y	N	Y	N	Y	Y
5 McNulty	Y	Y	Y	Y	Y	N	Y	N
ARKANSAS								
1 Alexander	Y	Y	?	?	N	?	?	X
2 *Bethune*	?	?	?	?	?	?	?	?
3 *Hammerschmidt*	?	?	?	?	?	?	?	?
4 Anthony	Y	Y	Y	Y	Y	N	Y	N
CALIFORNIA								
1 Bosco	Y	Y	Y	Y	Y	N	N	N
2 *Chappie*	N	N	Y	N	Y	Y	Y	Y
3 Matsui	Y	Y	Y	Y	N	N	Y	N
4 Fazio	Y	Y	Y	Y	N	N	Y	N
5 Burton	Y	Y	Y	Y	N	N	?	?
6 Boxer	Y	Y	Y	Y	N	N	Y	N
7 Miller	Y	Y	Y	Y	N	N	Y	N
8 Dellums	Y	Y	Y	Y	N	N	Y	N
9 Stark	Y	Y	Y	Y	N	N	Y	N
10 Edwards	Y	Y	Y	Y	N	N	Y	N
11 Lantos	Y	Y	Y	Y	N	N	Y	N
12 *Zschau*	N	N	N	N	N	Y	Y	Y
13 Mineta	Y	Y	Y	Y	N	N	Y	N
14 *Shumway*	N	N	Y	N	Y	N	Y	Y
15 Coelho	Y	Y	Y	Y	N	N	Y	N
16 Panetta	Y	Y	Y	Y	Y	N	Y	N
17 *Pashayan*	N	X	Y	Y	Y	Y	Y	Y
18 Lehman	Y	Y	Y	Y	N	N	Y	N
19 *Lagomarsino*	N	N	Y	N	Y	Y	Y	Y
20 *Thomas*	N	N	Y	N	Y	Y	Y	Y
21 *Fiedler*	N	N	Y	N	Y	Y	Y	Y
22 *Moorhead*	N	N	Y	N	Y	Y	N	Y
23 Beilenson	Y	N	N	Y	N	N	N	N
24 Waxman	Y	Y	Y	Y	N	N	Y	N
25 Roybal	Y	Y	Y	Y	N	N	Y	N
26 Berman	Y	Y	Y	Y	N	N	Y	N
27 Levine	Y	Y	Y	Y	N	N	Y	N
28 Dixon	Y	Y	Y	Y	N	N	Y	N
29 Hawkins	Y	Y	Y	Y	N	N	Y	N
30 Martinez	Y	Y	Y	Y	N	N	Y	N
31 Dymally	Y	Y	Y	Y	N	N	Y	N
32 Anderson	Y	Y	Y	Y	N	N	Y	N
33 *Dreier*	N	N	N	N	Y	N	Y	Y
34 Torres	Y	Y	Y	Y	N	N	Y	N
35 *Lewis*	N	N	Y	N	Y	Y	Y	Y
36 Brown	Y	Y	Y	Y	N	N	Y	N
37 *McCandless*	N	N	Y	N	Y	Y	Y	Y
38 Patterson	Y	Y	Y	Y	N	N	Y	N
39 *Dannemeyer*	N	N	Y	N	Y	Y	Y	N
40 *Badham*	N	N	N	N	Y	Y	Y	Y
41 *Lowery*	N	N	Y	N	Y	Y	Y	Y
42 *Lungren*	N	N	Y	N	Y	Y	Y	Y
43 *Packard*	N	Y	Y	N	Y	Y	Y	Y
44 Bates	Y	Y	Y	Y	Y	N	Y	N
45 *Hunter*	?	X	?	?	?	?	Y	Y
COLORADO								
1 Schroeder	N	N	Y	Y	Y	N	Y	N
2 Wirth	Y	Y	Y	Y	Y	N	Y	N
3 Kogovsek	?	?	Y	Y	Y	N	Y	N
4 *Brown*	N	N	N	N	Y	N	Y	N
5 *Kramer*	N	N	Y	N	Y	Y	Y	Y
6 *Schaefer*	N	N	Y	N	Y	Y	Y	Y
CONNECTICUT								
1 Kennelly	Y	Y	Y	Y	Y	N	Y	N
2 Gejdenson	Y	Y	Y	Y	N	N	?	N
3 Morrison	Y	Y	Y	Y	N	N	Y	N
4 *McKinney*	N	N	Y	N	Y	N	N	Y
5 Ratchford	Y	Y	Y	Y	Y	N	Y	N
6 *Johnson*	N	N	N	N	N	N	Y	Y
DELAWARE								
AL Carper	Y	Y	Y	N	Y	N	Y	Y
FLORIDA								
1 Hutto	Y	Y	Y	Y	Y	Y	N	Y
2 Fuqua	Y	Y	Y	N	Y	N	Y	Y
3 Bennett	Y	Y	Y	Y	Y	Y	Y	Y
4 Chappell	Y	Y	Y	N	Y	N	Y	Y
5 *McCollum*	N	N	Y	?	Y	Y	Y	Y
6 MacKay	Y	N	N	Y	N	Y	Y	Y
7 Gibbons	Y	Y	Y	Y	N	N	Y	Y
8 *Young*	N	N	Y	N	Y	Y	Y	Y
9 *Bilirakis*	N	N	Y	N	Y	Y	Y	Y
10 *Ireland*	N	N	N	N	Y	Y	Y	Y
11 Nelson	N	N	Y	N	Y	Y	Y	Y
12 *Lewis*	N	N	Y	N	Y	Y	Y	Y
13 *Mack*	N	N	N	N	Y	Y	N	Y
14 Mica	N	Y	Y	?	Y	Y	Y	Y
15 *Shaw*	N	N	Y	N	Y	Y	Y	Y
16 Smith	Y	Y	Y	Y	Y	N	N	N
17 Lehman	Y	Y	Y	Y	N	N	Y	N
18 Pepper	#	#	?	?	?	?	?	?
19 Fascell	Y	Y	Y	N	Y	N	N	Y
GEORGIA								
1 Thomas	Y	Y	Y	Y	Y	N	Y	N
2 Hatcher	?	?	?	?	?	?	?	?
3 Ray	N	N	?	N	Y	Y	Y	Y
4 Levitas	Y	N	Y	Y	Y	Y	Y	Y
5 Fowler	?	?	N	Y	Y	N	Y	N
6 *Gingrich*	N	N	Y	N	Y	Y	Y	Y
7 Darden	Y	Y	Y	N	Y	Y	Y	Y
8 Rowland	Y	Y	Y	Y	N	Y	N	Y
9 Jenkins	Y	Y	Y	Y	N	N	Y	N
10 Barnard	Y	Y	Y	N	Y	N	Y	N
HAWAII								
1 Heftel	Y	Y	Y	Y	Y	N	N	Y
2 Akaka	Y	Y	Y	Y	Y	N	Y	N
IDAHO								
1 *Craig*	N	N	N	N	Y	N	Y	N
2 *Hansen*	N	N	?	N	Y	Y	Y	N
ILLINOIS								
1 Hayes	Y	Y	Y	Y	N	N	Y	N
2 Savage	?	?	?	?	?	?	?	N
3 Russo	Y	Y	N	Y	N	N	Y	N
4 *O'Brien*	N	Y	Y	N	N	N	Y	Y
5 Lipinski	Y	Y	Y	Y	N	N	Y	N
6 *Hyde*	N	Y	Y	N	N	?	?	Y
7 Collins	Y	Y	Y	Y	N	N	Y	N
8 Rostenkowski	Y	Y	Y	Y	N	N	Y	N
9 Yates	Y	Y	Y	Y	N	N	Y	N
10 *Porter*	N	N	Y	N	Y	N	Y	N
11 Annunzio	Y	Y	Y	Y	N	N	Y	N
12 *Crane, P.*	N	N	N	N	Y	Y	Y	N
13 *Erlenborn*	N	N	N	N	Y	Y	N	Y
14 *Corcoran*	X	X	-	-	-	+	+	+
15 *Madigan*	N	?	Y	N	N	?	Y	Y
16 *Martin*	N	N	Y	N	N	Y	Y	Y
17 Evans	Y	Y	Y	Y	N	N	Y	N
18 *Michel*	N	N	N	?	Y	Y	Y	N
19 *Crane, D.*	N	N	N	N	Y	N	Y	N
20 Durbin	Y	Y	Y	Y	N	N	Y	Y
21 Price	Y	Y	Y	Y	N	N	Y	Y
22 Simon	?	?	?	?	?	?	?	?
INDIANA								
1 Hall	?	?	?	?	?	N	N	Y
2 Sharp	N	N	N	N	Y	Y	Y	Y
3 *Hiler*	N	N	N	N	Y	Y	Y	Y
4 *Coats*	N	N	N	N	Y	Y	Y	Y
5 Hillis	N	Y	Y	N	Y	Y	Y	Y

Corresponding to Congressional Record Votes 411, 412, 413, 415, 417, 418, 419, 420

	363	364	365	366	367	368	369	370
6 ***Burton***	N	N	N	N	Y	Y	Y	Y
7 ***Myers***	Y	Y	Y	N	Y	Y	Y	N
8 McCloskey	Y	Y	Y	Y	Y	N	Y	Y
9 Hamilton	N	Y	Y	Y	Y	Y	Y	Y
10 Jacobs	N	Y	N	Y	Y	Y	Y	N
IOWA								
1 ***Leach***	N	N	?	N	Y	Y	Y	Y
2 ***Tauke***	N	N	N	N	Y	Y	Y	Y
3 ***Evans***	N	N	?	N	Y	N	Y	Y
4 Smith	Y	Y	Y	Y	Y	N	Y	Y
5 Harkin	Y	Y	Y	Y	Y	N	Y	Y
6 Bedell	Y	Y	Y	Y	Y	N	Y	Y
KANSAS								
1 ***Roberts***	N	N	Y	N	Y	Y	Y	Y
2 Slattery	Y	N	Y	Y	Y	Y	N	Y
3 ***Winn***	N	N	Y	N	Y	N	Y	Y
4 Glickman	Y	Y	Y	Y	N	N	Y	N
5 ***Whittaker***	N	N	Y	N	Y	N	Y	Y
KENTUCKY								
1 Hubbard	N	N	N	Y	Y	N	N	Y
2 Natcher	Y	Y	Y	Y	N	N	Y	N
3 Mazzoli	N	Y	Y	N	Y	N	Y	Y
4 ***Snyder***	N	Y	Y	N	Y	N	Y	Y
5 ***Rogers***	N	N	Y	Y	Y	N	Y	Y
6 ***Hopkins***	N	N	N	N	Y	N	Y	Y
7 Vacancy								
LOUISIANA								
1 ***Livingston***	N	N	Y	N	N	N	Y	Y
2 Boggs	?	?	?	?	?	?	?	?
3 Tauzin	N	Y	Y	N	Y	Y	Y	Y
4 Roemer	N	N	Y	N	Y	Y	Y	Y
5 Huckaby	N	Y	Y	N	Y	Y	Y	Y
6 ***Moore***	N	N	Y	N	Y	Y	Y	Y
7 Breaux	X	?	Y	N	Y	Y	Y	Y
8 Long	Y	Y	Y	Y	N	N	Y	N
MAINE								
1 ***McKernan***	N	N	Y	N	Y	N	Y	Y
2 ***Snowe***	N	N	Y	N	Y	N	Y	Y
MARYLAND								
1 Dyson	Y	Y	Y	Y	Y	N	Y	Y
2 Long	Y	Y	Y	N	N	N	Y	Y
3 Mikulski	Y	Y	Y	Y	N	N	Y	N
4 ***Holt***	N	Y	Y	Y	Y	Y	N	Y
5 Hoyer	Y	Y	Y	Y	N	?	?	X
6 Byron	Y	Y	Y	Y	Y	?	Y	Y
7 Mitchell	Y	Y	Y	Y	N	N	Y	N
8 Barnes	Y	Y	Y	Y	N	N	Y	N
MASSACHUSETTS								
1 ***Conte***	N	Y	Y	N	N	N	Y	Y
2 Boland	Y	Y	Y	Y	N	N	Y	N
3 Early	Y	Y	Y	N	N	N	Y	N
4 Frank	Y	Y	Y	Y	N	N	Y	N
5 Shannon	Y	Y	N	Y	N	N	Y	N
6 Mavroules	Y	Y	Y	Y	N	N	Y	N
7 Markey	?	?	Y	Y	N	N	Y	N
8 O'Neill								
9 Moakley	Y	Y	Y	Y	N	N	Y	N
10 Studds	Y	Y	N	Y	N	N	Y	N
11 Donnelly	Y	Y	Y	Y	N	N	Y	N
MICHIGAN								
1 Conyers	Y	Y	Y	Y	N	N	Y	N
2 ***Pursell***	N	N	Y	N	Y	N	Y	Y
3 Wolpe	Y	Y	Y	Y	N	N	Y	N
4 ***Siljander***	N	N	Y	N	Y	Y	Y	Y
5 ***Sawyer***	N	N	N	N	Y	N	Y	Y
6 Carr	Y	Y	Y	Y	Y	N	Y	Y
7 Kildee	Y	Y	Y	Y	N	N	Y	N
8 Traxler	Y	Y	Y	Y	N	N	Y	N
9 ***Vander Jagt***	N	Y	Y	N	Y	Y	Y	Y
10 Albosta	Y	Y	Y	Y	Y	N	Y	Y
11 ***Davis***	Y	Y	Y	Y	Y	N	Y	Y
12 Bonior	?	?	Y	Y	N	N	N	N
13 Crockett	Y	Y	?	Y	Y	N	Y	N
14 Hertel	?	?	Y	Y	Y	N	Y	Y
15 Ford	Y	Y	Y	Y	N	N	Y	N
16 Dingell	Y	Y	Y	Y	N	N	Y	N
17 Levin	Y	Y	Y	Y	N	N	Y	N
18 ***Broomfield***	N	N	N	N	Y	N	Y	Y
MINNESOTA								
1 Penny	Y	Y	Y	Y	Y	Y	N	N
2 ***Weber***	N	N	N	N	Y	Y	Y	Y
3 ***Frenzel***	N	Y	N	N	Y	Y	Y	Y
4 Vento	Y	Y	Y	Y	N	N	Y	N
5 Sabo	Y	Y	Y	Y	N	N	Y	N
6 Sikorski	Y	Y	N	Y	Y	N	Y	N
7 ***Stangeland***	N	N	Y	N	Y	Y	Y	Y
8 Oberstar	Y	Y	Y	Y	N	N	Y	N
MISSISSIPPI								
1 Whitten	Y	Y	Y	Y	Y	N	Y	N
2 ***Franklin***	?	?	?	?	?	?	?	#
3 Montgomery	Y	Y	Y	N	Y	Y	N	Y
4 Dowdy	Y	Y	Y	Y	Y	N	Y	Y
5 ***Lott***	N	N	Y	N	Y	Y	Y	Y
MISSOURI								
1 Clay	Y	Y	Y	Y	N	N	Y	N
2 Young	Y	Y	Y	Y	Y	N	Y	Y
3 Gephardt	Y	Y	Y	Y	N	N	Y	N
4 Skelton	Y	Y	Y	Y	Y	N	Y	N
5 Wheat	Y	Y	Y	Y	N	N	Y	N
6 ***Coleman***	?	?	Y	N	Y	Y	Y	Y
7 ***Taylor***	N	N	Y	N	Y	N	Y	Y
8 ***Emerson***	N	Y	Y	Y	Y	N	Y	Y
9 Volkmer	Y	Y	Y	Y	Y	N	Y	Y
MONTANA								
1 Williams	Y	Y	Y	Y	Y	N	Y	N
2 ***Marlenee***	?	?	?	?	?	?	?	?
NEBRASKA								
1 ***Bereuter***	N	N	Y	Y	Y	N	Y	Y
2 ***Daub***	N	N	Y	N	Y	Y	Y	Y
3 ***Smith***	N	Y	Y	N	Y	Y	Y	Y
NEVADA								
1 Reid	Y	Y	Y	Y	N	N	Y	N
2 ***Vucanovich***	N	N	Y	N	Y	N	Y	Y
NEW HAMPSHIRE								
1 D'Amours	?	?	?	?	?	?	?	#
2 ***Gregg***	N	N	N	N	Y	Y	Y	Y
NEW JERSEY								
1 Florio	Y	Y	+	Y	N	N	Y	N
2 Hughes	Y	Y	Y	Y	Y	N	Y	N
3 Howard	Y	Y	Y	Y	N	N	Y	N
4 ***Smith***	N	Y	Y	Y	Y	N	Y	Y
5 ***Roukema***	N	N	Y	N	Y	N	Y	Y
6 Dwyer	Y	Y	Y	Y	N	Y	Y	Y
7 ***Rinaldo***	N	Y	Y	Y	Y	N	Y	Y
8 Roe	Y	Y	Y	Y	Y	N	Y	N
9 Torricelli	Y	Y	Y	Y	Y	N	Y	N
10 Rodino	Y	Y	Y	Y	N	N	Y	N
11 Minish	Y	Y	Y	Y	Y	N	Y	Y
12 ***Courter***	N	N	Y	N	Y	N	Y	Y
13 Vacancy								
14 Guarini	#	#	Y	Y	N	N	Y	X
NEW MEXICO								
1 ***Lujan***	N	N	Y	N	Y	Y	Y	Y
2 ***Skeen***	N	N	Y	N	Y	Y	Y	Y
3 Richardson	Y	Y	Y	Y	Y	N	Y	N
NEW YORK								
1 ***Carney***	N	N	Y	N	Y	N	Y	Y
2 Downey	Y	Y	Y	Y	N	N	Y	N
3 Mrazek	Y	Y	Y	Y	Y	N	Y	Y
4 ***Lent***	N	N	Y	N	N	N	Y	Y
5 ***McGrath***	X	X	?	?	?	?	?	#
6 Addabbo	Y	Y	Y	Y	N	N	Y	N
7 Ackerman	Y	Y	Y	Y	N	N	Y	N
8 Scheuer	Y	Y	Y	Y	N	N	Y	N
9 Ferraro	?	?	?	?	?	?	?	?
10 Schumer	Y	Y	Y	Y	N	N	Y	N
11 Towns	Y	Y	Y	Y	N	N	Y	N
12 Owens	Y	Y	Y	Y	N	N	Y	N
13 Solarz	Y	Y	Y	Y	N	N	Y	N
14 ***Molinari***	N	N	Y	N	Y	N	Y	Y
15 ***Green***	N	Y	N	N	N	N	Y	Y
16 Rangel	#	#	Y	Y	N	N	Y	N
17 Weiss	Y	Y	Y	Y	N	N	Y	N
18 Garcia	Y	Y	Y	Y	N	N	Y	N
19 Biaggi	Y	Y	Y	Y	N	N	Y	N
20 Ottinger	Y	Y	Y	Y	?	N	Y	N
21 ***Fish***	N	N	N	Y	Y	N	Y	Y
22 ***Gilman***	N	Y	Y	Y	N	N	Y	Y
23 Stratton	N	Y	Y	N	N	N	Y	Y
24 ***Solomon***	N	N	N	N	Y	N	Y	Y
25 ***Boehlert***	N	N	N	Y	Y	N	Y	Y
26 ***Martin***	N	N	Y	N	Y	N	Y	Y
27 ***Wortley***	N	N	N	N	Y	Y	Y	Y
28 McHugh	Y	Y	Y	Y	N	N	Y	Y
29 ***Horton***	N	Y	Y	Y	Y	N	Y	Y
30 ***Conable***	N	N	N	N	Y	Y	Y	Y
31 ***Kemp***	N	N	Y	N	N	N	Y	Y
32 LaFalce	Y	Y	Y	Y	N	N	Y	N
33 Nowak	Y	Y	Y	Y	Y	N	Y	N
34 Lundine	Y	Y	Y	N	Y	Y	Y	Y
NORTH CAROLINA								
1 Jones	Y	Y	Y	Y	Y	N	Y	N
2 Valentine	N	N	Y	N	Y	N	Y	Y
3 Whitley	Y	Y	Y	Y	Y	N	Y	Y
4 Andrews	N	N	Y	Y	Y	N	Y	Y
5 Neal	Y	Y	Y	Y	Y	N	Y	Y
6 Britt	Y	Y	Y	Y	Y	N	Y	Y
7 Rose	Y	Y	Y	Y	Y	N	Y	Y
8 Hefner	N	Y	Y	Y	Y	N	Y	Y
9 ***Martin***	?	?	?	?	?	?	?	?
10 ***Broyhill***	N	N	N	N	Y	Y	N	Y
11 Clarke	Y	Y	Y	Y	Y	N	Y	N
NORTH DAKOTA								
AL Dorgan	?	Y	Y	Y	Y	N	Y	N
OHIO								
1 Luken	Y	Y	Y	Y	Y	N	Y	Y
2 ***Gradison***	N	Y	N	N	Y	Y	N	Y
3 Hall	Y	Y	Y	Y	Y	N	Y	N
4 ***Oxley***	N	N	N	N	Y	Y	N	Y
5 ***Latta***	N	N	N	N	Y	Y	Y	Y
6 ***McEwen***	N	N	Y	N	Y	Y	Y	Y
7 ***DeWine***	N	N	Y	N	N	Y	Y	Y
8 ***Kindness***	N	N	Y	N	Y	Y	N	Y
9 Kaptur	N	Y	Y	Y	Y	N	Y	Y
10 ***Miller***	N	Y	Y	N	Y	Y	Y	Y
11 Eckart	Y	Y	?	Y	Y	N	Y	Y
12 ***Kasich***	N	N	Y	N	Y	Y	Y	Y
13 Pease	Y	Y	Y	Y	Y	N	Y	N
14 Seiberling	Y	Y	Y	Y	Y	N	Y	N
15 ***Wylie***	N	N	Y	N	Y	N	Y	Y
16 ***Regula***	N	N	Y	N	Y	N	Y	Y
17 ***Williams***	?	?	?	?	?	?	?	?
18 Applegate	N	Y	Y	Y	Y	N	Y	Y
19 Feighan	Y	Y	Y	Y	N	N	Y	N
20 Oakar	Y	Y	Y	Y	Y	N	Y	N
21 Stokes	Y	Y	Y	Y	N	N	Y	N
OKLAHOMA								
1 Jones	N	N	Y	N	Y	Y	Y	Y
2 Synar	Y	N	N	N	N	N	N	N
3 Watkins	Y	Y	Y	N	Y	N	Y	Y
4 McCurdy	N	N	Y	Y	Y	N	Y	Y
5 ***Edwards***	N	N	Y	N	N	Y	Y	Y
6 English	N	N	Y	N	Y	Y	Y	Y
OREGON								
1 AuCoin	Y	Y	Y	Y	Y	N	Y	Y
2 ***Smith, R.***	N	N	Y	N	Y	Y	Y	Y
3 Wyden	Y	Y	Y	Y	N	N	Y	N
4 Weaver	Y	Y	Y	Y	Y	N	Y	N
5 ***Smith, D.***	N	N	N	N	Y	Y	N	Y
PENNSYLVANIA								
1 Foglietta	Y	Y	Y	Y	N	N	Y	N
2 Gray	Y	Y	Y	Y	N	N	Y	N
3 Borski	Y	Y	Y	Y	N	N	Y	N
4 Kolter	Y	Y	Y	Y	Y	N	Y	N
5 ***Schulze***	?	?	?	?	Y	Y	Y	Y
6 Yatron	Y	Y	Y	Y	Y	N	Y	Y
7 Edgar	Y	Y	Y	Y	N	N	Y	N
8 Kostmayer	?	?	Y	Y	N	N	Y	Y
9 ***Shuster***	N	Y	Y	Y	Y	Y	Y	Y
10 ***McDade***	N	Y	Y	Y	N	N	Y	Y
11 Harrison	?	?	?	?	?	?	?	?
12 Murtha	Y	Y	Y	Y	N	N	Y	N
13 ***Coughlin***	N	N	N	N	N	N	Y	Y
14 Coyne	Y	Y	Y	Y	N	N	Y	N
15 ***Ritter***	?	?	?	?	?	Y	Y	Y
16 ***Walker***	N	N	N	N	Y	Y	Y	Y
17 ***Gekas***	N	Y	Y	N	Y	Y	Y	Y
18 Walgren	Y	Y	Y	Y	Y	N	Y	N
19 ***Goodling***	?	?	N	Y	Y	N	Y	Y
20 Gaydos	Y	Y	Y	Y	Y	N	Y	N
21 ***Ridge***	N	N	Y	N	Y	N	Y	Y
22 Murphy	Y	Y	Y	Y	Y	N	Y	N
23 ***Clinger***	?	?	Y	N	Y	Y	Y	Y
RHODE ISLAND								
1 St Germain	Y	Y	Y	Y	N	N	Y	N
2 ***Schneider***	N	N	Y	Y	Y	N	Y	Y
SOUTH CAROLINA								
1 ***Hartnett***	N	N	Y	Y	Y	Y	N	Y
2 ***Spence***	N	N	Y	N	Y	N	Y	Y
3 Derrick	Y	Y	Y	N	Y	N	Y	Y
4 ***Campbell***	N	N	Y	N	Y	Y	Y	Y
5 Spratt	Y	Y	Y	Y	Y	N	Y	N
6 Tallon	Y	Y	Y	N	Y	N	Y	Y
SOUTH DAKOTA								
AL Daschle	Y	Y	Y	Y	Y	N	?	N
TENNESSEE								
1 ***Quillen***	Y	Y	Y	Y	Y	N	Y	N
2 ***Duncan***	N	Y	Y	Y	Y	N	Y	Y
3 Lloyd	N	Y	Y	N	Y	N	Y	Y
4 Cooper	Y	Y	Y	Y	N	N	Y	N
5 Boner	Y	Y	Y	Y	Y	N	Y	N
6 Gore	Y	Y	Y	Y	Y	N	Y	N
7 ***Sundquist***	N	N	Y	N	Y	Y	Y	Y
8 Jones	Y	Y	Y	Y	Y	N	Y	N
9 Ford	Y	Y	Y	Y	Y	N	Y	N
TEXAS								
1 Hall, S.	Y	Y	Y	Y	Y	Y	Y	Y
2 Wilson	?	?	Y	Y	N	N	Y	Y
3 ***Bartlett***	N	N	N	N	Y	Y	N	Y
4 Hall, R.	N	Y	Y	Y	Y	N	Y	Y
5 Bryant	?	Y	Y	Y	N	N	Y	N
6 ***Gramm***	?	?	?	?	?	?	?	?
7 ***Archer***	N	N	N	N	Y	Y	Y	Y
8 ***Fields***	N	N	Y	N	Y	Y	Y	Y
9 Brooks	Y	Y	Y	Y	Y	N	Y	N
10 Pickle	Y	Y	Y	Y	Y	N	Y	Y
11 Leath	Y	Y	Y	Y	Y	Y	Y	Y
12 Wright	Y	Y	?	Y	N	N	Y	N
13 Hightower	Y	Y	Y	Y	Y	N	Y	Y
14 Patman	N	N	Y	N	Y	N	Y	Y
15 de la Garza	Y	Y	Y	Y	N	N	Y	N
16 Coleman	Y	Y	Y	Y	Y	N	Y	Y
17 Stenholm	N	N	Y	N	Y	Y	N	Y
18 Leland	#	#	?	?	?	?	?	X
19 Hance	Y	Y	Y	Y	Y	N	Y	Y
20 Gonzalez	Y	Y	Y	Y	N	N	Y	N
21 ***Loeffler***	N	N	N	N	Y	Y	Y	Y
22 ***Paul***	N	N	N	N	Y	Y	N	N
23 Kazen	Y	Y	Y	N	N	N	Y	N
24 Frost	Y	Y	Y	Y	N	N	Y	N
25 Andrews	Y	Y	Y	Y	Y	N	Y	N
26 Vandergriff	N	N	Y	Y	Y	N	Y	Y
27 Ortiz	Y	Y	Y	Y	N	N	Y	N
UTAH								
1 ***Hansen***	N	N	N	N	Y	Y	N	Y
2 ***Marriott***	N	N	Y	N	Y	Y	Y	Y
3 ***Nielson***	N	N	N	N	Y	Y	N	Y
VERMONT								
AL ***Jeffords***	N	Y	N	N	N	N	Y	Y
VIRGINIA								
1 ***Bateman***	N	Y	Y	N	Y	Y	Y	Y
2 ***Whitehurst***	N	Y	Y	N	Y	N	Y	Y
3 ***Bliley***	N	Y	Y	N	Y	Y	Y	Y
4 Sisisky	Y	Y	Y	Y	N	N	Y	Y
5 Daniel	Y	Y	N	N	Y	Y	N	Y
6 Olin	Y	N	N	Y	Y	Y	Y	Y
7 ***Robinson***	N	N	N	N	N	N	Y	Y
8 ***Parris***	N	Y	Y	N	Y	N	Y	Y
9 Boucher	Y	Y	Y	Y	?	N	Y	N
10 ***Wolf***	N	Y	Y	N	N	N	Y	Y
WASHINGTON								
1 ***Pritchard***	N	N	Y	Y	N	Y	Y	Y
2 Swift	Y	Y	Y	Y	N	N	Y	N
3 Bonker	Y	Y	Y	Y	N	N	Y	N
4 ***Morrison***	?	?	Y	Y	Y	N	Y	Y
5 Foley	Y	Y	Y	Y	N	N	Y	N
6 Dicks	Y	Y	Y	Y	Y	N	Y	N
7 Lowry	Y	Y	Y	Y	N	N	Y	N
8 ***Chandler***	N	N	Y	Y	Y	Y	Y	Y
WEST VIRGINIA								
1 Mollohan	Y	Y	Y	Y	Y	N	Y	N
2 Staggers	Y	Y	Y	Y	Y	N	Y	N
3 Wise	Y	Y	Y	Y	Y	N	Y	Y
4 Rahall	Y	Y	Y	Y	Y	N	Y	Y
WISCONSIN								
1 Aspin	Y	Y	Y	Y	N	N	Y	N
2 Kastenmeier	Y	N	N	Y	Y	N	Y	N
3 ***Gunderson***	N	N	Y	N	Y	Y	N	Y
4 Kleczka	Y	Y	Y	Y	Y	N	Y	N
5 Moody	Y	Y	Y	?	?	?	?	?
6 ***Petri***	N	N	N	N	Y	Y	Y	Y
7 Obey	Y	Y	N	Y	N	N	Y	N
8 ***Roth***	N	N	Y	N	Y	Y	Y	Y
9 ***Sensenbrenner***	N	N	N	N	Y	Y	Y	Y
WYOMING								
AL ***Cheney***	?	X	?	?	?	?	?	#

Southern states - Ala., Ark., Fla., Ga., Ky., La., Miss., N.C., Okla., S.C., Tenn., Texas, Va.

KEY

Y Voted for (yea).
\# Paired for.
+ Announced for.
N Voted against (nay).
X Paired against.
- Announced against.
P Voted "present".
C Voted "present" to avoid possible conflict of interest.
? Did not vote or otherwise make a position known.

Democrats *Republicans*

371. H J Res 648. Continuing Appropriations, Fiscal 1985. Passage of the joint resolution to provide interim funding for agencies and programs included in the nine regular fiscal 1985 appropriations bills that have not been signed into law. Passed 316-91: R 107-48; D 209-43 (ND 136-33, SD 73-10), Sept. 25, 1984.

372. S 2603. Older Americans Act Amendments. Adoption of the conference report on the bill to authorize $4 billion over fiscal years 1985-87 for programs of the Older Americans Act. Adopted 393-2: R 151-2; D 242-0 (ND 161-0, SD 81-0), Sept. 26, 1984.

	371	372
ALABAMA		
1 *Edwards*	Y	Y
2 *Dickinson*	Y	Y
3 Nichols	Y	Y
4 Bevill	Y	Y
5 Flippo	Y	Y
6 Erdreich	Y	Y
7 Shelby	Y	Y
ALASKA		
AL *Young*	Y	Y
ARIZONA		
1 *McCain*	Y	Y
2 Udall	Y	?
3 *Stump*	N	Y
4 *Rudd*	Y	Y
5 McNulty	Y	Y
ARKANSAS		
1 Alexander	?	?
2 *Bethune*	?	?
3 *Hammerschmidt*	?	?
4 Anthony	Y	Y
CALIFORNIA		
1 Bosco	Y	Y
2 *Chappie*	Y	Y
3 Matsui	Y	Y
4 Fazio	Y	Y
5 Burton	?	Y
6 Boxer	Y	Y
7 Miller	Y	Y
8 Dellums	N	Y
9 Stark	Y	Y
10 Edwards	N	Y
11 Lantos	Y	Y
12 *Zschau*	N	Y
13 Mineta	Y	Y
14 *Shumway*	N	Y
15 Coelho	Y	?
16 Panetta	N	?
17 *Pashayan*	Y	Y
18 Lehman	Y	Y
19 *Lagomarsino*	Y	Y
20 *Thomas*	Y	Y
21 *Fiedler*	Y	Y
22 *Moorhead*	Y	Y
23 Beilenson	N	Y
24 Waxman	N	Y
25 Roybal	Y	Y
26 Berman	Y	Y
27 Levine	Y	Y
28 Dixon	Y	Y
29 Hawkins	Y	Y
30 Martinez	Y	Y
31 Dymally	N	Y
32 Anderson	Y	?
33 *Dreier*	N	Y
34 Torres	Y	Y
35 *Lewis*	Y	Y
36 Brown	Y	Y
37 *McCandless*	Y	Y
38 Patterson	Y	Y
39 *Dannemeyer*	N	Y
40 *Badham*	Y	Y
41 *Lowery*	Y	Y
42 *Lungren*	Y	Y

	371	372
43 *Packard*	Y	Y
44 Bates	Y	Y
45 *Hunter*	Y	Y
COLORADO		
1 Schroeder	N	Y
2 Wirth	N	Y
3 Kogovsek	Y	Y
4 *Brown*	N	Y
5 *Kramer*	N	Y
6 *Schaefer*	N	Y
CONNECTICUT		
1 Kennelly	Y	Y
2 Gejdenson	Y	Y
3 Morrison	Y	Y
4 *McKinney*	Y	Y
5 Ratchford	Y	Y
6 *Johnson*	Y	Y
DELAWARE		
AL Carper	Y	Y
FLORIDA		
1 Hutto	Y	Y
2 Fuqua	Y	Y
3 Bennett	Y	Y
4 Chappell	Y	Y
5 *McCollum*	Y	Y
6 MacKay	N	Y
7 Gibbons	Y	Y
8 *Young*	Y	Y
9 *Bilirakis*	N	Y
10 *Ireland*	Y	Y
11 Nelson	N	Y
12 *Lewis*	N	Y
13 *Mack*	N	Y
14 Mica	Y	Y
15 *Shaw*	Y	Y
16 Smith	Y	?
17 Lehman	Y	Y
18 Pepper	?	?
19 Fascell	Y	Y
GEORGIA		
1 Thomas	Y	Y
2 Hatcher	?	?
3 Ray	Y	Y
4 Levitas	Y	Y
5 Fowler	Y	Y
6 *Gingrich*	Y	Y
7 Darden	Y	Y
8 Rowland	Y	Y
9 Jenkins	Y	Y
10 Barnard	Y	Y
HAWAII		
1 Heftel	Y	Y
2 Akaka	Y	Y
IDAHO		
1 *Craig*	N	Y
2 *Hansen*	N	Y
ILLINOIS		
1 Hayes	Y	Y
2 Savage	Y	Y
3 Russo	N	Y
4 *O'Brien*	Y	Y
5 Lipinski	Y	Y
6 *Hyde*	Y	Y
7 Collins	Y	?
8 Rostenkowski	Y	Y
9 Yates	Y	Y
10 *Porter*	Y	Y
11 Annunzio	Y	Y
12 *Crane, P.*	N	N
13 *Erlenborn*	N	Y
14 *Corcoran*	-	Y
15 *Madigan*	Y	Y
16 *Martin*	N	Y
17 Evans	Y	Y
18 *Michel*	Y	Y
19 *Crane, D.*	N	?
20 Durbin	Y	Y
21 Price	Y	Y
22 Simon	?	?
INDIANA		
1 Hall	Y	Y
2 Sharp	N	Y
3 *Hiler*	N	Y
4 *Coats*	N	Y
5 Hillis	Y	Y

ND - Northern Democrats   SD - Southern Democrats

	371	372
6 Burton	N	Y
7 Myers	Y	Y
8 McCloskey	Y	Y
9 Hamilton	Y	Y
10 Jacobs	N	Y
IOWA		
1 Leach	N	Y
2 Tauke	N	Y
3 Evans	N	Y
4 Smith	Y	Y
5 Harkin	Y	Y
6 Bedell	Y	Y
KANSAS		
1 Roberts	N	Y
2 Slattery	N	Y
3 Winn	Y	Y
4 Glickman	Y	Y
5 Whittaker	Y	Y
KENTUCKY		
1 Hubbard	N	Y
2 Natcher	Y	Y
3 Mazzoli	Y	Y
4 Snyder	Y	Y
5 Rogers	Y	Y
6 Hopkins	N	Y
7 Vacancy		
LOUISIANA		
1 Livingston	Y	Y
2 Boggs	?	?
3 Tauzin	Y	Y
4 Roemer	N	Y
5 Huckaby	Y	Y
6 Moore	Y	Y
7 Breaux	Y	?
8 Long	Y	Y
MAINE		
1 McKernan	Y	Y
2 Snowe	Y	Y
MARYLAND		
1 Dyson	Y	Y
2 Long	Y	Y
3 Mikulski	Y	Y
4 Holt	Y	Y
5 Hoyer	?	Y
6 Byron	Y	Y
7 Mitchell	N	Y
8 Barnes	Y	Y
MASSACHUSETTS		
1 Conte	Y	Y
2 Boland	Y	Y
3 Early	Y	Y
4 Frank	N	Y
5 Shannon	N	Y
6 Mavroules	Y	?
7 Markey	N	Y
8 O'Neill		
9 Moakley	Y	Y
10 Studds	Y	Y
11 Donnelly	Y	Y
MICHIGAN		
1 Conyers	N	Y
2 Pursell	N	Y
3 Wolpe	Y	Y
4 Siljander	Y	Y
5 Sawyer	Y	Y
6 Carr	Y	Y
7 Kildee	Y	Y
8 Traxler	Y	Y
9 Vander Jagt	Y	Y
10 Albosta	Y	Y
11 Davis	N	Y
12 Bonior	N	Y
13 Crockett	N	?
14 Hertel	N	Y
15 Ford	Y	Y
16 Dingell	Y	Y
17 Levin	Y	Y
18 Broomfield	N	Y
MINNESOTA		
1 Penny	Y	Y
2 Weber	Y	Y
3 Frenzel	N	Y
4 Vento	Y	Y
5 Sabo	Y	Y
6 Sikorski	Y	Y

	371	372
7 Stangeland	Y	Y
8 Oberstar	Y	Y
MISSISSIPPI		
1 Whitten	Y	Y
2 Franklin	?	Y
3 Montgomery	Y	Y
4 Dowdy	Y	Y
5 Lott	Y	?
MISSOURI		
1 Clay	N	Y
2 Young	Y	Y
3 Gephardt	Y	Y
4 Skelton	Y	Y
5 Wheat	N	Y
6 Coleman	Y	Y
7 Taylor	Y	Y
8 Emerson	Y	Y
9 Volkmer	Y	Y
MONTANA		
1 Williams	Y	Y
2 Marlenee	?	Y
NEBRASKA		
1 Bereuter	Y	Y
2 Daub	Y	Y
3 Smith	Y	Y
NEVADA		
1 Reid	Y	Y
2 Vucanovich	N	Y
NEW HAMPSHIRE		
1 D'Amours	?	Y
2 Gregg	N	Y
NEW JERSEY		
1 Florio	Y	Y
2 Hughes	N	Y
3 Howard	Y	Y
4 Smith	Y	Y
5 Roukema	Y	Y
6 Dwyer	Y	Y
7 Rinaldo	Y	Y
8 Roe	Y	Y
9 Torricelli	Y	Y
10 Rodino	N	Y
11 Minish	Y	Y
12 Courter	Y	Y
13 Vacancy		
14 Guarini	?	Y
NEW MEXICO		
1 Lujan	Y	Y
2 Skeen	Y	Y
3 Richardson	Y	Y
NEW YORK		
1 Carney	Y	Y
2 Downey	Y	Y
3 Mrazek	Y	Y
4 Lent	?	?
5 McGrath	?	?
6 Addabbo	Y	Y
7 Ackerman	Y	?
8 Scheuer	Y	Y
9 Ferraro	?	?
10 Schumer	Y	Y
11 Towns	Y	Y
12 Owens	Y	Y
13 Solarz	Y	Y
14 Molinari	Y	Y
15 Green	Y	Y
16 Rangel	Y	Y
17 Weiss	Y	Y
18 Garcia	Y	Y
19 Biaggi	Y	Y
20 Ottinger	Y	Y
21 Fish	Y	Y
22 Gilman	Y	Y
23 Stratton	Y	Y
24 Solomon	N	Y
25 Boehlert	Y	Y
26 Martin	Y	Y
27 Wortley	Y	Y
28 McHugh	Y	Y
29 Horton	Y	Y
30 Conable	N	Y
31 Kemp	Y	Y
32 LaFalce	Y	Y
33 Nowak	Y	Y
34 Lundine	Y	Y

	371	372
NORTH CAROLINA		
1 Jones	Y	?
2 Valentine	Y	Y
3 Whitley	Y	Y
4 Andrews	Y	Y
5 Neal	N	Y
6 Britt	Y	Y
7 Rose	Y	Y
8 Hefner	Y	Y
9 Martin	?	?
10 Broyhill	Y	Y
11 Clarke	Y	Y
NORTH DAKOTA		
AL Dorgan	N	Y
OHIO		
1 Luken	Y	Y
2 Gradison	N	Y
3 Hall	Y	Y
4 Oxley	Y	+
5 Latta	N	?
6 McEwen	N	Y
7 DeWine	Y	Y
8 Kindness	Y	Y
9 Kaptur	Y	Y
10 Miller	Y	Y
11 Eckart	Y	Y
12 Kasich	Y	Y
13 Pease	Y	Y
14 Seiberling	N	Y
15 Wylie	Y	Y
16 Regula	Y	?
17 Williams	?	Y
18 Applegate	N	Y
19 Feighan	Y	Y
20 Oakar	Y	Y
21 Stokes	Y	Y
OKLAHOMA		
1 Jones	Y	Y
2 Synar	N	Y
3 Watkins	Y	Y
4 McCurdy	Y	Y
5 Edwards	Y	Y
6 English	N	Y
OREGON		
1 AuCoin	N	?
2 Smith, R.	Y	Y
3 Wyden	Y	Y
4 Weaver	N	?
5 Smith, D.	N	Y
PENNSYLVANIA		
1 Foglietta	Y	Y
2 Gray	Y	Y
3 Borski	Y	Y
4 Kolter	Y	?
5 Schulze	Y	Y
6 Yatron	Y	Y
7 Edgar	Y	Y
8 Kostmayer	Y	Y
9 Shuster	Y	Y
10 McDade	Y	Y
11 Harrison	?	?
12 Murtha	Y	?
13 Coughlin	Y	Y
14 Coyne	Y	Y
15 Ritter	Y	Y
16 Walker	N	Y
17 Gekas	Y	Y
18 Walgren	Y	Y
19 Goodling	N	Y
20 Gaydos	Y	Y
21 Ridge	Y	Y
22 Murphy	Y	Y
23 Clinger	Y	Y
RHODE ISLAND		
1 St Germain	Y	?
2 Schneider	Y	Y
SOUTH CAROLINA		
1 Hartnett	N	Y
2 Spence	N	Y
3 Derrick	Y	Y
4 Campbell	Y	Y
5 Spratt	Y	Y
6 Tallon	Y	Y
SOUTH DAKOTA		
AL Daschle	N	Y

	371	372
TENNESSEE		
1 Quillen	Y	Y
2 Duncan	Y	?
3 Lloyd	Y	Y
4 Cooper	Y	Y
5 Boner	Y	Y
6 Gore	Y	Y
7 Sundquist	Y	Y
8 Jones	Y	Y
9 Ford	Y	Y
TEXAS		
1 Hall, S.	Y	Y
2 Wilson	Y	Y
3 Bartlett	Y	Y
4 Hall, R.	Y	Y
5 Bryant	Y	Y
6 Gramm	?	?
7 Archer	N	Y
8 Fields	Y	Y
9 Brooks	Y	Y
10 Pickle	Y	Y
11 Leath	Y	Y
12 Wright	Y	Y
13 Hightower	Y	Y
14 Patman	Y	Y
15 de la Garza	Y	Y
16 Coleman	Y	Y
17 Stenholm	N	Y
18 Leland	?	Y
19 Hance	Y	Y
20 Gonzalez	Y	Y
21 Loeffler	Y	Y
22 Paul	N	N
23 Kazen	Y	Y
24 Frost	Y	Y
25 Andrews	Y	Y
26 Vandergriff	N	Y
27 Ortiz	Y	Y
UTAH		
1 Hansen	N	Y
2 Marriott	N	Y
3 Nielson	N	Y
VERMONT		
AL Jeffords	Y	Y
VIRGINIA		
1 Bateman	Y	Y
2 Whitehurst	Y	Y
3 Bliley	Y	Y
4 Sisisky	Y	Y
5 Daniel	Y	Y
6 Olin	N	Y
7 Robinson	Y	Y
8 Parris	Y	Y
9 Boucher	Y	Y
10 Wolf	Y	Y
WASHINGTON		
1 Pritchard	?	Y
2 Swift	Y	Y
3 Bonker	Y	Y
4 Morrison	Y	Y
5 Foley	Y	Y
6 Dicks	Y	Y
7 Lowry	N	Y
8 Chandler	Y	Y
WEST VIRGINIA		
1 Mollohan	Y	Y
2 Staggers	Y	Y
3 Wise	Y	Y
4 Rahall	Y	Y
WISCONSIN		
1 Aspin	Y	Y
2 Kastenmeier	N	Y
3 Gunderson	N	Y
4 Kleczka	Y	Y
5 Moody	?	Y
6 Petri	N	Y
7 Obey	N	Y
8 Roth	Y	Y
9 Sensenbrenner	N	?
WYOMING		
AL Cheney	?	?

Southern states - Ala., Ark., Fla., Ga., Ky., La., Miss., N.C., Okla., S.C., Tenn., Texas, Va.

373. H J Res 653. Interim Continuing Appropriations, Fiscal 1985. Passage of the joint resolution to provide interim funding, until midnight Oct. 3, for programs and agencies under the nine appropriations bills not enacted into law by Oct. 1. Passed 240-79: R 54-65; D 186-14 (ND 125-7, SD 61-7), Oct. 1, 1984.

374. H Con Res 280. First Budget Resolution, Fiscal 1985. Jones, D-Okla., motion that the House concur in the Senate amendment and adopt the first budget resolution for fiscal 1985. The resolution sets fiscal 1985 spending and revenue ceilings as follows: budget authority, $1.021 trillion; outlays, $932 billion; revenues, $750.9 billion; it also projects a fiscal 1985 deficit of $181.1 billion. Motion agreed to 232-162: R 48-97; D 184-65 (ND 120-46, SD 64-19), Oct. 1, 1984.

375. HR 5361. Group Legal Services Exclusion. Rostenkowski, D-Ill., motion to suspend the rules and pass the bill to extend for one year, through 1985, the current law allowing employees to take advantage of employer-provided group legal service benefits without declaring the benefits as income. Motion agreed to 300-87: R 72-74; D 228-13 (ND 161-5, SD 67-8), Oct. 1, 1984. A two-thirds majority of those present and voting (258 in this case) is required for passage under suspension of the rules. A "nay" was a vote supporting the president's position.

376. HR 5538. Preventive Health Care. Waxman, D-Calif., motion to suspend the rules and pass the bill to authorize $701 million for fiscal years 1985-87 for preventive health programs, including childhood immunization, venereal disease and tuberculosis control, and for preventive health block grants. Motion agreed to 368-18: R 129-17; D 239-1 (ND 165-0, SD 74-1), Oct. 1, 1984. A two-thirds majority of those present and voting (258 in this case) is required for passage under suspension of the rules.

377. HR 6299. Social Security Cost-of-Living Adjustment. Rostenkowski, D-Ill., motion to suspend the rules and pass the bill to provide a cost-of-living adjustment equal to the rate of inflation in January 1985 to Social Security, disability and Supplemental Security Income beneficiaries and instructing the Social Security Administration to conduct a study of the cost-of-living adjustment. Motion agreed to 417-4: R 162-2; D 255-2 (ND 170-2, SD 85-0), Oct. 2, 1984. A two-thirds majority of those present and voting (281 in this case) is required for passage under suspension of the rules. A "yea" was a vote supporting the president's position.

378. HR 5790. Amusement Park Safety Act. Waxman, D-Calif., motion to suspend the rules and pass the bill to restore some federal oversight of amusement rides at fixed-park sites. Motion agreed to 300-119: R 67-97; D 233-22 (ND 166-4, SD 67-18), Oct. 2, 1984. A two-thirds majority of those present and voting (280 in this case) is required for passage under suspension of the rules.

379. HR 4712. Water Project Law Enforcement. Kazen, D-Texas, motion to suspend the rules and pass the bill to authorize the interior secretary to make cooperative agreements with state and local governments for law enforcement at federal water projects, to extend the service area of the San Luis Unit of the Central Valley Project to include the Pleasant Valley Water District, and authorize the energy secretary to enter into an agreement with respect to the Eklutna Lake hydropower project in Alaska. Motion rejected 19-402: R 2-162; D 17-240 (ND 12-160, SD 5-80), Oct. 2, 1984. A two-thirds majority of those present and voting (281 in this case) is required for passage under suspension of the rules. A "nay" was a vote supporting the president's position.

380. HR 4684. Nutritional Monitoring and Related Research Act. Fuqua, D-Fla., motion to suspend the rules and pass the bill to authorize $2 million in fiscal 1985 for a new, interagency "directorate" to coordinate nutrition surveys and research; and also to authorize $3 million annually for nine years to carry out the group's recommendations on coordinating national nutritional status monitoring, and grants for nutrition-related research. Motion rejected 265-157: R 34-130; D 231-27 (ND 164-9, SD 67-18), Oct. 2, 1984. A two-thirds majority of those present and voting (282 in this case) is required for passage under suspension of the rules. A "nay" was a vote supporting the president's position.

KEY

Y	Voted for (yea).
#	Paired for.
+	Announced for.
N	Voted against (nay).
X	Paired against.
-	Announced against.
P	Voted "present".
C	Voted "present" to avoid possible conflict of interest.
?	Did not vote or otherwise make a position known.

Democrats   *Republicans*

	373	374	375	376	377	378	379	380
ALABAMA								
1 *Edwards*	Y	Y	Y	Y	Y	Y	N	N
2 *Dickinson*	Y	Y	N	Y	Y	N	N	N
3 Nichols	Y	Y	Y	Y	Y	Y	N	N
4 Bevill	Y	Y	Y	Y	Y	Y	N	N
5 Flippo	Y	Y	Y	Y	Y	Y	N	Y
6 Erdreich	Y	N	Y	Y	Y	Y	N	N
7 Shelby	Y	N	Y	Y	Y	Y	N	Y
ALASKA								
AL *Young*	N	Y	Y	Y	Y	N	Y	N
ARIZONA								
1 *McCain*	?	?	?	?	Y	N	N	N
2 Udall	Y	Y	Y	Y	Y	Y	N	Y
3 *Stump*	N	N	N	N	Y	N	N	N
4 *Rudd*	Y	N	N	N	Y	N	N	N
5 McNulty	Y	Y	Y	Y	Y	Y	N	Y
ARKANSAS								
1 Alexander	?	#	?	?	?	?	?	?
2 *Bethune*	?	?	?	?	Y	N	N	N
3 *Hammerschmidt*	N	N	Y	Y	Y	N	N	N
4 Anthony	Y	Y	?	?	Y	Y	N	Y
CALIFORNIA								
1 Bosco	?	Y	Y	Y	Y	Y	N	Y
2 *Chappie*	N	N	?	Y	Y	N	N	N
3 Matsui	?	Y	Y	Y	Y	Y	N	Y
4 Fazio	Y	Y	Y	Y	Y	Y	Y	Y
5 Burton	Y	Y	Y	Y	Y	Y	N	Y
6 Boxer	Y	Y	Y	Y	Y	Y	N	Y
7 Miller	Y	Y	Y	Y	Y	Y	N	Y
8 Dellums	?	?	Y	Y	Y	Y	N	Y
9 Stark	Y	N	Y	Y	Y	Y	N	Y
10 Edwards	?	Y	Y	Y	Y	Y	N	Y
11 Lantos	Y	Y	Y	Y	Y	Y	N	Y
12 *Zschau*	N	N	N	Y	Y	N	N	N
13 Mineta	Y	Y	Y	Y	Y	Y	N	Y
14 *Shumway*	N	N	N	N	Y	N	N	N
15 Coelho	Y	Y	Y	Y	Y	Y	N	Y
16 Panetta	Y	Y	Y	Y	Y	N	N	Y
17 *Pashayan*	?	?	?	Y	Y	N	N	Y
18 Lehman	Y	Y	Y	Y	Y	Y	N	Y
19 *Lagomarsino*	Y	N	Y	Y	Y	Y	N	N
20 *Thomas*	N	N	Y	N	Y	N	N	N
21 *Fiedler*	?	?	Y	Y	Y	N	N	N
22 *Moorhead*	N	N	N	Y	Y	N	N	N
23 Beilenson	Y	Y	N	Y	N	Y	N	N
24 Waxman	Y	Y	Y	Y	Y	Y	N	Y
25 Roybal	Y	Y	Y	Y	Y	Y	Y	Y
26 Berman	Y	Y	Y	Y	?	?	?	Y
27 Levine	Y	Y	Y	Y	Y	Y	N	Y
28 Dixon	?	Y	Y	Y	Y	Y	N	Y
29 Hawkins	Y	Y	Y	Y	Y	Y	N	Y
30 Martinez	?	Y	Y	Y	Y	Y	N	Y
31 Dymally	Y	Y	Y	Y	?	?	?	?
32 Anderson	Y	N	N	Y	Y	Y	N	?
33 *Dreier*	N	N	N	N	Y	N	N	N
34 Torres	Y	Y	Y	Y	Y	Y	N	Y
35 *Lewis*	N	N	N	Y	Y	N	N	N
36 Brown	Y	Y	Y	Y	Y	Y	N	Y
37 *McCandless*	N	N	N	Y	Y	N	N	N
38 Patterson	Y	Y	Y	Y	Y	Y	N	Y
39 *Dannemeyer*	N	N	N	N	Y	N	N	N
40 *Badham*	N	N	N	N	Y	N	N	N
41 Lowery	Y	Y	Y	Y	Y	Y	N	N
42 *Lungren*	N	N	N	Y	Y	N	N	N

	373	374	375	376	377	378	379	380
43 *Packard*	N	N	N	Y	Y	N	N	N
44 Bates	Y	Y	Y	Y	Y	Y	N	Y
45 *Hunter*	Y	N	Y	Y	Y	N	N	N
COLORADO								
1 Schroeder	Y	N	Y	Y	Y	Y	N	Y
2 Wirth	Y	N	Y	Y	Y	Y	N	Y
3 Kogovsek	Y	Y	Y	Y	Y	Y	N	Y
4 *Brown*	N	N	N	N	Y	N	N	N
5 *Kramer*	N	N	Y	Y	Y	N	N	N
6 *Schaefer*	N	N	N	N	Y	N	N	N
CONNECTICUT								
1 Kennelly	Y	Y	Y	Y	Y	Y	N	Y
2 Gejdenson	Y	Y	Y	Y	Y	Y	N	Y
3 Morrison	+	X	+	+	+	+	-	+
4 *McKinney*	Y	Y	Y	Y	Y	Y	N	Y
5 Ratchford	Y	Y	Y	Y	Y	Y	N	Y
6 *Johnson*	Y	Y	Y	Y	Y	N	N	Y
DELAWARE								
AL Carper	Y	Y	Y	Y	Y	Y	N	Y
FLORIDA								
1 Hutto	Y	Y	Y	Y	N	Y	N	N
2 Fuqua	?	Y	Y	Y	Y	Y	N	Y
3 Bennett	Y	Y	Y	Y	Y	Y	N	Y
4 Chappell	Y	Y	Y	Y	Y	Y	N	Y
5 *McCollum*	?	N	Y	Y	Y	N	N	N
6 MacKay	Y	Y	?	Y	Y	Y	N	Y
7 Gibbons	?	?	?	?	Y	Y	N	Y
8 *Young*	?	N	Y	Y	Y	N	N	N
9 *Bilirakis*	N	N	Y	Y	Y	N	N	N
10 *Ireland*	Y	N	Y	Y	Y	N	N	N
11 Nelson	N	Y	Y	Y	Y	N	N	N
12 *Lewis*	-	N	Y	Y	Y	N	N	N
13 *Mack*	?	X	?	?	Y	N	N	N
14 Mica	Y	Y	Y	Y	Y	Y	N	Y
15 *Shaw*	N	N	N	Y	Y	N	N	N
16 Smith	?	Y	Y	Y	Y	Y	N	Y
17 Lehman	Y	Y	Y	Y	Y	Y	N	Y
18 Pepper	Y	Y	Y	Y	Y	Y	N	Y
19 Fascell	Y	?	?	?	Y	Y	N	Y
GEORGIA								
1 Thomas	Y	Y	Y	Y	Y	Y	N	N
2 Hatcher	Y	Y	Y	Y	Y	Y	N	Y
3 Ray	Y	N	Y	Y	Y	Y	N	Y
4 Levitas	?	N	Y	Y	Y	Y	N	Y
5 Fowler	?	Y	?	?	?	?	?	?
6 *Gingrich*	?	N	N	Y	Y	N	N	N
7 Darden	Y	N	Y	Y	Y	N	N	Y
8 Rowland	Y	Y	Y	Y	Y	Y	N	Y
9 Jenkins	Y	Y	Y	Y	Y	Y	N	Y
10 Barnard	Y	N	Y	Y	Y	N	N	Y
HAWAII								
1 Heftel	?	?	Y	Y	Y	Y	N	Y
2 Akaka	?	Y	Y	Y	Y	Y	N	Y
IDAHO								
1 *Craig*	N	N	N	Y	N	N	N	N
2 *Hansen*	N	N	N	N	Y	N	N	N
ILLINOIS								
1 Hayes	Y	N	Y	Y	Y	Y	N	Y
2 Savage	Y	Y	Y	Y	Y	Y	N	Y
3 Russo	N	Y	Y	Y	Y	Y	N	Y
4 *O'Brien*	Y	Y	Y	Y	Y	N	N	N
5 Lipinski	Y	Y	Y	Y	Y	Y	N	Y
6 *Hyde*	Y	N	Y	Y	Y	N	N	N
7 Collins	+	+	+	+	Y	Y	N	Y
8 Rostenkowski	Y	Y	Y	Y	Y	Y	N	Y
9 Yates	Y	N	Y	Y	Y	Y	N	Y
10 *Porter*	N	Y	Y	Y	Y	N	N	N
11 Annunzio	Y	Y	Y	Y	Y	Y	N	Y
12 *Crane, P.*	N	N	N	N	N	N	N	N
13 *Erlenborn*	?	Y	N	Y	Y	N	N	N
14 *Corcoran*	?	Y	Y	Y	Y	Y	N	N
15 *Madigan*	Y	Y	Y	Y	Y	N	N	N
16 *Martin*	N	?	Y	Y	Y	N	N	N
17 Evans	Y	Y	Y	Y	Y	Y	N	Y
18 *Michel*	Y	N	Y	Y	Y	N	N	N
19 *Crane, D.*	?	N	Y	Y	Y	N	N	N
20 Durbin	Y	N	Y	Y	Y	Y	N	Y
21 Price	Y	Y	Y	Y	Y	Y	N	Y
22 Simon	?	?	?	?	Y	Y	N	Y
INDIANA								
1 Hall	?	Y	Y	Y	Y	Y	N	Y
2 Sharp	Y	N	Y	Y	Y	Y	N	Y
3 *Hiler*	N	N	Y	Y	Y	N	N	N
4 *Coats*	N	N	N	Y	Y	N	N	N
5 *Hillis*	?	Y	N	Y	Y	Y	N	N

ND - Northern Democrats   SD - Southern Democrats

Corresponding to Congressional Record Votes 424, 425, 426, 427, 429, 430, 431, 432

	373	374	375	376	377	378	379	380
6 *Burton*	?	N	N	Y	Y	N	N	N
7 *Myers*	?	N	Y	Y	Y	N	N	N
8 McCloskey	?	Y	Y	Y	Y	Y	N	Y
9 Hamilton	Y	Y	Y	Y	Y	Y	N	Y
10 Jacobs	?	N	Y	Y	Y	Y	N	Y
IOWA								
1 *Leach*	N	N	N	Y	Y	Y	N	N
2 *Tauke*	N	N	N	Y	Y	Y	N	N
3 *Evans*	?	N	N	Y	Y	N	N	N
4 Smith	?	N	Y	Y	Y	Y	N	Y
5 Harkin	Y	N	Y	Y	Y	Y	N	Y
6 Bedell	Y	N	Y	Y	Y	Y	N	Y
KANSAS								
1 *Roberts*	N	N	N	Y	Y	N	N	N
2 Slattery	?	N	Y	Y	Y	Y	N	Y
3 *Winn*	N	N	N	Y	Y	Y	N	N
4 Glickman	Y	N	Y	Y	Y	Y	N	Y
5 *Whittaker*	?	N	N	Y	Y	Y	N	N
KENTUCKY								
1 Hubbard	N	N	Y	N	Y	N	N	N
2 Natcher	Y	Y	Y	Y	Y	Y	N	Y
3 Mazzoli	Y	Y	Y	Y	Y	Y	N	Y
4 *Snyder*	Y	N	Y	Y	Y	Y	N	Y
5 *Rogers*	Y	Y	Y	Y	Y	N	N	N
6 *Hopkins*	N	N	N	Y	Y	N	N	N
7 Vacancy								
LOUISIANA								
1 *Livingston*	Y	Y	Y	N	Y	N	N	N
2 Boggs	?	Y	Y	Y	Y	Y	N	Y
3 Tauzin	?	N	Y	Y	Y	Y	N	Y
4 Roemer	N	N	N	Y	Y	Y	N	Y
5 Huckaby	Y	Y	Y	Y	Y	Y	N	Y
6 *Moore*	Y	N	Y	Y	Y	Y	N	N
7 Breaux	?	X	?	?	Y	Y	N	Y
8 Long	Y	Y	Y	Y	Y	Y	N	Y
MAINE								
1 *McKernan*	Y	Y	Y	Y	Y	Y	N	Y
2 *Snowe*	Y	Y	Y	Y	Y	Y	N	Y
MARYLAND								
1 Dyson	?	N	Y	Y	Y	Y	N	Y
2 Long	Y	N	Y	Y	Y	Y	Y	Y
3 Mikulski	Y	Y	?	?	Y	Y	N	Y
4 *Holt*	Y	N	N	Y	Y	N	N	Y
5 Hoyer	Y	Y	Y	Y	Y	Y	N	Y
6 Byron	Y	Y	Y	Y	Y	Y	N	N
7 Mitchell	Y	Y	Y	Y	Y	Y	N	Y
8 Barnes	Y	Y	?	?	Y	Y	N	Y
MASSACHUSETTS								
1 *Conte*	Y	N	Y	Y	Y	Y	N	Y
2 Boland	?	Y	Y	Y	Y	Y	N	Y
3 Early	Y	N	Y	Y	Y	Y	N	Y
4 Frank	Y	N	Y	Y	Y	Y	N	Y
5 Shannon	Y	Y	Y	Y	Y	Y	N	Y
6 Mavroules	Y	Y	Y	Y	Y	Y	N	Y
7 Markey	Y	N	Y	Y	Y	Y	N	Y
8 O'Neill								
9 Moakley	Y	Y	Y	Y	Y	?	N	Y
10 Studds	Y	N	Y	Y	Y	Y	N	Y
11 Donnelly	?	Y	Y	Y	Y	Y	N	Y
MICHIGAN								
1 Conyers	Y	N	Y	Y	Y	Y	N	Y
2 *Pursell*	?	?	N	Y	Y	Y	N	Y
3 Wolpe	Y	Y	Y	Y	Y	Y	N	Y
4 *Siljander*	?	?	?	?	Y	N	N	Y
5 *Sawyer*	Y	Y	N	Y	Y	N	N	N
6 Carr	Y	N	Y	Y	Y	Y	N	N
7 Kildee	Y	Y	Y	Y	Y	Y	N	Y
8 Traxler	?	Y	Y	Y	Y	Y	N	Y
9 *Vander Jagt*	N	Y	Y	Y	Y	N	N	N
10 Albosta	?	Y	Y	Y	Y	Y	N	Y
11 *Davis*	?	?	Y	Y	Y	Y	N	Y
12 Bonior	Y	Y	Y	Y	Y	Y	Y	Y
13 Crockett	Y	N	Y	Y	Y	Y	N	Y
14 Hertel	N	N	Y	Y	Y	Y	N	Y
15 Ford	Y	Y	Y	Y	Y	Y	N	Y
16 Dingell	?	Y	Y	Y	Y	?	N	Y
17 Levin	Y	Y	Y	Y	Y	Y	N	Y
18 *Broomfield*	?	?	Y	Y	Y	Y	N	Y
MINNESOTA								
1 Penny	N	N	N	Y	Y	N	N	Y
2 *Weber*	N	N	N	Y	Y	N	N	N
3 *Frenzel*	N	Y	N	Y	Y	N	N	N
4 Vento	Y	N	Y	Y	Y	Y	N	Y
5 Sabo	?	Y	Y	Y	Y	Y	N	Y
6 Sikorski	N	N	Y	Y	Y	Y	N	Y

	373	374	375	376	377	378	379	380
7 *Stangeland*	?	Y	Y	Y	Y	Y	N	N
8 Oberstar	Y	Y	Y	Y	Y	Y	N	Y
MISSISSIPPI								
1 Whitten	Y	Y	Y	Y	Y	Y	N	Y
2 *Franklin*	?	?	?	?	Y	N	N	N
3 Montgomery	Y	Y	Y	Y	Y	N	N	N
4 Dowdy	?	Y	Y	Y	Y	Y	N	Y
5 *Lott*	?	?	?	?	Y	N	N	N
MISSOURI								
1 Clay	?	Y	Y	Y	Y	Y	N	Y
2 Young	Y	Y	Y	Y	Y	N	N	Y
3 Gephardt	Y	Y	Y	Y	Y	Y	Y	Y
4 Skelton	?	Y	Y	Y	Y	Y	N	Y
5 Wheat	Y	Y	Y	Y	Y	Y	N	Y
6 *Coleman*	Y	N	Y	Y	Y	Y	N	N
7 *Taylor*	Y	N	Y	Y	Y	N	N	N
8 *Emerson*	Y	N	Y	Y	Y	N	N	N
9 Volkmer	?	?	Y	Y	Y	Y	N	Y
MONTANA								
1 Williams	Y	Y	Y	Y	Y	Y	N	Y
2 *Marlenee*	N	N	Y	Y	Y	N	N	N
NEBRASKA								
1 *Bereuter*	N	Y	Y	Y	Y	Y	N	Y
2 *Daub*	N	N	N	Y	Y	N	N	N
3 *Smith*	Y	N	N	Y	Y	Y	N	N
NEVADA								
1 Reid	Y	Y	Y	Y	Y	N	N	Y
2 *Vucanovich*	N	N	N	N	Y	N	N	N
NEW HAMPSHIRE								
1 D'Amours	?	N	Y	Y	Y	Y	N	N
2 *Gregg*	N	Y	N	Y	Y	N	N	N
NEW JERSEY								
1 Florio	Y	Y	Y	Y	Y	Y	N	Y
2 Hughes	Y	Y	N	Y	Y	Y	Y	N
3 Howard	Y	Y	Y	Y	Y	Y	N	Y
4 *Smith*	?	?	Y	Y	Y	Y	N	Y
5 *Roukema*	Y	Y	Y	Y	Y	Y	N	N
6 Dwyer	Y	Y	Y	Y	Y	Y	N	Y
7 *Rinaldo*	Y	N	Y	Y	Y	Y	N	N
8 Roe	Y	Y	Y	Y	Y	Y	N	Y
9 Torricelli	Y	Y	?	?	Y	Y	N	Y
10 Rodino	?	Y	Y	Y	Y	Y	N	Y
11 Minish	Y	Y	Y	Y	Y	Y	N	Y
12 *Courter*	?	N	?	?	Y	Y	N	N
13 Vacancy								
14 Guarini	?	#	?	?	Y	Y	N	Y
NEW MEXICO								
1 *Lujan*	?	Y	Y	Y	Y	N	N	N
2 *Skeen*	N	N	N	Y	Y	N	N	N
3 Richardson	?	Y	Y	Y	Y	Y	N	Y
NEW YORK								
1 *Carney*	?	N	N	Y	Y	Y	N	N
2 Downey	Y	Y	Y	Y	Y	Y	N	Y
3 Mrazek	Y	Y	Y	Y	Y	Y	N	Y
4 *Lent*	N	Y	N	Y	Y	Y	N	N
5 *McGrath*	?	?	?	?	?	?	?	?
6 Addabbo	Y	Y	Y	Y	Y	Y	N	Y
7 Ackerman	Y	N	Y	Y	Y	Y	N	Y
8 Scheuer	?	N	Y	Y	Y	Y	N	Y
9 Ferraro	?	?	?	?	?	?	?	?
10 Schumer	?	N	Y	Y	Y	Y	N	Y
11 Towns	Y	Y	Y	Y	Y	Y	N	Y
12 Owens	?	Y	Y	Y	Y	Y	N	Y
13 Solarz	?	Y	Y	Y	Y	Y	N	Y
14 *Molinari*	N	N	N	Y	Y	Y	N	N
15 *Green*	Y	N	Y	Y	Y	Y	N	N
16 Rangel	Y	Y	Y	Y	Y	Y	N	Y
17 Weiss	Y	N	Y	Y	Y	Y	N	Y
18 Garcia	Y	Y	Y	Y	Y	Y	N	Y
19 Biaggi	?	Y	?	Y	Y	Y	N	Y
20 Ottinger	Y	Y	?	?	Y	Y	N	Y
21 *Fish*	?	Y	Y	Y	Y	Y	N	Y
22 *Gilman*	Y	N	Y	Y	Y	Y	N	Y
23 Stratton	Y	Y	Y	Y	Y	Y	N	Y
24 *Solomon*	?	?	N	Y	Y	Y	N	Y
25 *Boehlert*	?	Y	Y	Y	Y	Y	N	Y
26 *Martin*	?	Y	Y	Y	Y	Y	N	Y
27 *Wortley*	Y	N	N	Y	Y	Y	N	Y
28 McHugh	Y	Y	Y	Y	Y	Y	N	Y
29 *Horton*	Y	Y	Y	Y	Y	N	N	Y
30 *Conable*	Y	N	N	Y	Y	Y	N	Y
31 *Kemp*	?	N	?	?	Y	N	N	N
32 LaFalce	?	Y	Y	Y	Y	Y	N	Y
33 Nowak	Y	Y	Y	Y	Y	Y	N	Y
34 Lundine	Y	Y	Y	Y	Y	Y	N	Y

	373	374	375	376	377	378	379	380
NORTH CAROLINA								
1 Jones	Y	Y	?	?	Y	Y	N	Y
2 Valentine	Y	Y	?	?	Y	Y	N	Y
3 Whitley	Y	Y	Y	Y	Y	Y	N	Y
4 Andrews	Y	Y	Y	Y	Y	Y	Y	Y
5 Neal	Y	N	Y	Y	Y	Y	N	Y
6 Britt	?	Y	?	?	Y	Y	N	Y
7 Rose	Y	Y	Y	Y	Y	Y	N	Y
8 Hefner	?	?	?	?	Y	Y	N	Y
9 *Martin*	?	?	?	?	?	?	?	?
10 *Broyhill*	Y	Y	Y	Y	Y	Y	N	N
11 Clarke	Y	Y	Y	Y	Y	Y	N	Y
NORTH DAKOTA								
AL Dorgan	Y	N	Y	Y	Y	Y	N	Y
OHIO								
1 Luken	Y	Y	Y	Y	Y	Y	N	Y
2 *Gradison*	Y	Y	N	Y	Y	Y	N	N
3 Hall	Y	?	Y	Y	Y	Y	N	Y
4 *Oxley*	N	N	Y	Y	Y	N	N	N
5 *Latta*	N	N	N	Y	Y	N	N	N
6 *McEwen*	N	?	?	?	Y	N	N	N
7 *DeWine*	N	N	Y	Y	Y	Y	N	N
8 *Kindness*	N	N	N	Y	Y	N	N	N
9 Kaptur	?	N	Y	Y	Y	Y	N	N
10 *Miller*	N	N	N	Y	Y	N	N	N
11 Eckart	Y	N	Y	Y	Y	Y	N	N
12 *Kasich*	Y	N	Y	Y	Y	Y	N	N
13 Pease	Y	N	Y	Y	Y	Y	N	N
14 Seiberling	?	N	Y	Y	Y	Y	Y	Y
15 *Wylie*	?	N	Y	Y	Y	Y	N	N
16 *Regula*	N	N	Y	Y	Y	Y	N	N
17 *Williams*	Y	Y	Y	Y	Y	Y	N	Y
18 Applegate	N	?	Y	Y	Y	Y	N	N
19 Feighan	Y	N	Y	Y	Y	Y	N	Y
20 Oakar	Y	Y	Y	Y	Y	Y	N	Y
21 Stokes	Y	Y	Y	Y	Y	Y	N	Y
OKLAHOMA								
1 Jones	Y	Y	Y	Y	Y	Y	N	Y
2 Synar	Y	Y	Y	Y	Y	Y	N	Y
3 Watkins	Y	Y	Y	Y	Y	Y	N	Y
4 McCurdy	Y	Y	N	Y	Y	Y	N	Y
5 *Edwards*	Y	N	N	Y	Y	Y	N	N
6 English	Y	N	N	Y	Y	Y	N	N
OREGON								
1 AuCoin	N	N	Y	Y	Y	Y	N	Y
2 *Smith, R.*	N	N	N	Y	Y	N	N	N
3 Wyden	Y	N	Y	Y	Y	Y	N	Y
4 Weaver	N	N	Y	Y	Y	N	Y	Y
5 *Smith, D.*	N	N	N	N	Y	N	N	N
PENNSYLVANIA								
1 Foglietta	Y	Y	Y	Y	Y	Y	N	Y
2 Gray	Y	Y	Y	Y	Y	Y	N	Y
3 Borski	Y	Y	?	?	Y	Y	N	Y
4 Kolter	?	Y	Y	Y	Y	Y	N	Y
5 *Schulze*	Y	Y	N	Y	Y	Y	N	N
6 Yatron	Y	N	Y	Y	Y	Y	N	Y
7 Edgar	Y	Y	Y	Y	Y	Y	N	Y
8 Kostmayer	+	N	Y	Y	Y	Y	N	Y
9 *Shuster*	?	N	Y	Y	Y	Y	N	N
10 *McDade*	N	Y	Y	Y	Y	Y	N	Y
11 Harrison	?	Y	Y	Y	Y	Y	N	Y
12 Murtha	Y	Y	Y	Y	Y	Y	N	Y
13 *Coughlin*	Y	#	?	?	Y	Y	N	N
14 Coyne	Y	Y	Y	Y	Y	Y	N	Y
15 *Ritter*	?	N	Y	Y	Y	N	N	N
16 *Walker*	N	N	?	?	Y	N	N	N
17 *Gekas*	?	N	N	Y	Y	N	N	Y
18 Walgren	Y	N	Y	Y	Y	Y	Y	Y
19 *Goodling*	N	N	?	?	Y	Y	N	Y
20 Gaydos	Y	Y	Y	Y	Y	Y	N	Y
21 *Ridge*	Y	Y	Y	Y	Y	Y	N	Y
22 Murphy	?	N	Y	Y	Y	Y	Y	Y
23 *Clinger*	Y	Y	Y	Y	Y	N	N	Y
RHODE ISLAND								
1 St Germain	Y	Y	Y	Y	Y	Y	N	Y
2 *Schneider*	Y	Y	Y	Y	Y	Y	N	Y
SOUTH CAROLINA								
1 *Hartnett*	?	?	N	N	Y	N	N	N
2 *Spence*	?	N	Y	Y	Y	N	N	N
3 Derrick	Y	Y	Y	Y	Y	N	N	Y
4 *Campbell*	?	N	?	?	Y	N	N	N
5 Spratt	Y	Y	Y	Y	Y	Y	N	Y
6 Tallon	Y	N	Y	Y	Y	N	N	Y
SOUTH DAKOTA								
AL Daschle	Y	Y	Y	Y	Y	Y	N	Y

	373	374	375	376	377	378	379	380
TENNESSEE								
1 *Quillen*	Y	Y	Y	Y	Y	N	N	N
2 *Duncan*	N	Y	Y	Y	Y	N	N	Y
3 Lloyd	Y	N	Y	Y	Y	Y	N	Y
4 Cooper	Y	Y	Y	Y	?	?	?	?
5 Boner	Y	Y	Y	Y	Y	Y	N	Y
6 Gore	Y	Y	Y	Y	Y	Y	N	Y
7 *Sundquist*	Y	Y	Y	Y	Y	N	N	N
8 Jones	Y	Y	Y	Y	Y	Y	N	Y
9 Ford	Y	Y	Y	Y	Y	Y	N	Y
TEXAS								
1 Hall, S.	?	N	N	Y	Y	N	N	N
2 Wilson	?	Y	Y	Y	Y	Y	N	Y
3 *Bartlett*	Y	N	Y	N	Y	N	N	N
4 Hall, R.	Y	N	N	Y	Y	N	N	N
5 Bryant	Y	Y	Y	Y	Y	Y	N	Y
6 *Gramm*	?	?	?	?	?	?	?	?
7 *Archer*	N	N	N	Y	Y	N	N	N
8 *Fields*	N	N	N	Y	Y	Y	N	N
9 Brooks	?	Y	Y	Y	Y	Y	N	Y
10 Pickle	Y	Y	Y	Y	Y	Y	N	Y
11 Leath	Y	N	N	Y	Y	N	N	N
12 Wright	Y	Y	?	?	Y	Y	N	Y
13 Hightower	Y	Y	Y	Y	Y	Y	N	N
14 Patman	N	N	Y	Y	Y	N	Y	N
15 de la Garza	Y	Y	?	?	Y	Y	N	Y
16 Coleman	?	Y	Y	Y	Y	Y	N	Y
17 Stenholm	N	Y	N	Y	Y	N	N	N
18 Leland	Y	Y	Y	Y	Y	Y	N	Y
19 Hance	Y	Y	Y	Y	Y	N	N	N
20 Gonzalez	Y	Y	Y	Y	Y	N	N	Y
21 *Loeffler*	Y	Y	N	Y	Y	Y	N	N
22 *Paul*	?	N	Y	N	N	N	N	N
23 Kazen	Y	Y	Y	Y	Y	Y	Y	Y
24 Frost	Y	Y	Y	Y	Y	Y	N	Y
25 Andrews	Y	Y	Y	Y	Y	Y	N	Y
26 Vandergriff	N	N	Y	Y	Y	N	N	N
27 Ortiz	?	Y	Y	Y	Y	Y	Y	Y
UTAH								
1 *Hansen*	N	N	N	Y	Y	N	N	N
2 *Marriott*	N	N	Y	Y	Y	N	N	N
3 *Nielson*	N	N	N	Y	Y	N	N	N
VERMONT								
AL *Jeffords*	?	?	N	Y	Y	Y	N	Y
VIRGINIA								
1 *Bateman*	N	Y	Y	Y	Y	N	N	N
2 *Whitehurst*	Y	Y	?	?	Y	Y	N	N
3 *Bliley*	N	N	N	Y	Y	N	N	N
4 Sisisky	Y	Y	Y	Y	Y	N	N	Y
5 Daniel	N	N	Y	Y	Y	N	N	N
6 Olin	?	Y	Y	Y	Y	N	N	N
7 *Robinson*	Y	N	N	Y	Y	N	N	N
8 *Parris*	?	N	Y	Y	Y	N	N	N
9 Boucher	Y	Y	Y	Y	Y	Y	N	Y
10 *Wolf*	Y	N	?	?	Y	Y	N	N
WASHINGTON								
1 *Pritchard*	Y	Y	N	Y	Y	N	N	N
2 Swift	Y	Y	Y	Y	Y	Y	N	Y
3 Bonker	Y	Y	Y	Y	Y	Y	N	Y
4 *Morrison*	Y	Y	N	Y	Y	N	N	N
5 Foley	Y	Y	Y	Y	Y	Y	N	Y
6 Dicks	Y	Y	Y	Y	?	?	?	Y
7 Lowry	Y	Y	Y	Y	Y	Y	N	Y
8 *Chandler*	Y	Y	N	Y	Y	N	N	N
WEST VIRGINIA								
1 Mollohan	Y	Y	Y	Y	Y	Y	N	Y
2 Staggers	Y	Y	Y	Y	Y	Y	N	Y
3 Wise	Y	Y	Y	Y	Y	Y	N	Y
4 Rahall	Y	Y	Y	Y	Y	Y	N	Y
WISCONSIN								
1 Aspin	Y	Y	Y	Y	Y	Y	N	Y
2 Kastenmeier	?	Y	Y	Y	Y	Y	N	Y
3 *Gunderson*	Y	N	N	Y	Y	N	N	N
4 Kleczka	Y	Y	Y	Y	Y	Y	N	Y
5 Moody	Y	Y	Y	?	N	Y	N	Y
6 *Petri*	N	N	N	Y	Y	N	N	N
7 Obey	?	Y	Y	Y	Y	Y	N	Y
8 *Roth*	N	N	Y	Y	Y	Y	N	Y
9 *Sensenbrenner*	N	N	N	Y	Y	Y	N	N
WYOMING								
AL *Cheney*	?	?	?	?	Y	N	N	N

Southern states - Ala., Ark., Fla., Ga., Ky., La., Miss., N.C., Okla., S.C., Tenn., Texas, Va.

381. HR 6300. Balanced Budget. Jones, D-Okla., motion to suspend the rules and pass the bill to require both the president and congressional budget committees to submit balanced budgets, starting in fiscal 1986. Both also may propose budgets that do not show balance. Motion agreed to 411-11: R 155-9; D 256-2 (ND 172-2, SD 84-0), Oct. 2, 1984. A two-thirds majority of those present and voting (282 in this case) is required for passage under suspension of the rules.

382. HR 5690. Anti-Crime Act. Hughes, D-N.J., motion to suspend the rules and pass the omnibus anti-crime bill to revise federal sentencing procedures, permit pretrial detention of dangerous suspects, increase penalties for drug violations, tighten the insanity defense, create a program of anti-crime grants to states, establish a victims' compensation fund and make other changes in criminal law. Motion agreed to 406-16: R 160-3; D 246-13 (ND 163-11, SD 83-2), Oct. 2, 1984. A two-thirds majority of those present and voting (282 in this case) is required for passage under suspension of the rules.

383. H Res 599. Small Business Procurement. Mitchell, D-Md., motion to suspend the rules and adopt the resolution providing that the House concur in the Senate amendment to HR 4209, a bill to increase competition in federal procurement and enhance small business participation in the process, with an amendment, sending the bill back to the Senate. Motion agreed to 416-0: R 162-0; D 254-0 (ND 170-0, SD 84-0), Oct. 2, 1984. A two-thirds majority of those present and voting (278 in this case) is required for adoption under suspension of the rules.

384. HR 2848. Service Industries Commerce Development. Hall, D-Ohio, motion to order the previous question (thus ending debate and the possibility of amendment) on the rule (H Res 595) providing for House floor consideration of the bill to establish a program in the Commerce Department to assist service industries, such as banking and insurance, doing business overseas. The effect of the motion was to prevent Republican members from attaching a balanced-budget constitutional amendment to the bill. Motion agreed to 238-179: R 0-158; D 238-21 (ND 168-5, SD 70-16), Oct. 3, 1984.

385. HR 5377. U.S.-Israel Free Trade Area. Passage of the bill to authorize the president to negotiate an agreement establishing duty-free trade between the United States and Israel. Passed 416-6: R 162-1; D 254-5 (ND 171-3, SD 83-2), Oct. 3, 1984. A "yea" was a vote supporting the president's position.

386. HR 6301. Steel Import Stabilization. Passage of the bill to request that the president negotiate a voluntary agreement with steel-producing nations to limit shipments to the United States to 17 percent of the U.S. market. The agreement would be contingent on domestic steel producers' willingness to modernize plants and aid unemployed or laid-off workers. The bill also would extend for two years the Trade Adjustment Assistance Program, which provides government help to workers whose jobs are eliminated because of foreign competition. Passed 285-134: R 63-98, D 222-36 (ND 156-16, SD 66-20), Oct. 3, 1984.

387. HR 3795. Wine Equity and Export Expansion. Conable, R-N.Y., motion to recommit the bill to the Ways and Means Committee with instructions to remove the part of the measure that would extend import protection to grape growers. Motion rejected 178-239: R 100-59; D 78-180 (ND 35-135, SD 43-45), Oct. 3, 1984. A "yea" was a vote supporting the president's position.

388. HR 6023. Generalized System of Preferences Renewal Act. Gephardt, D-Mo., amendment to remove Taiwan, Hong Kong and South Korea from the list of countries eligible for duty-free treatment under the generalized system of preferences. Rejected 174-233: R 14-142; D 160-91 (ND 128-38, SD 32-53), Oct. 3, 1984. A "nay" was a vote supporting the president's position. (The bill subsequently was passed by voice vote.)

KEY

Y Voted for (yea).
\# Paired for.
\+ Announced for.
N Voted against (nay).
X Paired against.
\- Announced against.
P Voted "present".
C Voted "present" to avoid possible conflict of interest.
? Did not vote or otherwise make a position known.

Democrats ***Republicans***

	381	382	383	384	385	386	387	388
ALABAMA								
1 ***Edwards***	Y	Y	Y	N	Y	Y	Y	N
2 ***Dickinson***	Y	Y	Y	N	Y	N	Y	N
3 Nichols	Y	Y	Y	Y	N	Y	Y	N
4 Bevill	Y	Y	Y	?	Y	Y	Y	N
5 Flippo	Y	Y	Y	Y	Y	Y	Y	Y
6 Erdreich	Y	Y	Y	N	Y	Y	Y	Y
7 Shelby	Y	Y	Y	N	Y	Y	Y	Y
ALASKA								
AL ***Young***	Y	Y	Y	N	Y	N	?	?
ARIZONA								
1 ***McCain***	Y	Y	Y	N	Y	Y	N	N
2 Udall	Y	Y	Y	Y	Y	Y	N	?
3 ***Stump***	Y	Y	Y	N	Y	N	Y	N
4 ***Rudd***	Y	Y	Y	N	Y	?	?	?
5 McNulty	Y	Y	?	Y	Y	Y	N	?
ARKANSAS								
1 Alexander	?	?	?	Y	?	Y	Y	Y
2 ***Bethune***	N	Y	Y	N	Y	N	Y	N
3 ***Hammerschmidt***	Y	Y	Y	N	Y	N	N	N
4 Anthony	Y	Y	Y	Y	Y	N	Y	N
CALIFORNIA								
1 Bosco	Y	Y	Y	Y	Y	Y	N	Y
2 ***Chappie***	Y	Y	Y	N	Y	N	N	N
3 Matsui	Y	Y	Y	Y	Y	Y	N	Y
4 Fazio	Y	Y	Y	Y	Y	Y	N	Y
5 Burton	Y	Y	Y	Y	Y	Y	N	Y
6 Boxer	Y	Y	Y	Y	Y	Y	N	Y
7 Miller	Y	Y	Y	Y	Y	Y	N	Y
8 Dellums	Y	N	Y	Y	Y	Y	N	Y
9 Stark	Y	Y	Y	Y	Y	Y	P	Y
10 Edwards	Y	N	Y	Y	Y	Y	N	Y
11 Lantos	Y	Y	Y	Y	Y	Y	N	Y
12 ***Zschau***	Y	Y	Y	N	N	N	N	N
13 Mineta	Y	Y	Y	Y	Y	Y	N	Y
14 ***Shumway***	N	Y	Y	N	Y	N	N	N
15 Coelho	Y	Y	Y	Y	Y	Y	N	Y
16 Panetta	Y	Y	Y	Y	Y	N	N	Y
17 ***Pashayan***	Y	Y	Y	N	Y	N	N	N
18 Lehman	Y	Y	Y	Y	Y	Y	N	Y
19 ***Lagomarsino***	Y	Y	Y	N	Y	N	N	N
20 ***Thomas***	Y	?	Y	N	Y	N	N	N
21 ***Fiedler***	Y	Y	Y	N	Y	N	N	N
22 ***Moorhead***	Y	Y	Y	N	Y	N	N	N
23 Beilenson	Y	Y	Y	Y	Y	N	N	Y
24 Waxman	Y	Y	Y	Y	Y	N	N	N
25 Roybal	Y	Y	Y	Y	Y	Y	N	Y
26 Berman	Y	Y	Y	Y	Y	N	N	N
27 Levine	Y	Y	Y	Y	Y	N	N	Y
28 Dixon	Y	Y	Y	Y	Y	Y	N	N
29 Hawkins	Y	Y	Y	Y	Y	Y	N	Y
30 Martinez	Y	Y	Y	Y	Y	Y	N	N
31 Dymally	?	?	?	Y	Y	Y	N	N
32 Anderson	Y	Y	Y	N	Y	Y	N	N
33 ***Dreier***	Y	Y	Y	N	Y	N	N	N
34 Torres	Y	Y	Y	Y	Y	Y	N	Y
35 ***Lewis***	Y	Y	Y	N	Y	N	N	N
36 Brown	Y	Y	Y	Y	Y	Y	N	?
37 ***McCandless***	Y	Y	Y	?	Y	N	N	N
38 Patterson	Y	Y	Y	Y	Y	Y	N	N
39 ***Dannemeyer***	Y	Y	Y	N	Y	N	Y	N
40 ***Badham***	Y	Y	Y	N	Y	N	N	N
41 ***Lowery***	Y	Y	Y	N	Y	N	N	N
42 ***Lungren***	N	Y	Y	N	Y	N	Y	N
43 ***Packard***	Y	Y	Y	N	Y	N	N	N
44 Bates	Y	Y	Y	Y	Y	Y	N	Y
45 ***Hunter***	Y	Y	Y	N	Y	Y	Y	N
COLORADO								
1 Schroeder	Y	Y	Y	Y	Y	N	Y	N
2 Wirth	Y	Y	Y	Y	Y	Y	Y	N
3 Kogovsek	Y	Y	Y	Y	Y	Y	N	N
4 ***Brown***	Y	Y	Y	N	Y	N	Y	N
5 ***Kramer***	Y	Y	Y	N	Y	N	Y	N
6 ***Schaefer***	Y	Y	Y	N	Y	N	Y	N
CONNECTICUT								
1 Kennelly	Y	Y	Y	Y	Y	Y	Y	Y
2 Gejdenson	Y	Y	Y	Y	Y	Y	Y	Y
3 Morrison	+	+	+	Y	Y	Y	Y	Y
4 ***McKinney***	Y	Y	Y	N	Y	Y	Y	N
5 Ratchford	Y	Y	Y	Y	Y	Y	N	Y
6 ***Johnson***	Y	Y	Y	N	Y	Y	Y	N
DELAWARE								
AL Carper	Y	Y	Y	Y	Y	Y	N	Y
FLORIDA								
1 Hutto	Y	Y	Y	?	Y	N	Y	N
2 Fuqua	Y	Y	Y	Y	Y	Y	N	N
3 Bennett	Y	Y	Y	Y	Y	N	Y	N
4 Chappell	Y	Y	Y	Y	Y	Y	N	N
5 ***McCollum***	Y	N	Y	N	Y	N	Y	N
6 MacKay	Y	Y	Y	Y	Y	N	N	N
7 Gibbons	Y	Y	Y	Y	Y	?	N	N
8 ***Young***	Y	Y	Y	N	Y	Y	N	N
9 ***Bilirakis***	Y	Y	?	N	Y	Y	N	N
10 ***Ireland***	Y	Y	Y	N	Y	Y	N	N
11 Nelson	Y	Y	Y	N	Y	N	Y	N
12 ***Lewis***	Y	Y	Y	N	Y	N	Y	N
13 ***Mack***	N	Y	Y	N	Y	N	Y	N
14 Mica	Y	Y	Y	Y	Y	N	Y	N
15 ***Shaw***	Y	Y	Y	N	Y	N	Y	N
16 Smith	Y	Y	Y	Y	Y	Y	N	Y
17 Lehman	Y	Y	Y	Y	?	Y	N	Y
18 Pepper	Y	Y	Y	Y	Y	Y	N	Y
19 Fascell	Y	Y	Y	Y	Y	Y	N	Y
GEORGIA								
1 Thomas	Y	Y	Y	Y	Y	Y	N	N
2 Hatcher	Y	Y	Y	Y	Y	Y	N	Y
3 Ray	Y	Y	Y	N	Y	N	N	N
4 Levitas	Y	Y	Y	N	Y	Y	Y	N
5 Fowler	?	?	?	Y	Y	Y	N	N
6 ***Gingrich***	N	Y	Y	N	Y	N	Y	N
7 Durden	Y	Y	Y	N	Y	Y	N	N
8 Rowland	Y	Y	Y	Y	Y	Y	Y	N
9 Jenkins	Y	Y	Y	N	Y	Y	Y	Y
10 Barnard	Y	Y	Y	N	Y	Y	Y	?
HAWAII								
1 Heftel	Y	Y	Y	Y	Y	Y	Y	N
2 Akaka	Y	Y	Y	Y	Y	Y	N	Y
IDAHO								
1 ***Craig***	Y	Y	Y	N	Y	N	Y	N
2 ***Hansen***	Y	Y	Y	N	Y	N	Y	?
ILLINOIS								
1 Hayes	Y	Y	Y	Y	Y	Y	N	Y
2 Savage	Y	N	Y	Y	N	Y	N	Y
3 Russo	Y	Y	Y	Y	Y	Y	N	Y
4 ***O'Brien***	Y	Y	Y	N	Y	Y	Y	N
5 Lipinski	Y	Y	Y	Y	Y	Y	N	Y
6 ***Hyde***	N	Y	Y	N	Y	N	Y	N
7 Collins	Y	Y	Y	Y	Y	Y	N	Y
8 Rostenkowski	Y	Y	Y	Y	Y	Y	N	Y
9 Yates	Y	Y	Y	Y	Y	Y	Y	Y
10 ***Porter***	Y	Y	Y	N	Y	N	Y	N
11 Annunzio	Y	Y	Y	Y	Y	Y	N	Y
12 ***Crane, P.***	Y	Y	Y	?	Y	N	Y	N
13 ***Erlenborn***	Y	Y	Y	N	Y	?	?	?
14 ***Corcoran***	Y	Y	Y	N	Y	N	Y	N
15 ***Madigan***	Y	Y	Y	N	Y	Y	Y	N
16 ***Martin***	Y	Y	Y	N	Y	Y	Y	N
17 Evans	Y	Y	Y	Y	Y	Y	Y	Y
18 ***Michel***	Y	Y	Y	N	Y	N	Y	N
19 ***Crane, D.***	Y	Y	Y	N	Y	N	Y	N
20 Durbin	Y	Y	Y	Y	Y	Y	Y	Y
21 Price	Y	Y	Y	Y	Y	Y	N	Y
22 Simon	Y	Y	Y	?	?	?	?	?
INDIANA								
1 Hall	Y	Y	Y	Y	Y	Y	N	Y
2 Sharp	Y	Y	Y	Y	Y	Y	Y	N
3 ***Hiler***	Y	Y	Y	N	Y	N	Y	N
4 ***Coats***	Y	Y	Y	N	Y	N	Y	N
5 ***Hillis***	Y	Y	Y	N	Y	Y	Y	N

ND - Northern Democrats SD - Southern Democrats

Corresponding to Congressional Record Votes 433, 434, 435, 436, 437, 438, 439, 440

	381	382	383	384	385	386	387	388
6 ***Burton***	Y	Y	Y	N	Y	Y	Y	N
7 ***Myers***	Y	Y	Y	N	Y	Y	N	N
8 McCloskey	Y	Y	Y	Y	Y	Y	Y	Y
9 Hamilton	Y	Y	Y	Y	Y	Y	Y	N
10 Jacobs	Y	N	Y	N	Y	Y	N	Y
IOWA								
1 ***Leach***	Y	Y	Y	N	Y	N	Y	N
2 ***Tauke***	Y	Y	Y	N	Y	N	Y	?
3 ***Evans***	Y	Y	Y	N	Y	N	Y	N
4 Smith	Y	Y	Y	Y	Y	N	Y	Y
5 Harkin	Y	Y	Y	Y	Y	N	Y	N
6 Bedell	Y	Y	Y	Y	Y	N	Y	P
KANSAS								
1 ***Roberts***	Y	Y	Y	N	Y	N	Y	N
2 Slattery	Y	Y	Y	Y	Y	N	Y	Y
3 ***Winn***	Y	Y	Y	N	Y	N	Y	N
4 Glickman	Y	Y	Y	Y	Y	N	Y	Y
5 ***Whittaker***	Y	Y	Y	N	Y	N	Y	N
KENTUCKY								
1 Hubbard	Y	Y	Y	Y	Y	Y	Y	N
2 Natcher	Y	Y	Y	Y	Y	Y	N	Y
3 Mazzoli	Y	Y	Y	Y	Y	N	Y	N
4 ***Snyder***	Y	Y	Y	N	Y	Y	N	N
5 ***Rogers***	Y	Y	Y	N	Y	Y	N	N
6 ***Hopkins***	Y	Y	Y	N	Y	Y	Y	N
7 Vacancy								
LOUISIANA								
1 ***Livingston***	Y	Y	Y	N	Y	N	Y	N
2 Boggs	Y	Y	Y	Y	Y	Y	N	N
3 Tauzin	Y	Y	Y	Y	Y	Y	N	Y
4 Roemer	Y	Y	Y	Y	Y	N	Y	N
5 Huckaby	Y	Y	Y	Y	Y	N	Y	N
6 ***Moore***	Y	Y	Y	N	Y	N	Y	N
7 Breaux	Y	Y	Y	Y	?	Y	Y	N
8 Long	Y	Y	Y	Y	Y	Y	N	Y
MAINE								
1 ***McKernan***	Y	Y	Y	N	Y	Y	N	Y
2 ***Snowe***	Y	Y	Y	N	Y	Y	N	Y
MARYLAND								
1 Dyson	Y	Y	Y	Y	Y	Y	N	Y
2 Long	Y	Y	?	Y	Y	Y	N	N
3 Mikulski	Y	Y	Y	Y	Y	Y	N	Y
4 ***Holt***	Y	Y	Y	N	Y	Y	Y	N
5 Hoyer	Y	Y	Y	Y	Y	Y	N	Y
6 Byron	Y	Y	Y	Y	Y	Y	N	N
7 Mitchell	N	N	Y	Y	Y	Y	N	Y
8 Barnes	Y	Y	Y	#	Y	Y	Y	Y
MASSACHUSETTS								
1 ***Conte***	Y	Y	Y	N	Y	Y	N	Y
2 Boland	Y	Y	Y	Y	Y	Y	N	Y
3 Early	Y	Y	Y	Y	Y	Y	N	Y
4 Frank	Y	Y	Y	Y	Y	Y	N	Y
5 Shannon	Y	Y	Y	?	?	?	?	?
6 Mavroules	Y	Y	Y	Y	Y	Y	N	Y
7 Markey	Y	Y	?	Y	Y	Y	N	Y
8 O'Neill								
9 Moakley	Y	Y	Y	Y	Y	Y	N	Y
10 Studds	Y	Y	Y	Y	Y	Y	?	Y
11 Donnelly	Y	Y	Y	Y	Y	Y	N	Y
MICHIGAN								
1 Conyers	Y	N	Y	Y	Y	Y	N	Y
2 ***Pursell***	Y	Y	Y	N	Y	Y	Y	?
3 Wolpe	Y	Y	Y	Y	Y	Y	N	Y
4 ***Siljander***	Y	Y	Y	N	Y	N	N	N
5 ***Sawyer***	Y	Y	Y	N	Y	Y	Y	N
6 Carr	Y	Y	Y	Y	Y	Y	N	Y
7 Kildee	Y	Y	Y	Y	Y	Y	N	Y
8 Traxler	Y	Y	Y	Y	Y	Y	Y	Y
9 ***Vander Jagt***	Y	Y	Y	N	Y	Y	N	N
10 Albosta	Y	Y	Y	Y	Y	Y	N	Y
11 ***Davis***	Y	Y	Y	?	?	?	N	N
12 Bonior	Y	Y	Y	Y	N	Y	N	Y
13 Crockett	Y	N	Y	Y	N	Y	N	Y
14 Hertel	Y	Y	Y	Y	Y	Y	N	Y
15 Ford	Y	Y	Y	Y	Y	Y	N	Y
16 Dingell	Y	Y	Y	Y	Y	Y	N	Y
17 Levin	Y	Y	Y	Y	Y	Y	N	Y
18 ***Broomfield***	Y	Y	Y	N	Y	Y	N	N
MINNESOTA								
1 Penny	Y	Y	Y	Y	Y	N	Y	N
2 ***Weber***	Y	Y	Y	N	Y	N	Y	N
3 ***Frenzel***	Y	Y	Y	N	Y	N	Y	N
4 Vento	Y	Y	Y	Y	Y	Y	N	Y
5 Sabo	Y	Y	Y	Y	Y	Y	N	N
6 Sikorski	Y	Y	Y	Y	Y	Y	N	Y
7 ***Stangeland***	Y	Y	Y	N	Y	N	Y	N
8 Oberstar	Y	Y	Y	Y	Y	Y	N	Y
MISSISSIPPI								
1 Whitten	Y	Y	Y	Y	Y	Y	Y	Y
2 ***Franklin***	Y	Y	Y	N	Y	N	Y	N
3 Montgomery	Y	Y	Y	Y	Y	Y	Y	Y
4 Dowdy	Y	Y	Y	Y	Y	Y	Y	Y
5 ***Lott***	Y	Y	Y	N	Y	N	Y	N
MISSOURI								
1 Clay	Y	N	Y	Y	Y	Y	N	Y
2 Young	Y	Y	Y	Y	Y	Y	N	Y
3 Gephardt	Y	Y	Y	Y	Y	Y	N	Y
4 Skelton	Y	Y	Y	Y	Y	Y	Y	Y
5 Wheat	Y	Y	Y	Y	Y	Y	N	Y
6 ***Coleman***	Y	Y	Y	N	Y	N	Y	N
7 ***Taylor***	Y	Y	Y	N	Y	N	Y	N
8 ***Emerson***	Y	Y	Y	N	Y	N	Y	N
9 Volkmer	Y	Y	Y	N	Y	Y	Y	Y
MONTANA								
1 Williams	Y	Y	Y	Y	Y	Y	Y	?
2 ***Marlenee***	Y	Y	Y	N	Y	N	N	N
NEBRASKA								
1 ***Bereuter***	Y	Y	Y	N	Y	N	Y	N
2 ***Daub***	Y	Y	Y	N	Y	N	Y	N
3 ***Smith***	Y	Y	Y	N	Y	N	Y	N
NEVADA								
1 Reid	Y	Y	Y	Y	Y	Y	N	Y
2 ***Vucanovich***	Y	Y	Y	N	Y	N	N	N
NEW HAMPSHIRE								
1 D'Amours	Y	Y	Y	N	Y	Y	N	Y
2 ***Gregg***	Y	Y	Y	N	Y	N	Y	N
NEW JERSEY								
1 Florio	Y	Y	Y	Y	Y	Y	N	Y
2 Hughes	Y	Y	Y	Y	Y	Y	N	N
3 Howard	Y	Y	Y	Y	Y	Y	N	Y
4 ***Smith***	Y	Y	Y	N	Y	Y	Y	Y
5 ***Roukema***	Y	Y	Y	N	Y	N	Y	N
6 Dwyer	Y	Y	Y	Y	Y	Y	N	Y
7 ***Rinaldo***	Y	Y	Y	N	Y	Y	N	Y
8 Roe	Y	Y	Y	Y	Y	Y	N	Y
9 Torricelli	Y	Y	Y	Y	Y	Y	N	Y
10 Rodino	Y	Y	Y	Y	Y	Y	N	Y
11 Minish	Y	Y	Y	Y	Y	?	?	?
12 ***Courter***	Y	Y	Y	N	Y	N	Y	N
13 Vacancy								
14 Guarini	Y	Y	Y	Y	Y	Y	N	Y
NEW MEXICO								
1 ***Lujan***	Y	Y	Y	N	Y	N	?	N
2 ***Skeen***	Y	Y	Y	N	Y	N	Y	N
3 Richardson	Y	Y	Y	Y	Y	Y	N	Y
NEW YORK								
1 ***Carney***	Y	Y	Y	N	Y	N	Y	N
2 Downey	Y	Y	Y	Y	Y	Y	Y	N
3 Mrazek	Y	Y	Y	Y	Y	Y	Y	Y
4 ***Lent***	Y	Y	Y	N	Y	Y	N	N
5 ***McGrath***	?	?	?	X	?	?	?	?
6 Addabbo	Y	Y	Y	Y	Y	Y	N	Y
7 Ackerman	Y	Y	Y	Y	Y	Y	N	N
8 Scheuer	Y	Y	Y	Y	Y	Y	Y	N
9 Ferraro	?	?	?	?	?	?	?	?
10 Schumer	Y	Y	Y	Y	Y	Y	Y	Y
11 Towns	Y	N	Y	Y	Y	Y	N	Y
12 Owens	Y	Y	Y	Y	Y	Y	N	Y
13 Solarz	Y	Y	Y	Y	Y	Y	N	N
14 ***Molinari***	Y	Y	Y	N	Y	N	N	N
15 ***Green***	Y	Y	Y	N	Y	N	Y	N
16 Rangel	Y	Y	Y	Y	Y	Y	N	Y
17 Weiss	Y	N	Y	Y	Y	Y	N	N
18 Garcia	Y	Y	Y	Y	Y	Y	N	Y
19 Biaggi	Y	Y	Y	Y	Y	Y	N	N
20 Ottinger	N	N	Y	Y	Y	?	N	Y
21 ***Fish***	Y	Y	Y	N	Y	Y	N	?
22 ***Gilman***	Y	Y	Y	N	Y	Y	N	Y
23 Stratton	Y	Y	Y	Y	Y	Y	N	N
24 ***Solomon***	Y	Y	Y	N	Y	N	N	N
25 ***Boehlert***	Y	Y	Y	N	Y	Y	N	N
26 ***Martin***	Y	Y	Y	N	Y	N	N	N
27 ***Wortley***	Y	Y	Y	N	Y	N	N	N
28 McHugh	Y	Y	Y	Y	Y	N	N	N
29 ***Horton***	Y	Y	Y	N	Y	Y	N	N
30 ***Conable***	Y	Y	Y	N	Y	N	Y	N
31 ***Kemp***	N	Y	Y	N	Y	N	Y	N
32 LaFalce	Y	Y	Y	Y	Y	Y	N	?
33 Nowak	Y	Y	Y	Y	Y	Y	N	Y
34 Lundine	Y	Y	Y	Y	Y	Y	N	Y
NORTH CAROLINA								
1 Jones	Y	Y	Y	Y	Y	Y	N	?
2 Valentine	Y	Y	Y	Y	Y	N	Y	Y
3 Whitley	Y	Y	Y	Y	Y	Y	Y	N
4 Andrews	Y	Y	Y	N	Y	Y	Y	N
5 Neal	Y	Y	Y	Y	Y	N	N	N
6 Britt	Y	Y	Y	N	Y	Y	N	Y
7 Rose	Y	Y	Y	Y	Y	Y	Y	Y
8 Hefner	Y	Y	Y	N	Y	Y	Y	N
9 ***Martin***	?	?	?	?	?	?	?	?
10 ***Broyhill***	Y	Y	?	?	Y	Y	N	Y
11 Clarke	Y	Y	Y	Y	Y	N	N	Y
NORTH DAKOTA								
AL Dorgan	Y	Y	Y	Y	Y	N	Y	Y
OHIO								
1 Luken	Y	Y	Y	Y	Y	Y	N	Y
2 ***Gradison***	Y	Y	Y	N	Y	N	Y	N
3 Hall	Y	Y	Y	Y	Y	Y	N	Y
4 ***Oxley***	N	Y	Y	N	Y	N	Y	N
5 ***Latta***	Y	Y	Y	N	Y	N	Y	N
6 ***McEwen***	Y	Y	Y	N	Y	Y	Y	N
7 ***DeWine***	N	Y	Y	N	Y	Y	Y	N
8 ***Kindness***	Y	Y	Y	N	Y	N	Y	N
9 Kaptur	Y	Y	Y	Y	Y	Y	N	N
10 ***Miller***	Y	Y	Y	N	Y	Y	Y	N
11 Eckart	Y	Y	Y	Y	Y	Y	N	Y
12 ***Kasich***	Y	Y	Y	N	Y	Y	Y	Y
13 Pease	Y	Y	Y	Y	Y	Y	Y	N
14 Seiberling	Y	Y	Y	Y	Y	Y	Y	Y
15 ***Wylie***	Y	Y	Y	N	Y	Y	Y	N
16 ***Regula***	Y	Y	Y	N	Y	Y	N	Y
17 ***Williams***	Y	Y	Y	N	Y	Y	N	Y
18 Applegate	Y	Y	Y	Y	Y	Y	N	Y
19 Feighan	Y	Y	Y	Y	Y	Y	N	Y
20 Oakar	Y	Y	Y	Y	Y	Y	N	Y
21 Stokes	Y	Y	Y	Y	Y	Y	N	Y
OKLAHOMA								
1 Jones	Y	Y	Y	Y	Y	Y	Y	N
2 Synar	Y	Y	Y	Y	Y	Y	Y	N
3 Watkins	Y	Y	Y	Y	Y	Y	Y	N
4 McCurdy	Y	Y	Y	Y	Y	N	N	N
5 ***Edwards***	Y	Y	Y	N	Y	N	Y	N
6 English	Y	Y	Y	N	Y	N	Y	N
OREGON								
1 AuCoin	Y	Y	Y	Y	Y	Y	N	N
2 ***Smith, R.***	Y	Y	Y	N	Y	N	Y	N
3 Wyden	Y	Y	Y	Y	Y	N	N	N
4 Weaver	Y	Y	Y	Y	Y	Y	N	Y
5 ***Smith, D.***	Y	Y	Y	N	Y	N	Y	N
PENNSYLVANIA								
1 Foglietta	Y	Y	Y	Y	Y	Y	N	Y
2 Gray	Y	Y	Y	Y	Y	Y	N	Y
3 Borski	Y	Y	Y	Y	Y	Y	N	Y
4 Kolter	Y	Y	Y	Y	Y	Y	N	Y
5 ***Schulze***	Y	Y	Y	N	Y	Y	N	N
6 Yatron	Y	Y	Y	Y	Y	Y	?	?
7 Edgar	Y	Y	Y	Y	Y	Y	N	Y
8 Kostmayer	Y	Y	Y	Y	Y	Y	N	Y
9 ***Shuster***	Y	Y	Y	N	Y	Y	N	N
10 ***McDade***	Y	Y	Y	N	Y	Y	N	N
11 Harrison	Y	Y	Y	Y	Y	Y	N	Y
12 Murtha	Y	Y	?	Y	Y	Y	N	Y
13 ***Coughlin***	Y	Y	Y	N	Y	Y	N	N
14 Coyne	Y	Y	Y	Y	Y	Y	N	Y
15 ***Ritter***	Y	Y	Y	N	Y	Y	N	Y
16 ***Walker***	Y	Y	Y	N	Y	Y	N	N
17 ***Gekas***	Y	N	Y	N	Y	Y	N	N
18 Walgren	Y	Y	Y	Y	Y	Y	N	Y
19 ***Goodling***	Y	Y	Y	N	Y	Y	N	N
20 Gaydos	Y	Y	Y	Y	Y	Y	N	Y
21 ***Ridge***	Y	Y	Y	N	Y	Y	N	Y
22 Murphy	Y	Y	Y	Y	Y	Y	N	Y
23 ***Clinger***	Y	Y	Y	N	Y	Y	N	N
RHODE ISLAND								
1 St Germain	Y	Y	Y	Y	Y	Y	N	Y
2 ***Schneider***	Y	Y	Y	N	Y	Y	N	Y
SOUTH CAROLINA								
1 ***Hartnett***	Y	Y	Y	N	Y	N	Y	N
2 ***Spence***	Y	Y	Y	N	Y	N	Y	N
3 Derrick	Y	Y	Y	Y	Y	N	Y	N
4 ***Campbell***	Y	Y	Y	?	Y	N	Y	N
5 Spratt	Y	Y	Y	Y	Y	Y	N	N
6 Tallon	Y	Y	Y	Y	Y	Y	Y	N
SOUTH DAKOTA								
AL Daschle	Y	Y	Y	N	Y	Y	Y	N
TENNESSEE								
1 ***Quillen***	Y	Y	Y	N	Y	Y	Y	N
2 ***Duncan***	Y	Y	Y	N	Y	N	N	N
3 Lloyd	Y	Y	Y	N	Y	Y	Y	N
4 Cooper	?	?	?	Y	Y	Y	N	N
5 Boner	Y	Y	Y	Y	Y	Y	Y	Y
6 Gore	Y	Y	Y	Y	Y	Y	Y	Y
7 ***Sundquist***	Y	Y	Y	N	Y	N	Y	N
8 Jones	Y	Y	Y	Y	Y	Y	Y	Y
9 Ford	Y	Y	Y	Y	Y	Y	N	Y
TEXAS								
1 Hall, S.	Y	Y	Y	N	Y	Y	N	N
2 Wilson	Y	Y	Y	Y	Y	Y	N	?
3 ***Bartlett***	Y	Y	Y	N	Y	Y	Y	N
4 Hall, R.	?	Y	Y	N	Y	Y	N	N
5 Bryant	Y	Y	Y	Y	Y	Y	N	Y
6 ***Gramm***	?	?	?	?	Y	Y	?	?
7 ***Archer***	Y	Y	Y	N	Y	N	Y	N
8 ***Fields***	Y	Y	Y	N	Y	Y	Y	N
9 Brooks	Y	Y	Y	Y	Y	Y	N	Y
10 Pickle	Y	Y	Y	Y	Y	Y	N	N
11 Leath	Y	Y	Y	Y	Y	N	N	N
12 Wright	Y	Y	?	Y	Y	Y	N	N
13 Hightower	Y	Y	Y	Y	Y	Y	Y	N
14 Patman	Y	Y	Y	Y	N	Y	Y	Y
15 de la Garza	Y	Y	Y	Y	Y	Y	Y	N
16 Coleman	Y	Y	Y	Y	Y	?	N	N
17 Stenholm	Y	Y	Y	Y	Y	N	Y	N
18 Leland	Y	N	Y	Y	Y	Y	N	Y
19 Hance	Y	Y	Y	Y	Y	Y	N	N
20 Gonzalez	Y	N	Y	Y	Y	Y	N	Y
21 ***Loeffler***	Y	Y	Y	N	Y	Y	N	N
22 ***Paul***	Y	N	Y	N	Y	N	Y	N
23 Kazen	Y	Y	Y	Y	Y	Y	N	N
24 Frost	Y	Y	Y	Y	Y	Y	N	Y
25 Andrews	Y	Y	Y	Y	Y	Y	N	Y
26 Vandergriff	Y	Y	Y	N	Y	Y	N	N
27 Ortiz	Y	Y	Y	Y	Y	Y	N	N
UTAH								
1 ***Hansen***	Y	Y	Y	N	Y	Y	Y	N
2 ***Marriott***	Y	Y	Y	N	Y	Y	Y	N
3 ***Nielson***	Y	Y	Y	N	Y	Y	Y	N
VERMONT								
AL ***Jeffords***	Y	Y	Y	N	Y	N	Y	N
VIRGINIA								
1 ***Bateman***	Y	Y	Y	N	Y	N	Y	N
2 ***Whitehurst***	Y	Y	Y	N	Y	N	Y	N
3 ***Bliley***	Y	Y	Y	N	Y	N	Y	N
4 Sisisky	Y	Y	Y	Y	Y	Y	Y	N
5 Daniel	Y	Y	Y	Y	Y	N	N	N
6 Olin	Y	Y	Y	Y	Y	N	N	Y
7 ***Robinson***	Y	Y	Y	N	Y	N	Y	N
8 ***Parris***	Y	Y	Y	N	Y	N	Y	N
9 Boucher	Y	Y	Y	Y	Y	Y	N	N
10 ***Wolf***	Y	Y	Y	N	Y	N	Y	N
WASHINGTON								
1 ***Pritchard***	Y	Y	Y	N	Y	N	Y	N
2 Swift	Y	Y	Y	Y	Y	Y	N	N
3 Bonker	Y	Y	Y	Y	Y	Y	Y	N
4 ***Morrison***	Y	Y	Y	N	Y	N	N	N
5 Foley	Y	Y	Y	Y	Y	N	N	N
6 Dicks	Y	Y	Y	Y	Y	Y	N	N
7 Lowry	Y	Y	Y	Y	Y	Y	N	N
8 ***Chandler***	Y	Y	Y	N	Y	N	Y	N
WEST VIRGINIA								
1 Mollohan	Y	Y	Y	Y	Y	Y	N	Y
2 Staggers	Y	Y	Y	Y	Y	Y	N	Y
3 Wise	Y	Y	Y	Y	Y	Y	N	Y
4 Rahall	Y	Y	Y	Y	Y	Y	N	Y
WISCONSIN								
1 Aspin	Y	Y	Y	Y	Y	Y	Y	Y
2 Kastenmeier	Y	Y	Y	Y	Y	Y	Y	Y
3 ***Gunderson***	Y	Y	Y	N	Y	Y	N	N
4 Kleczka	Y	Y	Y	Y	Y	Y	Y	Y
5 Moody	Y	Y	Y	Y	Y	Y	N	Y
6 ***Petri***	Y	Y	Y	N	Y	N	Y	N
7 Obey	Y	Y	Y	Y	Y	Y	N	N
8 ***Roth***	Y	Y	Y	N	Y	Y	Y	N
9 ***Sensenbrenner***	Y	Y	Y	N	Y	Y	Y	N
WYOMING								
AL ***Cheney***	Y	Y	Y	?	?	?	?	?

Southern states - Ala., Ark., Fla., Ga., Ky., La., Miss., N.C., Okla., S.C., Tenn., Texas, Va.

389. Procedural Motion. Daub, R-Neb., motion to approve the House *Journal* of Wednesday, Oct. 3. Motion agreed to 333-28: R 128-15; D 205-13 (ND 131-11, SD 74-2), Oct. 4, 1984.

390. HR 5492. Atlantic Striped Bass Conservation. Bateman, R-Va., amendment to give the secretary of commerce greater discretion in carrying out the bill to reduce the annual catch of Atlantic striped bass by 55 percent in each Atlantic coastal state north of South Carolina. (The amendment would have made discretionary, instead of mandatory, a striped bass fishing moratorium to be imposed by the secretary on non-complying states.) Rejected 98-307: R 79-79; D 19-228 (ND 12-154, SD 7-74), Oct. 4, 1984.

391. H Res 603. Committee Ratios. Foley, D-Wash., motion to table (kill) the privileged resolution offered by Dannemeyer, R-Calif., requiring that membership on each House subcommittee should be proportionate to the membership of the two political parties on each House committee. Motion agreed to 251-158: R 0-158; D 251-0 (ND 169-0, SD 82-0), Oct. 4, 1984.

392. Procedural Motion. Solomon, R-N.Y., motion to approve the House *Journal* of Thursday, Oct. 4. Motion agreed to 321-28: R 121-14; D 200-14 (ND 122-13, SD 78-1), Oct. 5, 1984.

393. S 607. Public Broadcasting Authorizations. Dannemeyer, R-Calif., amendment to the Oxley, R-Ohio, substitute *(see vote 394, below)*, to limit increases in authorized funding for the Corporation for Public Broadcasting to 5 percent a year in fiscal 1987 through 1989. Rejected 68-328: R 61-88; D 7-240 (ND 0-168, SD 7-72), Oct. 5, 1984.

394. S 607. Public Broadcasting Authorizations. Oxley, R-Ohio, substitute to reduce the authorized funding for the Corporation for Public Broadcasting to $186 million in fiscal 1987, $214 million in fiscal 1988 and $246 million in fiscal 1989; and to reduce the authorized funding for the Public Telecommunications Facilities Program to $14 million in fiscal 1985, $16 million in fiscal 1986 and $18 million in fiscal 1987. Rejected 167-233: R 120-31; D 47-202 (ND 12-156, SD 35-46), Oct. 5, 1984. A "yea" was a vote supporting the president's position.

395. S 607. Public Broadcasting Authorizations. Passage of the bill to authorize for fiscal 1987-89 funding of $775 million for the Corporation for Public Broadcasting: $675 million for operations in fiscal years 1987-89 ($200 million in fiscal 1987, $225 million in fiscal 1988 and $250 million in fiscal 1989) and $100 million for construction under the Public Telecommunications Facilities Program in fiscal 1985-87 ($25 million in fiscal 1987, $35 million in fiscal 1988 and $40 million in fiscal 1989). Passed 308-86: R 72-76; D 236-10 (ND 163-2, SD 73-8), Oct. 5, 1984. A "nay" was a vote supporting the president's position.

396. HR 6163. Semiconductor Chip Protection/Trademark Clarification. Kastenmeier, D-Wis., motion to concur in the Senate amendments to the bill to grant 10 years of copyright-style legal protection to makers of semiconductor chips, clarify trademark definitions, establish a State Justice Institute to help state judicial systems, sharply reduce the types of civil cases entitled to speedy court action, revise a 1980 patent law designed to help educational and small business organizations, make technical corrections to a 1982 law creating the U.S. Court of Appeals for the Federal Circuit, and to establish new sites for holding federal court in certain states. Motion agreed to 363-0: R 141-0, D 222-0 (ND 145-0, SD 77-0), Oct. 9, 1984.

KEY

Y	Voted for (yea).
#	Paired for.
+	Announced for.
N	Voted against (nay).
X	Paired against.
-	Announced against.
P	Voted "present".
C	Voted "present" to avoid possible conflict of interest.
?	Did not vote or otherwise make a position known.

Democrats   *Republicans*

	389	390	391	392	393	394	395	396
ALABAMA								
1 *Edwards*	Y	?	N	Y	N	N	Y	Y
2 *Dickinson*	?	Y	N	?	Y	Y	N	?
3 Nichols	Y	N	Y	Y	N	Y	Y	Y
4 Bevill	Y	N	Y	Y	N	N	Y	Y
5 Flippo	Y	N	Y	Y	N	Y	Y	Y
6 Erdreich	Y	N	Y	Y	N	Y	Y	Y
7 Shelby	Y	N	Y	Y	N	N	Y	Y
ALASKA								
AL *Young*	?	Y	N	?	N	N	Y	Y
ARIZONA								
1 *McCain*	Y	N	N	?	?	?	?	Y
2 Udall	?	N	Y	N	N	Y	Y	Y
3 *Stump*	Y	N	N	Y	Y	Y	Y	Y
4 *Rudd*	?	?	?	?	?	?	?	Y
5 McNulty	Y	N	Y	Y	N	Y	Y	Y
ARKANSAS								
1 Alexander	Y	?	?	Y	?	N	Y	?
2 *Bethune*	Y	Y	N	Y	Y	Y	N	?
3 *Hammerschmidt*	Y	N	N	Y	Y	Y	Y	Y
4 Anthony	?	N	Y	N	N	Y	Y	Y
CALIFORNIA								
1 Bosco	Y	Y	Y	N	Y	N	Y	Y
2 *Chappie*	N	Y	N	N	Y	Y	Y	Y
3 Matsui	Y	N	Y	N	N	Y	Y	Y
4 Fazio	Y	?	Y	Y	N	N	Y	Y
5 Burton	Y	N	Y	N	N	Y	Y	Y
6 Boxer	Y	N	Y	Y	?	X	?	Y
7 Miller	?	N	Y	N	N	Y	Y	Y
8 Dellums	Y	N	Y	N	N	Y	Y	Y
9 Stark	?	N	Y	N	N	Y	Y	Y
10 Edwards	Y	N	Y	N	N	Y	Y	Y
11 Lantos	Y	N	Y	N	N	Y	Y	Y
12 *Zschau*	Y	Y	N	Y	N	Y	Y	Y
13 Mineta	Y	N	Y	N	N	Y	Y	Y
14 *Shumway*	Y	N	N	Y	Y	Y	N	Y
15 Coelho	?	N	Y	N	N	Y	Y	Y
16 Panetta	Y	N	Y	N	N	Y	Y	Y
17 *Pashayan*	?	Y	N	Y	N	Y	Y	Y
18 Lehman	Y	N	Y	P	N	Y	Y	Y
19 *Lagomarsino*	Y	Y	N	Y	N	W	N	Y
20 *Thomas*	Y	Y	N	Y	N	Y	Y	Y
21 *Fiedler*	Y	Y	N	Y	N	Y	Y	Y
22 *Moorhead*	Y	Y	N	Y	Y	Y	N	Y
23 Beilenson	Y	N	Y	?	N	N	?	Y
24 Waxman	Y	N	Y	?	N	N	Y	Y
25 Roybal	Y	N	Y	N	N	Y	Y	Y
26 Berman	Y	N	Y	N	N	Y	Y	Y
27 Levine	Y	N	Y	?	N	Y	Y	Y
28 Dixon	?	N	Y	Y	N	N	Y	?
29 Hawkins	N	N	Y	N	N	N	Y	Y
30 Martinez	Y	N	Y	Y	N	Y	Y	Y
31 Dymally	P	N	Y	P	N	N	Y	?
32 Anderson	Y	N	Y	N	N	Y	Y	Y
33 *Dreier*	Y	Y	N	Y	Y	Y	N	Y
34 Torres	Y	N	Y	N	N	Y	Y	Y
35 *Lewis*	Y	Y	N	?	N	Y	Y	Y
36 Brown	Y	N	Y	N	N	Y	Y	Y
37 *McCandless*	P	Y	N	Y	Y	Y	N	Y
38 Patterson	Y	N	Y	N	N	Y	Y	Y
39 *Dannemeyer*	N	Y	N	Y	Y	Y	N	Y
40 *Badham*	Y	Y	N	?	?	?	?	Y
41 *Lowery*	?	Y	N	?	N	Y	Y	?
42 *Lungren*	Y	N	N	?	Y	Y	N	Y

	389	390	391	392	393	394	395	396
43 *Packard*	Y	Y	N	Y	N	Y	N	Y
44 Bates	Y	N	Y	N	N	N	Y	Y
45 *Hunter*	Y	Y	N	?	Y	Y	Y	Y
COLORADO								
1 Schroeder	N	N	Y	N	N	N	Y	Y
2 Wirth	Y	N	Y	N	N	Y	Y	?
3 Kogovsek	Y	N	Y	N	N	N	Y	Y
4 *Brown*	N	N	N	Y	Y	Y	N	Y
5 *Kramer*	Y	N	N	Y	Y	Y	N	Y
6 *Schaefer*	Y	N	N	N	Y	Y	N	Y
CONNECTICUT								
1 Kennelly	Y	N	Y	Y	N	N	Y	Y
2 Gejdenson	N	N	Y	N	N	Y	Y	Y
3 Morrison	Y	N	Y	N	N	Y	Y	Y
4 *McKinney*	?	N	N	Y	N	N	Y	Y
5 Ratchford	Y	N	Y	N	N	Y	Y	Y
6 *Johnson*	Y	N	Y	N	Y	Y	Y	Y
DELAWARE								
AL *Carper*	Y	N	Y	?	N	Y	Y	Y
FLORIDA								
1 Hutto	Y	N	Y	Y	Y	Y	N	Y
2 Fuqua	Y	N	Y	?	?	?	#	Y
3 Bennett	Y	N	Y	N	Y	Y	N	Y
4 Chappell	Y	N	Y	N	N	N	Y	Y
5 *McCollum*	Y	N	Y	N	Y	N	N	Y
6 MacKay	Y	N	Y	N	N	N	Y	Y
7 Gibbons	Y	?	Y	Y	N	Y	Y	Y
8 *Young*	?	N	?	N	Y	N	Y	Y
9 *Bilirakis*	Y	N	Y	Y	N	Y	Y	Y
10 *Ireland*	Y	N	N	?	N	Y	Y	Y
11 Nelson	Y	N	Y	N	N	Y	Y	Y
12 *Lewis*	Y	N	N	Y	N	N	Y	Y
13 *Mack*	N	Y	N	Y	Y	Y	N	Y
14 Mica	Y	N	?	N	Y	?	Y	Y
15 *Shaw*	Y	N	N	Y	N	N	Y	Y
16 Smith	Y	N	?	Y	?	?	?	Y
17 Lehman	Y	N	Y	N	N	?	?	Y
18 Pepper	?	?	?	Y	N	N	Y	Y
19 Fascell	?	N	Y	N	N	Y	Y	Y
GEORGIA								
1 Thomas	Y	N	Y	N	N	N	Y	Y
2 Hatcher	Y	Y	Y	Y	?	N	Y	?
3 Ray	Y	N	Y	N	Y	Y	N	Y
4 Levitas	Y	N	Y	N	Y	N	Y	Y
5 Fowler	?	N	Y	Y	?	N	Y	Y
6 *Gingrich*	?	N	N	Y	Y	Y	Y	Y
7 Darden	Y	N	Y	N	Y	N	Y	Y
8 Rowland	Y	N	Y	N	N	Y	Y	Y
9 Jenkins	Y	N	Y	N	N	Y	Y	Y
10 Barnard	Y	N	Y	N	N	Y	Y	Y
HAWAII								
1 Heftel	?	N	Y	?	?	C	Y	?
2 Akaka	Y	N	Y	N	N	Y	Y	Y
IDAHO								
1 *Craig*	Y	N	N	N	Y	Y	N	Y
2 *Hansen*	Y	N	N	?	?	?	?	?
ILLINOIS								
1 Hayes	Y	N	Y	N	N	N	Y	Y
2 Savage	Y	?	Y	?	N	N	Y	Y
3 Russo	Y	N	Y	N	N	Y	Y	Y
4 *O'Brien*	?	Y	N	Y	N	Y	Y	Y
5 Lipinski	Y	N	Y	?	?	?	?	Y
6 *Hyde*	Y	N	Y	N	Y	Y	N	Y
7 Collins	?	N	Y	N	N	N	Y	Y
8 Rostenkowski	Y	N	Y	N	N	N	Y	Y
9 Yates	Y	N	Y	N	N	N	Y	Y
10 *Porter*	Y	N	N	Y	N	Y	N	Y
11 Annunzio	Y	N	Y	N	N	N	Y	Y
12 *Crane, P.*	Y	Y	N	N	Y	Y	N	Y
13 *Erlenborn*	?	?	?	?	?	?	?	Y
14 *Corcoran*	Y	N	N	Y	N	Y	N	?
15 *Madigan*	?	Y	N	Y	N	Y	N	Y
16 *Martin*	Y	N	Y	Y	N	Y	N	Y
17 Evans	Y	N	Y	N	Y	Y	N	?
18 *Michel*	Y	N	Y	Y	N	Y	N	Y
19 *Crane, D.*	Y	Y	N	Y	Y	Y	N	?
20 Durbin	N	N	Y	N	N	N	Y	Y
21 Price	Y	N	Y	N	N	N	Y	Y
22 Simon	?	?	?	?	?	?	?	?
INDIANA								
1 Hall	?	N	Y	N	N	N	Y	?
2 Sharp	Y	N	Y	N	N	N	Y	Y
3 *Hiler*	Y	Y	N	Y	N	Y	N	?
4 *Coats*	Y	N	N	N	Y	N	N	Y
5 Hillis	Y	N	N	Y	?	?	?	Y

ND - Northern Democrats   SD - Southern Democrats

Corresponding to Congressional Record Votes 441, 443, 444, 445, 447, 448, 449, 451

	389	390	391	392	393	394	395	396
6 ***Burton***	Y	Y	N	Y	Y	Y	N	Y
7 ***Myers***	Y	Y	N	Y	Y	Y	N	Y
8 McCloskey	Y	N	Y	Y	N	N	Y	Y
9 Hamilton	Y	N	Y	Y	N	N	Y	Y
10 Jacobs	N	N	Y	N	N	N	Y	Y
IOWA								
1 ***Leach***	Y	N	N	Y	N	N	Y	Y
2 ***Tauke***	?	?	?	Y	N	N	Y	?
3 ***Evans***	N	N	N	Y	N	N	Y	Y
4 Smith	Y	N	Y	Y	N	N	Y	Y
5 Harkin	N	N	Y	N	N	N	Y	?
6 Bedell	Y	N	Y	Y	N	N	Y	Y
KANSAS								
1 ***Roberts***	N	Y	N	N	N	Y	N	Y
2 Slattery	Y	N	Y	Y	N	N	Y	Y
3 ***Winn***	Y	?	N	Y	Y	Y	N	?
4 Glickman	Y	N	Y	Y	N	N	Y	Y
5 ***Whittaker***	?	Y	N	Y	Y	Y	N	Y
KENTUCKY								
1 Hubbard	Y	N	Y	Y	Y	Y	N	Y
2 Natcher	Y	N	Y	Y	N	N	Y	Y
3 Mazzoli	Y	N	Y	Y	N	N	Y	Y
4 ***Snyder***	Y	N	N	Y	Y	Y	Y	Y
5 ***Rogers***	Y	N	N	Y	N	N	Y	Y
6 ***Hopkins***	Y	N	N	Y	N	Y	Y	Y
7 Vacancy								
LOUISIANA								
1 ***Livingston***	Y	N	N	Y	Y	Y	N	Y
2 Boggs	?	N	Y	?	N	N	Y	Y
3 Tauzin	Y	N	Y	Y	N	N	Y	Y
4 Roemer	N	N	Y	N	Y	Y	N	Y
5 Huckaby	Y	N	?	Y	N	?	Y	Y
6 ***Moore***	Y	N	N	Y	N	Y	N	Y
7 Breaux	Y	N	Y	Y	N	N	Y	Y
8 Long	Y	N	Y	Y	N	N	Y	Y
MAINE								
1 ***McKernan***	Y	N	N	Y	N	N	Y	Y
2 ***Snowe***	Y	N	N	Y	N	N	Y	Y
MARYLAND								
1 Dyson	Y	Y	Y	?	N	Y	Y	Y
2 Long	?	N	?	Y	N	N	Y	Y
3 Mikulski	?	N	Y	P	N	N	?	Y
4 ***Holt***	Y	Y	N	N	N	Y	N	Y
5 Hoyer	Y	N	Y	Y	N	N	Y	Y
6 Byron	Y	Y	Y	?	N	N	Y	?
7 Mitchell	?	N	Y	?	N	N	Y	Y
8 Barnes	?	N	Y	Y	N	N	Y	Y
MASSACHUSETTS								
1 ***Conte***	Y	N	N	Y	N	N	Y	Y
2 Boland	Y	N	Y	Y	N	N	Y	Y
3 Early	Y	N	Y	Y	N	N	Y	Y
4 Frank	Y	?	Y	Y	N	N	Y	?
5 Shannon	?	N	Y	?	N	N	Y	Y
6 Mavroules	?	N	?	Y	N	N	Y	Y
7 Markey	N	N	Y	N	N	N	Y	Y
8 O'Neill								
9 Moakley	Y	N	Y	Y	N	N	Y	Y
10 Studds	Y	N	Y	Y	N	N	Y	Y
11 Donnelly	Y	N	Y	?	N	N	Y	Y
MICHIGAN								
1 Conyers	Y	N	Y	Y	N	N	Y	Y
2 ***Pursell***	Y	N	N	Y	N	Y	N	?
3 Wolpe	Y	N	Y	Y	N	N	Y	Y
4 ***Siljander***	Y	N	N	?	Y	Y	Y	Y
5 ***Sawyer***	Y	?	N	Y	N	Y	Y	Y
6 Carr	Y	N	Y	Y	N	N	Y	Y
7 Kildee	Y	N	Y	Y	N	N	Y	Y
8 Traxler	?	N	Y	Y	N	N	Y	Y
9 ***Vander Jagt***	Y	Y	N	Y	N	Y	N	Y
10 Albosta	Y	N	Y	Y	N	N	Y	Y
11 ***Davis***	?	Y	?	Y	N	N	Y	?
12 Bonior	Y	N	Y	?	?	?	?	Y
13 Crockett	?	N	Y	Y	N	N	Y	?
14 Hertel	Y	N	Y	Y	N	N	Y	Y
15 Ford	?	?	Y	?	N	N	Y	?
16 Dingell	Y	N	Y	?	N	N	Y	?
17 Levin	Y	N	Y	Y	N	N	Y	Y
18 ***Broomfield***	N	Y	N	?	N	Y	?	?
MINNESOTA								
1 Penny	N	N	Y	N	N	N	Y	Y
2 ***Weber***	Y	N	?	Y	N	Y	N	?
3 ***Frenzel***	Y	N	N	N	Y	Y	N	Y
4 Vento	Y	N	Y	Y	N	N	Y	Y
5 Sabo	N	N	Y	N	N	N	Y	Y
6 Sikorski	N	N	Y	N	N	N	Y	Y
7 ***Stangeland***	?	Y	N	Y	N	Y	Y	Y
8 Oberstar	?	N	Y	P	N	N	Y	Y
MISSISSIPPI								
1 Whitten	Y	N	Y	Y	N	N	Y	Y
2 ***Franklin***	Y	N	N	Y	Y	Y	Y	?
3 Montgomery	Y	N	Y	Y	N	Y	Y	Y
4 Dowdy	Y	N	Y	Y	N	Y	Y	Y
5 ***Lott***	Y	Y	N	Y	Y	Y	N	Y
MISSOURI								
1 Clay	N	N	Y	N	N	N	Y	Y
2 Young	Y	Y	Y	Y	N	N	Y	Y
3 Gephardt	Y	N	Y	Y	N	N	Y	Y
4 Skelton	Y	N	Y	Y	N	Y	Y	Y
5 Wheat	?	N	Y	Y	N	N	Y	Y
6 ***Coleman***	Y	Y	N	Y	N	N	Y	Y
7 ***Taylor***	Y	Y	N	Y	Y	Y	Y	Y
8 ***Emerson***	N	Y	N	N	N	N	Y	Y
9 Volkmer	Y	Y	Y	Y	N	N	Y	Y
MONTANA								
1 Williams	?	N	Y	Y	N	N	Y	?
2 ***Marlenee***	Y	Y	N	Y	N	Y	Y	Y
NEBRASKA								
1 ***Bereuter***	Y	N	N	Y	N	N	Y	Y
2 ***Daub***	Y	N	N	Y	Y	Y	Y	Y
3 ***Smith***	Y	N	N	Y	Y	Y	N	Y
NEVADA								
1 Reid	Y	N	Y	Y	N	N	Y	Y
2 ***Vucanovich***	?	Y	N	?	?	N	Y	Y
NEW HAMPSHIRE								
1 D'Amours	Y	N	Y	Y	N	N	Y	?
2 ***Gregg***	Y	N	N	Y	N	Y	N	Y
NEW JERSEY								
1 Florio	Y	N	Y	Y	N	N	Y	Y
2 Hughes	Y	N	Y	Y	N	Y	Y	?
3 Howard	?	?	?	?	?	?	?	?
4 ***Smith***	Y	N	N	Y	N	Y	Y	Y
5 ***Roukema***	Y	N	N	Y	N	Y	Y	Y
6 Dwyer	Y	N	Y	Y	N	N	Y	Y
7 ***Rinaldo***	?	N	N	Y	N	Y	Y	Y
8 Roe	Y	N	Y	Y	N	N	Y	Y
9 Torricelli	Y	N	Y	?	N	N	Y	?
10 Rodino	Y	N	Y	Y	N	N	Y	Y
11 Minish	Y	?	?	Y	N	N	Y	Y
12 ***Courter***	Y	N	N	?	?	#	?	Y
13 Vacancy								
14 Guarini	Y	N	Y	Y	N	N	Y	?
NEW MEXICO								
1 ***Lujan***	?	Y	N	Y	N	Y	Y	Y
2 ***Skeen***	Y	Y	N	Y	N	N	Y	Y
3 Richardson	Y	Y	Y	Y	N	N	Y	Y
NEW YORK								
1 ***Carney***	Y	N	N	?	Y	Y	N	Y
2 Downey	Y	N	Y	Y	N	N	Y	Y
3 Mrazek	Y	N	Y	?	N	N	Y	Y
4 ***Lent***	Y	N	N	?	N	Y	Y	Y
5 ***McGrath***	?	?	?	?	?	?	?	Y
6 Addabbo	Y	N	Y	Y	N	N	Y	Y
7 Ackerman	Y	N	Y	Y	N	N	?	Y
8 Scheuer	Y	N	Y	Y	N	N	Y	Y
9 Ferraro	?	?	?	?	?	?	?	?
10 Schumer	Y	N	Y	Y	N	N	Y	Y
11 Towns	Y	N	Y	?	N	N	Y	Y
12 Owens	Y	N	Y	?	N	N	Y	Y
13 Solarz	Y	N	Y	Y	N	N	Y	?
14 ***Molinari***	Y	N	N	Y	N	Y	N	Y
15 ***Green***	Y	N	N	Y	N	N	Y	Y
16 Rangel	Y	N	?	Y	N	N	Y	Y
17 Weiss	Y	N	Y	Y	N	N	Y	Y
18 Garcia	Y	N	Y	?	N	N	Y	?
19 Biaggi	?	N	Y	?	?	X	?	Y
20 Ottinger	?	Y	Y	?	?	?	?	?
21 ***Fish***	Y	N	N	Y	N	Y	Y	Y
22 ***Gilman***	Y	N	N	Y	N	Y	Y	Y
23 Stratton	Y	Y	Y	Y	N	N	Y	Y
24 ***Solomon***	N	N	N	N	N	Y	N	?
25 ***Boehlert***	Y	N	N	Y	N	N	Y	Y
26 ***Martin***	Y	N	N	Y	N	N	Y	Y
27 ***Wortley***	Y	N	N	Y	N	N	Y	Y
28 McHugh	Y	N	Y	Y	N	N	Y	Y
29 ***Horton***	Y	N	N	Y	N	N	Y	Y
30 ***Conable***	Y	Y	N	Y	Y	Y	Y	Y
31 ***Kemp***	Y	Y	N	Y	Y	Y	Y	Y
32 LaFalce	?	N	Y	P	N	N	Y	?
33 Nowak	Y	N	Y	Y	N	N	Y	Y
34 Lundine	Y	N	Y	Y	N	N	Y	?
NORTH CAROLINA								
1 Jones	P	N	Y	P	?	?	?	Y
2 Valentine	Y	N	Y	Y	N	Y	N	Y
3 Whitley	Y	N	Y	Y	N	Y	Y	Y
4 Andrews	Y	N	Y	Y	N	N	Y	Y
5 Neal	?	?	Y	Y	N	Y	Y	Y
6 Britt	Y	N	Y	Y	N	N	Y	Y
7 Rose	?	N	Y	Y	N	N	Y	Y
8 Hefner	Y	N	Y	Y	N	Y	Y	?
9 ***Martin***	?	?	?	?	?	?	?	?
10 ***Broyhill***	Y	Y	N	Y	Y	Y	N	Y
11 Clarke	Y	N	Y	Y	N	Y	Y	Y
NORTH DAKOTA								
AL Dorgan	Y	N	Y	N	N	N	Y	Y
OHIO								
1 Luken	Y	N	Y	Y	N	N	Y	Y
2 ***Gradison***	Y	N	N	Y	N	Y	N	Y
3 Hall	Y	N	Y	Y	N	N	Y	Y
4 ***Oxley***	Y	Y	N	Y	Y	Y	N	Y
5 ***Latta***	Y	Y	N	Y	Y	Y	N	?
6 ***McEwen***	Y	Y	N	?	?	?	?	?
7 ***DeWine***	Y	N	N	Y	N	Y	N	Y
8 ***Kindness***	Y	Y	N	Y	?	Y	N	Y
9 Kaptur	Y	N	Y	Y	N	N	Y	Y
10 ***Miller***	?	Y	N	N	N	Y	Y	Y
11 Eckart	Y	N	Y	Y	N	N	Y	Y
12 ***Kasich***	Y	Y	N	Y	Y	Y	N	Y
13 Pease	Y	N	Y	Y	N	N	Y	Y
14 Seiberling	Y	N	Y	Y	N	N	Y	Y
15 ***Wylie***	Y	Y	N	Y	N	N	Y	Y
16 ***Regula***	Y	Y	N	Y	N	Y	N	Y
17 ***Williams***	Y	N	N	?	N	N	Y	?
18 Applegate	?	Y	Y	Y	N	Y	N	Y
19 Feighan	?	N	Y	?	N	N	Y	?
20 Oakar	Y	N	Y	Y	N	N	Y	Y
21 Stokes	Y	N	Y	Y	N	N	Y	Y
OKLAHOMA								
1 Jones	Y	?	Y	Y	N	Y	Y	Y
2 Synar	Y	N	Y	Y	N	N	Y	Y
3 Watkins	Y	N	Y	Y	N	Y	Y	Y
4 McCurdy	Y	N	Y	?	N	N	Y	Y
5 ***Edwards***	Y	N	N	Y	Y	Y	Y	Y
6 English	Y	N	Y	Y	N	Y	Y	Y
OREGON								
1 AuCoin	Y	N	Y	?	N	N	Y	Y
2 ***Smith, R.***	Y	Y	N	Y	N	Y	N	Y
3 Wyden	Y	N	Y	Y	N	N	Y	Y
4 Weaver	Y	N	Y	?	N	N	?	?
5 ***Smith, D.***	N	Y	N	N	Y	Y	N	Y
PENNSYLVANIA								
1 Foglietta	Y	N	Y	Y	N	N	Y	Y
2 Gray	Y	N	Y	Y	N	N	Y	?
3 Borski	Y	N	Y	Y	N	N	Y	Y
4 Kolter	Y	N	Y	Y	N	Y	Y	Y
5 ***Schulze***	Y	N	N	?	?	?	?	Y
6 Yatron	Y	N	Y	Y	N	Y	Y	Y
7 Edgar	?	N	Y	Y	N	N	Y	?
8 Kostmayer	Y	N	Y	Y	N	N	Y	Y
9 ***Shuster***	Y	Y	N	Y	Y	Y	N	Y
10 ***McDade***	Y	Y	N	Y	N	Y	Y	Y
11 Harrison	?	?	?	?	N	N	Y	Y
12 Murtha	Y	N	Y	Y	N	N	Y	Y
13 ***Coughlin***	N	N	N	N	P	Y	Y	Y
14 Coyne	Y	N	Y	Y	N	N	Y	Y
15 ***Ritter***	Y	N	N	Y	N	Y	N	Y
16 ***Walker***	N	N	N	N	Y	Y	N	Y
17 ***Gekas***	Y	N	N	Y	N	Y	Y	Y
18 Walgren	?	Y	Y	?	N	N	Y	Y
19 ***Goodling***	N	Y	N	?	N	Y	N	Y
20 Gaydos	?	N	Y	Y	N	Y	Y	Y
21 ***Ridge***	N	Y	N	Y	N	N	Y	Y
22 Murphy	Y	Y	Y	Y	N	Y	Y	Y
23 ***Clinger***	Y	Y	N	Y	N	N	Y	+
RHODE ISLAND								
1 St Germain	P	N	Y	P	N	N	Y	Y
2 ***Schneider***	Y	N	N	Y	N	N	Y	Y
SOUTH CAROLINA								
1 ***Hartnett***	Y	Y	N	Y	Y	Y	N	Y
2 ***Spence***	Y	Y	N	Y	Y	Y	?	Y
3 Derrick	Y	N	Y	Y	N	N	Y	Y
4 ***Campbell***	Y	Y	N	?	?	#	X	Y
5 Spratt	Y	N	Y	Y	N	N	Y	Y
6 Tallon	Y	N	Y	Y	N	Y	Y	Y
SOUTH DAKOTA								
AL Daschle	Y	N	Y	Y	N	N	Y	Y
TENNESSEE								
1 ***Quillen***	Y	N	N	Y	Y	?	?	Y
2 ***Duncan***	Y	N	N	Y	N	Y	Y	Y
3 Lloyd	Y	Y	Y	Y	N	N	Y	Y
4 Cooper	Y	?	?	?	?	?	?	Y
5 Boner	Y	N	Y	?	?	X	?	?
6 Gore	Y	N	Y	?	N	N	Y	Y
7 ***Sundquist***	Y	N	N	Y	N	Y	Y	Y
8 Jones	Y	N	Y	Y	N	N	Y	Y
9 Ford	Y	N	Y	Y	N	?	Y	Y
TEXAS								
1 Hall, S.	Y	N	Y	Y	N	Y	N	Y
2 Wilson	?	?	Y	Y	N	N	Y	?
3 ***Bartlett***	Y	Y	N	Y	N	Y	N	Y
4 Hall, R.	Y	N	Y	Y	N	Y	Y	Y
5 Bryant	Y	N	Y	Y	N	N	Y	?
6 ***Gramm***	Y	N	N	?	?	?	?	?
7 ***Archer***	Y	N	N	Y	Y	Y	N	Y
8 ***Fields***	Y	Y	N	?	Y	Y	N	?
9 Brooks	?	N	Y	Y	?	N	Y	Y
10 Pickle	Y	N	Y	Y	N	N	Y	Y
11 Leath	Y	Y	Y	Y	N	Y	N	Y
12 Wright	Y	N	Y	Y	N	N	Y	Y
13 Hightower	Y	N	Y	Y	N	Y	Y	Y
14 Patman	?	N	Y	Y	Y	Y	Y	?
15 de la Garza	Y	N	Y	Y	N	Y	Y	Y
16 Coleman	Y	N	Y	Y	N	N	Y	Y
17 Stenholm	N	N	Y	Y	Y	Y	N	?
18 Leland	Y	N	Y	Y	N	N	Y	Y
19 Hance	Y	N	Y	Y	N	N	Y	Y
20 Gonzalez	Y	N	Y	Y	N	N	Y	Y
21 ***Loeffler***	Y	Y	N	Y	Y	Y	N	Y
22 ***Paul***	Y	Y	N	Y	Y	Y	N	?
23 Kazen	Y	N	Y	Y	N	Y	Y	Y
24 Frost	Y	N	Y	Y	N	N	Y	Y
25 Andrews	Y	N	Y	Y	N	N	Y	Y
26 Vandergriff	?	Y	Y	P	N	Y	Y	Y
27 Ortiz	Y	N	Y	Y	N	N	Y	?
UTAH								
1 ***Hansen***	Y	N	N	Y	Y	Y	N	Y
2 ***Marriott***	?	N	N	Y	Y	Y	N	?
3 ***Nielson***	Y	N	N	Y	Y	Y	N	Y
VERMONT								
AL ***Jeffords***	N	N	N	?	N	N	Y	Y
VIRGINIA								
1 ***Bateman***	Y	Y	N	Y	N	Y	Y	Y
2 ***Whitehurst***	Y	Y	N	?	?	?	?	Y
3 ***Bliley***	Y	Y	N	Y	Y	Y	N	Y
4 Sisisky	Y	Y	Y	Y	N	Y	Y	Y
5 Daniel	Y	Y	Y	Y	Y	Y	N	Y
6 Olin	Y	Y	Y	Y	Y	Y	Y	Y
7 ***Robinson***	Y	Y	N	Y	N	Y	N	Y
8 ***Parris***	Y	Y	N	Y	N	Y	Y	Y
9 Boucher	Y	N	Y	Y	N	N	Y	Y
10 ***Wolf***	Y	Y	N	Y	N	Y	Y	Y
WASHINGTON								
1 ***Pritchard***	Y	N	N	Y	N	N	Y	Y
2 Swift	Y	N	Y	Y	N	N	Y	Y
3 Bonker	Y	?	Y	Y	N	N	Y	Y
4 ***Morrison***	Y	N	N	Y	N	N	Y	Y
5 Foley	Y	?	Y	Y	N	N	Y	Y
6 Dicks	Y	N	Y	?	N	N	Y	Y
7 Lowry	Y	N	Y	Y	N	N	Y	Y
8 ***Chandler***	Y	Y	N	Y	N	N	Y	Y
WEST VIRGINIA								
1 Mollohan	Y	N	Y	Y	N	N	Y	Y
2 Staggers	Y	N	Y	Y	N	N	Y	Y
3 Wise	Y	N	Y	Y	N	Y	Y	Y
4 Rahall	Y	N	Y	?	N	N	Y	Y
WISCONSIN								
1 Aspin	?	N	Y	Y	N	N	Y	?
2 Kastenmeier	Y	N	Y	Y	N	N	Y	Y
3 ***Gunderson***	Y	N	N	Y	N	Y	N	Y
4 Kleczka	Y	N	Y	?	N	N	Y	Y
5 Moody	Y	Y	Y	Y	N	N	Y	Y
6 ***Petri***	Y	N	N	Y	Y	Y	N	Y
7 Obey	Y	N	Y	?	N	N	Y	?
8 ***Roth***	Y	N	N	Y	Y	Y	Y	?
9 ***Sensenbrenner***	Y	Y	N	Y	Y	Y	N	?
WYOMING								
AL ***Cheney***	?	?	?	?	?	#	?	?

Southern states - Ala., Ark., Fla., Ga., Ky., La., Miss., N.C., Okla., S.C., Tenn., Texas, Va.

397. HR 999. American Conservation Corps. Seiberling, D-Ohio, motion that the House concur in the Senate amendment to the bill to authorize $225 million over three years for a new program to provide jobs for unemployed youths on conservation projects. Motion agreed to 296-75: R 69-72; D 227-3 (ND 152-0, SD 75-3), Oct. 9, 1984. A "nay" was a vote supporting the president's position.

398. S 2565. Human Services Amendments. Passage of the bill to reauthorize Head Start, Low-Income Energy Assistance, Community Services Block Grants and other social services through fiscal 1986, and to establish state block grants to help expand child-care services and several new programs to promote excellence in education. Passed 376-6: R 138-6; D 238-0 (ND 158-0, SD 80-0), Oct. 9, 1984.

399. HR 3398. Tariff and Trade Act. Adoption of the conference report on the bill to alter tariffs and customs on more than 70 items, broaden the president's authority to respond to a wide range of unfair trade practices by foreign competitors, renew for eight and a half years duty-free treatment of exports from developing countries, enforce the president's voluntary restraints on steel imports, and aid the domestic shoe, copper and wine industries. Adopted 386-1: R 145-1; D 241-0 (ND 161-0, SD 80-0), Oct. 9, 1984. A "yea" was a vote supporting the president's position.

400. S 2574. Health Professions and Services. Waxman, D-Calif., motion to suspend the rules and pass the bill to reauthorize health professions programs, community and migrant health centers, the National Health Service Corps and certain other health programs. Motion agreed to 363-13: R 128-13; D 235-0 (ND 155-0, SD 80-0), Oct. 9, 1984. A two-thirds majority of those present and voting (251 in this case) is required for passage under suspension of the rules. A "nay" was a vote supporting the president's position.

401. HR 6027. Local Government Antitrust Act. Edwards, D-Calif., motion to suspend the rules and adopt the resolution (H Res 613) providing for agreeing, with an amendment, to the Senate amendment to the bill to protect local governments from monetary damage awards in antitrust lawsuits. Motion rejected 220-160: R 22-121; D 198-39 (ND 141-17, SD 57-22), Oct. 9, 1984. A two-thirds majority of those present and voting (254 in this case) is required for adoption under suspension of the rules.

402. HR 6028. Labor, Health and Human Services, Education Appropriations, Fiscal 1985. Adoption of the conference report on the bill to appropriate $93,514,124,000 for the Labor Department, the Department of Health and Human Services, the Education Department and related agencies in fiscal 1985, and $11,050,769,000 in advance funding for fiscal 1986-87 for certain programs. The bill continued to bar Medicaid funding for abortions except when the mother's life is endangered. Adopted 313-70: R 85-58; D 228-12 (ND 161-2, SD 67-10), Oct. 10, 1984. The president had requested $99,685,346,000 in new budget authority.

KEY

Y	Voted for (yea).
#	Paired for.
+	Announced for.
N	Voted against (nay).
X	Paired against.
-	Announced against.
P	Voted "present".
C	Voted "present" to avoid possible conflict of interest.
?	Did not vote or otherwise make a position known.

Democrats   *Republicans*

	397	398	399	400	401	402
ALABAMA						
1 Edwards	Y	Y	Y	Y	N	Y
2 *Dickinson*	?	?	?	?	?	N
3 Nichols	Y	Y	Y	Y	N	Y
4 Bevill	Y	Y	Y	Y	Y	Y
5 Flippo	Y	Y	Y	Y	Y	Y
6 Erdreich	Y	Y	Y	Y	Y	Y
7 Shelby	Y	Y	Y	Y	N	Y
ALASKA						
AL *Young*	Y	Y	Y	Y	N	Y
ARIZONA						
1 *McCain*	N	Y	Y	Y	N	Y
2 Udall	Y	Y	Y	Y	Y	Y
3 *Stump*	N	N	Y	N	Y	N
4 *Rudd*	N	Y	Y	N	Y	N
5 McNulty	Y	Y	Y	Y	Y	Y
ARKANSAS						
1 Alexander	?	?	Y	Y	Y	?
2 *Bethune*	?	?	?	?	?	?
3 *Hammerschmidt*	Y	Y	Y	Y	N	Y
4 Anthony	Y	Y	Y	Y	N	Y
CALIFORNIA						
1 Bosco	Y	Y	Y	Y	Y	Y
2 *Chappie*	N	Y	Y	Y	N	N
3 Matsui	Y	Y	Y	Y	Y	Y
4 Fazio	Y	Y	Y	Y	Y	Y
5 Burton	Y	Y	Y	Y	Y	Y
6 Boxer	Y	Y	Y	Y	Y	Y
7 Miller	Y	Y	Y	Y	Y	Y
8 Dellums	Y	Y	Y	Y	Y	Y
9 Stark	Y	Y	Y	Y	Y	Y
10 Edwards	Y	Y	Y	Y	Y	Y
11 Lantos	Y	Y	Y	Y	Y	Y
12 *Zschau*	N	Y	Y	Y	N	N
13 Mineta	Y	Y	Y	Y	Y	Y
14 *Shumway*	N	N	Y	N	N	N
15 Coelho	?	?	Y	Y	Y	Y
16 Panetta	Y	Y	Y	Y	Y	Y
17 *Pashayan*	Y	Y	Y	Y	N	Y
18 Lehman	Y	Y	Y	Y	Y	Y
19 *Lagomarsino*	Y	Y	Y	Y	N	Y
20 *Thomas*	Y	Y	Y	Y	N	Y
21 *Fiedler*	Y	Y	Y	Y	N	?
22 *Moorhead*	N	Y	Y	N	N	N
23 Beilenson	Y	Y	Y	Y	Y	Y
24 Waxman	Y	Y	Y	Y	Y	Y
25 Roybal	Y	Y	Y	Y	Y	Y
26 Berman	Y	Y	Y	Y	Y	Y
27 Levine	Y	Y	Y	Y	Y	Y
28 Dixon	?	Y	Y	Y	Y	Y
29 Hawkins	Y	Y	Y	Y	Y	?
30 Martinez	Y	Y	Y	Y	Y	Y
31 Dymally	?	?	?	?	?	Y
32 Anderson	Y	Y	Y	Y	Y	Y
33 *Dreier*	N	Y	Y	N	N	N
34 Torres	Y	Y	Y	Y	Y	Y
35 *Lewis*	N	Y	Y	?	?	Y
36 Brown	Y	Y	Y	Y	Y	Y
37 *McCandless*	N	Y	Y	Y	N	N
38 Patterson	Y	Y	Y	Y	Y	Y
39 *Dannemeyer*	N	N	Y	N	N	N
40 *Badham*	N	Y	Y	?	?	N
41 *Lowery*	Y	Y	Y	Y	Y	Y
42 *Lungren*	N	Y	Y	N	N	N
43 *Packard*	N	Y	Y	Y	N	N
44 Bates	Y	Y	Y	Y	N	Y
45 *Hunter*	N	Y	Y	Y	N	Y
COLORADO						
1 Schroeder	Y	Y	Y	Y	Y	N
2 Wirth	Y	Y	Y	Y	Y	Y
3 Kogovsek	Y	Y	Y	Y	Y	Y
4 *Brown*	N	Y	Y	N	N	N
5 *Kramer*	N	Y	Y	N	N	N
6 *Schaefer*	N	Y	Y	Y	N	N
CONNECTICUT						
1 Kennelly	Y	Y	Y	Y	Y	Y
2 Gejdenson	Y	Y	Y	Y	Y	Y
3 Morrison	Y	Y	Y	Y	Y	Y
4 *McKinney*	Y	Y	Y	Y	Y	Y
5 Ratchford	Y	Y	Y	Y	Y	Y
6 *Johnson*	Y	Y	Y	Y	N	Y
DELAWARE						
AL Carper	Y	Y	Y	Y	Y	Y
FLORIDA						
1 Hutto	Y	Y	Y	Y	Y	Y
2 Fuqua	Y	Y	Y	Y	Y	Y
3 Bennett	Y	Y	Y	Y	N	Y
4 Chappell	Y	Y	Y	Y	Y	Y
5 *McCollum*	N	Y	Y	Y	N	N
6 MacKay	Y	Y	Y	Y	Y	Y
7 Gibbons	Y	Y	Y	Y	Y	Y
8 *Young*	N	Y	Y	Y	N	Y
9 *Bilirakis*	N	Y	Y	Y	N	Y
10 *Ireland*	Y	Y	Y	Y	N	Y
11 Nelson	Y	Y	Y	Y	N	N
12 *Lewis*	Y	Y	Y	Y	N	Y
13 *Mack*	N	?	?	?	?	N
14 Mica	Y	Y	Y	Y	Y	Y
15 *Shaw*	N	Y	Y	Y	N	Y
16 Smith	Y	Y	Y	Y	Y	?
17 Lehman	Y	Y	Y	Y	Y	Y
18 Pepper	Y	Y	Y	Y	N	Y
19 Fascell	Y	Y	Y	Y	Y	Y
GEORGIA						
1 Thomas	Y	Y	Y	Y	Y	Y
2 Hatcher	Y	Y	Y	Y	Y	Y
3 Ray	Y	Y	Y	Y	Y	N
4 Levitas	Y	Y	Y	Y	N	Y
5 Fowler	Y	Y	Y	Y	Y	Y
6 *Gingrich*	Y	Y	Y	Y	N	N
7 Darden	Y	Y	Y	Y	Y	?
8 Rowland	Y	Y	Y	Y	Y	Y
9 Jenkins	?	?	?	?	?	Y
10 Barnard	Y	Y	Y	Y	Y	Y
HAWAII						
1 Heftel	?	?	?	Y	Y	Y
2 Akaka	Y	Y	Y	Y	Y	Y
IDAHO						
1 *Craig*	N	Y	Y	N	N	N
2 *Hansen*	?	?	?	?	?	?
ILLINOIS						
1 Hayes	Y	Y	Y	Y	Y	Y
2 Savage	Y	Y	Y	Y	Y	Y
3 Russo	Y	Y	Y	Y	Y	Y
4 *O'Brien*	Y	Y	Y	Y	N	Y
5 Lipinski	Y	Y	Y	Y	Y	?
6 *Hyde*	N	Y	Y	N	Y	N
7 Collins	Y	Y	Y	Y	N	Y
8 Rostenkowski	Y	Y	Y	Y	Y	Y
9 Yates	Y	Y	Y	Y	Y	Y
10 *Porter*	N	Y	Y	Y	Y	Y
11 Annunzio	Y	Y	Y	Y	Y	Y
12 *Crane, P.*	N	N	N	N	N	N
13 *Erlenborn*	?	Y	Y	Y	Y	?
14 *Corcoran*	N	Y	Y	Y	N	?
15 *Madigan*	Y	Y	Y	Y	N	Y
16 *Martin*	?	?	Y	Y	N	?
17 Evans	?	?	Y	Y	N	Y
18 *Michel*	N	Y	Y	Y	N	Y
19 *Crane, D.*	?	?	Y	N	N	N
20 Durbin	Y	Y	Y	Y	N	Y
21 Price	Y	Y	Y	Y	Y	Y
22 Simon	?	?	?	?	?	?
INDIANA						
1 Hall	?	?	Y	Y	Y	Y
2 Sharp	Y	Y	Y	Y	Y	Y
3 *Hiler*	N	Y	Y	Y	N	Y
4 *Coats*	Y	Y	Y	Y	N	Y
5 *Hillis*	Y	Y	Y	Y	N	Y

	397	398	399	400	401	402
6 ***Burton***	N	Y	?	?	?	N
7 ***Myers***	N	Y	Y	Y	N	Y
8 McCloskey	Y	Y	Y	Y	Y	Y
9 Hamilton	Y	Y	Y	Y	Y	Y
10 Jacobs	Y	Y	Y	Y	N	Y
IOWA						
1 ***Leach***	Y	Y	Y	Y	Y	N
2 ***Tauke***	?	?	Y	Y	N	N
3 ***Evans***	Y	Y	Y	Y	N	Y
4 Smith	Y	Y	Y	Y	Y	Y
5 Harkin	?	?	Y	Y	Y	Y
6 Bedell	Y	Y	Y	Y	Y	Y
KANSAS						
1 ***Roberts***	Y	Y	Y	Y	N	N
2 Slattery	Y	Y	Y	Y	Y	Y
3 ***Winn***	?	?	?	?	?	?
4 Glickman	Y	Y	Y	Y	Y	Y
5 ***Whittaker***	N	Y	Y	Y	N	Y
KENTUCKY						
1 Hubbard	N	Y	Y	Y	N	N
2 Natcher	Y	Y	Y	Y	Y	Y
3 Mazzoli	Y	Y	Y	Y	Y	Y
4 ***Snyder***	N	Y	Y	Y	N	Y
5 ***Rogers***	Y	Y	Y	Y	N	Y
6 ***Hopkins***	Y	Y	Y	Y	N	Y
7 Vacancy						
LOUISIANA						
1 ***Livingston***	N	Y	Y	Y	N	Y
2 Boggs	Y	Y	Y	Y	Y	Y
3 Tauzin	Y	Y	Y	Y	Y	Y
4 Roemer	Y	Y	Y	Y	Y	N
5 Huckaby	Y	Y	Y	Y	Y	Y
6 ***Moore***	N	Y	Y	Y	N	Y
7 Breaux	Y	Y	Y	Y	Y	Y
8 Long	?	Y	Y	Y	Y	Y
MAINE						
1 ***McKernan***	Y	Y	Y	Y	N	Y
2 ***Snowe***	Y	Y	Y	Y	N	Y
MARYLAND						
1 Dyson	Y	Y	Y	Y	Y	?
2 Long	Y	Y	Y	Y	Y	Y
3 Mikulski	Y	?	?	?	Y	Y
4 ***Holt***	N	?	?	?	N	?
5 Hoyer	Y	Y	Y	Y	Y	Y
6 Byron	Y	Y	Y	Y	Y	Y
7 Mitchell	Y	Y	Y	Y	Y	Y
8 Barnes	Y	Y	Y	Y	Y	Y
MASSACHUSETTS						
1 ***Conte***	Y	Y	Y	Y	Y	Y
2 Boland	Y	Y	Y	Y	Y	Y
3 Early	Y	Y	Y	Y	Y	Y
4 Frank	Y	Y	Y	Y	Y	Y
5 Shannon	?	Y	Y	Y	Y	Y
6 Mavroules	Y	Y	Y	Y	Y	?
7 Markey	Y	Y	Y	Y	Y	Y
8 O'Neill						
9 Moakley	Y	Y	Y	Y	Y	Y
10 Studds	Y	Y	Y	Y	Y	Y
11 Donnelly	Y	Y	Y	Y	Y	Y
MICHIGAN						
1 Conyers	Y	Y	Y	?	?	Y
2 ***Pursell***	?	?	?	?	?	#
3 Wolpe	Y	Y	Y	Y	?	Y
4 ***Siljander***	N	Y	Y	Y	N	?
5 ***Sawyer***	Y	Y	Y	Y	N	Y
6 Carr	Y	Y	Y	Y	Y	Y
7 Kildee	Y	Y	Y	Y	Y	Y
8 Traxler	Y	Y	Y	Y	Y	Y
9 ***Vander Jagt***	Y	Y	Y	Y	N	?
10 Albosta	Y	Y	Y	Y	Y	Y
11 ***Davis***	?	?	?	?	?	Y
12 Bonior	Y	Y	Y	Y	Y	Y
13 Crockett	Y	Y	?	?	?	Y
14 Hertel	Y	Y	Y	Y	Y	Y
15 Ford	?	?	?	?	?	Y
16 Dingell	Y	Y	Y	Y	Y	Y
17 Levin	Y	Y	Y	Y	Y	Y
18 ***Broomfield***	?	?	?	?	?	?
MINNESOTA						
1 Penny	Y	Y	Y	Y	Y	N
2 ***Weber***	?	Y	Y	Y	N	N
3 ***Frenzel***	N	Y	Y	Y	N	N
4 Vento	Y	Y	Y	Y	Y	Y
5 Sabo	Y	Y	Y	Y	Y	Y
6 Sikorski	Y	Y	Y	Y	Y	Y

	397	398	399	400	401	402
7 ***Stangeland***	Y	Y	Y	Y	N	Y
8 Oberstar	Y	Y	Y	Y	Y	Y
MISSISSIPPI						
1 Whitten	Y	Y	Y	Y	Y	Y
2 ***Franklin***	?	?	Y	Y	N	N
3 Montgomery	N	Y	Y	Y	N	N
4 Dowdy	Y	Y	Y	Y	N	Y
5 ***Lott***	N	Y	Y	Y	N	N
MISSOURI						
1 Clay	Y	Y	Y	?	?	Y
2 Young	Y	Y	Y	Y	Y	Y
3 Gephardt	Y	Y	Y	Y	Y	Y
4 Skelton	Y	Y	Y	Y	N	Y
5 Wheat	Y	Y	Y	Y	Y	Y
6 ***Coleman***	Y	Y	Y	Y	N	Y
7 ***Taylor***	N	Y	Y	Y	N	N
8 ***Emerson***	Y	Y	Y	Y	N	Y
9 Volkmer	Y	Y	Y	Y	Y	Y
MONTANA						
1 Williams	Y	Y	Y	Y	N	Y
2 ***Marlenee***	N	Y	Y	Y	N	N
NEBRASKA						
1 ***Bereuter***	Y	Y	Y	Y	N	Y
2 ***Daub***	N	Y	Y	Y	N	Y
3 ***Smith***	N	Y	Y	Y	N	Y
NEVADA						
1 Reid	Y	Y	Y	Y	Y	Y
2 ***Vucanovich***	N	Y	Y	Y	N	Y
NEW HAMPSHIRE						
1 D'Amours	?	Y	Y	Y	N	Y
2 ***Gregg***	N	Y	Y	Y	N	N
NEW JERSEY						
1 Florio	Y	Y	Y	Y	Y	Y
2 Hughes	Y	Y	Y	Y	Y	Y
3 Howard	?	?	?	?	?	?
4 ***Smith***	Y	Y	Y	Y	Y	Y
5 ***Roukema***	?	Y	Y	Y	Y	Y
6 Dwyer	Y	Y	Y	Y	Y	Y
7 ***Rinaldo***	?	Y	Y	Y	Y	Y
8 Roe	Y	Y	?	Y	Y	Y
9 Torricelli	?	?	?	?	?	Y
10 Rodino	Y	Y	Y	Y	Y	Y
11 Minish	Y	Y	Y	Y	Y	Y
12 ***Courter***	Y	Y	Y	Y	Y	Y
13 Vacancy						
14 Guarini	?	?	Y	Y	Y	Y
NEW MEXICO						
1 ***Lujan***	Y	Y	Y	Y	N	N
2 ***Skeen***	N	Y	Y	Y	N	N
3 Richardson	Y	Y	Y	Y	Y	Y
NEW YORK						
1 ***Carney***	N	Y	Y	Y	N	Y
2 Downey	Y	Y	Y	Y	Y	Y
3 Mrazek	Y	Y	Y	Y	Y	Y
4 ***Lent***	Y	Y	Y	Y	N	Y
5 ***McGrath***	Y	Y	Y	Y	N	Y
6 Addabbo	Y	Y	Y	?	Y	Y
7 Ackerman	Y	Y	Y	Y	Y	Y
8 Scheuer	Y	Y	Y	Y	Y	Y
9 Ferraro	?	?	?	?	?	?
10 Schumer	Y	Y	Y	Y	Y	Y
11 Towns	Y	Y	Y	Y	Y	Y
12 Owens	Y	Y	Y	Y	Y	Y
13 Solarz	?	Y	Y	?	?	Y
14 ***Molinari***	N	Y	Y	Y	N	Y
15 ***Green***	Y	Y	Y	Y	Y	Y
16 Rangel	?	?	?	?	?	Y
17 Weiss	Y	Y	Y	Y	Y	Y
18 Garcia	Y	Y	Y	?	?	Y
19 Biaggi	?	Y	Y	Y	Y	Y
20 Ottinger	?	?	?	?	?	Y
21 ***Fish***	Y	Y	Y	Y	N	Y
22 ***Gilman***	Y	Y	Y	Y	N	Y
23 Stratton	Y	Y	Y	Y	N	Y
24 ***Solomon***	?	Y	Y	Y	N	Y
25 ***Boehlert***	Y	Y	Y	Y	Y	Y
26 ***Martin***	Y	Y	Y	Y	N	Y
27 ***Wortley***	Y	Y	Y	Y	N	Y
28 McHugh	Y	Y	Y	Y	Y	Y
29 ***Horton***	Y	Y	Y	Y	N	Y
30 ***Conable***	?	?	?	?	?	?
31 ***Kemp***	N	Y	?	?	?	?
32 LaFalce	Y	Y	Y	Y	Y	?
33 Nowak	Y	Y	Y	Y	Y	Y
34 Lundine	?	Y	Y	Y	Y	Y

	397	398	399	400	401	402
NORTH CAROLINA						
1 Jones	Y	Y	Y	Y	Y	Y
2 Valentine	Y	Y	Y	Y	Y	Y
3 Whitley	Y	Y	Y	Y	N	Y
4 Andrews	?	Y	Y	Y	Y	?
5 Neal	Y	Y	Y	Y	Y	Y
6 Britt	Y	Y	Y	Y	Y	Y
7 Rose	?	?	?	?	?	?
8 Hefner	?	?	?	?	?	?
9 ***Martin***	?	?	?	?	?	?
10 ***Broyhill***	N	Y	Y	Y	N	N
11 Clarke	Y	Y	Y	Y	Y	Y
NORTH DAKOTA						
AL Dorgan	Y	Y	Y	Y	Y	Y
OHIO						
1 Luken	Y	Y	Y	Y	Y	Y
2 ***Gradison***	N	Y	Y	Y	N	N
3 Hall	Y	Y	Y	?	?	Y
4 ***Oxley***	N	Y	Y	Y	N	N
5 ***Latta***	N	Y	Y	Y	N	N
6 ***McEwen***	?	?	?	?	?	?
7 ***DeWine***	Y	Y	Y	Y	N	N
8 ***Kindness***	Y	Y	?	Y	N	N
9 Kaptur	Y	Y	Y	Y	Y	Y
10 ***Miller***	N	Y	Y	Y	N	Y
11 Eckart	Y	Y	Y	Y	Y	Y
12 ***Kasich***	Y	Y	Y	?	?	?
13 Pease	Y	Y	Y	Y	Y	Y
14 Seiberling	Y	Y	Y	Y	Y	Y
15 ***Wylie***	Y	Y	Y	Y	N	Y
16 ***Regula***	Y	Y	Y	Y	N	Y
17 ***Williams***	Y	Y	Y	Y	N	Y
18 Applegate	Y	Y	Y	?	N	Y
19 Feighan	Y	Y	Y	Y	Y	Y
20 Oakar	Y	Y	Y	Y	Y	Y
21 Stokes	Y	Y	Y	Y	Y	Y
OKLAHOMA						
1 Jones	Y	Y	Y	Y	Y	Y
2 Synar	Y	Y	Y	Y	Y	Y
3 Watkins	Y	Y	Y	Y	Y	Y
4 McCurdy	Y	Y	Y	Y	Y	?
5 ***Edwards***	N	Y	Y	Y	N	N
6 English	Y	Y	Y	Y	N	N
OREGON						
1 AuCoin	Y	Y	Y	Y	Y	Y
2 ***Smith, R.***	Y	Y	Y	Y	N	Y
3 Wyden	Y	Y	Y	Y	Y	Y
4 Weaver	?	?	?	?	?	Y
5 ***Smith, D.***	N	N	Y	N	N	N
PENNSYLVANIA						
1 Foglietta	Y	Y	Y	Y	Y	Y
2 Gray	?	?	?	?	?	?
3 Borski	Y	Y	Y	Y	Y	Y
4 Kolter	Y	Y	Y	Y	N	Y
5 ***Schulze***	Y	Y	Y	?	?	?
6 Yatron	Y	Y	Y	Y	N	Y
7 Edgar	?	?	?	?	?	?
8 Kostmayer	Y	Y	Y	Y	Y	Y
9 ***Shuster***	Y	Y	Y	Y	N	N
10 ***McDade***	Y	Y	Y	Y	Y	Y
11 Harrison	Y	Y	Y	Y	Y	?
12 Murtha	Y	Y	Y	?	Y	Y
13 ***Coughlin***	Y	Y	Y	Y	N	Y
14 Coyne	Y	Y	Y	Y	Y	Y
15 ***Ritter***	Y	Y	Y	Y	Y	Y
16 ***Walker***	N	Y	Y	Y	N	N
17 ***Gekas***	N	Y	Y	Y	Y	N
18 Walgren	Y	Y	Y	Y	Y	Y
19 ***Goodling***	Y	Y	Y	Y	N	Y
20 Gaydos	Y	Y	Y	Y	N	Y
21 ***Ridge***	Y	Y	Y	Y	Y	Y
22 Murphy	Y	Y	Y	Y	N	Y
23 ***Clinger***	Y	Y	Y	+	N	Y
RHODE ISLAND						
1 St Germain	Y	Y	Y	Y	Y	Y
2 ***Schneider***	Y	Y	Y	Y	Y	Y
SOUTH CAROLINA						
1 ***Hartnett***	?	?	?	?	?	N
2 ***Spence***	Y	Y	Y	Y	N	N
3 Derrick	Y	Y	Y	Y	Y	Y
4 ***Campbell***	Y	Y	Y	Y	N	X
5 Spratt	Y	Y	Y	Y	Y	Y
6 Tallon	Y	Y	Y	Y	Y	Y
SOUTH DAKOTA						
AL Daschle	Y	Y	Y	Y	Y	Y

	397	398	399	400	401	402
TENNESSEE						
1 ***Quillen***	N	Y	Y	Y	N	Y
2 ***Duncan***	Y	Y	Y	Y	N	Y
3 Lloyd	Y	Y	Y	Y	N	Y
4 Cooper	Y	Y	Y	Y	Y	Y
5 Boner	?	?	?	?	?	?
6 Gore	Y	Y	?	?	?	Y
7 ***Sundquist***	N	Y	Y	Y	N	Y
8 Jones	Y	Y	Y	Y	Y	Y
9 Ford	Y	Y	Y	Y	?	Y
TEXAS						
1 Hall, S.	Y	Y	Y	Y	N	N
2 Wilson	Y	Y	Y	Y	Y	Y
3 ***Bartlett***	N	Y	Y	Y	N	N
4 Hall, R.	Y	Y	Y	Y	N	N
5 Bryant	?	?	?	?	?	Y
6 ***Gramm***	?	?	?	?	?	?
7 ***Archer***	N	Y	Y	Y	N	N
8 ***Fields***	N	Y	Y	Y	N	N
9 Brooks	Y	Y	Y	Y	Y	Y
10 Pickle	Y	Y	Y	Y	Y	Y
11 Leath	N	Y	Y	Y	N	N
12 Wright	Y	Y	Y	Y	Y	Y
13 Hightower	Y	Y	Y	Y	N	Y
14 Patman	Y	Y	Y	Y	N	Y
15 de la Garza	Y	Y	Y	Y	Y	Y
16 Coleman	Y	Y	Y	Y	Y	Y
17 Stenholm	?	?	?	?	?	?
18 Leland	Y	Y	Y	Y	Y	Y
19 Hance	Y	Y	Y	Y	Y	?
20 Gonzalez	Y	Y	Y	Y	Y	Y
21 ***Loeffler***	N	Y	Y	Y	N	N
22 ***Paul***	?	?	?	?	?	X
23 Kazen	Y	Y	Y	Y	Y	Y
24 Frost	Y	Y	Y	Y	N	Y
25 Andrews	Y	Y	Y	Y	Y	Y
26 Vandergriff	Y	Y	Y	Y	N	Y
27 Ortiz	Y	Y	Y	Y	Y	Y
UTAH						
1 ***Hansen***	N	N	Y	N	N	N
2 ***Marriott***	?	?	?	?	?	?
3 ***Nielson***	N	Y	Y	Y	N	N
VERMONT						
AL ***Jeffords***	Y	Y	Y	Y	N	Y
VIRGINIA						
1 ***Bateman***	Y	Y	Y	Y	Y	Y
2 ***Whitehurst***	Y	Y	Y	Y	N	Y
3 ***Bliley***	N	Y	Y	Y	N	N
4 Sisisky	Y	Y	Y	Y	Y	Y
5 Daniel	Y	Y	Y	Y	N	N
6 Olin	Y	Y	Y	Y	N	?
7 ***Robinson***	N	Y	Y	Y	N	N
8 ***Parris***	N	Y	Y	?	?	?
9 Boucher	?	?	?	?	?	Y
10 ***Wolf***	Y	Y	Y	?	?	Y
WASHINGTON						
1 ***Pritchard***	?	Y	?	Y	Y	Y
2 Swift	Y	Y	Y	Y	Y	Y
3 Bonker	Y	Y	Y	Y	Y	?
4 ***Morrison***	Y	Y	Y	Y	Y	Y
5 Foley	Y	Y	Y	Y	Y	Y
6 Dicks	Y	Y	Y	Y	Y	Y
7 Lowry	Y	Y	Y	Y	Y	Y
8 ***Chandler***	Y	Y	Y	Y	Y	Y
WEST VIRGINIA						
1 Mollohan	Y	Y	Y	Y	Y	Y
2 Staggers	Y	Y	Y	Y	Y	Y
3 Wise	Y	Y	Y	Y	Y	Y
4 Rahall	Y	Y	Y	Y	Y	Y
WISCONSIN						
1 Aspin	?	?	?	?	?	?
2 Kastenmeier	Y	Y	Y	Y	Y	Y
3 ***Gunderson***	N	Y	Y	Y	N	Y
4 Kleczka	Y	Y	Y	Y	Y	Y
5 Moody	Y	Y	Y	Y	Y	Y
6 ***Petri***	Y	Y	Y	Y	Y	Y
7 Obey	?	Y	Y	Y	Y	Y
8 ***Roth***	?	?	Y	Y	N	Y
9 ***Sensenbrenner***	?	?	Y	N	N	N
WYOMING						
AL ***Cheney***	N	?	?	?	?	#

Southern states - Ala., Ark., Fla., Ga., Ky., La., Miss., N.C., Okla., S.C., Tenn., Texas, Va.

KEY

Y Voted for (yea).
Paired for.
+ Announced for.
N Voted against (nay).
X Paired against.
- Announced against.
P Voted "present".
C Voted "present" to avoid possible conflict of interest.
? Did not vote or otherwise make a position known.

Democrats   *Republicans*

403. H J Res 648. Continuing Appropriations, Fiscal 1985. Molinari, R-N.Y., motion to concur in the Senate amendment establishing a fund to be used to retire $33 million in past interest debt owed to the Treasury by the Kennedy Center for the Performing Arts, with an amendment to require higher repayments. Motion rejected 178-185: R 129-12; D 49-173 (ND 22-128, SD 27-45), Oct. 10, 1984.

404. H J Res 648. Continuing Appropriations, Fiscal 1985. Yates, D-Ill., motion that the House recede from its disagreement and concur with the Senate amendment to establish a fund to retire $33 million in past interest debt owed to the Treasury by the Kennedy Center for the Performing Arts. Motion agreed to 166-163: R 13-120; D 153-43 (ND 114-17, SD 39-26), Oct. 10, 1984.

405. HR 4230. Export Administration Act. Adoption of the rule (H Res 615) providing for House floor consideration of the bill reauthorizing for five years government authority to control U.S. exports to protect national security, promote foreign policy and prevent shortages of important commodities. Adopted 226-124: R 44-101; D 182-23 (ND 125-13, SD 57-10), Oct. 11, 1984.

406. HR 4230. Export Administration Act. Fascell, D-Fla., motion to concur in the Senate amendment with an amendment to ban U.S. commercial bank loans to the government of South Africa. Motion agreed to 269-62: R 96-50; D 173-12 (ND 121-2, SD 52-10), Oct. 11, 1984.

407. HR 6027. Local Government Antitrust Act. Wilson, D-Texas, motion to strike from the conference report on the bill a provision restoring the authority of the Federal Trade Commission to seek injunctions against local governments for alleged antitrust violations. Such authority had been severely curbed in the appropriations law (PL 98-411) funding the agency for fiscal 1985. HR 6027 amended antitrust law to give local governments immunity from monetary damage awards in antitrust lawsuits. Motion rejected 36-298: R 19-122; D 17-176 (ND 8-123, SD 9-53), Oct. 11, 1984.

408. HR 6027. Local Government Antitrust Act. Adoption of the conference report on the bill to give local governments immunity from monetary damage awards in antitrust lawsuits. Adopted 318-0: R 134-0; D 184-0 (ND 128-0, SD 56-0), Oct. 11, 1984.

	403	404	405	406	407	408
ALABAMA						
1 *Edwards*	N	Y	N	Y	N	Y
2 *Dickinson*	Y	N	?	?	?	?
3 Nichols	Y	N	?	N	N	Y
4 Bevill	N	Y	Y	Y	N	Y
5 Flippo	N	?	Y	Y	N	Y
6 Erdreich	Y	?	Y	Y	N	Y
7 Shelby	Y	N	N	Y	N	Y
ALASKA						
AL *Young*	Y	N	Y	Y	N	Y
ARIZONA						
1 *McCain*	Y	N	N	Y	N	?
2 Udall	N	Y	?	?	?	?
3 *Stump*	Y	N	N	N	Y	Y
4 *Rudd*	Y	N	?	?	?	?
5 McNulty	N	Y	?	?	?	?
ARKANSAS						
1 Alexander	?	?	?	?	?	?
2 *Bethune*	?	?	?	?	?	?
3 *Hammerschmidt*	Y	N	N	?	Y	Y
4 Anthony	Y	N	Y	Y	?	?
CALIFORNIA						
1 Bosco	?	?	Y	Y	N	Y
2 *Chappie*	Y	N	N	N	N	Y
3 Matsui	N	?	Y	Y	N	Y
4 Fazio	N	Y	Y	Y	N	Y
5 Burton	N	Y	Y	Y	N	Y
6 Boxer	N	Y	Y	Y	N	Y
7 Miller	N	Y	Y	Y	N	Y
8 Dellums	N	Y	N	P	N	Y
9 Stark	N	Y	Y	Y	?	Y
10 Edwards	N	Y	Y	Y	N	Y
11 Lantos	N	Y	Y	Y	N	?
12 *Zschau*	Y	N	Y	Y	N	Y
13 Mineta	N	Y	Y	Y	N	Y
14 *Shumway*	Y	N	N	N	N	Y
15 Coelho	N	Y	?	?	?	?
16 Panetta	N	Y	Y	Y	N	Y
17 *Pashayan*	Y	N	N	Y	N	Y
18 Lehman	N	?	Y	Y	N	Y
19 *Lagomarsino*	Y	N	N	N	N	Y
20 *Thomas*	Y	N	Y	Y	N	Y
21 *Fiedler*	Y	N	N	Y	N	Y
22 *Moorhead*	Y	N	N	N	N	Y
23 Beilenson	N	Y	Y	Y	N	Y
24 Waxman	?	?	#	?	?	?
25 Roybal	N	Y	?	?	?	?
26 Berman	N	?	Y	Y	?	?
27 Levine	N	?	Y	Y	N	Y
28 Dixon	N	Y	N	P	N	Y
29 Hawkins	?	?	N	P	N	Y
30 Martinez	N	?	Y	Y	N	Y
31 Dymally	N	Y	X	?	?	?
32 Anderson	N	Y	Y	Y	N	Y
33 *Dreier*	Y	N	N	N	Y	Y
34 Torres	N	Y	Y	Y	N	Y
35 *Lewis*	Y	N	N	Y	N	Y
36 Brown	N	Y	?	?	?	?
37 *McCandless*	Y	N	N	N	N	Y
38 Patterson	Y	N	#	?	?	?
39 *Dannemeyer*	Y	N	N	N	Y	Y
40 *Badham*	Y	N	N	N	N	Y
41 *Lowery*	Y	N	Y	Y	N	Y
42 *Lungren*	Y	N	N	Y	N	Y

	403	404	405	406	407	408
43 *Packard*	Y	N	?	?	?	?
44 Bates	Y	N	?	?	?	?
45 *Hunter*	Y	N	?	N	N	Y
COLORADO						
1 Schroeder	N	Y	?	?	?	?
2 Wirth	N	Y	Y	Y	N	Y
3 Kogovsek	N	Y	Y	Y	N	Y
4 *Brown*	Y	N	N	Y	N	Y
5 *Kramer*	Y	?	N	Y	N	Y
6 *Schaefer*	Y	?	N	N	N	Y
CONNECTICUT						
1 Kennelly	N	Y	Y	Y	N	Y
2 Gejdenson	N	?	Y	Y	N	Y
3 Morrison	N	Y	Y	?	?	?
4 *McKinney*	N	Y	Y	Y	N	Y
5 *Ratchford*	N	Y	?	?	?	?
6 *Johnson*	Y	N	N	Y	N	Y
DELAWARE						
AL Carper	N	Y	Y	Y	N	Y
FLORIDA						
1 Hutto	Y	Y	Y	N	N	Y
2 Fuqua	?	?	?	?	?	?
3 Bennett	N	Y	Y	N	N	Y
4 Chappell	N	Y	Y	Y	N	Y
5 *McCollum*	?	?	N	N	N	Y
6 MacKay	Y	N	#	?	?	?
7 Gibbons	N	?	Y	Y	N	?
8 *Young*	Y	N	N	N	N	Y
9 *Bilirakis*	Y	N	N	N	N	Y
10 *Ireland*	Y	N	N	N	N	Y
11 Nelson	Y	N	Y	Y	N	Y
12 *Lewis*	Y	N	N	-	N	Y
13 *Mack*	Y	N	N	N	N	Y
14 Mica	Y	N	Y	Y	N	Y
15 *Shaw*	Y	N	?	?	?	?
16 Smith	N	Y	Y	Y	N	Y
17 Lehman	N	?	Y	Y	Y	Y
18 Pepper	N	Y	Y	Y	N	Y
19 Fascell	N	Y	Y	Y	N	Y
GEORGIA						
1 Thomas	N	Y	Y	Y	N	Y
2 Hatcher	N	Y	Y	Y	?	?
3 Ray	Y	N	Y	Y	N	Y
4 Levitas	N	Y	Y	Y	N	Y
5 Fowler	?	?	Y	Y	N	Y
6 *Gingrich*	?	?	?	N	N	Y
7 Darden	?	?	Y	Y	N	Y
8 Rowland	N	Y	Y	Y	N	Y
9 Jenkins	?	?	?	?	?	?
10 Barnard	N	Y	N	N	N	Y
HAWAII						
1 Heftel	N	?	?	?	?	?
2 Akaka	N	Y	Y	Y	N	Y
IDAHO						
1 *Craig*	Y	N	?	Y	N	Y
2 *Hansen*	?	?	?	?	?	?
ILLINOIS						
1 Hayes	N	Y	N	P	N	Y
2 Savage	N	Y	N	P	N	Y
3 Russo	N	Y	Y	Y	N	Y
4 *O'Brien*	N	Y	N	Y	N	Y
5 Lipinski	?	?	?	?	?	?
6 *Hyde*	Y	N	N	N	N	Y
7 Collins	N	Y	N	P	N	Y
8 Rostenkowski	N	?	?	Y	N	Y
9 Yates	N	Y	Y	Y	N	Y
10 *Porter*	Y	N	N	Y	N	Y
11 Annunzio	N	Y	Y	Y	N	Y
12 *Crane, P.*	Y	N	N	N	Y	Y
13 *Erlenborn*	N	Y	N	Y	N	Y
14 *Corcoran*	Y	N	N	Y	N	Y
15 *Madigan*	?	?	N	Y	Y	?
16 *Martin*	Y	N	N	Y	?	?
17 Evans	N	Y	Y	Y	N	Y
18 *Michel*	Y	N	Y	Y	N	Y
19 *Crane, D.*	Y	N	N	N	Y	Y
20 Durbin	N	Y	Y	Y	N	Y
21 Price	N	Y	Y	Y	N	Y
22 Simon	?	?	?	?	?	?
INDIANA						
1 Hall	N	?	N	P	N	Y
2 Sharp	Y	N	Y	Y	N	Y
3 *Hiler*	Y	?	N	?	?	?
4 *Coats*	Y	N	Y	N	Y	Y
5 *Hillis*	Y	N	N	?	?	?

Corresponding to Congressional Record Votes 458, 459, 460, 461, 462, 463

	403	404	405	406	407	408
6 ***Burton***	Y	N	N	N	N	Y
7 ***Myers***	Y	N	N	Y	N	Y
8 McCloskey	N	Y	Y	Y	N	Y
9 Hamilton	Y	N	Y	Y	N	Y
10 Jacobs	Y	N	Y	Y	?	?
IOWA						
1 ***Leach***	Y	Y	Y	Y	N	Y
2 ***Tauke***	Y	N	Y	Y	N	Y
3 ***Evans***	Y	N	Y	Y	N	Y
4 Smith	Y	Y	Y	Y	N	Y
5 Harkin	?	?	?	?	?	?
6 Bedell	Y	Y	?	Y	N	Y
KANSAS						
1 ***Roberts***	Y	N	Y	Y	N	Y
2 Slattery	Y	N	Y	Y	N	Y
3 ***Winn***	?	?	Y	Y	N	Y
4 Glickman	N	Y	Y	Y	N	Y
5 ***Whittaker***	Y	N	Y	Y	N	Y
KENTUCKY						
1 Hubbard	Y	N	N	N	N	Y
2 Natcher	N	Y	Y	Y	N	Y
3 Mazzoli	Y	N	Y	Y	N	Y
4 ***Snyder***	Y	N	N	N	N	Y
5 ***Rogers***	Y	N	N	N	N	Y
6 ***Hopkins***	Y	N	N	N	N	Y
7 Vacancy						
LOUISIANA						
1 ***Livingston***	Y	N	N	N	Y	Y
2 Boggs	N	Y	N	P	Y	Y
3 Tauzin	Y	N	Y	Y	Y	Y
4 Roemer	Y	N	N	Y	N	Y
5 Huckaby	N	Y	Y	Y	N	?
6 ***Moore***	Y	N	N	Y	Y	Y
7 Breaux	?	?	?	?	?	?
8 Long	N	?	?	?	?	?
MAINE						
1 ***McKernan***	Y	N	Y	Y	N	Y
2 ***Snowe***	Y	N	Y	Y	N	Y
MARYLAND						
1 Dyson	N	Y	#	?	?	?
2 Long	N	Y	Y	Y	N	Y
3 Mikulski	N	?	#	?	?	?
4 ***Holt***	N	Y	N	Y	N	Y
5 Hoyer	N	Y	Y	Y	N	Y
6 Byron	Y	N	Y	Y	N	Y
7 Mitchell	?	?	X	P	N	Y
8 Barnes	N	Y	Y	Y	N	Y
MASSACHUSETTS						
1 ***Conte***	N	Y	Y	Y	N	Y
2 Boland	N	Y	Y	Y	N	Y
3 Early	N	Y	Y	?	?	?
4 Frank	?	?	Y	Y	?	?
5 Shannon	?	?	?	?	?	?
6 Mavroules	N	Y	Y	Y	N	Y
7 Markey	N	Y	Y	Y	N	Y
8 O'Neill						
9 Moakley	N	Y	Y	Y	N	Y
10 Studds	N	Y	Y	Y	N	Y
11 Donnelly	N	Y	Y	Y	N	Y
MICHIGAN						
1 Conyers	N	?	N	P	N	Y
2 ***Pursell***	?	?	?	?	?	?
3 Wolpe	N	Y	Y	Y	N	Y
4 ***Siljander***	?	?	?	?	?	?
5 ***Sawyer***	Y	Y	Y	?	N	Y
6 Carr	N	Y	Y	Y	N	Y
7 Kildee	N	Y	Y	Y	N	Y
8 Traxler	?	?	Y	Y	?	Y
9 ***Vander Jagt***	?	?	?	?	?	?
10 Albosta	N	?	?	?	?	?
11 ***Davis***	Y	N	Y	Y	N	Y
12 Bonior	?	?	?	?	?	?
13 Crockett	?	?	X	?	?	?
14 Hertel	N	N	Y	Y	N	Y
15 Ford	N	Y	Y	Y	N	Y
16 Dingell	Y	N	Y	Y	N	Y
17 Levin	N	Y	Y	Y	N	Y
18 ***Broomfield***	?	?	N	Y	N	Y
MINNESOTA						
1 Penny	Y	N	Y	Y	N	Y
2 ***Weber***	Y	N	Y	Y	N	Y
3 ***Frenzel***	Y	N	Y	Y	Y	Y
4 Vento	Y	?	Y	Y	N	Y
5 Sabo	N	Y	Y	Y	Y	Y
6 Sikorski	N	Y	Y	Y	Y	Y

	403	404	405	406	407	408
7 ***Stangeland***	Y	N	Y	Y	N	Y
8 Oberstar	N	Y	Y	Y	Y	Y
MISSISSIPPI						
1 Whitten	N	Y	Y	Y	N	Y
2 ***Franklin***	Y	N	N	Y	N	Y
3 Montgomery	?	?	?	?	?	?
4 Dowdy	Y	N	?	?	?	?
5 ***Lott***	?	?	N	N	N	?
MISSOURI						
1 Clay	N	Y	Y	P	N	Y
2 Young	N	Y	Y	Y	N	Y
3 Gephardt	?	?	?	?	?	?
4 Skelton	?	?	?	?	?	?
5 Wheat	N	Y	N	P	N	Y
6 ***Coleman***	N	?	N	Y	N	Y
7 ***Taylor***	Y	N	N	N	Y	Y
8 ***Emerson***	Y	N	Y	Y	N	Y
9 Volkmer	N	Y	Y	Y	N	Y
MONTANA						
1 Williams	?	?	Y	Y	Y	Y
2 ***Marlenee***	Y	N	N	Y	N	Y
NEBRASKA						
1 ***Bereuter***	Y	N	Y	Y	N	Y
2 ***Daub***	Y	N	Y	Y	N	Y
3 ***Smith***	Y	N	Y	Y	N	Y
NEVADA						
1 Reid	N	Y	Y	?	?	?
2 ***Vucanovich***	Y	N	N	Y	N	Y
NEW HAMPSHIRE						
1 D'Amours	Y	?	?	?	?	?
2 ***Gregg***	Y	?	N	Y	N	?
NEW JERSEY						
1 Florio	?	?	Y	Y	N	Y
2 Hughes	N	Y	Y	Y	N	Y
3 Howard	?	?	?	?	?	?
4 ***Smith***	Y	N	Y	Y	N	Y
5 ***Roukema***	Y	N	Y	Y	N	Y
6 Dwyer	N	Y	Y	Y	N	Y
7 ***Rinaldo***	Y	N	Y	Y	N	Y
8 Roe	N	Y	Y	Y	N	Y
9 Torricelli	N	Y	Y	Y	N	Y
10 Rodino	N	Y	Y	Y	N	Y
11 Minish	Y	N	Y	Y	N	Y
12 ***Courter***	Y	N	N	N	N	Y
13 Vacancy						
14 Guarini	N	Y	Y	Y	N	Y
NEW MEXICO						
1 ***Lujan***	Y	N	N	N	Y	Y
2 ***Skeen***	Y	N	N	N	Y	Y
3 Richardson	N	Y	Y	Y	N	Y
NEW YORK						
1 ***Carney***	Y	N	N	Y	Y	?
2 Downey	N	?	Y	Y	N	Y
3 Mrazek	N	Y	Y	Y	N	Y
4 ***Lent***	Y	N	N	N	N	Y
5 ***McGrath***	Y	N	N	Y	N	Y
6 Addabbo	N	Y	Y	Y	N	Y
7 Ackerman	N	Y	Y	Y	Y	Y
8 Scheuer	N	Y	Y	Y	N	Y
9 Ferraro	?	?	?	?	?	?
10 Schumer	?	?	Y	Y	Y	Y
11 Towns	N	Y	N	P	N	Y
12 Owens	?	?	N	P	N	Y
13 Solarz	N	Y	Y	Y	N	Y
14 ***Molinari***	Y	N	N	Y	N	Y
15 ***Green***	N	Y	Y	Y	N	Y
16 Rangel	N	Y	N	P	N	Y
17 Weiss	?	?	Y	Y	N	Y
18 Garcia	?	?	X	Y	N	Y
19 Biaggi	?	?	Y	Y	N	Y
20 Ottinger	?	?	?	?	?	?
21 ***Fish***	?	?	N	Y	N	Y
22 ***Gilman***	Y	N	N	Y	N	Y
23 Stratton	N	Y	Y	N	N	Y
24 ***Solomon***	Y	N	N	N	N	Y
25 ***Boehlert***	Y	?	Y	Y	N	?
26 ***Martin***	Y	N	N	Y	N	Y
27 ***Wortley***	Y	N	N	N	N	Y
28 McHugh	N	Y	Y	Y	N	Y
29 ***Horton***	Y	N	?	?	?	?
30 ***Conable***	Y	?	N	N	N	Y
31 ***Kemp***	?	?	N	Y	N	?
32 LaFalce	N	Y	Y	Y	N	Y
33 Nowak	N	Y	Y	Y	N	Y
34 Lundine	N	Y	?	?	?	?

	403	404	405	406	407	408
NORTH CAROLINA						
1 Jones	?	?	Y	Y	N	Y
2 Valentine	Y	N	Y	Y	N	Y
3 Whitley	N	Y	?	?	?	?
4 Andrews	N	Y	Y	Y	N	Y
5 Neal	N	Y	Y	Y	N	Y
6 Britt	N	Y	Y	Y	N	Y
7 Rose	?	?	Y	Y	N	Y
8 Hefner	?	?	?	?	?	?
9 ***Martin***	?	?	?	?	?	?
10 ***Broyhill***	Y	N	N	Y	N	Y
11 Clarke	N	Y	Y	?	?	?
NORTH DAKOTA						
AL Dorgan	N	Y	Y	Y	Y	Y
OHIO						
1 Luken	N	Y	Y	Y	N	Y
2 ***Gradison***	Y	N	Y	Y	N	Y
3 Hall	?	?	Y	Y	N	?
4 ***Oxley***	?	?	N	Y	N	Y
5 ***Latta***	Y	N	N	N	N	Y
6 ***McEwen***	?	?	?	?	?	?
7 ***DeWine***	Y	N	N	N	N	Y
8 ***Kindness***	Y	N	N	N	N	Y
9 Kaptur	N	?	?	?	?	?
10 ***Miller***	Y	N	N	N	N	Y
11 Eckart	Y	?	Y	Y	N	Y
12 ***Kasich***	Y	N	N	N	N	Y
13 Pease	N	Y	Y	Y	N	Y
14 Seiberling	N	Y	Y	Y	N	Y
15 ***Wylie***	Y	N	N	Y	N	Y
16 ***Regula***	N	Y	N	Y	N	Y
17 ***Williams***	?	?	?	?	?	?
18 Applegate	Y	N	Y	N	N	Y
19 Feighan	Y	?	Y	Y	N	Y
20 Oakar	N	?	?	?	?	?
21 Stokes	N	Y	N	P	N	Y
OKLAHOMA						
1 Jones	Y	N	Y	Y	N	Y
2 Synar	N	Y	Y	Y	N	Y
3 Watkins	Y	N	?	?	?	?
4 McCurdy	N	Y	?	?	?	?
5 ***Edwards***	Y	N	N	N	N	Y
6 English	Y	N	Y	Y	?	?
OREGON						
1 AuCoin	N	Y	Y	Y	N	Y
2 ***Smith, R.***	Y	?	Y	Y	N	Y
3 Wyden	N	Y	Y	Y	N	Y
4 Weaver	Y	N	?	?	?	?
5 ***Smith, D.***	Y	N	N	N	?	?
PENNSYLVANIA						
1 Foglietta	N	Y	?	?	?	?
2 Gray	?	?	X	?	?	?
3 Borski	N	Y	Y	Y	N	Y
4 Kolter	N	Y	Y	Y	N	Y
5 ***Schulze***	?	?	?	?	?	?
6 Yatron	N	Y	Y	Y	N	Y
7 Edgar	N	Y	Y	Y	N	?
8 Kostmayer	N	Y	Y	Y	N	Y
9 ***Shuster***	Y	N	N	N	Y	Y
10 ***McDade***	N	Y	N	Y	N	Y
11 Harrison	N	Y	Y	Y	N	Y
12 Murtha	N	Y	Y	Y	N	Y
13 ***Coughlin***	Y	N	Y	Y	N	Y
14 Coyne	N	Y	Y	Y	?	?
15 ***Ritter***	Y	N	N	Y	N	?
16 ***Walker***	Y	N	N	Y	N	Y
17 ***Gekas***	Y	N	N	N	N	Y
18 Walgren	N	Y	?	?	?	?
19 ***Goodling***	Y	N	N	Y	N	Y
20 Gaydos	N	Y	Y	Y	?	Y
21 ***Ridge***	Y	N	Y	Y	N	Y
22 Murphy	Y	N	Y	?	?	?
23 ***Clinger***	Y	N	Y	Y	N	Y
RHODE ISLAND						
1 St Germain	N	Y	Y	Y	N	Y
2 ***Schneider***	Y	N	Y	Y	Y	Y
SOUTH CAROLINA						
1 ***Hartnett***	Y	N	N	N	N	Y
2 ***Spence***	Y	N	N	N	N	Y
3 Derrick	N	Y	Y	?	?	?
4 ***Campbell***	?	?	N	Y	N	Y
5 Spratt	N	Y	Y	Y	N	Y
6 Tallon	Y	N	Y	?	?	?
SOUTH DAKOTA						
AL Daschle	N	Y	Y	Y	N	Y

	403	404	405	406	407	408
TENNESSEE						
1 ***Quillen***	Y	N	N	N	?	?
2 ***Duncan***	Y	N	N	Y	N	Y
3 Lloyd	Y	N	N	N	N	Y
4 Cooper	N	Y	Y	?	?	?
5 Boner	?	?	?	?	?	?
6 Gore	N	?	Y	Y	N	?
7 ***Sundquist***	Y	N	Y	Y	N	Y
8 Jones	N	Y	Y	Y	N	Y
9 Ford	N	Y	Y	P	N	?
TEXAS						
1 Hall, S.	Y	N	N	N	N	Y
2 Wilson	N	Y	?	Y	Y	?
3 ***Bartlett***	Y	N	N	Y	N	Y
4 Hall, R.	Y	N	N	N	Y	Y
5 Bryant	N	Y	Y	Y	N	Y
6 ***Gramm***	?	?	?	?	?	?
7 ***Archer***	Y	N	N	Y	N	Y
8 ***Fields***	Y	N	N	Y	N	Y
9 Brooks	N	Y	Y	Y	N	Y
10 Pickle	N	Y	Y	?	?	?
11 Leath	?	?	?	?	?	?
12 Wright	N	Y	?	Y	N	Y
13 Hightower	Y	N	Y	Y	N	Y
14 Patman	N	Y	Y	N	N	Y
15 de la Garza	N	Y	?	?	?	?
16 Coleman	N	Y	?	?	?	?
17 Stenholm	?	?	?	?	?	?
18 Leland	N	Y	N	P	N	Y
19 Hance	?	?	?	?	?	?
20 Gonzalez	N	Y	N	N	Y	P
21 ***Loeffler***	Y	N	N	Y	Y	Y
22 ***Paul***	?	?	?	?	?	?
23 Kazen	Y	N	Y	Y	Y	Y
24 Frost	?	?	Y	Y	Y	Y
25 Andrews	?	?	Y	Y	N	Y
26 Vandergriff	Y	N	Y	Y	N	Y
27 Ortiz	N	Y	Y	Y	N	Y
UTAH						
1 ***Hansen***	Y	N	N	N	N	Y
2 ***Marriott***	?	?	?	?	?	?
3 ***Nielson***	Y	N	N	N	N	Y
VERMONT						
AL ***Jeffords***	N	Y	Y	Y	N	Y
VIRGINIA						
1 ***Bateman***	Y	N	Y	N	N	Y
2 ***Whitehurst***	?	?	N	Y	N	Y
3 ***Bliley***	Y	N	Y	Y	N	Y
4 Sisisky	Y	N	Y	Y	N	Y
5 Daniel	N	N	Y	N	N	Y
6 Olin	Y	N	Y	Y	N	Y
7 ***Robinson***	Y	N	N	N	N	Y
8 ***Parris***	?	?	N	Y	N	Y
9 Boucher	N	?	Y	Y	N	Y
10 ***Wolf***	N	Y	N	Y	N	Y
WASHINGTON						
1 ***Pritchard***	?	?	N	Y	?	Y
2 Swift	N	Y	Y	Y	N	Y
3 Bonker	N	Y	Y	Y	N	Y
4 ***Morrison***	Y	N	Y	Y	N	Y
5 Foley	N	Y	Y	Y	N	Y
6 Dicks	N	Y	Y	Y	N	?
7 Lowry	N	Y	Y	Y	N	Y
8 ***Chandler***	Y	N	Y	Y	N	Y
WEST VIRGINIA						
1 Mollohan	Y	N	Y	Y	N	Y
2 Staggers	N	Y	Y	Y	N	Y
3 Wise	Y	N	Y	Y	N	Y
4 Rahall	N	Y	Y	Y	N	Y
WISCONSIN						
1 Aspin	?	?	?	?	?	?
2 Kastenmeier	N	Y	Y	Y	N	Y
3 ***Gunderson***	Y	N	Y	Y	N	Y
4 Kleczka	Y	N	Y	Y	N	Y
5 Moody	N	Y	Y	Y	N	Y
6 ***Petri***	Y	N	Y	Y	N	Y
7 Obey	N	Y	Y	Y	Y	Y
8 ***Roth***	Y	N	N	Y	N	Y
9 ***Sensenbrenner***	Y	N	N	Y	?	?
WYOMING						
AL ***Cheney***	?	?	?	N	?	?

Southern states - Ala., Ark., Fla., Ga., Ky., La., Miss., N.C., Okla., S.C., Tenn., Texas, Va.

House and Senate Roll-Call Index

Supreme Court ruling in *Grove City v. Bell*, 42-S, 43-S
Trademark Counterfeiting Act, 106-H
Victim compensation, 118-H
Water Projects Law Enforcement, 116-H
See also Immigration
Legal Services Corporation, 96-H
Appropriations, 29-S
Legislative Branch Appropriations, Fiscal 1985, 28-S, 60-H, 80-H
Library of Congress American Folklife Center, 96-H
Library Services and Construction Act, 6-H
Local Government Antitrust Act, 122-H, 124-H

Medicaid abortion funding, 41-S, 45-S, 122-H
Medical Technology assessment, 64-H
Medicare
Patient costs, 18-S
Physician fee freeze, 26-H
Recipient eligibility, 18-S
Spending cuts, exemptions and restorations, 16-S, 17-S, 18-S, 19-S, 28-S, 76-H
Metric system study, 32-H
Middle East, combat troops in the, 52-H
Military Construction and Appropriations, Fiscal 1985, 78-H, 80-H
Military Construction Authorization, 74-H
Minimum Drinking Age, 28-S
Motor Vehicle Safety/Minimum Drinking Age, 28-S
Municipal Antitrust Amendments, 96-H
MX missile, 24-S, 36-H, 44-H, 56-H, 58-H

National Advisory Committee on Oceans and Atmosphere, Burford appointment, 31-S, 90-H
National Aeronautics and Space Administration Authorizations, 18-H, 80-H
National Bureau of Standards
Authorization, 32-H
Conversion to metric system, 32-H
National Critical Materials Council, 30-H
National Debt. *See* Debt Limit
National Endowment for Democracy, 29-30-S
Funding, 56-H, 96-H
National Health Services Corps, 122-H
National Oceanic and Atmospheric Administration Authorization, 4-H
National Productivity and Innovation Act, 34-S
National Science Foundation and Authorization, 30-H
NATO
Alliance budget shares, 22-S, 27-S
U.S. troop reductions, 27-S
New Ireland Forum commendation, 48-H
Nicaragua
Covert aid to rebels, 12-S, 26-S, 28-S, 44-S, 45-S, 54-H, 94-H
Introduction of combat troops into, 25-S, 52-H, 54-H
Mining of territorial waters, 13-S, 26-H, 28-H
Nominations and appointments
Beaudin, Bruce D., 39-S
Burford, Anne M., 31-S, 90-H

Seger, Martha, 36-S
Wilkinson, J. Harvie, III, 21-S, 33-S, 37-S
Wilson, William A., 7-S
Nuclear materials
Export, 6-S
International agreements, 6-S
See also Arms control
Nutritional Monitoring and Related Research Act, 116-H
Ocean and Coastal Resources, 106-H
Office of the U.S. Trade Representative funding, 34-H
Older Americans Act, 96-H
Amendments, 114-H
Olympic Games, permanent site for, 25-S
Omnibus Defense Authorization, 22-27-S
Omnibus Budget Reconciliation Act, 12-S, 26-H
Oregon Wilderness, 62-H
Organ Transplant Act, 72-H
Organized crime, forfeiture of proceeds from, 3-S

Panama Canal Authorization, 24-H
Parklands. *See* Federal lands
Parole, prohibition against, 3-S
Pennsylvania Wilderness Act, 36-H
Petroleum industry
Competitive bidding on federal leases, 44-S
Oil company mergers, 6-S, 10-S
Oil exports, 6-S, 7-S, 25-S
Philippines
Food aid to, 11-S
Military assistance to, 40-H
Port-Cargo Diversion, 108-H
Postal Service
Appropriations, Fiscal 1985, 72-H, 78-H, 104-H
Protest against non-delivery of international mail in the Soviet Union, 70-H
Wages for new employees, 100-H
Presidential powers
Application of export controls, 7-S
Authority to veto line items in appropriations bills, 17-S, 2-H, 6-H
Budget cuts, 54-H
National security interests, 23-S
Response to unfair trade practices by foreign competitors, 40-S
Presidents, former, reduction of appropriations for, 78-H
Preventive Health Care, 116-H
Preventive Health Services, 64-H
Public Broadcasting Authorization, 86-H, 120-H
Public Debt. *See* Debt Limit
Public Utilities. *See* Energy
Puerto Rico Passenger Service, 44-H

Quadrennial Political Party Convention, 82-H, 84-H

Railroad Safety Improvement Act, 110-H
Reagan, Ronald
Abortion stand, 35-S
Budget recommendations, 20-H
Real Estate
Depreciation life, 15-S, 50-H
Penalties on certain seller-financed

transactions, 30-S, 46-S, 47-S
Credits for rehabilitation of old buildings, 15-S, 150-H
Shelters, 15-S
Reclamation Dam Safety, 16-H
Reform of Federal Intervention in State Proceedings Act, 10-S
Rehabilitation Act Amendments, 8-H
Religion
Constitutional Amendment on School Prayer, 8-9-S, 88-H
Equal access to school buildings by student religious groups, 8-S, 28-S, 44-H, 86-H
Research and Development
Arctic Research and Critical Materials Policy, 30-H
Joint Research and Development Antitrust Act, 34-H
Resources
National Critical Materials Council, 30-H
See also Energy; Water projects
Retirement Equity Act, 48-H
Rural Electrification Administration Financing, 12-H

Safe Drinking Water, 108-H
Sakharov, Andrei, protest against Soviet treatment of Yelena Bonner and, 20-S, 31-S, 82-H
Seger, Martha, appointment of, 36-S
Select Committee on Hunger, 10-H
Semiconductor Chip Protection, 64-H, 120-H
Senior citizens
Older Americans Act, 96-H
Amendments, 114-H
Retirement Equity Act, 148-H
See also Medicare; Social Security
Sentencing Reform Act, 3-S
Service Industries Commerce Development, 118-H
Sex discrimination
In educational institutions, 42-S, 43-S, 44-S, 74-H, 76-H
Wage difference for federal employees, 45-S, 74-H, 82-H
Shipping Antitrust Act, 5-S
Small Business and Federal Procurement Enhancement Act, 35-S
Small Business Authorization, 14-H
Small Business Procurement, 118-H
Social Security
Cost-of-Living Adjustments, 32-S, 116-H
Disability Amendments, 39-S, 110-H
Disability Reform Act, 16-H, 18-H
Identification number validation, 66-H
Income tax on benefits, 14-S
Spending cut exemptions, 16-S, 17-S
Withholding of wages of parents in arrears on child support, 16-S
Social Services
Community Services Block Grants, 62-H, 122-H
Emergency Food and Shelter Program, 35-S
Family Planning Block Grant Authorization, 64-H
Head Start, 62-H, 74-H, 122-H
Human Services Amendments, 62-H, 74-H
Legal Services Corporation, 96-H
Low-Income Energy Assistance, 122-H

INDEX

A

X, Y, Z